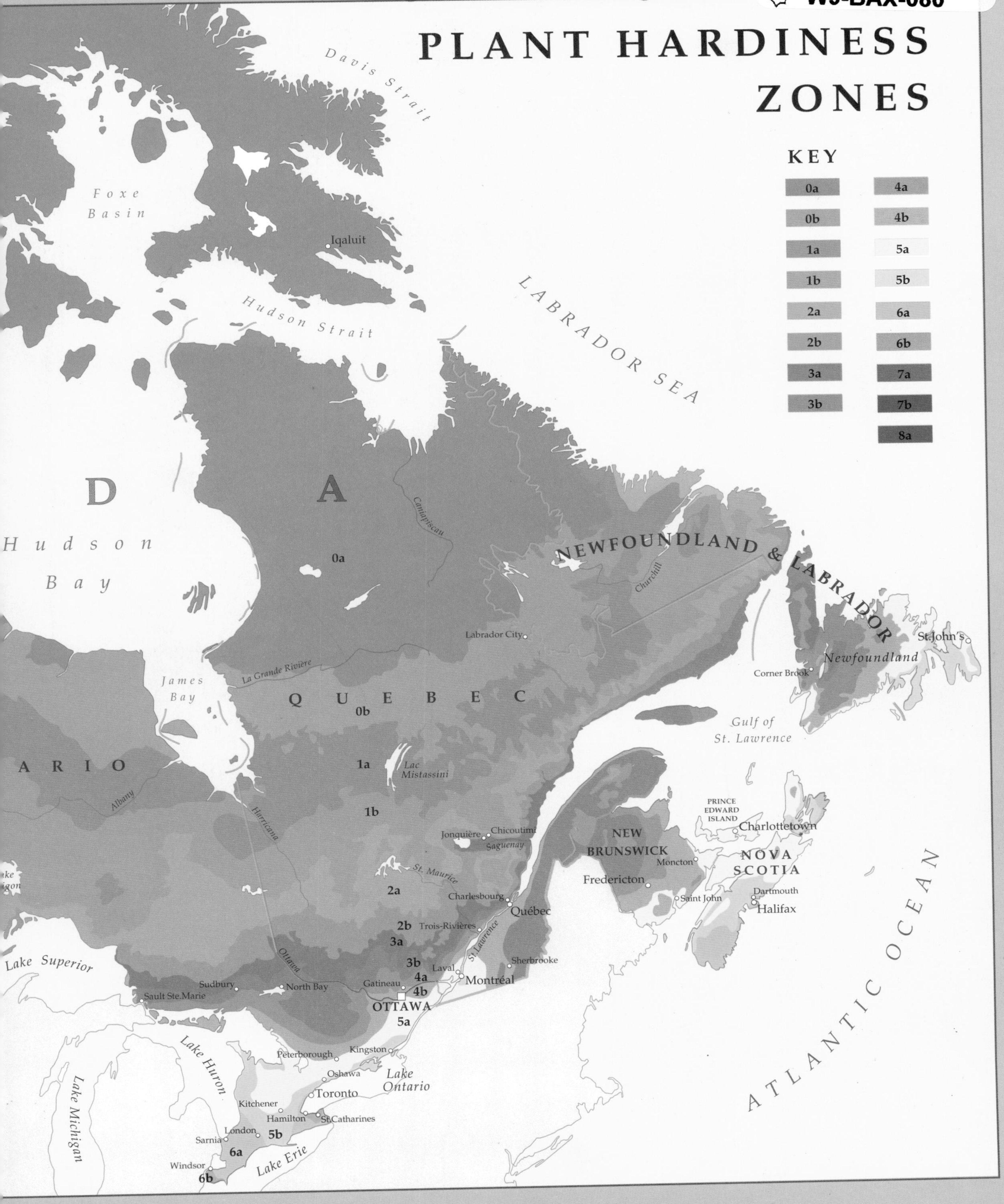
PLANT HARDINESS ZONES
KEY
0a
0b
1a
1b
2a
2b
3a
3b
4a
4b
5a
5b
6a
6b
7a
7b
8a
Davis Strait
Foxe Basin
Iqaluit
Hudson Strait
LABRADOR SEA
D
A
Hudson Bay
0a
Caniapiscau
NEWFOUNDLAND & LABRADOR
Churchill
Labrador City
St.John's
Newfoundland
Corner Brook
La Grande Rivière
James Bay
QUEBEC
0b
Gulf of St. Lawrence
ARIO
1a
Lac Mistassini
Albany
1b
Harricana
PRINCE EDWARD ISLAND
Charlottetown
Jonquière
Chicoutimi
Saguenay
NEW BRUNSWICK
Moncton
NOVA SCOTIA
St. Maurice
2a
Fredericton
Charlesbourg
Québec
Saint John
Dartmouth
Halifax
2b
Trois-Rivières
3a
St. Lawrence
Lake Superior
Ottawa
3b
Sherbrooke
Laval
4a
Montréal
Sudbury
North Bay
Gatineau
4b
Sault Ste.Marie
OTTAWA
5a
ATLANTIC OCEAN
Lake Huron
Peterborough
Kingston
Oshawa
Lake Ontario
Toronto
Lake Michigan
Kitchener
Hamilton
St.Catharines
London
5b
Sarnia
6a
Windsor
Lake Erie
6b

A-Z encyclopedia of GARDEN PLANTS

CANADIAN EDITION

A-Z encyclopedia of GARDEN PLANTS

CANADIAN EDITION

CHRISTOPHER BRICKELL
TREVOR COLE
Editors-in-Chief

DK

Editor, Canada Julia Roles
Project Manager Jill Hamilton
Editors Jennifer Williams, Deslie Lawrence, Nasim Mawji, Mary Sutherland
Editorial Assistants Myrsini Stephanides, Susanna Coates, John Searcy, Rip Noyes, Madeline Farbman
Art Director Dirk Kaufman
Art Editor Kirsten Cashman
Designer Tai Blanche
DTP Designer Milos Orlovic
Picture Researcher Chrissy McIntyre
Production Manager Chris Avgherinos
Project Director Sharon Lucas
Creative Director Tina Vaughan

DK Delhi
Editors Dipali Singh, Glenda Fernandes, Chumki Sen, Rohan Sinha
DTP Pankaj Sharma, Sunil Sharma
Manager Aparna Sharma

Cultivation Editors Cathy Buchanan, Lin Hawthorne, Andrew Mikolajski
Horticultural Advisors Peter Barnes, Roy Cheek, Sabina Knees, Nigel Rowland
Picture Researchers Denise Greig, Emily Hedges, Dr. Alan Hemsley
Illustrators Karen Cochrane, Martine Collings, Joanna Roy, Gill Tomblin

Canadian Edition, 2004

Dorling Kindersley is represented in Canada by Tourmaline Editions Inc.,
662 King Street West, Suite 304, Toronto, Ontario M5V 1M7

National Library of Canada Cataloguing in Publication

A-Z encyclopedia of garden plants / editor in chief, Christopher Brickell, editor in chief, Trevor Cole. -- 2nd Canadian ed.

Includes index.
ISBN 978-1-5536-3041-8

1. Plants, Ornamental--Encyclopedias. 2. Gardening--Encyclopedias.
I. Brickell, Christopher II. Cole, Trevor J.

SB403.2.A19 2004 635.9'03 C2004-902267-9

Color reproduction by GRB Editrice s.r.l., Italy
Printed and bound in China by Toppan Printing Co. Ltd. , Hong Kong

04 05 06 07 08 10 9 8 7 6 5 4 3 2

Discover more at
www.dk.com

CONTENTS

Editors-in-Chief

Christopher Brickell   Trevor Cole

Contributors and Consultants

Terry Aitken
Tim Alderton
Duke Benadom
Dick Bir
Edward Buyarski
Richard Craig
Arabella Dane
John T. Dickman, Ph.D.
Joyce Fingerut
Alan A. Fisher

Judith I. Jones
Richard Koogle
Victoria Koogle
Anthony Liberta, Ph.D.
Michael Ludwig
Harry E. Luther
Edith M. Malek
Susan Martin
Mark Miller
Ned Nash

Robert Nold
Susanne Warner Pierot
Ruth Rumsey
Luke Senior
Ann Walton
Russell Windle

Kathryn S. Andersen, Ph.D.
Miles D. Anderson
Susyn Andrews
Daniel Arcos
George Argent
Roger S. Aylett
David G. Barker
Larry Barlow
Peter Barnes
George Bartlett
Kenneth A. Beckett
Jeffrey Brande
Faye Brawner
A. Richard Brooks
Cathy Buchanan
David Burnie
Brian Burrow
Margaret Cass
Beth Reitz Castellon
Eric Catterall
A. R. Chase, Ph.D.
Roy Cheek
Ian Cooke
Allen J. Coombes
Dr. August De Hertogh
Christopher DeRosa, L. A.
Jack Elliott
Raymond J. Evison

John & Eileen Galbally
Richard W. Gilbert
Pippa Greenwood
Diana Grenfell
Dr. Christopher Grey-Wilson
Dr. Patricia Griggs
Mary Lou Gripshover
Peter Harkness
Lin Hawthorne
Brent Heath
Tony Hender
Betty Hotchkiss
Peter Hovenkamp
Clive Innes
Henry Jaworski
Clive Jermy
Hazel Key
Sabina G. Knees
Rand B. Lee
Bob Lilly
W. A. Lord
Robert J. Loughry, D. Ed.
Ann Lunn
Dr. Donald A. M. Mackay
Beverly B. Markels
Brian Mathew
Peter R. Maynard
Dr. Bruce McAlpin
Margaret E. McKendrick

Judith C. McKeon
Tim Miles
Rolf J. Nelson
Ralph B. & Jean C. Parks
Jim Pearce
Dr. Leonard P. Perry
Martin Rickard
Wilma Rittershausen
Frank L. Robinson
Peter Robinson
Peter Q. Rose
Keith Rushforth
Tony Schilling
W. George Schmid
Holly H. Shimizu
Ken Selody II
Christine Skelmersdale
David Small
Arthur Smith
Joyce Stewart
Dr. Sabina Mueller Sulgrove
Alex Summerville
Al J. Sydnor
Nigel Taylor
David Trehane
R. G. Turner, Jr.
Ray Waite
Dr. Trevor G. Walker

Photographers

Clive Boursnell
Deni Bown
Jonathan Buckley
Andrew Butler
Eric Crichton
Andrew de Lory
Christine M. Douglas

Derek Fell
John Fielding
Neil Fletcher
Roger Foley
John Glover
Harold E. Greer
Jerry Harpur
Sunniva Harte
C. Andrew Henley
Dency Kane

Andrew Lawson
Howard Rice
Bob Rundle
Steven M. Still
Joseph Strauch
Juliette Wade
Matthew Ward
Dave Watts
Tom Woodham
Steven Wooster

FOREWORD

The last thirty years have seen tremendous changes in gardening in Canada. The range of plants now available has greatly increased, and specialist nurseries have sprung up almost everywhere. Gone are the days when summer annuals were petunias, marigolds, or zinnias; now, new plants like the Australian fan flower (*Scaevola*) and Madagascar periwinkle (*Catharanthus*) are all the rage. The choice of perennials has increased tenfold, with new and exciting species and varieties becoming available each year. And trees and shrubs are no longer limited to just a few named forms.

So now is the perfect time for this Canadian edition. DK's *A–Z Encyclopedia of Garden Plants* has been extensively revised and updated to include all the latest developments and to tailor the information to the requirements of Canadian gardeners.

In addition to the ornamental trees, shrubs, ground covers, rock-garden plants, bulbs, annuals, grasses, herbaceous perennials, aquatics, and houseplants covered in the previous version, this Canadian edition contains new entries for vegetables, herbs, fruiting plants, and turf grasses. Recently established varieties of popular plants such as roses, daylilies, and African violets have replaced some of their predecessors. New introductions have been added and other existing descriptions have been revised. Within the pages of this outstanding volume are more than 2,000 genera and 15,000 individual plant entries, illustrated by nearly 6,000 photographs. In addition, there is detailed information on how to take care of all these plants, including advice on propagation, water and nutrient requirements, and disease and pest control.

Specialist plant societies have been consulted and have given valuable advice on the latest trends and innovations. The minimum temperature at which tender plants will survive is noted and, very importantly for Canadian gardeners, the hardiness zones now relate to the plant hardiness zones map researched and developed by Canadian authorities. For easy reference, this map is featured on the endpapers.

This is the book I will turn to first for information on unusual plants or to check on the cultural needs of not-so-familiar ones. The excellent colour photographs give an instant idea of the plant's form, while the detailed descriptions, written in an easy-to-understand way, add the salient points about each specific plant. It is a book that should be on the shelf of every gardener in Canada. You will soon come to wonder how you ever managed without it.

TREVOR COLE
Editor-in-Chief for Canada

How to use this encyclopedia

This encyclopedia is arranged in four main sections: an introduction to gardening; the alphabetical A–Z plant directory, in which more than 15,000 garden plants are listed by their current botanical names; an extensive glossary of horticultural terms that are used in the book; and a common name index. Scientific name synonyms are cross-referenced throughout the plant directory, occurring both in parentheses after the currently accepted scientific names and between genus entries, indicated by the ▷ symbol. A visual key to botanical and horticultural terms and symbols used throughout the plant entries appears in the visual glossary on pages 1080 and 1081, and the Canadian plant hardiness zones map is displayed on the endpapers.

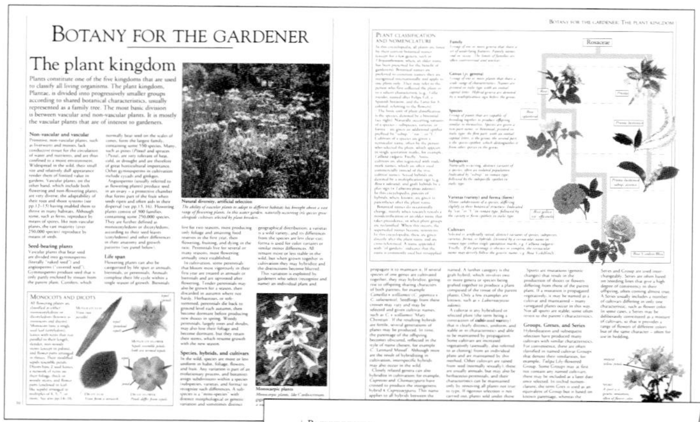

Introduction
Illustrated features outline the key elements of gardening, including plant classification and anatomy, outdoor and under-glass cultivation, propagation, and pruning, and provide a concise introduction to each of the major ornamental plant categories, from trees to grasses.

PHOTOGRAPHS
Plant portraits appear in alphabetical order within the genus text and illustrate different growth habits and ornamental features, as appropriate.

FEATURE PANELS
Close-up views of leaves or flowers may be grouped within major genera, allowing differences in form, color, or markings to be seen clearly. Panels read alphabetically from left to right.

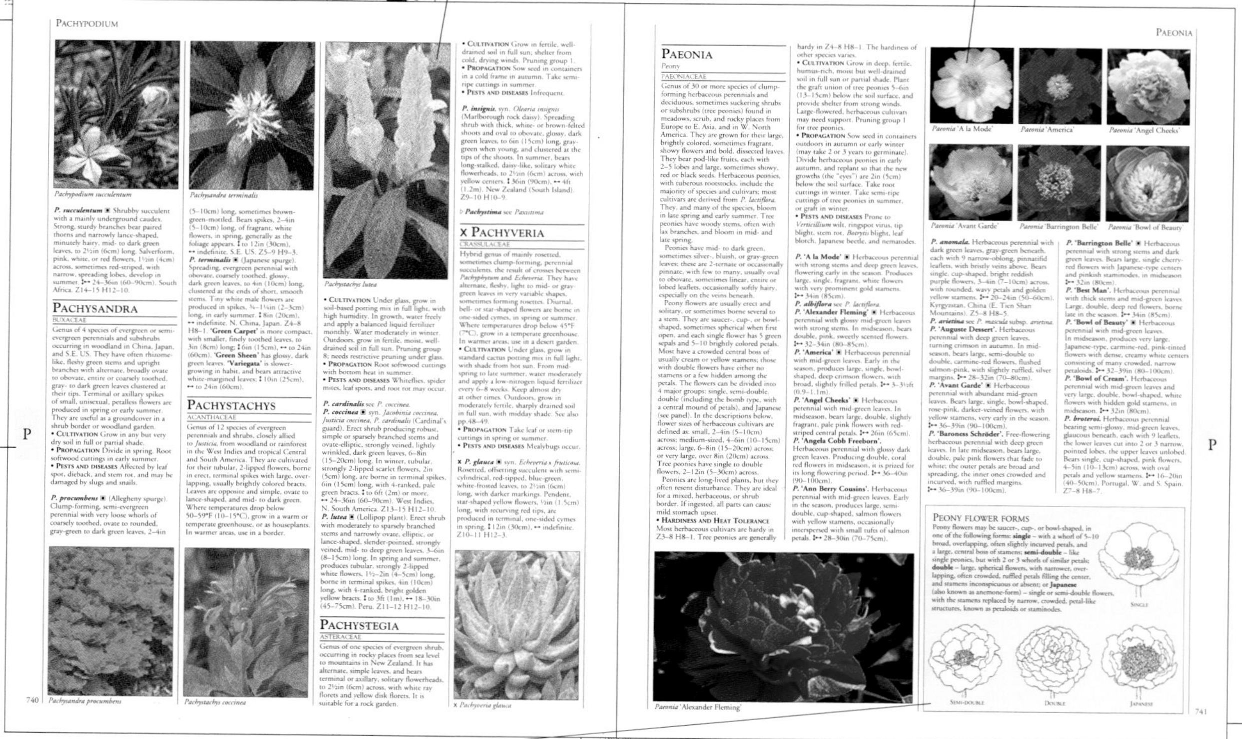

A–Z plant directory
All plants are arranged in alphabetical order within a genus entry, which consists of a short introduction followed by individual plant descriptions. Pictures appear near their relevant text; common names and synonyms are cross-referenced.

MARGINAL MARKERS
Colored tabs move down the margin with the alphabet, for quick location of the letter required.

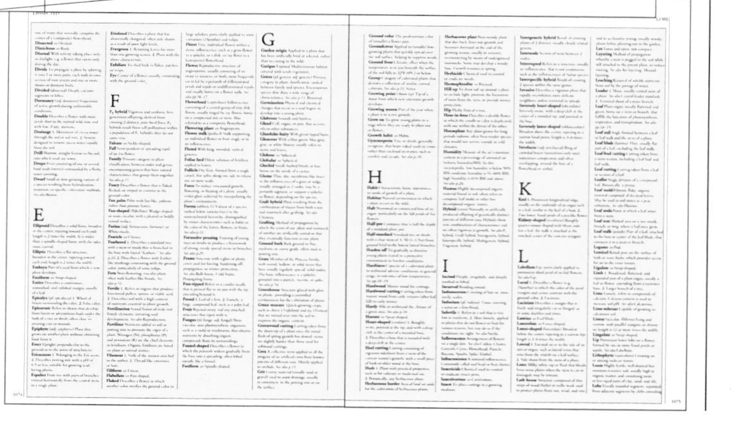

ARTWORKS
Distinctive or complex features of larger genera, such as variations in flower and leaf form, are illustrated and labeled for clearer understanding.

Visual glossary
Quick-reference, visual glossary to terms and concepts used in the plant entries appears on pages 1080 and 1081.

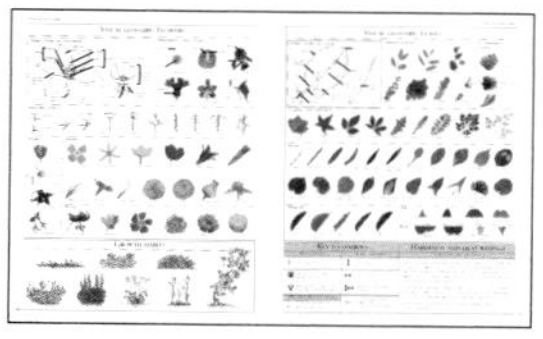

Glossary of terms
All horticultural and botanical terms used in the encyclopedia, as well as other terms used in gardening, are defined here. Some are cross-referenced to related topics in the glossary and the introduction.

THE GENUS ENTRY

All plants in the A–Z directory are described within a genus entry, the genus being a grouping of one or more species with similar characteristics (see p.11). Each entry includes an introduction to the entire genus, outlining its composition and extent, and the salient features of plants within it. Where information is common to all plants in the genus, it may be presented here but omitted from each individual plant entry. Sections on cultivation, propagation, and pests and diseases appear after the introduction, the advice given being applicable to all cultivated plants in the genus. Individual plant entries follow, under their own bold headings. Variants and cultivars of a species are presented under the main plant entry; only characteristics that distinguish them from the species are described. In all entries, perennials are assumed to be deciduous, and leaves simple and mid-green, unless otherwise stated. All measurements are rounded, for ease of use.

pink flowers, to ⅜in (9mm) long, with crimson veins, open from late spring to summer. ↕ ¾in (2cm), ↔ indefinite. South America. Zone 7b.

HYSSOPUS

Hyssop

LAMIACEAE

Genus of about 5 often variable species of aromatic herbaceous perennials and evergreen or semi-evergreen shrubs, occurring in dry, sandy, and rocky sites from the Mediterranean to C. Asia. The linear to lance-shaped, ovate, or oblong leaves are mid- or blue-green. Tubular, violet-blue to pink flowers are borne in whorls on narrow, spike-like, terminal inflorescences. *H. officinalis* and its cultivars are grown for their aromatic foliage and flowers, and are excellent for a rock garden or herb garden. They are also suitable for low hedging, and for growing at the base of a warm, sunny wall or in containers. The flowers are attractive to bees and butterflies; the foliage has culinary and medicinal uses.

- **CULTIVATION** Grow in fertile, well-drained, neutral to alkaline soil in full sun. Pruning group 10, in midspring.
- **PROPAGATION** Sow seed in containers in a cold frame in autumn. Root softwood cuttings in summer.
- **PESTS AND DISEASES** Infrequent.

H. officinalis ▣ (Hyssop). Dwarf, semi-evergreen, aromatic shrub with erect shoots and linear to narrowly lance-shaped, or oblong, mid-green leaves, to 2in (5cm) long. Slender spikes of whorled, funnel-shaped, 2-lipped, dark blue flowers, ½in (1.5cm) long, are produced from midsummer to early autumn. ↕ 24in (60cm), ↔ 3ft (1m). S. Europe. Zone 6. **f. *albus*** has white flowers. **subsp. *aristatus*** has a dense, upright habit, and bright green leaves. **f. *roseus*** bears pink flowers.

Hyssopus officinalis

GARDEN USE
Suitable sites for planting are suggested, either in the garden or, where applicable, under glass (see p.24 for definitions of the various greenhouse categories). Additional information on subjects such as attractiveness to wildlife, herbal uses, or potentially harmful qualities may also be included.

PROPAGATION
Propagation techniques give the most appropriate ways of increasing stock, including any special requirements.

SYMBOLS
Located after the plant name, ▣ indicates that the plant is pictured on that page or the facing page. ❀ indicates that the plant is tender and may be damaged by temperatures below freezing.

INDIVIDUAL PLANT ENTRY
Each entry begins with the botanical name, in bold type, with the genus name abbreviated. Most entries include a description of habit, leaf and flower characteristics, and other ornamental features, such as fruits, as appropriate.

GEOGRAPHICAL ORIGIN
The country or region from which the plant originates appears after the plant dimensions. "Garden origin" indicates that an interspecific hybrid has been artificially selected, rather than occurring naturally in the wild.

VARIANTS AND CULTIVARS
Subspecies, forma, varietas, and cultivar descriptions follow from the main plant entry. Their names appear in bold type, without the generic name or species epithet, and with "subsp.", "f.", and "var." disregarded for purposes of alphabetization. Only those characteristics that distinguish them from the species are described, including height and spread, hardiness, and geographical origin.

PICTURE CAPTION
Plants are identified by their full botanical names.

GENUS HEADING
The botanical genus name is followed by common names or synonyms for the genus.

FAMILY NAME
The botanical family to which the genus belongs appears after the genus heading.

GENUS INTRODUCTION
A broad description of the genus includes the number of species, plant categories, native habitat, geographical origin, and main characteristics of plants in the genus.

CULTIVATION
Care requirements are given for all cultivated plants in the genus. Pruning advice (for woody plants) refers to one of the 13 groups described on pp.26–27. For tender plants, suggestions for growing both outdoors and under glass (which may be in a greenhouse, an alpine house, a conservatory, or indoors) are included.

PESTS AND DISEASES
The pests, diseases, and disorders most likely to afflict plants in the genus are listed. "Infrequent" means the genus is seldom bothered by pests and diseases.

ALTERNATIVE NAMES
Synonyms and common names are listed directly after the plant name and any symbols. Parents of hybrids, where known, appear in parentheses. Synonyms are prefaced by "syn."

HEIGHT AND SPREAD
Unless otherwise specified, height (↕) and spread (↔) are for typical mature plants, cultivated in an appropriate site. Where height and spread are the same, only one measurement is given, after the combined symbol (↕↔). Where appropriate, height is of the plant in flower. Container-grown plants may be smaller than the dimensions given. For bulbous plants, PD *can be used as a guide to planting distance. Height is not given for floating or submerged aquatic plants; spread is not given for climbers.*

HARDINESS
Plant descriptions are accompanied by hardiness zones, except for tender plants and annuals. Minimum temperature is given for tender plants; individual plants may be able to withstand night temperatures lower than this, depending on local conditions and the maturity and health of the plant. Entries for tender orchids (for example, Cattleya*) include both a minimum and a maximum temperature that can be tolerated. See also pp.18–19, and the map on the endpapers.*

HAZARDOUS PLANTS

The majority of garden plants are safe to grow and handle. However, any plant substance is capable of causing an allergic reaction in some people, through either contact or ingestion, so care should always be taken. Warnings are included in the encyclopedia for plants known to have potentially harmful properties, but many plants have yet to be scientifically screened.

Children and animals are most at risk, since they are often attracted to brightly colored flowers, fruits, and also seed pods, which may cause stomach upset if ingested. Gardeners may also come into contact with plants whose foliage or sap may irritate skin, aggravate allergies, or cause photodermatitis (a sunlight-induced rash; reaction is not always immediate and may include itching, redness, or blistering).

If an adverse reaction to a plant occurs, seek immediate medical help and take a sample of the plant for examination. Do not force the affected person to vomit.

KEY TO SYMBOLS

- ▷ Cross-reference
- ▣ Plant is pictured (on same page as entry or facing page)
- ❀ Plant is tender and may be damaged by temperatures below freezing. The minimum temperature (min.) for cultivation appears after the symbol.

PLANT DIMENSIONS

- ↕ Typical height
- ↔ Typical spread
- ↕↔ Typical height and spread (if the same)
- PD Planting distance between bulbous plants

CROSS-REFERENCES

Synonyms (botanical names no longer considered valid) appear in alphabetical order, between genus entries and indicated with the ▷ symbol. Synonyms also occur along with the genus heading and within the relevant species entry, listed after the currently accepted name. Common names are listed within entries (in parentheses) and in an alphabetical list at the back of the book. Cross-references to synonyms of variants and cultivars of a species entry are included as appropriate within the entry but do not occur between genus entries.

The plant kingdom

Plants constitute one of the five kingdoms that are used to classify all living organisms. The plant kingdom, Plantae, is divided into progressively smaller groups according to shared botanical characteristics, usually represented as a family tree. The most basic division is between vascular and non-vascular plants. It is mostly the vascular plants that are of interest to gardeners.

Non-vascular and vascular

Primitive, non-vascular plants, such as liverworts and mosses, lack conductive tissue for the circulation of water and nutrients, and are thus confined to a moist environment. Widespread in the wild, their small size and relatively dull appearance render them of limited value in gardens. Vascular plants, on the other hand, which include both flowering and non-flowering plants, are very diverse, the adaptability of their root and shoot systems (see pp.12–13) having enabled them to thrive in many habitats. Although some, such as ferns, reproduce by means of spores, like non-vascular plants, the vast majority (over 250,000 species) reproduce by means of seeds.

Seed-bearing plants

Vascular plants that bear seed are divided into gymnosperms (literally "naked seed") and angiosperms ("covered seed"). Gymnosperms produce seed that is only partly enclosed by tissues from the parent plant. Conifers, which normally bear seed on the scales of cones, form the largest family, containing some 550 species. Many, such as pines (*Pinus*) and spruces (*Picea*), are very tolerant of heat, cold, or drought and are therefore of great horticultural importance. Other gymnosperms in cultivation include cycads and ginkgos.

Angiosperms (usually referred to as flowering plants) produce seed in an ovary – a protective chamber that forms part of the fruit when seeds ripen and often aids in their dispersal (see pp.13, 16). Flowering plants consist of 300 families, containing some 250,000 species. They are further defined as monocotyledons or dicotyledons, according to their seed leaves (cotyledons) and other differences in their anatomy and growth patterns (see panel below).

Life span

Flowering plants can also be categorized by life span as annuals, biennials, or perennials. Annuals complete their life cycle within a single season of growth. Biennials live for two seasons, most producing only foliage and amassing food reserves in the first year, then flowering, fruiting, and dying in the next. Perennials live for several or many seasons, most flowering annually once established.

In cultivation, some perennials that bloom most vigorously in their first year are treated as annuals or biennials and are uprooted after flowering. Tender perennials may also be grown for a season, then discarded in autumn where not hardy. Herbaceous, or soft-stemmed, perennials die back to ground level each autumn, then become dormant before producing new shoots in spring. Woody perennials, largely trees and shrubs, may also lose their foliage and become dormant, but they retain their stems, which resume growth with the new season.

Species, hybrids, and cultivars

In the wild, species are more or less uniform in habit, foliage, flowers, and fruit. Any variation is part of an evolutionary process, and botanists assign subdivisions within a species (subspecies, varietas, and forma) to recognize such differences. A sub-species is a "mini-species" with distinct morphological or genetic variation and sometimes distinct geographical distribution; a varietas is a wild variety, and its differences from the species are less clear-cut; forma is used for color variants or similar minor differences. All remain more or less stable in the wild, but when grown together in cultivation they may hybridize and the distinctions become blurred.

This variation is exploited by gardeners who select (recognize and name) an individual plant and

Natural diversity, artificial selection
The ability of vascular plants to adapt to different habitats has brought about a vast range of flowering plants. In this water garden, naturally occurring iris species grow alongside cultivars selected by plant breeders.

Monocarpic plants
Monocarpic plants, like Cardiocrinum giganteum *var.* yunnanense, *grow for a number of years, flower once, then die.*

MONOCOTS AND DICOTS

All flowering plants are classified as either monocotyledons or dicotyledons (known as monocots and dicots). Monocots have a single seed leaf (cotyledon), leaves with veins that run parallel to their length, slender, non-woody stems (except in palms), and flower parts arranged in threes. Their modified sepals resemble petals. Dicots have 2 seed leaves, a network of veins on their foliage, thick or woody stems, and flower parts (enclosed in leaf-like sepals) arranged in multiples of 4, 5, 7, or more. See also pp.14–16.

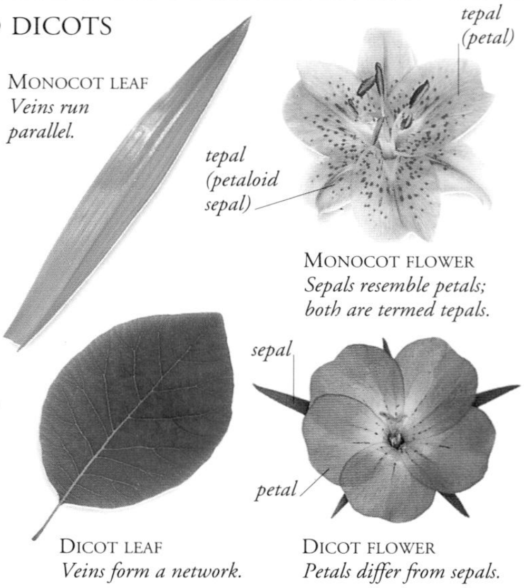
MONOCOT LEAF
Veins run parallel.
tepal (petal)
tepal (petaloid sepal)
MONOCOT FLOWER
Sepals resemble petals; both are termed tepals.
sepal
petal
DICOT LEAF
Veins form a network.
DICOT FLOWER
Petals differ from sepals.

PLANT CLASSIFICATION AND NOMENCLATURE

In this encyclopedia, all plants are listed by their current botanical names (except for a few genera, such as *Chrysanthemum*, where an older name has been preserved for the benefit of gardeners). Botanical names are preferred to common names; they are recognized internationally and apply to one plant only. They may refer to the person who first collected the plant or to a salient characteristic (e.g., *Gilia tricolor*, named after Felipe Gil, a Spanish botanist, and the Latin for 3-colored, referring to the flowers).

The basic unit of plant classification is the species, denoted by a binomial (see right). Naturally occurring variants of a species – subspecies, varietas, or forma – are given an additional epithet prefixed by "subsp.", "var.", or "f." Cultivars of a species are given a vernacular name, often by the person who selected the plant, which appears in single quotation marks, for example, *Calluna vulgaris* 'Firefly'. Some cultivars are also registered with trade-mark names, which are often used commercially instead of the true cultivar names. Sexual hybrids are denoted by a multiplication sign (e.g., *Rosa* x *odorata*), and graft hybrids by a plus sign (+ *Laburnocytisus adamii*). In this encyclopedia, parents of hybrids, where known, are given in parentheses after the plant name.

Botanical names do occasionally change, mainly when research reveals a misidentification or an older name that takes precedence, or when plant groups are reclassified. When this occurs, the superseded names become synonyms. In this encyclopedia, these are given directly after the plant name and are cross-referenced. A name appended with "of gardens" indicates that the name is commonly used but misapplied.

Family
Group of one or more genera that share a set of underlying features. Family names end in -aceae. The limits of families are often controversial and unclear.

Genus (*pl.* **genera**)
Group of one or more plants that share a wide range of characteristics. Names are printed in italic type with an initial capital letter. Hybrid genera are denoted by a multiplication sign before the genus.

Species
Group of plants that are capable of breeding together to produce offspring similar to themselves. Species are given a two-part name, or binomial, printed in italic type: the first part, with an initial capital letter, is the genus; the second part is the species epithet, which distinguishes it from other species in the genus.

Subspecies
Naturally occurring, distinct variant of a species, often an isolated population. Indicated by "subsp." *in roman type, followed by the subspecific epithet in italic type.*

Varietas (variety) and forma (form)
Minor subdivisions of a species, differing slightly in their botanical structure. Indicated by "var." *or* "f." *in roman type, followed by the variety or form epithets in italic type.*

Cultivars
Selected or artificially raised, distinct variants of species, subspecies, varietas, forma, or hybrids. Denoted by a vernacular name in roman type within single quotation marks, e.g. Calluna vulgaris 'Firefly'. *If the parentage is obscure or complex, the vernacular name may directly follow the generic name, e.g. Rosa* 'Goldfinch'.

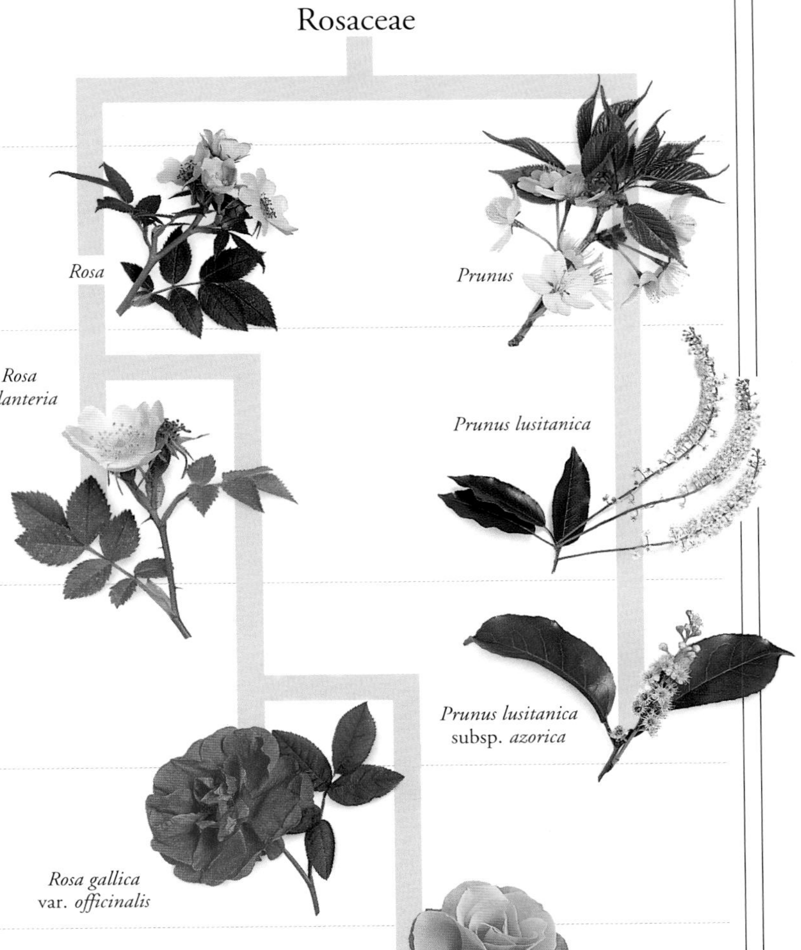

propagate it to maintain it. If several species of one genus are cultivated together, they may hybridize, giving rise to offspring sharing characters of both parents, for example *Camellia* x *williamsii* (*C. japonica* x *C. saluenensis*). Seedlings from these crosses may vary and may be selected and given cultivar names, such as *C.* x *williamsii* 'Mary Christian'. If the resulting hybrids are fertile, several generations of plants may be produced. In time, the parentage of the offspring becomes obscured, reflected in the style of name chosen, for example *C.* 'Leonard Messel'. Although most are the result of hybridizing in cultivation, interspecific hybrids may also occur in the wild.

Closely related genera can also hybridize in cultivation; for example, *Cupressus* and *Chamaecyparis* have crossed to produce the intergeneric hybrid x *Cupressocyparis*. This name applies to all hybrids between the two genera, and individual cultivars may be selected, propagated, and named. A further category is the graft hybrid, which involves two or more genera or species being grafted together to produce a plant composed of the tissue of the parent plants. Only a few examples are known, such as + *Laburnocytisus adamii*.

A cultivar is any hybridized or selected plant (the term being a contraction of **culti**vated **var**iety) that is clearly distinct, uniform, and stable in its characteristics and able to be maintained by propagation. Some cultivars are increased vegetatively (asexually, also referred to as cloning) from an individual plant and are maintained by this method. Other cultivars are raised from seed (normally sexually); these are usually annuals, but may also be herbaceous perennials, and their characteristics can be maintained only by removing all plants not true to type. If rigorous selection is not carried out, plants sold under those cultivar names may not have the expected characteristics.

Sports are mutations (genetic changes) that result in the production of shoots or flowers differing from those of the parent plant. If a mutation is propagated vegetatively, it may be named as a cultivar and maintained – many variegated plants occur in this way. Not all sports are stable; some often revert to the parent's characteristics.

Groups, Grexes, and Series

Hybridization and subsequent selection have produced many cultivars with similar characteristics. For convenience, these are often classified in named cultivar Groups that denote their similarities, for example, *Tulipa* Lily-flowered Group. Some Groups may at first not contain any named cultivars; these may be included at a later date once selected. In orchid nomenclature, the term Grex is used as an equivalent of Group but is based on known parentage, whereas the parentage in Groups may not be certain. Commercially, the terms Series and Group are used interchangeably. Series are often based on breeding lines that give a high degree of consistency in their offspring, often coming almost true. A Series usually includes a number of cultivars differing in only one characteristic, such as flower color. In some cases, a Series may be deliberately constituted as a mixture of cultivars, so that it provides a range of flowers of different colors but of the same character – often for use in bedding.

SPORT
A sport is a genetic mutation, often of flower color, as seen in the ray florets of this chrysanthemum.

The life of a plant

Flowering plants have evolved a range of strategies and structures that enable them to survive and reproduce in diverse habitats. Knowing how plants function and understanding their life cycle are vital to raising and maintaining healthy specimens, and to successfully increasing stocks, whether from seed or by other means.

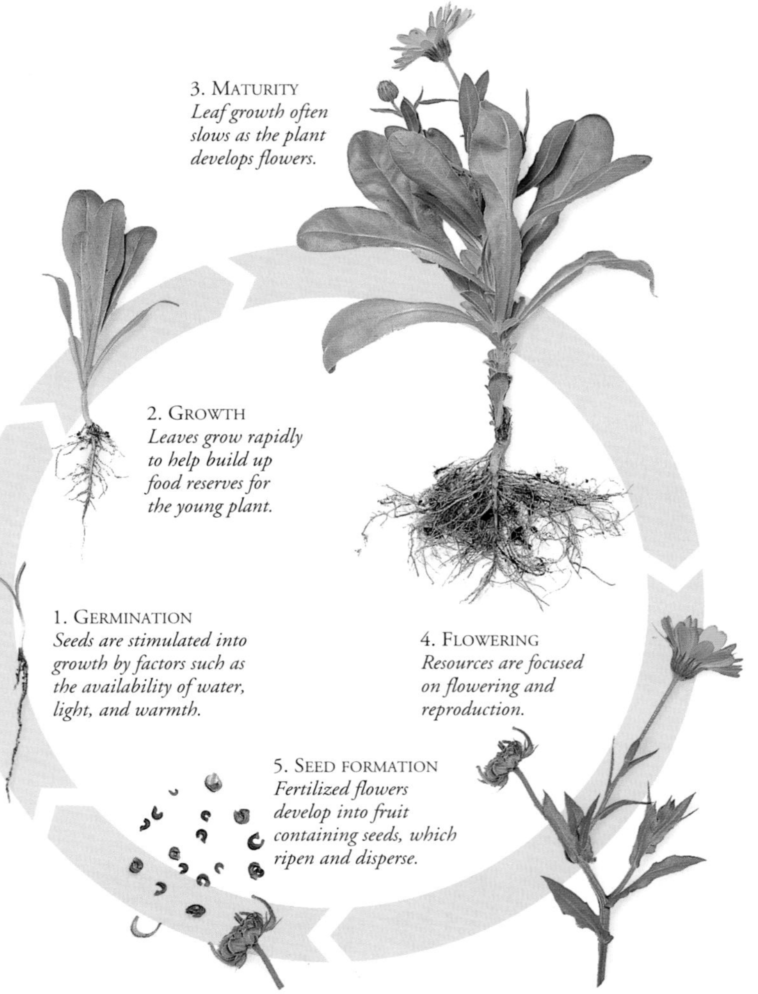

3. MATURITY
Leaf growth often slows as the plant develops flowers.
2. GROWTH
Leaves grow rapidly to help build up food reserves for the young plant.
1. GERMINATION
Seeds are stimulated into growth by factors such as the availability of water, light, and warmth.
4. FLOWERING
Resources are focused on flowering and reproduction.
5. SEED FORMATION
Fertilized flowers develop into fruit containing seeds, which ripen and disperse.

Life cycle of a flowering plant

The life cycle of an angiosperm has several phases, often regulated by seasonal variations such as water availability, air temperature, and day length. Germination is followed by a period of growth. The mature plant then flowers and sets seed. With annuals and biennials, this cycle occurs once; with most perennials, growth and flowering recurs for many years.

Seeds, shoots, and roots

Seeds are a plant's essential agent of reproduction. Each seed contains the embryo of a new plant and is genetically programmed to start into growth only when conditions are absolutely right. In temperate climates, for example, the soft growth of many flowering plants is unable to withstand severe winter cold. The seeds of plants from such areas remain dormant in the soil until spring, when they germinate, triggered mainly by water intake, but also by factors such as rising temperatures of air and soil, higher levels of light and humidity, and increasing day length.

Some seeds, such as those of many woody plants, must experience a period of cold before they will germinate. In cultivation, dormancy may be broken by stratification, which involves the intake of water by the seed, followed by a period of cold. The seeds must be sown outdoors in autumn, then exposed to winter cold, or kept warm and moist for a few days and then placed in a refrigerator for 3–18 weeks. For tough-coated seeds, dormancy may be broken by scarification: nicking or abrading the outer casing to encourage the seed to absorb water (see also p.28).

Successful germination is usually indicated by the emergence of seed leaves (cotyledons) – a single leaf in monocotyledons, a pair of leaves in dicotyledons. These first leaves and a stem rapidly develop into the mature shoot system. Its initial function is to gather energy from sunlight, which is essential for photosynthesis. During this process, the plant uses a complex series of chemical reactions to produce sugar, in the form of glucose, from carbon dioxide and water. Glucose provides the plant with energy for growth, but it is also a component in the manufacture of more complex substances. One of these is cellulose, a tough, fibrous material that gives strength and flexibility to cell walls. Another is starch, which is stored in the cells to provide a supply of energy later on. Once a plant has reached maturity, the resources of the shoot system are concentrated on forming the structures involved in reproduction: flowers, followed by fruits, which contain seeds for regeneration (see pp.16–17).

Hidden below ground, the root system also makes an essential contribution to a plant's health and vigor, not only anchoring the plant but also absorbing a constant supply of moisture and nutrients from the soil. Some plants develop a taproot system with one main root; others form a wide-spreading, fibrous root system in which there is no taproot. Microscopic root hairs fan out from just behind the root tips, vastly increasing the surface area of each root, and therefore the amount of water and nutrients it can take up. For a healthy root system, always prepare the ground thoroughly before sowing or planting: loose, well-aerated soil allows roots to spread widely in their search for food and water.

After it has entered through the roots, water is drawn up through the plant in a process known as transpiration, carrying minerals to the leaves, from which oxygen and water vapor escape through stomata (microscopic pores) in the leaf surface. Most moisture leaves the plant in this manner, although some

GROWTH HABITS

As with other organisms, the way a plant grows – whether it is stemless, climbing, or clump-forming, for example – is genetically determined, laid down in a blueprint carried in every cell. How well individual plants grow varies with availability of light, exposure to wind, and competition for food and space with other plants.

MAT-FORMING
Stems densely cover the ground; flowers extend above.

PROSTRATE AND TRAILING
Stems spread out on the ground; flowers are borne close to foliage.

CUSHION- OR MOUND-FORMING
Tightly packed stems form a low clump; flowers are close to foliage.

SPREADING
Stems extend horizontally and then ascend, forming a densely packed mass.

CLUMP-FORMING
Flower stems and leaf stalks arise at ground level to form a dense mass.

STEMLESS
Flower stems and leaf stalks arise at ground level.

ERECT
Stems stand upright and support leaves and flowers.

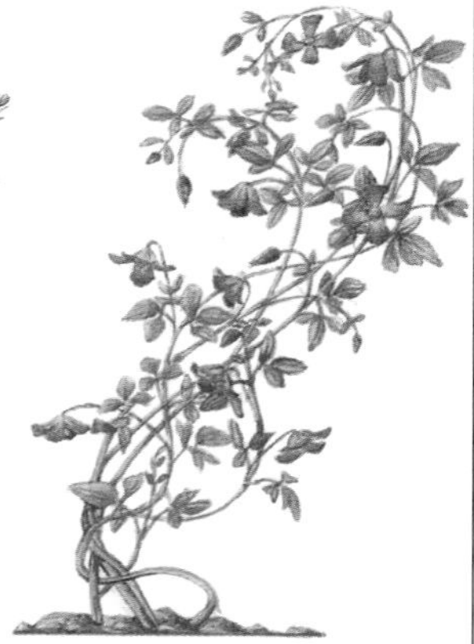

CLIMBING AND SCANDENT
Long, flexible stems are supported by other plants or structures.

MALE AND FEMALE

Most plants have bisexual (hermaphrodite) flowers, containing both male and female reproductive organs. These may pollinate themselves or be pollinated by another plant of the same species. Other plants produce unisexual flowers: on a monoecious plant, male and female flowers are borne separately; on a dioecious plant, the flowers are either all male or all female, so both male and female plants must be grown to produce fruit. A few species are polygamous, with both bisexual and unisexual flowers.

BISEXUAL (HERMAPHRODITE) PLANTS
Each flower contains both male and female organs. It may pollinate itself, or be pollinated by another plant of the species.

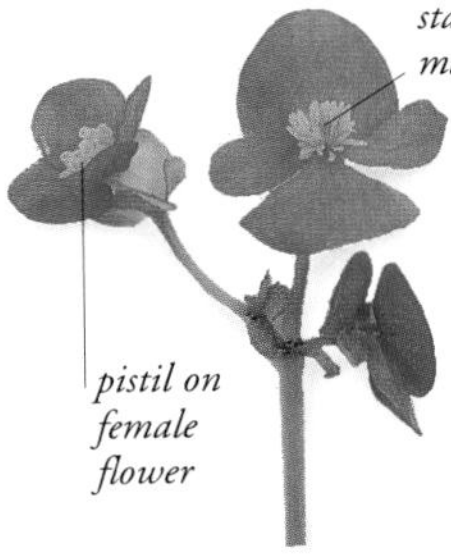

MONOECIOUS PLANTS
Flowers are either male or female, but are borne on the same plant.

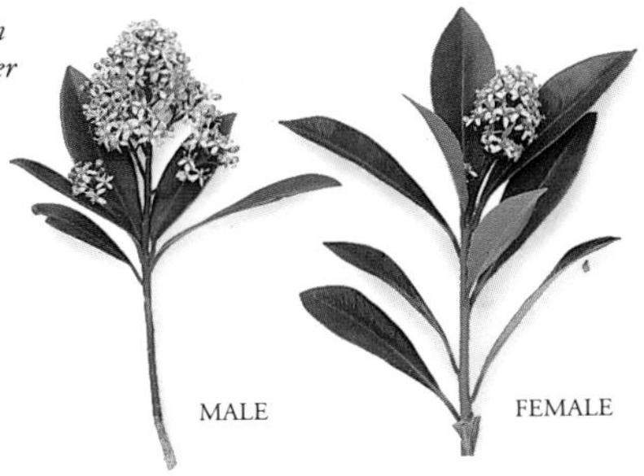

DIOECIOUS PLANTS
Male and female flowers form on separate plants; both are needed for fertilization.

FRUITS

Fruits are formed from the ovaries of flowering plants. They protect the seeds and often aid their dispersal. Soft, fleshy fruits are eaten by animals and birds, which disperse the seeds in the process; dry pods or capsules split open when ripe to scatter the seeds.

The cones of many conifers and other gymnosperms are not true fruits, since they are not formed by ovaries. However, conifers such as yews (*Taxus*) do produce soft, berry-like structures, but the flesh (the aril) is produced on the seed itself, rather than by the ovary of the parent plant.

BERRY
Non-splitting fruit with one to numerous seeds surrounded by soft flesh. Many soft, fleshy fruits are loosely referred to as berries.

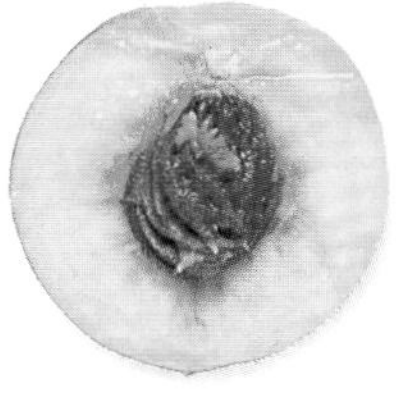

STONE FRUIT (drupe)
Non-splitting fruit with soft flesh surrounding one or several hard seeds (stones).

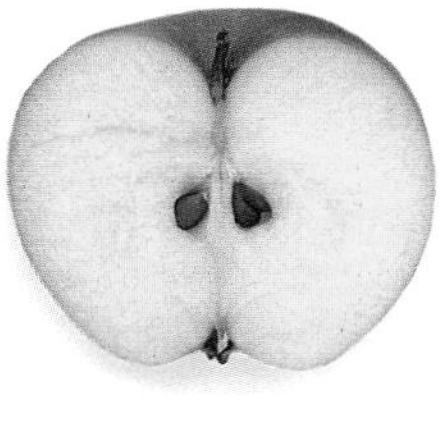

POME
Non-splitting fruit with firm flesh surrounding chambers containing seeds.

NUT
Non-splitting fruit with a hard casing surrounding a softer seed (kernel).

CAPSULE
Dry fruit that normally splits open when ripe to disperse seeds.

CONE
Not a true fruit. Woody scales part to release seeds when conditions are favorable.

POD (legume)
Usually firm or dry fruit that splits along 2 sides when ripe to release seeds.

is used as a raw material in photosynthesis. The movement of water through a plant also keeps its cells turgid (swollen), enabling the stem to stay upright. When water is in short supply, the stem quickly loses its rigidity (wilts) and the plant may die, particularly if transpiration is increased by hot, dry, or windy weather. In cultivation, therefore, provide plants – especially those that are grown under glass or in containers outdoors – with a regular supply of water, and food in the form of fertilizers. Too much water, however, may inhibit growth by waterlogging the soil or soil mix, so that oxygen intake is impossible and the roots rot and die. On the other hand, an excess of nutrients, mainly nitrogen, may encourage the strong growth of lush foliage at the expense of flower production.

Modified shoots

Many plants have evolved modified shoot and root systems in response to the conditions in their native environments. Above ground, the winding tendrils of climbing plants are stems or leaves that have become adapted for grasping a support in the upward quest for light. Thorns are modified branches that deter plant-eating animals. In plants that live in arid conditions, such as cacti, leaves are often reduced to spines to minimize water loss, while the swollen, succulent stems perform photosynthesis and store water. Similarly, the trunk of the tropical baobab tree (*Adansonia digitata*) swells with water-filled tissue, permitting vital functions and growth to continue even during long periods of sparse rainfall.

In some plants, a significant part of the shoot system develops below ground. Subterranean stems include swollen structures such as bulbs, corms, tubers, and rhizomes, which act as food stores. They also increase in number, by producing offsets or bulblets, for example. Such plants offer a simple means of propagation, since when dormant they may be lifted, divided, and replanted.

Unlike other swollen stems, rhizomes grow horizontally, often close to or at the surface of the soil. Adventitious roots arise at the nodes along the length of the rhizome, rather than from its base as with a conventional stem. The rhizomes of some perennials, such as certain irises, have a relatively slow growth rate. In others, however, such as the bamboo *Yushania anceps*, the rhizomes spread very vigorously, rapidly defeating more delicate competitors for available space, light, moisture, and nutrients. A knowledge of such growth habits is indispensable for gardeners, to prevent any one plant from becoming dominant or invasive.

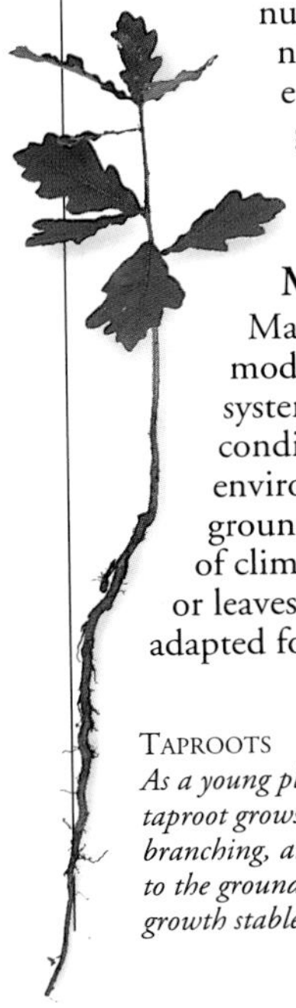

TAPROOTS
As a young plant develops, its taproot grows downward before branching, anchoring the plant to the ground and holding top-growth stable against wind-rock.

Alternative root systems

In the same way that shoots may sometimes develop below ground, roots may grow above it. Climbing plants such as ivies (*Hedera*) have adventitious, aerial roots arising from their stems. These roots cling to most surfaces and penetrate the smallest cracks and crevices, where they expand until the plant is securely attached to its support. Many low-growing plants of spreading habit, such as periwinkles (*Vinca*), produce adventitious roots from nodes on the stems. In cultivation, this is encouraged by layering (pinning stems down to root in the soil) for the purposes of propagation.

Aerial roots are also produced by epiphytic plants, which lodge on other plants and derive moisture and nutrients from the atmosphere, rather than from the soil. In tropical rainforest, epiphytes are often found in the higher branches of trees, where they benefit from increased levels of light near the upper canopy. In such plants, the root system is highly specialized for a permanent existence above ground. The plant is held secure by a network of generally thickened roots, which wrap themselves around twigs and branches in similar fashion to tendrils, and are able to take up rainwater.

A number of trees, such as screw pines (*Pandanus*) and banyans (*Ficus microcarpa, F. benghalensis*), develop additional roots above ground to support them when mature. Stilt roots, for example, are adventitious roots that arise from the trunk, whereas wide-spreading buttress roots are either outgrowths of the trunk or fused, adventitious, aerial roots, forming flanges that provide the tree with extra support; both are commonly found on trees in tropical rainforest, where the soil is relatively shallow or may be heavily saturated.

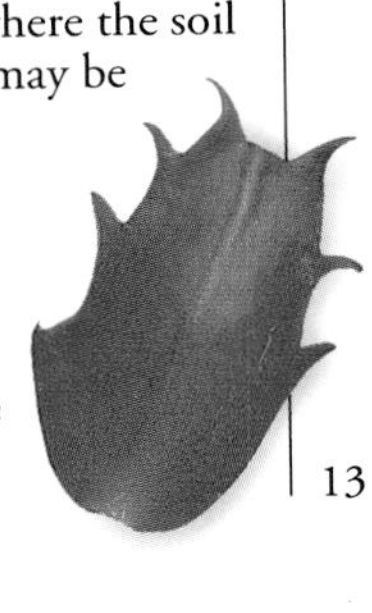

PHYLLOCLADE
The modified stems of some succulents, known as phylloclades, perform functions similar to those of leaves.

Leaves

Leaves fuel the growth of a plant by utilizing solar energy to manufacture food. They also control the passage of water through the plant, which gives it rigidity. The enormous diversity of leaf shapes, sizes, forms, and arrangements, as illustrated here, is the result of plants adapting to conditions in a vast range of habitats.

Structure and function

The basic component of a leaf is the blade (lamina). Simple leaves consist of one continuous blade, while compound leaves are divided into separate leaflets (see Lobing and division, right). Most leaves are attached to the stem by a slender stalk (petiole), but some, as in the case of many monocotyledons, are stalkless (sessile). The leaves (fronds) of ferns often have numerous divisions and uncurl as they grow. Reproductive, spore-bearing structures usually form on their undersides (see p.51). Some flowering plants have modified leaves, such as the tendrils of climbers (see p.13).

The veins on a leaf are extensions of the food and watering tissue (xylem and phloem) of the stem. The leaves of dicotyledons usually have a primary vein (midrib), with a subsidiary network of veins fanning out from it. In monocotyledons, the veins run parallel to the length of the leaf, and there is often no distinct midrib (see p.10).

The greatest division within leaf types lies between deciduous and evergreen foliage in trees and shrubs. Evergreen leaves are shed and replaced throughout the year, while deciduous leaves are all replaced annually, mostly falling in autumn to minimize moisture loss in winter.

A leaf's main functions are photosynthesis and transpiration (see pp.12–13). The first depends on the presence of chlorophyll (the pigment that makes most leaves green), and the second on stomata (minute pores) on the leaf surface.

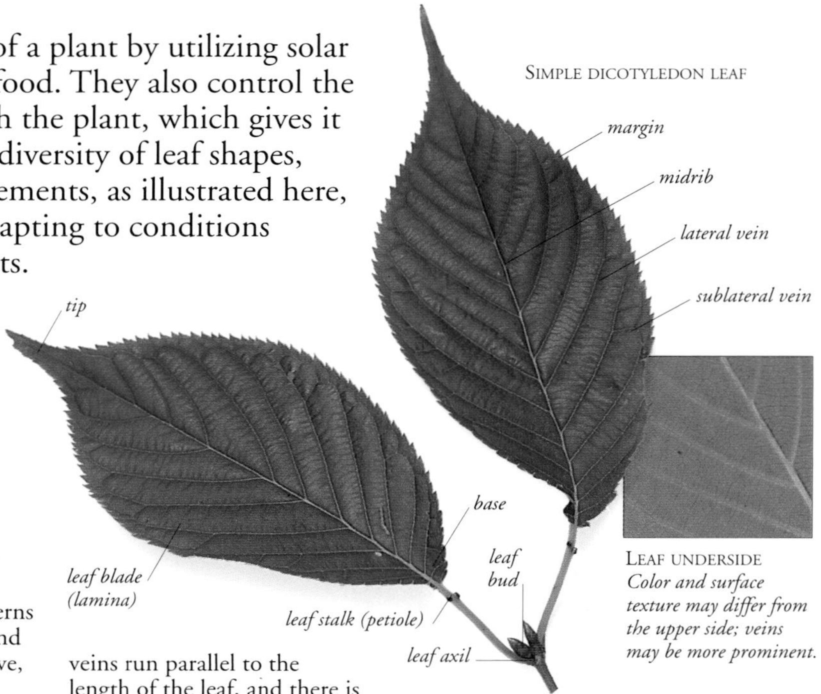

Leaf structure
Although some are divided into separate leaflets, the leaves of most dicotyledons and virtually all monocotyledons consist of a single, flat leaf blade.

CONIFER LEAVES

Most coniferous trees and shrubs have linear leaves, which are often needle-like or scale-like, and covered in a thick, waxy outer layer. These factors help to reduce moisture loss, especially useful in winter when roots cannot take up water from frozen soil. Leaves may be arranged singly, in pairs on either side of the stem (pectinate), or in whorls.

COMB-LIKE (pectinate)

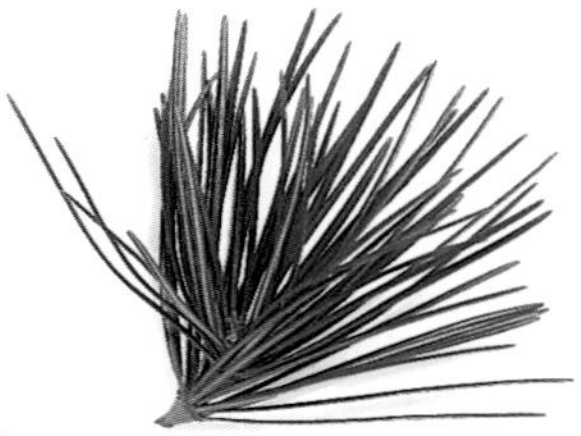
NEEDLE-LIKE (acicular)

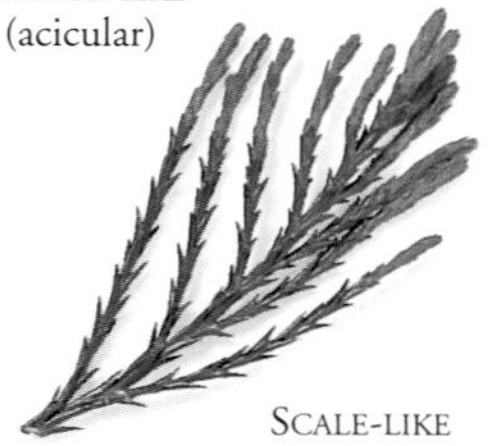
SCALE-LIKE

COLOR AND TEXTURE

Leaf color, which may be affected by surface texture, normally changes in deciduous plants as the leaf ages, due to the breakdown of pigments, especially chlorophyll. In variegated leaves, pigments are unevenly dispersed, usually due to a mutation.

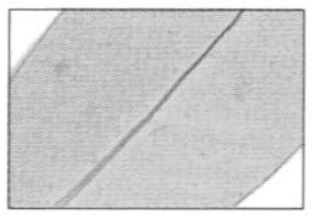
GLAUCOUS

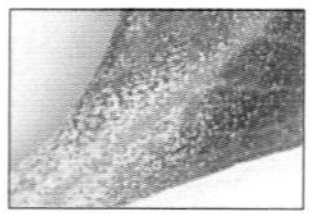
WHITE-MEALY (farinose)

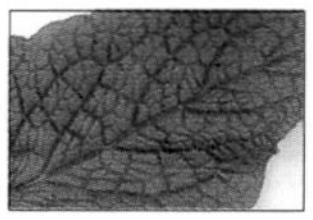
CORRUGATED (rugose)

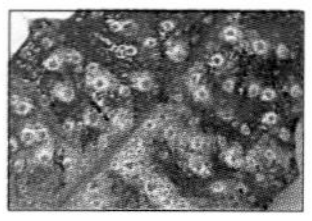
WARTY (pustulate)

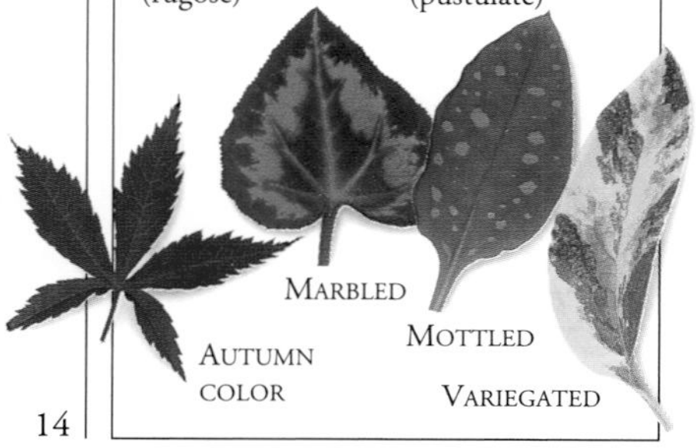
AUTUMN COLOR
MARBLED
MOTTLED
VARIEGATED

LEAF ARRANGEMENTS

The leaves of plants are arranged in a variety of ways to ensure maximum exposure to sunlight in different environments. In some cases, the leaf arrangement may help collect rain-water. Members of a genus or family often have a common arrangement.

In some species, leaves are densely packed at each leaf node (joint with the stem), forming a rosette or whorl. In others, leaves are borne individually or in pairs, separated by a length of bare stem (internode), as in opposite, alternate, and perfoliate arrangements. Some leaves are spirally arranged around the stem.

OPPOSITE
Leaves arranged in pairs on the same plane.

ALTERNATE
Leaves arranged singly on alternate sides of stem.

PERFOLIATE
Leaves arranged singly or in pairs, bases surrounding stem.

ROSETTE
Leaves densely packed, radiating from single point on stem or from base of plant.

WHORLED
Leaves in groups of 3 or more around stem.

2-RANKED (distichous)
Leaves arranged on stem in 2 flattened, opposite ranks.

4-RANKED (decussate)
Leaves arranged in pairs at alternate right angles.

SHAPE

Leaf shape may not be consistent within a species: in some, it depends on a leaf's position on the stem; in others, on whether plants are juvenile or adult. Certain aquatic plants produce one type of leaf under water, another type above the surface. This panel illustrates leaf shapes and terms, and characteristic length to width ratios.

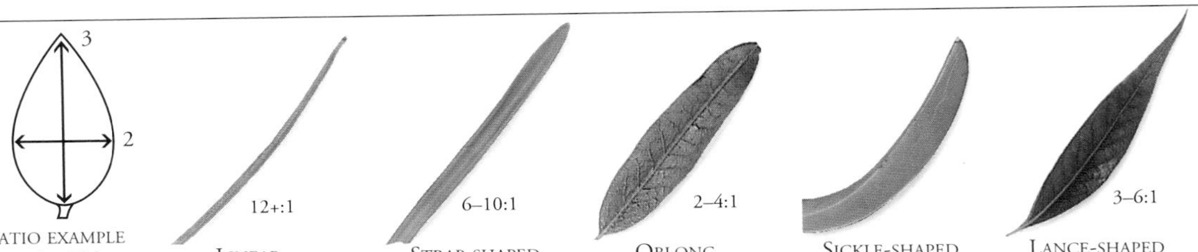

RATIO EXAMPLE *Length:width here is 3:2.*

LINEAR (acicular/filiform)

STRAP-SHAPED (ensiform/ligulate/lorate)

OBLONG

SICKLE-SHAPED (falcate)

LANCE-SHAPED (lanceolate)

INVERSELY LANCE-SHAPED (oblanceolate)

SPOON-SHAPED (spathulate)

OVAL

ELLIPTIC

OVATE

ROUNDED (orbicular)

HEART-SHAPED (cordate)

KIDNEY-SHAPED (reniform)

INVERSELY HEART-SHAPED (obcordate)

OBOVATE

DIAMOND-SHAPED (rhomboidal)

TRIANGULAR (deltoid)

SPEAR-SHAPED (hastate)

ARROW-SHAPED (sagittate)

FAN-SHAPED (flabellate)

PELTATE

LOBING AND DIVISION

Simple leaves consist of one blade with a continuous surface. This, however, does not preclude them from being lobed to varying degrees. Shallowly lobed and pinnatifid leaves have lobes cut no deeper than halfway to the midrib. Palmately lobed and pinnatisect leaves have deeper, more distinct lobes.

Compound leaves have blades that are fully divided into leaflets. In palmate leaves, leaflets arise from a single point at the top of the leaf stalk. In pinnate leaves, the leaflets arise on both sides of a main axis. The leaflets may be stalkless, and may themselves be subdivided. Two features can help to show that compound leaves are single entities, whatever their size or complexity: in many cases, they are shed as a single unit, and while buds form in the axil of a compound leaf, they do not occur in the axils of individual leaflets.

SHALLOWLY LOBED *With shallowly cut lobes.*

PALMATELY LOBED *With deeply cut lobes.*

3-PALMATE/TERNATE (trifoliolate) *With 3 leaflets.*

5-PALMATE (digitate) *With 5 leaflets.*

9-PALMATE *With 9 leaflets.*

PINNATIFID *Pairs of shallowly cut lobes on each side of midrib.*

PINNATISECT *Pairs of deeply cut lobes on each side of midrib.*

PINNATE *Fully divided into leaflets along a single axis.*

2-PINNATE (bipinnate) *Each division divided along 2 axes.*

3-PINNATE (tripinnate) *Each division divided along 3 axes.*

TIPS AND BASES

The tips and bases of leaves vary greatly. The leaves of monocotyledons are often linear, with rounded or pointed tips. Leaves of dicotyledons display greater diversity of tip and base shapes, including lobed bases that meet the leaf-stalk, and narrow "drip tips," which channel rainwater away from the plant. In a decurrent leaf, the leaf stalk, and sometimes the base of the leaf blade, is joined to the stem below the node. Some leaf bases partly sheathe the stem.

TIPS

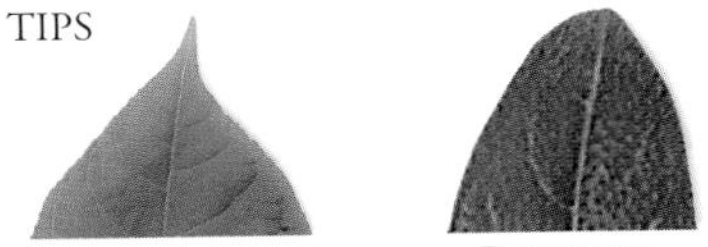

SHARPLY POINTED (acute)

ROUNDED (obtuse)

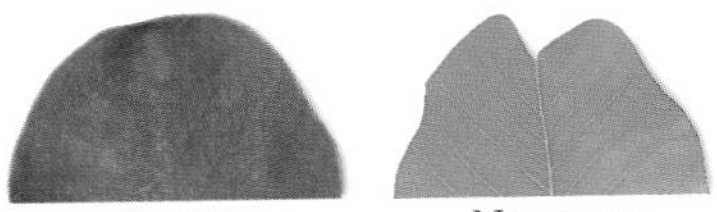

BLUNT (truncate)

NOTCHED (emarginate)

BASES

UNEVEN

HEART-SHAPED (cordate)

WEDGE-SHAPED (cuneate)

POINTED (acute)

MARGINS

Most monocotyledons have leaves with smooth margins, without indentations (entire). Many dicotyledons have more complex leaf margins: they may have sharply pointed teeth or be scalloped, lobed, or deeply incised, as if cut or torn. Most leaves have flat blades, but in some the margins are wavy or tightly rolled inward or outward. Ciliate leaves have marginal hairs.

ENTIRE

SCALLOPED (crenate)

FINELY TOOTHED (serrate)

TOOTHED (dentate)

WAVY (undulate)

SPINY (spinose)

Flowers

Flowers are unique structures that house the reproductive organs of angiosperm plants. Although all flowers share similar underlying features, which enable them to produce seed, they have evolved an enormous variety of shapes, sizes, colors, and fragrances. In cultivation, this diversity has been further enhanced by selective breeding.

Structure and function

All parts of a flower arise from the enlarged or elongated tip of a stem (the receptacle). Most flowers consist of a whorl of colorful petals (the corolla), surrounded by an outer whorl of leaf-like, often green sepals (the calyx). In most monocotyledons, the sepals look like the petals, and the two alternate around the rim of the flower; both are then known as tepals (or perianth segments in some genera).

At the center of a bisexual flower, male reproductive organs (stamens) surround the female part or parts (carpels – collectively known as pistils). Each stamen consists of a pollen-producing anther at the end of a slender stalk (filament). Flowers may have one or more carpels; each carpel has a stigma, which receives the pollen, connected by a stalk (style) to an ovary containing one or more ovules. Once the ovules have been fertilized by pollen, they develop into seeds, which contain food to sustain the embryo plant until its shoot and root systems can fuel growth.

Although many plants are able to pollinate themselves, most have mechanisms that encourage cross-pollination – the transfer of pollen from one plant to another. This increases the genetic diversity of the seeds, improving seedlings' chances of survival. In cultivation, cross-pollination is used to produce plants with new or improved traits (see p.11).

Ornamental attractions
Many insect-pollinated flowers, such as Lonicera periclymenum *'Serotina', have a sweet fragrance and attractive form that make them a popular choice among gardeners.*

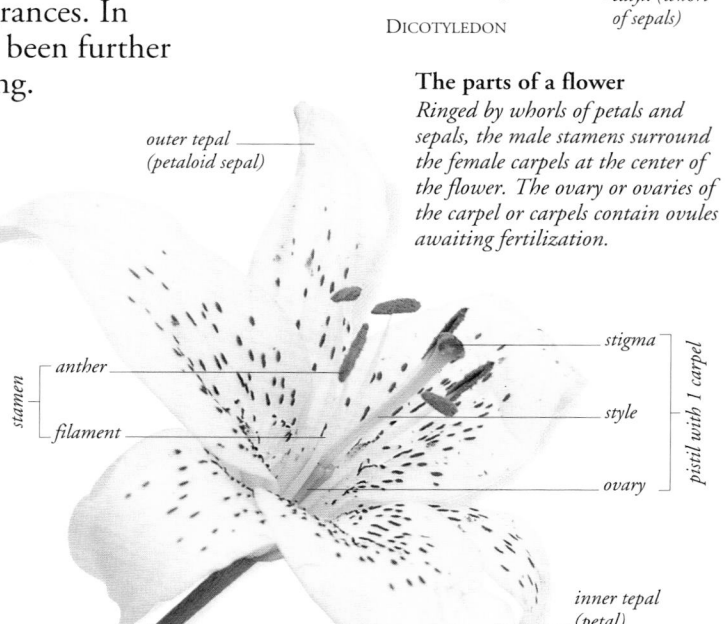

DICOTYLEDON

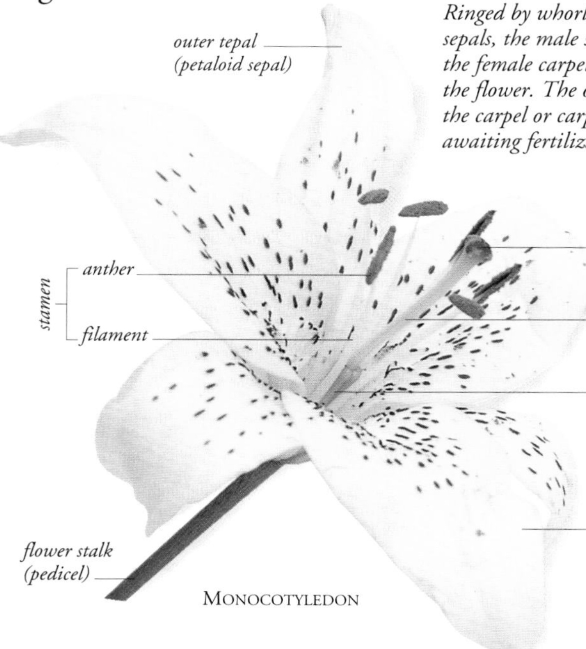

MONOCOTYLEDON

The parts of a flower
Ringed by whorls of petals and sepals, the male stamens surround the female carpels at the center of the flower. The ovary or ovaries of the carpel or carpels contain ovules awaiting fertilization.

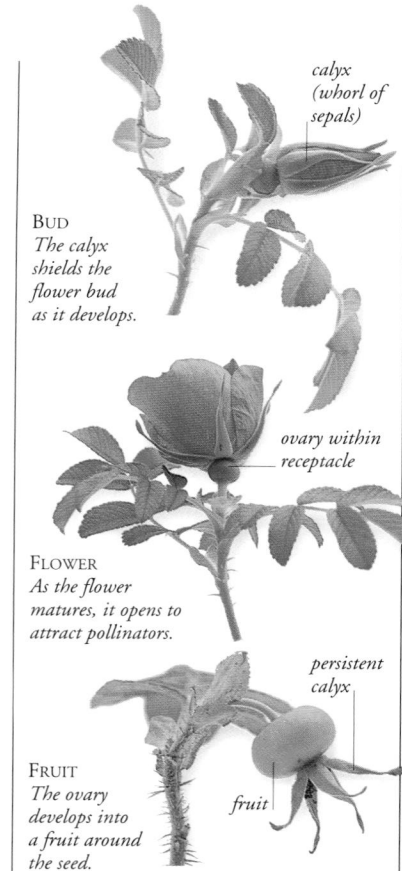

BUD
The calyx shields the flower bud as it develops.

FLOWER
As the flower matures, it opens to attract pollinators.

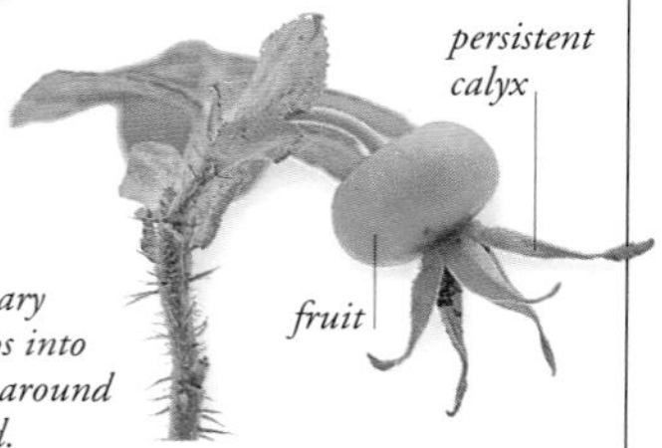

FRUIT
The ovary develops into a fruit around the seed.

Life cycle of a flower
The calyx protects the developing flower bud, which eventually matures to reveal its reproductive organs. Once ovules are fertilized by pollen, the ovary develops into a fruit containing one or more seeds capable of germination into new plants.

DIFFERENT STRUCTURES

Flowers have evolved innumerable forms in order to facilitate pollination – by insects and other animals, by wind, and, more rarely, by water. Flowers that are pollinated by insects or other animals are typically brightly colored and sweetly scented, often containing sugar-rich nectar. Some have specialized forms to encourage a particular pollinator; the flowers of certain orchids, for example, resemble female insects, which attract the males. Wind-pollinated flowers tend to be smaller and less conspicuous, although in plants such as grasses, they are often crowded into large inflorescences.

FLOWERHEAD (composite flower)
Inflorescence made up of usually 2 types of tiny florets (sometimes disk florets only).

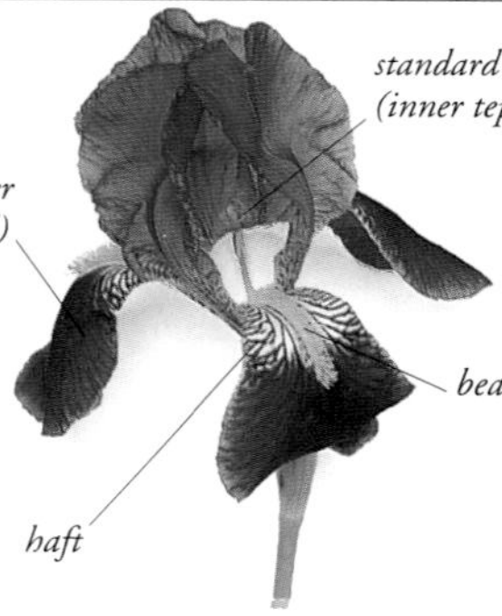

IRIS FLOWER
Flower with very distinct tepals (perianth segments) and parts in threes.

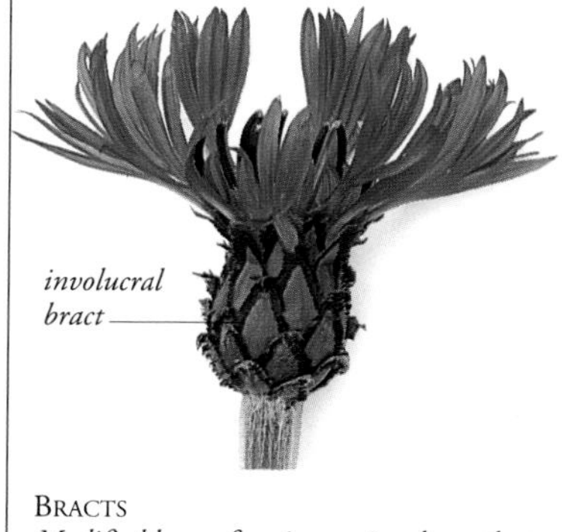

BRACTS
Modified leaves forming an involucre that surrounds the base of a flower or flowerhead.

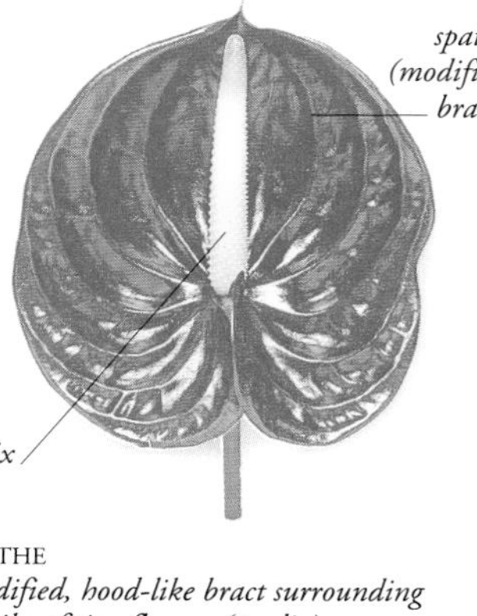

SPATHE
Modified, hood-like bract surrounding a spike of tiny flowers (spadix).

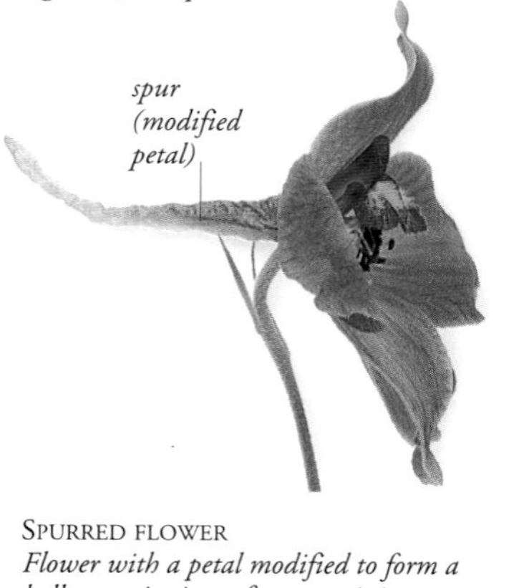

SPURRED FLOWER
Flower with a petal modified to form a hollow projection, often containing nectar.

INFLORESCENCES

Some plants bear solitary flowers, each on its own stem. In many others, flowers are grouped into inflorescences. The type of inflorescence may be identified by the way the flowers are arranged on the stem (the arrows in the diagrams indicate that the main axis may extend farther). Some compound flowerheads resemble a single flower.

TERMINAL
Borne at the end of a stem.

AXILLARY
Borne from a leaf axil.

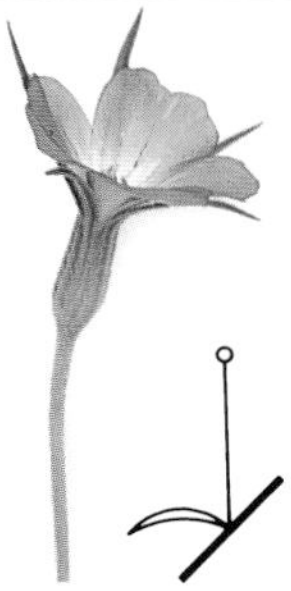

SOLITARY
Flowers are borne singly on a stem.

CLUSTER
Several stalked flowers arise from a single point on a stem.

FLOWERHEAD (capitulum)
Stalkless florets are densely packed on a disk-like pad.

UMBEL
Stalked flowers radiate from a single point at the top of a stem.

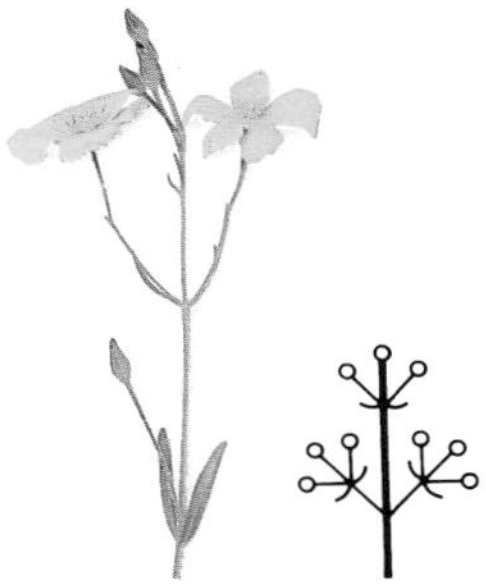

CYME
A flower terminates each branch, the oldest in the center.

SPIKE
Stalkless flowers radiate from an unbranched stem.

RACEME
Stalked flowers radiate from an unbranched stem.

CORYMB
Flat-topped or domed, stalked flowers alternate on the stem.

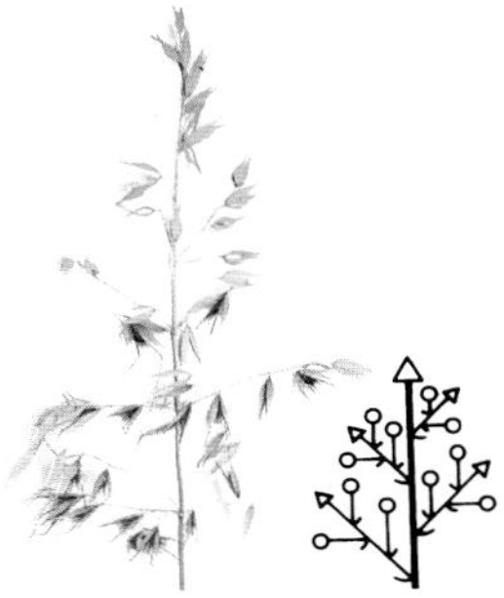

PANICLE
Branched raceme (or sometimes cyme or corymb) of stalked flowers.

SHAPE

Flower shapes are divided into 2 types: either regular or radially symmetrical and rounded in outline; or long and irregular or symmetrical along one axis only. Petals may be separate (free) or partly fused, forming a funnel-shaped or tubular flower. In composite flowers, the florets may be elongated, but the flowerhead is usually rounded.

CROSS-SHAPED (cruciform)

STAR-SHAPED (stellate)

SAUCER-SHAPED

CUP-SHAPED

BELL-SHAPED (campanulate)

TUBULAR

FUNNEL-SHAPED

SALVERFORM

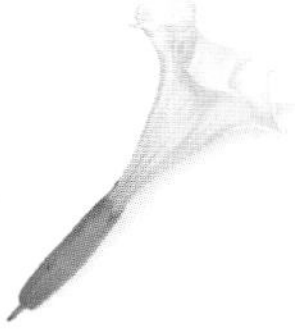

TRUMPET-SHAPED

ROSETTE

POMPON

PEA-LIKE

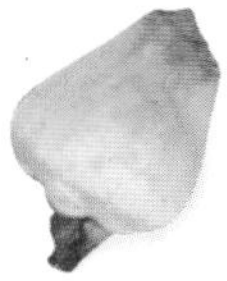

PITCHER-SHAPED

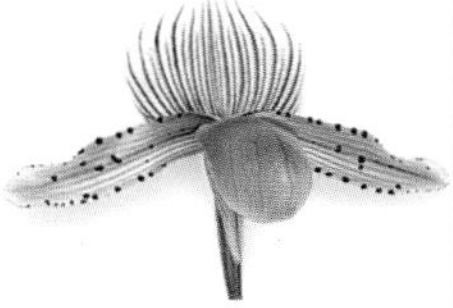

SLIPPER-SHAPED

PETAL ARRANGEMENTS

Virtually all flowers in the wild have a single whorl or fused group of 2–6 petals. A few may have more, but this is far more common in cultivated plants, occurring as mutations and perpetuated through selective breeding. Semi-double flowers generally have 2 or 3 whorls of petals, and double flowers have 3 or more whorls and few or no stamens (and sometimes no carpels). In many cases, the stamens have been modified into petal-like structures called staminodes. Doubling also occurs in many members of the Asteraceae, such as *Chrysanthemum* and *Dahlia*, but in this case the number of ray florets is increased, partially or completely replacing the disk florets.

SINGLE

SEMI-DOUBLE

DOUBLE

HABITS

The habit of a flower or an inflorescence describes its orientation on its stalk when mature. In some plants, this changes as the flower develops.

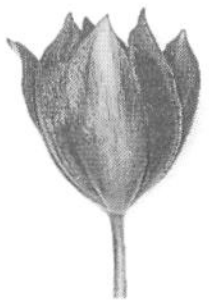

ERECT

HORIZONTAL

NODDING

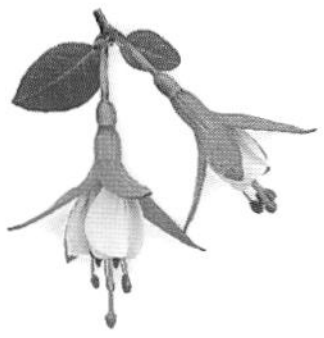

PENDENT

FLOWER COLOR

The colors and markings of flowers originally evolved to attract pollinators; in cultivation, many have been modified to extend their decorative value.

SELF-COLORED

BICOLORED

PICOTEE

STRIPED

Hardiness

Every plant is hardy in its natural, native habitat, since it has survived by adapting to the distinctive conditions that exist there. The concept of hardiness generally applies to cultivated plants, which almost invariably live in a different or an alien environment. In simple terms, hardiness is the capacity of a plant to withstand prevailing climatic conditions in a specific area all year round. In cold regions, it usually refers to the tolerance of low temperatures without protection; in hot climates, it often considers the resistance to such stresses as drought and extreme heat.

Hardiness and exposure
The plateau grasslands of South Africa (including Namaqualand, above) are divided into low veldt, middle veldt, and high veldt. Plants occurring at different altitudes are adapted to withstand different degrees of cold and exposure to wind.

Factors affecting hardiness

The ability of an individual plant to withstand severe conditions depends on a number of factors. In general, plants become increasingly hardy as they mature. The chief determinant of hardiness, however, is the degree of similarity between conditions in the garden and those in the plant's natural habitat, especially soil type and fertility, drainage, soil and air temperature, and levels of humidity, light, and rainfall. It is best, therefore, to select the right plant for the site, rather than to try to tailor the site to the plant's needs. Fortunately for gardeners, many plants readily acclimatize to new circumstances, although some will thrive only in their indigenous surroundings.

Adaptations for survival

Plants in the wild have developed a number of strategies to enable them to survive severe conditions. Many hardy plants become dormant in winter, restricting their growing period to those seasons when conditions of light, moisture, and temperature are favorable. Annuals complete their life cycle in a single season, leaving dormant seed to germinate the following spring. The top-growth of many perennials dies down in autumn; the roots, safely insulated below ground, store food in order to permit rapid growth when favorable conditions return. Woody, deciduous plants protect themselves by shedding their leaves, the parts most vulnerable to winter cold, in autumn; their buds remain dormant until triggered into growth by increasing warmth and light in spring. Many hardy evergreens produce small leaves with a reduced surface area, which is often leathery or covered with an insulating layer of hairs to minimize the drying effects of strong winds. These plants often root deeply to levels where the soil will not freeze. They may also adopt a ground-hugging habit or produce aromatic oils that help to conserve water and act in a similar way to antifreeze.

The relativity of hardiness
While not hardy in cold climates, cannas and dahlias (as shown in this summer border) are hardy in warmer areas and may be left in the ground over winter.

The effects of habitat

An understanding of a plant's natural habitat provides valuable clues to its needs in cultivation. For example, alpine plants that live in scree and rock crevices develop deep root systems that extend widely to take up moisture and the available nutrients. Beneath the rocks, the roots are insulated from extremes of both cold and heat. During winter, the top-growth is maintained at temperatures near freezing by a blanket of dry snow. Snowmelt in spring triggers a short but intense period of growth; many alpines bloom early so that they may set seed and become dormant before the snows return. In cultivation, therefore, alpine plants need a very free-draining, low-nutrient soil; a cool, deep root run; and shelter from high winter rainfall.

At another extreme, plants native to hot, desert-like areas are adapted to store moisture in succulent tissue, safeguarded against desiccation and the sun's heat by spines, hairs, or tough, waxy skin. In the dry season, succulents may lose up to 70

IN ARID AREAS, *cacti such as* Rebutia pygmaea *are resistant to cold, but they require protection in wetter climates.*

Gardening in different regions

Within Canada there is a wide variation in soils and climate. To a large extent, this determines the kinds of plants that will grow well in any given locality.

Atlantic Canada

From a horticultural perspective, this region consists of Newfoundland and Labrador, New Brunswick, Nova Scotia, Prince Edward Island, and the eastern seaboard of Quebec. The sea has a considerable influence on the coastal regions by reducing the extremes of temperature.

The growing season ranges from 130 frost-free days in southern Nova Scotia, to about 95 frost-free days in northern Newfoundland. In the interior, summers are hot and dry and water conservation is often required. Coastal areas often receive heavy rain, especially in spring and fall, which can lead to water-logged soils unless the drainage is improved. Wind is another factor near the coast. Winds blowing from a sea studded with pack ice can delay plant development, and salt-laden sprays can cause considerable damage to tender growth. In the eastern townships of Quebec, deep, reliable snow cover enables the survival of some plants not normally considered hardy, and the lack of summer humidity results in a great diversity of plants.

Soils tend to be acidic, are frequently shallow and rocky, and generally require frequent applications of organic matter, lime, and fertilizer. There are areas of good soil but these are frequently localized. The shallow nature of the soil in much of this region, coupled with frequent mid-winter thaws, often results in plants being heaved out of the soil by frost.

Central Canada

Comprising most of Quebec and the province of Ontario, gardening is mostly limited to the southern, more populated regions but is becoming more and more popular and the range of plants available has increased dramatically in recent years.

Temperatures fluctuate widely from winter to summer with lows of -10°F (-22°C) even in the milder areas and highs of 95°F (35°C) or more, often with high humidity. The most rapid change occurs in spring when in the space of a few days snow banks can melt and early spring bulbs burst into bloom. Spring is fleeting, however, and the slow succession of spring bulbs experienced in other regions may be compressed into a few weeks. The frost-free period ranges from about 110 days in the north to 165 in the Niagara peninsula. Rainfall is spread throughout the year but summer droughts are becoming increasingly common. Water conservation techniques are being used more often. Snow may be deep in the north but in the south, mid-winter thaws happen most years, exposing plants to the cold until the next snow fall.

Soils are generally alkaline, but there are areas with acidic peat-based soils that are widely used for market gardening since they warm quickly in spring. In parts of Quebec, there are considerable areas of sphagnum peat moss, on the sites of ancient dried-up lakes, that are harvested commercially.

The prairies

This region presents a challenge to gardeners because of the winter which can exceed six months in length. However, during the growing season, the long hours of daylight result in rapid growth.

The generally high elevation of this region, plus the mountains to the west, gives summers that are hot and dry. However nights are cool and the humidity is low, so most plants grow well. The growing season is short, with about 120 frost-free days in the more populated parts, and frost or snow are not uncommon at either end of this period. Most of the moisture falls in winter as snow and summer droughts are common. In winter, areas near the mountains and foothills often have warm winds from the west – Chinooks – that cause a dramatic increase in temperature and may encourage plants to break dormancy with disastrous results when the normal cold weather returns. Apart from in the south, soils are generally heavy clay, and slightly acidic to neutral. This soil is sticky in spring and bakes hard in summer, making it a difficult soil to work, but is very fertile and can be very productive if sufficient organic matter and coarse sand can be added. In the south, high alkalinity and, in some places, salinity, limit the number of plant species that will survive.

West coast

This region is greatly influenced by the warm winds off the sea and has the longest growing season and the greatest diversity of plants in all Canada. This warm climate is not without its problems, the humid winds give ideal conditions for the spread of some diseases and limit the popularity of some plants widely grown elsewhere.

Coastal regions have mild winters with temperatures rarely dropping as low as 0°F (-18°C), and summers when the temperature seldom gets above 91°F (33°C). The frost-free period is long, up to 280 days in Victoria, and occasional winters will see no below-freezing temperatures at all. The warm Pacific winds shed their moisture as they climb over the Rockies, and rainfall is up to 128in (3,200mm) in the western slopes but only 25 in (635mm) on the eastern. The mountains also greatly affect the climate and two gardens a short distance apart can have very different growing conditions. The hardiness zones map is of limited use in this mountainous region and local experts are trying to devise a more detailed one for here.

Soils are mostly acidic in the coastal areas, which, coupled with the climate, makes Rhododendrons very popular. Due to the high precipitation, mountain soils are often very thin and lacking in nutrients, needing generous applications of organic material. Soils in the Fraser valley are clay and difficult to work in this wet climate.

percent of their water content and may even experience severe cold. After the rains, plants swell and burst into bloom. When cultivated in a cool, wet climate, most succulents need the warmth of a heated greenhouse or must be grown as houseplants, with little or no watering outside their natural period of growth.

The effects of climate

The difference between continental and maritime (coastal) climates is a significant factor affecting plant hardiness. In continental interiors, most rainfall occurs in summer, and winters are relatively dry and often extremely cold. Seasonal differences are clearly defined: a large, sustained rise in temperature in spring is followed by a long, hot summer. These conditions are ideal for the maturation, or "ripening," of woody growth. Maturation causes internal cell walls to become firm and tough, yet flexible, ensuring that the plant is better able to withstand severe winter cold.

In maritime climates, rainfall is more evenly distributed throughout the year, and temperature extremes are modified by the presence of vast bodies of water. The fluctuation of temperatures in summer may prevent adequate maturation, leaving growth soft and more susceptible to cold damage. Persistent rainfall in winter may cause the roots of dormant or semi-dormant plants to rot. In spring, unusually mild weather induces premature growth, which tends to be extremely vulnerable to damage, even in light frost. For this reason, in a maritime climate, plants that are fully hardy in the extremes of a continental winter may not grow to their full stature, or may fail to thrive at all.

Hardiness in cultivation

Plants exposed to temperatures below their normal tolerances may experience impairment of their physiological processes. In severe cases, this can lead to injuries, such as damage to shoots, stems, and leaves, or even to plant death. Some of these injuries may be avoided by identifying and improving those conditions that cause stress to plants grown beyond their prescribed limits of hardiness.

Perhaps the most vital factor, certainly for evergreen plants, is protection against cold, drying winds; they increase the rate of transpiration from leaf surfaces, causing moisture to be lost more quickly than it can be replaced from the soil, especially in a severely cold spell. Protect plants, especially young specimens, with a wind-filtering hedge or belt of trees, or more locally with fine-grade netting.

Cold damage to roots may often be avoided by growing plants in deep, crumbly, easily worked, well-drained soil, into which roots may penetrate easily, and by applying a thick, dry winter mulch, which will also protect dormant plants from excessive moisture in winter.

Promote maturation of wood by positioning plants in a warm, sunny site (providing they are tolerant of full sun). A warm wall retains and reflects the sun's heat in summer, and so enhances maturation. In winter, the few added degrees of warmth may make the difference between success and failure.

Hardiness ratings

All plants in this encyclopedia are given a Canadian hardiness zone, except for tender plants (which are given a minimum temperature) and annuals. Hardiness may be modified through cultural practices; zones and temperature ranges should be viewed as guides and not as absolute dictates.

FROST-TENDER PLANTS, *such as* Hibiscus rosa-sinensis *'Crown of Bohemia', need winter protection in cold climates.*

The garden environment

Every garden contains a unique combination of light levels, exposure to wind and cold, soil type, and drainage. Understanding the prevailing conditions in a region and their small-scale variations in the garden is an important first step in devising a planting plan, since plants from similar natural habitats can then be used. By combining the advice presented here with good design practice, it is possible to develop an attractive garden using plants that will thrive in the sites chosen.

WATER IN THE SOIL

Rainfall is the main source of water for plants grown outdoors, and is vital for plant growth. Rain drains through the soil, where it is absorbed by plant root hairs, along with essential minerals. In order to be able to take up water and nutrients readily, most plants require an aerated soil that is moist but well-drained. Waterlogged soil lacks oxygen and is fatal to many plants, since the roots will rot if deprived of oxygen. These conditions are, however, ideal for cultivating plants that thrive in the saturated soil of such habitats as bogs, marshland, streambanks, and riversides.

SUNLIGHT AND GROWTH

All plants need light. It is the source of energy for photosynthesis, which fuels their growth. Heat from sunlight also warms the air and soil, and increases humidity through the evaporation of water. The rate of plant growth is largely dependent on the amount of light received, and therefore on day length and the extent of the growing season (determined, in turn, by latitude and altitude).

PELARGONIUM *'POLKA' thrives in sunny sites.*

Individual plants vary in their need for and response to sunlight. Those that need full sun grow pale and elongated (etiolated) in poor light. Conversely, the foliage of plants that are adapted to shaded conditions in their natural habitat will often scorch in strong sunlight.

In cold areas, plants from warm climates require a site in full sun, such as the base of a sunny wall. Summer warmth helps to increase a plant's food reserves and helps woody growth to mature, as well as roots, corms, bulbs, and tubers below ground. Plants with fully ripened tissue are better able to withstand winter cold.

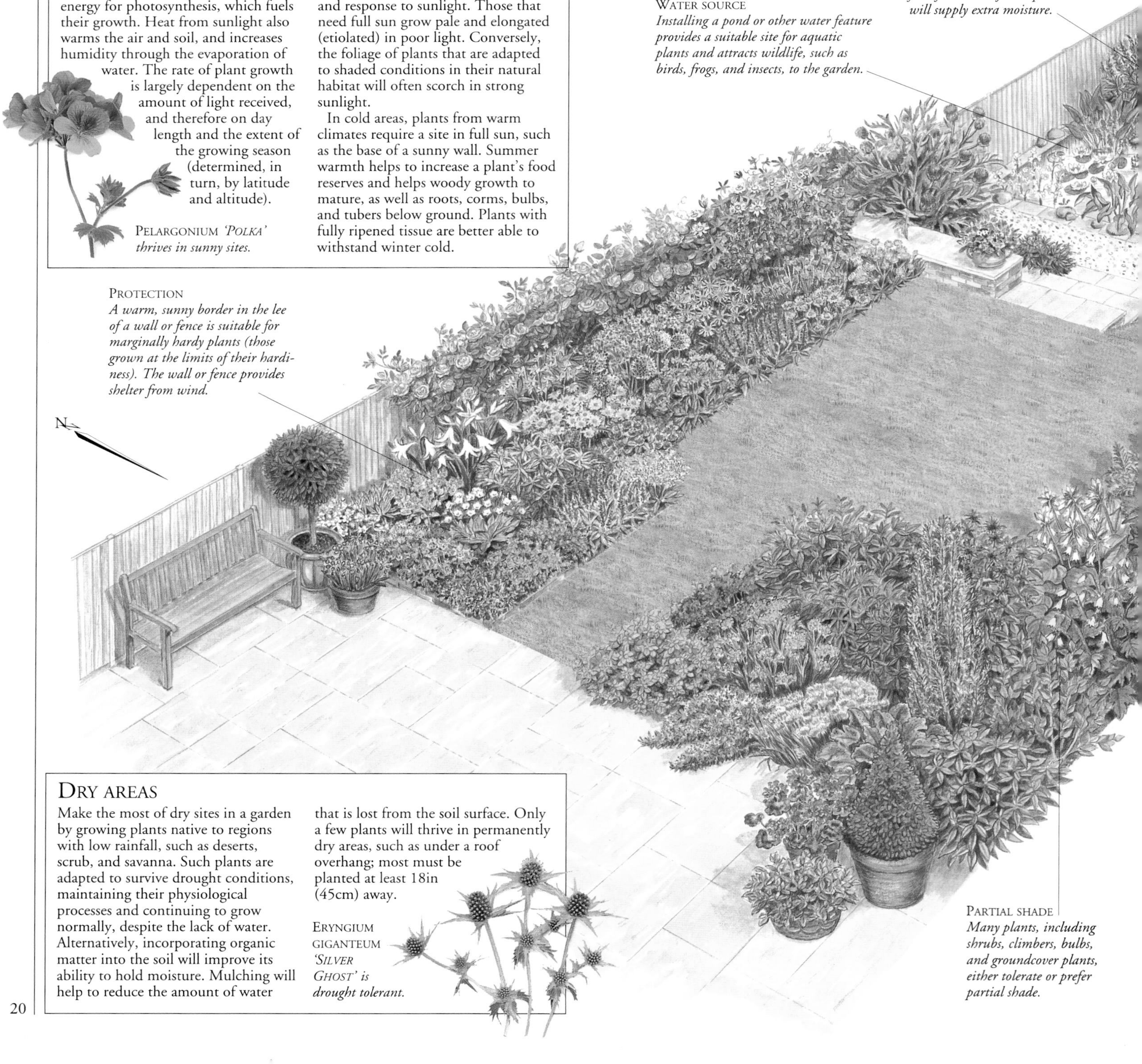

DAMP SOIL
Low-lying, damp soil is ideal for a bog garden; the overflow from an adjacent pond will supply extra moisture.

WATER SOURCE
Installing a pond or other water feature provides a suitable site for aquatic plants and attracts wildlife, such as birds, frogs, and insects, to the garden.

PROTECTION
A warm, sunny border in the lee of a wall or fence is suitable for marginally hardy plants (those grown at the limits of their hardiness). The wall or fence provides shelter from wind.

PARTIAL SHADE
Many plants, including shrubs, climbers, bulbs, and groundcover plants, either tolerate or prefer partial shade.

DRY AREAS

Make the most of dry sites in a garden by growing plants native to regions with low rainfall, such as deserts, scrub, and savanna. Such plants are adapted to survive drought conditions, maintaining their physiological processes and continuing to grow normally, despite the lack of water. Alternatively, incorporating organic matter into the soil will improve its ability to hold moisture. Mulching will help to reduce the amount of water that is lost from the soil surface. Only a few plants will thrive in permanently dry areas, such as under a roof overhang; most must be planted at least 18in (45cm) away.

ERYNGIUM GIGANTEUM *'SILVER GHOST' is drought tolerant.*

SHELTER FROM THE WIND

The movement of air over leaf surfaces increases the rate of water transpiration through a plant. If water loss is greater than uptake, however, the plant suffers leaf scorch and desiccation and, in extreme cases, will die. These effects are most severe in winter, particularly with evergreens, since water lost from the leaves cannot be replaced when the soil is frozen.

In coastal or exposed areas, strong, persistent winds may stunt the top-growth of woody plants, making them lopsided. Windbreaks, ideally using trees or hedges from maritime areas, provide shelter for a distance equal to up to 5 times their own height.

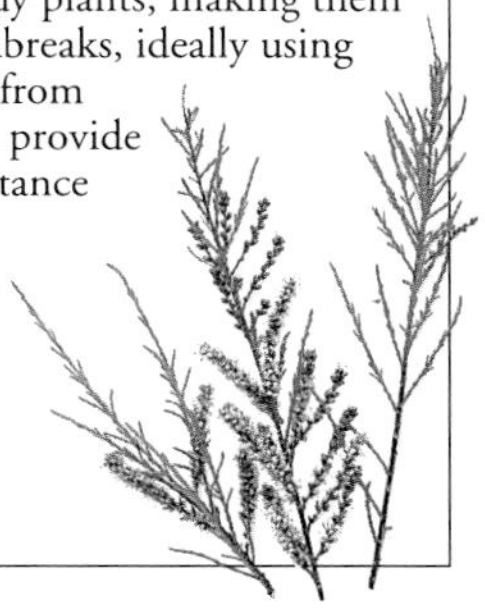

TAMARIX TETRANDRA *is wind resistant.*

WIND BARRIER *A hedge filters wind more effectively than a solid wall, which often creates turbulence on the leeward side.*

POOR SOIL *Soil that is low in nutrients is ideal for a patch of wild-flower meadow.*

FROST *In frost pockets, such as at the base of a slope, provide protection or use only fully hardy plants.*

DAPPLED SHADE *Woodland plants and many spring-flowering bulbs are excellent for growing in the shade of a tree.*

FROST

Frost occurs when cold air sinks, causing air or soil temperatures to fall below 32°F (0°C). Expansion and contraction (frost heaving) of soil during winter may lead to damage to plant roots from breakage and desiccation. A frost pocket forms if cold air is trapped at the bottom of a valley or hollow, or against a solid barrier such as a wall. Even hardy plants may be vulnerable to frost and cold damage, especially once new growth has developed in spring. Avoid planting in frost pockets, or use only fully hardy plants, ideally with top-growth emerging, when the risk of severe frosts has passed.

HELLEBORUS ORIENTALIS *is a frost-tolerant perennial.*

SHADY SITES

Shaded areas of the garden are often regarded as problematic. These sites are, however, ideal for plants that occur naturally in shaded habitats, such as woodland or the bottoms of ravines, and so tolerate lower light levels. There are several different degrees of shade. Light, dappled shade is similar to that found in light woodland, where patterns of shade and sunlight shift over the course of a day. Partial shade describes a site where shade is more or less constant throughout the day, as found beneath a canopy of deciduous trees. A deeply shaded site, such as beneath dense evergreen trees and shrubs or between cliffs or buildings, receives very little or no direct sunlight.

Spring ephemerals are herbaceous plants that emerge in spring, come into flower, produce seeds, and die back to resting structures before the overhead canopy of tree and shrub leaves fills in completely. Most ephemerals, including many well-known woodland wild-flowers, are ideally suited to shady sites. Genera include *Allium*, *Anemonella*, *Aquilegia*, *Arisaema*, *Claytonia*, *Clintonia*, *Dicentra*, *Dodecatheon*, *Erythronium*, *Mertensia*, *Phlox*, *Podophyllum*, *Sanguinaria*, and *Trillium*.

SOIL TYPES

Soils may be divided into mineral and organic types (although all have both mineral and organic components). Mineral soils, derived from weathered rock, are classified according to the size and composition of their particles.

Clay soils have tiny particles and are often very fertile. They are also heavy to dig, may become waterlogged after rainfall, and warm up slowly in spring. They are easily compacted when wet and are prone to surface-capping (baking hard), reducing the amount of air available to roots and seeds.

Silty soils are moderately fertile and hold less water than clay soils, but are also prone to compaction and capping.

Sandy soils contain particles up to 1,000 times larger than those of clay soils. They are light, free-draining, and easily worked, and warm up rapidly in spring, but are often of low fertility because nutrients are quickly leached away as water drains through the soil.

Loam soils are the best mineral soils for most purposes, since they have a balanced mix of particle sizes and combine good drainage and moisture retention with high fertility.

Calcareous (chalky) soils are shallow, free-draining, moderately fertile, and alkaline.

Organic soils, particularly those that contain peat, are formed by the decay of organic matter and are low in nutrients. They are suitable for plants from acidic habitats. A number of peat substitutes are available, based on such materials as leaf mold or coconut fiber, rather than natural peat.

MULCHES

Throughout the year, mulches play an important role in gardening by conserving moisture, moderating soil temperatures, and suppressing the growth of weeds. Most also are an attractive, unifying feature of the garden. The depth of the layer depends on the type of plant being mulched: alpines and other small, low-growing plants require only a very thin layer, whereas trees and shrubs will benefit from 6in (15cm) or more of an appropriate organic mulch. Apply summer mulches after the soil warms up in spring, and apply winter mulches after the soil surface has frozen. Never mulch excessively wet or dry soil.

Mulches occur in a wide range of organic and inorganic materials; some, such as cocoa shells, buckwheat and rice hulls, pine needles, and bagasse (ground sugar cane), may be locally plentiful. Organic mulches should be composted for at least a few months before using them; otherwise, bacteria from the soil will feed and multiply rapidly on the nitrogen content in the mulch and may consume much of the nitrogen in the soil as well. This will lead to yellowing of leaves and other problems. Also see p.23.

COMPOST

Compost is an excellent organic soil additive, helping to retain water and nutrients and improving aeration. It provides organic matter, which decomposes into humus; some nutrients (including trace elements); and many microorganisms, which are an essential part of healthy soil chemistry. It may also be used as a mulch, as an ingredient in soil mixes, and as a home for earthworms.

To make compost, assemble layers of grass clippings, leaves, weeds, straw, shredded paper, chipped branches, kitchen scraps, and similar organic material into a pile or in a bin. Avoid adding diseased plants, and also avoid meat and dairy products, which attract vermin. Chopping or shredding the ingredients will speed up the process. Add a few handfuls of soil (or compost starter) to introduce decay microorganisms, and water as needed to keep the pile moist. Turn occasionally to help aerate the pile. Properly maintained compost will generate considerable internal heat, so take care when handling an active pile. When heat is no longer being generated, the compost is ready to use. Finished compost is dark and crumbly with a pleasant, earthy odor.

IMPROVING THE SOIL

Few gardens have the fertile, well-drained, loamy soil that is ideal for most plants, but there are several ways in which soil can be improved. Incorporating organic matter, such as compost or manure, increases the humus content of soil, improving its structure. The presence of humus in clay and silty soils draws the fine particles together into larger, crumb-like structures, and improves the flow of air and water between them. If the soil is usually waterlogged, it may be necessary to install drainage pipes. Increasing humus in sandy soils improves their ability to hold both moisture and nutrients.

Soil fertility may be improved by applying fertilizer, either in liquid form or as solid slow-release pellets, powders, or concentrated granules.

The acidity or alkalinity of the soil is also important when considering what plants to grow. It is measured on the pH scale, which is numbered 1 to 14: acidic soils have a pH value below 7, and alkaline soils a pH value above 7; neutral soils are pH7. Adding lime will reduce acidity; incorporating organic matter will lower alkalinity to some extent. In the long term, however, it is better to select plants that thrive in a given soil type, rather than trying to change its pH radically. Many plants prefer neutral to slightly acidic soil. Others, such as heathers (*Calluna* and *Erica*) and almost all rhododendrons and azaleas (*Rhododendron*), prefer acidic conditions and will thrive in peaty soil; those needing alkaline conditions flourish in limestone-rich, chalky soils.

Outdoor cultivation

For successful outdoor cultivation, preparation is as important as routine maintenance. Wherever possible, select plants whose natural habitats are similar to the proposed planting site (see pp.20–21). Next, choose robust specimens that are free of pests and diseases. Finally, prepare the site carefully and plant out at the most favorable time of year.

A well-maintained and healthy border
For flourishing, vigorous growth, provide plants with well-cultivated soil and good drainage. Allow plenty of space for each plant to develop, and keep free from weeds. Many plants will flower freely over a long period if they are regularly deadheaded.

Choosing the right plant

When planning a garden, bear in mind the characteristics of the site. Try to find a plant from a similar habitat, although the match need not be exact, since many plants will tolerate a range of conditions.

It is important to acquire robust, well-grown plants. When buying plants, inspect for signs of pests or diseases, such as discolored foliage or dieback (see pp.30–31). With herbaceous perennials, look for vigorous top-growth, with strong, emergent shoots or plump, healthy buds, and an even network of established roots. Ensure that the potting mix is moist. A layer of moss or liverworts suggests a plant has been in its container for some time and may suffer from nutrient deficiency and waterlogging.

When buying a tree or shrub, make sure that it has a balanced framework of top-growth in proportion to the size of its root ball. Shrubs and trees are available either bare-root or balled-and-burlapped (with a ball of soil around the roots, wrapped in netting or burlap) in the dormant season, or in containers at any time of year. Select bare-root plants with well-developed, fibrous roots. With balled-and-burlapped plants, check that the root ball is firm and evenly moist, with the wrapping intact. Avoid plants with roots that are tightly coiled or that protrude from the base of the container.

Soil preparation and planting

Careful preparation of the planting site is critical for vigorous, healthy growth. First, clear the site of all weeds. Next, prepare the site by digging deeply or using a rototiller, and incorporating well-rotted organic matter to improve soil structure and fertility (see p.21). If possible, prepare the ground a season before planting.

Autumn or spring is the best time to plant herbaceous perennials. An autumn planting enables roots to become established while the soil is still warm. Herbaceous plants that are intolerant of cold and moisture when not established are better planted in spring.

Bare-root and balled-and-burlapped trees and shrubs should be planted as soon as possible after purchase, in mild spring or autumn weather; do not plant in wet or frozen soil.

Although container-grown plants may be planted at any time of year, spring and summer plantings need extra care, especially with watering; growth will be checked and the plant may die if the soil is allowed to dry out. Most trees and shrubs are best planted in autumn, at the start of the dormant season. Some, including certain evergreens, will establish better if planted in spring.

Watering

An adequate supply of water is essential for plant growth. For most plants grown in the open, rainfall is the main source of water. However, due to the unreliability of rainfall in most areas, some form of artificial watering is usually required. The amount needed varies between plants and also depends in part on soil type and structure (see p.21).

Most plants require more water when in active growth than at other times of the year. Plants that have a dormant period should be kept barely moist, but no more, when dormant. Newly planted or transplanted plants should be watered until they have become established.

Always water thoroughly, so that water is available deep in the soil; it is better to water infrequently in large quantities than to apply a little often. Water in the early morning or evening to reduce loss by evaporation.

CHOOSE PLANTS *that have vigorous, well-balanced top-growth and a firm, fibrous rootball.*

CONTAINER GARDENING

Use plants grown in containers to decorate paved areas, such as patios and courtyards, or as focal points in other areas of a garden. In frost-prone areas, many tender plants can be displayed in containers outdoors in summer, and moved under glass in winter.

In mixed plantings, it is important to group plants that grow at a similar rate and require similar conditions. Set containers in position before planting up, since they may be too heavy to move afterward. Plants may need watering twice daily in hot spells. If grown in a container for more than one season, plants should be top-dressed in spring by replacing the upper layer of soil mix with new mix.

For permanent plantings, use fertile, soil-based potting mix. Soilless mixes, lightweight in structure as well as being clean to use, are most suitable for short-term plantings, especially for hanging baskets. Most soilless mixes now contain slow-release fertilizer; if not, apply fertilizer regularly in the growing season. Do not allow the soil mix to dry out.

MIXED CONTAINER PLANTINGS *can provide a succession of ornamental features, with evergreen leaves providing prolonged interest and acting as a foil to the flowers.*

Staking

After planting, young trees usually require support for 1 or 2 years, sometimes more, until strong, anchoring roots are established. For most, a short stake is best, since it permits movement of the trunk, encouraging the tree to produce a tapered trunk from the ground up. Stake trees with slender or flexible stems, or ones over 12ft (4m) tall, as high as the base of the crown in the first year; reduce the height of the stake in the second year; remove it in the third.

To support large, newly planted trees, attach guy ropes or wires to low, sturdy stakes angled at 45° away from the tree. Space the guys and stakes evenly around the tree, securing them with eyebolts or U-bolts for easier adjustment as the tree grows. Wrap lengths of hose around the ropes or wires where they touch the tree to prevent damage.

Some perennials also need staking to prevent lax stems from overhanging other plants, as well as to protect them from wind damage. Stake plants well before they grow to their mature height; it is nearly impossible to attractively stake a wind-thrown plant.

Single stake
Insert a single stake to two-thirds of the mature height of a tall, single-stemmed plant, when it is 8in (20cm) high. Tie the stem to the stake using soft twine.

Ring stake
Use ring stakes for clump-forming plants of medium size; link stakes together for taller plants. Set stakes in place early in the season, and raise as the plants grow.

Mulching

Mulching soil has three purposes. It helps to prevent the germination of weed seeds, minimizes evaporation of water from the soil surface, and keeps plant roots cooler in summer and insulated in winter. Organic mulches, such as compost or well-rotted farmyard manure, also improve soil structure and fertility.

There are 2 main types of mulch: continuous sheet mulches and loose mulches consisting of material such as compost or farmyard manure, bark chips, cocoa shells, and many other products. In areas with severe winter cold, apply a deep, dry mulch of conifer branches, leaf mold, straw, or similar material to protect roots and dormant buds from alternate freezing and thawing.

Mulches should be applied annually in spring or autumn, to soil that is moist but not waterlogged. For effective control of weeds, lay the mulch at least 2–3in (5–8cm) deep. To provide adequate winter protection for the roots of plants growing at the limits of their hardiness, the mulch should be 4–6in (10–15cm) deep. A mulch should not be applied too close to the crown of a plant, since this will encourage rot and perhaps attract pests. Also see p.21.

Sheet mulches
Black plastic or woven-fiber sheeting, disguised with a material such as bark chips, controls weeds over a large area and may raise soil temperature slightly.

Loose mulches
Applying a loose mulch to soil regulates its temperature, improves moisture retention, and discourages the growth of weeds.

Routine garden maintenance

A number of routine operations should be carried out during the growing season. For some plants, both thinning (cutting out weak shoots early in the year in order to encourage healthy development of the rest) and pinching increase the number and quality of flowers in certain perennials. Deadheading prolongs flowering and prevents self-seeding. Cutting back dead, diseased, damaged, and flowered shoots and clearing residual weed growth in autumn help to maintain good hygiene, reduce risk of disease, and prevent rotting in winter, when plants are most vulnerable.

Pinching
As plants reach one-third of their final height, pinch out 1–2in (2.5–5cm) from the stem tip, to encourage shorter, sturdier stems and formation of flower buds in the upper leaf axils.

Deadheading
Removing dead or fading flowers diverts energy into growth, improving flowering potential for the following season. Break stems cleanly using finger and thumb, or use pruners for tougher stems.

Preventing seed formation
Remove flowered stems, especially of short-lived perennials, before they set seed. As well as helping to prolong the plant's life, this also reduces the nuisance of unwanted, self-sown seedlings.

Winter protection

Small plants, particularly immature ones, should be protected from excessive winter rain, frost, or snow in a cold or heated frame. Cloches or, where practical, propped panes of glass may be used to shelter mature plants.

Protect larger shrubs growing at the limits of their climatic tolerance by packing them with straw and wrapping them loosely in burlap or horticultural fleece. Frost-tender, wall-trained shrubs and climbers are best covered with screens of fleece or fine netting, stretched over a framework of laths or stakes. See also Mulching, above.

Barn cloche
A barn cloche is useful for protecting young seedlings, frost-tender perennials grown as annuals, and small shrubs. Close the ends with sheets of glass or plastic to protect plants from cold winds.

Cold frame
Use a cold frame to overwinter autumn-sown seedlings and to protect alpines and other plants from excess moisture in winter and summer. It is also ideal for hardening off young plants in spring.

Tunnel cloche
A tunnel cloche made of horticultural fleece protects spring- or autumn-sown annuals and biennials from light frost. It will also allow air to circulate and water to penetrate.

Care under glass

Cultivation under glass, whether in a greenhouse or conservatory, or as houseplants, greatly extends the range of plants that can be grown, especially in cool climates. In greenhouses in particular, the environment should be regulated to suit specific plants, using one of four distinct regimes (see panel below right).

Regulating the greenhouse environment
A greenhouse offers the most versatile means of maintaining a controlled growing environment, especially with regard to temperature, ventilation, and humidity. Areas may also be sectioned off to enable a range of regimes to be set up.

Environments under glass

As a rule, plants that are grown as houseplants must be able to tolerate less than ideal light levels, as well as the dry air associated with central heating. Conservatories provide good levels of light but may become too hot and dry in summer for some plants, since they often lack good ventilation or any means of shading or increasing humidity, and may be too cold in winter if unheated.

Conditions in a greenhouse are easier to control. Ventilation and temperature can be adjusted in most, and humidity increased by damping down or using a hand-held sprayer. Shade may be provided with shade netting or a shade wash. Alpine plants are best grown in a type of greenhouse known as an alpine house, which is designed to provide a level of ventilation two or three times greater than in a standard greenhouse (see p.41).

With all plants grown under glass, the need for light, moisture, and nutrients varies from season to season, according to whether the plant is in growth or dormant.

In this encyclopedia, it is assumed that plants grown under glass are in containers, unless otherwise stated.

Light levels

A number of different light levels may be provided under glass. Plants described as needing full light must have the maximum possible level of light all day; for those needing full light with shade from hot sun, use screens or blinds to protect them from scorching in strong sun. Bright filtered light is achieved using screens, blinds, or a shade wash. Bright indirect light, such as that found near a well-lit window, is suitable for plants that require good light but not direct sun. Place plants that prefer low light beneath staging or shade netting in a greenhouse; as houseplants, they should be sited away from windows.

Potting mixes

Container-grown plants require a potting mix that is suitable for the plants' specific needs, including water, fertility, and aeration around the roots. Therefore, a suitable mix provides proper water and fertilizer retention, promotes good aeration, and maintains its structure under the appropriate watering schedule. Both soil-based and soilless mixes are useful; the "correct" mix is the formulation that suits the plants best. Many different mixes are available commercially, or they may be made up from materials on hand.

Watering and feeding

When in growth, some plants need to be watered freely, which means that the potting mix should be kept evenly moist but not waterlogged. Others need only moderate watering; allow the soil mix to dry out partially before watering again. To water sparingly, allow the soil mix to dry almost completely between applications. When plants cease active growth, they need less water; most should be kept moist so the soil mix has just enough water to avoid desiccation. Some plants, such as many cacti and other succulents, must be kept totally (or almost totally) dry in winter or when dormant; resume watering as growth restarts.

Plants in containers are restricted in their quest for nutrients, and usually need fertilizer in the growing season. Most conveniently applied in liquid form, balanced commercial fertilizers contain the nutrients needed for plant growth – nitrogen, phosphorus, and potassium (NPK) – and a full range of trace elements.

Ventilation and humidity

Good ventilation serves to control temperature, maintains a flow of fresh air, and moderates levels of atmospheric humidity. Ventilation is particularly necessary with high humidity, to avoid stagnant air in which fungal diseases thrive. In this encyclopedia, low humidity is defined as less than 50% relative humidity (RH) – a percentage of saturation of the air. Moderate humidity is 51–60% RH, and high humidity 61% RH and above. If damping down is impractical, humidity may be increased locally by grouping plants on trays of moist gravel or expanded clay granules.

GREENHOUSE ENVIRONMENTS

TEMPERATURE REGIME	VENTILATION	HUMIDITY	SHADING
COLD Above freezing; 32°F (0°C).	Ventilate whenever necessary in summer (or during bright days in spring or autumn) to lower temperature and to prevent excessive humidity. During cold weather, ventilate whenever possible to prevent stagnant conditions; during severe cold, take care to ensure that the correct temperature is maintained, especially at night.	Natural levels of humidity are adequate.	Admit full light in winter; shade vulnerable plants in summer.
COOL Day: 41–50°F (5–10°C) Night: 36°F (2°C)		Damp down in summer to keep cool, with low humidity.	Admit full light in winter; shade vulnerable plants in summer.
TEMPERATE Day: 50–55°F (10–13°C) Night: 45°F (7°C)		Damp down in summer to keep cool, with moderate humidity.	Admit full light in winter; shade vulnerable plants in summer.
WARM Day: 55–64°F (13–18°C) or above Night: 55°F (13°C)		Provide high humidity in summer; reduce in winter.	Admit full light in winter; shade vulnerable plants in summer.

GARDENING UNDER LIGHTS

The light produced by fluorescent or incandescent tubes and bulbs (or a combination of the two) may be used to grow a wide range of plants.

Many gesneriads (such as African violets and episcias), begonias, succulents, ferns, and a host of other plants thrive under these conditions. Careful attention must be paid to watering and fertilizing, and pests and diseases may develop quickly. Light systems are also useful for starting seeds and for forcing bulbs. In all applications, it is essential to determine the most beneficial distance from the light units: germinating seeds may be placed directly under fluorescent tubes, whereas some gesneriads and ferns will thrive up to 18in (45cm) from the lights.

Shared needs
Where possible, plants under glass should be grouped with others that need similar levels of warmth, light, nutrients, water, and humidity.

Pruning

Woody plants are pruned for a number of reasons: to maintain good health by removing dead, diseased, or damaged wood; to encourage the formation of vigorous and bushy growth; to produce plants that have a sound structure when mature; and to shape and direct growth so that plants display their decorative features to optimum effect. Regular pruning also improves the supply of strong, young growth, which normally produces flowers and fruit in greater abundance and of better quality than does old or declining growth.

PRUNING CUTS

Different techniques are used to prune plants, depending on whether buds are alternately or oppositely arranged (see right). Keep tools clean and blades sharp so that they do not produce a ragged cut that is slow to heal. Use pruners to sever small branches up to about ½in (1cm) in diameter. For larger branches, use loppers or a pruning saw to avoid crushing plant tissue.

Alternate buds
For plants with alternate buds, angle the cut away from and just above an outward-facing bud.

Opposite buds
For plants with opposite buds, cut straight across immediately above a strong pair of buds.

Principles of pruning

Before making any cuts, assess the overall shape of the plant. Never cut indiscriminately. Begin by removing any wood that is dead, diseased, or damaged, since this helps to promote plant hygiene and good health. The timing and nature of subsequent pruning depend on the age and type of flowering wood, and also on an individual species' vigor and ability to produce new growth in response to pruning. Follow one of the 13 regimes set out on pp.26–27, as recommended in the introduction to each genus of woody plants.

Provided that a plant is healthy, has adequate nutrients, and tolerates drastic pruning, the harder a shoot is pruned, the more vigorously it will grow. Conversely, light pruning results in limited regrowth.

Woody plants that flower before midsummer usually bloom on the previous year's growth. They are therefore normally pruned after flowering, so that new growth has a full season in which to mature before blooming the following year. Most plants that bloom after midsummer flower on the current season's growth. They are pruned in winter or spring, then flower later in the season on new growth. Pruning in spring (when the sap is rising) should be avoided for plants that "bleed" (leak sap) when cut. Pruning of evergreens is best carried out in midspring, so that shoots develop after the danger of hard frost has passed.

Formative pruning

The aim of formative pruning is to produce a balanced framework of sturdy, well-spaced branches that permits maximum light and air to reach the entire plant. Most evergreen trees and shrubs require little formative pruning, but may need light shaping after planting, to ensure balanced growth. Formative pruning of deciduous species should be carried out in the dormant season, either at or soon after planting. For the vast majority of woody plants, formative pruning follows the procedure illustrated (center right). If a young shrub does not have a balanced framework, cut it back hard; then select the strongest, most evenly spaced branches from the resulting growth to form the new framework, and cut out the rest. Some plants (mainly those assigned pruning group 1) need only minimal pruning; they include slow-growing shrubs with an intricate, ornamental branch structure whose appearance is easily spoiled by cutting back.

Restrictive pruning

It is best to select plants whose natural size suits an allotted area in a garden, rather than prune to restrict size. Under glass, however, such pruning is often unavoidable. Follow the principles outlined above with regard to timing, referring also to the pruning group. However, the pruning should be more severe than usual, and in many cases must be performed every year. Aim to reduce the previous season's growth by one- to two-thirds of its length after flowering, retaining only the strongest shoots to maintain a well-spaced and open framework.

Renovation (renewal) pruning

Some old or overgrown shrubs – such as those that produce new shoots from the base or from old wood – may be rejuvenated by hard pruning. Renovate deciduous shrubs after flowering or when dormant, and evergreen shrubs in midspring. For drastic renovation, cut back all main stems to 12–18in (30–45cm) above the ground. Select the strongest shoots that then sprout to produce a new framework, and cut out the rest. However, for all but the most resilient shrubs, it is best to stagger pruning over 3 years, as illustrated (bottom right). After both types, mulch the soil to a depth of 2–4in (5–10cm); apply a slow-release, balanced fertilizer; and keep the plant well watered.

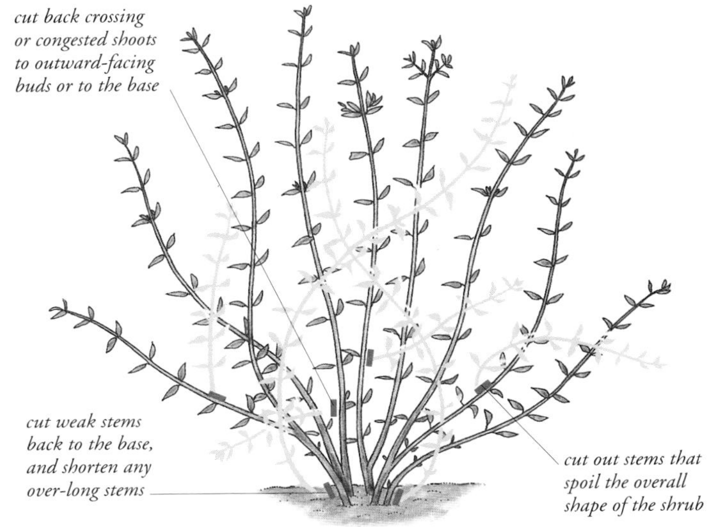

cut back crossing or congested shoots to outward-facing buds or to the base
cut weak stems back to the base, and shorten any over-long stems
cut out stems that spoil the overall shape of the shrub

Formative pruning
Formative pruning aims to produce a balanced framework of strong, evenly spaced stems. After planting, remove dead, diseased, and damaged wood. Cut out or shorten crossing, rubbing, or congested stems, and cut all weak growth back to the base.

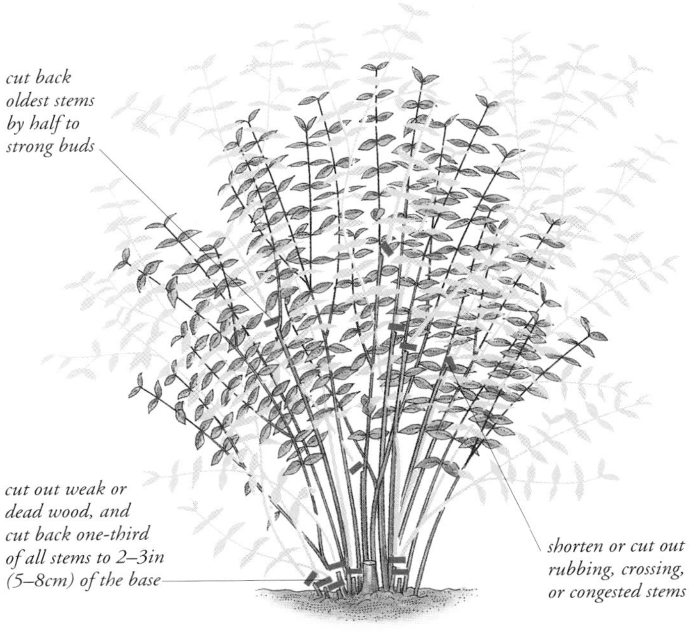

cut back oldest stems by half to strong buds
cut out weak or dead wood, and cut back one-third of all stems to 2–3in (5–8cm) of the base
shorten or cut out rubbing, crossing, or congested stems

Gradual renovation
To renovate a woody plant, remove dead wood and cut back up to one-third of the oldest stems close to the base. Of those that remain, shorten the oldest. Repeat in the following two years, cutting back the remaining old main stems.

Pruning groups

In this encyclopedia, all woody plants that require pruning are assigned to one of the groups outlined here (see relevant genus cultivation notes). An individual species may be assigned to a group different from that of the genus, or may be assigned more than one group if it can be grown in a variety of ways. Because all woody plants require routine removal of dead, diseased, and damaged wood, this is not stated for each group. In groups 10–13, the correct time to prune depends on the type of flowering wood: plants that flower on the previous year's growth usually bloom between early spring and early summer; those that bloom on the current year's growth usually flower after midsummer. In the illustrations, red cut marks show where to prune.

GROUP 1 e.g. *Acer palmatum*, *Hamamelis*, some *Magnolia* species

TYPE Evergreen and deciduous trees and some deciduous shrubs that flower on previous or current year's growth and need minimal pruning.

ACTION Remove wayward or crossing shoots to maintain permanent, healthy framework.

WHEN In late winter or early spring, when dormant; some in late summer or early autumn to prevent bleeding of sap.

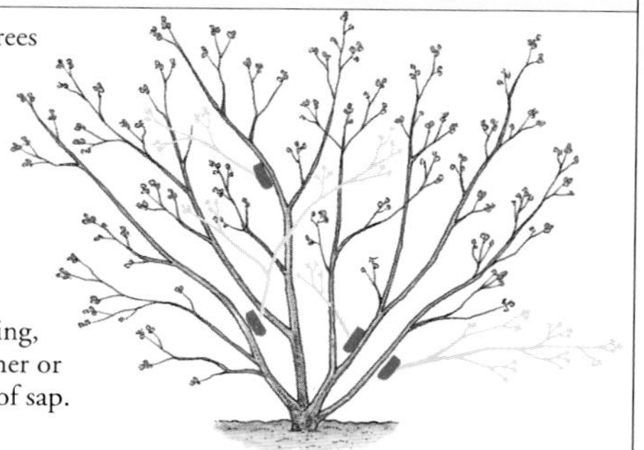

GROUP 2 e.g. *Buddleja alternifolia*, *Deutzia*, *Forsythia*, *Philadelphus*

TYPE Deciduous shrubs (and a few trees) that flower in spring or early summer on previous year's growth.

ACTION Cut back flowered shoots to strong buds or young lower or basal growth. On established plants, cut back about one-third to one-fifth of old shoots to the base, to promote replacement growth.

WHEN Annually, after flowering.

GROUP 3 e.g. *Cytisus scoparius* and hybrids, *Kerria*

TYPE Deciduous shrubs that flower in spring or early summer on previous year's growth and produce new growth at or near ground level.

ACTION Cut back flowered shoots to young sideshoots or to strong buds low down on branch framework, to encourage strong new growth.

WHEN Annually, after flowering.

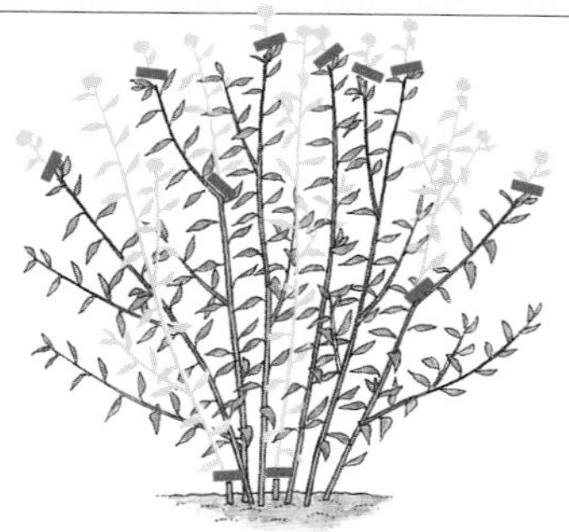

GROUP 4 e.g. *Hydrangea macrophylla*

TYPE Deciduous shrubs that flower in mid- or late summer to autumn on previous year's growth.

ACTION Trim off last season's flowerheads to the first bud or pair of buds beneath each flowerhead. With established plants, cut back about one-third to one-quarter of the oldest flowered shoots to the base, to promote replacement growth.

WHEN Annually, in early or midspring.

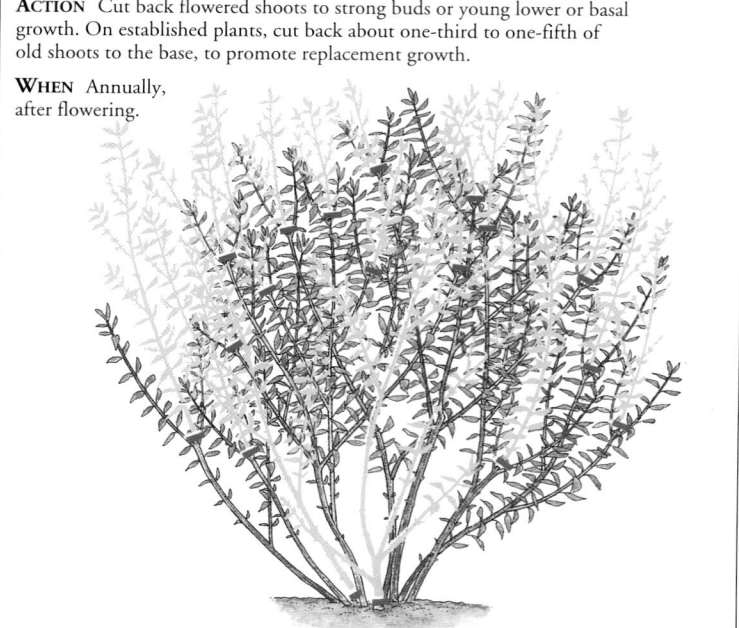

GROUP 5 e.g. *Prunus triloba*

TYPE Deciduous shrubs that flower between late winter and early spring on previous year's growth.

ACTION Cut back all stems to strong buds or to developing shoots close to the base of the plant, to promote replacement growth.

WHEN Annually, after flowering.

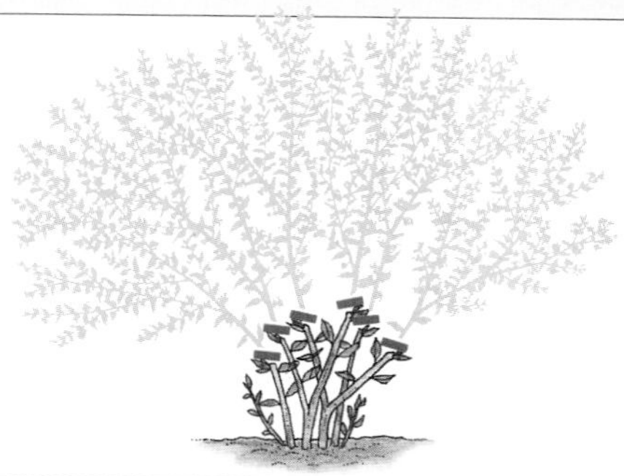

GROUP 6 e.g. *Buddleja davidii*, *Caryopteris*, *Perovskia*

TYPE Deciduous shrubs that flower in mid- or late summer to autumn on current year's growth.

ACTION Cut back to low permanent framework. For subshrubs, and for drastic renovation, cut back all flowered stems close to the base.

WHEN Annually, as buds begin to swell in early spring.

GROUP 7 e.g. *Cornus alba*, *Cotinus*, some *Eucalyptus* species, *Sambucus*

TYPE Deciduous trees and shrubs that, when pruned hard, produce colorful winter stems, or large or brightly hued foliage, as ornamental features. Plants that flower on previous year's wood do not bloom if pruned this way.

ACTION Cut back stems to within 2 or 3 buds of the base (suckering species close to base) or to permanent framework. Feed or apply well-rotted manure, and mulch to compensate for loss of vigorous wood.

WHEN Annually, in early spring.

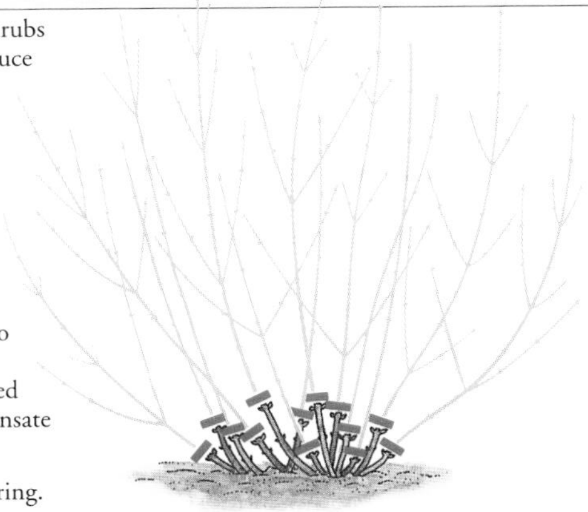

GROUP 8 e.g. *Camellia*, *Rhododendron*

TYPE Evergreen shrubs that flower between winter and early summer on previous or current year's growth and need minimal pruning.

ACTION Trim or lightly cut back shoots that spoil symmetry. Deadhead regularly if practical (unless fruit are desired).

WHEN Annually, after flowering. Remove dead and damaged growth in midspring.

GROUP 9 e.g. *Eucryphia*, *Prunus laurocerasus*, *P. lusitanica*

TYPE Evergreen shrubs that flower between midsummer and late autumn on previous or current year's growth, or that bear insignificant flowers, and that need minimal pruning.

ACTION Trim or lightly cut back shoots that spoil symmetry. Shrubs grown for foliage often tolerate harder pruning. Deadhead regularly if practical (unless fruit are desired).

WHEN Annually, or as necessary, in mid- or late spring.

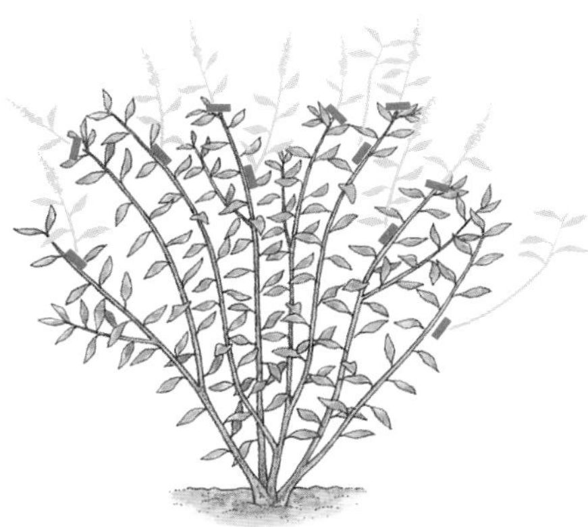

GROUP 10 e.g. *Calluna*, *Erica*, *Lavandula*

TYPE Evergreen shrubs that flower on previous year's growth in spring or early summer, or on current year's growth in late summer or autumn.

ACTION Cut back flowered shoots to within ½–1in (1.5–2.5cm) of previous year's growth.

WHEN Annually:
- after flowering, if flowering on previous year's growth.
- in early or midspring, if flowering on current year's growth.

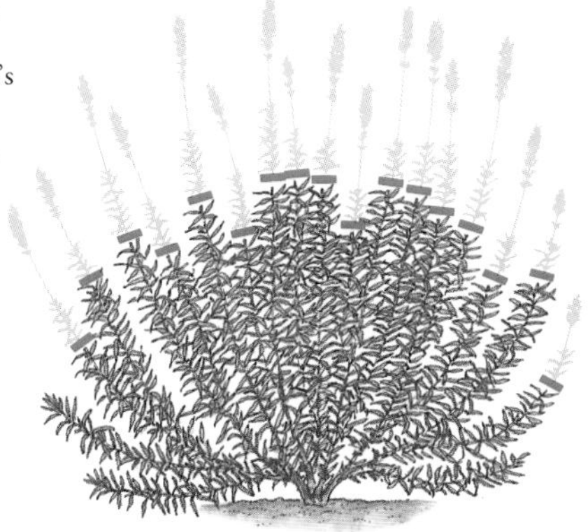

GROUP 11 e.g. *Akebia*, *Clematis montana*, *Fallopia baldschuanica*

TYPE Vigorous, deciduous and evergreen climbers that flower on previous or current year's growth and need no regular pruning.

ACTION Trim to fit available space; carry out renovation pruning as needed (see p.25).

WHEN Annually, or as needed:
- after flowering, if flowering on previous year's growth.
- from late winter to spring, if flowering on current year's growth.

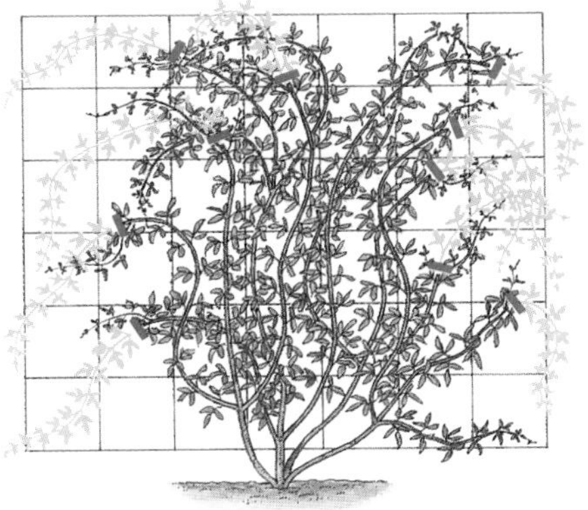

GROUP 12 e.g. *Bougainvillea*, *Solanum crispum*

TYPE Less vigorous, deciduous and evergreen climbers that flower on previous or current year's growth. (For *Wisteria*, see cultivation notes in genus introduction.)

ACTION "Spur prune" by cutting back sideshoots to within 3 or 4 buds of permanent framework. Thin out overcrowded shoots.

WHEN Annually:
- after flowering, if flowering on previous year's growth.
- in late winter or early spring, if flowering on current year's growth.

FORMING A SPUR *Cut back to within 3 or 4 buds of main stem.*

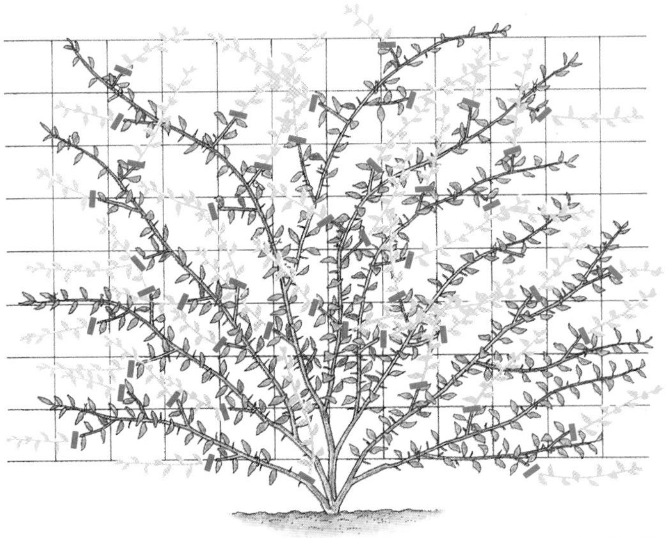

GROUP 13 e.g. *Ceanothus*, *Chaenomeles*

TYPE Wall-trained, deciduous and evergreen shrubs that flower on previous or current year's growth. (For *Cotoneaster* and *Pyracantha*, see cultivation notes in each genus introduction.)

ACTION Cut back flowered shoots to within 2–4 buds of permanent framework. Trim outward-facing shoots and those growing toward the wall.

WHEN Annually:
- after flowering, if flowering on previous year's growth.
- in late winter or early spring, if flowering on current year's growth.

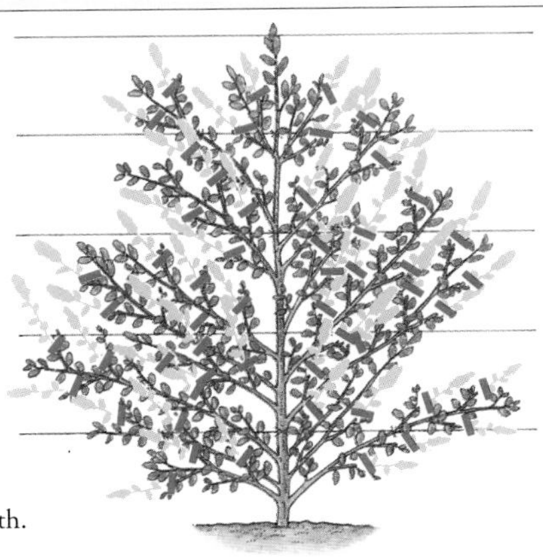

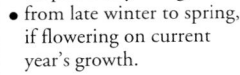

Propagation

Plants propagate naturally in ways that can be exploited by gardeners to increase stocks or preserve the distinct characteristics of individual plants. The cultivation notes for each genus described in this encyclopedia specify the methods that may be used. Techniques fall into two categories: propagation by seed or by vegetative means. Raising plants from seed is relatively simple, although variants of garden origin are unlikely to breed true from garden-collected seed (see p.11). Such plants should instead be increased by asexual, vegetative means, such as from suckers; by division, grafting, or layering; or by taking cuttings.

Propagation from seed

Most seed is best sown as soon as ripe. If necessary, soak fruits in water first, then extract seeds by rubbing the flesh, and allow to dry. Hard-coated seeds may need soaking or scarification before germination. Soak in recently boiled water for between 10 minutes and 72 hours, depending on the species; viable seeds will swell, and should then be sown immediately. To scarify small seeds, abrade with fine sandpaper; with large seeds, file the coats or chip (nick) with a knife. Some seeds need cold stratification to break dormancy: sow in a cold frame or open frame for exposure to winter cold. Alternatively, place in moist peat inside a plastic bag, and keep warm for 3 or 4 days, then place in a refrigerator at 34–41°F (1–5°C). Sow on germination – after 3–18 weeks, depending on the species.

Seed may be sown *in situ* or in a tray or seedbed. Sow thinly or in rows to lessen the danger of damping off, and, except for tiny seeds or seeds that need light, cover with soil, soil mix, perlite, or vermiculite. As a rule, maintain seeds of plants from the tropics at 66–75°F (19–24°C); from warm-temperate and subtropical areas at 55–64°F (13–18°C); from cool-temperate areas at 43–54°F (6–12°C).

Sowing in a seed tray
Sow seed thinly and evenly onto moist seed starting mix and cover, if required, to its own depth in sieved mix. Cover with glass, shade from hot sun, and keep at an appropriate temperature.

Pricking out
When seed leaves are strong enough to be handled, prick out singly into cell packs or small containers. Pot on when large enough, or harden off, then plant out in open ground.

Division

Division is the most rapid means of increasing perennials that have a spreading rootstock and produce new shoots annually from the crown, as well as rhizomatous plants and some tuberous ones. The term is also loosely used to describe the separation of offsets from clump-forming bulbous plants (see p.45).

Division is best carried out when the plant is dormant, normally between late autumn and early spring, but never in very wet or cold weather. However, fleshy-rooted plants, or those that are not fully hardy, are best divided in early spring, when young plants are less likely to suffer damage from cold.

Lift the parent plant and shake off excess soil from the roots. Separate the plant into sections, using forks, a spade, or a sharp knife, so that each part has a good root system and several new shoots or growth buds. Discard old, damaged, or unproductive pieces, and replant vigorous material immediately, at the original depth of soil. Small divisions may be potted up and grown on in a cold frame until established. For plants with thick rhizomes, cut the rhizomes into sections; retain at least one growing point on each section. Dust cut surfaces with fungicide before replanting at the original depth.

Loose, fleshy roots
Lift the parent plant and shake off surplus soil. Separate the plant into sections by hand. Replant vigorous, healthy sections, each with several new shoots, at their previous depth of soil.

Fibrous roots and woody crowns
Pry apart fibrous-rooted plants using two forks set back to back. To section plants with tough, woody crowns, use a spade or knife to cut through the roots, trying to avoid growth buds.

Layering, suckers, and grafting

Layering is a simple technique for increasing plants whose stems will produce roots if wounded: the stem is pegged to the ground and left to form roots, while still attached to the parent plant.

Suckering plants, such as *Cornus alba* and kerrias, naturally produce suckers that may be detached and inserted as already rooted plants.

Several trees, shrubs, and house- or greenhouse plants may be increased by air layering. Cut a slit in an aerial stem, pack the resulting tongue with a wad of damp sphagnum moss, and enclose it in a plastic sleeve. Once roots have grown into the moss, which may take up to 2 years, separate the layered stem from the parent plant and pot up.

Grafting involves taking the stem of one plant and uniting it with the rootstock of a closely related plant. It is used to increase stocks of newly bred woody cultivars and to improve the rate of development or flowering of slow-growing plants by joining them to more vigorous ones. The union is achieved by making a close-fitting join between woody parts of the rootstock (the plant with roots and stem) and the scion (the plant with top-growth). Budding is a form of grafting, in which a vegetative bud of one plant is grafted onto another plant.

Simple layering
Wound the underside of a pliable young stem. Apply rooting hormone, peg the wounded section down, and cover with soil. Bend the stem tip upright and tie to a stake. Sever when roots have formed.

Suckers
To detach a sucker, uncover its long suckering root and sever it close to the parent plant. Dig up the sucker with its own fibrous roots, replant, then cut back top-growth by half.

Taking cuttings

Raising plants from cuttings is one of the most common methods of vegetative propagation. In general, the technique involves taking a small piece of material from a living plant. After insertion in a rooting medium (usually in an enclosed area to maintain humidity), it develops new roots and may then be grown on until large enough to be planted out. There are three main types of cutting: stem, leaf, and root. Several types of stem cutting are used, differentiated by the ripeness of the wood. Instructions for propagation from each of the main types are given in the table below.

Two other types of cutting (not listed below) are also used. Semi-ripe leaf-bud cuttings are trimmed just above an axillary leaf bud and ¾in (2cm) below it. Wound ¼in (6mm) of the base, and insert in cutting mix with the leaf axil just above the surface. Heel cuttings are taken as other stem cuttings, using sideshoots with a heel (sliver) of old wood at the base.

Simple propagating case

Use a clear plastic bag, inflated and supported by stakes or wire hoops, as an alternative to a propagating case.

Cuttings from conifers

For most conifers, propagate from semi-ripe cuttings, choosing leaders or sideshoots typical of the parent plant.

GUIDE TO TAKING CUTTINGS

	Type of cutting	When to cut	Cutting material	Preparation	Rooting medium	Rooting environment
Trees, shrubs, and climbers (woody plants)	Softwood and greenwood cuttings 	Spring to early summer.	Soft, pliable tips of fast-growing, non-flowering shoots of current season's growth, with 3–5 pairs of leaves. Greenwood is slightly firmer.	Take early in morning, and seal in an opaque plastic bag to conserve moisture. Do not allow to wilt. Trim to 3–4in (8–10cm) long, with a straight cut just below a node. Remove leaves on lowest third of cutting.	Insert into standard cutting mix, or equal parts peat (or substitute) and perlite or sharp sand. Ensure that leaves do not touch. Water with fungicide solution.	Place in a mist unit or propagating case at 64–75°F (18–24°C). Remove fallen leaves daily. Apply fungicidal spray weekly.
	Semi-ripe and ripewood cuttings 	Semi-ripe: mid- or late summer, occasionally early autumn. Ripewood: early autumn to early winter.	Soft-tipped shoots of current season's growth, firm and woody at the base. Cut just below a node for nodal cuttings, or with a heel of older wood at the base.	Remove sideshoots. Trim nodal cuttings to 3–4in (8–10cm) long; heel cuttings to 2–3in (5–8cm) long; trim heel. Remove leaves on lowest third, and for semi-ripes also soft tips. Reduce large leaves by half. Wound 1–1½in (2.5–4cm) of the stem base.	Dip base of cutting in rooting hormone. Insert into standard cutting mix, or equal parts peat (or substitute) and perlite or sharp sand. Ensure that leaves do not touch. Water with fungicide solution.	Place in a mist unit or propagating case at 70°F (21°C), if bottom heat is needed, or use an insulated cold frame (vital for ripewood). Shade from hot sun. Remove fallen leaves daily. Once rooted, apply liquid fertilizer every 2 weeks.
	Hardwood cuttings 	Early autumn (after leaf fall) to early winter.	Leafless shoots of fully ripe current year's growth, cut at join with previous year's growth. On pithy stems, take with a heel of older wood at the base.	Trim to 6–9in (15–23cm) long, with the top cut just above a bud or pair of buds, and the bottom cut just below a bud or pair of buds. Make a wound in the stem base up to ½in (1.5cm) long, if difficult to root.	Dip base in rooting hormone. Insert in a trench in a prepared bed; line the bottom with coarse sand (vital in heavy soil) and cover with soil. Alternatively, insert in containers in a cold frame; use equal parts peat (or substitute) and sharp sand.	Firm into the trench with the top 1–2in (2.5–5cm) of the cutting visible above soil level; check and re-firm after frost. If slow-rooting, place in bundles in a sand bed in a cold frame; move to the trench in spring.
	Basal stem cuttings 	Early or mid-spring.	New shoots, when about 1½–2in (4–5cm) high, as first leaves unfurl, taken from close to the base or crown, with a heel of older, woody tissue at the base.	Trim to 1½–2in (4–5cm) long, with a straight cut at the base, and with a heel of basal tissue. Remove leaves on lowest third of cutting.	Dip base in rooting hormone. Insert singly or severally into standard cutting mix, or equal parts peat (or substitute) and perlite or sharp sand. Ensure that leaves do not touch. Water with fungicide solution.	Place in a propagating case or cold frame, or cover with a clear plastic bag supported by stakes or wire hoops.
Perennials (non-woody plants)	Stem-tip (soft-tip) cuttings 	Spring to autumn, or any time in growing season when suitable shoots are available.	Soft, pliable tips of fast-growing, non-flowering shoots, 3–5in (8–13cm) long, cut just above leaf nodes.	Take early in morning, and seal in an opaque plastic bag to conserve moisture. Do not allow to wilt. Trim to 2–3in (5–8cm) long, with a straight cut just below a node. Remove leaves on lowest third of cutting.	Insert into standard cutting mix, or equal parts peat (or substitute) and perlite or sharp sand. Ensure that leaves do not touch. Water with fungicide solution.	Place in a mist unit or propagating case, or cover with a clear plastic bag supported by stakes or wire hoops. Shade from hot sun. Remove fallen leaves daily.
	Root cuttings 	In dormant period, usually late winter.	Vigorous young roots, preferably at least ¼in (6mm) in diameter, taken from close to the crown of the parent plant.	Trim thick roots to 2–4in (5–10cm) long; thin roots to 3–5in (8–13cm) long. Make a straight cut at the proximal end (nearest to crown) and a slanted cut at the distal (opposite) end to ensure correct orientation. Remove fibrous roots. Dust with fungicide powder.	Insert thick roots upright in containers of moist standard cutting mix, the proximal end flush with the surface. Lay thin roots flat in trays; cover with mix. Top-dress with sharp sand.	Place in a cold frame or propagating case. Do not water until rooted.
	Leaf cuttings 	Any time of year.	Mature, healthy, undamaged leaves, cut off close to the bases of the leaf stalks.	Whole leaves, e.g., *Saintpaulia*: cut leaf stalk straight across, 1¼in (3cm) below leaf blade. Half-leaf sections, e.g., *Streptocarpus*: cut in half, removing the midrib. Scored leaf/leaf squares, e.g., Rex begonias: make ½in (1.5cm) cuts across undersides of main veins.	Use equal parts fine sand and peat (or substitute). Insert whole leaves upright, with leaf blades just above mix. Pin scored leaves or leaf squares flat on mix, cut side down. Insert half-leaf sections cut edge down. Water with fungicide solution.	Place in a propagating case at 64–75°F (18–24°C). Keep in bright indirect light; always shade from hot sun.

Plant problems

By following good gardening practices, many plant problems can be prevented before they arise. Yet even in the most carefully attended gardens, leaves may be eaten; a tree, shrub, or plant may wilt; buds may form, but fail to open; or weeds may grow. It often is easy to see the symptom of a plant problem, but it is more important to link that symptom with a specific source and then choose an appropriate method of control. By recognizing the plant problem in the early stage, treatment can be more effective.

LADYBUG

Pests

Pests are animals that cause damage to cultivated plants. Most are small invertebrates such as mites, nematodes, sowbugs, and millipedes; the largest group by far in this category are the insects. Larger animals, such as slugs, rabbits, and deer, also cause problems. Pests may damage or destroy any part of a plant or, in some cases, the entire plant. They feed in various ways – by sap sucking, leaf mining, defoliating, or tunneling. Sometimes they cause abnormal growths known as galls. Some pests also indirectly damage plants by spreading diseases. Many insects and animals are beneficial to gardens (see p.31).

Diseases

A plant disease is any pathological condition caused by other organisms, such as bacteria, fungi, or viruses. Symptoms vary considerably in appearance and severity, but the growth or health of the plant is almost always affected and, in severe attacks, the plant may be killed. The rate of infection is affected by factors such as weather and growing conditions. Symptoms such as discoloration, distortion, and wilting are typical signs of infection.

Disorders

Plant disorders usually result from nutritional deficiencies or from unsuitable growing or storage conditions. An inappropriate temperature range, inadequate or erratic water or food supply, poor light, or unsatisfactory atmospheric conditions may all lead to physiological plant disorders. The problems become apparent through symptoms such as discolored leaves and stunted growth. A plant that lacks water, food, or the appropriate environmental conditions not only will appear unhealthy, but also will be far less able to resist attack from either insect pests or diseases caused by fungi, viruses, or bacteria.

Weeds

Simply put, a weed is a plant growing where it is not wanted. Any plant, no matter how choice and rare initially, has the potential for becoming a weed if the site is favorable. Most common weeds germinate quickly and are fast-growing, and thus can outcompete desirable plants for space, water, light, and nutrients. Many are very adaptable, growing in a wide range of conditions, although some are site-specific. Most weeds produce seed freely or reproduce easily from tubers, rhizomes, or bits of root left in the ground.

Control weeds by hand-pulling, hoeing, mulching, or growing plants closely together to prevent the weeds from becoming established. They may also be treated with herbicides; although they are generally less toxic than insecticides, they must still be handled with care (see box above).

Preventing problems

Good cultivation practices and simple garden hygiene considerably reduce the risk of plant problems. Buy only vigorous, healthy plants with sound, uncongested root systems (see p.22), and try to grow pest- and disease-resistant cultivars wherever possible. To help prevent physiological disorders, select plants for sites in the garden where conditions match their specific needs (see pp.20–21). Thereafter, provide the correct amount of water (see p.22), and maintain adequate levels of nutrients in the soil (see p.21). Avoid over-watering and over-fertilizing; both can kill plants. Mulch beds and borders annually to suppress weeds (see p.23), and clear away all withered or damaged plant material, composting only healthy plant waste. Where feasible, grow annuals, vegetables, and bulbs in different sites each year to lessen the buildup of pests and diseases.

POTASSIUM DEFICIENCY

BLACKSPOT

Evaluating the problem

It is important to know the normal growth habit of the afflicted plant and thereby correct any environmental conditions or cultural practices. In assessing the extent of plant damage, determine whether treatment is timely and worthwhile. Application of any control may be too late to be effective or simply not necessary; for example, in a minor insect infestation, tolerance of slight damage might be best.

Methods of control

Once a problem occurs, it is always important to tackle it quickly. Two common strategies are chemical and biological control. Chemical control refers to the destruction of pests by applying a synthetic compound, such as a fungicide, an insecticide, or a weedkiller, to plants or the soil. Biological control involves attracting beneficial insects, bacteria, or fungi that attack specific pests; for example, to attract hoverflies, which feed on aphids, grow French marigolds (*Tagetes patula*). Beneficials may also be introduced (see p.31).

USING CHEMICALS SAFELY

Pesticide registration in Canada is the responsibility of Health Canada, but individual provinces can also ban the use of specific chemicals within their jurisdiction. Garden centres and nurseries in your region will only sell those that are approved for home gardeners to use. Many municipalities have, or are considering, banning the use of pesticides completely, so check locally before using them.

Pesticide labeling is determined by law, and the label is considered a legal document. Follow instructions on labels, and use only as indicated. For example, if a pesticide is labeled for use only as a wettable powder for spraying, it cannot be applied dry directly to the soil. If you have any questions about pesticides, consult the manufacturer or your supplier for help.

Always take precautions when using chemicals:

- Think before you spray: is it necessary?
- Choose the right chemical for the job.
- Heed the warnings on the label.
- Do not mix chemicals unless labeling indicates it is safe to do so.
- Apply the chemical at the frequency and rate stated on the label.
- Do not spray in the wind, to avoid drift and damage to nearby plants.
- Do not spray in hot weather or in bright sunlight, to avoid "scorching."
- Always wear protective clothing.
- Avoid contact with skin, eyes, nose, and mouth.
- Keep pets and children away.
- Never eat, drink, or smoke.
- After application, thoroughly wash any apparatus you intend to reuse.
- Wash hands and face thoroughly after use, or bathe or take a shower.
- Store chemicals in original containers with original labels and inserts.
- Wrap damaged apparatus and empty containers in paper, and dispose of according to local regulations.
- Never dump unused chemicals; dispose of them properly.

INVASIVE PLANTS

Many aggressively growing non-native plants have become established in North America, posing a threat to indigenous flora and ecosystems. Certain invaders, such as Norway maple, several honeysuckles, and common buckthorn, are already so well established over a broad area that eradication is nearly impossible.

Because prevention is far easier than cure, invasive plants need to be identified and controlled when their populations are small and localized. Invasive characteristics include rapid growth, abundant establishment along woodland edges, indifference to north- or south-facing slopes, ease of germination, and fruit eaten (and transported to new sites) by birds.

THE PURPLE MENACE
*Purple loosestrife (*Lythrum*) has displaced native plants and disturbed wetlands throughout much of North America.*

Organic issues and native plants

Gardens (and gardeners) do not exist separately from the rest of the natural world. Forgetting this essential fact can lead, in the short or long term, to disaster on a local or global scale. Recognizing this, many gardeners employ techniques variously termed organic, natural, eco-aware, or green. These techniques consider the complex balance among plants, animals, and humans, as well as the influence of regional factors such as soil, geology, climate, and weather.

Applying an organic approach

Organic controls use natural methods to help plants resist pests and disease. For the basic organic gardening approach to pest control, see Preventing problems, p.30.

The simplest solution to rid pests may sometimes be to physically remove them, for instance, taking gypsy moth egg cases from trees or hand-picking slugs from the soil. Install a fence around the garden to keep animals out. Also use sticky paper, metal plant collars, or other easily contructed organic traps. There are a few chemical preparations, like pyrethrum and sulfur dust, that originate from natural sources; however, they work on contact, rather than being systemic, and often require several applications to be effective. Caution is recommended for use of another botanical insecticide, rotenone, a nerve poison toxic to birds and fish. Other organic remedies include biodegradable soaps, diatomaceous earth, and dormant oils. Even homemade cures, like garlic-pepper solution, are effective against a wide range of insects and animals.

Growing a particular plant in the same ground for a number of years may also lead to problems such as "rose-sick soil," so rotate plantings where possible or bring in fresh soil and compost to rejuvenate the beds. Through companion planting, two or more kinds of plants may benefit from being situated near each other. Although more widely used in vegetable gardening, companion planting may also benefit ornamentals.

Employing biological pest control

Biological control involves the deliberate attraction or introduction of natural enemies such as predators, parasites, and diseases. This treatment can be effective outdoors or in the relatively controlled environment of the greenhouse, where pests may have developed resistance or even immunity to chemicals.

Specific biological controls include predatory mites (*Metaseiulus occidentalis* and *Amblyseius* species) for spider mites and thrips; the parasitic wasp (*Encarsia formosa*) for whiteflies; ladybugs (*Cryptolaemus* and other genera) for aphids, mealybugs, and soft scale insects; *Aphidoletes* flies for aphids; nematodes (*Heterorhabditis* species) for black vine weevil larvae; and various strains of the bacterial disease *Bacillus thuringiensis* (Bt) for caterpillars.

Biological controls rarely give 100 percent control, and it often takes a season for populations to reach effective levels. Avoid spraying pesticides when attempting to establish insects, mites, and nematodes; many beneficials can be wiped out with one pesticide application, whereas pests that have developed resistance to chemicals may survive.

Many creatures are beneficial throughout the garden. Raccoons, skunks, frogs, snakes, and toads feed on a wide range of plant pests. Earthworms and microorganisms break down organic matter in the soil. Although bats, birds, spiders, ants, and wasps can create damage to certain plants or become garden nuisances, they are often helpful because they prey on insects, thereby helping to keep insect populations in balance.

Maintaining a diversity of plants and even some weeds in the garden will provide food and shelter for beneficials, as will allowing a corner of the garden to remain "wild." Rock and brush piles, water features, and bird- and bat houses are particularly attractive to beneficial organisms. Plants that are attractive to beneficial insects include members of the Asteraceae, such as *Aster*, *Echinacea*, and *Solidago*; members of the Apiaceae, such as *Angelica*, *Anethum*, *Foeniculum*, and *Petroselinum*; and *Asclepias*, *Nepeta*, and *Sedum*.

Integrated Pest Management (IPM)

IPM employs a variety of techniques and information to reduce or maintain pest populations at tolerable levels (the threshold levels), while providing protection against hazards to humans, animals, and the environment. An effective IPM program typically contains the following elements:

1. Carefully recorded observations, on a regular basis, of pests, beneficial organisms, weather conditions, and plant growth.
2. Determination of acceptable levels of damage.
3. Selected treatments that are least disruptive to natural controls (including predators and diseases) and least hazardous to the environment. These treatments can be categorized as follows:

- Cultural practices, such as garden hygiene, plant rotation, mulching, and proper soil management.
- Mechanical practices, including hand-picking insect pests and diseased leaves, and using traps and physical barriers.
- Biocontrols, including the conservation and enhancement of predators and pathogens.
- Chemical control, starting with the least toxic pesticide, and only when damage exceeds the determined threshold.

Native and exotic plants

A "native" plant is indigenous to North America or a specific area (such as the central prairies or Newfoundland). An "exotic" plant is non-indigenous; thus a plant native to the Atlantic coast may be considered an exotic on the Pacific coast. Similarly, a "wildflower" can be a native plant or an exotic that has adapted to its surroundings. Many wildflowers are cultivated in natural-looking settings and may also be grown in more formal settings, such as cottage gardens, for a casual effect. See also p.43.

Native gardening

Native gardening is the culture of indigenous or native plants that are appropriate to the conditions and geography of a given area, to simulate a natural habitat. There are many different types of habitat, such as woodlands; grasslands, including prairies and meadows; wetlands; drylands; and coastal or maritime lands. Each of these has its own specific native plant communities, and several can occur within the same habitat. Through careful plant selection and maintenance, a native garden helps to preserve the diversity of local plants and provides an environment that also benefits wildlife.

Native gardening often considers the conservation of water and other resources. As a general rule, once established, a native garden is easier to maintain than more traditionally designed landscapes based on lawns and formally defined plantings.

RARE AND ENDANGERED PLANTS

For a variety of reasons, many of the world's plant species are facing imminent extinction and require remedial action to prevent their demise. Although the primary concern for these plants is often discussed in a global context, local, regional, and federal organizations promote the preservation of various species, including those that are being exploited commercially. Among the plants in this group are many ferns, clubmosses, orchids, cacti, and rhododendrons, to name a few.

As is true for animals, the best protection for the greatest number of plants is to preserve the habitats in which they thrive. Although attempting this is generally within the scope of only governments and large businesses, individual gardeners may do their part in several ways:

- Refuse to participate in the illegal trafficking of wild-collected plants. Some plants, including many orchids and cycads, are slow-growing and difficult to cultivate, making them economically unfeasible to produce from seed or division. Such plants offered for sale have almost certainly been collected from the wild.
- Refuse to buy from suppliers if they cannot document their sources.
- Propagate plants from legally obtained sources. Wildflower societies and enthusiasts are valuable resources.
- Participate in plant rescues at construction sites, and transplant the specimens into a suitable part of your garden or local preserve.

BUYER BEWARE
Many native orchids, such as this Cypripedium reginae, *are wild-collected.*

ORNAMENTAL PLANT GROUPS

Trees

As the largest and most prominent of all garden plants, trees establish the basic, long-term framework of a garden, and their forms and colors influence the selection of other plants. Since they originate from most regions of the world, there is an immense variety of ornamental trees suitable for almost any garden site.

An ideal specimen
The best specimen trees display a succession of ornamental features. Catalpa bignonioides *'Aurea' has bronze young foliage in midspring, soon turning bright yellow, and bears bell-shaped flowers in summer, followed by bean-like pods.*

What are trees?

Trees may be broadly defined as long-lived, woody perennial plants, deciduous or evergreen, each usually with a single stem, although some, such as birches (*Betula*), may have 2 or 3 stems and still be regarded as trees. They are generally quite distinct from shrubs, which produce several or many stems that branch from or near soil level. As a group, trees are larger than shrubs, but show great variation in shape and height, ranging from dwarf cultivars only 3ft (1m) high to specimens of 300ft (90m). In horticulture, a trained or grafted shrub that is grown as a standard, even if only 6ft (2m) or so high, is often referred to as tree-like.

Most trees are angiosperms (see p.10). Exceptions include conifers, which reproduce by means of naked ovules borne on the scales of cones. Many conifers can withstand extreme climatic conditions and have distinctive, regular branching, often conical crowns, and linear, needle-like leaves. They are popular as specimen trees and for hedging and screening. Dwarf conifers are ideal in beds and containers.

Shape and size

A tree's shape and size have a strong impact on the style of a garden. Tall, narrow trees can lend a formal air; trees that are open and spreading seem more informal. Weeping trees are graceful, whereas conical trees are strong and sculptural.

When choosing a tree, take note of its size at maturity and the proximity of other plants to ensure that it will be appropriate for the size and style of the garden. A weeping willow (*Salix* x *sepulcralis* 'Chrysocoma'), for example, would overwhelm a small garden and cause problems for other plants growing nearby, whereas the same tree would look magnificent in a larger area.

Ornamental features

The leaves of trees are often highly decorative and vary greatly in size, shape, surface texture, and color. Occurring in many shades of red, green, as well as yellow, purple, and other hues, their dense mass of color can complement other plants throughout the year. Some deciduous trees, especially those originating from W. North America and parts of China, produce spectacular autumn color, including *Acer, Cornus, Fraxinus, Ginkgo, Liquidambar, Liriodendron, Nyssa, Quercus, Stewartia, Tilia*, and *Zelkova*. Leaf textures, whether smooth and glossy, or hairy or woolly, add further interest. Some trees bear aromatic foliage.

Many trees are also cultivated for their attractive, often scented flowers, which range from the small, clustered flowers of crabapple (*Malus*) to the large single blooms of *Magnolia*. The berries, pods, or other fruits that follow the flowers, with their bold shapes and colors, often persist throughout autumn or winter. Some species bear fruit only in maturity, while dioecious trees, such as most hollies (*Ilex*), must be cross-pollinated by a second plant of the opposite sex before setting fruit. Bisexual and monoecious trees can usually set their own fruit (see p.13).

Bark can also provide fascinating patterns, textures, and colors (see panel, left). Some species may need to be pruned to the base or to major branch framework annually to stimulate vividly colored new growth.

Garden uses

Trees are most commonly grown in an open site as specimen plants, visible from all angles, generally on a lawn or underplanted with groundcover, or they may be grown in a large shrub border as a focal point. Single trees can also be used to mark an entrance to or change of levels in a garden. Ideally, a specimen tree will display one or more features at different times.

In larger gardens, trees can be planted in groups. Year-round interest is ensured if both evergreen and deciduous trees are included, since the branches of deciduous trees are bare for up to half the year in cold climates.

Trees may also be used as hedging, as wind or sound barriers, to screen eyesores, to frame a view, or to line a pathway. They can give shelter from sun or rain, as well as provide a home for wildlife.

A woodland of mature trees provides a naturalistic, shady, and

DECORATIVE BARK

Bark performs the essential function of protecting the sensitive growth tissue of the tree stem or branches beneath. As their girth expands with age, the bark may fissure or peel, sometimes resulting in patterns, textures, and hues with ornamental interest. Brightly colored bark is also produced on the young branches of some trees. Bark may be conspicuously marked with lenticels (pores), which provide access for air to the inner tissues.

ATTRACTIVELY COLORED
Betula ermanii

PEELING IN FLAKES
Betula nigra

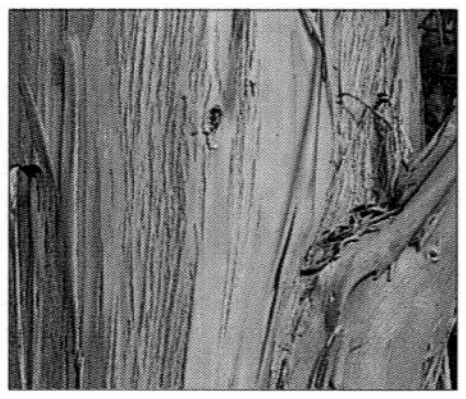

PEELING VERTICALLY
Eucalyptus johnstonii

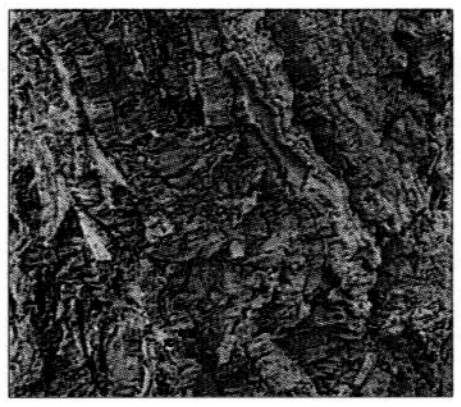

FISSURED
Quercus suber

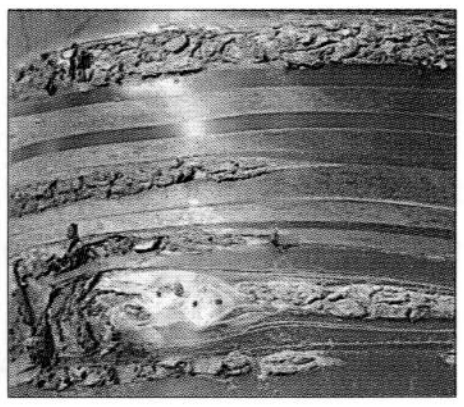

PEELING HORIZONTALLY
Prunus serrula

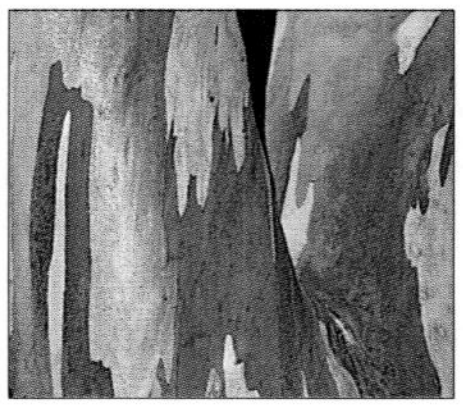

PEELING IN PATCHES
Eucalyptus pauciflora

FORMATIVE PRUNING

A young tree, particularly if deciduous, requires formative pruning in order to develop even growth. A "feathered" tree, with a stem branched to the base, can be trained either as a central-leader standard, with a clear stem and lateral branches tapering toward the bottom third of the trunk, or as a branched-head standard, with a clear stem and a more fully developed crown. Mature trees require little pruning, except to maintain their vigor and shape (see pp.26–27). More drastic pruning, such as for renewal, is described on p.25.

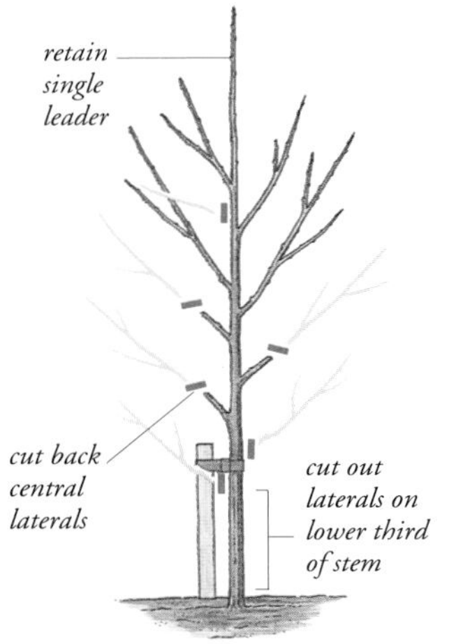

Central-leader standard
Remove the lower lateral branches and prune back all others to produce a clear stem, 6ft (1.8m) tall.

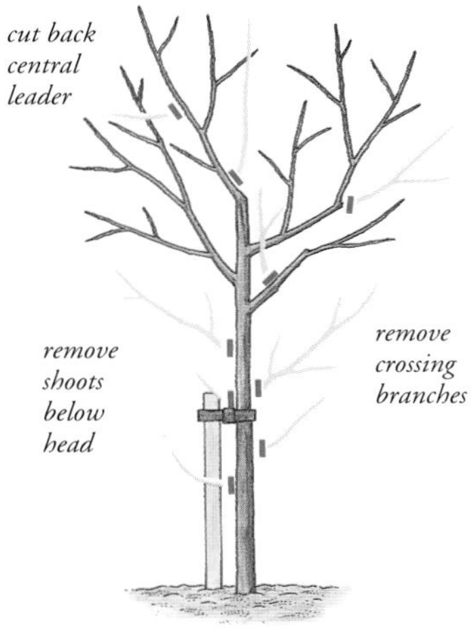

Branched-head standard
Train as a central-leader standard with a clear stem, 6ft (1.8m) tall, then cut back the leader to open the crown.

sheltered environment in which to nurture shrubs, perennials, and bulbs that grow best in dappled shade. Larger birches or oaks (*Quercus*) can provide an excellent canopy above smaller trees, such as some magnolias and maples (*Acer*).

Many trees are also tolerant of cultivation in containers; bonsai is the primary example of this. Since it is possible to move them around, they can be used in varied displays in areas such as patios and courtyard or rooftop gardens, or to flank steps or doorways. Container-grown trees can also be underplanted with annuals and trailing plants for color and variety. In cold climates, ensure that containers are frost-proof; tender trees can be moved under glass for protection in winter.

Bonsai
The Japanese art of restrictive pruning of roots and branches produces tiny trees for indoor and outdoor use, such as this Acer palmatum *'Schindeshojo'.*

Cultivation

Trees can thrive for decades, some even for centuries, if they are grown in the right soil and climate, and have adequate shelter, levels of light, and rainfall. Plant away from pipes, drains, cables, and usually walls and buildings, although some tender trees are best grown against a sunny wall. On slopes, plant trees halfway down, where it is warmer and less windy. In coastal zones, select trees that tolerate salt winds and spray.

Plant bare-root, usually deciduous trees in midautumn and midspring, but not in frosty weather; evergreen trees are best planted in autumn or midspring. Plant hardy trees with fleshy roots, whether evergreen or deciduous, in midautumn or in mid- or late spring; in cold areas, less hardy and evergreen trees should be planted only in midspring. Plant balled-and-burlapped trees in early or midautumn, or in early or midspring; deciduous balled-and-burlapped trees may be planted in winter when the weather is mild. Plant out container-grown trees at any time during the growing season, except during severe cold or drought.

STREET AND URBAN TREES

Beautification, shelter from the elements, and greenery for people and wildlife are among the benefits of growing trees along streets and in harsh urban conditions. Trees also help to clean and oxygenate the air. However, trees can have a difficult time surviving the usual stresses of drought and cold, not to mention road salt, dog feces and urine, injury from cars and trucks, root damage from street and sidewalk repairs, clumsy pruning, and irrational assaults.

Proper tree selection depends on assessing the reasons for planting the tree and evaluating the conditions of its proposed site. In addition to understanding the tree's adaptability to temperature, light, and soil conditions, many other characteristics determine whether a tree is suitable. For example, although the Norway maple (*Acer platanoides*) provides dense shade, its shallow roots tend to heave sidewalks. The ginkgo (*Ginkgo biloba*) tolerates dry, poor soil, but only males should be planted, because females produce foul-smelling fruit that litters sidewalks. The pin oak (*Quercus palustris*) tolerates dry soil, but develops chlorosis in alkaline soil. Because lime leaches from concrete sidewalks and construction rubble, urban soils tend to be alkaline; such soils reduce nutrient availability.

It is best not to seek the perfect street or urban tree, but rather to plant a variety of suitable trees in order to reduce the possibility of major disease and insect infestations and to lessen routine maintenance. Among many others, green ash (*Fraxinus pennsylvanica*), honey locust (*Gleditsia triacanthos* var. *inermis*), and Bradford pear (*Pyrus calleryana* 'Bradford') have proved their ability to survive in most street and urban conditions.

The single greatest stress to trees is the limited amount of room for their roots, which must share space with the infrastructure related to urban services: water, gas, other utility conduits, and underground transportation. In addition, urban soil is highly compacted, making it more difficult for trees to spread their roots. These factors explain the relatively short life of a street tree, typically 7–15 years.

Recent experiments show that tree roots and the urban environment can coexist. In a new planting medium for use in urban areas, clay loam is mixed with 1½in (4cm) pieces of crushed stone and moistened hydrogel, a water-holding compound, which serves as a glue to prevent the finer soil particles from washing out. The stone supports the sidewalk, and the soil and small air spaces within the mixture provide a good environment for root growth. Since this new mixture cannot replace existing tree-pit soil, it may be used along the sides of pits in trenches, covered with paving, so that the trees can have additional growing space.

A good choice
*The form, foliage, and fall color make sweet gum (*Liquidambar styraciflua*) cultivars excellent choices for street tree planting and for urban sites.*

Dig the planting hole 2 to 4 times as wide as the root ball, and 1½ times as deep, working organic matter into the base. If necessary, drive a stake off-center into the hole (see p.23). Plant the tree, backfill with soil mixed with organic matter, tread it in firmly, and water well, mulching thickly or top-dressing with bark chips or a similar organic mulch. Secure the tree to the stake and protect it with a stem guard. Until established, water young trees regularly, especially those on light, sandy soils; keep them free of weeds to a diameter of 3ft (1m) around the trunk. Provide a mulch. Remove suckers as they appear.

Feed and water trees grown in containers regularly, watering freely in hot, dry weather. In spring, replace the top 2in (5cm) of soil mix with fresh soil mix and apply a slow-release fertilizer. Pot on every 3 to 5 years.

Trees may be propagated by seed, cuttings, layering, or grafting (rarely used by amateur gardeners). Species are often grown from seed, although they take a long time to establish. Hybrids and cultivars rarely come true from seed and must be increased by vegetative means, usually from cuttings.

GINKGO BILOBA, *a deciduous conifer, has fan-shaped, mid-green leaves that turn golden yellow in autumn.*

Shrubs

Both deciduous and evergreen shrubs are prized as essential elements in most garden designs. The diversity of their ornamental features – architectural habits, fragrant flowers, striking fruits, or attractive foliage – and the year-round presence of their woody, often decorative stems offer an almost infinite choice for gardeners. Like trees, they occur in the wild in a broad spectrum of habitats, ensuring that there is a wide range of shrubs suitable for every soil and exposure.

Designing for a mature border
Positioned too close together, larger plants may compete for space, light, moisture, and nutrients. Here, Viburnum plicatum *'Mariesii' is centrally placed at the back of the border, with ample room for its spreading growth. Its magnificent white flowerheads cascade toward the bronze foliage of the perennial* Rodgersia podophylla.

What are shrubs?

Shrubs are woody-stemmed plants, usually freely branching from the base. Whereas a tree usually has a single stem (see p.32), a shrub has several or many stems arising from or near ground level. Most shrubs reach no more than 15–20ft (5–6m) in height, the majority of species and cultivars attaining considerably smaller stature. However, a degree of overlap occurs between shrubs and other plant groups. Larger shrubs that grow on a single stem, such as some viburnums, can be considered trees, although this depends on their size at maturity. Subshrubs (shrubs that are woody only at the base), such as *Perovskia*, and shrubs that die back annually as a result of winter cold, such as *Fuchsia*, are often cultivated as herbaceous perennials.

Container display
A shrub grown in a pot, such as this Pyracantha *'Golden Charmer', is ideal for a small, paved garden or formal area. Container-grown shrubs need careful watering and pruning.*

Essential framework

In every size and style of garden, shrubs are invaluable for their structural forms and their woody stems, which provide the garden with a long-term framework. They offer a variety of shapes and sizes, from prostrate, mat-, or clump-forming subshrubs, such as dwarf cultivars of *Erica carnea*, only 6in (15cm) high, to erect, tree-like shrubs like *Buddleja colvilei*, 20ft (6m) tall.

Ornamental features

Shrubs display an immense range of decorative features. They are often cultivated for their foliage, occurring in many shades of green, yellow, red, purple, silver, or gray.

Some are especially favored for their brilliant autumn coloration: Japanese maples (*Acer palmatum*) include numerous cultivars that turn from yellow through orange to shades of red, while the leaves of some *Cotinus* cultivars turn red between autumn and early winter. The notable autumn leaf color of witch hazels (*Hamamelis*) ranges from yellow to orange-red or purple.

The flowers of shrubs vary enormously in shape, size, and scent, and occur in almost every color. At one end of the spectrum are the abundant, tiny flowers of *Ceanothus*; at the other are the giant blooms of tree peonies (*Paeonia*). While numerous shrubs bloom for only a few weeks each year, others, including *Hypericum* and *Potentilla*, flower reliably over several months; shrubs of the latter type are valuable during periods when little else is in bloom. Some shrubs, such as Mexican orange blossom (*Choisya ternata*), are remontant, regularly flowering twice a year. Late-winter-flowering shrubs, such as *Viburnum* x *bodnantense*, often bear scented blooms over a long period.

Many popular shrubs, including *Cotoneaster*, holly (*Ilex*), *Pyracantha*, and *Viburnum*, bear vividly colored berries in autumn, which persist into winter. Other types of fruit range from those of *Dipelta*, which are covered by papery bracts, to the pendent, bean-like, deep blue pods of *Decaisnea fargesii*.

Some shrubs display brightly colored winter stems. In dogwoods (*Cornus*), the stems can be blazing red through to bright greenish yellow. They are usually coppiced to stimulate new growth for the best display of color (see pruning group 7, p.27).

Garden uses

Most shrubs are grown in a shrub border, or in a mixed border among annuals or perennials. When designing a border, it is advisable first to establish a theme. Consider whether the border is to display a selection of favorite species or to provide interest in a particular season or throughout the year, and whether plants should feature ornamental or scented flowers, decorative foliage, fruit, or various combinations of all these.

For an all-season shrub border, select larger shrubs that will flower in different seasons: for example, choose *Viburnum sargentii* to flower in spring, lilacs (*Syringa*) or *Philadelphus* for flowers in summer, and witch hazel (*Hamamelis*) or *Garrya elliptica* for autumn or late-winter blooms. For year-round foliage interest, include both deciduous and evergreen shrubs.

Shrub borders are usually designed with larger shrubs planted at the back of the border, and dwarf or groundcover shrubs, such as *Chaenomeles japonica*, at the front, although other arrangements can also be successful. It is particularly important to provide sufficient space for each shrub; as plants become established, they should not crowd one another. If necessary, any bare patches can be filled in with small, fast-growing shrubs, such as

RHODODENDRON KIUSIANUM *thrives only in acid soil.*

Topiary showpiece
Flowering shrubs can be grown as standards to produce a spectacular, and portable, display. This fuchsia has been trained for several years.

fuchsias, potentillas, or spireas, which can be removed when shrubs with a slower growth rate have reached maturity. Some shrubs are best trained against a warm, sunny wall, particularly tender shrubs, which may not thrive elsewhere in the garden; a few, such as *Ceanothus*, may grow to twice their usual height in this situation.

In a mixed border, cultivate shrubs alongside annuals, biennials, bulbs, or herbaceous perennials, seeking associations of color and texture of flowers and foliage, and contrasts in form and habit. When dividing (see p.28) or transplanting perennials within a mixed border, take care not to damage the roots of nearby plants.

Shrubs that exhibit a variety of ornamental features make excellent specimen plants and are ideally sited where they may be viewed from different angles. A specimen shrub should be appealing in habit and branch structure, particularly if it is deciduous, as well as in its foliage, flowers, or fruit. In a small garden, where a single specimen serves as a focal point throughout the year, versatility is essential; it is less important in a large garden that can accommodate a selection of shrubs of different sizes and features.

Growing in containers

Many shrubs thrive in containers and are excellent for a small garden, patio, or roof terrace. Use an isolated specimen in a decorative container as an arresting focal point, or group containers in different arrangements for variety.

Container growing also enables cultivation of shrubs that may not survive in the open garden due to the pH or drainage of the local soil, or an unsuitable climate. Tender plants can be grown outdoors in summer, and then moved indoors before the first frosts. Ensure that hardy plants kept outside are grown in frost-proof containers.

HEDGES AND SCREENS

Many shrubs can be used as boundary markers or screens, as low edging, or to divide areas within a garden. Those most suitable are robust, dense, and erect in habit and tolerate clipping.

Spiny-leaved or thorny shrubs, such as cultivars of *Berberis thunbergii*, *Ilex aquifolium*, and roses, as well as shrubs with dense growth, including many *Taxus* cultivars, are excellent for creating an impenetrable hedge. Dwarf shrubs, such as *Buxus sempervirens* 'Suffruticosa', are good for low edging. Herbs, such as lavender (*Lavandula*) and rosemary (*Rosmarinus*), make fragrant low hedges. In coastal areas, select plants resistant to wind and salt, such as *Elaeagnus* and *Griselinia*.

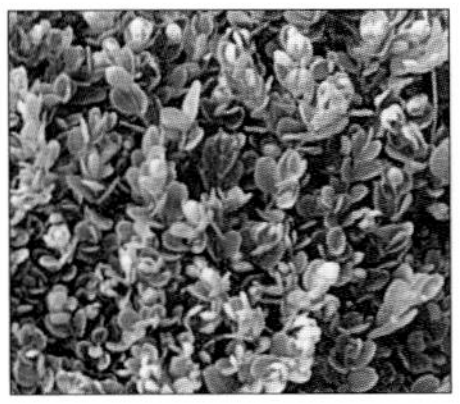

Buxus sempervirens 'Suffruticosa'

Ilex aquifolium 'Handsworth New Silver'

Taxus baccata 'Adpressa'

Berberis thunbergii 'Dart's Red Lady'

Rosa 'Buff Beauty'

Lavandula angustifolia 'Hidcote'

Wall-trained shrub
Many shrubs, such as this Ceanothus, *make extremely attractive garden features when trained against a wall. This technique may also be used to extend the hardiness of otherwise tender shrubs if grown in the open ground.*

Cultivation

Shrubs will thrive for many years, given the right growing conditions. The majority will grow in many types of garden soil, but generally prefer a fertile, well-drained but moisture-retentive loam. Plant bare-root and balled-and-burlapped shrubs in autumn or spring, although planting should be avoided if the ground is frozen. Container-grown plants can be planted at any time, but usually establish best if planted in autumn or spring.

For balled-and-burlapped or container-grown plants, make the planting hole 2 or 3 times the width of the root ball and deep enough for the roots to be buried to their original depth of soil. For bare-root plants, allow room for the roots to fan out fully around the shrub.

Plant the shrub, backfilling with a mixture of soil and organic matter, and firm in. In sandy soils, leave a depression around the shrub to retain moisture; in clay soils, plant the shrub slightly higher than the surrounding soil level so that water will readily drain off. Water and mulch well with compost or bark chips. Protect newly planted shrubs from cold, drying winds. Plant wall-trained shrubs about 18in (45cm) from the wall; lean the plant against the wall, and support it with stakes tied into wires. Young plants require regular watering until established. Apply fertilizer in early spring, and mulch thickly with bark chips or compost in spring or autumn.

SAMBUCUS NIGRA *'GUINCHO PURPLE' has ornamental foliage, flowers, and fruit for a long season of interest.*

From early spring to midsummer, water shrubs in containers freely and apply a quick-release fertilizer 2 or 3 times. In spring, replace the top 2–4in (5–10cm) of soil mix with fresh soil mix, mixed with a slow-release, balanced fertilizer. Pot on in late summer or autumn, when the root growth appears congested.

For all shrubs, remove suckers and cut out reverted (plain) shoots from variegated plants as soon as they appear. Deadhead regularly to encourage stronger growth.

General pruning advice and details of the pruning groups for each shrub genus in this encyclopedia are given on pp.25–27. Unless otherwise stated, coniferous shrubs do not require pruning.

Climbers

Gardeners value evergreen and deciduous climbing plants for their ability to cover walls, tree stumps, or buildings, or to grow through the branches of robust trees or shrubs. Many can be used as a groundcover or as living ornamental screens. Climbers provide diverse attractions of flowers, fruits, and foliage, and there is an ample choice of annuals, perennials, and woody plants.

Arching stems
The lax shoots of a scandent climber, such as Plumbago auriculata, *can be loosely tied in to a free-standing support for an attractively informal display.*

What are climbers?

Climbing plants may be self-clinging or twining, or scandent, scrambling, or trailing. Self-clinging plants use aerial roots or terminal adhesive pads to attach themselves to any surface that offers support, such as rock faces, tree trunks, or walls, and need only initial guidance. Twining climbers twine their stems, coil their tendrils, or use modified leaf stalks to wind through trees, shrubs, or a trellis. They will thread their way through shrubs and trees without additional support, but require wires or a trellis if wall-trained. If used as a groundcover, they need to be pinned down so that they root at the nodes. Scandent, scrambling, and trailing plants have long stems that attach themselves loosely, if at all, to their support. To climb, they must be tied in to their support, or they can be allowed to tumble over walls or banks.

HEDERA NEPALENSIS *'SUZANNE' is excellent for clothing a sheltered, shady wall.*

Garden uses

Evergreens, such as *Hedera helix* and its variegated cultivars, provide handsome foliage all year round. Deciduous climbers can display attractive foliage from their first bright new spring growth through to autumn, when many, such as *Parthenocissus tricuspidata*, provide brilliant autumn color. *Actinidia kolomikta* has decorative green foliage splashed pink and white.

Many climbers, including clematis, honeysuckle (*Lonicera*), and jasmine (*Jasminum*), are cultivated for their colorful or fragrant flowers. Some produce ornamental fruits: the silky seed heads of clematis often remain decorative for some time after the flowers have gone; many honeysuckles follow their blooms with red berries. Climbers grown mainly for their fruits include *Celastrus*, whose fruits split open in autumn, revealing brightly colored seeds.

Vigorous climbers, such as *Fallopia baldschuanica* or *Wisteria*, can be used to hide unsightly outbuildings. To cover low objects, such as old tree stumps, and for use as groundcover, choose self-clinging plants, such as ivies (*Hedera*), *Hydrangea petiolaris*, and Virginia creeper (*Parthenocissus*), which require no training or support. Climbers can also be trained to form attractive screening between various parts of a garden. For example, a trellis can be used to support a screen of fragrant annuals or can be covered with both climbing roses and honeysuckle.

Many climbers will easily twine through the branches of a tree, complementing the host tree's own features and extending its period of interest. Self-clinging climbers planted at the base of a tree will establish themselves against the trunk; twining or tendril climbers will need to be trained into the lower branches. *Clematis montana* and *C. armandii*, as well as honeysuckles, *Hydrangea petiolaris*, ivies, *Vitis coignetiae*, and *Wisteria*, can all be grown this way. Shade-loving honeysuckles flower beneath the foliage of the tree, while sun-loving clematis will flower only at the sunlit top of the canopy.

Pergolas and pillars are ideal for supporting climbers, since they can be admired from all sides. These structures also provide strong vertical elements in garden design.

Visual counterpoint
Here, climbers are used as the focus of a raised bed improvised from a well-head. The lush foliage of Humulus lupulus *and a clematis, trained over a wire loop, are offset by abundantly flowering roses, honeysuckle (*Lonicera*),* Clematis *'Nelly Moser', and* C. *'William Kennett'.*

HOW CLIMBERS ATTACH

Twining plants use tendrils or leaf stalks to coil their stems in spirals around a support; guide them into the branches of a tree or shrub, or train them on to a wire framework or wooden trellis against a wall. Self-clinging plants climb by using aerial roots or adhesive pads on their tendrils until they have become established against the trunk of a tree or a wall. Scandent and scrambling climbers need to be tied in to a support in order to climb, or they can be left to trail. All types can be used as a groundcover.

Twining tendrils
Passionflowers send out slender tendrils (modified stems) to curl around a support.

Twining leaf stalks
Clematis climb by spiraling modified leaf stalks around an appropriate support.

Twining stems
The flexible stems of Akebia *curl and extend around the support as they grow.*

Self-clinging aerial roots
Ivies fasten to a surface by means of their aerial roots (adventitious rootlets).

Self-clinging adhesive pads
Parthenocissus *cling to a surface using adhesive pads at the end of their tendrils.*

Short-term climbers

Climbing annuals, and perennials grown as annuals (such as *Eccremocarpus scaber*), are useful for providing temporary screens, for short-term cover on arches or a trellis until permanent plantings are established, or for providing shade during summer. The fragrant sweet pea (*Lathyrus odoratus*) is ideal for a cottage-style garden, with attractive flowers suitable for cutting. Slender perennial climbers, such as species of *Codonopsis*, can be used to twine through subshrubs. Herbaceous species, for example, *Tropaeolum speciosum*, *Lathyrus grandiflorus*, and *L. latifolius*, will scramble through robust shrubs. All die back in autumn, thereby avoiding problems with pruning among the host plants.

Choosing a climber

Consider the exposure of the intended site before choosing a climber. Many climbers, including *Actinidia*, *Clerodendrum*, and passionflowers (*Passiflora*), need a sunny wall to thrive, as does any climber grown at the limits of its climatic tolerance. *Akebia quinata*, *Jasminum officinale*, *Stauntonia hexaphylla*, and *Wisteria* tolerate a shaded wall, but flower and fruit more reliably in full sun. A few, like *Hydrangea petiolaris* and Virginia creeper, thrive in sun or shade. *Parthenocissus henryana* will color better in shade. For shaded walls, use a robust ivy or *Pileostegia viburnoides*, *Schizophragma hydrangeoides*, or *S. integrifolium*.

Take care to match the vigor of the chosen climber to the size and strength of the host tree or the scale of the building to be covered. Very vigorous climbers, such as *Fallopia baldschuanica*, or rampant ramblers, such as *Rosa wichurana* and *R. filipes* 'Kiftsgate', may cause an elderly or a small tree to topple, or may rapidly overwhelm a small structure.

Types of support

Choose a support that will accommodate the eventual height, spread, and vigor of the chosen climber. The main types are wooden or plastic trellis panels, wire or plastic mesh, and wires (usually plastic-covered) stretched between vine eyes. A trellis is the most reliable support for twining climbers; use wire or mesh for tendril climbers, and a trellis or wire framework for scandent or scrambling climbers.

Specifically built structures, such as pergolas and pillars, must be strong and durable to support plants throughout their life span.

Cultivation

When planting climbers against a wall or fence, position the plant at least 18in (45cm) from the base of the support. This allows the roots to receive sufficient rainwater, once established. After planting, water and apply mulch 2–3in (5–8cm) deep to a radius of about 24in (60cm) around the plant. Top-dress climbers in spring during their first two seasons, using 2–3oz (50–85g) of a balanced fertilizer, and apply a mulch each spring. Apply a slow-release fertilizer annually.

In hot, dry periods, water weekly. Deadhead plants regularly, unless fruits are desired. Tie in new shoots, and cut back overgrown plants (see p.25). Protect tender climbers grown outdoors in cold weather.

Where not hardy, climbers such as the tropical *Bougainvillea*, *Hoya*, *Mandevilla*, and *Pandorea* may be grown in a greenhouse or conservatory; some are suitable as houseplants. Climbers grown permanently under glass will outgrow their allotted space, so early restrictive pruning is essential (see p.25). Small climbers grown in containers with free-standing supports, such as stake tripods or trellis panels, can be moved outside during summer and returned under glass before autumn frosts. Plant vigorous species in large containers or in a greenhouse border. If they are allowed to grow very large, they may need to be replaced, since few respond to hard renovation pruning. Climbers in containers have to be repotted and fed regularly.

Climbing plants can be propagated by seed, by stem or root cuttings, or by layering. For species, seed is the most practical method, particularly for annuals and herbaceous species, although woody plants take some time to establish. Cultivars and hybrids do not come true from seed; take cuttings or layer.

Instant color
Parthenocissus tricuspidata *offers a spectacular display of autumn color, and is one of the best climbers for covering a bare wall rapidly.*

ESTABLISHING A CLIMBER

It is important that climbers become well established against their support early on. Plants with aerial roots or adhesive pads are best planted at the base of a wall without support and allowed to establish themselves.

To grow a climber that requires support against a wall, mount a wooden trellis or wire support 12in (30cm) above the soil, slightly away from the wall. Dig a hole 18in (45cm) from the foot of the wall, deep enough so that the top of the root ball, when planted, will be level with the soil. Drench the root ball, then place it at an angle of 45° to the support. Fan the roots away from the wall. Fill in the hole with soil, firm in, and water well. Remove the stake that comes with the plant, and fasten each main shoot to a new stake, attaching them to the lower rungs of the support. As new shoots appear, tie in to the support; do not damage the stems by tying too tightly. Cut out any weak or wayward shoots. Water freely until established.

Check the level of the root ball.

Tie to stakes attached to the support.

Perennials

Perennials reach maturity in as little as two seasons. A well-chosen selection rapidly forms a fine tableau of textures and colors, both foliage and flowers providing visual interest for months. They can be featured as specimen plants, massed in a traditional herbaceous border, or interspersed with shrubs, annuals, and biennials in a mixed border. For variety, they can be cultivated in containers or windowboxes, or grown among fruit and vegetables in a kitchen garden.

Mixed border
Shrubs and perennials have been planted here in a series of groupings, some of them providing color harmonies, others striking contrasts. Heights are unevenly arranged with taller plants such as alstroemerias, heleniums, salvias, and verbascums brought to the front, surrounding smaller plants such as Argyranthemum frutescens.

What are perennials?

Precisely defined, perennials are plants that live for 2 years or longer and, once mature, flower annually. In gardens, however, the term perennial is commonly applied to herbaceous plants that form flowering stems each year before seeding, then die back in autumn to ground level, sending up new growth in spring. The term is also used to describe some non-woody, evergreen plants, such as *Bergenia* and *Yucca*, as well as subshrubs like *Artemisia* and *Penstemon.*

Ornamental features

Perennials are probably the most diverse plant group, providing a huge variety of shape, form, color, texture, and scent with which to design a planting. They range in height from low, creeping plants, useful as groundcovers, to feature plants, such as *Rheum palmatum*, which is 8ft (2.5m) or more high.

Colorful foliage plants can add contrast to a predominantly mid-green backdrop, accentuating each plant's structural form. Possible choices include the glossy, dark green leaves of *Acanthus*, the purple foliage of some *Canna* species, the variegated leaves of *Hosta* cultivars, and the silvery foliage of *Onopordum.*

Perennials with unusual shapes, arrangements, or textures of leaf can also produce eye-catching effects, especially when used as accent plants (usually taller feature plants used to accentuate contrasts).

Flowers of perennials are extremely varied in color, size, and form, presenting the gardener with endless possibilities for contrasting, complementary, and single-color plantings. Well-chosen groupings can also provide form and structure, for example, the flat corymbs of *Achillea*, the tall spikes of lupines (*Lupinus*), or the tiered whorls of *Phlomis russeliana*. Popular fragrant perennials, attractive to bees and butterflies, include species of *Asclepias*, clematis, *Echinacea*, phlox, and verbenas.

Late-season interest
*Many perennials provide interest throughout autumn and winter. A fine clump of stonecrop (*Sedum *'Herbstfreude'), whose stems and seed heads remain attractive in winter, dominates the center of this planting, with* Caryopteris *and rosemary (*Rosmarinus*) at the rear. At the front, the deep red flowers of* Sedum *'Ruby Glow' contrast with the cool, silvery green foliage of various species of* Stachys *and* Senecio.

Borders

The traditional herbaceous border dates back to the nineteenth century and earlier. It was usually a large rectangular plot, set into a lawn or against a hedge or wall, filled with summer- and autumn-flowering perennials banked according to height. Today, herbaceous borders are frequently more modest in scale, often incorporating a carefully planned color scheme and using foliage as well as flowers for color, texture, and structure. Some gardeners still prefer a banked effect. Others choose to arrange plant heights unevenly.

Borders can be planned as a series of units (groupings of 3 or more plants) or as a progression of subtle associations along the border. Swathes of massed plants, at an oblique angle to the front of the border, have strong visual impact. Experiment with merging informal drifts of several different species and cultivars, or create intricate patterns using regularly spaced groups of a more limited number of plants.

For groundcovers, choose low, mat-forming, or creeping perennials displaying attractive foliage, such as *Lamium*, or flowering, clump-forming plants, such as geraniums; evergreens, such as *Bergenia* and some hellebores, can soften stark winter borders in cold areas (see also panel, far right).

SPECIALIST GROWING

The cultivation and exhibition of prodigious and flawless blooms can be a source of immense satisfaction to many gardeners. Popular hobby plants, such as chrysanthemums, dahlias, daylilies, irises, and peonies, can all be grown with other plants in garden beds and borders. Specialist growers, however, will often set aside a designated area for such plants, such as a side garden or in a greenhouse, to provide them with extra space and careful tending, and to protect them from damage from pests or diseases, or from adverse weather conditions. Specialist societies have been established to distribute information to enthusiasts about species, hybrids, and cultivars of their favored plants, and to give advice on sources, cultivation, and the exhibition of blooms and plants.

Show bloom
This Dahlia *'Hamari Accord' flower is ready for exhibition, demonstrating perfect form and ideal proportions.*

CULTIVATING HERBS ORNAMENTALLY

Generally speaking, herbs are plants grown for culinary or medicinal use, although many are also popular for their ornamental qualities. Many are of Mediterranean origin, preferring full sun and sharply drained soil, although mints (*Mentha*) thrive in moist soil and tolerate partial shade. A few, such as lavender (*Lavandula*) and chives (*Allium schoenoprasum*), bear showy flowers, and many have attractively colored or variegated leaves. Sow annual or biennial herbs in succession against a framework of perennials to provide a continual supply and to avoid gaps in the herb garden in late summer. Some medicinal herbs are of benefit only if prescribed by a qualified herbalist; unsupervised use may have harmful consequences.

Herbs for the kitchen and display
Going far beyond parsley, sage, rosemary, and thyme, herbs encompass a wide range of plants and may be grown in utilitarian beds or in more ornamental designs. These well-defined beds are attractive and make harvest easier.

Mixed borders of herbaceous perennials, shrubs, bulbs, climbers, annuals, and biennials are excellent for providing year-round interest. A careful selection of perennials and deciduous and evergreen shrubs that fill up to a third of the border will provide a balanced planting. Fill out the border with annuals until the perennials and shrubs mature. For extra interest in spring, many perennials, particularly those coming into growth in mid- or late spring, such as hostas, can be underplanted with bulbs or other early-flowering plants, such as tulips, anemones, and scillas. Tender perennials, such as dahlias, can be added to enhance a late-summer and autumn display.

Container ideas

Some hardy perennials are ideal for use in containers; ornamental grasses, for example, offer excellent choices of shape, structure, and color. Less hardy plants, such as *Agave*, *Cordyline*, *Melianthus major*, and variegated *Phormium* cultivars, are also attractive, but may need overwintering indoors. Perennial subshrubs in decorative containers, for example, *Argyranthemum* and lavender (*Lavandula*), can serve as focal points in paved areas. For a long floral display, choose summer- and autumn-flowering perennials, such as *Felicia* and geraniums.

Cutting and drying

Perennials include some of the best garden plants for cutting. Blooms often last well if they are cut early in the morning. Remove leaves from the bases of the stalks. To encourage them to take up water, bruise or slit the base of each stem, or plunge stems briefly in very warm water, before immersing them in warm water to the necks (where the flowers begin).

The flowers and seed heads of some perennials are also good for drying, particularly those that hold their shape and color well, such as *Achillea* and *Eryngium*. Some less rigid flowers with a higher water content may be air-dried if this is done quickly, by suspending small bunches in a dark and airy place. Flowers with papery petals can be dried in a commercial desiccant. Pick blooms as they begin to open. If picked too soon, the stems will not be sufficiently stiff; if picked too late, the color of the flowers will have deteriorated or the petals (or seed, in the case of grasses) will fall.

Cultivation

When planning a herbaceous or mixed border, match the needs of plants to the exposure and conditions of the chosen site. Plant in carefully prepared ground, usually in spring or autumn. Keep the surrounding area free of weeds, and water young plants regularly until established. Mature perennials require little watering except during prolonged dry periods. Apply an annual top-dressing of bone meal or a balanced, slow-release fertilizer, preferably in early spring after rain.

Most herbaceous plants produce vigorous shoots in spring, but some may be spindly. When the plant is one-quarter to one-third of its final height, pinch out or cut back weak shoots; the remaining sturdy shoots will usually bear larger flowers. This particularly benefits plants such as asters, delphiniums, and phlox. Plants that require support should be staked when young to ensure that lax stems remain upright (see p.23). Deadhead regularly.

In autumn, cut shoots down to the base, and remove dead and faded growth and weeds, leaving the border tidy in winter. In spring, when the ground is moist, apply a mulch of organic matter, such as mushroom compost or bark chips. Where practical, perennials grown in a border should be divided not only for propagation, but also to maintain vigor, ideally every 3 to 5 years. Take care when lifting and replanting not to damage the roots of surrounding trees and shrubs.

To appreciate grasses and other plants throughout the winter months, delay cutting and mulching until spring. In cold areas, leaving top-growth in place during winter will also offer some protection to the crown of a plant.

For container-grown perennials, use soil-based soil mix or lighter soilless mix mixed with a slow-release, balanced fertilizer. Although the extra weight of the soil adds stability, use soilless mixes in plastic containers for roof gardens or balconies where heavy containers may be too great a load; lighter containers are also easier to move.

Ensure that soil mix in containers does not dry out when plants are in growth; water daily in hot, dry weather. Plants in larger containers require less frequent watering, especially if moisture-retentive polymer granules have been added to the soil mix. Mulching also helps to retain moisture; replace mulch when dividing or repotting plants.

Perennials can be propagated by seed, division, cuttings, or grafting (rarely used by amateur gardeners). Sowing seed is preferable for species where large numbers of plants are required. Hybrids and cultivars do not come true from seed; divide or take cuttings.

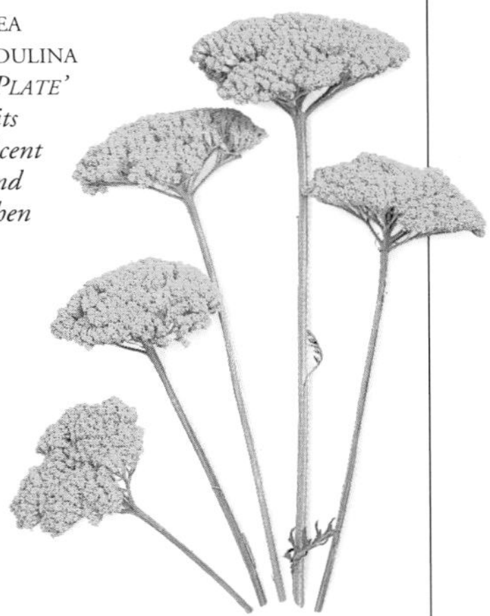

ACHILLEA FILIPENDULINA *'GOLD PLATE' retains its magnificent shape and color when dried.*

GROUNDCOVERS

A wide variety of perennials can be used as decorative, low-maintenance groundcovers, with the added benefit of reducing the labor of weeding. Geraniums are often chosen for their abundant flowers, while others, such as hostas, are grown mainly for their attractive foliage. Cerastiums prefer full sun, but many perennials, such as *Asarum*, hostas, *Lamium*, and *Persicaria*, also thrive in partial shade. Tiarellas prefer partial to deep shade.

Persicaria virginiana 'Painter's Palette'

Geranium asphodeloides

Lamium maculatum 'Beacon Silver'

Tiarella cordifolia

Hosta 'Shade Fanfare'

Cerastium tomentosum

Rock plants

As a group, rock plants represent an extensive range of hardy perennials, shrubs, and bulbous plants, many of which originate in mountain ranges. Delicate, simple, clear-colored flowers are often prolifically borne in spring and early summer. Many rock plants will flourish in a suitably well-drained site with an appropriate exposure; some require special conditions in the garden or in an alpine house.

GENTIANA VERNA *bears a profusion of blue flowers in early spring.*

What are rock plants?

The term rock plant is often used more or less interchangeably with alpine. In fact, true alpines are native to mountains in temperate, subtropical, and tropical regions, where they grow above the tree line in screes, rocky crevices, and grass. Subalpines occur just below the tree line. Most alpines are compact in habit and rarely over 6in (15cm) tall. This minimizes wind resistance and water loss at high altitudes.

When more broadly defined, a rock plant is any plant sufficiently dwarf in its habit to associate well with true alpines. Many rock plants are found in mountain pasture and woodland or on dry hillsides. A few occur on coastal cliffs and shores.

Adapted to growth in thin, rapidly draining soil, often at high altitudes, most alpines and rock plants will survive extremes of temperature but not excessive moisture. In cultivation, many prefer an environment that reproduces the exposure, light level, and moisture, wind, and soil conditions of their natural habitat. Rock gardens, raised beds, scree beds, and alpine houses (see panel opposite) will all provide suitable growing conditions. Other less specialized plants, like aubretias (*Aubrieta*), will thrive in any well-drained site with a suitable exposure.

Ornamental features and uses

Rock plants broadly encompass a diverse mixture of mat- or cushion-forming plants, dwarf shrubs and trees, and bulbous plants. Dwarf coniferous shrubs and trees, such as *Juniperus communis* 'Compressa', can provide height and structure in a planting, contrasting with specimens of more open or rounded habit like hebes. Lower-growing, tufted, or mat-forming plants, like sandworts (*Arenaria*), are useful as a groundcover or an edging.

Some rock plants, like houseleeks (*Sempervivum*), have fleshy, water-storing leaves. Others, like edelweiss (*Leontopodium*), have small, closely arranged, sometimes hairy leaves, which minimize water loss through transpiration. These provide a varied choice of foliage textures for garden plantings. Specimens like *Celmisia semicordata*, with its sword-shaped, silvery leaves, will offset rosette-forming, fleshy plants like stonecrops (*Sedum*) or those with feathery leaves, such as pulsatillas.

Many rock plants are evergreen and will provide year-round interest in the open garden. Spaces within a framework of miniature shrubs can be filled with rock plants; their tufts, clumps, or cushions of foliage are often as interesting as their blooms.

Rock plants flower mainly over a relatively short period in spring and early summer, but often produce a profusion of tiny, clear-colored blooms. Autumn- and late-winter-flowering bulbs, such as some cyclamen or crocuses, may be used to extend the flowering season.

Rock gardens

The most popularly constructed environment for rock plants is a rock garden. This is best located in an open, sunny site on a slope, clear from the shade cast by trees and sheltered from cold, drying winds. Where possible, include a source of water, such as a pond or stream, to enhance the basic design.

Construct the rock garden on a bed of coarse rubble, covered with standard rock garden soil (see right). Set rocks into the soil in a natural formation. Pockets between the rocks will accommodate the rock plants and provide them with a deep, cool root run. Top-dress the surface after planting with grit, gravel, or stone chips.

Mountain dwellers

True alpines, like this Aquilegia fragrans*, grow above the tree line in mountain ranges to over 10,000ft (3,000m) high. In the garden, such plants require conditions that replicate their high-altitude habitats: well-drained soil and a cool root run.*

A matter of scale

Rock gardens are not always composed of tiny, ground-hugging plants. This rock garden is planted with azaleas and other shrubs, dwarf and full-sized conifers, and large perennials, in addition to smaller perennials and bulbs.

GESNERIADS

A plant family of about 2,500 species, the Gesneriaceae are mainly evergreen perennials (some epiphytic) or shrubs, plus a few trees. Most are native to tropical or subtropical regions, with a few from temperate zones. Of the latter group, rock plants such as *Ramonda* and *Haberlea* are ideal for growing in the niches of a cool, shady wall or rock, or in a scree bed, where their rosettes will remain free of excess moisture. Often grown in an alpine house, *Jancaea heldreichii* will also thrive outdoors in tufa, in a shady site.

Haberlea ferdinandi-coburgii

Planting a trough
As with raised beds, carefully placed rocks can enhance the natural effect of a trough or sink planting. If using tufa, bore holes in them to fill with soil mix and appropriate small plants.

Niches or crevices in a wall, or between paving, can provide growing conditions similar to those of a rock garden. Some rosette-forming plants, such as *Lewisia* and *Ramonda*, are best planted on their sides in cracks in a wall, so that water drains away quickly from their collars.

Grow mat-forming plants like *Sedum acre* and *Dianthus deltoides* in pockets of soil on the top of a wall, or in vertical cracks, to produce a cascade of color. Use trailing or spreading plants, such as *Saponaria ocymoides* and *Saxifraga* 'Tumbling Waters', to soften the lines of a boundary wall or the retaining wall of a bank or raised bed.

Beds and containers

Raised beds and scree beds are ideal for growing plants on a level site. Rock plants that prefer very gritty soil and a well-drained root run, like alpine forget-me-nots (*Myosotis alpestris*), will grow best in a scree bed. If the bed is designed to be a free-standing feature, it should be slightly raised to assist drainage. A scree bed may also be constructed as part of a larger rock garden.

A raised bed can be constructed in a garden of any size and is useful where garden soil is heavy or slow-draining. Its added height improves drainage and brings the attractions of low-growing plants closer to eye-level. Grow species and cultivars that prefer acid soil, such as *Cassiope* and *Arctostaphylos*, in a peat bed or bog garden, which may be top-dressed with bark chips.

The retaining walls of a raised or scree bed can be constructed from natural or artificial stone, bricks, wooden logs, or railroad ties. As with a rock garden, all beds should have a rubble base, covered with a suitable soil mix and top-dressed with grit, stone chips, or gravel.

Rock plants will also flourish in containers such as sinks, troughs, and tubs. Provide a generous top-dressing of grit around the bases of the plants to improve drainage and reduce the evaporation of moisture from the soil mix.

Cultivation

In general, alpines and other rock plants prefer an open site in full sun, with moderately fertile soil, a cool, deep root run, and sharp drainage.

With some cushion-forming plants, like *Dionysia* and *Androsace*, the rotting of one or two rosettes may rapidly lead to the death of the whole plant. Such species and their cultivars are best grown within the controlled environment of an alpine house or cold frame. Some bulbous plants, like *Calochortus*, also benefit from a controlled environment since they require protection from moisture when dormant in summer.

In the open garden, shelter susceptible plants from moisture by providing very well-drained soil and a thick dressing of grit around the collar of each plant. Panes of glass or clear plastic can also be propped up over the plants, or they can be covered with an open-ended cloche of glass or transparent plastic.

At planting, incorporate a slow-release, balanced fertilizer into the soil or soil mix. Thereafter, apply a general-purpose fertilizer in spring, if vigorous growth is required. Plants grown in a free-draining scree bed may require watering until established. Rock plants grown in an alpine house, in raised beds, or in containers should be watered regularly. In an alpine house, soak the medium in which plants are plunged, as well as the individual plants. For species and cultivars that resent moisture from above, soak the plunging medium only.

Deadhead rock plants, where practical, to encourage further flowering, and remove withered or damaged growth immediately. Trim plants as required to maintain their neat, compact form and, where necessary, to restrict their spread.

Various propagation methods are used for rock plants; consult individual genus entries for the most appropriate method in each case.

SOIL MIXES

Special soil mixes aim to reproduce the media in which alpines and other rock plants grow in the wild. For acid-loving plants, use lime-free soil and grit, supplemented with granite or sandstone chips; for alkaline-loving plants, use limestone chips. Peat substitutes include decomposed bark, bracken litter, garden compost, and leaf mold.

ROCK GARDEN (STANDARD MIX)
2 parts soil mix (1 part sterilized loam; 1 part peat or peat substitute); 1 part sharp sand or grit.
SCREE BED
1 part sterilized loam; 1 part peat or substitute; 3 parts grit or stone chips (in dry areas, 2 parts grit or chips). Or 2 parts sterilized loam; 2 parts leaf mold; 1 part sharp sand; 4 parts grit or chips.
RAISED BED
3 parts sterilized loam; 2 parts peat or substitute; 1 or 2 parts sharp sand or coarse grit.
PEAT BED (< pH6.5)
1 part peat or substitute; 1 part acidic leaf mold; 1 part fibrous acidic loam; 1 part lime-free sharp sand or coarse grit. Add a slow-release, balanced fertilizer.
WALLS
3 parts sterilized loam; 2 parts peat or substitute; 1 or 2 parts sharp sand or coarse grit. Add extra sand, grit, or stone chips to improve drainage in crevices.
FOR ACID-LOVING PLANTS (< pH6.5)
4 parts acidic leaf mold, or peat or substitute (such as decomposed bark or compost); 1 part sharp sand.
FOR HIGH-ALTITUDE ALPINES
1 part standard mix; 1 part gravel or stone chips. Or 1 part sterilized loam; 1 part leaf mold, or peat or substitute (such as decomposed bark); 2 or 3 parts gravel or stone chips.
FOR CONTAINERS
3 parts standard mix; 1 part coarse grit. Add a slow-release, balanced fertilizer.

ALPINE HOUSES

The needs of moisture-sensitive rock plants are best met in an alpine house: a minimally heated greenhouse with maximum levels of ventilation, usually provided by a door at each end, and extra windows or louvered panels set into the sides, along the roof ridge, and below the staging. Most growers heat an alpine house just sufficiently to prevent hard-freezing of soil mixes, enabling the cultivation of a wide range of choice plants.

Most plants are grown in clay pots, plunged to the rims in sand on staging; this reduces the need for watering and offers some cold protection. Plants in plastic containers may not require plunging, but they risk dehydration if the growing medium freezes hard in winter. A raised bed allows for landscaping and provides a deep root run, but plants cannot then be moved.

To keep plants cool in summer, shade an alpine house (see p.24) from late spring to early autumn and, where possible, move containerized plants that have finished flowering to an open plunge bed or cold frame outdoors.

Maintaining healthy plants
In an alpine house, most rock plants are grown in clay pots, plunged to the rims in a layer of sand upon staging. In summer, maximum levels of ventilation reduce the risk of disease, while shade netting protects foliage and flowers from scorching.

Annuals and biennials

These versatile and free-flowering plants, though short-lived, are easy to grow from seed and require little maintenance. They are suitable for all gardening situations, being native to both temperate and subtropical climates. Annuals and biennials will quickly provide a vibrant display of color, enhancing a framework of trees, shrubs, and perennials, or grown by themselves in beds, containers, or hanging baskets.

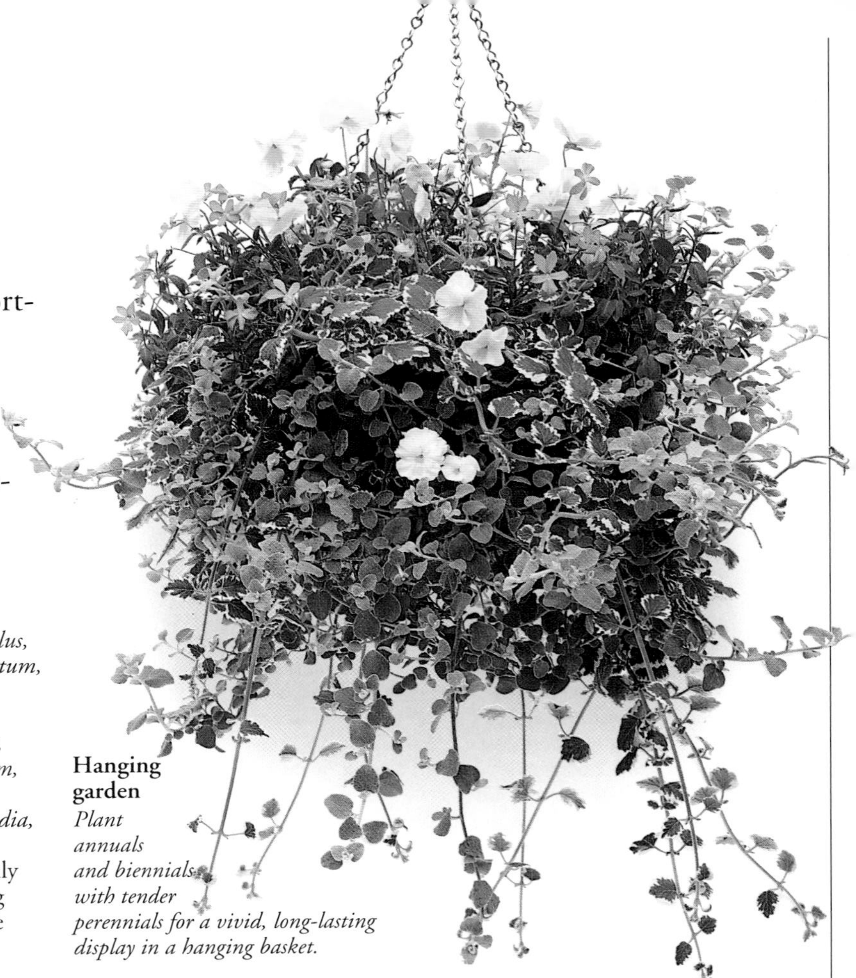

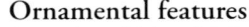

Hanging garden
Plant annuals and biennials with tender perennials for a vivid, long-lasting display in a hanging basket.

What are annuals and biennials?

Annuals are plants that germinate, flower, set seed, and die within one year. Certain members of other plant groups, such as perennials or subshrubs, which will often flower in their first year when raised from cuttings or seed, are also commonly grown as annuals. Some tender perennials, like *Cobaea, Impatiens,* and geraniums (*Pelargonium*), can be seed-raised each year to provide a display of flowers, and then discarded rather than overwintered under glass. Other genera containing perennial species grown as annuals include *Abelmoschus, Abutilon, Antirrhinum, Argyranthemum, Asclepias, Bacopa, Begonia, Browallia, Canna, Catharanthus, Celosia, Centaurea, Dahlia, Dianthus, Diascia, Eccremocarpus, Echinacea, Evolvulus, Felicia, Fuchsia, Gazania, Gerbera, Helichrysum, Heliotropium, Hibiscus, Hypoestes, Ipomoea, Lablab, Lantana, Leonotis, Limonium, Lobelia, Lobularia, Lotus, Mimulus, Mirabilis, Nierembergia, Pennisetum, Petunia, Plectranthus, Pueraria, Ratibida, Ricinus, Rudbeckia, Salvia, Scaevola, Senecio, Setaria, Solanum, Solenostemon, Teucrium, Thunbergia, Thymophylla, Tradescantia, Tropaeolum, Tweedia, Verbena,* and *Vinca.*

Biennials normally produce only foliage in their first year, bearing flowers and completing their life cycle in the following season.

New plants and names

Each year, new annual and biennial cultivars are introduced to stimulate or cater to commercial demand. They may be completely new plants or improvements on existing cultivars. In many species, breeding programs have increased the choice of flower colors, extended the flowering season, and developed a wider range of habits, often producing dwarf cultivars ideal for small gardens or pendent cultivars suitable for windowboxes and hanging baskets.

New introductions may have been obtained from the wild or selected from a batch of seedlings, or are the result of genetic mutation. Continual breeding and interbreeding of these selections blurs the parentage of many cultivars and results in a complicated (and often confusing) system of categorization.

Two or more cultivars are often crossed to produce a hybrid or group of hybrids. In these circumstances, where parentage becomes confused, or where several cultivars display very similar or common features, they may form a Group, the name of which is printed in roman rather than italic type, as in *Impatiens* New Guinea Group, or *Digitalis purpurea* Foxy Hybrids.

Cultivars that consistently share all but one of their characteristics (usually flower color) may be termed a Series, as in *Tropaeolum* Alaska Series. This distinguishing feature may also be used to identify further a plant within a Series; for example, *Tagetes* Antigua Series 'Antigua Gold' differs from other cultivars in the Series only in its golden yellow flowers.

Individual cultivars within a Group or Series may bear flowers of only one color (self-colored) or may produce flowers consisting of two colors (bicolored). A cultivar may also consistently bear flowers of the same color (single colors), or individual plants of the same cultivar may bear flowers in any one of a number of colors (mixes).

Annual beauty from tender perennials
Many tender perennials may also be grown as annuals. Combined here are the bright flowers of a Lantana *cultivar, the rich purple foliage of* Tradescantia pallida *'Purpurea', and the boldly striped leaves of* Canna *'Pretoria'.*

Ornamental features

Annuals and biennials have an exceptionally diverse range of habits, from low mat-formers to erect or climbing plants, allowing them to fulfill many roles in different areas of the garden. Most are cultivated for their brightly colored, sometimes very fragrant flowers, which are often freely borne over long periods during spring and summer. Some blooms, such as those of *Gypsophila*, china asters (*Callistephus*), and cornflowers (*Centaurea cyanus*), are excellent for cutting. "Everlasting" flowers, like statice (*Limonium sinuatum*) and strawflowers (*Bracteantha bracteata*), and the decorative seed heads of plants such as love-in-a-mist (*Nigella*) and *Scabiosa* are invaluable for dried arrangements (see p.39).

Several annuals and biennials are valued primarily for their attractively colored or textured foliage. These include silver-leaved plants, such as *Senecio cineraria* (a half-hardy perennial that is usually grown as an annual); coleus (*Solenostemon*), which have foliage in an extremely wide color range; and ornamental cabbages (*Brassica oleracea* cultivars), with their low-growing, crinkled leaves in muted to bright shades of pink, green, and white.

Garden uses

Annuals and biennials will provide a fast-growing display of color in a new garden, before a final planting design has been devised, or while slower-growing trees and shrubs become established. They may also be used to alter the color scheme or fill spaces within the long-term framework of a mature garden. Plants with scented blooms are best enjoyed close to the house or beside a seating area. Grow especially tender plants in a sheltered, sunny site at the base of a wall or fence.

Trailing annuals and biennials, such as nasturtiums (*Tropaeolum majus*), will provide rapid ground-cover and may be encouraged to tumble over the sides of window-boxes, hanging baskets, or other containers. Container-grown plants are of particular value where space is limited, such as on a balcony or patio. Annual climbers or those grown as annuals, like *Cobaea* and *Rhodochiton*, may also be trained through a tree or other support, or used to clothe a screen or barrier.

Tender annuals and biennials cultivated as specimen plants in a conservatory or temperate green-house, or as houseplants, can be moved outdoors in summer, either in their containers or as temporary bedding plants.

Planning displays

Because annuals and biennials are short-lived, use a succession of plants to provide flowers over a long period; some gardeners change their bedding design several times in a year. Group plants with shared cultivation needs, like *Impatiens* and Semperflorens (wax) begonias, both of which thrive in moist soil in dappled shade. To obtain a dense block of color, plant several plants of a single cultivar.

In an informal, cottage-style garden, use annuals and biennials among vegetables, herbs, perennials, shrubs, and trees. Arrange adjacent drifts with varying outlines and heights for an apparently random, flowing effect. In maturity, plants will overflow the edges of paths and lawns, and may self-seed profusely.

In a garden of formal design, use annuals and biennials in ordered or structured plantings to create a uniform display, to form a pattern, or to enhance or soften the edges of rigid lines of tiles, pathways, or hedges, such as boxwood (*Buxus*).

Informal border
*Annuals and biennials can provide waves of texture and color. In this border, the strong colors and abundant flowers of snapdragons (*Antirrhinum*),* Cosmos, *and* Tagetes *are balanced by the striking foliage of* Senecio cineraria *'Silver Dust'.*

Cultivation

Seed-raised annuals and biennials, depending on their hardiness and flowering season, may be sown *in situ* or under glass. Outdoors, the seeds of genera that dislike trans-planting, such as *Clarkia*, are best scattered where they are to flower. Sow the seeds of other annuals and biennials in drills, and thin out when seedlings have developed. Under glass, sow seed in containers or seed trays (see p.28) and plant out at the appropriate time.

Weed regularly, stake tall plants, and pinch out growing tips to promote bushiness (see p.23). On poor soils, apply a quick-release fertilizer as flower buds form. Water freely in hot weather, especially plants grown in containers. Deadhead regularly to avoid self-seeding. Clear plants away when the foliage starts to die down or when killed by frost.

Cutting gardens

Many annuals, and perennials grown as annuals, provide excellent cut flowers. Although they may be grown in massed beds or as part of a mixed border, plants raised for cut flowers are often best relegated to a cutting garden, where they may be given special attention to their needs, and where harvesting them will not leave gaps.

A site in full sun, protected from strong winds and close to a water supply, is ideal; many successful and productive cutting gardens are adjacent to a vegetable plot. Start plants from seed in cell packs under cover or sow *in situ*, and grow in rows or blocks for easy maintenance. Provide a trellis or twiggy branches for vining plants such as sweet peas, and grow plants that require support between 2 or 3 lengths of twine running along the rows. Water, fertilize, and control pests and diseases as needed.

When harvesting flowers, cut in the morning after the dew has evaporated, or in the evening after the heat of the day has passed. Strip off some of the lower leaves, split the cut end of the stem if thick or woody, and plunge into deep containers of almost-hot water. Allow the water to cool for at least a few hours or overnight to allow for water uptake, which will "harden" the stems and help prevent premature wilting.

ZINNIA ELEGANS
DREAMLAND SERIES 'DREAMLAND SCARLET'
is ideal for pots or bedding.

Genera (both herbaceous and woody) with members often grown for cut flowers include *Allium, Anemone, Antirrhinum, Calendula, Callistephus, Celosia, Centaurea, Chrysanthemum, Consolida, Cosmos, Dahlia, Dianthus, Echinacea, Gaillardia, Gerbera, Gladiolus, Gypsophila, Helianthus, Iris, Lathyrus, Leucanthemum, Lilium, Limonium, Matthiola, Moluccella, Narcissus, Paeonia, Papaver, Phlox, Polianthes, Rosa, Rudbeckia, Salvia, Scabiosa, Syringa, Tagetes, Tithonia, Trachymene, Tropaeolum, Tulipa, Verbena, Viola,* and *Zinnia.*

WILDFLOWERS

Many plants are regarded and beloved as "wildflowers," although a precise definition of the term is elusive and the subject of much debate. Whether defined as a specific group of plants that are native to a given area, or loosely meant to include worldwide plants with a given appearance and habit, wildflowers are popular and wide-ranging additions to the garden.

Wildflower gardening stems in part from a wish to conserve native species that are threatened by the decline of their natural habitats. While it is not possible to re-create such habitats exactly, growing even a small area of wildflowers contributes to their conservation and attracts a variety of insects (often beneficial) and other wildlife into the garden.

Natural planting
Depending on site and selection, wild-flowers give brief or extended displays of color and attract wildlife to the garden.

Creating a wildflower area is often the best way of using part of the garden that does not lend itself to more conventional cultivation, perhaps because it is too exposed, sloping, or dry, or has poor soil. It may also be the ideal way to cultivate a wooded area or boggy spot.

Wildflower habitats are extremely diverse and include meadows or flower-rich grasslands, alpine meadows, grainfields, wetlands, woodlands, and arid areas.

When planning a wildflower area, assess the site, taking into account climate, soil type, and drainage, and the degree of sun, shade, and shelter. The growing conditions will determine the plants that will thrive and look natural in the setting.

Observe the local wild flora, since this will indicate which species to grow, but never take plants from the wild without gaining permission from the landowner. Also, consider including some non-native plants that require the same conditions and are in keeping with the planting style.

Depending on the site and the selected plants, the main display may be planned for a particular season or to extend over a longer period. A wood-land habitat favors spring-flowering plants, for example, whereas a prairie generally peaks in summer.

Bulbous plants

Bulbous plants occur worldwide in habitats from scrub, meadows, and woodland to mountains and streamsides. Sometimes evergreen, bulbs are valued mainly for the beauty of their flowers, which can provide welcome color in early spring. Summer-flowering bulbs, like lilies and gladioli, are splendid in borders or integrated into a bedding design; their tall, showy blooms often last well when cut. Excellent in containers, bulbs can also be used to brighten the home or garden in winter.

Spring border
A burst of early-spring color is produced here by Crocus tommasinianus, *winter aconites (*Eranthis*),* Arum italicum *'Marmoratum', hellebores, and snowdrops.*

What are bulbous plants?

The term bulb is generally used to describe a range of different structures, including true bulbs, corms, tubers, and rhizomes. These fleshy storage organs enable bulbous plants to survive a long dormant period, often spent underground.

True bulbs have fleshy scales (swollen leaves or leaf bases), sometimes tightly overlapping, attached to a small basal plate. In plants such as daffodils (*Narcissus*), each bulb is encased in a thin, papery tunic; others, like lilies (*Lilium*), have loosely arranged, unclothed scales.

AGAPANTHUS INAPERTUS, *a tender bulbous plant, may be placed outdoors in summer in frost-prone areas.*

Corms are enlarged, compressed stems, often marked with leaf scars. The majority, including those of crocuses and gladioli, are sheathed in a papery or fibrous tunic. Each corm usually lasts for one year and is then replaced by a new one.

Tubers are swollen sections of stem or root, modified to store food. They are solid in form, like those of dahlias and cyclamen, and usually lack scales or tunics.

Rhizomes are stems that usually creep at or below ground level, often dividing as they spread. Ridged with leaf scars, rhizomes may be thin and wiry, as with lily-of-the-valley (*Convallaria*), or thick and fleshy, as with bearded irises.

A bulbous structure that has died down out of sight is often described as being dormant. Far from a state of low activity, however, this period represents a significant time in the plant's life cycle, when the bulb ripens and flower buds form, ready for the new season of active growth.

Woodland bulbs
Bulbous plants native to woodland soon naturalize when planted in the dappled shade of a tree. Here, Cyclamen hederifolium *has colonized a shady bank to form a carpet of color with its vivid autumn blooms.*

Ornamental features

Bulbous plants are grown mainly for their decorative and sometimes fragrant flowers, which can have the delicate appeal of tiny snowdrops (*Galanthus*) or the imposing effect of tall gladiolus spikes. Many, like those of irises and lilies, are good for cutting. Their floral parts are usually arranged in multiples of 3.

Most bulbous plants are monocotyledons (see p.10), having long, narrow to fairly broad, strap-shaped leaves with near-parallel veins along their length. Some, like cannas, are particularly valued for their foliage, which is erect or semi-erect, sometimes is attractively colored, and forms striking clumps.

Year-round interest

A spectacular array of flowering bulbs, from snowdrops and crocuses to daffodils, provides some of the first blooms of spring. Different species and cultivars may be interplanted with one another to create a rich display that will last for several months until perennials and shrubs come fully into flower.

Later-flowering bulbs can be used to provide highlights of seasonal color, extending interest throughout the year. Summer-flowering bulbs are often tall, robust plants, producing flowers in vivid colors, such as the brilliant red or yellow of montbretias (*Crocosmia*) or the purple globes of *Allium aflatunense.* Autumn-blooming bulbs, including colchicums and some crocuses, are dormant during summer, but provide a late flush of color with the onset of autumn rains.

STORAGE ORGANS

Gardeners commonly refer to any swollen, underground, food-storage organ as a bulb. True bulbs consist of fleshy scales attached to a basal plate, often within a papery tunic. Corms are swollen stem bases. Tubers are unevenly swollen stems or roots. Rhizomes are horizontal, swollen stems.

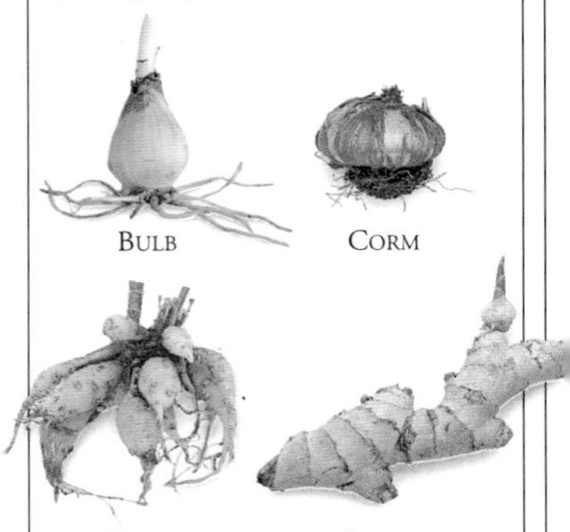

CROCUS SIEBERI *SUBSP.* SUBLIMIS *F.* TRICOLOR *blooms in early spring.*

For early color, grow bulbous plants such as *Chionodoxa, Crocus, Eranthis, Fritillaria, Galanthus, Iris, Leucojum, Muscari, Narcissus, Puschkinia, Scilla,* and *Tulipa.*

Where to grow

Interesting contrasts can be achieved by associating bulbs with other plants. Small bulbs, like autumn daffodils (*Sternbergia*), are ideal for growing among rock plants. Those with larger leaves and flowers, like lilies and *Crinum*, are good for infilling or naturalizing in a mixed or shrub border. After flowering, bulbs may be lifted to make room for new plantings or left in place to increase and flower the next year.

To encourage an abundant crop of flowers, plant bulbs originating from Mediterranean climates in a site where they will receive maximum sun. *Amaryllis,* nerines, and autumn daffodils can be planted at the base of a warm wall or fence.

Bulbs native to woodland habitats, such as some cyclamen, *Eranthis,* erythroniums, snowdrops, and many lilies, will thrive in the light shade of deciduous trees or large shrubs.

Some bulbs, including daffodils, scillas, and crocuses, can be planted in quantity in grass. Cease mowing when the noses of the bulbs appear in late summer or early autumn, and recommence only when the foliage has died down in late spring.

Bulbs are excellent for providing a display of flowers in windowboxes or in containers on a patio. Plant species with differing flowering times to extend the show.

Colorful display
A large pot of forced tulips can brighten the gray days of winter.

Cultivation

Many bulbs thrive outdoors without protection, even in areas of severe cold. Their main requirement is a near-neutral, well-drained soil in full sun, although bulbs of woodland origin prefer partial shade.

Improve the texture of heavy, wet soil by digging in grit, coarse sand, and organic matter. On poor soil, incorporate a balanced fertilizer on planting. Supplement very light soil with decomposed organic matter to assist moisture retention.

After flowering, allow the foliage to die down naturally; do not knot leaves together, since this reduces their ability to photosynthesize and thus store food in the bulb.

Bulbs from dry summer habitats may rot if subjected to summer rainfall. They are best grown in a raised bed to provide sharp drainage or in a bulb frame (a raised bed with a protective shelter). Small, rare bulbs with specialized needs are best grown in an alpine house (see p.41) or in a cool greenhouse (see p.24).

In frost-prone areas, plant summer-flowering, frost-tender bulbs in late spring; lift them in autumn and store in frost-free conditions. They may also be grown in a conservatory, a warm greenhouse, or indoors. Keep tender bulbs that are dormant in summer, like some nerines and *Hippeastrum,* in a cool, dry site; in early autumn, move them to a frost-free place, such as a sunny window-sill, to flower.

The atmosphere in a home may not be sufficiently humid to support bulbs for long periods. They can be brought indoors when in bud, but returned under glass for their foliage to mature and for their dormant period. When in growth, apply a potash-rich (tomato-type) liquid fertilizer twice monthly to bulbs grown in containers for more than one year. Water freely when in flower. When the leaves die back after flowering, allow bulbs to dry off, and keep warm and dry while dormant. At the end of this period, repot and water to stimulate growth.

Forcing

Forcing is the process of bringing a plant into flower out of season. Bulbs may be planted in either clay or plastic pots; water the soil mix less frequently in plastic pots than in clay pots. A piece of screening placed over drainage holes prevents soil from washing out.

Ideally, bulbs should be planted in pots at the same depths as bulbs grown outdoors. However, this is often not possible with larger bulbs, in which case make sure the pot is deep enough to allow at least 1in (2.5cm) of moist soil mix beneath the bulb. When filling the pot with soil mix, allow ½in (1.5cm) of space below the rim of the pot. Do not press the bulbs into the soil mix too firmly, since this may compress the soil just beneath the roots of the bulbs and impede their growth. Work more soil mix down between the bulbs and firm gently. Small bulbs should be covered completely, but tulips and daffodils may be left with the tip of the bulbs showing.

After planting, water and keep the pots in a cold frame or cold greenhouse. Bulbs in pots are particularly susceptible to cold damage; in severe winters, pots in a shallow cold frame or an unheated greenhouse may freeze solid. Protect them by sinking the pots in a plunge bed of coarse sand, perlite, or grit. Alternatively, the pots may be plunged in a straw-lined trench in the garden and covered with an insulating layer of straw, loosely packed leaves, or perlite. The lining and covering should be thick enough to prevent the pots from freezing in midwinter.

If only a few pots are being forced, they may be placed in a refrigerator, a root cellar, or a corner of a basement. The temperature should remain between 35–40°F (2–4°C).

Check periodically in winter for watering needs. After about 10 weeks, begin checking for pots ready to bring into gentle warmth. Early-flowering varieties need less cold treatment than later-flowering ones, which may need up to 16 weeks. When ready, new shoots are visible and roots show at the base of the container. Move the containers into a cool room or greenhouse, between 50–55°F (10–12°C), and keep them out of direct sunlight initially. Once the shoots turn green and elongate, move them into more light and warmer conditions, and keep moist but not wet. In the home, flowers will last longer if the pots are moved into a cool room at night.

Bulbs that have been forced into bloom should be planted in the garden once spring arrives or allowed to go dormant in their pots and then planted out in autumn. They will not force well again.

Suitable genera for forcing include *Chionodoxa, Crocus, Eranthis, Fritillaria, Galanthus, Hyacinthus, Iris, Leucojum, Lilium, Muscari, Narcissus, Scilla,* and *Tulipa.*

PLANTING BULBS

Bulbs must be planted at the correct depth (see below) and distance apart. In the individual plant entries in this encyclopedia, ideal planting distance is indicated after the "PD" symbol. Spreads of plants may be deduced from habit descriptions and leaf lengths.

Once planted, protect bulbs from extremes of temperature with a suitable loose mulch such as straw, pine needles, or shredded leaves. Rot-prone bulbs are best laid on sharp sand to improve drainage. Place bulbs with a hollow top, such as fritillarias, on their side, to prevent water from lying in the crown.

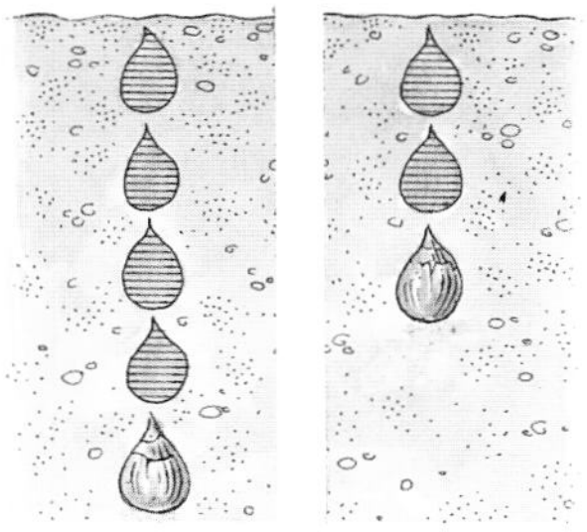

Planting depths
In cold areas and sandy soil, plant at 4 or 5 times bulb depth (left). Elsewhere, plant at 2 or 3 times bulb depth (right).

Orchids

All orchids belong to the huge Orchidaceae family, which contains 25,000 species and perhaps 100,000 hybrids in some 835 genera. They are evergreen or deciduous perennials; epiphytic, lithophytic (rock-dwelling), or terrestrial in habit; and distinguished by a unique flower structure that has diversified into numerous shapes and spectacular color combinations.

Orchids outdoors
In tropical climates, orchids thrive outdoors if shaded from strong sun by trees or a lath house. In cool areas, use the vivid color and unusual shape of orchid flowers for an exotic effect under glass, or grow hardier orchids from temperate zones outdoors.

What are orchids?

Most orchid species are rhizomatous epiphytes from tropical rainforest. They often bear fleshy aerial roots, which are fully or partially attached to the host tree and which absorb atmospheric moisture; some species are lithophytic. Most cultivated orchids are complex hybrids. The majority are grexes, denoted by a vernacular name in roman type, as in *Lycaste* Wyldfire (see also p.11).

Epiphytic orchids have two distinct patterns of growth. Sympodial epiphytes, mainly from rainforest at sea level or at low altitudes, arise from horizontal rhizomes. Each season, growing points (buds) on the rhizomes produce new pseudobulbs – erect, swollen stems that store water and food, and bear leaves and flowers. Active buds usually cease growth by flowering time, and any new growth occurs from lateral buds on older rhizomes. Backbulbs (pseudobulbs that no longer bear leaves) may be used for propagation (see panel); their removal reactivates dormant buds on the bulbs.

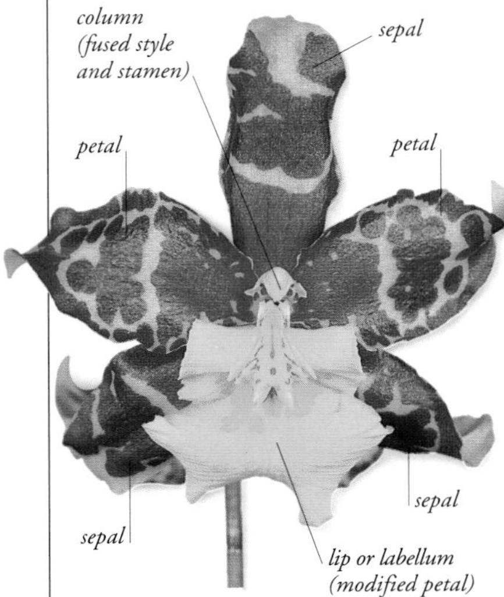

Flower structure
x Odontocidium *Tiger Hambühren clearly displays the typical anatomy and brilliant coloration of an orchid flower.*

Monopodial epiphytes are usually native to dense, steamy rainforest at higher altitudes. Instead of pseudobulbs, they have extended stems that produce new growth from the shoot tips and growing points.

Terrestrial orchids, mainly native to temperate regions, are distinct from epiphytes in that they have underground tubers or rhizomes. These bear a rosette of leaves from which flower stems arise.

Cultivation

All epiphytes, and a few terrestrials, require one of three controlled temperature zones – cool, intermediate, or warm (see panel below) – depending on their origins. Use shading in spring and summer to regulate temperatures and protect foliage from scorching (see p.24).

In hot climates, orchids of tropical origin provide a spectacular and colorful outdoor display. Epiphytes that need moist, shaded conditions, such as moth orchids (*Phalaenopsis*), are best grown in a lath house to protect them from strong sunlight.

In cool regions, terrestrial orchids from northern temperate zones, like lady's slipper orchids (*Cypripedium*), can be cultivated outdoors in a rock garden, in woodland, or on a peat bed. Most die back after flowering and undergo a dormant period.

Some epiphytic orchids may be mounted on slabs of bark, others on branches anchored to form an orchid "tree." Genera with pendent or semi-pendent flowers, such as *Stanhopea*, are best grown in open-slatted hanging baskets.

Both epiphytic and terrestrial orchids are suitable for growing in a conservatory, greenhouse, or, in certain cases, as houseplants. Grow houseplants in clay or plastic pots or wooden baskets, in humid but well-ventilated conditions. When the roots of a plant overflow its container, repot at the onset of the growing season into a container that has room for 2 years' new growth.

Orchids are not easily propagated from seed; in the wild, the tiny seeds usually germinate only with the help of a mycorrhizal fungus, which must be replicated in cultivation. Alternative methods of propagation are given below.

Illegal collecting is depleting wild orchid species, so it is vital that gardeners obtain only plants that have been raised in cultivation.

ORCHID PROPAGATION

Increase stocks by division, removal of backbulbs, or from stem cuttings. Professional growers also raise plants from seed or by meristem culture.

For division, select a plant that has outgrown its container, and split the rhizome so that each part retains at least 3 healthy pseudobulbs; cut out any dead roots, then pot up with the oldest pseudobulb against the rim. With backbulbs, detach from the rhizome, and pot up singly in a 2½in (6cm) container, the cut surface against the rim. For stem cuttings, use sections 3in (8cm) long, with at least 1 dormant bud. Store on moist moss in indirect light until rooted.

Selecting backbulbs
Choose firm backbulbs, such as the examples on this Cymbidium.

CULTIVATION REQUIREMENTS

TEMPERATURE REGIME	GROWING MEDIUM	LIGHT	HUMIDITY	WATERING	FERTILIZER
COOL Min. 50–55°F (10–13°C). Max. 70–75°F (21–24°C). INTERMEDIATE Min. 57–66°F (14–19°C). Max. 86–91°F (30–33°C). WARM Min. 68–75°F (20–24°C). Max. 86–91°F (30–33°C).	STANDARD EPIPHYTIC MEDIUM 3 parts bark chips (use fine-grade granulated bark for fine-rooted orchids); 1 part perlite; 1 part fine charcoal. STANDARD TERRESTRIAL MEDIUM 3 parts fibrous peat; 3 parts coarse grit; 1 part perlite; 1 part fine charcoal.	IN SUMMER Most need shade from direct sunlight: shade the greenhouse from early spring until early autumn. IN WINTER Provide full light.	IN SUMMER Damp down daily in early morning (tropical species also in late afternoon). Also mist foliage to reduce leaf temperature. Ventilate well. IN WINTER Do not damp down in cold, clammy conditions, except to counteract drying effects of heating in very cold weather.	IN GROWTH When new growth appears, water regularly in the early morning. Use rainwater or soft water at ambient temperature; medium should remain moist. Mist foliage. WHEN DORMANT Water species that retain leaves sufficiently to prevent dehydration; allow medium to dry out between applications. Keep orchids that lose their leaves dry.	IN GROWTH Apply commercial orchid fertilizer or ¼- to ½-strength balanced liquid fertilizer every 2 or 3 weeks, when watering. (Some growers use a high-nitrogen fertilizer for leaf growth, followed by a high-potash fertilizer for better flowering.) WHEN DORMANT Do not feed.

Bromeliads

Members of the Bromeliaceae family, bromeliads number over 2,800 species in 56 genera. Most grow wild from the southern states of the US to Central and South America, and in the West Indies. Producing striking inflorescences and colorful, often variegated leaves, they are easy to cultivate in a greenhouse, as houseplants, or even outdoors during the summer.

Rainforest epiphytes
In the wild, many epiphytes (here, Aechmea fasciata*) cling to the highest branches of trees to obtain maximum levels of moisture and light. In cultivation, such plants may be displayed on bare branches, secured with adhesive or wedged into notches.*

What are bromeliads?

Bromeliads are mainly rainforest plants, although some are found in mountainous or semi-desert areas, with a few in marshes and on seashores. Most are tropical epiphytes, thriving in humid conditions, rooted to trees or rocks with little soil around their roots. Others are terrestrial.

Most bromeliads are rosette-forming. They range greatly in size, from low-growing plants that form dense colonies, like *Bromelia balansae*, to tree-like species up to 15ft (5m) tall, such as *Puya berteroniana*. The erect or semi-prostrate rosettes consist of brightly colored or variegated, sometimes toothed or spiny-margined leaves, which are often adapted to absorb or conserve moisture. Some bromeliads, including air plants (*Tillandsia*), have leaves covered in tiny scales that enable them to retain and absorb moisture and nutrients from the atmosphere, often from mists and low, moisture-laden clouds. In other bromeliads, like *Guzmania*, *Vriesea*, and *Aechmea*, the center of the rosette forms a "cup" or "vase" that retains water and nutrients.

Water-retaining cup
The leaves of some bromeliads, such as Neoregelia, *form a cup, which should be wiped clean and refilled regularly.*

Brightly colored inflorescences of bracts and flowers are borne in the center of the rosettes or are set low in the central cup in certain bromeliads. As monocotyledons (see p.10), bromeliads have flower parts in groups of 3. After flowering, the rosettes begin to die, although new offsets are usully born from dormant buds in the basal leaf axils or on the rhizomes or roots. These offsets can be used for propagation (see below).

Cultivation

Bromeliads are best cultivated by simulating the conditions of their natural habitat (see panel below). Given the right growing environment, they require relatively little maintenance.

In cool areas, most rock-dwelling and terrestrial bromeliads will thrive in a greenhouse or conservatory, or as houseplants. In warmer climates, cultivate bromeliads outdoors, with protection from extremes of heat, sunlight, and rain. Most epiphytes require partial shade, both outdoors and under glass, since bright light may fade their foliage. In many terrestrial species, however, full light improves leaf coloration.

Epiphytes may be attached to a tree or branch, which can be secured in a container, or to a metal or wire framework covered in bark.

To propagate bromeliads, detach offsets from the base or leaf axils of mature plants. Pot up each offset individually into a mix of equal parts shredded peat (or substitute), leaf mold, and granitic grit. Water sparingly until new growth develops.

Sow seed as soon as ripe in a mix of 1 part each leaf mold and shredded peat (or substitute), and 3 parts sharp sand or fine granitic grit. Sow winged seeds (like those of air plants) on slabs of moistened wood or bark; place the slabs at regular intervals on a tray containing a mix of equal parts sharp sand and moist, chopped sphagnum moss.

Apply a commercial fungicide to prevent damping off, then place the containers or tray in a closed case with bottom heat at about 70°F (21°C). The slow-growing seedlings will be large enough to prick out and grow on after a few months.

CULTIVATION REQUIREMENTS

TYPE		TEMPERATURE REGIME	GROWING MEDIUM	LIGHT	HUMIDITY AND VENTILATION	WATERING	FERTILIZER
UNDER GLASS	EPIPHYTES	RAINFOREST SPECIES Min. 55–59°F (13–15°C). MOST OTHER SPECIES Min. 50°F (10°C); some hardy, alpine species can tolerate lower temperatures.	IN CONTAINERS Equal parts shredded peat or granulated bark; leaf mold; granitic grit. GROWN EPIPHYTICALLY Cover roots in moist sphagnum moss.	Most need bright filtered light.	Rainforest species need high humidity; all others need moderate humidity. Damp down daily in growth, less often when dormant. Ventilate well.	Mist daily, using rain-water or soft water; also mist moss around roots of epiphytes. Keep cup full of water, less so in winter.	IN GROWTH Apply ¼-strength commercial orchid foliar fertilizer every 4 or 5 weeks when misting. WHEN DORMANT Do not feed.
UNDER GLASS	TERRESTRIALS AND ROCK-DWELLERS		1 part peat or coconut fiber (coir); 1 part leaf mold; 3 parts granitic grit.	Most need full light.	Maintain low to moderate humidity. Ventilate well.	Water freely; allow the medium to dry partially between applications. Where appropriate, regularly replenish cup with fresh rainwater.	IN GROWTH Apply ½-strength low-nitrogen liquid feed every 3 or 4 weeks when watering. WHEN DORMANT Do not feed.
OUTDOORS	EPIPHYTES, TERRESTRIALS, AND ROCK-DWELLERS	Minimum temperatures as above.	Most prefer sharply drained, humus-rich soil.	Most epiphytes need partial shade; most terrestrials and rock-dwellers need full sun.	Rainforest epiphytes need high humidity. Terrestrials need low to moderate humidity.	Water as needed; light misting is advisable in extremely hot weather.	Feeding is not necessary but will improve size and vigor.

Cacti and other succulents

The fascinating shapes of cacti and other succulents are the result of the adverse conditions they endure in their natural habitats. They vary in habit from small cushions of rosetted leaves to the tall, branching columns of some desert cacti. Their unusual textures include smooth, waxy, hairy, or spiny surfaces. Many produce subtly or brightly colored flowers, enhancing their appeal in desert gardens and greenhouses, and as houseplants.

What are succulents?

Succulents are plants that have adapted to extreme conditions, particularly frequent periods of drought. Typical adaptations include reduced leaf size and the presence of fleshy, water-storing tissue in the stems, leaves, or roots. They are native to a range of habitats, from cold alpine climates, and semi-desert areas in temperate and subtropical zones, to moist rainforest; many may undergo a dormant period in either summer or winter. Succulents may be loosely grouped as stem succulents (including cacti), leaf succulents, root succulents, and caudiciform succulents.

CAUDICIFORM SUCCULENTS, *such as* Adenium obesum, *have swollen stem bases.*

Stem succulents

Stem succulents (most of which are cacti) have swollen, moisture-retaining stems, usually slender, oval, columnar, or spherical in shape. They may be climbing, pendent, or tree-like in habit; some resemble flat, leaf-like pads. Epiphytic succulents native to dry regions often produce aerial roots on their stems that absorb moisture from the atmosphere.

Cacti, which originate in North, Central, or South America (except for *Rhipsalis baccifera*), are distinguished from other stem succulents by their unique growing points, known as areoles. Although a few, such as *Pereskia*, have semi-succulent leaves, most lack foliage, thereby minimizing water loss through transpiration in very dry conditions; chlorophyll for photosynthesis is contained in the stems.

Most cacti have ribs arranged longitudinally on the stems, which expand or contract according to their water content. Along the ribs are the areoles, from which arise flowers, new growth, and spines. Cactus spines are modified leaves, borne as radials (around the edge of an areole) or as centrals (in the center of an areole). They condense moisture that drips onto the soil around the plant's roots. Epiphytic cacti from humid rainforests have flattened stems with broad surface areas to absorb as much of the limited available light as possible.

Some cacti, such as *Melocactus*, produce a terminal, head-like, almost woody structure, the cephalium, which produces a mass of woolly spines and flowers and stops further vegetative growth. In other genera, the cephalium is lateral, allowing growth in height to continue. It is then often referred to as a pseudocephalium.

Spiny cactus
Cacti like Oreocereus intertexta *(syn.* Matucana intertexta*) are stem succulents with characteristic growing points known as areoles.*

Leaf succulents

The foliage of leaf succulents is usually fleshy, very variable in shape, and downy, felted, glaucous, powdery, waxy, or glossy in texture. Many species have opaque areas at the leaf tips to diffuse the sun's rays. To lessen the rate of transpiration in a dry climate, leaves have a limited number of stomata (pores), which remain closed in the heat of the day.

Water-storage tissues inside the leaves enable the plants to survive in arid conditions. Leaves swell and shrink according to their water content, and usually drop away during periods of severe drought. In many species, the leaves form tight rosettes, which are borne on short stems. This minimizes evaporation both from the plant itself and from the soil beneath.

Root succulents

These succulents are usually found in places where the climate is harsh or the soil thin and poor. They have swollen roots, hidden below ground, that lose moisture relatively slowly. Most root succulents develop from

A desert garden
In warm, dry climates, dramatic effects can be achieved by contrasting the columnar habits of Cereus, Cleistocactus, *and* Haageocereus *species with the more complex outlines of such plants as* Agave, Aloe, *or* Opuntia *species.*

LEAF AND STEM SUCCULENTS

Leaf succulents have foliage but often lack a stem, whereas cacti and other stem succulents have a swollen stem but mostly lack leaves. In both types, stems or foliage expand when water is plentiful and contract or, in the case of foliage, drop away, in a drought. The fibrous root system of leaf and stem succulents extends over a wide area just below the surface level to maximize the collection of water. New root hairs are quickly formed to take up any available moisture from dew and passing rain showers.

LEAF SUCCULENT
Thick, fleshy leaves retain water.

STEM SUCCULENT
Stem contains water-storage tissue.

a normal root system, but some have a specialized rootstock, usually in the form of a tuber. Many also have deciduous succulent leaves or stems, which regenerate when good conditions for growth prevail.

Caudiciform succulents

Some succulents, such as certain species of *Adenium*, *Dioscorea*, *Euphorbia*, and *Pachypodium*, have a rootstock that may develop to large proportions and gradually emerge above ground to form a rounded, sometimes slightly flattened, bottle-shaped or tree-like growth, known as a caudex. The caudex is defined botanically as a swollen base formed at the junction of root and stem. More generally, any succulent with a swollen stem or root above ground is described as caudiciform. Many cactus and succulent specialists gradually lift caudiciform plants out of their growing media to encourage and expose the growth of attractive caudices.

Garden and indoor displays

Where climate allows, cacti and other succulents can provide an impressive outdoor display. Planted out or grouped in containers, their foliage, flowers, and unusual forms create an eye-catching feature on a sunny patio or terrace. Even in frost-prone areas, plants may be moved outdoors to a sheltered site during the hottest summer months. Some succulents from mountainous regions are hardy, particularly when protected from moisture in winter, and are ideal for cultivating outdoors in a raised bed. Those originating from cooler areas are best shaded from full sun. Cacti and other succulents are very popular as houseplants, individually or grouped in containers. They are often also grown in a temperate or warm greenhouse, where they may be displayed in containers, in indoor borders, or in raised beds.

Epiphytic succulents, such as *Epiphyllum* and *Schlumbergera*, require partial or dappled shade. They are particularly effective when used in plantings with epiphytic bromeliads (see p.47), which have similar cultivation requirements. Many epiphytic species can be wedged into the crevices of a wall or between roof tiles; those with pendent or trailing habits are suitable for hanging baskets. Some can be lodged in the branches of a tree, with moistened sphagnum moss wrapped around their roots, and held in place with fine wire or garden twine; the roots will eventually anchor themselves.

Hardy succulents
Members of several genera (including Opuntia, Sedum, *and* Sempervivum*) are hardy throughout much of North America. Shown here is* Sempervivum arachnoides, *the cobweb houseleek.*

Cultivation

The panel below gives details of the general growing requirements of cacti and other succulents.

Suitable containers for growing succulents include shallow pans or half-pots, which should contain a layer of coarse sand at the base to ensure sharp drainage. Plants should also be top-dressed with grit or stone chips to protect their collars from excess moisture, which tends to lead to fatal rotting.

PROPAGATION

Increase succulents by the following methods, or by offsets or grafts.

Divide clump-forming species and cultivars as soon as new growth appears, so that each part has a healthy bud or shoot and roots.

Take stem cuttings in early or mid-spring: trim a leaf-bearing stem to ½in (1.5cm), or cut sections of leaf-like or columnar cacti into lengths of 2–4in (5–10cm). Take leaf cuttings from spring to early summer, each with a sliver of stem at the base. Allow all cuttings to callus, then insert upright into equal parts peat (or substitute) and sharp grit or sand. Top-dress with grit or gravel and place in bright indirect light at 70°F (21°C). Spray with tepid water until rooted.

Sow seed as soon as ripe from late winter to late spring; cover with twice their depth of standard seed mix, top-dressed with fine grit. Keep moist and place in a closed case in indirect light. Upon germination, gradually admit more light and air. Maintain tender species at 70°F (21°C). Plunge containers of seed of hardy species in a cold frame. After pricking out, grow on at 59°F (15°C).

Division of rootstock
Split rootstock into sections; discard old or damaged material; repot each section.

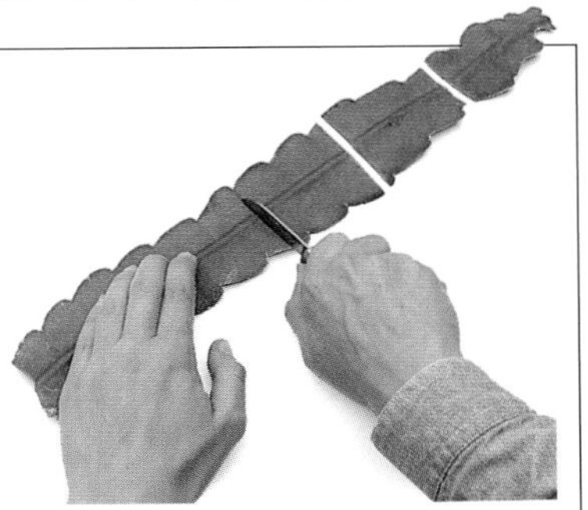

Stem cuttings
Cut leaf-like stems laterally into sections about 2–4in (5–10cm) long.

Leaf cuttings
Detach a healthy leaf with a small piece of stem attached to the base.

Cacti seedlings
Prick out seedlings as soon as they can be handled (several months after sowing).

CULTIVATION REQUIREMENTS

	TEMPERATURE REGIME	GROWING MEDIUM	LIGHT	HUMIDITY	WATERING	FERTILIZER
UNDER GLASS	MOST SPECIES Optimum day temp.: 59–86°F (15–30°C). Min. night temp.: 50–59°F (10–15°C). When dormant: 45–50°F (7–10°C). TROPICAL AND EQUATORIAL SPECIES Optimum day temp.: 70–90°F (21–32°C). Min. night temp.: 55–68°F (13–20°C). When dormant: 50–59°F (10–15°C).	Most need pH 6–7.5 and sharply drained soil. STANDARD CACTUS MEDIUM 3 parts soil-based mix or 2 parts soilless mix; 1 part ¼in (6mm) grit. Top-dress with grit, or apply limestone chips for species that require alkaline conditions. EPIPHYTIC CACTUS MEDIUM 3 parts soil-based compost or soilless mix; 2 parts ¼in (6mm) grit; 1 part leaf mold.	SUMMER Most species require full light with shade from hot sun. Epiphytes and trailing/climbing members of the Asclepiadaceae family require partial shade or bright filtered light. WINTER Provide full light in winter. Supplement light for winter-growing species, if possible.	Most require low humidity and good ventilation. Damp down in very hot weather. Many rainforest epiphytes require high humidity (*Rhipsalis* species need 80 percent humidity); mist on warm days. Shelter all from drafts.	IN GROWTH Soak thoroughly, using rain-water or soft water; allow medium to dry between applications; avoid wetting the foliage. Keep medium of tropical and epiphytic species just moist. WHEN DORMANT Keep most species dry; mist with tepid water at noon on warm days to prevent desiccation. Keep medium of tropical species and epiphytes just moist.	Add slow-release balanced fertilizer to medium. IN GROWTH Apply commercial cactus fertilizer or ½-strength balanced liquid fertilizer every 4 or 5 weeks when watering. WHEN DORMANT Do not feed when dormant or when medium is dry.
OUTDOORS	Min. temp. 50°F (10°C) for most. In frost-prone areas, move plants outdoors only in warm summer months (except for fully hardy species).	CONTAINERS AND RAISED BEDS 2 parts soilless mix, coconut fiber, or ground bark; 1 part ¼in (6mm) grit. Apply slow-release balanced fertilizer.	Most require full sun. Very succulent, smooth-skinned species require full sun with some midday shade.	Most require low humidity. Many rainforest epiphytes need high humidity.	Soak thoroughly; allow to dry. Many rainforest epiphytes require light misting on warm days.	Apply slow-release balanced fertilizer to soil, or use commercial cactus fertilizer (as above).

Palms and cycads

These evergreen trees or shrubs, with arching, divided leaves, are similar in appearance, yet botanically unrelated. Mainly from tropical and subtropical regions, palms and cycads cannot be grown outdoors permanently in Canada but may be placed outside during the summer. They are generally grown as houseplants or in a conservatory.

What are palms?

Palms range from usually unbranched large trees to dwarf shrubs that grow on the forest floor or in open, rocky sites. Some appear stemless; most have an upright trunk. Many have a distinctive crownshaft (a usually green, slightly swollen extension of the stem tip) formed from tightly rolled, flattened leaf stalks.

The leaves may be pinnate, palmately lobed, or semi-palmate. Palms with pinnate foliage, such as the coconut palm (*Cocos nucifera*), are known as feather palms. The leaflets may be lobed or cut, forming a 2-pinnate leaf, as in fish-tail palms (*Caryota*). The palmately lobed leaves of fan palms, such as *Trachycarpus*, are basically hand-shaped, sometimes with radiating lobes. Semi-palmate leaves, such as those of some species of *Livistona*, appear palmate, but have a short extension of the leaf stalks between each pair of leaflets.

Palm trees produce panicles of small flowers among the leaves or just beneath the lowest leaf. They are monocotyledons (see p.10), their floral parts occurring in multiples of 3. The variably sized fruits have moist flesh, as in the date palm (*Phoenix dactylifera*), or dry flesh, as in the coconut palm.

Cultivating palms

In summer, grow palms in moist but well-drained, neutral to slightly acidic soil in full sun to deep shade, depending on the species. Many require shelter from strong winds, although some, such as the coconut palm and *Trachycarpus*, are wind-tolerant.

Indoors or under glass, grow palms as dwarf or young specimens in soilless potting mix. Place them in bright, indirect light to minimize leaf scorch: those native to rain-forests are particularly sensitive to harsh light. From late spring to late summer, water moderately and apply a balanced liquid fertilizer monthly. At other times, water sparingly. Repot in spring. Palms rarely can be pruned.

Most palms are grown from seed, although some species may be divided, and a few produce suckers that may be transplanted. Sow fresh seed singly, as soon as ripe, in standard seed-starting mix in containers 3–3½in (8–9cm) in diameter. Cover each seed with its own depth in soil mix, although very large seeds should be only half-buried. Sow seed of tropical species at 72–86°F (22–30°C), and seed of temperate species at 55–64°F (13–18°C). Germination often occurs within 2 or 3 months, but may take from 10 days to 2 years. Grow seedlings in partial shade with moderate humidity.

Coconut palms
Cocos nucifera *(coconut palm) thrives in tropical climates, reaching a height of 70–100ft (20–30m). Young specimens are impressive as houseplants or grown under glass, and will last until they outgrow their site.*

What are cycads?

Cycads are primitive seed plants. Most have short, sometimes branched, occasionally tuber-like trunks, either fully or partly below ground. Some produce suckers. The foliage is pinnate or 2-pinnate, usually tough, leathery, and often rigid; the leaflets may be tipped or margined with spines.

The majority of cycads reproduce by means of primitive, unisexual, cone-like structures that bear either ovules or pollen sacs. *Cycas* species differ in bearing large, naked ovules along the margins of structures similar to reduced leaves. The ovules develop into nut-like seeds up to 3in (8cm) long, with a tough, woody casing, covered by a thin, sometimes bright red or orange pulp.

Cultivating cycads

Cycads, with their slow growth and elegant habit, are popular house-plants. They are becoming scarce in their native habitats, so always ensure that plants purchased have not been collected in the wild.

During the summer, grow cycads outdoors in well-drained, neutral to acidic soil in full sun or partial shade. Indoors or under glass, grow them in bright but indirect light, in a mix of 2 parts well-drained, soil-based potting mix, and 1 part grit or washed sand. Water plants sparingly except when in active growth, and keep dry in cooler temperatures. Apply a half-strength balanced liquid fertilizer monthly to container-grown plants when in growth. Repot in spring. Cycads rarely can be pruned.

CYCAD PROPAGATION

Cycads can be increased from seed or by transplanting suckers. Sow seed singly in small, deep containers. Use a standard, soil-based potting mix or a mix of equal parts gritty sand and peat (or substitute). Seeds should protrude slightly above the surface of the soil. Maintain at a temperature of 61–86°F (16–30°C). Germination, if successful, may take from 3 months to 2 years. The subsequent growth rate will also be slow, with each plantlet producing 1–3 leaves per year. To propagate from suckers, detach the suckers produced by mature plants in spring and pot them up separately.

MOST CYCADS, *like* Cycas revoluta, *can be propagated from seed or by detaching and potting up suckers of mature plants.*

SHAPE

Many palms produce a single, tall, unbranched stem, making them suitable for specimen and street-tree planting. Cycads are also generally single-stemmed, and make striking specimens. Multi-stemmed species occur in both groups and are also useful.

SINGLE-STEMMED
Roystonea regia

MULTI-STEMMED
Chamaedorea seifrizii

Ferns

Attractive foliage, year-round interest, and a general preference for damp, shaded areas where many flowering plants are unable to survive make ferns popular as houseplants, or for growing outdoors or under glass. Hardy ferns are especially effective in streamside and woodland settings, and frost-tender, tropical ferns are handsome plants for greenhouses or conservatories.

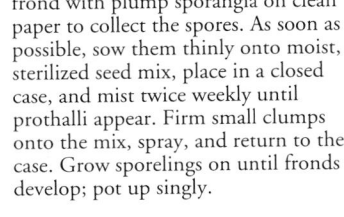

Planting for contrasts
Successful plantings of ferns often contrast textures, habits, and colors of foliage. Here, the glossy, strap-shaped leaves of Asplenium scolopendrium *arch over the feathery fronds of* Polypodium vulgare.

What are ferns?

Ferns are primitive plants that produce evergreen or deciduous leaf-like structures, known as fronds. Together with club mosses and horsetails, they belong to the Pteridophytes, a group of plants that lack flowers and reproduce by spores rather than seeds. Ferns are epiphytic (lodging on trees or rocks) or terrestrial (rooted in soil). Their reproductive spores are sometimes borne in sporangia, usually clustered within indusia (covers of epidermal tissue) on the underside of their fronds. After germination, spores form a ribbon of green tissue (prothallus), where both the male and the female reproductive organs are sited. Fertilization occurs on the underside of the prothallus.

Ornamental features

Ferns are highly valued for the elegant symmetry of their fronds and the textural contrasts of their lush, usually green foliage, varied in some species with displays of red, yellow, or gray. Fronds may also have brown scales at their bases or have silvery undersides.

Their diversity of habit presents a wide choice for the gardener. Shuttlecock ferns like *Matteuccia* have erect rhizomes, each bearing a crown of fronds. Creeping ferns, such as *Phlebodium*, are prostrate and provide good groundcover, producing single fronds at intervals along each rhizome. Tree ferns, such as *Dicksonia,* have erect, trunk-like rhizomes, ridged with scars left by the stalks of old fronds. Staghorn ferns (*Platycerium*) are tender epiphytes with some clasping fronds produced from the base of each plant, and some erect fronds, slightly arching outward.

If carefully chosen, ferns provide year-round garden interest. Most uncurl bright foliage in spring, the fronds of deciduous plants starting to fade by late summer and dying back after the first frosts. Evergreen ferns often remain attractive throughout autumn and winter.

Cultivation

Once established, ferns usually require little maintenance. The majority prefer conditions ranging from partial to deep shade. Some, such *Matteuccia*, *Onoclea*, and *Osmunda,* require damp soil. Others, such as *Asplenium*, *Polypodium*, and *Polystichum*, tolerate relatively dry sites. Dwarf species of *Asplenium* and ferns from desert areas, such as *Cheilanthes*, prefer full sun and are ideal in rock crevices. Most other hardy species will thrive outdoors in well-aerated, humus-rich soil.

Many ferns, particularly frost-tender species, may be grown in a conservatory or greenhouse, or as houseplants. They prefer bright indirect light. Species native to desert habitats, such as *Cheilanthes* and *Pellaea*, will thrive in full light in an alpine house (see p.41).

Water ferns only when soil mix is barely moist to the touch, since they are intolerant of excessive water. As a rule, they should be watered more freely in summer than in winter. Do not allow ferns in containers to remain standing in water.

Most ferns prefer high levels of humidity, which can be achieved indoors by standing containers on a tray of moistened, expanded clay granules or gravel, or by misting frequently. In winter, the humidity level may be reduced by the drying effects of central heating. This can be offset by keeping ferns in a cool room or hallway.

Grow terrestrial ferns in a mix of 1 part each of soil, medium-grade ground bark, and charcoal, 2 parts sharp sand, and 3 parts coarse leaf mold; add 1 part limestone chips for species that require alkaline conditions. Include a slow-release, balanced fertilizer in the mixture; alternatively, apply a half-strength, general-purpose or tomato-type liquid fertilizer every 3 or 4 weeks during growth. Grow epiphytic ferns in a mix of equal parts fine-grade ground bark, perlite, and charcoal, or on bark slabs.

Repot all container-grown ferns in spring or summer when their roots overfill the containers.

To propagate ferns, cut rhizomes into sections; or divide crowns, in spring; or use bulbils or spores (see panel).

PINNATE FOLIAGE *is typical of ferns; this frond of* Dryopteris affinis *shows the division into pinnae (leaflets), which are further divided into segments (pinnules).*

PROPAGATION BY BULBILS OR SPORES

To propagate from bulbils, sever a frond full of bulbils at the base. Peg it flat onto seed or cutting mix in a tray, water, label, and seal in an inflated plastic bag, and leave in a warm, light place until the bulbils have rooted. Grow on singly in 3in (8cm) containers of moist, soilless mix. To propagate from spores, place a frond with plump sporangia on clean paper to collect the spores. As soon as possible, sow them thinly onto moist, sterilized seed mix, place in a closed case, and mist twice weekly until prothalli appear. Firm small clumps onto the mix, spray, and return to the case. Grow sporelings on until fronds develop; pot up singly.

Ripe bulbils
Select a frond that is drooping under the weight of bulbils, which may have tiny green fronds emerging from them.

Ripe spores
Select fronds with sporangia that are neither rough (too old) nor still tightly wrapped in the indusium (too young).

Aquatic plants

Many aquatic plants, prized over the centuries for their beauty, can be cultivated in artificial or natural water features in the garden. Large and small ponds, formal or informal pools, streams, bog gardens, and even small barrel ponds all present different conditions and varying water depths that will support an exciting diversity of aquatic plant, insect, and animal life.

An emphasis on marginals

Marginals, bog plants, and moisture-loving plants link a pond with the rest of the garden and provide a habitat for wildlife. They are also useful in smaller ponds, leaving the water surface clear to reflect the colors and forms of the planting.

What are aquatic plants?

All plants that grow rooted, floating, or submerged in water are broadly termed aquatic plants. They are categorized as submerged, deep-water, surface-floating, marginal, bog, or moisture-loving plants, according to the depth of water in which they grow best. Depth is measured from the surface of the soil around a plant's roots to the surface of the water.

Most aquatic plants are both ornamental and functional. They produce attractive foliage and flowers, but also play a vital role in the ecosystem of water features, by providing a habitat for myriad microorganisms, insects, and wildlife, and by helping to suppress algal growth and maintain the clarity of water. A healthy balance of animal and plant life can be achieved only if a pond is stocked with an appropriate range of species.

Submerged and floating plants

Certain plants, such as *Lagarosiphon major* and milfoils (*Myriophyllum*), remain totally submerged in water. They are fast-growing and usually produce slender stems and leaves. Submerged plants are grown mainly for their ability to reduce algae by competing with them for mineral salts (released by the breakdown of organic matter, such as dead leaves) dissolved in the water. They are often called oxygenators, because they release oxygen into the water as a by-product of photosynthesis – an asset if fish are to be kept in a pool. The fine strands of submerged plant foliage also provide valuable shelter for fish fry.

Deep-water plants, like waterlilies (*Nymphaea*), grow with their root systems at depths of 12–36in (30–90cm) and with their foliage and flowers floating at surface level. The shade cast by their leaves reduces underwater light levels, which helps to control algal growth.

Surface-floating plants, such as *Azolla filiculoides*, usually have tiny leaves and spreading roots that absorb nutrients from the water. They multiply rapidly during summer, forming dense colonies.

Ideally, 50–70 percent of a pool's surface should be covered with the foliage of deep-water and floating plants to keep the water clear. In a new pond, this allows other aquatics to become established. If coverage is greater than 70 percent, insufficient light will filter through the water for submerged plants to survive.

Waterlily pond

*Deep-water plants, such as these waterlilies (*Nymphaea *'Escarboucle'), are ideal for larger ponds; they are complemented here by marginal clumps of sedges and rushes.*

Shallow-water and bog plants

Marginal plants tolerate conditions ranging from pure mud to water 12–18in (30–45cm) deep over their roots and are perhaps the most diverse of all aquatic plants. They are best used to conceal the artificial outline of an informal water feature, such as a wildlife pond or water-course, but also provide cover for birds and other wild creatures.

Bog plants are also marginal plants but prefer a site in shallower water. However, the term is commonly used to describe any plant that grows in saturated soil just beyond the water's edge, normally without a covering of water. Such plants represent the transition between true aquatics and plants that are simply moisture-loving. In nursery catalogs, the latter are sometimes referred to as bog plants, despite their intolerance of waterlogged ground and need for oxygen around their roots.

Planning a water feature

Formal and informal water features and their associated aquatic plants have been used throughout history as major elements of garden design. As with all plantings, water gardens should be designed to take advantage of the contrasts and similarities between plants, and provide a long succession of flowers and seed heads or decorative foliage throughout the year. In selecting aquatic plants, it is worth bearing in mind that many die back after frost, reducing winter interest in cold regions. Native plants provide food for insect life, such as dragonflies, which in turn fall prey to other creatures.

Always choose a water feature that is appropriate for the size and style of the garden, and take great care when deciding on its position. A pond is best sited in full sun, away from overhanging trees, and should not be constructed in an exposed site or a frost pocket. Since most gardens lack a brook or natural spring, a pond should lie near an accessible water source so that moisture lost through evaporation can be replaced easily.

A formal pond of any dimensions provides an impressive focal point

MOISTURE-LOVING PLANTS, *such as* Astilbe *'Bressingham Beauty', will thrive in damp, but not saturated soil, in a bog garden.*

PLANTING A POND

Aquatic plants are best introduced into a pond from late spring to midsummer. Slide surface-floaters onto the water with roots trailing downward. Plant deep-water, submerged, and marginal plants in an underwater bed or in containers, using heavy soil or a commercial aquatic mix that will not cloud the water. Containers will curb invasive species and allow easier relocation and division of plants.

Aquatic containers usually have solid sides with a few holes at the bottom. Some containers are open-sided, allowing a much freer passage of water and oxygen. Firm plants into the soil and top-dress with grit or pea gravel for ballast and to prevent fish from disturbing the roots. Apply a slow-release aquatic fertilizer in summer.

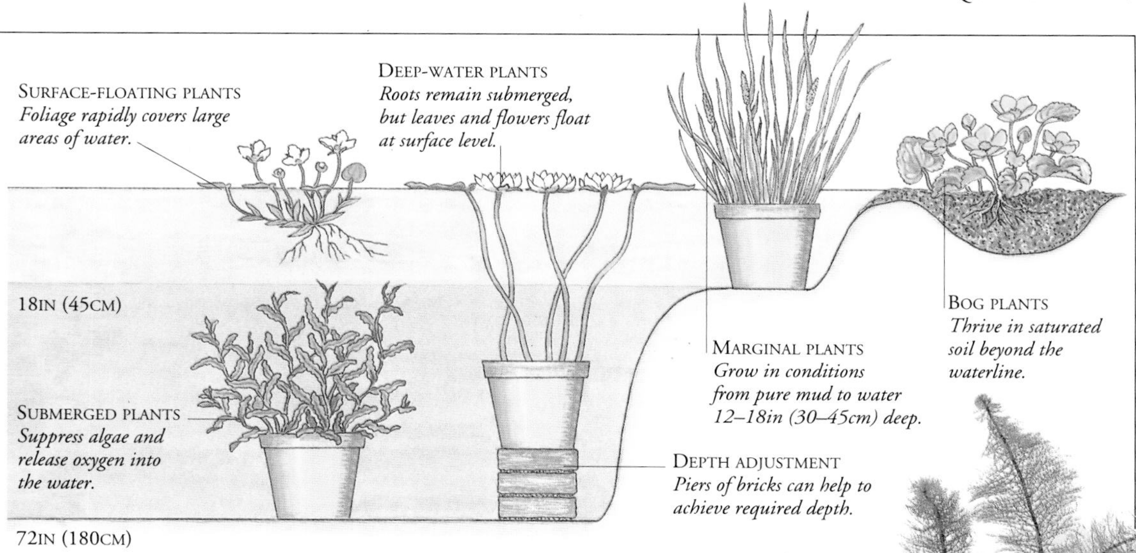
SURFACE-FLOATING PLANTS
Foliage rapidly covers large areas of water.
DEEP-WATER PLANTS
Roots remain submerged, but leaves and flowers float at surface level.
18IN (45CM)
SUBMERGED PLANTS
Suppress algae and release oxygen into the water.
72IN (180CM)
MARGINAL PLANTS
Grow in conditions from pure mud to water 12–18in (30–45cm) deep.
BOG PLANTS
Thrive in saturated soil beyond the waterline.
DEPTH ADJUSTMENT
Piers of bricks can help to achieve required depth.

within a garden. It may be sunken or raised, made from concrete or stone, and is usually geometric in shape, with straight sides. Use ornamental materials to decorate its perimeter, either as paving or in the form of a raised edge or seat.

A small formal pond will support a limited but choice range of species and cultivars. They are often best selected for their architectural interest. Ideal examples are water-lilies, with their spreading, rounded foliage and exquisite flowers, or water irises, like *Iris pseudacorus,* which have upright blooms on strongly erect stems.

Informal pools are mostly sunken and irregular in outline, often designed to attract native wildlife to a garden. To suit amphibians, the pool should ideally have a muddy bottom and gently sloping sides, dotted with large, flat stones. Birds and other wild creatures, such as turtles, will be attracted to the bathing and drinking facilities provided by an area of shallow beach. Soften or disguise the edges of an informal pool with natural materials, like rocks or turf, partially concealed by clumps of marginal and bog plants.

A bog garden is an attractive way of using waterlogged ground, and also provides good conditions for local wildlife. To create an artificial bog garden, place a perforated synthetic liner under soil next to a pool; this will retain sufficient moisture for bog plants.

Almost any water-tight container may be used to grow oxygenators, dwarf water lilies, and marginal plants. Metal containers must be painted with sealant or fitted with a synthetic liner to avoid poisoning either fish or plants. In cold regions, containers also enable frost-tender plants to be grown outdoors in summer, then overwintered indoors.

Corner feature
Even small gardens may be enlivened by a small pool and fountain, ringed with ferns and other moisture-loving plants.

Maintenance

Synthetic liners, plastic and fiber-glass modules, and electric pumps for filtering water have all simplified pond maintenance. Ensure that drainage is adequate for occasions when the pond may overflow. On sloping ground, a tumbling or split-level watercourse or waterfall may be constructed. If fish are kept, install a fountain or similar device to aerate the water during still summer nights, when oxygenating plants are unable to photosynthesize. Most aquatic plants are intolerant of splashing water, so they are best sited in more tranquil parts of the pond. In areas with cold winters, move fish that are normally kept in a container pond, such as a barrel, to a sunken pool, where they are more likely to survive.

Aquatic plants require little regular care, although submerged plants grown in a soil-bottomed pond need regular thinning. Remove damaged and diseased leaves throughout the growing season. In autumn, cut back any leaves or stems that would rot in the water. With wildlife ponds, however, foliage is best left until spring to provide winter cover for birds and animals.

CABOMBA CAROLINIANA
is an oxygenator with attractive feathery foliage, best displayed in an aquarium.

Aquarium plants

An indoor aquarium enables year-round cultivation of tender plants, and also displays the foliage of submerged plants and the feathery roots of surface-floaters to good effect. Grow aquatic plants from temperate regions in a cold-water aquarium. Tropical plants and fish must have a heated aquarium.

Line the base of the aquarium with an inert medium, such as grit, sand, or gravel. Maintain the balance of the water chemistry by growing a suitable range of oxygenating plants, and provide a good filtration system and correct temperature. Ensure that lighting is adequate but not too bright (excess light will encourage algal growth). Trim foliage as necessary, and occasionally apply commercial slow-release fertilizer tablets to the growing medium.

PROPAGATION

Aquatic plants can be propagated by seed, division, cuttings, turions (see below), offsets, and runners. Most are increased by division of the rootstock in summer; divide every 1 or 2 years, since roots soon become enmeshed.

Moisture-loving and some aquatic plants can be grown from ripe seed in summer or autumn. Sow on an inert medium and top-dress with fine grit. Keep submerged under glass in bright indirect light at 64°F (18°C). Prick out plantlets, retain under glass, and plant out in spring of the second year.

With submerged plants, take stem-tip cuttings in spring or summer. Trim to 4–6in (10–15cm) long, and insert singly or in bunches of 3–6 into submerged pots of soil; transplant when rooted. Alternatively, float weighted bunches on the water to root in the bottom of a soil-based pond.

Certain aquatic species bear turions: swollen buds that overwinter at the bottom of a pond. When they surface in spring, pot up singly as new plants.

Many surface-floating plants of tropical origin may be increased from offsets or runners, which form on long, adventitious shoots. If detached from the parent, these plantlets will multiply rapidly on the water's surface.

Planting cuttings in containers
Insert cuttings singly or in bunches in a container that is sufficiently large to accommodate the adult plant.

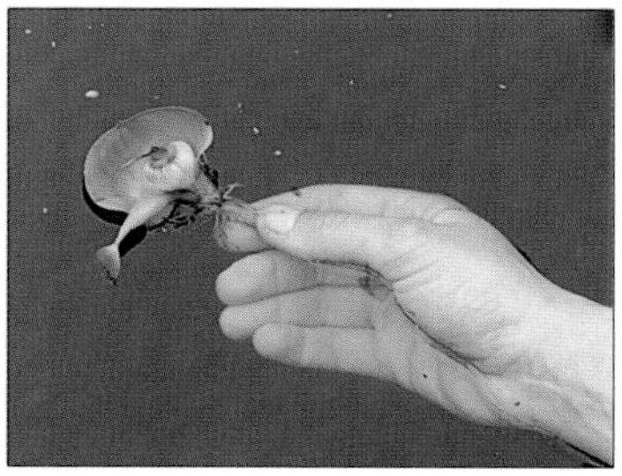

Offsets
Place offsets of floating plants directly on the surface of the water, supporting each one until it floats upright.

Grasses and bamboos

True grasses, including bamboos, are members of a vast family of plants that grows natively throughout the world. A few are very commonly grown as lawns, but many ornamental grasses are valued for their stately habit, feathery inflorescences, and slender, sometimes unusually colored leaves. Some bear decorative seed heads, many of which are suitable for drying.

Flashy grasses
Use grasses to give a border strong visual impact. Select for contrast in height and habit, as well as in the shape and texture of their inflorescences. Here, the arching Pennisetum setaceum *'Purpureum' is offset by silvery mounds of* Senecio cineraria.

What are grasses?

Grasses are evergreen or deciduous annuals or perennials belonging to the Poaceae family. Their erect or arching stems are usually round and hollow, with regularly spaced nodes, clearly seen in the jointed culms ("stems") of bamboos. The foliage is borne in 2 ranks from sheaths, which may be split or peeled back. Colors include yellow, silvery blue, and red, as well as shades of green. Numerous cultivated grasses have variegated leaves, with longitudinal stripes or cross-bands.

The delicate inflorescences, in the form of spikes, panicles, or racemes of tiny spikelets, are usually light and feathery, and subtle in color. Many are suitable for cutting and displaying indoors, either fresh or dried (see p.39).

In the garden, grasses have a variety of uses. Those of imposing habit, like pampas grass (*Cortaderia selloana*), are splendid as specimen plants, while some lower-growing grasses, such as hair grass (*Aira elegantissima*), provide excellent groundcover. Many grasses can also be used in a mixed border, where their soft curves and vertical lines contrast well with more rounded, broader-leaved plants.

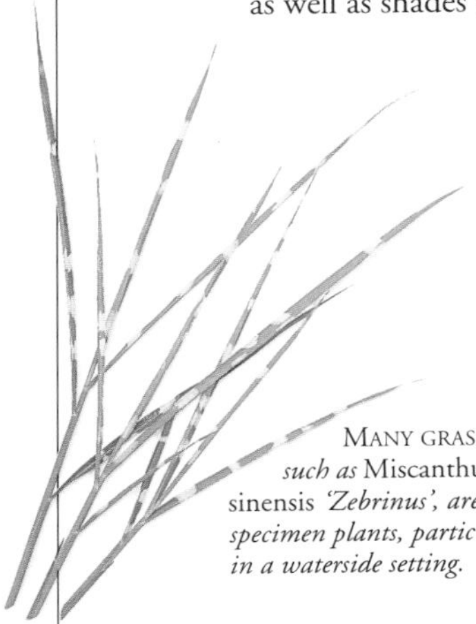

MANY GRASSES, *such as* Miscanthus sinensis *'Zebrinus', are fine specimen plants, particularly in a waterside setting.*

Cultivation

Once established, grasses need little maintenance. Most prefer full sun and moist but well-drained soil, not too rich in nutrients. Feeding is rarely required. Grow grasses that prefer damp soil near a water feature.

Plant hardy, container-grown grasses throughout the year. Tender grasses are best planted in spring; in areas with high rainfall, use sharply drained, gritty soil, and top-dress with stone chips in winter. Bamboos should be watered freely until well established.

Restrain vigorous and invasive grasses by growing in containers, or place a barrier, such as thick plastic sheeting, in the soil around them. Alternatively, cut back invasive roots with a spade when new growth appears in spring, and again in mid- or late summer. Cut perennials to ground level in autumn or early winter, but leave attractive foliage and seed heads until late winter. Cut back tender grasses in spring.

Propagate grasses by seed, sown as soon as ripe, or divide rhizomatous and clump-forming grasses in late spring or early summer. Divisions are often best potted up and established before planting out; use moist but well-drained soil mix, and keep cool in bright indirect light.

BAMBOOS

Most of these woody-culmed, perennial grasses originate in tropical and subtropical regions, particularly E. Asia. The majority are frost tender and evergreen; the few that are fully hardy are from temperate zones. Bamboos range in habit from low-growing plants like *Pleioblastus pygmaeus* var. *distichus* to those with a tall, almost tree-like habit, such as *Phyllostachys aureosulcata* 'Spectabilis'. Popularly grown as specimen or accent plants, for screening and hedging, or as decorative groundcovers, bamboos have elegant, ornamental foliage, which is sometimes variegated with green, cream, or yellow.

Sasa veitchii

Phyllostachys nigra

Phyllostachys aureosulcata 'Spectabilis'

Pleioblastus pygmaeus var. *distichus*

Grass border
Creating an all-grass border presents an exciting challenge for the gardener. To avoid monotony, choose species and cultivars with a variety of complementary sizes, shapes, textures, and colors.

THE A–Z PLANT DIRECTORY

A

ABELIA

CAPRIFOLIACEAE

Genus of about 30 species of deciduous and evergreen shrubs found on hillsides and in open woodland from the Himalayas to E. Asia, and in Mexico. They are cultivated for their attractive foliage and profusion of flowers, borne over a long period. The ovate to rounded leaves are opposite or occasionally in whorls of 3 or 4. Funnel-shaped or tubular flowers are borne in axillary cymes or terminal panicles on the current year's growth in summer and autumn; they have persistent calyces which, in several species, remain showy after the flowering period. Abelias are ideal for a sunny or partially shaded border, and many attract butterflies. Where marginally hardy, grow against a warm, sunny wall.

• **CULTIVATION** Grow in fertile, well-drained soil in full sun or partial shade, sheltered from wind. Pruning group 1 for deciduous shrubs (group 6, if very vigorous); group 8 for evergreen shrubs.

• **PROPAGATION** Root greenwood cuttings in early summer, or semi-ripe cuttings in late summer.

• **PESTS AND DISEASES** Anthracnose, *Cercospora* leaf spots, powdery mildew, and fungal root rots occur.

A. chinensis, syn. *A. rupestris* (Chinese abelia). Spreading, deciduous shrub with ovate, glossy, dark green leaves, to 1½in (4cm) long. From summer to autumn, bears terminal panicles of fragrant, funnel-shaped, pink-tinged white flowers, ¼in (6mm) long, with 5-lobed pink calyces. ↕ 5ft (1.5m), ↔ 8ft (2.5m). China. Zone 7.

***A.* 'Edward Goucher'**. Semi-evergreen shrub with arching branches and ovate, glossy, dark green leaves, to 2in (5cm) long, bronze when young. Trumpet-shaped, lilac-pink flowers, ¾in (2cm) long, with 2-lobed pink calyces, are

Abelia floribunda

Abelia x *grandiflora*

borne singly or in small axillary cymes from summer to autumn. ↕ 5ft (1.5m), ↔ 6ft (2m). Zone 5b.

A. floribunda ▣ Evergreen shrub with arching shoots and ovate, glossy, dark green leaves, to 2in (5cm) long. Pendent, tubular, bright cerise flowers, 1¼–2in (3–5cm) long, with 5-lobed green calyces, are borne in profuse terminal panicles in early summer. ↕ 10ft (3m), ↔ 12ft (4m). Mexico. Zone 8.

A.* x *grandiflora ▣ (*A. chinensis* x *A. uniflora*), syn. *A. rupestris* of gardens (Glossy abelia). Vigorous, rounded, evergreen or semi–evergreen shrub with arching branches which produce ovate, glossy, dark green leaves, to 2in (5cm) long. Axillary cymes and terminal panicles of funnel-shaped, fragrant, pink-tinged white flowers, ¾in (2cm) long, with 2- to 5-lobed pink calyces, are borne from midsummer to autumn. ↕ 10ft (3m), ↔ 12ft (4m). Garden origin. Zone 5b. **'Francis Mason'** is less vigorous, and has yellow leaves marked with dark green; ↕ 5ft (1.5m), ↔ 6ft (2m). **'Goldsport'**, syn. 'Gold Strike', has all-yellow foliage.

A. rupestris see *A. chinensis.*

***A. rupestris* of gardens** see *A.* x *grandiflora.*

A. schumannii ▣ Deciduous shrub with arching shoots and ovate, mid-green leaves, bronze when young, to 1¼in (3cm) long. Funnel-shaped, slightly scented, orange-marked, lilac-pink flowers, 1in (2.5cm) long, with 2-lobed, pinkish green calyces, are produced singly or in axillary cymes, from late summer to autumn. ↕ 6ft (2m), ↔ 10ft (3m). C. China. Zone 7.

Abelia schumannii

Abelia triflora

A. triflora ▣ Large shrub or small tree, vigorous and erect in habit, with deeply ridged bark and deciduous, ovate, dark green leaves, to 3in (8cm) long. Small, very fragrant, pink-tinged white flowers, ½in (1.5cm) long, with 5-lobed, bronze-red, narrowly segmented calyces, are produced in threes from the upper leaf axils, in clusters to 2in (5cm) across, in summer. ↕ 15ft (5m) or more, ↔ 10ft (3m). N.W. Himalayas. Zone 7b.

ABELIOPHYLLUM

White forsythia

OLEACEAE

Genus of one species of deciduous shrub occurring on open hillsides in Korea. Related to *Forsythia*, it is cultivated for its fragrant flowers, borne in late winter or early spring on the previous year's growth. Grow *A. distichum* in a sunny border or train against a warm wall.

• **CULTIVATION** Grow in fertile, well-drained soil in full sun. Pruning group 5, or group 13 if wall-trained.

• **PROPAGATION** Root greenwood or semi-ripe cuttings, or layer, in summer.

• **PESTS AND DISEASES** Infrequent.

A. distichum ▣ (Korean abelialeaf, White forsythia). Open, spreading shrub with opposite, ovate, matte, dark green leaves, to 3in (8cm) long, often turning purple in autumn. Long, axillary racemes of small, cross-shaped, 4-petaled, fragrant, white, sometimes pink-tinged flowers, with purple-tinged calyces and stalks, are produced in late winter or early spring. ↕↔ 5ft (1.5m). Korea. Zone 5b.

Abeliophyllum distichum

Abelmoschus moschatus 'Pacific Orange'

ABELMOSCHUS

MALVACEAE

Genus of 15 species of hairy annuals and perennials from meadows and wasteland in tropical Asia. They are grown mostly for their flowers, although some, such as *A. escalentes*, are tropical crops, grown for their edible pods (okra) and leaves. They have large, palmately lobed, toothed leaves, and 5-petaled flowers, usually yellow with purple centers, borne in terminal racemes or singly from the leaf axils. Grow *A. moschatus* as an annual in a mixed border, or in summer bedding, while *A. esculentes* is most often included in a vegetable garden.

• **CULTIVATION** Under glass, grow in soil-based potting mix, in full light. In the growing season, water freely and apply a balanced liquid fertilizer monthly; water more sparingly in winter. Outdoors, grow in fertile, well-drained soil in full sun.

• **PROPAGATION** Sow seed at 50–55°F (10–13°C) in late winter or early spring, or sow *in situ* in mid- or late spring, after any danger of frost has passed.

• **PESTS AND DISEASES** Susceptible to slugs, spider mites, and whiteflies. Some fungal diseases, including powdery mildew, can be a problem. Bacterial diseases are common, especially in the Southeast. Root rots are also a concern.

A. esculentes (Okra). Tropical annual, often grown as a vegetable. Palmately divided leaves 12in (30cm) long. Flowers have a white to yellow corolla with a red or purple base and are 3–7in (8–18cm) across. Edible pod fruit 3–4in (8–10cm) long. ↕ 6ft (2m), ↔ 2ft (60cm).

A. moschatus, syn. *Hibiscus abelmoschus* (Musk mallow). Bushy perennial, often grown as an annual, with broadly ovate, 3- to 7-lobed, coarsely hairy leaves, to 18in (45cm) long. Hibiscus-like flowers, to 4in (10cm) across, usually yellow with purple centers, sometimes pink, orange, or red with white centers, are borne singly or in terminal racemes from midsummer to autumn, followed by musk-scented seeds. ↕ 5ft (1.5m), ↔ 18in (45cm). Tropical Asia. ❄ (min. 41°F/5°C). **'Pacific Orange'** ▣ has single, orange blooms, to 3in (8cm) across. ↕ 12–15in (30–38cm).

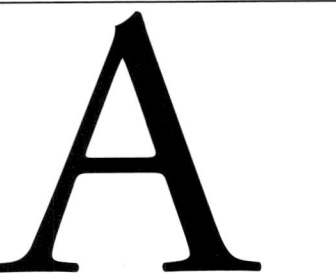

Abies balsamea 'Nana'

ABIES

Fir

PINACEAE

Genus of about 50 species of evergreen conifers from Europe, N. Africa, Asia, and North America, dominating northern and mountainous regions. The whorled branches bear linear, flattened, sometimes glossy, mid- to dark green leaves, often with 2 longitudinal silver bands beneath. The female cones are often purplish blue, erect, with occasionally protruding bracts, and are produced on the upper branches in late spring and early summer. After ripening in autumn, they break up to release the seeds, leaving the central stalk on the shoot. Male cones are pendent, green when young, usually purple, purplish blue, or brown when mature, and are borne throughout the crown. In the descriptions below, all the cones are female. Firs provide good shelter and screening, and also make fine specimens.

• **CULTIVATION** Grow in fertile, moist but well-drained, neutral to slightly acidic soil in full sun, with some shelter from wind. Most are shade tolerant and do best in areas with cool summers.

• **PROPAGATION** Sow seed in containers in a cold frame as soon as ripe or in late winter; stratify for 21 days to aid germination. Graft cultivars in winter.

• **PESTS AND DISEASES** Prone to adelgids, bark beetles, bagworms, woolly aphids, and spruce budworms. A wide variety of fungi cause needle blights and root rots. Rust diseases are especially common.

Abies cephalonica 'Meyer's Dwarf'

A. alba, syn. *A. pectinata* (European silver fir, Silver fir). Columnar tree with dark green leaves, silver beneath, to 1in (2.5cm) long, arranged on the shoots in a V-shape. Cylindrical cones are yellow-green ripening to brown, 4–6in (10–15cm) long, with protruding bracts. ↕80–150ft (25–45m), ↔ 12–20ft (4–6m). C. and S.E. Europe. Zone 4.

A. amabilis (Cascade fir, Pacific fir). Conical tree with shoots covered in pale hairs, and with small, spherical, resinous buds. Square-tipped, dark green leaves, silvery white beneath, ¾–1¼in (2–3cm) long, are densely borne on the upper surface of each shoot in neat, forward-pointing rows. Ovoid-cylindrical purple cones, 3½–6in (9–15cm) long, have hidden bracts. Grows best in cool, moist climates in acidic soil. ↕70–100ft (20–30m), ↔ 12–20ft (4–6m). S. Alaska to N. California. Zone 6.

A. balsamea (Balsam fir). Conical tree with smooth gray bark and fragrant resin blisters. Dark green leaves, whitish green beneath, and ½–1in (1.5–2.5cm) long, are semi-erect, forward pointing, and densely arranged on the shoots in a V-shape. Oblong-cylindrical, purplish blue cones, 2–3in (5–8cm) long, have hidden bracts. Needs a moist site. ↕to 50ft (15m), ↔ to 15ft (5m). C. and E. Canada, N.E. US. Zone 2. **'Nana'** ■ is rounded, with short leaves, ⅛–½in (3–15mm) long, arranged radially around the shoots; ↕↔ 3ft (1m).

A. bracteata, syn. *A. venusta* (Bristle-cone fir, Santa Lucia fir). Columnar tree with distinctive spindle-shaped, pointed, non-resinous buds. Sharp-pointed, glossy, dark green leaves, silvery green beneath, to 2in (5cm) long, spread from either side of each shoot in 3 or 4 ranks. Ovoid, golden brown cones, 3in (8cm) long, have large, protruding bracts, with long, narrow, reflexed points, and often exude resin. ↕80ft (25m), ↔ to 20ft (6m). California. Zone 7b.

Abies concolor 'Argentea'

A. cephalonica (Greek fir). Conical tree with a spreading crown in old age. Stiff, glossy, dark green leaves, greenish white beneath, ¾–1¼in (2–3cm) long, are arranged radially around each shoot, with a rounded, sucker-like pad at each leaf base. Cylindrical, tapering, resinous, green-brown cones, 4–6in (10–15cm) long, have protruding, reflexed bracts, and nipple-like apexes. ↕to 100ft (30m), ↔ 15–25ft (5–8m). C. and S. Greece. Zone 5. **'Meyer's Dwarf'** ■ syn. 'Nana', produces short leaves, ⅜–½in (0.8–1.5cm) long, and forms a low, spreading mound; ↕20in (50cm), ↔ 3–10ft (1–3m).

A. cilicia (Cilician fir). Columnar tree with lax, shiny, rich green leaves, dull white beneath, 1–1½in (2.5–4cm) long, spreading at the sides and pointing forward along the upper surface of each shoot. Cylindrical, green-brown cones are 2½–8in (6–20cm) long, rarely to 12in (30cm), with hidden bracts and nipple-like apexes. ↕to 100ft (30m), ↔ to 20ft (6m). S.E. Turkey, N. Syria, N. Lebanon. Zone 6.

A. concolor (White fir). Columnar tree with soft, lax, glaucous or bluish green leaves, 1½–2½in (4–6cm) long, pointing forward and upward along the shoots. Cylindrical cones, 3–5in (8–13cm) long, with hidden bracts, are mid-green, olive-green, yellow, or pale violet, ripening to brown. ↕80–130ft (25–40m), ↔ 15–22ft (5–7m). Oregon to N. Mexico. Zone 4. **'Argentea'** ■ syn. 'Candicans', is conical when young, later columnar, with silver-white leaves. **'Candicans'** see 'Argentea'. **'Compacta'**, syn. 'Glauca Compacta', is slow-growing, with gray foliage; ↕↔ to 10ft (3m). **'Glauca Compacta'** see 'Compacta'. **'Violacea'** has bluish white young foliage.

A. fargesii, syn. *A. sutchuenensis* (Farges fir). Columnar to conical tree with finely flaky, pale brown bark and deep purple, year-old shoots with conical, resinous purple buds. Shiny, dark green leaves, banded with silver beneath, to 1in (2.5cm) long, spread below and point forward above each shoot. Ovoid, slightly resinous cones, 2–3in (5–8cm) long, are violet-purple with protruding bracts. ↕30–50ft (10–15m), ↔ 10–12ft (3–4m). China. Zone 6.

A. firma (Momi fir, Japanese fir). Columnar tree with shining, dark green needles. The needles are spreading and more or less recurved. On young trees, the needles are distinctively notched at the apex. Branchlets are brown and downy when young; buds are small and ovoid. Yellow-green cones, 3–6in (8–15cm) long, ripen to brown. Scales are broadly kidney-shaped ↕to 160ft (50m), ↔ 25ft (8m). Japan. Zone 7.

A. fraseri (Fraser fir). Pyramidal tree with stiff, horizontal branches and very resinous, gray or pale yellowish brown stems. Shiny, downy, dark green leaves, ½–1in (1.5–2.5cm) long, are white-banded beneath, crowded, and directed forward. Cones, 1½–2¼in (4–5.5cm) long, have strongly protruding and

Abies grandis

downwardly turned bracts that almost hide the scales. ↕30–40ft (10–12m), ↔ 20–25ft (6–8m). Allegheny Mountains to Tennessee. Zone 5.

A. grandis ■ (Giant fir, Lowland fir). Very fast-growing, conical to columnar tree with smooth gray bark, cracked into squares on old trees, and small, conical, resinous buds. Produces soft, shiny, dark green leaves, 1¼–2in (3–5cm) long, with whitish green bands on the reverse, arranged like the teeth of a 2-sided comb. Cylindrical cones, 2–4½in (5–11cm) long, with hidden bracts, are green, ripening to brown. ↕80–200ft(25–60m), ↔ 15–25ft (5–8m). British Columbia, Oregon to Idaho. Zone 6.

A. koreana ■ (Korean fir). Small, conical tree with shiny, dark green leaves, silver beneath, ½–¾in (1–2cm)

Abies koreana

Abies lasiocarpa var. *arizonica* 'Compacta'

long, arranged radially but mainly on the upper surface of each shoot. From a young age, produces cylindrical, violet-blue cones, 2–3in (5–8cm) long, with either hidden or protruding bracts. ↕ 30ft (10m), ↔ to 20ft (6m). S. Korea. Zone 4. **'Silberlocke'** has leaves that twist above the fawn-colored shoots to reveal the silver undersides.

A. lasiocarpa (Alpine fir, Corkbark fir, Rocky Mountain fir). Small, narrowly pyramidal tree with corky bark. Densely arranged but spreading, 2-ranked, gray-green leaves, ½–1½in (1.5–4cm) long, have a waxy coating. Oblong-cylindrical cones, 3–4in (8–10cm) long, with hidden bracts, are dark purple, ripening to brown. ↕ to 90ft (25m), ↔ 10–12ft (3–4m). Alaska to Oregon, Wyoming

Abies nordmanniana

Abies nordmanniana 'Golden Spreader'

to N. Colorado. Zone 2b. **var. *arizonica*** has thicker, soft bark, silvery gray leaves, 1–1½in (2.5–4cm) long, and cones 2½–3in (6–8cm) long; Arizona, New Mexico. **var. *arizonica* 'Compacta'** ■ is slow-growing, forming a conical to oval tree with blue-gray leaves; ↕ 10–15ft (3–5m), ↔ 6–10ft (2–3m). **'Roger Watson'** is slow-growing, with gray-green leaves, reaching its full height after about 10 years; ↕↔ to 36in (90cm).

A. magnifica (Red fir). Columnar tree with a narrow crown and thick trunk. Leaves, 1½–2in (4–5cm) long, gray-green to bright blue-gray above, gray-banded beneath, lie flat along the upper surfaces of the shoots and are arranged like the teeth of a comb beneath. Barrel-shaped, golden green cones, 7–10in (18–25cm) long, have concealed bracts. ↕ 80–120ft (25–35m), ↔ 15–20ft (5–6m). S. Oregon to N. California. Zone 6.

A. nobilis see *A. procera.*

A. nordmanniana ■ (Nordmann fir). Columnar tree with tiered branches. Densely arranged, glossy, rich green leaves, dull white beneath, ¾–1¼in (2–3cm) long, point forward and overlap above on each shoot. Ovoid-cylindrical, greenish brown cones, to 6in (15cm) long, have protruding bracts. One of the best for areas with hot summers. ↕ to 130ft (40m), ↔ to 20ft (6m). Caucasus, N. Turkey. Zone 6. **'Golden Spreader'** ■ is slow-growing, and usually dwarf, with spreading branches and golden yellow leaves, pale yellowish white beneath; ↕ to 3ft (1m), ↔ to 5ft (1.5m), sometimes forms small tree.

Abies numidica

A. numidica ■ (Algerian fir). Conical tree with glossy, green shoots, tinged yellow or brown. Very dense, stiff leaves, ½–¾in (1–2cm) long, are twisted at the bases. Erect, cylindrical, violet-green cones, 4–7in (10–18cm) long, are broad scaled, to 1½in (4cm), with hidden bracts. ↕ to 120ft (35m), ↔ 20ft (6m). N.E. Algeria. Zone 5b.

A. pectinata see *A. alba.*

A. pinsapo (Spanish fir). Conical tree when young, later becoming irregular. Rigid, dark green to glaucous, gray-blue leaves, ½–¾in (1–2cm) long, are arranged radially around each shoot. Cylindrical cones, 4–6in (10–15cm) long, with hidden bracts, are green, ripening to brown. Tolerates dry, alkaline soils. ↕ to 80ft (25m), ↔ 15–25ft (5–8m). S. Spain. Zone 6b. **'Glauca'** has striking, glaucous, gray-blue leaves.

A. procera ■ syn. *A. nobilis* (Noble fir). Conical tree, later becoming broad and columnar, with whorled branches when young, and silvery gray bark. Gray-green to bright blue-gray leaves, ½–1½in (1–4cm) long, with narrow gray bands beneath, lie flat along the upper surfaces of the shoots, and are 2-ranked and slightly downward-curving below. Cylindrical, green and brown cones, 6–10in (15–25cm) long, with protruding, reflexed bracts, are borne on the uppermost branches when the tree is 20ft (6m) or more tall. ↕ 80–150ft (25–45m), ↔ 20–28ft (6–9m). Oregon, Washington. Zone 5. **'Glauca'** has glaucous, bright blue foliage and forms a tall tree or, if no leader develops, a spreading shrub.

A. sutchuenensis see *A. fargesii.*

Abies procera

A. veitchii (Veitch fir). Fast-growing, conical tree with soft, densely arranged, glossy, dark green leaves, to 1¼in (3cm) long, which curve upward and are silver on the reverse. Cylindrical, bright gray-blue cones, 2–3in (5–8cm) long, bear either protruding or hidden bracts. ↕ 50–70ft (15–20m), ↔ 12–20ft (4–6m). Japan. Zone 4.

A. vejarii (Vejar fir). Conical tree with olive-green shoots and forward- and upward-pointing, gray-green or glaucous leaves, gray-banded on the reverse, ¾–1in (2–2.5cm) long. Produces cylindrical or ovoid violet cones, 2½–6in (6–15cm) long, which have protruding bracts. Tolerates dry, alkaline soils. ↕ 30–70ft (10–20m), ↔ 10–15ft (3–5m). N.E. Mexico. Zone 7b.

A. venusta see *A. bracteata.*

ABROMEITIELLA

BROMELIACEAE

Genus of 2 or 3 species of low, mound-forming, terrestrial, evergreen perennials (bromeliads) occurring in dry, rocky sites in the Andes of Bolivia and Argentina. They form large mats or cushions of numerous small, dense rosettes of triangular, succulent, grayish green leaves, with spiny margins and tips. Short-branched inflorescences, made up of groups of 3 greenish yellow or green flowers with twisted petals, develop from the centers of the rosettes in summer, and are followed by dull, grayish green berries. Where temperatures fall below 41°F (5°C), grow in a cool or temperate greenhouse, or as houseplants; in warmer areas, they are excellent for a border or a rock garden.

• **CULTIVATION** Under glass, grow in terrestrial bromeliad potting mix in full light. Keep almost dry in winter; water moderately at all other times of the year. Excess water may cause rotting at temperatures below 41°F (5°C). Apply a low-nitrogen liquid fertilizer every 3–4 weeks from midspring to late autumn. Outdoors, grow in moderately fertile, acidic, well-drained soil in full sun. See also p.47.

• **PROPAGATION** Sow seed at 81°F (27°C) in spring. Detach and root rosettes in spring and summer.

• **PESTS AND DISEASES** Mealybugs may be a problem at flowering time.

A. brevifolia ■ syn. *A. chlorantha.* Terrestrial bromeliad with narrowly triangular, densely arranged leaves, ¾in

Abromeitiella brevifolia

Abromeitiella lorentziana

(2cm) long, toothed only at the bases, and with sharp-pointed tips. Cylindrical green flowers, 1¼in (3cm) long, with a white basal scale to each petal, are produced in summer. ↕ 6in (15cm) or more, ↔ indefinite. S.W. Bolivia, N.W. Argentina. ❀ (min. 41°F/5°C)

A. chlorantha see *A. brevifolia.*

A. lorentziana ■ Terrestrial bromeliad with triangular, spine-tipped, grayish green leaves, 1½–6in (4–15cm) long. In summer, bears long-tubed yellow, green-tipped flowers, to 1½in long (4cm). Very similar to *A. brevifolia*, but with leaves that are more spiny, and with a white-fringed basal scale to each petal. ↕ 10in (25cm) or more, ↔ indefinite. N.W. Argentina. ❀ (min. 41°F/5°C)

ABRONIA

Sand verbena

NYCTAGINACEAE

Genus of some 35 species of sprawling herbaceous annuals or perennials from coastal and desert areas of W. North America. Leaves are opposite, ovate to ovate-linear, unequal, and fleshy. They are grown for their fragrant, verbena-like flowers, borne in groups of 5–15 in a stalked head surrounded by bracts. Grow in the front of a border or trailing in a rock garden. Where not hardy, grow indoors or in a hanging basket.

• **CULTIVATION** Grow in moderately fertile, sandy soil in full sun. Under glass, grow in soil-based potting mix in full light. Apply a balanced liquid fertilizer and water moderately when in growth; water sparingly in winter.

• **PROPAGATION** Sow the seed of annuals *in situ* in autumn in warmer climates and in late spring in cooler climates, or sow in autumn in a cold frame or at 60°F (16°C) in spring. Before sowing, remove the outer seed husk and soak seed for 24 hours. Propagate perennials by softwood cuttings in sand in spring.

• **PESTS AND DISEASES** Downy mildew, rust, and leaf spot occur.

A. villosa. Trailing annual with usually softly hairy branches with ascending, ovate, mid- to dark green leaves, ½–2½in (1.5–6cm) long. Bears round, fragrant, vibrant purple to rose-pink flowers, ½in (1.5cm) across, in dense, verbena-like heads, to 3in (8cm) across. ↕ 2in (5cm), ↔ 4–6in (10–15cm). Arizona, Nevada, S. California, Baja California.

ABUTILON

Flowering maple, Indian mallow, Parlor maple

MALVACEAE

Genus of about 150 species of evergreen and deciduous shrubs, small trees, perennials, and annuals from tropical and subtropical regions of Africa, Asia, Australia, and North and South America. The leaves vary from simple to palmately 3- to 7-lobed. Abutilons are cultivated for their showy, mostly bell-, cup-, or bowl-shaped axillary flowers, some with highly colored calyces and stamens. The flowers are usually solitary and pendent, occasionally borne in racemes or panicles, and often produced continuously from spring to autumn. Some abutilons also have attractive variegated foliage. Where not hardy, grow in a conservatory or cool or temperate greenhouse, or as houseplants or large container plants (including standards), and set them outside in summer. Train marginally hardy abutilons of arching habit against a warm wall. In frost-free areas, grow tender abutilons in a shrub border.

• **CULTIVATION** Under glass, grow in soil-based potting mix in full light. In the growing season, water freely and apply a balanced liquid fertilizer every two weeks; water sparingly in winter. Outdoors, grow in moderately fertile, well-drained soil in full sun. Pruning group 1 or 6, as required, for deciduous shrubs; group 9 for evergreens. Pruning group 13 for wall-trained abutilons.

• **PROPAGATION** Sow seed at 59–64°F (15–18°C) in spring. Softwood cuttings may be rooted in spring, or greenwood cuttings in summer.

• **PESTS AND DISEASES** Whiteflies, spider mites, scale insects, and mealybugs may be problems under glass. Mushroom root rot can occur. Rust and abutilon mosaic virus as well as *Alternaria* and *Cercospora* leaf spots occur widely.

***A.* 'Ashford Red'.** Erect to spreading, evergreen shrub or small tree with broadly ovate to rounded, 3- to 5-lobed, pale to mid-green leaves, 4–8in (10–20cm) long. From spring to autumn, produces nodding to pendent, bell-shaped red flowers, 2½–3in (6–8cm) long. ↕↔ to 10ft (3m). Zone 8.

***A.* 'Boule de Neige'** ■ Vigorous, evergreen shrub or small tree, of erect to spreading habit, with broadly ovate to rounded, 3- to 5-lobed, mid-green leaves, 4–8in (10–20cm) long. From spring to autumn, bears pendent, bell-shaped white flowers, 2½–3in (6–8cm) long. ↕ to 12ft (4m), ↔ to 10ft (3m). Zone 8.

Abutilon 'Boule de Neige'

***A.* 'Canary Bird'.** Erect to spreading, evergreen shrub or small tree with broadly ovate to rounded, 3- to 5-lobed, mid-green leaves, 4–8in (10–20cm) long. From spring to autumn, produces pendent, bell-shaped, lemon-yellow flowers, 2½–3in (6–8cm) long. ↕↔ to 10ft (3m). Zone 8.

***A. globosum* of gardens** see *A.* x *hybridum.*

A.* x *hybridum (*A. darwinii* x *A. pictum* and other species) syn. *A. globosum* of gardens. Erect to spreading, evergreen shrub or small tree with ovate to rounded, 3- to 5-lobed, pale to mid-green leaves, 4–8in (10–20cm) long, which may be variegated. Bears pendent, bowl- or bell-shaped, white, yellow, red, or orange flowers, 2–3in (5–8cm) long, from spring to autumn. ↕ to 15ft (5m), ↔ 6–15ft (2–5m). Garden origin. Zone 8.

***A.* 'Kentish Belle'.** Evergreen or semi-evergreen shrub with slender, arching, dark purple-brown shoots and narrowly ovate, shallowly lobed, dark green leaves, to 1½in (4cm) long. Pendent, bell-shaped flowers, 2½–3in (6–8cm) long, with apricot-yellow petals and purple stamens, protruding from red calyces, are produced along the young shoots from summer to autumn. ↕↔ to 8ft (2.5m). Zone 8.

***A.* 'Louis Marignac'**, syn. *A.* 'Louise de Marignac'. Evergreen shrub or small tree, of erect to spreading habit, with ovate to rounded, 3- to 5-lobed, pale to mid-green leaves, 4–8in (10–20cm) long. Distinctive, pendent, bell-shaped, pale pink flowers, 2½–3in (6–8cm) long, are borne from spring to autumn. ↕↔ to 10ft (3m). Zone 8.

***A.* 'Louise de Marignac'** see *A.* 'Louis Marignac'.

A. megapotamicum ■ (Trailing abutilon). Evergreen or semi-evergreen shrub with slender, arching shoots and lance-shaped to ovate, bright green leaves, to 5in (13cm) long, sometimes shallowly lobed, and heart-shaped at the bases. Pendent, bell-shaped flowers, to 1½in (4cm) long, with yellow petals and purple stamens, protruding from red calyces, are borne along the young shoots from summer to autumn.

Abutilon megapotamicum

↕↔ 6ft (2m). Brazil. Zone 8.

'Variegatum' has leaves heavily mottled yellow.

A.* x *milleri (*A. megapotamicum* x *A. pictum*). Evergreen shrub with thin, arching shoots and narrowly ovate, bright green leaves, to 5in (13cm) long, with 3 long-pointed lobes. Pendent, bell-shaped flowers, to 1½in (4cm) long, with dusky pink calyces surrounding petals of dark apricot, flushed dark red inside the bases, are borne along the young shoots from summer to autumn. ↕↔ 8ft (2.5m). Garden origin. Zone 8.

***A.* 'Moonchimes'.** Evergreen shrub with maple-like, mid- to dark green leaves, to 5in (13cm) long, and large, bell-shaped, luminous yellow flowers, 3in (8cm) long, borne all year. Good as a garden annual, container plant, houseplant, or cut flower. ↕↔ to 6ft (2m). Zone 8.

***A.* 'Nabob'.** Erect to spreading, evergreen shrub or small tree. Leaves are ovate to rounded, 3- to 5-lobed, 4–8in (10–20cm) long, and rich green in color. From spring to autumn, bears large, nodding to pendent, open bowl-shaped, deep crimson flowers, to 3in (8cm) across. ↕↔ to 10ft (3m). Zone 8.

A. ochsenii. Fast-growing, upright, deciduous shrub, sometimes tree-like, with thick, gray-felted shoots and ovate, 3- to 5-lobed, dark green leaves, to 6in (15cm) long. Pendent, cup-shaped, violet-blue flowers, to 2½in (6cm) across, are borne on long stalks in late spring and early summer. ↕ 10ft (3m), ↔ 8ft (2.5m). Chile. Zone 8.

***A.* 'Patrick Synge'.** Very vigorous, evergreen shrub or small tree, of erect to spreading habit, bearing ovate to rounded, 3- to 5-lobed, pale to mid-green leaves, 4–8in (10–20cm) long. Bears pendent, open bowl-shaped flowers, to 3in (8cm) across, with slightly reflexed, flame-red petals, from spring to autumn. ↕↔ to 10ft (3m). Zone 8.

A. pictum, syn. *A. striatum* of gardens. Evergreen shrub or small tree, erect at first, then spreading, with ovate to rounded, 3- to 5-lobed, mid- to deep green leaves, to 6in (15cm) long. From spring to autumn, bears pendent, bell-shaped, yellow to orange flowers, 2½in (6cm) long, with dark red veins. ↕ 15ft (5m), ↔ 6–15ft (2–5m). Brazil. Zone 8.

'Thompsonii' ■ is erect, with 5- to 9-lobed, yellow-mottled leaves, and orange-flushed, salmon-pink flowers.

Abutilon pictum 'Thompsonii'

Abutilon 'Souvenir de Bonn'

***A.* 'Souvenir de Bonn'** ▣ Vigorous, erect, evergreen shrub or small tree with ovate to rounded, 3- to 5-lobed, pale to mid-green leaves, 4–8in (10–20cm) long, margined and occasionally mottled creamy white. From spring to autumn, bears pendent, bowl-shaped flowers, to 3in (8cm) across, soft orange with darker veins. ↕ to 10ft (3m), ↔ 6–10ft (2–3m). Zone 8.
***A. striatum* of gardens** see *A. pictum.*
A.* x *suntense (*A. ochsenii* x *A. vitifolium*). Fast-growing, upright, deciduous shrub with thick, gray-felted shoots and narrowly ovate, 3- to 5-lobed, gray-green leaves, to 5in (13cm) long, with toothed margins. In late spring and early summer, bears long-stalked, pendent, saucer-shaped, white to dark violet-blue flowers, to 2½in (6cm) across. ↕ 12ft (4m), ↔ 8ft (2.5m). Garden origin. Zone 8. **'Geoffrey Gorer'** has sprays of purple-blue flowers. **'Gorer's White'** has pure white flowers. **'Ralph Gould'** ▣ bears larger, flatter flowers, to 3in (8cm) wide. **'Violetta'** ▣ bears abundant dark violet-blue flowers.
A. vitifolium. Fast-growing, upright, deciduous shrub, sometimes tree-like, with thick, gray-felted shoots, and ovate, shallowly 3- to 5-lobed, toothed, softly gray-hairy leaves, to 6in (15cm) long. Bears long-stalked, pendent, saucer-shaped, white to purple-blue flowers, to 3in (8cm) across, with long stamens, in early summer. ↕ 15ft (5m), ↔ 8ft (2.5m). Chile. Zone 8. **var. *album*** has white flowers. **'Veronica Tennant'** ▣ bears profuse, mauve flowers, to 3½in (9cm) across.

Abutilon x *suntense* 'Ralph Gould'

Abutilon x *suntense* 'Violetta'

Abutilon vitifolium 'Veronica Tennant'

ACACIA
Mimosa, Wattle

FABACEAE

Genus of at least 1,100 species of deciduous and evergreen trees, shrubs, and climbers, cultivated mainly for their flowers, and sometimes foliage. Acacias are found in tropical to warm-temperate regions of Central and South America, Kenya, southern Africa, Polynesia, and Australia. Leaves are alternate and pinnate or 2-pinnate, or may be reduced to flattened leaf stalks known as phyllodes, mostly lance-shaped to ovate and entire. Tiny flowers, often sweetly scented, with 4 or 5 minute petals and long stamens, form either spherical heads, ¼–½in (6–15mm) across, in racemes or panicles, or are borne in short, cylindrical spikes, ½–3in (1.5–8cm) long. They are usually produced in winter or spring. These are followed by variously shaped seed pods, mostly green, sometimes flushed with red or purple. Grow in a cool or cold greenhouse; with a minimum temperature of 35–41°F (2–5°C) or grow as a houseplant. May possibly survive against a warm outside wall in parts of Zone 8.

• **CULTIVATION** Under glass, grow in soil-based potting mix in full light. In the growing season, water freely and apply a balanced liquid fertilizer monthly; water sparingly in winter. Outdoors, grow in moderately fertile, neutral to acidic soil in a sheltered site in full sun. Pruning group 1 for deciduous acacias; group 8 for evergreen acacias; and group 13 for wall-trained plants. Most acacias resent hard pruning.

Acacia baileyana

Acacia cultriformis

• **PROPAGATION** Sow seed in spring at not less than 64°F (18°C), after soaking in warm water until swollen. Root semi-ripe cuttings in summer.

• **PESTS AND DISEASES** Spider mites may be a problem under glass, and mimosa webworms, scale insects, and fungal leaf spots occur outdoors. Heart rot caused by *Armillaria*, and root rot caused by *Ganoderma*, are fatal.

A. armata see *A. paradoxa.*
A. baileyana ▣ (Cootamundra wattle). Small tree or large shrub with spreading, dense branches and fern-like, 2-pinnate, evergreen, silvery gray leaves, to 2in (5cm) long, composed of 16–40 tiny, linear leaflets. Spherical, bright yellow flowerheads, ¼in (6mm) across, open in dense axillary racemes, 3–4in (7–10cm) long, from winter to spring. ↕ 15–25ft (5–8m), ↔ 10–20ft (3–6m). New South Wales.
A. cultriformis ▣ (Knife acacia, Knife-leaf wattle). Erect, evergreen shrub, becoming bushy and spreading with age. Bluish green phyllodes are ½–1in (1–2.5cm) long, and lopsidedly oval to triangular. In spring, bears spherical, bright yellow flowerheads, ¼in (6mm) across, in axillary racemes, 1½–3in (4–8cm) long, which are crowded toward the tips of the stems. ↕↔ 6–12ft (2–4m). Queensland to New South Wales.
A. dealbata ▣ (Mimosa, Silver wattle). Open, evergreen tree with fern-like, 2-pinnate, hairy leaves, 5in (13cm) long, each with 40–80 linear, glaucous to silvery leaflets. Terminal racemes, 4–8in (10–20cm) long, of spherical, fragrant yellow flowerheads, ¼in (6mm) across, are borne from winter to spring. ↕ 50–100ft (15–30m), ↔ 20–30ft (6–10m). New South Wales to Tasmania.

Acacia dealbata

A. decurrens (Early black wattle, Green wattle). Spreading, evergreen large shrub or medium-sized tree with 2-pinnate, fern-like, dark green leaves, to 3in (8cm) long, composed of 60–80 linear leaflets. In spring, bears spherical, rich yellow flowerheads, ¼in (6mm) across, in profuse axillary racemes and panicles, 4–6in (10–15cm) long. ↕ 15–50ft (5–15m), ↔ 10–25ft (3–8m). New South Wales.
A. drummondii (Drummond's wattle). Open, spreading, evergreen shrub producing sparse, pinnate or 2-pinnate leaves, ¾–1¼in (2–3cm) long, with up to 12 oblong, mid-green or slightly glaucous leaflets. During late winter and spring, bright to rich yellow flowerheads, in the form of cylindrical spikes, ½–1¼in (1.5–3cm) long and ⅜–½in (9–15mm) across, are produced at the tips of short side branches. ↕ 2–6ft (0.6–1.8m), ↔ 3–5ft (0.9–1.5m). Western Australia.
A. farnesiana (Perfume acacia). Fast-growing, large, thorny, many-branched, evergreen shrub with 2-pinnate, fern-like leaves, to 3in (8cm) long, with 20–40 linear, blue-gray to blue-green leaflets. Very fragrant yellow flowerheads, ¼–½in (6–15mm) long, are borne singly or in groups of 2–3, in early spring. Useful in a desert garden and as a houseplant. ↕ to 22ft (7m), ↔ to 15–25ft (5–8m). Tropical America.
A. floribunda (White sallow wattle). Tall shrub or small tree, usually open in habit, but sometimes bushy. Evergreen, mid-green phyllodes, 2–5in (5–13cm) long, are linear to lance-shaped with slender, curved tips. Produces 1–3 spikes of loosely cylindrical, fragrant, pale yellow flowerheads, 1–2½in (2.5–6cm) long and ¼–½in (6–15mm) across, from each upper phyllode axil, in spring. ↕ 12–25ft (4–8m), ↔ 10–20ft (3–6m). Queensland to Victoria.
A. mearnsii (Black wattle). Spreading, evergreen tree producing 2-pinnate leaves, 3–6in (8–15cm) long, with 18–40 tiny, linear, gray-green leaflets. Bears many spherical, richly fragrant, pale yellow flowerheads, ¼in (6mm) across, in axillary racemes and panicles, 3–6in (8–15cm) long, in spring. ↕ 25–70ft (8–20m), ↔ 15–30ft (5–10m). New South Wales, Victoria.
A. melanoxylon (Blackwood). Evergreen tree or shrub with an erect to spreading habit and freely branching, angular stems. Tapered, matte, grayish green phyllodes, to 6in (15cm) long, are oblong to lance-

Acacia paradoxa

Acacia pravissima

shaped. From late winter to late spring, bears branched axillary racemes, 2–4in (5–10cm) long, of spherical, pale yellow flowerheads, ½in (1.5cm) across. ↕ 15–80ft (5–25m), ↔ 12–40ft (4–12m). South Australia, Queensland to Tasmania.
A. paradoxa ■ syn. *A. armata* (Kangaroo thorn). Evergreen shrub with erect, spiny stems and lance-shaped to oblong, deep green phyllodes, ½–1¼in (1–3cm) long, often with strongly wavy margins. Solitary, long-stalked, spherical, golden yellow flowerheads, ½in (1.5cm) across, are produced from the phyllode axils in spring. ↕↔ 6–12ft (2–4m). New South Wales.
A. pendula (Weeping myall). Bushy, broad-headed, evergreen tree with pendent branches. Bears lance- or slightly sickle-shaped, grayish green to glaucous phyllodes, to 4in (10cm) long. Short, branching racemes, ¾–2in (2–5cm) long, of spherical, pale yellow flowerheads, ½in (1.5cm) across; borne from the phyllode axils in winter. ↕ 20–30ft (6–10m), ↔ 20–22ft (6–7m). Queensland to Victoria.
A. podalyriifolia (Queensland silver wattle). Erect, loosely branched, evergreen, hairy shrub, often grown for its attractive foliage. Downy, white to blue-white phyllodes are ovate to oblong and ¾–1½in (2–4cm) long. Produces spherical, fragrant, rich yellow flowerheads, ½in (1.5cm) across, in terminal and axillary racemes, 3–6in (7–15cm) long, in spring. ↕ 10–15ft (3–5m), ↔ 10–12ft (3–4m). Queensland to New South Wales.
A. pravissima ■ (Ovens wattle). Large shrub or small tree, open to dense in habit, with short, pendent branches, crowded with lopsidedly triangular, evergreen, gray-green phyllodes, ¼–¾in (0.5–2cm) long. Spherical, fragrant, bright yellow flowerheads, ¼in (6mm) across, are profusely borne in axillary racemes, 2–4in (5–10cm) long, in late winter and spring. ↕ 10–25ft (3–8m), ↔ 10–22ft (3–7m). New South Wales, Victoria.
A. pulchella (Western prickly Moses). Bushy, evergreen, prickly shrub with 2-pinnate leaves, ½–¾in (1–2cm) long, composed of 4–22 narrowly oblong, deep green leaflets. Solitary, spherical, golden yellow flowerheads, to ½in (1.5cm) across, are produced from the phyllode axils in winter and spring. ↕ 2–5ft (0.6–1.5m), ↔ 3–6ft (1–2m). Western Australia.

Acacia retinodes

A. retinodes ■ (Silver wattle, Swamp wattle, Wirilda). Spreading, large shrub or small tree with slender, angular, often pendent stems, and linear to narrowly lance-shaped, evergreen, bluish green phyllodes, 4–8in (10–20cm) long. Short axillary racemes, ¾–1½in (2–4cm) long, of spherical, lemon-yellow flowerheads, ¼in (6mm) across, are produced periodically throughout the year. ↕ 12–25ft (4–8m), ↔ 10–22ft (3–7m). South Australia, Victoria, Tasmania.
A. verticillata (Prickly Moses). Tall, bushy, evergreen shrub or sometimes small tree, bearing linear, spine-tipped, dark green phyllodes, ¾in (2cm) long, usually in whorls, or scattered. Bears panicles, to ½in (1.5cm) long, of 1–3 ovoid to rod-shaped, lemon-yellow flowerheads, 1¼in (3cm) long, in spring. ↕ 6–25ft (2–8m), ↔ 10–25ft (3–8m). South Australia, New South Wales to Tasmania.

ACAENA

Bidi-bidi, New Zealand burr

ROSACEAE

Genus of about 100 species of mainly evergreen, creeping, mat-forming perennials and semi-prostrate subshrubs, widely distributed over the S. hemisphere, most from open habitats at high altitudes, cultivated for their variously colored, narrowly oblong-ovate, pinnate leaves, and petalless flowers, produced in stalked spikes or dense, ovoid or spherical heads, which develop into colorful, spiny burrs in mid- or late summer. The prostrate stems root where they touch the ground and rapidly form dense mats of foliage. The burrs may be a nuisance to pets. *A. microphylla* 'Kupferteppich' is an effective and restrained rock garden plant. Other acaenas are good groundcover plants, although often invasive in zone 7 or warmer.

• **CULTIVATION** Grow in moderately fertile, well-drained soil in sun or partial shade. Pull out rooted stems to restrict growth.
• **PROPAGATION** Sow seed in containers in an open frame in autumn. Separate rooted stems from the parent plant in autumn or early spring, or take softwood cuttings in late spring.
• **PESTS AND DISEASES** Powdery mildew and rust occur.

***A. anserinifolia* of gardens** see *A. novae-zelandiae.*

Acaena 'Blue Haze'

A. 'Blue Haze' ■ syn. *A.* 'Pewter'. Creeping, vigorous, evergreen perennial producing pinnate leaves, to 3in (8cm) long, gray-blue, shaded bronze at the margins, with 9–13 oval leaflets. Spherical flowerheads are followed by dark red burrs, to ¾in (2cm) across, with pinkish red spines, in midsummer. ↕ 4–6in (10–15cm), ↔ 3ft (1m). Zone 7.
A. caerulea see *A. caesiiglauca.*
A. caesiiglauca, syn. *A. caerulea.* Creeping, usually evergreen perennial with pinnate, glaucous blue leaves, to 4in (10cm) long, divided into 7–13 obovate leaflets. Spherical flowerheads are followed by reddish brown burrs, to ¾in (2cm) across, in late summer. ↕ 3–5in (8–13cm), ↔ to 3ft (1m). New Zealand. Zone 7.
***A. microphylla* 'Copper Carpet'** see *A. microphylla* 'Kupferteppich'.
***A. microphylla* 'Kupferteppich'** ■ syn. *A. microphylla* 'Copper Carpet'. Compact, creeping, usually evergreen perennial with pinnate bronze leaves, to 1¼in (3cm) long, with 9–15 rounded leaflets. Small, spherical flowerheads are followed by bright red burrs, 1in (2.5cm) across, in late summer. ↕ 1¼in (3cm), ↔ to 24in (60cm). Zone 7.
A. novae-zelandiae, syn. *A. anserinifolia* of gardens. Vigorous, creeping, evergreen perennial producing pinnate, gray-green or rich green leaves, to 4in (10cm) long, with 9–15 oblong leaflets. Small, ovoid to spherical flowerheads are followed by red burrs, ½in (1.5cm) across, in late summer. ↕ to 6in (15cm), ↔ 3ft (1m) or more. New Zealand. Zone 6.
A. 'Pewter' see *A.* 'Blue Haze'.

Acaena microphylla 'Kupferteppich'

ACALYPHA

EUPHORBIACEAE

Genus of about 430 species of evergreen shrubs and trees, and annuals, grown for their foliage and flowers. They are found in tropical and subtropical regions, from tropical woodland to open savanna. Their alternate leaves are oval to ovate, simple, and toothed. Tiny, petalless flowers are borne in terminal or axillary, catkin-like racemes, either small and insignificant, or large and brightly colored. Where temperatures fall below 50–55°F (10–13°C), grow in a warm greenhouse or as a houseplant. In warmer areas, grow in a border, or use for hedging or as specimen plants.

• **CULTIVATION** Under glass, grow in soilless potting mix in full or filtered light. Water freely in the growing season, applying a balanced liquid fertilizer monthly during summer; water moderately in winter. Pot on or top-dress in early spring or autumn. Outdoors, grow in fertile, humus-rich, moist but well-drained soil in sun or partial shade. Pruning group 9.

• **PROPAGATION** Divide rhizomatous or clump-forming species in spring. Root softwood cuttings in early spring, or semi-ripe cuttings in late summer, with bottom heat.

• **PESTS AND DISEASES** Scale insects, mealybugs, whiteflies, and spider mites may be problems under glass. Downy mildew, powdery mildew, rust, *Cercospora* leaf spots, and fungal root rots occur. Bacterial leaf spots are sometimes a problem in warm climates.

Acalypha wilkesiana (inset: leaf color variation)

A. hispida ■ (Chenille plant, Red-hot cat's-tail). Erect shrub, usually sparsely branched, with oval, rich green leaves, 4–10in (10–25cm) long. Bears thick, fluffy, deep crimson or bright red catkins, 10–20in (25–50cm) long, periodically during the year. Semi-trailing forms are available, suitable for a hanging basket. ↕ 6–10ft (2–3m), ↔ 3–6ft (1–2m). Malaysia, New Guinea. ❀ (min. 55°F/13°C). **'Alba'** has off-white catkins.

A. wilkesiana ■ (Copperleaf, Fire-dragon, Jacob's-coat, Match-me-if-you-can). Spreading shrub, with oval, multi-colored, mottled, and often variegated leaves, 4–8in (10–20cm) long. Bears catkin-like racemes, 4–8in (10–20cm) long, usually green- or copper-tinted, and often hidden among the leaves, periodically during the year. ↕ to 6ft (2m), ↔ 3–6ft (1–2m). Pacific islands. ❀ (min. 50°F/10°C). **'Ceylon'** has rounded, twisted, copper-maroon leaves with white to pink lobes bordering the margins. **'Hoffmana'** has slender, twisted leaves, margined with ivory lobes. **'Marginata'** produces leaves with crimson to white margins. **'Miltoniana'** has pendent, oblong leaves with variable white margins. **'Moorea'** has wide, scalloped, waxy, twisted, copper-tinged black leaves, and bears small, red-shaded green flowers. **'Musaica'** has foliage heavily mottled red and orange. **'Obovata'** produces bronze-tinged, green leaves with pink margins.

▷***Acanthocalycium*** see *Echinopsis*
▷***Acanthocalyx*** see *Morina*

Acalypha hispida

ACANTHOLIMON

Prickly thrift

PLUMBAGINACEAE

Genus of about 120 species of evergreen, mat-forming perennials, found in open, rocky areas at high altitudes, from the E. Mediterranean to C. Asia. They are grown for their dense, spiny rosettes of needle-like leaves, ½–3in (1.5–8cm) long, and short spikes or panicles of shallowly funnel-shaped flowers, borne in early and midsummer. Suitable for a scree bed or a wall, although in cold climates with high winter rainfall, most species are best grown in an alpine house or a cool greenhouse.

• **CULTIVATION** Outdoors, grow in moderately fertile, very well-drained soil in full sun; only *A. glumaceum* tolerates winter moisture. Under glass, grow in a mix of equal parts soil-based potting mix and sharp grit, with additional limestone chips; top-dress with grit. Established plants resent disturbance.

• **PROPAGATION** Sow seed, which may be slow to germinate, as soon as ripe in containers in an open frame. Root softwood cuttings in spring. Layer shoot tips in sandy potting mix in spring.

• **PESTS AND DISEASES** Spider mites may be a problem under glass. Fungal leaf spots occur occasionally.

Acantholimon glumaceum

A. glumaceum ■ Slow-growing perennial with crowded rosettes of stiff, linear-lance-shaped, spiny, dark green leaves, to 1in (2.5cm) long. In summer, dense spikes of 3–8 deep rose-pink flowers are produced on stems 1in (2.5cm) long. ↕ 2–3in (5–8cm), ↔ 8–12in (20–30cm). Caucasus, Armenia, Turkey. Zone 5.

A. venustum. Slow-growing perennial with rosettes of linear-lance-shaped, spiny, silver-margined, blue-gray leaves, ½–1½in (1.5–4cm) long. Bears spikes of up to 20 pink flowers on stems to 1¼in (3cm) long, in midsummer. ↕ 2–3in (5–8cm), ↔ 6–8in (15–20cm). Turkey, Syria, Iraq, Iran. Zone 6b.

▷***Acanthopanax ricinifolius*** see *Kalopanax septemlobus*
▷***Acanthopanax sieboldianus*** see *Eleutherococcus sieboldianus*

ACANTHOPHOENIX

Barbel palm

ARECACEAE

Genus of one very variable species of single-stemmed palm from coastal woodland in the Mascarene Islands in the Indian Ocean. Pinnate leaves are produced in a terminal tuft on the stem, and small, separate male and female flowers are borne in panicles just beneath them. In cool climates, grow young specimens as foliage plants in a conservatory or warm greenhouse. In warmer regions, barbel palms are fine specimen trees for growing outdoors.

• **CULTIVATION** Under glass, grow in soil-based potting mix, with additional sharp sand, in full light. In the growing season, water freely and apply a balanced liquid fertilizer monthly; water moderately in winter. Pot on or top-dress in spring. Outdoors, they are best grown in fertile, sandy soil in full sun.

• **PROPAGATION** Sow seed at 81°F (27°C) in spring.

• **PESTS AND DISEASES** Spider mites may be a problem under glass. Fungal leaf spots occur occasionally.

A. crinita see *A. rubra.*

A. rubra, syn. *A. crinita* (Barbel palm). Elegant palm with a slender trunk, swollen at the base and topped by a prominent crownshaft. The pinnate leaves, 6–12ft (2–4m) long, have prickly stalks and midribs, and are divided into many crowded, linear, rich green leaflets with cleft tips. Small, inconspicuous, dull white, yellow, pink, red, or purple flowers are produced in panicles, to 18in (45cm) long, during summer. ↕ to 60ft (18m), ↔ 12–25ft (4–8m). Mascarene Islands. ❀ (min. 50–55°F/10–13°C)

Acanthus hirsutus

ACANTHUS

Bear's breeches

ACANTHACEAE

Genus of about 30 species of perennials from dry, rocky sites, mostly in the Mediterranean. They are vigorous, architectural plants, with bold, striking foliage and flowers. The dark green, oblong-lance-shaped to broadly ovate, usually basal leaves, up to 36in (90cm) long, are variously lobed and toothed, sometimes spiny. The tubular, 2-lipped flowers are generally 1½–2in (3.5–5cm) long, usually with spiny bracts and sepals in combinations of white, green, yellow, pink, or purple. They are borne, sometimes in ranks of 4, in erect, terminal racemes, to 4ft (1.2m) tall. Grow bear's breeches in a spacious border; they are also good for cutting or drying. Where not hardy, grow *A. montanus* in a cool or temperate greenhouse or conservatory.

• **CULTIVATION** Under glass, grow in soil-based potting mix in full or filtered light. In the growing season, water moderately and apply a balanced liquid fertilizer monthly; keep just moist in winter. Outdoors, grow in any soil in sun or partial shade, although they thrive in deep, fertile, moist but well-drained loam.

• **PROPAGATION** Sow seed in containers in a cold frame in spring. Divide in spring or autumn. Take root cuttings in late autumn or early winter.

• **PESTS AND DISEASES** Powdery mildew and fungal and bacterial leaf spots may be problems.

Acanthus hungaricus

Acanthus mollis

A. balcanicus see *A. hungaricus.*

A. hirsutus ■ Clump-forming perennial with slender, semi-erect, lance-shaped, pinnatifid, weakly spiny, dark green leaves, 10–14in (25–35cm) long. Racemes, 6in (15cm) long, of pale yellow or greenish white flowers with hairy, weakly spiny, yellowish green bracts, are produced from late spring to midsummer. ↕ 6–14in (15–35cm), ↔ 12in (30cm). Turkey. Zone 8.

A. hirsutus* var. *syriacus see *A. syriacus.*

A. hungaricus ■ syn. *A. balcanicus, A. longifolius.* Clump-forming perennial with oblong-ovate, dark green leaves, 24–36in (60–90cm) long, with deep lobes narrowed at the bases, and wide, winged midribs between the main lobes. Bears racemes, 24–28in (65–70cm) long, of white or pale pink flowers with purple-shaded bracts, in early and midsummer. ↕ 24–48in (60–120cm), ↔ 24–36in (60–90cm). Balkans. Zone 7b.

A. longifolius see *A. hungaricus.*

A. mollis ■ Clump-forming perennial with obovate, deeply lobed, dark green leaves, shiny above, to 3ft (1m) long. In late summer, white flowers with purple-shaded bracts are borne in 3ft (1m) long racemes, often with purple-tinted stems. ↕ 5ft (1.5m), ↔ 36in (90cm). S.W. Europe, N.W. Africa. Zone 6b. **Latifolius Group** includes variants with broad, shallowly lobed, conspicuously veined, shiny, rich green leaves, to 4ft (1.2m) long.

A. montanus (Bears' breeches, Mountain thistle). Shrubby perennial with few branches; oblong-lance-shaped, pinnatifid, spiny, leathery leaves, 12in (30cm) long, are glossy and dark green, with silver markings and wavy margins. Bears racemes, 9–12in (23–30cm) long, of rose-pink or pale mauve flowers with spiny calyces in late summer and early autumn. ↕ 6ft (2m), ↔ 24in (60cm). W. Africa. Zone 8.

A. spinosissimus see *A. spinosus* Spinosissimus Group.

A. spinosus ■ Variable, clump-forming perennial producing narrowly oblong-ovate, arching, dark green leaves, to 3ft (1m) long, often deeply cut to the midribs, with spiny margins. Tall racemes, to 3ft (1m) long, of pure white flowers with purple bracts are produced from late spring to midsummer. ↕ 5ft (1.5m), ↔ 24–36in (60–90cm). Italy to W. Turkey. Zone 5. **Spinosissimus Group**, syn. *A. spinosissimus*, includes variants with deep grayish green leaves, 20in (50cm) long, deeply cut to the bold white midribs, and with white-spiny margins; ↕ 4ft (1.2m), ↔ 24in (60cm).

A. syriacus, syn. *A. hirsutus* var. *syriacus*. Clump-forming perennial with clusters of long-stalked, pinnatifid, lance-shaped, spiny, hairy, dark green leaves, to 8in (20cm) long. Racemes, 6–9in (15–23cm) long, of greenish white flowers with purple-shaded bracts, are produced from late spring to midsummer. ↕↔ 24in (60cm). Turkey, Syria, Jordan, Israel, Lebanon. Zone 8.

Acanthus spinosus

ACCA *syn.* FEIJOA

MYRTACEAE

Genus of 2 or 3 species of evergreen, opposite-leaved shrubs occurring in dry upland slopes, scrub, and open woodland in subtropical South America. They are cultivated for their attractive, shallowly cup-shaped flowers, which are produced singly from the upper leaf axils in midsummer. In hot climates, edible fruits may also be produced. To obtain fruit in areas where temperatures fall below 41°F (5°C), grow in a cool greenhouse. *A. sellowiana* is tolerant of salt and drought, and may be used as hedging in mild coastal areas.

• **CULTIVATION** Under glass, grow in soil-based potting mix in full light. During the growing season, water freely and apply a balanced liquid fertilizer monthly; water more sparingly in winter. Outdoors, grow in light, well-drained soil in full sun in a sheltered site.

• **PROPAGATION** Sow seed at 55–61°F (13–16°C) as soon as ripe. Take semi-ripe cuttings in summer.

• **PESTS AND DISEASES** Fungal leaf spots are common. Root rots caused by water molds and *Armillaria* are found in poorly drained sites.

A. sellowiana ■ (Pineapple guava). Bushy shrub with elliptic-oblong, gray-green leaves, to 3in (8cm) long, white-woolly beneath. In midsummer, bears flowers, 1½in (4cm) across, with long red stamens and purple-red petals, white on the margins and reverse, singly from the upper leaf axils; they are followed in warm climates by ovoid, red-tinged green berries, 2in (5cm) long. ↕ 6ft (2m), ↔ 8ft (2.5m). Brazil, Uruguay. **'Variegata'** has leaves with creamy white margins.

Acca sellowiana

A

ACER

Maple

ACERACEAE

Genus of about 150 species of evergreen and deciduous trees and shrubs from Europe, N. Africa, Asia, and North and Central America. Mainly woodland plants, they exist as large trees or grow as part of the understory. The opposite leaves are usually shallowly to deeply palmately lobed, but in some species and cultivars are unlobed or, more rarely, 3-palmate or pinnate. The small, often greenish yellow flowers are borne in generally pendent, occasionally upright racemes, panicles, or umbels, in early or midspring, and are followed by green to brown, occasionally colorful, winged fruits, joined in pairs. Maples are valued for their foliage, which may be variegated or have good autumn color; some also have attractive bark.

Acer campestre

Acer capillipes

Acer cappadocicum

Grow large maples as specimen trees; smaller trees and those of shrubby habit are well-suited to gardens of any size. Many are excellent choices for street and urban plantings. Some maples may be grown in large containers, although doing so will restrict their growth.

• **CULTIVATION** Grow in fertile, moist but well-drained soil, in sun or partial shade. Pruning group 1, but prune only from late autumn to midwinter. Train large species as central-leader standards.

• **PROPAGATION** Sow seed *in situ* or in containers outdoors as soon as ripe. Graft in late winter; bud in late summer.

• **PESTS AND DISEASES** Prone to aphids, scale insects, and caterpillars. Mites cause leaf and stem galls on several species. *Verticillium* wilt, tar spot, and numerous other fungal leaf spots and root rots are common. Branch cankers and heart and wood rots caused by fungi also occur.

A. buergerianum (Three-toothed maple, Trident maple). Spreading, deciduous tree with obovate, 3-lobed, glossy leaves, to 3½in (9cm) long, dark green above, blue-green beneath, turning orange and red in late autumn and early winter. Bears erect racemes of pale yellow flowers. Ideal in a small garden or large containers; also popular for bonsai work. ↕30ft (10m), ↔25ft (8m). E. China, Korea, Japan. Zone 5b.

A. caesium* subsp. *giraldii see *A. giraldii.*

A. campestre ▣ (Hedge maple). Slow-growing, rounded, dense, deciduous tree with dark green, ovate to rounded, 5-lobed leaves, 2–4in (5–10cm) long, composed of 3–5 rounded, entire lobes, softly hairy beneath, turning yellow in autumn. Bears corymbs of 5 green flowers, followed by flat, horizontal-winged fruit. Suitable as a large hedge. ↕↔25–35ft (8–11m). Europe, W. Asia. Zone 5. **'Compactum'** is dwarf, broader than tall, and multi-stemmed. Less hardy than the species; ↕2–4ft (60–120m), ↔3–5ft (1–1.5m).

A. capillipes ▣ (Snakebark maple). Deciduous tree with spreading, arching branches, streaked green and white, and with red young shoots. Broadly ovate, mid- to dark green leaves, to 5in (13cm) long, with 3 pointed lobes, turn bright red in autumn. Bears pendent racemes of greenish white flowers. ↕↔30ft (10m). Japan. Zone 6.

Acer carpinifolium

Acer circinatum (inset: autumn leaf color)

A. cappadocicum ▣ (Cappadocian maple, Caucasian maple, Coliseum maple). Spreading, deciduous tree with broadly ovate, bright green leaves, to 4in (10cm) long, with 5–7 tapered lobes, which turn yellow in autumn. Bears erect umbels of pale yellow flowers. ↕70ft (20m), ↔50ft (15m). Caucasus, N. Turkey, Iran, Himalayas, China. Zone 6b. **'Aureum'** has bright yellow young leaves, which turn green in summer, and yellow again in autumn; ↕50ft (15m), ↔30ft (10m). **subsp. *lobelii***, syn. *A. lobelii* (Lobel's maple), is narrow, with upright branches and dark green leaves, 3–5in (8–13cm) long, each with 3–5 wavy-margined lobes, on glaucous shoots; ↕70ft (20m), ↔20ft (6m); Italy. **var. *mono*** see *A. mono.* **'Rubrum'** has dark red young leaves on red shoots.

A. carpinifolium ▣ (Hornbeam maple). Bushy, spreading, deciduous tree with upright branches and simple, ovate to ovate-oblong, tapered, sharply toothed, prominently veined, mid-green leaves, to 6in (15cm) long, which turn golden brown in autumn. Green flowers are borne in short, pendent racemes. ↕↔30ft (10m). Japan. Zone 5.

A. circinatum ▣ (Vine maple). Spreading, bushy, sometimes shrubby, deciduous tree with rounded, deeply 7- to 9-lobed, light green leaves, to 5in (13cm) long, which turn orange and red in autumn. Bears pendent umbels of small, purple and white flowers. ↕15ft (5m), ↔20ft (6m). W. North America. Zone 6.

A. cissifolium (Ivy-leaved maple). Spreading, deciduous tree with deeply toothed, 3-palmate leaves, with oval or obovate leaflets, each to 3in (8cm) long, that open bronze, become dark green, then turn brilliant red in early autumn. Bears upright racemes of pale yellow flowers. Acidic or neutral soils give the best autumn color. ↕25ft (8m), ↔30ft (10m). Japan. Zone 5. **subsp. *henryi*** see *A. henryi.*

A. crataegifolium (Hawthorn maple). Spreading, deciduous tree with green- and white-streaked bark and arching branches. Ovate, shallowly 3-lobed, dark green leaves, to 3in (8cm) long, with toothed margins, turn orange in autumn. Produces pale yellow flowers in upright racemes. ↕↔30ft (10m). Japan. Zone 6. **'Veitchii'** ▣ has white-mottled leaves, sometimes also pink-mottled, which turn pink and purple in autumn; ↕↔20ft (6m).

Acer crataegifolium 'Veitchii'

Acer davidii 'George Forrest'

Acer davidii 'Madeline Spitta'

A. dasycarpum see *A. saccharinum.*
A. davidii (Père David's maple). Variable, deciduous tree with arching branches and green- and white-streaked bark. The ovate, unlobed or shallowly lobed, mid-green leaves, to 6in (15cm) long, turn orange to yellow in autumn, when pink-brown fruit are also borne. Bears pendent racemes of pale yellow flowers. ↕↔ 50ft (15m). China. Zone 6b. **'Ernest Wilson'** has pale green leaves that turn bright orange in autumn; ↕ 25ft (8m), ↔ 30ft (10m). **'George Forrest'** ■ is broadly upright, with large, mid- to dark green leaves, to 8in (20cm) long, but with poor, unreliable autumn color. **subsp. *grosseri*** syn. *A. grosseri, A. grosseri* var. *hersii, A. hersii,* has boldly streaked bark and triangular-ovate leaves, each with 3

Acer griseum

Acer heldreichii subsp. *trautvetteri*

shallow side lobes, which turn orange or yellow in autumn; N. China. **'Madeline Spitta'** ■ is narrowly erect, with glossy, dark green leaves, orange-red in autumn; ↕ 40ft (12m), ↔ 15ft (5m).
A. forrestii see *A. pectinatum* subsp. *forrestii.*
A. x freemanii (*A. rubrum* x *A. saccharinum*). Variable hybrid group between red maple and silver maple. Selections have been made for autumn color, growth rate, and habit. Zone 3b. **'Autumn Blaze'** is fast growing, with a dense, oval-rounded head, and a central leader with ascending branches. Bears deeply lobed, rich green leaves with persistent orange-red autumn color; ↕ 50ft (15m), ↔ 40ft (12m). **'Autumn Fantasy'** is upright and oval, with 5-lobed leaves more closely resembling silver maple than red maple, turning crimson in autumn; ↕ 40ft (12m), ↔ 30ft (10m). **'Celebration'** has upright, uniform growth and strong crotch angles. Dense foliage turns red, then gold in autumn. Does not bear fruit; ↕ 45ft (14m), ↔ 20–25ft (6–8m). **'Lee's Red'** has foliage not as deeply lobed as silver maple, turning brilliant red in autumn; ↕ 60ft (18m), ↔ 30ft (10m). **'Marmo'** is distinctly broad-columnar, with foliage that turns color early, dominated by red, with green patches, lasting 2–4 weeks; ↕ 70ft (20m), ↔ 35–40ft (11–12m).
A. ginnala see *A. tataricum* subsp. *ginnala.*
A. giraldii, syn. *A. caesium* subsp. *giraldii.* Spreading, deciduous tree with glaucous young shoots and broadly ovate, 3-lobed, glossy, dark green leaves, 5in (13cm) long, glaucous beneath, borne on thick red leaf stalks. Produces greenish white flowers in upright umbels. ↕↔ 50ft (15m). C. China. Zone 7b.
A. grandidentatum see *A. saccharum* subsp. *grandidentatum.*
A. griseum ■ (Paperbark maple). Slow-growing, oval to rounded, deciduous tree with highly ornamental, peeling, orange-brown bark. Dark green, 3-palmate leaves, to 4in (10cm) long, have ovate leaflets, and turn orange to red and scarlet in autumn. Bears yellow flowers in pendent racemes. Excellent small ornamental tree. ↕↔ 30ft (10m). C. China. Zone 6.
A. grosseri see *A. davidii* subsp. *grosseri.*
A. grosseri* var. *hersii see *A. davidii* subsp. *grosseri.*
A. heldreichii* subsp. *trautvetteri ■ (Greek maple, Red bud maple). Upright, deciduous tree with heart-shaped, deeply

Acer japonicum 'Aconitifolium'

5-lobed, dark green leaves, 4–6in (10–15cm) long, opening from red buds, turning dark yellow in autumn. Erect umbels of yellow flowers are followed by fruit that ripen to red. ↕↔ 50ft (15m). Caucasus, N. Turkey. Zone 7.
A. henryi, syn. *A. cissifolium* subsp. *henryi.* Spreading, deciduous tree producing 3-palmate, dark green leaves, to 4in (10cm) long, with entire or nearly entire, elliptic leaflets, which open bronze and turn brilliant red in early autumn. Produces green flowers in slender, pendent racemes. ↕ 25ft (8m), ↔ 30ft (10m). C. China. Zone 5b.
A. hersii see *A. davidii* subsp. *grosseri.*
A. japonicum (Full-moon maple). Spreading, bushy, deciduous tree or shrub with rounded, 7- to 11-lobed, toothed, mid-green leaves, 6–8in (15–20cm) long, turning red in autumn. Bears upright umbels of conspicuous, small, red-purple flowers. Leaves are prone to scorch during hot, dry summers. ↕↔ 30ft (10m). Japan. Zone 6. **'Aconitifolium'** ■ syn. 'Filicifolium', 'Laciniatum', has deeply lobed leaves and is very free flowering; ↕ 15ft (5m), ↔ 20ft (6m). **'Aureum'** see *A. shirasawanum* 'Aureum'. **'Filicifolium'** see 'Aconitifolium'. **'Laciniatum'** see 'Aconitifolium'. **'Vitifolium'** ■ has large, shallowly lobed leaves, 2–10in (5–25cm) long, with coarsely toothed margins, turning dark red in autumn.
A. laxiflorum, syn. *A. pectinatum* subsp. *laxiflorum.* Rounded, deciduous tree with arching branches and green- and white-streaked bark. Simple, ovate, leathery, glossy, mid-green leaves, to 3in (8cm) long, on red leaf stalks, turn orange in autumn. Bears brownish green flowers in slender, pendent racemes. ↕↔ 30ft (10m). W. China. Zone 7.
A. lobelii see *A. cappadocicum* subsp. *lobelii.*

Acer japonicum 'Vitifolium'

A. macrophyllum ■ (Big-leaf maple, Oregon maple). Vigorous, deciduous tree with broadly ovate, deeply 5-lobed, glossy, dark green leaves, 8–12in (20–30cm) long, which turn orange-brown in autumn. Yellow-green flowers, in long, pendent racemes, are followed by large, bristly, winged fruit. ↕↔ 70ft (20m). W. North America. Zone 7.
A. maximowiczianum, syn. *A. nikoense* (Nikko maple). Rounded, deciduous tree producing 3-palmate leaves, to 4in (10cm) long, with oval, entire or nearly entire leaflets, dark green above, glaucous and softly hairy beneath, which turn red in autumn. Bears yellow flowers in small umbels. ↕↔ 40ft (12m). Japan, China. Zone 7.
A. micranthum. Deciduous tree or shrub with upright, arching branches and red young shoots. Ovate, deeply 5-lobed, mid-green leaves, 2–3in (5–8cm) long, with lobes tapered and sharply toothed, turn yellow and red in autumn. Produces pendent racemes of greenish white flowers. ↕ 30ft (10m), ↔ 25ft (8m). Japan. Zone 7.
A. miyabei. Rounded, deciduous tree with corky bark and rounded, deeply 3- to 5-lobed, rich green leaves, 4–6in (10–15cm) long, heart-shaped at the base, turning clear yellow in autumn. Pendent racemes of yellow flowers open in spring, with the leaves. ↕↔ 40ft (12m). Japan. Zone 3.
A. mono ■ syn. *A. cappadocicum* var. *mono, A. pictum* (Painted maple). Rounded, deciduous tree with almost heart-shaped leaves, 3–6in (8–15cm) long, each with 5–7 tapered lobes, bright green, turning yellow in autumn. Bears erect umbels of greenish yellow flowers. ↕↔ 40ft (12m). China, Korea, Japan. Zone 5.

Acer macrophyllum

Acer mono

Acer negundo 'Flamingo'

A. monspessulanum (Montpellier maple). Variable, bushy, deciduous shrub or small, rounded tree bearing leathery, ovate, glossy, dark green leaves, 1¼–2in (3–5cm) long, with 3 rounded lobes. Bears a profusion of yellow-green flowers in pendent racemes, followed by red-winged fruit in midsummer. ↕↔ 25ft (8m). Mediterranean. Zone 7.
A. negundo (Ash-leaved maple, Box elder, Manitoba maple). Fast-growing, upright, deciduous tree, cultivated mostly as its variants. Pinnate leaves, 8in (20cm) or more long, have 3–9 ovate, light green leaflets, to 4in (10cm) long, turning yellow in autumn. Greenish yellow flowers are borne in pendent racemes, males and females on separate plants. May become weedy. ↕ 50ft (15m), ↔ 30ft (10m). North America.

Acer negundo 'Variegatum'

Acer palmatum f. *atropurpureum*

Acer palmatum 'Bloodgood'

Zone 2. **'Argenteovariegatum'** see 'Variegatum'. **'Auratum'** is slow-growing, with bright yellow leaves in spring, becoming paler in summer; ↕↔ 25ft (8m). **'Flamingo'** ■ has glaucous shoots and leaves with broad pink margins that turn white in summer. **'Variegatum'** ■ syn. 'Argenteovariegatum', has leaves broadly margined with white.
A. nikoense see *A. maximowiczianum.*
A. oliverianum. Graceful, deciduous tree with spreading, arching branches. Ovate, shallowly lobed, mid-green leaves, 2–5in (5–13cm) long, each with 5 tapered and finely toothed lobes, turn orange, red, and purple in autumn. Bears pale yellow flowers in long-stalked, upright, corymb-like umbels. ↕ 25ft (8m), ↔ 30ft (10m). China. Zone 8.

Acer palmatum 'Butterfly'

Acer palmatum 'Chitoseyama'

Acer palmatum 'Corallinum'

A. palmatum (Japanese maple). Round-headed, deciduous tree with rounded, shallowly to deeply 5- to 9-lobed, mid-green leaves, 2–5in (5–13cm) long, which turn orange to yellow or red in autumn. Tiny, purple-red flowers, produced in small, pendent corymbs, are followed by red-winged fruit in late summer. ↕ 25ft (8m), ↔ 30ft (10m). China, Korea, Japan. Zone 6, although a few cultivars and some seed-raised plants are hardy to Zone 5b. Most cultivars are low-growing and shrubby; taller ones form trees or large shrubs. Several, particularly var. *dissectum* and similar mound-forming cultivars with arching shoots, may be top-grafted to make miniature trees. Many are excellent choices for small gardens, large containers, and bonsai. **'Atrolineare'** see 'Linearilobum Atropurpureum'. **f. *atropurpureum*** ■ syn. 'Atropurpureum', has deeply lobed, red-purple leaves, turning brilliant red in autumn. **'Beni-kagami'** has pendent branches and very deeply cut, 5-lobed, red-purple leaves; ↕↔ 25ft (8m). **'Bloodgood'** ■ has deeply cut, 5-lobed, dark red-purple leaves, turning bright red in autumn, and red fruit; ↕↔ 15ft (5m). **'Burgundy Lace'** has very deeply cut, 5-lobed, dark red-purple leaves; ↕ 12ft (4m), ↔ 15ft (5m). **'Butterfly'** ■ is upright with small, shallowly 5-lobed, gray-green leaves, 1¼–2in (3–5cm) long, margined white and pink; ↕ 10ft (3m), ↔ 5ft (1.5m). **'Chishio'** see 'Shishio'. **'Chitoseyama'** ■ is mound-forming, with deeply 7-lobed, pale crimson-green leaves, turning purple-red in autumn; ↕ 6ft (2m), ↔ 10ft (3m).

Acer palmatum 'Garnet'

'Corallinum' ■ is slow-growing, with small, deeply lobed, pale green leaves, 1¼–3in (3–8cm) long, opening brilliant pink in spring; ↕ 4ft (1.2m), ↔ 3ft (1m). **'Crimson Queen'** has arching shoots and red-purple leaves divided into finely cut, deeply toothed lobes; ↕ 10ft (3m), ↔ 12ft (4m). **var. *dissectum*,** syn. *A.* 'Dissectum', is mound-forming, with arching shoots, and has 7- to 11-lobed leaves, each deeply and finely cut, turning gold in autumn; ↕ 6ft (2m), ↔ 10ft (3m). **'Dissectum Atropurpureum'** ■ is similar to var. *dissectum*, but has red-purple leaves. **'Dissectum Nigrum'**, syn. 'Ever Red', is similar to 'Dissectum Atropurpureum', but has dark red-purple leaves, silvery-hairy beneath when young. **'Dissectum Ornatum Variegatum'** is similar to var. *dissectum*, but has leaves with white markings. **'Ever Red'** see 'Dissectum Nigrum'. **'Filigree'** is similar to var. *dissectum*, but has very finely cut leaves, opening pale green mottled with cream, turning gold in autumn. **'Garnet'** ■ is similar to 'Dissectum Atropurpureum', but with leaves remaining red-purple into autumn. **var. *heptalobum*** ■ has leaves with 7–9 broad lobes, turning orange to red in autumn; ↕ 15ft (5m), ↔ 20ft (6m). **var. *heptalobum* 'Lutescens'** is similar to var. *heptalobum*, but has yellow-green leaves in spring, turning bright gold in autumn. **var. *heptalobum* 'Rubrum'** ■ is similar to var. *heptalobum*, but with dark red-purple leaves, turning red in autumn. **'Higasayama'** has small leaves, 2–3in (5–8cm) long, margined white and pink, turning yellow to red in autumn; ↕↔ 15ft (5m). **'Kagiri-nishiki'**, syn.

Acer palmatum 'Dissectum Atropurpureum'

A

Acer palmatum var. *heptalobum*

Acer palmatum var. *heptalobum* 'Rubrum'

'Roseomarginatum', has blue-green leaves with deeply cut, often curved lobes, margined white and pink, and turning pink and red in autumn; ↕↔ 10ft (3m). **'Linearilobum'** ■ syn. 'Scolopendrifolum', has deeply cut, bright green leaves with 7 long, slender lobes, turning yellow in autumn; ↕ 15ft (5m), ↔ 12ft (4m). **'Linearilobum Atropurpureum'**, syn. 'Atrolineare', is similar to 'Linearilobum', but with red-purple foliage. **'Osakazuki'** produces large, deeply 7-lobed leaves, 4–5in (10–13cm) long, which turn brilliant red in autumn; ↕↔ 20ft (6m). **'Red Pygmy'** is vase-shaped, with linear leaves, dark red in spring and gold in autumn; ↕↔ 5ft (1.5m). **'Ribesifolium'** see 'Shishigashira'. **'Roseomarginatum'** see 'Kagiri-nishiki'. **'Sango-kaku'** ■ syn. 'Senkaki', has bright coral-red shoots in winter and deeply 5-lobed leaves, 1¼–3in (3–8cm) long, opening orange-yellow, turning soft yellow in autumn; ↕ 20ft (6m), ↔ 15ft (5m). **'Scolopendrifolum'** see 'Linearilobum'. **'Senkaki'** see 'Sango-kaku'. **'Shindeshojo'** has 5- to 7-lobed leaves that are brilliant red when young, white- and pink-speckled green in summer, and orange and red in autumn. Less hardy than most other selections; ↕↔ 6ft (2m). **'Shishigashira'**, syn. 'Ribesifolium', is upright, with densely clustered leaves; ↕ 12ft (4m), ↔ 10ft (3m). **'Shishio'**, syn. 'Chishio', has 5-lobed leaves, bright red when young, green in summer, and red in autumn; ↕↔ 8ft (2.5m). **'Ukigumo'** has small, deeply cut, 5-lobed leaves,

Acer palmatum 'Linearilobum'

1¼–3in (3–8cm) long, irregularly mottled white and pink; ↕↔ 6ft (2m). **'Waterfall'** is similar to var. *dissectum*, but has slightly deeper cut, semi-pendent leaves.
A. pectinatum* subsp. *forrestii ■ syn. *A. forrestii*. Spreading, deciduous tree with arching branches, red when young, later becoming green-and-white-striped. Broadly ovate leaves, to 5in (13cm) long, each with 3, sometimes 5 lobes, open red-tinged green, turn dark green in summer, and orange-red in autumn. Produces pendent racemes of brownish green flowers. ↕↔ 30ft (10m). W. China. Zone 6.
A. pectinatum* subsp. *laxiflorum see *A. laxiflorum*.
A. pensylvanicum ■ (Moosewood, Striped maple). Broadly upright, deciduous tree with green-and-white-striped bark. Obovate, bright green leaves, to 8in (20cm) long, have 3 forward-pointing lobes, and turn clear yellow in autumn. Bears pendent panicles, 4–6in (10–15cm) long, of greenish yellow flowers. Often difficult to transplant and cultivate. ↕ 40ft (12m), ↔ 30ft (10m). E. North America. Zone 2b. **'Erythrocladum'** ■ has brilliant pink young shoots, striking in winter, which become orange-red with white stripes as they mature.
***A. pentaphyllum*.** Spreading, deciduous tree with slender shoots. The 5- to 7-palmate leaves, to 3in (8cm) long, with long red leaf stalks, are divided into narrow, oblong to lance-shaped, entire or nearly entire leaflets, which are glossy, light green above, and blue-green beneath. Bears upright corymbs of yellow-green flowers. ↕ 30ft (10m), ↔ 25ft (8m). S.W. China. Zone 8.
A. pictum see *A. mono*.
A. platanoides (Norway maple). Vigorous, spreading, deciduous tree with large, broadly ovate, dark green leaves, 3–6in (8–15cm) long, each with 3–5 lobes, ending in slender-pointed teeth, and turning clear yellow or (rarely) red, or falling green, in autumn. Bears small but conspicuous, upright corymbs of yellow flowers. Cultivars are widely grown as street trees, although they cast dense shade and out-compete

Acer pensylvanicum

Acer pensylvanicum 'Erythrocladum'

most plants for water and nutrients. May become weedy, particularly in wooded areas. ↕ 80ft (25m), ↔ 50ft (15m). Europe. Zone 4b. **'Cleveland'** is upright-oval to oval-rounded, bearing dense, dark green foliage with exceptional golden yellow autumn color; ↕ 40–50ft (12–15m), ↔ 30–40ft (10–12m). **'Columnarbroad'**, syn. 'Parkway', is compact and broadly upright, with an oval crown and bright yellow autumn color; ↕ 40ft (12m), ↔ 25ft (8m). **'Columnare'** is similar to 'Columnarbroad', but is taller and has a narrower spread; ↕ 70ft (20m), ↔ 20ft (6m). **'Crimson King'** ■ has dark red-purple foliage, maturing dark purple, and red-tinged yellow flowers. **'Crimson Sentry'** is narrowly upright,

Acer palmatum 'Sango-kaku'

Acer pectinatum subsp. *forrestii*

Acer platanoides 'Crimson King'

Acer platanoides 'Drummondii'

Acer pseudoplatanus 'Simon Louis Frères'

with red-purple foliage; ↕40ft (12m), ↔15ft (5m). **'Deborah'** has wavy-margined leaves, which open brilliant red, turn dark green in summer, and become orange-yellow in autumn. **'Drummondii'** ■ (Harlequin maple) has leaves broadly margined creamy white; ↕↔30–40ft (10–12m). **'Emerald Lustre'** is vigorous and well-branched, with red-tinged young leaves that mature to glossy, deep green with a wavy margin. **'Emerald Queen'** is fast-growing, with an oval-rounded outline, ascending branches, and bright yellow autumn color; ↕50ft (15m), ↔40ft (12m). **'Faassen's Black'** is similar to 'Crimson King', but has duller and darker red-purple leaves, turned up at the margins, turning bright red in autumn. **'Fairview'** has leaves opening dark red, then turning dark green in summer. **'Globosum'** has a dense, rounded head; ↕20ft (6m), ↔25ft (8m). **'Goldsworth Purple'** is similar to 'Crimson King', but has lighter red-purple leaves, wrinkled when young. **'Jade Glen'** is fast-growing, with an open head. **'Laciniatum'** (Eagle's claw maple) is upright, and has fan-shaped, deeply lobed leaves with claw-like lobes; ↕70ft (20m), ↔30ft (10m). **'Lorbergii'** see 'Palmatifidum'. **'Olmsted'** is dense and upright; ↕30ft (10m), ↔15ft (5m). **'Oregon Pride'** is fast-growing, with shallowly lobed leaves that turn golden bronze in autumn. **'Palmatifidum'**, syn. 'Lorbergii', has shallowly to deeply lobed leaves, the lobes ending in long, slender teeth. **'Parkway'** see 'Columnarbroad'. **'Schwedleri'** bears conspicuous, purplish yellow flowers before the leaves. The leaves open red at first, then turn dark purple-green in summer. **'Summershade'** grows rapidly, with an upright-rounded habit, and maintains a single leader. Foliage is more leathery and is retained later than other cultivars. Heat resistant; ↕60–80ft (18–25m), ↔50–65ft (15–20m). **'Superform'** is fast-growing, with a straight trunk and heavy, dark green foliage; ↕50ft (15m), ↔45ft (14m).

A. pseudoplatanus (Planetree maple, Sycamore maple). Fast-growing, spreading, rounded, deciduous tree producing ovate, 5-lobed, dark green leaves, 4–8in (10–20cm) long. Yellow-green flowers are borne in pendent panicles, to 5in (13cm) long, followed by green, sometimes red, winged fruit. ↕100ft (30m), ↔80ft (25m). Europe, S.W. Asia. Zone 5b. **'Atropurpureum'** has dark green leaves, dark red-purple beneath, with red leaf stalks. Bears clusters of red-winged fruit in late summer; ↕80ft (25m), ↔70ft (20m). **'Brilliantissimum'** ■ is slow-growing, with a dense head, and bright pink leaves that turn yellow, then green in summer. Requires protection from strong summer sun; ↕20ft (6m), ↔25ft (8m). **f. *erythrocarpum*** ■ produces fruit with bright red wings. **'Leopoldii'** has leaves that open pink, later turning yellow, then green speckled with yellow and pink; ↕↔30ft (10m). **'Nizetii'** produces leaves splashed and streaked with pale green and white above, red-purple beneath; ↕↔40ft (12m). **'Simon Louis Frères'** ■ is slow-growing, with leaves opening pink, then turning creamy green speckled with white, in summer. ↕↔30ft (10m).

A. pseudosieboldianum (Purplebloom). Small, rounded, deciduous tree with a bushy head and rounded, glossy, mid-green leaves, to 5in (13cm) long, with 9–11 finely toothed lobes. The leaves turn red, orange, or purple in autumn. Red-purple flowers are borne in erect corymbs. ↕↔20ft (6m). N.E. China, Korea. Zone 6.

A. rubrum (Red maple, Scarlet maple, Swamp maple). Round-headed to open-crowned, deciduous tree with 3- or 5-lobed, ovate, dark green leaves, to 4in (10cm) long, grayish white beneath, turning bright red in autumn. Produces erect clusters of tiny red flowers. Grow in acidic soil for best autumn color. Many make excellent shade, specimen, and street trees. ↕70ft (20m), ↔30ft (10m). E. North America. Zone 3. **'Armstrong'** is erect; ↔to 20ft (6m). **'Autumn Flame'** has foliage that turns brilliant red in early autumn. **'Bowhall'** is an upright form with a symmetrical, narrow, pyramidal head, wider than 'Armstrong'. Good yellowish red autumn color; ↕50ft (15m), ↔15ft (5m). **'Columnare'** ■ is narrow, with red-orange autumn color; ↔10ft (3m). **'Embers'** is narrow when young, maturing to a rounded outline. Bears lustrous green foliage turning consistently bright red in autumn. **'Gerling'** is conical when young; ↕25ft (8m), ↔30ft (10m). **'Indian Summer'** see 'Morgan'. **'Morgan'**, syn. 'Indian Summer', is vigorous and extremely

Acer pseudoplatanus 'Brilliantissimum'

Acer pseudoplatanus f. *erythrocarpum*

Acer rubrum 'Columnare'

Acer rubrum 'October Glory'

hardy, with leaves that turn brilliant orange-red in autumn. **'Northwood'** has a rounded-oval crown with branches ascending at 45-degree angles, and dark green foliage, turning orange-red in autumn. **'October Glory'** ▣ has glossy foliage, which turns brilliant red in early autumn. **'Red Sunset'** has bright red color very early in autumn. **'Scanlon'** ▣ is dense and columnar, and has foliage that turns red-orange in autumn; ↕ 50ft (15m), ↔ 15ft (5m). **'Scarlet Sentinel'** is vigorous and columnar, with leaves that turn orange-red in autumn; ↕ 40ft (12m). **'Schlesingeri'** ▣ has leaves that turn dark red very early in autumn.
A. rufinerve ▣ (Redvein maple). Arching, deciduous tree with glaucous young shoots, green-and-white-striped branches, and ovate, 3-lobed leaves, to 5in (13cm) long, turning red in autumn. Greenish yellow flowers are borne in erect racemes, followed by red-winged fruit. ↕↔ 30ft (10m). Japan. Zone 7. **f. *albolimbatum*** see 'Hatsuyuki'. **'Hatsuyuki'**, syn. f. *albolimbatum*, has leaves that are boldly mottled white.
A. saccharinum ▣ syn. *A. dasycarpum* (Silver maple, Soft maple). Spreading, fast-growing, deciduous tree, often with pendent branches. Sharply-toothed, shallowly to deeply 5-lobed leaves, 4–8in (10–20cm) long, are light green above, silvery white beneath, and turn yellow to orange or red in autumn. Greenish yellow flowers are borne in small, erect corymbs. Subject to damage from wind and ice storms. ↕ 80ft (25m), ↔ 50ft (15m). E. North America. Zone 3. **'Laciniatum Wieri'**, syn. 'Wieri', has pendent lower branches and very deeply cut leaves. **'Pyramidale'** is broadly upright, with deeply cut leaves. **'Silver Queen'** is broadly upright, with bright green leaves turning yellow in autumn, and produces few fruit. **'Wieri'** see 'Laciniatum Wieri'.
A. saccharum (Hard maple, Rock maple, Sugar maple). Deciduous tree with a dense, oval to rounded crown and large, broadly ovate, dull, mid-green leaves, 3–7in (8–18cm) long, with 3–5 blunt lobes, which turn brilliant orange to red and yellow in autumn. Greenish yellow flowers are borne in corymbs. Most make excellent shade trees, although not suitable for urban or polluted conditions. ↕ 70ft (20m), ↔ 40ft (12m). E. North America. Zone 4. **'Bonfire'** is vigorous, with glossy, mid-green leaves, turning bright red and orange in autumn. **'Columnare'** see 'Newton Sentry'. **'Commemoration'** is vigorous and fast-growing, with a dense, oval-rounded outline and glossy, heavily textured leaves that turn color earlier, from yellow to orange to red. Resistant to leaf tatter; ↕ 50ft (15m), ↔ 38ft (11.5m). **'Fairview'** is sturdy and broad-oval shaped, with emerald-green leaves, turning orange in autumn; ↕ 50ft (15m), ↔ 40ft (12m). **'Flax Mill Majesty'** is more densely branched and symmetrical, and is faster-growing than the species. Has large, thick, dark green leaves that turn red-orange in autumn. **'Goldspire'** is columnar in habit, with bright yellow-orange leaves in autumn. **subsp. *grandidentatum***, syn. *A. grandidentatum* (Canyon maple), is much smaller than *A. saccharum* and has glossy, mid-green leaves, 2½–5in (6–13cm) long, which turn brilliant scarlet, orange, or yellow in autumn. ↕↔ 30ft (10m). W. US. **'Green Mountain'** is upright, and suitable for hot, dry areas. **'Legacy'** has a denser crown, with thick, glossy, dark green leaves that turn red or yellow-orange in autumn. Drought resistant and well acclimated to warm climates. Resists leaf tatter better than most other sugar maples. **'Monumentale'** see 'Temple's Upright'. **'Newton Sentry'**, syn. 'Columnare', has upright branches, which have short, spur-like shoots, and lacks a central leader; ↕ 30ft (10m), ↔ 8ft (2.5m). **subsp. *nigrum* 'Green Column'** ▣ is broadly columnar, with leaves that turn bright yellow in autumn; ↕ 40ft (12m), ↔ 25ft (8m). **'Sweet Shadow'** has deeply lobed leaves, turning orange in autumn. **'Temple's Upright'** ▣ syn. 'Monumentale', is narrowly upright, and has ascending branches; ↕ 70ft (20m), ↔ 15ft (5m).
***A. shirasawanum* 'Aureum'** ▣ syn. *A. japonicum* 'Aureum'. Rounded, bushy, deciduous tree or shrub producing rounded, 7- to 11-lobed,

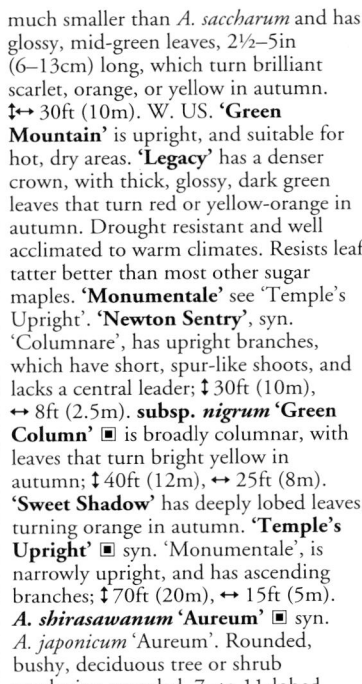

Acer rufinerve

Acer saccharum subsp. *nigrum* 'Green Column'

Acer rubrum 'Scanlon'

Acer rubrum 'Schlesingeri'

Acer saccharinum (inset: autumn leaf color)

Acer saccharum 'Temple's Upright'

Acer shirasawanum 'Aureum'

Acer tataricum subsp. *ginnala*

bright yellow leaves, 3–4in (7–10cm) long, which turn red in autumn. Tiny, red-purple flowers are borne in upright corymbs. ↕↔ 20ft (6m). Zone 5.
A. sieboldianum. Rounded, bushy, deciduous tree with rounded, 7- to 11-lobed, mid-green leaves, 2½–3½in (6–9cm) long, which turn orange-yellow to red in autumn. Bears small, nodding corymbs of tiny yellow flowers. ↕↔ 20ft (6m). Japan. Zone 6.
A. spicatum (Mountain maple). Deciduous shrub or tree with upright shoots, red-tinged when young, and ovate, shallowly 3-lobed, toothed, bright green leaves, to 5in (13cm) long, turning orange, purple, and red in autumn. Creamy white flowers are borne in slender, upright panicles. ↕ 25ft (8m), ↔ 15ft (5m). E. North America. Zone 2.
A. tataricum (Tatarian maple). Bushy, deciduous tree with a rounded crown. Produces broadly ovate, glossy, bright green leaves, to 4in (10cm) long, entire or with up to 3 lobes, and with toothed margins; the leaves turn red or yellow in autumn. Upright panicles of creamy white flowers are followed by red-winged fruit. ↕ 30ft (10m), ↔ 25ft (8m). S.E. Europe, S.W. Asia. Zone 2b. **subsp. *ginnala*** ■ syn. *A. ginnala* (Amur maple), has slender, arching branches and deeply 3-lobed leaves, which turn deep red in autumn. **subsp. *ginnala* 'Durand Dwarf'** is dense and shrubby, and has leaves, to 1½–3in (4–8cm) long, which turn light to dark red in early autumn; ↕ 5ft (1.5m), ↔ 6ft (2m). **subsp. *ginnala* 'Flame'** has red fruit in summer and bright red leaves in autumn.

Acer triflorum

Acer velutinum

A. tegmentosum. Spreading, deciduous tree with green-and-white-striped branches, and ovate, shallowly 3-lobed, bright green leaves, to 6in (15cm) long, yellow in autumn. Bears yellowish green flowers in pendent racemes. ↕ 25ft (8m), ↔ 30ft (10m). N.E. Asia. Zone 5b.
A. triflorum ■ (Threeflower maple). Broadly columnar to spreading, deciduous tree with peeling, light brown bark and unevenly toothed, 3-palmate, mid-green leaves, to 3in (8cm) long, with obovate to lance-shaped leaflets, often brilliant orange or red in autumn. Bears clusters of yellow-green flowers. ↕ 30ft (10m), ↔ 25ft (8m). N.E. Asia. Zone 4b.
A. truncatum (Purpleblow maple, Shantung maple). Compact, rounded, deciduous tree with a spreading head and glossy, mid-green, broadly ovate leaves, 3–5in (8–13cm) long, usually with 5 tapered lobes, turning yellow in autumn. Yellowish green flowers are produced in upright corymbs. ↕ 25ft (8m), ↔ 30ft (10m). N. China, Korea. Zone 4.
A. velutinum ■ (Persian maple). Vigorous, spreading, deciduous tree with ovate, 5-lobed, dark green leaves, 6–10in (15–25cm) long, downy on the reverse, on red leaf stalks. Bears upright, corymb-like panicles of yellow-green flowers. ↕ 70ft (20m), ↔ 50ft (15m). Caucasus, N. Iran. Zone 8. **var. *vanvolxemixi*** has large leaves, 8–12in (20–30cm) long, blue-green beneath.

▷***Aceriphyllum*** see *Mukdenia*

ACHILLEA

Yarrow

ASTERACEAE

Genus of about 85 species of mainly deciduous perennials from temperate regions of the N. hemisphere. Some, from mountainous regions, are low-growing and mat-forming. Other species, from grassland or dry waste-ground, are taller and herbaceous. The gray or green, often aromatic leaves are mostly 1- to 3-pinnate or pinnatifid, and fern-like, although some are entire. They are elliptic to lance-shaped, toothed, and 6–12in (15–30cm) long in most species, 2–5in (5–13cm) long in smaller-growing achilleas. The basal leaves are usually larger than the stem leaves. Most achilleas produce daisy-like flowerheads, ⅛–½in (3–15mm) across, in corymbs, 3–5in (7–13cm) across, in summer and autumn; the disk and ray florets are usually both white or both yellow. Newer cultivars and hybrids, including the Galaxy hybrids (*A. millefolium* x *A.* 'Taygetea'), offer a wide color range, and produce flower-heads in compound corymbs, 4–5in (10–13cm) across. Grow achilleas in a wildflower or rock garden; the taller ones are excellent for a mixed or herbaceous border, and for cutting and drying. Contact with foliage may aggravate skin allergies.
• **CULTIVATION** Grow in moist but well-drained soil in an open site in full sun, although most will tolerate a wide range of soils and conditions. *A. ageratum* 'W.B. Childs' and *A. ptarmica* cultivars require more moisture than other achilleas (but not waterlogged soils) and partial shade. *A. clavennae* and *A.* x *kellereri* will not tolerate winter moisture in poorly drained soils. Dwarf species and silver- and hairy-leaved alpine species must have sharp drainage.
• **PROPAGATION** Sow seed *in situ* or divide in spring. *A. clypeolata* is short-lived, so divide annually. Divide all others regularly to maintain vigor.
• **PESTS AND DISEASES** Aphids may be a problem. Powdery mildew is common on *A. ptarmica*, and rust occurs on several species. Several other foliar diseases caused by fungi occur.

***A. aegyptica* of gardens** see *A.* 'Taygetea'.
A. ageratifolia. Tufted perennial with linear to linear-lance-shaped, sharply toothed, softly hairy, silver-green leaves, to 1½in (4cm) long. In summer, bears white flowerheads in unbranched corymbs, 1½–2in (4–5cm) across. ↕ to 8in (20cm), ↔ 12in (30cm). N. Greece. Zone 3b. **subsp. *aizoon*** has linear to strap-shaped, finely scalloped or entire leaves and clustered flowerheads; ↕ 6in (15cm). Greece.
A. ageratum, syn. *A. decolorans*. Spreading perennial producing linear, pinnatifid, sharply toothed, gray-white leaves. Yellowish white flowerheads are borne in loose corymbs, 3in (8cm) wide, from midsummer to early autumn. ↕↔ 24in (60cm). Portugal, W. Mediterranean. Zone 5. **'W.B. Childs'** ■ bears many attractive white flowerheads with creamy white disk florets; ↕ 24–28in (60–70cm).
***A.* 'Apfelblüte'**, syn. 'Appleblossom'. Vigorous, compact Galaxy hybrid with foliage similar to *A. millefolium*, but with larger flowerheads and stronger

Achillea ageratum 'W.B. Childs'

Achillea clavennae

Achillea clypeolata

Achillea 'Coronation Gold'

Achillea 'Fanal'

Achillea filipendulina 'Gold Plate'

stems. Bears large corymbs, 2–3in (5–8cm) across, of lilac-pink flowerheads in summer. Flowers fade when temperatures rise above 80°F (27°C). ↕ 24–36in (60–90cm), ↔ 24in (60cm). Zone 4.

***A.* 'Appleblossom'** see *A.* 'Apfelblüte'.

A. argentea see *Tanacetum argenteum.*

***A. argentea* of gardens** see *A. clavennae.*

A. clavennae ■ syn. *A. argentea* of gardens. Mat-forming perennial with semi-evergreen, narrowly obovate, pinnatifid or pinnate, light gray-green, silver-hairy leaves. Bears clusters of up to 25 white flowerheads, in corymbs 1½–2in (4–5cm) across, in summer and early autumn. ↕ 6–8in (15–20cm), ↔ 12in (30cm) or more. E. European Alps. Zone 5.

A. clypeolata ■ Mat-forming perennial with ovate to lance-shaped, pinnatifid, silvery green leaves. Corymbs, 2–3in (5–8cm) across, of tiny, golden yellow flowerheads are produced from early to late summer. ↕ 18–24in (45–60cm), ↔ 12in (30cm). Balkans. Zone 5.

***A.* 'Coronation Gold'** ■ Clump-forming perennial with evergreen, oblong, pinnatifid, silvery gray leaves. Bears tiny, golden yellow flowerheads in corymbs, 4in (10cm) across, from mid-summer to early autumn. ↕ 30–36in (75–90cm), ↔ 18in (45cm). Zone 3.

***A.* Debutante Hybrids.** Clump-forming perennials with evergreen, fern-like, pinnatifid, gray-green leaves. In summer, produce corymbs, 6in (15cm) across, of remontant flowerheads in shades of ivory, yellow, rose, scarlet, salmon, lilac, and purple. ↕ 18in (45cm), ↔ 24in (60cm). Zone 3.

Achillea 'Forncett Candy'

Achillea x *lewisii* 'King Edward'

A. decolorans see *A. ageratum.*

A. eupatorium see *A. filipendulina.*

***A.* 'Fanal'** ■ syn. *A.* 'The Beacon'. Mat-forming Galaxy hybrid with broadly linear, 2-pinnate, slightly grayish green leaves. In early summer, bears corymbs, to 4in (10cm) across, of bright red flowerheads with yellow disk florets that fade with age. ↕ 30in (75cm), ↔ 24in (60cm). Zone 4.

A. filipendulina, syn. *A. eupatorium.* Clump-forming, evergreen perennial with rosettes of oblong, pinnate or 2-pinnate, mid- to gray-green leaves. Strong, leafy stems bear golden yellow flowerheads in flat corymbs, 5in (13cm) across, from early summer to early autumn. ↕ 4ft (1.2m), ↔ 18in (45cm). Caucasus. Zone 3. **'Altgold'** has gray-green leaves and corymbs of copper-tinged yellow flowerheads; ↕ 24in (60cm). **'Cloth of Gold'** has light green leaves and corymbs of deep golden yellow flowerheads; ↕ 5ft (1.5m). **'Gold Plate'** ■ has bright golden yellow flowerheads in slightly convex corymbs, 6in (15cm) across.

***A.* 'Flowers of Sulphur'** see *A.* 'Schwefelblüte'.

***A.* 'Forncett Candy'** ■ Clump-forming, evergreen perennial producing rosettes of fern-like, broadly linear, pinnatifid, gray-green leaves. In summer, freely branching stems bear a profusion of pale pink flowerheads in corymbs to 6in (15cm) across; the ray florets fade almost to white with age. ↕ 36in (90cm), ↔ 18in (45cm). Zone 4.

A. grandifolia (White yarrow). Clump-forming perennial with ovate, coarsely pinnate, grayish green leaves. Thick stems bear white flowerheads, in corymbs to 5in (13cm) across, from early summer to autumn. ↕ 36in (90cm), ↔ 24in (60cm). C. Balkans. Zone 5.

***A.* 'Great Expectations'** see *A.* 'Hoffnung'.

***A.* 'Hoffnung'**, syn. *A.* 'Great Expectations'. Compact, clump-forming Galaxy hybrid with broadly linear, 2-pinnate, mid-green leaves. In summer, freely bears corymbs, 4–5in (10–13cm) across, of cream flowerheads with disk florets that darken with age. ↕ 30in (75cm), ↔ 24in (60cm). Zone 4.

A.* x *kellereri (*A. ageratifolia* x *A. clypeolata*). Semi-evergreen perennial with lance-shaped, pinnatifid, gray-green leaves. In summer, bears loose clusters of 6–8 cream flowerheads, each ¾in (2cm) across, with darker disk florets. ↕ 6–8in (15–20cm), ↔ 12in (30cm) or more. Garden origin. Zone 5.

***A.* x *kolbiana* 'Weston'**, syn. *A. umbellata* 'Weston'. Mat-forming perennial with semi-evergreen, linear, pinnate, silver-gray leaves. Short-stemmed white flowerheads, ½–¾in (1–2cm) across, are borne in corymbs 1¼–4in (3–10cm) wide, in summer and early autumn. ↕ 4–6in (10–15cm), ↔ to 12in (30cm). Zone 7.

***A.* 'Lachsschönheit'**, syn. *A.* 'Salmon Beauty'. Clump-forming Galaxy hybrid with broadly linear, pinnatifid, dark green leaves. In summer, many-branched stems bear a profusion of light salmon-pink flowerheads, fading to pink-flushed, creamy white, in corymbs 5½in (14cm) across. ↕ 30–36in (75–90cm), ↔ 24in (60cm). Zone 4.

***A.* x *lewisii* 'King Edward'** ■ Woody-based, mat- to low-mound-forming perennial with semi-evergreen, linear, fern-like, pinnatifid, sharply toothed, soft gray-green leaves. Pale yellow flowerheads are borne in dense corymbs, to 4in (10cm) across, in early and midsummer. ↕ 3–5in (8–13cm) or more, ↔ 9in (23cm) or more. Zone 5.

***A. millefolium* cultivars.** Selections from this rhizomatous, mat-forming and invasive perennial have linear to lance-shaped, pinnatisect, mid-green leaves. Flowerheads are borne in flat corymbs 3–4in (7–10cm) across, from early to late summer. ↕↔ 24in (60cm). Zone 3. **'Cerise Queen'** ■ is very vigorous and forms a mat of dark green leaves; the bright magenta-pink flowerheads have white disk florets, fading with age. **'Fire King'** is vigorous and upright, with richer red flowerheads than 'Cerise Queen'. **'Lavender Beauty'** see 'Lilac Beauty'. **'Lilac Beauty'**, syn. 'Lavender Beauty', is very free flowering, with lilac flowerheads fading with age; ↕ 30in (75cm). **'Paprika'** bears orange-red flowerheads that fade with age. **'Red Beauty'** has bright scarlet flowers in summer; ↕ 24in (60cm).

***A.* 'Moonshine'** ■ Clump-forming perennial producing evergreen, linear to lance-shaped, pinnatifid, gray-green

Achillea millefolium 'Cerise Queen'

Achillea 'Moonshine'

leaves. Light yellow flowerheads with slightly darker disk florets are borne in corymbs, to 4in (10cm) across, from early summer to early autumn. ↕↔ 24in (60cm). Zone 3b.

***A.* 'Moonwalker'.** Clump-forming, aromatic perennial with linear to lance-shaped, pinnatifid, dark green leaves. In summer, bears flat corymbs, 4–6in (10–15cm) across, of scented, yellow, copper-tinged flowerheads that fade with age. ↕↔ 24in (60cm). Zone 3b.

A. ptarmica (Sneezewort). Strong, rhizomatous perennial with simple, linear-lance-shaped, finely toothed, dark green leaves. From early to late summer, bears loose corymbs, ¾–4in (2–10cm) across, of usually off-white flowerheads, ½–¾in (1.5–2cm) across. ↕ 12–36in (30–90cm), ↔ 24in (60cm). Europe, W. Asia. Zone 3. **'Angel's Breath'** has white flowers from early summer to autumn; ↕ 24in (60cm). **'Ballerina'** has small, double white flowerheads, which open to show disk florets that fade to gray; ↕ to 24in (60cm), ↔ 12in (30cm). **'Boule de Neige'** ■ syn. 'Schneeball', has double, pure white flowerheads; ↕ 18–24in (45–60cm). **'Perry's White'** has larger, double white flowerheads; ↕ 30–36in (75–90cm). **'Schneeball'** see 'Boule de Neige'. **'The Pearl'** has tight, button-like, double white flowerheads; the flowers may be variable when seed-raised; ↕ 30in (75cm).

***A.* 'Salmon Beauty'** see *A.* 'Lachsschönheit'.

***A.* 'Schwefelblüte'**, syn. *A.* 'Flowers of Sulphur', *A.* 'Sulphur Flowers'. Clump-forming perennial with broadly linear, pinnatifid, grayish green leaves. In early

Achillea ptarmica 'Boule de Neige'

Achillea 'Schwellenburg'

Achillea Summer Pastels

Achillea 'Summerwine'

and midsummer, bears corymbs, to 4in (10cm) across, of sulfur-yellow flowerheads, that fade to a paler shade of yellow with age. ↕ 24in (60cm), ↔ 18in (45cm). Zone 5.

***A.* 'Schwellenburg'** ■ Low-growing, spreading perennial producing oblong-ovate, pinnatifid, gray-green leaves. From early summer to early autumn, branched stems bear corymbs, 4–8in (10–20cm) across, of lemon-yellow flowerheads, opening from silvery buds. ↕ 18in (45cm), ↔ 24in (60cm). Zone 4.

***A.* 'Sulphur Flowers'** see *A.* 'Schwefelblüte'.

***A.* Summer Pastels** ■ Compact, heat- and drought-tolerant group, with colors that fade less than other *millefolium* selections. Colors include lavender, purple, white, apricot, cream, rose, and pink. May bloom the first year from seed. ↕↔ 24in (60cm). Zone 4.

***A.* 'Summerwine'** ■ Upright Galaxy hybrid with linear, pinnatifid, dark green leaves. Dark red flowerheads, ¾in (2cm) across, with white disk florets, are produced in corymbs, to 3in (8cm) across, in mid- and late summer. ↕↔ 24in (60cm). Zone 4.

***A.* 'Taygetea'** ■ syn. *A. aegyptica* of gardens. Clump-forming perennial with evergreen, linear, pinnatifid, grayish green leaves. In mid- and late summer, bears pale, creamy yellow flowerheads in corymbs, 2–4in (5–10cm) across. ↕ 24in (60cm), ↔ 18in (45cm). Zone 3b.

***A.* 'The Beacon'** see *A.* 'Fanal'.

A. tomentosa (Woolly yarrow). Mat-forming perennial with linear, pinnatifid, woolly, gray-green leaves. Bears dense corymbs, to 3in (8cm) across, of lemon-yellow flowerheads from early summer to early autumn. ↕ to 14in (35cm), ↔ 18in (45cm). S. Europe to W. Asia. Zone 4b. **'Aurea'**, syn. 'Maynard's Gold', is more compact, with brighter (but fewer) flowerheads in early summer; ↕ 8in (20cm). **'Maynard's Gold'** see 'Aurea'.

A. umbellata. Clump-forming, semi-evergreen perennial with ovate, pinnate, silver-gray, white-hairy leaves. Hairy stems bear umbels, 1¼in (3cm) across, of 3–6 white flowerheads, to ½in (1.5cm) across, in summer. ↕ to 8in (20cm), ↔ to 12in (30cm). Greece. Zone 7. **'Weston'** see *A.* x *kolbiana* 'Weston'.

***A.* 'Wesersandstein'** ■ Mat-forming, many-branched Galaxy hybrid with linear to lance-shaped, pinnatifid, mid-green leaves. In summer, bears corymbs, to 5in (13cm) across, of pinkish red flowerheads, fading to a creamy sand color. ↕ 18–24in (45–60cm), ↔ 24in (60cm). Zone 4.

x ACHIMENANTHA

GESNERIACEAE

Hybrid genus, a cross between *Achimenes* and *Smithiantha*, of upright, rhizomatous, herbaceous perennials, cultivated for their brightly colored flowers. The ovate to oval leaves are opposite and usually hairy. The axillary clusters of tubular flowers vary greatly in color. Where not hardy, grow in a warm greenhouse; in warmer regions, grow in a border.

• **CULTIVATION** Under glass, grow in soilless potting mix in bright filtered light and moderate humidity. Water sparingly in spring; in summer, water moderately and apply a quarter-strength balanced liquid fertilizer at each watering. After flowering, reduce water until growth has withered; remove any dead growth. Overwinter rhizomes in dry, frost-free conditions. Excellent for growing under lights. Outdoors, grow in fertile, humus-rich, moist but well-drained soil in partial shade.

• **PROPAGATION** Divide rhizomes or plant individual scales in containers in spring. The latter will produce flowering plants after a few years.

• **PESTS AND DISEASES** Aphids, spider mites, and thrips may be problems. Fungal leaf spots, root rots, and tobacco mosaic virus may occur.

x *A.* Hybrids. Upright, rhizomatous perennials with hairy, ovate to oval, mid- to dark green leaves, to 5in (13cm) long. In summer, they bear tubular, slightly nodding flowers, to 2in (5cm) long. ↕ to 14in (35cm), ↔ to 9in (23cm). Garden origin. ❄ (min. 60°F/16°C). **'Ginger Peachy'** is compact, with peach-pink flowers; ↕ 8in (20cm), ↔ 6in (15cm). **'Inferno'** ■ has bright red, yellow-centered, red-veined flowers. **'Rose Bouquet'** has small leaves, to 3in (8cm) long, and double magenta flowers.

ACHIMENES

Cupid's bower, Hot water plant

GESNERIACEAE

Genus of about 25 species of winter-dormant, rhizomatous perennials, grown for their flowers, occurring mainly in subtropical forest in Mexico and Central America. Each of the small, scaly rhizomes produces a single upright, spreading, or trailing stem, which may be either branched or unbranched. The simple, ovate, dark green leaves are opposite (sometimes in unequal pairs) or in whorls, have toothed margins, and are fleshy and usually hairy; the undersides are often red and less hairy. From summer to autumn, salverform flowers are borne singly, in pairs, or in cymes from the leaf axils. There are many cultivars, with flowers in a wide range of colors. Where not hardy, grow in containers or hanging baskets in a temperate greenhouse, as houseplants, or as summer bedding plants. In frost-free areas, grow in a border.

• **CULTIVATION** Under glass, grow in soilless or soil-based potting mix in bright filtered light and moderate humidity. Bring into growth at 60–64°F (16–18°C) in spring, and water sparingly. In summer, water freely and apply a quarter-strength balanced liquid fertilizer at each watering. In autumn, remove dead top growth, and store containers in a dry, frost-free place until spring. May be grown under lights. Outdoors, grow in fertile, humus-rich, moist but well-drained soil in full sun; needs partial shade in very hot areas. Do not allow to dry out during active growth, or premature dormancy may set in.

• **PROPAGATION** Divide rhizomes or take stem cuttings in spring.

• **PESTS AND DISEASES** See x *Achimenantha*.

Achillea 'Taygetea'

Achillea 'Wesersandstein'

x *Achimenantha* 'Inferno'

Achimenes 'Ambroise Verschaffelt'

***A.* 'Ambroise Verschaffelt'** ▣ Free-flowering perennial, trailing to 12in (30cm). Dark green leaves, usually in whorls of 3 or 4, sometimes opposite, are ovate to oblong, 2in (5cm) long, coarsely toothed, and sometimes red-tinted on the reverse. From summer to autumn, bears numerous solitary white flowers, 2in (5cm) across, with purple-red veins and dots in the yellowish throats. ↕ 10in (25cm), ↔ 14–16in (35–40cm). ❀ (min. 50–59°F/10–15°C)

A. antirrhina. Erect perennial with unequal pairs of ovate, toothed, downy, dark green leaves, 4in (10cm) long, red beneath. Solitary, cream or yellow flowers, to 1in (2.5cm) across, striped purple and spotted red in the throats, are borne from summer to autumn. ↕ 12in (30cm), ↔ 6in (15cm). Mexico, Guatemala. ❀ (min. 50–59°F/10–15°C)

A. coccinea see *A. erecta.*

A. erecta, syn. *A. coccinea, A. pulchella.* Long-stemmed perennial, trailing to 18in (45cm), with whorls of 3 ovate to elliptic, toothed, dark green leaves, 2½in (6cm) long, often red-flushed beneath. Bears numerous solitary, long-tubed, bright red, occasionally rose-pink flowers, ½in (1.5cm) across, from summer to autumn. ↕ 18in (45cm), ↔ 12in (30cm). Mexico to Panama. ❀ (min. 50–59°F/10–15°C)

A. grandiflora. Erect perennial bearing pairs of ovate, pointed, toothed leaves, 6–7in (15–18cm) long, hairy and dark green above, red-flushed beneath. From summer to autumn, produces solitary or paired, reddish purple flowers, to 2in (5cm) across, each with a white eye and a purple-dotted throat. ↕↔ 24in (60cm). Mexico to Honduras. ❀ (min. 50–59°F/10–15°C)

***A.* 'Little Beauty'.** Bushy perennial with 3-whorled, ovate, pointed, dark green leaves, 6–7in (15–18cm) long, with toothed margins. Solitary, deep pink flowers, 1¼in (3cm) across, with yellow eyes, are produced from summer to autumn. ↕ 10in (25cm), ↔ 12in (30cm). ❀ (min. 50–59°F/10–15°C)

A. longiflora. Erect perennial with whorls of 3 or 4 ovate to oblong, toothed, dark green leaves, to 3in (8cm) long, red-marked beneath. Bears solitary, violet-blue flowers, to 1½in (4cm) across, from summer to autumn. ↕↔ to 24in (60cm). Mexico to Panama. ❀ (min. 50–59°F/10–15°C). **'Dentoniana'** has pale purple flowers, to 1¼in (3cm) across, with yellow-blotched, red-spotted white throats.

***A.* 'Paul Arnold'** ▣ Erect, compact perennial producing whorls of 3 or 4 ovate, toothed, dark green leaves, 2½in (6cm) long, red-purple beneath. Attractive, solitary, deep purple-blue flowers, 2in (5cm) across, with white throats suffused with yellow and purple, are borne from summer to autumn. ↕↔ 16in (40cm). ❀ (min. 50–59°F/10–15°C)

***A.* 'Peach Blossom'.** Trailing perennial with whorls of usually 3 ovate, pointed, toothed, dark green leaves, 2½in (6cm) long. Solitary, magenta-pink flowers, 2in (5cm) across, each with a darker ring around the eye, are borne from summer to autumn. ↕↔ 8in(20cm). ❀ (min. 50–59°F/10–15°C)

A. pulchella see *A. erecta.*

***A.* 'Purple King'.** Vigorous, upright or spreading perennial, trailing to 16in(40cm), with whorls of 3 ovate, toothed, dark green leaves, red beneath. Solitary, ruffle-margined, reddish purple flowers, 2in (5cm) across, open from summer to autumn. ↕ 14–16in (35–40cm), ↔ 12in (30cm). ❀ (min. 50–59°F/10–15°C)

***A.* 'Yellow Beauty'.** Erect perennial with pairs of ovate, toothed, slightly hairy, dark green leaves, 2in (5cm) long. Solitary, primrose-yellow flowers, 1in (2.5cm) across, are produced from summer to autumn. ↕ 10in (25cm), ↔ 12in (30cm). ❀ (min. 50–59°F/10–15°C)

Achimenes 'Paul Arnold'

▷***Achnatherum*** see *Stipa*
▷***Acidanthera*** see *Gladiolus*

ACINOS

Calamint

LAMIACEAE

Genus of 10 species of annuals and evergreen or semi-evergreen, spreading, woody-stemmed perennials found in mountainous areas and open sites from Europe to Asia. They have small, aromatic, usually mid-green, opposite leaves, and tubular, 2-lipped flowers, borne in erect, spike-like whorls in midsummer. Grow in a rock garden or at the front of a border.

• **CULTIVATION** Grow in poor to moderately fertile, well-drained soil in full sun; they resent wet conditions.

• **PROPAGATION** Sow seed in containers in a cold frame in autumn or spring. Separate rooted stems, or root basal softwood cuttings, in late spring or summer.

Acinos arvensis

• **PESTS AND DISEASES** Aphids and spider mites may be problems under glass. *Pythium* root rot also can occur.

A. alpinus, syn. *Calamintha alpina* (Alpine calamint). Woody-based, low-growing, evergreen perennial with entire or slightly toothed, elliptic to rounded leaves, to ¾in (2cm) long, with pointed or blunt tips. In midsummer, produces spike-like whorls of 3–8 purple flowers, ½–¾in (1–2cm) long, marked white on the lower lips, from the upper leaf axils. ↕ 4–8in (10–20cm), ↔ 3–6in (8–15cm). S. and C. Europe. Zone 5.

A. arvensis ▣ syn. *Clinopodium acinos* (Basil thyme, Mother of thyme). Spreading, short-lived perennial or annual with ovate to elliptic leaves, to ½in (1.5cm) long, on erect, branching stems. In mid- and late summer, produces loose, axillary whorls of 3–8 violet flowers, ¼–½in (6–15mm) long, marked white on the lower lips. ↕ 8in (20cm), ↔ to 12in (30cm). N. Europe to W. Asia. Zone 8.

ACIPHYLLA

Bayonet plant, Speargrass

APIACEAE

Genus of about 40 species of evergreen, mostly dioecious perennials, mainly from New Zealand and a few from Australia. Most species are from sparse mountain grassland or alpine regions, but some are from lower altitudes. They form stiff, grassy clumps, the rosettes of flattened, linear, leathery leaves having divided, much-reduced leaf blades, large terminal spines, and usually conspicuous stipules, also spined. Aciphyllas bear terminal panicles of numerous compound umbels, ¾–1½in (2–4cm) across, of tiny, star-shaped, white or yellow-green flowers, to 1⁄16in (2mm) long, which are protected by spiny bracts, usually larger and more colorful than the flowers themselves. Most species seldom flower in cool climates. Both male and female plants are needed to produce fruit. Grow larger species in a mixed border and smaller species in a rock garden or as specimens in containers during the summer..

• **CULTIVATION** Grow in moist but well-drained, fertile, humus-rich, gritty soil in an open site in full sun.

• **PROPAGATION** Sow seed in containers in a cold frame as soon as ripe, although it may remain viable for up to one year. Plant out seedlings *in situ* as soon as possible, because the deep roots resent disturbance. Divide rhizomatous species, such as *A. pinnatifida,* in spring.

• **PESTS AND DISEASES** Slugs may damage young plants.

A. aurea. Rosette-forming perennial with narrowly strap-shaped, pinnate or 2-pinnate, spine-tipped, gray-green leaves, to 24in (60cm) long, with bold yellow margins and midribs. From early to late summer, bears numerous golden brown flowers. ↕↔ 3ft (1m). New Zealand. Zone 8.

A. colensoi (Speargrass, Wild Spaniard). Rosette-forming perennial with strap-shaped, pinnate or 2-pinnate, stiff, spiny, bluish green leaves, 12–20in (30–50cm) long, with toothed margins and red or reddish brown main veins. In summer, bears small, yellowish green flowers on prickly stems. ↕ to 8ft (2.5m), ↔ 5–6ft (1.5–2m). New Zealand. Zone 8.

A. glaucescens. Rosette-forming perennial producing very narrow, strap-shaped, 3-pinnate, spine-tipped, silvery gray leaves, to 3ft (1m) long; they have prominent, almost white midribs, toothed margins, and stipules divided into 3 unequal lengths. Yellow-green flowers are borne from early to late summer. ↕↔ 3ft (1m). New Zealand. Zone 8.

A. hectoris. Dwarf, rosette-forming, perennial producing flat, lance-shaped, dark green leaves, 8–10in (20–25cm) long, deeply divided into 3 slender segments; they have toothed, almost spineless, narrow, red-gold margins and shiny stipules. Pale yellow-green flowers are borne in midsummer. ↕↔ 6in (15cm). New Zealand. Zone 8.

A. pinnatifida. Low-growing, fern-like, rhizomatous perennial producing linear, deeply pinnatifid, spine-tipped, bronze-tinged, dark green leaves, 6–8in (15–20cm) long, with yellow midribs and shiny stipules. Bears off-white flowers in summer. ↕ 4–6in (10–15cm), ↔ 12in (30cm). New Zealand. Zone 8.

A. scott-thomsonii ▣ (Giant Spaniard). Rosette-forming perennial with linear, pinnate or 2-pinnate, sharply spined, glaucous, blue-green leaves, to 5ft (1.5m) long, with green or pale yellow midribs and finely toothed margins. Yellowish green flowers are produced from early to late summer. ↕ 10ft (3m) or more, ↔ 6ft (2m). New Zealand. ❀ (min. 41°F/5°C)

Aciphylla scott-thomsonii

A

ACMENA

MYRTACEAE

Genus of 7 species of evergreen trees, occurring in rainforest and moist woodland from Australia to New Guinea. The opposite leaves are oval to lance-shaped, simple, and entire. Small, 5-petaled flowers are borne in axillary racemes or terminal panicles, followed by colorful, succulent berries. Where not hardy, grow in a temperate greenhouse; in frost-free areas, grow as specimen trees.

• **CULTIVATION** Under glass, grow in soil-based potting mix in full light (they will also tolerate filtered light). Pot on or top-dress in early spring or autumn. In the growing season, water freely and apply a balanced liquid fertilizer monthly; water sparingly in winter. Outdoors, grow in moist but well-drained, moderately fertile soil in full sun. Pruning group 8, or 13 if wall-trained.

• **PROPAGATION** Sow seed at 55–64°F (13–18°C) as soon as ripe, or in spring. Root semi-ripe cuttings with bottom heat in late summer.

• **PESTS AND DISEASES** Whiteflies, scale insects, and aphids may be problems.

A. smithii, syn. *Eugenia smithii* (Lillypilly). Rounded, bushy tree producing ovate to lance-shaped, glossy, dark green leaves, 1½–4in (4–10cm) long, with long, slender tips. Terminal panicles, ¾–2in (2–5cm) long, of greenish white flowers are borne in late spring and early summer. Edible, white, pink, or red-purple berries, ½in (1.5cm) across, ripen in autumn. In cool areas, only established container plants will bear fruit. ↕ 25–50ft (8–15m), ↔ 20–30ft (6–10m). Northern Territory, Queensland to Victoria. ❄ (min. 41°F/5°C), although it may survive short periods at just above 32°F (0°C).

ACOELORRAPHE

Saw palm

ARECACEAE

Genus of one species of cluster-stemmed palm from moist forest and swampland in S. Florida, and from Mexico to Central America and the West Indies. Panicles of bowl-shaped, hermaphrodite flowers are borne among fan-shaped leaves, produced in terminal tufts. Where not hardy, grow young saw palms in a temperate or warm greenhouse; in frost-free areas, grow outdoors as specimen trees.

• **CULTIVATION** Under glass, grow in soilless or soil-based potting mix in full light. In the growing season, water freely and apply a balanced liquid fertilizer monthly; water sparingly in winter. Pot on or top-dress in spring. Outdoors, grow in fertile, well-drained soil in full sun. Tolerates wet soil.

• **PROPAGATION** Sow seed at 81°F (27°C) in spring.

• **PESTS AND DISEASES** Spider mites may be a problem under glass. *Ganoderma* butt rot occurs on landscape plantings. Tar spot, false smut, and *Stigmina* leaf spot are common.

A. wrightii ■ syn. *Paurotis wrightii* (Everglades palm, Saw cabbage palm, Silver saw palm). Compact-crowned palm with no crownshaft and 3–10 slender stems clothed with brown fibers and old leaf bases. Rounded, deeply cut, fan-like leaves, with spiny stalks, are glossy, mid-green above, light green to silvery beneath, and to 3ft (1m) long. In summer, bears small white flowers in slender panicles, to 3ft (1m) long, partly hidden by the leaves, followed by black fruit. ↕ 15–25ft (5–8m), ↔ 8–20ft (2.5–6m). Subtropical and tropical North America. ❄ (min. 50°F/10°C)

ACOKANTHERA

APOCYNACEAE

Genus of 5 species of evergreen trees and shrubs from arid to seasonally moist scrub in tropical to subtropical regions, from southern and eastern Africa to the Arabian Peninsula. They are cultivated mainly for their clusters of long-tubed, 5-petaled flowers, which are borne on the previous year's growth, and for their simple, leathery leaves, produced in opposite pairs. Where not hardy, grow in a temperate greenhouse; in frost-free areas, grow in a border. The sap and small, plum-like fruits that follow the flowers are highly toxic if ingested.

• **CULTIVATION** Under glass, grow in soil-based potting mix in full light; top-dress or pot on in autumn. From late spring to autumn, water freely and apply a balanced liquid fertilizer monthly; water sparingly in winter. Outdoors, grow in moderately fertile, well-drained soil in full sun. Pruning group 9; plants under glass may need restrictive pruning.

• **PROPAGATION** Sow seed at 66–75°F (19–24°C) in spring. Root semi-ripe cuttings with bottom heat in summer.

• **PESTS AND DISEASES** Mushroom root rot sometimes occurs outdoors.

A. oblongifolia ■ syn. *A. spectabilis*, *Carissa spectabilis* (Poison arrow plant, Wintersweet). Bushy shrub or small tree producing elliptic, glossy, dark green leaves, to 5in (13cm) long. Fragrant white flowers, ½–¾in (1.5–2cm) long, are borne in axillary clusters, 2–4in (5–10cm) long, from winter to spring. The flowers are followed by ellipsoid, purple-black fruit, to 1in (2.5cm) long. ↕ 10–20ft (3–6m), ↔ 5–12ft (1.5–4m). Mozambique, South Africa (KwaZulu/Natal, Northern Cape). ❄ (min. 41°F/5°C), although will survive short periods down to 36°F (2°C).

A. spectabilis see *A. oblongifolia.*

ACONITUM

Aconite, Monkshood

RANUNCULACEAE

Genus of 100 species of perennials and biennials, mainly from mountainous grassland or scrub in the N. hemisphere. Most have tuberous or occasionally fibrous roots and erect, sometimes twining stems. The stems bear shallowly to palmately lobed, kidney-shaped to rounded or ovate, usually rich green leaves, mostly 2–4in (5–10cm) long. The curious, hooded flowers, usually 1–2in (2.5–5cm) long, are borne in racemes or panicles, 12–24in (30–60cm) long, well above the leaves. Flower shape and color are provided by the sepals, because the petals are converted to nectaries under the "hood" of sepals. Ideal for a woodland garden and for borders; grow twining species through shrubs for support. Aconites are good for cutting, but contact with the foliage may irritate skin; all parts are highly toxic if ingested.

• **CULTIVATION** Best grown in cool, moist, fertile soil in partial shade, but will tolerate most soils and full sun. Taller aconites require staking.

• **PROPAGATION** Sow seed in containers in a cold frame in spring. Divide every third year in autumn or early spring to maintain vigor, although plants are sometimes slow to re-establish.

• **PESTS AND DISEASES** Prone to aphids, fungal stem rots, crown rot, and *Verticillium* wilt. Downy mildew, powdery mildew, and rusts also occur.

'Bressingham Spire'

A. anthora ■ Upright, usually hairy perennial with rounded, deeply lobed, dark green leaves. In mid- and late summer, produces compact racemes of pale yellow, sometimes blue-violet flowers. ↕ 24–30in (60–75cm), ↔ 12in (30cm). C., S., and E. Europe. Zone 6.

***A.* 'Bressingham Spire'** ■ Upright perennial with rounded, 3- to 5-lobed, glossy, dark green leaves. Tapering racemes of deep violet flowers are produced from midsummer to early autumn. ↕ 36in (90cm), ↔ 12in (30cm). Zone 3b.

***A.* x *cammarum* 'Bicolor'** ■ Erect perennial with ovate to rounded, deeply 3- to 7-lobed, glossy, dark green leaves. Bears loose panicles of blue and white flowers, 1½in (4cm) across, sometimes bicolored, on arching branches, in mid- and late summer. ↕ 4ft (1.2m), ↔ 12in (30cm). Zone 3b.

A. carmichaelii, syn. *A. fischeri* of gardens. Erect perennial with ovate, 3- to 5-lobed, leathery, dark green leaves. In early autumn, bears dense panicles of large, violet or blue flowers. ↕ 5–6ft (1.5–1.8m), ↔ 12–16in (30–40cm). Russia to China. Zone 3b. **'Arends'** see 'Arendsii'. **'Arendsii'** ■ syn. 'Arends', has sturdy stems and bears rich blue flowers in branched panicles in early and midautumn; ↕ to 4ft (1.2m), ↔ 12in (30cm). **'Barker's Variety'** produces deep violet flowers.

***A. compactum* 'Carneum'** see *A. napellus* 'Carneum'.

***A. fischeri* of gardens** see *A. carmichaelii.*

Acoelorraphe wrightii

Acokanthera oblongifolia

Aconitum anthora

Aconitum x *cammarum* 'Bicolor'

Aconitum carmichaelii 'Arendsii'

A. hemsleyanum ▣ Perennial, twining climber with ovate, 3- to 5-lobed leaves. Racemes of large violet flowers are borne from midsummer to early autumn. ↕6–10ft (2–3m). W. and C. China. Zone 6.
***A.* 'Ivorine'** ▣ syn. *A. septentrionale* 'Ivorine'. Upright, bushy perennial with rounded, deeply 3- to 7-lobed leaves. Dense racemes of ivory flowers are borne in late spring and early summer. The flowers are larger and clearer in color in cool, moist climates. ↕36in (90cm), ↔ 18in (45cm). Zone 4.
A. lamarckii see *A. lycoctonum* subsp. *neapolitanum.*
A. lycoctonum (Wolf's bane). Erect perennial with rounded, 5- to 7-lobed, dark green leaves and panicles of usually yellow, sometimes purple flowers borne in mid- and late summer. ↕3–5ft (1–1.5m), ↔ 12in (30cm). C. and S. Europe. Zone 5. **subsp. *lycoctonum*,** syn. *A. septentrionale*, has deeply lobed leaves and often scandent stems, bearing erect racemes of tall, narrowly hooded, pale yellow, cream, or purple flowers. W. Europe to Romania. **subsp. *neapolitanum*,** syn. *A. lamarckii*, *A. neapolitanum*, *A. pyrenaicum*, has 7- or 8-lobed leaves and yellow flowers in large racemes or panicles; ↕3–4ft (1–1.2m). Pyrenees to Balkans. **subsp. *vulparia*** ▣ syn. *A. orientale* of gardens, *A. vulparia*, has 5- to 9-lobed leaves and pale yellow flowers. C. and S. Europe.
A. napellus (Monkshood). Variable, erect perennial with rounded, deeply 5- to 7-lobed, dark green leaves, the lobes toothed or further divided.

Aconitum hemsleyanum

Aconitum 'Ivorine'

Aconitum lycoctonum subsp. *vulparia*

Aconitum 'Spark's Variety'

Bears dense racemes of indigo-blue flowers in mid- and late summer. ↕5ft (1.5m), ↔ 12in (30cm). N. and C. Europe. Zone 5b. **'Albidum'** bears gray-white flowers. **'Carneum',** syn. *A. compactum* 'Carneum', has leaves with deep, narrow lobes and dusty pink flowers, which are a clearer color in cool, moist climates.
A. neapolitanum see *A. lycoctonum* subsp. *neapolitanum.*
***A. orientale* of gardens** see *A. lycoctonum* subsp. *vulparia.*
A. pyrenaicum see *A. lycoctonum* subsp. *neapolitanum.*
A. septentrionale see *A. lycoctonum* subsp. *lycoctonum.*
***A. septentrionale* 'Ivorine'** see *A.* 'Ivorine'.
***A.* 'Spark's Variety'** ▣ Upright perennial with rounded, deeply 5- to 7-lobed leaves on thin stems. Large, widely branched panicles of deep violet flowers are produced in mid- and late summer. ↕4–5ft (1.2–1.5m), ↔ 18in (45cm). Zone 3b.
A. vulparia see *A. lycoctonum* subsp. *vulparia.*

▷***Aconogonon*** see *Persicaria*

ACORUS

ARACEAE

Genus of 2 species of rhizomatous, marginal aquatic perennials, one semi-evergreen and one deciduous, found in shallow water by streams and lakes throughout the N. hemisphere, particularly E. Asia. They have sheathed, radical, linear or strap-shaped leaves, which die off in autumn, leaving a small basal tuft of foliage that develops the following year. In midsummer, insignificant flowers, resembling small horns, 2–3in (5–8cm) long, are produced laterally just below the tips of central, leaf-like flower stems. They are excellent foliage plants for the shallow margins of a pool, for a bog garden, or for marshy areas. Some of the smaller cultivars of *A. gramineus* are useful aquarium plants.

• **CULTIVATION** Grow at pool margins in wet or very moist soil in full sun; use aquatic containers for *A. gramineus* and its cultivars, which thrive in shallow water, to 4in (10cm) deep. In an aquarium, grow *A. gramineus* and its cultivars in containers to avoid disturbing the roots. They are short-lived in an aquarium if the water temperature exceeds 72°F (22°C) for long periods. See also pp.52–53.
• **PROPAGATION** Divide rhizomes at the beginning of the growing season and pot up, planting out only when established; repeat every 3–4 years to prevent congestion.
• **PESTS AND DISEASES** Wet and dry root rots as well as rust and several fungal leaf spots occur.

***A. calamus* 'Variegatus'** ▣ (Variegated sweet flag). Spreading, deciduous, aquatic perennial with strap-shaped, aromatic, bright green leaves, 5ft (1.5m) long, longitudinally striped creamy white and cream, and with distinct midribs and occasionally wrinkled margins. Grows best in water no deeper than 9in (23cm). ↕5ft (1.5m), ↔ 24in (60cm). Zone 4.
A. gramineus (Grassy-leaved sweet flag). Semi-evergreen, aquatic perennial with fans of 2-ranked, linear, glossy, rich green leaves, 3–14in (8–35cm) long. ↕3–14in (8–35cm), ↔ 4–6in (10–15cm). E. Asia. ❀ (min. 41°F/5°C). **'Ogon',** syn. 'Wogon' (Japanese rush), has glossy, variegated leaves, striped with pale green and cream; ↕to 10in (25cm), ↔ 4–6in (10–15cm). **'Pusillus'** (Dwarf Japanese rush) is compact, and has stiff, dark green leaves, 1½–6in (4–15cm) long; ↕4in (10cm), ↔ 4–6in (10–15cm). **'Variegatus'** (Variegated Japanese rush) has leaves 3–12in (8–30cm) long, striped creamy white and green; ↕10in (25cm), ↔ 6in (15cm).
'Wogon' see 'Ogon'.

▷***Acroclinium*** see *Rhodanthe*

Acorus calamus 'Variegatus'

A

ACROCOMIA

Gru gru palm

ARECACEAE

Genus of up to 20 (or one very variable) species of single-stemmed, often spiny, palms from dry areas of Central America, the West Indies, and tropical South America. Pinnate leaves are produced in a terminal tuft, with the monoecious, bowl-shaped flowers borne in panicles among them. In cool areas, grow young acrocomias as foliage plants in a warm greenhouse. In tropical regions, use them as specimen trees.

• **CULTIVATION** Under glass, grow in soil-based potting mix in full light. Water freely and apply a balanced liquid fertilizer monthly in the growing season; water sparingly in winter. Outdoors, grow in fertile, moist but well-drained soil in full sun.

• **PROPAGATION** Sow seed at 77–86°F (25–30°C) in spring.

• **PESTS AND DISEASES** Spider mites may be a problem under glass.

A. aculeata. Single-stemmed palm with a slender trunk, sometimes thickened above, with no crownshaft, and ringed with spines. Pinnate, rich green leaves, 5–10ft (1.5–3m) long, have many narrow, downy-backed leaflets. Bears panicles of cream to yellow flowers in summer, followed by greenish yellow fruit. ↕ to 50ft (15m), ↔ to 20ft (6m). Dominica, Martinique.
❀ (min. 61–64°F/16–18°C)

ACTAEA

Baneberry

RANUNCULACEAE

Genus of 8 species of rhizomatous woodland perennials from temperate regions of the N. hemisphere. Grown mainly for their foliage and fruit, they have 2- or 3-ternate, toothed leaves and usually terminal, compact, fluffy, spherical to ovoid racemes of small white flowers with prominent stamens, followed by longer clusters of colorful berries. Grow in a woodland garden, or in a shady mixed or herbaceous border. The berries are highly toxic if ingested.

• **CULTIVATION** Grow in cool, moist, moderately fertile soil, enriched with leaf mold, in partial shade. Water thoroughly in very dry weather. *A. spicata* will thrive even in full shade and beneath conifers.

• **PROPAGATION** Sow seed in containers in a cold frame in autumn. Divide in early spring.

• **PESTS AND DISEASES** *Ramularia* and *Ascochyta* leaf spots and leaf smut occur.

A. alba ■ syn. *A. pachypoda* (Doll's eyes, White baneberry, White cohosh). Clump-forming perennial with leaves to 24in (60cm) long, composed of 3–12 ovate leaflets. White flowers are borne in spherical racemes, ¾–2in (2–5cm) long, in late spring and early summer, followed by spherical white berries, ⅜in (8mm) across, each with a black eye, on stalks that elongate, thicken, and turn red. ↕ 36in (90cm), ↔ 18–24in (45–60cm). E. North America. Zone 4.

A. asiatica. Clump-forming perennial with leaves to 22in (55cm) long, composed of 3–12 ovate, sharply

Actaea alba

toothed leaflets. In early summer, bears white flowers in spherical racemes, to 2½in (6cm) long; they are followed by spherical black berries, to ¼in (6mm) across, on horizontally held stalks that elongate, thicken, and turn red. ↕ to 28in (70cm), ↔ to 24in (60cm). China, Korea, Japan. Zone 5.

A. erythrocarpa, syn. *A. spicata* var. *rubra.* Clump-forming perennial with leaves to 16in (40cm) long, composed of 3–12 ovate to lance-shaped leaflets. White flowers in ovoid racemes, 1¼–2in (3–5cm) long, are borne in late spring and early summer; they are followed by spherical maroon berries, ¼–⅜in (7–9mm) across, on arching red stalks. ↕ 2ft (60cm), ↔ 18in (45cm). N. Europe to E. Asia. Zone 4.

***A. erythrocarpa* of gardens** see *A. rubra.*

A. nigra see *A. spicata.*

A. pachypoda see *A. alba.*

A. rubra ■ syn. *A. erythrocarpa* of gardens (Red baneberry, Snakeberry). Clump-forming perennial with leaves to 16in (40cm) long, composed of 3–15 ovate leaflets. From midspring to early summer, bears white flowers in ovoid racemes, 1¼–2in (3–5cm) long, followed by spikes of shiny red, spherical or ellipsoid berries, ¼–½in (6–15mm) across, on slender green stalks. ↕ 18in (45cm), ↔ 12in (30cm). C. and E. North America. Zone 4. **subsp. *arguta*** is smaller and has almost spherical red berries; ↕ 18in (45cm), ↔ 12in (30cm). **f. *neglecta*** has white berries to ½in (1.5cm) long; W. US.

A. spicata, syn. *A. nigra* (Herb Christopher). Clump-forming perennial producing leaves to 24in (60cm) long,

Actaea rubra

with 9–15 ovate leaflets. From midspring to early summer, bears white flowers in ovoid racemes, ¾–2½in (2–6cm) long, followed by ovoid black berries, to ½in (1.5cm) across, on slender green stalks. ↕↔ 18in (45cm). N. Europe, Asia. Zone 3. **var. *rubra*** see *A. erythrocarpa.*

ACTINIDIA

ACTINIDIACEAE

Genus of about 40 species of mainly deciduous, twining climbers with alternate, simple leaves, found among shrubs in areas of light forest in E. Asia. They are valued for their ornamental, sometimes variegated foliage, their cup-shaped, occasionally scented flowers, produced singly or in axillary cymes in summer, and their edible fruits, which ripen in autumn. Train against a wall, on a trellis, or into a tree. Both male and female plants are usually needed to obtain fruit, although some self-fertile cultivars are available for commercial fruit production. *A. deliciosa* will fruit if grown in a cool greenhouse.

• **CULTIVATION** Under glass, grow in soil-based potting mix in full light. During the growing season, water freely and apply a balanced liquid fertilizer monthly; keep moist in winter. Outdoors, grow in fertile, well-drained soil, with shelter from strong winds. Grow in full sun to maximize fruiting. Prune in late winter: if grown for fruit, pruning group 12; otherwise, pruning group 11.

• **PROPAGATION** Sow seed in containers in a cold frame in autumn or spring. Root semi-ripe cuttings, or graft cultivars, in late summer.

• **PESTS AND DISEASES** A wide variety of fungal diseases may occur.

A. arguta (Hardy kiwi, Tara vine). Deciduous climber with ovate to ovate-oblong, bristle-toothed, dark green leaves, to 5in (13cm) long. In early summer, bears clusters of 3 fragrant white flowers, each ¾in (2cm) wide. Female plants produce smooth-skinned, oblong, yellow-green fruit, 1in (2.5cm) long. ↕ 22ft (7m). E. Asia. Zone 4. **'Issai'** is self-fertile.

***A. chinensis* of gardens** see *A. deliciosa.*

A. coriacea. Vigorous, deciduous climber with oblong to ovate-oblong or lance-shaped, leathery, hairless, sharply toothed, mid-green leaves, to 6in (15cm) long, pale green beneath. Bears

Actinidia deliciosa

Actinidia kolomikta

clusters of a few red flowers, to ¾in (2cm) across, with concave petals and yellow anthers. Female plants bear ovoid to spherical brown fruit, to ¾in (2cm) across. ↕ to 25ft (8m). China. Zone 6.

A. deliciosa ■ syn. *A. chinensis* of gardens (Chinese gooseberry, Kiwi fruit). Vigorous, deciduous climber with thick shoots covered in red-brown hairs and broadly ovate, heart-shaped, mid-green leaves, to 8in (20cm) long. In early summer, bears clusters of 2 or 3 (occasionally more) creamy white, later yellow flowers, 1½in (4cm) across. Female plants produce ovoid-oblong, bristly-skinned, greenish brown fruit, to 3in (8cm) long. ↕ 30ft (10m). China. Zone 7. Several female cultivars, including **'Blake'** (which is self-fertile), **'Bruno'**, **'Hayward'**, and **'Saanichton'**, and several males, such as **'Matua'** and **'Tomuri'**, are available.

A. kolomikta ■ (Variegated kiwi vine). Deciduous climber with ovate-oblong, dark green leaves, to 6in (15cm) long, purple-tinged when young, becoming variegated with white and pink in the apical half. Bears clusters of 3 fragrant white flowers, ¾in (2cm) across, in early summer. Female plants produce smooth, ovoid-oblong, yellow-green fruit, 1in (2.5cm) long. ↕ 15ft (5m) or more. E. Asia. Zone 3. **'Arctic Beauty'** has leaves, purple at first, to 4in (10cm) long, becoming variegated with purple, pink, and green.

A. polygama (Silver vine). Deciduous climber with elliptic or ovate-oblong leaves, to 6in (15cm) long, dark green with silver-white tips, or silvery white in the apical half. Clusters of 3 fragrant white flowers, ¾in (2cm) across, open in early summer. Female plants bear smooth, ovoid, yellow-green fruit, 1in (2.5cm) long. ↕ 15ft (5m). Japan. Zone 5b.

ADA

ORCHIDACEAE

Genus of about 2 species of evergreen, epiphytic orchids, growing at an altitude of 8,000ft (2,500m) in Central and South America. They have short rhizomes and small, elliptic, compressed pseudobulbs with 1 or 2 narrowly oval leaves at the tips. In spring or summer, arching racemes of bell-shaped flowers are borne from the bases of the pseudobulbs. Grow in containers or epiphytically.

Ada aurantiaca

• **CULTIVATION** Cool-growing orchids. Grow epiphytically or in epiphytic orchid potting mix in the smallest possible containers. Supply high humidity and good ventilation. Provide bright filtered light in summer; in winter, remove shading. Water freely when in growth, more sparingly in winter. In summer, apply a half-strength liquid fertilizer at every third watering. See also p.46.
• **PROPAGATION** Divide when the plant overflows its container, or pot up back-bulbs separately.
• **PESTS AND DISEASES** Aphids, spider mites, mealybugs, and whiteflies may be problems.

A. aurantiaca ■ Evergreen, epiphytic orchid with 2 narrowly oval, dark green leaves, 4–12in (10–30cm) long. Produces basal racemes of bright orange flowers, 1in (2.5cm) long, in spring. ↕ 9in (23cm), ↔ 6–9in (15–23cm). Colombia, Venezuela. ❀ (min. 50°F/10°C; max. 75°F/24°C)

ADANSONIA

BOMBACACEAE

Genus of 9 or 10 species of mostly deciduous trees from tropical, semi-arid regions of Africa, the Comoros Islands, Madagascar, and N. and N.W. Australia. They have succulent, often swollen, urn-shaped trunks, which can reach 35ft (11m) across, and short, branched crowns. The simple to palmate (sometimes only palmately lobed) leaves are borne in summer. The large, solitary, pendent flowers are usually creamy white with 5 crinkled, waxy petals and "powder puffs" of numerous stamens; they are followed by spherical to oblong-obovoid, fleshy, often woody-coated, edible, velvety, pale brown fruits. Plant adansonias in containers to limit growth. Where temperatures fall below 61°F (16°C), grow in a warm greenhouse; in warmer climates, grow in a desert garden.
• **CULTIVATION** Under glass, grow in soil-based potting mix, with added grit or sharp sand, in full light. Water sparingly in spring and autumn, moderately in summer; keep dry in winter. In the growing season, apply a low-phosphate liquid fertilizer monthly. Outdoors, grow in well-drained, sandy, moderately fertile soil in full sun.
• **PROPAGATION** Sow seed as soon as ripe at 66–75°F (19–24°C).
• **PESTS AND DISEASES** A few fungal leaf spots as well as butt rot occur. Aphids may attack flower buds.

A. digitata (Baobab, Dead-rat tree, Monkey-bread tree). Deciduous tree with a thick, swollen, succulent trunk and short branches. These bear rounded, usually 5- to 9-palmate, occasionally only lobed leaves, to 7in (18cm) long. Pendent flowers, 4–5in (10–13cm) across, with partially reflexed white petals and extended, central balls of purple-anthered stamens, are produced on long stalks, with or just before the leaves, in summer. These are followed by woody, ovoid fruit, 10in (25cm) long, containing large black seeds. ↕ to 60ft (18m), ↔ 100ft (30m). S.W. Africa, N.E. South Africa, Comoros Islands, W. Madagascar. ❀ (min. 61°F/16°C)

ADENIA

PASSIFLORACEAE

Genus of over 90 species of deciduous, perennial succulents, sometimes semi-evergreen, with caudiciform rootstocks and vine-like climbers with thin, thorny, tendril-bearing stems; they are found in scrub or desert in Africa, Madagascar, and Burma. All have alternate, palmate or simple leaves. The axillary cymes of tiny, sometimes scented flowers, to ½in (1.5cm) across, are followed by conical to obovoid, capsular, yellow, green, or red fruits, ¾–1½in (2–4cm) long. Where temperatures fall below 59°F (15°C), grow in a warm greenhouse; in warmer regions, grow in a desert garden.
• **CULTIVATION** Under glass, grow in standard cactus potting mix in full light in dry, airy conditions. Water sparingly in spring and autumn, freely in summer; keep dry in winter. In the growing season, apply a balanced liquid fertilizer every 4–6 weeks. Outdoors, grow in well-drained soil in full sun. See also pp.48–49.
• **PROPAGATION** Sow seed at 66–75°F (19–24°C) as soon as ripe. Take cuttings from non-flowering stems in summer; small tubers develop about 3 months from rooting.
• **PESTS AND DISEASES** Vulnerable to mealybugs during the growing season.

A. buchananii see *A. digitata.*
A. digitata, syn. *A. buchananii, Modecca digitata.* Perennial succulent with a cylindrical gray caudex, to 12in (30cm) or more across, which tapers into an erect, slender stem, crowned by a cluster of 3- to 5-palmate, sometimes semi-evergreen, dark green leaves, 4in (10cm) or more long. Small, star-shaped yellow flowers open with the leaves in summer, followed by obovoid, yellow to red fruit. The sap may cause severe discomfort if ingested. ↕ 5ft (1.5m), ↔ to 3ft (1m). Mozambique, N.E. South Africa. ❀ (min. 59–61°F/15–16°C)
A. globosa ■ Perennial succulent with a spherical, grayish green caudex, to 3ft (1m) across. Interlaced, stiff, spiny, thick, grayish green branches have lance-shaped, warty, mid-green, deciduous leaves, ¼–½in (6–15mm) long. Small, star-shaped, scented, bright red flowers open in spring, followed by ovoid, green then orange fruit. ↕ to 5ft (1.5m), ↔ 3ft (1m). Kenya, Tanzania. ❀ (min. 59–61°F/15–16°C)
A. spinosa. Perennial succulent with a swollen, gray-green caudex, to 6ft (2m) wide, and stiff, sharply spiny branches with ovate to elliptic, mid-green, deciduous leaves, 1¼in (3cm) long. Small, tubular, creamy white flowers open in summer with the leaves; they are followed by obovoid yellow fruit. ↕ 10ft (3m), ↔ 3ft (1m). N.E. South Africa. ❀ (min. 59–61°F/15–16°C)

Adenia globosa

ADENIUM

Desert rose, Impala lily

APOCYNACEAE

Genus of one very variable species (sometimes considered to be 5 or 6 species) of perennial succulent found in semi-arid regions of the Arabian Peninsula and E. to S.W. Africa. The swollen caudex may be very low, with its base partly underground, or may grow taller and be widely bottle-shaped. The irregular, spineless branches bear glossy leaves in spiral, terminal clusters, with salverform flowers varying in color from rich red to pink or white. Where temperatures fall below 59°F (15°C), grow in a warm greenhouse or as house-plants; in warmer areas, grow in a desert garden. The milky sap that exudes from broken stems may irritate skin and cause severe discomfort if ingested.
• **CULTIVATION** Under glass, grow in soil-based potting mix with added sharp sand, in full light with shade from hot sun. When in growth, water moderately and apply a balanced liquid fertilizer 2 or 3 times; water more sparingly in winter. Outdoors, grow in well-drained, slightly alkaline, humus-rich soil in full sun with some midday shade. See also pp.48–49.
• **PROPAGATION** Sow seed as soon as ripe at 70°F (21°C). Root cuttings from non-flowering shoots in summer with bottom heat.
• **PESTS AND DISEASES** Prone to aphids at flowering time. Anthracnose and other fungal leaf diseases are common. Excess watering contributes to basal rots caused by both fungi and bacteria.

Adenium obesum

A. arabicum see *A. obesum.*
A. micranthum see *A. obesum.*
A. obesum ■ syn. *A. arabicum, A. micranthum, A. speciosum, Nerium obesum* (Desert rose). Variable, perennial succulent with a thick, usually bottle-shaped, twisted, grayish brown caudex, often more than 3ft (1m) long, and tapering to a many-branched tip. Upright, succulent brown branches produce ovate, gray-green leaves, to 4in (10cm) long. Red, pink, or, rarely, white flowers, to 1½–2½in (4–6cm) across, are borne in small terminal corymbs throughout summer, sometimes before the leaves. ↕ 5ft (1.5m), ↔ 3ft (1m). E. to S.W. Africa, Arabian Peninsula. ❀ (min. 59°F/15°C; optimum 70°F/21°C). **subsp. *oleifolium*** has an almost spherical or ovoid caudex and produces 1–5 slender branches with lance-shaped, gray-green leaves, to 6in (15cm) long, arranged in loose rosettes; ↕ 18in (45cm), ↔ 12in (30cm). S.W. Africa. **subsp. *somalense***, syn. *A. somalense*, has a tall, conical, white caudex, turning brown with age, longer blue-green leaves with wavy margins, and smaller flowers, to ¾in (2cm) across; ↕ to 9ft (2.5m). E. Africa.
A. somalense see *A. obesum* subsp. *somalense.*
A. speciosum see *A. obesum.*

ADENOCARPUS

FABACEAE

Genus of about 15 species of deciduous and evergreen, sometimes semi-evergreen shrubs, occasionally trees, found in scrub or light woodland in S.W. Europe, the Mediterranean, Canary Islands, and N. Africa. They have alternate, 3-palmate leaves and are valued for their broom-like yellow flowers, which are borne in terminal, sometimes congested racemes on the previous year's growth in spring or summer. Grow in a sunny shrub border in frost-free climates, or against a warm wall where marginally hardy.
• **CULTIVATION** Grow in light, moderately fertile, very well-drained soil in full sun; where not reliably hardy, protect from winter moisture and wind. Pruning group 8, or 13 if wall-trained.
• **PROPAGATION** Sow seed in containers in a cold frame in autumn or spring. Root semi-ripe cuttings in summer.
• **PESTS AND DISEASES** Infrequent.

A. complicatus. Variable, upright or spreading, deciduous shrub producing 3-palmate leaves with inversely lance-shaped leaflets, to 1in (2.5cm) long. In summer, bears dark yellow flowers, occasionally red-tinged, to ½in (1.5cm) long, in dense, arching terminal racemes, to 4–6in (10–15cm) long. ↕↔ 12ft (4m). Mediterranean, S.W. Europe. ❀ (min. 35°F/2°C)

Adenocarpus decorticans

A. decorticans ■ Stiff, horizontally branching, deciduous shrub with flaky gray to white bark and dense clusters of small, silver-hairy leaves with 3 narrowly elliptic leaflets, ¼–½in (0.5–1.5cm) long, with inrolled margins. Bright yellow flowers, to ½in (1.5cm) long, are borne in short, erect racemes, to 2½in (6cm) long, in late spring and early summer. ↕↔ 7ft (2.2m). Spain. ❄ (min. 35°F/2°C)

ADENOPHORA

CAMPANULACEAE

Genus of more than 40 species of fleshy-rooted perennials, similar to campanulas (differing in having disks at the bases of the styles). They are found in temperate woodland and grassland, sometimes at high altitudes, in Europe and Asia. They produce rounded basal leaves (dying back before flowering in some species) and small, lance-shaped to ovate, entire or toothed stem leaves, arranged alternately or, occasionally, in whorls. The pendent or semi-pendent, bell- or funnel-shaped flowers, ¼–¾in (0.5–2cm) long, with protruding styles, are pale to dark lavender-blue and are mostly produced in terminal racemes or panicles. Grow in a border or in open woodland; smaller species are suitable for a rock garden.

• **CULTIVATION** Grow in light, humus-rich, moist but well-drained soil in sun or partial shade. Plant seedlings when young, or plant from containers, to minimize disturbance of the deep roots.

• **PROPAGATION** Sow seed thinly in containers outdoors as soon as ripe or in late winter; plant out potfuls of seedlings to avoid disturbing the roots. Root cuttings of basal shoots in late spring. Seldom tolerates division.

• **PESTS AND DISEASES** Vine weevils may attack the fleshy roots. Slugs and snails may eat young growth.

Adenophora bulleyana

A. bulleyana ■ Erect perennial with alternate, lance-shaped, toothed stem leaves, to 3in (8cm) long. In late summer, bears spike-like racemes of nodding, narrowly funnel-shaped, pale to mid-blue flowers, ½in (1.5cm) long, often in groups of 3. ↕ 4ft (1.2m), ↔ 12in (30cm). W. China. Zone 4.

A. confusa, syn. *A. farreri* (Common ladybells). Upright perennial with toothed, scalloped leaves, to 3in (8cm) long. Bears few-branched panicles of nodding, bell-shaped, deep blue flowers, ¾in (2cm) across, that persist for 3–4 weeks. ↕ 24–30in (60–75cm), ↔ 24in (60cm). W. China. Zone 4.

A. farreri see *A. confusa.*

A. liliiflora see *A. liliifolia.*

A. liliifolia, syn. *A. liliiflora.* Erect perennial with alternate, lance-shaped, stalkless, toothed, hairy stem leaves, 2–3in (5–8cm) long; the basal leaves die back before flowering. Produces panicles of pendent, widely bell-shaped, fragrant, pale blue flowers, to ¾in (2cm) long, in midsummer. ↕ 18in (45cm), ↔ 12in (30cm). C. Europe to Siberia. Zone 4.

▷***Adhatoda duvernoia*** see *Justicia adhatoda*

ADENOSTOMA

ROSACEAE

Genus of 2 species of large evergreen shrubs and small trees, from dense thickets of the coastal hills of the W. US. They have alternate, linear, resinous, aromatic leaves. Adenostomas are grown for their small, scented white flowers, and for their attractive, peeling bark on older specimens. Grow in a shrub border or as a specimen.

• **CULTIVATION** Grow in moderately fertile, well-drained soil in full sun. Shelter from excessive winter moisture and wind. Where marginally hardy, grow against a south- or southwest-facing wall. Pruning group 1.

• **PROPAGATION** Sow seed *in situ* in spring, or root softwood cuttings in mid- or late spring.

• **PESTS AND DISEASES** Infrequent.

A. sparsifolium (Ribbonwood, Redshanks). Large shrub or small tree with green-yellow, peeling branches that become red-brown, and linear, mid-green leaves, to ¾in (2cm) long. In late summer, fragrant white flowers, to ¼in (6mm) across, are borne in open panicles, 4in (10cm) long. ↕ to 20ft (6m), ↔ to 10ft (3m). S. California, Baja California. ❄ (min. 41°F/5°C)

Adiantum aleuticum

ADIANTUM

Maidenhair fern

PTERIDACEAE

Genus of 200–250 species of evergreen, semi-evergreen, and deciduous ferns, many from tropical and subtropical areas of North and South America, but a few from temperate regions of Europe, Asia, Australasia, and North America. Most grow at woodland margins, in shady crevices in rocks, or at stream-sides; some prefer deeper forest shade. The fronds are 1- to 5-pinnate, with oblong or diamond-shaped to rounded segments and usually long, shiny black or deep purple-red stalks; these are produced from often many-branched, long- to short-creeping, sometimes erect rhizomes. Rounded or oblong sori form on the margins of the frond divisions and are covered by kidney-shaped or semicircular indusia. Adiantums are grown for their elegant foliage and, in many species, the purplish pink color of the croziers and young fronds. Grow tender species in a temperate or warm greenhouse (*A. formosum* in a cool greenhouse). Grow hardy species, or tender species in warmer regions, in woodland or in a shady border.

• **CULTIVATION** Under glass, grow in 1 part each of loam, medium-grade bark, charcoal, and limestone chips; 2 parts sharp sand; 3 parts leaf mold. Provide bright indirect light in summer (such as under benches or along a north wall), bright filtered light in winter, and medium to high humidity with good ventilation; water less if air flow is poor, and sparingly in winter. When in growth, apply a half-strength balanced liquid fertilizer monthly. Remove old, damaged fronds in spring. If moving plants from a humid to a drier environment, do so gradually to avoid wilting. They make good companion plants for many orchids. Outdoors, grow hardy species in moist but well-drained, moderately fertile soil in partial shade; *A. capillus-veneris* prefers moist, alkaline soil. Grow tender species in humus-rich, well-drained soil in a partially shaded, open site.

• **PROPAGATION** Sow spores as soon as ripe, at minimum 59°F (15°C) for hardy species and 70°F (21°C) for tender ones. Divide rhizomes in early spring. Root plantlets from *A. caudatum* and others that root at the frond tips. See also p.51.

• **PESTS AND DISEASES** Scale insects may be a problem under glass. Leaf spots can occur during production but are rarely a problem later. Fungal root rots can also occur but are rare.

A. aleuticum ■ syn. *A. pedatum* subsp. *aleuticum* (Aleutian maidenhair fern, Northern maidenhair fern). Deciduous or semi-evergreen fern with short rhizomes and broadly ovate to kidney-shaped, pedate, pale to mid-green fronds, 8–12in (20–30cm) long, with oblong segments, and black stalks and midribs. New fronds may be tinged pink when very young. Closely allied to *A. pedatum* but with shorter rhizome internodes. ↕↔ to 30in (75cm). W. North America, E. Asia. Zone 3. **'Japonicum'** has golden red new fronds,

Adiantum formosum

Adiantum pedatum

maturing to green. **var. *subpumilum***, syn. subsp. *subpumilum* (Dwarf maidenhair fern), has fronds 4–5in (10–13cm) long; ↕ to 6in (15cm), ↔ 12in (30cm).
A. capillus-veneris (Southern maidenhair fern). Evergreen fern, deciduous at around 28°F (-2°C), with short-creeping rhizomes. Triangular, 2- or 3-pinnate, light green fronds, 28in (70cm) long, with fan-shaped pinnae, are produced on glossy black stalks. ↕ 12in (30cm), ↔ 16in (40cm). Temperate and tropical regions worldwide. Zone 8.
A. caudatum (Trailing maidenhair fern, Walking fern). Evergreen fern, with short-creeping rhizomes, bearing ladder-like, linear, pinnate fronds, to 24in (60cm) long, with entire to shallowly lobed, sometimes deeply cut pinnae. Young fronds are pale green to pale pink with red-brown stalks that darken with age, and prominent veins. Plantlets are produced on the elongated frond tips. Ideal for hanging baskets. ↕ 4–16in (10–40cm), ↔ 24in (60cm). India to Philippines, New Guinea, Taiwan, China. ❄ (min. 50°F/10°C)
A. cuneatum see *A. raddianum.*
A. formosum ■ (Australian maidenhair fern, Giant maidenhair fern). Evergreen fern with erect, roughly triangular, 2- to 4-pinnate fronds, to 3ft (1m) long, on long purple-black stalks, arising from long-creeping rhizomes. Segments are triangular to diamond-shaped and deeply cut. Fronds are pale green when young, darkening with age. Grow in a cool greenhouse in cold climates. ↕ to 3ft (1m), ↔ 6ft (2m) or more. E. Australia, New Zealand. ❄ (min. 41°F/5°C)
A. pedatum ■ (American maidenhair fern). Deciduous fern with thick, creeping rhizomes, producing lance-shaped, broadly ovate to kidney-shaped, pinnate, mid-green fronds, to 14in (35cm) long, on glossy, dark brown or black stalks. The segments are oblong or obliquely triangular, and lobed or toothed on their upper margins. ↕↔ 12–16in (30–40cm). E. North America. Zone 4. **subsp. *aleuticum*** see *A. aleuticum.*
A. raddianum, syn. *A. cuneatum* (Delta maidenhair fern). Evergreen fern with short rhizomes and roughly triangular, 3- or 4-pinnate, black-stalked fronds, to 24in (60cm) long, with rounded to triangular, variably lobed segments. Fronds are pale green, darkening with age. ↕ to 24in (60cm), ↔ 32in (80cm). Tropical North and South America,

Adiantum raddianum 'Gracillimum'

West Indies. ❄ (min. 45°F/7°C). **'Fritz Luth'** has light green fronds with segments that arch downward or are held almost horizontally. **'Gracilis'** see 'Gracillimum'. **'Gracillimum'** ■ syn. 'Gracilis', has pendent, broadly triangular, much-dissected fronds, with oblong segments, tapered at the bases. Some variants are crested; young foliage may be pale pink; ↕ 32in (80cm). **'Grandiceps'** (Tassel maidenhair fern) is crested, with each frond tip forming a dissected fan. Use in a hanging basket. **'Micropinnulum'** has compact, mounded growth and tiny, dissected, thread-like pinnules. Suitable for a terrarium, greenhouse, or indoor garden; ↕ 5in (13cm). **'White Fritz Luth'** has fronds that unfold pure white and turn pale green.
A. tenerum ■ (Brittle maidenhair fern). Evergreen fern with broadly triangular, 1- to 3-pinnate, mid-green fronds, to 3ft (1m) long, borne on dark purple-brown to black stalks, arising from short rhizomes. Superficially similar to *A. raddianum*, but the segments are ovate and deeply cut, with jointed stalks, and softly hairy when young. ↕ to 24in (60cm), ↔ to 36in (90cm). S. US, Central America, N. South America. ❄ (min. 35°F/2°C). **'Farleyense'** (Barbados maidenhair fern, Glory fern) is a variable complex of large ferns with broadly fan-shaped, deeply cut segments, tinged bronze-pink when young and becoming light green with age; many of its selections are infertile; ↕ to 36in (90cm). **'Lady Moxham'** has pendent fronds with broad, fan-shaped segments. **'Pacific Maid'** has broadly

Adiantum tenerum

Adiantum venustum

fan-shaped segments with many narrow, deeply cut divisions; ↕ to 30in (75cm). **'Scutum Roseum'** has erect, 3-pinnate fronds with crowded, rhomboidal segments. Young fronds are rose-pink; ↕ 20in (50cm).
A. trapeziforme (Diamond maidenhair fern, Giant maidenhair fern). Evergreen fern with short rhizomes, producing erect to spreading, broadly triangular, 3-pinnate fronds, to 6ft (2m) or more long, on black stalks. Segments, to 2½in (6cm) long, vary from ovate-diamond-shaped to rhomboidal, and are mid-green, sometimes glaucous beneath. Excellent as a groundcover in shaded gardens in frost-free areas. ↕ to 6ft (2m) or more, ↔ 8ft (2.5m) or more. Tropical North and South America, West Indies, Cuba. ❄ (min. 57°F/14°C)
A. venustum ■ (Himalayan maidenhair fern). Evergreen fern, deciduous below 14°F (-10°C), with creeping rhizomes. Narrowly triangular, usually 3-pinnate, mid-green fronds, 6–12in (15–30cm) long, with narrowly fan-shaped segments, are produced on black stalks. New fronds emerge bright bronze-pink in late winter and early spring. ↕ 6in (15cm), ↔ indefinite. China, Himalayas. Zone 6.

ADLUMIA

FUMARIACEAE

Genus of one species of biennial climber found at the edges of moist woodland in temperate areas of Korea and E. North America, grown for its delicate foliage and flower panicles. The leaves are 2- to 4-pinnate, and form a basal rosette on the plant when young, becoming alternate as the flowering stem elongates in the second year. The flowers, borne in axillary, nodding to pendent panicles, each have 2 pairs of petals, the outer pair with basal pouches. *A. fungosa* is attractive grown over an arch or pergola, or through a large shrub.

- **CULTIVATION** Grow in any fertile, humus-rich, moist but well-drained soil in sun or partial shade, with shelter from strong winds.
- **PROPAGATION** Sow seed as soon as ripe or in spring, either in containers in a cold frame or *in situ.* May self-seed.
- **PESTS AND DISEASES** Prone to aphids.

A. cirrhosa see *A. fungosa.*
A. fungosa, syn. *A. cirrhosa* (Allegheny vine, Climbing fumitory, Mountain fringe). Slender biennial climber with leaf-stalk tendrils and 2- to 4-pinnate, light green, fern-like leaves, 4–10in (10–25cm) long. Green- or purple-tinted, pale pink or white flowers, ½in (1.5cm) long, are borne in panicles, 2–4in (5–10cm) long, from summer to autumn. As the flowers fade, the persistent petals enclose the developing seed pods. ↕ 10–15ft (3–5m), occasionally more. Korea, E. North America. Zone 5b.

▷ ***Adonidia merrillii*** see *Veitchia merrillii*

ADONIS

RANUNCULACEAE

Genus of about 20 species of annuals and perennials from Europe and Asia, mainly from alpine habitats. The fern-like foliage dies back by midsummer in some species. The solitary, terminal, anemone-like flowers are usually yellow in perennials and red in annuals; double-flowered cultivars have up to 30 petals. The Asiatic species are best grown in shady woodland and the European species in an open, rocky site.

- **CULTIVATION** *Adonis* species have varying cultivation requirements. These have been divided into the following groups:

1. Humus-rich, cool, moist, light, acidic soil in full shade.
2. Moist but well-drained, humus-rich soil in partial shade.
3. Well-drained, moderately fertile, alkaline soil in full sun.

- **PROPAGATION** Sow seed of perennials in containers in a cold frame as soon as ripe; germination in spring is slow and erratic, and seedling growth slow. Sow seed of annuals *in situ* in spring. Perennial species resent division, but if required, divide after flowering.
- **PESTS AND DISEASES** Susceptible to slug damage, especially *A. vernalis.*

A. aestivalis. Erect annual with 1 to 3-pinnate leaves, 1¼–2in (3–5cm) long, with linear to thread-like leaflets. In summer, has cup-shaped, dark-centered red flowers, ½–1in (1.5–2.5cm) wide, with 5 spreading petals, and sepals pressed to the petal backs. Cultivation group 3. ↕ 16in (40cm), ↔ 6–12in (15–30cm). C. and S. Europe.
A. amurensis ■ (Amur adonis). Clump-forming perennial producing triangular to ovate, 3-pinnate leaves, to 4in (10cm) long, with many linear

Adonis amurensis

leaflets with pointed lobes. Bowl-shaped yellow, sometimes bronze-backed flowers, 1¼–2in (3–5cm) across, with 20–30 petals, are borne in late winter and early spring, before the leaves emerge, on short stems that gradually lengthen. Cultivation group 1. ↕ 8–16in (20–40cm), ↔ 12in (30cm). China (Manchuria), Korea, Japan. Zone 5. **'Flore Pleno'** ▣ has double, green-tinged yellow flowers. **'Fukujukai'** has semi-double, sterile, bright yellow flowers, 2in (5cm) across. **'Hinomoto'** has orange-red, green-tinted flowers. **'Pleniflora'**, syn. 'Plena', produces neat, double yellow flowers, each with a prominent green eye.

A. annua (Pheasant's eye). Erect annual producing finely divided, 3-pinnate leaves, 1¼–2in (3–5cm) long, with linear leaflets. Cup-shaped, dark-centered scarlet flowers, ½–1in (1.5–2.5cm) across, are borne in early summer. The 5 almost erect petals are clearly separated from the sepals. Cultivation group 3. ↕ 18in (45cm), ↔ 6–12in (15–30cm). S. Europe to S.W. Asia.

Adonis amurensis 'Flore Pleno'

Adonis brevistyla

Adonis vernalis

A. brevistyla ▣ Clump-forming perennial producing narrowly ovate, pinnate or 2-pinnate leaves, 2–5in (5–13cm) long; the leaflets have pointed lobes. Shallowly cup-shaped flowers, to 2in (5cm) across, with 20 or more petals, usually white with blue on the outside, open in late spring. Cultivation group 1. ↕ 8–16in (20–40cm), ↔ 8in (20cm). China (Yunnan), S. Tibet, Bhutan. Zone 5.

A. chrysocyathus. Clump-forming perennial with triangular, 3-pinnate leaves, to 6in (15cm) long; the leaflets have long, flat, sharp-pointed lobes. Many cup-shaped, bright yellow flowers, to 2in (5cm) across, with 20–25 petals, are produced from early summer to early autumn. Cultivation group 2. ↕ 6–16in (15–40cm), ↔ 12in (30cm). W. Himalayas, Tibet. Zone 5.

A. vernalis ▣ (Pheasant's eye, Spring adonis). Clump-forming perennial producing 2- or 3-pinnate, bright green leaves, 1¼–2in (3–5cm) long, with linear leaflets, the lower ones scale-like. Shallowly cup-shaped, bright golden yellow flowers, to 3in (8cm) across, with up to 20 elliptic petals, open in mid- and late spring. Cultivation group 3. ↕ to 15in (38cm), ↔ 18in (45cm). Finland to Italy, E. Europe to the Urals. Zone 5.

ADROMISCHUS

CRASSULACEAE

Genus of about 30 species of stemless or short-stemmed perennial succulents, closely related to *Cotyledon*, from semi-arid areas of southern Africa. The thick, fleshy leaves (which may fall off readily if touched) are clustered or spirally arranged, and the small, tubular flowers, with spreading lobes, are borne in spike-like cymes, mainly in summer. Where temperatures fall below 45°F (7°C), grow in a temperate greenhouse or as houseplants; they tolerate short periods at 25°F (-4°C). In warmer areas, grow in a raised bed.

• **CULTIVATION** Under glass, grow in sharply drained standard cactus potting mix in full light with good ventilation. In summer, water only when the soil has become dry; at other times, water only in warm weather; excess watering may encourage root rot. Apply a low-nitrogen fertilizer 2 or 3 times in the growing season. Outdoors, grow in well-drained, fertile soil, enriched with leaf mold, in full sun. See also pp.48–49.

• **PROPAGATION** Sow seed at 66–75°F (19–24°C) in spring. Take stem or leaf cuttings in summer.

• **PESTS AND DISEASES** Susceptible to mealybugs and aphids.

A. clavifolius see *A. cooperi.*

A. cooperi, syn. *A. clavifolius, Cotyledon cooperi, Echeveria cooperi* (Plover eggs). Freely branching succulent with grayish brown stems and inversely lance-shaped, glossy, gray-green leaves, to 2in (5cm) long, often purple-marked above.

Adromischus marienae subsp. *herrere*

Tubular, green-and-red flowers, to ½in (1.5cm) long, with white-margined, pink or purple lobes, are borne in spike-like cymes, 10in (25cm) or more long, in summer. ↕ 4in (10cm), ↔ to 6in (15cm). South Africa (Eastern Cape, Western Cape). ❀ (min. 45°F/7°C)

A. cristatus* var. *zeyheri, syn. *Cotyledon zeyheri* (Crinkle-leaf plant). Perennial succulent with semi-erect stems and many aerial roots. Inversely lance-shaped to obovate, hairy, gray-green leaves, to 1½in (4cm) long, spotted purple-red, are fan-like and wavy near the tips. In summer, bears tubular, greenish red flowers, to ½in (1.5cm) long, with white and pink lobes, in spike-like cymes, to 5in (13cm) long. ↕ 4in (10cm), ↔ indefinite. South Africa (Eastern Cape). ❀ (min. 45°F/7°C)

A. maculatus, syn. *Cotyledon maculatus, Crassula maculata* (Calico hearts). Perennial succulent producing a sparsely branched brown caudex. Inversely lance-shaped, glossy, bright green leaves, to 2in (5cm) long, are mottled dark purplish red, and often have horny margins. Spike-like cymes, 10–12in (25–30cm) long, of tubular green flowers, to ½in (1.5cm) long, with pinkish white or pale purple lobes, are borne in summer. ↕ 6in (15cm), ↔ to 6in (15cm). South Africa (Eastern Cape, Western Cape). ❀ (min. 45°F/7°C)

A. marienae* subsp. *herrere ▣ Very rare, slow-growing succulent with about 7 very fleshy leaves. These are spirally arranged, greenish yellow tinged red or red brown, maturing to entirely rusty brown, covered with prominent tubercles, giving a wrinkled, granulated appearance. Elliptical outline tapers to a finely pointed apex, with the base tapering into a petiole. ↕ 3½in (9cm). ↔ ½–1⅜in (1.5–3.5cm). From a very localized area near the Buffels River, toward the S. end of Namaqualand; S. Africa into S. Namibia. ❀ (min. 45°F/7°C)

AECHMEA

BROMELIACEAE

Genus of nearly 200 species of rosette-forming, often rhizomatous, mostly epiphytic, evergreen perennials (bromeliads), mainly from rainforest in S. Mexico, Central America, South America, and the West Indies. Their arching leaves are narrowly strap-shaped to triangular. Terminal, simple or compound, spike-like inflorescences with long-lasting, brightly colored, tubular flowers and triangular bracts are produced in summer, and are often followed by persistent, fleshy, colorful fruits. *Aechmea* species are generally grown in a warm greenhouse or as houseplants. In warmer areas, grow epiphytically in a moist site.

• **CULTIVATION** Under glass, grow either epiphytically or in epiphytic bromeliad potting mix in bright filtered light with moderate to high humidity and excellent air circulation. In the growing season, water freely and apply a low- or no-nitrogen fertilizer monthly. Keep the central cup filled with water. Outdoors, grow epiphytically or in moist, gritty, humus-rich soil. See also p.47.

• **PROPAGATION** Sow seed at 68°F (20°C) when ripe. Remove the outer jelly from the seed before sowing on the surface of the medium. Root offsets in early summer.

• **PESTS AND DISEASES** Vulnerable to scale insects and mealybugs, especially when flowering. *Helminthosporium* leaf spot and crown rots caused by a variety of fungi and bacteria are very common during propagation and production. Excess watering and heavy potting media also contribute to fungal root rots.

A. bambusoides. Epiphytic perennial with narrowly funnel-shaped rosettes of strap-shaped, spiny, white-scaly, bright green leaves, to 24in (60cm) long. Narrow, lax, branched inflorescences, often over 3ft (1m) long, with many, well-separated, 1- or 2-flowered spikes, ½in (1.5cm) long, with bright yellow petals, and reddish brown bracts and sepals, are borne in summer, followed by ovoid green fruit. ↕ 4ft (1.2m), ↔ 15in (38cm). Brazil. ❀ (min. 50°F/10°C)

A. chantinii ▣ Epiphytic perennial with wide-spreading rosettes of strap-shaped, mid-green leaves, to 16in (40cm) long, margined with short brown spines and cross-banded in grayish white. Lax pyramidal inflorescences, 6in (15cm) long, with short spikes of up to 8 bright yellow to orange flowers, 1¼in (3cm) long, are borne on erect, white-scaly, red-bracted stems in summer. They are followed by ovoid, greenish red fruit. ↕ to 3ft (1m), ↔ to 32in (80cm). S.E. Colombia, N.E. Peru, N. Brazil. ❀ (min. 50°F/10°C), but tolerates brief periods of light frost.

A. cylindrata. Rhizomatous, epiphytic or terrestrial perennial with dense, flat, open rosettes of strap-shaped, gray-scaly,

Aechmea chantinii

Aechmea distichantha

Aechmea Foster's Favorite Group

Aechmea gamosepala

Aechmea nudicaulis

mid-green leaves, to 20in (50cm) long, with red tips and lilac-gray stripes. In summer, bears simple, cylindrical inflorescences, to 8in (20cm) long, composed of many rows of red-bracted flowers, ¾in (2cm) long, with blue petals and rose-red sepals. They are followed by ovoid, woolly white fruit. ↕ 24in (60cm), ↔ to 14in (35cm). S.E. Brazil. ❀ (min. 50°F/10°C)

A. distichantha ▣ Variable, epiphytic or terrestrial perennial with funnel-shaped rosettes of narrowly triangular to strap-shaped, gray-scaly, dull, mid-green leaves, 3ft (1m) long, with pointed tips and brown marginal spines. Pyramidal or ovoid inflorescences composed of erect to spreading spikes of 2–12 white-felted, pink-bracted, purple, blue, or white flowers, to 1¼in (3cm) long, are produced on white-woolly stems in summer. These are followed by cylindrical, woolly white fruit. ↕↔ 3ft (1m) or more. C. South America. ❀ (min. 50°F/10°C)

A. fasciata ▣ syn. *Billbergia rhodocyanea* (Urn plant, Vase plant). Rhizomatous, epiphytic perennial with funnel-shaped rosettes of strap-shaped, lilac-gray leaves, to 24in (60cm) long, cross-banded with gray scales, and with tiny brown marginal spines. In summer, densely white-woolly stems bear wide pyramidal inflorescences, 3in (8cm) long, consisting of dense flower clusters, 1½in (4cm) long, with blue petals, rose-pink bracts, and white-scaly, rose-pink sepals, followed by spherical, woolly white fruit. ↕ 16in (40cm) or more, ↔ to 20in (50cm). S.E. Brazil. ❀ (min. 50°F/10°C)

Aechmea fasciata

***A.* Foster's Favorite Group** ▣ Terrestrial perennial with erect rosettes of strap-shaped, wine-red leaves, 18in (45cm) long, with tiny marginal spines. Semi-pendent inflorescences, to 20in (50cm) long, of pink-tipped, red-bracted blue flowers, ¾in (2cm) long, are borne in summer, followed by pear-shaped red fruit. ↕↔ 12–24in (30–60cm). ❀ (min. 50°F/10°C)

A. fulgens ▣ Epiphytic perennial with funnel-shaped rosettes of broadly strap-shaped, bright green leaves, 16in (40cm) long, gray-waxy beneath, with marginal spines. In summer, red stems bear branched inflorescences, 8in (20cm) long, consisting of spikes of 2–5 flowers, ¾in (2cm) long, with red sepals and violet petals, fading to red; the bracts are absent or reduced to scales. The red fruit are spherical and stalked. ↕ to 20in (50cm), ↔ 16in (40cm). E. Brazil. ❀ (min. 50°F/10°C). **var. *discolor*** produces leaves purplish or brownish red beneath.

A. gamosepala ▣ Epiphytic or terrestrial perennial with erect, funnel-shaped rosettes of broadly strap-shaped, bright green leaves, 10–22in (25–55cm) long, gray-scaly beneath, with rounded, spiny tips. In summer, bears cylindrical inflorescences, to 10in (25cm) long, of flowers, ½in (1.5cm) long, with pale blue or purple petals, red or pink sepals, and reddish brown bracts. These are followed by spherical, rose-pink fruit. ↕ 20in (50cm), ↔ to 24in (60cm). S.E. Brazil. ❀ (min. 50°F/10°C)

A. marmorata see *Quesnelia marmorata*.

A. mexicana. Epiphytic or terrestrial perennial with wide funnel-shaped rosettes of broadly strap-shaped, spiny-margined, mid-green leaves, 3ft (1m) or more long, irregularly marked with darker green patches. In summer, bears pyramidal or cylindrical, branched inflorescences, to 28in (70cm) long, on gray-scaly stems; they consist of spikes of 5–10 red, lilac, or violet flowers, ½in (1.5cm) long, with rose-pink bracts, and are followed by spherical white fruit. ↕↔ 3ft (1m) or more. Mexico. ❀ (min. 50°F/10°C)

Aechmea fulgens

A. nudicaulis ▣ Variable, epiphytic or terrestrial perennial with rosettes of strap-shaped, gray-green leaves, 12–36in (30–90cm) long, cross-banded with darker gray-green beneath, and with black marginal spines. In summer, bears simple, cylindrical inflorescences, 2–10in (5–25cm) long, of 15–20 red-bracted yellow flowers, ¾in (2cm) long, followed by cylindrical, scaly green fruit. ↕ to 28in (70cm), ↔ 10in (25cm). Central America, N. and N.E. South America, West Indies. ❀ (min. 50°F/10°C). **var. *cuspidata*** has triangular yellow bracts; ↕ to 20in (50cm). Brazil.

A. orlandiana ▣ (Finger of God). Epiphytic perennial with funnel-shaped rosettes of strap-shaped, mid-green, gray-scaly leaves, 12in (30cm) long, spotted and banded dark purple, with purple marginal spines. In summer, red stems bear pyramidal inflorescences, to 4in (10cm) long, with spikes of 4–6 red-bracted, yellow-white flowers, ¾–1¼in (2–3cm) long; they are followed by ovoid, pale green fruit. ↕ to 20in (50cm), ↔ 16–20in (40–50cm). S.E. Brazil. ❀ (min. 50°F/10°C)

A. pineliana. Variable, mainly epiphytic perennial with funnel-shaped rosettes of strap-shaped, silvery gray-scaly, dark green leaves, to 28in (70cm) long, often cross-banded with silver-gray beneath, and with dark reddish brown marginal spines. In summer, slender, white-woolly stems bear cylindrical inflorescences, 3in (8cm) long, with clusters of brown bristles, and long-bracted yellow flowers, ½in (1.5cm) long, which gradually turn black. The white fruit is spherical and woolly. ↕ to 32in (80cm), ↔ 20in (50cm) or more. S.E. Brazil. ❀ (min. 50°F/10°C)

A. recurvata ▣ Variable, terrestrial perennial with dense, tubular rosettes of narrowly triangular, channeled, often strongly recurved, dark or mid-green leaves, 16in (40cm) long, with curved marginal spines; the central leaves turn red at flowering time and in strong sun.

Aechmea orlandiana

Ovoid inflorescences, 2½in (6cm) long, have red bracts almost hiding the pinkish white or purple flowers, 1½in (4cm) long; they are followed by ovoid white fruit. ↕ to 8in (20cm), ↔ to 20in (50cm). C. South America. ❀ (min. 50°F/10°C)

A. weilbachii. Epiphytic perennial with funnel-shaped rosettes of strap-shaped, almost smooth-margined, dark green leaves, to 24in (60cm) long, often tinged purple. In summer, red-bracted pink stems bear slender inflorescences, 6in (15cm) long, composed of spikes of 5–10 red-bracted, bluish purple flowers, ½in (1.5cm) long. They are followed by ellipsoid, rough, lilac-red fruit. ↕ to 28in (70cm), ↔ 12in (30cm). S.E. Brazil. ❀ (min. 50°F/10°C)

▷ ***Aegle*** see *Poncirus*

Aechmea recurvata

Aegopodium podagraria 'Variegatum'

AEGOPODIUM

Bishop's weed, Goutweed

APIACEAE

Genus of about 5 species of perennials, with invasive rhizomes, occurring in woodland in N. and C. Europe, Siberia, and W. Asia. The alternate, deep green leaves have 3 ovate leaflets, and the many-rayed umbels of white flowers are borne on branching, hairless stems. Very invasive; plant either in containers or as a groundcover in poor soil in a shady site, where little else flourishes and where they cannot spread into other plants. May be cut back completely in summer to produce fresh growth.

- **CULTIVATION** Grow in any soil in full or partial shade. Deadhead before the flowers set seed.
- **PROPAGATION** Separate rhizomes in autumn or spring.
- **PESTS AND DISEASES** Leaf blight may brown foliage off in summer.

***A. podagraria* 'Variegatum'** ▣ Ground-covering perennial with ternate or 2-ternate, toothed, deep green leaves, 4–8in (10–20cm) long, margined and splashed creamy white. Flat umbels, ¾–2½in (2–6cm) across, of tiny, creamy white flowers are borne in early summer. ↕ 12–24in (30–60cm), ↔ indefinite. Zone 4.

AEONIUM syn. MEGALONIUM

CRASSULACEAE

Genus of about 30 species of evergreen, perennial, occasionally biennial succulents, often subshrubby, mainly found on hillsides in Madeira, the Canary Islands, Cape Verde Islands, N. Africa, and the Mediterranean. Neat rosettes of fleshy leaves are produced at the ends of clustered basal shoots. Terminal cymes, panicles, or racemes of numerous star-shaped, many-petaled flowers, ⅜–½in (8–15mm) across, develop from the centers of the rosettes from spring to summer. In some species, the flowering branches die once the seeds have ripened. Where temperatures fall below 50°F (10°C), grow in a cool or temperate greenhouse or as houseplants; elsewhere, grow in a border.

- **CULTIVATION** Under glass, grow in standard cactus potting mix in filtered light. Water freely and apply a balanced liquid fertilizer 2 or 3 times during the growing season; allow the soil mix to dry out almost completely between waterings. Keep dry when dormant. Outdoors, grow in moderately fertile, well-drained soil in partial shade. Aeoniums generally grow actively in winter, especially in warmer areas. See also pp.48–49.
- **PROPAGATION** Sow seed at 66–75°F (19–24°C) in spring. Take rosette cuttings in early summer, wait until calluses have formed, then insert in sandy cactus cutting soil mix in moderate light, at 64°F (18°C), and keep barely moist until rooted.
- **PESTS AND DISEASES** Prone to aphids, especially while flowering, and to mealybugs in autumn and winter. Several fungal rots and spots occur during propagation.

A. arboreum, syn. *Sempervivum arboreum.* Erect, succulent subshrub with few branches, each bearing a tightly packed rosette, 8in (20cm) across, of spoon-shaped, light green leaves, to 6in (15cm) long, margined with fine hairs and sometimes mottled purplish green. Bears large, pyramidal panicles, to 12in (30cm) long, of many bright yellow flowers in late spring. ↕↔ to 6ft (2m). Morocco, but naturalized in other frost-free areas. ❄ (min. 50°F/10°C)
'Zwartkop' ▣ syn. 'Schwarzkopf', has dark, almost black-purple leaves.
A. bertoletianum see *A. tabuliforme.*
A. canariense, syn. *A. exsul* (Velvet rose). Short-stemmed, perennial succulent, often branching at the base. Produces rosettes, to 16in (40cm) across, of broadly spoon-shaped, dark green leaves, to 10in (25cm) long, with glandular, sticky white hairs. In spring, bears pale green and white flowers in pyramidal, leafy racemes, 20–28in (50–70cm) long. ↕ to 8in (20cm), ↔ 20in (50cm). Canary Islands (Tenerife). ❄ (min. 50°F/10°C)
***A. domesticum* 'Variegatum'** see *Aichryson* x *domesticum* 'Variegatum'.
A. exsul see *A. canariense.*
A. haworthii ▣ syn. *Sempervivum haworthii* (Pinwheel). Succulent subshrub with slender branches, each crowned by a rosette, 2½–6in (6–15cm) across, of spoon-shaped, pointed, toothed, bluish green leaves, to 3in (8cm) long, keeled beneath, and with red margins. Bears lax panicles, 4–6in (10–15cm) long, of pale yellow to pinkish white flowers in spring. ↕↔ 24in (60cm). Canary Islands (Tenerife). ❄ (min. 50°F/10°C)
A. lindleyi. Evergreen perennial succulent with densely branched shrublets. Predominantly erect, yellow to dark green leaves are spatula- to egg-shaped, and smooth or velvety fuzzy-textured, ¾–1¾in (2–4.5cm) long. Produces rosettes of 8–9 lance-shaped flowers, with golden-yellow petals, 2–2¾in (5–7mm) long, from terminal cymes; bears long, tapering, pubescent sepals. May be used as an antidote for painful Euphorbia latex in eyes or on skin. ↕ to 20in (50cm), ↔ 28in (70cm). Canary Islands (Tenerife). ❄ (min. 50°F/10°C)
A. nobile, syn. *Megalonium nobile, Sempervivum nobile.* Subshrubby, usually unbranched, short-stemmed succulent. Produces rosettes, 20in (50cm) across, of broadly obovate to rounded, very fleshy, often red-tinged, olive-green leaves, to 12in (30cm) long, with incurved margins. Bears large, pyramidal, flat-topped cymes, 8–16in (20–40cm) long, of copper-red or yellow flowers, lined with red, in late spring. The rosettes often die soon after flowering. ↕ 24in (60cm), ↔ 20in (50cm). Canary Islands (La Palma). ❄ (min. 50°F/10°C)
A. sedifolium, syn. *Aichryson sedifolium, Sempervivum masferreri.* Dense, succulent subshrub with slender, erect branches that later become pendent. Club-shaped, sticky, fleshy, mid-green to yellowish green, red-lined leaves, to ½in (1.5cm) long, are borne in rosettes, 2½in (6cm) across. Bears large, golden yellow flowers, in racemes, ¾–3in (2–8cm) long, in spring. ↕ 6–16in (15–40cm), ↔ 5in (13cm). Canary Islands (Tenerife). ❄ (min. 50°F/10°C)
A. tabuliforme ▣ syn. *A. bertoletianum, Sempervivum complanatum.* Biennial or perennial succulent with very short, unbranched stems bearing plate-like rosettes, to 20in (50cm) across, of many spoon-shaped, bright green leaves, to 10in (25cm) long, margined with fine hairs. Yellow flowers are produced in large panicles, 12in (30cm) or more long, in spring. ↕ 3–4in (8–10cm), ↔ to 20in (50cm). Canary Islands (Tenerife). ❄ (min. 50°F/10°C)

Aeonium haworthii

Aeonium tabuliforme

Aeonium arboreum 'Zwartkop'

AERANGIS

ORCHIDACEAE

Genus of about 35 species of evergreen, epiphytic (or rarely lithophytic), monopodial orchids, mostly from lowland forest and savanna or woodland in tropical Africa and Madagascar. The fleshy or leathery leaves are generally oval, obovate, or inversely lance-shaped, occasionally narrowly linear-oblong, and are arranged in 2 ranks. Racemes of white, sometimes red- or yellow-tinted, usually star-shaped, long-spurred flowers, in most cases night-scented, are borne at various times of the year, but mostly in winter or spring.

Aerangis luteoalba var. *rhodosticta*

• **CULTIVATION** Intermediate- to warm-growing orchids. Grow epiphytically on an orchid raft or cork slab; provide shade in summer and high humidity. Water freely throughout the year, more sparingly in winter. In spring and summer, apply a half-strength, balanced fertilizer at every third watering. Spray aerial roots with water once or twice daily in summer. See also p.46.
• **PROPAGATION** Not suitable for division, although cuttings or offshoots may be rooted successfully.
• **PESTS AND DISEASES** Aphids, spider mites, and mealybugs may be problems.

***A. ellisii* var. *grandiflora*.** Epiphytic orchid with leathery, oblong-obovate leaves, 8–10in (20–25cm) long, unequally 2-lobed at the tip. Pendent racemes, to 24in (60cm) long, of 9–20 star-shaped, fragrant, pure white flowers, 2in (5cm) across, with curved spurs, 7–11in (18–28cm) long, and tinted pale orange, are borne in winter. ↕ 10in (25cm), ↔ 12in (30cm). Madagascar. ❀ (min. 55–64°F/13–18°C; max. 86°F/30°C)
A. luteoalba* var. *rhodosticta ■ Epiphytic orchid with oblong-obovate leaves, to 6in (15cm) long. In winter, produces arching racemes, 4–12in (10–30cm) long, of 9–25 star-shaped, fragrant, white to creamy white flowers, 1¼in (3cm) across, with a striking bright red column and spurs, ¾–1½in (2–4cm) long. ↕↔ 6in (15cm). Cameroon, Ethiopia, Kenya, Tanzania. ❀ (min. 55–64°F/13–18°C; max. 86°F/30°C)

AERIDES

ORCHIDACEAE

Genus of about 40 species of evergreen, monopodial, epiphytic orchids from India, the Himalayas, and S.E. Asia, mostly found at low altitudes in tropical forest. Strap-shaped to linear, leathery leaves are borne alternately in 2 ranks, with moth-like, often fragrant flowers produced in dense, arching racemes from the leaf axils in summer. They develop numerous aerial roots, sometimes up to 3ft (1m) long.
• **CULTIVATION** Cool- to intermediate-growing orchids. Grow in epiphytic orchid potting mix in an orchid basket or epiphytically on slabs of bark. Provide high humidity and filtered light. Water freely throughout the year, more sparingly in winter. Apply a half-strength, balanced fertilizer at every third watering in spring and summer. They will bloom in spring and summer if grown suspended in a position with good light. See also p.46.
• **PROPAGATION** Not suitable for division, although cuttings or offshoots may be rooted successfully.
• **PESTS AND DISEASES** Aphids, whiteflies, spider mites, and mealybugs may be problems.

A. japonica see *Sedirea japonica*.
***A. odorata*.** Epiphytic orchid with linear leaves, to 14in (35cm) long. In summer, produces arching racemes, to 10in (25cm) long, of fragrant, white-tinted, rose-pink to purple, often spotted flowers, 1½in (4cm) long, with incurved green- or yellow-tipped spurs. ↕ 18in (45cm), ↔ 12in (30cm). India to Philippines. ❀ (min. 52–55°F/11–13°C; max. 86°F/30°C)
***A. rosea*.** Robust, epiphytic orchid with linear, deeply channeled leaves, to 14in (35cm) long. Many fragrant, white-spotted amethyst flowers, 1in (2.5cm) across, with white spurs, are produced in pendent racemes, to 24in (60cm) long, in early summer. ↕↔ 12in (30cm). Himalayas, Myanmar, Thailand, Vietnam. ❀ (min. 52–55°F/11–13°C; max. 86°F/30°C)

AESCHYNANTHUS

GESNERIACEAE

Genus of about 140 species, and many cultivars, of evergreen subshrubs, climbers, and trailing and semi-trailing perennials, most of which are epiphytic, from subtropical forest in the Himalayas, S. China, Malaysia, Indonesia, and New Guinea. They have ovate to lance-shaped, leathery, fleshy leaves in opposite pairs or whorls. From summer to winter, vividly colored flowers are produced in pairs from the leaf axils near the stem tips, or in terminal corymbs or clusters. The flowers often have prominent calyces, sometimes in a contrasting color, and long, tubular, often curved, sometimes hooded corollas, with protruding stamens and styles. Where they are not hardy, grow *Aeschynanthus* species and cultivars in hanging baskets in a warm conservatory or greenhouse; compact types are good houseplants. Elsewhere, grow outdoors in shade or semi-shade.
• **CULTIVATION** Under glass, grow in a peat/perlite mix with high humidity. Grow in bright filtered light to encourage flowering; the compact types are excellent under lights. Water freely during the growing season, more sparingly in winter; when established, apply a half-strength, balanced liquid fertilizer monthly. Outdoors, grow in humus-rich, well-drained soil in partial shade; they will tolerate a more sunny position if humidity is high.
• **PROPAGATION** Sow seed at 66–75°F (19–24°C) when ripe. Take cuttings of young shoots, 1¼–2in (3–5cm) long, in spring, or semi-ripe cuttings in summer; root in an open peat/perlite mix at 59–66°F (15–19°C).
• **PESTS AND DISEASES** Aphids and thrips may infest young growth and flowers. Scale insects and mealybugs are also problems. Many fungi cause leaf spots, and *Rhizoctonia* blight is common on cuttings as well as mature plants. Tobacco mosaic virus can occur.

***A.* 'Black Pagoda'** ■ Semi-trailing perennial producing elliptic leaves, to 4in (10cm) long, pale green with dark brown marbling above, and purple beneath. Terminal clusters of 3 or 4 deep yellow to red-orange flowers, to 2in (5cm) long, with green calyces, are borne from summer to winter. ↕ 24in (60cm), ↔ to 18in (45cm). ❀ (min. 59–64°F/15–18°C)
***A. bracteatus*.** Scrambling epiphyte, often growing on rocks in the wild, with elliptic to ovate, sharply pointed, dark green leaves, 4in (10cm) long. Produces terminal clusters of 4 or 5 scarlet flowers, to 2in (5cm) long, with dark purple calyces, from summer to winter. ↕ 6in (15cm), ↔ 24in (60cm). Himalayas. ❀ (min. 59–64°F/15–18°C)
A. hildebrandii, syn. *A.* 'Hillbrandii'. Small, epiphytic subshrub with ovate, dark green leaves, to 1in (2.5cm) long, tinged red at the margins. Periodically throughout the year, bears terminal clusters of 2 or 3 orange-red flowers, 2in (5cm) long, with green calyces. Grows well under lights. ↕ 8in (20cm), ↔ 12in (30cm) or more. Myanmar. ❀ (min. 59–64°F/15–18°C)
***A.* 'Hillbrandii'** see *A. hildebrandii*.
A. lobbianus ■ syn. *A. radicans* var. *lobbianus* (Lipstick plant). Spreading, trailing perennial with elliptic, dark green leaves, 1¾in (4.5cm) long, tinged purple at the margins. Bears terminal clusters of 2 or 3 red flowers, 2in (5cm) long, with purple calyces, from summer to winter. ↕ 8in (20cm), ↔ to 36in (90cm). Indonesia (Java). ❀ (min. 59–64°F/15–18°C)
***A. longicaulis*.** Semi-trailing perennial with lance-shaped, dark green leaves, 3in (8cm) long. Orange-red flowers, 2in (5cm) long, with green calyces, are produced in axillary and terminal clusters of 1–3 from summer to winter. ↕ 24in (60cm), ↔ to 36in (90cm). Malaysia. ❀ (min. 59–64°F/15–18°C)
A. marmoratus, syn. *A. zebrinus*. Semi-trailing perennial producing oval leaves,

Aeschynanthus 'Black Pagoda'

Aeschynanthus lobbianus

3–4in (8–10cm) long, light green with dark marbling above and red beneath. Solitary, axillary, greenish yellow flowers, 1½in (4cm) long, with maroon- or brown-tinged throats and deeply cut green calyces, are produced from summer to winter. ↕ 24in (60cm), ↔ 36in (90cm). Myanmar, Thailand, Malaysia. ❀ (min. 59–64°F/15–18°C)
A. pulcher (Lipstick plant, Red bugle vine, Scarlet basket vine). Epiphytic climber with thin, rooting branches and oval, slightly toothed, shiny, dark green leaves, 1¾in (4.5cm) long. From summer to winter, bears terminal corymbs of 6–8 hooded, bright red flowers, 2½in (6cm) long, with green calyces and yellow throats. ↕ 30in (75cm), ↔ 24in (60cm) or more. Indonesia (Java). ❀ (min. 59–64°F/15–18°C)
A. radicans* var. *lobbianus see *A. lobbianus*.
***A. speciosus*.** Trailing perennial with lance-shaped, pale green leaves, to 4in (10cm) long. From summer to winter, bright orange flowers, 4in (10cm) long, marked red across the lower lobes and with green calyces, are borne in terminal clusters of 6–20. ↕↔ 32in (80cm). Malaysia. ❀ (min. 59–64°F/15–18°C)
A. zebrinus see *A. marmoratus*.

AESCULUS

Buckeye, Horse chestnut

HIPPOCASTANACEAE

Genus of about 15 species of deciduous trees and shrubs, mainly from woodland in S.E. Europe, the Himalayas, E. Asia, and North America. They have opposite, palmate leaves, mostly mid- to dark green, some turning deep yellow or red in autumn. Large, upright, conical to cylindrical panicles of 4- or 5-petaled flowers, each ½–1¼in (1.5–3cm) across, with prominent stamens, are borne usually in late spring and early summer. The spiny or smooth-skinned, rounded to pear-shaped fruits contain 1 or 2 large, usually brown or blackish brown seeds. Most horse chestnuts are suitable only for large gardens, where they are best planted as specimen trees, although *A. parviflora* and *A. pavia* may be grown in a medium-sized garden. All parts may cause mild stomach upset if ingested.
• **CULTIVATION** Grow in deep, fertile, moist but well-drained soil in sun or

Aesculus californica

Aesculus hippocastanum

Aesculus x *neglecta* 'Erythroblastos'

Aesculus x *carnea* 'Briotii'

partial shade. Grow *A. californica* and *A. chinensis* in a hot (but not dry) sunny site for best results. Pruning group 1, when dormant; train trees as central leader standards.

- **PROPAGATION** Sow seed in a seedbed as soon as ripe. *A.* x *carnea* comes true from seed. Graft in late winter or bud in summer. Propagate *A. parviflora* from suckers or seed.
- **PESTS AND DISEASES** Prone to canker, coral spot, leaf blotch, Japanese beetles, and scale insects. Anthracnose, rust, and powdery mildew also occur.

A. californica ■ (California buckeye). Spreading, rounded, short-trunked tree with 5- to 7-palmate, mid-green leaves divided into narrowly ovate leaflets, 4in (10cm) or more long. Bears fragrant white or pink-tinged white flowers, with long, protruding stamens, in dense, cylindrical panicles, to 8in (20cm) tall, in early summer, followed by rough-skinned fruit, 2–3in (5–8cm) long. Grow in full sun. ↕25ft (8m), ↔ 30ft (10m). California. Zone 8.

A.* x *carnea (*A. hippocastanum* x *A. pavia*) (Red horse chestnut). Spreading tree with 5- to 7-palmate, dark green leaves composed of stalkless or short-stalked, often slightly twisted, obovate leaflets, 10in (25cm) long. Bears dark red or rose-red flowers with yellow centers in conical panicles, 8–12in (20–30cm) tall, from late spring to early summer, followed by spiny fruit. ↕70ft (20m), ↔ 50ft (15m). Garden origin. Zone 5b. **'Briotii'** ■ has glossy leaves and larger panicles of dark rose-red flowers.

A. chinensis ■ (Chinese horse chestnut). Slow-growing, spreading tree with 5-palmate (occasionally 7-palmate), glossy, mid-green leaves composed of narrowly oblong, finely pointed leaflets, 8in (20cm) or more long. White flowers with protruding stamens are produced in slender, cylindrical panicles, to 12in (30cm) tall, in midsummer, followed by rough-skinned fruit. ↕50ft (15m), ↔ 30ft (10m). N. China. Zone 7.

A. flava ■ syn. *A. octandra* (Yellow buckeye). Broadly oval-conical tree with 5- to 7-palmate, glossy, dark green leaves with obovate or ovate leaflets, 3in (8cm) or more long. Bears yellow flowers in conical panicles, to 7in (18cm) tall, in late spring, followed by smooth-skinned fruit. ↕50–80ft (15–25m), ↔ 30–50ft (10–15m). E. US. Zone 3b.

Aesculus chinensis

Aesculus flava

A. glabra (Ohio buckeye). Broadly conical-rounded tree with rough, fissured bark, bearing 5-palmate, glossy, light green leaves with obovate to ovate, long-pointed leaflets, 6in (15cm) or more long. In late spring, bears yellow-green flowers in conical panicles, to 6in (15cm) tall, followed by sparsely prickly fruit. ↕50ft (15m), ↔ 30ft (10m). C. and E. US. Zone 3.

A. hippocastanum ■ (Common horse chestnut). Vigorous, spreading, rounded tree with 5- to 7-palmate, mid-green leaves consisting of obovate leaflets, 12in (30cm) or more long. White flowers, with yellow, later pink marks, open in conical panicles, to 12in (30cm) tall, in late spring; flowers are followed by the well-known, spiny fruit, regionally known as "buckeyes." ↕80ft (25m), ↔ 70ft (20m). S.E. Europe. Zone 5. **'Baumannii'**, syn. 'Flore Pleno', has double flowers and does not bear fruit.

A. indica (Indian horse chestnut). Spreading, rounded tree with usually 7-palmate leaves composed of obovate to lance-shaped leaflets, 12in (30cm) or more long, opening bronze and turning glossy, mid-green. White or pink flowers, with central red and yellow marks, are borne in cylindrical panicles, 12–16in (30–40cm) tall, in summer, followed by smooth-skinned fruit. Prefers a cool, moderate climate. ↕↔ 50ft (15m). N.W. Himalayas. Zone 8. **'Sydney Pearce'** ■ is vigorous, with freely produced panicles of deep pink, yellow-centered flowers.

***A.* x *mutabilis* 'Induta'.** Small tree, sometimes shrubby, with 5- to 7-

Aesculus indica 'Sydney Pearce' (inset: flower detail)

Aesculus parviflora

palmate, mid-green leaves consisting of ovate leaflets, 8in (20cm) or more long. Bears profuse yellow-flushed pink flowers in panicles, to 8in (20cm) tall, in late spring and early summer. Does not bear fruit. ↕↔ 15ft (5m). Zone 5.

A.* x *neglecta (*A. flava* x *A. sylvatica*). Conical tree with 5-palmate, mid-green leaves composed of obovate to ovate leaflets, 6in (15cm) or more long. Bears yellow or yellow-flushed red flowers in conical panicles, to 6in (15cm) tall, in midsummer, followed by smooth-skinned fruit. ↕ 30ft (10m) or more, ↔ 25ft (8m). S.E. US. Zone 5. **'Erythroblastos'** ▣ (Sunrise horse chestnut) has red leaf stalks and leaves that unfold cream and bright pink, become yellow, then finally green.

A. octandra see *A. flava.*

A. parviflora ▣ (Bottlebrush buckeye). Suckering shrub with 5- to 7-palmate, mid- to dark green leaves divided into ovate leaflets, 9in (23cm) or more long, bronze when young and yellow in autumn. Bears spidery white flowers, with protruding stamens, in conical panicles to 12in (30cm) tall, in midsummer, followed by smooth-skinned fruit. Tolerant of all but very poorly drained sites. May be slow to establish. ↕ 10ft (3m), ↔ 15ft (5m). S.E. US. Zone 4b.

A. pavia, syn. *A. splendens* (Red buckeye). Conical shrub or small tree producing 5- to 7-palmate, lustrous dark green leaves with obovate to oblong to lance-shaped leaflets, 5in (13cm) or more long. Red, sometimes yellow-marked flowers are borne in conical panicles, to 6in (15cm) tall, in early summer, followed by smooth-skinned fruit. ↕ 15ft (5m), ↔ 10ft (3m). E. US. Zone 5b. **'Atrosanguinea'** ▣ has dark red flowers.

A. splendens see *A. pavia.*

A. turbinata (Japanese horse chestnut). Vigorous, spreading tree producing 5- to 7-palmate, mid-green leaves with obovate leaflets, 16in (40cm) or more long. White flowers, each with a yellow, later pink mark, are borne in cylindrical panicles, to 12in (30cm) tall, in early and midsummer, followed by smooth-skinned fruit. ↕ 70ft (20m), ↔ 40ft (12m). Japan. Zone 7.

Aesculus pavia 'Atrosanguinea'

AETHIONEMA

syn. EUNOMIA

Stone cress

BRASSICACEAE

Genus of more than 40 species of evergreen or semi-evergreen, dwarf subshrubs, woody-based perennials, and annuals from sunny, open sites, on limestone, in the mountains of Europe and W. Asia, particularly Turkey. They are grown for their dense to loose, terminal racemes of small, 4-petaled, cross-shaped, sometimes fragrant flowers, in red, pink, or creamy to pure white, profusely borne on stems ¾–1½in (2–4cm) long, usually from spring to early summer. The leaves are small, usually stalkless, fleshy, and arranged alternately, or sometimes in opposite pairs. Grow in a rock garden or wall crevice; *A. oppositifolium* prefers a scree bed or alpine house.

• **CULTIVATION** Grows best in fertile, well-drained, alkaline soil in full sun, but will tolerate poor, acidic soils.

• **PROPAGATION** Sow seed of perennials in containers in a cold frame in spring. Sow seed of annuals *in situ* as soon as ripe or in autumn. Seedlings grown from garden seed often prove to be hybrids. Root softwood cuttings in late spring or early summer.

• **PESTS AND DISEASES** Aphids and spider mites may be problems.

Aethionema armenum

A. armenum ▣ Short-lived, compact, evergreen or semi-evergreen subshrub with linear-oblong, blue- to gray-green leaves, ¼–½in (0.5–1.5cm) long. Dense racemes of small, pale pink flowers, ¼in (6mm) across, are borne in late spring. ↕↔ 6–8in (15–20cm). Caucasus, Turkey. Zone 5.

A. grandiflorum ▣ syn. *A. pulchellum* (Persian stone cress). Short-lived, evergreen or semi-evergreen, loosely branched subshrub or woody-based perennial with blunt-tipped, linear-oblong, blue-green leaves, to ½in (1.5cm) long. Bears pale to deep rose-pink flowers, to ¼in (6mm) wide, in loose racemes in late spring and early summer. ↕↔ 8–12in (20–30cm). Caucasus, Turkey, Iraq, Iran. Zone 5.

A. oppositifolium, syn. *Eunomia oppositifolia.* Mat- or cushion-forming, evergreen or semi-evergreen perennial with opposite, obovate, blue-gray leaves, ½in (1.5cm) long. Bears small racemes of lavender-pink flowers, ¼–⅜in (6–8mm) across, in late spring. ↕ to 2in (5cm), ↔ 4–6in (10–15cm). Caucasus, Turkey, Syria, Lebanon. Zone 6.

A. pulchellum see *A. grandiflorum.*

***A.* 'Warley Rose'** ▣ Short-lived, evergreen or semi-evergreen, compact subshrub with linear, blue-gray leaves, ½in (1.5cm) long. Profuse racemes of rich pink flowers, to ¼in (6mm) across, are produced in late spring and early summer. ↕↔ 6–8in (15–20cm). Zone 5b.

Aethionema grandiflorum

Aethionema 'Warley Rose'

AGAPANTHUS

African blue lily

LILIACEAE

Genus of about 10 species of vigorous perennials, some of them evergreen, from southern Africa. The evergreen species occur in coastal areas, the deciduous ones in moister, mountain grassland in inland regions. They form bold clumps of large, strap-shaped, usually arching, often deep green leaves, and bear rounded, intermediate, or pendent umbels of many tubular, bell- or trumpet-shaped, blue or white flowers. The inflorescences are good for cutting, and are followed by decorative seed heads. Grow in a border or in large containers. Most hybrids are deciduous and usually hardier than the species, with dense, rounded umbels, to 8in (20cm) across, of 1¼in (3cm) long flowers, and with leaves to 18in (45cm) long, sometimes more.

AGAPANTHUS INFLORESCENCES

Agapanthus flowers are borne in 3 main inflorescence types: rounded umbels of bell- to trumpet-shaped flowers; intermediate umbels of usually trumpet-shaped flowers; and pendent umbels of tubular flowers.

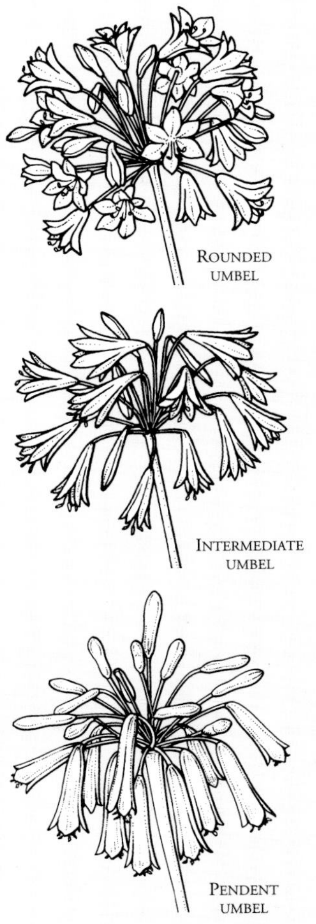

Agapanthus 'Blue Giant'

• **CULTIVATION** Grow in fertile, moist but well-drained soil in full sun. Where marginally hardy, grow against a wall and mulch in late autumn. In containers, grow in soil-based potting mix. Water freely when in growth, sparingly in winter. Apply a balanced liquid fertilizer monthly from spring until flowering. Overwinter in a cool, bright spot and water sparingly until growth resumes.
• **PROPAGATION** Sow seed at 55–59°F (13–15°C) when ripe or in spring; keep the seedlings in a frame for the first winter where marginally hardy. They will flower in 2–3 years. Most seedlings grown from garden seed do not come true. Divide in spring.
• **PESTS AND DISEASES** Slugs and snails may be a problem. Bacterial soft rot can be a problem during propagation.

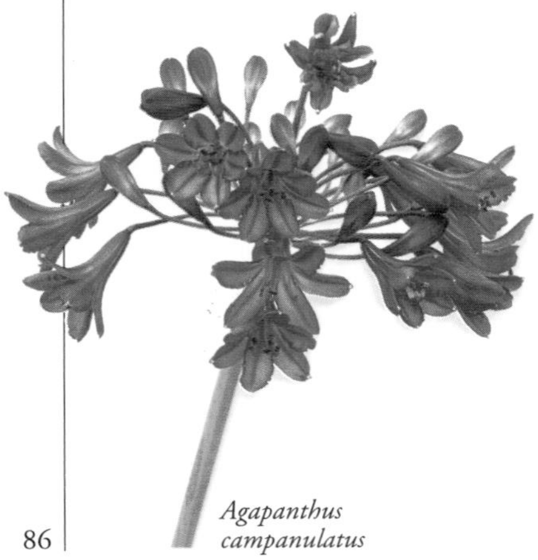

Agapanthus campanulatus

Phytophthora and *Phythium* root and bulb rots occur in poorly draining soils. Leaf spots can occur.

A. africanus (African lily). Clump-forming, evergreen perennial with strap-shaped leaves, to 12in (30cm) or more long. In late summer, bears trumpet-shaped, deep blue flowers, 1–2in (2.5–5cm) long, in rounded umbels, 6–12in (15–30cm) across. ↕ 24–36in (60–90cm), ↔ 18in (45cm). South Africa (Northern Cape, Western Cape, Eastern Cape). ❄ (min. 41°F/5°C). **'Peter Pan'** is dwarf, with profuse flowers; ↕ 18in (45cm).
***A.* 'Alice Gloucester'.** Clump-forming perennial that produces intermediate umbels of trumpet-shaped white flowers, the buds and pedicels tinged lilac, in mid- and late summer. ↕ 36in (90cm), ↔ 18in (45cm). Zone 7b.
***A.* 'Blue Giant'** ▣ Clump-forming perennial producing rounded umbels of open bell-shaped, rich blue flowers in mid- and late summer. ↕ 4ft (1.2m), ↔ 24in (60cm). Zone 7b.
***A.* 'Blue Triumphator'.** Clump-forming perennial producing rounded to intermediate umbels of open bell-shaped, clear blue flowers in mid- and late summer. ↕ 36in (90cm), ↔ 18in (45cm). Zone 7b.
***A.* 'Bressingham White'.** Clump-forming perennial bearing intermediate umbels of trumpet-shaped, pure white flowers in mid- and late summer. ↕ 36in (90cm), ↔ 24in (60cm). Zone 7b.
A. campanulatus ▣ Vigorous, clump-forming perennial producing narrow, strap-shaped, deciduous, grayish green leaves, 6–16in (15–40cm) long. Rounded umbels, 4–8in (10–20cm) across, of bell-shaped, pale to dark blue, sometimes white flowers, ¾–1½in (2–4cm) long, are borne on strong stems in mid- and late summer. ↕ 24–48in (60–120cm), ↔ 18in (45cm). South Africa (KwaZulu/Natal, Northern Cape). Zone 7b. **'Albovittatus'** ▣ is less vigorous and has broad leaves, boldly striped white. **'Isis'** produces dark blue flowers; ↕ 30in (75cm), ↔ 12in (30cm). **subsp. *patens*** bears light blue flowers, with shorter tubes and more open mouths than the species, in late summer and early autumn; ↕ to 18in (45cm), ↔ 12in (30cm); South Africa (Drakensberg Mountains to Northern Transvaal).
A. caulescens. Clump-forming perennial with a leek-like stem, bearing deciduous, narrowly strap-shaped lower leaves, to 6in (15cm) long, and broader upper leaves, to 24in (60cm) long. From midsummer to early autumn, produces open, rounded umbels, 6–10in (15–25cm) across, of bell-shaped violet-blue flowers, 1¼–2in (3–5cm) long, with tepals spreading at the mouths, and long, projecting stamens. ↕ 3–4ft (90–120cm), ↔ 24in (60cm). Swaziland. ❄ (min. 41°F/5°C)
***A.* Headbourne Hybrids.** Large, quite variable group of vigorous, clump-forming perennials with trumpet-shaped flowers ranging from deep violet to pale blue, 2–3in (5–8cm) long, in summer. Some are among the hardiest of the genus. Zone 7.
A. inapertus ▣ Clump-forming perennial with erect, strap-shaped leaves, to 28in (70cm) long. In late summer and early autumn, stiff, upright stems bear pendent umbels, 4–6in (10–15cm) across, of pendent, tubular blue flowers, narrowed at the mouths, and 1–1¾in (2.5–4.5cm) long. ↕ 3–5ft (90–150cm), ↔ 24in (60cm). South Africa (Northern Transvaal, Eastern Transvaal). ❄ (min. 41°F/5°C)
***A.* 'Lilliput'.** Clump-forming perennial bearing rounded to intermediate umbels of trumpet-shaped, deep blue flowers in mid- and late summer. ↕↔ 16in (40cm). Zone 7b.
A. orientalis see *A. praecox* subsp. *orientalis.*
A. praecox* subsp. *orientalis ▣ syn. *A. orientalis.* Clump-forming, evergreen perennial with broad, strap-shaped, dark green leaves, 12–28in (30–70cm) long. Bears large, rounded umbels, 6–12in (15–30cm) across, of trumpet-shaped, rich mid-blue flowers, 1½–2½in (4–6cm) long, in late summer and early autumn. ↕ 24–36in (60–90cm), ↔ 24in (60cm). South Africa. Zone 7.
***A.* 'Snowy Owl'** ▣ Clump-forming perennial with rounded umbels of bell-shaped white flowers in late summer. ↕ 4ft (1.2m), ↔ 24in (60cm). Zone 7b.

Agapanthus campanulatus 'Albovittatus'

Agapanthus praecox subsp. *orientalis*

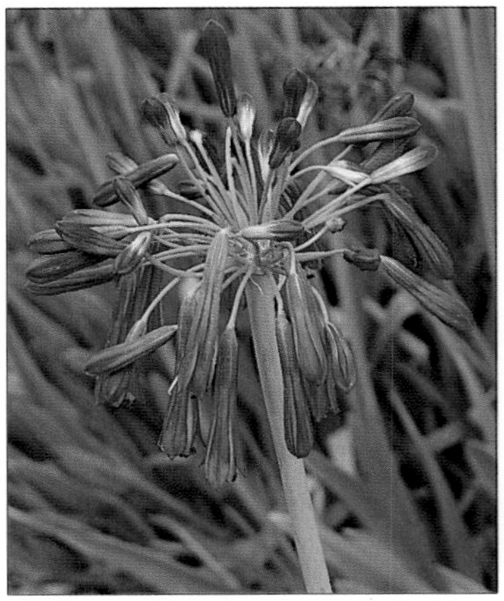

Agapanthus inapertus

Agapanthus 'Snowy Owl'

AGAPETES

ERICACEAE

Genus of about 95 species of spreading to erect or scandent shrubs, sometimes epiphytic in the wild, found in scrub and forest from warm-temperate regions of E. Asia to the western Pacific, including Australia. The evergreen, occasionally briefly deciduous leaves are simple, usually entire, and leathery, and are borne in opposite pairs. They are cultivated mainly for their solitary or clustered, pendent flowers, which are tubular, bell-, or urn-shaped, with 5 short petal lobes. Where not hardy, grow in a cool or temperate greenhouse; in frost-free areas, grow in a border or against a wall or arbor.

• **CULTIVATION** Under glass, grow in well-drained, acidic potting mix in bright filtered light. In the growing season, water freely and apply a balanced liquid fertilizer monthly; water sparingly in winter. Pot on or top-dress in late winter or spring. Outdoors, grow in moist but well-drained, neutral to acidic, moderately fertile soil, enriched with organic matter. These plants prefer partial shade, but tolerate some sun. Mulch in spring every other year. Pruning group 11; pruning is best kept to a minimum.

• **PROPAGATION** Root semi-ripe cuttings with bottom heat in late summer, or layer in spring.

• **PESTS AND DISEASES** Scale insects may be a problem.

A. incurvata ■ syn. *A. rugosa.* Sparsely branched shrub, which may be trained as a climber, with flexible, arching to pendent stems. Dark green leaves, to 4in (10cm) long, are broadly lance-shaped to ovate, shallowly toothed, and conspicuously veined. In summer, bears pendent clusters of up to 5 angular, narrowly urn-shaped white to pink, purple-veined flowers, ¾in (2cm) long, with prominent, ovate calyx lobes. ↕ to 3ft (1m), ↔ 3–6ft (1–2m) as a shrub; ↕ 6–10ft (2–3m) as a climber. E. Nepal to India. ❄ (min. 41–45°F/5–7°C). **var. *hookeri*** has yellow flowers.

***A.* 'Ludgvan Cross'** (*A. incurvata* x *A. serpens*). Pendent shrub with lance-shaped, mid- to dark green leaves, to 2in (5cm) long. From spring to summer, bears pendent clusters of up to 6 urn-shaped pink flowers, ¾–1¼in (2–3cm) long, with dark crimson veins. ↕↔ 4–5ft (1.2–1.5m). ❄ (min. 45°F/7°C)

Agapetes incurvata

Agapetes serpens

A. macrantha see *A. variegata* var. *macrantha.*

A. rugosa see *A. incurvata.*

A. serpens ■ Initially erect, then arching shrub, which may be trained as a climber. Small, crowded, lance-shaped leaves, to ¾in (2cm) long, are rich green and glossy. From late winter to spring, usually solitary, narrowly urn-shaped red flowers, ¾in (2cm) long, with V-shaped, darker red markings, are produced from the leaf axils. ↕ 24–36in (60–90cm), ↔ 6–10ft (2–3m); ↕ 6–10ft (2–3m) if grown as a climber. Nepal, Bhutan, India (Assam). ❄ (min. 41–45°F/5–7°C)

***A. variegata* var. *macrantha*,** syn. *A. macrantha.* Spreading, arching shrub with elliptic-lance-shaped, mid- to deep green leaves, 3–5in (8–13cm) long. From winter to spring, older stems bear clusters of up to 5 urn-shaped, white to pink flowers, 1½–2in (4–5cm) long, patterned with V-shaped red lines. ↕↔ 3–6ft (1–2m). N.E. India. ❄ (min. 45–50°F/7–10°C)

AGASTACHE

syn. BRITTONASTRUM

LAMIACEAE

Genus of about 30 species of aromatic perennials from dry, often hilly habitats in China, Japan, US, and Mexico. Most are stiffly erect, bushy plants, with lance-shaped to ovate, grayish green leaves, borne in opposite pairs. Spikes of long-lasting, small, 2-lipped, tubular flowers are borne in whorls from midsummer to autumn. Agastaches are suitable for an herb garden or a mixed border. They may also be grown as annuals and in containers where not hardy. Many are highly attractive to insects.

• **CULTIVATION** Grow in well-drained, fertile soil in full sun. In warmer areas, less hardy species should overwinter in a sheltered site.

• **PROPAGATION** Sow seed at 55–64°F (13–18°C) in early spring. Divide in spring. Root semi-ripe cuttings in late summer; overwinter young plants under cover where not hardy. Root semi-ripe cuttings of *A. mexicana* in early summer to maintain stocks.

• **PESTS AND DISEASES** Mildew and rust affect leaves in the dry summer months. Downy mildew and a few other fungal leaf diseases may occur.

A. aurantiaca. Erect, bushy, strongly mint-scented perennial with ovate to ovate-lance-shaped, gray-green leaves, 2in (5cm) long. Bears spikes, 12in (30cm) long, of orange-pink flowers in summer. ↕ 18–30in (45–75cm), ↔ 24in (60cm). S. US, Mexico. Zone 7b. **'Apricot Sunrise'** has pale orange flowers with purple-tinged calyces and stems.

A. anethiodora see *A. foeniculum.*

A. anisata see *A. foeniculum.*

A. barberi (Giant hummingbird's mint). Upright, bushy perennial with aromatic, ovate leaves, 1¼–2in (3–5cm) long. Loose spikes, to 12in (30cm) long, of rose to light magenta flowers are produced from midsummer to late autumn. ↕ 24in (60cm), ↔ 12in (30cm). S. US to N. Mexico. Zone 7.

A. cana (Hummingbird's mint, Mosquito plant, Wild hyssop). Erect, branched perennial with ovate leaves, ½–1¼in (1.5–3cm) long, scented of bubblegum and camphor. Bears loose spikes, to 12in (30cm) long, of dark pink to rose-purple flowers, in late summer to autumn. ↕ 24–36in (60–90cm), ↔ 18in (45cm). New Mexico, W. Texas. Zone 6.

***A.* 'Firebird'.** Erect, bushy, aromatic perennial with ovate, toothed leaves, 1½–2in (3–5cm) long. From midsummer to late autumn, copper-orange flowers are produced on loose spikes, to 12in (30cm) long. ↕ 2–6ft (0.6–2m), ↔ 12–36in (30–90cm). Zone 6b.

***A. foeniculum*,** syn. *A. anethiodora, A. anisata* (Anise hyssop). Erect, leafy, anise-scented perennial with ovate-lance-shaped, veined leaves, 2–3in (5–8cm) long, downy and whitish green beneath. Dense spikes, 1½–3in (4–8cm) long, of blue flowers, with violet bracts and calyces, are borne from midsummer to early autumn. Blooms the first year from seed and reseeds freely. ↕ 3–5ft (90–150cm), ↔ 12in (30cm). North America. Zone 6. **'Alabaster'** produces white flowers and a pleasant musky scent.

Agastache 'Tutti-Frutti'

***A. mexicana*,** syn. *Brittonastrum mexicanum, Cedronella mexicana* (Mexican giant hyssop). Bushy, lemon-scented, short-lived perennial with ovate to lance-shaped leaves, 1½–2½in (4–6cm) long. Edible rose-red flowers are produced in spikes, to 12in (30cm) long, in mid- and late summer. ↕ 24–36in (60–90cm), ↔ 12in (30cm). Mexico. Zone 7b.

***A.* 'Pink Panther'.** Erect perennial with lance-shaped to ovate-lance-shaped, purple-tinged, dark green leaves, 1½–2½in (4–6cm) long. From late spring to autumn, bears spikes, to 12in (30cm) long, of bright shell-pink flowers. ↕ 24in (60cm), ↔ 12in (30cm). Zone 6b.

A. rugosa (Wrinkled giant hyssop). Erect perennial with aromatic, ovate, toothed leaves, 2½–3in (6–8cm) long, often white-hairy below. Branching stems bear violet to pinkish purple flowers in short spikes, 2–4in (5–10cm) long, from midsummer to early autumn. ↕ 4ft (1.2m), ↔ 18in (45cm). China, Japan. Zone 7b.

A. scrophulariifolia (Purple giant hyssop). Erect, bushy perennial with ovate to ovate-lance-shaped, conspicuously hairy leaves, to 2in (5cm) long. In late summer and early autumn, produces rose to purple flowers on spikes, 4–10in (10–25cm) long. ↕ 4ft (1.2m), ↔ 12in (30cm). N.E. to C. US. Zone 5. **'Liquorice Blue'** bears blue flowers and strongly anise-scented foliage. **'Liquorice White'** produces white flowers. **Premium Series** cultivars produce long flower spikes, 8–10in (20–25cm) long, in blue, white, apricot, and bright reddish rose, the first year from seed.

***A.* 'Tutti-Frutti'** ■ Erect, bushy perennial with ovate, scented, toothed, gray-green leaves, 1½–2in (3–5cm) long. Produces raspberry-red flowers, on loose spikes, to 12in (30cm) long, from midsummer to late autumn. ↕ 2–6ft (0.6–2m), ↔ 12–36in (30–90cm). Zone 6.

▷ ***Agathaea*** see *Felicia*

AGATHIS *syn.* DAMMARA

Kauri pine

ARAUCARIACEAE

Genus of 13 species of evergreen, coniferous trees with broad, flat leaves, from tropical areas without a dry season, from Malaysia and the Philippines to New Guinea, Australia (Queensland), Fiji, and New Zealand. The male cones are cylindrical, the females spherical. They are monoecious, but may be dioecious when young. Where not hardy, grow young plants for their foliage in a cool greenhouse or conservatory. In frost-free areas, grow as specimen trees.

• **CULTIVATION** Under glass, grow in soil-based potting mix, in full light, with ample ventilation. When in growth, water freely and apply a balanced liquid fertilizer monthly; water sparingly in winter. Outdoors, grow in any moist

but well-drained soil in full sun, sheltered from cold winds.
• **PROPAGATION** Sow seed at 50–55°F (10–13°C) in early spring.
• **PESTS AND DISEASES** Infrequent.

A. australis (Dammar pine, Kauri pine). Coniferous tree, conical when young, with a massive spreading crown on a thick trunk when mature. Leathery leaves are opposite, lance-shaped, to 3in (8cm) long, and bright green when young, maturing to gray-green. Female cones, 2–3in (5–8cm) long, are woody and green; male cones are 1¼–1½in (3–4cm) long. ↕ 130ft (40m), ↔ to 50ft (15m). New Zealand (North Island). ❄ (min. 45°F/7°C)

AGAVE

AGAVACEAE

Genus of more than 200 species of rosette-forming, mostly monocarpic or sometimes perennial succulents from desert and mountain regions of the Americas. The leaves are often rigid and fleshy, usually having sharp terminal spines and toothed margins. The funnel-shaped, short-tubed flowers, each with 6 tepals, are borne in umbel-like clusters, racemes, or panicles on leafless stems from the centers of the rosettes. The ovoid or spherical, capsular fruits hold numerous flat black seeds. In most species, the rosettes die after flowering and fruiting, leaving offsets to mature and flower in subsequent years. Where not hardy, grow in a cool or temperate greenhouse; in frost-free areas, grow as specimen plants or in a border.

Agave americana 'Marginata'

Agave attenuata

Agave filifera

• **CULTIVATION** Under glass, grow in standard cactus potting mix in full light. In summer, water freely and apply a low-nitrogen fertilizer 3 or 4 times; reduce water in autumn; keep dry in winter. Outdoors, grow in slightly acidic, moderately fertile, sharply drained soil in full sun. See also pp.48–49.
• **PROPAGATION** Sow seed at 70°F (21°C) in early spring. Remove offsets in spring or autumn; if already rooted, treat as mature plants. Insert unrooted offsets, or plantlets of *A. americana* and other species, in a mix of equal parts peat and sharp sand until rooted.
• **PESTS AND DISEASES** Prone to scale insects and mealybugs, particularly on young growth. Many fungi cause leaf blights; root rot can occur in poorly draining soil. Bacterial soft rot occurs sometimes during propagation.

A. altissima see *A. americana.*
A. americana, syn. *A. altissima* (American aloe, Century plant). Monocarpic succulent producing basal rosettes of spreading, lance-shaped, spine-tipped and spiny-margined, gray-green leaves, often to 6ft (2m) long. In summer, bears clusters of yellowish green flowers, 3½–4in (9–10cm) long, in spreading panicles, to 25ft (8m) long. ↕ to 6ft (2m), ↔ to 10ft (3m). Mexico. ❄ (min. 41°F/5°C). **'Marginata'** ▣ produces pale yellow-margined leaves that often become white with age. **'Mediopicta'** has a broad, pale yellow central band along each leaf. **'Striata'** bears leaves that are vertically striped yellow or white.

Agave parryi

Agave parviflora

A. attenuata ▣ syn. *A. cernua, A. glaucescens.* Perennial succulent with a thick trunk, often branching at the base. The branches are crowned by rosettes of ovate, sometimes finely toothed, pale yellowish green or grayish green leaves, 20–28in (50–70cm) long, with no terminal spines. Recurving racemes, to 11ft (3.5m) or more long, bear greenish white flowers, 2½in (6cm) long, in summer. ↕ to 3ft (1m), ↔ to 6ft (2m). C. Mexico. ❄ (min. 50°F/10°C)
A. cernua see *A. attenuata.*
A. consideranti see *A. victoriae-reginae.*
A. cupreata. Basal-rosetted or short-stemmed, perennial succulent. Pointed, pale green leaves are ovate to obovate, 30in (75cm) long, with twisted, spiny, reddish brown marginal teeth, and brown terminal spines. Yellow flowers, 1½–3in (4–8cm) long, are produced in erect panicles, 24in (60cm) or more long, in summer. ↕ to 3ft (1m), ↔ 5ft (1.5m). W. Mexico. ❄ (min. 50°F/10°C)
A. dentiens see *A. deserti.*
A. deserti, syn. *A. dentiens, A. nelsonii, A. pringlei.* Variable, perennial succulent producing basal rosettes of thick, sharp-tipped, grayish green leaves, 6–16in (15–40cm) long. The concave to flat leaves are triangular to linear to lance-shaped, channeled above, sometimes banded, usually with spiny margins, occasionally entire. In summer, bears erect panicles, 6–22ft (2–7m) long, of silvery yellow flowers, to 2in (5cm) long. ↕ to 20in (50cm), ↔ to 3ft (1m). California, Arizona, N. Mexico. ❄ (min. 50°F/10°C)
A. ferox. Rosetted, perennial succulent with a thick stem. Oblong to spoon-shaped, rigid, fleshy, sharp-tipped, dark green leaves, 3ft (1m) long, have marginal hooked teeth, to ¾in (2cm) long, and terminal spines, to 3in (8cm) long. In summer, bears greenish yellow flowers, 3in (8cm) long, in erect then spreading panicles, to 30ft (10m) long. ↕ to 12–15ft (4–5m), ↔ to 6ft (2m). Mexico. ❄ (min. 50°F/10°C)
A. filifera ▣ Stoloniferous, perennial succulent with basal rosettes of slender, lance-shaped, dark green leaves, to 10in (25cm) long, margined with white threads, and each with a brown terminal spine. Erect, spike-like inflorescences, to 8ft (2.5m) long, with dense clusters of greenish yellow flowers, 2in (5cm) long, are borne in late summer and early autumn. ↕ 12–20in (30–50cm), ↔ 3ft (1m). C. Mexico. ❄ (min. 50°F/10°C)

Agave stricta

Agave utahensis

A. glaucescens see *A. attenuata.*
A. hartmanii see *A. parviflora.*
A. huachucensis see *A. parryi* var. *huachucensis.*
A. hystrix see *A. stricta.*
A. nelsonii see *A. deserti.*
A. neomexicana see *A. parryi.*
A. parryi ■ syn. *A. neomexicana* (Mescal). Perennial succulent producing a dense, compact, basal rosette of broadly oblong, spiny, gray-blue leaves, to 12in (30cm) long. Numerous creamy yellow flowers, pink- or red-tinged in bud, and 2½in (6cm) long, open in erect panicles, to 15ft (5m) long, in summer. ↕ 20in (50cm), ↔ to 3ft (1m). Mountains of Arizona to N. Mexico. ❄ (min. 41°F/5°C). **var. *huachucensis*,** syn. *A. huachucensis,* has broadly oblong leaves to 26in (65cm) long, and flowers 3in (8cm) long; S. Arizona.
A. parviflora ■ syn. *A. hartmanii.* Basal-rosetted, perennial succulent with narrowly lance-shaped, white-marked, dark green leaves, 1½–4in (4–10cm) long, margined with white threads, and each with a greenish brown terminal spine. Erect racemes, 3–6ft (1–1.8m) or more long, with clusters of pale yellow flowers, ½in (1.5cm) long, are borne in summer. ↕ 6in (15cm), ↔ 20in (50cm). S. Arizona to N. Mexico. ❄ (min. 50°F/10°C)
A. pringlei see *A. deserti.*
A. scaphoidea see *A. utahensis.*
***A. schidigera*,** syn. *A. vestita.* Basal-rosetted or short-stemmed, perennial succulent with lance-shaped, shiny, dark green or purplish green leaves, to 20in (50cm) long, margined with coiled white threads, and each with a brown terminal spine. Produces erect, spike-like inflorescences, 6–8ft (2–2.5m) long, with yellow-green or reddish brown flowers, 2in (5cm) long, in summer. ↕ to 20in (50cm), ↔ to 30in (75cm). C. Mexico. ❄ (min. 50°F/10°C)
A. stricta ■ syn. *A. hystrix* (Hedgehog agave). Short-stemmed, perennial succulent with rosettes of linear-lance-shaped, sharply tapered, mid-green leaves, to 14in (35cm) long, with red-brown terminal spines. In summer, bears red to purple-red flowers, ¾in (2cm) long, in dense, erect, spike-like racemes, 6–8ft (2–2.5m) long. ↕↔ 10–20in (25–50cm). S.E. Mexico. ❄ (min. 50°F/10°C)
A. utahensis ■ syn. *A. scaphoidea.* Variable, basal-rosetted, clump-forming, perennial succulent with linear to lance-shaped, gray-green leaves, to 12in (30cm) long, each with a long terminal spine; indented, wavy margins have hooked spines. In summer, bears yellow flowers, 1¼in (3cm) long, in erect panicles or racemes, 5–12ft (1.5–4m) long. ↕ 12in (30cm), ↔ indefinite. Utah. ❄ (min. 50°F/10°C)
A. vestita see *A. schidigera.*
A. victoriae-reginae ■ syn. *A. consideranti.* Variable, perennial succulent with basal rosettes of straight or incurved, triangular-oblong, white-marked, dark green leaves, 6–12in (15–30cm) long, with thick, rounded tips, and each with a brown terminal spine. The horny leaf margins are usually entire, but may have small white spines. In summer, bears erect or curved, spike-like racemes, 12–15ft (4–5m) long, of creamy white flowers, to 2in (5cm) long, sometimes tinged purple. ↕↔ to 20in (50cm). California, N. and W. Mexico. ❄ (min. 50°F/10°C)

Agave victoriae-reginae

▷***Ageratina*** see *Eupatorium*

AGERATUM

Floss flower

ASTERACEAE

Genus of about 40 species of annuals, perennials, and shrubs from diverse habitats in tropical and warm-temperate North and South America, some of which have become naturalized in many warm areas. They may be erect, spreading, or mound-forming, and have oval to lance-shaped, mid-green leaves. In summer and autumn, panicles of 30–50 small flowerheads form soft, rounded, brush-like clusters, varying in color from bright blue or gray-blue to pink or white; they attract butterflies. Ageratums are usually grown as annuals; use *A. houstonianum* and its cultivars for bedding or as edging in borders. They may also be grown in containers.

- **CULTIVATION** Grow in fertile, moist but well-drained soil in full sun to partial shade.
- **PROPAGATION** Sow seed at 61–64°F (16–18°C) in early spring, or sow in autumn and overwinter at 50°F (10°C).
- **PESTS AND DISEASES** Southern blight and crown and root rots occur. *Botrytis* blight is a problem during cool, wet weather, and powdery mildew and rust can be problems during dry summers.

Ageratum houstonianum 'Adriatic'

Ageratum houstonianum 'Bavaria'

Ageratum houstonianum 'Blue Mink'

***A. houstonianum* cultivars.** Selections from the fast-growing Mexican annual *A. houstonianum* are mostly compact, mound-forming, and of uniform habit. They have oval, downy leaves, 2–3in (5–8cm) long, heart-shaped at the bases. Rounded panicles, 2–4in (5–10cm) across, of 40 or more small flowerheads are borne just above the foliage from midsummer until first frost. ↕↔ 6–12in (15–30cm). **'Adriatic'** ■ is bushy, with clear, mid-blue flowerheads; ↕ 6–8in (15–20cm). **'Atlantic Plus'** has deep blue flowerheads; ↕ 6–8in (15–20cm). **'Bavaria'** ■ has blue-and-white flowerheads; ↕ 10in (25cm). **'Blue Danube'** bears many small, weather-resistant, lavender-blue flowerheads while plants are still young; ↕ 6–7in (15–18cm). **'Blue Horizon'** produces purple-blue, weather-resistant flowerheads on long, sturdy stems, good for cutting; ↕ 18in (45cm). **'Blue Mink'** ■ is vigorous and of relatively open habit, with powder-blue flowerheads; ↕ 8–12in (20–30cm). **Hawaii Series** includes uniform, compact plants, with deep to pale blue and white flowerheads. **'Hawaii White'** ■ has fluffy white flowerheads; ↕ to 6in (15cm). **'Pacific'** is neat, with tight clusters of deep violet-blue flowerheads; ↕ 8in (20cm). **'Swing Pink'** ■ is dwarf, with attractive pink flowerheads; ↕ 6–8in (15–20cm).

Ageratum houstonianum Hawaii Series 'Hawaii White'

Ageratum houstonianum 'Swing Pink'

AGLAONEMA

ARACEAE

Genus of about 20 species of usually rhizomatous, evergreen perennials from tropical forest in Asia. The leaf blades are borne on long, sheathing leaf stalks from a central growing point, and are variegated in many species. The stems are erect and cane-like, or short, decumbent, and creeping. Insignificant flowering spadices, enclosed in cream or greenish white spathes, are borne sporadically. Where not hardy, grow in a temperate or warm greenhouse or conservatory, or as houseplants; in frost-free areas, grow in a shady border.

- **CULTIVATION** Under glass, grow in well-drained, soilless or soil-based potting mix, in filtered light, with high humidity. Water moderately; allow some drying out between applications in winter; excess watering may encourage stem or root rot. Apply a balanced liquid fertilizer monthly in the growing season. Pot on every 2–3 years. Outdoors, grow in well-drained, moderately fertile, humus-rich soil in partial shade.

Aglaonema commutatum

• **PROPAGATION** Separate basal shoots with 3 or 4 leaves, ideally with roots attached, or divide in spring. Cuttings may be rooted in soil or water at any time.
• **PESTS AND DISEASES** Mealybugs and scale insects can be persistent problems. Bacterial and fungal stem rots are serious on overwatered plants. Fungal leaf spots are very common during propagation. Dasheen mosaic virus is sometimes present.

A. commutatum ▣ Erect perennial, becoming decumbent with age. Leaf stalks, to 6in (15cm) long, bear oblong-elliptic, dark green leaf blades, feathered and barred silver-gray, and 12in (30cm) long. ↕↔ 20in (50cm). Philippines, Indonesia (Sulawesi). ❀ (min. 55°F/13°C)
'Malay Beauty', syn. 'Pewter', has green-marbled white stems and yellow- and green-mottled leaf blades, 12in (30cm) long, with white veins; **'Pewter'** see 'Malay Beauty'. **'Pseudobracteatum'** ▣ produces narrowly elliptic leaf blades, 8in (20cm) long, which are mid- to dark green, with irregular white and pale green markings radiating from the leaf veins; ↕↔ 24in (60cm). **'Treubii'** ▣ is compact, with narrowly lance-shaped, pointed, gray-green leaf blades, 10in (25cm) long, irregularly marked with silver or pale green; ↕↔ 16in (40cm).
A. costatum. Rhizomatous, creeping perennial with leaf stalks to 5in (13cm) long, bearing ovate to lance-shaped, dark green leaf blades, 8in (20cm) long, with broad white midribs, and spotted white on both surfaces. ↕↔ 30in (75cm). Malaysia. ❀ (min. 55°F/13°C)
A. crispum, syn. *A. roebelinii* (Painted drop-tongue). Erect perennial with lance-shaped to elliptic, leathery, silvery gray-green leaf blades, 8in (20cm) long, with dark green margins, on leaf stalks to 10in (25cm) long. ↕↔ 4ft (1.2m). Philippines. ❀ (min. 55°F/13°C)
A. modestum. Erect perennial bearing lance-shaped to ovate, waxy, glossy, dark green leaf blades, 8in (20cm) long, with wavy margins, on leaf stalks 4–8in (10–20cm) long. ↕↔ 24in (60cm). S. China to N. Thailand. ❀ (min. 45°F/7°C)
A. nitidum. Erect perennial with leaf stalks, 4½–10in (11–25cm) long, and narrowly elliptic to narrowly lance-shaped dark green leaf blades, 18in (45cm) long, barred or blotched white.

Aglaonema commutatum 'Pseudobracteatum'

Aglaonema commutatum 'Treubii'

↕↔ 3ft (1m). S. Myanmar, Malaysia, Sumatra, Borneo. ❀ (min. 55°F/13°C)
'Cutisii' has leaves with silver-striped primary veins.
A. pictum ▣ Erect perennial producing narrowly elliptic to oval, wavy-margined leaf blades, 8in (20cm) long, lustrous bluish green in color, and irregularly marked with pale green and silvery gray, on leaf stalks 2–2½in (5–6cm) long. ↕↔ 24in (60cm). Indonesia (Sumatra). ❀ (min. 55°F/13°C)
A. roebelinii see *A. crispum.*
***A.* 'Silver King'.** Upright perennial bearing lance-shaped leaf blades, 12in (30cm) long, light to dark green, strongly suffused silver, and with short-pointed tips, on leaf stalks to 4in (10cm) long. ↕↔ 24in (60cm). ❀ (min. 55°F/13°C)

Aglaonema pictum

AGONIS

MYRTACEAE

Genus of 10–12 species of evergreen shrubs and small trees from dry to seasonally moist scrub., often near te sea, in Western Australia. they are grown mainly for their small, 5-petaled, fragrant flowers, which are produced in clusters from the upper leaf axils. The alternate leaves vary from ovate to lance-shaped. Where not hardy, overwinter in a cool greenhouse. In frost-free areas, grow *A. flexuosa* as an elegant specimen tree; smaller species are effective in a border or against a wall.
• **CULTIVATION** Under glass, grow in well-drained, acidic potting mix in full light, with good ventilation. In the growing season, water moderately and apply a balanced liquid fertilizer monthly; water more sparingly in winter. Outdoors, grow in moist but well-drained, moderately fertile, neutral to slightly acidic soil in full sun; established plants will tolerate partial shade and dry spells. Pruning group 8, but pruning is best kept to a minimum.
• **PROPAGATION** Sow seed at 61°F (16°C) in spring. Root semi-ripe cuttings with bottom heat in sumer.
• **PESTS AND DISEASES** Prone to scale insects and spider mites under glass.

A. flexuosa (Peppermint tree, Willow myrtle). Bushy tree, willow-like in growth, with pendent branches and lance-shaped, bright green leaves, 2–6in (5–15cm) long. Numerous axillary clusters of 2 or 3 white flowers, ½in (1.5cm) across, are produced in summer. ↕ 20–40ft (6–12m), ↔ 20–40ft (5–10m). S.W. Australia. ❀ (min. 45°F/7°C)

AGROPYRON

POACEAE

Genus of 40 species of coarse-textured, noncreeping, bud-type grasses, native to Eurasia, and adapted for hay and pasture. The leaves are 12in (30cm) long; pectinate spikelets are 2–14in (5–35cm) long.
• **CULTIVATION** Grow lawns in semi-arid conditions. These grasses are able to survive draught conditions because of their extensive, deep root system.
• **PROPAGATION** Sow grain 2¾in (7cm).
• **PESTS AND DISEASES** Infrequent.

A. cristatum (Fairway crested wheatgrass). ↕ 12in (30cm). Russia, Siberia. Zone 4.

AGROSTEMMA

Corn cockle

CARYOPHYLLACEAE

Genus of 2–4 species of erect, branching annuals from scrub, stony slopes, and cultivated fields in S. Europe, the Mediterranean, and W. Asia. They have linear, opposite leaves and, in summer, bear usually solitary, 5-petaled, open trumpet-shaped flowers with long-toothed calyces. The stems are slender and covered with a soft down. Grow in a border, a cottage garden, or in containers. *A. githago* is a noxious agricultural weed in some areas. The flowers are suitable for cutting and are attractive to bees. Seeds may cause severe discomfort if ingested.

Agrostemma githago 'Milas'

• **CULTIVATION** Grow in preferably poor, well-drained soil in full sun. The lax growth needs staking. Deadhead to prolong flowering.
• **PROPAGATION** Sow seed *in situ* as soon as ripe, or in early spring; thin seedlings to 9–12in (23–30cm) apart. For summer-flowering container plants, sow seed in autumn, overwinter in a cold frame, and then pot up the following spring.
• **PESTS AND DISEASES** Fungal leaf spots.

A. coeli-rosa see *Silene coeli-rosa.*
A. githago. Summer-flowering annual with linear to lance-shaped, gray-green leaves, to 3in (8cm) long. Produces magenta-purple, sometimes white-eyed, or white flowers, to 2in (5cm) across, with ribbed, hairy calyces. ↕ 24–36in (60–90cm), ↔ 12in (30cm). Mediterranean. **'Milas'** ▣ syn. 'Rose Queen', has deep plum-pink flowers. **'Milas Cerise'**, syn. 'Purple Queen', has cerise-pink flowers, darker than 'Milas'. **'Purple Queen'** see 'Milas Cerise'. **'Rose Queen'** see 'Milas'.

AGROSTIS

POACEAE

Genus of 120–150 species of annual and perennial grasses found at high altitudes in tropical regions and temperate zones; some species are important fodder grasses, while others are used in fine lawn-seed mixtures. A few annual species with light, airy panicles are suitable for a border and for cutting and drying. The perennial species are more commonly cultivated and are useful for the front of a border or a wildflower meadow.
• **CULTIVATION** Grow in well-drained soil in full sun. *A. canina* thrives in all but very dry soils in sun or partial shade. Deadhead before seed is set.
• **PROPAGATION** Divide between midspring and early summer.
• **PESTS AND DISEASES** Brown patch, slow decline, and rust are common. Powdery mildew and smut are widespread. Many other fungal diseases are also common.

A. canina (Brown bent, Velvet bent). Mat-forming, evergreen perennial with short stolons and erect, rounded stemsbearing flat, slightly rough, linear, mid-green leaves, 2½in (6cm) long. From early to late summer, bears slender panicles, to 4½in (11cm) long, of shiny, reddish brown spikelets. ↕ 2½in (6cm),

↔ 12in (30cm) or more. Europe, Asia, N.E. US. Zone 3. **'Silver Needles'** has leaf blades with silvery white margins.
A. stolonifera (Creeping bent). Evergreen, stoloniferous perennial grass with initially rolled then flat, rough, bluish green leaves, to 4in (10cm) long, and smooth, rounded stems. Airy, narrowly conical panicles, to 5in (13cm) long, of green to pink-purple spikelets are borne in mid- and late summer. ↕ to 30in (75cm), ↔ to 3ft (1m) or more. Europe, Asia, North America. Zone 3.
A. tenuis (Colonial bent, Rhode Island bent). Low-growing, cool-season grass with a small, dense terminal spray. Spikelets are not crowded; glumes are scabrous only on keels. Can be mowed to ¾in (2cm). ↕ 4in (10cm), ↔ ⅛in (3mm). Europe, Asia, North America. Zone 4.

AICHRYSON

CRASSULACEAE

Genus of about 10 annual or perennial succulents, mostly from hilly areas of the Azores, Madeira, and the Canary Islands. They have erect, often forked stems and rosettes of mid- to dark green, mainly alternate, hairy leaves, produced close to the stem tips. Panicles or cymes of star-shaped yellow or red flowers are borne from late spring to summer. Where not hardy, grow in a temperate greenhouse or as houseplants.
• **CULTIVATION** Under glass, grow in standard cactus potting mix or soil-based potting mix, with additional grit, in full or bright filtered light. Water moderately at all times, and apply a balanced liquid fertilizer 3 or 4 times when in growth. Outdoors, grow in an open site in poor to moderately fertile, well-drained soil in full sun. See also pp.48–49.
• **PROPAGATION** Sow seed at 66–75°F (19–24°C) in spring; flowers are usually borne after 2 years. Root cuttings of rosettes in spring or early summer.
• **PESTS AND DISEASES** Susceptible to mealybugs and aphids.

***A. x domesticum* 'Variegatum'** ■ syn. *Aeonium domesticum* 'Variegatum'. Shrubby, branching, perennial succulent with rosettes of diamond-shaped or obovate to ovate, finely hairy, dark green leaves, ¾–2in (2–5cm) long, margined and marbled white or creamy white. Occasionally produces shoots with only creamy white or white leaves. In early summer, bears panicles of bright yellow flowers, ½–¾in (1.5–2cm) wide. ↕ 6in (15cm) or more, ↔ 16in (40cm). ❄ (min. 45°F/7°C; optimum 55–79°F/13–26°C)
A. sedifolium see *Aeonium sedifolium.*
A. villosum. Densely branched, annual or short-lived perennial succulent with sticky, usually rough, white-hairy stems and diamond-shaped, mid-green leaves, to 1¼in (3cm) long, densely covered with long hairs. Produces cymes of yellow flowers, to ½in (1.5cm) wide, which are borne in late spring. ↕ 8in (20cm), ↔ to 16in (40cm). Azores, Madeira. ❄ (min. 45°F/7°C; optimum 55–79°F/13–26°C)

Aichryson x *domesticum* 'Variegatum'

AILANTHUS

SIMAROUBACEAE

Genus of 5 species of deciduous trees and shrubs occurring in woodland in China and from S.E. Asia to Australia, with large, alternate, pinnate leaves. *A. altissima* is sometimes grown as a specimen tree, for its striking foliage and colorful, winged fruit. Individual plants usually have either male or female flowers; both are needed to produce fruit. Male flowers are unpleasantly scented and their pollen may cause an allergic reaction.
• **CULTIVATION** Grow in deep, fertile, well-drained soil in sun or partial shade, although *A. altissima* is extremely tolerant of very poor soil and pollution and may be an option for planting where few other woody ornamentals would survive. Suckers and seedlings may be problems with *A. altissima.* Pruning group 1; train as a central leader standard or prune hard annually to grow as a large-leaved shrub.
• **PROPAGATION** Sow seed in containers in a cold frame as soon as ripe, or in spring. Remove and pot up suckers or take root cuttings in winter.
• **PESTS AND DISEASES** *Verticillium* wilt, fungal stem galls, and *Cristulariella* rust.

A. altissima ■ (Tree of heaven). Spreading tree with large, oblong-elliptic, pinnate, malodorous leaves, to 24in (60cm) long, composed of up to 30 ovate to lance-shaped leaflets, which open reddish green and later turn mid-green. Bears terminal panicles, to 12in (30cm) across, of small green flowers in summer, followed by red-brown fruit, similar to those of ash (*Fraxinus*). ↕ 80ft (25m), ↔ 50ft (15m). China, naturalized widely in United States. Zone 6.

Ailanthus altissima

Aiphanes caryotifolia

AIPHANES

Ruffle palm

ARECACEAE

Genus of about 40 species of single-stemmed, spiny, monoecious palms from dry forest in the West Indies and Central and South America. The pinnate leaves are arranged in terminal tufts, and small, cup-shaped flowers are borne in panicles among them. Where not hardy, grow young plants as foliage specimens in a temperate or warm greenhouse. In frost-free areas, grow as specimen trees.
• **CULTIVATION** Under glass, grow in soil-based potting mix, with additional leaf mold, in full light. When in growth, water freely and apply a balanced liquid fertilizer monthly; water more sparingly in winter. Outdoors, grow in fertile, moist but well-drained soil in full sun.
• **PROPAGATION** Sow seed at 77–86°F (25–30°C) in spring.
• **PESTS AND DISEASES** Spider mites may be a problem under glass. Many fungal leaf diseases, *Ganoderma* butt rot, and lethal yellowing are common.

A. caryotifolia ■ (Ruffle palm, Spine palm). Slender-stemmed palm, ringed with spines, and producing pinnate leaves, 3–10ft (1–3m) long, with prickly stalks and 4–10 strap-shaped, light to mid-green leaflets. In summer, bears yellow flowers in panicles, to 5ft (1.5m) long, followed by spherical red or yellow fruit. ↕ 20–40ft (6–12m), ↔ 8–10ft (2.5–3m). N. South America. ❄ (min. 45°F/7°C)

AIRA

Hair grass

POACEAE

Genus of 8 or 9 species of annual, sometimes biennial grasses from dry, open areas in Europe, the Mediterranean, N. Africa, and mountainous regions of tropical Africa, the Middle East, and N. and W. Asia. They have linear, often inrolled leaves. Several species are cultivated for their delicate, lax, finely branched flower panicles, and provide good cut or dried flowers. Grow hair grasses at the front of a border.
• **CULTIVATION** Grow in any well-drained soil in sun or partial shade.
• **PROPAGATION** Sow seed *in situ* from spring to early summer.
• **PESTS AND DISEASES** A few fungal diseases occur infrequently.

A. elegantissima (Hair grass). Tufted annual grass with linear, inrolled, mid-green leaves, to 2in (5cm) long. Open, diffuse panicles, to 4in (10cm) long, of small silvery or purple spikelets, ¹⁄₁₆–⅛in (2–3mm) long, are borne on hair-fine branches in late spring and early summer. ↕ 12in (30cm), ↔ 10in (25cm). Mediterranean.
A. flexuosa see *Deschampsia flexuosa.*

AJANIA

ASTERACEAE

Genus of 30 species of low-growing, mound-forming perennials, subshrubs, or shrubs from exposed, rocky hillsides in C. and E. Asia. The leaves are shallowly lobed to pinnatifid, and often white-woolly or silky. In summer and autumn, they bear attractive racemes or branched corymbs of buttonlike yellow flowerheads, with broadly bell-shaped involucres and tubular to cup-shaped disk florets. They make a suitable addition to a sunny rock garden or herbaceous border, particularly in areas with poor soil. They are also good for pot culture in an alpine house.
• **CULTIVATION** Grow in poor to moderately fertile, well-drained soil in full sun. They do not tolerate standing water in winter.
• **PROPAGATION** Sow seed in containers in a cold frame in spring. Divide runners in spring, or take basal cuttings in spring or summer.
• **PESTS AND DISEASES** Infrequent.

A. pacifica ■ syn. *Chrysanthemum pacificum, Dendranthema pacificum.* Low-mound-forming perennial or subshrub with short runners and lobed, ovate, silky-white, silver-margined, mid-green leaves to 2in (5cm) long. Small yellow flowerheads, to ¾in (2cm) across, are borne in branched corymbs, to 4in (10cm) across, in autumn. Needs a longer growing season to flower; otherwise, grow for foliage. ↕ 12in (30cm), ↔ 36in (90cm). C. and E. Asia. Zone 6.

Ajania pacifica

A

AJUGA

Bugleweed

LAMIACEAE

Genus of about 40 species of annuals and clump-forming or spreading, evergreen or semi-evergreen, usually rhizomatous perennials found in shady habitats throughout temperate Europe and Asia. The attractive leaves are opposite and entire, or occasionally toothed, and the 2-lipped, tubular, usually blue flowers are produced in whorls from the axils of leaf-like bracts from spring to early summer. Bugleweeds are excellent as a groundcover, spreading freely from rhizomes or stolons, especially in moist conditions.

• **CULTIVATION** Grow in any moist soil in partial shade or part-day sun, since the foliage may scorch in full sun. *A. reptans* and its cultivars will tolerate poor soils, even in full shade. *A. reptans* can invade lawns.

• **PROPAGATION** Separate rooted stems, or root cuttings, in early summer. Divide *A. pyramidalis* 'Metallica Crispa' every 2–3 years to maintain vigor.

• **PESTS AND DISEASES** Southern blight is very common. Various fungal leaf spots, crown rot, and occasionally a fungal root rot also occur.

A. genevensis ■ (Blue bugleweed, Upright bugleweed). Clump-forming, densely hairy to almost hairless, evergreen perennial, rhizomatous but without stolons, and with upright stems to 16in (40cm) long. Long-stalked, mid- or light green, obovate, basal leaves, to 5in (13cm) long, are shallowly lobed or toothed. In spring, bears spike-like whorls, to 4in (10cm) tall, of bright indigo-blue (sometimes pink or white) flowers, ¾in (2cm) long. ↕ 8–16in (20–40cm), ↔ 18in (45cm). S. Europe, S.W. Asia. Zone 3b.

A. metallica see *A. pyramidalis*.

A. pyramidalis, syn. *A. metallica* (Pyramidal bugleweed). Clump-forming,

Ajuga reptans

evergreen or semi-evergreen, rhizomatous perennial, without stolons, producing basal rosettes of obovate, slightly toothed, softly hairy, dark green leaves, to 4½in (11cm) long. Deep blue or pale violet-blue (sometimes pink or white) flowers, ¾in (2cm) long, are borne in dense, pyramidal, spike-like whorls, to 4in (10cm) tall, among purple-tinged bracts, from spring to early summer. ↕ 6–10in (15–25cm), sometimes to 12in (30cm), ↔ 18–24in (45–60cm). N. and C. Europe, Alps. Zone 3. **'Metallica Crispa'** forms tight cushions of crinkled and curled, metallic green-purple leaves; ↕ 6in (15cm), ↔ 12–16in (30–40cm).

A. reptans ■ (Carpet bugleweed, Common bugleweed). Creeping, evergreen, rhizomatous perennial, spreading rapidly by stolons, with partly hairy stems producing ovate to oblong-spoon-shaped, dark green leaves, 3½in (9cm) long. Dark blue flowers, ½in (1.5cm) long, are borne in spike-like whorls, to 6in (15cm) tall, in late spring and early summer. ↕ 6in (15cm), ↔ 24–36in (60–90cm) or more. Europe, Caucasus, Iran. Zone 3. **'Burgundy Glow'** has silvery green leaves suffused deep wine-red. **'Catlin's Giant'** has very large, dark bronze-purple leaves, to 6in (15cm) long, and produces inflorescences to 8in (20cm) long. **'Multicolor'** ■ syn. 'Rainbow', is mat-forming, with dark bronze-green leaves marked with cream and pink. **'Pink Elf'** is compact, with deep pink flowers on stems 2in (5cm) long. **'Rainbow'** see 'Multicolor'. **'Variegata'** is dense and slow spreading, with gray-green leaves margined and splashed cream.

AKEBIA

Chocolate vine

LARDIZABALACEAE

Genus of about 5 species of deciduous or semi-evergreen, twining climbers from forest margins in E. Asia, grown for their flowers and foliage. They have alternate, 3- to 5-, occasionally 7-palmate, mid-green leaves, often bronze-tinted when young. Racemes of self-sterile, shallowly cup-shaped flowers, with both sexes borne in each raceme, and with the larger, deeper-colored female flowers at the base, are produced in spring, followed by unusual, sausage-shaped, fleshy purple fruits. To ensure cross-pollination, grow 2 plants from the same species (not of the same clone). Grow against a wall or train into a tree or on an arbor or pergola. May become invasive.

• **CULTIVATION** Grow in moist but well-drained, fertile soil, in sun or partial shade. Pruning group 11, after flowering.

• **PROPAGATION** Sow seed in containers in a cold frame as soon as ripe. Root semi-ripe cuttings in summer. Layer in winter.

• **PESTS AND DISEASES** Twig dieback is sometimes a problem.

A. lobata see *A. trifoliata*.

A. x pentaphylla (*A. quinata* x *A. trifoliata*). Semi-evergreen climber with rounded leaves, 3in (8cm) long, divided into 3–5 (or more) ovate to obovate, sometimes shallowly lobed, mid-green leaflets, purple-tinged in winter. Fragrant purple flowers open in pendent racemes, to 5in (13cm) long, in early spring, followed by fruit, to 4in (10cm) long. ↕ 30ft (10m). Japan. Zone 6.

A. quinata ■ (Fiveleaf akebia, Chocolate vine). Semi-evergreen climber with rounded leaves, 1½–3in (4–8cm) long, composed of usually 5 oblong to obovate, entire leaflets, notched at the tips, dark green above, blue-green below, tinged purple in winter. Spicy-smelling, brownish purple flowers are borne in pendent racemes, to 5in (13cm) long, in early spring, followed by fruit to 4in (10cm) long. ↕ 30ft (10m). China, Korea, Japan. Zone 5b. **'Variegata'** has cream-splashed leaves.

A. trifoliata, syn. *A. lobata* (Three-leaf akebia). Deciduous climber with rounded leaves, 4in (10cm) long, composed of 3 broadly ovate, shallowly lobed leaflets, opening bronze, then turning glossy, dark green. Purple flowers are produced in pendent racemes, to 5in (13cm) long, in spring, and are followed by fruit, to 5in (13cm) long. ↕ 30ft (10m). China, Japan. Zone 6.

ALANGIUM

ALANGIACEAE

Genus of about 17 species of deciduous and evergreen trees, shrubs, and climbers from open scrub in tropical Africa and warm-temperate to tropical regions from E. Asia to E. Australia. *A. platanifolium*, the most commonly grown species, has attractive, alternate leaves and axillary cymes of unusual, tubular flowers. They are best grown in a shrub border.

• **CULTIVATION** Grow in fertile, well-drained soil in sun or partial shade. Where not reliably hardy, grow against a wall or among other plants for protection. Pruning group 1.

• **PROPAGATION** Sow seed in containers in a cold frame in autumn. Root semi-ripe cuttings in summer.

• **PESTS AND DISEASES** Infrequent.

A. platanifolium. Upright, deciduous shrub with rounded, maple-like, shallowly 3- to 7-lobed leaves, to 8in (20cm) long, dark green above and mid-green beneath. In summer, bears clusters of 4 (sometimes up to 7) tubular, fragrant white flowers, to 1½in (4cm) wide, with recurving petal lobes, followed by spherical to ovoid, deep purple-red fruit, to ½in (1.5cm) long. ↕ 10ft (3m), ↔ 6ft (2m). Korea, Japan. Zone 7.

ALBIZIA

syn. PARASERIANTHES

FABACEAE

Genus of about 150 species of deciduous trees, shrubs, and climbers, often found in poor soils, in tropical and subtropical regions from Africa and Asia to Australia. They are grown for their filigree foliage and attractive flowerheads of small florets with long stamens, which may be borne on plants only a few years old. The alternate, 2-pinnate leaves have numerous oblong-ovate to sickle-shaped leaflets. Where not hardy, overwinter in a cool greenhouse; elsewhere, grow as specimen plants.

• **CULTIVATION** Under glass, grow in soil-based potting mix in full light, with shade from hot sun. When in growth, water freely and apply a balanced liquid fertilizer monthly; water sparingly in winter. Pot on or top-dress in late winter. Outdoors, grow in poor to moderately fertile, well-drained soil in full sun. Pruning group 1, or 13 if wall-trained; plants under glass may need restrictive pruning in early spring.

Ajuga genevensis

Ajuga reptans 'Multicolor'

Akebia quinata

Albizia julibrissin var. *rosea*

• **PROPAGATION** Sow seed in spring, at not less than 59°F (15°C), after soaking for 24 hours in warm water. Root semi-ripe cuttings with bottom heat in summer. Take root cuttings in winter.
• **PESTS AND DISEASES** Spider mites and whiteflies may be problems under glass. A wide variety of fungi cause twig dieback and galls. In the landscape they may be prone to vascular wilts.

A. distachya see *A. lophantha.*
A. julibrissin (Mimosa, Silk tree). Large shrub or small tree with a domed crown when mature. Fern-like, light to mid-green leaves, 12–18in (30–45cm) long, have many small, sickle-shaped leaflets. Bears terminal clusters, 3–6in (7–15cm) wide, of spherical, pink or tannish pink flowerheads, 1½in (4cm) across, in summer. Grows quickly and is often short-lived. The numerous seedlings can become a nuisance. ↕ 20ft (6m), ↔ 12–20ft (4–6m). Iran to Japan. Zone 6. **var. *alba*** has white flowerheads. **var. *rosea*** ■ has clear pink flowerheads.
A. lophantha, syn. *A. distachya, Paraserianthes lophantha* (Cape wattle, Plume albizia, Swamp wattle). Erect to spreading, large shrub or small tree with fern-like, bright green leaves, 12in (30cm) long, with numerous small, oblong-ovate, lopsidedly pointed leaflets. In spring, tiny, yellow-green or gold flowerheads are produced in cylindrical, axillary spikes, 1¼–2½in (3–6cm) long. ↕ 6–30ft (2–10m), ↔ 3–10ft (1–3m). Western Australia. Zone 8.

ALBUCA

LILIACEAE

Genus of 30 species of bulbous perennials from grassland in the Middle East and Africa. Most of those cultivated come from South Africa, and have open tubular flowers and long, strap-shaped to lance-shaped or narrowly linear, deep green to gray-green, basal leaves. The narrowly bell-shaped or tubular flowers, ¾–1½in (2–4cm) across, are borne in loose racemes, and are usually white or yellow with a green or dull red central stripe on each tepal. Where not hardy, grow in a cool greenhouse; in frost-free areas, grow in an open, sunny site in a mixed border.
• **CULTIVATION** Plant bulbs 2in (5cm) deep in spring. Under glass, grow in sandy, soil-based potting mix in

Albuca humilis

full light. In the growing season, apply a balanced liquid fertilizer monthly. Water freely when flowering, more sparingly in spring and autumn; keep dry in winter. Pot on in spring, if required. Outdoors, grow in moderately fertile, well-drained soil in full sun.
• **PROPAGATION** Sow seed at 55–64°F (13–18°C) as soon as ripe, or remove offsets in autumn.
• **PESTS AND DISEASES** Infrequent.

A. canadensis, syn. *A. minor.* Bulbous perennial with 3–6 lance-shaped leaves, 6in (15cm) long. In late spring and early summer, produces up to 7 nodding, narrowly bell-shaped, pale yellow flowers, the tepals each with a wide green central stripe. ↕ 20in (50cm), PD8in (20cm). South Africa. ❄ (min. 45°F/7°C), although it may survive very brief spells to 23°F/-5°C.
A. humilis ■ Bulbous perennial with 1–3 narrowly linear leaves, 3–6in (7–15cm) long. Produces 1–3 narrowly bell-shaped white flowers in late spring and early summer. Outer tepals are green-striped; inner ones have yellow tips. ↕ 4in (10cm), PD2in (5cm). South Africa. ❄ (min. 41°F/5°C)
A. minor see *A. canadensis.*
A. nelsonii ■ Tall, bulbous perennial with 4–6 lance-shaped leaves, 3–4ft (90–120cm) long. In late spring and early summer, produces dense racemes of many, almost erect, tubular white flowers, the tepals each with a green, or occasionally dull red, central stripe. Good for cutting. ↕ 5ft (1.5m), PD8in (20cm). South Africa. ❄ (min. 45°F/7°C)

Albuca nelsonii

ALCEA

Hollyhock

MALVACEAE

Genus of about 60 species of biennials and short-lived perennials found in temperate regions of Europe and Asia, usually in rocky sites and on dry, grassy wasteland. They are cultivated for their tall, slender inflorescences of large, stalkless or short-stalked, funnel-shaped, 5-petaled, brightly colored flowers, often double in cultivars, which are borne in summer. Suitable for a mixed border, or for growing along a wall; they are attractive to butterflies and bees.
• **CULTIVATION** Grow in moderately fertile, well-drained soil in full sun. May require staking in exposed sites. Grow as annuals or biennials to limit the spread of hollyhock rust.
• **PROPAGATION** To grow as annuals, sow seed at 55°F (13°C) in late winter, or *in situ* in midspring. For biennials and perennials, sow seed *in situ* in midsummer. If required, transplant in early autumn, when 2 or 3 true leaves have developed.
• **PESTS AND DISEASES** Susceptible to hollyhock rust as well as bacterial and fungal leaf spots. Southern blight is quite common. Cutworms and slugs may damage young growth. Mallow flea beetles, aphids, Japanese beetles, and capsid bugs are sometimes problems.

A. ficifolia. Erect biennial or short-lived perennial with rounded, 5- to 7-lobed, conspicuously veined, rough, mid-green leaves, to 7in (18cm) long. Terminal spikes of single, sometimes double yellow flowers, 2–3in (5–8cm) across, are borne in early summer. ↕ to 8ft (2.5m), ↔ 36in (90cm). Siberia. Zone 3.
A. rosea, syn. *Althaea rosea* (Hollyhock). Vigorous, upright perennial producing rounded, roughly hairy, light green leaves, to 1½in (4cm) long, cut into 3–7 shallow lobes. Long, terminal racemes of single, purple, pink, white, or

Alcea rosea 'Chater's Double'

Alcea rosea 'Nigra'

yellow flowers, 2–4in (5–10cm) across, are borne in early and mid-summer. ↕ 5–8ft (1.5–2.5m), ↔ to 24in (60cm). Probably W. Asia. Zone 3. **'Chater's Double'** ■ bears double flowers in a range of bright colors and paler shades, including pink, apricot, red, white, lavender-blue, yellow, and purple; ↕ 6–8ft (2–2.5m). **'Indian Spring'** bears single, white, pink, or yellow flowers. **'Majorette'** is dwarf and bushy, bearing rosette-like, fringed, semi-double flowers in pale shades, including yellow, carmine, and apricot, in early summer, the first year from seed; ↕ 3ft (1m), ↔ to 12in (30cm). **'Nigra'** ■ has single, deep chocolate-maroon flowers with yellow throats; ↕ to 6ft (2m). **'Summer Carnival'** bears double flowers in colors such as pale yellow and red, in early summer, the first year from seed. Flowers are produced lower on the flowering stems than in other cultivars.

ALCHEMILLA

Lady's mantle

ROSACEAE

Genus of about 250 species of perennials from meadows and light woodland, some from rocky habitats, in N. temperate and arctic zones, and from mountain regions in tropical Africa, India, Sri Lanka, and Indonesia (Java). Alchemillas are valued for their attractive foliage and frothy sprays of flowers. Most have woody rhizomes and shallowly to palmately lobed, rounded or kidney-shaped, attractively pleated, often silky-haired leaves. The many-branched cymes of tiny, green or

Alchemilla alpina

yellowish green flowers, 1/16–1/8in (2–3mm) across, last long and are good for cutting. Alchemillas are suitable for a large rock garden, a border, or as a groundcover.

• **CULTIVATION** Grow in any moist, humus-rich soil in sun or partial shade. Deadhead *A. mollis* soon after flowering, since it self-seeds very freely. Cut back and water in summer to produce a fresh new flush of leaves in autumn.

• **PROPAGATION** Sow seed in containers in a cold frame in spring. Transplant seedlings while small. Divide in early spring or autumn.

• **PESTS AND DISEASES** Slugs and snails may damage young foliage.

A. alpina ■ (Alpine lady's mantle). Mat-forming perennial with a creeping, woody rootstock and rounded or kidney-shaped, very deeply 5- to 7-lobed leaves, to 1½in (4cm) long, deep green and smooth above, silver-hairy beneath, with toothed tips. Loose cymes of tiny, yellow-green flowers are borne on stems 3–5in (8–13cm) long, in summer. Often confused with *A. conjuncta*. ↕ 3–5in (8–13cm), ↔ to 20in (50cm). N. Europe, mountains of W. and C. Europe, Greenland. Zone 4.

A. conjuncta ■ Clump-forming, spreading perennial producing rounded, very deeply 7- to 9-lobed leaves, 1½–1¾in (4–4.5cm) long, blue-green above and silver-hairy beneath. Cymes of tiny, greenish yellow flowers are borne from early summer to early autumn. ↕ 16in (40cm), ↔ 12in (30cm). Jura Mountains, S.W. Alps. Zone 3.

Alchemilla conjuncta

Alchemilla mollis

A. ellenbeckii. Evergreen, mat-forming perennial with wiry red stems and small, kidney-shaped, deeply 5-lobed, pale green leaves, to ¾in (2cm) long. Bears tiny, yellow-green flowers in loose cymes in summer. Flowers resemble those of *A. alpina*, but are fewer, on shorter stems, and almost hidden by the foliage. Thrives in moist but well-drained soil. ↕ 1–2in (2.5–5cm), ↔ 12in (30cm) or more. Mountains of E. Africa. Zone 6b.

A. erythropoda. Clump-forming perennial with rounded, shallowly 7- to 9-lobed, sharp-toothed, hairy, bluish green leaves, 1¼–2in (3–5cm) long. Cymes of yellowish green flowers are produced from late spring to late summer. ↕ 8–12in (20–30cm), ↔ 8in (20cm). Carpathian and Balkan mountains, Caucasus, Turkey. Zone 4.

A. faeroensis. Clump-forming perennial producing kidney-shaped, deeply 7- to 9-lobed leaves, 1½–1¾in (4–4.5cm) long, blue-green above and silver-hairy beneath. Cymes of tiny, greenish yellow flowers are borne from early summer to early autumn. ↕ 16in (40cm), ↔ 12in (30cm). E. Iceland. Zone 3.

A. fulgens, syn. *A. splendens* of gardens. Spreading, rhizomatous perennial with rounded, shallowly 7- to 9-lobed, toothed, hairy leaves, 1¾–2in (4.5–5cm) long, blue-green above and silvery green beneath. Cymes of greenish yellow flowers are borne from early to late summer. ↕ 12in (30cm), ↔ 10in (25cm). Pyrenees. Zone 4b.

A. mollis ■ Clump-forming perennial with rounded, shallowly 9- to 11-lobed, toothed, densely softly hairy, pale green leaves, to 6in (15cm) long. Bears loose cymes of many tiny, greenish yellow flowers from early summer to early autumn. Drought tolerant. Excellent as a groundcover and for providing long-lasting cut flowers. ↕ 24in (60cm), ↔ 30in (75cm). E. Carpathians, Caucasus, Turkey. Zone 4b.

***A. splendens* of gardens** see *A. fulgens*.

A. xanthochlora. Clump-forming perennial producing kidney-shaped, shallowly 9- to 11-lobed, often yellowish green leaves, 2in (5cm) long, hairless above and hairy beneath, with hairy leaf stalks. Cymes of tiny, yellow-green flowers are borne in profusion from early to late summer. ↕ 20in (50cm), ↔ 24in (60cm). N.W. and C. Europe, Greece. Zone 4.

ALEURITES

EUPHORBIACEAE

Genus of 6 species of evergreen trees from tropical to subtropical rainforest and moist woodland in China, Indonesia, and W. Pacific islands. The usually alternate leaves are shallowly lobed or entire. The small, 5-petaled white flowers are borne in terminal, panicle-like cymes, followed by fruits containing oil-bearing seeds. Where temperatures fall below 45°F (7°C), grow in a cool greenhouse. In warmer areas, grow as shade or specimen trees.

• **CULTIVATION** Under glass, grow in acidic potting mix in full light. In the growing season, water freely and apply a balanced liquid fertilizer monthly; water sparingly in winter. Outdoors, grow in fertile, moist but well-drained, neutral to acidic soil in full sun; they will tolerate partial shade. Pruning group 1; plants under glass may need restrictive pruning.

• **PROPAGATION** Sow seed at 55–64°F (13–18°C) as soon as ripe or in spring. Root semi-ripe cuttings in late summer.

• **PESTS AND DISEASES** Prone to spider mites and whiteflies under glass. Branch canker and dieback caused by a variety of fungi are common.

A. fordii (China wood-oil tree, Tung-oil tree). Erect to spreading tree with ovate, pointed, 3-lobed, light green leaves, to 10in (25cm) long, mostly arranged in whorls. Red-tinted white flowers are borne in panicle-like cymes, 4–6in (10–15cm) long, in summer, followed by spherical, greenish brown fruit, 2½–3in (6–8cm) across. ↕ 15–22ft (5–7m), ↔ 10–20ft (3–6m). W. and C. China. ❄ (min. 45°F/7°C), although it may tolerate periods around 32°F (0°C).

x ALICEARA

ORCHIDACEAE

Hybrid genus of evergreen, epiphytic orchids that are crosses between *Brassia*, *Miltonia*, and *Oncidium*. Basal rhizomes produce groups of oval pseudobulbs, each pseudobulb bearing 2 narrowly oval, mid-green leaves with pointed tips. Up to 12 long-lasting, star-shaped flowers, varying in size and color, are borne in racemes from the bases of the pseudobulbs at various times.

• **CULTIVATION** Cool-growing orchids. Grow in epiphytic orchid potting mix in the smallest possible containers; they respond well to yearly repotting. Provide shady, well-ventilated conditions and high humidity in summer; remove shading in winter. Water moderately throughout the year, more sparingly in winter. In summer, spray the foliage lightly with water once or twice a day; apply a half-strength fertilizer at every third watering. See also p.46.

• **PROPAGATION** Divide before the plant overgrows its container.

• **PESTS AND DISEASES** Aphids, whiteflies, spider mites, and mealybugs may be problems. Bacterial soft rot, and basal stem and leaf rot caused by *Rhizoctonia*, can also occur.

***A.* 'Dark Warrior'** ■ Evergreen hybrid orchid with oval pseudobulbs and oval leaves, 9in (23cm) long. Racemes of up to 12 flowers, each 1½in (4cm) across, typically brown with cream lips, are borne throughout the year. ↕ 10in (25cm), ↔ 12in (30cm). ❄ (min. 52–55°F/11–13°C; max. 75°F/24°C)

Aliceara 'Dark Warrior'

ALISMA

Water plantain

ALISMATACEAE

Genus of 9 species of rhizomatous, deciduous, marginal aquatic perennials from temperate regions of the N. hemisphere, southern Africa, and from Australia. Basal rosettes of plantain-like leaves, with long leaf stalks and elliptic to lance-shaped leaf blades, are held above the water surface in spring. Whorled, umbel-like panicles of 3-petaled, saucer-shaped, white or pink flowers are borne above the foliage in mid- and late summer. Grow in large groups or drifts at pool margins. *A. plantago-aquatica* is ideal for a large pond and for naturalizing in a lake.

• **CULTIVATION** Flowering is most profuse in water 6in (15cm) deep; they will tolerate water up to 12in (30cm) deep. *A. plantago-aquatica* self-seeds freely; deadhead regularly once established. See also pp.52–53.

• **PROPAGATION** Sow seed as soon as ripe in seed trays or pots half submerged in shallow trays of water. Divide tuber-like rhizomes in late spring, or detach rooted plantlets that form along flowering stems.

• **PESTS AND DISEASES** Infrequent.

A. gramineum. Aquatic perennial with growth above the water surface, or submerged to a depth of 9in (23cm). Above water, the dark green leaves are elliptic to lance-shaped, and 4in (10cm) long; submerged, they are linear, and to 18in (45cm) long. White or pinkish white flowers, to ¼in (6mm) across, are borne in dense panicles, 5–6in (12–15cm) tall. ↕↔ 6–8in (15–20cm). Europe, N. Africa, W. Asia, North America. Zone 5.

A. lanceolatum. Aquatic perennial that thrives in water 8–9in (20–23cm) deep. Lance-shaped, bluish green leaves, to 12in (30cm) long, often smaller, grow above water. Bears panicles, 8–28in (20–70cm) tall, of purplish pink flowers, to ½in (1.5cm) across. ↕ 20–28in (50–70cm), ↔ 9in (23cm). Europe, Africa, C. and S.W. Asia. Zone 5b.

Alisma plantago-aquatica

A. plantago-aquatica ▣ (Mad-dog weed). Aquatic perennial with rosettes of elliptic to lance-shaped, grayish green leaves, to 12in (30cm) long, heart-shaped at the bases, with pointed tips, borne on long stalks above the water. Bears white or pinkish white flowers, to ½in (1.5cm) wide, in panicles 8–30in (20–75cm) tall. ↕ 24–30in (60–75cm), ↔ 18in (45cm). Europe, N. and southern Africa, E. Asia, North America. Zone 4.

ALKANNA

BORAGINACEAE

Genus of 30–40 species of annuals or evergreen, clump-forming perennials, mostly found in scree and rock crevices from S. Europe to Iran. Few species are cultivated. They have basal tufts of alternate leaves, 3–6in (8–15cm) long, which are usually entire and hairy. They are grown for their funnel-shaped or salverform, bright blue flowers, borne in erect, terminal cymes on leafy stems in early summer. Best grown in a raised scree bed or alpine house.

• **CULTIVATION** Outdoors, grow in sharply drained soil in a raised scree bed, protected from winter moisture; alternatively, grow in an alpine house in very gritty potting mix. Water moderately in the growing season; keep just moist in winter; avoid wetting the foliage.

• **PROPAGATION** Sow seed in containers in a cold frame in autumn, or root softwood cuttings in summer.

• **PESTS AND DISEASES** Prone to aphids and spider mites under glass.

A. incana. Low, mound-forming, evergreen perennial with linear to lance-shaped, very hairy, gray-green leaves, to 6in (15cm) long, and salverform, bright blue flowers, ½in (1.5cm) across, on stiff stems, to 1½–2in (4–5cm) long. Needs good drainage. ↕ 2–6in (5–15cm), ↔ 2–4in (5–10cm). Turkey. Zone 8.

ALLAMANDA

syn. ALLEMANDA

APOCYNACEAE

Genus of 12 species of evergreen shrubs and scandent climbers from scrub and forest in tropical North, Central, and South America. They have simple leaves, which may be alternate, opposite, or whorled, and are grown for their showy, usually terminal cymes of large, funnel- or trumpet-shaped flowers, each with 5 broad petal lobes. These are followed by spiny seed capsules. Where temperatures fall to 45°F (7°C), grow in a temperate or warm greenhouse or in a large container. In warmer areas, grow in a border or on a wall. Contact with sap may irritate skin; all parts may cause mild stomach upset if ingested.

• **CULTIVATION** Under glass, grow in soil-based potting mix in full light. Water freely when in growth, applying a balanced liquid fertilizer every 2–3 weeks; water sparingly in winter. Outdoors, grow in moist, fertile soil in full sun. Pruning group 11 or 12 in late winter or early spring.

• **PROPAGATION** Sow seed at 64–68°F (18–20°C) in spring. Root greenwood cuttings in late spring or early summer.

• **PESTS AND DISEASES** Spider mites and whiteflies are common problems. A variety of fungal leaf spots can occur.

A. blanchetii, syn. *A. violacea.* Erect shrub or semi-scandent climber, with whorls of 4 oblong-obovate leaves, 3–5in (8–13cm) long. From summer to autumn, produces axillary and terminal cymes of trumpet-shaped flowers, 2½–3½in (6–9cm) long, which are purplish pink, deeper toned inside. ↕↔ 6–10ft (2–3m). South America. ❄ (min. 45–50°F/7–10°C), although it may survive short spells at 32°F/0°C.
A. cathartica (Golden trumpet). Strong-growing climber with whorls of 3 or 4 lance-shaped to obovate leaves, 4–6in (10–15cm) long. Axillary and terminal cymes of yellow flowers, 5in (13cm) or more long, are borne from summer to autumn. ↕ 25–52ft (8–16m). Central and South America. ❄ (min. 45–50°F/7–10°C), although it may survive short spells at 32°F/0°C. **'Hendersonii'** ▣ has bronze-tinted buds that open to bright yellow flowers, sometimes white-flecked in the throats. **'Nobilis'** has large, whorled leaves and very large golden flowers.
A. violacea see *A. blanchetii.*

Allamanda cathartica 'Hendersonii'

ALLIUM

Onion

LILIACEAE

Genus of about 700 species of spring-, summer-, and autumn-flowering, bulbous and rhizomatous perennials, mainly from dry and mountainous areas of the N. hemisphere. In most species, a single bulb produces clusters of offset bulbs around it, which gradually form clumps. A few species have elongated bulbs, which develop on short, fleshy rhizomes; some produce bulbils in the flowerheads. The upright to spreading, sometimes cylindrical, linear to strap-shaped, basal or stem-clasping leaves have a pungent aroma when crushed; they are often withered by flowering time. The tubular-based flowers are bell-, star-, or cup-shaped; they are borne, few to many, in usually spherical, sometimes hemispherical or ovoid, occasionally pendent umbels, mostly ½–4in (1–10cm) across, sometimes to 12in (30cm) across. Excellent planted in groups in a border; some have flowerheads that dry well. Grow shorter species at the front of a border or in a rock garden. Many seed freely and will naturalize. Contact with the bulbs may irritate skin or aggravate some skin allergies. Several species have culinary uses, including *A. schoenoprasum* (chives) and *A. tuberosum* (Chinese chives). Related plants include onion (*A. cepa*) and garlic (*A. sativum*).

• **CULTIVATION** Grow in fertile, well-drained soil in full sun. Plant bulbs 2–4in (5–10cm) deep in autumn; plant clump-forming species with rhizomes at, or just below, the soil surface in spring. Alliums from areas with hot, dry summers may be best grown in sandy, soil-based potting mix in an alpine house; keep dry when dormant.

• **PROPAGATION** Sow seed in containers in a cold frame, when ripe or in spring; sow seed of *A. schoenoprasum* in drills *in situ.* Some may take 2 years to germinate. Remove offsets of bulbous species in autumn. Divide clump-forming, rhizomatous species in spring.

• **PESTS AND DISEASES** Bulb rots caused by soil-borne fungi are common under damp conditions, especially immediately following planting. White rot, mildew, rust, smut, and various fungal leaf spots (such as purple blotch and gray mold) can also occur. Susceptible to onion fly and thrips.

Allium acuminatum

Allium aflatunense

A. acuminatum ▣ Bulbous perennial with linear, channeled, mid-green basal and stem-clasping leaves, 4–8in (10–20cm) long. Hemispherical umbels, 1½–2½in (4–6cm) across, of 10–30 star-shaped, pinkish purple, occasionally white or pale pink flowers are produced in early summer. ↕ 4–12in (10–30cm), PD2in (5cm). W. North America. Zone 5.
A. aflatunense ▣ Bulbous perennial with slightly ribbed stems and linear, mid-green, basal leaves, 12–24in (30–60cm) long. Dense umbels, 4in (10cm) across, of many star-shaped, purplish pink flowers, are produced in summer. ↕ 3ft (1m), PD4in (10cm). C. Asia. Zone 4b.
***A. aflatunense* of gardens** see *A.* x *hollandicum.*
A. akaka. Bulbous perennial with oblong-elliptic, gray-green, basal leaves, to 8in (20cm) long. Virtually stemless umbels, 2½in (6cm) across, of 30–40 small, star-shaped, lilac-pink flowers are borne in spring. ↕ 5in (13cm), PD4in (10cm). Caucasus, Turkey, Iran. Zone 4b.
A. albopilosum see *A. cristophii.*
A. azureum see *A. caeruleum.*
A. beesianum. Bulbous perennial with linear, gray-green, basal leaves, 6–8in (15–20cm) long, and umbels, 1in (2.5cm) across, of 6–12 pendent, bell-shaped, blue or white flowers, with short stamens, from late summer to autumn. ↕ 6–8in (15–20cm), PD2in (5cm). W. China. Zone 7.
A. bulgaricum see *Nectaroscordum siculum* subsp. *bulgaricum.*
A. caeruleum ▣ syn. *A. azureum.* Bulbous perennial with linear, mid-green, stem-clasping leaves, 3in (8cm)

Allium caeruleum

long, which die back before flowering. Dense umbels, 1in (2.5cm) across, of 30–50 small, star-shaped, bright blue flowers are borne on stiff stems in early summer. ↕ 24in (60cm), PD1in (2.5cm). N. and C. Asia. Zone 2.

A. callimischon. Bulbous perennial with grass-like, linear, mid-green, stem-clasping leaves, to 12in (30cm) long. Wiry stems bear loose umbels, 1in (2.5cm) across, of 8–25 cup-shaped, white or pale pink flowers in autumn. ↕ 3½–14in(9–35cm), PD2in (5cm). Greece, W. Turkey. Zone 6. **subsp. *haemostictum*** has white or pale pink flowers with maroon spots; Crete.

A. campanulatum. Bulbous perennial with linear, mid-green, stem-clasping leaves, to 12in (30cm) long, which die back at flowering time. Bears dense umbels, 1¼–2½in (3–6cm) across, of up to 20 cup-shaped, rose-pink flowers in summer. ↕ 4–12in (10–30cm), PD2in (5cm). California, Nevada. Zone 8.

A. carinatum. Bulbous perennial with linear, mid-green basal and stem-clasping leaves, to 8in (20cm) long. Bears loose umbels, 2in (5cm) across, of up to 30 bell-shaped purple flowers in midsummer, usually accompanied by bulbils; the outer flowers are pendent. Spreads rapidly, so best in informal plantings. ↕ 12–24in (30–60cm), PD2in (5cm). C. and S. Europe, Turkey, former USSR. Zone 3. **subsp. *pulchellum***, syn. *A. pulchellum*, has rich purple flowers in dense, elongated umbels, 2½in (6cm) across, with no bulbils. Virtually evergreen, since new leaves are produced with the flowers. Rapidly forms clumps, but is not invasive. ↕ 12–18in (30–45cm), PD2in (5cm). S. Europe. **subsp. *pulchellum* f. *album*** has white flowers.

A. cepa ▣ Widely cultivated as a vegetable; grows year round. Flattened, pale green leaves and long flower stems that may have bulbils around the flowerhead. Produces bunching, mini, sweet, and storage onions that can be red, yellow, or white. ↕ 4ft (1.2m), ↔ 3ft (1m). Northern Hemisphere. Zone 4.

A. christophii see *A. cristophii.*

A. cowanii see *A. neapolitanum.*

A. cristophii ▣ syn. *A. albopilosum*, *A. christophii* (Stars of Persia). Bulbous perennial with ribbed stems and strap-shaped, gray-green, basal leaves, 6–16in (15–40cm) long, with stiff marginal hairs. The leaves start to wither before

Allium cristophii

large umbels, 8in (20cm) across, of up to 100 star-shaped, pinkish purple flowers with a metallic sheen are borne in early summer. The flowerheads dry well. ↕ 12–24in (30–60cm), PD6–7in (15–19cm). Turkey, C. Asia. Zone 5.

A. cyaneum. Bulbous perennial with short rhizomes and thread-like, dark green, basal leaves, to 6in (15cm) long. Produces small umbels, ¾in (2cm) across, of 6 or more bell-shaped blue flowers in summer. ↕ 4–10in (10–25cm), PD3in (8cm). China. Zone 5.

A. cyathophorum* var. *farreri ▣ syn. *A. farreri.* Vigorous, bulbous perennial with narrowly strap-shaped, mid-green, basal leaves, 7–10in (18–25cm) long. In summer, bears loose umbels, ½in (1.5cm) across, of 6–30 small, pendent, bell-shaped, deep violet-purple flowers. ↕ 6–12in (15–30cm), PD2in (5cm). China. Zone 5.

A. dichlamydeum. Bulbous perennial with narrowly strap-shaped, short, mid-green, basal leaves, 4–8in (10–20cm) long. Bears thick-stemmed, compact umbels, 1½in (4cm) across, of up to 20 large, bell-shaped, pinkish purple flowers in early summer. ↕ 4–10in (10–25cm), PD2in (5cm). California. Zone 4b.

A. elatum see *A. macleanii.*

A. farreri see *A. cyathophorum* var. *farreri.*

A. flavum ▣ Very variable, bulbous perennial with cylindrical, narrowly strap-shaped, glaucous, stem-clasping leaves, to 8in (20cm) long. In summer, produces loose umbels, ½in (1.5cm) across, of up to 60 bell-shaped, bright yellow flowers with prominent stamens.

Allium flavum

The flowers bend downward as they open. ↕ 4–14in (10–35cm), PD2in (5cm). Europe, W. Asia. Zone 4.

A. giganteum ▣ Bulbous perennial with large, strap-shaped, pale green, basal leaves, 12–36in (30–90cm) long, which wither before flowering. In summer, bears dense umbels, 4in (10cm) across, of 50 or more star-shaped, lilac-pink flowers with prominent stamens. ↕ 5–6ft (1.5–2m), PD6in (15cm). C. Asia. Zone 5.

***A.* 'Globemaster'** ▣ Bulbous perennial with star-shaped, gray-green, basal leaves, 14–36in (35–90cm) long. Large umbels, 6–8in (15–20cm) across, of numerous star-shaped, deep violet flowers, are produced in summer. ↕ 32in (80cm), PD8in (20cm). Zone 5.

A.* x *hollandicum, syn. *A. aflatunense* of gardens. Bulbous perennial with unribbed stems and strap-shaped, mid-green, basal leaves, 12–24in (30–60cm) long, dying back at flowering time. Numerous star-shaped, purplish pink flowers are borne in dense umbels, 4in (10cm) across, in summer. Excellent for drying. ↕ 3ft (1m), PD4in (10cm). Garden origin. Zone 4.

A. insubricum. Bulbous perennial with short rhizomes and narrowly strap-shaped, mid-green, stem-sheathing leaves, 5–8in (12–20cm) long. Umbels, 1in (2.5cm) across, of 3–5 pendent, bell-shaped, pink-purple flowers are produced in summer, and are followed by pendent seed heads. Often confused with *A. narcissiflorum*, which has more flowers and erect seed heads. ↕ 6–10in (15–25cm), PD2in (5cm). N. Italy. Zone 5.

A. kansuense see *A. sikkimense.*

Allium 'Globemaster'

A. karataviense ▣ Bulbous perennial grown for its pairs of elliptic, almost horizontal, red-margined, gray-green or grayish purple, basal leaves, 6–9in (15–23cm) long. In summer, bears umbels, 2–3in (5–8cm) across, of 50 or more star-shaped, pale pink flowers with purple midribs. ↕ 4–10in (10–25cm), PD4in (10cm). C. Asia. Zone 4.

A. lemmonii. Bulbous perennial with sickle-shaped, grass-like, mid-green, basal leaves, 4–8in (10–20cm) long. In early summer, bears numerous tiny, star-shaped, white to pink flowers in umbels, 1½in (4cm) across. ↕ 4–6in (10–15cm), PD2in (5cm). California. Zone 6b.

***A.* 'Lucy Ball'.** Robust, bulbous perennial with strap-shaped, pale green, basal leaves, to 3ft (1m) long. In early summer, bears 50 or more star-shaped, dark lilac flowers in tight umbels, 2–3in (5–8cm) across. ↕ 3ft (1m), PD6in (15cm). Zone 5.

A. macleanii, syn. *A. elatum.* Bulbous perennial with deeply ridged stems and strap-shaped, glossy, mid-green, basal leaves, to 12in (30cm) long. In summer, bears umbels, 2–3in (5–8cm) across, of 50 or more star-shaped violet flowers, fading to rose-pink. ↕ 2–3½ft (60–110cm), PD6in (15cm). C. and S.E. Asia. Zone 5.

A. macranthum, syn. *A. oviflorum.* Bulbous perennial with short rhizomes and channeled, linear, mid-green, basal leaves, 6–18in (15–45cm) long. Loose umbels, 3–4in (7–10cm) across, of up to 20 pendent, bell-shaped, deep plum-purple flowers are produced in summer. ↕ 8–12in (20–30cm), PD2in (5cm). India (Sikkim), W. China. Zone 5.

Allium cepa

Allium cyathophorum var. *farreri*

Allium giganteum

Allium karataviense

Allium moly

A. mairei. Slender, bulbous perennial with short rhizomes and linear, grass-like, mid-green, basal leaves, to 10in (25cm) long. In late summer, bears loose umbels, 1in (2.5cm) across, of up to 10 bell-shaped, pale to bright pink flowers with red spots. ↕ 6–10in (15–25cm), PD2in (5cm). S.W. China. Zone 4b.
A. moly ■ (Golden garlic, Lily leek). Bulbous perennial with lance-shaped, gray-green, basal leaves, 8–12in (20–30cm) long, usually produced in pairs. In summer, bears dense umbels, 2in (5cm) across, of up to 30 star-shaped, bright golden yellow flowers. Increases rapidly and is ideal for naturalizing in light woodland or around shrubs. ↕ 6–10in (15–25cm), PD2in (5cm). S.W. and S. Europe. Zone 3. **'Jeannine'** flowers in early summer and has larger umbels, 3in (8cm) across, on stiff stems; ↕ 12–16in (30–40cm), PD3in (8cm).
A. multibulbosum see *A. nigrum.*
A. murrayanum see *A. unifolium.*
A. narcissiflorum, syn. *A. pedemontanum* of gardens. Bulbous perennial with short rhizomes and strap-shaped, gray-green, stem-sheathing leaves, 3½–7in (9–18cm) long. Pendent umbels, 1in (2.5cm) across, of up to 10 relatively large, bell-shaped, pink-purple flowers are borne in summer, followed by erect seed heads. Often confused with *A. insubricum*, which has fewer flowers and pendent seed heads. ↕ 6–14in (15–35cm), PD2in (5cm). Portugal, France, N. Italy. Zone 4.
A. neapolitanum ■ syn. *A. cowanii.* Bulbous perennial with linear-lance-shaped, mid-green, stem-sheathing leaves, 3–14in (8–35cm) long, which wither before flowering time. Umbels, 2in (5cm) across, of up to 30 star-shaped, pure white flowers are produced in summer. Excellent for cut flowers. ↕ 8–16in (20–40cm), PD2in (5cm). S. Europe, N. Africa. Zone 5.
A. neriniflorum see *Caloscordum neriniflorum.*
A. nigrum, syn. *A. multibulbosum.* Bulbous perennial with lance-shaped, gray-green, basal leaves, to 20in (50cm) long. In summer, bears flattish umbels, 3in (8cm) across, of 20–35 large, open cup-shaped flowers, usually creamy white, sometimes pale lilac, each with a prominent dark green ovary. ↕ 16–36in (40–90cm), PD3in (8cm). Mediterranean. Zone 5.

Allium neapolitanum

A. obliquum. Bulbous perennial with short rhizomes and linear, gray-green, stem-clasping leaves, to 14in (35cm) long. In midsummer, stiff stems bear dense umbels, 1in (2.5cm) across, of up to 50 or more cup-shaped, pale yellow-green flowers with protruding stamens. ↕ 24in (60cm), PD2in (5cm). Romania, C. Asia, Siberia. Zone 3.
A. oreophilum ■ syn. *A. ostrowskianum.* Bulbous perennial with linear, mid-green leaves, 4–6in (10–15cm) long, sheathing the lower part of the stems. In early summer, produces loose umbels, 1½in (4cm) across, of up to 15 long-lasting, bell-shaped, bright pinkish purple flowers. Each tepal has a darker midrib. ↕ 2–8in (5–20cm), PD1¼in (3cm). Caucasus, C. Asia. Zone 4. **'Zwanenburg'** has brighter, carmine flowers.
A. ostrowskianum see *A. oreophilum.*
A. oviflorum see *A. macranthum.*
A. paniculatum. Vigorous, bulbous perennial with linear, mid-green leaves, 10in (25cm) long, sheathing the lower part of the stems. In summer, produces ovoid umbels, 2in (5cm) across, of up to 40 bell-shaped, white, pink, or yellowish brown flowers, with prominent stamens; the flowers become pendent as they open. ↕ 12–28in (30–70cm), PD2in (5cm). Europe, C. Asia. Zone 3.
***A. pedemontanum* of gardens** see *A. narcissiflorum.*
A. porrum ■ (Leek). Large, upright, non-bulbing onion. Leaves 12in (30cm) long. Produces pink to white simple flowers on 3in (7.5cm) scape. ↕ 12in (30cm), ↔ 6in (15cm). Europe, Asia. Zone 3.

Allium oreophilum

Allium porrum

A. pulchellum see *A. carinatum* subsp. *pulchellum.*
***A.* 'Purple Sensation'.** Bulbous perennial with long, strap-shaped, gray-green, basal leaves, 12–24in (30–60cm) long. In summer, bears umbels, 3in (8cm) across, of 50 or more star-shaped, deep violet flowers. Remove immature seed heads to prevent paler-flowered, self-sown seedlings. ↕ 3ft (1m), PD3in (8cm). Zone 4.
A. roseum (Rosy garlic). Very variable, bulbous perennial with linear, mid-green, basal leaves, 5–14in (12–35cm) long. In summer, produces small, loose umbels, ½in (1.5cm) across, of 5–25 cup-shaped, pale pink flowers, often with bulbils present. Few-flowered plants with many bulbils may be invasive and are best removed. ↕ 4–26in (10–65cm), PD2in (5cm). S. Europe, N. Africa, Turkey. Zone 6b.
A. schoenoprasum ■ (Chives). Bulbous perennial with short rhizomes and edible, cylindrical, hollow, dark green leaves, to 14in (35cm) long. Produces dense umbels, 1in (2.5cm) across, of up to 30 bell-shaped, pale purple or white flowers in summer. ↕ 12–24in (30–60cm), PD2in (5cm). Europe, Asia, North America. Zone 3. **'Forescate'** ■ is vigorous, and produces deep purplish pink flowers; ↕ 24in (60cm), PD3in (8cm).
A. schubertii. Bulbous perennial with strap-shaped, bright green, basal leaves, 8–16in (20–40cm) long, which die back before flowering. Umbels, to 12in (30cm) across, of up to 50 star-shaped, pale purple flowers are borne on stalks

Allium schoenoprasum

Allium schoenoprasum 'Forescate'

of differing lengths in early summer. ↕ 12–24in (30–60cm), PD8in (20cm). E. Mediterranean to C. Asia. Zone 4b.
A. senescens. Vigorous, bulbous perennial with short rhizomes and short strap-shaped, mid-green, basal leaves, 1½–12in (4–30cm) long. In mid- and late summer, bears dense umbels, ¾in (2cm) across, of up to 30 long-lasting, cup-shaped, pale to mid-purple-pink flowers. ↕ 3–24in (8–60cm), PD2in (5cm). Europe, N. Asia. Zone 5.
var. *calcareum* see subsp. *montanum.*
subsp. *montanum* ■ syn. var. *calcareum*, has gray-green, often twisted leaves, and pink flowers; ↕ 18in (45cm).
subsp. *montanum* var. *glaucum*, syn. *A. spiralis*, a variant of the subspecies, has twisted gray leaves and bears bright pink flowers; ↕ 6in (15cm).
A. siculum see *Nectaroscordum siculum.*
A. sikkimense, syn. *A. kansuense*, *A. tibeticum.* Slender, bulbous perennial with short rhizomes and linear, mid-green, basal leaves, 12in (30cm) long. In early summer, bears nodding umbels, 1in (2.5cm) across, of up to 10 small,

Allium senescens subsp. *montanum*

bell-shaped, bright blue, sometimes white flowers. ↕6–10in (15–25cm), PD4in (10cm). W. China, Tibet, Nepal, India (Sikkim). Zone 6b.
A. sphaerocephalon (Drumstick allium, Round-headed garlic). Bulbous perennial with linear, mid-green, basal leaves, to 14in (35cm) long. In summer, bears ovoid umbels, 1in (2.5cm) across, of up to 40 tightly packed, bell-shaped flowers, from green to pink to dark red-brown, sometimes with bulbils. ↕20–36in (50–90cm), PD3in (8cm). Europe, N. Africa, W. Asia. Zone 3.
A. spiralis see *A. senescens* subsp. *montanum* var. *glaucum.*
A. stellatum (Prairie onion). Bulbous perennial with clumped, flattened, linear leaves, to 12in (30cm) long, which die before the flowers appear and are keeled beneath. From midsummer to late autumn, bears hemispherical umbels, 1¼–2in (3–5cm) across, of many cup-shaped pink to rose flowers. ↕8–14in (20–35cm), PD2in (5cm). North America. Zone 4.
A. stipitatum. Bulbous perennial with ribbed stems and broadly strap-shaped, gray-green, basal leaves, 12–18in (30–45cm) long, hairy beneath. In early summer, produces tightly packed umbels, 4in (10cm) across, of 50 or more star-shaped, pale lilac flowers. Excellent for drying. Often confused with *A. rosenbachianum.* ↕4½ft (1.4m), PD4in (10cm). C. Asia. Zone 4. **'Album'** bears smaller heads of clear white flowers.
A. tibeticum see *A. sikkimense.*
A. triquetrum (Three-cornered leek). Bulbous perennial with triangular stems and narrowly linear, grooved leaves, to 20in (50cm) long, keeled beneath. In spring, drooping stems bear umbels, 1½–3in (4–8cm) across, of many bell-shaped flowers with white petals, striped green down the middle. ↕12in (30cm), PD2in (5cm). S. Europe. Zone 8.
A. tuberosum (Chinese chives, Garlic chives). Fast-growing, bulbous perennial with short rhizomes and solid, linear, keeled, edible, mid-green basal and stem-sheathing leaves, to 14in (35cm) long. From late summer to autumn, bears many star-shaped, fragrant white flowers in umbels, 2in (5cm) across. Self-sows vigorously. ↕10–20in (25–50cm), PD2in (5cm). S.E. Asia. Zone 4.
A. unifolium ■ syn. *A. murrayanum.* Bulbous perennial with short, linear, gray-green, basal leaves, 6–8in (15–20cm) long, that wither by flowering time. In spring, each stem produces a hemispherical umbel, 2½in (6cm) across, of up to 20 large, open bell-shaped, clear purple-pink flowers. ↕12in (30cm), PD2in (5cm). Oregon, California. Zone 4.
A. wallichii. Bulbous perennial with short rhizomes and linear, keeled, mid-green basal and stem-clasping leaves, 24–36in (60–90cm) long. Many star-shaped purple flowers are borne in loose umbels, 2–3in (5–8cm) across, in late summer and early autumn. Bulbs are slender and poorly developed. ↕12–36in (30–90cm), PD3in (8cm). Nepal to W. China. Zone 3.
A. zebdanense. Bulbous perennial producing strap-shaped, mid-green, basal leaves, 4–12in (10–30cm) long. In spring, bears umbels, 1¼in (3cm) across, of 6–10 large, bell-shaped, lightly scented white flowers. Reseeds freely. ↕10–16in (25–40cm), PD2in (5cm). Lebanon. Zone 4.

Allium unifolium

ALLUAUDIA

DIDIEREACEAE

Genus of about 6 species of tree-like, perennial succulents from dry regions of S.W. and S. Madagascar. They have mainly thick, fleshy trunks and often thorny stems. The fleshy leaves are shed in dry periods and are apparent only during the growing season. The unisexual flowers are borne in umbel-like cymes. Where temperatures fall below 59°F (15°C), grow in a temperate or warm greenhouse. In warmer climates, grow in a desert garden.
• **CULTIVATION** Under glass, grow in soil-based potting mix, with up to 10 percent each of added leaf mold and sharp sand, in full light. Water moderately in summer; keep almost dry at other times. Apply a balanced liquid fertilizer 2 or 3 times in the growing season. Outdoors, grow in sharply drained, humus-rich, slightly alkaline soil, with additional sharp sand, in partial shade. See also pp.48–49.
• **PROPAGATION** Sow seed at 66–75°F (19–24°C) as soon as ripe. Take stem cuttings in spring, and place in partial shade until rooted.
• **PESTS AND DISEASES** Spider mites.

A. ascendens Sparsely branched, tree-like succulents. Columnar stems and deciduous, nearly round leaves are reddish green in full sun. New leaves are produced first horizontally above the spines and then vertically, distinguishing each year's growth. Numerous white to dull reddish flowers are borne on the upper stem, with cymes spreading, peduncle short. ↕to 50ft (15m), ↔ to 20in (50cm). S. Madagascar. ❀ (min. 59°F/15°C)
A. comosa. Perennial succulent with 4 or 5 erect main branches and slender, twiggy, long-thorned stems bearing obovate to rounded, mid-green leaves, to ¾in (2cm) long. Minute white flowers in small cymes, 1½–3in (4–8cm) across, are produced directly from branches, below a thorn, in summer. ↕to 70ft (20m), ↔ 3ft (1m). S.W. and S. Madagascar. ❀ (min. 59°F/15°C)
A. procera. Small, tree-like perennial succulent, shrubby when young. Bears short-shoot, vertically-paired leaves. Primary stem branches near base and

Alluaudia procera

above; stems and branches are covered with spiraling rows of spines. Small white flowers emerge near apex of the stem. Cymes are highly branched, about 8in (20cm) across; peduncle is thick. Produces small nuts, enveloped by prophylls. ↕to 50ft (15m), ↔ to 20in (50cm). S. Madagascar. ❀ (min. 59°F/15°C)

ALNUS

Alder

BETULACEAE

Genus of about 35 species of deciduous trees and shrubs from all parts of the N. hemisphere, usually found in poor or wet soils. Alders have alternate, simple, toothed leaves, and bear male and female flowers in separate catkins on the same tree. The male catkins are conspicuous; the females are smaller, and after pollination develop into persistent, woody, cone-like green fruits, which turn brown in autumn. Some alders, such as *A. rubra* and selected forms of *A. cordata, A. glutinosa,* and *A. incana,* are grown for their ornamental foliage, and are particularly suitable planted close to water. Most alders, however, are notable for their ability to thrive in poor, wet soils, and are therefore widely used in land reclamation. *A. cordata, A. incana,* and *A. rubra* are fast-growing and valuable as windbreaks.
• **CULTIVATION** Alders thrive in moderately fertile, moist but well-drained to wet soil in full sun; *A. cordata* and *A. incana* tolerate dry soils. Pruning group 1, between leaf fall and midwinter.
• **PROPAGATION** Sow seed in a seedbed as soon as ripe. Root hardwood cuttings in winter. Bud in late summer.
• **PESTS AND DISEASES** Prone to *Phytophthora* root rot and mealybugs.

A. crispa see *A. viridis* subsp. *crispa.*
A. glutinosa (Black alder, Common alder). Broadly conical tree with ovate, dark green leaves, to 4in (10cm) long, sticky when young. Groups of 3–5 pendent, yellow-brown male catkins, 4in (10cm) long, are produced in late winter or early spring. Bears ovoid fruit, ½–¾in (1–2cm) long, in summer. ↕80ft (25m), ↔ 30ft (10m). Europe, N. Africa, W. Asia. Zone 4. **'Aurea'** has yellow leaves that mature to light green; ↕40ft (12m), ↔ 15ft (5m). **'Imperialis'** ■ has mid-green leaves

Alnus glutinosa 'Imperialis' (inset: leaf detail)

Alnus incana

with deeply cut lobes. **'Laciniata'** resembles 'Imperialis', but the leaves are more shallowly cut. **'Pyramidalis'** is stiffly erect, with upright branches and dark green leaves; ↕ 50ft (15m), ↔ 15ft (5m).
A. incana ▣ (Gray alder). Conical tree with ovate, dark green leaves, to 4in (10cm) long, gray-white and hairy beneath. Clusters of 3 or 4 pendent, yellow-brown male catkins, to 4in (10cm) long, are borne in late winter and early spring, before the leaves. Produces ovoid fruit, ½in (1.5cm) long, in summer. ↕ 70ft (20m), ↔ 30ft (10m). Europe, Caucasus. Zone 4.
'Aurea' ▣ has yellow leaves, pale green in summer, and orange shoots and catkins in winter; ↕ 30ft (10m), ↔ 15ft (5m). **'Laciniata'** has narrow-lobed leaves. **'Pendula'** has weeping branches; ↕ 30ft (10m), ↔ 20ft (6m). **'Ramulis Coccineis'** has yellow leaves in spring, red shoots and buds in winter, and orange catkins; ↕ 30ft (10m), ↔ 15ft (5m).
A. japonica (Japanese alder). Conical tree with narrowly ovate, glossy, dark green leaves, paler beneath, to 4in (10cm) long. Clusters of 4–8 pendent, yellow-brown male catkins, to 3in (8cm) long, open before the leaves in early spring. Ovoid fruit, ½–1in (1.5–2.5cm) long, are borne in summer. ↕ 70ft (20m), ↔ 25ft (8m). N. China, Korea, Japan. Zone 4.
A. oregona see *A. rubra.*
A. rhombifolia (White alder). Rounded tree with spreading branches and arching shoot-tips. Ovate, glossy, dark green leaves, to 4in (10cm) long, are

Alnus incana 'Aurea'

yellow-green beneath. Groups of 2–7 pendent, yellowish brown male catkins, to 4in (10cm) long, open before the leaves in early spring. Bears ovoid fruit, ½in (1.5cm) long, in summer. ↕ 80ft (25m), ↔ 70ft (20m). W. US. Zone 5.
A. rubra, syn. *A. oregona* (Oregon alder, Red alder). Very vigorous, conical tree with semi-pendent shoots and ovate, red-veined, glossy, dark green leaves, to 4in (10cm) or more long. Clusters of 2–5 pendent yellow male catkins, to 6in (15cm) long, open in early spring, followed by ovoid-oblong fruit, 1¼in (3cm) long, in summer. ↕ 80ft (25m), ↔ 30ft (10m). W. North America. Zone 5b.
A. sinuata (Sitka alder). Narrowly conical tree, sometimes shrubby, with ovate, light green leaves, to 6in (15cm) long, glossy beneath and sticky when young. In spring, produces clusters of 3–6 pendent, yellow male catkins, to 5in (13cm) long, after the leaves; they are followed in summer by ellipsoid fruit, ½in (1.5cm) long. ↕ 30ft (10m), ↔ 12ft (4m). N.W. North America. Zone 3.
A. tenuifolia (Mountain alder, Thinleaf alder). Spreading tree with a rounded head and red buds. Ovate leaves, to 4in (10cm) long, are dark green above and paler beneath. Pendent clusters of 3 or 4 small, yellow-brown male catkins, to 2½in (6cm) long, open in early spring, before the leaves. Produces narrowly ovoid fruit, ¾in (2cm) long, in summer. ↕↔ 25ft (8m). W. North America. Zone 6b.
A. viridis (Green alder). Upright shrub with ovate leaves, to 3½in (9cm) long, matte, mid-green above, glossy, yellow-green beneath. Groups of up to 10 thick, yellow-brown male catkins, to 3in (8cm) long, open in spring, erect at first, later pendent. In summer, bears ovoid fruit, to ½in (1.5cm) long. ↕ 10ft (3m), ↔ 6ft (2m). Europe. Zone 4.
subsp. *crispa*, syn. *A. crispa* (Mountain alder), has slightly larger, fine-toothed, bright green leaves, to 3in (8cm) long; Canada, N.E. US.

ALOCASIA

Elephant's ear

ARACEAE

Genus of about 70 species of large, evergreen, mainly rhizomatous, sometimes tuberous-rooted perennials, found in tropical forest and sunny, open or shaded, usually damp sites by streams and marshes in S. and S.E. Asia. They are cultivated for their large, usually peltate, heavily veined, oblong to ovate, arrow-shaped leaves, which are often marked with black, dark violet, or bronze, and have cylindrical leaf stalks. The relatively insignificant spathes, borne at any time of year, are followed by clusters of red or orange fruits. Where not hardy, grow in a warm greenhouse; some species are suitable as houseplants. In frost-free areas, grow in a shady border. Contact with sap may irritate skin; all parts may cause mild stomach upset if ingested.
• **CULTIVATION** Under glass, grow in a mix of equal parts composted bark, loam, and sand, in filtered light. In the growing season, provide high humidity, water freely, and apply a balanced liquid fertilizer every 2–3 weeks; water moderately in winter. Outdoors,

Alocasia cuprea

grow in moderately fertile, humus-rich, moist but well-drained soil in partial shade.
• **PROPAGATION** Sow seed at 73°F (23°C) as soon as ripe. Divide the rhizomes, or separate offsets, in spring or summer. Root stem cuttings from spring to early summer.
• **PESTS AND DISEASES** Mealybugs and scale insects may be problems. Fungal and bacterial leaf diseases are common under glass. Bacterial soft rot occurs during propagation.

A. cuprea ▣ (Giant caladium). Rhizomatous perennial with oblong-ovate leaf blades, 18in (45cm) long, and leaf stalks 24in (60cm) long. Upper leaf surfaces have dark green zones and midribs with copper-colored areas in between; the undersides are reddish violet. Produces purple spathes, to 6in (15cm) long. ↕ 3ft (1m), ↔ 30in (75cm). Malaysia, Borneo. ❀ (min. 59–64°F/15–18°C)
***A. indica* var. *metallica* of gardens** see *A. plumbea.*
A. lowii* var. *veitchii see *A. veitchii.*
A. macrorrhiza ▣ (Giant taro). Imposing, rhizomatous perennial with large, ovate, glossy, mid- to dark green leaves, arrow-shaped at the bases, with pale green veins, borne on "stems" to 6ft (2m) long. Each leaf blade is 3–4ft (1–1.2m) long and each leaf stalk 4ft (1.2m) long. Produces yellow-green spathes, to 8in (20cm) long. Widely cultivated in tropical areas for its edible rhizomes and shoots. ↕ 12–15ft (4–5m), ↔ 6–8ft (2–2.5m). India, Sri Lanka, Malaysia. ❀ (min. 59–64°F/15–18°C).

Alocasia macrorrhiza

Alocasia sanderiana

'Variegata' produces leaves variably blotched in cream-white, gray-green, or dark green. **'Violacea'** has violet-tinged leaves.
A. picta see *A. veitchii.*
A. plumbea, syn. *A. indica* var. *metallica* of gardens. Rhizomatous perennial producing purple or dark olive-green stems, and similarly colored, ovate leaves that are arrow-shaped at the bases, with wavy margins, purple veins, and silvery purple beneath. Each leaf blade is 3–4ft (1–1.2m) long, and each leaf stalk 4ft (1.2m) long. Produces white spathes, 6–7in (15–18cm) long. ↕ 12–15ft (4–5m), ↔ 6–8ft (2–2.5m). Indonesia (Java). ❀ (min. 59–64°F/15–18°C).
'Rubra' has red-tinted leaves.
A. sanderiana ▣ (Kris plant). Rhizomatous perennial with arrow-shaped, dark green leaves, sometimes purple beneath, with wavy or deeply lobed silver margins, a metallic sheen, and silver veins. Each leaf blade is 12–16in (30–40cm) long, the leaf stalk to 24in (60cm) long. The creamy white spathes are 5in (13cm) long. ↕ 6ft (2m), ↔ to 6ft (2m). Philippines (Mindanao). ❀ (min. 59–64°F/15–18°C)
A. veitchii, syn. *A. lowii* var. *veitchii*, *A. picta.* Rhizomatous perennial with very dark green, pointed, narrowly ovate-triangular leaves, arrow-shaped at the bases, with gray margins and veins, and red-purple beneath. Each leaf blade grows to 30in (75cm) long, the leaf stalk 4½ft (1.3m) long. Produces yellowish green spathes, 4½–5in (11–13cm) long. ↕ 6–7ft (2–2.2m), ↔ 4ft (1.2m). Borneo. ❀ (min. 59–64°F/15–18°C)
A. watsoniana. Rhizomatous perennial producing blue-green stems with similarly colored, elliptic-ovate leaves that are arrow-shaped at the bases, puckered, with silver-gray margins and veins, red-purple beneath. Each leaf blade and leaf stalk grows up to 36in (90cm) long. Bears yellowish white spathes, to 4½–5in (11–13cm) long. ↕↔ to 5ft (1.5m). Malaysia, Indonesia. ❀ (min. 59–64°F/15–18°C)

ALOE

LILIACEAE

Genus of about 300 species of small to large, rosetted, evergreen perennials. Some are shrub-like or climbing, a few tree-like. They are found at various altitudes in the Cape Verde Islands, tropical and southern Africa, Madagascar, and the Arabian Peninsula. Most have succulent leaves and axillary or terminal racemes or panicles of cylindrical to 3-angled, tubular, or bell-shaped flowers. The leaves of many *Aloe* species become suffused with red in poor soils and dry conditions. The cylindrical or spherical fruits are papery or woody, and contain many flat or angular seeds. When temperatures fall below 50°F (10°C), grow in a temperate greenhouse or as houseplants. In summer, grow in a desert garden or in a border. Most aloes are excellent choices for growing in a container.

• **CULTIVATION** Under glass, grow in soil-based potting mix, with added sharp sand or perlite, in full light with good ventilation. Water moderately throughout the year, but sparingly when dormant. In the growing season, apply a balanced liquid fertilizer 2 or 3 times. Outdoors, grow in fertile, well-drained soil in full sun. See also pp.48–49.

• **PROPAGATION** Sow seed at 70°F (21°C) as soon as ripe. Separate offsets in late spring or early summer. Insert unrooted offsets in standard cactus potting mix.

• **PESTS AND DISEASES** Prone to mealybugs and scale. *Pythium* root rot, bacterial soft rot, and fungal stem and leaf rots are common.

A. albiflora, syn. *Guillauminia albiflora.* Basal-rosetted, clump-forming succulent producing spirally arranged, linear, tapering, fleshy, dark green leaves, 5–6in (12–15cm) long, slightly grooved and rough, white-warty above and with small white marginal teeth. Terminal racemes, 24in (60cm) tall, of bell-shaped white flowers, to ½in (1.5cm) long, are borne in early summer. ‡ 6in (15cm), ↔ indefinite. Madagascar. ❄ (min. 50°F/10°C)
A. arabica see *A. vera.*
A. arborescens, syn. *A. perfoliata* var. *arborescens* (Candelabra plant). Tree-like, many-branched succulent with rosettes of sword-shaped, very fleshy, bright green leaves, to 24in (60cm)

Aloe arborescens 'Variegata'

Aloe aristata

long, partly concave above, with wavy, toothed margins. Each rosette produces terminal racemes, to 12in (30cm) long, of cylindrical red flowers, to 1½in (4cm) long, in late spring and early summer. ‡ 6–12ft (2–4m), ↔ 6ft (2m). Malawi, Mozambique, Zimbabwe, South Africa. ❄ (min. 50°F/10°C). **'Variegata'** ■ has yellow-striped leaves.
A. aristata ■ syn. *A. ellenbergeri* (Torch plant). Stemless, clump-forming succulent with a dense rosette of lance-shaped, minutely toothed, white-margined, dark green leaves, 3–4in (8–10cm) long, cross-banded with very small white spots and soft white spines, particularly on the undersides. Terminal panicles, to 20in (50cm) long, and usually 2- to 6-branched, bear cylindrical, orange-red flowers, to 1½in (4cm) long, in autumn. ‡ to 5in (13cm), ↔ indefinite. E. and S. South Africa. ❄ (min. 50°F/10°C)
A. atherstonei see *A. pluridens.*
A. ausana see *A. variegata.*
A. bakeri. Mat-forming succulent with clustered rosettes of very slender, linear, fleshy, white-mottled, greenish or reddish brown leaves, to 4in (10cm) long, sometimes partially banded red or pink, with softly toothed margins. In summer, bears tubular, green-tipped, scarlet or yellowish orange flowers, ¾in (2cm) long, in axillary racemes, 12in (30cm) long. ‡ 4–8in (10–20cm), ↔ 16in (40cm). Madagascar. ❄ (min. 50°F/10°C)
A. barbadensis see *A. vera.*
A. bellatula. Stemless, suckering succulent forming dense, rosetted clumps of linear to lance-shaped, grooved, warty, fleshy, dark green leaves, to 5in (13cm) long, spotted with pale green; the leaf margins are horny and minutely toothed. Terminal racemes, to 24in (60cm) long, of bell-shaped, coral-red flowers, to ½in (1.5cm) long, are produced throughout the summer. ‡ 6in (15cm), ↔ indefinite. Madagascar. ❄ (min. 50°F/10°C)
A. brevifolia, syn. *A. prolifera.* Stemless or short-stemmed succulent producing groups of compact rosettes with erect to spreading, triangular-lance-shaped, fleshy, glaucous leaves, 3–7in (7–18cm) long, with toothed margins. Each rosette bears an axillary raceme, 16–20in (40–50cm) long, of cylindrical red flowers, 1½in (4cm) long, in autumn. ‡ 4in (10cm), ↔ indefinite. South Africa (Western Cape). ❄ (min. 50°F/10°C)

Aloe distans

A. comptonii. Stemless or short-stemmed succulent with large, compact rosettes of upright, lance-shaped, fleshy, toothed, bluish green leaves, to 12in (30cm) long, concave above, keeled and spiny below. Terminal panicles, 32in (80cm) long, with 3–5 branches, bear pendent, cylindrical scarlet flowers, 1½in (4cm) long, in autumn. ‡ 16in (40cm), ↔ indefinite. South Africa (Eastern and Western Cape). ❄ (min. 50°F/10°C)
A. descoingsii. Stemless, clump-forming succulent with rosettes of ovate, tapered, dull green leaves, 1¼–1½in (3–4cm) long, with small white tubercles on both surfaces, and incurved, toothed margins. Flattened racemes, to 6in (15cm) long, terminate in cylindrical to bell-shaped, deep red and yellowish orange flowers, ⅜in (8mm) long, from spring to summer. ‡ 1½–2in (4–5cm), ↔ indefinite. Madagascar. ❄ (min. 50°F/10°C)
A. distans ■ Trailing succulent with stems often 6–10ft (2–3m) long, and rooting at the nodes. Lance-shaped to broadly ovate, fleshy, white-spotted, bluish green leaves, 3in (8cm) long, are sharply pointed and have horny yellow marginal teeth. In winter, panicles, 16–24in (40–60cm) long, with 3 or 4 branches, bear cylindrical, red and yellow flowers, 1½in (4cm) long, in terminal clusters. ‡ 20in (50cm), ↔ indefinite. South Africa (Western Cape). ❄ (min. 50°F/10°C)
A. ellenbergeri see *A. aristata.*
A. excelsa. Tree-like succulent with very thick stems bearing dense rosettes of lance-shaped, fleshy, dull green leaves, 24–26in (60–65cm) long, with toothed margins and undersides. Each rosette has 1 or 2 many-branched panicles, to 4½ft (1.3m) tall, bearing terminal clusters of cylindrical, orange-red to rich scarlet flowers, to 1¼in (3cm) long, in summer. ‡ 20–28ft (6–9m), ↔ 30in (75cm). Zimbabwe. ❄ (min. 50°F/10°C)
A. ferox ■ syn. *A. galpinii, A. socotrina, A. supralaevis* (Cape aloe). Single-stemmed, tree-like succulent crowned by a rosette of narrowly to broadly lance-shaped, fleshy, sometimes red-tinged, dull green leaves, to 3ft (1m) long, hairless or spiny above, spiny beneath, and with red marginal teeth. Erect, terminal panicles with 5–10 branches, 12–32in (30–80cm) long, covered with tubular, scarlet-orange flowers, ¾–1¼in (2–3cm) long, are

Aloe ferox

produced in summer. ↕ 6–10ft (2–3m), ↔ 5ft (1.5m). South Africa (Northern Cape, Eastern Cape, Western Cape). ❀ (min. 50°F/10°C)

A. galpinii see *A. ferox.*

A. haworthioides ■ syn. *Aloinella haworthioides.* Stemless, suckering succulent with dense rosettes of lance-shaped, fleshy, white-warty, gray-green leaves, 1¼–2½in (3–6cm) long, suffused red in dry conditions; each has a terminal spine and white marginal teeth. Bears terminal racemes, to 12in (30cm) long, of tubular orange flowers, ⅜in (8mm) long, with projecting stamens, in summer. ↕ 2½in (6cm), ↔ 4in (10cm). Madagascar. ❀ (min. 50°F/10°C)

A. indica see *A. vera.*

A. jucunda. Stemless or short-stemmed, clump-forming succulent with rosettes of ovate, recurved, fleshy, deep green leaves, 1½in (4cm) long. These are brown-tinged toward the tips and have pale green and white spots, and reddish brown marginal teeth. In summer, bears sublateral racemes, to 12in (30cm) long, of cylindrical, pale pink flowers, ¾in (2cm) long. ↕ to 2in (5cm), ↔ indefinite. Somalia. ❀ (min. 50°F/10°C)

A. marlothii. Tree-like succulent with persistent old leaves, on a thick stem crowned with a dense rosette of semi-erect, broadly lance-shaped, fleshy, mid-green or glaucous, gray-green leaves, 3ft (1m) long; both upper and lower surfaces and margins are spiny. Many-branched, dense, terminal panicles, to 32in (80cm) or more long, of cylindrical, yellowish orange flowers, to 1¼in (3cm) long, are borne in summer. ↕ to 12ft (4m), ↔ 5ft (1.5m). Botswana, E. South Africa. ❀ (min. 50°F/10°C)

A. mitriformis ■ syn. *A. xanthocantha* (Purple-crown). Variable, clump-forming succulent with thick, nearly erect or horizontal stems bearing terminal rosettes of ovate-lance-shaped, fleshy, bluish green leaves, 18in (45cm) long, keeled beneath, and suffused red in poor soil conditions. Both keel and leaf margins are yellow-toothed. In

Aloe haworthioides

Aloe mitriformis

winter, broadly conical, occasionally branched, axillary racemes, 16–24in (40–60cm) long, of tubular, dull scarlet flowers, 1½–2in (4–5cm) long, are borne on branched stems. ↕ to 6ft (2m), ↔ indefinite. South Africa (Western Cape). ❀ (min. 50°F/10°C)

A. paniculata see *A. striata.*

A. perfoliata* var. *arborescens see *A. arborescens.*

A. platyphylla see *A. zebrina.*

A. pluridens ■ syn. *A. atherstonei.* Tree-like succulent with simple or branching stems, each crowned by a dense rosette of strap-shaped, recurved, fleshy, pale green or yellowish green leaves, 28–32in (70–80cm) long, with horny, grooved white marginal teeth. Conical, axillary racemes, to 32in (80cm) long, of cylindrical, rose-pink to scarlet flowers, 1½–1¾in (4–4.5cm) long, are borne in spring. ↕ 6–10ft (2–3m), ↔ 3ft (1m). South Africa (Eastern Cape). ❀ (min. 50°F/10°C)

A. polyphylla. Stemless succulent with a dense rosette of diamond-shaped, fleshy, white-toothed, deep-purple-tipped, gray green leaves, 12in (30cm) long. The leaves are arranged in 5 rows, oriented in a clockwise or counterclockwise spiral. In autumn, produces sparsely branched racemes, 20–24in (50–60cm) long, of cylindrical, pale red flowers, 2½in (6cm) long. ↕ 20in (50cm), ↔ 24–32in (60–80cm). Lesotho, South Africa (Eastern Cape). ❀ (min. 50°F/10°C)

A. prolifera see *A. brevifolia.*

A. punctata see *A. variegata.*

A. rauhii. Stemless, clump-forming succulent with rosettes of spreading,

Aloe pluridens

Aloe saponaria

lance-shaped, fleshy, gray-green leaves, to 4in (10cm) long. They are sometimes tinged brown, with H-shaped markings and minute white marginal teeth. In summer, produces tubular, rose-scarlet flowers, 1in (2.5cm) long, in cylindrical, terminal racemes, to 12in (30cm) long. ↕ 4–6in (10–15cm), ↔ indefinite. Madagascar. ❀ (min. 50°F/10°C) **'Snowflake'** is heavily white-marked.

A. saponaria ■ Stemless or short-stemmed, suckering succulent with solitary or multiple rosettes of toothed, lance-shaped, pale to dark green leaves, 8in (20cm) or more long, with oblong white marks. In summer, produces terminal panicles, 16–24in (40–60cm) long, with up to 3 branches, of cylindrical red to yellow flowers, 1½–1¾in (4–4.5cm) long. ↕ 28in (70cm), ↔ indefinite. E. South Africa. ❀ (min. 50°F/10°C)

A. striata ■ syn. *A. paniculata.* Almost stemless succulent with a dense rosette of lance-shaped, fleshy, white-margined leaves, 18in (45cm) or more long. The leaves are often reddish green, indistinctly spotted and striped, and with a waxy white bloom. Corymb-like, many-branched, terminal panicles, to 3ft (1m) long, of tubular, orange-red flowers, 1in (2.5cm) long, are produced in summer. ↕ 3ft (1m), ↔ 3ft (1m). S.W. to southern Africa. ❀ (min. 50°F/10°C)

A. supralaevis see *A. ferox.*

A. variegata ■ syn. *A. ausana, A. punctata* (Partridge-breast). Stemless, stoloniferous succulent, forming dense clumps, with rosettes of semi-erect, overlapping, lance-shaped, fleshy, dark

Aloe striata

Aloe variegata

green leaves, 5in (13cm) long. They are V-shaped in cross-section, with irregular white cross-bands and small white marginal teeth. Each rosette produces axillary racemes, 12in (30cm) long, sometimes branched, of pendent, tubular, pink or scarlet flowers, 1¼–1¾in (3–4.5cm) long, in summer. ↕ 8in (20cm), ↔ indefinite. South Africa. ❀ (min. 50°F/10°C)

A. vera ■ syn. *A. arabica, A. barbadensis, A. indica* (Medicinal aloe). Clump-forming, suckering succulent producing basal rosettes of lance-shaped, fleshy, gray-green leaves, 18in (45cm) long, slightly grooved above, with toothed pink margins. In summer, bears tubular yellow flowers, to 1¼in (3cm) long, in terminal racemes, 36in (90cm) or more long, sometimes with up to 4 branches. ↕ 24in (60cm), ↔ indefinite. Origin unknown, but widespread in tropical and subtropical regions. ❀ (min. 50°F/10°C)

A. xanthocantha see *A. mitriformis.*

A. zebrina, syn. *A. platyphylla.* Usually stemless succulent with rosettes of linear-lance-shaped, fleshy, powdery glaucous, sometimes red-flushed, dark green leaves, to 12in (30cm) long, with thick brown marginal teeth and white-spotted cross-banding. Many-branched, erect, terminal panicles, 3–5ft (1–1.5m) long, of cylindrical, deep red or orange-red flowers, 1¼–1½in (3–4cm) long, are produced in spring. ↕ 12in (30cm), ↔ 32in (80cm). S.W. to southern Africa. ❀ (min. 50°F/10°C)

▷ ***Aloinella haworthioides*** see *Aloe haworthioides*

Aloe vera

Aloinopsis schooneesii

ALOINOPSIS

AIZOACEAE

Genus of 10–15 species of dwarf, fleshy- or tuberous-rooted, tufted, perennial succulents, closely related to *Nananthus* and *Titanopsis*, from low, hilly areas of South Africa. Most species have loose, basal rosettes of warty leaves and bear usually solitary, stalked, 2-bracted, many-petaled flowers in late autumn; the flowers open in late afternoon or early evening. Below 50°F (10°C), grow in a temperate greenhouse; in warm, dry areas, grow in a raised bed or border.

• **CULTIVATION** Under glass, grow in standard cactus potting mix in full light. In the growing season, water moderately and apply a half-strength, balanced liquid fertilizer 2 or 3 times; keep almost dry in winter. Outdoors, grow in sharply drained soil in full sun. See also pp.48–49.

• **PROPAGATION** Sow seed at 70°F (21°C) in early spring. Take stem or leaf cuttings in late spring or early summer; root in equal parts fine peat and sand in partial shade.

• **PESTS AND DISEASES** Vulnerable to mealybugs and root mealybugs.

A. rubrolineata, syn. *Nananthus rubrolineata.* Fleshy-rooted succulent producing rosettes of 4–6 ovate, slightly recurved, dull, mid-green leaves, 1in (2.5cm) long. Bears daisy-like yellow flowers, 1in (2.5cm) across, with a central red stripe along each petal. ↕ 1¼in (3cm), ↔ to 10in (25cm). South Africa. ❄ (min. 50°F/10°C)

A. schooneesii ■ syn. *Nananthus schooneesii.* Tuberous-rooted succulent with irregular rosettes of 8–10 roughly diamond-shaped, dark green leaves, to ½in (1.5cm) long. Yellow-red flowers, ½in (1.5cm) across, are silky and daisy-like. ↕ ¾in (2cm), ↔ 12in (30cm). South Africa. ❄ (min. 50°F/10°C)

ALONSOA

Mask flower

SCROPHULARIACEAE

Genus of about 12 species of evergreen shrubs, subshrubs, and perennials from stony slopes and scrub in tropical and subtropical W. South America. The leaves are arranged in opposite pairs or in whorls of 3, on 4-angled, branching, slender shoots, and often alternately on the flowering shoots. Delicate, spurred,

Alonsoa linearis

unequally 2-lipped, orange or red, sometimes white flowers are borne in spring and autumn in lax, terminal racemes. Use as colorful winter-flowering container plants in a temperate greenhouse or conservatory, as summer bedding, or in a mixed border. They also provide good cut flowers. Modern, compact-growing seed selections for bedding are now available. The species described are usually grown as annuals but will survive temperatures down to 30°F/-1°C for short periods.

• **CULTIVATION** Under glass, grow in soil-based potting mix in full light at a minimum of 50°F (10°C). Water moderately. Outdoors, grow in any fertile, well-drained soil in full sun.

• **PROPAGATION** Sow seed *in situ* after the last spring frost. Sow seed in late summer for winter-flowering container plants. Root semi-ripe cuttings in late summer.

• **PESTS AND DISEASES** Aphids may be a problem, particularly under glass.

A. acutifolia, syn. *A. myrtifolia.* Erect, spreading subshrub with lance-shaped, pointed, toothed, downy, dark green leaves, ¾–1¼in (2–3cm) long. Lax racemes of spurred, orange or deep red flowers, ¾–1in (2–2.5cm) across, are borne continuously throughout summer. ↕ 20–36in (50–90cm), ↔ 6–9in (15–23cm). Andes in Peru and Bolivia. **var. *candida***, syn. *A. albiflora* of gardens, has white flowers.

***A. albiflora* of gardens** see *A. acutifolia* var. *candida.*

A. caulialata see *A. meridionalis.*

A. grandiflora see *A. warscewiczii.*

A. linearis ■ syn. *A. linifolia.* Erect, moderately compact subshrub with linear to ovate to lance-shaped, pointed, entire or minutely toothed, dark green leaves, to 1½in (4cm) long. Lax racemes of spurred, brick-red flowers, ¾–1in (2–2.5cm) across, with black-spotted throats, are borne for much of the summer. Useful for cutting. ↕ to 3ft (1m), ↔ 12in (30cm). Peru, Chile.

A. linifolia see *A. linearis.*

A. meridionalis, syn. *A. caulialata.* Bushy, red-stemmed perennial or subshrub with ovate to lance-shaped, pointed, toothed, mid-green leaves, to 1½in (4cm) long. Lax racemes of spurred, orange or deep red flowers, to ¾in (2cm) across, are borne in summer. Useful for cut flowers. ↕ 12–36in (30–90cm), ↔ 12in (30cm). Colombia, Peru. **Firestone Jewels Series** produces scarlet, orange, salmon-pink, pink, or white flowers, with red shades predominating; selected cultivars are also available from seed.

A. myrtifolia see *A. acutifolia.*

A. warscewiczii, syn. *A. grandiflora.* Bushy, compact, red-stemmed perennial or subshrub with ovate to lance-shaped, toothed, dark green leaves, to 1½in (4cm) long, heart-shaped at the bases. From summer to autumn, bears lax racemes of spurred, scarlet, sometimes white flowers, ½–¾in (1.5–2cm) wide. ↕ 18–24in (45–60cm), ↔ 12in (30cm). Peru.

ALOPECURUS

Foxtail grass

POACEAE

Genus of 25–40 species of annual and perennial grasses from meadows and pastures, occasionally scree and rocky sites, in N. temperate regions. They produce tufts of usually flat, sometimes channeled leaves and dense, terminal panicles of cylindrical, single-flowered spikelets. Some are important fodder crops; several have ornamental foliage and are suitable for a rock garden or mixed border.

• **CULTIVATION** Grow in fertile, well-drained soil in sun or partial shade. *A. lanatus* does not tolerate wet conditions in winter. Clip back in spring for best foliage effect; in areas with hot summers, cut down in midsummer for new foliage in autumn.

• **PROPAGATION** Sow seed in containers in a cold frame when ripe, or in spring. Divide with care in spring or early summer.

• **PESTS AND DISEASES** Rust, smut, and leaf streak (brown stripe) can occur, as well as ergot occasionally. Anthracnose and leaf scald are also common.

A. lanatus (Woolly foxtail grass). Densely tufted perennial producing linear, often channeled, white-woolly, blue-green leaves, to 2in (5cm) long, appearing silvery gray overall. Bears ovoid-spherical, densely hairy, light green panicles, to ¾in (2cm) long by ½in (1.5cm) wide, from midspring to midsummer. ↕ to 4in (10cm), ↔ 5in (13cm). E. Mediterranean, Turkey. Zone 7.

***A. pratensis* 'Aureovariegatus'** ■ Spreading, but not invasive, perennial with striped, rich yellow and green, linear leaves, 2–2½in (5–6cm) long, arranged in basal tufts. Dense, cylindrical, pale green to purple panicles, to 4in (10cm) long by ½in (1.5cm) across, are produced from midspring to midsummer. ↕ to 4ft (1.2m), ↔ 16in (40cm) or more. Zone 4.

Alopecurus pratensis 'Aureovariegatus'

A. arundinaceus. Spreading perennial with linear, hairless to softly hairy, sharp-pointed, mid-green leaves, to 1¾in (4.5cm) long. Spherical, green-purple panicles, to 3in (8cm) long by ½in (1.5cm) across, are borne from midspring to midsummer. ↕ 3ft (1m), ↔ 10–15in (25–40cm). Temperate Eurasia. Zone 6b.

▷ ***Alophia lahue*** see *Herbertia lahue*

ALOYSIA

VERBENACEAE

Genus of 37 species of deciduous or evergreen shrubs from warm areas of North and South America, favoring dry, rocky soils. The simple leaves are aromatic, and opposite or whorled, and small, salverform flowers are borne in slender, spike-like panicles or racemes. *A. triphylla* (Lemon verbena) is cultivated for its strongly lemon-scented foliage, which is used for culinary purposes or in potpourri. Where not hardy, grow in a cool greenhouse. Where marginally hardy, grow at the base of a warm, sheltered wall. In frost-free areas, grow in a sunny border.

• **CULTIVATION** Under glass, grow in soil-based potting mix in full light. In the growing season, water moderately and apply a balanced liquid fertilizer monthly; keep just moist in winter. Outdoors, grow in well-drained, moderately fertile, dry soil in full sun. Mulch in autumn to protect the roots. Pick and dry leaves in summer before flowering. Pruning group 6, or 13 if wall-trained.

• **PROPAGATION** Root softwood or greenwood cuttings in summer.

• **PESTS AND DISEASES** Whiteflies are common. Root rot can occur but is rare.

A. citriodora see *A. triphylla.*

A. triphylla ■ syn. *A. citriodora, Lippia citriodora* (Lemon verbena). Bushy, upright, deciduous shrub with whorled, narrow, lance-shaped, lemon-scented, rough, bright green leaves, to 4in (10cm) long. Bears tiny, pale lilac to white flowers in slender panicles, to 5in (13cm) long, in late summer. Good in a container. ↕↔ 10ft (3m). Chile, Argentina. Zone 8.

Aloysia triphylla

ALPINIA

Ginger lily

ZINGIBERACEAE

Genus of about 200 species of rhizomatous, evergreen, clump-forming perennials from open forest and forest margins in moist tropical areas of India, China, S.E. Asia, and Australia. The ginger-scented rhizomes give rise to slender but strong, reed-like stems, to 10ft (3m) high, which bear 2-ranked, lance-shaped leaves and a panicle or raceme of showy, narrowly bell-shaped, slightly hooded flowers; these each have a 3-lobed calyx and a 3-petaled corolla, with a 2-lobed lip, enclosed in prominent bracts. The fruits are ovoid or spherical capsules. Where not hardy, grow smaller species in a warm greenhouse or conservatory, preferably in a border, so their growth is not restricted; they may be difficult to grow in containers. In frost-free areas, they are best grown in a shady border.

• **CULTIVATION** Under glass, grow in soil-based potting mix, with up to 25 percent each added leaf mold and composted bark, in bright filtered light. In the growing season, water freely and apply a balanced liquid fertilizer monthly; water moderately in winter. Pot on container-grown plants and cut out flowered stems in spring. Outdoors, grow in moist, fertile, humus-rich soil in partial shade.

• **PROPAGATION** Sow seed as soon as ripe at 68°F (20°C), or divide in spring. Treat plantlets produced in the inflorescences of *A. purpurata* as offsets.

• **PESTS AND DISEASES** Fungal leaf spots and root rots can occur. Under glass, spider mites may be a problem during drier months.

A. calcarata (Indian ginger). Slender, upright perennial with narrowly lance-shaped, stalkless, glossy, mid-green leaves, 12in (30cm) long, with minute, well-spaced bristles on the margins.

Alpinia zerumbet

Yellow flowers, 1½–2in (4–5cm) long, with lower petals veined dark red or maroon, are usually borne in pairs in spreading or more or less erect panicles, 4–5in (10–13cm) long, in summer. ↕3ft (1m), ↔ 12–24in (30–60cm). India, China. ❄ (min. 61°F/16°C)

A. galanga (Siamese ginger, Galangal). Upright, branched perennial with lance-shaped, minutely stalked, mid-green leaves, 20in (50cm) long, with downy margins. Pale green flowers, 1in (2.5cm) long, with pink-lined, white lips, are borne 3–5 per bract in branched, upright racemes, to 10in (25cm) long. ↕ to 6ft (2m), ↔ 3–4ft (1–1.2m). S.E. Asia. ❄ (min. 61°F/16°C)

A. japonica. Upright perennial with lance-shaped to oblong-lance-shaped, stalked, mid-green leaves, to 16in (40cm) long. Red-veined, white flowers, to 1in (2.5cm) long, are borne 1 or 2 per bract, in racemes, to 6in (15cm) long. ↕ to 24in (60cm), ↔ 12–24in (30–60cm). China, Taiwan, Japan. ❄ (min. 61°F/16°C)

A. nutans of gardens see *A. zerumbet.*

A. purpurata ▣ (Red ginger). Robust, upright perennial with stalked, hairless, lance-shaped, mid-green leaves, 32in (80cm) long. In summer, pendent to semi-erect racemes, to 36in (90cm) long, of many small white flowers, to 1in (2.5cm) long, are produced from the axils of persistent red bracts. ↕ 10–12ft (3–4m), ↔ 24–36in (60–90cm). S. Pacific islands. ❄ (min. 61°F/16°C)

A. sanderae of gardens see *A. vittata.*

A. speciosa see *A. zerumbet.*

A. vittata, syn. *A. sanderae* of gardens (Variegated ginger). Robust, upright perennial with almost stalkless, lance-shaped, mid-green leaves, 6in (15cm) long, striped with white and cream, and with bristly hairy margins. In summer, pale green flowers, ¾in (2cm) long, are borne in pendent racemes, 6in (15cm) long, from the axils of green, pink-tinged bracts. ↕ 5ft (1.5m), ↔ 24–36in (60–90cm). Solomon Islands. ❄ (min. 61°F/16°C)

A. zerumbet ▣ syn. *A. nutans* of gardens, *A. speciosa* (Pink porcelain lily, Shell ginger). Robust, upright perennial with stalkless, oblong-lance-shaped, mid-green leaves, to 24in (60cm) long. In summer, fragrant white, purple-tinged flowers, to 2–2½in (5–6cm) long, with yellow lips striped red and brown, are borne usually in pairs, in pendent racemes, to 16in (40cm) long. ↕ 10ft (3m), ↔ 3–4ft (1–1.2m). E. Asia. ❄ (min. 61°F/16°C). **'Variegata'** has dark green foliage, banded or striped pale yellow.

Alpinia purpurata

ALSOBIA

GESNERIACEAE

Genus of 2 species of perennials, related to *Episcia*, found in tropical forest and rocky habitats from Mexico to South America. Leaves are opposite, oblong to oblong-elliptic, hairy, often puckered, and produced in rosettes or whorls. The salverform flowers are 5-lobed and are borne singly or in few-flowered racemes from the leaf axils, from spring to autumn. Where not hardy, grow as houseplants, in a conservatory or terrarium, or in a hanging basket; elsewhere, use as a groundcover.

• **CULTIVATION** Under glass, grow in soilless potting mix with added perlite or vermiculite, in bright filtered light, with high humidity. When in growth, water moderately, applying a quarter-strength, balanced liquid fertilizer at each watering. Keep just moist in winter. Outdoors, grow in fertile, humus-rich, moist but sharply drained soil in partial shade.

Alsobia dianthiflora

• **PROPAGATION** Surface-sow seed at about 68–77°F (20–25°C) as soon as ripe or in early spring. Divide, separate plantlets, or root stem cuttings with bottom heat, in early or midsummer.

• **PESTS AND DISEASES** Susceptible to fungal spots and aerial blights, mealybugs, and aphids.

A. 'Cygnet', syn. *Episcia* 'Cygnet'. Vigorous, trailing, terrestrial perennial with elliptic to ovate, velvety, light green leaves, 4in (10cm) long. Purple-spotted white flowers, ¾in (2cm) across, are produced in twos in the leaf axils from spring to summer. ↕ 6in (15cm), ↔ 12in (30cm). ❄ (min. 55°F/13°C)

A. dianthiflora ▣ syn. *Episcia dianthiflora.* Creeping, terrestrial perennial bearing elliptic to ovate, toothed, dark green leaves, to 1½in (4cm) long, often veined purple-red. Solitary white flowers, to 1¼in (3cm) across, with purple spots at the bases and very deeply and finely fringed lobes, are produced from spring to summer. ↕ 6in (15cm), ↔ 12in (30cm). Mexico, Costa Rica. ❄ (min. 55°F/13°C)

▷ ***Alsophila*** see *Cyathea*

ALSTROEMERIA

Peruvian lily

LILIACEAE

Genus of about 50 species of perennials from open mountain screes and grassland in South America. The fleshy, sometimes rhizome-like tubers spread to form clumps, 12–24in (30–60cm) across. They produce erect stems with alternate or scattered, linear to lance-shaped, mid- to gray-green leaves, usually 3–5in (8–13cm) long, with twisted leaf stalks. Showy, funnel-shaped, 6-tepaled flowers, 1½–4in (4–10cm) long (smaller in the dwarf species), are borne in summer; they are produced in loose, often compound, few- to many-rayed, terminal umbels, 3–5in (8–13cm) across. They are ideal for a mixed or herbaceous border, although *A. pygmaea* and *A. hookeri* may be best grown in an alpine house. Many species are good for cut flowers. Contact with foliage may aggravate skin allergies.

• **CULTIVATION** Plant tubers 8in (20cm) deep in late summer or early autumn. Take care when handling. In an alpine house, grow in a mix of loam, leaf mold, and sharp sand. Most may also be grown in a cool greenhouse in soil-based potting mix. In the growing season, water freely and apply a balanced liquid fertilizer monthly; water sparingly in winter. Outdoors, grow in moist but well-drained, fertile soil in sun or partial shade. Mulch for the first 2 years; where not reliably hardy, protect with a dry mulch in winter, and grow at the base of a warm wall. *A. aurea* and *A. ligtu* and their hybrids will tolerate brief drops in temperature to 5°F (-15°C). Leave undisturbed to form clumps.

• **PROPAGATION** Sow seed in containers in a cold frame as soon as ripe. Plant out seedlings by the potful to avoid damaging the tubers. Divide established clumps in autumn or very early spring.

• **PESTS AND DISEASES** Gray mold on flowers can be a problem. A variety of virus diseases also occur. Prone to attack by spider mites and slugs.

Alstroemeria aurea

A. aurantiaca see *A. aurea.*
A. aurea ▣ syn. *A. aurantiaca.* Tuberous perennial bearing 3- to 7-rayed umbels, each ray with 1–3 bright orange or yellow flowers, the inner tepals streaked dark red, in summer. ↕ 3ft (1m), ↔ 18in (45cm). Chile. Zone 6. **'Dover Orange'** has deep orange flowers with paler orange inner tepals, streaked red. Among the hardiest. **'Lutea'** has bright yellow flowers with brown-spotted inner tepals.
***A.* 'Ballerina'.** Tuberous perennial producing 3- to 7-rayed umbels, each ray with 1–3 rose-pink flowers, with bronze-green tips and purple stripes, in summer. ↕ 3ft (1m), ↔ 30in (75cm). Zone 8.
***A.* 'Beatrix'**, syn. *A.* 'Stadoran'. Tuberous perennial bearing 3- to 8-rayed umbels of vivid orange flowers, 2 or 3 per ray, in summer. ↕ 3ft (1m), ↔ 30in (75cm). Zone 8.
A. gayana see *A. pelegrina.*
A. hookeri. Dwarf, tuberous perennial with gray-green leaves to 1in (2.5cm) long, and stems to 6in (15cm) long, bearing up to 6-rayed umbels, each ray with 1–3 pink flowers, in summer. The inner tepals have yellow flashes and are streaked with purple. ↕ 12–24in (30–60cm), ↔ to 24in (60cm). Peru. Zone 8.
A. ligtu. Tuberous perennial producing 3- to 8-rayed umbels, each ray with 2 or 3 flowers, varying in color from white to pale lilac or pinkish red, in summer. The obovate inner tepals are usually yellow with white, yellow, red, or purple markings; the stamens are shorter than the tepals. ↕ 20in (50cm), ↔ 30in (75cm). Chile, Argentina. Zone 7b. **Ligtu Hybrids** is a collective name given to seedlings derived mainly from crosses between *A. ligtu* and *A. haemantha.* Flower color varies considerably.
***A.* 'Orchid'** see *A.* 'Walter Fleming'.
***A.* 'Parigo Charm'** ▣ Tuberous perennial with 3- to 8-rayed umbels, each ray bearing 2 or 3 salmon-pink flowers, in summer. The inner tepals are primrose-yellow, marked carmine. ↕ 3ft (1m), ↔ 24in (60cm). Zone 8.

Alstroemeria 'Parigo Charm'

A. paupercula, syn. *A. violacea.* Tuberous perennial with 3- to 6-rayed umbels, each ray with 3–5 violet flowers, in summer; the inner tepals have white centers, spotted purple. ↕ 18–36in (45–90cm), ↔ 18in (45cm). N. Chile. Zone 8.
A. pelegrina ▣ syn. *A. gayana.* Tuberous perennial, similar to *A. hookeri*, producing white flowers, flushed pink or purple and with a darker central area, in summer. The inner tepals are yellow at the bases, with maroon flecks. Blooms are solitary or borne in 2- or 3-rayed umbels, with 1–3 flowers per ray. ↕ 12–24in (30–60cm), ↔ to 24in (60cm). Peru. Zone 8. **'Alba'** produces green-flushed white flowers, the inner tepals with yellow or green markings.
A. psittacina, syn. *A. pulchella.* Tuberous perennial with mauve-spotted stems bearing 4- to 6-rayed umbels, each ray with 1–3 green flowers, heavily overlaid with deep red, in summer. ↕ 3ft (1m), ↔ 18in (45cm). Brazil. Zone 8.
A. pulchella see *A. psittacina.*
A. pygmaea ▣ Dwarf, fleshy-rooted perennial producing gray-green leaves to 1in (2.5cm) long, and stems to 6in (15cm) long. In summer, solitary, deep yellow flowers, 2in (5cm) long, the inner tepals spotted with red, are borne in single-rayed umbels. Attractive species for a scree bed or cold greenhouse. ↕↔ 6–8in (15–20cm). Andes of Argentina, Bolivia, and Peru. Zone 8.
***A.* 'Regina'** see *A.* 'Victoria'.
***A.* 'Rosy Wings'.** Tuberous perennial producing 3- to 8-rayed umbels, each ray with 2 or 3 flowers, in summer. The outer tepals are red with green-marked tips, the inner ones are pink, marked with yellow and red. ↕ 36in (90cm), ↔ 20in (50cm). Zone 8.
***A.* 'Sonata'.** Tuberous perennial producing 3- to 8-rayed umbels of red flowers, with 2 or 3 blooms per ray, in summer; the tepals have green margins and yellow and purple markings. ↕ 36in (90cm), ↔ 36in (90cm). Zone 8.
***A.* 'Stadoran'** see *A.* 'Beatrix'.
***A.* 'Sweetheart'.** Tuberous perennial bearing 3- to 8-rayed umbels, each ray with 2 or 3 flowers, in summer. The outer tepals are pink, each with a darker central mark; the inner ones are paler, with red, yellow, and brown markings. ↕ 36in (90cm), ↔ 20in (50cm). Zone 8.
***A.* 'Victoria'**, syn. *A.* 'Regina'. Tuberous perennial bearing 3- to 6-rayed umbels, each ray with 2 or 3 pale pink flowers with bright yellow and red markings, in summer. ↕ 36in (90cm), ↔ 24in (60cm). Zone 8.
A. violacea see *A. paupercula.*
***A.* 'Walter Fleming'**, syn. *A.* 'Orchid'. Tuberous perennial producing 3- to 8-rayed umbels of yellow- and purple-marked cream flowers in summer. Each ray bears 2 or 3 blooms. ↕ 24in (60cm), ↔ 8in (20cm). Zone 8.

ALTERNANTHERA

AMARANTHACEAE

Genus of about 200 species of bushy annuals and perennials from moist, open forest areas in tropical and subtropical Central and South America. They are grown for their colorful leaves, which are opposite, linear to obovate, often toothed, and variable in size. They bear insignificant flowers in terminal or axillary spikes. Where not hardy, use as annuals in summer bedding, in knot gardens, or as edging, or grow in a cool or temperate greenhouse or conservatory; they are excellent massed in a hanging basket. In frost-free climates, use for bedding or as a groundcover.
• **CULTIVATION** Under glass, grow in soil-based potting mix in full light. In the growing season, water freely and apply a balanced liquid fertilizer monthly; in winter, water sparingly and keep well ventilated. Outdoors, plant out after any risk of frost has passed;

Alstroemeria pelegrina

Alstroemeria pygmaea

Alternanthera ficoidea var. *amoena*

grow in moist but well-drained soil, in full sun for best leaf color, or in partial shade. Clip to maintain compactness.
• **PROPAGATION** Sow seed at 55–64°F (13–18°C) as soon as ripe, or in spring; seedlings will vary in leaf color, making the plants less suitable for a uniform display. Divide in spring. Take softwood or greenwood cuttings in late summer. Overwinter young plants under glass.
• **PESTS AND DISEASES** Spider mites and *Fusarium* wilt may be problems.

A. amoena see *A. ficoidea* var. *amoena*.
A. bettzichiana (Calico plant). Mat-forming to erect annual or short-lived perennial with narrow, spoon-shaped, olive-green to yellow leaves, to 1in (2.5cm) long, mottled in combinations of red, purple, and bronze. Insignificant white flowers are borne in axillary spikes, ¼–½in (6–15mm) long, and are similar to those of *A. ficoidea*, of which this species is sometimes considered a variety. ↕ 2–8in (5–20cm), ↔ indefinite. Brazil. ❀ (min. 41°F/5°C)
A. ficoidea (Joseph's coat, Parrot leaf). Mat-forming to erect perennial with elliptic to obovate, pointed, mid-green leaves, 1in (2.5cm) long, marked with combinations of red, orange, purple, and yellow. Insignificant white flowers are produced in spherical to ovoid, axillary spikes, ⅛–½in (3–15mm) long. ↕ 8–12in (20–30cm), ↔ indefinite. Mexico, South America. ❀ (min. 41°F/5°C). **var. *amoena*** ■ syn. *A. amoena*, is dwarf, with lance-shaped to elliptic, mid-green leaves, heavily mottled and veined brown-red, orange, and purple; ↕ to 2in (5cm). **'Versicolor'**, syn. *A. versicolor*, is erect with bluntly spoon-shaped, copper or blood-red to maroon leaves; ↕↔ 12in (30cm). Many other color and leaf-shape variants exist.
A. versicolor see *A. ficoidea* 'Versicolor'.

ALTHAEA

MALVACEAE

Genus of about 12 species of annuals and perennials, similar to *Alcea* but with smaller, usually stalked flowers, found mainly in moist, often salt and brackish coastal habitats from W. Europe to C. Asia. They have strong, wiry stems that seldom need support, and broadly ovate, shallowly to deeply lobed, dark green leaves. Racemes or panicles of small, pink to bluish purple, 5-petaled flowers are produced from summer to autumn. They are suitable for a mixed or herbaceous border or wildflower garden.
• **CULTIVATION** They will tolerate a wide range of situations, but for best results grow in fertile, moist but well-drained soil in full sun.
• **PROPAGATION** Sow seed of annuals at 55°F (13°C) in late winter, or *in situ* in midspring. For perennials, sow seed in midsummer; transplant in early autumn, when 2 or 3 true leaves have developed.
• **PESTS AND DISEASES** Powdery mildew, white mold, and *Septoria* leaf spot occur. Flea beetles and Japanese beetles may be problems.

A. armeniaca. Erect, woody-based perennial with triangular-ovate, toothed or deeply 3- to 5-lobed leaves, to 6in (15cm) long, dark green above, paler

Althaea cannabina

beneath, and densely softly hairy. From midsummer to early autumn, produces leafy racemes of open funnel-shaped, deep rose-pink flowers, to 2in (5cm) across, on short stalks from the leaf axils. ↕ 4ft (1.2m), ↔ 12in (30cm). C. and S.W. Asia, S.E. Russia. Zone 4.
A. cannabina ■ Erect, woody-based perennial with rounded, hairy leaves, to 14in (35cm) long, each with 3–5 lobes, which are themselves lobed or toothed, and dark green above, paler beneath. Axillary clusters of small, cupped, lilac to deep pink flowers, 1¼–2in (3–5cm) across, sometimes with darker eyes, open from midsummer to early autumn. ↕ 6ft (2m), ↔ 24in (60cm). C., S., and E. Europe. Zone 4.
A. officinalis (Marsh mallow). Erect perennial producing softly hairy leaves with 3–5 shallow, toothed lobes. From midsummer to early autumn, bears pale lilac-pink flowers, ½–¾in (1.5–2cm) across, singly or in short axillary or terminal clusters. Grown for medicinal use. ↕ 6ft (2m), ↔ to 5ft (1.5m). C., S., and E. Europe. Zone 3.
A. rosea see *Alcea rosea*.

ALYOGYNE

MALVACEAE

Genus of 4 species of evergreen shrubs, formerly included in *Hibiscus*, growing wild in dry scrub in Australia (Northern Territory, Southern Australia, Western Australia). The leaves are alternate and entire to deeply lobed. They are valued for their large, attractive, hibiscus-like flowers, which are produced singly from the upper leaf axils from late spring to autumn. Where not hardy, grow in a cool greenhouse and move plants outdoors for the summer. In frost-free areas, grow in a border or at the base of a wall. Established plants will tolerate short periods of drought.
• **CULTIVATION** Under glass, grow in soilless or soil-based potting mix in full light. Pot on or top-dress in spring. In the growing season, water moderately and apply a balanced liquid fertilizer every 2–3 weeks; water sparingly in winter. Outdoors, grow in any well-drained soil in full sun. Pruning group 9, or 13 if wall-trained.
• **PROPAGATION** Sow seed in spring, at not less than 61°F (16°C). Root semi-ripe cuttings in late summer.
• **PESTS AND DISEASES** Aphids, whiteflies, and spider mites may be problems, especially under glass.

Alyogyne huegelii 'Santa Cruz'

A. huegelii, syn. *Hibiscus huegelii*. Erect, fast-growing shrub, spreading with age, bearing palmate, hairy, bright green leaves, 1¼–3in (3–8cm) long, each with 5 irregularly toothed lobes. Solitary, funnel-shaped, satiny, lilac, mauve, or purple flowers, to 4in (10cm) across, are produced from the leaf axils of young shoots from late spring to autumn. ↕↔ 3–6ft (1–2m). Western Australia. ❀ (min. 45°F/7°C). **'Santa Cruz'** ■ is a free-flowering, mauve-purple cultivar.

ALYSSUM

BRASSICACEAE

Genus of over 150 tufted, mat- or hummock-forming, sometimes erect annuals, and evergreen perennials and subshrubs, mostly found in open, rocky sites in C. and S. Europe, N. Africa, and S.W. and C. Asia. They have simple, alternate leaves, ⅛–1in (0.4–2.5cm) long, and are cultivated mainly for their corymb-like racemes of cross-shaped, 4-petaled yellow or white flowers, borne in early summer. They are suitable for growing in a rock garden, at the front or middle ground of a mixed border, or in wall crevices.
• **CULTIVATION** Grow in well-drained, moderately fertile, preferably gritty, loamy soil in full sun. Trim lightly after flowering to maintain compactness.
• **PROPAGATION** Sow seed in containers when ripe. Root greenwood cuttings in early summer.
• **PESTS AND DISEASES** Clubroot, downy mildew, basal stem rot, and root rot caused by fungi may occur. Aphids can also be a problem.

Alyssum wulfenianum

A. alpestre. Spreading, evergreen, mat-forming perennial with spoon-shaped, grayish green basal leaves, ¼in (6mm) long. Bears elongated clusters of numerous fragrant, tiny yellow flowers with notched petals, in summer. ↕ to 6in (15cm), ↔ indefinite. W. and C. Alps. Zone 5.
A. maritimum see *Lobularia maritima*.
***A. montanum* 'Berggold'**, syn. *A. montanum* 'Mountain Gold'. Evergreen, mat-forming perennial with prostrate stems and rosettes of small, oblong to obovate, gray leaves. Racemes of many fragrant, golden yellow flowers, each to ¼in (6mm) across, are borne in early summer. ↕ 4–6in (10–15cm), ↔ to 20in (50cm) or more. Zone 4.
***A. montanum* 'Mountain Gold'** see *A. montanum* 'Berggold'.
A. saxatile see *Aurinia saxatilis*.
A. spinosum, syn. *Ptilotrichum spinosum*. Compact, mounded, evergreen subshrub with densely branching, spine-tipped stems. Dense, corymb-like racemes of white flowers, each to ¼in (6mm) across, are borne in early summer above tiny, obovate, silvery gray leaves. ↕↔ 12–20in (30–50cm). S.E. France, S. Spain. Zone 4.
A. vesicaria see *Coluteocarpus vesicarius*.
A. wulfenianum ■ Erect or prostrate, tufted, evergreen perennial producing rosettes of small, oblong-obovate, gray- or white-hairy leaves. Corymbs of tiny pale yellow flowers, each to ¼in (6mm) across, are borne in early summer. ↕ 4–6in (10–15cm), ↔ to 20in (50cm). S.E. Alps. Zone 5.

▷***Amana edulis*** see *Tulipa edulis*

AMARANTHUS

AMARANTHACEAE

Genus of about 60 species of erect, spreading, or prostrate annuals or short-lived perennials, often invasive, from a range of habitats, including wasteland and fields, in temperate and tropical regions worldwide. They have alternate, entire, often colorful leaves, and bear large, upright or pendent, catkin-like cymes of numerous densely packed, small, red or green flowers in summer and early autumn. The flowers are followed by variously colored seed heads. Where not hardy, use as summer bedding, or grow in containers or hanging baskets; they may also be grown as short-lived houseplants or in a temperate greenhouse. *A. tricolor* cultivars are best grown under glass in cool climates. *A. caudatus* and *A. hypochondriacus* cultivars are good for cut or dried flowers.
• **CULTIVATION** Under glass, grow in soil-based potting mix in full light. Water freely in summer, and provide high humidity. Outdoors, grow in moderately fertile, humus-rich, moist soil in full sun. *A. caudatus* will tolerate poor soil. Water freely during dry periods in summer to prolong flowering.
• **PROPAGATION** Sow seed at 68°F (20°C) in midspring. *A. caudatus* may also be sown *in situ* in midspring; thin to 24in (60cm) apart.
• **PESTS AND DISEASES** White rust, brown rust, *Cercospora* leaf spot, and *Phyllosticta* leaf spot occur on foliage. Root rot can also be a problem. Prone to aster yellows and virus diseases, as well as aphids.

Amaranthus caudatus

A. caudatus ▣ (Love-lies-bleeding, Tassel flower). Bushy, erect annual or short-lived perennial with red, purple, or green stems, and ovate to ovate-oblong, light green leaves, to 6in (15cm) long. Some cultivars have red or purple-green leaves. Tassel-like, pendent, terminal and axillary panicles, 18–24in (45–60cm) long, of crimson-purple flowers are borne freely from summer to early autumn. ↕ 3–5ft (1–1.5m), ↔ 18–30in (45–75cm). Africa, India, Peru. **'Love Lies Bleeding'** is vigorous, with long, drooping, blood-red spikes. **'Viridis'** ▣ produces tassels of vivid green flowers, fading to greenish cream.

A. cruentus (Prince's feather, Purple amaranth, Red amaranth). Coarsely hairy, erect annual with ovate to lance-shaped, purplish green leaves, to 6in (15cm) long. Bears pendent, cylindrical, terminal cymes, to 24in (60cm) long, of tightly packed, red-suffused green flowers from summer to early autumn, followed by red-brown or purple, sometimes yellow seed heads. ↕ to 6ft (2m), ↔ 18in (45cm). Tropical North and South America. **'Golden Giant'** has prominent golden seed heads.

Amaranthus caudatus 'Viridis'

Amaranthus tricolor 'Illumination'

***A. hypochondriacus* cultivars.** Erect, bushy annuals with oblong-lance-shaped, dark purple-green leaves, 6in (15cm) long. From summer to early autumn, bears tiny crimson flowers in erect, plume-like, sometimes flattened, terminal cymes, to 6in (15cm) or more long. ↕ 3–4ft (0.9–1.2m), ↔ 12–18in (30–45cm). **'Green Thumb'** has much-divided cymes of brilliant yellow-green flowers; ↕ to 24in (60cm), ↔ 12in (30cm). **'Pygmy Torch'** is dwarf, with erect cymes of maroon flowers; ↕ 12–18in (30–45cm), ↔ 12in (30cm).

A. tricolor* cultivars** (Chinese spinach, Tampala). Erect, bushy annuals, grown for their ovate or elliptic, sometimes lance-shaped, multi-colored leaves, to 8in (20cm) or more long, which vary in color from green or purple to brilliant crimson or maroon, often suffused with gold, rose-pink, and bronze in the different cultivars. Insignificant green or red flowers are borne in often thickened and flattened, terminal or axillary cymes, from summer to early autumn. ↕ 4½ft (1.3m), ↔ 12–18in (30–45cm). **'Early Splendor'** has showy scarlet foliage; ↕ 3½–4ft (1.1–1.2m), ↔ 24–30in (60–75cm). **'Flaming Fountains'** has willow-like, lance-shaped leaves in carmine-red, crimson, and bronze. **'Illumination'** ▣ has ovate to elliptic, bright rose-red upper leaves topped with gold, and lower leaves in copper-brown; ↕ to 18in (45cm). **'Joseph's Coat'** has ovate to elliptic, gold and crimson upper leaves and a mix of green, yellow, and chocolate-brown lower leaves. **'Molten Fire'** has brown-red to maroon leaves. **var. *salicifolius has a pyramidal habit and pendulous leaves, to 7in (18cm) long.

x AMARCRINUM

syn. x CRINODONNA

AMARYLLIDACEAE

Hybrid genus of a single summer-flowering, evergreen, bulbous perennial, a cross between *Amaryllis* and *Crinum*. x *A. memoria-corsii* is similar to *Crinum* in both its growth and showy, funnel-shaped flowers. Where hardy, grow in a mixed or herbaceous border or at the base of a sheltered wall. In colder climates, grow in a cool greenhouse or conservatory.

• **CULTIVATION** Plant in late summer or spring, with the nose of the bulb just below soil level. Under glass, grow in well-drained, soil-based potting mix, with additional leaf mold and sharp sand, in full light. In the growing season, water moderately and apply a balanced liquid fertilizer monthly; reduce water after flowering and keep almost dry in winter. Outdoors, grow in moderately fertile, dry, well-drained soil in full sun. Protect foliage from prolonged cold.

• **PROPAGATION** Remove offsets from established plants in early spring; grow on under glass for 1–2 years before planting outside in spring.

• **PESTS AND DISEASES** Susceptible to slug damage; aphids and spider mites may be problems under glass.

x *Amarcrinum memoria-corsii*

x *A. howardii* see x *A. memoria-corsii.*

x *A. memoria-corsii* ▣ syn. x *A. howardii*, x *Crinodonna corsii.* Robust, bulbous perennial with semi-erect, wide, strap-shaped, basal leaves, to 24in (60cm) long. In late summer, thick stems bear loose umbels of up to 10 funnel-shaped, fragrant, rose-pink flowers, 2½–4in (6–10cm) long. ↕ 3ft (1m), PD24in (60cm). Garden origin. Zone 8.

x AMARYGIA

syn. x BRUNSDONNA

AMARYLLIDACEAE

Hybrid genus of a single bulbous perennial, a cross between *Amaryllis belladonna* and *Brunsvigia*, cultivated for its umbels of showy flowers, which are borne before the leaves from summer to autumn. Where hardy, grow in a mixed or herbaceous border or at the base of a warm, sheltered wall. In cooler areas, grow in a cool greenhouse or conservatory.

• **CULTIVATION** Plant from early to late summer with the neck of the bulb just above soil level. Under glass, grow in soil-based potting mix with additional leaf mold and sharp sand. Provide full light, but shade when flowering. Water moderately during the growing season, more sparingly when the leaves fade; keep dry while dormant. Allow the bulbs to become congested before potting on. Outdoors, grow in humus-rich, sandy, well-drained soil in full sun; protect foliage from prolonged cold.

• **PROPAGATION** Remove offsets from congested plants only, just before the plant comes into growth in summer.

• **PESTS AND DISEASES** Prone to leaf scorch. Narcissus nematode, narcissus bulb flies, aphids, mealybugs, whiteflies, and spider mites may be problems.

x *A. parkeri*, syn. x *Brunsdonna parkeri.* Robust, bulbous perennial bearing loose umbels of up to 12 large, funnel-shaped, frilled pink flowers, 2½–4in (6–10cm) long, on thick stems in summer. Semi-erect, strap-shaped, basal leaves, 12–18in (30–45cm) long, are borne after flowering. ↕ 3ft (1m), PD12in (30cm). Garden origin. ❀ (min. 41°F/5°C)

AMARYLLIS

AMARYLLIDACEAE

Genus of one species of deciduous, summer-flowering, bulbous perennial from coastal hills and streambanks in S. Western Cape, South Africa. It is cultivated for its showy flowers. Where not hardy, grow in a cool greenhouse; where not reliably hardy, grow against a sheltered wall.

• **CULTIVATION** Plant bulbs just below the surface after the foliage dies down in late spring. Under glass, grow in soil-based potting mix, with additional leaf mold and sharp sand, in full light. In growth, water moderately and apply a balanced liquid fertilizer monthly; keep dry when dormant. Outdoors, grow in moderately fertile, well-drained soil in full sun or partial shade.

• **PROPAGATION** Sow seed thinly in containers at 61°F (16°C) as soon as ripe; grow on under glass. Remove offsets when dormant, and grow on under glass for 1 or 2 seasons, before planting outdoors.

• **PESTS AND DISEASES** Leaf scorch (red blotch), *Cercospora* leaf spot, and Southern blight are common. Cucumber mosaic virus may be present. Slugs and narcissus bulb fliesmay be problems, as well as aphids and spider mites under glass.

A. belladonna ▣ (Magic lily, Naked ladies, Resurrection lily). Bulbous perennial producing thick, purple or purple-green stems with umbels of 6 or more funnel-shaped, scented pink flowers, 2½–4in (6–10cm) long, in summer. Strap-shaped, fleshy leaves, 9–16in (22–40cm) long, are produced in late fall or early spring and die down well before the flower stalks emerge. ↕ 24in (60cm), PD4in (10cm). South Africa. Zone 8. **'Barberton'** produces dark rose-pink flowers. **'Cape Town'** bears deep rose-red

Amaryllis belladonna

Amaryllis belladonna 'Hathor'

flowers. **'Hathor'** ▣ has white flowers, which are pink in bud. **'Johannesburg'** is free flowering, with pale pink flowers. **'Kimberley'** bears deep carmine-pink flowers with white centers.

AMBERBOA

Sweet sultan

ASTERACEAE

Genus of about 6 species of upright annuals or biennials found in gravelly and sandy soils from the Mediterranean to W. and C. Asia, with alternate, entire to deeply divided, pinnatifid, gray-green leaves. Attractive, solitary flowerheads, each with a thistle-like center of disk florets and soft, fringed rings of long, outer ray florets, are borne from spring to autumn. Grow sweet sultans in a border or cutting garden.

• **CULTIVATION** Grow in any moderately fertile, well-drained, neutral to alkaline soil in full sun. Provide plants with light, twiggy support when they reach 3–4in (7–10cm) high. Make successive sowings for continued bloom.

• **PROPAGATION** Sow seed thinly in containers in a cold frame or *in situ* in early spring; plant out *A. moschata* seedlings in potfuls to avoid root disturbance.

• **PESTS AND DISEASES** Powdery mildew may be a problem in dry summers.

A. moschata, syn. *Centaurea moschata* (Sweet sultan). Strongly branched annual with gray-green leaves, the basal leaves entire, to 4in (10cm) long, the stem leaves lobed or pinnatifid. Bears scented, fringed flowerheads, to 2in (5cm) across, resembling large corn-flowers, in white, yellow, pink, or purple, on erect stems, from spring to summer. ↕ to 24in (60cm), ↔ 9in (23cm). Turkey, Caucasus. **'Imperialis'** bears flowerheads in a range of colors, including white, yellow, pink, red, and purple. **'The Bride'** has pure white flowerheads.

▷ ***Amblyopetalum*** see *Tweedia*

AMELANCHIER

Juneberry, Shadbush, Snowy mespilus

ROSACEAE

Genus of about 25 species of deciduous trees and shrubs, often suckering, mostly from moist woodland and streambanks in Europe, Asia, and North America. Amelanchiers are cultivated for their racemes of 5-petaled, star-shaped, flat to very shallowly saucer-shaped, usually white or pink-flushed flowers, ½–¾in (1–2cm) across, borne from early to midspring, and for their fine autumn color and fruit. The alternate, ovate to oblong leaves are often silver or bronze when young, and open with the flowers. Grow at the edge of a woodland, in a shrub border, or as specimen plants. The spherical or pear-shaped, purple to maroon fruits, attractive to birds, ripen in summer and are edible.

• **CULTIVATION** Grow in acidic, fertile, moist but well-drained soil in sun or partial shade. *A. asiatica* and *A. alnifolia* tolerate alkaline soil. Pruning group 1.

• **PROPAGATION** Sow seed in a seedbed as soon as ripe; the species hybridize freely. Root greenwood or semi-ripe cuttings in summer. Remove suckers of stoloniferous species in winter.

• **PESTS AND DISEASES** Susceptible to fireblight and a variety of fungal leaf spots. *Gymnosporangium* rust and powdery mildew are common. Dieback and cankers caused by many different fungi occur.

Amelanchier arborea

A. alnifolia (Alder-leaved serviceberry, Saskatoon). Suckering shrub with oval to oblong leaves, ¾–2in (2–5cm) long, turning bright red or yellow in autumn. In late spring, pure white flowers are borne in racemes, to 3in (8cm) long, followed by small purple-black fruit, ½in (1.5cm) across. ↕↔ 12ft (4m). N.W. North America. Zone 2b. **'Regent'** is compact in habit and bears white flowers. Produces abundant, purple-black, very sweet fruit, excellent for jams, jellies, and attracting wildlife. ↕ 4–6ft (1.2–2m).

A. arborea ▣ (Downy serviceberry). Round-headed tree, sometimes multi-stemmed and shrubby, with ovate leaves, 1½– 4in (4–10cm) long, gray and hairy when young, mid-green in summer, turning yellow to red in autumn. Pendent racemes, 2–3in (5–8cm) long, of fragrant white flowers open in midspring, followed by red-purple fruit, ¼–½in (6–15mm) across. ↕ 25ft (8m), ↔ 30ft (10m). E. North America. Zone 2b.

A. asiatica (Asian serviceberry). Spreading tree with arching branches and ovate leaves, 1½–3in (4–8cm) long, white-hairy beneath when young, mid-green in summer, then orange to red in autumn. Bears scented white flowers in upright racemes, 1¼–2½in (3–6cm) long, in late spring, followed by blue-black fruit, ¼–½in (6–15mm) across. ↕ 25ft (8m), ↔ 30ft (10m). China, Korea, Japan. Zone 6.

A. canadensis (Shadblow, Shadbush). Dense, erect, suckering shrub with oblong-elliptic to obovate leaves, 1½–2in (4–5cm) long, white-hairy when young, becoming almost hairless when mature, and mid-green in summer, yellow to orange and red in autumn. Erect racemes, 1–2½in (2.5–6cm) long, of white flowers open in spring, followed by sweet, blue-black fruit, ¼–½in (6–15mm) across. ↕ 20ft (6m), ↔ 10ft (3m). E. North America. Zone 3b.

A. x grandiflora (*A. arborea* x *A. laevis*) (Apple serviceberry). Spreading, sometimes shrubby tree producing ovate

Amelanchier x *grandiflora* 'Ballerina'

Amelanchier laevis

leaves, 1¾–3in (4.5–8cm) long, bronze with hairy undersides, turning green in late spring, orange and red in autumn. Bears pendent racemes, 2½–3in (6–8cm) long, of white flowers in spring, followed by sweet, juicy, blue-black fruit, ¼–½in (6–15mm) across. ↕ 25ft (8m), ↔ 30ft (10m). Garden origin. Zone 4. **'Autumn Brilliance'** is vigorous, with brilliant red autumn color. **'Ballerina'** ▣ has foliage turning red and purple in autumn, and bears profuse flowers in arching racemes, to 6in (15cm) long. Highly resistant to fireblight. **'Cole Select'** has consistent autumn coloration. **'Princess Diana'** is relatively slow-growing, with red autumn color. **'Robin Hill'** is compact and broadly upright, with white flowers and pink-tinged buds; ↕ 25ft (8m), ↔ 15ft (5m). **'Rubescens'**, syn. *A. lamarckii* 'Rubescens', has dark pink buds and paler pink flowers. **'Strata'** has strongly horizontal branches. A good alternative to *Cornus florida*.

A. laevis ▣ (Allegheny serviceberry). Spreading, sometimes shrubby tree with ovate leaves, 1½–2½in (4–6cm) long, bronze and hairless when young, turning mid-green in summer, then orange or red in autumn. Bears pendent racemes, 1½–5in (4–13cm) long, of white flowers in midspring, followed by sweet, blue-black fruit, to ½in (1.5cm) long. ↕↔ 25ft (8m). North America. Zone 3b. **'Cumulus'** usually grows as a single-stemmed tree and is slightly larger, more open, and more disease resistant.

A. lamarckii ▣ Upright-stemmed shrub or small tree with white-haired young shoots and leaves, soon becoming hairless. Elliptic to oblong bronze leaves,

Amelanchier lamarckii

to 3in (8cm) long, turn dark green, then orange and red in autumn. In midspring, bears pendent racemes, 2½–5in (6–13cm) long, of white flowers, followed by sweet, juicy, purple-black fruit, ¼–½in (6–15mm) across. ↕ 30ft (10m), ↔ 40ft (12m). Uncertain origin. Zone 4.
'Rubescens' see *A.* x *grandiflora* 'Rubescens'.
A. stolonifera (Running serviceberry). Dense, erect, thicket-forming, suckering shrub with oval to rounded, mid-green leaves, ½–1¼in (1–3cm) long, white-hairy beneath when young, turning yellow to orange and red in autumn. Bears erect, compact racemes, to 1½in (4cm) long, of 4–10 white flowers in spring, followed by sweet, blue-black fruit, ¼–⅜in (6–8mm) across. ↕ 6ft (2m), ↔ 5ft (1.5m). E. North America. Zone 3b.

AMESIELLA

ORCHIDACEAE

Genus of one species of evergreen, epiphytic, monopodial orchid from the Philippines, where it grows in mountain forest at an altitude of 2,600ft (800m). Short stems, 1¼–2½in (3–6cm) long, bear 2-ranked leaves (usually no more than 4) and produce racemes of spurred, almost spherical flowers, mostly in autumn.
• **CULTIVATION** Intermediate-growing orchid. Grow in small pots or slatted baskets of epiphytic orchid potting mix, in filtered light and humid conditions. Water moderately throughout the year, applying fertilizer at every third watering in summer. See also p.46.
• **PROPAGATION** Not suitable for division, although cuttings or offshoots may be rooted successfully.
• **PESTS AND DISEASES** Prone to spider mites, aphids, and mealybugs.

A. philippinensis. Miniature, evergreen, epiphytic orchid with elliptic-oblong, fleshy leaves, to 2in (5cm) long. Short, axillary racemes of 1–3 almost spherical white flowers, 1¼in (3cm) across, each with a yellow stain on the lip, and spurs 1½in (4cm) long, are produced in autumn. ↕ 2½in (6cm), ↔ 4in (10cm). Philippines. ❀ (min. 61°F/16°C; max. 86°F/30°C)

AMHERSTIA

FABACEAE

Genus of one species of evergreen tree, found on riverbanks in tropical forest in Burma. It has alternate, large, pinnate leaves, and long racemes of 5-petaled, orchid-like flowers. Where temperatures fall below 61°F (16°C), grow *A. nobilis* in a warm greenhouse, although it rarely flowers in a container. In tropical areas, it is a spectacular specimen tree.
• **CULTIVATION** Under glass, grow in soil-based potting mix in bright filtered light and high humidity. In the growing season, water freely and apply a balanced liquid fertilizer monthly; water sparingly in winter. Outdoors, grow in moist, fertile soil in a sheltered, reasonably sunny site. Pruning group 1; plants under glass may need restrictive pruning in late winter or after flowering.
• **PROPAGATION** Sow seed in spring at a minimum temperature of 70–75°F (21–24°C). Root semi-ripe cuttings with bottom heat in summer, or layer in early to midautumn.
• **PESTS AND DISEASES** Spider mites may be a problem under glass.

Amherstia nobilis (inset: flower detail)

A. nobilis ■ (Orchid tree, Pride of Burma). Erect, open-branched tree producing pinnate leaves, 24–36in (60–90cm) long, divided into 8–18 copper-pink leaflets, which turn deep green with age. The orchid-like flowers, 2½–4in (6–10cm) across, are bright red, suffused pink and white, with yellow tips and protruding stamens, and are borne in pendent racemes, 16–36in (40–90cm) long, from winter to early summer. ↕ 30ft (10m), ↔ 50ft (15m). Burma. ❀ (min. 61°F/16°C)

AMICIA

FABACEAE

Genus of 7 species of upright, woody-based perennials found on riverbanks and in woodland in the mountains of Mexico and in the Andes. They are grown mainly for their alternate leaves, each with 2 pairs of leaflets and, when young, large, pale green stipules with purple veins. The pea-like autumn flowers may be damaged by early frosts, except in mild areas. Where temperatures fall below 14°F (-10°C), grow in containers in a cool greenhouse and move outdoors in summer. Elsewhere, grow in a mixed or herbaceous border.
• **CULTIVATION** Under glass, grow in soil-based potting mix in full light. In the growing season, water freely and apply a balanced liquid fertilizer monthly; keep just moist in winter. Outdoors, grow in well-drained, fertile soil in full sun; mulch in winter. Cut back nearly to the ground in spring.
• **PROPAGATION** Sow seed at 55–64°F (13–18°C) in spring. Root basal cuttings in late spring, or semi-ripe cuttings in summer.
• **PESTS AND DISEASES** Slugs and snails may be problems.

A. zygomeris ■ Woody-based perennial with mid-green leaves, 6–8in (15–20cm) long. Each leaf has 2 pairs of inversely heart-shaped leaflets with rounded, pale green stipules, to 1½in (4cm) across, veined purple and tinged reddish purple. Racemes of 3–10 pea-like yellow flowers, to 1¼in (3cm) across, with purple keels, are borne in autumn. ↕ 7ft (2.2m), ↔ 4ft (1.2m). Mexico. Zone 8.

Amicia zygomeris

AMMI

APIACEAE

Genus of about 10 species of slender, upright to spreading, summer-flowering annuals and biennials occurring in scrub in Europe, N. Africa, and W. Asia. They have pinnate to 3-pinnate or ternate to 3-ternate, fern-like leaves, and white or creamy white, lace-like flowers borne in large, rounded, branched umbels in summer. Suitable for a border or a cottage garden.
• **CULTIVATION** Grow in any moist but well-drained, fertile soil in sun or partial shade. Provide support when seedlings are 3–4in (7–10cm) high.
• **PROPAGATION** Sow seed *in situ* in spring.
• **PESTS AND DISEASES** Infrequent.

A. majus (Bishop's weed). Slender, upright, branched annual producing 2- or 3-pinnate, light green leaves, 6–8in (15–20cm) long, divided into many finely toothed, ovate to lance-shaped leaflets. Compound umbels with 30 or more rays, each with 10 or more small white flowers, resembling delicate lace-work, are borne in summer. Good for cutting. ↕ 12–36in (30–90cm), ↔ 12in (30cm). S. Europe, Turkey, N. Africa.

AMMOBIUM

Winged everlasting

ASTERACEAE

Genus of 2 or 3 upright, branched or unbranched perennials from grassland and open forest in E. Australia. The white-woolly, lance-shaped leaves are produced in broad, basal rosettes. Bright green flowering stems, winged and flattened, and usually branched, bear loose clusters of papery flowerheads, each to 1in (2.5cm) across. Suitable for an annual border; *A. alatum* is excellent for dried flower arrangements.
• **CULTIVATION** Grow in any light, well-drained soil, preferably low in nutrients, in full sun. May tolerate temperatures to 23°F (-5°C) in well-drained soil. Cut flowerheads for drying before fully open.
• **PROPAGATION** Sow seed at 55–61°F (13–16°C) in early spring, or *in situ* in midspring.
• **PESTS AND DISEASES** Infrequent.

A. alatum (Winged everlasting). Rosette-forming perennial, grown as an annual, with lance-shaped, white-woolly leaves, to 7in (18cm) long. In summer, winged, bright green stems bear clusters of flowerheads, to 1in (2.5cm) across, with orange or yellow disk florets and reflexed, papery, silvery outer bracts and scales. ↕ 18–36in (45–90cm), ↔ 18in (45cm). Queensland, New South Wales.

▷ ***Amomyrtus luma*** see *Myrtus lechleriana*

AMORPHA

FABACEAE

Genus of 15 species of deciduous shrubs from North America, found in dry, often sandy areas, such as prairies, scrub, and hills, and sometimes in woodland and on riverbanks. They are grown for their aromatic leaves, which are alternate and pinnate, consisting of 7–45 leaflets, and for their dense, erect racemes of

Amorpha fruticosa

small flowers, which have only a single petal (the standard). They are also valued for their ability to thrive in very poor, dry soils, particularly where temperatures fall to -22°F (-30°C) or below. Grow in a mixed or shrub border.
• **CULTIVATION** Grow in light, sandy, well-drained soil in sun or partial shade. Pruning group 6.
• **PROPAGATION** Sow pre-soaked or scarified seed in autumn in containers in an open frame. Separate rooted suckers of *A. fruticosa* in autumn or late winter.
• **PESTS AND DISEASES** Susceptible to powdery mildew and rust, as well as a few fungal leaf spots.

A. canescens (Lead plant). Rounded shrub producing hairy, gray-white shoots and pinnate leaves, 2½–6in (6–15cm) long, with 10–20 pairs of overlapping, ovate-oblong to elliptic leaflets. Small, pea-like, dark violet-purple flowers, to ¼in (6mm) long, with orange anthers, are borne in racemes, to 6in (15cm) long, in late summer and early autumn. ↕ 3ft (1m), ↔ 5ft (1.5m). C. North America. Zone 2b.
A. fruticosa ▣ (Bastard indigo, False indigo). Fast-growing, spreading shrub with pinnate leaves, to 12in (30cm) long, composed of 13–33 oval or oblong leaflets. Orange- or yellow-anthered, purple-blue flowers, ¾in (2cm) long, are produced in narrow racemes, to 6in (15cm) long, in summer. Can become weedy. ↕↔ to 15ft (5m). E. US. Zone 2b.

AMORPHOPHALLUS
Devil's tongue, Snake palm
ARACEAE

Genus of 90–100 species of perennials, with corm-like rhizomes, from moist, shaded habitats in tropical Africa and Asia, grown for their magnificent, deeply lobed leaves and bizarre flowers. The large, dramatic, purple-red to greenish white spathes, produced in summer, are usually unpleasantly scented. Outside tropical regions, grow in a warm greenhouse, although they may be moved outdoors in summer after any danger of frost has passed.
• **CULTIVATION** Plant dormant tubers 4in (10cm) deep in late winter or early spring. Under glass, grow in soil-based potting mix in containers 24–36in (60–90cm) wide, in filtered light. In the growing season, water freely and apply a balanced liquid fertilizer monthly.

Amorphophallus titanum

Reduce water as the foliage dies down; overwinter tubers in warm, barely moist conditions. Outdoors, grow in moist, humus-rich soil in partial shade.
• **PROPAGATION** Sow seed at 66–75°F (19–24°C) in autumn or early spring. Separate offsets when dormant.
• **PESTS AND DISEASES** Dasheen mosaic virus may occur. Bacterial soft rot and anthracnose are sometimes a problem.

A. konjac, syn. *A. rivieri* (Devil's tongue, Snake palm, Umbrella arum). Perennial with corm-like rhizomes, to 10in (25cm) across. Reddish purple spathes, to 16in (40cm) long, each with a protruding, dark brown spadix, are borne on stalks 24in (60cm) long, in summer. Each spathe is followed by a solitary, 2-pinnate leaf, to 4½ft (1.3m) long, with oblong-elliptic leaflets or lobes, on a brownish green, white-mottled leaf stalk, 3–4½ft (1–1.3m) long. ↕ 3–4½ft (1–1.3m), ↔ 3ft (1m). S.E. Asia. ❀ (min. 55–61°F/13–16°C)
A. rivieri see *A. konjac.*
A. titanum ▣ (Corpse flower). Perennial with huge, corm-like rhizomes, to 20in (50cm) across, and weighing up to 15lb (7kg) each. In summer, produces reddish purple spathes, 5ft (1.5m) long, each with a protruding white spadix, on stalks 3ft (1m) long. The spathes are followed by solitary, 3-parted, deeply lobed leaves, to 12ft (4m) across, borne on leaf stalks 14ft (4.5m) long. ↕ 15ft (5m), ↔ 12ft (4m). Indonesia (Sumatra). ❀ (min. 55–61°F/13–16°C)

AMPELOPSIS
VITACEAE

Genus of about 25 species of woody, deciduous climbers and a few shrubs from woodland in Asia and North America. They are cultivated for their attractive foliage, which often colors well, turning red and yellow in autumn; the leaves are alternate, simple, palmate or pinnate, often lobed or toothed, with clinging tendrils on the stems opposite the leaves. They are also valued for their sometimes ornamental, spherical or top-shaped berries, which develop from insignificant cymes of small green flowers. The climbers are excellent for covering a wall, fence, pergola, old tree stump, or tree. If grown on house walls, keep clear of gutters and shingles. *A. brevipedunculata* 'Elegans' may also be grown as a houseplant.
• **CULTIVATION** Under glass, grow in soil-based potting mix in bright filtered light. During the growing season, water freely and apply a balanced liquid fertilizer monthly; water sparingly in winter. Outdoors, grow in any moist but well-drained, fertile soil in sun or partial shade. Fruiting will be most reliable in a sunny site, especially where root growth can be restricted. Pruning group 11, in spring.
• **PROPAGATION** Sow seed in containers in an open frame in autumn, or stratify and sow in containers in a cold frame in spring. Root softwood cuttings in summer.
• **PESTS AND DISEASES** Fungal leaf spots, powdery mildew, and downy mildew sometimes occur. Flea beetles and Japanese beetles can cause severe damage.

A. aconitifolia, syn. *Vitis aconitifolia* (Monkshood vine). Vigorous, slender-stemmed climber with 3- or 5-palmate, glossy, dark green leaves, to 5in (13cm) long, composed of lance- to diamond-shaped, deeply lobed leaflets. In late summer, bears axillary cymes of small green flowers, followed by spherical orange fruit, to ¼in (6mm) across. ↕ 40ft (12m). Mongolia, N. China. Zone 2b.
A. brevipedunculata ▣ (Porcelain berry, Porcelain vine). Vigorous climber producing palmately 3-lobed, occasionally 5-lobed, dark green leaves, hairy beneath, and 2–6in (5–15cm) long. Branched, axillary cymes of small green flowers are borne in summer, followed by attractive, almost spherical fruit, ¼–⅜in (5–8mm) across, progressing from green to light blue to darker blue and purple shades, generally occuring at the same time. May become invasive. ↕ 15ft (5m). N.E. Asia. Zone 3. **'Elegans'** is less vigorous, and has dark green leaves, heavily mottled white and pink. **var. *maximowiczii***, syn. *A. heterophylla, Vitis heterophylla*, has very variable, slightly longer leaves than the species, sometimes broadly heart-shaped at the bases and shallowly lobed, or deeply cut into 3–5 lobes.

Ampelopsis brevipedunculata

A. heterophylla see *A. brevipedunculata* var. *maximowiczii.*
A. megalophylla. Vigorous climber with glaucous shoots and large, 2-pinnate, occasionally pinnate leaves, to 24in (60cm) long, composed of 7–9 ovate to ovate-oblong, dark green leaflets, glaucous on the reverse. Few-flowered, axillary cymes of green flowers are borne in late summer, followed by top-shaped black fruit, ¼in (6mm) across. ↕ 30ft (10m). W. China. Zone 6.
A. sempervirens see *Cissus striata.*
A. veitchii see *Parthenocissus tricuspidata* 'Veitchii'.

▷***Amphicome*** see *Incarvillea*

AMSONIA syn. RHAZYA
APOCYNACEAE

Genus of about 20 species of clump-forming perennials from light woodland or grassland in moist, stony or heavy soils in S.E. Europe, Turkey, Japan, and N.E. and C. US. They have alternate, lance-shaped or ovate to elliptic, entire leaves, which in several species turn yellow in autumn. Long-lasting cymes or panicles of narrowly funnel-shaped, distinctively blue flowers, with 5 spreading petal lobes, are borne from spring to summer. They are suitable for a mixed or herbaceous border, at the edge of a woodland, or in a wildflower garden. Contact with the milky sap may irritate skin.
• **CULTIVATION** Grow in any moist but well-drained soil in full sun to light shade. Will tolerate some drought.
• **PROPAGATION** Sow seed in containers in a cold frame in autumn or spring. Divide in spring. Root softwood or basal cuttings in early summer.
• **PESTS AND DISEASES** Susceptible to rust.

A. ciliata (Blue milkweed, Bluestar). Slow-growing, erect, clump-forming perennial with crowded, linear, thread-like leaves, 1–2in (2.5–5cm) long. Panicles of periwinkle-blue flowers, ½in (1.5cm) across, are produced in summer. ↕ 12–36in (30–90cm), ↔ 12in (30cm). North Carolina to Texas. Zone 6.
A. hubrectii. Clump-forming perennial with linear, willow-like, mid-green leaves, 1¼–3in (3–8cm) long, turning bright yellow in autumn. Produces panicles of sky-blue flowers, 2–3in (5–8cm) across, in late spring. ↕ 3ft (1m), ↔ 4ft (1.2m). C. and N.E. US. Zone 5b.
A. illustris. Clump-forming perennial with broadly ovate to lance-shaped or elliptic, glossy, bright green leaves, 1¼–3in (3–8cm) long. Open panicles of light blue flowers, to ½in (1.5cm) across, are borne on erect stems, in late spring and early summer. ↕ 4ft (1.2m), ↔ 18in (45cm). C. and S. US. Zone 6.
A. orientalis, syn. *Rhazya orientalis.* Clump-forming perennial with many erect stems rising from a woody rootstock, and with narrowly ovate to lance-shaped, willow-like, grayish green leaves, 1¼–3in (3–8cm) long. Short, compact or loose panicles of violet-blue flowers, ½–¾in (1–2cm) across, are produced in early and midsummer. ↕ 20–36in (50–90cm), ↔ 36in (90cm). N.E. Greece, N.W. Turkey. Zone 4.

Amsonia tabernaemontana

A. salicifolia see *A. tabernaemontana* var. *salicifolia.*
A. tabernaemontana ■ (Willow bluestar). Clump-forming perennial with many stems and small, ovate to elliptic or lance-shaped, matte, dark green leaves, 1¼–3in (3–8cm) long. Dense, rounded, cyme-like panicles of pale blue flowers, ½–¾in (1–2cm) across, are borne from late spring to mid-summer. ↕24in (60cm), ↔ 18in (45cm). E. US. Zone 4. **var. *salicifolia*,** syn. *A. salicifolia*, has much narrower leaves, glaucous beneath, and produces flowers in more open panicles.

▷***Amygdalus*** see *Prunus*

ANACAMPSEROS

PORTULACACEAE

Genus of about 50 species of perennial succulents, mainly from the most arid regions of Africa and Australia, with either minute leaves, often covered by hairs or hidden by stipules, or fleshy, ovoid to spherical, conspicuous leaves. In summer, the 5-petaled, white, pink, or red flowers, produced singly or in racemes, open only for a brief period, in full sun. Where not hardy, grow in a temperate greenhouse; in frost-free areas, grow in a desert garden.
• **CULTIVATION** Under glass, grow in standard cactus potting mix in full light with good ventilation. In the growing season, water moderately and apply a diluted liquid fertilizer monthly; keep almost dry when dormant in winter. Outdoors, grow in poor to moderately fertile, sharply drained soil in full sun. See also pp.48–49.
• **PROPAGATION** Sow seed as soon as ripe at 64°F (18°C), or take stem cuttings in spring and root at the same temperature.
• **PESTS AND DISEASES** Prone to aphids.

A. alstonii. Tufted, many-branched succulent with a tuberous rootstock, which, when exposed, is caudex-like. Tiny leaves are arranged in rows along the branches and are hidden by small, overlapping, triangular silver stipules, 1/16in (2mm) long. Solitary, open white flowers, 1¼in (3cm) across, are borne in summer. ↕ 1¼in (3cm), ↔ 3in (8cm). South Africa (Northern Cape). ❄ (min. 45°F/7°C)
A. comptonii. Succulent with a short, thick stem, much of which is buried, becoming swollen and caudex-like. The aerial stems produce spherical, olive-green or bronzed leaves, 1¼–2in (3–5cm) long, tapered at the tips, grooved above, and covered with white hairs. Solitary, open, red-purple, pink, or white flowers, ¼in (6mm) across, are borne in summer. ↕↔ 1in (2.5cm). Namibia, South Africa. ❄ (min. 45°F/7°C)
A. intermedia see *A. telephiastrum.*
***A. telephiastrum*,** syn. *A. intermedia*, *A. varians* (Sand rose). Mat-forming succulent, becoming tufted when mature, with ovoid, short-pointed, fleshy, brownish green leaves, ¾in (2cm) long. Racemes of 1–4 deep pink flowers, 1¼in (3cm) or more across, open in summer. ↕ 2in (5cm), ↔ 4in (10cm). South Africa (Western Cape). ❄ (min. 45°F/7°C)
A. varians see *A. telephiastrum.*

▷***Anacharis densa*** see *Egeria densa*

ANACYCLUS

ASTERACEAE

Genus of 9 species of annuals and herbaceous perennials from stony slopes and sandy and disturbed ground in the Mediterranean. The 2- or 3-pinnatisect leaves, with finely cut lobes, are produced on creeping stems radiating from a central rootstock. Solitary or paired, daisy-like flowerheads are borne on short stems in summer. Grow in an alpine house, rock garden, or wall.
• **CULTIVATION** Under glass, grow in a mix of equal parts loam, leaf mold, and sharp sand or grit, in full light. Outdoors, grow in well-drained soil in full sun, protected from excessive winter moisture.
• **PROPAGATION** Sow seed in containers in an open frame in autumn. Root softwood cuttings in spring or early summer.
• **PESTS AND DISEASES** Aphids may be a problem under glass.

A. depressus see *A. pyrethrum* var. *depressus.*
A. pyrethrum* var. *depressus ■ syn. *A. depressus* (Mt. Atlas daisy). Prostrate, mat-forming perennial with rosettes of 2- or 3-pinnatisect, gray-green leaves, 4–5½in (10–14cm) long. Bears numerous solitary flowerheads, 1–2in (2.5–5cm) across, with white ray florets; the ray florets are red on the reverse, each with a white stripe. ↕ 1–2in (2.5–5cm) or more, ↔ 4in (10cm). Atlas Mountains in Morocco, Algeria, and Tunisia. Zone 4.

Anacyclus pyrethrum var. *depressus*

Anagallis monellii 'Pacific Blue'

ANAGALLIS

Pimpernel

PRIMULACEAE

Genus of about 20 species of low-growing or creeping annuals and evergreen perennials, occurring in open meadows, bogs, and dry sites in the Mediterranean and W. Europe. The opposite or alternate leaves (occasionally borne in threes) are entire and smooth, with very short or no leaf stalks. The solitary, bell-shaped to open saucer-shaped flowers, each with 5 petals, are produced from the leaf axils. Easily cultivated, pimpernels provide colorful groundcover for a rock garden or the front of a border.
• **CULTIVATION** Under glass, grow in gritty, soil-based potting mix in full light. Outdoors, grow pimpernels in fertile, moist but well-drained soil in full sun; *A. monellii* needs moderately fertile, well-drained soil in full sun. Overwinter young plants in a cool greenhouse and plant out after danger of frost has passed. Pimpernels are often short-lived.
• **PROPAGATION** Sow seed in containers in a cold frame in spring, or divide in spring. Increase *A. tenella* 'Studland' and cultivars of *A. monellii* by soft tip-cuttings in spring or early summer.
• **PESTS AND DISEASES** Prone to aphids.

Anagallis tenella 'Studland'

A. collina see *A. monellii.*
A. linifolia see *A. monellii.*
***A. monellii*,** syn. *A. collina*, *A. linifolia* (Blue pimpernel). Low-growing perennial with branching stems bearing stalkless, lance-shaped to elliptic, mid-green leaves, to 1in (2.5cm) long, in opposite pairs or in threes. Open saucer-shaped flowers, to ½in (1.5cm) or more across, usually deep blue, sometimes reddish at the bases, are produced on long stalks in summer. Red- and pink-flowered variants are also available. ↕4–8in (10–20cm), ↔ to 16in (40cm). Mediterranean. Zone 7b. **'Pacific Blue'** ■ has gentian-blue flowers.
***A. tenella* 'Studland'** ■ Mat-forming perennial with alternate or opposite, stalkless, elliptic to rounded, bright green leaves, ⅛–⅜in (4–9mm) long. In late spring and early summer, the leaves are almost hidden by upright, bell-shaped, scented, deep pink flowers, ¼–½in (6–15mm) across. ↕ 2–4in (5–10cm), ↔ to 16in (40cm). Zone 6.

ANANAS

Pineapple

BROMELIACEAE

Genus of 5 or 6 species of evergreen, terrestrial perennials (bromeliads) from South America, occurring in habitats ranging from fairly dry to extremely humid, and from low terrain to mountains over 3,000ft (1,000m). They form rosettes of lance-shaped, spiny leaves and, in summer, produce showy flowers in dense, terminal, cone-like inflorescences on thick stems, giving rise to fleshy, swollen, edible fruits. In areas where temperatures fall below 59°F (15°C), grow pineapples as houseplants or in a warm greenhouse. In tropical climates, grow in a border.
• **CULTIVATION** Under glass, grow in terrestrial bromeliad potting mix in full light with low to moderate humidity and in draft-free conditions. Water freely during the growing and flowering season; reduce water slightly and apply a balanced liquid fertilizer weekly as the fruits begin to swell. Keep barely moist at other times of the year. Outside, grow in well-drained, fertile, humus-rich soil in full sun. See also p.47.

Ananas bracteatus 'Tricolor'

Ananas comosus 'Variegatus'

• **PROPAGATION** Root basal offsets in early summer; or carefully sever the leafy rosette at the top of the fruit, allow it a day or two to callus, then root it in a barely moist mix of peat and sand, in indirect light at 70°F (21°C).
• **PESTS AND DISEASES** Wet root rot caused by fungi is common. Fruit rot can also occur. Mealybugs and scale insects may be problems.

A. bracteatus (Red pineapple, Wild pineapple). Terrestrial bromeliad with green-brown, coarsely spiny leaves, 18in (45cm) or more long, the spines upward-pointing. In summer, bears red-bracted, yellowish red flowers in almost cylindrical inflorescences, to 6in (15cm) long, followed by edible but not very fleshy, greenish brown fruit, 6in (15cm) long. ↕ to 28in (70cm), ↔ 20in (50cm). Brazil, Paraguay, Argentina. ❀ (min. 59°F/15°C). **'Striatus'** see 'Tricolor'. **'Tricolor'** ■ syn. 'Striatus', var. *tricolor*, has deep green, yellow-striped leaves.
A. comosus (Commercial pineapple). Variable, terrestrial bromeliad with dense rosettes of slightly recurved, spiny-margined, dark green leaves, to 3ft (1m) long. In summer, produces oblong-ovoid inflorescences, 12in (30cm) or more long, of small, reddish yellow bracts and violet flowers, followed by bright red fruit, to 12in (30cm) long. ↕ 3ft (1m), ↔ 20in (50cm). Presumed to have originated in Brazil. ❀ (min. 59°F/15°C). **'Variegatus'** ■ syn. var. *variegatus*, has leaves longitudinally striped yellowish white, occasionally also with red stripes.
A. nanus. Terrestrial bromeliad resembling a miniature *A. comosus.* Slightly recurved, dark green leaves, to 24in (60cm) long, have upward-pointing marginal spines. Cone-shaped inflorescences, 4in (10cm) long, consisting of lilac-purple or red flowers with small yellow bracts, are produced in summer. They are followed by fruit to 4in (10cm) long, with a large crown. ↕ 18in (45cm), ↔ 24in (60cm). Surinam, Brazil. ❀ (min. 59°F/15°C)

ANAPHALIS

Pearly everlasting

ASTERACEAE

Genus of about 100 species of spreading to upright perennials, some evergreen, from dry slopes, dry forest, sunny riverbanks, or moist woodland in the N. hemisphere. They have woolly gray foliage and produce corymbs of papery everlasting white flowerheads, ¼–1in (0.6–2.5cm) across, which are good for cutting and drying. The larger species provide pale foliage contrast in borders too moist for most sun-loving, gray-leaved plants, while the smaller species are excellent, long-lasting rock-garden plants.
• **CULTIVATION** Grow in full sun in moderately fertile, reasonably well-drained soil that does not dry out in summer (very important for *A. nepalensis* and its variants). Most will also grow in partial shade.
• **PROPAGATION** Sow seed in containers in a cold frame in spring. Divide in early spring, or take basal or stem tip cuttings in spring or early summer.
• **PESTS AND DISEASES** Susceptible to stem rot, rust, and *Septoria* leaf spot.

A. cinnamomea see *A. margaritacea* var. *cinnamomea.*
A. margaritacea ■ Clump-forming, rhizomatous perennial with erect, leafy stems and lance-shaped, mid-green leaves, 3–5½in (7–14cm) long, white-woolly beneath. From midsummer to early autumn, bears dense corymbs, to 6in (15cm) across, of yellow flowerheads surrounded by white bracts. Tolerates drought better than others. ↕↔ 24in (60cm). N.E. Asia, North America. Zone 4. **var. *cinnamomea*,** syn. *A. cinnamomea*, has broader leaves, white or cinnamon-colored beneath, with 3 main veins, and flowerheads in tighter, rounder, many-branched corymbs; ↔ 18–20in (45–50cm). Mountains of India and Burma. **'New Snow'**, syn. 'Neuschnee', has silver-green leaves and white flowerheads. **var. *yedoensis*,** syn. *A. yedoensis*, has shorter, narrow, single-veined, white-woolly leaves, 2½in (6cm) long; Japan.
A. nepalensis ■ syn. *A. triplinervis* var. *intermedia.* Clump-forming perennial with lance-shaped, pale gray-green leaves, 1½–4in (3–10cm) long, white-woolly beneath, with 3 main veins, on short, silvery green stems. In late

Anaphalis margaritacea

Anaphalis nepalensis

summer and early autumn, produces solitary to several yellow flowerheads, surrounded by pointed white bracts, in rounded corymbs, ¾in (2cm) across. ↕ 12in (30cm), ↔ 6in (15cm) or more. Himalayas, W. China. Zone 5b. **var. *monocephala*,** syn. *A. nubigena*, has short, densely leafy, white-woolly stems, and inversely lance-shaped to linear-lance-shaped leaves, light gray-green above, white-woolly beneath, to 1in (2.5cm) long. Solitary to several, white or yellow flowerheads in corymbs, ½in (1.5cm) across, are borne in mid-summer; ↕ 4–8in (10–20cm), ↔ 12in (30cm). China (Yunnan) to Tibet.
A. nubigena see *A. nepalensis* var. *monocephala.*
A. sinica* subsp. *morii. Upright, evergreen, silvery gray, downy perennial, which is a dwarf variant of *A. sinica*, with linear-lance-shaped leaves, to ¾in (2cm) long. In late summer and early autumn, bears spherical corymbs, 1¼–3in (3–8cm) across, of white flowerheads surrounded by pointed white bracts. Tolerates heavy soils and partial shade. ↕ to 8in (20cm), ↔ to 24in (60cm). Mountainous areas of China, Korea, Japan (Kyushu). Zone 7b.
A. triplinervis. Clump-forming perennial with spoon-shaped to obovate-elliptic, pale gray-green, white-woolly leaves, 1¼–4in (3–10cm) long, with 3–5 main veins. Domed corymbs, 1½–2in (4–5cm) across, of white-bracted, yellow-centered flowerheads, are produced in mid- and late summer. ↕ 30–36in (75–90cm), ↔ 18–24in (45–60cm). Himalayas to S.W. China. Zone 3. **var. *intermedia*** see *A. nepalensis.* **'Sommerschnee'**, syn. 'Summer Snow', bears brilliant white bracts.
A. yedoensis see *A. margaritacea* var. *yedoensis.*

ANCHUSA

Alkanet

BORAGINACEAE

Genus of about 35 species of erect to spreading or mound-forming annuals, biennials, and perennials, often short-lived, occurring in sunny, dry sites, in temperate regions of Europe, Africa, and W. Asia. They have alternate, linear-lance-shaped to elliptic leaves, sometimes with a covering of bristly hairs, and are grown for their tubular, usually blue flowers with 5 spreading lobes, borne in terminal and axillary cymes. Grow dwarf species, such as *A. cespitosa*, in tufa or in a rock garden, raised bed, or trough. Taller species are ideal for a herbaceous border. The flowers are attractive to bees.
• **CULTIVATION** Grow in any moist but well-drained, moderately fertile soil in full sun. Tall species and cultivars may need staking when in flower. Many tend to be short lived; cut back top-growth after flowering to encourage the development of overwintering basal rosettes. Deadhead after the first flush of flowers to encourage a second flush. Most resent excessive winter moisture.
• **PROPAGATION** Sow seed of annuals at 55–61°F (13–16°C) in late winter or early spring. Sow seed of perennials in containers in a cold frame in spring. Root basal cuttings in spring, or insert root cuttings in late winter or early spring.
• **PESTS AND DISEASES** Rust, mildew, leaf scorch, and basal rot can occur but are not common. Cutworms, chafer grubs, and vine weevil larvae eat roots.

A. angustissima see *A. leptophylla* subsp. *incana.*
A. azurea, syn. *A. italica* (Blue bugloss, Italian alkanet). Erect, clump-forming perennial with mainly basal leaves, 4–16in (10–40cm) long, which are linear-elliptic to lance-shaped, mid- to dark green, and stiffly hairy. Branching panicles of gentian-blue flowers, to ½in (1.5cm) across, turning blue-purple with age, are borne in early summer. ↕ 3–5ft (0.9–1.5m), ↔ 24in (60cm). S. Europe, N. Africa, W. Asia. Zone 3b. **'Dropmore'** has large, lance-shaped, hairy, gray-green leaves and amethyst-blue flowers; ↕ 24–36in (60–90cm). **'Feltham Pride'** is compact, with clear, bright blue flowers. Often grown as a biennial; ↕ to 36in (90cm). **'Little John'** is long-lived and dwarf, with deep blue flowers. It is ideal for the front of a border or a rock garden; ↕ 18in (45cm), ↔ 12in (30cm). **'Loddon Royalist'** ■ is sturdy, so seldom needs staking, and has bright, deep blue flowers; ↕ 36in (90cm).

Anchusa azurea 'Loddon Royalist'

Anchusa capensis 'Blue Angel'

'Morning Glory' has flowers in a bright shade of deep blue; ↕ 3ft (1m). **'Opal'** has paler blue flowers than the other cultivars; ↕ 36in (90cm).
A. barrelieri. Erect, clump-forming perennial with elliptic or lance-shaped to oblong-spoon-shaped, wavy-margined or sometimes toothed, mid-green leaves, 2–3in (5–8cm) long. Panicles of white-eyed blue flowers, ¼–⅜in (6–8mm) across, similar to forget-me-nots, are borne in early summer. ↕ 24in (60cm), ↔ 12in (30cm). N. Balkans to Ukraine, Turkey. Zone 4.
A. caespitosa see *A. cespitosa.*
A. capensis. Erect biennial, usually grown as an annual, with rough, narrowly lance-shaped, mid-green leaves, to 5in (13cm) long, covered with bristly hairs. Bears a mass of terminal, open panicles of saucer-shaped, bright blue, white-throated flowers, ⅛–⅜in (4–8mm) across, in summer. ↕ 5–7in (12–18cm), ↔ 3½–5in (9–13cm). South Africa. **'Blue Angel'** ■ is upright and compact with ultramarine-blue flowers; ↕ 8in (20cm), ↔ 6in (15cm). **'Blue Bird'** has indigo-blue flowers; ↕ 18in (45cm), ↔ 6–9in (15–23cm). **'Dawn'** has blue, pink, or white flowers; ↕ 18in (45cm), ↔ 6–9in (15–23cm).
A. cespitosa ■ syn. *A. caespitosa.* Dense, mound-forming perennial with rosettes of narrowly linear, hairy, dark green leaves, to 2½in (6cm) long. Bears clusters of stemless, white-eyed, vivid blue flowers, to ½in (1.2cm) across, in summer. Needs sharp drainage. ↕ 2–4in (5–10cm), ↔ 6–8in (15–20cm). Mountain rocks in Greece (Crete). Zone 5b.

Anchusa cespitosa

A. italica see *A. azurea.*
***A. leptophylla* subsp. *incana*,** syn. *A. angustissima.* Upright, tufted, many-branched perennial with loose rosettes of narrowly lance-shaped, dark green leaves, 2½–4½in (6–11cm) long. Bears one-sided cymes of bright azure-blue, white-eyed flowers, ⅛–¼in (4–6mm) across, throughout the summer. ↕ to 12in (30cm), occasionally more, ↔ 8in (20cm). Turkey. Zone 6.
A. myosotidiflora see *Brunnera macrophylla.*
A. sempervirens see *Pentaglottis sempervirens.*

▷ ***Ancistrocactus*** see *Sclerocactus*

ANDROMEDA

Bog rosemary

ERICACEAE

Genus of 2 species of low-growing, wiry-stemmed, evergreen shrubs, found in acidic peat bogs in the arctic and cool-temperate regions of the N. hemisphere. The leaves are simple, alternate, and linear-lance-shaped to oblong; the small, urn-shaped flowers, produced in terminal umbels from spring to early summer, are white or pink. Grow with woodland plants; they are also suitable for a shady rock garden, or a damp border in acidic soil.
• **CULTIVATION** Grow in moist, acidic, humus-rich soil, in partial shade or full sun. Mulch annually in spring with leaf mold in dry sites.
• **PROPAGATION** Root softwood cuttings in early to midsummer; pot up suckers or rooted layers in autumn or spring.

Andromeda polifolia

Andromeda polifolia 'Alba'

Andromeda polifolia 'Compacta'

• **PESTS AND DISEASES** Susceptible to *Exobasidium* galls.

A. polifolia ■ syn. *A. rosmarinifolia* (Common bog rosemary, Marsh andromeda). Variable, erect or semi-prostrate shrub producing pointed, linear-oblong, leathery, dark green leaves, ½–1½in (1.5–4cm) long. White or pale pink flowers are borne on slender flower stalks, in 2- to 5-flowered umbels, to 1¼in (3cm) across, from spring to early summer. ↕ to 16in (40cm), ↔ to 24in (60cm). N. Europe. Zone 2. **'Alba'** ■ syn. 'Compacta Alba', is semi-prostrate and freely produces pure white flowers; ↕ 6in (15cm), ↔ 8in (20cm). **'Compacta'** ■ is a densely twiggy shrub, with broad, glaucous leaves and pink flowers; ↕ to 12in (30cm), ↔ to 8in (20cm). **'Compacta Alba'** see 'Alba'. **'Macrophylla'** is low-growing, with broad, ovate, dark green leaves, to 1¼in (3cm) long. It produces numerous deep pink and white flowers, which are slightly larger and more rounded than the species; ↕ 2–6in (5–15cm), ↔ 10in (25cm). **'Nikko'** is vigorous, compact, and rounded, with gray-green leaves to 1in (2.5cm) long, and umbels of clear pink flowers; ↕↔ 8–10in (20–25cm).
A. rosmarinifolia see *A. polifolia.*

ANDROPOGON

Beard grass, Bluestem

POACEAE

Genus of over 100 species of annual or perennial, rhizomatous and clump-forming grasses, mostly from grassland in tropical regions, but also from the temperate zones of both hemispheres. They have flat, sheathed, linear leaves and produce racemes of small spikelets, on erect, sometimes branching stems in summer or autumn. *A. gerardii,* which has colorful foliage and flower-heads, is of ornamental value; it is suitable for growing at the back of a herbaceous border. Andropogons are an essential part of prairie restoration.
• **CULTIVATION** Grow in light, fertile, well-drained, and preferably sandy soil, in full sun. *A. gerardii* does not tolerate excessive winter moisture. Cut back old stems to the ground in early spring before growth begins.
• **PROPAGATION** Divide from midspring to early summer. Sow seed in containers in a cold frame in spring.
• **PESTS AND DISEASES** Infrequent.

A. gerardii (Big bluestem, Turkey foot). Densely tufted perennial, with short rhizomes, producing erect clumps of arching, linear, blue-green leaves, to 12in (30cm) long, which turn bronze-red in autumn. Strong, erect stems, to 6ft (2m) tall, bear 3–6 terminal, finger-like, deep red-purple racemes, to 4in (10cm) long, in early and midautumn. ↕ to 6ft (2m), ↔ 24in (60cm). Canada to Mexico. Zone 3. **'Champ'** produces attractive autumn color. Grows well in sandy soils. **'Pawnee'** has a slightly pendulous habit. **'Roundtree'** is more upright and earlier blooming; ↕ 6–7ft (2–2.2m).
A. scoparius see *Schizachyrium scoparium.*

ANDROSACE

SYN. DOUGLASIA

Rock jasmine

PRIMULACEAE

Genus of about 100 species of annuals, biennials, and predominantly evergreen, mat- or cushion-forming perennials. They have small rosettes of hairy leaves and produce stemless or short-stemmed, tubular-based flowers, with flat or cup-shaped lobes, singly or in umbels from late spring to late summer. Most occur in the mountains of the N. hemisphere, growing in rock crevices, scree, or turf. The high-alpine (Aretian), cushion-forming species are superb for a well-ventilated alpine house; most of the remainder are ideal for a rock garden, scree bed, or trough.
• **CULTIVATION** Under glass, grow in pans in full light with good ventilation. Grow Aretian species in a very sharply drained mix of equal parts soil-based potting mix and grit, with a collar of grit around the neck of the plant. They are best watered from below to keep the plant neck and foliage dry; do not allow the soil mix to dry out. Outdoors, grow other species in a scree bed, in vertical crevices in rock-work, or in moist but gritty, well-drained soil in a trough in full sun. In areas with hot summers, provide shade from afternoon sun. The Aretian species need protection from excessive moisture, especially in winter. The smallest cushion-forming species also grow well in tufa.
• **PROPAGATION** Sow seed in containers in an open frame as soon as ripe or in autumn. Root rosettes in early or mid-summer. Keep moist, but water from below to avoid wetting the rosettes.

Androsace carnea

Androsace carnea subsp. *laggeri*

Androsace pyrenaica

Androsace vandellii

Androsace villosa var. *jacquemontii*

• **PESTS AND DISEASES** Downy mildew, leaf spot, and rust may occur. Remove dead rosettes to reduce the risk of disease. Susceptible to aphids, especially under glass.

A. carnea ▣ Tufted perennial with loose rosettes, ½–¾in (1.5–2cm) wide, of evergreen, hairy-margined, linear, fleshy, mid-green leaves, to ¾in (2cm) long. In late spring, bears umbels of 3–8 pink, yellow-eyed flowers, ¼–⅜in (5–8mm) across, on stems 1–2in (2.5–5cm) tall. ↕ 2in (5cm), ↔ 3–6in (8–15cm). Pyrenees, Alps, Tyrol. Zone 4. **subsp. *laggeri*** ▣ syn. *A. laggeri*, is more densely tufted, with smaller rosettes, ¼–½in (6–15mm) across, and deeper pink flowers; E. Pyrenees.
A. chamaejasme. Mat-forming, evergreen perennial with short stolons and open rosettes, ½–¾in (1.5–2cm) across, of oblong-lance-shaped to elliptic, silky-hairy, mid-green leaves, to ½in (1.5cm) long. In late spring, bears umbels of 2–8 pink or white, yellow-eyed flowers, to ⅜in (8mm) across, sometimes turning pink- or red-eyed with age, on stems to 2½in (6cm) tall. ↕ 1¼–2½in (3–6cm), occasionally to 5in (13cm), ↔ to 6–8in (15–20cm). Europe to North America. Zone 4.
A. ciliata. Cushion-forming Aretian with loose, evergreen rosettes, ½–1in (1.5–2.5cm) across, of inversely lance-shaped to ovate, hairy, glossy, mid-green leaves, to ½in (1.5cm) long. In late spring and early summer, pale to deep pink, yellow- to orange-eyed flowers, ⅜–½in (8–15mm) across, are borne singly above the cushions, on stems ½in (1.5cm) long. ↕ 1in (2.5cm), ↔ 2–3in (5–8cm). Pyrenees. Zone 6.
A. cylindrica. Compact, cushion-forming, evergreen Aretian with rosettes, ½–¾in (1.5–2cm) wide, of linear-elliptic, hairy-margined, gray-green leaves, to ½in (1.5cm) long. In mid- and late spring, bears white flowers, ½in (1.5cm) across, with greenish yellow eyes, singly on stems, to ½in (1.5cm) high. ↕ ½–¾in (1.5–2cm), ↔ 4–6in (10–15cm). Pyrenees. Zone 6.
A. hirtella. Evergreen, cushion-forming Aretian with tight rosettes, ½in (1.5cm) wide, of linear to oblong, dark green, white-hairy leaves, to ½in (1.5cm) long. In mid- and late spring, each rosette produces 1–2 almost stemless, almond-scented white flowers, ¼in (5–7mm) across. ↕ ½–¾ in (1–2cm), ↔ 4in (10cm). Pyrenees. Zone 6.
A. imbricata see *A. vandellii.*
A. jacquemontii see *A. villosa* var. *jacquemontii.*
A. laevigata, syn. *Douglasia laevigata.* Densely tufted, evergreen perennial with rosettes, ½–1½in (1.5–4cm) across, of oblong-lance-shaped, glossy, dark gray-green leaves, ½–¾in (1.5–2cm) long. Compact umbels of 2–10 deep rose-pink flowers, ½–¾in (1.5–2cm) across, are borne on stems ¾–3in (2–8cm) long, in early summer. ↕ 2in (5cm), ↔ to 8in (20cm). N.W. US. Zone 6.
A. laggeri see *A. carnea* subsp. *laggeri.*
A. lanuginosa ▣ Prostrate, evergreen, mat-forming perennial with trailing, reddish green stems and alternate, elliptic, silky-hairy, gray-green leaves, to ½in (1.5cm) long. Produces compact umbels of 10–15 pale pink flowers, ⅜–½in (8–15mm) across, with greenish yellow eyes, on stems 3–4in (8–10cm) long, in mid- and late summer. ↕ to 2in (5cm), sometimes to 4in (10cm), ↔ to 12in (30cm). Himalayas. Zone 3b.
A. muscoidea. Cushion-forming, evergreen Aretian with closely grouped, woolly rosettes, to ½in (1.5cm) across, of silvery gray-hairy, elliptic, dark green leaves, ¼in (6mm) long. In late spring, produces heads of 1–3 white, greenish yellow-eyed flowers, to ⅜in (9mm) across, often turning pink with age, on stems to ¹⁄₁₆in (2mm) long. ↕ to 1¼in (3cm), ↔ 4–6in (10–15cm). W. Himalayas. Zone 4b.
A. pubescens. Cushion-forming, evergreen perennial with dense rosettes, ⅜–½in (9–15mm) across, of elliptic to spoon-shaped, hairy, mid-green leaves, to ½in (1.5cm) long. Solitary white flowers, ¼–½in (6–15mm) across, with green or yellow eyes, are borne on stems to ¼in (6mm) long, in spring and early summer. ↕ to 2½in (6cm), ↔ to 4in (10cm). Pyrenees. Zone 6.
A. pyrenaica ▣ Compact, cushion-forming, evergreen perennial with dense rosettes, ⅛–¼in (4–6mm) across, of elliptic, hairy, gray-green leaves, to ⅛in (4mm) long. Solitary, almost stemless white flowers, ¼in (6mm) across, with yellow eyes, are borne in mid- and late spring. ↕ 1½–2in (4–5cm), ↔ 3–5in (7–13cm). Pyrenees. Zone 6.
A. sarmentosa. Mat-forming, stoloniferous, evergreen perennial, with rosettes, ½–1¼in (1.5–3cm) across, of narrowly to broadly elliptic, white-hairy, light green leaves, ½–1¼in (1.5–3cm) long. In late spring and early summer, stems to 4in (10cm) long, bear compact umbels of 3–8 pale to deep rose-pink flowers, ¼–⅜in (7–9mm) across, with greenish yellow eyes. Vigorous species for a rock garden. ↕ 2–4in (5–10cm), ↔ to 12in (30cm). Himalayas to W. China (Sichuan). Zone 5. **var. *chumbyi*** forms a tufted mat, densely covered with silver hairs, and produces very short flower stems; Himalayas.
A. sempervivoides ▣ Mat-forming, stoloniferous, evergreen perennial with open rosettes, ½–1in (1–2.5cm) across, of oblong to spoon-shaped, leathery, hairy-margined, mid-green leaves, ¼in (6mm) long. In mid- and late spring, umbels of 4–10 pink to mauve-pink, yellow-eyed, scented flowers, ⅜–½in (8–15mm) across, their eyes turning red with age, open on stems ¾–3in (2–8cm) long. ↕ 1–2in (2.5–5cm), ↔ 6–8in (15–20cm). N.W. Himalayas. Zone 4.
A. strigillosa. Vigorous, stoloniferous, evergreen perennial with loosely clustered rosettes, to 3in (8cm) across, of broadly elliptic, mid-green, downy leaves, to 2½in (6cm) long. In early and midsummer, bears open umbels of 5–15 usually white, purplish red-backed, yellow-eyed flowers, ¼in (6mm) across, on stems to 10in (25cm) tall. Variants with white or pink flowers are also grown. ↕ to 10in (25cm), ↔ to 6in (15cm). C. Himalayas. Zone 4b.
A. vandellii ▣ syn. *A. imbricata.* Evergreen, cushion-forming Aretian with dense rosettes, ¼–½in (6–15mm) wide, of linear to elliptic, silvery gray-hairy leaves, to ¼in (6mm) long. Produces attractive, white, yellow-eyed flowers, ⅛–⅜in (4–8mm) across, singly from the leaf axils on short stems, ¹⁄₁₆–¼in (2–6mm) long, in early and midspring. ↕ 1½–2in (4–5cm), ↔ 3–5in (8–13cm). Sierra Nevada, Pyrenees, Alps. Zone 4.
A. villosa ▣ Mat- or cushion-forming, evergreen perennial with densely silky-hairy rosettes, to ½in (1.5cm) across, of linear to broadly elliptic leaves, ¼in (5–7mm) long, mid-green above and covered in long, silky hairs beneath. In spring, bears tight umbels of 3–7 white flowers, ¼–½in (6–15mm) across, with yellow eyes, sometimes turning pink- and red-eyed with age, on stems ¾–1¼in (2–3cm) long. ↕ to 1½in (4cm), ↔ to 8in (20cm). W. Europe to W. Asia. Zone 4. **var. *jacquemontii*** ▣ syn. *A. jacquemontii*, is stoloniferous, with deep pink-purple, yellow- to green-eyed flowers; Himalayas.
A. vitaliana see *Vitaliana primuliflora.*

Androsace lanuginosa

Androsace sempervivoides

Androsace villosa

A

ANEMONE

Windflower

RANUNCULACEAE

Genus of about 120 species of variable perennials from a wide range of habitats in temperate regions, mainly of the N. but also of the S. hemisphere. Anemones have rhizomatous, tuberous, fleshy, or fibrous rootstocks. They may be divided into 3 main groups: spring-flowering species, some with tubers or rhizomes, which are found in woodland and alpine pastures; tuberous Mediterranean and C. Asian species from areas with hot, dry summers, flowering in spring or early summer; and larger, mainly tall, herbaceous species with fibrous roots, occurring in moist, open woodland and grassy sites, and flowering from late summer to autumn. Most anemones produce both basal and stem leaves. The basal leaves are rounded to oval, 3- to 7-palmate or palmately lobed, rarely entire, and mid- to dark green. The leaflets and lobes are often shallowly to deeply dissected or toothed, and may be either hairless or hairy. Smaller, stalkless or short-stalked stem leaves are often produced in a whorl beneath the flowers.

Anemones are grown for their open saucer-shaped to shallowly cup-shaped flowers, each with a central boss of stamens. The flowers are solitary or borne in cymes or umbels, on branched or unbranched stems. Larger species are ideal for a border, smaller species for a woodland or rock garden. Contact with the sap may irritate skin.

Anemone blanda 'Atrocaerulea'

Anemone blanda 'Violet Star'

• **CULTIVATION** Anemones have varying cultivation requirements. For ease of reference, these are grouped as follows:

1. Moist but well-drained, humus-rich soil in sun to partial shade, although drier conditions are tolerated when dormant in summer.
2. Light, sandy soil in full sun. Ensure a dry dormancy after flowering.
3. Moist, fertile, humus-rich soil in sun or partial shade. Some species may be invasive once established.

Most species are best planted in autumn, but plant *A. coronaria* selections in spring. Plant anemones with tubers 2–3in (5–8cm) below the surface of the soil.

• **PROPAGATION** Sow seed in containers in a cold frame as soon as ripe (use dry sand to rub hairs off the woolly-coated seeds); germination may be slow and erratic. Divide autumn-flowering anemones in early spring or autumn, growing on in containers for a year before planting out in spring. Take root cuttings of autumn-flowering anemones in spring. Separate the rhizomes of rhizomatous species in spring, or after the leaves have died down. Separate the tubers of tuberous species in summer, when dormant.

• **PESTS AND DISEASES** *Synchytrium* leaf gall, downy mildew, leaf and stem smut, *Septoria* leaf spot, powdery mildew, and rust are all very common. Viruses may also occur. Autumn-blooming anemones are prone to nematodes. All species are susceptible to caterpillars, slugs, and flea beetles.

A. altaica. Creeping perennial with slender yellow rhizomes and whorls of 3 rounded to oval, 3-palmate, toothed, mid- to dark green basal and stem leaves, ¾–1½in (2–4cm) long. Solitary flowers, to 1½in (4cm) across, with 8–10 white tepals, veined violet inside, are produced in spring. Cultivation group 1. ↕ 6–8in (15–20cm), ↔ 8–12in (20–30cm). N.E. Russia, N. Asia. Zone 3.

A. apennina (Apennine windflower). Perennial with short, creeping rhizomes and rounded to oval, 3-palmate, dark green basal and stem leaves, 1¼–3in (3–8cm) long, with hairy undersides, and toothed and lobed leaflets. Solitary, usually blue flowers, 1–1¼in (2.5–3cm) across, with 8–14 tepals, are borne in spring; white flowers, sometimes pink-flushed, also occur. Good for naturalizing. Cultivation group 1. ↕ 8in (20cm), ↔ 12in (30cm). S. Europe. Zone 5b.

A. baldensis. Clump-forming, fibrous-rooted perennial producing rounded, 3-palmate, dark green basal and stem leaves, 1¼–3in (3–8cm) long, with 3-lobed leaflets. Slightly nodding, solitary white flowers, 1–1½in (2.5–4cm) across, with 8–10 tepals, often flushed blue on the reverse, open in mid- and late spring. Cultivation group 1. ↕ 8in (20cm), ↔ 4–6in (10–15cm). Mountains of N. Italy, rocky sites in former Yugoslavia. Zone 5.

A. biflora. Tuberous perennial with rounded, 3-palmate, mid-green basal and stem leaves, 1¼–2in (3–5cm) long, with toothed and lobed leaflets. Red flowers, occasionally yellow or orange, 1¼–1½in (3–4cm) across, with 5 tepals, are produced in 2- or 3-flowered clusters in spring. Cultivation group 2. ↕ 5in (13cm), ↔ 4in (10cm). Iran. Zone 6.

Anemone coronaria 'Lord Lieutenant'

A. blanda (Grecian windflower). Spreading perennial with knobby tubers. Produces 1 or 2 broadly oval to triangular, 3-palmate, dark green basal and stem leaves, 1¼–4in (3–10cm) long, with irregularly lobed leaflets. In spring, solitary flowers, ¾–1½in (2–4cm) across, with 10–15 deep blue to white or pink tepals, are borne above the leaves. Excellent for naturalizing. Cultivation group 2. ↕↔ 6in (15cm). S.E. Europe, Turkey. Zone 5. **'Atrocaerulea'** ■ has deep blue flowers. **'Blue Star'** produces pale blue flowers. **'Charmer'** has deep pink flowers. **'Ingramii'** bears deep blue flowers with purple-backed tepals. **'Pink Star'** has bright pink flowers. **'Radar'** ■ bears magenta flowers with white centers. **'Violet Star'** ■ produces large, amethyst flowers with white backs. **'White Splendour'** ■ produces large white flowers with pink-tinged backs.

***A.* 'Bressingham Glow'** see *A. hupehensis* var. *japonica* 'Bressingham Glow'.

A. bucharica. Clump-forming perennial with knobby tubers and rounded, 3-palmate, light to dark green basal and stem leaves, 2–5in (5–13cm) long, with lobed and toothed leaflets. In spring, branched stems bear pairs of red or violet-red flowers, 1¼–1½in (3–4cm) across, with 5 tepals, hairy on the outside. Cultivation group 3. ↕ 8in (20cm), ↔ 4in (10cm). C. Asia. Zone 6.

Anemone blanda 'Radar'

Anemone blanda 'White Splendour'

Anemone coronaria 'The Bride'

Anemone x *fulgens*

Anemone hupehensis

A. canadensis, syn. *A. pennsylvanica* (Meadow anemone). Spreading, invasive rhizomatous perennial with diamond-shaped to ovate, 5- to 7-palmate, light green leaves, 1–5in (2–13cm) long, with toothed leaflets, hairy beneath. In summer, bears clusters of 1–3 upward facing, buttercup-like, yellow-centered white flowers, to 2in (5cm) across; with 5 or 6 tepals. Occurs naturally in low-lying areas; requires moist conditions to become established. Cultivation group 3. ↕ 12–24in (30–60cm), ↔ 12in (30cm). Labrador to Colorado. Zone 3.

A. coronaria (Poppy anemone). Erect perennial with knobby tubers, producing rounded to oval, 3-palmate, mid-green basal and stem leaves, 2–5in (5–13cm) long, with finely lobed leaflets. Solitary, showy, single, red, blue, or white flowers, 1¼–3in (3–8cm) across, with 5–8 tepals, are borne in spring. Cultivation group 2. ↕ 12–18in (30–45cm), ↔ 6in (15cm). Mediterranean. Zone 7b. There are many cultivars, both single- and double-flowered; all are useful as cut flowers. **De Caen Group** is a collective name for a group of single-flowered cultivars with 5–8 tepals. **'Lord Lieutenant'** ■ has semi-double, deep blue flowers. **'Mr. Fokker'** has single, violet-blue flowers. **St. Brigid Group** is a collective name for a group of double-flowered cultivars. **'The Admiral'** produces semi-double violet flowers. **'The Bride'** ■ has semi-double, pure white flowers.

A.* x *elegans see *A.* x *hybrida.*

A. flaccida. Erect, rhizomatous perennial forming mounds of oval, 3-palmate, fleshy basal and stem leaves, 1¼–4in (3–10cm) long, with lobed and toothed leaflets, bronze at first, later dark green with white-marked bases. In late spring, bears clusters of 1–3 creamy white, sometimes pink-flushed flowers, ½–1¼in (1.5–3cm) across, with 5–7 tepals. Cultivation group 1. ↕ to 8in (20cm), ↔ 6–8in (15–20cm). Mountain forest in Russia, China, Japan. Zone 6b.

A.* x *fulgens ■ (*A. hortensis* x *A. pavonina*). Tuberous perennial with rounded to oval, 3-palmate to deeply 3-lobed, mid-green basal and stem leaves, 1¼–5in (3–13cm) long, with lobed and toothed leaflets. In spring, bears solitary, narrow-petaled scarlet flowers, 2–3in (5–8cm) across, with 10–15 tepals. Cultivation group 2, but will tolerate summer rain without protection. ↕ 12in (30cm), ↔ 6in (15cm). Garden origin. Zone 7b. **'Annulata Grandiflora'** has large red flowers with yellow centers.

A. globosa see *A. multifida.*

A. heldreichiana ■ syn. *A. stellata* var. *heldreichii.* Slow-growing perennial with a tuber-like, congested rhizome. Produces rounded, 3-palmate, light green basal leaves, 1¼–3½in (3–6cm) long, and small, rounded stem leaves, ¼–½in (6–15mm) long, with lobed leaflets. Solitary flowers, ¾–1½in (2–4cm) across, with 8–14 tepals, gray-blue on the outside and white inside, are borne in spring. Cultivation group 2. ↕ 4–6in (10–15cm), ↔ to 4in (10cm). Greece (Crete). Zone 8.

A. hepatica see *Hepatica nobilis.*

A. hupehensis ■ (Chinese anemone). Erect perennial with a woody-based, fibrous rootstock and suckering shoots. Long-stalked, rounded to oval,

Anemone hupehensis var. *japonica* 'Bressingham Glow'

3-palmate, dark green basal leaves, 4–8in (10–20cm) long, and smaller stem leaves, are sharply toothed, and sparsely hairy beneath. From mid-summer to autumn, branched stems bear umbels of up to 15 white or pink flowers, 2–2½in (5–6cm) across, with 5–6 tepals, the outer ones often deep pink outside. Plant in masses or in a border. Cultivation group 3. ↕ 24–36in (60–90cm), ↔ 16in (40cm). W. and C. China. Zone 3. **'Hadspen Abundance'** ■ has flowers with dark reddish pink outer tepals. **var. *japonica*** (Japanese anemone) is taller than the species and has creamy pink flowers with 10–20 narrow tepals; ↕ 2–4ft (60–120cm), ↔ 18in (45cm); S. China, Japan. **var. *japonica* 'Bressingham Glow'** ■ syn. *A.* 'Bressingham Glow', has slightly darker pink flowers and longer tepals than var. *japonica*, the silky hairs on the outer surfaces producing a white sheen. **var. *japonica* 'Prinz Heinrich'**, syn. *A.* x *hybrida* 'Prince Henry', is very similar to var. *japonica* 'Bressingham Glow', but more invasive. **'Pink Shell'** see 'Rosenschale'. **'Rosenschale'**, syn. 'Pink Shell', is vigorous and produces flowers with large, overlapping, broad-based, dark rose-pink outer tepals. **'September Charm'** has uniform, pale pink flowers, 3½in (9cm) across.

A.* x *hybrida (*A. hupehensis* var. *japonica* x *A. vitifolia*) syn. *A.* x *elegans*, *A. japonica* of gardens (Japanese anemone). Vigorous, erect, woody-based perennial with suckering shoots and oval, usually 3-palmate, toothed, mid-green leaves, softly hairy beneath. Basal leaves are 4–8in (10–20cm) long; stem leaves are 2–5in (5–13cm) long. Branched stems bear umbels of 12–18 semi-double, pale pink flowers, to 3½in (9cm) across, with 6–11 (sometimes up to 15) tepals, from late summer to midautumn. Plant in masses or in a border. Cultivation group 3. ↕ 4–5ft (1.2–1.5m), ↔ indefinite. Garden origin. Zone 4. **'Géante des Blanches'** syn. 'White Giant', 'White Queen', is vigorous and has semi-double flowers with broad white tepals, shaded green on the reverse. **'Honorine Jobert'** ■ has single white flowers, pink-tinged on the reverse, with golden yellow stamens. **'Königin Charlotte'**, syn. 'Queen Charlotte', is vigorous with large, semi-double pink flowers, 4in (10cm) across, shaded purple on the reverse of the outer tepals; ↕ 5ft (1.5m).

Anemone heldreichiana

Anemone hupehensis 'Hadspen Abundance'

Anemone x *hybrida* 'Honorine Jobert'

Anemone x *hybrida* 'Luise Uhink'

'Kriemhilde' bears semi-double, pale purple-pink flowers, darker on the reverse of the tepals. **'Lady Gilmour'** see 'Margarete'. **'Luise Uhink'** ▣ is vigorous with large, semi-double white flowers. **'Margarete'**, syn. 'Lady Gilmour', 'Margaret', bears almost double, pale pink flowers. **'Max Vogel'** ▣ bears single, light pink flowers that become paler with age, the 3 or 4 outer tepals slightly darker than the 5 or 6 inner ones. **'Pamina'** has double, rose-red flowers; ↕ 24–36in (60–90cm). **'Prince Henry'** see *A. hupehensis* var. *japonica* 'Prinz Heinrich'. **'Profusion'** is vigorous with semi-double, rose-pink flowers, 2½–3in (6–8cm) across. **'Queen Charlotte'** see 'Königin Charlotte'. **'Whirlwind'** has semi-double white flowers, often with

Anemone x *hybrida* 'Max Vogel'

Anemone x *lipsiensis*

twisted, greenish white tepals at the centers. **'White Giant'** see 'Géante des Blanches'. **'White Queen'** see 'Géante des Blanches'.
A.* x *intermedia see *A.* x *lipsiensis.*
***A. japonica* of gardens** see *A.* x *hybrida.*
A.* x *lesseri (*A. multifida* x *A. sylvestris*). Erect, fibrous-rooted perennial forming clumps of large, rounded, 3- to 5-palmate, hairy, mid-green basal and stem leaves, 2–5in (5–13cm) long, with very finely lobed and toothed leaflets. In summer, bears reddish pink flowers, to 1¼in (3cm) across, with 5–8 tepals, singly or in umbels of 2 or 3. There are also variants with purple, yellow, or white flowers. Cultivation group 1. ↕ 16in (40cm), ↔ to 12in (30cm). Garden origin. Zone 4.
A.* x *lipsiensis ▣ (*A. nemorosa* x *A. ranunculoides*) syn. *A.* x *intermedia, A.* x *seemannii.* Vigorous perennial with slender brown rhizomes and rounded, 3-palmate, mid-green basal and stem leaves, 2–3in (5–8cm) long, with deeply lobed leaflets. Similar to *A. nemorosa,* but bears solitary, pale creamy yellow flowers, ½–¾in (1.5–2cm) across, with 6–8 tepals, in spring. Cultivation group 1. ↕ 2–6in (5–15cm), ↔ to 18in (45cm). Europe. Zone 6.
***A. magellanica* of gardens** see *A. multifida.*
A. multifida ▣ syn. *A. globosa, A. magellanica* of gardens. Vigorous, rhizomatous perennial with rounded, 3- to 5-palmate, mid-green basal and stem leaves, 1¼–3in (3–8cm) long, with finely lobed leaflets. In summer, bears umbels of 2 or 3 creamy yellow flowers, to 1in (2.5cm) across, with 5–9 tepals. Cultivation group 1. ↕ to 12in (30cm), ↔ to 6in (15cm). N. America. Zone 3.
A. narcissiflora ▣ Clump-forming perennial with a slightly woody rootstock. Rounded, 3- to 5-palmate, mid-green basal leaves, 3–6in (8–15cm) long, and smaller stem leaves, have deeply lobed and toothed leaflets. In late spring and early summer, bears umbels of 3–8 (sometimes 9 or 10) white flowers, ¾–1½in (2–4cm) across, occasionally flushed pink on the reverse of the 5–7 tepals. Cultivation group 1. ↕ 16in (40cm), ↔ 18in (45cm). Mountains of C. and S. Europe to Turkey, Caucasus, Siberia, W. North America. Zone 5.
A. nemorosa. Vigorous, low-growing, creeping perennial with slender brown rhizomes and rounded, 3-palmate, mid-

Anemone multifida

green basal and stem leaves, 2–5in (5–13cm) long, the narrow leaflets further lobed and toothed. In spring, bears solitary white, often pink-flushed flowers, ¾–1¼in (2–3cm) across, with 6–8 tepals. Foliage dies soon after flowering. Good for naturalizing. Cultivation group 1. ↕ 3–6in (8–15cm), ↔ 12in (30cm) or more. Woods and mountain pastures of Europe. Zone 4. **'Allenii'** produces deep lavender-blue flowers, 1½in (4cm) across, shaded paler blue on the outside of the tepals. **'Blue Bonnet'** is late flowering, with deep blue flowers, 1¼–1½in (3–4cm) across. **'Bracteata Pleniflora'** ▣ has semi-double flowers, each with a ruff of leaves below the narrow tepals, the inner tepals white or white with green tips and the outer ones green. **'Flore Pleno'**, syn.

Anemone narcissiflora

Anemone nemorosa 'Bracteata Pleniflora'

'Plena', has small, double white flowers, ¾–1¼in (2–3cm) across; **'Plena'** see 'Flore Pleno'. **'Robinsoniana'** ▣ has large, pale lavender-blue flowers, 1¼–1½in (3–4cm) across, with creamy gray backs. **'Rosea'** has slightly hairy leaves and elliptic, hairless, red-purple flowers, ½–¾in (1.5–2cm) across. **'Vestal'** bears double white flowers, ¾–1in (2–2½cm) across, with central buttons of symmetrically arranged tepals. **'Wilk's Giant'** produces single white flowers, 1½–2in (4–5cm) across, among the largest blooms of all *A. nemorosa* cultivars.
A. obtusiloba. Tufted, fibrous-rooted perennial with rounded, deeply lobed, mid-green basal and stem leaves, 2–5in (5–13cm) long, the 3 lobes subdivided and spreading. In late spring, produces umbels of 2 or 3 white, yellow, or deep blue flowers, ¾–1¼in (2–3cm) across, with 4–6 tepals. Cultivation group 1. ↕ 2in (5cm), ↔ to 10in (25cm). Himalayas, S.W. China. Zone 6.
A. pavonina ▣ Tuberous perennial with rounded, 3-palmate or deeply 3-lobed, dissected, sparsely toothed, mid- to dark green basal and stem leaves, 3–6in (8–15cm) long. In early spring, bears solitary, red, pink, or purple flowers, 1¼–4in (3–10cm) across, with 7–9 tepals, often with white tepal bases. Cultivation group 2. ↕ 10in (25cm), ↔ 6in (15cm). Mediterranean. Zone 8. **var. *ocellata*** bears scarlet flowers with white centers. **St. Bavo Group** produces large flowers, 4in (10cm) across, in shades of purple, pink, and salmon-pink.
A. pennsylvanica see *A. canadensis.*

Anemone nemorosa 'Robinsoniana'

Anemone pavonina

A. petiolulosa. Tuberous perennial, closely related to *A. biflora*, with rounded, 3-palmate, mid-green basal and stem leaves, 2–5in (5–13cm) long, with deeply lobed leaflets. In spring, bears clusters of up to 4 slightly pendent, yellow, red-backed flowers, ¾–1¾in (2–4.5cm) across, with 5 tepals. Cultivation group 2; best in a bulb frame. ↕ 6in (15cm), ↔ 4in (10cm). C. Asia. Zone 6b.
A. polyanthes. Clump-forming perennial with a woody-based, fibrous rootstock. Rounded, hairy, dark green basal and stem leaves, 6–12in (15–30cm) long, are shallowly 5- to 7-lobed, with rounded teeth. Umbels of 5 or more white, purple-blue, or reddish purple flowers, to 1¼in (3cm) across, with 4–6 tepals, are produced in late spring or early summer. Cultivation group 2. ↕ 20in (50cm), ↔ 18in (45cm). Pakistan to Bhutan. Zone 7.
A. ranunculoides ▣ Spreading perennial with yellow rhizomes and rounded, deeply 3-lobed, mid-green basal and stem leaves, 3–6in (8–15cm) long, each lobe also deeply divided. Solitary, deep yellow flowers, ¾–1¼in (2–3cm) across, with 5 or 6 tepals, open in spring. Good for naturalizing. Cultivation group 1. ↕ 2–4in (5–10cm), ↔ to 18in (45cm) or more. Woodland in Europe. Zone 4. **'Pleniflora'**, syn. 'Flore Pleno', has double flowers. **'Superba'** has bronze-green leaves.
A. rivularis ▣ Variable, clump-forming perennial with a woody-based fibrous rootstock and long-stalked, rounded, 3-palmate to deeply 3-lobed, softly hairy, dark green leaves, the lobes or

Anemone ranunculoides

Anemone rivularis

leaflets further divided and toothed. Basal leaves are 3–7in (8–18cm) long, stem leaves are slightly smaller. Umbels of 10–20 or more white flowers, 1½–3in (4–8cm) across, with 5–8 tepals, often blue on the reverse, are borne on long, spreading stalks from the branching stems, in late spring and early summer, and sometimes again in autumn. Cultivation group 1. ↕ 24–36in (60–90cm), ↔ 12in (30cm). India, S.W. China. Zone 7.
A. x seemannii see *A.* x *lipsiensis.*
A. stellata* var. *heldreichii see *A. heldreichiana.*
A. sylvestris ▣ (Snowdrop anemone). Perennial with a woody-based, fibrous rootstock, spreading rapidly by root suckers. Long-stalked, mid-green basal and stem leaves, 2–6in (5–15cm) long, are rounded to oval, and deeply 5-lobed, the lobes also deeply divided. In late spring, bears solitary, single, semi-pendent white flowers, 1–3in (2.5–8cm) across, with 5 or more tepals and golden yellow stamens. Cultivation group 1. ↕↔ 12–20in (30–50cm). S. Sweden, N.E. France, C. and E. Europe, Caucasus. Zone 3. **'Flore Pleno'** bears double white flowers. **'Macrantha'** has large, single white flowers.
A. tomentosa, syn. *A. vitifolia* of gardens, *A. vitifolia* 'Robustissima'. Clump-forming perennial with a woody-based, fibrous rootstock, spreading by underground shoots. Oval, toothed, mid-green basal and stem leaves, 4–8in (10–20cm) long, are 3- to 7-palmate, conspicuously veined, and white-woolly on the reverse. In late summer and early autumn, branched

Anemone sylvestris

Anemone trullifolia

stems bear clusters of 10 or more pale pink flowers, 2–3in (5–8cm) across, with 5 or 6 tepals. Good in a border. Cultivation group 3. ↕ 3–5ft (1–1.5m), ↔ 24in (60cm). N. and C. China. Zone 4. **'Superba'** is low-growing and has larger flowers, 3–4in (8–10cm) across; ↕ 3ft (1m).
A. trifolia. Creeping perennial with slender brown rhizomes and long-stalked, rounded to oval, 3-palmate, toothed, light green basal and stem leaves, 2–5in (5–13cm) long, with narrow leaflets. In spring, leafy stems bear solitary white flowers, sometimes pink on the reverse, ¾in (2cm) across, with 5–8 tepals and a conspicuous boss of blue or white anthers. Cultivation group 1. ↕ to 6in (15cm), ↔ to 12in (30cm). Woodland in S. Europe. Zone 6b.
A. trullifolia ▣ Compact, tufted, fibrous-rooted perennial, resembling *A. obtusiloba*, but producing wedge-shaped, deeply 3-lobed, mid-green basal and stem leaves, 2–5in (5–13cm) long, the lobes further divided and toothed. Solitary, blue, white, or yellow flowers, ¾in (2cm) across, with 4–6 tepals, are borne in late spring and early summer.

Anemone vitifolia

Cultivation group 1. ↕ to 6in (15cm), ↔ to 8in (20cm). E. Himalayas, S.W. China. Zone 5b.
A. tschaernjaewii. Tuberous perennial producing oval, 3-palmate, mid-green basal and stem leaves, 1¼–3in (3–8cm) long, the leaflets shallowly 3-lobed. In spring, each stem bears 1–3 white or pink flowers, ¾–1¾in (2–4.5cm) across, with purple centers and 5 tepals. Cultivation group 2; best grown in a bulb frame. ↕ 9in (23cm), ↔ 4in (10cm). C. Asia. Zone 5.
A. vitifolia ▣ (Grape-leaved anemone). Clump-forming perennial with a woody-based, fibrous rootstock and oval, shallowly 5-lobed, vine-like, dark green basal and stem leaves, 4–8in (10–20cm) long, the lobes conspicuously toothed and sparsely white-woolly beneath. Loose umbels of 3–7 white flowers, 1¼–3½in (3–6cm) across, with 5 or 6 tepals, are produced in late summer and early autumn. Cultivation group 3. ↕ 3ft (1m), ↔ indefinite. Afghanistan to W. China, Burma. Zone 4b. **'Robustissima'** see *A. tomentosa.*
***A. vitifolia* of gardens** see *A. tomentosa.*

ANEMONELLA

RANUNCULACEAE

Genus of one species of tuberous, clump-forming perennial occurring in woodland in E. North America. *A. thalictroides* is cultivated for its attractive flowers, and is suitable for growing in a woodland garden, or for underplanting in a shady shrub border or rock garden. Although slow to establish, it will eventually increase to form colonies 12in (30cm) across.

- **CULTIVATION** Grow in moist, moderately fertile, humus-rich soil in partial shade. Tubers may rot in very wet soils.
- **PROPAGATION** Sow seed in containers in a cold frame as soon as ripe, or divide young plants in early spring.
- **PESTS AND DISEASES** Susceptible to powdery mildew, leaf smut, and rust, as well as slugs.

A. thalictroides ▣ (Rue anemone). Tuberous perennial producing loose umbels of 2–4 fragile, cup-shaped, white or pale pink flowers, to ¾in (2cm) wide, on slender stems, from spring to early summer. Flowers are borne above 2- to 3-ternate, delicate, fern-like, dark bluish green leaves, 4–6in (10–15cm) long,

Anemonella thalictroides

Anemonella thalictroides 'Oscar Schoaf'

with 5–9 ovate leaflets, arising from clusters of small tubers. ↕ 4in (10cm), ↔ 12in (30cm). E. North America. Zone 5. **'Oscar Schoaf'** ■ syn. 'Flore Pleno', 'Schoaf's Double', 'Schoaf's Pink', has double pink flowers.

ANEMONOPSIS

RANUNCULACEAE

Genus of a single species of clump-forming perennial from woodland in Japan. It produces 2- or 3-ternate leaves with lobed or sharply toothed leaflets, and bears racemes or loose panicles of pendent, lilac and violet flowers. Grow *A. macrophylla* in a woodland garden.

• **CULTIVATION** Grow in deep, cool, moist, moderately fertile, humus-rich, preferably acidic soil, in partial shade. Grows well in areas with cool summers.

• **PROPAGATION** Sow seed in containers in a cold frame as soon as ripe; germination is unreliable. Carefully divide the thick, fleshy roots in spring.

• **PESTS AND DISEASES** Infrequent.

A. macrophylla ■ Clump-forming perennial with 2- or 3-ternate, glossy, hairless, dark green leaves, 2½–4in (6–10cm) long, with diamond-shaped to ovate or oblong, sharply toothed, often 3-lobed leaflets. Racemes of cup-shaped, nodding flowers, to 1¼in (3cm) across, each with 3 waxy lilac sepals and several rows of 7–10 smaller violet petals, are borne in mid- and late summer. ↕ 30in (75cm), ↔ 18in (45cm). Japan. Zone 5b.

Anemonopsis macrophylla

ANEMOPAEGMA

BIGNONIACEAE

Genus of over 40 species of evergreen, tendril climbers from moist forest in tropical North and South America. They are grown for their terminal or axillary racemes of showy, foxglove-like flowers. The leaves are opposite and 2- to 5-pinnate. Where not hardy, grow in a temperate or warm greenhouse. In warmer areas, they are ideal for growing on a house wall, pergola, arbor, or tree.

• **CULTIVATION** Under glass, grow in soil-based potting mix in full or bright filtered light. When in growth, water freely and apply a balanced liquid fertilizer monthly; water sparingly in winter. Outdoors, grow in fertile, moist but well-drained soil in sun or partial shade. Pruning group 11, or group 12 in a restricted site; prune in late winter or early spring.

• **PROPAGATION** Sow seed at minimum 61°F (16°C) in spring. Root cuttings of short-jointed, lateral shoots in summer.

• **PESTS AND DISEASES** Prone to spider mites, whiteflies, and mealybugs.

A. chamberlaynei. Vigorous climber, supporting itself by claw-like tendrils at the leaf tips. Ovate-lance-shaped, pinnate leaves, 2–5½in (5–14cm) long, have 2 large, lance-shaped or ovate, glossy, mid-green leaflets with wavy margins. Bears axillary racemes of 2–8 trumpet-like, pale yellow flowers, 2–3in (5–8cm) long, with purple-and-white-striped throats, from summer to early autumn. ↕ 12–20ft (4–6m). Brazil. ❅ (min. 45°F/7°C), although may survive short periods down to 36°F (2°C).

ANETHUM

Dill

APIACEAE

Genus of 2 species of scented annuals or biennials with smooth, branching stems, feathery, blue-green foliage, and umbels of small yellow flowers in summer. They are probably native to S.W. Asia and India, but *A. graveolens* has become widely naturalized on roadsides and wasteland in Europe and N. US. *A. graveolens* is grown in herb and vegetable gardens for its aromatic leaves and seeds, which have many culinary uses. Like others of its family, dill attracts beneficial insects, including wasps and other predators.

• **CULTIVATION** Grow in fertile, well-drained soil in full sun with shelter from strong winds. Water freely during the growing season to retard bolting. Often resprouts after cutting.

• **PROPAGATION** Sow seed *in situ* at monthly intervals from spring to midsummer to produce a succession of fresh foliage.

• **PESTS AND DISEASES** *Cercosporidium* leaf spot and a few other fungal leaf and root diseases sometimes occur.

Anethum graveolens

A. graveolens ■ syn. *Peucedanum graveolens* (Dill). Aromatic annual with hollow, finely ridged stems. It has 3- or 4-pinnate, obovate to oblong leaves, to 14in (35cm) long, finely divided into numerous thread-like, blue-green leaflets. In midsummer, produces flattened umbels, 3½in (9cm) across, of tiny, deep yellow, scented flowers. ↕ 24in (60cm) or more, ↔ 12in (30cm). Probably S.W. Asia and India.

ANGELICA

APIACEAE

Genus of 50 species of herbaceous perennials and biennials, some monocarpic, mainly from damp woodland, meadows, fens, and streambanks in the N. hemisphere. They are large, architectural plants producing alternate, 2- or 3-pinnate or 2- or 3-ternate, usually diamond-shaped leaves, 12–36in (30–90cm) long. They bear large umbels of small, white, greenish yellow, or purple flowers, followed by flat, ribbed brown fruit. Angelicas are excellent for a large border, as specimens in a woodland setting, or for growing by a pond or stream. *A. archangelica* also has culinary and medicinal uses, and is suitable for an herb garden.

• **CULTIVATION** Grow in deep, moist, fertile, loamy soil in full or partial shade, although most species will tolerate drier conditions; *A. sylvestris* prefers full sun. *A. archangelica* generally dies after flowering, but if flowering is prevented, or the spent flowers are removed before setting seed, it will often flower a second year or even more.

• **PROPAGATION** Sow seed in containers in a cold frame as soon as ripe; exposure to light is required for germination. Transplant the seedlings while small, since older plants resent disturbance. They normally flower within 2 or 3 years.

• **PESTS AND DISEASES** Susceptible to powdery mildew and several leaf spots. Prone to aphids, snails, slugs, carrot rust fly larvae, and leaf miners.

Angelica archangelica

A. archangelica ■ syn. *A. officinalis* (Archangel). Thick, upright, herbaceous or monocarpic perennial, often grown as a biennial, with 2- or 3-pinnate, mid-green leaves, to 24in (60cm) long, which have ovate-lance-shaped, toothed leaflets. Rounded umbels, to 10in (25cm) across, of greenish yellow flowers are borne on thick, ribbed stems in early and midsummer. ↕ 6ft (2m), ↔ 4ft (1.2m). N. Europe. Zone 4.

A. gigas ■ Clump-forming biennial or short-lived herbaceous perennial with toothed, tripartite, mid-green leaves, 12–16in (30–40cm) long, composed of diamond-shaped to ovate, lobed leaflets. Produces conspicuous, inflated, red-purple leaf sheaths and dense, purple-bracted umbels, 5in (13cm) across, of rich, dark purple flowers on dark red stems, in late summer and early autumn. Highly attractive to insects, especially bees. ↕ 3–6ft (1–2m), ↔ 4ft (1.2m). N. China, Korea, Japan. Zone 4.

A. montana see *A. sylvestris.*

A. officinalis see *A. archangelica.*

A. sylvestris, syn. *A. montana* (Wild angelica). Robust biennial or short-lived herbaceous perennial producing ridged, purple-flushed stems and 2- or 3-pinnate,

Angelica gigas

light green leaves, to 24in (60cm) long, divided into sharply toothed, oblong-ovate leaflets. Bears many white or pale pink flowers in rounded, compound umbels, to 6in (15cm) across, in late summer and early autumn. ↕ to 8ft (2.5m), ↔ 3ft (1m). Europe to C. Asia. Zone 5.

ANGELONIA

SCROPHULARIACEAE

Genus of about 30 species of small subshrubs and evergreen, soft-stemmed perennials from damp savanna in tropical and subtropical Central and South America. They have opposite or alternate, broadly to narrowly lance-shaped leaves. The 2-lipped, shallowly cup-shaped, white, pink, mauve, or blue flowers, with spreading lobes, are borne in terminal racemes or singly from the leaf axils. Where not hardy, grow as summer bedding annuals, in containers, or in a warm greenhouse; with minimum temperatures of 50°F/10°C.

• **CULTIVATION** Under glass, grow in soil-based potting mix in full light, with filtered light in summer. Water freely and apply a balanced liquid fertilizer monthly. Container-grown plants are best discarded after flowering. Outdoors, grow in moist but well-drained, fertile soil in full sun.

• **PROPAGATION** Sow seed in spring at 75°F (24°C). Divide or take softwood cuttings in spring, or at any time in frost-free areas.

• **PESTS AND DISEASES** Prone to aphids and powdery mildew.

A. angustifolia. Upright perennial with hairless stems and lance-shaped, sharp-pointed, toothed leaves, 1½–3in (4–8cm) long. Bears long, narrow racemes, 8in (20cm) high, of deep mauve to violet flowers, ¾in (2cm) across, in summer. ↕ 12–18in (30–45cm), ↔ 12in (30cm). Mexico, West Indies.

A. gardneri. Subshrubby perennial with stalkless, broadly lance-shaped, softly hairy leaves, 1½–2½in (4–6cm) long, with toothed margins. In summer, bears terminal racemes, to 6in (15cm) high, of purple flowers, ¾in (2cm) across, with red-spotted centers. ↕ 3ft (1m), ↔ 24in (60cm). Brazil.

ANGOPHORA

MYRTACEAE

Genus of about 8 species of evergreen trees and shrubs, closely related to *Eucalyptus*, found in dry to moist, tropical to warm-temperate woodland and thickets in Australia. The leathery leaves are simple and entire, opposite on mature plants, but often alternate on immature ones. The 5-petaled, creamy white flowers have a prominent crown of stamens, and are borne in terminal, corymb-like cymes. *A. hispida*, the most commonly grown species, is valued for its foliage, although flowers may be borne once the plant is 6–10ft (2–3m) tall. Where not hardy, grow in a cool greenhouse; in frost-free regions, use as handsome specimen trees.

• **CULTIVATION** Under glass, grow in soil-based potting mix, with additional sharp sand, in full light. In the growing season, water moderately and apply a balanced liquid fertilizer monthly; reduce water in winter. Outdoors, grow in fertile, well-drained soil in full sun. Pruning group 1; plants grown under glass need restrictive pruning.

• **PROPAGATION** Sow seed in spring at 66–75°F (19–24°C); pot on seedlings singly as soon as possible.

• **PESTS AND DISEASES** Infrequent.

A. cordifolia see *A. hispida*.

A. hispida, syn. *A. cordifolia* (Dwarf apple, Gum myrtle). Erect to spreading shrub or small tree with peeling gray to gray-brown bark, orange-brown when young, and young branchlets with red-brown hairs. The opposite, short-stalked or stalkless, elliptic to ovate, gray-green leaves, to 4in (10cm) long, dark purple-red when young, are heart-shaped at the bases, and have wavy, scalloped margins. From early to late summer, bears corymb-like cymes of 3–7 creamy white flowers, each ¾in (2cm) across. ↕ 10–25ft (3–8m), ↔ 10–20ft (3–6m). New South Wales. ❄ (min. 45°F/7°C)

ANGRAECUM

ORCHIDACEAE

Genus of about 200 species of mostly evergreen, epiphytic, monopodial orchids, found mainly in warm, humid regions at sea level or at low altitudes in Africa and Madagascar. They have semi-rigid, linear to oblong leaves, produced in 2 ranks, and bear white to green or yellowish green, spurred flowers, singly or in racemes from the leaf axils, at various times of the year.

• **CULTIVATION** Warm- to temperate-growing orchids. Grow epiphytically or in baskets of epiphytic orchid potting mix; provide humid conditions and full shade. Water freely all year, more sparingly in winter. In summer, apply a half-strength liquid fertilizer at every third watering and spray foliage lightly with water once or twice daily. See also p.46.

• **PROPAGATION** Not suitable for division, although robust species sometimes produce offsets, which may be detached after they have formed roots.

Angraecum sesquipedale

• **PESTS AND DISEASES** Fungal leaf spots, as well as cymbidium mosaic virus, can occur. Prone to spider mites, aphids, mealybugs, and whiteflies.

A. distichum. Miniature, evergreen, epiphytic orchid with broadly elliptic-oblong, curved, mid-green leaves, 3–5in (8–13cm) long, giving a chain-like appearance. Many stalkless, night-scented, pure white flowers, ½in (1.5cm) across, with spurs ⅜in (8mm) long, are produced singly from the leaf axils from summer to autumn. ↕↔ 6in (15cm). Tropical Africa, from Guinea to Uganda and Angola. ❄ (min. 64°F/18°C; max. 86°F/30°C)

A. eburneum, syn. *A. superbum*. Variable, robust, evergreen epiphytic orchid with rigid, strap-shaped, leathery, mid- to dark green leaves, 12–20in (30–50cm) long. Night-scented, light green flowers, 3in (8cm) long, with white lips and spurs, to 4in (10cm) long, are borne in one-sided axillary racemes, to 24in (60cm) long, from autumn to winter. ↕ 4ft (1.2m), ↔ 24in (60cm). E. tropical Africa, Madagascar, islands of the Indian Ocean. ❄ (min. 64°F/18°C; max. 86°F/30°C)

A. leonis. Dwarf to medium-sized evergreen epiphytic orchid with narrowly sickle-shaped mid-green leaves, 2–10in (5–25cm) long. In winter, produces erect or arching racemes, 3–4in (7–10cm) long, with 1–7 white flowers, 1½–2in (4–5cm) across, having compressed pedicels and linear, green-tinted spurs, 3–3½in (7–9cm) long; the racemes arise from leafless axils below the leaves. ↕↔ 8–12in (20–30cm). Madagascar. ❄ (min. 50–54°F/10–12°C; max. 86°F/30°C)

A. sesquipedale ▣ Robust, evergreen, epiphytic orchid with strap-shaped to oblong, dark green leaves, to 12in (30cm) long. In winter, bears axillary racemes, 10–12in (25–30cm) long, of 2–4 night-scented, waxy, ivory-white flowers, 7–9in (18–23cm) across, with spurs, 8–12in (20–30cm) long. ↕ 24in (60cm), ↔ 12in (30cm). Madagascar. ❄ (min. 64°F/18°C; max. 86°F/30°C)

A. superbum see *A. eburneum*.

ANGULOA

Cradle orchid, Tulip orchid

ORCHIDACEAE

Genus of about 10 species of deciduous, epiphytic or terrestrial orchids from South America, where they are found at high altitudes in the Andes. They have cylindrical to conical pseudobulbs, each of which produces 3 strongly ribbed and folded, broadly lance-shaped, soft-textured leaves. Anguloas are cultivated for their superb, tulip-like, solitary, fragrant flowers with waxy tepals, which are borne on basal stems in summer. Cradle or tulip orchids are closely related to, and hybridize readily with, the genus *Lycaste*.

• **CULTIVATION** Cool- to intermediate-growing orchids. Grow in containers of epiphytic or terrestrial orchid potting mix with high humidity and full shade in summer. In spring and summer, while the plants are in leaf, water freely and apply a half-strength liquid fertilizer at every third watering. Take care not to

Anguloa clowesii

wet new growth. In autumn, reduce water and temperature, and remove shading. Keep dry after the leaves have died away; resume watering and pot on when new growth develops. Avoid spraying the foliage, since this may encourage fungal diseases. See also p.46.

• **PROPAGATION** Remove the oldest pseudobulbs and pot up separately, but leave no fewer than 4 on the main plant.

• **PESTS AND DISEASES** Prone to spider mites, aphids, and mealybugs.

A. clowesii ▣ Deciduous, terrestrial orchid with conical pseudobulbs and folded, deep green leaves, 18–32in (45–80cm) long. Solitary, bright lemon-yellow flowers, 4in (10cm) long, are chocolate- and wintergreen-scented, and are produced on stems to 9in (23cm) long from spring to summer. ↕↔ 24in (60cm). Colombia, Venezuela. ❄ (min. 52°F/11°C; max. 86°F/30°C)

A. ruckeri. Deciduous, epiphytic or terrestrial orchid producing conical pseudobulbs and folded, deep green leaves, 18in (45cm) long. Solitary flowers, 3½in (9cm) long, are greenish brown on the outside and ochre, spotted red on the inside; they are borne on stems 9in (23cm) long in early summer. ↕↔ 24in (60cm). Colombia. ❄ (min. 52°F/11°C; max. 86°F/30°C)

ANGULOCASTE

ORCHIDACEAE

Bigeneric hybrid genus of deciduous orchids, a cross between *Anguloa* and *Lycaste*, with conical pseudobulbs and broadly lance-shaped, soft, folded leaves, to 24in (60cm) or more long. They are grown for their large, solitary, tulip-like, fragrant, often colorful flowers, which are borne in profusion in early summer.

• **CULTIVATION** Cool- to intermediate-growing orchids. Grow in epiphytic orchid potting mix in humid conditions with full shade in summer. In spring and summer, water freely and apply a half-strength liquid fertilizer at every

third watering. In autumn, when the pseudobulbs are fully formed, reduce water and temperature, and remove shading. Keep dry after the leaves have died; resume watering and pot on when new growth develops. Do not spray the foliage, since this encourages fungal diseases. See also p.46.
• **PROPAGATION** Remove oldest pseudobulbs and pot up separately, leaving at least 4 on the main plant, or divide when the plant overgrows its container.
• **PESTS AND DISEASES** Prone to spider mites, aphids, and mealybugs.

***A.* Apollo 'Goldcourt'.** Deciduous hybrid orchid with conical pseudobulbs and folded, dark green leaves, to 24in (60cm) long. In spring, bears numerous solitary, fragrant, deep yellow, red-flecked flowers, to 4in (10cm) across. ↕↔ 24in (60cm). ❄ (min. 52°F/11°C; max. 86°F/30°C)
***A.* Olympus 'Magnolia'.** Deciduous hybrid orchid with conical pseudobulbs and folded, dark green leaves, to 24in (60cm) long. In spring, bears many solitary, fragrant, creamy yellow flowers, 4in (10cm) across. ↕↔ 24in (60cm). ❄ (min. 52°F/11°C; max. 86°F/30°C)

▷ ***Anhalonium*** see *Ariocarpus*

ANIGOZANTHOS

Cat's paw, Kangaroo paw

HAEMODORACEAE

Genus of 11 species of evergreen, clump-forming perennials from a variety of habitats in S.W. Australia, including winter-wet swamps, sandy plains, open dry woodland, and coastal heathland. They have short rhizomes, fans of sheathing, lance- or strap-shaped, light to dark green leaves, and erect, slender, sometimes branched stems that bear terminal racemes or panicles of unusual, 2-lipped, tubular flowers, thought to resemble a kangaroo's paws. These are densely covered with red, orange, yellow, or green woolly hairs. They flower from spring to midsummer outdoors, but under glass may flower at any time of year. They hybridize freely, both in the wild and in cultivation. Where not hardy, grow in a cool greenhouse or conservatory. In frost-free regions, use to add interest to a border. They are also excellent for cut flowers.
• **CULTIVATION** Under glass, grow in 3 parts leaf mold and 1 part each loam and sharp sand in full light. Water freely in spring and summer, applying a balanced liquid fertilizer monthly; keep almost dry in winter. Outdoors, grow in moist but well-drained, humus-rich, sandy loam in full sun. Water freely during dry periods; mulch with straw or bark chips in autumn.
• **PROPAGATION** Sow seed at 55–64°F (13–18°C) as soon as ripe; carefully divide in spring.
• **PESTS AND DISEASES** Bacterial and fungal (ink spot) leaf diseases are rare.

A. bicolor (Little kangaroo paw). Clump-forming perennial with mid-green leaves, 12–16in (30–40cm) long, usually with bristly margins. Racemes, 1¼–4in (3–10cm) long, of 4–10 olive-green flowers, 1½–2½in (4–6cm) long, blue-green inside with red- or yellow-felted ovaries and reflexed lobes, are

Anigozanthos flavidus

borne from spring to summer. ↕ 28in (70cm), ↔ 16in (40cm). S.W. Australia. ❄ (min. 41°F/5°C)
***A.* Bush Gem Hybrids.** Clump-forming perennials bearing terminal racemes, 2–6in (5–15cm) long, of flowers in a range of colors, from late spring to midsummer. ❄ (min. 41°F/5°C)
'Bush Dawn' has dark green leaves, 9–18in (22–45cm) long, and bears racemes, 3–6in (8–15cm) long, of up to 100 yellow flowers, each 1¼–1½in (3–4cm) long, green inside and with reflexed lobes, on branched stems. ↕ 3–5ft (1–1.5m), ↔ 24in (60cm).
'Bush Emerald' has glaucous, blue-green leaves, to 14in (35cm) long, and racemes, 2–5in (5–13cm) long, of 12–15 yellow-green flowers, 2in (5cm) long, borne on red-purple, occasionally forked stems. ↕ 24–36in (60–90cm), ↔ 24in (60cm). Other cultivars include 'Bush Baby', 'Bush Ruby', and 'Bush Surprise'.
***A.* 'Dwarf Delight'.** Clump-forming perennial with bright green leaves, to 20in (50cm) long. From late spring to midsummer, erect stems bear panicles, 2–5in (5–13cm) long, of 5–15 greenish yellow flowers, 2–3in (5–8cm) long, covered with red hairs, appearing rich orange-red. ↕ 32in (80cm), ↔ 20in (50cm). ❄ (min. 45°F/7°C)
A. flavidus ■ Clump-forming, evergreen perennial with olive to mid-green leaves, 14–39in (35–100cm) long. From late spring to midsummer, panicles, 4–8cm (1½–3in) long, of 9–10 yellow-green to brownish red flowers, to 2in (5cm) or more long, the lobes not reflexed, are borne on widely branched stems. ↕ 3–10ft (1–3m),

Anigozanthos manglesii

↔ 24–32in (60–80cm). S.W. Australia. ❄ (min. 41°F/5°C)
A. humilis (Common cat's paw). Clump-forming perennial with light to mid-green leaves, 6–8in (15–20cm) long, with hairy margins. In early and midspring, bears racemes, 2–5in (5–13cm) long, of up to 15 yellow-green, yellow, orange, or red flowers, 2in (5cm) long, with lobes not reflexed. ↕ to 20in (50cm), ↔ to 12in (30cm). S.W. Australia. ❄ (min. 41°F/5°C)
A. manglesii ■ (Mangles' kangaroo paw). Clump-forming perennial with erect, gray-green leaves, 4–16in (10–40cm) long. From midspring to early summer, red-hairy, rarely branched stems bear racemes, 2–5½in (5–14cm) long, of up to 7 yellow-green flowers, 2½–4in (6–10cm) long, with reflexed lobes, grading to dark green with lime-green hairs outside and red, sometimes yellow or apricot-yellow hairs at the bases. ↕ 1–4ft (30–120cm), ↔ 16–24in (40–60cm). S.W. Australia. ❄ (min. 41°F/5°C)
A. pulcherrimus (Yellow kangaroo paw). Clump-forming perennial with gray-green, sometimes silky-haired leaves, 8–16in (20–40cm) long. From late spring to late summer, branched stems produce panicles, 1¼–3in (3–8cm) long, of 5–15 yellow flowers, 1½–2in (4–5cm) long, with spreading lobes and yellow hairs. ↕ to 3ft (1m), ↔ 16–24in (40–60cm). S.W. Australia. ❄ (min. 41°F/5°C)
A. rufus. Clump-forming perennial producing mid-green leaves, 8–16in (20–40cm) long, with rough, hairy margins. Broad panicles, 1¼–3½in (3–9cm) long, of 5–15 or more red or deep claret, purple-woolly flowers, to 1¾in (4.5cm) or more long, with lobes not reflexed, are produced on branched stems from midspring to midsummer. ↕ to 3ft (1m), ↔ 16–24in (40–60cm). S.W. Australia. ❄ (min. 41°F/5°C)
A. viridis (Green kangaroo paw). Clump-forming perennial with narrow, gray-green leaves, 4–20in (10–50cm) long. Racemes, 2–5½in (5–14cm) long, of up to 15 yellow-green flowers, 2–3in (5–8cm) long, with reflexed lobes and covered with greenish yellow hairs, are produced from early spring to early summer. ↕ to 3ft (1m), ↔ 16–24in (40–60cm). S.W. Australia. ❄ (min. 41°F/5°C)

ANISACANTHUS

ACANTHACEAE

Genus of 8 species of evergreen or deciduous subshrubs or shrubs, from rocky banks and flood plains of the S.W. US and N. Mexico. They have opposite or clustered, lance-shaped, and entire leaves, and are grown for their terminal spikes or axillary racemes of colorful flowers. *Anisacanthus* species are a colorful addition to a wild or desert garden. Where not hardy, grow in a warm greenhouse.
• **CULTIVATION** Outdoors, grow in moderately fertile, well-drained soil in full sun. Under glass, grow in soil-based potting mix in full light. Water freely when in growth; keep completely dry in winter. Pruning group 6.
• **PROPAGATION** Sow seed at 66–75°F (19–21°C) as soon as ripe, or root softwood and semi-ripe cuttings in sand.
• **PESTS AND DISEASES** Rust can occur.

A. thurberi (Chuparosa, Desert honeysuckle). Evergreen or deciduous shrub with opposite, light green leaves to 2in (5cm) long. Bears spikes of tubular, yellow-orange flowers, to 1½in (4cm) long, from spring to summer. Sometimes incorrectly offered as *Justicia leonardii*. ↕ to 4½ft (1.4m), ↔ 36in (90m). New Mexico, Arizona, N.W. Mexico. ❄ (min. 35°F/2°C)

ANISODONTEA

MALVACEAE

Genus of 19 species of woody-based perennials and shrubs from a variey of habitats in South Africa. The evergreen, alternate, usually toothed leaves vary from linear to elliptic or ovate and are sometimes lobed or 3-palmate. They are grown for their shallowly cup-shaped, 5-petaled flowers, borne singly or in racemes, corymbs, or cymes from spring to autumn. Where not hardy, grow in a cool greenhouse, moving plants outside or bedding them out in summer. Excellent for training into standards. In frost-free areas, grow in a border.
• **CULTIVATION** Under glass, grow in soil-based potting mix in full light. Pot on or top-dress in late winter. From spring to autumn, water freely and apply a balanced liquid fertilizer monthly; water sparingly in winter. Outdoors, grow in moderately fertile, well-drained soil in full sun. *A. capensis* and *A.* x *hypomadarum* may withstand spells to 23°F (-5°C). Tip-prune young plants to encourage a bushy habit. Pruning group 9.
• **PROPAGATION** Sow seed at 55–64°F (13–18°C) in spring. Root semi-ripe cuttings with bottom heat in summer.
• **PESTS AND DISEASES** Susceptible to spider mites, whiteflies, and aphids.

A. capensis ■ syn. *Malvastrum capensis.* Erect shrub with hairy stems and hairy, triangular to ovate, mid-green leaves, 1in (2.5cm) long, with 3–5 shallow to deep lobes, which may also be lobed and toothed. From summer to autumn, produces dark-veined, pale to deep red-purple flowers, 1in (2.5cm) wide, singly or in 2- or 3-flowered racemes from the leaf axils. ↕ 24–36in (60–90cm), ↔ 16–32in (40–80cm). South Africa. ❄ (min. 35°F/2°C)
A.* x *hypomadarum. Bushy shrub or subshrub, with slender, erect, densely hairy stems, and obovate to oblong, 3-lobed, toothed, mid- to deep green

Anisodontea capensis

leaves, to 1½in (4cm) long. From spring to autumn, produces purple-veined, pale pink flowers, 1–1¼in (2.5–3cm) wide, singly from the upper leaf axils. ↕5ft (1.5m), ↔3ft (1m). Garden origin. ❀ (min. 35°F/2°C)

▷***Anneliesia candida*** see *Miltonia candida*

ANODA
MALVACEAE

Genus of about 10 species of upright to spreading annuals, perennials, and subshrubs, widespread in moist soils in meadows and near streams, some from woodland or rocky areas, from S.W. US to Mexico, the West Indies, and N. South America. They have slightly hairy, unlobed, palmately lobed or palmate, lance-shaped to spear-shaped, mid-green leaves, and 5-petaled, mallow-like flowers borne singly or in racemes or panicles from summer to autumn. The short-lived perennials, usually grown as annuals, may survive mild winters with a mulch to protect the root system. They are suitable for a mixed or annual border.

• **CULTIVATION** Grow in any moist but well-drained soil, preferably low in nutrients, in full sun. Provide support early, when the seedlings are 3–4in (7–10cm) high. Deadhead to prolong flowering.

• **PROPAGATION** Sow seed at 55–59°F (13–15°C) in early spring, or *in situ* in midspring.

• **PESTS AND DISEASES** Powdery mildew and rust rarely occur.

A. cristata (Snowcup). Upright or spreading annual or short-lived perennial with ovate, unlobed to deeply 3- to 7-lobed, entire or toothed leaves, usually to 4in (10cm) long, but varying greatly in size and shape, even on the same plant. Saucer-shaped, white, lavender-blue, lilac, or purple-blue, veined flowers, ½–2in (1.5–5cm) across, are produced singly or in pairs from the upper leaf axils, from summer to autumn. ↕to 5ft (1.5m), ↔to 24in (60cm). S.W. US to Mexico, West Indies, N. South America. ❀ (min. 41°F/5°C). **'Opal Cup'** ▣ produces silver-lilac flowers with darker veins, and leaves sometimes marked purple. **'Silver Cup'** has pure white flowers.
A. wrightii. Variable annual with lance-shaped to spear-shaped, softly hairy leaves, to 1½in (4cm) long, and often with heart-shaped basal leaves. From summer to autumn, yellow to yellow-orange flowers, to ¾in (2cm) across, are produced singly or in pairs, with purple bases and triangular sepals. ↕to 24in (60cm), ↔to 12in (30cm). New Mexico, Arizona, Mexico.

▷***Anoiganthus*** see *Cyrtanthus*

ANOMATHECA
IRIDACEAE

Genus, closely related to *Freesia*, of 6 species of cormous perennials from upland grassland in C. and southern Africa. They have flat, broadly lance-shaped leaves, and bear terminal racemes of small, trumpet- to funnel-shaped flowers in late spring and early summer. The flowers are followed in autumn by brown capsules containing bright red seeds. Where not hardy, they are effective grown in containers in a cool or cold greenhouse. In frost-free regions, they are suitable for a sunny border.

• **CULTIVATION** Plant corms in spring, 2in (5cm) deep. Under glass, grow in sandy, soil-based potting mix in full light. In the growing season, water moderately and apply a balanced liquid fertilizer monthly; keep completely dry when dormant. Outdoors, grow in sandy, moderately fertile soil in full sun.

• **PROPAGATION** Sow seed at 55–61°F (13–16°C) in spring. Seedlings will flower in 2 years. Divide clumps in spring.

• **PESTS AND DISEASES** Infrequent.

Anoda cristata 'Opal Cup'

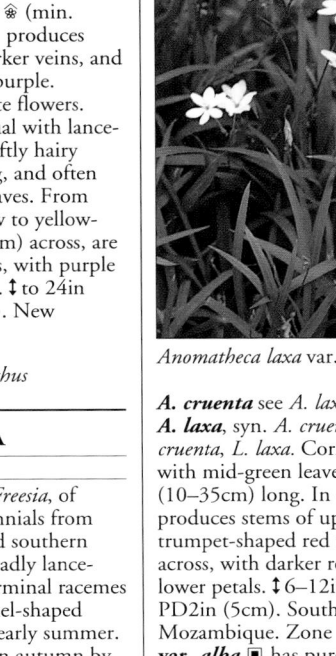

Anomatheca laxa var. *alba*

A. cruenta see *A. laxa*.
A. laxa, syn. *A. cruenta, Lapeirousia cruenta, L. laxa.* Cormous perennial with mid-green leaves, 4–14in (10–35cm) long. In early summer, produces stems of up to 6 open trumpet-shaped red flowers, ¾in (2cm) across, with darker red spots on the lower petals. ↕6–12in (15–30cm), PD2in (5cm). Southern Africa, Mozambique. Zone 8.
var. *alba* ▣ has pure white flowers.
A. viridis. Cormous perennial with mid-green leaves, 4–10in (10–25cm) long. In early summer, bears stems of 2–10 green flowers, to ¾in (2cm) across, shaped like curved funnels, with narrow, recurved petals. ↕12in (30cm), PD2in (5cm). South Africa (Northern Cape, Eastern Cape, Western Cape). Zone 8.

ANOPTERUS
ESCALLONIACEAE

Genus of 2 species of evergreen shrubs from moist forest in E. Australia and Tasmania. They have simple, alternate leaves and are cultivated for their attractive, terminal racemes of flowers. They are effective when planted in light woodland. Where not hardy, grow in a cool greenhouse and move outdoors during the summer.

• **CULTIVATION** Under glass, grow in acidic potting mix in full or filtered light. In the growing season, water freely and apply a balanced liquid fertilizer monthly; water sparingly in winter. Outdoors, grow in cool, moist, acidic, humus-rich soil in partial shade, ideally among trees and other shrubs for protection from wind. Pruning group 8.

• **PROPAGATION** Root semi-ripe cuttings in summer.

• **PESTS AND DISEASES** Infrequent.

Anopterus glandulosus

A. glandulosus ▣ (Tasmanian laurel). Upright, evergreen shrub with narrowly obovate, toothed, leathery, glossy, dark green leaves, to 5in (13cm) long. In mid- and late spring, bears cup-shaped white, sometimes pink-tinged flowers in terminal racemes, to 5in (13cm) long. ↕30ft (10m), ↔25ft (8m). Tasmania. ❀ (min. 41°F/5°C)

ANREDERA
syn. BOUSSINGAULTIA
BASELLACEAE

Genus of 10 species of tuberous-rooted, twining, evergreen climbers found in dry scrub and thickets in South America. The leaves are alternate, simple, and fleshy, often with bulbils produced in the leaf axils. Racemes of tiny, 5-petaled flowers are produced from the upper axils of long, young shoots. Where not hardy, grow *A. cordifolia* in a cool greenhouse. In frost-free areas, train over a support.

• **CULTIVATION** Under glass, grow in soil-based potting mix in full light. Water freely when in growth, applying a balanced liquid fertilizer monthly; water sparingly in winter. Outdoors, grow in any well-drained soil in full sun. Pruning group 11; prune in late winter or early spring.

• **PROPAGATION** Divide the tuberous roots in early spring. Root softwood cuttings in early summer. Collect tubers and bulbils in autumn and store in frost-free conditions; plant in early spring.

• **PESTS AND DISEASES** Prone to aphids and spider mites under glass.

A. cordifolia, syn. *Boussingaultia baselloides* of gardens (Madeira vine, Mignonette vine). Fast-growing twiner with reddish green stems and oblong, fleshy, bright green leaves, 1¼–4in (3–10cm) long, with heart-shaped bases. In autumn, bears numerous racemes, 12in (30cm) long, of sweetly scented white flowers. ↕12–20ft (4–6m). S. Brazil to N. Argentina. ❀ (min. 41°F/5°C)

ANTENNARIA
Cat's ears, Pussy-toes
ASTERACEAE

Genus of about 45 species of mostly evergreen or semi-evergreen, dioecious, mat-forming perennials from open habitats in the N. hemisphere. They have basal rosettes of hairy leaves and solitary or corymb-like heads of small, everlasting flowerheads on short stems. Use in a rock garden, as a low ground-cover at the front of a border, or in crevices in walls or paving. The flowerheads may be dried for use in flower arrangements.

• **CULTIVATION** Grow in any moderately fertile, well-drained soil in full sun to light shade.

• **PROPAGATION** Sow seed in containers in an open frame in spring or autumn. Divide in spring.

• **PESTS AND DISEASES** Susceptible to *Phyllosticta* and *Septoria* leaf spots, as well as powdery mildew and smut.

Antennaria dioica 'Rosea'

A. dioica. Semi-evergreen, mat-forming, stoloniferous perennial with gray-green, spoon-shaped leaves, to 1½in (4cm) long, densely white-hairy beneath. Bears corymbs of small, fluffy, white or pale pink flowerheads on stems ¾in (2cm) long in early summer. ↕ 2in (5cm), ↔ to 18in (45cm). Europe, N. Asia, North America. Zone 4. **'Nyewoods'** is compact, bearing deep pink flowerheads; ↔ to 8in (20cm). **'Rosea'** ■ has rose-pink flowerheads.

ANTHEMIS

ASTERACEAE

Genus of about 100 species of mat- or clump-forming, occasionally hummock-forming annuals and perennials from a wide range of well-drained, sunny habitats from Europe to N. Africa, Turkey, the Caucasus, and Iran. They are valued in a border or rock garden for their filigree foliage and extended flowering season, from late spring to late summer. They have usually pinnatisect to 3-pinnatisect, hairy, aromatic leaves and daisy-like, white or yellow flowerheads with yellow disk florets; some species are good for cutting.

Anthemis punctata subsp. *cupaniana*

Anthemis sancti-johannis

• **CULTIVATION** Grow in moderately fertile, well-drained, sandy or gravelly soil in full sun. Taller kinds normally need staking, or grow in self-supporting masses. *A. marschalliana* prefers partial shade with protection from winter moisture. *A. sancti-johannis* and *A. tinctoria* are often short-lived; to increase their longevity, cut back hard after flowering to encourage fresh growth and secondary flowering.
• **PROPAGATION** Sow seed in containers in a cold frame in spring. Divide in spring or root basal cuttings in spring and late summer.
• **PESTS AND DISEASES** A few fungal diseases, such as mildew, rarely occur. Prone to slug damage and aphids.

A. biebersteiniana see *A. marschalliana.*
A. marschalliana, syn. *A. biebersteiniana, A. rudolphiana.* Mat-forming perennial with obovate, 2-pinnatisect, silky gray leaves, to 3in (8cm) long, densely arranged on the stems. Solitary yellow flowerheads, ½in (1.5cm) across, with white-woolly, black-margined involucral bracts, are borne in early summer. ↕ 8–18in (20–45cm), ↔ 18–24in (45–60cm). Caucasus, N. Turkey. Zone 5.
A. nobilis see *Chamaemelum nobile.*
A. punctata* subsp. *cupaniana ■ Mat-forming perennial with ovate to obovate, pinnatisect or 2-pinnatisect, silvery gray leaves, 3–5in (8–13cm) long, turning dull gray-green in winter. In early summer, bears long-lasting white flowerheads, to 2½in (6cm) wide, with fewer blooms later. ↕ 12in (30cm), ↔ 36in (90cm). Italy (Sicily). Zone 7.
A. rudolphiana see *A. marschalliana.*
A. sancti-johannis ■ Clump-forming, short-lived perennial bearing oblong, pinnatisect, gray-hairy, white-tipped leaves, to 2in (5cm) long, and bright orange flowerheads, 1¼–2in (3–5cm) across, throughout summer. Hybridizes freely with *A. tinctoria*, and many plants offered under this name are hybrids. ↕ 24–36in (60–90cm), ↔ 24in (60cm). S.W. Bulgaria. Zone 4.
A. tinctoria (Golden marguerite, Ox-eye chamomile). Clump-forming, free-flowering perennial with inversely lance-shaped to obovate, 2- or 3-pinnatisect basal leaves, ½–2in (1–5cm) long, and smaller stem leaves. Leaves are mid-green above and gray-downy beneath. In summer, branching stems bear solitary, golden yellow to cream flowerheads, 1¼in (3cm) across, with gray-woolly involucral bracts. ↕↔ 36in (90cm). Europe, Caucasus, Turkey, Iran. Zone 3. The cultivars flower for many weeks, and are good in borders and for cutting; ↕↔ 24–36in (60–90cm) for most cultivars. **'Beauty of Grallach'** has orange-gold flowerheads. **'E.C. Buxton'** ■ produces attractive lemon-yellow flowerheads; ↕ 18–28in (45–70cm). **'Grallach Gold'** bears vivid gold flowerheads. **'Kelwayi'** has clear mid-yellow flowerheads; ↕↔ 24in (60cm). **'Moonlight'** has large, light yellow flowerheads that fade to near white; ↕ 30in (75cm), ↔ 20in (50cm).**'Sauce Hollandaise'** has very pale cream, almost white flowerheads, and dark green foliage; ↕ to 24in (60cm), ↔ 16–24in (40–60cm). **'Wargrave'** has pale yellow flowerheads.

Anthemis tinctoria 'E.C. Buxton'

ANTHERICUM

LILIACEAE

Genus of about 50 species of fleshy-rooted, rhizomatous perennials from grassy scrub on hillsides in Europe, Turkey, and Africa. They form clumps of narrow, linear, radical leaves and produce attractive, small, lily-like white flowers in racemes or panicles on slender stems, mainly in spring or summer, followed by decorative brown capsular fruits. They are ideal for a herbaceous border, or for naturalizing in grass; also excellent for cutting.
• **CULTIVATION** Grow in any fertile, well-drained soil in full sun.
• **PROPAGATION** Sow seed in containers in a cold frame in autumn or spring – they may flower within 3 years – or divide as growth begins in spring.
• **PESTS AND DISEASES** Susceptible to damage from rust, slugs, and snails.

***A. algeriense* 'Grandiflorum'** see *A. liliago* 'Major'.
A. graminifolium see *A. ramosum.*
A. liliago ■ (St. Bernard's lily). Rhizomatous perennial with grass-like,

Anthericum liliago

linear, mid-green leaves, to 16in (40cm) long. Open trumpet-shaped, lily-like white flowers, ¾–1¼in (2–3cm) across, with tepals to ¾in (2cm) long, are borne in racemes in late spring and early summer. ↕ 24–36in (60–90cm), PD12in (30cm). N., C., and S. Europe. Zone 7. **'Major'**, syn. *A. algeriense* 'Grandiflorum', has large, wide-opening flowers, to 1¼in (3cm) across.

A. ramosum, syn. *A. graminifolium.* Rhizomatous perennial with linear, gray-green leaves, to 16in (40cm) long. During early and midsummer, bears branched, open panicles of star-shaped, lily-like white flowers, to ½in (1.5cm) across, with tepals ½–¾in (1–2cm) long. ↕ 36in (90cm), PD12–24in (30–60cm). N. to S. Europe, Turkey, Crimea. Zone 4.

▷ ***Antholyza*** see *Crocosmia*

ANTHRISCUS

APIACEAE

Genus of about 12 species of annuals, biennials, and perennials from grassland, wasteland, and light woodland in temperate regions of the N. hemisphere. They have 2- or 3-pinnate, finely divided, light to mid-green leaves and tiny white flowers in umbels, 2–3in (5–8cm) across. Common chervil (*A. cerefolium*) has many culinary uses. Cow parsley (*A. sylvestris*) is attractive as a meadow plant. *A. sylvestris* 'Ravenswing' is useful for providing dark foliage contrast in a herbaceous border.

• **CULTIVATION** Grow in any well-drained soil in sun or partial shade. Water *A. cerefolium* in dry periods to retard bolting. *A. sylvestris* self-seeds prolifically if not deadheaded.

• **PROPAGATION** Sow *A. cerefolium* seed *in situ*, in succession from early spring to midsummer. Sow seed of perennials in containers in a cold frame in autumn or spring. Insert root cuttings in midwinter. Grown in isolation, *A. sylvestris* 'Ravenswing' produces many dark-leaved seedlings, but take care to select stock with dark, purple-brown foliage.

• **PESTS AND DISEASES** Slugs, snails, and caterpillars may damage young growth; powdery mildew may also be a problem.

A. cerefolium (Common chervil). Erect annual with 2- or 3-pinnate, anise-scented leaves, 1¼–2in (3–5cm) long, and hairy beneath, composed of ovate, toothed or pinnatifid leaflets. In midsummer, bears umbels of white flowers. ↕ to 20in (50cm), ↔ 10in (25cm). Europe, W. Asia.

A. sylvestris (Cow parsley, Queen Anne's lace). Clump-forming biennial or short-lived perennial with lacy, 3-pinnate leaves, 6–12in (15–30cm) long, composed of ovate, pinnatifid leaflets. Umbels of tiny white flowers open from midspring to early summer. ↕ 24–36in (60–90cm), ↔ 12in (30cm). Europe, Caucasus, Turkey, N.W. Africa. Zone 4. **'Ravenswing'** ■ has purple-brown leaves, and bears umbels of tiny white flowers with small pink bracts from late spring to summer; ↕ 3ft (1m).

Anthriscus sylvestris 'Ravenswing'

ANTHURIUM

Flamingo flower, Tail flower

ARACEAE

Large genus of 700–900 species of evergreen perennials, many epiphytic, with erect, sometimes climbing stems, from wet mountain forest in tropical and subtropical North and South America. They have large, entire or palmately lobed, often glossy leaves, and produce brightly colored, flat or concave spathes and cylindrical spadices, to 18in (45cm) long. The spadices usually taper evenly upward but may be pendent or contorted. The fruits are ovoid or spherical berries, which ripen to orange, red, or purple. Where not hardy, grow in containers or epiphytically on false "trees" in a warm greenhouse; species that tolerate drier conditions, such as *A. scherzerianum*, are suitable for use as houseplants. All provide excellent, long-lasting cut flowers. In humid, tropical areas, grow as epiphytes or in a border. If ingested, all parts may cause mild stomach disorder; contact with sap may irritate skin.

• **CULTIVATION** Plant with the crowns just above the soil surface and cover with a layer of sphagnum moss to protect the uppermost roots from drying out. Under glass, grow epiphytically or in a mix of 1 part fibrous loam, 1 part coarse sand, and 2–3 parts leaf mold, with additional charcoal. Provide high humidity and a constant temperature, with filtered light in summer and full light in winter. In the growing season, water freely and apply a balanced liquid fertilizer every 2–3 weeks; reduce humidity and water sparingly in winter. Top-dress annually and pot on every 2 years. Outdoors, grow epiphytically or in coarse, moist, fertile, humus-rich soil, enriched with leaf mold, in full or partial shade.

Anthurium andraeanum

Anthurium crystallinum

• **PROPAGATION** Sow seed at 75–81°F (24–27°C) as soon as ripe; they may take several months to germinate. Divide rootstock in winter. Root stem cuttings or offsets at 75–81°F (24–27°C) in spring or summer.

• **PESTS AND DISEASES** Mealybugs and scale insects may be problems. Fungal root rot, bacterial blight (*Xanthomonas*), fungal leaf spots, and bacterial soft rot are very common. Dasheen mosaic virus also occurs.

A. andraeanum ■ (Flamingo lily). Upright, epiphytic perennial with stems to 12in (30cm) tall, and ovate, reflexed, dark green leaves, which are arrow-shaped at the bases. Both leaf blades and leaf stalks grow to 12in (30cm) long. Erect, ovate to heart-shaped red spathes, 4–5in (10–13cm) long, often puckered, with yellow spadices, are produced throughout the year. Used extensively for hybridization. ↕ 24in (60cm), ↔ 8–12in (20–30cm). Colombia, Ecuador. ❀ (min. 61°F/16°C)

A. crystallinum ■ Upright, epiphytic perennial with stems 10in (25cm) tall, cultivated for its large, broadly ovate to elliptic, velvety, deep green leaves, which are pink-bronze when young. The leaf blades are sharply reflexed and 12–18in (30–45cm) long, with prominent white veins; the leaf stalks are 8in (20cm) long. Erect and spreading, narrow green spathes, 3in (8cm) long, with greenish yellow spadices, are produced intermittently throughout the year. ↕↔ 24in (60cm). Colombia. ❀ (min. 61°F/16°C)

A. x cultorum see *A. x ferrierense.*

A. x ferrierense (*A. andraeanum* x *A. nymphaeifolium*), syn. *A. x cultorum.* Upright, epiphytic perennial with dense growth. Stems are to 12in (30cm) tall; leaves are ovate, reflexed, bright to mid-green, and arrow-shaped at the bases.

Anthurium scherzerianum

The leaf blades are 14–16in (35–40cm) long, the leaf stalks 3ft (1m) long. Erect, fleshy, smooth, ovate to heart-shaped spathes, to 6in (15cm) long, varying in color from dark red to pink and orange-white, with curving yellow spadices, are borne at any time of year. ↕ 3ft (1m), ↔ 30in (75cm). Guatemala. ❀ (min. 61°F/16°C). **'Guatemala'** has broad, thick, bright red spathes with yellow spadices. **'Reidii'** produces large pink spathes, 6–8in (15–20cm) long.

A. 'Flamingo'. Upright, epiphytic perennial, similar to *A. andraeanum*, with reflexed, ovate, dark green leaf blades, arrow-shaped at the bases. Leaf blades and leaf stalks are both 12in (30cm) long. Erect, rounded-ovate, puckered, bright pink spathes, 7in (18cm) long, with white spadices, which turn yellow with age, are produced sporadically throughout the year. ↕ 24in (60cm), ↔ 8–12in (20–30cm). ❀ (min. 61°F/16°C)

A. scherzerianum ■ Variable, upright, epiphytic or terrestrial perennial with oblong-elliptic to lance-shaped, reflexed, leathery, dark green leaf blades, 6–8in (15–20cm) long, on leaf stalks to 10in (25cm) long. Broadly elliptic, reflexed, bright red spathes, 3–4in (8–10cm) long, with twisted, orange-red spadices, are borne intermittently throughout the year. ↕ 20–24in (50–60cm), ↔ 12in (30cm). Costa Rica, Guatemala. ❀ (min. 61°F/16°C). **'Rothschildianum'** ■ has red spathes with white spots and yellow spadices; **'Wardii'** has red stems and large, dark red spathes with long red spadices.

Anthurium scherzerianum 'Rothschildianum'

A. warocqueanum. Climbing, epiphytic perennial with narrowly ovate to lance-shaped, reflexed, velvet-textured, glossy, emerald green leaf blades, 20–36in (50–90cm) long; the leaf stalks are 6–24in (15–60cm) long. Bears narrow, reflexed green spathes, to 4in (10cm) long, with yellow-green spadices, at any time of year. ↕ 4ft (1.2m), ↔ 24–36in (60–90cm). Colombia. ❀ (min. 61°F/16°C)

Anthyllis

FABACEAE

Genus of about 20 species of annuals, perennials, and shrubs found on rocky cliffs or in open grassland, mainly in the Mediterranean. They have pinnate or 3-palmate leaves and bear racemes of pea-like, mostly yellow, cream, or red flowers in dense heads, occasionally in clusters or singly from the leaf axils. They thrive in areas with long, hot summers and tolerate poor, dry soils. Some species are suitable for a rock garden or the front of a mixed border.

- **Cultivation** Grow in well-drained, poor to moderately fertile soil in full sun. Trim plants after flowering.
- **Propagation** Sow seed in containers in a cold frame in autumn. Root semi-ripe cuttings in late summer.
- **Pests and diseases** Susceptible to fungal leaf spots.

A. hermanniae. Compact, rounded shrub with spiny, tangled branches and tiny 3-palmate leaves, to ½in (1.5cm) long, with oblong to lance-shaped, bright to gray-green leaflets, the 2 lateral leaflets sometimes very small. In early summer, bears a mass of bright golden yellow flowers, ¼–½in (6–15mm) long, in short, 2- to 8-flowered racemes, ¾–1¼in (2–3cm) long, with 2 large, leaf-like bracts. ↕ to 18in (45cm), ↔ to 24in (60cm) or more. Mediterranean, from Balearic Islands to Turkey. Zone 6. **'Minor'**, syn. 'Compacta', is compact; ↕ 4in (10cm), sometimes more, ↔ 12in (30cm).
A. montana ▣ Clump-forming, woody-based perennial with pinnate leaves, to 2½in (6cm) long, consisting of 8–15 or more pairs of narrowly elliptic to obovate-oblong, silky-haired, gray-green leaflets. During late spring and early summer, bears red, pink, or purple, white-tipped flowers, to ½in (1.5cm) long, in dense, spherical, clover-like heads, ¾–1¼in (2–3cm) across, above 2 deeply lobed, leaf-like bracts. Suitable for a rock garden or retaining wall. ↕ to 12in (30cm), ↔ to 24in (60cm). Alps and mountains of S. Europe. Zone 6. **'Rubra'** produces bright crimson flowers.
A. vulneraria (Kidney vetch). Very variable, spreading, silky-hairy annual or short-lived perennial with erect or spreading stems and pinnate, mid-green leaves, to 5½in (14cm) long, consisting of oblong to elliptic leaflets with a larger terminal leaflet. In summer, bears rounded, umbel-like clusters, to ½in (1.5cm) across, of cream or yellow, often purple-tipped flowers, ½in (1.5cm) long, surrounded by palmately lobed, silky, leaf-like bracts. Color variations from red, orange, and purple to white also occur. Suitable for a large rock garden or meadow planting. ↕ 8–24in (20–60cm), ↔ to 32in (80cm). Europe and North Africa to W. Asia. Zone 6. **var. *coccinea*** is the name applied to variants bearing bright red flowers.

Anthyllis montana

Antigonon

Corallita, Coral vine, Queen's wreath

POLYGONACEAE

Genus of 3 species of tendril climbers from Mexico and Central America, where they thrive in moist, tropical forest and scrub. They have tuberous roots and alternate, simple leaves, and are grown for their small, pink or white flowers, usually borne in panicles at the tips of the shoots. Where temperatures fall below 45°F (7°C), grow in a temperate greenhouse or conservatory. In warmer areas, train over a pergola, against a house wall, or through a tree.

- **Cultivation** Under glass, grow in soil-based potting mix in full light. From spring to autumn, water freely and apply a low-nitrogen liquid fertilizer monthly; keep just moist in winter. Outside, grow in moderately fertile, well-drained soil in full sun. Pruning group 11, in spring.
- **Propagation** Sow seed at 55–61°F (13–16°C) in spring. Root semi-ripe cuttings with bottom heat in summer.
- **Pests and diseases** Aphids, spider mites, and whiteflies may be problems under glass. Sometimes susceptible to fungal leaf spots.

A. leptopus ▣ (Confederate vine, Mexican creeper). Fast-growing climber with heart-shaped to almost triangular, bright green leaves, 2–5½in (5–14cm) long. From summer to autumn, bears coral-pink to red, occasionally white flowers, ½–¾in (1.5–2cm) across, in airy racemes and panicles, to 6in (15cm) or more long. The tuberous roots are edible. ↕ 25–40ft (8–12m). Mexico. ❀ (min. 45°F/7°C)

Antigonon leptopus

Antirrhinum

Snapdragon

SCROPHULARIACEAE

Genus of about 30–40 species of annuals, perennials, and semi-evergreen subshrubs from mainly rocky sites in Europe, US, and N. Africa. They are cultivated for their broadly tubular, 2-lipped flowers, with a characteristic hairy palate on the lower lip, which are produced from the leaf axils or in terminal racemes from early summer to autumn. The leaves, borne on branching stems, are linear-lance-shaped to ovate, and sometimes glandular. The common snapdragon, *A. majus*, is a short-lived perennial, usually grown as a bedding annual and for cut flowers. Shrubby perennial species are ideal for growing in a rock garden or retaining wall.

- **Cultivation** Grow *A. majus* cultivars in fertile, sharply drained soil in full sun. Deadhead to prolong flowering. First-year plants may survive the winter in Zones 5–7 if mulched deeply but loosely. Shrubby perennial species require very well-drained soil and shelter from wind; they are extremely brittle and sensitive to winter moisture.
- **Propagation** Sow seed of *A. majus* cultivars at 61–64°F (16–18°C) in winter. Where reliably winter hardy, sow seed in summer and set out plants in autumn. Root softwood cuttings of shrubby species in summer, or sow seed in containers in a cold frame in autumn or spring; they may not come true. Overwinter young plants under glass.
- **Pests and diseases** Gray mold, many fungal leaf spots (such as frogeye), rust, and root rots caused by *Pythium* and *Phytophora* are common. Seed-borne downy mildew is becoming a problem. Fungal wilt diseases and Southern blight sometimes occur. Aphids and leaf miners are problems in some areas.

A. asarina see *Asarina procumbens.*
A. braun-blanquettii. Erect, branched perennial with hairless stems and narrowly rounded, pointed leaves, 1–2½in (2.5–6cm) long. Bears spikes, 8in (20cm) long, of large, downy, creamy white flowers with yellow throats, from spring to autumn. ↕ 2–4ft (60–120cm), ↔ 12–24in (30–60cm). Portugal, Spain. Zone 7.

Antirrhinum majus 'Madame Butterfly'

A. glutinosum see *A. hispanicum.*
A. hispanicum, syn. *A. glutinosum.* Dwarf, branched shrub with lance-shaped to rounded, mid-green leaves, ¼–1½in (0.6–4cm) long. Bears loose racemes of yellowish white flowers, to ½in (1.5cm) across, with tiny red stripes, from midsummer to early autumn. ↕ 8–24in (20–60cm), ↔ 12in (30cm). Spain. Zone 7b. **'Album'** produces white flowers. **'Roseum'** has pink flowers.
A. majus. Variable, strongly branched, short-lived perennial, generally grown as an annual, often woody at the base, with mostly alternate, lance-shaped, glossy, deep green leaves, to 3in (8cm) long. Upright racemes of fragrant, 2-lipped flowers, 1¼–1¾in (3–4.5cm) across, with spreading, rounded, upper and lower lobes, vary in color in cultivated selections from white, yellow, and bronze, to purple, pink, and red, often including bicolors; they are borne all summer and into autumn. ↕ 9–72in (0.25–2m), ↔ 6–24in (15–60cm). S.W. Europe, Mediterranean. Zone 6b. Cultivars fall into 3 groups: tall, excellent for cut flowers and as fillers in a mixed border, ↕ 3ft (1m), ↔ to 18in (45cm) or more; intermediate, the most suitable for bedding, ↕ 12–24in (30–60cm), ↔ to 18in (45cm); and dwarf, for a small bed planting, edging, and containers, ↕ 8–12in (20–30cm), ↔ to 12in (30cm). **'Bells'** is dwarf and early flowering, with long-lasting, open-faced or hyacinth-like flowers, in purple, purple and white, red, rose-pink, pink, bronze, yellow, or white. **'Black Prince'** is intermediate and has bronze foliage and deep crimson flowers; ↕ 18in (48cm). **'Chimes'** is exceptionally dwarf and compact, producing flowers in a wide color range, including several bicolors; ↕ to 6in (15cm). **'Floral Showers'** is dwarf and early flowering, bearing flowers in many colors, including some bicolors. Tolerates wet weather; ↕ to 8in (20cm). **Liberty Series** cultivars are intermediate and bear long-blooming spikes in a wide range of colors; ↕ 24–36in (60–90cm). **Longshot Series** cultivars are intermediate, upright, and sturdy, bearing flowers in a wide range of colors, including some bicolors. Weather resistant; ↕ 24in (60cm). **'Madame Butterfly'** ▣ is a tall mixture with double, azalea-like flowers in a

Antirrhinum majus Sonnet Series

range of colors; ↕ 24–36in (60–90cm). **'Princess White with Purple Eye'** is a compact dwarf hybrid bearing bicolor flowers of pure white with a prominent purple spot; ↕ 14–24in (35–60cm). **Rocket Series** cultivars are vigorous, tall snapdragons, producing flowers in a broad color range; they are excellent for cut flowers; ↕ to 4ft (1.2m). **Sonnet Series** ■ cultivars are very early and free-flowering, intermediate snapdragons. They are bushy in habit, with good wet-weather tolerance, and produce bronze, pink, carmine-red, crimson, burgundy, white, and yellow flowers. **Tahiti Series** ■ cultivars are dwarf and rust-resistant, producing flowers in red, orange, rose-pink, and bronze, with a pink-and-white bicolor; ↕ to 8in (20cm).

Antirrhinum majus Tahiti Series

A. molle. Vigorous, dwarf subshrub with both procumbent and almost erect stems producing alternate, broadly ovate to elliptic, sticky-hairy, mid-green leaves, ½–¾in (1–2cm) long. White or pale pink flowers, 1–1¼in (2.5–3cm) long, with yellow palates, are produced from the upper leaf axils in early and midsummer. ↕ 6–8in (15–20cm), ↔ 8–12in (20–30cm). N.E. Spain, Portugal. Zone 8.

A. pulverulentum ■ Decumbent, dwarf shrub with opposite and alternate, ovate to elliptic, hairy, mid-green leaves, to 1¼in (3cm) long. Pale yellow flowers, ¾–1in (2–2.5cm) long, are produced from the upper leaf axils in early and midsummer. ↕ 6–8in (15–20cm), ↔ 8–12in (20–30cm). Chalky, alkaline soils in E. Spain. Zone 8.

Antirrhinum pulverulentum

A. sempervirens. Dwarf shrub, similar to *A. pulverulentum*, with trailing or erect, branching stems bearing opposite, oblong-ovate to elliptic, slightly sticky-hairy, mid-green leaves, ¼–½in (5–15mm) long. In early and midsummer, produces cream or white flowers, to 1in (2.5cm) long, with purple veins and yellow palates, from the upper leaf axils. ↕ 6–8in (15–20cm), ↔ 8–12in (20–30cm). Pyrenees, E. central Spain. Zone 8.

APHELANDRA

ACANTHACEAE

Genus of about 170 species of evergreen shrubs and subshrubs from moist woodland in tropical North, Central, and South America. They are grown for their attractive flowerheads and opposite pairs of simple, fleshy, glossy leaves produced on thick or slender stems. Terminal, occasionally axillary, 4-sided spikes with long-lasting, overlapping, brightly colored bracts and a succession of short-lived, tubular, red to yellow flowers are usually borne sporadically throughout the year. Where not hardy, grow in a temperate or warm greenhouse or as houseplants; elsewhere, use for bedding or for a border. Plants in containers may grow to only about a third of the dimensions given below.

• **CULTIVATION** Under glass, grow in soil-based potting mix, with additional leaf mold, one-third by volume; grow in full light, with filtered light in summer. Water freely during the growing season, more sparingly in winter. Apply a balanced liquid fertilizer every 2 weeks in summer, and monthly in winter. Outdoors, grow in moderately fertile, humus-rich, well-drained soil in partial shade.

• **PROPAGATION** After flowering, cut back the main stems to a strong pair of leaves to encourage sideshoots. When these are 3–4in (8–10cm) long, detach them and root at 70°F (21°C). Propagate regularly, since older specimens deteriorate rapidly.

• **PESTS AND DISEASES** Susceptible to many serious fungal diseases, including *Myrothecium* and *Corynespora* leaf spot and *Phytophthora* crown rot. Aphids, mealybugs, and scale insects may also be problems.

A. aurantiaca ■ syn. *A. fascinator.* Erect shrub with slender stems and ovate to elliptic, deep green leaves, 4–6in (10–15cm) long, flushed or mottled with silver. In winter, bears dense, terminal spikes, to 18in (45cm) long, of overlapping bracts and protruding, orange-scarlet or vermilion flowers, 1½–2in (4–5cm) long. ↕ 2½–4½ft (0.75–1.3m) ↔ 2–4ft (0.6–1.2m). Mexico to Colombia. ❄ (min. 45°F/7°C). **'Roezlii'** has wavy and puckered, gray-green leaves with bold silver markings, and scarlet flowers.

A. fascinator see *A. aurantiaca.*

A. squarrosa (Saffron-spike, Zebra plant). Compact shrub with thick stems and ovate to elliptic, dark green leaves, to 12in (30cm) long, with white, silver, or yellow veins and midribs. Bears terminal spikes, to 8in (20cm) long, of waxy yellow flowers, 1–1¼in (2.5–3cm) long, and maroon-tinged yellow bracts. ↕ 5–6ft (1.5–2m), ↔ 5ft (1.5m). Tropical

Aphelandra aurantiaca

and subtropical America. ❄ (min. 45–50°F/7–10°C; optimum 66°F/19°C). **'Dania'** has ovate to ovate-elliptic leaves with very prominent white veins that are feathered at the margins. Flowers, rarely produced, are yellow or orange-yellow and 1in (2.5cm) long; ↕↔ 12in (30cm). **'Louisae'** ■ has leaves with prominent white midribs and bold cross-bands of white around the veins. Bears spikes, 3–4in (8–10cm) long, of waxy, green-tipped, golden yellow flowers, resembling those of 'Dania'. Produces smaller flowerheads from the leaf axils just below the main spike; ↕ to 18in (45cm), ↔ 12in (30cm). **'Snow Queen'** is erect, with ovate, dark green leaves, which have silvery white veins. Flowers are pale lemon-yellow; ↕ to 18in (45cm), ↔ 12in (30cm).

A. tetragona. Spreading shrub with slender stems bearing broadly ovate, dark green leaves, 9in (23cm) long. Produces axillary and terminal spikes, 2–3in (5–8cm) long, of small orange bracts and hooded, bright red flowers, 1½–3in (4–8cm) long, with curved tubes. ↕↔ 4ft (1.2m). West Indies, Costa Rica, N. South America. ❄ (min. 45–50°F/7–10°C; optimum 66°F/19°C)

Aphelandra squarrosa 'Louisae'

APHYLLANTHES

LILIACEAE

Genus of one species of densely tufted or clump-forming perennial occurring on hot, dry hillsides in S.W. Europe and Morocco. It has rush-like stems, and leaves that are reduced to membranous, basal sheaths. Attractive, saucer-shaped, deep to pale blue flowers are borne on slender stems in early summer. *A. monspeliensis* is suitable for a rock garden or an alpine house.

• **CULTIVATION** Under glass, grow in a mix of 1 part each loam and grit with 2 parts leaf mold or peat. Water freely during the growing season; keep just moist when dormant. Outdoors, grow in sharply drained, sandy, peaty soil in full sun, with shelter from wind.

• **PROPAGATION** Sow seed in containers in a cold frame when ripe, or in spring; plant out seedlings as soon as possible, as young seedlings do not transplant well and larger plants resent disturbance. Divide with care in early spring.

• **PESTS AND DISEASES** Infrequent.

A. monspeliensis. Tufted or clump-forming, fibrous-rooted perennial with stiff, ribbed stems. In early summer, the stems bear deep blue to pale blue, dark-veined flowers, to 1in (2.5cm) across, singly or in groups of 2 or 3, above papery, reddish brown bracts. ↕ 4–10in (10–25cm), sometimes to 16in (40cm), PD4–6in (10–15cm). S.W. Europe, Morocco. ❀ (min. 41°F/5°C)

APIUM

Celery

APIACEAE

Genus of 20 species of celery with origins in Europe and temperate Asia. Biennial plants with fleshy bulbous roots bear compressed flowers, 3ft (90cm) tall; fruits are small, ribbed, elliptical to oval seeds. Traditional trench celery is demanding of soil conditions and requires attention throughout the 9-month growing season. Self-blanching celery is easier to grow, but not as hardy.

• **CULTIVATION** Grow in an open site in fertile, miost, but well-drained soil enriched with organic matter or lime acidic soil. Plant seedlings 10–12in (25–30cm) apart in a protected, sunny environment. Germinates best at 50–66°F (10–19°C).

Apium graveolens

• **PROPAGATION** Sow in spring *in situ* after all risk of frost after all risk of frost has passed, or indoors, for 12 weeks, roughly 80 days.

• **PESTS AND DISEASES** Susceptible to yellowing, leaf blight, slugs, and celery flies.

A. graveolens ▣ (Celery). Aromatic perennial with erect leaves and enlarged leaf stalks. Leaf segments, ½–2in (12–50mm) long, lance-shaped, lobed, on thick, long, grooved stalks. Bears compressed whitish flowers in compound umbels. ↕ 24–36in (60–90cm), ↔ 12–18in (30–45cm). Europe, Asia. ❀ (min. 35°F/2°C)

APONOGETON

APONOGETONACEAE

Genus of 44 species of rhizomatous, submerged aquatic perennials from temperate and tropical regions of Africa, S.E. Asia, and N. and E. Australia. The linear to elliptic or lance-shaped, floating leaves are produced from a tuber-like rhizome. Compound panicles or simple, forked racemes of tiny, often scented flowers, with 1–6 tepals and 6 or more stamens, are borne, mainly in summer, from a spathe-like bract just above the water surface. Some species will grow in water to 3ft (1m) deep. *A. distachyos* and *A. madagascariensis* are the most commonly cultivated species. In warmer climates, they are suitable for a pond outdoors. Where not hardy, grow in an aquarium.

• **CULTIVATION** Grow *A. distachyos* in soil at the bottom of a pond, or in aquatic containers, at least 12in (30cm) across, in water 12–36in (30–90cm) deep. Prefers full sun, but will tolerate partial shade. Grow *A. madagascariensis* outdoors in a shady pool in frost-free regions or, where not hardy, in an aquarium with filtered light, in water up to 20in (50cm) deep, at 73–82°F (23–28°C); the flowers last longer in the high humidity of a closed aquarium. Remove dying foliage after the growing season. See also pp.52–53.

• **PROPAGATION** Sow seed as soon as ripe, or seed that has been kept moist since collection, in small containers, covered by 2–3in (5–8cm) of water, at 55–61°F (13–16°C) for *A. distachyos* and 66–75°F (19–24°C) for *A. madagascariensis.* Divide rhizomes of large clumps when dormant.

• **PESTS AND DISEASES** Susceptible to a few fungal diseases. Young leaves are often eaten by water snails and the larvae of the brown china-mark moth. Algae may smother the delicate leaves.

A. distachyos ▣ (Cape pondweed, Water hawthorn). Aquatic perennial with oblong-lance-shaped, bright green floating leaves, to 8in (20cm) long, which are almost evergreen in mild winters. Small, scented white flowers, 1¼in (3cm) across, with purplish brown anthers, are enclosed in white spathes, to ¾in (2cm) long, and borne in racemes with forked branches, 4in (10cm) long, above the water surface in winter and spring. ↔ 4ft (1.2m). Southern Africa. Zone 4.

A. madagascariensis (Lace plant, Lattice leaf plant). Aquatic perennial with unusual, skeletonized foliage reduced to a network of veins with no tissue in between. Leaves, to 22in (55cm) long, with very long leaf stalks, are elliptic, light green, and submerged below the water surface. In summer, bears small white flowers, with white anthers, in compound panicles of white-spathed spikes, 1–2in (2.5–5cm) long. After fertilization, the flowers turn mauve. ↔ 12–14in (30–35cm). Madagascar. ❀ (min. 59°F/15°C)

Aponogeton distachyos

APOROCACTUS

Rat's tail cactus

CACTACEAE

Genus of 2 species of often epiphytic cacti found in sparsely wooded areas of S. Mexico and N. Central America. They are cultivated for their trailing stems, sometimes up to 6ft (2m) long, and colorful flowers. The pencil-like, pendent, fleshy stems have low ribs and closely arranged areoles bearing short, fine spines. The irregular, tubular to funnel-shaped, diurnal, bright red or purple flowers, with stamens longer than the petals, are borne singly, mainly on mature growth. They are followed by spherical, soft-bristly red berries containing numerous small, reddish brown seeds. Where not hardy, they are excellent for hanging baskets in a temperate greenhouse or conservatory. In frost-free areas, they are best grown outdoors in hanging baskets, epiphytically, or cascading over rocks.

• **CULTIVATION** Grow in epiphytic cactus potting mix in bright filtered light. During the growing season, water moderately and apply a high-potash liquid fertilizer monthly; keep just moist at other times of the year. Outdoors, grow in sharply drained, gritty, humus-rich soil in a sheltered site in partial shade. See also pp.48–49.

• **PROPAGATION** Sow seed at 70°F (21°C) as soon as ripe; keep just moist and provide filtered light. Root stem cuttings in early summer.

• **PESTS AND DISEASES** Susceptible to a few stem spots caused by fungi. New growth is particularly prone to mealybugs.

A. conzattii see *A. martianus.*

A. flagelliformis ▣ syn. *Cereus flagelliformis.* Pendent cactus producing grayish green stems with 10–14 ribs, and areoles each bearing reddish brown spines (8–12 radials and 3 or 4 centrals). Narrowly tubular, funnel-shaped, purple-red flowers, 3in (8cm) long, with narrow, reflexed outer petals and wider, spreading inner ones, are borne in late spring and early summer. ↕ 4in (10cm), ↔ to 5ft (1.5m). S. Mexico, N. Central America. ❀ (min. 50°F/10°C)

Aporocactus flagelliformis

A. mallisonii see x *Aporoheliocereus smithii.*

A. martianus, syn. *A. conzattii, Eriocereus martianus.* Pendent or creeping cactus producing gray-green stems with 8 ribs and yellow-spiny areoles, each bearing 6–8 radial spines and 2 or more centrals. Funnel-shaped, bright scarlet flowers, 4in (10cm) long, are borne in early summer. ↕ 4–5in (10–13cm), ↔ to 3ft (1m). S. Mexico. ❀ (min. 50°F/10°C)

x APOROHELIOCEREUS

CACTACEAE

Hybrid genus, a cross between *Aporocactus* and *Heliocereus,* of one creeping, pendent, cactus, whose parents originate from wooded areas in Mexico. It has pencil-like, fleshy stems, often up to 6ft (2m) long, closely set, fine-spiny areoles, and solitary, large, funnel-shaped flowers that form mainly on mature growth. Where not hardy, x *A. smithii* is excellent in a hanging basket in a temperate greenhouse or conservatory. In frost-free regions, it is effective trailing over a wall.

• **CULTIVATION** Under glass, grow in epiphytic cactus potting mix in bright filtered light. When in growth, water moderately and apply a high-potash liquid fertilizer monthly; keep just moist at other times. Outdoors, grow in sharply drained, gritty, humus-rich soil in a sheltered site in partial shade. See also pp.48–49.

• **PROPAGATION** Take stem cuttings in early summer.

• **PESTS AND DISEASES** Vulnerable to mealybugs.

x *A. mallisonii* see x *A. smithii.*

x *A. smithii*, syn. *Aporocactus mallisonii,* x *Aporoheliocereus mallisonii.* Pendent cactus producing dark green stems, with 6–8 prominent ribs, brown areoles, and radiating, dark yellow spines. In summer, funnel-shaped, diurnal red flowers, to 3in (8cm) long, are borne mainly on the upper parts of the stems. ↕ 6in (15cm), ↔ to 30in (75cm). Garden origin. ❀ (min. 50°F/10°C)

▷ ***Aprica arachnoidea*** see *Haworthia arachnoidea*

Arbutus x *andrachnoides* (inset: bark detail)

fruits, ½–1¼in (1–3cm) across. They are excellent for a large shrub border, for a woodland garden, or as specimen trees. Where not hardy, grow in a cool greenhouse.

• **CULTIVATION** Grow in fertile, humus-rich, well-drained soil, in a sheltered site in full sun. Protect from cold winds, even when mature. *A. andrachne*, *A.* x *andrachnoides*, and *A. unedo* will tolerate alkaline soils. *A. menziesii* (and other species) need acidic soils. Pruning group 1, but keep pruning to a minimum.

• **PROPAGATION** Sow seed in containers in a cold frame as soon as ripe. Root semi-ripe cuttings in late summer.

• **PESTS AND DISEASES** Algal leaf spot is common in S.E. US. Susceptible to a wide variety of fungal leaf spots. May attract tent caterpillars and scale insects.

Arbutus menziesii

A. andrachne (Grecian strawberry tree). Spreading, sometimes shrubby tree with smooth, peeling, red-brown bark. Ovate to ovate-oblong, glossy, dark green leaves, 2–4in (5–10cm) long, are usually entire, occasionally finely toothed. White flowers are produced in leafy, erect panicles, to 4in (10cm) long, in late spring, followed by spherical, warty, orange-red fruit, ½–¾in (1–2cm) across, which ripen in autumn the following year. ↕↔ 20ft (6m). S.E. Europe, Turkey, Lebanon. Zone 7b.

A.* x *andrachnoides ■ (*A. andrachne* x *A. unedo*). Broadly upright, then often spreading, sometimes shrubby tree with peeling, red-brown bark and ovate to lance-shaped, finely toothed, glossy, mid-green leaves, to 4in (10cm) long, and glaucous beneath. Semi-pendent panicles, to 3in (8cm) long, of small white flowers, sometimes pink-tinged, are borne from autumn to spring. Fruit are rarely produced. ↕↔ 25ft (8m). S.E. Europe, S.W. Asia. Zone 8.

Arbutus unedo

A. menziesii ■ (Madroño). Spreading, sometimes shrubby tree with peeling, red-brown bark. Oval, toothed leaves, 2–6in (5–15cm) long, are glossy, dark green, and glaucous beneath. White flowers in erect panicles, to 8in (20cm) tall, are borne freely in early summer, followed by spherical, warty, orange-red fruit, ½in (1.5cm) across, which ripen in autumn the following year. ↕↔ 50ft (15m). W. North America. Zone 7.

A. unedo ■ (Strawberry tree). Spreading, picturesque, sometimes shrubby tree with rough, shredding, red-brown bark and oval to obovate, shallowly toothed, glossy, mid-green leaves, to 4in (10cm) long. Small white flowers, sometimes pink-tinged, open in pendent panicles, to 2in (5cm) long, in autumn; spherical, warty red fruit, ¾in (2cm) across, ripen the following autumn. ↕↔ 25ft (8m). S.E. Europe, Turkey, Lebanon. Zone 7. **'Elfin King'** is compact, flowering and fruiting freely when small; ↕ 6ft (2m), ↔ 5ft (1.5m). **f. *rubra*** has dark pink flowers.

ARCHONTOPHOENIX

King palm

ARECACEAE

Genus of 2 species of single-stemmed palms from rainforest in E. Australia. Large, pinnate leaves are arranged in a terminal tuft above a prominent crownshaft, and large panicles or racemes of monoecious, cup-shaped flowers are borne beneath them. Grow young plants in a temperate greenhouse or conservatory; in warmer areas, grow as specimen trees.

• **CULTIVATION** Under glass, grow in soilless potting mix in bright, filtered light with moderate humidity. When in growth, water moderately and apply a balanced liquid fertilizer monthly; keep just moist in winter. Outdoors, grow in fertile, humus-rich, moist but well-drained soil in partial shade to prevent leaf scorch.

• **PROPAGATION** Sow seed in spring at 75–81°F (24–27°C).

• **PESTS AND DISEASES** Spider mites may be a problem under glass. Susceptible to *Helminthosporium* leaf spot when plants are young, as well as *Phytophthora* root rot and aerial blight.

Archontophoenix alexandrae

A. alexandrae ■ syn. *Ptychosperma alexandrae* (Alexander palm, Northern bangalow palm). Tall, fast-growing palm with a slender trunk, swollen at the base and covered with ring-like leaf scars. Arching, pinnate leaves, 6–12ft (2–4m) long, have numerous narrowly lance-shaped leaflets, pale green or purple-flushed above, silver to gray beneath. In summer, cream to yellow flowers open in large panicles, to 30in (75cm) long, followed by ellipsoid to almost spherical, pinkish red fruit. ↕ to 80ft (25m), ↔ 15–22ft (5–7m). Queensland. ❀ (min. 50°F/10°C)

A. cunninghamiana (Bangalow palm, Illawarra palm, Piccabeen palm, Seaforthia palm). Slender-stemmed palm with a ringed trunk, sheathed in greenish leaf bases, and arching, pinnate leaves, 6–12ft (2–4m) long, consisting of many lance-shaped, gray-green or light green leaflets. When mature, bears small lilac flowers in large, pendent racemes, to 24–36in (60–90cm) long, in summer, followed by ovoid red fruit. ↕ 50–70ft (15–20m), ↔ 6–15ft (2–5m). Queensland. ❀ (min. 50°F/10°C)

▷ ***Arcterica nana*** see *Pieris nana*

ARCTOSTAPHYLOS

syn. COMAROSTAPHYLIS

Bearberry, Manzanita

ERICACEAE

Genus of about 50 species of prostrate or upright shrubs, or small trees, all evergreen except for *A. alpina*, mainly from W. North America, particularly California. They are found in a range of moist or dry habitats, from coastal scrub to mountain slopes, pine forest, and high moors. They have alternate, simple, entire or toothed leaves, and terminal panicles or racemes of tiny, urn-shaped flowers, ⅛–¼in (4–6mm) long, followed by spherical fruits, ¼–½in (6–15mm) across. Use the prostrate and compact species as a groundcover or, where summers are cool, in a rock garden. The more upright species, with their often attractive bark, are effective in open areas of a woodland garden. Where not hardy, grow in a cool greenhouse.

• **CULTIVATION** Under glass, grow in acidic potting mix in full light. When in growth, water freely and apply a balanced liquid fertilizer monthly; water sparingly in winter. Outdoors, grow in moist but well-drained, moderately fertile, acidic soil in full sun or partial shade. Shelter less hardy species from wind.

• **PROPAGATION** Sow seed in containers in a cold frame in autumn (immerse seed in boiling water for 20 seconds before sowing), or root semi-ripe cuttings in summer. Layer in autumn. Prostrate species and hybrids often root at the nodes, providing rooted pieces that may be removed and potted up.

• **PESTS AND DISEASES** *Exobasidium* bud and leaf galls are common. Susceptible to a variety of other fungal diseases on leaves, stems, and fruit.

A. alpina, syn. *Arctous alpinus* (Alpine bearberry). Deciduous, creeping shrub with obovate to inversely lance-shaped, white-woolly, toothed leaves, ½–1¼in (1.5–3cm) long, bright green, turning red in autumn. In late spring, bears axillary racemes, ½–¾in (1–2cm) long, of pendent, pink-flushed white flowers, followed in autumn by small, spherical, red then purple-black fruit. ↕ 2in (5cm), ↔ to 8in (20cm). Mountain moors and heaths in N. circumpolar regions. Zone 4.
***A. densiflora* 'Howard McMinn'.** Dense, mound-forming shrub with smooth, dark red bark and elliptic, glossy, mid-green leaves, 1¼in (3cm) long. Pink-tinged white flowers are borne in small racemes, to 1½in (4cm) long, in spring. ↕ 5ft (1.5m), ↔ 6ft (2m). Zone 7b.
A. diversifolia, syn. *Comarostaphylis diversifolia* (Summer holly). Upright shrub with peeling or shredding bark and oblong to elliptic, toothed, glossy, dark green leaves, to 3in (8cm) long. Small white flowers are borne in racemes, to 2½in (6cm) long, in spring, and are followed by small, spherical, warty red fruit in autumn. ↕ 15ft (5m), ↔ 10ft (3m). California. Zone 8.
A. glandulosa (Eastwood manzanita). Rounded shrub with smooth, red-brown bark. Ovate to lance-shaped, leathery, matte green leaves, to 2in (5cm) long, are covered with sticky hairs on both sides when young, becoming hairless when mature. Bears small white flowers in racemes, to 1½in (4cm) long, in late winter and early spring, followed by small, flattened-spherical, sticky, red-brown fruit in summer. ↕↔ 6ft (2m). Oregon, California. Zone 8.
A. glauca (Bigberry manzanita). Rounded shrub, sometimes tree-like, with smooth, red-brown bark and elliptic to ovate, leathery, glaucous leaves, to 1½in (4cm) long. White or pink flowers open in racemes, to 3in (8cm) long, from spring to early summer, followed in late summer by spherical, sticky brown fruit. ↕↔ 20ft (6m). California. Zone 8.
***A. hookeri* 'Monterey Carpet'.** Low-growing, sometimes mat-forming shrub with purple-tinged branches and ovate to elliptic, narrow-pointed, glossy, pale

Arctostaphylos patula

Arctostaphylos pumila

green leaves, ¾–1½in (2–4cm) long. In early summer, produces racemes, 3in (8cm) long, of pinkish white flowers, followed by spherical scarlet fruit. ↕ to 8in (20cm), ↔ to 3ft (1m) or more. Zone 8.
A. manzanita (Manzanita, Parry manzanita). Upright shrub or small tree with smooth, red-brown bark and ovate, leathery, bright green to gray-green leaves, to 2in (5cm) long, sometimes hairy on both sides. Dark pink, sometimes white flowers in racemes, to 1½in (4cm) long, are produced in late winter and early spring, followed by flattened-spherical white fruit, ripening to red, in autumn. ↕ 12ft (4m), ↔ 10ft (3m). California. Zone 8.
***A. x media* 'Snow Camp'**, syn. *A. uva-ursi* 'Snow Camp'. Mat-forming shrub, closely resembling *A. uva-ursi*, with prostrate branches, erect or ascending stems, and obovate, dark green leaves, to 1¼in (3cm) long. In summer, bears a profusion of compact racemes, 2–4in (5–10cm) long, of pale pink flowers, followed by flattened-spherical red fruit. ↕ 4in (10cm), ↔ to 3ft (1m) or more. Zone 7.
A. nevadensis (Pine-mat manzanita). Prostrate, mat-forming shrub with spreading branches, often rooting at the nodes, and narrowly lance-shaped to obovate, sharply tipped, glossy, bright green leaves, ¾–1¼in (2–3cm) long. In early summer, bears erect, raceme-like clusters, 1½–3in (4–8cm) long, of white, sometimes pink-tinged flowers, followed by flattened-spherical, reddish brown fruit in autumn. ↕ to 12in (30cm), ↔ to 3ft (1m). California, W. Oregon. Zone 7b.
A. patula ■ (Greenleaf manzanita). Spreading shrub with smooth, red-brown bark and broadly ovate to rounded, leathery, hairless, bright green leaves, 1–1½in (2.5–4cm) long. Bears pink or white flowers in loose panicles, to 3in (8cm) long, from spring to early summer, followed by flattened-spherical, dark brown fruit in late summer. ↕↔ 6ft (2m). California. Zone 7.
A. pumila ■ (Dune manzanita). Trailing, dense, mat-forming shrub with upright branch tips and obovate to spoon-shaped, dark green leaves, ¾in (2cm) long, paler and sometimes white-downy beneath. Short, dense racemes, 1½–3in (4–8cm) long, of white flowers, sometimes pink-tinted, are borne in summer, followed by small, flattened-spherical, reddish brown fruit in

Arctostaphylos uva-ursi 'Wood's Red'

autumn. ↕ 12in (30cm), ↔ 16in (40cm), possibly reaching 30in (75cm) in cultivation. California. Zone 8.
A. uva-ursi (Common bearberry, Kinnikinick). Low-growing, intricately branched, often mat-forming shrub with small, obovate, leathery, dark green leaves, ¾–1½in (2–4cm) long. Small racemes, ¾–1¼in (2–3cm) long, of pink-tinted white flowers are borne in summer, followed by spherical, bright scarlet fruit in autumn. ↕ to 4in (10cm), ↔ to 20in (50cm). N. Eurasia, North America. Zone 1. **'Massachusetts'** is small and flat-growing, bearing abundant pinkish white flowers, followed by red fruit. Resistant to leaf spot and leaf gall. **'Snow Camp'** see *A.* x *media* 'Snow Camp'. **'Vancouver Jade'** is a low-growing, arching shrub with glossy leaves and small pink flowers; ↕ 6in (15cm), ↔ 18in (45cm). **'Wood's Red'** ■ is a dwarf cultivar with pink flowers and large, shiny red fruit.

ARCTOTHECA

ASTERACEAE

Genus of 4 species of low-growing, usually rosette-forming perennials from open, sandy areas in South Africa; some species have become naturalized in Portugal, Spain, and Australia. The leaves, often white-woolly, are pinnatifid with prominent lobes, toothed, or sometimes entire. The yellow, daisy-like flowerheads, with purplish black disk florets in some species, are often tinged with bronze or purple, especially on the undersides; they are mostly solitary, but sometimes borne in twos or threes, on

Arctotheca calendula

long, slender stems. Use for covering banks or for edging; usually treated as annuals where not hardy.
• **CULTIVATION** Grow in well-drained, moderately fertile soil in full sun.
• **PROPAGATION** Sow seed at 61–64°F (16–18°C), or divide in spring.
• **PESTS AND DISEASES** Infrequent.

A. calendula ■ syn. *Cryptostemma calendulaceum*. Low-growing, rhizomatous perennial with rosettes of oblong-obovate, pinnatifid, occasionally entire leaves, 6in (15cm) long, and white-woolly beneath. Flowerheads, to 1½in (4cm) across, with yellow ray florets, tinged purple on the undersides, and purplish black disk florets with yellow anthers, are borne in spring or early summer. ↕ 20in (50cm), ↔ indefinite. South Africa. ❄ (min. 45°F/7°C)
A. populifolia. Low-growing, rhizomatous perennial with alternate, elliptic to ovate, occasionally pinnatifid, mid-green leaves, 3in (8cm) long, and white-woolly beneath. From summer to autumn, bears flowerheads ½–¾in (1.5–2cm) across, with yellow ray florets and yellow disk florets. ↕ 12in (30cm), ↔ 24in (60cm). South Africa. ❄ (min. 45°F/7°C)

ARCTOTIS

syn. x VENIDIOARCTOTIS, VENIDIUM

African daisy

ASTERACEAE

Genus of about 50 species of erect to spreading annuals and perennials, occasionally subshrubs, found in dry, stony soils in South Africa. They form basal rosettes of entire to lobed, lance-shaped to elliptic, gray-green to silvery green leaves. Solitary, daisy-like, brightly colored flowerheads are borne on long, thick, ribbed stems from midsummer to early autumn. Grow as an annual in bedding, a gravel garden, or containers. The flowerheads of modern cultivars, bred for bedding display, tend to stay open longer than those of the original species, which close in the afternoon and in cloudy weather. They are attractive cut flowers, though short-lived.
• **CULTIVATION** Grow in sharply drained but relatively moist, light soil in full sun.
• **PROPAGATION** Sow seed at 61–64°F (16–18°C) in early spring or autumn. Prick out individually into 3½in (9cm) containers to avoid further root disturbance. Root softwood stem cuttings of good color selections.
• **PESTS AND DISEASES** Aphids and leaf miners may be problems. Susceptible to downy mildew, fungal leaf spots, and Southern blight.

A. fastuosa ■ syn. *Venidium fastuosum* (Monarch of the veldt). Spreading perennial, usually cultivated as a half-hardy annual, with elliptic, deeply lobed, silvery white leaves, 5in (13cm) long, with a dense covering of woolly hairs. Rich orange flowerheads, to 4in (10cm) across, with deep purple or black disk florets, are produced from midsummer to early autumn. ↕ 12–24in (30–60cm), ↔ 12in (30cm). South Africa. ❄ (min. 41°F/5°C)
'Zulu Prince' ■ has intensely silvery white foliage and creamy yellow flowerheads, with a small black triangle with orange margins at the base of each ray floret.

Arctotis fastuosa

A. Harlequin Hybrids, syn. *A.* x *hybrida*, x *Venidioarctotis*. Interspecific hybrids bred for cultivation as half-hardy annuals or perennials. They have elliptic, wavy-margined, lobed, felted, silvery green leaves, to 5in (13cm) long. From midsummer to early autumn, they bear pink, orange, white, carmine-red, or apricot-yellow flowerheads, 3–3½in (8–9cm) across, with dark disk florets, sometimes with darker markings on the ray florets. ↕ 18–20in (45–50cm), ↔ to 12in (30cm). ❄ (min. 41°F/5°C). A number of named cultivars, originally introduced under the name x *Venidioarctotis*, are very free-flowering and are propagated by cuttings; they include **'Bacchus'**, with reddish purple flowerheads, **'China Rose'**, with dusky pink flowerheads, and **'Flame'**, which has brilliant orange-red flowerheads.
A.* x *hybrida see *A.* Harlequin Hybrids.
A. stoechadifolia see *A. venusta*.
A. venusta, syn. *A. stoechadifolia* (Blue-eyed African daisy). Spreading perennial, often cultivated as an annual, with elliptic-obovate, wavy-margined, lobed leaves, to 5in (13cm) long, dark green above, and silvery green beneath. Creamy white flowerheads, to 3in (8cm) across, with blue disk florets, are borne from midsummer to early autumn. ↕ 24in (60cm), ↔ 16in (40cm). South Africa. ❄ (min. 41°F/5°C).
var. *grandis* is larger overall and is well suited for growing in a cool greenhouse in containers.

▷***Arctous alpinus*** see *Arctostaphylos alpina*

Arctotis fastuosa 'Zulu Prince'

ARDISIA

MYRSINACEAE

Genus of about 250 species of evergreen trees and shrubs from moist woodland in tropical and warm-temperate areas of Asia, Australasia, and North and South America. They are grown for their whorled or spiralled, mid- to dark green leaves, their panicles or umbel-like corymbs of white or pink flowers, and their showy red fruits. In frost-free areas, grow in woodland; *A. japonica* is a reliable groundcover where temperatures do not fall below 23°F (-5°C). Where not hardy, grow *A. crispa* in a temperate greenhouse or as a houseplant.
• **CULTIVATION** Under glass, grow *A. crispa* in soil-based potting mix in bright filtered light. When in growth, water freely and apply a balanced liquid fertilizer monthly; water moderately at all other times. Outdoors, grow in moist but well-drained, humus-rich soil, in a shady site, sheltered from strong winds. Pruning group 9; plants under glass need restrictive pruning.
• **PROPAGATION** Sow seed at 55°F (13°C) in spring. Root semi-ripe cuttings in summer. Divide runners of *A. japonica* in spring.
• **PESTS AND DISEASES** Susceptible to many fungal root rots, as well as a number of fungal stem and leaf diseases. Mealybugs can be a problem. Basal stem gall may occur when seeds germinate at excessively high temperatures.

A. crispa ■ Erect shrub with spiralled or alternate, lance-shaped, leathery, mid- to dark green leaves, 2–5½in (5–14cm) long, with shallowly scalloped margins. In summer, bears terminal, umbel-like corymbs, to 4in (10cm) long, of star-shaped pink flowers, ⅜–½in (9–12mm) across, followed by spherical red berries, to ¼in (6mm) wide. ↕ 2–5ft (0.6–1.5m), ↔ 18–24in (45–60cm). S.E. Asia. ❄ (min. 35°F/2°C)
A. japonica (Marlberry). Compact shrub with erect, clustered stems, underground runners, and whorls of toothed, ovate, glossy, mid- to dark green leaves, 1½–3½in (4–9cm) long. In summer, bears umbel-like corymbs, 1¼–3in (3–8cm) long, of pendent, star-shaped, white to pale pink flowers, ½in (1.5cm) across, followed by persistent, spherical red berries, ¼in (6mm) across. ↕ 18in (45cm), ↔ indefinite. China, Japan. Zone 8.

Ardisia crispa

ARECA

ARECACEAE

Genus of 50–60 species of single-stemmed, monoecious palms found growing in woodland in humid tropical forest from Malaysia and Indonesia to the Solomon Islands. They are grown for their linear or lance-shaped, 2-pinnate leaves, produced in a terminal tuft above a distinct crownshaft, with panicles of cup-shaped flowers borne beneath them. Where not hardy, grow young plants in containers in a temperate greenhouse. In frost-free climates, use arecas as specimen plants.
• **CULTIVATION** Under glass, grow in soilless potting mix in bright filtered light. During the growing season, water moderately and apply a balanced liquid fertilizer monthly; keep just moist in winter. Outdoors, grow in fertile, moist but well-drained soil in partial shade.
• **PROPAGATION** Sow seed at 75–81°F (24–27°C) in spring.
• **PESTS AND DISEASES** Susceptible to a few fungal leaf spots, *Ganoderma* butt rot, and spider mites.

A. catechu ■ (Betel nut palm, Pinang). Slender palm producing a trunk ringed with old leaf scars and topped by a crownshaft. Arching, pinnate leaves, 3–6ft (1–2m) long, have lance-shaped, soft-textured, truncate, mid-green leaflets. In summer, bears large panicles, to 24in (60cm) long, of pale yellow flowers; these are followed by orange to red fruit that contain betel nuts, chewed as a stimulant in India, Pakistan, and S.E. Asia. ↕ 70–80ft (20–25m), ↔ 6–12ft (2–4m). Probably mainland Malaysia, Singapore. ❄ (min. 55–59°F/13–15°C)
A. lutescens see *Chrysalidocarpus lutescens*.

▷***Arecastrum*** see *Syagrus*
▷***Aregelia*** see *Neoregelia*

Areca catechu

Arenaria balearica

ARENARIA

Sandwort

CARYOPHYLLACEAE

Genus of about 160 species of annuals and mainly low-growing perennials, some of which are evergreen, mostly from mountainous, arctic and temperate regions of the N. hemisphere. They have opposite pairs of small, linear to ovate leaves and bear solitary or few-flowered cymes of 5-petaled, usually white flowers. Several *Arenaria* species are attractive mat- or cushion-forming plants for a rock garden, alpine house, or scree bed, or for growing in the crevices of a wall or paving.
• **CULTIVATION** Grow in moist but well-drained, sandy, poor soil in full sun. *A. tetraquetra* requires very sharp drainage. *A. balearica* thrives in partial shade.
• **PROPAGATION** Sow seed in containers in an open frame in autumn, divide in spring, or root basal cuttings in summer.
• **PESTS AND DISEASES** Rust and anther smut occur.

A. balearica ■ (Corsican sandwort). Prostrate, mat-forming, evergreen perennial with broadly ovate, shiny, light green leaves, 1/16–⅛in (2–4mm) long. From late spring to summer, it is studded with solitary, star-shaped white flowers, ¼–½in (6–15mm) across. May seed itself excessively. ↕ ½in (1.5cm), ↔ 12in (30cm) or more. W. Mediterranean islands. Zone 5b.
A. montana ■ Vigorous, low-growing, evergreen perennial with wiry, prostrate stems and linear to lance-

Arenaria montana

Arenaria purpurascens

Arenaria tetraquetra

shaped, grayish green leaves, ½–¾in (1–2cm) long. Shallowly cup-shaped white flowers, ½–¾in (1.5–2cm) across, are freely borne, singly or in few-flowered cymes, in early summer. Easily grown in a rock garden, or in crevices in a wall or paving. ↕ ¾–2in (2–5cm), ↔ 12in (30cm). Mountains of S.W. Europe. Zone 4.
A. purpurascens ■ (Pink sandwort). Evergreen, mat- or cushion-forming perennial with elliptic to lance-shaped, sharp-pointed, glossy, dark green leaves, ¼–⅜in (6–9mm) long, with hairy margins. In midsummer, bears profuse cymes of 2–4 star-shaped, deep pink flowers, to ½in (1.5cm) across. ↕ ¾–2in (2–5cm), ↔ 8in (20cm). Pyrenees and mountains of N. Spain. Zone 4.
A. tetraquetra ■ Dense, cushion-forming, evergreen perennial with tiny, ovate, overlapping, gray-green leaves, 1⁄16–⅛in (1–4mm) long, profusely covered with solitary, very short-stemmed, star-shaped white flowers, ¼–½in (6–15mm) across, in spring. Suitable for a scree bed, a trough, or an alpine house. ↕ 1–2in (2.5–5cm), ↔ 6–8in (15–20cm). Pyrenees and mountains of N. Spain. Zone 4.

Arenga pinnata

ARENGA

ARECACEAE

Genus of 17 species of single- or cluster-stemmed palms from tropical lowland and hilly forest areas in S.E. Asia. Erect to arching, pinnate leaves are borne in a terminal tuft, with no crownshaft. The monoecious (rarely dioecious), cup-shaped flowers are produced only at the end of the tree's life, initially from the top leaf axils, then from all the lower ones. After fruiting, the tree usually dies. Where temperatures fall below 50–55°F (10–13°C), grow as a houseplant or in a temperate greenhouse. In tropical regions, grow as a specimen tree.
• **CULTIVATION** Under glass, grow in soilless potting mix in bright filtered light. In the growing season, water freely and apply a balanced fertilizer monthly; keep just moist in winter. Outdoors, grow in fertile, moist but well-drained soil, ideally in partial shade when young.
• **PROPAGATION** Sow seed at 75–81°F (24–27°C) in spring.
• **PESTS AND DISEASES** Susceptible to fungal leaf spots and false smut. Spider mites occur under glass.

A. pinnata ■ (Sugar palm). Tall, single-stemmed palm, trunk clothed with leaf bases and the remains of fibrous black sheaths. Pinnate leaves, 20ft (6m) or more long, composed of linear, green leaflets arranged in several ranks. Bears panicles, to 6ft (2m) long, of green to bronze flowers in summer, followed by black fruit. When tapped, flowering stems yield a sweet sap, which is the basis of palm sugar. ↕ to 70ft (20m), ↔ to 40ft (12m) or more. Malaysian islands. ❄ (min. 50–55°F/10–13°C)

▷ ***Arequipa hempeliana*** see *Oreocereus hempelianus*

ARGEMONE

Prickly poppy

PAPAVERACEAE

Genus of 28 species of vigorous, erect to spreading, usually prickly annuals, perennials, and one shrub, from scrub and wasteland in S. and S.E. US, Central America, and the West Indies. The fleshy roots produce large clusters of mostly basal, entire to deeply lobed, smooth to prickly, glaucous leaves. Paper-thin, poppy-like, white, yellow,

Argemone grandiflora

or mauve flowers are borne singly or in corymbs in a long succession from summer to autumn. The flowers are followed by very prickly seed pods; the seeds may cause severe discomfort if ingested. The stems, when cut, exude a pale yellow to orange latex. Although some species are perennial, they are often cultivated as annuals. Grow in a gravel garden or in a sunny mixed border. Prickly poppies self-seed freely.
• **CULTIVATION** Grow in very poor, gritty, or stony soil in full sun. Deadhead to prolong flowering.
• **PROPAGATION** Sow seed at 64°F (18°C) in early spring. Established plants resent disturbance.
• **PESTS AND DISEASES** Prone to downy mildew, anthracnose, and Texas root rot. Bacterial leaf spots can also be a problem in areas where rainfall is high.

A. grandiflora ■ Spreading, clump-forming annual or short-lived perennial with inversely lance-shaped to elliptic, deeply lobed, white-veined, blue-green leaves, to 5in (13cm) or more long; the leaves are often prickly beneath and have prickle-tipped margins. Showy, poppy-like, white or yellow flowers, to 4in

Argemone mexicana

(10cm) across, are borne singly or in few-flowered corymbs throughout the summer. ↕ to 5ft (1.5m), ↔ 12–16in (30–40cm). Mexico. Zone 8.
A. mexicana ■ (Devil's fig, Mexican poppy, Prickly poppy). Spreading, clump-forming annual with inversely lance-shaped to elliptic, deeply lobed, silver-veined, blue-green leaves, to 5in (13cm) long, with spine-tipped teeth. In late summer and early autumn, produces solitary, poppy-like, slightly scented, pale to deep yellow flowers, to 3in (8cm) across. ↕ to 3ft (1m), ↔ 12–16in (30–40cm). S. US to Central America. **'White Lustre'** has pure white blooms. **'Yellow Lustre'** has yellowish orange flowers.

ARGYRANTHEMUM

ASTERACEAE

Genus of 23 species of procumbent or spreading to erect, evergreen subshrubs (sometimes offered as chrysanthemums) from the Canary Islands and Madeira. They occur in a wide range of habitats, from coastal beaches to light woodland and volcanic mountains, 6,900ft (2,300m) high. The opposite or alternate leaves are entire to finely dissected or coarsely lobed, usually 2–4in (5–10cm) long, and vary from green to intensely glaucous. Loose corymbs of daisy-like, single, sometimes anemone-centered or double flowerheads, in white, rose-pink, yellow, or apricot, are freely borne from late spring to early autumn. They are excellent for bedding or borders, since they may flower almost continuously. Grow as summer bedding or in containers ❄ (min. 35°F/2°C).
• **CULTIVATION** Grow in well-drained, moderately fertile soil in full sun. Most species will tolerate sea winds. Where marginally hardy, apply a deep, dry winter mulch, and take cuttings as insurance against winter losses; even if top-growth is killed to the ground, plants often regenerate from the base

Argyranthemum foeniculaceum

Argyranthemum frutescens

in spring. Pinch out the growing tips to encourage a compact habit. Pruning group 10, in early to midspring; may be trained as standards.

• **PROPAGATION** Root greenwood or semi-ripe cuttings of non-flowering shoots, 2–4in (5–10cm) long, in late summer or midspring. Overwinter young plants in a cool greenhouse.

• **PESTS AND DISEASES** Coarse-leaved species and cultivars are prone to crown gall and chrysanthemum leaf miner.

***A.* 'Chelsea Girl'** see *A. gracile* 'Chelsea Girl'.
***A.* 'Cornish Gold'.** Compact subshrub producing pinnatisect, toothed, mid-green leaves and yellow flowerheads, 2in (5cm) across, with yellow disk florets. ↕↔ 24in (60cm).

Argyranthemum 'Mary Wootton'

A. foeniculaceum ■ Compact subshrub with 2- or 3-pinnatisect, finely dissected, blue-gray leaves. White flower-heads, 1¼in (3cm) across. Yellow disc florets. ↕↔ 32in (80cm). Canary Islands. **'Royal Haze'** has intensely blue-gray foliage.
A. frutescens ■ Variable, rounded subshrub producing pinnatisect or 2-pinnatisect, coarsely dissected, bright green leaves and profuse white flower-heads, to ¾in (2cm) across, with yellow disk florets. ↕↔ 28in (70cm). Canary Islands.
***A. gracile* 'Chelsea Girl'** ■ syn. *A.* 'Chelsea Girl'. Compact subshrub with pinnatisect, gray-green leaves with hair-like lobes. Bears white flowerheads, 1¼in (3cm) across, with yellow disk florets. ↕↔ 24in (60cm).
***A.* 'Jamaica Primrose'** ■ Open subshrub with pinnatisect, coarsely toothed, grayish green leaves. Long, branching stems bear primrose-yellow flowerheads, 2½in (6cm) across, with darker yellow disk florets. ↕ 3½ft (1.1m), ↔ 3ft (1m).
***A.* 'Jamaica Snowstorm'** see *A.* 'Snowstorm'.
A. maderense, syn. *A. ochroleucum.* Compact subshrub with pinnatisect, deeply toothed, grayish green leaves. Bears lemon-yellow flowerheads, 1¼in (3cm) across, with yellow disk florets. ↕ 12in (30cm), ↔ 20in (50cm). Canary Islands (N. Lanzarote).
***A.* 'Mary Cheek'.** Compact subshrub with pinnatisect, narrow-lobed, gray-green leaves. Produces double, hemi-spherical, light pink flowerheads, 1¼in (3cm) across, with pink disk florets. ↕↔ 16in (40cm).
***A.* 'Mary Wootton'** ■ Open subshrub with coarsely pinnatisect, grayish green leaves. Bears anemone-centered, light pink flowerheads, 2in (5cm) across, which fade almost to white, with pink disk florets. Easily trained as a standard. ↕ 3½ft (1.1m), ↔ 3ft (1m).
A. ochroleucum see *A. maderense.*
***A.* 'Petite Pink'**, syn. *A.* 'Pink Delight'. Neat, dome-shaped subshrub with finely pinnatisect, grayish green leaves and profuse, light pink flowerheads, 1in (2.5cm) across, with yellow disk florets. Excellent for bedding and containers. ↕↔ 12in (30cm).
***A.* 'Pink Delight'** see *A.* 'Petite Pink'.
***A.* 'Snowstorm'**, syn. *A.* 'Jamaica Snowstorm'. Compact subshrub with pinnatisect, gray-green leaves and white flowerheads, 1¼in (3cm) across, with yellow disk florets. ↕↔ 12in (30cm).
***A.* 'Vancouver'** ■ Compact subshrub producing coarsely pinnatisect, grayish green leaves. Double, anemone-centered flowerheads, 2in (5cm) across, have rose-pink disk florets and mid-pink outer ray florets fading to buff-pink. Easily trained as a standard. ↕ 36in (90cm), ↔ 32in (80cm).

Argyranthemum gracile 'Chelsea Girl'

Argyranthemum 'Jamaica Primrose'

Argyranthemum 'Vancouver' (inset: flower detail)

ARGYREIA

CONVOLVULACEAE

Genus of about 90 species of mainly woody-stemmed, evergreen climbers found in tropical rainforest and thickets from Asia to Queensland, Australia. The handsome, alternate leaves are large and usually broadly ovate; the funnel-shaped flowers are borne singly or in axillary cymes, followed by colorful berries. Where temperatures fall below 55°F (13°C), grow in a warm greenhouse. Elsewhere, grow on an arbor, pergola, or wall, or through a tree.

• **CULTIVATION** Under glass, grow in soil-based potting mix in full light. From spring to autumn, water freely and apply a balanced liquid fertilizer monthly; reduce water in winter. Outdoors, grow in moderately fertile, moist but well-drained soil in full sun. Pruning group 11, in late winter.

• **PROPAGATION** Sow seed at 64–70°F (18–21°C) in spring. Root softwood cuttings with bottom heat in spring.

• **PESTS AND DISEASES** Spider mites, whiteflies, and aphids can be problems under glass. Rust may also occur.

A. nervosa, syn. *A. speciosa* (Woolly morning glory). Twining climber with white-downy young shoots and broadly ovate, silver-backed leaves, 7–11in (18–28cm) long, with heart-shaped bases. From summer to autumn, bears axillary cymes, to 6in (15cm) long, of flowers 2½–3in (6–7cm) long, which are white-downy in bud, opening lavender-blue with darker bases, and flushed red-purple inside. Berries are rich brown. ↕ 25–30ft (8–10m). India (Assam), Bangladesh. ❀ (min. 55°F/13°C)
A. speciosa see *A. nervosa.*

▷***Argyrocytisus*** see *Cytisus*

ARGYRODERMA

AIZOACEAE

Genus of about 10 species of dwarf, stemless, sometimes clustered, perennial succulents occurring in arid regions of South Africa. They have finger-like or kidney-shaped, fleshy, evergreen leaves, arranged in pairs; some species are briefly deciduous, the new leaves forming quickly as the old leaves die away. Solitary, short-stalked or stalkless, daisy-like, yellow, purple, red, or white flowers are borne in late summer. Where not hardy, grow in a cool or temperate greenhouse; in dry, frost-free areas, use in a desert garden.

• **CULTIVATION** Under glass, grow in standard cactus potting mix in full light with low humidity. In summer, water moderately and apply a balanced liquid fertilizer monthly; water very sparingly in spring and autumn; keep dry in

Argyroderma delaetii

Argyroderma fissum

winter. Outdoors, grow in poor, sharply drained soil in full sun. Hardy to 20°F (-7°C) for short periods if kept dry. See also pp.48–49.
• **PROPAGATION** Sow seed at 70°F (21°C) in early spring; provide partial shade until germinated, then give more light but keep temperature consistent.
• **PESTS AND DISEASES** Mealybugs and aphids may be problems.

A. aureum see *A. delaetii.*
A. blandum see *A. delaetii.*
A. brevipes see *A. fissum.*
A. delaetii ▣ syn. *A. aureum, A. blandum.* Usually unbranched succulent with a single pair of deciduous, kidney-shaped, silvery gray or bluish gray leaves, ¾–2in (2–5cm) long, united at the bases and partly sunken in the ground. The inner leaf surface is flat, and the outer one convex. In late summer, bears white, pink-purple, or yellow flowers, 2in (5cm) across. ↕ 1¼in (3cm), ↔ 2in (5cm). South Africa. ❀ (min. 45°F/7°C)
A. fissum ▣ syn. *A. brevipes.* Clump-forming succulent with pairs of finger-shaped, erect, deciduous, usually whitish green or gray-blue leaves, 2–4in (5–10cm) long, the upper surfaces rounded and smooth, and often red-tipped. Produces flowers 1½in (4cm) across, with white or yellow inner petals, and red or purple outer petals, in late summer. ↕ 5in (13cm), ↔ indefinite. South Africa. ❀ (min. 45°F/7°C)
A. pearsonii ▣ syn. *A. schlechteri.* Usually unbranched succulent with a single pair of kidney-shaped, deciduous, greenish or brownish gray leaves, ¾in (2cm) or more long, united near their bases, each with a flattish inner surface and a rounded and partly keeled outer one. In summer, produces flowers 1¼in (3cm) across, varying from violet or violet-white to yellow flushed with violet or orange. ↕ 1¼in (3cm), ↔ 2in (5cm). South Africa. ❀ (min. 45°F/7°C)
A. schlechteri see *A. pearsonii.*

ARIOCARPUS

CACTACEAE

Genus of 5 or 6 species of slow-growing, spineless cacti from desert in Mexico. They have a long taproot and a spherical, flat-topped stem, covered with lateral to semi-erect rosettes of triangular, rock-like tubercles. Solitary, funnel-shaped, diurnal, white, pink, yellow, or reddish purple flowers are borne in the centers of the crowns from autumn to winter, followed by ovoid green berries containing black seeds. Grow in a temperate greenhouse where not hardy; elsewhere, grow in a desert garden.
• **CULTIVATION** Under glass, grow in standard cactus potting mix in full light. When in growth, water moderately and apply a balanced liquid fertilizer monthly; keep dry at other times. Outdoors, grow in poor, sharply drained soil in full sun. See also pp.48–49.
• **PROPAGATION** Sow seed at 75°F (24°C) in early spring.
• **PESTS AND DISEASES** Mealybugs may be a problem.

A. fissuratus, syn. *Roseocactus fissuratus* (Living rock). Flat-topped cactus with blunt-tipped, gray-green tubercles, 1in (2.5cm) long and 1in (2.5cm) wide at the bases. In autumn, bears pink flowers to 1½in (4cm) across. ↕ 4in (10cm), ↔ to 6in (15cm). Mexico. ❀ (min. 50°F/10°C)
A. kotschoubeyanus. Flat-topped, dark olive-green furrowed cactus, with central depression. Shrinks well below surface during dry periods. Tubercles are laterally divergent, elongated at the base, and becoming broadly triangular and flattened. Areoles with central woolly furrows extend the length of the tubercle, with no spines or glochids. Bears magenta or white flowers, ½in–1in (1.5–2.5cm), and elongated fruits, 3–4in (8–10cm). ↔ 1¼–2¾in (3–7cm). Coahuila S. into Querétaro, Mexico. ❀ (min. 50°F/10°C)
A. retusus ▣ syn. *Anhalonium retusum.* Flat-topped cactus with gray-green tubercles, ½–1½in (1.5–4cm) long and ½–1¼in (1–3cm) wide. White to pink flowers, 1½–2in (4–5cm) across, are produced in autumn. ↕ 3½in 9cm), ↔ to 10in (25cm). Mexico. ❀ (min. 50°F/10°C)

ARISAEMA

ARACEAE

Genus of about 150 species of spring- or summer-flowering, tuberous or rhizomatous perennials from moist woodland and rocky wasteland. The species in cultivation are mainly from the Himalayas, China, Japan, and North America. They are cultivated for their attractive, sometimes unusually shaped spathes and simple, palmately lobed or palmate, mid-green leaves. Insignificant flowers are borne at the bases of slender, sometimes striking spadices, and are followed by dense clusters of spherical to

Arisaema consanguineum

oblong, red to orange berries. They are best grown outdoors in partial shade, but are suitable for a cold greenhouse where not hardy.
• **CULTIVATION** Plant tubers or rhizomes 2–10in (5–25cm) deep in autumn or spring. Under glass, grow in deep clay containers in equal parts loam, leaf mold, and grit in bright indirect light. Water freely when in growth, applying a balanced liquid fertilizer monthly; keep cool and barely moist in winter when dormant. Outdoors, grow in moist but well-drained, neutral to acidic, humus-rich soil in a cool, partially shaded site. *A. candidissimum, A. consanguineum,* and *A. flavum* will tolerate more sun. Mulch in winter; protect the leaves of early-flowering species from late frosts. Do not allow dormant tubers to dry out completely.
• **PROPAGATION** Sow seed in containers in a cold frame in autumn or spring. Most species produce offsets, which may be removed in autumn.
• **PESTS AND DISEASES** Protect from slugs and vine weevils. Susceptible to rust, anthracnose, leaf blight (*Streptobotrys*), and dasheen mosaic virus.

A. amurense. Tuberous perennial with a purple stem and usually a solitary leaf, divided into 5 radiating, oblong to linear-lance-shaped leaflets, 4–7in (10–18cm) long. In spring, bears hooded spathes, 3–5in (8–13cm) long, with dark purple and white stripes. ↕ 18in (45cm), PD6in (15cm). N. Asia. Zone 4.
A. atrorubens see *A. triphyllum.*
A. candidissimum ▣ Tuberous perennial bearing a conspicuous, sweetly

Argyroderma pearsonii

Ariocarpus retusus

Arisaema candidissimum

Arisaema costatum

Arisaema flavum

Arisaema jacquemontii

Arisaema triphyllum

scented, pink-striped white spathe, 3–6in (8–15cm) long, in early summer, followed by a solitary, 3-palmate leaf with broadly ovate leaflets, 4–8in (10–20cm) long. ↕16in (40cm), PD6in (15cm). W. China. Zone 6.
A. consanguineum ■ Tuberous perennial producing a hooded, white-striped, brown-tinged green spathe, 4–8in (10–20cm) long, in summer, followed by a large cluster of red berries. The spathe appears below a solitary leaf with 11–20 broadly to narrowly ovate leaflets, to 8in (20cm) or more long. ↕3ft (1m), PD6in (15cm). E. Himalayas to C. China. Zone 6.
A. costatum ■ Tuberous perennial with a single red-margined leaf divided into 3 ovate leaflets, to 16in (40cm) long. In early summer, produces a hooded, deep purple-brown spathe with white stripes, 4–6in (10–15cm) long, and a long, twisted spadix. ↕14–20in (35–50cm), PD6in (15cm). Nepal. Zone 8.
A. dracontium (Dragon root). Tuberous perennial bearing a single pedate leaf, 4–8in (10–20cm) long, deeply divided into 7–15 lance-shaped lobes. Produces a narrow, hooded green spathe, 2–3in (5–7cm) long, in spring. ↕32in (80cm), PD6in (15cm). E. North America. Zone 5b.
A. flavum ■ Tuberous perennial with 2 palmate leaves composed of 5–11 ovate to lance-shaped leaflets, 2–5in (5–13cm) long. Small but conspicuous, greenish yellow to bright yellow spathes, ¾–1½in (2–4cm) long, are borne in summer. ↕4–18in (10–45cm), PD6in (15cm). Yemen to W. China. Zone 4.
A. griffithii. Tuberous perennial with 2 large leaves, divided into 3 ovate to diamond-shaped leaflets, to 8in (20cm) long. In early summer, bears a spathe, 4–10in (10–25cm) long, just above the ground; it is purple or green, heavily veined, and hooded like a cobra. ↕24in (60cm), PD6in (15cm). E. Himalayas. Zone 6.
A. helleborifolium see *A. tortuosum.*
A. jacquemontii ■ Tuberous perennial producing a narrow, hooded, white-striped, light green spathe, 4–6in (10–15cm) long, in early summer. This is borne above the 1 or 2 palmate leaves, each divided into 3–9 ovate to inversely lance-shaped leaflets, 2–6in (5–15cm) long. ↕6–28in (15–70cm), PD6in (15cm). Himalayas. Zone 7.
A. japonicum see *A. serratum.*
A. ringens. Tuberous perennial with 2 glossy leaves, each composed of 3 elliptic to ovate leaflets, 6–8in (15–20cm) long, with long points. Bears a large, hooded and curled, green-and-purple-striped, purple-lipped spathe, 4–6in (10–15cm) long, below the leaves in early summer. ↕12in (30cm), PD8in (20cm). China, Korea, Japan. Zone 6.
A. robustum. Tuberous perennial with 1 or 2 pedate leaves, each divided into 5 ovate leaflets, to 6in (15cm) long. In early summer, bears tapered, white- or dark purple-striped, mid-green spathes, 2½in (6cm) long, dark purple inside. ↕to 24in (60cm), PD6in (15cm). Russia (Sakhalin), Japan, Korea. Zone 6.
A. serratum, syn. *A. japonicum.* Tall, tuberous perennial with 2 pedate leaves, each with 7–20 elliptic to lance-shaped lobes, 2–5in (5–13cm) long, on a mottled stem. In spring, bears a hooded spathe, 3–5in (8–13cm) long, varying from green to purple, and sometimes spotted or striped. ↕3ft (1m), PD6in (15cm). China, Korea, Japan. Zone 5b.
A. sikokianum ■ Tuberous perennial with usually 2 pedate leaves, one 3- and one 5-lobed, the divisions broadly ovate and 2–6in (5–15cm) long, sometimes variegated with silver. In spring, bears a large, purple-brown spathe, 8in (20cm) long, which is open at the mouth, revealing the club-like white spadix. ↕12–20in (30–50cm), PD6in (15cm). Japan. Zone 5.
A. speciosum. Tuberous perennial with a hooded, trailing, white-striped purple spathe, 4–6in (10–15cm) long, borne in spring or early summer below a solitary 3-palmate leaf on a mottled stem. The leaf has ovate to lance-shaped leaflets, 8–18in (20–45cm) long. ↕24in (60cm), PD6in (15cm). E. Himalayas. Zone 8.
A. tortuosum, syn. *A. helleborifolium.* Tuberous perennial with 2 or 3 pedate leaves, each divided into 5–17 elliptic leaflets, 6–8in (15–20cm) long. Hooded green spathes, 4–7in (10–18cm) long, with long, erect then outward-curving, purple or sometimes green spadices, are borne above the leaves in spring or early summer. ↕to 5ft (1.5m), PD8in (20cm). Himalayas. Zone 6.
A. triphyllum ■ syn. *A. atrorubens* (Jack-in-the-pulpit). Tuberous perennial producing 1 or 2 leaves, each divided into 3 narrow, oblong to ovate leaflets, 3–6in (8–15cm) long. Bears hooded, green, often dark purple-striped spathes, 4–6in (10–15cm) long, from spring to early summer, followed by large, showy clusters of red berries in autumn. Several subspecies are recognized by some authorities. ↕6–24in (15–60cm), PD6in (15cm). E. North America. Zone 4.

Arisaema sikokianum

ARISARUM

ARACEAE

Genus of 3 species of rhizomatous or tuberous perennials from moist woodland or rocky ground and wasteland in Europe. They are grown for their small, hooded, tubular spathes, developing in winter or early to midspring, which enclose spadices that have minute flowers. The densely arranged, radical, ovate to arrow-shaped leaves, on long leaf stalks, sometimes obscure the inflorescences. Ideal for an alpine house, or for a woodland garden.
• **CULTIVATION** Plant tubers or rhizomes 3in (8cm) deep in autumn. Under glass, grow in gritty, humus-rich, soilless potting mix in filtered light. Outdoors, *A. proboscideum* requires humus-rich, moist soil in partial shade. *A. vulgare* needs a more open site in full sun, in well-drained soil that is dry in summer.
• **PROPAGATION** Sow seed in containers in a cold frame in spring, or divide in autumn or winter.
• **PESTS AND DISEASES** Infrequent.

A. proboscideum ■ (Mouse plant). Rhizomatous perennial with mats of arrow-shaped, glossy, dark green leaves, 2½–6in (6–15cm) long. In spring, produces hooded, dark brown-purple spathes, 1¼–2in (3–5cm) long, each with a long, thin, curled tip, to 6in (15cm) long, which looks like a mouse's tail; the spadices are insignificant. Often forms large colonies. ↕6in (15cm), ↔ to 10in (25cm) or more. Italy, Spain. Zone 7b.
A. vulgare (Friar's cowl). Tuberous perennial with arrow-shaped, mid- to yellowish green leaves, 2–5in (5–13cm) long, sometimes mottled with purple. In winter or early spring, produces small, hooded green spathes, 1–2in (2.5–5cm) long, striped brown or purple, with blackish brown spadices. ↕6in (15cm), ↔ to 4in (10cm) or more. Mediterranean. Zone 8.

Arisarum proboscideum

ARISTEA

IRIDACEAE

Genus of 50 species of rhizomatous, evergreen, clump-forming, mainly spring- or summer-flowering perennials from coastal and mountain sites in W. and E. Africa, Madagascar, and South Africa. They have slender stems bearing spike-like, terminal panicles with lateral clusters of saucer-shaped flowers, each lasting only one day. The basal leaves, 4–28in (10–70cm) long, are erect and 2-ranked, and longer than the stem-clasping leaves.
Where not hardy, grow in a cool greenhouse; in frost-free areas, grow in a border.
• **CULTIVATION** Under glass, grow in soilless potting mix in bright filtered light. When in growth, water freely and apply a balanced liquid fertilizer monthly; keep moist at other times. Outdoors, grow in well-drained, moderately fertile, humus-rich soil in full sun. They resent root disturbance.
• **PROPAGATION** Sow seed thinly at 55–61°F (13–16°C) in spring.
• **PESTS AND DISEASES** Infrequent.

Aristea major

A. ecklonii. Robust, clump-forming, evergreen, rhizomatous perennial with tufts of linear basal leaves, 12–18in (30–45cm) long, and smaller, linear stem-clasping leaves. Loose, spike-like panicles of saucer-shaped blue flowers, ¾in (2cm) across, are borne in summer. ↕ 3ft (1m), ↔ 18in (45cm). C. Africa, South Africa. ❀ (min. 35°F/2°C)
A. major ▣ syn. *A. thyrsiflora.* Clump-forming, evergreen, rhizomatous perennial with dense, spike-like panicles of saucer-shaped, blue or purple flowers, 1¼–1½in (3–4cm) across, in summer. Basal leaves are lance-shaped and 12–20in (30–50cm) long; stem leaves are linear and smaller. ↕ 3–5ft (1–1.5m), ↔ 18in (45cm). South Africa. ❀ (min. 35°F/2°C)
A. thyrsiflora see *A. major.*

ARISTOLOCHIA

Dutchman's pipe

ARISTOLOCHIACEAE

Genus of about 300 species of evergreen and deciduous climbers, occasionally shrubs or scandent perennials, mostly from moist woodland in temperate and tropical regions of both hemispheres. The leaves are entire or lobed, and often heart-shaped. The petalless flowers, mostly in white, purple, liver-brown, or maroon, veined or mottled with darker hues, have a curved or S-shaped calyx with an inflated base, resembling the shape of a Dutch pipe. Aristolochias are unusual and useful climbing plants for screening, but some have unpleasantly scented flowers and are best grown away from residential buildings. Where not hardy, grow in a temperate or warm greenhouse. Some species were formerly included in the genus *Isotrema.*

• **CULTIVATION** Under glass, grow in soilless potting mix in bright filtered light. During the growing season, water freely and apply a balanced liquid fertilizer monthly; water more sparingly in winter. Outdoors, grow in fertile, well-drained soil in sun or partial shade. Hardy species overwinter most successfully in dry soils. Climbing species require strong support. Pruning group 11 or 12; prune after flowering.

• **PROPAGATION** Sow seed of hardy species at 55–61°F (13–16°C) and tender species at 70–75°F (21–24°C), as soon as ripe or in spring. Divide perennials in spring, or insert root cuttings in winter. Root softwood

Aristolochia gigantea

cuttings of climbing or scandent species grown under glass in early spring, and of hardy species in midsummer.

• **PESTS AND DISEASES** *Cercospora* leaf spot, gray mold, Southern blight, and *Pythium* root rot can occur. Aphids may be a problem under glass.

A. clematitis (Birthwort). Deciduous perennial with creeping, branched rhizomes, and heart-shaped, mid- to dark green leaves, 2½–6in (6–15cm) long, on erect, then scandent stems. Axillary clusters of 3–8 narrow, tubular, pale yellow, brown, or yellowish brown flowers, ¾–1¼in (2–3cm) long, with pointed, curved upper lips, are borne from late spring to midsummer. Sap may irritate skin. ↕ 36in (90cm), ↔ 24in (60cm). Europe. Zone 7.

A. durior see *A. macrophylla.*
A. elegans see *A. littoralis.*
A. gigantea ▣ Evergreen twiner with broadly triangular, dark green leaves, 2–4in (5–10cm) long. In summer, bears solitary, rounded, white, purple-veined flowers, white- or ivory-mottled maroon inside, to 6in (15cm) across. ↕ 30ft (10m). Panama. ❀ (min. 50°F/10°C)
A. gigas see *A. grandiflora.*
A. grandiflora, syn. *A. gigas* (Pelican flower). Vigorous, evergreen twiner with heart-shaped, dark green leaves, 8–10in (20–25cm) long. Solitary, rounded, long-tailed white flowers, 6–7in (15–18cm) across, with brownish purple veins and dark purple eyes, are borne in summer. ↕ to 30ft (10m) or more. Mexico to Panama, West Indies. ❀ (min. 50°F/10°C)
A. littoralis ▣ syn. *A. elegans* (Calico flower). Evergreen twiner with kidney- to heart-shaped, glaucous, pale green leaves, 2–4in (5–10cm) long. Solitary, rounded, purple-brown flowers, 4in (10cm) across, with white markings and veins, are borne in summer. ↕ 15–25ft (5–8m). Brazil. ❀ (min. 45°F/7°C)
A. macrophylla, syn. *A. durior, A. sipho* (Dutchman's pipe). Strong-growing, deciduous twiner with broadly heart-shaped leaves, dark green above, lighter beneath, and 4–12in (10–30cm) long. In summer, bears solitary, rounded, mid-green flowers, 1in (2.5cm) across, mottled with yellow, purple, and brown, that are hidden among the leaves. ↕ 25–30ft (8–10m). S.E. US. Zone 5.
A. sipho see *A. macrophylla.*

Aristolochia littoralis

ARMERIA

Sea pink, Thrift

PLUMBAGINACEAE

Genus of about 80 species of tufted or hummock- or cushion-forming, evergreen perennials or subshrubs, distributed widely from sea cliffs to mountainous areas in Europe, Turkey, N. Africa, and the Pacific coast of North and South America. They produce dense rosettes of linear to strap-shaped leaves and compact, spherical heads of small, saucer- or cup-shaped flowers on slender stems. They are ideal for a rock garden or trough, or for the front of a border.

• **CULTIVATION** Grow in well-drained, poor to moderately fertile soil in an open site in full sun.

• **PROPAGATION** Sow seed in containers in a cold frame in autumn or spring; the species cross freely and hybrids may result. Divide in early spring. Root semi-ripe, basal cuttings in summer.

• **PESTS AND DISEASES** Rarely susceptible to rust and Southern blight. In areas with hot summers, plants may rot out in the center. Prone to spider mites and aphids under glass.

A. alliacea, syn. *A. arenaria, A. plantaginea.* Robust, clump-forming perennial with narrow, inversely lance-shaped to linear, dark green leaves, to 6in (15cm) long. In summer, bears white to deep red-purple flowerheads, to ¾in (2cm) across, on wiry stems, 8–20in (20–50cm) long. ↕↔ to 20in (50cm). Mountains of W. Europe. Zone 7b.
A. arenaria see *A. alliacea.*
A. atrosanguinea of gardens see *A. pseudarmeria.*
A. 'Bee's Ruby' ▣ Tufted, woody-based perennial with broadly strap-shaped, dark green leaves, to 6in (15cm) long. Bears deep, bright pink flowerheads, 1¼–1½in (3–4cm) across, on strong stems, 8–12in (20–30cm) long, in early summer. ↕ 12in (30cm), ↔ 10in (25cm). Zone 5.

Armeria 'Bee's Ruby'

Armeria juniperifolia

A. caespitosa see *A. juniperifolia.*
A. juniperifolia ■ syn. *A. caespitosa.* Hummock-forming subshrub with rosettes of linear, hairy, spine-tipped, gray-green leaves, to ½in (1.5cm) long. Purplish pink to white flowerheads, to ½in (1.5cm) across, are produced on stems, ½–¾in (1–2cm) long, in late spring. ↕ 2–3in (5–8cm), ↔ to 6in (15cm). Mountain pastures or rock crevices in C. Spain. Zone 5.
'Alba' has pure white flowerheads. **'Bevan's Variety'** is compact, with deep rose-pink flowerheads on very short stems; ↕ to 2in (5cm). **'Rubra'** has very deep pink flowerheads.
A. latifolia see *A. pseudarmeria.*
A. maritima (Sea thrift). Variable, clump-forming perennial with linear, dark green leaves, 1½–5in (4–13cm) long. Stiff stems, to 8in (20cm) long, bear profuse, white, pink, or red-purple flowerheads, to 1in (2.5cm) wide, from late spring to summer. ↕ to 8in (20cm), ↔ to 12in (30cm). Mountain and coastal areas in N. hemisphere. Zone 4. **'Alba'** has white flowerheads. **'Bloodstone'** has dark, blood-red flowerheads. **'Dusseldorf Pride'** has rose-pink flowerheads. **'Laucheana'** has deep rose-pink flowerheads. **'Vindictive'** ■ has stems to 6in (15cm) long, and pink flowerheads to ¾in (2cm) wide.
A. plantaginea see *A. alliacea.*
A. pseudarmeria ■ syn. *A. atrosanguinea* of gardens, *A. latifolia.* Clump-forming subshrub with lance-shaped, mid-green leaves, to 8in (20cm) long. In summer, bears white or pale pink flowerheads, 1¼–1½in (3–4cm) across, on stems 10–20in (25–50cm) long. ↕ to 20in

Armeria maritima 'Vindictive'

Armeria pseudarmeria

(50cm), ↔ 12in (30cm). Coastal pastures in W. Portugal. Zone 5. **'Royal Rose'** has rose-pink flowerheads.

ARMORACIA

BRASSICACEAE

Genus of 3 species of erect perennials from a range of habitats at low altitudes, including wasteland, streamsides, and roadsides, in Eurasia and E. US. Simple or pinnatifid, dock-like, toothed, coarse, basal leaves arise from deep, woody or fleshy taproots. Small, cruciform, 4-petaled white flowers are borne in large, terminal racemes or panicles on leafy, branching stems from late spring to late summer, followed by oblong to obovate fruits. *A.rusticana* (Common horseradish) is widely grown for its pungent, fleshy roots, often used in sauces and relishes.
• **CULTIVATION** Grow in full sun in light, fertile, moist but well-drained soil. Water freely when in growth to prevent roots from becoming woody.
• **PROPAGATION** Divide or take root cuttings in winter.
• **PESTS AND DISEASES** Powdery mildew, downy mildew, and *Alternaria* and *Cercospora* leaf spots occur. Root rot, is a problem in some areas. Also prone to black rot, clubroot, and turnip mosaic.

A. rusticana, syn. *Cochlearia armoracia* (Horseradish, Red cole). Clump-forming perennial with long-stalked, ovate-oblong, toothed, puckered, dark green leaves, 12–20in (30–50cm) long, arising from fleshy, branching, cream-colored roots. Leafy, branched stems bear terminal panicles of white flowers, ¼–⅜in (5–8mm) across, late spring to late summer. Contact with sap may irritate skin. ↕ 3ft (1m), ↔ 18in (45cm) or more. S.E. Europe, but naturalized widely. Zone 5b. **'Variegata'** has cream-marbled leaves.

Arnebia pulchra

ARNEBIA

BORAGINACEAE

Genus of about 25 species of erect to spreading annuals and perennials found in woodland and dry, rocky areas, or on grassy slopes, from N. Africa to C. Asia. Simple or branching stems produce hairy leaves, 1¼–6in (3–15cm) long. Blue to purple or yellow to cream flowers are borne in short, coiled, usually terminal cymes.
• **CULTIVATION** *A. pulchra* is best in partial shade in moist but well-drained soil; will tolerate full sun if kept moist. Most other species prefer more sharply drained soil in an open, sunny site.
• **PROPAGATION** Sow seed in containers in a cold frame as soon as ripe.
• **PESTS AND DISEASES** Susceptible to aphids and spider mites under glass.

A. echioides see *A. pulchra.*
A. pulchra ■ syn. *A. echioides, Echioides longiflorum, Macrotomia echioides* (Prophet flower). Clump-forming perennial with lance-shaped to oblong, stiffly hairy, light green leaves, to 6in (15cm) long. In summer, unbranched stems bear terminal cymes of trumpet-shaped yellow flowers, to1in (2.5cm) across; each petal has a brown basal spot that fades with age. ↕↔ to 12in (30cm). Caucasus, Turkey, N. Iran. Zone 7.

ARNICA

ASTERACEAE

Genus of about 32 species of clump-forming and rhizomatous perennials from pasture and open woodland in N. temperate and arctic regions. They have mainly basal leaves, 4½–8in (11–20cm) long, and daisy-like flowerheads borne on unbranched stems. All parts may cause severe discomfort if ingested, and contact with sap may aggravate skin allergies.
• **CULTIVATION** Grow in moist but well-drained, humus-rich soil in full sun.
• **PROPAGATION** Sow seed in a cold frame in autumn, or divide in spring.
• **PESTS AND DISEASES** Caterpillars and slugs may be problems. Powdery mildew, rusts, and and white smuts are common.

A. chamissonis. Erect perennial with slightly toothed, lance-shaped leaves ↕ 36in (90cm). Produces bright yellow flowerheads 1¼–2in (3–5cm) mid-spring. Alaska to New Mexico. Zone 2b.

A. montana. Clump-forming perennial with mainly basal, broadly obovate to inversely lance-shaped leaves to 6in (15cm) long. In summer, produces solitary (occasionally 2 or 3), deep yellow or orange-yellow flowerheads, each 2–3in (5–8cm) across, on stems 10–20in (25–50cm) long. ↕ to 20in (50cm), ↔ 12in (30cm). Europe, W. Asia. Zone 5b.

ARONIA

Chokeberry

ROSACEAE

Genus of 2 species of deciduous, suckering shrubs, sometimes classified as *Photinia*, from woodland clearings, scrub, and swamps in E. North America. They are grown for their white, sometimes pink-tinged flowers, borne in late spring in corymbs, to 2½in (6cm) wide; for their colorful autumn leaves, which are alternate, simple, fine-toothed, and 3–4in (8–10cm) long; and for their spherical red or black fruits.
• **CULTIVATION** Grow in any moist but well-drained soil (except shallow, alkaline soil) in sun or partial shade. Pruning group 1 or 2. Aronias tolerate wet and dry soil.
• **PROPAGATION** Sow seed in a seedbed in autumn. Root softwood cuttings in early summer.
• **PESTS AND DISEASES** *Mycosphaerella* and *Cercospora* leaf spots, as well as rusts, are common.

A. arbutifolia ■ (Red chokeberry). Erect shrub with narrowly ovate, matte, dark green leaves, densely gray-hairy beneath, turns orange, red, and yellow in autumn. Corymbs of white, often pink-tinged flowers, to ½in (1.5cm) across, are borne in late spring, followed by persistent, showy red berries, to ¼in (6mm) across. ↕ 10ft (3m), ↔ 5ft (1.5m). E. North America. Zone 4.
'Brilliant' see *A. x prunifolia* 'Brilliant'. **'Brilliantissima'** has lustrous, dark green leaves that turn brilliant scarlet in autumn. Bears more flowers and glossier, larger, more abundant fruit; ↕ 6–8ft (2–2.5m).
A. melanocarpa (Black chokeberry). Upright shrub with obqvate, hairless, glossy, mid-green leaves, which turn dark purple-red in autumn. Corymbs of white, occasionally pink-tinged flowers, to 1in (1.5cm) across, are born in late

Aronia arbutifolia

Aronia x *prunifolia*

spring and early summer, and are followed by black berries, to 1in (1.5cm) across. ↕ 6ft (2m), ↔ 10ft (3m). E. North America. Zone 4.
'Autumn Magic' has good autumn leaf color and larger, shinier, and more persistent black fruit, which remain long after the leaves. **'Brilliant'** see *A.* x *prunifolia* 'Brilliant'.
A.* x *prunifolia ▣ (*A. arbutifolia* x *A. melanocarpa*) (Purple chokeberry). Variable, erect shrub producing obovate, matte, dark green leaves, gray-hairy beneath, which turn dark purple-red in autumn. Corymbs of white, sometimes pink-tinged flowers, to ½in (1.5cm) across, are borne in late spring, and are followed by purple-black berries, to ⅜in (8mm) across. ↕ 10ft (3m), ↔ 8ft (2.5m). E. North America. Zone 4b.
'Brilliant', syn. *A. arbutifolia* 'Brilliant', *A. melanocarpa* 'Brilliant', has bright red leaves and abundant fruit in autumn.

ARRABIDAEA

BIGNONIACEAE

Genus of about 50 species of evergreen, tendril climbers occurring in tropical and subtropical rainforest from Mexico to Argentina and the West Indies. They are cultivated mainly for their attractive flowers, which are salverform to bell-shaped, each with 5 petal lobes, often reddish purple or pink, and borne in terminal or axillary panicles. The opposite leaves are 3-palmate, or consist of a pair of leaflets with a tendril between them. Where not hardy, grow in a temperate or warm greenhouse. In warmer climates, train on a pergola or wall, or through a tree.
• **CULTIVATION** Under glass, grow in soilless potting mix in full light. During the growing season, water freely and apply a balanced liquid fertilizer monthly; reduce water in winter. Outdoors, grow in moist but well-drained, reasonably fertile soil in sun or partial shade. Pruning group 11; prune in early spring or after flowering.
• **PROPAGATION** Sow seed in spring at 61–64°F (16–18°C). Root semi-ripe cuttings in summer. Layer in spring.
• **PESTS AND DISEASES** Spider mites may be a problem under glass.

A. corallina. Vigorous climber with mid-green leaves divided into 3 ovate leaflets, 1¼–4½in (3–11cm) long. In summer, produces terminal panicles, 4–12in (10–30cm) long, of bell-shaped, red-purple to lilac flowers, 2in (5cm) long, with spreading lobes and white throats. ↕ 15–25ft (5–8m). Mexico to Argentina. ❀ (min. 50°F/10°C)
A. magnifica see *Saritaea magnifica.*

ARRHENATHERUM

Oat grass

POACEAE

Genus of 6 species of deciduous, loosely tufted, perennial grasses from meadows and grassland in Europe, N. Africa, and N. and W. Asia. While most species have unattractive, coarse foliage, and some are invasive, *A. elatius* subsp. *bulbosum* 'Variegatum' is useful for planting as a groundcover in front of a border.
• **CULTIVATION** Grow in well-drained, fertile soil in full sun or partial shade. Cut to ground level in midsummer; in fertile soil, a second flush of leaves will follow when nights become cooler.
• **PROPAGATION** Every third year, divide plants in spring to maintain stocks.
• **PESTS AND DISEASES** *Cercosporidium* leaf streak, rust, ergot, and anthracnose are common in many areas.

***A. elatius* subsp. *bulbosum* 'Variegatum'** (Bulbous oat grass). Loosely tufted perennial producing chains of small, usually pear-shaped "bulbs" (swollen stem bases), ½in (1.5cm) across, and erect, narrow, linear, gray-green leaves, to 10in (25cm) long, with white-striped margins. Narrow, silvery green panicles, 8–12in (20–30cm) long, with open, oat-like spikelets, ½in (1.5cm) long, are borne from midsummer to early autumn. ↕↔ to 12in (30cm). Zone 4b.

ARROJADOA

CACTACEAE

Genus of 9 species of columnar cacti from hillsides in Brazil. Slender stems bear clusters of pinkish to reddish or yellow, tubular, bird-pollinated flowers borne near stem tips, which open during the day in summer. These plants are suitable for landscape or pot culture.
• **CULTIVATION** Under glass, grow in standard cactus potting mix in full light. Water moderately in growth; keep dry at all other times of the year. Outdoors, grow in sharply drained, gritty, poor soil in full sun.
• **PROPAGATION** Sow seed at 55–61°F (13–16°C) in spring, or root semi-ripe cuttings in summer. Propagation by seed is difficult and extremely slow. Offsets may be grafted, but expect atypical growth.
• **PESTS AND DISEASES** Mealybugs and root mealybugs may be problems, especially under glass.

A. rhodanthus. Basal-branching cactus with jointed dark green stems bearing 10–12 fairly shallow ribs. Spines are produced by areoles (5–6 stout central and 20 radial). Purple to pink flowers are borne from tops of uppermost stems. ↕ 6ft (2m), ↔ ¾in–2in (2–5cm). Bahia, Brazil. ❀ (min. 35°F/2°C)

ARTEMISIA

Mugwort, Sagebrush, Wormwood

ASTERACEAE

Genus of about 300 species of evergreen and deciduous shrubs, perennials, and annuals found in dry fields, prairies, and scrub in the N. hemisphere, with a few from South Africa and W. South America. Artemisias are cultivated for their alternate, variously shaped, often pinnatisect, usually aromatic, gray or silver leaves; the cylindrical flowerheads, 1⁄16–⅜in (2–8mm) across, occasionally solitary, but usually in terminal panicles or racemes, are generally of little interest. They are suitable for a rock garden or border; The silver-foliaged forms are excellent foils for many bright and pastel colors. Some have culinary uses and are grown in herb gardens.
• **CULTIVATION** Grow in well-drained, fertile soil in full sun. A few, such as *A. lactiflora*, require fairly moist soil. Most species die back in heavy, poorly drained soils and may be short-lived. Cut perennials to the bases in autumn; if necessary, cut shrubby species and cultivars back hard in spring to maintain a compact habit. Some may become invasive.
• **PROPAGATION** Sow seed in containers in a cold frame in autumn or spring. Divide in spring or autumn. Root greenwood cuttings or heel cuttings of side-shoots in early summer. *A.* 'Powis Castle' is often unreliably hardy; maintain stocks by regular propagation from cuttings.
• **PESTS AND DISEASES** White rust, downy mildew, powdery mildew, many rusts, and a variety of other fungal leaf and stem diseases are common.

A. abrotanum ▣ (Lad's love, Old man, Southernwood). Erect, deciduous to semi-evergreen shrub producing aromatic, pinnatisect to 3-pinnatisect, gray-green leaves, to 2in (5cm) long, with thread-like lobes, gray-hairy beneath. Yellowish gray flowerheads are borne in dense panicles, 4–12in (10–30cm) long, in late summer. ↕↔ 3ft (1m). S. Europe. Zone 4.
A. absinthium (Absinth, Wormwood). Clump-forming, woody-based perennial producing 2- or 3-pinnatisect, aromatic, silky-hairy, silvery gray leaves, 2½–4in (6–10cm) long, with oblong lobes. Loose panicles, 2–5in (5–13cm) long,

Artemisia abrotanum

Artemisia alba 'Canescens'

of grayish yellow flowerheads are borne in late summer. ↕ 36in (90cm), ↔ 24in (60cm). Europe, temperate Asia. Zone 5. **'Lambrook Silver'** has deeply divided silver foliage; ↕ to 30in (75cm).
***A. alba* 'Canescens'** ▣ syn. *A. canescens, A. splendens, A. vulgaris* 'Canescens'. Clump-forming, semi-evergreen perennial producing pinnatisect to 3-pinnatisect silver leaves, ⅛–½in (3–15mm) long, with slender, curling lobes. Insignificant, brownish yellow flowerheads are borne in panicles, 2–8in (5–20cm) long, in late summer. ↕ 18in (45cm), ↔ 12in (30cm). Zone 5.
A. annua (Sweet Annie, Sweet wormwood). Upright, hairless annual with pinnatisect to 3-pinnatisect, sweetly fragrant, bright green leaves, 1–2½in (2.5–6cm) long, with linear-lance-shaped, entire or toothed lobes. Bears loose panicles, to 18in (45cm) long, of yellow flowerheads, from summer to autumn. May become weedy. ↕ to 6ft (2m), ↔ 30in (75cm). S.E. Europe to Iran.
A. arborescens ▣ Upright, evergreen shrub with pinnatisect or 2-pinnatisect, aromatic, fern-like, silvery white leaves, to 4in (10cm) long, with linear lobes. Small yellow flowerheads, borne in one-sided panicles, 12in (30cm) long, in summer and autumn, are initially semi-pendent and later erect. Grow against a warm wall in cold areas. ↕ 3ft (1m), ↔ 5ft (1.5m). Mediterranean. Zone 4. **'Brass Band'** see *A.* 'Powis Castle'.
A. canescens see *A. alba* 'Canescens'.
A. dracunculus (Tarragon). Clump-forming, subshrubby perennial with aromatic, lance-shaped, light to mid-green leaves, 4in (10cm) long.

Artemisia arborescens

Artemisia lactiflora

Insignificant, nodding, yellowish white flowerheads are borne in loose panicles, 2–14in (5–35cm) long, in late summer. The leaves are used for seasoning; European (French) tarragon has a finer flavor than the hardier and more vigorous Russian tarragon. French tarragon is almost always propagated from cuttings. ↕4ft (1.2m), ↔ 12in (30cm). C. and E. Europe, S. Russia. Zone 4.
***A. kitadakensis* 'Guizhou'** see *A. lactiflora* 'Guizhou'.
A. lactiflora ▣ (White mugwort). Clump-forming perennial producing jaggedly cut, pinnatisect, dark green leaves, 8–10in (20–25cm) long, with broadly lance-shaped segments. Spreading panicles, to 24in (60cm) long, of long-lasting, creamy white flowerheads are borne from late summer to mid-autumn. Excellent for a border and for cut or dried flowers. ↕5ft (1.5m), ↔ 24in (60cm). W. China. Zone 5. **'Guizhou'**, syn. *A. kitadakensis* 'Guizhou', has purple-flushed stems and young leaves, and bears widely branched white flowerheads.
A. lanata see *A. pedemontana.*

Artemisia ludoviciana var. *albula*

Artemisia ludoviciana 'Silver Queen'

A. ludoviciana, syn. *A. palmeri, A. purshiana* (Western mugwort). Rhizomatous, clump-forming perennial with lance-shaped, downy, silvery white leaves, 4–5in (10–13cm) long, which become greener with age. Densely white-woolly panicles, to 8in (20cm) long, of brownish yellow flowerheads are produced from midsummer to autumn. ↕4ft (1.2m), ↔ 24in (60cm) or more. Often invasive. W. North America to Mexico. Zone 4b. **var. *albula*** ▣ has white-woolly leaves. **'Silver King'** is compact, with lance-shaped, white-woolly leaves, to ¾in (2cm) long, that turn red in autumn; bears mostly male flowerheads. **'Silver Queen'** ▣ produces slightly larger leaves than *A. ludoviciana*, and flowers less freely; ↕30in (75cm). **'Valerie Finnis'** has silvery gray leaves with sharply cut margins; ↕24in (60cm).
A. nutans see *Seriphidium nutans.*
A. palmeri see *A. ludoviciana.*
A. pontica ▣ Vigorous, rhizomatous, aromatic, evergreen perennial forming a dense dome of erect, unbranched stems, with pinnatifid or 2-pinnatifid, woolly, grayish green leaves, 1¼–1½in (3–4cm) long, with narrow, linear lobes. In early summer, grayish yellow flowerheads are produced in panicles 2–8in (5–20cm) long. It is excellent as a groundcover in poor soils in full sun. Highly invasive. ↕16–32in (40–80cm), ↔ indefinite. C. and E. Europe. Zone 5b.
***A.* 'Powis Castle'** ▣ syn. *A. arborescens* 'Brass Band'. Woody-based perennial forming a dense, billowing clump of

Artemisia pontica

Artemisia 'Powis Castle'

pinnatisect or 2-pinnatisect, feathery, silver-gray leaves, 2½in (6cm) long, with linear lobes. Panicles, to 6in (15cm) long, of silver, yellow-tinged flowerheads may be produced in late summer, but are best cut off. ↕24in (60cm), ↔ 36in (90cm). Zone 5b.
A. purshiana see *A. ludoviciana.*
A. schmidtiana (Silvermound). Low, rhizomatous, evergreen, tufted perennial, forming a silver carpet of 2-pinnatisect, silky-hairy leaves, 1¼–1¾in (3–4.5cm) long, with very fine linear lobes. Panicles,to 4in (10cm) long, of small yellow flowerheads are produced in summer. ↕12in (30cm), ↔ to 18in (45cm). Japan. Zone 4. **'Nana'** ▣ is very similar, but smaller and more compact;↕3in (8cm), ↔ 12in (30cm).
A. splendens see *A. alba* 'Canescens'.
***A. stelleriana* 'Boughton Silver'** ▣ syn. *A. stelleriana* 'Mori', *A. stelleriana* 'Silver Brocade'. Compact, almost prostrate, rhizomatous, evergreen perennial with stalkless, deeply toothed or pinnatifid, white-hairy, silvery gray leaves, 2–4in (5–10cm) long. Panicles, 1¼–3in (3–8cm) long, of insignificant yellow flowerheads are borne on erect white stems in late summer and early autumn. ↕to 6in (15cm), ↔ 12–18in (30–45cm). Zone 4b.
***A. stelleriana* 'Mori'** see *A. stelleriana* 'Boughton Silver'.
***A. stelleriana* 'Silver Brocade'** see *A. stelleriana* 'Boughton Silver'.
A. tridentata see *Seriphidium tridentatum.*
***A. vulgaris* 'Canescens'** see *A. alba* 'Canescens'.

Artemisia schmidtiana 'Nana'

Artemisia stelleriana 'Boughton Silver'

ARTHROPODIUM

LILIACEAE

Genus of 12 species of evergreen or deciduous, rhizomatous, tufted perennials, found in a variety of open habitats, mainly in New Zealand and S. Australia. The radical, basally sheathing leaves are simple, entire, and linear to lance-shaped. Loose panicles or racemes of small flowers, with 6 spreading tepals and hairy anthers and filaments, are borne in summer. The hardier species, such as *A. candidum* and *A. milleflorum*, are excellent for a sunny rock garden. Grow marginally hardy species in a cool greenhouse or conservatory.

• **CULTIVATION** Under glass, grow in soil-based potting mix with added sharp sand, in full light. Water moderately when in growth, applying a balanced liquid fertilizer monthly; water sparingly in winter. Outdoors, grow in fertile, well-drained, gritty soil in full sun; grow at the base of a warm, sunny wall where unreliably hardy.
• **PROPAGATION** Sow seed in containers in a cold frame in autumn or early spring, or divide in spring. Overwinter young plants under glass.
• **PESTS AND DISEASES** New growth is particularly vulnerable to slugs.

A. candidum, syn. *A. reflexum.* Deciduous, tuberous-rooted perennial with linear, mid-green leaves, 6–8in (15–20cm) long. In early and midsummer, bears small, rounded white flowers, ⅜in (8mm) across, with white-hairy anthers and white filaments, in panicles or racemes, 2–4in (5–10cm) long. ↕to 8in (20cm), PD to 4in (10cm). New Zealand. Zone 8. **'Maculatum'** and **'Purpureum'** are names applied to variants that produce bronze foliage when raised from seed.
A. cirratum, syn. *A. cirrhatum.* Tufted, evergreen perennial with short rhizomes and linear to lance-shaped, channeled, gray-green leaves, 12–24in (30–60cm) long. Nodding, star-shaped white flowers, 1in (2.5cm) across, flecked purple and yellow, with white anthers and filaments are borne in lax panicles, 12in (30cm) long, in early summer. ↕36in (90cm), PD12in (30cm). New Zealand. Zone 8.
A. cirrhatum see *A. cirratum.*

Arthropodium milleflorum

A. milleflorum ■ syn. *A. millefoliatum*, *A. paniculatum*. Deciduous perennial with short rhizomes, fibrous roots, and lance-shaped, blue- or gray-green leaves, to 10in (25cm) or more long. In midsummer, bears loose, branched panicles, 12–24in (30–60cm) long, of star-shaped, pale violet or blue flowers, ½in (1.5cm) across, with creamy white filaments and deep violet anthers. ↕ to 20in (50cm), PD to 8in (20cm). S.E. Australia, Tasmania. ❄ (min. 41°F/5°C)
A. millefoliatum see *A. milleflorum*.
A. paniculatum see *A. milleflorum*.
A. reflexum see *A. candidum*.

ARUM

Lords and ladies

ARACEAE

Genus of 26 species of mainly spring-flowering, tuberous perennials found in a range of partially shaded habitats in S. Europe, N. Africa, and W. Asia to the W. Himalayas. They have often attractively marked leaves, which may be spear-, arrow-, or heart-shaped, and which are normally produced in late autumn or winter. Large spathes enclose thin spadices of tiny flowers, either sweetly or unpleasantly scented; these are followed by spikes of red or orange berries. All parts may cause severe discomfort if ingested, and contact with sap may irritate skin. Some species are good foliage plants for growing with shrubs. The leaves of *A. italicum* 'Marmoratum' are often used in flower arrangements. Marginally hardy species are best grown under glass.

• **CULTIVATION** Plant tubers 4–6in (10–15cm) deep in autumn or spring. Under glass, grow in coarse, soilless potting mix with additional grit, in full or filtered light. In the growing season, water freely and apply a balanced liquid fertilizer monthly; reduce water as the leaves wither, and keep almost dry when dormant. Outdoors, grow in well-drained, humus-rich soil in a sheltered site in sun or partial shade.

• **PROPAGATION** Sow seed in autumn: remove the outer pulp from the berries (it may be caustic) and sow seed in containers in a cold frame. Divide clumps of tubers after flowering.

• **PESTS AND DISEASES** Infrequent.

Arum creticum

A. creticum ■ Tuberous perennial bearing showy, creamy white or deep yellow spathes, 6–10in (15–25cm) long, in spring; they recurve at the tip to reveal thick, pale to deep yellow, sweetly scented spadices. The arrow-shaped leaves, 7–10in (18–25cm) long, are unmarked and dark green. Needs sun. ↕ 12–20in (30–50cm), PD6in (15cm). Greece (Crete). Zone 8.
A. dioscoridis. Variable, tuberous perennial bearing large, deep purple or pale green spathes, 6–14in (15–35cm) long, in spring; they are stained or spotted dark maroon-purple and have unpleasantly scented spadices. Narrow, arrow- to spear-shaped leaves, 11–18in (27–45cm) long, are dark green. Requires full sun. ↕ 8–12in (20–30cm), PD6in (15cm). E. Mediterranean. Zone 7b.
A. dracunculus see *Dracunculus vulgaris*.
A. hygrophilum. Tuberous perennial bearing green spathes, 2–5in (5–13cm) long, with purple-flushed margins and deep purple spadices, in late spring. The variable, spear-shaped leaves, 5½–18in (14–45cm) long,are light to mid-green. Best in a cool greenhouse where not hardy. ↕ 6in (15cm), PD6in (15cm). Morocco, Cyprus, Lebanon. ❄ (min. 41°F/5°C)
A. italicum. Tuberous perennial with arrow- to spear-shaped, mid-green, white-veined leaves, to 14in (35cm) long, lasting to late spring, then withering away. In early summer, bears pale greenish white spathes, 6–16in (15–40cm) long, followed by spikes of bright orange-red berries, which may last until new leaves develop. Produces largest leaves in a partially shaded site; needs an open, sunny site to flower well. ↕ 12in (30cm), PD6in (15cm). Europe, Turkey, N. Africa. Zone 5b. **subsp. *albispathum*** has plain green leaves, to 8in (20cm) long, and white spathes; Crimea, Caucasus. **'Marmoratum'** ■ syn. 'Pictum', has pale green or cream-veined leaves. **'Pictum'** see 'Marmoratum'.
A. pictum (Black calla). Tuberous perennial bearing blackish purple spathes, 6–10in (15–25cm) long, with short spadices, in autumn. Arrow- to heart-shaped leaves, 12in (30cm) long, are leathery, glossy, dark green, often with fine creamy white veins. Grow in an alpine house where not hardy. ↕ 6–10in (15–25cm), PD6in (15cm). Balearic Islands, France (Corsica), W. central Italy, Sardinia. Zone 7b.

Arum italicum 'Marmoratum'

ARUNCUS

ROSACEAE

Genus of 2 or 3 species of clump-forming perennials with short rhizomes, closely related to *Filipendula* and *Spiraea*, from moist, shady woodland, often in mountainous areas, in the N. hemisphere. They have alternate, pinnate leaves with long leaf stalks and conspicuously veined, toothed leaflets. Tiny, unisexual (occasionally bisexual), white or creamy white flowers, to ¼in (6mm) across, are borne in terminal panicles above the leaves, and are useful for cutting and drying. Grow in a moist border or rock garden, or woodland garden, or along streams or ponds.

• **CULTIVATION** Grow in moist, fertile soil in full or partial shade. *A. dioicus* will tolerate drier conditions in full sun.

• **PROPAGATION** Sow seed in containers in a cold frame in autumn or spring; will self-seed freely unless deadheaded. Divide in early spring or autumn.

• **PESTS AND DISEASES** Fly larvae and tarnished plant bugs may be problems.

A. aethusifolius ■ Compact perennial with 3- or 4-pinnate, mid-green leaves, to 10in (25cm) long, with ovate, deeply cut leaflets, turning yellow in autumn. Bears panicles, 2–6in (5–15cm) long, of numerous tiny, creamy white flowers in early and midsummer. Makes a good groundcover. ↕↔ 10–16in (25–40cm). Korea. Zone 4.
A. dioicus, syn. *A. sylvester*, *Spiraea aruncus* (Goatsbeard). Dioecious perennial with 2-pinnate, toothed,

Aruncus aethusifolius

Aruncus dioicus 'Kneiffii'

hairless, fern-like, mid-green leaves, to 3ft (1m) long, with ovate leaflets. Flowers are borne in loose, pyramidal panicles, to 20in (50cm) long, in early and midsummer. The male inflorescences are creamy white; the females are more pendent and greenish white. ↕ to 6ft (2m), ↔ 4ft (1.2m). Europe to E. Siberia, E. North America. Zone 3b. **'Kneiffii'** ▣ has very finely divided, fern-like leaves, and bears tiny, nodding cream flowers on arching, wiry stems; ↕ 4ft (1.2m), ↔ 18in (45cm).
A. sylvester see *A. dioicus.*

ARUNDINARIA

POACEAE

Genus of 1 or 2 species of bamboo from swampy areas in S.E. US. They have spreading rhizomes and thick, rigid culms, 5–30ft (1.5–10m) high, which are simple in the first year, then branching in the second. The persistent culm sheaths produce 3–6 leafy branches from each node. Lateral panicles of 5–15 flower spikelets are borne among the branches at various times of the year. Grow as a dense hedge or screen.
• **CULTIVATION** Grow in moist, fertile, humus-rich soil in a sheltered position in sun or partial shade. They are useful for creating a tropical effect but may be highly invasive.
• **PROPAGATION** Divide in spring.
• **PESTS AND DISEASES** Many different fungi may cause spots and dieback of culms. Rust sometimes occurs.

A. anceps see *Yushania anceps.*
A. auricoma see *Pleioblastus auricomus.*
A. disticha see *Pleioblastus pygmaeus* var. *distichus.*
A. falconeri see *Himalayacalamus falconeri.*
A. fastuosa see *Semiarundinaria fastuosa.*
A. fortunei see *Pleioblastus variegatus.*
A. gigantea, syn. *A. macrosperma, A. tecta* (Canebrake). Rapidly spreading bamboo with yellow-green culms, lance-shaped leaves, to 8in (20cm) long, and lateral panicles of purple spikelets. Shorter plants to 6ft (2m) that develop flowering panicles directly from the rhizomes are sometimes also sold as *A. gigantea* subsp. *tecta* (Switchcane). ↕ to 30ft (10m), ↔ indefinite. S.E. US. Zone 6b.
A. humilis see *Pleioblastus humilis.*
A. jaunsarensis see *Yushiana anceps.*
A. macrosperma see *A. gigantea.*
A. murieliae see *Fargesia murieliae.*
A. nitida see *Fargesia nitida.*
A. pygmaea see *Pleioblastus pygmaeus.*
A. quadrangularis see *Chimonobambusa quadrangularis.*
***A. simonii* 'Variegata'** see *Pleioblastus simonii* 'Variegatus'.
A. tecta see *A. gigantea.*
A. vagans see *Sasa ramosa.*
A. variegata see *Pleioblastus variegatus.*
A. viridistriata see *Pleioblastus auricomus.*

ARUNDO

POACEAE

Genus of 2 or possibly 3 species of evergreen, rhizomatous perennial grasses from riversides and ditches in warm-temperate regions of the N. hemisphere. They have alternate, broadly linear, flat leaves, borne on thick, reed-like stems, and terminal, feathery flower panicles.

Arundo donax var. *versicolor*

A. donax is grown for its attractive, bamboo-like foliage. Where not hardy, the variegated cultivars are ideal for a cool conservatory or greenhouse, or for large containers. In warmer areas, use as specimen plants or at the back of a large border.
• **CULTIVATION** Under glass, grow variegated cultivars in permanently moist, soilless potting mix in full light. Outdoors, *A. donax* grows well in any soil, but thrives in moist conditions in full sun, with protection from strong winds. For best foliage, cut back annually to the bases, avoiding contact with the sharp leaf margins.
• **PROPAGATION** Sow seed of *A. donax* in containers in a cold frame in spring. Divide the rootstock in midspring. Root sections of stems in a water-filled tray from midspring to midsummer; pot up and keep moist.
• **PESTS AND DISEASES** Rust is sometimes a problem.

A. conspicua see *Chionochloa conspicua.*
A. donax (Giant reed). Clump-forming, rhizomatous perennial with thick stems and arching, broadly linear, mid-green, glaucous leaves, to 24in (60cm) long. In mid- and late autumn, produces terminal panicles of light green to purple spikelets, to 24in (60cm) long. ↕ 15ft (5m), ↔ 5ft (1.5m) or more. S. Europe. Zone 7; variegated cultivars are generally hardy to Zone 7b. **'Variegata'** see var. *versicolor.* **'Variegata Superba'** has wide leaves, 1½–2½in (4–6cm) across, and to 12in (30cm) long, striped and margined white; ↕ to 3ft (1m), ↔ indefinite. **var. *versicolor*** ▣ syn. 'Variegata', produces white-striped leaves; ↕ to 6ft (1.8m), more in mild climates, ↔ 24in (60cm).

ASARINA

SCROPHULARIACEAE

Genus of one species of trailing, evergreen perennial, with softly sticky-hairy leaves, occurring among shaded rocks in the Pyrenees. *A. procumbens* is cultivated for its attractive, 2-lipped flowers, which strongly resemble those of snapdragons (*Antirrhinum*). They are produced singly from the upper leaf axils over long periods in summer. It will trail effectively over walls or rocks, the side of a raised bed, or a bank.
• **CULTIVATION** Grow in fertile, well-drained, sandy soil in sun or partial shade.

Asarina procumbens

• **PROPAGATION** Sow seed at 61°F (16°C) in early spring, or root tip cuttings in summer. It often self-sows.
• **PESTS AND DISEASES** Infrequent.

A. antirrhiniflora see *Maurandella antirrhiniflora.*
A. barclayana see *Maurandya barclayana.*
A. erubescens see *Lophospermum erubescens.*
A. procumbens ▣ syn. *Antirrhinum asarina* (Climbing snapdragon). Trailing, evergreen perennial with opposite pairs of shallowly lobed, kidney-shaped, hairy, gray-green leaves, to 2½in (6cm) long, on brittle stems. Pale yellow "snapdragon" flowers, to 1½in (4cm) long, with deep yellow throats and light purple veining, are produced in summer. Tolerates partial shade. ↕ 2in (5cm), ↔ to 24in (60cm). Pyrenees. Zone 5. **'Iberian Trail'** is a seed-raised cultivar of the species.
A. purpusii see *Maurandya purpusii.*

ASARUM

syn. HETEROTROPA, HEXASTYLIS
Wild ginger

ARISTOLOCHIACEAE

Genus of about 70 species of mainly evergreen, low-growing, rhizomatous perennials occurring in woodland in Europe, E. Asia, and North America. Asarums have large, usually glossy, sometimes marbled leaves, concealing mildly malodorous, pitcher-shaped flowers, some with 3 slender, tail-like petal tips. Use as a groundcover at the edge of a shady border or grow in a woodland garden. The evergreen species may shed their leaves in unusually cold, snowless winters. The rhizomes are aromatic, smelling somewhat like ginger.
• **CULTIVATION** Grow in partial to full shade in moderately fertile, humus-rich, moist but well-drained, preferably neutral to acidic soil.
• **PROPAGATION** Sow seed in containers in a cold frame as soon as ripe. Some species self-seed freely. Divide carefully in early spring.
• **PESTS AND DISEASES** Slugs and snails may be problems, especially in spring. Leaf gall and rust also occur.

A. canadense (Canadian wild ginger). Deciduous perennial with leaves up to 2–4in (6–10cm) long, held on softly hairy leaf stalks, 6–12in (15–30cm) long. Produces concealed, bell-shaped,

Asarum europaeum

brownish purple flowers, 1in (2.5cm) across, in spring. ↕↔ to 6in (15cm). New Brunswick to North Carolina. Zone 3.
A. europaeum ▣ (European wild ginger). Evergreen, creeping, rhizomatous perennial, forming carpets of kidney-shaped, glossy, dark green leaves, 2–3in (5–8cm) long. These conceal small, greenish purple then brown, narrowly bell-shaped, short-lobed flowers, ½–¾in (1.5–2cm) long, borne in late spring. Ideal as a groundcover. ↕ 3in (8cm), ↔ to 12in (30cm) or more. W. Europe. Zone 4. **var. *caucasicum*** has tapered and extended leaf tips.
A. hartwegii, syn. *A. marmoratum.* Evergreen, prostrate, rhizomatous perennial with heart-shaped, pointed, dark green-bronze leaves, 2½–5in (6–13cm) long, attractively marbled silvery green along the veins. Broadly tubular, brownish purple flowers, to 2in (5cm) or more long, with long, slender lobes, are borne in early summer. ↕ 3in (8cm), ↔ to 12in (30cm) or more. California, Oregon. Zone 6.
A. marmoratum see *A. hartwegii.*
A. shuttleworthii. Evergreen, prostrate, rhizomatous perennial with broadly heart-shaped, shiny, dark green, often silver-marbled leaves, 1–4in (2.5–10cm) long. Broadly tubular, purple-brown flowers, ½–1½in (1.5–4cm) long, with triangular lobes, patterned purple-red and cream within, are produced in early summer. ↕ 3in (8cm), ↔ to 12in (30cm) or more. S.E. US. Zone 6. **'Callaway'** ▣ is a vigorous cultivar; the leaves are more mottled than the species.

Asarum shuttleworthii 'Callaway'

A

ASCLEPIAS

Milkweed, Silkweed

ASCLEPIADACEAE

Genus of about 110 species of evergreen or deciduous, clump-forming, sometimes spreading perennials, and a few subshrubs and shrubs, mainly from well-drained soils in scrub or grassland, some from marsh, wet scrub, and lakeside areas, in South Africa, temperate North America, and tropical North and South America. They have simple, narrowly elliptic to lance-shaped or ovate, opposite or alternate, sometimes spirally arranged leaves and umbel-like cymes of numerous small flowers, to 1in (2.5cm) across. The corolla lobes reflex to display the unusual, upright, horn-like, staminal appendages. The flowers are followed by pairs of spindle-shaped green fruits, variable in length, which ripen to yellowish brown, and split open to expose rows of seeds with long, silky white hairs, giving rise to the common name, silkweed. *Asclepias* species are attractive to bees and butterflies and are showy plants for a border, meadow, or wildflower garden. Contact with the milky sap may irritate skin.

• **CULTIVATION** Outdoors, grow in fertile, well-drained, loamy soil in full sun, although *A. incarnata* and *A. speciosa* prefer more moisture and will thrive near a pond or stream. Some are slow to begin growth in spring.

• **PROPAGATION** Sow seed of tender species at 61–64°F (16–18°C) in late winter. Sow seed of perennials in containers in a cold frame in early spring, or divide in spring. Root basal cuttings in spring.

• **PESTS AND DISEASES** Whiteflies and spider mites may be problems under glass. Aphids and mealybugs are common when flowering. Rust and bacterial and fungal leaf spots are quite common in the S.E. US.

A. curassavica ▣ (Blood flower, Indian root, Swallow-wort). Evergreen subshrub, often grown as an annual and sometimes under glass, with upright branches and opposite, elliptic-lance-shaped, mid-green leaves, to 6in (15cm) long. Axillary or near-terminal, umbel-like cymes, 2–4in (5–10cm) across, of red or orange-red flowers, sometimes yellow or white, with orange-yellow hoods, are borne from summer to autumn. They are followed by erect

Asclepias curassavica

Asclepias incarnata

fruit, to 3in (8cm) long. ↕ 3ft (1m), ↔ 24in (60cm). South America. ❄ (min. 45°F/7°C)

A. fruticosa see *Gomphocarpus fruticosus.*

A. hallii. Vigorous perennial with upright stems, spreading, fleshy roots, and alternate, lance-shaped, dark green leaves, 5in (13cm) long. Semi-pendent, terminal cymes, 2–3in (5–8cm) across, of deep pink flowers, are produced in mid- and late summer. The flowers are followed by erect fruit, to 6in (15cm) long. ↕ 36in (90cm), ↔ 24in (60cm). W. US. Zone 6.

A. incarnata ▣ (Swamp milkweed). Thick-stemmed perennial with dense branches and opposite, narrowly elliptic to ovate, mid-green leaves, 3–6in (7–15cm) long. Clustered, umbel-like cymes, 2in (5cm) across, of pinkish purple flowers, with paler "horns," are produced from the upper leaf axils from midsummer to early autumn. The flowers are followed by erect fruit, to 3in (8cm) long. ↕ 4ft (1.2m), ↔ 24in (60cm). N.E. to S.E. US. Zone 4.

A. lanceolata. Erect, tuberous perennial with slender stems and opposite, lance-shaped, mid-green leaves, to 10in (25cm) long. Bears terminal, umbel-like cymes, 3–4in (8–10cm) across, of bright

Asclepias tuberosa

red flowers – orange or yellow in some garden cultivars – in mid- and late summer. They are followed by erect fruit, to 4in (10cm) across. ↕ 5ft (1.5m), ↔ 30in (75cm). S.W. US. Zone 3.

A. physocarpa see *Gomphocarpus physocarpus.*

A. speciosa. Erect, softly hairy perennial with opposite, oblong-ovate, gray-white, woolly leaves, 3–8in (8–20cm) long. Numerous axillary, umbel-like cymes, 1¼–3in (3–8cm) across, of purple-pink flowers are borne in summer, and are followed by densely hairy, semi-pendent or pendent fruit, 2½–4in (6–10cm) long. ↕ 30in (75cm), ↔ 24in (60cm). W. and C. North America. Zone 4.

A. syriaca (Common milkweed). Vigorous, softly hairy perennial with spreading, fleshy roots and upright stems with opposite, oblong-ovate leaves, 4–10in (10–25cm) long, mid-green above and blue-green beneath. In summer, bears scented, greenish purple and pink, occasionally white flowers in axillary, nodding, umbel-like cymes, 2in (5cm) across. These are followed by pendent, softly spiny fruit, to 5in (13cm) long. Sometimes grown as host plants for Monarch butterfly caterpillars. May become weedy. ↕ to 6ft (2m), ↔ indefinite. E. North America. Zone 4.

A. tuberosa ▣ (Butterfly weed). Tuberous, hairy perennial with thick, unbranched stems bearing numerous spirally arranged, lance-shaped to oblong-ovate, light to mid-green leaves, 4–5½in (10–14cm) long. Bears axillary and terminal, umbel-like cymes, 1½–2in (4–5cm) across, of orange, sometimes orange-red or yellow flowers, from midsummer to early autumn; they are followed by fruit 3½–5in (9–13cm) long, on nodding stalks. ↕ 36in (90cm), ↔ 12in (30cm). E. and S. North America. Zone 4. **'Gay Butterflies'** has yellow, red, and orange flowers.

ASCOCENDA

ORCHIDACEAE

Bigeneric hybrid genus, a cross between *Ascocentrum* and *Vanda*, of several hundred compact, evergreen, epiphytic orchids, derived from species originally growing wild in Burma, India, and the Philippines. They have upright rhizomes producing semi-rigid, narrowly oval, light to mid-green leaves. The axillary racemes of 6–8 or more delicate, open flowers, are borne freely over long periods of the year, although mainly in winter. The flowers are often richly colored and attractively overlaid with contrasting colors.

• **CULTIVATION** Warm-growing orchids. Grow in epiphytic orchid potting mix, ideally in slatted baskets. Provide full light and high humidity throughout the year, with shade from hot sun in spring and summer. In summer, water freely, mist twice daily, and apply a balanced liquid fertilizer at every third watering; water moderately in winter. See also p.46.

• **PROPAGATION** Plants occasionally produce basal shoots, which can be separated when rooted.

• **PESTS AND DISEASES** Susceptible to a number of fungal and bacterial leaf rots as well as cymbidium mosaic virus. Aphids, spider mites, whiteflies, and mealybugs may be problems.

Ascocenda Dong Tarn

***A.* Dong Tarn** ▣ (*A.* Eileen Beauty x *A.* Medasand). Compact, evergreen, epiphytic orchid producing alternate, 2-ranked, mid-green leaves. In winter, bears upright racemes of many maroon-flecked, bright red flowers, 2½in (6cm) across, touched magenta and yellow. ↕ 12in (30cm), ↔ 9in (23cm). ❄ (min. 64°F/18°C; max. 86°F/30°C)

ASIMINA

ANNONACEAE

Genus of 8 species of deciduous and evergreen shrubs or small trees found in rich, moist soils in thickets and woodland, mainly in southern parts of E. North America. Their leaves are entire and alternate. *A. triloba*, the only species commonly cultivated, is grown for its striking foliage; unusual, solitary flowers, borne on the previous year's shoots; and edible fruit. It is suitable for a shrub border or a sunny woodland clearing. In cooler climates, *A. triloba* is cultivated as a multi-stemmed foliage shrub.

• **CULTIVATION** Grow in moist but well-drained, fertile, humus-rich, neutral to acidic soil, in full sun. Can be difficult to transplant, so is best transplanted as a small balled-and-burlapped or container plant.

• **PROPAGATION** Sow seed in autumn in a seedbed, or stratify in moist sand at 41°F (5°C) for 90 days, and sow in spring. Alternatively, layer in autumn or insert root cuttings in winter.

• **PESTS AND DISEASES** Leaf blotch, eye spot, and other fungal leaf diseases may occur.

Asimina triloba

A. triloba ■ (Pawpaw). Deciduous shrub or small tree with obovate, mid-green leaves, to 12in (30cm) long, turning yellow to coppery red in autumn. Cup-shaped flowers, 1¼–2in (3–5cm) across, each with 3 large calyx lobes surrounding 6 purple-brown petals (3 large and 3 small), are borne singly or in small clusters in late spring. Ovoid to bottle-shaped, edible, sweet fruit, to 5in (13cm) long, are yellow-green, ripening to yellow-brown. ↕↔ 20ft (6m). E. US. Zone 5b.

ASPARAGUS

LILIACEAE

Genus of about 300 species of evergreen and deciduous perennials, climbers, and subshrubs from sandy and coastal sites in Europe, Asia, and Africa. They usually have spindle-shaped tubers or tuber-like rootstocks. Arching and spreading or climbing stems bear scale-like true leaves and more prominent leaf-like stems, which in some species have straight or curved spines. Slightly scented, white or pink flowers, borne singly or in racemes or small clusters, are followed by red, orange, or purple berries, ½in (1.5cm) across. Where not hardy, grow as houseplants or in a cool or temperate greenhouse. In frost-free climates, grow in a border, or train climbers on a trellis. The foliage is useful for floral arrangements.

• **CULTIVATION** Under glass, grow in soil-based potting mix in bright filtered light, with shade from hot sun. Water freely from early spring to midautumn, applying a balanced liquid fertilizer monthly; water more sparingly in winter. Pot on in spring. Provide support for climbers. Outdoors, grow in fertile, moist but well-drained soil in a sheltered site in partial shade.

• **PROPAGATION** Sow seed at 61°F (16°C) in autumn or early spring. Divide clusters of tubers in early spring.

• **PESTS AND DISEASES** *Fusarium* crown rot and *Helminthosporium* and *Cercospora* leaf spots are common. Rust, anthracnose, and canker occur. Slugs, spider mites, and aphids are problems.

A. densiflorus (Asparagus fern). Evergreen, arching, tuberous perennial with feathery, linear, leaf-like, light green stems, to ½in (1.5cm) long. In summer, bears axillary racemes of small white flowers, followed by bright red berries. ↕ 24–36in (60–90cm), ↔ 3–4ft (1–1.2m). South Africa. ❄ (min.

Asparagus densiflorus 'Myersii'

Asparagus scandens

45°F/7°C). **'Myersii'** ■ syn. *A. meyeri*, *A.* 'Myers' (Foxtail fern), has dense, arching, foxtail-like fronds, 12–16in (30–40cm) long, of needle-like, leaf-like stems, each ¾–1in (2–2.5cm) long; ↕ 16in (40cm). **'Sprengeri'**, syn. *A. sprengeri* (Emerald feather, Emerald fern), has arching then pendent stems, giving an open, loose appearance, and needle-like, leaf-like stems, ¼–½in (5–15mm) long, borne in groups of 3.

A. meyeri see *A. densiflorus* 'Myersii'.

***A.* 'Myers'** see *A. densiflorus* 'Myersii'.

A. officinalis (Asparagus). Herbaceous, erect, many-branched perennial with clusters of 4–25 leaf-like stems, ½in (1.5cm) long. Clusters of 1–4 green-white, drooping, axillary flowers become bright red berries, ¼–½in (6–15mm) long. Site where it will not be disturbed. ↕ to 3ft (1m), ↔ 4ft (1.2m). E. Mediterranean. Zone 4.

A. plumosus see *A. setaceus*.

A. scandens ■ Scrambling or climbing perennial producing fern-like foliage, with whorls of 2or 3, lance- to sickle-shaped, light green, leaf-like stems, to ½in (1.5cm) long. Tiny, nodding,white, sometimes pink-flushed flowers are produced singly from the leaf axils in summer, and followed by red berries. ↕ 6ft (2m). South Africa. ❄ (min. 45°F/7°C)

A. schoberoides. Herbaceous, erect to arching perennial producing fern-like foliage, with clusters of 6–12 leaf-like stems, ½in (1.5cm) long. In early summer, bears axillary clusters of tiny, creamy white flowers, followed by red berries. ↕↔ 18–24in (45–60cm). Asia. Zone 7.

A. setaceus, syn. *A. plumosus* (Asparagus fern). Bushy, then twining climber, with feathery foliage, consisting of clusters of up to 20 bristle-like, leaf-like, deep green stems, ½in (1.5cm) long. Bears solitary, tiny, nodding white flowers from the leaf axils in summer, followed by purple-black berries. ↕ 10ft (3m). South Africa. ❄ (min. 45°F/7°C)

A. sprengeri see *A. densiflorus* 'Sprengeri'.

ASPERULA

Woodruff

RUBIACEAE

Genus of about 100 species of annuals, evergreen or deciduous perennials, and dwarf shrubs, from woodland and mountain sites, mainly in Europe and Asia. The stalkless leaves are opposite or whorled. Tubular or funnel-shaped

Asperula suberosa

flowers, with widely spreading lobes, are borne in branched, terminal or axillary panicles or cymes in spring or summer. Grow dwarf shrub or perennial species in an alpine house, or in a rock garden, a trough, tufa, or a scree bed. *A. orientalis* is useful for an annual border or groundcover, and for cut flowers.

• **CULTIVATION** Under glass, grow perennials and dwarf shrubs in gritty, soil-based potting mix. Outdoors, grow in sharply drained, moderately fertile soil in sun or partial shade. All tolerate alkaline soils. Protect from excessive winter moisture. Some perennials, especially *A. suberosa*, are very brittle.

• **PROPAGATION** Sow seed of perennials in an open frame in autumn; sow seed of annuals *in situ* in spring. Divide in spring or autumn, or root softwood cuttings in early summer.

• **PESTS AND DISEASES** Susceptible to aphids and spider mites under glass.

A. aristata* subsp. *thessala see *A. sintenisii*.

***A. athoa* of gardens** see *A. suberosa*.

A. azurea see *A. orientalis*.

A. gussonii. Densely tufted, mat-forming, woody-based, evergreen perennial with whorls of narrowly ovate-oblong to linear, glaucous green leaves, ¼–½in (6–15mm) long. Bears clusters of tubular, deep pink flowers, to ¼in (6mm) long, in late spring and early summer. ↕ to 2in (5cm), ↔ to 6in (15cm). Italy (mountains in Sicily). Zone 5.

A. nitida (Woodruff). Tufted, cushion-forming, evergreen perennial with rosettes of whorled, linear to lance-shaped, rich green leaves, to ½in (1.5cm) long. Few-flowered, terminal cymes of narrowly tubular pink flowers, to ⅜in (8mm) long, are produced in early summer. ↕ 4in (10cm), ↔ to 8in (20cm). Mountains of Greece and Turkey. Zone 7b. **subsp. *hirtella***, syn. subsp. *puberula*, is very similar to the species, but has leaves fringed with fine hairs. It is sometimes confused with *A. sintenisii*.

A. odorata see *Galium odoratum*.

A. orientalis, syn. *A. azurea*. Upright, then spreading annual with whorls of obovate to oblong-lance-shaped, bristly, mid-green leaves, to 1in (2.5cm) long. Powderpuff-like, flattened cymes of sweetly scented, tubular, bright blue, occasionally white flowers, ⅜in (9mm) long, are borne in summer. ↕ 12in (30cm), ↔ 3–4in (8–10cm). Caucasus, Syria, Iran, Iraq.

A. sintenisii, syn. *A. aristata* subsp. *thessala*. Tufted, cushion-forming, evergreen perennial with rosettes of whorled, linear to oblong, glaucous, blue-green leaves, ⅛–⅜in (4–8mm) long. Bears paired or solitary, short-stemmed, narrowly tubular pink flowers, to ½in (1.5cm) long, in early summer. ↕ 4in (10cm), ↔ to 8in (20cm). Mountains of Turkey. Zone 7.

A. suberosa ■ syn. *A. athoa* of gardens. Clump-forming, evergreen perennial with whorled, inversely lance-shaped, white-hairy, glaucous leaves, ⅛–½in (3–15mm) long. Profuse clusters of tubular, bright pink flowers, to ¼in (6mm) long, are produced in early summer. ↕ to 3in (8cm), ↔ to 8in (20cm). Mountains of Greece, Bulgaria. Zone 5b.

Asphodeline lutea

ASPHODELINE

Jacob's rod

LILIACEAE

Genus of up to 20 species of biennials and perennials from sunny, rocky meadows and scrub on dry slopes from the Mediterranean and Turkey to the Caucasus. They have clustered, fleshy or fibrous rhizomes, grass-like basal and stem leaves, and star-shaped, yellow or white flowers in erect, narrow racemes on erect, unbranched stems. Grow in a border or on a dry, sunny bank.

• **CULTIVATION** Grow in moderately fertile, well-drained, sandy, loamy, deep soil in full sun. Mulch in autumn at the northern hardiness limit.

• **PROPAGATION** Sow seed in containers in a cold frame in spring. Divide in late summer and early autumn: tease apart the fleshy rhizomes, retaining 2 or 3 growing points on each piece.

• **PESTS AND DISEASES** Slugs, snails, and aphids may be problems.

A. liburnica. Clump-forming perennial with narrowly triangular, blue-green leaves, to 10in (25cm) long, borne only on the lower part of the flower stems. In midsummer, bears slender racemes, 6–9in (15–22cm) long, of pale yellow flowers, 2in (5cm) wide, the backs of the tepals striped green, with narrowly ovate to lance-shaped bracts, ½in (1.5cm) long. ↕ 3ft (1m), PD12in (30cm). S.E. Europe, E. Mediterranean. Zone 6.

A. lutea ▣ (King's spear, Yellow asphodel). Clump-forming perennial with furrowed, narrowly triangular, blue-green leaves, 14in (35cm) long, produced all along the flower stems. In late spring, bears dense racemes, to 8in (20cm) long, of fragrant, bright yellow flowers, 1¼in (3cm) wide, with large, ovate bracts, 1in (2.5cm) long. ↕ 5ft (1.5m), PD12in (30cm). C. and E. Mediterranean, W. Turkey. Zone 6.

ASPHODELUS

Asphodel

LILIACEAE

Genus of 12 species of annuals and perennials found in open woodland, meadows, and scrub in well-drained, sometimes barren, rocky soils from C. Europe and the Mediterranean to the Himalayas. They have fleshy, congested rhizomes and dense tufts of radical,

Asphodelus albus

linear, flat or cylindrical, sometimes keeled, basal leaves, 6–24in (15–60cm) long. Leafless stems bear dense racemes or panicles of flowers, mostly 1¼–1½in (3–4cm) across, surrounded by persistent, scaly, white or brown bracts. The white or pink tepals have green or brown central veins. The taller perennial species are striking in a sunny border or wild garden; grow *A. acaulis* in a scree bed or in an alpine house.

• **CULTIVATION** Grow in deep, well-drained, moderately fertile, sandy loam in a warm, sunny, dry site. May also be naturalized in thin grass. Under glass, grow *A. acaulis* in gritty, soil-based potting mix; outdoors, grow in a scree bed in full sun.

• **PROPAGATION** Sow seed in containers in a cold frame in spring, or divide in early spring. Raise the short-lived *A. fistulosus* annually from seed.

• **PESTS AND DISEASES** Prone to aphids.

A. acaulis. Evergreen, rhizomatous, stemless perennial with rosettes of flat, linear, light green leaves, to 8in (20cm) long. In late winter and early spring, produces congested racemes of open funnel-shaped, pale pink or white, green-veined flowers, to 1½in (4cm) wide, with white bracts, on short stems in the center of the leaf rosettes. ↕ to 6in (15cm), PD to 8in (20cm). Atlas Mountains. ❄ (min. 35°F/2°C)

A. aestivus, syn. *A. microcarpus.* Clump-forming perennial with broad, linear, flat, thick and leathery, mid-green leaves, 8–16in (20–40cm) long. In mid- and late spring, bears star-shaped, white, sometimes pink-flushed flowers, 2–3in (5–8cm) across, with brown central veins and greenish white bracts, in branched panicles. ↕ 3ft (1m), PD12in (30cm). Mediterranean, W. Turkey. Zone 7b.

A. albus ▣ Clump-forming perennial with linear, flat but keeled, mid-green leaves, 12–24in (30–60cm) long, and leafless flowering stems. Star-shaped white flowers, ¾–1½in (2–4cm) across, with pink central veins and white or brown bracts (depending on the subspecies), are borne in occasionally branched racemes in early summer. ↕ 36in (90cm), PD12in (30cm). C. and S. Europe, N. Africa. Zone 7b.

A. fistulosus, syn. *A. tenuifolius.* Annual or short-lived perennial with a dense, basal clump of narrow, cylindrical, keeled, mid-green leaves, to 14in (35cm) long. In mid- and late summer, hollow, usually branched stems bear panicles of star-shaped, pinkish white flowers, to 1in (2.5cm) across, with brown central veins, surrounded by white bracts. ↕ 18in (45cm), PD8in (20cm). S.W. Europe to S.W. Asia. Zone 8.

A. microcarpus see *A. aestivus.*

A. tenuifolius see *A. fistulosus.*

ASPIDISTRA

LILIACEAE

Genus of 3 or more species of evergreen, rhizomatous perennials from woodland in the Himalayas, China, and Japan. The long-lasting, leathery, glossy, basal leaves are elliptic to lance-shaped, pointed at the tips, and narrowed at the bases into long, slightly winged leaf stalks. Solitary, 6- to 8-lobed, purple or gray-white flowers with purple markings, borne on the rhizomes at soil level, are pollinated by snails or slugs and mostly hidden by the foliage. Aspidistras are valued for their tolerance of deep shade, fluctuating temperatures, and neglect. Although commonly grown as houseplants, they are also useful as a groundcover in mild climates.

• **CULTIVATION** Under glass, grow in soil-based potting mix in bright filtered light. Water moderately when in growth, sparingly in winter. Once established, apply a balanced liquid fertilizer monthly (variegated cultivars tend to revert if overfed). Grows best with a minimum of 45–50°F (7–10°C). Outdoors, grow in moist but well-drained, fertile, sandy loam with added leaf mold, in a sheltered site in full or partial shade.

• **PROPAGATION** Divide in spring.

• **PESTS AND DISEASES** Relatively disease-free under most conditions. Sometimes susceptible to anthracnose, fungal leaf spots, and nonparasitic conditions (algal leaf spot and slime molds) due to slow growth. Mealybugs, scale insects, spider mites, and vine weevil larvae may sometimes be problems.

Aspidistra elatior 'Variegata'

A. elatior (Cast-iron plant). Rhizomatous perennial, usually grown as a houseplant, with ovate to lance-shaped, glossy, dark green leaves, 12–20in (30–50cm) long, produced singly at short intervals along the rhizomes. Erect, fleshy, broadly bell-shaped, 8-lobed cream flowers, ¾–1¼in (2–3cm) across, and maroon inside, are borne singly along the rhizomes in early summer. ↕↔ to 24in (60cm). China. ❄ (min. 35°F/2°C). **'Milky Way'** has white-speckled foliage. **'Variegata'** ▣ has elliptic leaves, to 28in (70cm) long, with creamy white stripes or wider cream bands along the margins and down the leaf stalks. Variegated areas on older leaves often turn brown in bright light.

***A. lurida* 'Irish Mist'.** Rhizomatous perennial with stiff, lance-shaped, dark green leaves, 6–8in (15–20cm) long, 2 or 3 per node. Leaves develop yellow markings when mature. Bears solitary, bell-shaped, 8-lobed, deep purple-red flowers, ¾–1¼in (2–3cm) across, along the rhizomes in early summer. ↕↔ 6–8in (15–20cm). ❄ (min. 35°F/2°C)

ASPLENIUM

syn. CETERACH, PHYLLITIS

ASPLENIACEAE

Genus of over 700 species of evergreen or semi-evergreen, terrestrial and epiphytic ferns found in diverse habitats on all continents except Antarctica. Short, erect, occasionally creeping rhizomes produce tufts of fronds, which may be simple, or pinnate to 4-pinnate, or pinnatifid. Some are "bird's-nest" ferns with long, entire fronds overlapping to form a "nest" in which organic matter collects. Sori are linear, and usually run parallel to each other from the midribs toward the margins of the fronds. Use smaller species in wall crevices, a rock garden, or an alpine trough. Grow larger species in woodland or among shrubs in a shady border. Where not hardy, grow as houseplants or in a cool or temperate greenhouse.

Asplenium bulbiferum

• **CULTIVATION** Under glass, grow in a mix of equal parts loam, coarse leaf mold or peat substitute (or peat), sharp sand, and charcoal. Provide bright filtered light and moderate humidity. When in growth, water moderately and apply a half-strength balanced liquid fertilizer monthly; water sparingly in winter. Outdoors, grow in humus-rich, moist but well-drained soil, with added grit, in partial shade. *A. rhizophyllum* needs alkaline soil; *A. ceterach, A. scolopendrium,* and *A. trichomanes* prefer alkaline conditions, but most other terrestrial species must be kept acidic.

• **PROPAGATION** Sow spores as soon as they are ripe at 59°F (15°C) for hardy species and at 70°F (21°C) for tender species. Divide hardy species in spring. Some species, such as *A. bulbiferum,* produce plantlets that may be potted up when 3 or 4 leaves have formed. See also p.51.

• **PESTS AND DISEASES** Frequently affected by scale insects, mealybugs, deformation due to over-fertilization, and bacterial leaf diseases. Foliar nematode is also common.

A. antiquum. Often epiphytic fern. Upright, glossy green. Its fronds are more compact, narrower, and uniform than in nidus, but with the same rounded keel on the back of the rachis or midrib. Found in evenly moist conditions. ↕ 24–36in (60–90cm). Taiwan and Japan. ❀ (min. 50°F/10°C)

A. australasicum. Often epiphytic fern. Upright vase shape, similar in appearance to nidus, but with a keeled, rather than rounded midrib. Found in evenly moist woods. ↕ 2–6ft (0.6–2m). Australia and Pacific Islands. ❀ (min. 50°F/10°C)

A. bulbiferum ▣ (Hen-and-chicken fern, Mother spleenwort). Evergreen or semi-evergreen, terrestrial or epiphytic fern with short, erect rhizomes and 2- or 3-pinnate, ovate, triangular, or lance-shaped to oblong, dark green fronds, 4ft (1.2m) long. The lance-shaped to oblong segments bear numerous plantlets that fall off and may eventually form large colonies. ↕↔ 4ft (1.2m). Australia, New Zealand. Zone 8.

Asplenium scolopendrium

A. musifolium. Evergreen, epiphytic fern with short, erect rhizomes, producing "nests" of simple, broadly ovate to lance-shaped, glossy, bright green fronds, 4ft (1.2m) long, similar to those of *A. nidus,* but much wider. ↕ to 7ft (2.2m), ↔ 5ft (1.5m). Tropical S.E. Asia. ❀ (min. 50°F/10°C)

A. nidus ▣ (Bird's-nest fern). Slow-growing, evergreen, epiphytic fern with "nests" of ovate to lance-shaped, entire, glossy, bright green fronds, 5ft (1.5m) long, and short, erect rhizomes. Commonly cultivated, especially as a houseplant, and has given rise to a number of cultivars. Several species have similar frond characteristics and may be confused with *A. nidus.* ↕ to 5ft (1.5m), ↔ 3ft (1m). Widespread in tropical areas. ❀ (min. 50°F/10°C)

A. oblongifolium (Shining spleenwort). Evergreen, terrestrial or epiphytic fern with short, erect rhizomes and ovate to elliptic, pinnate, mid-green fronds, 24in (60cm) long, with elongated, ovate to elliptic pinnae, borne on purplish black stalks. ↕ to 18–28in (45–70cm), ↔ 24in (60cm). New Zealand. ❀ (min. 45°F/7°C)

Asplenium nidus

Asplenium scolopendrium 'Crispum'

A. platyneuron (Ebony spleenwort). Evergreen, terrestrial fern with a short, erect rhizome, producing upright, linear-oblong, dark green fronds, 10in (25cm) long, with oblong-linear, leathery pinnae on purplish brown stalks. ↕↔ 10in (25cm). North America. Zone 4.

A. rhizophyllum, syn. *Camptosorus rhizophyllus* (Walking fern). Semi-evergreen or deciduous, terrestrial fern with short, erect rhizomes. Tapered, triangular-lance-shaped or linear, simple fronds, are 12in (30cm) long, heart-shaped, and sometimes pinnatifid at the bases, with short, reddish green stalks. The elongated frond tips curve over and root where they touch the ground, quickly producing new plantlets and forming large colonies. ↕ to 9in (23cm), ↔ indefinite. North America. Zone 4.

A. scolopendrium ▣ syn. *Phyllitis scolopendrium, Scolopendrium vulgare* (Hart's tongue fern). Terrestrial, evergreen fern with erect to short, creeping rhizomes. It produces irregular, shuttlecock-like crowns of strap-shaped, leathery, glossy, bright green fronds, to 16in (40cm) or more long, which are heart-shaped at the bases and often have wavy margins. Sori are arranged in herringbone fashion. ↕ 18–28in (45–70cm), ↔ 24in (60cm). Europe, W. Asia, North America (as var. *americanum*). Zone 7. **'Crispum'** ▣ has mid-green fronds with strongly wavy margins, and is usually sterile. **Cristatum Group** cultivars have fronds that are fertile and crested at the tips. ↕ 24in (60cm), ↔ 32in (80cm). **'Kaye's Lacerate'** is a horizontally arching fern. Edges of simple glassy green blade cut into jagged segments. ↕ 6in (15cm), ↔ 4in (10cm). England. **Marginatum Group** contains variants that have fertile fronds with toothed or irregular margins and often fleshy ridges of tissue running along the undersides, close to the margins; ↕ 14in (35cm), ↔ 24in (45cm). **Ramocristatum Group** cultivars produce many-branched fronds, with each division lightly crested at the tip, eventually forming a ball of shiny green foliage; ↕ 12in (30cm), ↔ 20in (50cm). **Ramomarginatum Group** cultivars have branched fronds with toothed or irregular margins, often with fleshy ridges running along the under-sides, close to the margins; ↕ 12in (30cm), ↔ 20in (50cm). **'Undulatum'** has fertile fronds with wavy margins, less regular than those of 'Crispum'; ↕ 12in (30cm), ↔ 20in (50cm).

A. trichomanes ▣ (Maidenhair spleen-wort). Evergreen or semi-evergreen, terrestrial fern with erect, sometimes creeping rhizomes producing narrowly lance-shaped, pinnate, dark green fronds, usually 4–8in (10–20cm) long, on glossy black or dark brown stalks. Pinnae are distinctly stalked, elliptic or oblong, and rounded at the tips. ↕ 6in (15cm), ↔ 8in (20cm). Most temperate regions. Zone 4. **subsp. *quadrivalens*** has fronds with short-stalked pinnae, which are squarer at the tips, and closer together.

Asplenium trichomanes

A

ASTELIA

LILIACEAE

Genus of about 25 species of evergreen perennials with short rhizomes, mostly from subalpine or mountainous areas, in boggy, peaty soil, in New Guinea, Australasia, Hawaii, and southern areas of South America. They form large, striking, clumps of arching, usually keeled, linear leaves covered in silvery white scales, sometimes losing these at maturity. In spring or summer, they bear panicles of small, unisexual, pale-hued, often green, yellow, or brownish purple flowers. The 6 tepals may be spreading or reflexed, and often persist below the orange or red berries.
A. chathamica and *A. nervosa* have particularly attractive foliage.
In frost-free climates, grow in a peat bed or rock garden. Where not hardy, they are best grown in a cool greenhouse or conservatory.
• **CULTIVATION** Under glass, grow in soilless potting mix in full light with shade from hot sun and with good ventilation. Water freely during the growing season; keep just moist in winter. Outdoors, grow in moist, fertile, peaty soil in sun or partial shade.
• **PROPAGATION** Sow seed in containers in a cold frame as soon as ripe, or divide in spring.
• **PESTS AND DISEASES** Infrequent.

A. chathamica ■ syn. *A. nervosa* var. *chathamica*. Clump-forming perennial producing arching, leathery, silver-scaly leaves, to 5ft (1.5m) long. Long-stalked panicles of pale yellowish green flowers, ⅜in (8mm) across, with reflexed tepals, are borne in mid- and late spring. The flowers are followed by orange berries on female plants. ↕4ft (1.2m), ↔ to 6ft (2m). New Zealand (Chatham Islands). ❁ (min. 45°F/7°C)
A. nervosa. Clump-forming perennial with tufts of arching foliage, green and silver-woolly above, bronze to white and scaly beneath, with green midribs. Leaves are usually 24in (60cm) long, sometimes to 6ft (2m). Long-stalked, open panicles of greenish yellow or brownish purple flowers, ¼–⅜in (7–8mm) across, with spreading tepals, are borne in summer; female plants produce orange or red berries. ↕24in (60cm), ↔ to 6ft (2m). New Zealand. ❁ (min. 45°F/7°C). **var. *chathamica*** see *A. chathamica*.

Astelia chathamica

ASTER

ASTERACEAE

Genus of about 250 species of annuals, biennials, perennials, and subshrubs from a variety of habitats, including well-drained, mountainous sites to moist woodland, particularly in North America. The few shrubby species are mainly from South Africa. Most asters have alternate, entire, simple, lance-shaped leaves, some hairless, some softly hairy. The daisy-like flowerheads are either solitary or borne in terminal corymbs, racemes, or panicles on erect to spreading, usually branched stems; they have strap-shaped, female ray florets in white, pink, blue, or purple, and tubular, hermaphrodite, usually yellow disk florets. There are asters for almost all garden sites, including borders and rock gardens, streamsides, dry sites, and wildflower gardens. Where not hardy, grow the tender, shrubby species in a cool greenhouse.
• **CULTIVATION** Asters have varying cultivation requirements. For ease of reference, these are grouped as follows:
1. Well-cultivated, fertile, moist soil in sun or partial shade.
2. Well-drained, open, moderately fertile soil in full sun.
3. Moist, moderately fertile soil in partial shade.
Stake taller perennials, 30–36in (75–90cm) or more high, in early spring. Taller asters may be cut back by up to one-half of their height in late spring or early summer to control their mature height and encourage bushiness. To maintain vigor and flower quality, divide cultivars of *A. novae-angliae* and *A. novi-belgii* every second or third year.
• **PROPAGATION** Sow seed in containers in a cold frame in spring or autumn. Divide or separate runners, preferably in spring, otherwise in autumn; replant only vigorous, young shoots. Root basal cuttings of *A. amellus*, *A.* x *frikartii*, and *A. thomsonii* in spring.

Aster amellus 'Sonia'

Aster linosyris

• **PESTS AND DISEASES** *Verticillium* wilt, gray mold, powdery mildew, rusts, white smut, aster yellows, and many fungal leaf spots and stem cankers are common. Prone to rosy blister gall, aphids, tarsonemid mites, slugs, snails, and nematodes.

A. acris see *A. sedifolius*.
A. alpinus ■ (Alpine aster). Spreading, clump-forming perennial with short-stalked, spoon-shaped to narrowly lance-shaped, mid-green leaves, to 3½in (9cm) long. Bears solitary violet flowerheads, to 2in (5cm) across, with deep yellow disk florets, on erect stems in early and mid-summer. Suitable for the front of a border or large rock garden. Cultivation group 2. ↕ to 10in (25cm), ↔ 18in (45cm). Alps. Zone 4. **'Beechwood'** bears lavender flowerheads. **'Dark Beauty'** see 'Dunkle Schöne'. **'Dunkle Schöne'**, syn. 'Dark Beauty', has deep purple flowerheads. **'Wargrave Variety'**, syn. 'Wargrave Park', has pale pink, purple-tinged flowerheads. **'White Beauty'** has white flowerheads.
A. amelloides see *Felicia amelloides*.
A. amellus (Italian aster). Clump-forming, erect or semi-decumbent, hairy perennial with lance-shaped, mid-green leaves, 1¼–2in (3–5cm) long. Loose corymbs, to 6in (15cm) across, of lilac-blue flowerheads, each 1¼–2in (3–5cm) wide, with yellow disk florets, open from late summer to autumn. Cultivation group 2; thrives in alkaline soil. ↕12–24in (30–60cm), ↔ 18in (45cm). C. and E. Europe to W. Russia and Turkey. Zone 4. **'King George'** ■ has large violet-blue flowerheads; ↕18in (45cm). **'Mauve Beauty'** has large violet flowerheads; ↕24–36in (60–90cm). **'Nocturne'** ■ has deep lilac flowerheads; ↕30in (75cm). **'Rudolph Goethe'** bears deep lavender-blue flowerheads. **'Sonia'** ■ has light pink flowerheads. **'Veilchenkönigin'**, syn. 'Violet Queen', produces violet-purple flowerheads. **'Violet Queen'** see 'Veilchenkönigin'.
A. capensis see *Felicia amelloides*.
A. carolinianus. Climbing, densely gray-woolly subshrub with arching stems and oblong-lance-shaped, mid-green leaves, 2–4in (5–10cm) long. Produces terminal, solitary, pale pink or purple flowerheads, to 1in (2.5cm) across, with yellow disk florets, in autumn. Cultivation group 1. ↕ to 13ft (4.5m). S.E. US. Zone 8.
A. coelestis see *Felicia amelloides*.
A. cordifolius (Blue wood aster). Clump-forming, erect perennial with long-stalked, broadly ovate to heart-shaped, mid-green leaves, to 5in (13cm) long. From late summer to midautumn, produces loose panicles, 10in (25cm) across, of pale to deep blue flowerheads, to ¾in (2cm) across, with yellow disk florets. Cultivation group 3. ↕2–5ft (0.6–1.5m), ↔ 18in (45cm). E. North America. Zone 5. **'Silver Spray'** ■ has pale pink, white-tinged flowerheads, to 1¼in (3cm) across; ↕4ft (1.2m).
A. corymbosus see *A. divaricatus*.
A. diffusus see *A. lateriflorus*.
A. divaricatus, syn. *A. corymbosus* (White wood aster). Clump-forming, rhizomatous perennial with arching, wiry, blackish purple stems bearing mid-green leaves, 2½–5in (6–13cm) long, the upper ones ovate-lance-shaped, the lower ones heart-shaped. Bears loose corymbs, 4in (10cm) across, of white flowerheads, to ½in (1.5cm) across, with brownish yellow disk florets, from midsummer to midautumn. Cultivation group 3. ↕↔ 24in (60cm). E. North America. Zone 4.
A. ericoides (Heath aster). Clump-forming, bushy perennial with slender, freely branched stems and small, linear-lance-shaped, mid-green leaves, to 3in (8cm) long. Bears white flowerheads, to ½in (1.5cm) across, sometimes shaded pink or blue, with yellow disk florets, in loose panicles, 8in (20cm) across, from late summer to late autumn. Cultivation group 2. ↕36in (90cm), ↔ 12in (30cm). Canada, C. and E. US. Zone 5. **'Blue Star'** has blue-tinged white flowerheads. **'Esther'** is bushy, with small pink flowerheads; ↕28in (70cm).

Aster novae-angliae 'Purple Dome'

'Golden Spray' ■ is bushy, bearing pink-tinged white flowerheads with bold, golden yellow disk florets. **'White Heather'** is upright, with compact panicles of white flowerheads.
A.* x *frikartii (*A. amellus* x *A thomsonii*). Upright perennial with oblong-ovate, rough, dark green leaves, 2–3in (5–8cm) long. In late summer and early autumn, bears loose corymbs, 8in (20cm) across, of light to dark violet-blue flowerheads, 2–3in (5–8cm) across, with orange disk florets. Cultivation group 2. ↕ 28in (70cm), ↔ 16in (45cm). Garden origin. Zone 4. **'Jungfrau'** has long-lasting blue flowerheads with yellow disk florets; ↕ 24–36in (60–90cm), ↔ 36in (90cm). **'Mönch'** ■ has long-lasting, clear lavender-blue flowerheads on thick stems; ↕ 28in (70cm), ↔ 14–16in (35–40cm). **'Wunder von Stäfa'** is similar to 'Mönch', with thick stems and long-lasting blue flowerheads; ↕ 28in (70cm), ↔ 14–16in (35–40cm).
A. laevis (Smooth aster). Clump-forming perennial with stalkless, stem-clasping, elliptic-lance-shaped, smooth, glaucous-green leaves, to 5in (13cm) long. In late summer and early autumn, bears raceme-like panicles, 6in (15cm) across, of blue or pale purple flowerheads, to 1in (2.5cm) across, with golden yellow disk florets. Cultivation group 2. ↕ to 3½ft (1.1m), ↔ 18in (45cm). C. and E. North America. Zone 4.
A. lateriflorus, syn. *A. diffusus*, *A. vimineus*. Clump-forming perennial with slender, hairy stems, spreading branches, and linear- to oblong-lance-shaped, mid-green leaves, to 6in (15cm) long. Corymbs, to 6in (15cm) across, of white to pale lilac flowerheads, to ½in (1.5cm) across, with rose-pink disk florets, are produced from midsummer to midautumn. Cultivation group 3. ↕ 4ft (1.2m), ↔ 12in (30cm). North America. Zone 4. **'Horizontalis'** ■ has widely spreading branches and small leaves, to 3in (8cm) long. It bears white, sometimes pink-tinged flowerheads with pink-brown disk florets; ↕ 24in (60cm). **'Lovely'** has pink flowerheads. **'Prince'** forms a shrub-like mound, with twiggy, horizontal branches and tiny, purplish green leaves, to 1½in (4cm) long, turning plum-purple in autumn. Bears white flowerheads with raspberry-red disk florets, in autumn; ↕ 30in (75cm).
A. linariifolius (Stiff aster). Clump-forming perennial with wiry, hairy stems and linear, stiff, bristle-margined, dark green leaves, to 1½in (4cm) long. In early and midautumn, bears violet flowerheads, 1in (2.5cm) across, with golden disk florets, solitary or in corymbs, to 4in (15cm) across. Cultivation group 2. ↕ to 24in (60cm), ↔ 12in (30cm). C. and E. North America. Zone 4.
A. linosyris ■ (Goldilocks). Clump-forming perennial with unbranched, erect stems and linear, mid-green leaves, 2–3in (5–8cm) long. In late summer or early autumn, bears tiny flowerheads, 1/16–⅛in (2–4mm) across, with golden yellow disk florets and no ray florets, in dense corymbs, 1¼–6in (3–15cm) across. Cultivation group 2. ↕ 28in (70cm), ↔ 12in (30cm). Europe. Zone 4.
***A.* 'Little Carlow'** ■ Clump-forming, erect perennial, a hybrid of *A. cordifolius*, with ovate to heart-shaped, toothed, dark green leaves, 4–5in (10–13cm) long. Bears loose panicles, 8in (20cm) across, of violet-blue flowers, to ¾in (2cm) across, with yellow disk florets, in early and mid-autumn. Cultivation group 3, but tolerates well-drained soil in full sun. ↕ 36in (90cm), ↔ 18in (45cm). Zone 4.
A. natalensis see *Felicia rosulata.*
A. novae-angliae (New England aster). Clump-forming, hairy perennial with short rhizomes and thick stems, densely covered with stalkless, stem-clasping, lance-shaped, mid-green leaves, to 5in (13cm) long. From late summer to midautumn, strong, almost woody stems bear terminal, corymb-like sprays, to 10in (25cm) across, of violet-purple flowerheads, to 2in (5cm) across, with yellow disk florets. Cultivation group 1. ↕ to 5ft (1.5m), ↔ 24in (60cm). North Dakota to New Mexico east to Vermont and Alabama. Zone 4. **'Andenken an Alma Pötschke'** ■ syn. 'Alma Pötschke', produces bright salmon-pink flowerheads; ↕ 4ft (1.2m). **'Barr's Pink'** ■ has semi-double, bright rose-pink flowerheads in early autumn; ↕ 4½ft (1.3m). **'Harrington's Pink'** ■ has clear, light pink flowerheads; ↕ 4ft (1.2m). **'Hella Lacy'** is very heavily branched with prolific purple flowerheads; ↕ 3½ft (1.2m), ↔ 30in (75cm). **'Honeysong Pink'** has rich pink flowerheads with lemon-yellow disk florets; ↕ 3½ft (1.1m). **'Purple Dome'** ■ is dwarf and bears semi-double, deep purple flowers, 1½in (4cm) across. Mildew resistant; ↕ 18in (45cm), ↔ 30in (75cm). **'Septemberrubin'**, syn. 'September Ruby', bears deep rose-pink flowerheads; ↕ 4ft (1.2m). **'September Ruby'** see 'Septemberrubin'. **'Wedding Lace'** has pure white flowerheads; ↕ 3–4ft (1–1.2m).
A. novi-belgii (Michaelmas daisy, New York aster). Clump-forming, rhizomatous, hairless perennial with slender, branched stems and stalkless, lance-shaped, mid-green leaves, 2–4in (5–10cm) long. From late summer to midautumn, bears corymb-like panicles, 4–12in (10–30cm) across, of violet flowerheads, to 2½in (6cm) across, with yellow disk florets. Cultivation group 1. ↕ 4ft (1.2m), ↔ 36in (90cm). E. North America. Zone 3. **'Ada Ballard'** bears large, lavender-blue flowerheads, 3in (8cm) across; ↕ 36in (90cm). **'Alert'** has semi-double ruby-red flowerheads; ↕ 12in (30cm). **'Alice Haslam'** has rose-red flowerheads; ↕ 10in (25cm), ↔ 18in (45cm). **'Apple Blossom'** ■ has flowerheads in creamy pink; ↕ 36in (90cm). **'Audrey'** bears lavender-blue flowerheads; ↕ 14in (35cm), ↔ 18in (45cm). **'Bonningale White'** bears double white flowerheads; ↕ 3½ft (1.1m). **'Chequers'** ■ has purple flowerheads; ↕ 24in (60cm). **'Crimson Brocade'** has semi-double crimson flowerheads; ↕ 36in (90cm). **'Ernest Ballard'** has large, carmine-red flowerheads; ↕ 36in (90cm). **'Eventide'** has semi-double purple flowerheads; ↕ 36in (90cm). **'Fellowship'** bears large, double, deep pink flowerheads, 3in (8cm) across; ↕ 36in (90cm). **'Freda Ballard'** has semi-double, rich rose-red flowerheads; ↕ 36in (90cm). **'Jenny'** has double, red-purple flowerheads; ↕ 12in (30cm), ↔ 18in (45cm). **'Kristina'** ■ has large, semi-double white flowerheads; ↕ 12in (30cm), ↔ 18in (45cm). **'Lady in Blue'** bears powder-blue flowerheads; ↕ 16in (40cm). **'Lassie'** ■ has large, clear pink flowerheads;

Aster alpinus

Aster amellus 'King George'

Aster amellus 'Nocturne'

Aster cordifolius 'Silver Spray'

Aster ericoides 'Golden Spray'

Aster x *frikartii* 'Mönch'

Aster lateriflorus 'Horizontalis'

Aster 'Little Carlow'

Aster novae-angliae 'Andenken an Alma Pötschke'

Aster novae-angliae 'Barr's Pink'

Aster novae-angliae 'Harrington's Pink'

Aster novi-belgii 'Apple Blossom'

Aster novi-belgii 'Chequers'

Aster novi-belgii 'Kristina'

Aster novi-belgii 'Lassie'

Aster novi-belgii 'Patricia Ballard'

Aster novi-belgii 'Peace'

Aster novi-belgii 'Professor Anton Kippenberg'

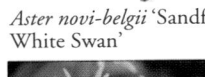

Aster novi-belgii 'Royal Velvet'

Aster novi-belgii 'Sandford White Swan'

Aster 'Ringdove'

Aster sedifolius

Aster thomsonii 'Nanus'

Aster turbinellus

↕ 36in (90cm), ↔ 18in (45cm). **'Little Pink Beauty'** has semi-double, soft pink flowerheads; ↕ 12in (30cm), ↔ 18in (45cm). **'Margaret Rose'** has light pink flowerheads; ↕ 12in (30cm), ↔ 18in (45cm). **'Marie Ballard'** has double, pale blue flowerheads; ↕ 36in (90cm). **'Melbourne Belle'** bears bright pink flowerheads; ↕ 30in (75cm). **'Mount Everest'** has white flowerheads; ↕ 36in (90cm). **'Niobe'** is compact with pure white flowerheads; ↕ 10–12in (25–30cm). **'Orlando'** has deep pink flowerheads with golden yellow disk florets; ↕ 36in (90cm). **'Patricia Ballard'** ■ has semi-double, dark pink flowerheads; ↕ 36in (90cm). **'Peace'** ■ produces mauve flowerheads, 3in (8cm) across. **'Percy Thrower'** has double, deep violet-blue flowerheads; ↕ 36in (90cm). **'Peter Harrison'** produces pink flowerheads; ↕ 16in (40cm). **'Professor Anton Kippenberg'** ■ bears mid-blue flowerheads; ↕ 14in (35cm), ↔ 18in (45cm). **'Prosperity'** produces large, semi-double flowerheads, 3in (8cm) across, in rose-pink; ↕ 3½ft (1.1m). **'Raspberry Ripple'** bears cerise flowerheads; ↕ 30in (75cm). **'Red Star'** has rose-maroon flowerheads; ↕ 12–16in (30–40cm). **'Rosenwichtel'** produces deep pink flowerheads; ↕ 8in (20cm), ↔ 14in (35cm). **'Royal Opal'** has large, light blue flowerheads; ↕ 16in (40cm). **'Royal Ruby'** produces semi-double, rich red flowerheads; ↕ 20in (50cm). **'Royal Velvet'** ■ produces deep violet flowerheads. **'Sandford White Swan'** ■ bears white flowerheads; ↕ 36in (90cm). **'Sarah Ballard'** has narrow, pointed violet flowerheads; ↕ 36in (90cm). **'Schneekissen'**, syn. 'Snow Cushion', has white flowerheads; ↕ 12in (30cm), ↔ 18in (45cm). **'Schöne von Dietlikon'** is early, and bears mid-blue-violet flowerheads; ↕ 30in (75cm). **'Snowball'** has a mounded habit and bears small white flowerheads with yellow disk florets; ↕ 10in (25cm). **'Snow Cushion'** see 'Schneekissen'. **'Snow Flurry'** produces large white flowerheads; ↕ 18in (45cm). **'Snowsprite'** has pink buds opening white; ↕ 10–12in (25–30cm), ↔ 18in (45cm). **'The Cardinal'** produces deep rose-red flowerheads. **'Thundercloud'** produces deep purple flowerheads; ↕ 36in (90cm). **'White Ladies'** has dark green foliage, and bears white flowers; 4ft (1.2m). **'Winston S. Churchill'** has double, dark ruby-red flowerheads; ↕ 36in (90cm).

A. pappei see *Felicia amoena*.

***A. pringlei* 'Monte Cassino'** ■ Clump-forming perennial producing sparsely branched, upright stems and narrowly oblong to lance-shaped, pale to mid-green leaves, to 3in (8cm) long. From late summer to late autumn, bears open sprays, to 4in (10cm) long, of white flowerheads, ⅜–½in (9–15mm) across, with yellow disk florets. Cultivation group 1 or 3. ↕ to 36in (90cm), ↔ 12in (30cm). Zone 4.

***A.* 'Ringdove'** ■ Clump-forming, erect perennial, a hybrid of *A. ericoides*, with linear-lance-shaped, stalkless, mid-green leaves, to 3in (8cm) long. Produces numerous pale mauve flowerheads, to ½in (1.5cm) across, with yellowish brown disk florets, in panicles to 7in (18cm) long, in autumn. Cultivation group 2. ↕ 36in (90cm), ↔ 12in (30cm). Zone 3.

A. sedifolius ■ syn. *A. acris* (Rhone aster). Clump-forming perennial with weakly branched stems and stalkless, lance-shaped, mid-green leaves, 2–2½in (5–6cm) long. Terminal sprays, 2–6in (5–15cm) wide, of flowerheads to 1½in (4cm) across, are borne in late summer and early autumn. Ray florets are widely spaced and blue-purple, lilac, or lilac-pink, disk florets are yellow. Cultivation group 2. ↕ to 4ft (1.2m), ↔ 24in (60cm), ↔ indefinite. C., S., and E. Europe. Zone 4. **'Nanus'** is compact in habit, bearing flowerheads with darker blue ray florets; ↕ 18in (45cm).

A. tataricus ■ (Tatarian aster). Spreading perennial with lance-shaped, elliptic leaves, to 24in (60cm) long. Bears lavender-blue flowerheads, about 1–1¼in (2.5–3cm) across, in large, often elongated corymbs, in mid- and late autumn. Cultivation group 1. ↕ to 8ft (2.5m). Siberia, China, Korea, Japan. Zone 4. **'Jindai'** has light blue flowerheads; ↕ 4–5ft (1.2–1.5m).

A. thomsonii. Clump-forming perennial with erect, slender stems and ovate to elliptic, coarsely toothed, mid-green leaves, to 4in (10cm) long. Bears lilac-blue flowerheads, 1½–2in (4–5cm) across, with yellow disk florets, in terminal sprays, 2–6in (5–15cm) across, from midsummer to early autumn. Cultivation group 3. ↕ 24–30in (60–75cm), ↔ 20in (50cm). W. Himalayas. Zone 4. **'Nanus'** ■ has long-lasting, star-shaped, lilac-blue flowerheads; ↕ 18in (45cm), ↔ 10in (25cm).

A. tongolensis (East Indies aster). Rhizomatous, mat-forming perennial with elliptic, softly hairy, mostly basal, dark green leaves, to 3½in (9cm) long. In early summer, erect, thick, almost leafless stems bear solitary flowerheads, to 2½in (6cm) across, with violet-blue ray florets and orange-yellow disk florets. Cultivation group 2, but will

Aster tataricus

tolerate moist soil. ↕ 18in (45cm), ↔ 12in (30cm). W. China, Himalayas. Zone 4. The following cultivars bear profuse, large flowerheads, to 3in (8cm) across, which are useful for cutting. **'Berggarten'** has flowerheads with lavender-blue ray florets and orange disk florets; ↕ 16in (40cm). **'Lavender Star'** bears lavender-blue flowerheads; ↕ to 12in (30cm). **'Leuchtenburg'**, syn. 'Shining Mountain', has flowerheads with amethyst-violet ray florets and bright orange disk florets. **'Napsbury'** has flowerheads with violet-blue ray florets and bright orange disk florets; ↕ 20in (50cm). **'Shining Mountain'** see 'Leuchtenburg'. **'Wartburg Star'** is mound-forming with deep violet-blue flowerheads; ↕ to 36in (90cm).

A. turbinellus ■ Clump-forming perennial with slender, erect, dark green stems and lance-shaped, mid-green leaves, 3–4in (8–10cm) long. In early and midautumn, bears airy panicles, to 6in (15cm) wide, of pale violet flowerheads, to ¾in (2cm) across, with yellow disk florets. Cultivation group 2. ↕ 4ft (1.2m), ↔ 24in (60cm). C. and E. US. Zone 4b.

A. vimineus see *A. lateriflorus*.

Aster pringlei 'Monte Cassino'

ASTERANTHERA

GESNERIACEAE

Genus of one species of evergreen, climbing or creeping shrub from humid, temperate forest in Chile and Argentina. Grown for its brightly colored flowers, *A. ovata* is best trained against a shady wall, or grown in woodland against a tree trunk. In cold areas, grow in a cool greenhouse or conservatory.

• **CULTIVATION** Under glass, grow in acidic potting mix in full light, shaded from hot sun. Provide moderate humidity. When in growth, water freely and apply a balanced liquid fertilizer monthly; water sparingly in winter. Outdoors, grow in moist, lime-free, moderately fertile, humus-rich soil in partial shade; shelter from cold, drying winds.

• **PROPAGATION** Surface-sow seed in containers in a cold frame in autumn. Root semi-ripe cuttings in late summer. Detach and pot up rooted pieces in spring.

• **PESTS AND DISEASES** Infrequent.

A. ovata. Freely branching, evergreen, climbing or creeping shrub with opposite, ovate-rounded, toothed, bristly, deep green leaves, to 1½in (4cm) long, on white-hairy stems. Solitary, long-tubed, bright deep reddish pink flowers, to 2½in (6cm) long, each with 5 spreading lobes forming a 2-lipped mouth, are produced from the leaf axils in summer. ↕ 12ft (4m), ↔ 6ft (2m). Chile, Argentina. Zone 8.

ASTILBE

SAXIFRAGACEAE

Genus of about 12 species of densely clump-forming, rhizomatous perennials from moist sites in mountain ravines, woodland, and streambanks in S.E. Asia and North America, grown for their striking, plume-like panicles, 7–18in (18–45cm) long, of tiny, red, pink, purple, or white flowers, borne mainly in summer. The dry flowerheads fade to decorative shades of brown in autumn, providing continued landscape interest through winter. They are attractive cut flowers, but quickly fade. The handsome leaves, usually 9–30in (23–75cm) long, are 2- or 3-ternate, with each leaflet further divided into 3–5 toothed lobes. Grow in a damp border or a woodland garden, or use for waterside plantings or a shady rock garden.

Numerous *Astilbe* hybrids have been raised. They are the result of complex crosses between several species. *A.* x *arendsii* hybrids are 1½–4ft (45–120cm) tall, with ovate to lance-shaped, 2- or 3-ternate leaves, 8–28in (20–75cm) long, and panicles to 18in (45cm) long. *A. chinensis* and *A. chinensis* var. *davidii* hybrids are either low-growing, 6–10in (15–25cm) high; or tall, growing to 30–54in (75–130cm) high. They have elliptic-ovate, 3-ternate leaves, 6–20in (15–50cm) long, and slender panicles, 4–8in (10–20cm) long. *A. japonica* hybrids are 20–36in (50–90cm) tall, with ovate to ovate-lance-shaped, 2- or 3-ternate leaves, 6–24in (15–60cm) long, and erect, branched panicles, 4–8in (10–20cm) long. *A. simplicifolia* hybrids are usually 12–24in (30–60cm) tall, occasionally dwarf, with ovate to narrowly ovate, 2-ternate leaves, 5–22in (13–55cm) long, and small, arched panicles, 4–8in (10–20cm) long. *A. thunbergii* hybrids are 20–48in (50–120cm) tall, with ovate to lance-shaped, 2-ternate leaves, 8–22in (20–55cm) long, and open panicles, 8–12in (20–30cm) long, of white or pink flowers.

• **CULTIVATION** Grow in moist, humus-rich soil or boggy sites in full sun; in drier soils, grow in partial shade and provide extra water in dry spells. Astilbes prefer fertile soil and will not thrive in alkaline or clay soils that dry out in summer. Divide and replant every 3 or 4 years to maintain vigor and flower quality, discarding old, woody rhizomes.

• **PROPAGATION** Divide in early spring when dormant; either replant the divisions immediately or pot them up to plant out in early summer when re-established.

• **PESTS AND DISEASES** Tarnished plant bug, powdery mildew, bacterial leaf spots, and *Cercospora* leaf spots occur.

***A.* 'Amethyst'.** Tall *A.* x *arendsii* hybrid with 3-ternate, mid-green leaves and open panicles of lilac-pink flowers in early summer. ↕ 30–36in (75–90cm), ↔ 24–36in (60–90cm). Zone 3b.

***A.* 'Aphrodite'** ▣ Clump-forming *A. simplicifolia* hybrid bearing panicles of red flowers above bronze foliage in midsummer. ↕ 16–24in (40–60cm), ↔ 24in (60cm). Zone 3b.

A. biternata (False goatsbeard). Large perennial with ovate, basally rounded, sharply toothed leaves, to 5in (13cm) long and 24in (60cm) across. Bears long, drooping spikes, 4ft (1.2m) long, of minutely petaled or apetalous white or yellowish white flowers, in summer. The only North American astilbe. ↕ to 6ft (2m), ↔ 3–4ft (1–1.2m). Kentucky and Virginia to Georgia. Zone 5b.

***A.* 'Brautschleier'**, syn. *A.* 'Bridal Veil'. Clump-forming *A.* x *arendsii* hybrid producing elegant sprays of nodding white flowers. They open in mid-summer from bright green buds above bright green leaves, and fade to creamy yellow. ↕↔ 30in (75cm). Zone 3b.

***A.* 'Bressingham Beauty'.** Tall *A.* x *arendsii* hybrid with spreading, bronze-flushed, mid-green leaves and panicles of bright pink flowers in midsummer. ↕ 36in (90cm), ↔ 24in (60cm). Zone 3b.

***A.* 'Bridal Veil'** see *A.* 'Brautschleier'.

Astilbe 'Aphrodite'

***A.* 'Bronce Elegans'**, syn. *A.* 'Bronze Elegance'. Clump-forming *A. simplicifolia* hybrid with dark green leaves. Panicles of pink-red flowers are produced on reddish green stems in late summer. ↕ 12in (30cm), ↔ 10in (25cm). Zone 3b.

***A.* 'Bronze Elegance'** see *A.* 'Bronce Elegans'.

***A.* 'Cattleya'.** Tall *A.* x *arendsii* hybrid bearing graceful panicles of big, open, crimson-pink flowers, in midsummer and sometimes again in early autumn. ↕↔ 36in (90cm). Zone 3b.

A. chinensis. Vigorous perennial with 3-ternate, toothed, softly hairy, dark green leaves. In late summer, bears panicles of pinkish white flowers. ↕↔ to 24in (60cm). Siberia, China, Korea. Zone 3b. **var. *davidii***, syn. *A. davidii*, has bronze-tinted leaves and slender panicles of erect branches bearing purple-pink flowers. Thrives in sun or shade and tolerates drought better than most; ↕ to 6ft (2m), ↔ 24in (60cm). China. **var. *pumila*** is dwarf, with red-green leaves and broad, dense, conical panicles of reddish pink flowers; ↕ to 10in (25cm), ↔ to 8in (20cm). **var. *taquetii* 'Purpurlanze'** see *A.* 'Purpurlanze'. **var. *taquetti* 'Superba'** ▣ bears dense, crinkled, bronze-green leaves and larger, narrower, conical panicles of small magenta or reddish purple flowers; tolerates drought and sun; ↕ 4ft (1.2m), ↔ 24in (60cm). Zone 3b.

***A.* x *crispa* 'Gnom'** see *A.* 'Gnom'.

***A.* x *crispa* 'Perkeo'** see *A.* 'Perkeo'.

A. davidii see *A. chinensis* var. *davidii.*

***A.* 'Deutschland'** ▣ Clump-forming *A. japonica* hybrid with erect panicles of pure white flowers above bright green foliage in late spring. ↕ 20in (50cm), ↔ 12in (30cm). Zone 3b.

***A.* 'Diamont'**, syn. *A.* 'Diamond'. Clump-forming *A.* x *arendsii* hybrid bearing slender panicles of pure white flowers above mid-green foliage, in midsummer. ↕ 30in (75cm), ↔ 24in (60cm). Zone 4.

***A.* 'Drayton Glory'** see *A.* 'Peach Blossom'.

***A.* 'Erica'.** Clump-forming *A.* x *arendsii* hybrid bearing slender panicles of mid-pink flowers above bronze leaves, in midsummer. ↕ 36in (90cm), ↔ 24in (60cm). Zone 3b.

***A.* 'Etna'.** Clump-forming *A. japonica* hybrid bearing panicles of dark red flowers above mid-green leaves, in early summer. ↕ 24in (60cm), ↔ 18in (45cm). Zone 3b.

Astilbe chinensis var. *taquetti* 'Superba'

Astilbe 'Deutschland'

***A.* 'Europa'.** Clump-forming *A. japonica* hybrid with mid-green leaves and dense panicles of light pink flowers in late spring and early summer. ↕ 24in (60cm), ↔ 18in (45cm). Zone 3b.

***A.* 'Fanal'** ▣ Clump-forming *A.* x *arendsii* hybrid producing dark green foliage. Bears dense panicles of dark crimson flowers in early summer. ↕ 24in (60cm), ↔ 18in (45cm). Zone 3b.

***A.* 'Federsee'.** Strong-growing *A.* x *arendsii* hybrid bearing dense, conical panicles of deep rose-pink flowers over mid-green foliage in mid- and late summer. ↕ 24in (60cm), ↔ 18in (45cm). Zone 3b.

***A.* 'Feuer'**, syn. *A.* 'Fire'. Clump-forming *A.* x *arendsii* hybrid bearing narrow panicles of carmine-red flowers in late summer. ↕ 36in (90cm), ↔ 24in (60cm). Zone 3b.

***A.* 'Fire'** see *A.* 'Feuer'.

***A.* 'Gladstone'.** Clump-forming *A. japonica* hybrid bearing panicles of white flowers above mid-green leaves, in early summer. ↕ 20in (50cm), ↔ 18in (45cm). Zone 3b.

***A.* 'Glow'** see *A.* 'Glut'.

***A.* 'Glut'**, syn. *A.* 'Glow'. Clump-forming *A.* x *arendsii* hybrid bearing panicles of dark ruby-red flowers above mid-green leaves, in late summer. ↕ 36in (90cm), ↔ 24in (60cm). Zone 3b.

***A.* 'Gnom'**, syn. *A.* x *crispa* 'Gnom', *A. simplicifolia* 'Gnome'. Arching, clump-forming *A. simplicifolia* hybrid with basal rosettes of deeply cut, reddish green leaves with wavy leaflets. In summer, bears tiny pink flowers in dense spikes, 6in (15cm) long. ↕ to 6in (15cm), ↔ to 8in (20cm). Zone 3b.

Astilbe 'Fanal'

Astilbe 'Irrlicht'

A. 'Granat'. *A.* x *arendsii* hybrid with panicles of deep red flowers above dark green foliage in midsummer. ↕24in (60cm), ↔ 18in (45cm). Zone 3b.
A. 'Hennie Graafland'. Clump-forming *A. simplicifolia* hybrid bearing panicles of rose-pink flowers above shiny, dark bronze-green leaves, in mid- and late summer. ↕16in (40cm), ↔ 12in (30cm). Zone 3b.
A. 'Hyazinth', syn. *A.* 'Hyacinth'. *A.* x *arendsii* hybrid with compact panicles of lilac-pink flowers over bright green foliage in mid- and late summer. ↕36in (90cm), ↔ 18in (45cm). Zone 3b.
A. 'Inshriach Pink'. Dwarf *A. simplicifolia* hybrid bearing panicles of pendent, pale pink flowers above reddish green leaves, in late summer. ↕↔ 12in (30cm). Zone 3b.

Astilbe 'Perkeo'

A. 'Irrlicht' ▣ Clump-forming *A.* x *arendsii* hybrid bearing elegant panicles of white flowers over dark green foliage in late spring and early summer. ↕↔ 18in (50cm). Zone 3b.
A. 'Koblenz'. Clump-forming *A. japonica* hybrid with bronze-tinted, dark green leaves and open panicles of deep salmon-pink flowers in midsummer. ↕24in (60cm), ↔ 20in (50cm). Zone 3b.
A. 'Montgomery'. Clump-forming *A. japonica* hybrid bearing tapering panicles of deep red flowers over finely cut, dark red-bronze foliage in midsummer. ↕24–28in (60–70cm), ↔ 18in (45cm). Zone 3b.
A. 'Ostrich Plume' see *A.* 'Straussenfeder'.
A. 'Peach Blossom', syn. *A.* 'Drayton Glory'. *A. japonica* hybrid producing

Astilbe 'Professor van der Wielen'

Astilbe 'Sprite'

peach-pink flower panicles over mid-green foliage in midsummer. ↕24in (60cm), ↔ 18in (45cm). Zone 3b.
A. 'Perkeo' ▣ syn. *A.* x *crispa* 'Perkeo'. Compact, clump-forming perennial with finely cut, dark green leaves, bronze-tinted when young. Bears pyramidal spires, 6–8in (15–20cm) long, of small, deep pink flowers in summer. ↕↔ to 8in (20cm). Zone 3b.
A. 'Professor van der Wielen' ▣ Graceful *A. thunbergii* hybrid with open, arching plumes of white flowers over mid-green foliage in midsummer. ↕4ft (1.2m), ↔ to 36in (90cm). Zone 3b.
A. 'Purple Lance' see *A.* 'Purpurlanze'.
A. 'Purpurlanze', syn. *A. chinensis* var. *taquetii* 'Purpurlanze', *A.* 'Purple Lance'. Vigorous hybrid bearing panicles of purple-red flowers over mid-green foliage in late summer and early autumn. Tolerates drought better than most. ↕4ft (1.2m), ↔ 36in (90cm). Zone 3b.
A. 'Red Sentinel'. Clump-forming *A. japonica* hybrid producing panicles of deep crimson-red flowers over dark green foliage in early summer. ↕36in (90cm), ↔ 20in (50cm). Zone 3b.
A. 'Rheinland'. Clump-forming *A. japonica* hybrid with mid-green foliage, and compact, upright panicles of rich pink flowers in summer. ↕20in (50cm), ↔ 18in (45cm). Zone 3b.
***A. simplicifolia* 'Gnome'** see *A.* 'Gnom'.
A. 'Snowdrift'. Dwarf *A. simplicifolia* hybrid bearing panicles of white flowers over mid-green foliage, in mid- and late summer. ↕↔ 12in (30cm). Zone 3b.
A. 'Sprite' ▣ Clump-forming *A. simplicifolia* hybrid with broad, mid-green leaves composed of narrow

Astilbe 'Straussenfeder'

Astilbe 'Venus'

leaflets. Bears feathery spikes of small, shell-pink flowers in summer. ↕20in (50cm), ↔ to 36in (90cm). Zone 3b.
A. 'Straussenfeder' ▣ syn. *A.* 'Ostrich Plume'. Vigorous *A. thunbergii* hybrid with bronze-tinted young foliage and open, arching sprays of rich coral-pink flowers in late summer and early autumn. Requires ample moisture in the growing season. ↕36in (90cm), ↔ 24in (60cm). Zone 3b.
A. 'Venus' ▣ Tall *A.* x *arendsii* hybrid bearing tapering, feathery panicles of bright pink flowers over bright green foliage in early summer. ↕36in (90cm), ↔ 18in (45cm). Zone 3b.
A. 'Weisse Gloria', syn. *A.* 'White Glory'. Strong-growing *A.* x *arendsii* hybrid with mid-green leaves, and large panicles of white flowers in late summer and early autumn. ↕36in (90cm), ↔ 18in (45cm). Zone 3b.
A. 'White Glory' see *A.* 'Weisse Gloria'.
A. 'William Buchanan' ▣ Dwarf *A. simplicifolia* hybrid producing red-tinted leaves, and panicles of white flowers with red stamens, appearing pink overall, in mid- and late summer. ↕9–12in (23–30cm), ↔ 8in (20cm). Zone 3b.

Astilbe 'William Buchanan'

Astilboides tabularis

ASTILBOIDES

SAXIFRAGACEAE

Genus of one species of perennial from moist woodland on the banks of lakes and streams in E. Asia. It produces panicles to 5ft (1.5m) tall, of numerous small, creamy white flowers above rounded clumps of large, lobed leaves.

• **CULTIVATION** Grow in cool, moist, humus-rich soil in partial shade. If grown beside water, plant with the roots above water level.

• **PROPAGATION** Sow seed in containers in a cold frame in autumn, or divide in spring as growth begins.

• **PESTS AND DISEASES** Slugs may eat the large resting buds.

A. tabularis ■ syn. *Rodgersia tabularis.* Clump-forming perennial with long-stalked, rounded, peltate, shallowly but often sharply lobed, softly hairy, light green leaves, to 36in (90cm) long. In early and midsummer, bears plume-like panicles of numerous tiny, creamy white flowers. ↕ 5ft (1.5m), ↔ 4ft (1.2m). N.E. China, N. Korea. Zone 4.

ASTRAGALUS

Milk vetch

FABACEAE

Genus of some 2,200 species of annuals, perennials, and deciduous shrubs from prairie to desert, tundra, coastal dunes, open woodland, and grassland of the N. temperate zone. They have alternate, regularly or irregularly pinnate leaves with entire, softly white-hairy leaflets. Milk vetches are grown for their white, pink, purple, or yellow flowers, attractive to bees and butterflies, and for their finely divided, silvery foliage. Mat-forming *Astragalus* species are ideal for a rock garden or raised bed.

• **CULTIVATION** Outdoors, grow in moderately fertile, sharply drained soil in full sun.

• **PROPAGATION** Sow seed in containers in a cold frame, or as soon as ripe, in early spring, after stratification. Root basal-shoot cuttings in spring or summer, or take softwood cuttings after flowering in late summer. Division is not advised.

• **PESTS AND DISEASES** Rust, downy mildew, powdery mildew, smut, *Septoria* leaf spot, and several other leaf spots.

A. ceramicus. Mat-forming, weak-stemmed perennial with long, slender stems to 20in (50cm), which produce a few tiny leaflets, borne on long petioles. Tiny white-pink flowers arise on tips of stems. followed by bladder-like, crimson and cream seedpods, to 2in (5cm) long. ↕ 15in (38cm) ↔ 15–20in (38–50cm). Great Plains. Zone 3.

A. tridactylicus. Stemless, tufted, mat-forming perennial with pinnate, silky leaves, to 2½in (6cm) long, and inversely lance-shaped leaflets, to ¾in (2cm) long. Racemes of 2–10 tubular, pink-purple flowers, to ½in (1.5cm) long, are borne in summer. ↕ to 2in (5cm), ↔ indefinite. Wyoming, Colorado. Zone 7b.

A. utahensis. Mat-forming, prostrate perennial with gray-green, hairy foliage, leaflets to 1–5in (3–5cm). Magenta or pink-purple, pea-flower in early spring, followed by pods, covered with shaggy, silky, cream-colored hairs. ↕ 6–8in (15–20cm) ↔ to 12in (30cm). Utah, Idaho, Wyoming, Nevada. Zone 3.

ASTRANTIA

Hattie's pincushion, Masterwort

APIACEAE

Genus of about 10 species of clump-forming perennials found in alpine woods and meadows from Europe to W. Asia. They have loose, basal rosettes of palmately lobed or palmate leaves. Erect umbels of small, 5-petaled flowers, surrounded by ruff-like involucres of showy, papery bracts, are borne in sprays above the foliage. Astrantias will thrive in a woodland garden, on a streambank, or in a moist border. The flowerheads are useful for dried flower arrangements.

• **CULTIVATION** Grow in moist, fertile, preferably humus-rich soil in sun or partial shade. Most variants of *A. major* will tolerate drier conditions. *A. major* 'Sunningdale Variegated' needs full sun to obtain the best leaf color.

• **PROPAGATION** Sow seed in containers as soon as ripe. Divide in spring.

• **PESTS AND DISEASES** Gray mold, mildew, slugs, and aphids can occur.

A. major ■ (Masterwort). Clump-forming, variable perennial with deeply 3- to 7-lobed, toothed, basal leaves, 3–6in (8–15cm) long. Green-veined white or pink-tinted bracts, surround the small, green or pink, occasionally deep purple-red flowers, which are produced in umbels, ¾–1¼in (2–3cm) across, in early and midsummer. ↕ 12–36in (30–90cm), ↔ 18in (45cm). C. and E. Europe. Zone 5.

Astrantia major

Astrantia major 'Hadspen Blood'

subsp. *carinthiaca* see subsp. *involucrata.* **'Hadspen Blood'** ■ has dark red bracts and flowers. **subsp. *involucrata*** ■ syn. subsp. *carinthiaca,* var. *involucrata,* has green-and-white bracts, twice as long as the umbel width. **'Margery Fish'** see 'Shaggy'. **'Rosensinfonie'** has rose-pink flowerheads. **'Rubra'** has maroon flowerheads; ↕ 28in (70cm). **'Shaggy'**, syn. 'Margery Fish', has very long bracts with prominent green tips, and deeply cut leaves. **'Sunningdale Variegated'** ■ has pale pink bracts andleaves unevenly margined creamy yellow.

A. maxima. Clump-forming perennial producing basal leaves, 1¼–4in (3–10cm) long, deeply divided into 3–5, almost separate lobes. Umbels, 1½–2½in (4–6cm) across, with sharp-pointed, broad pink bracts, each to 1¼in (3cm) long, surrounding tiny, soft pink flowers, are borne singly, or in twos or threes, in early and midsummer. ↕ 24in (60cm), ↔ 12in (30cm). Caucasus, Turkey, Iran. Zone 5.

Astrantia major subsp. *involucrata*

Astrantia major 'Sunningdale Variegated'

ASTROPHYTUM

CACTACEAE

Genus of 4–6 species of slow-growing cacti of the dry, arid areas of S. Texas, and N. and C. Mexico. Their spherical, hemispherical, or distinctively angular, ribbed stems, may become columnar when mature, with woolly, occasionally spiny areoles. Solitary, large, funnel-shaped, diurnal yellow flowers, some with red-tinted throats, are borne in spring and summer, followed by ovoid, green or red berries containing boat-shaped, black or brown seeds. If falls below 50°F (10°C), grow in a temperate greenhouse, although they are hardy outdoors to 20°F (-7°C) for short periods if kept dry. In warmer climates, grow in a desert garden.

• **CULTIVATION** Under glass, grow in standard cactus potting mix, with added limestone chips, in bright filtered light. During the growing season, water moderately; keep almost dry when dormant. Apply a low-nitrogen liquid fertilizer monthly from midspring to late summer. Outdoors, grow in sharply drained, poor, slightly alkaline soil in full sun. See also pp.48–49.

• **PROPAGATION** Sow seed at 70°F (21°C) in early spring.

• **PESTS AND DISEASES** *Bipolaris* scab, root rot, and mealybugs.

A. asterias ■ syn. *Echinocactus asterias* (Sand dollar cactus, Sea urchin cactus). Hemispherical cactus with 6–10 flat, mid-green to purplish brown ribs with usually straight, sometimes slightly spiralled, grooves between. Prominent, spineless white areoles are set along the ribs. Red-throated, bright yellow flowers, 1¼–3in (3–8cm) long, are borne in summer. ↕↔ 4in (10cm). Texas, N.E. Mexico. ❄ (min. 50°F/10°C)

A. capricorne, syn. *Echinocactus capricornis* (Goat's horn cactus). Spherical to ovoid cactus with 7–9 white-flecked, pale green ribs, with deep grooves between. Areoles bear long, twisted, yellowish brown spines, fading to light to mid-gray. Bears red-centered yellow flowers, 2½–4in (6–10cm) long, in summer. ↕ 8–10in (20–25cm), ↔ 4in (10cm). N. Mexico. ❄ (min. 50°F/10°C)

Astrophytum asterias

Astrophytum myriostigma

Astrophytum ornatum

A. hybrids. *Astrophytum* species have been extensively crossed with each other, producing a wide range of highly variable progeny, showing characteristics intermediate between the parents. For example, *A. asterias* x *A. capricorne* selections are spineless and flattened (like *A. asterias*) and bear fewer, larger areoles (like *A. capricorne*).
A. myriostigma ■ syn. *Echinocactus myriostigma* (Bishop's cap). Spherical or occasionally columnar cactus with usually 4–8 ribs covered with minute, white-woolly scales. Areoles are brown and spineless. Yellow, often red-centered flowers, 1½–2½in (4–6cm) long, are produced in summer. ↕9in (23cm), ↔ 8–12in (20–30cm). N.E. Mexico. ❄ (min. 50°F/10°C)
A. ornatum ■ syn. *Echinocactus ornatus.* Spherical to columnar cactus with 6–8 ribs, straight or occasionally spiralled, and cross-banded with woolly scales. Close-set areoles bear brown or yellow spines. Bears yellow flowers, 3–4in (7–10cm) long, in summer. ↕14in (35cm) or more, ↔ 6in (15cm). Central E. Mexico. ❄ (min. 50°F/10°C)

▷***Asystasia*** see *Mackaya*

ATHEROSPERMA

MONIMIACEAE

Genus of one species of evergreen tree occurring in woodland in S.E. Australia, including Tasmania. In its natural habitat, *A. moschatum* grows to 70–100ft (20–30m) tall, but it is much smaller in cultivation, when it is best grown in sheltered woodland. Both the opposite, simple, aromatic leaves and the white flowers produced in spring (the male and female blooms on different plants) are attractive. In cold areas, grow in a cool greenhouse.
• **CULTIVATION** Under glass, grow in acidic potting mix in full light, shaded from hot sun. Provide good ventilation. Water freely when in growth, applying a balanced liquid fertilizer monthly; water more sparingly in winter. Outdoors, grow in moderately fertile, moist but well-drained, humus-rich, acidic soil in sun or partial shade, sheltered from cold, drying winds. Pruning group 1; may need restrictive pruning under glass.
• **PROPAGATION** Sow seed at 50–55°F (10–13°C) in spring. Root semi-ripe cuttings in summer.
• **PESTS AND DISEASES** Infrequent.

A. moschatum (Australian sassafras). Conical tree with lance-shaped, nutmeg-scented, dark green leaves, to 4in (10cm) long, glaucous on the reverse. Bears solitary, saucer-shaped, fragrant, creamy white flowers, 1in (2.5cm) across, in the upper leaf axils in early spring. ↕20ft (6m), ↔ 10ft (3m) in cultivation. S.E. Australia, including Tasmania. ❄ (min. 45°F/7°C)

ATHROTAXIS

Tasmanian cedar

TAXODIACEAE

Genus of 2 species and 1 natural hybrid of evergreen, coniferous trees, restricted to mountainous areas of W. Tasmania, where they grow in rocky gullies, on exposed ridges, or around lakes. They have fissured, shredding, red- to gray-brown bark, and scale-like or ovate leaves, arranged in spirals, and lying flat to the shoots or spreading. Cones are spherical or ovoid, and green, ripening to brown at the end of the first year. The female cones have 10–16 scales. Useful as small specimen trees, they thrive in areas with cool, humid summers.
• **CULTIVATION** Grow in moist but well-drained, moderately fertile, humus-rich, preferably slightly acidic soil in full sun, with shelter from cold, dry winds. They grow best in mild, moist areas.
• **PROPAGATION** Sow seed in a seedbed or in containers in a cold frame in late winter or early spring. Root semi-ripe cuttings in late summer.
• **PESTS AND DISEASES** Infrequent.

A. x laxifolia ■ (*A. cupressoides* x *A. selaginoides*) (Summit cedar, Tasmanian cedar). Coniferous, narrowly to broadly conical tree with an open crown and shaggy, fissured reddish brown bark. Glossy, dark green leaves, yellowish green when young, are ovate, ⅛–¼in (4–6mm) long, spreading and horizontally arranged along the shoots. Bright green, ovoid cones, ¾–1in (2–2.5cm) long, turn orange-yellow then brown as they ripen. ↕30–70ft (10–20m), ↔ 12–20ft (4–6m). W. Tasmania. ❄ (min. 41°F/5°C)
A. selaginoides (King William pine). Conical, coniferous tree with an open crown and fissured, shredding, reddish brown bark. Similar to *A.* x *laxifolia*, except that the ovate leaves, to ½in (1.5cm) long, spread more widely, and are bright green with blue-white bands along their length; the bark is thicker; and the spherical cones are larger, to 1¼in (3cm) long, becoming orange-brown when ripe. It requires a more moist site than *A.* x *laxifolia.* ↕50–100ft (15–30m), ↔ 12–25ft (4–8m). W. Tasmania. ❄ (min. 41°F/5°C)

Athrotaxis x *laxifolia* (inset: cone detail)

ATHYRIUM

DRYOPTERIDACEAE

Genus of 180 species of deciduous, terrestrial ferns found mainly in moist woodland or forest in temperate and tropical regions of the world. They have erect or creeping, sometimes branched rhizomes. Fronds are normally pinnate to 3-pinnate or pinnatifid, but in a few species are simple. Sori form in 2 rows and are usually covered by J-shaped indusia. They are useful for a range of sites, from a shady border to a woodland setting. Where not hardy, grow as houseplants or in a warm greenhouse.
• **CULTIVATION** Under glass, grow in 1 part each of loam, medium-grade bark, and charcoal; 2 parts sharp sand; and 3 parts coarse leaf mold. Provide bright filtered light and high humidity. In growth, water freely and apply a half-strength fertilizer monthly; water sparingly in winter. Outdoors, grow in moist, fertile, neutral to acidic soil, enriched with leaf mold or compost.
• **PROPAGATION** Sow spores as soon as ripe, at 70°F (21°C) for tender species and 59–61°F (15–16°C) for hardy ones. Divide in spring. See also p.51.
• **PESTS AND DISEASES** Prone to rust.

A. filix-femina (Lady fern). Variable, deciduous fern with erect rhizomes and usually lance-shaped, 2- or 3-pinnate or pinnatifid, light green fronds, 3ft (1m) long, sometimes with red-brown stalks, borne like upright shuttlecocks and arching outward with age. Pinnae are variably sized, but usually elliptic with long, pointed tips; segments are lance-shaped to oblong. ↕ to 4ft (1.2m), ↔ 24–36in (60–90cm). Widespread in temperate regions of N. hemisphere. Zone 4. **var. *angustum* 'Lady in Red'** more brilliant ruby red than typically found among the red-stemmed northern lady ferns. Found in moist woods. NE US. Cultivars of **Cruciatum Group** have crested fronds, 12–20in (30–50cm) long, with each pinna branching at the midrib, producing the effect of a row of crosses. They are often sold incorrectly as 'Victoriae' (Queen Victoria's lady

Athyrium filix-femina 'Frizelliae'

Athyrium niponicum var. *pictum*

fern), a cultivar with pinnae and segments branching to form crosses; ↕ 3ft (1m). **'Frizelliae'** ■ (Mrs. Frizell's lady fern, Tatting fern) has fronds 4–8in (10–20cm) long, and pinnae reduced to rounded lobes along each side of the midribs, resembling tatting (handmade lace); ↕ 8in (20cm), ↔ 12in (30cm). **'Minutissimum'** is smaller than the species, and forms dense clumps; ↕ 12in (30cm), ↔ 16in (40cm). Cultivars of **Plumosum Group** have 3- or 4-pinnate fronds with finely cut segments; ↕ 4ft (1.2m), ↔ 3ft (1m). **'Vernoniae Cristatum'** is an arching cultivar. with a reddish stipe and rachis. Pinnules are crispate and wedge-shaped; pinnae and apex have repeatedly forked tips (crests). ↕↔ 24in (60cm). England.
A. goeringianum see *A. niponicum.*
A. niponicum syn. *A. goeringianum, A. nipponicum* (Japanese painted fern). Deciduous fern with creeping red-brown rhizomes and 2- or 3-pinnate to pinnatifid, lance-shaped, silvery gray-green or mid-green fronds, to 14in (35cm) long, with red-purple midribs. Plants grown from spores show variable coloration; this species hybridizes freely with other athyriums. Segments are lance-shaped to oblong or ovate, sometimes with notched or lobed margins. Makes an excellent, tough groundcover. ↕ 8–12in (20–30cm), ↔ indefinite. Japan. Zone 5. **var. *pictum*** ■ syn. 'Pictum', f. *metallicum*, has fronds with purplish red stalks and silver-gray segments, sometimes flushed purple-red.

▷ ***Atragene*** see *Clematis*

ATRIPLEX

CHENOPODIACEAE

Genus of about 100 species of evergreen or semi-evergreen shrubs, subshrubs, annuals, and perennials, found on coasts and in saltmarshes, salt flats, and deserts worldwide. They have alternate or opposite, often gray or silver leaves and insignificant flowers. *A. halimus* is an attractive foliage shrub for a border, and also useful for hedging in coastal areas. Use the edible leaves of colored variants of *A. hortensis* to provide contrast in summer bedding, or as a colorful addition to salads.

• **CULTIVATION** Grow shrubs in well-drained, dry, poor to moderately fertile soil in full sun, sheltered from cold, dry winds. Pruning group 1. Grow *A. hortensis* in moist but well-drained, fertile soil in full sun; water freely during dry periods to inhibit bolting.

• **PROPAGATION** Sow seed of *A. hortensis in situ* in succession from spring to early summer. Root softwood cuttings of shrubs in summer.

• **PESTS AND DISEASES** Rust diseases, powdery mildew, and *Ramularia* leaf spot occur.

A. canescens (Four-wing saltbush). Erect, dioecious shrub with alternate, narrowly oblong, gray leaves, to 2in (5cm), with backward-rolled margins. In summer, produces greenish white flowers in clustered spikes, to 2in (5cm) long, followed by fruit with 4 conspicuous, longitudinal wings or crests. Tolerates wind and salt. Useful in fire-retardant areas around buildings. ↕ to 6ft (2m), ↔ to 8ft (2.5m). W. North America. Zone 7b.
A. halimus (Sea orache, Tree purslane). Dense, semi-evergreen shrub with alternate, ovate or diamond-shaped, sometimes toothed, leathery, silvery gray leaves, to 2½in (6cm) long. In late summer, bears tiny, greenish white flowers in terminal panicles, to 12in (30cm) long. Tolerates full exposure to sea winds. ↕ 6ft (2m), ↔ 8ft (2.5m). S. Europe. Zone 7b.
A. hortensis (Mountain spinach, Orache). Erect annual grown for its spinach-like, succulent, alternate or opposite, lance-shaped, green to purple-brown leaves, to 7in (18cm) long; they are slightly downy when young, and may be shallowly toothed or entire. Green or red-brown flowers are borne in tall, foxtail-like, terminal racemes, to 8in (20cm) long, in summer. ↕ 4ft (1.2m), ↔ 12in (30cm). Asia, also naturalized widely in Europe and North America. **Plume Series** contains variants selected for their yellow, green, or burgundy-red flowerheads and foliage. **var. *rubra*** has blood-red or purple-red foliage and flowering spikes.

AUBRIETA

Aubretia

BRASSICACEAE

Genus of about 12 species of evergreen, mound- or mat-forming perennials, occurring among rocks, in scree, and in coniferous woodland from Europe to C. Asia. They have small, obovate to oblong, entire or toothed, hairy, mid-green leaves, and few-flowered racemes of cross-shaped, 4-petaled, colorful

Aubrieta x *cultorum* 'Argenteovariegata'

Aubrieta x *cultorum* 'Aureovariegata'

flowers, usually borne in abundance in spring. Grow on walls, as a groundcover on a sunny bank, or in a rock garden.

• **CULTIVATION** Grow in moderately fertile, well-drained, preferably neutral or alkaline soil in full sun. Cut back after flowering to maintain compactness. Generally short-lived in areas with hot summers.

• **PROPAGATION** Sow seed in containers in a cold frame in autumn or spring; seed germinates freely, but rarely comes true from cultivated plants. Root softwood cuttings in early summer, or semi-ripe cuttings in midsummer. Division of clumps in autumn is less successful than taking cuttings.

• **PESTS AND DISEASES** Prone to aphids, nematodes, flea beetles, and white blister.

A. x cultorum. Mat-forming perennials of complex hybrid origin, usually grown in preference to the species. They are available in a wide range of colors, with single or double flowers, to ½in (1.5cm) across, borne in profusion in spring. All are often listed under *A. deltoidea.* ↕ 2in (5cm), ↔ to 24in (60cm) or more. Zone 4. **'Albomarginata'** see 'Argenteo-variegata'. **'Argenteovariegata'** ■ syn. 'Albomarginata', has soft, mid-green leaves, margined silvery white, and single, pinkish mauve flowers. **'Aureovariegata'** ■ is similar to 'Argenteovariegata', but has irregularly gold-margined leaves and single mauve-pink flowers. **'Barker's Double'** has double, pink-tinged purple flowers. **'Bressingham Pink'** bears large heads of double pink flowers. **'Carnival'** see 'Hartswood Purple'. **'Greencourt Purple'** has single purple flowers. **'Hartswood Purple'**, syn. 'Carnival', produces large, single violet flowers. **'Joy'** ■ bears double mauve flowers on short stems. **'Leichtlinii'** is spreading, with masses of bright red flowers; ↕ 4in (10cm), ↔ 18in (45cm). **'Royal Velvet'** has large, frilly flowers of rich violet-purple, showing a definite two-tone effect as the blossoms age. **'Whitewell Gem'** bears hundreds of violet-purple blooms, ¾in (2cm) long; ↕ to 8in (20cm).

Aubrieta x *cultorum* 'Joy'

AUCUBA

CORNACEAE

Genus of 3 or 4 species of evergreen, dioecious shrubs from a wide variety of habitats from the Himalayas to E. Asia. While cultivated for their bold, alternate leaves and large fruits, aucubas are most valued for their tolerance of full shade, dry soils, pollution, and salt winds. Use as specimen plants, for hedges and screens, or to fill a dark corner where little else will flourish. They are also suitable for containers outdoors and as large houseplants.

• **CULTIVATION** Grow in any but waterlogged soil, in full sun or partial or full shade; variegated plants prefer partial shade. All are best in shade where summers are very hot, and all should be protected from winter sun and wind at the northern limit of hardiness. In containers, grow in soil-based potting mix. When in growth, water freely and apply a balanced liquid fertilizer monthly; water sparingly in winter. Pruning group 1. Trim hedges and cut back shrubs hard in spring.

• **PROPAGATION** Sow seed in containers in a cold frame in autumn or root semi-ripe cuttings in summer.

• **PESTS AND DISEASES** Wet root rot, Southern blight, and fungal leaf spots may occur.

A. japonica ■ (Japanese laurel). Rounded, evergreen shrub with elliptic to ovate, glossy, mid-green leaves, to 8in (20cm) long, usually with a few marginal teeth. In midspring, bears small, red-purple flowers, the males with yellow anthers, in erect panicles to 4in (10cm) long. Female plants produce bright red berries, to ½in (1.5cm) across, in autumn. All parts may cause mild stomach upset if ingested. ↕↔ 10ft (3m). Japan. Zone 7. **'Crassifolia'** is male, with large, leathery, dark green leaves, to 10in (25cm) long.

Aucuba japonica

Aucuba japonica 'Crotonifolia'

'Crotonifolia' ■ is female, with yellow-speckled leaves. **'Gold Dust'** is female, with leaves heavily speckled golden yellow. **'Hillieri'** is female, with glossy, dark green leaves, to 10in (25cm) long. **'Lance Leaf'** is male, with lance-shaped, entire leaves. **'Mr. Goldstrike'** is male, more upright, and has gold-splashed leaves; ↕↔ 4–6ft (1.2–2m). **'Picturata'** is female, and produces leaves marked yellow in the centers; it often reverts. **'Rozannie'** is compact in habit, with broadly elliptic, dark green leaves and bisexual flowers; ↕ 36in (90cm). **'Salicifolia'** is female, with slender leaves. **'Sulfurea Marginata'** is female, with yellow-margined leaves. **'Variegata'** (Gold-dust plant) has leaves spotted with yellow.

AURINIA

BRASSICACEAE

Genus, closely allied to *Alyssum*, of 7 species of clump-forming biennials or woody-based, evergreen perennials, found in rocky, mountainous areas from C. and S. Europe, eastward to Russia and Turkey. They bear rosettes of hairy, usually inversely lance-shaped to spoon-shaped leaves, and racemes or panicles of 4-petaled, yellow or white flowers. They are robust plants for a rock garden, the front of a border, or a sunny bank.

• **CULTIVATION** Grow in moderately fertile soil in full sun. Ensure good drainage. Cut back after flowering to maintain compactness; untrimmed plants quickly become leggy.

• **PROPAGATION** Sow seed in containers in a cold frame in spring or autumn, or root softwood cuttings in early summer.

Aurinia saxatilis

Aurinia saxatilis 'Dudley Nevill'

Aurinia saxatilis 'Variegata'

• **PESTS AND DISEASES** Prone to aphids.

A. saxatilis ■ syn. *Alyssum saxatile* (Basket of gold, Cloth of gold, Gold dust). Evergreen, mound-forming perennial with rosetted, obovate, occasionally pinnatifid, toothed, hairy, gray-green leaves, 1¼–3in (3–8cm) long, sometimes to 5in (13cm) long. Dense panicles of bright yellow flowers, to ½in (1.5cm) across, are produced in late spring and early summer. ↕ 8in (20cm), ↔ to 12in (30cm). C. and S.E. Europe. Zone 3b. **'Citrina'** bears abundant panicles of lemon-yellow flowers. **'Dudley Nevill'** ■ bears soft yellowish buff flowers. **'Variegata'** ■ has leaves with irregular creamy margins.

AUSTROCEDRUS

CUPRESSACEAE

Genus of one species of evergreen, coniferous tree from the Andes of Chile and Argentina, where it grows on steep, dry mountain slopes with winter rain or snow and a prolonged dry season. *A. chilensis* forms a small, columnar tree, with flattened, moss- or fern-like sprays of foliage, similar to *Calocedrus*. The solitary cones each have 4 scales, hinged at the bases; only the central pair are fertile. Grow as a specimen tree.

• **CULTIVATION** Grow in any moist but well-drained, moderately fertile soil in full sun, with shelter from wind.

• **PROPAGATION** Sow seed in containers in a cold frame or in a seedbed in late winter or early spring. Root semi-ripe cuttings in late summer.

• **PESTS AND DISEASES** Infrequent.

Australocedrus chilensis

A. chilensis ■ syn. *Libocedrus chilensis* (Chilean incense cedar). Narrowly columnar, densely branched tree with grayish green foliage and dark brown to orange-gray bark. Scale-like leaves are to ¼in (6mm) long, with long, decurrent bases, and are arranged in sets of 2 unequal pairs, often with glaucous bands on the reverse. Produces ovoid-oblong brown cones, to ½in (1.5cm) long. ↕ to 50ft (15m), ↔ to 12ft (4m). Andes of Chile and Argentina. ❀ (min. 35°F/2°C)

▷ ***Avena*** see *Helictotrichon*
▷ ***Azalea*** see *Rhododendron*

AZARA

FLACOURTIACEAE

Genus of 10 species of evergreen shrubs and small trees from South America, found at woodland margins and lakesides. They have simple, usually glossy leaves, alternate or in unequal pairs, and entire or toothed. The fragrant flowers are small and petalless, but have showy stamens and are borne in axillary spikes, clusters, or corymbs. They are followed by mauve or white berries, to ¼in (6mm) across. Grow in a sheltered, sunny site, against a wall or in a cool greenhouse, min. 35–41°F/2–5°C, for short periods.

• **CULTIVATION** Under glass, grow in soil-based potting mix in full light with shade from hot sun. Water freely when in growth, applying a balanced liquid fertilizer monthly; water sparingly in winter. Outdoors, grow in moist, fertile, humus-rich soil, in sun or partial shade, sheltered from cold winds. Pruning group 8, or 13 if wall-trained.

Azara integrifolia

• **PROPAGATION** Root semi-ripe cuttings in summer.

• **PESTS AND DISEASES** Infrequent.

A. dentata. Arching, evergreen shrub or small tree with ovate, toothed, glossy, dark green leaves, to 1½in (4cm) long, densely hairy beneath. In late spring, bears branching, dense corymbs, to 1½in (4cm) across, of fragrant, dark yellow flowers. ↕↔ 10ft (3m). Chile.

A. integrifolia ■ (Goldspire). Upright, evergreen shrub or small tree with obovate or diamond-shaped, usually entire, hairless, glossy, dark green leaves, to 2in (5cm) long. From midwinter to early spring, bears fragrant yellow flowerheads in mimosa-like clusters, ½in (1.5cm) wide. ↕ 15ft (5m), ↔ 10ft (3m) or more. Chile, Argentina.

A. lanceolata ■ Evergreen shrub with arching, fern-like branches and lance-shaped, sharply toothed, hairless, bright green leaves, to 2½in (6cm) long. Bears fragrant, bright yellow flowers in small, rounded, corymb-like clusters, to ¾in (2cm) across, in mid- and late spring. ↕↔ 15ft (5m). Chile, Argentina.

A. microphylla. Upright, evergreen tree or large shrub with semi-pendent shoots

Azara lanceolata

and small, obovate, entire or toothed, hairless, very dark green leaves, to 1in (2.5cm) long. In late winter and spring, produces tiny, vanilla-scented, greenish yellow flowers in clusters, to ½in (1.5cm) across, from leaf axils on the undersides of the shoots. Tolerates full shade and grows well against a wall. ↕ 30ft (10m), ↔ 12ft (4m). Chile, Argentina.

A. petiolaris. Arching, evergreen shrub or sometimes small tree, bearing ovate, leathery, hairless, dark green leaves, to 3in (8cm) long, with a few large marginal teeth. In mid- and late spring, bears fragrant, pale creamy yellow flowers in nodding, catkin-like racemes, to 1in (2.5cm) long. ↕ 15ft (5m), ↔ 12ft (4m). Chile.

A. serrata. Evergreen shrub with downy branches and oval, toothed, glossy, dark green leaves, hairless beneath, to 2½in (6cm) long. Fragrant, dark yellow flowers open in dense, spherical, umbel-like corymbs, to ¾in (2cm) across, in mid-summer. ↕ 12ft (4m), ↔ 10ft (3m). Chile.

AZOLLA

AZOLLACEAE

Genus of 8 species of floating, aquatic ferns found in lakes, ponds, and slow-flowing streams in both hemispheres. They have pinnately branched, floating rhizomes, with frail roots, producing 2-lobed, light green, scale-like fronds, which turn reddish brown in autumn. On a pool, they provide fast-growing surface cover, which partially suppresses algae and helps clear the water. They may quickly become invasive, however, particularly where summers are hot. Where not hardy, only *A. filiculoides* is suitable for outdoor pools; grow tender species in indoor pools in a cool or temperate conservatory or terrarium.

• **CULTIVATION** Under glass, scatter plants on the water surface in spring and provide full light. Outdoors, scatter on the pool surface when any danger of frost has passed, in full sun or partial shade. Where temperatures do not fall below 23°F (-5°C), plants overwinter as resting buds that sink to the pool bottom after the foliage is frosted, rising to the surface in spring. Where not hardy, remove before the first frost and overwinter in frost-free conditions in a saucer of moist soil. See also pp.52–53.

• **PROPAGATION** Scatter small bunches on the water surface in early summer.

• **PESTS AND DISEASES** May be eaten by waterfowl.

Azolla filiculoides

A. caroliniana see *A. filiculoides.*

A. filiculoides ■ syn. *A. caroliniana* (Fairy moss, Mosquito fern). Aquatic perennial forming an attractive cover of soft foliage on the water surface. Pairs of delicate, lacy, light green fronds, reddish green in full sun, 1/16in (2mm) long, are 2-ranked, and support single strands of fine roots, to ½in (1.5cm) long. North and South America. Zone 7.

A. pinnata. Aquatic perennial with broadly ovate, firm-textured, red-brown fronds, ½–1in (1.5–2.5cm) long, more slender and feathery than those of *A. filiculoides.* S.E. Asia, southern Africa. ❄ (min. 41°F/5°C)

AZORELLA

APIACEAE

Genus of about 70 species of evergreen, mat- or cushion-forming perennials from open, rocky areas in New Zealand and South America. They produce attractive mounds of foliage, consisting of rosettes of toothed or lobed, leathery leaves, ¼–½in (0.5–1.5cm) long. Umbels of small flowers are borne in late spring or summer. Grow in a raised bed or scree bed, or in an alpine house. Often confused with the genus *Bolax.*

• **CULTIVATION** Grow in gritty, soil-based potting mix in an alpine house in full light. Outdoors, grow in gritty, poor to moderately fertile, sharply drained soil in full sun.

• **PROPAGATION** Sow seed in containers in an open frame in autumn, or root rosettes as cuttings in spring.

• **PESTS AND DISEASES** Prone to aphids and spider mites under glass.

A. glebaria see *Bolax gummifera.*

A. nivalis see *A. trifurcata.*

A. trifurcata ■ syn. *A. nivalis.* Dense, cushion-forming perennial with rosettes of overlapping, glossy, dark green leaves, to ½in (1.5cm) long, deeply cut into 3 (occasionally 5) sharp-tipped, triangular lobes. Inconspicuous umbels of tiny, creamy white flowers are borne in summer. ↕ to 4in (10cm) or more, ↔ to 8in (20cm). Chile, Argentina. Zone 7.

AZORINA

CAMPANULACEAE

Genus of one species of erect, sparsely branched, evergreen shrub from volcanic cliffs or scree in the Azores. It has ridged stems and alternate, mid-green leaves,

Azorella trifurcata

Azorina vidalii

and bears racemes of bell-shaped flowers in late summer. Where not hardy, *A. vidalii* is an attractive plant for a cool conservatory or greenhouse. In frost-free climates, it is best grown among shrubs or in a border.

• **CULTIVATION** Under glass, grow in soil-based potting mix in bright filtered light. Provide good ventilation. In the growing season, water freely and apply a balanced liquid fertilizer monthly; keep just moist in winter. Outdoors, grow in fertile, moist but well-drained soil in full sun with some midday shade.

• **PROPAGATION** Sow seed at 55–61°F (13–16°C) in spring, or root softwood or semi-ripe cuttings in summer.

• **PESTS AND DISEASES** Infrequent.

A. vidalii ■ syn. *Campanula vidalii.* Soft-stemmed, evergreen shrub with spoon-shaped, toothed, veined, glossy, mid-green leaves, 2–6in (5–15cm) long, crowded toward the stem tips. In late summer, bears loose racemes of up to 50 pendent, waisted, bell-shaped, white or pink flowers, 2in (5cm) long, with orange bases. ↕↔ 16–24in (40–60cm). Azores. ❄ (min. 41°F/5°C)

AZTEKIUM

CACTACEAE

Genus of two species of very slow-growing, tuberous-rooted cacti, occurring on scree slopes in N.E. Mexico. They have prominently ribbed stems and produce areoles in rows along the ribs. They occasionally form compact colonies. Where not hardy, grow in a temperate greenhouse; in frost-free climates, they are suitable for a desert garden.

• **CULTIVATION** Under glass, grow in standard cactus potting mix in full light. Water moderately in growth; keep dry at all other times of the year. Outdoors, grow in sharply drained, gritty, poor soil in full sun. See also pp.48–49.

• **PROPAGATION** Sow seed at 55–61°F (13–16°C) in spring, or root semi-ripe

Aztekium hintonii

cuttings in summer. Propagation by seed is difficult and extremely slow. Offsets may be grafted, but expect atypical growth.

• **PESTS AND DISEASES** Mealybugs and root mealybugs may be problems, especially under glass.

A. hintonii ■. Solitary, globose to short columnar cactus with 10–15 pronounced ribs. Rows of areoles each produce 3 strongly curved spines, ½in (13mm) long. Bears magenta flowers, ⅜in–1¼in (1–3cm). ↕↔ 4in (10cm). Sierra Madre Oriental, Nuevo Leon, Mexico. ❄ (min. 50°F/10°C)

A. ritteri ■ syn. *Echinocactus ritteri.* Cactus with a flattened-spherical, 8- to 11-ribbed, minutely furrowed, olive-green stem. Tiny areoles each bear 1–4 flat, papery, curved, yellow to gray spines, which fall once an areole produces flowers. Funnel-shaped, diurnal, white or pink flowers, ½in (1.5cm) long, are borne from new areoles at the center of the stem from spring to autumn. ↕↔ 2in (5cm). N.E. Mexico. ❄ (min. 50°F/10°C)

▷ ***Azureocereus*** see *Browningia*

Aztekium ritteri

B

BABIANA

IRIDACEAE

Genus of 50–60 species of cormous perennials from open grassland and hillsides in South Africa. They have ribbed or pleated, often hairy, lance-shaped, mid- to bright green leaves and spikes of funnel-shaped, often strongly scented flowers, ¾–1½in (2–4cm) across, borne mainly in spring. Where not hardy, grow in a cool greenhouse; in warmer climates, plant in a sunny border.

• **CULTIVATION** Under glass, plant corms in autumn in soil-based potting mix, and grow in full light. When in growth, water freely and apply a weak balanced liquid fertilizer every 3 weeks before flowering; dry off as the leaves die down in summer. Outdoors, plant 8in (20cm) deep, in light, rich, well-drained soil in full sun in autumn. Dormant corms are sometimes offered for spring planting to bloom in summer. If left in the soil, they will revert to winter growing (if they survive).

• **PROPAGATION** Sow seed at 55–59°F (13–15°C) as soon as ripe. Remove offsets when dormant.

• **PESTS AND DISEASES** Spider mites may be a problem.

B. disticha see *B. plicata*.

B. plicata, syn. *B. disticha*. Cormous perennial with hairy leaves, 3–5in (8–13cm) long. Spikes of 4–10 scented, pale lilac to violet flowers, often with a paler mark on the lower lobes, are borne in spring. ↕ 3–8in (7–20cm), PD2in (5cm). South Africa. ❅ (min. 41°F/5°C)

B. rubrocyanea ▣ Cormous perennial with hairy leaves, to 6in (15cm) long. In spring, bears spikes of 5–10 scarlet and blue flowers. ↕ 2–8in (5–20cm), PD2in (5cm). South Africa. ❅ (min. 41°F/5°C)

B. stricta ▣ Variable, cormous perennial with hairy leaves, 1½–5in (4–13cm) long. In spring, bears spikes of 4–8 sometimes scented, purple, mauve, blue, or yellow

Babiana rubrocyanea

Babiana stricta

flowers, occasionally with dark red centers. ↕ 4–12in (10–30cm), PD2in (5cm). South Africa. ❅ (min. 41°F/5°C). **'Zwanenburg's Glory'** has alternate blue and white flower segments.

B. villosa. Cormous perennial with hairy leaves, 2–5in (5–13cm) long. In spring, bears spikes of 4–8 deep red flowers, with large, purple-black anthers. ↕ 5–8in (12–20cm), PD2in (5cm). South Africa. ❅ (min. 41°F/5°C)

BACCHARIS

ASTERACEAE

Genus of about 350 species of dioecious, deciduous or evergreen shrubs and herbaceous perennials from coasts, salt marshes, riverbanks, mountains, and woodland margins in North and South America. Leaves are alternate or absent; flowerheads are borne singly or in axillary panicles or corymbs. Where not hardy, grow in a cool greenhouse. *B. halimifolia* is valued as a windbreak, especially near the sea, and for its silver seed heads.

• **CULTIVATION** Grow in fertile soil in full sun. Pruning group 1 or 4.

• **PROPAGATION** Sow seed in containers in a cold frame in spring. Root softwood cuttings in summer.

• **PESTS AND DISEASES** Rusts and some fungal leaf spots occur.

B. halimifolia (Groundsel bush, Sea myrtle). Vigorous, upright, deciduous shrub with obovate to oval, gray-green leaves, to 3in (8cm) long, with large marginal teeth. In autumn, bears axillary clusters of small white flowerheads in corymbs to 6in (15cm) across. Female plants produce thistle-like, silky, white fruit. ↕↔ 12ft (4m). E. US, S. central US, Mexico, West Indies. Zone 4.

B. magellanica. Prostrate to erect shrub with spoon-shaped, hairless, mid-green leaves, 2–3½in (5–9cm) long. Bears terminal, solitary, yellow flowerheads, to 1in (2.5cm) across, in summer. ↕ to 12in (30cm), ↔ 8–10in (20–25 cm). S. South America. Zone 7.

BACKHOUSIA

MYRTACEAE

Genus of 7 species of evergreen shrubs and trees found mainly in subtropical and tropical rainforest in Australia. Ovate, elliptic, or lance-shaped, aromatic leaves are borne in opposite pairs. Small flowers, with 4 petals and conspicuous stamens, are borne in cymes, umbels, or panicles. Where not hardy, grow in a temperate greenhouse; elsewhere, grow in a border.

• **CULTIVATION** Under glass, grow in equal parts loam, peat, and sand in full light. Pot on or top-dress in spring. When in growth, water freely and apply a balanced liquid fertilizer monthly; water sparingly in winter. Outdoors, grow in fertile, humus-rich, neutral to acidic soil in full sun. Pruning group 9.

• **PROPAGATION** Surface-sow seed at 55–59°F (13–15°C) in spring. Root semi-ripe cuttings in summer.

• **PESTS AND DISEASES** Infrequent.

B. citriodora (Lemon ironwood, Lemon-scented myrtle). Shrub or bushy tree with broadly lance-shaped, hairy, reddish green leaves, 2–5in (5–13cm) long, maturing to glossy, deep green. From summer to autumn, bears umbels, 4–6in (10–15cm) or more across, of creamy white flowers. ↕ 10–50ft (3–15m), ↔ 6–20ft (2–6m). Queensland. ❅ (min. 41–45°F/5–7°C)

BACOPA

Water Hyssop

SCROPHULARIACEAE

Genus of about 56 species of mostly aquatic or semi-aquatic perennials, from shallow water, marshes, pond margins, and slow-moving streams of warm-temperate and tropical regions in Asia, Africa, Australia, and North and South America. Low, spreading to upright, often succulent, stems bear opposite, toothed, ovate to spoon-shaped leaves. Blue or white flowers are borne in clusters of 1–3, from the leaf axils, and are bell-shaped. Where not hardy, grow in an indoor aquarium.

• **CULTIVATION** Outdoors, grow in shallow mud or damp gravel in full sun. In frost-prone areas, grow in unwashed river sand mixed with a small amount of clay, in full light. See also pp.52–53.

• **PROPAGATION** Sow seed when ripe, or divide or take softwood cuttings in spring and early summer.

• **PESTS AND DISEASES** Occasionally subject to fungal stem rot at plant base.

B. caroliniana. Stoloniferous, aquatic perennial with spreading to ascending, softly hairy stems and ovate, palmately-veined, lemon-scented, mid-green leaves, to 1in (2.5cm) long. In summer, bears solitary, bell-shaped, blue flowers, to ⅜in (9mm) across. ↕ to 2in (5cm), ↔ to 24in (60cm). North America. Zone 8.

***B.* 'Snowflake'.** Spreading, terrestrial perennial, usually grown as an annual, with rounded, toothed, mid-green leaves, to ¾in (2cm) long. Open star-shaped, 5-lobed white flowers, ½in (1.5cm) across, are borne singly. Ideal for hanging baskets. ↕ 3in (8cm), ↔ 12–20in (30–50cm). ❅ (min. 41°F/5°C)

BAECKEA

MYRTACEAE

Genus of about 70 species of evergreen shrubs and small trees occurring in scrub in subtropical to subalpine areas in China, Malaysia, Australia, and New Caledonia. Linear to narrowly lance-shaped, usually entire leaves are borne in opposite pairs. Saucer-shaped, 5-petaled flowers are produced singly or in umbels in summer. Where not hardy, grow in a cool greenhouse. In warmer climates, grow in a border, at the base of a warm, sunny wall, or as a groundcover.

• **CULTIVATION** Under glass, grow in neutral to acidic, soil-based potting mix in bright light, with some shade from hot sun. In the growing season, water freely and apply a balanced liquid fertilizer monthly; water sparingly in winter. Pot on or top-dress in late winter. Outdoors, grow in neutral to acidic, well-drained soil in full sun. Pruning group 9.

• **PROPAGATION** Surface-sow seed at 55–59°F (13–15°C) in spring, and keep moist. Root semi-ripe cuttings in a propagating case in late summer.

• **PESTS AND DISEASES** Infrequent.

B. virgata (Twiggy baeckea). Prostrate to erect, bushy shrub or small tree with narrowly oblong to lance-shaped, dark green leaves, to 1in (2.5cm) long. In summer, numerous white flowers, to ¼in (6mm) across, are produced in umbels of 2–9 near the ends of the branchlets. ↕ 1–10ft (0.3–3m) or more, ↔ 3–10ft (1–3m). E. Australia. ❅ (min. 41°F/5°C)

BALLOTA

LAMIACEAE

Genus of 30–35 species of clump- or mat-forming perennials and evergreen subshrubs from rocky and waste ground in the Mediterranean, Europe, and W. Asia. The leaves are opposite, toothed to scalloped, and aromatic, sometimes unpleasantly so. Whorls of 2-lipped flowers, often with prominent, saucer- or funnel-shaped calyces, are produced from the leaf axils of terminal shoots. Grow in a sunny border.

• **CULTIVATION** Grow in poor, dry, well-drained soil in full sun. Cut back subshrubs in spring to keep compact.

• **PROPAGATION** Divide perennials in spring. For subshrubs, root softwood

Ballota 'All Hallows Green'

Ballota pseudodictamnus

cuttings in late spring or early summer, or semi-ripe cuttings in early summer.
• **PESTS AND DISEASES** Infrequent.

B. acetabulosa. Compact, bushy, evergreen subshrub with upright, white-woolly shoots and heart-shaped, round-toothed, gray-green leaves, to 2in (5cm) long. Small, 2-lipped, white-marked, purple-pink flowers, to ¾in (2cm) long, with open funnel-shaped green calyces, to ¾in (2cm) across, are produced in mid- and late summer. ↕ 24in (60cm), ↔ 30in (75cm). S.E. Greece, Crete, W. Turkey. Zone 8.
***B.* 'All Hallows Green'** ▣ Bushy, evergreen subshrub with heart-shaped, woolly, lime-green leaves, to 2in (5cm) long. Small, 2-lipped, pale green flowers with open funnel-shaped calyces, to ¾in (2cm) across, are produced in mid- and late summer. ↕ 24in (60cm), ↔ 30in (75cm). Zone 8.
B. nigra (Black Horehound). Hairy perennial with ovate leaves, 1–2in (2.5–5cm) long, that exude an unpleasant smell if handled. Bears tubular, white or lilac-pink flowers, ½in (1.5cm) long, from early summer to early autumn. ↕ 4ft (1.2m), ↔ 10in (25cm). Europe, N. Africa. Zone 8. **'Archer's Variety'**, syn. 'Variegata', has leaves spotted and streaked white, and purple flowers.
B. pseudodictamnus ▣ Mound-forming, evergreen subshrub with ovate, yellowish gray-green leaves, to 1¼in (3cm) long, on sparsely branched, erect, woody-based, white-woolly stems. Tubular, 2-lipped, white or pinkish white flowers, ½in (1.5cm) long, with pale green calyces, ¾in (2cm) wide, are borne in late spring and early summer. ↕ 18in (45cm), ↔ 24in (60cm). Greece, Crete, W. Turkey. Zone 8.

▷ ***Balsamita*** see *Tanacetum*

BALSAMORHIZA

Balsam root

ASTERACEAE

Genus of 10–14 species of perennials with fleshy, balsam-scented roots, from gravelly banks and cliffs in W. North America. Erect stems bear opposite, simple or pinnate leaves, mainly in basal rosettes, and solitary yellow flowerheads. Grow in a border or rock garden.
• **CULTIVATION** Grow in well-drained, moderately fertile soil in full sun. Liable to die back in wet winters.
• **PROPAGATION** Sow seed in a cold frame in autumn. Divide in spring.
• **PESTS AND DISEASES** Prone to rust.

B. sagittata. Clump-forming perennial with simple, heart- to arrow-shaped, entire, very white-hairy leaves, 6–20in (15–50cm) long, later almost hairless, with conspicuous midribs and long leaf stalks. Flowerheads, 3–4in (8–10cm) across, with yellow disk and ray florets, and white-woolly involucres, are borne in late spring and early summer. ↕ 10–24in (25–60cm), ↔ 12in (30cm). Canada, N.W. US. Zone 7b.

BAMBUSA

Bamboo

POACEAE

Genus of 100–120 species of clump-forming, evergreen bamboos, occurring in forest and woodland in tropical and subtropical Africa, Asia, and Central and South America. Smooth, usually hollow culms produce slender branches at each node, bearing linear-lance-shaped leaves. They are cultivated for their foliage and, in some species, such as *B. ventricosa*, for their unusual, swollen internodes. Where not hardy, grow in a temperate green-house or conservatory. In frost-free climates, *B. multiplex* is useful as a hedge or windbreak.
• **CULTIVATION** Under glass, grow in soilless potting mix in bright indirect light. Maintain high humidity, and water moderately. To produce the swollen internodes, confine *B. ventricosa* and its allies to 5–7in (13–18cm) containers; water and fertilize sparingly.

Bambusa multiplex 'Alphonse Karr'

Outdoors, grow in moist, fertile, humus-rich soil, in a sheltered site in full sun or partial shade.
• **PROPAGATION** Divide in spring.
• **PESTS AND DISEASES** Newly emerging shoots are susceptible to slugs. Fungal leaf spot, rust, and dieback may occur.

B. glaucescens see *B. multiplex.*
B. multiplex, syn. *B. glaucescens* (Hedge bamboo). Variable bamboo with slender, arching, yellow or striped culms, and up to 20 crowded, paired, linear-lance-shaped, mid-green leaves, to 6in (15cm) long, silvery beneath. ↕ 10–50ft (3–15m) much smaller in containers, ↔ indefinite. China. Zone 7b. **'Alphonse Karr'** ▣ has upright, yellow culms with bright green stripes and smooth leaves, green-blue beneath. **'Fernleaf'**, syn. 'Wang Tsai', has fern-like whorls of about 20 leaves, 1–1¾in (2.5–4.5cm) long.
B. oldhamii (Giant timber bamboo). Vigorous, spreading bamboo with upright, soft green culms and wide green leaves, to 10in (25cm) long, on short branches. Prefers full sun. ↕ 55ft (17m). ↔ indefinite. China. ❄ (min. 35°F/-2°C)
B. ventricosa (Buddha's belly bamboo). Very vigorous bamboo with strong culms bearing whorls of 10–20 linear-lance-shaped, dark green leaves, to 5in (13cm) long. The internodes swell decoratively under poor growing conditions or if potbound. ↕ 15–80ft (5–25m) outdoors, 8ft (2.5m) or more in containers, ↔ indefinite. S. China. ❄ (min. 41°F/5°C)
B. vulgaris (Common bamboo). Vigorous, clump-forming bamboo with upright, smooth, soft green culms and linear-lance-shaped leaves, to 8in (20cm) long. ↕ 50ft (15m), ↔ indefinite. China. ❄ (min. 41°F/5°C). **'Vittata'** has yellow culms with green stripes and soft green leaves with some variegation.

BANKSIA

PROTEACEAE

Genus of about 70 species of evergreen trees and shrubs, occurring in temperate to tropical scrub and forest, mainly in Australia, with one in New Guinea. They are cultivated for their foliage and flowers. Alternate or whorled, linear to ovate or pinnate, leathery leaves are often boldly lobed or toothed. Cone-like flowerheads of crowded, slender florets are followed by woody fruit. Where not hardy, grow in a cool greenhouse. In frost-free areas, grow in a border or as specimen plants.
• **CULTIVATION** Under glass, grow in equal parts soil-based potting mix, grit, and peat (or peat substitute) in full light and with good ventilation. In the growing season, water moderately and apply a half-strength, phosphate-free liquid fertilizer monthly; water sparingly in winter. Pot on or top-dress in spring. Outdoors, grow in well-drained, neutral to acidic soil, low in phosphates and nitrates, in full sun. Many will survive short spells around 32°F (0°C). Pruning group 1 or 8.
• **PROPAGATION** Sow seed singly in small containers at 64°F (18°C) in spring. Root semi-ripe cuttings of smooth-leaved species in summer.
• **PESTS AND DISEASES** Outdoors, *Phytophthora* root rot may be fatal; plants may become chlorotic if soil is excessively alkaline or contains too much phosphorus.

B. attenuata (Slender banksia). Spreading shrub or tree with broadly linear to linear-lance-shaped, toothed, mid-green leaves, 3–5½in (8–14cm) long, hairy beneath. Cylindrical, greenish yellow flowerheads, to 10in (25cm) long, are borne from late spring to summer. ↕↔ 6–30ft (2–10m). Western Australia. ❄ (min. 35°F/2°C)
B. baxteri ▣ Dense to loosely spreading shrub with alternate, fan-shaped leaves, 3–7in (7–17cm) long, with acutely triangular, brownish red lobes, maturing to deep green. From summer to autumn, produces spherical, greenish yellow flowerheads, 2–3in (5–8cm) across. ↕↔ 6–12ft (2–4m). Western Australia. ❄ (min. 41°F/5°C)
B. coccinea (Scarlet banksia). Erect, sparsely branched shrub with alternate, broadly heart-shaped, oblong to inversely heart-shaped, toothed leaves, to 4in (10cm) long, deep green above, white-downy beneath. Cylindrical scarlet flowerheads, to 3in (8cm) long, are produced from spring to summer. ↕ 12–25ft (4–8m), ↔ 5–12ft (1.5–4m). Western Australia. ❄ (min. 35°F/2°C)
B. ericifolia ▣ (Heath banksia). Bushy shrub with crowded, alternate, linear, entire leaves, ¾in (2cm) long, glossy, mid- to deep green above, silvery beneath. Cylindrical, orange-yellow to orange-red or russet flowerheads, to 8in (20cm) long, are produced in autumn or winter. ↕ 10–20ft (3–6m), ↔ 6–12ft (2–4m). New South Wales. ❄ (min. 41°F/5°C)

Banksia baxteri

Banksia ericifolia

B

Banksia integrifolia (inset: flower detail)

B. integrifolia ■ (Coast banksia). Variable, vigorous, erect shrub or large tree, sparsely to moderately branched. Whorled, elliptic to obovate, entire, velvety, light brown leaves, to 4in (10cm) long, turn mid-green above, white beneath. Cylindrical, pale yellow flowerheads, to 5in (13cm) long, are borne from late summer to autumn. ↕ 15–80ft (5–25m), ↔ 10–25ft (3–8m). Queensland to Victoria. ❀ (min. 45°F/7°C)
B. menziesii (Firewood banksia, Menzies' banksia). Erect, then spreading, bushy shrub or tree with very downy young stems. Thick, alternate, narrowly oblong leaves, 6–12in (15–30cm) long, with shallow, irregular teeth and rust-red hairs, mature to semi-glossy or matte, deep or gray-green. From autumn to late spring, produces short, cylindrical to broadly ovoid flowerheads, 4–6in (10–15cm) long, varying from red aging to yellow, to pink or bronze. ↕ 15–50ft (5–15m), ↔ 15–30ft (5–10m). Western Australia. ❀ (min. 37–41°F/3–5°C)
B. serrata ■ (Saw banksia). Erect then spreading shrub or tree with alternate, narrowly obovate to oblong, toothed leaves, 3–6in (8–15cm) long, downy and light red or reddish brown at first, then leathery, smooth, and semi-glossy, deep green. Cylindrical, greenish yellow to creamy gray flowerheads, 3½–6in (9–15cm) long, are produced from summer to late autumn. ↕ 10–70ft (3–20m), ↔ 6–25ft (2–8m). New South Wales, Victoria. ❀ (min. 45°F/7°C)

Banksia serrata

BAPTISIA

False indigo, Wild indigo

FABACEAE

Genus of 20 or more species of erect or spreading perennials occurring in poor, gravelly soils in dry woodland and grassland in E. and S. US, with a few in river valleys. They have alternate, fully divided, 3-palmate leaves and tall, branched stems bearing terminal or axillary racemes of pea-like flowers. The flowers are followed by large, often inflated pods. Grow in an informal border, open, hillside site, wild garden, or on a dry, sunny bank.
• **CULTIVATION** Grow in open, porous, preferably sandy soil in full sun. Deadhead after flowering.
• **PROPAGATION** Sow seed in containers in a cold frame as soon as ripe. Divide in early spring.

Baptisia australis

• **PESTS AND DISEASES** Seeds may be eaten by weevils. Fungal leaf spots, powdery mildew, and rust occur.

B. alba. Erect, bushy perennial bearing palmate leaves, consisting of 3 obovate to narrowly elliptic-lance-shaped, glaucous leaflets, 2in (2–5cm) long. In early summer, bears racemes of up to 20 white flowers, to ¾in (2cm) long, sometimes with purple-marked standard petals. ↕ 2–4ft (60–120cm), ↔ 24in (60cm). S.E. US. Zone 4.
B. australis ■ (Plains false indigo). Gently spreading to erect perennial with glaucous stems and palmate, mid- to deep green leaves, each with 3 ovate to inversely lance-shaped leaflets, to 1½in (4cm) long. In early summer, bears many-flowered racemes of dark blue flowers, to 1¼in (3cm) long, often flecked white or cream, followed by black seed pods. Useful in flower arrangements. ↕ 5ft (1.5m), ↔ 24in (60cm). E. US. Zone 3b.
B. lactea (White false indigo). Herbaceous perennial with hairless, often glaucous, purple-tinged stems, and palmate, mid-green leaves, divided into 3 elliptic-obovate leaflets, to 3in (8cm) long. In early summer, produces terminal, many-flowered racemes of creamy white flowers, to 1in (2.5cm) across, followed by pendent, pea-like, olive-green, seed pods that turn black. ↕ to 36in (90cm), ↔ to 24in (60in). E. US. Zone 5.
B. pendula ■ Erect, bushy perennial with purple-blue-tinted, gray-green stems and palmate, blue-gray leaves, each with 3 ovate leaflets, 1½–3in (4–8cm) long. In late spring, produces erect, terminal racemes of many white flowers, to 1in (2.5cm) across, followed by pendent, black seed pods. Useful in the back of a border as a contrast to shorter, spring-blooming perennials. ↕ to 3½ft (1.1m), ↔ 30in (75cm). E. North America. Zone 5b.
B. perfoliata. Erect perennial with hairless, glaucous, densely branched stems and simple, perfoliate, gray-green leaves, to 3in (8cm) long. Bears axillary, solitary, bright yellow flowers, to ½in (1.5cm) across, in summer. ↕ to 12in (30cm), ↔ 4ft (1.2m). South Carolina to Florida. Zone 5b.

▷ ***Barbacenia elegans*** see *Vellozia elegans*

BARBAREA

St. Barbara's herb

BRASSICACEAE

Genus of about 12 species of biennials and perennials found in damp habitats in fertile, slightly acidic to moderately alkaline soils, in temperate regions of the N. hemisphere. They have basal rosettes of entire or pinnatisect, radical leaves and clasping stem leaves, and produce terminal racemes of cross-shaped, 4-petaled yellow flowers. A few are used as salad plants, and the double-flowered and variegated cultivars of *B. vulgaris* may be grown as ornamental plants at the front of a border. A few have become weedy in some areas.
• **CULTIVATION** Grow in any moist but well-drained soil in full sun or partial shade.
• **PROPAGATION** Sow seed of biennials *in situ* as soon as ripe. Divide perennials in spring, or root softwood or semi-ripe cuttings in early summer. *B. vulgaris* 'Variegata' breeds almost true from seed; discard green-leaved plants.
• **PESTS AND DISEASES** Flea beetles feed on leaves. White rust, downy mildew, and *Ramularia* leaf spot occur.

***B. vulgaris* 'Variegata'** (Variegated winter cress). Rosette-forming biennial or short-lived perennial with 4- to 10-lobed basal leaves and simple stem leaves, both 2–5in (5–13cm) long, and mid- to deep green, variably splashed yellow. Cross-shaped yellow flowers are produced in racemes from early spring to early summer. Remove flowers unless seed is required. ↕ 10–18in (25–45cm), ↔ to 8in (20cm). Zone 5.

Baptisia pendula

BARKERIA

ORCHIDACEAE

Genus of about 10 species of deciduous, epiphytic orchids growing in altitudes of 6,200–8,000ft (1,900–2,500m) in Central America. They produce stem-like, cylindrical or spindle-shaped pseudobulbs, with alternate, broadly linear to broadly ovate, slightly fleshy leaves and copious aerial roots. Flowers are borne in narrowly pyramidal or cylindrical, terminal racemes, rarely panicles, in early summer.

• **CULTIVATION** Cool-growing orchids. They require perfect drainage: grow in epiphytic orchid potting mix in a slatted basket or pot. Good under lights. In summer, provide moist, shady conditions, water freely, applying half-strength fertilizer at every third watering, and mist once or twice a day. Admit full light and keep dry in winter. See also p.46.

• **PROPAGATION** Divide when the plant fills the pot and flows over the sides.

• **PESTS AND DISEASES** Prone to spider mites, aphids, and mealybugs.

B. lindleyana. Epiphytic orchid with cylindrical pseudobulbs and linear-lance-shaped to oblong-lance-shaped, gray-green leaves, 6in (15cm) long, with sharp-pointed tips. Bears white, lilac, or deep purple flowers, 2½–3in (6–8cm) across, in loose terminal racemes in winter. ↕ to 36in (90cm), generally shorter, ↔ 6in (15cm). Mexico to Costa Rica. ❀ (min. 52–55°F/11–13°C; max. 86°F/30°C)

B. skinneri. Epiphytic orchid with cylindrical pseudobulbs and elliptic to elliptic-lance-shaped, long, sharp-pointed, pale green leaves, 6in (15cm) long. Bears rich magenta to lilac flowers with yellow keels, 1½in (4cm) across, in terminal racemes or panicles, in winter. ↕ 20in (50cm), ↔ 6in (15cm). Guatemala. ❀ (min. 52–55°F/11–13°C; max. 86°F/30°C)

BARLERIA

ACANTHACEAE

Genus of about 250 species of evergreen perennials and shrubs occurring in scrub and forest in tropical and subtropical Africa and Asia, grown mainly for their spikes of tubular, 2-lipped flowers, which frequently have spiny bracts. The leaves are oblong, elliptic, or lance-shaped and are borne in opposite pairs. Where not hardy, grow in a temperate greenhouse. In frost-free areas, grow in a border or against a warm, sunny wall.

• **CULTIVATION** Under glass, grow in soil-based potting mix with additional well-rotted compost, in full light, but shaded from the hottest sunlight. When in growth, water freely and apply a balanced liquid fertilizer monthly; water sparingly in winter. Pot on or top-dress in spring. Outdoors, grow in fertile, moist but well-drained soil in a sunny site. Pruning group 2.

• **PROPAGATION** Sow seed at 61°F (16°C) in spring. Root softwood or semi-ripe cuttings from non-flowering shoots in summer, with bottom heat.

• **PESTS AND DISEASES** Aphids, spider mites, whiteflies, bacterial leaf spots, fungal spots, and stem galls are problems.

Barleria cristata

B. cristata ■ (Philippine violet). Erect to spreading, bushy, bristly-hairy shrub with oblong-elliptic, mid- to deep green leaves, to 4in (10cm) long. Bears small, stalkless, axillary spikes of light violet-blue, pink, or white flowers in summer. ↕ 3–4ft (90–120cm), ↔ 18–28in (45–70cm). India, Burma. ❀ (min. 50°F/10°C)

▷ ***Bartlettina sordidum*** see *Eupatorium sordidum*

▷ ***Bartonia aurea*** see *Mentzelia lindleyi*

BASSIA

CHENOPODIACEAE

Genus of about 26 species of annuals and perennials from disturbed land in S. Europe, Asia, and North America. They are cultivated for their habit, the feathery effect created by their alternate, very narrow, usually entire leaves, and their autumn coloration. The flowers are inconspicuous. Plant in small groups in a bedding design, or to make a temporary low screen.

• **CULTIVATION** Grow in fertile, well-drained soil in a sheltered site in full sun. Trim untidy plants in summer. May become weedy in warmer climates.

• **PROPAGATION** Surface-sow seed at 61°F (16°C) in early or midspring, or sow *in situ* in late spring.

• **PESTS AND DISEASES** Infrequent.

B. scoparia* f. *trichophylla, syn. *Kochia trichophylla* (Burning bush, Summer cypress). Fast-growing, bushy, cone-shaped annual with close-set, narrowly lance-shaped to oblong, light green leaves, 2–3in (5–8cm) long, turning bright red or purple in late summer or autumn. ↕ 1–5ft (0.3–1.5m), ↔ 12–18in (30–45cm). Asia, North America. Variegated and more compact selections are also available.

BAUERA

CUNONIACEAE

Genus of 3 species of evergreen shrubs occurring in light woodland in E. Australia. They are erect or prostrate, with slender, sometimes hairy branches bearing opposite, fully divided, 3-palmate, mid- or deep green leaves. Baueras are cultivated for their small, bowl-shaped, 4- to 10-petaled flowers, which are produced singly from the upper leaf axils. Where not hardy, grow in a cool greenhouse. In frost-free climates, they make a good groundcover around shrubs and beneath trees.

• **CULTIVATION** Under glass, grow in a mix of equal parts loam, leaf mold, and sharp sand, in full light with shade from hot sun. During the growing season, water moderately and apply a balanced liquid fertilizer monthly. Water sparingly in winter. Pot on or top-dress in late winter. Outdoors, grow in humus-rich, neutral to acidic soil in partial shade. Pruning group 8.

• **PROPAGATION** Sow seed at 68–75°F (20–24°C) in spring. Root semi-ripe cuttings in late summer. Layer in spring.

• **PESTS AND DISEASES** Infrequent.

B. rubioides. Mat-forming to low, spreading, bushy, evergreen shrub bearing glossy, 3-palmate, deep green leaves, to 1½in (4cm) long, consisting of oblong to lance-shaped, often toothed leaflets. Solitary, bowl-shaped pink or white flowers, to ¾in (2cm) across, are produced on long flower stalks from the upper leaf axils, mainly from spring to summer. ↕ ½–10ft (0.15–3m), ↔ 2–10ft (0.6–3m). Queensland to Tasmania. ❀ (min. 37–41°F/3–5°C)

BAUHINIA

FABACEAE

Genus of at least 250 species of evergreen or deciduous trees, shrubs, and perennial climbers from damp to dry forest and grassland in tropical and subtropical regions, grown mainly for their orchid-like flowers with 5 irregular petals. Leaves are alternate, simple, and often 2-lobed. Where not hardy, grow in a warm greenhouse; elsewhere, use as specimen plants or in a border.

• **CULTIVATION** Under glass, grow in soil-based potting mix in full light. When in full growth, water freely and apply a balanced liquid fertilizer monthly; reduce water in winter. Pot on or top-dress in late winter. Outdoors, grow in fertile, moist but well-drained soil in full sun. Water freely during drought. Pruning group 12 for climbers; pruning group 1 (or 13 if wall-grown) for trees and shrubs.

• **PROPAGATION** Sow seed at 61°F (16°C) in spring. Root semi-ripe cuttings in summer with bottom heat. Layer in spring.

• **PESTS AND DISEASES** Spider mites, whiteflies, aphids, mealybugs, fungal leaf spots, stem galls, and root rots occur.

Bauhinia galpinii

Bauhinia variegata

B. corymbosa (Phanera). Evergreen, tendril climber with rust-red-hairy young shoots. Leaves, to 1½in (4cm) long, are rounded with heart-shaped bases and deeply 2-lobed tips, mid-green above, pale green beneath. In summer, produces dense, terminal racemes of fragrant white or pink flowers, 1¼in (3cm) across. ↕ 12ft (4m) or more. S. China. ❀ (min. 45°F/7°C)

B. galpinii ■ syn. *B. punctata*. Spreading or semi-climbing, evergreen shrub with oval, notched or 2-lobed, light green leaves, 2in (5cm) long. Produces orange or red flowers, to 3in (8cm) across, in short, axillary racemes from spring to autumn. ↕ 6–10ft (2–3m), ↔ 3–10ft (1–3m). South Africa. ❀ (min. 45°F/7°C)

B. punctata see *B. galpinii*.

B. variegata ■ (Mountain ebony, Orchid tree). Spreading, deciduous tree bearing rounded, rich green leaves, 4–8in (10–20cm) long, with heart-shaped bases and deeply 2-lobed tips. From winter to summer, produces short, terminal racemes of light magenta to purple-blue flowers, 3–5in (8–13cm) across, sometimes white-variegated. ↕ 25–40ft (8–12m), ↔ 10–25ft (3–8m). E. Asia. ❀ (min. 45°F/7°C). **'Candida'** bears pure white flowers, occasionally suffused green.

BEAUCARNEA

AGAVACEAE

Genus of about 24 species of evergreen shrubs and trees found in semi-desert and scrub from S. US to Guatemala. Most have unbranched, palm-like stems with an expanded base, and a terminal tuft of strap-shaped, leathery leaves. They bear 6-tepaled flowers in terminal panicles. Where not hardy, grow in a temperate greenhouse. In frost-free, dry climates, grow as specimen plants.

• **CULTIVATION** Under glass, grow in soil-based potting mix in full light. Water moderately in growth, sparingly in winter. Top-dress or pot on in spring. Outdoors, grow in moderately fertile, sharply drained soil in full sun.

• **PROPAGATION** Sow seed at 64–70°F (18–21°C) or root offsets in spring.

• **PESTS AND DISEASES** Spider mites and scale insects are problems under glass and indoors. Sensitive to a number of fungal spots and stem rots as well as bacterial leaf streak and bacterial soft rot.

Beaucarnea recurvata

B. recurvata ▣ syn. *Nolina recurvata, N. tuberculata* (Ponytail palm). Evergreen tree with a flaring to flask-shaped base; the trunk branches sparingly with age. Rosetted, mid- to deep green leaves, to 6ft (1.8m) long, are channeled and recurved, and sometimes twisted. Bears tiny, mauve-tinted, creamy white flowers, in panicles 3ft (1m) long, in summer. Makes a handsome large houseplant. ↕ 12–25ft (4–8m), ↔ 6–12ft (2–4m). S.E. Mexico. ❀ (min. 45°F/7°C)

BEAUFORTIA

MYRTACEAE

Genus of 18 species of evergreen shrubs occurring mainly on poor soils in scrub and forest in warm-temperate areas of Australia. They are cultivated for their terminal, brush-like heads of numerous small flowers. Leaves are small, simple, and borne in opposite pairs, in most species tightly packed and overlapping. Where not hardy, grow beaufortias in a cool greenhouse. In frost-free climates, plant in a border; they may also be used as low windbreaks.

• **CULTIVATION** Under glass, grow in a mix of equal parts loam, peat, and sand in full light. Water freely during the growing season, sparingly in winter. Pot on or top-dress in early spring, and apply a half-strength, balanced liquid fertilizer monthly from spring to autumn. Outdoors, grow in poor, well-drained, neutral to acidic soil in full sun. Pruning group 9.

• **PROPAGATION** Surface-sow seed at 55–61°F (13–16°C) in spring. Root semi-ripe cuttings in summer.

Beaufortia sparsa

• **PESTS AND DISEASES** Prone to chlorosis and dieback in phosphate-rich soil.

B. sparsa ▣ (Swamp bottlebrush). Erect to spreading, evergreen shrub with upright to recurved, oval, mid- to deep green leaves, ½in (1.5cm) long. Bright orange-red flowerheads, 2–3in (5–8cm) long, are produced from summer to autumn. ↕ 6–10ft (2–3m), ↔ 3–6ft (1–2m). Western Australia. ❀ (min. 41°F/5°C)

BEAUMONTIA

APOCYNACEAE

Genus of 9 species of evergreen climbers occurring in temperate and tropical forest and scrub in China and from India to Vietnam. They are cultivated for their foliage and attractive, scented flowers. The leaves are opposite, entire, and usually oblong-ovate to ovate. The large, trumpet-shaped or bell-shaped flowers are produced in terminal or axillary corymbs, from late spring to summer. Where not hardy, grow in a temperate or warm greenhouse. In frost-free regions, train them over a pergola, against a house wall, or through a tree.

• **CULTIVATION** Under glass, grow in soil-based potting mix in full light. When in growth, water freely and apply a balanced liquid fertilizer monthly; water sparingly in winter. Top-dress in spring. Keep warm and humid in summer, but cool in winter, with night temperatures down to 45°F (7°C) to initiate flower-bud formation. Outdoors, grow in moist, fertile, humus-rich soil in full sun. Prune after flowering; pruning group 11 or 12.

• **PROPAGATION** Sow seed at 61°F (16°C) in spring. Root semi-ripe cuttings, preferably with a heel, in a propagating case with bottom heat in late summer. Layer in autumn or spring.

• **PESTS AND DISEASES** Spider mites may be a problem under glass.

B. grandiflora ▣ (Herald's trumpet, Nepal trumpet flower). Vigorous, evergreen, twining climber with broadly oblong-ovate, downy, reddish brown leaves, 4–10in (10–25cm) long, maturing to glossy, deep green. Trumpet-shaped, fragrant white flowers, 3–5in (8–13cm) long, with green bases, are borne in corymbs from late spring to summer. ↕ 15–50ft (5–15m). India to Vietnam. ❀ (min. 41°F/5°C), although it may survive down to 32°F (0°C).

Beaumontia grandiflora

BEGONIA

BEGONIACEAE

Genus of about 1,300 species and numerous cultivars of more or less fleshy annuals, herbaceous perennials, shrubs, and climbers, including some succulents and epiphytes. They are widespread in tropical and subtropical regions, between approximately 15°N. and 15°S. of the equator. Begonias are fibrous-rooted, rhizomatous, or tuberous, the tubers becoming dormant in winter. Variable in habit, some are grown for their colorful flowers and others for their decorative, alternate, usually asymmetric, simple to compound leaves. Most begonias have flowers of both sexes on the same plant, although not necessarily at the same time. A few are dioecious. Where not hardy, grow begonias as houseplants or in a greenhouse; the Semperflorens and Tuberhybrida groups may be used for summer bedding. Most begonias are suitable for permanent outdoor cultivation only in relatively humid, tropical or subtropical regions.

• **CULTIVATION** Under glass, grow all begonias in a light, well-drained, neutral to slightly acidic, peat- or soil-based potting mix, in bright light, but with shade from direct sun. Water moderately when in growth, reduce water in winter, and always avoid wet or waterlogged soil. Feed with a balanced liquid fertilizer at alternate waterings when in full growth. Winter-flowering begonias with many rhizomes will benefit from a low- or no-nitrogen, high-phosphorus fertilizer. Repot annually in spring. For optimum growth, maintain at 66–73°F (19–23°C), with moderate humidity. Most will survive short periods at or just below 50°F (10°C), especially in a dry soil mix, but all growth will cease and many will shed their leaves. Succulent begonias require a more porous medium, higher light levels, and drier conditions. The smallest begonias, including *B. imperialis, B. prismatocarpa,* and *B. pustulata,* thrive in the high humidity and diffused light of a terrarium. Many begonias, especially rex-cultorum hybrids and other smaller and shorter kinds, grow very well indoors under fluorescent lights. Place begonias near the center of a bank of tubes, 6–10in (15–25cm) below the tubes.

Rex-cultorum hybrids will have the most radiant foliage when grown under lights, and they appreciate the additional warmth that the lights generate. Set the plants on a pebble tray to provide extra humidity, especially thin- and velvety-leaved cultivars.

Outdoors, grow begonias in fertile, well-drained, humus-rich, neutral to slightly acidic soil in partial shade, or in good light, but out of direct sun. Some cane-stemmed begonias appreciate higher light levels. Further cultivation details may be found under the groups that follow.

• **PROPAGATION** Sow seed of species as soon as ripe, and seed of Tuberhybrida and Semperflorens hybrids in early spring. Root stem, tip, or leaf cuttings in spring or summer in a propagating case, in light shade. Take rhizome cuttings in summer. Take basal cuttings from tuberous begonias in spring, or from winter-flowering types in early summer. Surface sow bulbils onto damp peat in spring. For further information, see the individual groups.

• **PESTS AND DISEASES** Vulnerable to mealybugs, mites, thrips, whiteflies, powdery mildew, stem rot, rhizome rot, and nematode invasion.

For ease of reference, begonias are divided into 7 informal groupings, based broadly on their growth habit and slightly differing cultivation needs:

Cane-stemmed begonias
Woody, fibrous-rooted, usually upright, evergreen perennials, with many species from Brazil. They have slender, bamboo-like stems, with regularly spaced, swollen nodes, and broad, asymmetrical, often deeply toothed to lobed leaves. Showy flowers are borne in terminal or axillary cymes, 4–8in (10–20cm) across, in early spring and summer. These begonias are grown for their habit, foliage, and flowers. Few tolerate continuous, direct sunlight. They tend to shed their lower leaves, especially if overwatered. To keep clothed to the base, cut back over-long canes to 2 or 3 buds in spring or early summer. Propagate by division or tip or stem cuttings.

Rex-cultorum begonias
Mainly evergreen, usually rhizomatous perennials of variable habit, derived from crosses with *B. rex* and related species. Some involve crosses with tuberous begonias, and are not truly rhizomatous, showing a tendency to winter dormancy. The brilliantly colored, obliquely ovate to ovate-lance-shaped leaves sometimes have spirally arranged basal lobes. Single, relatively inconspicuous flowers, ½–1in (1.5–2.5cm) across, are borne in early spring. These begonias are grown for their foliage. They need bright, indirect light, and an optimum of 70–75°F (21–24°C). Bright light deepens red leaf coloration, and lower light enhances the metallic sheen of many cultivars. To minimize risk of rhizome rot, water by immersion of the pots, and drain thoroughly. Remove the small, single flowers as they appear. Propagate by ripe seed, or by rhizome or leaf cuttings.

Rhizomatous begonias
Variable, mostly evergreen perennials with creeping, erect, or subsurface rhizomes, and small, single flowers, borne solitary or in large cymes, on 6–12in (15–30cm) flower stalks, in winter or early spring. Leaves, 1–12in (2.5–30cm) long, sometimes have spiralled basal lobes, and may be smooth, crested, or puckered, in shades of green or brown, often marked with silver. Hybrids derived from *B. bowerae,* the "eyelash begonias," have colored leaves with prominently fringe-haired margins, and those derived from *B. imperialis* have unusual leaf surfaces and colors. Rhizomatous begonias are grown for their foliage and flowers. They need bright, filtered light with shade in summer, and an optimum range of 58–72°F (14–22°C). To minimize risk of rhizome rot, water by immersion of the pots, and drain thoroughly. Some grow actively throughout the year; if so, continue watering moderately. Propagate by seed, or leaf or rhizome cuttings.

Semperflorens begonias
Bushy, usually compact, fibrous-rooted, evergreen hybrids, derived from *B. cucullata* var. *hookeri*, *B. schmidtiana*, and other species, with freely branching, soft, succulent stems and generally rounded, bronze or green leaves, 1¼–4in (3–10cm) long. Cymes of rounded, single or double flowers, ½–1in (1–2.5cm) across, are produced throughout summer. Semperflorens begonias are grown for their leaves and flowers. In cold climates, set out bedding plants when risk of frost has passed, planting into fertile, well-drained, humus-rich soil. They flower well in light shade to full sun; the bronze-leaved varieties are more suited to full-day sun. Keep potted plants fairly dry and well-ventilated in winter, at 50–59°F (10–15°C). In frost-free climates, treat as perennials and provide similar conditions outdoors, but lift and divide annually in spring. Propagate by seed or well-branched basal cuttings.
Shrub-like begonias
Mostly bushy, sometimes succulent, evergreen perennials with freely branching, erect, or semi-erect stems. They are grown mainly for their leaves, which are smooth to pustular with glossy or hairy surfaces. The often fragrant flowers are borne in cymes. Blooming period is highly varied: begonias in this group are seasonal, everblooming, or occasional. Under glass, maintain a winter minimum of 63°F (17°C), and provide moderate to bright winter light to enhance foliage color; hairless or glaucous species and cultivars tolerate higher light levels than those with hairy leaves; all need shade from direct summer sun. To encourage compact growth, pinch out the growing tips twice in the growing season. Propagate by seed, or by tip or stem cuttings.
Tuberous begonias (including the Tuberhybrida Group, Multiflora Group, and Pendula Group)
Mostly upright, bushy, tuberous winter-dormant perennials. The Tuberhybrida Group begonias (*B.* x *tuberhybrida*) are derived from Andean species, including *B. boliviensis*, *B. gracilis*, *B. pearcei*, and *B. veitchii*. They vary from pendent to upright, with sparsely branched, succulent stems and pointed, glossy, bright to dark green leaves. Most are summer-flowering and double-flowered. Several poorly defined groups are sometimes recognized (for example, the Multifloras, with many small, single to double flowers, and the Pendula Group with trailing or pendulous stems). Flowers are borne in cymes of 2 small female flowers and one showy, often double, male flower. They bear flowers and top growth annually from winter-dormant tubers. Tuberous begonias are grown for their flowers. Under glass, provide bright, filtered light and good ventilation. Reduce humidity when flowering, and pinch out small female flowers to prolong flowering. Treat bedding plants as for the Semperflorens Group, but lift tubers in autumn before the first hard frost, and dry off. Dust with fungicide, and store dormant tubers at 41–45°F (5–7°C). In spring, replant tubers, hollow side up, in free-draining potting soil at 61–64°F (16–18°C). Propagate by basal cuttings,

BEGONIA GROUPS

Begonias are very varied in habit. The genus includes trailing, pendent, shrub-like, upright, and climbing species. Based partly on these habits, they may be divided into 7 broad groups.

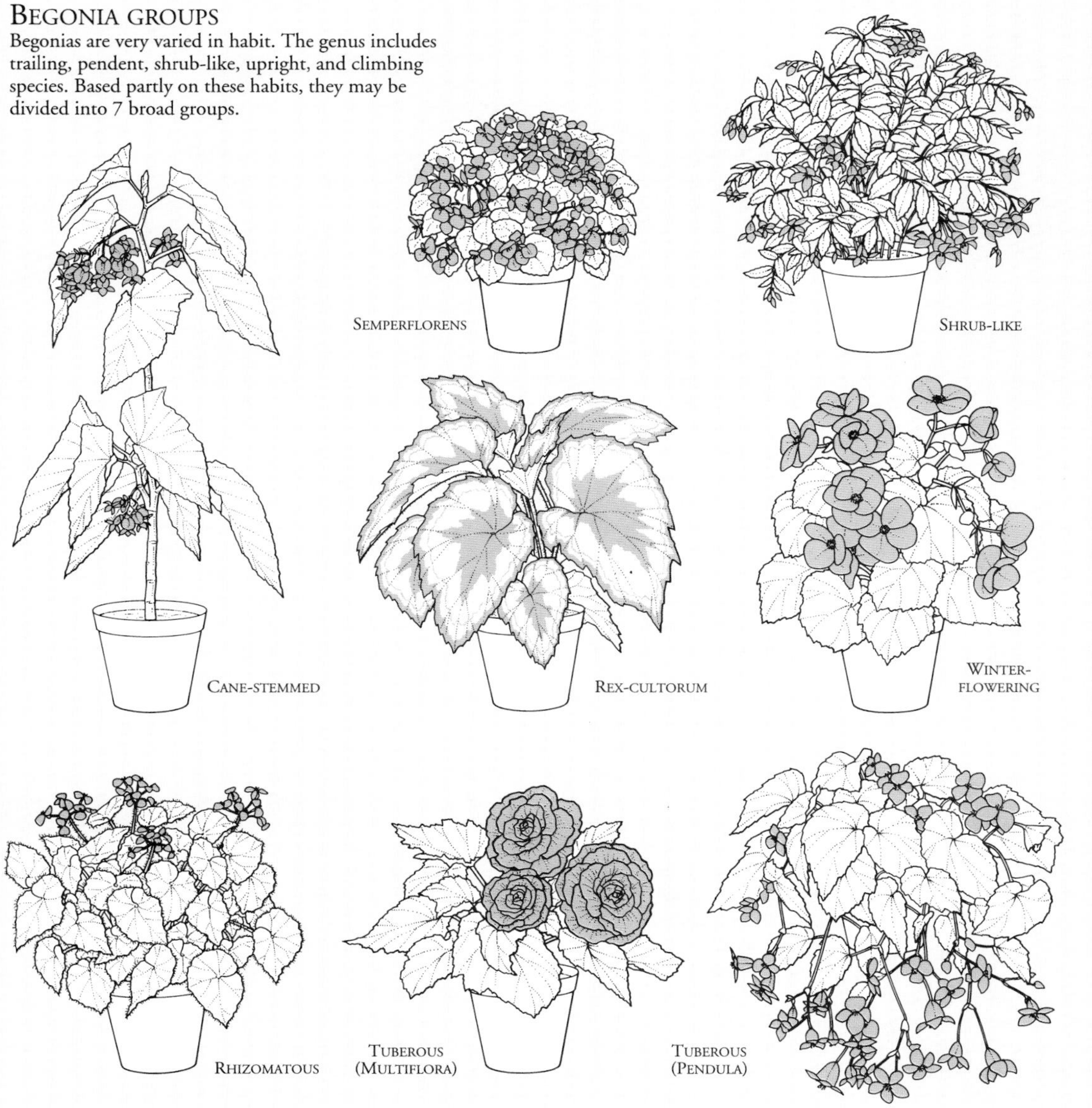

stem cuttings of side shoots, or seed. The species *B. grandis* and its varieties may be increased by bulbils produced from the upper leaf axils.
Winter-flowering begonias
Low-growing, compact, evergreen perennials, usually fibrous-rooted but sometimes swollen into tuber-like bases, with slender, succulent stems and green or bronze-flushed leaves, about 2–3in (5–8cm) long. They bear a profusion of single, semi-double, or double flowers from late autumn to early spring.
Two broad groups are recognized: *B.* x *cheimantha* (*B. socotrana* x *B. dregei*), the Lorraine, Cheimantha, or Christmas begonias, have rounded, often heart-shaped leaves, and usually single flowers. The Elatior begonias (*B.* x *hiemalis*), which include the Rieger hybrids, result from crosses between *B. socotrana* and various Tuberhybrida hybrids. All are bushy plants with asymmetric leaves and masses of single or double flowers throughout winter. They are grown primarily for their flowers. They thrive in bright, filtered light, with the maximum available light in winter; an optimum of 59–68°F (15–20°C), or a few degrees cooler for tuberous types; relatively low humidity; and good ventilation. Propagate by basal cuttings. Some are very prone to mildew; water early in the day, when possible, to allow the leaves to dry before the onset of cooler night temperatures.

B. aconitifolia, syn. *B. sceptrum* (Holly-leaf begonia). Cane-stemmed begonia with ovate, 4- to 6-palmate, dark green leaves, 8in (20cm) long, splashed with silver, with sunken red veins beneath. About 15 pendent, pale pink or white flowers, to 2in (5cm) across, are produced in cymes in autumn. ↕ 36in (1m), ↔ 12in (30cm). Brazil. ❀ (min. 50°F/10°C).
'Hildegard Schneider' has bronze-tinted leaves with red undersides and pronounced silver markings.
B. albopicta. Semi-pendent to upright, freely branching, cane-stemmed begonia. Ovate to lance-shaped, wavy-margined leaves, 3in (8cm) long, are glossy green above, covered in silver spots, and pale green beneath. Pendent, green-white flowers, to ¾in (2cm) across, are borne in cymes in summer. ↕ 24–36in (60–100cm), ↔ 12in (30cm). Brazil. ❀ (min. 50°F/10°C)
***B.* 'All Around'.** Semperflorens begonia, producing rounded, green leaves. Single flowers, ¾in (2cm) across, in a wide range of colors, are produced in summer. Excellent cultivar for a mass planting or hanging basket. ↕↔ to 16in (40cm). ❀ (min. 55–59°F/10–15°C)
***B.* 'Ambassador'.** Semperflorens begonia with rounded, rich green leaves. Bears early, single flowers in a range of colors, including scarlet, salmon, pink, rose-pink, coral-pink, or white, throughout summer. ↕↔ to 8in (20cm). ❀ (min. 55–59°F/10–15°C)
B. angularis. Many-branched, cane-stemmed begonia with somewhat angular stems in cross-section. Produces ovate, silky-sheened, gray-green leaves, 8in (20cm) long, with slightly wavy, toothed margins, silver bands highlighting the veins, purple-green beneath. White flowers, ½in (1.5cm) across, are sparsely borne in pendent cymes from late winter to early spring. ↕ 4ft (1.2m), ↔ 12in (30cm). Brazil. ❀ (min. 50°F/10°C)
***B.* 'Anniversary'.** Upright, strongly branched Tuberhybrida Group begonia, with ovate leaves, to 5in (13cm) long. Bears golden flowers, 7in (18cm) across, with many broad, overlapping, slightly serrated petals, in summer. ↕ 24in

Begonia 'Azotus'

Begonia Cocktail Series

Begonia 'Ginny'

(60cm), ↔ 18in (45cm). ❄ (min. 50°F/10°C)

***B.* 'Apricot Cascade'** ■ Pendent, Tuberhybrida Group begonia with oval, emerald-green leaves, to 8in (20cm) long. Double, pale orange flowers, 3in (8cm) across, with serrated petals, are produced from early summer to midautumn. ↕↔ 24in (60cm). ❄ (min. 50°F/10°C)

B.* x *argenteoguttata ■ (*B. albopicta* x *B. olbia*) (Trout-leaved begonia). Shrub-like begonia with slender, strongly branched stems, and obovate, toothed, dark green leaves, to 6in (15cm) long, covered with silver spots above. Cream flowers, to 1¼–1½in (3–4cm) across, are freely produced in cymes, to 2½in (6cm) across, from spring to autumn. Garden origin. ↕ 30in (75cm), ↔ 24in (60cm). ❄ (min. 50°F/10°C)

***B.* 'Azotus'** ■ Winter-flowering begonia with ovate leaves. A double cerise-pink flower, to 1½in (4cm) across, is produced from late autumn to early spring. ↕ 8in (20cm), ↔ 6in (15cm). ❄ (min. 50°F/10°C)

***B.* 'Baby Perfection'.** Small, rhizomatous begonia with a creeping rhizome and small, peltate, ovate, deeply lobed, chartreuse-green leaves, ½in (1.5cm) across, margined with black. Light pink flowers, ¼in (6mm) across, are profusely borne in spring. ↕ 4in (10cm), ↔ 7in (18cm). ❄ (min. 50°F/10°C)

***B.* 'Barcos'** ■ Winter-flowering begonia with ovate, very dark green leaves. Fully double, dark crimson flowers, to 1½in (4cm) across, are produced from late autumn to early spring. ↕ 9in (23cm), ↔ 8in (20cm). ❄ (min. 50°F/10°C)

***B.* 'Bethlehem Star'** ■ Small rhizomatous begonia with ovate, entire leaves, 2in (5cm) long, almost black, with a cream star at the centers. Light pink flowers, to 1¼in (3cm) across, are freely borne in winter. ↕ 10in (25cm), ↔ 12in (30cm). ❄ (min. 50°F/10°C)

***B.* 'Billie Langdon'** ■ Upright Tuberhybrida begonia with oval, mid-green leaves, to 8in (20cm) long. Pure white flowers, 7in (18cm) across, with broad, attractively veined petals, are freely borne in summer. ↕ 24in (60cm), ↔ 18in (45cm). ❄ (min. 50°F/10°C)

***B.* 'Bokit',** syn. *B.* 'Bowkit'. Rhizomatous begonia with ovate, palmate leaves, 3in (8cm) long, striped with yellow and brown and spirally arranged on basal lobes. Pinkish white flowers, ½in (1.5cm) across, are sparsely borne in winter. ↕ 10in (25cm), ↔ 14in (35cm). ❄ (min. 50°F/10°C)

***B.* 'Boomer'** ■ Vigorous, shrub-like begonia with thick stems and rounded, lobed, puckered, bronze-green leaves, 6–10in (15–25cm) across, with pale green veins and many stiff, short hairs. Cymes of white flowers, ½in (1.5cm) across, are produced on flower stalks, 8–12in (20–30cm) long, in summer. ↕ 3–5ft (1–1.5m), ↔ 3–4ft (1–1.2m). ❄ (min. 50°F/10°C)

B. bowerae ■ (Eyelash begonia). Rhizomatous begonia with ovate, entire, light green leaves, to 1in (2.5cm) long, marked with dark brown and fringed with hairs. White flowers, ½in (1.5cm) across, are produced from winter to early spring. ↕ 10in (25cm), ↔ 7in (18cm). Mexico. ❄ (min. 50°F/10°C)

***B.* 'Bowkit'** see *B.* 'Bokit'.

***B.* 'Buttercup'** (*B. prismatocarpa* x *B. ficicola*). Creeping rhizomatous begonia with green stems covered in fine, white hairs and pustular, peltate, mid- to dark green leaves, to 2in (5cm) long. Bears yellow-orange, ever-blooming flowers, ½in (1.5cm) across. Ideal in a terrarium. ↕ 6in (15cm), ↔ indefinite. ❄ (min. 50°F/10°C)

***B.* 'Can-Can'** ■ Upright begonia from the Tuberhybrida Group, with oval, green leaves, to 8in (20cm) long. Rich yellow flowers, 7in (18cm) across, composed of serrated petals with heavy, red-picotee margins, are produced in summer. ↕ 36in (90cm), ↔ 18in (45cm). ❄ (min. 50°F/10°C)

***B.* 'Caravan',** syn. *B.* 'Serlis'. Shrub-like begonia with upright stems and peltate, soft, ovate, bronze-green leaves, 8in (20cm) long, with a slightly felted appearance and veins marked pale green. Insignificant white flowers, ½in (1.5cm) across, are produced from early spring to autumn. ↕ 18in (45cm), ↔ 8in (20cm). ❄ (min. 50°F/10°C)

***B.* 'Christmas Candy'.** Sturdy, semi-erect Semperflorens begonia with hairless, red-blushed, mid-green stems and elliptic, entire, deep green leaves, 2½–3in (6–8cm) long, with fine red edges. Bears everblooming, abundant, vivid red flowers, 2in (5cm) across, with red-and-white ovaries. Provide full light for the most intense flower color. ↕ 12–14in (30–35cm), ↔ 24in (60cm). ❄ (min. 50°F/10°C)

***B.* 'City of Ballarat'** ■ Strong-growing, upright Tuberhybrida begonia with oval, mid-green leaves, to 8in (20cm) long. In summer, produces bright orange flowers, 7in (18cm) across, with broad, slightly wavy, glaucous petals. ↕ 24in (60cm), ↔ 18in (45cm). ❄ (min. 50°F/10°C)

B. coccinea (Angelwing begonia). Cane-stemmed begonia; a parent of many hybrids. Ovate leaves, to 6in (15cm) long, are green on both sides with red margins above. Coral-red flowers, to 1¼in (3cm) across, are profusely borne in red-stalked, pendent cymes in spring. ↕ 4ft (1.2m), ↔ 12in (30cm). Brazil. ❄ (min. 50°F/10°C)

***B.* Cocktail Series** ■ Semperflorens begonias with rounded bronze leaves. Single flowers in a wide range of colors, including single colors and bicolors, are produced in summer. Sun resistant. ↕ 8–12in (20–30cm), ↔ 12in (30cm). ❄ (min. 55°F/13°C)

***B.* 'Corallina de Lucerna'** see *B.* 'Lucerna'.

B. crassicaulis. Rhizomatous begonia producing thick, brown-scaled stems, with rough, brown, spine-like hairs and deeply lobed, mid- to dark green leaves, 5–10in (13–25cm) long, which drop in autumn. In winter, bears cymes, to 9in (23cm) across, of white flowers, to 1in (2.5cm) across. ↕ 12–24in (30–60cm), ↔ 24–36in (60–90cm). Guatemala. ❄ (min. 55°F/13°C)

***B.* 'Crestabruchii'** (Lettuce-leaf begonia). Rhizomatous begonia with ovate, acute, bronze-green leaves, 8in (20cm) long, with heavily crested margins, edged in red hairs. Insignificant pink flowers, ¾in (2cm) across, are produced in late winter. ↕↔ 10in (25cm). ❄ (min. 50°F/10°C)

B. dichroa. Low-growing, somewhat pendent, cane-stemmed begonia with ovate, bright green leaves, 5in (13cm) long. Orange flowers, 1¼in (3cm) across, are borne in profusion throughout the year. Attractive in a hanging basket. ↕ 14in (35cm), ↔ 10in (25cm). Brazil. ❄ (min. 50°F/10°C)

B. disticha see *B. stipulacea.*

B. dregei ■ (Grape-leaf begonia, Maple-leaf begonia). Semi-tuberous begonia with tall, flexible stems and maple-leaf-like leaves, to 3in (8cm) long, mid-green with purple veins above, red beneath, some spotted with silver. Bears many single white flowers, to ½in (1.5cm) across, in late summer. Prone to mildew. Requires staking. Excellent as a bonsai. ↕ 30in (75cm), ↔ 24in (60cm). South Africa. ❄ (min. 50°F/10°C)

***B.* 'Duartei'** ■ Rex-cultorum begonia with spirally arranged, obovate, red-hairy, dark green leaves, 7in (18cm) long, with darker green margins and a banding of silver streaks. Pink flowers are produced in spring. ↕↔ 24in (60cm). ❄ (min. 50°F/10°C)

***B.* 'Emerald Giant'.** Rex-cultorum begonia with a creeping rhizome and ovate, vibrant green leaves, 18in (45cm) long, banded with shades of brown. Pink flowers are produced in summer. ↕↔ 30in (75cm). ❄ (min. 50°F/10°C)

***B.* 'Erythrophylla',** syn. *B.* 'Feastii' (Beefsteak begonia). Rhizomatous begonia with thick, rounded, hairless leaves, 6in (15cm) long, glossy green above and dark reddish brown beneath. Light pink flowers, to ¾in (2cm) across, are produced well above the foliage in late winter or early spring. ↕ 8in (20cm), ↔ 12in (30cm). ❄ (min. 50°F/10°C)

***B.* 'Esther Albertine'** ■ Large cane-stemmed begonia with deeply cut, silver-splashed, apple-green leaves, 8–11in (20–28cm) long. Huge cymes of everblooming, light pink flowers, 1in (2.5cm) across, are borne in profusion. ↕ to 8ft (2.5m), ↔ to 6ft (2m). ❄ (min. 50°F/10°C)

***B.* 'Feastii'** see *B.* 'Erythrophylla'.

B. foliosa ■ (Fern-leaf begonia). Shrub-like begonia with pendent stems, 18in (45cm) long, densely clothed with ovate, notched leaves, ⅜in (9mm) long. White flowers, to ½in (1.5cm) across, are produced in autumn and spring. ↕ 18in (45cm), ↔ 12in (30cm). Colombia, Venezuela. ❄ (min. 50°F/10°C)

B. fuchsioides (Fuchsia begonia). Shrub-like begonia with slender stems and oblong-ovate to sickle-shaped, toothed, shiny, mid-green leaves, 1in (2.5cm) long. Produces fuchsia-like, pink to red flowers, to 1¼in (3cm) across, in winter. ↕ 30in (75cm), ↔ 18in (45cm). Mexico. ❄ (min. 50°F/10°C)

***B.* 'Gay Star'.** Miniature rhizomatous begonia with white-haired, red-marked, green stems. Star-shaped, maroon-edged apple-green leaves, 1in (2.5cm) long, have thick white eyelashes. In mid-winter, bears apricot flowers, ⅜in (9mm) across. Ideal on a windowsill, in a terrarium, or under lights. ↕ 3in (8cm), ↔ 6in (15cm). ❄ (min. 55°F/13°C)

***B.* 'Ginny'** ■ Shrub-like begonia with white-haired, red stems and narrow, shiny, sparsely white-haired, red-veined, deep green leaves, blushed red on the undersides. Everblooming, red-hairy, pale pink flowers, 1½in (4cm) across, are borne in profusion. Immature

flowers are shocking pink, opening to 2-toned pink, with bright yellow centers. ↕ 4ft (1.2m), ↔ 30in (75cm). ❀ (min. 50°F/10°C)
B. glabra ■ Trailing begonia with glabrous, green to red, trailing stems, to 3ft (1m) long, and oval- to heart-shaped, waxy, bright green leaves, 3in (8cm) long, with the tip ends somewhat toothed. Bears profuse white flowers, ½in (1.5cm) across, from winter to spring. Excellent as a climber and groundcover. West Indies, Mexico to Ecuador. ↕ 3ft (1m), ↔ 6ft (2m). ❀ (min. 50°F/10°C)
B. glaziovii see *B. soli-mutata.*
***B.* 'Gloire de Lorraine'.** Winter-flowering begonia of the Lorraine Group, with inversely lance-shaped, shiny, bright green leaves. Bears cymes, 6in (15cm) long, of mostly male, single, clear pink flowers, 1in (2.5cm) long, in winter. ↕ 18in (45cm), ↔ 24in (60cm). ❀ (min. 50°F/10°C)
B. goegoensis (Fire-king begonia). Rhizomatous begonia with a horizontal rhizome and erect stems. Ovate-rounded, peltate, puckered, bronze-green leaves, over 6in (15cm) long, have lighter green veins. Bears pink flowers, 1in (2.5cm) across, from summer to autumn. ↕ 10in (25cm), ↔ 12in (30cm). Sumatra (Goego Island). ❀ (min. 50°F/10°C)
***B. gracilis* var. *martiana*,** syn. *B. martiana* (Hollyhock begonia). Tuberous begonia with sparsely branched stems and obliquely heart-shaped, sharp-pointed, toothed, brownish green leaves, 1½in (4cm) long. Fragrant, rose-pink or white flowers, to 2in (5cm) across, are produced over much of the summer. ↕ 30in (75cm), ↔ 14in (35cm). Mexico, Guatemala. ❀ (min. 50°F/10°C)
B. grandis* subsp. *evansiana (Hardy begonia). Bulbous begonia, classified as tuberous, with branched stems bearing

Begonia Illumination Series 'Illumination Orange'

ovate, notched, olive-green leaves, 4in (10cm) long, pale green, sometimes red, beneath. Pendent cymes of fragrant pink or white flowers, to 1¼in (3cm) across, are borne in summer. ↕ 24in (60cm), ↔ 18in (45cm). Zone 7. **var. *alba*** has pinkish white flowers.
***B.* 'Helen Lewis'** ■ Upright, rex-cultorum begonia with ovate, dark wine-red leaves, to 6in (15cm) long, margined with an isolated band of silver. Creamy white flowers with white hairs are produced in summer. ↕ 24in (60cm), ↔ 14in (35cm). ❀ (min. 50°F/10°C)
B. heracleifolia (Star-leaved begonia). Rhizomatous begonia with a short, thick rhizome and rounded, palmately 7-lobed, mid-green leaves, 6in (15cm) long. Fragrant, pinkish white flowers, 1–1½in (2.5–4cm) across, are profusely borne in cymes from spring to autumn. ↕ 18in (45cm), ↔ 14in (35cm). Mexico, Guatemala, El Salvador, Honduras. ❀ (min. 50°F/10°C). **'Sunderbruchii'** has bronze-streaked leaves with green along the veins, dark purple beneath, and pink flowers from winter to spring.
***B.* Illumination Series.** Pendulous, tuberous begonias with branched stems and slender, mid- to dark green leaves, 5in (13cm) long. Double, slightly flattened, pale pink or orange flowers, 3in (8cm) across, are borne in arching cymes in summer. Better heat resistance than many others. ↕ 10in (26cm), ↔ 20in (52cm). ❀ (min. 50°F/10°C) **'Illumination Orange'** ■ has vivid orange flowers.
B. imperialis ■ Rhizomatous begonia with ovate, toothed, light green leaves, 4in (10cm) long, with silver-green splashes along the main veins; the warty upper surfaces are covered with very fine hairs. Bears sparse white flowers, to ½in (1.5cm) across, in winter. ↕ 5in (13cm), ↔ 9in (23cm). Mexico. ❀ (min. 50°F/10°C)
B. incana see *B. peltata.*
***B.* 'Ingramii'** ■ Shrub-like begonia with erect, slender stems, pendent at the tips, and slender, ovate-lance-shaped, toothed, shiny, mid-green leaves, 3in (8cm) long. Produces dark pink flowers, to 1¼in (3cm) across, more or less continuously if grown in good light. Foliage burns if the light intensity is too high. ↕ 30in (75cm), ↔ 18in (45cm). ❀ (min. 50°F/10°C)
***B.* 'Irene Nuss'** ■ Cane-stemmed begonia with ovate-oblique, wavy-margined, palmate leaves, 8in (20cm) long, bronze above and red beneath. Dark coral-pink flowers, to 1½in (4cm) across, are freely produced in large pendent cymes throughout summer. ↕ 30in (75cm), ↔ 24in (60cm). ❀ (min. 50°F/10°C)
***B.* 'Iron Cross'** see *B. masoniana.*
***B.* 'Jill Adair'.** Very compact, shrub-like begonia with ovate-acute, slightly pleated, rich dark green leaves, 4–5in (10–13cm) long, red-tinted beneath. Small white flowers, ½in (1.5cm) across, are freely produced in cymes well above the foliage intermittently throughout the year. ↕↔ 12in (30cm). ❀ (min. 50°F/10°C)
***B.* 'Kathleen Meyer'.** Miniature cane-stemmed begonia with ovate-lance-shaped, lobed, mid-green leaves, 2in (5cm) long. Salmon-red flowers, 2–3in (5–8cm) across, are borne intermittently throughout the year. ↕ 14in (35cm), ↔ 9in (23cm). ❀ (min. 50°F/10°C)
***B.* 'Lime Swirl'.** Very compact, rhizomatous begonia with spirally arranged, deeply cut, bright green leaves, 5in (13cm) long, with wavy margins. Light pink flowers, 1–1½in (2.5–4cm) across, are freely produced in cymes, about 6in (15cm) across, in very early spring. ↕ 14in (35cm), ↔ 12in (30cm). ❀ (min. 50°F/10°C)
***B.* 'Looking Glass'.** Cane-stemmed begonia with ovate, gently wavy-margined leaves, 6in (15cm) long, shallowly lobed, especially when young; the leaves are silver-bronze above, with contrasting olive-green veins, and burgundy-red beneath. Pink flowers, to ¾in (2cm) across, are sparsely borne in early summer. ↕ 36in (90cm), ↔ 18in (45cm). ❀ (min. 50°F/10°C)
***B.* 'Love Me'.** Tuberous Cheimantha begonia, an F1 hybrid grown from seed, with obovate, mid-green leaves. Single, coral-pink flowers, ¾–1½in (2–4cm) across, are profusely borne from late autumn to early spring. ↕ 18in (45cm), ↔ 10in (25cm). ❀ (min. 50°F/10°C)
***B.* 'Lucerna',** syn. *B.* 'Corallina de Lucerna'. Vigorous, cane-stemmed begonia with ovate, olive-green leaves, 8in (20cm) long, heavily marked with silver-white spots. Huge cymes, 10in (25cm) or more across, of single, rose-pink flowers, to 1½in (4cm) across, are produced in summer. ↕ 6–7ft (2–2.2m), ↔ 14in (35cm). ❀ (min. 50°F/10°C)

Begonia 'Apricot Cascade'

Begonia x *argenteoguttata*

Begonia 'Barcos'

Begonia 'Bethlehem Star'

Begonia 'Billie Langdon'

Begonia 'Boomer'

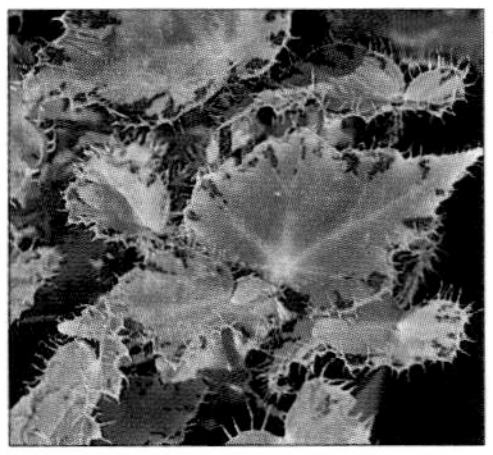
Begonia bowerae

Begonia 'Can-Can'

Begonia 'City of Ballarat'

Begonia dregei

Begonia 'Duartei'

Begonia 'Esther Albertine'

Begonia foliosa

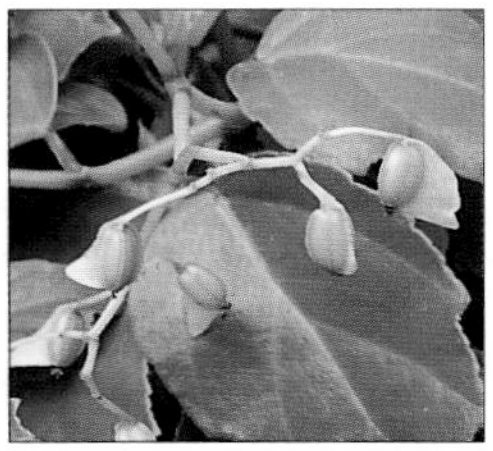
Begonia glabra

Begonia 'Helen Lewis'

Begonia imperialis

Begonia 'Ingramii'

Begonia 'Irene Nuss'

Begonia manicata

B. luxurians (Palm-leaf begonia). Shrub-like begonia with slightly hairy, compound, mid-green leaves, 10in (25cm) across, consisting of up to 16 lance-shaped leaflets, to 6in (15cm) long. They are umbrella-like, produced at the top of an erect, largely unbranched stalk, to 10in (25cm) tall. Produces cymes, 4in (10cm) across, of many slightly fragrant, yellowish white flowers, ¼in (6mm) across, in spring and summer. Difficult to grow, but magnificent. ↕ 5ft (1.5m), ↔ 3ft (1m), often much smaller as a container plant. Brazil. ❄ (min. 55°F/13°C)
***B.* 'Magic Lace'** ▣ (Grape-leaf begonia). Rhizomatous begonia with spirally arranged, ovate, copper leaves, 4in (10cm) long, splashed with silvery green. Light pink flowers, to ½in (1.5cm) across, are produced from winter to early spring. ↕ 10in (25cm), ↔ 12in (30cm). ❄ (min. 50°F/10°C)
B. manicata ▣ Upright, rhizomatous begonia, characterized by a collar of red hairs around the stalk below the leaf blade. Bears toothed, ovate to heart-shaped, shiny green leaves, 6in (15cm) long, fringed with hairs. Small cymes, to 2in (5cm) across, of pale pink flowers, to ½in (1.5cm) across, are produced well above the foliage in late winter. ↕ 24in (60cm), ↔ 14in (35cm). Mexico. ❄ (min. 50°F/10°C). **'Aurea Cristata'** see Aureomaculata Crispa'. **'Aureomaculata'** has leaves splashed with yellow. **'Aureomaculata Crispa'**, syn 'Aurea Cristata', has ruffle-edged, yellow-marbled, pale green leaves, pink in sunlight. **'Crispa',** syn. 'Cristata', has crested and fringed leaves. **'Cristata'** see 'Crispa'.
B. martiana see *B. gracilis* var. *martiana.*
B. masoniana ▣ syn. *B.* 'Iron Cross' (Iron-cross begonia). Rhizomatous begonia with long, ovate, sharp-pointed, warty, apple-green leaves, 8in (20cm) long, overlaid with a black-brown mark resembling the German Iron Cross. Cymes of green-white flowers, to ¾in (2cm) across, are freely produced in spring to summer. ↕ 20in (50cm), ↔ 18in (45cm). China. ❄ (min. 50°F/10°C)
B. mazae. Rhizomatous begonia resembling many shrub-like begonias, with very slender, spreading, pendent stems, creating a trailing effect. Ovate, sharp-pointed, bronze-green leaves, 3in (8cm) long, have pronounced red-brown markings along the veins. In early spring, bears cymes, to 4in (10cm) long, of fragrant pink flowers, to ½in (1.5cm) across. ↕ 10in (25cm), ↔ indefinite. Mexico. ❄ (min. 50°F/10°C). **f. *viridis*** (Stitched-leaf begonia) has light green leaves with a pronounced, stitch-like, dark brown mark where each vein meets the margin.
***B.* Memory Series.** Tuberous begonias with double white, yellow, pink, orange, and red flowers, 6in (15cm) across, throughout the year. ❄ (min. 50°F/10°C)
***B.* 'Merry Christmas'** ▣ syn. *B.* 'Ruhrtal'. Rex-cultorum begonia with ovate, glossy, bright red leaves, 8in (20cm) long, outlined in emerald green, with darker red centers and margins. Pale rose-pink flowers are produced from autumn to early winter. ↕ 10in (25cm), ↔ 12in (30cm). ❄ (min. 50°F/10°C)
B. metallica ▣ (Metallic-leaf begonia). Shrub-like begonia with ovate, red-hairy, dark green leaves, 7in (18cm) long, with a bright metallic sheen and sunken, dark reddish brown veins. Red-hairy, pink flowers, to 1½in (3.5cm) across, are produced in autumn. ↕ 36in (90cm), ↔ 24in (60cm). Brazil. ❄ (min. 50°F/10°C)
***B.* 'Midnight Sun'** ▣ Compact, shrub-like begonia with centrally produced, ovate leaves, 4in (10cm) long, translucent pink with green veins when young; they mature to moss-green as outer leaves. Cymes of white flowers, to ½in (1.5cm) across, are produced in summer. ↕ 12in (30cm), ↔ 18in (45cm). ❄ (min. 50°F/10°C)
***B.* 'Mini Merry'.** Miniature rex-cultorum begonia with ovate, bright red leaves, barely 3in (8cm) long, outlined in emerald-green, with darker red centers and margins. Pink flowers are borne in autumn. ↕ 5in (13cm), ↔ 6in (15cm). ❄ (min. 50°F/10°C)
***B.* 'Munchkin'** ▣ Rhizomatous begonia with ovate leaves, 5in (13cm) long, bronze with dark green veins above, red beneath, and with crested margins covered in fine white hairs. Small pink flowers, to ½–¾in (1.5–2cm) across, are produced in cymes, to 4in (10cm) across, above the foliage in early spring. ↕↔ 8in (20cm). ❄ (min. 50°F/10°C)
B. nelumbiifolia ▣ (Lily-pad begonia). Rhizomatous begonia with rounded, peltate, mid-green leaves, to 12in (30cm) long. Pinkish white flowers, to

Begonia masoniana

½in (1.5cm) across, are produced in cymes on flower stalks 24in (60cm) tall, in late winter. ↕ 18in (45cm), ↔ 24in (60cm). Mexico to Colombia. ❄ (min. 50°F/10°C).
***B.* 'Non Stop'** ▣ Upright, compact begonia from the Tuberhybrida Group, with heart-shaped, mid-green leaves, 4–6in (10–15cm) long. Solitary, double flowers, to 3in (8cm) across, in apricot, bright red, orange, pink, white, or yellow, are borne in summer. ↕↔ 12in (30cm). ❄ (min. 50°F/10°C)
***B.* 'Oliver Twist'** ▣ Rhizomatous begonia with ovate, crested, ruffled,

Begonia 'Magic Lace'

Begonia 'Merry Christmas'

Begonia metallica

Begonia 'Midnight Sun'

Begonia 'Munchkin'

Begonia nelumbiifolia

Begonia 'Non Stop'

Begonia 'Oliver Twist'

Begonia olsoniae

Begonia 'Olympia White'

Begonia 'Orange Rubra'

Begonia 'Orpha C. Fox'

Begonia 'Pin-up'

Begonia 'Potpourri'

Begonia 'Princess Hanover'

Begonia pustulata 'Argentea'

Begonia scharffii

Begonia schmidtiana

mid-green leaves, 6in (15cm) long, with brown markings along the veins. Pink flowers crown the plant from winter to spring. ↕ 18in (45cm), ↔ 10in (25cm). ❄ (min. 50°F/10°C)

B. olsoniae ▣ Compact, shrub-like begonia with ovate, blunt-based, bronze-tinted, lush green leaves, 5–8in (12–20cm) long, with prominent, creamy white veins culminating in an ivory and brownish red reverse. Pinkish white flowers, to 1¼in (3cm) across, are borne in cymes, 2in (5cm) across, well above the foliage at almost any time of year. ↕ 9in (23cm), ↔ 12in (30cm). Brazil. ❄ (min. 50°F/10°C)

***B.* 'Olympia White'** ▣ Vigorous, compact, mound-forming Semperflorens begonia with rounded, mid-green leaves. Bears single, pure white flowers, to 1½in (4cm) across, in summer. Sun and rain resistant. ↕↔ 8in (20cm). ❄ (min. 55°F/13°C)

***B.* 'Orange Cascade'.** Pendent, tuberous begonia with very freely branching stems and ovate, mid-green leaves, to 6in (15cm) long. Fully double, bright orange to apricot-orange flowers, 3in (8cm) across, are profusely borne in summer. ↕↔ 24in (60cm). ❄ (min. 50°F/10°C)

***B.* 'Orange Rubra'** ▣ Striking cane-stemmed begonia with lance-shaped, emerald-green leaves, 5in (13cm) long, sometimes faintly spotted with silver. Vivid orange flowers, ¾–1¼in (2–3cm) across, are produced in cymes at any time of year. ↕ 24in (60cm), ↔ 18in (45cm). ❄ (min. 50°F/10°C)

***B.* 'Orpha C. Fox'** ▣ Cane-stemmed begonia with ovate leaves, 6in (15cm) long, gray-green splashed with silver, and maroon beneath. Single, rose-pink flowers, to 1¼in (3cm) across, are produced throughout the year, but mainly in summer. ↕ 36in (90cm), ↔ 12in (30cm). ❄ (min. 50°F/10°C)

***B.* 'Othello'.** Rhizomatous begonia with white-hairy, red-dotted, light green stems and rounded, eyelashed, deep green-black leaves, 2–4in (5–10cm) long, with a double curl at the sinus. Bears many branches of white flowers, ½in (1.5cm) across, above the compact foliage in early spring. Grows well under lights. Allow to dry between waterings. ↕ 6–8in (15–20cm), ↔ 10–12in (25–30cm). ❄ (min. 55°F/13°C)

***B.* 'Pandora'.** Rex-cultorum begonia with spectacular, ovate, deep emerald-green leaves, 5in (13cm) long, splashed with topaz, ruby, and silver. Produces pink flowers in autumn. ↕ 10in (25cm), ↔ 9in (23cm). ❄ (min. 50°F/10°C)

B. partita. Semi-tuberous begonia with a greenish brown, silver-sheened, bulbous base and a thick, woody stem. Produces tiny, pointed, deeply 3-lobed, mid-green leaves, to 1in (2.5cm) long. White flowers, ½in (1.5cm) across, are borne from spring to autumn. ↕↔ 12–16in (30–40cm). South Africa. ❄ (min. 50°F/10°C)

***B.* Party Fun Series.** Tall-growing, well-branched, open Semperflorens begonias with large, rounded, bronze to mid-green leaves, to 5in (13cm) long. Single flowers, to 1½in (4cm) across, in a wide range of single and mixed colors, are produced in summer. ↕↔ 12in (30cm). ❄ (min. 55°F/13°C)

B. paulensis. Rhizomatous begonia with rounded, peltate, glossy, mid-green

Begonia serratipetala

leaves, 10in (25cm) long, with the surfaces between the radial veins raised and covered with cross-veins in a spider web pattern. Cymes, to 4in (10cm) across, of creamy white flowers, 1½–2in (3.5–5cm) across, with red hairs, are produced in spring. ↕↔ to 10–12in (25–30cm). ❄ (min. 55°F/13°C)

B. peltata, syn. *B. incana.* Fibrous-rooted begonia with somewhat bottle-shaped, erect, succulent stems. Peltate, fleshy, ovate, mid-green leaves, 8in (20cm) long, have small, well-spaced marginal teeth, and are densely white-hairy beneath. White or pink-flushed flowers, to 1in (2.5cm) across, are borne in pendent cymes from autumn to spring. ↕ 24in (60cm), ↔ 16in (40cm). Mexico, Guatemala. ❄ (min. 50°F/10°C)

***B.* 'Phyllomanica'** (Crazy plant). Fibrous-rooted, shrub-like begonia with thick, branched, shaggy-hairy stems and obliquely heart-shaped, toothed leaves, 6in (15cm) long, fringed with hairs, light green above, paler and with a few red hairs beneath. Pale pink flowers, to ¾in (2cm) across, are produced in cymes, 3in (8cm) across, in winter or early spring. ↕ 36in (90cm), ↔ 18in (45cm). ❄ (min. 50°F/10°C)

***B.* 'Pickobeth'.** Fairly compact, cane-stemmed begonia with ovate leaves, to 6in (15cm) long, heavily freckled with white spots, and bunched together along the stems. Rose-pink flowers, to 4in (10cm) across, are borne in cymes from winter to late spring. ↕ 30in (75cm), ↔ 14in (35cm). ❄ (min. 50°F/10°C)

***B.* 'Pin-up'** ▣ Erect, compact, tuberous begonia with ovate, mid- to dark green leaves, to 6in (15cm) long. Single flowers, 3–5in (8–13cm) across, composed of 4 white petals with dark pink picotee margins and yellow centers, are profusely borne in summer. Grows best in full or partial shade. ↕ 10in (25cm), ↔ 8in (20cm). ❄ (min. 55°F/13°C)

***B.* 'Pink Avalanche'.** Loose, cascading Semperflorens begonia with rounded,

Begonia 'Silvermist'

mid-green leaves. Sterile, single, pink flowers, to 1½in (4cm) across, are profusely and continuously produced throughout summer. Extremely heat tolerant. Suitable for sun or shade. Ideal in a hanging basket or windowbox. ↕↔ 12in (30cm). ❄ (min. 55°F/13°C)

***B.* 'Potpourri'** ▣ Trailing, pendent begonia with stems to 36in (90cm) long, and heart-shaped, vivid green leaves, 3in (8cm) long. Cascading cymes of fragrant white flowers, 1¼in (3cm) across, suffused salmon-pink toward the margins, are borne in winter. ↕↔ 12in (30cm). ❄ (min. 50°F/10°C)

***B.* 'Princess Hanover'** ▣ Rex-cultorum begonia with spirally arranged, ovate, dark green leaves, 8in (20cm) long, each with a broad band of silver-white spots. Insignificant, pale pink flowers are produced in autumn. Sport of 'Queen of Hanover'. ↕↔ 10–12in (25–30cm). ❄ (min. 50°F/10°C)

B. prismatocarpa. Rhizomatous begonia with obliquely ovate, lobed, bright green leaves, 1¼in (3cm) long. Bears small yellow flowers, ⅜in (9mm) across, throughout the year. ↕ 6–8in (15–20cm), ↔ 8–10in (20–25cm). Tropical West Africa. ❄ (min. 50°F/10°C) **'Variegation'** is neat and creeping, producing pale red stems with sparse white hairs and small, creamy white-dappled leaves, ½–1in (1.5–2.5cm) long at maturity. Requires high humidity. ❄ (min. 60°F/16°C)

B. procumbens see *B. radicans.*

B. pustulata. Rhizomatous begonia with broadly ovate, dark green, warty, basal leaves, to 6in (15cm) long, covered with tiny white hairs. Bears rose-pink flowers, to ½in (1.5cm) across, in cymes in early summer. ↕ 6–8in (15–20cm), ↔ 8–10in (20–25cm). Mexico, Guatemala. ❄ (min. 50°F/10°C) **'Argentea'** ▣ syn. *B.* 'Silver', is more common and has leaves with silvery white markings, and white flowers.

B. radicans, syn. *B. procumbens.* Trailing rhizomatous begonia with slender stems, to 18in (45cm) long, and ovate to heart-shaped, acute, shiny green leaves, 3in (8cm) across, with slightly wavy margins. Cymes, to 4in (10cm) across, of coral-red flowers, 1in (2.5cm) across, are produced in midwinter. Pinch out growing tips to encourage branching. ↕ 18in (45cm), ↔ 12in (30cm). Brazil. ❄ (min. 50°F/10°C)

***B.* 'Rajah'.** Low-growing, compact, rhizomatous begonia with broad, heart-shaped, glossy, mid-green leaves, 4in (10cm) long, with raised copper spots and red undersides. Bears small pink flowers, ¼in (6mm) across, on red stems, intermittently. Requires warmth and high humidity. ↕ 4–5in (10–13cm), ↔ 6–10in (15–25cm). Malay Peninsula. ❄ (min. 60°F/16°C)

B. rex. Rhizomatous begonia, parent of the rex-cultorum begonias, and now very rare. Ovate leaves, 8in (20cm) long, are warty, fringed with hairs, and dark green, margined with a broad band of silvery gray-green, with individual splashes of color on the leaf surface between the veins. Pink flowers, 1¼in (3cm) across, are produced in winter. ↕ 10in (25cm), ↔ 12in (30cm). N. India (Himalayas). ❄ (min. 50°F/10°C)

***B.* 'Ruhrtal'** see *B.* 'Merry Christmas'.

B. sceptrum see *B. aconitifolia.*

B. scharffii ▣ Shrub-like begonia with obovate, tapered, white-silky, olive-green leaves, 10in (25cm) long, with red undersides. Bears prolific, pink-haired, pinkish white flowers, 3in (8cm) across, in cascading cymes from winter to spring. ↕ 4ft (1.2m), ↔ 24in (60cm). Brazil. ❄ (min. 50°F/10°C)

B. schmidtiana ▣ Semperflorens begonia with stems in shades of green to red with many soft, white hairs and ovate, hairy, toothed, olive-green leaves, to 1in (2.5cm) long. White, pink-tinged flowers, ½in (1.5cm) across, are borne continuously. Excellent on an east- or west-facing windowsill, in a hanging basket, or under lights. ↕↔ 6–12in (15–30cm). Brazil. ❄ (min. 50°F/10°C)

***B.* 'Serlis'** see *B.* 'Caravan'.

B. serratipetala ▣ Shrub-like begonia bearing ovate, deeply serrated, olive-green leaves, 3in (8cm) long, with wavy margins, a slightly arched main vein, and vibrant deep pink markings. Single, rose-pink flowers, ¾–1¼in (2–3cm) across, are sparsely borne throughout the year. Water sparingly. ↕↔ 18in (45cm). New Guinea. ❄ (min. 55°F/13°C)

***B.* 'Silver'** see *B. pustulata* 'Argentea'.

***B.* 'Silvermist'** ▣ Vigorous, cane-like, Superba-type begonia with glabrous, white-marked, green stems and wavy, lobed, mid-green leaves, 12in (30cm) long, with heavy splashes of silver. Large clusters of light pink flowers, 1½in

(4cm) across, are borne intermittently all year. Requires staking. ↕ to 5ft (1.5m), with staking, ↔ to 3ft (90cm). ❄ (min. 50°F/10°C)

***B.* 'Silver Queen'** ■ Rex-cultorum begonia with ovate, mainly silver leaves, 8in (20cm) long, with metallic green centers, produced from an erect rhizome. The leaves become dull purple in bright light. Pink flowers appear in autumn. ↕ 12in (30cm), ↔ 18in (45cm). ❄ (min. 50°F/10°C)

***B.* 'Small Change'.** Dwarf rhizomatous begonia with small, frilly-edged, crested, platinum leaves, ¾in (2cm) long, edged in deep green with red undersides. White flowers, ½in (1.5cm) across, are borne in late winter. Excellent on a windowsill or under lights. ↕↔ to 4in (10cm). ❄ (min. 55°F/13°C)

B. solananthera. Trailing-scandent begonia with flattened, glabrous, mid-green stems and wavy, acute, heart-shaped, mid-green leaves, 2½in (6cm) long. Orange-scented, red-centered, white flowers, ¾in (2cm) across, are profusely borne from midwinter to spring. Ideal in a hanging basket. ↕↔ to 36in (90cm). Brazil. ❄ (min. 50°F/10°C)

B. soli-mutata ■ syn. *B. glaziovii.* Rhizomatous begonia with oblong, shiny, warty, mid-green leaves, 4in (10cm) long, red beneath. Bears white flowers, ½in (1.5cm) across, well above the foliage in spring. Leaves turn brown in full light. ↕ 30in (75cm), ↔ 24in (60cm). Brazil. ❄ (min. 45°F/7°C)

***B.* 'Sophie Cecile'.** Cane-stemmed, Superba-type begonia with ovate-acute, deeply or palmately 7– to 9- lobed, glossy green leaves, 8in (20cm) long, with slightly wavy margins and splashed with silver. Slightly fragrant pink flowers, to 2in (5cm) across, are freely produced in large cymes in spring and summer. ↕ 4½ft (1.3m), ↔ 24in (60cm). ❄ (min. 50°F/10°C)

B. stipulacea, syn. *B. disticha, B. zebrina.* Cane-stemmed begonia with slender, angular stems. Ovate, sharp-pointed, bright green leaves, 4–6in (10–15cm) long, are paler beneath, slightly toothed, and fringed with hairs. White flowers, to ½in (1.5cm) across, are freely produced throughout the year. Requires staking to remain erect. ↕ 24in (60cm), ↔ 18in (45cm). Brazil. ❄ (min. 50°F/10°C)

Begonia 'Silver Queen'

B. sutherlandii ■ Tuberous begonia with long, slender stems and ovate-lance-shaped, slightly toothed, bright green leaves, to 6in (15cm) long, often with red veins. Small orange flowers, to 1in (2.5cm) across, are freely produced in pendent sprays throughout summer. ↕ 4ft (1.2m), ↔ 18in (45cm). South Africa (KwaZulu, Natal), Tanzania. ❄ (min. 50°F/10°C)

***B.* 'Thurstonii'** ■ Shrub-like begonia bearing ovate, sharp-pointed, very glossy, green leaves, 6in (15cm) long, rich reddish brown beneath and with sunken main veins. Insignificant, single pink flowers, are sparsely produced in summer. Leaf color fades or disappears in excessive light. ↕ 6ft (2m), ↔ 18in (45cm). ❄ (min. 50°F/10°C)

Begonia soli-mutata

Begonia 'Thurstonii'

Begonia 'Tiny Bright'

Begonia venosa

Begonia 'Weltoniensis'

Begonia 'Yellow Melody'

***B.* 'Tingley Mallet'.** Cane-stemmed begonia with ovate, toothed, reddish brown leaves, to 5in (13cm) long, with somewhat puckered surfaces, brown shading, a covering of fine hairs, and, frequently, silver-pink spots. Produces dark pink flowers, to 2in (5cm) across, in cymes in early summer. ↕ 18in (45cm), ↔ 12in (30cm). ❄ (min. 50°F/10°C)

***B.* 'Tiny Bright'** ■ Dwarf rex-cultorum begonia with ovate-acute leaves, 3in (8cm) long, marked with red, green, and bronze bands. Pale pink flowers are sparsely produced from late summer to autumn. ↕ 4in (10cm), ↔ 5in (13cm). ❄ (min. 50°F/10°C)

***B.* 'Tiny Gem'.** Shrub-like, trailing begonia with narrowly ovate, wavy-edged, pointed, light green leaves, to 1½in (4cm) long. Bears continous, cascading cymes of deep pink flowers, ½in (1.5cm) across, throughout the year. Delightful in a hanging basket. ↕ 12in (30cm), ↔ 9in (23cm). ❄ (min. 50°F/10°C)

***B.* 'Tweed'.** Rex-cultorum begonia bearing ovate leaves, 5in (13cm) long, with gently wavy and slightly lobed margins. A broad silver band separates the dark green center of each leaf from a green-red marginal area, and the surface is covered with fine silver hairs. Pink flowers are sparsely produced from late summer to autumn. ↕ 9in (22cm), ↔ 10in (25cm). ❄ (min. 50°F/10°C)

B. venosa ■ Atypical shrub-like begonia, branching from the base, with thick, succulent stems covered with

Begonia sutherlandii

persistent, veined stipules, and slightly convex, kidney-shaped, fleshy, white-hairy leaves, 4–6in (10–15cm) long. Long-stalked, spicy-scented, white flowers, ½in (1.5cm) or more long, are produced in cymes, mainly from late summer to spring. ↕ 24–30in (60–90cm), ↔ 24in (60cm). Brazil. ❄ (min. 50°F/10°C)

B. versicolor (Fairy-carpet begonia). Rhizomatous begonia with ovate leaves, to 4in (10cm) long, with overlapping basal lobes, both surfaces a blend of reddish brown, apple-green, and silver, with veins marked dark maroon, and very fine red hairs. Produces small cymes of salmon-pink flowers, to ¼in (6mm) across, sparsely and intermittently throughout the year. ↕ 6in (15cm), ↔ 12in (30cm). China. ❄ (min. 64°F/18°C)

***B.* Victory Series.** Semperflorens begonias with rounded, mid-green leaves. Single flowers, to 1½in (4cm) across, are available in pink, rose-pink, scarlet, and white, or in a mix of these colors, and are borne in summer. ↕↔ to 10in (25cm). ❄ (min. 55°F/13°C)

***B.* 'Weltoniensis'** ■ (Maple-leaf begonia). Upright, semi-tuberous begonia with lance-shaped, bright green leaves, 3in (8cm) long, resembling maple leaves, with purple-red veining. Single pink flowers, to 1¼in (3cm) across, are profusely borne from early summer to midautumn. ↕ 18in (45cm), ↔ 12in (30cm). ❄ (min. 50°F/10°C)

B. williamsii see *B. wollnyi.*

B. wollnyi, syn. *B. williamsii.* Semi-tuberous begonia with thickened stems, swollen at the bases, and peltate, irregularly star-shaped, palmately 3- to 7-lobed, mid-green leaves, to 4in (10cm) long, with red veins and silver splotches. In winter, produces cymes of light green flowers, to ½in (1.5cm) across, with occasional pink streaks and deep orange anthers. May go semi-dormant in winter, dropping leaves and going into bloom. ↕ 18in (45cm), ↔ 36in (90cm). Bolivia. ❄ (min. 52°F/11°C)

***B.* 'Yellow Melody'** ■ Winter-flowering begonia of the Elatior Group, with ovate, mid-green leaves, to 6in (15cm) long. Single, primrose-yellow flowers, 2in (5cm) across, with dark orange-yellow centers, are produced from late autumn to early spring. ↕ 8in (20cm), ↔ 7in (18cm). ❄ (min. 50°F/10°C)

B. zebrina see *B. stipulacea.*

B

Belamcanda chinensis

Bellevalia pycnantha

BELAMCANDA

IRIDACEAE

Genus of 2 species of short-lived perennials with slender rhizomes, from sandy, coastal meadows and grassland in India, China, former USSR, and Japan. They have fans of sword-shaped leaves and branching stems that bear showy flowers with 6 tepals. Grow in a herbaceous border or large rock garden.

• **CULTIVATION** Grow in moist but well-drained soil that does not dry out in summer, in full sun or partial shade.

• **PROPAGATION** Sow seed in a cold frame in spring. Divide in spring.

• **PESTS AND DISEASES** Susceptible to bacterial crown rot, rust, *Cladosporium* leaf spot, and anthracnose.

B. chinensis ■ (Blackberry lily, Leopard lily). Clump-forming, rhizomatous perennial with sword-shaped, mid- to deep green leaves, 8in (20cm) long. In summer, bears a succession of many wide-opening flowers, 1½in (4cm) across, bright yellow to orange-red with maroon spots, followed by beige capsules that open to reveal large black seeds. ↕ 18–36in (45–90cm), ↔ 8in (20cm). India, China, E. former USSR, Japan. Zone 5b.

BELLEVALIA

LILIACEAE

Genus of 45 species of bulbous perennials from scrub and maquis in S. Europe and Asia, with strap-shaped, mid- to gray-green, basal leaves. Their racemes of bell-shaped flowers, similar to grape hyacinths (*Muscari*), are borne in spring and are mostly white, lilac, or violet-blue, often fading to brown. Grow bellevalias in a rock garden or sunny border.

• **CULTIVATION** Plant 2in (5cm) deep in autumn in any well-drained soil in full sun. Divide congested clumps to maintain vigor. Most prefer to be kept dry in summer. *B. hyacinthoides* grows best in a bulb frame.

• **PROPAGATION** Sow seed in a cold frame in autumn. Remove offsets from mature bulbs, or divide clumps, while dormant in summer.

• **PESTS AND DISEASES** Infrequent.

B. hyacinthoides, syn. *Strangweja spicata.* Bulbous perennial with strap-shaped, fleshy, mid-green leaves, 6–18in (15–45cm) long, during autumn and winter. In spring, produces loose racemes of a few wide-opening flowers, ¼–½in (6–15mm) long, pale blue with deeper blue veins. ↕ 2–6in (5–15cm), PD2in (5cm). Greece. Zone 5.

B. pycnantha ■ syn. *Muscari paradoxum* of gardens, *M. pycnantha.* Robust, bulbous perennial with strap-shaped, grayish green leaves, 6–18in (15–45cm) long. Navy-blue flowers, ¼in (7mm) long, with yellowish white rims, are produced in spring. ↕ 12in (30cm), PD2in (5cm). Caucasus, E. Turkey, Iraq, Iran. Zone 6.

B. romana, syn. *Hyacinthus romanus.* Bulbous perennial with strap-shaped, mid-green leaves, 6–12in (15–30cm) long. Loose, conical racemes of white flowers, to ⅜in (8mm) long, tinged green or brown, are produced in spring. ↕ 12in (30cm), PD2in (5cm). Mediterranean (S. France to Greece). Zone 7b.

BELLIS

Daisy

ASTERACEAE

Genus of 15 species of rosette-forming, carpeting perennials from grassland and woodland glades. They have oval to spoon-shaped leaves and solitary, long-stalked white, pink, or deep reddish pink flowerheads. The English daisy (*B. perennis*) has given rise to a range of cultivars, most commonly grown as biennials for spring bedding displays or as container plants.

• **CULTIVATION** Grow in well-drained, reasonably fertile soil in full sun or partial shade. Deadhead to avoid self-seeding. They grow best in areas with cool summers. Provide winter mulch in colder areas. For winter-flowering container plants, grow in soil-based potting mix, water moderately, and maintain at 39–45°F (4–7°C).

• **PROPAGATION** Sow seed in shallow drills outdoors in early summer, or at 50–55°F (10–13°C) in early spring. Divide in early spring or after flowering.

• **PESTS AND DISEASES** Susceptible to a few fungal leaf spots.

B. perennis (English daisy). Stoloniferous perennial with inversely lance-shaped to obovate or spoon-shaped, bright green leaves, ½–2½in (1–6cm) long. From late winter to late summer, produces flowerheads, ½–1¼in (1–3cm) across, with white ray florets, often tinged maroon or pink, and yellow disk florets. ↕↔ 2–8in (5–20cm). Europe, Turkey. Zone 5b. **'Aucubifolia'** bears leaves variegated green and gold. **Habanera Series** cultivars bear pink, white, or red, long-petaled flowerheads, to 2½in (6cm) across, in early summer. **Pomponette Series** cultivars bear double pink, white, or red flowerheads, to 1½in (4cm) across, with quilled petals. **Roggli Series** cultivars flower early and prolifically, with semi-double red, rose-pink, salmon-pink, or white flowerheads, to 1¼in (3cm). **'Shrewly Gold'** has gold leaves and single flowerheads. **Super Enorma Series** cultivars have everblooming, double flowers, 3in (8cm) across, in many colors. **Tasso Series** ■ cultivars bear double, pink, white, or red flowerheads, to 2½in (6cm) across, with quilled petals.

Bellis perennis Tasso Series

▷ ***Beloperone*** see *Justicia*

BELLIUM

ASTERACEAE

Genus of 4 species of small spreading annuals and perennials from seaside outcroppings or moist, sandy regions of Europe and the Mediterranean. They have alternate or whorled, mid-green, basal leaves and are grown for their tiny white flowerheads with yellow disks. Perfect for a rock garden or trough. Where not hardy, grow in a cool greenhouse.

• **CULTIVATION** Grow in fertile, sharply drained but moist soil in full sun with some midday shade. Protect with a dry winter mulch.

• **PROPAGATION** Sow seed in containers in a cold frame in spring, or divide in spring.

• **PESTS AND DISEASES** Infrequent.

B. bellidioides. Small, trailing perennial with thread-like, elliptic leaves, to ½in (1.5cm) long. In summer, produces white to pinkish white flowerheads, to ¾in (2cm) across. ↕ to 5½in (14cm), ↔ indefinite. W. Mediterranean islands. Zone 7.

B. crassifolium. Small, trailing perennial with rounded to elliptic-spoon-shaped, fleshy, hairless or softly hairy leaves, ⅜–½in (0.9–1.5cm) long. In summer, bears white flowerheads, ½–¾in (1.5–2cm) across. ↕ to 4in (10cm), ↔ indefinite. Italy (Sardinia). Zone 7.

B. minutum. Tiny, trailing annual with sparsely softly hairy scapes and thread-like elliptic-obovate leaves, to ⅜in (9mm) long. Bears white flowerheads, to ½in (1.5cm) across, in summer. ↕ 3in (8cm), ↔ indefinite. E. Mediterranean islands.

BERBERIDOPSIS

FLACOURTIACEAE

Genus of one species of woody, evergreen, scandent climber from moist woodland in Chile, cultivated mainly for its clusters and racemes of spherical flowers. The leaves are ovate or heart-shaped, spiny, and alternate. Grow against a wall or train into a tree.

• **CULTIVATION** Grow in humus-rich, neutral to acidic, moist but well-drained soil, in a partially shaded, sheltered site. Protect the roots in winter with a deep, loose mulch. Remove dead or damaged wood in spring.

• **PROPAGATION** Sow seed in containers in a cold frame in spring. Root semi-ripe cuttings in late summer. Layer in autumn.

• **PESTS AND DISEASES** Infrequent.

B. corallina ■ (Coral plant). Weakly twining climber with ovate or heart-shaped, dark green leaves, to 4in (10cm) long, glaucous beneath, with small marginal spines. Spherical, dark red flowers, ½in (1.5cm) across, with stalks 2in (5cm) long, are produced both in pendent, terminal racemes and in 2- or 3-flowered clusters from the upper leaf axils from summer to early autumn. ↕ 15ft (5m). Chile. Zone 8.

Berberidopsis corallina

B

BERBERIS

Barberry

BERBERIDACEAE

Genus of about 450 species of evergreen or deciduous shrubs from all parts of the N. hemisphere, N. and tropical Africa, and South America, that prefer rocky soils in mountain areas. Linear to very broadly ovate or obovate, entire or spine-toothed leaves are produced in the axils of stem spines, which are often borne in groups of 3, and persist on old, leafless stems. Barberries are cultivated for their foliage (ornamental or giving good autumn color); racemes, panicles, or axillary clusters of yellow to dark orange flowers, cup-shaped with usually reflexed sepals; and colorful autumn fruits. They range from dwarf species and cultivars to large shrubs that are effective in a border, as specimen shrubs, or as a hedge. All parts may cause mild stomach upset if ingested; contact with the spines may irritate skin.

• **CULTIVATION** Grow in almost any well-drained soil in full sun or partial shade. Fruiting and autumn color are better in sun. Evergreen species, pruning group 8; deciduous species, pruning group 2. Trim hedges after flowering.

• **PROPAGATION** Sow seed in a seedbed in early spring; many species cross freely in gardens, so seed-raised plants are often hybrids. Root softwood cuttings of deciduous barberries in summer; take semi-ripe cuttings of deciduous and evergreen ones in summer.

• **PESTS AND DISEASES** Scale insects, mites, and Japanese weevils can be problems. Prone to canker and dieback, fungal leaf spots, powdery mildew, root rot, *Verticillium* wilt, and a wide variety of rust diseases. Many *Berberis* species are the alternate hosts of wheat rust; their culture is banned in Canada and parts of the US.

B. aggregata. Compact, deciduous shrub with oblong-ovate, olive-green leaves, to 1¼in (3cm) long, sparsely toothed at the tips, blue-green beneath, and turning red in autumn. Pale yellow flowers, ¼in (6mm) across, are borne in dense axillary panicles, to 1½in (4cm) long, in late spring and early summer, followed by spherical to ovoid, gray-glaucous, red fruit, to ¼in (6mm) long. ↕ 5ft (1.5m), ↔ 6ft (2m). W. China (Gansu, Sichuan). Zone 6b.

Berberis x *bristolensis*

Berberis buxifolia (inset: flower detail)

B.* x *bristolensis ■ (*B. calliantha* x *B. verruculosa*). Dense, mound-forming, evergreen shrub with elliptic, spine-toothed leaves, to 1½in (4cm) long, glossy, dark green above, intensely glaucous beneath, some turning red in autumn or winter. Yellow flowers, ½in (1.5cm) or more across, are produced singly or in twos or threes from the leaf axils in late spring, followed by oblong-ovoid, blue-black fruit, ⅜in (9mm) long. ↕ 5ft (1.5m), ↔ 6ft (2m). Garden origin. Zone 6.

B. buxifolia ■ (Magellan barberry). Upright, evergreen or semi-evergreen shrub with arching branches and elliptic, spine-tipped, leathery, dark green leaves, to 1in (2.5cm) long. In mid- and late spring, dark orange-yellow flowers, to ½in (1.5cm) across, are produced singly or in pairs from the upper leaf axils, on stalks ¾–1in (2–2.5cm) long. They are followed by spherical, dark purple fruit, to ¼–⅜in (6–8mm) across. ↕ 8ft (2.5m), ↔ 10ft (3m). Chile, Argentina. Zone 5b. **'Pygmaea'**, syn. var. *nana* of gardens, is compact, lacks spines, has leaves to 1¼in (3cm) long, and rarely produces flowers; ↕ 12in (30cm), ↔ 18in (45cm).

B. calliantha. Compact, evergreen shrub with holly-like, elliptic to oblong, spine-toothed leaves, to 2½in (6cm) long, that are glossy, dark green above, waxy-white beneath, and borne on red young shoots. Pale yellow flowers, to 1in (2.5cm) across, are produced singly, occasionally in twos or threes, from the upper leaf axils in late spring, followed by ovoid, blue-glaucous, black fruit, ½in (1.5cm) or more long. ↕ 30in (75cm), ↔ 36in (90cm). China (S.E. Tibet). Zone 7b.

B. candidula. Dense, mound-forming, evergreen shrub with elliptic to ovate, entire, spine-tipped, glossy, dark green leaves, to 1¼in (3cm) long, with inrolled margins, and waxy-white beneath. Bears solitary, bright yellow flowers, to ½in (1.5cm) across, from the upper leaf axils in late spring, followed by ovoid, white-glaucous, purple fruit, to ½in (1.5cm) long. ↕ 24in (60cm), ↔ 4ft (1.2m). W. China (Hubei). Zone 7.

B.* x *carminea (*B. aggregata* x *B. wilsoniae*). Vigorous, semi-evergreen shrub with arching branches and narrowly obovate, slightly spiny, often grayish green leaves, to 1¼in (3cm) long. Bears spherical yellow flowers, to ¼in (6mm) across, in 10- to 16-flowered panicles, to 2in (5cm) long, in late spring and early summer, followed by dense clusters of ovoid-spherical, usually red or orange fruit, ½in (1.5cm) across. Garden origin. ↕ 5ft (1.5m), ↔ 8ft (2.5m). Zone 7. **'Barbarossa'** has bright red fruit. **'Buccaneer'** bears spherical, glowing red fruit. **'Pirate King'** ■ bears bright scarlet-red fruit.

Berberis x *carminea* 'Pirate King'

***B.* 'Chenaultii'**, syn. *B.* 'Chenault'. Spreading, dense, evergreen shrub with lance-shaped, wavy-margined, spine-toothed leaves, to 1½in (4cm) long, that are glossy, dark green above and glaucous beneath, often turning bronze-red in winter. Spherical yellow flowers, ½in (1.5cm) across, are produced in axillary clusters of 2–4 in late spring, followed by ovoid, blue-black fruit, ½in (1.5cm) long. ↕↔ 5ft (1.5m). Zone 5b.

***B.* 'Cherry Ripe'.** Rounded, deciduous shrub with obovate, mainly entire leaves, to 1in (2.5cm) long, dull green above, gray-green beneath. Umbel-like clusters, to 4in (10cm) across, of 2–8 yellow flowers, to ½in (1.5cm) across, are produced freely in early summer. Broadly ovoid, creamy pink fruit, to ½in (1.5cm) long, turn bright cerise and last well into winter. ↕ 5ft (1.5m), ↔ 6ft (2m). Zone 7.

B. coxii. Vigorous, dense, evergreen shrub with elliptic to ovate-elliptic, spine-toothed leaves, to 2in (5cm) long, that are glossy, dark green above and intensely glaucous beneath. Produces clusters of 3–6 pale yellow flowers, to ½in (1.5cm) across, in late spring, followed by oblong-ovoid, blue-glaucous, black fruit, ½in (1.5cm) long. ↕ 6ft (2m) or more, ↔ 10ft (3m). N.E. Burma. Zone 7b.

B. darwinii ■ Vigorous, upright, evergreen shrub with obovate, spine-toothed, glossy, dark green leaves, ¾–1½in (2–4cm) long. Pendent racemes, to 2in (5cm) long, of 10–30 dark orange flowers, ¼in (6mm) across, are borne profusely in mid- and late spring, sometimes again in autumn, and are succeeded by spherical, blue-glaucous, black fruit, ¼in (6mm) across. ↕↔ 10ft (3m). Chile, Argentina. Zone 7. **'Flame'** has broad leaves, to ¾in (2cm) long, and produces rich orange-red flowers; ↕↔ 5ft (1.5m).

B. dictyophylla ■ Vigorous, upright, deciduous shrub with reddish brown shoots covered in white bloom, and obovate to elliptic, entire or sometimes spine-toothed leaves, to ¾in (2cm) long, mid-green above, white beneath, and turning red in autumn. Bears pale yellow flowers, to ½in (1.5cm) across, singly or in twos from the upper leaf axils in late spring, followed by ellipsoid, white-glaucous, red fruit, to ½in (1.5cm) long. ↕ 6ft (2m), ↔ 5ft (1.5m). W. China (Yunnan, W. Sichuan). Zone 7.

B. empetrifolia ■ Spreading, evergreen shrub with arching shoots and linear-

Berberis darwinii

B

Berberis dictyophylla

elliptic, spine-tipped leaves, to 1in (2.5cm) long, dark green above, grayish beneath. Deep golden yellow flowers, ½in (1.5cm) across, are borne singly or in twos from the upper leaf axils in late spring, followed by spherical, blue-glaucous, black fruit, ¼in (6mm) across. ↕ 18in (45cm), ↔ 24in (60cm). Chile, Argentina. Zone 7b.

***B.* x *frikartii* 'Amstelveen'** (*B. candidula* x *B. verruculosa*). Vigorous, compact, evergreen shrub with arching shoots and lance-shaped, glossy leaves, to 1¼in (3cm) long, dark green above, gray-white beneath. Yellow flowers, ½in (1.5cm) across, are borne in clusters of 2–4 from the upper leaf axils in late spring, followed by ovoid, blue-glaucous, black fruit, ½in (1.5cm) long. ↕ 3ft (1m), ↔ 5ft (1.5m). Zone 5b. **'Telstar'** is flat-topped when mature; ↕ to 4ft (1.2m).

***B. gagnepainii* of gardens** see *B. gagnepainii* var. *lanceifolia*.

B. gagnepainii* var. *lanceifolia ▣ syn. *B. gagnepainii* of gardens. Dense, evergreen shrub with spreading, semi-pendent branches and linear-lance-shaped, dark green leaves, to 4in (10cm) long, spine-toothed and wavy at the margins. Golden yellow flowers, ½in (1.5cm) across, are produced in clusters of 2–5 from the upper leaf axils in late spring and early summer, followed by oblong-ovoid, blue-black fruit, to ½in (1.5cm) long. Useful for hedging. ↕ 5ft (1.5m), ↔ 6ft (2m). W. China (Hubei, Sichuan). Zone 7.

***B.* x *gladwynensis* 'William Penn'** ▣ Dense, mound-forming, evergreen shrub with arching branches and elliptic

Berberis empetrifolia

Berberis gagnepainii var. *lanceifolia*

to ovate-lance-shaped, lustrous, dark green leaves, 1¼–4in (3–10cm) long, turning bronze in winter. In spring, bears clusters of yellow flowers, ½in (1.5cm) across, followed by ovoid purple-yellow fruit, to ½in (1.5cm) long. ↕↔ 3–4ft (1–1.2m). Zone 6.

***B.* 'Goldilocks'** ▣ Very vigorous, upright then spreading, evergreen shrub with oblong-ovate, entire or slightly toothed leaves, to 2in (5cm) long, glossy, dark green above, paler beneath. Red-stalked, dark golden yellow flowers, ⅛in (4mm) across, are profusely borne in dense clusters, to 1½in (4cm) across, in mid- and late spring, followed by spherical, blue-black fruit, ⅜in (8mm) across. ↕ 12ft (4m), ↔ 10ft (3m). Zone 6b.

***B.* x *hybrido-gagnepainii* cultivars** (*B. candidula* x *B. gagnepainii*). Evergreen shrubs with ovate to oblong-ovate or lance-shaped, bright green leaves, ¾–2in (2–5cm) long, sometimes tinted bluish or reddish green beneath. Clusters of yellow flowers, to ½in (1.5cm) across, are produced in late spring, followed by ovoid, gray-glaucous, black fruit, to ¼in (6mm) long. ↕ to 5ft (1.5m), ↔ to 6ft (2m). Zone 7. **'Minikin'** is compact, with slightly twisted, lance-shaped, bright green leaves, to ¾in (2cm) long, that are white beneath; ↕ 20in (50cm), ↔ 32in (80cm). **'Tottenham'** is more vigorous than 'Minikin', with arching shoots and oblong-ovate leaves, to 1½in (4cm) long, some turning red in autumn; ↔ 5ft (1.5m).

***B.* x *interposita* 'Wallich's Purple'.** Densely mound-forming, evergreen

Berberis x *gladwynensis* 'William Penn'

Berberis 'Goldilocks'

shrub with arching shoots and elliptic, sparsely spiny, glossy, mid-green leaves, to 1in (2.5cm) long, gray-green beneath, bronze-purple when young. Clusters of yellow flowers, ½in (1.5cm) across, are produced in late spring, followed by ellipsoid, slightly blue-glaucous, black fruit, 2in (5cm) long. ↕ 5ft (1.5m), ↔ 6ft (2m). Zone 7b.

B. jamesiana. Vigorous, upright, deciduous shrub with ovate, entire to finely toothed, olive-green leaves, to 4in (10cm) long, glaucous gray beneath, turning red in autumn. Pendent racemes, to 4in (10cm) long, of 20–40 yellow flowers, ¼in (6mm) across, are borne in early summer, followed by spherical, coral-red fruit, ½in (1.5cm) across. ↕ 6ft (2m), ↔ 5ft (1.5m). W. China (N.W. Yunnan). Zone 7b.

B. julianae ▣ (Wintergreen barberry). Dense, upright, evergreen shrub with rigid, obovate to elliptic leaves, to 1½–3in (4–8cm) long, that are glossy, deep green above, pale green beneath, with strongly spined margins. Up to 20 yellow or red-tinged flowers, ½in (1.5cm) across, are produced in clusters in late spring, and are succeeded by oblong, white-glaucous, black fruit, ⅜in (8mm) long. ↕↔ 10ft (3m). China. Zone 6. **'Lombart's Red'** has leaves tinged with red beneath.

B. koreana ▣ (Korean barberry). Dense, multi-stemmed, deciduous shrub bearing alternate, oblong-ovate, mid- to dark green leaves, 1–3in (2.5–8cm) long, rounded at the apex, and strongly veined beneath. Deep reddish purple autumn color persists late into the season. Showy yellow flowers, ¼in (6mm) across, are borne on pendent racemes, 3–4in (8–10cm) long, in midspring, followed by ovoid, bright red fruit, ¼–⅜in (6–9mm) long, with a waxy bloom. Forms large colonies. ↕ 4–6ft (1.2–2m), ↔ 3–5ft (1–1.5m). Korea. Zone 4.

B. linearifolia. Upright, stiffly branched, evergreen shrub with obovate to inversely lance-shaped, glossy, dark green leaves, to 2in (5cm) long. Bears clusters of 2–4 rich orange to apricot flowers, ¾in (2cm) across, in late spring, followed by ellipsoid, blue-glaucous, black fruit, ½in (1.5cm) long. Chile, Argentina. ↕ 6ft (2m), ↔ 5ft (1.5m). Zone 5b. **'Jewel'** has clusters of 4–6 dark orange flowers that open from scarlet buds. **'Orange King'** is vigorous, with arching shoots, leaves to 2½in (6cm) long, and less deeply colored,

Berberis julianae

Berberis koreana

slightly larger flowers than 'Jewel'; ↕↔ 8ft (2.5m).

B.* x *lologensis (*B. darwinii* x *B. linearifolia*). Strong-growing, spreading, evergreen shrub with arching shoots and spoon-shaped, spine-toothed, glossy, dark green leaves, to 2in (5cm) long. Clusters of 8–12 rich orange flowers, 1¼in (3cm) across, are produced in late spring, and often again from summer to autumn, followed by spherical, blue-black fruit, to ¼in (6mm) across. ↕↔ 12ft (4m). Argentina. Zone 7. **'Apricot Queen'** bears umbel-like racemes, to 2in (5cm) long, of 3–7 dark orange flowers in late spring and sporadically throughout summer; ↔ 10ft (3m). **'Mystery Fire'** bears abundant bright orange-yellow flowers. **'Stapehill'** ▣ bears abundant rich orange flowers.

Berberis x *lologensis* 'Stapehill'

Berberis x *ottawensis* 'Silver Mile'

Berberis x *stenophylla*

Berberis thunbergii f. *atropurpurea*

B.* x *mentorensis (Mentor barberry). Fast-growing, upright, rounded, semi-evergreen shrub with slender, stiff shoots and alternate, simple, elliptic, dark green leaves, 1–2in (2.5–5cm) long, toothed at the tips, pale green beneath, turning yellow to orange to red in late autumn. In spring, produces yellow flowers, ⅜–½in (0.8–1.5cm) across, solitary or in pairs, followed by red-brown fruit. Excellent for hedging. ↕ 5ft (1.5m), ↔ 5–7ft (1.5–2.2m). Garden origin. Zone 4.

B.* x *ottawensis (*B. thunbergii* x *B. vulgaris*). Rounded, deciduous shrub with obovate, mainly entire, mid-green leaves, to 1¼in (3cm) long. Clusters of up to 10 red-tinged, pale yellow flowers, ⅜in (8mm) across, are produced in spring, and are succeeded by ovoid red berries, ⅜in (8mm) long. ↕↔ 8ft (2.5m). Zone 5. **'Purpurea'** see 'Superba'. **'Silver Mile'** ▣ has dark red-purple leaves, flushed silvery gray, turning red in autumn. **'Superba'** ▣ syn. 'Purpurea', is very vigorous, with red-purple leaves turning crimson in autumn.

B. panlanensis see *B. sanguinea*.

***B.* 'Park Jewel'** see *B.* 'Parkjuweel'.

***B.* 'Parkjuweel'**, syn. *B.* 'Park Jewel'. Compact, semi-evergreen shrub with oblong-ovate, entire or slightly toothed, very glossy, dark to mid-green leaves, to 1¼in (3cm) long, some turning red in autumn. In late spring, bears yellow flowers, ⅜in (8mm) across, singly or in small clusters to 1in (2.5cm) across. ↕ 6ft (2m), ↔ 8ft (2.5m). Zone 7.

***B. polyantha* of gardens** see *B. prattii*.

B. prattii, syn. *B. polyantha* of gardens. Deciduous shrub with arching branches and densely clustered, obovate leaves, to 1¼in (3cm) long, that are glossy, mid-green above, gray beneath, with spine-tipped teeth. Bears lax, upright panicles, to 8in (20cm) long, of 8 yellow flowers in summer, followed by long-lasting, spherical, bright pink fruit, to ¼in (6mm) long. ↕↔ 10ft (3m). W. China (Sichuan). Zone 7.

***B.* 'Red Jewel'.** Compact, semi-evergreen shrub with oblong-ovate, entire or slightly toothed leaves, to 1¼in (3cm) long, dark bronze-red when young, dark to mid-green when mature. Yellow flowers, ⅜in (8mm) across, borne singly or in small clusters, to 1in (2.5cm) across, are produced in late spring. A sport of 'Parkjuweel'. ↕ 6ft (2m), ↔ 8ft (2.5m). Zone 7.

B.* x *rubrostilla see *B.* 'Rubrostilla'.

***B.* 'Rubrostilla'**, syn. *B.* x *rubrostilla*. Rounded, deciduous shrub with narrow, obovate, light mid-green leaves, to 1¼in (3cm) long, with small marginal spines. Umbel-like racemes of 2–4 yellow flowers, ¼–⅜in (7–9mm) across, on stalks 1in (2.5cm) long, are borne in profusion along the branches in summer, followed by oblong-ovoid, translucent, coral-red fruit, ½in (1.5cm) long. ↕ 5ft (1.5m), ↔ 8ft (2.5m). Zone 7b.

B. sanguinea, syn. *B. panlanensis*. Slow-growing, very dense, evergreen shrub with arching shoots and linear-lance-shaped, spine-toothed, gray-green leaves, to 2½in (6cm) long. Yellow flowers, to ½in (1.5cm) across, are borne in clusters of 2–7 in spring, followed by oblong black fruit, to ⅜in (8mm) long. ↕ 8ft (2.5m), ↔ 12ft (4m). W. China (Sichuan). Zone 7b.

B. sargentiana. Dense, upright, evergreen shrub with rigid, narrowly elliptic to oblong, strongly spined, glossy leaves, to 4in (10cm) long, dark green above and yellowish green beneath. Greenish yellow, sometimes red-tinged flowers, to ½in (1.5cm) across, are produced in clusters of 4–8 in late spring, and are succeeded by oblong-ellipsoid, blue-black fruit, to ¼in (6mm) long. ↕↔ 6ft (2m). W. China (Sichuan, Hubei). Zone 7b.

B.* x *stenophylla ▣ (*B. darwinii* x *B. empetrifolia*). Vigorous, evergreen shrub with long, arching branches and linear to narrowly elliptic, spine-tipped, dark green leaves, to 1in (2.5cm) long. Short, clustered racemes of 7–14 deep yellow flowers, to ½in (1.5cm) across, are borne profusely along the branches in late spring, followed by spherical, blue-glaucous, black fruit, to ¼in (6mm) long. An excellent plant for hedging. ↕ 10ft (3m), ↔ 15ft (5m). Garden origin. Zone 6b. **'Claret Cascade'** produces red young shoots and bronze-green young leaves; ↕↔ 4ft (1.2m). **'Coccinea'** is compact, with red flower buds and red-tinged flowers borne in clusters of 4–8; ↕ 4ft (1.2m), ↔ 5ft (1.5m). **'Corallina Compacta'** ▣ is compact, with leaves ¼–⅜in (6–8mm) long, and bears red-budded, light orange flowers; ↕↔ to 12in (30cm). **'Cornish Cream'** see 'Lemon Queen'. **'Cream Showers'** see 'Lemon Queen'. **'Irwinii'** is compact, with sharply toothed, glossy leaves and orange flowers; ↕↔ 5ft (1.5m). **'Lemon Queen'**, syn. 'Cornish Cream', 'Cream Showers', has dark green leaves and produces creamy white flowers. **'Pink Pearl'** has leaves variegated white and pink, and pink flowers. Cut out reverted shoots as they occur; ↕↔ 5ft (1.5m).

B. temolaica. Arching, deciduous shrub with white-glaucous stems, turning purple, and obovate to oblong, entire or few-spined, gray-green leaves, to 1¾in (4.5cm) long. Solitary, pale yellow flowers, ½in (1.5cm) across, are produced on stalks ½in (1.5cm) long, in late spring, and are succeeded by ellipsoid, white-glaucous, red fruit, ½in (1.5cm) long. ↕ 6ft (2m), ↔ 10ft (3m). China (S.E. Tibet). Zone 6b.

B. thunbergii (Japanese barberry). Dense, rounded, deciduous shrub with obovate, entire leaves, to 1¼in (3cm) long, fresh green above and bluish green

Berberis x *ottawensis* 'Superba'

Berberis x *stenophylla* 'Corallina Compacta'

Berberis thunbergii 'Aurea'

Berberis thunbergii 'Bagatelle'

Berberis thunbergii 'Helmond Pillar'

Berberis verruculosa

Berberis wilsoniae

beneath, turning orange and red in autumn. Umbel-like racemes of 2–5, rarely solitary, red-tinged, pale yellow flowers, ½in (1.5cm) long, are produced along the branches in midspring, and are succeeded by ellipsoid, glossy red fruit, to ⅜in (8mm) long. Excellent for hedging and urban conditions. ↕ 3ft (1m), occasionally more, ↔ 8ft (2.5m). Japan. Zone 4b. **f. *atropurpurea*** ■ produces dark red-purple or purplish bronze foliage, turning red in autumn. **'Atropurpurea Nana'**, syn. 'Crimson Pygmy', 'Little Favourite', has red-purple foliage; ↕ 24in (60cm), ↔ 30in (75cm). **'Aurea'** ■ has bright yellow young foliage; ↕ 5ft (1.5m), ↔ 6ft (2m). **'Bagatelle'** ■ is very compact, with deep red-purple foliage; ↕ 12in (30cm), ↔ 16in (40cm). **'Crimson Pygmy'** see 'Atropurpurea Nana'. **'Dart's Red Lady'** ■ has very dark red-purple foliage, turning bright red in autumn. **'Erecta'** is upright when young, becoming open with age; ↕↔ 5ft (1.5m). **'Golden Ring'** ■ has purple leaves, narrowly margined with golden yellow, that turn red in autumn, and produces red fruit. **'Green Ornament'** is similar in habit to 'Erecta', with bronze young foliage and a profusion of red fruit. **'Helmond Pillar'** ■ is narrowly upright and has dark red-purple foliage; ↕ 5ft (1.5m), ↔ 24in (60cm). **'Kobold'** is very compact and fruits freely; ↕ 16in (40cm), ↔ 24in (60cm). **'Little Favourite'** see 'Atropurpurea Nana'. **'Pink Queen'** is similar to 'Rose Glow', but with more conspicuously variegated foliage. **'Red Pillar'** is similar in habit to 'Erecta', and has red-purple foliage. **'Rose Glow'** ■ has red-purple leaves flecked with white; but the first growth of the season shows no variegation. **'Silver Beauty'** is slow-growing, with leaves mottled creamy white; ↕ 24in (60cm), ↔ 36in (90cm). **'Sparkle'** is compact, with arching branches and good autumn color, and fruits freely; ↕ 4ft (1.2m), ↔ 5ft (1.5m).

B. verruculosa ■ (Warty barberry). Compact, evergreen shrub with arching shoots and obovate to elliptic, spine-tipped leaves, ¾–1¼in (2–3cm) long, glossy, dark green above, gray-white beneath. Bears solitary, golden yellow flowers, ¾in (2cm) across, in late spring, followed by oblong-ovoid, white-glaucous, dark purple fruit, to ½in (1.5cm) long. ↕↔ 5ft (1.5m). W. China. Zone 5.

Berberis thunbergii 'Dart's Red Lady'

Berberis thunbergii 'Golden Ring'

Berberis thunbergii 'Rose Glow' (inset: leaf detail)

B. wilsoniae ■ Dense, mound-forming, very spiny, semi-evergreen shrub with spreading, arching branches and obovate-spoon-shaped, usually entire, gray-green leaves, to 1in (2.5cm) long, that turn red and orange in autumn. Bears short panicles or clusters of 4–7 pale yellow flowers, ¼–½in (6–15mm) across, in summer, followed by spherical, translucent, coral-pink to pinkish red fruit, to ¼in (6mm) across. ↕ 3ft (1m), ↔ 6ft (2m). W. China (W. Sichuan, Yunnan). Zone 6. **'Orangeade'** produces striking, carmine-red and orange-red fruit, ½in (1.5cm) across.

B. x wisleyensis (Threespine barberry). Open, evergreen shrub with stems having 3-parted spines and alternate, simple, linear, bright green leaves, 1–2in (2.5–5cm) long, glaucous beneath. Older leaves turn reddish purple in winter. Bears clusters of pale yellow flowers, tinged red, to ¾in (2cm) across, followed by glaucous, bluish black fruit, to ⅜in (9mm) across. Sometimes offered as *B. triacanthophora*. ↕↔ 3–5ft (1–1.5m). C. China. Zone 6.

BERCHEMIA

RHAMNACEAE

Genus of about 12 species of deciduous climbers, rarely shrubs, from woodland in E. Africa, E. Asia, and North and Central America. They have attractively veined, alternate, ovate to elliptic leaves, and terminal or axillary panicles of small flowers in summer, followed by fleshy fruits. Train against a wall, fence, or pergola, or into a small tree.

• **CULTIVATION** Grow in fertile soil in full sun or partial shade. Pruning group 11, in late winter or early spring.

• **PROPAGATION** Sow seed in containers in a cold frame in autumn or spring. Root semi-ripe cuttings in summer or take root cuttings in winter. Layer in autumn or winter.

• **PESTS AND DISEASES** Infrequent.

B. racemosa. Twining, woody climber or spreading shrub, bearing ovate leaves, to 3in (8cm) long, dark green above, lighter or bluish green beneath, each with 7–9 pairs of prominent, parallel veins. Produces panicles, to 6in (15cm) long, of tiny green flowers in summer, followed by oblong red fruit, ½in (15mm) long, that ripen to black. ↕ 12ft (4m). Japan. Zone 7. **'Variegata'** has white-variegated leaves.
B. scandens (Rattan vine, Supple Jack). Vigorous, twining, woody climber bearing ovate, mid-green leaves, to 3in (8cm) long, each with 9–12 pairs of prominent, parallel veins. Bears panicles, 2in (5cm) long, of tiny green flowers in summer, followed by oblong, blue-black fruit, to ⅜in (8mm) long. ↕ 15ft (5m). S. US to Central America. Zone 7.

BERGENIA *syn.* MEGASEA
Elephant's ears, Pigsqueak

SAXIFRAGACEAE

Genus of 6–8 species of clump-forming, evergreen perennials from meadows, rocky moorland, and moist woodland in Central and E. Asia. They have tough, thick rhizomes and distinctive rosettes of alternate, simple, entire or toothed, obovate or oblong to broadly ovate, leathery, glossy leaves, many coloring well in winter. Panicle-like cymes of shallowly funnel-shaped to bell-shaped, 5-petaled flowers, usually ½–1in (1.5–2.5cm) across, on short, branched, often red or purple flower stems, are produced mainly in spring. Grow in a woodland garden or border, or as a groundcover.

- **CULTIVATION** Grow in humus-rich, moist but well-drained soil in full sun or partial shade. Most dislike extremes of heat and drought, but will tolerate exposure and poor soil, which enhances their winter leaf color. Mulch in autumn. Frost may damage early flowers, and the foliage of some species may die back in winter.
- **PROPAGATION** Seed-raised plants in gardens usually produce hybrids. Divide deteriorating clumps, or root rhizome sections from them, every 3–5 years in autumn or spring. Root sections of young rhizomes with one or more leaf rosettes after flowering or in autumn, in a sand frame or the open ground.
- **PESTS AND DISEASES** Sometimes troubled by fungal leaf spots and rhizome rot. Prone to weevils, slugs and snails, caterpillars, and foliar nematode.

Bergenia 'Ballawley'

Bergenia ciliata

***B.* 'Abendglut'**, syn. *B.* 'Evening Glow'. Clump-forming perennial with obovate, red-tinted, mid- to dark green leaves, 6in (15cm) long, ruby-red beneath, rich maroon in winter. Produces semi-double, magenta-crimson flowers on red flower stems in mid- and late spring. ↕ 8–12in (20–30cm), ↔ 18–24in (45–60cm). Zone 3b.
***B.* 'Baby Doll'.** Clump-forming perennial with obovate, bronze-tinted, mid-green leaves, 4in (10cm) long. Bears soft pink flowers that darken with age, in mid- and late spring. ↕ 12in (30cm), ↔ 18–24in (45–60cm). Zone 3b.
***B.* 'Ballawley'** ▣ Clump-forming perennial with very broadly ovate, glossy, mid-green leaves, to 12in (30cm) long, turning bronze-purple in winter. Red flower stems bear bright crimson flowers in mid- and late spring. Prefers a sheltered site. ↕ 24in (60cm), ↔ 18–24in (45–60cm). Zone 3b.
B. beesiana see *B. purpurascens.*
***B.* 'Beethoven'.** Free-flowering perennial with spoon-shaped, mid-green leaves, 10in (25cm) long. Produces white flowers, with red to greenish pink calyces, in mid- and late spring. ↕ 12–18in (30–45cm), ↔ 18–24in (45–60cm). Zone 3b.
***B.* 'Bell Tower'** see *B.* 'Glockenturm'.
***B.* 'Bressingham Bountiful'.** Compact perennial with broadly obovate to ovate, thin, dark green leaves, 7in (18cm) long, liable to frost damage but attractively margined with maroon, especially in winter. Bears nodding, rose-pink flowers in mid- and late spring, darkening as they age. ↕ 12–18in (30–45cm), ↔ 18–24in (45–60cm). Zone 3b.
***B.* 'Bressingham Ruby'.** Clump-forming perennial with rounded to obovate, deep green leaves, 7–8in (18–20cm) long, rich maroon beneath and turning beet-red in winter. Bears intensely red flowers in nodding cymes in spring. ↕ 14in (35cm), ↔ 12in (30cm). Zone 3b.
***B.* 'Bressingham Salmon'.** Clump-forming perennial with obovate, bronze-tinted, deep green leaves, 6–7in (15–18cm) long, turning dark red in winter. Produces bright salmon-pink flowers in mid- and late spring. ↕ 12–18in (30–45cm), ↔ 18–24in (45–60cm). Zone 3b.
***B.* 'Bressingham White'.** Clump-forming perennial with robust, broadly obovate, deep green leaves, 6–7in (15–18cm) long. Pure white flowers are freely produced in mid- and late spring. ↕ 12–18in (30–45cm), ↔ 18–24in (45–60cm). Zone 3b.
B. ciliata ▣ (Winter begonia). Clump-forming perennial with very broadly obovate, hairy, mid-green leaves, to 14in (35cm) long. In early spring, flower stems bear more or less erect flowers that are pink, or white fading to pinkish white, with rose-pink calyces. ↕ 12in (30cm), ↔ 18in (45cm). Himalayas, India (Assam). Zone 6. **'Leichtlinii'** has red-tinted leaves and rose flowers. **f. *ligulata*** has leaves with hairy margins and almost hairless surfaces, and bears very pale pink flowers with rose-red calyces. **'Rosea'** has deep rose flowers.
B. cordifolia. Clump-forming perennial with rounded to heart-shaped, sometimes puckered, deep to mid-green leaves, 12in (30cm) long, tinted purple in winter. Bears pale rose-red to dark pink flowers on red flower stems in late winter and early spring. ↕ 24in (60cm), ↔ 30in (75cm). Russia (Siberia). Zone 3b. **'Purpurea'** has magenta-purple flowers and thicker, redder leaves. **'Redstart'** bears vibrant red flowers in late spring. **'Rotblum'** has red flowers and red leaves in winter; ↕ 18in (45cm).
B. crassifolia (Siberian tea). Clump-forming perennial with oblong, obovate or broadly ovate, mid-green leaves, 3½–7in (9–18cm) long, with toothed margins, becoming red-tinged in exposed sites, especially in winter. Branched, reddish green flower stems bear nodding, pinkish purple flowers in late winter and early spring. ↕↔ 18in (45cm). Russia (Siberia), E. former USSR. Zone 3b. **'Aureo-Marginata'** has purple-green leaves edged with cream. **var. *pacifica*** has slightly broader leaves and larger, red-purple flowers; ↕ 12in (30cm), ↔ 8in (20cm); Russia (Sikhote Alin Mountains).
***B.* 'Eric Smith'.** Vigorous perennial with rounded-ovate, puckered, bronze-flushed, mid-green leaves, 8in (20cm) long, turning bronze-red in winter. Bears deep coral-pink flowers on strong, upright flower stems in mid- and late spring. ↕ 12–18in (30–45cm), ↔ 18–24in (45–60cm). Zone 3b.
***B.* 'Evening Glow'** see *B.* 'Abendglut'.
***B.* 'Glockenturm'**, syn. *B.* 'Bell Tower'. Free-flowering perennial with obovate-oblong, mid-green leaves, 6–7in (15–18cm) long. Deep reddish pink flowers are produced in mid- and late spring. ↕ 12–18in (30–45cm), ↔ 18–24in (45–60cm). Zone 3b.
B. milesii see *B. stracheyi.*

Bergenia x *schmidtii*

***B.* 'Morgenröte'**, syn. *B.* 'Morning Red'. Clump-forming perennial with broadly obovate, deep green leaves, 5–6in (13–15cm) long. Bright reddish pink flowers are borne on strong red flower stems in mid- and late spring; repeat-flowering in cool summers. ↕ 12–18in (30–45cm), ↔ 18–24in (45–60cm). Zone 3b.
***B.* 'Morning Red'** see *B.* 'Morgenröte'.
***B.* 'Opal'.** Clump-forming perennial with red stems and rounded to oval leaves, 7–8in (18–20cm) long. Bears lilac-rose flowers from early to late spring. ↕ 16in (40cm), ↔ 18–24in (45–60cm). Zone 3b.
***B.* 'Pinneberg'.** Clump-forming perennial with erect, oblong leaves, 7–8in (18–20cm) long, turning bright red in the fall. Carmine-red flowers are produced in spring. ↕ 12–16in (30–40cm), ↔ 18–24in (45–60cm). Zone 3b.
***B.* 'Pugsley's Pink'.** Clump-forming perennial with obovate leaves, 6in (15cm) long, mid-green above, reddish green beneath. Produces pink flowers, with brownish pink calyces, in mid- and late spring. ↕ 12–18in (30–45cm), ↔ 18–24in (45–60cm). Zone 3b.
B. purpurascens, syn. *B. beesiana.* Clump-forming perennial with elliptic or ovate-elliptic, deep green leaves, 3–10in (7–25cm) long, purple-red beneath, turning deep purple or beet-red in winter. Upright, reddish brown flower stems bear nodding to pendent, rich purple-red flowers in mid- and late spring. ↕ 18in (45cm), ↔ 12in (30cm). E. Himalayas, W. China, N. Burma. Zone 3b.
***B.* 'Purple King'** see *B.* 'Purpurkönigin'.
***B.* 'Purpurkönigin'**, syn. *B.* 'Purple King.' Clump-forming perennial with rounded-ovate, mid-green leaves, 3½–7in (9–18cm) long. Bears salmon-tinted, rose-red flowers from early to late spring. ↕ 12–16in (30–40cm), ↔ 18–24in (45–60cm). Zone 3b.
B.* x *schmidtii ▣ (*B. ciliata* x *B. crassifolia*). Vigorous perennial with broadly obovate to obovate-elliptic, rich green leaves, to 10in (25cm) long, narrowed at the base, with toothed margins, very sparsely fringed with hairs, and long leaf stalks. Bright rose-pink flowers, nodding at first, then horizontal to erect, are produced in dense, short, panicle-like cymes in late winter and early spring. ↕ 12in (30cm), ↔ 24in (60cm). Garden origin. Zone 3b.

Bergenia stracheyi

Bergenia 'Sunningdale'

***B.* 'Schneekönigin'**, syn. *B.* 'Snow Queen'. Clump-forming perennial with rounded-obovate, mid-green leaves, 7–8in (18–20cm) long, with irregularly curled margins. Pale pink flowers are borne profusely in early and midspring and darken as they age. ↕ 12–18in (30–45cm), ↔ 18–24in (45–60cm). Zone 3b.
***B.* 'Silberlicht'**, syn. *B.* 'Silver Light'. Clump-forming perennial with broadly obovate, mid-green leaves, to 8in (20cm) long, with shallowly scalloped margins. Bears white flowers, aging to pink, with pink sepals, in early and midspring. ↕ 12–18in (30–45cm), ↔ 18–24in (45–60cm). Zone 3b.
***B.* 'Silver Light'** see *B.* 'Silberlicht'.
***B.* 'Snow Queen'** see *B.* 'Schneekönigin'.
B. stracheyi ■ syn. *B. milesii*. Clump-forming perennial with erect, obovate, mid-green leaves, 2½–8in (6–20cm) long, wedge-shaped at the bases and hairy-margined. Nodding, fragrant pink flowers are produced on short flower stems in early spring. ↕ 6–12in (15–30cm), ↔ 12in (30cm). Tajikistan, Afghanistan, W. Himalayas. Zone 3b.
f. *alba*, syn. 'Alba', bears white flowers.
***B.* 'Sunningdale'** ■ Clump-forming perennial with rounded-obovate, mid- to deep green leaves, 6–7in (15–18cm) long, red beneath, becoming copper-red in winter, especially in a sunny, exposed site. Rich lilac-magenta flowers are borne on red flower stems in early and midspring. ↕ 12–18in (30–45cm), ↔ 18–24in (45–60cm). Zone 3b.
***B.* 'Winter Fairy Tale'** see *B.* 'Wintermärchen'.
***B.* 'Wintermärchen'**, syn. *B.* 'Winter Fairy Tale'. Clump-forming perennial with obovate to narrowly ovate, deep green leaves, 6in (15cm) long, red-purple beneath, with slightly twisted leaf blades, becoming red-tinged in winter. Bears dark rose-red flowers in early and midspring. ↕ 12–18in (30–45cm), ↔ 18–24in (45–60cm). Zone 3b.

BERGEROCACTUS

CACTACEAE

Genus of one species of cactus from semi-desert areas of S. California and N.W. Mexico. It has funnel-shaped flowers produced laterally from the upper part of the stems in summer, and spherical, spiny fruit. Where not hardy, grow *B. emoryi* in a warm greenhouse for its golden-spined shoots; elsewhere, use in a desert garden.
• **CULTIVATION** Under glass, grow in standard cactus potting mix with additional sharp sand, in full light. During the growing season, water moderately and apply a nitrogen- and potash-based liquid fertilizer monthly; keep completely dry in winter. Outdoors, grow in slightly enriched, sharply drained soil in full sun. See also pp.48–49.
• **PROPAGATION** Sow seed at 75°F (24°C) in early spring. Root 6in- (15cm-) long basal cuttings of new shoots in early or midspring, with bottom heat; keep barely moist.
• **PESTS AND DISEASES** Susceptible to mealybugs and root mealybugs.

B. emoryi, syn. *Cereus emoryi*. Cactus branching freely from the base. Slender, erect or decumbent, pale green stems produce 14–20 or more, densely spiny, slightly warty ribs. Close-set areoles each produce 10–30 golden yellow spines, including 1–4 centrals. In summer, bears diurnal yellow flowers, ¾–1½in (2–4cm) across, with wool and spines in the axils of the ovaries and the short, scaly tubes. ↕ 24in (60cm), ↔ 18in (45cm). S. California, N.W. Mexico. ❀ (min. 61°F/16°C)

BERKHEYA

ASTERACEAE

Genus of about 80 species of rosette-forming, often spiny-leaved, biennials, perennials, evergreen subshrubs, and shrubs, found in open grassland and rocky areas in tropical Africa and South Africa. They are grown for their unusual foliage and long flowering period. Berkheyas are woody-based or tap-rooted, with pinnatisect, pinnatifid, or pinnate, prickly, thistle-like leaves, often white-hairy beneath, and spiny, involucral bracts. The daisy-like flowerheads are usually yellow. Grow in a sunny border or against a warm wall.

Berkheya macrocephala

• **CULTIVATION** Grow in fertile, well-drained soil, in a sheltered site in full sun. Protect from winter moisture.
• **PROPAGATION** Sow seed in containers in a cold frame in autumn. Divide in spring; the divisions re-establish slowly.
• **PESTS AND DISEASES** Infrequent.

B. macrocephala ■ Rosette-forming perennial with pinnatisect, narrowly oblong-ovate, very spiny, mid-green leaves, 12–18in (30–45cm) long, pale green beneath. In midsummer, erect, branched stems bear bright yellow flowerheads, 4in (10cm) across, with paler yellow disk florets and spiny bracts. ↕↔ 20–36in (50–90cm). South Africa. ❀ (min. 41°F/5°C)
B. purpurea. Rosette-forming perennial with oblong-lance-shaped, pinnatifid, spiny, mid-green basal leaves, to 18in (45cm) long, white-woolly beneath; upper stem leaves are pale green beneath and only slightly woolly. In midsummer, bears corymbs of purple flowerheads, 3in (8cm) across. ↕↔ 16–30in (40–75cm). South Africa, Lesotho. ❀ (min. 41°F/5°C)

BERLANDIERA

Green-eyes

ASTERACEAE

Genus of about 7 species of perennials native to open fields of S. US and Mexico. The alternate leaves are scalloped or pinnatifid. They are grown for their colorful flowerheads, which have yellow ray florets and brown or yellow disk florets. Grow green-eyes in a wildflower or native plant garden.
• **CULTIVATION** Grow in well-drained, moderately fertile soil in full sun.
• **PROPAGATION** Sow seed *in situ* when ripe.
• **PESTS AND DISEASES** Infrequent.

B. lyrata. Erect, branched perennial with oblong, mid-green leaves, to 7in (18cm) long, pinnatifid at base, whitish green beneath. In spring and summer, bears yellow flowerheads, 1in (2.5cm) across, brown-tinged beneath, with maroon disk florets. ↕ to 8in (20cm), ↔ 6in (15cm). Arizona to Arkansas. Zone 7b.

BERTOLONIA

MELASTOMATACEAE

Genus of about 14 species of low-growing, often creeping, evergreen perennials from forest in tropical South America, grown primarily for their variegated foliage. The leaves are simple, stalked, mostly ovate or ovate-oblong, prominently veined, velvety, and colorful, with scalloped margins. Shallowly cup- or saucer-shaped flowers, with 4 or 5 petals, are borne in corymb-like, terminal cymes. Where not hardy, grow in a terrarium or warm greenhouse; elsewhere, use as a low groundcover in a border.
• **CULTIVATION** Under glass, grow in soilless potting mix with added grit, in bright filtered light. In growth, water freely and maintain high humidity, but keep foliage as dry as possible. Outdoors, grow in humus-rich soil in partial shade.
• **PROPAGATION** Sow seed at 66–75°F (19–24°C) in spring. Root tip cuttings in spring, in a closed propagating case with bottom heat.
• **PESTS AND DISEASES** Infrequent.

B. marmorata. Decumbent or mound-forming perennial with ovate-oblong, hairy, bright green leaves, 2–3in (5–8cm) long, irregularly marked or banded with white, and deep purple beneath. Leaves may also be copper-green. Cymes, 4–5in (10–13cm) long, of saucer-shaped purple flowers, ¾in (2cm) across, are produced irregularly throughout the year. ↕ 4–6in (10–15cm), ↔ 10in (25cm) or more. Brazil. ❀ (min. 61–66°F/16–19°C)

BESCHORNERIA

AGAVACEAE

Genus of about 7 species of clump-forming, rosetted, perennial succulents from semi-arid areas of Mexico. Leaves are linear to lance-shaped, arching, and often glaucous, with fleshy keels and very fine marginal teeth. Slightly arching, red-bracted racemes or panicles of pendent, tubular flowers are borne in late spring or summer. Where not hardy, grow in a temperate greenhouse; elsewhere, grow as specimen plants.
• **CULTIVATION** Under glass, grow in standard cactus potting mix in full light. From late spring to autumn, water moderately and apply a balanced liquid fertilizer monthly; water sparingly in winter. Outdoors, grow in sharply drained, humus-rich loam in full sun. May tolerate short periods of 32°F (0°C). See also pp.48–49.
• **PROPAGATION** Sow seed at 70°F (21°C) in early spring. Root offsets in early spring.
• **PESTS AND DISEASES** Scale insects may be a problem.

B. tubiflora. Perennial succulent with compact rosettes of slender, lance-shaped, fleshy, grayish green leaves, to 12in (30cm) long, roughened on both surfaces. Racemes, to 3ft (1m) long, with purplish red bracts and reddish green flowers, 1½in (4cm) long, are borne in late spring. ↕ 3ft (1m), ↔ 26in (65cm). Mexico. ❀ (min. 45°F/7°C)
B. yuccoides ■ Perennial succulent with compact rosettes of lance-shaped, fleshy, gray-green leaves, 20in (50cm) long, becoming glaucous with age. In summer, produces panicles, 3–5ft (1–1.5m) or more long, with vivid red bracts and yellow-tinted, bright green flowers, 3in (8cm) or more long, with spreading lobes. ↕ 5ft (1.5m), ↔ 3ft (1m) or more. Mexico. ❀ (min. 45°F/7°C)

Beschorneria yuccoides

Bessera

LILIACEAE

Genus of 2 species of cormous perennials from rocky slopes, scrub, and grassland in Mexico. They are grown for their pendent, conical, brightly colored flowers, produced in terminal umbels in summer or autumn. Leaves are basal and narrowly linear. Where not hardy, grow in a cool conservatory or at the base of a warm, sunny wall. In frost-free areas, grow in a sunny, open border.

• **Cultivation** Under glass, grow in soil-based potting mix in full light. Water moderately in the growing season; keep dry in winter. Outdoors, plant 2½in (6cm) deep in well-drained soil in full sun in spring. Keep dormant corms dry in winter.

• **Propagation** Sow seed at 55–61°F (13–16°C) in spring, or remove offsets in autumn or winter.

• **Pests and diseases** Infrequent.

B. elegans (Coral drops). Cormous perennial with linear leaves, 24–32in (60–80cm) long. In late summer or autumn, bears umbels of up to 9 bright scarlet flowers, 1¼–1½in (3–4cm) across, creamy white within and with projecting stamens. ↕ 24in (60cm), PD2in (5cm). S.W. and S. central Mexico. ❄ (min. 41°F/5°C)

Beta

CHENOPODIACEAE

Genus of 5 or 6 species of rosette-forming perennials and biennials from grassland and seashores in Europe and the Mediterranean. They have ovate to triangular-ovate, glossy, light or mid-green or reddish purple basal leaves, and lance-shaped stem leaves produced on thick leaf stalks. Spike-like cymes of insignificant green flowers are produced in summer, with flowering accelerated by hot, dry conditions. The most commonly cultivated species are grown as annual vegetables (such as beet and chard) or fodder plants, forming massively swollen roots. Some selections of *B. vulgaris* subsp. *cicla* produce attractive, ornamental foliage, and are useful for summer and winter color contrast in a mixed border or in annual bedding.

• **Cultivation** Grow in rich, light but moisture-retentive soil in full sun or partial shade. Water thoroughly during periods of drought to reduce the likelihood of bolting.

• **Propagation** Sow seed *in situ* in early spring or late summer.

• **Pests and diseases** Prone to fungal leaf spots, downy mildew, powdery mildew, damping off, and root rots caused by *Pythium* and *Phytophthora*. Leaf miners, aphids, and caterpillars can be problems.

B. vulgaris* subsp. *cicla (Swiss chard). Ornamental biennial, often grown as an annual for its decorative foliage. Bears clusters of initially upright then arching, narrow, sometimes puckered, glossy, light or mid-green leaves, 9–12in (23–30cm) long, with bright red or yellow midribs and, in some selections, with red or purple-red leaf blades. ↕ 9in (23cm), ↔ to 18in (45cm).

Beta vulgaris subsp. *cicla* 'MacGregor's Favourite'

'MacGregor's Favourite' ■ has brilliant blood-red foliage and is less liable to bolt than most other cultivars. **'Bright Lights'** has midribs of red, yellow, pink, orange, purple, gold, or white.

▷ ***Betonica*** see *Stachys*

Betula

Birch

BETULACEAE

Genus of about 60 species of deciduous trees and shrubs found in diverse habitats, including woodland, moors, mountains, and heathland, throughout the N. hemisphere. Leaves are alternate, toothed, usually ovate, and mid- to dark green. Male and female flowers are borne in separate catkins on the same plant in spring, the male catkins are usually yellow-brown, pendent, and longer than the females, which are erect at first, becoming pendent. Birches are grown for their ornamental bark, colorful autumn foliage, attractive male catkins, and graceful, open habit. Many are suitable for a small garden, either as isolated specimens or in small groups.

• **Cultivation** Grow in moderately fertile, moist but well-drained soil in full sun or light, dappled shade. *B. alleghaniensis*, *B. grossa*, *B. lenta*, and *B. maximowicziana* prefer sheltered, woodland conditions. Pruning group 1.

• **Propagation** Sow seed, of known wild origin only (most seed from cultivated plants will produce hybrids), in a seedbed in autumn. Root softwood cuttings in summer, or graft in winter.

• **Pests and diseases** Canker and twig dieback are caused by many different fungi. Susceptible to leaf spots, viruses, anthracnose, rust, and wood-rotting fungi. Borers (especially bronze birch borer), leaf miners, aphids, skeletonizers, leafhoppers, and caterpillars, including gypsy moth larvae, are common.

B. albosinensis (Chinese paper birch). Conical tree with peeling, orange-brown or brown bark, cream when newly exposed, often covered with a white glaucous bloom when young. Ovate, tapered, glossy leaves, to 3in (8cm) long, are deep green above, lighter beneath, turning yellow in autumn. Yellow-brown male catkins, to 2½in (6cm) long, open with the young leaves. ↕ 80ft (25m), ↔ 30ft (10m). W. China. Zone 3.

Betula ermanii

var. *septentrionalis* has orange-brown bark and paler, dull leaves.

B. alleghaniensis, syn. *B. lutea* (Yellow birch). Conical tree with peeling, yellow-brown bark. Ovate, matte, yellow-green leaves, to 5½in (14cm) long, become yellow in autumn and are borne on aromatic shoots. Yellow-brown male catkins, to 4in (10cm) long, are borne in early spring. ↕ 80ft (25m), ↔ 30ft (10m). E. North America. Zone 3b.

***B. costata* of gardens** see *B. ermanii* 'Grayswood Hill'.

B. ermanii ■ (Erman's birch). Conical tree with rough, warty shoots and pinkish or creamy white bark with conspicuous lenticels. Ovate, tapered, dull, dark green leaves, 4in (10cm) long, are glandular beneath and turn yellow in autumn. Yellow-brown male catkins, to 4in (10cm) long, open as the young leaves emerge. ↕ 70ft (20m), ↔ 40ft (12m). Russia (Kamchatka), Japan, Korea. Zone 5.

'Grayswood Hill', syn. *B. costata* of gardens, is a vigorous clone, with pure white bark.

B. grossa (Japanese cherry birch). Conical tree with peeling, reddish gray bark, becoming dark gray on mature plants. Ovate, sharply toothed, matte, dark green leaves, to 4in (10cm) long, are borne on aromatic shoots and turn golden yellow in autumn. Produces yellow-brown male catkins, to 3in (8cm) long, in early spring. ↕ 80ft (25m), ↔ 30ft (10m). Japan. Zone 5.

B. jacquemontii see *B. utilis* var. *jacquemontii*.

B. lenta ■ (Cherry birch, Sweet birch). Conical tree with dark red bark that becomes gray and scaly in maturity. Aromatic shoots bear ovate, matte, yellow-green leaves, to 4in (10cm) long, which turn yellow in autumn. Produces yellow-brown male catkins, to 3in (8cm) long, in early spring. ↕ 50ft (15m), ↔ 40ft (12m). E. US. Zone 4b.

B. lutea see *B. alleghaniensis*.

B. maximowicziana (Monarch birch). Broadly conical tree with pink-tinged, gray-white bark, peeling in horizontal strips, with conspicuous lenticels. Heart-shaped, deep green leaves, to 6in (15cm) long, turn yellow in autumn. Yellow-brown male catkins, to 5in (13cm) long, are produced in early spring. ↕ 80ft (25m), ↔ 40ft (12m). Russia (Kurile Islands), Japan. Zone 5b.

Betula lenta

Betula medwedewii

B. medwedewii ■ (Transcaucasian birch). Compact shrub with upright branches spreading with age and bearing conspicuous, pointed, glossy winter buds. Ovate, glossy, dark green leaves, to 4in (10cm) long, turn yellow to yellow-brown in autumn. In spring, produces yellow-brown male catkins, to 4in (10cm) long. ↕↔ 15ft (5m). Caucasus. Zone 5b.
B. nana ■ (Arctic birch, Dwarf birch). Spreading shrub with rounded to kidney-shaped, finely toothed, glossy, mid-green leaves, to ¾in (2cm) long, turning yellow or red in autumn. Bears yellow-brown male catkins, to ½in (1.5cm) long, in spring. ↕ 24in (60cm), ↔ 4ft (1.2m). Subarctic North America and Eurasia. Zone 2.
B. nigra ■ (Black birch, River birch). Conical to spreading tree with shaggy, red-brown bark, peeling in layers when young, becoming blackish or gray-white and fissured on old trees. Diamond-shaped, glossy, mid- to dark green leaves, to 3in (8cm) long, glaucous beneath, turn yellow in autumn. Bears yellow-brown male catkins, to 3in (8cm) long, in early spring. ↕ 60ft (18m), ↔ 40ft (12m). E. US. Zone 3.
'Heritage' is vigorous and exfoliates at an early age; the white to salmon-white young bark darkens to orange-brown. The leaves are larger and glossier than the species, and less prone to leaf spot. Heat tolerant. Shows superior tolerance to bronze birch borer; Zone 4.
'Little King' is a multi-stemmed, dwarf selection, with bark that exfoliates at an early age to orange-brown; ↕ 10ft (3m), ↔ 12ft (4m).

B. papyrifera ■ (Canoe birch, Paper birch). Conical tree with white bark, peeling in thin layers and pale orange-brown when newly exposed. Ovate, dark green leaves, to 4in (10cm) long, turn yellow to orange in autumn. Produces yellow male catkins, to 4in (10cm) long, in early spring. Grows best in cooler climates. ↕ 70ft (20m) or more, ↔ 30ft (10m). North America. Zone 2.
B. pendula, syn. *B. verrucosa* (European white birch). Narrowly conical tree with pendent, warty branchlets and peeling white bark, which becomes marked with dark, rugged cracks at the base on older trees. Diamond-shaped, sharply toothed, mid-green leaves, to 2½in (6cm) long, turn yellow in autumn. Bears yellow-brown male catkins, to 2½in (6cm) long, in early spring. Grows best in cooler climates. Very susceptible to bronze birch borer, and often short-lived. ↕ 80ft (25m), ↔ 30ft (10m). Europe, Russia (W. Siberia) Zone 2.
'Dalecarlica' of gardens see 'Laciniata'.
'Fastigiata' has upright branches; ↕ 70ft (20m), ↔ 20ft (6m). **'Golden Cloud'** has yellow foliage. Hot sun may scorch the leaves; ↕ 20ft (6m), ↔ 15ft (5m).
'Gracilis' has pendulous branches in clusters resembling witches' brooms, with finely dissected leaves. Lacks a central leader; ↕ 15–20ft (5–6m).
'Laciniata', syn. 'Dalecarlica' of gardens, has very pendulous branchlets and deeply cut leaves. **'Purple Rain'** has rich purple-green leaves. **'Purpurea'** has purple-tinged bark and dark purple leaves; ↕ 30ft (10m), ↔ 10ft (3m).
'Tristis' ■ has slender branchlets and bark remaining white at the base; Zone 2. **'Trost's Dwarf'** is bushy and dwarf, with thread-like, deep green leaves; ↕ 3–4ft (1–1.2m). **'Youngii'** ■ (Young's weeping birch) is dome-shaped; ↕ 25ft (8m); Zone 2.
B. platyphylla* var. *japonica (Asian white birch). Narrowly conical tree with slightly pendent, warty branchlets, and bark creamy white to the base. Diamond-shaped, sharply toothed, yellowish green leaves, to 4in (10cm) long, are hairless beneath, and turn yellow in autumn. Bears yellow-brown male catkins, to 3in (8cm) long, in early spring. ↕ 70ft (20m), ↔ 40ft (12m). Japan. Zone 3.
var. *szechuanica* see *B. szechuanica.*
'Whitespire' is conical, with chalk-white bark and darker green leaves. It has shown superior resistance to bronze birch borer.

B. populifolia (Gray birch). Narrowly conical, sometimes multi-stemmed tree, which is fast-growing, but usually short-lived. Branchlets are pendent and warty, and the gray-white bark, remaining white at the base, does not peel. Diamond-shaped, sharply toothed, glossy, yellowish green leaves, to 4in (10cm) long, end in long, slender points,

Betula papyrifera

Betula pendula 'Tristis'

Betula nana

Betula nigra (inset: bark detail)

Betula pendula 'Youngii'

Betula utilis var. *jacquemontii* 'Jermyns'

and turn yellow in autumn. Bears yellow-brown male catkins, to 3in (8cm) long, in early spring. Good for naturalizing in poor soils. ↕30ft (10m), ↔ 10ft (3m). E. North America. Zone 3.
B. pubescens (Downy birch). Narrowly conical tree with ascending branches, downy shoots, and peeling bark with conspicuous lenticels; bark remains white at the base. Diamond-shaped, sharply toothed, mid-green leaves, to 2½in (6cm) long, turn yellow in autumn. Produces pendent, yellow-brown male catkins, to 2½in (6cm) long, in early spring. Tolerates poor or wet, acidic soils. ↕70ft (20m), ↔ 30ft (10m). Europe, N. Asia. Zone 3.
B. schmidtii (Schmidt birch). Rounded tree with brownish black bark, exfoliating in irregular plates. Ovate, toothed, dark green leaves, 1½–3in (4–8cm) long, turn golden yellow in autumn. In early spring, produces yellow-brown male catkins, 3½in (9cm) long. ↕20–40ft (6–12m), ↔ 10–20ft (3–6m). Manchuria, Korea, Japan. Zone 5.
B. szechuanica, syn. *B. platyphylla* var. *szechuanica* (Szechuan birch). Vigorous, conical tree with chalk-white bark when mature, and ovate, leathery, dark bluish green leaves, to 4in (10cm) long, turning golden yellow in autumn. Produces yellow-green male catkins, to 3in (8cm) long, in early spring. ↕70ft (20m), ↔ 30ft (10m). S.W. China. Zone 4.
***B.* 'Trost's Dwarf'.** Slender-stemmed shrub with gracefully arching branches and ovate, mid-green leaves, to 2in (5cm) long, finely cut and divided into long, slender lobes. Not known to produce catkins. Often grafted as a standard. ↕↔ 5ft (1.5m). Zone 3.
B. utilis (Himalayan birch). Variable tree with peeling, copper-brown or pinkish bark and ovate to oblong, tapered, dark green leaves, to 5in (13cm) long, that turn yellow in autumn. In early spring, produces yellow-brown male catkins, to 5in (13cm) long. ↕60ft (18m), ↔ 30ft (10m). China, Himalayas. Zone 3. Most often grown in one of the following forms: **var. *jacquemontii***, syn. *B. jacquemontii* (White barked Himalayan birch) has white bark; Himalayas. **var. *jacquemontii* 'Grayswood Ghost'** has brilliant white bark and very glossy leaves. **var. *jacquemontii* 'Jermyns'** ▣ is a vigorous clone, with pure white bark and larger catkins, 6in (15cm) long. **var. *jacquemontii* 'Silver Shadow'** ▣ has bright white bark and pendent, dark green leaves, to 5in (13cm) long.
B. verrucosa see *B. pendula*.

Betula utilis var. *jacquemontii* 'Silver Shadow' (inset: bark detail)

BIARUM

ARACEAE

Genus of 15 species of small, tuberous perennials from open ground and maquis in the Mediterranean region and W. Asia. In autumn, they produce hooded, often malodorous spathes at ground level, followed by broadly ovate to spoon-shaped or lance-shaped leaves. They are best grown in a bulb frame or cold greenhouse, except *B. tenuifolium*, which may be grown outside at the base of a sunny wall, and increases rapidly.
• **CULTIVATION** Plant dormant tubers 2in (5cm) deep in summer. Under glass, grow in equal parts loam, leaf mold, and sharp sand or grit, in full light. Keep warm and dry when dormant in summer; water regularly but sparingly when in leaf. Tubers may rot if overwatered. *B. tenuifolium* may be grown outside in light, open, sharply drained soil in full sun.
• **PROPAGATION** Sow seed at 55°F (13°C) in autumn or spring, and prick out seedlings as soon as possible. Separate tubers in summer.
• **PESTS AND DISEASES** Infrequent.

B. davisii ▣ Tuberous perennial producing open flask-shaped, sweet-scented, pink-spotted cream spathes, 2–2½in (5–6cm) long, enclosing slightly protruding, reddish brown spadices, in autumn. Spathes are followed by ovate, wavy-margined leaves, 3in (8cm) long. ↕3in (8cm), PD2in (5cm). Crete, Turkey. Zone 7b.
B. eximium. Tuberous perennial bearing almost prostrate, recurved, deep purple spathes, 4–6in (10–15cm) long, revealing nearly black spadices, in autumn. Spathes are followed by narrowly ovate leaves, 7in (18cm) long. ↕3–4in (8–10cm), PD2in (5cm). S. Turkey. Zone 7b.
B. tenuifolium. Tuberous perennial bearing narrow, often twisted, purple-flushed, pale green spathes, to 4in (10cm) long, and nearly black spadices, in autumn, followed by lance-shaped to spoon-shaped leaves, 2–8in (5–20cm) long. ↕4–8in (10–20cm), PD2in (5cm). Mediterranean. Zone 7.

Biarum davisii

Bidens ferulifolia

BIDENS

ASTERACEAE

Genus of about 200 species of annuals, perennials, and deciduous shrubs occurring in grassland and wasteland, and among shrubs in Europe, tropical Africa, Asia, Australia, and temperate and tropical America. They have erect or spreading, opposite, simple or pinnate leaves, and flowerheads that are often terminal, or branched and cyme-like. Suitable for a container, hanging basket, gravel garden, or border. Where not hardy, grow as annuals.
• **CULTIVATION** Grow in reasonably fertile, moist but well-drained soil in full sun. Under glass, container plants will flower from midspring to winter if grown in frost-free conditions.
• **PROPAGATION** Sow seed at 55–64°F (13–18°C) in spring. Root stem cuttings of perennials in spring or autumn, or divide when growth begins in spring.
• **PESTS AND DISEASES** Prone to mottle virus, *Cercospora* leaf spot, white smut, downy mildew, powdery mildew, and rust. Leaf miners and aphids can occur.

B. atrosanguinea see *Cosmos atrosanguineus*.
B. ferulifolia ▣ Short-lived perennial, with 1- to 3-pinnate, fresh green leaves, to 3in (8cm) long, with lance-shaped leaflets. Slender, spreading stems produce daisy-like, golden yellow flowerheads, 1¼–1½in (3–4cm) across, from midsummer to autumn. ↕ to 12in (30cm), ↔ indefinite. S. US, Mexico. Zone 8. **'Golden Goddess'** has leaves with more slender segments and bears flowerheads 2in (5cm) across.

BIGNONIA *syn.* DOXANTHA

Cross vine

BIGNONIACEAE

Genus of one species of evergreen climber from moist forest of North America. It is grown for its cymes of 2–5 trumpet-shaped flowers. Train on a wall or over a pergola or tree; where not hardy, grow in a cool greenhouse.
• **CULTIVATION** Under glass, grow in soil-based potting mix in full light. When in growth, water freely and apply a balanced liquid fertilizer monthly; water sparingly in winter. Pot on or top-dress in spring. Outdoors, grow in fertile, moist but well-drained soil in full sun. Pruning group 11.

• **PROPAGATION** Sow seed at 64°F (18°C) in spring. Root leaf-bud cuttings in summer. Layer in autumn or spring.
• **PESTS AND DISEASES** Black mildew, powdery mildew, and *Cercospora* leaf spot are common in the S.E. US. *Botryosphaeria* dieback can occur. Mealybugs and spider mites can be problems under glass.

B. capensis see *Tecoma capensis.*
B. capreolata, syn. *Doxantha capreolata* (Cross vine). Vigorous climber with opposite leaves, to 7in (18cm) long, usually consisting of 2 oblong-ovate to lance-shaped, wavy-margined leaflets and one tendril. In late spring, bears fragrant flowers, 1½–2in (4–5cm) long; flowers are red-brown outside and yellow-orange inside. ↕ 30ft (10m) or more. S. Ontario, E. US. Zone 6.
B. grandiflora see *Campsis grandiflora.*
B. jasminoides see *Pandorea jasminoides.*
B. pandorana see *Pandorea pandorana.*
B. radicans see *Campsis radicans.*
B. stans see *Tecoma stans.*
B. unguis-cati see *Macfadyena unguis-cati.*

▷ ***Bilderdykia*** see *Fallopia*

BILLARDIERA

PITTOSPORACEAE

Genus of 8 species of evergreen, twining, perennial climbers occurring at forest margins and in moist to dry scrub in temperate to subtropical regions of Australia. They are cultivated for their usually bell-shaped, 5-petaled flowers, produced on the current year's growth, either singly or in small clusters in the upper leaf axils, and for their beautifully colored berries. Leaves are alternate, small, entire, and often lance-shaped. Where not hardy, grow in a cool greenhouse or conservatory; elsewhere, grow over a pergola or against a house wall, or allow to scramble over vigorous shrubs.
• **CULTIVATION** Under glass, grow in acidic potting mix in bright filtered light. Water freely from spring to autumn, applying a balanced liquid fertilizer monthly; water sparingly in winter. Top-dress or pot on in late winter. Outdoors, grow in humus-rich, moist but well-drained, neutral to acidic soil in a sunny or partially shaded, sheltered site. Survives short periods of 32°F (0°C), but may lose some leaves. Pruning group 11, after fruiting.

Billardiera longiflora

• **PROPAGATION** Sow seed at 55–59°F (13–15°C), ideally as soon as ripe in autumn, or in spring. Root softwood cuttings in early summer with bottom heat, or semi-ripe cuttings in late summer, both in a propagating case. Layer in autumn or spring.
• **PESTS AND DISEASES** Spider mites may be troublesome under glass.

B. longiflora ▣ (Climbing blueberry, Purple apple berry). Slender, wiry-stemmed climber with linear-lance-shaped, deep green leaves, ½–1¾in (1.5–4.5cm) long. In summer, produces solitary, pendent, narrowly bell-shaped, pale green flowers, ¾–1¼in (2–3cm) long, followed by oblong-ovoid berries, ¾in (2cm) long, usually deep purple-blue, but sometimes purple, red, pink, or white. ↕ 6–10ft (2–3m). New South Wales to Tasmania. ❄ (min. 41°F/5°C)
B. scandens (Common apple berry). Wiry-stemmed climber with ovate-lance-shaped, wavy-margined, deep green leaves, ½–2in (1–5cm) long. Solitary, bell-shaped, greenish yellow or violet to purple flowers, ½–1in (1.5–2.5cm) long, are produced mainly in late spring and early summer, followed by ellipsoid, olive-green berries, ¾–1¼in (2–3cm) long, which are occasionally flushed red. ↕ 6–15ft (2–5m). E. Australia. ❄ (min. 41°F/5°C)

BILLBERGIA

BROMELIACEAE

Genus of about 60 species of rosette-forming, rhizomatous or suckering, evergreen, mainly epiphytic or rock-dwelling perennials (bromeliads) from scrub, woodland, and forest, up to an altitude of 5,500ft (1,700m), in S. Mexico, Central America, and N., E., and C. South America. They are cultivated for their erect or arching panicles or racemes of tubular, colorful but short-lived flowers. Many also have attractive leaves. Where not hardy, grow in a temperate greenhouse or as houseplants; in warm, humid areas, grow in a border or epiphytically.
• **CULTIVATION** Under glass, grow epiphytically or in containers of epiphytic bromeliad potting mix in bright indirect light. Keep the central funnel filled with fresh water. In the growing season, water freely and apply a low-nitrogen liquid fertilizer monthly; at other times, spray plants once a week. Outdoors, grow epiphytically or in humus-rich, sharply drained soil in partial shade. See also p.47.
• **PROPAGATION** Sow seed at 81°F (27°C) as soon as ripe. Root offsets in summer.
• **PESTS AND DISEASES** Scale insects, mealybugs, and some fungal spots may be troublesome.

B. amoena. Variable, rhizomatous bromeliad, generally epiphytic, with neat, tubular rosettes of 8–10 strap-shaped, mid-green, often white-spotted, sometimes red-flushed leaves, 12–24in (30–60cm) long. In summer, branched, arching, terminal inflorescences, 18in (45cm) long, with showy, deep red bracts, produce blue-tipped, green flowers, to ½in (1.5cm) long. ↕ to 24in (60cm), ↔ to 8in (20cm). E. Brazil. ❄ (min. 45°F/7°C)

Billbergia Fantasia Group

B. distachia. Epiphytic bromeliad with short rhizomes and erect, cylindrical rosettes of 4 or 5 linear to lance-shaped, mid-green leaves, 10–36in (25–90cm) long, flushed purple, with short, widely spaced, marginal prickles. In summer, slightly arching panicles, 12in (30cm) long, bear short, lax branches of 7 or 8 green flowers, to 2in (5cm) long, with blue-tipped petals and sepals. ↕↔ 20in (50cm). E. Brazil. ❄ (min. 45°F/7°C)
B. elegans. Epiphytic perennial with a vase-like rosette of 8–10 broadly lance-shaped, light green leaves, to 16in (40cm) long, with conspicuous silver scales and marginal brown spines. Pendulous, white-scaped inflorescences, to 16in (40cm) long, with pyramidal pink bracts, bear lax, blue-tipped, yellow-green flowers, to 1½in (4cm) long, in summer. ↕↔ 16in (40cm). Brazil. ❄ (min. 45°F/7°C)
B. euphemiae. Epiphytic perennial with a tubular rosette of 8–10 lance-shaped gray-green leaves, 12in (30cm) long, faintly silver-banded outside with inconspicuous spines. In summer, produces pendulous, pink-scaped inflorescences, to 16in (40cm) long, bearing clusters of blue-petaled flowers, to 1in (2.5cm) long, among pink bracts. ↕↔ 12in (30cm). S. Brazil. ❄ (min. 45°F/7°C) **var. *purpurea*** has reddish purple leaves without bands. **var. *saundersioides*** has white and pink spots on narrow leaves.
***B.* Fantasia Group** ▣ (Marbled rainbow plant). Epiphytic bromeliads with urn-shaped rosettes of 6–8 narrowly lance-shaped, copper-green leaves, 12–18in (30–45cm) long, marbled creamy white and pink. Erect, white-felted, red-stalked inflorescences, to 16in (40cm) long, with red bracts, terminate in panicles, 5in (13cm) long, of violet-blue flowers, 2½–3in (6–8cm) long, in summer. ↕ 20in (50cm), ↔ 18in (45cm). ❄ (min. 45°F/7°C)

Billbergia nutans

Billbergia pyramidalis

B. nutans ▣ (Friendship plant, Queen's tears). Variable, epiphytic bromeliad with short rhizomes and narrowly funnel-shaped rosettes of 12–15 linear or strap-shaped, pointed, sometimes red-flushed, gray-green leaves, to 28in (70cm) long, with smooth or finely toothed margins. In summer, slender, short-branched, red-bracted flower stems, to 6in (15cm) long, bear panicles, to 2in (5cm) long, of flowers with pale green petals margined blue and tipped darker green, and reflexed, rose-pink sepals with greenish blue margins. ↕ 20in (50cm), ↔ indefinite. S. Brazil, Paraguay, N. Argentina, Uruguay. ❄ (min. 45°F/7°C)
B. porteana. Epiphytic bromeliad with short rhizomes and sturdy, tubular rosettes of 6–8 strap-shaped, gray-mottled, gray-green leaves, to 36in (90cm) long, with white cross-banding beneath and frequently spotted yellow. In summer, pendent, white-mealy racemes, to 16in (40cm) long, with papery red bracts, produce tubular, yellowish green flowers, 3in (8cm) long, with purple styles and stamens. ↕ 3ft (1m) or more, ↔ 20in (50cm). Brazil, Paraguay. ❄ (min. 45°F/7°C)
B. pyramidalis ▣ Epiphytic bromeliad with tubular rosettes of 5–13 strap-shaped, minutely toothed, fresh green leaves, to 20in (50cm) long. Bears dense panicles of erect, pale red flowers, ½–¾in (1.5–2cm) long, with reflexed blue tips, terminally on white-mealy flower stems, to 5in (13cm) long, in summer. ↕ 20in (50cm), ↔ 10in (25cm). Brazil. ❄ (min. 45°F/7°C). **var. *concolor*** has deeper red flowers without any blue coloration.
B. rhodocyanea see *Aechmea fasciata.*
B. vittata. Epiphytic bromeliad with tubular rosettes of 8–10 lance- to strap-shaped, olive-green or gray-green leaves, 16–36in (40–90cm) or more long, with reflexed, spiny tips and gray cross-banding. In summer, narrowly pyramidal, pendent, red- or orange-bracted inflorescences, to 30in (75cm) long, bear 20 or more flowers, to 2½in (6cm) long, with orange sepals, white or pale green petals, and dark blue tips. ↕ to 3ft (1m), ↔ 16in (40cm). S.E. Brazil. ❄ (min. 45°F/7°C)

▷ ***Biota orientalis*** see *Thuja orientalis*
▷ ***Bistorta*** see *Persicaria*

BIXA

BIXACEAE

Genus of one species of evergreen tree from rich soil along the edges of forest in tropical North and South America. It has alternate leaves and corymb-like panicles of rose-like flowers, followed by bristly fruits. Where not hardy, grow *B. orellana* in a warm greenhouse for its attractive, bright red fruit. In warmer climates, grow as a hedge or specimen tree, for the flowers, which are an excellent source of nectar for honeybees, and for the seeds, which yield a dye used in cosmetics and food. Bixa is a source of red body paint for some tropical Native American tribes.

• **CULTIVATION** Under glass, grow in soil-based potting mix in full light. Water freely when in growth, sparingly in winter. Outdoors, grow in fertile, well-drained, humus-rich loam in full sun. Clip hedges in early spring before new growth begins. Pruning group 8 or 9 under glass; group 1 when grown outdoors as a tree.

• **PROPAGATION** Sow seed at 66–75°F (19–24°C) in spring, or root semi-ripe cuttings in summer.

• **PESTS AND DISEASES** Algal leaf spot, a few fungal leaf spots, and powdery mildew can occur.

B. orellana ■ (Achiote, Annatto, Lipstick tree). Intricately branched tree with broad, ovate-heart-shaped, slender-pointed, smooth, mid-green leaves, to 8in (20cm) long. From late summer to autumn, bears terminal panicles of 3–5 or more, open cup-shaped, 5-petaled, purple-tinted, white or pink flowers, to 2in (5cm) across, followed by ovoid, bristly, bright red or dark pink fruit, 2in (5cm) long, containing many dark red seeds. ↕ 22–30ft (7–10m), ↔ 10–15ft (3–5m), much shorter under glass. Florida, West Indies, Central America, tropical South America. ❄ (min. 61–64°F/16–18°C)

Bixa orellana

Blandfordia grandiflora

BLANDFORDIA

Christmas bells

LILIACEAE

Genus of 4 species of rhizomatous perennials from swampy areas, acidic heaths, and bogs on the Australian mainland and in Tasmania. They are cultivated for their racemes of showy, tubular flowers, produced in summer. The leaves are linear, sharp-pointed, and gray-green. Where not hardy, grow in a cool or temperate greenhouse. In frost-free areas, grow in a rock garden.

• **CULTIVATION** Under glass, plant rhizomes 2in (5cm) deep in autumn in clay pots filled with acidic potting mix, with additional sharp sand. Provide full light and good ventilation. When in growth, water moderately and apply a balanced liquid fertilizer monthly. Keep dry during winter dormancy. Outdoors, grow in well-drained, humus-rich, acidic soil in full sun.

• **PROPAGATION** Sow seed at 55–61°F (13–16°C) in spring. Remove offsets after flowering.

• **PESTS AND DISEASES** Infrequent.

B. grandiflora ■ Rhizomatous perennial producing linear leaves, to 28in (70cm) long, and, in early summer, loose racemes of up to 10 red or red-and-yellow flowers, 1½–2½in (4–6cm) long. ↕ 24in (60cm), PD6in (15cm). Australia. ❄ (min. 41°F/5°C)

B. punicea (Tasmanian Christmas bells). Rhizomatous perennial with linear leaves, to 14in (35cm) long. In summer, produces loose racemes of up to 25 flowers, 2in (5cm) long, pinkish red with yellow tips outside, yellow inside. ↕ 32–36in (80–90cm), PD9in (23cm). Tasmania. ❄ (min. 41°F/5°C)

BLECHNUM

Hard fern

BLECHNACEAE

Genus of 150–200 species of usually evergreen, rhizomatous, terrestrial ferns found mostly in moist, sheltered, acidic sites in temperate and tropical regions. The rhizomes are erect or creeping, often densely covered with black scales, and bear pinnate or pinnatifid, rarely simple, usually leathery fronds. Fertile fronds are generally erect, in the centers of the frond rosettes. Linear sori are arranged in 2 rows along the midrib of each frond lobe or segment. Some

Blechnum gibbum

species form small "trunks." Some hard ferns are monomorphic, with sterile and fertile fronds identical, and some are dimorphic, with sterile and fertile fronds somewhat different. Grow in woodland, in a shady herbaceous border, or in a rock garden. Where not hardy, grow in a warm greenhouse or conservatory.

• **CULTIVATION** Under glass, grow in a mix of 1 part each acidic loam, medium-grade bark, and charcoal; 2 parts sharp sand; and 3 parts coarse leaf mold. Provide bright filtered or indirect light, and moderate to high humidity with good ventilation. Fronds discolor if air circulation is poor, and in a dry atmosphere, they may scorch in full sun. Water freely when in growth, moderately in winter. Outdoors, grow in moist, humus-rich, acidic soil in humid, partial or deep shade.

• **PROPAGATION** Sow spores in late summer. Divide *B. penna-marina* and *B. spicant* in spring; divisions of other species take some time to re-establish. See also p.51.

• **PESTS AND DISEASES** Prone to leaf spot and rust, as well as scale insects, mealybugs, and caterpillars.

B. alpinum see *B. penna-marina*.

B. appendiculatum. Slightly arching, colonizing fern. Lance-shaped pinnate dark green fronds have reddish stipe and rachis. Similar to occidentale, but has hairs on the lower surface of the rachis and new growth reddish instead of pinkish. Moist shade. Southern US, American tropics. ↕ 15in (37.5cm). ❄ (min. 45°F/7°C)

B. australe. Slightly arching, colonizing fern, in uneven clusters. Linear pinnate midgreen fronds have reddish stipes and rachis. New growth is yellowish. Found in semi-shady, moist woods. ↕ 15in (30cm). South Africa, Madagascar, S. Atlantic Islands. ❄ (min. 45°F/7°C)

B. brasiliense. Evergreen fern with upright, trunk-like rhizomes, to 12in (30cm) tall, and oblong-lance-shaped, pinnate, mid- to dark green fronds, 3ft (1m) tall, with finely toothed, linear pinnae. Fronds are reddish green when young. Similar to *B. gibbum*, but the fronds are narrower and the fertile fronds are similar to the sterile ones. ↕↔ 3–5ft (1–1.5m). Peru, Brazil. ❄ (min. 50°F/10°C)

B. chilense, syn. *B. cordatum*, *B. magellanicum*. Evergreen fern with a

Blechnum penna-marina

creeping rhizome, which may become erect and trunk-like. Ovate-lance-shaped, pinnate, dark green fronds, to 3ft (1m) long, have long, brown-scaly stalks. Sterile fronds have oblong, toothed pinnae; fertile ones have linear-lance-shaped pinnae. Often confused with *B. tabulare.* ↕ 3–6ft (1–2m), ↔ indefinite. Chile, Argentina. ❀ (min. 50°F/10°C)
B. cordatum see *B. chilense.*
B. gibbum ▣ syn. *Lomaria gibba.* Evergreen fern with upright, trunk-like rhizomes, to 3ft (1m) tall. Oblong-lance-shaped, pinnatisect, black-scaled, bright green fronds are usually 3ft (1m) long, but may reach 6ft (2m). Narrowly linear, entire lobes are erect, then spreading, each pair forming a V-shape along the frond. Sterile fronds have broader lobes than fertile ones. ↕↔ to 36in (90cm) or more. Fiji. ❀ (min. 50°F/10°C)
B. magellanicum see *B. chilense.*
B. nudum. Evergreen fern with erect, occasionally trunk-like rhizomes, to 36in (90cm) tall, and ovate-lance-shaped, pinnate, mid- to dark green fronds. Sterile fronds are 16–36in (40–90cm) long, with narrowly linear pinnae. Fertile fronds are 8–28in (20–70cm) long, and are narrower, with more slender pinnae. Similar to *B. gibbum,* but pinnae are nearly perpendicular to the midribs. Sometimes united with the closely related *B. discolor.* ↕↔ to 3ft (1m). Australia. ❀ (min. 41°F/5°C)
B. occidentale (Hammock fern). Evergreen fern with erect or ascending, brown rhizomes, 24in (60cm) tall, producing pinnate to pinnatisect, linear-oblong or lance-shaped, mid-green sterile fronds, 9–18in (23–45cm) long, with linear-oblong or narrowly triangular pinnae. Fertile fronds are slightly longer. ↕↔ 9–18in (23–45cm). Central America and tropical South America, West Indies. ❀ (min. 45°F/7°C)
B. penna-marina ▣ syn. *B. alpinum.* Evergreen fern with linear, pinnate or pinnatifid fronds arising in tufts from creeping rhizomes. Sterile fronds have oblong to triangular pinnae; fertile fronds have more widely spaced, narrowly linear to oblong pinnae. ↕ 4–8in (10–20cm), ↔ indefinite. Australia, S. South America. ❀ (min. 50°F/10°C). At least 2 subspecies are cultivated: **subsp. *penna-marina*** with glossy, dark green fronds, 8in (20cm) tall; **subsp. *alpina*** smaller, 4–6in (10–15cm) tall, with matte, dark green fronds, which are reddish green when young. There is also a crested cultivar of the smaller form, **subsp. *alpina* 'Cristatum'** ↕ 4–8in (10–20cm), ↔ indefinite. Australasia, S. South America. ❀ (min. 50°F/10°C)
B. spicant (Deer fern). Evergreen fern with short, creeping rhizomes. Produces tufts of narrowly lance-shaped, pinnate, sometimes partly pinnatifid, dark green sterile fronds, 8–20in (20–50cm) long, with oblong pinnae. As they age, sterile fronds spread semi-horizontally to form a rosette around the taller fertile fronds; these are 12–24in (30–60cm) long, and have very narrowly linear, well-separated pinnae. ↕ 8–20in (20–50cm), ↔ 24in (60cm) or more. Europe, N. Asia, North America. Zone 5. **'Crispum'** is evergreen, with closely set, crinkled pinnae. ↕ 10in (25cm). Washington. **'Cristatum'** is evergreen and has forked blade tips. ↕ 10in (25cm). England. **'Rickard's Serrate'** is evergreen with pinnae edges that are neatly lobed, making the blade nearly pinnate. ↕ 15in (37.5cm). England.
B. wattsii. Arching, colonizing fern. Broadly ovate pinnate dark green blades have bronzy red new growth. Pinnae ¾in (2cm) across. Prefers partial shade, evenly moist conditions. ↕ 12in (30cm). Australia. ❀ (min. 45°F/7°C)

BLETILLA
ORCHIDACEAE

Genus of 9 or 10 species of deciduous, terrestrial orchids occurring in cool to temperate regions of China, Taiwan, and Japan. They have short rhizomes that develop corm-like pseudobulbs, partially underground, each pseudobulb producing 3 or 4 linear to obovate, folded leaves. Upright, terminal racemes of up to 12 narrowly bell-shaped flowers are borne from spring to early summer. Grow outdoors in a woodland garden or lath house, or in an alpine house or a cold greenhouse.
• **CULTIVATION** Under glass, grow in soil-based potting mix with added leaf mold, in bright filtered or bright indirect light. In summer, water freely, applying a quarter-strength balanced liquid fertilizer at every third watering. Keep dry in winter. Outdoors, grow in moist, well-drained, humus-rich soil in a sheltered site, with partial shade in summer. Mulch in winter, or lift and store dry and frost-free. See also p.46.
• **PROPAGATION** Divide in early spring.
• **PESTS AND DISEASES** Spider mites, aphids, whiteflies, and mealybugs may be troublesome.

B. hyacinthina see *B. striata.*
B. striata ▣ syn. *B. hyacinthina.* Terrestrial orchid with flattened pseudobulbs and oblong-lance-shaped, dark green leaves, 12–18in (30–45cm) long. Produces magenta flowers, 1in (2.5cm) across, from spring to early summer. ↕↔ 12–24in (30–60cm). China, Japan. Zone 5b. **f. *alba*** has white flowers. There are also creamy white- to pale yellow-flowered forms, and selections with longitudinally white-variegated foliage.

Bletilla striata

BLOOMERIA
LILIACEAE

Genus, related to *Allium* and *Brodiaea,* of 3 species of cormous perennials from scrub in North America. They have linear leaves with keeled tips and bear umbels of flattish, star-shaped flowers on leafless stems. Grow in a rock garden, in a raised bed, or in an alpine house.
• **CULTIVATION** Plant corms 3in (8cm) deep in autumn in light, fertile, sandy soil in full sun or partial shade. Provide ample water while in growth; keep dry in summer after flowering. Excessive moisture encourages corms to rot. Under glass, grow in a mix of equal parts loam, leaf mold, and sharp sand.
• **PROPAGATION** Sow seed in containers in a cold frame as soon as ripe. Remove offsets in autumn.
• **PESTS AND DISEASES** Infrequent.

B. crocea. Cormous perennial with linear leaves, 4–6in (10–15cm) long, that may die down at flowering time. In late spring and early summer, bears large, lax, spherical umbels of deep golden yellow flowers, ½–¾in (1.5–2cm) across, with a green or purple midrib on each tepal. ↕ 6–12in (15–30cm), PD3in (8cm). California. Zone 8.

BLOSSFELDIA
CACTACEAE

Genus, closely related to *Parodia,* of one species of miniature cactus from rocky hills in semi-desert regions of the Bolivian and Argentinian Andes. It has tuberous rootstocks and flattened-spherical stems, which frequently offset to form cushions. Spineless areoles are scattered across the ribless stems and, in summer, those close to the crown produce funnel-shaped, diurnal flowers.

Blossfeldia liliputana

These are followed by spherical fruits containing tiny, brownish red seeds. Where not hardy, grow *B. liliputana* in a temperate greenhouse. In frost-free areas, grow in a desert garden.
• **CULTIVATION** Under glass, grow in standard cactus potting mix in full light. When in growth, water moderately, applying half-strength, low-nitrogen fertilizer monthly; keep just moist from midautumn to early spring. Excess moisture may encourage root rot. Outdoors, grow in gritty, loamy soil in partial shade. See also pp.48–49.
• **PROPAGATION** Sow seed in early spring or remove offsets in late spring or early summer; keep both at 70°F (21°C). Most blossfeldias in cultivation have been grafted.
• **PESTS AND DISEASES** Mealybugs.

B. liliputana ▣ syn. *Parodia liliputana.* Cushion-forming cactus with grayish or dark green stems, ¾in (2cm) high, and minute, woolly gray areoles. Open funnel-shaped, yellowish white flowers, ½in (1.5cm) across, are produced in summer. ↕ 1¼–2in (3–5cm), ↔ to 2½in (6cm). Bolivia, Argentina. ❀ (min. 63°F/17°C)

▷ ***Bocconia*** see *Macleaya*

BOENNINGHAUSENIA
RUTACEAE

Genus of one species of deciduous subshrub from woodland in the mountains of E. Asia. It is grown for its visually attractive, although unpleasantly scented leaves and its terminal panicles of small, delicate, 4-petaled flowers. Grow in a sheltered rock garden, in a shrub border or woodland garden, or against a warm wall.
• **CULTIVATION** Grow in well-drained soil in full sun. Where not reliably hardy, apply a deep winter mulch in autumn. Cut out dead shoots in spring.
• **PROPAGATION** Sow seed in containers in a cold frame in autumn. Root softwood cuttings in summer.
• **PESTS AND DISEASES** Infrequent.

B. albiflora. Upright subshrub with alternate, 2- or 3-pinnate, dark green leaves, to 6in (15cm) long, consisting of 10–80 obovate leaflets. In late summer, bears cup-shaped, white or creamy white flowers, ½in (1.5cm) across, in panicles to 12in (30cm) long. ↕↔ 3ft (1m). Himalayas, China, Japan. Zone 6.

B

Bolax gummifera

BOLAX

APIACEAE

Genus of 2 or 3 species of dense, cushion-forming, evergreen perennials, allied to *Azorella*, occurring in open, rocky areas of S. South America. They have tight rosettes of alternate, simple, very deeply 3-lobed leaves and umbels of insignificant, greenish white flowers. In the wild, they form large hummocks, to 24in (60cm) or more tall, by 4ft (1.2m) across, but seldom attain this size in cultivation. Grow as foliage plants in an alpine house, in a scree bed, or in tufa.
• **CULTIVATION** Grow in any very sharply drained soil in full sun.
• **PROPAGATION** Sow seed (although seldom produced) in containers in a cold frame as soon as ripe. Remove and pot up offsets in spring.
• **PESTS AND DISEASES** Susceptible to spider mites and aphids under glass.

B. glebaria see *B. gummifera*.
B. gummifera ◼ syn. *Azorella glebaria*, *B. glebaria*. Slow-growing, compact perennial with rosettes of very deeply 3-lobed, leathery, dark blue-green leaves, to ¼in (6mm) long. Umbels, consisting of 3–20 tiny, greenish white flowers, borne in summer, are rarely produced. ↕ to 2in (5cm), sometimes to 6in (15cm), ↔ to 6in (15cm), sometimes to 10in (25cm). S. Chile, S. Argentina, Falkland Islands. Zone 5b.

BOLBITIS

LOMARIOPSIDACEAE

Genus of over 40 species of terrestrial, or almost scandent, epiphytic ferns usually found in riverine sites in tropical forest in Africa, Asia, and Central and South America. Creeping rhizomes produce entire and simple to pinnatifid or pinnate sterile fronds, often with plantlets near the tips. Fertile fronds are usually taller and narrower than sterile fronds, with black sporangia beneath. Where not hardy, they are best grown in the border of a warm greenhouse, to allow a free root-run, but may also be grown in containers. In frost-free areas, grow in a bog garden or by a stream.
• **CULTIVATION** Under glass, grow in a mix of 1 part each of loam, medium-grade bark, and charcoal; 2 parts sharp sand; and 3 parts coarse leaf mold. Provide low light and high humidity. Water freely when in growth, sparingly

Bolbitis heteroclita

in winter. Outdoors, grow in moist, humus-rich soil in partial or deep shade, in a sheltered, humid site.
• **PROPAGATION** Sow spores at 70°F (21°C) as soon as ripe. Root plantlets as soon as they appear. See also p.51.
• **PESTS AND DISEASES** Infrequent.

B. heteroclita ◼ Variable, evergreen, rhizomatous, terrestrial or semi-epiphytic fern. Sterile, bright mid-green fronds, to 24in (60cm) or more long and usually elliptic, are simple, or pinnate with elliptic pinnae; most have a long, strongly developed, ovate-lance-shaped terminal segment that produces a plantlet or roots down at the tip of the fertile fronds. Fertile fronds, 5½–30in (14–75cm) long, are usually pinnate, sometimes simple, with narrower pinnae than on sterile fronds; the lower surface is covered with felt-like sporangia. ↕ to 3ft (1m), ↔ 24in (60cm) or more. Tropical Asia. ❀ (min. 61–70°F/16–21°C)

BOLLEA

ORCHIDACEAE

Genus of 6 species of evergreen, epiphytic orchids, without pseudobulbs, from high forest of Ecuador, Colombia, and Brazil at 6,600ft (2,000m). They have oblong-lance-shaped leaves, and bear solitary, rounded, fleshy flowers, from small sheathing bracts at the pendent, triangular nodes of the inflorescences.
• **CULTIVATION** Intermediate-growing orchids. Grow in epiphytic orchid potting mix in partial shade and high humidity. Water freely and apply a balanced liquid fertilizer every 3 weeks when in growth; water sparingly in winter. See also p.46.
• **PROPAGATION** Divide when the plant fills the pot and flows over the sides; laboratory conditions required if grown from seed.
• **PESTS AND DISEASES** Infrequent.

B. violacea. Epiphytic orchid with 6–10 oblong-lance-shaped, mid- to dark green leaves, 6–12in (15–30cm) long. At various times, produces inflorescences, 4–10in (10–25cm) long, of solitary, rounded, fleshy, violet flowers, 3–5in (8–13cm) across, with purple calluses and narrow apexes on the lips. ↕↔ 12in (30cm). Ecuador, Colombia, Brazil. ❀ (min. 54°F/12°C; max. 77°F/25°C)

BOLTONIA

ASTERACEAE

Genus of about 8 species of perennials from sunny, moist sites in North America. Erect, hairless stems branch toward the apex and bear alternate, lance-shaped, stalkless, sometimes finely toothed, blue-green or mid-green leaves. Small flowerheads of white, lilac, or pinkish purple ray florets and yellow disk florets are borne in panicles. Grow in a border or wild garden, or for cut flowers.
• **CULTIVATION** Grow in fertile, moist but well-drained soil in full sun or partial shade. Divide every 2 or 3 years.
• **PROPAGATION** Sow seed in a cold frame in autumn. Divide in early spring.
• **PESTS AND DISEASES** Anthracnose, rust, powdery mildew, and leaf spot occur.

B. asteroides ◼ Upright perennial with strong stems and inversely lance-shaped, finely toothed, slightly glaucous, blue-green leaves, 5in (13cm) long, becoming greener as they age. From late summer to midautumn, bears inflorescences of many panicles, 4–6in (10–15cm) across, of flowerheads, ¾in (2cm) across, with white, lilac, or pinkish purple ray florets. ↕ 6ft (2m), ↔ 3ft (1m). C. and E. US. Zone 4. **var. *latisquama***, syn. *B. latisquama*, has flowerheads ¾–1¼in (2–3cm) across, with deep lilac-purple or white ray florets. **var. *latisquama* 'Pink Beauty'** has pink ray florets. **'Snowbank'** has pure white ray florets; ↕ to 5ft (1.5m), ↔ to 3ft (90cm).
B. latisquama see *B. asteroides* var. *latisquama*.

Boltonia asteroides

BOLUSANTHUS

South African wisteria

FABACEAE

Genus of one species of deciduous tree from scrub and forest in Africa, grown mainly for its clustered racemes of brightly colored, pea-like flowers. The alternate, pinnate leaves unfold after the flowers open. Where not hardy, grow *B. speciosus* in a cool greenhouse; it rarely flowers well in a container. In warmer regions, use as a specimen tree.
• **CULTIVATION** Under glass, grow in soil-based potting mix in full light. When in growth, water moderately and apply a balanced liquid fertilizer monthly; keep just moist in winter. Top-dress in late winter. Outdoors, grow in moderately fertile, well-drained soil in full sun. May survive short spells at 32°F (0°C). Pruning group 1.
• **PROPAGATION** Sow seed at 55–61°F (13–16°C) in spring.
• **PESTS AND DISEASES** Spider mites may be troublesome under glass.

B. speciosus (Elephantwood). Spreading tree, briefly deciduous from late winter to spring, with silky-hairy, yellow-green leaves, to 6in (15cm) long, composed of 7–15 ovate-lance-shaped leaflets, maturing to glossy, pale green. Blue-violet flowers, ¾in (2cm) long, open in clustered racemes, to 10in (25cm) long, from late winter to spring. ↕ 12–20ft (4–6m), ↔ 8–12ft (2.5–4m). Angola, Zimbabwe, Mozambique, South Africa. ❀ (min. 41°F/5°C)

BOMAREA

LILIACEAE

Genus of about 120 species of tuberous-rooted, usually deciduous, rarely semi-evergreen, twining and scandent climbers from scrub and forest margins in Mexico and South America. Leaves are alternate or spiralling, simple, and generally narrow. Tubular to bell-shaped, 6-tepaled flowers are borne in showy, terminal racemes or umbels. Where not hardy, grow in a cool greenhouse; elsewhere, use to clothe a pergola, arbor, or house wall. The naming of cultivated species is confused.
• **CULTIVATION** Under glass, grow in soil-based potting mix with added sharp sand, in full light with shade from hot sun. Provide support. When in growth, water freely and apply a balanced liquid fertilizer monthly; keep just moist in winter. Pot on or top-dress in early spring. Outdoors, grow in fertile, moist but well-drained soil in full sun. Cut back dead growth and flowered stems to ground level in winter.
• **PROPAGATION** Sow seed at 55–61°F (13–16°C) in spring. Divide established plants in late winter or in early spring as growth begins.
• **PESTS AND DISEASES** Prey to spider mites, whiteflies, and aphids under glass.

B. andimarcana, syn. *B. pubigera* of gardens. Scandent, erect, deciduous climber with lance-shaped, white-downy leaves, 2–5in (5–13cm) long, which appear almost gray. Bears umbels of up to 10 pendent, tubular, pale yellow flowers, 1½–2in (4–5cm) long, suffused with light red and tipped with soft green,

Bracteantha bracteata Monstrosum Series

Bracteantha bracteata 'Silvery Rose'

colors; ↕ 36in (90cm). **'Silvery Rose'** ▣ has double, silvery rose-pink flowerheads; ↕ to 30in (75cm). **'Sky Net'** has pink-flushed, creamy white flowerheads, to 3in (8cm) across. Cultivars of **Tetraploid Double Series** are very vigorous and bear pink, crimson-red, yellow, orange, or white flowerheads, to 3in (8cm) across; ↕ 5ft (1.5m).

BRAHEA

Hesper palm

ARECACEAE

Genus of 16 species of usually single-stemmed palms occurring on dry, open forest slopes in S. California, and from Mexico to Guatemala. Long panicles of 3-petaled, bell-shaped flowers develop among dense, terminal heads of fan-like leaves. Where not hardy, grow young specimens for their foliage, as houseplants or in a temperate greenhouse or conservatory. In warmer regions, use as specimen trees.

• **CULTIVATION** Under glass, grow in soil-based potting mix in full light. When in growth, water moderately and apply a balanced liquid fertilizer monthly; water sparingly in winter. Pot on or top-dress in spring. Outdoors, grow in well-drained soil in full sun; will tolerate poor, dry soil. Can withstand short periods at 32°F (0°C).

• **PROPAGATION** Sow seed at 73–81°F (23–27°C) in spring.

• **PESTS AND DISEASES** Spider mites and scale insects can be problems under glass. *Ganoderma* butt rot, false smut, and anthracnose occur.

B. armata ▣ (Blue-fan palm, Blue hesper palm, Gray goddess palm). Erect palm with the trunk clothed in fibrous leaf bases. Bears fan-like, waxy-textured, blue-green leaves, 3–6ft (1–2m) across, with about 50 slender lobes, on long, spiny stalks. In summer, bears arching panicles, 12ft (4m) long, of small yellow flowers. ↕ to 50ft (15m), ↔ to 22ft (7m). S. California, Mexico. ❀ (min. 41–59°F/5–15°C)

Brahea armata

B. brandegeei (San Jose hesper palm). Slender palm with a tapered trunk. Fan-like leaves, 3ft (1m) or more across, with about 50 narrow lobes, rich green above, tinted blue-gray beneath, on long, spiny stalks. In summer, bears small cream flowers in narrow panicles that are as long as the leaves. ↕ to 40ft (12m), ↔ to 15ft (5m). S. California. ❀ (min. 41–59°F/5–15°C)

B. dulcis. Small palm with rounded, mid-green blades, 3–5ft (1–1.5m) across, that are divided into 36–50 linear, long, sharp-pointed, semi-rigid lobes and are borne on stalks with short, recurved spines. In summer, bears cream flowers in panicles, to 10ft (3m) long. ↕ to 20ft (6m), ↔ to 8ft (2.5m). S. Mexico. ❀ (min. 45°F/7°C)

BRASILIOPUNTIA

CACTACEAE (OPUNTIOIDEA)

Genus of 5 species of cactus from varied habitats in Brazil. Produces dimorphic shoots. Flowers are characterized by a ring of hair-like staminodes between the perianth parts and the stamens.

• **CULTIVATION** Under glass, grow in standard cactus potting mix in full light or bright filtered light. Large species are best planted directly into a greenhouse border. From early spring to mid-autumn, water only when approaching dryness and apply a balanced liquid fertilizer, diluted one quarter to half strength, 3 or 4 times. Keep reasonably dry at other times. Outdoors, grow in moderately fertile, sharply well drained, gritty, humus-rich soil in full sun.

• **PROPAGATION** Sow pre-soaked seed at 70°F (21°C) in spring. Separate, detach, and root stem segments. Handle plants using newspaper; dispose of it after use.

• **PESTS AND DISEASES** Cladode rots, zonate leaf spot, black spot, mealybugs, and scale insects are common. Bacterial soft rot and several viruses also occur.

B. braziliensis. Tree-like cactus with thick, bright green stems, cylindrical branches, and flat, oblong segments, 2–5in (5–13cm) long, each with pale brown glochids and one spine, which is red at first, then brown. Bears wide-spreading, funnel-shaped yellow flowers, 1¼–1½in (3–4cm) across, in summer, and edible, ovoid, spineless, purplish red fruit, 2in (5cm) long. ↕ to 50ft (15m), ↔ to 10ft (3m). Brazil. ❀ (min. 50°F/10°C)

▷ ***Brassaia*** see *Schefflera*

BRASSAVOLA

ORCHIDACEAE

Genus of up to 20 species of evergreen, upright or horizontal to pendent, epiphytic or lithophytic orchids, found from sea level to 6,000ft (1,800m) in Central and South America. They have woody, creeping rhizomes that produce stem-like, narrowly cylindrical pseudobulbs, each with one cylindrical, apical leaf. Long-lasting, night-scented, white, ivory-white, or green flowers are borne singly or in short, often pendent racemes of up to 7 blooms from the base of the leaf, usually in summer.

Brassavola nodosa

• **CULTIVATION** Cool- to intermediate-growing orchids. Grow in epiphytic orchid potting mix in a slatted basket, or epiphytically on a bark slab. Provide moist, unshaded conditions all year. In summer, water freely, applying fertilizer at every third watering, and mist twice daily. Keep dry in winter. See also p.46.

• **PROPAGATION** Divide when plants fill their pots and flow over the sides.

• **PESTS AND DISEASES** Prone to a large number of fungal spots as well as virus diseases. Under glass, whiteflies, mealybugs, scale insects, and spider mites can be a problem.

B. nodosa ▣ Epiphytic or lithophytic orchid with very small, stem-like pseudobulbs and thick, upright, cylindrical-linear, mid-green leaves, to 7in (18cm) long. In summer, produces racemes, to 6in (15cm) long, of 3–5 light green, ivory, or white flowers, 3in (8cm) across, with white lips and maroon-spotted throats. ↕↔ 7in (18cm). Mexico to Panama, Venezuela. ❀ (min. 55°F/13°C; max. 86°F/30°C)

BRASSIA

ORCHIDACEAE

Genus of about 50 species of evergreen, epiphytic orchids, found at altitudes of 2,500–5,200ft (750–1,600m) in tropical regions of North, Central, and South America. They have horizontal to upright rhizomes and compressed, ovoid-spherical to cylindrical pseudo-bulbs, each with 1–3 strap-shaped to oblong-lance-shaped leaves. Racemes of up to 12 or more spider-like, fragrant, long-petaled, yellow to green flowers are borne laterally from the pseudobulb bases from spring to early summer.

• **CULTIVATION** Cool-growing orchids. Grow in epiphytic orchid potting mix in a pot or slatted basket, or epiphytically on a bark slab. In summer, provide moist, partially shaded, well-ventilated conditions; water freely, applying fertilizer at every third watering; and mist twice daily. Keep lightly shaded and almost dry in winter. See also p.46.
• **PROPAGATION** Divide when the plant fills the pot and flows over the sides, or pot up backbulbs separately.
• **PESTS AND DISEASES** Prone to spider mites, mealybugs, scale insects, and aphids. Fungal leaf diseases and virus diseases are common.

B. verrucosa. Epiphytic orchid with narrowly ovoid to oblong pseudobulbs and 2 elliptic-oblong to inversely lance-shaped, bright green leaves, 12in (30cm) long. In early summer, bears upright then arching racemes, to 30in (75cm) long, of yellow to green flowers, spotted red-brown, with white lips spotted dark green or red-brown. ↕↔ 30in (75cm). S. Mexico to Venezuela. ❄ (min. 52–55°F/11–13°C; max 86°F/30°C)

BRASSICA

BRASSICACEAE

Genus of 30 species of annuals and evergreen biennials, perennials, or rarely subshrubs, occurring on rocky slopes, and waste and disturbed ground from the Mediterranean to temperate Asia. Most are erect, branching, taprooted plants, with oblong-ovate to rounded, entire or pinnately lobed, hairless, more or less glaucous leaves. They bear terminal racemes of cross-shaped, yellow or white flowers with 4 clawed petals, followed by long, narrow, beaked fruits. *Brassica* species have been developed to produce many edible vegetables, including cabbage, Brussels sprouts, cauliflower, and broccoli (all variants of *B. oleracea*), and turnip, Chinese cabbage, and canola. Most are grown in the vegetable garden, although some ornamental cabbages – with variegated pink, white, or green foliage – are used in a border or for a bedding display.
• **CULTIVATION** Grow in fertile, well-drained, ideally lime-rich soil in full sun.
• **PROPAGATION** Sow seed *in situ* in spring, or under glass in early spring.
• **PESTS AND DISEASES** Pests include leaf miners, caterpillars, aphids, harlequin bugs, root maggots, nematodes, cabbage white butterfly, and flea beetles. Susceptible to black leg, white rust, black leaf spot (*Xanthomonas*), downy mildew, powdery mildew, damping off, white mold, clubroot, and root knot nematodes. Magnesium, boron, and potassium deficiency can occur.

B. juncea (Leaf mustard). Cool-season annual with thin, curled leaves, to 10in (25cm) long, cannot withstand temperatures above 85°F (29°C). In spring produces bright yellow flowers, to 1¼in (3cm) long, that develop into sickle-shaped green seed pods. ↕ to 4ft (1.2m), ↔ to 1.5 ft (30cm). Asia. ❄ (min. 35°F/2°C)
***B. oleracea* cultivars.** Ornamental cabbage and kale cultivars grown as annuals for their rounded, loose rosettes of variously colored foliage, suitable either for autumn or winter bedding or for containers. They are usually available as seed mixtures of rounded to ovate, plain or fringed, white, red, or pink leaves. The most vivid coloration is produced after temperatures fall below 50°F (10°C). ↕↔ to 12–18in (45cm). **'Osaka'** ▣ is fast-growing with wavy, bluish green outer leaves and compact, pink or red centers; ↕ to 12in (30cm). **Peacock Series** cultivars are hybrids with feathery, finely toothed, red or white leaves. In cooler temperatures, the webbing of color expands and becomes deeper in tone. **'Tokyo'** has neat, rounded, blue-green outer leaves and soft, pink, red, or white centers; ↕ to 10in (25cm).
B. rapa ▣ (Turnip). Winter annual with light to medium green, bristly leaves, 12–20in (30–50cm) long. Bears yellow flowers, 2–3in (5–8cm) long from May to August; seeds ripen from July to September. ↕ 2½–4ft (75–120cm), ↔ 12–18in (30–45cm). Asia.

BRASSOCATTLEYA

ORCHIDACEAE

Bigeneric hybrid genus, a cross of *Brassavola* and *Cattleya*, consisting of several hundred evergreen, epiphytic orchids derived from Central American species. They have thick, club-shaped, sheathed pseudobulbs and 1 or 2 semi-rigid, oblong to oblong-lance-shaped, leathery leaves. Showy, fragrant flowers, with frilled lips, are borne in racemes arising from sheaths at the leaf bases in spring or autumn; each scape produces 1 or 2 flowers.
• **CULTIVATION** Cool- to intermediate-growing orchids. Grow in epiphytic orchid potting mix in containers. In summer, provide moist, partially shaded conditions and water when mix is almost dry, applying fertilizer at every third watering. Keep lightly shaded and almost dry in winter. See also p.46.
• **PROPAGATION** Divide when the plant fills the pot and flows over the sides, or pot up backbulbs, preferably in groups of 3.
• **PESTS AND DISEASES** Scale insects, mealybugs, spider mites, and aphids are troublesome under glass. Prone to virus diseases and many fungal and bacterial diseases of leaves and roots.

***B.* Mount Adams** ▣ (*B.* Déesse x *Cattleya* Bob Betts). Epiphytic orchid with thick pseudobulbs and oblong-lance-shaped, light green leaves, 6in (15cm) long. Light rose-mauve flowers, 6in (15cm) across, with purple- and yellow-striped throats, are produced, usually in pairs, in spring or autumn. ↕ 12in (30cm), ↔ 18in (45cm). ❄ (min. 55°F/13°C; max 82°F/28°C)

BRASSOLAELIO-CATTLEYA

ORCHIDACEAE

Trigeneric hybrid genus, a cross of *Brassavola*, *Laelia*, and *Cattleya*, consisting of several hundred evergreen, epiphytic orchids derived from Central and South American species. They have thick, club-shaped, sheathed pseudobulbs and 1 or 2 semi-rigid, oblong to oblong-lance-shaped, leathery leaves. Colorful, fragrant flowers are produced in short inflorescences arising from sheaths at the leaf bases. Brassolaeliocattleyas resemble brassocattleyas, with which they are often associated.
• **CULTIVATION** As for *Brassocattleya*.
• **PROPAGATION** Scale insects, mealybugs, spider mites, and aphids are problems under glass. Prone to viral, bacterial, and fungal diseases.
• **PESTS AND DISEASES** As for *Brassocattleya*.

***B.* Hetherington Horace 'Coronation'** ▣ Epiphytic orchid with 1 or 2 oblong-lance-shaped, light-green leaves, 6in (15cm) long. Soft lilac flowers, to 5in (13cm) across, with deep mauve lips and white-margined yellow throats, are produced in spring or autumn. ↕↔ 18in (45cm). ❄ (min. 55°F/13°C; max 82°F/28°C)
***B.* St. Helier** ▣ (*B.* Norman's Bay x *B.* Sussex). Epiphytic orchid with 1 or 2 oblong-lance-shaped, mid-green leaves, 6in (15cm) long. Rich magenta flowers, 6–7in (15–18cm) across, 2 or 3 together, with mauve-purple and golden yellow lips, are produced in spring. ↕↔ 18in (45cm). ❄ (min. 55°F/13°C; max 82°F/28°C)

▷ ***Bravoa geminiflora*** see *Polianthes geminiflora*
▷ ***Brevoortia*** see *Dichelostemma*

BREYNIA

EUPHORBIACEAE

Genus of about 25 species of evergreen shrubs and trees occurring in tropical forest and scrub in Asia, Australia, and the Pacific islands from New Caledonia to Hawaii. They are grown for their alternate, small, simple, colorful leaves, often in flattened, frond-like sprays. Tiny, petal-less flowers are followed by red berries. Where not hardy, grow as houseplants or in a warm greenhouse; in warmer climates, plant in a border.
• **CULTIVATION** Under glass, grow in soil-based potting mix in bright filtered light. In growth, water freely and apply a balanced liquid fertilizer monthly; water sparingly in winter. Pot on or top-dress in spring. Outdoors, grow in fertile, humus-rich soil, preferably in partial or light dappled shade, at least during the hottest months. Pinch out stem tips when young to promote branching.
• **PROPAGATION** Root softwood cuttings in summer in a propagating case with bottom heat.

Brassica rapa

Brassocattleya Mount Adams

Brassolaeliocattleya Hetherington Horace 'Coronation'

Brassolaeliocattleya St. Helier

Breynia disticha

• **PESTS AND DISEASES** Spider mites, whiteflies, and aphids may be problems under glass.

B. disticha ▣ syn. *B. nivosa*, *Phyllanthus nivosus* (Snow bush). Slender, evergreen shrub with zigzagged, pink or red stems bearing ovate, dark green leaves, ¾–2in (2–5cm) long, with bold white variegation. Will drop leaves if soil is allowed to become dry. ↕ 3ft (1m) or more, ↔ 2–3ft (60–90cm). Pacific islands. ❄ (min. 59°F/15°C). **'Roseopicta'** has white- and pink-mottled leaves.
B. nivosa see *B. disticha*.

▷ ***Bridgesia spicata*** see *Ercilla volubilis*

BRIGGSIA

GESNERIACEAE

Genus of at least 20 species of evergreen perennials from moist woodland in India, S. China, and S.E. Tibet. They produce basal rosettes of obovate or narrowly elliptic to lance-shaped, hairy leaves. Axillary, tubular flowers with 5 short petal lobes are borne singly or in cymes. Where not hardy, grow in an alpine house or cool greenhouse. In frost-free areas, grow in a rock garden.
• **CULTIVATION** Under glass, grow in soil-based potting mix with additional leaf mold, in bright indirect light and with good ventilation. Water freely in summer; keep moist in winter. Outdoors, grow in moist but well-drained, humus-rich soil in partial shade.
• **PROPAGATION** Surface-sow seed in containers of peaty seed starting mix in a cold frame in partial shade, in spring.
• **PESTS AND DISEASES** Susceptible to neck rot in winter, as well as aphids.

B. muscicola. Evergreen perennial with narrowly elliptic to lance-shaped, scalloped, pale green leaves, to 3in (8cm) long, clothed in silvery white hairs. In early summer, arching stems bear loose cymes of 2–6 tubular, soft yellow to orange-yellow flowers, to ¾in (2cm) long, marked purple within. ↕ 2–3in (5–8cm), ↔ to 6in (15cm). Bhutan, India (Assam), W. China. ❄ (min. 36°F/2°C)

BRIMEURA

LILIACEAE

Genus of 2 species of bulbous perennials from meadows, maquis, and garigue in S.E. Europe. They are cultivated for their slender-stalked racemes of bell-shaped flowers, which are produced in spring. Leaves are basal and linear. Grow in a rock garden, beneath shrubs, or in an alpine house.
• **CULTIVATION** Plant bulbs 2in (5cm) deep in autumn. Grow in fertile, humus-rich, well-drained soil in full sun or partial shade.
• **PROPAGATION** Sow seed in containers in a cold frame as soon as ripe. Divide clumps in summer.
• **PESTS AND DISEASES** Infrequent.

B. amethystina ▣ syn. *Hyacinthus amethystinus*. Bulbous perennial with linear, channeled, bright green leaves, 4–12in (10–30cm) long. Bears loose, slender racemes of tubular-bell-shaped, pale to dark blue flowers, ½in (1.5cm)

Brimeura amethystina

long, in spring. ↕ 4–8in (10–20cm), PD2in (5cm). Pyrenees. Zone 5.
var. *alba* bears white flowers.

▷ ***Brittonastrum*** see *Agastache*

BRIZA

Quaking grass

POACEAE

Genus of 12–20 species of tufted, annual and perennial grasses occurring in open scrub and on a range of natural grassland in temperate regions of Europe and S.W. Asia. Attractive, long-lasting, loose or dense racemes or panicles of pendent, 4- to 20-flowered spikelets, animated by the slightest wind, are borne mostly in summer. The leaves are linear. Grow in a mixed or herbaceous border, or in a rock garden. The flowerheads are very popular for dried flower arrangements, used either in their natural color or, very often, dyed.
• **CULTIVATION** Grow annuals in any well-drained soil in full sun. Perennials tolerate a wide range of well-drained soil types in sun or partial shade.
• **PROPAGATION** Sow seed *in situ* in spring or autumn. Divide perennials from midspring to midsummer.
• **PESTS AND DISEASES** Infrequent.

B. maxima ▣ (Big quaking grass, Puffed wheat). Loosely tufted, erect, annual grass with linear, finely bristle-margined, pale green then straw-colored leaves, to 8in (20cm) long. From late spring to late summer, produces loose, open panicles, to 4in (10cm) long, of 7- to 20-flowered, ovate to heart-shaped

Briza maxima

green spikelets, to ½in (1.5cm) long, which are tinged red-brown or purplish gray and become straw-colored when ripe; they hang from hair-fine stalks. ↕ 18–24in (45–60cm), ↔ 10in (25cm). Mediterranean.
B. media (Common quaking grass, Trembling grass). Perennial grass forming a dense tuft of linear, finely bristle-margined, blue-green leaves, to 6in (15cm) long. From late spring to midsummer, erect stems produce open, pyramidal panicles, to 7in (18cm) long, of 4- to 12-flowered, nodding, heart-shaped spikelets, to ½in (1.5cm) long; purple-tinted green at first, they later turn straw-colored and are arranged like a rattlesnake's tail. ↕ 24–36in (60–90cm), ↔ 12in (30cm). Europe, W. Asia. Zone 4b.
B. minor (Little quaking grass). Erect, loosely tufted, annual grass with linear, finely bristle-margined, pale green then straw-colored leaves, to 6in (15cm) long. From early summer to early autumn, produces slender-stemmed panicles, to 8in (20cm) long, of 4- to 8-flowered, ovate spikelets, to ¼in (5mm) long; pale green initially and frequently purple-tinted, they later turn straw-colored. ↕ to 18in (45cm), ↔ 10in (25cm). Europe, W. Asia.

BRODIAEA

LILIACEAE

Genus of 15 species of cormous perennials occurring in grassland and dry woodland or scrub in W. US and Mexico. They are cultivated for their funnel-shaped flowers, 1–1¾in (2.5–4.5cm) long, borne in umbels in spring or early summer. Basal leaves, 2–6in (5–15cm) long, are linear and blue-green or mid-green, and often die back before the flowers are produced. Many similar cormous perennials, once listed as *Brodiaea*, are now classified under *Bloomeria*, *Dichelostemma*, and *Triteleia*. Suitable for a herbaceous border or rock garden, or an alpine house or bulb frame.
• **CULTIVATION** Plant corms in groups 3in (8cm) deep in autumn. Grow in well-drained, light, fertile, sandy loam in full sun or partial shade. Water freely when in growth; keep warm and dry in summer when the corms have died down. Where not reliably hardy, protect with a winter mulch.
• **PROPAGATION** Sow seed at 55–61°F (13–16°C) as soon as ripe. Remove offsets once they have become dormant.
• **PESTS AND DISEASES** Sometimes susceptible to rust.

B. californica ▣ Cormous perennial producing large umbels of up to 12 widely funnel-shaped, violet, lilac, or pink flowers, on stalks 5in (13cm) long, in early summer. ↕ 20in (50cm), PD3in (8cm). N. California. Zone 8.
B. capitata see *Dichelostemma pulchellum*.
B. congesta see *Dichelostemma congestum*.
B. coronaria, syn. *B. grandiflora*. Cormous perennial bearing umbels of a few funnel-shaped, pale to deep purple flowers, with conspicuous cream stamens, on stalks to 2in (5cm) long, in early summer. ↕ 2–10in (5–25cm), PD2in (5cm). W. US. Zone 8.
B. elegans. Cormous perennial producing umbels of up to 12 funnel-

Brodiaea californica

shaped, deep purple flowers, with strongly recurved tips, on stalks ¼in (5mm) long, in early summer. ↕ 4–20in (10–50cm), PD2in (5cm). W. US. Zone 8.
B. grandiflora see *B. coronaria*.
B. hyacinthina see *Triteleia hyacinthina*.
B. ida-maia see *Dichelostemma ida-maia*.
B. ixioides see *Triteleia ixioides*.
B. lactea see *Triteleia hyacinthina*.
B. laxa see *Triteleia laxa*.
B. lutea see *Triteleia ixioides*.
B. pulchella see *Dichelostemma pulchellum*.
B. volubilis see *Dichelostemma volubile*.

BROMELIA

BROMELIACEAE

Genus of at least 50 species of evergreen, rhizomatous or suckering, terrestrial, or rarely epiphytic perennials (bromeliads) occurring in woodland, scrub, or rocky areas, up to an altitude of 6,000ft (1,800m), in Central America, the West Indies, and South America. They form colonies of dense rosettes of linear to elliptic, rigid leaves with large, curved, marginal spines. Dense, cylindrical or conical inflorescences of white, red, or purple flowers are produced from the centers of the rosettes in summer, and are followed by ovoid yellow fruits containing large brown seeds. Where temperatures drop below 59°F (15°C), grow in a warm greenhouse. In frost-free climates, they are suitable for a shady site or desert garden.
• **CULTIVATION** Under glass, grow in terrestrial bromeliad potting mix in full light. From spring to late autumn, water freely and apply a low-nitrogen fertilizer 2 or 3 times; keep just moist at other times. Outdoors, grow in gritty, humus-rich, neutral to acidic, well-drained soil in full sun, with some midday shade in summer. See also p.47.
• **PROPAGATION** Sow seed at 81°F (27°C) as soon as ripe. Divide in late spring or early summer.
• **PESTS AND DISEASES** Scale insects and fungal leaf spots may be troublesome.

B. agavifolia. Rhizomatous, terrestrial bromeliad with rosettes of linear, brown-scaly, laxly spiny, dark green leaves, to 2in (5cm) long, and scarlet inner leaves. In summer, produces rounded, panicle-like inflorescences, to 6ft (2m) long, of tubular or cylindrical purple and white flowers, to 2½in (6cm) long, with red-flushed apexes. ↕↔ to 6ft (2m). N.E. South America. ❄ (min. 59°F/15°C)

Bromelia balansae

B. balansae ■ (Heart of flame). Variable, terrestrial bromeliad with rosettes of 25–30 linear, wide-spreading, laxly spiny, often red-suffused, gray-green leaves, 3ft (1m) or more long, hairless above, with pale scales beneath. In summer, bears short-branched, cylindrical inflorescences, to 10in (25cm) long, of erect, tubular or cylindrical, white-margined maroon-violet flowers, 1¾in (4.5cm) long. ↕ to 3ft (1m), ↔ indefinite. Colombia, Brazil, Bolivia, Paraguay, N. Argentina. ❀ (min. 59°F/15°C)
B. humilis. Rhizomatous, terrestrial bromeliad with a dense rosette of bright green, narrowly triangular semi-succulent leaves 10–16in (25–40cm) long, 1in (2cm) across; become red toward the center at anthesis. Pungent marginals have curved spines 1/16–1/8in (2–3mm) long. Inflorescence nearly sessile, central with red and white bracts, purple and white petals. Useful as a border or groundcover. ↕ 8–14in (20–35cm), ↔ 16–24in (40–60cm). Venezuela. ❀ (min. 59°F/15°C)
B. plumieri. Rhizomatous, terrestrial bromeliad with rosettes of linear, aromatic, coarsely spiny, mid-green leaves, 5–10ft (1.5–3m) long, with tiny scales beneath and red inner leaves. In summer, bears flat panicles, 12–24in (30–60cm) long, of erect, tubular or cylindrical, white-margined, rose-pink or purple flowers, to 2in (5cm) long. ↕↔ to 10ft (3m). West Indies, Mexico to Brazil and Ecuador. ❀ (min. 59°F/15°C)

BROUGHTONIA

ORCHIDACEAE

Genus of 5 species (possibly only one variable one) of evergreen, epiphytic orchids from Jamaica and Cuba, where they grow from sea level to 2,600ft (800m). They have 2 semi-rigid, narrowly oblong, dark green leaves, very short rhizomes, and tightly clustered and flattened-spherical to cylindrical pseudobulbs. In summer, racemes of brilliant crimson flowers are borne on long stems from the base of the leaves.
• **CULTIVATION** Cool- to intermediate-growing orchids. Grow in epiphytic orchid potting mix in a small container or epiphytically on a bark slab. In summer, provide moist conditions in bright filtered light, and water freely when in active growth, applying fertilizer at every third watering. Keep almost dry in winter. See also p.46.
• **PROPAGATION** Divide when the plant fills the pot and flows over the sides.
• **PESTS AND DISEASES** Susceptible to spider mites, aphids, mealybugs, and cymbidium mosaic virus.

B. sanguinea. Epiphytic orchid with flattened, subcylindrical pseudobulbs and 2 narrowly oblong, dark green leaves, 6–7in (15–18cm) long. In summer, stems to 20in (50cm) long produce up to 15 bright crimson, occasionally white or yellow flowers, 1in (2.5cm) across, with rose-purple lips. ↕ 20in (50cm), ↔ 6in (15cm). Jamaica. ❀ (min. 55°F/13°C; max. 86°F/30°C)

BROUSSONETIA

MORACEAE

Genus of about 7 species of deciduous trees and shrubs from woodland in E. Asia and Polynesia. They have alternate, entire or lobed, toothed leaves. Male and female flowers are borne on separate plants. *B. papyrifera*, the only widely cultivated species, is grown for its large leaves, pendent male catkins, and unusual fruit. Its tolerance of pollution, heat, and poor soil has made it a popular tree for urban locations, although it may become weedy. In areas with cool summers, it grows as a large shrub and is suitable for a shrub border.
• **CULTIVATION** Grow in almost any well-drained soil in full sun, sheltered from wind. Pruning group 1. To produce unusually large leaves, grow coppiced or pollarded; pruning group 7.
• **PROPAGATION** Sow seed in containers in a cold frame in autumn. Insert semi-ripe cuttings in late summer, and hardwood or root cuttings in winter. Transplant suckers in winter.
• **PESTS AND DISEASES** Susceptible to a variety of cankers and leaf spots.

B. papyrifera ■ (Paper mulberry). Rounded, suckering tree or large shrub with ovate to deeply lobed, gray-green leaves, to 8in (20cm) long, which are roughly hairy above, softly hairy below. Male flowers with creamy anthers are borne in thick, pendent catkins, to 3in (8cm) long, in late spring and early summer. Female flowers, with slender purple stigmas, are produced in spherical heads, to ¾in (2cm) across, and develop into mulberry-like, sweet-tasting, orange-red fruit in autumn. ↕↔ 25ft (8m). China, Korea, Japan. Zone 6b.

Broussonetia papyrifera

Browallia speciosa 'Vanja'

BROWALLIA

Amethyst violet, Bush violet

SOLANACEAE

Genus of 6 upright, bushy annuals and subshrubby perennials from damp, shady areas and woodland in N. South America and the West Indies. They have slender, ovate to elliptic leaves and salverform, violet, purple, blue, or white flowers, with 5 broad, unequal lobes. Where not hardy, grow as container plants in a conservatory or in the home, or in an annual or mixed herbaceous border. In tropical climates, grow in a border or container.
• **CULTIVATION** Under glass, grow in soil-based potting mix in full light, with shade from hot sun and good ventilation. When in full growth, water moderately and apply a low-nitrogen liquid fertilizer monthly; keep just moist in winter. Pinch out the growing tips to encourage bushy plants. Outdoors, grow in fertile, well-drained soil in full sun or partial shade.
• **PROPAGATION** Sow seed at 64°F (18°C) in early spring for summer-flowering plants and in late summer for winter- to spring-flowering plants.
• **PESTS AND DISEASES** Aphids and whiteflies are common. Tomato spotted wilt virus and fungal leaf spots can occur.

Browallia speciosa 'White Troll'

B. americana, syn. *B. elata*. Variable, erect, bushy annual with usually ovate, pointed or blunt, slightly sticky, matte leaves, to 4in (10cm) long. In summer, bears single- or several-flowered, axillary inflorescences of violet to blue or white flowers, 2in (5cm) across. ↕↔ to 24in (60cm). Tropical South America. ❀ (min. 59–61°F/13–16°C)
B. elata see *B. americana*.
B. speciosa (Bush violet, Sapphire flower). Woody-based, bushy perennial, usually grown as an annual, with ovate or elliptic, rounded or pointed, slightly sticky, matte leaves, 4in (10cm) long. In summer, violet, blue, or white flowers, 2in (5cm) across, are borne singly or in small clusters from the leaf axils. ↕ 24in (60cm), ↔ 10in (25cm). Tropical South America. ❀ (min. 59–61°F/13–16°C). **'Blue Bells'** is compact, with violet-blue flowers; ↕ to 8in (20cm). **'Blue Troll'** is compact, with clear blue flowers; ↕ to 10in (25cm). **'Dawn Blue'** is shorter and bears pale lilac-blue flowers; ↕ 18in (45cm). **'Heavenly Bells'** bears pale sky-blue flowers, 2½–3in (6–8cm) across; ↕ 12in (30cm). **'Marine Bells'** bears deep violet-blue flowers. **'Silver Bells'** is compact, with white flowers; ↔ 10–12in (25–30cm). **'Vanja'** ■ has deep blue flowers, to 3in (8cm) across, with white eyes. **'White Bell'** is compact and bushy, with white flowers. **'White Troll'** ■ has pure white flowers; ↕ to 10in (25cm).

Brownea ariza

BROWNEA

FABACEAE

Genus of at least 25 species of evergreen shrubs and trees found in tropical forest in South America, grown for their foliage and attractive flowerheads. Large, opposite, pinnate leaves emerge pink or red, speckled white, later turning deep green. Small, 4- or 5-petaled flowers are mixed with large colored bracts in pompon-like, terminal inflorescences. Where not hardy, grow in a warm greenhouse; elsewhere, grow as specimens.

• **CULTIVATION** Under glass, grow in soil-based potting mix in full light. They need a large container to flower. When in growth, water freely and apply a balanced liquid fertilizer monthly; keep just moist in winter. Pot on or top-dress in early spring. Outdoors, grow in fertile, moist but well-drained soil in light, dappled shade. Pruning group 1, but need restrictive pruning under glass.

• **PROPAGATION** Sow seed at 61°F (16°C) in spring. Root semi-ripe cuttings with bottom heat in summer. Layer in spring.

• **PESTS AND DISEASES** Spider mites, mealybugs, and whiteflies may be problems under glass.

B. ariza ■ syn. *B. grandiceps*, *B. princeps* (Rose of Venezuela). Erect to spreading tree with pinnate leaves, 8–16in (20–40cm) long, consisting of 12 or more pairs of elliptic, bronze-red leaflets, pendent at first, then spreading. Bears rounded, orange to red flowerheads, to 10in (25cm) across, in summer, each with up to 50 flowers. ↕ 22–30ft (7–10m), ↔ 10–22ft (3–7m). Colombia. ❄ (min. 59°F/15°C)

B. grandiceps see *B. ariza*.

B. princeps see *B. ariza*.

BROWNINGIA

syn. AZUREOCEREUS

CACTACEAE

Genus of about 10 species of erect, tree-like cacti from hilly or low mountainous regions, principally in Peru and Chile. They branch freely toward the trunk base or from nearer the crown, like candelabra, with semi-pendent branches. The tubercled ribs produce prominently spiny areoles. Funnel-shaped, nocturnal flowers have short, rounded petals and densely scaly, often curved tubes. They are followed by spherical to ovoid, dry or juicy, green fruits containing brown or black seeds. Where not hardy, grow in a conservatory or warm greenhouse; in warmer areas, use in a mixed cactus border or desert garden. They are large, architectural specimens when mature.

• **CULTIVATION** Under glass, grow in a mix of 4 parts standard cactus potting mix and 1 part limestone chips, in full light. During the growing season, water freely and apply a low-nitrogen fertilizer every 3–4 weeks; keep completely dry at other times. Outdoors, grow in sharply drained, alkaline soil in full sun. See also pp.48–49.

• **PROPAGATION** Sow seed at 66–75°F (19–24°C) in early spring.

• **PESTS AND DISEASES** Mealybugs occur.

B. hertlingiana, syn. *Azureocereus hertlingianus*. Slow-growing cactus with a trunk, to 12in (30cm) thick, that generally branches, once it is 3ft (1m) tall, into thick, ascending, bluish green branches with 18 or more ribs. Tufted, gray-felted, yellowish brown areoles produce pale brown spines (4–7 radials, 1–3 centrals). Funnel-shaped purple flowers, 2in (5cm) across, white inside, are borne from the areoles near the stem tips in summer. ↕ 25ft (8m), ↔ to 5ft (1.5m). Peru, Chile. ❄ (min. 55°F/13°C)

BRUCKENTHALIA

ERICACEAE

Genus of one species of small, evergreen shrub occurring on acidic soils in woodland and subalpine pastures in S.E. Europe. It has needle-like foliage, and bears terminal racemes of bell-shaped flowers from late spring to summer. Cultivated for its neat habit and attractive flowers, *B. spiculifolia* is suitable for a rock garden, and associates well with heathers (*Calluna*, *Erica*), to which it is closely related.

• **CULTIVATION** Grow in moist but well-drained, peaty, acidic soil in full sun. Mulch with softwood boughs to protect from wind and extended low temperatures. Pruning group 10, after flowering.

• **PROPAGATION** Sow seed in containers in a cold frame in spring. Root semi-ripe cuttings in a closed propagating case with gentle bottom heat in summer.

• **PESTS AND DISEASES** Infrequent.

B. spiculifolia (Spike heath). Compact, evergreen shrub with whorls of linear, glossy, dark green leaves, to ¼in (5mm) long, which are borne on stiff, sparsely branched, upright stems. Dense, terminal racemes, to 1¼in (3cm) long, of bell-shaped, pale to deep pink, occasionally white flowers, ¾–1¼in (2–3cm) long, are produced from late spring to summer. Balkans. ↕ 6in (15cm), ↔ to 8in (20cm). Zone 5b. **'Balkan Rose'** has deep pink flowers.

BRUGMANSIA

Angels' trumpets

SOLANACEAE

Genus of 5 species of evergreen shrubs and trees found in scrub and along streamsides from S. US to South America. They are cultivated for their large, usually scented, solitary, pendent, tubular or trumpet-shaped flowers, with 5 usually reflexed, pointed lobes, borne

Brugmansia aurea

from late spring to autumn. The leaves are alternate, simple, often toothed, and sometimes lobed. Where not hardy, grow in a temperate greenhouse or conservatory, and move containers outside or plunge in a border for the summer. In milder areas, grow as specimen plants. All parts are highly toxic if ingested.

• **CULTIVATION** Under glass, grow in soil-based potting mix in full light. From spring to autumn, water freely and apply a balanced liquid fertilizer every 3–4 weeks; keep just moist in winter. Outdoors, grow in fertile, moist but well-drained soil in full sun. Pruning group 9, or 7 if required.

• **PROPAGATION** Sow seed at 61°F (16°C) in spring. Root semi-ripe cuttings with bottom heat in summer.

• **PESTS AND DISEASES** Spider mites, whiteflies, and mealybugs may be problems under glass.

B. arborea, syn. *B. versicolor* of gardens, *Datura arborea* (Common angels' trumpets). Open shrub or tree with robust stems and elliptic-oblong to ovate, entire or coarsely toothed leaves, 6–12in (15–30cm) long. Trumpet-shaped, scented white flowers, to 6in (15cm) long, are borne from late spring to autumn. ↕ 6–12ft (2–4m) or more, ↔ 5–8ft (1.5–2.5m). Ecuador to N. Chile (Andes). ❄ (min. 45°F/7°C)

B. aurea ■ syn. *Datura aurea*. Open shrub or tree with ovate leaves, 6–10in (15–25cm) long, coarsely toothed on young plants, entire on mature ones. Trumpet-shaped, night-scented, golden yellow to white flowers, to 10in (25cm) long, are borne mainly from summer to autumn. ↕ 15–30ft (5–10m), ↔ 6–12ft (2–4m). Colombia to Ecuador (Andes). ❄ (min. 45°F/7°C)

B. × candida (*B. aurea* × *B. versicolor*), syn. *Datura* × *candida*. Open shrub or tree with oblong-elliptic, entire to coarsely toothed, wavy-margined leaves, 12–24in (30–60cm) long. From summer to autumn, bears trumpet-shaped, night-scented flowers, to 12in (30cm) long, that may be white or soft yellow aging to white or, rarely, pink. ↕ 10–15ft (3–5m), ↔ 5–8ft (1.5–2.5m). Garden origin. ❄ (min. 45°F/7°C). **'Double White'** bears double white flowers. **'Grand Marnier'** ■ bears apricot flowers. **'Knightii'**, syn. 'Plena', bears hose-in-hose blooms. **'Plena'** see 'Knightii'.

***B. rosei* of gardens** see *B. sanguinea*.

Brugmansia × *candida* 'Grand Marnier'

Brugmansia sanguinea

B. sanguinea ■ syn. *B. rosei* of gardens, *Datura rosei* of gardens (Red angels' trumpets). Open shrub or tree with ovate-oblong, wavy-margined, coarsely toothed to entire leaves, to 7in (18cm) long. Tubular, unscented flowers, 6–10in (15–25cm) long, orange-red with yellow veins, are borne from late spring to autumn. ↕ 10–30ft (3–10m), ↔ 6–10ft (2–3m). Colombia to N. Chile. ❄ (min. 45°F/7°C)

B. suaveolens. Vigorous shrub or tree with ovate-oblong to narrowly elliptic, entire leaves, to 8in (20cm) long. Tubular-bell-shaped, night-scented, white, yellow, or pink flowers, 12in (30cm) long, are produced from early summer to autumn. ↕ to 15ft (5m), ↔ 8–10ft (2.5–3m). S.E. Brazil. ❄ (min. 45°F/7°C)

***B. versicolor* of gardens** see *B. arborea*.

B

BRUNFELSIA

SOLANACEAE

Genus of approximately 40 species of evergreen shrubs and small trees growing in light woodland and thickets in tropical North, Central, and South America. They are cultivated for their large, tubular, salverform flowers, each with 5 broad petal lobes. The alternate, simple leaves are elliptic to ovate, oblong, or spoon-shaped. Where not hardy, grow in a cool or temperate greenhouse. In frost-free climates, plant in a border.

• **CULTIVATION** Under glass, grow in soil-based potting mix in bright indirect or filtered light. When in growth, water freely and apply a balanced liquid fertilizer every 3–4 weeks; water sparingly in winter. Pot on or top-dress in late winter. Outdoors, grow in fertile, humus-rich, moist but well-drained soil, in full sun with some midday shade. Pruning group 8; pinch out stem tips of young plants to promote branching.
• **PROPAGATION** Root softwood cuttings in spring or summer.
• **PESTS AND DISEASES** Susceptible to spider mites and mealybugs under glass.

B. americana (Lady of the night). Erect to spreading shrub or small tree with elliptic to obovate, mid- to deep green leaves, 2–5in (5–13cm) long. Solitary, night-scented flowers, 3in (8cm) long, which age from white to creamy yellow, are produced during summer. ↕ 6–15ft (2–5m), ↔ 3–10ft (1–3m). West Indies. ❄ (min. 45°F/7°C)
B. calycina see *B. pauciflora.*
B. eximia see *B. pauciflora.*
B. pauciflora, syn. *B. calycina, B. eximia* (Yesterday, today, and tomorrow). Bushy shrub with elliptic to oblong-lance-shaped, leathery, glossy, deep green leaves, 3–6in (7–15cm) long. Terminal or axillary cymes of up to 10 wavy-margined, pansy-like flowers, 1½–2in (3.5–5cm) across, opening purple and aging almost to white, are borne from spring to summer. ↕ 3–10ft (1–3m), ↔ 1½–5ft (0.5–1.5m). Brazil. ❄ (min. 45°F/7°C). **'Floribunda'** is spreading, with freely borne flowers that open violet and age to purple; ↕ to 5ft (1.5m). **'Floribunda Compacta'** has a smaller, compact habit and is very floriferous; ↕ 3–4ft (1–1.2m). **'Macrantha'** ▣ has very large flowers, to 3in (8cm) across.

Brunfelsia pauciflora 'Macrantha'

Brunnera macrophylla

BRUNNERA

BORAGINACEAE

Genus of 3 species of rhizomatous perennials from woodland in E. Europe and N.W. Asia, valued for their flowers and ground-covering foliage. They have usually ovate, rough-hairy basal leaves and lance-shaped to ovate stem leaves. Terminal, cyme-like panicles of purple-blue, rarely white flowers are produced in spring. Grow in woodland, as a groundcover, or in a border.

• **CULTIVATION** Grow in moderately fertile, humus-rich, moist but well-drained soil.
• **PROPAGATION** In early spring, sow seed in containers in a cold frame, or divide. Take root cuttings of *B. macrophylla* in winter.
• **PESTS AND DISEASES** Infrequent.

B. macrophylla ▣ syn. *Anchusa myosotidiflora* (Siberian bugloss). Rhizomatous perennial with softly hairy, mid- to deep green leaves. Basal leaves are ovate-heart-shaped, sharp-pointed, and 2–8in (5–20cm) long, with long leaf stalks; stem leaves are lance-shaped to elliptic-ovate. In mid- and late spring, produces bright blue flowers, to ¼in (7mm) across, in panicles 8in (20cm) or more long. ↕ 18in (45cm), ↔ 24in (60cm). Caucasus. Zone 3b. **'Dawson's White'**, syn. 'Variegata', has wide, irregular, creamy white leaf margins. **'Hadspen Cream'** has irregular, creamy white leaf margins, narrower than those of 'Dawson's White'. **'Variegata'** see 'Dawson's White'.

▷**x *Brunsdonna*** see x *Amarygia*

BUCHLOE

Buffalo grass

GRAMINEAE

Genus of one species of grass native from Western Minnesota to Mexico, which grows in dry, exposed sites. It can be used for lawns or banks.

• **CULTIVATION** Thrives with as little as 12–25 in (30–64cm) of rainfall per year.
• **PROPAGATION** Sow 2lbs of seed per 1,000 square feet (4.4kg/93sq m). Fertilize with 1–2lbs nitrogen per 100sq.ft (2.2–4.4kg/9.3sq.m).
• **PESTS AND DISEASES** None.

B. dactyloides ▣ (Buffalo grass). This grass forms a dense turf that can take hard wear and look fairly good with little summer watering. Leaves are gray-green and grow to 4in (10cm). Both male and female plants bear yellow to golden flowers. Zone 5.

Buchloe dactyloides

BUDDLEJA syn. BUDDLEIA

LOGANIACEAE

Genus of about 100 species of evergreen, semi-evergreen, and deciduous shrubs, sometimes trees and climbers, and a few herbaceous perennials, from riversides, rocky areas, and scrub in Asia, Africa, and North and South America. They are cultivated for their panicles of small, tubular, usually fragrant flowers, and sometimes for their lance-shaped to broadly ovate, usually opposite leaves. All except the climbers are suitable for a mixed or shrub border, or as specimens. Where not hardy, grow in a cool greenhouse. *B. davidii* and several others, such as *B. alternifolia, B. crispa,* and *B.* 'Lochinch', are attractive to many insects, especially butterflies.

• **CULTIVATION** Under glass, grow in soil-based potting mix in full light with good ventilation. Water freely when in growth, sparingly in winter. Outdoors, grow in fertile, well-drained soil in full sun. Pruning group 6 for most; group 2 for *B. alternifolia, B. colvilei,* and *B. globosa* (although the last 2 need minimal pruning). Pruning group 13 for wall-trained plants: after flowering for those that bloom in spring or early summer, in spring for late-summer and autumn-flowering species.
• **PROPAGATION** Sow seed at 66–75°F (19–24°C) in spring. Root semi-ripe cuttings in summer. Root hardwood cuttings of *B. davidii* in autumn.
• **PESTS AND DISEASES** Susceptible to capsid bug, caterpillars, weevils, mullein moth, and spider mites. Fungal leaf spots and diebacks can occur.

Buddleja alternifolia

B. alternifolia ▣ Deciduous shrub or small tree with slender, arching shoots and alternate, lance-shaped, dark green, occasionally silvery green leaves, to 3in (8cm) long. Dense, rounded clusters, 1½in (4cm) long, of intensely fragrant lilac flowers clothe the branches of the

BUDDLEJA INFLORESCENCES

Flowers are usually borne in dense, conical panicles, but are also produced in whorled or cyme-like panicles, and in intermediate forms.

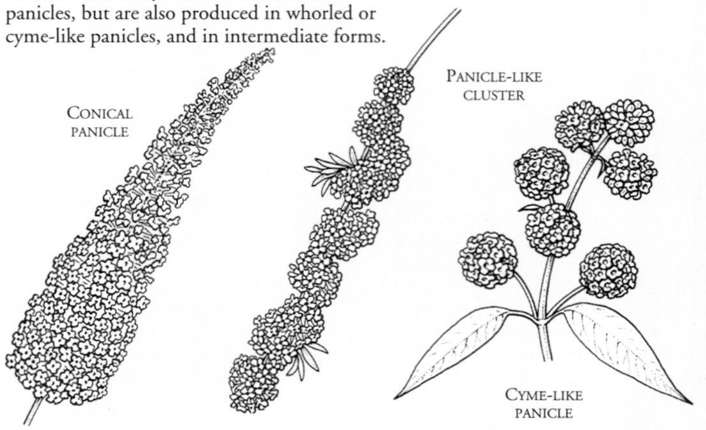

Buddleja colvilei 'Kewensis'

previous year's growth in early summer. Trained as a standard, it makes an excellent specimen plant. ↕↔ 12ft (4m). China. Zone 4.

B. asiatica. Evergreen shrub with arching white- or gray-woolly shoots and lance-shaped, dark green leaves, to 12in (30cm) long. Fragrant white flowers are produced in cyme-like panicles, to 10in (25cm) long, in late winter and early spring. ↕↔ 10ft (3m). Himalayas to S.E. Asia. Zone 8.

B. colvilei. Upright, stoutly branched, deciduous (sometimes semi-evergreen) shrub or small tree with elliptic-lance-shaped, dark green leaves, 5in (13cm) or more long. Bears tight, pendent, terminal, occasionally axillary panicles, to 8in (20cm) long, of dark pink or red flowers in early summer. ↕↔ 20ft (6m). Himalayas. ❄ (min. 35°F/2°C). **'Kewensis'** ■ bears dark red flowers.

B. crispa ■ Arching, deciduous shrub with white-woolly young shoots and broadly ovate-triangular, white-hairy leaves, to 5in (13cm) long. Fragrant, lilac-pink flowers are produced in dense, whorled, cyme-like, terminal and axillary panicles, to 4in (10cm) long, in mid- and late summer. ↕↔ 10ft (3m). Himalayas. ❄ (min. 35°F/2°C)

B. davidii (Butterfly bush, Summer lilac). Variable, fast-growing, deciduous shrub with long, arching shoots and lance-shaped, pointed, mid-green to gray-green leaves, to 10in (25cm) long. From summer to autumn, bears dense panicles, 12in (30cm) or more long, of fragrant, lilac to purple flowers, often with orange or yellow eyes. ↕ 10ft (3m), ↔ 15ft (5m). China, Japan. Zone 5b.

Buddleja crispa

Buddleja davidii 'Empire Blue'

'African Queen' has dark violet panicles, 7–9in (18–23cm) long. **'Black Knight'** bears dark purple-blue flowers. **'Border Beauty'** is strongly branched and low-growing with profuse, deep lilac-purple flowers; ↕ to 6ft (2m). **'Charming'** bears lavender-pink flowers. **'Darkness'** is wide-spreading and arching with deep blue to purple-blue flowers. **'Dartmoor'** has slender leaves with deeply cut margins and reddish purple flowers in atypical, open-branched panicles. **'Deep Lavender'** bears heavily ruffled and fringed, deep lavender-lilac flowers with orange eyes, in broad panicles. **'Dubonnet'** is upright with panicles, to 14in (35cm) long, of dark purple flowers with orange eyes. **'Empire Blue'** ■ has violet-blue flowers with orange eyes. **'Fascinating'** ■ bears lilac-pink flowers in broad, tight panicles, 4in (10cm) or more across. **'Fortune'** bears soft lilac-blue flowers in slender panicles, to 16in (40cm) long. **'Harlequin'** ■ has leaves that are yellow-margined when young, cream-margined when mature, and dark red-purple flowers. **'Ile de France'** has light green leaves and panicles, to 28in (70cm) long, of profuse, dark violet flowers with yellow eyes. **'Nanho Blue'**, syn. 'Petite Indigo', has slender leaves and narrow panicles, to 6in (15cm) long, of pale lilac-blue flowers; ↕↔ 4–5ft (1.2–1.5m). **'Nanho Purple'** is very compact in habit and bears bright purple flowers; ↕ 4–5ft (1.2–1.5m). **'Nanho White'** is very compact with white flowers; ↕ 4–5ft (1.2–1.5m). **'Opera'** is bushy and has bright fuchsia-pink panicles, 12–24in

Buddleja davidii 'Fascinating'

Buddleja davidii 'Harlequin' (inset: flower detail)

(30–60cm) long. **'Orchid Beauty'** has a spreading, low habit and tight, narrow panicles of ruffled lilac flowers with no eyes. **'Peace'** produces panicles, to 20in (50cm) long, of white flowers with orange eyes. **'Petite Indigo'** see 'Nanho Blue'. **'Petite Plum'** has dark green, persistent leaves and bears red-purple flowers with orange eyes. **'Pink Delight'** has deep green leaves and produces very large, broad, dense panicles, to 18in (45cm) long, of bright pink flowers with orange eyes. **'Pink Pearl'** has lilac-pink flowers with orange eyes. **'Princeton Purple'** has full, broad, conical panicles of blue-purple flowers that open from top to bottom, at almost the same time.**'Raspberry Wine'** has full panicles of slightly ruffled, dusky, deep mauve flowers with deep golden yellow eyes. **'Royal Red'** ■ has dark red-purple flowers in panicles to 20in (50cm) long. **'Snow Bank'** has pure white flowers. **'Summer Beauty'** is compact, with silver leaves and very deep rose-pink flowers; ↕ 5–6ft (1.5–2m), ↔ 6–8ft (2–2.5m). **'White Bouquet'** bears panicles, 8–12in (20–30cm) long, of white flowers with orange eyes. **'White Harlequin'** has leaves margined creamy white, and white flowers. **'White Profusion'** ■ has yellow-eyed white flowers in panicles, to 16in (40cm) long.

B. fallowiana. Deciduous shrub with arching stems and lance-shaped, gray-white leaves, to 5in (13cm) long, mid-green beneath, and densely white-felted, particularly when young. Bears panicles,

Buddleja davidii 'Royal Red'

Buddleja davidii 'White Profusion'

Buddleja globosa

to 6in (15cm) long, of very fragrant, pale lavender-blue flowers, with orange eyes, in late summer and early autumn. ↕ 6ft (2m), ↔ 10ft (3m). W. China. Zone 7b. **var. *alba*** has white flowers.
B. globosa ■ (Orange ball tree). Rounded, stiffly branched, deciduous or semi-evergreen shrub with lance-shaped, deeply veined, dark green leaves, to 8in (20cm) long. Bears dense, rounded clusters, to ¾in (2cm) across, of fragrant, dark orange and yellow flowers in open panicles in early summer. ↕↔ 15ft (5m). Chile, Argentina. Zone 8.
B. lindleyana ■ Upright, somewhat arching, slender-branched, deciduous shrub with ovate, dark green leaves, 4in (10cm) long, borne on square stems. Distinctly curved, dark violet flowers, ¾in (2cm) long, are borne in nodding panicles, to 8in (20cm) long, in late summer. ↕↔ 6ft (2m). China. Zone 8.
***B.* 'Lochinch'.** Spreading, vigorous, deciduous shrub with long, arching, gray-hairy shoots and lance-shaped, white-hairy, mid-green leaves, to 8in (20cm) long, that become greener with age. From late summer to autumn, bears fragrant, orange-eyed, violet-blue flowers in panicles to 8in (20cm) long. ↕ 8ft (2.5m), ↔ 10ft (3m). Zone 6.
B. madagascariensis ■ syn. *B. nicodemia, Nicodemia madagascariensis.* Vigorous, strongly branched, evergreen shrub or lax climber with lance-shaped, deep green leaves, 2–5½in (5–14cm) long, white-felted beneath. Produces bright orange-yellow flowers in slender,

Buddleja lindleyana

Buddleja madagascariensis

terminal panicles, 6–10in (15–25cm) long, from autumn to spring, sometimes followed by small, amethyst-purple berries. ↕↔ 6–12ft (2–4m). Madagascar. ❄ (min. 41–45°F/5–7°C)
B. nicodemia see *B. madagascariensis.*
B. nivea. Vigorous, upright, deciduous shrub with thick, densely white-woolly shoots and narrowly ovate leaves, to 8in (20cm) long, dark green above, white below. Produces slender panicles, to 6in (15cm) long, of pale lilac-blue or violet-blue flowers, in late summer. ↕ 10ft (3m), ↔ 8ft (2.5m). China. Zone 7b.
B. officinalis. Upright, evergreen or semi-evergreen shrub with arching shoots and narrowly lance-shaped, dark green leaves, 6in (15cm) long, gray beneath. From winter to early spring, bears fragrant, yellow-eyed, lilac-pink flowers in arching panicles, to 12in (30cm) long. ↕↔ 8ft (2.5m). China. ❄ (min. 41°F/5°C)
***B.* x *pikei* 'Hever'.** Spreading, branched, deciduous shrub with slender, arching shoots and opposite or alternate, ovate to oblong, gray-green leaves, to 6in (15cm) long, maturing to dark green. Fragrant, lilac-mauve flowers, with orange centers, are produced in arching panicles, to 12in (30cm) long, in late summer. ↕↔ 10ft (3m). Zone 7b.
***B.* 'West Hill'** ■ Vigorous, deciduous shrub with long, arching, gray-hairy shoots and lance-shaped, white-hairy, mid-green leaves, 8in (20cm) long. Fragrant, orange-eyed, pale lavender-blue flowers are produced in slender, arching panicles, to 8in (20cm)

Buddleja 'West Hill'

Buddleja x *weyeriana* 'Sungold'

long, from late summer to autumn. ↕ 8ft (2.5m), ↔ 10ft (3m). Zone 7b.
B.* x *weyeriana (*B. davidii* x *B. globosa*). Spreading, deciduous shrub with long, arching shoots and lance-shaped, mid-green leaves, to 8in (20cm) long, both gray-hairy when young. Rounded clusters of fragrant yellow to violet flowers are produced in open, terminal panicles, to 12in (30cm) long, from summer to autumn. ↕ 12ft (4m), ↔ 10ft (3m). Garden origin. Zone 7. **'Golden Glow'** is vigorous, with loose clusters of mauve-flushed, orange-yellow flowers. **'Sungold'** ■ has dense heads of dark orange-yellow flowers.

BUGLOSSOIDES

BORAGINACEAE

Genus, similar to *Lithospermum*, of about 15 species of hairy annuals, perennials, and evergreen or semi-evergreen subshrubs from sunny scrub and rocky slopes in W. and S. Europe, Africa, and parts of W. Asia. They have erect or decumbent stems, which sometimes root at the tips, and produce variable, simple, rough-hairy, mid- to dark green leaves and terminal cymes of small, salverform flowers. Grow in a border, rock garden, or wild garden.
• **CULTIVATION** Grow in well-drained, fertile, neutral to alkaline soil in full sun with some midday shade.
• **PROPAGATION** Sow seed of annuals and perennials in containers in a cold frame in autumn or spring. Divide perennials in early spring. Root softwood cuttings of subshrubs in midsummer.
• **PESTS AND DISEASES** Infrequent.

B. annua. Succulent annual with basal clusters of 12–20 linear, fleshy, mid-green leaves, 8–12in (20–30cm) long. Lax racemes, 6–9in (15–23cm) long, of 10–15 star-shaped, bright yellow flowers, ¼–⅜in (7–9mm) across, are borne in summer. ↕↔ to 9in (23cm). South Africa.
B. gastonii. Rhizomatous perennial with erect stems and ovate-lance-shaped to lance-shaped, rough, mid-green leaves, to 2½in (6cm) long. In early summer, produces cymes of initially purple, later blue flowers, to ½in (1.5cm) long, with white throats. ↕ 12–18in (30–45cm), ↔ 12in (30cm). W. Pyrenees. Zone 7.
B. purpurocaerulea ■ syn. *Lithospermum purpureocaeruleum.* Rhizomatous perennial with tip-rooting,

Buglossoides purpurocaerulea

decumbent, non-flowering stems and lance-shaped, dark green leaves, to 3in (8cm) long. In late spring and early summer, erect stems bear cymes of initially purple, later gentian-blue flowers, ½–¾in (1–2cm) long. ↕ to 24in (60cm), ↔ variable. W. Europe to N. Iran. Zone 7.

BULBINE

LILIACEAE

Genus of about 30 species of clump-forming, succulent and non-succulent, occasionally slightly woody-stemmed, sometimes bulbous or tuberous perennials, and one annual, occurring in desert grasslands in E. and South Africa, and Australia. They have linear to broadly lance-shaped, mid- to blue-green, basal leaves. Dense, terminal racemes of small, star-shaped to shallowly cup-shaped flowers, with conspicuously hairy stamens, are borne in spring or summer. Where not hardy, grow in a cool greenhouse. In frost-free areas, grow in a rock garden.
• **CULTIVATION** Under glass, grow in soil-based potting mix with additional sharp sand, in full light with good ventilation. Water freely when in growth; keep dry in winter. Outdoors, grow in well-drained, sandy loam in full sun. Bulbines are tolerant of poor, dry soil, and some withstand occasional light frost.
• **PROPAGATION** Sow seed at 55–64°F (13–18°C) in early spring. Divide or root offsets in spring. Root stem cuttings of *B. frutescens* in summer.
• **PESTS AND DISEASES** Infrequent.

B. alooides. Clump-forming perennial with compact rosettes of lance-shaped, fleshy, mid-green leaves, 6–9in (15–23cm) long. Racemes, 8–12in (20–30cm) long, of star-shaped yellow flowers, to ⅛in (4mm) across, are produced in late spring. ↕ 12in (30cm), PD6in (15cm). South Africa. ❄ (min. 41°F/5°C)
B. caulescens see *B. frutescens.*
B. frutescens, syn. *B. caulescens.* Succulent, branching, slightly woody-stemmed perennial with lance-shaped, blue-green, basal leaves, 1½–9in (4–23cm) long. Racemes, 6–12in (15–30cm) long, of star-shaped yellow flowers, ¼–½in (6–15mm) across, are borne in summer. ↕↔ 16in (40cm). South Africa. ❄ (min. 41°F/5°C)

Bulbinella hookeri

Bulbocodium vernum

BULBINELLA

LILIACEAE

Genus of 20 species of robust perennials from grassland in South Africa and New Zealand. They have fleshy roots, and basal rosettes of succulent, grass-like leaves, 6–18in (15–45cm) long. In late winter, spring, or summer, they bear dense, terminal racemes of star-shaped or shallowly cup-shaped, occasionally monoecious flowers, usually to ½in (1.5cm) across. Grow in a rock garden or peat garden. Where not hardy, grow *B. cauda-felis* in an alpine house.

• **CULTIVATION** Grow in moist but well-drained, neutral to acidic soil in full sun or partial shade. *B. hookeri* is more tolerant of dry soils. Mulch with leaf mold in winter. In an alpine house, grow in a mix of equal parts loam, leaf mold, and sharp sand.

• **PROPAGATION** Sow seed in a cold frame as soon as ripe. Divide in autumn.

• **PESTS AND DISEASES** Prey to whiteflies, spider mites, and aphids under glass.

B. cauda-felis, syn. *B. setosa.* Robust perennial with leaves to 8in (20cm) long and racemes of bisexual yellow flowers, aging to reddish brown, borne in late winter and early spring. ↕ 12in (30cm), PD6in (15cm). South Africa. Zone 8.

B. hookeri ■ Robust perennial with leaves 12in (30cm) long and racemes of bisexual yellow flowers borne from spring to summer. ↕ 24in (60cm), PD12in (30cm). New Zealand. Zone 8.

B. rossii. Robust perennial with leaves to 12in (30cm) long and racemes of unisexual yellow flowers produced in spring. ↕ 4ft (1.2m), PD18in (45cm). New Zealand. Zone 8.

B. setosa see *B. cauda-felis.*

BULBOCODIUM

LILIACEAE

Genus, related to *Colchicum,* of 2 species of cormous perennials from alpine meadows and dry grassland in S. and E. Europe. The open funnel-shaped flowers, each with a single style, divided at the tip, and 6 free, clawed tepals, are borne in spring, just before or with the linear to lance-shaped, dark green leaves. Grow bulbocodiums in a rock garden, or naturalize in thin grass.

• **CULTIVATION** Plant corms 3in (8cm) deep in autumn in humus-rich, well-drained soil in full sun.

• **PROPAGATION** Sow seed in containers in a cold frame in autumn or spring. Remove offsets in summer.

• **PESTS AND DISEASES** Infrequent.

B. vernum ■ (Spring meadow saffron). Cormous perennial with 2 narrowly linear, glossy, dark green leaves, to 6in (15cm) long. Crocus-like, pinkish purple flowers, occasionally white, 1½–3in (4–8cm) long, are produced in spring. ↕ 1½–3in (4–8cm), PD2in (5cm). Pyrenees, S.W. and W. central Alps. Zone 5.

BULBOPHYLLUM

ORCHIDACEAE

Genus of 1,000–1,200 species of very variable, evergreen, epiphytic orchids from a range of habitats throughout tropical and subtropical regions. They have creeping or pendent rhizomes with prominent pseudobulbs bearing 1 or 2 apical, ovate, oval, oblong-oval, or lance-shaped leaves. Flowers are produced at various times of the year, in basal racemes or umbels, occasionally singly. A number of them are pungent or sweet-smelling. Minute species, visible only with a lens, grow on leaf surfaces of other plants.

• **CULTIVATION** Cool- to intermediate-growing orchids. Grow in epiphytic orchid potting mix in a half-pot or slatted basket, or epiphytically on bark. In summer, provide high humidity and partial shade; water freely, applying fertilizer at every third watering, and mist twice daily. In winter, give full light and keep dry. See also p.46.

Bulbophyllum careyanum

• **PROPAGATION** Divide when the plant fills the pot and flows over the sides.

• **PESTS AND DISEASES** Susceptible to spider mites, aphids, and mealybugs.

B. careyanum ■ Epiphytic orchid with spherical to oblong pseudobulbs, each with one oblong or linear-oblong leaf, to 10in (25cm) long. In summer, bears dense, cylindrical, arching to pendent racemes, to 8in (20cm) long, of tiny, fragrant, orange-yellow or green flowers, suffused red-brown or purple, with violet lips. ↕ 10in (25cm), ↔ 12in (30cm). E. Himalayas, Myanmar, Thailand. ❀ (min. 55°F/13°C; max 86°F/30°C)

B. guttulatum, syn. *Cirrhopetalum guttulatum.* Epiphytic orchid with ovoid pseudobulbs, each with one narrowly ovate leaf, 4in (10cm) long. Upright, umbel-like panicles, 6–10in (15–25cm) tall, of several tiny, purple-spotted, straw-yellow or green flowers, with pale purple lips, are produced in summer. ↕↔ 10in (25cm). India. ❀ (min. 55°F/13°C; max 86°F/30°C)

B. medusae, syn. *Cirrhopetalum medusae.* Epiphytic orchid with ovoid pseudobulbs, each with one narrowly lance-shaped leaf, 6in (15cm) long. In summer, produces erect or arching flower stems bearing terminal umbels, to 6in (15cm) long, of small, white or cream flowers, spotted red or yellow. A well-grown specimen is a stunning reminder of its namesake. ↕ 8in (20cm), ↔ 9in (23cm). Thailand, Malaysia to Borneo and the Philippines. ❀ (min. 55°F/13°C; max 86°F/30°C)

BUPHTHALMUM

ASTERACEAE

Genus of 2 species of perennials found on rocky slopes, open woodland, and meadows in Europe and W. Asia. They have alternate, lance-shaped to obovate, entire or toothed leaves, and produce daisy-like, yellow flowerheads from early summer to early autumn. Suitable for a border, wild garden, or cutting garden.

• **CULTIVATION** Grow in moist, well-drained soil in full sun.

• **PROPAGATION** Sow seed in containers in a cold frame in spring, or divide in early spring.

• **PESTS AND DISEASES** Infrequent.

B. salicifolium ■ Clump-forming perennial with narrowly obovate to lance-shaped, willow-like, dark green leaves, to 4in (10cm) long. From midsummer to early autumn, erect, slender stems produce deep yellow flowerheads, 2–3in (5–8cm) across; these last well when cut. ↕ 24in (60cm), ↔ 18in (45cm). C. Europe. Zone 3b.

B. speciosum see *Telekia speciosa.*

Buphthalmum salicifolium

BUPLEURUM

Thorow-wax

APIACEAE

Genus of about 100 species of annuals, perennials, and evergreen or semi-evergreen shrubs. They are widely distributed in the N. hemisphere, with some species in southern Africa, and occur on dry, upland scrub, in moist areas, and among rocks. The variably shaped leaves are alternate, simple, and entire, often with conspicuous parallel veins. Umbels of star-shaped, yellow or green flowers are usually surrounded by involucres of leafy bracts. Grow in a flower or shrub border. *B. fruticosum* is an excellent cut flower. Plant smaller species in a rock garden.

• **CULTIVATION** Grow in any well-drained soil in full sun. Deadhead to avoid self-seeding. Grow *B. fruticosum* in a warm, sheltered site; cut back hard in spring if required.

• **PROPAGATION** Sow seed in containers in a cold frame in spring. Divide perennials in spring. Root semi-ripe cuttings of shrubs in summer.

• **PESTS AND DISEASES** Infrequent.

B. angulosum. Clump-forming, semi-evergreen perennial with linear-lance-shaped, blue-green basal leaves, 4–14in (10–35cm) long, and broader, heart-shaped, blue-green stem leaves, to 2in (5cm) long, clasping the upright, branching stems with their bases. In mid- and late summer, bears terminal umbels, ½in (1.5cm) across, consisting of rings of 4–6 ovate, jade-green bracts surrounding clusters of tiny, star-shaped, yellowish or creamy green flowers. ↕↔ to 12in (30cm). Pyrenees, N.E. Spain. Zone 5.

B. fruticosum ■ (Shrubby hare's ear). Open, spreading but dense, evergreen shrub with long, slender, mainly unbranched, erect shoots and narrowly obovate, blue-green leaves, to 3in (8cm) long. Small, star-shaped yellow flowers are borne in domed, terminal umbels, to 1½in (4cm) across, from midsummer to early autumn. Suitable for a coastal garden. ↕ 6ft (2m), ↔ 8ft (2.5m). Mediterranean. Zone 7b.

Bupleurum fruticosum

B. rotundifolium. Bushy, yellow-stemmed annual or short-lived perennial with stem-clasping, ovate to elliptic, or rounded, glaucous, mid-green leaves, ¾–2in (2–5cm) long, slightly pink-flushed when young. In summer, bears umbels, to 1¼in (3cm) across, of 4–8 greenish yellow bracts surrounding tiny, star-shaped, yellow-green flowers. ↕ 18–24in (45–60cm), ↔ 12in (30cm). C. and S. Europe, C. Asia. Zone 5. **'Green Gold'**, syn. 'Leprechaun Green Gold', has light green leaves and yellow flowers; ↕ to 18in (45cm).

BURCHARDIA
Milkmaids

LILIACEAE

Genus of 5 species of perennials from dry woodland and swamps in temperate Australia, grown for their umbels of 5–20, sometimes fragrant, star-shaped flowers. They have small corms, thick tuberous roots, and 1–5 linear, basal leaves, with a few leaves on the scapes in some species. Where not hardy, grow in a warm greenhouse or conservatory, or grow outdoors in a sunny border and lift and pot for winter storage. In warmer climates, grow in a border.

• **CULTIVATION** Under glass, grow in equal parts loam, leaf mold, and sharp sand in full light. Water freely when in growth, then sparingly as leaves wither, to store dry in winter. Pot on in spring. Outdoors, grow in humus-rich, moist but well-drained soil in full sun.

• **PROPAGATION** In spring, sow seed at 59–64°F (15–18°C) or pot up offsets.

• **PESTS AND DISEASES** Infrequent.

B. umbellata. Fleshy-rooted perennial with 1 or 2 linear, basal leaves, 1¾–2½in (4.5–6cm) long. In late spring and early summer, bears umbels of 2–9 fragrant, greenish white to white flowers, often tinged red outside, with purple anthers. ↕ 4–26in (10–65cm), PD4–6in (10–15cm). Australia (except Northern Territory). ❄ (min. 50–55°F/10–13°C)

BURCHELLIA
Buffalo-wood

RUBIACEAE

Genus of one species of evergreen shrub from warm-temperate forest of South Africa, grown for its small, terminal heads of flowers. The leaves are opposite and ovate. Where not hardy, grow *B. bubalina* in a cool greenhouse; in warmer areas, grow in a border.

• **CULTIVATION** Under glass, grow in soil-based potting mix with full light and good ventilation. Water moderately throughout the year, applying a balanced liquid fertilizer monthly from spring to autumn. Pot on or top-dress in late winter. Outdoors, grow in moist but well-drained, fertile soil in full sun. Will tolerate short spells around 32°F (0°C). Pruning group 8.

• **PROPAGATION** Root semi-ripe cuttings in a propagating case in summer, with gentle bottom heat.

• **PESTS AND DISEASES** Spider mites, whiteflies, aphids, and mealybugs occur.

B. bubalina ■ syn. *B. capensis* (Wild pomegranate). Erect to spreading shrub with ovate, glossy, dark green leaves, to

Burchellia bubalina

5in (13cm) long. From spring to summer, bears terminal clusters of 3–12 narrowly bell-shaped or tubular flowers, 1in (2.5cm) long, with 5 orange or scarlet petal lobes, aging to red. These are followed by spherical, red to brown berries, ½in (1.5cm) across. ↕ 6–15ft (2–5m), ↔ 3–10ft (1–3m). South Africa. ❄ (min. 41°F/5°C)

B. capensis see *B. bubalina.*

BURSERA

BURSERACEAE

Genus of about 40 species of variable, semi-evergreen, shrub- and tree-like perennials found in low, often hilly terrain from the Colorado Desert, south to tropical Central America. They usually have thick trunks or stems with deep cherry-red bark; the succulent species are relatively fleshy. Pinnate, alternate leaves are clustered near the stem tips. Insignificant, usually white flowers are borne singly or in few-flowered cymes at the stem tips in summer, followed by single-seeded, capsular or fleshy fruits. Burseras may be treated as bonsai plants or conventional container plants. Where not hardy, grow in a temperate greenhouse; in warmer areas, use in a desert garden.

• **CULTIVATION** Under glass, grow in a mix of 4 parts standard cactus potting mix and 1 part limestone chips in full light. When in growth, water freely and apply half-strength balanced liquid fertilizer monthly; keep completely dry in winter. Outdoors, grow in sharply drained, ideally alkaline soil in full sun. See also pp.48–49.

• **PROPAGATION** Sow seed at 70°F (21°C) in early spring. Root stem cuttings in late spring or early summer with bottom heat.

• **PESTS AND DISEASES** Aphids and mealybugs may be problems. Sensitive to a variety of fungal diseases.

B. microphylla (Elephant tree). Tree-like, perennial succulent with a thick, fleshy trunk, branches that become cherry red as they mature, and papery white bark, which readily peels off and exudes a milky white sap. Fern-like, pinnate leaves, 3–4in (7–10cm) long, have 30 or more oblong-linear leaflets, in opposite pairs. Bears cymes of star-shaped, yellow or white flowers, ½in (1.5cm) across, in summer. ↕ to 15ft (5m), ↔ to 5ft (1.5m). Colorado Desert. ❄ (min. 45–50°F/7–10°C)

BUTEA

FABACEAE

Genus of 4 species of deciduous trees, shrubs, and climbers from tropical forest in India, Sri Lanka, Myanmar, and Malaysia. They have large, long-stalked, alternate, fully divided, 3-palmate leaves and colorful, pea-like flowers in showy, terminal racemes or panicles. Only the trees are usually grown. Where not hardy, grow in a warm greenhouse; in warmer climates, use as specimen plants.

• **CULTIVATION** Under glass, grow in soil-based potting mix in full light with high humidity. When in growth, water moderately and apply a balanced liquid fertilizer monthly; keep just moist in winter. Top-dress or pot on in spring. Outdoors, grow in moderately fertile soil in full sun. Pruning group 1, but need restrictive pruning under glass.

• **PROPAGATION** Sow seed at 64–75°F (18–24°C) in spring. Root semi-ripe cuttings in a propagating case with bottom heat in summer.

• **PESTS AND DISEASES** Spider mites may be a problem under glass.

B. frondosa see *B. monosperma.*

B. monosperma, syn. *B. frondosa* (Dhak, Flame of the forest, Palas). Strongly branched tree, twisting with age. Leathery, silky-backed leaves consist of 3 diamond-shaped to rounded leaflets, 4–8in (10–20cm) long, borne on stalks almost as long. Racemes, to 6in (15cm) long, of silver-hairy, rich vermilion flowers, 1¼–1½in (3–4cm) long, are borne along the bare branches from winter to spring. ↕ to 50ft (15m), ↔ 10–15ft (3–5m). India, Sri Lanka, Myanmar. ❄ (min. 61°F/16°C)

BUTIA

ARECACEAE

Genus of 8–12 species of monoecious, single-stemmed palms from cool, dry areas of S. Brazil, Paraguay, Uruguay, and Argentina. They bear panicles of 3-petaled, male and female flowers among dense, terminal heads of pinnate leaves. Where not hardy, grow young butias as houseplants or in a cool greenhouse or conservatory. In frost-free areas, grow as specimen trees.

• **CULTIVATION** Under glass, grow in soil-based potting mix in bright filtered light. When in growth, water moderately and apply a balanced liquid fertilizer monthly. Keep just moist in winter. Pot on or top-dress in spring. Outdoors, grow in well-drained soil in full sun or partial shade. They withstand short periods near 32°F (0°C) in very dry, sunny climates.

• **PROPAGATION** Sow seed at 75–84°F (24–29°C) in spring.

• **PESTS AND DISEASES** Tar spot, false smut, *Ganoderma* butt rot, and other fungal leaf diseases are common. Spider mites and scale insects may be problems.

B. capitata ■ syn. *Cocos capitata* (Jelly palm). Slow-growing palm with a sturdy trunk often clothed with leaf bases. Strongly arching, narrowly elliptic to elliptic, blue-green-tinted, gray-green leaves, 6ft (2m) or more long, consist of many slender, leathery leaflets. Yellow

Butia capitata

flowers are borne in panicles, to 5ft (1.5m) long, in summer, followed by spherical to ovoid, yellow to purple fruit. ↕ 12–20ft (4–6m), ↔ 10–15ft (3–5m). S. Brazil, Uruguay, Argentina. ❄ (min. 41–50°F/5–10°C). **var. *nehrlingiana*** has red-purple, female flowers and red fruit. **var. *pulposa*** has pulpy, edible yellow fruit.

BUTOMUS
Flowering rush, Water gladiolus

BUTOMACEAE

Genus of one species of rhizomatous, aquatic perennial widely distributed in Europe, W. Asia, and North America, often found at the margins of ponds or in shallow water with cattails (*Typha*). It produces long, twisted leaves and fragrant flowers. *B. umbellatus* is ideal for a large pond or wildlife pool.

• **CULTIVATION** Grow in rich mud at the margins of ponds, or in water to 10in (25cm) deep, in full sun. If grown in a container, divide regularly to maintain free flowering. See also pp.52–53.

• **PROPAGATION** Sow seed in moist soil in a container half submerged in shallow water, in summer; after germination,

Butomus umbellatus

submerge the seedlings to a depth of ½in (1.5cm). Divide rhizomes in early spring when dormant. Remove root bulbils of divided plants in early spring and grow on in small containers of soil half submerged in water.
• **PESTS AND DISEASES** Waterlily aphid may be troublesome.

B. umbellatus ■ Rush-like, marginal, aquatic perennial with long, twisted, radical, dark-green leaves, ½in (1.5cm) wide, turning bronze-purple then dark green as they extend, with sheathed, triangular bases. Spreading umbels, to 4in (10cm) across, of many cup-shaped, fragrant, rose-pink flowers, ½–1in (1–2.5cm) across, are borne well above the water in late summer. ↕ to 5ft (1.5m), ↔ 18in (45cm). Eurasia, North America. Zone 4.

BUXUS

Box, Boxwood

BUXACEAE

Genus of about 70 species of evergreen shrubs and trees found in habitats ranging from rocky hills to woodland in Europe, Asia, Africa, and Central America. The leaves are opposite, linear-lance-shaped to almost rounded, entire, and leathery. In spring, small, axillary, star-shaped, yellow-green flowers of both sexes are borne on the same plant; several male flowers, with conspicuous yellow anthers, surround one female. Boxwoods are grown mainly for their foliage, which may be variegated, and for their ability to withstand clipping, which makes them ideal for hedging and topiary. Use dwarf boxwoods for edging, as a groundcover, or in a rock garden. Contact with sap may irritate skin.
• **CULTIVATION** Grow in any fertile, well-drained soil, preferably in partial shade. They are tolerant of sun, but the combination of full sun and dry soil may encourage poor, dull foliage color or scorching. Pruning group 8; trim hedges and edging plants in summer. Tolerant of hard, rejuvenative pruning in late spring, if followed by an application of fertilizer and a mulch.
• **PROPAGATION** Sow seed in containers in a cold frame in autumn. Root semi-ripe cuttings in summer. Graft in winter.
• **PESTS AND DISEASES** Powdery mildew, *Pythium* root rot, canker, dieback, and leaf spots are common problems. Leaf miners, scale insects, lesion nematodes, caterpillars, psyllids, and mites occur.

Buxus microphylla 'Green Pillow'

***B. harlandii* of gardens** ■ syn. *B. microphylla* var. *japonica* (Japanese boxwood). Slow-growing, very dense, upright shrub with narrowly lance-shaped, mid- to deep green leaves, to 1¼in (3cm) long. The plant grown under this name is not the true *B. harlandii*, which is tender and native to S. China and Hong Kong. ↕ 5ft (1.5m), ↔ 4ft (1.2m). Zone 6b.
B. microphylla (Small-leaved boxwood). Slow-growing, dense, rounded shrub with elliptic-oblong to inversely lance-shaped, dark green leaves, to ¾in (2cm) long, turning bronze in winter. ↕ 30in (75cm), ↔ 5ft (1.5m). Probably of garden origin. Zone 5. **'Compacta'** is very compact, dense, and slow-growing, with obovate, slightly recurved leaves, to ¼in (5mm) long; ↕↔ to 12in (30cm). **'Curly Locks'** has an open habit and pale green leaves on twisted shoots; ↕ 3ft (1m), ↔ 4ft (1.2m). **'Green Jade'** has broadly ovate to rounded, pale green leaves, deeply notched at the tips; ↕ 24in (60cm), ↔ 3ft (1m). **'Green Pillow'** ■ is very compact, dense, and slow-growing, with obovate, slightly recurved leaves; ↕ 18in (45cm), ↔ 3ft (1m). **var. *japonica*** see *B. harlandii* of gardens. **'Kingsville Dwarf'** is compact and slow-growing. **var. *koreana***, syn. *B. sinica* var. *insularis*, is very hardy; ↕ 24in (60cm), ↔ 30in (75cm); Korea, China. **var. *koreana* x *B. sempervirens* Hybrids** possess the hardiness and compactness of var. *koreana* and the leaf color of *B. sempervirens*, which they retain well. **var. *koreana* x *B. sempervirens* 'Green Gem'** is slow-growing and forms a deep green mound

Buxus sempervirens 'Latifolia Maculata'

that retains its color through winter; ↕↔ 24in (60cm). **var. *koreana* x *B. sempervirens* 'Green Mound'** is mounded and has dark green leaves; ↕↔ 3ft (1m). **var. *koreana* x *B. sempervirens* 'Green Mountain'** is upright and pyramidal-oval in shape, with dark green leaves; ↕ 5ft (1.5m), ↔ 3ft (1m). **'Morris Dwarf'** is slow-growing, forming a low, compact mound; ↕ 12in (30cm), ↔ 18in (45cm). **'Wintergreen'** is very hardy and retains the dark green color of its foliage in winter.
B. sempervirens (Common boxwood). Bushy, rounded shrub or small tree with ovate to oblong, glossy, dark green leaves, to 1¼in (3cm) long, notched at the tips. ↕ 15ft (5m), ↔ 15ft (5m) or more. Europe, N. Africa, Turkey. Zone 6. **'Aureomarginata'** see 'Marginata'. **'Bullata'**, syn. 'Latifolia Bullata' is low-growing with short, blunt, dark green leaves; ↕ 8ft (2.5m), ↔ 10ft (3m). **'Elegantissima'** is very dense, with narrow, white-margined leaves, to ¾in (2cm) long; ↕↔ 5ft (1.5m). **'Handsworthensis'** ■ is dense and upright in habit, with leaves to 1½in (4cm) long. Very good as a hedge. **'Latifolia Bullata'** see 'Bullata'. **'Latifolia Maculata'** ■ is compact, with bright yellow young foliage, maturing to dark green marked yellow; ↕ 8ft (2.5m), ↔ 6ft (2m). **'Marginata'** ■ syn. 'Aureomarginata', has yellow-margined, dark green leaves; ↕ 8ft (2.5m), ↔ 10ft (3m). **'Myrtifolia'** is low-growing; ↕ 4–5ft (1.2–1.5m). **'Newport Blue'** is dwarf and rounded, with blue-green leaves; ↕ 18in (45cm), ↔ 3ft (1m). **'Northland'** is hardy, with dark green leaves all winter; ↕ 4ft (1.2m), ↔ 5ft (1.5m). **'Pendula'** has weeping branches and becomes a small tree. **'Pullman'** is very vigorous, compact, and rounded; ↕ 6ft (2m), ↔ 5ft (1.5m); **'Rosmarinifolia'** is low-growing and has very small leaves, ¼in (6mm) long; ↕ 4–5ft (1.2–1.5m), ↔ 5ft (1.5m). **'Suffruticosa'** ■ (Edging boxwood) is compact and very slow-growing. Excellent as a hedge; ↕ 6ft (2m), ↔ 9ft (2.5m). **'Vardar Valley'** forms a flat-topped mound, with dark green leaves; ↕ 5ft (1.5m). **'Welleri'** is compact and broad in habit, with green leaves throughout winter; ↕ 3ft (1m), ↔ 5ft (1.5m).
B. sinica* var. *insularis see *B. microphylla* var. *koreana*.

Buxus sempervirens 'Marginata'

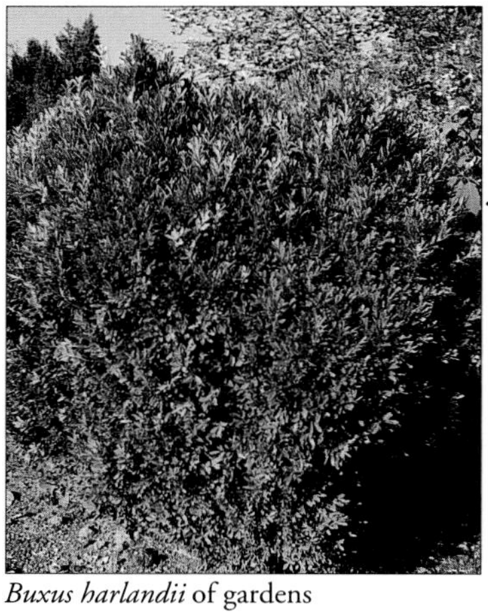

Buxus harlandii of gardens

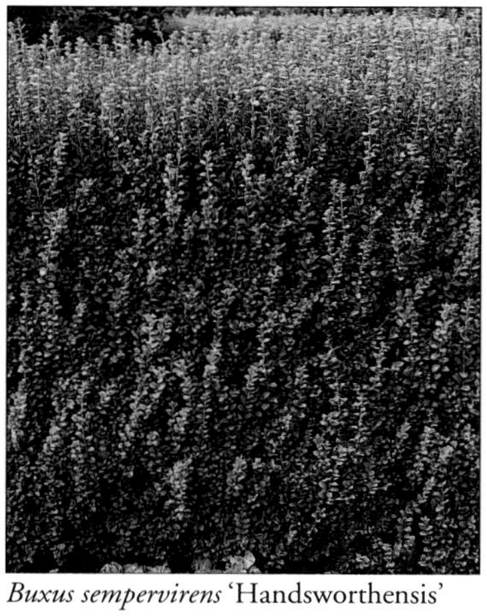

Buxus sempervirens 'Handsworthensis'

Buxus sempervirens 'Suffruticosa'

C

CABOMBA

CABOMBACEAE

Genus of 7 species of submerged aquatic perennials found in still water in North and South America. Long, thin, branching stems produce opposite or whorled sub-merged leaves, divided into linear lobes, and alternate, peltate floating leaves with broadly ovate to narrowly elliptic leaf blades. The solitary flowers, ½–1½in (1–4cm) across, are borne above the water on long stems. They are valued for their feathery foliage and, like other submerged aquatics, they absorb nutrients out of the water, helping to reduce algae levels, thereby making the water clearer.

• **CULTIVATION** In an aquarium, grow in full light in pots of coarse sand, in water without air-diffusers, since they dislike water movement. See also pp.52–53.

• **PROPAGATION** Take stem- tip cuttings, to 12in (30cm) long, in spring or early summer. Insert bunches of 5 or 6 cuttings into the aquarium soil.

• **PESTS AND DISEASES** Infrequent.

C. caroliniana ■ (Carolina water shield, Fanwort). Aquatic perennial with fan-shaped, sharp-pointed, dark green sub-merged leaves, to 3in (8cm) long, divided into 5 leaflets. The ovate, inversely lance-shaped to linear-oblong, sharp-pointed, mid-green floating leaves are ¾in (2cm) long. In summer, saucer-shaped, white or purple-pink flowers, 1¼–1½in (3–4cm) across, with 2 yellow spots at the base of each petal, are produced singly from the leaf axils, just above the water. ↔ indefinite. E. US. Zone 7.

▷ ***Cacalia*** see *Emilia*

Cabomba caroliniana

Caesalpinia pulcherrima

CAESALPINIA

FABACEAE

Genus of 70 or more evergreen species of trees, scandent to climbing shrubs, and perennials found in scrub and lowland rainforest, and on rocky mountain slopes in tropical and subtropical areas. They are grown for their terminal racemes or panicles of 30–40 flowers, each 5-petaled and with protruding stamens, 2–3in (5–8cm) long, and for their alternate, 2-pinnate, fern-like leaves. Where not hardy, grow in a cool or temperate greenhouse. In frost-free regions, grow as specimen plants or in a large shrub border.

• **CULTIVATION** Under glass, grow in soil-based potting mix, with additional leaf mold, in full light. In the growing season, water moderately and apply a balanced liquid fertilizer monthly; water sparingly in winter. Pot on or top-dress in early spring. Outdoors, grow in moist but well-drained, fertile soil in full sun. *C. gilliesii* and *C. pulcherrima* may survive short spells around 32°F (0°C). Pruning group 8, or group 13 if wall-trained; plants under glass may need restrictive pruning after the first flush of flowers.

• **PROPAGATION** Sow seed at 55–64°F (13–18°C) in spring, after soaking in warm water for 24 hours. Root soft-wood cuttings in spring or greenwood cuttings in summer.

• **PESTS AND DISEASES** Fungal canker and dieback can occur. Spider mites, whiteflies, and mealybugs are problems under glass.

C. gilliesii, syn. *Poinciana gilliesii* (Bird of paradise shrub). Erect to spreading shrub or small tree with 2-pinnate, mid- to dark green leaves, 8in (20cm) long, consisting of numerous oblong leaflets, ⅜in (9mm) long. Erect racemes, 6–12in (15–30cm) long, of up to 40 yellow flowers, to 1½in (4cm) across, with scarlet stamens, are borne in summer. ↕ 6–10ft (2–3m) or more, ↔ 3–8ft (1–2.5m). Argentina, Uruguay. ❀ (min. 45°F/7°C)

C. pulcherrima ■ syn. *Poinciana pulcherrima* (Barbados pride). Erect shrub or small tree with long-stalked, 2-pinnate, light green leaves, 12in (30cm) or more long, composed of numerous elliptic to obovate leaflets, ⅜in (9mm) long. From spring to autumn, bears erect racemes, to 8in (20cm) long, of up to 40 irregularly bowl-shaped flowers, 1¼–1½in (3–4cm) across, with orange-yellow or yellow petals, orange-red sepals, and red stamens. ↕ 10–20ft (3–6m), ↔ 6–12ft (2–4m). Probably West Indies. ❀ (min. 45°F/7°C)

CALADIUM

ARACEAE

Genus of 7 species of tuberous-rooted perennials from woodland margins in tropical South America. They are grown for their long-stalked, peltate, ovate to elliptic, broadly arrow- or lance-shaped leaves, which are variegated white, pink, or red. The greenish white spathes and spadices with green flowers are followed by white berries. Where not hardy, grow in a warm greenhouse; outdoors, use in bedding or as grouped specimens in containers. Contact with all parts may irritate skin, and may cause mild stomach upset if ingested.

• **CULTIVATION** Under glass, grow in soilless potting mix in bright filtered light. Pot up tubers in spring and provide high humidity at 70°F (21°C), not less than 55°F (13°C) when leaves develop. During the growing season, maintain high humidity, water freely, and apply a balanced liquid fertilizer monthly; reduce water in autumn. Keep dormant tubers almost dry at 55–61°F (13–16°C). Outdoors, grow in moist but well-drained, humus-rich, slightly acidic soil in partial to full shade. Lift for the winter and start again in spring as for culture under glass.

• **PROPAGATION** Divide tubers in spring; dust cut portions with fungicide.

• **PESTS AND DISEASES** Tuber rot, Southern blight, bacterial and fungal leaf spot, and root-knot nematodes are problems. Under glass, aphids and spider mites can be troublesome.

C. bicolor, syn. *C.* x *hortulanum* (Angel wings, Elephant's ears, Heart of Jesus, Mother-in-law plant). Tuberous-rooted perennial, the spherical tubers producing slender stems, 6in (15cm) long, with peltate, arrow- or lance-shaped, dark green leaves, 6–12in (15–30cm) long, streaked or spotted white, pink, or red. In spring, bears greenish white spathes, to 9in (23cm) long. ↕↔ to 24in (60cm). Garden origin. ❀ (min. 55°F/13°C). **'Candidum'** has white foliage with dark green veins. **'Fanny Munson'** has narrowly green-edged, pale pink leaves with green veins and deep pink midribs. **'Freida Hemple'** has leaves with bright red centers and wide green margins. **'Gingerland'** has gray leaves with white ribs, dark green edges, and maroon spots. **'John Peed'** has leaves with dark red centers fading to broad, dark green margins. **'June Bride'** has silvery white leaves with green veins. **'Little Miss Muffet'** has smaller, lime-green leaves with burgundy-red speckles and variably colored, bright red veins; ↕ 8–12in (20–30cm). **'Pink Beauty'** ■ has red-veined leaves, pink in the centers, with bright green, pink-speckled margins. **'Pink Symphony'** has less pronounced, arrow-like, pale pink leaves with bright green midribs and veins. **'Red Flash'** has white-marked green leaves with red veins and wide green margins. **'Rosebud'** has pink-centered leaves, shading to white, then green with pink midribs. **'White Christmas'** has broad, snow-white leaves with mid-green veins. **'White Queen'** has white leaves, gradually shading toward the deep green margins, and red veins that bleed slightly.

C.* x *hortulanum see *C. bicolor*.

C. humboldtii. Clump-forming, tuberous-rooted perennial with peltate, ovate to oblong, arrow-shaped, white-blotched, dull green leaves, 1–4in (2.5–10cm) long. Inflorescences are insignificant. May be grown in long-fiber sphagnum moss in standing water. ↕ 10in (25cm), ↔ indefinite. Venezuela, Brazil. ❀ (min. 55°F/13°C)

Caladium bicolor 'Pink Beauty'

CALAMAGROSTIS

Reed grass, Smallweed

POACEAE

Genus of about 250 species of sturdy, tufted, rhizomatous, perennial grasses widely distributed in temperate zones of the N. hemisphere, where they occur in marshland and damp woodland. They have linear, flat or channeled leaves and dense inflorescences borne in branching panicles. Ornamental cultivars are useful in a herbaceous or mixed border for their long-lasting, elegant inflorescences and architectural form. Some species may be invasive.

• **CULTIVATION** Grow in moist, humus-rich soil in sun or partial shade, although they will tolerate all but the poorest soils. In early spring, before new growth begins, cut down to the ground all stems that were left for winter effect.

• **PROPAGATION** Divide in midspring.

• **PESTS AND DISEASES** Ergot, powdery mildew, tar spot, rust, smut, leaf streak, red eye spot, scald, char spot, speckle, and foot rot can occur.

C.* x *acutiflora (*C. arundinacea* x *C. epigejos*) (Feather reed grass). Slow-spreading, clump-forming, perennial grass with arching, linear, flat, slightly glossy, mid-green leaves, 18–36in (45–90cm) long. Stiff, erect, unbranched stems bear soft, silvery bronze to pale purple-brown inflorescences in narrow panicles, 6–12in (15–30cm) long, in mid- and late summer; these persist throughout winter. ↕ 2–6ft (0.6–1.8m), ↔ 2–4ft (0.6–1.2m). Europe, Russia. Zone 4. **'Karl Foerster'** has pink-bronze inflorescences that fade to buff or pale brown. Often confused with 'Stricta',

Calamagrostis x *acutiflora* 'Overdam'

whose habit is identical in mild climates. In colder climates, 'Karl Foerster' is compact and blooms 2 or 3 weeks earlier; ↕ to 6ft (1.8m), ↔ 24in (60cm).
'Overdam' ▣ has leaves with pale yellow margins and stripes, which fade to pink-flushed white with age. Produces purplish brown inflorescences that become grayish pink. Forms looser clumps than 'Karl Foerster'; ↕ to 4ft (1.2m).

CALAMINTHA

Calamint

LAMIACEAE

Genus of 8 or more species of aromatic, sometimes rhizomatous perennials, some woody-based, found in grassland, scrub, and woodland in N. temperate regions. They have ovate to oblong, usually toothed leaves and bear axillary cymes of tubular, 2-lipped flowers, mainly in shades of blue, but pink or white in some species. Grow calamints in a border, or an open woodland garden. The flowers are attractive to bees.

• **CULTIVATION** Grow in moist but well-drained soil in sun or partial shade.

• **PROPAGATION** Sow seed in containers in a cold frame in spring, or divide in early spring.

• **PESTS AND DISEASES** Powdery mildew may be a problem.

C. alpina see *Acinos alpinus.*
C. corsica see *Acinos corsicus.*
C. grandiflora, syn. *Clinopodium grandiflorum.* Rhizomatous, many-branched, bushy perennial with ovate, toothed leaves, 2in (5cm) long, dark green above and pale green beneath. Lax cymes of up to 5 pink flowers, 1–1½in (2.5–4cm) long, are borne in summer. Thrives in dappled shade. ↕↔ 18in (45cm). S. and S.E. Europe to Caucasus, Russia (Crimea), Turkey, Iran. Zone 5.
C. nepeta ▣ (Lesser calamint). Aromatic, slow-growing, erect perennial with ovate, often shallowly toothed, hairy, dark green leaves, to 1½in (4cm)

Calamintha nepeta

long. In summer, bears branched cymes of 5 to 15 mauve, occasionally pink flowers, to ¼in (6mm) long. ↕ to 18in (45cm), ↔ 20–30in (50–75cm). S. and C. Europe, N.W. Africa, N. Turkey, Caucasus, Russia (Crimea). Zone 5.

CALAMUS

ARECACEAE

Genus of about 370 species of spiny, evergreen, usually climbing, occasionally shrub-like, dioecious palms found in tropical forest in Africa and Asia, New Guinea, and from N.E. Australia to Fiji. The leaves are pinnate, sometimes ending in barbed whips, and have lance-shaped leaflets. The inflorescences, borne among the leaf sheaths, have tubular, spiny, persistent bracts. Male flowers are solitary and symmetrical; female flowers are paired with sterile males and are often larger and followed by spherical yellow fruits, ½–1¼in (1–3cm) across. Many species are used in the construction of rattan furniture. Where not hardy, grow young plants in a temperate greenhouse, or as houseplants. In warmer areas, grow through shrubs or trees.

• **CULTIVATION** Under glass, grow in soil-based potting mix in bright filtered light and high humidity. Throughout the summer, water freely and apply a balanced liquid fertilizer monthly; water more sparingly in winter. Outdoors, grow in moist but well-drained soil in partial shade.

• **PROPAGATION** Sow seed at 66–75°F (19–24°C) in spring.

• **PESTS AND DISEASES** Infrequent.

C. rotang (Rattan cane). Erect or climbing palm with solitary or clustered stems and alternate or nearly opposite, pinnate, light to mid-green leaves, 32in (80cm) long, composed of lance-shaped leaflets. Star-shaped, 3-pointed cream flowers, ½in (1.5cm) long, may be produced at any time during the year. ↕ 30ft (10m), ↔ 20–30ft (6–10m). S. India, Sri Lanka. ❀ (min. 50°F/10°C)

CALANDRINIA

PORTULACACEAE

Genus of about 150 species of annuals and short-lived, tufted to clump-forming, evergreen perennials, a few of which are succulent. They occur in hot, dry, open, rocky areas, and sometimes grassy or bare alpine steppe or scree, in W. North America, Central America to N.W. and W. South America, and also S. Australia. Although they often appear rosetted, the narrow, entire, usually fleshy leaves are alternate. The 5- to 7-petaled flowers, with 2 large sepals, are usually red, reddish purple, or white, and may be solitary or borne in semi-erect or pendent racemes or panicles on long stalks. Where not hardy, treat calandrinias as annuals, or grow in a cool greenhouse. Elsewhere, grow on a sunny bank, or in a border, rock garden, scree bed, or alpine house.

• **CULTIVATION** Under glass, grow in a mix of equal parts loam, peat, leaf mold, and sand in full light. Water moderately when in growth (the high-alpine species in particular are very sensitive to excess water) and apply a dilute, balanced liquid fertilizer monthly in summer; keep just moist in winter. Outdoors, grow in slightly acidic, humus-rich, sharply drained soil in full sun. See also pp.48–49.

• **PROPAGATION** Sow seed at 61–64°F (16–18°C) in early spring or autumn, or take stem cuttings in spring.

• **PESTS AND DISEASES** Prone to aphids and spider mites under glass. Young plants are vulnerable to slugs and snails.

C. caespitosa. Cushion-forming, variable, evergreen perennial with fleshy, linear to inversely lance-shaped, mid-green leaves, ¼–1¼in (0.5–3cm) long. The best variants have compact cushions of small-leaved rosettes, and bear cup-shaped, glossy magenta flowers, ½in (1.5cm) across, with greenish gold disk florets, singly on short stems in summer. Less compact variants with golden orange or pale pink flowers also occur. ↕ to 3in (8cm), ↔ to 4in (10cm). Chile, Argentina, Tierra del Fuego. ❀ (min. 43°F/6°C)
C. ciliata (Redmaids). Semi-prostrate to semi-erect annual with fleshy, linear to spoon-shaped, gray-green leaves, 1½in (4cm) long, purple beneath, on spreading, erect stems. In late summer, bears solitary, purple, red, pink, or white flowers, to ¾in (2cm) across. Needs light soil in a sheltered site in full sun. ↕↔ to 12in (30cm). Ecuador, Peru.
C. grandiflora. Clump-forming perennial succulent, often grown as an annual, with thick, elliptic, pointed, flat, smooth-margined, bright green leaves, to 8in (20cm) long. Racemes of numerous cup-shaped, pale reddish purple to magenta flowers, to 1¼in (3cm) across, are borne in summer. ↕ to 3ft (1m), ↔ 18in (45cm). Chile. ❀ (min. 43°F/6°C)
C. megarhiza* var. *nivalis see *Claytonia megarhiza* var. *nivalis.*
C. spectabilis. Shrubby, tufted perennial producing succulent branches, stems, and foliage. Pointed, softly hairy, smooth-margined, light to mid-green leaves, 1¼–1½in (3–4cm) long, are diamond- or spoon- to lance-shaped. In summer, bears solitary or paired, cup-shaped, vivid purple-red flowers, 2in (5cm) across. ↕ 24in (60cm), ↔ 18in (45cm). Chile. ❀ (min. 43°F/6°C)
C. umbellata ▣ (Rock purslane). Variable, loose, mound-forming, evergreen perennial, often treated as an annual, with semi-upright, branching stems and linear to linear-lance-shaped, very hairy, blue- or gray-green leaves, ¾–1½in (2–4cm) long. Produces loose panicles of 6–30 upturned, cup-shaped, crimson-magenta flowers, to ¾in (2cm) across, in summer. ↕↔ 6–8in (15–20cm). Chile, Argentina. Zone 7b.

CALANTHE

ORCHIDACEAE

Genus of 120–150 species of evergreen, semi-evergreen, or deciduous, rhizomatous, terrestrial, occasionally epiphytic orchids from sites in tropical and temperate Asia, Polynesia, and Madagascar, ranging from sea level and lowland forest to altitudes over 10,000ft (3,000m). The deciduous species are usually found in woodland or among shaded rocks. They have corm-like, sometimes angular, oblong-ellipsoid pseudobulbs, often partially exposed above the soil surface, and basal clusters of 2–5 mid- to dark green, folded leaves. Erect, loose to dense-flowered racemes of spurred flowers, each with a 3-lobed lip, are borne in spring, summer, or winter. *C. discolor* and *C. discolor* var. *bicolor* are suitable for a rock garden or woodland garden; grow tender species in a warm greenhouse.

Calandrinia umbellata

C

Calanthe vestita

• **CULTIVATION** Cool- and warm-growing orchids. Under glass, grow in terrestrial orchid potting mix in bright filtered light and high humidity. In summer, water freely and apply a half-strength liquid fertilizer at every second or third watering. Avoid spraying the foliage, since it may become spotted. Water evergreen species sparingly in winter. Keep deciduous species completely dry when dormant, with a minimum of 50°F (10°C). Pot on annually. Outdoors, grow in coarse, well-drained, humus-rich soil in a sheltered site in partial or dappled shade. See also p.46.
• **PROPAGATION** For spring-flowering plants, divide pseudobulbs after flowering; otherwise, divide in early spring as new growth appears.
• **PESTS AND DISEASES** Spider mites, mealybugs, aphids, and whiteflies are problems under glass. Prone to fungal spots as well as cymbidium mosaic virus.

C. discolor. Evergreen or semi-evergreen, terrestrial orchid producing narrowly obovate to oblong leaves, 8–12in (20–30cm) long. In spring, bears up to 10 purple-brown to green flowers, 1–1½in (2.5–4cm) across, with pale rose-pink or white lips, in erect racemes, 16in (40cm) long. ↕ 6–12in (15–30cm), ↔ 12in (30cm). Japan. Zone 7b. **var. *bicolor***, syn. *C. striata*, *C. striata* var. *bicolor*, produces flowers 1¼–1½in (3–4cm) across, the tepals sometimes suffused yellow. **f. *sieboldii***, syn. *C. sieboldii*, *C. sieboldii* var. *flava*, *C. striata* f. *sieboldii*, has bright, clear yellow flowers.
C. sieboldii see *C. discolor* f. *sieboldii*.
C. sieboldii* var. *flava see *C. discolor* f. *sieboldii*.
C. striata see *C. discolor* var. *bicolor*.
C. striata* var. *bicolor see *C. discolor* var. *bicolor*.
C. striata* f. *sieboldii see *C. discolor* f. *sieboldii*.
C. tricarinata. Evergreen or semi-evergreen, terrestrial orchid producing broadly inversely lance-shaped to elliptic, strongly ribbed leaves, 7–12in (18–30cm) long. Racemes, 12–16in (30–40cm) long, of up to 15 nodding or pendent flowers, ¾–1½in (2–4cm) across, with greenish yellow to brown-green tepals, the lips purplish brown or red-brown, are borne from the leaf axils in spring. ↕↔ 20in (50cm). Himalayas, China, Japan, Taiwan. ❄ (min. 48°F/9°C; max. 81°F/27°C)

C. vestita ▣ Deciduous, terrestrial orchid with large, narrowly ovate to broadly lance-shaped leaves, to 36in (90cm) long. Arching racemes, to 36in (90cm) long, of up to 12 white or pale rose-pink flowers, 2in (5cm) across, with red to rose-pink or magenta lips, are borne in winter, before the leaves emerge. ↕ 3½ft (1.1m), ↔ 3ft (1m). Burma, Thailand, Cambodia, Laos, Vietnam, Indonesia (Sulawesi). ❄ (min. 64°F/18°C; max. 86°F/30°C)

CALATHEA

MARANTACEAE

Genus of about 300 species of evergreen, rhizomatous perennials found in humid forest and at forest margins in tropical Central and South America, and the West Indies. Most are clump-forming, with ovate to elliptic, shiny, long-stalked, pale to dark green leaves, often attractively patterned and red on the reverse; young plants may differ from mature plants in the size and color of their foliage. Pairs of small flowers, rarely produced in cultivation, are tubular with extended upper and lower lips, and are borne in racemes or dense spikes, accompanied by sheathed bracts, in summer. Where not hardy, grow in a warm or temperate greenhouse, or as houseplants; they will tolerate fairly low light levels. In warmer areas, grow in a border or among shrubs.
• **CULTIVATION** Under glass, grow in soilless or soil-based potting mix in bright indirect or filtered light, with high humidity, draft-free conditions, and a constant temperature. When in growth, water freely and apply a balanced liquid fertilizer monthly; water moderately in winter. Pot on annually in late spring. Outdoors, grow in moist but well-drained, humus-rich soil in partial shade.
• **PROPAGATION** Divide clumps in late spring; keep plants in warm, humid conditions until re-established.
• **PESTS AND DISEASES** Very prone to spider mites, bud mites, mealybugs, and aphids. Sensitive to fluoride toxicity, and low humidity can cause marginal leaf necrosis. Fungal and bacterial leaf spots are common.

***C. burle-marxii* 'Ice Blue'.** Clump-forming perennial with slightly arching or spreading, ovate leaf blades, to 30in (75cm) long, on leaf stalks to 12in (30cm) long. The leaves are bright green above with yellow-green midribs, and gray-green beneath with yellow midribs. Well-established plants bear ovoid flower spikes, 5–7in (12–18cm) long, with blue bracts and purple flowers. ↕ 2½–5ft (75–150cm), ↔ 4ft (1.2m). ❄ (min. 61–70°F/16–21°C)
C. discolor see *C. lutea*.
C. insignis see *C. lancifolia*.
C. lancifolia, syn. *C. insignis* (Rattlesnake plant). Clump-forming perennial with erect, linear to lance-shaped, wavy-margined leaf blades, to 18in (45cm) long, on leaf stalks to 12in (30cm) long. Leaves are pale green above, with darker green patches on either side of the midribs, and deep red-purple beneath. Yellow flowers are borne in conical spikes, 2–4in (5–10cm) long, in summer. ↕ 18–30in (45–75cm), ↔ 24in (60cm). Brazil. ❄ (min. 61–70°F/16–21°C)

Calathea louisae

C. lindeniana. Clump-forming perennial producing elliptic leaf blades, 12–16in (30–40cm) long, on leaf stalks to 12in (30cm) long. Leaves are dark green above with olive-green patches on each side of the midribs, green and red beneath. Bears pale yellow flowers in ellipsoid spikes, to 4in (10cm) long. ↕ to 36in (90cm), ↔ 24in (60cm). Peru, N.W. Brazil. ❄ (min. 61–70°F/16–21°C)
C. louisae ▣ Clump-forming perennial producing elliptic-ovate, dark green leaf blades, red beneath, and 6in (15cm) long, with silver-green feathering around the midribs, on leaf stalks to 8in (20cm) long. White flowers are borne in conical spikes, 1¼–2½in (3–6cm) long. ↕ to 36in (90cm), ↔ 18in (45cm). Tropical Central and South America. ❄ (min. 61–70°F/16–21°C)

C. lutea, syn. *C. discolor*. Clump-forming perennial producing ovate to obovate leaf blades, 5½ft (1.7m) long, bright green above, gray beneath, with raised lateral veins, on leaf stalks to 6in (15cm) long. Yellow flowers are borne in ovoid spikes, 3–5in (8–13cm) long. ↕ to 6ft (2m), ↔ 4ft (1.2m). Tropical Central and South America. ❄ (min. 61–70°F/16–21°C)
***C. majestica* 'Roseolineata'**, syn. *C. ornata* 'Roseolineata'. Robust, clump-forming perennial, producing elliptic, unequal-sided leaf blades, 12–16in (30–40cm) long, erect at first, then spreading, on leaf stalks 8in (20cm) or more long. Leaves are deep olive-green above, with pairs of thin, rose-red, lateral stripes on opposite sides of the midribs, becoming white with age; the undersides are purple. Bears ovoid spikes, 2–3in (5–8cm) long, of white flowers with violet petal lobes. ↕ 6ft (2m), ↔ to 3ft (1m). ❄ (min. 61–70°F/16–21°C)
***C. majestica* 'Sanderiana'** see *C. sanderiana*.
C. makoyana ▣ syn. *Maranta makoyana* (Cathedral windows, Peacock plant). Clump-forming, stemless perennial with erect, ovate leaf blades, 8–12in (20–30cm) long, on leaf stalks 6in (15cm) or more long. Leaves are pale green above, with oblong patches and fine lines of dark green along the lateral veins; the undersides are purple-tinged, with similar purple markings. Bears ovoid spikes, to 2½in (6cm) long, of white and purple flowers. ↕ 18in (45cm), ↔ 9in (23cm). E. Brazil. ❄ (min. 61–70°F/16–21°C)

Calathea makoyana

Calathea sanderiana

C. oppenheimiana see *Ctenanthe oppenheimiana.*
***C. ornata* 'Roseolineata'** see *C. majestica* 'Roseolineata'.
C. ornata* var. *sanderiana see *C. sanderiana.*
C. picturata. Clump-forming perennial with elliptic leaf blades, 8–10in (20–25cm) long, on leaf stalks 8in (20cm) long. Leaves are deep olive-green above, marked with a wide silver line along each side of the midribs, and with a narrower, jagged silver line near the margins; the undersides are purple. White flowers are borne in cylindrical spikes, 4in (10cm) long. ↕↔ 14–16in (35–40cm). N.W. Brazil. ❀ (min. 61–70°F/16–21°C). **'Argentea'** produces leaves silvery white above, bright rich purple beneath; they have dark green margins.
C. roseopicta. Clump-forming perennial with rounded leaf blades, to 8in (20cm) long, on leaf stalks 1¼–4in (3–10cm) long. Leaves are dark green with pink midribs and feathered, pink or cream stripes between the midribs and margins; the undersides are red. Bears cylindrical spikes, 3½in (9cm) long, of white and violet flowers. ↕ 10in (25cm), ↔ 6in (15cm). N.W. Brazil. ❀ (min. 61–70°F/16–21°C)
***C.* 'Sanderiana'** see *C. sanderiana.*
C. sanderiana ▣ syn. *C. majestica* 'Sanderiana', *C. ornata* var. *sanderiana*, *C.* 'Sanderiana'. Robust, clump-forming perennial with broadly elliptic, unequal-sided leaf blades, 24in (60cm) long, on leaf stalks 8in (20cm) or more long. Deep olive-green leaves have pairs of thin, rose-red, lateral stripes on either side of the midribs, becoming white on older leaves; the undersides are purple. White and violet flowers are borne in conical spikes, 2–3in (5–8cm) long, in summer. ↕ 6ft (3m), ↔ 3ft (1m). Peru. ❀ (min. 61–70°F/16–21°C)
C. veitchiana. Clump-forming perennial with ovate-elliptic, unequal-sided leaf blades, 12in (30cm) long, on leaf stalks 4–8in (10–20cm) or more long. Dark green leaves have feathery markings in shades of green, and red undersides. Violet-flecked white flowers are borne in conical spikes, 3in (8cm) long. ↕ 3ft (1m), ↔ 24in (60cm). S.E. Brazil. ❀ (min. 61–70°F/16–21°C)
C. zebrina ▣ (Zebra plant). Clump-forming perennial with oblong-ovate to elliptic leaf blades, 18in (45cm) or more long, on leaf stalks 12in (30cm) long. Leaves are dark green and velvety above, purple-red beneath; they have yellow-green midribs, margins, and veins. Bears white to violet flowers in almost spherical spikes, 3–4in (7–10cm) long. ↕ 3ft (1m), ↔ 24in (60cm). S.E. Brazil. ❀ (min. 61–70°F/16–21°C). **'Humilior'** is compact in habit, producing leaves with areas around the lateral veins that are olive-green above, gray-green beneath.

Calathea zebrina

CALCEOLARIA

Pouch flower, Slipper flower, Slipperwort

SCROPHULARIACEAE

Genus of some 300 species of annuals, biennials, perennials, and shrubs, some of them scandent, from diverse habitats ranging from dry scrub to alpine regions. They occur in temperate and tropical areas of Mexico, Central and South America (many in Peru and Chile), with some from the Falkland Islands. Leaves are opposite and whorled or in rosettes. The slipper-like flowers are solitary or borne in few- to many-flowered panicles, racemes, corymbs, or cymes. They are usually yellow or purple, often heavily spotted in one or more contrasting colors, and 2-lipped, the upper lip small but often inflated, the lower lip large and pouched. Where not hardy, grow annuals, biennials, and shrubs in a temperate greenhouse or as summer bedding. The hardier, low-growing perennials (alpine species) are ideal for a rock garden or alpine house.
• **CULTIVATION** Under glass, grow in soil-based potting mix in bright filtered light with good ventilation. In the growing season, water freely and apply a balanced liquid fertilizer every 3–4 weeks; water sparingly in winter. Outdoors, grow in light, moderately fertile, acidic soil in sun or partial shade. They require cool, moist conditions to flower freely. Grow alpine species outdoors in moist but well-drained, very gritty soil in partial shade; protect from winter moisture. In an alpine house, grow in soil-based potting mix or in a mix of equal parts loam, leaf mold, and sharp sand; top-dress with grit. Pot on every second year in late spring.
• **PROPAGATION** Sow seed of hardy species in containers in a cold frame in autumn or early spring, or divide in spring. Root individual rosettes in early summer. Sow seed of *C. integrifolia* in spring or autumn, and seed of *C. mexicana* in late winter or early spring. Surface-sow seed of *C.* Herbeohybrida Group cultivars at 64°F (18°C) in late summer or spring. Root softwood cuttings of shrubby species in late spring or summer; increase good color variants of *C. integrifolia* by rooting semi-ripe cuttings in late summer.
• **PESTS AND DISEASES** Prone to spider mites, whiteflies, aphids, and slugs. Gray mold, white mold, wilt, and a few fungal spots occur.

Calceolaria arachnoidea

C. acutifolia see *C. polyrrhiza.*
C. arachnoidea ▣ Evergreen, rhizomatous, cushion- or mat-forming perennial with rosettes of lance-shaped to oblong-spoon-shaped, white-hairy leaves, 1½–4in (4–10cm) long, with winged leaf stalks. Compact cymes of 2–5 deep purple flowers, to ½in (1.5cm) long, are produced on slender, branching stems, from summer to autumn. Best in an alpine house. ↕ 8–10in (20–25cm), ↔ to 6in (15cm). Chile. ❀ (min. 35°F/2°C)
C. biflora, syn. *C. plantaginea.* Evergreen, mat-forming, rhizomatous perennial with rosettes of ovate-lance-shaped to oblong, obovate, or diamond-shaped, toothed, dark green leaves, 1–4in (2.5–10cm) long. Bears loose racemes of 2–8 short-stemmed, bright yellow flowers, each to ¾in (2cm) long, over several months in summer. Suitable for a shaded rock garden. ↕ 6–10in (15–25cm), ↔ to 8in (20cm). Chile, Argentina. ❀ (min. 45°F/7°C)
C. darwinii, syn. *C. uniflora* var. *darwinii.* Rhizomatous, evergreen, rosetted perennial with oblong-spoon-shaped to diamond-shaped, wrinkled, glossy, dark green leaves, 1¼–1½in (3–4cm) long. In early summer, bears solitary yellow flowers, 1–1½in (2.5–4cm) long, each with a deep yellow lower lip, heavily freckled red-brown, and with a wide, horizontal white band at the junction of the throat and pouch. Best in an alpine house. ↕ 3–4in (7–10cm), ↔ to 5in (13cm). Argentina (S. Patagonia), Tierra del Fuego. Zone 7b.
***C.* Fruticohybrida Group** see *C. integrifolia* Fruticohybrida Group.
***C.* Herbeohybrida Group.** Bushy, compact biennials, normally grown as spring- or summer-flowering container plants, with opposite, ovate, softly hairy, mid-green leaves, 3–5in (8–13cm) or more long. ↕ 8–18in (20–45cm), ↔ 6–12in (15–30cm). There are 2 main subgroups: Grandiflora group cultivars have compact cymes of 5–15 flowers, to 3in (8cm) long, in red, yellow, orange, and bicolors, often marked with purple, red, or other colors; Multiflora group cultivars have cymes of 3–12 smaller, more numerous flowers, to 2in (5cm) long, in a range of colors. **Anytime Series** (Multiflora group) are compact and flower in less than 16 weeks from sowing, at any time of year, given suitable conditions; ↕ to 8in (20cm). **'Bright Bikinis'** ▣ (Multiflora group) bears dense cymes of yellow, orange, or red flowers in summer; ↕↔ 8in (20cm). **'Monarch'** (Grandiflora group) has light green leaves and bears red or yellow flowers, often marked orange-red or maroon; ↕ 12in (30cm), ↔ 10in (25cm).
C. integrifolia, syn. *C. rugosa.* Evergreen, subshrubby perennial, usually grown as an annual, with softly hairy young shoots. The opposite, linear-lance-shaped to ovate-lance-shaped leaves are finely toothed, gray-green, and 2in (5cm) or more long, frequently with reddish hairs beneath. Panicle-like cymes of 10–35 yellow flowers, to 1in (2.5cm) long, are borne over several months in summer. ↕ to 4ft (1.2m), ↔ 9–12in (23–30cm). Mexico. ❀ (min. 45°F/7°C). This species is the

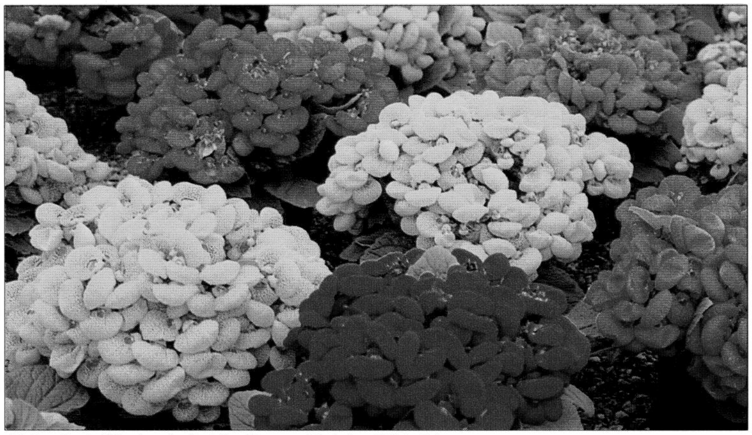

Calceolaria Herbeohybrida Group 'Bright Bikinis'

Calceolaria polyrrhiza

main parent of the **Fruticohybrida Group** of cultivars described below. **'Goldcut'** is tall-growing, and good for cut flowers; ↕ 12–16in (30–40cm). **'Golden Bunch'** is compact, with pale golden yellow flowers in early summer; excellent for containers or as bedding; ↕ to 10in (25cm). **'Midas'** is upright, bearing deep yellow, weather-resistant flowers in early summer; good for hanging baskets; ↕ to 10in (25cm). **'Sunshine'** is similar to 'Midas', but flowers in midsummer. Useful for bedding, hanging baskets, or containers; ↕ to 12in (30cm).

C. mexicana. Bushy, erect to spreading, softly hairy annual with opposite, ovate to lance-shaped, pinnatifid, mid-green leaves, ¾–3in (2–8cm) long, often tinged purple beneath. Cymes of 3–5 pale to bright yellow, unspotted flowers, to ½in (1.5cm) long, are produced in summer. ↕ 8–20in (20–50cm), ↔ to 12in (30cm). Mexico to Bolivia.

C. pavonii. Scandent, woody-based, evergreen, perennial climber with woolly stems. Winged leaf stalks bear opposite, triangular-ovate, irregularly toothed, softly hairy, mid- to dark green leaves, 3–8in (8–20cm) long, heart-shaped at

Calceolaria tenella

Calceolaria 'Walter Shrimpton'

the bases. Cymes of 4–20 sulfur-yellow flowers, ¾in (2cm) long, with purple-marked throats, are borne in summer. ↕ 5–10ft (1.5–3m). Ecuador, Peru. ❄ (min. 45°F/7°C)

C. plantaginea see *C. biflora.*

C. polyrrhiza ■ syn. *C. acutifolia.* Rhizomatous, mat-forming, evergreen perennial with opposite, oblong-ovate or lance-shaped, shallowly toothed, mid-green leaves, to 1¾in (4.5cm) long, crowded on the stems. In summer, bears cymes of 4–6 red-spotted yellow flowers, to 1in (2.5cm) long. ↕ 2in (5cm), ↔ to 8in (20cm). Chile, Argentina. Zone 6.

C. rugosa see *C. integrifolia.*

C. scabiosifolia see *C. tripartita.*

***C.* Sunset Series.** Compact, rounded, evergreen, many-branched, sturdy-stemmed perennials producing opposite, ovate-lance-shaped, dark gray-green leaves, 4in (10cm) long. They produce red, yellow, orange, or bi-colored flowers, ¾in (2cm) long, from midspring to midsummer. ↕ to 12in (30cm), ↔ 9–12in (23–30cm). ❄ (min. 45°F/7°C)

C. tenella ■ Mat-forming, creeping, evergreen perennial with slender stems clothed in broadly ovate, finely toothed, pale yellowish green leaves, to ½in (1.5cm) long. In summer, produces solitary or branched cymes of 3 broadly pouched, red-spotted yellow flowers, ¼–⅜in (7–9mm) long. ↕ 2in (5cm), ↔ to 12in (30cm) or more. Chile. Zone 7b.

C. tripartita, syn. *C. scabiosifolia.* Erect, evergreen perennial, usually grown as an annual, with softly hairy stems and leaves. The opposite, ovate, pinnatifid, toothed, mid-green leaves are ¾–3½in (2–9cm) long. Cymes of 5–12 pale to bright to deep yellow, unspotted flowers, ¼in (6mm) long, are produced in summer. ↕ 24in (60cm), ↔ 12in (30cm). Mexico to Peru. ❄ (min. 41°F/5°C)

C. uniflora* var. *darwinii see *C. darwinii.*

***C.* 'Walter Shrimpton'** ■ Evergreen perennial, similar to *C. darwinii*, with rosettes of spoon- to diamond-shaped, glossy dark green leaves, 1¼–2in (3–5cm) long. In summer, bears cymes of 2–5 bronze-yellow flowers, to 1in (2.5cm) long, spotted rich brown, each with a horizontal white band at the junction of the throat and pouch, broader and bolder than in *C. darwinii.* ↕ 4in (10cm), ↔ 9in (23cm). Zone 7b.

CALENDULA

ASTERACEAE

Genus of 20–30 species of bushy, fast-growing annuals and woody-based, evergreen perennials, occurring in arable land, wasteland, and rocky habitats from S. Europe to North Africa. Leaves are alternate, simple, and aromatic. Daisy-like flowerheads, with orange or yellow ray florets and yellow, orange, violet, purple, or brown disk florets, are borne over a long period, and throughout autumn into mild winters. Many of the cultivars are excellent annuals for an informal border; the flowers last well when cut. They are also suitable for growing in containers.

- **CULTIVATION** Grow in well-drained, moderately fertile soil in sun or partial shade. Deadhead to prolong flowering.
- **PROPAGATION** Sow seed *in situ* in spring or autumn. Provide protection for autumn-sown seedlings where not reliably hardy.
- **PESTS AND DISEASES** White smut, rust, gray mold, cucumber mosaic virus, aster yellows, powdery mildew, and fungal leaf spots occur. Aphids, whiteflies, snails, and slugs can be problems.

***C. officinalis* cultivars** (English marigold, Pot marigold). Fast-growing, erect, sometimes spreading annuals with inversely lance-shaped to spoon-shaped, softly hairy, aromatic leaves, to 6in (15cm) long. Daisy-like, single or double, orange, yellow, gold, cream, or apricot flowerheads, to 4in (10cm) across, many with dark disk florets, are borne profusely from summer to autumn. ↕ 12–30in (30–75cm), ↔ 12–18in (30–45cm). **'Art Shades'** has cream, apricot, or orange flowerheads with contrasting highlights; ↕ to 24in (60cm). **'Bon Bon'** is dwarf and compact, with flowerheads 2½–3in (6–8cm) across; ↕ 12in (30cm). **'Fiesta Gitana'** ■ is dwarf, with usually double flowerheads in pastel orange and yellow, including bicolors; ↕ to 12in (30cm). **'Hen and Chicks'** see 'Prolifera'. **'Indian Prince'** has dark orange flowerheads, tinted reddish brown on the petals; good for cutting; ↕ 30in (75cm). **Kablouna Series** cultivars are tall, with double orange, gold, or yellow flowerheads, each with a crested disk floret of quilled petals; ↕ to 24in (60cm). **'Orange King'** has double, deep orange flowerheads;

Calendula officinalis Pacific Beauty Series 'Lemon Queen'

↕ to 18in (45cm). **Pacific Beauty Series** cultivars have double flowerheads in an unusual color range, including apricot-orange, primrose-yellow, cream, and bicolors, with red-brown disk florets; ↕ to 24in (60cm); **Pacific Beauty Series 'Lemon Queen'** ■ has double, lemon-yellow flowerheads; ↕ to 18in (45cm). **Prince Series** cultivars have double, golden yellow or orange flowerheads. **'Prolifera'**, syn. 'Hen and Chicks', bears orange flowerheads, each encircled by miniature flowerheads. **'Touch of Red'** has flowerheads 2½in (6cm) across, in pastel shades, tipped and backed brownish red; ↕ 18in (45cm).

CALIBANUS

AGAVACEAE

Genus of one species of very slow-growing, perennial succulent from rocky grassland in C. and E. Mexico. It has a large, fibrous-rooted, spherical, corky-barked caudex, which, in the wild, sometimes grows partially above ground. The caudex develops tufts of grass-like, arching foliage, among which pinkish purple panicles of tiny flowers are borne. Where not hardy, grow *C. hookeri* in a temperate greenhouse or in containers outdoors during summer. In warmer areas, grow outdoors in a desert garden.

- **CULTIVATION** Under glass, grow in standard cactus potting mix, with an additional 25 percent sharp sand, in full light. In the growing season, water freely and apply a low-nitrogen fertilizer monthly; keep just moist in winter.

Calendula officinalis 'Fiesta Gitana'

Calibanus hookeri

Outdoors, grow in very well-drained, gritty, alkaline, humus-rich soil in full sun. See also pp.48–49.
• **PROPAGATION** Sow seed at 66–75°F (19–24°C) in spring; keep moist.
• **PESTS AND DISEASES** Susceptible to scale insects in summer.

C. hookeri ■ syn. *Dasylirion hartwegianum.* Perennial succulent with a spherical caudex, 12in (30cm) or more across, covered in thick, corky bark. Rosettes of 10–15 upright, then recurved, linear leaves are 12in (30cm) long. Bears panicles, 20–24in (50–60cm) long, of cup-shaped, pinkish purple flowers, ¼–⅜in (6–9mm) across, in summer. ↕ to 36in (90cm), ↔ 12in (30cm) or more. C. and E. Mexico. ❄ (min. 41°F/5°C)

CALLA

ARACEAE

Genus of one species of deciduous or semi-evergreen, marginal aquatic perennial from swamps, and lake and stream edges, in temperate regions of the N. hemisphere. *C. palustris* has glossy, dark green leaves and bears showy spathes, followed by dull red berries. It seldom exceeds 8–10in (20–25cm) in height and is excellent for softening the margins of a small to medium-sized pool, or in a bog garden. At depths of 2–3in (5–8cm), it spreads through shallow water or mud by creeping rhizomes, which may extend to 6–20in (15–50cm) and thicken to 1¼in (3cm) in diameter. Contact with the foliage may aggravate skin allergies.
• **CULTIVATION** Grow in aquatic containers in humus-rich, acidic soil, or in mud in shallow, still or slow-moving water no deeper than 10in (25cm). Position in full sun to encourage flowering and fruiting. See also pp.52–53.
• **PROPAGATION** Sow seed in late summer in containers submerged to the rims in water. Divide rhizomes in spring.
• **PESTS AND DISEASES** Infrequent.

Calla palustris

C. palustris ■ (Bog arum). Aquatic, rhizomatous perennial with upright, alternate, glossy, dark green leaves, to 8in (20cm) long, broadly ovate with heart-shaped bases. The basal leaves are arranged in 2 ranks on slender leaf stalks growing from the rhizomes. In midsummer, bears white-spathed inflorescences, 10in (25cm) tall; the spathes surround insignificant flower clusters. They are followed by clusters of dull red berries in autumn. ↕ 10in (25cm), ↔ 24in (60cm). N. and C. Europe, Asia, North America. Zone 4.

CALLIANDRA

Powderpuff tree

FABACEAE

Genus of about 200 species of evergreen perennials, shrubs, and small trees from W. Africa, Madagascar, India, and tropical and subtropical North and South America, mainly found in dry sites at forest margins. Only the shrubs and trees are usually cultivated: they are valued for their attractive, alternate, pinnate or 2-pinnate leaves, and their spherical heads of few to many small, bell- or funnel-shaped flowers, which have 10–100 colorful stamens, ½–1½in (1–4cm) long. Where not hardy, grow in a warm greenhouse; in warmer regions, grow in a shrub border.
• **CULTIVATION** Under glass, grow in soil-based potting mix in full light with shade from hot sun. From early summer to autumn, water freely and apply a balanced liquid fertilizer monthly; water sparingly in winter. Outdoors, grow in well-drained, fertile soil in full sun. Pruning group 1, after flowering; plants under glass may need restrictive pruning.
• **PROPAGATION** Sow seed at 61–64°F (16–18°C) in spring. Root semi-ripe cuttings in summer. Layer in spring.
• **PESTS AND DISEASES** Prone to spider mites and mealybugs under glass. Dieback and fungal leaf spots can occur.

C. eriophylla. Low-growing shrub or small tree producing 2-pinnate leaves, 3–5in (7–13cm) long, each pinna subdivided into 1 or 2 pairs of elliptic to ovate, dark green leaflets, often softly hairy beneath. In summer, bears axillary, spherical heads, to 1¼in (3cm) across, of pale to deep pink flowers, ½in (1.5cm) long, with reddish purple, sometimes white stamens. ↕ 3ft (1m), ↔ 32in (80cm). N. South America. ❄ (min. 55°F/13°C)

Calliandra haematocephala (inset: variant with white stamens)

C. haematocephala ■ syn. *C. inaequilatera.* Large, many-branched, spreading shrub or small tree with pinnate or 2-pinnate leaves, 12–18in (30–45cm) long; each leaf is composed of 5–10 pairs of sickle-shaped to elliptic, glossy, dark green leaflets. Axillary, spherical heads, to 3in (8cm) across, of usually red, sometimes pink or white flowers, ¼–⅜in (7–9mm) long, with prominent, bright red, pink, or white stamens, are borne in summer. ↕ 10–20ft (3–6m), ↔ 6–12ft (2–4m). Bolivia. ❄ (min. 55°F/13°C)
C. inaequilatera see *C. haematocephala.*
C. surinamensis. Large, spreading shrub or small tree with 2-pinnate, pale green leaves, 4in (10cm) or more long, each pinna subdivided into 7–12 pairs of oblong-lance-shaped leaflets. Axillary heads, 2–3in (5–8cm) across, of yellow-green flowers, to ¼in (6mm) long, with conspicuous, white-based, deep red stamens, are produced from the leaf axils in summer. ↕ 10–25ft (3–8m), ↔ 6–15ft (2–5m). N. South America. ❄ (min. 55°F/13°C)
C. tweedii (Mexican flame bush). Large shrub or small tree producing 2-pinnate, mid-green leaves, 4–6in (10–15cm) long, each pinna divided into 15–20 pairs of narrowly oblong, often curved leaflets. Green or white flowers, to ¼in (6mm) long, with red stamens, are borne in axillary, spherical heads, 2–3in (5–8cm) across, from winter to spring. ↕ 6–15ft (2–5m), ↔ 5–6ft (1.5–2m), sometimes more. Brazil to Uruguay. ❄ (min. 55°F/13°C)

CALLIANTHEMUM

RANUNCULACEAE

Genus of about 10 species of perennials from alpine grassland, stony slopes, or coniferous forest in the mountains of C. Asia and C. and S. Europe. They have short rhizomes and produce rosettes of finely divided, pinnate leaves. In late spring, they bear white, pink, or mauve, buttercup-like flowers with 5–20 petals, usually solitary, but sometimes in 2- or 3-flowered racemes. Grow in a rock garden, scree bed, or alpine house.
• **CULTIVATION** Under glass, grow in soil-based potting mix with additional grit. Outdoors, grow in moist, humus-rich, gritty soil in full sun.
• **PROPAGATION** Sow seed as soon as ripe in containers in a cold frame; keep cool and shaded until germination. Divide as growth begins in spring.
• **PESTS AND DISEASES** Prone to aphids and spider mites under glass.

C. coriandrifolium, syn. *C. rutifolium.* Prostrate perennial with erect rhizomes and rosettes of long-stalked, ovate-elliptic, pinnate leaves, 2–5in (5–13cm) long, with 5–7 linear-oblong, blue-green leaflets. In late spring, erect stems bear solitary (occasionally 2 or 3), 9- to 13-petaled white flowers, ¾–1¼in (2–3cm) wide, sometimes flushed pink outside, with greenish yellow centers. ↕↔ 4–8in (10–20cm). Mountains from N.W. Spain to S. Carpathians. Zone 5.
C. rutifolium see *C. coriandrifolium.*

CALLICARPA

Beautyberry

VERBENACEAE

Genus of about 140 species of evergreen and deciduous shrubs and trees from woodland in mainly tropical and subtropical regions. They have opposite, simple leaves and bear dense, axillary cymes or panicles of numerous tiny, white, pink, red, or purple flowers in summer. Grown mainly for their clusters of small but often highly colorful, spherical, bead-like fruits, 1/16–1/8in (2–3mm) across, they are ideal for a shrub border; they fruit most prolifically in long, hot summers and if planted in groups. Where not hardy, grow in a cool greenhouse and move outdoors in summer.
• **CULTIVATION** Under glass, grow in soil-based potting mix in full or bright filtered light. In the growing season,

Callicarpa bodinieri var. *giraldii* 'Profusion'

water freely and apply a balanced liquid fertilizer monthly; water sparingly in winter. Outdoors, grow in fertile, well-drained soil in sun or dappled shade. Pruning group 6.

• **PROPAGATION** Sow seed in containers in a cold frame in autumn or spring. Root softwood cuttings in spring, or semi-ripe cuttings with bottom heat in summer.

• **PESTS AND DISEASES** Cottony camellia scale, black mildew, dieback, leaf scorch, and fungal leaf spots (*Cercospora*) occur.

C. americana (French mulberry, Beautyberry). Loose, open, deciduous shrub with ovate, toothed, mid-green leaves, to 6in (15cm) long, densely white- or rust-woolly beneath. Produces lavender-pink flowers in axillary cymes, to 1½in (4cm) across, in late spring to early summer, followed by violet fruit. ↕ to 6ft (2m), ↔ 5ft (1.5m). Virginia to Texas, West Indies. Zone 6. **var. *lactea*** has white fruit.
***C. bodinieri* var. *giraldii*.** Bushy, upright, deciduous shrub with elliptic to obovate, tapered, dark green leaves, to 7in (18cm) long. In midsummer, produces small pink flowers in cymes, to 1½in (4cm) across, from the leaf axils, followed by violet fruit in autumn. ↕ 10ft (3m), ↔ 8ft (2.5m). W. and C. China. Zone 6b. **'Profusion'** ■ has bronze young leaves and pale pink flowers; it freely produces dark violet fruit.
C. dichotoma ■ (Purple beautyberry). Dense, upright, deciduous shrub with ovate to elliptic, tapered, bright green leaves, to 4in (10cm) long. Pale pink flowers are borne in axillary cymes, ½–¾in (1–2cm) across, in summer, followed by bright purple fruit. ↕↔ 4ft (1.2m). China, Korea, Japan. Zone 6b.
***C. japonica*.** Bushy, deciduous shrub with narrowly oval to lance-shaped, tapered, light to mid-green leaves, to 5in (13cm) long. Pink or white flowers are borne in axillary cymes, to 1¼in (3cm) across, in late summer, followed by purple fruit. ↕↔ 6ft (2m). Zone 6b. **'Leucocarpa'** has white fruit.
***C. rubella*.** Evergreen or semi-evergreen, erect, open shrub with obovate to lance-shaped, yellow-green leaves, 4–6in (10–15cm) long, and downy beneath. Bears axillary cymes, to 2in (5cm) across, of small, purplish pink flowers in summer, followed by bright pinkish purple fruit. ↕ 3–10ft (1–3m), ↔ 3–6ft (1–2m). India to China, Malaysia. Zone 7b.

▷ ***Calliopsis tinctoria*** see *Coreopsis tinctoria*

CALLIRHOE

Poppy mallow

MALVACEAE

Genus of 8 species of annuals and taprooted perennials from prairies and grassland in the US and Mexico. Their leaves are alternate and deeply palmately lobed. They are grown for their 5-petaled, cup-shaped, mallow-like, brightly colored flowers, produced from the upper leaf axils either singly or in short racemes. Poppy mallows will thrive in a hot, dry site in a border or rock garden; they are also suitable for a wildflower or native garden.

• **CULTIVATION** Grow in well-drained, sandy soil in full sun. Protect from winter moisture. Avoid damage to the taproot when planting.

• **PROPAGATION** Sow seed of annuals *in situ* in spring, and of perennials *in situ* in early spring. Root softwood cuttings in early summer.

• **PESTS AND DISEASES** Rust diseases, powdery mildew, aphids, and spider mites may be problems.

C. involucrata ■ (Prairie poppy mallow). Low-growing perennial with a carrot-like taproot, giving rise to procumbent, hairy stems, 6in (15cm) or more long, with rounded, 3- to 7-lobed leaves, 1–2in (2.5–5cm) long. From late spring to midsummer, long flower stalks bear numerous erect, axillary, usually solitary flowers, 1¾–2½in (4.5–6cm) across, the petals cerise to purplish red with white bases. ↕↔ 12in (30cm). Missouri to Texas. Zone 5.

CALLISIA *syn.* PHYODINA

COMMELINACEAE

Genus, related to *Tradescantia*, of about 20 species of creeping, spreading, or suberect, evergreen perennials, and (rarely) annuals, from forest margins in S.E. US, Mexico, and tropical North and South America. They are valued for their attractive, alternate, succulent leaves. The flowers, borne in paired curled cymes or terminal panicles, are white or pink, with 3 sepals and 3 petals. Where not hardy, grow in hanging baskets in a temperate greenhouse or as houseplants; elsewhere, use as a groundcover in a border.

• **CULTIVATION** Under glass, grow in 2 parts soil-based potting mix to 1 part coarse grit in bright filtered or indirect light. In the growing season, water moderately and apply a balanced liquid fertilizer monthly; water sparingly in winter. Pot on only when very root-bound. Outdoors, grow in gritty, well-drained soil in partial shade.

• **PROPAGATION** Root tip cuttings, 2½–3in (6–8cm) long, in spring. Pot up several cuttings in a container to produce dense foliage cover quickly.

• **PESTS AND DISEASES** Susceptible to a wide variety of fungal leaf spots.

C. elegans, syn. *Setcreasea striata* (Striped inch plant). Decumbent, succulent perennial with 2-ranked, oval, pointed, olive-green leaves, 2–4in (5–10cm) long, purple beneath, and with longitudinal white stripes. Bears white flowers, ½in (1.5cm) across, in terminal panicles or curled cymes, to 6in (15cm) long, from autumn to winter. ↕ 6in (15cm), ↔ to 3ft (1m). Guatemala, Honduras. ❀ (min. 50°F/10°C)
C. fragrans, syn. *Spironema fragrans* (Chain plant). Stoloniferous, succulent perennial with 2-ranked, elliptic to lance-shaped, shiny, light green leaves, purple beneath, and to 10in (25cm) long. Fragrant white flowers, ½in (1.5cm) across, are borne in terminal panicles, 3in (8cm) long, from winter to spring. ↕↔ 5ft (1.5m). Mexico. ❀ (min. 50°F/10°C). **'Melnickoff'** produces pale-striped leaves.
C. navicularis, syn. *Tradescantia navicularis* (Chain plant). Slow-growing, succulent perennial with tufts of dense foliage and long, trailing shoots rooting at the internodes. Broadly ovate to lance-shaped leaves, 1in (2.5cm) long, are dull copper-green above and purple-striped beneath. From summer to autumn, bears bright magenta flowers, ½–¾in (1.5–2cm) across, in curled cymes, 2in (5cm) long. ↕ 4in (10cm), ↔ to 12in (30cm). N.E. and E. Mexico. ❀ (min. 50°F/10°C)
C. repens ■ Variable, trailing perennial with stems rooting at the nodes to form mats of broadly ovate, bright green leaves, ½–1½in (1–4cm) long. White flowers, to ½in (1.5cm) across, are borne in spike-like, curled cymes, 1¼in (3cm) long, in autumn. ↕ 4in (10cm), ↔ to 3ft (1m). Texas to Argentina. ❀ (min. 50°F/10°C)
***C. rosea*.** Upright or climbing succulent perennial with tufted stems and linear to linear-lance-shaped, mid-green leaves, 2–10in (5–25cm) long. In summer, produces pink flowers, ½–1in (1.5–2.5cm) across, in curled cymes, to 1½in (4cm) long. ↕↔ to 16in (40cm). Virginia to Florida. Zone 7b.

CALLISTEMON

Bottlebrush

MYRTACEAE

Genus of 25 species or more of evergreen trees and shrubs from Australia, most occurring in moist soil in open or woodland sites. The simple, alternate, leathery leaves are cylindrical to broadly lance-shaped. Callistemons are grown for their colorful, terminal or axillary, bottlebrush-like spikes of numerous tiny, 5-petaled, long-stamened flowers, which may be red, purple, pink, white, green, or yellow. Grow at the base of a house wall or in a shrub border. Where not hardy, grow in a cool greenhouse.

• **CULTIVATION** Under glass, grow in soil-based potting mix in full light with good ventilation. In the growing season, water freely and apply a balanced liquid fertilizer monthly; water more sparingly in winter. Pot on or top-dress in early spring. Outdoors, grow in moist but well-drained, neutral to acidic, moderately fertile soil in full sun. Pruning group 8; tolerates hard pruning.

Callicarpa dichotoma

Callirhoe involucrata

Callisia repens

Callistemon citrinus 'Austraflora Firebrand'

• **PROPAGATION** Surface-sow seed onto moist soil mix at 61–64°F (16–18°C) in spring. Root semi-ripe cuttings in late summer.
• **PESTS AND DISEASES** Spider mites, thornbugs, and scale insects can be problems. Fungal stem galls and cankers, witches' broom, and leaf spots occur.

***C.* 'Captain Cook'**, syn. *C. viminalis* 'Captain Cook'. Dense, rounded shrub with lance-shaped, mid-green leaves, 1–1¾in (2.5–4.5cm) long. Bright red flowers are borne in spikes, 4–6in (10–15cm) long, from early summer to autumn. ↕↔ 6ft (2m). ❄ (min. 45°F/7°C)
C. citrinus (Crimson bottlebrush). Variable shrub, often with arching branches, producing lance-shaped, dark green leaves, to 4in (10cm) long, with prominent oil glands. Brilliant crimson-red flowers in spikes, 2–6in (5–15cm) long, are borne freely in spring and summer. ↕↔ 5–25ft (1.5–8m). New South Wales, Victoria. ❄ (min. 45°F/7°C). **'Austraflora Firebrand'** ■ is low and spreading, producing silvery pink young shoots and bright crimson flowers; ↕ 5–6ft (1.5–2m), ↔ 10–12ft (3–4m). **'Splendens'** ■ has silky, pinkish red young shoots, broad leaves, and crimson flowers; ↕ 6–25ft (2–8m), ↔ 5–20ft (1.5–6m).
C. linearis (Narrow-leaved bottlebrush). Spreading, dense to open shrub with linear, rigid, sharp-pointed, thick, dark green leaves, to 5in (13cm) long. Bears rich, matte red flowers in spikes, to 5in (13cm) long, from late spring to autumn. ↕ 6–12ft (2–4m), ↔ 10–15ft (3–5m). New South Wales. ❄ (min. 45°F/7°C)
C. macropunctatus (Scarlet bottle-brush). Spreading, dense to open shrub with linear to narrowly oblong, pointed, glandular, mid-green leaves, 1¼–3in (3–8cm) long. Red flowers are borne in spikes, 4in (10cm) long, from early summer to autumn. ↕↔ 6–12ft (2–4m). South Australia, New South Wales, Victoria. ❄ (min. 45°F/7°C)

Callistemon 'Mauve Mist'

***C.* 'Mauve Mist'** ■ Spreading shrub with narrowly oblong, mid-green leaves, 1½–2½in (3–6cm) long, tapered at each end. Mauve-pink flowers, fading with age, are borne in spikes, 4in (10cm) long, in summer. ↕↔ 6–12ft (2–4m). ❄ (min. 45°F/7°C)
C. pallidus ■ (Lemon bottlebrush). Erect to spreading shrub producing downy shoots and lance-shaped to broadly lance-shaped, densely glandular, dark green or gray-green leaves, to 4in (10cm) long. Cream to greenish yellow flowers are borne in spikes, 4in (10cm) long, from late spring to midsummer. ↕↔ 6–12ft (2–4m). Queensland to Tasmania. ❄ (min. 45°F/7°C)
C. paludosus see *C. sieberi.*
C. pinifolius (Pine bottlebrush). Spreading shrub with rigid, linear, sharply pointed, dark green leaves, to 4in (10cm) long. In summer, bears yellow flowers in spikes, 2–3in (5–8cm) long. ↕ 5ft (1.5m), ↔ 8ft (2.5m). New South Wales. ❄ (min. 45°F/7°C)
C. pityoides (Alpine bottlebrush). Compact, usually upright shrub with densely arranged, linear, sharply pointed, dark green leaves, 1–1½in (2.5–4cm) long. Yellow flowers are produced in short spikes, ¾–1½in (2–4cm) long, in mid- and late summer. ↕ 5ft (1.5m), ↔ 3ft (1m). S.E. Australia. ❄ (min. 41°F/5°C)
C. rigidus (Stiff bottlebrush). Bushy, stiff-stemmed shrub with linear to lance-

Callistemon pallidus

shaped, matte, dark green leaves, to 6in (15cm) long. In summer, bears deep red flowers in numerous spikes, to 2in (5cm) long. ↕ 3–8ft (1–2.5m), ↔ 6–10ft (2–3m). Queensland, New South Wales. ❄ (min. 45°F/7°C)
C. salignus (White bottlebrush, Willow bottlebrush). Erect to spreading shrub or small tree with papery white bark and willow-like, narrowly lance-shaped, pale green leaves, to 4in (10cm) long. Bears green or white, sometimes red, pink, or mauve flowers in spikes, 1¼–2in (3–5cm) long, from late spring to midsummer. ↕ 15–50ft (5–15m), ↔ 10–15ft (3–5m). South Australia, New South Wales. ❄ (min. 45°F/7°C)
C. sieberi, syn. *C. paludosus* (Alpine bottlebrush). Small, spreading to semi-erect shrub with crowded, linear, rigid, dark green leaves, 1½in (4cm) long, with hard points. Bears creamy yellow flowers in spikes, 1½–6in (4–15cm) long, from late spring to summer. ↕↔ 3–6ft (1–2m). Queensland to Victoria. ❄ (min. 41°F/5°C)
C. speciosus (Albany bottlebrush). Erect, open shrub with lance-shaped to broadly lance-shaped, mid- to dark green leaves, to 6in (15cm) long. Deep red flowers are borne in dense spikes, to 6in (15cm) long, from late spring to autumn. ↕ 6–12ft (2–4m), ↔ 3–6ft (1–2m). Western Australia. ❄ (min. 41°F/5°C)
C. subulatus (Tonghi bottlebrush). Evergreen shrub with arching shoots and linear, pointed, bright green leaves, to 1½in (4cm) long. Bright red flowers are borne in spikes, to 2in (5cm) long, in mid- and late summer. ↕ 5ft (1.5m), ↔ 6ft (2m). S.E. Australia. ❄ (min. 41°F/5°C)

Callistemon citrinus 'Splendens' (inset: flower detail)

Callistemon viminalis 'Rose Opal'

C. viminalis (Weeping bottlebrush). Bushy shrub or small tree with arching or weeping stems and lance-shaped, glandular, mid- to dark green leaves, ¾–2½in (2–6cm) long. Bright red flowers are produced in spikes, 4–8in (10–20cm) long, from late spring to midsummer. ↕ 6–30ft (2–10m), ↔ 5–12ft (1.5–4m). Queensland, New South Wales. ❄ (min. 45°F/7°C) **'Captain Cook'** see *C.* 'Captain Cook'. **'Rose Opal'** ■ is compact, producing narrow leaves and spikes of deep red flowers that fade to rose-pink; ↕ 5–6ft (1.5–2m).
C. viridiflorus (Green bottlebrush). Compact shrub, usually of arching habit, with linear, sharply pointed, mid- to dark green leaves, ¾–1¼in (2–3cm) long, densely arranged around the stems. Yellow-green flowers are borne in dense spikes, to 3in (8cm) long, in mid- and late summer. ↕ 5ft (1.5m), ↔ 6ft (2m). Tasmania. ❄ (min. 41°F/5°C)

CALLISTEPHUS
China aster

ASTERACEAE

Genus of one species of erect, bushy, fast-growing annual from stony slopes, wasteland, and cultivated fields in China. It has alternate, ovate-triangular or ovate, coarsely toothed leaves and solitary, daisy-like, single, semi-double, or double flowerheads, borne from late summer to autumn. Modern cultivars are available in a wide range of flower-head forms and colors. Use for bedding, in annual or informal borders, or in containers. In a frost-free site, they will bloom until midwinter. The cultivars provide long-lasting cut flowers.
• **CULTIVATION** Grow in a sheltered site in fertile, neutral to alkaline, moist but well-drained soil in full sun. Water in dry periods. Deadhead to prolong flowering. Tall cultivars require staking. Grow medium and dwarf cultivars for autumn flowering in 5–7in (13–18cm) containers of soil-based potting mix in cool, well-ventilated conditions, with ample water.
• **PROPAGATION** Sow seed at 61°F (16°C) in early spring, or *in situ* in midspring, in succession for an extended period of bloom. Sow seed for autumn-flowering container plants in early summer.
• **PESTS AND DISEASES** Aster yellows, tomato spotted wilt virus, anthracnose, powdery mildew, stem wilt (yellows), rust, and *Septoria* leaf spot are common. Aphids, rosy blister gall, blister beetles, and spider mites can occur.

***C. chinensis* cultivars.** Selections from *C. chinensis* are fast-growing, bushy annuals with ovate-triangular or ovate, coarsely toothed, mid-green leaves, to 3in (8cm) long. From summer to autumn, they bear branching stems of single to fully double, chrysanthemum-like flowerheads, 3–5in (7–13cm) across, sometimes with quilled ray florets, mainly in shades of purple- and violet-blue, but also in crimson, rose-pink, white, or occasionally yellow. ↕ 8–36in (20–90cm), ↔ 10–18in (25–45cm). **Comet Series** cultivars are dwarf and early flowering, with large, spreading, quill-petaled, double flowerheads in a range of colors,

C

Callistephus chinensis Compliment Series 'Compliment Light Blue'

including white, pink, blue, purple, scarlet, and yellow; good for containers; ↕ to 10in (25cm), ↔ 8in (20cm). **Compliment Series** cultivars produce large, spreading, quill-petaled, long-stemmed, double flowerheads in salmon-pink, light blue, violet-blue, and white; ↕ 28in (70cm), ↔ 8in (20cm); **'Compliment Light Blue'** ■ has double, pale violet-blue flowerheads with yellow disk florets. **'Crego Improved'** has tall, upright stems with large, feathery flowerheads in a range of white, pink, blue, and purple; ↕ 30in (75cm). **'Florette Champagne'** is sturdy and upright, with large, quilled flowerheads of soft cream-pink; ↕ 20–24in (50–60cm). **'Matsumoto'** is tall and erect, bearing semi-double flowerheads with yellow disk florets; it is good for cutting, weather-resistant, and partially wilt-resistant; ↕ to 30in (75cm). **Milady Series** ■ cultivars are sturdy-branched, bearing rounded, double flowerheads in rose-pink, rose-red, scarlet, blue, white, and mixed colors; they are ideal for bedding and wilt-resistant; ↕ to 12in (30cm), ↔ 10in (25cm). **Ostrich Plume Series** ■ cultivars have long stems and bear spreading, feathery, reflexed, double flowerheads, mainly in pinks and crimsons, as well as blue and white shades, from late summer to late autumn; wilt-resistant; ↕ to 24in (60cm), ↔ 12in (30cm). **Pinocchio Series** cultivars bear incurved, rounded, dense, double flowerheads in a wide color range; good for bedding and edging; ↕ to 8in (20cm), ↔ 8in (20cm). **'Powder Puff Mix'** is tall, upright, sturdy, and well-branched, with uniform, dense flowerheads, 2½–3in (6–8cm) across, in shades of pink, purple, lavender, and white; ↕ 24in

Callistephus chinensis Milady Series

Callistephus chinensis Ostrich Plume Series

Callistephus chinensis Princess Series 'Giant Princess'

(60cm). **Princess Series** cultivars produce slightly incurved, semi- to fully double, quill-petaled flowerheads in a wide color range; wilt-resistant; ↕ to 24in (60cm), ↔ 12in (30cm); **Princess Series 'Giant Princess'** ■ is taller, with long-stemmed, red-purple flowerheads, their disk florets tipped with yellow; ↕ 30in (75cm). **Thousand Wonder Series** cultivars are compact and produce fully double flowers in a variety of colors; ↕ 8in (20cm).

CALLITRICHE

Water starwort

CALLITRICHACEAE

Genus of 25 species of aquatic, sometimes terrestrial, herbaceous perennials from bogs and marshes in Europe, Asia, and North America. They grow in tight, submerged clumps or form a turf-like surface on wet soil. The floating leaves are opposite, and linear or spoon-shaped to rounded. The tangled submerged leaves are linear, and almost translucent in deeper water. The name "starwort" arises from the rosette-like arrangement of the leaves of some species. Minute, solitary flowers are produced in summer from the axils of both the floating and submerged leaves. Grow as oxygenating plants in ponds and cold-water aquaria.
• **CULTIVATION** To control spread, grow in baskets of loamy soil or soil-based potting mix, topped with a layer of gravel, submerged 18–24in (45–60cm) deep, in sun or partial shade. In cold-water aquaria, grow in an inert medium in full light. See also pp.52–53.

Callitris rhomboidea (inset: foliage detail)

• **PROPAGATION** In summer, take softwood cuttings of terminal shoots, 6–8in (15–20cm) long; bunch and weight them near the bases, and insert them into an aquatic container or at the muddy bottom of a pond.
• **PESTS AND DISEASES** Infrequent.

C. autumnalis see *C. hermaphroditica.*
C. hermaphroditica, syn. *C. autumnalis* (Autumn starwort). Submerged aquatic perennial producing linear, light green leaves, 1¼in (3cm) long, on thin, branching stems, to 20in (50cm) long. Does not develop floating rosettes and grows mainly toward the bottom of a pool. ↔ indefinite. Europe, North America. Zone 5b.

CALLITRIS

Cypress pine

CUPRESSACEAE

Genus of 14–17 species of evergreen, monoecious, coniferous large shrubs or trees from forest in Australia and New Caledonia. The scale-like adult leaves, 1/16–1/8in (2–3mm) long, have free tips but lie flat along the shoots in whorls of 3; the decurrent parts of the leaves form ridges and furrows on the shoots. Young leaves, 3/8–1/2in (0.8–1.5cm) long, are needle-like and arranged in whorls. The small, ovoid-conical to spherical female cones of most species each have a single whorl of 6 scales, hinged at the bases; male cones are cylindrical or oblong and are borne singly or in groups of 2 or 3. Where not hardy, grow in a cool greenhouse or conservatory. In frost-free areas, grow as windbreaks or specimen trees. They tolerate drought, coastal conditions, and saline soils, and thrive in dry, temperate or Mediterranean climates.
• **CULTIVATION** Under glass, grow in soil-based potting mix in full light, shaded from hot sun. When in growth, water freely and apply a balanced liquid fertilizer monthly; water sparingly in winter. Outdoors, grow in well-drained, sandy soil in full sun.
• **PROPAGATION** Sow seed at 55–64°F (13–18°C) in spring, or take root cuttings in late summer.
• **PESTS AND DISEASES** Twig dieback and needle blight sometimes occur.

C. cupressiformis see *C. rhomboidea.*
C. gunnii see *C. oblonga.*
C. oblonga, syn. *C. gunnii* (Tasmanian cypress pine). Symmetrical shrub or small tree with erect branches, a dense crown, and blue-green or mid-green, keeled leaves. Ovoid-conical, shiny black female cones, 1/2–3/4in (1.5–2cm) long, with thick scales, are borne singly or in groups. ↕ to 25ft (8m), ↔ 6–10ft (2–3m). Tasmania. ❄ (min. 45°F/7°C)
C. rhomboidea ■ syn. *C. cupressiformis, C. tasmanica* (Oyster Bay cypress pine). Narrow, dense-crowned, large shrub or tree with bright green or blue-green leaves. Flattened-spherical, gray-brown female cones, 3/8–1/2in (0.8–1.5cm) across, with thick scales, are borne singly or in groups. ↕ 28–50ft (9–15m), ↔ 6–10ft (2–3m). Queensland to Tasmania, South Australia. ❄ (min. 45°F/7°C)
C. tasmanica see *C. rhomboidea.*

CALLUNA

Heather, Ling

ERICACEAE

Genus of one species of evergreen shrub found on moorland and heaths from N. and W. Europe to Siberia, Turkey, Morocco, and the Azores. It bears dense racemes of small, usually bell-shaped flowers with the corolla completely enclosed by long, colored sepals, in shades of red, purple, pink, or white, which produce the dominant color effect (as distinct from *Erica* species, in which sepals are short and color of the corolla is apparent). Flowers of some cultivars stay in the bud stage; others open late in the season to reveal stamens and corolla; others produce long-lasting, rose-like double flowers. Racemes on young plants may be short, ½–2in (1–5cm) long; medium, 2–4in (5–10cm); or long, over 4in (10cm). As plants age, the racemes become shorter. The tiny, scale-like leaves, borne in opposite and overlapping pairs, sometimes hairy, give the plant a gray color. Leaves become purple-tinged in winter, with red-orange coloration especially noticeable in yellow-foliaged cultivars that bear colorful flowers. There are more than 500 cultivars, all of which are good groundcover and rock garden plants and very attractive to bees.

• **CULTIVATION** Grow in an open site in well-drained, humus-rich, acidic soil in full sun. Where snow cover is unreliable, mulch and cover with pine boughs. Pruning group 10, in spring.

• **PROPAGATION** Root semi-ripe cuttings, 2in (5cm) long, in midsummer, or layer in spring.

• **PESTS AND DISEASES** Spider mites may be a problem during hot summers.

C. vulgaris, syn. *Erica vulgaris* (Ling, Scotch heather). Variable, prostrate to erect shrub with green to gray, hairless or hairy leaves, 1⁄16–1⁄8in (2–3mm) long. Bell-shaped or tubular flowers, to 1⁄8in (3mm) long, are borne in short to long racemes from midsummer to late autumn. ↕ 4–24in (10–60cm), ↔ to 30in (75cm). N. and W. Europe to Russia (Siberia), Turkey, Morocco, the Azores. Zone 4, although they may survive in Zone 3 with winter protection or sufficient snow cover. Unless stated otherwise, the following cultivars are erect, with dark green leaves and single flowers. **'Alison Yates'** is compact but vigorous, with silvery gray foliage and long racemes of white flowers; ↕ 18in (45cm), ↔ 24in (60cm). **'Allegro'** is compact and vigorous, with medium racemes of ruby-red flowers; ↕ 20in (50cm), ↔ 24in (60cm). **'Annemarie'** bears long racemes of double, rose-pink flowers, good for cutting; ↕ 20in (50cm), ↔ 24in (60cm). **'Anthony Davis'** ■ has green-gray leaves and long racemes of white flowers, good for cutting; ↕ 18in (45cm). **'Barbara Fleur'** has medium racemes of pale crimson flowers; ↕ 18in (45cm), ↔ 22in (55cm). **'Beoley Gold'** ■ has yellow foliage and medium racemes of white flowers; ↕ 14in (35cm). **'Beoley Silver'** has softly hairy silver foliage and medium racemes of white flowers; ↕ 16in (40cm), ↔ 24in (60cm). **'Blazeaway'** ■ has gold foliage, turning bright red in winter, and medium racemes of lilac-mauve flowers; ↕ 14in (35cm), ↔ 24in (60cm). **'Boskoop'** ■ has gold leaves, red-tinted orange in winter, and medium racemes of lilac-pink flowers. **'Clare Carpet'** is prostrate, with light green foliage, and produces short racemes of pale pink flowers; ↕ 2in (5cm), ↔ 18in (45cm). **'County Wicklow'** ■ is compact and semi-prostrate, with mid-green leaves and large, double, pale pink flowers in long racemes; ↕ 10in (25cm), ↔ 14in (35cm). **'Darkness'** ■ has short racemes of crimson flowers; ↕ 10in (25cm), ↔ 14in (35cm). **'Dark Star'** is compact, with short racemes of semi-double, crimson flowers; ↕ 8in (20cm), ↔ 14in (35cm). **'Drum-ra'** has light green foliage and short racemes of white flowers; ↕ 8in (20cm). **'Elsie Purnell'** ■ has gray-green leaves and long racemes of double, pale pink flowers, good for cutting; ↕ 16in (40cm), ↔ 30in (75cm). **'Firefly'** ■ has terracotta foliage in summer, brick-red in winter, with short racemes of deep mauve flowers; ↕ 18in (45cm). **'Foxii Nana'** ■ forms tight mounds of bright green foliage with short racemes of mauve flowers; ↕ 6in (15cm), ↔ 12in (30cm). **'Glenfiddich'** has copper-red leaves, turning bronze-red in winter, and medium racemes of mauve flowers; ↔ 16in (40cm).

Calluna vulgaris 'Firefly'

'Golden Feather' ■ has gold foliage, turning reddish orange in winter, and bears short racemes of mauve flowers; ↕ 10in (25cm), ↔ 28in (70cm). **'Gold Haze'** ■ has pale yellow foliage and medium racemes of white flowers; ↔ 18in (45cm). **'Hamlet Green'** has yellowish gray-green leaves, becoming orange-yellow and green in winter, and short racemes of mauve flowers. **'Hammondii Aureifolia'** has light green foliage tipped with yellow from spring to early summer, and short racemes of white flowers; ↔ 16in (40cm). **'H.E. Beale'** has long racemes of double, pale pink flowers, good for cutting. **'Hirta'** is prostrate, with golden yellow foliage, yellow-green in winter, and bears short racemes of pink flowers; ↕ 4in (10cm), ↔ 12in (30cm). **'Inshriach Bronze'** has lemon-yellow leaves in spring, gold in summer, and bronze in winter, and bears medium racemes of lilac-pink flowers; ↕ 10in (25cm), ↔ 14in (35cm). **'J.H. Hamilton'** ■ is dwarf, with medium racemes of double, deep pink flowers; ↕ 4in (10cm), ↔ 10in (25cm). **'John F. Letts'** is prostrate, with gold foliage, turning bronze then red and orange, and short racemes of pale lilac flowers; ↕ 4in (10cm), ↔ 10in (25cm). **'Johnson's Variety'** has mid-green leaves and medium racemes of purple-pink flowers from midautumn to mid-winter; ↔ 24in (60cm). **'Joy Vanstone'** has straw-colored foliage, turning orange in winter, and medium racemes of pink flowers. **'Kerstin'** has downy, deep lilac-gray leaves in winter, tipped pale yellow and red in spring, and short racemes of mauve flowers; ↔ 18in (45cm). **'Kinlochruel'** ■ has bright green foliage, turning bronze in winter, and long racemes of double white flowers; ↕ 10in (25cm), ↔ 16in (40cm). **'Mair's Variety'** has mid-green leaves and bears long racemes of white flowers, good for cutting; ↕ 16in (40cm). **'Marleen'** has medium racemes of purple-tipped white buds that do not open but persist late into autumn.

Calluna vulgaris 'Anthony Davis'

Calluna vulgaris 'Beoley Gold'

Calluna vulgaris 'Blazeaway'

Calluna vulgaris 'Boskoop'

Calluna vulgaris 'County Wicklow'

Calluna vulgaris 'Darkness'

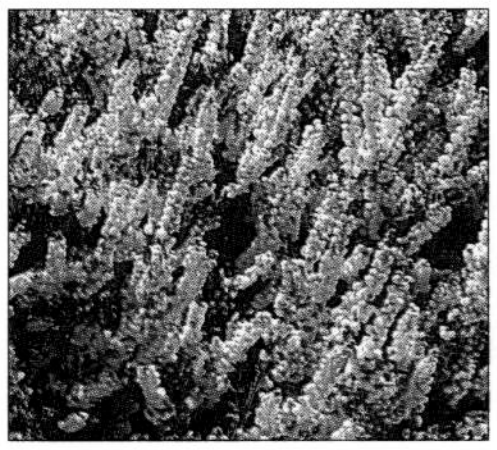

Calluna vulgaris 'Elsie Purnell'

Calluna vulgaris 'Foxii Nana'

Calluna vulgaris 'Golden Feather'

Calluna vulgaris 'Gold Haze'

Calluna vulgaris 'J.H. Hamilton'

Calluna vulgaris 'Kinlochruel'

Calluna vulgaris 'Silver Knight'

'Martha Hermann' is compact with vivid green foliage and white flowers with faint traces of pink; ↕ 12in (30cm), ↔ 16in (40cm). **'Mullion'** has short racemes of lilac-pink flowers; ↕ 8in (20cm). **'Multicolor'** ▣ is compact with copper foliage, usually flecked orange and red, and short racemes of mauve flowers; ↕ 4in (10cm), ↔ 10in (25cm). **'My Dream'** ▣ bears long racemes of double white flowers, good for cutting; ↕ 18in (45cm). **'Orange Queen'** has bronze foliage in autumn, orange in winter, turning gold in summer, and bears short racemes of pink flowers. **'Peter Sparkes'** ▣ bears long racemes of double, rose-pink flowers, good for cutting, into late autumn; ↔ 22in (55cm). **'Red Carpet'** is semi-prostrate, and chiefly grown for its foliage, which is orange-red in winter, gold in summer; it produces short racemes of mauve-pink flowers; ↕ 8in (20cm), ↔ 18in (45cm). **'Red Fred'** has brilliant red foliage in spring, persisting well into summer, and bears medium racemes of lilac-pink flowers; ↕ 14in (35cm), ↔ 18in (45cm). **'Red Star'** has medium racemes of double, deep lilac-pink flowers in autumn; ↕ 16in (40cm), ↔ 24in (60cm). **'Robert Chapman'** ▣ has gold foliage in summer, turning red in winter and spring, and produces medium racemes of purple flowers; ↕ 10in (25cm), ↔ 26in (65cm). **'Roland Haagen'** is grown for its golden yellow foliage, turning bright orange in winter; it produces medium racemes of lilac-pink flowers; ↕ 6in (15cm), ↔ 14in (35cm). **'Rosalind, Underwood's Variety'** has yellow-green foliage, with yellow tips in autumn, winter, and spring, and bears medium racemes of pink flowers; ↔ 22in (55cm). **'Serlei Aurea'** has dense, yellow-green foliage, tipped yellow in summer and autumn, and produces short racemes of white flowers; ↔ 16in (40cm). **'Silver Knight'** ▣ has downy gray foliage, deepening to purple-gray in winter, and bears medium racemes of mauve-pink flowers; ↕ 16in (40cm). **'Silver Queen'** is spreading, with downy, silvery gray leaves, and short racemes of pale mauve flowers; ↕ 16in (40cm), ↔ 22in (55cm). **'Silver Rose'** has silvery gray foliage and produces medium racemes of lilac-pink flowers; ↕ 16in (40cm). **'Sir John Charrington'** has golden yellow foliage in summer, turning orange and red in winter, and produces short racemes of mauve-pink flowers; ↕ 16in (40cm). **'Sirsson'** has gold leaves, turning bright orange-red in winter in cold, open sites, and bears medium racemes of pink flowers. **'Sister Anne'** is compact and spreading, with gray-green foliage, becoming dull bronze in winter; it bears short racemes of mauve flowers; ↕ 4in (10cm), ↔ 10in (25cm). **'Spring Cream'** ▣ is compact, with mid-green leaves, cream-tipped in spring, and short racemes of white flowers; ↕ 14in (35cm), ↔ 18in (45cm). **'Spring Torch'** produces mid-green leaves with cream, orange, and red tips in spring, and short racemes of mauve flowers; ↕ 16in (40cm), ↔ 24in (60cm). **'Sunset'** has golden yellow leaves in spring, turning orange in summer and red in winter, and bears short racemes of mauve-pink flowers; ↕ 10in (25cm). **'Tib'** ▣ is fairly open in habit, producing long racemes of double flowers in midsummer; ↔ 16in (40cm). **'Velvet Fascination'** has silvery gray foliage and produces medium racemes of pure white flowers; ↕ 20in (50cm), ↔ 28in (70cm). **'White Lawn'** is prostrate and trailing, producing bright green foliage and medium racemes of white flowers; ↕ 2in (5cm), ↔ 16in (40cm). **'Wickwar Flame'** has gold leaves, turning red in winter, and bears medium racemes of mauve-pink flowers; ↕ 20in (50cm), ↔ 26in (65cm).

Calluna vulgaris 'Multicolor'

Calluna vulgaris 'My Dream'

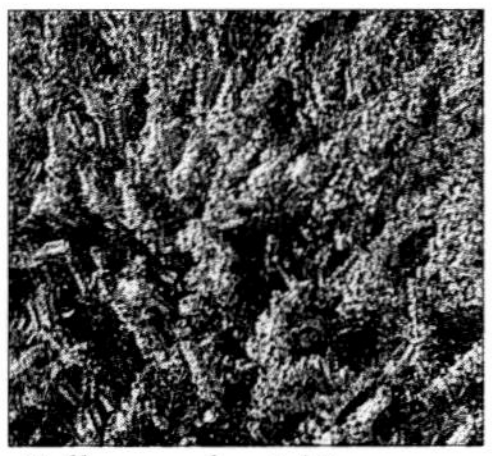

Calluna vulgaris 'Peter Sparkes'

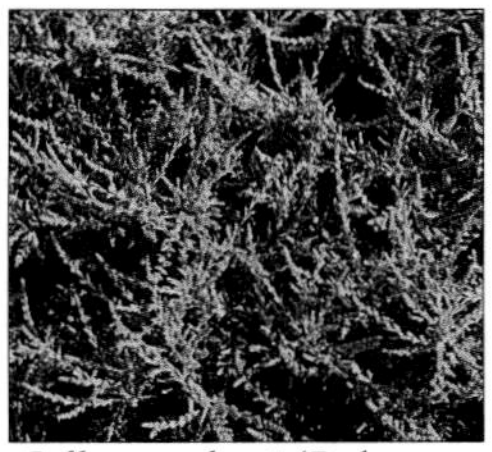

Calluna vulgaris 'Robert Chapman'

Calluna vulgaris 'Spring Cream'

Calluna vulgaris 'Tib'

Calocedrus decurrens

CALOCEDRUS

Incense cedar

CUPRESSACEAE

Genus of 3 species of evergreen, monoecious conifers from dry, warm-temperate forest in S. China, Taiwan, Vietnam, and W. North America. The branchlets are arranged in 2 flattened rows; the decurrent, scale-like leaves appear 4-ranked, but are arranged in 2 pairs. The female cones have 6 scales, hinged at the bases, of which only the central pair is fertile, each scale bearing 2 seeds. Grow as specimen trees. Where not hardy, grow in a cool greenhouse.

- **CULTIVATION** Grow in any well-drained soil in sun or partial shade.
- **PROPAGATION** Sow seed in containers in a cold frame in spring, or root semi-ripe cuttings in late summer.
- **PESTS AND DISEASES** Rust may occur.

C. decurrens ▣ syn. *Heyderia decurrens*, *Libocedrus decurrens* (Incense cedar). Narrow-crowned, columnar tree in cultivation, but often with a wide crown and horizontal branches in the wild. Produces flat sprays of linear, glossy, dark green leaves, to ⅜in (9mm) long, with free tips. Pendent shoots bear erect, ovoid, yellow-brown female cones, ¾–1in (2–2.5cm) long, ripening red-brown. ↕ 70–130ft (20–40m), ↔ 6–28ft (2–9m). Oregon to Mexico (Baja California). Zone 6b. **'Maupin Glow'** is a columnar plant with bright yellow foliage year-round. ↕ 10–12ft (3–4m), ↔ 4ft (1.2m).
C. macrolepis. Narrow, conical tree with slightly larger and flatter, linear leaves than those of *C. decurrens*; they are ½in (1.5cm) long, bright green above, and glaucous beneath. Erect, ellipsoid, purple-tinted orange female cones, to ½in (1.5cm) long, are borne on pendent shoots. ↕ 100ft (30m), ↔ 25ft (8m). China (Yunnan, Hainan). Zone 6b.

▷ ***Calocephalus*** see *Leucophyta*

CALOCHONE

RUBIACEAE

Genus of 2 evergreen species, one a perennial climber, the other a shrub (not usually cultivated), found in forest in W. Africa. They have simple leaves, in opposite pairs, and are valued for their showy, tubular-based, 5-petaled flowers, which are borne in spherical heads at the ends of the shoots. Grow *C. redingii* in a warm greenhouse; in subtropical and tropical areas, it is suitable for training over large shrubs, through trees, or on house walls.

- **CULTIVATION** Under glass, grow in soil-based potting mix in full light with shade from hot sun. In the growing season, water freely and apply a balanced liquid fertilizer monthly; water sparingly in winter. Pot on or top-dress in spring. Outdoors, grow in moist but well-drained, humus-rich, fertile soil in full sun. Pruning group 11, after flowering.
- **PROPAGATION** Root semi-ripe cuttings in summer.
- **PESTS AND DISEASES** Spider mites may be a problem under glass.

C. redingii. Vigorous, twining climber producing ovate, bristly hairy leaves, 6–8in (15–20cm) long, heart-shaped at the bases, and with wavy margins. Bears a profusion of flowers, ¾in (2cm) across, with greenish yellow tubes and bright-pink petals, from winter to spring. ↕ 30ft (10m) or more. Zaire. ❀ (min. 59°F/15°C)

CALOCHORTUS

Fairy lantern, Mariposa

LILIACEAE

Genus of about 60 species of bulbous perennials from grassland and open woodland in W. North America and Mexico. They are cultivated for their showy, tulip-like flowers, borne mainly in spring or early summer. The flowers have a distinctive nectary near the base of each inner petal, often with striking basal marks and conspicuous hairs inside. *C. luteus*, *C. superbus*, *C. venustus*, and *C. vestae* appear very similar, but differ in the shape of their nectaries. The leaves are mid- to gray-green: lower stem leaves are 8–28in (20–70cm) long, narrow, and linear to lance-shaped; upper stem leaves are shorter, 4–12in (10–30cm) long. Often grown in a cold greenhouse or bulb

Calochortus albus

Calochortus amabilis

frame since they are intolerant of moisture when dormant in winter. In dry climates, grow in a mixed or herbaceous border.

• **CULTIVATION** Plant bulbs 4–6in (10–15cm) deep in autumn. Under glass, grow in soil-based potting mix with added grit, in full light. Water freely when in growth; water sparingly as the leaves die back; provide dry conditions when dormant (in summer for spring-flowering bulbs). Pot on just before growth begins in autumn. Outdoors, grow in an open site, in well-drained, sandy, loam soil in full sun. Lift and store corms dry to protect them from rain when dormant and in winter.

• **PROPAGATION** Sow seed in containers in a cold frame as soon as ripe or remove offsets in late summer. Some species produce bulbils in the leaf axils; plant these in late spring or early summer.

• **PESTS AND DISEASES** Infrequent.

C. albus ■ (Fairy lantern). Bulbous perennial with leaves 12–28in (30–70cm) long. From spring to early summer, branched stems bear 2 or more nodding, spherical to bell-shaped, sparsely hairy white flowers, ¾–1¼in (2–3cm) long, with crescent-shaped nectaries. ↕4–20in (10–50cm), PD2in (5cm). California. Zone 7.

C. amabilis ■ Bulbous perennial producing leaves 8–20in (20–50cm) long. Branched stems bear 2 or more nodding, spherical to bell-shaped, deep yellow flowers, ½–¾in (1.5–2cm) long, from spring to early summer; the conspicuous tepals, occasionally tinged green, have deeply crescent-shaped

Calochortus luteus

Calochortus superbus

nectaries. ↕4–20in (10–50cm), PD2in (5cm). California. Zone 7.

C. barbatus, syn. *Cyclobothra lutea.* Bulbous perennial with leaves 4–18in (10–45cm) long. In summer, branched, spreading stems bear 1 or 2 open cup-shaped flowers, ¾–1¼in (2–3cm) wide, usually mustard-yellow with purple hairs, but varying from yellow to purplish yellow. The nectaries are semi-circular. Sometimes produces bulbils. ↕6–12in (15–30cm), PD2in (5cm). Mexico. Zone 7.

C. luteus ■ (Yellow mariposa). Bulbous perennial with leaves 4–18in (10–45cm) long. In spring, branched stems bear 1–7 open bell-shaped flowers, 1½–2½in (4–6cm) across. Flowers are deep yellow; the insides have sparse, slender hairs and red-brown lines and marks. The nectaries are crescent-shaped. ↕8–20in (20–50cm), PD3in (8cm). California. Zone 6b.

C. macrocarpus (Green-banded mariposa). Bulbous perennial with leaves 8–20in (20–50cm) long. In summer, unbranched stems bear up to 3 erect, open cup-shaped purple flowers, 2½–3½in (6–9cm) across, usually with a deep purple ring inside, toward the bases of the petals. Narrow sepals extend beyond the petals. The nectaries are triangular. ↕8–20in (20–50cm), PD2in (5cm). W. US. Zone 7.

C. superbus ■ Bulbous perennial producing leaves 4–16in (10–40cm) long. In late spring, branching stems bear 1–3 erect, cup-shaped, sparsely hairy, white, cream, lavender-blue, or yellow flowers, 2–3in (5–8cm) across, with a brown mark above the yellow base of each petal. The nectaries are V-shaped. ↕16–24in (40–60cm), PD3in (8cm). California. Zone 6.

C. uniflorus. Bulbous perennial with very narrow leaves, 4–16in (10–40cm) long. Up to 5 erect, saucer-shaped, pale

Calochortus venustus

Calochortus vestae

lilac flowers, 1½–1¾in (3.5–4.5cm) across, sparsely hairy and often with darker lilac marks inside, are produced on long, unbranched stems in summer. Has oblong nectaries. ↕4–6in (10–15cm), PD2in (5cm). W. US. Zone 7.

C. venustus ■ (White mariposa). Bulbous perennial with leaves 4–16in (10–40cm) long. From late spring to summer, branched stems bear 1–3 erect, cup-shaped flowers, 2–3in (5–8cm) across, varying from white to yellow, purple, or dark red, each with a yellow-ringed, dark red mark inside. The nectaries are rounded or diamond-shaped. ↕8–24in (20–60cm), PD3in (8cm). California. Zone 7.

C. vestae ■ Bulbous perennial with leaves 6–18in (15–45cm) long. From late spring to summer, branched stems bear 1–6 erect, cup-shaped white flowers, 2–3in (5–8cm) across, sometimes tinged purple, with a yellow-ringed maroon mark at the base of each petal. The nectaries are double crescent-shaped. ↕12–20in (30–50cm), PD3in (8cm). California. Zone 6.

CALOMERIA syn. HUMEA

Incense plant

ASTERACEAE

Genus of about 14 species of strongly aromatic annuals and perennials found in varying habitats, from coastal mudflats to mountain forest, in Africa, Madagascar, and S. Australia. They have simple, alternate leaves and, in summer, bear large, branched, pyramidal panicles of tiny, tubular flowerheads. Where not hardy, grow as biennials in a cool conservatory or greenhouse, or use for summer bedding. In warmer regions, grow in a border or in specimen groups.

• **CULTIVATION** Under glass, grow in borders or containers of soil-based potting mix in full light with good ventilation. When in growth, water moderately and apply a balanced liquid fertilizer every 3–4 weeks. Mist over to release fragrance. Keep just moist in winter. Outdoors, grow in fertile, well-drained soil in full sun.

• **PROPAGATION** Sow seed at 55–64°F (13–18°C) as soon as ripe. Production of seed is very low or nonexistent in some years.

• **PESTS AND DISEASES** Infrequent.

C. amaranthoides ■ syn. *Humea elegans* (Incense plant, Plume plant). Erect, branching, smooth to slightly hairy, aromatic perennial, usually grown as a biennial, with almost stem-clasping, ovate to lance-shaped leaves, to 10in (25cm) long. In summer, bears feathery panicles, to 4ft (1.2m) tall, of tiny, brownish pink to red flowerheads. Contact with the leaves may aggravate skin allergies. ↕4–6ft (1.2–2m), ↔ to 3ft (1m). New South Wales, Victoria. ❄ (min. 39°F/4°C)

Calomeria amaranthoides

▷ ***Calonyction aculeatum*** see *Ipomoea alba*

CALOSCORDUM

LILIACEAE

Genus, related to *Allium*, of one species of bulbous perennial from mountainous regions of Asia. It has narrow leaves and bears umbels of tiny flowers in late summer, but does not have a pungent odor. *C. neriniflorum* is best grown in a sunny rock garden, or in an alpine house. In mild or frost-free areas, grow in thin grass on a sunny bank.

• **CULTIVATION** Plant bulbs 3in (8cm) deep in spring. Grow in well-drained soil in full sun. Protect from excess winter moisture.

• **PROPAGATION** Sow seed in containers in a cold frame in spring. Remove offsets after flowering.

• **PESTS AND DISEASES** Infrequent.

C. neriniflorum, syn. *Allium neriniflorum, Nothoscordum neriniflorum.* Bulbous perennial with 2–6 linear, channeled, pale green leaves, 3–6in (8–15cm) long, which die back as flowers are produced in late summer. Up to 20 star-shaped flowers, ⅛–¼in (4–6mm) across, the petals bright pink with dark midribs, are borne in erect, loose umbels, 2–3in (5–8cm) across. ↕10in (25cm), PD2in (5cm). C. Asia, N. and W. China, Russia (Siberia). Zone 6.

CALOTHAMNUS

Net bush, One-sided bottlebrush

MYRTACEAE

Genus of about 25 species of evergreen shrubs found in Western Australia, usually in dry scrub and open forest. They are cultivated for their nodding flowers, ½–1½in (1–4cm) long, which have tiny petals and prominent, flattened bundles of long red stamens; they are produced in one-sided spikes or clusters, ¾–10in (2–25cm) long. The leaves are needle-like and leathery, and crowded on the stems, either irregularly or in whorls. Where not hardy, grow in a cool greenhouse; in frost-free regions, grow in a shrub border.

Calothamnus quadrifidus

• **Cultivation** Under glass, grow in soil-based potting mix in full light with good ventilation. In the growing season, water moderately and apply a phosphate-free fertilizer every 4–6 weeks; water sparingly in winter. Pot on or top-dress in early spring. Outdoors, grow in well-drained, moderately fertile soil (very fertile soil diminishes flower production) in full sun. Pruning group 8, although pruning is seldom needed.
• **Propagation** Surface-sow seed at 61–64°F (16–18°C) in spring. Root semi-ripe cuttings in late summer.
• **Pests and diseases** Scale insects occur.

C. quadrifidus ▣ (Common net bush). Erect to spreading shrub with linear, grayish to dark green or gray leaves, 1¼in (3cm) long. Bears irregular, axillary, one-sided spikes of rich red flowers, 1in (2.5cm) long, from late spring to autumn, often forming clusters, 8in (20cm) or more across, around the stems. ↕ 6–12ft (2–4m), ↔ 6–15ft (2–5m). Western Australia. ❄ (min. 41°F/5°C)

Calpurnia

FABACEAE

Genus of 10 or more species of evergreen shrubs and small trees from mountain forest in Africa and India. They are cultivated for their pendent racemes of yellow, pea-like flowers, which are produced from the leaf axils or at the ends of the shoots. The leaves are alternate and pinnate, with 3 to many pairs of leaflets. Where not hardy, grow in a temperate greenhouse. Elsewhere, use as specimen plants or as an addition to a shrub border.
• **Cultivation** Under glass, grow in soil-based potting mix in full light. During growth, water freely and apply a balanced liquid fertilizer monthly; water sparingly in winter. Pot on or top-dress in spring. Outdoors, grow in well-drained, fertile soil in full sun. Pruning group 8; plants under glass may need restrictive pruning.
• **Propagation** Sow seed at 55–64°F (13–18°C) in spring; prick out seedlings as soon as possible.
• **Pests and diseases** Spider mites may be a problem under glass.

C. aurea (East African laburnum, Natal laburnum). Erect shrub or small tree, usually spreading in habit, with pinnate leaves, 4–10in (10–25cm) long, composed of 3–12 pairs of ovate, fine-tipped leaflets, dark green above, paler beneath. Racemes, 3–7in (8–18cm) long, of up to 30 bright yellow flowers are borne from winter to spring. ↕ 6–30ft (2–10m), ↔ 3–12ft (1–4m). South Africa (mainly Eastern Cape), S. India. ❄ (min. 45°F/7°C)

Caltha

Kingcup, Marsh marigold

RANUNCULACEAE

Genus of about 10 species of rhizomatous, marshland or marginal aquatic perennials and herbaceous, moisture-loving perennials, widespread in temperate and cold regions. The leaves are generally heart- or kidney-shaped. Those grown as marginal water plants provide a display of cup-shaped, yellow or white flowers in spring. They are borne in terminal or axillary corymbs before the dense clumps of foliage are produced; a second flush of flowers is often produced in late summer. Although they are best grown at the water's edge, several will thrive in a mixed or herbaceous border, if the soil is kept moist. *C. introloba* is suitable for a trough or alpine house.
• **Cultivation** Grow in an open site in rich, boggy soil in full sun at the water's edge; marsh marigolds will tolerate root restriction in aquatic containers. *C. introloba* needs moist but well-drained, humus-rich soil in a cool site in partial shade. See also pp.52–53.
• **Propagation** Sow seed as soon as ripe on permanently damp soil mix in a partially shaded cold frame. Divide in late summer or very early spring.
• **Pests and diseases** Powdery mildew and rust are common in summer.

C. dioneaefolia. Compact, cushion-forming, marshland perennial with upright, branching rhizomes that produce ovate to rounded, 2-lobed, mid-green leaves, to ⅛in (3mm) long. Bears pale yellow flowers, to 1in (2.5cm) across, in autumn and winter. ↕ to 2in (5cm), ↔ to 4in (10cm). S. Chile, Argentina. Zone 7.
C. introloba. Dwarf, tufted, marshland perennial with arrow-shaped, glossy, mid-green leaves, ¾–1in (2–2.5cm) long. In late winter, produces large, almost stemless white flowers, to 1in (2.5cm) across, flushed purple on the outside. ↕ 1in (2.5cm), ↔ to 3in (8cm). Mountains of Australia. Zone 6.

Caltha leptosepala

Caltha palustris

C. laeta see *C. palustris* var. *palustris*.
C. leptosepala ▣ (Alpine marsh marigold). Marginal aquatic perennial with heart-shaped, radical, dark green leaves, to 2½in (6cm) long. Silvery white flowers, ¾–1¼in (2–3cm) across, open on leafless stems, 6–8in (15–20cm) tall, in spring. ↕↔ 12in (30cm). Alaska to Alberta, south to New Mexico. Zone 3. **subsp. *howellii*** is compact, with broad leaves, to 3in (8cm) long, and white flowers, often in pairs; ↕ 8in (20cm); Alaska to California.
C. palustris ▣ (Kingcup, Marsh marigold). Variable, marginal aquatic perennial with decumbent rhizomes that produce kidney-shaped, toothed, dark green leaves, 1½–4in (4–10cm) long. In spring, stems 12–18in (30–45cm) tall, bear waxy yellow flowers, 1½in (4cm) across. May grow in water to 9in (23cm) deep for short periods, but prefers very shallow water or bog conditions. ↕ 4–16in (10–40cm), ↔ 18in (45cm). N. temperate regions. Zone 3. **var. *alba***, syn. 'Alba', is compact, bearing solitary white flowers with yellow stamens in early spring, often before the glossy foliage develops; ↕ 9in (23cm), ↔ 12in (30cm). **'Flore Pleno'** ▣ has double yellow flowers; ↕↔ 10in (25cm). **var. *palustris***, syn. *C. laeta*, *C. polypetala* of gardens (Giant marsh marigold), has creeping or decumbent rhizomes, rounded leaves, heart-shaped at the bases, and bears flowers to 3in (8cm) across; ↕ 24in (60cm), ↔ 28–30in (70–75cm). Alaska to Oregon.
***C. polypetala* of gardens** see *C. palustris* var. *palustris*.

Caltha palustris 'Flore Pleno'

Calycanthus

CALYCANTHACEAE

Genus of 2 or 3 species of deciduous shrubs from woodland and streambanks in the US. They are cultivated for their unusual, fragrant flowers, which have narrowly lance-shaped to elliptic petals and sepals, and resemble tiny waterlilies; they are solitary and are produced terminally or from the axils of the current year's shoots. The opposite, dark green leaves, 2–8in (5–20cm) long, have a camphor- or clove-like scent when crushed. Grow in a shrub border or as specimen plants.
• **Cultivation** Grow in fertile, moist, humus-rich soil in sun or, in warm climates, in partial shade. Pruning group 6.
• **Propagation** Sow seed as soon as ripe or in autumn in an open frame. Root softwood cuttings in summer, layer in autumn, or remove suckers in spring.
• **Pests and diseases** Fungal leaf spots, powdery mildew, and dieback occur.

C. chinensis see *Sinocalycanthus chinensis*.
C. floridus (Carolina allspice, Common sweetshrub, Strawberry shrub). Bushy, spreading shrub with oval or oblong, dark green leaves, to 5in (13cm) long, rough above, and sometimes turning yellow in autumn. Flowers, 1½–2in (4–5cm) across, with numerous strap-shaped, dark red petals, fading to brown at the tips, are borne in summer. ↕ 8ft (2.5m), ↔ 10ft (3m). S.E. US. Zone 5. **'Athens'** has deeply fragrant, yellow flowers.

Calycanthus occidentalis

C. occidentalis ■ (California allspice). Vigorous, spreading shrub with ovate to oblong-lance-shaped, dark green leaves, to 8in (20cm) long, rough above, and sometimes turning yellow in autumn. Dark red flowers, 2in (5cm) across, with linear, brown-tipped petals, are borne in summer. ↕ 10ft (3m), ↔ 12ft (4m). California. Zone 6b.

CALYMMANTHIUM

CACTACEAE

Genus of 2 species of columnar cacti from hilly lowlands in Peru. The pale green stems, occasionally many-branched, have 3- to 5-angled, warty or scalloped ribs and small, spiny areoles. Tubular-bell-shaped, nocturnal, white to red flowers develop from a small, stem-like, fleshy receptacle tube bearing spiny areoles. This tube encloses the inner parts of the flower, and is split by the emerging perianth. Elongated, 4- or 5-angled, pale green fruits contain ovoid seeds. Where not hardy, grow in a warm greenhouse; elsewhere, use in a semi-desert garden.

• **CULTIVATION** Under glass, grow in standard cactus potting mix in full light with shade from hot sun. In growth, water moderately and apply a low-nitrogen liquid fertilizer monthly; keep dry at other times. Outdoors, grow in sharply drained, humus-rich soil in full sun. They will tolerate short periods of temperatures just above freezing if kept dry. See also pp.48–49.

• **PROPAGATION** Sow seed at 66–75°F (19–24°C) in late spring, or root stem cuttings in summer.

• **PESTS AND DISEASES** Vulnerable to scale insects, mealybugs, and aphids.

C. substerile. Shrub-like cactus with ribbed stems bearing white areoles, each with 3–8 white or pale yellow radials, to ½in (1.5cm) long, and 1–6 white centrals, ½–2in (1–5cm) long. Bears nocturnal white flowers, to 4½in (11cm) long, with reddish brown outer petals, in summer. ↕ 25ft (8m), ↔ 30in (75cm). N. Peru. ❀ (min. 55°F/13°C)

CALYPSO

ORCHIDACEAE

Genus of one species of deciduous, terrestrial orchid from Europe, Asia, and North America, found in damp woodland, bogs, and marshes. The ovoid corm produces a single, pleated leaf. In summer, bears solitary, terminal, slipper-shaped flowers. Where not hardy, grow in a cold greenhouse or alpine house. Use in a rock, bog, or woodland garden.

• **CULTIVATION** Cool-growing orchid, often difficult in cultivation. Under glass, grow in terrestrial orchid potting mix with added leaf mold and charcoal, in filtered light. Top-dress annually. Water freely in the growing season, more sparingly in winter. Outdoors, grow in moist, neutral to acidic soil, enriched with coniferous leaf mold or bark chips, in partial shade. See also p.46.

• **PROPAGATION** Separate corms with great care in early spring.

• **PESTS AND DISEASES** Infrequent.

C. bulbosa ■ (Fairy slippers). Small, terrestrial orchid with one elliptic to oblong leaf, 5in (13cm) long.

Calypso bulbosa

In summer, a slender stem, 4–8in (10–20cm) tall, bears a solitary, nodding, fragrant flower, 1in (2.5cm) across; the reflexed sepals and petals are usually reddish purple, occasionally white; the lips are white. ↕ 8in (20cm), ↔ 6in (15cm). Scandinavia, Russia, North America. Zone 5.

CALYTRIX

Starflower

MYRTACEAE

Genus of about 70 species of prostrate to erect, evergreen shrubs, usually found in open scrub or light eucalyptus forest in Australia. The crowded, tiny leaves are alternate, opposite, or whorled. The star-shaped, 5-petaled, white to pink, purple, or yellow flowers, are borne singly from the leaf axils, and are often clustered at the branch ends. Where not hardy, grow in a cool greenhouse; elsewhere, use in a shrub border or as a groundcover.

• **CULTIVATION** Under glass, grow in soil-based potting mix in full light with good ventilation. In the growing season, water freely, applying a phosphate-free liquid fertilizer monthly; water sparingly in winter. Pot on or top-dress in early spring. Outdoors, grow in well-drained, neutral to acidic soil in full sun. Pruning group 10, after flowering.

• **PROPAGATION** Root semi-ripe cuttings with bottom heat in summer.

• **PESTS AND DISEASES** Infrequent.

C. alpestris (Snow myrtle). Many-branched, arching shrub with linear, spreading or sometimes reflexed, hairy, dark green leaves, 1/16–¼in (2–6mm) long. Profuse, often pink-budded white flowers, ¼–½in (6–15mm) across, are produced from late spring to summer. ↕ 6–10ft (2–3m), ↔ 6–12ft (2–4m). South Australia, Victoria. ❀ (min. 45°F/7°C)

CAMASSIA

Quamash

LILIACEAE

Genus of 5 or 6 species of bulbous perennials occurring in damp, fertile meadowland in North America. Large, ovoid to spherical bulbs give rise to erect, narrow, linear, keeled, channeled, gray-green, basal leaves. Loose or dense, terminal racemes of large, showy, star-shaped or cup-shaped, blue, purple, or white flowers, each with 6 tepals, are borne on leafless stems among the leaves from late spring to summer; the dead tepals sometimes persist after capsules develop. Grow in a border or a wild-flower meadow, or in containers. Good for long-lasting cut flowers. The cooked bulbs of *C. quamash* were once an important source of food for native Americans.

• **CULTIVATION** Plant bulbs 4in (10cm) deep in autumn, in moist but well-drained, fertile, humus-rich soil in sun or partial shade. Do not allow soil to become waterlogged.

• **PROPAGATION** Sow seed in containers in a cold frame as soon as ripe. Remove offsets when dormant in summer.

• **PESTS AND DISEASES** Leaf smut and a few fungal leaf spots occur.

C. cusickii (Camass). Bulbous perennial bearing large racemes, 8–16in (20–40cm) long, of shallowly cup-shaped, pale to deep steel-blue flowers, 2in (5cm) across, in late spring. The wavy-margined, linear leaves are 16–32in (40–80cm) long. ↕ 24–32in (60–80cm), PD4in (10cm). N.E. Oregon. Zone 4. **'Zwanenburg'** ■ has deep blue flowers.

C. esculenta see *C. quamash.*

C. fraseri see *C. scilloides.*

C. leichtlinii ■ Bulbous perennial with linear leaves, 8–24in (20–60cm) long. In late spring, bears racemes, 4–12in (10–30cm) long, of star-shaped, creamy white flowers, 2–3in (5–8cm) wide; the flower segments twist together as they fade. ↕ 2–4½ft (60–130cm), PD4in (10cm). W. Oregon. Zone 4. **'Semiplena'** ■ is sterile and bears dense racemes, 8–20in (20–50cm) long, of semi-double, creamy white flowers. **subsp. *suksdorfii*** has blue to violet flowers; British Columbia to California. **subsp. *suksdorfii* 'Blau Donau'**, syn. 'Blue Danube', has violet flowers.

C. quamash, syn. *C. esculenta* (Quamash). Bulbous perennial with linear leaves, 8–20in (20–50cm) long. Racemes, to 12in (30cm) long, of

Camassia cusickii 'Zwanenburg'

Camassia leichtlinii

shallowly cup-shaped, bright blue flowers, 1¼–2in (3–5cm) across, are borne in late spring. Rapidly forms large clumps and is easily naturalized in grass, provided the soil is moist. ↕ 8–32in (20–80cm), PD2in (5cm). S.W. Canada to N.W. US. Zone 4b. **'Orion'** produces larger racemes, 4–16in (10–40cm) long, of dark blue flowers; ↕ 24–32in (60–80cm).

C. scilloides, syn. *C. fraseri* (Wild hyacinth). Bulbous perennial producing linear leaves, 8–24in (20–60cm) long. Racemes, 3–6in (8–15cm) long, of star-shaped, violet, blue, or white flowers, ¾–1¼in (2–3cm) across, are produced in late summer. ↕ 8–32in (20–80cm), PD4in (10cm). C. and E. US. Zone 4b.

Camassia leichtlinii 'Semiplena'

CAMELLIA

THEACEAE

Genus of over 250 species of long-lived, evergreen shrubs and small trees, 3–70ft (1–20m) tall. They are found in acidic soil in woodland areas from N. India and the Himalayas to China and Japan, and south to N. Indonesia, Java, and Sumatra. The usually glossy, mid- to dark green leaves are simple, alternate, and lance-shaped to elliptic, with toothed margins. Popular for their bold foliage and abundance of showy, white, pink, red, or (rarely) yellow flowers, camellias have been extensively hybridized to produce a range of flower types (see panel, right). The flowers are usually solitary, sometimes paired or clustered, and are rarely fragrant. In the following descriptions, flower sizes of cultivars have been defined as follows: miniature, to 2½in (6cm); small, 2½–3in (6–8cm); medium, 3–4in (8–10cm); large, 4–5in (10–13cm); very large, 5in (13cm) or more across.

Blooming period has been defined as follows: early season (before January 1); midseason (January 1–March 1); late season (later than March 1). These designations are estimations based on typical environmental factors found in the S. US. Average blooming time may be influenced by latitude and weather fluctuations, including temperature and amount of rainfall.

Camellias are elegant shrubs for a border or a woodland garden; they also make excellent specimen plants, both outdoors in open ground or in containers. Where not hardy, grow in a cool greenhouse. The flowers are suitable for cutting and exhibition.

• **CULTIVATION** Under glass, grow in well-drained, acidic potting mix in bright filtered light. When in growth, water freely; water more sparingly in winter. Apply a balanced fertilizer in midspring and again in early summer. Top-dress annually with shredded bark. Container-grown plants may be moved outdoors in summer to a partially shaded, sheltered site. Outdoors, grow in moist but well-drained, humus-rich, acidic (pH5.5–6.5) soil; maintain a mulch, 2–3in (5–8cm) deep, of leaf mold or shredded bark.

Do not plant too deep; the top of the root ball should be level with the firmed soil. Position in partial or dappled shade, in a site sheltered from cold, dry winds and early morning sun; buds and flowers may be damaged by cold winds and late frosts. *C. sasanqua* cultivars will thrive in full sun once established, provided that the roots are kept cool. Water established plants in dry weather to prevent bud drop. Apply a balanced fertilizer in midspring and again, if necessary, in early summer; do not overfeed. Protect from prolonged winter cold with a thatch of straw or similar loose material. Pruning group 8; camellias tolerate hard pruning.

• **PROPAGATION** Root leaf bud or semi-ripe cuttings of the current year's growth from midsummer to late winter, or graft in late winter. Air-layer in late spring.

• **PESTS AND DISEASES** Canker, dieback, viruses, *Exobasidium* gall, root rot, algal leaf spot, and anthracnose can be troublesome. Camellia Petal Blight *(Ciborinia camellia)* is caused by a fungus which damages camellia blooms. Other problems include bud and spider mites, scale insects, weevils, planthoppers, and sometimes aphids. Sooty mold frequently grows on droppings from scale insects and aphids.

CAMELLIA FLOWER FORMS

Camellia flowers may be **single**, with one row of up to 8 petals and prominent stamens, forming usually saucer-shaped, occasionally cup- or trumpet-shaped flowers; **semi-double**, with 2 or more rows of large outer petals, the center regular, irregular, or composed of loose petals and stamens; **anemone-form**, with one or more rows of outer petals, and intermingling petaloids and stamens in the center; **peony-form**, with a convex mass of irregular petaloids, petals, and stamens, or with irregular petals and petaloids and hidden stamens; **rose-form double**, with overlapping petals showing stamens in a concave center when fully open; or **formal double**, with rows of overlapping petals and no stamens visible.

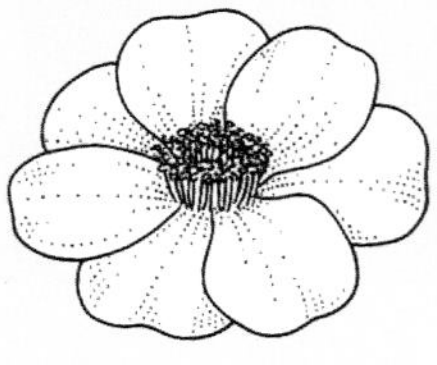
SINGLE

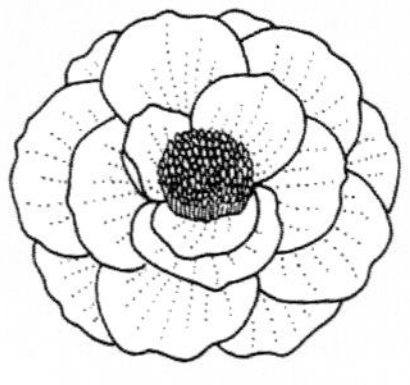
SEMI-DOUBLE

ANEMONE-FORM

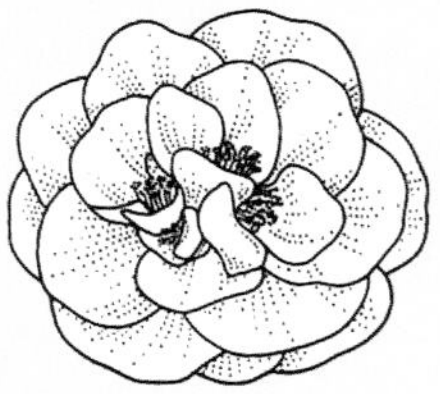
PEONY-FORM

ROSE-FORM DOUBLE

FORMAL DOUBLE

***C.* 'Anticipation'** ■ Narrow, upright shrub with elliptic to broadly elliptic, bright green leaves, 2½–4in (6-10cm) across. Bears very large, peony-form crimson flowers in midseason. ↕ 12ft (4m), ↔ 6ft (2m). Zone 8.

***C.* 'Black Lace'** ■ Slow-growing, dense, upright shrub with ovate, dark green leaves, 3in (8cm) long, and large, formal, double, black-red flowers, borne in mid- and late season. ↕ 5–8ft (1.5–2.5m), ↔ 3–8ft (1–2.5m). Zone 8.

C. chekiangoleosa. Excellent landscaping plant with clear, striking red flowers. Closely related to *C. japonica.* Field-tested to -10° F with no damage. Hybridizes readily with other species. ↕ 6ft (2m), ↔ 4–8ft (1.2–2.5m). Zone 8.

C. chrysantha see *C. nitidissima.*

***C.* 'Cinnamon Cindy'.** Open shrub with lance-shaped, light green leaves, 2in (5cm) long. Bears miniature, fragrant, peony-form flowers with white centers and rose-pink outer petals, in early and midseason. ↕ 10–15ft (3–5m), ↔ 4–8ft (1.2–2.5m). Zone 8.

***C. cuspidata* 'Spring Festival'.** Narrow, upright shrub with elliptic, dark green leaves, 3–5in (8–13cm) long. In mid- and late spring, bears small, formal double pink flowers. ↕ 6–12ft (2–4m), ↔ 2–6ft (0.6–2m). Zone 8.

***C.* 'Donation'** ■ Compact and erect shrub with elliptic to broadly elliptic, bright green leaves, 2½–4in (6-10cm) across, and large, semi-double pink flowers in midseason. In partial shade, its flowers are deeper in color and last longer; ↕ 15ft (5m), ↔ 8ft (2.5m). Zone 8.

***C.* 'Dream Boat'** ■ Spreading shrub, with elliptic to broadly elliptic, bright green leaves, 2½–4in (6–10cm) across, and medium, formal double, pale purplish pink flowers, with incurved petals, in midseason. ↕ 20ft (6m), ↔ 6–12ft (2–4m). Zone 8.

***C.* 'E.G. Waterhouse'** ■ Narrow, upright shrub with elliptic to broadly elliptic, pale green leaves, 2½–4in (6–10cm) across, and medium, formal double, pale pink flowers borne in mid- and late season. ↕ 20ft (6m), ↔ 6–12ft (2–4m). Zone 7.

***C.* 'Elsie Jury'.** Tall and upright shrub with well-spaced, spreading branches, elliptic to broadly elliptic, bright green leaves, 2½–4in (6–10cm) across, and large, full peony-form pink flowers borne in mid- and late season. ↕ 20ft (6m), ↔ 6–12ft (2–4m). Zone 8.

***C.* 'Fragrant Pink'** ■ Open shrub with lance-shaped, light green leaves, 2½in (6cm) long, and miniature, fragrant, peony-form, deep pink flowers, borne in early to late season. ↕ 10–15ft (3–5m), ↔ 4–8ft (1.2–2.5m). Zone 8.

C. fraterna. Dense shrub with small, elliptic, dark green leaves, 1½–3in (4–8cm) long, and fragrant, single, lilac-tinted white flowers, ¾–1¼in (2–3cm) across, in mid- and late season. ↕ 15ft (5m), ↔ 3–10ft (1–3m). China. Zone 8.

Camellia 'Anticipation'

Camellia 'Black Lace'

Camellia 'Donation'

Camellia 'Dream Boat'

Camellia 'E.G. Waterhouse'

Camellia 'Fragant Pink'

Camellia 'Freedom Bell'

Camellia granthamiana

Camellia hiemalis 'Dazzler'

Camellia hiemalis 'Shishigashira'

Camellia japonica 'Adolphe Audusson'

Camellia japonica 'Alexander Hunter'

C. **'Freedom Bell'** ■ Small, dense, rounded shrub with oval, glossy, dark green leaves, 3½in (9cm) long. Bears medium, deeply cup-shaped, semi-double, bright red flowers in early and midseason. Excellent for a small garden. ↕↔ 7ft (2.2m). Zone 8.
C. **'Garden Glory'.** Rounded and upright shrub, with elliptic to broadly elliptic, bright green leaves, 2½–4in (6–10cm) across, and formal double or rose-form double, rich pink flowers produced from early to late season. ↕ 6–15ft (2–5m), ↔ 3–10ft (1–3m). Zone 8.
C. **'Gay Time'.** Upright shrub, with elliptic to broadly elliptic, bright green leaves, 2½–4in (6–10cm) across, and large, semi-double to loose peony-form, bright pink flowers, darker on the petal margins, produced in midseason. ↕ 6–15ft (2–5m), ↔ 3–10ft (1–3m). Zone 8.
C. granthamiana ■ Large shrub or small tree bearing distinctive, elliptic, dark green leaves, to 4in (10cm) long, with deeply impressed veins. Single white flowers, 5–5½in (12–14cm) across, open from brown buds early in the season. ↕ 10ft (3m), ↔ 6ft (2m). Hong Kong. Zone 8.
C. grijsii. Bushy shrub with elliptic to oval, dark green leaves, to 3in (8cm) long. Bears single white flowers, ¾–1¼in (2–3cm) across, sometimes scented, with 2-lobed petals, in late winter. ↕ 3–10ft (1–3m), ↔ 2½–6ft (0.75–2m). China. Zone 8.
C. hiemalis. Upright shrub with elliptic, dark green leaves, 1½–2in (4–5cm) long, light green beneath. Bears single to peony-form, small, pink flowers, 2½in (6cm) across, early in the season. ↕ to 8ft (2.5m), ↔ to 6ft (2m). Origin unknown. Zone 8. **'Chansonette'** is a strong-growing shrub with elliptic, dark green leaves, 3in (8cm) long. Bears miniature, formal double, bright pink flowers early in the season; ↕ 10–12ft (3–4m), ↔ 6–12ft (2–4m). **'Dazzler'** ■ has fan-shaped branches and elliptic, dark green leaves, 2–3in (5–8cm) long. Medium, semi-double to loose peony-form, rose-red flowers are borne early in the season; ↕ 6–10ft (2–3m), ↔ 3–6ft (1–2m). **'Shishigashira'** ■ has small, semi-double to rose-form double, pinkish red flowers,

Camellia 'April Tryst'

early in the season; ↕ to 20ft (6m), ↔ to 10ft (3m).
C. japonica (Common camellia). Upright to spreading shrub or small tree with broadly elliptic, glossy, dark green leaves, 2–3in (5–8cm) long, and single red flowers, 1¼–1¾in (3–4.5cm) across. The species flowers in winter and early spring, its cultivars over a much longer period, in mid- and late spring. ↕ 10–20ft (3–6m), ↔ 3–10ft (1–3m). China, Korea, Japan. Zone 8. **'Adolphe Audusson'** ■ is compact, bearing large, semi-double red flowers in midseason. **'Akashigata'**, syn. 'Lady Clare', is a dense, strong-growing, rounded shrub with very large, semi-double, deep pink flowers with yellow stamens, borne in early and midseason. **'Alba Plena'** is erect, with light green foliage and produces medium, formal double white flowers, early in the season. **'Alexander Hunter'** ■ is upright, with upward-sweeping branches, bearing medium, single or semi-double crimson flowers with yellow stamens in early and midspring. **'Ann Blair Brown'** is an upright shrub bearing very large, anemone-form, light pink flowers, with dark pink petaloids shading to lavender, in midseason. **'April Blush'** is cold-hardy to nearly 0°F (-18°C), has average spreading growth, and bears rose pink, medium to large flowers. **'April Remembered'** ■ has vigorous growth, is cold-hardy to 0°F (-18°C), and bears magenta to rose large, semi-double flowers. **'April Tryst'** ■ has average, upright growth; is cold-hardy to nearly 0°F (-18°C); and bears currant-red, medium to large, anemone-form flowers. **Ave Maria'** ■ is upright, with downward-sweeping branches, and bears miniature, formal double, soft pink flowers in early and midseason. **'Berenice Boddy'** ■ is a strong, bushy shrub of arching habit. The large, semi-double, clear pink flowers are darker on the outer petals and are borne in mid-season. **'Betty Sheffield Supreme'** ■ is erect, with lance-shaped, slightly glossy leaves, 3–4in (8–10cm) long, and large, irregular, double white flowers, each petal margined in shades of rose-pink, borne in midseason. **'Blood of China'**, syn. 'Victor Emmanuel', is a vigorous, compact shrub producing medium-sized, semi-double to loose peony-form, deep salmon-red flowers, late in the season. **'Bob Hope'** is a large, upright shrub with vigorous, dense growth and large, semi-double or loose peony-form, dark red flowers; in midseason. **'Bob's Tinsie'** ■ has a dense, upright habit, and bears miniature, anemone-form, brilliant red flowers in midseason. **'Bokuhan'**, syn. 'Tinsie', is dwarf with spreading branches, and miniature, anemone-form flowers with red petals around a center of white petaloids, borne in early and midseason; ↕ 3ft (1m), ↔ 24in (60cm). **'Campari'** ■ is a vigorous, upright shrub with medium-sized, formal double, crimson-striped and -flecked, light pink flowers, borne in mid- and late season. **'Carter's Sunburst'** is spreading, with very large semi--double to peony-form to formal double, pale pink flowers, striped deep pink, borne from early to late season. **'Chandler's Elegans'** see 'Elegans'. **'Charlie Bettes'** is a large, dense, fast-growing shrub, producing large semi-double white flowers, with bright yellow stamens, early in the season. **'Cherries Jubilee'** is upright and compact, and bears large, semi-double to rose-form double, burgundy-red flowers with red and white petaloids, in midseason. **'China Doll'** ■ is a compact shrub with large, loose peony-form, coral-pink-edged, blush-pink flowers, with fluted petals, borne in midseason. **'Coquettii'** ■ syn.'Glen 40', is an upright, slow-growing shrub with downward-sweeping branches. In mid- and late season, bears profuse, medium to large, deep red flowers, sometimes formal double, sometimes peony- or anemone-form. **'Dahlohnega'** is upright and slow-growing, and produces medium-sized, formal double, light creamy yellow flowers, in midseason. **'Daikagura'**, syn. 'Idaten-Shibori', is compact and slow-growing, with large, peony-form, white-splotched, rose-pink flowers early in the season. **'Debutante'**, syn. 'Sara C. Hastie', is a vigorous, upright shrub with medium-sized, full peony-form, light pink flowers, borne in early and midseason. **'Dixie Knight'** is strong and bushy, with large, loose peony-form, dark red flowers, borne in mid- and late season. **'Dr. Burnside'** is moderately vigorous, with medium to large, semi-double or loose peony-form, dark red flowers, freely borne in midseason. **'Dr. Tinsley'** is compact and upright, bearing medium white flowers, suffused light pink, more strongly toward the petal margins. The flowers vary from semi-double to loose peony-form or formal double, and open from pink buds in midseason. **'Elegans'** ■ syn. 'Chandler's Elegans', has spreading branches with wavy leaves, and bears large, anemone-form, rose-pink flowers. Leading branches should not be cut back. **'Elegans Champagne'** ■ is an upright, open shrub bearing large, anemone-form, white flowers with creamy white to yellow petaloids, in early and midseason. **'Elegans Supreme'** ■ is similar to 'Elegans', with wavy leaves and very large, anemone-form, deep salmon-pink flowers, in early and midseason. **'Elizabeth Weaver'** is upright, and bears large, formal double, coral-pink flowers in early and midseason. **'Fimbriata'** is similar to 'Alba Plena', with medium, formal double white flowers with fringe-margined petals, borne early in the season. **'Francis Eugene Phillips'** is upright and vigorous with light green leaves having unusual, holly-like serations, and large, soft pink, loose peony-form flowers. **'Glen 40'** see 'Coquettii'. **'Gloire de Nantes'** ■ is compact and upright, with medium, semi-double to

C

Camellia japonica 'April Remembered'

Camellia japonica 'Ave Maria'

Camellia japonica 'Berenice Boddy'

Camellia japonica 'Betty Sheffield Supreme'

Camellia japonica 'Bob's Tinsie'

Camellia japonica 'Campari'

Camellia japonica 'China Doll'

Camellia japonica 'Coquettii'

Camellia japonica 'Elegans'

Camellia japonica 'Elegans Champagne'

Camellia japonica 'Elegans Supreme'

Camellia japonica 'Gloire de Nantes'

Camellia japonica 'Janet Waterhouse'

incomplete double, rose-red flowers, borne from late autumn to late spring. **'Governor Mouton'** is vigorous, with medium, semi-double or loose peony-form red flowers, often marked white, in midseason. **'Grace Albritton'** is upright, with small, formal double, light pink flowers with dark pink-tipped petals, produced in midseason. **'Granada'** ■ is a vigorous, upright shrub, and bears very large, semi-double to peony-form, vivid red flowers, in midseason. **'Grand Prix'** is vigorous, with very large, semi-double, brilliant red flowers with yellow stamens, borne in midseason. **'Grand Slam'** is strong and upright, with large, mostly anemone-form, sometimes semi-double, dark red flowers, in midseason. **'Guilio Nuccio'** ■ is a strong-growing, many-branched shrub with leaves 5–7in (12–18cm) long, and very large, semi-double, salmon-red flowers, with mustard-yellow stamens, in midseason. **'Hagoromo'** is erect, bearing medium, semi-double, pale pink flowers in mid- and late season. **'Helen Bower'** is vigorous and open, bearing very large, rose-form double, purple-shaded, rose-red flowers, in mid- and late season. **'Herme'**, syn. 'Hikaru Genji', 'Jordan's Pride', is vigorous and upright, and bears medium-sized, semi-double, light pink flowers with white borders and dark pink stripes, in midseason. **'Hikaru Genji'** see 'Herme'. **'Holly Bright'** is a compact shrub with unusual, crinkled, holly-like foliage and large, semi-double, glossy salmon-red flowers, borne in midseason. **'Idaten-Shibori'** see 'Daikagura'. **'Ivory Tower'** is compact, bearing very large, formal double, white flowers with high centers, in midseason. **'Janet Waterhouse'** ■ is sturdy and upright, with medium white flowers, semi-double in hot climates or formal double in cooler conditions, borne in midseason. **'Jordan's Pride'** see 'Herme'. **'Julia Drayton'** ■ syn. 'Mathotiana Purple King', 'Mathotiana Rubra', is upright and bears large, rose-form double or formal double crimson, purple-tinted flowers, in mid- and late season. **'Julia France'** is upright, with bold leaves, 3–5in (8–13cm) long, and large, semi-double, light pink flowers in midseason. **'Kramer's Supreme'** ■ is compact and upright, bearing large to very large, flat, fragrant, full peony-form, rose-red flowers in late autumn and again in midseason. **'Lady Clare'** see 'Akashigata'. **'Lady Laura'** is upright, and produces large, peony-form, pink flowers, striped and streaked with rose, in midseason. **'Lady Loch'** ■ is a leafy, rounded shrub, bearing medium, peony-form pink flowers, with white picotee-margined petals, in early and midseason. **'Lady Vansittart'** ■ is upright, with leaves 3–5in (8–13cm) long and medium, semi-double white flowers with rose-pink stripes; many specimens have stripes in 5 different colors, varying from white to red, on one shrub. The flowers are borne in mid- and late season. **'Lavinia Maggi'** ■ syn. 'Contessa Lavinia Maggi', is a vigorous, spreading shrub, bearing medium, formal double white flowers, with red and pink stripes, in early and midspring. **Lovelight'** ■ is vigorous and upright, with large leaves and large semi-double white flowers, composed of broad petals around a small tuft of white and yellow stamens, in mid- and late-

Camellia japonica 'Lovelight'

season. **'Man Size'** is spreading, and produces tiny, anemone-form white flowers in mid-season. **'Margaret Davis Picotee'** ■ is upright, producing peony-form or formal double white flowers with a narrow red margin to each petal, in early and midseason. **'Marie Bracey'**, syn. 'Spellbound', is compact and upright, producing very large, semi-double to loose peony-form, coral-rose flowers, in early and midseason. **'Mary Alice Cox'** is upright and bears very large, formal double, white flowers, in early and midseason. **'Mathotiana Purple King'** see 'Julia Drayton' **'Mathotiana Rubra'** see 'Julia Drayton'. **'Melissa Anne'** ■ has vigorous, dense growth with white large to very large, loose to full peony-form flowers produced early- and late season. **'Miss Charleston'** is upright, bearing large, rich red flowers, peony-form in cool climates or semi-double in warmer areas, in mid- and late season. **'Miss Charleston Var.'** ■ is identical to 'Miss Charleston' except that its flowers are white-splotched. **'Miss Universe'** ■ has a dense, spreading to upright habit, and in mid- and late season bears large white flowers, which are formal double with notched petals in cool climates, and peony-form elsewhere. **'Mrs. D.W. Davis'** ■ is a broad, strong, upright shrub with very large, nodding, semi-double, soft pink flowers, produced in midseason. **'Nuccio's Bella Rossa'** has upright, dense growth with large red, formal double flowers, and is an excellent land-scaping plant. **'Nuccio's Gem'** ■ is upright and dense in habit, producing large, formal double white flowers, with spirally arranged petals, in early and midseason; outdoors, the flowers are often irregular peony-form or semi-double. **'Pink Perfection'** see *C. rusticana* 'Otome'. **'Professor Charles S. Sargent'** is a vigorous, compact, upright shrub producing medium-sized, full peony-form, dark red flowers, produced in midseason. **'R.L. Wheeler'** ■ is a vigorous,

Camellia japonica 'Granada'

Camellia japonica 'Giulio Nuccio'

Camellia japonica 'Julia Drayton'

Camellia japonica 'Kramer's Supreme'

Camellia japonica 'Lady Loch'

Camellia japonica 'Lady Vansittart'

Camellia japonica 'Lavinia Maggi'

Camellia japonica 'Margaret Davis Picotee'

Camellia japonica 'Melissa Anne'

Camellia japonica 'Miss Charleston Var.'

Camellia japonica 'Miss Universe'

Camellia japonica 'Mrs. D.W. Davis'

rounded, open shrub with large, widely spaced leaves and very large, anemone-form or semi-double to incomplete double, brilliant red flowers, borne in early and midseason. **'Royal Velvet'** is an upright, dense, fast-growing shrub with very large, semi-double, dark velvet-red flowers, produced in midseason. **'Rubescens Major'** ■ is dense and upright, with distinctive, broad, rounded leaves and large, formal double or rose-form double crimson flowers, produced in midspring. **'Sara C. Hastie'** see 'Debutante'. **'Show Time'** is upright and fast-growing, and produces very large, semi-double, clear light pink flowers with fluted petals, in midseason. **'Sieboldii'** see 'Tricolor'. **'Snowman'** is a vigorous, upright, spreading shrub bearing very large, semi-double, white flowers with curled inner petals, in midseason. **'Something Beautiful'** is a strong, dense, erect shrub with miniature, formal double, pale pink flowers, the petals margined with burgundy-red, borne from early to late season. **'Spellbound'** see 'Marie Bracey'. **'Tama-No-Ura'** is vigorous and upright, and bears medium-sized, single, white-bordered, red flowers, in midseason. **'Tinsie'** see 'Bokuhan'. **'Tomorrow'** is vigorous and open, with very large, semi-double to peony-form, strawberry-red flowers, borne in early and mid-season. **'Tomorrow Var.'** ■ is identical to 'Tomorrow' except that its flowers bear white splotches. **'Tricolor'** ■ syn. 'Sieboldii', has bright green, crinkled, holly-like leaves and produces medium, single or semi-double red flowers, striped pink and white, in midseason. Breeds almost true from seed. **'Victor Emmanuel'** see 'Blood of China'. **'Ville de Nantes'** ■ is slow-growing and bushy, producing medium to large, semi-double red flowers with deeply fringed, white-marked petals, in mid- and late season. **'White Nun'** ■ is a strong-growing shrub with slightly corrugated leaves, and very large, flat, semi-double, pure white flowers, borne in midseason.

***C.* 'J.C. Williams'** ■ Spreading shrub with wide-sweeping branches and elliptic to broadly elliptic, glossy, bright green leaves, 2½–4in (6–10cm) long. Bears medium, single, pale pink flowers, with darker shading, from early to late season. Good for training on a partially shaded wall. ↕6–15ft (2–5m), ↔3–10ft (1–3m). Zone 8.

***C.* 'Julia Hamiter'** ■ Open, spreading shrub with elliptic to broadly elliptic, glossy, bright green leaves, 2½–4in (6–10cm) long. Bears flat, medium, rose-form double flowers, in midseason. The flowers have pink-flushed white petals, greenish white at the bases, surrounding cream petaloids. Similar to 'Donation'. ↕6–15ft (2–5m), ↔3–10ft (1–3m). Zone 8.

***C.* 'Julie'.** Upright, dense shrub with elliptic, pointed, dark green leaves, 3½in (9cm) long. Bears medium-sized, peony-form to rose-form double, salmon-pink to peach-pink flowers, in midseason. ↕20ft (6m), ↔10ft (3m). Zone 8.

***C.* 'Jury's Yellow'** ■ Narrow and erect shrub, with elliptic to broadly elliptic, glossy, bright green leaves, 2½–4in (6–10cm) long. Bears medium, anemone-form white flowers, with centers of yellow petaloids, from early to late season. ↕6–15ft (2–5m), ↔3–10ft (1–3m). Zone 8.

C. lutchuensis* 'Cinnamon Cindy' (*C. japon* x *C. lutch.*).** Open shrub with lance-shaped, light green leaves, 2in (5cm) long. Bears miniature, fragrant peony-form flowers with white centers and rose-pink outer petals, in early and midseason. ↕10–15ft (3–5m), ↔4–8ft (1.2–2.5m). Zone 8. **'Fragrant Pink' *C. japon* subsp. *rusticana* x *C. lutch is an open shrub with lance-shaped, light green leaves, 2½in (6cm) long, and miniature, fragrant peony-form deep pink flowers, borne from early to late season. with white centers and rose-pink outer petals, in early and midseason.

***C.* x *maliflora*,** syn. *C. maliiflora.* Leafy shrub with elliptic, dark green leaves, 1½–2in (3.5–5cm) long. Bears peony-form flowers, ½–¾in (1.5–2cm) across, in 2 shades of pink, in mid- and late season. Good for training against a wall. ↕8ft (2.5m), ↔6ft (2m). Garden origin. Zone 8.

C. maliiflora see *C.* x *maliflora.*

***C.* 'Mary Christian'** ■ Upright shrub with elliptic to broadly elliptic, dull, dark green leaves, 2½–4in (6–10cm) long. Trumpet-shaped, single, carmine-pink flowers, 2–3in (5–8cm) across, are borne in midseason. ↕6–15ft (2–5m), ↔3–10ft (1–3m). Zone 8.

Camellia japonica 'Ville de Nantes'

***C.* 'Mary Phoebe Taylor'.** Strong-growing shrub, with downward- and outward-sweeping branches and elliptic to broadly elliptic, bright green leaves, 2½–4in (6–10cm) long. Large, peony-form or semi-double, clear pink flowers are borne in early and midseason. ↕6–15ft (2–5m), ↔3–10ft (1–3m). Zone 8.

***C.* 'Mona Jury'** ■ Open shrub with elliptic to broadly elliptic, dull, dark green leaves, 2½–4in (6–10cm) long, and medium, loose peony-form, apricot-pink flowers from early to late season. ↕6–15ft (2–5m), ↔3–10ft (1–3m). Zone 8.

***C.* 'Nicky Crisp'.** Compact, slow-growing, rounded shrub with elliptic, dark green leaves, 3in (8cm) long, and large, semi-double, lavender-pink flowers borne from early to late season. ↕↔3–6ft (1–2m). Zone 8.

***C.* 'Night Rider'.** Upright shrub with narrowly elliptic, dark green leaves, 3in (8cm) long. Produces small, semi-double, dark red flowers in mid- and late season; the yellow stamens remain after the petals drop. Unusual in appearance, the plant seems to be suffused red, although the leaves are green. ↕6–12ft (2–4m), ↔4–8ft (1.2–2.5m). Zone 8.

C. nitidissima ■ syn. *C. chrysantha.* Large shrub producing oval, dark green leaves, 3–4½in (8–11cm) long, with deeply indented veins. Fragrant, single yellow flowers, 1–2in (2.5–5cm) across, are borne from the leaf axils in mid- and late season. Requires a warm, humid site in partial shade. ↕6–10ft (2–3m), ↔10ft (3m). S. China, Vietnam. ❀ (min. 45°F/7°C)

C. oleifera. Small, erect tree with slender branches and elliptic, oblong-elliptic, or obovate leaves, 1½–3½in (3.5–9cm) long, dark green above, light green beneath. In early season, bears scented, single white flowers, 2–2½in (5–6cm) across, occasionally 3–3½in (8–9cm) across. ↕22ft (7m), ↔10–12ft (3–4m). China. Zone 8.

Camellia japonica 'Nuccio's Gem'

Camellia japonica 'R.L. Wheeler'

Camellia japonica 'Rubescens Major'

Camellia japonica 'Tomorrow Var.'

Camellia japonica 'Tricolor'

Camellia japonica 'White Nun'

Camellia 'J.C. Williams'

Camellia 'Julia Hamiter'

Camellia 'Jury's Yellow'

Camellia 'Mary Christian'

Camellia 'Mona Jury'

Camellia nitidissima

C. reticulata. Open-branched small tree or large shrub with broadly elliptic to oblong-elliptic, leathery leaves, 3–4½in (8–11cm) long, dark green above, paler beneath. In spring, bears single, rose-red flowers, to 4½in (11cm) across. ↕ to 20ft (15m), ↔ 15ft (5m). China. Zone 8. Flowers of cultivars vary from single to semi-double to peony-form, and are pink, red, or white. **'Captain Rawes'** ▣ is a large, spreading shrub or small tree with very large, semi-double to loose peony-form, carmine-rose flowers, 5½–7in (14–18cm) across, borne in late season; ↕ to 30ft (10m), ↔ 20ft (6m). **'Curtain Call'** is a strong, spreading shrub with large, semi-double, deep coral-pink flowers, 6–7in (15–18cm) across, produced in mid- and late season; ↕↔ 20ft (6m). **'Dr. Clifford Parks'** ▣ is upright, with oval, dark green leaves, 5½in (14cm) long, and very large, peony- or anemone-form, dark rose-red flowers, produced in midseason; ↕ 12ft (4m), ↔ 8ft (2.5m). **'Dream Girl'** is a spreading shrub bearing elliptic, dark green leaves, 6in (15cm) long. Large to very large, strongly scented, semi-double, salmon-pink flowers are borne from early to late season. Best grown in full sun; ↕ 6–12ft (2–4m), ↔ 4–8ft (1.2–2.5m). **'Flower Girl'** is an upright shrub with elliptic, dark green leaves, 5–7in (12–18cm) long, and large, scented, semi-double pink flowers, produced from early to late season. ↕ 6–12ft (2–4m), ↔ 4–8ft (1.2–2.5m). **'Francie L'** ▣ bears long, fan-shaped branches, ideal for training against a wall. Bears lance-shaped, dark green leaves, 2½–4in (6–10cm) long, and large, semi-double, salmon-red to deep rose-red flowers, in midseason; ↕ 15ft (5m), ↔ 20ft (6m). **'Frank Houser'** ▣ is an upright, open, spreading shrub bears very large, semi-double to loose peony-form, glowing pink to red flowers with darker veins, in early and mid-season; ↕↔ 20ft (6m). **'Harold L. Paige'** is upright, with large, oval, dark green leaves, 5in (13cm) long; bears very large, rose-form double, bright red flowers in late season; ↕ 6–12ft (2–4m), ↔ 5–10ft (1.5–3m). **'Jean Pursel'** is vigorous and upright; bears very large, semi-double to peony-form, light purplish pink flowers, in mid- and late season; ↕↔ 20ft (6m). **'Lasca Beauty'** is an open, stiffly branched, upright shrub with elliptic, dark green leaves, 5in (13cm) long, and very large, semi-double, pale pink flowers, borne in midseason; ↕ 6–15ft (2–5m), ↔ 5–10ft (1.5–3m). **'Lila Naff'** ▣ is a strong, spreading shrub with smooth, elliptic to oval, dark green leaves, 4in (10cm) long. In midseason, bears very large, semi-double, clear silvery pink flowers; ↕ 6–22ft (2–7m), ↔ 4–8ft (1.2–2.5m). **'Mandalay Queen'** is a large, widely branching, erect shrub with broad leaves, and large, semi-double, deep rose-pink flowers, to 5½in (14cm) wide, in mid- and late season; ↕↔ 20ft (6m). **'Miss Tulare'** ▣ is a large, strong-growing, many-branched shrub, bearing large, peony-form or rose-form double flowers, to 5in (13cm) across, with waxy, brilliant rose-red petals in early and midseason; ↕↔ 20ft (6m). **'Royalty'** ▣ is open, with elliptic, glossy, dark green leaves, 4½in (11cm) long. In midseason, bears very large, semi-double, light red flowers. Train against a shady wall; ↕ 3ft (1m), ↔ 24in (60cm). **'Valentine Day'** is vigorous and upright, bearing very large, very deep, formal double, salmon-pink flowers with rosebud centers, in midseason; ↕↔ 20ft (6m). **'William Hertrich'** is a tall, open-growing shrub with very large, semi-double to loose peony-form, dark cherry-red flowers, to 7in (18cm) across, in midseason; ↕↔ 20ft (6m).

C. rosiflora. Shrub of open, lax habit, producing elliptic to broadly elliptic leaves, 1¾–3in (4.5–8cm) long, dark green above, paler beneath. Single pink flowers, to 1½in (4cm) across, are borne in midseason. ↕ 8ft (2.5m), ↔ 3–6ft (1–2m). China. Zone 8.

***C. rusticana* cultivars**, syn. *C. japonica* subsp. *rusticana* cultivars (Snow camellia). Selections from the Japanese species *C. rusticana* have an erect to spreading habit and elliptic, dark green leaves, 2–5in (5–13cm) long. They bear single or double flowers, 1¼–1½in (3–4cm) across. ↕ 6–12ft (2–4m), ↔ 3–10ft (1–3m). Zone 8. **'Otome'**, syn. *C. japonica* 'Pink Perfection', *C. rusticana* 'Frau Minna Seidel', 'Pink Pearl', 'Usuôtome', bears many-petaled, formal double, pale pink flowers from early to late season. **'Reigyoku'** has variegated leaves with distinctive gold "feathers," and bears small, single red flowers in midseason.

C. saluenensis. Freely branching shrub with narrowly ovate, glossy, dark green leaves, to 3in (8cm) long. In mid- and late season, bears single, white, pink, pink-and-white, or pinkish red flowers, 1½–2in (3.5–5cm) across. ↕↔ 3–15ft (1–5m). China (Yunnan). Zone 8. **'Water Lily'** is a vigorous, compact plant with upright growth and medium lavender-tinted, bright pink, formal double flowers. **'Wilber Foss'** is a vigorous plant with upright growth and large, pinkish red, full peony-form flowers.

C. sasanqua. Upright to spreading shrub or small tree with elliptic, oblong-elliptic, or broadly elliptic leaves, to 3in (8cm) long, dark green above, paler beneath. Bears fragrant, single, cup-shaped white flowers, 2–3in (5–8cm) across, early in the season. Will tolerate sun; in cold areas may be grown in containers and taken indoors to flower. ↕ to 20ft (6m), ↔ to 10ft (3m). Japan. Zone 8. **'Bonanza'** is strong-growing and upright, producing ovate, dark green leaves, 2½in (6cm) long, and medium, loose peony-form red flowers; ↕ 6–10ft (1.8–3m), ↔ 3–6ft (1–2m). **'Mine-No-Yuki'** is vigorous, with a willowy, spreading habit, and dark green leaves, 1½in (4cm) long. Bears small, double white flowers. **'Narumi-gata'** ▣ is erect, with small, fragrant, single white, pink-tinged flowers. **'Sparkling Burgundy'** is a spreading shrub, with narrowly ovate, dark green leaves, 3–5in (8–13cm) long. Bears medium, peony-form, ruby-red flowers; ↕ 5–10ft (1.5–3m), ↔ 3–6ft (1–2m). **'Yuletide'** has dense foliage and bears a profusion of single red flowers, with bright yellow stamens.

***C.* 'Snow Flurry'.** Dense, spreading, pendulous shrub with elliptic, dark green leaves, 3in (8cm) long, and small, anemone-form, white flowers, produced early in the season. One of a group of cold-hardy camellias. ↕ 10–15ft (3–5m), ↔ 5–10ft (1.5–3m). Zone 7.

***C.* 'Spring Festival'** ▣ Narrow, upright shrub with elliptic, dark green leaves, 3–5in (8–13cm) long. In mid- and late spring, bears small, formal double pink flowers. ↕ 6–12ft (2–4m), ↔ 2–6ft (0.6–2m). Zone 8.

C. sinensis. Shrub growing into a tree up to 53ft (17m) with white flowers. Elliptic leaves with rounded apex constitute the tea of commerce. Zone 8.

C. taliensis. Spreading shrub or small tree with elliptic to broadly elliptic, bright green leaves, 3½–6in (9–15cm) long. From midwinter to late spring, bears single white flowers, 2–2½in (5–6cm) across. ↕ 6–22ft (2–7m), ↔ 6–12ft (2–4m). China (Yunnan). Zone 8.

C. tsaii. Large, pendent shrub or small tree with oblong-elliptic, glossy, dark green leaves with wavy margins, to 3½in (9cm) long. Miniature, cup-shaped, single white flowers, ¾in (2cm) across, are produced from the leaf axils in mid- and late winter. ↕ to 30ft (10m), ↔ to 15ft (5m). W. China, Burma, N. Vietnam. Zone 8.

***C.* x *vernalis* cultivars.** Selections from *C.* x *vernalis* are erect to spreading shrubs with elliptic, dark green leaves, 2–5½in (5–14cm) long, and bear semi-double to double flowers, 2½–3in (6–8cm) across, early in the season. ↕ 6–15ft (2–5m), ↔ 3–12ft (1–4m). Zone 8. **'Dawn'** see 'Ginryû'. **'Egao'** bears semi-double, deep pink flowers with bold yellow stamens. **'Ginryû'**, syn. 'Dawn', has semi-double or formal double, pink-tinged white flowers. **'Star above Star'** ▣ bears semi-double flowers, with layers of reflexed, white or lavender-pink petals.

***C.* 'Water Lily'** ▣ Upright shrub with elliptic to broadly elliptic, glossy, bright green leaves, 2½–4in (6–10cm) long. Large, formal double, deep rose-pink flowers are borne in early and midseason. ↕ to 15ft (5m), ↔ to 10ft (3m). Zone 8.

***C.* 'Wilber Foss'** ▣ Rounded shrub with elliptic to broadly elliptic, dark green leaves, 2½–4in (6–10cm) long, and large, broad, peony-form, dark red flowers, borne from early to late season. ↕ to 20ft (6m), ↔ to 15ft (5m). Zone 8.

C. yuhsienensis. Rounded shrub or small tree with elliptic to oval, dark green leaves, to 3½in (9cm) long. Small, very fragrant, single white flowers, 2–3in (5–8cm) across, are produced in mid-season. ↕ to 10ft (3m), ↔ 2½–6ft (0.75–2m). China (Hunan). Zone 8.

Camellia reticulata 'Captain Rawes'

Camellia reticulata 'Dr. Clifford Parks'

Camellia reticulata 'Francie L'

Camellia reticulata 'Frank Houser'

Camellia reticulata 'Lila Naff'

Camellia reticulata 'Miss Tulare'

Camellia reticulata 'Royalty'

Camellia sasanqua 'Narumi-gata'

Camellia 'Spring Festival'

Camellia x *vernalis* 'Star above Star'

Camellia 'Water Lily'

Camellia 'Wilber Foss'

CAMPANULA syn. AZORINA

Bellflower

CAMPANULACEAE

Genus of about 300 species of annuals, biennials, and perennials, some of which are evergreen. They are distributed widely throughout temperate zones of the N. hemisphere, particularly in S. Europe and Turkey, and grow in diverse habitats, from high alpine rock crevices and scree to moorland, meadows, and woodland. Most species are easily cultivated and provide a long flowering display, blooming from late spring to late summer. The flowers are usually borne in panicles, racemes, or clustered heads, but are sometimes solitary. They vary from tubular to bell- or star-shaped, and may also be cup- or saucer-shaped. The entire or toothed leaves are alternate. Campanulas vary in habit from mat-forming, dwarf perennials to herbaceous species, 6ft (2m) tall.

Dwarf campanulas are ideal for a rock garden or alpine house, and many grow well on a wall or sunny bank. The taller perennials are excellent for a mixed or herbaceous border, or for naturalizing in a wildflower or woodland garden. Grow tender species, such as *C. isophylla*, as annuals in a conservatory or cool greenhouse, or outdoors.

• **CULTIVATION** For ease of reference, campanulas have been divided into the following cultivation groups:

1. Campanulas that need fertile, neutral to alkaline, moist but well-drained soil, in sun or (especially in areas with hot summers) partial shade; the delicate flower colors are best preserved in shade. *C. pyramidalis*, *C. sarmatica*, and *C. trachelium* thrive in dry soils, the first two in full sun, the last in partial shade. Taller species require staking. Cut back after flowering to prevent self-seeding and to encourage a second, less profuse, flush of flowers.

2. Robust rock-garden species, requiring moist but well-drained soil in sun or partial shade. Some thrive on a sunny wall or bank.

3. Species that enjoy the winter protection of deep, dry snow cover in their natural habitat and, in cultivation, will not tolerate winter moisture. Grow in a scree bed or trough, in gritty, moist but sharply drained soil, or in an alpine house in soil-based potting mix with up to one-third by volume of grit.

4. Tender perennials. Where not hardy, grow under glass in soil-based potting mix, in bright filtered light with good ventilation. In growth, water moderately and apply a balanced liquid fertilizer monthly; keep moist in winter. In frost-free areas, grow outdoors in an open site in well-drained, fertile soil in sun or partial shade. Cut dead stems to the base before winter.

• **PROPAGATION** Sow seed in containers in a cold frame in spring, except for alpines, which should be sown in an open frame in autumn. Divide in spring or autumn. Take basal cuttings of perennials in spring. To increase smaller species, take cuttings of new growth in early summer, or root rosettes of rosette-forming species in spring. Root tip cuttings of *C. isophylla* in early spring.

• **PESTS AND DISEASES** Prone to slugs, snails, vine weevils, spider mites, and aphids. Susceptible to powdery mildew, rust, *Septoria* and *Ramularia* leaf spots, and Southern blight.

Campanula alliariifolia

Campanula barbata

Campanula 'Birch Hybrid'

C. acutangula see *C. arvatica.*

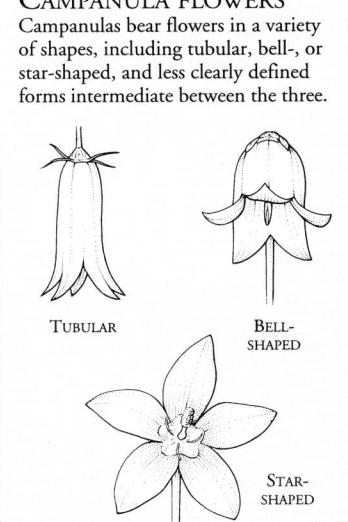

C. alliariifolia ▣ (Ivory bells). Vigorous, clump-forming perennial with heart-shaped, toothed, gray-hairy basal leaves, 3in (8cm) long. Leafy stems bear one-sided racemes of pendent, tubular-bell-shaped white flowers, ¾in (2cm) long, with sharply pointed petals, from midsummer to early autumn. Cultivation group 1. ↕ 12–24in (30–60cm), ↔ 18in (45cm). Caucasus, Turkey. Zone 4.

***C. amabilis* 'Planiflora'** see *C. persicifolia* var. *planiflora.*

C. americana. Upright annual or biennial with basal rosettes of ovate-heart-shaped, scalloped, softly hairy leaves, and narrowly lance-shaped, toothed, mid-green upper leaves, to 6in (15cm) long. In summer, bears racemes of flat, star-shaped, 5-lobed, pale blue flowers, to 1½in (4cm) across, with a paler ring at the throats. Cultivation group 1, but allow to self-seed. ↕ to 5½ft (1.7m), ↔ 12in (30cm). Great Lakes region to N. Florida. Zone 4.

C. arvatica, syn. *C. acutangula.* Mat-forming perennial with underground runners, and tufts of broadly ovate-heart-shaped, toothed, mid-green leaves, ¼–⅜in (6–9mm) long. Solitary, upturned, shallowly funnel-shaped, violet, pale blue, or white flowers, ¾–1½in (2–4cm) long, are borne on short stems in summer. Cultivation group 2. ↕ 3–4in (8–10cm), ↔ to 8in (20cm). N. Spain. Zone 6b.

C. barbata ▣ (Bearded bellflower). Short-lived perennial or biennial with rosettes of narrowly lance-shaped to oblong, slightly toothed, hairy, pale to mid-green leaves, 2½–3in (6–8cm) long. In early summer, erect stems bear one-sided racemes of pendent, bell-shaped, lavender-blue, sometimes white flowers, ¾–1¼in (2–3cm) long, the petals fringed with white hairs. Cultivation group 2. ↕ to 12in (30cm), ↔ 8in (20cm). Mountains of Norway, Alps. Zone 5.

C. bellardii see *C. cochleariifolia.*

C. betulaefolia see *C. betulifolia.*

C. betulifolia, syn. *C. betulaefolia*, *C. denticulata.* Tufted to clump-forming perennial with ovate to broadly ovate, toothed, dark green, purple-tinged leaves, 2–2½in (5–6cm) long. In early summer, produces corymbs of bell-shaped, pink-flushed white flowers, 1–1½in (2.5–4cm) long, with reflexed petal tips, that open from pink or red buds. Cultivation group 2 or 3. ↕ to 3in (8cm), ↔ to 8in (20cm). Turkey (Anatolia). Zone 5.

***C.* 'Birch Hybrid'** ▣ Vigorous, prostrate, evergreen perennial with underground runners, and small, ovate-heart-shaped, toothed, bright green leaves, ½in (1.5cm) long. Bears abundant, short racemes of open bell-shaped, mauve-blue flowers, ¾in (2cm) across, in summer. Cultivation group 2. ↕ 4in (10cm), ↔ to 20in (50cm) or more. Zone 4b.

CAMPANULA HABITS

Campanulas vary greatly in size and habit. They may be low, with a tufted, clump- or mat-forming, trailing, or spreading habit; or they may be tall and erect.

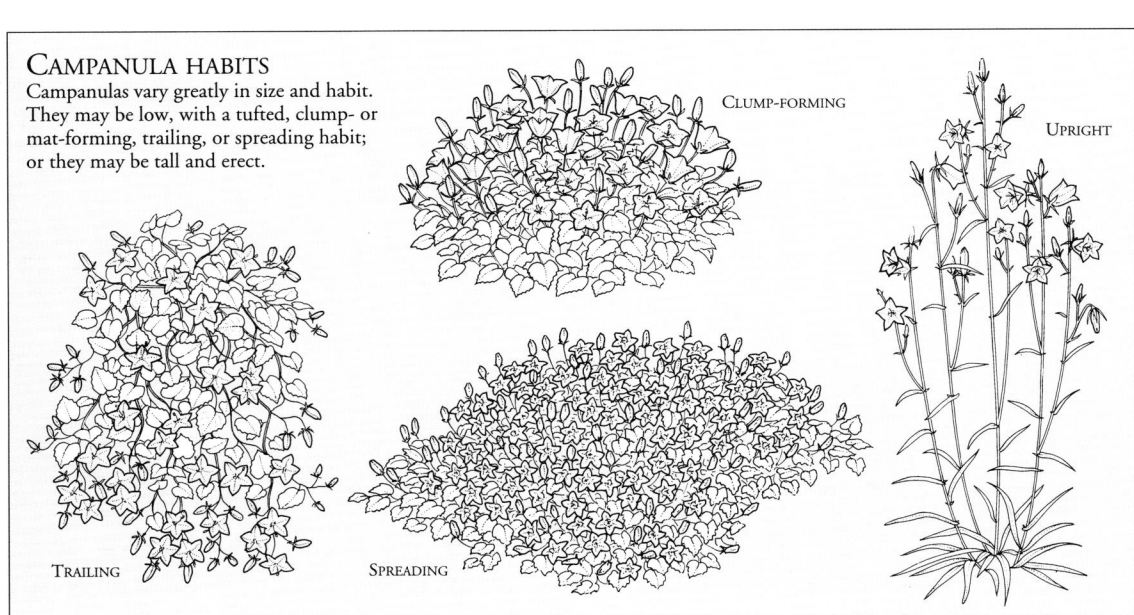

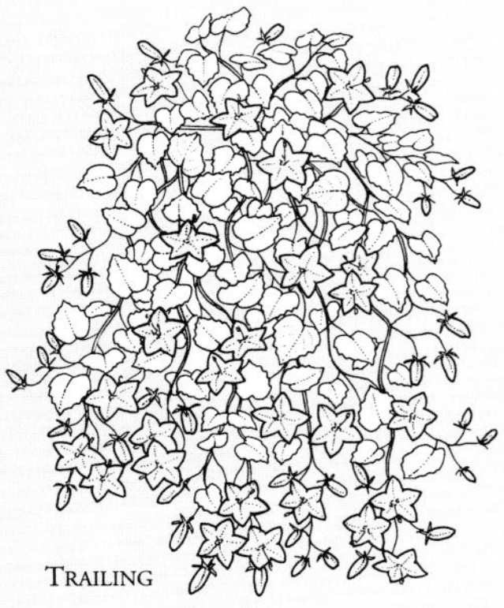

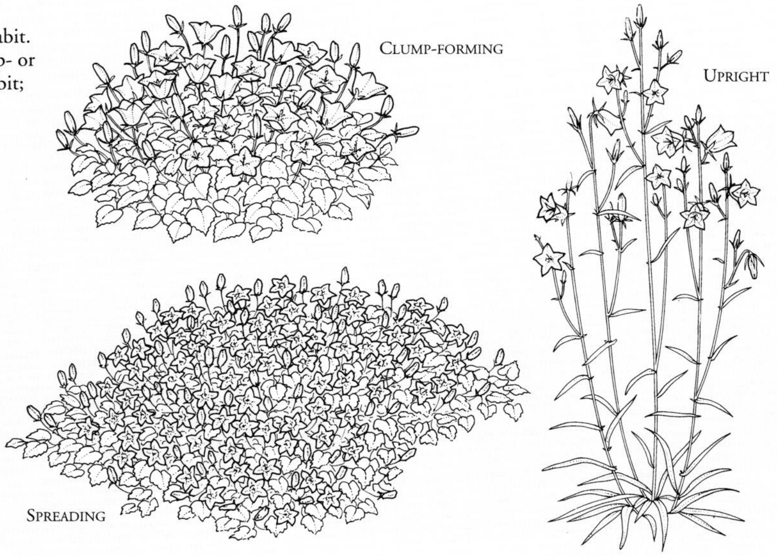

CAMPANULA FLOWERS

Campanulas bear flowers in a variety of shapes, including tubular, bell-, or star-shaped, and less clearly defined forms intermediate between the three.

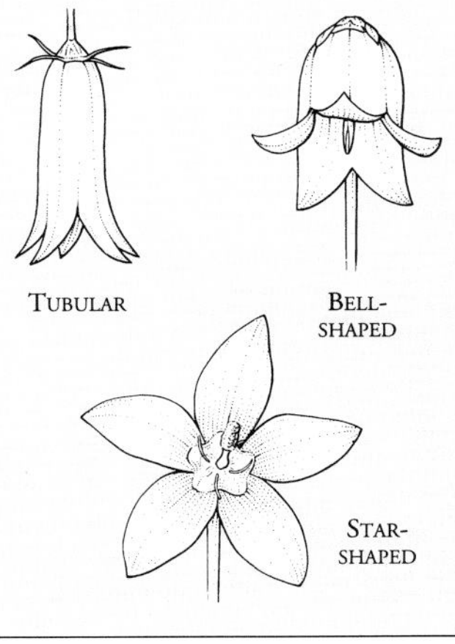

C

Campanula 'Burghaltii'

Campanula carpatica 'Jewel'

Campanula cochleariifolia

Campanula cochleariifolia 'Elizabeth Oliver'

***C.* 'Burghaltii'** ■ (*C. latifolia* x *C. punctata*). Mound-forming perennial with stalked, heart-shaped, toothed, mid-green basal leaves, to 3½in (9cm) long, and stalkless, much narrower stem leaves. In midsummer, bears racemes of pendent, tubular-bell-shaped flowers, to 4in (10cm) long, in a grayish lavender-blue. Cultivation group 1. ↕ 24in (60cm), ↔ 12in (30cm). Zone 4.
C. carpatica. Clump-forming, variable perennial with rounded to ovate or heart-shaped, toothed, mid-green, basal leaves, 1–2in (2.5–5cm) long. Many long, branched stems bear usually solitary, large, upturned, open bell-shaped, blue, violet-purple, or white flowers, 1¼in (3cm) or more across, over several months in summer. Cultivation group 2. ↕ to 12in (30cm), ↔ 12–24in (30–60cm) or more. C. Europe (Carpathians). Zone 4.
'Blue Clips', syn. 'Blaue Clips', is compact, with larger blue flowers, to 2in (5cm) across; ↕ 6–9in (15–23cm). **'Bressingham White'** ■ has large, pure white flowers, suffused blue-green at the bases; ↕ 6in (15cm). **'Jewel'** ■ is low-growing and compact, with bright purple-blue flowers; ↕ 4–6in (10–15cm). **'Turbinata'**, syn. var. *turbinata*, *C. turbinata*, is dwarf, with pale lavender-blue flowers borne singly on unbranched stems; ↕ 4–6in (10–15cm). **'Weisse Clips'**, syn. 'White Clips', produces abundant white flowers, and comes almost true from seed; ↕ 8in (20cm).
C. cashmeriana. Delicate, tufted, woody-based perennial with obovate to oblong, toothed, very hairy, gray-green leaves, to ½in (1.5cm) long, on slender, semi-erect, zigzagged, freely branching stems. Nodding, narrowly bell-shaped, pale lilac to gray-blue flowers, ½–1in (1–2.5cm) long, are produced singly from the leaf axils in summer. Best grown in an alpine house. Cultivation group 2 or 3. ↕ 4–6in (10–15cm), ↔ 6in (15cm). Afghanistan, India (Kashmir, Uttar Pradesh). Zone 4.
C. chamissonis, syn. *C. dasyantha*, *C. pilosa*, *C. pilosa* var. *dasyantha*. Variable, rhizomatous perennial with rosettes of spoon-shaped to inversely lance-shaped, finely toothed, pale green leaves, to 1½in (4cm) long. In early summer, erect stems bear bell-shaped to tubular, white-streaked blue flowers, ¾–1½in (2–4cm) long, usually singly but occasionally in few-flowered clusters. Cultivation group 2 or 3. ↕ 2–6in (5–15cm), ↔ to 8in (20cm). Japan to Alaska. Zone 3. **'Superba'** ■ syn. 'Major', is very compact, with pale purple-blue flowers, to 1½in (4cm) long; ↕ 2in (5cm), ↔ 8in (20cm).
C. cochleariifolia ■ syn. *C. bellardii*, *C. pusilla* (Fairies' thimbles). Creeping, tufted, rosette-forming perennial with slender rhizomes and oval to rounded-heart-shaped, toothed, bright green leaves, to ¾in (2cm) long. In summer, bears solitary, pendent, bell-shaped, white to lavender- or slate-blue flowers, ½in (1.5cm) long. Cultivation group 2. ↕ to 3in (8cm), ↔ to 12in (30cm) or more. European mountains. Zone 3. **'Elizabeth Oliver'** ■ produces double, pale lavender-blue flowers. **'Miranda'** bears single, gray-blue flowers. **'Miss Willmott'** has single, pale blue flowers, margined with silver.
C. collina. Upright perennial with creeping, underground rootstocks, softly hairy stems, and broadly lance-shaped, scalloped, basal leaves and narrowly lance-shaped, mid-green upper leaves, 2–3in (5–8cm) long. In summer, bears pendent, broadly bell-shaped, dark purple to blue-violet flowers, to 1½in (4cm) long, singly or in clusters or racemes. Cultivation group 1. ↕ to 12in (30cm), ↔ indefinite. Caucasus. Zone 5.
C. dasyantha see *C. chamissonis.*
C. denticulata see *C. betulifolia.*
C. elatines* var. *garganica see *C. garganica.*

Campanula carpatica 'Bressingham White'

Campanula chamissonis 'Superba'

Campanula 'Elizabeth'

Campanula 'G.F. Wilson'

***C.* 'Elizabeth'** ■ syn. *C. takesimana* 'Elizabeth'. Rhizomatous perennial with rosettes of heart-shaped, toothed, mid-green leaves, 3in (8cm) long. In mid- and late summer, bears racemes of pendent, bell-shaped cream flowers, 2in (5cm) or more long, flushed reddish purple outside and spotted red inside. Cultivation group 1. ↕ 14–16in (35–40cm), ↔ 16in (40cm). Zone 5.
C. excisa. Creeping, loose mat-forming perennial with upright, wiry stems bearing linear-lance-shaped, slender-pointed, entire, light green leaves, ¾in (2cm) long. In midsummer, produces solitary (sometimes 2 or 3), pendent, bell-shaped, violet to lilac flowers, to 1in (2.5cm) long, with a round hole at the base of each lobe. Cultivation group 2 or 3. ↕ to 4in (10cm), ↔ to 8in (20cm). S.W. and S. Central Alps. Zone 5b.
C. garganica, syn. *C. elatines* var. *garganica* (Adriatic bellflower). Spreading perennial with small, kidney-shaped or ovate-heart-shaped, toothed, mid-green basal leaves, 1–1½in (2.5–4cm) long, and heart-shaped, toothed stem leaves. Profuse racemes of star-shaped, bright blue to lilac flowers, ½–¾in (1–2cm) across, are produced in summer. Cultivation group 2. ↕ 2in (5cm), occasionally more, ↔ 12in (30cm) or more. S. Europe. Zone 4. **'Dickson's Gold'**, syn. 'Aurea', produces yellow leaves and blue flowers. **'W.H. Paine'** bears deep lavender-blue flowers with white centers.
***C.* 'G.F. Wilson'** ■ Compact, mound-forming perennial with slender runners and oval, toothed, pale yellow-green leaves, 1–2in (2.5–5cm) long. Bears

Campanula glomerata 'Superba'

solitary, semi-erect or nodding, cup-shaped, deep violet flowers, to 1in (2.5cm) across, in mid- and late summer. Cultivation group 2. ↕ to 4in (10cm), ↔ to 8in (20cm). Zone 4.
C. glomerata (Clustered bellflower). Vigorous, variable, rhizomatous, hairy perennial, spreading to form clumps of erect, stiff stems and bearing numerous ovate to lance-shaped, round-toothed, dark green leaves, 2–4in (5–10cm) long. Dense, terminal racemes of tubular-bell-shaped flowers, ½–1½in (1.5–4cm) long, varying from violet to lavender-blue, or white, are borne throughout summer. Cut back after flowering to encourage a second flush. Cultivation group 1. ↕ 4–18in (10–45cm) or more, ↔ indefinite. Europe (excluding extreme N.), Turkey, W., C., and S. Asia. Zone 3. **'Crown of Snow'** see 'Schneekrone'. **var. *dahurica*** ■ has wide, deep purple flowers; ↕ to 30in (75cm). **'Joan Elliott'** has large violet flowers in early summer; ↕ 16in (40cm). **'Schneekrone'**, syn. 'Crown of Snow', bears dense clusters of white flowers and breeds virtually true from seed; ↕ 20in (50cm). **'Superba'** ■ is vigorous, with purple-violet flowers; ↕ 24in (60cm).

Campanula isophylla Kristal Hybrids 'Stella Blue'

C.* x *haylodgensis see *C.* x *haylodgensis* 'Plena'.
***C.* x *haylodgensis* 'Plena'**, syn. *C.* x *haylodgensis*. Spreading perennial with rounded to ovate or heart-shaped, toothed, mid-green leaves, ½–¾in (1–2cm) long. In mid- and late summer, bears clusters of rounded-bell-shaped, double, deep lavender-blue flowers, to 1in (2.5cm) across. Cultivation group 2. ↕ to 3in (8cm), ↔ 6in (15cm). Garden origin. Zone 6. **'Warley White'**, syn. *C. warleyensis*, has open, semi-double or double white flowers, to 1½in (4cm) across.
C. isophylla (Falling stars, Italian bellflower, Star of Bethlehem). Trailing perennial with soft stems, becoming slightly woody at the bases, and small, heart-shaped, toothed, light green leaves, 2½in (6cm) long. Loose corymbs of numerous upright, saucer-shaped, pale blue or pure white flowers, 1½in (4cm) across, are produced in mid-summer; flowers for 2 or 3 months. Excellent for containers and hanging baskets. Cultivation group 4, usually as an annual. ↕ 6–8in (15–20cm), ↔ to 12in (30cm). N. Italy. ❄ (min. 35°F/2°C). **'Alba'** ■ has pure white flowers. **Kristal Hybrids** are compact, long-blooming, and very free-flowering, producing strong stems and large flowers; they flower in early summer from late-winter sowings. **'Stella Blue'** ■ is a compact Kristal Hybrid, producing star-shaped, bright violet-blue flowers; it is often cultivated as an annual for hanging baskets. **'Stella White'** is a Kristal Hybrid with star-shaped white flowers.

Campanula lactiflora 'Loddon Anna'

***C.* 'Joe Elliott'.** Small, mound-forming perennial producing rounded-heart-shaped, slightly toothed, hairy, grayish green leaves, to ½in (1.5cm) long. Upright, bell- to funnel-shaped, lavender-blue flowers, ¾–1¼in (2–3cm) long, are borne singly or in small clusters of 2 or 3, just above the foliage in summer. Cultivation group 3. ↕ 3in (8cm), ↔ 8in (20cm). Zone 5.
C. lactiflora ■ (Milky bellflower). Upright perennial producing thin, ovate to ovate-oblong, toothed, mid-green leaves, 2–5in (5–13cm) or more long. Conical panicles of open bell-shaped flowers, ½–1in (1.5–2.5cm) across, are borne on strongly branched, leafy stems from early summer to early autumn. The flowers are usually white to pale blue, sometimes lavender-blue, deep lilac-blue, or violet. Self-seeds freely, producing seedlings with some color variation. Often requires staking. Cultivation group 1. ↕ 4–5ft (1.2–1.5m), ↔ 24in (60cm). Caucasus, Turkey. Zone 3. **'Alba'** produces pure white flowers. **'Loddon Anna'** ■ bears soft lilac-pink flowers. **'Pouffe'** is dwarf, forming a tight mound of foliage covered with profuse, pale lavender-blue flowers; ↕ 10in (25cm), ↔ 18in (45cm). **'Prichard's Variety'** ■ produces dark violet-blue flowers; ↕ to 30in (75cm). **'White Pouffe'** is similar to 'Pouffe', but with white flowers.
C. latifolia. Vigorous, upright perennial with thick, unbranched stems arising from basal clumps of ovate-oblong, long-stalked, rough-textured, toothed, mid-green leaves, 3–5in

Campanula glomerata var. *dahurica*

Campanula isophylla 'Alba'

Campanula lactiflora

Campanula lactiflora 'Prichard's Variety'

C

Campanula latifolia 'Brantwood'

(8–13cm) long. Stem leaves are similar but stalkless and sharply pointed, decreasing in size toward the tops of the stems. In summer, flowers are produced singly or in twos or threes, from the axils of the upper leaves, forming narrow, leafy, spike-like racemes. The flowers are broadly tubular-bell-shaped, 1½–2½in (4–6cm) long, pale to deep violet or white, and have wide-spreading corolla lobes. Cultivation group 1. ↕ to 4ft (1.2m), ↔ 24in (60cm). Europe (except for the extreme N. and Mediterranean region), Caucasus, Turkey, Iran, W. Asia to India (Kashmir). Zone 4. **'Brantwood'** ■ bears deep violet flowers and breeds almost true from seed; ↕ 30in (75cm). **'Gloaming'** produces pale smoke-blue flowers; ↕ 24in (60cm). **var. *macrantha*** has sparse foliage and dark blue flowers; ↕ 3ft (1m); Caucasus.

C. latiloba, syn. *C. persicifolia* subsp. *sessiliflora*. Clump-forming perennial with basal rosettes of broadly lance-shaped, toothed, mid-green leaves, 3–5in (8–13cm) long, and thick, erect stems. Short racemes of stalkless, shallowly cup-shaped, rich lavender-blue flowers, 1¼–2in (3–5cm) across, are borne in mid- and late summer. Cultivation group 1. ↕ 36in (90cm), ↔ 18in (45cm). N. Turkey. Zone 4. **'Hidcote Amethyst'** ■ has pale amethyst flowers with deeper purple shading. **'Percy Piper'** produces rich lavender-blue flowers; ↕ 30in (75cm).

C. medium (Canterbury bells). Slow-growing, clump-forming, downy biennial producing lance-shaped to elliptic, toothed, mid-green basal leaves,

Campanula latiloba 'Hidcote Amethyst'

Campanula medium 'Bells of Holland'

5–6in (12–15cm) long, and smaller stem leaves. Lax racemes of single or double, bell-shaped, white, pink, or blue flowers, 1–1½in (2.5–4cm) long, open from spring to summer. Cultivation group 1. ↕ 24–36in (60–90cm), ↔ 12in (30cm). S. Europe. Zone 5. **'Bells of Holland'** ■ is dwarf, bearing single flowers in a variety of colors. May be grown as an annual; ↕ 16–18in (40–45cm). **'Calycanthema'**, syn. var. *calycanthema* (Canterbury bells, Cup and saucer) has single or double flowers, each surrounded by a large calyx the same color as the petals. An additional, flattened, lobed corolla forms a saucer-like rim at the base of the cup-like flowers; ↕ to 30in (75cm).

C. morettiana. Small, tufted perennial with finely hairy, broadly ovate, coarsely toothed, mid-green leaves, to ¾in (2cm) long. Arching stems bear usually solitary, erect, tubular-bell-shaped, violet-blue flowers, ¾–1¼in (2–3cm) long, in late spring and early summer. Prefers alkaline soil. Cultivation group 3. ↕ 2in (5cm), ↔ to 4in (10cm). Rock crevices, mountains of N. Italy, W. Austria (Tyrol). Zone 5b.

C. muralis see *C. portenschlagiana.*

C. nitida see *C. persicifolia* var. *planiflora.*

***C. nitida* 'Planiflora'** see *C. persicifolia* var. *planiflora.*

C. ossetica see *Symphyandra pendula.*

C. persicifolia (Peach-leaved bellflower). Rosette-forming perennial with slender white rhizomes and narrow, lance-shaped to oblong-obovate, toothed, evergreen, bright green, basal leaves, 4–6in (10–15cm) long. Short, terminal racemes of 2 or 3, occasionally solitary, slightly pendent, cup-shaped flowers, to 2in (5cm) across, varying from white to lilac-blue, are produced on slender stems, or from the leaf axils, in early and midsummer. Cultivation group 1. ↕ 36in (90cm), ↔ 12in (30cm). S. Europe, to C. and S. Russia, W. and N. Asia. Zone 3b. **'Alba Coronata'**, syn. 'Alba Plena', bears semi-double flowers with 2 or 3 rows of petals and enlarged, petaloid stamens; ↕ 18in (45cm). **'Boule de Neige'** bears double white flowers; ↕ 24in (60cm). **'Chettle Charm'** has snow-white flowers, 1in (2.5cm) across, margined with pale violet-blue, from late spring through summer; ↕ to 36in (90cm). **'Fleur de Neige'** produces large, shallowly cup-shaped white flowers with 3 rows of petals and petaloid stamens; ↕ 28in (70cm). **var. *planiflora***, syn. *C. amabilis* 'Planiflora', *C. nitida*, *C. nitida* 'Planiflora', *C. planiflora* (Willow-bell), is dwarf, with dense rosettes of inversely lance-shaped, wavy-margined, glossy, very dark green leaves, to 1¼in (3cm) long. In summer, bears erect racemes of widely bell-shaped blue flowers, ¾–1½in (2–4cm) across.

Campanula persicifolia 'Telham Beauty'

Cultivation group 2; ↕↔ 6in (15cm). **'Planiflora Alba'** has white flowers. Cultivation group 2; ↕↔ 6in (15cm). **'Pride of Exmouth'** bears semi-double, cup-in-cup, purple-blue flowers, and is remontant; ↕ 24in (60cm). **subsp. *sessiliflora*** see *C. latiloba.* **'Telham Beauty'** ■ has light blue flowers, 3in (8cm) across; ↔ 36in (90cm).

C. pilosa see *C. chamissonis.*

C. pilosa* var. *dasyantha see *C. chamissonis.*

C. piperi. Slow-growing, tufted, rhizomatous perennial with rosettes of spoon- to lance-shaped, toothed, glossy mid-green leaves, to 1in (2.5cm) long. Solitary, shallowly bowl-shaped, bright blue flowers, ¾in (2cm) across, with red anthers, are borne in summer. Best grown in an alpine house. Cultivation group 3. ↕ to 2in (5cm), ↔ to 6in (15cm). Rock crevices in N.W. Olympic Mountains. Zone 7b.

C. planiflora see *C. persicifolia* var. *planiflora.*

C. portenschlagiana ■ syn. *C. muralis* (Dalmatian bellflower). Robust, mound-forming, evergreen perennial with broadly kidney-shaped to ovate-heart-shaped, irregularly toothed, mid-green leaves, ¾–1½in (2–4cm) long. Erect or spreading, loosely branched panicles of tubular to funnel-shaped, deep purple flowers, to ¾in (2cm) long, are borne in mid- and late summer. Cultivation group 2. ↕ to 6in (15cm), ↔ 20in (50cm) or more. Mountains of Croatia. Zone 3.

C. poscharskyana ■ Vigorous perennial, spreading by underground runners, with toothed, rounded to ovate, mid-green leaves, to 1in (2.5cm) long, heart-shaped at the bases. Panicles of star-shaped, pale lavender flowers, ¾–1in (2–2.5cm) across, with white centers, are borne from summer to autumn. Cultivation group 2. ↕ to 6in (15cm), ↔ to 24in (60cm). Mountains of Croatia, Bosnia, Herzegovina. Zone 3. **'Stella'** has bright violet flowers.

C.* x *pseudoraineri (*C. carpatica* 'Turbinata' x *C. raineri*). Variable, dense, clump-forming perennial, resembling *C. carpatica*, with ovate to rounded or heart-shaped, toothed, hairy, gray-green, basal leaves, ½–1in (1–2.5cm) long. Bears solitary, large, upturned, open bell-shaped blue flowers, 1¼in (3cm) across, on erect stems throughout summer. Cultivation group 2. ↕ to 5in (13cm), ↔ to 6in (15cm). Garden origin. Zone 4.

Campanula portenschlagiana

Campanula poscharskyana

C. pulla. Spreading perennial with underground runners and small rosettes of shallowly toothed, rounded-spoon-shaped, shiny, mid-green, basal leaves. Solitary, pendent, tubular-bell-shaped, deep violet or purple-blue flowers, to ¾in (2cm) long, are borne in late spring and early summer. Cultivation group 2 or 3. ↕ to 2in (5cm), ↔ to 12in (30cm). N.E. Alps, Austria. Zone 5.
C. punctata ▣ Clump-forming perennial with creeping rhizomes and rosettes of ovate, toothed, slightly hairy, dark green leaves, 4–5in (10–13cm) long, heart-shaped at the bases. In early summer, erect stems bear short racemes of pendent, tubular-bell-shaped, creamy white to dusky pink flowers, 2in (5cm) long, red-spotted and hairy inside. Will thrive in fertile, sandy loam. Cultivation group 1. ↕ 12in (30cm), ↔ 16in (40cm). Russia (Siberia), Japan. Zone 4.
C. pusilla see *C. cochleariifolia.*
C. pyramidalis (Chimney bellflower). Short-lived, erect perennial, best grown as a biennial. Loose rosettes of ovate-lance-shaped, toothed, light to mid-green leaves, 3–6in (7–15cm) long, give rise to tall stems with stalkless, lance-shaped leaves. Pyramidal racemes of cup-shaped, fragrant, light blue or white flowers, 1½in (4cm) across, are borne from late spring to summer. Prefers rich soil. Cultivation group 1. ↕ to 10ft (3m), ↔ 24in (60cm). N. Italy, N.W. Balkans. Zone 5. **'Alba'** has white flowers.
C. raineri ▣ Slow-spreading perennial with underground runners and obovate, toothed, hairy, gray-green leaves, ½–1in (1–2.5cm) long. In summer, bears solitary, upturned, open bell-shaped,

Campanula punctata

Campanula raineri

pale lavender flowers, 1¼–1½in (3–4cm) across. Cultivation group 3. ↕ 2–3in (5–8cm), ↔ to 8in (20cm). Mountains of Switzerland, Italy. Zone 5.
C. rotundifolia (Bluebell, Harebell). Variable perennial with underground runners, and long-stalked, rounded to heart-shaped, finely toothed, light green basal leaves, ½in (1.5cm) long, and linear stem leaves. In summer, erect, slender stems bear lax, branched panicles of nodding, bell-shaped, dark blue to white flowers, to ¾in (2cm) long. May be naturalized in short grass. Cultivation group 2. ↕↔ 5–12in (12–30cm). Temperate N. hemisphere. Zone 3. **'Olympica'** has toothed, dark green leaves; ↕ 9in (23cm).
C. sarmatica. Clump-forming perennial, similar to *C. alliariifolia* but less vigorous, with elongated, triangular-ovate, heart-shaped, toothed, wrinkled, gray-woolly, basal leaves, to 3in (8cm) long, with long leaf stalks. Erect, unbranched, grayish green stems bear lax racemes of bell-shaped, hairy, light gray-blue flowers, 1¼–2in (3–5cm) long, from late spring to midsummer. Cultivation group 1. ↕ 20in (50cm), ↔ 16in (40cm). Caucasus. Zone 5.
C. saxatilis. Tufted perennial with erect or spreading stems arising from a thick rootstock, and rosettes of spoon-shaped to inversely lance-shaped, entire or round-toothed, mid-green leaves, to 2in (5cm) long. In summer, long stems bear loose spikes or clusters of tubular, pale blue flowers, to ¾in (2cm) long, with darker veins. Cultivation group 3. ↕ 3in (8cm) or more, ↔ to 8in (20cm). Crete (in rock crevices). Zone 7b.

Campanula trachelium

Campanula zoysii

C. takesimana. Rapidly spreading, rhizomatous perennial with heart-shaped, toothed, glossy, mid-green leaves, to 3in (8cm) long, with winged leaf stalks. In summer, bears arching, branched sprays of pendent, bell-shaped white flowers, 1½–3in (4–8cm) long, pink-flushed, and spotted maroon inside. Cultivation group 1. ↕ to 20in (50cm), ↔ to 36in (90cm). Korea. Zone 6. **'Elizabeth'** see *C.* 'Elizabeth'.
C. thyrsoides. Rosette-forming, bristly, biennial or monocarpic perennial with lance-shaped, wavy-margined, entire, mid-green leaves, 3–5in (8–13cm) long, the upper ones much narrower and stem-clasping. Dense, blunt-tipped, cylindrical spikes of cup-shaped, fragrant, lemon-yellow or creamy yellow flowers, ½–1in (1.5–2.5cm) long, are borne in mid- and late summer. Prefers light, alkaline soil. Cultivation group 1. ↕ 12–20in (30–50cm) or more, ↔ 9–12in (23–30cm). S. Europe. Zone 5.
C. trachelium ▣ (Bats-in-the-belfry, Nettle-leaved bellflower, Throatwort). Upright, woody-based perennial with ovate, sharply toothed, nettle-like, bristly, mid-green leaves, 2–5in (5–13cm) long. Thick, sometimes red-tinged stems bear short racemes of tubular, short-stalked, mid-blue to lilac, or white flowers, ¾–1¼in (2–3cm) long, from the leaf axils, in mid- and late summer. Cultivation group 1. ↕ 18–36in (45–90cm), ↔ 12in (30cm). Europe to Turkey and W. Asia, also N. Africa. Zone 5. **'Alba Flore Pleno'** produces semi-double white flowers. **'Bernice'** bears double, lilac-blue flowers.
C. turbinata see *C. carpatica* 'Turbinata'.
***C.* 'Van-Houttei'.** Clump-forming perennial with deeply notched, ovate to lance-shaped, scalloped, mid-green leaves, 3½–4in (9–10cm) long, with conspicuous veins. Pendent, tubular-bell-shaped mauve flowers, to 2½in (6cm) long, are produced on erect stems in early and midsummer. Cultivation group 1. ↕ 24in (60cm), ↔ 12in (30cm). Zone 4.
C. vidalii see *Azorina vidalii.*
C. waldsteiniana. Tufted, clump-forming perennial with small, ovate-elliptic, toothed, bright green leaves, ½in (1.5cm) long. In late summer and early autumn, bears loose racemes of 3–5 upturned, star-shaped, mid-blue flowers, ¾in (2cm) across, on wiry stems. Cultivation group 3. ↕ to 4in (10cm), ↔ to 8in (20cm). Rock crevices and mountains in S. Croatia. Zone 5.
C. wanneri see *Symphyandra wanneri.*
C. warleyensis see *C.* x *haylodgensis* 'Warley White'.
C. zoysii ▣ Cushion-forming, tufted perennial producing small, obovate to ovate, toothed, glossy, mid-green leaves, ¼–½in (6–15mm) long. Erect stems each bear several pendent, tubular, clear blue to pale lavender-blue flowers, ½–¾in (1.5–2cm) long, contracted at the mouths, in midsummer. Needs very gritty, alkaline soil. Cultivation group 3. ↕ to 2in (5cm), ↔ to 4in (10cm). S.E. Alps. Zone 5b.

▷ ***Campelia zanonia*** see *Tradescantia zanonia*

CAMPSIS
Trumpet creeper, Trumpet vine
BIGNONIACEAE

Genus of 2 species of vigorous, woody, deciduous climbers, usually climbing by aerial roots, found in woodland in China and North America. They have opposite, pinnate leaves, with ovate leaflets. From late summer to autumn, they bear showy, trumpet-shaped or funnel-shaped flowers, 2½–3in (6–8cm) long, that are attractive to hummingbirds, in terminal panicles or cymes. Train against a wall or fence, or up a pillar, or on a tree.
• **CULTIVATION** Grow in any moderately fertile, moist but well-drained soil; they tolerate poor soil and restricted roots. Where marginally hardy, trumpet creepers are best grown against a warm wall in full sun. Elsewhere, they will tolerate a wide range of exposures. Provide a sturdy, large support; many *Campsis* species can pull down an inadequate support or overwhelm a small tree. Pruning group 12, in late winter or early spring. It may take 2 or 3 seasons to establish the main framework; train and tie in the shoots until the aerial roots have taken hold.
• **PROPAGATION** Sow seed in containers in a cold frame in autumn. Root leaf-bud cuttings in spring or semi-ripe cuttings in summer. Graft or insert root cuttings in winter.
• **PESTS AND DISEASES** Prone to many fungal leaf spots, powdery mildew, scale insects, mealybugs, and whiteflies.

C. chinensis see *C. grandiflora.*
C. grandiflora, syn. *Bignonia grandiflora, C. chinensis, Tecoma grandiflora* (Chinese trumpet creeper, Chinese trumpet vine). Vigorous climber with pinnate, mid- to dark green leaves, to 12in (30cm) long, composed of 7–9 ovate, coarsely toothed leaflets. Pendent, terminal panicles of 6–12 open funnel-shaped, dark orange to red flowers, with spreading lobes, are borne from late summer to autumn. It produces relatively few aerial roots and may need to be tied permanently to its support. ↕ 30ft (10m). China. Zone 7b.
C. radicans, syn. *Bignonia radicans, Tecoma radicans* (Trumpet creeper). Vigorous climber with ovate, pinnate, dark green leaves, 1–4in

Campsis x *tagliabuana* 'Mme. Galen'

(2.5–10cm) long, composed of 7–11 ovate, toothed leaflets. Bears terminal cymes of 4–12 slender, tubular-trumpet-shaped, orange to red flowers from late summer to autumn. ↕ 30ft (10m) or more. S.E. US. Zone 5b. **f. *flava*,** syn. 'Yellow Trumpet', has yellow flowers.
***C.* x *tagliabuana* 'Mme. Galen'** ▣ Vigorous climber with pinnate, dark green leaves, to 12in (30cm) long, composed of 7–11 ovate leaflets. From late summer to autumn, bears terminal panicles of 6–12 trumpet-shaped, orange-red flowers. ↕ 30ft (10m) or more. Zone 6.

▷ ***Camptosorus rhizophyllus*** see *Asplenium rhizophyllum*

CAMPYLOTROPIS

FABACEAE

Genus of 65 species of deciduous shrubs or subshrubs commonly found in disturbed areas, on open hillsides, and in mountain scrub of E. Asia. They have alternate, fully divided, 3-palmate leaves with elliptic to ovate leaflets, and are grown for their heavily flowered racemes of pink to purple flowers. In temperate climates, they are an attractive addition to a warm, sunny border. Where not hardy, grow in a cool greenhouse.
• **CULTIVATION** Under glass, grow in soil-based potting mix in full light. Water freely when in the growing season and apply a balanced liquid fertilizer monthly. Water sparingly in winter. Outdoors, grow in deep, well-drained, moderately fertile soil in full sun. Cut back cold-damaged young shoots in spring, to the ground, if necessary. Protect with a winter mulch. Pruning group 6.
• **PROPAGATION** Sow seed *in situ* in autumn. Root softwood cuttings in spring to summer in a closed propagating case. Root semi-ripe heel cuttings in summer or autumn in a cold frame.
• **PESTS AND DISEASES** Infrequent.

C. macrocarpa. Deciduous shrub with 3-palmate, mid-green leaves, to 5in (13cm) long, silky beneath, divided into oblong leaflets, to 2in (5cm) long. Produces dense racemes, to 3in (8cm) long, of pea-like purple flowers, ¼in (6mm) across, from late summer to autumn, followed by small, ellipsoid fruit, ½in (1.5cm) long. ↕↔ to 3ft (1m). N. and C. China. Zone 7b.

CANARINA

CAMPANULACEAE

Genus of 3 species of herbaceous climbers, with thick, tuberous roots, found in forest and at forest margins in the Canary Islands and E. Africa. The leaves are opposite and simple or lobed. Canarinas are valued for their pendent, bell-shaped flowers, with 6 petal lobes, produced singly or in clusters from the upper leaf axils. Where not hardy, grow in a container or border in a cool greenhouse or conservatory; elsewhere, grow against a house wall or allow to scramble through low shrubs.
• **CULTIVATION** Under glass, grow in soil-based potting mix in bright filtered light with good ventilation. Keep completely dry when foliage yellows in late spring; pot on in late summer while dormant and keep just moist until new growth begins; when in growth, water freely and apply a balanced liquid fertilizer every 2–3 weeks. Provide support. Outdoors, grow in fertile, well-drained soil in partial shade. Protect from summer rain when growth yellows, and keep the crowns dry until autumn.
• **PROPAGATION** Sow seed at 59–64°F (15–18°C) in autumn or spring. Take basal cuttings flush with the tubers in late winter or early spring as shoots are produced; root in a propagating case.
• **PESTS AND DISEASES** May become infested with whiteflies.

C. campanula see *C. canariensis.*
C. canariensis ▣ syn. *C. campanula* (Canary bellflower). Scrambling, deciduous climber producing branching, scandent, robust stems and lance-shaped or 3-angled, shallowly lobed, mid-green leaves, 1½–3in (4–8cm) long. The bell-shaped, orange-red to orange-yellow flowers, 1¼–2½in (3–6cm) long, are attractively veined, and borne singly from the upper leaf axils from late winter to late spring. ↕ 3–5ft (1–1.5m), ↔ 24–36in (60–90cm). Canary Islands. ❄ (min. 41°F/5°C)

Canarina canariensis

▷ ***Candollea*** see *Hibbertia*

CANISTRUM

BROMELIACEAE

Genus of 7 species of epiphytic or terrestrial, evergreen perennials (bromeliads) from forest in Brazil. The funnel-shaped leaf rosettes consist of strap-shaped, spiny-margined leaves, which are fine-scaly on the undersides. Dense, compound cymes, each consisting of a rounded flowerhead of green, yellowish green to white, yellow, or occasionally blue flowers in a cup of large, colorful bracts, are borne in summer. They are followed by spherical, greenish white fruits containing spindle-shaped seeds. Where not hardy, grow in a warm conservatory or greenhouse; in warmer areas, grow outdoors in a moist, shady site.
• **CULTIVATION** Under glass, grow epiphytically, or in epiphytic bromeliad potting mix, in bright filtered light with moderate humidity. In the growing season, water freely, applying a low-nitrogen fertilizer 3 or 4 times; keep just moist at other times. Outdoors, grow epiphytically on a tree or in humus-rich, sandy soil in partial shade. See also p.47.
• **PROPAGATION** Sow seed at 81°F (27°C) as soon as ripe. Remove offsets in early summer.
• **PESTS AND DISEASES** Scale insects may be a problem.

C. lindenii. Variable, epiphytic bromeliad with funnel-shaped rosettes, to 3ft (1m) across, of mid-green leaves, to 32in (80cm) long, often marked darker green. In summer, bears dense cymes of about 100 narrowly funnel-shaped, white-tipped green flowers surrounded by a cup of yellowish white or green bracts. ↕ to 3ft (1m) or more, ↔ 2–4ft (60–120cm). Brazil. ❄ (min. 61°F/16°C). **var. *roseum*** ▣ has rose-pink to light red bracts.

Canistrum lindenii var. *roseum*

CANNA

Indian shot

CANNACEAE

Genus of about 50 species of rhizomatous herbaceous perennials, mainly from forest margins and moist, open areas in forest in Asia and tropical North and South America. Cannas are grown for their large, alternate, paddle-shaped leaves, 12–24in (30–60cm) long in most species and cultivars; they are pinnately veined and sheathed at the bases. The racemes or panicles of brightly colored flowers are also attractive; each asymmetric flower having 3 petals joined into a tube at the bases, 3 sepals, and showy stamens. Hundreds of hybrids have resulted from complex crosses between various species; they are often grouped under the names *C.* x *generalis* and *C.* x *orchioides.* Because the distinctions between these hybrid groups have been blurred by further interbreeding, these names have not been used in the descriptions below.

Where not hardy, use cannas in summer bedding and lift for winter, or grow in containers or in a cool conservatory or greenhouse. In warmer areas, grow in a border.
• **HARDINESS** Cannas are not normally hardy but may be left *in situ* during winter, protected with a deep, dry mulch in the warmest parts of British Columbia. ❄ (min. 35°F/2°C)
• **CULTIVATION** Under glass, grow in soilless potting mix in full light with shade from hot sun. In growth, water freely and apply a phosphate-rich liquid fertilizer monthly. Outdoors, grow in fertile soil in full sun; water freely in dry spells. Deadhead to promote continued flowering. Plant out in early summer. After autumn frost blackens the foliage, remove the stems and leaves, and lift the rhizomes for winter storage; store in barely moist peat or leaf mold in frost-free conditions.
• **PROPAGATION** Sow seed at 70°F (21°C) in spring or autumn. Chip seed or soak in warm water for 24 hours before sowing. Divide rhizomes into sections, each with a prominent "eye," in spring. Pot up and start into growth at 61°F (16°C); water sparingly at first.
• **PESTS AND DISEASES** Slugs, snails, spider mites, and caterpillars may be problems. Rust, fungal leaf spot, and bacterial blight are common. Bean yellow mosaic and tomato spotted wilt viruses can occur.

Canna 'Assaut'

C. 'Assault' see *C.* 'Assaut'.
C. 'Assaut' ▣ syn. *C.* 'Assault'. Upright, rhizomatous perennial bearing purple-brown leaves, and racemes of orange-scarlet flowers, 3in (8cm) across, from midsummer to autumn. ↕ 6ft (1.8m), ↔ 20in (50cm).
C. 'Black Knight'. Erect, rhizomatous perennial producing bronze foliage. From midsummer to late autumn, bears large racemes of very dark red flowers, 3in (8cm) across, with wavy petals. ↕ 6ft (1.8m), ↔ 20in (50cm).
C. 'Durban'. Erect, rhizomatous perennial producing elliptic, bronze foliage with orange, yellow, and red striations. From midsummer to early autumn, bears racemes of tomato-red flowers, 3in (8cm) across. Excellent in large containers. ↕ 4–5ft (1.2–1.5m), ↔ 20in (50cm).
C. edulis see *C. indica.*
C. 'Endeavour' ▣ Erect, rhizomatous perennial producing blue-green leaves. Racemes of bright soft red flowers, 2in (5cm) across, are borne from midsummer to early autumn. ↕ 5–7ft (1.5–2.2m), ↔ 20in (50cm).
C. Grand Opera Series. Upright, rhizomatous perennials with elliptic, mid-green foliage. From midsummer to early autumn, they bear racemes of flowers, 3in (8cm) across, in shades of peach, pink, or rose. ↕ 5–6ft (1.5–2m), ↔ 20in (50cm).
C. indica, syn. *C. edulis.* Rhizomatous perennial with ovate-lance-shaped to oblong, dark green, often bronze-tinted leaves, to 20in (50cm) long. Racemes or panicles of bright red or soft orange flowers, 2–3in (5–8cm) across, are borne from midsummer to midautumn. ↕ 5–7ft (1.5–2.2m), ↔ 20in (50cm). Tropical and subtropical South America. **'Purpurea'** has dark purple leaves.
C. iridiflora. Upright, rhizomatous perennial with broadly elliptic, dark bluish green leaves, to 3ft (1m) long. Pendent panicles of trumpet-shaped, bright cerise-pink flowers, 4½in (11cm) across, open from midsummer to early autumn. ↕ 10ft (3m), ↔ 20in (50cm). Peru. **'Ehemannii'** ▣ has dark blue-green leaves with red margins, and bears panicles of waxy, bright pinkish red flowers, to 6in (15cm) across; ↕ 6ft (2m), ↔ 24in (60cm).
C. 'King Humbert' see *C.* 'Roi Humbert'.
C. 'King Midas' ▣ Erect, rhizomatous perennial with dark green leaves. Sturdy racemes of golden yellow, orange-

Canna iridiflora 'Ehemannii'

marked flowers, 3in (8cm) across, are borne from midsummer to early autumn. ↕ 5ft (1.5m), ↔ 20in (50cm).
***C. malawiensis* 'Variegata'** see *C.* 'Striata'.
C. 'Pfitzer's Chinese Coral'. Upright, rhizomatous perennial with gray-green leaves. Abundant racemes of coral-pink flowers, 3in (8cm) wide, are borne from midsummer to early autumn. ↕ 32in (80cm), ↔ 20in (50cm).
C. 'President'. Erect, rhizomatous perennial with glossy, blue-green leaves and racemes of rich scarlet flowers, 3in (8cm) across, borne from midsummer to early autumn. ↕ 4ft (1.2m), ↔ 20in (50cm).
C. 'Pretoria' ▣ Erect, rhizomatous perennial producing mid-green leaves with yellow striations. From midsummer to early autumn, bears racemes of orange flowers, 2½–3in (6–8cm) across. ↕ 6ft (2m), ↔ 20in (50cm).
C. 'Red King Humbert' see *C.* 'Roi Humbert'.
C. 'Roi Humbert', syn. *C.* 'King Humbert', *C.* 'Red King Humbert'. Erect, rhizomatous perennial with elliptic, bronze-purple leaves. Bears racemes of red flowers, 3in (8cm) across,

Canna 'Pretoria'

from midsummer to early autumn. ↕ to 8ft (2.5m), ↔ 20in (50cm).
C. 'Rosemond Coles' ▣ Upright, rhizomatous perennial with large, mid-green leaves. From midsummer to early autumn, bears racemes of red flowers, 3in (8cm) across, with yellow margins and yellow-spotted throats; the undersides of the petals are golden. ↕ 5ft (1.5m), ↔ 20in (50cm).
C. 'Striata', syn. *C. malawiensis* 'Variegata'. Erect, rhizomatous perennial with dark red-purple stems and light green to yellow-green leaves, 10–20in (25–50cm) long, with bright yellow veins. Racemes of orange flowers, 3in (8cm) across, are produced from midsummer to early autumn. ↕ 5ft (1.5m), ↔ 20in (50cm).

Canna 'Rosemond Coles'

C. 'Stuttgart'. Upright, rhizomatous perennial producing narrowly elliptic, mid-green leaves with dark green, grayish green, and cream variegation and white stripes. The foliage may burn under hot, dry conditions. From midsummer to early autumn, produces racemes of flowers, 2in (5cm) across. The flowers have pale pink sepals, each with a central green stripe, and red-flushed, yellow-orange petals. ↕ 5–7ft (1.5–2.2m), ↔ 36in (90cm).
C. 'Tropical Rose' ▣ Upright, rhizomatous perennial with elliptic, mid-green leaves. Racemes of rose-pink flowers, 2–3in (5–8cm) across, are produced from midsummer to early autumn. Blooms the first year from seed. ↕ 20–24in (50–60cm), ↔ 20in (50cm).
C. 'TyTy Red'. Erect, rhizomatous perennial with elliptic-paddle-shaped, bronze-purple leaves. Bears racemes of orange-red flowers, 3in (8cm) across, from midsummer to early autumn. ↕ 6ft (2m), ↔ 20in (50cm).
C. 'Wyoming'. Upright, rhizomatous perennial producing brown-purple leaves with darker purple veins. From midsummer to early autumn, bears racemes of frilled orange flowers, 4in (10cm) across, with apricot feathering and darker orange margins. ↕ 6ft (2m), ↔ 20in (50cm).
C. 'Yellow King Humbert'. Upright, rhizomatous perennial with elliptic, mid-green foliage. Racemes of red-splashed, yellow flowers, 3in (8cm) across, are produced from midsummer to early autumn. ↕ 3–4ft (1–1.2m), ↔ 20in (50cm).

Canna 'Endeavour'

Canna 'King Midas'

Canna 'Tropical Rose'

CANTUA

POLEMONIACEAE

Genus of 6 species of evergreen, small trees and shrubs of arching, sometimes scandent habit, usually found in mountainous areas of South America. The alternate leaves are simple and borne on short leaf stalks. The showy, tubular, 5-lobed flowers, borne in terminal corymbs, are red, purple, violet, or white. Where not hardy, grow cantuas in a cool greenhouse. In frost-free climates, they are suitable for growing against a wall or pillar, or in a shrub border, allowed to climb and scramble through other plants.

• **CULTIVATION** Under glass, grow in soil-based potting mix in full light. Water freely during the growing season, applying a balanced liquid fertilizer monthly; water more sparingly in winter. Stand containers outdoors in summer. Top-dress or pot on in spring. The long, flexible stems require support. Outdoors, grow in fertile, moist but well-drained soil in a warm, sheltered site in full sun. *C. buxifolia* can withstand short periods of 32°F (0°C) if grown in a warm, sheltered position. Pruning group 11, after flowering.

• **PROPAGATION** Sow seed at 59–64°F (15–18°C) in spring. Root semi-ripe cuttings in summer.

• **PESTS AND DISEASES** Spider mites and whiteflies may be problems, particularly under glass.

C. buxifolia ▣ syn. *C. dependens* (Sacred flower of the Incas). Upright, often semi-scandent shrub with elliptic to lance-shaped, lobed, softly hairy, mid-green leaves, 1–2in (2.5–5cm) long. In spring, bears terminal corymbs of long-tubed, pendent flowers, 2½–3in (6–8cm) long, the tubes pink to purple, the petal lobes red. ↕ 6–15ft (2–5m), ↔ 5–8ft (1.5–2.5m). Peru, Bolivia, N. Chile. ❄ (min. 45°F/7°C)
C. dependens see *C. buxifolia.*

Cantua buxifolia

CAPSICUM

Chili pepper, Pepper

SOLANACEAE

Genus of up to 10 species of erect or spreading, many-branched annuals and perennials from wasteland and lowland forest margins in tropical North and South America. They have entire leaves, which are alternate or borne in groups of 2 or 3 at the nodes. Star- to bell-shaped, yellow, white, greenish white, purple, or purple-tinged flowers are produced singly or in clusters of 2 or 3 from the leaf axils. Capsicums are cultivated as crop plants and ornamentals for their shiny, chambered, many-seeded, variably shaped fruits, which are green at first, often ripening to yellow, orange, purple, or red. The genus includes bell peppers as well as hot chili peppers. Where not hardy, capsicums are used ornamentally as houseplants, for windowboxes, bedding, and patio containers, or for a warm greenhouse or conservatory.

• **CULTIVATION** Under glass, grow in soil-based potting mix in bright filtered light. When in growth, water freely and apply a balanced liquid fertilizer every 10 days until fruit begins to color. Provide tall cultivars with support. In summer, maintain high humidity and temperatures of at least 70–77°F (21–25°C). Mist flowers daily with water to encourage fruiting. Outdoors, grow in fertile, well-drained soil enriched with compost or manure, in full sun. Pinch out the growing tips of young plants to promote branching.

• **PROPAGATION** Sow seed at 70°F (21°C) in late winter.

• **PESTS AND DISEASES** Spider mites and aphids are a problem under glass. Bacterial and fungal spots (anthracnose) and wilt diseases are common. Gray mold, stem and root rots, Southern blight, and fruit rot also occur.

C. annuum (Chili pepper, Paprika). Annual or short-lived perennial with alternate, lance-shaped to ovate, mid-green leaves, to 5in (13cm) long. Solitary, star- to bell-shaped, white or yellow flowers, to ½in (1.5cm) across, are produced from the leaf axils in summer, or all year round, depending on the climate. The pendent, narrowly conical fruit, to 6in (15cm) long, are used fresh or dried. ↕ 5ft (1.5m), ↔ 20in (50cm). Tropical North and South America. ❄ (min. 39°F/4°C). Many cultivars, including forms with dark purple and white-variegated leaves, and a wide diversity of fruit shape and color, are available. They are divided into 5 main groups, varying in shape, color, and flavor. **Cerasiforme Group 'Birdseye'** is well branched and dense with narrow, bright green leaves and profuse white flowers; **Cerasiforme Group 'Holiday Cheer'** is bushy and well branched, with cream-colored fruit that turn yellow, brushed with purple, then red. **Conioides Group 'Thai Hot'** is compact, with many, very hot-flavored, tiny green fruit, maturing to red; ↕ 8in (20cm). **Fasciculatum Group** (Red cone pepper) cultivars bear hot-flavored, clustered, upright, conical, bright red fruit, to 3in (8cm) long; **Fasciculatum Group 'Fips'** is compact, with dark green foliage and conical red fruit, 2½in (6cm) long; ↕ 10–12in (25–30cm). **Grossum Group** (Bell pepper) cultivars bear sweet, irregularly ovoid-bell-shaped green fruit, 4–5in (10–13cm) long, which ripen to yellow, crimson, or deep purple. **Longum Group 'Hot Pepper'** (Cayenne pepper, Chili pepper) cultivars bear very hot-tasting, pendent, tapered fruit, 6–12in (15–30cm) long, in shades from red to black-purple; some have variegated leaves; **Longum Group 'Fiesta'** is compact and bushy with narrow, curved, cream-colored fruit, turning orange, then red.

Capsicum annum 'Hot Pepper'

CARAGANA

Peashrub

FABACEAE

Genus of 80 species of deciduous, often spiny shrubs or small trees found on dry soils in exposed sites from E. Europe to China. They are cultivated for their leaves, which are alternate, pinnate, and often clustered, and their pea-like flowers, which are usually yellow, but sometimes white or pink. Flowers are followed in autumn by slender brown pods, ¾–2½in (2–6cm) long. Grow in a shrub border or as windbreaks.

Caragana brevispina

• **CULTIVATION** Grow in well-drained, moderately fertile soil in full sun. Will thrive even in poor, dry soils in cold and exposed positions. May become weedy. Pruning group 1.

• **PROPAGATION** Sow seed in containers in an open frame as soon as ripe; pre-soak spring-sown seed in warm water. Root greenwood cuttings in late spring. Graft in late winter; *C. arborescens* 'Pendula' is usually top-grafted.

• **PESTS AND DISEASES** Infrequent.

C. arborescens (Siberian pea tree). Erect, thorny shrub with pinnate, light green leaves, to 3in (8cm) long, composed of up to 12 elliptic leaflets. Pale yellow flowers, to ¾in (2cm) long, are borne singly or in small clusters in late spring. ↕ 20ft (6m), ↔ 12ft (4m). Russia (Siberia), N. China. Zone 2. **'Lorbergii'** has elegant leaves, with 10–14 long, linear-lance-shaped leaflets, and small flowers, to ½in (1.5cm) long. **'Nana'** ▣ has a dwarf, congested habit and twisted shoots; ↕ 5ft (1.5m), ↔ 3ft (1m). **'Pendula'** has stiff, pendent shoots; ↕ 5ft (1.5m), ↔ 4ft (1.2m). **'Walker'** has fern-like leaves on pendent shoots; ↕ 5ft (1.5m), ↔ 3ft (1m).

Caragana arborescens 'Nana'

C. brevispina ▣ Spiny shrub with long, arching shoots, pink-tinged when young. Pinnate, softly hairy, mid-green leaves, to 4in (10cm) long, have up to 10 oblong to lance-shaped leaflets. In spring, produces clusters of 3 or 4 yellowish green flowers, to ¾in (2cm) long, becoming reddish yellow with age. ↕6–10ft (2–3m), ↔ 12ft (4m). N.W. Himalayas. Zone 6b.
C. frutex (Russian pea shrub). Shrub with upright, slender shoots and pinnate, dark green leaves, to 1in (2.5cm) long, each consisting of 2 pairs of stalkless, ovate leaflets. Bright yellow flowers, to 1in (2.5cm) long, are produced singly from the leaf axils in late spring and early summer. ↕10ft (3m), ↔ 8ft (2.5m). S. former USSR, C. Asia. Zone 2.
C. pygmaea. Low-growing, spiny shrub with arching or prostrate shoots and pinnate, mid-green leaves, ¾–1¼in (2–3cm) long, consisting of 2 pairs of inversely lance-shaped leaflets. From late spring to summer, bears pendent yellow flowers, to 1in (2.5cm) long, singly along the shoots. ↕3ft (1m), ↔ 5ft (1.5m). Caucasus to E. Russia (Siberia) and China (Tibet). Zone 2b.

CARALLUMA *syn.* FREREA

ASCLEPIADACEAE

Genus of 80–100 species of tufted or clump-forming, often stoloniferous, perennial succulents from dry areas of the Mediterranean, Africa, Socotra, the Arabian Peninsula, India, and Myanmar. The succulent stems bear leaves that are just scales in most species. The open bell-shaped, 5-lobed, axillary or terminal flowers, solitary or in umbels, often exude a pungent odor. Tufted seeds are contained in cylindrical, grayish green follicles. Where not hardy, grow in a warm greenhouse; in warm, dry climates, use outdoors in a semi-desert garden.
• **CULTIVATION** Under glass, grow in standard cactus potting mix in bright filtered light in summer and full light in winter. In growth, water moderately and apply a low-nitrogen fertilizer monthly; to avoid desiccation, water very sparingly in winter. Outdoors, grow in sharply drained, humus-rich, sandy soil in partial shade. See also pp.48–49.
• **PROPAGATION** Sow seed at 64–70°F (18–21°C) in late spring or early summer. Take stem cuttings in spring, allow calluses to form, then root in partial shade.

Caralluma joannis

• **PESTS AND DISEASES** Prone to scale insects, mealybugs, root mealybugs, and fungal rots.

C. albocastanea see *Orbeopsis albocastanea.*
C. burchardii. Cushion-forming, leafless succulent with 4-angled, gray- green to bluish green stems with deep marginal teeth. Terminal umbels of up to 6 olive-green or reddish brown flowers, each to ½in (1.5cm) across, with white-hairy corolla lobes, are borne in summer. Canary Islands, Morocco. ↕to 8in (20cm), ↔ to 7in (18cm). ❀ (min. 50°F/10°C)
C. dummeri see *Pachycymbium dummeri.*
C. europaea, syn. *Stapelia europaea.* Variable, leafless succulent with 4-angled, blunt-margined, gray-green stems, often spotted pale red. In summer, bears terminal umbels of 10 or more greenish yellow or reddish brown flowers, to ½in (1.5cm) across, the pointed yellow corolla lobes with reddish brown tips and purple stripes. ↕5in (13cm), ↔ to 8in (20cm). S. Italy, Spain, N. Africa. ❀ (min. 50°F/10°C)
C. frerei, syn. *Frerea indica.* Succulent with rounded, few-branched, prostrate or pendent, fleshy, pale green stems. The persistent, opposite, fleshy leaves, ¾–1¼in (2–3cm) long, are oblong or ovoid. In summer, bears solitary or paired, terminal, red-brown or maroon flowers, ¾in (2cm) across, with yellow- or white-marked lobes. ↕↔ to 5in (13cm). E. India. ❀ (min. 50°F/10°C)
C. joannis ▣ Leafless succulent with erect or pendent, square to rounded, minutely toothed, purple-green stems. In summer, bears umbels of 2–10 flowers, each to 1in (2.5cm) across, with red-spotted, olive-yellow tubes and velvety purple lobes tipped with fine hairs. ↕4in (10cm) or more, ↔ 5in (13cm). Morocco. ❀ (min. 50°F/10°C)
C. lutea see *Orbeopsis lutea.*
C. pillansii see *Quaqua pillansii.*

CARDAMINE *syn.* DENTARIA

Bittercress

BRASSICACEAE

Genus of about 150 species of annuals and perennials from cool, shady, damp habitats almost worldwide, but chiefly in the N. hemisphere. Some of the annuals are invasive garden weeds. The rootstock is fibrous or has scaly rhizomes. Cardamines have simple,

Cardamine enneaphyllos

Cardamine pentaphyllos

pinnate or palmate leaves and unbranched stems bearing panicles or racemes (some short and congested) of 4-petaled, white, yellow, pink, lilac, or reddish violet flowers. Grow in a border, a rock garden, a woodland, or a bog.
• **CULTIVATION** Grow in humus-rich, moist soil in full or partial shade.
• **PROPAGATION** Sow seed in containers in a cold frame in autumn or spring. Divide in spring or after flowering. Root leaf-tip cuttings of *C. pratensis* in midsummer; they may also form bulbils or plantlets in the axils of the leaflets.
• **PESTS AND DISEASES** White rust, downy mildew, powdery mildew, and rust. Flea beetles may damage leaves.

C. asarifolia. Stoloniferous, clump-forming perennial producing prostrate, rooting stems and simple, kidney-shaped, mid-green leaves, 4–6in (10–15cm) long. Compact racemes of white flowers, each ¼–½in (6–15mm) across, with violet anthers, are borne in late spring and early summer. ↕12–18in (30–45cm), ↔ to 24in (60cm). S. France, N. Italy. Zone 6.
C. enneaphyllos ▣ syn. *Dentaria enneaphyllos.* Spreading, rhizomatous

Cardamine pratensis 'Flore Pleno'

Cardamine trifolia

perennial producing whorls of 2- to 4-ternate or 3- to 5-palmate, toothed, mid-green leaves, 4–5in (10–13cm) long, composed of ovate to lance- shaped leaflets. Lax panicles of pendent, white or yellowish white flowers, ¾in (2cm) or more across are produced in late spring. ↕8–16in (20–40cm), ↔ 18–24in (45–60cm). W. Carpathians and E. Alps to S. Italy, N.W. Balkans. Zone 6.
C. latifolia see *C. raphanifolia.*
C. pentaphyllos ▣ syn. *Dentaria digitata, D. pentaphyllos.* Clump-forming, rhizomatous perennial with toothed, 5-palmate, mid-green leaves, 4–5in (10–13cm) long, composed of lance-shaped leaflets. Loose racemes of white, pale purple, or lilac flowers, to 1in (2.5cm) across, in late spring and early summer. ↕12–20in (30–50cm), ↔ 12in (30cm). Pyrenees to S. Germany and N.W. Balkans. Zone 6.
C. pratensis (Cuckoo flower, Lady's smock). Variable perennial with short rhizomes and rosettes of pinnate, gray-green to glossy, dark green leaves, to 6in (15cm) long, composed of 2–8 pairs of ovate to rounded or kidney-shaped leaflets, often producing plantlets. Panicles of purple, lilac, or white flowers, ½–1¼in (1–3cm) across, are produced in late spring. ↕12–18in (30–45cm), ↔ 12in (30cm). Europe, N. Asia, North America. Zone 5. **'Edith'** has pink buds, opening to double flowers that fade to white; ↕8in (20cm). **'Flore Pleno'** ▣ forms compact clumps and freely produces plantlets in the basal leaf clusters; it has double, lilac-pink flowers; ↕8in (20cm).
C. raphanifolia, syn. *C. latifolia.* Rhizomatous, spreading perennial with pinnate, dark green leaves, 4–6in (10–15cm) long, composed of 1–6 pairs of ovate to rounded, toothed leaflets. Panicles of lilac, reddish violet, or white flowers, ½–¾in (1–2cm) across, are borne in early summer. ↕18–32in (45–80cm), ↔ 24in (60cm). Mountains of S. Europe. Zone 4.
C. trifolia ▣ (Trifoliate bittercress). Creeping perennial with short rhizomes and 3-palmate, dark green leaves, ¾–1¼in (2–3cm) long, each with 3 rounded to diamond-shaped leaflets, red-tinted beneath. In late spring, produces short, congested racemes of open cup-shaped, yellow-anthered, white, occasionally pink flowers, ½–¾in (1–2cm) across. ↕to 6in (15cm), ↔ to 12in (30cm). Mountainous, wooded areas in C. and S. Europe. Zone 6.

CARDIOCRINUM

Giant lily

LILIACEAE

Genus of 3 species of large, bulbous, monocarpic perennials found in scrub and forest in the Himalayas, Japan, and China. They are cultivated for their spectacular, lily-like, trumpet-shaped flowers, borne in summer, and their attractive, heart-shaped, veined leaves. The flowers are followed by large, decorative, upright, oblong-ovoid, pale brown seed capsules, 2–2½in (5–6cm) long. The bulbs take several years to reach maturity and die after flowering, leaving numerous offsets. Grow in a woodland garden or in a shaded, sheltered border.

• **CULTIVATION** Plant bulbs just below the soil surface in autumn, in a cool, partially shaded, sheltered site in deep, fertile, humus-rich, moist but well-drained soil. Water freely in dry periods, but do not allow to become waterlogged; they are intolerant of hot or dry conditions. Apply a balanced liquid fertilizer 2 or 3 times when in growth, to encourage the development of offsets. Top-dress annually with leaf mold. Provide a deep winter mulch.

• **PROPAGATION** Sow seed in deep trays in a cool, shaded bulb frame as soon as ripe. Remove offsets after flowering. Offsets may take 4–5 years to flower; seed-raised plants take 7 years or more.

• **PESTS AND DISEASES** Prone to lily viruses and slug damage.

C. cordatum, syn. *Lilium cordatum*. Bulbous perennial with broad, heart-shaped, dark green leaves, to 12in (30cm) long, stained maroon when young, borne on the lower part of the stems. In summer, thick, hollow stems bear congested, terminal racemes of 4–10, occasionally up to 20, trumpet-shaped, scented, creamy white flowers, to 6in (15cm) long, with purple marks on the lower tepals. ↕4–6ft (1.2–2m), PD12in (30cm). Japan, Russia (Sakhalin). Zone 7b.

C. giganteum ▣ syn. *Lilium giganteum*. Bulbous perennial with basal rosettes of large, broadly ovate, glossy, dark green leaves, to 18in (45cm) long. Smaller leaves are produced on the tall, thick flower stems, which in summer bear racemes of up to 20 large, nodding, trumpet-shaped, strongly scented white flowers, 6–8in (15–20cm) long, with

Cardiocrinum giganteum

Cardiocrinum giganteum var. *yunnanense*

maroon stripes inside. ↕5–12ft (1.5–4m), PD18in (45cm). Himalayas, N.W. Myanmar, S.W. China. Zone 7.

var. *yunnanense* ▣ has bronze-purple stems, leaves, and young shoots; the flowers are often tinted green; W. and C. China.

CARDIOSPERMUM

SAPINDACEAE

Genus of 14 species of evergreen, perennial, woody-stemmed tendril climbers from forest margins in tropical Africa, India, and North and South America. They are cultivated for their attractive, fern-like foliage and decorative, swollen seed pods. The alternate, 2-ternate leaves have deeply toothed or pinnatifid leaflets. Small flowers, with 4 unequal petals, are borne in stalked, axillary corymbs, each with a pair of opposite tendrils. Where not hardy, grow outdoors as annuals, or in a temperate greenhouse. In warmer regions, train over a tall tree stump, archway, pergola, or arbor.

• **CULTIVATION** Under glass, grow in soil-based potting mix in bright filtered light. In the growing season, water freely and apply a liquid fertilizer monthly; keep just moist in winter. Pot on or top-dress in spring. Outdoors, grow in fertile, moist but well-drained soil in full sun. Provide support. In early spring, thin out congested growth of plants grown as perennials.

• **PROPAGATION** Sow seed at 64–70°F (18–21°C) in spring. Root softwood cuttings in summer.

• **PESTS AND DISEASES** Aphids and whiteflies may be problems.

C. halicacabum (Balloon vine, Heart seed, Love-in-a-puff). Slender, woody-based, evergreen tendril climber, normally grown as an annual or biennial. Leaves 6–8in (15–20cm) long are divided into 7–9 oblong-ovate, deeply toothed to pinnatifid, bright green leaflets. Bears tiny, greenish white flowers, ¼in (6mm) across, from summer to autumn. They are followed by ovoid, membranous, 3-angled, balloon-like capsules, ¾–1¼in (2–3cm) long, which mature from light green to brown. ↕10–12ft (3–4m). Tropical Africa, India, North and South America. ❀ (min. 45–50°F/7–10°C)

CAREX

Sedge

CYPERACEAE

Vast genus of 1,500 or more species of deciduous and evergreen, rhizomatous or tufted perennials from temperate and arctic zones, as well as high altitudes in tropical regions. Most species occur in bog, moorland, or damp woodland, or by water. Sedges are mainly cultivated for their variegated or colorful foliage, although some species have attractive inflorescences. The generally grass-like leaves are usually linear, 3-ranked, and with leaf bases sheathing the triangular stems, which are solid and without nodes. Sedges are mainly monoecious, occasionally dioecious, and bear panicles of small, grass-like flowers in short spikes. There are sedges for nearly every site in the garden.

• **CULTIVATION** Sedges have varying cultivation requirements. These are grouped as follows:

1. Most soils in sun or partial shade. Avoid extremes of wet or dry.
2. Fertile, moist but well-drained soil in sun or partial shade.
3. Fertile, moist or wet soil in sun or partial shade.

In summer, cut out any dead leaves on evergreen species.

• **PROPAGATION** Sow seed of New Zealand species at 50–55°F (10–13°C) in early spring; expose those from Europe and North America to winter cold in a cold frame. Divide between midspring and early summer.

• **PESTS AND DISEASES** Rust, smuts, and many fungal leaf spots are common. Aphids are sometimes present.

Carex elata 'Aurea'

C. berggrenii. Miniature, evergreen perennial with short rhizomes, spreading slowly and forming loose tufts of short, blunt, blue-green, metallic-gray, or reddish brown leaves, to 2in (5cm) long. Small brown flower spikes, to ¼in (6mm) long, are borne on stems to 4in (10cm) long in midsummer. Cultivation group 2. ↕4in (10cm), ↔6in (15cm). New Zealand. Zone 6.

C. buchananii (Leatherleaf sedge). Densely tufted, evergreen perennial of symmetrical, arching habit, with short rhizomes and orange-brown leaves, to 18in (45cm) long, curled at the tips. In mid- and late summer, produces brown flower spikes, ¼–1¼in (0.5–3cm) long, on lax stems, to 20in (50cm) long. Cultivation group 1. ↕20–30in (50–75cm), ↔36in (90cm). New Zealand. Zone 6.

C. comans (New England hair sedge). Densely tufted, evergreen perennial forming tussocks of hair-like, pale yellow-green, pale gray, or reddish brown leaves, 10in (25cm) or more long. Inconspicuous brown flower spikes, ¼–1in (0.5–2.5cm) long, are produced on stems to 10in (25cm) long in mid- and late summer. Variants with warm brown foliage have been selected. Cultivation group 1. ↕10–14in (25–35cm), ↔30in (75cm). New Zealand. Zone 6b.

***C. conica* 'Hime-kan-suge'** see *C. conica* 'Snowline'.

***C. conica* 'Snowline'**, syn. *C. conica* 'Hime-kan-suge'. Small, tufted, evergreen perennial with dark green, white-margined leaves, to 6in (15cm) long, forming dense, low, arching tufts. Small, dark brown-purple flower spikes, ½–1in (1–2.5cm) long, are produced on stems to 6in (15cm) long, in early summer. Cultivation group 2. ↕6in (15cm), ↔10in (25cm). Zone 5b.

***C. elata* 'Aurea'** ▣ syn. *C. stricta* 'Aurea' (Bowles' golden sedge). Deciduous perennial with short rhizomes, forming a dense clump of gently arching, rich yellow leaves, 16–24in (40–60cm) long, narrowly margined in green. In late spring and early summer, stems 20in (50cm) or more long bear brown male flower spikes, to 1in (2.5cm) long, above 2 or 3 stalkless green female spikes, ½–1½in (1.5–4cm) long. Cultivation group 3. ↕to 28in (70cm), ↔18in (45cm). Zone 5.

C. flagellifera ▣ Densely tufted, evergreen perennial with short rhizomes.

Carex flagellifera

C

Carex grayi

Carex pendula

Carex siderosticha 'Variegata'

It is similar to *C. comans*, but taller and with broader green or reddish brown leaves, 16–28in (40–70cm) long. Stems bearing light brown flower spikes, ¼–1in (0.5–2.5cm) long, elongate to over 36in (90cm) as the red-brown fruit mature. Variants in cultivation often have red-brown foliage. Cultivation group 1. ↕ 3½ft (1.1m), ↔ 36in (90cm). New Zealand. Zone 6.

***C.* 'Frosted Curls'.** Densely tufted, evergreen perennial with short rhizomes and arching, narrow, shiny, pale silvery green leaves, to 24in (60cm) long, curling at the tips. From early to late summer, bears small, cylindrical green flower spikes, ¼–½in (6–15mm) long, on stems 18–24in (45–60cm) long. Cultivation group 1. ↕ 24in (60cm), ↔ 18in (45cm). Zone 5.

C. grayi ▣ (Gray's sedge). Deciduous, densely tufted perennial, with short rhizomes, forming strong, erect clumps of broad, rich green leaves, to 24in (60cm) long. Stems 24in (60cm) long bear mid-green flower spikes, ½–¾in (1.5–2cm) long, from early to late summer, followed by star-like, pale green seed heads; these resemble spiked clubs and are good for flower arranging. Cultivation group 3. ↕ to 30in (75cm), ↔ 24in (60cm). North America. Zone 4.

***C. hachijoensis* 'Evergold'** ▣ syn. *C. oshimensis* 'Evergold'. Tufted, evergreen perennial, with short rhizomes, forming a low mound of dark green leaves, to 10in (25cm) long, each with a broad, creamy yellow central stripe. In mid- and late spring, bears brown flower spikes, ½–1¼in (1–3cm) long, on stems to 6in (15cm) long. Often confused with *C. morrowii*. Cultivation group 2. ↕ 12in (30cm), ↔ 14in (35cm). Zone 6b.

***C. morrowii* cultivars.** Clump-forming, evergreen perennials with broad, stiff, shiny, mid-green leaves, 16in (40cm) long. Panicles of green-and-brown flower spikes, ¾–2in (2–5cm) long, are borne on stems to 18in (45cm) long, in late spring. Cultivation group 2. ↕ 18–20in (45–50cm), ↔ 12in (30cm). Zone 5. **'Fisher'**, syn. *C. morrowii* 'Fisher's Form', has conspicuously cream-striped and cream-margined leaves. **'Variegata'** (Silver variegated Japanese sedge) has lightly variegated and narrowly silver-margined leaves. Zone 7b.

***C. morrowii* 'Fisher's Form'** see *C. morrowii* 'Fisher'.

C. muskingumensis (Palm branch sedge). Loosely tufted, deciduous, gently spreading perennial with erect stems that bear horizontally held, bright green leaves, to 30in (75cm) long. In early and midsummer, produces golden brown flower spikes, ½–1in (1.5–2.5cm) long, on stems 24–30in (60–75cm) long. Cultivation group 3. ↕ 28in (75cm), ↔ 18in (45cm). North America. Zone 4.

C. nigra. Clump-forming or tufted evergreen perennial with slender or occasionally absent rhizomes and mid-green leaves, 4–24in (10–60cm) long. Stems, 4–24in (10–60cm) long, bear dark black-brown or red-brown flower spikes, ¼–1½in (.6–4cm) long, in early summer. Cultivation group 2. ↕↔ 6–9in (15–22cm). Europe. Zone 4b.

C. ornithopoda (Bird's foot sedge). Clump-forming, dense, evergreen perennial with short rhizomes, and keeled, light green leaves, 2–8in (5–20cm) long. In late spring, bears slender, orange-brown flower spikes, ¼–1in (6–15mm) long, becoming curved and claw-like, on stems 2–6in (5–15cm) long. Cultivation group 2. ↕↔ 2–6in (5–15cm). N.W. Europe. Zone 4. **'Variegata'** has narrowly white-striped leaves.

***C. oshimensis* 'Evergold'** see *C. hachijoensis* 'Evergold'.

C. pendula ▣ (Drooping sedge, Pendulous sedge, Weeping sedge). Tufted, evergreen perennial forming dense clumps of relatively wide, keeled, shiny, mid-green leaves, to 36in (90cm) long, and blue-green beneath. In late spring and early summer, arching stems, to 4½ft (1.4m) long, bear cylindrical, catkin-like, dark brown flower spikes, to 6in (15cm) long; erect at first, they become pendent with age. Cultivation group 3. ↕ to 4½ft (1.4m), ↔ to 5ft (1.5m). Europe, N. Africa. Zone 4.

C. petriei. Densely tufted, evergreen perennial with short rhizomes and erect or arching, pale pinkish brown leaves, to 12in (30cm) long, with curled tips. In early and midsummer, produces stubby, red-brown flower spikes, ½–1¼in (1–3cm) long, on stems to 10in (25cm) long. Cultivation group 1. ↕ 10in (25cm), ↔ 6in (15cm). New Zealand. Zone 7b.

***C. pilulifera* 'Tinney's Princess'.** Deciduous perennial, similar to, but more delicate than *C. hachijoensis* 'Evergold'. The leaves, to 4in (10cm) long, have broad, creamy yellow central stripes and narrow, dark green margins. In midspring, stems to 6in (15cm) long each bear a single, terminal, cylindrical brown male spike, ¾–1½in (2–4cm) long, and several red-brown female spikes, ¾–1½in (2–4cm) long, clustered just below the male. Cultivation group 5. ↕↔ 6in (15cm). Zone 7b.

C. plantaginea. Clump-forming evergreen perennial with flat-spreading, many-veined, mid-green leaves, 16in (40cm) long. In spring, bears narrow, long-stalked, brownish black flower spikes, to 4in (10cm) long, on stems 8in (20cm) long. Cultivation group 1. ↕ 12–24in (30–60cm), ↔ 24–30in (60–75cm). North America. Zone 5.

***C. siderosticha* 'Variegata'** ▣ Slowly spreading, deciduous, rhizomatous perennial, forming clumps of relatively broad, linear-lance-shaped, pale green leaves, to 10in (25cm) long, margined and narrowly striped white, and pink-flushed at the bases. Slender, pale brown flower spikes, ⅛–¼in (3–6mm) long, open on stems to 12in (30cm) long, in late spring. Cultivation group 3. ↕ 12in (30cm), ↔ 16in (40cm) or more. Zone 5.

***C. stricta* 'Aurea'** see *C. elata* 'Aurea'.

C. sylvatica (Forest sedge, Wood sedge). Tufted, evergreen perennial with narrow, flat to furrowed, yellow-green leaves, to 3ft (1m) long. In midspring, bears pale green spikes, ½–3in (1–8cm) long, on thin stems, 2–10in (5–25cm) long. Cultivation group 3. ↕ to 6ft (2m), ↔ 16–36in (15–90cm). Europe. Zone 4.

C. testacea. Densely tufted, evergreen perennial with arching, pale olive-green leaves, to 24in (60cm) long, orange-brown on the surfaces that receive full light. Bears cylindrical, pale to dark brown flower spikes, to 1in (2.5cm) long, on stems 20–24in (50–60cm) long, in midsummer; stems later elongate in fruit to 5ft (1.5m). Cultivation group 1. ↕ to 5ft (1.5m), ↔ 24in (60cm). New Zealand. ❀ (min. 41°F/5°C)

Carex hachijoensis 'Evergold'

Carissa macrocarpa

CARISSA

APOCYNACEAE

Genus of about 20 species of evergreen, often spiny shrubs and small trees from dry, open woodland in tropical and subtropical Africa and Asia. The leaves are opposite, entire, and leathery. The tubular flowers, with 5 spreading petal lobes, are borne singly or in terminal or axillary cymes, and are followed by red or black, fleshy fruits. Although the flesh of these is edible and used for jam-making, the seeds are poisonous. Where not hardy, grow in a cool greenhouse. In frost-free areas, grow outdoors in a shrub border, or as hedging.

• **CULTIVATION** Under glass, grow in soil-based potting mix in bright filtered light. When in growth, water moderately and apply a balanced liquid fertilizer monthly; water sparingly in winter. Top-dress or pot on in spring. Outdoors, grow in moderately fertile, well-drained soil in full sun; partial shade is tolerated. Pruning group 8; plants under glass may need restrictive pruning. Trim hedges after flowering.

• **PROPAGATION** Sow seed at 59–64°F (15–18°C) as soon as ripe or in spring. Root semi-ripe cuttings in summer.

• **PESTS AND DISEASES** Anthracnose, stem galls, and dieback are common.

C. grandiflora see *C. macrocarpa*.

C. macrocarpa ■ syn. *C. grandiflora* (Natal plum). Many-branched, spiny shrub with ovate, rich green leaves, to 3in (8cm) long. Fragrant, waxy, white, jasmine-like flowers, 2in (5cm) wide, are borne in terminal or axillary cymes, to 4in (10cm) long, in late spring; they are followed by plum-like, ovoid-ellipsoid, red to purple-black fruit, 2in (5cm) long. ↕ 6–10ft (2–3m) or more, ↔ 10ft (3m) or more. South Africa (KwaZulu/Natal). ❀ (min. 45°F/7°C). Various cultivars have been selected, including **'Fancy'**, which is erect and very free-flowering, with glossy, dark green leaves and orange-red fruit, and **'Tuttlei'** ■ which is dwarf, semi-prostrate, and dense, and useful as a groundcover or for containers; ↕ 3ft (1m), ↔ to 6ft (2m).

C. spectabilis see *Acokanthera oblongifolia*.

Carissa macrocarpa 'Tuttlei'

CARLINA

Carline thistle

ASTERACEAE

Genus of about 28 species of annuals and perennials occurring in poor soils in Europe and Asia. The leaves form basal rosettes and are spiny and entire to pinnatisect. Large, solitary or cyme-like, occasionally stemless flowerheads are borne in summer; these have shiny, papery bracts and, in most species, are good for drying. The smaller species are suitable for a rock garden.

• **CULTIVATION** Grow in poor, well-drained soil in full sun; soil must not become waterlogged or the stems will rot. The compact, stemless habit of *C. acaulis* is lost on fertile soils.

• **PROPAGATION** Sow seed in autumn *in situ*, or in containers in a cold frame.

• **PESTS AND DISEASES** Infrequent.

C. acaulis (Stemless carline thistle). Clump-forming, short-lived perennial or monocarpic biennial with rosetted, pinnatifid to pinnatisect, elliptic-oblong, spiny-margined leaves, to 12in (30cm) long. Stemless flowerheads, to 4in (10cm) across, with silvery, off-white (sometimes pink-flushed) bracts surrounding a pale brown central disk, are borne in the center of the rosettes in mid- and late summer. ↕ to 4in (10cm), ↔ to 10in (25cm). Alpine pastures of S. and E. Europe. Zone 4b.

CARLUDOVICA

CYCLANTHACEAE

Genus of 3 species of short-stemmed or stemless, palm-like perennials from woodland in tropical North and South America. The very long-stalked, rounded leaves are divided into several fan-like segments, each one deeply and narrowly lobed. Insignificant, fleshy, unisexual flowers are borne in cone-like spadices produced from the leaf axils in summer; they develop into showy red berries. Where not hardy, grow in a temperate or warm greenhouse, or plant outdoors in summer to lend a tropical effect to summer bedding. In tropical and subtropical regions, use in shady sites, especially beneath trees, where the handsome foliage may be displayed to best advantage. The large leaves are used to make Panama hats.

• **CULTIVATION** Under glass, grow in soilless potting mix in full light with shade from hot sun. When in growth, water freely and apply a balanced liquid fertilizer monthly; water sparingly in winter. Pot on or top-dress in spring. Outdoors, grow in well-drained soil, ideally with some midday shade or in partial shade.

Carludovica palmata

• **PROPAGATION** Sow seed at 64–70°F (18–21°C) in spring. Divide in spring.

• **PESTS AND DISEASES** Spider mites may be a problem under glass.

C. palmata ■ (Panama hat palm). Stemless, palm-like perennial with erect or suberect leaf stalks, 5–10ft (1.5–3m) tall, and rounded leaf blades, 16–32in (40–80cm) long. The leaf blades have 3–5 segments, each with several rich green lobes, which are pendent at the tips. In summer, bears cylindrical to ellipsoid spathes enclosing yellowish to brownish green spadices that consist of groups of fleshy male flowers around individual female flowers. The spathes mature in autumn to about 6in (15cm) long, before they separate to disclose the bright red fruit. ↕ 6–10ft (2–3m), ↔ 5–10ft (1.5–3m). Central America to Bolivia. ❀ (min. 55–59°F/13–15°C)

CARMICHAELIA

FABACEAE

Genus of about 40 species of deciduous shrubs, occasionally small trees, from New Zealand and Lord Howe Island. They are found in diverse habitats from coastal to mountain areas, including sand dunes, swamps, grassland, rocky places, woodland margins, streambanks, and lakesides. The seedlings have pinnate leaves, but mature plants are leafless or lose their leaves quickly. They are grown for their small, but usually profuse, often fragrant, pea-like flowers, borne in summer, sometimes singly, but mostly in dense, short racemes of 5–15, on cylindrical or flattened green shoots. They are attractive and unusual shrubs for a border or, in cooler areas, against a warm wall. Dwarf species, such as *C. enysii*, are suitable for a rock garden. Where not hardy, grow in a cool greenhouse.

• **CULTIVATION** Grow in humus-rich, well-drained but not too dry soil, in sun or partial shade; *C. glabrata* requires acidic soil. Shelter from cold winds, either against a wall or among other shrubs. Pruning group 1.

• **PROPAGATION** Sow seed in a cold frame in autumn; or sow seed, scarified or pre-soaked in hot water, in spring. Root semi-ripe cuttings in summer.

• **PESTS AND DISEASES** Infrequent.

C. enysii ■ Dwarf, many-branched shrub, leafless when mature, with flattened, finely and longitudinally grooved shoots, to 1/16in (2mm) wide, which form a compact mound. Fragrant purple flowers, to ¼in (6mm) long, with dark purple veins, are borne singly or in 2- to 5-flowered racemes, to 2½in (6cm) long, in midsummer. ↕ 2in (5cm), ↔ 2–12in (5–30cm). New Zealand (South Island). ❀ (min. 41°F/5°C)

C. glabrata. Bushy, spreading shrub, leafy only when young, with flattened, pendent shoots, to ⅛in (3mm) across. Small, fragrant, purple-and-white flowers, to ¼in (6mm) long, are borne in dense racemes, to 10in (25cm) long, in summer. ↕ 6ft (2m), ↔ 8ft (2.5m). New Zealand (South Island). ❀ (min. 41°F/5°C)

Carmichaelia enysii

CARNEGIEA

Saguaro

CACTACEAE

Genus of one species of slow-growing, giant cactus from desert areas in the US and N.W. Mexico. It generally attains only 3ft (1m) in height after 30 years; branching and flowering may not occur until plants reach 10–12ft (3–4m) tall. *C. gigantea* has a large, ribbed trunk, which adapts to fluctuating desert moisture conditions by expanding and contracting. The large, funnel- to bell-shaped flowers, borne in early summer, open in the morning and last until the next day. They are followed by edible, ovoid-oblong, scaly, often spiny green fruit containing juicy red pulp and glossy black seeds. Where not hardy, grow in a warm greenhouse; in warm, dry climates, grow in a desert garden.

• **CULTIVATION** Under glass, grow in a mix of 3 parts standard cactus potting mix and 1 part limestone chips in full light, shaded from hot sun. During the growing season, water freely and apply a low-nitrogen liquid fertilizer monthly; keep dry from midautumn to early spring. Outdoors, grow in sharply drained, humus-rich, gritty, slightly alkaline soil in full sun. Survives brief periods of 20°F (-7°C). See also pp.48–49.

• **PROPAGATION** Sow seed at 70°F (21°C) in early spring. *C. gigantea* rarely survives transplanting from the wild.

• **PESTS AND DISEASES** Many fungi can cause stem rot or seedling rot. Bacterial soft rot and saguaro virus can occur.

Carnegiea gigantea

C. gigantea ▣ (Saguaro). Columnar, erect, slow-growing cactus with a tree-like trunk that eventually produces multiple ascending branches with 12–24 (occasionally up to 30) ribs. The areoles bear needle-shaped to awl-shaped, gray, brown, or yellow spines (12–16 radials and 3–6 centrals). In early summer, solitary, funnel- to bell-shaped, many-petaled white flowers, to 5in (13cm) long and across, are borne from felted, spineless areoles at the tips of the stems. The flowers are followed by ovoid-oblong, often spiny green fruit, 2–3in (5–8cm) long, which erupt upon ripening, exposing bright red pulp. ↕ to 50ft (15m), ↔ to 10ft (3m). S. California, Arizona, N.W. Mexico. ❀ (min. 50°F/10°C)

CARPENTARIA

ARECACEAE

Genus of one species of single-stemmed palm from Queensland, Australia, found along riverbanks in rainforest. The prominent crownshaft bears dense, terminal clusters of pinnate leaves, and spreading or semi-pendent, many-branched panicles of 3-petaled flowers. Where not hardy, grow *C. acuminata* in a warm greenhouse, or use young specimens as houseplants. In frost-free climates, grow as a handsome specimen tree; it is frequently used as a street tree in N.E. Australia and Florida.

• **CULTIVATION** Under glass, grow young plants in soil-based potting mix in bright filtered light with high humidity. Water freely in growth, applying a balanced liquid fertilizer monthly; water sparingly in winter. Pot on or top-dress in spring. Outdoors, grow in fertile, humus-rich, moist but well-drained soil in full sun, but screen from hot sun when young.

• **PROPAGATION** Sow seed at 81°F (27°C) in spring.

• **PESTS AND DISEASES** Prone to scale insects and spider mites. Susceptible to many fungal leaf spots.

Carpentaria acuminata

C. acuminata ▣ syn. *Kentia acuminata.* Medium-sized palm with a slender, smooth trunk ringed by old leaf scars. Arching, pinnate, dark green leaves, 6–12ft (2–4m) long, consist of many narrow, linear, abrupt- or ragged-ended leaflets. From spring to summer, bears cup-shaped cream flowers in panicles to 5ft (1.5m) long, followed by crimson fruit in persistent yellow calyces. ↕ 30–50ft (10–15m), ↔ 10–22ft (3–7m). Queensland. ❀ (min.55–59°F/13–15°C)

CARPENTERIA

HYDRANGEACEAE

Genus of one species of evergreen shrub found in scrub on dry slopes and ridges, and in pine forest, in California. It is valued mainly for its handsome leaves, which are opposite, leathery, and entire, and for its shallowly cup-shaped white flowers. *C. californica* is ideal for a shrub border or for growing against a wall.

• **CULTIVATION** Grow in well-drained, not too dry soil in full sun; shelter from cold, dry, and strong winds. Pruning group 8; remove the oldest flowered shoots occasionally from the base.

• **PROPAGATION** Sow seed at 55–64°F (13–18°C) in autumn or spring. Root greenwood or semi-ripe cuttings in summer.

• **PESTS AND DISEASES** Fungal leaf spot may be a problem.

C. californica ▣ Upright, open shrub with peeling, pale brown bark and lance-shaped to narrowly ovate-oblong, glossy, dark green leaves, 4–5in (10–13cm) long. Cup-shaped, fragrant white flowers, 1½–3in (4–8cm) across, with central bosses of yellow stamens, are produced singly or in short terminal cymes from the upper leaf axils in early and midsummer. ↕ 6ft (2m), or more if trained against a wall, ↔ 6ft (2m). California. Zone 8. **'Elizabeth'** is compact, bearing flowers to 1in (2.5cm) across. **'Ladham's Variety'** produces large flowers, to 3in (8cm) across.

CARPINUS

Hornbeam

BETULACEAE

Genus of 35–40 species of deciduous trees from woodland in Europe, Asia, and North America. They have alternate, prominently veined, entire or toothed leaves and, in spring, produce unisexual flowers in catkins; both male and female catkins are borne on the same plant. Hornbeams are cultivated for their elegant habit, ornamental foliage, autumn color, and pendent, leafy-bracted racemes of fruit. They are attractive specimen trees for a park or woodland, and are excellent for hedging.

• **CULTIVATION** Grow in moderately fertile, well-drained soil in sun or partial shade. Pruning group 1. Trim hedges of *C. betulus* in late summer. Hornbeams can withstand very hard pruning.

• **PROPAGATION** Sow seed in a seedbed in autumn. Root greenwood cuttings in early summer or bud in late summer. Graft in winter; top-graft *C. betulus* 'Pendula' to display its weeping habit.

• **PESTS AND DISEASES** Susceptible to powdery mildew, cankers and dieback, and wood-rotting fungi.

C. betulus (Hornbeam). Pyramidal, later irregularly rounded tree with fluted, smooth gray bark and ovate, unequally toothed, mid-green leaves, 3–5in (8–13cm) long, turning yellow to orange in autumn. In spring, bears yellow male catkins, to 1¼in (3cm) long, and greenish female catkins, to 5in (13cm) long. Female catkins are followed by racemes, 1¼–2½in (3–6cm) long, of green fruit with prominent, 3-lobed bracts, maturing to yellow-brown. ↕ 80ft (25m), ↔ 70ft (20m). Europe, Turkey, Ukraine. Zone 5. **'Aspleniifolia'** has toothed leaves with deeply cut lobes. **'Columnaris'** is a slow-growing, densely branched, compact tree, spire-like when young; it becomes ovoid with age, but retains its

Carpenteria californica

C

C

Carpinus betulus 'Fastigiata'

central leader; ↕30ft (10m), ↔ 20ft (6m). **'Fastigiata'** ■ syn. 'Pyramidalis', is narrow and upright, becoming broadly conical and more open with age; ↕50ft (15m), ↔ 40ft (12m). **'Frans Fontaine'** is similar to 'Fastigiata', but narrower when mature; ↕50ft (15m), ↔ 20ft (6m). **'Pendula'** is mound-forming, with pendent branches, and is best grown as a top-grafted standard; ↕8ft (2.5m), ↔ 12ft (4m). **'Pyramidalis'** see 'Fastigiata'.

C. caroliniana ■ (American hornbeam, Blue beech, Ironwood). Spreading, occasionally shrubby tree with fluted, smooth gray bark. Ovate, sharply (sometimes doubly) toothed, slightly glaucous, blue-green leaves, 5in (13cm) long, are rounded or heart-shaped at the bases, turning yellow to orange-red in autumn. Male catkins are yellow and to 1½in (4cm) long. Mid-green female catkins, to 4in (10cm) long, are followed by racemes, 2–4in (5–10cm) long, of green fruit, maturing yellow-brown, with irregularly 3-lobed bracts; the central lobe is to 1in (2.5cm) wide. ↕40ft (12m), ↔ 50ft (15m). E. North America, Mexico. Zone 3b.

C. tschonoskii. Spreading tree with pendent branch tips and ovate, sharp-pointed, double-toothed, glossy leaves, to 3in (8cm) long, dark green above, mid-green beneath, and yellow in autumn. Male catkins are green and ½–¾in (1–2cm) long; female catkins are yellow-green, to 2in (5cm) long, and followed by pendent, green, later yellow-brown racemes of fruit, 2–3in (5–8cm) long, with ovate, toothed bracts. ↕↔ 40ft (12m). China, Korea, Japan. Zone 6.

Carpinus caroliniana

Carpinus turczaninowii (inset: leaf detail)

C. turczaninowii ■ Small, elegant tree, upright when young and later rounded, with slender shoots and ovate to broadly ovate, double-toothed, glossy, dark green leaves, to 2in (5cm) long, turning orange in autumn. Male catkins are green and ½–1in (1–2.5cm) long. Female catkins are yellow-green and to 2in (5cm) long; they are followed by racemes, 1–2in (2.5–5cm) long, of pendent, green, later yellow-brown fruit with ovate, unequal bracts, toothed on one side. ↕20–40ft (6–12m), ↔ 30ft (10m). China, Korea, Japan. Zone 6.

CARPOBROTUS

AIZOACEAE

Genus of 20–25 species of creeping, perennial succulents, mainly occurring in dry regions of South Africa, Australia (including Tasmania), Chile, and Mexico. They have prostrate, fleshy stems and pairs of finger-like, 3-angled, opposite, fleshy, smooth, sometimes spotted leaves, which are joined at the bases and usually keeled. Colorful, solitary, daisy-like, many-petaled, diurnal flowers are borne from late spring to early autumn and are followed by pear-shaped, fleshy fruits; those of *C. edulis* are used in preserves. Where not hardy, grow in a cool or temperate greenhouse, or treat as annuals. In warmer areas, use as a groundcover on a sandy, sunny bank, or grow in a desert garden. They are useful for binding and stabilizing sandy soils, including those found in coastal areas.

• **CULTIVATION** Under glass, grow in a mix of 2 parts each loam and sharp sand and 1 part leaf mold in full light. In the growing season, water freely, and apply a balanced liquid fertilizer once annually, in early summer. Water very sparingly in winter. Outdoors, grow in poor, sharply drained, sandy, humus-rich soil in full sun. See also pp.48–49.

• **PROPAGATION** Sow seed at 59°F (15°C) in early spring, or root stem cuttings in spring or summer.

• **PESTS AND DISEASES** Susceptible to mealybugs.

C. acinaciformis. Succulent producing trailing stems, to 5ft (1.5m) or more long, with short, lateral branches. Sickle-shaped, strongly keeled, grayish green leaves, 3½in (9cm) long, have "blisters" at the bases of the upper sides. Daisy-like, bright reddish purple flowers, 5in (13cm) across, open after midday and are produced freely from late spring to early autumn. ↕6in (15cm), ↔ indefinite. South Africa (Eastern Cape, Western Cape, KwaZulu/Natal). ❄ (min. 41°F/5°C)

C. edulis ■ (Hottentot fig, Kaffir fig). Widely spreading succulent with prostrate stems, 6ft (2m) or more long, rooting at intervals along their length, and sickle-shaped, slightly curved, dull, gray-green leaves, to 3in (8cm) long. Numerous, daisy-like yellow flowers, 3–5in (8–13cm) across, opening after noon and turning pinkish later in the day, are borne from late spring to early autumn. Produces edible, fig-like brown fruit. ↕6in (15cm), ↔ indefinite. South Africa (Eastern Cape, Western Cape, KwaZulu/Natal). ❄ (min. 45°F/7°C)

Carpobrotus edulis

CARTHAMUS

Safflower

ASTERACEAE

Genus of 14 species of upright, hairy annuals and herbaceous perennials found in dry, open, sunny habitats in the Mediterranean and W. Asia. They have alternate, pinnatifid to pinnatisect, occasionally simple and shallowly lobed, spiny-margined leaves, and thistle-like, yellow, pink, purple, or violet flower-heads. *C. tinctorius* is the only widely cultivated species, and has been used for centuries as a source of red and yellow dye. It is a good everlasting flower for use in dried flower arrangements and is also excellent for growing in a border or herb garden.

• **CULTIVATION** Grow in any light, well-drained soil in full sun.

• **PROPAGATION** Sow seed at 50–59°F (10–15°C) from early to late spring.

• **PESTS AND DISEASES** Root and stem rots, rust, powdery mildew, *Alternaria* leaf spot, and wilt can occur.

C. tinctorius (False saffron, Safflower). Erect annual producing simple, ovate to linear, wavy-margined or pinnatifid, often spiny-toothed, light grayish green basal leaves, 1¼–3½in (3–9cm) long; stem leaves are narrowly linear-lance-shaped and stem-clasping. In summer, bears loose corymbs of thistle-like flowerheads, to 1½in (4cm) across, with large basal cups of stiff green bracts, from which tasselled tufts of red, orange, or yellow ray florets emerge. ↕12–24in (30–60cm), ↔ 12in (30cm). Probably W. Asia. **'Lasting White'** bears creamy white flowers. **'Orange Ball'** has orange flowers. **'Summer Sun'** produces bright yellow flowers.

CARUM

Caraway

APIACEAE

Genus of about 30 species of taprooted, upright biennials and perennials with 2- to 4-pinnate leaves and compound umbels of small white flowers. *C. carvi*, the only species widely cultivated, occurs in meadows, grassland, and wasteland from Europe and North Africa to Siberia, Russia. It is grown in herb gardens for its fern-like foliage and distinctively flavored seeds.

• **CULTIVATION** Grow in deep, fertile, well-drained soil in full sun; caraway will tolerate heavier soils. Seed is borne in the second summer; harvest before it begins to darken, to avoid self-seeding. *C. carvi* self-seeds very freely.

• **PROPAGATION** Sow seed in rows *in situ* in late spring or late summer. Seedlings may be transplanted, but will bolt unless moved when very small.

• **PESTS AND DISEASES** Infrequent.

C. carvi (Caraway). Aromatic biennial with slender, ribbed stems and feathery, 2- or 3-pinnate, bright green leaves, 3–6in (8–15cm) long, consisting of linear to linear-lance-shaped leaflets. Small white flowers are borne in compound umbels, to 1½in (4cm) across, in midsummer, followed by 5-ribbed fruit, ⅛–¼in (3–6mm) long, containing the seeds. ↕24in (60cm), ↔ 12in (30cm). Europe to W. Asia. Zone 4.

CARYA

Hickory, Pecan

JUGLANDACEAE

Genus of about 25 species of deciduous trees, mostly found in woodland in E. Asia and North America. Hickories are valued for their foliage, which is pinnate and alternate, and often colors well in autumn, and for their sometimes ornamental bark. Flowers of both sexes are borne separately on the same plant in late spring and early summer: the males are produced in branched, pendent, yellow-green catkins, the females in small, terminal green spikes. The autumn fruits are hard-shelled nuts, which in some species contain edible kernels. Use hickories and pecans as specimen trees for a lawn or a woodland garden, or for attracting wildlife.

• **CULTIVATION** Grow in deep, fertile, moist but well-drained, humus-rich soil in sun or partial shade. Seedlings quickly develop a deep taproot and resent transplanting. Pruning group 1.

• **PROPAGATION** Sow seed *in situ* as soon as ripe; if sowing in a seedbed transplant seedlings as soon as possible. Graft cultivars of *C. illinoinensis* in winter.

• **PESTS AND DISEASES** Prone to a wide variety of fungal leaf spots including nursery blight. Powdery mildew, crown gall, and catkin blight may also occur.

C. cordiformis ■ (Bitternut, Bitternut hickory, Swamp hickory). Broadly columnar tree with ornamental, ridged gray bark. Pinnate, mid-green leaves, 6–10in (15–25cm) or more long, with 5–9 ovate-lance-shaped leaflets, turn yellow in autumn. Produces unpalatable, thick-shelled, spherical nuts, to 1½in (4cm) long. ↕ 80ft (25m), ↔ 50ft (15m). E. North America. Zone 4.

C. glabra (Hognut, Pignut, Pignut hickory). Spreading tree with ornamental, furrowed gray bark. Pinnate, mid-green leaves, 8–12in (20–30cm) long, with usually 5–7 ovate-lance-shaped to obovate leaflets, turn yellow in autumn. Produces obovoid, bitter-tasting, thin-shelled nuts, to 2in (5cm) long. ↕ 80ft (25m), ↔ 70ft (20m). E. US. Zone 5.

C. illinoinensis (Pecan). Rounded tree with ornamental, furrowed gray bark. Pinnate, mid-green leaves, 12–20in (30–50cm) long, with usually 11–17 curved, oblong-lance-shaped leaflets, turn yellow in autumn. Oblong, thick-shelled nuts, to 2½in (6cm) long, are edible when ripe. In areas with warm summers, many cultivars are grown for their edible nuts. ↕ 100ft (30m), ↔ 70ft (20m). S. US. Zone 5b.

C. ovata (Shagbark hickory). Broadly conical tree with ornamental, peeling, gray to brown bark. The pinnate, mid-green leaves, 8–14in (20–35cm) long, have usually 5 leaflets, the upper 3 obovate and the lower 2 ovate-lance-shaped to ovate; the leaves turn golden yellow in autumn. Thick-shelled nuts, to 2½in (6cm) long, are edible when ripe. The wood chips are used commercially in smoking processes to flavor ham and bacon. ↕ 80ft (25m), ↔ 50ft (15m). E. North America. Zone 4b.

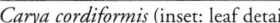

Carya cordiformis (inset: leaf detail)

CARYOPTERIS

VERBENACEAE

Genus of 6 species of aromatic, deciduous shrubs and perennials from a variety of habitats, including dry, hot slopes and woodland, in the Himalayas and mountains of E. Asia. They have opposite, simple, entire to toothed leaves and small, usually blue flowers, borne in terminal or axillary panicles or cymes. Cultivated for their attractive, aromatic foliage and flowers, which are borne from late summer to autumn on the current year's shoots, they are ideal for a mixed or shrub border.

• **CULTIVATION** Grow in moderately fertile, light, well-drained soil in full sun or light shade.

• **PROPAGATION** Sow seed in autumn in containers in a cold frame. Root softwood cuttings in late spring or greenwood cuttings in early summer.

• **PESTS AND DISEASES** Capsid bugs may cause leaf distortion.

***C. x clandonensis* cultivars** Selections derived from the dense, mound-forming shrub *C. x clandonensis* have ovate-lance-shaped, slightly toothed, gray-green leaves, to 2in (5cm) long, silver-hairy beneath. They bear axillary and terminal cymes of blue or purple-blue flowers, to ½in (1.5cm) across, in late summer and early autumn. ↕ 3ft (1m), ↔ 5ft (1.5m). Zone 6. **'Arthur Simmonds'** has dull, dark green leaves, silvery gray beneath, and bears bright purplish blue flowers. **'Blue Mist'** produces powder-blue blooms. **'Dark Knight'** has silvery gray leaves and very dark blue flowers. **'Heavenly Blue'** is erect, with intensely dark blue flowers. **'Kew Blue'** ■ has gray-green leaves, dull, dark green above, silvery gray beneath, and bears dark blue flowers. **'Longwood Blue'** has silvery gray leaves and violet-blue flowers. **'Worcester Gold'** ■ has warm yellow foliage and lavender-blue flowers.

C. incana, syn. *C. mastacanthus*. Dense, mound-forming shrub with aromatic, ovate, gray-green leaves, to 3in (8cm) long, sharply toothed at the margins. Bright violet-blue, occasionally white flowers, ¼–⅜in (6–9mm) across, are produced in rounded cymes from the upper leaf axils in autumn. ↕ 4ft (1.2m), ↔ 5ft (1.5m). China, Japan. Zone 7b.

C. mastacanthus see *C. incana*.

Caryopteris x clandonensis 'Kew Blue'

Caryopteris x clandonensis 'Worcester Gold'

CARYOTA

Fishtail palm

ARECACEAE

Genus of 12 species of single- and cluster-stemmed, monoecious, sometimes monocarpic palms from India and Sri Lanka to S.E. Asia, N. Australia, and the Solomon Islands. They occur in forest from sea level to 7,000ft (2,000m) in humid or monsoon climates. Huge, 2-pinnate leaves, each with a prominent, sheathing base, are arranged in spirals on the upper part of each stem. The 3-petaled, cup-shaped flowers are borne in large, pendent panicles just below the lowest leaf. Where not hardy, grow in a temperate or warm greenhouse, or use young specimens as houseplants. In tropical regions, fishtail palms are used as ornamental specimen trees; where they occur naturally, they provide sago, palm wine, and building materials.

• **CULTIVATION** Under glass, grow in soil-based potting mix in bright filtered light and high humidity. Water freely during the growing season, applying a balanced liquid fertilizer monthly; water sparingly in winter. Pot on or top-dress in spring. Outdoors, grow in fertile, humus-rich, moist but well-drained soil with midday shade.

• **PROPAGATION** Sow seed at 81°F (27°C) in spring.

• **PESTS AND DISEASES** Prone to spider mites and scale insects, as well as fungal leaf spots. Lethal yellowing and false smut sometimes occur.

C. mitis ■ (Burmese fishtail palm, Clustered fishtail palm). Small to medium-sized palm with clustered

Caryota mitis

C

stems, at first clothed with fibrous leaf bases, later bare. The broadly linear, 2-pinnate, rich green leaves are 6–12ft (2–4m) long, with 6–60, fishtail-like, asymmetrically 3-angled leaflets. Pendent panicles, 12in (30cm) or more long, of cream flowers, to ¾in (2cm) across, are borne in summer. ↕ 10–40ft (3–12m), ↔ 10–22ft (3–7m). Myanmar to Malaysian peninsula, Indonesia (Java), Philippines. ❀ (min. 59°F/15°C)
C. urens (Jaggery palm, Sago palm, Toddy palm, Wine palm). Medium-sized to large, fast-growing, monocarpic palm with a single, sturdy stem clothed with fibrous leaf bases. Arching, broadly linear, 2-pinnate, dark green leaves, to 20ft (6m) long, have 6–50 obliquely wedge-shaped leaflets, to 12in (30cm) long. Panicles, 6–12ft (2–4m) long, of cream flowers, ½–1¼in (1–3cm) across, are produced at the end of the tree's life, first at the top of the tree, then from each leaf axil downward. The sugary sap is boiled down to make crude sugar (jaggery), or is distilled into toddy. ↕ 40–80ft (12–25m), ↔ to 30ft (10m). India, Sri Lanka, Malaysian peninsula. ❀ (min. 59°F/15°C)

▷ ***Cassandra*** see *Chamaedaphne*

CASSIA

FABACEAE

Genus of over 500 species of annuals and perennials, and deciduous, semi-evergreen, and evergreen shrubs and trees from moist woodland, riverbanks, and scrub in tropical areas worldwide. Cassias have pinnate leaves and 5-petaled, loosely bowl-shaped flowers, produced in open panicles or racemes, or occasionally singly. Where not hardy, grow in a temperate or warm conservatory or greenhouse. In warmer areas, grow in a shrub or mixed border; use the trees as specimen plants.

• **CULTIVATION** Under glass, grow in soil-based potting mix in full light. In the growing season, water freely and apply a balanced liquid fertilizer monthly. Top-dress or pot on in early spring. Outdoors, grow in deep, well-drained, moderately fertile soil in full sun. Pruning group 1; plants under glass need restrictive pruning after flowering.
• **PROPAGATION** Sow pre-soaked seed at 64–70°F (18–21°C) in spring. Root semi-ripe cuttings in summer.
• **PESTS AND DISEASES** Prone to spider mites, scale insects, and whiteflies under glass. Leaf spots (such as tar spot), dieback, powdery mildew, rusts, and a variety of viral diseases can occur.

Cassia fistula

C. alata see *Senna alata.*
C. armata. Bushy, deciduous shrub having yellow-green, softly silver-woolly stems, leafless most of the year, and mid-green leaves, 8–36in (20–90cm) long, with 2–8 oblong leaflets. Dense, terminal racemes, to 6in (15cm) long, of yellow flowers, to 6in (15cm) long, are borne in late summer. ↕ to 5ft (1.5m), ↔ 2–7ft (.6–2.2m). California, Arizona. ❀ (min. 45°F/7°C)
C. artemisioides see *Senna artemisioides.*
C. corymbosa see *Senna corymbosa.*
C. corymbosa* var. *plurijuga see *Senna* x *floribunda.*
C. didymobotrya see *Senna didymobotrya.*
C. fistula ■ (Golden shower tree, Purging cassia). Spreading, semi-evergreen to deciduous tree producing bright green leaves, to 24in (60cm) long, with 6–16 ovate leaflets; the older leaves are shed in winter or in drought. Fragrant, bright yellow flowers, to 1½in (4cm) across, are borne freely in pendent racemes, 8–16in (20–40cm) long, from spring to summer. ↕ 25–40ft (8–12m), ↔ 10–15ft (3–5m). S.E. Asia, Pacific islands, Central and South America. ❀ (min. 59°F/15°C)
C.* x *floribunda see *Senna* x *floribunda.*
C. javanica (Appleblossom senna). Many-branched, spreading, usually deciduous tree with densely downy young growth. The leaves, 16in (40cm) long, have 16–34 elliptic to oblong-elliptic leaflets. Profuse pale pink, crimson, or buff-pink flowers, to 1½in (4cm) across, are borne in rigid racemes, 4in (10cm) or more long, from spring to summer. ↕ to 80ft (25m) or more, ↔ 10–20ft (3–6m). S.E. Asia. ❀ (min. 61°F/16°C)
C. marilandica (Wild senna). Many-stemmed, erect to arching perennial with yellow-green leaves, 5–11in (13–28cm) long, with 10–18 sharply pointed, oblong leaflets. Bears racemes, to 6in (15cm) long, of yellow flowers, ¾in (2cm) across, in mid- and late summer. ↕ to 4ft (1.2m), ↔ 2–6ft (0.6–2m). Kansas to Pennsylvania south to Texas and Florida. Zone 5b.
C. siamea see *Senna siamea.*
C. spectabilis. Deciduous shrub or tree, having softly hairy branchlets, with glossy green leaves, to 3in (8cm) long, paler and hairy beneath, with 16–40 oblong leaflets. Produces racemes, to 24in (60cm) long, of bright yellow flowers, 1½in (4cm) across, in late summer. ↕ to 60ft (18m), ↔ 10–15ft (3–5m). C. and tropical South America. ❀ (min. 45°F/7°C)

CASSINIA

ASTERACEAE

Genus of about 20 species of heather-like, evergreen shrubs, occasionally soft-stemmed, from Australia, New Zealand, and South Africa. In the wild, they are found from coastal areas to scrub and grassland in the mountains. Cassinias are cultivated for their neat leaves, which are alternate, narrow, and entire, and for their small heads of often fragrant flowers, borne in terminal corymbs. They are suitable for a shrub border or heather garden.

Cassinia leptophylla subsp. *vauvilliersii*

• **CULTIVATION** Grow in moderately fertile, well-drained, humus-rich soil in full sun. Pruning group 10, in spring.
• **PROPAGATION** Root semi-ripe cuttings in summer.
• **PESTS AND DISEASES** Infrequent.

C. fulvida see *C. leptophylla* subsp. *fulvida.*
C. leptophylla. Bushy, rounded, evergreen shrub with tiny, linear to spoon-shaped, dark green leaves, ⅛–⅜in (3–15mm) long, white- or yellowish white-hairy beneath, on sticky, white- or yellowish white-hairy shoots. In midsummer, produces small heads of tiny, funnel-shaped white flowers in terminal corymbs, to 3in (8cm) across. ↕ 6ft (2m), ↔ 8ft (2.5m). New Zealand. ❀ (min. 35°F/2°C). **subsp. *fulvida*,** syn. *C. fulvida* (Golden heather) has dark green leaves, yellow beneath, on sticky yellow shoots, giving the plant an overall golden appearance. **subsp. *vauvilliersii*** ■ syn. *C. vauvilliersii*, has narrowly spoon-shaped to oblong-ovate leaves, and pure white flowers, to 3in (8cm) across; ↕↔ to 10ft (3m). **subsp. *vauvilliersii* var. *albida*** (Silver heather) has densely silver-white-hairy shoots and dark green leaves, densely silver-white-hairy beneath; white flowerheads are borne in dense corymbs, to 2in (5cm) across, in mid- and late summer; ↔ 5ft (1.5m); ❀ (min. 35°F/2°C)
C. vauvilliersii see *C. leptophylla* subsp. *vauvilliersii.*

CASSIOPE

ERICACEAE

Genus of 12 species of dwarf, evergreen shrubs from diverse habitats in arctic and alpine regions of N. Europe, N. Asia, and North America. They have 4 rows of tiny, overlapping, scale-like leaves, pressed flat to the whipcord-like stems, and bear solitary, axillary, bell- or urn-shaped flowers in late spring and early summer. Grow in a rock garden or in open areas in woodland.

• **CULTIVATION** Grow in a sheltered site in moist, acidic, humus-rich soil in partial shade or in an open, sunny site. *C. tetragona* tolerates some alkalinity.
• **PROPAGATION** Sow seed in autumn in containers in an open frame. Root greenwood or semi-ripe cuttings in summer, preferably under mist. Prostrate species may be layered in autumn or early spring.
• **PESTS AND DISEASES** *Exobasidium* gall (witches' broom) is common.

***C.* 'Edinburgh'.** Upright shrub with few-branched stems clothed in closely overlapping, lance-shaped, hairy-margined, dark green leaves, 1/16–⅛in (2–3mm) long, and slightly furrowed beneath. Nodding, bell-shaped white flowers, to ⅜in (9mm) across, with reflexed lobes and greenish brown calyces, are produced at the stem tips in late spring. ↕↔ to 10in (25cm). Zone 7b.
C. fastigiata. Lax, erect shrub bearing furrowed, lance-shaped, dark green leaves, to ⅛in (3mm) long, with fringed, silvery margins. In late spring, produces bell-shaped white flowers, ⅜in (9mm) across, with slightly reflexed lobes and green or red calyces. ↕ to 10in (25cm), ↔ to 8in (20cm). Himalayas. Zone 3.
C. lycopodioides ■ Mat-forming shrub with slender, tangled stems and tiny, ovate, dark green leaves, to 1/16in (2mm) long. In late spring, bears axillary, short-stemmed, tubular-bell-shaped white flowers, ¼in (6mm) across, with red calyces and red leaf stalks. ↕ to 3in (8cm), ↔ to 10in (25cm). Japan to Alaska. Zone 3.
C. mertensiana ■ Dense, upright shrub with ovate-lance-shaped, dark green leaves, to ¼in (6mm) long. The bell-shaped, creamy white flowers, ¼–⅜in (6–9mm) across, have red or green calyces, and are produced from the leaf axils in spring. ↕ to 6in (15cm), ↔ to 10in (25cm). California to Alaska. Zone 6. **var. *gracilis*** is mound-forming, slender, and free-flowering.
C. selaginoides. Many-branched shrub with stems densely clothed in minute, narrowly oblong, deeply furrowed, dark green leaves, to 1/16in (2mm) long. In late spring, pendent, bell-shaped white flowers, to ½in (1.5cm) across, with red calyces, are borne on long green flower stalks, mainly at the stem tips. ↕↔ to 6in (15cm). W. China. Zone 7.
C. tetragona. Upright shrub with 4-angled shoots clothed in oblong-lance-shaped, scale-like, leathery, dark green

Cassiope lycopodioides

Cassiope mertensiana

leaves, ⅛–¼in (3–6mm) long. Bears pendent, bell-shaped white flowers, to ¼in (6mm) across, with red calyces, in late spring. ↕ to 10in (25cm), ↔ to 8in (20cm). Arctic, subarctic Europe and North America. Zone 3.
C. wardii. Lax, semi-upright shrub with 4-angled, few-branched stems and lance-shaped, hairy-margined, dark green leaves, to ¼in (6mm) long. Pendent, urn-shaped white flowers, ½in (1.5cm) across, flushed red inside at the bases, are borne close to the stem tips in late spring. Best grown in partial shade. ↕↔ to 6in (15cm). Tibet. Zone 4.

CASTANEA
Chestnut
FAGACEAE

Genus of about 12 species of deciduous trees and shrubs from woodland in S. Europe, Asia, North America, and N. Africa. They have alternate, oblong to oblong-elliptic or oval, veined, toothed leaves, and, in summer, bear small, strongly scented cream flowers in showy catkins from the leaf axils of young shoots. Chestnuts are valued for their bold foliage and spiny-husked, sometimes edible nuts, ¾–2½in (2–6cm) across. Grow them as specimen trees or in woodland.
• **CULTIVATION** Grow in deep, well-drained, slightly acidic, loam soil in sun or partial shade. Most species tolerate dry, sandy soils; with the exception of *C. sativa*, they grow best in climates with long, hot summers. Pruning group 1.
• **PROPAGATION** Sow seed in a seedbed as soon as ripe. Graft in late winter, or bud in summer.
• **PESTS AND DISEASES** Chestnut blight (*Endothia parasitica*), which appeared in the E. US in 1906, spread rapidly throughout forested and urban areas. It wiped out most American chestnuts (*C. dentata*), and is still a serious problem throughout the US. Dieback, stem canker, heart rot, powdery mildew, fungal blights (such as anthracnose or eye spot), and leaf scorch can occur.

C. mollissima (Chinese chestnut). Vigorous, spreading tree with spirally furrowed bark when old, and oblong to oval, toothed, glossy, mid-green leaves, to 8in (20cm) long, often softly downy beneath. Grown for its edible fruit, borne in autumn. ↕↔ 70ft (20m). China. Zone 5b.

Castanea sativa 'Albomarginata'

C. pumila (Chinquapin). Large shrub to small tree with coarsely toothed, oblong-ovate, dark green leaves, to 5in (13cm) long, densely white-woolly beneath. Edible fruit ripen in autumn, attracting a wide variety of wildlife. ↕ 20–25ft (6–8m), ↔ 5–8ft (1.5–2.5m). Missouri to New Jersey south to Texas and Florida. Zone 6.
C. sativa (Spanish chestnut, Sweet chestnut). Vigorous, broadly columnar tree with spiral furrows in the bark when mature, and oblong, toothed, glossy, dark green leaves, to 8in (20cm) long. Edible fruit ripen in autumn. ↕ 100ft (30m), ↔ 50ft (15m). S. Europe, N. Africa, S.W. Asia. Zone 5b. **'Albomarginata'** ■ syn. 'Argenteo-marginata', has leaves margined creamy white. **'Aspleniifolia'** has leaves deeply cut into slender lobes. Some cultivars, such as **'Marron de Lyon'**, are grown for their fruit.

CASTANOPSIS
FAGACEAE

Genus of about 110 species of evergreen trees and shrubs related to chestnuts (*Castanea*) and oaks (*Quercus*), from forest in warm regions of S.E. Asia. The leathery leaves are alternate and entire or toothed. The flowers are borne in erect, unisexual catkins, and are followed by nuts that develop inside prickly cases. They are useful specimen trees but may remain shrubby and achieve tree stature only in continental climates.
• **CULTIVATION** Grow in fertile, moist but well-drained, slightly acidic soil in sun; shelter from cold, dry winds. Tolerates partial shade in areas with long, hot summers. Pruning group 1.
• **PROPAGATION** Sow seed in containers in a cold frame as soon as ripe.
• **PESTS AND DISEASES** Similar to those found on *Castanea*.

C. chrysophylla see *Chrysolepis chrysophylla*.
C. cuspidata (Japanese chinquapin). Spreading tree, often shrubby in cultivation, with attractive, pendent branches and ovate to oblong, tapered, usually entire leaves, to 4in (10cm) long, glossy, dark green above, bronze beneath. Small white flowers are borne in erect catkins, 2–3in (5–8cm) long, in summer. Acorn-like nuts enclosed in downy husks ripen in 2 years. ↕ 25ft (8m), ↔ 25ft (8m) or more. China, Japan. ❄ (min. 41°F/5°C)

CASTANOSPERMUM
FABACEAE

Genus of one species of evergreen tree from rainforest in Australia. It produces alternate, oval to lance-shaped, pinnate leaves and bears short, dense racemes of pea-like flowers. Where not hardy, grow in a temperate greenhouse; in warmer areas, it is a majestic specimen or shade tree, especially beside a water feature.
• **CULTIVATION** Under glass, grow in soil-based potting mix in full light, shaded from hot sun, in moderate humidity. In growth, water freely and apply a balanced fertilizer monthly; water sparingly in winter. Pot on or top-dress in spring. Outdoors, grow in deep, fertile, moist but well-drained soil in sun or partial shade. Tolerates short periods of 32°F (0°C). Pruning group 1; may need restrictive pruning under glass.
• **PROPAGATION** Sow seed at 55–64°F (13–18°C) as soon as ripe or in spring.
• **PESTS AND DISEASES** Infrequent.

C. australe (Black bean tree, Moreton Bay chestnut). Open, spreading tree with lustrous, dark green leaves, 12–18in (30–45cm) long, composed of 9–17 elliptic-oblong, slightly curved leaflets. Bears racemes of yellow, orange, or red flowers, 1¼–1½in (3–4cm) long, from late spring to late summer, followed by thick pods, 4–10in (10–25cm) long, with chestnut-like black seeds. ↕ 30–100ft (10–30m), ↔ 15–40ft (5–12m). N.E. Australia. ❄ (min. 45°F/7°C)

CASUARINA
Australian pine, She oak
CASUARINACEAE

Genus of 40–70 species of evergreen, conifer-like trees and shrubs from Australia and the Pacific islands, where they thrive in a range of habitats, from semi-desert to swamp forest. They are cultivated for their foliage, which is modified into minute scales or teeth arranged in a collar-like ring at each node. The tiny, petalless flowers are borne in single-sexed, cone-like spikes. Some species have nitrogen-fixing bacterial nodules on their roots. Where not hardy, grow young plants in a cool or temperate conservatory or greenhouse, or as houseplants. In frost-free climates, use Australian pines as specimen trees, windbreaks, or screens. They are tolerant of strong winds, coastal conditions, and wet or dry soils.
• **CULTIVATION** Under glass, grow in soil-based potting mix, with added sharp sand, in full light. When in growth, water freely and apply a balanced liquid fertilizer monthly; water more sparingly in winter. Pot on or top-dress in late winter. Outdoors, grow in fertile, moist but well-drained soil in full sun. Pruning group 1.
• **PROPAGATION** Sow seed at 55–64°F (13–18°C) in spring. Root semi-ripe cuttings in mid- or late summer.
• **PESTS AND DISEASES** Mushroom root rot, scale insects, and needle blight may occur.

C. equisetifolia (Horsetail tree). Erect to spreading, open tree with pendent branch tips, gray-green shoots, and scale-like leaves, 1/16in (2mm) long, arranged in whorls of 6–8. The cylindrical to ovoid flower cones are ¼in (6mm) long. ↕ 15–50ft (5–15m), sometimes to 80ft (25m), ↔ 10–25ft (3–8m). E. Australia, Pacific islands. ❄ (min. 37–41°F/3–5°C)
C. torulosa ■ (Forest oak). Slender, erect to spreading tree, sometimes with pendent shoots, and with corky bark. Scale-like leaves, ⅛–⅜in (3–9mm) long, arranged in whorls of 4, are pinkish when young, maturing to mid- or dark green. Some variants have light bronze to black-bronze foliage. Semi-spherical to cylindrical, bronze-green flower cones are ¼–½in (6–15mm) long. ↕ 25–80ft (8–25m), ↔ 15–30ft (5–10m). Queensland, New South Wales. ❄ (min. 37–41°F/3–5°C)

Casuarina torulosa (inset: leaf detail)

C

C

CATALPA

BIGNONIACEAE

Genus of 11 species of deciduous trees from E. Asia and North America, usually found on riverbanks and in woodland. Their large leaves are opposite or in whorls of 3. Catalpas are grown for their handsome foliage; for their large, bell-shaped, 2-lipped flowers, borne in upright, terminal panicles or racemes in mid- and late summer; and for their pendent, bean-like, narrowly cylindrical seed pods, which develop in autumn. Their wide-spreading habit and conspicuous flower panicles are seen to best advantage when they are grown as specimen trees. Those with colored foliage are also effective in a large shrub border; if pollarded or coppiced annually or biennially, they produce large, ornamental leaves.

• **CULTIVATION** Grow in fertile, moist but well-drained soil in full sun, sheltered from strong winds. Pruning group 1, or group 7 if grown as a coppice or pollard.

• **PROPAGATION** Sow seed in a seedbed or in containers in an open frame in autumn. Root softwood cuttings in late spring or summer. Graft or insert root cuttings in winter. Bud in late summer.

• **PESTS AND DISEASES** Diseases include powdery mildew, white rot, dieback, leaf spots, and anthracnose. Mealybugs, whiteflies, scale insects, and aphids can be problems.

C. bignonioides ■ (Indian bean tree, Southern catalpa). Spreading tree with broadly ovate, entire, mid-green leaves, heart-shaped at the bases, and to 10in (25cm) long. White flowers, to 2in (5cm) across, marked with yellow and purple-brown, are borne in upright panicles, 8–12in (20–30cm) tall. They are followed by slender pods, to 16in (40cm) long. ↕↔ 50ft (15m). S.E. US. Zone 5. **'Aurea'** ■ has bright yellow foliage, bronze when young; ↕↔ 30ft (10m). **'Nana'** is a round-headed tree or shrub and rarely flowers; ↕ 6ft (1.8m), ↔ 5ft (1.5m). **'Purpurea'** see *C.* x *erubescens* 'Purpurea'.

***C.* x *erubescens* 'Purpurea'**, syn. *C. bignonioides* 'Purpurea'. Spreading tree with broadly ovate leaves, 10–16in (25–40cm) long, with 3 shallow, tapered lobes, dark blackish purple when young, maturing to dark green. Bears white flowers, marked yellow and purple, to 2in (5cm) across, in large, upright panicles, to 12in (30cm) tall. They are followed by slender pods, to 16in (40cm) long. ↕↔ 50ft (15m). Zone 5.

C. ovata (Chinese catalpa). Spreading tree with broadly ovate, often 3-lobed, pale green leaves, to 10in (25cm) long. Upright panicles, to 10in (25cm) tall, of orange- and purple-marked, yellowish white flowers, to 1¼in (3cm) across, are followed by slender pods, to 12in (30cm) long. ↕↔ 30ft (10m). China. Zone 4.

C. speciosa ■ (Northern catalpa, Western catalpa). Spreading tree with broadly ovate, glossy, dark green leaves, to 12in (30cm) long, usually with 3 finely tapered lobes, densely hairy beneath. Large white flowers, to 2½in (6cm) across, marked with yellow and purple, are sparsely borne in upright panicles, 6–8in (15–20cm) tall. They are followed by slender pods, to 20in (50cm) or more long. ↕↔ 50ft (15m). US. Zone 5.

Catalpa bignonioides

Catalpa speciosa

Catalpa bignonioides 'Aurea'

CATANANCHE

Blue cupidone, Cupid's dart

ASTERACEAE

Genus of 5 species of cornflower-like annuals and perennials occurring in dry meadows of the Mediterranean. They have linear to inversely lance-shaped, grayish green leaves, mainly in basal tufts, and are grown for their solitary flowerheads with strap-shaped, blue, yellow, or white ray florets and paper-like, silvery white bracts. Ideal for a sunny border; the flowers are also good for cutting and drying. *C. caespitosa* is best grown in an alpine house.

• **CULTIVATION** Grow in any well-drained soil in full sun; *C. caerulea* is often short-lived in heavy soil. In an alpine house, grow *C. caespitosa* in soil-based potting mix, with additional grit, in full light.

• **PROPAGATION** Sow seed in containers in a cold frame in early spring or *in situ* in midspring. *C. caerulea* is best treated as an annual or a biennial, flowering more freely in its second year. Divide in spring, or insert root cuttings in winter.

• **PESTS AND DISEASES** Powdery mildew may be a problem.

C. caerulea (Cupid's dart). Short-lived perennial with clumps of linear, grass-like, hairy leaves, to 12in (30cm) long.

Catananche caerulea 'Bicolor'

Catananche caerulea 'Major'

From midsummer to autumn, bears solitary, dark-centered, blue to lilac-blue flowerheads, 1¼–2in (3–5cm) across. ↕ 20–36in (50–90cm), ↔ 12in (30cm). S.W. Europe, Italy. Zone 4. **'Alba'** has silvery white flowerheads. **'Bicolor'** ■ has white flowerheads with purple centers. **'Major'** ■ has dark-centered, lilac-blue flowerheads, 2in (5cm) across; ↕ 18–20in (45–50cm). **'Perry's White'** has white flowerheads with cream centers.

C. caespitosa. Dwarf, mound-forming perennial with rosettes of hairy, linear leaves, to 3in (8cm) long. Produces solitary flowerheads, to 1¼in (3cm) across, with many pale to deep yellow ray florets, on short stems in spring. ↕ 2–4in (5–10cm), ↔ 6–8in (15–20cm). Morocco (Atlas Mountains). Zone 4.

CATASETUM

ORCHIDACEAE

Genus of about 50 species of deciduous, mainly epiphytic orchids from Central and South America, found from sea level to altitudes of 6,000ft (1,800m). They have thick, fleshy, ovoid to spindle-shaped pseudobulbs producing several alternately ranked, soft-textured, elliptic-lance-shaped to inversely lance-shaped, mid-green leaves. Lateral, erect or pendent racemes of male and female flowers are borne on separate inflorescences from summer to autumn; flowers of both sexes are occasionally found on the same inflorescence.

• **CULTIVATION** Intermediate-growing orchids. Grow in epiphytic orchid potting mix in containers or slatted baskets. During summer, provide bright filtered light and high humidity with good ventilation. Water freely and apply a balanced liquid fertilizer at every third watering. In winter, remove shading and keep almost completely dry. Do not spray foliage, since this may cause spotting and disease. See also p.46.

• **PROPAGATION** Divide when the plant overflows its container.

• **PESTS AND DISEASES** Spider mites, aphids, whiteflies, and mealybugs may be problems. Fungal and bacterial leaf and bulb rots, as well as viral diseases, can occur.

C. macrocarpum. Large, deciduous, epiphytic orchid with conical to spindle-shaped pseudobulbs and lance-shaped, sharp-pointed leaves, 10–25in (25–60cm) long. Fragrant, variable, greenish yellow male flowers, 3–4in (8–13cm) across, spotted purple, are produced in racemes, 7–13in (15–30cm) long, in summer. ↕12in (30cm), ↔ 18in (45cm). Trinidad, Venezuela, Guyana, Brazil. ❀ (min. 54–59°F/12–15°C; max. 75°F/24°C)

C. pileatum. Deciduous, epiphytic orchid with ovoid to spindle-shaped pseudobulbs and lance-shaped leaves, 12in (30cm) long. Fragrant, pale yellow or creamy white flowers, 4in (10cm) across, sometimes flecked purple or red, are produced in racemes, to 16in (40cm) long, in summer. ↕12in (30cm), ↔ 18in (45cm). Ecuador, Colombia, Venezuela, Trinidad, Brazil. ❀ (min. 64°F/18°C; max. 86°F/30°C)

CATHARANTHUS

Madagascar periwinkle, Vinca

APOCYNACEAE

Genus of 8 species of annuals and perennials from Madagascar, occurring in open scrub and at forest margins. The opposite leaves are simple and entire, and the 5-petaled, periwinkle-like flowers are solitary or borne in terminal cymes. Only *C. roseus* is widely cultivated. Where not hardy, grow as annual bedding, in containers, in a cool greenhouse or conservatory, or as a houseplant. In frost-free regions, grow in a bed or border.

• **CULTIVATION** Under glass, grow in soil-based potting mix in full light with good ventilation. During the growing season, water moderately and apply a balanced liquid fertilizer monthly; water more sparingly in winter. Pot on or top-dress in late winter. Outdoors, grow in moderately fertile, well-drained soil in full sun or partial shade.

Catharanthus roseus Pacifica Series 'Pacifica Punch'

Catharanthus roseus 'Parasol'

Catharanthus roseus Pretty Series 'Pretty in Rose'

• **PROPAGATION** Sow seed at 55–64°F (13–18°C) in early spring. Root softwood cuttings in late spring or semi-ripe cuttings in summer.

• **PESTS AND DISEASES** Aerial blights, stem rot, leaf spots, aster yellows, and tomato spotted wilt virus occur. Dodder is regionally common. Spider mites and whiteflies also occur under glass.

C. roseus, syn. *Vinca rosea* (Madagascar periwinkle, Old maid). Woody-based, fleshy, evergreen perennial, usually grown as an annual, erect at first, then spreading. It has stiff but slightly untidy stems and opposite, oblong-ovate, glossy, mid- to dark green leaves, to 2in (5cm) long, with paler midribs. Salverform, pink, rose-pink, red, or white flowers, to 1½in (4cm) across, are produced singly from the upper leaf axils, mainly from spring to summer. All parts may cause severe discomfort if ingested. ↕↔ 12–24in (30–60cm). Madagascar. ❀ (min. 41–45°F/5–7°C). **Cooler Series** cultivars are compact and branching, producing pastel to deep rose-pink and white flowers with broad, overlapping petals. **Pacifica Series** cultivars branch from the base, and bear large, lilac, pale pink, or white flowers in spring; some have white flowers with red eyes; ↕12–14in (30–35cm); **'Pacifica Punch'** ▣ produces red, white, or rose-red flowers with deeper red centers. **'Parasol'** ▣ is vigorous and upright, having overlapping petals on large, white flowers, 2in (5cm) across, with deep red eyes; ↕6–8in (15–20cm). **Pretty Series** cultivars bear flowers in shades of red, pink, and white, from early summer to first frost; **Pretty Series 'Pretty in Rose'** ▣ bears pink flowers.

▷ ***Cathcartia villosa*** see *Meconopsis villosa*

CATOPSIS

BROMELIACEAE

Genus, closely related to *Tillandsia*, of over 20 species of evergreen, epiphytic perennials (bromeliads) from lowland woodland and rainforest. They occur up to altitudes of 6,500ft (2,000m) in S. North America, Central America, W., N., and E. South America, and the West Indies. The prominently sheathed leaves form funnel-shaped rosettes and are lance-shaped, smooth-margined, and often white-mealy. In summer, produces

Catopsis hahnii

erect, arching, or pendent panicles of small, white or pale yellow flowers. Both male and female plants are needed to obtain fruit. Where not hardy, grow in a warm greenhouse or as houseplants. In warmer regions, grow outdoors in a moist, humid site.

• **CULTIVATION** Under glass, grow epiphytically on bark or wood slabs, or in epiphytic bromeliad potting mix in bright filtered light. In summer, water moderately, mist frequently, apply a quarter-strength foliar fertilizer monthly and provide high humidity. Water sparingly at other times. Outdoors, grow epiphytically in humid conditions in partial shade. See also p.47.

• **PROPAGATION** Sow seed at 81°F (27°C) as soon as ripe. Root offsets in late spring with bottom heat in partial shade.

• **PESTS AND DISEASES** Susceptible to mealybugs and scale insects.

C. hahnii ▣ Epiphytic bromeliad with dense rosettes of 12 or more white-mealy leaves, to 14in (35cm) long, tapering to fine tips. In summer, bears erect or arching panicles, 4–10in (10–25cm) long, with yellow bracts and white flowers, ¼–⅜in (7–9mm) long. ↕20in (50cm) or more, ↔ 8in (20cm). Mexico, Guatemala, El Salvador, Honduras, Nicaragua. ❀ (min. 61°F/16°C)

CATTLEYA

ORCHIDACEAE

Genus of about 40 species of evergreen, epiphytic orchids from dry coastal areas to altitudes of 7,000ft (2,000m), often found along mountain streams, in Central and South America. They produce erect, thick to slender pseudobulbs on short rhizomes, and 1 or 2 semi-rigid, leathery, oblong to broadly obovate, occasionally glaucous, mid- to dark green leaves. Large, showy flowers, with 3-lobed or entire lips, are borne in terminal racemes, or sometimes singly, and emerge from thick, bract-like sheaths. Many hundreds of hybrids exist.

Cattleya aurantiaca

• **CULTIVATION** Warm to intermediate-growing orchids. Grow in epiphytic orchid potting mix in containers or orchid baskets. Provide high humidity, good ventilation, and bright filtered light or full light with shade from hot sun; foliage will bleach out if given too much sun. In summer, water freely and apply a balanced liquid fertilizer at every third watering. In winter, remove shading and water more sparingly. See also p.46.

• **PROPAGATION** Divide when the plant overflows its container, or remove at least 4 backbulbs and pot up separately.

• **PESTS AND DISEASES** Scale insects, spider mites, whiteflies, aphids, and mealybugs occur. Fungal and bacterial pseudobulb and leaf rots are common, as well as viral diseases.

C. aurantiaca ▣ Variable, epiphytic orchid with slender, narrowly cylindrical or spindle-shaped pseudobulbs and 2 ovate to elliptic leaves, 4–8in (10–20cm) long. Numerous bright orange, sometimes red or pale gold flowers, 1½in (4cm) across, often with dark red spots or streaks on the lips, are produced in racemes in summer. ↕↔ 12in (30cm). Central America. ❀ (min. 53°F/12°C; max. 86°F/30°C)

C. bicolor ▣ Epiphytic orchid with cylindrical pseudobulbs producing 2 oblong leaves, 5–8in (12–20cm) long. Racemes of fragrant, yellow-green or brown flowers, 4in (10cm) across, with crimson lips, fading to pink at the edges, are borne from summer to autumn. ↕30in (75cm), ↔ 18in (45cm). Brazil. ❀ (min. 41°F/5°C; max. 86°F/30°C)

Cattleya bicolor

Cattleya bowringiana

C. bowringiana ■ Epiphytic or terrestrial orchid producing cylindrical pseudobulbs and 2 narrowly oblong or elliptic-oblong, dark green leaves, 5–8in (12–20cm) long, glaucous at first. Long racemes of glossy, rose to magenta flowers, 3in (8cm) across, with pale rose-purple and dark purple lips, and white throats, are borne from autumn to winter. ↕ 3ft (1m), ↔ 18in (45cm). Guatemala, Belize. ❀ (min. 41°F/5°C; max. 86°F/30°C)
***C.* Chocolate Drop.** Epiphytic orchid with slender, oblong pseudobulbs and 2 oval leaves, 4–6in (10–15cm) long. In autumn, bears variable, chocolate-brown to reddish orange flowers, 2in (5cm) across, some with darker lips. ↕ 18in (45cm), ↔ 12in (30cm). ❀ (min. 41°F/5°C; max. 86°F/30°C)
C. dowiana. Epiphytic orchid with thick, oblong pseudobulbs producing one oblong leaf, to 12in (30cm) long. Racemes of fragrant yellow flowers, 5in (13cm) across, with crimson, gold-veined lips, are borne in autumn. ↕↔ 12in (30cm). Costa Rica, Colombia. ❀ (min. 41°F/5°C; max. 86°F/30°C)
C. forbesii. Epiphytic orchid with slender, oblong to cylindrical pseudobulbs and 2 oblong or narrowly elliptic leaves, to 6in (15cm) long. From spring to summer, bears racemes of fragrant, tawny pink to light green flowers, 3in (8cm) across, with yellow throats and a yellow stripe on the lips. ↕↔ 12in (30cm). Brazil. ❀ (min. 41°F/5°C; max. 86°F/30°C)
C. guttata. Epiphytic orchid producing cylindrical pseudobulbs and 2 lance-shaped or elliptic-oblong leaves, to 10in

Cattleya J.A. Carbone

Cattleya José Marti

(25cm) long. In winter, produces racemes of yellow- to lime-green flowers, to 3in (8cm) across, spotted red-brown, or banded purple; the 3-lobed lips are rose-purple to magenta. ↕ 4ft (1.2m), ↔ 24in (60cm). Brazil. ❀ (min. 41°F/5°C; max. 86°F/30°C)
***C.* J.A. Carbone** ■ Epiphytic orchid with club-shaped pseudobulbs and one oblong leaf, 6in (15cm) long. In early summer, bears fragrant mauve flowers, 5in (13cm) across, with darker mauve lips. ↕ 8in (20cm), ↔ 18in (45cm). ❀ (min. 41°F/5°C; max. 86°F/30°C)
***C.* José Marti** ■ syn. *C.* Mother's Favourite 'José Marti'. Epiphytic orchid with club-shaped pseudobulbs and one oblong leaf, 6in (15cm) long. Fragrant white flowers, 5in (13cm) across, open in spring. ↕ 8in (20cm), ↔ 18in (45cm). ❀ (min. 41°F/5°C; max. 86°F/30°C)
C. labiata (Autumn cattleya). Epiphytic orchid with club-shaped pseudobulbs and one oblong leaf, to 12in (30cm) long. Racemes of ruffled, pale rose-pink to lilac-magenta flowers, 6in (15cm) across, with purple, yellow-veined lips, are produced in autumn. ↕↔ 12in (30cm). Brazil. ❀ (min. 41°F/5°C; max. 86°F/30°C)
C. mossiae. Epiphytic orchid with club-shaped pseudobulbs and one oblong to ovate-oblong leaf, to 12in (30cm) long. In early summer, bears fragrant, light mauve, pink, or magenta flowers, 6in (15cm) across, with yellow-centered, white to lilac lips. ↕↔ 12in (30cm). Venezuela. ❀ (min. 41°F/5°C; max. 86°F/30°C)
***C.* Mother's Favourite 'José Marti'** see *C.* José Marti.
***C.* Portia 'Coerulea'.** Epiphytic orchid with club-shaped pseudobulbs and 1 or 2 oblong leaves, 6in (15cm) long. Bears blue-lilac flowers, 4in (10cm) across, in early summer. ↕↔ 12in (30cm). ❀ (min. 41°F/5°C; max. 86°F/30°C)
C. skinneri. Epiphytic orchid with cylindrical pseudobulbs and 2 oblong or elliptic-oblong leaves, to 12in (30cm) long. From winter to spring, bears many small, rose-purple to bright purple flowers, to 4in (10cm) across, the lips often white or cream. ↕↔ 12in (30cm). Mexico to Costa Rica, Guatemala. ❀ (min. 41°F/5°C; max. 86°F/30°C)
C. trianae. Epiphytic orchid with club-shaped pseudobulbs and one oblong leaf, 12in (30cm) long. Racemes of pure white or rose-white flowers, 8in (20cm) across, often purple-suffused, with pink and magenta lips, are borne from winter to spring. ↕↔ 12in (30cm). Colombia. ❀ (min. 41°F/5°C; max. 86°F/30°C)
C. walkeriana. Epiphytic orchid with thick, spindle-shaped pseudobulbs and one oblong leaf, 2–4in (5–10cm) long. Solitary (occasionally 2 or 3), rich amethyst or white flowers, 4in (10cm) across, with rose-pink or light magenta lips, are produced in spring. ↕ 5in (13cm), ↔ 6in (15cm). Brazil. ❀ (min. 41°F/5°C; max. 86°F/30°C)

CAULOPHYLLUM

BERBERIDACEAE

Genus of 2 (possibly only one) species of rhizomatous perennials found in mountain woodland, one in E. North America, the other in Japan. They bear racemes or panicles of small flowers, with sepals much larger than the petals. The fruits split open early to reveal berry-like seeds that turn from green to blue. The leaves, which emerge dark purple and later turn green, develop with the flowers or just after they open, and immediately below them. Each leaf has 3 leaflets, which are ovate to obovate, 3-lobed, and conspicuously veined; they are occasionally 2-ternate. Grow in a woodland garden for their foliage and berries.
• **CULTIVATION** Grow in moist, humus-rich, acidic soil in partial or deep shade.
• **PROPAGATION** Sow seed in containers in an open frame as soon as ripe; germination may be slow and erratic. Divide in spring, before growth begins, or after flowering. Very slow to increase.
• **PESTS AND DISEASES** Fungal spots sometimes occur.

C. thalictroides (Blue cohosh). Rhizomatous perennial with 3-palmate, mid-green leaves, produced singly or in pairs. In mid- and late spring, bears green-brown or yellow-brown flowers, ½in (1.5cm) across, with 6 long sepals and 6 short petals, the latter reduced to nectaries. Spherical seeds, to ½in (1.5cm) across, are deep, bright blue, sometimes glaucous. ↕ to 30in (75cm), ↔ 7in (18cm). New Brunswick to Tennessee and South Carolina. Zone 4.

CAUTLEYA

ZINGIBERACEAE

Genus of 5 or 6 species of rhizomatous perennials from shaded ravines among low, grassy vegetation and shrubs in the Himalayas. They have 2-ranked, lance-shaped to oblong leaves, and bear lax, terminal, spike-like racemes of complex, 2-lipped yellow flowers, with bold red bracts and sepals. Grow in a shaded mixed or herbaceous border, or in a woodland garden.
• **CULTIVATION** Plant rhizomes 6in (15cm) deep in spring. Grow in moist, humus-rich soil in partial shade. Water freely when dry, and apply a thick mulch in autumn where marginally hardy.
• **PROPAGATION** Sow seed at 55–64°F (13–18°C) in early spring, or divide in late spring after growth has just begun.
• **PESTS AND DISEASES** Slugs may damage the leaves.

C. gracilis. Rhizomatous perennial with lance-shaped, hairless, mid-green leaves, 8in (20cm) long, purple- or red-brown-striped beneath. In summer, bears spikes of 2-lipped yellow flowers, 1in (2.5cm) long, with green bracts and wine-red calyces that are longer than the bracts. ↕ to 16in (40cm), ↔ 12in (30cm). Himalayas. Zone 7b.

Cautleya spicata

C. spicata ■ Rhizomatous perennial with broadly lance-shaped, hairless, mid-green leaves, to 14in (35cm) long. In late summer, produces stiff spikes of 2-lipped yellow flowers, 1in (2.5cm) long, with reddish green to maroon bracts. ↕ 24–36in (60–90cm), ↔ 18in (45cm). Himalayas. Zone 7b.

CAVENDISHIA

ERICACEAE

Genus of about 100 species of evergreen, small trees or shrubs from cloud forest in tropical South America. The leathery leaves are alternate, simple, and entire. They are cultivated mainly for their bell-shaped or tubular flowers, borne in axillary or terminal, simple or branched racemes. Where not hardy, grow in a cool or temperate greenhouse. In frost-free regions, grow in a shrub border or at the base of a house wall.
• **CULTIVATION** Under glass, grow in acidic potting mix in bright filtered light. In the growing season, water moderately and apply a balanced liquid fertilizer monthly; water more sparingly in winter. Top-dress or pot on in early spring. Outdoors, grow in moist but well-drained, humus-rich, neutral to acidic soil in partial shade or screened from full sun. Pruning group 8 or 9, but regular pruning is not necessary.
• **PROPAGATION** Sow seed at 59–64°F (15–18°C) in spring. Root semi-ripe cuttings in summer. Layer in spring or autumn.
• **PESTS AND DISEASES** Spider mites and scale insects may be problems under glass.

C. acuminata. Spreading shrub with arching to pendent branches, and ovate to oblong or lance-shaped leaves, 2–3in (5–8cm) long, pink when young but maturing to glossy, dark green. From autumn to early winter, produces clustered racemes, 1¼–2½in (3–6cm) long, of narrowly bell-shaped or tubular, crimson to scarlet flowers with green lobes, which are shielded in bud by large scarlet bracts. ↕ 3–6ft (1–2m), ↔ 3ft (1m). Colombia, Ecuador. ❀ (min. 41°F/5°C)

▷ ***Cayratia thomsonii*** see *Parthenocissus thomsonii*

CEANOTHUS

California lilac

RHAMNACEAE

Genus of about 55 species of deciduous and evergreen shrubs, more rarely small trees, mostly from W. North America, in particular California, but also from E. US and Mexico, occurring from the coast to the mountains, usually in scrub and woodland on dry slopes. They have opposite or alternate, usually toothed leaves, and are cultivated for their small but profuse, blue, white, or pink flowers, to ⅛in (3mm) across, borne in terminal, lateral, or axillary cymes, racemes, or panicles. They are suitable for growing in a shrub border or against a sunny wall. Low-growing or prostrate species and cultivars are excellent as a groundcover or in a large rock garden.

• **CULTIVATION** Grow in fertile, well-drained soil in full sun, sheltered from strong, cold winds. California lilacs are lime tolerant, but may become chlorotic on shallow alkaline soils. Most may be trained against a wall, where they can reach twice the height they would in an open site. As a group, California lilacs are short-lived in the landscape; expect 5–10 years for a typical lifespan. Pruning group 8, after flowering, for evergreens; group 6, in early spring, for deciduous plants; group 13 if wall-trained. Mulch and apply a balanced fertilizer after pruning.

• **PROPAGATION** Sow seed in a seedbed, or in containers in an open frame, in autumn; most species hybridize readily. Root greenwood cuttings of deciduous plants, and semi-ripe cuttings of evergreens, in mid- or late summer.

• **PESTS AND DISEASES** Dieback, powdery mildew, mushroom root rot, fungal leaf spots, and *Verticillium* wilt are somewhat common. Caterpillars, scale insects, lacebug, and mealybugs occur.

C. americanus (Mountain sweet, New Jersey tea, Redroot, Wild snowball). Low-growing, broad, compact, deciduous shrub with alternate, ovate to obovate, irregularly toothed, dark green leaves, 2–3in (5–8cm) long, softly hairy or nearly hairless beneath. In early summer, bears white flowers in terminal panicles, 1–2in (2.5–5cm) long. Tolerates poor growing conditions. ↕3–4ft (1–1.2m), ↔3–5ft (1–1.5m). Manitoba to Maine south to Alabama and Florida. Zone 4b.

Ceanothus arboreus 'Trewithen Blue'

Ceanothus 'Autumnal Blue'

***C. arboreus* 'Trewithen Blue'** ■ Vigorous, wide-spreading, evergreen shrub with alternate, broadly oval to rounded, shallowly toothed, dark green leaves, to 4in (10cm) long. In spring and early summer, bears fragrant, mid-blue flowers in large, pyramidal, terminal and lateral panicles, to 5in (13cm) long. ↕20ft (6m), ↔25ft (8m). Zone 8.

***C.* 'A.T. Johnson'.** Vigorous, bushy, spreading, evergreen shrub with alternate, ovate, shallowly toothed, light green leaves, to 1¼in (3cm) long. Rich blue flowers are produced in lateral and terminal panicles, 2–2½in (5–6cm) long, over a long period in late spring and again from late summer to autumn. ↕↔8ft (2.5m). Zone 8.

***C.* 'Autumnal Blue'** ■ Upright, evergreen shrub with alternate, elliptic, finely toothed, glossy, bright green leaves, to 2in (5cm) long. Rich sky-blue flowers are borne in large, lateral panicles, 3in (8cm) long, from late summer to autumn. ↕↔10ft (3m). Zone 8.

***C.* 'Blue Jeans'.** Spreading, evergreen shrub with opposite, oblong, toothed, leathery, dark green leaves, ¾–1½in (2–4cm) long. Mid-blue flowers are

Ceanothus 'Cascade'

freely borne in lateral and terminal, rounded cymes, to ¾in (2cm) across, in late spring. ↕↔8ft (2.5m). Zone 8.

***C.* 'Blue Mound'** ■ Mound-forming, evergreen shrub with alternate, oblong, very finely toothed, glossy, dark green leaves, to 1¼in (3cm) long. In late spring, produces dark blue flowers in large, lateral cymes, 2½–3in (6–8cm) long. ↕5ft (1.5m), ↔6ft (2m). Zone 8.

***C.* 'Burkwoodii'.** Bushy, compact, evergreen shrub with opposite, oval, toothed, glossy, dark green leaves, to 1¼in (3cm) long, and grayish beneath. Bright blue flowers are produced in dense lateral and terminal panicles, to 2½in (6cm) long, from late summer to autumn. ↕5ft (1.5m), ↔6ft (2m). Zone 8.

***C.* 'Burtonensis'.** Spreading, evergreen shrub with alternate, rounded, crinkled, dark green leaves, to ¾in (2cm) long. In late spring and early summer, bears dark blue flowers in dense, rounded, terminal and lateral cymes, to 1¼in (3cm) across. ↕6ft (2m), ↔12ft (4m). Zone 8.

***C.* 'Cascade'** ■ Vigorous, evergreen, open shrub with arching branches and alternate, oblong, finely toothed, glossy,

Ceanothus 'Blue Mound' (inset: flower detail)

Ceanothus 'Concha'

dark green leaves, to 2in (5cm) long. Bears a mass of powder-blue flowers in large, terminal and lateral panicles, to 2½in (6cm) long, from spring to early summer. ↕↔12ft (4m). Zone 8.

***C.* 'Concha'** ■ Dense, evergreen shrub with arching branches and alternate, oblong-elliptic, finely toothed, dark green leaves, to 2in (5cm) long. In late spring, reddish purple buds open to dark blue flowers in numerous rounded, terminal and lateral cymes, to 1¼in (3cm) across. ↕↔10ft (3m). Zone 8.

***C.* 'Cynthia Postan'** ■ syn. *C.* x *regius* 'Cynthia Postan'. Dense, rounded, evergreen shrub with alternate, oblong, finely toothed, glossy, dark green leaves, to 1½in (4cm) long, gray-green beneath. Rich blue flowers are profusely borne in dense, lateral cymes, 1½–2in (4–5cm) long, in late spring and early summer. ↕↔8ft (2.5m). Zone 8.

***C.* 'Dark Star'.** Arching, evergreen shrub with alternate, ovate, toothed, dark green leaves, to ½in (1.5cm) long, with deeply impressed veins. Honey-scented, dark purplish blue flowers are borne in rounded, terminal and lateral cymes, to 1¼in (3cm) across, in late spring. ↕6ft (2m), ↔10ft (3m). Zone 8.

***C.* 'Delight'.** Vigorous, bushy, evergreen shrub with alternate, oblong, glossy, dark green leaves, to 1in (2.5cm) long. Dark blue flowers are produced in terminal and lateral panicles, to 2½in (6cm) long, in mid- and late spring. ↕10ft (3m), ↔15ft (5m). Zone 8.

***C.* x *delileanus* 'Gloire de Versailles'** see *C.* 'Gloire de Versailles'.

Ceanothus 'Cynthia Postan'

C

Ceanothus 'Gloire de Versailles'

C. dentatus. Densely branched, spreading, evergreen shrub with rigid shoots and alternate, tightly clustered, small, oblong-elliptic, toothed, dark green leaves, to ½in (1.5cm) long. In late spring, bears dark blue flowers in small, rounded, terminal or lateral cymes, to ¾in (2cm) across. ↕ 5ft (1.5m), ↔ 6ft (2m). California. Zone 8. **var. *floribundus*** has broader leaves and more densely clustered flowers.
C. divergens. Spreading, evergreen shrub with rigid, slender shoots and opposite, flat, holly-like, dark green leaves, to 1in (2.5cm) long, with smooth margins. In spring, purple-blue flowers open from red-purple buds in dense, rounded, lateral, umbel-like cymes, to ¾in (2cm) across. ↕ 3ft (1m), ↔ 5ft (1.5m). California. Zone 8.
***C.* 'Edinburgh'.** Vigorous, dense, upright, evergreen shrub with alternate, oblong-ovate, toothed, olive-green leaves, to 3in (8cm) long. Produces rich blue flowers in lateral cymes, to 2in (5cm) long, from spring to early summer. ↕ 10ft (3m), ↔ 8ft (2.5m). Zone 8.
***C.* 'Gentian Plume'.** Open, spreading, evergreen shrub with alternate, ovate-oblong, strongly veined, shallowly toothed, mid-green leaves, 3in (8cm) or more long. Deep sky-blue flowers are borne in large, open, terminal and axillary panicles, 5in (13cm) or more long, in late spring and often again in autumn. ↕↔ 12ft (4m). Zone 8.
***C.* 'Gloire de Versailles'** ■ syn. *C.* x *delileanus* 'Gloire de Versailles'. Bushy, deciduous shrub with alternate, oval, finely toothed, dark green leaves, to 3in (8cm) long. From midsummer to autumn, bears pale blue flowers in large, terminal and axillary panicles, to 4in (10cm) or more long. ↕↔ 5ft (1.5m). Zone 7b.
C. gloriosus (Point Reyes creeper). Prostrate or decumbent, evergreen shrub with opposite, oblong-elliptic, holly-like, leathery leaves, to 1½in (4cm) long, dark green and hairless above, gray-hairy beneath, with strongly toothed margins. In late spring and early summer, bears deep blue to purple flowers in rounded, terminal, umbel-like cymes, to 2in (5cm) across. ↕ 12in (30cm), ↔ 10–12ft (3–4m). California. Zone 7b. **'Anchor Bay'** has dense growth and dark blue flowers; ↕ 20in (50cm), ↔ 6ft (2m). **'Emily Brown'** has small, very strongly toothed leaves, to 1in (2.5cm) long, and dark indigo flowers; ↕ 3ft (1m), ↔ 12ft (4m).
C. griseus (Carmel ceanothus). Vigorous, evergreen shrub producing alternate, ovate, glossy, dark green leaves, to 2in (5cm) long, gray-hairy beneath. Pale to dark blue flowers are borne in large, rounded, terminal and lateral panicles, to 3in (8cm) across, in late spring and early summer. ↕↔ 10ft (3m). California. Zone 8. **var. *horizontalis* 'Yankee Point'** bears profuse bright blue flowers; ↕ 24–36in (60–90cm), ↔ 10ft (3m). **'Santa Ana'** is low-growing, with very dark blue flowers; ↕ 5ft (1.5m), ↔ 15ft (5m).
C. hearstiorum. Prostrate, evergreen shrub with alternate, deeply veined, oblong, toothed, dark green leaves, to 1¼in (3cm) long, white-hairy beneath. Bears rich, dark blue flowers in rounded, terminal and lateral cymes, 1in (2.5cm) across, in late spring and early summer. ↕ 12in (30cm), ↔ 6ft (2m). California. Zone 8.
***C.* 'Henri Désfosse'.** Bushy, deciduous shrub with alternate, oval, toothed, mid-green leaves, to 3in (8cm) long. From midsummer to autumn, bears dark blue flowers in large, terminal and lateral panicles, 3–5in (8–13cm) across. ↕↔ 5ft (1.5m). Zone 8.
C. impressus (Santa Barbara ceanothus). Spreading, evergreen shrub with small, alternate, rounded to elliptic, deeply veined, dark green leaves, to ½in (1.5cm) long. Dark blue flowers are produced in rounded, terminal cymes, to 1in (2.5cm) across, in mid- and late spring. ↕ 5ft (1.5m), ↔ 8ft (2.5m). California. Zone 8. **'Puget Blue'** is vigorous, with larger, elliptic-oblong leaves, to ¾in (2cm) long, and profuse dark blue flowers, borne in cymes to 1¼in (3cm) long; ↕↔ 10ft (3m).
C. incanus ■ (Coast whitethorn). Spreading, stoutly branched, evergreen shrub with spiny, glaucous-gray shoots and alternate, ovate or broadly elliptic, entire or slightly toothed, gray-green leaves, to 2½in (6cm) long. In mid- and late spring, slightly fragrant, creamy white flowers are borne in lateral panicles, to 3in (8cm) long. ↕ 10ft (3m), ↔ 12ft (4m). California. Zone 8.
***C.* 'Italian Skies'.** Spreading, evergreen shrub with alternate, ovate, finely toothed, glossy, mid-green leaves, to ¾in (2cm) long. Bright blue flowers are borne in dense, conical, terminal and lateral cymes, to 3in (8cm) long, in late spring. ↕ 5ft (1.5m), ↔ 10ft (3m). Zone 8.
***C.* 'Julia Phelps'.** Rounded, evergreen shrub producing small, alternate, oblong-elliptic, finely toothed, dark green leaves, to 1in (2.5cm) long. Violet flowers, opening from red-purple buds, are borne in dense, rounded, terminal and lateral cymes, to 1¼in (3cm) across, in late spring and early summer. ↕ 6ft (2m), ↔ 8ft (2.5m). Zone 8.
***C.* 'Marie Simon'.** Upright, bushy, deciduous shrub with alternate, oval, toothed leaves, to 2in (5cm) long, borne on red stems. Pale pink flowers open in terminal panicles, to 3in (8cm) or more long, from midsummer to autumn. ↕↔ 5ft (1.5m). Zone 8.
C. papillosus* var. *roweanus. Bushy, spreading, evergreen shrub with slender, alternate, oblong to linear, dark green leaves, to 2in (5cm) long, covered on the margins of the upper surfaces with sticky glands. Dark blue to purple-blue flowers are produced in terminal and axillary racemes, 1¼–1½in (3–4cm) long, in mid- and late spring. ↕ 5ft (1.5m), ↔ 10ft (3m). California. Zone 8.

Ceanothus incanus (inset: flower detail)

Ceanothus 'Perle Rose'

***C.* 'Perle Rose'** ■ Bushy, deciduous shrub with alternate, oval, toothed, pale green leaves, to 2in (5cm) long. From midsummer to autumn, bears carmine-pink flowers in many terminal and lateral panicles, to 2½in (6cm) or more long. ↕↔ 5ft (1.5m). Zone 8.
***C.* 'Pin Cushion'** ■ Rounded, evergreen shrub with oblong-elliptic, dark green leaves, to 1½in (4cm) long. Mid- to light blue flowers are borne freely in terminal and axillary panicles, 2in (5cm) long, in late spring. ↕↔ to 6ft (2m). Zone 8.
C. purpureus (Hollyleaf ceanothus). Spreading, evergreen shrub with rigid shoots and opposite, holly-like, broadly elliptic to rounded, wavy-margined, spine-toothed, glossy, dark green leaves, to ¾in (2cm) long. In spring, red-purple buds open to purple-blue flowers in dense, lateral, umbel-like cymes, to 1½in (4cm) across. ↕ 4ft (1.2m), ↔ 6ft (1.8m). California. Zone 8.
***C.* x *regius* 'Cynthia Postan'** see *C.* 'Cynthia Postan'.
C. repens see *C. thyrsiflorus* var. *repens.*
C. rigidus (Monterey ceanothus). Intricately branched, evergreen shrub producing small, opposite, wedge-shaped to rounded, obovate, toothed leaves, to ½in (1.5cm) long, glossy, mid-green above and softly downy beneath, clustered on rigid shoots. Bright blue to purple-blue flowers are borne in dense, lateral, umbel-like cymes, to ¾in (2cm)

Ceanothus 'Pin Cushion'

Ceanothus 'Skylark'

across, during late spring and early summer. ↕ 4ft (1.2m), ↔ 6ft (2m). California. Zone 8. **'Snowball'** has white flowers.

***C.* 'Skylark'** ■ Bushy, evergreen shrub with alternate, oblong-elliptic, finely toothed, glossy, mid-green leaves, to 2in (5cm) long. Dark blue flowers are borne in profuse, open, terminal and lateral panicles, 2½–3in (6–8cm) long, in late spring and early summer. ↕ 6ft (2m), ↔ 5ft (1.5m). Zone 8.

***C.* 'Snow Flurries'.** Vigorous, upright, evergreen shrub with opposite, obovate, toothed, dark green leaves, ¼–½in (0.6–1.5cm) long, paler green beneath. Fragrant white flowers are borne in axillary panicles, 2in (5cm) long, from midspring to early summer. ↕↔ 4ft (1.2m). Zone 8.

***C.* 'Southmead'.** Compact, bushy, evergreen shrub with alternate, oblong, finely toothed, dark green leaves, to 1¼in (3cm) long. In late spring and early summer, bears dark, rich blue flowers in oblong, lateral cymes, to 1¼in (3cm) long. ↕↔ 5ft (1.5m). Zone 8.

C. thyrsiflorus (Blueblossom). Vigorous, upright, evergreen shrub with arching branches and alternate, ovate, toothed, glossy, mid-green leaves, to 1½in (4cm) long. In spring, bears pale to dark blue flowers in large, terminal and lateral panicles, 1¼–3in (3–8cm) long. ↕↔ 20ft (6m). California, Oregon. Zone 8. **'Millerton Point'** has spreading branches and bears honey-scented, creamy white flowers in panicles to 3½in (9cm) long. **var. *repens***, syn. *C. repens* (Creeping blueblossom), is low and spreading; ↕ 3ft (1m), ↔ 8ft (2.5m); coastal N. California. **var. *repens* 'Ken Taylor'** is more prostrate; ↕ to 12in (30cm).

***C.* 'Topaze'.** Bushy, deciduous shrub producing alternate, oval, dark green leaves, to 3in (8cm) long. From midsummer to autumn, bears dark indigo-blue flowers in large, terminal and axillary panicles, to 3in (8cm) long. ↕↔ 5ft (1.5m). Zone 8.

C.* x *veitchianus (*C. griseus* x *C. rigidus*). Spreading, rigidly branched, evergreen shrub with small, alternate or opposite, wedge-shaped, toothed leaves, to ¾in (2cm) long, glossy, dark green above and gray-green-hairy beneath. Bears dark blue flowers in dense, rounded, lateral cymes, to 1¼in (3cm) long, in mid- and late spring. ↕↔ 10ft (3m). California. Zone 8.

▷ ***Cedrela sinensis*** see *Toona sinensis*

Cedronella canariensis

CEDRONELLA

LAMIACEAE

Genus of one species of short-lived, woody-based perennial found on sunny, rocky slopes in the Canary Islands. It has alternate, 3-palmate leaves and 2-lipped flowers borne in long, terminal, whorled racemes. It is cultivated for its aromatic foliage, which is sometimes used in potpourri and herb teas. Where not hardy, grow *C. canariensis* in a cool conservatory or greenhouse, or outdoors in containers as an annual. In warmer areas, grow cedronella in a scented or herb garden.

• **CULTIVATION** Under glass, grow in soil-based potting mix in full light. From spring to autumn, water moderately and apply a balanced liquid fertilizer monthly; water more sparingly in winter. Outdoors, grow in well-drained, fertile soil in full sun.

• **PROPAGATION** Sow seed at 59–64°F (15–18°C) in early spring. Root soft-wood cuttings in late spring.

• **PESTS AND DISEASES** Whiteflies may be a problem under glass.

C. canariensis ■ syn. *C. triphylla* (Balm of Gilead). Erect, woody-based, slender-stemmed perennial with aromatic, 3-palmate, mid-green leaves, 3–5in (8–13cm) long, emitting a cedar-like scent when touched. In midsummer, bears whorls of 2-lipped, white, pink, or lilac flowers, to ¾in (2cm) long. ↕ to 4ft (1.2m), ↔ 24in (60cm). Canary Islands. ❄ (min. 41°F/5°C)

C. mexicana see *Agastache mexicana*.

C. triphylla see *C. canariensis*.

CEDRUS

Cedar

PINACEAE

Genus of 4 species of monoecious, evergreen, coniferous trees found in forest in the W. Himalayas and the Mediterranean. Some authorities give *C. atlantica* and *C. brevifolia* subspecific rank under *C. libani*, but they are maintained here as species. The needle-like foliage is arranged in clusters on short shoots, which develop new whorls each year. Cones are produced terminally on short shoots. The male cones, borne in autumn, are erect, cylindrical, light brown, and to 3in (8cm) long. The female cones are erect, ovoid to oblong, cylindrical or barrel-shaped, green then brown, and to 5in (13cm) long; they ripen slowly over 2 years, then break up to release the seeds. With their large, spreading branches, cedars are majestic specimen trees, but they need ample space if they are to achieve their full potential.

• **CULTIVATION** Grow in a sunny, open site, in any well-drained soil. Pruning group 1. If double leaders are produced, the weaker shoot should be cut out in autumn.

• **PROPAGATION** Sow seed in spring, after 21 days' moist pre-chill at 32–34°F (0–1°C). Graft selected cultivars in late summer or winter.

• **PESTS AND DISEASES** Pinewood nematode, root rot, needle blights, stem cankers, dieback, scale insects, pine sawfly, mealybugs, and caterpillars are problems. Boron toxicity causes yellowing and bronzing of needles.

C. atlantica, syn. *C. libani* subsp. *atlantica* (Atlas cedar). Conical, coniferous tree, later becoming more open, with fissured, silvery gray bark. Produces sharply pointed, roughly 4-sided, dark green to glaucous blue leaves, to 1in (2.5cm) long, in whorls of 30–45. Female cones, 2½–4in (6–10cm) long, are barrel-shaped and green, becoming pale brown. ↕ to 130ft (40m), ↔ to 30ft (10m). Morocco (Atlas Mountains). Zone 6. **'Aurea'** is a slow-growing, conical tree with golden yellow foliage when young, maturing green. **f. *fastigiata*** is an upright, narrow-crowned tree with bluish green leaves. **f. *glauca*** ■ (Blue Atlas cedar) has vivid, glaucous blue foliage, silvery white at first. **'Glauca Pendula'** has pendent, glaucous, blue-green foliage.

C. brevifolia, syn. *C. libani* subsp. *brevifolia* (Cyprus cedar). Open-crowned, coniferous tree with a narrow habit when young, becoming broader with age, and with fissured, silvery gray bark. Sharply pointed leaves, to ½in (1.5cm) long, are gray-green to mid-green, sometimes bluish green, and borne in whorls of 20–30. Cylindrical, green then pale brown female cones are 3–4in (7–10cm) long. ↕ 50–80ft (15–25m), ↔ to 40ft (12m). Cyprus. Zone 6.

C. deodara (Deodar cedar). Conical, coniferous tree with spreading branches, pendent shoot tips, and dark brown or black bark. The needle-like leaves, 1½–2in (4–5cm) long, are bright to glaucous, mid-green, and borne in whorls of 20–30. Glaucous, barrel-shaped female cones, 3–5in (8–13cm) long, are first green, ripening to brown. ↕ to 130ft (40m), ↔ to 30ft (10m). W. Himalayas. Zone 7. **'Aurea'** ■ is slow-growing, with golden yellow foliage, becoming greener as it matures; ↕ 15ft (5m). **'Cream Puff'** has a conical habit and creamy white foliage. ↕ to 6ft (2m), ↔ to 4ft (1.2m). **'Pendula'** has long, drooping branches. **'Shalimar'** has rich blue-green leaves and is much hardier than the species; Zone 6.

C. libani ■ (Cedar of Lebanon). Coniferous tree with wide-spreading branches, conical when young, flat-topped when old. The bark is black or brown with scaly fissures and ridges. Slightly flattened, 4-sided, sharply

Cedrus deodara 'Aurea'

Cedrus atlantica f. *glauca*

Cedrus libani

C

Cedrus libani 'Sargentii'

pointed, dark green to gray-green leaves, to 1in (2.5cm) long, are borne in whorls of 10–20. Barrel-shaped, dull green to brown female cones, broadest below the middle, are 3–5in (8–13cm) long. ↕↔ to 100ft (30m). Lebanon to Turkey. Zone 7. **subsp. *atlantica*** see *C. atlantica*. **subsp. *brevifolia*** see *C. brevifolia*. **'Sargentii'** ■ is slow-growing, with a pendent habit, and may be trained to make a rounded bush.

CEIBA

BOMBACACEAE

Genus of 4 species of large, spiny-trunked, deciduous trees from tropical North and South America, Africa, and Asia, favoring moist sites in forest and rainforest. The handsome leaves are alternate and palmate, with entire or finely toothed leaflets. Conspicuous, 5-petaled flowers are borne singly or in axillary clusters on bare stems, and are followed by large seed pods containing seeds padded with white floss (kapok). In cool climates, grow young specimens as foliage plants in a warm greenhouse. In tropical regions, they make splendid specimen and shade trees.

Ceiba pentandra

• **CULTIVATION** Under glass, grow in soil-based potting mix in full light shaded from hot sun. In growth, provide high humidity, water freely, and apply a balanced fertilizer monthly; water sparingly when leafless. Outdoors, grow in fertile, humus-rich, moist but well-drained soil in full sun. Pruning group 1; may need restrictive pruning under glass.
• **PROPAGATION** Sow seed at 70–75°F (21–24°C) in spring. Root semi-ripe cuttings in summer.
• **PESTS AND DISEASES** Spider mites often infest plants under glass.

C. pentandra ■ (Kapok, White silk cotton tree). Tall tree, erect at first then spreading, with a spiny trunk that eventually forms buttresses. Palmate, mid-green leaves, 3–6in (8–15cm) long, consist of 5–8 oblong-lance-shaped, entire leaflets. Clusters of cup-shaped, yellow, white, or pink flowers, 2½in (6cm) across, are borne from late winter to early spring. ↕ 80–230ft (25–70m), ↔ 15–80ft (5–25m). W. Africa (possibly introduced from South America). ❀ (min. 61°F/16°C)

CELASTRUS

Bittersweet, Staff vine

CELASTRACEAE

Genus of about 30 species of deciduous, rarely evergreen shrubs and twining, woody climbers, with alternate, simple, usually toothed leaves. They are found worldwide but occur mainly in thickets and woodland in warm-temperate or subtropical regions. Their attraction as garden plants lies in their ornamental autumn fruits, which split when ripe to reveal colorful seeds. Male and female flowers, in terminal or axillary racemes, panicles, or cymes, are often borne on separate plants. Train against a wall, fence, or pergola, or up a tree.
• **CULTIVATION** Grow in well-drained soil in full sun; will tolerate partial shade. Plant at least one male with several females to ensure fruit production on dioecious types. The vigorous species need strong support; if grown up trees, these should be at least 30ft (10m) tall. Pruning group 11, in winter or early spring.
• **PROPAGATION** Sow seed in containers in an open frame as soon as ripe, or in spring. Insert root cuttings in winter, or semi-ripe cuttings in summer.
• **PESTS AND DISEASES** Powdery mildew, *Nectria* canker, and fungal leaf spots occur.

Celastrus orbiculatus

C. articulatus see *C. orbiculatus*.
C. orbiculatus ■ syn. *C. articulatus* (Oriental bittersweet, Staff vine). Vigorous, woody, deciduous climber with broadly elliptic to rounded, scalloped to toothed, mid-green leaves, to 4in (10cm) long, turning yellow in autumn. Axillary cymes of small green flowers open in summer, followed by clusters of bead-like yellow fruit that open to expose pink to red seeds. Has become a weed in some areas. ↕ 46ft (14m). E. Asia. Zone 4.
C. scandens (American bittersweet, Climbing bittersweet, Staff tree, Staff vine). Woody, deciduous climber with oval to ovate, toothed, mid-green leaves, 4in (10cm) long. In summer, bears small, yellow-green flowers in terminal panicles or racemes, followed by clusters of orange-yellow fruit with red seeds. ↕ 30ft (10m). E. North America. Zone 3.

CELMISIA

New Zealand daisy

ASTERACEAE

Genus of about 60 species of evergreen, mat- or rosette-forming perennials and subshrubs, mostly from grassland, moors, or scree at high altitudes in New Zealand and S.E. Australia. They often have silky, silvery foliage, and bear daisy-like, solitary flowerheads, usually with white ray florets (occasionally flushed lilac or pale yellow) and yellow disk florets, in late spring and summer. They are excellent free-flowering foliage plants for a rock garden or for growing among small shrubs; grow smaller species as specimens in pans in an alpine house. Celmisias thrive in cool, moist climates.
• **CULTIVATION** Grow in moist but well-drained, slightly acidic, humus-rich soil in sun or partial shade. Some species, especially *C. argentea* and *C. sessiliflora*, need protection from winter moisture. In dry areas, shade from hot sun, and spray regularly during dry periods. In an alpine house, grow in a mix of equal parts acidic loam, leaf mold, and sharp sand. Move container-grown plants to a cool outdoor site in summer.
• **PROPAGATION** Sow seed in containers in an open frame as soon as ripe. Celmisias hybridize freely but often produce only a few viable seeds. Divide in spring, or root individual rosettes as cuttings in spring.
• **PESTS AND DISEASES** Prone to aphids and spider mites under glass.

Celmisia ramulosa

C. argentea. Cushion-forming perennial with densely packed, silver-woolly rosettes of linear leaves, to ½in (1.5cm) long. In late spring and early summer, bears almost stemless flowerheads, to 1in (2.5cm) across, with narrow, widely spaced white ray florets, and yellow disk florets. ↕ 1in (2.5cm), ↔ to 4in (10cm). New Zealand (South Island). Zone 8.
C. bellidioides. Mat-forming perennial with rooting stems and small rosettes of obovate-oblong or spoon-shaped, dark green, leathery leaves, to ½in (1.5cm) long. In early summer, bears white-rayed flowerheads, to 1in (2.5cm) wide, with yellow disk florets, on green stems to 1½in (4cm) long. ↕ to 2in (5cm), ↔ to 12in (30cm). New Zealand (South Island). Zone 8.
***C. coriacea* of gardens** see *C. semicordata*.
C. gracilenta. Tufted perennial with erect to semi-prostrate, very narrow, linear leaves, to 4in (10cm) long, with recurved margins; they are dark green, mottled brown above, and silky white beneath. Flowerheads, to ¾in (2cm) across, with white ray florets and yellow disk florets, are borne on densely gray-woolly stems, to 8in (20cm) tall, in early summer. ↕↔ 8in (20cm). New Zealand. Zone 8.
C. incana. Clump-forming subshrub with rosettes of obovate-oblong, brilliant white, silky-hairy leaves, 1¼–2in (3–5cm) long. Flowerheads, to 1½in (4cm) across, with numerous white ray florets and yellow disk florets, are produced on white-woolly stems, to 4in (10cm) long, in early summer. ↕ to 6in (15cm), ↔ to 8in (20cm). New Zealand. Zone 8.
C. ramulosa ■ Subshrub with branching stems and erect, overlapping, linear-oblong leaves, ⅜–½in (9–15mm) long, dark green above, densely white-woolly beneath. In late spring and early summer, bears flowerheads, 1in (2.5cm) across, with many white ray florets and pale yellow disk florets, on slender, sticky, whitish stems, 1½–2in (4–5cm) high. ↕↔ to 10in (25cm). New Zealand (South Island). Zone 7b.
C. semicordata ■ syn. *C. coriacea* of gardens. Clump-forming perennial with short rhizomes and erect, then recurved, sword- to lance-shaped, leathery, silky-hairy leaves, gray-green above, white beneath, to 12in (30cm) long. White-rayed flowerheads, to 3in (8cm) across, with yellow disk florets, are borne on

Celmisia semicordata

Celmisia spectabilis

Celosia argentea 'Apricot Brandy' (top) and 'New Look' (bottom)

Celosia argentea Century Series 'Century Yellow'

erect, whitish green stems, 12–16in (30–40cm) tall, in early and mid-summer. ↕ to 20in (50cm), ↔ to 12in (30cm). New Zealand (South Island). Zone 8.

C. sessiliflora. Cushion-forming perennial with rosettes of densely silver-woolly, sometimes olive-green, stiff, linear leaves, to ½in (1.5cm) long. Flowerheads, to 1¼in (3cm) across, with white ray florets and yellow disk florets, are produced on whitish green stems, 1–2in (2.5–5cm) long, in early summer. ↕ to 2in (5cm), ↔ to 8in (20cm). New Zealand (South Island). Zone 8.

C. spectabilis ▣ Tufted, clump-forming perennial with short rhizomes and narrowly oblong-lance-shaped, wide-spreading, leathery leaves, to 10in (25cm) long, glossy, dark green to silvery green above, and densely white- to buff-woolly beneath. Flowerheads, to 2in (5cm) across, with long white ray florets and yellow disk florets, are borne on densely whitish-woolly stems, 4–10in (10–25cm) long, in early summer. ↕↔ to 12in (30cm). New Zealand. Zone 8.

C. walkeri ▣ syn. *C. webbiana.* Sub-shrub with spreading, semi-decumbent, woody stems and terminal rosettes of linear-oblong, leathery, gray-green leaves, to 2in (5cm) long, densely white-woolly beneath. In early summer, white-rayed flowerheads, to 1½in (4cm) wide, with yellowish white disk florets, are borne on slender, sticky green stems, to 8in (20cm) tall. ↕↔ to 12in (30cm). New Zealand (South Island). Zone 8.

C. webbiana see *C. walkeri.*

Celmisia walkeri

CELOSIA

Cockscomb

AMARANTHACEAE

Genus of 50–60 species of erect annuals, perennials, and shrubs from dry slopes, stony soils, and scrub in subtropical and tropical Asia, Africa, and North, Central, and South America. Celosias have alternate, lobed or simple, oval to lance-shaped leaves and brightly colored, terminal or axillary cymes of tiny flowers. The cultivars often have plume-like (Plumosa group) or crested (Cristata group) inflorescences: the upright plumes of Plumosa group cultivars are frequently used for summer bedding, while Cristata group cultivars, with their tightly clustered flowerheads, make interesting subjects for growing in containers. Both groups are treated as annuals; they provide good cut flowers, either fresh or dried.

• **CULTIVATION** Under glass, grow in soil-based potting mix in full light with good ventilation; when in bloom, admit only bright filtered light to prolong flowering. Once the roots fill the container, water moderately but regularly, mist lightly, and apply a balanced liquid fertilizer every 2 weeks. Outdoors, after any danger of frost has passed, plant in moist but well-drained, fertile soil in a sheltered position in full sun; water freely in dry weather.

• **PROPAGATION** Sow seed at 64°F (18°C) from early to late spring. Transplant as soon as possible to prevent stunted growth and premature flowering.

• **PESTS AND DISEASES** Prone to foot and root rot, and fungal leaf spot diseases. Spider mites, whiteflies, and aphids may be problems under glass.

C. argentea. Upright, branching perennial, usually grown as an annual, with oval to lance-shaped, pale green leaves, to 6in (15cm) long. Flowers are silvery white, and produced in dense, terminal spikes, 2–4in (5–10cm) long, in summer. ↕ to 24in (60cm), ↔ to 18in (45cm). Equatorial tropics in Asia, Africa, and North, Central, and South America. Cultivars are available in shades and combinations of red, orange, yellow, and cream. Plumosa group cultivars have open, feathery, pyramidal flowerheads, 4–10in (10–25cm) long; those in the Cristata group are compact plants with crested, coral-like heads of tightly clustered flowers, 3–12in (8–30cm) across. **'Apricot Brandy'** ▣ (Plumosa group) is a many-branched cultivar producing deep orange flowerheads; ↕ to 20in (50cm). **Big Chief Mix** (Cristata group) is tall, and bears large, cauliflower-shaped flowerheads, 6in (15cm) across, in shades of pink, red, and yellow; ↕ 3ft (1m). Cultivars of **Century Series** (Plumosa group) produce vivid red, rose-pink, or yellow flowerheads; **'Century Yellow'** ▣ is a vigorous cultivar with golden yellow flowerheads suitable for drying; ↕ to 18in (45cm). **'Fairy Fountains'** (Plumosa group) bears flowerheads in a range of pastel colors, including pink, salmon-pink, and creamy yellow; ↕ to 16in (40cm). **Jewel Box Mix** (Cristata group) has green-and-bronze foliage and flower-heads in bright colors, including yellow, pink, salmon, bronze, and deep red, with sometimes 2 or 3 colors on an individual head; ↕ 6–8in (15–20cm). Cultivars of **Kimono Series** (Plumosa group) are exceptionally dwarf, producing disproportionately large flowerheads in bright colors, including salmon-pink, rose-red, yellow, and creamy white; ↕ to 8in (20cm). Cultivars of **Kurume Series** (Cristata group) are available in a wide color range, including gold, yellow, rose-pink, orange, scarlet, orange-red, and red-and-gold bicolors; the flowerheads, good for cutting, are to 8in (20cm) across; ↕ 4ft (1.2m). **'New Look'** ▣ (Plumosa group) has dark purple-green foliage and bears deep red flowerheads; ↕ to 18in (45cm). **Olympia Series** ▣ (Cristata group) cultivars are dwarf, and bear flowerheads in many colors including golden yellow, scarlet, light red, deep cerise, and purple; ↕ to 8in (20cm).

***C. spicata* Flamingo Series.** Cultivars from this series of annuals are upright and branching, with lance-shaped, mid-green leaves, 2½–5in (6–13cm) long. In summer, they produce compact, erect, and cylindrical, barley-like spikes of flowers, 4–5in (10–13cm) long, pink toward the tips and silvery white at the bases. The flowerheads are excellent for both cutting and drying. ↕ to 7in (18cm), ↔ to 6in (15cm).

▷ ***Celsia*** see *Verbascum*

Celosia argentea Olympia Series

CELTIS

Hackberry, Nettle tree

ULMACEAE

Genus of about 70 species of deciduous and evergreen trees and shrubs from temperate and tropical regions in both hemispheres, usually found in woodland, on rocky slopes, or on riverbanks. Hackberries are grown for their form, habit, and foliage, which often colors well in autumn. They have alternate and usually toothed leaves. The small green, unisexual flowers are borne in spring; male flowers are produced in clusters at the base of twigs, while the females are produced singly or in twos or threes from the leaf axils, and are followed in autumn by spherical, fleshy berries. Use hackberries as lawn specimens or in a woodland garden. They grow best in continental climates with hot summers; in cool, maritime climates they often form small, multi-stemmed trees.

• **CULTIVATION** In warm climates, grow in deep, fertile, well-drained soil in sun or partial shade. In cooler areas, hackberries thrive in dry soils and need a warm site in full sun. Pruning group 1.

• **PROPAGATION** Sow seed in a seedbed or open frame in autumn.

• **PESTS AND DISEASES** Powdery mildew, downy mildew, mushroom root rot, fungal root rot, and leaf spot are common. Hackberry psyllid leaf gall and hackberry witches' broom are common. Eriophyid mites and nematodes occur.

Celtis occidentalis

C. australis ▣ (European nettle tree). Spreading, deciduous tree producing ovate to lance-shaped, rough, coarsely toothed leaves, to 6in (15cm) long; they are dark green above, downy and light green beneath, turning yellow in autumn. Bears edible red fruit, to ½in (1.5cm) across, ripening blackish brown. ↕↔ 70ft (20m). Mediterranean, S.W. Asia. Zone 7.

C. laevigata (Common hackberry, Mississippi hackberry, Sugar hackberry). Spreading, deciduous tree with ovate to lance-shaped, entire or sparsely toothed leaves, to 4in (10cm) long, dark green and hairless above, paler and softly hairy on the veins beneath. Sweet, edible, orange-red fruit, to ¼in (6mm) across, ripen to purple-black. ↕↔ 40ft (12m). S. US. Zone 2b.

C. occidentalis ▣ (Hackberry, Sugarberry). Spreading, deciduous tree with broadly ovate to ovate-lance-shaped, sharply toothed leaves, to 5in (13cm) long, rounded to heart-shaped at the bases; they are glossy, mid-green above, paler and sparsely softly hairy on the veins beneath. Edible fruit, to ½in (1.5cm) across, ripen from yellow or red to purple. ↕ 70ft (20m), ↔ 50ft (15m). E. North America. Zone 2b. **'Prairie Pride'** has a uniform, compact, oval crown and produces thick, leathery, shiny, dark green leaves.

C. reticulata (Western hackberry, Sugarberry). Spreading, deciduous tree or shrub producing thick, oblong to ovate, usually entire but sometimes toothed, dark green leaves, to 4in (10cm) long, bright green above, darker with downy veins beneath. Sweet, edible, orange-red fruit, to ½in (1.5cm) across, ripen to deep purple. ↕↔ 25ft (8m). S.W. US. Zone 5.

C. sinensis (Japanese hackberry). Spreading, deciduous tree producing oblong to ovate leaves, to 3in (8cm) long, shallowly blunt-toothed except at the bases, glossy, dark green above, duller beneath, and hairless on both sides. Sweet, edible fruit, to ½in (1.5cm) across, are dark orange, ripening to red-brown. ↕↔ 40ft (12m). E. China, Korea, Japan. Zone 7b.

Celtis australis (inset: leaf detail)

CENTAUREA

Hardheads, Knapweed

ASTERACEAE

Genus of about 450 species of annuals, biennials, perennials, and subshrubs found in dry sites, including woodland, rocky mountain slopes, subalpine meadows, and sand dunes. They occur mainly in Europe and the Mediterranean, with a few in Asia, Australia, and North America. The simple leaves are pinnatisect or pinnatifid, and sometimes silver-hairy. They bear spherical or hemispherical flowerheads with tubular, usually deeply lobed florets, the outer ones often longer and more spreading than the rest. Each flowerhead has a conspicuous involucre, the bracts overlapping, fringed, and often with toothed or spiny, silvery white or black tips. Grow in a border or rock garden; some are ideal for naturalizing in grass or in a wildflower garden. Some perennials are grown as summer bedding annuals. For winter flowering, grow *C. cyanus* in containers. All are attractive to bees and butterflies, and many produce excellent cut flowers.

• **CULTIVATION** Grow in well-drained soil in full sun. *C. macrocephala* and *C. montana* and its cultivars require moist but well-drained soil in sun or partial shade; other perennials will tolerate some drought.

• **PROPAGATION** Sow seed of annuals *in situ* in spring, or in peat pots to avoid root disturbance; in all but extremely cold climates, seed of *C. cyanus* may be sown in early autumn to flower early the next year. Sow seed of perennials in containers in a cold frame in spring, and divide in spring or autumn. Sow seed of *C. montana* in late summer, or insert root cuttings in winter.

• **PESTS AND DISEASES** White mold, rust, downy and powdery mildew, thread blight, and Southern blight may occur.

Centaurea cyanus

C. americana (Basket flower, Cardo-del-valle). Thick, erect annual with rough, lance-shaped leaves, 4in (10cm) long. Bears large, rose-lilac to white flowerheads, 4–6in (10–15cm) across, with densely webbed buds, throughout the summer. Flowerheads close at night. ↕ 3–5ft (1–1.5m), 30–36in (75–90cm). S. central to S.E. US. **'Alaska'** produces white flowers. **'Aloha'** has lilac flowers with pale centers.

C. bella. Clump-forming perennial with densely white-woolly stems and obovate to fiddle-shaped, pinnatifid, feathery, light green leaves, to 5in (13cm) long, with elliptic to obovate lobes, the terminal lobes larger than the rest. Leaf undersides and flower stems are covered in fine white hairs. Pale pink to purple-pink flowerheads, to 1¾in (4.5cm) across, are borne in midsummer. ↕ 8–12in (20–30cm), ↔ 18in (45cm). Caucasus. Zone 4.

C. cineraria, syn. *C. maritima* (Dusty miller). Mound-forming, evergreen subshrub, often grown as an annual, with variable, oblong-ovate, pinnatisect or pinnatifid, felted, silvery gray leaves, to 3–6in (8–15cm) long. Loose,

Centaurea dealbata 'Steenbergii'

Centaurea hypoleuca 'John Coutts'

branching cymes of mustard-yellow flowerheads, ½–1in (1–2.5cm) across, are produced in midsummer; remove them to preserve the foliage effect. ↕ 8–24in (20–60cm), ↔ to 12in (30cm) or more. W. and S. Italy. Zone 7b. Cultivars have a range of foliage characteristics, and are useful summer bedding annuals. **'Cirrus'** has rounded, finely toothed, almost entire, silvery green to white leaves; ↕ to 12in (30cm). **'Silver Dust'** produces very deeply divided, lacy, almost white leaves; ↕ 14–24in (35–60cm).

C. cyanus ■ (Bachelor's buttons, Bluebottle, Cornflower). Erect annual with lance-shaped, entire leaves, 4–8in (10–20cm) long, the lower leaves with a few pinnatifid lobes, and woolly-hairy beneath. Bears dark blue flowerheads, 1–1½in (2.5–4cm) across, with violet-blue inner florets, from late spring to midsummer. ↕ 8–32in (20–80cm), ↔ 6in (15cm). N. temperate regions. Cultivars of **Ball Series** are mauve, pink, red, and white, and are long-lasting when cut; ↕ 30in (75cm). The series includes **'Black Ball'**, which produces warm brown flowerheads. **Boy Series** cultivars have bright green leaves and early-blooming, fully double flowerheads in shades of red, pink, blue, and white; ↕ 3ft (1m), ↔ 30in (75cm). The series includes **'Blue Boy'**, which is bright blue, **'Pinkie'**, which has bright pink flowerheads, and **'Snow Man'**, which has pure white flowerheads. **'Emperor William'** is robust, with gray-green foliage; produces single, vivid, dark blue flowerheads over a long period; ↕ 3ft (1m), ↔ 24in (60cm). **Florence Series** cultivars are compact, uniform, and many-branched, with flowerheads in cherry-red, pink, or white; ↕ to 14in (35cm), ↔ to 10in (25cm). **'Frosted Queen'** is a tall, double bicolor with blue, white, or crimson flowerheads and paler edges; ↕ 3ft (1m), ↔ 24in (60cm). **'Jubilee Gem'** has double, rich blue flowerheads; ↕↔ 10–16in (25–40cm).

Centaurea macrocephala

C. dealbata. Clump-forming perennial with obovate, pinnatisect leaves, to 8in (20cm) long, light green above and gray-green beneath. White-centered pink flowerheads, to 1½in (4cm) across, are borne in midsummer. Requires staking, but easy to grow. Good for cutting. ↕ 36in (90cm), ↔ 24in (60cm). Caucasus. Zone 4. **'Steenbergii'** ■ has dark carmine-pink flowerheads with white-tinged disk florets; ↕ 24in (60cm).

C. hypoleuca. Clump-forming perennial with gently spreading roots and elliptic-lance-shaped, pinnatifid, wavy-margined leaves, 6–8in (15–20cm) long, light green above and gray-white beneath. Bears long-lasting, fragrant, pale to deep pink flowerheads, 2½in (6cm) across, in summer. ↕ 24in (60cm), ↔ 18in (45cm). Caucasus, Turkey, Iran. Zone 5. **'John Coutts'** ■ has deep rose-pink flowerheads.

C. macrocephala ■ (Giant knapweed). Clump-forming, robust perennial with broadly lance-shaped, pinnatifid, mid-green leaves, 6–8in (15–20cm) long, and stiff, leafy stems. In mid- and late summer, buds with fringed, glossy brown involucral bracts, open to deep yellow flowerheads, 1¾–2in (4.5–5cm) across. ↕ to 5ft (1.5m), ↔ 24in (60cm). Caucasus, Turkey. Zone 3.

C. maritima see *C. cineraria.*

C. montana ■ (Mountain bluet). Rhizomatous, mat-forming perennial with ovate to broadly lance-shaped, entire to pinnatifid, sometimes slightly toothed, mid-green leaves, 2½in (6cm) long, woolly beneath, with densely woolly stems. Blue flowerheads, 2in (5cm) across, with reddish violet florets, open from late spring to midsummer. Often needs staking. Self-seeds readily. ↕ 18in (45cm), ↔ 24in (60cm). Mountains of C. Europe. Zone 3. **f. *alba*** has white flowerheads. **'Carnea'**, syn. 'Rosea', produces pink flowerheads. **'Rosea'** see 'Carnea'.

Centaurea montana

Centaurea pulcherrima

C. moschata see *Amberboa moschata.*

C. pulcherrima ■ Clump-forming perennial with lance-shaped to broadly lance-shaped, pinnatifid, silvery green leaves, to 10in (25cm) long. In midsummer, stiff, slender stems each bear a solitary flowerhead, to 2in (5cm) across, with silvery yellow involucral bracts and rose-pink or purple-pink florets. ↕ 12–16in (30–40cm), ↔ 24in (60cm). Caucasus, Turkey. Zone 4.

***C.* 'Pulchra Major'**, syn. *Leuzea centauroides.* Clump-forming perennial with numerous pinnatisect, narrowly ovate leaves, 6–18in (15–45cm) long, dark green above and gray-green beneath. In midsummer, tall stems bear striking buds, with bristly, glossy, silvery green bracts, which open to flowerheads, 3in (8cm) across, with bright purplish red florets. ↕ 4ft (1.2m), ↔ 24in (60cm). Zone 4.

C. rothrockii. Multi-stemmed hardy annual or biennial with lance-shaped, usually hairless leaves, to 5in (13cm) long. Produces pale purple to pink flowerheads, 4–5in (10–13cm) across, with off-white to yellow centers, from summer to autumn. The basket-like seedheads are attractive in arrangements. ↕ 3–5ft (1–1.5m), ↔ 3ft (1m). S.W. US, N. Mexico. Zone 7.

C. simplicicaulis. Rhizomatous perennial forming a dense mat of 2-pinnate, hairy, mid-green leaves, 2in (5cm) long, with 1–4 pairs of elliptic to rounded leaflets. In late spring and early summer, elongated buds, with white-tipped involucral bracts, open to silvery rose-pink flowerheads, 2in (5cm) across, on stiff, slender stems. ↕ to 10in (25cm), ↔ 24in (60cm). S. Caucasus, N. Turkey. Zone 3b.

C. triumfettii* subsp. *stricta. Perennial with short rhizomes and narrowly lance-shaped, entire or slightly toothed, densely gray-woolly leaves, 4in (10cm) long. Solitary, terminal flowerheads, to 1in (2.5cm) across, with clear blue outer florets, reddish violet central florets, and brown, white-tipped bracts, are produced on axillary branches in early summer. ↕ 12in (30cm), ↔ 24in (60cm). C. and E. Europe, N. Balkans. Zone 4.

CENTAURIUM

syn. ERYTHRAEA
Centaury
GENTIANACEAE

Widely distributed genus of about 30 species of rosette-forming or tufted annuals, biennials, and perennials, from Europe, N. Africa, Australia, Chile, the US, and W. Asia, often found in seaside habitats. Their leaves are mostly obovate to elliptic, gray-green to pale green, and ½–2in (1–5cm) long. Flat-topped cymes of upright, shallowly bell-shaped or salverform flowers are borne from early to late summer. Centauries are suitable for a rock garden, trough, or alpine house.

• **CULTIVATION** Grow in any moist but well-drained soil in full sun. They are often short-lived, so propagate regularly.

• **PROPAGATION** Sow seed in containers in a cold frame, as soon as ripe or in autumn. Divide in spring.

• **PESTS AND DISEASES** Powdery mildew, dieback, rust, and fungal spots occur.

C. erythraea (Common centaury). Variable, rosetted biennial or short-lived perennial with solitary or branching stems, and mostly basal, obovate to elliptic, gray-green leaves, ½–2in (1–5cm) long, with 3–7 prominent, parallel veins. In summer, stems 1¼–3in (3–8cm) long bear branched, flat-topped cymes of pink or pink-purple, salverform flowers, each to ½in (1.5cm) across. Thrives in sun or partial shade. ↕ to 3in (8cm), ↔ 1in (2.5cm). Dry grassland in Europe and W. Asia. Zone 8.

C

CENTRADENIA

MELASTOMATACEAE

Genus of 4 or 5 species of evergreen perennials and small shrubs found at forest margins and in moist scrub in Mexico and Central America. They are grown mainly for their small, 4-petaled pink flowers, borne abundantly in terminal or axillary racemes or panicles, and for their attractive foliage. The leaves are entire, often strongly 3-veined, and arranged in opposite pairs; one leaf of each pair is usually smaller than the other. Where not hardy, grow in a warm greenhouse. In warmer areas, use in a shrub border.

• **CULTIVATION** Under glass, grow in soil-based potting mix in bright filtered light. During the growing season, provide high humidity, water freely, and apply a balanced liquid fertilizer monthly; water moderately in winter. Top-dress or pot on in spring. Outdoors, grow in fertile, humus-rich, moist but well-drained soil in partial shade. Trim annually after flowering.

• **PROPAGATION** Sow seed at 64–70°F (18–21°C) in spring. Root softwood cuttings in spring.

• **PESTS AND DISEASES** Infrequent.

C. floribunda. Small, softly hairy shrub of open habit with lance-shaped leaves, 1–2in (2.5–5cm) long, mid- to dark green above and glaucous beneath, with reddish green veins. From winter to spring, bears small, lilac-pink flowers, white within, and ⅜in (8mm) across, in terminal panicles, to 4in (10cm) across. ↕↔ 12–36in (30–90cm). Mexico to Guatemala. ❀ (min. 55°F/13°C)

Centranthus ruber

CENTRANTHUS

Valerian

VALERIANACEAE

Genus of 8–12 species of annuals and perennials, a few subshrubby, from dry, sunny slopes, often on alkaline soils, in S. Europe, the Mediterranean, N.W. Africa, and S.W. Asia. They have erect, branched stems; simple or pinnate, opposite leaves; and funnel-shaped, red or white flowers, borne in terminal and axillary cymes. *C. ruber*, the only species in common cultivation, is free- and long-flowering. It is suitable for a border but grows best in walls and on stony banks. It is attractive to bees and other insects.

• **CULTIVATION** Grow in well-drained, poor to moderately fertile, preferably alkaline soil in full sun. Deadhead regularly and replace every 3 or 4 years.

• **PROPAGATION** Sow seed in containers in a cold frame in spring. Divide perennials with care in early spring.

• **PESTS AND DISEASES** Infrequent.

C. ruber ▣ (Jupiter's beard, Keys of heaven, Red valerian). Clump-forming, woody-based, many-branched perennial producing simple, lance-shaped to ovate, slightly toothed or entire, fairly fleshy, glaucous, deep to mid-green leaves, to 3in (8cm) long. Dense cymes of small, funnel-shaped, fragrant, white, pale rose-pink, or dark crimson flowers, ½in (1.5cm) long, are borne from late spring to late summer. Self-seeds freely. ↕↔ to 3ft (1m). Mediterranean (S. Europe and N. Africa to Turkey). Zone 4.
'Albus' (White Valerian) is compact and bushy, with dense white flower clusters along the stems; ↕ 24in (60cm).
'Coccineus' has large, carmine-red to deep crimson flowers; ↕ 24in (60cm).
'Roseus' bears rose-pink flowers.

CEPHALANTHUS

RUBIACEAE

Widely distributed genus of about 10 species of deciduous and evergreen trees and shrubs found mainly by rivers in temperate and tropical regions of Africa, Asia, and North and Central America. They are grown for their ball-like, terminal or axillary heads of small, fragrant flowers. The leaves are opposite or whorled. Suitable for a shrub border; grow frost-tender species in a temperate greenhouse. The foliage may cause severe discomfort if ingested.

• **CULTIVATION** Grow in fertile, humus-rich, moist but well-drained, neutral to acidic soil in full sun. Pruning group 6.

• **PROPAGATION** Sow seed of hardy species in containers in a cold frame in autumn. Take semi-ripe cuttings in summer, or hardwood cuttings in winter.

• **PESTS AND DISEASES** Infrequent.

C. occidentalis (Buttonbush, Button willow, Honey balls). Open-branched, deciduous shrub or small tree with oval to elliptic-lance-shaped leaves, to 7in (18cm) long. The glossy, mid-green leaves, with red veins and red midribs beneath, are opposite or arranged in whorls of 3, and emerge in late spring. Dense, rounded heads, to 1in (2.5cm) across, of small, very fragrant, tubular-funnel-shaped, white or cream flowers, are produced in late summer and early autumn. ↕ 6ft (2m), ↔ 8ft (2.5m), occasionally to 15ft (5m). New Brunswick south to C. California and Florida, Mexico, Cuba. Zone 4b.
var. *pubescens* has oblong to ovate-lance-shaped leaves and bears large flowerheads, to 2in (5cm) across; Indiana to Texas.

CEPHALARIA

DIPSACACEAE

Genus of about 65 species of annuals and perennials, occurring in habitats ranging from meadows to mountain pastures, from Europe and Africa to C. Asia. They have opposite, pinnatifid or pinnatisect, toothed leaves and scabiosa-like, terminal flowerheads, usually pale yellow or white, with several rows of stiff involucral bracts. *C. gigantea* is cultivated for its imposing stature in a large herbaceous border, as well as for its dark foliage and pastel-yellow flowers. Sturdy enough to stand upright without staking, and tolerant of a range of soils, it is a good choice for a mass planting in an urban setting or wild garden.

• **CULTIVATION** Grow in fertile, moist, well-drained soil in sun or partial shade.

• **PROPAGATION** Sow seed in containers in a cold frame in early spring. Divide in early or midspring.

• **PESTS AND DISEASES** Infrequent.

C. alpina, syn. *Scabiosa alpina*. Clump-forming perennial with elliptic, pinnate or pinnatisect, basal leaves, 6–16in (15–40cm) long, consisting of 3–8 pairs of oblong-lance-shaped, toothed leaflets or lobes. Bears long-stalked, pale yellow flowerheads, 1¼in (3cm) or more wide, the outer florets larger than the rest, in early and midsummer. ↕ to 6ft (2m), ↔ 24in (60cm). Jura mountains, S.W. and C. Alps, N. Apennines. Zone 4.
C. gigantea ▣ syn. *C. tatarica*, *Scabiosa gigantea*, *S. tatarica*. (Giant scabious, Yellow scabious). Clump-forming perennial producing pinnatisect, basal leaves, to 16in (40cm) long, with oblong to broadly lance-shaped, coarsely toothed lobes. In summer, thick, few-branched stems bear primrose-yellow flowerheads, 1½–2½in (4–6cm) across, the outer florets larger than the rest. ↕ to 8ft (2.5m), ↔ 24in (60cm). Caucasus, N. Turkey. Zone 3.
C. tatarica see *C. gigantea*.

Cephalaria gigantea (inset: flowerhead detail)

Cephalocereus senilis

CEPHALOCEREUS

CACTACEAE

Genus of 3 species of columnar, erect, occasionally branching, hairy cacti from rocky areas of C. Mexico. Many species once included in this genus have been transferred to other genera. They have ribbed stems with closely set areoles and numerous spines. Mature plants develop woody growths that bear funnel-shaped flowers in summer, followed by ovoid, dry, hairy red fruits. Where not hardy, grow in a warm greenhouse or conservatory, or use as houseplants. In warm, dry climates, grow outdoors in a desert garden.

• **CULTIVATION** Under glass, grow in a mix of 3 parts standard cactus potting mix and 1 part limestone chips in full light. During the growing season, water moderately and apply a low-nitrogen liquid fertilizer monthly; keep plants completely dry in winter. Outdoors, grow in sharply drained, poor to moderately fertile, slightly alkaline soil in full sun. See also pp.48–49.

• **PROPAGATION** Sow seed at 66–75°F (19–24°C) in spring.

• **PESTS AND DISEASES** Susceptible to root mealybugs and root rot.

C. euphorbioides see *Neobuxbaumia euphorbioides*.
C. senilis ▣ syn. *Pilosocereus senilis* (Old man cactus). Columnar cactus with 20–30 ribs. The areoles bear long, twisting, bristly white hairs that lengthen as the plant ages and almost cover the gray spines (3–5 centrals and 20–30 radials). Nocturnal pink flowers, 2in (5cm) long, are borne in summer. ↕ 40ft (12m), ↔ to 6ft (2m). C. Mexico. ❀ (min. 50°F/10°C)

CEPHALOPHYLLUM

AIZOACEAE

Genus of about 60 species of creeping, clump-forming or spreading, perennial succulents from sandy coastal regions of S.W. Africa and South Africa. They have fleshy, cylindrical to 3-angled leaves. Branched cymes of up to 3 many-petaled, large, daisy-like flowers, with yellow, red, purple, or white petals, and often with colorful stamens, open at about midday in summer. Where not hardy, grow in a cool or temperate greenhouse. In warm, dry regions, use as a groundcover.

Cephalophyllum alstonii

• **CULTIVATION** Under glass, grow in a mix of 2 parts each loam and sharp sand and 1 part leaf mold in full light; provide shade from hot sun and good ventilation. When in growth, water moderately and apply a low-nitrogen liquid fertilizer monthly. Keep plants almost dry at other times. Outdoors, grow in poor to moderately fertile, sharply drained, humus-rich soil in full sun. Some tolerate brief periods of temperatures to 18°F (-8°C). See also pp.48–49.
• **PROPAGATION** Sow seed at 55–64°F (13–18°C) or root cuttings in spring.
• **PESTS AND DISEASES** Susceptible to aphids while flowering.

C. alstonii ▣ Prostrate succulent with gray-green branches, 20in (50cm) or more long, and cylindrical, recurved, semi-erect, spotted, grayish green leaves, to 3in (8cm) long, the upper surfaces flattened. In summer, produces long-stemmed, ruby-red flowers, to 3in (8cm) across, with violet stamens. ↕ 4in (10cm), ↔ indefinite. South Africa (Western Cape). ❀ (min. 45°F/7°C)

CEPHALOTAXUS

Plum yew

CEPHALOTAXACEAE

Genus of up to 9 species of evergreen, normally dioecious, occasionally monoecious, coniferous, small trees or shrubs from forest understory in N.E. India, Burma, Vietnam, China, Korea, Japan, and Taiwan. The dark or mid-green foliage is yew-like, spreading, and 2-ranked on either side of the green shoots; the undersurfaces of the leaves have glaucous or silver bands. Female plants produce fleshy, green, plum-like fruits. Plum yews grow well in shaded sites and are useful as hedging.
• **CULTIVATION** Grow in fertile, moist but well-drained soil in partial shade, or in sun in cool, moist climates. Shelter from wind. Pruning group 9. Trim hedges in early summer. Tolerant of hard clipping.
• **PROPAGATION** Sow seed in containers in a cold frame in autumn, or in spring after stratification. Root greenwood or semi-ripe cuttings of terminal shoots in summer or autumn; cuttings from sideshoots seldom develop normally.
• **PESTS AND DISEASES** Infrequent.

C. fortunei (Fortune plum yew). Shrub or narrow-crowned, small, coniferous tree with whorled branches and

Cephalotaxus harringtonii var. *harringtonii* (inset: fruit detail)

shredding or scaly, red-brown bark. Linear or slightly curved, mid-green leaves, 1½–3½in (4–9cm) long, with 2 white bands beneath, are borne in flat or slightly V-shaped sprays. Ovoid to elliptic, olive-green fruit, to 1in (2.5cm) long, ripening to purple-brown, are borne on short stalks on female plants. ↕ to 30ft (10m), ↔ to 15ft (5m). C. and E. China. Zone 7.
C. harringtonii. (Cowtail pine, Plum yew). Coniferous shrub, occasionally a small tree, with sharp-pointed, slightly curved or linear, dark green leaves, 1½–2½in (4–6cm) long, rising either side of the shoots in a wide V-shape. Female plants produce ovoid to obovoid, olive-green fruit, 1¼in (3cm) long, in autumn. ↕ 10–30ft (3–10m), ↔ 10–20ft (3–6m). Korea, Japan. Zone 6b. **var. *harringtonii*** ▣ is a small tree with a wide, rounded crown and narrowly furrowed, partially peeling, dark gray bark. The leaves, 1–1½in (2.5–4cm) long, are arranged on each shoot in 2 ranks in a V-shape; ↔ 3–15ft (1–5m); Japan, C. and W. China. **'Fastigiata'** is a shrub, with erect branches and radially arranged leaves, to 3in (8cm) long; ↕↔ 15ft (5m). **'Prostrata'** is spreading and low-growing; ↕↔ 2–5ft (0.6–1.5m).

CERARIA

PORTULACACEAE

Genus of 5 or 6 species of succulent, sometimes deciduous shrubs from hilly areas of Namibia and South Africa, with short, swollen trunks and often with waxy bark. They are grown for their thick, fleshy leaves, which are usually opposite, occasionally alternate, and for their small, funnel-shaped, white or pink flowers, borne singly or in clusters of 2–6 in summer. Both male and female plants are needed to obtain fruit. Where not hardy, grow in a temperate conservatory or greenhouse, or as house-plants. In warm, dry areas, grow in a border or desert garden.

• **CULTIVATION** Under glass, grow in a mix of 3 parts standard cactus potting mix and 1 part leaf mold in full light with shade from hot sun. When in growth, water moderately and apply a low-nitrogen fertilizer monthly. Keep almost dry at other times. Outdoors, grow in well-drained, poor to moderately fertile, humus-rich soil in a sheltered, sunny site. See also pp.48–49.
• **PROPAGATION** Sow seed at 66–75°F (19–24°C) as soon as ripe, or root stem cuttings in spring.
• **PESTS AND DISEASES** Aphids can occur.

C. pygmaea. Dwarf, succulent shrub with a short caudex bearing spreading, stiff, fleshy, often down-curving stems covered with thick, ovoid, fleshy, bluish green or yellow-green leaves, to ½in (1.5cm) long. Clusters of 2–5 pale pink flowers, ⅛–¼in (3–6mm) across, are produced in summer. ↕ 8in (20cm), ↔ 12in (30cm). Namibia, South Africa (Western Cape, Northern Cape). ❀ (min. 61°F/16°C)

CERASTIUM

CARYOPHYLLACEAE

Genus of up to 100 annuals and mainly mat-forming or tufted perennials from temperate and arctic of Europe and North America. They are generally hairy, with tiny, star-shaped white flowers with 5 petals, deeply indented or cleft in 2, borne singly or in cymes. The leaves are usually simple, opposite, and entire. *Cerastium* species include many weeds and potential weeds; the species in cultivation are mainly vigorous and mat-forming. Grow at the front of a border, on a wall, in a large rock garden, or as a groundcover.
• **CULTIVATION** Grow in any well-drained soil in full sun. *C. tomentosum* is useful for poor soil on dry, sunny banks.
• **PROPAGATION** Sow seed in containers in an open frame in autumn. Divide in spring; root stem-tip cuttings in summer.
• **PESTS AND DISEASES** Infrequent.

Cerastium tomentosum

C. tomentosum ▣ (Snow in summer). Rampant, mat-forming perennial producing linear or linear-lance-shaped, white- or silver-woolly leaves, ½–1¼in (1–3cm) long. Profuse cymes of star-shaped white flowers, to 1in (2.5cm) across, are produced in late spring and summer. ↕ 2–3in (5–8cm), ↔ indefinite. Italy, including Sicily, and widely naturalized elsewhere in Europe. Zone 4.

CERATOPETALUM

CUNONIACEAE

Genus of 5 species of evergreen shrubs and trees from open woodland and rainforest in Australia and New Guinea. They are valued for their terminal and axillary panicles of 4- or 5-petaled flowers. After flowering, the calyces enlarge and become brightly colored, producing a second, showier display. Leaves are simple or 3-palmate, and borne in opposite pairs. Where not hardy, grow in a cool greenhouse. In frost-free climates, use as unusual specimen plants for a small garden.
• **CULTIVATION** Under glass, grow in soil-based potting mix with additional leaf mold and sharp sand, in full light, with shade from hot sun. In the growing season, water moderately and apply a balanced liquid fertilizer monthly; reduce water in winter. Top-dress or pot on in spring. Outdoors, grow in moderately fertile, moist but well-drained soil in sun or partial shade. Pruning group 1; plants under glass may need restrictive pruning, after flowering.
• **PROPAGATION** Sow seed at 55–64°F (13–18°C) in spring. Root semi-ripe cuttings in summer (rooting may be rather slow).
• **PESTS AND DISEASES** Infrequent.

C. gummiferum (New South Wales Christmas tree). Large shrub or small, bushy tree, erect at first then spreading, with 3-palmate leaves composed of narrowly oblong, shallowly toothed leaflets, to 3in (8cm) long, dark green above, paler beneath. Panicles, to 4in (10cm) or more long, of white flowers, ¼in (6mm) across, with enlarged, bright red calyces, to ½in (1.5cm) across, are borne in spring. ↕ 10–30ft (3–10m), ↔ 6–20ft (2–6m). New South Wales. ❀ (min. 41°F/5°C). **'Christmas Snow'** bears flowers with white calyces. **'White Christmas'** is similar to 'Christmas Snow', but has white-variegated leaves.

CERATOPHYLLUM

Hornwort

CERATOPHYLLACEAE

Genus of about 30 species of almost rootless, submerged aquatic perennials from Eurasia, N. and tropical Africa, and S. and E. US, producing whorls of delicate, stalkless, linear, dark green leaves, ½–1½in (1–4cm) long, often crowded near the growing points. The minute, unisexual flowers are enclosed in axillary bracts, with both male and female flowers borne on the same plant. Hornworts are grown in cold-water aquaria for their delicate foliage, and are good oxygenators for a garden pool; they are very useful for keeping algae in check by outcompeting them for nutrients. They tolerate a wide range of water conditions.

• **CULTIVATION** Grow in water 24–36in (60–90cm) deep in full sun; hornworts will, however, tolerate shade. Grow in a pool, tub, or aquarium in full light. The almost rootless stems spread freely; some shoots may root in mud at the bottom of the water. *C. demersum* overwinters by modified terminal buds (turions), which sink to the bottom until spring, when they develop into young plants. See also pp.52–53.

• **PROPAGATION** Detach small pieces of stem, or turions, and float in water. Cuttings may also be submerged and anchored in sand topped with an inch of pea gravel.

• **PESTS AND DISEASES** Algae may swamp the fragile lower leaves.

C. demersum (Hornwort). Submerged aquatic perennial producing slender, often rootless stems, 12–24in (30–60cm) long, with whorls of forked, brittle, dark green leaves, often borne more densely near the growing points. Tiny, cup-shaped flowers, the males white and ⅛in (3mm) across, the females green and 1⁄16in (2mm) across, are borne from the leaf axils in summer. ↔ indefinite. E. central Europe, Mediterranean, tropical Africa. Zone 7.

CERATOPTERIS

PARKERIACEAE

Genus of 4 species of variable deciduous and semi-evergreen, submerged or floating, aquatic annual and perennial ferns from W. Asia, Indonesia, tropical Africa, tropical North and South America, and N. Australia, occurring in shallow water in lakes and very slow-moving waterways. They are cultivated for their rosettes of lobed or feathery fronds, which are succulent and simple to pinnatifid or pinnate to 4-pinnate. *Ceratopteris* species are good nutrient removers, helping to keep algae growth in check.

• **CULTIVATION** Outdoors, float or grow in the shallow, muddy margins of a pool, tub, or warm-water aquarium in partial shade. Under glass, grow in an aquarium with ample light, at 68–72°F (20–22°C). Grows equally well free-floating or rooted into gravel or peat, in water to 12in (30cm) deep. See also pp.52–53.

• **PROPAGATION** Remove the numerous plantlets that develop along the edges of mature leaves and insert in the substrate, or allow to float on a shallow pan of peaty soil, submerged to its rim, at a minimum temperature of 65°F (18°C).

• **PESTS AND DISEASES** Infrequent.

C. thalictroides (Water fern). Semi-evergreen, floating aquatic annual fern, with sterile fronds that are oblong, 4–8in (10–20cm) long, and simple or only slightly divided. Bears ovate, 2- or 3-pinnate, fertile fronds, 18in (45cm) long, that break off easily. For best effect, plant in aquarium substrate. ↕ 6–8in (15–20cm), ↔ indefinite. Pantropical. ❄ (min. 50°F/10°C)

CERATOSTIGMA

PLUMBAGINACEAE

Genus of about 8 species of deciduous and evergreen subshrubs and herbaceous perennials found in dry, open situations in N.E. tropical Africa, the Himalayas, China, and S.E. Asia. They are grown for their 5-lobed, salverform blue flowers, borne in terminal and axillary, spike-like clusters from late summer to autumn, and for their simple, alternate leaves, which turn red or bronze in autumn. Grow in a mixed or shrub border, or against a warm, sunny wall. *C. plumbaginoides* is also suitable as a groundcover and for a rock garden. Where not hardy, grow *Ceratostigma* species in a cold or cool greenhouse.

• **CULTIVATION** Grow in moderately fertile, light, moist but well-drained soil in full sun. Pruning group 10, for shrubby species, in early to midspring.

• **PROPAGATION** Root softwood cuttings in spring or semi-ripe cuttings in summer. Remove suckers in autumn or spring. Layer in autumn. Overwinter young plants in frost-free conditions.

• **PESTS AND DISEASES** Powdery mildew may be a problem.

C. minus. Open-branched, deciduous shrub with slender, bristly, mid-green stems. Obovate to spoon-shaped, mid-green leaves, to 2in (5cm) long, are rounded at the tips and almost hairless above, but have bristly margins; they turn red in autumn. From late summer to autumn, bears dense, terminal or axillary, spike-like clusters of bright blue or purple-blue flowers, to ¾in (2cm) across and red-purple at the bases. ↕ 3ft (1m), ↔ 5ft (1.5m). W. China. ❄ (min. 35°F/2°C)

C. plumbaginoides ▣ syn. *Plumbago larpentiae.* Rhizomatous, spreading,

Ceratostigma plumbaginoides

Ceratostigma willmottianum

woody-based perennial with upright, slender red stems and obovate, bright green leaves, to 3½in (9cm) long, with bristly, wavy margins, richly red-tinted in autumn. In late summer, bears terminal, spike-like clusters of brilliant blue flowers, to ¾in (2cm) across. ↕ to 18in (45cm), ↔ to 12in (30cm) or more. W. China. Zone 6.

C. willmottianum ▣ (Chinese plumbago). Open-branched, spreading, deciduous shrub with slender, bristly, mid-green stems. Lance-shaped to obovate, pointed, bristly, mid- to dark green, purple-margined leaves, to 2in (5cm) long, turn red in autumn. Terminal or axillary, spike-like clusters of pale to mid-blue flowers, 1in (2.5cm) across, with red-purple tubes, are produced from late summer to autumn. ↕ 3ft (1m), ↔ 5ft (1.5m). W. China. Zone 7.

CERATOZAMIA

ZAMIACEAE

Genus of 9 species of dioecious, evergreen cycads found in cloud forest, on dry upland, and among dense, tangled brushwood, from Mexico to Belize. They are palm-like in habit, with short, swollen trunks and rigid, pinnate, leathery leaves in lax, terminal rosettes or whorls. Cone-like male and female inflorescences are borne on mature plants in summer: female cones are solitary, cylindrical, and dull green; male cones are slightly narrower and gray-green. Where not hardy, grow as houseplants or in a temperate or warm greenhouse. In warmer areas, use as specimen plants on a lawn or patio.

• **CULTIVATION** Under glass, grow in deep containers in a mix of equal parts loam, coarse sand, soil mix, and ground bark in bright filtered or indirect light. In the growing season, water freely and apply a balanced liquid fertilizer monthly; water sparingly in winter. Pot on or top-dress in spring. Outdoors, grow in fertile, humus-rich, moist but well-drained, neutral to acidic soil in partial or dappled shade.

• **PROPAGATION** Sow seed at 70–86°F (21–30°C) in spring. If offsets develop, detach and pot them up in spring.

• **PESTS AND DISEASES** Prone to scale insects and mealybugs under glass.

C. mexicana ▣ (Mexican horncone). Large cycad with almost columnar, usually single caudices. The arching,

Ceratozamia mexicana

pinnate leaves are erect to spreading, 3–10ft (1–3m) long, and have up to 150 narrowly to broadly lance-shaped, light green leaflets. Flowering cones are borne in summer: green female cones, to 12in (30cm) long, have prominently horned scales; gray-green male cones, to 20in (50cm) long, have only rudimentary horns. ↕ to 6ft (2m), ↔ to 12ft (4m). Mexico. ❄ (min. 61°F/16°C)

CERCIDIPHYLLUM

CERCIDIPHYLLACEAE

Genus of one species of deciduous tree from woodland in China and Japan. Tiny red flowers are borne in early spring, before the leaves; male and female flowers are produced on separate plants. *C. japonicum* is cultivated for its foliage, which provides good autumn color; it is best grown as a specimen tree in a spacious setting, or as a street tree.

• **CULTIVATION** Grow in deep, fertile, humus-rich, moist but well-drained soil, preferably neutral to acidic, in sun or dappled shade, sheltered from cold, dry winds. Plants often develop several main stems, but may be trained as central-leader standards. Pruning group 1.

• **PROPAGATION** Sow seed in containers in an open frame as soon as ripe. Take basal cuttings in late spring and semi-ripe cuttings in midsummer.

• **PESTS AND DISEASES** Infrequent.

C. japonicum ▣ (Katsura tree). Pyramidal, later rounded and sometimes very wide-spreading, deciduous tree with *Cercis*-like, opposite, sometimes alternate, ovate to rounded leaves, to 4in

Cercidiphyllum japonicum

(10cm) long. Bronze when young, the mid-green leaves turn yellow, orange, and red in autumn and color best on acidic soils. Fallen leaves smell of burnt sugar. ↕70ft (20m), ↔ 50ft (15m). China, Japan. Zone 5. **var. *magnificum***, syn. *C. magnificum*, is smaller, but with larger leaves, to 5in (13cm) long; ↕30ft (10m), ↔ 25ft (8m). Japan. **f. *pendulum***, syn. 'Pendulum', has a weeping habit, with slender, pendent branches; ↕20ft (6m), ↔ 25ft (8m).
C. magnificum see *C. japonicum* var. *magnificum*.

▷ ***Cercidium floridum*** see *Parkinsonia florida*

CERCIS

FABACEAE

Genus of about 6 species of deciduous trees and shrubs found in woodland, at woodland margins, and on rocky hillsides in the Mediterranean, C. and E. Asia, and North America. They have alternate, heart-shaped, entire leaves and bear brightly colored, pea-like flowers in stalkless clusters or short racemes in spring, followed by flattened pods. The flowers are normally produced on the previous year's wood, either before or as the leaves unfold, but they may also be borne on wood that is several years old. Larger species are excellent specimen plants; grow smaller ones in a shrub border, or train against a wall.
• **CULTIVATION** Grow in fertile, deep, moist but well-drained, preferably loam soil in full sun or dappled shade. Plant in the final location when young; older

Cercis canadensis var. *alba*

Cercis canadensis 'Forest Pansy'

Cercis chinensis

plants resent transplanting. Pruning group 1; also group 7 for *C. canadensis* 'Forest Pansy'. For large foliage, pollard well-established plants in early spring.
• **PROPAGATION** Sow seed in containers in a cold frame in autumn. Root semi-ripe cuttings or bud selected clones in summer.
• **PESTS AND DISEASES** Scale insects, weevils, caterpillars, whiteflies, and leafhoppers can cause problems. Leaf spots, blights, downy mildew, canker, dieback, and *Verticillium* wilt occur.

C. canadensis (Eastern redbud). Spreading, often multi-stemmed tree with heart-shaped leaves, pointed at the tips, to 4in (10cm) long, bronze when young, turning yellow in autumn. Deep crimson, purple to pink, or occasionally white flowers, to ½in (1.5cm) long, are borne in clusters of 2–8 on bare stems, before the leaves. ↕↔ 30ft (10m). North America. Zone 5b. **var. *alba*** ■ has white flowers. **'Forest Pansy'** ■ has dark red-purple leaves. **'Royal White'** bears a profusion of pure white flowers. **'Silver Cloud'** has irregularly white-variegated foliage; grow in shade. **var. *texensis* 'Oklahoma'**, syn. *C. reniformis* 'Oklahoma', has waxy, glossy, rich green leaves with rounded tips, and dark wine-red flowers; ↕↔ 15ft (5m). Zone 6b.
C. chinensis ■ (Chinese redbud). Densely branched shrub or small tree with erect shoots and rounded, glossy, leathery, rich green leaves, to 5in (13cm) long, with pointed tips, turning yellow in autumn. Bears clusters of 3–8 deep pink to lavender-pink flowers, to ½in (1.5cm) across, before the leaves. ↕20ft (6m), ↔ 15ft (5m). C. China. Zone 6. **'Avondale'** is compact, with abundant dark purple-pink flowers; ↕to 10ft (3m).

Cercis siliquastrum 'Bodnant'

C. occidentalis (California redbud, Western redbud). Spreading shrub or small tree, often multi-stemmed, with kidney-shaped, bluish green leaves, to 4in (10cm) long, that have rounded or notched tips, bronze at first, turning yellow in autumn. Dark purple-pink flowers, to ½in (1.5cm) across, are borne in clusters of 5 or 6, usually on year-old wood, before the leaves. ↕15ft (5m), ↔ 12ft (4m). S.W. US. Zone 7b.
***C. reniformis* 'Oklahoma'** see *C. canadensis* var. *texensis* 'Oklahoma'.
C. siliquastrum (Judas tree). Spreading, sometimes multi-stemmed tree with inversely heart-shaped to kidney-shaped, glaucous, blue-green leaves, to 4in (10cm) long, with notched tips, bronze when young, turning yellow in autumn. Bears clusters of magenta to pink, occasionally white flowers, ½–¾in (1.5–2cm) long, before and with the leaves, often on the main branches. ↕↔ 30ft (10m). S.E. Europe, S.W. Asia. Zone 7. **f. *albida***, syn. 'Alba', has white flowers. **'Bodnant'** ■ has dark purple-pink flowers.

CERCOCARPUS

Mountain mahogany

ROSACEAE

Genus of about 6 species of evergreen or semi-evergreen shrubs or small trees from dry, craggy, mountainous regions in W. North America. The leaves are alternate, and entire, scalloped, or toothed, and often clustered. *Cercocarpus* species bear axillary or terminal, solitary or clustered flowers, which are 5-lobed, cup-shaped, and petalless, followed by small, cylindrical fruits with feathery tails. *C. montanus* is salt tolerant and highly suitable for a seaside garden.
• **CULTIVATION** Grow in well-drained soil in full sun. Pruning group 6 or 10.
• **PROPAGATION** Sow seed *in situ* when ripe. Take semi-ripe cuttings in summer.
• **PESTS AND DISEASES** Leaf spots and wood rots can occur.

C. montanus. Erect, open, evergreen shrub with brown bark and obovate, coarsely toothed, leathery, mid-green leaves, to 1in (2.5cm) long, densely woolly beneath. From spring to summer, bears ivory to dull yellow flowers, ¼in (6mm) across, solitary or in clusters of 2 or 3, followed by cylindrical fruit, to 2½in (6cm) long, each with a silky tail. ↕↔ 4–9ft (1.2–2.5m). Washington to California. Zone 7.

CEREUS

CACTACEAE

Genus of about 25 species of tree-like or columnar cacti, mainly from rocky terrain in South America and the West Indies. They usually have 3–14 thick ribs and often woolly areoles bearing thick spines. Nocturnal, widely cup- or funnel-shaped flowers are borne from summer to early autumn, and are followed by ovoid, fleshy, red or yellow fruits containing glossy black seeds. Where not hardy, grow in a temperate greenhouse or conservatory. In warm, dry climates, use in a desert garden.
• **CULTIVATION** Under glass, grow in standard cactus potting mix in full light. In the growing season, water freely and

Cereus validus

apply a low-nitrogen liquid fertilizer monthly; keep almost dry in winter. Outdoors, grow in sharply drained, poor to moderately fertile, humus-rich, slightly acidic soil in full sun. They tolerate short periods to 25°F (-4°C). See also pp.48–49.
• **PROPAGATION** Sow seed at 66–75°F (19–24°C) in early spring, or root cuttings of young branches in late spring or early summer.
• **PESTS AND DISEASES** Dry stem rot and bacterial soft rot are common, especially on small specimens. Prone to scale insects and mealybugs.

C. chalybaeus. Columnar cactus with 5- or 6-ribbed, few-branched, often purple-tinged, glaucous, dark green stems. Brown-woolly areoles bear red then black spines (7–9 radials and 3 or 4 longer, thicker centrals). In summer, bears funnel-shaped flowers, to 8in (20cm) long; the inner petals are white, the perianth tubes and backs of the outer petals are purple or red. ↕10ft (3m), ↔ 28in (70cm). N. Argentina, Uruguay. ❀ (min. 45–50°F/7–10°C)
C. emoryi see *Bergerocactus emoryi.*
C. flagelliformis see *Aporocactus flagelliformis.*
C. forbesii see *C. validus.*
***C. peruvianus* of gardens** see *C. uruguayanus.*
C. silvestrii see *Echinopsis chamaecereus.*
C. spachianus see *Echinopsis spachiana.*
C. uruguayanus, syn. *C. peruvianus* of gardens (Apple cactus). Tree-like, columnar cactus with 5- to 9-ribbed, few-branched, glaucous, dark green stems. Rounded, furrowed ribs bear brown areoles with reddish brown to black, occasionally yellowish spines (4–7 radials and 1 or 2 longer, thicker centrals). In summer, produces funnel-shaped flowers, 6in (15cm) long, with white inner petals and green-, brown-, or red-tipped white outer petals. ↕to 15ft (5m), ↔ 28in (70cm). S.E. Brazil to N. Argentina. ❀ (min. 45–50°F/7–10°C)
C. validus ■ syn. *C. forbesii.* Tree-like, columnar cactus producing dull bluish green then gray-green stems, with 4–7 often notched ribs. White-woolly areoles bear dark brown spines (5–7 radials and 1 or 2 longer, thicker centrals). Cup-shaped flowers, 10in (25cm) long, with white inner and red-pink outer petals, are borne in early autumn. ↕12ft (4m), ↔ 24in (60cm). Argentina. ❀ (min. 45–50°F/7–10°C)

C

CEROPEGIA

ASCLEPIADACEAE

Genus of up to 200 or more species of evergreen or semi-evergreen, erect, pendent, or climbing perennials from deserts to rainforests in tropical and subtropical areas of the Canary Islands, Africa, Madagascar, Asia, and Australia. Many are succulent, with fleshy, tuber-like caudices. The leaves are opposite and in whorls of 3, varying from ovate-heart-shaped to lance-shaped or linear. The flowers are borne singly or in cymes in summer, and are often widely flared at the tips in the form of parachutes or lanterns. The fruits are cylindrical to lance-shaped, and the flat, silk-tufted seeds are contained in hairless follicles. Where not hardy, grow in a warm greenhouse or as houseplants, using pendent species in hanging baskets. In warm, dry climates, grow outdoors in a desert garden; train climbing species on a trellis, pergola, or other support.

• **CULTIVATION** Under glass, grow in a mix of 2 parts sharp sand and 1 part each loam, peat, and leaf mold, in bright filtered light. During the growing season, water moderately and apply a low-nitrogen liquid fertilizer 2 or 3 times. Keep plants dry at other times; overwatering and low temperatures will lead to basal rot of the caudices. Outdoors, grow in sharply drained, poor, humus-rich, loam soil, with shelter from full sun. See also pp.48–49.

• **PROPAGATION** Sow seed at 66–75°F (19–24°C) in early spring. Increase *C. linearis* subsp. *woodii* from stem bulbils. Take stem cuttings, 4–6in (10–15cm) long, in early summer; root in a sand and peat mix at 72–77°F (22–25°C), and keep moist.

• **PESTS AND DISEASES** Prone to aphids, scale insects, and sometimes mealybugs.

C. dichotoma. Erect, semi-evergreen succulent producing gray-green stems, 12–36in (30–90cm) long, with linear, slightly fleshy, gray-green leaves, 1–3in (2.5–8cm) long. Bright yellow flowers with slightly curved, paler yellow tubes, 1¼in (3cm) long, and fully united lobes, to ½in (1.5cm) long, are borne singly or in cymes in summer. ↕ 3ft (1m), ↔ 24in (60cm). Canary Islands (Tenerife). ❄ (min. 50°F/10°C)

C. linearis* subsp. *woodii ▣ syn. *C. woodii* (Hearts on a string, Rosary vine, Sweetheart vine). Pendent, evergreen, tuberous-rooted succulent with slender twining stems, to 3ft (1m) long. The heart-shaped, fleshy, mid-green leaves, to ½in (1.5cm) long, are purple beneath, and often have gray-green or purple markings above. Frequently produces bulbils from the leaf axils. Lantern-like, purplish brown flowers, ½–¾in (1–2cm) long, with pinkish green tubes margined with fine purple hairs, are borne singly in summer. ↕ 4in (10cm), ↔ indefinite. Zimbabwe to South Africa (Eastern Cape). ❄ (min. 50°F/10°C)

C. nilotica. Twining, semi-evergreen succulent with rounded or 4-angled, fleshy, grayish green stems, 12–36in (30–90cm) long, and ovate, finely toothed, grayish green leaves, ½–1½in (2–4cm) long. In summer, bears cymes of flowers, 1¼–1½in (3–4cm) long, with yellowish white or pale green tubes, and triangular, purple-brown lobes, yellow-blotched at the bases. ↕ 30in (75cm), ↔ 24in (60cm). Sudan, Ethiopia, Kenya. ❄ (min. 50°F/10°C)

C. sandersoniae see *C. sandersonii.*

C. sandersonii, syn. *C. sandersoniae* (Fountain flower, Parachute plant). Twining, evergreen succulent with ovate-heart-shaped, fresh green leaves, 1½–2in (4–5cm) long, on light green stems, 18–54in (45–140cm) long. In summer, produces solitary, parachute-like, short-stalked green flowers, with broadly funnel-shaped tubes, to 2in (5cm) long, mottled darker green; the narrow lobes widen to unite at their upturned, white-haired margins, forming canopies, to 1in (2.5cm) across. ↕ 4ft (1.2m), ↔ 24in (60cm). Mozambique, South Africa (KwaZulu/Natal). ❄ (min. 50°F/10°C)

C. woodii see *C. linearis* subsp. *woodii.*

Ceropegia linearis subsp. *woodii*

CESTRUM

SOLANACEAE

Genus of about 175 species of evergreen and deciduous shrubs with alternate, simple, usually unpleasantly scented leaves, from woodland in Mexico and Central and South America. They are grown for their tubular to funnel-shaped, often fragrant flowers, borne in terminal or axillary cymes, followed by white, purple-red, or red berries. Grow in a sheltered border or against a sunny wall. Where not hardy, grow in a temperate or warm greenhouse or conservatory; container-grown plants may be moved outdoors in summer.

Cestrum elegans

• **CULTIVATION** Under glass, grow in soil-based potting mix in full light, with shade from hot sun and good ventilation. In the growing season, water moderately and apply a balanced liquid fertilizer monthly; water sparingly in winter. Outdoors, grow in fertile, well-drained soil in sun or partial shade. Provide support for scrambling species. Pruning group 8 for early-flowering evergreens; group 9 for late-flowering evergreens; and group 6 for deciduous plants. Plants under glass may need restrictive pruning; prune *C. aurantiacum* and *C. parqui* close to their bases annually in early spring.

• **PROPAGATION** Sow seed of frost-hardy species in containers in a cold frame in autumn; sow seed of tender species at 55–64°F (13–18°C) in spring. Root softwood cuttings of frost-hardy species and semi-ripe cuttings of tender species in summer.

• **PESTS AND DISEASES** Magnesium deficiency, rust, powdery mildew, fungal leaf spots, and dieback are sometimes problems, as well as several scale insects.

C. aurantiacum ▣ Evergreen shrub, becoming scandent if not regularly pruned, with ovate to lance-shaped, smooth, light green leaves, to 4½in (11cm) long. Axillary and terminal, panicle-like cymes, to 4in (10cm) across, of tubular, bright orange flowers, to 1¼in (3cm) long, are produced from spring to early summer; they are followed by spherical, fleshy white berries. ↕ 6–10ft (2–3m), ↔ 5–6ft (1.5–2m). Venezuela to Guatemala. ❄ (min. 41°F/5°C)

Cestrum aurantiacum

Cestrum parqui

C. elegans ▣ syn. *C. purpureum.* Vigorous, evergreen shrub with arching branches and ovate-oblong to lance-shaped, matte, mid-green leaves, to 4in (10cm) long. From summer to autumn, bears tubular, crimson to purple-red or pink flowers, to ¾in (2cm) long, in pendent, terminal, compound, panicle-like cymes, 4in (10cm) across; they are followed by purple-red berries. ↕↔ 10ft (3m). Mexico. ❄ (min. 41°F/5°C)

C. fasciculatum. Strong-growing, evergreen shrub with arching branches and ovate to lance-shaped, wavy-margined, dark green leaves, to 3in (8cm) long. Bears tubular, bright red flowers, to ¾in (2cm) long, in terminal, pendent cymes, to 3in (8cm) across, from spring to early summer, followed by purple-red berries. ↕↔ 6ft (2m). Mexico. ❄ (min. 41°F/5°C)

C. 'Newellii'. Vigorous, evergreen shrub with arching branches and narrowly ovate, dark green leaves, to 4in (10cm) long. From summer to autumn, bears tubular crimson flowers, to ¾in (2cm) long, in dense, terminal, compound panicles, 3–5in (8–13cm) across, sometimes followed by purple-red berries. ↕↔ 10ft (3m). ❄ (min. 41°F/5°C)

C. parqui ▣ (Willow-leaved jessamine). Upright, deciduous shrub, herbaceous where marginally hardy, with linear-lance-shaped to elliptic, mid-green leaves, to 5in (13cm) long. From summer to autumn, produces night-scented, tubular, bright yellow-green flowers, to 1in (2.5cm) long, with star-shaped mouths, in large, terminal and axillary cymes, to 5in (13cm) across; they are followed by violet-brown berries. ↕↔ 6ft (2m). Chile. Zone 8.

C. psittacinum. Scandent, evergreen shrub with alternate, elliptic to oblong, softly hairy, mid-green leaves, 2–5in (5–13cm) long, heart-shaped or rounded at the bases. Bears axillary and terminal cymes of tubular to funnel-shaped, vivid orange flowers, ½in (1.5cm) long, in autumn, followed by ovoid black berries. ↕ 10ft (3m), ↔ 18in (45cm). Central America. ❄ (min. 50°F/10°C)

C. purpureum see *C. elegans.*

C. roseum. Erect, evergreen shrub with oblong to ovate, wavy-margined, softly hairy, mid-green leaves, to 4in (10cm) long. In summer, bears terminal cymes of tubular-funnel-shaped, rose-pink flowers, to 1¼in (3cm) long, with spreading lobes, followed by red berries. ↕↔ 6ft (2m). Mexico. Zone 8.

▷ ***Ceterach*** see *Asplenium*

CHAENOMELES

Flowering quince

ROSACEAE

Genus of 3 species of deciduous, often spiny shrubs, one sometimes a small tree, from mountain woodland in China and Japan. They are cultivated for their early flowers, which are 5-petaled, cup-shaped, single to double, borne singly or in dense clusters, and for their apple-like, edible, aromatic, yellow to green or purplish green fruits, produced in autumn, and palatable when cooked. The flowers are borne both before and with the alternately arranged, simple, toothed leaves. Grow in a shrub border or on a bank, or train against a wall. Some flowering quinces, such as *C. japonica*, are useful as a groundcover or low hedging.

• **CULTIVATION** Grow in moderately fertile, well-drained soil in sun or partial shade. Suitable for a lightly shaded wall, but bloom and fruit best in sun. They tolerate alkalinity, but may become chlorotic on very alkaline soils. Also tolerant of pollution and urban environments. Pruning group 2, or 13 if wall-trained.

• **PROPAGATION** Sow seed in containers in an open frame, or in a seedbed, in autumn. Root semi-ripe cuttings in summer. Layer in autumn.

• **PESTS AND DISEASES** Prone to fireblight, canker, rust, apple mosaic virus, and scale insects.

***C. x californica* 'Enchantress'** ▣ Compact, spiny, upright shrub with lance-shaped, mid-green leaves, to 3in (8cm) long, light brown-woolly beneath when young. Dark rose-pink flowers, 2in (5cm) across, are produced in profuse clusters in spring, followed by large yellow fruit, to 2½in (6cm) long. ↕8ft (2.5m), ↔6ft (2m). Zone 6b.

C. cathayensis. Vigorous, upright shrub or small tree with spiny shoots and lance-shaped, pointed, mid-green leaves,

Chaenomeles speciosa 'Moerloosei'

to 5in (13cm) long, often red-downy beneath when young. White, pink-flushed flowers, to 1½in (4cm) across, are borne in clusters of 2 or 3 blooms in early and midspring; they are followed by large, yellow-green fruit, to 6in (15cm) long. ↕↔10ft (3m). China. Zone 7.

C. japonica, syn. *C. maulei* (Japonica, Japanese flowering quince). Spreading, thorny shrub with obovate to rounded, glossy, mid-green leaves, to 2in (5cm) long. Abundant clusters of orange to red flowers, 1½in (4cm) across, are borne in spring, followed by yellow or yellow-flushed red fruit, 1–1½in (2.5–4cm) long. ↕3ft (1m), ↔6ft (2m). Japan. Zone 5. **'Jet Trail'** produces white flowers. **'Minerva'** bears large, velvety, cherry-red flowers. **'Orange Delight'** is low-growing and spreading in habit, and produces orange-red flowers; ↕24–36in (60–90cm).

C. lagenaria see *C. speciosa.*

C. maulei see *C. japonica.*

C. speciosa, syn. *C. lagenaria, Cydonia speciosa, Pyrus japonica.* Vigorous, wide-spreading shrub with tangled, spiny branches and oval, glossy, dark green leaves, 1½–3½in (4–9cm) long. In

Chaenomeles x *californica* 'Enchantress' (inset: flower detail)

Chaenomeles x *superba* 'Crimson and Gold'

spring, bears clusters of 2–4 scarlet to crimson flowers, 1¾in (4.5cm) across, followed by aromatic, green-yellow fruit, to 2½in (6cm) long. ↕8ft (2.5m), ↔15ft (5m). China. Zone 5b. **'Apple Blossom'** see 'Moerloosei'. **'Cardinalis'** bears crimson flowers, 1½in (4cm) across. **'Dwarf Orange'** is low-growing, with orange flowers; ↕4–6ft (1.2–2m). **'Dwarf White'** is low-growing and spreading, and bears white flowers; ↕4–6ft (1.2–2m). **'Falconnet Charlet'** has double, salmon-pink flowers. **'Moerloosei'** ▣ syn. 'Apple Blossom', bears large white flowers, flushed dark pink. **'Nekanashiki'** is an improved form of 'Toyo Nishiki', with more varied flowers. **'Nivalis'** has pure white flowers. **'Phylis Moore'** has large clusters of semi-double, light pink flowers. **'Port Eliot'** produces large red flowers. **'Red'** is rounded and thornless, with red flowers. **'Red Chief'** is compact, with double, bright red flowers. **'Simonii'** has large, double, dark blood-red flowers; ↕3ft (1m), ↔6ft (2m). **'Snow'** bears large white flowers. **'Spitfire'** has deep red flowers. **'Toyo Nishiki'** is upright, with pink, white, and red flowers on the same branches. **'Umbilicata'** bears dark pink flowers. **'White'** is rounded in habit, and one of the hardiest white-flowered quinces.

C. x superba (*C. japonica* x *C. speciosa*). Rounded shrub with spiny, spreading branches and narrowly to broadly ovate or ovate-oblong, glossy, mid-green leaves, to 2½in (6cm) long. From spring to summer, bears clusters of cup-shaped, white, pink, orange-scarlet, or crimson

Chaenomeles x *superba* 'Nicoline'

Chaenomeles x *superba* 'Pink Lady'

to orange flowers, 1¼–1¾in (3–4.5cm) across; they are followed by green fruit, 2–3in (5–8cm) long, ripening to yellow. ↕5ft (1.5m), ↔6ft (2m). Zone 5b. **'Cameo'** is thornless with double, peach-pink flowers. **'Crimson and Gold'** ▣ is compact and spreading, and has dark red flowers with golden yellow anthers; ↕3ft (1m). **'Elly Mossel'** has large scarlet flowers. **'Etna'** is spreading, with dark scarlet flowers; ↔10ft (3m). **'Fire Dance'** is spreading, with large, bright red flowers. **'Hollandia'** bears large red flowers over a long period and blooms again in autumn. **'Jet Trail'** is compact and low-growing, with masses of white flowers; ↕3–5ft (1–1.5m). **'Knap Hill Scarlet'** has large, bright red flowers. **'Nicoline'** ▣ bears abundant large, sometimes semi-double scarlet flowers. **'Pink Lady'** ▣ is thornless and has very early, dark pink flowers. **'Rowallane'** is low-growing and spreading, with scarlet flowers; ↕3ft (1m). **'Texas Scarlet'** is compact and spreading, with profusely borne, tomato-red flowers.

CHAENORHINUM

Dwarf snapdragon

SCROPHULARIACEAE

Genus of about 20 species of annuals and perennials from dry, often stony soils in the Mediterranean region and in Turkey. They have branching, erect or spreading stems; 2-lipped, snapdragon-like flowers, produced either singly from the leaf axils or in terminal racemes; and opposite, simple, entire leaves. They are suitable for a rock garden, scree bed, or alpine house.

• **CULTIVATION** Grow in well-drained soil in full sun. Protect from winter moisture.

• **PROPAGATION** Sow seed in containers in a cold frame in autumn. Separate rooted runners in spring.

• **PESTS AND DISEASES** Young growth is prone to damage from slugs and snails.

C. glareosum, syn. *Linaria glareosum.* Prostrate to upright, mat-forming perennial, spreading by runners, with scale-like, ovate to rounded, hairy, bluish green leaves, to ½in (1.5cm) long. Racemes of pale pinkish violet flowers, ½–1in (1.5–2.5cm) long, with yellow spurs and throats, are borne from early to late summer. ↕2in (5cm) if prostrate, ↕6–8in (15–20cm) when upright, ↔ to 8in (20cm). S. Spain. ❄ (min. 41°F/5°C)

C

Chaerophyllum hirsutum 'Roseum'

CHAEROPHYLLUM

APIACEAE

Genus of about 35 species of taprooted or tuberous annuals, biennials, and perennials from meadows, hedgerows, and open woodland in N. temperate regions. They have fern-like, pinnate to 3-pinnate leaves, and produce compound umbels of small, white, pink, or yellow flowers. Use in a border or a woodland garden; the leaves or roots of some have culinary uses.

• **CULTIVATION** Grow in moist, fertile soil in sun or partial shade.

• **PROPAGATION** Sow seed in containers in a cold frame as soon as ripe or in early spring.

• **PESTS AND DISEASES** Susceptible to damage from aphids, slugs, and snails. Powdery mildew may be a problem in dry spells.

C. aureum (Golden chervil). Clump-forming perennial with erect stems and mildly anise-flavored, 3-pinnate, yellow-green leaves, 1/2–1 1/2in (1–4cm) long, composed of lance-shaped, toothed or lobed leaflets. Umbels of white flowers, 2–4in (5–10cm) across, are borne in early summer. ↕ to 4ft (1.2m), ↔ 18in (45cm). C. and S. Europe, S.W. Asia. Zone 5.

C. hirsutum. Upright, hairy perennial producing 2- or 3-pinnate, apple-scented, mid-green, sometimes purple-flushed leaves, 5–12in (12–30cm) long, with ovate to heart-shaped, toothed leaflets. Umbels of white flowers, 2 1/2in (6cm) across, are borne from late spring to midsummer. ↕ 24in (60cm), ↔ 12in (30cm). Spain and France to S.W. Russia. Zone 6b. **'Roseum'** ■ syn. 'Rubrifolium', produces umbels of pink flowers.

▷ ***Chamaecereus silvestrii*** see *Echinopsis chamaecereus*

CHAMAECYPARIS

False cypress

CUPRESSACEAE

Genus of 7 species of monoecious, evergreen, coniferous trees from forest in Taiwan, Japan, and North America. They have flattened sprays of scale-like, overlapping adult leaves, 1/16–1/4in (2–6mm) long, and larger, ovate to linear juvenile leaves, 1/16–3/8in (2–9mm) long. The spherical or angular female cones have 2, occasionally 3–5 seeds on each shield-like scale, and most ripen in the first autumn. The spherical or ovoid male cones, usually 1/16–1/4in (2–6mm) long, are borne in spring. False cypresses are used as specimen trees and for hedging; they have given rise to a vast number of cultivars, many dwarf or slow-growing and suitable for rock gardens or bonsai. Contact with the foliage may aggravate skin allergies.

• **CULTIVATION** Tolerant of alkaline soils but best grown in moist but well-drained, preferably neutral to slightly acidic soil in full sun. Trim hedges from late spring to early autumn, but do not cut into older wood.

• **PROPAGATION** Sow seed in a seedbed outdoors in spring, or root semi-ripe cuttings in late summer. Dwarf cultivars, especially those of *C. obtusa*, should be grafted in late winter or spring.

• **PESTS AND DISEASES** Spruce mite, twig blight, root rot, and needle blights can be problems.

C. lawsoniana, syn. *Cupressus lawsoniana* (Lawson false cypress). Narrowly columnar, coniferous tree with a dense crown, a pendent leading shoot, and reddish brown bark forming rounded, scaly plates. Bright green mature leaves are arranged in opposite pairs; they are sharply pointed, with incurved tips and translucent central glands. Oblong male cones, 1/4–3/8in (6–9mm) long, are bluish black in bud, opening brick-red. The wrinkled, reddish brown, sometimes glaucous female cones, to 1/2in (1.5cm) across, each have 8 scales. ↕ 50–130ft (15–40m),

Chamaecyparis lawsoniana 'Columnaris'

Chamaecyparis lawsoniana 'Gnome'

↔ 6–15ft (2–5m). W. North America. Zone 6. **'Alumii'** has a narrow, conical habit, with erect sprays of blue-gray leaves, forming a billowing skirt of foliage at the base; ↕ 20–50ft (6–15m). **'Columnaris'** ■ has a columnar crown of pale blue-gray leaves; ↕ to 30ft (10m), ↔ 3ft (1m). **'Ellwoodii'** is a dense, conical shrub with erect branches and ovate, blue-gray young leaves; ↕ 10ft (3m). **'Fletcheri'** is similar to 'Ellwoodii' but larger, with grayer foliage; ↕ to 40ft (12m). **'Gnome'** ■ is rounded and spreading, with bluish green foliage; ↕ 3ft (1m). **'Intertexta'** ■ has hard, gray-green foliage in lax, pendent sprays. It eventually forms a tall tree and develops a crown with erratic, spreading branches. **'Lane'** ■ syn. 'Lanei', is narrowly conical, with leaves golden yellow above and green-yellow beneath. **'Lutea'** is narrowly columnar or conical, slow-growing at first, with pendent sprays of golden yellow foliage; ↕ 50–70ft (15–20m). **'Minima'** ■ has a very dwarf, rounded to conical habit, with upswept branches and rounded sprays of bluish green foliage; ↕ to 5ft (1.5m). **'Nana'** is similar to 'Minima' but forms a central trunk with yellow leaves; ↕ to 6ft (2m). **'Pembury Blue'** ■ is a conical tree producing pendent sprays of bright blue-gray foliage; ↕ to 50ft (15m). **'Stardust'** is a slow-growing, narrowly to broadly conical tree with fern-like yellow foliage. **'Winston Churchill'** is a narrowly conical tree with golden foliage. **'Wisselii'** ■ is a narrowly conical tree with 3-dimensional sprays of blue-gray

Chamaecyparis lawsoniana 'Intertexta'

Chamaecyparis lawsoniana 'Lane'

Chamaecyparis lawsoniana 'Minima'

Chamaecyparis lawsoniana 'Pembury Blue'

Chamaecyparis lawsoniana 'Wisselii'

Chamaecyparis nootkatensis 'Pendula' (inset: cone detail)

Chamaecyparis obtusa 'Tetragona Aurea'

Chamaecyparis pisifera 'Filifera Aurea'

or blue-green foliage; it bears a mass of male cones in spring; ↕ 70–80ft (20–25m). ***C. nootkatensis***, syn. *Cupressus nootkatensis* (Alaska cedar, Nootka false cypress). Conical, occasionally columnar, coniferous tree with brown-gray bark, peeling in large plates, and sharply pointed, free-tipped, scale-like, dark green mature leaves arranged in long, pendent sprays. Green female cones, ½in (1.5cm) long, with a recurved central hook on each of the 4–6 scales, ripen in spring. Male cones are ovoid, brownish green, and ⅛in (3mm) long. ↕ to 100ft (30m), ↔ to 25ft (8m). Alaska to Oregon. Zone 5b. **'Aurea'** has yellow foliage when young, maturing to yellow-green. **'Green Arrow'** has a very narrow spire with downward-sweeping branches and pendulous branchlets. Very dramatic specimen plant. ↕ 20ft (6m), ↔ 12in (30cm). **'Pendula'** ▣ is pendent, with vertical sprays of hanging foliage, and an open crown when mature. ↕ 35ft (11m), ↔ 20ft (6m). ***C. obtusa*** syn. *Cupressus obtusa* (Hinoki cypress). Broad, conical, coniferous tree with soft, stringy bark. Glandless, blunt, dark green mature leaves, bright white-banded beneath, are borne in 2 unequal pairs. The green, then brown, female cones are ½–¾in (1–2cm) across, and have 8–12 scales. Male cones are spherical, orange-brown, and ⅜–½in (8–15mm) across. ↕ to 70ft (20m), ↔ to 20ft (6m). S. Japan. Zone 5. **'Coralliformis'** is compact and slow-growing, with contorted branchlets and twisted foliage; ↕↔ 20in (50cm). **'Crippsii'** ▣ syn. 'Crippsii Aurea', is slow-growing with rich golden foliage. A fine specimen tree, best planted in full sun; ↕ 50ft (15m), ↔ 25ft (8m). **'Elf'** is a dwarf globe with very bright, tiny, emerald green foliage. ↕ 24in (60cm). **'Fernspray Gold'** is slow-growing, the branches clothed with short, rich golden yellow, fern-like leaves. **'Gracilis'** is pyramidal with dark green leaves. **'Minima'** (Golfball cypress) is dwarf, slow-growing, and spherical; ↔ to 16in (40cm). **'Nana Aurea'** ▣ is a flat-topped, dwarf shrub with golden yellow foliage, greener when grown in shade; ↕ 6ft (2m). **'Nana Gracilis'** has a dense, pyramidal habit with rich green foliage; ↕ 10ft (3m). **'Opaal'** is a dwarf form with a very tight upright growth habit. Deep green foliage is tinged with bright yellow on top. **'Pygmaea'** is a rounded, dwarf shrub with red-brown shoots and fan-shaped, bright green foliage, becoming brown over winter; ↕ 5ft (1.5m). **'Tempelhof'** is an ovoid or conical, dwarf shrub with yellow-green foliage, turning bronze in winter; ↕ 8ft (2.5m) **'Tetragona Aurea'** ▣ has 4-ranked, golden yellow to bronze-yellow leaves, which are greener when grown in shade; ↕ to 30ft (10m). ***C. pisifera***, syn. *Cupressus pisifera* (Sawara cypress). Initially broad, conical, coniferous tree with an open crown and hard, fissured, finely peeling, red-brown bark. Pairs of sharp-pointed, bright green mature leaves, marked white beneath, with small glands and free-spreading tips, are produced in flattened sprays. Angular female cones, to ¼in (6mm) long, are green, maturing to deep brown, with 6–8 scales. Black male cones are spherical, to ¼in (6mm) across. ↕ to 70ft (20m), ↔ to 15ft (5m). S. Japan. Zone 4b. **'Boulevard'** has soft, blue-green foliage. Needs a moist site; ↕ 30ft (10m). **'Filifera'** has slender, whip-like shoots, which are mostly unbranched, and dark green leaves. **'Filifera Aurea'** ▣ is similar to 'Filifera' but has golden yellow leaves and is slower-growing; ↕ 40ft (12m). **'Plumosa'** is erect and broadly conical with billowing foliage. The yellowish gray-green, semi-juvenile leaves, 1/16–⅛in (2–3mm) long, have free tips; ↔ 25ft (8m). **'Squarrosa'** ▣ syn. 'Squarrosa Veitchii', has soft young leaves, ¼–⅜in (6–9mm) long, with free tips. It is similar in habit to 'Plumosa' but tends to open up, losing the inner foliage.

Chamaecyparis obtusa 'Crippsii'

Chamaecyparis obtusa 'Nana Aurea'

Chamaecyparis pisifera 'Squarrosa'

Chamaecyparis thyoides

C. thyoides ■ syn. *Cupressus thyoides* (White cedar, White false cypress). Narrowly conical, coniferous tree with dull red-brown or gray-brown bark. Sharply pointed, dark gray-green, sometimes glaucous mature leaves, generally turning brown-green in the second year, with incurved tips and central glands, are produced on erratic sprays of fine shoots. The angular female cones, to ¼in (6mm) across, are purple-black to red-brown, initially glaucous, and have 6–10 scales. Spherical male cones are brown, and to ¼in (6mm) across. ↕ to 50ft (15m), ↔ to 12ft (4m). E. US. Zone 4. **'Andelyensis'** is a neat, conical shrub with linear, bluish green leaves; ↕ to 10ft (3m). **'Red Star'** is a very dwarf, upright conical form with blue-gray juvenile foliage. Needles form star shape at branch tips. Plant turns purple in winter. ↕ 15–25ft (5–8m).

CHAMAECYTISUS

FABACEAE

Genus of about 30 species of evergreen and deciduous, occasionally spiny, small trees, shrubs, and subshrubs found mainly on hillsides and in open woodland from sea level to 7,000ft (2,000m) in Europe and the Canary Islands. Some species were previously included in the genus *Cytisus*. They have alternate, 3-palmate leaves, sometimes with softly hairy leaflets, and are grown for their pea-like, usually yellow, sometimes purple-pink or white flowers, borne on short, axillary shoots or in terminal racemes or clusters. Grow on a sunny bank or in a shrub border, rock garden,

Chamaecytisus purpureus f. *albus*

trough, or raised bed. *C. purpureus* is top-grafted onto *Laburnum anagyroides* understock to produce the bigeneric graft hybrid, +*Laburnocytisus adamii*, a small standard tree. (See also p.586.) Where not hardy, grow in a cool greenhouse or conservatory.
• **CULTIVATION** Tolerant of a range of soil types, including poor, dry soils, but not shallow, alkaline soils. Best in moderately fertile, well-drained soil in full sun. They resent root disturbance, so plant out directly from containers into the final location as soon as possible. Pruning group 3 or 10, after flowering, or in spring for *C. supinus*. *C. demissus* needs little pruning. Do not cut back hard, since plants seldom recover fully.
• **PROPAGATION** Sow seed in containers in a cold frame in autumn or spring. Root semi-ripe cuttings in summer.
• **PESTS AND DISEASES** Spider mites may be a problem under glass.

C. demissus, syn. *C. hirsutus* var. *demissus*. Slow-growing, prostrate, hairy shrublet with deciduous, 3-palmate, mid-green leaves, ¼–½in (0.6–1.5cm) long, silky-hairy beneath, composed of oblong-obovate to inversely lance-shaped leaflets. Axillary clusters of 2–4 yellow flowers, to 1¼in (3cm) across, with brown keels and an involucre of brown bracts, are produced in late spring and early summer. Suitable for a rock garden or trough. ↕ 3in (8cm), ↔ 8in (20cm) or more. Greece. Zone 6b.
C. hirsutus* var. *demissus see *C. demissus*.
C. purpureus, syn. *Cytisus purpureus* (Purple broom). Deciduous, dense, semi-erect shrub with smooth, branching stems and 3-palmate, dark green leaves, to 1in (2.5cm) long, with obovate leaflets. In early summer, bears axillary clusters of 2 or 3 pale pink to deep lilac flowers, to 1in (2.5cm) across, with darker throats. ↕ 18in (45cm), ↔ 24in (60cm). S.E. Europe. Zone 6. **f. *albus*** ■ has white flowers.
C. supinus, syn. *Cytisus supinus*. Bushy, rounded, deciduous shrub producing shoots covered with long, spreading hairs, and 3-palmate, mid-green leaves, to 1½in (4cm) long, with oblong-elliptic leaflets. Clusters of 2–8 bright yellow flowers, to 1in (2.5cm) across, are borne at the ends of the shoots from mid-summer to autumn. ↕↔ 3ft (1m). C. and S. Europe. Zone 5.

CHAMAEDAPHNE

syn. CASSANDRA

ERICACEAE

Genus of one species of evergreen shrub found in moist, peaty soil, in bogs and at pond margins in N. temperate regions of Europe, Asia, and North America. It is grown for its alternate, glossy, dark green leaves and its urn-shaped white flowers. *C. calyculata* is suitable for a woodland garden.
• **CULTIVATION** Grow in moist, peaty, acidic soil in sun or dappled shade.
• **PROPAGATION** Root semi-ripe cuttings in summer.
• **PESTS AND DISEASES** Rust, dieback, *Exobasidium* galls, and leaf spots occur.

C. calyculata (Leatherleaf). Evergreen shrub with slender, arching shoots and obovate to oblong, leathery, glossy, dark green leaves, to 2in (5cm) long, scaly beneath. In spring, bears small, urn-shaped white flowers in arching, one-sided, leafy racemes, 1½–5in (4–13cm) long, at the ends of the shoots. ↕ 30in (75cm), ↔ 36in (90cm). N. Europe, N. Asia, North America. Zone 3. **'Nana'** is compact and free-flowering; ↕ 18in (45cm), ↔ 30in (75cm).

CHAMAEDOREA

ARECACEAE

Genus of about 100 species of mainly small palms from rainforest in Mexico and Central and South America. They are valued for their leaves, which are pinnate or resemble a fish's tail, often arching, either tufted or alternate, and borne on erect and flexible, sometimes scandent stems. Insignificant, 3-petaled flowers are borne in spikes or panicles, followed by small fruits, ¼–½in (0.6–1.5cm) across. Where not hardy, grow young specimens as houseplants, or in containers or borders in a warm conservatory or greenhouse. In warmer areas, grow in a shaded border, patio, or courtyard.
• **CULTIVATION** Under glass, grow in soilless potting mix in bright filtered or indirect light, shaded from hot sun. In the growing season, water freely and apply a balanced liquid fertilizer monthly; water sparingly in winter. Pot on or top-dress in spring. Outdoors, grow in humus-rich, moist but well-drained, neutral to acidic soil, in full or partial shade.

Chamaedorea elegans

• **PROPAGATION** Sow seed in spring at not less than 77°F (25°C).
• **PESTS AND DISEASES** Prone to spider mites, mealybugs, and scale insects. Fungal leaf spots, root rot, and stem cankers are common.

C. elegans ■ syn. *Neanthe bella* (Parlor palm). Slender-stemmed palm with a terminal tuft of pinnate, rich green leaves, to 24in (60cm) long, composed of 21–40 linear to lance-shaped leaflets. Tiny yellow flowers are borne in erect, simple or branched panicles, 8–12in (15–30cm) long, from spring to autumn, followed by small, spherical black fruit. ↕ 6–10ft (2–3m), ↔ 3–6ft (1–2m). Mexico, Guatemala. ❀ (min. 61°F/16°C). **'Bella'** has a more compact tuft of leaves, and flowers freely.
C. metallica (Miniature fishtail palm). Very small palm with a single, cane-like stem and a terminal tuft of foliage. The semi-lustrous, deep bluish green leaves, 12–20in (30–50cm) long, are slightly puckered and shaped like a fish's tail. In summer, produces orange to red flowers in panicles 8–14in (20–35cm) long, just below the leaves, followed by small, ovoid black fruit. ↕ to 3ft (1m), ↔ to 20in (50cm). Mexico. ❀ (min. 61°F/16°C)
C. microspadix ■ Small palm with groups of cane-like stems. Alternate, pinnate, blue-green leaves, 8–16in (20–40cm) long, have tubular basal sheaths and 14–18 lance-shaped leaflets. In summer, cream to white flowers are borne in arching to pendent panicles, 6–9in (15–23cm) long, followed by small, spherical, orange-red fruit. ↕ to 10ft (3m), ↔ to 5ft (1.5m). E. Mexico. ❀ (min. 61°F/16°C)
C. seifrizii ■ (Reed palm). Small, clump-forming palm with flexible, cane-like stems that may be semi-scandent in mature or large specimens. Alternate or loosely clustered, pinnate, rich green leaves, to 24in (60cm) long, have 24–28 narrowly lance-shaped leaflets. Yellow flowers are borne in erect panicles,

Chamaedorea microspadix

Chamaedorea seifrizii

6–10in (15–25cm) long, either on stalks or just above the foliage. The small, spherical fruit are black. ↕ 3–6ft (1–2m), ↔ 3–5ft (1–1.5m). Mexico (Yucatan). ❄ (min. 61°F/16°C)

CHAMAELIRIUM

LILIACEAE

Genus of one species of tuberous, dioecious perennial native to moist woodland in E. North America. *C. luteum* is grown for its rosettes of narrow, obovate to spoon-shaped, glossy, rich green basal leaves, 2–8in (5–20cm) long, and for its spikes of cream flowers, which are borne in summer. It is suitable for growing in a woodland or bog garden.

• **CULTIVATION** Grow in moist, peaty soil in partial shade.

• **PROPAGATION** Divide in spring or sow seed in autumn (male and female plants are required for seed production).

• **PESTS AND DISEASES** Susceptible to damage by slugs.

C. luteum (Fairy wand). Tuberous, dioecious perennial with narrow, obovate to spoon-shaped, glossy, rich green basal leaves, 2–8in (5–20cm) long, and smaller, lance-shaped stem leaves. Dense cylindrical racemes of cream flowers, ¼in (6mm) across, are borne in early and mid-summer. Male flowering spikes, 1½–5in (4–13cm) long, are denser, shorter, and more yellow than the female ones, which are creamy white and to 12in (30cm) long. ↕ 18in (45cm), ↔ 12in (30cm). E. North America. Zone 4.

CHAMAEMELUM

Chamomile

ASTERACEAE

Genus of 4 species of aromatic annuals and perennials from grassy pastures and wasteland in Europe. The leaves are feathery, alternate, and pinnate then pinnatisect. The flowerheads are daisy-like, with yellow disk florets and white ray florets. *C. nobile* is grown for its medicinal flowers and for its foliage, which releases an apple-like fragrance when crushed. The leaves and flower-heads are suitable for drying; the leaves for use in potpourri, the flowerheads for herbal tea. The leaves may be harvested at any time; the flowerheads should be picked when completely open, and then dried as entire heads. Where heavy foot

Chamaemelum nobile 'Flore Pleno'

traffic and wear will not be a problem, plant closely together to produce an ornamental lawn for a courtyard or patio. The dwarf, non-flowering cultivar *C. nobile* 'Treneague' is best for that purpose. It is also suitable as edging at the front of a border or along a walk-way, or at the margins of a pond or water garden.

• **CULTIVATION** Grow in an open site in well-drained, preferably light, sandy soil in full sun. To produce a lawn or seat, plant 5–6in (12–15cm) apart, and water freely until established. Cut the plants back regularly to encourage dense, compact growth; occasional rolling of lawns will help to maintain an even surface.

• **PROPAGATION** Sow seed *in situ* or divide in spring. Increase *C. nobile* 'Treneague' by division.

• **PESTS AND DISEASES** Infrequent.

C. nobile, syn. *Anthemis nobilis* (Lawn chamomile, Roman chamomile). Mat-forming, hairy, aromatic perennial with stalkless, oblong, fresh green leaves, to 2in (5cm) long, divided into thread-like segments. In summer, bears daisy-like flowerheads, ¼–½in (0.7–1.5cm) across, singly on long stalks. May be invasive. Contact with foliage may aggravate skin allergies. ↕ 12in (30cm), ↔ 18in (45cm). W. Europe. Zone 6. **'Flore Pleno'** ▣ has double, button-like flowerheads and is ideal for edging an herb border; ↕ 6in (15cm), ↔ 18in (45cm). **'Treneague'** is a low, tufted, non-flowering cultivar that roots where the decumbent stems touch the soil. It has strongly scented foliage, and is less vigorous than the species; ↕ 4in (10cm), ↔ 18in (45cm).

▷ ***Chamaenerion angustifolium* f. *album*** see *Epilobium angustifolium* f. *album*

CHAMAEROPS

Dwarf fan palm

ARECACEAE

Genus of one species of shrubby palm from dry scrub and rocky or sandy slopes in the W. Mediterranean region. Its pinnate leaves are densely borne in tufts or rosettes, and the tiny, 3-petaled flowers are produced in panicles from the lower leaf axils. Where not hardy, *C. humilis* is best grown in a cool green-house or as a houseplant. In warmer areas, use as a specimen plant.

• **CULTIVATION** Under glass, grow in soil-based potting mix in full to bright

Chamaerops humilis

indirect light. When in growth, water moderately and apply a balanced liquid fertilizer monthly; water sparingly in winter. Pot on or top-dress in spring. Outdoors, grow in well-drained, moderately fertile soil in full sun; tolerates poor soil and partial shade. May survive short spells just below 32°F (0°C).

• **PROPAGATION** Sow seed at not less than 72°F (22°C) in spring, or separate suckers in late spring.

• **PESTS AND DISEASES** *Ganoderma* butt rot, false smut, and spider mites can occur.

C. humilis ▣ (European fan palm). Bushy palm, producing suckers when mature, with broad, pinnate, bluish or grayish green leaves, 24–36in (60–90cm) long, composed of 12–15 linear leaflets. Bears yellow flowers in dense, almost hidden panicles, to 14in (35cm) long, from spring to summer. ↕ 6–10ft (2–3m), ↔ 3–6ft (1–2m). Mediterranean. ❄ (min. 45°F/7°C)

▷ ***Chamaespartium*** see *Genista*

CHAMELAUCIUM

MYRTACEAE

Genus of 21 species of evergreen shrubs from Western Australia, found on sandy heaths and in seasonally dry scrub. The narrow, needle-like leaves are usually borne in opposite pairs, and the small, clustered flowers, for which these plants are valued, each have 5 rounded, spreading petals and a cup-shaped center. Where not hardy, grow in a cool greenhouse or conservatory, or in

Chamelaucium uncinatum 'Album'

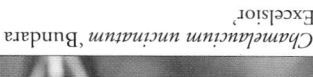

Chamelaucium uncinatum 'Bundara Excelsior'

containers. In warmer climates, use to add color and character to a shrub border or grow against a house wall; also useful for hedging.

• **CULTIVATION** Under glass, grow in acidic potting mix in full light with shade from hot sun. During the growing season, water moderately and apply a balanced liquid fertilizer monthly to well-established plants; water sparingly in winter. Pot on or top-dress in late winter. Outdoors, grow in sharply drained, neutral to acidic, poor to moderately fertile, sandy soil in full sun. Pruning group 8; plants under glass may need restrictive pruning.

• **PROPAGATION** Surface-sow seed at 55–64°F (13–18°C) in spring. Root greenwood cuttings in early summer or semi-ripe cuttings in late summer.

• **PESTS AND DISEASES** Root-rotting fungi may be a problem outdoors.

C. uncinatum (Waxflower). Large, erect to spreading, open shrub producing linear, 3-angled, dark green leaves, ¾–1½in (2–4cm) long, with hooked tips. Purple, mauve, red, pink, or white flowers, to 1in (2.5cm) across, are borne in abundant clusters 2–4in (5–10cm) across, from spring to summer. Excellent for cut flowers; drought tolerant. ↕ 6–15ft (2–5m), ↔ 6–12ft (2–4m). Western Australia. ❄ (min. 45°F/7°C). **'Album'** ▣ bears pure white flowers. **'Bundara Excelsior'** ▣ bears large pink blooms. **'Purple Pride'** has red-purple flowers. **'University'** is less vigorous, with red-tinged young stems, and bears flowers opening rose-purple, darkening to purple-violet, then to purple. ↕↔ 6–8ft (2–2.5m).

CHASMANTHE

IRIDACEAE

Genus of 3 species of cormous perennials, related to *Crocosmia*, from semi-shaded sites in South Africa. They are valued for their attractive, spike-like racemes of hooded, tubular, yellow, orange, or red flowers, borne from spring to summer. Their narrow, linear, lance- or sword-shaped, mid-green leaves form a flat, basal fan. Excellent for a mixed or herbaceous border.

• **CULTIVATION** Grow in fertile, moist but well-drained soil in sun or partial shade. Cut down in late winter, before new growth begins.

C

• **PROPAGATION** Sow seed at 55–61°F (13–16°C) in spring, or divide in spring.
• **PESTS AND DISEASES** Infrequent.

C. aethiopica. Clump-forming, cormous perennial with lance-shaped or linear leaves, 16–24in (40–60cm) long. From spring to early summer, bears spike-like, one-sided racemes, 6–7in (15–18cm) long, of red or orange flowers, 3in (8cm) long, with maroon throats and yellow-striped tubes. ↕ to 28in (70cm), PD2in (5cm). South Africa. ❄ (min. 41°F/5°C)
C. floribunda. Clump-forming, cormous perennial producing lance-shaped leaves, 12–20in (30–50cm) long. Numerous bright orange or yellow flowers, to 3in (8cm) long, arranged in 2 ranks, are borne on branched spikes, 12in (30cm) long, in summer. ↕ 20–60in (0.5–1.5m), PD6in (15cm). South Africa. ❄ (min. 45°F/7°C)

CHASMANTHIUM

POACEAE

Genus of about 6 species of perennial grasses, mostly from woodland in E. and C. US, Mexico, and Central America. The leaf blades are linear to narrowly lance-shaped, and the flowers are borne in panicles or racemes of 2- to 10-flowered spikelets. *C. latifolium* is the most often cultivated species, and produces oat-like flowerheads that may be dried if cut before they reach full maturity. Grow in a mixed or herbaceous border, or in a woodland garden.
• **CULTIVATION** Grow in fertile, moist but well-drained soil in sun or partial shade. Cut down in late winter.
• **PROPAGATION** Sow seed in containers in a cold frame in spring, or divide between midspring and early summer.
• **PESTS AND DISEASES** Infrequent.

C. latifolium ▣ syn. *Uniola latifolia* (Northern sea oats, Spangle grass, Wild oats). Loosely tufted, spreading, perennial grass with broadly lance-shaped, arching, mid-green leaves, 4–10in (10–25cm) long, that turn yellow in winter. In late summer and early autumn, bears open, oat-like panicles of flat, oblong-lance-shaped to broadly ovate green spikelets, ½in (1.5cm) long, aging to bronze, and breaking up at maturity. ↕ 3ft (1m), ↔ 24in (60cm). E. US, N. Mexico. Zone 5b.

CHEILANTHES

Lip fern

ADIANTACEAE

Genus of 150 or more species of mainly evergreen ferns, distributed worldwide. They are among the most drought-resistant of ferns, often growing between rocks, frequently in deserts or near-deserts; the fronds shrivel in periods of drought and recover after rain. They have erect or creeping rhizomes, producing dense clumps of small, pinnate to 3-pinnate, usually dull green fronds on shiny black stalks. The undersides of the leaf blades may be white-mealy and covered with minute hairs or scales. Spores are formed at the margins of the frond segments, which curl under to protect them. In dry climates, grow in a scree bed, rock garden, or in a stone wall. Elsewhere, grow in containers in a cool or temperate greenhouse.
• **CULTIVATION** Under glass, grow in a mix of equal parts soil-based potting mix, charcoal, and limestone chips for open aerated, free-draining medium, in full light. Provide low humidity and good ventilation. In the growing season, water copiously in the morning so that foliage is dry by night, and apply a half-strength, balanced liquid fertilizer monthly; keep the pots slightly moist in winter. Pot on every 2 or 3 years in spring, into containers nearly as wide as they are deep, and groom regularly to maintain air circulation. Outdoors, grow in sharply drained, gritty, humus-rich soil in full sun, and allow plants to dehisce naturally. Protect *C. tomentosa* from winter moisture.
• **PROPAGATION** Sow spores at 61°F (16°C) as soon as ripe. Division of plants is possible in spring, but is less likely to be successful than sowing spores, because the rhizomes resent disturbance. See also p.51.
• **PESTS AND DISEASES** Fungal root rot may be a problem under glass.

C. argentea ▣ Evergreen fern with erect or creeping rhizomes and long-stalked, 3-angled, 2- or 3-pinnate, dull green fronds, 6–10in (15–25cm) long, with linear segments; the undersides are white-mealy. ↕ 8in (20cm), ↔ 12in (30cm). E. Asia. ❄ (min. 45°F/7°C)
C. eatoni. Upright, semi-evergreen, colonizing fern. Gray-green to whitish-green lanceolate 3–4 pinnate oblong fronds whose pinnules are oval to bead-like and hairy on both surfaces. The lower side becomes fawn-colored with age. One of the most cold-hardy species, depending on the geographic origin of the stock. Thrives in partial sun to light shade; protect from excessive winter wet by tucking under rock ledge or open cover. Found on rock slopes and ledges. ↕ 6–12in (15–30cm). Southern US, Mexico, Costa Rica. ❄ (min. 41°F/5°C)
C. fendleri 3–4 pinnate, ovate triangular blades and lobed bead-like pinnules. Blade surfaces are nearly hairless, but stipes are densely scaly. Found on rocky ledges, slopes, and crevices. SW US, Mexico. ❄ (min. 41°F/5°C)
C. lendigera. Upright, arching, colonizing fern. Medium-green tripinnate blades with triangular-lanceolate, bead-like pinnules. Upper surface is smooth; long tawny hairs underneath. Thrives on rocky ledges. ↕ 12in (30cm). SW US to S America and W Indies. ❄ (min. 41°F/5°C)
C. tomentosa (Hairy lip fern). Evergreen fern with erect rhizomes. Lance-shaped, pinnatifid to 2-pinnate fronds, 6–12in (15–30cm) long, have rounded, dark gray-green segments, covered with silvery scales beneath. Stalks are purplish black with hair-like scales. ↕ 12in (30cm), ↔ 16in (40cm). S. Pennsylvania to New Mexico (on neutral or acidic rocks). Zone 6b.

▷ ***Cheiranthus*** see *Erysimum*

CHEIRIDOPSIS

AIZOACEAE

Genus of about 100 species of dwarf, clump-forming, perennial succulents from periodically semi-arid regions of Namibia and South Africa. Smooth, velvety, fleshy leaves are borne in pairs, either entirely free or partially joined along most of their length. The daisy-like, solitary, mainly stalked flowers, borne in summer, are followed by ovoid green fruits, which contain pale brown seeds. Where not hardy, grow in a temperate greenhouse. In warm, dry climates, use in a border or raised bed.
• **CULTIVATION** Under glass, grow in 2 parts each loam and sharp sand and 1 part leaf mold, in full light with low humidity. Water sparingly from summer to midautumn, applying a dilute, low-nitrogen liquid fertilizer at the beginning and end of this period; keep dry at other times. Old leaves must be completely dry before watering, especially with species having two or more different forms of leaf on the same plant. Outdoors, grow in gritty, humus-rich, sharply drained soil in full sun; protect from rain, except when in full growth. See also pp.48–49.
• **PROPAGATION** Sow seed at 66–75°F (19–24°C), or root stem cuttings, in late spring or early summer.
• **PESTS AND DISEASES** Susceptible to mealybugs in dry weather.

C. candidissima see *C. denticulata.*
C. denticulata ▣ syn. *C. candidissima.* Clump-forming succulent with paired, cylindrical, suberect, thick, grayish white leaves, to 4in (10cm) long, partially joined at the bases. Bears stalked yellow flowers, to 3in (8cm) across. ↕ 4in (10cm), ↔ indefinite. South Africa (Western Cape). ❄ (min. 41°F/5°C)
C. purpurata see *C. purpurea.*
C. purpurea, syn. *C. purpurata.* Clump-forming succulent with pairs of angular, bluish or pinkish green leaves, to 2½in (6cm) long, flat on the upper surfaces and rounded and keeled beneath. Bears short-stalked, purplish pink or yellow flowers, 1½in (4cm) across. ↕ 4in (10cm), ↔ indefinite. South Africa, possibly Namibia. ❄ (min. 45°F/7°C)

CHELIDONIUM

PAPAVERACEAE

Genus of one species of variable biennial or short-lived perennial from woodland, scrub, wasteland, and rocky slopes in Europe and W. Asia. It has deeply pinnatifid or pinnatisect, hairless leaves, and bears umbels of poppy-like, bowl-shaped yellow flowers in summer. It is suitable for naturalizing in a wild garden or in light woodland, but it may become invasive. Contact with the orange-yellow sap may cause skin blisters.
• **CULTIVATION** Easy to grow in any soil and in almost any situation, but prefers woodland conditions.
• **PROPAGATION** Sow seed *in situ* in spring.
• **PESTS AND DISEASES** Infrequent.

C. majus (Greater celandine). Clump-forming perennial with lobed to deeply pinnatifid or pinnatisect, scalloped, pale or slightly bluish green leaves, 4–10in (10–25cm) long. In summer, bears loose, terminal umbels of 4-petaled yellow flowers, ¾–1in (2–2.5cm) across, on upright, brittle stems. Self-seeds profusely. ↕ to 24in (60cm), ↔ 8in (20cm). Europe, W. Asia. Zone 4. **'Flore Pleno'** ▣ has double yellow flowers.

Chasmanthium latifolium

Cheilanthes argentea

Cheiridopsis denticulata

Chelidonium majus 'Flore Pleno'

Chelone obliqua

CHELONE

Turtlehead

SCROPHULARIACEAE

Genus of about 6 species of perennials from moist woodland, prairies, and mountains of North America, valued for their strong growth and weather-resistant flowers. Turtleheads have a stiff, upright habit and produce opposite pairs of simple, toothed, hairless leaves. The white, pink, or purple flowers, produced in short, dense, terminal racemes, from late summer to midautumn, are tubular and 2-lipped, with a beard on the inside of each lower lip. They are showy plants for a late-summer border.

• **CULTIVATION** Grow in deep, fertile, moist soil in an open site in partial shade or sun. Turtleheads tolerate heavy clay soil and will also grow in a bog garden. Mulch in midspring with well-rotted manure or compost.

• **PROPAGATION** Sow seed in containers in a cold frame in early spring. Divide in spring. Root soft-tip cuttings in late spring or early summer.

• **PESTS AND DISEASES** Prone to powdery mildew, rust, fungal leaf spots, and damage from slugs and snails.

C. glabra, syn. *C. obliqua* var. *alba* (Snakeshead, Turtlehead). Erect perennial with square stems and short-stalked, ovate to lance-shaped, mid-green leaves, 2–8in (5–20cm) long. Bears white or pink-tinged white flowers, 1in (2.5cm) long, with white beards. ↕ 24–36in (60–90cm), ↔ 18in (45cm). E. and S. North America. Zone 4.

C. lyonii. Erect perennial with square stems and long-stalked, ovate to elliptic, toothed, mid-green leaves, 2–6in (5–15cm) long. Produces purple-pink flowers, 1in (2.5cm) long, with yellow beards. ↕ to 4ft (1.2m), ↔ 24in (60cm). Mountains of S.E. US. Zone 3b.

C. obliqua ▣ Erect perennial with more rounded stems than other species, and short-stalked, broadly lance-shaped to elliptic-lance-shaped, toothed or incised, boldly veined, dark green leaves, 2–8in (5–20cm) long. Bears dark pink or purple flowers, to ¾in (2cm) long, with sparse yellow beards. ↕ 16–24in (40–60cm), ↔ 12in (30cm). C. and S.E. US. Zone 5. **var. *alba*** see *C. glabra*.

▷ ***Chiapasia nelsonii*** see *Disocactus nelsonii*

Chiastophyllum oppositifolium

CHIASTOPHYLLUM

CRASSULACEAE

Genus of one species of mat-forming, rhizomatous, succulent, evergreen perennial from shady, mountain habitats in the Caucasus. It is grown for its attractive, fleshy foliage and tiny yellow flowers in pendent racemes. Grow in a rock garden, border, or shaded rock and wall crevices.

• **CULTIVATION** Grow in moist but well-drained, poor to moderately fertile soil in partial shade.

• **PROPAGATION** Sow seed in containers in a cold frame in autumn, or root sideshoot cuttings in early summer.

• **PESTS AND DISEASES** Susceptible to damage by slugs and snails.

C. oppositifolium ▣ syn. *C. simplicifolium, Cotyledon simplicifolia.* Spreading, rhizomatous, evergreen perennial forming dense mats of ovate to rounded, scalloped or wavy-margined, fleshy, pale green leaves, 1½–5in (4–13cm) long. In late spring and early summer, long stems bear bell-shaped, deep yellow flowers, to ¼in (6mm) long, in dense, arching, branched racemes. ↕ 6–8in (15–20cm), ↔ 6in (15cm). Caucasus. Zone 5.

C. simplicifolium see *C. oppositifolium.*

CHILIOTRICHUM

ASTERACEAE

Genus of 2 species of evergreen shrubs from temperate regions of South America, where they are found from sea level to the mountains. *C. diffusum* is grown for its rosemary-like leaves and daisy-like flowerheads, and is best suited to a sheltered, sunny shrub border. It thrives in coastal gardens.

• **CULTIVATION** Grow in fertile, well-drained soil in full sun, with shelter from cold, dry winds. Pruning group 8.

• **PROPAGATION** Root semi-ripe cuttings in summer.

• **PESTS AND DISEASES** Infrequent.

C. amelloides see *C. diffusum.*

C. diffusum, syn. *C. amelloides.* Evergreen shrub with erect shoots and usually linear, oblong-lance-shaped to elliptic, glossy, dark green leaves, to 1½in (4cm) long, densely and alternately arranged around the stems. White flowerheads, to 2in (5cm) across, with yellow centers, are borne on flower stalks to 4in (10cm) long, in late spring and early summer. ↕ 3ft (1m), ↔ 5ft (1.5m). S. Chile, S.W. Argentina, Falkland Islands. ❄ (min. 45°F/7°C)

CHILOPSIS

Desert willow

BIGNONIACEAE

Genus of one species of evergreen shrub or tree from sandy riverbanks and desert areas of S.W. US and Mexico. It has alternate, linear, mid-green leaves and produces racemes of white to purple-red flowers, followed by elongated fruit. *C. linearis* is useful in a border in warm, dry areas; where not hardy, grow in containers or in a warm greenhouse.

• **CULTIVATION** Under glass, grow in soil-based potting mix in full light, with low humidity. When in growth, water sparingly and apply a balanced liquid fertilizer monthly; keep just moist in winter. Outdoors, grow in well-drained soil in full sun. Pruning group 8.

• **PROPAGATION** Sow seed at 70–79°F (21–26°C) as soon as ripe or take soft- or hardwood cuttings in spring or summer.

• **PESTS AND DISEASES** Seedlings are sometimes prone to root rot.

C. linearis. Upright, densely branched shrub or tree with linear, entire, often curved leaves, to 8in (20cm) long. Bears terminal racemes of large, trumpet-shaped, yellow-mottled, white, pink, lilac, lavender, or purple flowers, to 2in (5cm) long, sporadically throughout the summer. Drought tolerant. ↕↔ 6–25ft (2–8m). S. California, S. Nevada, Texas to Mexico. ❄ (min. 41°F/5°C)

CHIMAPHILA

Prince's pine

PYROLACEAE

Genus of about 6 species of evergreen, creeping perennials, related to *Pyrola*, found in cool-temperate woodland in Europe, Asia, and North America. They have slender, upright stems, and produce opposite or whorls of leathery leaves and nodding, white to pink flowers in terminal corymbs or umbels. They grow best in cool climates, and are ideal for a woodland garden or for shaded areas in a rock garden.

• **CULTIVATION** Grow in moist but well-drained, humus-rich, acidic soil, enriched with leaf mold, in a cool site in partial or dappled shade. Not easy to establish.

• **PROPAGATION** Sow seed as soon as ripe onto acidic seed-starting mix topped with damp sphagnum moss; keep in a cool, shaded frame until germination.

• **PESTS AND DISEASES** Prone to damage by slugs and snails.

C. japonica. Evergreen perennial with upright, unbranched stems and opposite or whorled, broadly lance-shaped, hairless, slightly toothed, dark green leaves, to 1½in (4cm) long, with white midribs. In summer, bears upright umbels of 1 or 2 white flowers, to 1in (2.5cm) across. ↕ to 4in (10cm), ↔ indefinite. E. Asia. Zone 5b.

C. maculata (Spotted wintergreen, Striped Pipsissewa). Evergreen perennial, with a creeping, woody rootstock producing ovate to lance-shaped, leathery, white-veined, dark green leaves, to 3in (8cm) long, usually arranged in whorls of 3. Umbels of 3–5 open cup-shaped, white or pale pink flowers, to ½in (1.5cm) across, are produced on pendent flower stalks in early summer. ↕ to 10in (25cm), ↔ to 8in (20cm). E. North America. Zone 5b.

C. umbellata (Western prince's pine). Evergreen perennial with simple or branched, hairless stems and whorled, inversely lance-shaped, toothed, mid-green leaves, 1¼–3in (3–8cm) long. In summer, bears densely hairy umbels of 3–10 white, pink, or red flowers, to ½in (1.5cm) across. ↕ to 14in (35cm), ↔ indefinite. N. and C. Europe, N. Asia, Japan, E. North America. Zone 4.

CHIMONANTHUS

Wintersweet

CALYCANTHACEAE

Genus of 6 species of deciduous and evergreen shrubs occurring in woodland in China. They are cultivated for their unusual, many-petaled, open bowl-shaped, waxy, and very fragrant flowers, which are borne in winter before the young leaves emerge. Grow wintersweets as specimen plants or in a shrub border. They may also be trained against a sunny wall.

• **CULTIVATION** Grow in any fertile, well-drained soil in full sun. Pruning group 1, or group 13 if wall-trained; prune plants immediately after flowering.

• **PROPAGATION** Sow seed in containers in a cold frame as soon as ripe. Root softwood cuttings in summer.

• **PESTS AND DISEASES** Infrequent.

C. praecox ▣ (Wintersweet). Vigorous, broadly upright, deciduous shrub with entire, lance-shaped, glossy, mid-green leaves, to 8in (20cm) long, rough above, smooth beneath, arranged in opposite pairs. Pendent, fragrant, sulfur-yellow flowers, 1in (2.5cm) across, stained brown or purple inside, are produced on the bare shoots in winter. ↕ 12ft (4m), ↔ 10ft (3m). China. Zone 7.

'Concolor' see 'Luteus'.

Chimonanthus praecox

Chimonanthus praecox 'Grandiflorus'

'Grandiflorus' ▣ has larger, deep yellow flowers, to 1¾in (4.5cm) long, conspicuously striped maroon inside.
'Luteus', syn. 'Concolor', bears clear yellow flowers which open widely.
'Parviflorus' has pale yellow flowers to ½in (1.5cm) across.

CHIMONOBAMBUSA

POACEAE

Genus of 6–20 species of small- to medium-sized bamboos from deciduous woodland in S. and E. Asia, with running rhizomes, bright green leaves, and flowers borne in spike-like racemes. They are useful for planting as a screen or hedge, and grow well in a woodland garden. *C. quadrangularis* is cultivated for its unusual square culms, and elegant shape and foliage. Where not hardy, grow in a cool or temperate greenhouse or conservatory.
• **CULTIVATION** Grow in fertile, humus-rich, moist but well-drained soil in partial shade, with shelter from winds.
• **PROPAGATION** Divide clumps, or take cuttings of sections of young rhizomes, in spring.
• **PESTS AND DISEASES** Emerging shoots are vulnerable to slug damage.

C. quadrangularis, syn. *Arundinaria quadrangularis* (Square-stemmed bamboo). Vigorous, spreading, rhizomatous bamboo, forming loose clumps of erect culms, often with sparse, small spines. Attractive, pendent, lance-shaped, dark green leaves, 8in (20cm) long, are produced from the prominent culm nodes. Older culms become square in cross-section, especially at the bases. ↕ to 28ft (9m), ↔ 3–6ft (1–2m). S.E. China, Taiwan. ❀ (min. 50°F/10°C)

CHIONANTHUS

Fringe tree

OLEACEAE

Genus of 10 or more species of evergreen and deciduous trees and shrubs found in a variety of habitats, including woodland and scrub, and on streambanks and rocky outcrops. They occur mainly in tropical regions, including E. Asia, Korea, Japan, and E. US. Cultivated for their terminal panicles of flowers, which have 4 slender white petals, and for their blue-purple or blue-black fruits, *Chionanthus* species are late-leafing, attractive specimen plants. They are also suitable for a shrub

Chionanthus virginicus

border. Some plants have only male or only female flowers, and therefore may not produce fruit.
• **CULTIVATION** Grow in any fertile, well-drained soil in full sun. Flowering and fruiting is best in areas with long, hot summers. Pruning group 1; remove the lower branches of *C. virginicus* to encourage a tree-like habit.
• **PROPAGATION** Sow seed in containers in a cold frame in autumn; germination may take up to 18 months.
• **PESTS AND DISEASES** Infrequent.

C. retusus (Chinese fringe tree). Spreading, deciduous shrub or small tree with peeling or deeply furrowed bark and opposite, usually elliptic, glossy leaves, 1½–4in (4–10cm) long, bright green above, softly white-hairy beneath. Fragrant white flowers are borne in erect panicles, 4–7in (10–18cm) long, in summer, followed by blue-black fruit, ½in (1.5cm) long. ↕↔ 10ft (3m). China, Taiwan. Zone 6.
C. virginicus ▣ (Fringe tree, Old man's beard). Spreading, deciduous shrub, or sometimes small tree, with opposite, usually elliptic, glossy, dark green leaves, to 8in (20cm) long. Fragrant white flowers are borne in pendent panicles, to 8in (20cm) long, in summer; they are followed by small, blue-black fruit, ½in (1.5cm) long. ↕ 10ft (3m), ↔ 10ft (3m) or more. E. US. Zone 5.

CHIONOCHLOA

POACEAE

Genus of about 20 species of evergreen, coarse, erect, tufted perennial grasses, mostly from New Zealand, found in alpine and subalpine grassland. The narrowly linear, deeply ridged leaves have persistent sheaths, similar to those of pampas grass (*Cortaderia*), to which this genus is related. The inflorescences bear several-flowered spikelets in loose, graceful panicles. *Chionochloa* species are cultivated for their strong, elegant shape, colorful foliage, and attractive flower-heads, which are excellent for dried flower arrangements if cut before fully mature. Grow as feature plants in a border or use as specimen plants.
• **CULTIVATION** Grow in a sheltered site in light, fertile, moist but well-drained soil. Protect crowns from excessive winter moisture. Cut out old, flowered stems at the bases in early winter. *C. conspicua* will withstand drops in temperature to 14°F (-10°C).

Chionochloa conspicua

• **PROPAGATION** Sow seed in containers in a cold frame in spring. Divide in early and midspring.
• **PESTS AND DISEASES** Infrequent.

C. conspicua ▣ syn. *Arundo conspicua*, *Cortaderia conspicua* (Plumed tussock grass). Robust, densely tufted, perennial grass, forming tussocks of stiff, arching, linear, red-brown-tinted, mid-green leaves, to 4ft (1.2m) long, often fringed with fine hairs at the bases. Strong, arching or erect stems bear large, open, pendent panicles, to 18in (45cm) long, of 3- to 7-flowered spikelets of creamy white flowers, each to ½in (1.5cm) long, in mid- and late summer. ↕ to 6ft (2m), ↔ 3ft (1m). New Zealand. Zone 7b.

CHIONODOXA

Glory of the snow

LILIACEAE

Genus, related to *Scilla*, of 6 species of small, bulbous perennials from open mountainsides and forest in Crete, W. Turkey, and Cyprus. They bear racemes of star-shaped flowers in early spring, above linear, sometimes channeled, mid-green, basal leaves, to 11in (28cm) long. Grow in a rock garden, raised bed, or trough; most may also be grown under shrubs or trees, where they can spread. They self-seed freely.
• **CULTIVATION** Plant bulbs 3in (8cm) deep in autumn, in well-drained soil in full sun. *C. nana* dislikes winter moisture.
• **PROPAGATION** Sow seed in containers in a cold frame as soon as ripe. Remove offsets in summer.
• **PESTS AND DISEASES** Infrequent.

C. cretica see *C. nana.*
C. forbesii ▣ syn. *C. luciliae* of gardens, *C. siehei*, *C. tmolusi.* Bulbous perennial producing erect to spreading leaves, 3–11in (7–28cm) long. In early spring, bears racemes of 4–12 star-shaped blue flowers, ½–¾in (1–2cm) across, with white centers. ↕ 4–8in (10–20cm), PD1in (2.5cm). W. Turkey. Zone 3.
'Alba' produces white flowers.
'Pink Giant' ▣ has pink flowers, ½in (1.5cm) across, with white centers.
C. gigantea see *C. luciliae.*
C. luciliae ▣ syn. *C. gigantea.* Bulbous perennial with often recurved leaves, 3–8in (7–20cm) long. In early spring, racemes are produced with up to 3 star-shaped blue flowers, ½–¾in (1–2cm) across, with white centers. Similar to *C. forbesii* but produces fewer

Chionodoxa forbesii

Chionodoxa forbesii 'Pink Giant'

Chionodoxa luciliae

flowers, with slightly wider tepals. ↕ 6in (15cm), PD1in (2.5cm). W. Turkey. Zone 3.
***C. luciliae* of gardens** see *C. forbesii.*
C. nana, syn. *C. cretica.* Delicate, bulbous perennial with spreading leaves, 3–7in (8–18cm) long. In early spring, bears racemes of up to 3 star-shaped blue flowers, ¼–½in (6–15mm) across, with white centers. ↕ 6in (15cm), PD1in (2.5cm). Greece (Crete). Zone 7b.
C. sardensis. Bulbous perennial with erect or spreading leaves, 3–8in (7–20cm) long. In early spring, produces racemes of up to 12 slightly pendent, star-shaped, deep clear blue flowers, ⅜–½in (9–15mm) across, with blue centers. ↕ 4–8in (10–20cm), PD1in (2.5cm). W. Turkey. Zone 3.
C. siehei see *C. forbesii.*
C. tmolusi see *C. forbesii.*

x CHIONOSCILLA

LILIACEAE

Genus of one hybrid bulbous perennial, a cross between *Chionodoxa forbesii* and *Scilla bifolia*, with semi-erect, narrow, inversely lance-shaped, dark green basal leaves. Grown for its short racemes of brilliant blue flowers in spring, it is suitable for a rock garden, trough, or raised bed, and for planting beneath trees or shrubs.
• **CULTIVATION** Plant bulbs 3in (8cm) deep in autumn, in any well-drained soil in sun or partial shade.
• **PROPAGATION** Remove offsets in summer.
• **PESTS AND DISEASES** Infrequent.

x *Chionoscilla allenii*

x *C. allenii* ■ Bulbous perennial with basal leaves 3–6in (7–15cm) long, and short racemes, 2½–5in (6–13cm) long, of variable, star-shaped, mid- to deep blue flowers, ½in (1.5cm) across, borne in spring. Natural hybrid. ↕ 4–8in (10–20cm), PD1in (2.5cm). Zone 3. **'Fra Angelico'** produces deep bright blue flowers.

CHIRITA

GESNERIACEAE

Genus of about 100 species of upright or mat-forming annuals and evergreen perennials from damp, semi-shaded sites in tropical Asia. They have fleshy stems and downy or bristly leaves in opposite pairs or whorls. The tubular or funnel-shaped flowers are either solitary or borne in many-flowered clusters from the leaf axils in summer and autumn. Where not hardy, grow in a warm greenhouse or conservatory; in tropical climates, grow in a damp, shady border.
• **CULTIVATION** Under glass, grow in soilless potting mix in bright filtered light, with high humidity and good air circulation. In growth, water moderately and apply a half-strength, balanced liquid fertilizer monthly. Water perennials more sparingly in winter. Outdoors, grow in well-drained, humus-rich, gritty soil in partial shade.
• **PROPAGATION** Sow seed at 66–75°F (19–24°C) in early spring; seed of *C. lavandulacea* may be sown in succession from late winter. *C. sinensis* may be increased by leaf cuttings, inserted in moist, sandy mix in a propagating case.
• **PESTS AND DISEASES** Prone to stem rot in damp conditions; water on the leaves causes discoloration and fungal rot.

C. lavandulacea ■ Fast-growing, erect, usually unbranched annual with pairs of oblong-elliptic, softly hairy, light green leaves, 8in (20cm) long. In summer and autumn, bears a profusion of tubular, pale lavender-blue flowers, 1–1½in (2.5–4cm) across; each flower lasts only 2 or 3 days. ↕ 3ft (1m), ↔ 12in (30cm). Asia. ❀ (min. 55–70°F/13–21°C)
C. sinensis. Evergreen perennial forming flat rosettes of thick, ovate-lance-shaped or elliptic, bristly-hairy, dark green leaves, sometimes heavily veined silver, 6–8in (15–20cm) long; they appear quilted, particularly at the margins. Occasionally produces tubular white flowers, 1¼in (3cm) long, marked yellow and suffused

Chirita lavandulacea

purple-pink. ↕ 2in (5cm), ↔ 14in (35cm). Himalayas, China, Hong Kong. ❀ (min. 55–70°F/13–21°C). **'Hisako'** has a very regular whorl of lance-shaped, toothed, distinctly white-netted leaves.

CHLIDANTHUS

AMARYLLIDACEAE

Genus of one species of bulbous perennial found in the Andes in Peru. It is grown for its strongly scented flowers, borne in summer. Where not hardy, it is best grown in a cool or temperate greenhouse or conservatory. In areas that are virtually frost free, grow in a sheltered site outdoors, such as at the base of a sunny wall.
• **CULTIVATION** Plant with the nose of the bulb just above the soil surface in spring. Under glass, grow in soil-based potting mix in full light. Water freely when in growth, reducing water as leaves wither; keep cool and dry in winter. Container-grown plants may be plunged outdoors in summer. Outdoors, grow in humus-rich, sandy, well-drained soil in a sheltered position; apply a dry mulch in winter.
• **PROPAGATION** Sow seed at 55–64°F (13–18°C) or remove offsets, in spring.
• **PESTS AND DISEASES** Infrequent.

C. fragrans ■ Bulbous perennial with semi-erect, narrow, linear, gray-green, basal leaves, 6–16in (15–40cm) long. In summer, leafless stems bear umbels of 3–5 trumpet-shaped, strongly scented, golden yellow flowers, 2in (5cm) wide. ↕ 12in (30cm), PD3in (8cm). Peru (Andes). ❀ (min. 41–50°F/5–10°C)

Chlidanthus fragrans

CHLOROPHYTUM

LILIACEAE

Genus of about 250 species of evergreen, rhizomatous perennials with fibrous or fleshy roots. Those in cultivation are from a variety of habitats in South Africa and W. Africa, and are clump-forming, with linear, lance-shaped, ovate, or strap-shaped, basal leaves. In summer, they bear arching racemes or panicles of small, 6-petaled flowers, and often produce plantlets. Where not hardy, grow in containers and hanging baskets in a cool or temperate conservatory; they are also popular foliage houseplants, tolerant of a wide range of conditions. In warmer areas, use in a border or as a groundcover.
• **CULTIVATION** Under glass, grow in soil-based potting mix in bright indirect to full light, shaded from hot sun. Water freely in growth, moderately at other times. Outdoors, grow in any soil in sun or partial shade.
• **PROPAGATION** Sow seed at 64–68°F (18–20°C) in spring. Root plantlets, or divide, at any time except winter.
• **PESTS AND DISEASES** Prone to tip burn from excess salts, fluoride, or dry soil.

C. capense. Clump-forming perennial with lance- or strap-shaped, bright green leaves, 10–24in (25–60cm) long. Bears small white flowers in racemes to 24in (60cm) long. Does not produce plantlets. ↕ 12in (30cm), ↔ 24in (60cm). South Africa. ❀ (min. 45°F/7°C)
***C. capense* of gardens** see *C. comosum.*
C. comosum, syn. *C. capense* of gardens (Ribbon plant, Spider plant). Clump-forming perennial with linear to linear-lance-shaped, fresh green leaves, 12in (30cm) long. Small white flowers are borne in racemes, to 24in (60cm) long. Produces plantlets. ↕ 6–8in (15–20cm), ↔ 6–12in (15–30cm). South Africa. ❀ (min. 45°F/7°C). **'Variegatum'** produces leaves with white margins. **'Vittatum'** ■ has leaves with white or cream central stripes.
C. orchidastrum. Clump-forming perennial with oblong to inversely lance-shaped, often wavy-margined, glossy, mid-green leaves, 8–11in (21–28cm) long. Small, white, green-tinged flowers are borne in lax racemes, 10–16in (25–40cm) long. Does not produce plantlets. ↕ 6–8in (15–20cm), ↔ 6–12in (15–30cm). Sierra Leone. ❀ (min. 45°F/7°C)

Chlorophytum comosum 'Vittatum'

C

CHOISYA

Mexican orange blossom

RUTACEAE

Genus of about 8 species of evergreen shrubs from canyons and rocky slopes in S.W. US and Mexico. Choisyas are valued for their attractive, opposite, palmate, aromatic leaves, and for their fragrant, star-shaped white flowers, which are occasionally solitary, more often borne in terminal or axillary cymes or corymbs. They are best grown in a shrub border or against a wall. Where not hardy, grow in a cool greenhouse.

• **CULTIVATION** Under glass, grow in soil-based potting mix in full light. In the growing season, water freely and apply a balanced liquid fertilizer weekly; water sparingly in winter. Outdoors, grow in fertile, well-drained soil, preferably in full sun; less hardy species benefit from the shelter of a wall. Pruning group 8.

• **PROPAGATION** Root semi-ripe cuttings in summer.

• **PESTS AND DISEASES** Prone to damage from slugs and snails.

C. arizonica. Erect shrub with slender branches, warty shoots, and mid- to dark green leaves composed of 5–10 linear, gland-margined leaflets, to 2in (5cm) long. In late spring, bears axillary corymbs of many pink-tinged white flowers, ¾–1¼in (2–3cm) across. ↕↔ 3ft (1m). S. Arizona. Zone 7b.

***C.* 'Aztec Pearl'** ■ Compact shrub with dark green leaves composed of 3–5 linear leaflets, to 3in (8cm) long. Pink-tinged white flowers, ¾–1¼in (2–3cm) across, are borne in axillary cymes of 3–6 blooms in late spring, and again in late summer and autumn. ↕↔ 8ft (2.5m). Zone 7b.

Choisya 'Aztec Pearl'

Choisya ternata

Choisya ternata 'Sundance'

C. ternata ■ (Mexican orange blossom). Compact shrub with dark green leaves consisting of 3 stalkless, obovate leaflets, 1½–3in (4–8cm) long. Axillary corymbs of 3–6 fragrant white flowers, 1–1¼in (2.5–3cm) across, are borne in late spring, and again in late summer and autumn. ↕↔ 8ft (2.5m). Mexico. Zone 7b. **'Sundance'** ■ has bright yellow young foliage, yellow-green when grown in partial shade; it rarely flowers.

▷ ***Chondrosum gracile*** see *Bouteloua gracilis*

CHORISIA

BOMBACACEAE

Genus of 2 species of semi-evergreen or deciduous, succulent trees from low-lying areas in the Windward Islands, Brazil, and Argentina. They have spiny, extremely fleshy trunks, alternate, 5- to 7-palmate leaves, and open funnel-shaped flowers borne in autumn. Where not hardy, grow in a warm greenhouse; elsewhere, use as specimen trees.

• **CULTIVATION** Under glass, grow in soil-based potting mix in full light, shaded from hot sun, with good ventilation. Water moderately in growth, applying a balanced liquid fertilizer 2 or 3 times; keep dry at other times. Outdoors, grow in well-drained, neutral to acidic, humus-rich soil in sun. Pruning group 1; plants under glass may need restrictive pruning in early spring.

• **PROPAGATION** Sow seed at 66–75°F (19–24°C) from spring to early summer.

• **PESTS AND DISEASES** Young plants are prone to scale insects. Leaf spots caused by a variety of fungi are common.

C. speciosa (Floss silk tree). Broadly conical, slow-growing, semi-evergreen tree with long-stalked, pinnate leaves, to 5in (13cm) long, composed of 5–7 lance-shaped, often toothed leaflets. Open funnel-shaped, cream or white flowers, 4in (10cm) or more across, the upper parts of the petals reddish violet or yellowish white, are produced singly from the leaf axils in autumn. The pear-shaped, green then brown fruit contain seeds encased in silky floss. ↕ to 50ft (15m), ↔ to 5ft (1.5m). Brazil, Argentina. ❄ (min. 61°F/16°C)

CHORIZEMA

FABACEAE

Genus of 18 species of evergreen, small shrubs and twining and scandent climbers found in semi-arid scrub and open woodland in Australia. They are cultivated for their brightly colored, small, pea-like flowers, borne mostly in terminal racemes. The leathery leaves are usually alternate, and may be entire or prickle-toothed. Where not hardy, grow in a cool conservatory or greenhouse. In warmer areas, grow in a shrub border or as a groundcover. Train climbing species over arches, arbors, or larger shrubs.

• **CULTIVATION** Under glass, grow in soilless or soil-based potting mix, with additional sharp sand. Provide full light, with shade from hot sun, and good ventilation. When in growth, water moderately and apply a balanced liquid fertilizer monthly; water more sparingly in winter. Pot on in early spring. Outdoors, grow in humus-rich, neutral to slightly acidic, moist but well-drained soil in full sun. *C. cordatum* and *C. ilicifolium* may survive brief spells close to 32°F (0°C). Pruning group 8, or group 11 for climbing species; prune after flowering.

• **PROPAGATION** Sow seed at 55–64°F (13–18°C) in spring, after soaking in hot water. Root semi-ripe cuttings in summer.

• **PESTS AND DISEASES** Spider mites may be a problem under glass.

C. cordatum (Heart-leaved flame pea). Dense, low shrub or semi-scandent climber with ovate, leathery, mid- to dark green leaves, ¾–2in (2–5cm) long, heart-shaped at the bases, and with spine-like teeth. From late winter to late summer, freely bears orange-red and yellow flowers, ½in (1.5cm) across, with purplish pink keels, in terminal racemes, 3–6in (8–15cm) long. ↕↔ to 4ft (1.2m) or more. Western Australia. ❄ (min. 41–50°F/5–10°C)

C. ilicifolium ■ (Holly flame pea). Spreading, open shrub with slender branches and narrowly to broadly ovate, dark green leaves, 2–3in (5–8cm) long, with wavy, prickle-toothed margins. Orange-red and yellow flowers, ½in (1.5cm) across, with purplish pink keels, are produced in terminal and axillary racemes, 3–6in (8–15cm) long, from late winter to late summer. ↕↔ 3–10ft (1–3m). Western Australia. ❄ (min. 41–50°F/5–10°C)

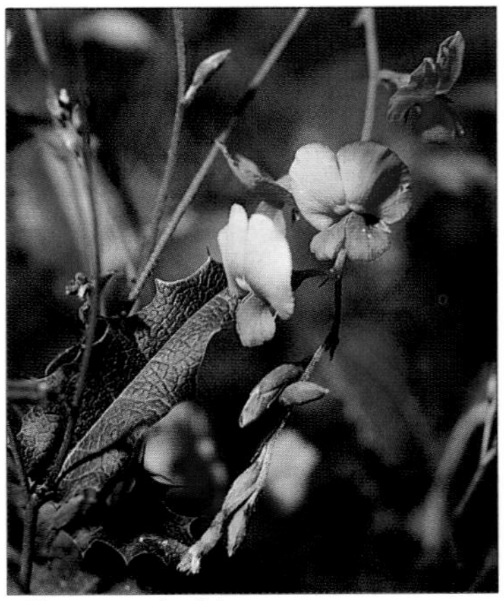

Chorizema ilicifolium

Chrysalidocarpus lutescens

CHRYSALIDOCARPUS

Yellow palm

ARECACEAE

Genus of about 20 species of single- and cluster-stemmed palms from forest in areas with high rainfall in Madagascar and adjacent islands. The pinnate, arching leaves are arranged in terminal clusters; panicles of small, 3-petaled flowers are borne among them. Where not hardy, grow in a temperate or warm greenhouse, or as houseplants. In tropical or subtropical regions, grow as elegant specimen trees.

• **CULTIVATION** Under glass, grow in soil-based potting mix in bright filtered or full light with shade from hot sun. Water freely when in growth, applying a balanced liquid fertilizer monthly; water sparingly in winter. Pot on or top-dress in spring. Outdoors, grow in fertile, moist but well-drained soil in sun or partial shade.

• **PROPAGATION** Sow seed at not less than 79°F (26°C) in spring, or remove rooted suckers.

• **PESTS AND DISEASES** Prone to spider mites, whiteflies, and scale insects, as well as foliar and root mealybugs. Young plants are prone to many fungal leaf spots. Lethal yellowing, *Ganoderma* butt rot, false smut, and *Phytophthora* bud rot occur outdoors.

C. lutescens ■ syn. *Areca lutescens* (Areca palm, Butterfly palm, Golden feather palm). Small palm producing clustered stems, at first covered with yellow leaf bases. The leaves, 3–6ft (1–2m) long, have numerous slender, lance-shaped, usually yellow-green leaflets. In summer, bears yellow flowers in panicles to 24in (60cm) long. ↕ to 28ft (9m), ↔ to 20ft (6m). Madagascar. ❄ (min. 50–59°F/10–15°C)

C. madagascariensis. Small palm with many obscurely ringed, gray-brown stems. The leaves, to 10ft (3m) long, each have at least 200 lance-shaped, mid-green leaflets, arranged in groups and in several planes. In summer, bears densely rust-woolly panicles, to 24in (60cm) long, of yellow flowers. ↕ to 30ft (10m), ↔ to 20ft (6m). Madagascar. ❄ (min. 50–59°F/10–15°C).

var. *lucubensis* bears solitary stems. **var. *madagascariensis*** has only a few stems, arranged in clumps.

▷ ***Chrysanthemopsis*** see *Rhodanthemum*

CHRYSANTHEMUM

ASTERACEAE

Genus of about 20 species of upright, bushy annuals and herbaceous perennials (some with woody bases), now almost all attributed by botanists to the genus *Dendranthema*, but here maintained under *Chrysanthemum* for the benefit of gardeners. The annual species come from the Mediterranean region, where they grow in dry fields and wasteland; the herbaceous perennials are from the Arctic, parts of N. and C. Russia, China, and Japan. The aromatic, alternate, ovate to lance-shaped, dark green leaves, 2–7in (5–18cm) long, are shallowly to deeply lobed or pinnatisect, occasionally entire, and often feathery.

Chrysanthemums are grown primarily for their showy flowerheads, 1–12in (2.5–30cm) across, which consist of ray florets in a variety of colors, including yellow, bronze, white, pink, purple, and red, with yellow disk florets; they are cultivated in a multiplicity of forms.

For ease of reference in this book, chrysanthemums have been divided into the following groups:

Exhibition chrysanthemums
These perennial cultivars are available in a wide range of forms and colors, and are grown for exhibition, garden use, and cutting. They are often categorized according to their flowerhead form (see panel below), their flowering season – early (late summer and early autumn), midseason (midautumn), or late (midautumn to early winter) – and whether they are disbudded or non-disbudded. Disbudded chrysanthemums are classified by exhibitors into size groups. Non-disbudded chrysanthemums are categorized by both size and habit.

The early-flowering spray chrysanthemums, reflexed cultivars, and pompon chrysanthemums are the best groups for outdoor use. Some midseason reflexed cultivars are suitable for garden use, but most require protection from rain and frost. Late-flowering cultivars are brought into bloom in a temperate or warm greenhouse. ❀ (min. 35°F/2°C)

Disbudded – Disbudded chrysanthemums have all the flower buds on each shoot removed except for the terminal bud, in order to increase the size of the remaining bloom. For exhibition, those with incurved, intermediate, or reflexed flowers are restricted to 2 blooms per plant; in gardens, 4 or 5 blooms are allowed to develop. Single and anemone-centered flowers are reduced to 4–8 blooms for exhibition, and 10 or more for garden use and for cutting.

Non-disbudded – In non-disbudded chrysanthemums, the buds are usually allowed to develop freely. Non-disbudded chrysanthemums are grouped according to the following habits. **Spray chrysanthemums** produce several blooms per stem in a variety of flower forms: single, intermediate, reflexed, anemone-centered, pompon, spoon-shaped, or quill-shaped. They are grown mainly for garden decoration and for cutting. For exhibition, one flowerhead must be retained per pedicel, and the terminal flowerhead must be present, each with 5 or more adjacent flowerheads. Commercially, the central bud of the spray is usually removed to give a more rounded outline. **Charm chrysanthemums** have a dwarf, bushy, domed to almost spherical habit, and bear hundreds of single flowerheads, to 1in (2.5cm) across. They do not need stopping or training, and are grown for indoor decoration, for exhibition, and as bonsai plants. **Cascade chrysanthemums** have similar flowerheads to charms but are trained as fans, pillars, pyramids, or cascades. They are grown for indoor decoration, for exhibition, and as bonsai plants. **Pompon chrysanthemums** are dwarf and bushy, producing 50 or more dense, spherical or occasionally hemi-spherical flowerheads per plant. They are suitable for a herbaceous border.

Rubellum Group chrysanthemums
These clump-forming, bushy perennials, with woody stem bases, are all named hybrids of *C. rubellum*, syn. *Dendranthema zawadskii*. They have pinnatisect leaves, often with a silvery cast, and bear single, semi-double, or double, yellow-centered flowerheads in a range of colors. Flowering in late summer and early autumn, they are excellent for a herbaceous border and for cutting. Zone 4.

Garden chrysanthemums
These chrysanthemums have a bushy, branched habit and bear clusters of flowerheads in a wide variety of colors. Commercial suppliers divide these into garden types, which are more upright, and cushion types, which tend to grow into a mound. They flower over a long period, normally during early or midseason, and are suitable for an annual border, or for a herbaceous border. *C. segetum* is also suitable for a wildflower garden. Zone 5 or 6.

• **CULTIVATION** Grow early-flowering and midseason exhibition chrysanthemums outdoors in a sheltered site in full sun in fertile, moist but well-drained, neutral to slightly acidic soil, enriched with well-rotted manure. Apply a top-dressing of balanced fertilizer before planting, and plant out when any danger of frost has passed. Provide support and tie stems in with soft twine as growth proceeds. Eventual height of most types is highly variable, depending on fertility and pruning practices. Stop plants at 6–8in (15–20cm) tall, by pinching out the growing tips to encourage the early production of flowering laterals. A second stop will produce greater numbers of smaller blooms. For exhibition purposes, select the required number of strong laterals and remove the remainder. Disbud gradually, removing unwanted flower buds as laterals reach about ¾in (2cm) long. The timing of stopping and disbudding varies with climate and growing conditions; generally, pinching should be discontinued by July 15 in cooler climates and by July 25 in warmer ones.

Water freely in dry weather, and apply a balanced liquid fertilizer every 7–10 days from midsummer until buds begin to show color. After flowering, cut back flowered stems to 6–9in (15–23cm). Lift crowns and store over winter in soilless potting mix in frost-free conditions. In areas experiencing only light frosts, leave *in situ*, apply a deep, dry winter mulch, and cut back in early spring. Protect early and midseason exhibition cultivars from rain and frost. Large-flowered cultivars, as well as early and midseason exhibition cultivars, are

CHRYSANTHEMUM FLOWERHEAD FORMS

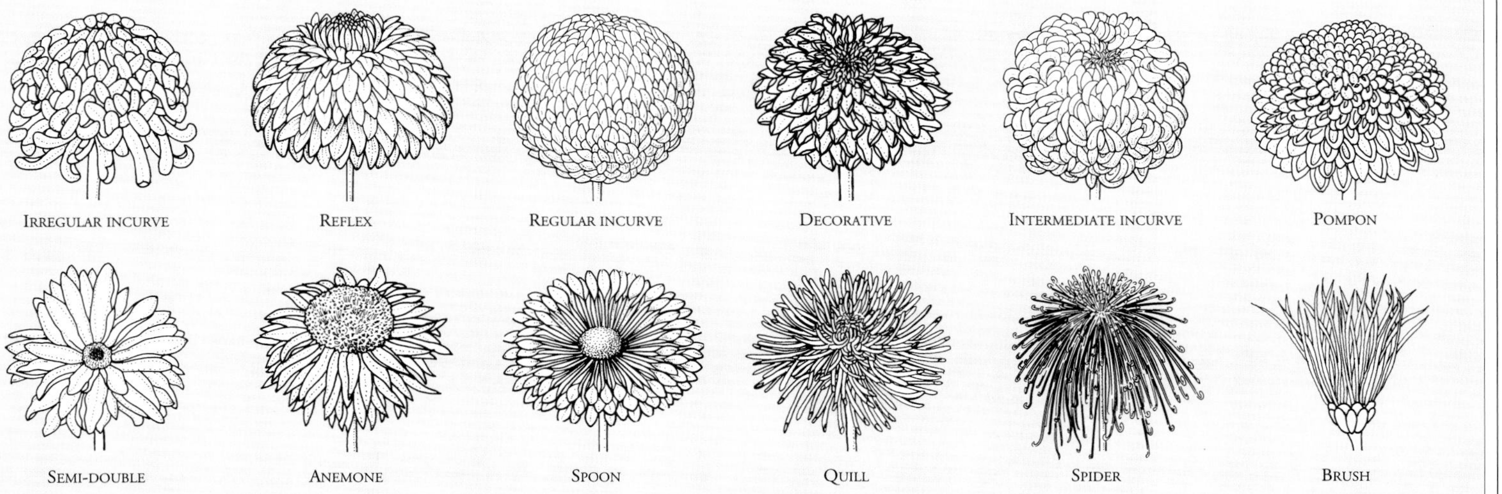

Irregular Incurve–Fully double, particularly large flowerheads with loosely upturned ray florets. The lower florets are not incurved, forming a skirt-like ring at the base of the flowerhead.
Reflex–Fully double flowerheads, each with a flattened top and downward-curving, overlapping ray florets that resemble bird plumage.
Regular Incurve–Fully double, spherical flowerheads with uniformly incurved ray florets.
Decorative–Fully double, flat-topped and short-petaled flowerheads; the upper ray florets tend to incurve, the lower ray florets usually reflex.
Intermediate Incurve–Fully double flowerheads, smaller and more open than irregular incurve; the ray florets are partially upturned.
Pompon–Fully double, small and spherical flowerheads, flattened when young and fully rounded when mature. Sizes range from small button types to large disbudded blooms.
Single and Semi-double–Daisy-like flowerheads with a prominent central disk and one (single) or more (semi-double) rows of ray florets.
Anemone–Semi-double flowerheads, each with a raised, preferably rounded, cushion-like center.
Spoon–Semi-double flowerheads; the ray florets are regularly arranged and spoon-shaped at the tips.
Quill–Fully double flowerheads that have tubular ray florets with open tips.
Spider–Fully double flowerheads with fine to coarse ray florets, which are long, tubular, and may coil or hook at the ends; florets drape gracefully in full bloom.
Brush or Thistle–Single flowerheads with upright, fine, tubular ray florets.
Unclassified–Flowerheads that do not fit in any of the other classes, or those showing characteristics of two classes. They often have twisted ray florets.

Chrysanthemum 'Alison Kirk'

Chrysanthemum 'Bronze Hedgerow'

Chrysanthemum 'Buckeye'

Chrysanthemum 'Carillon'

Chrysanthemum carinatum 'Court Jesters'

Chrysanthemum 'Cheers'

Chrysanthemum 'Cherry Chintz'

Chrysanthemum 'Clara Curtis'

Chrysanthemum 'Day's End'

Chrysanthemum 'Derek Bircumshaw'

Chrysanthemum 'Discovery'

Chrysanthemum 'Duke of Kent'

Chrysanthemum 'Edwin Painter'

Chrysanthemum 'Fairweather'

Chrysanthemum 'Fortune'

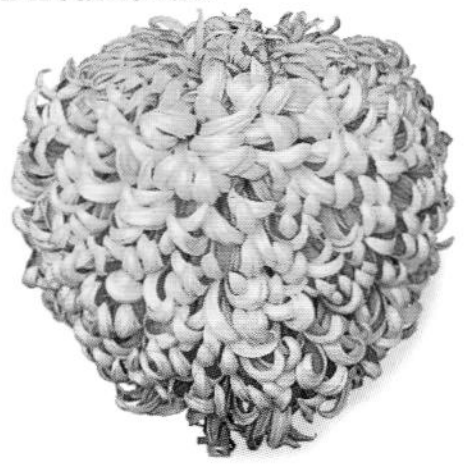
Chrysanthemum 'Golden Gigantic'

Chrysanthemum 'Green Satin'

Chrysanthemum 'Heather James'

best grown under an open-sided, plastic-covered lath house or in a cold greenhouse.

Grow late-flowering exhibition chrysanthemums, including charms, cascades, and late-flowering sprays, in porous, slightly acidic, soil-based potting mix, with added manure, in 3in (7.5cm) containers, and pot on successionally to flower in 9–12in (23–30cm) containers with the support of stakes. Allow about 10 days between repotting and disbudding. Grow in a cold frame, bring into a warm greenhouse in early autumn, and provide bright filtered light with good ventilation and a winter minimum of 50°F (10°C). From midsummer onward, water moderately and apply a balanced liquid fertilizer weekly.

Grow Rubellum Group and annual chrysanthemums in well-drained, moderately fertile soil in full sun.

• **PROPAGATION** Sow seed of charms and cascades at 55–61°F (13–16°C) in late winter or spring. Sow seed of Rubellum Group at 55–61°F (13–16°C) in spring, or divide in autumn or in early spring. Sow seed of annuals in containers in a cold frame in early spring, or *in situ* from spring to early summer; in frost-free areas, sow *in situ* in autumn for early flowering. Take basal cuttings of exhibition chrysanthemums from overwintered stocks: for late-flowering cultivars, take cuttings in early or midwinter; for other groups, take in early spring. Root cuttings in soilless potting mix with dry sand on the surface, at around 61°F (16°C). Place in a cold frame after first potting; protect from cold and ventilate as weather allows. Harden off in midspring.

• **PESTS AND DISEASES** Vulnerable to aphids, earwigs, nematodes, capsid bugs, leaf miners, spider mites, and whiteflies. Prone to fungal rot, gray mold (*Botrytis*), powdery mildew, and white rust. Viruses may cause stunting, yellow markings, and puckering of leaves.

***C.* 'Adrienne Mechen'.** Low-growing, anemone exhibition chrysanthemum with pink-centered, white flowerheads, 4in (10cm) across when disbudded, produced late in the season. Good for containers.

***C.* 'Alabama'** ■ Spoon exhibition chrysanthemum with deep red flowerheads, 4–6in (10–15cm) across when disbudded, borne late in the season.

***C.* 'Alexis'.** Intermediate incurve exhibition chrysanthemum producing pink flowerheads, 6in (15cm) or more across when disbudded, borne in midseason.

***C.* 'Alison Kirk'** ■ Regular incurve exhibition chrysanthemum with white flowerheads, 4–6in (10–15cm) across when disbudded, produced early in the season.

Chrysanthemum 'Alabama'

***C.* 'Aloha'.** Irregular incurve exhibition chrysanthemum with light bronze flowerheads, 6–8in (15–20cm) across when disbudded, borne late in the season.

C. alpinum see *Leucanthemopsis alpina.*

***C.* 'Amethyst'.** Reflex exhibition chrysanthemum with purple blooms, 6–8in (15–20cm) across when disbudded, borne late in the season.

***C.* 'Anita'** see *C.* 'Cottonball'.

***C.* 'Anzac'.** Low-growing, anemone exhibition chrysanthemum with bronze blooms, 4in (5cm) or more across when disbudded, borne in midseason. Suitable for containers.

***C.* 'Apricot Moneymaker'.** Anemone spray chrysanthemum bearing light bronze flowerheads, to 2in (5cm) across, in midseason.

C. atlanticum see *Rhodanthemum atlanticum.*

C. atratum see *Leucanthemum atratum.*

C. balsamita see *Tanacetum balsamita.*

***C.* 'Barbara'** ■ Upright, decorative garden chrysanthemum with purple flowerheads, to 3in (8cm) across, produced early in the season. Ideal for containers and hanging baskets.

***C.* 'Bill Bye'.** Reflex exhibition chrysanthemum with yellow flowerheads, 8in (20cm) or more across when disbudded, borne late in the season.

***C.* 'Bill Ferris'.** Quill exhibition chrysanthemum with pink flowerheads, 6in (15cm) or more across when disbudded, borne late in the season.

***C.* 'Black Magic'.** Reflex exhibition chrysanthemum bearing dark red flowerheads, 4–6in (10–15cm) across when disbudded, early in the season.

***C.* 'Blushing Christine'.** Upright, decorative garden chrysanthemum with light bronze flowerheads, to 3in (8cm) across, produced early in the season.

***C.* 'Bob Dear'.** Intermediate incurve exhibition chrysanthemum with yellow flowerheads, 6in (15cm) across when disbudded, borne in midseason.

***C.* 'Bola de Oro'.** Irregular incurve exhibition chrysanthemum with yellow flowerheads, 6–8in (15–20cm) across when disbudded, produced late in the season.

***C.* 'Bonton'.** Pompon spray chrysanthemum bearing bronze flowerheads, to 1in (2.5cm) across, in midseason.

***C.* 'Bright Golden Anne'.** Decorative exhibition chrysanthemum with intense yellow flowerheads, 5in (13cm) or more across when disbudded, borne in midseason.

***C.* 'Bronze Calvalcade'.** Intermediate incurve exhibition chrysanthemum with bronze flowerheads, 4–6in (10–15cm) across when disbudded, produced in midseason.

***C.* 'Bronze Hedgerow'** ■ Single exhibition chrysanthemum with bronze flowerheads, 2–4in (5–10cm) across when disbudded, produced late in the season.

***C.* 'Buckeye'** ■ Cushion-forming, semi-double garden chrysanthemum bearing red flowerheads, to 2in (5cm) across, early in the season. Excellent for containers.

***C.* 'Burna'.** Spoon exhibition chrysanthemum with bronze flowerheads, 4in (10cm) across or more when disbudded, borne in midseason.

***C.* 'Carillon'** ■ Pompon spray chrysanthemum producing pink flowerheads, 1–3in (2.5–8cm) across, late in the season.

C. carinatum, syn. *C. tricolor* (Painted daisy). Erect, fast-growing, branched annual chrysanthemum with almost succulent, pinnatisect, bright green leaves, to 4in (10cm) long. Long, stiff stems bear solitary, daisy-like, single,

purple-eyed flowerheads, to 4in (10cm) across, from summer to early autumn. The flowerheads typically have yellow or white ray florets, tinged red, with white zoning; a number of cultivars are available with flowerheads in shades of red, yellow, white, or purple, often with bold zoning on the ray florets. ↕ 24in (60cm), ↔ 12in (30cm). Morocco.
'Court Jesters' ▣ bears flowerheads to 3in (8cm) across, in brilliant colors from white and yellow to orange, scarlet, and maroon, zoned in orange or red.
'Polar Star' has pale yellow flowerheads, zoned in orange.
C. catananche see *Rhodanthemum catananche.*
***C.* 'Charm'.** Decorative exhibition chrysanthemum bearing pink flowerheads, 3–5in (8–13cm) across when disbudded, early in the season.
***C.* 'Cheers'** ▣ Cushion-forming, pompon garden chrysanthemum bearing yellow flowerheads, to 1in (2.5cm) across, in midseason.
***C.* 'Cherry Chintz'** ▣ Reflex exhibition chrysanthemum with red flowerheads, 6–8in (15–20cm) across when disbudded, produced in midseason.
***C.* 'Cherry Venice'.** Reflex exhibition chrysanthemum with red flowerheads, 6–8in (15–20cm) across when disbudded, borne in midseason.
***C.* 'Chidori'.** Single spray exhibition chrysanthemum with white flowerheads, to 2in (5cm) across, borne in midseason. Good in hanging baskets or as a bonsai.
***C.* 'Christine'.** Upright, decorative garden chrysanthemum with pink flowerheads, to 3in (8cm) across, borne early in the season. Good in containers.
***C.* 'Cindy'.** Brush or thistle spray chrysanthemum bearing pink flowerheads, to 2in (5cm) across, in midseason. Good for exhibition.
***C.* 'Clara Curtis'** ▣ Rubellum Group chrysanthemum freely bearing long-lasting, single to semi-double, pink flowerheads, to 2in (5cm) across, early in the season. The flowers are pleasantly scented, with centers that turn from green to yellow as the disk florets open. ↕ 30in (75cm), ↔ 24in (60cm).

Chrysanthemum 'Barbara'

Chrysanthemum 'Dusky Queen'

C. coccineum see *Tanacetum coccineum.*
C. coronarium. Erect, vigorous, many-branched annual chrysanthemum with pinnatisect, fern-like, light green leaves, 2–3in (5–8cm) long. From spring to summer, bears daisy-like, single yellow flowerheads, to 2in (5cm) across. ↕ to 32in (80cm), ↔ to 16in (40cm). Mediterranean. **'Primrose Gem'** has primrose-yellow, golden-eyed flowerheads; ↕ to 12–18in (30–45cm).
***C.* 'Cossack'.** Reflex exhibition chrysanthemum with red flowerheads, 8in (20cm) or more across when disbudded, borne late in the season.
***C.* 'Cottonball'**, syn. *C.* 'Anita'. Pompon spray exhibition chrysanthemum bearing white flowerheads, to 1in (2.5cm) across, in midseason.
***C.* 'Crimson Glory'.** Single exhibition chrysanthemum, with red flowerheads, 4in (10cm) or more across when disbudded, borne in midseason.
***C.* 'Day's End'** ▣ Low-growing, anemone exhibition chrysanthemum with red flowerheads, 4in (10cm) or more across when disbudded, produced in midseason. Suitable for containers.
C. densum see *Tanacetum densum* subsp. *amani.*
***C.* 'Derek Bircumshaw'** ▣ Regular incurve exhibition chrysanthemum with yellow flowerheads, 5–6in (13–15cm) across when disbudded, borne early in the season.
***C.* 'Discovery'** ▣ Low-growing, decorative exhibition chrysanthemum with yellow flowerheads, 3–5in (8–13cm) across when disbudded, borne in midseason. Excellent in containers.
***C.* 'Dorridge Sun'.** Regular incurve exhibition chrysanthemum with yellow flowerheads, 4–6in (10–15cm) across when disbudded, borne in midseason.
***C.* 'Dr. Ira B. Cross'.** Spider exhibition chrysanthemum with green flowerheads, to 6in (15cm) across when disbudded, borne late in the season.
***C.* 'Duke of Kent'** ▣ Reflex exhibition chrysanthemum with white flowerheads, 8in (20cm) or more across when disbudded, produced late in the season.
***C.* 'Dusky Queen'** ▣ Spider exhibition chrysanthemum with light bronze flowerheads, 6in (15cm) or more across when disbudded, borne late in the season.
***C.* 'Ed Hodgson'.** Intermediate incurve exhibition chrysanthemum with white flowerheads, 6in (15cm) or more across when disbudded, borne in midseason.
***C.* 'Edwin Painter'** ▣ Single exhibition chrysanthemum with yellow flowerheads, 4in (10cm) or more across when disbudded, produced in midseason.
***C.* 'Enbee Wedding'.** Single spray chrysanthemum producing pink flowerheads, to 2in (5cm) across, early in the season.
***C.* 'Engagement'.** Quill exhibition chrysanthemum with pink flowerheads, 6in (15cm) or more across when disbudded, borne early in the season.
***C.* 'Erie'.** Anemone spray chrysanthemum bearing yellow flowerheads, to 2in (5cm) across, in midseason.
***C.* 'Fairweather'** ▣ Regular incurve exhibition chrysanthemum with pink flowerheads, 4–6in (10–15cm) across when disbudded, produced late in the season.
***C.* 'Flame Symbol'.** Reflex exhibition chrysanthemum with bronze flowerheads, 4–6in (10–15cm) across when disbudded, produced in midseason.
***C.* 'Fontana'.** Quill exhibition chrysanthemum with yellow flowerheads, 4–6in (10–15cm) across when disbudded, borne early in the season.
***C.* 'Fortune'** ▣ Cushion-forming, decorative garden chrysanthemum with yellow flowerheads, to 2in (5cm) across, borne early in the season. Also suitable in containers.
***C.* 'Fred Shoesmith'.** Regular incurve exhibition chrysanthemum bearing white flowerheads, 6in (15cm) or more across when disbudded, produced in midseason.
C. gayanum see *Rhodanthemum gayanum.*
***C.* 'Georgia Girl'.** Spider exhibition chrysanthemum with white flowerheads, 6in (15cm) or more across when disbudded, borne late in the season.
***C.* 'Gigantic'.** Irregular incurve exhibition chrysanthemum, with bronze flowerheads, 8–11in (20–28cm) across when disbudded, borne in midseason. Its form depends on the amount of warmth provided.
***C.* 'Gillette'.** Regular incurve exhibition chrysanthemum with white flowerheads, 4–6in (10–15cm) across when disbudded, borne early in the season.
***C.* 'Ginger Nut'.** Regular incurve exhibition chrysanthemum with bronze flowerheads, 4–6in (10–15cm) across when disbudded, early in the season.
***C.* 'Golden Chalice'** ▣ Mound-forming, single charm chrysanthemum bearing yellow flowerheads, to 2in (5cm) across, in midseason. Good for exhibition.
***C.* 'Golden Gigantic'** ▣ Irregular incurve exhibition chrysanthemum with light bronze flowerheads, 8in (20cm) or more across when disbudded, produced late in the season.
***C.* 'Grandchild'.** Cushion-forming, decorative garden chrysanthemum producing pink flowerheads, to 3in (8cm) across, early in the season.
***C.* 'Green Satin'** ▣ Intermediate incurve exhibition chrysanthemum with green flowerheads, 6in (15cm) or more across when disbudded, borne late in the season. Green color fades in bright light.
C. haradjanii see *Tanacetum haradjanii.*
***C.* 'Harry James'.** Intermediate incurve exhibition chrysanthemum with red flowerheads, 6in (15cm) or more across when disbudded, produced early in the season.
***C.* 'Hatsune'.** Compact, anemone bonsai chrysanthemum bearing yellow flowerheads, to 2in (5cm) across, in midseason. Good in containers or as bonsai.
***C.* 'Heather James'** ▣ Regular incurve exhibition chrysanthemum with bronze flowerheads, 4–6in (10–15cm) across when disbudded, borne in midseason.
***C.* 'Hedgerow'.** Single spray chrysanthemum producing pink flowerheads, to 2in (5cm) across, late in the season.
***C.* 'Heyward Horry'.** Anemone spray chrysanthemum bearing pink flowerheads, to 2in (5cm) across, late in the season. Excellent as a tree or cascade. Good for exhibition.
C. hosmariense see *Rhodanthemum hosmariense.*
***C.* 'Idris'.** Reflex exhibition chrysanthemum with bronze flowerheads, 8in (20cm) or more across when disbudded, borne late in the season.
***C.* 'Jessie Habgood'.** Reflex exhibition chrysanthemum producing large white flowerheads, 8in (20cm) or more across when disbudded, late in the season.
***C.* 'John Hughes'.** Regular incurve exhibition chrysanthemum with white flowerheads, 4–6in (10–15cm) across when disbudded, produced in midseason.
***C.* 'John Wingfield'.** Reflex exhibition chrysanthemum with white, often

Chrysanthemum 'Golden Chalice'

pink-flushed flowerheads, 4–6in (10–15cm) across when disbudded, produced in midseason.
C. 'Keith Luxford' ▣ Reflex exhibition chrysanthemum with pink flowerheads, 8in (20cm) or more across when disbudded, produced late in the season.
C. 'Kelvin Mandarin'. Pompon spray chrysanthemum bearing bronze flowerheads, 1–3in (2.5–8cm) across, late in the season. Good for exhibition.
C. 'Kenbu'. Irregular incurve exhibition chrysanthemum with white flowerheads, 6–8in (15–20cm) across when disbudded, produced in midseason. When immature, flowerhead appears as a spider form.
C. 'Kokka Hougiku'. Irregular incurve exhibition chrysanthemum with purple flowerheads, 6–8in (15–20cm) across when disbudded, produced late in the season.
C. 'Kotoi No Kaori'. Anemone bonsai chrysanthemum bearing light bronze flowerheads, to 1in (2.5cm) across, late in the season. Excellent in containers.
C. 'Lakeside'. Pompon spray chrysanthemum producing bright yellow flowerheads, 1–3in (2.5–8cm), late in the season. Good for exhibition.
C. leucanthemum see *Leucanthemum vulgare.*
C. 'Lilac Moneymaker'. Tall-growing, anemone spray chrysanthemum bearing pink to lilac flowerheads, 2–4in (5–10cm) across, early in the season.
C. 'Linda'. Decorative garden chrysanthemum producing white flowerheads, to 3in (8cm) across, early in the season.
C. 'Luna', syn. *C.* 'Yellow Gull'. Regular incurve exhibition chrysanthemum with pale yellow flowerheads, 4–6in (10–15cm) across when disbudded, borne in midseason.
C. 'Majestic'. Decorative exhibition chrysanthemum bearing purple flowerheads, 3–5in (8–13cm) across when disbudded, early in the season.
C. 'Malcolm Perkins'. Intermediate incurve exhibition chrysanthemum with yellow flowerheads, 6in (15cm) or more across when disbudded, produced early in the season.
C. 'Mandalay'. Decorative spray chrysanthemum producing bronze flowerheads, to 3in (8cm) across, in midseason. Good for exhibition.
C. maresii see *Rhodanthemum maresii.*
C. 'Margaret'. Decorative spray chrysanthemum bearing pink flowerheads, to 3in (8cm) across, in midseason.
C. 'Marguerita'. Single spray chrysanthemum with white flowerheads, to 4in (10cm) across, borne in midseason. Good for exhibition.
C. 'Marlene Jones'. Irregular incurve exhibition chrysanthemum with yellow flowerheads, 8in (13cm) or more across when disbudded, early in the season.
C. 'Mary Stoker' ▣ Rubellum Group chrysanthemum bearing single, rose-tinted, apricot-yellow flowerheads, 2in (5cm) across, early in the season. The centers turn from green to yellow as the disk florets open. ↕ 30in (75cm), ↔ 24in (60cm).
C. 'Mason's Bronze'. Semi-double exhibition chrysanthemum with bronze flowerheads, 2–4in (5–10cm) across when disbudded, borne in midseason.
C. 'Matlock'. Reflex exhibition chrysanthemum with red flowerheads, 4–6in (10–15cm) across when disbudded, borne early in the season.
***C. maximum* of gardens** see *Leucanthemum* x *superbum.*
C. 'Max Riley'. Regular incurve exhibition chrysanthemum with yellow flowerheads, 4–6in (10–15cm) across when disbudded, produced early in the season.
C. 'May Shoesmith'. Regular incurve exhibition chrysanthemum with white flowerheads, 6in (15cm) or more across when disbudded, produced late in the season.
C. 'Mechen Reward'. Anemone exhibition chrysanthemum with light bronze flowerheads, 4in (10cm) or more across when disbudded, produced late in the season.

Chrysanthemum 'Mary Stoker'

C. 'Michael Fish'. Intermediate incurve exhibition chrysanthemum with white flowerheads, 6in (15cm) or more across when disbudded, borne early in the season.
C. 'Morning Star'. Mound-forming, single charm chrysanthemum bearing yellow flowerheads, to 2in (5cm) across, in midseason.
C. 'Mount Shasta'. Irregular incurve exhibition chrysanthemum with white flowerheads, 6–8in (15–20cm) across when disbudded, produced late in the season.
C. 'My Love' ▣ Semi-double exhibition chrysanthemum with light bronze flowerheads, 4in (10cm) or more across when disbudded, produced late in the season.
C. 'Nancye Furneaux' ▣ Reflex exhibition chrysanthemum with yellow flowerheads, 6–8in (15–20cm) across when disbudded, borne late in the season.
C. 'Nightingale'. Spider exhibition chrysanthemum with yellow-green flowerheads, 4–6in (10–15cm) across when disbudded, produced late in the season.
C. 'Nob Hill'. Irregular incurve exhibition chrysanthemum with white flowerheads, 6–8in (15–20cm) across when disbudded, borne in midseason.
C. 'November Wedding'. Decorative exhibition chrysanthemum with delicate pink flowerheads, 5in (13cm) or more across when disbudded, produced in midseason.
C. 'Otome Pink'. Decorative exhibition chrysanthemum with pale pink flowerheads, 3–5in (8–13cm) across when disbudded, borne in midseason.
C. pacificum see *Ajania pacifica.*
C. 'Paint Box'. Reflex exhibition chrysanthemum with bronze flowerheads, 4–6in (10–15cm) across when disbudded, borne early in the season.
C. 'Palisade' ▣ Intermediate incurve exhibition chrysanthemum with white flowerheads, 6in (15cm) or more across when disbudded, produced early in the season.
C. paludosum see *Leucanthemum paludosum.*
C. 'Parador'. Reflex exhibition chrysanthemum with purple flowerheads, 6–8in (15–20cm) across when disbudded, borne early in the season.
C. parthenium see *Tanacetum parthenium.*
C. 'Patricia Millar'. Reflex exhibition chrysanthemum bearing pink flowerheads, 4–6in (10–15cm) across when disbudded, early in the season.
C. 'Pavilion'. Intermediate incurve exhibition chrysanthemum with white flowerheads, 6in (15cm) or more across when disbudded, early in the season.
C. 'Peachy Lynn'. Decorative garden chrysanthemum bearing light bronze flowerheads, to 3in (8cm) across, early in the season.
C. 'Peacock'. Decorative exhibition chrysanthemum with pink flowerheads, 5in (13cm) or more across when disbudded, produced in midseason.
C. 'Pearl Celebration'. Reflex exhibition chrysanthemum with large, pink flowerheads, 6–8in (15–20cm) across when disbudded, borne in midseason.
C. 'Peggy Ann Hoover'. Quill exhibition chrysanthemum with pale pink flowerheads, 6in (15cm) or more across when disbudded, with very delicate florets, borne in midseason.
C. 'Pelee'. Single garden chrysanthemum with red-bronze flowerheads, 2–4in (5–10cm) across, borne early in the season.
C. 'Pennine Jewel'. Anemone spray chrysanthemum producing white flowerheads, to 2in (5cm) across, in midseason.
C. 'Pennine Oriel' ▣ Anemone spray chrysanthemum bearing yellow-centered cream flowerheads, 2–4in (5–10cm) across, early in the season.
C. 'Peter Rowe'. Regular incurve exhibition chrysanthemum with yellow flowerheads, 4–6in (10–15cm) across when disbudded, early in the season.
C. 'Ping Pong' ▣ Pompon spray chrysanthemum bearing white flowerheads, 1–3in (2.5–8cm) across, late in the season.
C. 'Pink Daphne'. Single cascade chrysanthemum bearing pink flowerheads, to 2in (5cm) across, in midseason.
C. 'Pink Gin'. Decorative exhibition chrysanthemum with reflexed, pale pink flowerheads, 3–5in (8–13cm) across when disbudded, borne in midseason.
C. 'Pink Splendor'. Spider exhibition chrysanthemum with pink flowerheads, 6in (15cm) or more across when disbudded, borne late in the season.
C. 'Powder Puff' ▣ Anemone exhibition chrysanthemum with yellow-centered, white flowerheads, 4in (10cm) or more across when disbudded, borne late in the season.
C. 'Primrose John Hughes'. Regular incurve exhibition chrysanthemum bearing pale yellow flowerheads, 4–6in (10–15cm) across when disbudded, in midseason.
C. 'Primrose West Bromwich'. Reflex exhibition chrysanthemum with yellow flowerheads, 6–8in (15–20cm) across when disbudded, borne in midseason.
C. 'Princess Anne'. Decorative exhibition chrysanthemum with pink flowerheads, 5in (8cm) or more across when disbudded, late in the season.
C. 'Promenade'. Intermediate incurve exhibition chrysanthemum with pink flowerheads, 6in (15cm) or more across when disbudded, borne in midseason.
C. 'Prom Queen'. Anemone exhibition chrysanthemum with pink flowerheads, 4in (10cm) or more across when disbudded, borne early in the season.
C. 'Purple Waters'. Cushion-forming, decorative garden chrysanthemum bearing purple flowerheads, to 3in (8cm) across, early in the season.
C. 'Quarterback'. Intermediate incurve exhibition chrysanthemum with pink flowerheads, 6in (15cm) or more across when disbudded, produced early in the season.
C. radicans see *Leucanthemopsis pectinata.*
C. 'Raquel'. Decorative garden chrysanthemum with red flowerheads, to 3in (8cm) across, borne early in the season.
C. 'Raya'. Spoon exhibition chrysanthemum with light bronze flowerheads, 2–4in (5–10cm) across when disbudded, borne in midseason.
C. 'Raymond Mounsey'. Anemone exhibition chrysanthemum with red flowerheads, 4in (10cm) or more across when disbudded, borne late in the season.

Chrysanthemum 'Keith Luxford'

Chrysanthemum 'My Love'

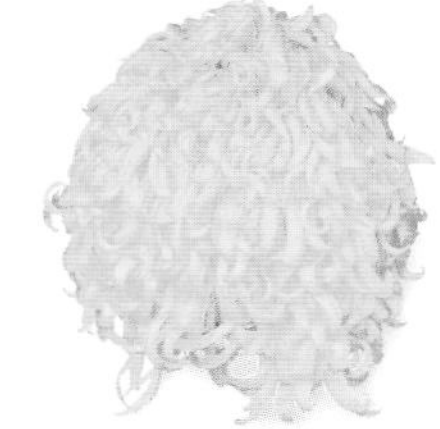

Chrysanthemum 'Nancye Furneaux'

Chrysanthemum 'Palisade'

Chrysanthemum 'Pennine Oriel'

Chrysanthemum 'Ping Pong'

Chrysanthemum 'Powder Puff'

Chrysanthemum 'Red Headliner'

Chrysanthemum 'Royal Touch'

Chrysanthemum 'Salmon Fairie'

Chrysanthemum 'Satin Pink Gin'

Chrysanthemum 'Shamrock'

***C.* 'Rebecca Walker'.** Intermediate incurve exhibition chrysanthemum with large yellow flowerheads, 6in (15cm) or more across when disbudded, borne in midseason.
***C.* 'Red Amethyst'.** Reflex exhibition chrysanthemum with red flowerheads, 8in (20cm) or more across when disbudded, produced late in the season.
***C.* 'Redding'.** Decorative exhibition chrysanthemum with red flowerheads, 3–5in (8–13cm) across when disbudded, borne in midseason.
***C.* 'Red Headliner'** ▣ Decorative garden chrysanthemum with red flowerheads, 3–5in (8–13cm) across, produced early in the season.
***C.* 'Red Remarkable'.** Cushion-forming, decorative garden chrysanthemum bearing red flowerheads, to 3in (8cm) across, in midseason.
***C.* 'Red Rover'.** Low-growing, single exhibition chrysanthemum with red-tipped yellow flowerheads, 4in (10cm) or more across when disbudded, borne in midseason. Suitable for containers.
***C.* 'Ringdove'.** Mound-forming, single charm chrysanthemum bearing pink flowerheads, to 2in (5cm) across, in midseason.
***C.* 'Robeam'.** Decorative spray chrysanthemum bearing yellow flowerheads, to 3in (8cm) across, late in the season.
***C.* 'Robin'** ▣ Pompon garden chrysanthemum producing bronze flowerheads, to 1in (2.5cm) across, early in the season.
***C.* 'Romance'.** Irregular incurve exhibition chrysanthemum with white flowerheads, 6–8in (15–20cm) across when disbudded, produced late in the season.
***C.* 'Rose My Love'.** Semi-double exhibition chrysanthemum with pink flowerheads, 4in (10cm) across when disbudded, borne in midseason.
***C.* 'Royal Champagne'.** Decorative garden chrysanthemum producing pink flowerheads, to 3in (8cm) across, in midseason.
***C.* 'Royal Touch'** ▣ Intermediate incurve exhibition chrysanthemum with pink flowerheads, 6in (15cm) or more across when disbudded, produced late in the season.
***C.* 'Roy Coopland'.** Intermediate incurve exhibition chrysanthemum with bronze flowerheads, 4–6in (10–15cm) across when disbudded, borne late in the season.
***C.* 'Ryflash'.** Single spray chrysanthemum producing red flowerheads, to 2in (5cm) across, in midseason.
***C.* 'Rynoon'.** Single spray chrysanthemum bearing pink flowerheads, to 2in (5cm) across, in midseason.
***C.* 'Rytorch'.** Single spray chrysanthemum bearing bronze flowerheads, to 2in (5cm) across, in midseason.
***C.* 'Saga No Yuki'.** Brush or thistle spray chrysanthemum producing white flowerheads, to 2in (5cm) across, late in the season.
***C.* 'Salmon Fairie'** ▣ Pompon garden chrysanthemum bearing bronze flowerheads, to 1in (2.5cm) across, early in the season.
***C.* 'Salmon Fairweather'.** Regular incurve exhibition chrysanthemum with bronze flowerheads, 4–6in (10–15cm) across when disbudded, borne late in the season.
***C.* 'Salmon Tracy Waller'.** Reflex exhibition chrysanthemum with pink flowerheads, 6–8in (15–20cm) across when disbudded, borne in midseason.
***C.* 'Sam Oldham'.** Reflex exhibition chrysanthemum with red flowerheads, to 4–6in (10–15cm) across when disbudded, produced early in the season.
***C.* 'San Ramon'.** Anemone exhibition chrysanthemum with bronze-red flowerheads, 4in (10cm) or more across when disbudded, borne late in the season.
***C.* 'Satin Pink Gin'** ▣ Decorative spray chrysanthemum bearing reflexed pink flowerheads, to 3in (8cm) across, in midseason.
***C.* 'Satin Ribbon'.** Semi-double, incurve exhibition chrysanthemum with pink flowerheads, 6in (15cm) or more across when disbudded, borne in midseason.
***C.* 'Seaton's Galaxy'.** Spider exhibition chrysanthemum with purple flowerheads, 6in (15cm) or more across when disbudded, borne late in the season.
C. segetum ▣ (Corn marigold). Fast-growing, erect, fleshy annual chrysanthemum with oblong to obovate, gray-green leaves, 1¼–2in (3–5cm) long, entire toward the stem tips, pinnatisect lower down the stems. Solitary, single, daisy-like yellow flowerheads, to 2in (5cm) across, are produced in summer. Often included in wildflower seed mixtures. ↕ to 32in (80cm), ↔ 12in (30cm). Mediterranean. **'Eastern Star'** bears primrose-yellow flowerheads with brown central disks. **'Prado'** has large, golden yellow flowerheads, to 3in (8cm) across, with dark brown central disks.
***C.* 'Senkyo Emaki'.** Spider exhibition chrysanthemum with light pink flowerheads, 6in (15cm) or more across when disbudded, borne late in the season.
C. serotinum see *Leucanthemella serotina.*
***C.* 'Seychelles'.** Reflex exhibition chrysanthemum with pink flowerheads, 6–8in (15–20cm) across when disbudded, produced in midseason.
***C.* 'Shamrock'** ▣ Quill exhibition chrysanthemum with greenish yellow flowerheads, 6in (15cm) or more across when disbudded, borne in midseason.

Chrysanthemum 'Robin'

Chrysanthemum segetum

Chrysanthemum 'Skater's Waltz'

Chrysanthemum 'Splendor'

Chrysanthemum 'Storm King'

Chrysanthemum 'Sundoro'

Chrysanthemum 'Wildfire'

Chrysanthemum 'Yellow John Hughes'

***C.* 'Silver Gigantic'.** Irregular incurve exhibition chrysanthemum with light bronze flowerheads, 6–8in (15–20cm) across when disbudded, borne in midseason.
***C.* 'Skater's Waltz'** ■ Intermediate incurve exhibition chrysanthemum with pink flowerheads, 6in (15cm) or more across when disbudded, borne in midseason.
***C.* 'Small Wonder'.** Cushion-forming, pompon garden chrysanthemum, bearing purple flowerheads, 1in (2.5cm) across, early in the season.
C.* x *superbum see *Leucanthemum* x *superbum.*
***C.* 'Snow Ball'.** Irregular incurve exhibition chrysanthemum with white flowerheads, 6–8in (15–20cm) across when disbudded, produced late in the season.
***C.* 'Snow Crystal'.** Decorative exhibition chrysanthemum with fringed, white flowerheads, 3–5in (8–13cm) across when disbudded, produced in midseason.
***C.* 'Snowdon'.** Intermediate incurve exhibition chrysanthemum with white flowerheads, 6in (15cm) or more across when disbudded, produced in midseason.
***C.* 'Snowflake'.** Decorative exhibition chrysanthemum with white flowerheads, 5in (13cm) across when disbudded, borne early in the season.
***C.* 'Sophia'.** Cushion-forming, decorative garden chrysanthemum bearing pink flowerheads, to 3in (8cm) across, early in the season.
***C.* 'Space Hall'.** Unclassified exhibition chrysanthemum with pink-centered, white-tipped flowerheads, 4–6in (10–15cm) across when disbudded, borne in midseason.
***C.* 'Speckles'.** Brush or thistle spray chrysanthemum producing white-speckled, purple flowerheads, to 2in (5cm) across, late in the season.
***C.* 'Splendor'** ■ Semi-double exhibition chrysanthemum with pink flowerheads, 4in (10cm) or more across when disbudded, borne in midseason.

Chrysanthemum 'Tracy'

***C.* 'Spring Delano'.** Decorative exhibition chrysanthemum with pink-centered, white-tipped flowerheads, 3–5in (8–13cm) across when disbudded, borne in midseason. Good in containers.
***C.* 'Starburst'.** Decorative exhibition chrysanthemum with bronze flowerheads, 3–5in (8–13cm) across when disbudded, produced in midseason.
***C.* 'Stardom'.** Cushion-forming, single garden chrysanthemum producing pink flowerheads, to 2in (5cm) across when disbudded, early in the season.
***C.* 'Statesman'.** Pompon spray chrysanthemum bearing yellow flowerheads, to 1in (2.5cm) across, in midseason.
***C.* 'Storm King'** ■ Decorative exhibition chrysanthemum with white flowerheads, 3–5in (8–13cm) across when disbudded, produced early in the season.
***C.* 'Subaru'.** Single spray chrysanthemum bearing yellow-centered, red flowerheads, to 2in (5cm) across, in midseason. Good in containers.
***C.* 'Sundoro'** ■ Cushion-forming, decorative garden chrysanthemum bearing pink flowerheads, to 3in (8cm) across, early in the season.
***C.* 'Sunny Morning'.** Cushion-forming, decorative garden chrysanthemum producing yellow flowerheads, to 3in (8cm) across, early in the season.
***C.* 'Super Cal'.** Irregular incurve exhibition chrysanthemum with yellow flowerheads, 6–8in (15–20cm) across when disbudded, produced late in the season.
***C.* 'Super White'.** Spider exhibition chrysanthemum with white flowerheads, 6in (15cm) or more across when disbudded, borne in midseason.
***C.* 'Susan Freestone'.** Reflex exhibition chrysanthemum with yellow flowerheads, 4–6in (10–15cm) across when disbudded, borne early in the season.
***C.* 'Susuki'.** Quill exhibition chrysanthemum with purple flowerheads, 4–6in (10–15cm) across when disbudded, borne early in the season.
***C.* 'Symphony'.** Spider exhibition chrysanthemum with bronze flowerheads, 6in (15cm) or more across when disbudded, borne in midseason.
***C.* 'Taiho Ginka'.** Irregular incurve exhibition chrysanthemum with white flowerheads, 6–8in (15–20cm) across when disbudded, borne late in the season.
***C.* 'Tanfastic'.** Cushion-forming, pompon garden chrysanthemum bearing bronze flowerheads, to 1in (2.5cm) across, late in the season.
***C.* 'Tayrona'.** Decorative spray chrysanthemum producing white flowerheads, to 3in (8cm) across, early in the season.
***C.* 'Tempo'.** Decorative exhibition chrysanthemum with purple flowerheads, 3–5in (8–13cm) across when disbudded, borne in midseason. Good for containers.
***C.* 'Tennis'.** Intermediate incurve exhibition chrysanthemum with white flowerheads, 4–6in (10–15cm) across when disbudded, borne in midseason.
***C.* 'Tolima'.** Cushion-forming, decorative garden chrysanthemum bearing white flowerheads, to 3in (8cm) across, in midseason.
***C.* 'Tom Blackshaw'.** Intermediate incurve exhibition chrysanthemum with yellow flowerheads, 6in (15cm) or more across when disbudded, produced early in the season.
***C.* 'Tom Statham'.** Reflex exhibition chrysanthemum with red flowerheads, 6–8in (15–20cm) across when disbudded, produced late in the season.
***C.* 'Universiade'.** Intermediate incurve exhibition chrysanthemum with bronze flowerheads, 6in (15cm) or more across when disbudded, produced late in the season.
***C.* 'Tracy'** ■ Cushion-forming, single to semi-double garden chrysanthemum, bearing white flowerheads, to 2in (5cm) across, early in the season.
C. tricolor see *C. carinatum.*
C. uliginosum see *Leucanthemella serotina.*
***C.* 'Universe'.** Spider exhibition chrysanthemum with purple flowerheads, 6in (15cm) or more across when disbudded, borne in midseason.
***C.* 'Valentine'.** Irregular incurve exhibition chrysanthemum with pale pink flowerheads, 6–8in (15–20cm) across when disbudded, borne late in the season.
***C.* 'Valley Forge'.** Spider exhibition chrysanthemum with purple flowerheads, 6in (15cm) or more across when disbudded, borne in midseason.
***C.* 'Venice'.** Reflex exhibition chrysanthemum with pink flowerheads, 4–6in (10–15cm) across when disbudded, borne in midseason.
***C.* 'Vicksburg'.** Spoon exhibition chrysanthemum with yellow flowerheads, 4in (10cm) or more across when disbudded, borne late in the season.
***C.* 'Vienna Waltz'.** Spider exhibition chrysanthemum with delicate, pink flowerheads, 6in (15cm) or more across when disbudded, borne in midseason.
***C.* 'Violet Cymbal'.** Intermediate incurve exhibition chrysanthemum with purple flowerheads, 6in (15cm) or more across when disbudded, produced early in the season. Good in containers.
C. vulgare see *Tanacetum vulgare.*
***C.* 'Walnut Queen'.** Spider exhibition chrysanthemum with bronze flowerheads, 6in (15cm) or more across when disbudded, produced in midseason.
***C.* 'Warm Megan'.** Upright, decorative garden chrysanthemum bearing bronze flowerheads, to 3in (8cm) across, early in the season.
***C.* 'West Bromwich'.** Reflex exhibition chrysanthemum with white flowerheads, 6–8in (15–20cm) across when disbudded, produced in midseason.
***C.* 'Westland Pink'.** Quill exhibition chrysanthemum with pink flowerheads, 4–6in (10–15cm) across when disbudded, produced in midseason.
C. weyrichii see *Dendranthema weyrichii.*
***C.* 'White Fairweather'.** Regular incurve exhibition chrysanthemum with white flowerheads, 4–6in (10–15cm) across when disbudded, produced late in the season.
***C.* 'Wildfire'** ■ Decorative exhibition chrysanthemum with bronze flowerheads, 3–5in (8–13cm) across when disbudded, borne in midseason.
***C.* 'Wild Honey'.** Low-growing, decorative exhibition chrysanthemum with light bronze flowerheads, 3–5in (8–13cm) across when disbudded, borne in midseason. Good for containers.
***C.* 'William Turner'.** Irregular incurve exhibition chrysanthemum with white

Chrysanthemum 'Wisley Bronze'

flowerheads, 8in (20cm) or more across when disbudded, produced in midseason. Favors cooler temperatures.

***C.* 'Windchime'.** Spider exhibition chrysanthemum with purple flowerheads, 6in (15cm) or more across when disbudded, produced late in the season.

***C.* 'Winter Carnival'.** Decorative exhibition chrysanthemum with white flowerheads, 6in (15cm) or more across when disbudded, borne late in the season.

***C.* 'Wisley Bronze'** ■ Cascade spray chrysanthemum bearing single bronze flowerheads, 2½in (6cm) across, late in the season.

***C.* 'Wisp of Pink'.** Brush or thistle spray chrysanthemum bearing pink flowerheads, to 2in (5cm) across, late in the season.

Chrysanthemum 'Yellow Knight'

***C.* 'Wooley Pride'.** Reflex exhibition chrysanthemum with bronze flowerheads, 4–6in (10–15cm) across when disbudded, borne in midseason.

***C.* 'Woolman's Prince'.** Regular incurve exhibition chrysanthemum with yellow flowerheads, 6in (15cm) or more across when disbudded, in midseason.

***C.* 'World of Sport'.** Decorative exhibition chrysanthemum with pale pink flowerheads, 5in (13cm) or more across when disbudded, in midseason.

***C.* 'Yellow Gull'** see *C.* 'Luna'.

***C.* 'Yellow Hammer'.** Mound-forming, single charm chrysanthemum bearing yellow flowerheads, to 2in (5cm) across, in midseason.

***C.* 'Yellow Jacket'.** Cushion-forming, single garden chrysanthemum producing yellow flowerheads, to 2in (5cm) across, in midseason.

***C.* 'Yellow John Hughes'** ■ Regular incurve exhibition chrysanthemum with yellow flowerheads, 4–6in (10–15cm) across when disbudded, produced in midseason.

***C.* 'Yellow Knight'** ■ Spider exhibition chrysanthemum with yellow flowerheads, 6in (15cm) or more across when disbudded, borne late in the season.

***C.* 'Yellow Nob Hill'.** Irregular incurve exhibition chrysanthemum with yellow flowerheads, 6–8in (15–20cm) across when disbudded, produced late in the season.

***C.* 'Yellow Palisade'.** Intermediate incurve exhibition chrysanthemum with yellow flowerheads, 6in (15cm) or more across when disbudded, borne late in the season.

***C.* 'Yukari'.** Single, bonsai chrysanthemum bearing pink flowerheads, to 2in (5cm) across, in midseason.

CHRYSOGONUM

ASTERACEAE

Genus of one species of rhizomatous perennial, with leafy runners, occurring in rich woodland soils in E. US. The flowerheads resemble those of small, single zinnias, and are produced over a long period from early spring into summer. *C. virginianum* is cultivated as a groundcover.

• **CULTIVATION** Grow in moist but well-drained, humus-rich soil in sun or partial shade.

• **PROPAGATION** Sow seed in containers in a cold frame as soon as ripe. Divide or separate runners in spring or autumn.

• **PESTS AND DISEASES** Infrequent.

Chrysogonum virginianum

C. virginianum ■ (Goldenstar). Creeping perennial with long, reddish green leaf stalks and opposite, heart-shaped to ovate-oblong, hairy, mid-green leaves, 1–4in (2.5–10cm) long, with scalloped to toothed margins. From early spring to summer, branched stems bear solitary, star-shaped yellow flowerheads, 1½in (4cm) across, from the upper leaf axils; they each have 5 large, triangular ray florets around the central disk florets. Evergreen in mild winters. ↕ 10in (25cm), ↔ 24in (60cm). E. US. Zone 3. **'Pierre'** is long-blooming and clump-forming, with soft green leaves; ↕ 6in (15cm).

CHRYSOLEPIS

FAGACEAE

Genus of 2 species of evergreen trees and shrubs from hill and mountain slopes from California to Washington. They are grown mainly for their handsome foliage and attractive catkins and fruits. They grow best in maritime climates, and are excellent specimen plants for a large lawn.

• **CULTIVATION** Grow in fertile, moist but well-drained, neutral or acidic soil in sun or partial shade, sheltered from strong, cold, or dry winds. Pruning group 8, or 1 for trees.

• **PROPAGATION** Sow seed as soon as ripe in a seedbed outdoors or in containers in an open frame.

• **PESTS AND DISEASES** Infrequent.

C. chrysophylla, syn. *Castanopsis chrysophylla* (Golden chinkapin). Conical tree producing narrowly oval, tapered, dark green leaves, to 6in (15cm) long, densely golden hairy beneath. Fragrant, creamy white catkins are borne in summer, and are followed by spiny, chestnut-like fruit, produced in the following summer. ↕ 40ft (12m), ↔ 40–100ft (12–30m). W. Oregon, California. Zone 7b. **'Obtusata'** has shorter, blunt-tipped leaves, 2in (5cm) long, and produces abundant fruit.

▷ ***Chrysopsis*** see *Heterotheca*

CHRYSOSPLENIUM

Golden saxifrage

SAXIFRAGACEAE

Genus of about 55 species of creeping annuals and perennials from Europe, Asia, and North America, often found in moist woodland and close to streams. They have rounded or kidney-shaped, toothed, light to dark green leaves, and flat, terminal cymes of shallowly cup-shaped flowers above leafy bracts. They are useful as a groundcover in a shady border, bog garden, or woodland garden.

• **CULTIVATION** Grow in moist, poor to moderately fertile, humus-rich soil in a shady site.

• **PROPAGATION** Divide, or take soft tip cuttings, in spring.

• **PESTS AND DISEASES** Susceptible to damage by slugs and snails.

C. davidianum ■ Rhizomatous, mat-forming perennial with erect, red-hairy stems. Broadly ovate-oblong leaves, ¾–1¼in (2–3cm) long, with scalloped margins, are mid- to dark green, densely white-hairy beneath, less so above. In late spring and early summer, bears

Chrysosplenium davidianum

greenish yellow flowers in cymes 1¼–2in (3–5cm) across, above pale green, leaf-like bracts. ↕ to 3in (8cm), ↔ 10in (25cm) or more. W. China. Zone 6b.

CHRYSOTHEMIS

GESNERIACEAE

Genus of 7 species of tuberous, herbaceous perennials from damp, semi-shaded areas in tropical North and South America. They have opposite and equal, usually toothed leaves. They are grown for their axillary cymes of tubular or bell-shaped flowers and persistent calyces. In subtropical and tropical regions, use in bedding or in a border. Where not hardy, grow in a warm greenhouse.

• **CULTIVATION** Under glass, grow in soilless potting mix with added coarse grit or perlite, in bright filtered light at high humidity. Water freely in the growing season, sparingly in winter. Apply a half-strength balanced liquid fertilizer every other week. Outdoors, grow in humus-rich, well-drained, gritty soil in partial shade.

• **PROPAGATION** Sow seed at 68–77°F (20–25°C) as soon as ripe. Root leaf cuttings or stem cuttings below a leaf node in moist, sandy rooting mix at high humidity. Divide by sectioning tubers, each with a growth eye. Pot up with the eye just above the surface.

• **PESTS AND DISEASES** Infrequent.

C. pulchella. Erect, tuberous perennial with oblong to lance-shaped, mid-green leaves, to 12in (30cm) long, pale green beneath. In summer, bears cymes of 3 or more bell-shaped red flowers, to ½in (1.5cm) across. ↕ to 12in (30cm), ↔ 8in (20cm). West Indies, Panama, N.E. South America to Brazil. ❄ (min. 50–59°F/10–15°C). **'Bronze'** produces heavily quilted, toothed, dark bronze leaves, maroon beneath, and solitary, orange-yellow flowers, with persistent orange calyces.

C

Chusquea culeou

Cibotium glaucum

Cicerbita alpina

Cichorium endivia

Cichorium intybus

CHUSQUEA

POACEAE

Genus of 90–100 species of evergreen, clump-forming bamboos occurring in upland woodland from Mexico to Chile. Chusqueas have cylindrical, smooth, glossy, pith-filled culms with 3 primary branches, borne alternately at the nodes, each branching densely and bearing linear to ovate or oval, pointed, mid- to dark green leaves. Use as specimen plants for a lawn or woodland garden.
• **CULTIVATION** Grow in humus-rich, leafy, moist but well-drained soil in sun or partial shade.
• **PROPAGATION** Sow seed at 55–64°F (13–18°C) in spring. Divide clumps, or remove sections of rhizome with a stem and root, in spring.
• **PESTS AND DISEASES** Emerging shoots are prone to slug damage.

C. culeou ▣ Graceful, erect bamboo, forming dense clumps of glossy, cylindrical, yellow-green to olive-green culms, to 1¼in (3cm) across, with long, tapered, papery white leaf sheaths; these are persistent for the first year, giving a striped appearance to the young culms. Clustered branches, 4–32in (10–80cm) long, arise alternately and almost encircle the white-waxy nodes; they bear numerous linear, checkered, mid-green leaves, to 3in (8cm) long. As old leaves fall, branches and leaf stalks persist, giving a whiskered look to the lower culms. ↕ to 20ft (6m), ↔ 8ft (2.5m) or more. Chile. ❄ (min. 41°F/5°C)
C. nigricans. Clump-forming, arching, solid-stemmed bamboo with one dominant, smooth, mid-green culm, ½in (15mm) across. Clustered branches, to 36in (90cm) long, arise from prominently swollen, mid-culm nodes; they bear numerous linear, smooth, mid-green leaves, 3–4in (8–10cm) long. ↕ 15ft (5m), ↔ 12ft (4m). S. Chile. Zone 6b.

CIBOTIUM

DICKSONIACEAE

Genus of about 10 species of evergreen tree ferns from forest in tropical and subtropical to warm-temperate regions. They have very large, finely divided, ovate to triangular fronds, growing in tufts from an erect, trunk-like rhizome, covered with golden brown hairs. Where not hardy, grow in a large, temperate or warm greenhouse. Elsewhere, grow outdoors as imposing specimen plants.
• **CULTIVATION** Under glass, grow in 1 part each of loam, medium-grade bark, and charcoal; 2 parts sharp sand, and 3 parts coarse leaf mold. Provide bright filtered light and moderate humidity. In growth, water freely and apply a high-nitrogen liquid fertilizer monthly; in winter, water sparingly and admit maximum light. Top-dress or pot on in spring. If plants outgrow their site, they may be reduced in height by air-layering the upper part of the rhizome. Outdoors, grow in humus-rich, moist but well-drained soil in partial shade.
• **PROPAGATION** Sow spores at 70°F (21°C) when ripe.
• **PESTS AND DISEASES** Occasionally affected by leaf spots.

C. glaucum ▣ (Hawaiian tree fern). Tree fern with an erect stem bearing ovate-triangular, 2-pinnate, mid-green fronds, 6–10ft (2–3m) long, glaucous beneath, with lance-shaped segments. The stem tips and bases of the frond stalks are covered with golden hairs. ↕ 6–20ft (2–6m), ↔ 10–12ft (3–4m). Hawaii. ❄ (min. 50°F/10°C)
C. regale. Tree fern with an erect stem crowned with ovate-triangular, 2-pinnate, yellowish green fronds, 10–12ft (3–4m) long, glaucous beneath, divided into lance-shaped segments. The stem tips and bases of the frond stalks are hairy. ↕ to 12ft (4m), ↔ 10–25ft (3–8m). Central America. ❄ (min. 50°F/10°C)

CICERBITA

ASTERACEAE

Genus of about 20 species of erect perennials found in N. temperate zones in wooded ravines, and subalpine and moist, grassy meadows. They have pinnatifid to pinnatisect, mid-green leaves, each with a large, 3-angled terminal lobe, and smaller, sharply pointed lateral lobes. The basal leaves are stalked, and the smaller stem leaves are stalkless and stem-clasping; their sap is milky. Cicerbitas are grown for their corymb-like panicles of numerous dandelion-like flowers; these have strap-shaped ray florets in blue, violet, lilac, or occasionally yellow, and are borne on branched stems from midsummer to early autumn. They are suitable for a large mixed or herbaceous border, or for naturalizing in a wild garden.
• **CULTIVATION** Grow in moist, fertile, humus-rich, neutral to acidic soil in sun or partial shade.
• **PROPAGATION** Sow seed in containers in early spring, or divide in early spring.
• **PESTS AND DISEASES** Mildew occurs.

C. alpina ▣ syn. *Lactuca alpina, Mulgedium alpinum* (Mountain sow thistle). Clump-forming perennial producing mid-green, basal leaves, 3–10in (8–25cm) long, blue-green beneath. Erect, branching, softly hairy, reddish green stems bear elongated panicles of violet-blue flowerheads, ¾in (2cm) across, from midsummer to early autumn. ↕ to 8ft (2.5m), ↔ 24in (60cm). Norway, Scotland, Pyrenees, Alps, Apennines, mountains of Bulgaria, Carpathians. Zone 5.
C. plumieri, syn. *Lactuca plumieri, Mulgedium plumieri.* Clump-forming, hairless perennial with mid-green, basal leaves, 2–24in (5–60cm) long, blue-green beneath. Erect, branching stems bear panicles of blue flowerheads, 1¼in (3cm) across, from midsummer to early autumn. ↕ to 4½ft (1.3m), ↔ 18in (45cm). Pyrenees, mountains of France, W. central Europe, S.W. Bulgaria. Zone 5.

CICHORIUM

Chicory, Endive

ASTERACEAE

Genus of about 8 species of annuals and perennials from dry, sunny sites in Europe, the Mediterranean, temperate Asia, and Ethiopia. They have large, variably toothed or pinnatifid, mid-green leaves, milky sap, and stems that branch at flowering to bear numerous thistle- or dandelion-like, usually blue, occasionally pink or white flowerheads, which close by midday. Cultivated forms include the salad greens radicchio and Belgian endive; chicory root is often used as a coffee substitute. Contact with all parts of the plants may irritate skin or aggravate skin allergies.
• **CULTIVATION** Grow in fertile, well-drained soil in full sun. *C. spinosum* needs sharply drained soil and protection from excessive winter moisture.
• **PROPAGATION** Sow seed in containers in a cold frame in autumn or spring.
• **PESTS AND DISEASES** Prone to bacterial soft rot and spot, powdery mildew, rust, leaf spot, damping off, Southern blight, and a variety of viruses.

C. endivia (Endive). Clump-forming perennial bears curly, crisp, broad leaves in rosette form. Often grown under a pot or other covering to blanche the heart, making it less bitter. Flowers are violet-blue. ↕ 10–12in (25–30cm), ↔ 24in (60cm). ❄ (min. 41°F/5°C)
C. intybus ▣ (Chicory). Clump-forming perennial with a large taproot and inversely lance-shaped, toothed, basal leaves, 3–12in (7–30cm) long. In summer, branched stems bear dandelion-like, terminal and axillary, clear blue, occasionally white or pink flowerheads, to 1½in (4cm) across. ↕ 4ft (1.2m), ↔ 24in (60cm). Mediterranean; widely naturalized in North America. Zone 4.
C. spinosum. Dwarf perennial with a woody rootstock. Branching stems terminating in long green spines bear inversely lance-shaped, pinnatifid, glossy leaves, to 2in (5cm) long. In summer, produces thistle-like blue flowerheads, to ¾in (2cm) across, singly from the leaf axils, or in few-flowered terminal clusters. Best in an alpine house. ↕↔ to 8in (20cm). Mediterranean. Zone 6.

CIMICIFUGA

Bugbane, Cohosh

RANUNCULACEAE

Genus of 18 species of erect, clump-forming perennials from N. temperate regions, usually found in moist, shady grassland, woodland, or scrub. They have alternate, ternate to 3-ternate leaves. The numerous, white or cream flowers, occasionally pink-tinged, and usually ½–¾in (1.5–2cm) long, have 2–5 small petals and prominent tufts of stamens. They are crowded together in slender, bottlebrush-like racemes or panicles, which are followed by greenish white, then brown, star-shaped follicles. Some are unpleasantly scented. They are suitable for a moist border or woodland.

• **CULTIVATION** Grow in moist, fertile, preferably humus-rich soil in partial shade. Provide support.

• **PROPAGATION** Sow seed in containers in a cold frame as soon as ripe, to germinate the following spring. Divide in spring.

• **PESTS AND DISEASES** Can be affected by rust and leaf-feeding insects such as tarnished plant bug.

C. acerina see *C. japonica.*

C. americana. Clump-forming perennial producing 2- or 3-ternate, toothed, basal leaves, to 20in (50cm) long, with 3-lobed, ovate to oblong leaflets, dark green above, mid-green beneath. Bears red-tinted white flowers, ¼–½in (5–12mm) long, in lax, branched racemes, to 20in (50cm) long, from late summer to midautumn. ↕2–8ft (0.6–2.5m), ↔ 20–36in (50–90cm). E. US. Zone 4.

C. dahurica. Clump-forming perennial with 2- or 3-ternate, ovate, toothed, basal leaves, to 24in (60cm) long, with pinnatifid or lobed bases and heart-shaped terminal leaflets. From summer to autumn, bears cream-white flowers, ¼–½in (5–12mm) long, in simple or compound racemes, to 20in (50cm) long. ↕ to 5ft (1.5m), ↔ 24–36in (60–90cm). E. Siberia, Mongolia, China to Japan. Zone 3b.

C. foetida. Clump-forming perennial with 2- or 3-ternate, toothed, mid-green, basal leaves, to 3ft (1m) long, usually with 3-lobed, oval or broadly ovate to elliptic leaflets. Pure white flowers, ¼–½in (5–12mm) long, are borne in branched racemes, to 24in (60cm) long, from late summer to midautumn. ↕2–6ft (0.6–2m), ↔ 20–32in (50–80cm). Russia (Siberia) to N. Mongolia. Zone 3.

C. japonica, syn. *C. acerina, C. japonica* var. *acerina.* Clump-forming perennial producing long-stalked, ternate or 2-ternate, toothed, hairy, dark green, basal leaves, 12–30in (30–75cm) long, with 3- to 5-lobed, ovate to broadly ovate leaflets. Pure white flowers, ¼–½in (0.6–1.5cm) long, are borne in erect racemes, to 14in (35cm) long, from late summer to midautumn. ↕24–36in (60–90cm), ↔ 24in (60cm). Japan. Zone 4. **var. *acerina*** see *C. japonica.*

C. racemosa (Black cohosh, Black snakeroot). Clump-forming perennial producing 2- or 3-ternate, occasionally ternate, dark green, basal leaves, to 16in (40cm) long, with oblong, often lobed or sharply toothed leaflets. In mid-summer, slender, branched stems bear racemes, 24in (60cm) long, sometimes curved, of unpleasantly scented white flowers, ¼–½in (0.5–1.5cm) long. ↕4–7ft (1.2–2.2m), ↔ 24in (60cm). E. North America. Zone 3. **var. *cordifolia*** see *C. rubifolia.*

C. rubifolia, syn. *C. racemosa* var. *cordifolia.* Clump-forming perennial with ternate or 2-ternate, dark green, basal leaves, to 24in (60cm) long, composed of 3–17 broadly obovate leaflets, heart-shaped at the bases. In late summer, bears branched, sometimes curved racemes, to 24in (60cm) long, of creamy white flowers, to ½in (1.5cm) long. ↕1–4½ft (30–140cm), ↔ 24in (60cm). E. North America. Zone 4.

Cimicifuga simplex

Cimicifuga simplex 'Brunette'

C. simplex ▣ (Autumn snakeroot). Clump-forming perennial with 3-ternate, light green to purplish green, basal leaves, 12–30in (30–75cm) long, composed of numerous ovate to rounded, irregularly lobed leaflets. In early and midautumn, unbranched, or occasionally branched, often arching stems bear white flowers, ¾in (2cm) long, in racemes 2½–12in (6–30cm) long. ↕3–4ft (1–1.2m), ↔ 24in (60cm). Russia (Kamchatka, Sakhalin, Siberia), China (W. China, Manchuria), Mongolia, Korea, Japan. Zone 4. **'Braunlaub'** has very dark green leaves; ↕24–36in (60–90cm). **'Brunette'** ▣ has very dark, brownish purple foliage, purple stems, and compact racemes, to 8in (20cm) long, of purple-tinted, off-white flowers. **'Elstead'** produces purple-tinted buds that open to white flowers later than in other cultivars; ↕24–36in (60–90cm). **'White Pearl'** has arching stems with narrow racemes of green buds opening to white flowers; ↕24–36in (60–90cm).

▷ ***Cineraria cruentus* of gardens** see *Pericallis* x *hybrida*

▷ ***Cineraria* x *hybrida*** see *Pericallis* x *hybrida*

▷ ***Cineraria maritima*** see *Senecio cineraria*

CINNAMOMUM

LAURACEAE

Genus of about 250 species of evergreen trees and shrubs found in forest in E. and S.E. Asia and Australia. The opposite or almost opposite leaves are simple, leathery, and aromatic; the small, insignificant, 6-lobed flowers are borne in axillary or terminal panicles. Where not hardy, grow in a temperate greenhouse. In frost-free areas, grow outdoors as shade or specimen trees.

• **CULTIVATION** Under glass, grow in soil-based potting mix in full light with shade from hot sun. During the growing season, water freely and apply a balanced liquid fertilizer monthly; water more sparingly in winter. Pot on or top-dress in early spring. Outdoors, grow in fertile, moist but well-drained soil in sun or partial shade. Pruning group 1; plants under glass may need restrictive pruning after flowering or in spring.

• **PROPAGATION** Sow seed at 55–64°F (13–18°C) as soon as ripe, or in spring. Root semi-ripe cuttings in summer.

• **PESTS AND DISEASES** Aphids, scale, canker, root rot, and leaf spots occur.

C. camphora (Camphor tree). Erect to spreading tree with narrowly ovate, boldly veined, glossy leaves, to 4in (10cm) long, greenish red when young, then rich green. Small, bowl-shaped, greenish yellow flowers are borne in clusters, 2–3in (5–8cm) across, from spring to summer, followed by black berries, ¼–½in (6–15mm) across. ↕70ft (20m) or more, ↔ 15–30ft (5–10m). Tropical S.E. and E. Asia, including Japan and Malaysia. ❄ (min. 50°F/10°C); tolerates brief periods to 32°F (0°C).

▷ ***Cirrhopetalum*** see *Bulbophyllum*

Cirsium rivulare 'Atropurpureum'

CIRSIUM

ASTERACEAE

Genus of about 200 species of biennials and perennials from a variety of habitats in N. temperate regions, including grassy mountain slopes, streamsides or moorland meadows, and dry or moist alpine and subalpine meadows. They have spiny leaves and bear heads of tubular, purple, red, yellow, or sometimes white flowers. Many are invasive, spreading by means of rhizomes, or self-seeding. Those listed here are useful border plants or suitable for damp meadows in a wild garden.

• **CULTIVATION** Grow in moist but well-drained soil in full sun. Deadhead to prevent self-seeding.

• **PROPAGATION** Sow seed in containers in a cold frame in spring. Divide perennials from autumn to spring.

• **PESTS AND DISEASES** Powdery mildew and rust can be problems.

C. japonicum. Clump-forming biennial or perennial producing oblong-obovate, pointed, deeply lobed to pinnate, spiny, toothed, mid- to dark green leaves, to 12in (30cm) long. In late summer and early autumn, bears thistle-like, rose-pink to lilac flowerheads, 2in (5cm) across. ↕3–6ft (1–2m), ↔ 24in (60cm). Japan. Zone 6. **'Rose Beauty'** has deep carmine-red flowerheads.

C. rivulare. Clump-forming, spreading perennial with narrowly elliptic to oblong-lance-shaped, entire to pinnatifid, prickly, dark green leaves, to 18in (45cm) long, softly hairy beneath. Erect stems bear spherical, pincushion-like, crimson-purple to purple flowerheads, 1¼in (3cm) across, in early and mid-summer. ↕4ft (1.2m), ↔ 24in (60cm). C. Europe into Russia, S.W. Europe. Zone 5. **'Atropurpureum'** ▣ has deep crimson flowerheads.

CISSUS

VITACEAE

Genus of about 350 species of evergreen perennials, shrubs, and climbers, some with succulent stems or roots, occurring in tropical and subtropical regions, at forest margins and in thickets. The leaves are alternate and may be simple, shallowly to deeply lobed, or 3- to 7-palmate. Insignificant, 4-petaled flowers are produced in compound, umbel-like cymes opposite the leaves or at the ends

Cissus antarctica

Cissus quadrangularis

of the shoots. Dry, usually unpalatable berries, ⅛–1¼in (0.3–3cm) across, ripen to blue, red, purple, or black. Where not hardy, grow as foliage houseplants, or in a cool or warm conservatory; most are suitable for hanging baskets. In warmer climates, use climbing species to clothe pergolas, arbors, walls, or tree stumps.

• **CULTIVATION** Under glass, grow non-succulents in soil-based potting mix in bright filtered or indirect light. Water freely in growth, applying a balanced liquid fertilizer monthly; water sparingly in winter. Grow succulent species in soil-based potting mix with added grit (up to one-third by volume) and full light. Water succulents moderately when in growth and keep them dry in winter. Outdoors, grow non-succulents in fertile, moist but well-drained soil in sun or partial shade; succulents need sharply drained soil and full sun. Pruning group 11, in spring; pinch out young plants to encourage a bushy habit. See also pp.48–49.

• **PROPAGATION** Root hardwood or greenwood cuttings in summer. For succulents, sow seed at 70°F (21°C) in spring, or take stem cuttings in summer.

Cissus discolor

• **PESTS AND DISEASES** Spider mites, whiteflies, mealybugs, powdery and downy mildew, aerial blight, stem and root rot, and leaf spots occur.

C. antarctica ■ (Kangaroo vine). Climber with tendrils and broadly ovate, toothed, leathery, glossy, rich green leaves, to 5in (13cm) long. Bears small green flowers in dense, axillary cymes, 1¼in (3cm) long, from spring to summer, followed by spherical black berries, ½in (1.5cm) across. ↕ 15–50ft (5–15m). N. Australia. ❄ (min. 41°F/5°C)
C. bainesii see *Cyphostemma bainesii.*
C. capensis see *Rhoicissus capensis.*
C. discolor ■ Slender climber with red stems and tendrils. Ovate to lance-shaped leaves, 3–10in (8–25cm) long, with heart-shaped bases, are deep green, zoned silver, gray, or pink above, and maroon beneath. In summer, bears red-tinted green flowers in small panicles, 2½in (5cm) long, followed by spherical, dark red fruit, ⅜in (9mm) across. ↕ 6–10ft (2–3m). S.E. Asia. ❄ (min. 41°F/5°C)
C. hypoglauca (Water vine). Vigorous, scandent climber with 5-palmate leaves, 2–3in (5–8cm) long, composed of ovate to lance-shaped leaflets, pale to deep green above, glaucous beneath. Small yellow flowers open in dense, axillary cymes, 1½–2½in (4–6cm) long, in summer, followed by blue-black berries, ½–¾in (1–2cm) across. ↕ 30–80ft (10–25m). New South Wales, Victoria. ❄ (min. 45°F/7°C)
C. juttae see *Cyphostemma juttae.*
C. quadrangularis ■ Few-leaved, succulent climber with tendrils, thick, 4-angled stems, and thinner, wavy-margined, horny branches constricted at the nodes. Entire to 3-lobed, ovate to triangular, coarsely toothed, fleshy, mid-green leaves, 8in (20cm) or more long, develop from the nodes and opposite the tendrils. Small, green or yellow flowers open in cymes, 2in (5cm) long, in summer, followed by ovoid, reddish black fruit, ⅛–¼in (4–6mm) across. ↕ 10ft (3m). Tropical Africa, Arabian peninsula, E. India. ❄ (min. 59°F/15°C)
C. rhombifolia ■ syn. *Rhoicissus rhombifolia* (Grape ivy). Vigorous climber producing forked tendrils and 3-palmate, dark green leaves, to 6in (15cm) long, with ovate to diamond-shaped leaflets, boldly veined and coarsely toothed, with rust-red hairs beneath. In summer, bears hairy green flowers in cymes 1¼–3in (3–8cm) long, opposite the leaves, followed by blue-black berries, ¼–½in (0.5–1.5cm) across. ↕ 10ft (3m) or more. Tropical America. ❄ (min. 41°F/5°C). **'Ellen Danica'** is bushy, with larger, deeply lobed leaflets; ↕ 3ft (1m).
C. striata, syn. *Ampelopsis sempervirens, Parthenocissus striata, Vitis striata* (Ivy of Uruguay). Slender, vigorous climber with tendrils and 3- to 5-palmate leaves, 1½–3in (4–8cm) long, composed of obovate, leathery, glossy, mid-green leaflets. In summer, bears green flowers in small cymes, 1¼in (3cm) long, opposite the leaves, followed by glossy black berries, ¼–½in (6–15mm) across. ↕ 30ft (10m). S. Brazil to Chile. ❄ (min. 45°F/7°C)
C. voinieriana see *Tetrastigma voinierianum.*

Cissus rhombifolia

CISTUS

Rock rose, Sun rose

CISTACEAE

Genus of about 20 species of evergreen shrubs occurring on dry, stony or rocky soils in the Canary Islands, N. Africa, Turkey, and S. Europe. They are grown for their showy, saucer-shaped, usually 5-petaled, white to dark pink flowers, borne singly or in terminal or axillary cymes from early to late summer; each bloom lasts only one day. They have opposite leaves. Rock roses are suitable for growing in a shrub border, on sunny banks, at the base of a wall, around paved areas, or in containers. They are often short-lived.

• **CULTIVATION** Grow in poor to moderately fertile, well-drained soil in a sheltered site in full sun, planting after any danger of hard frosts has passed. Rock roses generally tolerate alkaline soils, but may become chlorotic with age on very alkaline soils. Pinch back young plants after flowering to encourage a bushy habit. Old, leggy plants are best replaced; they do not respond well to hard pruning.

• **PROPAGATION** Sow seed in containers in a cold frame as soon as ripe or in spring. Root softwood or greenwood cuttings in summer.

• **PESTS AND DISEASES** Infrequent.

C.* x *aguilarii (*C. ladanifer* x *C. populifolius*). Rounded shrub with lance-shaped, 3-veined, wavy-margined, sticky, bright green leaves, to 4in (10cm) long. Solitary white flowers, to 3in (8cm) across, with golden yellow stamens, are borne in summer. ↕↔ 4ft (1.2m). S.W. Europe, N. Africa. ❄ (min. 41°F/5°C). **'Maculatus'** has sticky leaves and flowers with a dark red mark at the base of each petal.
C. albidus. Dense, bushy shrub with ovate to oblong, 3-veined, gray-white leaves, to 2in (5cm) long. Terminal cymes of 3–8 dark lilac-pink flowers, 2in (5cm) across, with yellow centers, are produced in summer. ↕↔ 3ft (1m). S.W. Europe, N. Africa. Zone 7.
C. algarvensis see *Halimium ocymoides.*
***C.* 'Anne Palmer'.** Bushy shrub with erect, red-flushed shoots and lance-shaped, wavy-margined, deeply veined, dark green leaves, to 2in (5cm) long. Soft rose-pink flowers, to 3in (8cm) across, are borne singly or in small, terminal cymes of 2–4 blooms in summer. ↕↔ 3ft (1m). ❄ (min. 41°F/5°C)

Cistus 'Peggy Sammons'

Cistus x *corbariensis*

Cistus creticus

Cistus x *cyprius*

Cistus x *dansereaui* 'Decumbens'

Cistus monspeliensis

Cistus x *skanbergii*

***C.* 'Blanche'.** Bushy shrub with lance-shaped leaves, 1½–3in (4–8cm) long, dark green above and gray-green beneath. Pure white flowers, to 4in (10cm) across, are produced singly from the leaf axils or in terminal cymes in summer. ↕↔ 5ft (1.5m). Zone 7b.
C. clusii, syn. *C. rosmarinifolius.* Mound-forming shrub with linear leaves, to 1in (2.5cm) long, dark green above and white beneath. Small white flowers, 1in (2.5cm) across, with yellow stamens, open in few-flowered, terminal cymes in summer. ↕ 12in (30cm), ↔ 24in (60cm). W. Mediterranean. ❄ (min. 41°F/5°C)
C.* x *corbariensis ■ (*C. populifolius* x *C. salviifolius*) syn. *C.* x *hybridus.* Dense, bushy shrub with ovate, wavy-margined, dark green leaves, to 2in (5cm) long. From late spring to summer, red buds open to white flowers, 1½in (4cm) across, with yellow centers and stamens, borne singly or in terminal cymes of 2 or 3 blooms. ↕ 3ft (1m), ↔ 5ft (1.5m). S. Europe. Zone 7b.
C. creticus ■ syn. *C. incanus* subsp. *creticus.* Compact shrub with ovate to obovate, wavy-margined, deeply veined, mid-green leaves, to 3in (8cm) long. In summer, bears terminal cymes of 3–5 purple-pink flowers, to 2½in (6cm) across, with yellow stamens. ↕↔ 3ft (1m). E. Mediterranean. ❄ (min. 35°F/2°C)
C. crispus. Rounded, bushy shrub with oblong to elliptic, gray-green leaves, to 1½in (4cm) long, deeply veined and wavy margined. In summer, bears terminal cymes of 2–5 purple-red flowers, to 2½in (6cm) across, with yellow stamens. ↕ 24in (60cm), ↔ 36in (90cm). W. Mediterranean. ❄ (min. 45°F/7°C). **'Sunset'** see *C.* x *pulverulentus* 'Sunset'.
C.* x *cyprius ■ (*C. ladanifer* x *C. laurifolius*). Bushy shrub with narrowly lance-shaped to oblong-lance-shaped, slightly wavy-margined, sticky, dark green leaves, to 4in (10cm) long. In summer, bears terminal cymes of 3–6 white flowers, to 3in (8cm) across, with yellow and crimson marks at the bases of the petals, and yellow stamens. ↕↔ 5ft (1.5m). S.W. Europe. Zone 7b.
C.* x *dansereaui (*C. hirsutus* x *C. ladanifer*) syn. *C.* x *lusitanicus* of gardens. Upright shrub with sticky shoots and oblong-lance-shaped, dark green leaves, to 2½in (6cm) long. Terminal cymes of 3–6 white flowers, to 3in (8cm) across, with faint yellow and crimson marks at the base of each petal, are borne in summer. ↕↔ 3ft (1m). S.W. Europe. ❄ (min. 41°F/5°C).
'Decumbens' ■ is low and spreading; ↕ 24in (60cm).
***C.* 'Elma'.** Vigorous, bushy shrub with lance-shaped, glossy, deep green leaves, to 4in (10cm) long. In summer, bears terminal cymes of 3–6 white flowers, to 4in (10cm) across, with yellow stamens. ↕↔ 6ft (2m). ❄ (min. 41°F/5°C)
C.* x *florentinus (*C. monspeliensis* x *C. salviifolius*). Compact shrub with lance-shaped to elliptic-lance-shaped, wavy-margined, gray-green leaves, to 1½in (4cm) long. White flowers, 1½in (4cm) across, with yellow centers, are borne in few-flowered, terminal cymes in summer. ↕ 3ft (1m), ↔ 5ft (1.5m). S. Europe, N. Africa. ❄ (min. 45°F/7°C)
C. hirsutus. Mound-forming shrub with dense branches. Shoots and ovate to elliptic, dark green leaves, to 2½in (6cm) long, are covered with long white hairs. In summer, bears terminal cymes of 3–8 white flowers, 1½in (4cm) across, with yellow centers. ↕ 3ft (1m), ↔ 5ft (1.5m). S.W. Europe. ❄ (min. 45°F/7°C)
C.* x *hybridus see *C.* x *corbariensis.*
C. incanus* subsp. *creticus see *C. creticus.*
C. ingwerseniana see x *Halimiocistus* 'Ingwersenii'.
C. ladanifer, syn. *C. ladaniferus* (Common gum cistus, Laudanum). Upright shrub with linear-lance-shaped, sticky, aromatic, dark green leaves, to 4in (10cm) long. White flowers, to 4in (10cm) across, with yellow centers, sometimes with crimson marks at the base of each petal, are borne singly at the ends of short sideshoots in summer. ↕ 6ft (2m), ↔ 5ft (1.5m). S.W. Europe to N. Africa. Zone 7b.
C. ladaniferus see *C. ladanifer.*
C. laurifolius. Upright shrub with ovate, sticky, aromatic, dark blue-green leaves, to 3in (8cm) long. In summer, bears erect, branched cymes of 3–8 white flowers, to 3in (8cm) across, with yellow centers. ↕↔ 6ft (2m). S.W. Europe. Zone 7.
***C.* x *lusitanicus* of gardens** see *C.* x *dansereaui.*
C. monspeliensis ■ (Montpellier rock rose). Bushy shrub with linear to lance-shaped, deeply veined, dark green leaves, to 2in (5cm) long. Crowded, terminal and axillary cymes of 3–6 saucer-shaped white flowers, to 1in (2.5cm) across, with yellow stamens, are borne in summer. ↕ 3ft (1m), ↔ 5ft (1.5m). S.W. Europe, N. Africa. Zone 7b.
C. parviflorus. Compact shrub with ovate, deeply veined, gray-green leaves, to 1¼in (3cm) long. Terminal and axillary cymes of 3–8 clear pink flowers, to 1in (2.5cm) across, are produced in summer. ↕ 3ft (1m), ↔ 5ft (1.5m). E. Mediterranean. Zone 7.
***C.* 'Peggy Sammons'** ■ Bushy, upright shrub with oval, gray-green leaves, to 2½in (6cm) long. In summer, bears profuse, terminal cymes of 3–8 pale purplish pink flowers, 2½in (6cm) across. ↕↔ 3ft (1m). ❄ (min. 45°F/7°C)
C. populifolius. Rounded shrub with broadly ovate to heart-shaped, dark green leaves, to 3½in (9cm) long. In summer, produces cymes of 2–5 white flowers, to 2in (5cm) across, with yellow centers, from the upper leaf axils. ↕↔ 6ft (2m). S.W. Europe. Zone 7b.
***C.* x *pulverulentus* 'Sunset'**, syn. *C. crispus* 'Sunset'. Compact, spreading shrub with oblong, wavy-margined, grayish green leaves, to 2in (5cm) long. Profuse terminal cymes of 3–6 rose-pink flowers, 2in (5cm) across, with yellow centers, are borne in summer. ↕ 24in (60cm), ↔ 36in (90cm). Zone 7b.
C.* x *purpureus (*C. creticus* x *C. ladanifer*). Rounded shrub with upright, sticky, red-flushed shoots and narrowly oblong-lance-shaped to obovate, slightly wavy-margined, dark green leaves, to 2in (5cm) long. In summer, produces terminal cymes of 3 crinkled, dark pink flowers, to 3in (8cm) across, with maroon marks at the bases of the petals. ↕↔ 3ft (1m). S. Europe. Zone 7b. **'Betty Taudevin'** has narrow, less wavy-margined leaves and bears brighter pink flowers, to 3½in (9cm) across.
***C. revolii* of gardens** see x *Halimiocistus sahucii.*
C. rosmarinifolius see *C. clusii.*
C. salviifolius. Bushy shrub with ovate, deeply veined, gray-green leaves, to 1½in (4cm) long. White flowers, to 2in (5cm) across, with yellow centers, are borne singly, or occasionally in few-flowered, axillary cymes in summer. ↕ 30in (75cm), ↔ 36in (90cm). S. Europe. Zone 7. **'Prostratus'** is low and spreading, with smaller leaves, ¾in (2cm) long; ↕ 6–10in (15–25cm), ↔ 24–36in (60–90cm).
***C.* 'Silver Pink'.** Mound-forming shrub with lance-shaped, dark green leaves, to 3in (8cm) long, gray-green beneath. Silvery pink flowers, 3in (8cm) across, almost white in the centers, with prominent golden stamens, are borne in erect, terminal cymes of 3–5 blooms in summer. ↕ 30in (75cm), ↔ 36in (90cm). Zone 7b.
C.* x *skanbergii ■ (*C. monspeliensis* x *C. parviflorus*). Compact shrub with narrowly oblong-lance-shaped, slightly wavy-margined, gray-green leaves, to 2in (5cm) long. In summer, profusely bears terminal cymes of 3–6 pale pink flowers, 1in (2.5cm) across. ↕ 30in (75cm), ↔ 36in (90cm). Greece. Zone 7b.
C. wintonensis see x *Halimiocistus wintonensis.*

x CITROFORTUNELLA

RUTACEAE

Hybrid genus of evergreen shrubs and trees, crosses of *Citrus* and *Fortunella.* The alternate, simple, leathery leaves may have narrow wings on the stalks. Saucer-shaped or shallowly cup-shaped, 5-petaled, waxy flowers are borne singly or in twos or threes from the leaf axils, and are followed by small, orange-like fruits. Where not hardy, grow in a cool or temperate greenhouse, or as houseplants; elsewhere, grow outdoors as specimen plants.

• **CULTIVATION** Under glass, grow in soil-based potting mix in full light, with shade from hot sun, and good ventilation. When in growth, mist daily, water freely, and apply a balanced liquid fertilizer every 2–3 weeks; water sparingly in winter. Pot on or top-dress in winter. Outdoors, grow in neutral to acidic, loamy, well-drained soil in full sun. Pruning group 1; plants under glass may need restrictive pruning in late winter or early spring.

• **PROPAGATION** Root semi-ripe cuttings in summer. Layer in early spring.

• **PESTS AND DISEASES** Collar and foot rot, dieback, tristeza virus, and anthracnose can occur. Scale insects and spider mites are also problems, especially under glass.

x *C. microcarpa* ■ syn. x *C. mitis*, *Citrus mitis* (Calamondin, Panama orange). Large shrub or small, bushy tree, sometimes with a few short spines, and elliptic to broadly ovate, bright green leaves, 1½–4in (4–10cm) long. Bears white flowers, ½in (1.5cm) across, from spring to summer, followed by spherical orange fruit, 1–1½in (2.5–4cm) across. ↕ 10–20ft (3–6m), ↔ 6–10ft (2–3m). ❄ (min. 41°F/5°C). **'Tiger'** has leaves margined and streaked with white. **'Variegata'** has white-mottled leaves and green-variegated fruit.
x *C. mitis* see x *C. microcarpa.*

x *Citrofortunella microcarpa*

Citrullus lanatus

CITRULLUS

CUCURBITACEAE

Genus of 3 species of annual, spreading, herbaceous vines, with pinnate leaves. Single staminate flowers produce fleshy, succulent fruits, including the widely cultivated watermelon.

• **CULTIVATION** Grow in well-drained, neutral, sandy soil in full sun. Requires at least 70–75 warm days. Harvest 10 to 14 weeks after sowing.

• **PROPAGATION** Sow seed in early spring when soil has warmed to 72°F (22°C). Thin to 1 plant every 3–5ft (1–1.5m).

• **PESTS AND DISEASES** Aphids, powdery mildew, and mosaic virus may occur.

C. lanatus* var. *lanatus ▣ (Watermelon). Annual vine with large, green, lobed leaves. Bears single bright to medium yellow flowers, and round or oblong, green or cream, striped or mottled fruits, to 24in (60cm) across, on spreading stems, to 12ft (4m) long. Edible, tasty flesh inside hard rind ranges from pink to red, yellow, or orange; seeds are white to black, to ½in (4cm). ↕ 6–12in (15–30cm), ↔ 4–6ft (1.2–1.8m). Tropics, Africa.

CITRUS

RUTACEAE

Genus of about 16 species of evergreen, often spiny, trees and shrubs from open forest, thickets, and scrub in S.E. Asia and the larger islands in the E. Pacific. The leaves are alternate and simple, usually with winged stalks. Shallowly cup-shaped, 5-petaled, often scented white flowers, 1–2in (2–5cm) across, are borne in small, axillary racemes or corymbs. The fruits take about one year to mature. Where not hardy, grow in a cool or temperate greenhouse or conservatory. In warmer areas, grow as specimens or in a fruit garden.

• **CULTIVATION** Under glass, grow in soil-based potting mix in full light, shaded from hot sun. In growth, water freely, mist daily, and apply a balanced liquid fertilizer every 2–3 weeks; water sparingly in winter. Pot on or top-dress in late winter. Outdoors, grow in moist but well-drained, neutral to slightly acidic soil in full sun. Most citrus survive short spells just below freezing. Pruning group 1; may need restrictive pruning in winter or early spring under glass.

Citrus aurantiifolia

• **PROPAGATION** Sow seed at 61°F (16°C) in spring; seedlings do not come true to type. Root semi-ripe cuttings in summer.

• **PESTS AND DISEASES** *Phytophthora* foot rot, gummosis, sooty mold (associated with scale insects), scab, greasy spot, mushroom root rot, heart rot, canker, and anthracnose can affect many *Citrus* species. Pests include scale insects, many nematodes, plant bugs, weevils, aphids, mealybugs, spider mites, and whiteflies.

C. aurantiifolia ▣ (Lime). Large shrub or small tree with an irregular, bushy habit, spiny stems, and elliptic to oblong-ovate, scalloped, mid- to light green leaves, 1½–3in (4–8cm) long. Small racemes of white flowers, 1¼–3in (3–8cm) across, open from spring to summer, followed by spherical to ovoid, green-yellow fruit, 1¼–2½in (3–6cm) long. ↕ 10–15ft (3–5m), ↔ 5–10ft (1.5–3m). E. Africa, Himalayas, Malaysia. ❄ (min. 37–41°F/3–5°C)
C. limon ▣ (Lemon). Large shrub or small, freely branching, spiny tree with narrowly ovate, finely toothed, light green leaves, 2–4in (5–10cm) long. From spring to summer, fragrant white flowers, 1½–2in (4–5cm) across, borne singly or in small cymes, open from red- or purple-tinted buds; they are followed by broadly ovoid yellow fruit, 3–6in (7–15cm) long. ↕ 6–22ft (2–7m), ↔ 5–10ft (1.5–3m). Asia. ❄ (min. 37–41°F/3–5°C). **'Improved Meyer'** is more cold- and disease-resistant than Meyer'. **'Meyer'**, syn. *C.* x *meyeri* (Meyer's lemon) is a compact hybrid of *C. limon*, with fragrant flowers and small, spherical fruit. **'Ponderosa'** is a dwarf tree with large, waxy, fragrant white flowers, followed by grapefruit-sized fruit.
C. medica (Citron). Large shrub or small, spiny tree with elliptic-ovate, toothed, rich green leaves, 4–7in (10–18cm) long. Short racemes of white, purple-tinted flowers, 1½in (4cm) wide, open from spring to autumn, followed by ovoid to oblong, lemon-yellow fruit, to 12in (30cm) long. ↕ 10–15ft (3–5m), ↔ 6–10ft (2–3m). Probably S.W. Asia. ❄ (min. 37–41°F/3–5°C)
C.* x *meyeri see *C. limon* 'Meyer'.
C. mitis see x *Citrofortunella microcarpa.*
C. reticulata (Clementine, Mandarin, Tangerine). Rounded, sometimes spiny, large shrub or small tree with ovate to lance-shaped, deep green leaves, 1¼–1¾in (3–4cm) long. In spring, bears very fragrant white flowers, 1–1½in (2.5–4cm) across, in short racemes. Spherical orange fruit, 1½–3in (4–8cm) long, are borne from autumn to spring. ↕ 6–25ft (2–8m), ↔ 5–10ft (1.5–3m). S.E. Asia. ❄ (min. 37–41°F/3–5°C). **Satsuma Group** cultivars are more cold-resistant than other variants and have thin-peeled, very sweet orange fruit, to 2in (5cm) long.
***C. sinensis* 'Washington'** (Sweet orange). Large, rounded, bushy shrub or small tree with oval to elliptic, dark green leaves, 2–6in (5–15cm) long. In spring, bears fragrant white flowers, 1½in (4cm) across, singly or in racemes. Sweet orange fruit, 2½–4in (6–10cm) long, each with a secondary, embryonic fruit embedded at the apex, are borne in winter. ↕ 20–40ft (6–12m), ↔ 10–15ft ❄ (min. 37–41°F/3–5°C)

CLADRASTIS

FABACEAE

Genus of 5 species of deciduous trees found in woodland and on limestone cliffs in China, Japan, and the US. They are grown for their terminal, erect or pendent panicles of pea-like flowers and colorful autumn foliage. The light to mid-green leaves are alternate and pinnate. They make fine specimen trees.

• **CULTIVATION** Grow in fertile, well-drained soil in full sun; shelter from strong winds, since the wood is brittle. Pruning group 1, after flowering, or in late autumn or early winter.

• **PROPAGATION** Sow scarified seed outdoors in containers in an open frame, or in a seedbed, in autumn. Insert root cuttings in winter.

• **PESTS AND DISEASES** Infrequent.

C. kentukea see *C. lutea.*
C. lutea ▣ syn. *C. kentukea* (Yellowwood). Spreading tree with bright, light green leaves, to 12in (30cm) long, composed of 7–9 ovate or obovate leaflets, turning clear yellow in autumn. Pendent panicles of fragrant, wisteria-like, white, yellow-marked flowers, to 1¼in (3cm) long, are borne in late spring and early summer, often only in alternate years. ↕ 40ft (12m), ↔ 30ft (10m). S.E. US. Zone 4b. **'Rosea'** has pink-tinged flowers.
C. platycarpa (Japanese Yellowwood). Rounded tree with light green leaves, to 12in (30cm) long, composed of 8–13 ovate-oblong, short-stalked leaflets, turning yellow to orange in autumn. In summer, bears erect panicles, to 10in (25cm) long, of white flowers, ½in (1.5cm) long, each with a yellow spot at the base. ↕ 40ft (12m), ↔ 30ft (10m). Japan, China. Zone 5.
C. sinensis. Rounded tree with mid-green, softly hairy leaves, to 12in (30cm) long, gray-tinged beneath, composed of 9–13 ovate to oval leaflets, turning bright yellow in autumn. In summer, bears upright, pyramidal panicles of pink-flushed, white flowers, ½in (1.5cm) across. ↕ 70ft (20m), ↔ 20–30ft (6–10m). China. Zone 6.

Citrus limon

Cladrastis lutea

CLARKIA
syn. EUCHARIDIUM, GODETIA

ONAGRACEAE

Genus of about 36 species of vigorous, mostly slender-stemmed annuals found on dry, open slopes, from sea level to 8,000ft (2,400m), in W. North America and South America. They have oval or linear to elliptic, sometimes toothed leaves. Spreading, funnel-shaped, paper-thin flowers, with a satin-like texture, are borne in upright, leafy racemes in summer. Grow in an annual border. *Clarkia* species and cultivars are also good for cut flowers.

• **CULTIVATION** Grow in moderately fertile, moist but well-drained, slightly acidic soil in sun or partial shade. Very fertile soil encourages growth of foliage at the expense of flowers. They dislike hot, humid conditions.

• **PROPAGATION** Sow seed *in situ* in autumn or spring. Protect autumn-sown seedlings over winter; avoid transplanting.

• **PESTS AND DISEASES** Downy mildew, rust, *Botrytis* leaf spot, and root rot sometimes occur.

C. amoena, syn. *Godetia amoena, G. grandiflora* (Satin flower). Erect annual with lance-shaped, sometimes toothed leaves, to 2½in (6cm) long. Bears fluted, single or double, lilac to reddish pink flowers, 2in (5cm) across, in raceme-like clusters at the tips of long, leafy shoots in summer. ↕ to 30in (75cm), ↔ 12in (30cm). California. Cultivars of **Grace Series** have single, lavender-pink, red, salmon-pink, or pink flowers with contrasting centers; ↕ to 20in (50cm). **Satin Series** cultivars are dwarf and bushy, with single flowers in various colors, many with white margins or contrasting centers; ↕ to 8in (20cm). **'Sybil Sherwood'** ▣ has single, salmon-pink flowers, fading to white at the margins; ↕ to 18in (45cm).
***C. breweri* 'Pink Ribbons'** ▣ syn. *Eucharidium breweri* 'Pink Ribbons'.

Clarkia amoena 'Sybil Sherwood'

Clarkia breweri 'Pink Ribbons'

Erect to spreading annual bearing lance-shaped to linear, sometimes toothed leaves, to 2in (5cm) long. Scented, purplish pink flowers, to 2in (5cm) across, with 3-lobed, ribbon-like petals, are borne in raceme-like clusters at the tips of leafy shoots in summer. ↕ to 12in (30cm), ↔ to 9in (23cm). California.
C. elegans see *C. unguiculata.*
C. unguiculata, syn. *C. elegans.* Erect annual with lance-shaped, elliptic, or ovate leaves. In summer, bears solitary, lavender- to salmon-pink, purplish red, or dark red-purple, rarely white flowers, ½–1½in (1.5–4cm) across, from the upper leaf axils. ↕ 12–36in (30–90cm), ↔ 8in (20cm). California. **Royal Bouquet Series** cultivars produce racemes, to 12in (30cm) long, resembling small hollyhocks, of evenly spaced, frilly, double, pink, red, or mauve flowers, to 2in (5cm) across, sometimes darker or paler at the bases; ↕ to 36in (90cm), ↔ to 12in (30cm).

CLAYTONIA
Spring beauty

PORTULACACEAE

Genus of about 15 species of deciduous and evergreen, succulent perennials and some annuals or short-lived perennials. They occur mainly in mountainous areas, often in scree, in Australasia and W. North America. They have rosettes of fleshy, stalked basal leaves, and opposite, stalkless, often stem-clasping upper leaves. Small, 5-petaled, cup- or bowl-shaped, pink or white flowers are borne in terminal racemes in summer. Grow in an alpine house or a scree bed.

Claytonia megarhiza var. *nivalis*

Claytonia virginica

• **CULTIVATION** Grow in gritty, humus-rich, sharply drained soil in full sun. Protect from excessive winter moisture.

• **PROPAGATION** Sow seed in containers in an open frame in autumn.

• **PESTS AND DISEASES** Downy mildew, rust, and aphids may be problems.

C. caroliniana (Carolina spring beauty). Small, weak-stemmed, succulent perennial with broad, oval to oblong, dark green leaves, to 2in (5cm) long. Bears racemes of 2–15 pink to white flowers, to 1in (2.5cm) across, marked with pink, in spring. ↕ to 12in (30cm), ↔ 8in (20cm). C. to E. North America. Zone 4.
C. megarhiza* var. *nivalis ▣ syn. *Calandrinia megarhiza* var. *nivalis.* Short-lived, taprooted, evergreen perennial with spoon-shaped, fleshy, gray-green or deep green basal leaves, to 6in (15cm) long, and smaller, inversely lance-shaped to linear upper leaves. In early summer, shallowly cup-shaped, deep rose-pink flowers, ¾–1¼in (2–3cm) across, occasionally suffused yellow, are produced in dense racemes on short, branching stems. ↕ to 2in (5cm), ↔ to 6in (15cm). Rocky Mountains. Zone 4.
C. virginica ▣ (Spring beauty). Low-growing, succulent perennial with opposite, paired, linear to lance-shaped, dark green leaves, to 6in (15cm) long. In spring, up to 15 pink-tinged, white flowers, ½–¾in (1.5–2cm) across, are produced in racemes. Produces sweet, edible corms. ↕ to 12in (30cm), ↔ 8in (20cm). E. North America. Zone 4.

CLEISTOCACTUS

CACTACEAE

Genus of about 50 species of columnar cacti from mountainous areas, to 10,000ft (3,000m), in Peru, Bolivia, Paraguay, Argentina, and Uruguay. They have cylindrical, fleshy stems bearing rounded ribs and dense spines. As they reach maturity (some in only 3 or 4 years), many species branch from the base and produce tubular, diurnal flowers. Where not hardy, grow in a warm greenhouse. In warmer climates, grow in a border or desert garden with other cacti and succulents.

• **CULTIVATION** Under glass, grow in standard cactus potting mix in full light and with low humidity. In the growing season, water freely and apply a half-strength balanced liquid fertilizer every

Cleistocactus strausii

5–6 weeks. Keep completely dry from midautumn to spring. Outdoors, grow in sharply drained, low-fertility, humus-rich soil in full sun. See also pp.48–49.

• **PROPAGATION** Sow seed at 70°F (21°C) in early spring or summer. Root stem cuttings in early summer.

• **PESTS AND DISEASES** Mealybugs and root rot may be problems.

C. brookei, syn. *C. wendlandiorum.* Semi-erect or spreading cactus with 22- to 25-ribbed, mid-green stems, 1½–2½in (4–6cm) thick, densely covered with bristle-like, slightly yellowish or grayish white spines. Red or orange flowers, 2in (5cm) long, are borne in summer. ↕ 26in (65cm), ↔ indefinite. Bolivia. ❀ (min. 50°F/10°C)
C. hyalacanthus, syn. *C. jujuyensis.* Erect cactus branching freely from the base. Grayish green stems, 1½–2½in (4–6cm) thick, have 17–25 ribs and are covered with bristle-like, hairy, brownish yellow or yellowish white spines. Bears pale red flowers, to 1½in (4cm) long, in summer. ↕ 3ft (1m) or more, ↔ 24in (60cm) or more. Bolivia, N.W. Argentina. ❀ (min. 50°F/10°C)
C. jujuyensis see *C. hyalacanthus.*
C. smaragdiflorus. Erect, then decumbent cactus with 12- to 16-ribbed, mid-green stems, 1½–2½in (4–6cm) thick. Closely set areoles produce long, bristly, pale to dark brown spines. Green-tipped red flowers, to 2in (5cm) long, are borne in summer. ↕ 6ft (2m), ↔ indefinite. Bolivia, Paraguay, Argentina, Uruguay. ❀ (min. 50°F/10°C)
C. strausii ▣ (Silver torch). Erect cactus branching freely from the base. Light green stems, 1½–3in (4–8cm) thick, have about 25 ribs with densely arranged, bristle-like, snow-white spines. Bears carmine-red flowers, 3–3½in (8–9cm) long, in summer. ↕↔ 3ft (1m) or more. Bolivia. ❀ (min. 50°F/10°C); will tolerate periods of 25°F (-4°C) if protected and kept dry in winter.
C. wendlandiorum see *C. brookei.*

CLEMATIS syn. ATRAGENE

Old man's beard, Traveler's joy, Virgin's bower

RANUNCULACEAE

Genus of more than 250 species of evergreen or deciduous, mainly semi-woody to woody, twining leaf-climbers and woody-based herbaceous perennials from the N. and S. hemispheres, including Europe, the Himalayas, China, Australasia, North America, and Central America. More than 2,500 mainly large-flowered cultivars are in cultivation. Due to the diversity of the species – which include short-growing herbaceous perennials, scandent or trailing shrubs, and climbers reaching 30ft (10m) in height – habit and leaf form vary greatly. The opposite, occasionally alternate, hairy to hairless leaves are simple, 3-palmate, or pinnate or 2-pinnate, with entire to irregularly cut margins. Climbing species attach to host plants or supporting structures by means of their leaf stalks. More specific leaf information is given in the group descriptions below. The mostly bisexual, rarely unisexual flowers are borne singly or in cymes or panicles. They have 4–10 tepals (often referred to as sepals) and vary greatly in shape and size (see panel below). Clematis are grown for their abundant flowers, often followed by decorative, filamentous, silvery gray seed heads. Some, such as *C. recta*, are scented. Use climbing species to clothe a wall, arbor, trellis, or pergola; they can also be grown over large shrubs or small trees. Grow herbaceous species in a mixed or herbaceous border.

For ease of reference, clematis may be divided into the following 3 groups, based on their cultivation requirements:

Group 1

Early-flowering species – bear flowers on the previous year's shoots in winter and early spring. They prefer a sheltered, sunny site with well-drained soil. Mid-green leaves are evergreen and glossy, or deciduous, usually divided into 3 leaflets, and either lance-shaped, to 5in (13cm) long, or simple, oblong, and fern-like, 2in (5cm) long. Flowers are single and either bell-shaped or open bell-shaped, ¾–2in (2–5cm) long, or saucer-shaped, 1½–2in (4–5cm) across.

C. alpina, C. macropetala, *and their cultivars* – bear flowers on the previous year's shoots in spring and occasionally on new growth in summer. *C. alpina* and its variants are ideal for cold, exposed sites. They are deciduous, having pale to mid-green leaves, 1¼–2in (3–5cm) long, with 3–5 lance-shaped to broadly oblong, toothed leaflets. Single, semi-double, or double, bell-shaped to open bell-shaped flowers, 1¼–3in (3–8cm) across, are followed by attractive seed heads from summer to autumn.

C. montana *and its cultivars* – bear flowers on the previous year's ripened shoots in late spring. They are very vigorous deciduous climbers, useful for clothing a large tree or building. Mid- to purplish green leaves, 2–3in (5–8cm) long, have 3 lance-shaped leaflets with pointed tips. Flowers are almost flat to saucer-shaped, and usually single, 2–3in (5–8cm) across.

Group 2

Early to midseason, large-flowered cultivars – bear flowers in late spring and early summer on sideshoots arising from the previous year's growth, and in mid- and late summer at the tips of the current year's shoots. They are deciduous, with pale to mid-green leaves, usually 4–6in (10–15cm) long and divided into 3 ovate or lance-shaped leaflets, or simple and ovate, to 4in (10cm) long. Flowers are upright; single, semi-double, or fully double; and mostly saucer-shaped, 4–8in (10–20cm) across.

Group 3

Late, large-flowered cultivars – bear flowers on the current year's shoots in summer and early autumn. They are deciduous with pale to mid-green leaves, mostly 4–6in (10–15cm) long with 3 ovate or lance-shaped leaflets, or simple and ovate, to 4in (10cm) long. Flowers are single, outward-facing, and usually saucer-shaped, 3–6in (7–15cm) across.

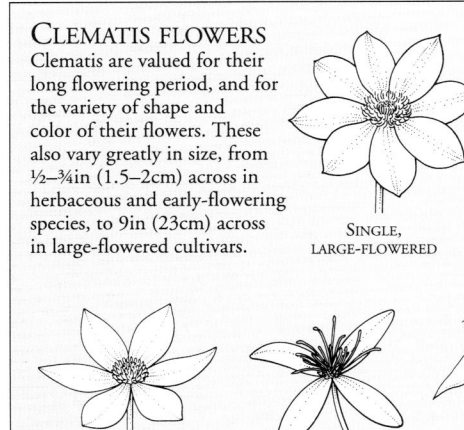

Late-flowering species and small-flowered cultivars – flower on the current year's shoots from summer to late autumn. They are generally deciduous, with pale to dark green or gray-green leaves, ¾–6in (2–15cm) long, and are either pinnate or 2-pinnate, with lance-shaped leaflets, or simple and lance-shaped. Blooms are single or double, and saucer-shaped, star-shaped, bell-shaped, open bell-shaped, tulip-shaped, or tubular, ½–4in (1–10cm) across.

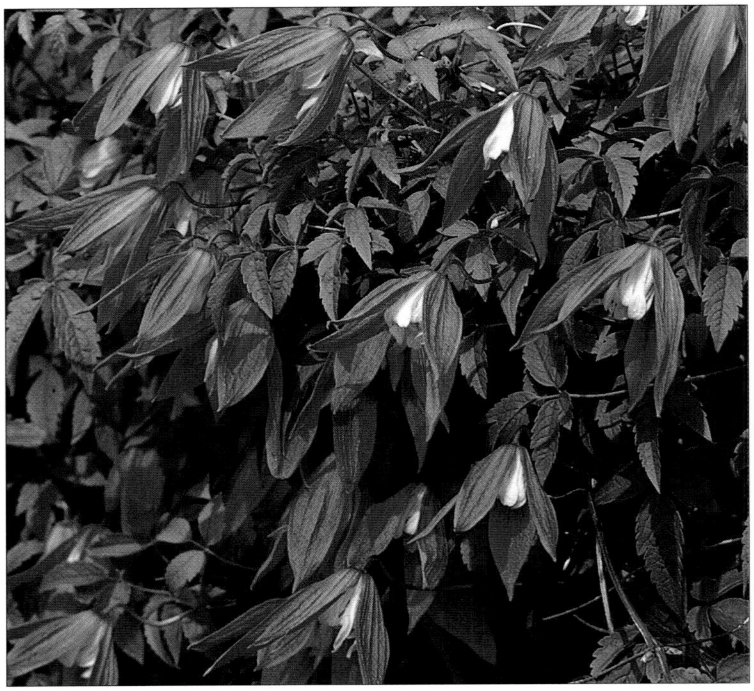

Clematis alpina

Herbaceous species and cultivars – bear flowers on the current year's shoots from midsummer to late autumn. They are suitable for a mixed border with perennials. The leaves are mid- to dark green or grayish green, and either simple and lance-shaped to ovate or heart-shaped, 1–6in (2.5–15cm) long, some with toothed margins, or 1–3in (2.5–8cm) long with 3–5 lance-shaped to ovate leaflets. Single flowers are either saucer-shaped, ½–¾in (1–2cm) across, or bell-shaped or tubular, ½–1½in (1–4cm) long.

• **CULTIVATION** Grow in fertile, humus-rich, well-drained soil in sun or partial shade, with the roots and base of the plant in shade. Herbaceous species prefer full sun. Mulch all clematis in late winter with compost or well-rotted manure, avoiding the crown. Plant climbing clematis with the top of the root ball about 3in (8cm) below the soil surface, to reduce risk of clematis wilt and encourage production of strong shoots from below soil level. After planting, cut back top growth of deciduous climbers to a strong pair of buds about 12in (30cm) above soil level. Provide strong support and tie in initially until plants begin to climb by themselves. Support herbaceous species and cultivars with twiggy brushwood.

Prune Group 1 clematis after flowering, removing dead or damaged stems and shortening others to their allotted space. This encourages production of new growth to flower in the following season. For Group 2 clematis, remove dead and damaged stems before growth begins in early spring, trimming all remaining stems back to where strong buds are visible. These buds provide a framework of second-year shoots, which, in turn, produce sideshoots that flower in late spring and early summer. The flowers may then be removed. Young shoots bear more flowers later in the summer. For Group 3 clematis, cut back all the previous year's stems to a pair of strong buds, 6–8in (15–20cm) above soil level, before growth begins in early spring.

• **PROPAGATION** Sow seed of species as soon as ripe in containers in a cold frame. Divide or take basal cuttings of herbaceous species in spring. Root softwood cuttings in spring, or semi-ripe cuttings in early summer. Layer in late winter or early spring.

• **PESTS AND DISEASES** Scale insects, whiteflies, earwigs, and aphids can be problems. Wilt, powdery mildew, rust, fungal spots, and stem cankers are common.

CLEMATIS FLOWERS

Clematis are valued for their long flowering period, and for the variety of shape and color of their flowers. These also vary greatly in size, from ½–¾in (1.5–2cm) across in herbaceous and early-flowering species, to 9in (23cm) across in large-flowered cultivars.

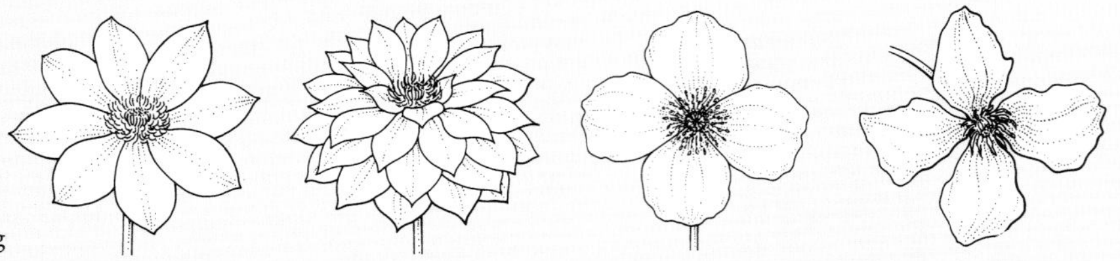

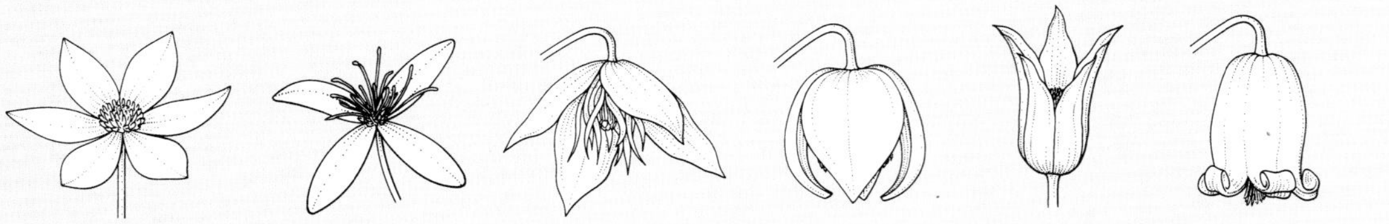

***C.* 'Abundance'** ■ syn. *C. viticella* 'Abundance'. (Group 3) Late, small-flowered climber with light green leaves. From midsummer to late autumn, bears open bell-shaped, single, 4-tepaled, wine-red flowers, 2½in (6cm) across, with cream anthers. ↕ 10ft (3m), ↔ 3ft (1m). Zone 4.

***C.* 'Alba Luxurians'** ■ syn. *C. viticella* 'Alba Luxurians'. (Group 3) Late, small-

Clematis 'Ascotiensis'

flowered climber with slightly gray-green foliage. From midsummer to late autumn, bears open bell-shaped, single flowers, 2–3in (5–8cm) across, with 4–6 green-tipped white tepals, sometimes faintly mauve-tinged when young, and small black anthers. ↕ 12ft (4m), ↔ 5ft (1.5m). Zone 4.

C. alpina ▣ (Alpine clematis). (Group 1) Early-flowering climber. Bears solitary, usually single, open bell-shaped blue flowers, 1½–3in (4–8cm) across, with white centers, from spring to early summer (occasionally also in mid- and late summer), followed by fluffy seed heads from late summer to autumn. ↕ 6–10ft (2–3m), ↔ 5ft (1.5m). Europe. Zone 4. **'Constance'** has semi-double, deep purplish pink flowers. **'Frances Rivis'** has slightly twisted, mid-blue flowers. **'Helsingborg'** bears flowers with pointed, deep blue-purple tepals and light brown-purple petaloid stamens. **'Pamela Jackman'** has deep blue flowers with blue and cream anthers. **'Pink Flamingo'** is free-flowering, and has semi-double, pale pink flowers with veins darkening toward the bases, and cream anthers. **'Willy'** has pale pink flowers, the tepals darkening toward the bases, deeper pink undersides, and cream anthers.

C. armandii ▣ (Group 1) Vigorous, evergreen, early-flowering climber bearing saucer-shaped, scented white flowers, 2in (5cm) across, with cream anthers, in axillary cymes in early spring. ↕ 10–15ft (3–5m), ↔ 6–10ft (2–3m). China. Zone 6. **'Apple Blossom'** has pink-tinged white flowers, with deeper pink undersides, fading to pinkish white, 1½–2in (4–6cm) across.

***C.* 'Asao'.** (Group 2) Compact, early, large-flowered climber producing single, creamy pink flowers, 4–5in (10–13cm) across, with deep pink tepal margins and yellow anthers, in late spring. Prefers partial shade. ↕ 6ft (2m), ↔ 3ft (1m). Zone 4.

***C.* 'Ascotiensis'** ▣ (Group 3) Vigorous, late, small- to large-flowered climber. Bears single, bright violet-blue flowers, 3½–5in (9–13cm) across, with pointed tepals and brownish green anthers, in summer. ↕ 10–12ft (3–4m), ↔ 3ft (1m). Zone 4.

***C.* 'Barbara Jackman'.** (Group 2) Early, large-flowered climber bearing single, mauve-blue flowers, 4in (10cm) across, with a magenta central band on each tepal and creamy yellow anthers, in summer. Fades in strong sun. ↕ 8–10ft (2.5–3m), ↔ 3ft (1m). Zone 3b.

***C.* 'Bees Jubilee'** ▣ (Group 2) Compact, early, large-flowered climber flowering freely in late spring and early summer. Single flowers, 4–5in (10–13cm) across, are deep pink, fading with age, with a darker central band on each tepal and light brown anthers. Prefers partial shade. ↕ 8ft (2.5m), ↔ 3ft (1m). Zone 3b.

***C.* 'Belle of Woking'.** (Group 2) Early, large-flowered climber flowering from late spring to late summer. Double, bluish white flowers, 3–5in (8–13cm) across, have cream anthers and sometimes green outer tepals. Prefers full sun. ↕ 8ft (2.5m), ↔ 3ft (1m). Zone 3b.

***C.* 'Betty Corning'**, syn. *C. viticella* 'Betty Corning'. (Group 3) Late, small-flowered climber producing bell-shaped, slightly scented, single, pale lilac flowers, 2in (5cm) long, with recurved tips and cream anthers, from midsummer to late autumn. ↕ 6ft (2m), ↔ 3ft (1m). Zone 4.

***C.* 'Bill MacKenzie'** ▣ syn. *C. orientalis* 'Bill MacKenzie'. (Group 3) Vigorous, late, small-flowered climber (thought to be a hybrid between *C. orientalis* and *C. tangutica*). From midsummer to late autumn, bears abundant open bell-shaped, single yellow flowers, 3in (8cm) across, with red anthers, followed by large, fluffy seed heads. ↕ 22ft (7m), ↔ 6–10ft (2–3m). Zone 4.

***C.* 'Carnaby'** ▣ (Group 2) Compact, early, large-flowered climber. Single, mid- to dark pink flowers, 3–4in (8–10cm) across, with a darker central band on each tepal and red anthers, are produced in summer. From late summer to autumn, flowers have lighter bases and darker central bands. Fades in strong sun. ↕ 8ft (2.5m), ↔ 3ft (1m). Zone 4.

C. cirrhosa ▣ (Group 1) Evergreen, early-flowering climber with leaves slightly bronze beneath. Produces open cup-shaped cream flowers, to 2½in (6cm) long, sometimes red-flecked, either singly or in clusters, in late winter and early spring, followed by attractive seed heads. ↕ 8–10ft (2.5–3m), ↔ 5ft (1.5m). Europe. Zone 5. **var. *balearica*** has fragrant, pale cream flowers, speckled reddish brown; Balearic Islands. **'Freckles'** has creamy pink flowers, heavily speckled red inside.

***C.* 'Comtesse de Bouchaud'.** (Group 3) Strong-growing, late, large-flowered climber bearing single, bright mauve-pink flowers, 3–4in (8–10cm) across, with pale yellow anthers, in summer. ↕ 6–10ft (2–3m), ↔ 3ft (1m). Zone 3.

***C.* 'Corona'.** (Group 2) Compact, early, large-flowered climber bearing single, light purplish pink flowers, 4–5in (10–13cm) across, with red anthers, in late spring and early summer. ↕ 6ft (2m), ↔ 3ft (1m). Zone 4.

***C.* 'Countess of Lovelace'.** (Group 2) Early, large-flowered climber producing double, bluish lilac flowers, 4in (10cm) across, with cream anthers, in early summer. Single flowers, with pointed tepals, are produced on new shoots in late summer. ↕ 6ft (2m), ↔ 3ft (1m). Zone 4.

C. crispa (Blue jasmine, Marsh clematis). (Group 3) Deciduous, late-flowering climber. In summer, bears solitary, bell-shaped, single, lavender-blue flowers, 1½–2in (4–5cm) across, with white margins and recurved tips to the tepals, and cream anthers. ↕ 8ft (2.5m), ↔ 3ft (1m). S.E. US. Zone 6b.

***C.* 'Dr. Ruppel'** ▣ (Group 2) Early, large-flowered climber. The single flowers, 4–6in (10–15cm) across, with deep rose-pink tepals with darker central bands, and light chocolate anthers, are freely produced throughout summer. ↕ 8ft (2.5m), ↔ 3ft (1m). Zone 4.

***C.* 'Duchess of Albany'** ▣ syn. *C. texensis* 'Duchess of Albany'. (Group 3) Deciduous, late, small-flowered climber. From midsummer to autumn, bears tulip-shaped, deep pink flowers, 2in (5cm) long, with slightly darker central bands inside. ↕ 8ft (2.5m), ↔ 5ft (1.5m). Zone 2.

***C.* 'Duchess of Edinburgh'** ▣ (Group 2) Deciduous, large-flowered climber with yellowish green leaves. Double, white flowers, 4–5in (10–13 cm) across, have cream-colored anthers, often with green outer tepals. 1/16–1/8in (2–3mm) ↕ 6–8ft (2–2.5m), ↔ 3ft (1m). Zone 3b.

***C.* x *durandii*.** (Group 3) Non-clinging, long-flowering, herbaceous perennial that requires staking. Solitary, saucer-shaped, single, deep indigo-blue flowers, 2½–3in (6–8cm) across, with distinctive, golden yellow anthers, are produced in summer. ↕ 3–6ft (1–2m), ↔ 3ft (1m). Garden origin. Zone 5.

***C.* 'Edomurasaki'.** (Group 2) Vigorous, mid-season, large-flowered climber. In summer, bears single, dark violet-blue flowers, 5–6in (12–15cm) across, with deep red anthers. ↕ 10ft (3m), ↔ 3ft (1m). Zone 4.

***C.* 'Elsa Späth'** ▣ syn. *C.* 'Xerxes'. (Group 2) Early, large-flowered climber bearing single flowers, 5–6in (12–15cm) across, with overlapping, rich mauve-blue tepals and red anthers, from late spring to summer. ↕ 6–10ft (2–3m), ↔ 3ft (1m). Zone 4b.

***C.* 'Ernest Markham'.** (Group 3) Vigorous, late, small- to large-flowered climber. In summer, produces abundant rich, vivid magenta flowers, 4in (10cm) across, with blunt-tipped tepals and light chocolate anthers. Prefers full sun. ↕ 10–12ft (3–4m), ↔ 3ft (1m). Zone 3b.

***C.* 'Etoile Violette'** ▣ syn. *C. viticella* 'Etoile Violette'. (Group 3) Late, small-flowered climber freely producing single, nodding, saucer-shaped, violet-purple flowers, 3in (8cm) across, with contrasting yellow anthers, from midsummer to late autumn. ↕ 10–15ft (3–5m), ↔ 5ft (1.5m). Zone 4.

Clematis 'Abundance'

Clematis 'Alba Luxurians'

Clematis armandii

Clematis 'Bees Jubilee'

Clematis 'Bill MacKenzie'

Clematis 'Carnaby'

Clematis cirrhosa

Clematis 'Dr. Ruppel'

Clematis 'Duchess of Albany'

Clematis 'Duchess of Edinburgh'

Clematis 'Elsa Späth'

Clematis 'Etoile Violette'

C

C

Clematis 'Gillian Blades'

Clematis 'Gravetye Beauty'

Clematis 'Hagley Hybrid'

Clematis 'Henryi'

Clematis heracleifolia var. *davidiana* 'Wyevale'

Clematis 'Huldine'

Clematis integrifolia

Clematis 'Jackmanii'

Clematis 'Jackmanii Rubra'

Clematis 'John Warren'

Clematis 'Kathleen Dunford'

Clematis 'Lasurstern'

Clematis 'Lincoln Star'

Clematis macropetala

Clematis 'Minuet'

Clematis 'Mme. Edouard André'

Clematis 'Mme. Julia Correvon'

Clematis montana

Clematis montana f. *grandiflora*

Clematis montana var. *rubens*

Clematis montana 'Tetrarose'

***C.* x *fargesioides* 'Paul Farges'** ■ syn. *C.* 'Summer Snow'. (Group 3) Very vigorous, late, small-flowered climber. Star-shaped flowers, 1½in (4cm) across, with white tepals and anthers, are produced from midsummer to autumn. ↕ 21–28ft (7–9m), ↔ 10ft (3m). Zone 2.

C. flammula. (Group 3) Semi-evergreen or deciduous, late-flowering climber. Star-shaped, heavily scented white flowers, 1¼in (3cm) across, with cream anthers, are freely produced in panicle-like cymes from midsummer to autumn. Foliage is sometimes glaucous. Prefers a well-drained, sheltered, sunny site. ↕ 20ft (6m), ↔ 3ft (1m). S. Europe, N. Africa, W. Syria, Turkey. Zone 7.

***C.* 'General Sikorski'.** (Group 2) Vigorous, mid-season, large-flowered climber. In early summer, bears single flowers, 4–6in (10–15cm) across, with overlapping blue tepals and creamy anthers. ↕ 10ft (3m), ↔ 3ft (1m). Zone 4.

***C.* 'Gillian Blades'** ■ (Group 2) Early, large-flowered climber. Single white flowers, 5–6in (12–15cm) across, with overlapping, wavy-margined tepals and cream anthers, appear in summer. ↕ 8ft (2.5m), ↔ 3ft (1m). Zone 4.

***C.* 'Gipsy Queen'.** (Group 3) Vigorous, late, large-flowered climber. Single flowers, 4–5in (10–13cm) across, with overlapping, velvety, violet-purple tepals and deep red anthers, are borne in summer. ↕ 10ft (3m), ↔ 3ft (1m). Zone 3.

***C.* 'Gravetye Beauty'** ■ syn. *C. texensis* 'Gravetye Beauty'. (Group 3) The late, small-flowered climber producing tulip-shaped, rich crimson-red flowers, 2in (5cm) long, with paler bands outside, from midsummer to autumn. ↕ 8ft (2.5m), ↔ 3ft (1m). Zone 3.

***C.* 'Hagley Hybrid'** ■ syn. 'Pink Chiffon'. (Group 3) Vigorous, compact, late, large-flowered climber. Single flowers, 3–4in (8–10cm) across, with boat-shaped, pinkish mauve tepals and red anthers, are produced in summer. Fades in strong sun. ↕ 6ft (2m), ↔ 3ft (1m). Zone 3.

***C.* 'Henryi'** ■ (Group 2) Vigorous, mid-season, large-flowered climber. Single flowers, 6–8in (16–20cm) across, with pointed, creamy white tepals and brown anthers, are borne in summer. ↕ 10ft (3m), ↔ 3ft (1m). Zone 4.

***C. heracleifolia* var. *davidiana*.** (Group 3) Woody-based perennial of open habit, with toothed, deeply 3-lobed, light green leaves, 4–6in (10–15cm) long. Scented, tubular, light to mid-blue flowers, 1¼in (4cm) long, are produced in whorled racemes in summer. Needs support. ↕ 30in (75cm), ↔ 3ft (1m). China. Zone 5. **'Wyevale'** ■ has more prominent yellow stamens.

***C.* 'H.F. Young'** ■ (Group 2) Very free-flowering, compact, early, large-flowered climber. Produces single, warm blue flowers, 4in (10cm) across, with overlapping, violet-tinged tepals and cream anthers, in early summer. ↕ 8ft (2.5m), ↔ 3ft (1m). Zone 4.

***C.* 'Honora'** ■ Deciduous, large flowered climber with green, palmate leaves. Produces single, raspberry-violet flowers, 5–7in (13–18cm) across, with gappy tepals and red anthers. ↕ 6–8ft (2–2.5m), ↔ 3ft (1m). Zone 4.

***C.* 'Huldine'** ■ (Group 3) Very vigorous, late, small-flowered climber producing cup-shaped white flowers, 2½in (6cm) across, mauve beneath, with short creamy anthers, in summer. ↕ 10–15ft (3–5m), ↔ 6ft (2m). Zone 3.

C. integrifolia ■ (Group 3) Herbaceous perennial with usually simple, inversely lance-shaped to elliptic leaves. Solitary, bell-shaped, mid-blue flowers, 2in (5cm) long, with 4 slightly twisted tepals and cream anthers, are borne in summer, followed by silvery brown seed heads. ↕↔ 24in (60cm). C. Europe. Zone 5.

***C.* 'Jackmanii'** ■ (Group 3) Late, large-flowered climber. In mid- and late summer, s abundant single, velvety, dark purple flowers, 3–4in (8–10cm) across, with light greenish brown anthers. ↕ 10ft (3m), ↔ 3ft (1m). Zone 2.

***C.* 'Jackmanii Alba'.** (Group 2) Vigorous, early, large-flowered climber. In early summer, produces semi-double flowers, 6in (15cm) across, with blue-tinged, milk-white, pointed tepals (and occasionally bluish gray-green outer tepals), and light brown anthers. Late-summer flowers are single and off-white. ↕ 10ft (3m), ↔ 3ft (1m). Zone 4.

***C.* 'Jackmanii Rubra'** ■ (Group 2) Early, large-flowered climber. Semi-double flowers, 5in (13cm) across, with crimson-purple tepals and yellow anthers, are produced in early summer, and single flowers are borne in mid- and late summer. ↕ 8ft (2.5m), ↔ 3ft (1m). Zone 3.

***C.* 'John Warren'** ■ (Group 2) Early, large-flowered climber. In early summer, produces single flowers, 6–7in (15–18cm) across, with pointed, overlapping, pinkish gray tepals, with deep carmine-red veins and margins, and red anthers. ↕ 8–10ft (2.5–3m), ↔ 3ft (1m). Zone 4b.

***C.* 'Kakio'** see *C.* 'Pink Champagne'.

***C.* 'Kathleen Dunford'** ■ (Group 2) Early, large-flowered climber. Single or semi-double mauve flowers, 5in (13cm) across, with pointed tepals and red anthers, are borne throughout summer. ↕ 8ft (2.5m), ↔ 3ft (1m). Zone 4.

***C.* 'Lady Betty Balfour'.** (Group 3) Very vigorous, late, large-flowered climber producing single flowers, 5–6in (12–15cm) across, with rich

Clematis 'Honora'

Clematis x *fargesioides* 'Paul Farges' (inset: flower detail)

purple tepals fading to purple-blue, and contrasting yellow anthers, in late summer and early autumn. Needs full sun. ↕ 10ft (3m), ↔ 3ft (1m). Zone 3b.

***C. lanuginosa* 'Candida'.** (Group 2) Early-flowering, deciduous climber with ovate, leathery, dark green leaves, 4in (10cm) long. From spring to autumn, produces large, flat, 4–8 tepaled, white flowers, 3–8in (8–20cm) across, with pale yellow stamens. ↕ to 15ft (5m), ↔ variable. China. Zone 5b.

***C.* 'Lasurstern'** ▣ (Group 2) Early, large-flowered climber. Single blue flowers, 5–6in (12–15cm) across, with wavy-margined, overlapping tepals and cream anthers, are produced in early summer. ↕ 8ft (2.5m), ↔ 3ft (1m). Zone 4.

***C.* 'Lemon Chiffon'.** (Group 1) Deciduous, large-flowered climber. Single, cream yellow flowers 6–7in (15–18cm) blend with yellow anthers. ↕ 6–8ft (2–2.5m), ↔ 3ft (1m). Zone 4.

***C.* 'Lincoln Star'** ▣ (Group 2) Early, large-flowered climber. Single flowers, 4–5in (10–13cm) across, with raspberry-pink tepals and red anthers, are produced in early summer. Later in the summer, flowers are much paler, with central bands of pink and pale margins. Flower color fades in strong sun. ↕ 6–8ft (2–2.5m), ↔ 3ft (1m). Zone 4.

***C.* 'Lord Nevill'.** (Group 2) Early, large-flowered climber. In early summer, bears single flowers, 4–6in (10–15cm) across, with overlapping, deep blue tepals, minutely scalloped at the margins, and purple-red anthers. ↕ 6–10ft (2–3m), ↔ 3ft (1m). Zone 3b.

C. macropetala ▣ (Group 1) Early-flowering, deciduous climber that produces solitary, open bell-shaped, blue or violet-blue flowers, to 4in (10cm) across, from spring to early summer (may rebloom from summer to early autumn), followed by silver seed heads. Flowers appear semi-double, having 4 long tepals with shorter petaloid stamens within: the outer stamens are blue and the inner ones cream. ↕ 6–10ft (2–3m), ↔ 5ft (1.5m). Russia (Siberia), Mongolia, China (Gansu). Zone 1. **'Blue Bird'** has open, semi-nodding, mauve-blue flowers, to 5in (13cm) across. **'Jan Lindmark'** has mauve flowers. **'Markham's Pink'** ▣ has sugar-pink flowers and pale to mid-green foliage. **'Rosy O'Grady'** has open, semi-nodding, pink-mauve flowers, 3in (8cm) across, with white petaloid stamens. **'White Swan'**, syn. *C.* 'White Swan', is compact, with white flowers, to 3in (8cm) across, with cream petaloid stamens; ↔ 3ft (1m).

***C.* 'Margaret Hunt'.** (Group 3) Vigorous, deciduous, large-flowered climber with pale green, pinnate leaves. Single flowers are dusky pink, 4–6in (10–15 cm) across, with pointed tepals and red anthers. ↕ 8–10ft (2.5–3m), ↔ 3ft (1m). Zone 4

***C.* 'Margaret Wood'.** (Group 2) Early, large-flowered climber. Single, white, blue-tinged flowers, 6–8in (15–20cm) across, with red stamens, are produced in early summer and in early autumn. ↕ 8–12ft (2.5–4m), ↔ 3ft (1m). Zone 4.

***C.* 'Marie Boisselot'.** (Group 2) Vigorous, mid-season, large-flowered climber. Single flowers, 6–7in (15–18cm) across, with overlapping white tepals and cream anthers, are produced from midsummer to late autumn. ↕ 10ft (3m), ↔ 3ft (1m). Zone 4.

***C.* 'Minuet'** ▣ syn. *C. viticella* 'Minuet'. (Group 3) Late, small-flowered climber bearing open bell-shaped, single white flowers, 2in (5cm) across, with pinkish purple veins and dark anthers, from midsummer to late autumn. ↕ 10ft (3m), ↔ 3ft (1m). Zone 2.

***C.* 'Miss Bateman'.** (Group 2) Compact, free-flowering, early, large-flowered climber. Rounded, single white flowers, 3–4in (8–10cm) across, with red anthers, are produced in early summer. ↕ 8ft (2.5m), ↔ 3ft (1m). Zone 4.

***C.* 'Mme. Baron Veillard'.** (Group 3) Very vigorous, late, large-flowered climber. Single, satin-like, lilac- to rose-pink flowers, 4in (10cm) across, with greenish, light brown anthers, are borne in late summer and early autumn. Needs full sun. ↕ 10–12ft (3–4m), ↔ 3ft (1m). Zone 4.

***C.* 'Mme. Edouard André'** ▣ (Group 3) Late, large-flowered climber. Single, deep red flowers, 3–4in (8–10cm) across, with pointed tepals with silver undersides, and yellow anthers, are produced freely in midsummer. ↕ 8ft (2.5m), ↔ 3ft (1m). Zone 4.

***C.* 'Mme. Grangé'.** (Group 3) Late, large-flowered climber. Single flowers, 4–5in (10–13cm) across, with boat-shaped, dusky purple tepals with silver undersides, and dark brown anthers, are produced in midsummer. Best against a light background. ↕ 10ft (3m), ↔ 3ft (1m). Zone 4.

***C.* 'Mme. Julia Correvon'** ▣ syn. *C. viticella* 'Mme Julia Correvon'. (Group 3) Late, small-flowered climber. From midsummer to late autumn, produces open bell-shaped, single, bright wine-red flowers, 3in (8cm) across, with slightly twisted tepals and yellow anthers. ↕ 10ft (3m), ↔ 5ft (1.5m). Zone 3.

***C.* 'Mme. le Coultre'** see *C.* 'Marie Boisselot'.

C. montana ▣ (Group 1) Early-flowering, very vigorous climber. Single white flowers, 2in (5cm) across, with creamy yellow anthers, either solitary or in short cymes, are produced very freely for about 4 weeks during late spring and early summer. ↕ 15–46ft (5–14m), ↔ 6–10ft (2–3m). W. and C. China, Himalayas. Zone 5b. **'Alexander'** has large, light green leaves and produces white flowers, 3–4in (8–10cm) across. Prefers full sun; ↕ 22ft (7m), ↔ 10ft (3m). **'Elizabeth'** has large, purple-flushed, mid-green leaves and strongly scented, pale pink flowers, 3in (8cm) across, with yellow anthers; ↕ 22ft (7m), ↔ 10ft (3m). **f. *grandiflora*** ▣ syn. 'Grandiflora', is very vigorous, with dark green leaves. Produces white flowers, 3–4in (8–10cm) across, with cream anthers; ↕ 30ft (10m), ↔ 12ft (4m). **'Mayleen'** has bronze-tinted leaves and produces large pink flowers, to 3in (8cm) across, with gold tepals. **'Pink Perfection'** has purple-flushed, mid-green leaves and produces rounded, strongly scented pink flowers, 2–3in (5–8cm) across, with yellow anthers; ↕ 22ft (7m), ↔ 10ft (3m). **var. *rubens*** ▣ has purple-flushed, mid-green foliage and pink flowers, with cream anthers; ↕ 30ft (10m); China. **'Tetrarose'** ▣ has purplish green leaflets, with toothed margins, and produces satin-like pink flowers, 3½in (9cm) across, with large bosses of yellow anthers; ↕ 15ft (5m).

***C.* 'Mrs. Cholmondeley'.** (Group 2) Early, large-flowered climber. The single, light lavender-blue flowers, 6–7in (15–18cm) across, with widely spaced tepals and light chocolate anthers, are produced in early summer. ↕ 6–10ft (2–3m), ↔ 3ft (1m). Zone 3b.

Clematis 'H.F. Young'

***C.* 'George Jackman'.** (Group 2 or 3) Deciduous, large-flowered climber. Produces single or semi-double, ivory flowers, 5–7in (13–18 cm) across, with beige anthers. ↕ 6–8ft (2–2.5m), ↔ 3ft (1m). Zone 4.

***C.* 'Mrs. N. Thompson'.** (Group 2) Compact, early, large-flowered climber. Single, deep violet flowers, 4in (10cm) across, with vivid scarlet central bands and red anthers, are freely produced in early summer. ↕ 8ft (2.5m), ↔ 3ft (1m). Zone 3b.

***C.* 'Mrs. P.B. Truax'.** (Group 2) Compact, early, large-flowered climber. Produces single, periwinkle-blue flowers, 4–5in (10–13cm) across, with cream anthers, during early summer. ↕ 8ft (2.5m), ↔ 3ft (1m). Zone 4.

***C.* 'Multi-blue'.** (Group 1) Deciduous, large-flowered climber with green, simple or ternate leaves. Bears long-lasting double, lavender-blue flowers, 4–5in (10–13 cm) across, with cream anthers. ↕ 6–8ft (2–2.5m), ↔ 3ft (1m). Zone 4.

Clematis macropetala 'Markham's Pink'

C. 'Nelly Moser' ■ (Group 2) Compact, early, large-flowered climber. Single, pinkish mauve flowers, 5–6in (12–15cm) across, with darker central bands and red anthers, are borne in early summer. Flowers are paler in late summer. Fades in strong sun. ↕ 6–10ft (2–3m), ↔ 3ft (1m). Zone 3b.
C. 'Niobe'. (Group 2) Compact, early, large-flowered climber. Single, rich deep red flowers, 4–6in (10–15cm) across, with pointed tepals and yellow anthers, are freely borne throughout summer. ↕ 6–10ft (2–3m), ↔ 3ft (1m). Zone 4.
***C. orientalis* 'Bill MacKenzie'** see *C.* 'Bill MacKenzie'.
***C. orientalis* 'Orange Peel'** see *C. tibetana* subsp. *vernayi* 'Orange Peel'.
C. paniculata see *C. terniflora*.
C. 'Perle d'Azur' ■ (Group 3) Vigorous, very free-flowering, late, small-flowered climber. Open bell-shaped flowers, 3in (8cm) across, with azure-blue tepals, recurved at the tips, and creamy green anthers, are borne from midsummer to autumn. ↕ 10ft (3m), ↔ 3ft (1m). Zone 3.
C. 'Perrin's Pride' ■ (Group 3) Deciduous, large-flowered climber. Single, deep purple flowers, 5in (13cm) across, have overlapping tepals and yellow anthers. ↕ 6–8ft (2–2.5m), ↔ 3ft (1m). Zone 4.
C. 'Piilu' ■ Very compact, deciduous, large-flowered climber with dark green, ternate leaves. Produces double and single, pink-mauve flowers, 4–5in (10–13 cm) across, with magenta bar and yellow anthers. ↕ 6ft (2m), ↔ 24in (60cm). Zone 3b.
C. 'Pink Champagne' syn. 'Kakio'. Deciduous, large-flowered climber with yellowish green, ternate leaves. Bears deep pink flowers, 6–8in (15–20cm) across, with a lighter central bar and yellow anthers. Fades in strong sun. ↕ 6–8ft (2–2.5m), ↔ 3ft (1m). Zone 4.
C. 'Pink Chiffon' see *C.* 'Hagley Hybrid'.
C. 'Polish Spirit', syn. *C. viticella* 'Polish Spirit'. (Group 3) Late, small-flowered climber with dark green leaves. Saucer-shaped, single, rich purple-blue flowers, 2–3in (5–8cm) across, with red anthers, are freely borne from mid-summer to late autumn. ↕ 15ft (5m), ↔ 6ft (2m). Zone 2.
C. 'Proteus' ■ (Group 2) Early, large-flowered climber. Double, mauve-pink flowers, 6in (15cm) across, paler toward the centers, with green outer tepals and cream anthers, are produced in early summer. From midsummer, flowers are single and pale mauve. ↕ 8–10ft (2.5–3m), ↔ 3ft (1m). Zone 4.
C. 'Purpurea Plena Elegans' see *C. viticella* 'Purpurea Plena Elegans'.

Clematis 'Nelly Moser'

Clematis 'Piilu'

Clematis 'Proteus'

Clematis recta

Clematis 'Richard Pennell'

Clematis 'Rouge Cardinal'

Clematis 'Silver Moon'

Clematis tangutica

Clematis 'The President'

Clematis 'Venosa Violacea'

Clematis 'Ville de Lyon'

Clematis viticella 'Purpurea Plena Elegans'

C. 'Ramona'. (Group 2) Vigorous, early, large-flowered climber. Pale blue flowers, 4–6in (10–15cm) across, with dark red anthers, are produced in midsummer and sometimes again in autumn. Prefers full sun. ↕ 10ft (3m), ↔ 3ft (1m). Zone 3b.
C. recta ■ (Group 3) Late-flowering, clump-forming, herbaceous perennial with gray-green foliage. Terminal panicles of small, star-shaped, heavily scented white flowers, ¾in (2cm) across, with cream anthers, are produced from midsummer to autumn, followed by attractive seed heads. Needs support. ↕ 3–6ft (1–2m), ↔ 30in (75cm). C. and S. Europe. Zone 4. **'Purpurea'** has purple young foliage.
C. 'Richard Pennell' ■ (Group 2) Early, large-flowered climber bearing single, rich purple-blue flowers, 4–5in (10–13cm) across, with golden yellow anthers, in early summer. ↕ 6–10ft (2–3m), ↔ 3ft (1m). Zone 4.
C. 'Rouge Cardinal' ■ (Group 3) Late, large-flowered climber bearing single, glowing velvet-crimson flowers, 4in (10cm) across, with reddish brown anthers, in midsummer. Prefers to be sited in full sun. ↕ 6–10ft (2–3m), ↔ 3ft (1m). Zone 4.
C. 'Sealand Gem'. (Group 2 or 3) Deciduous, large-flowered climber with green, simple and ternate leaves. Bears single, mauve-violet flowers, 4–6in (10–15cm) across, with darker central bar and reddish anthers. ↕ 6–8ft (2–2.5m), ↔ 3ft (1m). Zone 4.
C. 'Shoun'. (Group 3) Late, large-flowered climber. From summer to early autumn, bears single flowers, to 8in (20cm) across, with broad, overlapping tepals of a uniformly soft lavender, with darker veins, and white stamens. ↕ to 12ft (4m), ↔ 3ft (1m). Zone 4.
C. 'Silver Moon' ■ (Group 2) Very compact, early, large-flowered climber. In early summer, produces single flowers, 4–6in (10–15cm) across, with overlapping, silver-mauve tepals and cream anthers. ↕ 6ft (2m), ↔ 3ft (1m). Zone 4.
C. 'Snow Queen'. (Group 2) Early, large-flowered climber. Single flowers, 6–7in (15–18cm) across, with pointed white tepals, tinged bluish pink, and red anthers, are borne in early summer. Late-summer flowers have hints of pink. ↕ 8ft (2.5m), ↔ 3ft (1m). Zone 4.
C. 'Star of India'. (Group 3) Vigorous, late, large-flowered climber. Deep purple-blue flowers, 3–4in (8–10cm) across, with deep carmine-red central bands and light brown anthers, are produced in midsummer. ↕ 10ft (3m), ↔ 3ft (1m). Zone 4.
C. 'Summer Snow' see *C.* x *fargesioides* 'Paul Farges'.
C. 'Sunset'. (Group 3) Late, large-flowered climber bearing single, bright red flowers, 4–5in (10–13cm) across, with yellow anthers, in midsummer. ↕ 8ft (2.5m), ↔ 3ft (1m). Zone 4.
C. tangutica ■ (Russian virgin's bower). (Group 3) Vigorous, late-flowering climber. Abundant, solitary, bell-shaped yellow flowers, 1½in (4cm) long, are produced from midsummer to late autumn, followed by fluffy seed heads. ↕ 15–20ft (5–6m), ↔ 6–10ft (2–3m). W. China. Zone 1b.
C. terniflora, syn. *C. dioscoreifolia*, *C. maximowicziana*, *C. paniculata*

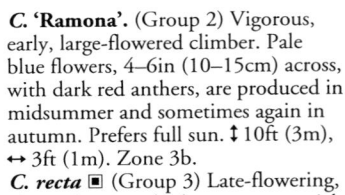

Clematis 'Perrin's Pride'

(Sweet autumn clematis). (Group 3) Deciduous or semi-evergreen, late-flowering climber with deep green leaves, sometimes with silver central bands. Numerous, fragrant, star-shaped white flowers, ¾–1¼in (2–3cm) across, are borne in panicles from late summer to autumn, followed by attractive seed heads. Prefers full sun. ↕ 15–20ft (5–6m), ↔ 6–10ft (2–3m). Japan. Zone 2.
C. texensis (Leather flower, Scarlet clematis, Texas clematis). (Group 3) Late-flowering climber with fully divided, 4- to 8-palmate, hairless, blue-green leaves. In summer, bears solitary, bell-shaped, reddish orange to scarlet flowers, ¾–1in (2–2.5cm) across, with thick tepals. ↕ 6–15ft (2–5m), ↔ 20in (50cm). S.W. US. Zone 2. Many of the cultivars ascribed to *C. texensis* are of hybrid origin, and are listed here under their cultivar names. **'Duchess of Albany'** see *C.* 'Duchess of Albany'. **'Gravetye Beauty'** see *C.* 'Gravetye Beauty'. **'Sir Trevor Lawrence'** is a semi-herbaceous, small-flowered climber with green, pinnate or ternate leaves. Tulip-shaped, deep carmine flowers, 2in (5cm) long, with yellow anthers. Prefers sun. ↕ 6–8ft (2–2.5m), ↔ 3ft (1m).

Clematis 'Perle d'Azur'

Clematis 'Walter Pennell'

***C.* 'The First Lady'.** (Group 2) Free-flowering, early, large-flowered climber producing silvery blue flowers, 8–12in (20–30cm) across, with magenta-red anthers, in early summer and early autumn. ↕ 7–9ft (2.2–2.5m), ↔ 3ft (1m). Zone 4.
***C.* 'The President'** ■ (Group 2) Free-flowering, early, large-flowered climber bearing single, rich purple flowers, 4–6in (10–15cm) across, with silver undersides and red anthers, in early summer. ↕ 6–10ft (2–3m), ↔ 3ft (1m). Zone 3b.
***C. tibetana* subsp. *vernayi* 'Orange Peel'**, syn. *C. orientalis* 'Orange Peel'. (Group 3) Vigorous, late, small-flowered climber. Bell-shaped, nodding flowers, 1½in (4cm) long, each with 4 thick yellow tepals and a dark center, are produced from midsummer. Flowers are followed by attractive seed heads from late summer to winter. Often confused with other selections from the original collection in the wild. ↕ 20ft (6m), ↔ 6ft (2m). Zone 5.
***C.* 'Venosa Violacea'** ■ syn. *C. viticella* 'Venosa Violacea'. (Group 3) Late, small-flowered climber. Single, saucer-shaped, purple-veined white flowers, 3in (8cm) across, with boat-shaped tepals and bluish black anthers, are produced from midsummer to late autumn. ↕ 10ft (3m), ↔ 3ft (1m). Zone 2.
***C.* 'Victoria'.** (Group 3) Vigorous, late, large-flowered climber producing single, pinkish mauve flowers, 4in (10cm) across, with 4–6 tepals and light greenish brown anthers, in midsummer. ↕ 10ft (3m), ↔ 3ft (1m). Zone 3.

Clematis 'Westerplatte'

***C.* 'Ville de Lyon'** ■ (Group 3) Late, large-flowered climber. In midsummer, produces bright carmine-red flowers, 4–5in (10–13cm) across, with deeper-colored tepal margins and yellow anthers. Best grown through an evergreen shrub, since lower foliage may be scorched by late summer. ↕ 6–10ft (2–3m), ↔ 3ft (1m). Zone 3b.
***C.* 'Vino'.** (Group 2) Early, large-flowered climber. Single, purple-red flowers, 6in (15cm) across, with overlapping tepals and yellow anthers, are produced in early summer. ↕ 6–10ft (2–3m), ↔ 3ft (1m). Zone 4.
C. viticella. (Group 3) Late, small-flowered, semi-woody climber. Solitary, open bell-shaped, blue, purple, or rose-red flowers, 1½in (4cm) across, with pale yellow anthers, are produced from midsummer to early autumn. ↕ 6–12ft (2–4m), ↔ 5ft (1.5m). Central S. Europe. Zone 3. Many of the cultivars ascribed to *C. viticella* are of hybrid origin, and are listed here under their cultivar names. **'Abundance'** see *C.* 'Abundance'. **'Alba Luxurians'** see *C.* 'Alba Luxurians'. **'Betty Corning'** see *C.* 'Betty Corning'. **'Blue Belle'** Vigorous, free-flowering, deciduous, with gray-green, pinnate leaves. Bears single, deep purple flowers, 3–4in (8–10cm) across, with yellow anthers. ↕ 7–10ft (2.2–3m), ↔ 3ft (1m). **'Etoile Violette'** see *C.* 'Etoile Violette'. **'Little Nell'.** Deciduous, small-flowered climber with green, pinnate leaves. Bears single, deep purple flowers, 3–4in (8–10cm) across, with yellow anthers. ↕ 7–10ft (2.2–3m), ↔ 3ft (1m). **'Margot Koster'** Vigorous, free-flowering, deciduous, small-flowered climber with green, pinnate leaves. Bears single, bright pink flowers, 3–4in (8–10cm) across, with twisted tepals and green anthers. ↕ 6–9ft (2–2.5m), ↔ 3ft (1m). **'Minuet'** see *C.* 'Minuet'. **'Mme. Julia Correvon'** see *C.* 'Mme. Julia Correvon'. **'Polish Spirit'** see *C.* 'Polish Spirit'. **'Purpurea Plena Elegans'** ■ syn. *C.* 'Purpurea Plena Elegans', bears abundant double flowers, 2–3in (5–8cm) across, with many purplish mauve tepals, occasionally green outer tepals, and no anthers, midsummer to late autumn; ↕ 10ft (3m), ↔ 3ft (1m). **'Venosa Violacea'** see *C.* 'Venosa Violacea'.
***C.* 'Voluceau'.** (Group 3) Deciduous, large-flowered climber with green, ternate leaves. Single, dark red flowers, 6–7in (15–18cm) across, with a reddish purple bar and yellow anthers are produced. ↕ 6–9ft (2–2.5m), ↔ 3ft (1m). Zone 4.
***C.* 'Vyvyan Pennell'.** (Group 2) Early, large-flowered climber. In early summer, bears double lilac flowers, 4–5in (10–13cm) across, with central, lavender-blue rosettes, golden yellow anthers, and occasionally green outer tepals. Midsummer flowers are blue-mauve. ↕ 6–10ft (2–3m), ↔ 3ft (1m). Zone 3b.
***C.* 'Walter Pennell'** ■ (Group 2) Deciduous, large-flowered climber with green, ternate leaves. Produces double and single, mauve-pink flowers, 5–7in (13–18cm) across, with a darker bar and buff anthers. ↕ 6–8ft (2–2.5m), ↔ 3ft (1m). Zone 4.
***C.* 'Warsaw Nike'** see *C.* 'Warszawska Nike'.
***C.* 'Warszawska Nike'**, syn. *C.* 'Warsaw Nike'. (Group 3) Late, large-flowered climber, freely producing rich velvet-purple flowers, 4in (10cm) across, with yellow anthers, in midsummer. ↕ 6–10ft (2–3m), ↔ 3ft (1m). Zone 4.
***C.* 'W.E. Gladstone'.** (Group 2 or 3) Deciduous, large-flowered climber with green, ternate and simple leaves. Bears single, lilac blue flowers, 6–8in (15–20cm) across, with red anthers. ↕ 6–8ft (2–2.5m), ↔ 3ft (1m). Zone 4.
***C.* 'Westerplatte'** ■ Compact, deciduous, large-flowered climber. Single, velvet red flowers, 4–5in (10–13cm) across, have overlapping tepals and red anthers. ↕ 6ft (2m), ↔ 3ft (1m). Zone 3b.
***C.* 'White Swan'** see *C. macropetala* 'White Swan'.
***C.* 'Will Goodwin'.** (Group 2) Deciduous, large-flowered climber with green, simple and ternate leaves. Bears single, pale lavender blue flowers, 6–8in (15–20cm) across, with wavy-edged tepals and cream anthers. ↕ 6–8ft (2–2.5m), ↔ 3ft (1m). Zone 4.
***C.* 'William Kennett'.** (Group 2 or 3)Deciduous, large-flowered climber with green, simple and ternate leaves. Bears single, pale lavender blue flowers, 7–8in (18–20cm) across, with reddish purple anthers. ↕ 6–8ft (2–2.5m), ↔ 3ft (1m). Zone 3b.

CLEOME

Spider flower

CAPPARIDACEAE

Genus of 150 species of robust annuals and evergreen shrubs from sandy, free-draining soils on plains and in mountain valleys in tropical and subtropical zones worldwide. Only the annuals are commonly cultivated; they are valued for their terminal racemes of spider-like, 4-petaled flowers, with prominent stamens, which are borne above 3- to 7-palmate leaves. Grow in a summer flower border or as a seasonal filler for a mixed or herbaceous border. May self-seed and become invasive in warm climates. Flowers for cutting in summer may also be grown in a cool greenhouse.
• **CULTIVATION** Under glass, grow in soil-based potting mix in full light. In the growing season, water freely and apply a balanced liquid fertilizer every 3–4 weeks. Outdoors, grow in light, fertile, preferably sandy, free-draining soil in full sun. Water freely in dry weather.
• **PROPAGATION** Sow seed at 64°F (18°C) or *in situ* in spring. Harden off and plant out after danger of frost has passed.
• **PESTS AND DISEASES** Prone to caterpillars, aphids, spider mites, and whiteflies, as well as a variety of fungal spots, rust, and sometimes powdery or downy mildew.

Cleome hassleriana 'Rose Queen'

C. hassleriana, syn. *C. pungens* of gardens, *C. spinosa* of gardens (Spider flower). Erect annual with hairy stems and 5- to 7-palmate, minutely toothed, glandular-hairy leaves, to 5in (13cm) long, with ovate to lance-shaped leaflets and spines at the base of each leaf stalk. Strongly scented, white to pink or purple flowers, to 1¼in (3cm) across, with oblong to rounded petals, are produced in dense, terminal racemes in summer. ↕ to 5ft (1.5m), ↔ to 18in (45cm). S. Brazil, Paraguay, Argentina, Uruguay. ❀ (min. 39°F/4°C). **'Colour Fountain'** has delicate, narrow-petaled, scented, pink, violet-pink, rose-red, or white flowers, to 4in (10cm) across; ↕ to 4ft (1.2m). **'Helen Campbell'** has white flowers. **'Pink Queen'** produces free-flowering, fragrant, non-fading pink flowers. **'Rose Queen'** ■ bears abundant open, spidery, fragrant, non-fading rose-pink flowers, 5–6in (13–15cm) across.
***C. pungens* of gardens** see *C. hassleriana.*
***C. spinosa* of gardens** see *C. hassleriana.*

CLERODENDRUM

VERBENACEAE

Genus of about 400 species of deciduous and evergreen trees, shrubs, and climbers, mainly found in woodland in tropical and subtropical regions, particularly in Africa and Asia. They are cultivated for their terminal or axillary cymes, panicles, or corymbs of showy, usually salverform, often fragrant flowers with cylindrical tubes and protruding stamens. The leaves are arranged in whorls or opposite pairs. The shrubs are suitable for a border. Train the climbers over a trellis, pergola, or other support. Where not hardy, grow in a warm greenhouse or conservatory.
• **CULTIVATION** Under glass, grow in large barrels of soil-based potting mix in full light, with shade from hot sun and good ventilation in summer. In growth, water freely and apply a balanced liquid fertilizer monthly; water sparingly in winter. Outdoors, grow in fertile, humus-rich, moist but well-drained soil in full sun. May become invasive by suckering. Pruning group 11 for climbers (immediately after flowering); group 1 for deciduous shrubs or trees; group 9 for evergreen shrubs; group 6 for *C. bungei.* Shrubs under glass may need restrictive pruning.
• **PROPAGATION** Sow seed at 55–64°F (13–18°C) in spring. Remove suckers from shrubs or trees in autumn or spring. Root semi-ripe cuttings with bottom heat in summer. Insert root cuttings in winter.
• **PESTS AND DISEASES** Whiteflies, mealybugs, and aphids are common. Galls, cankers, and a few leaf spots can occur.

C

Clerodendrum bungei

C. bungei ■ (Glory bower). Deciduous, suckering shrub producing upright shoots and opposite, ovate, toothed, dark green leaves, to 8in (20cm) long, tinged with purple when young. Salverform, very fragrant, dark pink flowers, each with 5 spreading lobes, are borne in rounded, terminal panicles, 5–6in (12–15cm) across, from late summer to autumn. ↕↔ 6ft (2m) or more. China. Zone 8.
C. fallax see *C. speciosissimum.*
***C. fragrans* 'Pleniflorum'** see *C. philippinum.*
***C. myricoides* 'Ugandense'** see *C. ugandense.*
C. paniculatum (Pagoda flower). Erect, open, evergreen shrub bearing opposite, ovate, 5-lobed, deep green leaves, 4–6in (10–15cm) long, with heart-shaped bases; the upper leaves are toothed or entire. Salverform, long-tubed scarlet flowers are produced in terminal panicles, to 12in (30cm) long, from summer to autumn. ↕ 3–4½ft (1–1.3m), ↔ 24–36in (60–90cm). S.E. Asia. ❄ (min. 50–55°F/10–13°C)
C. philippinum, syn. *C. fragrans* 'Pleniflorum' (Glory bower). Erect, evergreen shrub with angular, downy stems and opposite, broadly ovate, toothed, mid- to deep green leaves, to 10in (25cm) long. Terminal corymbs, 3–4in (7–10cm) across, of many fragrant, salverform, double, pink or white flowers, sometimes blue-tinted, are produced in summer. ↕ 6–10ft (2–3m), ↔ 5–8ft (1.5–2.5m). S. China. ❄ (min. 50–55°F/10–13°C)
C. speciosissimum, syn. *C. fallax* (Glory bower, Java glorybean). Erect, open,

Clerodendrum thomsoniae

Clerodendrum trichotomum

evergreen shrub with opposite, heart-shaped, corrugated, toothed, rich green leaves, to 12in (30cm) long. Bears tiered, terminal panicles, 8–12in (20–30cm) long, of salverform, bright scarlet flowers from summer to autumn. Bean-like fruit are dark blue. ↕ 3–12ft (1–4m), ↔ 3–6ft (1–2m). Indonesia (Java). ❄ (min. 50–55°F/10–13°C)
C. splendens. Twining, evergreen climber with opposite, ovate to elliptic, entire, more or less glossy, rich green leaves, to 7in (18cm) long. Salverform, bright scarlet flowers are produced in dense, terminal panicles, 4–5in (10–13cm) long, mainly in summer. ↕ 10ft (3m) or more. Tropical W. Africa. ❄ (min. 50–55°F/10–13°C)
C. thomsoniae ■ (Glory bower). Twining, evergreen climber with opposite, ovate, entire, rich green leaves, to 7in (18cm) long. Terminal and axillary panicles, 4in (10cm) across, of flowers with bell-shaped, pure white calyces and rich crimson petals are produced freely in summer. ↕ to 12ft (4m). Tropical W. Africa. ❄ (min. 50–55°F/10–13°C)
C. trichotomum ■ Upright, bushy, deciduous shrub or small tree with opposite, ovate, entire or sparsely toothed, dark green leaves, to 8in (20cm) long. From late summer to midautumn, bears salverform, fragrant white flowers with red sepals in erect, axillary cymes, to 8in (20cm) across; berries are bright blue. ↕↔ 15–20ft (5–6m). China, Japan. Zone 6.
var. *fargesii* has bronze young leaves, and flowers with green sepals; China.
C. ugandense ■ syn. *C. myricoides* 'Ugandense' (Blue glory bower). Scandent, evergreen climber with opposite, elliptic to narrowly obovate, boldly toothed, bright green leaves, 3–4in (7–10cm) long. Bears terminal panicles, 4–6in (10–15cm) long, of 5-petaled, blue to violet, sometimes blue and white flowers, each with long lower lips, from summer to autumn. ↕ 10–12ft (3–4m). Tropical Africa. ❄ (min. 50°F/10°C)

CLETHRA

Summersweet, Sweet pepperbush, White alder

CLETHRACEAE

Genus of more than 60 species of deciduous and evergreen trees and shrubs, occurring in woodland, swamps, and rocky places in E. Asia and North America, with one species (*C. arborea*) from Madeira. The leaves are alternate, simple, obovate to oblong, rarely lance-shaped, finely to coarsely toothed, and mid- to dark green. Clethras are grown for their fragrant, bell- to cup-shaped, white or yellowish white flowers, borne in racemes or panicles, and are suitable for a woodland garden or a mixed border. Where not hardy, grow *C. arborea* in a cool greenhouse or conservatory; it may be moved outdoors during summer.
• **CULTIVATION** Under glass, grow in acidic potting mix in bright filtered light. In growth, water freely and apply a balanced liquid fertilizer monthly; water sparingly in winter. Outdoors, grow in acidic, fertile, humus-rich,

Clerodendrum ugandense

Clethra alnifolia

moist but well-drained soil in partial or dappled shade. Pruning group 1 for deciduous species. For *C. alnifolia*, remove some of the oldest wood from the base in winter, leaving the strongest shoots as replacement growth. Pruning group 9 for *C. arborea*; needs restrictive pruning under glass.
• **PROPAGATION** Sow seed at 43–54°F (6–12°C) in spring or autumn, or sow seed of hardy species in containers outdoors in spring or autumn. Root greenwood cuttings of deciduous species in early summer, and semi-ripe cuttings of evergreens in mid- or late summer.
• **PESTS AND DISEASES** Fungal dieback and root rot can occur.

C. acuminata (Cinnamon clethra). Medium-sized, suckering shrub or small tree with cinnamon-brown bark and alternate, elliptic to oblong, simple, lustrous dark green leaves, 3–6in (8–15cm) long. In midsummer, bears long, solitary, terminal racemes, 3–8in (8–20cm) long, of fragrant white flowers, ¼in (6mm) across. ↕↔ 8–12ft (2.5–4m). West Virginia to Alabama. Zone 6.
C. alnifolia ■ (Sweet pepperbush). Upright, suckering, deciduous shrub with oval, mid-green leaves, often turning yellow in autumn, to 4in (10cm) long. In late summer and early autumn, bears bell-shaped, fragrant white flowers, to ½in (1.5cm) across, in dense, upright, terminal racemes, to 6in (15cm) long. ↕↔ 8ft (2.5m). E. US. Zone 5. **'Hummingbird'** is compact; ↕ 24–36in (60–90cm).
'Paniculata', syn. *C. paniculata*, bears

Clethra arborea

Clethra delavayi

abundant white flowers in broad panicles, to 4in (10cm) across. **'Pink Spires'** has flowers with rose buds, opening to soft pink.
C. arborea ▣ (Lily of the valley tree). Broadly conical, evergreen shrub or tree with red young shoots and oval, dark green leaves, to 6in (15cm) long. Cup-shaped, very fragrant white flowers, to ⅜in (8mm) across, are produced in lax, terminal racemes, to 6in (15cm) long, from late summer to midautumn. ↕ 25ft (8m), ↔ 20ft (6m). Madeira. ❁ (min. 45°F/7°C)
C. barbinervis. Upright, deciduous shrub with attractive, peeling bark when mature, and obovate-elliptic, dark green leaves, to 5in (13cm) long, turning red and yellow in autumn. Bell-shaped white flowers, to ⅜in (8mm) across, are produced in arching, terminal racemes, to 6in (15cm) long, from late summer to autumn. ↕↔ 10ft (3m). E. China to Japan. Zone 7.
C. delavayi ▣ Upright, deciduous shrub with arching shoots and lance-shaped, rich blue-green leaves, to 6in (15cm) long. Nodding, cup-shaped white flowers, ½in (1.5cm) across, produced in dense, terminal racemes, to 10in (25cm) long, open from pink buds in midsummer. ↕↔ 12ft (4m). W. China. Zone 7b.
C. paniculata see *C. alnifolia* 'Paniculata'.

CLEYERA

THEACEAE

Genus of about 17 species of evergreen and deciduous trees and shrubs found in woodland from the Himalayas to Japan, and from Mexico to Central America. They have alternate, leathery, usually linear to ovate-oblong, mid- to dark green leaves. *Cleyera* species and cultivars are grown for their attractive foliage and bowl-shaped, pale yellow to creamy white flowers, which may be borne singly or in clusters from the leaf axils of the previous year's wood. Suitable for a shrub border or for growing against a wall. Where not hardy, grow *C. japonica* 'Tricolor' in a cool greenhouse.
• **CULTIVATION** Under glass, grow in acidic potting mix in full light, with shade from hot sun. In growth, water freely and apply a balanced liquid fertilizer monthly; water sparingly in winter. Outdoors, grow in acidic, moderately fertile, humus-rich, moist but well-drained soil in sun or partial shade, sheltered from cold, dry winds. Pruning group 8; may need restrictive pruning under glass.
• **PROPAGATION** Root semi-ripe cuttings in summer.
• **PESTS AND DISEASES** Root rot and leaf spot can occur.

***C. fortunei* 'Variegata'** see *C. japonica* 'Tricolor'.
C. japonica. Bushy, evergreen shrub with narrowly oblong to ovate-oblong, glossy, dark green leaves, to 4in (10cm) long. Bowl-shaped, fragrant, creamy white flowers, ½in (1.5cm) across, are produced singly or in threes from the leaf axils in summer, occasionally followed in autumn by small red fruit, ¼–⅜in (6–9mm) across, ripening to black. ↕↔ 10ft (3m). Burma, China, Korea, Japan. ❁ (min. 45°F/7°C). **'Tricolor'**, syn. *C. fortunei* 'Variegata', has young leaves tinged with pink, maturing to green with creamy white margins; ↕↔ 6ft (2m).

CLIANTHUS

FABACEAE

Genus of 2 species of evergreen, trailing or climbing shrubs or subshrubs found in semi-desert or warm-temperate scrub or woodland in Australia and New Zealand. They have alternate, pinnate, mid- to dark green leaves and showy flowers resembling lobsters' claws. Where not hardy, *C. formosus* is excellent for a hanging basket in a temperate greenhouse or conservatory; in warmer areas, grow in a raised bed or terrace planting. *C. puniceus* is suitable for training against a wall; where not hardy, it needs the protection of a cool greenhouse or conservatory.
• **CULTIVATION** Under glass, grow in soil-based potting mix, with additional grit, in full light. In the growing season, provide moderate humidity, water freely (avoiding the foliage), and apply a balanced liquid fertilizer monthly; water sparingly and maintain low humidity in winter. Outdoors, grow in well-drained soil in full sun with shelter from cold, drying winds. If damaged by winter cold, *C. puniceus* often sprouts from the base in spring; provide a deep, dry winter mulch. Generally best with little pruning. *C. formosus* requires little regular pruning (except trimming). Pruning group 11 (or 13 if wall grown) for *C. puniceus* and cultivars, immediately

Clianthus formosus

Clianthus puniceus f. *albus*

after flowering; cut back flowered shoots by no more than one-third their length.
• **PROPAGATION** Sow seed at 55–64°F (13–18°C) in spring. Root semi-ripe cuttings of *C. puniceus* in summer. For hanging baskets, *C. formosus* is best grafted onto *Colutea arborescens* seedling rootstock in spring; on its own roots, it is very sensitive to overwatering.
• **PESTS AND DISEASES** Infrequent.

C. dampieri see *C. formosus.*
C. formosus ▣ syn. *C. dampieri* (Glory pea, Sturt's desert pea). Prostrate annual or short-lived perennial subshrub with densely silky-gray and downy leaves, 5–7in (12–18cm) long, with 9–21 oval leaflets. In summer, bears elongated, lobsterclaw-like, brilliant crimson and black flowers, 2–3in (5–8cm) long, in racemes 3–5in (8–13cm) long. ↕ to 8in (20cm), ↔ 3ft (1m) or more. N. Australia. ❁ (min. 45–50°F/7–10°C)
C. puniceus (Glory pea, Lobster claw, Parrot's bill). Evergreen shrub with climbing shoots and dark green leaves, to 6in (15cm) long, with 13–25 narrowly oblong leaflets. From spring to early summer, bears lobsterclaw-like, brilliant red flowers, to 3in (8cm) long, in pendent racemes, to 6in (15cm) long. ↕ 12ft (4m), ↔ 10ft (3m). New Zealand (North Island). Zone 8. **f. *albus*** ▣ has white flowers often flushed green. **f. *albus* 'White Heron'** bears abundant pure white flowers. **'Flamingo'** see 'Roseus'. **'Red Cardinal'** has brilliant scarlet flowers. **'Roseus'**, syn. 'Flamingo', has dark rose-pink flowers.

▷ ***Clinopodium acinos*** see *Acinos arvensis*
▷ ***Clinopodium grandiflorum*** see *Calamintha grandiflora*

CLINTONIA

LILIACEAE

Genus of 5 species of rhizomatous herbaceous perennials from woodland in the Himalayas, E. Asia, and North America. They have basal clumps of elliptic to broadly ovate, entire, glossy, pale to mid-green leaves. Bell- to star-shaped flowers are borne on upright stems in racemes or umbels, or occasionally singly; they are followed by spherical, fleshy berries. Grow in a woodland garden.
• **CULTIVATION** Grow in leafy, fertile, humus-rich, moist, neutral to acidic soil in partial or full shade. Mulch with leaf mold or compost in spring.

Clintonia andrewsiana

Clintonia borealis

• **PROPAGATION** Sow seed in containers of soilless seed-starting mix in a cold frame in autumn. Divide in spring; plants may be slow to re-establish.
• **PESTS AND DISEASES** Slugs and snails often attack new growth, and rust may be a problem.

C. alpina see *C. udensis.*
C. andrewsiana ▣ Clump-forming perennial with elliptic to broadly ovate, hairy-margined, glossy, rich green leaves, to 10in (25cm) long. In early summer, bears bell-shaped, pink-purple flowers, ¾–1in (2–2.5cm) long, in terminal umbels, sometimes with secondary umbels beneath, followed by deep blue berries. ↕ to 24in (60cm), ↔ to 10in (25cm). California. Zone 6.
C. borealis ▣ (Bluebead lily, Corn lily). Clump-forming perennial with inversely lance-shaped to obovate, glossy, pale green leaves, 4–12in (10–30cm) long, fringed with minute hairs. Bears loose, terminal umbels of nodding, bell-shaped, greenish yellow flowers, ½–¾in (1–2cm) long, in late spring and early summer, followed by blue or white berries. ↕ to 12in (30cm), ↔ to 8in (20cm). E. North America. Zone 4.
C. udensis, syn. *C. alpina.* Clump-forming perennial with inversely lance-shaped to obovate or oblong, hairy-margined, glossy, mid-green leaves, 3–14in (8–35cm) long. In summer, bears bell-shaped, white, yellow-green, or pale lilac flowers, to ½in (1.5cm) long, in lax, terminal, umbel-like racemes, followed by deep blue-purple berries. ↕ to 12in (30cm), ↔ to 8in

(20cm). Russia (Siberia), E. Himalayas, Japan. Zone 6.

C. uniflora (Bride's bonnet, Queencup). Spreading perennial with inversely lance-shaped to obovate, glossy, mid-green leaves, 3–6in (7–15cm) long, hairy beneath. Erect, star-shaped, pure white flowers, to 1in (2.5cm) across, are produced singly in the upper leaf axils in late spring, followed by blue-black berries. ↕ 8in (20cm), ↔ 6in (15cm). W. North America. Zone 5.

CLITORIA

FABACEAE

Genus of 70 species of mainly evergreen perennials, shrubs, and climbers found in forest margins, thickets, and scrub in tropical regions. The leaves are alternate and pinnate or 3-palmate. Pea-like flowers, with incurved, keeled petals, are borne singly or in racemes from the leaf axils. Where temperatures fall below 61°F (16°C), grow in a warm greenhouse or conservatory; in warmer areas, grow on a trellis or through a vigorous tree or shrub.

• **CULTIVATION** Under glass, grow in soil-based potting mix in full light. During the growing season, water moderately and apply a balanced liquid fertilizer monthly. Water sparingly in winter. Pot on or top-dress in spring. Outdoors, grow in fertile, moist but well-drained, loamy soil in full sun. Provide support for climbers. Pruning group 11, in spring.

• **PROPAGATION** Sow seed at 66–75°F (19–24°C) in spring.

• **PESTS AND DISEASES** Prone to spider mites, whiteflies, and sometimes bacterial soft rot and anthracnose.

C. ternatea (Blue pea, Butterfly pea). Slender, trailing or scandent, evergreen climber, sometimes a short-lived perennial but often treated as an annual or biennial. Pinnate leaves, 2½–5in (6–13cm) long, each have 5–9 elliptic to ovate, rich green leaflets. Bears clear blue flowers, 1¼–2in (3–5cm) across, with yellow-tinted white centers, singly or in pairs, from summer to autumn. ↕ to 10ft (3m), ↔ 6ft (2m) as a trailer. Tropical Asia. ❀ (min. 61°F/16°C)

CLIVIA

AMARYLLIDACEAE

Genus of 4 species of evergreen perennials from low-lying woodland, often by streams, in South Africa. They have swollen, bulb-like bases and are grown for their arching, narrowly lance-shaped to strap-shaped, dark green, basal leaves and robust, tubular to trumpet-shaped, colorful flowers, borne in umbels on thick stems. Where not hardy, grow in a conservatory or warm greenhouse, or as houseplants. In hot climates, grow in a border or bed, or among shrubs. All parts of *C. miniata* may cause mild stomach upset if ingested, and the sap may irritate skin.

• **CULTIVATION** Under glass, grow in soil-based potting mix, with additional leaf mold and grit, in bright filtered or indirect light. In the growing season, water freely, applying a balanced liquid fertilizer weekly until the flower buds form; water very sparingly in winter.

Clivia miniata

Outdoors, grow in fertile, humus-rich, well-drained soil in partial shade. Established clivias resent root disturbance and need a restricted root run to encourage flowering.

• **PROPAGATION** Sow seed at 61–70°F (16–21°C) as soon as ripe. Divide in late winter or early spring.

• **PESTS AND DISEASES** Bacterial and fungal spots are common, as well as virus-like diseases. Mealybugs can occur.

C. caulescens. Evergreen perennial with strap-shaped leaves, to 6ft (1.8m) long. Umbels of 15–20 pendent, narrowly funnel-shaped, orange, red, or pinkish red flowers, 1½–1¾in (4–4.5cm) long, are produced from spring to summer. ↕ 20in (50cm), ↔ 12in (30cm). South Africa. ❀ (min. 50°F/10°C)

C. × cyrtanthiflora (*C. miniata* × *C. nobilis*). Evergreen perennial with strap-shaped leaves, 12–24in (30–60cm) long. From summer to autumn, bears umbels of 40–60 semi-pendent, trumpet-shaped, rich salmon-pink to yellowish green flowers, 1½–3in (4–8cm) long. ↕ 12–16in (30–40cm), ↔ 12in (30cm). South Africa. ❀ (min. 50°F/10°C)

Clivia miniata 'Aurea'

C. gardenii. Evergreen perennial with narrowly lance-shaped leaves, 30in (75cm) long. Umbels of 10–20 pendent, narrowly funnel-shaped, often strongly curved, orange or red flowers, 1½–2½in (4–6cm) long, tipped with green, are produced from winter to spring. ↕ 18–30in (45–75cm), ↔ 12in (30cm). South Africa. ❀ (min. 50°F/10°C)

C. miniata ▣ Evergreen perennial with strap-shaped leaves, to 24in (60cm) long. Bears large umbels of up to 20 semi-pendent, open tubular to funnel-shaped, yellow, red, or orange flowers, 2–3in (5–8cm) long, from spring to summer. ↕ 18in (45cm), ↔ 12in (30cm). South Africa. ❀ (min. 50°F/10°C). **'Aurea'** ▣ produces yellow flowers; several different color selections are offered under this name.

C. nobilis ▣ Evergreen perennial bearing strap-shaped leaves, 18in (45cm) long. In spring and summer, produces umbels of 40–60 semi-pendent, narrowly trumpet-shaped, red and yellow flowers, 1–1½in (2.5–4cm) long, tipped with green. ↕ 16in (40cm), ↔ 12in (30cm). South Africa. ❀ (min. 50°F/10°C)

Clivia nobilis

CLUSIA

CLUSIACEAE

Genus of about 145 species of evergreen trees and shrubs, some epiphytic. Their simple, leathery leaves are borne in opposite pairs, and 4- to 9-petaled, magnolia-like flowers, are borne singly or in terminal clusters. Where not hardy, grow as foliage houseplants or in a warm or temperate greenhouse. In humid tropical climates, use them in a coastal garden or a shrub border, or for specimen planting.

• **CULTIVATION** Under glass, grow in soil-based potting mix, with additional sharp sand, in bright filtered light, with high humidity. Water freely and apply a balanced liquid fertilizer monthly from early summer to autumn; water moderately in winter. Top-dress or pot on in spring. Outdoors, grow in fertile, moist but well-drained soil in partial shade. Pruning group 1.

• **PROPAGATION** Sow seed at 66–75°F (19–24°C) in spring. Root softwood cuttings with bottom heat in summer. Air layer in spring or summer.

• **PESTS AND DISEASES** Root rot and leaf spot are common.

C. major. (Autograph tree, Balsam apple). Open, semi-epiphytic shrub or small tree with short-stalked, obovate, glossy, deep green leaves, 3–7in (8–18cm) long. Produces funnel-shaped, pink or creamy white flowers, 2–3in (5–8cm) across, in clusters of 1–3 in summer. ↕ 6–10ft (2–3m), ↔ 3–6ft (1–2m). Central to South America, W. Indies. ❀ (min. 61–64°F/16–18°C)

CNICUS

ASTERACEAE

Genus of one species of annual forb with spiny leaves and thistle-like flowers, grows in wasteland.

• **CULTIVATION** Grown as a winter or summer curiosity annual in herb gardens or natural areas. It may seed freely if not dead-headed and can become invasive.

• **PROPAGATION** Sow seeds in situ in midspring, blooms in late summer.

• **PESTS AND DISEASES** Infrequent.

C. benedictus (Blessed thistle). Branching, robust forb, with alternate, deeply toothed, spiny, white-veined leaves on a sturdy stem. The yellow thistle-like flowers are solitary, with large bracts. Mediterranean, Near East. ↕ 16–24in (40–60cm) ↔ 12in (30cm). Asia.

CLYTOSTOMA

BIGNONIACEAE

Genus of 9 species of evergreen, perennial climbers found in forests in tropical North and South America. The mid- to dark green leaves, borne in opposite pairs, are composed of 2 leaflets and a tendril. They are cultivated for their flowers, borne in pairs or clusters from the leaf axils. In warmer areas, grow as a groundcover or climber.

• **CULTIVATION** Under glass, grow in soil-based potting mix, with added leaf mold and sharp sand; provide full light, with shade from hot sun and moderate humidity. In growth, water freely and

Clytostoma callistegioides

apply a balanced liquid fertilizer monthly; water moderately in winter. Pot on in late winter or spring. Outdoors, grow in fertile, moist but well-drained soil in partial shade or full sun with some mid-day shade. Pruning group 11.
• **PROPAGATION** Sow seed at 55–64°F (13–18°C) in spring. Root short-jointed, lateral shoots in summer.
• **PESTS AND DISEASES** Spider mites, whiteflies, and mealybugs under glass.

C. callistegioides ■ Vigorous, open climber, with oblong-elliptic, lustrous, deep green leaves, 3–4in (8–10cm) long. Two-lipped purple flowers, 3in (8cm) long, with lilac-veined, often pale yellow tubes, in summer. ↕ to 30ft (10m). S. Brazil to Argentina. ❄ (min. 45–50°F/7–10°C)

COBAEA

POLEMONIACEAE

Genus of about 20 species of woody, evergreen and herbaceous climbers found in forest and thickets from Mexico to tropical South America. They have alternate, pinnate leaves, each with a terminal, branched tendril. Large, 5-lobed, bell-shaped flowers are borne singly from the upper leaf axils. Where not hardy, grow in a cool greenhouse or conservatory, or as annuals. In warmer areas, use to clothe a pergola or tree.

Cobaea scandens

• **CULTIVATION** Under glass, grow in soil-based potting mix in full light. In the growing season, water freely and apply a low-nitrogen liquid fertilizer monthly; water sparingly in winter. Top-dress or pot on in spring. Outdoors, grow in moderately fertile, moist but well-drained soil in a sheltered site in full sun. Pruning group 11, after flowering or in late winter or early spring.
• **PROPAGATION** Sow seed at 64°F (18°C) in spring; plant out when danger of frost has passed. Root softwood cuttings with bottom heat in summer.
• **PESTS AND DISEASES** Susceptible to spider mites under glass.

C. scandens ■ (Cathedral bell, Cup and saucer vine). Vigorous, erect, dense, semi-woody, evergreen, perennial climber, grown as an annual. Each leaf, to 4½in (11cm) long, has 4 oblong-elliptic, rich green leaflets, 2 basal stipules, and a large, branched tendril with tiny hooks. From summer to autumn, bears fragrant flowers, 2in (5cm) long, opening creamy green and aging to purple. ↕ 30–70ft (10–20m). Mexico. ❄ (min. 41°F/5°C), although may survive short periods near 32°F (0°C). **f. *alba*** has white flowers, aging to creamy white.

COCCOLOBA

Sea grape

POLYGONACEAE

Genus of 150 species of dioecious trees, shrubs, and climbers, mainly evergreen, from sandy seashores and humid regions of tropical and subtropical North, Central, and South America. They have alternate, variable, entire leaves. Their racemes, spikes, or panicles of green-white flowers are followed by grape-like, fleshy, black, brown, or purple fruits. Grow as a hedge, street tree, or specimen plant.
• **CULTIVATION** Under glass, grow in soil-based potting mix with added sand in full light at high humidity. In the growing season, water freely and apply a balanced liquid fertilizer weekly; water sparingly in winter. Outdoors, grow in moderately fertile, moist but well-drained soil in full sun. Pruning group 8; may need restrictive pruning under glass.
• **PROPAGATION** Sow seed at 70°F (20°C) in spring. Root softwood cuttings in a closed case with bottom heat in mid- or late spring, or layer.
• **PESTS AND DISEASES** Mushroom root rot, tip dieback, fungal and algal leaf spots, butt rot, gall midge, and aphids can be problems.

C. uvifera (Sea grape). Evergreen tree with rounded to heart-shaped, leathery, glossy, red-veined, bright green leaves, to 8in (20cm) long. From spring to summer, bears dense racemes, to 10in (25cm) long, of fragrant white flowers, to 2in (5cm) across, followed by clusters of grape-like, edible, spherical, purple fruit. Tolerates wind, strong sun, and salt spray. ↕ to 20ft (6m), ↔ 15–20ft (5–6m). S. Florida to South America. ❄ (min. 45°F/7°C)

COCCOTHRINAX

Thatch palm

ARECACEAE

Genus of 30–50 species of usually single-stemmed (rarely cluster-stemmed) palms occurring in dunes, scrub, and pine forest in Florida and the Caribbean. The flowers (with the 3 petals and sepals fused into 6-pointed, star-like disks) are borne in panicles among terminal clusters of stalked, fan-shaped leaves, with many slender, radiating lobes. Where not hardy, grow in a warm or temperate greenhouse, or as houseplants. Elsewhere, grow as specimen trees.
• **CULTIVATION** Under glass, grow in soil-based potting mix in full light, with shade from hot sun. In the growing season, water freely, and apply a balanced liquid fertilizer monthly; water sparingly in winter. Pot on or top-dress in spring. Outdoors, grow in neutral to alkaline, fertile, moist but well-drained soil in full sun.
• **PROPAGATION** Sow seed at 75–81°F (24–27°C) in spring.
• **PESTS AND DISEASES** Spider mites and scale insects, as well as false smut.

C. argentata (Florida silver palm). Single-stemmed palm with an erect gray trunk. Leaf stalks, to 24in (60cm) long, bear lustrous, yellow-green leaf blades, silvery white beneath, to 24in (60cm) across. Produces white flowers, ¼–½in (6–15mm) across, in panicles to 10ft (3m) long, in summer. ↕ to 25ft (8m), ↔ 6–10ft (2–3m). Florida, Bahamas. ❄ (min. 55°F/13°C)
C. fragrans (Silver thatch). Single-stemmed palm with a slender trunk, at first bearing a fibrous webbing of old leaf bases, then smooth. The leaf blades are light green above and silvery gray beneath, 16–24in (40–60cm) across, and borne on stalks of the same length. Produces fragrant yellow flowers, ¼–⅜in (6–8mm) across, in panicles to 6ft (2m) or more long, in summer. ↕ to 15ft (5m), ↔ 5–8ft (1.5–2.5m). Haiti, E. Cuba. ❄ (min. 55°F/13°C)
▷ ***Cochlearia armoracia*** see *Armoracia rusticana*

COCCULUS

MENISPERMACEAE

Genus of 11 species of deciduous and evergreen shrubs, trees, and climbing plants found in tropical areas of Africa, S. and E. Asia, and North America. They are grown for their glossy foliage and spherical red or black autumn fruits. Useful for covering a trellis or fence, but can be grown in a cool greenhouse.
• **CULTIVATION** Under glass, grow in soil-based potting mix in full light. Water freely in the growing season and apply a balanced liquid fertilizer monthly; water sparingly in winter. Outdoors, grow in moderately fertile, moist but well-drained soil in full sun to partial shade. Pruning group 1 for trees and shrubs; group 11 for climbers.
• **PROPAGATION** Sow seed *in situ* as soon as ripe. Root semi-ripe cuttings in a closed case, or take root cuttings of climbing species.
• **PESTS AND DISEASES** Leaf spots sometimes occur.

C. carolinus (Carolina moonseed). Climbing deciduous shrub with ovate to heart-shaped, mid-green leaves, to 4in (10cm) long, softly hairy beneath. In summer, bears tiny, greenish white flowers, ¼in (6mm) long, in panicles or racemes, to 5in (13cm) long, followed by dense clusters of spherical, bright red fruit, ¼in (6mm) across. ↕ to 12ft (4m), ↔ indefinite. S.E. US. Zone 6.

COCHLIODA

ORCHIDACEAE

Genus of about 6 species of evergreen, epiphytic orchids found at high altitudes in the Andes of Ecuador and Peru. One or two linear, dark green leaves, to 8in (20cm) long, are borne at the tip of each ovoid to conical pseudobulb. From late spring to summer, usually large, scarlet or bright pink flowers are borne in tall or short, arching racemes arising from the base of the pseudobulb.
• **CULTIVATION** Cool-growing orchids. Grow in epiphytic orchid potting mix in pots or slatted baskets. In summer, provide humid conditions with bright filtered light and good ventilation. Water freely, applying fertilizer at every third watering, and mist once or twice a day. In winter, admit full light and water sparingly. See also p.46.
• **PROPAGATION** Divide when the plant fills the container and flows over the sides.
• **PESTS AND DISEASES** Susceptible to spider mites, aphids, and mealybugs.

C. noezliana. Epiphytic orchid with ovoid, compressed pseudobulbs. Racemes, 6–18in (15–45cm) long, of up to 12 rich scarlet flowers, 1½in (4cm) across, are produced in summer. ↕ 5in (13cm), ↔ 10in (25cm). Peru. ❄ (min. 55°F/13°C; max 75°F/24°C)
C. rosea. Epiphytic orchid with ovoid, compressed pseudobulbs. Bears racemes, 5–16in (13–40cm) long, of up to 12 deep rose-pink flowers, 1½in (4cm) across, from spring to summer. ↕ 5in (13cm), ↔ 10in (25cm). Ecuador, Peru. ❄ (min. 55°F/13°C; max 75°F/24°C)

COCOS

Coconut

ARECACEAE

Genus of one species of single-stemmed palm from coastal tropical regions worldwide, possibly originating in the W. Pacific. Arching, pinnate leaves are borne in terminal heads. The 3-petaled flowers are produced in panicles from the leaf axils, followed by coconuts encased in thick, fibrous husks. Where not hardy, grow young specimens of *C. nucifera* as short-lived foliage plants in a warm greenhouse or conservatory, or as houseplants. In warmer areas, grow as a specimen or street tree.

• **CULTIVATION** Under glass, grow in soil-based potting mix with additional sharp sand and fibrous organic matter, in full or bright filtered light with moderate humidity. In the growing season, water moderately and apply a balanced liquid fertilizer monthly; water sparingly in winter. Pot on or top-dress in spring. Outdoors, grow in fertile, humus-rich, moist but well-drained soil in full sun.

• **PROPAGATION** Sow seed at 81–86°F (27–30°C) in spring.

• **PESTS AND DISEASES** Prone to scale insects and spider mites. Lethal yellows, tar spot, butt rot, false smut, other fungal spots, and viral diseases are common.

C. capitata see *Butia capitata.*

C. nucifera (Coconut). Large palm with a swollen, tapered base, an often-leaning gray trunk, and pinnate, bright green leaves, 12–20ft (4–6m) long, with many linear leaflets. Small, bowl-shaped, fragrant, cream to yellow flowers are borne at intervals throughout the year, followed by ovoid fruit, each with a green to ochre-yellow or orange-red exterior covering a fibrous brown husk. ↕70–100ft (20–30m), ↔ to 40ft (12m). Coastal tropical regions. ❀ (min. 64°F/18°C). **'Nino'** is dwarf and compact, with very narrow, lustrous leaflets; ↕ to 10ft (3m), ↔ 3ft (1m).

CODIAEUM

Croton

EUPHORBIACEAE

Genus of 6 species of evergreen shrubs, trees, and perennials from Malaysia and the larger islands in the E. Pacific, found in open forest, thickets, and scrub. They produce attractive, alternate, linear to broadly ovate, simple or shallowly to deeply lobed, leathery, often variegated leaves. Tiny, star-shaped yellow flowers are produced in axillary racemes intermittently throughout summer. Where not hardy, grow in a warm or temperate greenhouse, or as houseplants. In tropical or subtropical climates, grow in a shrub border or a courtyard garden, or as an informal hedge or screen. Contact with the foliage may aggravate skin allergies.

• **CULTIVATION** Under glass, grow in soil-based potting mix in full light, with shade from hot sun and high humidity. In growth, mist regularly, water freely, and apply a balanced liquid fertilizer every 2–3 weeks; water sparingly with tepid water in winter. Drafts and fluctuating temperatures cause leaf drop. Top-dress or pot on in spring.

Codiaeum 'Baronne de Rothschild'

Outdoors, grow in fertile, humus-rich, moist but well-drained soil in sun or partial shade. Pruning group 9; under glass, cut back leggy plants to within 3–5in (8–13cm) of soil level, and dust wounds with powdered charcoal.

• **PROPAGATION** Root softwood cuttings with bottom heat in summer, dipping the bases in charcoal to stop bleeding. Air layer in spring.

• **PESTS AND DISEASES** Prone to spider mites, scale insects, mealybugs, and caterpillars. Stem galls, root rot, and a wide variety of fungal and bacterial leaf spots are common.

***C.* 'Baronne de Rothschild'** ▣ Upright, woody-based perennial with ovate or lance-shaped leaves, 8in (20cm) long, green and yellow when young, maturing to rich red. Produces white flowers, ¼in (6mm) across, in summer. Rarely flowers in cultivation. ↕↔ to 5ft (1.5m). ❀ (min. 46°F/8°C)

***C.* 'Flamingo'** ▣ Upright, evergreen shrub or woody-based perennial with ovate leaves, 6–10in (15–25cm) long. Young leaves are mid-green, with cream veins, turning yellow and maturing to red or purple. Produces yellow flowers, ¼in (6mm) across, in summer. Rarely flowers in cultivation. ↕ 3–6ft (1–2m), ↔ to 3ft (1m). ❀ (min. 46°F/8°C)

***C. variegatum* var. *pictum*.** Upright, woody-based perennial with thick, ovate to linear, leathery leaves, to 12in (30cm) long, often deeply lobed, in various colors, usually green and yellow when young, maturing to shades of red. White flowers, ¼in (6mm) across, are borne in summer. ↕ 3–6ft (1–2m), ↔ 2–5ft (0.6–1.5m). ❀ (min. 50–55°F/10–13°C). **'Andreanum'** is compact and bushy, with oval, pointed, copper-flushed leaves, 4–8in (10–20cm) long, with yellow veins and margins, maturing to reddish orange; ↕ to 3ft (1m) or more, ↔ to 24in (60cm). **'Commotion'** has oval, slightly lobed or fiddle-shaped, rich bluish and bright green leaves, 4–8in (10–20cm) long, variegated pink, yellow, and cream, and maturing to crimson; ↔ 2–4ft (60–120cm). **'Evening Embers'** is dense and strong-growing, with oval, shallowly lobed, bluish black leaves, 6–10in (15–25cm) long, suffused and splashed red and green, with dark red veins; ↕ 5–6ft (1.5–2m), ↔ 2½–5ft (75–150cm). **'Imperiale'** is bushy, with elliptic leaves, 3–6in (8–15cm) long, which are almost entirely yellow at first, turning orange to

Codiaeum 'Flamingo'

red with green midribs; ↕ to 3ft (1m), ↔ to 30in (75cm). **'Majesticum'** has arching to pendent branches and linear, deep to olive-green leaves, to 10in (25cm) long, with yellow midribs, maturing to crimson; ↕↔ 3ft (1m) or more. **'Mrs. Iceton'** has oval, blackish green leaves, 4–6in (10–15cm) long, with yellow markings between the veins, aging to red and pink. **'Sunrise'** is strong-growing, with narrowly lance-shaped, rich green leaves, 4–8in (10–20cm) long, boldly veined and margined yellow, maturing to orange-red; ↔ 3–5ft (1–1.5m). **'Tortile'** has ribbon-like, spirally twisted, dark green leaves, 6–12in (15–30cm) long, variegated with orange-red; ↕↔ to 3ft (1m).

CODONANTHE

GESNERIACEAE

Genus of 13 species of epiphytic, creeping, evergreen shrubs and perennials found on forested hillsides from Mexico to S. Brazil. They have mainly elliptic to ovate or narrowly ovate, usually entire, fleshy leaves borne in opposite, equal- or very unequal-sized pairs. Flowers have curved corolla tubes, with wide yellow, sometimes red-speckled throats broadening to 5 petal lobes of white, pink, or pale or deep purple; they are solitary or borne in axillary cymes, and are followed by spherical, pink, red, or orange fruits. In the wild, ants collect the tiny, egg-like seeds and deposit them in their fertile nest walls, where they germinate quickly. Where not hardy, grow in a temperate green-house, or as houseplants in a container or hanging basket. In tropical areas, grow epiphytically or beneath shrubs in a shady border.

• **CULTIVATION** Under glass, grow in soilless potting mix in bright filtered light, with moderate to high humidity. In the growing season, mist regularly, water freely, and apply a half-strength balanced liquid fertilizer monthly; water moderately in winter. Outdoors, grow in moist, open, moderately fertile, humus-rich soil in partial shade. Prune only to restrict size.

• **PROPAGATION** Divide or root stem-tip cuttings at any time of year.

• **PESTS AND DISEASES** Mealybugs may be a problem.

***C. crassifolia*.** Epiphytic perennial with stems that are either prostrate and rooting at the nodes, or pendent. Elliptic to ovate, waxy, mid- to deep green leaves, 2in (5cm) or more long, have red glands beneath. Axillary cymes of 1–4 white flowers, ¾–1in (2–2.5cm) long, with yellow throats and sometimes pink-tinted petal lobes, are borne from spring to summer. ↕ 12in (30cm) or more, ↔ 24in (60cm) or more. Mexico to Brazil. ❀ (min. 59°F/15°C)

C. gracilis ▣ Epiphytic shrub with slender, prostrate or erect stems, bearing narrowly elliptic to ovate, stiffly and often sparsely hairy, mid- to deep green leaves, 1–1½in (2.5–4cm) long. In spring and summer, produces axillary cymes of 1 or 2 red- or maroon-spotted white flowers, ¾in (2cm) long, sometimes yellow at the bases. ↕↔ 12–36in (30–90cm). Brazil. ❀ (min. 59°F/15°C)

Codonanthe gracilis (inset: flower detail)

C

CODONOPSIS

CAMPANULACEAE

Genus of about 30 species of scandent or twining, mostly herbaceous perennials found on rocky mountain slopes or in alpine scrub from the Himalayas to Japan. Leaves are opposite or alternate, ovate or oblong to lance-shaped, and often malodorous when crushed. The flowers are usually solitary, terminal or axillary, nodding, and bell- or saucer-shaped, sometimes intricately marked inside. Grow smaller species in a rock garden, larger species in a herbaceous border or woodland garden, and scandent and twining species through small shrubs.

• **CULTIVATION** Grow in light, fertile, humus-rich, moist but well-drained soil in sun or partial shade, with shelter from strong winds to protect the slender, brittle shoots, especially those of *C. convolvulacea.* Most species need light, twiggy support. Where marginally hardy, mulch in winter.

• **PROPAGATION** Sow seed in containers in a cold frame in autumn or spring.

• **PESTS AND DISEASES** Susceptible to attack by slugs and snails. Spider mites may be a problem under glass.

C. clematidea ▣ Twining, herbaceous perennial climber with branching stems and alternate, narrowly ovate, slender-pointed, gray-green leaves, to 1in (2.5cm) long. Bears solitary, terminal, nodding, bell-shaped, pale greenish blue flowers, 1in (2.5cm) long, with yellow, blue, and black markings inside, in late summer. ↕ to 5ft (1.5m). C. Asia. Zone 6.

C. convolvulacea. Slender, twining, herbaceous perennial climber bearing opposite, ovate-lance-shaped to lance-shaped, mid-green leaves, ½–2in (1–5cm) long. Solitary, terminal, open bell- to saucer-shaped, violet-blue, occasionally white flowers, 1¼–2in (3–5cm) across, are produced in summer. ↕ to 6ft (2m). Himalayas, W. China. Zone 4.

C. meleagris. Upright, scandent herbaceous perennial with ovate, wavy, finely hairy, deep green leaves, ¾–3in (2–8cm) long, usually forming a basal rosette. In summer, branching stems bear solitary, axillary or terminal, nodding, bell-shaped, greenish blue flowers, heavily checkered purple and brown inside, 1–1½in (2.5–4cm) long. ↕↔ to 12in (30cm). China. Zone 7b.

Codonopsis clematidea

Codonopsis pilosula

C. ovata. Upright, non-twining herbaceous perennial with fleshy roots and mostly basal, opposite, ovate, very hairy, mid-green leaves, ½–1¼in (1–3cm) long. Solitary, terminal, tubular-bell-shaped, greenish blue flowers, 1–1¼in (2.5–3cm) long, checkered darker blue inside, are produced on slender stalks in mid- and late summer. Needs support. ↕↔ to 12in (30cm). W. Himalayas. Zone 7b.

C. pilosula ▣ Scandent, herbaceous, cool-weather perennial with large palmate leaves to 3in (8cm) long. Pendent, bell-shaped flowers are greenish white, often flushed mauve, prominent stamen. Vines can become invasive; training on a trellis or wall is recommended. Flowers in late summer give off a skunky smell. Roots (Dang Shen) are used in Chinese medicine. ↕ to 10ft (3m) ↔ 6–8in (15–20cm). Asia. Zone 6b.

C. tangshen. Herbaceous perennial climber with twining stems and alternate, broadly lance-shaped, fleshy, toothed, mid-green leaves, 1–2½in (2.5–6cm) long. Solitary, axillary or terminal, bell-shaped, yellow to olive-green flowers, with purple veins and spots inside, are produced in summer. ↕ 6ft (2m). W. China. Zone 4.

C. vinciflora. Twining, herbaceous perennial climber with alternate or opposite, lance-shaped to ovate, thin-textured, mid-green leaves, ½–1½in (1.5–4cm) long, glaucous blue beneath. In early and midsummer, solitary, saucer-shaped, blue to bluish lilac flowers, 1¼–1¾in (3–4.5cm) across, are produced terminally or on short lateral shoots. ↕ 3ft (1m). China. Zone 7b.

COELIA *syn.* BOTHRIOCHILUS

ORCHIDACEAE

Genus of 5 species of evergreen, epiphytic, terrestrial, or lithophytic orchids from Mexico to Panama, where they occur at altitudes up to 3,900ft (1,200m). They have short rhizomes and clusters of ovoid or ellipsoid, olive-green pseudobulbs; each produces up to 5 narrowly to broadly lance-shaped, folded, pale to mid-green leaves at the tip. The inflorescence is a short, basal raceme bearing 6 or more tubular-bell-shaped, fleshy, fragrant, cream, ivory-white, or buff flowers, with pink or violet marks.

• **CULTIVATION** Intermediate-growing orchids. Pot tightly in containers of epiphytic orchid potting mix. In summer, provide high humidity and bright filtered light, with generous ventilation; water moderately, applying fertilizer at every third watering. In winter, admit full light, and water more sparingly. See also p.46.

• **PROPAGATION** Divide when the plant fills the container and flows over the sides.

• **PESTS AND DISEASES** Susceptible to spider mites, aphids, and mealybugs.

C. bella, syn. *Bothriochilus bellus.* Epiphytic orchid with spherical to ovoid pseudobulbs, each producing 3 or 4 narrowly lance-shaped, pale green leaves, 18in (45cm) long. In early summer, up to 6 purple-tipped, ivory-white flowers, 1in (2.5cm) across, with lips marked golden orange, are produced in racemes, 4–6in (10–15cm) long. ↕↔ 18in (45cm). Mexico, Guatemala, Honduras. ❄ (min. 55°F/13°C; max 86°F/30°C)

COELOGYNE

ORCHIDACEAE

Genus of more than 100 species of evergreen, epiphytic orchids occurring from lowland forest to high altitudes in mountainous regions from India and S.E. Asia to the Pacific islands. They vary greatly in size, producing pseudobulbs with 2 narrow to broadly elliptic, leathery, pleated, generally mid-green leaves. Flowers are borne in racemes, mainly from the center of new growth, usually from spring to summer. Many species are fragrant. *C. cristata* may be grown as a houseplant.

• **CULTIVATION** Cool- to intermediate-growing orchids. Grow in epiphytic orchid potting mix in a container or slatted basket. In summer, provide moderate to high humidity, good ventilation, and bright filtered light; water freely, apply fertilizer at every third watering, and mist once or twice daily. In winter, admit full light and keep completely dry. Tropical species, such as *C. dayana* and *C. speciosa*, should be kept moist at a minimum temperature of 59°F (15°C) throughout the year. See also p.46.

• **PROPAGATION** Divide when the plant fills the container and flows over the sides, or remove backbulbs after flowering and pot them up separately.

• **PESTS AND DISEASES** Susceptible to spider mites, aphids, and mealybugs.

Coelogyne cristata

C. barbata. Epiphytic orchid with conical pseudobulbs and oblong-lance-shaped, semi-rigid leaves, to 18in (45cm) long. In summer, produces a succession of pure white flowers, 2in (5cm) across, with brown and white, fringed lips, in upright racemes. ↕↔ 18in (45cm). Bhutan,N.E. India. ❄ (min. 50°F/10°C; max 86°F/30°C)

***C.* Burfordiense** (*C. asperata* x *C. pandurata*). Epiphytic orchid with flattened, ribbed pseudobulbs and elliptic-lance-shaped, semi-rigid, folded leaves, 24in (60cm) long. Many apple-green flowers, 4in (10cm) across, with black lacing on the lips, are borne in arching racemes in summer. ↕ 30in (75cm), ↔ 36in (90cm). ❄ (min. 50°F/10°C; max 86°F/30°C)

C. cristata ▣ Epiphytic orchid with rounded pseudobulbs and lance-shaped leaves, to 12in (30cm) long. Pendent racemes of pure white, strongly fragrant flowers, 3in (8cm) across, with yellow-marked lips, are produced from winter to spring. ↕ 12in (30cm), ↔ 24in (60cm). E. Himalayas. ❄ (min. 50°F/10°C; max 86°F/30°C)

C. dayana. Epiphytic orchid with conical pseudobulbs and lance-shaped, semi-rigid leaves, to 30in (75cm) long. From winter to spring, bears pendent racemes of many fragrant, pale yellow flowers, 2in (5cm) across, marked dark brown, with white-veined lips. ↕↔ 24in (60cm). Malaysia, Sumatra, Java, Borneo. ❄ (min. 59°F/15°C; max 86°F/30°C)

C. flaccida ▣ Epiphytic orchid with conical pseudobulbs and lance-shaped, semi-rigid leaves, 8in (20cm) long. From winter to early summer, bears racemes of strongly fragrant white flowers, 1½in (4cm) across, marked yellow on the central lobe of each lip and reddish brown on the lateral lobes. ↕ 10in (25cm), ↔ 12in (30cm). Himalayas. ❄ (min. 50°F/10°C; max 86°F/30°C)

C. massangeana. Epiphytic orchid with conical pseudobulbs and elliptic-ovate, semi-rigid leaves, to 18in (45cm) long. From spring to early

Coelogyne flaccida

Coelogyne nitida

summer, fragrant, pale yellow flowers, 2in (5cm) across, with brown and yellow lips, are borne in pendent racemes. ↕↔ 24in (60cm). Malaysia, Sumatra, Java. ❀ (min. 59°F/15°C; max 86°F/30°C)

C. nitida ■ syn. *C. ochracea.* Epiphytic orchid with oblong, shining pseudobulbs and elliptic-lance-shaped, dark green leaves, to 12in (30cm) long. From spring to early summer, bears racemes of strongly fragrant, pure white flowers, 1in (2.5cm) across, with orange and yellow lip markings. ↕ 10in (25cm), ↔ 12in (30cm). W. Himalayas, China, Burma, Thailand, Laos. ❀ (min. 50°F/10°C; max 86°F/30°C)

C. ochracea see *C. nitida.*

C. pandurata. Epiphytic orchid with flattened, ribbed pseudobulbs and producing elliptic-lance-shaped, semi-rigid, folded leaves, to 24in (60cm) long. Pale green, fragrant flowers, 3in (8cm) or more across, with black lip markings, are borne in long, arching racemes of 7 to 15 in summer. ↕ 30in (75cm), ↔ 36in (90cm). Malaysia, Borneo, Sumatra. ❀ (min. 59°F/15°C; max 86°F/30°C)

C. speciosa ■ Epiphytic orchid with conical pseudobulbs and elliptic or lance-shaped leaves, to 14in (35cm) long. Bears tawny green-yellow to pale salmon-pink flowers, 3in (8cm) across, with reddish brown lips, in pendent racemes in any season. ↕ 12in (30cm), ↔ 24in (60cm). Sumatra, Java. ❀ (min. 59°F/15°C; max 86°F/30°C). **var. *salmonicolor*** has spindle-shaped pseudobulbs, wavy-edged leaves, and salmon-pink flowers with brown-checkered lips.

Coelogyne speciosa

Coix lacryma-jobi

COIX

POACEAE

Genus of about 5 species of monoecious, annual or perennial, often rhizomatous grasses, originating in E. Asia but widely naturalized in tropical regions throughout the world. The leaves are flat and narrowly lance-shaped. *Coix* species produce compound inflorescences, which consist of many racemes of separate male and female spikelets, and are borne in the upper leaf axils. Female flowers of *C. lacryma-jobi*, the only species commonly cultivated, produce hard, bead-like seeds, which are frequently used in the manufacture of rosaries and necklaces. The teardrop-like shape of the seeds gives rise to the common names, Christ's or Job's tears. *C. lacryma-jobi* may be grown outdoors in both warm- and cool-temperate climates, but it needs a long, hot summer to flower well. It is suitable for an annual border or for massing in a herbaceous border.

• **CULTIVATION** Grow in light to medium, fertile, moist but well-drained soil in a sheltered site in full sun. During the growing season, water freely.

• **PROPAGATION** Sow seed at 55–61°F (13–16°C) in late winter or early spring, and plant out when danger of frost has passed. In warm areas, sow seed *in situ* in spring.

• **PESTS AND DISEASES** Infrequent.

C. lacryma-jobi ■ (Christ's tears, Job's tears). Loosely tufted, annual grass with erect stems bearing bright green leaves, to 24in (60cm) long. In early autumn, produces long-stalked, arching inflorescences with racemes of separate male and female spikelets, the latter giving rise to hard, shiny, ovoid-spherical seeds, to ½in (1.5cm) long, which are green at first, becoming pearly purple-gray when ripe. ↕ 18–36in (45–90cm), ↔ 12in (30cm) or more. S.E. Asia.

COLCHICUM

Autumn crocus, Meadow saffron

LILIACEAE

Genus of about 45 species of cormous perennials from alpine and subalpine meadows and stony hillsides in Europe, N. Africa, W. and C. Asia, N. India, and W. China. The basal, linear, strap-shaped, lance-shaped, or elliptic-ovate leaves, often ribbed or pleated, develop with or after the flowers. Conspicuous, usually goblet-shaped, sometimes fragrant flowers, with perianth tubes ½–3in (1.5–8cm) long, are borne in late summer, autumn, winter, or spring. Many large-flowered colchicums, with attractively checkered flowers, bloom in autumn, usually long before the large leaves, which emerge in early spring and persist until summer.

Grow large-leaved species among deciduous shrubs; *C. autumnale*, *C. speciosum*, and several other robust species may be naturalized in grass or among a groundcover. The smaller species are suitable for a rock garden, scree bed, raised bed, or trough. Those with leaves present at flowering time are best grown in a bulb frame or alpine house to protect them from excessive summer rainfall. All parts are highly toxic if ingested and, if in contact with skin, may cause irritation.

• **CULTIVATION** Plant 4in (10cm) deep in summer or early autumn. Colchicums have varying cultivation requirements, which, for ease of reference, may be grouped as follows:

1. Deep, fertile, well-drained soil that is not too dry, in an open site in full sun.

2. Gritty, sharply drained soil in a sunny raised bed or scree bed. In a bulb frame or alpine house, use a mix of equal parts loam, leaf mold, sharp sand, and grit in full light. Apply a low-nitrogen liquid fertilizer at the beginning of the growing season. Water moderately when in growth, avoiding the foliage and flowers; keep completely dry when dormant.

• **PROPAGATION** Sow seed in containers in an open frame as soon as ripe. Separate corms when dormant in summer.

• **PESTS AND DISEASES** Gray mold (*Botrytis*) and slugs may be problems.

C. agrippinum ■ Cormous perennial, probably a hybrid between *C. autumnale* and *C. variegatum*, with semi-erect, linear-lance-shaped or strap-shaped, slightly wavy leaves, 3½–6in (9–15cm) long. In early autumn, produces 1 or 2 narrowly funnel-shaped, heavily checkered, deep purplish pink flowers with tepals 2in (5cm) long. Cultivation group 1. ↕ 3–4in (8–10cm), PD3in (8cm). Unknown origin. Zone 5b.

C. alpinum. Cormous perennial with semi-erect, strap-shaped to linear-lance-shaped leaves, 3–6in (8–15cm) long. From late summer to autumn, produces 1 or 2 goblet-shaped, pale pink flowers with tepals ½–1¼in (1.5–3cm) long. Cultivation group 1 or 2. ↕ 2½in (6cm), PD3in (8cm). France (including Corsica), Switzerland, Italy (including Sardinia). Zone 5.

C. atropurpureum. Cormous perennial with erect, strap-shaped to narrowly lance-shaped leaves, 3½–7in (9–18cm) long. In autumn, bears 1–3 cup-shaped flowers, opening white then turning dark magenta-red, with tepals 1¼–2in (3–5cm) long. Cultivation group 1 or 2. ↕ and PD2in (5cm). Unknown origin, probably Balkans. Zone 5.

C. autumnale ■ (Meadow saffron). Vigorous, cormous perennial bearing erect, linear-lance-shaped to broadly lance-shaped leaves, 5½–14in (14–35cm) long. In autumn, produces 1–6 goblet-shaped, lavender-pink flowers, with tepals 1½–2½in (4–6cm)

Colchicum agrippinum

Colchicum autumnale

Colchicum bivonae

Colchicum byzantinum

Colchicum cilicicum

Colchicum kesselringii

Colchicum luteum

Colchicum 'The Giant'

Colchicum 'Waterlily'

long. Cultivation group 1. ↕ 4–6in (10–15cm), PD3in (8cm). Europe. Zone 4. **'Alboplenum'** has double white flowers with numerous narrow tepals. **f. *album*** has white flowers. **'Major'** see *C. byzantinum*. **'Pleniflorum'**, syn. 'Plenum', 'Roseum Plenum', produces neat, rounded, double, pinkish lilac flowers, with tepals 2–3in (5–8cm) long. **'Plenum'** see 'Pleniflorum'. **'Roseum Plenum'** see 'Pleniflorum'.

***C.* 'Autumn Queen'.** Cormous perennial with semi-erect, broadly lance-shaped leaves, 7–10in (18–25cm) long. In early autumn, produces 1–4 goblet-shaped, fragrant flowers, with long perianth tubes, white throats, and rose-pink tepals, 1½–3in (4–8cm) long, strongly checkered with deep purple. Cultivation group 1. ↕ 6in (15cm), PD4in (10cm). Zone 4.

***C. baytopiorum*.** Cormous perennial with a horizontal corm and semi-erect, narrowly lance-shaped leaves, to 3in (8cm) long at flowering, 8–12in (20–30cm) long when mature. In autumn, produces 1–5 goblet-shaped, pinkish purple flowers, with tepals ¾–1½in (2–4.5cm) long. Cultivation group 1 or 2; best in an alpine house. ↕ PD3in (8cm). W. Turkey. Zone 6.

C. bivonae ▣ syn. *C. bowlesianum*, *C. sibthorpii*. Robust, cormous perennial with semi-erect, strap-shaped or linear-lance-shaped leaves, 5–12in (12–30cm) long. In autumn, produces 1–6 goblet-shaped, often fragrant, strongly checkered, purplish pink flowers, with tepals 1½–3½in (4–9cm) long, often with white bases. Cultivation group 1. ↕ 6in (15cm), PD4in (10cm). Italy to W. Turkey. Zone 5b.

C. boissieri, syn. *C. procurrens*. Cormous perennial with a horizontal corm and erect, narrowly linear leaves, 4½–9in (11–23cm) long. In autumn, produces 1 or 2 slender, goblet-shaped, pinkish lilac flowers, with tepals 1–2in (2.5–5cm) long. Cultivation group 2; best in a bulb frame. ↕ 1¼in (3cm), PD2in (5cm). S. Greece, W. Turkey. Zone 5b.

***C. bornmuelleri*.** Cormous perennial with semi-erect, narrowly elliptic leaves, 7–10in (17–25cm) long. In autumn, produces 1–6 funnel-shaped, pale to deep purplish pink flowers, with tepals 1¾–3in (4.5–8cm) long, and with purple-brown anthers. Often confused with *C. speciosum*, which has yellow anthers. Cultivation group 1. ↕ 6in (15cm), PD4in (10cm). Turkey. Zone 5b.

***C. bornmuelleri* of gardens** see *C. speciosum*.

C. bowlesianum see *C. bivonae*.

C. byzantinum ▣ syn. *C. autumnale* 'Major'. Vigorous, cormous perennial, probably a hybrid of *C. cilicicum*, with erect, strongly ribbed, elliptic or lance-shaped leaves, to 12in (30cm) long. In autumn, bears up to 20 open funnel-shaped, soft lilac flowers, with tepals 2in (5cm) long. Cultivation group 1. ↕ 5in (13cm), PD4in (10cm). Origin unknown. Zone 4.

C. cilicicum ▣ Cormous perennial bearing semi-erect, narrowly elliptic to elliptic-lance-shaped leaves, 12–16in (30–40cm) long. In autumn, produces 3–25 widely funnel-shaped, purplish pink flowers with blunt tepals, 1½–3in (4–7.5cm) long, sometimes deeper in

Colchicum speciosum 'Album'

color toward the tips. Cultivation group 1. ↕ 4in (10cm), PD3in (8cm). Turkey, Syria, Lebanon. Zone 6.

***C.* 'Conquest'** see *C.* 'Glory of Heemstede'.

C. crociflorum see *C. kesselringii*.

***C. cupanii*.** Cormous perennial with semi-erect, linear to linear-lance-shaped, very glossy leaves, 4in (10cm) long at flowering, to 6in (15cm) long when mature. Produces 1–12 widely goblet-shaped, pale to deep purplish pink flowers, with tepals ¾–1in (2–2.5cm) long, in autumn. Cultivation group 2; best in a bulb frame or alpine house. ↕ 1½in (4cm), PD2in (5cm). S. France, Italy, Greece (including Crete), N. Africa. Zone 6.

C. doerfleri see *C. hungaricum*.

***C.* 'Glory of Heemstede'**, syn. *C.* 'Conquest'. Robust, cormous perennial with semi-erect, narrowly ovate leaves, 7–10in (18–25cm) long. Produces 1–6 goblet-shaped, strongly checkered, fragrant, bright reddish purple flowers, with tepals 1¼– 2½in (3–6cm) long, in autumn. Cultivation group 1. ↕ 7in (18cm), PD4in (10cm). Zone 4.

C. hungaricum, syn. *C. doerfleri*. Cormous perennial with erect, narrowly linear-lance-shaped, hairy leaves, 1¼–4in (3–10cm) long at flowering, to 12in (30cm) long when mature. In late winter and early spring, produces up to 8 goblet-shaped, white or pinkish lilac flowers, with tepals ¾–1¼in (2–3cm) long. Cultivation group 2; best in an alpine house. ↕ 3in (8cm), PD2in (5cm). Hungary, Balkans. Zone 4b.

C. kesselringii ▣ syn. *C. crociflorum*. Cormous perennial with semi-erect, linear-lance-shaped leaves, ½–¾in (1–2cm) long at flowering, 3–4in (7–10cm) long when mature. Produces up to 4 funnel-shaped white flowers, with tepals ½–1¼in (1.5–3cm) long, striped or suffused purple outside, in late winter and early spring. Cultivation group 2; best in an alpine house. ↕ PD1in (2.5cm). C. Asia. Zone 5b.

***C.* 'Lilac Wonder'.** Robust, free-flowering cormous perennial with semi-erect, narrowly ovate leaves, 7–10in (18–25cm) long. Produces 4–10 goblet-shaped, deep lilac-pink flowers, with narrow tepals, 1½–2½in (4–6cm) long, in autumn. Cultivation group 1. ↕ 6in (15cm), PD4in (10cm). Zone 4.

C. luteum ▣ Cormous perennial with semi-erect, linear-lance-shaped leaves, ½–1¼in (1–3cm) long at flowering, 4–12in (10–30cm) long when mature. Produces up to 4 goblet-shaped golden flowers, with tepals ½–1in (1.5–2.5cm) long, in early spring. Cultivation group 2; best in a bulb frame. ↕ PD3in (8cm). Afghanistan, N. India, Tibet. Zone 6.

C. procurrens see *C. boissieri*.

***C.* 'Rosy Dawn'.** Robust, cormous perennial with semi-erect, ovate leaves, 7–10in (18–25cm) long. In autumn, produces 1–6 goblet-shaped then open trumpet-shaped, fragrant, pinkish violet flowers. Lightly checkered tepals, 2½–3in (6–8cm) long, have prominent white centers. Cultivation group 1. ↕ 6in (15cm), PD4in (10cm). Zone 4.

C. sibthorpii see *C. bivonae*.

C. speciosum, syn *C. bornmuelleri* of gardens. Vigorous, cormous perennial producing semi-erect, narrowly elliptic to oblong-lance-shaped leaves, 7–10in (18–25cm) long. In autumn, bears 1–3 goblet-shaped, pale to deep pinkish purple flowers, with yellow anthers, often white throats, and tepals 1¾–3in (4.5–8cm) long. Cultivation group 1. ↕ 7in (18cm), PD4in (10cm). Caucasus, Turkey, Iran. Zone 4. **'Album'** ▣ has weather-resistant white flowers.

***C.* 'The Giant'** ▣ Robust, cormous perennial with semi-erect, narrowly ovate leaves, 7–10in (18–25cm) long. In autumn, produces a succession of up to 5 somewhat goblet-shaped, purplish violet flowers, with lightly checkered tepals, to 3in (8cm) long, and white bases. Cultivation group 1. ↕ 8in (20cm), PD4in (10cm). Zone 4.

***C. variegatum*.** Cormous perennial with horizontal, linear-lance-shaped or strap-shaped, wavy leaves, 3½–6in (9–15cm) long. In autumn, bears 1–3 widely funnel-shaped, short-tubed, strongly checkered, violet-purple to pinkish purple flowers, with tepals ¾–1in (2–2.5cm) long. Cultivation group 2. ↕ PD4in (10cm). Greece, S.W. Turkey. Zone 6.

***C.* 'Violet Queen'.** Cormous perennial with semi-erect, broadly lance-shaped leaves, 7–10in (18–25cm) long. In early autumn, bears 1–5 funnel-shaped, strongly checkered, fragrant, pinkish violet flowers with pointed tepals, 1½–2½in (4–6cm) long. Cultivation group 1. ↕ 6in (15cm), PD4in (10cm). Zone 4.

***C.* 'Waterlily'** ▣ Cormous perennial with semi-erect, narrowly ovate leaves, 7–10in (18–25cm) long. In autumn, produces up to 5 fully double, many-tepaled, pinkish lilac flowers, with tepals 1½–3in (4–8cm) long. Looks best where its blooms are supported by neighboring plants. Cultivation group 1. ↕ 5in (13cm), PD4in (10cm). Zone 4.

COLEONEMA

RUTACEAE

Genus of 8 species of evergreen shrubs from open heathland and rocky slopes in South Africa. The alternate, usually short, linear to oblong or narrowly lance-shaped leaves are crowded on the stems, producing a feathery, heath-like effect. Small, star-shaped, 5-petaled flowers are produced singly, often profusely, at the ends of the shoots and from the leaf axils. Where not hardy, grow in a conservatory or cool greenhouse. In warmer climates, grow in a shrub border.

• **CULTIVATION** Under glass, grow in acidic potting mix in full light, with low humidity. Water moderately and apply a balanced liquid fertilizer monthly from spring to autumn; water sparingly in winter. Top-dress or pot on in spring. Outdoors, grow in moderately fertile, moist but well-drained, neutral to acidic soil in full sun. Pruning group 10, after flowering.

• **PROPAGATION** Surface-sow seed at 55–61°F (13–16°C) in spring. Root semi-ripe cuttings with bottom heat in summer.

• **PESTS AND DISEASES** Infrequent.

***C. pulchrum*.** Freely branching shrub, erect at first then spreading, with linear, bright green leaves, ¾–1½in (2–4cm)

Coleonema pulchrum 'Golden Sunset'

long. Bears terminal and axillary, red or pink flowers, 3½–5in (9–13cm) across, with reflexed petals and darker eyes, from late spring to summer. ↕↔ 3–4ft (1–1.2m). South Africa. ❄ (min. 37–41°F/3–5°C), although it tolerates 32°F (0°C). **'Golden Sunset'** ■ syn. 'Sunset Gold', has glowing, yellow-green leaves and white flowers.

▷ ***Coleus blumei* var. *verschaffeltii*** see *Solenostemon scutellarioides*

▷ ***Coleus thyrsoideus*** see *Plectranthus thyrsoideus*

COLLETIA

RHAMNACEAE

Genus of 17 species of deciduous shrubs occurring in hillside scrub in temperate South America. The modified branches form succulent, cylindrical or flat, triangular, mid- to blue-green or gray-green spines, which point outward from the shoots, with one terminal spine to each branch. The opposite leaves are either sparse or wholly absent, particularly on mature plants; both the stems and leaves photosynthesize. Small, tubular or bell-shaped flowers, with tiny petals and conspicuous calyces, are produced singly or in many-flowered clusters, either on or below the spines. Suitable for a sheltered shrub border or growing against a warm, sunny wall. Where not hardy, grow in a cool greenhouse.

• **CULTIVATION** Under glass, grow in soil-based potting mix in full light, with good ventilation. During the growing season, water moderately and apply a balanced liquid fertilizer monthly; water sparingly in winter. Outdoors, grow in moderately fertile, well-drained soil in an open site in full sun, sheltered from cold, dry winds. Pruning group 1; tip-prune young plants to encourage bushiness. Will tolerate moderately hard pruning.

• **PROPAGATION** Root semi-ripe cuttings of short sideshoots in late summer.

• **PESTS AND DISEASES** Infrequent.

Colletia paradoxa

C. armata see *C. hystrix.*

C. cruciata see *C. paradoxa.*

C. hystrix, syn. *C. armata.* Stiffly branched, rounded, almost leafless shrub with cylindrical, sharp-pointed, gray-green spines, to 1in (2.5cm) long. Bears clusters of tubular, fragrant white flowers, ⅛in (3mm) long, on the spines, in late summer and early autumn. ↕↔ 10ft (3m). Chile. Zone 7b. **'Rosea'** has white flowers opening from pink buds.

C. paradoxa ■ syn. *C. cruciata.* Spreading shrub with flattened, blue-gray spines, to 1½in (4cm) across, and few or no leaves. In autumn, clusters of tubular, fragrant white flowers, to ⅛in (3mm) long, are borne below the spines. ↕ 10ft (3m), ↔ 15ft (5m). Brazil, Uruguay. Zone 7b.

COLLINSIA

SCROPHULARIACEAE

Genus of 25 species of erect to spreading, slender-stemmed annuals from open woodland, fields, and low valleys in North America and Mexico. They produce opposite, ovate, oblong, or lance-shaped, sometimes softly hairy leaves. Whorled, asymmetrically

Collinsia bicolor

Collinsia grandiflora

2-lipped, pink, white, blue, or bicolored flowers are borne in racemes from spring to summer. Grow in an annual or mixed border, or in a wild garden; they provide long-lasting cut flowers.

• **CULTIVATION** Grow in fertile, humus-rich, moist but well-drained soil in a sheltered, sunny to partially shaded site. Provide light, twiggy support. Water in dry weather to prolong flowering.

• **PROPAGATION** Sow seed *in situ* in autumn or early spring, but delay thinning autumn sowings until the following spring.

• **PESTS AND DISEASES** Powdery mildew, downy mildew, rust, and white smut are common.

C. bicolor ■ syn. *C. heterophylla* (Chinese houses). Erect to spreading, weak-stemmed annual with ovate to lance-shaped, sometimes toothed, mid- to purplish green leaves, to 3in (8cm) long, heart-shaped at the bases. In summer, produces whorled racemes of flowers, to 1¼in (3cm) long, with upright, 2-lobed white upper lips and lilac to pinkish purple lower lips, slanting outward. ↕ to 24in (60cm), ↔ to 12in (30cm). California. **'Candidissima'** has pure white flowers. **'Multicolor'** has flowers marked white, lilac, and purplish pink.

C. grandiflora ■ Erect, bushy, slender-stemmed annual with oval to lance-shaped or linear, toothed or entire, mid-green leaves, 1¾in (4.5cm) long. From spring to summer, bears whorled racemes of flowers, to 1in (2.5cm) long, with erect, 2-lobed, pale pinkish purple to pale purple upper lips, and deeper blue-purple lower lips, slanting outward. ↕ 6–12in (15–30cm), ↔ 8–12in (20–30cm). British Columbia to California.

C. heterophylla see *C. bicolor.*

COLLOMIA

POLEMONIACEAE

Genus of 15 species of erect to spreading annuals and perennials found in habitats ranging from woodland to mountain screes, in North and South America. They are cultivated for their ovate to lance-shaped, entire to lobed leaves, and their small, funnel- to trumpet-shaped or tubular, 5-lobed, red, purple, blue, or pinkish yellow flowers, borne singly or in terminal cymes in summer. Grow *C. biflora* in an annual or mixed border. The flowers are attractive to bees.

• **CULTIVATION** Grow in fertile, well-drained soil in full sun. During dry spells, water freely to prolong flowering.

• **PROPAGATION** Sow seed *in situ* in autumn or spring. Provide autumn-sown seedlings with protection where marginally hardy.

• **PESTS AND DISEASES** Powdery mildew, downy mildew, rust, and *Septoria* leaf spot are common.

C. biflora, syn. *C. cavanillesii.* Variable, softly hairy annual with lance-shaped leaves, to 2½in (6cm) long, toothed at the tips. Clusters of tubular scarlet flowers, to ½in (1.5cm) across, with 5 spreading lobes, are produced from the leaf axils at the stem tips in summer. ↕ to 24in (60cm), ↔ to 18in (45cm). Bolivia, Chile, Argentina.

C. cavanillesii see *C. biflora.*

COLOCASIA

Taro

ARACEAE

Genus of 6 species of tuberous, deciduous or more or less evergreen perennials occurring in swampy or moist areas in tropical Asia, and widely grown there as a staple food. The upright, tuberous rootstocks produce rounded to arrow-shaped, mostly dark green leaves, sometimes with prominent veins. The inflorescences, which are rarely borne on cultivated plants, consist of small white spathes with spadices that develop fleshy, single-seeded, glossy green berries. Where not hardy, grow in a warm greenhouse, either in containers or at the margins of an indoor pool in water to 12in (30cm) deep; or grow outdoors as annuals, either in the ground or in large aquatic containers. In warmer areas, grow in moist conditions as foliage plants. All parts may cause mild stomach upset if ingested without cooking, and contact with the sap may irritate the skin.

• **CULTIVATION** Under glass, pot up tubers in spring in soilless potting mix, and bring into growth at 64°F (18°C). Provide bright filtered light and high humidity. In the growing season, water freely, applying a balanced liquid fertilizer monthly. Outdoors, grow in fertile, humus-rich, moist or wet, slightly acidic soil in partial shade. Keep tubers dry and frost-free when dormant. See also pp.52–53.

• **PROPAGATION** Divide in winter or early spring.

Colocasia esculenta 'Fontanesii'

• **PESTS AND DISEASES** Soft rot, bacterial blight, corm and root rot, and dasheen mosaic virus are common. Aphids, whiteflies, and spider mites occur.

C. antiquorum see *C. esculenta.*
C. esculenta, syn. *C. antiquorum* (Cocoyam, Dasheen, Taro). Marginal aquatic perennial with ovate-heart-shaped to arrow-shaped, dark green leaf blades, 24in (60cm) long, with leaf stalks to 3ft (1m) long. ↕ 5ft (1.5m), PD24in (60cm). Tropical E. Asia. ❀ (min. 45°F/7°C). **'Fontanesii'** ▣ has leaves with dark red to purple stalks, veins, and margins. **'Illustris'** (Imperial taro) has violet leaf stalks and light green leaf blades, marked blackish purple between the veins.

COLQUHOUNIA

LAMIACEAE

Genus of 3 species of evergreen or semi-evergreen shrubs and subshrubs found in scrub and thickets in the Himalayas and China. The simple leaves, borne in opposite pairs, are finely toothed and light to dark green. Terminal spikes of showy, tubular, 2-lipped flowers are produced in axillary whorls. Grow *C. coccinea* against a warm, sunny wall, or in a sheltered mixed border.
• **CULTIVATION** Grow in poor to moderately fertile, well-drained soil in full sun. May die to the ground in winter, but will usually re-sprout from the base. Provide a deep, dry winter mulch. Pruning group 6.
• **PROPAGATION** Root softwood cuttings in summer.
• **PESTS AND DISEASES** Infrequent.

C. coccinea ▣ Upright, evergreen or semi-evergreen subshrub with ovate-lance-shaped, finely toothed, aromatic, sage-green leaves, to 8in (20cm) long, woolly beneath. Bears whorls of tubular, 2-lipped, yellow to scarlet flowers, to 1in (2.5cm) long, in terminal spikes in late summer. ↕↔ 8ft (2.5m). Himalayas, W. China. ❀ (min. 41°F/5°C)

Colquhounia coccinea

COLUMNEA

GESNERIACEAE

Genus of over 150 species of evergreen shrubs or subshrubs, with trailing or pendent shoots, and occasionally scandent climbers, found in moist woodland, rainforest, or cloud forest in the West Indies, Mexico, Central America, and tropical South America. The taxonomy of this genus is complex; many species are often considered members of the genera *Dahlbergeria, Pentadenia,* and *Trichantha.* In the wild, they are frequently epiphytic, and often branch where the stems are rooted into the leaf litter; in cultivation, the stems tend to remain unbranched. They have pairs of usually ovate to elliptic, often hairy, dark green leaves. From spring to autumn, tubular flowers are borne singly or in small clusters from the leaf axils; they are 5-lobed, with the upper 2 petals joined to form a hood, and the stamens and style projecting beyond the hood. Where not hardy, grow as houseplants or in a warm greenhouse. In warm, humid areas, grow in a shaded position among trees and shrubs, or epiphytically.
• **CULTIVATION** Under glass, grow in a moss-lined hanging basket or half-pot in soilless potting mix, in bright filtered or indirect light. Mist regularly with tepid water to maintain high humidity. When in full growth, water freely, applying quarter-strength, high-potash fertilizer at each watering. Overwatering may encourage root and stem rot. In winter, provide full light, water moderately, and avoid wetting the foliage. For maximum production of flowers, water sparingly during the 6–8 weeks before the formation of flower buds; resume normal watering as flower buds appear. Outdoors, grow in coarse, open, moderately fertile, humus-rich soil in partial shade. To maintain vigorous growth, propagate every 2 or 3 years.
• **PROPAGATION** Root tip cuttings with bottom heat in spring.
• **PESTS AND DISEASES** Aphids, spider mites, bud mites, fungal spots, and tobacco mosaic virus occur.

C. x banksii ▣ (*C. schiedeana* x *C. oerstediana*). Trailing subshrub with ovate to oblong-ovate, smooth, shiny, dark green leaves, 1½in (4cm) long, sparsely hairy beneath. Throughout the year, produces solitary, hairy, scarlet

Columnea x *banksii*

Columnea crassifolia

flowers, 2½in (6cm) long, with faint yellow lines in the throats. ↕ to 6in (15cm), ↔ trails to 4ft (1.2m). Garden origin. ❀ (min. 59°F/15°C)
C. crassifolia ▣ Erect subshrub with narrowly elliptic, shiny leaves, dark green above, pale yellow-green and sparsely hairy beneath, to 4in (10cm) long. Bears solitary, hairy, bright scarlet flowers, to 4in (10cm) long, from spring to summer. ↕↔ 12in (30cm). Mexico, Guatemala. ❀ (min. 59°F/15°C)
C. erythrophaea. Semi-upright to trailing subshrub with elliptic, glossy, pointed-tipped, dark green leaves, to 2½in (6cm) long. Throughout the year, clusters of 3 or more narrow, yellow to burnt orange flowers, 2in (5cm) long, are produced from the leaf axils. ↕ 6in (15cm), ↔ 20in (50cm). Mexico. ❀ (min. 59°F/15°C)
C. gloriosa. Trailing subshrub with slender stems branching only at the base. Ovate or ovate-oblong, dark green leaves, 1in (2.5cm) long, are densely covered in fine purple hairs; the margins of the leaves are turned under, giving them a thickened appearance. From spring to summer, and intermittently throughout the rest of the year, bears

Columnea microphylla 'Variegata'

Columnea 'Robin'

solitary, hairy, fiery red flowers, 3in (8cm) long, with yellow throats. ↕ 6in (15cm), ↔ trails to 3ft (1m). Central America. ❀ (min. 59°F/15°C)
C. 'Julia'. Trailing subshrub with slender stems and ovate to elliptic, sharp-pointed, red-hairy-margined, mid-green leaves, to 1in (2.5cm) long, red-tinged beneath. Solitary, orange-red flowers, to 2½in (6cm) long, are borne throughout the year. ↕ 4in (10cm), ↔ 20in (50cm). ❀ (min. 59°F/15°C)
C. microphylla. Trailing subshrub with thin stems bearing close-set, ovate to rounded, dark green leaves, to ½in (1.5cm) long, covered in red-brown hairs. Bears solitary, hairy, scarlet flowers, 2–3in (5–8cm) long, with yellow throats, from spring to summer, and intermittently throughout the rest of the year. ↕ 6in (15cm), ↔ trails to 6ft (2m). Costa Rica. ❀ (min. 59°F/15°C). **'Variegata'** ▣ has gray-green leaves with narrow cream margins.
C. 'Robin' ▣ Vigorous, trailing subshrub with ovate, hairy, dark green leaves, ¾–1¼in (2–3cm) long. Numerous solitary, bright red flowers, 2–3in (5–8cm) long, are borne from early to late summer. ↕ 14in (35cm), ↔ 24in (60cm). ❀ (min. 59°F/15°C)
C. scandens. Trailing subshrub with slender stems bearing oblong to narrowly oblong or ovate-elliptic, dark green leaves, 2in (5cm) long, with red hairs at the margins. Bears sparsely hairy, red or yellow flowers, 2½in (6cm) long, either singly or in pairs, from spring to summer. ↕ to 6in (15cm), ↔ trails to 3ft (1m). Lesser Antilles. ❀ (min. 59°F/15°C)
C. schiedeana. Stiffly spreading subshrub with lance-shaped to oblong, pale-green-hairy, mid-green leaves, to 5in (13cm) long, red or red-veined beneath. From spring to autumn, bears red-tinged yellow flowers, to 2½in (6cm) long, with maroon spots and lines, singly or in pairs, on red-hairy flower stalks. ↕ to 3ft (1m), ↔ 20in (50cm). Mexico. ❀ (min. 59°F/15°C)
C. 'Stavanger' (*C. microphylla* x *C.* x *vedrariensis*) (Norse fire plant). Very vigorous, freely branching, trailing subshrub bearing oval, lustrous, dark green leaves, ¾in (2cm) long. Solitary, hairy, bright scarlet flowers, 3–4in (8–10cm) long, are produced from spring to summer, and intermittently throughout the rest of the year. ↕ to 6in (15cm), ↔ to 24in (60cm). Mexico. ❀ (min. 59°F/15°C)

COLUTEA

Bladder senna

FABACEAE

Genus of about 25 species of deciduous shrubs, sometimes trees, found in dry soils in woodland and thickets, from S. Europe, E. Africa, Turkey, Iran, C. Asia, Afghanistan, Pakistan, and the Himalayas. They are grown for their pinnate leaves, with entire, usually elliptic to obovate leaflets; their pea-like, yellow to red-brown flowers, borne in few-flowered, axillary, long-stalked racemes; and their unusual, inflated, membranous, bladder-like fruits. Coluteas are suitable for a shrub border; those described here are useful for an exposed site or dry, sunny bank. They tolerate poor, dry soils, coastal conditions, and urban pollution. Some may become weedy. Seeds may cause mild stomach upset if ingested.

Colutea arborescens

• **CULTIVATION** Grow in moderately fertile, well-drained soil in full sun. Pruning group 1 or 6; *C. arborescens* may be trained as a standard.
• **PROPAGATION** Sow seed in containers in a cold frame in autumn or spring. Root greenwood cuttings in summer.
• **PESTS AND DISEASES** Powdery mildew, rust, and root rot sometimes occur.

C. arborescens ▣ (Bladder senna). Vigorous shrub (rarely tree-like) with pinnate, pale green leaves, to 6in (15cm) long, with 5–6 pairs of broadly elliptic to ovate leaflets. Produces 3–8 yellow flowers, to ¾in (2cm) long, in racemes to 5in (13cm) long, over a long period in summer, followed by green, then translucent seed pods, to 3in (8cm) long. ↕↔ 10ft (3m). S. Europe. Zone 4.
C. x media ▣ (*C. arborescens* x *C. orientalis*). Vigorous, bushy shrub with pinnate, blue-green leaves, to 6in (15cm) long, with 3–6 pairs of elliptic leaflets. From early to late summer, produces orange-brown flowers, to ¾in (1.5cm) long, sometimes flushed yellow in the centers, in racemes to 4in (10cm) long. Seed pods, to 3in (8cm) long, are greenish brown at first, then translucent. ↕↔ 10ft (3m). Garden origin. Zone 4.
C. orientalis. Bushy, rounded shrub with pinnate, bluish green leaves, to 4in (10cm) long, with 3 or 4 pairs of obovate leaflets. In summer, produces 2–5 copper-red flowers, to ½in (1.5cm) long, with yellow markings, in racemes to 2½in (6cm) long, followed by pale brown then translucent seed pods, to 2in (5cm) long. ↕↔ 6ft (2m). Caucasus, N. Iran. Zone 4.

Colutea x *media* (inset: flower detail)

COLUTEOCARPUS

BRASSICACEAE

Genus of one species of dwarf, tufted perennial, closely related to *Alyssum*, occurring in dry, rocky areas in the E. Mediterranean and Turkey. It has basal rosettes of oblong to lance-shaped leaves, terminal cymes of cross-shaped flowers, and inflated seed pods. *C. vesicarius* is suitable for an alpine house or scree bed. In cool, damp areas, seed pods are more reliably produced in an alpine house.
• **CULTIVATION** Outdoors, grow in poor to moderately fertile, gritty, humus-rich, sharply drained soil in full sun. Protect from excessive moisture. In an alpine house, grow in equal parts loam, leaf mold, and grit.
• **PROPAGATION** Sow seed in containers in a cold frame in autumn.
• **PESTS AND DISEASES** Susceptible to aphids and spider mites under glass.

C. reticulatus see *C. vesicarius.*
C. vesicarius, syn. *Alyssum vesicaria*, *C. reticulatus.* Cushion-forming perennial with stiff, sharply toothed, glossy, mid-green leaves, to 3in (8cm) long. Loose, flat-topped, terminal cymes of golden yellow flowers, ½in (1.5cm) across, are produced on short stems in late spring, followed by papery, pale green seed pods, to 1¼in (3cm) long. ↕ to 3in (8cm), ↔ to 6in (15cm). E. Mediterranean. Zone 7b.

COLVILLEA

FABACEAE

Genus of one species of evergreen tree from forest in Madagascar. It has large, alternate, 2-pinnate leaves and produces showy, pea-like flowers in conspicuous, pendent racemes. Where not hardy, grow *C. racemosa* in a temperate greenhouse. In warmer climates, grow as a specimen tree.
• **CULTIVATION** Under glass, grow in soil-based potting mix in full light, with shade from hot sun and moderate humidity. During the growing season, water freely and apply a balanced liquid fertilizer monthly; water sparingly in winter. Top-dress or pot on in spring. Outdoors, grow in fertile, moist but well-drained soil in full sun. Pruning group 1; needs restrictive pruning under glass, immediately after flowering.
• **PROPAGATION** Sow seed at 64°F (18°C) in spring.
• **PESTS AND DISEASES** Spider mites may be a problem under glass.

C. racemosa. Erect tree, often with a long trunk and spreading branches. Fern-like, 2-pinnate leaves, to 36in (90cm) long, have many small, elliptic to oblong leaflets. From late autumn to winter, bears scarlet flowers, 1¾in (4.5cm) across, in racemes to 12in (30cm) long. ↕ 25–50ft (8–15m), ↔ 10–15ft (3–5m). Madagascar. ❀ (min. 45°F/7°C)

▷ ***Comarostaphylis*** see *Arctostaphylos*
▷ ***Comarum*** see *Potentilla*

COMBRETUM

COMBRETACEAE

Genus of about 250 species of evergreen or semi-evergreen, sometimes briefly deciduous trees and shrubs, some more or less scandent, occurring in forest and thickets in tropical regions worldwide (except Australia). Leaves, borne in opposite pairs or in whorls, are mainly ovate, or oblong to elliptic, and entire. They are cultivated for their mostly small, tubular, 4- or 5-lobed flowers, borne in terminal and axillary racemes and panicles. Where not hardy, grow in a warm greenhouse. In warmer climates, train onto a trellis or pergola.
• **CULTIVATION** Under glass, grow in a border or in large containers of soilless potting mix in bright filtered light, with full light in winter. Mist with tepid water as flower buds form. From spring to autumn, water freely and apply a balanced liquid fertilizer monthly; water moderately in winter. Top-dress or pot on in spring. Outdoors, grow in fertile, humus-rich, moist but well-drained soil, in partial shade. Pruning group 11 or 12, immediately after flowering.
• **PROPAGATION** Root semi-ripe cuttings with bottom heat in summer.
• **PESTS AND DISEASES** Spider mites may be a problem under glass.

C. grandiflorum. Evergreen, more or less scandent shrub or semi-climber with ovate-elliptic, slender-pointed, smooth or downy leaves, 4–6in (10–15cm) long. Produces many short, dense, one-sided racemes of bright red flowers, ¾in (2cm) long, from autumn to winter. ↕ 12–20ft (4–6m), ↔ 6–12ft (2–4m). Gambia to Ghana. ❀ (min. 61°F/16°C)
C. paniculatum. Vigorous, usually open, semi-evergreen or briefly deciduous, scandent shrub or climber. The stems bear short spines and broadly elliptic to oblong, papery leaves, to 7in (18cm) long. Panicles of many red flowers, 1½in (4cm) long, are produced in autumn. ↕ 30ft (10m) or more, ↔ 10–15ft (3–5m). Tropical Africa. ❀ (min. 61°F/16°C)

COMMELINA

Day flower, Spiderwort, Widow's tears

COMMELINACEAE

Genus of 100 species of mat-forming or clump-forming annuals and fibrous- or tuberous-rooted perennials from forest floors in tropical and subtropical regions of southern Africa, Asia, and North, Central, and South America. The leaves are alternate and ovate, lance-shaped, or linear. Most species root at the leaf nodes as they spread. One-sided cymes of small, saucer-shaped, 3-petaled flowers are enclosed in folded, terminal, spathe-like bracts; flowers emerge one at a time, each lasting less than a day. Use *Commelina* species as a groundcover. Where not hardy, grow in a cool greenhouse or outdoors in an annual border; hardy species are suitable for a herbaceous border. Some species are weedy.
• **CULTIVATION** Under glass, grow in soil-based potting mix in bright filtered light. In growth, water moderately and apply a balanced liquid fertilizer monthly; water sparingly in winter. Outdoors, grow in fertile, well-drained

soil in a warm, sheltered site in sun or partial shade. Provide a deep, dry, winter mulch. Where not hardy, lift plants before the first frost and overwinter in barely moist, frost-free conditions. Start into growth again in gentle heat in spring.
• **PROPAGATION** Sow seed at 55–64°F (13–18°C) in spring, or divide in spring.
• **PESTS AND DISEASES** Numerous viral diseases, rust, slugs, and leafminers are common in landscape plantings.

C. benghalensis. Creeping, fibrous-rooted perennial bearing ovate-lance-shaped to ovate leaves, to 3in (8cm) long. Cymes of blue or violet flowers, ½in (1.5cm) across, are borne in the upper leaf axils in summer. ↕ to 10in (25cm), ↔ indefinite. Tropical Asia, southern Africa. ❄ (min. 34°F/1°C)
C. coelestis ■ (Blue spiderwort). Vigorous, clump-forming, erect, tuberous perennial with hairy, fleshy stems bearing ovate-lance-shaped to oblong-lance-shaped, clasping leaves, 3–7in (8–18cm) long. From late summer to midautumn, freely produces cymes of vivid blue flowers, ¾–1¼in (2–3cm) across. Related to (and sometimes included in) *C. tuberosa.* ↕ to 36in (90cm), ↔ 18in (45cm). Central and South America. ❄ (min. 34°F/1°C).
var. *alba* bears white flowers.
C. tuberosa. Mat-forming, procumbent, tuberous perennial bearing narrowly lance-shaped leaves, to 3½in (9cm) long. Cymes of green flowers, 1¼in (3cm) across, streaked with dark blue-purple, are produced in summer. ↕ to 8in (20cm), ↔ indefinite. Central and South America. ❄ (min. 34°F/1°C)

Commelina coelestis

Comptonia peregrina

COMPTONIA

MYRICACEAE

Genus of one species of spreading, deciduous shrub from sandy, peaty, infertile soils of E. North America. It is grown for its alternate or clustered, linear to lance-shaped, fern-like leaves, aromatic on hot days or when crushed. Grow in a wild or native garden.
• **CULTIVATION** Grow in poor or moderately fertile, moist but well-drained, acidic soil, in partial shade or full sun. Resents transplanting and rarely requires pruning.
• **PROPAGATION** Sow seed *in situ* in autumn. Remove rooted suckers in late winter or early spring, or layer in spring.
• **PESTS AND DISEASES** Gall rust and twig dieback occur.

C. peregrina ■ (Sweet fern). Suckering shrub with hairless, spreading, rust to gray stems and deeply pinnatifid, linear to lance-shaped, softly hairy, light to dark green leaves, 2½–5in (6–13cm) long. Catkin-like, yellow-green male flowers, to 1½in (4cm) long, and rounded female inflorescences, to 1in (2.5cm) across, are produced in summer, followed by narrowly ellipsoid fruit. ↕ to 24–36in (60–90cm), ↔ indefinite. Nova Scotia to Virginia. Zone 4.

CONANDRON

GESNERIACEAE

Genus of one species of rosette-forming, tuberous-rooted, evergreen perennial from Japan, found on wet, rocky cliffs in mountainous areas. Leaves are elliptic-ovate, coarsely toothed, wrinkled, and fleshy. Tubular flowers, with prominent stamens, are borne in nodding cymes on leafless stems in midsummer. In dry, cool-temperate climates, grow in shaded, vertical crevices in a rock garden. In areas with cool, wet winters, grow in an alpine house.
• **CULTIVATION** In an alpine house, grow in soil-based potting mix with additional grit and leaf mold, in bright filtered light. In the growing season, water moderately, and apply a half-strength balanced liquid fertilizer monthly. Water sparingly in winter. Outdoors, grow in moderately fertile, gritty, humus-rich, moist but well-drained, acidic soil in partial shade. Protect from excessive winter moisture.
• **PROPAGATION** Surface-sow seed in containers in a cold frame in spring; water seedlings from below by plunging pots to their rims in water. Root leaf cuttings in early summer.
• **PESTS AND DISEASES** Spider mites and aphids may be troublesome under glass.

C. ramondoides. Hummock-forming perennial with glossy, mid-green leaves, to 12in (30cm) long. In midsummer, bears loose cymes of 10–40 tubular, deeply 5-lobed, white, lilac, or deep blue-purple flowers, to ½in (1.5cm) across, with orange centers, on stems to 8in (20cm) long. ↕ to 10in (25cm), ↔ to 8in (20cm). Japan (Honshu). Zone 7b.

CONGEA

VERBENACEAE

Genus of 7 species of evergreen, scandent shrubs and twining climbers, found in forest and thickets in S.E. Asia. The leaves are opposite, entire, and ovate to elliptic or oblong. Congeas bear terminal panicles of tiny, tubular, 2-lipped flowers, borne in small clusters, ringed by several petal-like bracts. Where not hardy, grow in a warm greenhouse or conservatory. In warmer areas, grow on a trellis, pillar, or pergola.
• **CULTIVATION** Under glass, grow in soil-based potting mix in full light, with shade from hot sun, and with good ventilation. In the growing season, water freely and apply a balanced liquid fertilizer monthly; water moderately in winter. Top-dress or pot on in spring. Provide support for the climbing stems. Outdoors, grow in fertile, humus-rich, moist but well-drained soil in full sun. Pruning group 11, immediately after flowering.
• **PROPAGATION** Sow seed at 61–68°F (16–20°C) in spring. Root semi-ripe cuttings in summer with bottom heat. Layer in spring.
• **PESTS AND DISEASES** Spider mites may be a problem under glass.

C. tomentosa (Shower orchid). Evergreen climber with downy, purple and green, scandent or climbing stems. Leaves are ovate to elliptic or oblong, and lightly hairy, to 8in (20cm) long. From winter to spring, bears panicles of white flowers in dense clusters, 2in (5cm) across, within groups of ovate to elliptic-oblong, violet or white bracts, densely covered with white hairs. ↕ 10–15ft (3–5m). Burma, Thailand. ❄ (min. 59°F/15°C)

CONICOSIA

AIZOACEAE

Genus of 10 species of semi-evergreen, spreading, perennial (in rare cases, biennial) succulents from arid regions of South Africa's Northern Cape, Eastern Cape, and Western Cape. The long, narrow, 3-angled to semi-cylindrical, fleshy, tufted, often dark-spotted leaves dry up after flowering, but persist after the solitary, long-stalked, daisy-like yellow flowers have faded. Green berries contain spherical, slightly keeled, smooth seeds. Where not hardy, grow in a temperate greenhouse; in warm, dry climates, grow in a desert garden.
• **CULTIVATION** Under glass, grow in a mix of 2 parts each loam and sharp sand

Conicosia pugioniformis

and 1 part leaf mold, in full light and with low humidity. At the beginning of the growing season, apply a balanced liquid fertilizer. Water moderately from early summer to autumn, and keep completely dry at other times of the year. Outdoors, grow in humus-rich, not too fertile, well-drained soil in full sun. See also pp.48–49.
• **PROPAGATION** Sow seed at 70°F (21°C) in midspring.
• **PESTS AND DISEASES** Aphids may prove troublesome.

C. capensis. Perennial succulent with stems to 6in (15cm) or more long. These are crowned by 3-angled, grooved, spotted, bluish green leaves, to 16in (40cm) long, which are shorter on the prostrate, floral branches. Bears pale yellow flowers, 3in (8cm) across, in summer. ↕ 10in (25cm), ↔ 12in (30cm). South Africa (Northern Cape, Western Cape). ❄ (min. 45°F/7°C)
C. pugioniformis ■ Perennial succulent with stems to 12in (30cm) long. These are crowned by 3-angled, grayish green leaves, to 8in (20cm) long, with grooved upper surfaces, reddish green at the bases. In late summer, bears glistening, bright yellow flowers, 3in (8cm) across. ↕ 16in (40cm), ↔ 12in (30cm). South Africa (Northern Cape, Western Cape). ❄ (min. 45°F/7°C)

CONIOGRAMME

ADIANTACEAE

Genus of 20 species of clump-forming, evergreen, semi-evergreen, or deciduous, terrestrial ferns from moist woodland in Asia. Creeping rhizomes produce pinnate to 3-pinnate, pale to dark green fronds with strap-shaped to ovate or oblong pinnae, pointed at the tips. Sporangia, not protected by indusia, are borne in rows on the undersides of the fronds. Suitable for a shady border or woodland garden; where not hardy, grow in a cool greenhouse or conservatory.
• **CULTIVATION** Under glass, grow in 1 part each of loam, medium-grade bark, and charcoal; 2 parts sharp sand; and 3 parts coarse leaf mold. Provide bright filtered or indirect light and moderate humidity. In the growing season, water freely, applying a half-strength balanced liquid fertilizer monthly; in winter, water moderately, keeping the foliage dry. Outdoors, grow in moist but well-drained, fertile, neutral to acidic, leafy

soil in partial shade. Provide shelter from strong winds.
• **PROPAGATION** Sow spores at 61°F (16°C) as soon as ripe. Divide rhizomes of well-established colonies in late spring. See also p.51.
• **PESTS AND DISEASES** Prone to slugs.

C

C. japonica (Bamboo fern). Deciduous, sometimes semi-evergreen fern with oblong to linear-lance-shaped fronds, 20–24in (50–60cm) long, pinnate at the tips and 2-pinnate at the bases. Narrowly ovate, pale green pinnae may have central yellow marks. ↕ 30in (75cm), ↔ 32in (80cm). E. Asia. Zone 7.

▷ ***Conoclinium coelestinum*** see *Eupatorium coelestinum*

CONOPHYTUM

AIZOACEAE

Genus of 290 species of dwarf, often slow-growing, clump-forming, perennial succulents, frequently with long roots, found in semi-desert areas with winter rainfall in Namibia and South Africa. Small, fleshy bodies consist of 2 united leaves with a central fissure, from which solitary, daisy-like flowers are produced, followed by small, ovoid, fleshy green fruits. After the flowers fade, the leaves gradually shrivel to papery sheaths; new leaves develop through the sheaths after the dormant period. In most climates, they are grown in a warm greenhouse, since they will not tolerate summer rainfall. In suitable regions, grow in a raised or scree bed, or in a desert garden.
• **CULTIVATION** Under glass, grow in a mix of 2 parts loam to 1 part each sharp sand and leaf mold, in full light with low humidity. Water sparingly from late summer to early winter and again in spring; additional fertilizer is not needed. Keep completely dry from late spring to midsummer. Outdoors, grow in gritty, humus-rich, low-fertility soil in full sun. Many tolerate temperatures to 25°F (-4°C). See also pp.48–49.
• **PROPAGATION** Surface-sow seed in late winter at 68–77°F (20–25°C) in moist, shady conditions; gradually increase light and reduce humidity after they germinate. Root bodies in summer.
• **PESTS AND DISEASES** Susceptible to aphids under glass.

C. bilobum ■ Perennial succulent with flattened, heart-shaped, grayish green bodies, 1in (2.5cm) across, branching

Conophytum bilobum

Conophytum notabile

with age to form clusters. Bears yellow flowers, to 1¼in (3cm) across, in late summer. ↕ 2in (5cm), ↔ 6in (15cm). South Africa (Northern Cape, Western Cape). ❄ (min. 50°F/10°C)
C. longum see *Ophthalmophyllum longum.*
C. nanum. Perennial succulent with fleshy, minutely papillose, bright green leaves forming spherical bodies, to ¼in (6mm) across. Red-tipped white flowers, ½in (1.5cm) across, are produced in late summer. ↕ ¾in (2cm), ↔ 3in (8cm). South Africa (Northern Cape). ❄ (min. 50°F/10°C)
C. notabile ■ Mat-forming, perennial succulent with generally ellipsoid, rounded, pale bluish green bodies, to ½in (1.5cm) across, each with a red dot on either side of the fissure. In late summer, produces brownish orange flowers, ¾in (2cm) across. ↕ 1in (2.5cm), ↔ ¾in (2cm). South Africa (Northern Cape, Western Cape). ❄ (min. 50°F/10°C)
C. pillansii ■ Perennial succulent with 1–3 joined, depressed obovoid, pale yellowish green bodies, ¾in (2cm) or more across, the tops marked with translucent green dots, the sides sometimes slightly reddened. In late summer, bears pinkish purple flowers, 1in (2.5cm) across, sometimes with white or lighter pinkish purple bases. ↕ ¾in (2cm), ↔ to 3in (8cm). South Africa (Western Cape). ❄ (min. 50°F/10°C)
C. truncatum ■ Variable, cushion-forming, perennial succulent with inversely conical, dark-spotted, grayish to bluish green bodies, ½in (1.5cm) across, with wide fissures. Yellowish or

Conophytum pillansii

Conophytum truncatum

creamy white flowers, ½in (1.5cm) across, are produced in autumn. ↕ ½in (1.5cm), ↔ to 6in (15cm). South Africa (Eastern Cape, Western Cape). ❄ (min. 50°F/10°C)

▷ ***Consolea falcata*** see *Opuntia falcata*

CONSOLIDA

Larkspur

RANUNCULACEAE

Genus of about 40 species of erect, slender-stemmed annuals, closely related to and sometimes included in the genus *Delphinium.* Larkspurs occur in fallow fields and on stony slopes and steppes in S.E. Europe and from the W. Mediterranean region to C. Asia. The feathery, softly downy, mid- to dark green, usually rounded leaves are deeply pinnatisect, or palmate with numerous slender leaflets. Spurred, delphinium-like, pink, blue, or white flowers are produced in racemes or panicles in summer. The taller cultivars provide long-lasting cut flowers, which may also be dried. All are excellent for a cottage garden or annual border. Larkspur seeds are poisonous.

Consolida ajacis Dwarf Rocket Series

• **CULTIVATION** Grow in light, fertile, well-drained soil in full sun. Water freely in dry weather. Provide twiggy support for tall cultivars. Deadhead to prolong flowering.
• **PROPAGATION** Sow seed *in situ* from early spring to early summer, or in autumn with protection where marginally hardy.
• **PESTS AND DISEASES** Slugs, snails, powdery mildew, and crown rot may cause problems.

C. ajacis, syn. *C. ambigua, Delphinium consolida* (Larkspur). Sparsely to well-branched annual with finely dissected, almost fern-like, palmate leaves, to 4in (10cm) long, with oblong to linear leaflets. In summer, bears upright, simple or branching, open to densely packed spikes, to 24in (60cm) tall, of spurred, single or rosette-like, double flowers, to 1½in (4cm) across, in rich tones or pastel shades of pink, white, or violet-blue. ↕ 1–4ft (30–120cm), ↔ 9–12in (23–30cm). Mediterranean. **Dwarf Hyacinth Series** cultivars do not branch strongly from the bases, and bear double flowers in densely packed, blunt-tipped racemes. Grow in an exposed garden; ↕ 12–18in (30–45cm). Cultivars of **Dwarf Rocket Series** ■ are compact, with double, blue, purple, white, or pink flowers; ↕ 12–20in (30–50cm), ↔ 6–10in (15–25cm). Cultivars of **Giant Imperial Series** branch strongly from the bases and produce racemes of double flowers on long, straight stems. Good for cut flowers. ↕ 24–36in (60–90cm), ↔ 14in (35cm).
C. ambigua see *C. ajacis.*

CONVALLARIA

Lily-of-the-valley

LILIACEAE

Genus of 3 species, sometimes considered to be one variable species, of rhizomatous perennials found in light woodland, scrub, or alpine meadows in N. temperate regions. They have ovate-lance-shaped to elliptic, stalked, basal leaves. Pendent, bell-shaped, fragrant, mostly white flowers are produced in arching racemes. Grow in a woodland garden, or use as a groundcover in a damp, shady border. The seeds of *C. majalis* may cause mild stomach upset if ingested.
• **CULTIVATION** Grow in leafy, fertile, humus-rich, moist soil in full sun to full shade. Top-dress with leaf mold in

Convallaria majalis

Convallaria majalis 'Albostriata'

autumn. For a fragrant indoor display, lift and pot up rhizomes in autumn, and force gently or allow them to grow at their own pace. Replant outdoors after flowering.
• **PROPAGATION** Sow seed in containers in a cold frame as soon as ripe, removing the flesh from the seeds before sowing. Separate rhizomes in autumn, keeping moist until established.
• **PESTS AND DISEASES** Anthracnose, white mold, and gray mold can be common.

C. majalis ■ Vigorous, rhizomatous perennial producing tough, slender, creeping, branching rhizomes bearing pairs of ovate-lance-shaped to elliptic, stalked, hairless, basal leaves, 1½–8in (4–20cm) long. Arching racemes of pendent, spherical-bell-shaped, strongly scented, waxy white flowers, ¼–½in (0.6–1.5cm) across, are produced on leafless stems in spring. ↕ 9in (23cm), ↔ indefinite. N. temperate regions. Zone 2. **'Albostriata'** ■ has leaves longitudinally striped creamy white. **'Aureovariegata'** has narrowly yellow-striped leaves. **'Flore Pleno'** has double white flowers. **'Fortin's Giant'** is vigorous, with wide leaves, and flowers ⅜–½in (8–15mm) across; ↕ 12in (30cm). **'Hardwick Hall'** has broad leaves with very narrow, pale green margins, and flowers ⅜–½in (9–15mm) across; ↕ 10in (25cm). **'Prolificans'** has panicle-like, branched inflorescences of sometimes slightly malformed flowers. **var. *rosea*** ■ produces pale mauve-pink flowers; ↕ 8in (20cm). **'Variegata'** has white-dappled leaves.

Convallaria majalis var. *rosea*

CONVOLVULUS

Bindweed, Morning glory

CONVOLVULACEAE

Genus of about 250 species of upright, climbing, or scrambling annuals and perennials, and evergreen shrubs or subshrubs, occurring in diverse habitats in subtropical and temperate areas. They have mostly entire leaves and produce solitary or clustered, funnel- or trumpet-shaped flowers. Grow in a rock garden, on a sunny bank, or in a mixed or herbaceous border. Where not hardy, grow in a temperate greenhouse. In areas with cold, wet winters, grow *C. cneorum* and *C. sabatius* in containers, and move them into a cold greenhouse in winter. Some species with running rootstocks, such as *C. arvensis* (Field bindweed), are highly invasive and difficult to control.
• **CULTIVATION** Grow in poor to moderately fertile, gritty, well-drained soil in a sheltered site in full sun. Deadhead annuals to prolong flowering. Confine potentially invasive species by planting in a container plunged into the soil. In containers, use a soil-based potting mix, and water freely when in growth; keep just moist during winter.
• **PROPAGATION** Sow seed of annuals *in situ* in midspring, or in autumn with protection where marginally hardy. For perennials, shrubs, and subshrubs, sow seed at 55–64°F (13–18°C) in spring; root softwood cuttings in late spring or greenwood cuttings in summer. Divide perennials in spring.
• **PESTS AND DISEASES** Rust, *Septoria* leaf spot (and others), spider mites, and aphids cause problems under glass.

C. althaeoides. Vigorous, slender, climbing or trailing perennial with ovate to heart-shaped, shallowly to deeply lobed, hairy, silvery green leaves, to 1¼in (3cm) long. Axillary clusters of 1–3 widely funnel-shaped, clear pink flowers, to 1½in (4cm) across, are produced in mid- and late summer. Invasive, but suitable for a container. ↕ to 6in (15cm), ↔ indefinite. S. Europe. Zone 7. **subsp. *tenuissimus***, syn. *C. elegantissimus*, has more finely dissected leaves with a covering of dense, soft, silvery hairs.
C. boissieri ■ syn. *C. nitidus.* Creeping, mat- or cushion-forming perennial with clustered, ovate, silky-hairy, silvery gray leaves, to 1¼in (3cm) long. Bears short-stemmed, axillary clusters of 1–4 funnel-

Convolvulus boissieri

Convolvulus cneorum

shaped white, sometimes pink-flushed flowers, to ¾in (2cm) across, with small yellow centers, in early summer. ↕ to 3in (8cm), ↔ 16in (40cm) or more. Spain. Zone 7b.
C. cneorum ■ (Silverbush). Compact, rounded, bushy shrub with inversely lance-shaped to linear, silky, silver-green leaves, 1¼–2½in (3–6cm) long. Funnel-shaped white flowers, to 1½in (4cm) across, with yellow centers, are borne from pink buds in axillary clusters from late spring to summer. ↕ 24in (60cm), ↔ 36in (90cm). C. and W. Mediterranean. Zone 8.
C. elegantissimus see *C. althaeoides* subsp. *tenuissimus.*
C. mauritanicus see *C. sabatius.*
C. minor see *C. tricolor.*

Convolvulus tricolor 'Royal Ensign'

C. nitidus see *C. boissieri.*
C. purpureus see *Ipomoea purpurea.*
C. sabatius ■ syn. *C. mauritanicus.* Trailing, slender-stemmed, woody-based perennial with oblong to broadly ovate, mid-green leaves, to 1¼in (3cm) long. Produces a profusion of shallowly funnel-shaped, pale to deep lavender-blue flowers, ½–1in (1.5–2.5cm) across, in clusters of 1–3 from the leaf axils, from summer to early autumn. ↕ 6in (15cm), ↔ to 20in (50cm). Spain, Italy, North Africa. Zone 8.
C. tricolor, syn. *C. minor.* Bushy, upright then spreading, red-stemmed annual or short-lived perennial with ovate to lance-shaped, dark green leaves, to 1½in (4cm) long. Solitary, open funnel-shaped, royal blue flowers, to 1½in (4cm) across, feathered white and with yellow eyes, are borne in long succession in summer; each bloom lasts only a day. ↕ 12–16in (30–40cm), ↔ 9–12in (23–30cm). Portugal to Greece, N. Africa. ❄ (min. 41°F/5°C). **'Royal Ensign'** ■ produces deep blue flowers, to 2in (5cm) across; grow in a hanging basket; ↕ to 12in (30cm).

▷ ***Cooperia*** see *Zephyranthes*

Convolvulus sabatius

COPERNICIA

Wax palm

ARECACEAE

Genus of about 24 species of slow-growing, single-stemmed palms from savanna and forest, often in dry areas prone to periodic flooding, in Cuba, Hispaniola, and South America. Leaves, borne in dense, terminal clusters, are pinnate, with 10–60 leaflets arranged so that the leaves appear to be palmately lobed. On fading, the leaves remain in place, hanging down and forming a thatch-like skirt. The bowl-shaped, 3-petaled flowers are borne in panicles between the leaves. Where not hardy, grow as houseplants or in a warm greenhouse or conservatory. In warmer areas, use as specimen trees.

• **CULTIVATION** Under glass, grow in soil-based potting mix in full light, with shade from hot sun. In the growing season, water freely and apply a balanced liquid fertilizer monthly; water sparingly in winter. Pot on or top-dress in spring. Outdoors, grow in fertile, moist but well-drained soil in sun or partial shade.

• **PROPAGATION** Sow seed at 73–81°F (23–27°C) in spring.

• **PESTS AND DISEASES** Fungal leaf spots and spider mites sometimes occur.

C. macroglossa ■ (Petticoat palm). Single-stemmed palm with pinnate leaves, consisting of wedge-shaped, stalkless or very short-stalked, usually deep green leaflets, to 4½ft (1.4m) long, the outer ones with spiny margins. Very small, greenish white flowers are borne in panicles that protrude beyond the leaf tips in summer. ↕ 15–22ft (5–7m), ↔ to 10ft (3m). Cuba. ❄ (min. 55°F/13°C)
C. prunifera (Carnauba palm). Single-stemmed palm with rounded, palmately lobed, waxy, mid-green leaves, 6ft (2m) long. In summer, bears panicles, to 9ft (2.5m) long, of small, greenish white flowers. ↕ 45ft (14m), ↔ to 15ft (5m). N.E. Brazil. ❄ (min. 55°F/13°C)

Copernicia macroglossa

COPIAPOA

CACTACEAE

Genus of 10–20 species of slow-growing, solitary or clustered, mound-forming cacti from coastal deserts of N. Chile. The stems have warty ribs and spiny areoles. Funnel-shaped, diurnal flowers, mostly in shades of yellow, rarely in shades of red, are borne from the densely woolly crowns in summer; they are followed by spherical to turban-shaped green fruits with glossy black-brown seeds. Where temperatures fall below 50°F (10°C), grow as houseplants or in a warm greenhouse. In warmer areas, grow in a desert garden.

• **CULTIVATION** Under glass, grow in a mix of 3 parts standard cactus potting mix and 1 part perlite, in bright filtered light. From spring to early autumn, water moderately, applying a balanced liquid fertilizer monthly. Keep dry at other times. Outdoors, grow in gritty, poor soil in full sun, with some midday shade. See also pp.48–49.

• **PROPAGATION** Sow seed at 66–75°F (19–24°C) in early spring. Remove offsets in summer.

• **PESTS AND DISEASES** Mealybugs may be a problem under glass.

C. barquitensis see *C. hypogaea.*
C. cinerea ■ Solitary or clump-forming cactus producing spherical then cylindrical, 14- to 30-ribbed, grayish white stems, to 8in (20cm) across. Dark brown areoles bear 1 or 2 black or gray spines. Bright yellow flowers, 1½in (4cm) long, are produced in summer. ↕ to 28in (70cm), rarely taller, ↔ to 16in (40cm). N. Chile. ❄ (min. 50°F/10°C). **var. *gigantea***, syn. *C. haseltoniana*, bears completely gray stems with 20 or more very prominent ribs and dark brown spines; ↔ 8in (20cm).
C. haseltoniana see *C. cinerea* var. *gigantea.*
C. hypogaea, syn. *C. barquitensis.* Solitary or clump-forming cactus with flattened-spherical, dark brownish green stems, 2½–3in (6–8cm) across, with 12 or more ribs. White-woolly areoles bear a few white radial spines. Yellow flowers, ¾in (2cm) long, are borne in summer. ↕ 1½–3in (4–8cm), ↔ 5in (13cm). N. Chile. ❄ (min. 50°F/10°C)
C. krainziana ■ Clump-forming cactus with spherical, 13- to 24-ribbed, grayish green stems, to 5in (13cm) across. Gray areoles bear gray spines

Copiapoa cinerea

Copiapoa krainziana

(10–12 radials and 14–20 centrals). Golden yellow flowers, 1½in (4cm) long, are produced in summer. ↕ 4in (10cm) or more, ↔ to 3ft (1m). N. Chile. ❄ (min. 50°F/10°C)

COPROSMA

RUBIACEAE

Genus of about 90 species of evergreen shrubs and small trees found in forest, swamp, grassland, and rocky areas, from Indonesia to Australia, New Zealand, and the Pacific islands. The opposite leaves are simple, linear to rounded, often leathery, and light to dark green, purple, or brown. The inconspicuous, usually dioecious, tubular or narrowly funnel-shaped flowers are borne singly or in cymes or clusters. Coprosmas are valued for their handsome foliage and for their mainly spherical, brightly colored, succulent berries, ⅛–½in (3–15mm) across, usually borne in autumn. Best grown in a cool greenhouse or conservatory with a minimum temperature of 41°F/5°C.

• **CULTIVATION** Under glass, grow in soil-based potting mix in bright filtered light, with good ventilation. In growth, water freely and apply a balanced liquid fertilizer monthly; water moderately at other times. Outdoors, grow in neutral to slightly acidic, moderately fertile, moist but well-drained soil in sun or partial shade. Pruning group 8.

• **PROPAGATION** Sow seed in containers in a cold frame in spring. Root semi-ripe cuttings in late summer.

• **PESTS AND DISEASES** Occasionally damaged by root rot and scale insects.

Coprosma 'Coppershine'

Coprosma x *kirkii* 'Variegata'

C. acerosa* f. *brunnea see *C. brunnea.*
C. baueri see *C. repens.*
C. baueriana see *C. repens.*
***C.* 'Beatson's Gold'.** Compact, rounded, female shrub with spreading branches and ovate, bright green leaves, to ½in (1.5cm) long, splashed yellow in the centers. Bright red berries are borne in autumn. ↕↔ 5ft (1.5m). ❄ (min. 35°F/2°C)
***C.* 'Blue Pearls'.** Mat-forming female shrub with rigid, spreading branches and inversely lance-shaped, dark green leaves, to ½in (1.5cm) long. Translucent blue berries are produced in summer. ↕ 18in (45cm), ↔ 36in (90cm). ❄ (min. 35°F/2°C)
***C.* 'Brunette'.** Bushy female shrub with ovate-oblong, glossy bronze leaves, 1in (2.5cm) long. Orange berries are borne in autumn. ↕↔ 3ft (1m). ❄ (min. 35°F/2°C)
C. brunnea, syn. *C. acerosa* f. *brunnea.* Mat-forming, dioecious shrub with spreading, tangled, wiry shoots and slender, linear, brownish green leaves, to ½in (1.5cm) long. Translucent blue berries are produced on female plants in autumn. ↕ 18in (45cm), ↔ 6ft (2m). New Zealand.
***C.* 'Chocolate Soldier'.** Upright, bushy, male shrub with oblong to oblong-ovate, very glossy, chocolate-brown to dark green leaves, ½–¾in (1–2cm) long. ↕ 3ft (1m), ↔ 18in (45cm).
***C.* 'Coppershine'** ■ Bushy male shrub with narrowly ovate-oblong, glossy, dark green to purple leaves, suffused copper, 1in (2.5cm) long. ↕↔ 3ft (1m).
C.* x *kirkii (*C. acerosa* x *C. repens*). Variants of this hybrid have an irregular,

Coprosma repens

Coprosma repens 'Marble Queen'

spreading habit. Arching branches bear linear-oblong, narrowly obovate, or lance-shaped, dark green leaves, to 1½in (4cm) long. In autumn, produces oblong-spherical, translucent or white berries, flushed or flecked red. ↕ 5ft (1.5m), ↔ 6ft (2m). New Zealand. **'Variegata'** ■ is a spreading, female shrub, with white-margined, gray-green leaves and white berries; ↕ 30in (75cm), ↔ 5ft (1.5m).
***C.* 'Kiwi-gold'.** Prostrate male shrub with elliptic to oblong, glossy, mid-green leaves, 1¼in (3cm) long, boldly splashed yellow. ↕ 10in (25cm), ↔ 3ft (1m).
C. repens ■ syn. *C. baueri*, *C. baueriana* (Looking-glass plant). Large, dioecious shrub or small tree, sometimes prostrate, with broadly ovate-oblong, fleshy, glossy, deep green leaves, ¾–3in (2–8cm) long. Bears obovoid, orange-red berries, to ½in (1.5cm) long, from late summer to autumn. ↕ 2–25ft (0.6–8m), ↔ 3–10ft (1–3m). New Zealand. **'Exotica'** is a female version of 'Picturata'. **'Marble Queen'** ■ is male, with leaves splashed creamy white. **'Picturata'** ■ is male, and has leaves with deep cream to yellow centers and orange berries.
C. robusta. Vigorous, usually dioecious, erect then spreading shrub with elliptic, semi-glossy, dark green leaves, 3–5in (8–13cm) long. Ovoid, deep orange to yellow berries are produced in autumn. ↕ 12–20ft (4–6m), ↔ 6–12ft (2–4m). New Zealand. **'Variegata'** is male, with a central yellow blaze on each leaf. **'Williamsii Variegata'**, syn. 'Williamsii', is bisexual, with dark and light green marbled leaves, margined creamy yellow, and orange berries.

Coprosma repens 'Picturata'

COPTIS

Goldthread

RANUNCULACEAE

Genus of 10 species of low-growing, evergreen perennials from temperate, usually coniferous woodland and bogs in the N. hemisphere. They produce slender yellow rhizomes and basal, 3- to 5-palmate or finely palmately lobed leaves. Goldthreads are also grown for their star-shaped flowers, borne on leafless stems above the foliage. Grow in a woodland garden.
• **CULTIVATION** Grow in moderately fertile, humus-rich, moist but well-drained, slightly acidic soil in a sheltered site in full or partial shade.
• **PROPAGATION** Sow seed in a cold frame as soon as ripe, or divide in spring.
• **PESTS AND DISEASES** Commonly affected by *Septoria* leaf spot.

C. quinquefolia. Rhizomatous, spreading, delicate perennial with long-stalked, 5-palmate leaves, to 1in (2.5cm) long, with obovate or diamond-shaped leaflets. Solitary, upturned white flowers are produced on stems 3–5in (8–13cm) long, in spring. ↕ to 5in (13cm), ↔ to 8in (20cm). Japan, Taiwan. Zone 6.
C. trifolia* subsp. *groenlandica (Cankerroot). Small, rhizomatous, spreading perennial with 3-palmate, basal leaves, 1in (2.5cm) long, with wedge-shaped, scalloped-toothed leaflets. From spring to summer, bears solitary white flowers, ½in (1.5cm) across, on stems 3–6in (8–15cm) long. Used as an herbal remedy and yellow dye. ↕ 2–6in (5–15cm), ↔ to 8in (20cm). Greenland, N.E. North America. Zone 2.

CORDIA

BORAGINACEAE

Genus of 300 species of deciduous or evergreen shrubs, trees, and climbers from dry slopes near waterways in tropical Africa, the Middle East, Asia, and Central and South America. They usually have alternate, simple leaves and are grown for their fragrant, showy, terminal flowers. *Cordia* species are outstanding as specimen plants. Where not hardy, grow in a temperate or warm greenhouse or conservatory.
• **CULTIVATION** Under glass, grow in soil-based potting mix mixed with added organic matter and coarse sand, with full light and high humidity. Water freely during the growing season, sparingly in winter. Outdoors, grow in moderately fertile, moist but well-drained soil, in full sun and high humidity. Pruning group 10.
• **PROPAGATION** Sow seed *in situ* at 55–64°F (13–18°C), or take semi-ripe cuttings in mid- or late summer.
• **PESTS AND DISEASES** Mushroom root rot, leaf spots, and rust may occur.

C. boisseri. Small evergreen tree with ovate, entire to minutely scalloped, velvety-hairy leaves, to 5in (13cm) long. In spring, produces terminal cymes of tubular to funnel-shaped, silky-hairy white flowers, 1in (2.5cm) across, with yellow centers, followed by ovoid, bright red-brown fruit. ↕ to 8–10ft (2.5–3m), ↔ 6–8ft (2–2.5m). S. New Mexico, Texas to Mexico. ❀ (min. 45°F/7°C)

CORDYLINE

Cabbage palm, Cabbage tree

AGAVACEAE

Genus of 15 species of evergreen shrubs or tree-like, woody-stemmed perennials, the larger ones resembling palms, found on open hillsides and in scrub and open forest in S.E. Asia and the Pacific, including Australasia. The tufted or rosetted, leathery leaves are simple, entire, and lance-shaped to linear. Sweetly scented, shallowly cup-shaped, 6-tepaled flowers, ¼–½in (6–15mm) across, are produced in sometimes large, conspicuous, terminal panicles, followed by spherical, white, red, blue, or purple berries, ⅛–⅜in (3–9mm) across. Where not hardy, grow as houseplants or in a cool, temperate, or warm greenhouse or conservatory. In warmer areas, grow as specimen plants, in a mixed or shrub border, or in a courtyard garden.
• **CULTIVATION** Under glass, grow in soilless or soil-based potting mix, with full light for green-leaved species, and bright filtered or indirect light for variants with colored foliage. In growth, water moderately and apply a balanced liquid fertilizer monthly; water sparingly in winter. Top-dress or pot on in spring. Outdoors, grow in fertile, well-drained soil in sun or partial shade.
• **PROPAGATION** Sow seed at 61°F (16°C) in spring. Remove well-rooted suckers in spring.
• **PESTS AND DISEASES** Prone to scale insects, spider mites, and mealybugs. Bacterial and fungal spots, bacterial soft rot, and root rot can occur. Fluoride toxicity can be a problem.

C. australis, syn. *Dracaena australis* (Giant dracaena, New Zealand cabbage palm). Erect, palm-like tree, branching sparingly with age. Arching, lance-shaped to linear leaves, 12–36in (30–90cm) long, are light green to almost yellow-green. In summer, mature trees bear tiny, creamy white flowers in broad panicles, 3ft (1m) or more long, followed by white or blue-tinted berries. ↕ 10–30ft (3–10m) or more, ↔ 3–12ft (1–4m). New Zealand. ❀ (min. 50°F/10°C). **'Albertii'** ■ has matte green leaves with red midribs, cream stripes, and pink margins. **'Atropurpurea'** has leaves flushed purple at the bases and on the main veins beneath. **'Doucettii'** has leaves with creamy white stripes and pink-flushed margins. **'Purple Tower'** has broad leaves, heavily flushed plum-purple. **'Torbay Dazzler'** produces leaves with bold cream stripes and margins. **'Variegata'** ■ has leaves longitudinally striped creamy white. **'Veitchii'** has leaves strongly flushed crimson at the bases and on the main veins beneath.
C. banksii. Sparingly clump-forming or single-stemmed, erect shrub or, rarely, small tree with few branches and a crown of arching, strap-shaped, mid- to yellow-green leaves, 3ft (1m) or more long. White flowers are borne in broadly pyramidal panicles, 3–6ft (1–2m) long, in summer, followed by white or blue-tinted fruit. ↕ 10–12ft (3–4m), ↔ 6–10ft (2–3m). New Zealand. ❀ (min. 45°F/7°C)
C. fruticosa, syn. *C. terminalis* (Good luck tree, Ti tree). Erect, suckering, clump-forming shrub with generally unbranched stems and strap-shaped, deep green leaves, 12–24in (30–60cm) long. In summer, produces white to purple flowers in loose panicles, 12–20in (30–50cm) long, followed by bright red berries. ↕ 6–15ft (2–5m), ↔ 3–8ft (1–2.5m). Tropical S.E. Asia, E. Australia, larger Pacific islands. ❀ (min. 55°F/13°C). **'Amabilis'** has broad, glossy, bronze and red leaves, with flecks of white and pink when mature. **'Baby Ti'** has leaf margins suffused copper-red; ↕↔ to 24in (60cm). **'Baptistii'** has broad, strongly recurved leaves streaked yellow and pink. **'Firebrand'**, syn. 'Red Dracaena', has compact heads of foliage, flushed deep red-purple. **'Guilfoylei'** has strongly tapered, recurved leaves streaked red,

Cordyline australis 'Albertii'

Cordyline australis 'Variegata'

C

Cordyline fruticosa 'Tricolor'

pink, and white, with white bases. **'Hawaiian Bonsai'** is compact, with dark crimson leaves; ↕ to 3ft (1m), ↔ to 24in (60cm). **'Margaret Storey'** is compact, with copper-flushed leaves splashed red and pink; ↕↔ 3ft (1m) or more. **'Mayi'** has red leaves when young, becoming deep green with red margins with age. **'Negri'** has deep copper-maroon foliage. **'Red Dracaena'** see 'Firebrand'. **'Tricolor'** ▣ has broad leaves boldly and very irregularly streaked and splashed in shades of red, pink, and cream.
C. indivisa ▣ syn. *Dracaena indivisa.* Thick-stemmed tree with a few branches at the top when mature. Each branch bears a tuft of narrowly lance-shaped, mid- to light green leaves, 3–6ft (1–2m) long, with red veins above and suffused blue-white beneath. Cream flowers are borne in dense panicles, to 5½ft (1.6m) long, in summer, followed by bluish purple berries. ↕ 20–30ft (6–10m), ↔ 6–12ft (2–4m). Mountain forest in New Zealand. ❀ (min. 45°F/7°C). **'Purpurea'** has leaves suffused bronze-purple.
C. stricta. Erect, suckering shrub with low-arching, linear, toothed, deep green leaves, 8–24in (20–60cm) long. In summer, bears lilac to violet flowers, with reflexed petals, in loose, pyramidal panicles, to 24in (60cm) long, followed by purple or almost black berries. ↕ 6–10ft (2–3m), ↔ 3–6ft (1–2m). Rainforest in Queensland to New South Wales. ❀ (min. 55°F/13°C). **'Discolor'** has bronze-purple leaves. **'Grandis'** is larger and more robust; ↕ to 11ft (3.5m). **'Rubra'** has foliage suffused copper-red.
C. terminalis see *C. fruticosa.*

Cordyline indivisa

COREOPSIS

Tickseed

ASTERACEAE

Genus of 80–100 species of hairless or softly hairy annuals and perennials, some becoming woody at the bases. They occur on prairies and in woodland in North and Central America, and Mexico. Most have upright stems and produce opposite leaves, which may be either simple and entire, pinnate, or palmate (either palmately lobed or fully divided, 3-palmate). Daisy-like, pink or yellow flowerheads are borne on long stalks; they are good for cut flowers (generally produced over a very long period), and are attractive to bees. Grow in an annual, herbaceous, or mixed border. Some cultivars, though perennial, are grown as annuals; most flower freely in their first year from seed.
• **CULTIVATION** Outdoors, grow in fertile, well-drained soil in full sun or partial shade. Deadhead to prolong flowering. Support taller cultivars.
• **PROPAGATION** Sow seed of annuals *in situ*, in succession from early spring to early summer; sow perennials in a seedbed in midspring. Alternatively, sow seed at 55–61°F (13–16°C) in mid- or late winter; perennials will flower in the first year. Divide perennials in early spring. Root basal cuttings in spring.
• **PESTS AND DISEASES** Slugs and snails feed on plants outdoors. Bacterial spot, rust, *Botrytis* flower blight, aster yellows, powdery mildew, downy mildew, and many fungal spots also occur.

C. auriculata. Rhizomatous perennial with erect, softly hairy stems bearing ovate to elliptic, entire or palmately lobed, mid-green leaves, to 5in (13cm) long. Solitary, bright yellow flowerheads, 2in (5cm) across, are borne in early and midsummer. ↕ to 32in (80cm), ↔ 24in (60cm). S.E. US. Zone 5. **'Cutting Gold'** see 'Schnittgold'. **'Nana'** is low-growing and tufted, bearing yellow-orange flowerheads, 1½in (4cm) across, from late spring to summer, and often to autumn; ↕ 8in (20cm). **'Schnittgold'**, syn. 'Cutting Gold', has vivid gold flowerheads. **'Superba'** produces bright orange-yellow flowerheads, 2½in (6cm) across, with maroon basal marks, from early to late summer; ↕ to 18in (45cm).
C. bigelovii. Erect annual with pinnate or 2-pinnate, clustered, mid-green leaves, to 4½in (11cm) long. Bears solitary yellow flowerheads, ½–1¾in (1.5–4.5cm) across, from spring to summer. ↕ to 16in (40cm), ↔ to 12in (30cm). California.
C. californica. Erect, branched, almost hairless annual with lance-shaped, entire to shallowly lobed, mostly basal, dark green leaves, to 6in (15cm) long. Produces solitary yellow flowerheads, to 1½in (4cm) across, in summer. ↕ to 18in (45cm), ↔ 9–12in (23–30cm). California, S. Arizona, N.W. Mexico.
C. grandiflora. Clump-forming, almost hairless perennial, often grown as an annual, with simple, lance-shaped or palmately lobed lower leaves, to 4in (10cm) long. Flowering stems produce 3- to 5-pinnate leaves with linear leaflets. From late spring to late summer, produces solitary flowerheads, to 2½in (6cm) across, consisting of golden yellow ray florets, with unevenly cut outer margins, and darker yellow disk florets. Excellent for cutting. ↕ 18–36in (45–90cm), ↔ 18in (45cm). C. and S.E. US. Zone 4. **'Badengold'** ▣ produces deep yellow flowerheads with orange centers; ↕ to 36in (90cm). **'Domino'** is a dwarf cultivar, producing yellow flowerheads; ↕ 16in (40cm). **'Early Sunrise'** ▣ is usually grown as an annual, and bears semi-double, deep yellow flowerheads, each flushed orange-yellow near the center; ↕ to 18in (45cm). **'Rotkehlchen'**, syn. *C.* 'Ruby Throat', is dwarf and bears double golden yellow flowerheads with rust-red eyes; ↕ 12in (30cm). **'Sunburst'** has double, rich yellow flowerheads. **'Sunray'**, usually grown as an annual, has double, deep yellow flowerheads; ↕ 20–30in (50–75cm).

Coreopsis grandiflora 'Badengold'

C. lanceolata ▣ Clump-forming, hairless perennial with usually entire, lance-shaped to inversely lance-shaped, mid-green leaves, to 6in (15cm) long. Flowering stems, with leaves only at the bases, produce solitary yellow flowerheads, 1½–2½in (4–6cm) across, from late spring to midsummer. ↕ to 24in (60cm), ↔ 18in (45cm). C. and S. US. Zone 4. **'Baby Gold'** has clear gold flowerheads; ↕ to 16in (40cm). **'Baby Sun'** see 'Sonnenkind'. **'Brown Eyes'** produces yellow flowerheads with maroon central rings; ↕ to 24in (60cm). **'Double Sunburst'** produces semi-double yellow-gold flowerheads with visible central disks. **'Goldfink'** is a dwarf cultivar, bearing golden yellow flowerheads; ↕ to 10in (25cm). **'Sonnenkind'**, syn. 'Baby Sun', bears golden yellow flowerheads; ↕ 16in (40cm). **'Sterntaler'** has yellow flowerheads with brown centers; ↕ to 16in (40cm). **'Sunburst'** bears double yellow flowerheads; ↕ to 30in (75cm).

Coreopsis grandiflora 'Early Sunrise'

***C.* 'Moonbeam'** ▣ syn. *C. verticillata* 'Moonbeam'. Upright perennial with 3-pinnate leaves, to 2½in (6cm) long, with linear, thread-like, deep green leaflets. Bears lemon-yellow flowerheads, ½–¾in (1.5–2cm) across, from early summer to autumn. ↕↔ 18in (45cm). Zone 3b.
C. palmata (Stiff tickseed). Upright perennial with 3-palmate, stiff, sometimes erect, thick, mid-green leaves, to 3in (8cm) long, with irregularly 2- or 3-lobed, oblong-linear leaflets. Yellow flowerheads, 2½in (6cm) across, are produced in summer. ↕ 18–30in (45–75cm), ↔ 24in (60cm). Minnesota to N. Louisiana. Zone 5.
C. rosea. Clump-forming perennial with linear or palmately 2- to 3-lobed, bright green leaves, to 2in (5cm) long. Produces mauve-pink flowerheads, 1in (2.5cm) across, from summer to early autumn. Good groundcover for a dry slope. ↕ to 24in (60cm), ↔ 12in (30cm). Nova Scotia to Delaware. Zone 4. **'Nana'** is dwarf; ↕ 8–10in (20–25cm).
***C.* 'Ruby Throat'** see *C. grandiflora* 'Rotkehlchen'.
C. tinctoria, syn. *Calliopsis tinctoria* (Calliopsis). Erect, hairless, stiff-stemmed annual bearing mostly basal, mid- to dark green leaves, to 4in (10cm) long. Leaves are lance-shaped and either entire, or pinnate or 2-pinnate with linear leaflets. In summer, produces solitary, bright yellow flowerheads, to 2in (5cm) across, shading to brown-red at the bases, with dark red disk florets. Dark red, purple, and brown variants also occur. ↕ to 4ft (1.2m), ↔ 12–18in (30–45cm). North America. **'Mahogany Midget'** is a dwarf cultivar, with yellow-centered, rich mahogany-scarlet flowerheads; ↕ to 12in (30cm). **'Nana'** has a compact, dwarf habit. **'Tiger Flower'** is a dwarf cultivar, bearing flowerheads that vary from pure crimson to golden yellow, many of them speckled and striped with both colors; ↕ to 9in (23cm), ↔ to 8in (20cm).
C. tripteris (Atlantic coreopsis). Erect, stout perennial with branched stems and 3-palmate, mid-green leaves, 8in (20cm) long, with linear to oblong-lance-shaped leaflets. From summer to autumn, bears pale yellow flowerheads, 2in (5cm) across, with yellow disk florets, becoming

Coreopsis lanceolata

Coreopsis 'Moonbeam'

brown or purple. ↕ 4–8ft (1.2–2.5m), ↔ 24in (60cm). Michigan, Iowa, Louisiana to Pennsylvania. Zone 4.

C. verticillata (Thread-leaved tickseed). Bushy, rhizomatous, slowly spreading, hairless perennial with numerous branched stems. Leaves are 3-pinnate, to 2½in (6cm) long, with linear, mid-green leaflets. Bears yellow flowerheads, to 2in (5cm) across, in loose corymbs in early summer. ↕ 24–32in (60–80cm), ↔ 18in (45cm). S.E. US. Zone 3b. **'Golden Shower'** see 'Grandiflora'. **'Grandiflora'**, syn. 'Golden Shower', has dark yellow flowerheads. **'Moonbeam'** see *C.* 'Moonbeam'. **'Zagreb'** has golden yellow flowerheads. Drought-resistant; ↕ 10–12in (25–30cm), ↔ to 12in (30cm).

CORIANDRUM

Cilantro, Coriander

APIACEAE

Genus of 2 species of annuals, with hairless, strongly aromatic foliage, occurring in scrub, wasteland, fallow fields, or steppes in the E. Mediterranean region. The rosettes of basal leaves are ovate and either pinnatisect or pinnate to 3-pinnate, with toothed, linear or oblong leaflets; the upper leaves are pinnate to 3-pinnate, with linear leaflets. Terminal, compound umbels of small, cup-shaped, white or purple-flushed sterile flowers, surrounded by larger fertile flowers, are followed by spherical, ribbed fruits. Grow in an herb garden for the leaves (Chinese parsley or cilantro) and seeds (coriander), which are used in cooking.

• **CULTIVATION** Grow in light, fertile, well-drained soil, in full sun for seed production or in partial shade for best leaf growth. Pick leaves throughout the growing season. Harvest seed when the fruits begin to change color and become pleasantly aromatic.

• **PROPAGATION** Sow seed *in situ* at intervals starting in spring. Bolts and self-seeds readily.

• **PESTS AND DISEASES** Susceptible to fungal wilt.

C. sativum. Aromatic annual with long-stalked, glossy, bright green leaves, ½in (1.5cm) long. From midsummer to autumn, 5-petaled, white or pale purple flowers are produced in umbels to ½in (1.5cm) across, followed by pale golden brown fruit. ↕ 20in (50cm), ↔ 8in (20cm). E. Mediterranean.

CORIARIA

CORIARIACEAE

Genus of about 8 species of small trees or shrubs, usually deciduous, and rhizomatous, herbaceous or subshrubby perennials, which occur in warm-temperate climates in grassland, scrub, and woodland, often in mountainous regions. They are cultivated for their attractive habit, foliage, and fruits. Arching shoots bear opposite, simple, entire leaves. Small, insignificant green flowers are produced in terminal or axillary racemes in spring, and followed by ornamental, fleshy, black, purplish black, red, or yellow fruits. In some species, male and female flowers are borne on different plants. *Coriaria* species are suitable for a shrub border or rock garden. Where not hardy, grow in a cool greenhouse. The leaves and fruits of some species may cause severe stomach upset if ingested; in other species, the fruits are edible, although the seeds are thought to be poisonous.

• **CULTIVATION** Grow in deep, moderately fertile, well-drained soil in a sheltered site in full sun. Mulch in winter where marginally hardy. Pruning group 1 or 2.

• **PROPAGATION** Sow seed in containers in a cold frame as soon as ripe. Sow seed of tender species at 55–61°F (13–16°C) in spring. Divide rhizomatous species in spring. Root greenwood cuttings in summer.

• **PESTS AND DISEASES** Infrequent.

C. terminalis. Deciduous, rhizomatous subshrub with arching shoots bearing broadly lance-shaped, mid-green leaves, to 3in (8cm) long, turning red in autumn. Small green flowers are borne in terminal racemes, to 6in (15cm) long, in late spring, followed in late summer by spherical, fleshy, dark blackish red fruit, to ½in (1.5cm) across. ↕ 3ft (1m), ↔ 6ft (2m). W. China, Himalayas. ❄ (min. 45°F/7°C). **var. *xanthocarpa*** ■ has translucent yellow fruit.

Coriaria terminalis var. *xanthocarpa*

CORNUS

Cornel, Dogwood

CORNACEAE

Genus of about 45 species of mainly deciduous shrubs and small trees, and a few woody-based perennials, from grassland, thickets, woodland, rocky slopes, and swamps, mostly in N. temperate areas. The usually opposite, sometimes alternate leaves are ovate-lance-shaped to broadly ovate, and mid- to dark green. Small, star-shaped flowers are borne in terminal cymes, with or without bracts; in dense umbels with yellowish bracts that fall as the flowers open; or in dense clusters with conspicuous white or pink bracts. Those borne in cymes or umbels are followed by loose clusters of berries; those borne in clusters are followed by tight clusters of berries or are united into compound, fleshy fruits.

Dogwoods are grown for their showy bracts, elegant habit, fruits, and colorful autumn leaves; some are effective specimen trees or shrubs, especially in a woodland garden. Those with colorful winter shoots, sometimes coppiced or pollarded, are useful for many situations, from a shrub border to a waterside garden. Use *C. canadensis* in woodland or as a groundcover in a shrub border. The fruits of some species may cause mild stomach upset if ingested; contact with the leaf hairs may irritate skin.

• **CULTIVATION** Grow flowering dogwoods (those having large bracts), such as *C. florida*, *C. kousa*, *C. nuttallii*, and their hybrids, in fertile, humus-rich, well-drained, neutral to acidic soil in sun or partial shade. *C. canadensis* prefers moist, acidic soil. Others tolerate a range of soils and locations. Those grown for winter stems color best in full sun. Pruning group 1; best with minimal pruning. Pruning group 7 for *C. alba*, *C. sanguinea*, and *C. stolonifera*.

• **PROPAGATION** Sow seed in a seedbed in autumn, or stratify and sow in spring. Divide *C. canadensis* in spring or autumn. Graft cultivars in winter. Root greenwood cuttings in summer. Take hardwood cuttings of those grown for winter stems in autumn.

• **PESTS AND DISEASES** Spot anthracnose (dogwood blight), powdery mildew, *Discula* blight, canker, bacterial leaf spot, and mushroom root rot occur. Twig borers, weevils, sawfly, scale insects, aphids, leafhoppers, root knot nematodes, and thrips are common.

Cornus alba 'Elegantissima'

Cornus alba 'Kesselringii'

C. alba (Redtwig dogwood). Vigorous, upright, deciduous shrub with red winter shoots and ovate-elliptic, dark green leaves, to 4in (10cm) long, which turn red or orange in autumn. White flowers in flat cymes, to 2in (5cm) across, are borne in late spring and early summer. Ellipsoid fruit are white, often tinged blue. ↕↔ 10ft (3m). Siberia, N. China to Korea. Zone 2. **'Aurea'** has yellow leaves. **'Elegantissima'** ■ has gray-green leaves, irregularly margined white. **'Gouchaultii'** produces pink-flushed, yellow-margined leaves. **'Kesselringii'** ■ has blackish purple winter shoots and red and purple autumn leaves. **'Sibirica'** ■ has bright red winter shoots and red autumn leaves. **'Spaethii'** ■ has broadly yellow-margined leaves.

Cornus alba 'Sibirica'

Cornus alba 'Spaethii'

C

Cornus alternifolia 'Argentea'

Cornus canadensis

Cornus controversa 'Variegata' (inset: leaf detail)

Cornus florida 'Cherokee Chief'

Cornus florida 'Spring Song'

C. alternifolia (Green osier, Pagoda dogwood). Deciduous tree or multi-stemmed shrub with spreading, tiered branches. Alternate, ovate-elliptic, mid-green leaves, to 5in (13cm) long, turn red and purple in autumn. Small white flowers are borne in flat cymes, to 2in (5cm) across, in early summer, followed by spherical blue-black fruit. Best in moist soil in partial shade. ↕↔ 20ft (6m). E. North America. Zone 4.
'Argentea' ■ syn. 'Variegata', is a tiered shrub or small tree with white-margined leaves, to 3in (8cm) long; ↕ 10ft (3m), ↔ 8ft (2.5m).
C. amomum (Silky dogwood). Vigorous, spreading, deciduous shrub with dull red-purple winter shoots and ovate-elliptic, dark green leaves, to 5in (13cm) long, turning orange, red, or purple in autumn. White flowers are produced in arching cymes, to 2½in (6cm) across, in late spring and early summer, followed by spherical, metallic gray-blue fruit. ↕ 10ft (3m), ↔ 12ft (4m). E. North America. Zone 4.
***C.* 'Ascona'**, syn. *C. nuttallii* 'Ascona'. Spreading, deciduous shrub producing purple winter shoots and ovate, mid-green leaves, to 5in (13cm) long, which turn orange, red, or purple in autumn. In late spring, green flowers are produced in flowerheads, ¾in (2cm) across, surrounded by 4 ovate, pointed white bracts, to 3in (8cm) long. ↕ 15ft (5m), ↔ 20ft (6m). Zone 7.
C. canadensis ■ (Bunchberry, Creeping dogwood, Dwarf cornel). Spreading, rhizomatous subshrub with terminal whorls of oval or obovate to lance-shaped, mid-green leaves, ¾–1½in (2–4cm) long. In late spring and early summer, green flowers are borne in cymes, ½in (1.5cm) across, surrounded by 4–6 white, sometimes pink-flushed bracts, ½–¾in (1–2cm) long; flowers are followed by spherical, fleshy, bright red fruit. May be difficult to establish; prefers cool summers. ↕ to 6in (15cm), ↔ indefinite. N. Asia, North America, Greenland. Zone 2.
C. capitata ■ Spreading, bushy, evergreen tree or shrub with ovate to lance-shaped, gray-green leaves, to 5in (13cm) long. In summer, green flowers are produced in small, hemispherical heads, ½in (1.5cm) across, surrounded by 4–6 obovate, creamy white or yellowish white bracts, 1½–2in (4–5cm) long; flowers are followed by pendent, strawberry-like fruit. ↕↔ 40ft (12m). China, Himalayas. Zone 8.
C. controversa (Giant dogwood). Rounded, deciduous tree bearing spreading, tiered branches. Alternate, elliptic leaves, to 6in (15cm) long, glossy, dark green above and glaucous beneath, turn rich red and purple in autumn. White flowers are borne in large, flattened cymes, to 7in (18cm) across, in early summer, followed by spherical, blue-black fruit. ↕↔ 50ft (15m). China, Himalayas, Japan. Zone 5. **'Variegata'** ■ produces leaves with bold, creamy white margins; ↕↔ 25ft (8m).
***C.* 'Eddie's White Wonder'** ■ Broadly conical, deciduous tree or multi-stemmed shrub with ovate, mid-green leaves, to 5in (13cm) long, turning

Cornus capitata

Cornus 'Eddie's White Wonder'

Cornus florida

Cornus florida 'Welchii'

Cornus kousa 'China Girl'

Cornus kousa 'Satomi'

Cornus mas

Cornus nuttallii 'Colrigo Giant'

orange, red, and purple in autumn. In late spring, purplish green flowers are borne in flowerheads, to ½in (1.5cm) across, surrounded by 4–6 ovate white bracts, to 3in (8cm) long. ↕20ft (6m), ↔ 15ft (5m). Zone 7.
C. florida ■ (Flowering dogwood). Conical, deciduous tree or shrub with broadly oval to ovate, often slightly twisted or curled, mid-green leaves, to 6in (15cm) long, which turn red and purple in autumn. In late spring, green flowers, tipped with yellow, are borne in flowerheads, to ½in (1.5cm) across, surrounded by 4 obovate, white to pink bracts, 1½–2in (4–5cm) long, followed by clusters of usually 3 or 4 bright red, ovoid fruit. ↕20ft (6m), ↔ 25ft (8m). E. North America. Zone 5b. **'Cherokee Chief'** ■ has very dark ruby-pink bracts. **'Cherokee Daybreak'** produces green and white leaves that turn pink to deep red in autumn. **'Cherokee Princess'** produces abundant flowerheads with large white bracts, 2½in (6cm) long. **'Cloud Nine'** has large, overlapping white bracts, 2½in (6cm) long; it flowers freely, even when young. **'First Lady'** has yellow-variegated leaves. **'Hohman's Gold'** has leaves margined golden yellow, turning red-purple with scarlet margins in autumn, and produces white bracts; ↕10ft (3m), ↔ 12ft (4m). **'Pendula'** has weeping branches. **'Pluribracteata'** has 6–8 large bracts with smaller bracts at the centers. **'Purple Glory'** has purple leaves, turning black-purple in autumn, and bears dark red bracts. **'Rainbow'** is similar to 'Hohman's Gold', but compact and upright; ↕10ft (3m), ↔ 8ft (2.5m). **f. *rubra*** has pink bracts; flowers may be slightly less cold hardy. **'Spring Song'** ■ has deep rose-pink bracts. **'Springtime'** bears large, white, overlapping bracts, 5in (13cm) across. **'Tricolor'** see 'Welchii'. **'Welchii'** ■ syn. 'Tricolor', is slow-growing, with white- and pink-margined, gray-green leaves, turning bronze-purple with rose-red margins in autumn, and white bracts. **'White Cloud'** is very free-flowering, and bears creamy white bracts.
C. kousa (Kousa dogwood). Broadly conical, deciduous tree with mottled bark and ovate, wavy-margined, dark green leaves, to 3in (8cm) long, turning deep crimson-purple in autumn. In early summer, green flowers are produced in flowerheads, to ½in (1.5cm) across, surrounded by 4 ovate-lance-shaped to ovate white bracts, 1–2in (2.5–5cm) long; flowers are followed by raspberry-like, fleshy red fruit. ↕22ft (7m), ↔ 15ft (5m). Korea, Japan. Zone 6. **'China Girl'** ■ is very free-flowering, even when young. **var. *chinensis*** ■ has smooth-margined leaves and large, tapered bracts, to 2in (5cm) long, which open creamy white and then turn white and eventually red-pink. **var. *chinensis* 'Elizabeth Lustgarten'** is weeping. **'Gold Star'** is shrubby, with leaves marked dark yellow in the centers, turning red with purple margins in autumn; bracts are white on opening, later becoming pink; ↕8ft (2.5m), ↔ 6ft (2m). **'Milky Way'** flowers and fruits profusely. **'Satomi'** ■ has dark red-purple autumn foliage and dark pink bracts. **'Snowboy'** has gray-green leaves with broad white margins, the leaves turn pink and red in autumn; ↕8ft (2.5m), ↔ 6ft (2m). **'Summer Stars'** has leaves that turn maroon in autumn, and bears a profusion of persistent flowers.
C. macrophylla ■ Broadly conical, deciduous tree with ovate, glossy, mid-green leaves, to 7in (18cm) long. Creamy white flowers are produced in broad, flattened heads, to 7in (18cm) across, in late summer; flowers are followed by spherical, blue-black fruit. ↕40ft (12m), ↔ 25ft (8m). China, Himalayas, Japan. Zone 7b.
C. mas ■ (Cornelian cherry). Vigorous, spreading, deciduous shrub or small tree with ovate, dark green leaves, to 4in (10cm) long, turning red-purple in autumn. Yellow flowers are produced in small umbels, to ¾in (2cm) across, in late winter, before the leaves. Oblong-ellipsoid, fleshy, bright red fruit are produced in late summer, and are edible when ripe. ↕↔ 15ft (5m). Europe, W. Asia. Zone 4b. **'Aurea'** has yellow juvenile leaves, maturing to mid-green. **'Aureoelegantissima'**, syn. 'Elegantissima', has leaves broadly margined yellow and pink; ↕6ft (2m), ↔ 10ft (3m). **'Elegantissima'** see 'Aureoelegantissima'. **'Variegata'** is compact, with white leaf margins and abundant fruit; ↕8ft (2.5m), ↔ 6ft (2m).
C. nuttallii (Pacific dogwood). Conical, deciduous tree with oval to obovate, mid-green leaves, to 5in (13cm) long, sometimes turning red in autumn. In late spring, purple and green flowers are produced in flowerheads, to ½in (1.5cm) across, surrounded by 4–6, occasionally up to 8, broadly ovate to obovate, white or pink-tinged bracts, 1½–3in (4–8cm) long; flowers are followed by spherical, orange-red fruit. ↕40ft (12m), ↔ 25ft (8m). W. North America. Zone 7. **'Ascona'** see *C.* 'Ascona'. **'Colrigo Giant'** ■ is very vigorous, with thick shoots, leaves to 6in (15cm) long, and spherical flowerheads with 6–8 bracts. **'Gold Spot'** has yellow-marked leaves.
C. officinalis. Vigorous, spreading, deciduous shrub with rough, flaking brown bark and ovate to elliptic, dark green leaves, to 4in (10cm) long, turning red-purple in autumn. Yellow flowers are produced in loose umbels, ¾in (2cm) or more across, in late winter, before the leaves open; they are followed by oblong-ellipsoid, edible, bright red fruit. ↕↔ 15ft (5m). China, Korea, Japan. Zone 6b.

Cornus kousa var. *chinensis*

Cornus macrophylla (inset: flower detail)

Cornus 'Porlock'

Cornus x *rutgersensis* Stellar Series 'Ruth Ellen'

***C.* 'Porlock'** ■ Spreading, semi-evergreen tree with elliptic to obovate, mid-green leaves, 2–3in (5–8cm) long. In late spring, purple and green flowers are produced in flowerheads, ½in (1.5cm) across, surrounded by ovate, white then pink-red bracts, 3in (8cm) long. ↕ 30ft (10m), ↔ 15ft (5m). Zone 6.
C. racemosa (Gray dogwood). Multi-stemmed, upright, suckering, deciduous shrub with red-brown young stems, gray when mature, and ovate-lance-shaped, gray-green to dark green leaves, 2–4in (5–10cm) long, turning purplish red in autumn. In late spring, bears white flowers in flat cymes, 2in (5cm) across, followed by white fruit. ↕↔ 10–15ft (3–5m). Minnesota to Maine, south to Nebraska and Georgia. Zone 2b.
***C.* x *rutgersensis* Stellar Series.** Vigorous trees with elliptic to ovate, dark green leaves, 2–5in (5–13cm) long, turning bright red in autumn. In late spring, green-white flowers are profusely borne in heads, 1in (2.5cm) across, surrounded by large, rounded, creamy white or pink bracts, 1–2in (2.5–5cm) long, followed by spherical to ovoid, red fruit. Highly resistant to common dogwood borer and anthracnose. Zone 6. **'Aurora'** is upright, blooming in spring about a week after most *C. florida* specimens have finished; ↕↔ 20–25ft (6–8m). **'Ruth Ellen'** ■ is spreading, with branches close to the ground; ↕ 20–25ft (6–8m), ↔ 25–30ft (8–10m).
C. sanguinea (Bloodtwig dogwood). Upright, deciduous shrub with reddish green, sometimes entirely green, winter shoots and ovate, mid-green leaves, to 4in (10cm) long, turning red in autumn. In summer, bears white flowers in dense, flat cymes, to 2in (5cm) across, followed by spherical, dull blue-black fruit. ↕ 10ft (3m), ↔ 8ft (2.5m). Europe. Zone 4. **'Viridissima'** has green winter shoots. **'Winter Beauty'**, syn. 'Winter Flame', has orange-yellow and red winter shoots. **'Winter Flame'** see 'Winter Beauty'.
C. sericea see *C. stolonifera*.
C. stolonifera, syn. *C. sericea* (Red osier dogwood). Vigorous, suckering, deciduous shrub with dark red winter shoots. Ovate to lance-shaped, dark green leaves, to 5in (13cm) long, turn red or orange in autumn. In late spring and early summer, white flowers are produced in flat cymes, to 2in (5cm) across, followed by white fruit, often tinged blue. Tolerates wet soils. ↕ 6ft (2m), ↔ 12ft (4m). E. North America. Zone 2. **'Flaviramea'** ■ has bright yellow-green winter shoots. **'Isanti'** is dense and compact, with bright red stems; ↕ 5–6ft (1.5–2m). **'Kelseyi'**, syn. 'Kelsey's Dwarf', 'Nana', is compact, with red-tipped, yellow-green winter shoots; ↕ 30in (75cm), ↔ 5ft (1.5m). **'Nana'** see 'Kelseyi'. **'Silver and Gold'** has yellow stems and cream-edged leaves.

Cornus stolonifera 'Flaviramea'

COROKIA

CORNACEAE

Genus of 3 species of evergreen shrubs occurring in forest and rocky areas in New Zealand. They have alternate, linear to obovate leaves. Star-shaped, 5-petaled yellow flowers, ⅜–½in (0.9–1.5cm) across, are produced singly from the leaf axils or in short, terminal racemes, panicles, or clusters, followed by colorful autumn fruits. Where not hardy, grow *Corokia* species and cultivars as specimen plants in a sheltered shrub border or against a wall. In warmer coastal regions, they will tolerate an open site or partial shade, and may be used for hedging.

- **CULTIVATION** Grow in fertile, well-drained soil, preferably in full sun, sheltered from cold, dry winds. Pruning group 8; will tolerate hard pruning to restrict growth, if required.
- **PROPAGATION** Root greenwood cuttings in early summer, or take semi-ripe cuttings in mid- or late summer.
- **PESTS AND DISEASES** Infrequent.

C. buddlejoides (Korokio). Upright shrub with elliptic to linear-lance-shaped, glossy, dark green leaves, to 6in (15cm) long. Bears small, fragrant yellow flowers in terminal panicles, ¾–2in (2–5cm) long, in spring, followed by spherical, bright red-black fruit. ↕ 10ft (3m), ↔ 6ft (2m). New Zealand (North Island). ❄ (min. 41°F/5°C)
C. cotoneaster ■ (Wire-netting bush). Rounded, intricately branched shrub bearing interlacing shoots and broadly ovate to obovate, dark green leaves, to ½in (1.5cm) long. In late spring, small, fragrant yellow flowers are produced singly or in clusters of up to 4, from the leaf axils, followed by oblong-ellipsoid, red or yellow fruit. ↕↔ 8ft (2.5m). New Zealand. Zone 7b.
C. macrocarpa. Upright shrub with lance-shaped, leathery leaves, gray-green above and silvery beneath, to 3in (8cm) long. In early summer, small yellow flowers are borne in short racemes, to 1½in (4cm) long, from the leaf axils, followed by oblong-ellipsoid red fruit. ↕↔ 6ft (2m) or more. New Zealand (Chatham Island). ❄ (min. 41°F/5°C)
C.* x *virgata ■ (*C. cotoneaster* x *C. buddlejoides*). Upright shrub with spoon-shaped to inversely lance-shaped leaves, glossy, dark green above and white beneath, to 2in (5cm) long. In late spring, small, fragrant yellow flowers are produced in clusters of 3 from the leaf axils, followed by ovoid, yellow or orange fruit. ↕↔ 10ft (3m). New Zealand (North Island). ❄ (min. 35°F/2°C). **'Bronze King'** has bronze-tinged foliage. **'Bronze Lady'** has dark bronze leaves, to 1½in (4cm) long, and bright red fruit. **'Yellow Wonder'** is vigorous and bears golden yellow fruit.

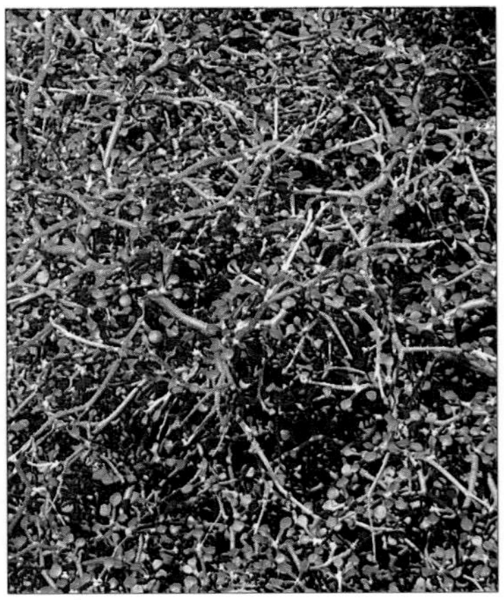

Corokia cotoneaster

Corokia x *virgata*

CORONILLA

FABACEAE

Genus of about 20 species of annuals, herbaceous perennials, and evergreen and deciduous shrubs from Europe and N. Africa, where they occur in habitats ranging from meadows to scrub, woodland and woodland margins, and cliffs. They are cultivated for their alternate, usually pinnate leaves and their often fragrant, pea-like flowers, borne in axillary umbels. Grow in a shrub border or at the base of a warm, sunny wall.

- **CULTIVATION** Grow in light, moderately fertile, well-drained soil in full sun, sheltered from winds. Pruning group 1; cut back leggy plants almost to the bases to rejuvenate them in spring.

Coronilla valentina subsp. *glauca*

Coronilla valentina subsp. *glauca* 'Variegata'

• **PROPAGATION** Sow seed in containers in a cold frame as soon as ripe, or stratify and sow at 50–55°F (10–13°C) in spring. Root greenwood cuttings in early summer or semi-ripe cuttings in late summer.
• **PESTS AND DISEASES** Anthracnose can be a problem.

C. emerus, syn. *Hippocrepis emerus* (Scorpion senna). Bushy, rounded, deciduous shrub with mid-green shoots and pinnate leaves, to 2½in (6cm) long, with up to 9 obovate leaflets. Slender-stalked, axillary umbels of 2 or 3 pale yellow flowers, ¾in (2cm) long, are produced from late spring to autumn, followed by slender, segmented pods, to 4in (10cm) long. ↕↔ 6ft (2m). C. and S. Europe. Zone 7b.
C. glauca see *C. valentina* subsp. *glauca.*
C. valentina. Dense, rounded, bushy, evergreen shrub with pinnate, bright green leaves, to 2in (5cm) long, with up to 13 obovate leaflets. Bears axillary umbels of 4–14 fragrant, bright yellow flowers, ½in (1.5cm) long, in late winter and early spring, and in late summer, followed by slender pods, to 2in (5cm) long. ↕↔ 5ft (1.5m). S. Portugal, Spain to Croatia (Dalmatia). Zone 8. **subsp. *glauca*** ■ syn. *C. glauca*, is often more compact, and bears blue-green leaves with 5–7 leaflets; ↕↔ 32in (80cm). **subsp. *glauca* 'Citrina'** has pale yellow flowers. **subsp. *glauca* 'Variegata'** ■ has leaves margined creamy white.
C. varia (Crown vetch). Creeping herbaceous perennial with pinnate, mid-green leaves, to 11in (28cm) long, with up to 14 oblong leaflets. From summer to autumn, bears umbels of 4–20 white, purple, or pink flowers, ½in (1.5cm) long, followed by slender, segmented pods, 2–8in (5–20cm) long. ↕ 8in (20cm), ↔ indefinite. C. and S. Europe. Zone 5. **'Penngift'** has a neater habit, with creeping stems and pink flowers. Used for erosion control and bank plantings; ↕ to 24in (60cm).

CORREA

Australian fuchsia

RUTACEAE

Genus of about 20 species of evergreen shrubs and small trees found in scrub and open woodland in Australia. The opposite, simple leaves have star-shaped hairs and are aromatic when bruised. The mainly pendent, tubular to bell-shaped flowers, with 4 spreading or

Correa backhouseana

reflexed lobes, are produced singly or in few-flowered clusters. Where not hardy, grow in a cool greenhouse or conservatory. In warmer areas, grow in a shrub border or courtyard garden, or at the base of a house wall.
• **CULTIVATION** Under glass, grow in acidic potting mix in full light, with shade from hot sun, and with good ventilation. In the growing season, water moderately and apply a balanced liquid fertilizer monthly; water sparingly in winter. Top-dress or pot on in spring. Minimum temperature 41°F/5°C but may survive brief periods of 30°F/-1°C. *C. pulchella* and *C. reflexa* tolerate mildly alkaline soil. Pruning group 8.
• **PROPAGATION** Sow seed at 55–64°F (13–18°C) in spring. Root semi-ripe cuttings with bottom heat in summer.
• **PESTS AND DISEASES** Scale insects may be a problem under glass.

C. alba. Freely branching shrub with ovate, rich green leaves, ¾–1½in (2–4cm) long, smooth above, finely hairy beneath. From early summer to late autumn, bears short, bell-shaped, sometimes pink-tinted, waxy white flowers, to ½in (1.5cm) long, in few-flowered clusters. ↕ 6ft (2m), ↔ 3–6ft (1–2m). South Australia, New South Wales, Victoria, Tasmania.
C. backhouseana ■ Dense, spreading shrub with hairy, rust-red twigs and oval, dark green leaves, ¾–1¼in (2–3cm) long, smooth above and hairy beneath. Produces small clusters of tubular, pale or reddish green or cream flowers, to 1in (2.5cm) long, from late

Correa 'Dusky Bells'

Correa pulchella

autumn to late spring. ↕ 3–6ft (1–2m), ↔ 5–8ft (1.5–2.5m). Victoria, Tasmania.
***C.* 'Carmine Bells'** see *C.* 'Dusky Bells'.
***C.* 'Dusky Bells'** ■ syn. *C.* 'Carmine Bells', *C.* 'Pink Bells', *C.* 'Rubra'. Wide-spreading shrub with reddish brown stems and oval, mid- to deep green leaves, to 1½in (4cm) long. Tubular, dusky carmine-red flowers, to 1in (2.5cm) long, are borne in small clusters from autumn to spring. ↕ 12–36in (30–90cm), ↔ 5–10ft (1.5–3m).
***C.* 'Harrisii'** see *C.* 'Mannii'.
***C.* 'Ivory Bells'.** Bushy, vigorous shrub with spreading, densely hairy stems and elliptic to ovate, matte, deep green leaves, ¾–1¼in (2–3cm) long. Clusters of tubular, ivory-white flowers, to ¾in (2cm) long, with recurved lobes, aging to tan, are mainly produced from winter to summer. ↕ 3–6ft (1–2m), ↔ 6–10ft (2–3m).
***C.* 'Mannii'**, syn. *C.* 'Harrisii'. Spreading shrub with broadly ovate leaves, ¾–1¼in (2–3cm) long, heart-shaped at the bases and dark green above, paler beneath. Tubular red flowers, to 1in (2.5cm) long, with reflexed petal tips, are borne in small clusters from autumn to spring. ↕ 3–8ft (1–2.5m), ↔ 6–10ft (2–3m).
***C.* 'Pink Bells'** see *C.* 'Dusky Bells'.
C. pulchella ■ Freely branching, prostrate to almost erect shrub with oval to elliptic, smooth, bright green leaves, ½–¾in (1–2cm) long. Bears tubular, vermilion, orange, or pink to white flowers, to 1in (2.5cm) long, in small clusters from autumn to spring. ↕ 1–5ft (30–150cm), ↔ 3–8ft (0.9–2.5m). South Australia.
C. reflexa, syn. *C. speciosa.* Erect to prostrate, loosely to compactly branched shrub bearing obovate-oblong to lance-shaped, rich green leaves, to 2in (5cm) long, white-felted beneath. Tubular to narrowly bell-shaped flowers are green, white, pink, or red, ¾–1in (2–2.5cm) long, sometimes with green or cream reflexed petal tips; they are produced in small clusters, mainly from autumn to spring. ↕ 1–10ft (0.3–3m), ↔ 3–10ft (1–3m). Australia (except Northern Territory).
***C.* 'Rubra'** see *C.* 'Dusky Bells'.
C. speciosa see *C. reflexa.*

CORRYOCACTUS

syn. ERDISIA

CACTACEAE

Genus of about 20 species of trailing or erect, shrub-like cacti from semi-arid areas of S. and C. Peru, Bolivia, and N. Chile. Many branch from the bases to form large clumps, with cylindrical, ribbed stems bearing evenly spaced, spiny areoles. Solitary, funnel-shaped, diurnal, orange, red, or vivid yellow flowers are borne in summer, followed by spherical, spiny green fruits with small black or brown seeds. Where not hardy, grow in a temperate greenhouse, with a minimum temperature of 50°F (10°C). In warmer areas, grow in a desert garden.
• **CULTIVATION** Under glass, grow in standard cactus potting mix in full light, with shade from hot sun. From spring to summer, water moderately and apply a dilute, low-nitrogen liquid fertilizer monthly; keep completely dry at other times. Outdoors, grow in low-fertility, sharply drained, gritty, humus-rich soil in full sun. See also pp.48–49.
• **PROPAGATION** Sow seed at 70°F (21°C) in spring. Root stem cuttings in late spring or early summer.
• **PESTS AND DISEASES** Mealybugs, and occasionally aphids, may be problems.

C. brachypetalus. Erect, clump-forming cactus with 7- or 8-ribbed, dull green stems branching from the base. White areoles bear 15–20 brownish black spines. Deep orange flowers, 1½–2½in (4–6cm) across, are produced in summer. ↕ 6–12ft (2–4m), ↔ 3ft (1m). S. Peru. ❄ (min. 50°F/10°C)
C. erectus ■ syn. *Erdisia erecta.* Usually erect, clump-forming cactus with 5- or 6-ribbed, mid-green stems branching from the base, and pale brown or white areoles bearing yellowish white spines (10 or more radials and 1 or 2 centrals). Produces carmine-red or scarlet flowers, 1½–2in (4–5cm) across, in summer.

Corryocactus erectus

C

↕ 3ft (1m) or more, ↔ 24in (60cm). S. Peru. ❀ (min. 50°F/10°C)
C. squarrosus, syn. *Erdisia squarrosa.* Erect, clump-forming cactus with 5- to 8-ribbed, deep green stems and brown areoles, each with about 11 yellow spines (1 central and 10 radials). Bright red, sometimes yellowish red flowers, 1½in (4cm) across, are produced in summer. ↕ 20in (50cm), ↔ 3ft (1m) or more. C. Peru. ❀ (min. 50°F/10°C)

C

CORTADERIA

Pampas grass, Tussock grass

POACEAE

Genus of about 23 species of evergreen or semi-evergreen, perennial grasses from grassland, often near water, in New Zealand, New Guinea, and South America. They form dense tussocks of stiff, flat, narrowly linear, often glaucous leaves with rough or sharp margins, and bear thick-stemmed, plume-like, silver, gold, or pale rose-pink flower panicles (usually with male and female spikelets on separate plants, but occasionally hermaphroditic). Female spikelets have long, silky hairs at the bases. The plumes may be used in fresh or dried flower arrangements. Grow at the back of a border or as free-standing specimens.

• **CULTIVATION** Grow in fertile, well-drained soil in full sun, with ample space to develop. Protect crowns of young plants during winter. Cut and comb out the previous year's stems and dead foliage annually, in late winter or early spring, taking care to avoid the sharp leaf margins, which can inflict severe cuts.

Cortaderia selloana 'Sunningdale Silver'

• **PROPAGATION** Sow seed at 55–64°F (13–18°C) in spring. Divide in spring.
• **PESTS AND DISEASES** *Helminthosporium* leaf spots are common.

C. argentea see *C. selloana.*
C. conspicua see *Chionochloa conspicua.*
C. richardii (Toe toe). Densely tufted, clump-forming, evergreen, perennial grass with recurved, leathery, pale olive-green leaves, to 4ft (1.2m) long. In early and midsummer, arching stems, to 9ft (2.5m) tall, bear shaggy, pyramidal, creamy white or silvery white panicles, 24in (60cm) long, which persist into winter. ↕ to 9ft (2.5m), ↔ 6ft (1.8m). New Zealand. Zone 7b.
C. selloana, syn. *C. argentea* (Pampas grass). Densely tufted, clump-forming, evergreen, perennial grass with arching, glaucous, mid-green leaves, to 8ft (2.5m) or more long. In late summer, silky, silver, often pink- or purple-flushed spikelets are borne in pyramidal to oblong panicles, 18–36in (45–90cm) long, on erect stems. ↕ 8–10ft (2.5–3m), ↔ 5ft (1.5m) or more. Temperate South America. Zone 7. **'Albolineata'**, syn. 'Silver Stripe', is slow-growing and compact, with white-margined leaves and silvery white plumes; ↕ to 6ft (2m). **'Aureolineata'** ▣ syn. 'Gold Band', has rich yellow-margined leaves, aging to dark golden yellow; ↕ to 7ft (2.2m). **'Gold Band'** see 'Aureolineata'. **'Pumila'** has mid-green leaves and produces masses of erect, silvery yellow plumes; ↕ to 5ft (1.5m), ↔ 4ft (1.2m). **'Rendatleri'** has purplish pink panicles; ↕↔ to 8ft (2.5m). **'Rosa Feder'** see 'Rosea'. **'Rosea'**, syn 'Rosa Feder', produces lightly pink-tinted panicles. **'Silver Stripe'** see 'Albolineata'. **'Sunningdale Silver'** ▣ has strong, erect stems and dense, weather-resistant, silvery white plumes; ↕ 10ft (3m) or more, ↔ to 8ft (2.5m).

Cortaderia selloana 'Aureolineata'

CORTUSA

PRIMULACEAE

Genus of 8 species of herbaceous perennials occurring in mountain woodland from W. and C. Europe to N. Asia. They produce long-stalked, rounded to heart-shaped, basal leaves. One-sided umbels of funnel- to bell-shaped flowers are produced on slender stems above the foliage. *Cortusa* species are suitable for a woodland or rock garden; they will not thrive in hot, dry climates.

• **CULTIVATION** Grow in moderately fertile, humus-rich, reliably moist but well-drained, slightly acidic or alkaline soil in a cool position in partial shade.
• **PROPAGATION** Sow seed in containers in an open frame as soon as ripe. Divide in spring.
• **PESTS AND DISEASES** Slugs and snails may be problems.

C. matthioli ▣ Clump-forming perennial with kidney-shaped to rounded, crinkled, rust-hairy, deep green leaves, 5in (13cm) or more across, with coarsely toothed lobes. Pendent, broadly bell-shaped, magenta or purple-violet, occasionally white flowers, ½in (1.5cm) long, are borne in one-sided umbels on hairy stems, in late spring and early summer. ↕ 8–12in (20–30cm), ↔ to 6in (15cm). W. Europe. Zone 5.

Cortusa matthioli

CORYDALIS

syn. PSEUDOFUMARIA

PAPAVERACEAE

Genus of about 300 species of fibrous- or fleshy-rooted annuals and biennials, and tuberous or rhizomatous perennials. Most are herbaceous; a few are evergreen. They occur in a range of habitats, with many from woodland or rocky, mountain sites, mostly in N. temperate regions. They have opposite or alternate stem leaves, which are compound, usually ternate to 3-ternate, sometimes pinnate to 3-pinnate, and sometimes triangular in outline. The leaflets are often finely divided, producing a fern-like appearance. Tubular flowers, borne in mostly terminal, sometimes axillary racemes, usually above the foliage, each have 4 petals: the outer pair with a spur and reflexed tips, the inner pair incurved to cover the stamens and style.

The sun-loving species are suitable for a rock garden or alpine house; grow shade-loving species in a rock or woodland garden, or as an underplanting in a shrub border. Some species need a period of dry dormancy in summer and protection from excessive winter moisture; these are best grown in a bulb frame or alpine house.

• **CULTIVATION** *Corydalis* species have varying cultivation requirements, which, for ease of reference, are grouped as follows:
1. Full sun or partial shade and fertile, well-drained soil. Often self-seed freely.
2. Full sun and sharply drained, moderately fertile soil in a rock garden. May tolerate partial shade.
3. Partial shade and moderately fertile, humus-rich, moist but well-drained soil.
4. Grow in a bulb frame or alpine house, in equal parts loam, leaf mold, and grit. Resent excessive moisture.
• **PROPAGATION** Sow seed in containers in an open frame as soon as ripe; germination may be erratic. Divide spring-flowering species in autumn, and summer-flowering species in spring.
• **PESTS AND DISEASES** Downy mildew and rust occur. Slugs and snails can damage plants, and aphids and spider mites are common under glass.

***C. ambigua* of gardens** see *C. fumariifolia.*
***C. bulbosa* of gardens** see *C. cava.*
C. cashmeriana. Tufted perennial with clusters of ovoid tubers. Produces

Corydalis cheilanthifolia

Corydalis diphylla

ternate, bright green leaves, to 3in (8cm) long, with ovate leaflets finely divided into oblong or elliptic lobes. Dense racemes of 3–8 brilliant blue flowers, ½in (1.5cm) long, with curved spurs, are borne in summer. Prefers cool, moist climates. Cultivation group 3. ↕ 4–10in (10–25cm), ↔ 3–6in (8–15cm). Himalayas. Zone 5b.

C. cava, syn. *C. bulbosa* of gardens (Fumewort). Hollow-tubered perennial with 2-ternate, pale green leaves, to 4in (10cm) long, composed of wedge-shaped, lobed leaflets. In early spring, produces dense racemes of purple or white flowers, to 1in (2.5cm) long, with downward-curving spurs, to ½in (1.5cm) long, and entire, scale-like bracts. Cultivation group 3. ↕ 4–8in (10–20cm), ↔ 4in (10cm). Europe. Zone 6b.

C. cheilanthifolia ■ Evergreen, fibrous-rooted, rosette-forming perennial with fern-like, 2- or 3-pinnate, bronze-tinted, light to mid-green leaves, 6–18in (15–45cm) long, with linear or linear-lance-shaped leaflets. Dense, spike-like racemes of straight-spurred, deep yellow flowers, to ½in (1.5cm) long, are borne from spring to summer. Self-seeds freely. Cultivation group 1. ↕ to 12in (30cm), ↔ to 10in (25cm). W. and C. China. Zone 6.

C. diphylla ■ Tuberous perennial with semi-erect, long-stalked, 2- or 3-ternate, glaucous, mid-green leaves, to 3in (8cm) long, consisting of linear-lance-shaped leaflets. In spring, produces loose, terminal racemes of 6–10 pale violet flowers, ¾–1¼in (2–3cm) long, with deeper violet or red-violet lips and upward-pointing white spurs, to ½in (1.5cm) long. Cultivation group 2. ↕ to 6in (15cm), ↔ to 4in (10cm). W. Himalayas. Zone 6.

C. flexuosa ■ Erect, summer-dormant perennial with slender, fibrous rootstocks with small bulbils, and 2-ternate leaves, to 6in (15cm) long, with ovate, glaucous, light green leaflets, sometimes flushed purple. From late spring to summer, produces dense, terminal and axillary racemes of slender-tubed, brilliant blue flowers, to 1in (2.5cm) long, with white throats. Cultivation group 3. ↕ to 12in (30cm), ↔ 8in (20cm) or more. China (W. Sichuan). Zone 5. **'Blue Panda'** is compact and free-flowering, with gentian-blue flowers; ↕ 8in (20cm). **'Pere David'** bears whorls of turquoise-blue flowers.

C. fumariifolia, syn. *C. ambigua* of gardens. Tuberous perennial with 2-ternate, slightly glaucous, mid-green leaves, to 3in (8cm) long, with entire, oval to obovate leaflets. From spring to early summer, bears loose, spike-like racemes of azure-blue, occasionally purple flowers, ¾–1¼in (2–3cm) long, with flattened, triangular spurs. Cultivation group 3. ↕ to 6in (15cm), ↔ to 4in (10cm). Russia (Kamchatka), China, Japan. Zone 5.

C. halleri see *C. solida.*

C. lutea ■ syn. *Pseudofumaria lutea.* Rhizomatous, mound-forming, evergreen perennial with fern-like, 2-ternate or 2- or 3-pinnate, arching leaves, 4–6in (10–15cm) long, with obovate, 3-lobed leaflets, pale green above, glaucous beneath. Bluntly spurred, golden yellow flowers, ½–¾in (1–2cm) long, are borne in terminal and axillary racemes of 6–16, in a long succession from late spring to early autumn. Self-seeds freely. Cultivation group 1, 2, or 3. ↕ 16in (40cm), ↔ 12in (30cm). Widespread in Europe. Zone 4.

C. nobilis. Rhizomatous, robust, deep-rooting perennial with much-divided, more or less stalkless, bluish green leaves, to 12in (30cm) long; the leaves are 2-pinnate at the bases, with wedge-shaped leaflets. In late spring, the upright stems bear dense, terminal racemes of up to 30 light yellow flowers, ¾–1in (2–2.5cm) long, each with a brown spot and a short, downward-pointing spur, and deeper yellow at the tips. Cultivation group 1. ↕ 24in (60cm), ↔ 18in (45cm). Russia (Siberia), E. Kazakhstan, N.W. China, Mongolia. Zone 5.

Corydalis flexuosa

Corydalis lutea

Corydalis ochroleuca

C. ochotensis. Mound-forming, tap-rooted biennial bearing few long-stalked, 2- or 3-pinnate, light green leaves, 6in (15cm) long, with obovate to wedge-shaped, usually 2- or 3-lobed leaflets. From midsummer to late autumn, bears simple or branched racemes of up to 10 yellow flowers, ½–¾in (1.5–2cm) long, maroon at the tips, with tapering, downward-curving spurs. Cultivation group 1 or 3. ↕ 24in (60cm), ↔ 12in (30cm). N. China, Korea, Japan. Zone 5.

C. ochroleuca ■ Evergreen, fibrous-rooted, clump-forming perennial with 2- or 3-pinnate, light green leaves, to 5in (13cm) long, with obovate leaflets. Compact, axillary racemes of creamy white flowers, to ½in (1.5cm) long, with yellow throats and downward-curving spurs, are produced from late spring to summer. Self-seeds freely. Cultivation group 1. ↕↔ to 12in (30cm). S.E. Europe. Zone 6.

C. popovii. Tuberous perennial with 2- or 3-ternate, blue-green leaves, to 6in (15cm) long, with 3–9 ovate leaflets. In late spring, produces loose, upright racemes of outward-facing, pale violet to white flowers, to 1¾in (4.5cm) long, with deep red-purple lips and downward-curving spurs, to 1in (2.5cm) long. Cultivation group 4. ↕ to 6in (15cm), ↔ to 5in (13cm). C. Asia. Zone 7b.

C. rutifolia. Variable, tuberous perennial with tufted, 2-ternate, gray-green leaves, to 4in (10cm) long, with entire or finely cleft leaflets. In spring, bears violet flowers, to 1in (2.5cm) long, with dark purple lips and ascending, inflated spurs, in loose racemes just above or among the leaves. Cultivation group 4. ↕ 3in (8cm), ↔ to 5in (13cm). Greece (Crete), Cyprus, E. Turkey, Lebanon, Iraq. Zone 5.

C. saxicola, syn. *C. thalictrifolia.* Rhizomatous perennial with 2- or 3-pinnate, shiny, mid-green leaves, 14in (35cm) long, with obovate or ovate leaflets. Spreading racemes of short-spurred yellow flowers, to 1in (2.5cm) long, are produced from late spring to summer. Cultivation group 2 or 4. ↕ to 12in (30cm), ↔ to 8in (20cm). C. China. Zone 6.

C. solida, syn. *C. halleri*, *C. transsylvanica* of gardens (Fumewort). Variable, tuberous perennial with 2- or 3-ternate, gray-green leaves, to 3in (8cm) long, with deeply and unevenly dissected, narrowly to broadly ovate leaflets. In spring, produces dense, upright, spike-like racemes of numerous pale mauve-pink to red-purple or white flowers, to ¾in (2cm) long, with tapered, downward-curving spurs and lobed bracts. Cultivation group 2 (tolerates partial shade). ↕ to 10in (25cm), ↔ to 8in (20cm). N. Europe, Asia. Zone 4. **'George Baker'** ■ syn. 'G.P. Baker', produces deep reddish

Corydalis solida 'George Baker'

Corydalis wilsonii

salmon-pink flowers. Many similar seedlings from pink- or red-flowered variants of *C. solida* have recently been raised and named.
C. thalictrifolia see *C. saxicola.*
***C. transsylvanica* of gardens** see *C. solida.*
C. wilsonii ■ Evergreen perennial with a fleshy, taprooted rootstock and rosettes of pinnate, smooth, blue-green leaves, to 3in (8cm) long, with broadly oblong-elliptic leaflets. Loose racemes of short-spurred, green-tipped, canary-yellow flowers, to ¾in (2cm) long, are produced in spring. Suitable for an alpine house or shady wall. Cultivation group 4. ↕↔ 4–8in (10–20cm). C. China. Zone 6.

CORYLOPSIS

Winter hazel

HAMAMELIDACEAE

Genus of 7–10 species of deciduous shrubs and small trees found in woodland and scrub in the E. Himalayas, China, Taiwan, and Japan. They have alternate, simple, ovate to broadly ovate, toothed, pale to dark green leaves. Pendent racemes of 6–20 bell-shaped, fragrant yellow flowers are produced in spring, before the young leaves emerge. Grow in a woodland garden or in a shrub or mixed border.
• **CULTIVATION** Grow in fertile, moist but well-drained, acidic soil in partial shade. Pruning group 1; prune immediately after flowering if required.
• **PROPAGATION** Sow seed in containers in an open frame in autumn. Insert greenwood cuttings in summer. Layer in autumn.
• **PESTS AND DISEASES** Infrequent.

C. glabrescens ■ Open, spreading shrub with broadly ovate leaves, dark green above and blue-green beneath, to 4in (10cm) long. Pale yellow flowers are borne in pendent racemes, to 1in (2.5cm) long, in midspring. ↕↔ 15ft (5m). Korea, Japan. Zone 7.
C. pauciflora (Buttercup winter hazel). Bushy, spreading shrub with ovate, bright green leaves, to 3in (8cm) long, bronze when young. Bears abundant pale yellow flowers in few-flowered, pendent racemes, to 1¼in (3cm) long, in early and midspring. ↕ 5ft (1.5m), ↔ 8ft (2.5m). Japan, Taiwan. Zone 7.
C. sinensis ■ syn. *C. willmottiae.* Vigorous, open, upright to spreading

Corylopsis glabrescens

shrub with obovate to oblong leaves, to 4in (10cm) long, dark green above and blue-green beneath. Lemon-yellow flowers are produced in pendent racemes, to 3in (8cm) long, in midspring. ↕↔ 12ft (4m). China. Zone 7. **var. *calvescens* f. *veitchiana***, syn. *C. veitchiana*, is upright, and produces pendent racemes, 3½in (9cm) long, of mid-yellow flowers with brick-red anthers; ↔ 8ft (2.5m). **'Spring Purple'** has dark plum-purple young foliage.
C. spicata. Open, spreading shrub with ovate to obovate leaves, dark green above and glaucous beneath, to 4in (10cm) long. Bears bright yellow flowers, with red to purple anthers, in slender, pendent racemes, to 6in (15cm) long, in spring. ↕ 6ft (2m), ↔ 10ft (3m). Japan. Zone 6.
C. veitchiana see *C. sinensis* var. *calvescens* f. *veitchiana.*
C. willmottiae see *C. sinensis.*
***C.* 'Winterthur'.** Compact, dense shrub with pleated young foliage, unfolding to heart-shaped, bright green leaves, to 4in (10cm) long. Bears bright yellow flowers in pendent racemes, to 3in (8cm) long, in early spring. ↕ to 6ft (2m), ↔ 12ft (4m). Zone 6.

CORYLUS

Filbert, Hazel

BETULACEAE

Genus of 10–15 species of deciduous trees and shrubs from N. temperate regions, usually found in woodland. They have alternate, rounded or oval to ovate leaves, sometimes with heart-shaped bases. Hazels are grown for their foliage and yellow male catkins. Cultivars of several species listed below also produce edible nuts. Smaller hazels are best grown in a shrub border; the larger species and cultivars are excellent specimen trees.
• **CULTIVATION** Grow in fertile, well-drained soil in sun or partial shade; they are ideal for alkaline soils. Grow variants with colored leaves in full sun. Remove suckers, which are produced particularly on grafted plants. Pruning group 1; also group 7 for *C. avellana* and *C. maxima.*
• **PROPAGATION** Sow seed in a seedbed as soon as ripe. Layer cultivars in autumn; graft in winter.
• **PESTS AND DISEASES** Powdery mildew, blight, canker, dieback, mushroom root rot, fungal spots, *Gymnosporangium* rust, bud mites, tent caterpillars, and webworms occur.

C. americana (American filbert). Multi-stemmed, deciduous shrub with heart-shaped to ovate, sharply pointed, toothed, dark green leaves, to 5in (13cm) long, sparsely hairy above and downy beneath. In early spring, bears pendent yellowish brown catkins, to 3in (8cm). In autumn, edible nuts, ½in (1.5cm) long, ripen in softly hairy, notched husks. ↕ 10–15ft (3–5m), ↔ 7–12ft (2.2–4m). E. US. Zone 2b.
***C. avellana* cultivars.** Upright or tree-like shrubs with broadly heart-shaped, round-tipped, toothed, mid-green leaves, to 4in (10cm) long. Pendent yellow catkins, 1½–2½in (4–6cm) long, are borne in late winter and early spring. ↕↔ 15ft (5m). Europe, Turkey. Zone 3. **'Aurea'** has bright yellow young foliage, becoming yellow-green when mature. **'Contorta'** ■ (Corkscrew hazel, Harry Lauder's walking stick) has strongly twisted shoots, which are particularly effective in winter and are useful for flower arrangements.
C. colurna ■ (Turkish hazel). Conical tree with broadly oval, shallowly lobed, dark green leaves, to 5in (13cm) long, turning yellow in autumn. Pendent

Corylus avellana 'Contorta'

yellow catkins, 2–3in (5–8cm) long, are borne in late winter. Produces edible nuts, enclosed in deeply fringed husks, in autumn. ↕ 70ft (20m), ↔ 22ft (7m). S.E. Europe, W. Asia. Zone 5.
C. cornuta (Beaked filbert). Upright, deciduous shrub with ovate, toothed, mid-green leaves, 1½–4½in (4–11cm) long. In early spring, bears pendent, yellowish brown catkins, ½–1in (1.5–2.5cm) long. In autumn, produces edible nuts, ½in (1.5cm) long, with husks forming narrow beaks, extending 1–1½in (2.5–4cm) beyond the nut. ↕↔ 4–8ft (1.2–2.5m). Saskatchewan to Quebec, south to Missouri and Georgia. Zone 5.
C. maxima (Filbert). Upright shrub or tree with heart-shaped, mid-green leaves, to 5½in (14cm) long. Pendent

Corylopsis sinensis

Corylus colurna

Corylus maxima 'Purpurea'

yellow catkins, 2–3in (5–8cm) long, are borne in late winter. Produces edible nuts, enclosed in tubular husks, that ripen in autumn. ↕ 20ft (6m), ↔ 15ft (5m). S.E. Europe to Caucasus. Zone 5. **'Purpurea'** ▣ has dark purple foliage, and purple-tinged catkins and fruit husks; grow in full sun.

CORYNOCARPUS

CORYNOCARPACEAE

Genus of 48 species of evergreen trees from Australasia, New Guinea, Vanuatu, and New Caledonia, occurring in open woodland and thickets. Simple, entire, leathery leaves are arranged alternately or in spirals along the stems. Small, tubular, 5-petaled flowers are borne in terminal panicles or racemes, followed by plum-like fruits. Where not hardy, grow *Corynocarpus* species and cultivars in a temperate or warm greenhouse; in warmer climates, use as specimen trees, screens, or windbreaks, especially in a coastal garden.

• **CULTIVATION** Under glass, grow in soil-based potting mix in full or bright filtered light, with good ventilation. In the growing season, water moderately and apply a balanced liquid fertilizer monthly; water sparingly in winter. Top-dress or pot on in spring. Outdoors, grow in fertile, moist but well-drained soil in sun or partial shade. Pruning group 1; plants under glass may need restrictive pruning.

• **PROPAGATION** Sow seed at not less than 59°F (15°C) in spring. Root semi-ripe cuttings with bottom heat in summer.

Corynocarpus laevigatus

• **PESTS AND DISEASES** Prone to scale insects, aphids, and spider mites, especially under glass.

C. laevigatus ▣ (Karaka). Erect and bushy, then spreading tree with obovate to elliptic-oblong, lustrous, deep green leaves, 4–8in (10–20cm) long. When mature, produces tiny, greenish yellow flowers in stiff panicles, 4–8in (10–20cm) long, from spring to summer. Narrowly ovoid orange fruit, 1½in (4cm) long, ripen in autumn. ↕ 30–50ft (10–15m), ↔ 6–15ft (2–5m). Vanuatu, New Zealand. ❀ (min. 50°F/10°C). **'Albovariegatus'** has leaves with white margins. **'Variegatus'** has yellow-margined leaves.

CORYPHA

ARECACEAE

Genus of 8 species of monocarpic, single-stemmed palms from tropical Asia to N. Australia and the Malaysian islands. Pinnate leaves, which appear to be palmate, are borne in dense clusters. Bowl-shaped, 3-petaled flowers are produced in spectacular, terminal panicles. Where not hardy, grow as foliage houseplants or in a warm greenhouse; in warmer areas, grow as free-standing specimens on a lawn.

• **CULTIVATION** Under glass, grow in soil-based potting mix in bright filtered light with moderate humidity. In the growing season, water moderately and apply a balanced liquid fertilizer monthly; water sparingly in winter. Pot on or top-dress in spring. Outdoors, grow in fertile, moist but well-drained soil in full sun.

• **PROPAGATION** Sow seed at 75–84°F (24–29°C) in spring.

• **PESTS AND DISEASES** Spider mites and scale insects may be problems.

C. umbraculifera ▣ (Talipot palm). Medium-sized to large palm with a sturdy trunk clad in old leaf bases. Leaf stalks are 6–10ft (2–3m) long, with short, spiny teeth; the lustrous, rich green blades, 8–15ft (2.5–5m) across, have 70–120 segments. Creamy white flowers are produced in panicles 20–25ft (6–8m) tall – the largest of all palm inflorescences; they first appear in spring at the end of the tree's life (usually between 20 and 30 years old). ↕ 50–80ft (15–25m), ↔ 22–46ft (7–14m). S. India, Sri Lanka. ❀ (min. 59°F/15°C)

CORYPHANTHA

CACTACEAE

Genus of 45 species of mostly spherical, occasionally cylindrical, warty, spiny cacti, occurring in semi-arid areas of S.W. US and Mexico. In summer, solitary, funnel-shaped, diurnal flowers are produced from the bases of the furrows in the tubercle axils; these are followed by cylindrical green seed pods, which contain ovoid to kidney-shaped brown seeds. Where not hardy, grow *Coryphantha* species as houseplants or in a warm greenhouse; in warmer climates, grow in a desert garden.

• **CULTIVATION** Under glass, grow in standard cactus potting mix in full light. In the growing season, water freely and apply a low-nitrogen liquid fertilizer monthly; keep completely dry at other times. Outdoors, grow in low-fertility, humus-rich, gritty, sharply drained soil in full sun. See also pp.48–49.

• **PROPAGATION** Sow seed at 66–75°F (19–24°C) in spring or early summer.

• **PESTS AND DISEASES** Mealybugs may be a problem under glass.

C. conoidea see *Neolloydia conoidea.*
C. cornifera ▣ Cactus with spherical then columnar, dark to gray-green stems, covered with angular tubercles, each with an areole bearing curved, yellowish brown spines (7–12 radials and 1 central). Yellow flowers, 2½in (6cm) across, are produced in summer. ↕ to 5in (13cm), ↔ 3in (8cm). C. Mexico. ❀ (min. 50°F/10°C)

Corypha umbraculifera

Coryphantha cornifera

C. elephantidens ▣ Cactus with flattened-spherical, glossy, mid-green stems, covered with long, very thick, furrowed and felted tubercles, and with white wool in the tubercle axils and at the crown. Each areole produces 6–8 curved, yellowish brown radial spines (no centrals). Deep pink flowers, 3–4in (8–10cm) across, with redder bases and mid-stripes, are produced in summer. ↕ 6in (15cm), ↔ to 8in (20cm). S.W. Mexico. ❀ (min. 50°F/10°C)
C. hesteri. Clump-forming cactus with spherical, dark green stems covered with conical tubercles. The areoles have stiff, white to brown spines (14–16 radials, 0–4 centrals). Bell-shaped, light purple flowers, ¾–1¼in (2–3cm) across, are borne in summer. ↕ 1½in (4cm), ↔ to 8in (20cm). W. Texas. ❀ (min. 41°F/5°C)
C. macromeris. Variable, clump-forming cactus with spherical, grayish green stems with cylindrical tubercles. The areoles have straight or curved spines (15 red radials and 1–4 dark brown centrals). Deep pink to purple-red flowers, 3in (8cm) across, are produced in summer. ↕ 6in (15cm), ↔ 12in (30cm). S.W. US, Mexico. ❀ (min. 50°F/10°C)
C. scheeri. Cactus with oblong-ovoid to spherical, mid-green stems with cylindrical tubercles. The areoles have straight or curved, thick, red-tipped, straw-colored spines (6–16 radials and 1–5 centrals). In summer, produces yellow, pink, or white flowers, 2–3in (5–8cm) across. ↕ 4–7in (10–18cm), ↔ to 8in (20cm). S.W. US, N. Mexico. ❀ (min. 41°F/5°C)
C. vivipara see *Escobaria vivipara.*

Coryphantha elephantidens

C

COSMOS

ASTERACEAE

Genus of about 25 species of erect to spreading, freely branched annuals and perennials, found in scrub and meadows in S. US and Central America. The leaves, borne in opposite pairs, may be simple, lobed, or pinnatisect to 3-pinnatisect or pinnate. *Cosmos* species and cultivars are grown for their large, showy, yellow, orange, crimson-red, pink, or white flowerheads, which may be saucer-, bowl-, or open cup-shaped, and are borne on long stems, mainly in summer. Grow annual species and cultivars in an annual border or cutting garden, or as fillers in a herbaceous border. Perennial species are excellent container or border plants.

• **CULTIVATION** Grow in moderately fertile, moist but well-drained soil in full sun. Deadhead to prolong flowering, leaving a few flowerheads on annual species, which often self-seed. Mulch *C. atrosanguineus* in autumn or lift tubers before first frosts and keep frost-free during winter, packed in barely moist peat.

• **PROPAGATION** Sow seed at 61°F (16°C) in midspring, or *in situ* in late spring. Root basal cuttings of *C. atrosanguineus* with bottom heat in early spring.

• **PESTS AND DISEASES** Stem canker, powdery mildew, *Rhizoctonia* stem rot, and sometimes gray mold can cause problems. Aphids also occur.

C. atrosanguineus ■ syn. *Bidens atrosanguinea*. Erect then spreading, tuberous perennial with reddish brown stems and spoon-shaped, pinnate to 2-pinnate, dark green leaves, 3–6in (7–15cm) long, with ovate-diamond-shaped, entire or toothed leaflets. Solitary, shallowly cup-shaped, lightly chocolate-scented, velvet-textured, maroon flowerheads, 1¾in (4.5cm) across, with slightly darker brown disk florets, are produced from midsummer to autumn. ↕ 30in (75cm), ↔ 18in (45cm). Mexico. Zone 7b.

C. bipinnatus. Erect, freely branching annual with pinnatisect, mid-green leaves, to 12in (30cm) long, with linear segments. Produces solitary, bowl- or saucer-shaped, white, pink, or crimson flowerheads, 3in (8cm) across, with yellow centers, throughout summer. ↕ to 5ft (1.5m), ↔ 18in (45cm). Mexico.

Cosmos atrosanguineus

Cosmos bipinnatus 'Sea Shells'

'Daydream' has white flowerheads, each with a pink central zone; ↕ to 36in (90cm). **'Picotee'** has white flowerheads with a variable, dark crimson picotee margin to each floret, some also flecked in crimson, and with the occasional pure crimson bloom; ↕ to 30in (75cm). **'Sea Shells'** ■ has carmine-red, pink, or white flowerheads, with florets curiously quilled (rolled into tubes); ↕ to 36in (90cm). **Sensation Series** cultivars bear pink or white flowerheads, sometimes more than 3½in (9cm) across; ↕ to 36in (90cm). Cultivars of **Sonata Series** are dwarf, with flowerheads in carmine-red, pink, or white; ↕↔ 12in (30cm). The series includes **'Sonata White'** ■, which has pure white flowers; ↕ to 18in (45cm), ↔ 12in (30cm).

C. sulfureus. Erect, bushy, hairy-stemmed annual with 2- or 3-pinnatisect, mid-green leaves, to 7in (18cm) long, with linear lobes. Open bowl-shaped, orange or yellowish red flowerheads, 1½–2½in (3.5–6cm) across, are borne in few-flowered clusters, throughout summer. ↕ 6ft (2m), ↔ 18in (45cm). Mexico. **'Bright Lights'** is a mixture of early-flowering and semi-double selections. **'Butterkist'**, syn. 'Lemon Cream', 'Lemon Peel', 'Yellow Garden', bears semi-double yellow flowerheads,

Cosmos bipinnatus 'Sonata White'

Cosmos sulfureus Ladybird Series

to 2½in (6cm) across, in late summer or early autumn; ↕ to 30in (75cm). **Klondike Series 'Sunny Gold'** is dwarf, bearing semi-double yellow flowers, to 2in (5cm) across; ↕ 14–18in (35–45cm). **Klondike Series 'Sunny Orange-Red'** is a dwarf selection with orange-red flowers; ↕ 12in (30cm). **Ladybird Series** ■ cultivars have less feathery foliage and semi-double flowerheads, 1½–3in (4–8cm) across, in yellow, orange, or scarlet; ↕ 12–16in (30–40cm), ↔ 8in (20cm). **'Lemon Cream'** see 'Butterkist'. **'Lemon Peel'** see 'Butterkist'. **'Yellow Garden'** see 'Butterkist'.

COSTUS

ZINGIBERACEAE

Genus of over 90 species of mostly clump-forming, rhizomatous perennials with an open, lax habit, found on forest floors in tropical Africa, Asia, Australia, and North, Central, and South America. The spirally arranged, somewhat fleshy leaves are inversely lance-shaped, lance-shaped, or elliptic. *Costus* species are cultivated for their showy, solitary or paired, white, yellow, orange, pink, or red flowers with basal bracts, usually produced in dense, terminal heads on leafy shoots or sometimes on leafless shoots. The flowers are tubular, each with 3, usually equal-sized petals. Where temperatures fall below 64°F (18°C), grow in a warm greenhouse. In humid tropical climates, grow in a shady border.

• **CULTIVATION** Under glass, grow in acidic potting mix, ideally in a border, in bright indirect light with high humidity. From spring to summer, water freely and apply a balanced liquid fertilizer monthly; reduce water in autumn, and water sparingly in winter. Pot on or replant in spring. Outdoors, grow in moist but well-drained, fertile, acidic soil in full or partial shade.

• **PROPAGATION** Sow seed at 68°F (20°C) as soon as ripe. Divide in spring.

• **PESTS AND DISEASES** Prone to leaf spots and anthracnose.

C. cuspidatus see *C. igneus.*

C. igneus, syn. *C. cuspidatus* (Fiery costus). Erect then spreading perennial producing elliptic, long-pointed leaves, 4–8in (10–20cm) long, dark green above and reddish green beneath. Bears terminal, deep yellow or orange flowers, 2in (5cm) across, at any time of year. ↕ 16in (40cm), ↔ 18in (45cm). Brazil. ❄ (min. 64°F/18°C)

Costus malortieanus

C. malortieanus ■ (Spiral ginger). Erect perennial with broadly elliptic or obovate, mid-green leaves, to 8in (20cm) long, with darker bands or stripes above, and shiny pale green beneath. Deep yellow flowers, 2in (5cm) across, with brown- or red-banded lips, are produced in dense, terminal heads at any time of year. ↕↔ 3ft (1m). Central America. ❄ (min. 64°F/18°C)

C. speciosus (Crepe ginger). Erect perennial with narrowly elliptic, mid-green leaves, 5–10in (12–25cm) long. Orange- or yellow-centered, white or pink flowers, 2in (5cm) across, are produced in terminal heads, 5in (13cm) long, with red bracts, at any time of year. ↕ 8ft (2.5m), ↔ 3ft (1m). S.E. Asia to New Guinea. ❄ (min. 64°F/18°C)

C. spicatus. Erect perennial with cane-like stems and narrowly elliptic, mid-green leaves, 12in (30cm) long. Yellow and pink flowers, 2in (5cm) across, with red to yellow lips, are produced in terminal heads at any time of year. ↕ 8ft (2.5m), ↔ 3ft (1m). West Indies (Hispaniola). ❄ (min. 64°F/18°C)

COTINUS

Smoke tree

ANACARDIACEAE

Genus of 2 species of deciduous trees and shrubs occurring in rocky habitats from the Mediterranean region to China and in S. US. They are cultivated for their alternate, broadly elliptic to rounded, green or purple leaves, which color well in autumn, and for their hairy, plume-like panicles, which appear in summer, producing a smoke-like

Cotinus coggygria 'Notcutt's Variety'

Cotinus coggygria f. *purpureus*

effect. The flowers and small, ovoid fruits are inconspicuous. Grow in a shrub border or as specimen plants, or plant in groups.

• **CULTIVATION** Grow in moderately fertile, moist but well-drained soil in full sun or partial shade. Purple-leaved forms color best in full sun. Pruning group 1; group 7 to produce large foliage.

• **PROPAGATION** Sow seed in containers in autumn. Layer in spring. Root softwood cuttings in summer.

• **PESTS AND DISEASES** Susceptible to *Verticillium* wilt. Powdery mildew may affect purple-leaved forms.

C. americanus see *C. obovatus.*

C. coggygria, syn. *Rhus cotinus* (Smoke bush, Venetian sumac). Bushy tree or shrub with oval, mid-green leaves, to 3in (8cm) long, turning yellow to orange and red in autumn. Fruiting panicles, to 6in (15cm) long, are green at first, becoming fawn then gray as they mature. ↕↔ 15ft (5m). S. Europe to C. China. Zone 4b. **'Daydream'** is dense in habit, and bears abundant, airy, brownish pink inflorescences. **'Flame'** see *C.* 'Flame'. **'Notcutt's Variety'** ■ has wine-red foliage and purple-pink fruiting panicles. **'Pink Champagne'** bears an abundance of beige-pink inflorescences; ↕ 10ft (3m). **f. *purpureus*** ■ has light to mid-green leaves, turning orange to red in autumn, and purplish pink inflorescences. **'Royal Purple'** has dark red-purple foliage, turning scarlet in autumn. **'Velvet Cloak'** produces dark purple leaves, turning reddish purple in autumn.

***C.* 'Flame'** ■ syn. *C. coggygria* 'Flame'. Vigorous, bushy, small tree or shrub producing oval, light green leaves, to 4in (10cm) long, which turn brilliant orange-red in autumn. Fruiting panicles are purple-pink. ↕ 20ft (6m), ↔ 15ft (5m). Zone 5.

C. obovatus, syn. *C. americanus, Rhus cotinoides* (American smoke tree, Chittamwood). Broadly conical shrub or small tree with attractive, plate-like, gray to gray-brown bark and obovate to oval leaves, to 5in (13cm) or more long, pinkish bronze when young, turning brilliant orange, red, and purple in autumn. Large, plume-like, pinkish gray fruiting panicles, to 12in (30cm) long, are borne in summer and persist into autumn. Tolerates alkaline soils. ↕ 30ft (10m), ↔ 25ft (8m). S.E. US. Zone 5.

Cotinus 'Flame'

COTONEASTER

ROSACEAE

Genus of more than 200 species of deciduous, semi-evergreen, or evergreen shrubs and trees from woodland and rocky areas in N. temperate regions of Europe, Asia, and N. Africa. They have alternate, lance-shaped to narrowly elliptic, broadly ovate, or rounded leaves. Saucer- to shallowly cup-shaped, white to deep pink flowers, borne singly or in cymes from spring to summer, are followed in autumn by ornamental, spherical to ovoid or obovoid fruits. Grow in a shrub border or as a hedge or screen; some are ideal for wall training. Dwarf species are suitable for a rock garden. Many prostrate species provide good groundcover; some may be trained as weeping standards. Seeds may cause mild stomach upset if ingested.

• **CULTIVATION** Grow in moderately fertile, well-drained soil; most will tolerate dry positions. Deciduous species prefer full sun. Large and medium-sized evergreens thrive in sun or partial shade. Dwarf evergreens fruit more prolifically in full sun. Most need little regular pruning but will tolerate hard pruning to produce tight hedges or to renovate. Pruning group 1 for deciduous species; group 8 for evergreens; group 13 for wall-trained shrubs. Prune formal hedges and wall-trained plants back to the fading flowers or nearest berry cluster in mid- or late summer. Trim again lightly in early autumn if fresh growth obscures fruit display.

• **PROPAGATION** Sow seed in containers in a cold frame as soon as ripe, in autumn; some species are apomictic and come true from seed. Root semi-ripe cuttings of evergreen and semi-evergreen species in late summer; root greenwood cuttings of deciduous species in early summer.

• **PESTS AND DISEASES** Sensitive to rust, powdery mildew, stem cankers, and fire blight. Scale insects, rose slugs, spider mites, slugs, and snails cause problems.

C. acutifolius (Peking cotoneaster). Upright, deciduous shrub with arching shoots and ovate, dark green leaves, to 2in (5cm) long. Short cymes of pink-tinged white flowers are borne in summer, followed by obovoid red fruit, ⅜–½in (9–15mm) long. ↕↔ 10ft (3m). China. Zone 2.

C. adpressus ■ Prostrate, deciduous shrub with broadly ovate to obovate, wavy-margined, dull green leaves, ½in (1.5cm) long, turning red in autumn. In summer, bears red-tinged white flowers, singly or in pairs, followed by spherical, bright red fruit, to ¼in (6mm) long. ↕ 12in (30cm), ↔ 6ft (2m). W. China. Zone 4. **var. *praecox*** see *C. nanshan.*

C. affinis. Vigorous, rounded to broadly columnar, deciduous shrub or small tree with peeling bark and elliptic, dark green leaves, 1½–4in (4–10cm) long. White flowers, borne in large cymes in early summer, are followed by cylindrical, dark purple-black fruit, ⅜–½in (0.9–1.5cm) long. ↕ 15ft (5m), ↔ 12ft (4m). Himalayas. Zone 7b.

C. apiculatus (Cranberry cotoneaster). Vigorous, more or less prostrate, deciduous shrub bearing rounded, wavy-margined, glossy, mid-green leaves, ½–¾in (1–2cm) long, turning red to

Cotoneaster adpressus

purple-red in autumn. Solitary, red-tinged white flowers are borne in summer, followed by spherical red fruit, ½in (1.5cm) long. ↕ 3ft (1m), ↔ 8ft (2.5m). China (Sichuan). Zone 4.

C. atropurpureus. Compact, prostrate or ascending, deciduous shrub with arching branches, and broadly ovate, slightly wavy-margined, glossy, mid-green leaves, to ½in (1.5cm) long, turning dark red-purple in autumn. Solitary, black-based red flowers are borne in summer, followed by almost spherical, bright orange-red fruit, ⅛–¼in (3–6mm) long. ↕ 20–36in (50–90cm), ↔ 8ft (2.5m). China (Hubei). Zone 4b. **'Variegatus'**, syn. *C. horizontalis* 'Variegatus', is less vigorous, with white-margined leaves, turning pink and red in autumn; ↕ 18in (45cm), ↔ 36in (90cm).

***C.* 'Autumn Fire'** see *C.* 'Herbstfeuer'.

C. bullatus* var. *macrophyllus see *C. rehderi.*

C. cashmiriensis ■ syn. *C. cochleatus* of gardens, *C. melanotrichus, C. microphyllus* var. *cochleatus* of gardens. Compact, prostrate, evergreen shrub with elliptic, glossy, dark green leaves, to ½in (1.5cm) long. Bears usually solitary white flowers, pink in bud, in summer, followed by almost spherical, dark red fruit, ¼–⅜in (6–9mm) long. Ideal as a groundcover. ↕ 12in (30cm), ↔ 6ft (2m). Himalayas (Kashmir). Zone 5.

***C. cochleatus* of gardens** see *C. cashmiriensis.*

C. congestus, syn. *C. pyrenaicus.* Dense, mound-forming or prostrate, evergreen shrub with obovate, dull pale green leaves, ¼–½in (6–15mm) long. Solitary

Cotoneaster cashmiriensis

C

C

Cotoneaster conspicuus

white flowers are borne in summer, followed by spherical, bright red fruit, ¼–½in (6–15mm) long. Excellent in a rock garden. ↕ 28in (70cm), ↔ 36in (90cm). Himalayas. Zone 5b.
C. conspicuus ▣ syn. *C. conspicuus* var. *decorus* (Wintergreen cotoneaster). Dense, mound-forming, evergreen shrub with narrowly elliptic, slightly shiny, dark green leaves, ¼–¾in (0.5–2cm) long. White flowers are produced singly or occasionally in cymes of up to 5 in summer; they are followed by spherical, shiny red fruit, ¼–⅜in (7–9mm) long, which often last well into winter. ↕ 5ft (1.5m), ↔ 6–8ft (2–2.5m). S.E. Tibet. Zone 6.
'Red Glory' is erect and vigorous, producing dark red fruit; ↕ 6ft (2m).
C. conspicuus* var. *decorus see *C. conspicuus.*
***C.* 'Coral Beauty'.** Dense, mound-forming, evergreen shrub with arching branches and obovate to oblong, glossy, dark green leaves, to ½in (1.5cm) long. Cymes of white flowers are borne in summer, followed by profuse, spherical, bright orange fruit, to ⅜in (9mm) long. Ideal as a groundcover. ↕ 3ft (1m), ↔ 6ft (2m). Zone 4.

Cotoneaster divaricatus

***C.* 'Cornubia'** ▣ Vigorous, arching, semi-evergreen shrub or tree bearing narrowly elliptic, dark green leaves, to 5in (13cm) long, some of which turn bronze in winter. Cymes of white flowers are produced in summer, followed by abundant, almost spherical, bright red fruit, to ¼in (6mm) long. ↕↔ 20ft (6m). Zone 6b.
C. dammeri. Vigorous, prostrate, evergreen shrub with long, spreading shoots and broadly obovate to elliptic, mid- to dark green leaves, ½–1¼in (1.5–3cm) long. White flowers are borne in 2- to 4-flowered cymes in early summer, followed in autumn by almost spherical red fruit, to ¼in (6mm) long. ↕ 8in (20cm), ↔ 6ft (2m). China (Hubei). Zone 4. **'Major'** has rounded, dark green leaves, to 1½in (4cm) long.
'Streibs Findling' see *C. procumbens.*
C. dielsianus. Erect, deciduous, occasionally semi-evergreen shrub with slender, arching shoots bearing ovate to obovate leaves, to 1½in (4cm) long, dark green above and yellowish gray-hairy beneath, turning red in autumn. In summer, produces cymes of 3–7 pink-tinged white flowers, followed by almost spherical, glossy red fruit, ¼in (6mm) long. ↕↔ 8ft (2.5m). China. Zone 3.
C. distichus see *C. nitidus.*
C. divaricatus ▣ (Spreading cotoneaster). Densely branched, erect, rounded, deciduous shrub with ovate to elliptic, glossy, dark green leaves, ⅜–1in (0.8–2.5cm) long, turning red in autumn. Pink-tinged white flowers are solitary or produced in 2- to 4-flowered cymes in summer, followed by ellipsoid to cylindrical, dark red fruit, ¼–⅜in (7–9mm) long. ↕ 8ft (2.5m), ↔ 10ft (3m). China (Hubei). Zone 5.
***C.* 'Exburiensis'.** Vigorous, arching, evergreen shrub with narrowly pointed, elliptic-lance-shaped, deeply veined, mid-green leaves, to 5in (13cm) long. Large cymes of white flowers, borne in early summer, are followed by almost spherical, pale yellow fruit, ¼in (6mm) long, becoming pink-tinged in winter. ↕↔ 15ft (5m). Zone 6.
***C. floccosus* of gardens** see *C. salicifolius.*
C. franchetii. Spreading to erect, evergreen or semi-evergreen shrub with arching branches, and elliptic to ovate leaves, to 1½in (4cm) long, gray-green above and white beneath. White flowers, suffused red, with erect petals, are borne in 5- to 15-flowered cymes in summer, followed by obovoid, bright orange-red fruit, ¼–⅜in (6–9mm) long. ↕↔ 10ft (3m). China (Yunnan). Zone 7.
var. *sternianus* see *C. sternianus.*
C. frigidus ▣ Deciduous tree or large shrub, upright when young, later spreading, with peeling bark and narrowly elliptic to obovate, wavy-margined, dull green leaves, to 6in (15cm) long. Large cymes of 20–60 white flowers are borne in summer, followed by almost spherical, bright red fruit, ¼in (6mm) long. ↕↔ 30ft (10m). Himalayas. Zone 7.
'Fructu Luteo' ▣ produces creamy yellow fruit.
C. glaucophyllus. Spreading, evergreen or semi-evergreen shrub with ovate or elliptic, mid-green leaves, 1¼–3in (3–8cm) long, glaucous beneath. Cymes of 15–40 white flowers are produced in midsummer, followed in late autumn by obovoid, orange-red fruit, to ¼in (6mm) long. ↕↔ 10ft (3m). China (Yunnan). Zone 7.
***C.* 'Gnom'** ▣ syn. *C.* 'Gnome', *C. salicifolius* 'Gnom'. Prostrate, dense, evergreen shrub bearing narrowly lance-shaped, dark green leaves, to 1¼in (3cm) long. Cymes of white flowers are produced in early summer, followed by spherical red fruit, to ¼in (6mm) long. Excellent as a groundcover. ↕ 12in (30cm), ↔ 6ft (2m). Zone 5.
***C.* 'Gnome'** see *C.* 'Gnom'.
***C.* 'Herbstfeuer'**, syn. *C.* 'Autumn Fire'. Evergreen shrub, prostrate at first, later mound-forming, with lance-shaped, dark green leaves, to 2½in (6cm) long, some turning bright red in autumn. Cymes of 5–12 white flowers are produced in early summer, followed by spherical, bright red fruit, to ¼in (6mm) long. ↕ 3ft (1m), ↔ 10ft (3m). Zone 5.
C. horizontalis ▣ (Rockspray). Spreading, deciduous shrub with branches forming a herringbone pattern. Rounded to broadly elliptic, glossy, dark green leaves, to ½in (1.5cm) long, turn red in autumn. In late spring, bears

Cotoneaster 'Cornubia' (inset: fruit detail)

Cotoneaster frigidus

pink-tinged white flowers singly or in pairs. Spherical fruit, to ¼in (6mm) long, are bright red. ↕ 3ft (1m), ↔ 5ft (1.5m). W. China. Zone 5.
var. *perpusillus* see *C. perpusillus.*
'Variegatus' see *C. atropurpureus* 'Variegatus'.
C. hupehensis. Deciduous shrub with slender, arching branches and elliptic to ovate, dark green leaves, to 1½in (4cm) long. Cymes of 5–10 white flowers are borne from late spring to summer, followed by spherical, bright red fruit, to ½in (1.5cm) or more long. ↕ 8ft (2.5m), ↔ 12ft (4m). W. China (Hubei). Zone 6.
***C.* 'Hybridus Pendulus'.** Prostrate, evergreen or semi-evergreen shrub with elliptic-lance-shaped, dark green leaves, to 3in (8cm) long. Small cymes of white flowers are borne in early summer, followed by almost spherical, bright red fruit, ¼in (6mm) long. Forms a small tree with weeping branches when grown as a standard. ↕↔ 6ft (2m). Zone 6b.
C. hylmoei, syn. *C. salicifolius* var. *rugosus* of gardens. Rounded, evergreen shrub with arching shoots and elliptic-lance-shaped, deeply veined, tapered, dark green leaves, to 3in (8cm) long. Cymes of small white flowers, opening from pink buds, are borne in summer, followed by long-lasting, spherical, bright red fruit, ¼–⅜in (6–9mm) long. ↕ 8ft (2.5m), ↔ 12ft (4m). W. China. Zone 6b.
C. integrifolius, syn. *C. microphyllus* of gardens, *C. thymifolius.* Stiffly branched, compact, evergreen shrub with obovate to oblong, glossy, dark green leaves, to ½in (1.5cm) long. Solitary white flowers

Cotoneaster frigidus 'Fructu Luteo'

Cotoneaster 'Gnom' (inset: fruit detail)

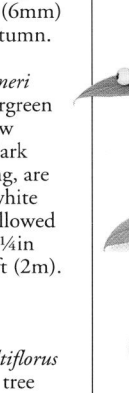

are borne in early summer, followed by spherical, dark reddish pink fruit, ⅜–½in (8–15mm) long. ↕ 3ft (1m), ↔ 5ft (1.5m). Himalayas. Zone 6b.
C. lacteus ▣ Dense, evergreen shrub with arching branches bearing obovate or broadly elliptic, deeply veined leaves, 1½–3½in (3.5–9cm) long, dark green above and yellow-white felted beneath. Bears cymes of up to 100 milky white flowers in summer, followed by obovoid red fruit, ¼in (6mm) long, which persist over winter. May be grown as a hedge. ↕↔ 12ft (4m). China (Yunnan). Zone 7b.
C. linearifolius, syn. *C. microphyllus* var. *thymifolius* of gardens. Compact, rounded, evergreen shrub with rigid branches, and oblong to inversely lance-shaped, glossy, dark green leaves, ⅛–¼in (3–6mm) long, glaucous beneath and notched at the tips. Bears solitary white flowers, pink in bud, in early summer, followed by spherical, dark red fruit, ⅛–¼in (3–6mm) long. ↕↔ 24–36in (60–90cm). Nepal. Zone 6b.
C. lucidus. (Hedge cotoneaster). Upright, rounded, evergreen shrub with spreading branches and elliptic-ovate to oblong-ovate, shiny, dark green leaves, ¾–2in (2–5cm) long, slightly softly hairy beneath. In mid- and late spring, bears 2- to 5-flowered cymes of pinkish white flowers, followed by persistent, spherical black fruit, ¼in (6mm) long. ↕↔ 6–10ft (2–3m). Siberia. Zone 2.
C. melanotrichus see *C. cashmiriensis.*
***C. microphyllus* var. *cochleatus* of gardens** see *C. cashmiriensis.*
***C. microphyllus* of gardens** see *C. integrifolius.*
***C. microphyllus* var. *thymifolius* of gardens** see *C. linearifolius.*
C. multiflorus. Vigorous, deciduous shrub with long, arching branches and ovate to rounded leaves, to 2in (5cm) long, dull yellowish green above and sparsely hairy, mid-green beneath. Cymes of 10–20 white flowers are borne in late spring, followed by abundant spherical red fruit, to ½in (1.5cm) long, from late summer to autumn. ↕↔ 15ft (5m). Kazakhstan. Zone 5b.
***C. multiflorus* of gardens** see *C. purpurascens.*
C. nanshan, syn. *C. adpressus* var. *praecox.* Prostrate, spreading, deciduous shrub with rounded, very wavy-margined, mid-green leaves, ½–1in (1–2.5cm) long, turning red in autumn.

Cotoneaster horizontalis

Cotoneaster lacteus

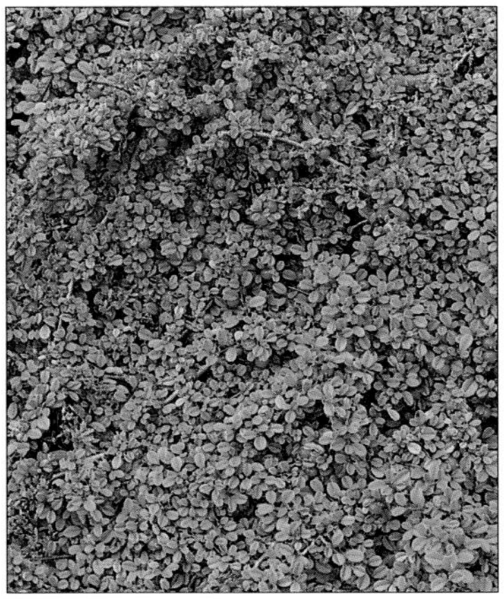

Cotoneaster procumbens

Paired or single, pinkish white or red-flushed white flowers are produced in late spring, followed by large, almost spherical, bright red fruit, to ½in (1.5cm) long. ↕ 3ft (1m), ↔ 6ft (2m). W. China (Sichuan, Yunnan). Zone 3. **'Boer'** bears larger, persistent fruit that turn color earlier in autumn.
C. nitidus, syn. *C. distichus.* Wide-spreading or erect, deciduous or semi-evergreen shrub with stiff branches bearing rounded, glossy, dark green leaves, to ½in (1.5cm) long. Solitary, pink-tinged white flowers are produced in summer; flowers are followed by long-lasting, obovoid to almost spherical, bright red fruit, to ¼in (6mm) long. ↕ 8ft (2.5m), ↔ 12ft (4m). China (Yunnan), Himalayas. Zone 7b.
C. perpusillus, syn. *C. horizontalis* var. *perpusillus.* Prostrate, deciduous shrub with branches forming a herringbone pattern. Rounded, glossy, dark green leaves, to ⅜in (9mm) long, turn red in autumn, and usually remain longer than those of *C. horizontalis.* In summer, bears solitary, pink-tinged white flowers. Almost spherical fruit, ⅛–¼in (3–6mm) long, are bright red. ↕ 12in (30cm), ↔ 6ft (2m). China (Hubei). Zone 6.
***C.* 'Pink Champagne'.** Vigorous, arching, evergreen shrub with narrowly elliptic-lance-shaped, pointed, deeply veined, mid-green leaves, to 5in (13cm) long. Large cymes of white flowers are borne in early summer, followed by spherical, pale yellow fruit, ¼in (6mm) long, which turn pink in late autumn. ↕↔ 15ft (5m). Zone 6b.
C. procumbens ▣ syn. *C. dammeri* 'Streibs Findling'. Prostrate, evergreen shrub, occasionally forming a low mound. Broadly obovate, dull dark green leaves, to ½in (1.5cm) long, are purplish when young. Solitary white flowers are borne in summer, followed by almost spherical red fruit, to ¼in (6mm) long. ↕ 4in (10cm), ↔ 6ft (2m). China. Zone 4.
***C. prostratus* of gardens** see *C. rotundifolius.*
C. purpurascens ▣ syn. *C. multiflorus* of gardens. Erect shrub or small tree with arching branches and ovate to rounded, mid-green leaves, ¾–2½in (2–6cm) long, paler beneath, and hairy when young. In mid- and late spring, bears cymes of white flowers, followed by long-lasting, pear-shaped or spherical red fruit, ¼in (6mm) long. ↕↔ 10–12ft (3–4m). Russia (Siberia), China. Zone 5b.

Cotoneaster purpurascens

C. pyrenaicus see *C. congestus.*
C. rehderi, syn. *C. bullatus* var. *macrophyllus.* Vigorous, deciduous shrub with long, arching shoots and ovate to oblong-elliptic, pointed, deeply veined, dark green leaves, to 6in (15cm) long, turning red in autumn. Cymes of up to 30 pink-tinged white flowers are borne in early summer, followed by obovoid to almost spherical, bright red fruit, ⅜–½in (9–15mm) long. ↕ 15ft (5m), ↔ 10ft (3m). China (Sichuan). Zone 6b.
***C.* 'Rothschildianus'** ▣ Vigorous, arching, evergreen shrub with narrowly elliptic-lance-shaped, tapered, deeply veined, pale green leaves, to 4in (10cm) long. Bears large cymes of white flowers in early summer, followed by spherical, golden yellow fruit, ¼in (6mm) long, produced over a long period in autumn. ↕↔ 15ft (5m). Zone 6b.
C. rotundifolius, syn. *C. prostratus* of gardens. Spreading, evergreen shrub with arching branches and broadly elliptic to obovate-elliptic, glossy, dark green leaves, to ¾in (2cm) long. Solitary flowers are borne in late spring, followed by spherical, dark pinkish red fruit, ¼–½in (6–15mm) long. ↕ 5ft (1.5m), ↔ 10ft (3m). Himalayas. Zone 7b. **'Ruby'** has glossy, slightly white-variegated, dark green leaves, pale to blue-green beneath. ↕ to 3ft (1m).
***C.* 'Sabrina'** see *C. splendens.*

Cotoneaster 'Rothschildianus'

Cotoneaster salicifolius

C. salicifolius ▣ syn. *C. floccosus* of gardens. Vigorous, evergreen shrub with arching branches and elliptic-lance-shaped, dark green leaves, to 4in (10cm) long. Bears cymes of 30–100 white flowers in summer, followed by almost spherical, shiny, bright red fruit, ¼in (6mm) long. ↕↔ 15ft (5m). China. Zone 5b. **'Emerald Carpet'** is dense and compact, and has smaller leaves. **var. *floccosus*** is semi-evergreen in cold climates and has smaller, shiny leaves, ¾–2½in (2–6cm) long, and fruit to ½in (1.5cm) across. **'Gnom'** see *C.* 'Gnom'. **var. *rugosus* of gardens** see *C. hylmoei.*
C. serotinus. Arching, open, evergreen shrub or small tree with elliptic or obovate-elliptic leaves, 1–3in (2.5–8cm) long, dark green above and pale green (softly downy at first) beneath. Cymes of up to 40 white flowers are borne in mid- and late summer, followed in autumn by obovoid to almost spherical, bright red fruit, ¼in (6mm) long. ↕ 30ft (10m), ↔ 10–12ft (3–4m). W. China (Yunnan). Zone 7b.
C. simonsii ▣ Upright, deciduous or semi-evergreen shrub. Broadly ovate, glossy, dark green leaves, to 1¼in (3cm) long, turn red in autumn. Bears pink-tinged white flowers singly or in few-flowered cymes in summer. Obovoid fruit, ⅜–½in (9–15mm) long, are bright orange-red. ↕ 8ft (2.5m), ↔ 6ft (2m). India (Sikkim), Bhutan. Zone 4.
***C.* 'Skogholm'**, syn. *C.* 'Skogsholmen'. More or less prostrate, evergreen shrub with ovate to oblong, glossy, dark green leaves, to ¾in (2cm) long. White flowers are borne singly or in few-flowered cymes in late spring, followed by sparse,

Cotoneaster simonsii

Cotoneaster sternianus

spherical, bright red fruit, ¼–⅜in (6–9mm) long. Good as a groundcover. ↕ 24in (60cm), ↔ 10ft (3m). Zone 5.
***C.* 'Skogsholmen'** see *C.* 'Skogholm'.
C. splendens, syn. *C.* 'Sabrina'. Rounded, deciduous shrub with arching branches bearing broadly elliptic to rounded, glossy, mid-green leaves, to ¾in (2cm) long, turning red in autumn. Bears cymes of 3 (occasionally up to 7) pink-suffused white flowers, margined rose-pink, in early summer, followed by almost spherical, bright orange fruit, ⅜–½in (9–15mm) long. ↕ 6ft (2m), ↔ 8ft (2.5m). China (Sichuan). Zone 4b.
C. sternianus ▣ syn. *C. franchetii* var. *sternianus.* Vigorous, upright, evergreen or semi-evergreen shrub with arching branches and elliptic, glossy, dark green leaves, 1–2½in (2.5–6cm) long, white-woolly beneath. Erect cymes of up to 15 pink-tinged white flowers are produced in summer, followed by spherical, bright, deep orange-red fruit, ⅜–½in (9–15mm) long. ↕↔ 10ft (3m). China (Yunnan). Zone 6.
C. thymifolius see *C. integrifolius.*
***C.* 'Valkenburg'.** Dense, spreading, semi-evergreen shrub with ovate, glossy, mid-green leaves, to ¾in (2cm) long, turning orange, red, and yellow in autumn. In late spring, pink-suffused white flowers are produced singly or in few-flowered cymes, followed by ellipsoid to cylindrical red fruit, ¼–⅜in (7–9mm) long. ↕ 6ft (2m), ↔ 12ft (4m). Zone 6b.
***C.* x *watereri* 'John Waterer'** ▣ Vigorous, evergreen or semi-evergreen shrub or small tree with arching branches and lance-shaped, dark green leaves, to 4in (10cm) long. Large cymes of 30–50 white flowers are borne in summer, followed by almost spherical red fruit, ⅜in (9mm) long. ↕↔ 15ft (5m). Zone 6b.

Cotoneaster x *watereri* 'John Waterer'

COTULA

ASTERACEAE

Genus of about 55 species of prostrate, tufted, or creeping, rhizomatous annuals and perennials, mostly found in moist areas in N. and E. Africa, South Africa, Australia, Mexico, and South America. They are grown mainly for their aster-like flowerheads. In some species, the male and female florets are borne in separate heads. *Cotula* species are also grown for their mainly alternate, sometimes opposite or rosette-forming leaves, which are usually pinnate or lobed, occasionally entire, and mostly silver or fresh green. *C. coronopifolia* is suitable for a pond margin, a bog garden, or a damp border; where not hardy, grow as an annual. Alpine species are suitable for a rock garden.

- **CULTIVATION** Grow in moist, humus-rich, moderately fertile soil in full sun. Deadhead to prolong flowering.
- **PROPAGATION** Surface-sow seed at 55–64°F (13–18°C) in spring. Lift and divide plants in autumn; where not hardy, overwinter in a cold frame.
- **PESTS AND DISEASES** Infrequent.

C. atrata see *Leptinella atrata.*
C. coronopifolia (Brass buttons). Moisture-loving annual or short-lived perennial with numerous creeping, semi-prostrate, hairless, succulent stems and linear, lobed or coarsely toothed, strongly scented, fresh green leaves, 2–5in (5–13cm) long. Bears button-like, bright yellow flowerheads, ½in (1.5cm) across, on slender stalks in summer. May be grown in water to 6in (15cm) deep. ↕ 6in (15cm), ↔ 12in (30cm). South Africa. Zone 7b.
C. squalida see *Leptinella squalida.*

COTYLEDON

CRASSULACEAE

Genus of 9 species of compact, often clump-forming, perennial succulents and evergreen subshrubs from desert or shaded areas in E. Africa, the Arabian Peninsula, and southern Africa. They are grown for their foliage and flowers. The stalked, fleshy leaves are borne in

Cotyledon ladismithensis

Cotyledon orbiculata

opposite pairs. Tubular to bell-shaped, generally pendent, red, yellow, or orange flowers are borne in crowded, terminal panicles, mostly in late summer and autumn. Where not hardy, grow in a temperate greenhouse or as houseplants. Elsewhere, grow in a desert garden.

- **CULTIVATION** Under glass, grow in standard cactus potting mix in full light, with shade from hot sun. In the growing season, water moderately, avoiding the foliage, and apply a dilute, low-nitrogen liquid fertilizer monthly; keep completely dry in winter. Outdoors, grow in gritty, low-fertility, humus-rich, sharply drained soil in full sun with some midday shade. Many species will tolerate brief periods to 25°F (-4°C). See also pp.48–49.
- **PROPAGATION** Sow seed at 66–75°F (19–24°C), or root stem cuttings, in spring or summer.
- **PESTS AND DISEASES** Susceptible to aphids while flowering.

C. cooperi see *Adromischus cooperi.*
C. ladismithensis ▣ syn. *C. tomentosa* var. *ladismithensis.* Bushy, often semi-prostrate succulent with many branches, fleshy and hairy above, woody beneath. Thick, oblong, round-tipped, softly hairy, mid-green leaves, 2in (5cm) long, have 2–4 soft teeth. In autumn, bears tubular, brownish red flowers, to ½in (1.5cm) long, in a fleshy inflorescence, 3½in (9cm) long. Often considered a variety of *C. tomentosa.* ↕ 12in (30cm), ↔ to 8in (20cm). South Africa (Western Cape). ❄ (min. 45°F/7°C)
C. maculata see *Adromischus maculatus.*
C. oblonga see *C. orbiculata* var. *oblonga.*

Cotyledon orbiculata var. *oblonga*

C. orbiculata ■ Shrubby, erect, freely branching succulent with thick, fleshy stems and ovoid, white-frosted, waxy, white or gray leaves, to 5½in (14cm) long. Bears tubular, red or yellowish red flowers, ½–¾in (1.5–2cm) long, in fleshy inflorescences, to 28in (70cm) long, from late summer to autumn. ↕ to 3ft (1m), ↔ 20in (50cm). Angola, Namibia, South Africa (Northern Cape, Western Cape). ❄ (min. 45°F/7°C). **var. *oblonga*** ■ syn. *C. oblonga*, *C. undulata*, is decumbent to suberect, with densely packed, obovate to inversely lance-shaped, thick, fleshy, wavy-margined, white-frosted leaves and yellowish red or orange flowers.
C. paniculata see *Tylecodon paniculatus.*
C. reticulata see *Tylecodon reticulatus.*
C. simplicifolia see *Chiastophyllum oppositifolium.*
C. tomentosa. Compact, woody-based, perennial succulent with slender, loose stems and thick, obovoid, gray-green leaves, to 2in (5cm) long, covered with a dense felt of dark hairs at the tips. From late summer to autumn, bears pendent, tubular red flowers, to ½in (1.5cm) long, with long, recurved lobes, in panicles to 8in (20cm) long. ↕ to 12in (30cm), ↔ 5in (13cm). South Africa (Western Cape). ❄ (min. 45°F/7°C). **var. *ladismithensis*** see *C. ladismithensis.*
C. undulata see *C. orbiculata* var. *oblonga.*
C. wallichii see *Tylecodon papillaris* subsp. *wallichii.*
C. zeyheri see *Adromischus cristatus* var. *zeyheri.*

CRAMBE

BRASSICACEAE

Genus of about 20 species of imposing, often woody-based annuals and perennials from rocky mountain slopes, coastal sand dunes, and open grassland, in Europe, Turkey, C. Asia, and tropical Africa. They have large, simple to pinnatisect basal leaves and erect, often thick stems, which are usually leafless or bear smaller leaves. Numerous tiny, scented, cross-shaped, white or pale yellow flowers are borne in large racemes or panicles. *Crambe* species are cultivated for their handsome foliage and elegant inflorescences, which are attractive to bees. The enormous span of their leaves requires siting in a large herbaceous border. They also thrive in wild or woodland gardens, and in coastal sites. The leafy stems of *C. maritima* are often eaten as a vegetable; developing stems may be blanched from late winter to spring.
• **CULTIVATION** Grow in deep, fertile, well-drained soil in full sun, although they will tolerate poor soils and partial shade. Provide shelter from strong winds.
• **PROPAGATION** Sow seed in containers in a cold frame in spring or autumn. Divide in early spring, or insert root cuttings in winter.
• **PESTS AND DISEASES** Susceptible to clubroot and soil-borne black rot (especially *C. maritima*).

C. cordifolia ■ (Colewort). Mound-forming perennial with long-stalked, kidney-shaped to ovate, puckered, toothed, bristly, dark green leaves, to 14in (35cm) or more across, which die down in mid- or late summer. Strong stems bear white flowers in many-branched panicles, to 5ft (1.5m) across, in late spring and midsummer. ↕ to 8ft (2.5m), ↔ 5ft (1.5m). Caucasus. Zone 5.
C. maritima (Sea kale). Spreading, mound-forming perennial with ovate, irregularly shallowly lobed to pinnatifid, twisted, glaucous, blue-green leaves, to 12in (30cm) long. Thick stems bear white flowers in dense racemes, to 24in (60cm) across, in early summer. ↕ 30in (75cm), ↔ 24in (60cm). Coastal N. and W. Europe, Black Sea. Zone 5.

Crambe cordifolia

CRASPEDIA

Bachelor's buttons, Billy buttons

ASTERACEAE

Genus of 8 species of annuals and perennials from mountainous regions of Australia, Tasmania, and New Zealand. They are grown mainly for their dense, hemispherical flowerheads of tiny, cup-shaped flowers, surrounded by leafy bracts and borne on stiff, unbranched stems. They are also cultivated for their basal rosettes of elliptic, obovate, spoon-shaped, or linear, hairy, mid-green to silvery white leaves. Grow perennial species in a rock garden or scree bed. In colder, wetter areas, most are best in an alpine house; grow *C. globosa* in an annual border. The flowerheads are useful for dried flower arrangements.
• **CULTIVATION** Grow annuals in any well-drained soil in full sun. Grow perennials in sharply drained, low-fertility, humus-rich, gritty soil in full sun; protect from excessive winter moisture. Under glass, grow in a mix of equal parts loam, leaf mold, and sharp sand, with a top-dressing of grit. Water freely in growth (avoiding the foliage) and keep just moist in winter.
• **PROPAGATION** Sow seed of perennials and annuals at 55–64°F (13–18°C) in spring. Divide perennials in spring.
• **PESTS AND DISEASES** Slugs and snails may attack young growth. Spider mites may be troublesome under glass.

C. glauca, syn. *C. richea.* Tufted, rosette-forming perennial with inversely lance-shaped to linear, usually white-hairy, gray-green leaves, to 6in (15cm) long. Solitary flowerheads, to 1¼in (3cm) across, of yellow or cream florets, are borne on stiff stems in summer. ↕ 16in (40cm) or more, ↔ 8in (20cm). S. Australia. ❄ (min. 45°F/7°C)
C. globosa (Bachelor's buttons, Drumsticks). Rosette-forming, white-woolly perennial, usually grown as an annual, with narrowly strap-shaped, light green leaves, to 12in (30cm) long, covered in white hairs. Mustard-yellow flowerheads, to 1¼in (3cm) across, are produced in summer at the tips of long, rigid, hairy stems. ↕ 24–36in (60–90cm), ↔ to 5in (13cm). W. Victoria, New South Wales. ❄ (min. 45°F/7°C)
C. incana. Densely white-woolly perennial bearing basal rosettes of obovate to spoon-shaped, mid-green leaves, to 4in (10cm) long. In summer, bears dense, bright yellow flowerheads, to 1¼in (3cm) across. ↕ 8–12in (20–30cm), ↔ 6in (15cm). New Zealand. ❄ (min. 45°F/7°C)
C. richea see *C. glauca.*
C. uniflora ■ (Bachelor's buttons). Rosette-forming annual or perennial with long-stalked, woolly, obovate or lance-shaped, mid-green basal leaves, to 5in (13cm) long, and white-woolly, lance-shaped, clasping stem leaves, 2½in (6cm) long. Clear yellow flowerheads, to 1½in (4cm) across, are produced in summer. ↕ to 18in (45cm), ↔ 14in (35cm). S. Australia, Tasmania, New Zealand. ❄ (min. 45°F/7°C)

Craspedia uniflora

CRASSULA

CRASSULACEAE

Genus of about 150 species of annual and perennial succulents and evergreen, succulent shrubs and subshrubs, ranging from dwarf to tall, tree-like plants, and found in dry to moist, high to low areas in Africa, Madagascar, and Asia, but mostly in South Africa. They are grown mainly for their fleshy, usually opposite leaves, which vary greatly in shape, size, and texture. They are also cultivated for their tubular or star- or funnel-shaped flowers, borne in dense, terminal, cyme-like inflorescences. Where not hardy, grow as houseplants, or in a cool or temperate greenhouse. In warm, dry climates, grow in a border with other succulents or in a desert garden.
• **CULTIVATION** Under glass, grow in standard cactus potting mix in full light; a few need bright filtered or indirect light. From spring to autumn, apply a balanced liquid fertilizer monthly and water moderately; water sparingly in winter. Outdoors, grow in moderately fertile to poor, humus-rich, sharply drained soil in full sun; *C. capitella* subsp. *thyrsiflora*, *C. hemisphaerica*, and *C. schmidtii* prefer partial shade. See also pp.48–49.
• **PROPAGATION** Sow seed at 59–64°F (15–18°C) in early spring. Root stem or leaf cuttings in spring or summer.
• **PESTS AND DISEASES** Aphids and mealybugs may be problems. Powdery mildew, fungal leaf spots, stem rot, and root rot are common.

C. arborescens ■ (Silver jade plant). Shrub-like succulent with a thick, branched stem and broadly elliptic to obovate, grayish green leaves, 1½–3in (3.5–8cm) long, often with red margins, or red-spotted above. From autumn to winter, bears star-shaped pink flowers, to ½in (1.5cm) across. ↕ 12ft (4m), ↔ to 6ft (2m). South Africa (Western Cape, Eastern Cape, KwaZulu/Natal). ❄ (min. 41–45°F/5–7°C)
***C. arborescens* of gardens** see *C. ovata.*

Crassula arborescens

Crassula deceptor

***C. argentea* of gardens** see *C. ovata.*
***C. capitella* subsp. *thyrsiflora*,** syn. *C. corymbosula, C. thyrsiflora.* Variable, erect, sparingly branched, perennial succulent. Ovate to linear-lance-shaped, hairy-margined, gray-green leaves, 1¼–3in (3–8cm) long, are spotted dark green or red. Star-shaped white flowers, ¼–⅜in (6–9mm) across, are produced in autumn. ↕ to 12in (30cm), ↔ 6in (15cm). Namibia, South Africa (Eastern Transvaal, Orange Free State, KwaZulu/ Natal, Northern Cape, Eastern Cape). ❄ (min. 41–45°F/5–7°C)
***C. coccinea*,** syn. *Rochea coccinea.* Erect, succulent subshrub with elliptic to ovate, pointed, dull green, often red-tinged leaves, to 1in (2.5cm) long, densely arranged in 4 rows on red stems. Tubular, bright red, occasionally white flowers, to 1¾in (4.5cm) long, are borne from summer to autumn. ↕ 24in (60cm), ↔ to 16in (40cm). South Africa (Northern Cape, Western Cape, Eastern Cape). ❄ (min. 41–45°F/5–7°C)
C. corymbosula see *C. capitella* subsp. *thyrsiflora.*
C. deceptor ■ syn. *C. deceptrix.* Perennial succulent, sometimes branching from the base, with 4-ranked, thick, ovate, greenish gray leaves, ½in (1.5cm) long, with minute, raised dots and lines. Bears funnel-shaped, cream to pale yellow or pink flowers, to ¼in (6mm) across, in spring. ↕↔ 4in (10cm). South Africa (Northern Cape, Western Cape). ❄ (min. 41–45°F/5–7°C)
C. deceptrix see *C. deceptor.*
C. falcata see *C. perfoliata* var. *minor.*
C. hemisphaerica. Tufted, perennial succulent with a short stem, crowned by a dense, hemispherical rosette of 4-ranked, obovate, recurved, gray-green leaves, ½–2in (1–5cm) long, with fine white hairs. Bears tubular white flowers, ⅛in across (3mm), in spring. ↕ 2–6in (5–15cm), ↔ to 7in (18cm). South Africa (Northern Cape, Western Cape). ❄ (min. 41–45°F/5–7°C)

Crassula multicava

Crassula ovata

C. lactea. Semi-erect or prostrate, succulent subshrub. Short branches bear inversely lance-shaped, pointed, glossy, dark green leaves, 1¼–3in (3–8cm) long, margined with white dots. Small, star-shaped, scented, yellowish white, pink-flushed flowers, to ¼in (6mm) across, are produced in winter. ↕ 8–12in (20–30cm), ↔ 3ft (1m) or more. South Africa (Eastern Cape, KwaZulu/Natal). ❄ (min. 41–45°F/5–7°C)
C. lycopodioides see *C. muscosa.*
C. maculata see *Adromischus maculatus.*
***C.* 'Morgan's Beauty'.** Clump-forming perennial succulent with rosettes of elliptic, pointed, grayish white leaves, 1in (2.5cm) long. In spring, produces short, dense panicles of star-shaped, reddish pink flowers, 1–2in (2.5–5cm) across. ↕ to 6in (15cm), ↔ 4–6in (10–15cm). ❄ (min. 41–45°F/5–7°C)
C. multicava ■ Freely branching, bushy or prostrate, perennial succulent with oblong-ovate to elliptic, minutely spotted and pitted, gray-green or glossy, mid-green leaves, ¾–3in (2–8cm) long. Star-shaped, pinkish white flowers, to ¼in (6mm) or more across, are produced in spring. ↕ 12–16in (30–40cm), ↔ to 3ft (1m). South Africa (Northern Transvaal, Eastern Transvaal, KwaZulu/Natal). ❄ (min. 41–45°F/5–7°C)

Crassula perfoliata var. *minor*

Crassula sarcocaulis

***C. muscosa*,** syn. *C. lycopodioides* (Rattail). Spreading, perennial succulent, forming a dense bush, with triangular to ovate, scale-like, densely 4-ranked, mid-green leaves, tinged yellow, gray, or brown, 1/16–⅜in (2–9mm) long. Bears minute, tubular, greenish yellow flowers, to ⅛in (3mm) across, sometimes tipped reddish brown, singly or in few-flowered clusters from the leaf axils, in spring. ↕ 4–12in (10–30cm), ↔ 8in (20cm). South Africa (Northern Cape, Western Cape). ❄ (min. 41–45°F/5–7°C)
***C. orbicularis*,** syn. *C. rosularis.* Tufted, perennial succulent with flat rosettes of elliptic to inversely lance-shaped, hairy-margined, glossy, mid-green leaves, ½–2in (1.5–5cm) long. Star-shaped white flowers, ⅛–⅜in (3–9mm) across, are produced from summer to autumn. ↕ 6–10in (15–25cm), ↔ to 12in (30cm). South Africa (KwaZulu/Natal). ❄ (min. 41–45°F/5–7°C)
C. ovata ■ syn. *C. arborescens* of gardens, *C. argentea* of gardens, *C. portulacea* (Jade plant, Jade tree). Erect, many-branched, succulent shrub with a thick, fleshy stem and elliptic, glossy, mid-green leaves, sometimes red-margined, ¾–1½in (2–4cm) long. Bears star-shaped, white to pale pink flowers, to ⅜in (9mm) across, in spring. ↕ 6ft (2m) or more, ↔ 3ft (1m) or more. South Africa (Northern Cape, Western Cape, Eastern Cape, KwaZulu/Natal, Northern Transvaal, Eastern Transvaal). ❄ (min. 41–45°F/5–7°C)
C. perfoliata* var. *falcata see *C. perfoliata* var. *minor.*
C. perfoliata* var. *minor ■ syn. *C. falcata, C. perfoliata* var. *falcata, Rochea falcata* (Propeller plant). Erect, perennial succulent with fleshy stems and thick, triangular-lance-shaped, curving gray leaves, 4in (10cm) long. Star-shaped, scented, scarlet, pink, or white flowers, to ½in (1.5cm) across, are borne in late summer. ↕ 3ft (1m), ↔ 30in (75cm). South Africa (Eastern Cape). ❄ (min. 41–45°F/5–7°C)

Crassula schmidtii

C. portulacea see *C. ovata.*
C. pyramidalis. Semi-erect, perennial succulent with stems forming leafy columns and 4 neat ranks of ovate, flat, mid-green leaves, 1½–5in (4–13cm) long. In autumn, each stem is crowned by creamy white flowers, to ½in (1.5cm) across. ↕ 1¼–3in (3–8cm) or more, ↔ 4in (10cm). South Africa (Northern Cape). ❄ (min. 41–45°F/5–7°C)
C. rosularis see *C. orbicularis.*
C. rupestris. Erect, spreading, or semi-prostrate, perennial succulent with thick, ovate-lance-shaped, brownish red leaves, ⅛–½in (3–15mm) long, often with red margins. In summer, bears star-shaped, white or pink flowers, to ¼in (6mm) across, in axillary cymes. ↕ 20in (50cm), ↔ 16in (40cm). South Africa (Northern Cape, Western Cape, Eastern Cape). ❄ (min. 41–45°F/5–7°C)
C. sarcocaulis ■ syn. *Sedum sarcocaule.* Bushy, perennial succulent with fleshy stems and branches, bearing elliptic-lance-shaped, sharply tapering, red-tinted, mid-green leaves, ½–1¼in (1–3cm) long. Star-shaped, malodorous, white or pink flowers, ⅛–¼in (3–6mm) across, are produced in summer. ↕ 12in (30cm) or more, ↔ 12in (30cm). South Africa (Eastern Cape, KwaZulu/ Natal), Lesotho. ❄ (min. 41–45°F/5–7°C)
C. schmidtii ■ Mat-forming, perennial succulent with erect, hairy, green or red stems bearing loose rosettes of narrowly lance-shaped, flat, pitted and spotted, dark green leaves, 1¼–1½in (3–4cm) long, margined with white hairs. Star-shaped, bright purplish pink flowers, to ⅛in (3mm) across, are produced in winter. ↕ 4in (10cm),

Crassula socialis

↔ 12in (30cm). South Africa (Western Cape, Eastern Cape, Kwazulu/Natal). ❄ (min. 41–45°F/5–7°C)
C. socialis ■ Tufted, perennial succulent bearing short, dense rosettes of 4-ranked, obovate to ovate, horny-margined, light green leaves, ¼in (6mm) long, with rounded undersides. Bears star-shaped white flowers, to ¼in (6mm) across, in spring. ↕ 2½in (6cm), ↔ indefinite. South Africa (Eastern Cape). ❄ (min. 41–45°F/5–7°C)
C. thyrsiflora see *C. capitella* subsp. *thrysiflora.*

CRATAEGUS

Hawthorn

ROSACEAE

Genus of 200 or more species of usually thorny, deciduous, sometimes semi-evergreen trees and shrubs occurring in woodland and scrub in N. temperate regions. The leaves are alternate, simple or lobed, mostly ovate or obovate, and mid- to dark green; a few species produce good autumn color. The white to deep pink flowers are usually shallowly cup-shaped and mostly borne in flat or rounded corymbs at the ends of short, leafy shoots, although (rarely) they may be solitary. Fruits, produced in autumn, consist of fleshy exteriors with bony nutlets; they are mostly red but may also be black, yellow, or bluish green. Hawthorns are valued for their long season of interest and for attracting wildlife. They are particularly useful specimen trees, for hedging, and for an urban, coastal, or exposed garden. The seeds may cause mild stomach upset if ingested.

• **CULTIVATION** Grow in any (except waterlogged) soil, in full sun or partial shade. Pruning group 1. Trim hedges after flowering or in autumn.

• **PROPAGATION** Remove seed from flesh as soon as ripe and sow in a seedbed or in containers in an open frame. Stratify and sow seed in a seedbed in spring (germination may take 18 months). Bud cultivars in midsummer, or graft in winter.

• **PESTS AND DISEASES** Tree borer, caterpillars, leafminers, skeletonizer, and scale insects are common. Fire blight, cankers, cedar-apple rust, powdery mildew, apple scab, and a variety of fungal spots each occur regularly in some locations.

C. cordata see *C. phaenopyrum.*

Crataegus laciniata

C. crus-galli (Cockspur hawthorn). Spreading, deciduous tree with curved thorns, 1¼–3in (3–8cm) long. Obovate, leathery, glossy, dark green leaves, to 4in (10cm) long, turn bright crimson in autumn. Bears many-flowered corymbs of white flowers, to ½in (1.5cm) across, with pink anthers, in early summer, followed by long-lasting, spherical, dark red fruit, to ½in (1.5cm) across. ↕ 25ft (8m), ↔ 30ft (10m). E. US. Zone 2b. **var. *inermis*** is thornless and more drought resistant than the species.
C. ellwangeriana. Spreading, thorny, deciduous tree with ovate, sharply toothed and lobed, mid-green leaves, to 3in (8cm) long, turning orange and red in autumn. Corymbs of 9–10 white flowers, to ¾in (2cm) across, with red anthers, are produced in late spring, followed by oblong-ellipsoid, glossy crimson fruit, to ½in (1.5cm) long. ↕↔ 20ft (6m). E. US. Zone 6.
C. flava (Yellow hawthorn). Spreading, thorny, deciduous shrub or small tree with ovate to obovate, often 3-lobed, dark green leaves, to 2in (5cm) long. Corymbs of 3–7 white flowers, ½in (1.5cm) across, are borne in late spring and early summer, followed by spherical or pear-shaped, yellow-green fruit, to ½in (1.5cm) across. ↕ 20ft (6m), ↔ 25ft (8m). E. US. Zone 7b.
C. laciniata ■ syn. *C. orientalis.* Compact, spreading, sparsely thorny, deciduous tree with triangular to diamond-shaped, 5- to 9-lobed, dark green leaves, to 2in (5cm) long. In late spring and early summer, bears corymbs of up to 12 white flowers, to ½in (1.5cm) across, with red anthers, followed by spherical, downy, orange-red to red fruit, to ½in (1.5cm) across. ↕↔ 20ft (6m). S.E. Europe, W. Asia. Zone 6b.
C. laevigata, syn. *C. oxyacantha* of gardens (English hawthorn). Rounded, thorny, deciduous tree with ovate, shallowly 3- to 5-lobed, glossy, mid-green leaves, to 2in (5cm) long. Corymbs of up to 10 white to pink flowers, ½in (1.5cm) across, are borne in late spring, followed by spherical to ovoid red fruit, ¼–½in (0.6–1.5cm) long. ↕↔ to 25ft (8m). Europe to India, N. Africa. Zone 6. **'Coccinea Plena'** see 'Paul's Scarlet'. **'Crimson Cloud'** has large, bright red flowers, ¾in (2cm) across, with white centers. **'Paul's Scarlet'** ■ syn. 'Coccinea Plena', bears profuse, double, dark pink flowers. **'Plena'** has double white flowers, aging to pink. **'Rosea Flore Pleno'** bears double pink flowers.
***C. x lavallei* 'Carrierei'.** Strong-growing, spreading, thorny, semi-evergreen tree with obovate, toothed, glossy, dark green leaves, to 4in (10cm), long, turning red in late autumn. In summer, bears erect, many-flowered corymbs of white flowers, to ¾in (2cm) across. Long-lasting, ellipsoid or spherical, orange-red fruit, ¾in (2cm) long, ripen in late autumn. ↕ 22ft (7m), ↔ 30ft (10m). Zone 5.
C. macrosperma* var. *acutiloba ■ Spreading, thorny, deciduous tree with ovate to elliptic, sharply toothed, dark green leaves, to 3in (8cm) long, with 5 broadly triangular, toothed lobes. Corymbs of 5–12 white flowers, to ½in (1.5cm) across, with red anthers, are produced in late spring; they are followed by obovoid, bright red fruit, ½in (1.5cm) long. ↕ 20ft (6m), ↔ 25ft (8m). E. North America. Zone 3b.

Crataegus laevigata 'Paul's Scarlet'

C. mollis (Downy hawthorn). Rounded, spreading, variably thorny, deciduous tree with white-hairy young shoots. The broadly ovate leaves are toothed, shallowly lobed, softly hairy, mid-green, and 2–4in (5–10cm) long, turning yellow to bronze-red in autumn. Densely woolly corymbs of white flowers, 1in (2.5cm) across, are produced in early spring, followed by pear-shaped, softly hairy, red fruit, ¾–1in (2–2.5cm) across. ↕ 30–45ft (10–14m), ↔ 25ft (8m). C. North America. Zone 2b.
C. monogyna (Singleseed hawthorn). Rounded, deciduous tree with numerous thorns and broadly ovate to diamond-shaped, deeply 3- to 7-lobed, glossy leaves, to 2in (5cm) long, dark green above and paler beneath. Flat corymbs of 6–12 fragrant white flowers, to ½in (1.5cm) across, with pink anthers, are borne in late spring, followed by spherical, ovoid, or ellipsoid, glossy, dark red fruit, ¼in (6mm) long. Suitable as a hedge. ↕ 30ft (10m), ↔ 25ft (8m). Europe. Zone 3. **'Biflora'** (Glastonbury thorn) produces both foliage and flowers in mild winter weather, as well as in spring. **'Stricta'** is narrow and columnar, with erect branches; ↔ 12ft (4m).
***C. x mordenensis* cultivars.** Compact, rounded, almost thornless, deciduous trees with obovate, deeply 2- to 4-lobed, glossy, mid-green leaves, to 3in (8cm) long. In late spring, bear many-flowered corymbs of white or pink flowers, ½in (1.5cm) across. Spherical, red-pink fruit, to ½in (1.5cm) long, are sparsely produced. ↕↔ 20ft (6m). Zone 3. **'Snowbird'** has fragrant, double white flowers. **'Toba'** produces pink-tinged white flowers, aging to pink.

Crataegus macrosperma var. *acutiloba*

Crataegus pedicellata

C. x nitida (*C. crus-galli* x *C. viridis)* (Glossy hawthorn). Dense, rounded, thornless deciduous tree with elliptic to obovate, coarsely toothed, slightly lobed, lustrous, dark green leaves, ¾–3in (2–8cm) long, turning orange to red in autumn. Corymbs of small white flowers, ½in (1.5cm) across, are borne in mid- to late spring, followed by ovoid, long-lasting, dull red fruit, ½in (1.5cm) across. ↕ to 30ft (10m), ↔ 25ft (8m). Ohio to Arkansas. Zone 4.
C. orientalis see *C. laciniata.*
***C. oxyacantha* of gardens** see *C. laevigata.*
C. pedicellata ■ Spreading, thorny, deciduous tree. Broadly ovate, dark green leaves, to 4in (10cm) long, with 4 or 5 pairs of shallow, sharply toothed lobes, turn orange and red in autumn. Loose, many-flowered corymbs of white flowers, to ¾in (2cm) across, with red anthers, are produced in late spring, followed by pear-shaped, bright red fruit, ¾in (2cm) long. ↕↔ 20ft (6m). E. North America. Zone 6b.
***C. persimilis* 'Prunifolia'**, syn. *C.* x *prunifolia.* Rounded, deciduous tree producing thick thorns and obovate, glossy, deep green leaves, to 3in (8cm) long, which turn orange and red in autumn. In early summer, produces dense, rounded, many-flowered corymbs of white flowers, to ¾in (2cm) across, with pink anthers, followed by spherical, bright red fruit, ½in (1.5cm) long. ↕ 25ft (8m), ↔ 30ft (10m). Zone 6b.
C. phaenopyrum, syn. *C. cordata* (Washington hawthorn). Rounded, slender, thorny, deciduous tree. The maple-like, deeply 3-lobed leaves, to 3in (8cm) long, are triangular with heart-shaped bases, and glossy mid-green, turning orange to red in autumn. In early and midsummer, bears many-flowered corymbs of white flowers, ½in (1.5cm) across, with pink anthers, followed by long-lasting, spherical, glossy, bright red fruit, ¼in (6mm) long. ↕↔ 30ft (10m). S.E. US. Zone 5.
C. x prunifolia see *C. persimilis* 'Prunifolia'.
***C. punctata* 'Ohio Pioneer'.** Spreading, almost thornless, deciduous tree with obovate, dark green leaves, to

Crataegus viridis 'Winter King'

4in (10cm) long. Many-flowered corymbs of white flowers, ¾in (2cm) across, with pink anthers, are borne in spring, followed by slightly pear-shaped to spherical, dark red fruit, ¾–1in (2–2.5cm) long. ↕25ft (8m), ↔ 30ft (10m). Zone 5.

C. tanacetifolia (Tansy-leaved hawthorn). Rounded to broadly upright, usually thornless, deciduous tree with thick shoots and obovate to diamond-shaped, gray-green leaves, to 1in (2.5cm) long, with 5–7 narrowly oblong, finely divided lobes. Rounded corymbs of 6–8 fragrant white flowers, to 1in (2.5cm) across, with red anthers, are borne in midsummer, followed by spherical, aromatic, orange-yellow fruit, ¾–1in (2–2.5cm) across. ↕30ft (10m), ↔ 25ft (8m). W. Asia. Zone 3.

***C. viridis* 'Winter King'** ■ Round-headed, deciduous tree with few slender thorns. The ovate or oblong, toothed or shallowly lobed, glossy, mid-green leaves, to 2½in (6cm) long, turn red in autumn. In late spring, bears many-flowered corymbs of white flowers, to ¾in (2cm) across, with pale yellow anthers, followed by spherical red fruit, ¼–⅜in (6–9mm) long, which often last through winter. ↕40ft (12m), ↔ 20ft (6m). Zone 4.

▷ ***Crawfurdia speciosa*** see *Gentiana speciosa*

CREPIS
Hawk's beard

ASTERACEAE

Genus of about 200 species of annuals and perennials found in dry grassland, on stony slopes, and among mountain screes and rocks throughout the N. hemisphere. Although some species are persistent weeds, others are cultivated for their dandelion-like flowerheads, borne singly or in simple or compound, many-flowered racemes, corymbs, or panicles. They have one or several, mainly branched stems, and usually produce flattened, basal rosettes of entire to pinnatifid leaves. Those species grown as ornamental plants are suitable for a large rock garden.

• **CULTIVATION** Grow in any well-drained soil in full sun.

• **PROPAGATION** Sow seed in an open frame as soon as ripe. Insert root cuttings from lateral roots (not taproots) in winter. Most species self-seed freely.

• **PESTS AND DISEASES** Commonly affected by powdery mildew and rust.

C. aurea ■ Rosette-forming, taprooted perennial with obovate to inversely lance-shaped, toothed or cleft, light green leaves, to 4in (10cm) long. Usually solitary, golden orange flowerheads, 1¼in (3cm) across, are borne on stems clothed in black and white hairs, from summer to autumn. ↕4–12in (10–30cm), ↔ to 12in (30cm). Alps, mountainous areas of Italy, S. and W. Balkans. Zone 5.

C. incana (Pink dandelion). Rosette-forming perennial with inversely lance-shaped, pinnatisect, usually densely gray-hairy leaves, 1¼–5in (3–13cm) long. In late summer, bears bright, clear pink to magenta-pink flowerheads, 1¼in (3cm) across, in many-flowered corymbs. Needs full sun. ↕↔ to 12in (30cm). S. and S.E. Greece. Zone 6.

C. jacquinii. Rosette-forming perennial with inversely lance-shaped to linear, entire to pinnatifid, hairless or slightly hairy, light green leaves, to 6in (15cm) long. In summer, bears racemes of 1–6 bright yellow flowerheads, 1¼in (3cm) across, on stiff, scape-like or branched, densely woolly stems. ↕to 16in (40cm), ↔ 6in (15cm). E. Alps, Carpathians, N.W. Balkans. Zone 6.

C. rubra. Rosette-forming annual or short-lived perennial with mostly basal, inversely lance-shaped, toothed, slightly puckered and hairy, pale green leaves, to 6in (15cm) long. Pinkish red flowerheads, to 1in (2.5cm) across, are borne singly or in pairs on stiff, slightly arching stems from spring to summer. ↕12–16in (30–40cm), ↔ 6in (15cm). Balkans, S. Italy, Greece (Crete). Zone 5b. **var. *alba*** has white flowers.

Crepis aurea

CRINODENDRON

ELAEOCARPACEAE

Genus of 2 species of evergreen shrubs and trees from forest in Chile. They are cultivated for their foliage and flowers. The alternate, dark green leaves are narrowly elliptic to narrowly oblong or ovate. Pendent, bell-, lantern-, or urn-shaped, red or white flowers are borne singly or in pairs. Grow in a sheltered woodland garden or against a sheltered wall; they will tolerate an exposed site in mild areas. They may also be grown in a cool greenhouse or conservatory, where they will flower earlier.

• **CULTIVATION** Grow in fertile, moist but well-drained, humus-rich, acidic soil in partial shade, or in full sun with the roots kept cool and shaded. *C. patagua* tolerates drier conditions and prefers full sun. Shelter from wind. Restrict pruning to removal of dead wood in late spring. Pruning group 9 for *C. patagua*; group 8 for *C. hookerianum.*

• **PROPAGATION** Root greenwood cuttings in early summer, or take semi-ripe cuttings in late summer.

• **PESTS AND DISEASES** Infrequent.

C. hookerianum ■ syn. *Tricuspidaria lanceolata* (Lantern tree). Stiffly branched shrub, rarely a small tree, with upright shoots bearing narrowly elliptic to narrowly oblong, pointed, toothed, dark green leaves, to 4in (10cm) long. Lantern- or urn-shaped, fleshy-petaled, scarlet to deep carmine-pink flowers, ¾–1in (2–2.5cm) long, are produced from late spring to late summer. ↕20ft (6m), ↔ 15ft (5m). Chile. ❀ (min. 45°F/7°C)

C. patagua. Vigorous, upright shrub, rarely a small tree, bearing ovate, glossy, dark green leaves, to 3in (8cm) long. Bell-shaped, scented flowers, 1in (2.5cm) long, with fringed white petals, are produced in late summer. ↕25ft (8m), ↔ 15ft (5m). Chile. ❀ (min. 45°F/7°C)

▷ **x *Crinodonna*** *see* x *Amarcrinum*

Crinum asiaticum

CRINUM

AMARYLLIDACEAE

Genus of approximately 130 species of deciduous or evergreen, bulbous perennials found at streamsides and lake margins throughout tropical regions and South Africa. They are grown for their umbels of large, showy, funnel-shaped, long-tubed, often scented flowers, borne on leafless stems from spring to autumn. Leaves are basal, usually long, strap-shaped, and light to mid-green. Grow in a warm, sheltered border. Where not hardy, grow in a temperate or warm greenhouse. All parts may cause severe discomfort if ingested; contact with the sap may irritate skin.

• **CULTIVATION** Plant in spring, with the neck of the bulb just above soil level. Under glass, grow in soil-based potting mix with additional sharp sand and well-rotted manure, in full or bright filtered light. Water freely when in growth; keep moist after flowering. Pot on only when absolutely necessary, in early spring. Outdoors, grow in deep, fertile, humus-rich, moist but well-drained soil in full sun.

Crinodendron hookerianum (inset: flower detail)

Crinum x *powellii* 'Album'

• **PROPAGATION** Sow seed at 70°F (21°C) as soon as ripe. Remove offsets in spring.
• **PESTS AND DISEASES** Sensitive to mosaic viruses, red leaf spot, and anthracnose.

C. americanum (Southern swamp lily). Deciduous, clump-forming, bulbous perennial, spreading by stolons, with curved, sparingly toothed, mid-green leaves, to 30in (75cm) long. Umbels of up to 6 white flowers, 4–5in (10–13cm) long, with purple or brown backs, are borne from spring to autumn. ↕20in (50cm), PD6in (15cm). S. US. ❀ (min. 50°F/10°C). **'Miss Elsie'** has leaves to 4ft (1.2m) long, and produces flowers with brown-flushed backs from spring to summer.
C. asiaticum ▣ (Poison bulb). Deciduous, clump-forming, bulbous perennial with semi-erect, mid-green leaves, to 4ft (1.2m) long, grouped at the top of a false stem. Bears umbels of 20 or more narrow-tepaled, fragrant white flowers, 4in (10cm) long, from spring to summer. ↕24in (60cm), PD6in (15cm). Tropical S.E. Asia. ❀ (min. 41°F/5°C)
C. macowanii. Deciduous, bulbous perennial with curved, mid-green leaves, 36in (90cm) long, with wavy margins. In autumn, bears umbels of 10–15 fragrant, white or pink flowers, to 4in (10cm) long, flared at the tips, with a dark red central stripe on each tepal. ↕24in (60cm), PD6in (15cm). C. and E. Africa, South Africa. ❀ (min. 45°F/7°C)
C. x powellii (*C. bulbispermum* x *C. moorei*). Deciduous, bulbous perennial with a long bulb neck bearing arching, light to mid-green leaves, to 5ft (1.5m) long. Umbels of up to 10 widely flared, fragrant, pale to mid-pink flowers, to 4in (10cm) long, are borne from late summer to autumn. ↕5ft (1.5m), PD12in (30cm). Garden origin. Zone 8. **'Album'** ▣ has pure white flowers.

CROCOSMIA

syn. ANTHOLYZA, CURTONUS, MONTBRETIA

IRIDACEAE

Genus of 7 species of clump-forming, cormous perennials from grassland in South Africa. Erect, linear-lance-shaped leaves are mostly ribbed or sometimes pleated, mainly mid-green, sometimes pale green or brownish green, usually 24–36in (60–100cm) long. They are grown for their funnel-shaped, brightly colored flowers, borne in mid- and late summer in often branched spikes on wiry stems. Grow at the edge of a shrub border or in clumps in a herbaceous border. They make excellent cut flowers.
• **CULTIVATION** Plant 3–4in (8–10cm) deep in spring, in moderately fertile, humus-rich, moist but well-drained soil in sun or partial shade. Where not reliably hardy, plant near a wall; mulch in winter. Lift and divide congested clumps in spring to maintain vigor.
• **PROPAGATION** Sow seed in containers in a cold frame as soon as ripe. Divide in spring, just before growth starts.
• **PESTS AND DISEASES** Spider mites may be troublesome.

C. aurea. Cormous perennial with pale green leaves, 20–28in (50–70cm) long. Erect or occasionally branched spikes of pale to dark orange flowers, 2in (5cm) long, arranged in 2 rows, are produced in early summer. ↕32–36in (80–90cm), PD3in (8cm). South Africa. Zone 6.
***C.* 'Bressingham Blaze'.** Cormous perennial with large clumps of pleated, mid-green leaves. In late summer, produces brilliant orange-red flowers, 2–2½in (5–6cm) long, with yellow throats, in spikes 24–32in (60–80cm) long. ↕30–36in (75–90cm), PD3in (8cm). Zone 6.
***C.* 'Citronella' of gardens** see *C.* 'Golden Fleece'.
C. x crocosmiiflora (*C. aurea* x *C. pottsii*) (Montbretia). Robust, sometimes invasive, variable cormous perennial with pale green leaves, 24–32in (60–80cm) long. Thin, slightly arching, sometimes branched spikes of orange or yellow flowers, 1¼–2in (3–5cm) long, are produced in summer. ↕24in (60cm), PD3in (8cm). South Africa. Zone 6.
***C.* 'Emberglow'.** Cormous perennial with mid-green leaves. Dark red flowers, 2–3in (5–8cm) long, arranged in 2 rows in arching, freely branching spikes, are produced in summer. ↕24–30in (60–75cm), PD3in (8cm). Zone 6.
***C.* 'Emily McKenzie'**, syn. *C.* 'Lady McKenzie'. Cormous perennial with mid-green leaves. In late summer, bears branched spikes of slightly downward-facing, broad-petaled, bright orange flowers, 1½–2in (4–5cm) long, with mahogany throat markings. ↕24in (60cm), PD3in (8cm). Zone 6.
***C.* 'Fire King' of gardens** see *C.* 'Jackanapes'.
***C.* 'George Davison' of gardens** see *C.* 'Golden Fleece'.

Crocosmia 'Golden Fleece'

Crocosmia 'Jackanapes'

***C.* 'Golden Fleece'** ▣ syn. *C.* 'Citronella' of gardens, *C.* 'George Davison' of gardens. Cormous perennial with mid-green leaves. In late summer, bears slightly arching, freely branching spikes of lemon-yellow flowers, to 2in (5cm) long. ↕24–30in (60–75cm), PD3in (8cm). Zone 6.
***C.* 'Jackanapes'** ▣ syn. *C.* 'Fire King' of gardens. Cormous perennial with mid-green leaves. Arching, many-branched stems of bicolored, orange-red and yellow flowers, ¾–1¼in (2–3cm) long, are produced in late summer. ↕16–24in (40–60cm), PD3in (8cm). Zone 6.
***C.* 'Lady Hamilton'.** Cormous perennial with mid-green leaves. In late summer, golden yellow flowers, 1¼–1½in (3–4cm) long, with apricot-

Crocosmia masoniorum

yellow centers, are produced in erect, branched spikes. ↕24–30in (60–75cm), PD3in (8cm). Zone 6.
***C.* 'Lady McKenzie'** see *C.* 'Emily McKenzie'.
***C.* 'Lucifer'** ▣ Robust, cormous perennial bearing pleated, mid-green leaves. Upward-facing, bright red flowers, to 2in (5cm) long, are borne in bold, slightly arching, sparsely branched spikes in midsummer. ↕3–4ft (1–1.2m), PD3in (8cm). Zone 5.
C. masoniorum ▣ Robust, cormous perennial producing pleated, mid-green leaves, 24–36in (60–90cm) long. In midsummer, bears upward-facing, orange-red flowers, 2in (5cm) long, in arching, usually unbranched spikes. ↕4ft (1.2m), PD3in (8cm). South Africa. Zone 8.

Crocosmia 'Lucifer'

Crocosmia 'Solfatare'

C. paniculata, syn. *Antholyza paniculata, Curtonus paniculatus.* Cormous perennial producing strongly pleated, olive-green leaves, to 3ft (1m) long. In late summer, downward-curved orange flowers, to 2½in (6cm) long, are borne alternately on branched, zigzagged stems. ↕5ft (1.5m), PD4in (10cm). South Africa. Zone 6.
C. rosea see *Tritonia disticha.*
***C.* 'Solfatare'** ▣ syn. *C.* 'Solfaterre'. Cormous perennial with bronze leaves. Apricot-yellow flowers, 1¼in (3cm) long, are borne on arching, branched stems in midsummer. ↕24–28in (60–70cm), PD3in (8cm). Zone 6.
***C.* 'Solfaterre'** see *C.* 'Solfatare'.
***C.* 'Spitfire'.** Cormous perennial with mid-green leaves. Upward-facing, bright orange-red flowers, 1½in (3.5cm) long, are borne on arching, branched stems in late summer. ↕28–36in (70–90cm), PD3in (8cm). Zone 6.
***C.* 'Star of the East'** ▣ Cormous perennial with mid-green leaves. From late summer to early autumn, produces outward-facing, clear orange flowers, 1½in (3.5cm) long, each with a paler orange center, on branched stems. ↕28in (70cm), PD3in (8cm). Zone 6.

Crocosmia 'Star of the East'

CROCUS

IRIDACEAE

Genus of about 80 species of dwarf, cormous, clump-forming perennials found in a wide range of habitats, including woodland, scrub, and meadows, from coastal to subalpine areas in C. and S. Europe, N. Africa, the Middle East, C. Asia, and W. China. The small, mainly goblet-shaped flowers (1 to 4 or more per corm) open in autumn or early spring to reveal inner tepals, often in contrasting colors. The 6 tepals forming the bowl of the flower are usually each ¾–2in (2–5cm) long, while the perianth tube may be up to 6in (15cm) long. The styles are either 3-branched (with expanded or frilled ends), 6-branched, or multi-branched (with more than 6 branches). Semi-erect, linear to linear-lance-shaped leaves, mostly mid-green with pale silvery green central stripes, usually appear at the same time as or soon after the flowers and elongate markedly as the flowers fade. In some autumn-flowering species, flowers appear before the leaves.

Grow crocuses in drifts in a mixed or herbaceous border, or in a rock garden, raised bed, or trough; the most vigorous are useful for naturalizing in short grass. Some need a dry summer dormancy, and these are best grown in a bulb frame or alpine house.

• **CULTIVATION** Plant crocuses 3–4in (8–10cm) deep: spring-flowering ones in autumn, and autumn-flowering ones in late summer. Crocuses have varying cultivation requirements, which, for ease of reference, are grouped as follows:
1. Full sun and gritty, poor to moderately fertile, well-drained soil.
2. Full light in a bulb frame or alpine house, in a mix of equal parts loam, leaf mold, and grit or sharp sand. In the growing season, water freely and apply a low-nitrogen fertilizer monthly; keep completely dry in summer dormancy.
3. Sun or partial shade and moderately fertile, humus-rich, moderately moist but well-drained soil.

• **PROPAGATION** Collect seed as soon as ripe, just before the seed capsule splits, and sow immediately in containers in a cold frame. Leave seedlings in containers for 2 years before planting out. Many crocuses self-seed freely. Remove cormlets during dormancy.

• **PESTS AND DISEASES** Mice, voles, and squirrels may feed on the corms. Birds sometimes pick off flowers. Corms in storage are prone to rots and molds.

***C. aerius* of gardens** see *C. biflorus* subsp. *pulchricolor.*
C. ancyrensis ▣ (Golden bunch). Late winter- and early spring-flowering crocus, producing 5 or more, rounded, bright yellow or orange flowers, ½–1¼in (1.5–3cm) long, which have long perianth tubes. Cultivation group 1. ↕2in (5cm), PD2in (5cm). C. and N. Turkey, W. China (Tien Shan). Zone 4.
C. angustifolius, syn. *C. susianus* (Cloth-of-gold crocus). Spring-flowering crocus producing gray-green leaves and 1 or 2 narrow, orange-yellow flowers, ½–1½in (1.5–3.5cm) long. Outer tepals are suffused or almost wholly marked deep bronze, and recurve

Crocus chrysanthus 'Gipsy Girl'

strongly when flowers are fully open. Cultivation group 1 or 2. ↕2in (5cm), PD2in (5cm). S. Ukraine (including Crimea), Armenia. Zone 3.
C. asturicus see *C. serotinus* subsp. *salzmannii.*
C. aureus see *C. flavus.*
C. banaticus ▣ syn. *C. iridiflorus.* Early autumn-flowering crocus with very distinctive, solitary flowers. Large, lilac to purple outer tepals, to 2in (5cm) long, open wide; smaller inner tepals, to 1¼in (3cm) long, remain erect and are usually paler. The style is divided into a mass of lilac or white branches. Dark green leaves, without central stripes, are borne after the flowers. Slow to increase, and best propagated by seed. Cultivation group 3. ↕4in (10cm), PD2in (5cm). N.E. former Yugoslavia, Romania, S.W. Ukraine. Zone 4.
C. baytopiorum. Spring-flowering crocus with 1 or 2 rounded, clear blue-turquoise flowers, ¾–1¼in (2–3cm) long. Cultivation group 2. ↕2in (5cm), PD1in (2.5cm). S.W. Turkey. Zone 4.
C. biflorus ▣ (Scotch crocus). Very variable, early spring-flowering crocus producing 1–4 yellow-throated flowers, to 1¼in (3cm) long, in shades of lilac-blue or white, the outer tepals sometimes striped purple or brownish purple. Cultivation group 1. ↕2½in (6cm), PD2in (5cm). Italy, Balkans, Iran, S. Ukraine, Caucasus. Zone 4. **subsp. *alexandri*** has white flowers, the outer tepals heavily marked deep purple; S.W. Bulgaria, former Yugoslavia. **subsp. *pulchricolor***, syn. *C. aerius* of gardens, has rich blue-purple flowers, stained dark violet near the bases, with deep yellow throats; N.W. Turkey. **subsp. *weldenii* 'Fairy'** has white flowers, the outer tepals dusted violet.
C. boryi. Autumn-flowering crocus producing up to 4 rounded, creamy white flowers, to 2in (5cm) long, sometimes veined or flushed mauve outside, with the leaves. Cultivation group 2. ↕3in (8cm), PD2in (5cm). Greece (including Crete). Zone 5.

C. cancellatus. Very variable, autumn-flowering crocus with 1–3 slender, pale blue flowers, to 2½in (6cm) long, striped violet outside. Gray-green leaves are usually absent but may just be visible at flowering. Cultivation group 2. This description applies to subsp. *cancellatus*, the most commonly cultivated variant, found in S. Turkey, Lebanon, and S. Israel; other subspecies occur in Greece, S. former Yugoslavia, Lebanon, Jordan, Iraq, and Iran. ↕2in (5cm), PD2in (5cm). Zone 6.
C. cartwrightianus ▣ Autumn- and early winter-flowering crocus with 1–5 open goblet-shaped, fragrant, pale to deep lilac or white flowers, ½–1¼in (1.5–3cm) long, veined dark purple. Leaves appear with or shortly after the flowers. Cultivation group 2, but may be grown outside in a sunny, very well-drained situation. ↕2in (5cm), PD2in(5cm). Greece (including Crete). Zone 6. **f. *albus*** has white flowers.
C. chrysanthus. Late winter- and early spring-flowering crocus with dull green leaves and up to 4 rounded, scented flowers, ½–1½in (1.5–4cm) long, which vary from cream to deep golden yellow, often suffused or veined bronze-maroon outside. Cultivation group 1. ↕2in (5cm), PD1½in (4cm). Balkans. Zone 3. **Chrysanthus Hybrids** (often called snow crocuses) are selections of *C. chrysanthus* or *C. biflorus*, or hybrids between these two species. They have gray- to mid-green leaves, eventually to 12in (30cm) long, first appearing with the flowers. Up to 4 flowers, each 2–4in (5–10cm) long, are produced in early spring. Cultivation group 1. Zone 3. **'Advance'** produces several pale yellow flowers, suffused violet-bronze outside and golden yellow inside; ↕3in (7cm), PD2in (5cm). **'Blue Bird'** has pale blue flowers, heavily marked violet outside, with golden yellow throats; ↕3in (7cm), PD2in (5cm). **'Blue Pearl'** produces yellow-throated white flowers with soft lilac-blue outer tepals; ↕3in (7cm), PD2in (5cm). **'Cream Beauty'** bears

rich cream flowers with pale greenish brown bases and deep golden yellow throats; ↕3in (7cm), PD2in (5cm). **'E.A. Bowles'** ■ produces compact, rich lemon-yellow flowers, the outer tepals with bronze-green bases and purple feathering; ↕3in (7cm), PD2in (5cm). **'Elegance'** grows taller than most, bearing large, bright golden yellow flowers with large brown marks outside; ↕3–4in (8–10cm), PD2in (5cm). **'Eyecatcher'** has gray-white flowers, heavily marked deep purple outside; ↕3in (7cm), PD2in (5cm). **'Gipsy Girl'** ■ produces large yellow flowers with purple stripes and feathering outside; ↕3in (7cm), PD2in (5cm). **'Ladykiller'** ■ bears white flowers heavily marked deep purple outside; ↕3in (7cm), PD2in (5cm). **'Prinses Beatrix'**, syn. *C.* 'Princess Beatrix', is compact, and bears clear blue flowers with yellow bases; ↕3in (7cm), PD2in (5cm). **'Skyline'** produces clear blue flowers, lightly veined darker blue outside; ↕3in (7cm), PD2in (5cm). **'Snow Bunting'** ■ has white flowers, lightly feathered gray-blue outside; ↕3in (7cm), PD2in (5cm). **'Spring Pearl'** bears bronze-yellow flowers, feathered purple-brown outside; ↕3in (7cm), PD2in (5cm). **'Zwanenburg Bronze'** has yellow flowers, almost completely suffused dark reddish brown outside; ↕3in (7cm), PD2in (5cm).

C. clusii see *C. serotinus* subsp. *clusii.*

C. corsicus ■ Spring-flowering crocus with 1 or 2 slender, scented flowers, ¾–1½in (2–3.5cm) long, bright lilac inside and paler lilac, striped violet or purple outside, with bright orange styles. Leaves are deep green. Cultivation group 1 or 2. ↕3–4in (8–10cm), PD1½in (4cm). France (Corsica). Zone 6b.

C. cvijicii ■ Spring-flowering crocus producing solitary flowers, ¾–1½in (2–4cm) long, usually golden yellow but sometimes white or cream. Leaves are only just visible at flowering. Cultivation group 2. ↕4in (10cm), PD1½in (4cm). S. former Yugoslavia, N. Greece, E. Albania. Zone 4.

C. dalmaticus ■ Late winter- and early spring-flowering crocus with solitary, rounded, pale lilac flowers, ½–1½in (1.5–3.5cm) long. Outer tepals have a silver or light brown overlay, lightly veined with purple. Cultivation group 1. ↕3in (8cm), PD1½in (4cm). Former Yugoslavia, N. Albania. Zone 4.

***C.* 'Dutch Yellow'**, syn. *C.* 'Golden Yellow', *C.* x *luteus* 'Dutch Yellow'. Vigorous, spring-flowering crocus with 2–5 orange-yellow flowers, 1¼–2in (3–5cm) long. Suitable for naturalizing in grass. Cultivation group 1. ↕3–4in (8–10cm), PD2in (5cm). Zone 3.

***C. etruscus* 'Zwanenburg'** ■ Late winter- and spring-flowering crocus with 1 or 2 lilac-blue flowers, 1¼–1½in (3–4cm) long, the outsides washed silver or light brown with faint purple veining. Cultivation group 1. ↕3in (8cm), PD1½in (4cm). Zone 4.

C. flavus, syn. *C. aureus.* Spring-flowering crocus producing 1–4 scented, orange-yellow flowers, ¾–1½in (2–3.5cm) long. Cultivation group 1. ↕3in (8cm), PD2in (5cm). S. former Yugoslavia, C. and N. Greece, N.W. and W. Turkey, Romania. Zone 5.

C. gargaricus. Spring-flowering crocus with tiny corms, ¼in (5mm) across, and solitary, slender, bright orange-yellow flowers, ½–1¾in (1.5–4.5cm) long. Cultivation group 3; may be difficult to grow. ↕1½in (4cm), PD1in (2.5cm). N.W. Turkey. Zone 5. **subsp. *herbertii*** ■ increases by stolons and may form large clumps. Cultivation group 2 or 3; easier to grow.

***C.* 'Golden Yellow'** see *C.* 'Dutch Yellow'.

C. goulimyi ■ Autumn-flowering crocus producing 1–3 rounded, scented, lilac flowers, ½–1½in (1.5–4cm) long, with long, slender perianth tubes. Leaves are borne with the flowers. Cultivation group 1 or 2. ↕4in (10cm), PD2in (5cm). S. Greece. Zone 4.

C. hadriaticus, syn. *C. hadriaticus* var. *chrysobelonicus.* Autumn-flowering crocus producing 1–3 white flowers, ¾–1¾in (2–4.5cm) long, with the leaves. Flowers have conspicuous yellow throats and may be lightly feathered with lilac at the bases; the style is divided into 3 bright red branches. Cultivation group 1 or 2. ↕3in (8cm), PD1½in (4cm). Greece. Zone 6.

C. hadriaticus* var. *chrysobelonicus see *C. hadriaticus.*

***C. imperati* 'De Jager'** ■ Late winter- and early spring-flowering crocus with 1 or 2 flowers, 1¼–1¾in (3–4.5cm) long, with long perianth tubes. Flowers are rich violet-purple inside and light brown outside, with pronounced violet stripes. Leaves are shiny and dark green. Cultivation group 1. ↕4in (10cm), PD1½in (4cm). Zone 5.

C. iridiflorus see *C. banaticus.*

C. korolkowii (Celandine crocus). Late winter- and early spring-flowering crocus with 3–5 slender, scented, shiny, golden yellow flowers, ¾–1½in (2–3.5cm) long. Cultivation group 2, although may be grown outside. Needs a dry summer dormancy. ↕4in (10cm), PD2in (5cm). Uzbekistan, Tajikistan, N. and E. Afghanistan, N. Pakistan. Zone 5.

C. kotschyanus ■ syn. *C. zonatus.* Vigorous, autumn-flowering crocus with large, irregular, flattened corms. Produces solitary, long-tubed, pale lilac flowers, 1¼–1¾in (3–4.5cm) long, before the leaves. Each short-stemmed flower has a ring of yellow dots around the throat, and creamy white stamens. Cultivation group 1 or 2. Needs a dry summer dormancy. ↕2½–3in (6–8cm), PD2in (5cm). Turkey, N.W. Syria, Lebanon. Zone 3. **var. *leucopharynx*** has flowers with white throats.

C. laevigatus. Late autumn- and early winter-flowering crocus with 1–3 often fragrant, white to lilac flowers, ½–1¼in (1.5–3cm) long, sometimes yellow or light brown outside, often heavily feathered with deep violet-purple. Deep green leaves are borne with the flowers. Suitable for naturalizing in grass. Cultivation group 1 or 2. ↕1½–3in (4–8cm), PD1½in (4cm). Greece (including Crete). Zone 6.

C. longiflorus ■ Autumn-flowering crocus with 1 or 2 pale to deep lilac, strongly fragrant flowers, ¾–1¾in (2–4.5cm) long, often lightly feathered outside, with bright orange-red styles. Leaves, with white central stripes, appear with the flowers. Cultivation group 2. ↕3–4in (8–10cm), PD1¼in (3cm). S.W. Italy (including Sicily), Malta. Zone 6.

***C.* x *luteus* 'Dutch Yellow'** see *C.* 'Dutch Yellow'.

C. malyi ■ Spring-flowering crocus with slightly gray-green leaves and 1 or 2 white flowers with long perianth tubes, yellow throats, and pointed tepals, ¾–1½in (2–4cm) long, sometimes faintly suffused purple at the bases. Cultivation group 2. ↕3in (8cm), PD1½in (4cm). W. former Yugoslavia. Zone 4.

C. medius ■ Late autumn-flowering crocus producing solitary, vivid purple, or sometimes paler flowers, 1–2in (2.5–5cm) long, with long perianth tubes and bright orange-red styles; flowers appear just before the leaves. Cultivation group 1. ↕3in (8cm), PD1in (2.5cm). S.E. France, N.W. Italy. Zone 5.

C

Crocus ancyrensis

Crocus banaticus

Crocus biflorus

Crocus cartwrightianus

Crocus chrysanthus 'E.A. Bowles'

Crocus chrysanthus 'Ladykiller'

Crocus chrysanthus 'Snow Bunting'

Crocus corsicus

Crocus cvijicii

Crocus dalmaticus

Crocus etruscus 'Zwanenburg'

Crocus gargaricus subsp. *herbertii*

Crocus goulimyi

Crocus imperati 'De Jager'

Crocus kotschyanus

Crocus longiflorus

Crocus malyi

Crocus medius

Crocus pulchellus

Crocus sieberi 'Hubert Edelsten'

Crocus sieberi subsp. *sublimis* f. *tricolor*

Crocus speciosus 'Oxonian'

C. minimus ■ Late spring-flowering crocus with 1 or 2 mid- to deep lilac-purple flowers, ¾–1¼in (2–3cm) long, with long perianth tubes. Outer tepals are veined, stained, or feathered with dark violet, often on a buff or yellow base. Cultivation group 1. ↕3in (8cm), PD1in (2.5cm). France (S. Corsica), Italy (Sardinia). Zone 4.
C. niveus. Autumn-flowering crocus bearing 1 or 2 yellow-throated, white to lilac flowers, 1¼–2½in (3–6cm) long, as the leaves emerge. They have white, yellow, or purple-brown perianth tubes and conspicuous, much-divided, orange styles. Cultivation group 2; may be grown outside. Needs a dry summer dormancy. ↕4–6in (10–15cm), PD1½in (4cm). S. Greece. Zone 6.
C. nudiflorus. Autumn-flowering crocus producing solitary, long-tubed, rich purple flowers, 1¼–2½in (3–6cm) long, before the leaves. Spreads by stolons and is suitable for naturalizing in grass. Cultivation group 3. ↕6–10in (15–26cm), PD2in (5cm). S.W. France, N. and E. Spain. Zone 4.
C. ochroleucus ■ Late autumn-flowering crocus producing 1–3 creamy white flowers, ¾–1½in (2–3.5cm) long, with conspicuous yellow throats and long perianth tubes. Leaves appear with, or shortly after, the flowers. Increases freely by offsets and is suitable for naturalizing in grass. Cultivation group 1 or 2. ↕2in (5cm), PD1in (2.5cm). S.W. Syria, Lebanon, N. Israel. Zone 6.

C. olivieri. Spring-flowering crocus with spreading leaves, producing 1–4 long-tubed, pale lemon-yellow to deep orange flowers, ½–1½in (1.5–3.5cm) long, with undivided styles. Cultivation group 1. ↕2in (5cm), PD1½in (4cm). Balkans. Zone 5. **subsp. *balansae*** has much-divided styles, and outer tepals striped or heavily suffused bronze; Greece (Sámos, Chíos), W. Turkey.
C. oreocreticus. Autumn-flowering crocus producing 1–5 rich lilac flowers, ½–1¼in (1.5–3cm) long, each with dark purple veins and a silvery wash on the outside. Leaves are barely present at flowering. Increases easily from seed. Cultivation group 2. ↕2in (5cm), PD2in (5cm). Greece (Crete). Zone 6.
C. pallasii* subsp. *pallasii. Autumn-flowering crocus producing 1–6 pale pinkish lilac to deep lilac-blue flowers, to 2in (5cm) across, veined darker, with white or lilac throats, yellow anthers, and red styles. The leaves begin to appear at flowering. Cultivation group 2. ↕3–4in (8–10cm), PD1½in (4cm). Balkans, Crimea, Lebanon, Israel. Zone 6b.
***C.* 'Princess Beatrix'** see *C. chrysanthus* Chrysanthus Hybrids 'Prinses Beatrix'.
C. pulchellus ■ Autumn- to early winter-flowering crocus producing 1, occasionally 2, long-tubed, goblet-shaped flowers, 1¼–2½in (3–6cm) long, before the leaves. Flowers are pale lilac-blue, lightly veined violet, with deep yellow throats and white anthers.

Crocus minimus

Crocus ochroleucus

Crocus sieberi 'Bowles' White'

Crocus tommasinianus 'Ruby Giant'

Crocus vernus subsp. *albiflorus*

Crocus vernus 'Purpureus Grandiflorus'

Very similar to *C. speciosus*, with which it hybridizes. Suitable for naturalizing in grass. Cultivation group 1. ↕4–5in (10–12cm), PD1½in (4cm). S. former Yugoslavia, N. Greece, S. Bulgaria, Turkey. Zone 4. **'Zephyr'** see *C.* 'Zephyr'.
C. reticulatus. Late winter- and early spring-flowering crocus producing 1 or 2 cup-shaped, fragrant, white or lilac flowers, ½–1½in (1.5–3.5cm) long, with light yellow throats inside. Outer tepals have 3–5 longitudinal, deep violet bands. Gray-green leaves have white central stripes. Cultivation group 2. ↕to 4in (10cm), PD3in (8cm). N.E. Italy to S. Turkey and N. Caucasus. Zone 6.
C. salzmannii see *C. serotinus* subsp. *salzmannii.*
C. sativus, syn. *C. sativus* var. *cashmirianus* (Saffron crocus). Autumn-flowering crocus producing 1–5 widely open, rich lilac flowers, to 2in (5cm) long, with dark purple veins. Dull green leaves are borne with or shortly after the flowers. Saffron is obtained from the long, conspicuous, 3-branched, deep red style. Sterile, increasing only by division. Cultivation group 1 or 2; generally fails to flower in cool, wet areas. ↕2in (5cm), PD2in (5cm). Origin uncertain; it is probably an ancient selection of *C. cartwrightianus*. Zone 6b.
var. *cashmirianus* see *C. sativus.*
C. serotinus. Autumn-flowering crocus with solitary, pale to deep lilac flowers, 1–1½in (2.5–4cm) long, sometimes veined darker lilac, with long perianth tubes and white or very pale yellow throats. Dark green leaves are sometimes present at flowering. Cultivation group 2. ↕2–3in (5–8cm), PD1½in (4cm). S. Portugal. Zone 6. **subsp. *clusii***, syn. *C. clusii*, produces leaves as the flowers fade; cultivation group 1, with added organic matter; ↕2–3in (5–8cm), PD1½in (4cm); Portugal, N.W. and S.W. Spain. **subsp. *salzmannii***, syn. *C. asturicus*, *C. salzmannii*, flowers earlier, producing larger, pale lilac flowers when leaves are only just present; N., C., and S. Spain, Gibraltar, N. Africa.
C. sieberi. Vigorous, late winter- and early spring-flowering crocus with 1–3 scented, rich pinkish lilac-blue, yellow-throated flowers, ¾–1¼in (2–3cm) long. Cultivation group 1. ↕2–3in (5–8cm), PD1in (2.5cm). Greece. Zone 3. **'Albus'** see 'Bowles' White'. **'Bowles' White'** ■ syn. 'Albus', produces white flowers, 1¼–1¾in (3–4.5cm) long, with deep golden yellow throats, in early spring. **'Firefly'** produces abundant lilac flowers. **'Hubert Edelsten'** ■ has pale lilac flowers, 1¼–1¾in (3–4.5cm) long, with rich purple outer tepals, each with a bold white line. **subsp. *sieberi*** produces white flowers, marked purple outside, from spring to early summer; cultivation group 2; ↕1½in (4cm); Greece (Crete). **subsp. *sublimis* f. *tricolor*** ■ has narrow flowers, each with 3 distinct bands of lilac, white, and golden yellow. **'Violet Queen'** has deep violet flowers with pointed tips.
C. speciosus. Autumn-flowering crocus producing solitary flowers before the leaves. Long-tubed flowers, 1¼–2½in (3–6cm) long, in shades of violet-blue with deeper blue veins, have much-divided, bright orange styles. Increases rapidly by seed and offsets; suitable for naturalizing in grass. Cultivation group 1. ↕4–6in (10–15cm), PD2in (5cm). N. and C. Turkey, N. Iran, S. Ukraine (Crimea), Caucasus, C. Asia. Zone 4. **'Aitchisonii'** bears large, pale lilac flowers with darker veins. **f. *albus***, syn. 'Albus', has pure white flowers. **'Conqueror'** has deep blue flowers, 1½–3in (4–7cm) long. **'Oxonian'** ■ has violet-mauve flowers with dark violet bases and tubes.
C. susianus see *C. angustifolius.*
C. tommasinianus. Late winter- to spring-flowering crocus producing 1 or 2 slender flowers, ¾–1¾in (2–4.5cm) long, with long white perianth tubes. Flowers vary from pale silvery lilac to shades of reddish purple; outer tepals are often overlaid silver. Increases freely by seed and offsets; suitable for naturalizing in grass. Cultivation group 1. ↕3–4in (8–10cm), PD1in (2.5cm). S. Hungary, S. former Yugoslavia, N.W. Bulgaria. Zone 4. **f. *albus*** ■ has white flowers. **'Barr's Purple'** has purple flowers, silvery outside. **'Ruby Giant'** ■ is clump-forming, with sterile, rich reddish purple flowers. **'Whitewell Purple'** increases rapidly and has reddish purple flowers, silver-mauve inside.
C. tournefortii. Late autumn- to winter-flowering crocus. Solitary, long-tubed, widely open, pale lilac flowers, ½–1½in (1.5–3.5cm) long, have much-divided orange styles and white anthers. Flowers, borne with the leaves, remain open at night. Cultivation group 1 or 2. ↕2–3in (5–8cm), PD1½in (4cm). S. Greece (including Crete, Cyclades). Zone 6.

Crocus tommasinianus f. *albus*

C. vernus (Dutch crocus). Spring- to early summer-flowering crocus producing solitary flowers, 1¼–2½in (3–6cm) long, in white or shades of lilac or purple. Suitable for naturalizing in grass. Cultivation group 1. ↕4–5in (10–12cm), PD2in (5cm). Italy to W. Russia. Zone 3. **subsp. *albiflorus*** ■ produces pointed, white or occasionally purple flowers, and is more difficult to cultivate than the species; Spain to Germany to Albania. **'Early Perfection'** has violet-purple to blue flowers with dark edges. **'Flower Record'** has pale violet flowers. **'Haarlem Gem'** has lilac flowers, silvery gray outside. **'Jeanne d'Arc'**, syn. 'Joan of Arc', has white flowers with deep purple bases and faint purple feathering. **'Joan of Arc'** see 'Jeanne d'Arc'. **'Kathleen Parlow'** has white flowers with purple bases. **'King of the Striped'** has violet flowers, striped light purple. **'Pickwick'** ■ has white flowers, striped pale and dark lilac, with dark purple bases. **'Purpureus Grandiflorus'** ■ has abundant violet flowers with purple bases. **'Queen of the Blues'** has lilac-blue flowers. **'Remembrance'** bears shiny violet flowers. **'Striped Beauty'** bears mauve-striped, pale silver-gray flowers with violet-purple bases. **'Vanguard'** produces pale lilac flowers, gray outside, in late winter.
***C.* 'Zephyr'**, syn. *C. pulchellus* 'Zephyr'. Autumn-flowering crocus producing solitary, long-tubed, pale lilac flowers, ¾–1½in (2–4cm) long, before the leaves. Cultivation group 1. ↕4–5in (10–12cm), PD2in (5cm). Zone 4b.
C. zonatus see *C. kotschyanus.*

Crocus vernus 'Pickwick'

CROSSANDRA

ACANTHACEAE

Genus of about 50 species of evergreen shrubs and subshrubs from forest margins of the Arabian Peninsula, tropical Africa, Madagascar, India, and Sri Lanka. They have whorls of hairless or softly hairy, usually entire, obovate, ovate, elliptic, or lance-shaped leaves. Fan-shaped, salverform flowers, each with a long corolla tube and 5 usually orange or red lobes, are produced in terminal or axillary, 4-sided spikes with prominent bracts. Where not hardy, grow in a temperate or warm greenhouse; a few may be used as houseplants. In tropical areas, grow as bedding or in a shrub border.
• **CULTIVATION** Under glass, grow in soilless or soil-based potting mix in full light from autumn to spring, and in bright filtered light in summer. Provide moderate to high humidity. During the growing season, water freely and apply a balanced liquid fertilizer monthly; water sparingly in winter. Pinch out growing points when young to encourage bushy growth. Outdoors, grow in fertile, humus-rich, well-drained soil in full sun. Pruning group 8; plants under glass may need restrictive pruning in late winter.
• **PROPAGATION** Sow seed at 61°F (16°C) in early spring. Root semi-ripe cuttings with bottom heat in early spring.
• **PESTS AND DISEASES** Plants are prone to stem and root rot, and flowers are sometimes attacked by gray mold. Aphids, thrips, and whiteflies can be problems.

Crossandra infundibuliformis

Crossandra nilotica

C. infundibuliformis ■ syn. *C. undulifolia* (Firecracker flower). Erect subshrub with slender stems and ovate to lance-shaped, wavy-margined, glossy, mid-green leaves, 2–5in (5–12cm) long. Fan-shaped, orange-yellow to salmon-pink flowers, to 1¼in (3cm) across, are borne in usually axillary, pinecone-like spikes, 4in (10cm) long, with downy bracts, at any time of year. ↕3ft (1m), ↔ 24in (60cm). S. India, Sri Lanka. ❄ (min. 59°F/15°C). **'Mona Walhead'** is much more compact, with lustrous green leaves and deep salmon-pink flowers; ↕20in (50cm), ↔ 12in (30cm).
C. nilotica ■ Erect subshrub with elliptic, softly hairy, mid-green leaves, the few basal leaves 2½in (6cm) long, and the stem leaves 4in (10cm) long. Fan-shaped, vivid red to orange flowers, 1in (2.5cm) across, are produced in dense, axillary or terminal spikes, to 3in (7cm) long, with hairy bracts, at any time of year. ↕12–24in (30–60cm), ↔ to 14in (35cm). Tropical Africa. ❄ (min. 59°F/15°C)
C. pungens. Dense subshrub with oblong, white-veined, dull green leaves, 2–5½in (5–14cm) long. Produces fan-shaped orange flowers, to 1½in (4cm) across, in congested, axillary or terminal spikes, 4in (10cm) long, with bristly, sometimes spiny bracts, at any time of year. ↕24in (60cm), ↔ 20in (50cm). Tropical Africa. ❄ (min. 59°F/15°C)
C. undulifolia see *C. infundibuliformis.*

CROTALARIA

Rattlebox

FABACEAE

Genus of about 600 species of annuals, perennials, and evergreen shrubs from scrub, grassland, and open forest in tropical and subtropical zones worldwide, particularly in E. and S. tropical Africa. The alternate leaves are simple or 3- to 7-palmate. Pea-like flowers are borne in terminal or axillary racemes, followed by inflated seed pods. Where not hardy, grow the perennials and shrubs in a temperate greenhouse. In warm, dry climates, grow against a warm, sunny wall or in a border. Annuals are easy to cultivate in a border.
• **CULTIVATION** Under glass, grow in soil-based potting mix in full light with shade from hot sun, and with good ventilation. In the growing season, water freely, and apply a balanced liquid fertilizer monthly; water sparingly in winter. Top-dress or pot on in spring.

Crotalaria agatiflora

Outdoors, grow in fertile, moist but well-drained soil in full sun. Pruning group 8; plants under glass need restrictive pruning after flowering.
• **PROPAGATION** Sow seed at 59–64°F (15–18°C) in spring. Root semi-ripe cuttings with bottom heat in summer.
• **PESTS AND DISEASES** Susceptible to collar rot, root rot, powdery mildew, thread blight, *Cercospora* leaf spot, *Fusarium* wilt, anthracnose, and a variety of viruses. Spider mites and whiteflies are problems under glass.

C. agatiflora ■ (Canary bush). Erect to spreading shrub with 3-palmate leaves, 2–3in (5–8cm) long, consisting of ovate to elliptic-lance-shaped, mid- to deep green leaflets. Yellow- to olive-green flowers, 1½–2in (3.5–5cm) long, are borne in terminal racemes, 10–16in (25–40cm) long, mainly in summer, followed by large, rattle-like seed pods. ↕6–10ft (2–3m), ↔ 3–6ft (1–2m). Uganda to Zimbabwe, highlands of Kenya. ❄ (min. 45–50°F/7–10°C)

CROWEA

RUTACEAE

Genus of 3 species of evergreen shrubs and woody-based perennials found in scrub and open woodland in Australia. The alternate, linear to elliptic leaves are simple and glandular. The usually solitary, sometimes paired, axillary or terminal, star-shaped flowers have 5 wide, spreading petals. Where not hardy, grow in a cool greenhouse or conservatory; in warmer climates, use in a shrub border or courtyard garden.

Crowea exalata

• **CULTIVATION** Under glass, grow in soil-based potting mix in full light with shade from hot sun, and with good ventilation. During the growing season, water moderately, applying a balanced liquid fertilizer monthly from spring to autumn; water sparingly in winter. Top-dress or pot on in spring. Outdoors, grow in fertile, moist but well-drained soil in full sun, with some midday shade, or in partial shade. Pruning group 10, after flowering.
• **PROPAGATION** Sow seed at 61–64°F (16–18°C) in early spring. Root semi-ripe cuttings with bottom heat in late spring or summer.
• **PESTS AND DISEASES** Scale insects may be a problem under glass.

C. exalata ■ Open-branched shrub with linear to narrowly obovate, mid-green leaves, ¾–2in (2–5cm) long, smelling of anise when bruised. Bears abundant solitary, pink or, rarely, white flowers, ¾in (2cm) across, from the leaf axils, from late spring to autumn. ↕ 12–36in (30–90cm), ↔ 20–60in (0.5–1.5m). New South Wales, Victoria. ❀ (min. 41°F/5°C); can survive short periods near 32°F (0°C).
C. saligna. Open-branched shrub with slender stems bearing narrowly elliptic, deep green leaves, 1½–3in (4–8cm) long, with recurved margins. From summer to late autumn, produces solitary, waxy pink flowers, 1½in (3.5cm) across, from the leaf axils. ↕↔ 3–5ft (1–1.5m). New South Wales. ❀ (min. 41°F/5°C)

▷ ***Crucianella*** see *Phuopsis*
▷ ***Cryptanthopsis navioides*** see *Orthophytum navioides*

CRYPTANTHUS

Earth star, Starfish plant

BROMELIACEAE

Genus of over 50 species of mostly stemless, evergreen, mainly dwarf, terrestrial perennials (bromeliads) found in soil or on rocks in moist to dry, forest regions, at altitudes up to 5,000ft (1,600m), in E. Brazil. The strap- to spoon-shaped, wavy-margined, sometimes attractively zoned leaves are borne in flat, star-like rosettes. In some species, offsets form in the leaf axils; others produce them from stolons. In summer, inconspicuous, star-shaped, often scented, white or greenish white

Cryptanthus bivittatus

flowers are produced in sunken, corymb-like inflorescences in the center of each rosette. Where temperatures fall below 59–68°F (15–20°C), grow in a warm greenhouse, as houseplants, or in a bottle garden; in humid, tropical areas, grow in a bed or border.
• **CULTIVATION** Under glass, grow in terrestrial bromeliad potting mix, in full or bright filtered light with moderate to high humidity. In the growing season, water moderately but carefully, mist regularly with tepid water, and apply a dilute fertilizer monthly; reduce water slightly in winter. Outdoors, grow in moist but well-drained, moderately fertile, acidic soil, enriched with fibrous organic matter, in partial or dappled shade. See also p.47.
• **PROPAGATION** Sow seed at 81°F (27°C) as soon as ripe. Remove offsets in early summer.
• **PESTS AND DISEASES** Prone to scale insects and mealybugs.

C. acaulis (Green earth star). Stemless or short-stemmed, clump-forming bromeliad with rosettes of 10–15 narrowly lance-shaped, wavy-margined, minutely toothed leaves, 5in (13cm) long; leaves are mid-green and scaly above, densely white-scaly beneath. Corymbs of 6 or more, scented white flowers, 1½in (4cm) long, are borne in summer. ↕ to 4in (10cm), ↔ indefinite. E. Brazil. ❀ (min. 68°F/20°C). **var. ruber** has leaves tinged brownish red.
C. beuckeri. Stemless or very short-stemmed, clump-forming bromeliad with loose, often irregular rosettes of

Cryptanthus bivittatus 'Pink Starlight'

Cryptanthus osirus 'Tricolor'

10–20 broadly lance-shaped to narrowly ovate, tapering, wavy-margined, toothed, pink-flushed, dull green leaves, to 6in (15cm) long, white-mottled above and gray-scaly beneath. Corymbs of 3–6 white or greenish white flowers, 1¼in (3cm) long, are produced in summer. ↕↔ to 6in (15cm). E. Brazil. ❀ (min. 68°F/20°C)
C. bivittatus ■ Stemless bromeliad with low, spreading rosettes of about 20 strap-shaped, wavy-margined, toothed, dark green leaves, to 7in (18cm) long, striped white or pink. Few-flowered corymbs of white flowers, 1in (2.5cm) long, are produced in summer. ↕ to 4in (10cm), ↔ to 10in (25cm). E. Brazil. ❀ (min. 68°F/20°C). **var. *atropurpureus*** has red-banded, red-flushed leaves. **var. *bivittatus*** has mainly green leaves. **'Pink Starlight'** ■ has rosettes of about 15 leaves, to in (8cm) long, striped olive-green and white, and strongly suffused deep pink. In summer, inconspicuous, slightly scented flowers, 1¼in (3cm) long. ↕ 8in (20cm), ↔ 14in (35cm) or more.
C. fosterianus. Stemless or short-stemmed bromeliad with almost flat, widely spreading rosettes of up to 12 strap-shaped, long-pointed, wavy-margined, toothed, brownish green or reddish brown leaves, to 12in (30cm) long. The leaves are cross-banded purplish brown or grayish brown above and gray-scaly beneath. In summer, bears white flowers, ½in (1cm) long, in corymbs, each consisting of a 3- or 4-flowered outer cluster and

Cryptanthus zonatus 'Zebrinus'

2-flowered inner cluster. ↕ to 5in (12cm), ↔ to 24in (60cm). E. Brazil. ❀ (min. 68°F/20°C)
C. osirus. Short-stemmed, stoloniferous bromeliad with rosettes of 10–20 strap-shaped, minutely toothed, stiff, olive-green to bronze leaves, to 14in (35cm) long, often wavy-margined, and stems to 24in (60cm) long. Dense corymbs of white flowers, 1½in (4cm) long, are borne in summer. ↕ 12–16in (30–40cm), ↔ indefinite. E. Brazil. ❀ (min. 68°F/20°C). **'Tricolor'** ■ syn. var. *tricolor* (Rainbow star), has olive-green leaves with white and red longitudinal stripes.
C. zonatus (Zebra plant). Stemless bromeliad with rosettes of 8–15 strap-shaped, mid-green leaves, to 8in (20cm) long, with gray-brown cross-banding above, and densely white-scaly beneath. White flowers, 1¼in (3cm) long, are produced in few-flowered corymbs in summer. ↕ to 5in (12cm), ↔ to 16in (40cm). E. Brazil. ❀ (min. 68°F/20°C). **'Zebrinus'** ■ has dark gray-green leaves with pronounced white cross-banding.

x CRYPTBERGIA

BROMELIACEAE

Hybrid genus, between *Cryptanthus* and *Billbergia*, of rosette-forming, evergreen, terrestrial perennials (bromeliads). The narrowly triangular, arching, olive-green to bronze outer leaves (shading to wine-red in the center in some variants) are much longer than the inner ones, which tend to form a cup. In summer, cryptbergias usually produce small corymbs of tubular white flowers, with spreading lobes, from the centers of the rosettes. Most offset freely. Where not hardy, grow in a warm greenhouse or conservatory, or as foliage houseplants; in warmer climates, grow in a bed or at the front of a border.
• **CULTIVATION** Under glass, grow in terrestrial bromeliad potting mix in bright filtered light, with moderate humidity. In the growing season, water freely, applying a dilute fertilizer monthly; water sparingly at other times. Outdoors, grow in moist but well-drained, moderately fertile, acidic soil, enriched with fibrous organic matter, in partial shade. See also p.47.
• **PROPAGATION** Remove offsets in spring.
• **PESTS AND DISEASES** Whiteflies and scale insects may prove troublesome under glass.

x *Cryptbergia* 'Red Burst'

x *C.* 'Red Burst' ■ Clump-forming bromeliad producing basal rosettes of dark green leaves, to 20in (50cm) long, turning copper-red in the lower halves, and with minutely scaly undersurfaces. In full light, the foliage intensifies to bronze-red. Small clusters of short-lived white flowers, to ½in (1cm) across, are occasionally produced in summer. ↕↔ 12in (30cm). ❄ (min. 55°F/13°C)

▷ ***Cryptocereus anthonyanus*** see *Selenicereus anthonyanus*

CRYPTOCORYNE

Water trumpet

ARACEAE

Genus of 50 species of slow-growing, rhizomatous, evergreen, marginal aquatic perennials from tropical S. and S.E. Asia. They are grown for their stiff, broadly ovate to lance-shaped, leathery leaves, which are mostly submerged. Minute, orange, red, or purple to almost black flowers are produced in a tubular spathe that projects above the surface of the water in mature plants. The flowers contain olfactory glands that give off a dung-like scent; this attracts insects, which crawl down the inside of the spathe, where they become trapped and pollinate the female flowers. Where not hardy, grow in a tropical aquarium or in the margins of an indoor pool in a warm greenhouse. In warmer areas, grow in the margins of an outdoor pool.

• **CULTIVATION** In an indoor pool, grow in aquatic containers of inert medium, in full light, in water 6–12in (15–30cm) deep, and feed with commercial aquatic plant fertilizer. In an outdoor pool, grow in baskets of humus-rich, sandy soil, or plant directly into the mud at the pond margin, in full sun or partial shade. In an aquarium, grow in containers of sharp sand and leave undisturbed. Provide full light until established; thereafter, they will tolerate bright filtered light. Maintain the water temperature at 68–86°F (20–30°C). See also pp.52–53.

• **PROPAGATION** Remove offsets in spring, or divide rhizomes in spring or summer, and plant ½–¾in (1.5–2cm) deep. Sow seed at 64–70°F (18–21°C) as soon as ripe.

• **PESTS AND DISEASES** Changes in external conditions, such as light and temperature, or in the balance of water chemistry, may cause the leaves to become soft and translucent.

C. beckettii. Submerged aquatic perennial with narrowly ovate to ovate, olive-green to dark brown leaves, 6in (15cm) long, with violet leaf stalks. The twisted flower spathes, to 5in (13cm) tall, dull yellow on the outside and purplish brown inside, with blackish purple collars, are produced intermittently, only when growth is above the water surface, but most often in winter. ↕↔ 6in (15cm). S. and S.E. Asia. ❄ (min. 45°F/7°C)

C. spiralis. Submerged aquatic perennial, variable in habit, with linear-lance-shaped, dark green leaves, 4–6in (10–15cm) long. The purple spathes, to 10in (25cm) tall, are twisted at first, later becoming straight, and are produced intermittently throughout the year. ↕ 10in (25cm), ↔ 6in (15cm). India. ❄ (min. 45°F/7°C)

Cryptomeria japonica (inset: fruit detail)

CRYPTOMERIA

Japanese cedar

TAXODIACEAE

Genus of 1 (possibly 2) species of evergreen, monoecious, coniferous tree from forest in China and Japan. It is cultivated for its conical or columnar habit; its thick, fibrous, red-brown bark; and its narrowly wedge-shaped, light to dark green leaves, which point forward in 5-ranked spirals around the shoots. Solitary, spherical female cones, ½–1¼in (1.5–3cm) long, have shield-like scales, each with a central point and triangular teeth. The ovoid male cones, ½in (1.5cm) long, are clustered at the shoot tips. Use larger forms as specimens or for screening. The dwarf cultivars are effective accent plants for a conifer collection or in a large rock garden. *Cryptomeria* is one of the few conifer genera that will coppice successfully.

• **CULTIVATION** Tolerates most well-drained soils, although it grows best in deep, fertile, moist but well-drained, humus-rich soil in a sheltered site in full sun or partial shade. Pruning group 1. To coppice or restore ungainly specimens, cut back to within 24–36in (60–90cm) of ground level in spring.

• **PROPAGATION** Sow seed in containers in a cold frame or in a seedbed in spring. Root ripewood cuttings in late summer or early autumn.

• **PESTS AND DISEASES** Needle necrosis, branch dieback, and root rot may occur on young plants. Nematodes can cause stunting.

Cryptomeria japonica 'Cristata'

Cryptomeria japonica 'Elegans Compacta'

Cryptomeria japonica 'Spiralis'

C. fortunei see *C. japonica* var. *sinensis.*

C. japonica ■ (Japanese cedar). Conical or columnar, coniferous tree with mid-to deep green leaves, ¼–½in (0.6–1.5cm) long, turning bronze to brown in winter. Bears brown female cones, each scale with 3–5 seeds. ↕ to 80ft (25m), ↔ to 20ft (6m). Japan. Zone 6. **'Bandai-sugi'** is a rounded, irregular shrub, with dense foliage; ↕ 6ft (2m). **'Compacta'** is a compact, conical tree with short, stiff, bluish green leaves; ↕ to 45ft (14m). **'Cristata'** ■ syn. 'Sekka-sugi', is narrow and conical, with several shoots fused and flattened into "cockscombs;" ↕ 25ft (8m), ↔ 15ft (5m). **'Elegans'** has soft, bluish green juvenile foliage, to 1in (2.5cm) long; leaves are well spaced on the shoots but create a dense overall effect; ↕ 20–30ft (6–10m). **'Elegans Compacta'** ■ is a conical shrub producing soft, glossy, dark green juvenile foliage; ↕ 6–12ft (2–4m). **'Lycopodiodes'** is open in habit, with long, thin, serpentine branches. **'Pyramidata'** is narrowly columnar in habit; ↕ to 12ft (4m), ↔ 16in (40cm). **'Sekkan-sugi'** is moderately slow-growing, producing creamy yellow leaves, turning almost white in winter. **'Sekka-sugi'** see 'Cristata'. **var. *sinensis*,** syn. *C. fortunei*, is conical, becoming rounded when mature, with an open crown and billowing branches (more pendent than those of *C. japonica*), and yellow-green leaves; female cones have only 2 seeds per fertile scale; S. China. **'Spiralis'** ■ syn. 'Yore-sugi', is a dense shrub or small tree, with spirally curved and twisted, inward-pointing leaves; ↕ to 20ft (6m). **'Yore-sugi'** see 'Spiralis'. **'Yoshino'** grows more quickly than the species, with bright blue-green leaves, becoming bronze-green in cold weather; ↕ 30–40ft (10–12m).

▷ ***Cryptostemma calendulaceum*** see *Arctotheca calendula*

CTENANTHE

MARANTACEAE

Genus of about 15 species of rosette-forming, evergreen, rhizomatous perennials from damp forest floors and thickets in Costa Rica and Brazil. They are grown for their ovate to obovate, lance-shaped, or inversely lance-shaped, yellowish to dark green leaves, marked dark or light green, silver, or yellow. The basal leaves have longer stalks than the stem leaves.

Ctenanthe burle-marxii

Irregularly shaped, tubular, white or yellow flowers are produced in short, terminal racemes or spikes. Where not hardy, grow in a warm greenhouse or conservatory, or as houseplants; in tropical and subtropical areas, grow in a shaded bed or border.

• **CULTIVATION** Under glass, grow in soilless or soil-based potting mix in bright filtered or bright indirect light, with high humidity. Maintain constant temperatures and draft-free conditions. In the growing season, mist regularly, water freely, and apply a balanced liquid fertilizer every 3 or 4 weeks. Water moderately in winter. Repot annually in late spring or early summer. Outdoors, grow in moist, fertile, humus-rich soil in partial shade.

• **PROPAGATION** Sow seed at 66–75°F (19–24°C) as soon as ripe or in spring. Divide in spring.

• **PESTS AND DISEASES** Mealybugs, spider mites, and root knot nematode can cause problems. Sensitive to fertilizer imbalance and drought, especially indoors.

C. burle-marxii ▣ Evergreen perennial with softly hairy, purple-tinged green stems. Ovate to obovate-oblong, hairless leaves, pale green above and deep purple beneath, have sickle-shaped, dark green markings, prominent main veins, and leaf bases of unequal size. The stem leaves, 5½in (14cm) long, are much larger than the basal leaves. White flowers are borne in inconspicuous spikes intermittently throughout the year. ↕ to 24in (60cm), ↔ 14in (35cm). Brazil. ❀ (min. 55°F/13°C)

Ctenanthe oppenheimiana 'Tricolor'

C. compressa. Evergreen perennial with wiry stems and slender-pointed, linear-oblong to oblong-ovate, waxy leaves, 14in (35cm) long, mid-green above and grayish green beneath. Spikes of yellowish green flowers are produced irregularly throughout the year. ↕ 24in (60cm), ↔ 14in (35cm). S.E. Brazil. ❀ (min. 55°F/13°C)

C. oppenheimiana, syn. *Calathea oppenheimiana.* Vigorous, bushy, evergreen perennial with lance-shaped, leathery leaves, 16in (40cm) long, dark green with V-shaped silver patterns above and wine-red beneath. Spikes of white flowers appear irregularly throughout the year. ↕ 3ft (1m), ↔ 24in (60cm). E. Brazil. ❀ (min. 55°F/13°C). **'Tricolor'** ▣ (Never-never plant) has foliage with irregular, creamy white and pale and dark green markings.

C. setosa. Vigorous, evergreen perennial with inversely lance-shaped, mid-green leaves, 5–7in (12–18cm) long, with the tips bent over, sometimes margined or sparsely striped white. Inconspicuous, pale yellow flowers are borne in spikes at any time of year. ↕ 5ft (1.5m), ↔ 3ft (1m). S.E. Brazil. ❀ (min. 55°F/13°C)

▷ ***Cudrania*** see *Maclura*

CUCURBITA

CUCURBITACEAE

Genus of about 27 species of warm-weather, annual, tendril-bearing vines. Leaves are simple, usually large, lobed or heart-shaped, and are often prickly. Male and female, bell-shaped flowers, to 6in (15cm) long, grow on the same vines, which may run for 10–30ft (3–9m); bush forms are compact and rarely grow larger than 2–4ft (60–120cm).

• **CULTIVATION** Grow in moderately fertile, well-drained, but moisture-retentive, soil in full sun or partial shade. None can withstand frost and all thrive in hot weather.

• **PROPAGATION** Sow seed *in situ* when soil is warm (60–75°F/16–23°C).

• **PESTS AND DISEASES** Slugs, aphids, and beetles may be problems.

C. moschata (Winter squash). Mostly trailing or spreading to bushy forms; hard angular stems have soft hairs. Leaves are shallow, rounded, and lobed, some with white markings. Sizes are highly variable. ↕ 1–2½ft (30–75cm). North America.

C. pepo (Summer squash). Trailing or bushy forms with hard stems, heart-shaped, deeply lobed, midgreen leaves. Produces yellow to orange flowers and cylindrical fruits, to 12in (30cm) long. North America. ***var. maxima*** (Pumpkin) cultivars have soft, hairy, spongy stems with large, roundish leaves and yellow flowers. ↕↔ 1–3ft (30–90cm). North America.

CUNNINGHAMIA

China fir

TAXODIACEAE

Genus of 2 or 3 species of evergreen, monoecious, coniferous trees from forest in China and Taiwan with thick, fibrous, red-brown bark and stiff, sharply pointed, narrowly lance-shaped, mid- to dark green leaves, densely arranged in 2 ranks in the same plane. Solitary female cones are brown and spherical to ovoid-conical; spherical, yellow-brown male cones are borne in clusters. Cunninghamias are closely related to the redwoods (*Sequoia*), although the foliage is similar to that of the monkey puzzle tree (*Araucaria araucana*). Grow as a specimen tree.

• **CULTIVATION** Grow in any moist but well-drained soil, in full sun or dappled shade. Shelter from strong winds. Best in a moist climate; otherwise, old foliage may turn brown and persist. Pruning group 1; needs no formal pruning but tolerates coppicing. Young plants may be slow to form a leader; if so, grow as a multi-stemmed specimen, or cut back in spring and train in the strongest resulting shoot as the new leader.

• **PROPAGATION** Sow seed in containers in a cold frame in spring. Root cuttings in early winter: those taken from side-shoots will be wide-spreading, and those from vertical shoots will be upright.

• **PESTS AND DISEASES** Leaf spot occurs.

C. lanceolata ▣ syn. *C. lanceolata* var. *sinensis* (China fir). Narrowly to broadly upright or conical, coniferous tree, developing a rounded, domed top. Lance-shaped, glossy, bright green leaves, to 3in (7cm) long, each with a raised midrib and 2 white bands beneath, are decurrent on the green shoots. Ovoid-conical, green-brown female cones are 1¼–1½in (3–4cm) long. ↕ to 70ft (20m) or more, ↔ to 20ft (6m). China. Zone 7b. **'Glauca'** has soft, blue-bloomed leaves and is slightly less hardy than the species. **var. *sinensis*** see *C. lanceolata.*

Cunninghamia lanceolata (inset: leaf detail)

CUNONIA

CUNONIACEAE

Genus of 15 species of evergreen trees occurring in damp sites in South Africa and New Caledonia. The pinnate or 3-palmate, thick, leathery, mid- to dark green leaves are borne in opposite pairs. Star-shaped, 5-petaled flowers are produced in dense, axillary racemes. Where not hardy, grow *C. capensis* as a foliage plant in a temperate greenhouse or conservatory; in warmer areas, it is an effective specimen or shade tree.

• **CULTIVATION** Under glass, grow in soil-based potting mix in full light, with shade from hot sun. In the growing season, water moderately and apply a balanced liquid fertilizer monthly from spring to autumn. Water sparingly in winter. Top-dress or pot on in spring. Outdoors, grow in fertile, moist but well-drained soil in full sun. Pruning group 1; may need restrictive pruning under glass in late winter or early spring.

• **PROPAGATION** Sow seed at 55–64°F (13–18°C) in spring. Root semi-ripe cuttings with bottom heat in summer.

• **PESTS AND DISEASES** Infrequent.

Cunonia capensis

C. capensis ■ (African red alder). Freely branched tree with pinnate, rich green leaves, 8–16in (20–40cm) long, with 5–9 lance-shaped to oblong, toothed leaflets, to 4in (10cm) long. Bears fragrant, cream to white flowers in opposite, paired racemes, to 6in (15cm) long, in late summer. ↕ 30–60ft (10–18m), ↔ 10–20ft (3–6m). South Africa. ❄ (min. 45°F/7°C)

CUPHEA

LYTHRACEAE

Genus of more than 250 species of annuals, short-lived, sometimes sub-shrubby evergreen perennials, and evergreen shrubs, from woodland clearings and pasture in S.E. US, Mexico, and subtropical and tropical Central and South America. Many species have sticky, glandular hairs. Mainly opposite, ovate to lance-shaped, entire or slightly toothed leaves are mid- to dark green. Irregularly shaped, tubular flowers are borne singly or in often-leafy racemes or panicles. Where not hardy, grow as houseplants or in a temperate greenhouse or conservatory, or use as annuals and grow in summer bedding or an annual border. Elsewhere, grow in a shrub border or bed.

• **CULTIVATION** Under glass, grow in soil-based potting mix in full light with shade from sun, in moderate humidity. In growth, water freely and apply a balanced liquid fertilizer every 3 or 4 weeks; water sparingly in winter. Outdoors, grow in moderately fertile, well-drained soil in full sun or partial shade. Pruning group 10, in spring.

Cuphea cyanea

Cuphea hyssopifolia

• **PROPAGATION** Sow seed at 55–61°F (13–16°C) in early spring or *in situ* in late spring. Divide, or root softwood cuttings of perennials with bottom heat, in late spring.

• **PESTS AND DISEASES** Whiteflies and aphids can be problems. Prone to root rot, stem galls, dieback, powdery mildew, and a few leaf spots.

C. cyanea ■ Freely branching, soft-stemmed shrub or subshrub with sticky, glandular-hairy shoots and long-stalked, ovate, mid- to deep green leaves, 2–3in (5–8cm) long. Bears terminal racemes of green-tipped, orange-red flowers, ¾–1¼in (2–3cm) long, each with 2 small, deep violet-blue petals, from late spring to autumn. ↕↔ to 3ft (1m) or more. Mexico. ❄ (min. 45°F/7°C)

C. hyssopifolia ■ (Elfin herb, False heather, Hawaiian heather). Bushy, rounded shrub with slender, downy stems and densely borne, narrowly lance-shaped, mid- to dark green leaves, to 1in (2.5cm) long. Bears short racemes of 1–3 light pink-purple, pink, or white flowers, to ½in (1cm) long, with 6 spreading petals, from the upper leaf axils, mainly from summer to autumn. ↕ 12–24in (30–60cm), ↔ 8–32in (20–80cm). Mexico, Guatemala. ❄ (min. 45°F/7°C)

C. ignea ■ syn. *C. platycentra* (Cigar flower). Spreading, freely branching, soft-stemmed shrub or subshrub, often grown as an annual, with lance-shaped to narrowly oblong, glossy, bright green leaves, 1¼–3in (3–8cm) long. From late spring to autumn, slender, deep red flowers, ¾–1¼in (2–3cm) long, each with a dark red band, a white rim, and 2 tiny black-purple petals, are borne singly from the upper leaf axils. ↕ 12–30in (30–75cm), ↔ 12–36in (30–90cm). Mexico to Jamaica. ❄ (min. 41°F/5°C). **'Variegata'** has mid-green leaves flecked cream and lime-green.

C. lanceolata. Bushy, purple-stemmed subshrub with sticky, glandular-hairy stems and foliage. Lance-shaped to oval, pointed leaves are mid-green and white-hairy, to 3in (8cm) long. Solitary, 6-petaled, deep violet flowers, to 1½in (4cm) long, constricted at the necks, then flaring into unequally sized upper and lower lips, are borne from the upper leaf axils from summer to autumn. ↕ to 26in (65cm), ↔ to 18in (45cm) (in containers). C. Mexico. ❄ (min. 41°F/5°C)

C. llavea* var. *miniata. Bushy subshrub with bristly stems and ovate to lance-

Cuphea ignea

shaped, mid-green leaves, to 3in (8cm) long. In early summer, bears terminal racemes of 2-petaled, vermilion flowers, 1½in (3.5cm) long, flared at the mouths, with greenish purple calyces. ↕ 18in (45cm), ↔ 6in (15cm). Mexico. ❄ (min. 45°F/7°C)

C. llavea* var. *miniata of gardens see *C.* x *purpurea.*

***C. llavea* of gardens** see *C.* x *purpurea.*

C. micropetala. Freely branching subshrub with densely borne, lance-shaped, slightly scaly, mid-green leaves, to 6in (15cm) long. From summer to autumn, bears terminal racemes of softly hairy flowers, to 1½in (4cm) long, each with a green-yellow-shaded, red tube and up to 6 tiny red, white, or yellow petals. ↕ to 36in (90cm), ↔ 12–36in (30–90cm). Mexico. ❄ (min. 45°F/7°C)

***C. miniata* of gardens** see *C.* x *purpurea.*

C. platycentra see *C. ignea.*

C.* x *purpurea (*C. llavea* x *C. procumbens*), syn. *C. llavea* of gardens, *C. miniata* of gardens. Bushy subshrub, often grown as an annual, with sticky, glandular-hairy stems and foliage. Red stems bear ovate to lance-shaped, pointed, dark green leaves, to 3in (8cm) long. From spring to autumn, produces terminal racemes of 2-petaled, pink to red flowers, to 1¼in (3cm) long, which flare at the mouths. ↕ 1–2ft (30–60cm), ↔ 9–18in (23–45cm). Garden origin. ❄ (min. 41°F/5°C). **'Avalon'** has purple flowers. **'Firefly'** has cherry-red flowers.

x CUPRESSOCYPARIS

CUPRESSACEAE

Hybrid genus, between *Chamaecyparis* and *Cupressus*, of fast-growing, columnar, evergreen, coniferous trees. They produce flattened sprays of scale-like, dark green leaves, to ⅛in (3mm) long. Female cones are spherical; male cones are ovoid, yellow, and 1/16–⅛in (2–3mm) long. Grow as specimen trees or use for hedging. Contact with the foliage may aggravate skin allergies.

• **CULTIVATION** Grow in any deep, well-drained soil in full sun or partial shade. Pruning group 1: trim hedges 2 or 3 times in growth (without cutting back into the old wood), with the last cut in late summer or early autumn.

• **PROPAGATION** Root semi-ripe cuttings in late summer.

• **PESTS AND DISEASES** *Coryneum* canker, tip and branch dieback, root rot, and needle blights are common. Bark beetles,

x *Cupressocyparis leylandii* 'Castlewellan'

x *Cupressocyparis leylandii* 'Haggerston Grey'

scale insects, caterpillars, and sawfly can cause problems in the landscape.

x *C. leylandii*, syn. *Cupressus leylandii* (Leyland cypress). Dense, tapering, coniferous tree with flat sprays of pointed, dark green, gray-tinged leaves; smooth bark grows stringy with age. Bears dark brown female cones, to ¾in (2cm) across, each with 8 scales. ↕ to 120ft (35m), ↔ to 15ft (5m). Garden origin. Zone 7. **'Castlewellan'** ■ syn. 'Galway Gold', bears plume-like sprays of yellow foliage; ↕ 80ft (25m). **'Galway Gold'** see 'Castlewellan'. **'Gold Rider'** is compact and upright with bright yellow foliage all year long. ↕ 8–10ft (2.5–3m). **'Haggerston Grey'** ■ has gray-green

x *Cupressocyparis leylandii* 'Harlequin'

foliage. **'Harlequin'** ■ syn. 'Variegata', a sport of 'Haggerston Grey', has patches of ivory-white foliage. **'Leighton Green'** is narrow, with fresh green foliage. **'Naylor's Blue'** has blue-gray foliage, which is especially attractive after rain. **'Robinson's Gold'** has bronze-yellow foliage in spring, maturing to golden yellow and lime-green. **'Variegata'** see 'Harlequin'.
x *C. notabilis.* Narrowly conical, coniferous tree with upswept branches, red-brown bark, and pointed, blue-gray leaves, produced in sparse sprays. Purple female cones, ½in (1.5cm) across, each have 4–8 scales. ↕ to 50ft (15m), ↔ to 20ft (6m). Garden origin. Zone 7.

Cupressus

Cypress

CUPRESSACEAE

Genus of about 24 species of evergreen, monoecious, coniferous trees from the Northern Hemisphere, found in dry, open hillside forest. Paired, overlapping, forward-pointing, scale-like leaves vary from rounded to pointed at the tips. The mature bark often breaks off into curling or rounded scales. Small, spherical to ovoid female cones, to 1½in (4cm) long, ripen in the second year but usually persist on the tree, and have 5–20 seeds per scale. Ovoid, green male cones, to ⅛in (3mm) long, are borne at the shoot tips. Cypresses tolerate dry conditions and are excellent specimen trees. *C. macrocarpa* may be used as a hedge or screen. Where not hardy, grow in a cool greenhouse or conservatory.

• **Cultivation** Under glass, grow in soil-based potting mix in full light, with good ventilation. Outdoors, grow in any well-drained soil (including alkaline and acidic soils) in full sun. Shelter from cold, drying winds. Pruning group 1: trim hedges in late spring; do not cut back into old wood.

• **Propagation** Sow seed in a seedbed or in containers in a cold frame in spring. Root cuttings in late autumn or early winter.

• **Pests and diseases** *Coryneum* canker, tip and branch dieback, root rot, and needle blights are common. Bark beetles, scale insects, caterpillars, and sawfly can cause problems.

C. abramsiana. Vigorous, conical, coniferous tree with deeply furrowed, dark gray bark and sparse sprays of pointed, bright green, glandless leaves, 1/16in (2mm) long. Spherical, shiny brown to gray-buff female cones, to 1½in (3.5cm) across, each have 6 scales. ↕ to 70ft (20m), ↔ to 20ft (6m). California. Zone 7.

Cupressus arizonica var. *glabra*

C. arizonica* var. *glabra ■ syn. *C. glabra* (Smooth cypress). Conical, coniferous tree with smooth, reddish purple bark. Pointed, glaucous, blue-gray leaves, 1/16in (2mm) long, are arranged in dense sprays. Dorsal resin glands form white flecks on the foliage. Spherical, prickly brown female cones, 1in (2.5cm) across, each have 6 or 8 scales. ↕ 30–50ft (10–15m), ↔ 12–15ft (4–5m). S.W. US. Zone 7b. **'Glauca'** has very blue young leaves.
C. bakeri (Baker cypress). Conical, coniferous tree with reddish gray or gray bark, splitting into thin scales. Pointed, aromatic, gray-green leaves, 1/16in (2mm) long, with prominent, dorsal resin glands, are borne in sparse sprays. Spherical, grayish brown female cones, ½in (1.5cm) across, each have 6–8 scales and prominent curved prickles. ↕ to 50ft (15m), ↔ to 15ft (5m). Oregon, N. California. Zone 7.
C. cashmeriana see *C. torulosa* 'Cashmeriana'.
C. glabra see *C. arizonica* var. *glabra.*
C. goveniana* var. *pygmaea. Shrubby, narrowly conical to columnar, coniferous tree with exfoliating, rough, gray or brown bark. Pointed, dark green, glandless leaves, 1/16in (2mm) long, are lemon-scented when crushed, and borne in plume-like sprays. Spherical, prickly brown female cones, less than ¾in (2cm) across, usually have 6 scales each. ↕ to 30ft (10m), ↔ to 12ft (4m). California (Mendocino County). Zone 8.
C. guadalupensis (Guadalupe cypress). Narrowly conical then ovoid, coniferous tree with red-brown bark that cracks into small flakes. Slender, blunt or pointed, blue-green leaves, ⅛in (3mm) long, borne in slender sprays; resin glands are fragrant when crushed. Spherical brown female cones, to 1½in (4cm) across, each have 8–10 scales and a prominent dorsal prickle. ↕ to 50ft (15m), ↔ 10–12ft (3–4m). S. California. Zone 8. **'Glauca'** has glaucous, gray-green leaves.
C. lawsoniana see *Chamaecyparis lawsoniana.*
C. leylandii see x *Cupressocyparis leylandii.*
C. lindleyi see *C. lusitanica.*
C. lusitanica, syn. *C. lindleyi* (Cedar of Goa, Mexican cypress). Conical to columnar, coniferous tree with brown bark, shallowly fissured into fibrous spirals. Bears glandless, gray-green or blue-green leaves, to ⅛in (3mm) long, with free, pointed tips, in spreading sprays. Spherical, glaucous blue then shiny brown female cones, ½in (1.5cm) across, each have 6–8 scales and conical prickles. ↕ to 70ft (20m), ↔ to 20ft (6m). Mexico to Guatemala. ❀ (min. 41°F/5°C) **'Glauca Pendula'** has pendent sprays of bright blue-green foliage.
C. macrocarpa (Monterey cypress). Coniferous tree, narrowly conical to columnar and spiky when young; wide-spreading with age, with shallowly ridged bark. Pointed, dark to bright green, glandless, lemon-scented leaves, 1/16in (2mm) long; borne in erect or spreading, plume-like sprays. Spherical brown female cones, to 1¼in (–3cm) across, each have 8–10 scales that lack a prominent prickle. ↕ to 100ft (30m), ↔ 12–40ft (4–12m). California. Zone 7b. **'Goldcrest'** ■ is narrowly conical, with dense, golden yellow foliage. ↕ to 16ft (5m), ↔ 8ft (2.5m).
C. nootkatensis see *Chamaecyparis nootkatensis.*

Cupressus macrocarpa 'Goldcrest'

Cupressus torulosa 'Cashmeriana'

C. obtusa see *Chamaecyparis obtusa.*
C. pisifera see *Chamaecyparis pisifera.*
C. sempervirens (Italian cypress, Mediterranean cypress). Narrowly conical or columnar to broadly spreading, coniferous tree. Horizontal branches bear dense sprays of gray-green or dark green, glandless leaves, to 1/16in (1mm) long, usually with rounded, abruptly pointed tips (but with free, pointed tips on strong shoots). Produces spherical to ovoid, prickly brown female cones, 1–1½in (2.5–3.5cm) long, each have 8–14 scales. ↕ to 70ft (20m), ↔ 3–20ft (1–6m). E. Mediterranean to Iran. Zone 7b. **'Stricta'** is narrowly upright, sometimes forming a very narrow, almost pencil-like tree, with fused and flattened branches; ↔ to 10ft (3m). **'Swane's Gold'** is narrowly upright, with pale yellow or greenish yellow leaves; ↕ to 20ft (6m), ↔ 3ft (1m).
C. thyoides see *Chamaecyparis thyoides.*
***C. torulosa* 'Cashmeriana'** ■ syn. *C. cashmeriana* (Kashmir cypress). Coniferous tree, conical when young, becoming broad and columnar when mature, with fibrous, red-brown bark. Bright, glaucous blue, glandless leaves, 1/16–⅛in (2–3mm) long, with free, pointed tips, to 1/16in (2mm) long, are borne in long, flat, pendent sprays. Spherical, prickly, green-brown female cones, ½in (1.5cm) across, each have 8–10 scales. ↕ to 100ft (30m), ↔ to 30ft (10m). Probably Himalayas. Zone 7.

Curcuma

ZINGIBERACEAE

Genus of 40 species of reed-like, rhizomatous perennials, which often have fleshy roots and thick, aromatic rhizomes. They are found in seasonally drought-prone areas of tropical Asia and Australia. The leaves are narrowly ovate to oblong. Cone-like, terminal inflorescences are formed from often colorful bracts. Very small, 3-petaled,

Curcuma roscoeana

tubular flowers are often obscured by the bracts. Where temperatures fall below 64°F (18°C), grow in a warm greenhouse; in tropical areas, use as a groundcover. The rhizomes of some species are used as spices and in cooking.
• **CULTIVATION** Under glass, grow in soil-based potting mix in bright filtered light, with moderate humidity. In growth, water freely and apply a balanced liquid fertilizer monthly. When dormant, keep almost dry at 54°F (12°C). Pot on in spring. Outdoors, grow in fertile, moist but well-drained soil in partial shade.
• **PROPAGATION** Sow seed at 68°F (20°C) as soon as ripe. Divide in spring.
• **PESTS AND DISEASES** Infrequent.

C. petiolata (Queen lily). Upright perennial with brownish yellow rhizome, pale yellow inside, and up to 6 oblong leaves, 10in (25cm) long, with leaf stalks of almost equal length. Yellow and white flowers, ½in (1cm) long, are produced at any time of year in terminal spikes, 6in (15cm) long, with deep violet upper bracts and green, occasionally violet lower bracts. ↕ 24in (60cm), ↔ 18in (45cm). Malaysia. ❀ (min. 64°F/18°C)
C. roscoeana ■ Erect perennial with a brown rhizome, white inside, and ovate, shiny, mid-green leaves, 6–12in (15–30cm) long, with deep green veins. In summer, bears bright yellow flowers, ½in (1cm) long, with orange bracts, in terminal spikes, 8in (20cm) long. ↕ to 3ft (90cm), ↔ 1½ft (45cm). Malaysia. ❀ (min. 64°F/18°C)

▷ ***Curtonus*** see *Crocosmia*

Cyananthus lobatus

CYANANTHUS

CAMPANULACEAE

Genus of about 25 species of tufted perennials occurring in cool, moist, mountainous areas in the Himalayas and W. China. They have prostrate stems radiating from a cluster of thick, almost woody roots, and alternate, linear to broadly rounded leaves, which are toothed, lobed, or entire, and often hairy. Terminal, usually solitary, broadly funnel-shaped, blue, violet, or yellow, occasionally white flowers each have 5 spreading lobes and short tubes. Grow in a rock garden, scree bed, or trough, or in an alpine house.
• **CULTIVATION** Grow in poor to moderately fertile, humus-rich, moist but well-drained, preferably neutral to slightly acidic soil in partial shade. Will tolerate high levels of summer rainfall. In an alpine house, grow in soil-based potting mix with added grit and leaf mold; keep plants cool and shaded in summer.
• **PROPAGATION** Sow seed in containers in an open frame as soon as ripe or in early spring. Root softwood cuttings in late spring or early summer.
• **PESTS AND DISEASES** Susceptible to spider mites and aphids under glass.

***C. integer* of gardens** see *C. microphyllus*.
C. lobatus ■ Spreading perennial with obovate, deeply lobed, fleshy, dull green leaves, ½in (1cm) long, with wedge-shaped bases. In late summer, produces solitary, bright blue-purple flowers, ¾–1½in (2–4cm) across, with spreading lobes and dark brown, shaggy-hairy calyces. ↕ 2in (5cm), ↔ to 12in (30cm). Himalayas to China (Yunnan). Zone 7.
C. microphyllus, syn. *C. integer* of gardens. Mat-forming perennial with slender red stems, clothed in ovate to oblong-elliptic, dark green leaves, ¹⁄₁₆–⅜in (2–8mm) long, with the margins rolled under. In late summer, bears solitary, violet-blue flowers, 1in (2.5cm) across, with tufts of white hair at the throats. ↕ to 1in (2.5cm), ↔ to 10in (25cm). Nepal to S.W. Tibet. Zone 6.

CYANOTIS

COMMELINACEAE

Genus of about 30 species of low-growing, evergreen perennials, related to *Tradescantia*, but more succulent and with greater tolerance of dry conditions. They occur in upland forest and rocky areas in Africa and Asia. The trailing stems, to 12in (30cm) long, are almost hidden by hairy, densely 2-ranked, lance-shaped to broadly ovate or oblong leaves. One-sided cymes of short-lived, shallowly cup-shaped, 3-petaled, purple, violet, or blue flowers are borne in summer. Where not hardy, grow in a temperate greenhouse or conservatory, in hanging baskets, or as houseplants. In warmer climates, grow in a herbaceous bed or border.
• **CULTIVATION** Under glass, grow in soil-based potting mix in full light, with shade from hot sun, and with low humidity. Water moderately at all times. During active growth, apply a balanced liquid fertilizer monthly; excessive feeding causes soft, untypical growth. Outdoors, grow in sharply drained, moderately fertile soil in full sun, with some midday shade.
• **PROPAGATION** Root stem-tip cuttings with bottom heat in spring.
• **PESTS AND DISEASES** Infrequent.

C. kewensis (Teddy bear plant). Spreading perennial with lance-shaped, fleshy leaves, to 2in (5cm) long, dark green above and red beneath, densely covered with short, felted, ginger-brown hairs. Cymes of up to 8 pink-purple flowers, ⅜in (8mm) across, are borne in summer. ↕ 5in (12cm), ↔ 12in (30cm). S. India. ❀ (min. 50°F/10°C)
C. somaliensis ■ (Pussy ears). Spreading perennial with oblong-linear, pointed, arching, leathery, deep olive-green leaves, 1½in (4cm) long, slightly purple-flushed and with whisker-like white hairs. Bears cymes of mauve-blue flowers, ¼in (5mm) across, with prominent golden stamens, in summer, although these are only occasionally produced in cultivation. ↕ 6in (15cm), ↔ 16in (40cm). Somalia. ❀ (min. 50°F/10°C)

Cyanotis somaliensis

CYATHEA

syn. ALSOPHILA, SPHAEOPTERIS
Tree fern

CYATHEACEAE

Genus of 600 or more species of evergreen tree ferns, mainly from forested mountain ranges in tropical and subtropical regions of the S. hemisphere. Cyatheas may reach over 70ft (20m) tall, some relatively quickly. They have a pole-like, fibrous trunk, consisting of an erect rhizome clad in roots, topped by large, pinnate, 2-pinnate, or pinnatifid fronds, which develop in flushes; the crowns of uncurling fronds are densely covered in white, brown, or black scales. The stems bear characteristic scars of old fronds. Grow as specimen plants in a shady site. Where not hardy, grow in a cool, temperate, or warm greenhouse.
• **CULTIVATION** Under glass, grow in large containers in a potting mix of 1 part each of loam, sharp sand, and charcoal, and 3 parts coarse leaf mold or peat. Provide bright filtered light and moderate to high humidity. During the growing season, water freely, applying a balanced liquid fertilizer monthly; water sparingly in winter. Outdoors, grow in fertile, moist but well-drained soil in dappled or partial shade, or full sun in moist soil. Outdoors and under glass, damp down trunk and leaves regularly on hot days.
• **PROPAGATION** Sow spores at 59–64°F (15–18°C) as soon as ripe.
• **PESTS AND DISEASES** *Rhizoctonia* may be a problem on young plants.

C. australis, syn. *Alsophila australis*. Tree fern producing a stem covered withfrond scars and, toward the base, dense wiry roots. Ovate, 2-pinnate, dark green fronds, to 12ft (4m) long, have lance-shaped or linear segments and shiny brown scales. ↕ 3–10ft (1–3m), ↔ 10–15ft (3–5m). E. Australia. ❀ (min. 45°F/7°C)
C. cooperi ■ syn. *Sphaeopteris cooperi*. Fast-growing tree fern with a slender

Cyathea cooperi

Cyathea dealbata

Fast-growing tree fern with a slender stem. Narrowly ovate, 2-pinnate, mid-green fronds, to 12ft (4m) long, lance-shaped or linear segments. Scales on the frond stalks are white. ↕ 6–15ft (2–5m), ↔ 10–12ft (3–4m). Australia. ❀ (min. 50°F/10°C)

C. dealbata ■ Tree fern with an attractive glaucous bloom, both on the frond bases covering the stem and on the undersides of the fronds. Narrowly ovate, 2-pinnate, mid- to deep green fronds, to 10ft (3m) long, have oblong-lance-shaped segments. Scales are shining, dark brown. ↕ to 30ft (10m), ↔ 3–10ft (1–3m). New Zealand. ❀ (min. 45°F/7°C)

C. howeana. Tree fern with a slender trunk and narrowly ovate, 2-pinnate, scaly-hairy, light green fronds, to 10ft (3m) long, with deeply toothed or pinnatifid segments. ↕ to 6ft (2m), ↔ 10–12ft (3–4m). Australia (Lord Howe Island). ❀ (min. 45°F/7°C)

C. medullaris ■ (Black tree fern, Sago fern). Wide-spreading tree fern with a black stem and a rosette of 2- or 3-pinnate fronds, 10–20ft (3–6m) long, deep green above and paler beneath, with narrowly oblong, finely tapering segments. Black stalks are scaly-hairy. ↕ 30–50ft (10–15m), ↔ 10–20ft (3–6m). Victoria to Tasmania, New Zealand. ❀ (min. 45°F/7°C)

C. smithii. Upright tree fern with a thick, tapering stem and a rosette of oblong-lance-shaped, 2- or 3-pinnate fronds, 3–6ft (1–2m) long, with yellow-green stalks and toothed, narrowly oblong segments, bright mid-green above and pale green beneath. ↕ to 25ft (8m), ↔ to 12ft (4m). New Zealand. ❀ (min. 45°F/7°C).

Cyathea medullaris

CYATHODES

EPACRIDACEAE

Genus of about 175 species of heath-like evergreen shrubs and small trees found in alpine and subalpine regions of Australia, Tasmania, and New Zealand, and in various habitats in Malaysia, New Guinea, and Polynesia. They have usually small, overlapping, linear, linear-oblong to lance-shaped, elliptic, or inversely lance-shaped leaves, the new growth often flushed pink or bronze. Small, tubular, unisexual or bisexual flowers are either solitary or borne in terminal racemes; they are followed by fleshy, colorful fruits, ⅜–½in (9–15mm) across, although fruiting is not always reliable in cultivation. Some species, including *C. colensoi*, are suitable for a rock garden or a shrub border. Where not hardy, grow in a cool or temperate greenhouse.

• **CULTIVATION** Grow in moist but well-drained, fertile, humus-rich, acidic soil in partial shade, although they will tolerate full sun in cooler climates, where soil remains reliably moist in the growing season. Provide shelter from cold, drying winds. Pruning group 8.

• **PROPAGATION** Sow seed in containers in a cold frame in autumn; germination may take up to 3 years. Root greenwood cuttings in early summer, or take semi-ripe cuttings in late summer.

• **PESTS AND DISEASES** Infrequent.

C. colensoi, syn. *Leucopogon colensoi*, *Styphelia colensoi*. Prostrate or decumbent shrub with stiff, upright shoots clothed in narrowly oblong, smooth, gray-green leaves, to ⅜in (9mm) long, fringed with fine hairs. White flowers, ¼in (6mm) long, are borne in erect racemes at the tips of young growth in spring, occasionally followed by spherical, white to deep crimson fruit, ⅛–¼in (3–6mm) across. ↕↔ 12in (30cm). New Zealand. ❀ (min. 41°F/5°C)

C. fraseri see *Leucopogon fraseri.*

CYBISTAX

BIGNONIACEAE

Genus of 3 species of deciduous or semi-evergreen trees and shrubs occurring in forest from Mexico to Paraguay. The palmate leaves, with 5–7 short-stalked leaflets, are borne in opposite pairs. Funnel-shaped, 5-lobed flowers are borne in showy, terminal panicles. Where not hardy, grow in a temperate or warm greenhouse or conservatory. In warmer climates, grow as specimen or shade trees.

• **CULTIVATION** Under glass, plant directly into a greenhouse border in soil-based potting mix in full light, and with moderate to high humidity. In the growing season, water freely and apply a balanced liquid fertilizer monthly; water sparingly in winter. Top-dress or pot on in spring. Outdoors, grow in fertile, moist but well-drained soil in full sun. Pruning group 1; plants under glass need restrictive pruning, when leafless or immediately after flowering.

• **PROPAGATION** Sow seed at 59–64°F (15–18°C) in spring. Root semi-ripe cuttings with bottom heat in summer. Air layer in early spring.

• **PESTS AND DISEASES** Susceptible to spider mites and whiteflies under glass.

C. donnell-smithii, syn. *Tabebuia donnell-smithii* (Primavera). Spreading to round-headed, deciduous tree, with 5- to 7-palmate, mid- to light green leaves, to 14in (35cm) long. Lax panicles, 6–12in (15–30cm) long, of foxglove-like yellow flowers, 1¼–1½in (3–4cm) long, are borne on the bare branches in spring. ↕ 60–80ft (18–25m), ↔ 15–30ft (5–10m). Mexico, Guatemala. ❀ (min. 50–59°F/10–15°C)

CYCAS

Fern palm, Sago palm

CYCADACEAE

Genus of about 15 species of cycads found mainly on dry, stony slopes and in semi-desert and dry, open woodland (and, rarely, at rainforest margins) from Madagascar to S. and S.E. Asia, Australia, and the Pacific islands. They have whorls of pinnate, stiff, leathery leaves, with linear-lance-shaped to sickle-shaped leaflets. Dioecious inflorescences arise from the centers of the leaf rosettes. The large male inflorescences are cone-like, up to 32in (80cm) tall, and usually covered in woolly hairs; the female inflorescences consist of loosely arranged, modified leaves, to 12in (30cm) long, bearing ovules on the margins. *Cycas* species are grown for their palm-like appearance, and are also cultivated as a source of starch after the removal of carcinogenic alkaloids. Where not hardy, grow in a temperate or warm greenhouse, or as foliage houseplants. In warmer climates, they make excellent specimen plants.

• **CULTIVATION** Under glass, grow in a mix of equal parts loam, compost, and coarse bark with additional grit and charcoal, and a slow-release fertilizer. Provide full light, with shade from hot sun, and moderate humidity. In the growing season, water moderately; reduce humidity and water in winter. Pot on or top-dress in spring. Outdoors, grow in fertile, moist but well-drained soil in full sun.

• **PROPAGATION** Sow seed at 59–84°F (15–29°C) in spring. Remove and pot up suckers in spring.

• **PESTS AND DISEASES** Spider mites, mealybugs, and scale insects are common. Many fungi cause leaf spots and root rots. Prone to magnesium deficiency.

C. circinalis ■ (False sago, Fern palm, Sago palm). Erect cycad with a robust stem, thickened toward the base and bearing pale bands of old leaf scars. Leaves are pinnate, 5–10ft (1.5–3m) long, with up to 100 narrowly lance-shaped, glossy, rich green leaflets. Cone-like inflorescences are brown; the males to 18in (45cm) long, females to 12in (30cm) long. Female inflorescences produce ovoid red fruit, to 2½in (6cm) long. ↕ to 20ft (6m), ↔ 10–20ft (3–6m). S.E. India. ❀ (min. 55°F/13°C)

C. media (Zamia palm). Erect cycad with a robust stem, rarely branched, bearing rings of pale leaf scars. Spreading leaves, ascending at first, are pinnate, to 5ft (1.5m) long, consisting of linear, bright green leaflets. Cone-like inflorescences are brown; the males to 20in (50cm) long, the females to 16in

Cycas circinalis

(40cm) long. Female inflorescences produce broadly ellipsoid, orange-red fruit, ¾–1½in (2–4cm) long. ↕ to 15ft (5m), ↔ to 10ft (3m). Queensland. ❀ (min. 55°F/13°C)

C. revoluta ■ (Japanese sago palm). Robust-stemmed cycad, erect at first but gradually reclining with age, and suckering and branching when mature. Arching leaves, 30–60in (0.75–1.5m) long, are pinnate, with up to 125 sickle-shaped, glossy, dark green leaflets. Ovoid, woolly, golden brown inflorescences are produced on mature plants but seldom on those grown in containers. The male inflorescences, to 16in (40cm) long, are pineapple-scented; females, 8in (20cm) long, produce ovoid yellow fruit, 1¼–1½in (3–4cm) long. ↕ 3–6ft (1–2m) or more, ↔ 3–6ft (1–2m) or more. Japan (including Ryukyu Islands). ❀ (min. 45–50°F/7–10°C), although it will survive short periods to 32°F (0°C) if given some protection.

C. rumphii. Erect cycad with a robust stem, becoming slightly lax with age, and bearing pale bands of old leaf scars. Leaves are pinnate, 5–10ft (1.5–3m) long, with up to 100 narrowly lance-shaped, dull, dark green leaflets, with swollen or slightly wavy margins. Cone-like inflorescences are brown; the males to 18in (45cm) long, the females to 12in (30cm) long. Female inflorescences produce almost spherical, red fruit, to 3in (8cm) long. ↕ to 25ft (8m), ↔ 10–20ft (3–6m). Coastal S.E. Asia, Micronesia, Madagascar, E. Africa. ❀ (min. 55°F/13°C)

Cycas revoluta

CYCLAMEN

PRIMULACEAE

Genus of about 19 species of tuberous perennials found in habitats ranging from alpine woodland and damp woods to dry sands and maquis, from the Mediterranean east to Iran and south to Somalia. Leaves are rounded to heart-shaped, sometimes toothed or lobed, often with silver zones or light and dark patterns above, and purplish red below. Leaves of autumn-flowering species last through winter to spring. The nodding, sometimes fragrant flowers, ½–1¼in (1–3cm) long, each have 5 reflexed, twisted petals, varying from white to pink and carmine-red, often with darker mouths (perianth tube rims). Flowers may be borne at almost any time of year, depending on the species. In most species, the flower stalk coils onto the soil surface after flowering to release the ripe seeds. *C. persicum* has been selected extensively to produce a wide color and size range, the flowers often much larger than those of the wild species.

Grow hardy species and cultivars in a rock garden, border, or raised bed. Frost-tender cyclamens (with the exception of *C. parviflorum*) need a warm, dry summer dormancy; outside Mediterranean climates, they are best grown in a cool greenhouse, alpine house, or bulb frame. Cultivars of *C. persicum* are excellent conservatory plants and houseplants. All parts may cause severe discomfort if ingested.

• **CULTIVATION** For ease of reference, cultivation requirements may be divided into 3 groups, as follows:

1. Plant 1¼–2in (3–5cm) deep. Grow in moderately fertile, humus-rich, well-drained soil in partial shade, ideally under trees or shrubs. Mulch annually with leaf mold as leaves wither; where marginally hardy, provide a deep, loose mulch. Do not allow *C. parviflorum* or *C. purpurascens* to dry out.

2. Plant ¾–1in (2–2.5cm) deep or with the tops of the tubers just at the soil surface. Grow in a mix of equal parts loam, leaf mold, peat, and sharp sand, in an alpine house or bulb frame; grow tender species in a cool greenhouse, in bright filtered light with moderate humidity. In growth, water moderately. Reduce water and humidity as leaves fade; keep completely dry in dormancy. Apply a low-nitrogen liquid fertilizer every 6–8 weeks when in full leaf.

3. (*C. persicum* and its cultivars). Plant with the tops of the tubers just above the soil surface. Grow in soil-based potting mix in bright filtered light (full light in winter), with moderate humidity and an even winter temperature of 55–61°F (13–16°C). Avoid drafts and hot, dry air. When in full leaf, water moderately (avoiding the crown), and apply a low-nitrogen liquid fertilizer every 2 weeks. Reduce water as leaves wither after flowering; keep dry when dormant (about 2–3 months). Resume watering and feeding as new growth appears. When tubers fill the pot, repot when dormant.

• **PROPAGATION** Sow seed as soon as ripe, in darkness, at 43–54°F (6–12°C). Sow seed of *C. persicum* at 54–59°F (12–15°C): sow seed of open-pollinated cultivars in late summer to flower in about 14 months; sow seed of other cultivars from late winter to midspring to flower in autumn of the same year. Before sowing, soak all seed in water for at least 12 hours and rinse thoroughly.

• **PESTS AND DISEASES** Mice or squirrels may be a problem. Prone to spider mites, vine weevil, cyclamen mite, and gray mold (*Botrytis*) under glass.

C. abchasicum see *C. coum* subsp. *caucasicum*.

C. africanum ■ Tuberous perennial with heart-shaped, bright green leaves, to 4in (10cm) long, with paler green markings. Produces flowers, ¾–1½in (2–4cm) long, in shades of pink with deep maroon mouths, just before the leaves in autumn. Cultivation group 2; cool greenhouse. ↕ 5–6in (12–15cm), PD9in (23cm). Algeria. ❄ (min. 35°F/2°C)

C. balearicum. Tuberous perennial with scallop-margined, heart-shaped, mid-green or gray-green leaves, heavily silvered above, maroon beneath, to 3½in (9cm) long, usually smaller. Delicate, strongly fragrant, white or pale pink flowers, to ½in (1.5cm) long, with fine pink veins, are borne with the leaves in spring. Cultivation group 2. ↕ 2in (5cm), PD2–3in (5–8cm). Balearic Islands. ❄ (min. 35°F/2°C)

C. caucasicum see *C. coum* subsp. *caucasicum*.

C. cilicium ■ Tuberous perennial with rounded or heart-shaped, strongly patterned, mid-green leaves, ½–2in (1.5–5cm) long, often purplish beneath. Slender, white or pink flowers, ½–¾in (1–2cm) long, stained dark carmine-red

Cyclamen coum f. *albissimum*

at the mouths, are produced with the leaves in autumn. Cultivation group 1 or 2. ↕ 2in (5cm), PD3in (8cm). S. Turkey. Zone 6. **f. *album*** has white flowers.

C. coum. Tuberous perennial with rounded leaves, 1–2½in (2.5–6cm) long, either shiny, unmarked, and deep green, or deep green with silver patterns. Compact flowers, ⅜–½in (0.8–1.5cm) long, varying from white to shades of pink and carmine-red, with dark carmine-red stains above white-rimmed mouths, are produced with the leaves in winter or early spring. Cultivation group 1. ↕ 2–3in (5–8cm), PD4in (10cm). Bulgaria, Caucasus, Turkey, Lebanon. Zone 5. **f. *albissimum*** ■ syn. 'Album', bears white flowers with dark carmine-red marks at the mouths. **subsp. *caucasicum***, syn. *C. abchasicum*, *C. caucasicum*, has pinkish lilac flowers, to ½in (1.5cm) long, and heart-shaped, silver-marked leaves with scalloped margins. **Pewter Group** ■ is a variable, vigorous selection with leaves almost entirely silvered above.

C. creticum. Tuberous perennial with heart-shaped, grayish green leaves, to 1½in (4cm) long, with silver markings. Slender, fragrant, white or very pale

Cyclamen hederifolium

pink flowers, ½–1in (1.5–2.5cm) long, are borne with the leaves in spring. Cultivation group 2. ↕ 2–3in (5–8cm), PD3–4in (8–10cm). Greece (Crete). Zone 7b.

C. cyprium. Tuberous perennial with heart-shaped, toothed leaves, to 2in (5cm) or more long, patterned light gray-green. Bears very fragrant white flowers, to 1in (2.5cm) long, marked carmine-red at the mouths, with the leaves in autumn. Cultivation group 2. ↕ 2–3in (5–8cm), PD6in (15cm). Cyprus. Zone 7b.

C. europaeum see *C. purpurascens*.

C. fatrense see *C. purpurascens*.

C. graecum. Tuberous perennial with long, fleshy roots and heart-shaped, deep green leaves, 2–5½in (5–14cm) long, marked silver and light green. Pink to carmine-red flowers, ½–1in (1.5–2.5cm) long, with darker markings at the mouths, are borne just before the leaves in autumn. Cultivation group 2; best in a large container. ↕ 3–4in (8–10cm), PD6in (15cm). Greece, Aegean Islands, Turkey, Cyprus. Zone 6b. **f. *album*** has pure white flowers.

C. hederifolium ■ syn. *C. neapolitanum* (Baby cyclamen). Tuberous perennial

Cyclamen coum Pewter Group

Cyclamen africanum

Cyclamen cilicium

Cyclamen libanoticum

with large, flattened tubers and clumps of very variable, triangular to heart-shaped, pointed, patterned, mid- to dark green leaves, 2–6in (5–15cm) long, often purplish green beneath. Frequently scented flowers, to 1in (2.5cm) long, in shades of pink, with deep maroon marks at the apexes of the mouths, are produced in mid- and late autumn before the leaves. Self-seeds freely. Cultivation group 1. ↕4–5in (10–13cm), PD6in (15cm). Mediterranean (Italy to Turkey). Zone 7. **f. *albiflorum*** has pure white flowers without basal marks.
C. libanoticum ■ Tuberous perennial bearing rounded-heart-shaped, shallowly lobed, dull green leaves, 3in (8cm) long, patterned with lighter green, in winter.

Cyclamen mirabile

Cyclamen persicum

Cyclamen persicum Sierra Series 'Sierra White'

Pale to mid-pink flowers, to 1¼in (3cm) long, white at the bases, with bold carmine-red marks at the mouths, are produced with the leaves from winter to early spring. Cultivation group 2; cool greenhouse. ↕4in (10cm), PD6in (15cm). Lebanon. ❄ (min. 41°F/5°C)
C. mirabile ■ Tuberous perennial with heart-shaped leaves, to 1½in (4cm) long, with scalloped margins, mid-green above and purplish red beneath; they often have pink marks on the upper surfaces when they first expand. Slender, pale pink flowers, to ¾in (2cm) long, with fringed petals and maroon marks at the mouths, are produced with the leaves in autumn. Cultivation group 2. ↕3in (8cm), PD3–4in (8–10cm). S.W. Turkey. ❄ (min. 35°F/2°C)
C. neapolitanum see *C. hederifolium.*
C. parviflorum. Tuberous perennial with rounded, dull, deep green leaves, to 1½in (4cm) long, often smaller. Bears pink flowers, to ½in (1.5cm) long, the mouths stained dark pink, with the leaves in early spring. Cultivation group 1 or 2. ↕1–1½in (2.5–4cm), PD2–3in (5–8cm). N.E. Turkey. Zone 7b.
C. persicum ■ (Florist's cyclamen). Tuberous perennial with heart-shaped leaves, 1–5½in (2.5–14cm) long, deep green, often silver-marbled above and pale or purplish green beneath. Sweet-scented, pink, red, or white flowers, ½–¾in (1–2cm) or more long, are produced on tall, slender stems, with the leaves, from early winter to early spring. Cultivation group 2 if grown outdoors; cultivation group 3 under glass and for all cultivars. ↕to 8in (20cm), PD6in

Cyclamen pseudibericum

Cyclamen repandum subsp. *peloponnesiacum*

(15cm). S.E. Mediterranean, N. Africa. ❄ (min. 50°F/10°C). **Mirabelle Series** cultivars have small flowers, to 1½in (4cm) across, in deep or light salmon-pink, lilac, purple, scarlet, or white; ↕6in (15cm). **Miracle Series** cultivars have pink, salmon-pink, scarlet, or white flowers, 2–3in (5–8cm) long; ↕to 6in (15cm). **'Scentsation'** is open-pollinated and produces strongly scented flowers, 2–3in (5–8cm) long, in pink, carmine-red, or crimson; ↕6in (15cm), PD9in (23cm). **Sierra Series** cultivars have marbled foliage and flower in late winter, bearing flowers 2–3in (5–8cm) long, in colors including white, pink, salmon-pink, scarlet, lilac, or purple; ↕9in (23cm), PD8in (20cm); the series includes **'Sierra White'** ■ with clear white flowers. **'Victoria'** is open-pollinated, and has ruffled white flowers, 2–3in (5–8cm) long, with bright cherry-red margins and mouths; ↕to 12in (30cm), PD12in (30cm).
C. pseudibericum ■ Tuberous perennial with heart-shaped, silvery, dark green leaves, to 3in (8cm) long, lightly to conspicuously marked with silvery gray or gray-green. Fragrant, bright magenta flowers, to 1in (2.5cm) long, with darker, white-rimmed mouths, are borne with the leaves from winter to spring. Cultivation group 2. ↕4–6in (10–15cm), PD3–4in (8–10cm). Turkey. ❄ (min. 35°F/2°C)
C. purpurascens, syn. *C. europaeum, C. fatrense.* Evergreen, sometimes deciduous, tuberous perennial with rounded to heart-shaped, shiny, dark green leaves, to 3in (8cm) long, sometimes faintly mottled silvery green above, and purplish red below. Broad-mouthed, very strongly scented, rich to pale carmine-red flowers, to ¾in (2cm) long, are produced with the leaves in mid- and late summer. Prefers alkaline conditions. Cultivation group 1 or 2. ↕4in (10cm), PD3–4in (8–10cm). C. and E. Europe. Zone 6.
C. repandum. Tuberous perennial bearing heart-shaped to triangular leaves, to 5in (13cm) long, dark green with gray-green patterning or speckles. Slender, fragrant, rich carmine-red flowers, to ¾in (2cm) long, are borne with the leaves in mid- and late spring. Cultivation group 1 or 2. ↕4–6in (10–15cm), PD4–5in (10–13cm). S. France (including Corsica), Italy, former Yugoslavia, Greece. Zone 8. **subsp. *peloponnesiacum*** ■ has scalloped-margined leaves with heavy silver speckling, and paler pink flowers with darker pink zones around the mouths.
C. rohlfsianum. Tuberous perennial with heart-shaped, strongly scalloped, shiny, bright green leaves, to 4½in (11cm) long, patterned silvery green. Scented pink flowers, to 1in (2.5cm) long, with deep maroon mouths and projecting anthers, are produced with the leaves in autumn. Cultivation group 2; cool greenhouse. ↕4–5in (10–13cm), PD6in (15cm). Libya. ❄ (min. 35°F/2°C)

▷ ***Cyclobothra lutea*** see *Calochortus barbatus*

CYCNOCHES

Swan orchid

ORCHIDACEAE

Genus of about 12 species of deciduous, epiphytic orchids from Central and South America, occurring at altitudes to 3,250ft (1,000m). They have elongated, spindle-shaped to cylindrical, fleshy pseudobulbs, and produce soft, folded, strap-shaped to ovate, light to mid-green leaves in summer. Swan-like flowers, which may be male or female, are borne in arching or pendent racemes from nodes on the upper portion of the pseudobulbs, in early summer. The sex of the flowers is determined by the light level: in poor light, inflorescences of male flowers are usually produced. Female inflorescences develop in brighter conditions.

• **CULTIVATION** Warm-growing orchids. Grow in epiphytic orchid potting mix in deep containers or baskets. In summer, provide bright filtered light and moderate humidity; water moderately, applying fertilizer at every second watering, and keep foliage dry. Provide full light in winter; keep completely dry when dormant. See also p.46.

• **PROPAGATION** Divide pseudobulbs when growth recommences in spring.

• **PESTS AND DISEASES** Spider mites, mealybugs, and whiteflies are problems under glass. Cymbidium mosaic virus, leaf spots, root rot, and sometimes pseudobulb rot can occur.

C. egertonianum. Epiphytic orchid with cylindrical to spindle-shaped pseudobulbs and strap-shaped, light green leaves, 3–8in (7–21cm) long. From summer to autumn, bears racemes of brown- or purple-spotted, green or greenish brown, sometimes yellow or white, rarely pink female flowers, 2in (5cm) across. Dark purple male flowers are smaller. ↕16in (40cm), ↔18in (45cm). Belize, Costa Rica, Guatemala, Nicaragua. ❄ (min. 64–68°F/18–20°C; max. 86°F/30°C)
C. ventricosum. Large, epiphytic orchid with cylindrical to spindle-shaped pseudobulbs and elliptic to linear-lance-shaped, sharp-pointed, mid- to light green leaves, to 14in (35cm) long. In summer, produces arching to pendent racemes of scented, greenish white male flowers, 3–4in (8–10cm) across, with white lips and black calluses. Female flowers are similar to the males, but with stouter, shorter columns. ↕24in (60cm), ↔30in (75cm). Mexico to Panama. ❄ (min. 64–68°F/18–20°C; max. 86°F/30°C)

Cydonia oblonga 'Vranja'

CYDONIA

Quince

ROSACEAE

Genus of one species of deciduous tree or shrub occurring at woodland margins and on rocky slopes in S.W. Asia. The elliptic to ovate leaves are arranged alternately. Attractive, shallowly bowl-shaped flowers are followed by pear-like, ornamental fruit, which are edible when cooked. *C. oblonga* should not be confused with the flowering quinces (*Chaenomeles*), which bear smaller fruit. In regions with cool summers or winter temperatures that fall below 5°F (-15°C), fan train *C. oblonga* against a wall. Elsewhere, it is excellent free-standing and fruits best with long, hot summers.

• **CULTIVATION** Grow in fertile, moist but well-drained soil in full sun. Pruning group 1; group 13 in winter, if fan-trained. In the first 3 or 4 winters, establish a framework of fruiting spurs; thereafter, prune only to remove badly placed shoots or to relieve overcrowding.

• **PROPAGATION** Sow seed of the species in a seedbed in autumn. Insert greenwood cuttings in early summer, or semi-ripe cuttings in mid- or late summer. May also be propagated from hardwood cuttings in autumn or early winter. Bud cultivars in summer, or bottom graft on-to seedling quince stocks in late winter.

• **PESTS AND DISEASES** Prone to scale insects, caterpillars, mealybugs, aphids, and Japanese beetles. Fire blight, powdery mildew, brown rot, *Gymnosporangium* rust, and crown gall affect quince.

C. oblonga (Common quince). Rounded tree or shrub with crowded branches bearing broadly ovate, dark green leaves, gray-downy beneath, to 4in (10cm) long. Solitary, pale pink to white flowers, 2in (5cm) across, are produced from the leaf axils in late spring. Aromatic, edible, light golden yellow fruit, 3in (8cm) long, which ripen in autumn, are used for flavoring and in preserves. ↕↔ 15ft (5m). S.W. Asia. Zone 6. **'Lusitanica'**, syn. 'Portugal', is vigorous, producing dark yellow fruit, 4in (10cm) long, covered in gray down. **'Maliformis'** produces almost spherical fruit. **'Portugal'** see 'Lusitanica'. **'Vranja'** ■ has very fragrant, pale green fruit, which ripen to golden yellow.
C. sinensis see *Pseudocydonia sinensis.*
C. speciosa see *Chaenomeles speciosa.*

CYLINDROPUNTIA

syn. OPUNTIA

CACTACEAE

Genus of 33 species of arborescent, erect, many-branched cacti of varied habitat, including desert, grasslands, and woodlands of the S.W. and S. US, south through Mexico to Mexico City. Spines are partly enclosed in a papery sheath, eventually falling away with age, and those of many species are dangerously sharp. Stem segments are cylindrical. Blooms can be yellow-green, yellow, bronze, red, or magenta. Fruit cylindrical to subspherical, sometimes club-shaped, and green, yellow, or red and fleshy or tan to brown and dry.

• **CULTIVATION** nder glass, grow in standard cactus potting mix in full light or bright filtered light. Large species are best planted directly into a greenhouse border. From early spring to mid-autumn, water only when approaching dryness and apply a balanced liquid fertilizer, diluted to one-quarter to half strength, 3 or 4 times. Keep reasonably dry at other times. Outdoors, grow in moderately fertile, sharply well drained, gritty, humus-rich soil in full sun.

• **PROPAGATION** Sow pre-soaked seed at 70°F (21°C) in spring. Separate, detach, and root stem segments. Handle plants with newspaper; dispose of it after use.

• **PESTS AND DISEASES** Cladode rots, zonate leaf spot, black spot, mealybugs, and scale insects are common. Bacterial soft rot and several viruses also occur.

C. echinocarpa (Silver cholla). Tree-like or shrubby cactus with many branches. The stems are obscured by interlaced spines (6–22) on most areoles. Flowers are light green to yellowish green, ¾–1in (2–2.3cm) long. The obconical or spherical tan fruit is densely spiny. The spines are difficult and painful to remove, ⅛–¾in (0.5–2cm), ↔ 1¼–3in (3–7.5cm). Arizona, Nevada, California, Baja California, Sonora, Mexico. ❄ (min. 55°F/13°C)
C. ramosissima (Diamond-plated pencil cholla). True to this cactus genus, ramosissima means "many branches." Mostly distal areoles bear 1–5 tan to reddish brown or deep purple spines that turn gray with age. Spines are dangerously sharp and long, to 2½in (6cm), but are sometimes absent. In early summer, produces rose-tinted bronze red flowers. Fruit is ovate, tan when dry. ↕ 8–20in (20–50cm), ⅛–⅜in (0.4–1cm). Arizona, Nevada, California, Baja California, and Sonora, Mexico. ❄ (min. 55°F/13°C)
C. tunicata see *Opuntia tunicata*

CYMBIDIUM

ORCHIDACEAE

Genus of about 50 species of evergreen, epiphytic, lithophytic, or terrestrial orchids from temperate and tropical areas in India, China, Japan, S.E. Asia, and Australia. They have spherical to elongated pseudobulbs and 8–10 long, narrowly oval to linear, light to mid-green leaves. Flowers are borne in long or short racemes from the bases, mainly in spring. Many hundreds of winter- or spring-flowering hybrids have been produced. Grow as houseplants or in a cool or temperate greenhouse; in Mediterranean climates, they may also be grown in a lath house. Contact with the foliage may aggravate skin allergies.

• **CULTIVATION** Cool-growing orchids. Some of the larger species and hybrids will tolerate short periods of 25°F (-4°C). Pot firmly into epiphytic or terrestrial orchid potting mix with added charcoal and bone meal. In summer, provide bright filtered light and good ventilation. Water moderately, applying fertilizer at every third watering, and mist once or twice a day. In winter, place in full light and water sparingly. See also p.46.

• **PROPAGATION** Divide in early and midspring when pot-bound, or remove backbulbs and pot up after flowering.

• **PESTS AND DISEASES** Cymbidium mosaic and ringspot viruses, Odontoglossum ringspot virus, root rot, gray mold, bacterial soft rot, and various pseudobulb rots can be serious. Prone to spider mites, scale insects, and mealybugs.

C. aloifolium, syn. *C. pendulum.* Epiphytic orchid with small, ovoid pseudobulbs and fleshy, semi-rigid, linear leaves, 12–24in (30–60cm) long. Numerous pale yellow to cream flowers, 1¾in (4.5cm) across, with dark red stripes on the tepals and lips, are produced in pendent racemes from late winter to spring. ↕ 12in (30cm), ↔ 18in (45cm). E. Himalayas to S. China and Malaysia. ❄ (min. 50°F/10°C; max. 75°F/24°C)
C. eburneum. Epiphytic orchid with very small pseudobulbs and linear leaves, 16–24in (40–60cm) long. In winter, bears upright racemes of white flowers, sometimes edged with pink, 3in (8cm) across, with yellow-stained lips. ↕ 20in (50cm), ↔ 24in (60cm). Himalayas, N. Myanmar, S.W. China. ❄ (min. 50°F/10°C; max. 75°F/24°C)
C. ensifolium. Lithophytic or terrestrial orchid with ovoid pseudobulbs and linear leaves, 12–24in (30–60cm) long. In summer, produces upright racemes of greenish yellow flowers, 1in (2.5cm) across, with white lips irregularly spotted red-brown. ↕↔ 12in (30cm). India, China, Japan, S.E. Asia. ❄ (min. 50°F/10°C; max. 75°F/24°C)
C. grandiflorum see *C. hookerianum.*
C. hookerianum ■ syn. *C. grandiflorum.* Epiphytic or lithophytic orchid with ovoid pseudobulbs and linear leaves, 24in (60cm) long. In early winter, bears fragrant, deep apple-green flowers, 3½–5in (9–13cm) across, with purple- or yellow-spotted white lips, in arching racemes. ↕ 24in (60cm), ↔ 36in (90cm). Himalayas, S.W. China. ❄ (min. 50°F/10°C; max. 75°F/24°C)
'Miniature Yellow' ■ has yellow flowers marked dark red on the lips.
C. insigne. Terrestrial or hemi-epiphytic orchid. Grassy, upright foliage is thinner than that of most cymbidiums. In late winter to early spring, bears nearly white to light pink blooms 4–5in (10-13cm), of typical "orchid" shape, with a lip or labellum that may be spotted and marked with dark red over color slightly darker than petals and sepals. Inflorescences are upright, to 3in (8cm), bearing 8–12 long-lasting flowers, for 6 weeks or more in cool conditions. Virus and other diseases may spread quickly in garden beds, so it is often best grown in pots, countersinking into the desired garden locations when in bloom. Prefers bright, warm summers with nights below 55°F (12.7°C). ❄ (min. 50°F/10°C; max. 75°F/24°C). **'Mrs. Carl Holmes'** ■ produces dark pink blooms in spring.
***C.* King's Loch** (*C.* King Arthur x *C.* Loch Lomond). Terrestrial orchid with ovoid pseudobulbs and linear leaves, 30in (75cm) long. Numerous green flowers, 3in (8cm) across, are borne in upright racemes in winter. ↕ 24in (60cm), ↔ 36in (90cm). ❄ (min. 50°F/10°C; max. 75°F/24°C)

Cymbidium hookerianum

Cymbidium insigne 'Mrs. Carl Holmes'

Cymbidium hookerianum 'Miniature Yellow'

C

C

Cymbidium Lisa Rose

C. Lisa Rose ■ (*C.* Keera x *C.* Sylvania). Terrestrial orchid with ovoid pseudobulbs and linear leaves, 30in (75cm) long. Up to 12 rose-pink flowers, 4in (10cm) across, with yellowish white and deep red lips, are borne in upright racemes in winter. ↕24in (60cm), ↔36in (90cm). ❄ (min. 50°F/10°C; max. 75°F/24°C)
C. lowianum. Epiphytic orchid with ovoid pseudobulbs and linear leaves, 24–30in (60–75cm) long. Greenish yellow flowers, 3½–5in (9–13cm) across, with red-banded lips, are borne in arching racemes in spring. ↕↔36in (90cm). Myanmar, Thailand, S.W. China. ❄ (min. 50°F/10°C; max. 75°F/24°C)
C. New Dimension (*C.* Mavourneen x *C.* Sussex Moor). Terrestrial orchid with ovoid pseudobulbs and narrowly oval leaves, 30in (75cm) long. Pale green flowers, 4in (10cm) across, are produced in upright racemes in winter. ↕24in (60cm), ↔36in (90cm). ❄ (min. 50°F/10°C; max. 75°F/24°C). **'Standard White'** ■ has white flowers with pink-flushed petals, and yellow and white lips with red markings.
C. pendulum see *C. aloifolium.*
C. Pontac 'Mont Millais' ■ (*C.* Hamsey x *C.* Memoria Doctor Borg). Terrestrial orchid with ovoid pseudo-bulbs and linear leaves, 30in (75cm) long. Bears

Cymbidium New Dimension 'Standard White'

Cymbidium Pontac 'Mont Millais'

dark red flowers, 4in (10cm) across, with red-banded white lips, in long, upright racemes in winter. ↕↔36in (90cm). ❄ (min. 50°F/10°C; max. 75°F/24°C)
C. Portelet Bay ■ (*C.* Caithness x *C.* Snowsprite). Terrestrial orchid with ovoid pseudobulbs and linear leaves, 30in (75cm) long. White flowers, 3in (8cm) across, with white-based, deep red lips, are borne in upright racemes in winter. ↕24in (60cm), ↔36in (90cm). ❄ (min. 50°F/10°C; max. 75°F/24°C)
C. Rosehill (*C.* Hamsey x *C.* Vieux Rose). Terrestrial orchid with ovoid pseudobulbs and linear leaves, 30in (75cm) long. Deep pink flowers, 4in (10cm) across, are borne in upright racemes in winter. ↕24in (60cm), ↔36in (90cm). ❄ (min. 50°F/10°C; max. 75°F/24°C)
C. Showgirl ■ (*C.* Alexanderi x *C.* Sweetheart). Terrestrial orchid with spherical pseudobulbs and linear leaves, to 18in (45cm) long. Pink-flushed white flowers, 2½in (6cm) across, with red flecks and stripes on the lips, are borne in upright racemes from winter to spring. ↕↔18in (45cm). ❄ (min. 50°F/10°C; max. 75°F/24°C)
C. St. Helier 'Trinity' (*C.* Mavourneen x *C.* New Dimension). Terrestrial orchid with ovoid pseudobulbs and narrowly oval leaves, 30in (75cm) long. Yellow-green flowers, 4in (10cm) across, with clear white lips, are produced in upright racemes from winter to spring. ↕↔36in (90cm). ❄ (min. 50°F/10°C; max. 75°F/24°C)
C. Strathbraan ■ (*C.* New Dimension x *C.* Putana). Terrestrial orchid with spherical pseudobulbs and linear leaves, to 18in (45cm) long. Very pale pink to

Cymbidium Portelet Bay

Cymbidium Showgirl

rose-pink flowers, 2½in (6cm) across, with red flecks and margins on the lips, are borne in upright racemes in winter. ↕↔18in (45cm). ❄ (min. 50°F/10°C; max. 75°F/24°C)
C. Strathdon 'Cooksbridge Noel' ■ (*C.* Kurun x *C.* Nip). Terrestrial orchid with spherical pseudobulbs and linear leaves, to 18in (45cm) long. Dusky red-pink flowers, 2½in (6cm) across, with yellow lips marked deep red and pale pink, are borne in upright racemes in winter. ↕↔18in (45cm). ❄ (min. 50°F/10°C; max. 75°F/24°C)
C. Strathkanaid (*C.* Hamsey x *C.* Nip). Terrestrial orchid with rounded pseudo-bulbs and linear leaves, to 18in (45cm) long. Upright racemes of dark pinkish red flowers, 2½in (6cm) across, are produced in winter. ↕↔18in (45cm). ❄ (min. 50°F/10°C; max. 75°F/24°C)
C. Thurso ■ (*C.* Miretta x *C.* York Meredith). Terrestrial orchid with ovoid pseudobulbs and linear leaves, 30in (75cm) long. Bears upright racemes of mid-green flowers, 4in (10cm) across, with red stripes and flecks on the lips, in winter. ↕24in (60cm), ↔36in (90cm). ❄ (min. 50°F/10°C; max. 75°F/24°C)
C. Tiger Tail (*C.* Alexanderi x *C. tigrinum*). Terrestrial orchid with ovoid pseudobulbs and linear leaves, 12in (30cm) long. Brown-shaded, lemon-yellow flowers, 2½in (6cm) across, are borne in upright racemes in early winter. ↕↔12in (30cm). ❄ (min. 50°F/10°C; max. 75°F/24°C)
C. tigrinum. Lithophytic orchid with almost spherical pseudobulbs and narrowly oval leaves, 9in (23cm) long. Olive-green to yellow flowers, to 2in (5cm) across, with purple lines, spots,

Cymbidium Strathbraan

Cymbidium Strathdon 'Cooksbridge Noel'

Cymbidium Thurso

and margins on the lips, are produced in upright racemes of 3 to 6 flowers in autumn. ↕10in (25cm), ↔6in (15cm). Burma, N.E. India. ❄ (min. 50°F/10°C; max. 75°F/24°C)
C. tracyanum ■ Epiphytic orchid with ovoid pseudobulbs and linear leaves, 24–30in (60–75cm) long. Strongly fragrant, yellow-green flowers, 3½in (9cm) across, boldly striped brown, with cream or yellow lips flecked purple-brown, are borne in arching racemes of 15 to 20 flowers in autumn. ↕↔36in (90cm). N. Burma, N. Thailand, China (S. Yunnan). ❄ (min. 50°F/10°C; max. 75°F/24°C)
C. Vieux Rose 'Del Park' (*C.* Babylon x *C.* Rio Rita). Terrestrial orchid with

Cymbidium tracyanum

ovoid pseudobulbs and linear leaves, 30in (75cm) long. Bears light pink flowers, 4in (10cm) across, with heavily red-spotted lips in upright racemes in spring. ↕↔ 36in (90cm). ❀ (min. 50°F/10°C; max. 75°F/24°C)

CYMBOPOGON

POACEAE

Genus of about 40 species of sturdy, aromatic, tufted, evergreen, perennial grasses, occurring in warm-temperate, subtropical, and tropical Africa and Asia, often in savanna grassland. They are grown for their linear to lance-shaped, mid- to bluish green leaves, and their loose or compact, many-branched flowering panicles, borne at the ends of the branches. The panicles consist of spikelets borne in short, paired, spike-like racemes, which are enclosed in spathe-like bracts. Where not hardy, grow in a conservatory or warm green-house and move outdoors in summer; in warmer climates, use in a mixed or grass border. *Cymbopogon* species contain essential oils that have medicinal, culinary, and cosmetic uses.

• **CULTIVATION** Under glass, grow in soil- based potting mix in full light, with moderate humidity. In the growing season, water freely; water sparingly in winter. Repot in early spring. Outdoors, grow in fertile, moist but well-drained soil in full sun.

• **PROPAGATION** Sow seed at 55–64°F (13–18°C) in early spring. Divide in late spring.

• **PESTS AND DISEASES** Infrequent.

C. citratus (Indian lemon grass). Densely tufted, clump-forming, perennial grass with hollow, cane-like stems and erect to arching, linear, rough-margined, strongly lemon-scented, pale blue-green leaves, to 36in (90cm) long. In late summer and early autumn, bears loose, branching flowering panicles, to 2in (5cm) long. Does not flower freely under glass. ↕ 24–36in (60–90cm), ↔ 36in (90cm). S. India, Sri Lanka. Very frost-sensitive; winter indoors. ❀ (min. 50°F/10°C)

CYNARA

ASTERACEAE

Genus of about 11 species of clump-forming, thistle-like perennials found on well-drained, sunny slopes and grass-land in the Mediterranean region, N.W. Africa, and the Canary Islands. Many are imposing plants, with pinnatifid or 2-pinnatifid, silvery or grayish green leaves and tall, spherical flowerheads, borne singly or in corymbs. *Cynara* species are statuesque plants, suitable for a herbaceous border. The flowerhead bracts and leaf stalks and midribs of some species are edible. The thistle-like flowerheads are also useful for dried flower arrangements, and attract insects.

• **CULTIVATION** Grow in fertile, well-drained soil in full sun, sheltered from strong winds. For best foliage effects, remove the flowering stems as they emerge in summer. Where temperatures fall below 5°F (-15°C), protect the rootstock with a dry winter mulch.

• **PROPAGATION** Sow seed in containers in a cold frame in red soil, or divide in spring. Insert root cuttings in winter.

• **PESTS AND DISEASES** Gray mold, root rot, slugs, and aphids can occur.

Cynara cardunculus

C. cardunculus ■ (Cardoon). Clump-forming perennial with pinnatifid or 2-pinnatifid, usually spiny, silvery gray leaves, to 20in (50cm) long, with ovate to linear-lance-shaped segments and deep basal lobes. From early summer to early autumn, purplish blue flowerheads, 1½–3in (4–8cm) across, are borne on gray-woolly stems. Blanched leaf stalks and midribs are edible. ↕ 6–8ft (3–2.4m), ↔ 4ft (1.2m). S.W. Mediterranean, Morocco. Zone 7b.

C. scolymus (Globe artichoke). Clump-forming perennial with deeply lobed or pinnatifid, gray-green leaves, to 32in (80cm) long, with pointed segments, gray-hairy above, densely white-woolly beneath. In early autumn, bears purple flowerheads, 3–6in (8–15cm) across, with large involucral bracts. The flower-heads (in bud) are eaten as a vegetable. Probably a variant of *C. cardunculus,* but horticulturally distinct. ↕ to 6ft (2m), ↔ 4ft (1.2m). Zone 7b.

CYNODON

Bermudagrass

POACEAE

Genus of about 8 species of tropical and subtropical grasses, used as lawns and best adapted to lower elevations in the Southwest US. Once established, they can be invasive.

• **CULTIVATION** Mow at ½–1in (1.5–2.5cm) and apply a nitrogen fertilizer, 4lb/1,000sq.ft (1.8kg/92sq.m).

• **PROPAGATION** Sown as seed or planted as sterile clones.

• **PESTS AND DISEASES** Infrequent.

C. dactylon. Vigorous spreading grass with strong stems that interweave, forming a dense ground cover. Flower spikes to 16in (40cm). Zone 7b.

CYNOGLOSSUM

Hound's tongue

BORAGINACEAE

Genus of about 55 species of annuals, biennials, and short-lived perennials from grassy places and rocky slopes in temperate regions and tropical uplands. The leaves are alternate, narrowly lance-shaped to oblong or ovate, and rough, often clasping the stems, the lower ones stalked. Cultivated for their usually blue, sometimes purple, rose-pink, or white flowers, similar to forget-me-nots (*Myosotis*), each has a short, tubular corolla and 5 widely spreading lobes, in

Cynoglossum amabile 'Firmament'

one-sided, terminal cymes over a long period from spring to autumn. Grow in a mixed, herbaceous, or annual border.

• **CULTIVATION** Grow in moderately fertile, moist but well-drained soil in sun or partial shade. Plants become coarse and leafy and may not flower well in soil that is too fertile; they do not thrive in heavy clay soils.

• **PROPAGATION** Sow seed of perennials in containers in a cold frame in autumn or spring. Sow seed of annuals and biennials *in situ* in midspring. Divide perennials in spring.

• **PESTS AND DISEASES** Root and stem rot, downy mildew, and powdery mildew sometimes occur.

C. amabile (Chinese forget-me-not). Slow-growing, upright, bushy annual or biennial with obovate to lance-shaped, hairy, gray-green leaves, to 8in (20cm) long. In late summer, bears terminal cymes of pendent, sky-blue, sometimes white or pale pink flowers, ¼–½in (6–15mm) across. ↕ 18–24in (45–60cm), ↔ to 12in (30cm). E. Asia. Zone 6. **'Firmament'** ■ is compact, with deep blue flowers and gray-hairy leaves; ↕ to 16in (40cm).

C. longiflorum see *Lindelofia longiflora.*

C. nervosum ■ (Hound's tongue). Clump-forming, erect, bushy perennial with bristly stems and narrowly oblong-lance-shaped, softly hairy or bristly, bright green leaves; the basal leaves to 1½in (4cm) long, the lower stem leaves to 5in (13cm). Bears many-flowered cymes of azure-blue flowers, ½in (1.5cm) across, from mid-spring to midsummer. ↕↔ 24in (60cm). W. Pakistan, N.W. India (including Kashmir). Zone 6.

Cynoglossum nervosum

C. officinale (Hound's tongue). Softly hairy biennial that in its first year forms a basal rosette of elliptic-oblong, gray-green leaves, 5in (13cm) long. In the second summer, ascending, leafy stems bear loose cymes of dull, dark purple flowers, ¼in (6mm) across. ↕ 20–28in (50–70cm), ↔ 12–20in (30–50cm). Europe, W. Asia. Zone 5.

C. zeylanicum. Upright, bushy annual or biennial with elliptic to oblong, densely brown- or yellow-hairy, mid-green leaves, to 8in (20cm) long. Bears terminal cymes of pendent, blue to white flowers, to ¼in (6mm) across, in summer. ↕ to 34in (85cm), ↔ to 18in (45cm). Afghanistan to Sri Lanka and Japan. Zone 6.

CYPELLA

IRIDACEAE

Genus of 15 species of bulbous perennials occurring in grassland and woodland, often near streams, in Central and South America. They are cultivated for their curious, iris-like flowers, each with 3 spreading outer tepals and 3 much smaller, incurved inner ones, borne singly or in terminal corymbs. Individual flowers are short-lived but are produced in succession over long periods in winter or summer. Leaves are linear-lance-shaped and pleated. Where not hardy, grow in a cool greenhouse; in warmer climates, grow at the base of a warm wall or in a rock garden.

• **CULTIVATION** Plant 3in (8cm) deep. Under glass, grow in 2 parts soil-based potting mix to 1 part grit, in bright filtered light with good ventilation. In the growing season, water freely and apply a low-nitrogen liquid fertilizer monthly until flowers begin to form; keep dry and frost-free when dormant. Outdoors, grow in humus-rich, sandy soil, in a warm, sunny site. Either plant in autumn and protect with a mulch in winter, or plant in spring. Alternatively, in cold areas, lift bulbs after flowering and store in a frost-free place over winter.

• **PROPAGATION** Sow seed as soon as ripe at 45–55°F (7–13°C). Remove offsets when dormant, in late winter or spring if outdoors, or in summer or autumn, just before growth begins, if under glass.

• **PESTS AND DISEASES** Infrequent.

C. herbertii ■ Bulbous perennial with linear-lance-shaped, pleated leaves, 6–12in (15–30cm) long, borne on the

Cypella herbertii

lower part of the stem. A succession of flowers, 1½–2½in (4–6cm) across, with broad, mustard-yellow outer tepals and purple-spotted or lined inner ones, is produced in summer. ↕ 12–20in (30–50cm), PD2in (5cm). Argentina, Uruguay. ❄ (min. 41°F/5°C)

CYPERUS

CYPERACEAE

Genus of about 500–600 species of sedge- or grass-like annuals and evergreen, rhizomatous perennials, found almost exclusively in wet habitats throughout tropical and subtropical areas, with a small number in cool-temperate regions. They are grown for their foliage and unusual inflorescences. The cylindrical, 3-angled, or winged, often leafy stems, bear grass-like, linear leaves. Terminal, usually linear spikelets of hermaphroditic flowers have leaf-like bracts beneath, which in most species give the inflorescence a typically umbrella-like form. Grow at the margins of a pool or in a bog garden, or in large containers. Where not hardy, grow as houseplants, in a temperate greenhouse or conservatory, or as marginal plants in an indoor pool.

• **CULTIVATION** Under glass, grow in soil-based potting mix in bright filtered light. Stand containers in shallow trays of water to ensure ample moisture and high humidity at all times. In summer, apply a balanced liquid fertilizer monthly. To grow as a marginal in an indoor pool, grow in a watertight barrel or bowl of loamy soil, top-dressed with a 1in (2.5cm) layer of gravel. Set at the pond edge with the gravel surface about 1–2in (2.5–5cm) below water level. Outdoors, *C. eragrostis* thrives in most soils, not necessarily wet ones, in sun or partial shade. It will usually self-seed, even if the parent plant is killed in extreme cold. Grow *C. longus* as a marginal plant, in water 6–12in (15–30cm) deep, or in moist soil in a sunny or partially shaded border. Cut back dead material in late autumn. In subtropical and tropical areas, grow all species outdoors as for *C. longus*.

• **PROPAGATION** Sow seed in permanently moist seed-starting mix in spring; hardy species in containers in a cold frame, tender species at 64–70°F (18–21°C). Divide both tender and hardy species in spring. Plantlets will develop on the leafy inflorescences of some tender species if they are placed upside down in water, or pinned onto the surface of consistently moist perlite or potting mix.

• **PESTS AND DISEASES** Black band, tar spot, rust, and smut occur.

Cyperus eragrostis

C. albostriatus, syn. *C. diffusus* of gardens, *C. elegans* of gardens. Densely tufted perennial with slender, woody rhizomes and firm, thin, winged stems. Mid-green leaves, to 24in (60cm) long, have pale, prominent veins. From mid-summer to early autumn, bears pale greenish yellow to pale brown spikelets in loose, compound umbels, 2–8in (5–20cm) across, above 6–9 leafy bracts, ⅜–½in (0.8–1.5cm) long. ↕ 24in (60cm), ↔ 12in (30cm). Southern Africa. ❄ (min. 50°F/10°C). **'Variegatus'** has stems, leaves, and bracts conspicuously variegated with white stripes of varying widths; ↕ 24–36in (60–90cm).

C. alternifolius (Umbrella plant). Densely tufted perennial with woody rhizomes and no basal leaves. Numerous winged, dark green stems each produce a terminal whorl of 11–25 deep green, arching, leaf-like bracts, 4–6in (10–15cm) long. From summer to autumn, the stems are topped by small spikelets of pale yellow-brown flowers in compound umbels, to 5in (13cm) across. ↕ 18–36in (45–90cm), ↔ 16in (40cm). Madagascar. ❄ (min. 41°F/5°C)

***C. alternifolius* of gardens** see *C. involucratus*.

***C. diffusus* of gardens** see *C. albostriatus*.

***C. elegans* of gardens** see *C. albostriatus*.

C. eragrostis ■ syn. *C. vegetus* (American galingale). Loosely tufted, shortly rhizomatous perennial with thick, winged stems bearing net-veined, rough-margined, bright green leaves, to 36in (90cm) long, which are V-shaped in section. From midsummer to early autumn, produces spherical clusters of pale green spikelets in spreading, compound umbels, 1in (2.5cm) across, above 5–8 linear bracts, 3–4in (8–10cm) long. Good for drying. ↕ 24–36in (60–90cm), ↔ 18in (45cm). W. US, warm-temperate South America. ❄ (min. 35°F/2°C)

Cyperus involucratus

Cyperus papyrus

C. flabelliformis see *C. involucratus*.

C. haspans see *C. profiler*.

C. involucratus ■ syn. *C. alternifolius* of gardens, *C. flabelliformis* (Umbrella grass). Clump-forming, tufted perennial with 12–28 leafy bracts in an umbrella-spoke arrangement, on 3-angled stems. Short, basal leaves are reduced to sheaths, 2in (5cm) long. In summer, produces 14–32 rays bearing tiny clusters of yellow flowers, which turn brown after producing pollen. ↕↔ 24–30in (60–75cm). Widely cultivated and naturalized throughout Africa. ❄ (min. 41–50°F/5–10°C)

C. isocladus see *C. profiler*.

C. longus (Galingale). Loosely tufted perennial with long, knotted rhizomes and stiff, erect, 3-angled stems. Each stem produces 2 or 3 arching, rough-margined, glossy, bright green leaves, 2–5ft (0.6–1.5m) long, grooved above, paler and sharply keeled beneath. In late summer and early autumn, bears red-brown spikelets in loose umbels, to 3in (8cm) across, above 2–6 leaf-like bracts that are often longer than the inflorescence. ↕ 2–5ft (0.6–1.5m), ↔ 3ft (1m) or more. Europe, N. Africa, S.W. and C. Asia. Zone 7b.

C. papyrus ■ (Egyptian paper rush, Papyrus). Clump-forming perennial with tall, 3-angled, pithy, leafless stems. Globe-like compound umbels of 100–200 thread-like rays, 5–12in (12–30cm) long, each ending in a tiny brown flower, become pendent with age. Ancient Egyptians flattened and dried the stems to make a form of paper. Needs high humidity. ↕ 6ft (2m), ↔ 2–4ft (0.6–1.2m). Egypt to tropical Africa. ❄ (min. 41–50°F/5–10°C). **'Nanus'** see *C. profiler*.

C. profiler, syn. *C. haspans*, *C. isocladus*, *C. papyrus* 'Nanus' (Dwarf papyrus). Small, clump-forming perennial with a brown, scaly, creeping rhizome and 3-angled or round, leafless stems. In summer, bears glossy green umbels, 3–4in (8–10cm) across, of persistent, brown spikelets, above tiny, thread-like bracts that are ⅛–⅜in (3–9mm) long. Attractive for use in dried arrangements. ↕ to 24–36in (60–90cm), ↔ 18–24in (45–60cm). S. Africa. ❄ (min. 35°F/2°C)

C. vegetus see *C. eragrostis*.

CYPHOMANDRA

Tree tomato

SOLANACEAE

Genus of about 30 species of perennials and evergreen shrubs, trees, and climbers from the margins of dry forest in tropical America. Leaves are simple, occasionally 3-lobed, or compound, and arranged alternately. Star-, bowl-, or saucer-shaped flowers, each with 5 petal lobes, may be produced singly or in racemes or panicles from the upper leaf axils. Tomato-like, spherical to oblong-ellipsoid fruits, produced from summer to winter, are palatable only when fully ripe. Where not hardy, grow in a cool or temperate greenhouse; in warmer areas, use in a shrub border, courtyard garden, or fruit garden.

• **CULTIVATION** Under glass, grow in soil-based potting mix in full or bright filtered light, with moderate humidity. In the growing season, water freely, applying a balanced liquid fertilizer monthly; water sparingly in winter. Top-dress or pot on in spring. Outdoors, grow in fertile, moist but well-drained soil in sun or partial shade. Pruning group 8; tip-prune when young. Plants under glass need restrictive pruning in late winter.

• **PROPAGATION** Sow seed at 55–64°F (13–18°C) in spring. Root greenwood cuttings with bottom heat in late spring or early summer.

• **PESTS AND DISEASES** Susceptible to whiteflies and spider mites under glass.

C. betacea ■ syn. *C. crassicaulis*. Sparingly, robustly branched, small tree or large shrub with ovate to heart-shaped, softly downy, almost fleshy, mid- to deep green leaves, to 12in

Cyphomandra betacea

C

(30cm) long. From spring to summer, star- or bowl-shaped, white to pale buff-pink flowers, 1in (2.5cm) across, are produced in axillary racemes, 4–6in (10–15cm) long, followed by ellipsoid, brick- to orange-red, edible fruit, 2–2½in (5–6cm) long. ↕ 6–10ft (2–3m), ↔ 3–6ft (1–2m). Peru. ❀ (min. 41–45°F/5–7°C)
C. crassicaulis see *C. betacea.*

CYPHOSTEMMA

VITACEAE

Genus of about 150 species of prostrate or climbing, often deciduous, perennial succulents from semi-desert areas of Africa and Madagascar. They sometimes have trunk-like caudices, often with peeling "bark," and produce fleshy branches, with the leaves clustered at their tips. The leaves may be pinnate or 3- to 7-palmate, occasionally simple. In some species, resin exudes from the leaf undersides. Corymbs of pendent, cup-shaped to cylindrical flowers are borne in summer, followed by ovoid fruits, which usually contain only one seed each. Where not hardy, grow in a warm greenhouse; in warmer climates, grow in a desert garden.

• **CULTIVATION** Under glass, grow in standard cactus potting mix in full light with low humidity. During the growing season, water sparingly, and apply a low-nitrogen fertilizer 2 or 3 times; keep completely dry once the leaves have fallen. Outdoors, grow in poor to moderately fertile, humus-rich, sharply drained soil, in full sun. See also pp.48–49.

• **PROPAGATION** Sow seed at 64–70°F (18–21°C) in spring. Root basal cuttings in spring.

• **PESTS AND DISEASES** Mealybugs may be a problem under glass.

C. bainesii, syn. *Cissus bainesii.* Deciduous, perennial succulent with a spherical or bottle-shaped caudex, which is often divided into 2 thick branches with peeling, pale yellow or green bark. Resinous, usually 3-pinnate leaves, to 5in (13cm) long, with lance-shaped, toothed, fleshy, silvery green leaflets, are silver-hairy when young. Flat-topped cymes of cup-shaped, yellowish green flowers, ½in (1.5cm) across, are produced in summer, followed by red fruit. ↕↔ 24in (60cm). S.W. Africa. ❀ (min. 50°F/10°C)
C. cirrhosa. Deciduous, perennial succulent with an elongated caudex, forming tuberous roots and peeling gray bark. Pinnate, resinous, mid-green leaves, 4in (10cm) long, have 3–6 oval leaflets. Bears corymbs of pendent, cup-shaped, yellowish green flowers, ½in (1.5cm) across, in summer, followed by red fruit. ↕↔ to 20in (50cm). South Africa. ❀ (min. 50°F/10°C)
C. juttae ▣ syn. *Cissus juttae.* Deciduous, perennial succulent with very swollen stems and branches, which have peeling, yellowish green bark. Oval, 3-palmate, coarsely toothed, resinous, glossy, mid-green leaves, to 6in (15cm) long, are often red-tinted. Cymes of cylindrical, yellowish green flowers, ½in (1.5cm) across, are produced in summer, followed by red fruit. ↕↔ 6ft (2m). S. Namibia. ❀ (min. 50°F/10°C)
C. uter. Deciduous, tree-like, perennial succulent with many-branched stems and white, peeling bark. Triangular, mid-green leaves, 3in (8cm) across, appear at the ends of the branches. In summer, bears loose panicles of green flowers, ½in (1.5cm) across, followed by red fruit. ↕↔ 5ft (1.5m). Angola. ❀ (min. 50°F/10°C)

CYPRIPEDIUM

Lady's slipper orchid

ORCHIDACEAE

Genus of about 45 species of deciduous, terrestrial orchids found in dry wood-land or marshy places in temperate areas of the N. hemisphere, and in S. Asia and Mexico. They have slender rhizomes and several soft, folded, ovate to fan-shaped leaves, which are either spirally arranged or borne in opposite pairs. The flowers, produced singly or in terminal racemes of up to 12 flowers in summer, each have 3 spreading, white, pink, red, or purple tepals, and a slipper-shaped, yellow, white, pink, or dark purple pouch (an adaptation of the lip), hence the common name. *Cypripedium* species are suitable for a shady rock garden or woodland garden.

• **CULTIVATION** Grow in moist, fertile, leafy, humus-rich, neutral to acidic soil, in a sheltered site in light dappled or partial shade. *C. calceolus* prefers slightly alkaline soil; most others prefer acidic soil. Provide a winter mulch of leaf mold. See also p.46.

• **PROPAGATION** Divide carefully in early or midspring, and replant immediately. Some of the soil from the root ball, which contains beneficial fungal mycorrhizae, should be planted with each division.

• **PESTS AND DISEASES** Susceptible to gray mold (*Botrytis*), rust, *Cercospora* leaf spot, and slug damage.

Cypripedium calceolus

C. acaule ▣ Terrestrial orchid with 2 elliptic leaves, 4–9in (10–23cm) long. In summer, bears solitary, nodding, light greenish brown flowers, 2in (5cm) long, with pink lips, on upright stems. ↕↔ 9in (23cm). Canada, E. US. Zone 4.
C. calceolus ▣ (Yellow lady's slipper orchid). Terrestrial orchid with 3–5 ovate to elliptic leaves, 2–8in (5–20cm) long. In summer, bears purple-brown flowers, 3½in (9cm) long, with twisted petals and large, deep yellow lips, singly or in pairs on upright stems. ↕↔ 16in (40cm). Europe, Asia, North America. Zone 4.
C. macranthon ▣ Terrestrial orchid with 3 or 4 ovate to elliptic leaves, 3–6in (8–15cm) long. Usually solitary, violet to purple-red or greenish brown flowers, 3in (8cm) across, with arching and downward-pointing tepals, are borne on upright stems in summer. ↕ 18in (45cm), ↔ 12in (30cm). N. Mongolia, N. and W. China, Korea, Japan. Zone 5b.
C. reginae ▣ (Showy lady's slipper orchid). Terrestrial orchid with 3–7 ovate to lance-shaped leaves, 4–9in (10–23cm) long. White flowers, almost 4in (10cm) long, with rose-pink lips, are borne singly or in pairs on upright stems in summer. ↕ 30in (75cm), ↔ 12in (30cm). E. North America. Zone 3.

Cyphostemma juttae

Cypripedium acaule

Cypripedium macranthon

Cypripedium reginae

CYRILLA

CYRILLACEAE

Genus of one species of spreading, deciduous, semi-evergreen, or evergreen shrub or tree, found in moist woodland from S.E. US to N. South America and Brazil. It is grown for its attractive foliage, often colorful in autumn, arranged alternately or occasionally in whorls, and for its long racemes of small, cup-shaped flowers, ¼in (6mm) long. *C. racemiflora* varies in hardiness according to its origin. It is important to select stock from the northerly parts of the range to ensure that plants are hardy. Grow cyrilla in a shrub or mixed border.

• **CULTIVATION** Grow in fertile, humus-rich, moist but well-drained, acidic soil in sun or partial shade, sheltered from cold, drying winds. Pruning group 9.

• **PROPAGATION** Sow seed in containers in a cold frame as soon as ripe in autumn. Root semi-ripe cuttings in summer. Insert root cuttings in winter.

• **PESTS AND DISEASES** Sometimes affected by leaf spot and scale insects.

C. racemiflora (Leatherwood). Rounded shrub or, rarely, small tree with inversely lance-shaped to obovate, glossy, dark green leaves, to 4in (10cm) long, turning orange and red in autumn. From late summer to autumn, produces small, fragrant white flowers in slender, axillary racemes, to 6in (15cm) long. ↕↔ 4ft (1.2m). S.E. US to Brazil (including West Indies). Zone 7 for plants from S.E. US; ❀ (min. 45°F/7°C) for plants from Brazil.

CYRTANTHUS

Fire lily

AMARYLLIDACEAE

Genus of about 50 species of clump-forming, bulbous perennials from grassland to forest and cliffs in Africa. Most cultivated species are from South Africa. Usually deciduous, sometimes semi-evergreen, lance- to strap-shaped, mostly mid-green, basal leaves may be present or absent at flowering. Umbels of showy, tubular or tubular-bell-shaped to funnel-shaped flowers are produced on leafless stems mainly from spring to autumn. Where not hardy, grow in a cool or temperate greenhouse, or as houseplants. Elsewhere, grow in a border or at the base of a warm, sunny wall.

• **CULTIVATION** Under glass, plant bulbs with the neck at soil level in soil-based potting mix, with added leaf mold and sharp sand, in bright filtered or full light with shade from hot sun. Water freely when in active growth, sparingly in winter; when dormant, keep deciduous species barely moist at not less than 41–50°F (5–10°C). In summer, apply a dilute, balanced liquid fertilizer every 2–3 weeks. Outdoors, plant at twice the bulb's depth in moderately fertile, humus-rich, well-drained soil in full sun.

• **PROPAGATION** Sow seed at 55–64°F (13–18°C) when ripe. Remove offsets in spring.

• **PESTS AND DISEASES** Infrequent.

C. brachyscyphus ■ syn. *C. parviflorus.* Deciduous perennial with semi-erect, lance-shaped, bright green leaves, 12in

Cyrtanthus brachyscyphus

(30cm) long. From spring to summer, produces 6–12 narrowly tubular, slightly curved red flowers, 1–1¼in (2.5–3cm) long. ↕ 8–12in (20–30cm), PD4in (10cm). South Africa (S. KwaZulu/Natal, Eastern Cape). ❀ (min. 45°F/7°C)

C. breviflorus, syn. *Anoiganthus breviflorus, A. luteus.* Deciduous perennial with erect, lance-shaped leaves, 8in (20cm) long. Up to 20 bell-shaped yellow flowers, to 1¼in (3cm) long, are produced at any time of year. ↕ 8in (20cm), PD4in (10cm). South Africa (widespread). ❀ (min. 45°F/7°C)

C. elatus ■ syn. *C. purpureus, Vallota speciosa* (Scarborough lily). Deciduous perennial with erect, strap-shaped leaves, 8–18in (20–45cm) long. Produces up to 9 open funnel-shaped, bright scarlet flowers, 3–4in (7–10cm) long, in late summer. Easily grown on an east- or south-facing windowsill if given enough room. ↕ 12–24in (30–60cm), PD4in (10cm). South Africa (Western Cape). ❀ (min. 45°F/7°C). **'Delicata'** bears soft salmon-pink flowers.

C. falcatus. Deciduous perennial with broadly strap-shaped, curved leaves, to 10in (25cm) long. Up to 10 pendent, funnel-shaped red flowers, 2½in (6cm) long, are produced in spring. ↕ 12in (30cm), PD4in (10cm). South Africa. ❀ (min. 45°F/7°C)

C. mackenii* var. *cooperi ■ Deciduous perennial with semi-erect, linear leaves, to 12in (30cm) long. Produces 4–10 narrowly tubular, scented, yellow or cream flowers, 2in (5cm) long, from spring to summer. ↕ 8–12in (20–30cm), PD4in (10cm). South Africa (Eastern Cape). ❀ (min. 41°F/5°C)

Cyrtanthus elatus

Cyrtanthus mackenii var. *cooperi*

C. obliquus. Deciduous perennial with strap-shaped, curved leaves, 8–24in (20–60cm) long. Umbels of 6–12 funnel-shaped, bicolored yellow and red, slightly green-tinged flowers, 3in (8cm) long, are produced from winter to early summer. ↕ 12–24in (30–60cm), PD3in (8cm). South Africa (S. KwaZulu/Natal, Eastern Cape). ❀ (min. 45°F/7°C)

C. parviflorus see *C. brachyscyphus.*

C. purpureus see *C. elatus.*

C. sanguineus. Deciduous perennial with semi-erect, strap-shaped leaves, to 16in (40cm) long. In summer, produces 1 or 2, rarely 3, open funnel-shaped, bright scarlet flowers, 3–4in (8–10cm) long. ↕ 12–20in (30–50cm), PD4in (10cm). South Africa. ❀ (min. 45°F/7°C)

▷ ***Cyrtochilum macranthum*** see *Oncidium macranthum*

CYRTOMIUM

syn. PHANEROPHLEBIA

DRYOPTERIDACEAE

Genus of 12 species of evergreen or deciduous ferns from often moist, rocky areas or woodland in C. and E. Asia. They have erect rhizomes and pinnate, leathery fronds with sickle-shaped, sharp-pointed pinnae. Sori, each with a peltate indusium, are scattered over the undersides of the pinnae. Most species have distinctive fronds, which provide strong contrast to more lacy ferns. Grow in a shady border or a rock garden. *C. falcatum* is a handsome houseplant.

• **CULTIVATION** Grow in moderately fertile, humus-rich, moist but well-drained soil in partial to full shade. Where marginally hardy, plant *C. falcatum* in the shelter of a rock and cover the crown with straw in winter. Under glass, grow in 1 part each loam, medium-grade bark, and charcoal, 2 parts sharp sand, and 3 parts coarse leaf mold, in bright indirect light. In growth, water freely and apply a dilute liquid fertilizer every 2 weeks; water moderately in winter.

• **PROPAGATION** Sow spores at 61°F (16°C) in late summer. See also p.51.

• **PESTS AND DISEASES** Fungal spots, root rot, and scale insects are common.

Cyrtomium falcatum

C. falcatum ■ syn. *Phanerophlebia falcata* (Japanese holly fern). Evergreen fern, deciduous in colder climates. Spreading, glossy, dark green fronds, 8–24in (20–60cm) long, have holly-like pinnae, 1½–2½in (4–6cm) long. ↕ 24in (60cm), ↔ 3½ft (1.1m). Japan. Zone 6b. **'Cristatum'**, syn. 'Mayi', has heavily crested frond tips and twisted pinnae tips. **'Mayi'** see 'Cristatum'. **'Rochfordianum'** has pinnae with deeply cut margins.

C. fortunei, syn. *Phanerophlebia fortunei.* Evergreen fern with erect, dull, pale green fronds, 12–24in (30–60cm) long, with broadly sickle-shaped pinnae, 1–2in (2.5–5cm) long. ↕ 24in (60cm), ↔ 16in (40cm). E. Asia. Zone 7b.

C. macrophyllum (Large-leaved holly fern). Evergreen fern with spreading, broad, mid-green fronds, 8–20in (20–50cm) long, with ovate to ovate-oblong pinnae, 4–8in (10–20cm) long. ↕ 18in (45cm), ↔ 24in (60cm). E. Asia. Zone 8.

CYRTOSTACHYS

ARECACEAE

Genus of 8 or 9 species of single- or cluster-stemmed palms occurring in swampy ground and tropical forest from Malaysia, Indonesia (Sumatra), and Borneo to New Guinea and the Solomon Islands. Terminal clusters of ascending, pinnate leaves are borne

Cyrtostachys lakka

above distinct crownshafts. Small, bowl-shaped, 3-petaled flowers are produced in panicles between the leaf clusters. Where not hardy, grow *C. lakka* as a houseplant or in a warm greenhouse; in humid tropical areas, use as a specimen tree or in a courtyard garden.
• **CULTIVATION** Under glass, grow in soilless or soil-based potting mix in bright filtered light, with moderate humidity. In growth, water freely, applying a balanced liquid fertilizer monthly; water moderately in winter. Pot on or top-dress in spring. Outdoors, grow in fertile, moist, well-drained soil in sun or partial shade.
• **PROPAGATION** Sow seed at 81°F (27°C) in spring. Remove and pot up suckers in spring.
• **PESTS AND DISEASES** Scale insects and spider mites may be problems under glass.

C. lakka ■ (Lipstick palm, Sealing wax palm). Clump-forming, cluster-stemmed palm with erect, slender stems. Each stem is topped by a scarlet crownshaft and a head of erect to ascending leaves, to 5ft (1.5m) long, with scarlet stalks and midribs, and many linear, mid-green leaflets, gray-tinted beneath. Panicles of bowl-shaped green flowers, ½in (1.5cm) long, are produced in summer. ↕ to 15ft (5m), ↔ to 10ft (3m). Malaysian Peninsula, Indonesia (Sumatra), Borneo. ❀ (min. 61°F/16°C)

CYSTOPTERIS
Bladder fern

DRYOPTERIDACEAE

Genus of 10–20 species of deciduous, rhizomatous ferns found among calcareous rocks in temperate and subtropical areas. Very finely divided, lance-shaped or triangular fronds, usually pinnate or 2- to 4-pinnate to pinnatifid, arise from creeping or erect rhizomes; the sori are protected by bladder-shaped indusia, giving rise to the common name. Grow in a rock garden or shady fern border, or in an alpine house.
• **CULTIVATION** Grow in fertile, moist but well-drained soil in partial shade. Shelter from wind. Under glass, grow in 1 part each of loam, medium-grade bark, charcoal, and limestone chips, 2 parts sharp sand, and 3 parts coarse leaf mold.
• **PROPAGATION** Sow spores at 61°F (16°C) or plant bulbils in late summer. Alternatively, divide rhizomes in spring. See also p.51.
• **PESTS AND DISEASES** Leaf gall and rust can occur.

C. bulbifera. Delicate, rosette-forming fern with erect rhizomes and tufts of erect, lance-shaped, 2-pinnate, pale green fronds, to 30in (75cm) long, with lance-shaped to linear-oblong segments. Bulbils develop beneath the often red-tinged midribs. Establishes quickly. ↕ 12in (30cm), ↔ 8in (20cm). North America. Zone 4.
C. dickieana (Dickie's fern). Clump-forming fern with erect rhizomes and tufts of lance-shaped, 2- or 3-pinnate, gray-green fronds, 4–10in (10–25cm) or more long, with rounded lobes at the tips, and overlapping, ovate to oblong-lance-shaped segments. ↕ 6in (15cm), ↔ 8in (20cm). Europe. Zone 3.
C. fragilis ■ (Brittle fern). Clump-forming fern with erect rhizomes and tufts of lance-shaped, 2- or 3-pinnate, pale gray-green fronds, 6–18in (15–45cm) long, with oblong-lance-shaped segments, sharply pointed at the frond tips; frond segments do not overlap. ↕↔ 8in (20cm). Mainly N. temperate regions, Chile. Zone 4.
C. protrusa (Lowland brittle fern). Deciduous, terrestrial fern with a long, creeping rhizome producing a tuft of lance-shaped, 2- or 3-pinnate, mid-green fronds, 16in (40cm) long, with oblong-lance-shaped segments and wedge-shaped, stalked bases on the lowest segments. The growing points of the leaves extend ¾–2in (2–5cm) beyond the leaves. Keep moist during dry periods. ↕ 32in (80cm), ↔ 12in (30cm). North America. Zone 4.

▷ ***Cytisophyllum sessilifolium*** see *Cytisus sessilifolius*

CYTISUS syn. ARGYROCYTISUS
Broom

FABACEAE

Genus of about 50 species, similar to *Genista*, of deciduous to evergreen shrubs, rarely small trees, from Europe, W. Asia, and N. Africa, found in well-drained soils, usually in open sites, from high mountains to scrub and heathland at lower altitudes. Brooms have alternate, usually 3-palmate, occasionally simple, mostly mid-green leaves, but are occasionally leafless when mature. They are cultivated for their abundant pea-like, sometimes very fragrant flowers, borne singly or in terminal or leafy, axillary racemes or clusters. Flowers are followed by linear or oblong, usually mid-green, often hairy or downy seed

Cytisus battandieri (inset: flower detail)

pods. The smaller species and cultivars are suitable for a rock garden or raised bed. Grow larger brooms in a shrub border; use prostrate variants as a groundcover. Where not hardy, grow *C.* x *spachianus* as a houseplant, or in a conservatory or cool greenhouse. All parts, especially the seeds, may cause mild stomach upset if ingested.
• **CULTIVATION** Under glass, grow in soil-based potting mix in full light. In the growing season, water freely and apply a balanced liquid fertilizer monthly; water sparingly in winter. Outdoors, grow in moderately fertile, well-drained soil in full sun. Provide less hardy species with shelter from cold, drying winds. Brooms thrive in poor, acidic soils. Most are also lime-tolerant, but often become chlorotic on shallow alkaline soils. Plant directly from containers when small; they resent transplanting. Pruning group 1 or 3; do not cut into the old wood. Prune *C. nigricans* in early spring. Prostrate and decumbent species generally need minimal pruning.
• **PROPAGATION** Sow seed in containers in a cold frame in autumn or spring. Root ripewood cuttings in midsummer, and semi-ripe cuttings in late summer.
• **PESTS AND DISEASES** Gray mold (*Botrytis*), dieback, root rot, and spider mites occur.

***C. albus* of gardens** see *C. multiflorus.*
C. ardoinoi ■ Semi-prostrate, hummock-forming, deciduous shrub with arching, ridged stems and 3-palmate leaves, ⅜in (9mm) long. Axillary clusters of 1–3 bright yellow flowers, ½in (1.5cm) long, are borne from late spring to summer. ↕↔ 8–24in (20–60cm). Maritime Alps. Zone 7.
C. battandieri ■ syn. *Argyrocytisus battandieri* (Pineapple broom). Vigorous, upright, tree-like deciduous shrub, spreading with age, with 3-palmate, silvery gray leaves, to 4in (10cm) long. Dense, upright, terminal racemes, to 6in (15cm) long, of pineapple-scented yellow flowers, ½–¾in (1.5–2cm) long, are produced in mid- and late summer. Will not tolerate an exposed position. Pruning group 1. ↕↔ 15ft (5m). Morocco. Zone 7.
C.* x *beanii ■ (*C. ardoinoi* x *C. purgans*). Semi-procumbent, deciduous shrub with arching, cylindrical stems and simple, linear, hairy leaves, to ½in (1.5cm) long. In spring, rich yellow flowers, ⅜–½in (0.8–1.5cm) long, are produced in axillary clusters of 1–3. ↕ to 24in (60cm), ↔ to 3ft (1m). Garden origin. Zone 5b.
***C.* 'Burkwoodii'.** Rounded, bushy, deciduous shrub with slender shoots and 3-palmate leaves, ½–¾in (1–2cm) long. Dark pink flowers, ½in (2cm) long, with yellow-margined crimson wings, are produced in axillary clusters in late spring and early summer. ↕↔ 5ft (1.5m). Zone 6.
***C. canariensis* of gardens** see *C.* x *spachianus.*
***C.* 'Cornish Cream'.** Bushy, spreading, deciduous shrub with slender, arching shoots and 3-palmate leaves, ½–¾in (1–2cm) long. In late spring and early summer, abundant flowers, 1in (2.5cm)

Cystopteris fragilis

Cytisus ardoinoi

Cytisus x *beanii*

C

Cytisus 'Hollandia'

Cytisus nigricans

Cytisus x *praecox* 'Allgold'

long, in a mixture of creamy yellow and white, are produced in axillary clusters. ↕↔ 5ft (1.5m). Zone 6.

C. decumbens, syn. *Genista decumbens*. Ascending or prostrate, deciduous shrub with wiry, branching stems and simple, oblong, finely hairy, stalkless leaves, ¼–¾in (0.6–2cm) long. Produces axillary clusters of 1–3 brilliant yellow flowers, ⅜–½in (0.9–1.5cm) long, in late spring and early summer. ↕ 4–12in (10–30cm), ↔ to 3ft (1m). S. Alps, Italy (Apennines). Zone 4.

***C.* 'Dragonfly'.** Compact, deciduous shrub with slender, arching shoots and 3-palmate leaves, to ½in (1.5cm) long. Dark yellow flowers, ½in (1.5cm) long, with crimson wings, are produced in axillary clusters in late spring and early summer. ↕↔ 5ft (1.5m). Zone 6.

***C.* 'Firefly'.** Rounded, bushy, deciduous shrub with slender, arching shoots and 3-palmate leaves, ½–¾in (1–2cm) long. In late spring and early summer, bears axillary racemes of abundant yellow flowers, ½in (1.5cm) long, with wings marked dark bronze-red. ↕↔ 5ft (1.5m). Zone 6.

***C.* 'Golden Sunlight'.** Rounded, deciduous shrub producing slender, arching branches and 3-palmate leaves, ½–¾in (1–2cm) long. Axillary racemes of abundant pale gold flowers, ½in (1.5cm) long, are produced in late spring and early summer. ↕↔ 5ft (1.5m). Zone 6.

***C.* 'Hollandia'** ■ Rounded, deciduous shrub with slender, arching branches and 3-palmate leaves, ½–¾in (1–2cm) long. Abundant cream and dark pink flowers, ½in (1.5cm) long, are borne in axillary clusters in late spring and early summer. ↕↔ 5ft (1.5m). Zone 4b.

C.* x *kewensis (*C. ardoinoi* x *C. multiflorus*). Prostrate, deciduous shrub with arching stems, clothed in 3-palmate, softly hairy leaves, to ¾in (2cm) long. Bears axillary racemes of 1–3 cream flowers, ½in (1.5cm) long, along the lengths of downy branches in late spring. ↕ 12in (30cm), ↔ to 5ft (1.5m). Garden origin. Zone 6b.

***C.* 'Killiney Red'.** Compact, deciduous shrub with arching branches and 3-palmate leaves, ½–¾in (1–2cm) long. Abundant rich red flowers, ½in (1.5cm) long, with darker wings, are borne in axillary clusters in late spring and early summer. ↕ 4ft (1.2m), ↔ 5ft (1.5m). Zone 6.

***C.* 'Lena'.** Compact, spreading, deciduous shrub with 3-palmate leaves, ⅜–½in (0.8–1.5cm) long. In late spring and early summer, produces axillary clusters of dark yellow flowers, to ¾in (2cm) long, with the backs of the standards and wings bright red. ↕ 4ft (1.2m), ↔ 5ft (1.5m). Zone 6.

C. leucanthus see *C. multiflorus*.

***C.* 'Maria Burkwood'.** Vigorous, spreading, deciduous shrub with slender, arching shoots and 3-palmate leaves, ½–¾in (1–2cm) long. Carmine-red flowers, ½in (1.5cm) long, with copper-bronze wings, are produced in axillary clusters in late spring and early summer. ↕↔ 5ft (1.5m). Zone 6.

C. multiflorus ■ syn. *C. albus* of gardens, *C. leucanthus* (Portuguese broom, White Spanish broom). Upright then spreading, deciduous shrub with 3-palmate or simple, linear-oblong leaves, to ½in (1.5cm) long. Abundant white flowers, to ½in (1.5cm) long, are borne in axillary clusters in late spring and early summer. ↕ 10ft (3m), ↔ 8ft (2.5m). Portugal, Spain. Zone 7b.

C. nigrescens see *C. nigricans*.

C. nigricans ■ syn. *C. nigrescens*, *Lembrotropis nigricans*. Erect, deciduous shrub with upright shoots and 3-palmate leaves, to 1in (2.5cm) long. Yellow flowers, ½in (1.5cm) long, are produced in slender, terminal racemes in late summer. ↕ 5ft (1.5m), ↔ 3ft (1m). C. and S.E. Europe. Zone 3b.

***C.* 'Porlock'.** Vigorous, arching, semi-evergreen shrub with upright shoots and 3-palmate leaves, ½–¾in (1–2cm) long. Terminal racemes of very fragrant, clear yellow flowers, ¾in (2cm) long, are produced in spring and, rarely, in mild weather in winter. ↕↔ 10ft (3m). Zone 6.

C.* x *praecox (*C. multiflorus* x *C. purgans*). Compact, deciduous shrub with arching shoots and simple leaves, to ¾in (2cm) long. Produces axillary clusters of abundant pale yellow flowers, ½–¾in (1–2cm) long, in mid- and late spring. ↕ 4ft (1.2m), ↔ 5ft (1.5m). Garden origin. Zone 6. **'Allgold'** ■ produces dark yellow flowers. **'Warminster'** ■ (Warminster broom) has creamy yellow flowers.

C. purpureus see *Chamaecytisus purpureus*.

C. scoparius (Scotch broom). Upright, deciduous shrub with slender, arching shoots and usually 3-palmate leaves, ½–¾in (1–2cm) long. Abundant bright yellow flowers, ½–1in (1.5–2.5cm) long, are produced in axillary clusters in late spring. ↕↔ 5ft (1.5m). W. Europe. Zone 6. **f. *andreanus*** (Normandy broom) has yellow flowers splashed red on the backs of the wings. **subsp. *maritimus***, syn. var. *prostratus*, is low-growing, forming a dense mound, with gray-green leaves; ↕ 8in (20cm), ↔ 5ft (1.5m). **'Moonlight'** is compact, with large, pale sulfur-yellow flowers, ½in (1.5cm) long; ↕↔ 30in (75cm).

var. *prostratus* see subsp. *maritimus*.

C. sessilifolius, syn. *Cytisophyllum sessilifolium*. Bushy, deciduous shrub with angled shoots and more or less stalkless, 3-palmate leaves, ⅜–¾in (0.8–2cm) long. Yellow flowers, ½in (1.5cm) long, are produced in short, terminal racemes in early summer. ↕↔ 5ft (1.5m). S. France, E. Spain, Italy. Zone 5.

C.* x *spachianus (*C. canariensis* x *C. stenopetalus*), syn. *C. canariensis* of gardens, *Genista fragrans* of gardens, *G.* x *spachiana*. Vigorous, evergreen shrub with upright, later arching branches and 3-palmate leaves, to 1½in (4cm) long. Bears slender, terminal racemes of very fragrant, golden yellow flowers, ½in (1.5cm) long, in late winter and early spring. ↕↔ 10ft (3m). Garden origin. ❄ (min. 35°F/2°C)

C. supinus see *Chamaecytisus supinus*.

***C.* 'Zeelandia'.** Rounded, bushy, deciduous shrub with slender, arching shoots and 3-palmate leaves, ½–¾in (1–2cm) long. Abundant creamy white and lilac-pink flowers, to ¾in (2cm) long, are borne in axillary clusters in late spring and early summer. ↕↔ 5ft (1.5m). Zone 6.

Cytisus multiflorus

Cytisus x *praecox* 'Warminster'

D

DABOECIA

ERICACEAE

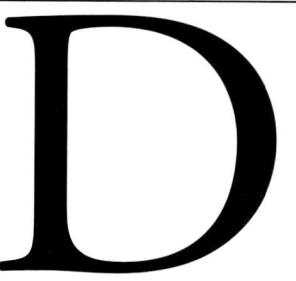

Genus of 2 species of evergreen shrubs from W. Ireland, W. France, N.W. Spain, N. Portugal, and the Azores, found from coastal cliffs to mountain heathland. Urn-shaped flowers are borne in racemes above alternate, lance-shaped to elliptic, usually dark green leaves. Grow as a groundcover in a heather garden or among other ericaceous shrubs; where not hardy, grow in a cool greenhouse.

• **CULTIVATION** Outdoors, grow in well-drained, acidic soil in full sun; will tolerate neutral soil and partial shade. Avoid frost pockets and provide winter protection, such as a loose covering of pine needles. Under glass, grow in acidic potting mix in full light. During growth, water freely and apply a balanced liquid fertilizer monthly. Water sparingly in winter. Pruning group 10, in early and midspring.

• **PROPAGATION** Root semi-ripe cuttings in midsummer; layer in autumn.

• **PESTS AND DISEASES** Susceptible to *Phytophthora* root rot when heavily watered or grown under *Eucalyptus*.

D. azorica, syn. *D. cantabrica* subsp. *azorica* (Azores heath). Compact shrub bearing narrowly elliptic leaves, ¼–⅜in (5–9mm) long, with recurved margins, dark green above and silvery gray beneath. Racemes, 2in (5cm) long, of spherical-urn-shaped, ruby-crimson flowers, ⅜in (9mm) long, sometimes paler, are borne in early summer. ↕ 8in (20cm), ↔ 16in

Daboecia cantabrica 'Bicolor'

Daboecia cantabrica 'Snowdrift'

(40cm). Azores. ❄ (min. 41°F/5°C).
f. *albiflora* has white flowers.
D. cantabrica, syn. *D. polifolia* (Cantabrian heath, Irish heath, St. Daboec's heath). Prostrate to erect shrub with lance-shaped to oval leaves, ¼–½in (6–15mm) long, usually dark green and lustrous above, densely silver-hairy beneath. Bears ovoid-urn-shaped, pinkish purple flowers, ½in (1.5cm) long, in racemes 4in (10cm) long from early summer to midautumn. ↕ 10–16in (25–40cm), ↔ 26in (65cm). W. Europe. Zone 6. **'Atropurpurea'** has dark green foliage and deep purple flowers; ↕↔ 18in (45cm). **subsp. *azorica*** see *D. azorica*. **'Bicolor'** ▣ has white, pink, and beet-red flowers, some striped, often on the same raceme. **'Cinderella'** is a bicolor with white and pale shell pink flowers; ↕ 16in (40cm), ↔ 18in (45cm). **'Praegerae'** has mid-green foliage, which may be deciduous in hard winters, and glowing, deep cerise flowers; ↕ 16in (40cm), ↔ 28in (70cm). **'Rubra'** has dark green foliage and deep purple flowers; ↕ 10in (25cm), ↔ 16in (40cm). **'Snowdrift'** ▣ has white flowers and bright green leaves. **'Waley's Red'**, syn. 'Whalley', has glowing, deep magenta flowers; ↔ 20in (50cm).
D. polifolia see *D. cantabrica*.
D. x scotica (*D. azorica* x *D. cantabrica*). Compact shrub with elliptic to elliptic-ovate, dark green leaves, ¼–⅜in (6–9mm) long. Racemes, 4in (10cm) long, of ovoid-urn-shaped, crimson to lilac-pink or white flowers, ⅜in (9mm) long, are produced from late spring to midautumn. ↕ 10in (25cm), ↔ 16in (40cm). Garden origin. Zone 6; young

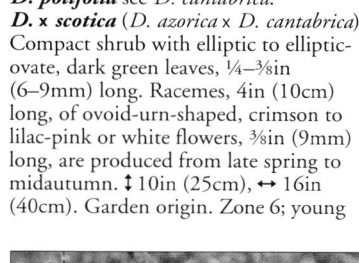

Daboecia x *scotica* 'William Buchanan'

plants may be more cold-tolerant than older, woodier specimens. **'Jack Drake'** has dark green foliage and ruby flowers; ↕ 10in (25cm), ↔ 12in (30cm). **'Silverwells'** has mid-green foliage and white flowers; ↕ 6in (15cm), ↔ 14in (35cm). **'William Buchanan'** ▣ has purple-crimson flowers; ↕ 14in (35cm), ↔ 22in (55cm). **'William Buchanan Gold'** has dark red and gold foliage with yellow flecks and bears crimson flowers; ↕ 10in (25cm), ↔ 20in (50cm).

DACRYDIUM

PODOCARPACEAE

Genus of about 20 species of dioecious, evergreen, coniferous trees and shrubs found in habitats ranging from swamps to dry, mountainous areas in subtropical S.E. Asia, W. Pacific islands, and New Zealand. They have linear juvenile leaves and spirally arranged, scale-like adult leaves lying flat along the shoots. The male cones are cylindrical and borne in short, axillary spikes; female cones are erect and terminal. In areas with humid summers and mild, damp winters, grow as specimen plants or in a shrub border; where not hardy, grow in a cool greenhouse or conservatory.

• **CULTIVATION** Under glass, grow in soil-based potting mix in full or bright filtered light, with high humidity. In summer, water freely and apply a balanced liquid fertilizer monthly; water sparingly in winter. Outdoors, grow in moist but well-drained, humus-rich soil in sun or partial shade.

• **PROPAGATION** Sow seed in containers in a cold frame or root semi-ripe cuttings from mid- to late summer.

• **PESTS AND DISEASES** Infrequent.

D. cupressinum (Rimu). Conical, later rounded, coniferous tree with dark green foliage: pointed, linear juvenile leaves, to ¼in (6mm) long, are arching or pendent; scale-like adult leaves are up to ⅛in (3mm) long. Female cones each contain a single, blue-black seed with a red or orange aril. ↕ to 30ft (10m), ↔ 10–30ft (3–10m). New Zealand. ❄ (min. 45°F/7°C)

DACTYLIS

POACEAE

Genus of 2 species of evergreen, perennial grasses from open grassland in Europe, N. Africa, and Asia. They have linear leaves and one-sided panicles of compressed, pale green spikelets. *D. glomerata* 'Variegata' looks best at the front of a border or in a rock garden.

• **CULTIVATION** Plant in fertile, well-drained soil in sun or partial shade.

• **PROPAGATION** Divide in early and midspring or in early autumn.

• **PESTS AND DISEASES** Several leaf diseases are common.

***D. glomerata* 'Variegata'.** Densely tufted, clump-forming, perennial grass with linear, white-variegated leaves, to 6in (15cm) long. Fluffy, pale green spikelets in one-sided panicles, 2in (5cm) long, are borne on stems 10in (25cm) long throughout summer. May be suitable as a groundcover in limited space. Remove shoots that revert to the green form. ↕ to 18in (45cm) in flower, ↔ 10in (25cm). Zone 6.

DACTYLORHIZA

Marsh orchid, Spotted orchid

ORCHIDACEAE

Genus of about 30 species of tuberous, deciduous, terrestrial orchids found in meadows, heathland, or marshy stream-sides in Europe, N. Africa, Asia, and North America. They have finger-like, flattened tubers and linear to lance-shaped, fleshy, usually mid-green, sometimes spotted leaves, 4–8in (10–20cm) long. Purple, lilac-purple, red, pink, or white flowers, with green, sometimes purplish bracts, are borne in dense, upright, terminal racemes, mostly 2–6in (5–15cm) long. Grow in a rock or woodland garden, or in a meadow planting.

• **CULTIVATION** Grow in moist but well-drained, humus-rich, leafy soil in partial shade. See also p.46.

• **PROPAGATION** Divide in early spring.

• **PESTS AND DISEASES** Infrequent.

D. elata, syn. *Orchis elata* (Robust marsh orchid). Terrestrial orchid with 6–10 linear to ovate-lance-shaped, sometimes brown- or purple-spotted leaves. Deep purple flowers, with long protruding bracts, are produced in racemes, 4–10in (10–25cm) long, in late spring. ↕ to 24in (60cm), ↔ 6in (15cm). S.W. Europe. Zone 6b.
D. foliosa ▣ syn. *D. maderensis*, *Orchis maderensis*. Robust, terrestrial orchid with 4–6 lance-shaped leaves, some-times brown- or purple-spotted. Pink to bright purple flowers, with bracts protruding or just hidden, in racemes 2–5in (5–13cm) long, are produced in late spring and early summer. ↕ 24in (60cm), ↔ 6in (15cm). Madeira. Zone 7.
D. fuchsii, syn. *D. maculata* subsp. *fuchsii*. Terrestrial orchid with 8–12 lance-shaped, purple-spotted leaves. Pale pink to white or mauve flowers, marked deep red or purple, are produced in late spring and early summer. ↕ 8–24in (20–60cm), ↔ 4in (10cm). Europe, W. Asia. Zone 6.
D. maculata (Heath spotted orchid). Terrestrial orchid with 5–12 lance-shaped, plain or brown- or purple-spotted leaves. Bears white, rose-pink, red, or mauve flowers from midspring to late summer. ↕ 6–24in (15–60cm), ↔ 6in (15cm). Europe, N. Africa. Zone 6. **subsp. *fuchsii*** see *D. fuchsii*.
D. maderensis see *D. foliosa*.

Dactylorhiza foliosa

DAHLIA

ASTERACEAE

Genus of about 30 species and some 20,000 cultivars of bushy, often tuberous-rooted, perennials from mountainous areas of Central America, grown for their blooms (flowerheads) in a variety of forms, colors, and patterns. Leaves are pinnate, sometimes pinnatifid to pinnatisect, and divided into oval leaflets with toothed margins and rounded tips, 8–20in (20–50cm) long, proportionate in size to the blooms, and are mid- to dark green. Cactus and laciniated blooms often have more delicate, finely cut leaves. Almost all currently grown cultivars have strong, straight stems and attractive foliage. Dahlias flower from midsummer to first frost, when many other plants are past their best. All are good for garden display and cutting; many, especially the giant-flowered dahlias, are suitable for exhibition. Plant different types in a bed, or group them in threes or fives in a mixed or herbaceous border. Those for exhibition or cut flowers are best grown in rows on their own. Bedding dahlias are low-growing and may be raised from seed and treated as annuals. They bloom from early or midsummer to autumn, especially if deadheaded; use for massed plantings, edging a border, and in containers.

Dahlias are first classified by bloom size as follows (commonly used designations and abbreviations in parentheses):

Size Categories

Giant (AA): over 10in (25cm) in diameter, at least 5in (13cm) in depth.
Large (A): 8–10in (20–25cm) in diameter, at least 4in (10cm) in depth.
Medium (B): 6–8in (15–20cm) in diameter, at least 3in (8cm) in depth.
Small (BB): 4–6in (10–15cm) in diameter, Ball varieties over 3½in (9cm).
Miniature (Min): 2–4in (5–10cm) in diameter, Miniature Ball varieties are 2–3½in (5–9cm).
Mignon: to 2in (5cm) in diameter, including Pompons and Mignon singles.

Fully double blooms, which show no central disk, are then classified by the following formations:

Decorative dahlias
Formal decorative (FD) dahlias have flat or nearly flat ray florets, regularly arranged, and tending to recurve toward the stem. Informal decorative (ID) dahlias have twisted, curled, or wavy ray florets, which may have an irregular arrangement.

Cactus dahlias
Semi-cactus dahlias (SC) have ray florets with revolute or downward-curled margins for up to one-half their length, which may be straight, incurved, or recurved. Straight cactus dahlias (C) have ray florets with revolute or downward-curled margins for more than half their length; the ray florets radiate in all directions from the center and may be straight or recurved. Incurved cactus dahlias (IC) have ray florets similar to straight cactus dahlias, but with pronounced curvature of the petals toward the center of the flowerhead.

Laciniated dahlias (LC)
Flowerheads composed of ray florets split at least ⅙ of their length and twisted, giving a fringed or fimbriated effect.

Ball (Ba), Miniature ball (Mba), Pompon dahlias (P)
Flowerheads ball-shaped or slightly flattened at the face. Ball dahlias have ray florets with fully involute or inward-curled margins for at least half their length, while pompon dahlias have ray florets that are involute their entire length.

Waterlily dahlias (WL)
Flowerheads composed of broad, slightly cupped outer florets. Side view of blooms is flat to saucer-shaped.

Other dahlia types, most of which are eight-petaled, single blooms, are also classified by formation:

Anemone dahlias
Flowerheads composed of ray florets around a center of tubular disk florets, presenting a pincushion appearance.

Collarette dahlias
Flowerheads composed of a single row of ray florets around an inner ring of shorter florets forming a collar around the disk.

Orchid dahlias
Flowerheads composed of a single row of ray florets around the disk, with involute or inward-curling margins for at least two-thirds of their length.

Peony dahlias
Flowerheads composed of two or more rows of ray florets surrounding the disk. Those adjacent to the disk may be twisted or curled.

Single and Mignon single dahlias
Flowerheads composed of a single row of uniform, evenly spaced ray florets in a flat plane surrounding the disk. Mignon singles are less than 2in (5cm) across.

Stellar dahlias (ST)
Flowerheads with ray florets that break gradually from immature florets to fully developed outer ray florets. Outer florets shouldl be narrow and involute, with a slight recurve to the stem.

Novelty dahlias (NO)
Dahlias with characteristics distinct and different from the present classifications with open centers (Novelty open dahlias, NO) or with closed centers (Novelty fully double dahlias, NX).

• **HARDINESS** *Dahlia* foliage blackens with the first frost, but tubers may be covered with a deep, dry mulch and left in the ground in the mildest parts of Zone 8. Elsewhere, lift plants for the winter (see below).

• **CULTIVATION** Grow in humus-rich, well-drained soil, in full sun. Use a high-nitrogen liquid fertilizer weekly in early summer, then a high-potassium liquid fertilizer weekly from midsummer to early autumn. Bedding dahlias need no staking or disbudding: just pinch out the growing point to encourage bushiness, and deadhead as the flowers fade. For taller dahlias, insert stakes at planting time. Moderately pinch, disbranch, and disbud, and deadhead to produce a showy display for three months or more. Dahlias thrive in the cool, moist climates of the Pacific Coast, where the blooms may be an inch larger and deeper than in hotter, drier climates. Plants grow 4–6ft (1.2–2m) tall, except for the low-growing, bedder types, but careful plant grooming can produce shorter, bushier plants. In midautumn, preferably when the foliage has been nipped by the first frost, cut back stems to 6in (15cm), and lift the tubers. Gently brush off the soil, and leave upside down to dry naturally. Dust with fungicide, then pack in boxes of vermiculite or dry sand, and store over winter in a well-ventilated, frost-free place. Check periodically for fungal infection, pare out any damaged tissue, and treat again with fungicide before returning to storage.

• **PROPAGATION** Take basal shoot cuttings from tubers started into growth in late winter or early spring in a greenhouse, and root under plastic cover or in a mist tent, with bottom heat. Alternatively, start clumps into growth in early spring, and when shoots are ¾in (2cm) long, divide clumps into 2 or more pieces, each with a shoot, and plant out 5in (13cm) deep after all danger of frost has passed. Sow seed of bedding dahlias in trays in early spring, in warmth; harden off, and plant out when all danger of frost has passed.

• **PESTS AND DISEASES** Aphids, stem borers, spider mites, caterpillars, earwigs, cucumber beetles, capsid bugs, flower thrips, planthoppers, and slugs may be troublesome. Also prone to powdery mildew, impatiens necrotic spot, dahlia mosaic viruses, smut, fungal leaf spots, soft rot, crown gall, blossom blights (especially gray mold), and tomato spotted wilt virus.

***D.* 'Akita No Hikari'** ▣ Medium-flowered novelty dahlia with deep, blood-red blooms. Flowerhead like a large double chrysanthemum.
***D.* 'Alfred Grille'** ▣ Medium-flowered incurved cactus dahlia with yellow and pink blooms.
***D.* 'Allie White'.** Tall-growing dahlia whose clear bright small informal blooms have excellent substance.
***D.* 'Allie Yellow'.** Low-growing dahlia with bright yellow miniature formal decorative blooms.
***D.* 'Alloway Candy'** ▣ Miniature-flowered stellar dahlia bearing deep pink blooms with an unusual cluster of tubular ray florets.
***D.* 'Alpen Cherub'.** Miniature-flowered collarette dahlia bearing white blooms with a white collar.
***D.* 'Alpen Fury'.** Anemone-flowered dahlia with red ray florets and a pincushion of flame-colored red and yellow elongated tubular disk florets.
***D.* 'Alta Bishop'.** Miniature-flowered single dahlia bearing striking red blooms with yellow centers. Good for flower arrangements.
***D.* 'Altara Majesty'.** Giant-flowered semi-cactus dahlia with light yellow petals and outstanding form.
***D.* 'Alva's Supreme'** ▣ Large-flowered formal decorative dahlia bearing light yellow blooms with flat ray florets.
***D.* 'Amberglow'.** Relatively low-growing dahlia with bronze-orange miniature ball blooms of excellent form.

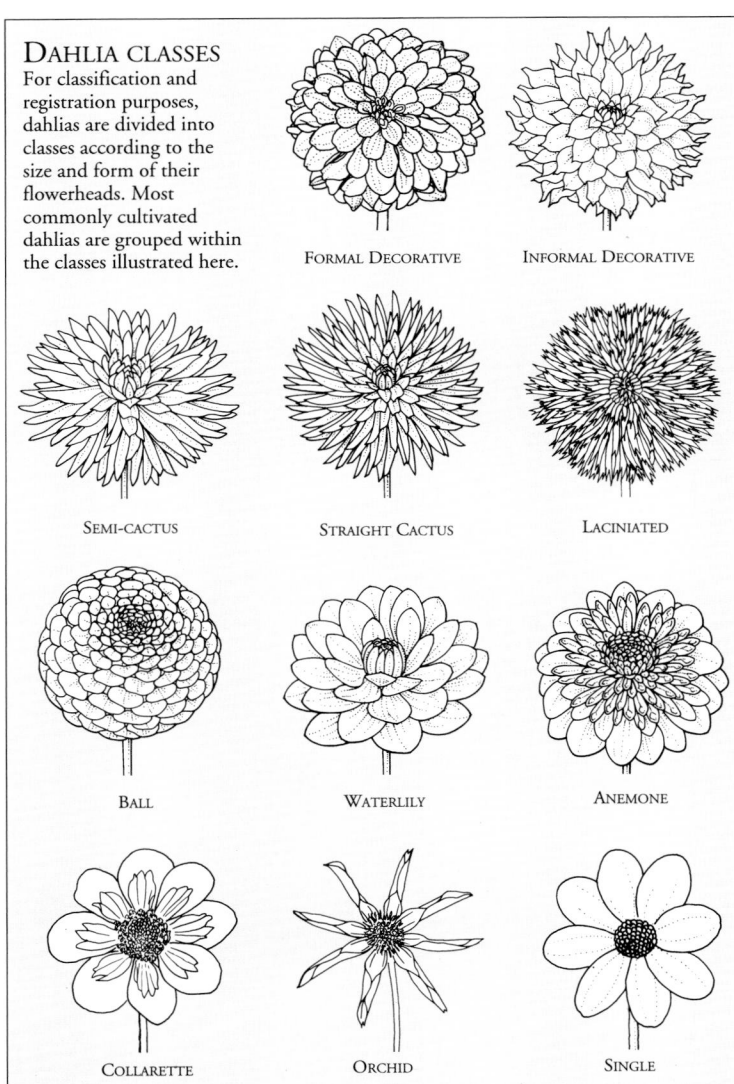

DAHLIA CLASSES

For classification and registration purposes, dahlias are divided into classes according to the size and form of their flowerheads. Most commonly cultivated dahlias are grouped within the classes illustrated here.

FORMAL DECORATIVE

INFORMAL DECORATIVE

SEMI-CACTUS

STRAIGHT CACTUS

LACINIATED

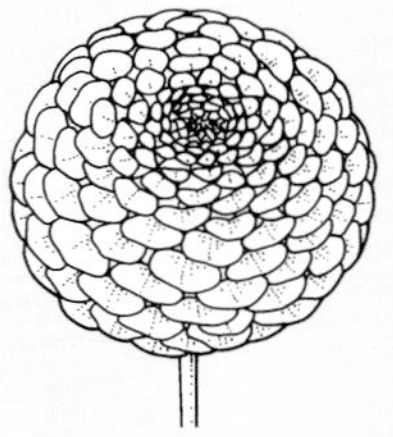
BALL

WATERLILY

ANEMONE

COLLARETTE

ORCHID

SINGLE

D

Dahlia 'Akita No Hikari'

Dahlia 'Alfred Grille'

Dahlia 'Alloway Candy'

Dahlia 'Color Magic'

***D.* 'Amy K'** ▣ Medium-flowered semi-cactus dahlia bearing many pink on white blooms over a long season.
***D.* 'April Dawn'** ▣ Medium-flowered informal decorative dahlia with carmine-rose and white blooms of perfect form. Excellent for exhibition.
***D.* 'Athalie'.** Small-flowered semi-cactus dahlia bearing medium to dark pink blooms with a touch of bronze.
***D.* 'Aurora's Kiss'** ▣ Miniature ball dahlia with darkest red blooms.
***D.* 'Azuma Kagami'.** Miniature-flowered anemone dahlia with dark red ray florets and dark red elongated pincushion centers.
***D.* 'Barbarry Gem'.** Miniature ball dahlia with a prolific dark red blooms.
***D.* 'Barbarry Red Baron'.** Miniature formal decorative dahlia; dark red blooms.
***D.* 'Bella S'.** Giant informal decorative dahlia with very large lavender blooms.
***D.* 'Bert Pitt'.** Medium-flowered informal decorative dahlia bearing deep red blooms with white tips.
***D.* 'Bishop of Llandaff'** ▣ Miniature-flowered peony dahlia with black-red foliage. Bears dark red blooms with black centers and yellow ray floret bases.
***D.* 'B.J. Beauty'** ▣ Medium- to large-flowered informal decorative dahlia with creamy white blooms.
***D.* 'Blended Beauty'.** Miniature-flowered straight cactus dahlia with dark purple-red and white blooms.
***D.* 'Bonaventure'.** Giant-flowered formal decorative dahlia with blooms in blends of primrose-yellow and orange.
***D.* 'Bonne Esperance'.** Mignon-flowered single dahlia bearing many daisy-like, pale shell-pink blooms on bushy 24in (60cm) plants.
***D.* 'Brenda Sue'.** Peony dahlia with orange blooms.
***D.* 'Brian R'.** Medium formal decorative dahlia with lavender blooms that reflex to the stem.
***D.* 'Bright Star'.** Small-flowered incurved cactus dahlia producing tangerine blooms with distinct, striking "elbows."
***D.* 'Bristol Fleck'.** Prolific blooming dahlia with variegated small formal blooms of white splashed with purple.
***D.* 'Bristol Karma'.** Dahlia with small semi-cactus pink blooms.
***D.* 'Bristol Sunny'.** Dahlia with miniature semi-cactus yellow blooms.
***D.* 'Brookside Cheri'.** Small-flowered straight cactus dahlia bearing dark pink blooms with a yellow center and bronze-green foliage on strong stems.
***D.* 'Brookside J. Cooley'.** Miniature-flowered informal decorative dahlia. Many perfect, blocky-shaped, light primrose-yellow blooms raised well above the foliage.
***D.* 'Brookside Snowball'.** Small-flowered ball dahlia with white blooms.
***D.* 'Camano Cloud'.** Small-flowered semi-cactus dahlia in shades of pink.
***D.* 'Camano Messenger'.** Large-flowered cactus dahlia bearing soft pink and yellow blooms on long stems.
***D.* 'Camano Pet'.** Tall-growing dahlia with many blooms of small stellar form, a blend of yellow with orange toward the outer portions. Direct sun brings out the most vivid color of the blooms.
***D.* 'Camano Shadows'.** Medium-flowered incurved cactus dahlia bearing spiky, purple and white blooms.
***D.* 'Camano Sitka'** ▣ Dahlia with large incurved cactus blooms in striking combination of yellow and bronze.
***D.* 'Cameo'.** Small-flowered waterlily dahlia bearing very pale yellow blooms with wide, cupped ray florets.
***D.* 'Campo's Hush'.** Medium-flowered semi-cactus dahlia; pale yellow blooms have perfect form and firm substance.
***D.* 'CG Coral'.** Vigorous cactus dahlia with numerous small dark pink blooms.
***D.* 'Charlie Two'** ▣ Medium-flowered formal decorative dahlia. Bears pale yellow blooms with slightly incurved ray florets.
***D.* 'Cherwell Goldcrest'.** Semi-cactus dahlia with small bronze blooms, often with yellow in the center portions.
***D.* 'Chilson's Pride'.** Small-flowered informal decorative dahlia bearing blooms in blends of white and pink with notched, scalloped ray florets.
***D.* 'Chimacum Katie'.** Dahlia with small formal decorative lavender blooms.
***D.* 'Chimacum Pumpkin'.** Low-growing pompom dahlia with orange blooms of outstanding form and color.
***D.* 'Chimacum Troy'.** Dahlia with miniature purple blooms.
***D.* 'Christmas Carol'.** Miniature-flowered collarette dahlia bearing blooms with 8 bright red ray florets surrounding red collars.
***D.* 'Clara Huston'.** Giant incurved cactus dahlia with vivid orange blooms.
***D.* 'Clearview Arla'** ▣ Miniature-flowered dahlia with semi-cactus vivid lavender blooms.
***D.* 'Clearview David'** ▣ Small formal decorative dahlia with pointed vivid lavender blooms and lighter-colored portions in the interior of the petals.
***D.* 'Clyde's Choice'.** Giant-flowered formal decorative dahlia; orange blooms.
***D.* 'Color Magic'** ▣ Large-flowered semi-cactus dahlia bearing gold, orange-splashed blooms with slashed ray florets.
***D.* 'Comet'.** Miniature-flowered anemone dahlia with dark red ray florets and a pincushion of dark red elongated tubular disk florets.
***D.* 'Connecticut Dancer'.** Small-flowered formal decorative dahlia bearing white blooms evenly splashed dark red.
***D.* 'Cornel'.** Ball-flowered dahlia with dark red petals of outstanding form.
***D.* 'Creve Coeur'** ▣ Giant-flowered semi-cactus dahlia with brilliant crimson blooms on strong stems.
***D.* 'Crichton Honey'.** Small-flowered ball dahlia with honey-bronze blooms.
***D.* 'Daisy'.** Mignon-flowered single dahlia bearing daisy-like blooms of pink ray florets around a dark pink disk.
***D.* 'Danum Meteor'** ▣ Relatively low-growing semi-cactus dahlia with giant dark red blooms.

Dahlia 'Alva's Supreme'

Dahlia 'Amy K'

Dahlia 'April Dawn'

Dahlia 'Aurora's Kiss'

Dahlia 'Bishop of Llandaff'

Dahlia 'B.J. Beauty'

Dahlia 'Camano Sitka'

Dahlia 'Charlie Two'

Dahlia 'Clearview Arla'

Dahlia 'Clearview David'

Dahlia 'Creve Coeur'

Dahlia 'Danum Meteor'

Dahlia 'Formby Perfection'

***D.* 'Dark Magic'.** Small-flowered informal decorative deep purple and white blooms.
***D.* 'Delta Red'.** Single dahlia with 8 red ray florets around a yellow disk center.
***D.* 'Devon Citation'.** Medium-size semi-cactus dahlia with clean bright white blooms of exceptionalform.
***D.* 'Downham Royale'.** Miniature-flowered ball dahlia; dark purple blooms.
***D.* 'Duet'.** Medium-flowered formal decorative dahlia bearing dark red blooms with white-tipped ray florets.
***D.* 'Edna C'.** Medium-flowered formal decorative dahlia with fully recurved, lemon-yellow blooms.
***D.* 'Elizabeth Hammett'.** Miniature-flowered formal decorative dahlia bearing pale, lavender-blushed blooms with white edges.
***D.* 'Elma Elizabeth'** ■ Large-flowered formal decorative dahlia with glistening pinkish lavender ray florets.
***D.* 'Elsie Huston'.** Large-flowered informal decorative dahlia with abundant, prominent, watermelon-pink blooms.
***D.* 'Elvira'.** Dahlia with dark pink peony blooms.
***D.* 'Embrace'** ■ Relatively low-growing semi-cactus dahlia with small yellowish bronze blooms.
***D.* 'Fidalgo Splash'.** Medium-flowered informal decorative dahlia with eye-catching, purple and white blooms.
***D.* 'Figurine'.** Small-flowered waterlily dahlia with dainty, pale pink blooms on long stems.
***D.* 'Formby Perfection'** ■ Medium-flowered formal decorative dahlia with perfectly arranged, magenta-lavender ray florets, recurved to the stems.
***D.* 'Gallery Art Deco'.** Dwarf early-flowering dahlia, orange stellar blooms.
***D.* 'Gallery Rembrandt'.** Dwarf early-blooming dahlia with miniature formal decorative purple and white blooms.
***D.* 'Gateshead Festival'** ■ Small-flowered formal decorative dahlia with blooms in blends of peach, orange, and yellow.
***D.* 'Gay Princess'** ■ Small-flowered informal decorative dahlia with blooms in blends of white and lilac-pink.
***D.* 'Gitt's Attention'.** Small-flowered dahlia with informal decorative white blooms.
***D.* 'Gitt's Perfection'.** Relatively low-growing dahlia with large informal decorative lavender and white blooms.
***D.* 'Glenbank Twinkle'.** Miniature-flowered straight cactus dahlia bearing fully globular, pink-tipped, blue-white blooms with spiky ray florets.
***D.* 'Glenplace'.** Pompon dahlia bearing deep purple blooms of tiny balls on long, stiff stems.
***D.* 'Glorisa'.** Tall-growing dahlia with medium formal decorative blooms in an attractive variegated combination of yellow overlaid with red.
***D.* 'Goldie Gull'** ■ Miniature-flowered anemone dahlia with pink outer ray florets and a pincushion of yellow elongated, tubular disk florets.
***D.* 'Goldilocks'.** Small-flowered informal decorative dahlia bearing canary-yellow blooms with full, twisted ray florets that give a tousled appearance.
***D.* 'Grenidor Pastelle'** ■ Medium-flowered semi-cactus dahlia bearing salmon-pink blooms with cream bases well above the foliage.
***D.* 'GW's Babe'.** Miniature semi-cactus dahlia with attractive blooms in a light blend of yellow and dark pink.
***D.* 'Hallmark'** ■ Dahlia with dark pink pompon blooms of outstanding form.
***D.* 'Hamari Accord'** ■ Medium-flowered semi-cactus dahlia with butter-yellow blooms.
***D.* 'Hamari Gold'** ■ Large-flowered informal decorative dahlia with deep gold-bronze blooms.
***D.* 'Hamari Sunshine'.** Medium-flowered dahlia with informal decorative bright yellow blooms with an attractive twist at the ends of the petals. In cool climates, produces large blooms.
***D.* 'Hamilton Lillian'.** Small-flowered formal decorative dahlia with very uniform, bronze-orange blooms on strong, straight stems.
***D.* 'Hillcrest Jessica J.'.** Dahlia with medium bright purple semi-cactus blooms.
***D.* 'Hillcrest Kismet'** ■ Small-flowered dahlia with formal decorative pink blooms that reflex to the stem. In cool climates, bears medium-size blooms.
***D.* 'Hollyhill Electra'** ■ Large-flowered dahlia with incurved cactus reddish orange blooms, which appear dark pink in some climates.
***D.* 'Hollyhill Purely Purple'.** Dahlia with miniature formal decorative vivid purple blooms.
***D.* 'Honka'** ■ Miniature-flowered orchid dahlia bearing lemon-yellow blooms with ray florets arranged in an eight-pointed star.
***D.* 'Horse Feathers'** ■ Prolific blooming dahlia with fully double white blooms in which each petal has spurs or thistles, accounting for its classification as a fully double novelty.
***D.* 'Hy Clown'.** Small dahlia with formal decorative blooms in a vivid blend of yellow and bronze. The petals reflex to the stem; depth sometimes exceeds diameter of the blooms.
***D.* 'Hy Mom'.** Giant incurved dahlia with bright white blooms that achieve great depth, especially in cool, moist climates.
***D.* 'Hy Pimento'.** Tall-growing semi-cactus dahlia with small variegated, red-splashed yellow blooms of excellent form. In cool climates, produces medium-size blooms.
***D.* 'Hy Sockeye'.** Formal decorative dahlia bearing vivid red blooms.
***D.* 'Hy Suntan'.** Dahlia with bronze-colored miniature ball blooms.
D. imperialis ■ Tender perennial or subshrub with glaucous, red-tinged or green stems bearing 2- or 3-pinnate leaves, 24–36in (60–90cm) long, consisting of ovate to elliptic, toothed, softly hairy leaflets. Bears terminal panicles, 18in (45cm) long, of pale pink, lavender, or white blooms with yellow disks, from late autumn to early winter. Ideal as a seasonal specimen plant. ↕ 12–18ft (4–5.5m), ↔ 4–6ft (1.2m–2m). Guatemala to Colombia.
***D.* 'Inflammation'.** Mignon-flowered single dahlia with bright tangerine blooms on low-growing plants.
***D.* 'Inland Dynasty'.** Giant-flowered semi-cactus dahlia with spectacular pale yellow to canary-yellow blooms.

Dahlia 'Elma Elizabeth'

Dahlia 'Embrace'

Dahlia 'Gateshead Festival'

Dahlia 'Gay Princess'

Dahlia 'Goldie Gull'

Dahlia 'Grenidor Pastelle'

Dahlia 'Hallmark'

Dahlia 'Hamari Accord'

Dahlia 'Hamari Gold'

Dahlia 'Hillcrest Kismet'

Dahlia 'Hollyhill Electra'

Dahlia 'Honka'

Dahlia imperialis

***D.* 'Irene's Pride'.** Giant-flowered semi-cactus dahlia producing bronze-toned blooms.
***D.* 'Islander'.** Large-flowered informal decorative dahlia with abundant, deep salmon-pink blooms.
***D.* 'Ivory Palaces'.** Relatively low-growing dahlia with giant informal decorative pale yellow blooms, often set close to the first set of leaves.
***D.* 'Janal Amy'.** Relatively low-growing semi-cactus dahlia with large bright yellow blooms.
***D.* 'Jennie'** ■ Medium-flowered laciniated dahlia with white, lavender-pink-tipped blooms.
***D.* 'Jessica'** ■ Small-flowered straight cactus dahlia bearing distinctive, canary-yellow blooms with red-tipped ray florets.
***D.* 'Jessie G'.** Small-flowered ball dahlia bearing deep, royal purple blooms with perfect form. Strong grower.
***D.* 'Joe K'.** Miniature-flowered formal decorative dahlia with perfect, deep crimson blooms, recurved to the stems.
***D.* 'Jomanda'.** Small formal decorative dahlia with vivid orange blooms; in cool weather, late in the season, often acquires a ball form.
***D.* 'Joshua Juul'** ■ Single-flowered dahlia with vivid blooms of white toward the edge, blending to a purple center, with yellow central disk flowers.
***D.* 'Juanita'.** Medium-flowered straight cactus dahlia with dark red blooms.
***D.* 'Just Married'.** Dahlia with medium laciniated lavender and white blooms.
***D.* 'Just Peachy'.** Small-flowered semi-cactus dahlia with blooms in blends of peach, gold, and yellow.
***D.* 'Juul's Lotus'** ■ Waterlily dahlia with attractive blooms of a blend of white with lavender near the petal tips.
***D.* 'Juul's Star'.** Miniature-flowered orchid dahlia with star-like, white blooms.
***D.* 'K-Andy'.** Miniature orchid-flowered dahlia with dark red petaloids and dark red ray florets arranged in an 8-pointed star.
***D.* 'Karenglen'.** Miniature formal decorative dahlia with red blooms of exceptional form.
***D.* 'Karris 150'** ■ Small cactus dahlia with white blooms of excellent form and depth.
***D.* 'Kathy's Choice'.** Miniature cactus dahlia with bright yellow blooms.
***D.* 'Kelvin Floodlight'.** Older, easy-to-grow dahlia with giant formal decorative yellow blooms, but with less depth than in the newer cultivars.
***D.* 'Kenora Challenger'.** Medium-size semi-cactus dahlia with pure white blooms. Does best in a cool climate, bearing large blooms.
***D.* 'Kenora Clyde'.** Giant-flowered semi-cactus dahlia bearing glistening, creamy white blooms.
***D.* 'Kenora Fireball'.** Small-flowered ball dahlia bearing crimson blooms with lighter reverses and ray florets with tightly involute or upward-curled margins.
***D.* 'Kenora Jubilee'.** Large semi-cactus dahlia with bright white blooms of exceptional form.
***D.* 'Kenora Lisa'** ■ Medium-flowered formal decorative dahlia with abundant, vivid, purple-rose blooms.
***D.* 'Kenora Majestica'** ■ Medium-flowered cactus dahlia of exceptional form, with bright lavender blooms, set against white toward the center petals.
***D.* 'Kenora Moonbeam'.** Small-flowered informal decorative dahlia bearing pale, creamy yellow blooms.
***D.* 'Kenora Spirit'.** Medium-flowered dahlia with laciniated bright white petals.
***D.* 'Kenora Sunset'.** Medium-flowered semi-cactus dahlia with vivid flame-colored blooms, bright yellow in the center, blending to vivid red toward the edges of the petals.
***D.* 'Kenora Wildfire'** ■ Large-flowered semi-cactus dahlia with striking, deep red to brilliant crimson blooms.

Dahlia 'Jessica'

***D.* 'Ken's Flame'.** Small-flowered waterlily dahlia with brilliant blooms in blends of bright scarlet and yellow.
***D.* 'Kidd's Climax'.** Large-flowered formal decorative dahlia with pink blooms suffused with gold.
***D.* 'Kiwi Gloria'** ■ Small-flowered straight cactus dahlia with many blooms in blends of white and lavender-pink.
***D.* 'K-K-K Katie'.** Miniature orchid-flowered dahlia with petals orange on both the front and reverse, and ray florets arranged in an 8-pointed star.
***D.* 'Lady Darlene'** ■ Medium-flowered formal decorative dahlia bearing blooms in blends of crimson and golden yellow.
***D.* 'L'Ancresse'.** Small-flowered ball dahlia with perfectly formed, white, lavender-edged blooms.
***D.* 'Lavender Athalie'** ■ Small-flowered semi-cactus dahlia with lavender-pink blooms held well above the foliage.
***D.* 'Lavid'.** Dahlia with small informal decorative lavender blooms.
***D.* 'Light Accord',** a sport of 'Hamari Accord'. Medium-flowered semi-cactus dahlia with very pale yellow blooms that can appear white in bright sunlight.
***D.* 'Lismore Moonlight'.** Dahlia with yellow pompon blooms.
***D.* 'Little Willow'.** Pompon dahlia with bright white blooms.
***D.* 'Lois V'.** Medium-flowered laciniated dahlia with canary-yellow blooms.
***D.* 'Lupin Dixie'.** Small-flowered straight cactus dahlia with lilac blooms.
***D.* 'Lupin Sheila'** ■ Miniature-flowered orchid dahlia with ray florets arranged in an 8-pointed star, in a flat plane surrounding yellow-centered disk flowers. Ray florets are dark pink on the reverse; their white fronts are seen only partially.

Dahlia 'Horse Feathers'

Dahlia 'Jennie'

Dahlia 'Joshua Juul'

Dahlia 'Juul's Lotus'

Dahlia 'Karris 150'

Dahlia 'Kenora Lisa'

Dahlia 'Kenora Majestica'

Dahlia 'Kenora Wildfire'

Dahlia 'Kiwi Gloria'

Dahlia 'Lady Darlene'

Dahlia 'Lavender Athalie'

Dahlia 'Lupin Sheila'

***D.* 'Madame de Rosa'.** Tall-growing medium-flowered cactus dahlia with yellow blooms of excellent form. From South Africa.
***D.* 'Magic Moment'** ▣ Medium-flowered semi-cactus dahlia bearing white, lavender-edged blooms with twisted, fringed ray florets.
***D.* 'Maisey Mooney'.** Large informal decorative dahlia with vivid bright white blooms of exceptional depth and form.
***D.* 'Majestic Kerkrade'** ▣ Small-flowered straight cactus dahlia bearing salmon-pink blooms with yellow bases.
***D.* 'Manor Sunset'.** Medium-flowered semi-cactus dahlia with abundant, flame-orange and yellow blooms.
***D.* 'Marie Schnugg'** ▣ Miniature-flowered orchid dahlia; dark red blooms.
***D.* 'Mary'.** Dahlia with attractive. formal lavender and white blooms. Produces medium blooms in cool climates, small in warmer climates.
***D.* 'Mary's Jomanda'.** ▣ Miniature-flowered semi-cactus dahlia bearing well-formed, peach-pink blooms.
***D.* 'Matthew Juul'.** Dwarf mignon single dahlia with 8 petals of orange and dark red blend, surrounding yellow central disk flowers.
***D.* 'Minerva Magic'.** Medium laciniated dahlia with bright white blooms of excellent form and depth.
***D.* 'Mingus Whitney'.** Relatively low-growing dahlia with giant informal decorative bright white blooms.
***D.* 'Michael J'.** Miniature-flowered formal decorative dahlia bearing red-freckled, yellow blooms.
***D.* 'Mini Red'.** Miniature-flowered straight cactus dahlia bearing crimson blooms with excellent form.
***D.* 'Mi Wong'** ▣ Pompon dahlia bearing white blooms, suffused pink.
***D.* 'Mom and Dad'.** Giant-flowered informal decorative dahlia with blooms in blends of pastel pink and yellow.
***D.* 'Moonlight Sonata'.** Vigorous-growing dahlia with informal decorative blooms in a striking blend of dark pink, yellow, and orange. In cool climates, produce medium blooms, and sometimes of large or giant size.
***D.* 'Moorplace'** ▣ Pompon dahlia with dark red blooms; excellent form.
***D.* 'Moray Susan'** ▣ Waterlily dahlia with blooms in a beautiful dark blend of red and yellow, of exceptional form.
***D.* 'My Beverly'.** Small-flowered dahlia with laciniated vivid yellow blooms, with dark pink tips.
***D.* 'My Wife'.** Medium-flowered dahlia with laciniated red blooms.
***D.* 'Nargold'** ▣ South African-raised medium-flowered laciniated dahlia with flame-colored blooms.
***D.* 'Nenekazi'** ▣ South African-raised dahlia with medium laciniated vivid red and pink blooms.
***D.* 'Nepos'** ▣ Small-flowered waterlily dahlia with blooms in blends of white and lavender, on strong stems.
***D.* 'Nettie'.** Miniature-flowered ball dahlia with many lemon-yellow blooms.
***D.* 'Nicole C'.** Miniature-flowered straight cactus dahlia bearing light tangerine blooms above delicate foliage.
***D.* 'Night Life'.** Small-flowered straight cactus dahlia with bright crimson, gold-tipped blooms.
***D.* 'Nina Chester'** ▣ Small-flowered formal decorative dahlia bearing white lilac-tipped blooms.
***D.* 'Nita'.** Medium-flowered straight cactus dahlia bearing fully double lavender blooms with red variegation.
***D.* 'Northwest Cosmos'.** Single-flowered dahlia with 8 ray florets in a dark blend of lavender running purple near the center, surrounding bright yellow disk flowers.

Dahlia 'Mary Jomanda'

***D.* 'Odyssey'** ▣ Dahlia with miniature ball blooms in lavender and white.
***D.* 'Paisley Gem'** ▣ Small-flowered formal decorative dahlia with purple-splashed, lavender blooms.
***D.* 'Pam Howden'** ▣ Small-flowered waterlily dahlia of finest form with bright orange blooms, often with yellow toward the center.
***D.* 'Peaches-n-Cream'** ▣ Miniature-flowered formal decorative dahlia bearing soft peach and cream blooms.
***D.* 'Pineapple Lollipop'.** Miniature-flowered formal decorative dahlia bearing yellow-ochre blooms.
***D.* 'Pink Jupiter'** ▣ Large-flowered semi-cactus dahlia bearing clear pink blooms with lighter, flatter, yellow-based central ray florets.
***D.* 'Pink Shirley Alliance'.** Small-flowered straight cactus dahlia bearing lilac-pink blooms.
***D.* 'Pocrates'.** Miniature-flowered ball dahlia with pure white blooms.
***D.* 'Polventon Supreme'.** Tall-growing dahlia with light yellow ball bloom.
***D.* 'Pooh'.** Collarette dahlia with bicolored orange and yellow ray florets surrounding yellow petaloids.
***D.* 'Porcelain'.** Medium-flowered waterlily dahlia with white blooms tinged pale lavender.
***D.* 'Powder Gull'.** Low-growing dahlia with bright pink peony blooms; a few rows of formal decorative petals surround yellow disk flowers.
***D.* 'Poppet'.** Pompon dahlia bearing tiny, tangerine blooms.
***D.* 'Preston Park'** ▣ Miniature-flowered single dahlia bearing bright scarlet blooms with nearly black foliage, on short stems. Attracts butterflies.
***D.* 'Primrose Pet'.** Small-flowered dahlia producing stellar bright yellow blooms.
***D.* 'Prom Queen'.** Miniature-flowered informal decorative dahlia producing abundant blooms in blends of soft pink and white.

Dahlia 'Magic Moment'

Dahlia 'Majestic Kerkrade'

Dahlia 'Marie Schnugg'

Dahlia 'Mi Wong'

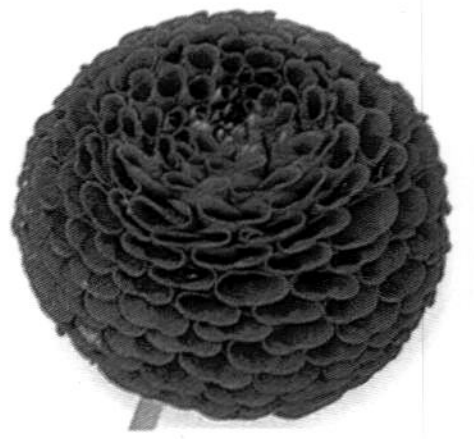
Dahlia 'Moorplace'

Dahlia 'Moray Susan'

Dahlia 'Nargold'

Dahlia 'Nenekazi'

Dahlia 'Nepos'

Dahlia 'Nina Chester'

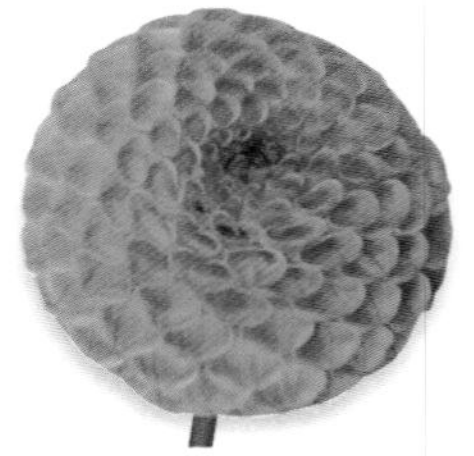
Dahlia 'Odyssey'

Dahlia 'Paisley Gem'

Dahlia 'Pam Howden'

Dahlia 'Peaches-n-Cream'

Dahlia 'Pink Jupiter'

Dahlia 'Preston Park'

Dahlia 'Ruskin Diane'

Dahlia 'Ruskin Marigold'

***D.* 'Rebecca Lynn'.** Miniature-flowered formal decorative dahlia bearing deep pink blooms, often with darker stripes, on short stems.
***D.* 'Redskin'.** Miniature-flowered dahlia, grown as an annual, bearing blooms in a range of colors, including scarlet-red, lilac-pink, and orange, above bronze foliage. ‡↔ 18–24in (45–60cm).
***D.* 'Red Velvet'.** Small-flowered waterlily dahlia bearing vibrant scarlet blooms with yellow near the centers.
***D.* 'Rejman's Polish Kid'.** Miniature formal decorative dahlia has bicolored petals with striking red with white tips.
***D.* 'Rembrandt'.** Dwarf mignon-flowered single dahlia producing black-red blooms.
***D.* 'Robann's Royal'.** Tall-growing lavender dahlia with miniature ball blooms.
***D.* 'Robin Hood'.** Ball dahlia with blooms of excellent form in blends of red-orange to pink, on strong stems.
***D.* 'Rokewood Opal'.** Cactus dahlia with small lavender ball blooms.
***D.* 'Rose Toscano'.** Miniature-flowered formal decorative dahlia with soft peach blooms and clean foliage.
***D.* 'Ruskin Diane'** ■ Small-flowered formal decorative dahlia with butter-yellow blooms.
***D.* 'Ruskin Marigold'** ■ Small cactus dahlia with bright orange blooms of exceptional color and form.
***D.* 'Sam Huston'.** Tall-growing lavender dahlia with miniature ball blooms.
***D.* 'Santa Claus'** ■ Small-flowered informal decorative dahlia with white blooms edged in candy-cane red.
***D.* 'Sean C'. Collarette'.** Dahlia with purple ray florets surrounding dark purple and white petaloids.
***D.* 'Shea's Rainbow'** ■ Miniature cactus dahlia with attractive variegated pink and yellow blooms.
***D.* 'Shinkyoku'.** Striking dahlia with fully double novelty blooms in vivid purple, whose form is similar to that of a spider chrysanthemum.
***D.* 'Shipley Spot Lenny'** ■ Small-flowered formal decorative dahlia; white-tipped, scarlet blooms on strong stems.
***D.* 'Show 'N' Tell'** ■ Large-flowered semi-cactus dahlia bearing crimson-tipped, gold blooms with twisted ray florets, giving a tousled appearance.
***D.* 'Sir Alf Ramsey'** ■ Vigorous dahlia with exceptionally sizable giant informal decorative lavender and white blooms.
***D.* 'Snoho Doris'** ■ Ball dahlia with dark bronze and red blooms.
***D.* 'Snoho Peggy'.** Small-flowered ball dahlia bearing perfectly formed, deep pink blooms over a long season.
***D.* 'Spartacus'.** Large-flowered informal decorative dahlia bearing recurved, perfectly formed, blood-red blooms.
***D.* 'Stellyvonne'.** Large-flowered laciniated dahlia with bright canary-yellow blooms.
***D.* 'Sterling Silver'.** Medium-flowered formal decorative dahlia with late, almost ball-shaped, white blooms.
***D.* 'Stoneleigh Joyce'.** Pompon dahlia with red blooms of excellent form.
***D.* 'Sugartown Sunrise'** ■ Tall-growing dahlia with exceptional formal decorative pink and creamy yellow blooms, 3½–5in (9–13cm) across. In cool climates, bears small flowers; miniature in areas with hotter summers.
***D.* 'Taratahi Lilac'.** Cactus dahlia with incurved lavender and white blooms.
***D.* 'Taratahi Ruby'** ■ Waterlily dahlia with outstanding red blooms.
***D.* 'Tarahahi Sunrise'.** Waterlily dahlia of exceptional form with attractive yellow and orange blooms.
***D.* 'Taylor Nelson'.** Small-flowered semi-cactus dahlia bearing well-formed, recurved, cardinal-red blooms.
***D.* 'Ted's Choice'.** Small-flowered formal decorative dahlia bearing blooms of lavender and purple.
***D.* 'The Baron'.** Small-flowered formal decorative dahlia with purple blooms.
***D.* 'The Queen'.** Small-flowered semi-cactus dahlia with mauve-pink blooms.
***D.* 'Thistle'.** Small-flowered novelty dahlia bearing bronze blooms with small extensions on the ray florets, giving a prickly appearance.
***D.* 'Tom Yano'.** Large-flowered semi-cactus dahlia bearing striking, deep blood-red blooms.
***D.* 'Trelyn Kiwi'** ■ Small cactus dahlia with white blooms flushed with pink or lavender. In shade, blooms pure white.
***D.* 'Tui Avis'.** Low-growing cactus dahlia with miniature pink blooms.
***D.* 'Ukraine'.** Giant-flowered informal decorative dahlia bearing bright yellow blooms with twisted ray florets.
***D.* 'Urchin'** ■ Small laciniated cactus dahlia with dark red blooms.
***D.* 'Valley Porcupine'.** Unusual novelty dahlia with miniature involute petals.
***D.* 'Verda'** ■ Vigorous comparatively low-growing semi-cactus dahlia with pure white large blooms.
***D.* 'Vernon Rose'** ■ Small-flowered formal decorative dahlia with pink blooms splashed dark red.
***D.* 'Vicki'** ■ Vigorous tall-growing semi-cactus dahlia with yellow blooms.
***D.* 'Victor D'.** Miniature-flowered ball dahlia bearing yellow-touched, deep pink blooms.
***D.* 'Walter Hardisty'.** Giant-flowered informal decorative dahlia bearing snow-white blooms.
***D.* 'Weston Pirate'** ■ Miniature cactus dahlia with attractive large red blooms.
***D.* 'Weston Spanish Dancer'** ■ Miniature cactus dahlia with striking flame red blooms around yellow center.
***D.* 'Wiggles'.** Miniature-flowered straight cactus dahlia bearing cadmium-

Dahlia 'Woodland's Uptown Girl'

orange blooms with incurved ray florets.
***D.* 'Wildwood Marie'.** Waterlily dahlia with dark pink blooms.
***D.* 'Windhaven Blush'** ■ Large semi-cactus dahlia whose yellow blooms have a red blush in full sunlight.
***D.* 'Windhaven Highlight'.** Tall-growing cactus dahlia with medium incurved rich yellow blooms.
***D.* 'Wine Frost'.** Miniature-flowered orchid dahlia bearing dark purple-red blooms with white reverses.
***D.* 'Woodland's Uptown Girl'** ■ Miniature dahlia with formal decorative red blooms.
***D.* 'Woodland Wildthing'.** Semi-cactus dahlia with medium-size orange blooms; the petals can have unusual twists.
***D.* 'Wootton Cupid'** ■ Small-flowered ball dahlia with abundant, dark pink blooms on strong stems.
***D.* 'Yellow Baby'.** Pompon dahlia with yellow blooms, a popular variety.
***D.* 'Zorro'** ■ Giant-flowered informal decorative dahlia with dark red blooms.

Dahlia 'Santa Claus'

Dahlia 'Shea's Rainbow'

Dahlia 'Shipley Spot Lenny'

Dahlia 'Show 'N' Tell'

Dahlia 'Sir Alf Ramsey'

Dahlia 'Snoho Doris'

Dahlia 'Sugartown Sunrise'

Dahlia 'Taratahi Ruby'

Dahlia 'Trelyn Kiwi'

Dahlia 'Urchin'

Dahlia 'Verda'

Dahlia 'Vernon Rose'

Dahlia 'Vicki'

Dahlia 'Weston Pirate'

Dahlia 'Weston Spanish Dancer'

Dahlia 'Windhaven Blush'

Dahlia 'Wootton Cupid'

Dahlia 'Zorro'

D

Dais cotinifolia (inset: flower detail)

DAIS

THYMELAEACEAE

Genus of 2 species of deciduous or evergreen shrubs and trees from forest margins and damp, wooded slopes in Madagascar and South Africa. They produce alternate or opposite, obovate to oblong-elliptic leaves, and are grown for their terminal umbels of tubular flowers. Where not hardy, grow in a cool greenhouse. In warmer climates, grow in a border or as a specimen plant.
• **CULTIVATION** Under glass, grow in soil-based potting mix in full light. In growth, water freely and apply balanced liquid fertilizer monthly; keep just moist in winter. Outdoors, grow in fertile, moist soil in full sun. Pruning group 1.
• **PROPAGATION** Sow seed at 61–64°F (16–18°C) in spring. Root semi-ripe cuttings in summer.
• **PESTS AND DISEASES** Spider mites may infest greenhouse plants.

D. cotinifolia ■ Bushy, rounded shrub or small tree, deciduous in cool climates, evergreen in warm areas, with obovate to ovate or oblong, glossy, bluish green leaves, 1½–3in (4–8cm) long. In summer, bears erect, rounded umbels, 1¼–2in (3–5cm) across, of up to 15 fragrant lilac or lilac-pink flowers, ½in (1.5cm) long. ↕ 5–10ft (1.5–3m), ↔ 6–12ft (2–4m). South Africa, Madagascar. ❀ (min. 45°F/7°C)

▷ ***Daiswa*** see *Paris*

DALEA

Indigo bush

FABACEAE

Genus of 160 species of evergreen or deciduous shrubs and monocarpic perennials from high, dry, desert or alluvial regions in North and South America. They produce pinnate leaves terminating in a single leaflet; stems, leaves, and flowers are dotted with blister-like glands. They are grown for their loose to dense spikes or racemes of small, pea-like flowers, which are followed by single-seeded, obovoid to kidney-shaped fruit. Daleas are well suited for a wild or desert garden.
• **CULTIVATION** Outdoors, grow in moderately fertile, well-drained soil in full sun.
• **PROPAGATION** Sow seed *in situ* or grow on in pots until planting out in their final sites in the garden.
• **PESTS AND DISEASES** Rust may be a problem.

D. gattingeri. Herbaceous perennial with short, sparse, decumbent stems, and pinnate leaves, to 1½in (4cm) long, of 5–7 blunt, flat or inrolled, linear to elliptic leaflets. In summer, produces small, vivid rose-purple, 3 or 4 ranked flowers, ½in (1.5cm) across, in dense flower spikes, to 3½in (9cm) long. ↕ to 14in (35cm), ↔ to 12in (30cm). Tennessee to N.W. Alabama. ❀ (min. 41°F/5°C)
D. greggii (Trailing indigo bush). Fast-growing, recumbent shrub with pinnate, gray leaves, to 1in (2.5cm) long. Bears spikes, to 3in (8cm) long, of tiny purple flowers, to ½in (1.5cm) across, in spring. ↕ to 2in (5cm), ↔ to 3ft (1m). W. Texas to S. Mexico. ❀ (min. 35°F/2°C)
D. oaxacana. Low-growing, deciduous shrub with tiny, pinnate, gray-green leaves, to 1in (2.5cm) long. Bears spikes, to 3in (8cm) long, of tiny, pea-shaped, purple flowers, to ½in (1.5cm) across, in autumn. ↕ 12–18in (30–45cm), ↔ 12in (30cm). W. Texas to S. Mexico. ❀ (min. 41°F/5°C)
D. purpurea. Herbaceous perennial with upright, slender, ribbed stems and pinnate, downy, glaucous, gray or dark green leaves with thread-like, inversely lance-shaped leaflets, ½–1in (1.5–2.5cm) long. Bears spikes, to ½in (1.5cm) across, of rose-purple flowers, 3½–5½in (9–14cm), in summer. ↕ 8–36in (20–90cm), ↔ 24in (60cm). North and South America. ❀ (min. 41°F/5°C)

DAMASONIUM

ALISMATACEAE

Genus of 6 species of marginal aquatic, herbaceous perennials occurring in the N. hemisphere and Australia. The long-stalked, linear-oblong, often floating leaves have prominent midribs. Whorls of shallowly cup-shaped, white or pink flowers are borne in umbels, racemes, or panicles. The clusters of ellipsoid fruits grow in radiating, star-like whorls. Damasoniums are particularly decorative when planted in groups in the shallow margins of a small pool.
• **CULTIVATION** Grow in full sun, in water no deeper than 6in (15cm), or in wet mud at the side of still water.
• **PROPAGATION** Sow seed in seed trays or containers half submerged in shallow trays of water, as soon as ripe or in the following spring if kept damp. Divide rhizomes when dormant.
• **PESTS AND DISEASES** Larvae of certain moths may feed on the leaves.

D. alisma. Variable, marginal aquatic perennial with oblong or ovate-oblong, floating leaves, 3in (8cm) long. Numerous white flowers, ¼–⅜in (6–9mm) across, with a yellow spot at the base of each petal, are produced in whorled panicles, 1¼–3in (3–8cm) long, in late spring and early summer. The star-shaped fruit is ¼–½in (6–12mm) across. ↕↔ 6–8in (15–20cm). W., S., and S.E. Europe. Zone 7b.
D. californicum. Marginal aquatic, rhizomatous perennial with linear-oblong to ovate leaves, 4in (10cm) long, that are erect or floating. Numerous white or pink flowers, ⅛–¼in (4–6mm) across, are borne in whorled panicles, to 18in (45cm) long, in late spring and early summer. ↕ 18in (45cm), ↔ 16in (40cm). S. US. Zone 7b.

▷ ***Dammara*** see *Agathis*

DAMPIERA

GOODENIACEAE

Genus of about 70 species of herbaceous perennials or deciduous or evergreen subshrubs from heath to high mountains in Australia. The variable, alternate leaves are often densely woolly. Flowers are usually blue and have a split corolla tube, the 3 lower petals spreading, the upper 2 widely separated and erect; they are solitary or borne in cymes, panicles, or racemes. Grow suckering species as a groundcover. Where not hardy, grow in a temperate greenhouse.
• **CULTIVATION** Under glass, grow in soil-based potting mix in full light with some midday shade. In growth, water freely, applying a balanced liquid fertilizer monthly; keep just moist in winter. Outdoors, grow in well-drained, neutral to acid soil in sun or partial shade.
• **PROPAGATION** Divide rootstocks and separate suckers of perennials in spring; root semi-ripe cuttings in summer.
• **PESTS AND DISEASES** Infrequent.

Dampiera diversifolia

D. diversifolia ■ Densely branched, suckering, prostrate perennial. The lance-shaped to inversely lance-shaped, hairless, leathery leaves, to 1¼in (3cm) long, are entire or minutely toothed. Solitary, dark blue flowers, ½in (1.5cm) across, on short peduncles, are produced from the leaf axils in summer. ↕ 3ft (1m), ↔ 6ft (2m). Western Australia. ❀ (min. 45°F/7°C)
D. hederacea. Procumbent perennial with ovate, often lobed, hairless leaves, to 1½in (4cm) long, broadly ovate to heart-shaped at the bases, densely woolly beneath. The upper leaves are smaller. Bears slender cymes, to 2in (5cm) long, of 3–7 pale to rich blue or white flowers, to ½in (1.5cm) long, softly hairy on the outside, from midwinter to midsummer. ↕ 12in (30cm), ↔ 3ft (1m). Western Australia. ❀ (min. 45°F/7°C)
D. rosmarinifolia (Wild rosemary). Erect or procumbent, suckering, evergreen subshrub with densely woolly stems and blunt-tipped, linear-oblong or oblong, entire, silver leaves, 1in (2.5cm) long. Bears solitary, deep blue, rarely pink flowers, ½in (1.5cm) across, in summer. ↕ 20in (50cm), ↔ 3ft (1m). South Australia, Victoria. ❀ (min. 50°F/10°C)

DANA

LILIACEAE

Genus of one species of clump-forming, shrub-like, evergreen, rhizomatous perennial found in woodland in Turkey and Iran. Upright then arching, branched shoots bear flattened, leaf-like stems. Small, greenish yellow flowers, which appear to be growing directly on the leaf-like stems, are followed by shiny red berries. *D. racemosa* has attractive "foliage," stems, and fruit, and is suitable for a woodland margin or a shrub border. The "foliage" makes a long-lasting addition to floral arrangements.
• **CULTIVATION** Grow in fertile, moist but well-drained soil in partial shade; "foliage" may burn in full sun. Shelter from strong winds. Cut old shoots back to ground level in spring.
• **PROPAGATION** Sow seed in containers in a cold frame in autumn. Divide from autumn to early spring.
• **PESTS AND DISEASES** Infrequent.

D. racemosa (Alexandrian laurel). Shrub-like perennial with slender green shoots and alternate, lance-shaped to ovate-lance-shaped, tapering, glossy, leaf-like stems, to 4in (10cm) long. Terminal racemes, 2in (5cm) long, of 5–8 small, greenish yellow flowers are borne in early summer. Berries are orange-red or red, ¼in (6mm) across. ↕↔ 3ft (1m). Turkey, Iran. Zone 6b.

DAPHNE

THYMELAEACEAE

Genus of about 50 species of deciduous, semi-evergreen, or evergreen shrubs from Europe, N. Africa, and temperate and subtropical Asia, in habitats ranging from lowland woodland to mountains. They are grown mainly for their 4-lobed, tubular, usually fragrant, terminal or axillary flowers, borne singly or in short racemes or clustered heads, and varying from red-purple to pink, lavender-pink, lilac, yellow, and white. Daphnes are also sometimes grown for their foliage, fruit, or upright, rounded, or prostrate habit. The simple, linear to ovate, entire leaves are alternate, rarely opposite, and hairless to softly hairy; and the spherical to ovoid, white, pink, orange, red, or purple-black fruits, 1/16–½in (2–15mm) across, are fleshy or dry. Grow in a rock garden, a shrub border, or in woodland. All parts, including the seeds, are highly toxic if ingested, and contact with the sap may irritate skin.

• **CULTIVATION** Grow in moderately fertile, humus-rich, well-drained but not dry soil. Mulch to keep roots cool. Most prefer slightly alkaline to slightly acidic soil in sun or partial shade. *D. arbuscula* and *D. genkwa* need full sun, while *D. laureola* and *D. pontica* tolerate deep shade. All resent transplanting and so are best transplanted from containers. Mature specimens may die suddenly for no apparent reason. Pruning group 1 or 8; keep to a minimum.

• **PROPAGATION** Sow seed in containers in a cold frame as soon as ripe. Insert softwood cuttings in early and mid-summer, and semi-ripe and evergreen cuttings in mid- or late summer. Graft in winter or layer in spring.

• **PESTS AND DISEASES** Fasciation, Southern blight, tobacco ringspot virus, *Verticillium* wilt, crown and root rot, *Botrytis* twig blight, aphids, and scale insects are common.

D. acutiloba. Erect, sometimes spreading, evergreen shrub with oblong-lance-shaped to inversely lance-shaped, leathery, glossy, bright green leaves, to 4in (10cm) long. In summer, bears terminal clusters of 5–7 white, usually scented flowers, to ½in (1.5cm) across, followed by fleshy, spherical red fruit. ↕↔ 5ft (1.5m). W. and C. China. ❀ (min. 35°F/2°C)

Daphne bholua 'Gurkha'

D. alpina ■ Upright, compact, deciduous shrub with downy shoots and obovate to inversely lance-shaped, hairy, gray-green leaves, ½–1½in (1–4cm) long. Bears terminal clusters of 4–10 fragrant white flowers, to ½in (1.5cm) across, in late spring and early summer, followed by fleshy, spherical, orange-red fruit. ↕↔ to 24in (60cm). C. and S. Europe. Zone 5b.

D. arbuscula. Dwarf, semi-prostrate, evergreen shrub with linear to linear-oblong, leathery, glossy, dark green leaves, to ¾in (2cm) long. In late spring and early summer, produces dense terminal clusters of 3–30 very fragrant, deep pink flowers, to ½in (1.5cm) across, followed by dry, ovoid, grayish white fruit. ↕ to 6in (15cm), ↔ to 18in (45cm). Czech Republic and Slovakia (Carpathian Mountains). Zone 6.

D. bholua. Upright, rarely spreading, deciduous or evergreen shrub with narrowly elliptic to inversely lance-shaped, leathery, dark green leaves, to 4in (10cm) long. Terminal clusters of 7–15 richly fragrant white flowers, to ½in (1.5cm) across, flushed purple-pink, are produced in late winter, followed by fleshy, spherical, blackish purple fruit. ↕ 6–12ft (2–4m), ↔ 5ft (1.5m). E. Himalayas. ❀ (min. 35°F/2°C). **'Gurkha'** ■ is deciduous. **'Jacqueline Postill'** ■ is evergreen, with intensely fragrant flowers, to ¾in (2cm) across, purple-pink outside and white within.

D. blagayana ■ Prostrate, trailing, evergreen or semi-evergreen shrub with broadly ovate to obovate, leathery, dark green leaves, 1¼–2in (3–5cm) long. In spring, bears terminal clusters of 20–30 fragrant, creamy white flowers, to ½in (1.5cm) across, followed by fleshy, spherical white or pink fruit. ↕ to 16in (40cm), ↔ 3ft (1m). Balkans. Zone 7b.

Daphne blagayana

***D.* x *burkwoodii* cultivars.** Upright, densely branched, semi-evergreen shrubs with linear to inversely lance-shaped, mid-green leaves, to 1½in (4cm) long. Bears terminal clusters of up to 16 fragrant white flowers, ⅜in (8mm) across, flushed pink to pale purplish pink, in late spring, and sometimes again in autumn. ↕↔ 3–5ft (1–1.5m). Zone 5. **'Albert Burkwood'** is rounded, usually broader than tall, and has pink-flushed white flowers; ↕ 30in (75cm), ↔ 3ft (1m). **'Astrid'** has narrow, creamy white leaf margins. **'Carol Mackie'** ■ has leaves margined golden yellow, later creamy white. **'G.K. Argles'** has leaves with golden yellow margins. **'Lavenirii'** is spreading and has deep purple-pink flowers with light pink lobes and deep pink throats; ↕ 3ft (1m), ↔ 4½ft (1.3m). **'Somerset'** ■ is vase-shaped and has purple-pink flowers with light pink lobes; ↕ 5ft (1.5m), ↔ 3ft (1m). **'Somerset Variegated'** has bright gold leaf margins.

D. caucasica. Upright, deciduous shrub with inversely lance-shaped to linear-lance-shaped, hairless, pale green leaves, to 3in (8cm) long. Produces terminal and axillary clusters of up to 20 fragrant white flowers, to ½in (1.5cm) across, in spring and intermittently until frost. The fleshy, spherical fruit are black (or red in one variant). Excellent in a sunny or shady mixed border. ↕↔ 4ft (1.2m). Caucasus. Zone 6.

Daphne x *burkwoodii* 'Carol Mackie'

Daphne x *burkwoodii* 'Somerset'

D. cneorum ■ (Garland flower). Low-growing, evergreen shrub with trailing, branching stems and smooth, inversely lance-shaped leaves, ½–¾in (1–2cm) long, dark green above, gray-green beneath. Bears abundant dense, terminal clusters of 6–20 strongly scented, pale to deep rose-pink, sometimes white flowers, to ½in (1.5cm) long, in late spring. ↕ 6in (15cm) or more, ↔ to 4ft (1.2m). Mountains of C. and S. Europe. Zone 3. **'Eximia'** is vigorous, with crimson buds and deep rose-pink flowers, to ½in (1.5cm) long; ↕ to 8in (20cm). **var. *pygmaea*** is very compact, with leaves ¼–⅜in (6–8mm) long; ↕ to 4in (10cm), ↔ to 12in (30cm). Alps (S.E. France, N. Italy).**'Ruby Glow'** has ruby-red flowers. **var. *variegata*** has yellow-edged leaves.

Daphne alpina

Daphne bholua 'Jacqueline Postill'

Daphne cneorum

Daphne genkwa

D. collina, syn. *D. sericea.* Collina Group. Domed, many-branched, dense, evergreen shrub with obovate, glossy, mid-green leaves, ¾–1½in (2–4cm) long, hairy beneath. In late spring and early summer, bears terminal clusters of up to 15 strongly fragrant flowers, to ⅜in (8mm) across, deep purplish pink, becoming paler with age, and with silky-haired tubes. The fleshy, spherical fruit are orange-red. ↕↔ to 20in (50cm). S. Italy. Zone 7b.
D. genkwa ▣ Upright, open, deciduous shrub with opposite, occasionally alternate, lance-shaped to ovate, mid-green, initially silky leaves, to 3in (8cm) long. Produces axillary clusters of 2–7 fragrant lilac flowers, ¼–¾in (0.6–2cm) across, in mid- and late spring, before the leaves. The dry, ovoid fruit are grayish white. ↕↔ 4ft (1.2m). China (W. Hubei). Zone 7.

Daphne x *houtteana*

Daphne jasminea

D. giraldii. Upright, bushy, deciduous shrub with inversely lance-shaped, slightly glaucous, pale green leaves, to 2½in (6cm) long. Bears terminal clusters of 4–8 fragrant, golden yellow flowers, ⅜in (8mm) across, in early summer; the fleshy, spherical fruit are red. ↕↔ 24in (60cm). China. Zone 5.
D. glandulosa see *D. oleoides.*
D. gnidium. Upright, evergreen shrub with linear to obovate-oblong, pointed, leathery, gray-green leaves, to 2in (5cm) long. Bears terminal and axillary panicles of 10 or more fragrant, creamy white flowers, to ¼in (6mm) across, from late spring to autumn, followed by fleshy, spherical red fruit. ↕ 5ft (1.5m), ↔ 4ft (1.2m). Coastal areas of Spain to Greece, N. Africa, Canary Islands. ❀ (min. 41°F/5°C)
D. x houtteana ▣ (*D. laureola* x *D. mezereum*) (Purple-leaved daphne). Erect, semi-evergreen shrub with inversely lance-shaped, purple-suffused, glossy, dark green leaves, to 3½in (9cm) long. Bears axillary clusters of 2–5 purple-pink flowers, ¼in (6mm) across, in early spring. ↕ 4ft (1.2m), ↔ 5ft (1.5m). Garden origin. Zone 7.
D. jasminea ▣ Semi-prostrate, occasionally upright, many-branched evergreen shrub with scattered, oblong-obovate, hairless, gray-green or blue-green leaves, to ½in (1.5cm) long. Terminal pink buds, in pairs (rarely in groups of 3), open to fragrant, sometimes pink-flushed, white or cream flowers, to ⅜in (8mm) across, from late spring to summer. ↕ 4–12in (10–30cm), ↔ to 12in (30cm). S.E. Greece including Crete, Libya. Zone 7b.
D. jezoensis ▣ Slow-growing, rounded, upright, summer-deciduous shrub with inversely lance-shaped leaves, to 3½in (9cm) long, slightly shiny above, pale green at first, later mid-green. Bears up to 10 fragrant, golden yellow flowers, to ½in (1.5cm) across, in terminal clusters, from winter to early spring, followed by fleshy, spherical red fruit. ↕ 18in (45cm), ↔ 24in (60cm). N. Japan. Zone 7.
***D.* 'Kilmeston'.** Semi-prostrate, evergreen shrub with narrowly ovate, leathery, dark green leaves, ½in (1.5cm) long. Terminal clusters of 6–12 fragrant, mid-pink flowers, ⅜–½in (8–12mm) across, are produced in early and midspring and sporadically in early and midsummer. ↕ 12in (30cm), ↔ 16in (40cm). Zone 7b.

Daphne jezoensis

Daphne laureola subsp. *philippi* (inset: flower detail)

D. laureola (Spurge laurel). Bushy, evergreen shrub with obovate to inversely lance-shaped, leathery, glossy, dark green leaves, to 3in (8cm) long. In late winter and early spring, bears axillary clusters of up to 10 slightly fragrant, pale green or yellow-green flowers, to ⅜in (8mm) across, followed by fleshy, ovoid black fruit. ↕ 3ft (1m), ↔ 5ft (1.5m). W. to S.E. Europe, Sicily, Corsica, North Africa, Azores. Zone 7b. **subsp. *philippi*** ▣ is semi-prostrate, mildly suckering, and compact, with leaves to 2½in (6cm) long and flowers, to ¼in (6mm) across; ↕ 18in (45cm), ↔ 24in (60cm). Pyrenees.
D. longilobata. Erect, sometimes spreading, evergreen shrub with oblong-lance-shaped to inversely lance-shaped, leathery, glossy, mid-green leaves, to 4in (10cm) long. Bears terminal clusters of 5–7 fragrant, softly hairy, white flowers, ½in (1.5cm) across, above new growth in early summer, followed by abundant, fleshy, spherical, glossy red fruit. ↕↔ 5ft (1.5m). W. China, S.E. Tibet. Zone 7. **'Peter Moore'** has gray-green leaves with creamy white margins.
***D. x mantensiana* 'Manten'.** Dwarf, rounded, evergreen shrub with oblong to obovate, glossy, mid-green leaves, to 1½in (4cm) long. Terminal clusters of up to 12 fragrant, purple-pink flowers, to ½in (1.5cm) across, paler within, are borne in late spring and early summer, and often again from summer to autumn. ↕↔ 30in (75cm). Zone 6.
D. mezereum ▣ (February daphne, Mezereon). Upright, deciduous shrub with inversely lance-shaped, pale green to soft gray-green leaves, to 5in (13cm) long. Lateral clusters of 2–4 fragrant pink to purplish pink flowers, to ¼in (6mm) long, are borne before the leaves, in late winter and early spring, followed by fleshy, spherical red fruit. ↕ 4ft (1.2m), ↔ 3ft (1m). Europe, Caucasus, Turkey, Siberia. Zone 5. **f. *alba*** has creamy white flowers and yellow fruit; **'Bowles' Variety'** ▣ syn. 'Bowles' White', is very vigorous and upright, with pure white flowers and yellow fruit; ↕ to 6ft (2m).
D. x napolitana (*D. cneorum* x *D. sericea*), syn. *D. neapolitana.* Compact, densely branched, evergreen shrub with inversely lance-shaped to narrowly obovate, glossy, dark green leaves, to 1½in (4cm) long, grayish green beneath. Bears terminal clusters of 6–8 (occasionally up to 16) fragrant,

Daphne mezereum

Daphne mezereum 'Bowles' Variety'

rose-pink flowers, to 3/8in (8mm) across, in spring, with flushes from summer to autumn. ↕↔ 30in (75cm). Garden origin. ❀ (min. 41°F/5°C)
D. neapolitana see *D.* x *napolitana.*
D. odora (Winter daphne). Rounded, evergreen shrub with inversely lance-shaped to narrowly oval, leathery, glossy, deep green leaves, to 3in (8cm) long. Bears fragrant, deep purple-pink and white flowers, to ½in (1.5cm) across, in terminal, sometimes axillary clusters of 10–15 or more, from midwinter to early spring, followed by fleshy, spherical red fruit. ↕↔ 4ft (1.2m). China, Japan. Zone 6. **f. *alba***, syn. var. *leucantha*, bears white or creamy white flowers. **'Aureomarginata'**, syn. 'Marginata', has leaves with narrow, irregular yellow margins, and red-purple flowers, paler and sometimes almost white within. **var. *leucantha*** see f. *alba.* **'Marginata'** see 'Aureomarginata'. **'Mazelli'** produces terminal clusters of pinkish white flowers that are paler or white within.
D. oleoides, syn. *D. glandulosa.* Slow-growing, variable, evergreen shrub with spreading branches and elliptic to obovate, leathery, gray-green leaves, ½–1¾in (1–4.5cm) long. Produces terminal clusters of up to 8 usually scented, sometimes pink-tinged, creamy white flowers, to ½in (1.5cm) across, in early summer, followed by downy, fleshy, orange fruit. ↕ 8in (20cm), ↔ to 10in (25cm). S. Europe, N. Africa, Turkey, Caucasus. ❀ (min. 35°F/2°C)
***D. petraea* 'Grandiflora'** ▣ Slow-growing, very compact, many-branched, evergreen shrub with narrowly spoon-shaped, leathery, shiny, dark green leaves, to ½in (1.5cm) long. Bears dense, terminal clusters of 3–5 or more scented, deep rose-pink flowers, to ½in (1.5cm) across, in late spring. ↕ 4in (10cm), ↔ to 10in (25cm). Zone 6.
D. pontica. Spreading, evergreen shrub with obovate, pointed, glossy, dark green leaves, to 4in (10cm) long. Clusters of up to 10 pairs of fragrant,

Daphne petraea 'Grandiflora'

yellow-green flowers, to ¾in (2cm) across, with slender, pointed lobes, are borne at the base of overlapping shoots, in mid- and late spring, followed by fleshy, ovoid black fruit. ↕ 3ft (1m), ↔ 5ft (1.5m). S.E. Europe, N. Turkey, S.E. Bulgaria, Caucasus. Zone 7b.
D. retusa ▣ syn. *D. tangutica.* Retusa Group. Compact, dwarf, evergreen shrub with inversely lance-shaped to elliptic, leathery, glossy, dark green leaves, to 2in (5cm) long, notched at the tips. Terminal clusters of up to 10 or more fragrant flowers, to ½in (1.5cm) across, purple-red outside, white within, are produced in late spring and early summer; flowers are followed by fleshy, spherical red fruit. ↕↔ 30in (75cm). W. China (W. Sichuan, Yunnan). Zone 7b.
D. sericea. Compact or open, rounded, evergreen shrub with inversely lance-shaped, obovate, or narrowly elliptic, dark green leaves, to 2in (5cm) long, glossy above, softly hairy beneath. Terminal and axillary clusters of up to 15 fragrant, purple-pink and white flowers, to ½in (1.5cm) across, fading to buff, are produced in late spring. ↕↔ 20in (50cm). Italy including Sicily, Greece (Crete), S. and W. Turkey, Syria, Caucasus. ❀ (min. 35°F/2°C).
Collina Group see *D. collina.*
D. tangutica. Upright, open to dense, evergreen shrub with inversely lance-shaped, oblong or elliptic, leathery, dull, dark green leaves, to 3in (8cm) long, with pointed or notched tips. Terminal clusters of 6–8 fragrant, purple- or pink-flushed white flowers, to ½in (1.5cm) across, are produced in late spring and early summer, followed by fleshy, spherical red fruit. ↕↔ 3ft (1m). Tibet, China (Gansu, Hubei, Sichuan), possibly Taiwan. Zone 6.
Retusa Group see *D. retusa.*

Daphne retusa

DAPHNIPHYLLUM

DAPHNIPHYLLACEAE

Genus of about 15 species of evergreen trees and shrubs found in woodland in E. Asia, grown for their handsome foliage. The alternate, rhododendron-like leaves often appear whorled at the ends of the shoots. Inconspicuous, petalless pink, green, or yellow flowers are borne in short racemes, the male and female on separate plants. The rounded or ovoid fruits are fleshy, with large, hard, blue-black seeds. Grow in a large shrub border or woodland garden. Where not hardy, grow in a temperate greenhouse or in containers indoors.
• **CULTIVATION** Grow in moist but well-drained, humus-rich soil in sun or partial shade, sheltered from cold, drying winds. Pruning group 8; tolerates hard pruning.
• **PROPAGATION** Insert semi-ripe or evergreen cuttings in late summer.
• **PESTS AND DISEASES** Infrequent.

D. himalense* subsp. *macropodum see *D. macropodum.*
D. macropodum, syn. *D. himalense* subsp. *macropodum.* Dense, rounded shrub or small tree with narrowly oval to oblong, leathery, dark green leaves, to 8in (20cm) long, glaucous beneath. Bears axillary racemes of small, petalless, deep purple-pink male or green female flowers on separate plants, in late spring and early summer. ↕↔ 20ft (6m). China, Korea, Japan. Zone 7b.

DARMERA *syn.* PELTIPHYLLUM

SAXIFRAGACEAE

Genus of one species of rhizomatous perennial from mountain streamsides in woodland in W. US. With its large, bold, peltate leaves, which appear after the star-shaped, white to pink flowers, *D. peltata* forms an umbrella-like clump suitable for a pond or streambank.
• **CULTIVATION** Grow in moist or boggy soil (although it will tolerate drier conditions), in sun or partial shade.
• **PROPAGATION** Sow seed in containers in a cold frame in spring or autumn, or divide in spring.
• **PESTS AND DISEASES** Infrequent.

Darmera peltata

D. peltata ▣ syn. *Peltiphyllum peltatum.* Slowly spreading, rhizomatous perennial with leaf stalks to 4ft (1.2m) long, and peltate, rounded, deeply lobed, coarsely toothed, conspicuously veined, dark green leaves, to 24in (60cm) across, that turn red in autumn. Rounded cymes of numerous 5-petaled, white to bright pink flowers, to ½in (1.5cm) across, are borne on flower stems to 6ft (2m) long in late spring. ↕ to 4ft (1.2m), ↔ 3ft (1m) or more. S.W. Oregon to N.W. California. Zone 6.

DARWINIA

Scent myrtle

MYRTACEAE

Genus of at least 60 species of evergreen, heather-like shrubs found on heaths, on sandy plains, and in scrub in S.W. Australia. They are grown for their dense terminal heads of tiny, petalless flowers, enclosed by sometimes large, petal-like, colorful bracts. The crowded, opposite, linear to rounded leaves are small and sometimes aromatic. Where not hardy, grow in a cool greenhouse; elsewhere, plant at the base of a wall or in a border.
• **CULTIVATION** Under glass, grow in sandy, well-drained, soilless potting mix in full light, with shade from hot sun, and good ventilation. In growing season, water moderately, applying a low-nitrogen liquid fertilizer monthly; keep just moist in winter. Top-dress or pot on in spring. Outdoors, grow in well-drained, humus-rich, sandy soil in full sun. Trim after flowering to keep compact.
• **PROPAGATION** Sow seed at not less than 61°F (16°C) in spring. Root semi-ripe cuttings in summer, with bottom heat. Layer in spring.
• **PESTS AND DISEASES** Scale insects may be a problem.

D. citriodora ▣ (Lemon-scented myrtle). Erect to spreading, bushy shrub with narrowly ovate to lance-shaped, lemon-scented, gray-green leaves, ½–¾in (1–2cm) long, sometimes heart-shaped at the bases, with slightly recurved margins. Pendent to erect flowerheads, 1–1¼in (2.5–3cm) across, with prominent, bell-shaped, orange-red and green outer bracts, are usually produced in spring. ↕ 20–72in (0.5–2m), ↔ 3–8ft (1–2.5m). Western Australia. ❀ (min. 41°F/5°C)

Darwinia citriodora

DASYLIRION

AGAVACEAE

Genus of 18 species of yucca-like, evergreen shrubs, trees, and perennial succulents found in dry, mountainous areas and deserts in S. US and Mexico. They have thick, woody stems and bear narrowly lance-shaped, mostly spiny-margined leaves, usually about 3ft (1m) long, in dense, terminal rosettes. Mature plants bear star- or bell-shaped flowers, to 1/16 in (2mm) across, in long, narrow panicles intermittently throughout summer. Male and female flowers are borne on separate plants. Mature plants may withstand several degrees below freezing if kept dry. Where not hardy, grow in a temperate or warm greenhouse or conservatory. Elsewhere, use at the base of a wall or as a focal feature on a large lawn or in a desert garden.

• **CULTIVATION** Under glass, grow in a mix of 2 parts each loam and sand and 1 part each leaf mold and peat (or peat substitute). Provide full light with low humidity. From early spring to autumn, water freely, applying a balanced liquid fertilizer monthly; water sparingly in winter. In summer, move containerized specimens outside. Outdoors, grow in well-drained soil in a sheltered site in full sun. See also pp.48–49.

• **PROPAGATION** Sow seed at 70°F (21°C) in spring.

• **PESTS AND DISEASES** Prone to scale insects and occasionally to leaf spot and canker.

Dasylirion acrotrichum

D. acrotrichum ▣ syn. *D. gracile.* Evergreen shrub, eventually forming a trunk 3–5ft (0.9–1.5m) high. Upright then arching, fibrous-tipped, pale green leaves are margined with hooked yellow spines. In summer bears dense, narrow inflorescences, 8–12ft (2.5–4m) long, of star-shaped white flowers. ↕ 11–20ft (3.5–6m), ↔ to 7ft (2.2m). Mexico. ❀ (min. 50°F/10°C)

D. gracile see *D. acrotrichum.*

D. hartwegianum see *Calibanus hookeri.*

D. longissimum (Mexican grass plant). Tree-like succulent with erect then spreading, entire, 4-angled, stiff, slightly fleshy, olive-green leaves, 5ft (1.5m) or more long, on a trunk 3–6ft (1–2m) tall. In summer bears dense inflorescences, to 6ft (1.8m) long, of bell-shaped white flowers. ↕ to 12ft (4m), ↔ 5ft (1.5m). E. Mexico. ❀ (min. 45°F/7°C)

D. texanum. Tall, evergreen shrub with semi-pendent, glossy, mid-green leaves margined with yellow spines, fading to brown. Leaves persist when dead, usually concealing the trunk, 10ft (3m) tall. In early summer bears dense inflorescences, to 5ft (1.5m) long, of bell-shaped white flowers. ↕ to 15ft (5m), ↔ to 10ft (3m). Texas, N. Mexico. ❀ (min. 45°F/7°C)

▷ ***Datura*** see *Brugmansia*

▷ ***Daubentonia*** see *Sesbania*

DAUCUS

APIACEAE

Genus of about 25 species of biennials, usually grown for food and forage. If allowed to remain *in situ,* bear white, umbrella-shaped flowers, which rise 12in (30cm) above the leaves.

• **CULTIVATION** Grow in light, fertile soil, in full sun. Work in organic matter in the fall or apply fertilizer a few times during growth.

• **PROPAGATION** Sow seeds *in situ* in early spring as soon as soil can be worked. Zone 7.

• **PESTS AND DISEASES** Carrot rust fly, wireworms, leaf aphids may occur.

D. carota* var. *sativum (Carrots). Herbaceous, cool-season biennial with lacy, pinnate lower leaves. Carpels form tiny seeds covered with a spiny, hooked, and slightly curved mericarp. Taproots, 2–36in (5–90cm) long, can be long and tapered or round to oblong. Zone 7.

DAVALLIA

DAVALLIACEAE

Genus of 34 species of mostly epiphytic ferns, found by streams or on rocks in W. Mediterranean, N. Africa, China to Japan, and tropical Asia to Australia and the Pacific islands. Creeping surface rhizomes, densely covered with scales, produce triangular, usually finely dissected, shiny fronds, which, in many species, are short-lived and deciduous. The sori are marginal or submarginal, with tubular to urn-shaped indusia. Where not hardy, grow *Davallia* species in a warm or cool greenhouse; they look effective in a hanging basket, and their cut fronds may also be used in flower arrangements. Elsewhere, they are suitable for a moist, shaded site.

• **CULTIVATION** Under glass, grow in equal parts peat, moss, bark, grit, and pine needles in bright indirect light with high humidity. Water moderately and

Davallia fejeensis

mist frequently in summer; water sparingly in winter. Outdoors, grow epiphytically or in moist, open, leafy soil in partial shade.

• **PROPAGATION** Sow spores of hardy species at 59°F (15°C) and tender ones at 70°F (21°C), as soon as ripe. Divide rhizomes in spring, making sure each division has roots. See also p.51.

• **PESTS AND DISEASES** Susceptible to scale insects, foliar nematodes, gray mold (*Botrytis*), and aerial blight.

D. canariensis (Deer's foot fern, Hare's foot fern). Deciduous or semi-evergreen fern with thick, succulent rhizomes covered with dark brown scales. Produces broad, 3- or 4-pinnate, mid-green fronds, 8–20in (20–50cm) long, with narrowly triangular or linear segments. ↕ 8–20in (20–50cm), ↔ 1–3ft (30–100cm). S.W. Europe, N.W. Africa. ❀ (min. 45°F/7°C)

D. fejeensis ▣ (Rabbit's foot fern). Evergreen fern with thick, tough rhizomes covered with mid- to dark brown scales pressed tightly to the surface, with long, curly hairs on the margins. Produces very broad, 3- or 4-pinnate, mid-green fronds, 8–39in (20–100cm) long, with linear segments. ↕ 8–39in (20–100cm), ↔ 16–60in (40–150cm). Fiji. ❀ (min. 45°F/7°C) **'Dwarf Ripple'** is dwarf, with very finely cut fronds; ↕ 8–16in (20–40cm). **'Major'** produces fronds 2–4ft (60–120cm) long; ↔ to 4ft (1.2m). **'Plumosa'** has slender fronds with feather-like segments.

D. mariesii ▣ (Squirrel's foot fern). Deciduous fern with thin, creeping rhizomes covered with brown scales. Broad, very finely cut, 3- or 4-pinnate, mid-green fronds, 8–12in (20–30cm) long, have narrowly triangular or linear segments. ↕ 6in (15cm), ↔ indefinite. E. Asia, Japan. ❀ (min. 41°F/5°C)

D. solida (Polynesian davallia). Evergreen fern with short, creeping rhizomes, covered with dark brown scales. Bears arching, broadly triangular, 3-pinnate, mid-green fronds, 28in (70cm) long, with triangular, soft, leathery segments. ↕ 20in (50cm), ↔ indefinite. Malaysia, Polynesia. ❀ (min. 41°F/5°C). **'Ornata'** has wide segments. **'Ruffled Ornata'** has wide, irregularly curled and twisted segments.

D. tyermanii. Epiphytic, evergreen fern, with slow-growing, arching, creeping, exposed rhizomes, covered with whitish scales. Waxy triangular blades are tripinnate. ↕ 8–12in (20–30cm). China. ❀ (min. 41°F/5°C)

DAVIDIA

Dove tree, Ghost tree, Handkerchief tree

NYSSACEAE

Genus of one species of deciduous tree found in woodland in China, with small ellipsoid flowerheads surrounded by showy white bracts, which give rise to the common names. Its bark is smooth and mid-gray, and the leaves are simple, alternate, and broadly ovate. Grow *D. involucrata* as a specimen tree.

• **CULTIVATION** Grow in fertile, moist but well-drained soil in sun or partial shade, with shelter from strong winds. Pruning group 1; maintain a strong central leader in the formative years.

• **PROPAGATION** Sow the whole fruit in a seedbed or in containers in an open frame as soon as ripe. Germination normally occurs in spring after 2 winters outdoors. Seed-raised plants may not flower for up to 20 years. Insert leaf-bud cuttings in early autumn or hardwood cuttings in winter.

• **PESTS AND DISEASES** Infrequent.

D. involucrata ▣ Broadly pyramidal tree with broadly ovate, sharp-pointed, toothed, red-stalked leaves, to 6in (15cm) long, with heart-shaped bases, mid-green above and softly hairy beneath. In late spring, produces dense, pendent, ellipsoid heads, to 3/4in (2cm) across, of small male flowers, each with red-purple anthers and a single, ovoid green ovary. Each flower is surrounded by a pair of leafy, showy white bracts of

Davallia mariesii

Davidia involucrata

unequal size. The pendent fruit are ridged and greenish brown, 1½in (4cm) across. ↕ 50ft (15m), ↔ 30ft (10m). S.W. China. Zone 7. **var. *vilmoriniana*** has almost hairless leaves, glaucous or yellow-green beneath.

DECAISNEA

LARDIZABALACEAE

Genus of 2 species of deciduous shrubs from woodland in W. China and the Himalayas, grown for their bold, pinnate leaves, borne alternately on stout shoots, and their unusual, bean-like, pendent fruit. The bell-shaped flowers are petalless. Grow *D. fargesii* in a shrub border or woodland garden.

• **CULTIVATION** Grow in fertile, moist but well-drained soil in sun or partial shade, with shelter from strong winds. Pruning group 1.

• **PROPAGATION** Sow seed in containers in an open frame in autumn.

• **PESTS AND DISEASES** Infrequent.

Decaisnea fargesii

D. fargesii ▣ Upright, sparsely branched shrub with stout, hairless shoots and pinnate leaves, to 36in (90cm) long, dark green above, glaucous green beneath, with 13–25 ovate to elliptic leaflets. Bears pendent panicles, to 18in (45cm) long, of bell-shaped, petalless green or yellow-green flowers in early summer, followed by pendent, cylindrical, dull, deep blue fruit, to 4in (10cm) long, in autumn. ↕↔ 20ft (6m). W. China. Zone 6b.

DECARYA

DIDIEREACEAE

Genus of one species of deciduous, succulent shrub or small tree occurring from sea level to 1,600ft (500m) or more in Madagascar. It has zigzag twigs, borne on spreading branches, which produce a small, inversely heart-shaped leaf and 2 spines from each node, and a single cyme of small, cup-shaped white flowers in summer. Where not hardy, grow in a warm greenhouse; elsewhere, plant at the base of a wall.

• **CULTIVATION** Under glass, grow in soil-based potting mix with additional grit, in full light and low humidity. In growth, water moderately, applying a low-nitrogen liquid fertilizer monthly; keep just moist at other times. Outdoors, grow in sharply drained soil in full sun. See also pp.48–49.

• **PROPAGATION** Sow seed at 70°F (21°C) or take stem cuttings from spring to summer.

• **PESTS AND DISEASES** Susceptible to scale insects.

D. madagascariensis. Succulent shrub or small tree with a straight, brownish green trunk branching from the sides and base, and inversely heart-shaped, fleshy, spiny, dull, mid-green leaves, to ¼in (6mm) long. Produces cymes, 2–3in (5–8cm) long, of small white flowers in summer. ↕ to 25ft (8m), ↔ indefinite. S.W. Madagascar ❀ (min. 55°F/13°C)

DECUMARIA

HYDRANGEACEAE

Genus of 2 species of woody, evergreen or deciduous climbers from China and S.E. US, where they grow on forest trees. They climb by aerial roots and produce opposite pairs of attractive, ovate to oblong, glossy, dark green leaves. Slightly fragrant white or yellowish white flowers, with 10 small petals and 20–30 stamens in a "brush," are borne in terminal corymbs or panicles. Grow at the base of a sheltered wall or train into a tree. *D. barbara* is also good as a groundcover.

• **CULTIVATION** Grow in reasonably fertile, preferably loamy, well-drained soil in sun or partial shade. Provide shelter in all but mild areas. Pruning group 13, if wall-grown; otherwise needs minimal pruning.

• **PROPAGATION** Root semi-ripe cuttings in late summer or early autumn.

• **PESTS AND DISEASES** Infrequent.

D. barbara (Climbing hydrangea, Wood-vamp). Deciduous climber with ovate to ovate-oblong, glossy, dark green leaves, to 4in (10cm) long. In summer, white flowers are produced in corymbs, to 3in (8cm) across. ↕ 30ft (10m). S.E. US. Zone 7.

D. sinensis. Evergreen climber with narrowly obovate to ovate, glossy, dark green leaves, to 3in (8cm) long. Bears pyramidal panicles, to 3in (8cm) across, of yellow or creamy white flowers in late spring and early summer. ↕ 6ft (2m) or more. C. China. Zone 7b.

DEINANTHE

HYDRANGEACEAE

Genus of 2 species of perennials, related to hydrangeas, found in moist, shady woodland in China and Japan. They have short rhizomes and upright stems. The opposite leaves are ovate or obovate to elliptic, toothed, crinkled, hairy, slightly glossy, and mid- to dark green. Terminal panicles of showy, pendent, cup-shaped, waxy, fertile flowers with 5 fleshy petals and numerous stamens, and a few sterile outer flowers without petals, are produced in mid- and late summer. Their slowly spreading mats of attractive foliage and flowers make them suitable for a woodland garden, a rock garden, or an alpine house.

• **CULTIVATION** Under glass, grow in a mix of equal parts loam, leaf mold, and sharp sand. In growth, water freely; keep just moist in winter. Outdoors, grow in moist but well-drained, acidic, humus-rich soil in partial shade. Will not tolerate heat or drought.

Deinanthe caerulea

• **PROPAGATION** Sow seed in containers in a cold frame as soon as ripe, although germination is uncertain and seedlings take several years to reach flowering size. Divide in early spring; divisions are slow to re-establish.

• **PESTS AND DISEASES** Slugs may damage young shoots.

D. bifida. Clump-forming, rhizomatous perennial with obovate to elliptic, mid-green leaves, to 8in (20cm) long, distinctly notched at the tips, and white flowers, ½–¾in (1–2cm) across, with yellow stamens. ↕ 16in (40cm), ↔ 18in (45cm). Japan. Zone 6.

D. caerulea ▣ Clump-forming rhizomatous perennial usually with 2 pairs of ovate to elliptic, sharp-pointed, conspicuously veined, mid- to dark green leaves, to 6in (15cm) long. Bears mauve to violet-blue flowers, ¾–1½in (2–4cm) across, with gray-blue or blue stamens. ↕↔ 18in (45cm). C. China (Hubei). Zone 6.

▷ ***Delairea odorata*** see *Senecio mikanioides*

DELONIX

FABACEAE

Genus of 10 species of deciduous, semi-evergreen, or evergreen trees from open, dry forest in Madagascar, tropical Africa, and India. They have elegant, alternate, 2-pinnate, fern-like leaves, and produce large, terminal, corymb-like racemes of irregularly shaped, 5-petaled flowers. Where not hardy, grow in a temperate greenhouse as foliage plants, since they rarely flower in a container. In warmer areas, they make effective specimen or shade trees.

• **CULTIVATION** Under glass, grow in soil-based potting mix in full light. In the growing season, water freely, applying a balanced liquid fertilizer monthly; keep just moist in winter. Top-dress or pot on in spring. Outdoors, grow in fertile, moist but well-drained soil in full sun, with shelter from strong winds. Pruning group 1; tolerates hard pruning under glass.

• **PROPAGATION** Sow seed at 64–70°F (18–21°C) in spring. Root semi-ripe cuttings in summer, with bottom heat.

• **PESTS AND DISEASES** Prone to whiteflies and spider mites under glass, and thornbugs, crown gall, mushroom root rot, wood rot, leaf spots, and dieback outdoors.

D

Delonix regia

D. regia ▣ syn. *Poinciana regia* (Flamboyant tree, Flame tree, Royal poinciana). Semi-evergreen tree, fully deciduous in areas with a long dry season. It has a wide-spreading, dome-shaped crown and broadly ovate, 2-pinnate, bright green leaves, 12–20in (30–50cm) long, each pinna divided into 10–25 pairs of elliptic to oblong leaflets. From spring to summer, bears many scarlet flowers, 4–5in (10–13cm) across; the standard petals are pale yellow and striped with red. ↕ to 30ft (10m), ↔ 15–30ft (5–10m). Madagascar. ❄ (min. 45°F/7°C)

DELOSPERMA

AIZOACEAE

Genus of about 150 or more species of evergreen or semi-evergreen, succulent shrubs and mat-forming, succulent perennials (some with annual shoots from a tuberous caudex) from hilly lowlands in C., E., and southern Africa. The triangular to cylindrical, fleshy leaves are borne in opposite pairs, and the daisy-like flowers are produced singly or in open cymes in summer. Where not hardy, grow in a temperate greenhouse or as houseplants; elsewhere, use in a desert or rock garden or border.

• **CULTIVATION** Under glass, grow in standard cactus potting mix in full light, with good but draft-free ventilation. In the growing season, water moderately, applying fertilizer every 3 weeks; keep dry at other times. Outdoors, grow in sharply drained soil in a sheltered site in full sun. See also pp.48–49.

• **PROPAGATION** Sow seed at 70°F (21°C), or take stem cuttings in spring or summer.

• **PESTS AND DISEASES** Vulnerable to mealybugs and aphids.

Delosperma aberdeenense

D. aberdeenense ▣ Dense, evergreen, succulent shrub with minutely warty, often prostrate branches with thick, semi-cylindrical, pointed, mid-green leaves, ½–¾in (1–2cm) long. Solitary, purplish red flowers, ½in (1.5cm) across, are freely produced in summer. ↕ to 5in (13cm), ↔ indefinite. South Africa (Western Cape, Eastern Cape). ❄ (min. 41°F/5°C)

D. cooperi. Creeping, mat-forming, subshrubby, succulent perennial with cylindrical, warty, light green leaves, to 2in (5cm) long. Solitary, glossy magenta flowers, to 2in (5cm) across, with white anthers, are produced in mid- and late summer. ↕ 2in (5cm), ↔ 24in (60cm) or more. South Africa (Orange Free State). ❄ (min. 35°F/2°C)

D. nubigerum. Creeping, mat-forming, subshrubby, succulent perennial with oblong-elliptic or linear, warty, mid-green leaves, to 1½in (4cm) long. Solitary orange-red flowers, ¾in (2cm) across, are produced in summer. ↕ 2in (5cm), ↔ indefinite. South Africa (Orange Free State). Zone 6b.

D. velutinum. Compact, bushy, semi-evergreen, succulent shrub with curved, warty-bristly branches and broadly cylindrical, tapering, pale green leaves, to ½in (1.5cm) long, keeled beneath. Solitary white flowers, ½in (1.5cm) across, are produced in summer. ↕ 2in (5cm), ↔ indefinite. South Africa (KwaZulu/Natal). ❄ (min. 41°F/5°C)

DELPHINIUM

RANUNCULACEAE

Genus of about 250 species of annuals, biennials, and perennials found mainly in mountainous areas worldwide, except Australia and the polar regions. They are grown for their spikes, racemes, or occasionally panicles of shallowly cup-shaped, sometimes hooded, spurred, single to fully double flowers, often termed "florets." Most have fibrous or fleshy roots, although some are tuberous. The basal leaves, mostly to 8in (20cm) long, are toothed and deeply or shallowly 3- to 5-lobed, occasionally 7-lobed. Grow tall delphiniums in a mixed border or island bed, and dwarf ones in a rock garden. All parts may cause severe discomfort if ingested, and contact with foliage may irritate skin.

Belladonna Group
Upright, branching perennials with palmately lobed leaves. Wiry stems bear loose, branched spikes of elf-cap-shaped, single flowers, ¾in (2cm) or more across, with spurs up to 1¼in (3cm) long, in early and late summer. ↕ 3–4ft (1–1.2m), ↔ to 18in (45cm).

Elatum Group
Clump-forming perennials with fleshy crowns producing flowering spikes in early and midsummer, and sometimes again in autumn, if cut back. The spikes bear numerous single, semi-double, or double flowers, with 5 large outer sepals and a "bee" formed by 8 inner sepals. The flowers, at least 2½in (6cm) across, are usually larger at the base of the spike. Each stem also bears lateral shoots, flowering after the main spike, with slightly smaller flowers. Elatum Group cultivars are the most spectacular garden delphiniums, and generally require considerable effort to produce the best results (see CULTIVATION). They fall into 3 height categories: small, to 5ft (1.5m); medium, 5½ft (1.7m); and tall, 6ft (2m). Spreads are usually in the range of 24–36in (60–90cm).

Pacific Hybrids
Similar to Elatum Group cultivars, but grown as annuals or biennials. At one time, they were raised from hand-pollinated, line-bred seed to produce selections with clear, brightly colored flowers; today, they are cross-pollinated and less uniform. The short-lived flowers are large, to 3in (8cm) across, and semi-double, and are produced on spikes in early and midsummer. ↕ 5½ft (1.7m), ↔ to 30in (75cm).

• **HARDINESS** Most cultivars are hardy in Zone 4; species vary widely.

• **CULTIVATION** Grow in fertile, well-drained soil in full sun, with shelter from strong winds. Except for dwarf perennials, most delphiniums need staking: low-growing cultivars, with twiggy, brushwood support; taller, large-flowered ones, with sturdy stakes. Insert supports no later than midspring, or when the plants reach 12in (30cm) high. To ensure good-quality flower spikes, thin shoots when 3in (8cm) high; leave a minimum of 2 or 3 shoots on young plants, and 5–7 strong shoots on well-established ones. In growth, water all plants freely, applying a balanced liquid fertilizer every 2 or 3 weeks. Deadhead by cutting spent flower spikes back to small, flowering sideshoots. Cut all growth to ground level after it has withered in autumn.

• **PROPAGATION** Sow seed at 55°F (13°C) in early spring. For Elatum and Belladonna Group cultivars, take pencil-thick basal cuttings, 3–4in (7–10cm) long, with solid heels, from close to the crown, in early spring.

• **PESTS AND DISEASES** Susceptible to slugs and snails as well as cyclamen mites. Powdery mildew, Southern blight, bacterial and fungal spots, gray mold (*Botrytis*), crown and root rot, white rot, rust, white smut, leaf smut, and damping off occur.

***D.* 'Alice Artindale'.** Small Elatum with neat, button-like, fully double mauve flowers, margined with blue, on narrow spikes. Good for cut flowers.

***D.* 'Andenken an August Koenemann'** see *D.* 'Wendy'.

***D.* 'Astolat'.** Pacific Hybrid with lilac and pink flowers.

***D.* 'Bellamosum'** ▣ Belladonna with deep gentian-blue flowers.

***D.* 'Berghimmel'.** Tall Elatum with short, slim, wind-resistant stems bearing single, clear sky-blue flowers with white

DELPHINIUM INFLORESCENCES

Delphiniums are grown for their showy spikes of colorful summer flowers. The spikes are variable in height and shape: those produced by the Belladonna Group hybrids are loose and branched, while the tallest spikes, to 6ft (2m) high or more, are produced by hybrids of the Elatum Group. Pacific Hybrids are similar to Elatum Group cultivars, although they are not as tall.

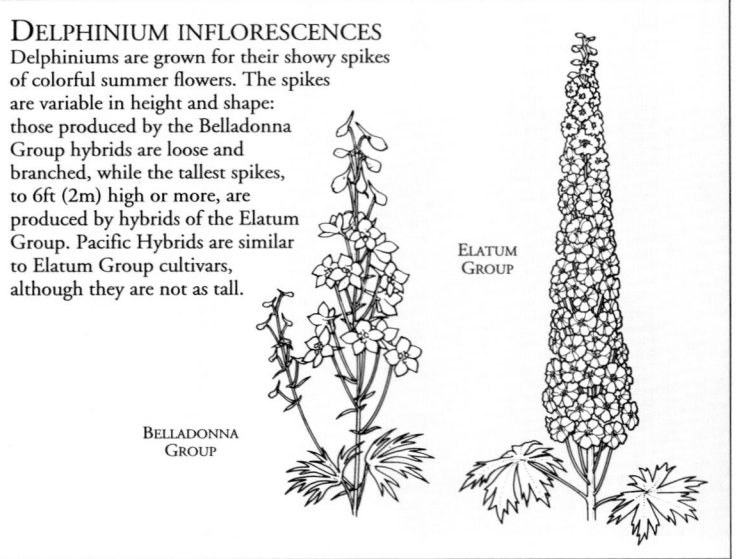

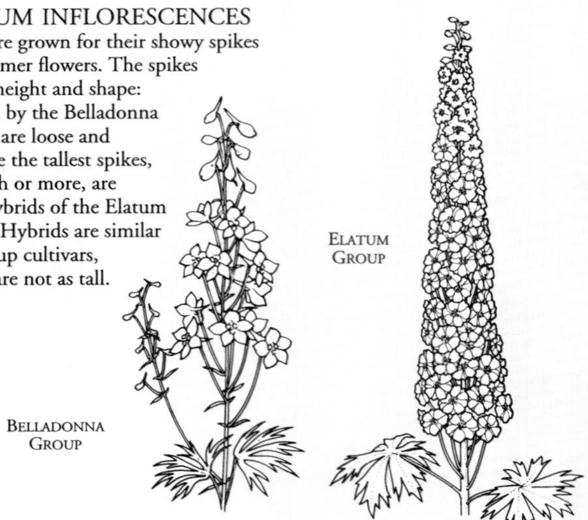

Delphinium 'Bellamosum'

Delphinium 'Blue Nile'

Delphinium cardinale

Delphinium 'Cliveden Beauty'

Delphinium 'Conspicuous'

Delphinium 'Emily Hawkins'

bees; the lower florets often still in good condition as the top ones open.
***D.* 'Black Knight'.** Pacific Hybrid with deep purple flowers with black bees.
***D.* 'Blue Bees'** ■ Belladonna producing clear blue flowers with white centers.
***D.* 'Blue Bird'.** Pacific Hybrid bearing mid-blue flowers with white bees.
***D.* 'Blue Dawn'.** Medium Elatum bearing semi-double, pale blue flowers, with a touch of pink, and small, brown-black bees.
***D.* 'Blue Jay'.** Pacific Hybrid with deep blue flowers.
***D.* 'Blue Nile'** ■ Medium Elatum bearing semi-double, bright, mid-blue flowers with white bees.
***D.* 'Boningale Glory'.** Tall Elatum bearing semi-double, mid-blue flowers with mauve inner petals.
***D.* 'Bruce'** ■ Tall Elatum bearing semi-double, violet-purple flowers, paler toward the centers, with brown bees.
D. brunonianum. Upright perennial with hairy stems and deeply 3- to 5-lobed leaves. In early summer, bears racemes of hooded, short-spurred, hairy, single flowers, 1¼–2in (3–5cm) wide, blue to purple with black-purple bees, and heavily veined. ↕↔ 8in (20cm). Pakistan to S.W. Tibet. Zone 4.
***D.* 'Butterball'** ■ Small Elatum producing semi-double, rich light cream flowers with deep yellow bees.
***D.* 'Cameliard'.** Pacific Hybrid with deep purple flowers, shading to blue at the frilly sepal margins, and cream bees.
***D.* 'Can-can'.** Small Elatum producing fully double flowers. Light mauve sepals are veined with dark mauve and have frilled margins; the outer sepals have dark blue margins.
D. cardinale ■ Short-lived perennial with deeply 3- to 5-lobed leaves. Bears loose racemes of elf-cap-shaped, stout-spurred, single scarlet flowers, ¾in (2cm) across, with yellow centers, in early summer. ↕ 6ft (2m), ↔ 18in (45cm). California to Mexico (Baja California). Zone 7b.
***D.* 'Casa Blanca'.** Belladonna with white flowers.
D. cashmerianum. Perennial with rounded, toothed, shallowly 5- to 7-lobed leaves. From early to late summer, bears single, dark purple-blue flowers, 1¼–1½in (3–4cm) across, in open panicles. ↕ 12–16in (30–40cm), ↔ 6in (15cm). N. India to China. Zone 6.
***D.* 'Cassius'.** Medium Elatum with semi-double, deep blue flowers overlaid with purple; bees are brown-tinged.
***D.* 'Chelsea Star'.** Medium Elatum bearing semi-double, velvety, rich violet flowers with white bees.
D. chinense see *D. grandiflorum.*
***D.* 'Cliveden Beauty'** ■ Belladonna with sky-blue flowers.
***D.* Connecticut Yankee Series 'Blue Fountains'.** Belladonna producing single flowers in white and shades of blue and mauve. Zone 4.
D. consolida see *Consolida ajacis.*
***D.* 'Conspicuous'** ■ Small Elatum bearing semi-double, lilac-mauve flowers with prominent brown bees.
***D.* 'Crown Jewel'.** Small Elatum bearing semi-double, pink-tinged, pale blue flowers with prominent brown bees.
***D.* 'Emily Hawkins'** ■ Medium Elatum producing neat, semi-double, light violet flowers with fawn bees.

Delphinium 'Blue Bees'

Delphinium 'Bruce'

Delphinium 'Butterball'

Dendrobium Malones 'Hope'

D. lindleyi, syn. *D. aggregatum*. Evergreen, epiphytic orchid with dwarf, compressed pseudobulbs each bearing a single, oval leaf, 2–3in (5–8cm) long. Bright yellow or pale golden yellow flowers, to 1½in (4cm) across, in pendent racemes, 4–12in (10–30cm) long, are produced in spring. ↕ 4in (10cm), ↔ 6in (15cm). Himalayas, Laos, Vietnam, Cambodia, S.W. China, Burma, Thailand. ❄ (min. 50°F/10°C; max. 86°F/30°C)
D. loddigesii. Deciduous, epiphytic orchid with cylindrical pseudobulbs, becoming pendent, and oblong, fleshy leaves, 3in (8cm) long. Pale rose-pink flowers, 2in (5cm) across, each with an orange disk on the fringed lip, are produced singly from the nodes in spring, usually after the leaves have fallen. ↕↔ 6in (15cm). S.W. China. ❄ (min. 50°F/10°C; max. 86°F/30°C)
D. longicornu. Semi-evergreen, epiphytic orchid with slender, black-hairy pseudobulbs and linear-lance-shaped leaves, 3in (8cm) long. In autumn, bears racemes of 1–3 fragrant white flowers, 2in (5cm) across, with red and yellow markings on the fringed lips, from the upper halves of the leafy stems. ↕ 12in (30cm), ↔ 6in (15cm). Himalayas, Burma, Thailand. ❄ (min. 50°F/10°C; max. 86°F/30°C)
***D.* Malones 'Hope'** ▣ Deciduous nobile hybrid orchid with erect pseudobulbs and oblong leaves, 4in (10cm) long. Dark pink flowers, 3in (8cm) across, with white-margined yellow lips, are produced in pairs in spring. ↕ 24in (60cm), ↔ 12in (30cm). ❄ (min. 50°F/10°C; max. 86°F/30°C)

Dendrobium nobile

***D.* Momozono 'Princess'** ▣ Deciduous nobile hybrid orchid with pseudobulbs and oblong leaves, 4in (10cm) long. Bears dark pink flowers, 3in (8cm) across, fading to white in the centers, and with white and pink marks on the lips, in pairs in spring. ↕ 24in (60cm), ↔ 12in (30cm). ❄ (min. 50°F/10°C; max. 86°F/30°C)
D. moschatum. Evergreen, epiphytic orchid with cylindrical pseudobulbs and lance-shaped leaves, to 6in (15cm) long. In spring, bears pale yellow flowers, 3in (8cm) across, with a pink flush and 2 maroon marks on each cupped lip, in racemes to 8in (20cm) long, from the upper nodes. ↕ 3–6ft (1–2m), ↔ 24in (60cm). Himalayas, Burma, Thailand, Laos. ❄ (min. 50°F/10°C; max. 86°F/30°C)
D. nobile ▣ Semi-evergreen, epiphytic orchid with cylindrical to club-shaped pseudobulbs and lance-shaped to ovate-lance-shaped leaves, 3–5in (8–13cm) long. Pale rose-pink flowers, 2½in (6cm) across, tipped with amethyst, and with a maroon mark on each lip, are produced in pairs in spring. ↕ 18in (45cm), ↔ 6in (15cm). Himalayas, S. China, Taiwan. ❄ (min. 50°F/10°C; max. 86°F/30°C)

D. ochreatum. Deciduous, epiphytic orchid with long, knotted, decumbent pseudobulbs, 4–5in (10–13cm) long, and lance-shaped leaves, 4–7in (10–18cm) long. Rich golden yellow flowers, 3in (8cm) across, with a maroon mark on each lip, are produced in pairs in spring. ↕↔ 6in (15cm). E. Himalayas, Burma, Thailand, Laos. ❄ (min. 50°F/10°C; max. 86°F/30°C)
***D.* Oriental Paradise** ▣ Deciduous nobile hybrid orchid with pseudobulbs and oblong leaves, 4in (10cm) long. Bears white flowers, 3in (8cm) across, with dark pink notches on the petals, and red and yellow marks on the lips, in pairs, in spring. ↕ 24in (60cm), ↔ 12in (30cm). ❄ (min. 50°F/10°C; max. 86°F/30°C)
D. phalaenopsis see *D. bigibbum* var. *phalaenopsis.*
D. pierardii see *D. aphyllum.*
D. speciosum (Rock lily). Evergreen, semi-epiphytic orchid with stout, cylindrical or club-shaped pseudobulbs bearing ovate or oblong leaves, to 10in (25cm) long, at the apexes. In spring, produces fragrant, purple-marked, creamy white flowers, to 3in (8cm) across, that do not open widely, in dense racemes, to 24in (60cm) long, from the pseudobulb tips. ↕ 18in (45cm), ↔ 12in (30cm). Australia (New South Wales, Queensland, Victoria). ❄ (min. 55°F/13°C; max. 86°F/30°C)
***D.* Spiral Gem 'Universal Topaz'** ▣ Evergreen orchid with cylindrical pseudobulbs and narrowly ovate leaves, 4–10in (10–25cm) long. Bears racemes, 16in (40cm) long, of 6–9 green-yellow flowers, ⅜–½in (8–12mm) across, with red lips, from winter to spring. ↕ 10–14in (25–35cm), ↔ 3ft (1m). ❄ (min. 50°F/10°C; max. 86°F/30°C)
D. wardianum. Deciduous, epiphytic orchid with jointed, cylindrical pseudobulbs, becoming pendent, and lance-shaped leaves, 3–5in (8–13cm) long. From spring to autumn, white flowers, to 4in (10cm) across, with purple-tipped segments, and yellow and maroon marks on the lips, are produced in pairs. ↕ 12in (30cm), ↔ 6in (15cm). E. Himalayas, Bhutan, S.W. China, Burma, Thailand. ❄ (min. 50°F/10°C; max. 86°F/30°C)

Dendrobium Momozono 'Princess'

Dendrobium Oriental Paradise

Dendrobium Spiral Gem 'Universal Topaz'

DENDROCALAMUS

POACEAE

Genus of about 30 species of giant, clump-forming, evergreen, rhizomatous bamboos from tropical and subtropical S. and E. Asia. They have thick culms and lance-shaped, downy or bristly leaf-blades. In their native regions, these huge bamboos are used in construction; the hollowed stems are used in irrigation and to make paper pulp. They are suitable for specimen plantings or may be used for making a bamboo grove. Where not hardy, they can be grown in a warm greenhouse or in interior landscapes.

- **CULTIVATION** Under glass, grow in soil-based potting mix, enriched with leaf mold, in bright filtered light with high humidity. Water freely in summer, moderately in winter. Outdoors, grow in fertile, humus-rich, moist but well-drained soil in sun or partial shade. Most are frost-tender; some will tolerate 30°F (-1°C).
- **PROPAGATION** Divide established clumps in spring. Cut sections of young culms in spring, placing them horizontally in sphagnum moss in a closed, heated propagating case.
- **PESTS AND DISEASES** Infrequent.

D. giganteus, syn. *Sinocalamus giganteus* (Giant bamboo, Kyo-Chiku). Robust, clump-forming bamboo producing rapidly spreading rhizomes and erect then gracefully arching, hairy-jointed culms, eventually reaching 12in (30cm) wide. Lance-shaped, smooth, minutely toothed leaf blades, to 22in (55cm) long, arise from the culm joints and clasp the culms at their bases. ↕ 80–100ft (25–30m). S.E. Asia. ❄ (min. 45°F/7°C)

DENDROCHILUM

Golden chain orchid

ORCHIDACEAE

Genus of about 120–150 species of evergreen, epiphytic orchids from S.E. Asia and New Guinea, often found on trees and rocks by rivers at altitudes of 2,300–7,000ft (700–2,000m). Ovoid to cylindrical pseudobulbs produce 1 or 2 elliptic-lance-shaped leaves. They are valued for their chain-like racemes of

D

Delphinium 'Bellamosum'

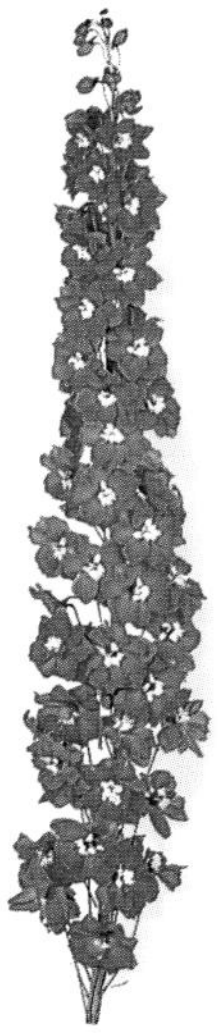

Delphinium 'Blue Nile'

Delphinium cardinale

Delphinium 'Cliveden Beauty'

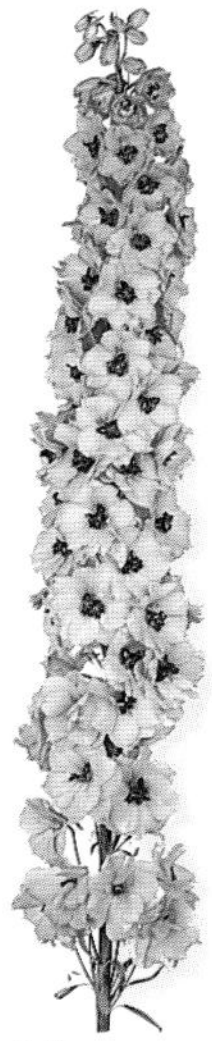

Delphinium 'Conspicuous'

Delphinium 'Emily Hawkins'

bees; the lower florets often still in good condition as the top ones open.
***D.* 'Black Knight'.** Pacific Hybrid with deep purple flowers with black bees.
***D.* 'Blue Bees'** ■ Belladonna producing clear blue flowers with white centers.
***D.* 'Blue Bird'.** Pacific Hybrid bearing mid-blue flowers with white bees.
***D.* 'Blue Dawn'.** Medium Elatum bearing semi-double, pale blue flowers, with a touch of pink, and small, brown-black bees.
***D.* 'Blue Jay'.** Pacific Hybrid with deep blue flowers.
***D.* 'Blue Nile'** ■ Medium Elatum bearing semi-double, bright, mid-blue flowers with white bees.
***D.* 'Boningale Glory'.** Tall Elatum bearing semi-double, mid-blue flowers with mauve inner petals.
***D.* 'Bruce'** ■ Tall Elatum bearing semi-double, violet-purple flowers, paler toward the centers, with brown bees.
D. brunonianum. Upright perennial with hairy stems and deeply 3- to 5-lobed leaves. In early summer, bears racemes of hooded, short-spurred, hairy, single flowers, 1¼–2in (3–5cm) wide, blue to purple with black-purple bees, and heavily veined. ↕↔ 8in (20cm). Pakistan to S.W. Tibet. Zone 4.
***D.* 'Butterball'** ■ Small Elatum producing semi-double, rich light cream flowers with deep yellow bees.
***D.* 'Cameliard'.** Pacific Hybrid with deep purple flowers, shading to blue at the frilly sepal margins, and cream bees.
***D.* 'Can-can'.** Small Elatum producing fully double flowers. Light mauve sepals are veined with dark mauve and have frilled margins; the outer sepals have dark blue margins.
D. cardinale ■ Short-lived perennial with deeply 3- to 5-lobed leaves. Bears loose racemes of elf-cap-shaped, stout-spurred, single scarlet flowers, ¾in (2cm) across, with yellow centers, in early summer. ↕ 6ft (2m), ↔ 18in (45cm). California to Mexico (Baja California). Zone 7b.
***D.* 'Casa Blanca'.** Belladonna with white flowers.
D. cashmerianum. Perennial with rounded, toothed, shallowly 5- to 7-lobed leaves. From early to late summer, bears single, dark purple-blue flowers, 1¼–1½in (3–4cm) across, in open panicles. ↕ 12–16in (30–40cm), ↔ 6in (15cm). N. India to China. Zone 6.
***D.* 'Cassius'.** Medium Elatum with semi-double, deep blue flowers overlaid with purple; bees are brown-tinged.
***D.* 'Chelsea Star'.** Medium Elatum bearing semi-double, velvety, rich violet flowers with white bees.
D. chinense see *D. grandiflorum.*
***D.* 'Cliveden Beauty'** ■ Belladonna with sky-blue flowers.
***D.* Connecticut Yankee Series 'Blue Fountains'.** Belladonna producing single flowers in white and shades of blue and mauve. Zone 4.
D. consolida see *Consolida ajacis.*
***D.* 'Conspicuous'** ■ Small Elatum bearing semi-double, lilac-mauve flowers with prominent brown bees.
***D.* 'Crown Jewel'.** Small Elatum bearing semi-double, pink-tinged, pale blue flowers with prominent brown bees.
***D.* 'Emily Hawkins'** ■ Medium Elatum producing neat, semi-double, light violet flowers with fawn bees.

Delphinium 'Blue Bees'

Delphinium 'Bruce'

Delphinium 'Butterball'

Delphinium 'Fanfare'

Delphinium grandiflorum 'Blue Butterfly'

Delphinium 'Langdon's Royal Flush'

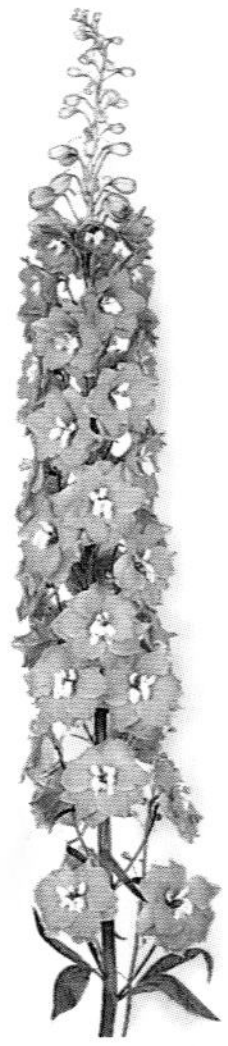
Delphinium 'Lord Butler'

Delphinium 'Mighty Atom'

Delphinium nudicaule

***D.* 'Fanfare'** ▣ Unusually tall Elatum bearing semi-double, silvery mauve flowers with white bees. ↕7ft (2.2m).
***D.* Fantasia Hybrids.** Semi-dwarf hybrid strain producing white, lavender, and blue flowers with white bees. ↕28in (70cm).
***D.* 'Faust'.** Tall Elatum with semi-double flowers of deep cornflower-blue, overlaid with purple, and indigo bees.
***D.* 'Fenella'.** Small Elatum bearing semi-double, gentian-blue flowers with black bees.
***D.* 'Finsteraarhorn'.** Medium Elatum with short, slim, wind-resistant stems and single, dark gentian-blue flowers with black bees. The lower florets are often still in good condition as the top ones open.
***D.* 'Galahad'.** Pacific Hybrid with pure white flowers.
***D.* 'Gillian Dallas'.** Small Elatum bearing semi-double, mauve-tinged, slate-gray flowers with white bees.
***D.* 'Giotto'.** Medium Elatum with semi-double flowers. The inner sepals are clear violet, the outer ones are gentian-blue, and the bees are light yellowish brown.
***D.* 'Gletscher Wasser'.** Medium Elatum with short, slim, wind-resistant stems and single, light ice-blue flowers. The lower florets are often still in good condition as the top ones open.
***D.* 'Gordon Forsyth'.** Tall Elatum producing semi-double, amethyst-purple flowers with gray-brown bees.
D. grandiflorum, syn. *D. chinense.* Short-lived perennial usually grown as an annual. The elf-cap-shaped, single blue, violet, or white flowers, 1½in (4cm) across, are produced in open panicles in early summer. Leaves are 5-lobed, with each lobe further divided into narrow segments. ↕8–20in (20–50cm), ↔ 9–12in (23–30cm). Siberia, Mongolia, China, Japan. Zone 4. **'Album'** produces white flowers. **'Blauer Zwerg'** is upright in habit, bearing gentian-blue flowers; ↕ to 8in (20cm). **'Blue Butterfly'** ▣ is stocky, and bears bright blue flowers. **'Sky Blue'** produces almost pure white sepals, turning very pale blue, with dark veins beneath.
***D.* 'Guinevere'.** Pacific Hybrid bearing pink-tinged, pale purple flowers with white bees.
***D.* 'Jubelruf'.** Tall Elatum producing short, slim, wind-resistant stems that bear semi-double, bright mid-blue flowers with white bees. The lower florets are often still in good condition as the top ones open.
***D.* 'King Arthur'.** Pacific Hybrid bearing plum flowers with white bees.
***D.* 'Lancelot'.** Pacific Hybrid with purplish pink flowers.
***D.* 'Langdon's Royal Flush'** ▣ Small Elatum bearing semi-double, pale mauve-pink flowers with white or pale yellow bees.
***D.* 'Loch Leven'.** Medium Elatum bearing semi-double, light blue flowers with white bees.
***D.* 'Lord Butler'** ▣ Small Elatum with semi-double, mid-blue flowers, flushed mauve at the centers, with white bees.
***D.* Mid-century Hybrids.** Hybrid strain producing flowers in various shades, on strong stems. Mildew resistant. ↕4–5ft (1.2–1.5m). **'Ivory Towers'** produces white flowers. **'Moody Blues'** is pale blue. **'Rose Future'** produces pink flowers. **'Ultra Violet'** is deep blue-purple.
***D.* 'Mighty Atom'** ▣ Small Elatum bearing semi-double, mid-violet flowers with brown-streaked bees. May develop fused and flattened stems, especially if overfertilized.
***D.* 'Min'.** Medium Elatum bearing semi-double, very pale purple flowers, suffused and veined with deeper purple; the brown bees are striped with pale purple.
***D.* 'Moerheimii'.** Belladonna with white flowers.
***D.* 'Mother of Pearl'** see *D.* 'Perlmutterbaum'.
D. muscosum. Perennial with rounded, 3- to 7-lobed, finely divided, softly hairy leaves, on long stalks. Bears single, dark blue to dark violet flowers, 1¼–1½in (3–4cm) across, in racemes in early and midsummer. ↕↔ 4–6in (10–15cm). Bhutan. Zone 5.
***D.* 'Nachtwache'.** Tall Elatum with short, slim, wind-resistant stems and semi-double, violet-blue flowers with white bees. The lower florets remain in good condition as the top ones open.
D. nudicaule ▣ Short-lived perennial, often grown as an annual, with fleshy, 3- to 5-lobed leaves on long stalks. Half-closed, funnel-shaped, single, bright vermilion-red, orange-red, or yellow flowers, to ¾in (2cm) across, with red to yellow throats, are produced in open panicles on sturdy, unbranched stems in midsummer. ↕8–24in (20–60cm), ↔ 8in (20cm). California. Zone 5.
***D.* Pennant Hybrids.** Hybrid strain producing double, blue, lavender, pink, and white flowers with white and dark bees. ↕18in (45cm).
***D.* 'Percival'.** Pacific Hybrid that produces white flowers with black bees.
***D.* 'Pericles'.** Medium Elatum producing semi-double, pale sky-blue flowers with white bees that have a few creamy white hairs.
***D.* 'Perlmutterbaum'**, syn. *D.* 'Mother of Pearl'. Tall Elatum producing semi-double, light blue and soft pink, bicolored flowers, with brown bees, on

Delphinium 'Princess Caroline'

Delphinium requienii

Delphinium 'Rosemary Brock'

Delphinium 'Sandpiper'

Delphinium 'Sungleam'

Delphinium tatsienense

short, slim, wind-resistant stems. The lower florets are often still in good condition as the top ones open.
***D.* 'Piccolo'**. Belladonna with bright gentian-blue flowers.
***D.* 'Princess Caroline'** ■ Perennial selected from hybrids of *D. cardinale*, *D. elatum*, and *D. nudicaule* cultivars. Bears semi-double, coral-pink flowers, 1¼–2½in (3–6cm) across, in short racemes in early summer. ↕ 3½ft (1.1m), ↔ 24in (60cm).
D. requienii ■ Vigorous annual or biennial with 5- to 7-lobed, glossy leaves. In early summer, produces many branched spikes of elf-cap-shaped, green and mauve-gray flowers, ½in (1.5cm) across, with prominent purple anthers. ↕ 12–39in (30–100cm), ↔ 18in (45cm). S. France (including Iles d'Hyères and Corsica), Italy (Sardinia). Zone 7b.
***D.* 'Rosemary Brock'** ■ Small Elatum bearing semi-double, deep dusky pink flowers, with darker sepal tips and margins, and brown bees with yellow hairs.
***D.* x *ruysii* 'Pink Sensation'**. Short-lived, upright perennial with small, glossy, finely divided, 3- to 5-lobed leaves. Nodding, yellowish pink buds, on short, straight, slim spikes, open to elf-cap-shaped, dusty pink flowers, ¾in (2cm) across, from summer to autumn. ↕ 3ft (1m), ↔ 24in (60cm).
***D.* 'Sandpiper'** ■ Small Elatum producing semi-double white flowers with dark brown bees.
D. semibarbatum, syn. *D. zalil*. Short-lived, tuberous perennial with 5-lobed leaves, further divided into narrow segments. In early and mid-summer, produces unbranched spikes of elf-cap-shaped, sulfur-yellow flowers, ½in (1.5cm) across, with orange-tipped central sepals. ↕ 3ft (1m), ↔ 9in (23cm). Afghanistan, Iran. ❀ (min. 41°F/5°C)
***D.* 'Skyline'**. Small Elatum with semi-double, sky-blue flowers tinged pink near the centers, the large white bees tinted blue.
***D.* 'Spindrift'**. Medium Elatum with semi-double, pale cobalt-blue flowers with creamy white bees; sepals and bees are suffused with lilac. Variable in color; sepals often have conspicuous turquoise and green tinges.
***D.* 'Summer Skies'**. Pacific Hybrid producing light sky-blue flowers.
***D.* 'Sungleam'** ■ Small Elatum bearing semi-double cream flowers, deeper cream near the margins, with pale sulfur-yellow bees.
D. tatsienense ■ Perennial with deeply divided, 3- to 7-lobed leaves. In early and midsummer, bears panicles of elf-cap-shaped, bright cornflower-blue flowers, 1–2in (2.5–5cm) across, with hooded bees and azure-tipped sepals, on branched stems. ↕ 8–24in (20–60cm), ↔ 12in (30cm). W. China (including E. Tibet). Zone 7.
***D.* 'Tiddles'**. Small Elatum with fully double, slate-mauve flowers.
***D.* 'Turkish Delight'**. Medium Elatum producing semi-double, pale pinkish mauve flowers, with white bees.
***D.* 'Völkerfrieden'**. Strong-growing Belladonna with deep blue flowers.
***D.* 'Wendy'**, syn. *D.* 'Andenken an August Koenemann'. Belladonna with gentian-blue flowers.
D. zalil see *D. semibarbatum*.

DENDRANTHEMA

ASTERACEAE

Genus of 20 species of erect perennials from Europe and C. and E. Asia, occurring in very variable habitats, from seashore to mountain top. They were previously included in and commonly grown as *Chrysanthemum*, but are now considered distinct. Alternate, mostly rounded, aromatic, fleshy, mid- to dark green leaves are palmately 5-lobed. Disk- or bowl-shaped white, yellow, pink, or purple flowerheads, ½–3in (1–8cm) across, are produced singly or in loose corymbs. Grow in a herbaceous or mixed border, a rock garden, or a scree bed. All parts may cause mild stomach upset if ingested, and contact with foliage may aggravate skin allergies.
• **CULTIVATION** Grow in fertile, sandy, moist but well-drained soil in full sun. Short-lived when grown in heavy soil.
• **PROPAGATION** Sow seed in containers in an open frame in autumn. Divide after flowering in autumn, or in spring.
• **PESTS AND DISEASES** Infrequent.

D. pacificum see *Ajania pacifica*.
D. weyrichii, syn. *Chrysanthemum weyrichii*. Mat-forming, rhizomatous perennial with rounded, 5-lobed, fleshy, mid- to dark green leaves, 2–4in (5–10cm) long. The smaller stem leaves are lance-shaped and usually pinnatifid. Daisy-like flowerheads, to 2in (5cm) across, with pink or white ray florets and yellow disk florets, are produced in autumn. ↕ to 12in (30cm), ↔ 18in (45cm). Russia (Kamchatka, Sakhalin). Zone 4. Both of the following cultivars make attractive, mounded cushions: **'Pink Bomb'** produces pink flowerheads; ↕ 10in (25cm). **'White Bomb'** has pink-tinged, white flowerheads.

DENDROBIUM

ORCHIDACEAE

Genus of about 900 species of deciduous, semi-evergreen, or evergreen, epiphytic and terrestrial orchids widely spread from India and S.E. Asia to New Guinea, Australia, and the Pacific islands; they occur in low-altitude rain-forest or montane forest over 7,000ft (2,000m). Elongated, stem-like pseudobulbs, sometimes branched, bear linear or lance-shaped to ovate leaves, either at the ends of the stems or 2-ranked. Single- to many-flowered racemes or panicles of showy flowers are produced from nodes along the stems, mainly in spring.
• **CULTIVATION** Temperate-growing orchids. Grow epiphytically on a bark slab, or in epiphytic orchid potting mix in a container or slatted basket. From late spring to summer, grow in humid, partial shade; water freely, adding half-strength fertilizer at every third watering, and mist twice daily. Admit full light from autumn to early spring; keep dry in winter. They resent disturbance and flower best in small containers. Support flowering stems. See also p.46.
• **PROPAGATION** Divide when plant fills and overflows the container. Plant offsets when roots are actively growing. For deciduous species, take stem cuttings of the older stems, each with one or more dormant buds, and lay them on damp moss in humid conditions. Pot up individually when rooted, usually after a few months.
• **PESTS AND DISEASES** Spider mites, aphids, whiteflies, and mealybugs are troublesome. Prone to a number of viruses, bacterial and fungal bulb rots, leaf spots, petal blights such as gray mold (*Botrytis*), and soft rot.

D. aggregatum see *D. lindleyi*.
D. amethystoglossum. Semi-evergreen, epiphytic orchid with upright pseudobulbs and oval-oblong leaves, 4in (10cm) long. Produces crowded, drooping racemes, 5in (13cm) long, of white flowers, to 1¼in (3cm) across, with bright amethyst lips, from winter to spring. ↕ 24–36in (60–90cm), ↔ 6in (15cm). Philippines. ❀ (min. 50°F/10°C; max. 86°F/30°C)
D. aphyllum ■ syn. *D. pierardii*. Deciduous, epiphytic orchid with pendent, slender pseudobulbs and lance-shaped to linear-lance-shaped, fleshy leaves, 5in (13cm) long. Pale mauve-pink flowers, 2in (5cm) across, with primrose-yellow lips, are borne in pairs in spring. ↕ 3ft (1m), ↔ 6in (15cm). Himalayas, S.W. China to Malaysia. ❀ (min. 50°F/10°C; max. 86°F/30°C)
D. bigibbum. Semi-evergreen, epiphytic orchid with upright pseudobulbs and oblong-lance-shaped, leathery leaves, to 5in (13cm) long. White, lilac-purple, purple, mauve, or pink flowers, to 2½in (6cm) across, are produced in racemes 4–16in (10–40cm) long, from the upper nodes in spring. ↕ 3ft (1m) or more, ↔ 6in (15cm). Australia (Queensland). ❀ (min. 55°F/13°C; max. 86°F/30°C). **var. *phalaenopsis***, syn. *D. phalaenopsis*, has white flowers, flushed light pinkish mauve at the tips and on the lips.
D. chrysanthum ■ Evergreen, epiphytic orchid producing pendent pseudobulbs, 3ft (1m) long, with lance-shaped leaves, 4–8in (10–20cm) long, along their lengths. Deep golden yellow flowers, 1½in (4cm) across, with fringed deep orange or yellow lips, are borne in pendent racemes, 1½–8in (4–20cm) long, in summer or autumn. ↕ 3–6ft (1–2m), ↔ 18in (45cm). E. Himalayas to Burma, Thailand. ❀ (min. 50°F/10°C; max. 86°F/30°C)
D. densiflorum. Evergreen, epiphytic orchid with 4-angled pseudobulbs and narrowly elliptic or lance-shaped leaves, to 6in (15cm) long. In spring, bears golden yellow flowers, 2in (5cm) across, with darker, downy, lips, in dense, pendent racemes, to 10in (25cm) long, from the upper nodes. ↕↔ 12in (30cm). Himalayas, Burma, Vietnam, Thailand. ❀ (min. 50°F/10°C; max. 86°F/30°C)
D. fimbriatum. Evergreen, epiphytic orchid with slender, spindle-shaped pseudobulbs and oblong to lance-shaped, pointed leaves, 3–6in (8–15cm) long. In spring, produces golden or orange-yellow flowers, to 2½in (6cm) across, with fringed lips, in pendent racemes, to 7in (18cm) long, from the upper nodes. ↕ 2–4ft (60–120cm), ↔ 12in (30cm). Himalayas, Burma, Thailand, Malaysia, Vietnam, Laos, S. China. ❀ (min. 50°F/10°C; max. 86°F/30°C)
D. infundibulum ■ Semi-evergreen, epiphytic orchid with cylindrical, hairy pseudobulbs and ovate-oblong leaves, 3in (8cm) long. Pure white flowers, 3in (8cm) across, with yellow markings in the throats, are produced in racemes, to 8in (20cm) long, from the upper halves of the pseudobulbs, from spring to summer. ↕ 24in (60cm), ↔ 6in (15cm). Burma, Thailand. ❀ (min. 50°F/10°C; max. 86°F/30°C)
D. kingianum. Evergreen, epiphytic orchid with narrowly ovate to narrowly obovate leaves, to 4in (10cm) long, produced from the upper portions of the short, thick, pointed pseudobulbs. In spring, fragrant white, pink, mauve, purple, or red flowers, to 1½in (4cm) across, are borne in racemes, 3–6in (7–15cm) long, from the pseudobulb tips. ↕↔ 6in (15cm). Australia (New South Wales, Queensland). ❀ (min. 50°F/10°C; max. 86°F/30°C)

Dendrobium chrysanthum

Dendrobium aphyllum

Dendrobium infundibulum

Dendrobium Malones 'Hope'

D. lindleyi, syn. *D. aggregatum*. Evergreen, epiphytic orchid with dwarf, compressed pseudobulbs each bearing a single, oval leaf, 2–3in (5–8cm) long. Bright yellow or pale golden yellow flowers, to 1½in (4cm) across, in pendent racemes, 4–12in (10–30cm) long, are produced in spring. ↕4in (10cm), ↔6in (15cm). Himalayas, Laos, Vietnam, Cambodia, S.W. China, Burma, Thailand. ❀ (min. 50°F/10°C; max. 86°F/30°C)
D. loddigesii. Deciduous, epiphytic orchid with cylindrical pseudobulbs, becoming pendent, and oblong, fleshy leaves, 3in (8cm) long. Pale rose-pink flowers, 2in (5cm) across, each with an orange disk on the fringed lip, are produced singly from the nodes in spring, usually after the leaves have fallen. ↕↔6in (15cm). S.W. China. ❀ (min. 50°F/10°C; max. 86°F/30°C)
D. longicornu. Semi-evergreen, epiphytic orchid with slender, black-hairy pseudobulbs and linear-lance-shaped leaves, 3in (8cm) long. In autumn, bears racemes of 1–3 fragrant white flowers, 2in (5cm) across, with red and yellow markings on the fringed lips, from the upper halves of the leafy stems. ↕12in (30cm), ↔6in (15cm). Himalayas, Burma, Thailand. ❀ (min. 50°F/10°C; max. 86°F/30°C)
***D.* Malones 'Hope'** ▣ Deciduous nobile hybrid orchid with erect pseudobulbs and oblong leaves, 4in (10cm) long. Dark pink flowers, 3in (8cm) across, with white-margined yellow lips, are produced in pairs in spring. ↕24in (60cm), ↔12in (30cm). ❀ (min. 50°F/10°C; max. 86°F/30°C)

Dendrobium Momozono 'Princess'

Dendrobium nobile

***D.* Momozono 'Princess'** ▣ Deciduous nobile hybrid orchid with pseudobulbs and oblong leaves, 4in (10cm) long. Bears dark pink flowers, 3in (8cm) across, fading to white in the centers, and with white and pink marks on the lips, in pairs in spring. ↕24in (60cm), ↔12in (30cm). ❀ (min. 50°F/10°C; max. 86°F/30°C)
D. moschatum. Evergreen, epiphytic orchid with cylindrical pseudobulbs and lance-shaped leaves, to 6in (15cm) long. In spring, bears pale yellow flowers, 3in (8cm) across, with a pink flush and 2 maroon marks on each cupped lip, in racemes to 8in (20cm) long, from the upper nodes. ↕3–6ft (1–2m), ↔24in (60cm). Himalayas, Burma, Thailand, Laos. ❀ (min. 50°F/10°C; max. 86°F/30°C)
D. nobile ▣ Semi-evergreen, epiphytic orchid with cylindrical to club-shaped pseudobulbs and lance-shaped to ovate-lance-shaped leaves, 3–5in (8–13cm) long. Pale rose-pink flowers, 2½in (6cm) across, tipped with amethyst, and with a maroon mark on each lip, are produced in pairs in spring. ↕18in (45cm), ↔6in (15cm). Himalayas, S. China, Taiwan. ❀ (min. 50°F/10°C; max. 86°F/30°C)

Dendrobium Oriental Paradise

D. ochreatum. Deciduous, epiphytic orchid with long, knotted, decumbent pseudobulbs, 4–5in (10–13cm) long, and lance-shaped leaves, 4–7in (10–18cm) long. Rich golden yellow flowers, 3in (8cm) across, with a maroon mark on each lip, are produced in pairs in spring. ↕↔6in (15cm). E. Himalayas, Burma, Thailand, Laos. ❀ (min. 50°F/10°C; max. 86°F/30°C)
***D.* Oriental Paradise** ▣ Deciduous nobile hybrid orchid with pseudobulbs and oblong leaves, 4in (10cm) long. Bears white flowers, 3in (8cm) across, with dark pink notches on the petals, and red and yellow marks on the lips, in pairs, in spring. ↕24in (60cm), ↔12in (30cm). ❀ (min. 50°F/10°C; max. 86°F/30°C)
D. phalaenopsis see *D. bigibbum* var. *phalaenopsis*.
D. pierardii see *D. aphyllum*.
D. speciosum (Rock lily). Evergreen, semi-epiphytic orchid with stout, cylindrical or club-shaped pseudobulbs bearing ovate or oblong leaves, to 10in (25cm) long, at the apexes. In spring, produces fragrant, purple-marked, creamy white flowers, to 3in (8cm) across, that do not open widely, in dense racemes, to 24in (60cm) long, from the pseudobulb tips. ↕18in (45cm), ↔12in (30cm). Australia (New South Wales, Queensland, Victoria). ❀ (min. 55°F/13°C; max. 86°F/30°C)

Dendrobium Spiral Gem 'Universal Topaz'

***D.* Spiral Gem 'Universal Topaz'** ▣ Evergreen orchid with cylindrical pseudobulbs and narrowly ovate leaves, 4–10in (10–25cm) long. Bears racemes, 16in (40cm) long, of 6–9 green-yellow flowers, ⅜–½in (8–12mm) across, with red lips, from winter to spring. ↕10–14in (25–35cm), ↔3ft (1m). ❀ (min. 50°F/10°C; max. 86°F/30°C)
D. wardianum. Deciduous, epiphytic orchid with jointed, cylindrical pseudobulbs, becoming pendent, and lance-shaped leaves, 3–5in (8–13cm) long. From spring to autumn, white flowers, to 4in (10cm) across, with purple-tipped segments, and yellow and maroon marks on the lips, are produced in pairs. ↕12in (30cm), ↔6in (15cm). E. Himalayas, Bhutan, S.W. China, Burma, Thailand. ❀ (min. 50°F/10°C; max. 86°F/30°C)

DENDROCALAMUS

POACEAE

Genus of about 30 species of giant, clump-forming, evergreen, rhizomatous bamboos from tropical and subtropical S. and E. Asia. They have thick culms and lance-shaped, downy or bristly leaf-blades. In their native regions, these huge bamboos are used in construction; the hollowed stems are used in irrigation and to make paper pulp. They are suitable for specimen plantings or may be used for making a bamboo grove. Where not hardy, they can be grown in a warm greenhouse or in interior landscapes.
• **CULTIVATION** Under glass, grow in soil-based potting mix, enriched with leaf mold, in bright filtered light with high humidity. Water freely in summer, moderately in winter. Outdoors, grow in fertile, humus-rich, moist but well-drained soil in sun or partial shade. Most are frost-tender; some will tolerate 30°F (-1°C).
• **PROPAGATION** Divide established clumps in spring. Cut sections of young culms in spring, placing them horizontally in sphagnum moss in a closed, heated propagating case.
• **PESTS AND DISEASES** Infrequent.

D. giganteus, syn. *Sinocalamus giganteus* (Giant bamboo, Kyo-Chiku). Robust, clump-forming bamboo producing rapidly spreading rhizomes and erect then gracefully arching, hairy-jointed culms, eventually reaching 12in (30cm) wide. Lance-shaped, smooth, minutely toothed leaf blades, to 22in (55cm) long, arise from the culm joints and clasp the culms at their bases. ↕80–100ft (25–30m). S.E. Asia. ❀ (min. 45°F/7°C)

DENDROCHILUM

Golden chain orchid

ORCHIDACEAE

Genus of about 120–150 species of evergreen, epiphytic orchids from S.E. Asia and New Guinea, often found on trees and rocks by rivers at altitudes of 2,300–7,000ft (700–2,000m). Ovoid to cylindrical pseudobulbs produce 1 or 2 elliptic-lance-shaped leaves. They are valued for their chain-like racemes of

fragrant, dainty, star-shaped flowers, borne in early summer.
• **CULTIVATION** Cool-growing orchids. Grow in epiphytic orchid potting mix in a container. In summer, provide humid, shaded conditions and water freely, applying fertilizer at every third watering. In winter, admit full light and water sparingly. See also p.46.
• **PROPAGATION** Divide when plant overflows the container, or remove backbulbs and pot up separately.
• **PESTS AND DISEASES** Susceptible to spider mites, aphids, and mealybugs.

D. glumaceum (Hay-scented orchid). Epiphytic orchid with ovoid pseudobulbs, 1–2in (2.5–5cm) long, each with one narrowly elliptic leaf, to 12in (30cm) long. Star-shaped white flowers, to ¾in (2cm) across, do not open widely. They are produced densely from the axils of conspicuous white bracts, in 2 rows on pendent racemes, from the center of the new growth. ↕ to 20in (50cm), ↔ 12in (30cm). Philippines. ❀ (min. 55°F/13°C; max. 86°F/30°C)

DENDROMECON
Tree poppy
PAPAVERACEAE

Genus of 1 or 2 species of evergreen shrubs and small trees found in scrub on dry, rocky slopes in S.W. US and Mexico. *D. rigida* is cultivated for its lance-shaped, simple, leathery, glaucous leaves, arranged alternately along the stems, and for its showy, poppy-like, fragrant flowers. It looks best grown against a wall, but may be used in a cool greenhouse in cold regions.
• **CULTIVATION** Grow in well-drained soil in full sun. Pruning group 13, if wall-trained.
• **PROPAGATION** Sow seed at 50–55°F (10–13°C) in autumn or spring. Insert softwood cuttings in summer or insert root cuttings in winter.
• **PESTS AND DISEASES** Infrequent.

Dendromecon rigida

D. rigida ■ Spreading shrub with rigid, upright shoots and lance-shaped, leathery, glaucous, gray-green leaves, to 4in (10cm) long. Solitary, poppy-like, fragrant yellow flowers, to 3in (8cm) across, are produced from spring to autumn. ↕↔ 10ft (3m). California, Mexico. ❀ (min. 41°F/5°C)

DENMOZA
CACTACEAE

Genus of 2 species of spherical to columnar cacti from hillsides in Argentina. They have very thick stems and densely spiny ribs. Tubular flowers are produced mainly near the top of the stems, the style and stamens protruding in a cluster from each almost-closed throat. Spherical, scaly fruits have woolly tufts, which later fall, and large, helmet-shaped black seeds. Where not hardy, grow in a warm greenhouse; in warmer climates, grow in a border with other succulents.
• **CULTIVATION** Under glass, grow in standard cactus potting mix, in full light and low humidity. In growing season, water moderately and apply fertilizer monthly; keep completely dry at other times. Outdoors, grow in sharply drained, gritty soil in full sun. Some species tolerate 21°F (-6°C) if kept dry in winter. See also pp.48–49.
• **PROPAGATION** Sow seed at 70°F (21°C) in spring or early summer.
• **PESTS AND DISEASES** Vulnerable to mealybugs and root mealybugs, especially in containers.

D. rhodacantha. Spherical cactus with 15–30 deeply furrowed ribs. Areoles have brownish red spines (8–10 radials and usually one central). Bears diurnal, tubular red flowers, 3in (8cm) long, in summer. ↕↔ 6–12in (15–30cm). N.W. and W. Argentina. ❀ (min. 50°F/10°C)

DENNSTAEDTIA
DENNSTAEDTIACEAE

Genus of about 70 species of deciduous ferns found mainly in woodland in tropical regions. In spring, erect, lance-shaped or roughly triangular fronds, usually 2- or 3-pinnate, arise from a creeping rhizome, soon forming colonies that may become invasive. Sori develop along the margins of the frond segments, covered by cup-shaped indusia. Use *Dennstaedtia* species to provide groundcover in a shady border, although *D. punctiloba* may become invasive. Where not hardy, grow in a cool or warm greenhouse; tropical species may also become invasive.
• **CULTIVATION** Under glass, grow in an acidic, soilless potting mix in bright filtered light. Water freely when in growth, sparingly in winter. Outdoors, grow in moist, humus-rich, acidic soil in partial to deep shade.
• **PROPAGATION** Sow spores at 59°F (15°C) for hardier species, and 70°F (21°C) for tender species, as soon as ripe. Divide in spring. See also p.51.
• **PESTS AND DISEASES** Slugs and snails may be problems.

D. davallioides (Lacy ground fern). Spreading fern with long-creeping rhizomes. Broadly triangular, mid-green fronds, 16–28in (40–70cm) long, are 4- or 5-pinnate with linear segments. ↕ 30in (75cm), ↔ 32–60in (80–150cm). Australia (Queensland, New South Wales, Victoria). ❀ (min. 35°F/2°C)
D. punctiloba (North American hay-scented fern). Fern with long-creeping rhizomes. Yellow-green fronds, 6–18in (15–45cm) long, are erect to arching, lance-shaped and 2- or 3-pinnate, with linear segments. ↕ 18in (45cm), ↔ indefinite. North America. Zone 4.

▷ ***Dentaria*** see *Cardamine*
▷ ***Derwentia*** see *Parahebe*

DESCHAMPSIA
Hair grass
POACEAE

Genus of about 50 species of tufted or tussock-forming, herbaceous or evergreen, perennial grasses widely distributed in arctic and temperate zones, found in damp meadows, moorland, and woodland clearings, and on high mountains in tropical regions. The leaves are thread-like, linear, or oblong. Grown for their habit and graceful, airy panicles, they are suitable for a mixed, herbaceous, or shrub border, and also appropriate for a wildflower garden. The flowerheads of the taller species are useful in fresh or dried arrangements.
• **CULTIVATION** Grow in dry to damp, neutral to acidic soil in sun or partial shade. Incorporate compost before planting in dry soils. Remove previous year's growth before new growth begins.
• **PROPAGATION** Sow seed *in situ* in spring or autumn, or divide in midspring and early summer.
• **PESTS AND DISEASES** Infrequent.

D. cespitosa (Tufted hair grass, Tussock grass). Dense, tussock-forming, evergreen grass with rigid, linear, rough, mid-green leaves, to 24in (60cm) long. Produces airy, arching panicles, to 18in (45cm) long, of glistening, silver-tinted purple spikelets, from early to late summer. ↕ to 6ft (2m), ↔ 4–5ft (1.2–1.5m). Eurasia, tropical Africa. Zone 4. **'Bronzeschleier'**, syn. 'Bronze Veil', has larger, bronze-tinted panicles. **'Fairy's Joke'** see var. *vivipara*. **'Golden Dew'** see 'Goldtau'. **'Golden Veil'** see 'Goldschleier'. **'Goldgehänge'** has golden yellow panicles and is later flowering. **'Goldschleier'**, syn. 'Golden Veil', has dark green leaves and spikelets that age to bright silvery yellow; ↕↔ to

Deschampsia cespitosa 'Goldtau'

Deschampsia flexuosa 'Tatra Gold'

4ft (1.2m). **'Goldtau'** ■ syn. 'Golden Dew', is more compact, with silvery reddish brown spikelets that age to golden yellow; ↕↔ to 30in (75cm). **var. *vivipara***, syn. 'Fairy's Joke', produces young plantlets in place of seed, eventually weighing the slender culms to the ground; ↕↔ to 4ft (1.2m).
D. flexuosa, syn. *Aira flexuosa* (Crinkled hair grass). Tufted, often rhizomatous, evergreen grass with thread-like, smooth, bluish green leaves, to 8in (20cm) long. Open panicles, to 5in (13cm) long, of glistening, silver-tinted purple or brown spikelets are borne on wavy stalks in early and midsummer. Prefers acidic soil. ↕ to 24in (60cm), ↔ 12in (30cm). Europe, Asia, N.E. US, South America. Zone 5. **'Tatra Gold'** ■ syn. 'Aurea', produces arching, bright yellow-green leaves and bronze-tinted inflorescences; ↕ 20in (50cm).

DESFONTAINIA
LOGANIACEAE

Genus of one species of evergreen shrub from rainforest and mountain slopes in the Andes, cultivated for its holly-like, opposite leaves and its showy, solitary, tubular flowers. In areas of high rainfall, *D. spinosa* will tolerate open situations, but in drier places a cool, sheltered shrub border or peat garden is essential.
• **CULTIVATION** Grow in moist, peaty, acidic soil in cool, dappled shade, with shelter from cold, drying winds. Pruning group 9.
• **PROPAGATION** Insert semi-ripe cuttings in summer.
• **PESTS AND DISEASES** Infrequent.

D

Desfontainia spinosa

D. spinosa ■ Dense, bushy shrub with oval or ovate, spiny, glossy, dark green leaves, to 2½in (6cm) long. Bears pendent, yellow-tipped red flowers, to 1½in (4cm) long, from the upper leaf axils from midsummer to late autumn. ↕↔ 6ft (2m). Andes (from Colombia to Strait of Magellan). ❄ (min. 35°F/2°C)

DESMODIUM

FABACEAE

Genus of more than 450 species of deciduous shrubs, subshrubs, and herbaceous perennials, mainly from tropical and subtropical regions. They are grown for their loose terminal or axillary panicles or racemes of small, pea-like white to purple flowers. The leaves, arranged alternately, are pinnate to 3-palmate. Where marginally hardy, grow against a wall; where not hardy, grow in a temperate greenhouse.

• **CULTIVATION** Grow in well-drained soil in full sun. Pruning group 4 or 6.

• **PROPAGATION** Sow seed in containers in a cold frame in autumn. Insert softwood cuttings in late spring.

• **PESTS AND DISEASES** Powdery mildew, black mildew, rust and other fungal leaf spots, and heart rot are common.

D. elegans ■ syn. *D. tiliifolium.* Upright subshrub with leaves, to 10in (25cm) long, composed of 3 obovate leaflets, dark green above and gray and hairy beneath. Terminal panicles, 8in (20cm) long, of pea-like lilac to deep pink flowers are produced from late summer to autumn. ↕↔ 5ft (1.5m). Himalayas, China. ❄ (min. 35°F/2°C)

Desmodium elegans

D. praestans see *D. yunnanense.*
D. tiliifolium see *D. elegans.*
D. yunnanense, syn. *D. praestans.* Vigorous, spreading shrub with pale green leaves, 4–8in (10–20cm) long, downy, gray-green beneath, composed of one broadly ovate central leaflet and two much smaller lateral ones; they are occasionally reduced to a single, large, central leaflet. Pea-like, purple flowers are produced in terminal panicles, to 16in (40cm) long, in late summer. ↕↔ 12ft (4m). S.W. China. ❄ (min. 41°F/5°C)

DEUTZIA

HYDRANGEACEAE

Genus of about 60 species of mainly deciduous shrubs found in scrub and woodland, from the Himalayas to E. Asia. Many have peeling bark, especially when mature. Leaves, usually to 3in (8cm) long, are opposite, ovate to lance-shaped, and mainly toothed. Numerous 5-petaled, cup- to star-shaped, often fragrant white to pink flowers are borne in axillary or terminal racemes, panicles, cymes, or corymbs from midspring to midsummer. All are suitable for a shrub border; the larger ones are also good specimen plants. Where marginally hardy, plant against a wall or among trees and other shrubs.

• **CULTIVATION** Grow in reasonably fertile, not too dry soil, preferably in full sun; some will tolerate partial shade. Pruning group 2.

• **PROPAGATION** Sow seed in containers in a cold frame in autumn. Insert softwood cuttings in summer, and root hardwood cuttings in autumn.

• **PESTS AND DISEASES** A few fungal leaf spots sometimes occur.

D. chunii see *D. ningpoensis.*
D. compacta. Spreading shrub with lance-shaped to inversely lance-shaped, tapered leaves, to 2½in (6cm) long, dark green above, gray-green beneath. In midsummer, produces compact, corymb-like panicles, 2in (5cm) across, of cup-shaped, fragrant white flowers, ½in (1.5cm) across. ↕ 6ft (2m), ↔ 8ft (2.5m). China. Zone 7. **'Lavender Time'** produces lilac flowers, fading with age.
***D.* 'Contraste'.** Bushy shrub with arching branches and narrowly ovate, dark green leaves. Star-shaped, wavy-petaled, yellow-anthered pink to purplish pink flowers, to 1in (2.5cm) across, with deep pink bands on the backs of the petals, are produced in corymb-like panicles, 2–3in (5–8cm) across, in early summer. ↕ 5ft (1.5m), ↔ 4ft (1.2m). Zone 7.

Deutzia crenata var. *nakaiana* 'Nikko'

Deutzia x *elegantissima* 'Rosealind'

***D. crenata* var. *nakaiana* 'Nikko'** ■ Compact shrub with lance-shaped, rich green leaves, 1¼–2½in (3–6cm) long, turning red-purple in autumn. Produces racemes or panicles, 4–6in (10–15cm) long, of star-shaped white flowers, ½in (1.5cm) across, in late spring. Good for a rock garden or as a groundcover. ↕ 24in (60cm), ↔ 4ft (1.2m). Zone 5b.
***D. discolor* 'Major'.** Spreading shrub with arching branches and narrowly ovate-oblong, mid-green leaves, to 4in (10cm) long. Star-shaped, pink-flushed white flowers, ½–1in (1.5–2.5cm) across, in corymbs, 3in (8cm) across, in late spring and early summer. ↕ 5ft (1.5m), ↔ 6ft (2m). Zone 6.
***D.* x *elegantissima* 'Rosealind'** ■ Compact, rounded, upright shrub with ovate to ovate-oblong, dull, mid-green leaves. Star-shaped, pink-flushed white flowers, ¾in (2cm) across, are produced in corymb-like cymes, 1½–3in (4–8cm) across, in late spring and early summer. ↕ 4ft (1.2m), ↔ 5ft (1.5m). Zone 5b.
D. gracilis ■ (Slender deutzia). Bushy, erect shrub with lance-shaped to ovate, tapered, bright green leaves, to 2½in (6cm) long. Fragrant, star-shaped white flowers, to ¾in (2cm) across, are borne in upright racemes, 2–3in (5–8cm) long, from spring to early summer. ↕↔ 3ft (1m). Japan. Zone 5b.
***D.* 'Joconde'.** Bushy, upright shrub with narrowly ovate, long-pointed, mid-green leaves. Panicles, 2–3in (5–8cm) long, of cup-shaped, yellow-anthered white flowers (purple in bud), 1–1¼in (2.5–3cm) across, streaked purple on the backs of the wavy petals, are produced in summer. ↕↔ 5ft (1.5m). Zone 6.

Deutzia gracilis

D.* x *kalmiiflora (*D. parviflora* x *D. purpurascens*). Open shrub with arching branches and narrowly oval, mid-green leaves, 1½–3in (4–8cm) long. Bears star-shaped, deep pink flowers, to ¾in (2cm) across, paler inside, in upright panicles, 2–3in (5–8cm) long, in early summer. ↕↔ 5ft (1.5m). Garden origin. Zone 6b.
***D.* x *lemoinei*.** (*D. gracilis* x *D. parviflora*). Upright shrub with elliptic-lance-shaped, long-pointed leaves, 1¼–2½in (3–6cm) long, hairy beneath. Bears panicles or pyramidal corymbs, to 3in (8cm) long,

Deutzia longifolia 'Veitchii'

Deutzia x *magnifica* 'Staphyleoides'

Deutzia monbeigii

of abundant white flowers, to ¾in (2cm) across, in early summer. ↕↔ to 6ft (2m). Garden origin. Zone 5. **'Avalanche'** has arching branches and profuse white flowers. **'Compacta'** has a tight habit and wide-opening flowers.

D. longifolia. Spreading shrub with arching branches and lance-shaped, gray-green leaves, to 5in (13cm) long. Panicle-like cymes, 2–3in (5–8cm) long, of star-shaped white flowers, to 1in (2.5cm) across, purple-pink on the backs of the petals, are borne in early and midsummer. ↕ 6ft (2m), ↔ 10ft (3m). W. China (Sichuan, Yunnan). Zone 7b. **'Veitchii'** ▣ has deep lilac-pink flowers, to 1¼in (3cm) across, with white margins.

***D.* 'Magicien'.** Bushy, upright shrub with narrowly ovate, mid-green leaves.

Deutzia 'Mont Rose'

Deutzia ningpoensis

Deutzia x *rosea*

In early summer, produces panicles, 2–3in (5–8cm) long, of cup-shaped flowers, 1in (2.5cm) across, pink inside, white with deep pink stripes outside, and with yellow anthers. ↕↔ 5ft (1.5m). Zone 6.

***D.* x *magnifica* 'Staphyleoides'** ▣ Vigorous, upright shrub with arching branches and ovate-oblong, bright green leaves, to 4in (10cm) long, densely hairy beneath. Star-shaped white flowers, ¾–1in (2–2.5cm) across, with recurved petals, are borne in panicles, 4in (10cm) long, in early summer. ↕ 10ft (3m), ↔ 6ft (2m). Zone 6b.

D. monbeigii ▣ Graceful, arching shrub with slender shoots and ovate-lance-shaped, dark green leaves, to 2in (5cm) long, white hairy beneath. Produces star-shaped white flowers, to ½in (1.5cm) across, in corymbs, 2½in (6cm) across, in early and midsummer. ↕ 4ft (1.2m), ↔ 5ft (1.5m). S.W. China (Yunnan). Zone 6b.

***D.* 'Mont Rose'** ▣ Bushy, upright shrub with narrowly ovate, dark green leaves. Star-shaped, purple-pink flowers, to ½in (1.5cm) across, with wavy petals and yellow anthers, are produced in panicles, ¾–1¼in (2–3cm) long, in early summer. ↕↔ 4ft (1.2m). Zone 6.

D. ningpoensis ▣ syn. *D. chunii.* Open shrub with slender, lance-shaped to ovate, generally entire, mid-green leaves, densely hairy beneath. Panicles, to 4in (10cm) long, of star-shaped white or pink-tinged flowers, to ½in (1.5cm) across, are produced in summer. ↕↔ 6ft (2m). E. China (Zhejiang, Anhui). Zone 7.

Deutzia scabra

Deutzia setchuenensis var. *corymbiflora*

D. pulchra. Upright shrub with arching branches, peeling, orange-brown bark, and lance-shaped to narrowly ovate, entire or toothed, densely hairy, dark green leaves, to 4in (10cm) long. Star-shaped, pink-tinged white flowers, to ¾in (2cm) across, are produced in slender, pendent panicles, to 5in (13cm) long, in late spring and early summer. ↕ 8ft (2.5m), ↔ 6ft (2m). Taiwan, Philippines. Zone 7b.

D.* x *rosea ▣ (*D. gracilis* x *D. purpurascens*). Compact, rounded, bushy shrub with ovate-lance-shaped to ovate-oblong, dark green leaves. In early summer, produces a profusion of star-shaped white flowers, to ½in (1.5cm) across, pink- to red-tinged outside, in broad, corymb-like panicles, 2–3in (5–8cm) long. ↕↔ 4ft (1.2m). Garden origin. Zone 6. **'Campanulata'** has bell-shaped white flowers, ¾in (2cm) across. **'Carminea'** has red-pink flowers.

D. scabra ▣ (Fuzzy deutzia). Upright shrub with arching shoots, peeling, pale brown bark when mature, and broadly ovate, dark green leaves, to 3in (8cm) long. Produces dense, upright, cylindrical panicles, 3–6in (8–15cm) long, of star-shaped, honey-scented, single white or pink-tinged flowers, to ½in (1.5cm) across, in early and midsummer. ↕ 10ft (3m), ↔ 6ft (2m). China, Japan. Zone 6. **'Candidissima'** produces double white flowers. **'Codsall Pink'** has peeling, orange-brown bark and bears pink flowers. **'Pride of Rochester'** has double white flowers tinged with pink. **'Variegata'** produces leaves splashed with white.

D. setchuenensis* var. *corymbiflora ▣ Upright shrub with peeling, pale brown bark when mature and ovate to lance-shaped, long-pointed, gray-green leaves, to 4½in (11cm) long. In early or midsummer, cup-shaped white flowers, to ½in (1.5cm) across, are produced in corymbs, 3–4in (7–10cm) across. ↕ 6ft (2m), ↔ 5ft (1.5m). W. China. Zone 6b.

DIANELLA

Flax lily

LILIACEAE

Genus of 25–30 species of variable, evergreen, rhizomatous perennials, sometimes with fibrous roots, found in subtropical and temperate woodland, heath, or more open areas in E. Africa, Madagascar, E. Asia, W. Pacific, and Australasia. They are grown for their loose panicles of slightly pendent, star-shaped, usually blue flowers, followed by spherical or oblong-ovoid berries. Grass-like, linear to lance-shaped leaves are radical or borne in 2 ranks on the stems, which are usually 16–32in (40–80cm) tall; they may reach 6ft (2m). Grow in a woodland garden or a warm, sheltered border. Where not hardy, grow in a cool greenhouse.

• **CULTIVATION** Under glass, grow in soil-based potting mix, in full light with shade from hot sun. In growth, water freely and apply a balanced liquid fertilizer weekly; keep just moist in winter. Outdoors, grow in moderately fertile, humus-rich, well-drained, neutral to acidic soil in a sheltered site in sun or partial shade.

• **PROPAGATION** Sow seed at 55–61°F (13–16°C) or divide in spring.

• **PESTS AND DISEASES** Black mildew and leaf spot can occur.

D. caerulea. Tufted or mat-forming perennial with broadly lance-shaped, keeled, stiff leaves, to 30in (75cm) long, with rough margins. In early summer, bears panicles, to 12in (30cm) long, of pendent, star-shaped, blue, blue-green, or white flowers, ½–¾in (1–2cm) long, with conspicuous yellow anthers, followed by spherical, shiny blue berries, ¼–½in (7–12mm) long. ↕ 24in (60cm), ↔ 12in (30cm). E. Australia, New Guinea. ❀ (min. 45°F/7°C)

D. tasmanica ▣ Tufted perennial forming clumps of strap-shaped, stiff, rough-margined leaves, to 4ft (1.2m) long, sometimes also producing tall, cane-like stems with tufts of smaller leaves at the top. Branching panicles, to 24in (60cm) long, of star-shaped, lavender-blue to violet flowers, to ¾in (2cm) across, with pale yellow anthers, are borne in early summer, followed by persistent, oblong-ovoid, dark blue berries, to ¾in (2cm) long. ↕ to 4ft (1.2m), ↔ 18in (45cm). S.E. Australia, including Tasmania. ❀ (min. 45°F/7°C)

Dianella tasmanica

D

DIANTHUS

Carnation, Pink

CARYOPHYLLACEAE

Genus of over 300 species of mostly evergreen, low-growing subshrubs, annuals, and biennials from the mountains and meadows of S., C., and E. Europe, and N. Asia to Japan, plus one species native to North America. Tens of thousands of cultivars have been bred for garden use and commercial greenhouse production. These are divided into several subgroups, described below. The leaves of all types of dianthus are linear to lance-shaped, mostly pointed, and often blue-gray or gray-green with a waxy bloom. The leaves of the rock garden species are approximately ½in (1.5cm) long, while those of the carnations and larger pinks may be up to 5in (13cm) long.

Carnations and pinks are similar in habit and flower, although pinks are usually smaller in stature and frequently have fewer petals. Carnations and pinks are grown primarily for their flowers, which are produced in profusion over a long period in spring and summer, and are long-lasting when cut. The flowers are often fragrant (usually referred to as "clove-scented"), and are solitary or borne in few- to many-flowered clusters (cyme-like umbels). Flowers may be "single," possessing one row of petals, generally five in number; "double," bearing two or more rows of petals; or "semi-double," the intermediate form. Individual flowers have a tubular base, composed of the calyx and the shorter epicalyx, and up to 60 wide-spreading petals, sometimes toothed or fringed, or bearded with tiny hairs.

Carnations and pinks are grouped according to the coloring and marking of their flowers (see panel below). *Dianthus* species and cultivars are also divided into the following subgroups:

Border carnations
Evergreen perennial border plants good for cutting. Each stem bears 5 or more double flowers, to 3in (8cm) across, in summer. These are of the self, fancy, and picotee types, and may be clove-scented. ↕ 4–24in (10–60cm), ↔ 6–24in (15–60cm).

Perpetual-flowering carnations
Perennial hybrid group particularly cultivated under glass for their constant production of large, double flowers, 2–4in (5–10cm) across. ↕ 6–48in (15–120cm), ↔ 8–24in (20–60cm). These are the florists' carnations. **Malmaison carnations** are a subgroup, grown for their intensely fragrant, immense, 5in (13cm), double blooms. ↕ 24–48in (60–120cm), ↔ 24–36in (60–90cm). These and the perpetual-flowering carnations often produce unattractive, "split-calyx" blooms unless a small plastic band is placed around the calyx before the flowers open fully.

Border pinks
Perennials, usually evergreen, most forming compact mounds, grown for border decoration, cut flowers, and containers. From spring to summer, they bear single to double, often clove-scented flowers, 1–2½in (2.5–6cm) across, borne 1–6 per stem, and may be selfs, bicolors, fancies, or laced. ↕ 8–18in (20–45cm), ↔ 15in (38cm). **Antique border pinks** include all pinks introduced before 1920. They are often relaxed and open in habit, and are frequently prized for their fragrance, blooming for about 2 weeks in early summer. **Modern border pinks** are compact and long-flowering, often with multiple flushes of bloom, from late spring to autumn.

Rock garden pinks
Evergreen perennials, mat- or cushion-forming, useful for the edge of a border or in a raised bed, trough, or rocky scree. Many have attractive gray foliage. Flowers, ½–1½in (1–4cm) across, are borne singly or in few-flowered clusters, in spring and summer. ↕↔ variable.

China pinks and their hybrids
D. chinensis, a frost-tender perennial, has been developed into a wide range of long-blooming, scentless, and brilliantly colored bedding pinks. They are heat-tolerant, quick to bloom in nursery packs, and easily propagated from seed. ↕ 6–24in (15–60cm), ↔ 6–12in (15–30cm). Most commonly available are the **tender perennial China pinks**, which are widely used for bedding and nearly always treated as annuals, although they often survive mild winters. **Hardy hybrid China pinks** (*D. barbatus* x *D. chinensis*) are recently developed, short-lived perennials that are produced and marketed to bloom abundantly the first year.

Clusterhead pinks
Includes many of the species dianthuses, such as *D. carthusianorum*, *D. giganteus*, and the most famous, *D. barbatus*, the sweet William. Clusterheads are different in appearance from carnations and pinks, because the flowers are held in a flat or rounded group, topping a stem. Flowers in the head are usually small and scentless. Held just under the flowers are tiny leaflets, bracts, or awns, sometimes prominent. ↕ 4–36in (10–90cm), ↔ 4–24in (10–60cm).

Species pinks
Although numerous species pinks have been used in producing cultivars, there are many that are charming in their own right, such as *D. alpinus*, *D. arenarius*, *D. knappii*, and *D. superbus*. Very variable in flower and foliage color, fragrance, height, and hardiness, most are informal in habit; the alpine types are suitable for rock gardens, and the taller types are best suited to borders and wildflower gardens. Many may be grown to perfection in containers. Most species set seed readily but rarely become weedy.

CARNATIONS AND PINKS

For descriptive purposes, carnations and pinks are classified as follows: self-colored (**selfs**), which are of any one color; **fancies**, with stripes, flakes, or flecks that contrast with the ground color; **picotee** carnations, usually white or yellow, each petal margined with a contrasting color; **bicolor** pinks, which have a central zone or eye of contrasting color; and **laced** pinks, which have a contrasting center and each petal margined in the same color.

• **HARDINESS** Hardiness varies widely; see individual entries. Where frost penetration is typically deep and snow cover variable, apply a loose winter covering of ever-green boughs. Good drainage and air circulation also help. Heat and humidity tolerance is as important as cold hardiness, which is why many pinks grow poorly in humid regions. This hardiness can be extended by using tender perennials as annuals.

• **CULTIVATION** Most species and cultivars prefer full sun and well-drained, neutral to slightly alkaline soil. *D. glacialis*, *D. microlepis*, and *D. pavonius* prefer acidic conditions. Rock garden species particularly benefit from the sharp drainage of a raised bed, wall, or trough. Poor drainage, especially standing water in winter, is the primary cause of failure in *Dianthus* cultivation. Plant young border carnations and pinks in soil lightened with sand or gravel and enriched with well-rotted, finely sifted manure or compost. For acidic soils, dig in a sprink-ling of horticultural lime. When planting, do not bury the lowest leaves, and when cultivating, take care not to damage the plants' feeder roots, which lie close to the surface. In spring, side-dress established plants with a balanced low-nitrogen fertilizer. Avoid organic mulches, since they encourage fungal diseases; instead, use stone chips, gravel, or sand to keep foliage from contact with the soil. Support border carnations as the stems elongate in the spring. Generally, flowering is prolonged in cooler climates and by judicious deadheading. In hot climates, provide protection from afternoon sun.

Where not hardy, overwinter perpetual-flowering carnations under glass at 45–50°F (7–10°C) in soil-based potting mix. Admit full light in winter with good ventilation and low humidity, and water sparingly. Deadhead all species and cultivars to maintain a compact habit or to prolong flowering.

• **PROPAGATION** Sow seed of annuals, biennials, and rock garden species in containers in a cold frame from autumn to early spring. Sow seed of annuals at 55–59°F (13–15°C) in early spring. Sow biennials *in situ* in summer to flower the following year. Take cuttings from nonflowering shoots of all perennial *Dianthus* species and pinks in summer. Layer border carnations after flowering.

• **PESTS AND DISEASES** Slugs, sow bugs, grasshoppers, chipmunks, squirrels, and deer are the most common pests. In the West, blister beetles can be a problem. Fungal diseases such as crown rot and rusts are prevalent in humid regions and poorly drained soils. Under glass, aphids and spider mites are common.

***D.* 'Agatha'.** Durable modern border pink bearing semi-double to double, fragrant, light purple flowers with fringed petals and dark, red-purple eyes. Zone 5.

***D.* 'Aldridge Yellow'.** Self-colored border carnation producing double, pale yellow flowers on stiff stems. Zone 6.

***D.* 'Alice'** ▣ Modern bicolor pink. Clove-scented, semi-double, ivory-white flowers have dark crimson eyes. Zone 5.

D. alpinus (Alpine pink). Short-lived, loose cushion-forming species pink with glossy, dark green leaves, to 1¼in (3cm) long. Bears solitary, single, pale-spotted, deep pink to crimson flowers, 1–1½in (2.5–4cm) across, with bearded, toothed petals, in summer. Prefers humus-rich soil. ↕ 3in (8cm), ↔ to 4in (10cm). S.E. European Alps. Zone 3. **'Joan's Blood'** ▣ has deep crimson flowers with very dark centers.

D. amurensis. Short-lived, upright, mat-forming, loosely branched species pink with bright green leaves, to 2in (5cm) long. Terminal cymes of 1–3 single, deep purplish pink to mauve flowers, ½–1in (1–2.5cm) across, with darker centers and deeply toothed, bearded petals, are produced in summer. ↕ to 16in (40cm), ↔ to 12in (30cm). E. Asia. Zone 4.

***D.* 'Annabelle'.** Rock garden pink bearing masses of solitary, clove-scented, double, cerise-pink flowers. Zone 5.

***D.* 'Aqua'.** Open, modern border pink with dense blue-green foliage. Bears double, strongly clove-scented, white flowers. Zone 5b.

D. arenarius. Tufted, slender species pink with bright green leaves, to 1½in (4cm) long. Produces solitary, single, deeply fringed, bearded white flowers, to 1in (2.5cm) across, often purple at the bases, in summer. ↕↔ to 12in (30cm). N. and E. Europe. Zone 4. **'Snow Flurries'** is compact; ↕ to 8in (20cm).

D. armeria (Deptford pink). Basal rosette-forming, stiffly hairy annual or biennial species pink, with dark green leaves, 2in (5cm) long. In summer, bears dense, terminal cymes, 3–6in (1¼–2½cm) across, of numerous single, toothed, bearded, bright rose-pink flowers, to ½in (1.5cm) across, with prominent bracts, dotted pale pink at

the bases. ↕ to 16in (40cm), ↔ 18in (45cm). Europe, W. Asia. Zone 4.
D. barbatus (Sweet William). Bushy clusterhead pink, grown as a biennial, with light to mid-green leaves, sometimes deep bronze-green, to 4in (10cm) long. In late spring and early summer, leafy bracts surround dense, flat terminal clusters, 3–5in (8–13cm) across, of many small, single, sweet-scented, purple-red, pink, salmon-pink, or white flowers, sometimes bicolored, each petal bearded and dotted in a paler color at the base. ↕ to 28in (70cm), ↔ to 12in (30cm). S. Europe. Zone 4. **'Dunnet's Dark Crimson'** has deep bronze-green foliage and blood-red flowers; ↕ to 24in (60cm). Cultivars of **Electron Strain** bear tightly held clusters, 3in (8cm) across, of single selfs and bicolors in red, pink, rose, and white with rose eyes, on strong stems, in summer. Suitable for cutting; ↕ to 24in (60cm). **Roundabout Series** ▣ cultivars are bushy, with flowers in a range of single colors and bicolors, and may be grown as hardy annuals; ↕ 8in (20cm). **'Wee Willie'** produces crimson, rose-pink, or white flowers, and may be grown as an annual; ↕ 4–6in (10–15cm). Zone 4.
D. 'Bath's Pink'. Floriferous rock garden pink with blue-green mounded foliage. Bears single, scented, soft pink flowers, 1in (2.5cm) across, with darker eyes, from spring to summer. Tolerant of heat, drought, and high humidity; ↕ 10in (25cm), ↔ 12in (30cm). Zone 5.
D. 'Bat's Double Red', syn. *D.* 'Double Ruby Pink'. Antique border pink with grass-like, deep blue-green foliage. Bears double, bluntly toothed, slightly scented, ruby-red flowers. Zone 5b.
D. 'Beatrix'. Antique border pink with grass-like, dark green leaves. Bears clusters of double, pink, cinnamon-scented blooms in summer. Zone 5b.
D. 'Becky Robinson'. Laced modern border pink bearing clove-scented, double, warm pink flowers with ruby-red centers and margins. Zone 5.
D. 'Berry Burst'. Modern border pink bearing single, scented, toothed, purple-pink flowers, splashed with deeper purple-red. Zone 5.
D. bicolor see *D. seguieri.*
D. 'Bookham Fancy' ▣ Fancy border carnation producing double, bright yellow flowers, with red-purple margins and flecks, on short, stiff stems. Zone 6b.
D. brevicaulis (Mt. Taurus pink). Cushion-forming species pink with very short, flat, pointed, toothed, gray-green leaves, ¾in (2cm) long. Bears profuse, irregularly toothed, bearded, rose-pink flowers, ½in (1.5cm) across, yellow beneath with purple calyces, from spring to summer. ↕ 2–3in (5–8cm), ↔ 6–12in (15–30cm). Turkey. Zone 5b.
D. 'Brympton Red'. Laced antique border pink with single, bright crimson flowers, with deeper crimson stripes. Zone 5b.
D. caesius see *D. gratianopolitanus.*
D. carthusianorum (Carthusian pink). Tufted clusterhead pink with pale to mid-green leaves, ¾in (2cm) long. In summer, bears flattened, terminal clusters, 1¼–2in (3–5cm) across, of toothed, bearded, single, deep red-pink, occasionally white flowers, to ¾in (2cm) across, on slender stems. ↕ to 16in (40cm), ↔ to 8in (20cm). S. and C. Europe. Zone 6.
D. caryophyllus (Wild carnation). Loosely tufted species pink with flattened, soft mid-green leaves, to 6in (15cm) long, with conspicuous sheaths. Bears loose cymes, 2in (5cm) across, of 1–5 single, strongly fragrant, toothed, bright pink-purple flowers, to 1in (2.5cm) across, on stiff stems in summer. ↕ to 32in (80cm), ↔ 12–24in (30–60cm). Mediterranean. Zone 5. This species has been bred and selected extensively to produce a large range of cultivar groups, including the following: **Chabaud Series** cultivars are border carnations that bloom five months from sowing. In summer, they produce double, fringed, scented flowers in shades of red, pink, white, yellow, and salmon, and bicolors. Good for greenhouse culture and cutting; ↕↔ to 24in (60cm). Zone 6. **Fragrance Strain**, syn. *D.* 'Dwarf Fragrance', cultivars are dwarf and compact, bearing mostly double, long-blooming, clove-scented flowers, 2½in (6cm) across, in mixed colors on stems suitable for cutting; ↕ to 14in (35cm), ↔ 12in (30cm). Zone 6. Cultivars of **Grenadin Series** bear mostly double, fringed, clove-scented flowers, 2in (5cm) across, in shades of red, yellow, and white, and bicolors, from spring to summer. They bloom the second year from seed; ↕ 20–24in (50–60cm), ↔ 30in (75cm); dwarf strains ↕ to 15in (38cm), ↔ 12–24in (30–60cm). Zone 6. **Knight Series** ▣ cultivars are dwarf, very bushy, and grown as annuals, with double flowers, in colors including crimson, yellow, white, and orange, with some picotees; ↕ to 12in (30cm), ↔ to 9in (23cm). Zone 6. Cultivars of **Monarch Series** are annual border carnations with a compact, vigorous branching habit. Easier to flower than Knight Series, bearing double flowers up to 3in (8cm) across in salmon, pink, purple, scarlet, and white, in summer. Excellent as container or bedding plants; ↕ 6–8in (15–20cm), ↔ 6in (15cm). Zone 6.
D. caucasicus see *D. seguieri.*
D. 'Charles Musgrave' see *D.* 'Musgrave's Pink'.
D. chinensis (China pink, Indian pink). Bushy, short-lived perennial or biennial species pink, usually grown as an annual from seed. Leaves are pale to mid-green and up to 3in (8cm) long. In summer, produces loose terminal cymes, to 3in (8cm) across, of up to 15 single, basically scentless pink, red, or white flowers, often with purple eyes, fringed to nearly half their lengths and often intricately patterned. ↕ to 28in (70cm), ↔ 6–9in (16–23cm). China. Zone 7b. **Baby Doll Series** cultivars have large, single, patterned flowers in mainly crimson to white; ↕ 6–8in (15–20cm). Cultivars of **Carpet Series** have single, self-colored flowers available in shades of crimson, rose-pink, or white. **'Fire Carpet'** ▣ has scarlet flowers; ↕ to 8in (20cm). **Heddewigii Group 'Color Magician'** is compact and free-flowering, with small, single flowers that age from clear white to pink to deep rose-pink; ↕ to 10in (25cm). **'Parfait'** has small, weather-resistant, single, lightly fringed flowers, in a color range including bicolors, borne throughout summer; ↕ to 12in (30cm).
D. 'Christopher'. Modern border self pink with long-blooming, double, clove-scented, dark orange-pink flowers. ↕ 12–16in (30–40cm). Zone 5b.
D. 'Clara' ▣ Fancy perpetual-flowering carnation bearing clear yellow flowers, striped salmon-pink. ❀ (min. 35°F/2°C)
D. 'Constance Finnis' see *D.* 'Fair Folly'.
D. 'Coronation Ruby' ▣ Modern laced pink with clove-scented, double, warm pink flowers, with ruby-red margins and centers. Zone 5b.
D. 'Crimson Treasure'. Rock garden pink with compact gray-green foliage. Bears very striking crimson flowers, spotted white, continuously in spring. Tolerates partial shade. ↕ 5–8in (13–20cm), ↔ 12in (30cm). Zone 5.
D. 'Crompton Princess' ▣ Perpetual-flowering carnation producing perfectly formed, pure white flowers. Zone 7.
D. 'Dad's Favourite' ▣ syn. *D.* 'Dad's Favorite'. Laced antique border pink with semi-double, red-margined, purple-centered, white flowers. Zone 4.
D. 'Danielle Marie', syn. *D.* 'Danielle'. Modern border pink, sport of *D.* 'Doris', with close-knit, gray-green foliage. In summer, bears scented, double, salmon-orange to coral-red flowers with toothed petals, on long stems. ↕ 10–12in (25–30cm), ↔ 12in (30cm). Zone 5.
D. deltoides (Maiden pink). Mat-forming species pink with narrow, dark green leaves, to ½in (1.5cm) long, bearing usually solitary, scentless, single flowers, to ¾in (2cm) across, with toothed, bearded petals, on upright, leafy stems in summer. The flowers are white, deep pink, or red, often with darker eyes. Good for bedding and rock gardens, but it self-sows prolifically. Seed strains are particularly variable as to height and width. ↕ to 8in (20cm), ↔ 12in (30cm) or more. Europe, Asia. Zone 4. **'Fanal'** has bronze foliage and single, cardinal-red flowers; ↕ 8in (20cm). **'Flashing Light'** ▣ has profuse, brilliant cerise flowers. **'Zing Rose'** produces single, bright rose-red flowers.
D. 'Desmond'. Floriferous modern border pink with deep blue-green foliage and moderately scented, double, crimson flowers. Good for cutting. ↕ to 12in (30cm). Zone 5b.
D. 'Doris' ▣ Modern border bicolor pink bearing scented, semi-double, salmon-pink flowers with scarlet eyes. Zone 4.
D. 'Dottie'. Rock garden pink bearing single white flowers with maroon eyes, from spring to summer. Good companion to *D.* 'Spotty'. ↕ to 4in (10cm). Zone 4.

Dianthus 'Alice'

Dianthus alpinus 'Joan's Blood'

Dianthus barbatus Roundabout Series

Dianthus 'Bookham Fancy'

Dianthus caryophyllus Knight Series

Dianthus chinensis Carpet Series 'Fire Carpet'

Dianthus 'Clara'

Dianthus 'Coronation Ruby'

Dianthus 'Crompton Princess'

Dianthus 'Dad's Favourite'

Dianthus deltoides 'Flashing Light'

Dianthus 'Doris'

D

Dianthus erinaceus

***D.* 'Duchess of Westminster'** ▣ Strong-growing Malmaison carnation with salmon-pink flowers. Zone 6.
***D.* 'Earl of Essex'.** Bicolor antique border pink bearing double, rose-pink flowers with darker eyes. Zone 5b.
***D.* 'Emile Paré'.** Antique border pink with bright green foliage and clusters of semi-double, salmon-pink flowers. Zone 5b.
D. erinaceus ▣ Cushion-forming species pink with stiff mid-green leaves, to ¾in (2cm) long. Solitary, occasionally paired, pink flowers, ½in (1.5cm) across, with toothed, bearded petals, are produced on short stems in summer. Flowers are generally sparsely produced in cool climates. ↕ 2in (5cm), ↔ 20in (50cm) or more. Mountainous regions in Turkey. Zone 4.
***D.* 'Essex Witch'.** Rock garden pink. Produces finely fringed, scented, semi-double, rose-pink flowers with darker zones. Intolerant of high temperatures. ↕ 5–8in (12–20cm). Zone 5.
***D.* 'Evangeline'.** Sturdy-stemmed modern border pink bearing spicy, double, smooth-edged, pink flowers from spring to summer. ↕ 8–12in (20–30cm). Zone 4.
***D.* 'Fair Folly'**, syn. *D.* 'Constance Finnis', 'Fair Folley'. Antique border laced pink bearing single white flowers, with strawberry-pink centers and margins. Zone 5b.
***D.* 'Feuerhexe'** see *D.* 'Fire Witch'.
***D.* 'Fire Witch'**, syn. *D.* 'Feuerhexe', *D.* 'Firewitch'. Rock garden pink forming deep blue-green mats. Produces single, toothed, bright carmine-magenta flowers. ↕ to 6in (15cm). Zone 5.
D. gallicus (Gallic pink). Tufted, mat-forming species pink with broad, blue-green leaves, to 2in (5cm) long. In spring, bears 1–3 strongly fragrant, single pink flowers, 1in (2.5cm) across, with finely fringed, overlapping petals. Suitable for a rock garden. ↕ to 9–20in (23–50cm), ↔ 12in (30cm). Coastal Portugal, Spain, France. Zone 5.
D. giganteus. Robust, variable, upright species pink with flat, narrow, pointed, green or glaucous-green leaves, 4in (10cm) long. Bears a single, dense head 1–2in (2.5–5cm) across, of up to 40 single, toothed, scentless, reddish purple flowers, ½in (1.5cm) across, opening throughout summer. Thrives in sandy soil. Excellent in a wild or prairie garden. ↕ 8–40in (20cm–100cm), ↔ 12in (30cm). Romania, Bulgaria, Turkey. Zone 4b.
D. glacialis. Compact, densely tufted, cushion-forming species pink with soft, glossy, dark green leaves, to ½in (1.5cm) long. In summer, bears usually solitary, short-stemmed, single, pale to deep pink flowers, to ¾in (2cm) across, with finely toothed, bearded petals. ↕ 2in (5cm), ↔ 6in (15cm). E. Alps. Zone 4.
***D.* 'Gold Dust'.** Mounded, rock garden pink with striking blue-gray leaves. Produces toothed, slightly scented, velvety, single, dark red flowers, lightly flecked with gold. ↕ 6–8in (15–20cm), ↔ 12in (30cm). Zone 4.
***D.* 'Gran's Favourite'** ▣ Modern laced border pink with short-stemmed, clove-scented, semi-double, white flowers, with mauve centers and margins. Zone 5b.
D. gratianopolitanus, syn. *D. caesius* (Cheddar pink). Mat-forming species pink with gray-green leaves, to 2in (5cm) long. Solitary, very fragrant, single, deep pink flowers, to 1¼in (3cm) across, with slightly bearded, toothed petals, are produced in summer. ↕ to 6in (15cm), ↔ to 16in (40cm). N.W. and C. Europe. Zone 4. **'Petite'** bears very compact mounds of small, single, bright pink flowers from spring to summer; ↕ 3–4in (8–10cm). Zone 4.
D. haematocalyx. Compact, cushion-forming species pink with gray-green leaves, 1–2in (2.5–5cm) long. In summer, bears terminal clusters,

Dianthus Ideal Series 'Cherry Picotee'

¾–2½in (2–6cm) across, of 1–4 single, toothed, bearded, deep pink flowers, ½–1in (1.5–2.5cm) across, with yellow-tinged reverses. ↕ to 5in (13cm), ↔ to 8in (20cm). Balkan Peninsula, mountains in N. Greece. Zone 4b.
***D.* 'Her Majesty'.** Antique border pink bearing powerfully fragrant, double, white, fringed flowers. Good for cutting. ↕ 8–10in (20–25cm). Zone 5b.
***D.* 'Horatio'.** Rock garden pink with compact, mounded, blue-green foliage. Bears moderately scented, double, bright rose-pink flowers with maroon eyes. Drought resistant. ↕ 6–8in (15–20cm), ↔ 24in (60cm). Zone 4.
***D.* 'Houndspool Cheryl'.** Modern border pink with double, currant-red flowers. Zone 4.
***D.* 'Ian'.** Modern border pink with double, scented, deep crimson flowers, borne from spring to summer. Good for cutting. ↕ to 18in (45cm). Zone 4b.
***D.* Ideal Series** (*D. barbatus* x *D. chinensis*). Bushy, dwarf, short-lived, hardy hybrid China pinks, usually grown as annuals or sometimes biennials, with bright green leaves, 3–5in (8–13cm) long. In summer, bear terminal clusters, 4–5in (10–13cm) across, of small, single self-colored flowers, in a vivid range including crimson-red and deep violet-blue, some marked with a different color. **'Cherry Picotee'** ▣ has flowers with white picotee margins and cherry-red eyes. **'Ideal Violet'** ▣ bears richly colored red-purple flowers; ↕ 8–14in (20–35cm), ↔ 9in (23cm).
***D.* 'Inchmery'.** Self-colored, antique border pink with shapely, semi-double, pale pink flowers. Zone 5.
D. inodorus see *D. sylvestris.*
***D.* 'Inshriach Dazzler'.** Rock garden pink bearing solitary, short-stemmed, single, deep carmine flowers with fringed petals. Zone 5.
***D.* 'Itsaul White'.** Modern border pink with bluish green foliage. Bears vanilla-scented, single white flowers that open from brown buds, from spring to summer. More heat tolerant than many pinks. ↕ 8–12in (20–30cm). Zone 4.
***D. japonicus* Ginza Series.** Bushy, erect, short-lived perennials, usually grown as annuals, with blunt-tipped, light to mid-green leaves, 1½–2in (4–5cm) long. Dense, flat, terminal clusters, 3–5in (8–13cm) across, of small, toothed, single, lilac to deep rose-pink flowers are produced in summer. ↕↔ 18in (45cm). Zone 6b.
***D.* 'Karlik'**, syn. *D.* 'Karliks'. Mat-forming rock garden pink bearing single, rose-pink, very fragrant, fringed flowers, 1in (2.5cm) across. ↕ 6–8in (15–20cm), ↔ 8in (20cm). Zone 4.
D. knappii. Species pink with mid-green leaves, 2–2½in (5–6cm) long, and small, solitary, toothed, single sulfur-yellow flowers, ½in (1.5cm) across. Striking beside *D. carthusianorum.* Ideal for a prairie garden or informal border. ↕↔ to 16in (40cm). Zone 4. **'Yellow Harmony'** is a seed-strain selection, with a more upright, tidier habit and larger flowers; Zone 4.
***D.* 'La Bourboule'** ▣ syn. *D.* 'La Bourbille', *D.* 'La Bourbrille'. Rock garden pink bearing clusters of clove-scented, single, clear pink flowers with fringed petals. Zone 4.
***D.* 'Laced Hero'.** Laced modern border pink with blue-gray foliage. Bears very striking, scented, semi-double to double white flowers, laced dark reddish purple and zoned black. ↕ 12in (30cm), ↔ 12in (30cm). Zone 5b.
***D.* 'Laced Monarch'** ▣ Laced modern border pink producing double pink flowers with deep red centers and margins. Zone 5b.
***D.* 'Lady Granville'**, syn. *D.* 'Lady Glanville'. Antique border pink with very fragrant, semi-double white flowers, with crimson edges and eyes. ↕ 1–10in (2.5–25cm). Zone 5.

Dianthus 'Duchess of Westminster'

Dianthus 'Gran's Favourite'

Dianthus Ideal Series 'Ideal Violet'

Dianthus 'La Bourboule'

Dianthus 'Laced Monarch'

Dianthus 'Little Jock'

Dianthus 'London Delight'

Dianthus 'Monica Wyatt'

Dianthus 'Mrs. Sinkins'

Dianthus 'Musgrave's Pink'

Dianthus myrtinervius

Dianthus 'Valda Wyatt'

Dianthus microlepis

***D.* 'Little Bobby'.** Rock garden pink with blue-green foliage. Produces clove-scented, single, raspberry-colored flowers with darker eyes, from spring to summer. ↕ to 6in (15cm). Zone 4.
***D.* 'Little Jock'** ■ Rock garden pink with very short-stemmed, clove-scented, single flowers, with deeply fringed petals, pale pink with maroon eyes. Zone 5.
***D.* 'London Delight'** ■ Laced modern border pink bearing clove-scented, semi-double, pale pink flowers with maroon centers and margins. Zone 5.
***D.* 'Loveliness'**, syn. *D.* Rainbow Loveliness Strain. Short-lived modern border pink bearing loose clusters of deep-fringed, very sweet-scented, single flowers, 1½in (4cm) across, in white, pink, and deep rose-pink, with contrasting edges, central zones, and eyes. Blooms the first year from seed. Protect from direct sun. Zone 4.
***D.* 'Margaret Curtis'.** Modern border pink bearing unfringed, scented, single white flowers with deep burgundy eyes. ↕ 6–8in (15–20cm). Zone 4.
D. microlepis ■ Neat, cushion-forming species pink with tufts of silvery gray to green leaves, to ¾in (2cm) long. Bears solitary, slightly toothed, single pink or purple flowers, ½in (1.5cm) across, just above the leaves in early summer. ↕ 2in (5cm), ↔ to 6in (15cm). Mountains in Bulgaria. Zone 5.
***D.* 'Monica Wyatt'** ■ Bicolor modern border pink with clove-scented, double, pale lavender-pink flowers, centered magenta. Zone 5b.
D. monspessulanus. Loosely tufted species pink with soft, gray-green leaves, to ½in (1.5cm) long. Terminal cymes, ¾–2½in (2–5.5cm) across, of 2–7 fragrant, white or pink flowers, with deeply fringed petals, are borne on slender stems in summer. ↕ to 20in (50cm), ↔ to 8in (20cm). E. Europe. Zone 4.
***D.* 'Mrs. Holt'.** Tightly cushioned rock garden pink with single, pink flowers. ↕ to 6in (15cm). Zone 4.
***D.* 'Mrs. Sinkins'** ■ Antique pink with double, shaggy, fringed white flowers with split calyces. Grown for its powerful scent. Zone 5b.
***D.* 'Musgrave's Pink'** ■ syn. *D.* 'Charles Musgrave'. Bicolor antique pink bearing clove-scented, single white flowers with green eyes. Zone 5.
D. myrtinervius ■ Dense, mat-forming species pink with bright green leaves, to ¼in (6mm) long, and numerous solitary, single, deep pink flowers, ½in (1.5cm) across, with pale eyes, borne just above the leaves in summer. Best on a scree. ↕ to 2in (5cm), ↔ to 8in (20cm). Balkans, Macedonia, N. Greece. Zone 4.
D. neglectus see *D. pavonius.*
***D. nitidus* of gardens** see *D. scardicus.*
D. noeanus see *D. petraeus.*
D. pavonius, syn. *D. neglectus.* Mat-forming species pink with gray-green basal leaves, to 1½in (4cm) long. Bears usually solitary, toothed, bearded, single, pale to deep pink flowers, to 1¼in (3cm) across, buff-colored beneath, in summer. ↕ 3in (8cm), ↔ to 8in (20cm). S.W. Alps. Zone 4.
***D.* 'Peppermint Patty'.** Modern border pink producing spicy-scented, toothed, self-colored, pale pink flowers. ↕ to 8in (20cm). Zone 4.
D. petraeus, syn. *D. noeanus.* Mat-forming species pink with stiff, mid-green basal leaves, to 1in (2.5cm) long. Usually solitary, fragrant, single white flowers, ⅜–½in (9–15mm) across, with toothed or notched petals, are produced in summer. ↕ 6in (15cm), ↔ to 8in (20cm). S.E. Europe, Balkan peninsula, Romania. Zone 4.
***D.* 'Pike's Pink'.** Rock garden pink with solitary, clove-scented, double, pale pink flowers, darker zoned at the bases. ↕ 6in (15cm). Zone 5b.
***D.* 'Pink Feather'**, syn. *D.* 'Rosafeder', *D.* 'Rose Feather'. Rock garden pink with scented, very feathery pink flowers, ↕ to 9in (23cm). Zone 5.
***D.* 'Pink Princess'.** Floriferous modern border pink producing very fragrant, fringed, salmon-pink flowers. ↕ 12–16in (30–40cm). Zone 5.
***D. plumarius* cultivars.** Modern border pinks, with green to blue-gray leaves, 2–4in (5–10cm) long. From spring to summer, bear scented, toothed flowers. ↕ 12–16in (30–40cm), ↔ 24in (60cm). **Ballade Strain**, syn. *D.* 'Ballad Blend', cultivars produce mixed colors with contrasting central zones, the best colors are often the last to germinate; Zone 5. **Spring Beauty Strain** cultivars bear mixed single and semi-double flowers, 1½in (4cm) across, in white and rose shades; Zone 4.
***D.* 'Prairie Pink'.** Long-blooming modern border pink bearing blue-green foliage and large, scented, toothed, double, fuchsia-pink flowers. ↕ to 18in (45cm). Zone 4.
***D.* 'Queen of Sheba'.** Antique border pink bearing clove-scented, toothed, single, ivory-white flowers, laced or flecked magenta. Zone 5b.
***D.* Rainbow Loveliness Strain** see *D.* 'Loveliness'.
***D.* 'Raspberry Tart'.** Modern border pink with semi-double, spicy, toothed, raspberry-red flowers with maroon centers, from spring to summer. ↕ 8–10in (20–25cm). Zone 4.
D. repens. Mat-forming species pink, with straight, pointed, gray-green leaves, ¾–1½in (2–4cm) long. In summer, bears solitary, pink flowers, to ½in (1.5cm) across, with very small, rounded teeth, and often purple-tinged calyces. ↕ 2–8in (5–20cm), ↔ 4–12in (10–30cm). Russia, arctic Asia, Alaska. Zone 2.
***D.* 'Robespierre'.** Modern border pink with double, salmon flowers, streaked red. ↕ 8–10in (5–20cm). Zone 5b.

Dianthus subacaulis

***D.* 'Rosafeder'** see *D.* 'Pink Feather'.
***D.* 'Rose de Mai'**, syn. *D.* 'Rose du Mai'. Long-blooming antique border pink with drought-tolerant blue-green foliage. Bears double, strongly scented, creamy mauve flowers, zoned slightly darker. Zone 5.
***D.* 'Rose Feather'** see *D.* 'Pink Feather'.
***D.* 'Salmon Unique'.** Compact modern border pink producing unusual, double salmon-coral flowers from spring to summer. ↕ 10–12in (25–30cm). Zone 5.
D. scardicus, syn. *D. nitidus* of gardens. Domed, cushion-forming species pink with dark green leaves, ¾in (2cm) long. In summer, produces solitary, single pink flowers, to ½in (1.5cm) across, on short stems. ↕ 4in (10cm), ↔ to 6in (15cm). Mountains in Slovenia and E. Albania. Zone 4.
D. seguieri, syn. *D. bicolor, D. caucasicus.* Loosely tufted, slender species pink with flat, lance-shaped, dark grass-green leaves, ¾–3in (2–8cm) long. In early summer, produces solitary or loose clusters of bearded, single, reddish pink flowers, ½–1in (1.5–2.5cm) across, often basally spotted white, with almost cylindrical calyces. ↕ 12–24in (30–60cm), ↔ 6–12in (15–30cm). S.W. and W. central Europe. Zone 4.
D. simulans, syn. *D.* 'Simulans'. Mound-forming species pink with very short, gray to olive foliage, to ¾in (2cm) across. Tiny, single, rose-colored flowers, ¼–½in (0.6–1.5cm) across, are produced in spring. Perfect for a small rock garden. ↕ 3in (8cm), ↔ 5in (13cm). Mountains in E. Europe. Zone 5.
***D.* 'Simulans'** see *D. simulans.*
***D.* 'Spottii'** see *D.* 'Spotty'.
***D.* 'Spotty'**, syn. *D.* 'Spotti', *D.* 'Spottii'. Mound-forming rock garden pink with blue-gray foliage. Bears many small, scented, single rose-red flowers, edged and spotted silvery white. ↕ 2–6in (5–15cm). Zone 3.
D. subacaulis ■ Mat-forming or densely tufted species pink with dark green basal leaves, to ½in (1.5cm) long. In summer, produces solitary, single, deep pink flowers, ½–¾in (1.5–2cm) across, with entire or finely toothed, rounded petals. ↕ 2in (5cm), ↔ to 4in (10cm). Mountains in S.W. Europe. Zone 4.
D. superbus. Loosely tufted species pink with mid-green leaves, to 3in (8cm) long. In summer, bears solitary or pairs of single, fragrant, purplish pink flowers, 1½–2½in (4–6cm) across, with deeply fringed petals. ↕↔ to 8in (20cm). Mountains in Europe and Asia. Zone 3.
***D.* 'Swarthmore'.** Rock garden pink with gray-green foliage. From spring to summer, bears fringed, scented, single white flowers, eyed and edged raspberry-red. ↕ to 8in (20cm). Zone 5.
D. sylvestris, syn. *D. inodorus.* Densely matted, tufted perennial species pink with many narrow, mid-green basal leaves, 2in (5cm) long. In summer, bears single, sometimes toothed, pink to rose flowers, 1in (2.5cm) across. ↕↔ to 16in (40cm). Spain to France, Greece. Zone 5b.
***D.* Telstar Series** (*D. barbatus* x *D. chinensis*). Bushy, dwarf, hardy hybrid China pinks, usually grown as annuals or biennials, with dark green leaves, 2–3in (5–8cm) long. In summer, they bear terminal clusters, 2–3in (5–8cm) across, of small, weather-resistant, single flowers, in separate, strong shades of pink, red, or white, including some bicolors and picotees. ↕ 8–14in (20–35cm), ↔ 9in (23cm). Zone 5. **'Telstar Crimson'** ■ produces deep, blood red flowers. **'Telstar Picotee'** is a very free-flowering red picotee. **'Telstar White'** bears white flowers with a slight pink blush.
***D.* 'Tiny Rubies'**, syn. *D.* 'Tiny Ruby'. Rock garden pink producing tiny, fragrant, rose-colored flowers, ½in (1.5cm) across. Good for candying. ↕ 4in (10cm), ↔ 12in (30cm). Zone 5.
***D.* 'Ursula Le Grove'**, syn. *D.* 'Ursula La Grave'. Antique border pink bearing long-blooming, very fragrant, single, white flowers with maroon eyes and markings. ↕ to 12in (30cm). Zone 5.
***D.* 'Valda Wyatt'** ■ Modern bicolor border pink with clove-scented, double, lavender-pink flowers, slightly deeper in color at the centers. Zone 5b.
***D.* 'Waithman's Beauty'.** Compact, rock garden pink bearing pink-splashed, ruby-red flowers. Zone 5.
***D.* 'War Bonnet'.** Border carnation bearing double, shallowly toothed, cinnamon-scented, purplish red flowers, becoming white-edged with age. Zone 5.
***D.* 'Whatfield Gem'.** Compact, mound-forming rock garden pink with silver foliage. Bears double, smooth-margined, scented pink flowers, laced maroon. ↕ 3–6in (8–15cm). Zone 5.

Dianthus Telstar Series 'Telstar Crimson'

DIASCIA

SCROPHULARIACEAE

Genus of about 50 species of annuals and semi-evergreen, occasionally evergreen, sometimes suckering, perennials found mainly in mountains in southern Africa. Erect, semi-erect, or prostrate stems bear opposite, ovate or heart-shaped to elliptic or linear, toothed, mainly mid-green leaves. They produce terminal racemes of tubular, 5-lobed flowers, the lower lobes broad, the paired upper lobes having 2 backward-pointing spurs and a translucent yellow "window" at each base. Use at the front of a border, on a sunny bank, in a rock garden, or in containers.

• **CULTIVATION** Grow in fertile, moist but well-drained soil in full sun. Water in dry periods. Many fail to bloom during hot summers. Deadhead often.

• **PROPAGATION** Sow seed at 61°F (16°C) as soon as ripe or in early spring. Divide suckering species in spring. Take softwood cuttings in spring or semi-ripe cuttings in summer. Overwinter young plants under glass.

• **PESTS AND DISEASES** May be damaged by slugs and snails.

***D. barberae* cultivars.** Mat-forming perennials with narrowly heart-shaped, tapering leaves, ¾–1¼in (2–3cm) long. Bears loose racemes of flowers, ½–¾in (1.5–2cm) across, with small, narrow "windows" and almost straight, downward-pointing spurs, from summer to autumn. ↕ 10in (25cm), ↔ to 20in (50cm). Zone 7. **'Blackthorn Apricot'** ■ has apricot flowers. **'Pink Queen'** has slender spikes of shell-pink flowers.

D. cordata ■ Mat-forming perennial with branching stems and heart-shaped, tapering, pale green leaves, ½–¾in (1.5–2cm) long. Loose racemes of long-stalked, deep pink flowers, ¾in (2cm) across, with small, narrow, very concave "windows" and slightly curved, downward-pointing spurs, are borne from early summer to early autumn. ↕ 6in (15cm), ↔ to 20in (50cm). South Africa. Zone 8.

D. elegans see *D. vigilis.*

D. felthamii see *D. fetcaniensis.*

D. fetcaniensis, syn. *D. felthamii.* Creeping perennial with ovate, hairy leaves, 1in (2.5cm) long, heart-shaped at the bases. Loose racemes of rose-pink flowers, ¾in (2cm) long, with concave "windows" and incurved, downward-pointing spurs, are produced from summer to early autumn. ↕ 10in (25cm), ↔ to 20in (50cm). South Africa, Lesotho. Zone 8.

***D.* 'Hector Harrison'** see *D.* 'Salmon Supreme'.

D. integerrima, syn. *D. integrifolia.* Creeping perennial with slender, wiry, upright stems bearing linear to oblong-lance-shaped, sparsely toothed leaves, ¾–1in (2–2.5cm) long. Loose racemes of purplish pink flowers, ¾in (2cm) long, with broad, horizontal lower lips, concave "windows," and downward-pointing, incurved spurs, are borne in summer. ↕ 12in (30cm) or more, ↔ to 20in (50cm). South Africa. Zone 8.

D. integrifolia see *D. integerrima.*

D. rigescens ■ Trailing perennial with stiff, erect and semi-erect, branching stems and heart-shaped, deeply toothed, mainly stalkless leaves, 1½in (4cm) long. Produces tall, dense racemes of mid- to deep pink flowers, ¾in (2cm) across, with small, round "windows" and short, incurved spurs, in summer. ↕ 12in (30cm), ↔ to 20in (50cm). South Africa. Zone 6b.

Diascia cordata

Diascia barberae 'Blackthorn Apricot'

Diascia rigescens

Diascia 'Salmon Supreme'

***D.* 'Ruby Field'.** Mat-forming perennial with short, wiry stems clothed in heart-shaped leaves, 1–1½in (2.5–4cm) long. Masses of rich salmon-pink flowers, ½in (1.5cm) long, with small, narrow "windows" and spurs curving inward and downward, are produced from summer to autumn. ↕ 10in (25cm), ↔ to 24in (60cm). Zone 7.

***D.* 'Rupert Lambert'.** Mat-forming perennial with narrowly elliptic to ovate, pointed, shallowly toothed leaves, 1–1½in (2.5–4cm) long. Bears long racemes of deep pink flowers, 1in (2.5cm) long, with double "windows" and long, parallel spurs, from summer to autumn. ↕ 10in (25cm), ↔ to 20in (50cm). Zone 7.

***D.* 'Salmon Supreme'** ■ syn. *D.* 'Hector Harrison'. Mat-forming perennial with heart-shaped, sparsely toothed leaves, 1–1½in (2.5–4cm) long. Dense racemes of pale apricot flowers, ½in (1.5cm) long, with very small, deeply concave "windows" and short, straight, downward-pointing spurs, are produced from summer to autumn. ↕ 6in (15cm), ↔ to 20in (50cm). Zone 7.

D. vigilis, syn. *D. elegans.* Vigorous, creeping, prostrate perennial with ovate-lance-shaped, fleshy, deeply toothed leaves, 1–1½in (2.5–4cm) long. Loose racemes of clear pink flowers, ¾–1in (2–2.5cm) long, with deep-set yellow and maroon "windows" and short, incurved spurs, are borne from early summer to early autumn. One of the hardier and most floriferous species. ↕ 12in (30cm), ↔ to 24in (60cm). South Africa and Lesotho. Zone 7b.

DICENTRA

FUMARIACEAE

Genus of 20 or more species of annuals and perennials from Asia and North America, often found in moist habitats, including woodland, especially in mountainous areas. The perennial species may be rhizomatous or tuberous, or have fleshy taproots. The hairless, sometimes silvery gray leaves are fern-like and much divided. Pendent, heart-shaped flowers, in red, pink, white, purple, or yellow, are borne in panicles or racemes, often arching, or are occasionally solitary. Some species are excellent woodland plants or are useful shady border plants; the smaller species look best in a rock garden or alpine house. All parts of the plant may cause mild stomach upset if ingested. Contact with the foliage may aggravate skin allergies.

• **CULTIVATION** Grow most species and cultivars in moist, fertile, humus-rich soil, preferably neutral or slightly alkaline, in partial shade, where they will self-seed freely. *D. chrysantha* needs a dry, sunny site; *D. spectabilis* tolerates sun in reliably moist soil. Grow alpine species in sharply drained, volcanic soil or very gritty potting mix in a scree bed or alpine house.

• **PROPAGATION** Sow seed in containers in a cold frame as soon as ripe or in spring. Divide carefully in early spring or after the leaves have died down. Insert root cuttings of *D. spectabilis* in winter. Hybrids may produce a wide range of seedlings that vary in foliage and flower characteristics.

• **PESTS AND DISEASES** Downy mildew, *Verticillium* wilt, viruses, rust, and fungal leaf spot can occur. Slugs and snails can attack new growth.

***D.* 'Adrian Bloom'.** Clump-forming, rhizomatous perennial with pinnate, gray-green leaves, 4–20in (10–50cm) long. Nodding racemes of narrow, dark carmine-red flowers, 1¼in (3cm) long, are produced in late spring and intermittently to early autumn. ↕ 14in (35cm), ↔ 18in (45cm). Zone 3.

***D.* 'Bacchanal'** ■ Rhizomatous perennial with finely lobed, gray-green leaves, ½–¾in (1–2cm) long. Racemes of dusk-crimson flowers, 1in (2.5cm) long, are borne in mid- and late spring. ↕ 18in (45cm), ↔ 24in (60cm). Zone 3.

Dicentra 'Bacchanal'

Dicentra cucullaria

***D.* 'Boothman's Variety'** see *D.* 'Stuart Boothman'.
***D.* 'Bountiful'.** Clump-forming, rhizomatous perennial with red-tinged stems bearing pinnate, mid-green leaves, 4–20in (10–50cm) long. In late spring and intermittently to early autumn, bears nodding racemes or panicles of purplish pink flowers, ½–1in (1.5–2.5cm) long. ↕ 12in (30cm), ↔ 18in (45cm). Zone 3.
D. canadensis (Squirrel corn). Rhizomatous perennial with fern-like, pinnate, broadly triangular basal leaves, to 10in (25cm) long, with linear-elliptic to linear-obovate leaflets. In spring, bears racemes of 3–12 heart-shaped, white flowers, tinged mauve, ½in (15mm) long. ↕↔ to 12in (30cm). Minnesota to Quebec south to Missouri and North Carolina. Zone 4.
D. chrysantha (Golden eardrops). Upright perennial with 2-pinnate, glaucous, mid-green leaves, 4–18in (10–45cm) long, with linear, lobed leaflets. Numerous golden yellow flowers, ½–¾in (1–2cm) long, are produced in upright panicles, to 12in (30cm) long, from midsummer to early autumn. ↕ 3–5ft (1–1.5m), ↔ 18in (45cm). S. Oregon to dry chaparral of S. California. Zone 6b.
D. cucullaria ▣ (Dutchman's breeches). Compact, clump-forming, tuberous perennial with 3-ternate, blue-green leaves, 4–10in (10–25cm) long, deeply lobed or divided into linear to elliptic leaflets. Racemes of white, rarely pink-flushed, yellow-tipped flowers, ½–¾in (1–2cm) long, on arching stems, are borne in early spring. Needs humus-rich soil in partial shade. Dies down quickly after flowering and should be kept almost dry in summer, when dormant. ↕ to 8in (20cm), ↔ to 10in (25cm). Nova Scotia to Kansas and North Carolina. Zone 4.
D. eximia (Fringed bleeding heart, Turkey corn). Clump-forming, rhizomatous perennial with red-tinged stems bearing pinnate, mid- to gray-green leaves, 6–20in (15–50cm) long, with lance-shaped to oblong or ovate lobes. In late spring and intermittently to early autumn, nodding racemes or panicles of deep rose-pink buds open to narrow pink, purple-pink, or white flowers, ½–1¼in (1.5–3cm) long, with reflexed outer petals. Self-sows readily. ↕ 24in (60cm), ↔ 18in (45cm). E. US. Zone 4. **'Alba'** has

Dicentra scandens (inset: flower detail)

white flowers and deeply divided foliage; ↕ 16in (40cm). **'Snowdrift'** has everblooming, larger pure white flowers.
***D. eximia* of gardens** see *D. formosa.*
D. formosa, syn. *D. eximia* of gardens (Western bleeding heart). Wide-spreading, rhizomatous perennial with abundant, lobed, basal leaves, 6–20in (15–50cm) long, mid-green above, glaucous beneath. Deep rose-pink buds, borne high above the foliage in branching racemes, open to pink flowers, ½–1in (1–2.5cm) long, fading almost to white, in late spring and early summer. Self-seeds freely. ↕ 18in (45cm), ↔ 24–36in (60–90cm). W. North America. Zone 4. **var. *alba*** has white flowers.**subsp. *oregona***, syn. *D. oregona*, has more glaucous leaves and soft bluish pink flowers; Oregon, California. **'Zestful'** has everblooming deep rose flowers and soft gray-green foliage; ↕ 12in (30cm).
***D.* 'Langtrees'.** Vigorous, rhizomatous perennial with abundant, lobed, silvery gray leaves, to 12in (30cm) long. Bears pink-tinted white flowers, ½–¾in (1–2cm) long, in racemes from midspring to midsummer. ↕ 12in (30cm), ↔ 18in (45cm). Zone 3.
***D.* 'Luxuriant'.** Spreading perennial with lobed, mid- to deep green leaves, to 12in (30cm) long. Racemes of red flowers, ½–1in (1.5–2.5cm) long, are produced from midspring to early or midsummer. ↕ 12in (30cm), ↔ 18in (45cm). Zone 4.
D. macrantha. Spreading perennial with 2-ternate, coarsely toothed, pale to yellow-green leaves, 8–12in (20–30cm) long, divided into ovate leaflets, produced on yellowish green stalks. Bears narrow, creamy yellow flowers, 3in (8cm) long, solitary or in short racemes, in late spring. May be damaged by cold, dry winds and late frosts. ↕ 24in (60cm), ↔ 18in (45cm). E. China. Zone 4b.
D. oregona see *D. formosa* subsp. *oregona.*
D. scandens ▣ syn. *D. thalictrifolia.* Climbing perennial with slender stems and deeply lobed, mid-green leaves, 6–14in (15–35cm) long, divided into ovate to lance-shaped leaflets. White or yellow, sometimes purple- or pink-tipped flowers, ¾–1in (2–2.5cm) long, are borne in long racemes on leafy peduncles in summer. ↕↔ 3ft (1m). Himalayas. Zone 6b.

Dicentra 'Stuart Boothman'

***D.* 'Silver Smith'.** Clump-forming, rhizomatous perennial with pinnate, blue-green leaves, 4–20in (10–50cm) long. In late spring and intermittently to early autumn, bears nodding racemes or panicles of pink-flushed, creamy white flowers, ½–¾in (1.5–2cm) long. ↕↔ 18in (45cm). Zone 4.
D. spectabilis ▣ (Bleeding heart, Lyre flower). Clump-forming perennial with thick, fleshy roots and 2-ternate, pale green leaves, 6–16in (15–40cm) long, with ovate, sometimes cut or lobed leaflets. Arching, fleshy stems bear racemes of flowers ¾–1¼in (2–3cm) long, with rose-pink outer petals and white inner ones, in late spring and early summer. Protect from early frosts and high winds. Usually dies down to the ground in midsummer. ↕ to 4ft (1.2m), ↔ 18in (45cm). Siberia, N. China, Korea. Zone 3.
f. *alba* ▣ has white flowers.
***D.* 'Spring Morning'.** Clump-forming, rhizomatous perennial with finely cut, mid- to dark green leaves, 4–20in (10–50cm) long. Produces nodding racemes or panicles of light pink flowers, ¾–1¼in (2–3cm) long, in late summer, intermittently to early autumn. ↕ 12in (30cm), ↔ 18in (45cm). Zone 4.
***D.* 'Stuart Boothman'** ▣ syn. *D.* 'Boothman's Variety'. Spreading, rhizomatous perennial with ternate, blue-gray leaves, 4–8in (10–20cm) long, with narrow leaflets. Deep pink flowers, ½–1in (1.5–2.5cm) long, are produced from midspring to midsummer. ↕ 12in (30cm), ↔ 16in (40cm). Zone 4.
D. thalictrifolia see *D. scandens.*

Dicentra spectabilis

Dicentra spectabilis f. *alba*

DICHELOSTEMMA

syn. BREVOORTIA

LILIACEAE

Genus of 7 species of cormous perennials found in grassland and chaparral in W. North America. They are grown for their umbels or racemes of tubular to bell-shaped flowers, clustered at the ends of long, thin stems. Narrow, grass-like leaves, 12in (30cm) long, produced in spring, die off as the flowers open. Grow in a warm, sheltered border or, in cool climates with damp summers, in a bulb frame or cold greenhouse to ensure a warm, dry dormancy.

• **CULTIVATION** Plant 4in (10cm) deep in autumn, in well-drained soil in full sun. Keep warm and dry after flowering.

• **PROPAGATION** Sow seed at 55–61°F (13–16°C) as soon as ripe, or remove offsets in late summer.

• **PESTS AND DISEASES** Prone to rust.

D. congestum, syn. *Brodiaea congesta.* Cormous perennial producing dense racemes, 2in (5cm) across, of numerous tubular, lilac-blue flowers, ¾in (2cm) long, in early summer. Similar to *D. pulchellum*, but flower stalks are joined at the base. ↕ 16–36in (40–90cm), PD2in (5cm). Washington, Oregon, California. Zone 6b.

D. ida-maia ■ syn. *Brodiaea ida-maia* (Firecracker flower). Cormous perennial bearing umbels, 2½in (6cm) across, of up to 8 pendent, narrowly tubular, crimson flowers, ¾–1¼in (2–3cm) long, with short, reflexed sepals with greenish yellow tips, in summer. Excellent for cutting. Requires a dormant season to ripen the corm, so best grown in an alpine house or cold frame in moist climates. ↕ 8–12in (20–30cm), PD2in (5cm). Oregon, California. Zone 6b.

D. pulchellum, syn. *Brodiaea capitata, B. pulchella* (Blue-dicks). Cormous perennial bearing dense umbels, 2in (5cm) across, of many tubular, lilac-blue flowers, ½in (1.5cm) long, in early summer. ↕ 12–24in (30–60cm), PD2in (5cm). Oregon, California. Zone 6b.

D. volubile, syn. *Brodiaea volubilis* (Twining brodiaea). Scrambling, cormous perennial producing umbels, 3in (8cm) across, of many tubular pink or pinkish mauve flowers, ¾in (2cm) long, in summer. Needs support. ↕ to 5ft (1.5m), PD2in (5cm). California. Zone 6b.

Dichelostemma ida-maia

Dichondra micrantha

DICHONDRA

CONVOLVULACEAE

Genus of about 10 species of prostrate, creeping perennials from tropical and subtropical regions of E. Asia. The leaves are heart- to kidney-shaped and entire. Solitary flowers are borne in the axils and have ovate-spoon-shaped sepals and tiny, 5-lobed corollas. *D. micrantha* is most often used as a groundcover or substitute for lawn grass.

• **CULTIVATION** Grow in moderately fertile, well-drained, slightly acidic soil in full sun or partial shade. Apply a slow-release fertilizer before sowing. Mow, water, and fertilize regularly. Dichondras will not tolerate regular foot traffic, especially when covered with frost; trodden leaves will turn black as they thaw.

• **PROPAGATION** Sow seed *in situ* in spring or plant plugs of *Dichondra* 3in (8cm) apart.

• **PESTS AND DISEASES** Dichondra flea beetles may be a problem.

D. carolinensis see *D. micrantha.*

D. micrantha ■ syn. *D. carolinensis, D. repens.* Prostrate perennial groundcover with rooting surface runners, slender, hairy stems, and small, spoon-shaped, softly hairy leaves, ¼–1¼in (.5–3cm) long. Bears tiny, white, green or yellow-green flowers from summer to autumn. ↕ 20in (50cm), ↔ indefinite. E. Asia. ❀ (min. 45°F/7°C)

D. repens see *D. micrantha.*

DICHORISANDRA

COMMELINACEAE

Genus of about 25 species of robust, erect, soft-stemmed, evergreen perennials from woodland in tropical North, Central, and South America. The linear to elliptic leaves are spirally arranged or 2-ranked, and the angular, cup-shaped flowers, with 3 sepals and 3 unequally sized, intense blue or sometimes white petals, are produced in terminal or axillary racemes, followed by fleshy, orange-red fruit. Where not hardy, grow in a warm greenhouse or as a houseplant; in warmer climates, use in a border.

• **CULTIVATION** Under glass, grow in soil-based potting mix in bright filtered light and high humidity. In the growing season, water freely and apply a balanced liquid fertilizer monthly; keep just moist

Dichorisandra reginae

in winter. Outdoors, grow in well-drained, fertile soil in partial shade.

• **PROPAGATION** Divide or root stem cuttings at any time.

• **PESTS AND DISEASES** Anthracnose, crown rot, Southern blight, and mealybugs can occur.

D. reginae ■ (Queen's spiderwort). Erect perennial having fleshy, rhizomatous roots and 2-ranked, elliptic, dark green leaves, 7in (18cm) long, that are suffused with reddish purple when young, often streaked with silver, and purple beneath. White flowers, to ¾in (2cm) across, violet-blue on the upper half of the petals, are produced in compact racemes, 6–8in (15–20cm) long, from summer to autumn. ↕↔ 12in (30cm). Peru. ❀ (min. 54°F/12°C)

D. thyrsiflora. Erect perennial with short, rhizomatous roots and spirally arranged, elliptic-lance-shaped, lustrous, dark green leaves, 8–12in (20–30cm) long. Deep violet flowers, ½–¾in (1–2cm) across, are produced in dense racemes, 5–8in (13–20cm) long, in autumn. ↕ 8ft (2.5m), ↔ 3ft (1m). Brazil. ❀ (min. 54°F/12°C)

DICKSONIA

DICKSONIACEAE

Genus of about 25 species of evergreen or semi-evergreen ferns, usually with upright, trunk-like rhizomes or caudices, but occasionally creeping in habit. They are found in sheltered, upland forest in temperate and tropical regions of S.E. Asia, Australasia, and South America. The often massive rhizomes or caudices are usually clothed in old leaf bases and fibrous roots, and crowned with spreading, 2- to 4-pinnate or pinnatifid, leathery fronds. The sori are round and form along the margins of the segments, on the underside, each protected by an indusium. *Dicksonia* species are fine specimen plants, whether in a cool greenhouse or conservatory, or outdoors in frost-free areas. They are suitable for growing in large containers.

• **CULTIVATION** Under glass, grow in a mix of 1 part each loam and coarse bark, 2 parts sharp sand, and 3 parts leaf mold, in bright filtered light and moderate humidity; if possible, move the plants outside during summer. In the growing season, water freely and apply a high-nitrogen liquid fertilizer monthly; keep just moist and admit full light in winter. Top-dress or pot on annually in spring. Outdoors, grow in humus-rich, acidic soil in partial or full shade. Hose the rhizomes or caudices with water daily in hot, dry weather. Take care not to damage the growing tips; damaged plants will fail to generate new growth and will eventually die. They thrive in the subtropical regions of North America and in Hawaii.

• **PROPAGATION** Sow spores at 59–61°F (15–16°C) as soon as ripe. See also p. 51.

• **PESTS AND DISEASES** Infrequent.

D. antarctica ■ (Man fern, Tasmanian tree fern, Woolly tree fern). Tree-like fern, evergreen in mild climates, with a massive, trunk-like rhizome, 24in (60cm) across, covered with a thick mat

Dicksonia antarctica

of roots. The fronds are 2- or 3-pinnate, to 10ft (3m) long, and pale green when young, darkening with age. ↕ to 20ft (6m) (usually considerably less), ↔ 12ft (4m). E. Australia, including Tasmania. ❀ (min. 45°F/7°C)

D. fibrosa. Upright to horizontally arching fern, with reddish brown fronds, 6–8ft (2–2.5m) long 30in (75cm) wide. Blades are smaller, glossier, and more prickly than *D. antarctica.* Old fronds form a skirt on the trunk for protection against frost and drying winds. Grows in lowland to montane forests or in open areas. Trunk ↕ 10–20ft (3–6m), ↔ 24in (60cm). New Zealand. ❀ (min. 41°F/5°C)

D. squarrosa. Tree-like, upright, arching fern. Lance-shaped fronds, silvery green above to glaucous underneath, and nearly tripinnate with abundant dark hairs on the stipe and rachis, 3–6ft (1–2m) long and 18in (45cm) wide. The slender, black trunk will produce side crowns and runners underground. Trunk ↕ 10–20ft (3–6m) ↔ 3–4in (8–10cm). Grows in lowland forests. New Zealand. ❀ (min. 41°F/5°C)

DICLIPTERA

ACANTHACEAE

Genus of 150 species of annuals, soft-stemmed or woody, evergreen perennials, subshrubs, and climbers with angled stems, found in many tropical or warm temperate regions. They are grown for their opposite, lance-shaped to almost circular, velvety, gray-green leaves and their slender, tubular, 2-lipped, colorful flowers, borne in terminal and axillary clusters with prominent bracts. Grow in a border; where not hardy, grow as a houseplant or in a warm greenhouse.

- **CULTIVATION** Under glass, grow in soil-based potting mix in full light with shade from hot sun. In growth, water freely and apply a balanced liquid fertilizer monthly; keep just moist in winter. Outdoors, grow in moderately fertile, well-drained soil in sun or partial shade. Cut back leggy plants after flowering.
- **PROPAGATION** Root softwood cuttings in spring or summer.
- **PESTS AND DISEASES** Prone to rust.

D. suberecta ■ syn. *Jacobinia suberecta, Justicia suberecta.* Erect or arching subshrub with slender stems and ovate, dull, mid-green leaves, 1½–3in (4–8cm) long, covered in gray down. In summer, orange-red flowers, 1½in (4cm) long,

Dicliptera suberecta

Dictamnus albus var. *purpureus*

are produced in axillary and terminal clusters. ↕ 24in (60cm), ↔ 18in (45cm). Uruguay. ❀ (min. 55°F/13°C)

DICTAMNUS

RUTACEAE

Genus of one species of woody-based perennial, native to open woodland, dry grassland, and rocky sites, in C. and S. Europe, and from S. and C. Asia to China and Korea. It has pinnate, ash-like, alternate leaves, each with 3–6 pairs of leaflets and a single terminal one. Bears 5-petaled, asymmetrical flowers, with long, projecting stamens, in long, open racemes. They, and the unripe fruit, produce a volatile oil, which may be ignited in hot, windless weather. *D. albus* is suitable for a border. Its foliage, roots, and seeds may cause mild stomach upset if ingested; contact with the foliage may cause photodermatitis.

- **CULTIVATION** Grow in any dry, well-drained, moderately fertile soil in full sun or partial shade. Dislikes disturbance.
- **PROPAGATION** Sow seed in containers in a cold frame as soon as ripe. Divide in autumn or spring, although the woody rootstock does not re-establish easily.
- **PESTS AND DISEASES** Infrequent.

D. albus, syn. *D. fraxinella* (Burning bush, Dittany, Gas plant). Clump-forming perennial with pinnate, leathery, lemon-scented leaves, to 14in (35cm) long, with lance-shaped to ovate leaflets. White or pinkish white flowers, ¾–1in (2–2.5cm) across, with darker veins, are produced in early summer. ↕ 16–36in (40–90cm), ↔ 24in (60cm). C. and S. Europe to N. China, Korea. Zone 3. **var. *purpureus*** ■ has purple-mauve flowers with darker veins.

D. fraxinella see *D. albus.*

DICTYOSPERMA

Princess palm

ARECACEAE

Genus of one species of monoecious, single-stemmed palm from Mauritius and Réunion. Pinnate leaves are produced in a terminal head above a distinct crownshaft, and 3-petaled, cup-shaped flowers, arranged in groups of 3 (2 male and 1 female), develop in simple panicles between them. *D. album* is an effective specimen tree. Where not hardy, grow in a warm greenhouse.

- **CULTIVATION** Under glass, grow in soil-based potting mix in bright filtered

Dictyosperma album

light. In the growing season, water freely, applying a balanced liquid fertilizer monthly; keep just moist in winter. Pot on or top-dress in spring. Outdoors, grow in fertile, moist but well-drained soil in sun or partial shade.
- **PROPAGATION** Sow seed at 75–84°F (24–29°C) in spring.
- **PESTS AND DISEASES** Frizzle top (manganese deficiency), lethal yellowing, butt rot, and fungal spots are common. Prone to spider mites and scale insects.

D. album ■ Single-stemmed palm with a closely ringed, dark brown to gray trunk, sometimes wider at the base, with a woolly, red-brown to whitish gray crownshaft. Arching, pinnate leaves, to 10ft (3m) long, have up to 140 lance-shaped, often divided, mid- to dark green leaflets, with yellow midribs and dark veins when young. Leaf stalks are orange-yellow above, yellow-striped beneath. Bears yellow male flowers in panicles, to 3ft (1m) long, in summer, followed by ovoid, purplish black fruit, to ¾in (2cm) long. ↕ 70ft (20m), ↔ to 20ft (6m). Mauritius, Réunion. ❀ (min. 61°F/16°C). **var. *conjugatum*** has maroon to red male flowers.

▷ ***Didiscus*** see *Trachymene*

DIDYMOCHLAENA

DRYOPTERIDACEAE

Genus of one species of evergreen fern from tropical Africa, America, and Polynesia, occurring in woodland and by streams. It produces tufts of glossy, mid-green fronds, tinged with rose-pink or red when young. Grow *D. truncatula* in a shady border; where not hardy, grow in a warm greenhouse.

- **CULTIVATION** Under glass, grow in soil-based potting mix, with additional leaf mold and granulated bark, in bright filtered light and high humidity. In the growing season, water freely, applying a balanced liquid fertilizer monthly; keep just moist in winter. Outdoors, grow in moist, humus-rich soil in partial shade.
- **PROPAGATION** Sow spores at 70°F (21°C) as soon as ripe; divide established plants in spring. See also p.51.
- **PESTS AND DISEASES** Mealybugs and soft scale may be troublesome.

D. lunulata see *D. truncatula.*

D. truncatula ■ syn. *D. lunulata.* Evergreen fern with erect rhizomes and triangular, 2-pinnate fronds, 2–5ft (60–150cm) long, with simple, obliquely ovoid-diamond-shaped segments. ↕↔ to 3ft (1m). Tropical and southern Africa, Fiji, Argentina. ❀ (min. 50°F/10°C)

DIEFFENBACHIA

Dumb cane, Mother-in-law's tongue

ARACEAE

Genus of about 30 species of evergreen perennials from tropical forest in North and South America and the West Indies. Most cultivars are derived from *D. seguine*, now thought to include *D. maculata*, a name still used commercially. They are grown for their handsome, large, mainly paddle-shaped, oblong, or ovate, fleshy leaves, often heavily marked yellow or white and borne on sheathed stalks. As the lower leaves are shed, scars are left on the erect, thick, cane-like stems, although some modern cultivars are virtually stemless. Inflorescences with creamy spathes are produced intermittently throughout the year, although seldom in cultivation. Where not hardy, grow in a warm greenhouse, or as houseplants; elsewhere, grow in a border. All parts may cause severe discomfort if ingested; contact with sap may irritate skin.

- **CULTIVATION** Under glass, grow in soil-based potting mix in bright filtered light and high humidity. In the growing season, water moderately, applying a balanced liquid fertilizer monthly; mist daily in summer. Water sparingly and admit full light in winter. Pot on each spring. Outdoors, grow in fertile, moist but well-drained soil in partial shade.
- **PROPAGATION** Root tip cuttings in spring or summer; or take stem sections,

Didymochlaena truncatula

D

Dieffenbachia seguine 'Amoena'

each with a growth bud, and lay flat on the surface of the soil mix. Alternatively, increase by air layering.

• **PESTS AND DISEASES** Spider mites, aphids, mealybugs, and scale insects are common. Fungal spot, stem rot, and root rot, as well as bacterial blight and soft rot, also occur frequently. Dasheen mosaic virus was prevalent in the past.

***D. amoena* of gardens** see *D. seguine* 'Amoena'.
***D.* 'Exotica'** see *D. seguine* 'Exotica'.
D. maculata see *D. seguine, D. seguine* 'Maculata'.
***D. maculata* 'Hi-color'** see *D. seguine* 'Tropic Snow'.
***D. maculata* 'Snow Queen'** see *D. seguine* 'Tropic Snow'.
***D. maculata* 'Tropic Topaz'** see *D. seguine* 'Tropic Snow'.
***D.* 'Memoria'** see *D. seguine* 'Memoria Corsii'.
D.* x *memoria-corsii see *D. seguine* 'Memoria Corsii'.
***D.* 'Pia'** see *D. seguine* 'Pia'.
D. picta see *D. seguine.*
D. seguine, syn. *D. maculata, D. picta.* Robust perennial with alternate, broadly ovate to oblong or lance-shaped leaves, 12–18in (30–45cm) long, evenly spread along the stem. They are glossy, dark green, sparsely spotted white, with white midribs. ↕ 3–10ft (1–3m), ↔ 24in (60cm). Brazil. ❀ (min. 59°F/15°C). **'Amoena'** ▣ syn. *D. amoena* of gardens, has oblong-ovate leaves, 6–14in (15–35cm) long, with creamy white bands and marbling between the veins; ↕ to 6ft (2m). **'Exotica'** ▣ syn. *D.* 'Exotica', *D. maculata* 'Exotica', is virtually

Dieffenbachia seguine 'Exotica'

Dieffenbachia seguine 'Rudolph Roehrs'

stemless, with oblong-ovate leaves, heavily and irregularly white-variegated between the veins and on the midribs; ↕ 3ft (1m), ↔ 16in (40cm). **'Maculata'**, syn. *D. maculata*, has bright green leaves, 10in (25cm) long, heavily veined and spotted creamy white, and mottled leaf stalks; ↕ 4ft (1.2m) or more, ↔ 3ft (1m). **'Memoria'** see 'Memoria Corsii'. **'Memoria Corsii'**, syn. *D.* 'Memoria', *D.* x *memoria-corsii*, 'Memoria', has elliptic to oblong, gray-green leaves, that darken with age, with large, dark green patches, darker veining, and sparse white spots; ↕ 3ft (1m), ↔ 16in (40cm). **'Pia'**, syn. *D. maculata* 'Pia', *D.* 'Pia', is virtually stemless, with oblong-lance-shaped white leaves, tinged pale green, and deep green margins; ↕ 16in (40cm), ↔ 12in (30cm). **'Roehrsii'** see 'Rudolph Roehrs'. **'Rudolph Roehrs'** ▣ syn. *D. maculata* 'Rudolph Roehrs', 'Roehrsii', has ovate to elliptic leaves, mostly creamy yellow or chartreuse-green, spotted white, with dark green midribs and margins; ↕ 3ft (1m) or more, ↔ 16in (40cm). **'Tropic Snow'**, syn. *D. maculata* 'Hi-color', *D. maculata* 'Snow Queen', *D. maculata* 'Tropic Snow', *D. maculata* 'Tropic Topaz', *D.* 'Tropic Snow', is virtually stemless, with thick, ovate, mid-green leaves, with sage-green markings and cream feathering; ↕ 4ft (1.2m).
***D.* 'Tropic Snow'** see *D. seguine* 'Tropic Snow'.

DIERAMA

Angel's fishing rod, Wand flower

IRIDACEAE

Genus of 44 species of evergreen, cormous perennials usually found in moist, mountainous or submountainous grassland in Ethiopia, E. and S. tropical Africa, and South Africa. Gladiolus-like corms, produced annually, form chains of old corms on top of one another. Basal tufts of semi-erect to erect, thin, grass-like, mid- to gray-green leaves, to 36in (90cm) long, are overtopped in summer by a succession of pendent, funnel- or bell-shaped flowers, borne in spikes on long, slender, arching stems. Hybrids between *D. dracomontanum* and *D. pulcherrimum* are sometimes known as Slieve Donard Hybrids, a name wrongly applied to mixed seedlings. Where not hardy, grow *Dierama* in a cool greenhouse. Elsewhere, grow tall species at the back of a border or by a pool or stream, and dwarf species in a rock garden or at the front of a border.

Dierama dracomontanum

• **CULTIVATION** Plant corms 3–5in (8–13cm) deep in spring. Under glass, grow in soil-based potting mix in full light. In the growing season, water freely. Outdoors, grow in humus-rich, well-drained soil in full sun in a sheltered site, watering freely in the growing season. Divisions and young plants take some time to establish, but once settled are trouble free.

• **PROPAGATION** Sow seed in a seedbed or in containers in a cold frame as soon as ripe, or divide in spring.

• **PESTS AND DISEASES** Infrequent.

D. dracomontanum ▣ syn. *D. pumilum* of gardens. Clump-forming, cormous perennial. Produces arching stems of bell-shaped, light pink, rose-pink, coral-pink, red, purple-pink, or mauve flowers, ¾–1¼in (2–3cm) long, in summer. ↕ 24in (60cm), occasionally to 3ft (1m), PD12in (30cm). South Africa. Zone 7b.
D. ensifolium see *D. pendulum.*
D. grandiflorum. Cormous perennial bearing bell-shaped, light mauve flowers, 2in (5cm) long, with darker markings, in late spring and early summer. Withstands drought once established. ↕ 36in (90cm), PD12in (30cm). South Africa (Eastern Cape). Zone 8.
D. luteoalbidum. Cormous perennial that produces narrowly bell-shaped, white or creamy yellow flowers, 1¼–2in (3–5cm) long, in summer. ↕ 24–36in (60–90cm), PD12in (30cm). South Africa (KwaZulu/Natal). Zone 7b.
***D.* 'Miranda'** ▣ Clump-forming, cormous perennial. Bears bell-shaped,

Dierama 'Miranda'

Dierama pulcherrimum

bright pink flowers, 1¼–1½in (3–4cm) long, in summer. ↕ 30–36in (75–90cm), PD12in (30cm). Zone 7b.
D. pendulum, syn. *D. ensifolium* (Grassy bells). Tufted, clump-forming, cormous perennial bearing clustered spikes of wide, open bell-shaped, purple-pink flowers, 1¼–2in (3–5cm) long, in summer. ↕ 3–6ft (1–2m), PD24in (60cm). South Africa (Western Cape, Eastern Cape). Zone 7b.
D. pulcherrimum ▣ Cormous perennial bearing dense, pendent spikes of tubular-bell-shaped, pale to deep magenta-pink, occasionally purple-red or white flowers, 1½–2½in (3.5–6cm) long, in summer. ↕ 3–5ft (1–1.5m), PD24in (60cm). Zimbabwe, South Africa. Zone 7b. **'Blackbird'** has deep wine-purple flowers, 1½–2in (4–5cm) long.
***D. pumilum* of gardens** see *D. dracomontanum.*
***D.* 'Titania'.** Clump-forming, cormous perennial producing bell-shaped, pale pinkish red flowers, 1¼in–2in (3–5cm) long, in summer. ↕ 24in (60cm), PD12in (30cm). Zone 7.

DIERVILLA

Bush honeysuckle

CAPRIFOLIACEAE

Genus of 3 species of suckering, deciduous shrubs from North America, found in open woodland. They are valued for their attractive habit and tubular, 2-lipped yellow flowers, which are produced in axillary or terminal cymes. Leaves are simple, oblong-lance-shaped to ovate, toothed, and opposite. Grow in a shrub border or open woodland garden.

• **CULTIVATION** Grow in fertile, well-drained soil in sun or partial shade. Mulch well. Pruning group 6.

• **PROPAGATION** Separate suckers in early and midspring. Root softwood cuttings in summer.

• **PESTS AND DISEASES** Powdery mildew and fungal spot occur.

D. sessilifolia (Southern bush honeysuckle). Thicket-forming shrub, spreading by suckers. Ovate-lance-shaped, mid-green leaves, 2½–7in (6–18cm) long, are tapered at the tips and bronze-tinged when young. Sulfur-yellow flowers, to ½in (1.5cm) long, are produced in terminal cymes, to 3in (8cm) across, in summer. ↕ 3–5ft (1–1.5m), ↔ 5ft (1.5m). S.E. US. Zone 4.

DIETES

IRIDACEAE

Genus of 6 species of evergreen, rhizomatous perennials from C., E., and S.E. tropical Africa, South Africa, and Lord Howe Island, Australia, occurring in open grassland, dry bushland, moist forest margins, and mountain cliffs. They have erect, linear to sword-shaped, leathery, basal leaves. Branching stems bear a succession of flat, short-lived, iris-like flowers, from spring to summer. Where not hardy, grow in a cool greenhouse or conservatory. In warmer climates, grow outdoors in a border.

• **CULTIVATION** Under glass, grow in soil-based potting mix in full light. In growth, water freely, applying a balanced liquid fertilizer monthly; reduce water after flowering to keep just moist when dormant. Outdoors, grow in moist but well-drained soil in sun or partial shade. Tolerates poor, dry soils. The flowering stems of *D. iridioides* should not be cut back after flowering.

• **PROPAGATION** Sow seed at 55–59°F (13–15°C) in autumn or spring. Divide rhizomes after flowering, although they may be difficult to establish.

• **PESTS AND DISEASES** Rust and crown and root rot are common.

D. bicolor ■ Rhizomatous perennial with narrowly sword-shaped, pale green, basal leaves, 24in (60cm) long. Bears pale to deep yellow flowers, 1½in (4cm) across, from spring to summer. The 3 larger tepals each have a brown mark at the base. ↕ 24–36in (60–90cm), ↔ 12in (30cm). South Africa. ❄ (min. 41°F/5°C)
D. grandiflora (Wild iris). Rhizomatous perennial with sword-shaped, dark green leaves, to 28in (70cm) long. From spring to summer, bears white flowers, 3–4in (8–11cm) across, with a yellow mark at the base of the 3 larger tepals, and a brown mark at the base of the 3 smaller tepals. ↕ 3–4ft (1–1.2m), ↔ 24–36in (60–90cm). South Africa. ❄ (min. 41°F/5°C)
D. iridioides, syn. *D. vegeta*. Rhizomatous perennial with a fan of sword-shaped, dark green, basal leaves, 24in (60cm) long. White flowers, 2–2½in (5–6cm) across, with a yellow mark at the center of each of the 3 larger tepals, are produced from spring to summer. ↕ 12–24in (30–60cm), ↔ 12in (30cm). South Africa, E. Africa to Kenya. ❄ (min. 41°F/5°C)
D. vegeta see *D. iridioides*.

Dietes bicolor

DIGITALIS

Foxglove

SCROPHULARIACEAE

Genus of about 22 species of biennials and short-lived perennials from Europe, N.W. Africa, and C. Asia, found in open woodland, with a few occurring in subalpine meadows and on stony, grassy slopes. They produce simple, mainly oblong to lance-shaped to obovate, entire or toothed, mostly mid-green leaves. They have one or more basal leaf rosettes with smaller, alternate stem leaves. Inflated, tubular-bell-shaped, somewhat 2-lipped flowers, often spotted inside, are produced in tall, sometimes branched, often closely packed racemes, usually on one side of the stems. Most foxgloves are handsome, suitable for a border or rock garden, or for naturalizing in woodland. All parts may cause severe discomfort if ingested. Contact with foliage may irritate skin.

• **CULTIVATION** Grow in almost any soil and situation, except very wet or very dry soil; most prefer humus-rich soil in partial shade. Some species self-seed profusely, so deadhead after flowering unless seedlings are desired.

• **PROPAGATION** Sow seed *in situ* or in containers in a cold frame in late spring. Divide perennials in spring or autumn.

• **PESTS AND DISEASES** Southern blight, anthracnose, and fungal leaf spots may be problems.

D. ambigua see *D. grandiflora*.
D. davisiana ■ Rhizomatous perennial with linear-lance-shaped, finely toothed, hairless, mid-green leaves, 3–5in (8–13cm) long. Bears pale yellow flowers, 1¼–1½in (3–4cm) long, with orange veins, in loose-flowered racemes in early summer. ↕ to 28in (70cm), ↔ 18in (45cm). Turkey. Zone 8.
D. dubia. Rosette-forming perennial with lance-shaped, wrinkled, entire or shallowly toothed, dark green leaves, 1¼–5in (3–13cm) long, hairless above and downy beneath. Bears few-flowered racemes of purplish pink or white flowers, 1¼–1½in (3.5–4cm) long, heavily spotted inside, in early summer. ↕ 18in (45cm), ↔ 12in (30cm). Spain (Balearic Islands). ❄ (min. 35°F/2°C)
D. eriostachya see *D. lutea*.
D. ferruginea (Rusty foxglove). Rosette-forming, robust biennial or perennial with oblong to oblong-lance-shaped, entire, dark green leaves, 2–8in (5–20cm) long, sometimes slightly hairy beneath. Bears racemes of golden brown flowers, 1½in (4cm) long, with red-brown veins inside and sepals with translucent margins, in midsummer. ↕ to 4ft (1.2m), ↔ 18in (45cm). S. and S.E. Europe, Hungary, Balkans, Turkey, Lebanon, Caucasus. Zone 4.
D. grandiflora ■ syn. *D. ambigua*, *D. orientalis* (Yellow foxglove). Clump-forming biennial or perennial with ovate-oblong, finely toothed, conspicuously veined, usually hairless, often glossy, mid-green leaves, 3–10in (7–25cm) long. Racemes of well-spaced, pale yellow flowers, 1½–2in (4–5cm) long, with brown veins inside, are produced in early and midsummer. ↕ to 3ft (1m), ↔ 18in (45cm). C. and S. Europe to Siberia, Turkey. Zone 3.

Digitalis davisiana (inset: flower detail)

D. kishinskyi see *D. parviflora*.
D. laevigata. Clump-forming, hairless perennial with obovate, mid-green basal leaves and linear-lance-shaped stem leaves, 2–10in (5–25cm) long. Loose racemes of horizontally borne, brown-yellow flowers, to 1½in (4cm) long, each with a white lower lip, and reddish brown veins and speckles inside, open in midsummer. ↕ to 3ft (1m), ↔ 18in (45cm). W. and C. Balkans. Zone 6.
D. lanata (Grecian foxglove). Clump-forming biennial or perennial with oblong-lance-shaped or inversely lance-shaped, mid-green leaves, to 5in (13cm) long, hairless beneath or with toothed margins. Dense, leafy racemes of pale cream or fawn flowers, 1¼in (3cm) long, each with brown or violet-brown veins and a lighter cream lower lip, are produced in mid- and late summer. ↕ 24in (60cm), ↔ 12in (30cm). Italy, Balkans, Hungary, Turkey. Zone 5.
D. lutea, syn. *D. eriostachya*. Clump-forming perennial with oblong to inversely-lance-shaped, toothed to almost entire, hairless, glossy, dark green leaves, 2–8in (5–20cm) long. Bears thin racemes of narrow, pale yellow flowers, ½–1in (1–2.5cm) long, in summer. Prefers alkaline soil. ↕ 24in (60cm), ↔ 12in (30cm). S.W. central Europe to Italy, N.W. Africa. Zone 3b.
D. x mertonensis ■ (*D. grandiflora* x *D. purpurea*). Robust, clump-forming perennial with ovate-lance-shaped to lance-shaped, toothed, conspicuously veined, glossy, dark green leaves, 3–12in (7–30cm) long, slightly hairy beneath. Bears racemes of pinkish buff flowers, to

Digitalis grandiflora

Digitalis x *mertonensis*

Digitalis obscura

2½in (6cm) long, in late spring and early summer. Comes true from seed. ↕ to 36in (90cm), ↔ 12in (30cm). Garden origin. Zone 3.

D. obscura ■ Subshrubby perennial with lance-shaped to linear, entire, hairless, gray-green leaves, 3–6in (8–15cm) long. Racemes of rust-brown to yellow or orange-yellow flowers, ¾–1¼in (2–3cm) long, with red veins and spotting inside, are produced from late spring to midsummer. ↕ 12–48in (30–120cm), ↔ 18in (45cm). Spain. Zone 4.

D. orientalis see *D. grandiflora.*

D. parviflora, syn. D. kishinskyi. Clump-forming perennial with oblong to inversely lance-shaped to lance-shaped, entire or slightly toothed, leathery, softly hairy, dark green leaves, 3–8in (8–20cm) long. Dense racemes of dark orange-brown flowers, ½–¾in (1–2cm) long, each with a purple-brown lip, are produced in early summer. ↕ 24in (60cm), ↔ 12in (30cm). N. Spain. Zone 4.

D. purpurea (Common foxglove). Rosette-forming, very variable, hairy biennial or short-lived perennial with ovate to lance-shaped, usually toothed, dark green, sometimes white-woolly leaves, 4–10in (10–25cm) long. Tall, one-sided spikes of purple, pink, or white flowers, to 2½in (6cm) long, spotted maroon to purple inside, are produced in early summer. Best grown annually from seed; often self-sows. ↕ 3–6ft (1–2m), ↔ to 24in (60cm). S.W. and W. central Europe. Zone 4. **f. *albiflora*** ■ has white flowers. **'Dwarf Sensation'** is compact, with densely packed flowers, to 3in (8cm) long; ↕ 4ft (1.2m). **Excelsior Hybrids** ■ produce horizontally held flowers, arranged evenly around each spike, in pastel shades of creamy yellow, white, purple, or pink. Good for cut flowers. **Foxy Hybrids** produce flowers in carmine-red, pink, creamy yellow, or white, heavily spotted maroon, and may be grown as annuals; ↕ to 36in (90cm). **'Giant Shirley'** has huge, bell-shaped white, shell-pink, and deep rose spikes, 3ft (1m) long, many dotted crimson or chocolate. **'Gloxinioides'** has horizontally held, wide-open, frilly-margined flowers in salmon-pink, creamy yellow, purple, or pink, richly spotted and blotched inside; ↕ 6ft (2m) or more. **'Sutton's Apricot'** has apricot-pink flowers.

Digitalis purpurea f. *albiflora*

Digitalis purpurea Excelsior Hybrids

Dillenia indica

Dillenia

DILLENIACEAE

Genus of about 60 species of magnolia-like, evergreen or briefly deciduous shrubs and trees usually found in forest from Asia to Australia. They are grown for their flowers and their large, alternate, usually ovate to rounded, conspicuously veined leaves. The 5-petaled, saucer- to cup-shaped flowers are solitary or borne in racemes or panicles; they are followed by edible, fleshy, star-shaped to spherical fruits in enlarged calyces. Where not hardy, grow *D. indica* in a temperate or warm greenhouse; in warmer regions, it makes an attractive specimen or medium-sized shade tree.

• **Cultivation** Under glass, grow in soil-based potting mix, with additional sharp sand, in full light. In growth, water freely and apply a balanced liquid fertilizer monthly; water sparingly in winter. Top-dress or pot on in spring. Outdoors, grow in fertile, humus-rich, moist but well-drained, neutral to acidic soil in full sun. Pruning group 1; under glass, may need light restrictive pruning after flowering.

• **Propagation** Sow seed at 61–64°F (16–18°C) in spring. Root semi-ripe cuttings with bottom heat in summer.

• **Pests and diseases** Infrequent.

D. indica ■ (Chulta). Bushy shrub or spreading tree with elliptic-oblong, toothed, lustrous, bright, dark green leaves, 12in (30cm) or more long, boldly patterned with sunken veins. Solitary, cup-shaped white flowers, 8in (20cm) or more across, are produced from the upper leaf axils in summer, followed by spherical, yellowish green fruit, to 4in (10cm) across. ↕ 50ft (15m), ↔ 30–50ft (10–15m). India to Java. ❄ (min. 59°F/15°C)

Dillwynia

FABACEAE

Genus of 15 species of evergreen shrubs from dry scrub, heath, and sandy plains in Australia. They are grown for their pea-like flowers, with large wing petals, which are borne singly, or in terminal or axillary racemes or corymbs. The small, alternate, linear leaves are often crowded. Grow in a border or rock garden. Where not hardy, grow in a cool greenhouse.

• **Cultivation** Under glass, grow in soil-based potting mix with additional sharp sand, in full light and with good ventilation. In the growing season, water moderately and apply a balanced liquid fertilizer monthly; water sparingly in winter. Top-dress or pot on in spring. Outdoors, grow in moist but well-drained, poor to moderately fertile soil in sun or partial shade. Pruning group 10, after flowering.

• **Propagation** Sow seed at 64–70°F (18–21°C) in spring after soaking in hot water. Root semi-ripe cuttings with bottom heat in summer.

• **Pests and diseases** Spider mites may infest greenhouse plants.

D. floribunda. Freely branching, softly hairy shrub with crowded, linear, warty, mid- to deep green leaves, ¼–½in (5–15mm) long. Produces a profusion of yellow or yellow-and-orange flowers, ¼in (6mm) across, in leafy, spike-like, terminal and axillary racemes, mainly from spring to summer. ↕↔ 3–5ft (1–1.5m). Queensland, New South Wales. ❄ (min. 45°F/7°C)

D. sericea. Erect, freely branching shrub with silky-white-hairy shoots bearing linear, warty, mid- to deep green leaves, ¼–½in (7–12mm) long. Bears spike-like terminal racemes of single or paired flowers, ½in (1.5cm) across, in shades of yellow and red, apricot, orange, or pink, from spring to summer. ↕ 2–4ft (60–120cm), ↔ 3–5ft (0.9–1.5m). Queensland to South Australia and Tasmania. ❄ (min. 45°F/7°C)

Dimorphotheca

African daisy

ASTERACEAE

Genus of 7 species of low-branching, erect annuals or evergreen, subshrubby perennials occurring in open, semi-arid, sandy areas in tropical Africa and South Africa, closely related to *Osteospermum* and at one time considered to include species now placed in that genus. All produce alternate, obovate to inversely lance-shaped, entire to pinnatisect, often wavy-margined to toothed leaves, and daisy-like flowerheads, on stiff stems, that close in cloudy weather. They are attractive container, bedding, or border plants, flowering from summer until first frost. The perennial species may be treated as annuals.

• **Cultivation** Grow in light, well-drained, fertile soil in full sun, in a

Dimorphotheca pluvialis

sheltered position. Deadhead regularly to prolong flowering.
• **PROPAGATION** Sow seed at 64°F (18°C) in early spring and plant out seedlings when danger of frost has passed, or sow *in situ* in midspring.
• **PESTS AND DISEASES** Rust, gray mold (*Botrytis*), *Fusarium* wilt, and *Verticillium* wilt may be problems.

D. annua see *D. pluvialis.*
***D. aurantiaca* of gardens** see *D. sinuata.*
***D. barberae* of gardens** see *Osteospermum jucundum.*
D. ecklonis see *Osteospermum ecklonis.*
D. pluvialis ■ syn. *D. annua* (Rain daisy, Weather prophet). Erect, hairy annual with obovate to inversely lance-shaped, coarsely toothed or pinnatifid, aromatic, dark green leaves, to 4in (10cm) long. In summer, produces single white flowerheads, to 2½in (6cm) across, violet-blue beneath, with violet-purple zoning at the bases of the ray petals and violet-brown central disks. Flowers do not open if rain is imminent. ↕ to 16in (40cm), ↔ 6–12in (15–30cm). Namibia, South Africa. ❀ (min. 41°F/5°C). **'Glistening White'** has white flowerheads, tinged with violet. **'Tetra Polar Star'** has white flowerheads, to 3in (8cm) across, with violet-blue central disks.
D. sinuata, syn. *D. aurantiaca* of gardens (Star of the veldt). Erect annual with oblong to lance-shaped, coarsely toothed, aromatic, mid-green leaves, to 4in (10cm) long. In summer, bears white, yellow, orange, or pink flowerheads, to 1½in (4cm) across, often tinged violet-blue, with violet-brown central disks. ↕↔ to 12in (30cm). South Africa. ❀ (min. 41°F/5°C)

DIONAEA

Venus flytrap

DROSERACEAE

Genus of one species of insectivorous perennial found in bogs in coastal areas of North and South Carolina. It has hinged, rounded, 2-lobed leaves, with stiff marginal spines and 3 or 4 sensitive hairs in the center of each lobe. When an insect, attracted by the plant's nectar, touches the hairs, the hinge mechanism is triggered, and the leaves close, trapping the insect. Cup-shaped flowers are borne in umbel-like cymes. Where not hardy, grow *D. muscipula* in a terrarium or in a cool greenhouse; elsewhere, grow in a bog garden.

Dionaea muscipula

• **CULTIVATION** Under glass, grow in an acidic mix of equal parts peat moss and sand in full or bright filtered light, or in a terrarium in bright light. Keep wet by standing in a saucer with ½in (1.5cm) of water. Growth ceases in autumn, leaving swollen leaf bases in a bulb-like structure below soil level; keep just moist when dormant. Pot on each spring as new growth appears. Outdoors, grow in moist, acidic soil in full sun. To encourage trap production, pinch out emerging flower stems and remove dead traps.
• **PROPAGATION** Sow seed at 50–55°F (10–13°C) in spring; place the container in a water tray to keep the potting mix moist. Germination is often very slow. Divide in spring, or take leaf cuttings in late spring or early summer.
• **PESTS AND DISEASES** Anthracnose, leaf spot, and crown rot are common.

D. muscipula ■ (Venus flytrap). Very variable, rosette-forming perennial with rounded, yellow-green to red leaves with winged stalks. Each leaf has 2 hinged lobes with 15–20 stiff, marginal spines. Winter and early summer leaves are 3in (8cm) long, with traps 1in (2.5cm) long; many plants also produce summer leaves, to 6in (15cm) long, with traps 1¼in (3cm) long and flatter, narrower stalks. In early and midsummer, bears 3–10 white flowers, ½in (1.5cm) across, in umbel-like cymes on bare stems, 12in (30cm) or more tall. ↕ 6–18in (15–45cm), ↔ 6in (15cm). North and South Carolina. ❀ (min. 35°F/2°C)

DIONYSIA

PRIMULACEAE

Genus of 42 species of tufted or cushion-forming, subshrubby, evergreen perennials found on shady cliffs in arid mountainous areas of C. Asia. The leaves, usually oblong to spoon-shaped, often with a woolly coating (farina) beneath, are borne in rosettes at the ends of branching shoots. Long-tubed, 5-petaled, salverform flowers, with spreading lobes, are solitary or borne in umbels in spring or early summer. Except for *D. involucrata,* variants with long or short pistils (pin- or thrum-eyed) must be grown together to produce seed. Grow *Dionysia* species in an alpine house or outdoors in tufa, protected from excess rainfall.
• **CULTIVATION** Under glass, grow in a mix of 3 parts grit and 1 part each loam and leaf mold, with a deep collar of grit

Dionysia aretioides

around the neck of the plant; provide full light and good ventilation. During the growing season, water freely from below, keeping the collar dry; water sparingly in winter. Outdoors, plunge pots into a cold frame in full sun. Carefully water the material into which the plants are plunged; the leaves and plant collar must be kept dry.
• **PROPAGATION** Sow seed in containers in a cold frame as soon as ripe. Take cuttings of single rosettes in summer, and root in a propagating case, watering only from below.
• **PESTS AND DISEASES** Very susceptible to gray mold (*Botrytis*), especially if overwatered or poorly ventilated. May be infested with aphids.

D. aretioides ■ Cushion-forming perennial with dense rosettes of linear-oblong to narrowly spoon-shaped, softly hairy, gray-green leaves, to ¼in (6mm) long, with turned-back margins, yellow- or white-mealy beneath. Produces numerous solitary, stemless, scented, bright yellow flowers, to ½in (1.5cm) across, with notched petals, in early spring. ↕ 3in (8cm), ↔ to 12in (30cm). N. Iran. Zone 7b.
D. involucrata. Dense, cushion-forming perennial with obovate to broadly spoon-shaped, finely toothed, dark green leaves, ⅛–½in (4–12mm) long. In early summer, bears stalked umbels of violet or violet-purple flowers, ¼–½in (7–15mm) across, with white eyes that darken with age. ↕ 3in (8cm), ↔ to 4in (10cm). N.E. Afghanistan and Tajikistan (Pamir Mountains). Zone 7b.

Dionysia michauxii

Dionysia tapetodes

D. michauxii ■ Dense, cushion-forming perennial with tight, rounded rosettes of oblong to oblong-spoon-shaped, silver-gray-hairy leaves, to ⅛in (3mm) long. In spring, the cushions are studded with stemless yellow flowers, to ¼in (6mm) across. ↕ 2in (5cm), ↔ to 6in (15cm). S.W. Iran. Zone 7b.
D. microphylla. Dense, cushion-forming perennial with hard, compact rosettes of entire, obovate to rounded, often sharp-pointed, gray-green leaves, to 1/16 in (2mm) long, with a mealy yellow coating beneath. In early summer, bears short-stemmed umbels of white-eyed, pale to deep violet flowers, to ½in (1.5cm) across, with darker petal bases. ↕ 2in (5cm), ↔ to 6in (15cm). N.W. Afghanistan. Zone 7b.
D. tapetodes ■ Tight, cushion-forming perennial with rosettes of oblong, obovate, or spoon-shaped, glandular, mid-green leaves, to ⅛in (3mm) long, sometimes with a dense, woolly white or yellow farina beneath. Bears masses of solitary, stemless, long-tubed, sometimes scented yellow flowers, to ½in (1.5cm) across, in late spring and early summer. Relatively easy to grow. ↕ 2in (5cm), ↔ to 8in (20cm). Turkmenistan, N.E. Iran, C. Afghanistan. Zone 7b.

DIOON

ZAMIACEAE

Genus of 10 species of dioecious, evergreen, palm-like cycads, with strong, woody stems, found on steep, rocky slopes or in open woodland in Central America. The stiff, leathery leaves are pinnate with many slender leaflets. Large, elliptic-ovoid, woolly, female cones are produced in the center of the terminal leaf rosettes; the male cones are cylindrical and smaller. Grow as specimen plants. Where not hardy, *Dioon* species need the protection of a temperate or warm greenhouse.
• **CULTIVATION** Under glass, grow in a mix of equal parts fibrous loam, coarse bark, and compost, in full light with shade from hot sun. In the growing season, water *D. edule* freely and *D. spinulosum* moderately, applying a balanced liquid fertilizer monthly. Water sparingly in winter. Top-dress or pot on in spring. Outdoors, grow most species in fertile, moist but well-drained, humus-rich, neutral to acidic soil in full sun. *D. spinulosum* prefers partial shade, high humidity, and neutral to slightly alkaline soil.

D

D

Dioon edule

• **PROPAGATION** Sow seed at 75–90°F (24–32°C) in spring in very sandy potting mix.
• **PESTS AND DISEASES** Scale insects, fungal leaf spot, crown rot, and root rot are common.

D. edule ▣ (Chestnut dioon, Mexican fern palm). Very slow-growing cycad with robust, solitary stems, which incline with age. Semi-erect leaves, 3–5ft (0.9–1.5m) long, have up to 200 linear-lance-shaped, sharp-tipped, hairy, gray- to bluish green leaflets, the lower ones almost spine-like. Female cones, to 12in (30cm) long, are rarely produced in cultivation. ↕ to 6ft (1.8m), ↔ 5–8ft (1.5–2.5m). Mexico. ❀ (min. 55°F/13°C)

DIOSCOREA

DIOSCOREACEAE

Genus of 600 species of tuberous, deciduous or evergreen, monoecious or dioecious, climbing perennials, some of which are succulent, from tropical forest and relatively dry, often arid areas in tropical and subtropical regions, and from woodland and open scrub in temperate areas. In a few species, the tubers are at or above ground level and covered with layers of corky bark, resembling a caudex. The stems are mostly woody based and often become vine-like, with alternate, occasionally opposite, simple or palmate leaves, and axillary racemes of small, bell-shaped, 6-tepaled flowers. Some species produce bulbils in the leaf axils. Use to clothe a pillar or pergola; *D. elephantipes* is also suitable for a desert garden. Where not hardy, grow in a temperate or warm greenhouse or conservatory.
• **CULTIVATION** Under glass, grow in soil-based potting mix in bright filtered light. Provide support. In the growing season, water freely, applying a balanced liquid fertilizer monthly; keep just moist at other times. Outdoors, grow in fertile, humus-rich soil in partial shade. Under glass, *D. elephantipes* needs full light and gritty, sharply drained potting mix, top-dressed with grit. In the growing season, water moderately; reduce water as stems wither, to keep completely dry when dormant. Outdoors, provide sharply drained soil in full sun.
• **PROPAGATION** Sow seed at 66–75°F (19–24°C) or plant bulbils in spring. Divide tubers when dormant. Root cuttings of young shoots as they arise from the tuber in spring.

Dioscorea discolor

• **PESTS AND DISEASES** Viral diseases, fungal spot, and aphids can occur.

D. batatas (Chinese yam, Cinnamon vine). Deciduous, annual climbing vine, with heart-shaped, opposite, simple, bright green leaves, 3–4in (7–10cm). Clockwise-twining stems bear green-yellow-white cinnamon-scented flowers. In the US, grown on trellises or with support in containers for the decorative foliage and flowers. ↕ 20ft (6m), ↔ 24in (60cm). China. Zone 6.
D. discolor ▣ (Ornamental yam). Moderately vigorous, erect, evergreen, twining climber with slightly angled stems. Heart-shaped or ovate, pointed leaves, 4–6in (10–15cm) long, are velvety olive-green, mottled with lighter green and silver, with silvery pink veins above and purple beneath. Racemes of green flowers, ¹⁄₁₆ in (2mm) across, are produced in summer. ↕ 6–10ft (2–3m). Tropical South America. ❀ (min. 55–59°F/13–15°C)
D. elephantipes ▣ syn. *Testudinaria elephantipes* (Elephant's foot). Slow-growing, deciduous, climbing perennial with a partially buried, pyramidal or hemispherical, woody tuber, to 36in (90cm) across, divided into angled, corrugated fissures. Blue-green leaves, to 2½in (6cm) long, are heart- or kidney-shaped. Bears racemes of dark-spotted, greenish yellow flowers, ⅛in (3mm) across, in spring. ↕↔ 3ft (1m). Grows in winter and is summer dormant. South Africa. ❀ (min. 45–50°F/7–10°C)

▷ ***Diosphaera*** *see Trachelium*

Dioscorea elephantipes

DIOSPYROS

EBENACEAE

Genus of 475 species of deciduous or evergreen trees and shrubs found in forest in tropical, subtropical, and warm-temperate regions worldwide. They are grown for their attractive habit; their bold, alternate, lance-shaped to broadly ovate, simple, often glossy leaves (sometimes with heart-shaped bases); and their fleshy fruits. Bell- or urn-shaped, male and female flowers are usually borne on separate plants, on the previous year's wood. Although some female cultivars of *D. kaki* produce fruit without a male, pollination will generally result in larger crops. In cool-temperate climates, the species and cultivars described here make attractive specimen trees, but most need long, warm summers to fruit well. If growing for fruit, train *D. kaki* as an espalier on a warm, sunny wall; where not hardy, grow in a cool greenhouse.
• **CULTIVATION** Under glass, grow in soil-based potting mix in full light. In the growing season, water freely, applying a balanced liquid fertilizer monthly; water sparingly in winter. Outdoors, grow in deep, fertile, well-drained, loamy soil in full sun, preferably sheltered from cold, drying winds and late frosts. Pruning group 1.
• **PROPAGATION** Sow seed in containers in an open frame as soon as ripe. Graft cultivars of *D. kaki* in winter.
• **PESTS AND DISEASES** Under glass, scale insects, leaf rollers, and mealybugs are problems. Fruit rot, wood rot, anthracnose, *Acremonium* wilt, powdery mildew, and a variety of fungal spots and blights are common.

D. kaki (Chinese persimmon, Japanese persimmon, Kaki). Spreading, deciduous tree with oval, glossy, dark green leaves, to 8in (20cm) long, which turn yellow to orange-red and purple in autumn. Small, bell-shaped, pale yellow flowers, to ½in (1.5cm) across, are produced in summer. Female plants bear edible, conical to spherical yellow to orange fruit, to 3in (8cm) across. ↕ 30ft (10m), ↔ 22ft (7m). China. Zone 6. Many cultivars exist. **'Hachiya'** ▣ is female, with conical, orange-red fruit, 3in (8cm) long.
D. lotus (Date plum) Spreading, deciduous tree with lance-shaped, elliptic, or oval, glossy, dark green leaves, to 5in (13cm) long. Bears tiny, bell-shaped, red-tinged green flowers in mid- and late summer, followed (on female plants) by unpalatable, spherical to ovoid yellow to purple fruit, to ¾in (2cm) across. ↕ 30ft (10m), ↔ 20ft (6m). S.W. Asia to China. Zone 7.
D. virginiana (American persimmon, Possumwood). Large, spreading, deciduous tree with distinctive "alligator-hide" bark and elliptic to oblong, glossy, dark green leaves, to 5in (13cm) long, paler beneath, which turn red in autumn. Bears greenish yellow flowers, ⅜–¾in (0.9–2cm) long, both male and female on the same tree, or dioecious, followed by sweet, spherical, yellow-orange fruit, 1–1½in (2.5–4cm) across. ↕ to 70ft (20m), ↔ to 35ft (11m). E. US. Zone 6.

Diospyros kaki 'Hachiya' (inset: fruit detail)

DIPCADI

LILIACEAE

Genus of 55 species of small, bulbous perennials found in dry, rocky areas in S. and W. Europe and N. and southern Africa. Leaves are linear to strap-shaped, and the narrowly bell-shaped or tubular flowers are borne in loose racemes. Grow in a rock garden; where winters are cold and wet, grow in an alpine house or bulb frame.
• **CULTIVATION** Plant bulbs 2in (5cm) deep in winter or early spring. Under glass, grow in a mix of equal parts loam, leaf mold, and sharp sand in full light. In growth, water freely; reduce water as leaves wither, and keep dry during summer dormancy. Outdoors, grow in light, well-drained soil in full sun.
• **PROPAGATION** Sow seed in containers in a cold frame as soon as ripe. Remove offsets during summer dormancy.
• **PESTS AND DISEASES** Infrequent.

D. serotinum. Bulbous perennial with narrowly linear, gray- or light green, basal leaves, to 12in (30cm) long. In spring, bears racemes of tubular, bronze, green, or dull orange-red flowers, 1in (2.5cm) long, with spreading or reflexing tips, on leafless stems, 18in (45cm) long. ↕ 4–18in (10–45cm), PD2in (5cm). S.W. Europe, N. Africa. ❀ (min. 35°F/2°C)

DIPELTA

CAPRIFOLIACEAE

Genus of 4 species of deciduous shrubs found in scrub and woodland in C. and W. China. They are valued for their peeling bark; their fragrant, tubular to bell-shaped flowers, borne singly or in short corymbs; and for the papery bracts that surround the fruits. The simple, ovate to oval-lance-shaped, pointed leaves are borne in opposite pairs. Grow as a specimen or in a large shrub border.
• **CULTIVATION** Grow in fertile, well-drained, preferably alkaline soil in sun or partial shade. Pruning group 2.
• **PROPAGATION** Sow seed in a seedbed in autumn or spring. Root softwood cuttings in summer.
• **PESTS AND DISEASES** Infrequent.

D. floribunda ▣ Upright, multi-stemmed shrub with pale brown bark and ovate to oval-lance-shaped, sharp-pointed, pale green leaves, to 4in (10cm) long. Produces terminal and axillary corymbs of 1–6 tubular, yellow-marked, pale pink flowers, to 1¼in (3cm) long, in late spring and early summer. ↕↔ 12ft (4m). C. and W. China. Zone 7.

D. yunnanensis. Arching shrub with pale brown bark and ovate-lance-shaped, pointed, glossy, mid-green leaves, to 5in (13cm) long. Corymbs of 1–4 tubular, orange-marked white flowers, to 1in (2.5cm) long, are borne on short, leafy stems in late spring. ↕ 10ft (3m), ↔ 12ft (4m). W. China. Zone 7b.

Dipelta floribunda

DIPHYLLEIA

BERBERIDACEAE

Genus of 2 or 3 species of rhizomatous perennials found in woodland and by mountain streams in Japan and North America. They produce large, peltate, dark green leaves and terminal cymes of 6-petaled, bowl-shaped white flowers that quickly lose their petals. Grow in a woodland garden.
• **CULTIVATION** Grow in moist, leafy or humus-rich soil in full or partial shade, preferably sheltered from wind.
• **PROPAGATION** Sow seed in containers in a cold frame as soon as ripe. Divide rhizomes in spring.
• **PESTS AND DISEASES** Slugs and snails eat resting buds and young growth.

D. cymosa (Umbrella leaf). Rhizomatous perennial with cleft radical leaves, 12–24in (30–60cm) across, each segment with 5–7 shallow, pointed, toothed lobes. Upright flowering stems each bear 2 deeply 2-lobed leaves, to 16in (40cm) across. Bears flowers to ¾in (2cm) across in umbel-like cymes in late spring and early summer, followed by blue berries, ½in (1.5cm) across, on red stalks. ↕ to 3ft (1m), ↔ 12in (30cm). S. Appalachians. Zone 7b.

▷ ***Diplacus*** see *Mimulus*
▷ ***Dipladenia*** see *Mandevilla*

DIPLARRHENA

syn. DIPLARRENA

IRIDACEAE

Genus of 2 species of rhizomatous, evergreen perennials from moist, grassy mountain slopes in S.E. Australia and Tasmania. They form basal tufts of long, flat, linear to sword-shaped leaves. The usually unbranched flowering stems produce clusters of fragrant, short-lived, iris-like flowers, enclosed by 2 bracts. Grow in a sheltered herbaceous border, at the base of a house wall, or in a cool greenhouse or conservatory.
• **CULTIVATION** Under glass, grow in soilless potting mix in bright filtered light. Water freely when in growth, sparingly in winter. Outdoors, grow in moist but well-drained, sandy, humus-rich, neutral to acidic soil in full sun, or partial shade in a hot site.
• **PROPAGATION** Sow seed in containers in a cold frame in autumn or spring, or divide in spring.
• **PESTS AND DISEASES** Infrequent.

D. moraea ▣ Tufted perennial with short rhizomes and linear to sword-shaped, dark green to slightly glaucous, basal leaves, 18in (45cm) long. Bears a succession of 3–6 white flowers,

Diplarrhena moraea

1½–2½in (4–6cm) across, the inner tepals marked with yellow and purple, in late spring and early summer. ↕ 24in (60cm), PD9in (23cm). S.E. Australia, Tasmania. ❀ (min. 41°F/5°C)

DIPLAZIUM

DRYOPTERIDACEAE

Genus of about 350 terrestrial or epiphytic, evergreen ferns, often with trunk-like rhizomes, found worldwide in tropical and warm- or cool-temperate forest. The 1- to 3-pinnate or simple fronds arise from erect or sometimes creeping rhizomes. Spores, formed in single or often V-shaped, double lines along the veins on the lower frond surfaces, are covered by indusia when young. Where not hardy, grow in a warm greenhouse; elsewhere, use in a moist, sheltered site.
• **CULTIVATION** Under glass, grow in a mix of 1 part each loam and ground bark, 3 parts leaf mold, and 2 parts sharp sand. Provide bright filtered light and high humidity. Water freely when in growth, sparingly in winter. Pot on annually in spring. Outdoors, grow in moist but well-drained, humus-rich soil in partial shade.
• **PROPAGATION** Sow spores at 70°F (21°C) as soon as ripe. Separate underground runners in spring.
• **PESTS AND DISEASES** Snails, slugs, and various insects often cause serious damage to tender young fronds.

D. esculentum ▣ (Vegetable fern). Evergreen fern, which spreads by underground runners. Ovate-triangular,

Diplazium esculentum

pinnate or 2-pinnate, leathery, dark green fronds, to 2ft (60cm) long, with oblong-lance-shaped segments, grow in tufts from an erect, stem-like rhizome. ↕↔ to 3ft (1m). S.E. Asia, Polynesia. ❀ (min. 46–50°F/8–10°C)

DIPLOCYCLOS

CUCURBITACEAE

Genus of 4 species of monoecious, climbing, herbaceous perennials, from tropical Africa, Asia, Australia, and the Pacific islands. They have climbing tendrils and palmately 3- to 5-lobed leaves, and bear small white to pale yellow flowers, in clusters from the leaf axils, followed by ovoid, fleshy green to red berries. Excellent for covering a trellis.
• **CULTIVATION** Under glass, grow in soil-based potting mix in bright filtered light, with high humidity, and water freely in the growing season. Apply a balanced liquid fertilizer every 2 weeks. Outdoors, grow in fertile, well-drained soil in full sun.
• **PROPAGATION** Sow seed at 68°F (20°C) in spring, and plant out seedlings after risk of frost has passed.
• **PESTS AND DISEASES** Spider mites may be a problem.

D. palmatus (Marble vine). Climbing perennial, grown as an annual, with broadly ovate, 3- to 5-lobed, wavy-margined or entire, mid-green leaves, to 5½in (14cm) long. In summer, bears clusters of tiny white or pale yellow flowers, followed by ovoid, white-striped, green to red fruit, to 1in (2.5cm) across. ↕ 20ft (6m). Tropical Africa and Asia to N. Australia. ❀ (min. 45°F/7°C)

▷ ***Diplocyathus ciliata*** see *Orbea ciliata*

DIPSACUS

Teasel

DIPSACACEAE

Genus of 15 species of hairy or prickly biennials or short-lived perennials from damp grassland and woodland in Europe, N. Africa, and Asia. The simple or pinnatifid, toothed or cut leaves are borne in opposite pairs. In the second summer, teasels bear cone-shaped flowerheads on long, upright, branching stems. Grow in a wild garden.
• **CULTIVATION** Grow in any moderately fertile soil, including heavy clays, in sun or partial shade. Harvest flowerheads for air-drying in mid- and late summer.
• **PROPAGATION** Sow seed *in situ* in autumn or spring.
• **PESTS AND DISEASES** Infrequent.

D. fullonum, syn. *D. sylvestris* (Fuller's teasel). Prickly biennial with a basal rosette of simple, oblong-lance-shaped, toothed, dark green leaves, 12in (30cm) or more long, covered in spiny pustules. Paired lance-shaped leaves are borne on upright stems in the second summer, joined at their bases to form a cup. Oblong-ovoid, thistle-like, pinkish purple or white flowerheads, 1¼–3in (3–8cm) long, with stiff, curved, prickly bracts, are produced in mid- and late summer. ↕ 5–6ft (1.5–2m), ↔ 12–32in (30–80cm). Europe, Asia. Zone 4.
D. sylvestris see *D. fullonum.*

▷ ***Dipteracanthus*** see *Ruellia*

D

D

DIPTERONIA

ACERACEAE

Genus of 2 species of deciduous trees and shrubs found in woodland in C. and S. China. *D. sinensis* is grown for its pinnate leaves, produced in opposite pairs, and for its large clusters of winged, red-brown fruit. Small, greenish white flowers are produced in erect terminal panicles in summer. Grow in a large shrub border or woodland garden.

• **CULTIVATION** Grow in fertile, moist but well-drained, loamy soil in sun or partial shade. Pruning group 1.

• **PROPAGATION** Sow seed in a seedbed in autumn. Layer in late spring or early summer; shoots often layer naturally. Insert softwood cuttings in summer.

• **PESTS AND DISEASES** Infrequent.

D. sinensis. Spreading tree or shrub with pinnate leaves, to 12in (30cm) long, with 7–11 ovate or lance-shaped, toothed leaflets. Bears erect, pyramidal panicles, 6–12in (15–30cm) long, of small, greenish white flowers in summer, followed by large clusters of flat, winged, red-brown fruit, 1in (2.5cm) across, ripening to brown-red in autumn. ↕↔ 30ft (10m). C. China. ❀ (min. 35°F/2°C)

DIRCA

THYMELEACEAE

Genus of 2 species of deciduous shrubs found in woodland in E. North America and on wet slopes in evergreen forest on rocky hills in California. The oval to obovate or broadly elliptic leaves are simple, entire, and alternate. They are cultivated for their early, *Daphne*-like flowers, borne on bare branches in axillary clusters of 2 or 3 in early spring. Grow in a sheltered shrub border.

• **CULTIVATION** Grow in moist but well-drained, humus-rich soil in partial shade. Pruning group 1.

• **PROPAGATION** Sow seed in a seedbed in autumn. Layer in autumn or spring.

• **PESTS AND DISEASES** Infrequent.

D. palustris (Leatherwood). Upright shrub with fibrous bark and very flexible shoots (which may literally be tied into knots), bearing oval to obovate leaves, to 3in (7cm) long, mid-green above, blue-green beneath, often clear tawny yellow in autumn. Narrowly funnel-shaped, pale yellow flowers, ½in (1.5cm) long, are produced in clusters of 3 in early spring. ↕↔ 5ft (1.5m). E. North America. Zone 4.

DISA

ORCHIDACEAE

Genus of approximately 130 species of deciduous, occasionally evergreen, terrestrial orchids found at low to high altitudes, often by running water, in tropical C. and E. Africa, South Africa, and Madagascar. They have tuberous, sometimes stoloniferous roots. The erect stems, with ovate to lance-shaped or linear leaves, bear one to many richly colored flowers, with hooded upper and spreading lower perianth segments, in terminal racemes or corymbs.

• **CULTIVATION** Cool-growing orchids. Grow in a mix of equal parts peat, perlite, and chopped sphagnum moss, and cover the surface with sphagnum moss. In summer, provide cool, humid, shady conditions. Water freely to keep the roots continually moist when in active growth, but avoid wetting the leaves, which are prone to black rot; keep cool and dry in winter. Do not fertilize. Repot annually after new growth has started. See also p.46.

• **PROPAGATION** Divide plants when repotting.

• **PESTS AND DISEASES** Spider mites may be troublesome.

Disa uniflora

D. grandiflora see *D. uniflora.*

D. Kirstenbosch Pride (*D. cardinalis* x *D. uniflora*). Hybrid terrestrial orchid producing a basal rosette of lance-shaped leaves, 3–6in (7–15cm) long. Racemes of up to 8 scarlet and orange-red flowers, 3in (7cm) across, are produced on tall stems in late summer. ↕ 36in (90cm), ↔ 8in (20cm). ❀ (min. 41°F/5°C; max. 75°F/24°C)

D. uniflora ■ syn. *D. grandiflora.* Terrestrial orchid with lance-shaped leaves, to 10in (25cm) long. Produces short racemes of up to 3, or very rarely 5, brilliant scarlet flowers, 3–5in (8–13cm) across, with red and gold veining, in midsummer. ↕ 24in (60cm), ↔ 8in (20cm). South Africa (Northern Cape, Western Cape, Eastern Cape). ❀ (min. 41°F/5°C; max. 75°F/24°C)

DISANTHUS

HAMAMELIDACEAE

Genus of one species of deciduous shrub found in woodland and mountains in China and Japan. It is grown for its striking autumn color, graduating from yellow through red to purple, and displaying all these shades at once. The ovate to rounded leaves are alternate, and the slightly fragrant, spidery flowers are borne in pairs in midautumn as the leaves fall. Grow *D. cercidifolius* as a specimen in a woodland garden, or in a shrub border.

• **CULTIVATION** Grow in humus-rich, moist but well-drained, acidic soil in sun or partial shade, sheltered from strong winds. Pruning group 1.

• **PROPAGATION** Sow seed in a seedbed in autumn or spring. Layer in spring.

• **PESTS AND DISEASES** Infrequent.

D. cercidifolius ■ Rounded shrub with ovate to almost circular, glaucous blue-green leaves, to 4in (10cm) long, with heart-shaped bases, turning yellow, orange, red, and purple in autumn. Slightly fragrant, axillary, spidery, bright rose-red flowers, ¾in (2cm) across, are produced in midautumn. ↕↔ 10ft (3m). C. China, Japan. Zone 7.

Disanthus cercidifolius (inset: leaf detail)

DISCARIA

RHAMNACEAE

Genus of about 15 species of spiny, deciduous shrubs and small trees from Australia, New Zealand, and temperate South America, found in rocky places and scrub, and closely allied to *Colletia.* They produce opposite or clustered, mainly elliptic to obovate or oblong leaves; opposite pairs of spines on stiff or flexuous branches; and star- or bell-shaped flowers, often without petals. *Discaria* species are grown for their numerous thick spines and their abundant, densely clustered flowers. In warm climates, they are suitable for an open shrub border; in cooler conditions, they grow best at the base of a warm, sunny, sheltered wall.

• **CULTIVATION** Grow in fertile, well-drained soil in full sun. Provide shelter from cold, drying winds. Pruning group 1, after flowering.

• **PROPAGATION** Sow seed in containers in a cold frame in spring. Insert softwood or semi-ripe cuttings in summer.

• **PESTS AND DISEASES** Infrequent.

D. toumatou (Wild Irishman). Large shrub or small tree bearing cylindrical, flexuous, slender green stems; numerous slender, opposite green spines, to 2in (5cm) long, are borne at right angles to the stems. Obovate to narrowly oblong, glossy leaves, to ¾in (2cm) long, borne below the spines on year-old shoots, fall early. Bears dense clusters of star-shaped, greenish white flowers, ⅛in (3mm) across, composed of 4 or 5 small sepals, in late spring. ↕ 8ft (2.5m), ↔ 10ft (3m). New Zealand. ❀ (min. 35°F/2°C)

DISCHIDIA

ASCLEPIADACEAE

Genus of about 80 species of trailing-scandent, epiphytic herbaceous perennials, from W. Asia to W. Pacific. As myrmecophilous or ant-loving plants, several dischidas are particularly intriguing. Ants inhabit the inflated, often hollow leaves, using them as nurseries for their young and as garbage dumps. The plants benefit from the ants' carbon dioxide and waste products. Dischidias also bear small flowers. Excellent in a terrarium.

• **CULTIVATION** Under glass, grow in epiphytic bromeliad mix in bright filtered light. In growth, mist frequently, foliar-fertilize, and water freely; water sparingly in winter. Keep potbound.

• **PROPAGATION** Take semi-ripe cuttings and grow on in a shaded, closed case with gentle bottom heat, or layer.

• **PESTS AND DISEASES** Mealybugs can be a problem under glass.

D. rafflesiana. Climbing or twining epiphytic perennial with whorls of evergreen, ovate-rounded, waxy green-yellow leaves, to 1in (2.5cm) long, often modified to 2–5in (5–13cm) long. India to Australia. ↕ 10ft (3m). ❀ (min. 55°F/13°C; max. 82°F/28°C)

DISCOCACTUS

CACTACEAE

Genus of 5–7 species of ribbed, spherical cacti from hilly lowlands in Brazil, E. Bolivia, and N. Paraguay. Most have prominent areoles and strong, often horny spines. Mature plants develop a woolly and bristly-spiny cephalium, from which funnel-shaped or tubular, salverform, scented white or sometimes pinkish white flowers, 2–4in (5–10cm) long, are produced at night in summer. The berries contain minute black seeds. Suitable for a desert garden. Where not hardy, grow in a warm greenhouse or as houseplants.

• **CULTIVATION** Under glass, grow in standard cactus potting mix in full light. In the growing season, water moderately, applying a nitrogen- and potassium-based fertilizer every 3 weeks. Mist in hot weather, but keep soil completely dry from autumn to early spring. Outdoors, grow in sharply drained mineral soil, low in organic matter, in full sun. See also pp.48–49.

• **PROPAGATION** Sow seed at 70–75°F (21–24°C) in spring or early summer.

• **PESTS AND DISEASES** Sometimes affected by mealybugs and basal rot.

D. hartmannii, syn. *Echinocactus hartmannii.* Flattened-spherical to spherical cactus with a white-woolly, tufted cephalium, 15–22 dark green ribs, and well-spaced areoles bearing blackish brown spines (6–12 radials and one central). Funnel-shaped, many-petaled white flowers, to 4in (10cm) across, are produced in summer. ↕4in (10cm), ↔ to 10in (25cm). Brazil, N. Paraguay. ❀ (min. 61°F/16°C)

D. horstii ■ Flattened-spherical cactus with a white-woolly cephalium, 15–22 prominent, brownish green to purple-brown ribs, and close-set areoles, each bearing 8–10 minute, grayish white to chalky white radial spines. Open funnel-shaped white flowers, to 3in (8cm) across, are produced in summer. ↕¾–1¼in (2–3cm), ↔ to 2½in (6cm). E. Brazil. ❀ (min. 61°F/16°C)

D. placentiformis, syn. *D. tricornis.* Flattened-spherical cactus, sometimes producing offsets, with a white-woolly cephalium, 10–16 light to dark green or blue-green ribs, and few areoles, bearing brownish white spines (3–8 curved radials and often a shorter, straight central). Funnel-shaped white flowers, to 3½in (9cm) across, are borne in summer. ↕ to 3in (7cm), ↔ 4in (10cm). E. Brazil. ❀ (min. 61°F/16°C)

D. tricornis see *D. placentiformis.*

Discocactus horstii

DISOCACTUS

CACTACEAE

Genus of 10 species of freely branching, epiphytic or rock-dwelling cacti, found in rainforest in subtropical and tropical North and South America, and the West Indies. They have cylindrical primary stems, rounded in cross-section, and flattened lateral stems. Funnel-shaped or tubular, diurnal flowers, sometimes sweetly scented, are borne on marginal areoles, followed by spherical to ovoid, usually white or greenish white fruits with black seeds. Where not hardy, grow in a container or hanging basket in a warm greenhouse; in warmer regions, grow epiphytically.

• **CULTIVATION** Under glass, grow in acidic, epiphytic cactus potting mix in bright filtered light and low humidity. In the growing season, water freely, applying fertilizer in spring and again in late autumn; keep just moist in winter. Outdoors, grow epiphytically in partial shade. See also pp.48–49.

• **PROPAGATION** Sow seed at 81°F (27°C) as soon as ripe in soilless seed-starting mix, in a closed case and filtered light; keep the mix moist. Root stem cuttings in late spring.

• **PESTS AND DISEASES** Sometimes affected by mealybugs and basal rot.

D. alatus, syn. *Pseudorhipsalis alata.* Freely branching cactus with pendent primary stems, to 15ft (5m) across, and broadly linear to lance-shaped or oblong, leaf-like, flat, scalloped-wavy lateral stems. Open funnel-shaped, yellowish cream or greenish white flowers, ½in (1.5cm) across, are borne in late spring. ↕12in (30cm), ↔ 6in (15cm). Jamaica. ❀ (min. 61°F/16°C)

D. amazonicus, syn. *Wittia amazonica, Wittiocactus amazonicus.* Freely branching cactus bearing oblong-lance-shaped, leaf-like flattened stems, 6–12in (15–30cm) long, with coarsely toothed margins and prominent midribs. Bears tubular magenta flowers, ¾–1¼in (2–3cm) across, in late spring. ↕18in (45cm), ↔ 8in (20cm). N.W. Peru, Colombia. ❀ (min. 61°F/16°C)

D. biformis, syn. *Phyllocactus biformis.* Freely branching cactus bearing cylindrical primary stems, to 8in (20cm) long, and linear or narrowly oblong lateral stems with toothed margins. Narrowly funnel-shaped, deep red to magenta flowers, 2–2½in (5–6cm) long, are produced in early spring. ↕↔ 8in (20cm). Guatemala, Honduras. ❀ (min. 61°F/16°C)

D. macranthus, syn. *Pseudorhipsalis macrantha.* Bushy cactus with a cylindrical base and pendent, strap-shaped, slightly toothed stems, to 36in (90cm) across. Tubular-salverform, sweetly scented flowers, 2½in (6cm) across, pink-purple at the bases, with pale orange-brown outer tepals, lemon-yellow inside, are freely borne in late winter and early spring. ↕36in (90cm), ↔ 12in (30cm). S. Mexico. ❀ (min. 61°F/16°C)

D. nelsonii ■ syn. *Chiapasia nelsonii.* Freely branching cactus with cylindrical primary stems, to 5ft (1.5m) long, and pendent, inversely lance-shaped, slightly toothed, flattened lateral stems. Funnel-shaped, scented, purplish pink flowers, 3½–4½in (9–11cm) across, are borne from spring to early summer. ↕20in (50cm) or more, ↔ 10in (25cm). Mexico to Honduras. ❀ (min. 61°F/16°C)

D. quezaltecus, syn. *Bonifazia quezalteca.* Freely branching cactus with primary stems, to 32in (80cm) long, flattened at the top, and toothed, leaf-like lateral stems. Tubular-salverform, pale purple to purple-red flowers, 3½in (9cm) across, are borne from spring to early summer. ↕24in (60cm), ↔ 12in (30cm). Guatemala. ❀ (min. 61°F/16°C)

D. ramulosus. Freely branching cactus with cylindrical primary stems, to 3in (8cm) long, usually flattened and broad at the top, and flat, linear or narrowly lance-shaped lateral stems with cylindrical, toothed, often purple bases. In spring, bears salverform, pink- or green-tinged, yellow-white flowers, ¼–½in (6–15mm) across. ↕↔ to 12in (30cm). West Indies, Mexico to Brazil and Bolivia. ❀ (min. 61°F/16°C)

Disocactus nelsonii

D

DISPOROPSIS

LILIACEAE

Genus of 4 species, closely allied to *Polygonatum*, of rhizomatous, evergreen perennials, occurring in upland forest in S.E. China. Mottled, dark green stems bear elliptic-lance-shaped, waxy leaves, which gradually die back as new growth is fully formed. Pendent, narrowly bell-shaped flowers are solitary or produced in pairs from the leaf axils. Grow in a woodland garden or border.

• **CULTIVATION** Grow in moist but well-drained, humus-rich soil in partial shade.

• **PROPAGATION** Sow seed in containers in a cold frame in autumn or spring, or divide rhizomes in spring.

• **PESTS AND DISEASES** Infrequent.

D. pernyi ■ syn. *Polygonatum cyrtonema* of gardens. Rhizomatous perennial with lance-shaped to elliptic, glossy, dark green leaves, to 5in (13cm) long. Lemon-scented white flowers, ¾in (2cm) long, with pale green outer tips that are slightly reflexed, are borne singly or in pairs in early summer. ↕16in (40cm), ↔ 12–16in (30–40cm). S.E. China. Zone 7b.

Disporopsis pernyi

DISPORUM syn. PROSARTES

Fairy bells

LILIACEAE

Genus of 10–20 species of rhizomatous perennials occurring in woodland in the Himalayas, E. and S.E. Asia, and temperate North America. The mid- to dark green leaves are ovate to lance-shaped, stalkless or with short stalks, usually hairless, and borne alternately on sparsely branched stems. Often pendent, narrowly bell-shaped, tubular, open trumpet-shaped, or cup-shaped, white to green-yellow, purple-red, or brown-red flowers, ½–1¼in (1–3cm) long, are usually borne in few-flowered umbels, occasionally singly. They are followed by orange, red, or black berries. Grow in a woodland garden or shady mixed or herbaceous border.

• **Cultivation** Grow in cool, moist, well-drained, humus-rich soil in partial shade. *D. smithii* tolerates deep shade.

• **Propagation** Sow seed in containers in a cold frame in autumn; alternatively, divide rhizomes in early spring.

• **Pests and diseases** Fungal spots, slugs, and vine weevils may occur.

D. cantoniense. Clump-forming, rhizomatous perennial bearing lance-shaped leaves, 2–6in (5–15cm) long. Bears umbels of 3–6 pendent, tubular, purplish red, brownish red, or white flowers, on short stalks, in late spring and early summer, followed in early autumn by black-red berries. ↕ to 36in (90cm), ↔ 12in (30cm). Himalayas, China, S.E. Asia. Zone 5.

Disporum sessile 'Variegatum'

D. flavens. Clump-forming, rhizomatous perennial bearing lance-shaped leaves, 2–6in (5–15cm) long. In early spring, 1–3 pendent, tubular, soft yellow flowers are produced on axillary stalks, followed in early autumn by black berries. ↕ to 30in (75cm), ↔ 12in (30cm). Korea. Zone 5.

D. hookeri. Clump-forming, rhizomatous perennial bearing ovate to lance-shaped leaves, 1¼–5½in (3–14cm) long, with heart-shaped bases, hairy on the margins and on the veins beneath. Umbels of up to 3 pendent, tubular-bell-shaped, greenish cream flowers, with slightly spreading tepals, are produced in spring, followed in autumn by orange-red berries. ↕ to 36in (90cm), ↔ 18in (45cm). N.W. US. Zone 5.

D. lanuginosum. Clump-forming, rhizomatous perennial with ovate-lance-shaped leaves, 1¼–5in (3–13cm) long, with narrow, pointed tips, downy beneath. Umbels of up to 3 open trumpet-shaped, pale yellowish white or greenish white flowers, with narrow tepals, are borne in late spring, followed in early autumn by black or red berries. ↕ 12–36in (30–90cm), ↔ 12in (30cm). E. central US. Zone 6.

D. sessile. Spreading, rhizomatous perennial with almost stalkless, oblong or oblong-lance-shaped leaves, 2–6in (5–15cm) long. Each stem produces 2 or 3 flower stalks, each bearing up to 3 pendent, tubular, green-tipped, white or very pale cream flowers in late spring and early summer, followed in early autumn by black berries. ↕ 24in (60cm), ↔ 24in (60cm) or more. Japan. Zone 5. **'Variegatum'** ■ has leaves broadly and variously striped white; ↕ 18in (45cm), ↔ 36in (90cm) or more.

D. smilacinum. Sparsely branched, rhizomatous perennial with oblong to elliptic-ovate leaves, 1½–3in (4–7cm) long. Stems, 6–16in (15–40cm) long, produce 1 or 2 pendent or semi-pendent, cup-shaped white flowers in mid- and late spring. ↕ to 16in (40cm), ↔ 12in (30cm). Korea, Japan. Zone 5.

D. smithii ■ Clump-forming, rhizomatous perennial with red-tinged stems and ovate to ovate-lance-shaped leaves, 2–5in (5–13cm) long, rounded to heart-shaped at the bases. From early to late spring, bears umbels of 2–6 pendent, tubular-bell-shaped, greenish white flowers, followed in late summer by orange berries. ↕ 12–24in (30–60cm), ↔ 12in (30cm). British Columbia to California. Zone 6.

Disporum smithii

Distictis buccinatoria

DISTICTIS

BIGNONIACEAE

Genus of 9 species of climbing, evergreen perennials from Mexico and the West Indies, usually among thickets and at forest margins. They are valued for their colorful, tubular to trumpet-shaped or salverform flowers, produced in small, terminal racemes or panicles. The opposite leaves consist of 2 ovate-lance-shaped leaflets and a 3-branched tendril. Where not hardy, grow in a cool greenhouse; in warmer regions, train on a pergola or wall, or grow through trees.

• **Cultivation** Under glass, grow in soil-based potting mix in full light. Support with wires or a trellis and tie in as growth proceeds. When in growth, water freely, applying fertilizer monthly; water sparingly in winter. Top-dress or pot on in spring. Outdoors, grow in fertile, moist but well-drained soil in full sun. Pruning group 11, in early spring.

• **Propagation** Sow seed at 61–64°F (16–18°C) in spring. Root semi-ripe cuttings with bottom heat in summer. Layer in early spring.

• **Pests and diseases** Spider mites and whiteflies may be troublesome.

D. buccinatoria ■ syn. *Phaedranthus buccinatorius.* Vigorous climber bearing ovate-lance-shaped, mid- to deep green leaflets, to 4in (10cm) long. Tubular-salverform, purple-red flowers, to 3in (8cm) long, with yellow toward the bases, are borne in racemes, 6–10in (15–25cm) long, from summer to autumn. ↕ 30–80ft (10–25m). Mexico. ❄ (min. 45°F/7°C)

DISTYLIUM

HAMAMELIDACEAE

Genus of about 6–8 species of evergreen shrubs and trees found in woodland in E. Asia. They have alternate, obovate or ovate to lance-shaped, leathery, usually dark green leaves, and petalless, male and bisexual flowers in axillary spikes or racemes. *D. racemosum* is valued for its simple, glossy foliage, borne on arching branches, and for its unusual flowers. Grow in a sheltered position among trees and other shrubs.

• **Cultivation** Grow in moist but well-drained, humus-rich soil in partial shade, sheltered from strong, cold, drying winds. Pruning group 1, but pruning is usually not required.

• **Propagation** Sow seed in containers in a cold frame as soon as ripe. Insert semi-ripe cuttings in summer.

• **Pests and diseases** Infrequent.

D. racemosum. Spreading shrub or tree with obovate to narrowly oblong, leathery, glossy, dark green leaves, 1¼–3in (3–7cm) long. Small flowers, produced in upright racemes, 1–2in (2.5–5cm) long, in late spring and early summer, lack petals but have conspicuous, 5-parted red calyces and purple stamens. ↕ 6–10ft (2–3m) (to 80ft/25m in the wild), ↔ 10ft (3m). S. Japan. Zone 7b.

▷ ***Dizygotheca elegantissima*** see *Schefflera elegantissima*

DOCYNIA

ROSACEAE

Genus of 2 species of evergreen, semi-evergreen, or deciduous trees and shrubs, occurring in woodland in the Himalayas and E. Asia. The oblong to ovate or lance-shaped leaves, borne alternately, are either entire or toothed. Bowl-shaped white or pinkish white flowers are produced in umbels of 2–6. *D. delavayi* is an attractive flowering specimen tree or shrub, suitable for a sheltered site.

• **Cultivation** Grow in fertile, well-drained soil in sun or partial shade. Provide protection from strong winds. Pruning group 1, when necessary.

• **Propagation** Sow seed in containers in a cold frame in autumn or spring.

• **Pests and diseases** Susceptible to fireblight. Caterpillars may also be troublesome.

D. delavayi. Spreading, semi-evergreen to deciduous tree with tiered branches, spiny, blackish green shoots, and alternate, narrowly to broadly ovate-lance-shaped, entire or toothed, dark green leaves, to 3in (7cm) long. (On young seedlings, leaves are hawthorn-like and deeply lobed.) Produces clusters of 2–4 bowl-shaped white flowers, to 1in (2.5cm) across, from pink buds in spring, followed by small, apple-like yellow fruit, 1½in (4cm) across, in autumn. ↕↔ 25ft (8m). China (Sichuan, Yunnan). ❄ (min. 35°F/2°C)

DODECATHEON

Shooting stars

PRIMULACEAE

Genus of 14 species of perennials mostly found in damp grassland or high alpine meadows, occasionally in woodland, in North America. They have basal rosettes of ovate to inversely lance-shaped, spoon-shaped, or oblong, usually hairless leaves. Umbels of pendent, cyclamen-like flowers are borne on arching stems, the petals acutely reflexed, displaying long, pointed styles. They go dormant in summer, after flowering, and are suitable for a woodland or rock garden.

• **Cultivation** Grow in moist but well-drained, humus-rich soil in sun or partial shade, with abundant moisture in the growing season; grow *D. dentatum* and *D. pulchellum* in moist shade. During summer dormancy, keep *D. clevelandii* and *D. hendersonii* in a bulb frame.

Dodecatheon clevelandii

• **PROPAGATION** Sow seed in containers in an open frame as soon as ripe; the seed needs exposure to cold before it will germinate. Divide in spring.
• **PESTS AND DISEASES** Leaves may be eaten by slugs and snails. Rust is common.

D. amethystinum see *D. pulchellum.*
D. clevelandii ■ Rosette-forming perennial with spoon-shaped to ovate, irregularly toothed, fleshy, pale green leaves, to 2½in (6cm) long. In early spring, bears umbels of up to 20 reddish purple flowers, to ¾in (2cm) long, with yellow tubes, spotted purple at the throats. ↕ to 16in (40cm), ↔ to 6in (15cm). California. Zone 6b. **subsp. *insulare*** flowers later and is slightly hardier.
D. dentatum ■ Clump-forming perennial with rosettes of long-stalked, oblong-lance-shaped, sometimes toothed, pale to mid-green leaves, to 3in (8cm) long. In late spring, bears umbels of 2–5 slender-stemmed white flowers, ½–¾in (1–2cm) long, sometimes purple-spotted at the petal bases, with prominent, dark purple anthers. ↕↔ to 8in (20cm). W. North America. Zone 8.

Dodecatheon dentatum

Dodecatheon pulchellum 'Red Wings'

D. hendersonii, syn. *D. latifolium* (Mosquito bills, Sailor caps). Rosette-forming perennial with oblong-ovate, fleshy, dark green leaves, to 2½in (6cm) long. Sturdy stems produce umbels of 1–5 dark-centered, purplish pink flowers, ½–1in (1.5–2.5cm) long, each with a white ring at the base, in early summer. ↕ 16in (40cm), ↔ 10in (25cm). California. Zone 6b.
D. latifolium see *D. hendersonii.*
D. meadia, syn. *D. pauciflorum* (Shooting stars). Variable, clump-forming perennial with ovate, toothed, pale to mid-green leaves, to 10in (25cm) long. Umbels of up to 15 magenta-pink flowers, ½–¾in (1.5–2cm) long, are borne on strong stems in mid- and late spring. ↕ 16in (40cm), ↔ 10in (25cm). N.W. US. Zone 5. **f. *album*** has creamy white flowers with dark centers, and yellow styles and anthers.
D. pauciflorum see *D. meadia.*
***D. pauciflorum* of gardens** see *D. pulchellum.*
D. pulchellum, syn. *D. amethystinum, D. pauciflorum* of gardens, *D. radicatum.* Clump-forming perennial with ovate-spoon-shaped, mid-green leaves, to 8in (20cm) long. Umbels of up to 20 dark-centered, deep cerise-pink flowers, ½–¾in (1–2cm) long, are produced in mid- and late spring. ↕ to 14in (35cm), ↔ to 6in (15cm). High altitudes in W. North America. Zone 5. **'Red Wings'** ■ has oblong-ovate, soft, pale green leaves, and produces deep magenta-pink flowers, ½–¾in (1–2cm) long, on strong stems in late spring and early summer; ↔ 8in (20cm).
D. radicatum see *D. pulchellum.*

DODONAEA

SAPINDACEAE

Genus of 50–60 species of evergreen shrubs and small trees found in tropical and subtropical regions, primarily in Australia, where they grow in dry, open forest, thickets, and scrub. They are grown mainly for their needle-like or oblong to broadly ovate or obovate, simple or pinnate, leathery leaves, dotted with glands and spiralling or scattered along the stems. The insignificant, petal-less flowers, with 3- to 5-lobed calyces, are borne in terminal and axillary cymes, male and female on separate plants. The fruits are membranous, 3-angled or 3-winged (sometimes up to 6-winged), often colorful capsules. Where not hardy, grow in a cool greenhouse; in warmer climates, use as a hedge or in a border. *D. viscosa* tolerates drought and exposure to wind, salt, and pollution.

Dodonaea viscosa 'Purpurea'

• **CULTIVATION** Under glass, grow in soil-based potting mix in full light. In growth, water freely and apply a balanced liquid fertilizer monthly; water sparingly in winter. Top-dress or pot on in spring. Outdoors, grow in moderately fertile, moist but well-drained soil in full sun. Pinch out tips of young shoots to encourage bushy growth. Shear hedges lightly in spring; avoid cutting into old wood.
• **PROPAGATION** Sow seed at no less than 64°F (18°C) in spring. Root semi-ripe cuttings with bottom heat in summer.
• **PESTS AND DISEASES** Spider mites may infest greenhouse plants.

D. viscosa (Hop bush). Vigorous, erect to spreading shrub or small tree with elliptic to almost obovate, simple, yellow to mid-green leaves, 3–5in (7–13cm) long, with irregular, wavy margins. Bears 2- or 3-winged pink to reddish brown, light brown, purple, or yellow capsules, ¾–1in (2–2.5cm) across, from summer to autumn. ↕ 3–15ft (1–5m), ↔ 3–10ft (1–3m). Coastal regions in tropics and subtropics worldwide. ❄ (min. 41°F/5°C). **'Purpurea'** ■ has leaves strongly suffused purplish red.

▷ ***Dolichos*** see *Lablab*
▷ ***Dolichothele*** see *Mammillaria*

DOMBEYA

STERCULIACEAE

Genus of 200–300 species of evergreen or deciduous shrubs and trees from Africa and Madagascar to the Mascarene Islands, found in habitats ranging from tropical woodland to upland scrub. Leaves are alternate, simple, and lobed or unlobed, often heart-shaped, with long stalks. Dombeyas are grown mainly for their 5-petaled white, pink, yellow, or red flowers, resembling those of mallows (*Malva*); they are produced in dense, axillary, terminal, or umbel-like cymes on long, nodding or pendent stalks. Where not hardy, grow in a warm greenhouse; elsewhere, use outdoors as a specimen or in a border.
• **CULTIVATION** Under glass, grow in soil-based potting mix, in bright filtered light or in full light with shade from hot sun. In growth, water freely, applying a balanced liquid fertilizer monthly; water sparingly in winter. Top-dress or pot on in spring. Outdoors, grow in fertile, moist but well-drained soil in sun or partial shade. Pruning group 6 (deciduous), 8 (evergreen); plants under glass may need restrictive pruning.
• **PROPAGATION** Sow seed at 64–70°F (18–21°C) in spring. Root semi-ripe cuttings with bottom heat in summer.
• **PESTS AND DISEASES** Spider mites, whiteflies, canker, and stem galls occur.

D. burgessiae, syn. *D. mastersii.* Strong-growing, open, evergreen shrub with softly hairy young stems, and broadly ovate to almost circular (heart-shaped at the bases), 3- to 5-lobed, or unlobed, downy, mid-green leaves, 4½–9in (11–23cm) long. Axillary corymbs or cymes, 4in (10cm) or more across, of fragrant, red- or pink-veined white flowers, 2–3in (5–8cm) across, are borne from late summer to autumn. ↕ 6–12ft (2–4m), ↔ 5–10ft (1.5–3m). Kenya to South Africa. ❄ (min. 50°F/10°C)
D. x cayeuxii ■ (*D. burgessiae* x *D. wallichii*). Vigorous, evergreen shrub or small tree with bristly hairy stems and ovate to heart-shaped, acute, toothed, hairy, mid- to dark green leaves, 8–12in (20–30cm) long. Produces pink flowers, 1¼–1½in (3–4cm) across, in many-flowered, spherical, umbel-like cymes, 4–5in (10–13cm) across, usually from autumn to spring. ↕ 10–15ft (3–5m), ↔ 6–10ft (2–3m). Garden origin. ❄ (min. 50°F/10°C)
D. mastersii see *D. burgessiae.*
D. spectabilis. Vigorous, deciduous shrub or tree, with softly red-hairy stems and ovate to rounded, unlobed, leathery, slightly toothed, mid-green leaves, to 7in (18cm) long. From winter to spring, produces white to pink flowers, to ¾in (9mm) across, in axillary, panicle-like cymes, 4–5in (10–13cm) across, before the leaves appear. ↕ to 45ft (14m), ↔ 15–20ft (5–6m). Madagascar. ❄ (min. 50°F/10°C)
D. wallichii. Evergreen shrub or tree of variable habit but generally freely branching, with sturdy, downy stems. The broadly ovate to circular, toothed, bright green leaves, 6–8in (15–20cm) long, softly hairy beneath, have pointed tips and heart-shaped bases. Deep pink or red flowers, 1¼–2in (3–5cm) across, are borne in dense, umbel-like cymes, 4–6in (10–15cm) across, mainly from winter to spring. ↕ 20–30ft (6–10m), ↔ 8–15ft (2.5–5m). E. Africa, Madagascar. ❄ (min. 50°F/10°C)

▷ ***Dondia*** see *Hacquetia*

Dombeya x *cayeuxii*

D

DOODIA

BLECHNACEAE

Genus of about 11 species of usually evergreen, terrestrial ferns found mainly in damp, sunny or partially shaded sites, often rocky woodland margins, in Australasia. Fronds, produced in tufts from short, creeping rhizomes, are lance-shaped, pinnate or pinnatifid, and usually pink-tinged when young. Fertile fronds are often more erect than sterile fronds, with slightly narrower divisions. The sori are covered by curved indusia. *Doodia* species are easy to grow in a rock garden or sheltered border; where not hardy, grow in a cool greenhouse.

• **CULTIVATION** Under glass, grow in a mix of 1 part loam, 2 parts sharp sand, and 3 parts leaf mold, in bright filtered light, with moderate humidity. Water freely when in growth. In winter, admit full light and water sparingly. Outdoors, grow in moist, acidic soil in sheltered site in partial shade. Where marginally hardy, cover with a straw mulch in winter.

• **PROPAGATION** Sow spores at 59°F (15°C) as soon as ripe. Divide in spring. See also p.51.

• **PESTS AND DISEASES** Infrequent.

D. caudata (Small rasp fern). Tufted, evergreen fern with erect rhizomes and upright, lance-shaped, mid- to pale green fertile fronds, 3–12 in (8–30cm) long, with linear pinnae, ½in (1.5cm) long. Sterile fronds are shorter, fewer, and decumbent, with sharply toothed pinnae. ↕↔ 3–12in (8–30cm). Australia, New Zealand, Polynesia. ❄ (min. 41°F/5°C)

D. media (Common rasp fern). Tufted, evergreen fern with suberect rhizomes, and lance-shaped to inversely lance-shaped, leathery, dark green fronds, 12–24in (30–60cm) long, pinnatifid at the tips and pinnate toward the bases, often with brown midribs. Ovate-heart-shaped pinnae have a firm, prickly texture and very finely toothed margins. ↕ 12–16in (30–40cm), ↔ 20–39in (50–100cm). Australia, New Zealand, Pacific Islands to Hawaii. ❄ (min. 41°F/5°C)

DORONICUM

Leopard's bane

ASTERACEAE

Genus of about 35 species of deciduous, rhizomatous or tuberous perennials found in woodland, scrub, meadows, heathland, and rocky sites in Europe, S.W. Asia, and Siberia. They have simple, alternate, elliptic to ovate basal leaves, with heart-shaped bases, and lance-shaped to ovate or oblong stem leaves. The daisy-like yellow flowerheads are produced singly or in cyme-like corymbs. Grow in a border or naturalize in a woodland garden. The flowers are also good for cutting.

• **CULTIVATION** Grow in moist, humus-rich soil in partial or light, dappled shade. Doronicums do best in reasonably fertile, moist but well-drained, preferably sandy soil in partial shade; they go completely dormant in summer. They do not tolerate drought.

• **PROPAGATION** Sow seed in containers in a cold frame in spring. Alternatively, divide in early autumn.

Doronicum columnae 'Miss Mason'

• **PESTS AND DISEASES** Leaf spot and root rot (especially on *D. orientale*) may be troublesome, and some species are susceptible to powdery mildew.

D. austriacum. Clump-forming, rhizomatous perennial bearing ovate-oblong, toothed, hairy basal leaves, 5in (13cm) long, heart-shaped at the bases, usually at or just after flowering; the stem leaves are smaller, narrower, and either entire or minutely toothed. In late spring and early summer, corymbs of yellow flowerheads, 1½–2½in (3.5–6cm) across, are borne on slender, branched stems. ↕↔ to 4ft (1.2m). Mountain woodland in C. and S. Europe, Turkey. Zone 6.

D. caucasicum see *D. orientale.*

Doronicum x *excelsum* 'Harpur Crewe'

D. columnae, syn. *D. cordatum.* Clump-forming, rhizomatous perennial bearing clustered, ovate-rounded to heart-shaped, toothed, hairy or hairless, scalloped basal leaves, 1¼–3in (3–8cm) long, and elliptic to ovate-lance-shaped stem leaves. Slender stems bear solitary yellow flowerheads, ¾–3in (2–7cm) across, from midspring to early summer. ↕ 5–24in (12–60cm), ↔ 12in (30cm). Mountains of S. and E. Europe. Zone 4. **'Miss Mason'** ■ has bright yellow flowerheads, 3in (8cm) across, held well above the foliage, in mid- and late spring; ↔ 24in (60cm).

D. cordatum see *D. columnae, D. pardalianches.*

***D.* x *excelsum* 'Harpur Crewe'** ■ syn. *D. plantagineum* 'Excelsum', *D. plantagineum* 'Harpur Crewe'. Rhizomatous perennial producing ovate-elliptic, entire, softly hairy basal leaves, to 5in (13cm) long, heart-shaped at the bases; the stem leaves are ovate-lance-shaped and toothed. In spring, branched stems bear 3 or 4 golden yellow flowerheads, to 4in (10cm) across. ↕↔ to 24in (60cm). Zone 5.

D. orientale, syn. *D. caucasicum.* Slowly spreading, rhizomatous perennial with ovate-elliptic, gently scalloped, sparsely

Doronicum orientale 'Frühlingspracht'

Doronicum pardalianches

hairy basal leaves, 2½–4in (6–10cm) long, with heart-shaped bases, and a few elliptic to ovate-lance-shaped stem leaves. Produces solitary, golden yellow flowerheads, 1–2in (2.5–5cm) across, on slender stems in mid- and late spring. ↕ to 24in (60cm), ↔ 36in (90cm). S.E. Europe, Caucasus, Turkey, Lebanon. Zone 4. **'Finesse'** has slender ray florets and long stems; comes true from seed, and is good for cutting; ↕ to 20in (50cm). **'Frühlingspracht'** ■ syn. 'Spring Beauty', has double flowerheads; ↕ to 16in (40cm). **'Gerhard'** produces double, lemon-yellow flowerheads with greenish yellow centers. **'Goldzwerg'** has golden yellow ray florets; ↕ 10in (25cm). **'Magnificum'** has flowerheads 1½–2in (4–5cm) across, and comes true from seed; ↕ 20in (50cm). **'Spring Beauty'** see 'Frühlingspracht'.

D. pardalianches ■ syn. *D. cordatum* (Great leopard's bane). Spreading, rhizomatous perennial with ovate to almost circular, toothed, softly hairy basal leaves, 3–5in (8–13cm) long, with heart-shaped bases, and ovate to lance-shaped stem leaves. Branching, softly hairy stems bear corymbs of light yellow flowerheads, 1¼–2in (3–5cm) across, from late spring to midsummer. ↕ 36in (90cm), ↔ 24–36in (60–90cm) or more. W. and C. Europe to S. central Europe. Zone 4. **'Goldstrauss'** flowers very freely.

D. plantagineum. Spreading, rhizomatous perennial with ovate-elliptic, entire or weakly toothed, hairy basal leaves, 2–4½in (5–11cm) long, and lance-shaped stem leaves. Branched stems bear golden yellow flowerheads, 1¼–2in (3–5cm) across, in late spring. Leaves die back soon after flowering. ↕ 32in (80cm), ↔ 18in (45cm). W. Europe to N. France. Zone 4. **'Excelsum'** see *D.* x *excelsum* 'Harpur Crewe'. **'Harpur Crewe'** see *D.* x *excelsum* 'Harpur Crewe'. **'Strahlengold'** has summer-persistent foliage, and flowers freely from spring to summer. Resists mildew and root rot.

DOROTHEANTHUS

Ice plant, Livingstone daisy

AIZOACEAE

Genus of 10 species of low-growing, basally branching, succulent annuals from open, sandy or rocky areas in South Africa. They have opposite or alternate, narrowly linear to spoon-shaped leaves, glistening with small, crystal-like structures. In summer, they produce numerous long-stalked, daisy-like white, yellow, orange, pink, or red flowers that close in cloudy weather. Grow as border edging, to fill gaps in paving, or on a dry slope.

• **CULTIVATION** Grow in well-drained, preferably low-fertility, sandy soil in full sun. Deadhead to prolong flowering.

• **PROPAGATION** Sow seed at 61–66°F (16–19°C) in late winter or early spring.

• **PESTS AND DISEASES** Slugs, aphids, snails, and foot rot may be troublesome.

D. bellidiformis, syn. *D. littlewoodii, Mesembryanthemum criniflorum* (Livingstone daisy). Low-growing annual bearing alternate, cylindrical, obovate to spoon-shaped, fleshy, light green leaves, to 3in (7cm) long. Solitary flowers, to 1½in (4cm) across, in white, crimson, rose-red, orange-gold, or buff-yellow, some zoned in a contrasting color, are freely borne in summer. Plants with striped, light pink flowers, to 1in (2.5cm) across, and white throats, are sometimes listed as *D. littlewoodii.* ↕ to 6in (15cm), ↔ 12in (30cm). South Africa (Western Cape). ❄ (min. 50°F/10°C).
'Lunette', syn. 'Yellow Ice', produces red-centered, soft yellow flowers. **'Magic Carpet'** ■ has pink, purple, cream, orange, or white flowers. **'Yellow Ice'** see 'Lunette'.
D. gramineus, syn. *Mesembryanthemum tricolor.* Erect, red-stemmed annual with opposite, linear, bright green leaves, to 2in (5cm) long, rounded on the lower surfaces. Bears solitary, crimson to deep rose-pink or white flowers, to 1in (2.5cm) across, with a dark central disk, in summer. ↕ 4in (10cm), ↔ to 12in (30cm). South Africa (Western Cape). ❄ (min. 50°F/10°C)
D. littlewoodii see *D. bellidiformis.*

Dorotheanthus bellidiformis 'Magic Carpet'

DORSTENIA

MORACEAE

Genus of about 170 species of rhizomatous or shrubby perennials, a small number of which are succulent, from lowlands in the Arabian Peninsula, N.E. Africa, Madagascar, India, and tropical South and Central America. In many species, the rhizome is thick and tuber-like, and the caudex fleshy and thick, with leaves that are sometimes scale-like, especially on the upper nodes. The insignificant, petalless flowers, and later, ovoid green fruits, are embedded in disk-shaped receptacles, produced from the upper leaf axils. Where not hardy, grow in a temperate greenhouse for their bonsai-like growth or use as a groundcover beneath greenhouse staging. In warmer climates, grow in a desert garden. All parts of dorstenias are harmful if ingested.

• **CULTIVATION** Under glass, grow in a mix of equal parts loam, peat (or peat substitute), leaf mold, and gritty sand, in full light. In the growing season, water freely, applying fertilizer monthly; keep just moist in winter. Outdoors, grow in sharply drained, gritty, humus-rich soil in full sun. See also pp.48–49.

• **PROPAGATION** Sow seed at 70–75°F (21–24°C) in spring or summer.

• **PESTS AND DISEASES** Susceptible to scale insects.

D. foetida ■ Erect or semi-prostrate, subshrubby succulent with a flattened caudex, thick, fleshy branches, and oblong-lance-shaped or obovate, spirally arranged leaves, 1¼–5½in (3–14cm) long. Circular, greenish white "flowers," ¾in (2cm) across, shaped like starfish, with 6–15 bract-like "tentacles," are

Dorstenia foetida

produced in summer. ↕ 12–16in (30–40cm), ↔ 10–12in (25–30cm). Saudi Arabia. ❄ (min. 61°F/16°C)
D. gigas. Shrubby perennial. Leaves are inversely lance-shaped with rounded tips and lateral veins in 10–24 pairs. The solitary flowers have a nearly round flowering face, with a rim around the periphery and an outer row of 4–8 appendages. Ripe seeds are ejected with force from flower structures. ↕ to 5ft (1.5m). Socotra, island S. of Yemen. ❄ (min. 61°F/16°C)

DORYANTHES

Spear lily

LILIACEAE

Genus of 2 species of perennial succulents mainly from coastal, open *Eucalyptus* forest of E. Australia. They are grown for their loosely rosetted, linear to lance-shaped leaves, with long, cylindrical points, and huge, terminal inflorescences of tubular flowers, with spreading tips, borne on mature plants. Grow as specimen plants. Where temperatures fall below 35°F (2°C), grow on a patio (overwinter under glass) or in a cool greenhouse.

• **CULTIVATION** Under glass, grow in soil-based potting mix in full light. During the growing season, water freely, applying a balanced liquid fertilizer monthly; keep just moist in winter. Outdoors, grow in humus-rich, well-drained soil in sun, with plenty of water in the growing season, although they will tolerate poor soils, some drought, and partial shade. See also pp.48–49.

• **PROPAGATION** Sow seed at 50–55°F (10–13°C) in spring. Sow bulbils, occasionally produced on flower stems, when mature. Separate suckers produced after flowering.

• **PESTS AND DISEASES** Infrequent.

D. excelsa. Succulent with erect clusters of curving, linear or lance-shaped, dark green leaves, to 8ft (2.5m) long. Flowering stems to 15ft (5m) long bear many short, erect, linear-lance-shaped leaves and dense, spherical, terminal racemes, to 28in (70cm) across, of tubular red flowers, 4in (10cm) long, within leafy bracts, in late summer. ↕ 15–20ft (5–6m), ↔ to 8ft (2.5m). New South Wales. ❄ (min. 35°F/2°C)
D. palmeri ■ Succulent with rosettes of upright then arching, linear or lance-shaped, lush, bright green leaves, 8–10ft (2.5–3m) long. Flowering stems, to 8ft

Doryanthes palmeri

(2.5m) long, are also erect then arching. Along the upper halves, they bear smaller, linear-lance-shaped leaves and dense, oblong, terminal panicles, 10–12ft (3–4m) long, of tubular, rich red or red-brown flowers, 1½–2½in (4–6cm) long, pale red or white inside, enclosed in deep red bracts, in late spring. ↕ 8ft (2.5m), ↔ to 10ft (3m). Queensland, N. New South Wales. ❄ (min. 35°F/2°C)

▷ ***Dorycnium*** see *Lotus*

DORYOPTERIS

PTERIDACEAE

Genus of about 25 species of evergreen ferns from dry, open areas or woodland in tropical regions. The tufted fronds, borne on erect or creeping rhizomes, have arrow-shaped, pedate, or palmate, sometimes pinnatifid blades on long, shiny, black stalks. Grow in a shady, sheltered border. Where not hardy, grow in a warm greenhouse or as houseplants.

• **CULTIVATION** Under glass, grow in a mix of 1 part loam, 2 parts sharp sand, and 3 parts leaf mold, in bright filtered light and moderate humidity. Water moderately when in full growth, sparingly in winter. Outdoors, grow in well-drained soil in partial shade.

• **PROPAGATION** Sow spores at 70°F (21°C) as soon as ripe, or divide mature plants in spring. Pot up "bulblets" from fronds of *D. palmata* when 1¼–1½in (3–4cm) across. See also p.51.

• **PESTS AND DISEASES** Leaf spots and Southern blight can occur. Scale may infest the stalks.

D. palmata, syn. *D. pedata* var. *palmata.* Evergreen fern bearing broadly ovate, dark green fronds, 8–24in (20–60cm) long, very deeply palmately lobed with 10–15 or more lobes. Proliferous buds ("bulblets") are produced at the frond bases. ↕ to 14in (35cm), ↔ 12–20in (30–50cm). West Indies, C. and W. tropical South America to Peru and Brazil. ❄ (min. 46–50°F/8–10°C)
D. pedata* var. *palmata see *D. palmata.*

▷ ***Douglasia laevigata*** see *Androsace laevigata*

▷ ***Douglasia vitaliana*** see *Vitaliana primuliflora*

▷ ***Doxantha capreolata*** see *Bignonia capreolata*

▷ ***Doxantha unguis-cati*** see *Macfadyena unguis-cati*

DRABA

BRASSICACEAE

Genus of about 300 species of annuals and mat- or cushion-forming, evergreen or semi-evergreen perennials found in scree and other rocky, mountainous areas in arctic and northern temperate regions and temperate South America. They have rosettes of mainly linear to ovate, oblong, or spoon-shaped leaves, and small, cross-shaped flowers, borne in terminal racemes, in spring or early summer. Grow in a rock garden, scree bed, or alpine house, or in tufa.

• **CULTIVATION** Grow in gritty, sharply drained soil in full sun. Protect from excessive winter rain. For optimum form, grow the densest cushion plants in an alpine house, in a mix of equal parts loam, leaf mold, and grit, with a layer of grit or small stones around the neck of the plant. Avoid wetting the foliage at all times.

• **PROPAGATION** Sow seed in containers in an open frame in autumn; they need exposure to cold to germinate. Root rosettes of larger species in late spring.

• **PESTS AND DISEASES** Susceptible to aphids and spider mites under glass. Rust, white rust, and mildew can occur.

D. aizoides (Yellow whitlow grass). Mat- or cushion-forming, semi-evergreen perennial bearing rosettes of linear-lance-shaped, bristle-margined, dark green leaves, to ½in (1.5cm) long. Dense racemes of 4–18 bright yellow flowers, ⅜–½in (8–12mm) across, are produced on stems 2–4in (5–10cm) long, in late spring. ↕ 4in (10cm), ↔ to 10in (25cm). UK, C. and S. Europe to Carpathians. Zone 4.

D. bryoides see *D. rigida* var. *bryoides*.

D. dedeana ■ Woody-based, cushion-forming, evergreen perennial with dense rosettes of linear-oblong, fringed and bristle-tipped, gray-green or bright green leaves, to ¼in (6mm) long. From spring to early summer, bears dense racemes of 3–10 white flowers, ⅜–½in (9–15mm) across, flushed pale violet at the bases, on stems to 3in (8cm) long. ↕ to 3in (8cm), ↔ to 6in (15cm). N. and E. Spain (mountains). Zone 4.

D. longisiliqua. Cushion-forming, evergreen perennial with firm rosettes of obovate, gray-hairy leaves, ¼–⅜in (6–8mm) long. Bears short, dense racemes of 3–14 yellow flowers, to ½in (1.5cm) across, on stems 2–3in (5–8cm) long, in spring. ↕ 3½in (9cm), ↔ to 10in (25cm). Caucasus. Zone 4.

Draba dedeana

Draba mollissima

D. mollissima ■ Hummock-forming, evergreen perennial with rosettes of oblong, very hairy, gray-green leaves, to ¼in (6mm) long, forming a dense, domed cushion. In late spring, produces tight racemes of 6–8 bright yellow flowers, to ⅜in (8mm) across, on stems to 3in (8cm) long. ↕ 3in (8cm), ↔ to 8in (20cm). Caucasus. Zone 4.

D. rigida. Hummock-forming, evergreen perennial with rosettes of linear to obovate, spreading, dark green, hairy-margined leaves, ⅛–¼in (3–6mm) long. In late spring, bears corymb-like racemes of 5–20 bright yellow flowers, ⅛–¼in (3–6mm) across, on stems to 2in (5cm) long. ↕ to 2in (5cm), ↔ to 8in (20cm). Turkey (Anatolia). Zone 4.

var. *bryoides*, syn. *D. bryoides*, has smaller rosettes; leaves, to 1/16 in (2mm) long, have inrolled margins; ↕ 1¼in (3cm), ↔ to 6in (15cm). Caucasus.

DRACAENA

DRACAENACEAE

Genus of 40 species of sparsely branched, evergreen shrubs and trees from forest, scrub, and dry, open slopes. They occur in the Canary Islands and throughout tropical Africa, but mainly in W. Africa, with one species in South America. These striking architectural plants produce usually lance- to strap-shaped, leathery, glossy leaves, which are spirally arranged and often crowded at the stem tips. Small flowers, with tubular bases and 6 spreading tepals, are borne in terminal panicles, followed by red or yellow berries. Grow as specimen plants or in a border. Where not hardy, grow in a warm or temperate greenhouse, or as houseplants.

Dracaena draco

Dracaena fragrans Deremensis Group 'Warneckei'

• **CULTIVATION** Under glass, grow in soil-based potting mix in full light with shade from hot sun and moderate humidity. Green-leaved plants tolerate slightly lower light levels. From spring to autumn, water freely, applying a balanced liquid fertilizer monthly; water sparingly in winter. Top-dress or pot on in spring. Outdoors, grow in moderately fertile, moist but well-drained soil in full sun. Regular pruning is not necessary. If growth is weak, cut back to within 6in (15cm) of the base in spring.

• **PROPAGATION** Sow seed at 64–70°F (18–21°C) in spring, although variegated cultivars will not come true. Root semi-ripe cuttings and leafless stem sections with bottom heat in summer.

• **PESTS AND DISEASES** Spider mites, scale insects, and mealybugs are common under glass. Very sensitive to excess fluoride, and to boron and calcium deficiency.

D. australis see *Cordyline australis.*

D. deremensis see *D. fragrans* Deremensis Group.

***D. deremensis* 'Souvenir de Schrijver'** see *D. fragrans* Deremensis Group 'Warneckei'.

D. draco ■ (Dragon tree). Robust, slow-growing, eventually widely branched tree, resembling an inside-out umbrella in outline when mature. Tufted or rosetted, glaucous, mid- to dark green leaves, 12–24in (30–60cm) long, are linear-lance-shaped and spine-tipped. Mature plants produce terminal panicles, to 12in (30cm) long, of white-tinged green flowers in summer, followed by large, spherical, orange-red fruit. ↕ 10–30ft (3–10m) or more, ↔ 6–25ft (2–8m) or more. Canary Islands. ❀ (min. 55°F/13°C)

D. fragrans. Erect, evergreen shrub or small tree, very sparsely branched when young, with spreading to strongly arching, inversely lance-shaped, keeled, mid-green leaves, 8–48in (20–120cm) long, confined to upper parts of the stems. When mature, bears strongly scented white flowers in erect to arching, branched or unbranched, terminal panicles, to 20in (50cm) long,

Dracaena marginata

Dracaena marginata 'Tricolor'

in summer, followed by spherical, orange-red fruit. ↕ 15–50ft (5–15m), ↔ 3–10ft (1–3m). W., C., and E. Africa. ❀ (min. 55°F/13°C)
Deremensis Group, syn. *D. deremensis*, includes cultivars with different patterns of longitudinal leaf striations of varying colors and widths. **Deremensis Group 'Warneckei'** ▣ syn. *D. deremensis* 'Souvenir de Schrijver', *D. deremensis* 'Warneckei', has dark gray-green leaves, 16–24in (40–60cm) long, with narrow lighter streaks, dark green margins, and near-central, longitudinal white stripes. **'Massangeana'** has recurved, dull green leaves, 8–24in (20–60cm) long, with grayish green streaks and a broad, longitudinal, yellow-green band, interspersed with narrow, gray-green stripes.
D. indivisa see *Cordyline indivisa*.
D. marginata ▣ Erect, slow-growing shrub or small tree, often unbranched at first, then branching and spreading. Spreading, linear-lance-shaped, recurved, red-margined, dark green leaves, 12–24in (30–60cm) long, are densely borne on upper parts of the stems. Mature plants produce terminal panicles, 16–20in (40–50cm) across, of white flowers in summer, followed by yellow berries. ↕ 6–15ft (2–5m), ↔ 3–10ft (1–3m). Réunion Island. ❀ (min. 55°F/13°C). **'Tricolor'** ▣ has leaves with cream marginal stripes shaded red.
D. sanderiana ▣ (Ribbon plant). Slender, erect shrub with cane-like stems that branch sparingly to moderately from the base. Arching, slightly wavy, lance-shaped, glossy, rich green leaves, 6–10in (15–25cm) long, tapering to false stalks, have bold, longitudinal, silvery white stripes. Not known to flower in cultivation. ↕ to 5ft (1.5m), ↔ 16–32in (40–80cm). Cameroon. ❀ (min. 55°F/13°C)

Dracaena sanderiana

DRACOCEPHALUM

Dragon's head

LAMIACEAE

Genus of 50 species of annuals, perennials, and dwarf, evergreen shrubs found in a range of habitats, from dry, sunny steppes and rocky, grassy slopes to dry woodland, mostly in Eurasia, but also in N. Africa and N. US. They are grown for their whorls of tubular, 2-lipped flowers produced in upright, terminal or axillary racemes, 3–12in (7–30cm) or more long, in summer. They have square stems and opposite, often aromatic, mainly linear to broadly ovate, entire or toothed, lobed or pinnatisect, mid-green leaves, usually ½–3in (1.5–8cm) long. Grow in a border or rock garden; some species are also suitable for naturalizing in partial shade. Annuals may be used to fill gaps in mixed plantings.
• **CULTIVATION** Grow in well-drained, moderately fertile soil in full sun with some midday shade. *D. forrestii* requires sharply drained soil with protection from excessive winter moisture. *D. ruyschiana* tolerates dry soils.
• **PROPAGATION** Sow seed of annuals *in situ* in midspring, thinning as required. Divide or sow seed of perennials in containers in a cold frame in autumn or spring, or root basal cuttings of young growth in mid- or late spring.
• **PESTS AND DISEASES** Occasionally affected by rust, mildew, and Southern blight. Spider mites may be a problem.

D. argunense ▣ syn. *D. ruyschiana* var. *speciosum*, *D. speciosum*. Clump-forming perennial with oblong-lance-shaped to linear-lance-shaped, entire, minutely glandular, hairy leaves, 2–3in (5–7cm) long. Bluish purple flowers, to 1¾in (4.5cm) long, are borne in softly hairy, whorled, terminal racemes among ovate-lance-shaped stem leaves in midsummer. ↕ 18in (45cm), ↔ 12in (30cm). China, N.E. Asia. Zone 4.
D. forrestii. Rhizomatous perennial with obovate, pinnatisect leaves, ½–¾in (1.5–2cm) long, with 2 or 3 pairs of linear segments, tightly inrolled. Slender, very leafy, white-hairy stems bear dense, whorled racemes of softly white-hairy, deep purple-blue flowers, ¾–1¼in (2–3cm) long, from late summer to midautumn. ↕ to 20in (50cm), ↔ 12in (30cm). China (Yunnan). Zone 5.

Dracocephalum argunense

D. govanianum see *Nepeta govaniana*.
D. grandiflorum. Upright, rhizomatous perennial with long-stalked, oblong-elliptic, toothed radical leaves, ¾–2in (2–5cm) long, and smaller, broadly ovate, scalloped, stalkless stem leaves. Bears short, spike-like racemes of hooded, intense blue flowers, to 1½in (4cm) long, with darker spots on the lower lips, in summer. ↕ 12in (30cm), ↔ 8in (20cm). Siberia. Zone 4.
D. moldavica (Moldavian balm). Erect, bushy, slightly hairy, aromatic annual with oblong-lance-shaped to ovate-triangular, toothed, gray-green leaves, ½–1½in (1.5–4cm) long. Bears slender, spike-like racemes of whorled, unevenly 2-lipped, hairy, violet-blue to purple flowers, to 1in (2.5cm) long, in summer. ↕ 12–24in (30–60cm), ↔ 12in (30cm). E. and C. Europe, C. Asia, Siberia, China. Zone 5. **f. album** has white flowers.
D. ruyschiana, syn. *D. ruyschianum* (Siberian dragon's head). Clump-forming, bushy perennial with linear-lance-shaped, entire, inrolled, hairless leaves, 1½–2½in (3.5–6cm) long, and erect, often downy stems. Bears short spikes of blue-purple flowers, to 1in (2.5cm) long, in mid- and late summer. ↕ to 24in (60cm), ↔ 12in (30cm). C. Europe to Siberia. Zone 4.
var. *japonicum* has white flowers shaded blue; Japan. **var. *speciosum*** see *D. argunense*.
D. ruyschianum see *D. ruyschiana*.
D. sibiricum see *Nepeta sibirica*.
D. speciosum see *D. argunense*.
D. tanguticum. Clump-forming, variable perennial bearing ovate, pinnatisect, aromatic leaves, 1–3in (2.5–8cm) long, with 5–7 narrowly linear divisions. Produces whorled, spike-like racemes of long-lasting, deep violet-blue flowers, ¾–1¼in (2–3cm) long, from midsummer to early autumn. ↕ 16in (40cm), ↔ 12in (30cm). S.W. China. Zone 4.

DRACULA

ORCHIDACEAE

Genus of about 60 species of evergreen, epiphytic orchids from around 7,000ft (2,000m) in the Andean regions of South America and adjacent highlands of Central America. They produce short, slender stems along creeping rhizomes, each stem having a single, lance-shaped to obovate, thin-textured, slightly folded, dark green leaf with a prominent midrib. The flowers are borne singly or in erect, or more commonly pendent, arching racemes. The sepals are fused into wide, star-shaped cups, with the free parts of the sepals resembling long tails. The lip has a short claw and a cup (or pouched blade).
• **CULTIVATION** Cool-growing orchids. Grow in epiphytic orchid potting mix in a slatted basket. In summer, provide humid, shady conditions, and water moderately with rainwater if possible, applying half-strength fertilizer at every third watering. Water sparingly in winter to avoid root rot. See also p.46.
• **PROPAGATION** Divide when the plant fills the pot and flows over the sides.
• **PESTS AND DISEASES** Prey to spider mites, aphids, whiteflies, and mealybugs.

D. bella. Epiphytic orchid with oblong to lance-shaped leaves, 5–8in (12–20cm) long. Flowers, 4–10in (10–25cm) long, densely spotted brown, with greenish yellow bases, long-tailed sepals, and small white lips, are borne singly, from winter to summer. ↕↔ 10in (25cm). Colombia. ❀ (min. 50°F/10°C; max. 75°F/24°C)
D. chimaera. Robust, epiphytic or lithophytic orchid with elliptic to obovate leaves, 6–10in (15–25cm) long. In winter, the erect or ascending stems each bear a succession of 3–8 densely spotted, dark maroon flowers, 5in (13cm) long, with yellow or greenish yellow bases, long-tailed sepals, and small cream lips. ↕ to 24in (60cm), ↔ 8in (20cm). Colombia. ❀ (min. 50°F/10°C; max. 75°F/24°C)
D. erythrochaete. Epiphytic orchid with elliptic to obovate to linear-lanceolate leaves, 6–10in (15–25cm) long. Bears 1–3 cream flowers, 4in (10cm) across, with red-purple spotting and purple tails, on long, erect to pendent stems, from autumn to winter. ↕ 16–24in (40–60cm), ↔ 8in (20cm). Costa Rica to Colombia. ❀ (min. 50°F/10°C; max. 75°F/24°C)

DRACUNCULUS

ARACEAE

Genus of 3 species of tuberous perennials from the Mediterranean, Madeira, and the Canary Islands, found on waste ground, in rocky areas, and on hillsides, with pedate, sometimes white-mottled, dark green leaves. They are grown for their distinctive but foul-smelling, often very large, flat or curved spathes, borne in spring or summer. Although not reliably hardy, they grow well in open glades in sheltered woodland or at the base of a sunny wall.
• **CULTIVATION** Plant tubers 6in (15cm) deep in autumn or spring in humus-rich, well-drained soil that dries out in summer. Grows best in full sun but will tolerate partial shade. Protect with a loose winter mulch.
• **PROPAGATION** Separate offsets in autumn or spring.
• **PESTS AND DISEASES** Infrequent.

D. vulgaris ▣ syn. *Arum dracunculus* (Dragon arum). Tuberous perennial with pedate, dark green basal leaves,

Dracunculus vulgaris

D

12in (30cm) or more long, marked purple-brown. In spring or summer, foul-smelling, maroon-purple spathes, 24–39in (60–100cm) long, with erect, near-black spadices, are produced above the leaves. ↕ to 5ft (1.5m), ↔ 24in (60cm). C. and E. Mediterranean. ❄ (min. 35°F/2°C)

DREGEA *syn.* WATTAKAKA

ASCLEPIADACEAE

Genus of 3 or more species of twining, woody, evergreen climbers found in tropical forest from South Africa to China, with opposite, heart-shaped to pointed ovate or lance-shaped leaves. They are cultivated for their small, bowl-shaped, fragrant yellow or white flowers, produced in stalked umbels from the leaf axils. Where marginally hardy, grow *D. sinensis* against a sheltered wall.

• **CULTIVATION** Grow in well-drained soil in sun or partial shade. Tie young shoots to their supports until they begin to twine. Pruning group 11, after flowering; remove dead wood in early spring.

• **PROPAGATION** Sow seed in containers in a cold frame in spring. Take stem cuttings in summer or autumn.

• **PESTS AND DISEASES** Infrequent.

D. sinensis, syn. *Wattakaka sinensis.* Twining climber with ovate-heart-shaped leaves, to 4in (10cm) long, mid-green above and gray-downy beneath. Produces fragrant, creamy white flowers, to ½in (1.5cm) across, pale pink and speckled red within, in umbels 2½in (6cm) across, in summer, followed by slender, paired seed pods, to 3in (7cm) long. ↕ 10ft (3m). China. ❄ (min. 41°F/5°C)

▷ ***Drejerella*** see *Justicia*
▷ ***Drepanostachyum falconeri*** see *Himalayacalamus falconeri*

DRIMYS *syn.* TASMANNIA

WINTERACEAE

Genus of about 30 species of evergreen shrubs and trees from woodland and mountains in Malaysia, Australasia, and Central and South America. They are grown for their handsome, usually elliptic to inversely lance-shaped, aromatic leaves, arranged alternately on the branches, and terminal, umbel-like clusters of small, star-shaped, sometimes unisexual flowers. Grow in a woodland garden or in a sheltered position among other trees and shrubs.

• **CULTIVATION** Grow in fertile, moist but well-drained soil in sun or partial shade. Shelter from cold, drying winds. Pruning group 8; cut out dead or damaged wood in spring.

• **PROPAGATION** Sow seed in containers in a cold frame in autumn. Insert semi-ripe cuttings in summer.

• **PESTS AND DISEASES** Infrequent.

D. aromatica see *D. lanceolata.*
D. colorata see *Pseudowintera colorata.*
D. lanceolata, syn. *D. aromatica, Tasmannia aromatica* (Pepper tree). Dense, upright shrub or tree with deep red shoots and elliptic to inversely lance-shaped, leathery, glossy, dark green leaves, to 3in (8cm) long. Clusters of 7–18 white flowers, ½in (1.5cm) across, are produced in mid- and late spring.

Drimys winteri

↕ 12ft (4m), ↔ 8ft (2.5m). S.E. Australia, Tasmania. ❄ (min. 41°F/5°C)
D. winteri ■ syn. *Wintera aromatica* (Winter's bark). Vigorous, upright tree or shrub with aromatic bark and oblong-elliptic to narrowly inversely lance-shaped, leathery leaves, to 8in (20cm) long, dark green above, blue-white beneath. Produces large umbels of 5–20 fragrant, ivory-white flowers, 1in (2.5cm) across, from spring to early summer, followed by edible, aromatic, glossy black berries. Suitable for hedging. ↕ 50ft (15m), ↔ 30ft (10m). Mexico, Chile, Argentina. ❄ (min. 35°F/2°C). **var. *andina*** is dwarf and flowers when 12–16in (30–40cm) tall; ↕↔ 36–39in (90–100cm). Andes of Chile, Argentina.

DROSANTHEMUM

AIZOACEAE

Genus of about 90 species of erect or prostrate, succulent shrubs from semi-desert regions of Namibia and South Africa. They have slender, rough stems clad in minute, fine hairs, and leaves, triangular to cylindrical in cross-section, densely covered with papillae. Daisy-like white or red flowers, solitary or in threes, open after midday in summer. Where not hardy, grow in a cool greenhouse and transfer outdoors in summer; elsewhere, grow in a desert garden or border with other succulents.

• **CULTIVATION** Under glass, grow in standard cactus potting mix in full light. In growth, water freely, applying fertilizer monthly; keep just moist at other times. Outdoors, grow in sharply drained soil in full sun. See also pp.48–49.

• **PROPAGATION** Sow seed at 61–66°F (16–19°C) or take stem cuttings from spring to summer.

• **PESTS AND DISEASES** Susceptible to aphids while flowering.

Drosanthemum hispidum

D. hispidum ■ Bushy, succulent shrub with erect then spreading, roughly hairy branches, which frequently root where they touch the ground. Cylindrical, fleshy, glossy, pale green to reddish green leaves, to 1in (2.5cm) long, are covered with transparent papillae. In summer, bears solitary, glossy-petaled, deep purplish red flowers, to 1¼in (3cm) across. ↕ 6in (15cm), ↔ 3ft (1m). Namibia, South Africa (Western Cape). ❄ (min. 41°F/5°C)
D. speciosum. Bushy, succulent shrub with erect, spotted stems and curved, semi-cylindrical, fleshy leaves, ½in (1.5cm) long, covered with glistening papillae. Solitary, orange-red flowers, to 2in (5cm) across, with green centers, are produced in summer. South Africa (Western Cape). ↕ 12–16in (30–40cm), ↔ 12in (30cm). ❄ (min. 41°F/5°C)

DROSERA

Sundew

DROSERACEAE

Genus of about 100 species of rosette-forming or scrambling, evergreen or herbaceous, insectivorous perennials, also including some annuals, found in poor, acidic, boggy soil throughout the world, but mainly in Australia. Leaves are alternate or whorled, often long stalked, and linear to almost circular, the blades covered and fringed with gland-tipped, red or green hairs, which trap and digest insects. The small flowers are usually 5-petaled, most often white, pink, or purple, and are borne singly or in racemes or panicles. Where not hardy, grow in a cool greenhouse; in warmer climates, use in a bog garden.

• **CULTIVATION** Under glass, grow in a mix of equal parts peat (or peat substitute) and sand in full light, with shade from hot sun. Keep continually moist by standing in a saucer of soft (acidic) water. Outdoors, grow in wet, peaty, acidic, nutritionally poor soil in full sun.

• **PROPAGATION** Sow seed at 50–55°F (10–13°C) as soon as ripe. Take cuttings from young, fully developed leaves, or take root cuttings when dormant.

• **PESTS AND DISEASES** Infrequent.

D. capensis (Cape sundew). Evergreen perennial with loose basal rosettes of linear-oblong to spoon-shaped leaves, 1¼–2½in (3–6cm) long, covered in glandular red or green hairs. Racemes of 6–20 rounded, rose-pink flowers, ¾in (2cm) across, are borne from spring to autumn, and sometimes into winter. ↕ 8–12in (20–30cm), ↔ to 6in (15cm). Southern Africa. ❄ (min. 35°F/2°C)
D. intermedia (Love nest sundew). Evergreen perennial with obovate leaves, ¼in (6mm) long, in a basal rosette or scattered along the stems. Bears racemes of 3–20 small white flowers, ½in (1.5cm) across, in early summer. ↕↔ to 6in (15cm). N. Eurasia, S. North America, West Indies, N. South America. Zone 6.
D. linearis. Evergreen perennial with straight, erect leaves, ¾–2in (2–5cm) long, forming a loose basal rosette. Bears racemes of 1–4 white flowers, ½in (1.5cm) across, in summer. Tolerates alkaline soil. ↕ to 5in (13cm), ↔ to 6in (15cm). N.E. North America. Zone 4.
D. rotundifolia (Round-leaved sundew). Rosette-forming annual with rounded leaves, ¼–½in (.6–1.5cm) long, usually wider than long. Bears racemes of 1–25 white to pink flowers, ½in (1.5cm) across, in summer. ↕ to 4in (10cm), ↔ to 6in (15cm). Circumboreal.

DRYANDRA

PROTEACEAE

Genus of about 60 species of evergreen shrubs and small trees found on sandy heath, on dry, rocky and sandy coasts, and in scrub in Australia. They are grown for their foliage and their very colorful flowerheads, both of which are suitable for dried flower arrangements. Leaves are alternate, sometimes whorled, linear to ovate, leathery, usually boldly toothed, and often pinnatifid. Spherical to ovoid, often thistle-like flowerheads, borne at the ends of the shoots, consist of many slender, usually yellow florets enclosed by overlapping, sometimes colorful bracts. Where not hardy, grow in a cool greenhouse; elsewhere, grow in a border, against a warm wall, or in a sunny courtyard. Survives short periods near 32°F (0°C).

• **CULTIVATION** Under glass, use 1 part soil-based potting mix and 3 parts of a

Dryandra formosa

50/50 mix of grit and peat (or peat substitute), and grow in full light. In growth, water moderately, applying half-strength, phosphate-free fertilizer monthly; water sparingly in winter. Top-dress or pot on in spring. Outdoors, grow in sharply drained, neutral to acidic soil of low fertility (or at least low in phosphates and nitrates), in full sun. Pruning group 1 or 8.
• **PROPAGATION** Sow seed at not less than 64°F (18°C) in spring, ideally singly, in small containers. Root softwood cuttings with bottom heat in summer; rooting may be slow.
• **PESTS AND DISEASES** In warm areas, *Phytophthora* root rot may be fatal. In soil containing too much phosphorus or too little nitrogen, plants may become chlorotic.

D. formosa ■ (Showy dryandra). Erect, moderately bushy shrub or small tree. Crowded, linear, mid- to dark green leaves, to 8in (20cm) long, with triangular, teeth-like lobes, are sometimes downy beneath. Spherical, bright yellow-orange flowerheads, to 4in (10cm) across, are produced from spring to early summer. ↕ 6–10ft (2–3m), ↔ 6–15ft (2–5m). Western Australia (Stirling Range to Albany Mountains). ❄ (min. 45°F/7°C)

DRYAS

Mountain avens

ROSACEAE

Genus of 3 species of prostrate, evergreen subshrubs found on cliffs and rock ledges in alpine and arctic regions of the N. hemisphere. They are grown for their oak-like, leathery, wrinkled, dark green leaves, 1¼–1½in (3–4cm) long, and white downy beneath. Solitary, cup- to bell-shaped, 8-petaled flowers are followed by fluffy seed heads. They are easily cultivated carpeting plants, useful for a rock garden, wall, or border edge.
• **CULTIVATION** Grow in well-drained, humus-rich, slightly acidic, preferably gritty soil in sun or partial shade.
• **PROPAGATION** Sow seed in containers in a cold frame as soon as ripe, or take softwood cuttings in early summer. Lift and transplant rooted stems in spring.
• **PESTS AND DISEASES** Infrequent.

D. drummondii. Mat-forming subshrub with elliptic to obovate, coarsely scalloped leaves, to 1½in (4cm) long, and nodding, bell-shaped, pale

Dryas octopetala

yellow flowers, ½–1in (1.5–2.5cm) across, in early summer. ↕ 4in (10cm), ↔ 36in (90cm) or more. North America. Zone 3. **'Grandiflora'** bears large flowers, to 1in (2.5cm) across.
D. octopetala ■ (Mountain avens). Mat-forming subshrub with oblong-elliptic to ovate, scalloped leaves, to 1½in (4cm) long. Upward-facing, cup-shaped, creamy white flowers, to 1½in (4cm) across, with yellow stamens, are produced in late spring and early summer. ↕ 4in (10cm), ↔ 36in (90cm) or more. N. Europe. Zone 3.
D. x suendermannii (*D. drummondii* x *D. octopetala*). Mat-forming subshrub with oblong-elliptic to ovate, scalloped leaves, to 1½in (4cm) long. Produces slightly nodding, cup-shaped flowers, to 1¼in (3cm) across, pale yellow in bud, becoming pale creamy yellow, from spring to early summer. ↕ 4in (10cm), ↔ 36in (90cm) or more. Garden origin. Zone 3.

DRYNARIA

POLYPODIACEAE

Genus of 20 epiphytic, evergreen ferns found in tropical forest and scrub in tropical Africa, S.E. Asia, and Australia, with thick, creeping rhizomes and two types of frond. Basal fronds are papery, oak-like in shape, stalkless, and sterile. They turn brown quickly and form a "nest" in which organic matter collects. The more upright fertile fronds remain green and are taller, stalked, more deeply pinnate, and have linear pinnae; these produce spores in small groups on the lower surfaces. The pinnae are often

Drynaria rigidula

shed in dry periods and may leave long, bare midribs. All fronds, even when fresh, have a thin, leathery texture. Where not hardy, grow in a warm greenhouse; in warmer climates, grow epiphytically.
• **CULTIVATION** Under glass, grow in a mix of equal parts ground bark, perlite, and charcoal, in a hanging basket, or epiphytically on bark or a tree-fern slab, with a moss pad at the base. In summer, provide bright filtered light, high humidity, and good ventilation, and water freely. Admit full light and water sparingly in winter. Repot in early spring. Outdoors, grow epiphytically on a tree trunk in humid, partial shade.
• **PROPAGATION** *D. rigidula* increases readily from spores, sown at 70°F (21°C) as soon as ripe; other species are not as easy to propagate from spores. Divide the rhizomes of large specimens in spring, ensuring that each portion has at least one growing tip. See also p.51.
• **PESTS AND DISEASES** Scale insects may infest fronds.

D. quercifolia. Clump-forming, epiphytic fern with ovate, shallowly lobed basal fronds, and narrowly ovate, deeply pinnatisect, dark green fertile fronds, to 3ft (1m) tall, with linear-lance-shaped pinnae. Spores are formed in small sori in double rows running from midrib to margins. ↕↔ to 3ft (1m). S.E. Asia, Australia. ❄ (min. 45°F/7°C)
D. rigidula ■ Clump-forming, epiphytic fern producing elongated, deeply lobed basal fronds, and ovate, pinnate, dark green fertile fronds, to 5ft (1.5m) tall. Young fronds are covered with soft down, which often persists until the fronds wither. Spores are formed in sori in a single row between midrib and margins. ↕ to 3ft (1m), ↔ to 5ft (1.5m). India, S. China, Polynesia, New Guinea, Australia. ❄ (min. 45°F/7°C). **'Whitei'** has broader pinnae, which are lacerate to irregularly lobed.

DRYOPTERIS

Buckler fern

DRYOPTERIDACEAE

Genus of about 200 species of terrestrial ferns found mainly in temperate regions of the N. hemisphere, where they grow in woodland, by streams or lakes, and among mountain rocks. Most are deciduous, but in mild winters some stay green in sheltered sites. Pinnate to 4-pinnate, sometimes pinnatisect fronds

Dryopteris affinis

Dryopteris affinis Polydactyla Group 'Mapplebeck'

form shuttlecocks in most cultivated species. Spores are produced in kidney-shaped sori. The foliage looks effective with most herbaceous plants and shrubs; where not hardy, grow in a cool greenhouse.
• **CULTIVATION** Grow in moist, humus-rich soil in partial shade and a sheltered site. *D. affinis* and its cultivars will tolerate more sun and wind than other species.
• **PROPAGATION** Sow spores at 59°F (15°C) as soon as ripe. Except in *D. affinis,* sporelings of cultivars differ in appearance from the parent. Divide mature plants in spring or autumn. See also p.51.
• **PESTS AND DISEASES** Rust, leaf gall, and fungal spots occur.

D. affinis ■ syn. *D. borreri, D. pseudomas* (Golden male fern). Virtually evergreen fern producing a shuttlecock of lance-shaped, 2-pinnate or pinnatisect fronds, 8–32in (20–80cm) tall, from an erect rhizome. Fronds are pale green as they unfurl in spring, in striking contrast to the scaly, golden brown midribs; they mature to dark green and often remain green through winter. Distinguished from *D. filix-mas* by a dark spot where each pinna joins the midrib. ↕↔ 36in (90cm). Europe to Himalayas. Zone 7. **'Crispa Congesta'** see 'Crispa Gracilis'.**'Crispa Gracilis'**, syn. 'Crispa Congesta', is dwarf and evergreen, with congested fronds and pinnae twisted at the tips; ↕↔ 12in (30cm). **'Cristata'**, syn. 'Cristata The King', has arching fronds, 4–6in (10–15cm) across, with crested tips and pinnae, and is the most handsome of numerous selected forms. **'Cristata Angustata'** is similar to 'Cristata', but the fronds are 2in (5cm) wide. **'Cristata The King'** see 'Cristata'. **Polydactyla Group 'Mapplebeck'** ■ has semi-erect fronds, with large, fingered crests at the tips, broader than the fronds; pinnae are also finger crested; ↕↔ 4ft (1.2m).
***D. atrata* of gardens** see *D. cycadina.*
D. austriaca see *D. dilatata.*
D. borreri see *D. affinis.*
D. carthusiana (Narrow buckler fern). Usually deciduous, delicate fern with a slowly creeping rhizome producing a tuft of narrowly lance-shaped, 2- or 3-pinnate, pale green fronds, to 24in (60cm) long, with uniformly pale scales on the midribs. ↕ to 24in (60cm), ↔ 12in (30cm). Europe. Zone 6. **'Cristata'** has crested pinnae and frond tips.

D

D. x complexa (*D. affinis* x *D. filix-mas*). Semi-evergreen fern, similar to *D. affinis*, with fronds 36in (90cm) tall. ↕↔ 36in (90cm). Garden origin. Zone 7. **'Crispa Angustata'** has crisped fronds; ↕ 24in (60cm), ↔ 18in (45cm). **'Robust'** has arching fronds, 4–5ft (1.2–1.5m) with wider blades. Pinnules are larger with ruffled edges and overlap one another. Moist to dryish woods, Europe.

D. cycadina, syn. *D. atrata* of gardens. Deciduous fern with an erect rhizome bearing a shuttlecock of lance-shaped, pinnate, bright green fronds, 18in (45cm) tall, with green midribs. ↕ 24in (60cm), ↔ 18in (45cm). N. India to China, Taiwan, Japan. ❄ (min. 35°F/2°C)

D. dilatata, syn. *D. austriaca* (Broad buckler fern). Usually deciduous fern with a shuttlecock of broadly triangular-lance-shaped, 2- or 3-pinnate, dark green fronds, to 5ft (1.5m) tall and 15in (38cm) wide, arising from an erect rhizome. Frond midribs and stalks are covered in conspicuous, dark brown scales with darker centers. ↕ 36in (90cm), ↔ 4ft (1.2m). N.W. and C. Europe. Zone 5. **'Crispa Whiteside'** has prettily crisped fronds. **'Jimmy Dyce'** has closely set pinnae with ruffled edges, more blue-green than others of the species. ↕ 24in (60cm). Isle of Ayran. **'Lepidota Cristata'** is crested, with narrower fronds, 8in (20cm) wide, more finely divided pinnules, and paler brown scales; ↕ 24–36in (60–90cm), ↔ 18in (45cm).

D. erythrosora ■ Usually deciduous fern with a slow-creeping rhizome producing a tuft of triangular, 2- or 3-pinnate fronds, 10–24in (25–60cm) long; these are copper-red when young, slowly turning slightly shiny, dark green. Undersides of fronds bear conspicuous red sori; midribs are green. A striking border fern; grow in a protected, moist site. ↕ 24in (60cm), ↔ 15in (38cm). Japan. Zone 6.

D. filix-mas (Male fern). Deciduous fern forming a large clump of lance-shaped, 2-pinnate or pinnatifid, mid-green fronds, 3–4ft (1–1.2m) tall, with green midribs, arising from a crown of large rhizomes. ↕↔ 3ft (1m). Europe, North America. Zone 4. **'Barnesii'** has long, narrow fronds; ↕↔ 4ft (1.2m). **'Crispa Cristata'** has crested fronds and pinnae, and the pinnae are also crisped; ↕ 24in (60cm). **'Cristata Martindale'** is a distinctive selection with small crests. The pinnae curve toward frond apexes; ↕ 24in (60cm). **'Grandiceps Wills'** is a striking plant: the tip of each frond has a heavy crest as wide as the frond, and the pinnae are also finely crested; ↕↔ 36in (90cm). **Linearis Group** cultivars have narrower pinna divisions than the species, giving a delicate, airy look.

D. goldieana (Giant wood fern, Goldie's fern). Deciduous fern with a slow-creeping rhizome producing tufts of long-stalked, broadly oval, 2-pinnate, pale green fronds, 4ft (1.2m) tall, with green midribs. ↕ 4ft (1.2m), ↔ 24in (60cm). North America. Zone 5.

D. marginalis (Marginal wood fern, Evergreen fern, Leather wood fern). Evergreen fern with a short, erect rhizome bearing a cluster of upright, lance-shaped, pinnatifid or pinnate or 2-pinnate, leathery, grayish green fronds, 10–20in (25–50cm) long. Shady hillsides. ↕↔ 24in (60cm). Quebec to Kansas and S.W. Virginia. Zone 4.

D. pseudomas see *D. affinis*.

D. wallichiana (Wallich's wood fern). Deciduous fern producing an erect rhizome and a shuttlecock of lance-shaped, 2-pinnate or pinnatisect, dark green fronds, yellow-green when young, 36in (90cm) or more long. Midribs are covered with dark brown or black scales, providing striking color contrasts in spring. ↕ 36in (90cm), sometimes to 6ft (1.8m), ↔ 30in (75cm). Himalayas. ❄ (min. 45°F/7°C). **subsp. *nepalensis* 'Molten Lava'** has a shiny-textured blade and more widely spaced pinnae; new growth has an orangy-brown color that matures to a more yellowish green. ↕ 3–4ft (1–1.2m).

Dryopteris erythrosora

DUCHESNEA

ROSACEAE

Genus of 6 species of low-growing, more or less evergreen perennials from damp, shady woodland and streamsides in S. and E. Asia. Duchesneas are grown for their 5-petaled flowers, which are yellow and strawberry-like, as are the fruits that follow, although these are unpalatable. Rooting runners may be invasive in warm areas, but the fully divided, 3-palmate, conspicuously veined, toothed, strawberry-like leaves are a good groundcover. *D. indica* looks especially attractive when grown as a houseplant in a hanging basket.

• **CULTIVATION** Grow in any soil and position, although they prefer humus-rich soil in full or partial shade.

Duchesnea indica

• **PROPAGATION** Sow seed in containers in a cold frame in autumn or spring, or detach and replant rooted plantlets at almost any time of year.

• **PESTS AND DISEASES** Slugs, snails, and birds may eat the fruits.

D. indica ■ syn. *Fragaria indica* (Indian strawberry, Mock strawberry). Rosette-forming, more or less evergreen perennial producing numerous short runners that root at the nodes. The 3-palmate, hairy leaves, to 4in (10cm) long, have obovate leaflets. Solitary, 5-petaled yellow flowers, to 1in (2.5cm) across, surrounded by large green calyces and epicalyces, in early and late summer, are followed by unpalatable, bright red fruit, to ¾in (2cm) long. ↕ 4in (10cm), ↔ 4ft (1.2m) or more. India, China, Japan. Zone 4. **'Harlequin'** has red-tinged foliage, speckled white.

DUDLEYA

CRASSULACEAE

Genus of 40 species of basal-rosetted, perennial succulents mainly from hilly and low mountainous areas of S. and S.W. US and N. and N.W. Mexico, closely related to *Echeveria*. Often low-growing, they form dense rosettes of ovate to linear, succulent leaves. Tubular, bell-, or star-shaped, yellow, white, or red flowers are borne in panicles from the leaf axils in spring or early summer. Where not hardy, grow as houseplants or in a cool or temperate greenhouse; in warmer climates, use in a border.

• **CULTIVATION** Under glass, grow in standard cactus potting mix in full or bright filtered light. In growth, water moderately, applying fertilizer monthly; water sparingly in summer when plants are semi-dormant. Outdoors, grow in sharply drained, humus-rich, moderately fertile soil in full sun. See also pp.48–49.

• **PROPAGATION** Sow seed at 61°F (16°C) in early spring, or take stem cuttings from spring to summer.

• **PESTS AND DISEASES** Mealybugs.

Dudleya pulverulenta

D. attenuata. Variable, perennial succulent with stems branching to form large rosettes of slender, linear-inversely lance-shaped, fleshy, silvery gray leaves, ¾–4in (2–10cm) long; the stem leaves are linear-lance shaped. Bears tubular, yellowish red flowers, ¾in (2cm) across, in panicles, 2–8in (5–20cm) high, in spring or early summer. ↕ to 4–6in (10–15cm), ↔ to 16in (40cm). California, Mexico. ❄ (min. 45°F/7°C)

D. pulverulenta ■ (Chalk lettuce). Variable, perennial succulent with an unbranched, silvery gray stem, often very thick and fleshy. Oblong to obovate-spoon-shaped, tapering, fleshy, silvery gray leaves are 3–12in (7–30cm) long. Star-shaped red to yellow flowers, ¾–1¼in (2–3cm) across, are borne in panicles, 12–39in (30–100cm) tall, in spring or early summer. ↕ 12in (30cm) or more, ↔ to 22in (55cm). California, N. Mexico. ❄ (min. 45°F/7°C)

D. traskiae. Perennial succulent with a short, branching stem, and oblong, pointed, fleshy, silvery gray leaves, 1½–6in (4–15cm) long. Bears star-shaped yellow flowers, ¾in (2cm) across, in panicles, to 12in (30cm) high, in spring or early summer. ↕ to 8in (20cm), ↔ 10in (25cm). California (Santa Barbara Island). ❄ (min. 45°F/7°C)

DURANTA

VERBENACEAE

Genus of about 30 species of evergreen trees and shrubs found in tropical S. US and Central and South America, in scrub, thickets, and open woodland. Simple, mainly ovate, often toothed leaves are opposite or sometimes in whorls. They are grown for their salver-form flowers, borne in terminal or axillary racemes or panicles, followed by attractive, spherical berries. Where not hardy, grow in a temperate greenhouse; in warmer climates, use in a border, or as a hedge or windbreak.

• **CULTIVATION** Under glass, grow in soil-based potting mix in full light, with shade from hot sun. During growth, water

Duranta erecta

freely, applying a balanced liquid fertilizer every 2 weeks; water sparingly in winter. Top-dress or pot on in spring. Outdoors, grow in moist but well-drained, moderately fertile soil in full sun. Pruning group 1; plants under glass may need restrictive pruning in late winter.
• **PROPAGATION** Sow seed at 64–70°F (18–21°C) in spring. Root semi-ripe cuttings with bottom heat in summer. Layer in early spring.
• **PESTS AND DISEASES** Susceptible to spider mites, mealybugs, and whiteflies under glass. Leaf spot and damping off can occur.

D. erecta ▣ syn. *D. plumieri, D. repens* (Golden dewdrop, Pigeon berry, Sky flower). Erect to spreading, bushy shrub or small tree with ovate to obovate, sparsely to boldly toothed, usually rich green leaves, to 3in (7cm) long. Bears axillary, pendent panicles, 4–6in (10–15cm) long, of small blue, lilac-blue, purple, or white flowers, mainly in summer, followed by yellow fruit, to ½in (1.5cm) across. ↕ 10–20ft (3–6m), ↔ 6–10ft (2–3m). Florida to Brazil. ❄ (min. 50°F/10°C)
D. plumieri see *D. erecta.*
D. repens see *D. erecta.*

DUVALIA

ASCLEPIADACEAE

Genus of about 19 species of prostrate or semi-erect, mainly leafless, clump-forming, perennial succulents from hilly lowlands of the Arabian Peninsula, E. Africa, and southern Africa. They have toothed stems, each with 4–6

Duvalia corderoyi

Duvalia sulcata

blunt, warty ribs separated by transverse furrows. Star-shaped, stalked flowers have 5 fleshy lobes, recurved at the tips, and are solitary or produced in clusters at the base of the stems, from late spring to summer. Where not hardy, grow in a warm greenhouse; in warmer climates, grow outdoors with other succulents.
• **CULTIVATION** Under glass, grow in standard cactus potting mix in bright filtered light. In the growing season, water moderately, and apply fertilizer monthly; keep almost completely dry when dormant. Overwatering may encourage black rot. Outdoors, grow in sharply drained, humus-rich, gritty soil in partial shade. See also pp.48–49.
• **PROPAGATION** Sow seed at 70–75°F (21–24°C) or take stem cuttings from spring to summer.
• **PESTS AND DISEASES** Mealybugs.

D. corderoyi ▣ Semi-erect succulent with short, somewhat rounded, 6-ribbed, leafless green or purple stems. Produces 2–4 dull olive-green flowers, to 2in (5cm) across, covered with soft purple hairs, in summer. ↕ to 2in (5cm), ↔ indefinite. South Africa (Northern Cape). ❄ (min. 50°F/10°C)
D. maculata. Prostrate succulent with oblong, leafless, dark green stems, each with 4 or 5 ribs and prominent, pointed teeth. Bears 4–8 olive-green or dark reddish brown flowers, ¾in (2cm) across, with lobes spotted red-brown, and the white tubes spotted maroon, in summer. ↕ to 2in (5cm), ↔ indefinite. Namibia, South Africa (Western Cape). ❄ (min. 50°F/10°C)
D. sulcata ▣ Prostrate succulent with 4-ribbed, leafless, whitish green stems, purple-spotted and prominently toothed. From late spring to summer, bears clusters of 1–3 reddish brown flowers, 1¾in (4.5cm) across, with 5-furrowed, hairy-based lobes, covered with pale reddish hairs. ↕ to 3in (7cm), ↔ indefinite. Arabian Peninsula. ❄ (min. 50°F/10°C)

▷ ***Duvernoia*** see *Justicia*

DYCKIA

BROMELIACEAE

Genus of over 120 species of rosette-forming, evergreen, succulent, terrestrial perennials (bromeliads) from South America, found in rocky areas, especially near coasts, and in mountainous regions, at altitudes up to 6,500ft (2,000m). They have linear to lance-shaped or short, triangular, spiny-margined, stiff, often gray-scaly leaves, and tubular, sulfur-yellow to orange flowers, produced laterally from the rosettes in racemes or panicles, generally in spring. Many species develop a thickened, trunk-like stem, while some are mat-forming. Where not hardy, grow as houseplants or in a temperate greenhouse; elsewhere, they are suitable for a desert garden.
• **CULTIVATION** Under glass, grow in extremely well-drained succulent potting mix in full light. From late spring to autumn, water moderately, applying fertilizer monthly; keep completely dry in winter. Outdoors, grow in sharply drained, gritty, humus-rich soil in full sun. See also p.47.
• **PROPAGATION** Sow seed at 81°F (27°C) in early spring, or divide clumps in late spring or early summer.
• **PESTS AND DISEASES** Scale insects occur.

D. argentea see *Hechtia argentea.*
D. fosteriana ▣ Bromeliad with dense, flat rosettes of lance-shaped, gray-scaly leaves, 3½–7in (9–18cm) long, with sharp, recurved marginal spines. Densely scaly racemes, 18in (45cm) long, of bright orange flowers, 1in (2.5cm) long, are produced in late spring. ↕ to 8in (20cm), ↔ 5in (13cm). E. Brazil. ❄ (min. 50°F/10°C)
D. platyphylla. Bromeliad with spreading rosettes of thick, narrowly triangular, dark green leaves, to 9in (23cm) long, hairless above, with white scales pressed flat against the undersides. The lax racemes, 11in (28cm) long, of bright yellow flowers, 1in (2.5cm) long, are produced in late spring. ↕ to 32in (80cm), ↔ 16in (40cm). E. Brazil. ❄ (min. 50°F/10°C)
D. remotiflora ▣ Bromeliad with dense rosettes of very narrowly triangular, arching, dark green leaves, 4–10in (10–25cm) long, covered with gray scales, especially on the undersides, and with hooked marginal spines. Loose, sparsely hairy panicles, to 36in (90cm) long, with lateral spikes of dark orange flowers, ¾in (2cm) long, are produced in late spring. ↕ 12in (30cm), ↔ 12–20in (30–50cm). S. Brazil, Uruguay. ❄ (min. 50°F/10°C), although it will tolerate brief periods near freezing if dry.

Dyckia remotiflora

▷ ***Dysosma pleiantha*** see *Podophyllum pleianthum*
▷ ***Dyssodia*** see *Thymophylla*

Dyckia fosteriana

E

E

EBRACTEOLA

AIZOACEAE

Genus of 5 species of very fleshy, mat- or clump-forming, perennial succulents from low-lying hills in Namibia. They have extremely thick rootstocks and 3-sided, sometimes spotted, bluish green leaves. Solitary, almost stalkless, daisy-like, terminal flowerheads are borne in summer. Where not hardy, grow as a groundcover in a warm greenhouse; in warm, dry climates, grow in a desert garden or in a raised bed.

• **CULTIVATION** Under glass, grow in standard cactus potting mix in full light. During the growing season, water moderately and apply a low-nitrogen liquid fertilizer monthly; keep dry at other times. Outdoors, grow in sharply drained soil in full sun. See also pp.48–49.

• **PROPAGATION** Sow seed at 66–75°F (19–24°C) in spring or summer, or take cuttings of stem sections in early summer.

• **PESTS AND DISEASES** Infrequent.

E. derenbergiana, syn. *Mesembryanthemum derenbergianum, Ruschia derenbergiana.* Mat- or cushion-forming succulent with a very thick taproot, 8in (20cm) long, producing fleshy stems, each with 2 or 3 pairs of 3-sided, densely spotted, light blue-green leaves, 1¼–1½in (3–4cm) long, bluntly margined, with the sides hatchet-shaped above. Daisy-like, pale pink flowers, ¾–1in (2–2.5cm) across, are borne in summer. ↕ to 3in (8cm), ↔ indefinite. Namibia. ❀ (min. 50°F/10°C)

ECBALLIUM

Squirting cucumber

CUCURBITACEAE

Genus of one species of trailing or bushy, bristly-hairy, monoecious perennial found in rough, dry ground from the Mediterranean to S. Russia. The female flowers give rise to touch-sensitive fruit that squirt out seeds over great distances when ripe. Usually grown for the curiosity value of its fruit; it needs an open, sunny site. Where not hardy, treat as an annual.

• **CULTIVATION** Grow in well-drained, poor to moderately fertile soil in full sun.

• **PROPAGATION** Sow seed at 64°F (18°C) in early spring, and plant out seedlings when risk of frosts has passed.

• **PESTS AND DISEASES** Under glass, aphids and spider mites may be problems.

E. elaterium ■ Bushy or trailing perennial with long, bristly-hairy stems, and ovate-triangular, palmately 5-lobed, dark grayish green leaves, 2–6in (5–15cm) long, with shallow, wavy-margined lobes, rough-textured above, downy on the undersides. In summer,

Ecballium elaterium

produces widely funnel-shaped, pale yellow flowers, to 1in (2.5cm) across, sometimes with deeper yellow centers. Male flowers are produced in racemes; female flowers are solitary. Ovoid to cylindrical, hairy, blue-green fruit, to 2in (5cm) long, enclose many seeds in watery mucilage. ↕ to 20in (50cm), ↔ 3ft (1m) or more. Mediterranean. ❀ (min. 35°F/2°C)

▷ ***Eccremocactus bradei*** see *Weberocereus bradei*

ECCREMOCARPUS

Chilean glory flower

BIGNONIACEAE

Genus of 5 species of evergreen or herbaceous, climbing perennials from scrub and forest margins in Chile and Peru. They are grown for their colorful, terminal racemes of lopsidedly tubular flowers, which bloom in succession throughout the entire growing season. The leaves are opposite and 2-pinnate, each with a terminal, branched tendril. Where not hardy, grow in a cool greenhouse, or outside as annuals. In warmer areas, grow as short-lived perennials, to clothe an arch, pergola, or house wall, or to clamber through a large shrub or small tree.

• **CULTIVATION** Under glass, grow in well-drained, soil-based potting mix in full light. When in growth, water freely and apply a balanced liquid fertilizer monthly; water sparingly in winter. Outdoors, grow in fertile, well-drained soil in full sun. Provide support. Pruning group 11, in early spring.

• **PROPAGATION** Sow seed at 55–61°F (13–16°C) in late winter or early spring. Root tip cuttings with bottom heat in spring or summer.

• **PESTS AND DISEASES** Prone to spider mites and whiteflies under glass.

E. scaber ■ (Chilean glory flower). Slender, fast-growing, evergreen climber with sharply 4-angled stems, erect at first, then branching and spreading. Pinnate leaves, 2–3in (5–8cm) long, have small, ovate, boldly veined, light green, sometimes gray-tinted leaflets. From late spring to autumn, bears tubular, orange-red flowers, to 1in (2.5cm) long, swollen near the mouths, in racemes 4–6in (10–15cm) long. ↕ 10–15ft (3–5m), sometimes more. Chile. ❀ (min. 45°F/7°C). **Anglia Hybrids** is a mixed color selection with

Eccremocarpus scaber

red, pink, orange, or yellow flowers. **f. *aureus*** has golden yellow blooms. **f. *carmineus***, syn. 'Ruber', has carmine-red flowers. **f. *roseus*** has bright pink to light red flowers. **'Ruber'** see f. *carmineus.*

ECHEVERIA

CRASSULACEAE

Genus of about 150 species of evergreen and occasionally deciduous succulents and subshrubs found in dry, often semi-desert areas in Texas, Mexico, and from Central America to the Andes. The often spectacularly colorful leaves, usually in rosettes, are fleshy, alternate, and may be linear to cylindrical, spoon-shaped, or broadly triangular. The flowers have erect or spreading petal lobes, often slightly spreading at the tips or constricted at the mouths, and occasionally angled or keeled tubes. They are produced in racemes, cymes, or panicles, on long stalks from the leaf axils. Where not hardy, grow as houseplants or in a temperate greenhouse. Compact species may be used as annuals in carpet bedding. In warmer climates, plant outdoors in a border with other succulents. Some species tolerate short periods to 20°F (-7°C).

• **CULTIVATION** Under glass, grow in standard cactus potting mix in full light. While in growth, water moderately and apply a half-strength balanced liquid fertilizer monthly; keep just moist in winter. Place containerized plants outdoors during the frost-free months. Outdoors, grow in moderately fertile to poor, well-drained soil in full sun. See also pp.48–49.

• **PROPAGATION** Sow seed at 61–66°F (16–19°C) as soon as ripe. Root stem or leaf cuttings in late spring, or separate offsets in spring.

• **PESTS AND DISEASES** Prone to mealybugs, soft rot, and leaf and stem rots caused by a variety of fungi.

E. agavoides ■ Often clump-forming, very short-stemmed succulent with solitary or tufted rosettes of thick, ovate to ovate-triangular, sharply pointed, waxy, pale green leaves, 1¼–3½in (3–9cm) long, with transparent, often reddish brown margins. From spring to early summer, bears ovoid, yellow-tipped red flowers, to ½in (1.5cm) long, yellow inside, in one-sided cymes, to 20in (50cm) long. ↕ 6in (15cm), ↔ 12in (30cm) or more. Mexico. ❀ (min. 45°F/7°C)

E. ciliata. Short-stemmed, hairy succulent with dense rosettes of wedge-shaped to obovate, bristle-tipped, dark green leaves, to 2in (5cm) long, often margined red. In early summer, bears ovoid, green then red or yellow-red flowers, ½in (1.5cm) long, in one-sided cymes, 1½–5½in (4–14cm) long. ↕ to 7in (18cm), ↔ to 4in (10cm). Mexico. ❀ (min. 45°F/7°C)

E. cooperi see *Adromischus cooperi.*

E. crenulata. Short-stemmed succulent with loose rosettes of broadly obovate-diamond-shaped, pointed, pale green leaves, to 12in (30cm) long, with or without bristle tips, and with wavy or flat, red or red-brown margins. From early summer to winter, bears ovoid, yellowish red flowers, ½in (1.5cm) long, yellow inside, in panicle-like cymes, to 3ft (90cm) long. ↕ 12in (30cm) or more, ↔ 20in (50cm). Mexico. ❀ (min. 45°F/7°C)

E. derenbergii (Painted lady). Short-stemmed succulent with dense tufts or rosettes of wedge-shaped to obovate, thick, bristle-tipped, intensely white-frosted, light green leaves, to 1½in (4cm) long, tipped and margined red. From late winter to early summer, produces racemes, to 4in (10cm) long, of ovoid-bell-shaped yellow flowers, to ½in (1.5cm) long, with red petal lobes. ↕ 4in (10cm), ↔ to 12in (30cm). Mexico. ❀ (min. 45°F/7°C)

E. elegans ■ (Mexican gem). Stemless or short-stemmed, clump-forming succulent with rounded rosettes of obovate to spoon-shaped, sometimes red-margined, silvery blue leaves, 1¼–2½in (3–6cm) long. From late winter to early summer, produces solitary, one-sided cymes, to 10in (25cm) long, of ovoid, yellow-tipped pink flowers, ½in (1.5cm) long, yellow-orange inside. ↕ 2in (5cm), ↔ 20in (50cm). Mexico. ❀ (min. 45°F/7°C)

E.* x *fruticosa see X *Pachyveria glauca.*

E. gibbiflora. Simple-stemmed or few-branched succulent that produces terminal rosettes of obovate-spoon-shaped, pointed, wavy-margined, gray-green leaves, to 14in (35cm) long, often tinged reddish brown. Panicle-like cymes, to 3ft (1m) long, of ovoid-bell-shaped, pale red flowers, to ¾in (2cm) long, yellow inside, are borne from late summer to winter. ↕ 12in (30cm), ↔ 6in (15cm). Mexico. ❀ (min. 45°F/7°C) **'Carunculata'** has wart-like protuberances on the upper leaf surfaces, causing the margins to curl and twist. **'Metallica'** bears white- or red-margined, purple-green leaves maturing to green-bronze.

E. goldieana. Stemless or very short-stemmed, clump-forming succulent with dense rosettes of broadly obovate, thick, glossy, mid-green leaves, to 1½in (4cm) long, blunt with small points. From spring to early summer, produces racemes, 16in (40cm) long, of pitcher-shaped, nodding pink flowers, to ½in (1.5cm) long, with greenish yellow tips. ↕ 2½in (6cm), ↔ to 5in (13cm). Mexico. ❀ (min. 45°F/7°C)

E. harmsii, syn. *Oliveranthus elegans.* Bushy succulent with softly hairy branches, each branch crowned with a rosette of narrow, inversely lance-shaped, pointed, slightly hairy, red-margined, light green leaves, ¾–2in

Echeveria agavoides

Echeveria elegans

(2–5cm) long. In spring, produces urn-shaped, orange-tipped red flowers, 1¼in (3cm) long, yellow inside, in racemes to 8in (20cm) long. ↕↔ 12in (30cm). Mexico. ❀ (min. 45°F/7°C)

E. nodulosa. Erect then prostrate succulent covered in minute, prickly-tipped white papillae. Thick, obovate-spoon-shaped leaves, 2in (5cm) long, light green with red margins and keels, are arranged in loose rosettes or scattered. From early summer to autumn, produces ovoid-angular, yellow-tipped red flowers, ½in (1.5cm) long, yellow inside, in racemes to 12in (30cm) long. ↕ 12in (30cm), ↔ to 16in (40cm). S. Mexico. ❀ (min. 45°F/7°C)

E. peacockii (Peacock echeveria). Stemless or short-stemmed succulent producing dense rosettes of obovate-oblong, slightly tapering, pointed or bristle-tipped, white-frosted leaves, to 3in (8cm) long, with red tips and margins. In early summer, bears ovoid, deep red or red-pink flowers, to ½in (1.5cm) long, in one-sided cymes, 12in (30cm) or more long. ↕ to 5in (13cm), ↔ 10in (25cm). Mexico. ❀ (min. 45°F/7°C)

E. pilosa ■ Short-stemmed, sparsely branched or unbranched succulent,

Echeveria pilosa

Echeveria pulvinata

densely covered with white hairs. Loose rosettes of thick, spoon-shaped, mid-green leaves, 3in (8cm) long, with wedge-shaped ends, are borne on reddish brown stems. From spring to summer, produces ovoid flowers, to ½in (1.5cm) long, dull orange-red outside, yellow inside and on the tips, in raceme-like cymes, 12in (30cm) long. ↕ 4in (10cm), ↔ 16in (40cm). Mexico. ❀ (min. 45°F/7°C)

E. pulvinata ■ (Plush plant). Bushy succulent with brown-felted stems, each producing a lax rosette of spoon-shaped-obovate, fine-pointed, thick, softly white-hairy, mid-green leaves, 1–2½in (2.5–6cm) long, the margins turning red in autumn. From winter to early summer, produces loose panicles, 8–12in (20–30cm) long, of ovoid to urn-shaped, red-keeled, yellow or yellow-red flowers, to ¾in (2cm) long. ↕ 12in (30cm), ↔ 20in (50cm). S. Mexico. ❀ (min. 45°F/7°C). **'Ruby'** bears densely hairy, light red leaves.

E. secunda ■ Short-stemmed, clump-forming succulent with often decumbent, dense, basal rosettes of spoon- to wedge-shaped, blunt, bristle-tipped, glaucous, pale green to gray leaves, to 2in (5cm) long, with red tips and margins. In late spring and early summer, bears ovoid red flowers, to ½in (1.5cm) long, yellow inside, in one-sided cymes, to 12in (30cm) long. ↕ 1½in (4cm), ↔ 12in (30cm). Mexico. ❀ (min. 45°F/7°C). **var. *pumila*** produces very tiny leaves, to only ½in (1.5cm) across.

E. setosa (Mexican firecracker). Stemless succulent with dense, nearly spherical rosettes of inversely lance-shaped to

Echeveria secunda

spoon-shaped, pointed, bristle-tipped, mid-green leaves, 3in (8cm) long, densely covered with white hairs. From late spring to summer, urn-shaped, yellow-tipped red flowers, ½in (1.5cm) or more long, yellow inside, are produced in one-sided cymes, to 12in (30cm) long. ↕ 1½in (4cm), ↔ 12in (30cm). Mexico. ❀ (min. 45°F/7°C)

ECHIDNOPSIS

ASCLEPIADACEAE

Genus of about 20 species of very variable, perennial succulents from low hillsides in Saudi Arabia, Oman, Yemen, and tropical E. Africa and South Africa. They have branching, prostrate to erect, spherical to short-columnar stems, each with 6- to 20-angled, dark green ribs, usually divided into hexagonal tubercles. Tiny, gray-green leaves are short-lived, sometimes persisting as white spines on the tubercles. Saucer- to bell-shaped, 5-lobed, fleshy flowers, with whorled, cup-shaped corollas, are borne in clusters, mainly at the stem tips. Where not hardy, grow as houseplants or in a warm greenhouse; in warm, dry climates, grow outdoors in a border with other succulents.

• **CULTIVATION** Under glass, grow in equal parts of soil-based potting mix and grit, in full light and with good ventilation. In growth, water moderately and apply a balanced liquid fertilizer monthly; water very sparingly in winter. Outdoors, grow in moderately fertile, sharply drained soil in full sun. See also pp.48–49.

• **PROPAGATION** In spring or summer, sow seed at 70–75°F (21–24°C), or take stem cuttings, ensuring the cut surface forms a complete callus before inserting.

• **PESTS AND DISEASES** Vulnerable to black rot if overwatered, especially if temperatures fall below 61°F (16°C).

E. chrysantha see *E. scutellata* subsp. *planiflora.*

E. dammanniana. Erect or curved succulent with 8-angled, ribbed stems, each rib divided into small, irregular tubercles. From late spring to summer, produces clusters of 2–5 flowers, to ½in (1.5cm) wide; the cup-shaped corollas and spreading lobes vary from yellow, densely spotted with purplish maroon, to purplish maroon; the coronas are yellowish purple. ↕ 8in (20cm), ↔ to 10in (25cm). N. Ethiopia. ❀ (min. 61°F/16°C)

E. scutellata. Erect or prostrate succulent with 8- or 9-angled, ribbed stems, each rib divided into hexagonal-conical tubercles. In late spring, bears solitary or paired flowers, to ½in (1.5cm) wide: the saucer- to bell-shaped corollas are yellow or yellowish green (often with purple mottling on the exterior), with triangular to ovoid-triangular, minutely warty lobes; the coronas are yellow, with red-spotted throats. ↕ to 12in (30cm), ↔ indefinite. Saudi Arabia, Yemen, Somalia. ❀ (min. 61°F/16°C). **subsp. *planiflora,*** syn. *E. chrysantha,* has 8- to 15-angled, ribbed stems, and flowers varying in color from brown, suffused yellow near the centers, to bright yellow with pale green outsides; coronas vary from yellow to red-brown; Ethiopia, Djibouti, Somalia.

E

ECHINACEA

Coneflower

ASTERACEAE

Genus of about 5 species of bold, stiff perennials from dry prairies, gravelly hillsides, and open woodland in C. and E. North America, usually with thick, black rootstocks and short rhizomes. Erect, hairy stems bear linear-lance-shaped to ovate, entire, toothed, or deeply pinnatifid, bristly, dark green leaves. Solitary, daisy-like, purple, red, pink, or white flowerheads, with pointed, stiff scales on the undersides and prominent, ovoid or cone-shaped, brownish yellow to orange central disks, are produced terminally on thick, sometimes sparsely branched stems. Grow in a herbaceous border or in open woodland.

• **CULTIVATION** Grow in deep, well-drained, humus-rich soil in full sun, although they will tolerate some shade. Cut back stems as the blooms fade to encourage further flower production and to prevent excessive self-seeding.

• **PROPAGATION** Sow seed at 55°F (13°C) in spring. Divide clumps in spring every 3 or 4 years. Insert root cuttings from late autumn to early winter. Deadheading prolongs flowering.

• **PESTS AND DISEASES** Leaf miners, powdery mildew, bacterial spots, and gray mold are problems. Vine weevils may attack roots.

Echinacea purpurea 'White Lustre'

E. angustifolia. Erect perennial with lance-shaped to linear, hairy, entire leaves, to 6in (15cm) long, the stem leaves stalkless. In early summer, produces flowerheads, to 6in (15cm) across, with conical, orange-brown disks and narrow, arching, pink or purple-pink, occasionally white ray florets, 1¼–1¾in (3–4.5cm) long. ↕ to 4ft (1.2m), ↔ 18in (45cm). S. Canada to Texas. Zone 5.

E. pallida (Pink coneflower). Erect perennial with linear-lance-shaped to elliptic, entire leaves, to 8in (20cm) long. In summer, bears flowerheads, 4–6in (10–15cm) across, with conical, orange-brown disks, and narrow, pendulous, pink, rose, or white ray florets, 1½–3½in (4–9cm) long. ↕ 3–4ft (1–1.2m), ↔ 24in (60cm). S. central US. Zone 4.

E. purpurea syn. *Rudbeckia purpurea.* Erect perennial with smooth, sometimes rough-hairy, red-tinted green stems, ovate, toothed, rough-hairy basal leaves, 6in (15cm) long, and ovate-lance-shaped, toothed stem leaves. From mid-summer to early autumn, bears flower-heads to 5in (13cm) across, with conical, golden brown disks and partly reflexed, purplish red ray florets, 1¼–3in (3–8cm) long. ↕ to 5ft (1.5m), ↔ 18in (45cm). Michigan and Virginia to Louisiana and Georgia. Zone 3b. **'Bravado'** has flowerheads, 4–4½in (10–11cm) across, with horizontal, rose-red ray florets; ↕ 24in (60cm). **'Bright Star'** see 'Leuchtstern'. **'Finale White'** has single, creamy white flowerheads, 4in (10cm) across, with greenish brown disks; ↕ 12–16in (30–40cm), ↔ 16–18in (40–45cm). **'Leuchtstern'**, syn. 'Bright Star', has purple-red flowerheads; ↕ to 32in (80cm). **'Magnus'** has flowerheads to 7in (18cm) across, with dark orange disks, the ray florets deep purple and more horizontal than in other cultivars. **'Robert Bloom'** ▣ has prominent, dark orange-brown disks and mauve-crimson ray florets. **'The King'** has arching, pinkish crimson ray florets and ovate, orange-brown disks. **'White Lustre'** ▣ has creamy white flowerheads with orange-brown disks; ↕ to 32in (80cm). **'White Swan'** has white flowerheads, to 4½in (11cm) across, with orange-brown disks; ↕ to 24in (60cm).

E. tennesseensis (Tennessee coneflower). Erect perennial with linear leaves, 4–6in (10–15cm) long. In summer, produces flowerheads, to 4in (10cm) across, with conical, greenish pink disks, and upturned, dark mauve ray florets, 1¼in (3cm) long. May be overrun by more aggressive plants. ↕ 24–36in (60–90cm), ↔ 18in (45cm). S.E. US. Zone 5.

Echinacea purpurea 'Robert Bloom'

ECHINOCACTUS

CACTACEAE

Genus of about 15 species of slow-growing, spherical, barrel-shaped or columnar cacti from low, open scrubland in S.W. US and Mexico. They have prominent, heavily spined ribs and large areoles forming densely woolly crowns, from which rings of diurnal, bell-shaped, yellow, pink, red, or magenta flowers develop in summer on mature plants. Ovoid, white-woolly fruits contain large black or dark brown seeds. Where not hardy, grow in a warm greenhouse; elsewhere, plant in a desert garden.

• **HARDINESS** Mature specimens of all species are hardy to 20°F (-7°C), and some tolerate brief periods to 10°F (-12°C). Immature specimens, however, are hardy only to 50°F (10°C).

• **CULTIVATION** Under glass, grow in standard cactus potting mix in full light. From midspring to early autumn, water freely and apply a half-strength balanced liquid fertilizer every 4 weeks; keep totally dry at other times of the year. Outdoors, grow in fertile, well-drained soil in full sun. See also pp.48–49.

• **PROPAGATION** Sow seed at 70°F (21°C) in spring.

• **PESTS AND DISEASES** Basal stem rot, soft rot, and mealybugs are common on small plants.

E. asterias see *Astrophytum asterias.*

E. capricornis see *Astrophytum capricorne.*

E. chilensis see *Neoporteria chilensis.*

E. grusonii ▣ (Golden barrel cactus, Mother-in-law's cushion). Spherical, eventually elongating cactus with a bright green stem bearing 20–40 sharply angled ribs. Yellow areoles produce golden yellow spines (8–10 radials and 3–5 centrals). Bears bright yellow flowers, 1½–2½in (4–6cm) long, in summer. ↕ to 24in (60cm), ↔ to 32in (80cm). C. Mexico.

E. hartmannii see *Discocactus hartmannii.*

E. horizonthalonius (Mule-crippler cactus). Spherical to columnar cactus with a blue-green or gray-green stem bearing 7–13 often spirally arranged ribs. Brown areoles produce brown spines (6–9 radials and 1 central). Rose-red or pink flowers, 2–3in (5–8cm) long, darker near their bases, are produced in summer. ↕ to 10in (25cm), ↔ to 16in (40cm). W. Texas, New Mexico, N. Mexico.

E. ingens see *E. platyacanthus.*

E. myriostigma see *Astrophytum myriostigma.*

E. ornatus see *Astrophytum ornatum.*

E. platyacanthus, syn. *E. ingens.* Spherical cactus with a fresh green stem bearing 20–60 very pronounced ribs. Gray areoles produce grayish brown or yellow-brown spines (about 4 radials and 3 or 4 centrals). In summer, bears golden yellow flowers, 1¼–2½in (3–6cm) long, with brown-tipped outer tepals. ↕↔ to 3ft (1m). C. and N. Mexico.

E. polycephalus ▣ Spherical, often elongating, clump-forming cactus with

Echinocactus grusonii

Echinocactus polycephalus

13- to 21-ribbed, gray-green stems. Whitish gray areoles bear reddish brown spines (4–8 flattish radials and 4 centrals). In summer, produces yellow flowers, 2–2½in (5–6cm) long, the outer tepals with pink midribs. ↕ to 28in (70cm), ↔ 10in (25cm). California, S. Utah, N. Arizona, N. Mexico.
E. ritteri see *Aztekium ritteri*.
E. scheerii see *Sclerocactus scheerii*.
E. texensis, syn. *Homalocephala texensis*. Flattened-spherical or barrel-shaped cactus with a 13- to 27-ribbed, grayish green stem. Well-spaced, white-woolly areoles bear red-brown spines (6 or 7 radials and 1 thicker central). Bears satiny, pale reddish pink flowers, 2–2½in (5–6cm) long, with pink to orange-red throats and paler, irregular margins, in summer. ↕ to 6in (15cm), ↔ to 12in (30cm). Texas, S. New Mexico, N.E. Mexico.
E. uncinatus see *Sclerocactus uncinatus*.

ECHINOCEREUS

CACTACEAE

Genus of about 45 species of solitary or clump-forming cacti found in lowland deserts to open, dry uplands in S. and S.W. US and Mexico. They produce spherical to cylindrical, prominently ribbed stems and are noted for their very colorful, diurnal flowers, which are generally large and usually funnel- or bell-shaped. Where not hardy, grow on a sunny windowsill or in a cool or temperate greenhouse; in warmer areas, plant in a desert garden.

• **CULTIVATION** Under glass, grow in standard cactus potting mix in full light. From midspring to early autumn, water freely and apply a half-strength balanced liquid fertilizer monthly; keep totally dry at other times. Outdoors, grow in well-drained soil in full sun. Some tolerate brief periods to 20°F (-7°C), making them among the hardiest species in the Cactaceae. See also pp.48–49.

• **PROPAGATION** Sow seed at 70°F (21°C) in early spring. Root stem cuttings in spring or summer.

• **PESTS AND DISEASES** Stem rot, soft rot, scale insects, and mealybugs are common on small plants.

E. baileyi see *E. reichenbachii* var. *baileyi*.
E. brandegeei. Erect or decumbent, clump-forming cactus with cylindrical, 6- to 8-ribbed, warty, dull, pale green stems, 1½–2½in (4–6cm) thick.

Echinocereus leucanthus

Yellowish green areoles bear yellowish red or yellowish white spines (12 radials and 4 centrals). Produces bell-shaped, purplish pink flowers, to 3in (8cm) long, with red throats, in early summer. ↕ 3ft (1m), ↔ to 20in (50cm). Mexico (Baja California). ❄ (min. 45°F/7°C)
E. cinerascens. Clump-forming cactus with spherical to cylindrical, 5- to 12-ribbed, sometimes warty, bright green stems, 1½–3in (4–8cm) thick. Bright green areoles bear yellowish white or red spines (8–10 radials and 1–4 centrals). Funnel-shaped, bright pink or purple flowers, 2½–4in (6–10cm) across, with paler, greenish pink throats, are borne in early summer. ↕ 4–24in (10–60cm), ↔ to 3ft (1m). N., C., and E. Mexico. ❄ (min. 45°F/7°C)
E. engelmannii. Semi-erect, clump-forming cactus with cylindrical, 10- to 14-ribbed, densely spiny, mid-green stems, 1½–3in (4–8cm) thick. Large, mid-green areoles bear variously colored spines (10–12 radials and 2–6 longer centrals). Produces broadly funnel-shaped, purple-red to magenta or lavender-pink flowers, 3in (8cm) across, in early summer. ↕ 2–24in (5–60cm), ↔ to 18in (45cm). S.W. US, N.W. Mexico. ❄ (min. 45°F/7°C)
E. fendleri. Solitary or clump-forming cactus with ovoid to cylindrical, variably warty, 9- to 18-ribbed, dull or brownish green stems, 1½–3in (4–8cm) thick. Green areoles bear brown spines (about 8 radials and 1 longer central). From spring to early summer, produces broadly bell-shaped, purplish violet or purple-magenta to white flowers, 3½in (9cm) long, which darken toward the sometimes green-tinged centers and have jagged petal margins. ↕ 3–20in (8–50cm), ↔ to 12in (30cm). S. Utah, Arizona, New Mexico, N.W. Mexico. ❄ (min. 45°F/7°C)
E. knippelianus. Erect, solitary or clustering cactus with spherical, almost ovoid, dark green stems, to 3in (8cm) thick, offsetting from the base, with 5–8 rounded ribs divided by broad furrows. Small green areoles bear 1–3 bristly, short-lived, yellow radial spines. Funnel-shaped, pink, lavender-pink, purple, or white flowers, to 1½in (4cm) long, are produced from spring to early summer. ↕ to 8in (20cm), usually smaller, ↔ 6in (15cm). N.E. Mexico. ❄ (min. 45°F/7°C)
E. leucanthus ■ syn. *Wilcoxia albiflora*. Clambering cactus, freely branching from the base, with cylindrical, 8- to 12-ribbed, dark green stems, to ¼in (6mm) thick. Brown areoles bear 10–12 yellow, sometimes almost black radial spines. Wide-spreading, funnel-shaped white flowers, ¾–1½in (2–4cm) long, with greenish brown throats, and sometimes pale pink midstripes, are borne in early summer. ↕ to 3ft (1m), ↔ 12in (30cm). N.W. Mexico. ❄ (min. 45°F/7°C)
E. maritimus. Variable, erect, clump-forming cactus with spherical or slightly cylindrical, 8- to 10-ribbed, greenish gray stems, 1in (2.5cm) thick. Bright green areoles bear grayish white or red, later grayish yellow to gray spines (9 or 10 radials and 1–4 longer centrals). Funnel-shaped, brown- or red-tinged yellow flowers, 1½in (4cm) long, are produced in early summer. ↕ 6in (15cm), ↔ indefinite. N.W. Mexico. ❄ (min. 45°F/7°C)
E. pectinatus. Erect, solitary or eventually sparsely branched cactus with spherical or cylindrical, 12- to 23-ribbed, mid-green stems, 3–4in (8–10cm) thick. Mid-green areoles produce comb-like, pinkish white spines (up to 30 radials and 3 shorter centrals). In late spring and early summer, bears funnel-shaped, pale pinkish lavender, sometimes magenta or yellow flowers, 3–5in (8–13cm) long, green at the bases, with white or maroon throats. ↕ 3–14in (8–35cm), ↔ 8in (20cm). S.W. US, N. Mexico. ❄ (min. 45°F/7°C)
E. pentalophus ■ syn. *E. procumbens*. Prostrate or erect, clump-forming cactus with cylindrical, 4- to 8-ribbed, pale to dark green stems, ¾in (2cm) thick. White areoles bear about 6 yellow or white radial spines. Bears bell-shaped,

Echinocereus pentalophus

Echinocereus pulchellus

lilac to carmine-red or bright pink-magenta flowers, to 4in (10cm) long, with white or yellow throats, rarely entirely white, in early summer. ↕ 8in (20cm), ↔ 24in (60cm). Texas, E. and N.E. Mexico. ❄ (min. 45°F/7°C)
E. procumbens see *E. pentalophus*.
E. pulchellus ■ Erect, solitary or clustering cactus that branches at the base. Spherical or hemispherical, gray to bluish green stems, 1½–2in (4–5cm) thick, have 11–13 low, warty ribs. White areoles bear 3 or 4 yellow to gray radial spines. Widely spreading, funnel-shaped, bright rose-pink, pink, magenta, or white flowers, 1½in (4cm) long, with white margins, are produced in late spring and early summer. ↕ 2in (5cm), ↔ 6in (15cm). N. and S. central Mexico. ❄ (min. 45°F/7°C)
E. reichenbachii (Lace cactus). Variable, erect cactus with usually solitary, spherical to cylindrical, light to dark green stems, to 4in (10cm) thick, with up to 19 ribs. Light to dark green areoles bear 12–40 white or brown radial spines. Bears broadly funnel-shaped, pink to purple or magenta flowers, 3in (8cm) across, with darker throats, from spring to early summer. ↕ to 14in (35cm), ↔ 8in (20cm). Kansas, Oklahoma, Texas, N. Mexico. ❄ (min. 45°F/7°C). **var. *baileyi***, syn. *E. baileyi*, is sparsely branched, with 12–15 ribs. Areoles produce up to 14 radials and sometimes 1–3 centrals. Rich pink flowers have darker petal bases. ↕↔ to 8in (20cm). Oklahoma, Texas.
E. rigidissimus ■ Usually solitary, globose to cylindrical cactus with no central spines; 15–35 radial spines are

Echinocereus rigidissimus

E

Echinocereus triglochidiatus var. *paucispinus*

flattened against the stems, often with bands of red, white, and yellowish to brownish around stems. Funnel-shaped flowers break through the epidermis at the sides of stem; brilliant pinkish red to magenta with white throats, 2½–2¾in (6–7cm) long, 2½–3½in (6–9cm) in diameter. Produces ovoid, green to red, fleshy fruit, with heavy spination. It grows well in pots, in very bright light. ↕ to 12in (30cm), ↔ to 4½in (11cm). Arizona, New Mexico, Sonora, Mexico. **var. *rubispinus*** has 30–35 radial spines flattened against its stems. ↕ to 4½in (11cm), ↔ 2½in (6cm). Chihuahua, Mexico. ❀ (min. 45°F/7°C)

E. subinermis. Erect, solitary or sparsely clustered cactus with spherical then cylindrical, 5- to 8-ribbed, shallow-furrowed, bluish green or dark green stems, 3–3½in (7–9cm) thick at the bases. Dark green areoles bear yellow spines (3–8 radials and often 1 central). Produces broadly funnel-shaped, bright yellow flowers, 3in (8cm) long, in early summer. ↕↔ to 12in (30cm). N., N.W., and C. Mexico. ❀ (min. 45°F/7°C)

E. triglochidiatus. Very variable, erect, solitary or clustering cactus with ovoid to cylindrical, 6- to 12-ribbed, sometimes warty, dark green stems, 2–6in (5–15cm) thick. Dark green, woolly areoles bear pale brown spines (3–16 radials and often 1 central). Funnel-shaped, bright red flowers, to 3in (8cm) long, are produced from spring to early summer. ↕ 12in (30cm), ↔ 6in (15cm). S. US, N. Mexico. ❀ (min. 45°F/7°C). **var. *paucispinus*** ■ has 6- or 7-ribbed stems, 4in (10cm) thick. Areoles bear 4–6 radial spines and no centrals. Orange-red flowers, 3in (8cm) long, are borne in spring; ↕ 8in (20cm), ↔ to 20in (50cm). Texas.

▷ ***Echinofossulocactus*** see *Stenocactus*

ECHINOMASTUS

CACTACEAE

Genus of 7 species of usually solitary small globose or short cylindrical cacti from the deserts of the S.W. US and N. Mexico. Their distinct, spiny tubercles often obscure the stems. The stem tips bear flowers that can be purple to pinkish to white. The elongated fruit is scaly and dry at maturity, each one dehiscing by a basal pore.

• **CULTIVATION** Under glass, grow in a mix of 4 parts standard cactus potting mix and 1 part limestone chips, in full light. From spring to summer, water freely and apply a balanced liquid fertilizer every 4-5 weeks. Keep nearly dry at other times. Outdoors, grow in moderately fertile, slightly alkaline, sharply drained, humus-rich soil in full sun. See also pp.48–49.

• **PROPAGATION** Sow seed at 70°F (21°C) in spring or summer.

• **PESTS AND DISEASES** Scale occurs.

E. johnsonii. Ovoid or cylindrical cactus densely covered with spines, bearing 17–21 ribs, strongly indented above each tubercle. Areoles bear pinkish to reddish spines (4–9 central, 9–10 lighter-colored radial, half as thick). Funnel-like flowers are magenta, pink, or greenish yellow, 2–2½in (5–6cm) long; 2–3in (5–7.5cm) across. ↕ 4–10in (10–25cm), ↔ 2–4in (5–10cm). E. California, S. Nevada, W. Arizona. ❀ (min. 50°F/10°C)

E. macdowellii see *Thelocactus macdowellii*

E. unguispinus. Solitary, globose or short cylindrical, bluish green cactus, densely covered with spines with 18–21 ribs. Areoles bear short spines (3–9 central, 15–30 irregularly spreading radial). Produces brownish red funnel-shaped flowers, to 1in (2.5cm) long. ↔ 8–14cm), ↔ 2¾–4½in (7–11cm). Chihuahua, Coahuila, Durango, Zacatecas, San Luis Potosi, Mexico. ❀ (min. 50°F/10°C)

ECHINOPS

Globe thistle

ASTERACEAE

Genus of approximately 120 species of perennials, biennials, and annuals found in hot, gravelly slopes and dry grassland from C. and S. Europe to C. Asia, India, and the mountains of tropical Africa. Globe thistles have simple, entire or pinnatifid to pinnatisect, spiny foliage, usually grayish white and woolly. They bear spherical, white, gray, or blue terminal flowerheads with bristly bracts. Undemanding plants, they are suitable for a large border or wild garden. They are also good for cutting and drying.

• **CULTIVATION** Best grown in poor, well-drained soil in full sun, but will grow in almost any soil in full sun or partial shade. Deadhead to prevent self-seeding.

• **PROPAGATION** Sow seed in a seedbed in midspring. Divide perennials from

Echinops bannaticus

Echinops ritro 'Veitch's Blue'

autumn to spring, or insert root cuttings in autumn.

• **PESTS AND DISEASES** Susceptible to infestation by aphids.

E. bannaticus ■ Clump-forming perennial with densely gray-woolly stems and ovate to elliptic, subentire to 2-pinnatisect, spiny, hairy, gray-green leaves, to 10in (25cm) long. Spherical, blue-gray to blue flowerheads, 1–2in (2.5–5cm) across, are borne in mid- and late summer. ↕ 1½–4ft (0.5–1.2m), ↔ 24in (60cm). S.E. Europe. Zone 3b. **'Blue Globe'** bears dark blue flowerheads, 2½in (6cm) across, and blooms again if stems are cut back after flowering; ↕ to 3ft (1m). **'Taplow Blue'** has bright blue flowerheads.

E. giganteus. Imposing perennial with erect, woolly stems and obovate to lance-shaped, pinnatifid, bristly leaves, 18in (45cm) long, which are white-hairy beneath. In midsummer, produces solitary, sometimes multiple, spherical, grayish blue flowerheads, 8in (20cm) across. ↕ to 15ft (5m), ↔ 30in (75cm). Ethiopia. Zone 4.

E. niveus. Slender but sturdy, clump-forming perennial with lance-shaped to

Echinops sphaerocephalus

elliptic, deeply pinnatisect, spiny leaves, 3–8in (7–20cm) long, with linear segments, mid-green above, densely white-woolly beneath. In late summer, gray stems bear spherical, blue-gray or white flowerheads, 1½–3in (3.5–8cm) across. ↕ to 6ft (1.8m), ↔ 24in (60cm). W. Himalayas. Zone 4.

E. ritro (Small globe thistle). Compact, clump-forming perennial with oblong-elliptic, pinnatifid to pinnatisect, stiff, spiny leaves, to 8in (20cm) long, dark green and cobweb-like above, white-downy beneath. In late summer, bears spherical flowerheads, 1–1¾in (2.5–4.5cm) across, metallic-blue before the florets open, maturing to a brighter blue. ↕ to 24in (60cm), ↔ 18in (45cm). S. central and S.E. Europe to C. Asia. Zone 3. **'Veitch's Blue'** ■ is remontant, with slightly darker blue flowerheads, and is good for cutting; ↕ to 3ft (90cm).

E. sphaerocephalus ■ Vigorous, clump-forming perennial with oblong-elliptic, pinnatifid or 2-pinnatifid to pinnatisect, spiny, gray-green leaves, to 14in (35cm) long, hairy beneath. Spherical, silvery gray flowerheads, 1¼–2½in (3–6cm) across, are borne on thick gray stems in mid- and late summer. ↕ to 6ft (2m), ↔ 3ft (1m). C. and S. Europe, Caucasus, Russia (Siberia). Zone 3b.

ECHINOPSIS

CACTACEAE

Genus of 50–120 species of sometimes shrubby or tree-like, perennial cacti occurring in South America, in habitats ranging from lowland deserts to upland dry scrub. They have mainly spherical stems with straight ribs and spiny areoles. Large, trumpet-shaped to almost bell-shaped flowers are produced laterally or near the ends of the stems from spring to summer. On species native to mountainous regions to 10,000ft (3,000m) high, the flowers are white, yellow, red, purple, or pink, and open during the day; on plants that grow naturally at much lower altitudes, the flowers are mainly white or pale pink, and open at night. Where not hardy, grow as houseplants or in a temperate or warm greenhouse. In warmer areas, grow in a desert garden.

• **CULTIVATION** Under glass, grow in standard cactus potting mix in full light. In the growing season, water freely and apply a nitrogen- and potassium-based fertilizer monthly; keep completely dry in winter. Outdoors, grow in well-drained soil in full sun. Many species tolerate brief periods to 20°F (-7°C). See also pp.48–49.

• **PROPAGATION** Sow seed at 70°F (21°C) in spring, or remove offsets in spring or summer.

• **PESTS AND DISEASES** Prone to mealybugs, stem rot, and soft rot.

E. backebergii ■ syn. *Lobivia backebergii.* Solitary or clump-forming cactus with spherical to obovoid, mid- to dark green stems, 1½–2in (4–5cm) thick, bearing about 15 spirally notched ribs. White-woolly areoles produce 3–7 red-brown, later gray radial spines, sometimes curved or hooked. In summer, produces diurnal, carmine-red or violet flowers, 2in (5cm)

Echinopsis backebergii

long, with paler throats. ↕ 2in (5cm), ↔ indefinite. E. Bolivia, S. Peru. ❀ (min. 50°F/10°C)

E. candicans ▣ syn. *Trichocereus candicans*. Erect or semi-prostrate, clump-forming cactus with cylindrical to hemispherical, bright, light green stems, 6in (15cm) thick, bearing 9–11 prominent ribs. Large white areoles bear yellowish brown spines (10–14 radials and 1 or more centrals). Nocturnal, fragrant white flowers, 7–10in (18–25cm) long, are borne in summer. ↕ to 24in (60cm), ↔ to 20in (50cm). W. Argentina. ❀ (min. 50°F/10°C)

E. cinnabarina, syn. *Lobivia cinnabarina*. Solitary cactus with flattened-spherical to spherical, dark green stems, to 6in (15cm) thick, bearing about 20 notched, acutely warty ribs. White areoles produce light brownish gray spines (8–12 radials and 2 or 3 stouter centrals). Diurnal, short-tubed, rich scarlet flowers, 1½in (4cm) long, are produced from spring to summer. ↕↔ to 6in (15cm). Bolivia. ❀ (min. 50°F/10°C)

E. ferox, syn. *Lobivia ferox*. Solitary cactus with spherical, 15- to 30-ribbed, pale gray-green stems, to 12in (30cm)

Echinopsis candicans

Echinopsis lageniformis

thick. Gray areoles bear initially brown, then gray spines (8–12 radials and about 3 centrals). Diurnal white, rarely pink, flowers, 3–4½in (7–11cm) long, are produced in summer. ↕↔ 12in (30cm) or more. Bolivia to N. Argentina. ❀ (min. 50°F/10°C)

E. huascha, syn. *Trichocereus huascha, T. grandiflorus*. Offsetting, erect to semi-prostrate cactus with many-branched, 12- to 18-ribbed, dark green stems, 2–3in (5–8cm) thick. Whitish brown areoles bear dark yellow to brown spines (9–11 radials and 1 or 2 centrals). Diurnal, golden yellow or red flowers, 3–4in (7–10cm) long, are produced in summer. ↕↔ to 3ft (1m). Argentina. ❀ (min. 50°F/10°C)

E. lageniformis ▣ syn. *Trichocereus bridgesii*. Tree-like cactus with columnar, glaucous, pale to dark green stems, to 6in (15cm) thick, bearing 4–8 rounded ribs. Gray areoles produce 2–6 yellow radial spines. Nocturnal white flowers, 7in (18cm) long, are produced in summer. ↕ 6ft (2m) or more, ↔ 8in (20cm) or more. Bolivia. ❀ (min. 50°F/10°C)

E. maximiliana, syn. *Lobivia caespitosa*. Clump-forming cactus with depressed-spherical to obovoid or cylindrical, pale green stems, 2½–3in (6–8cm) thick, each with 12–17 ribs divided by cross-furrows into hatchet-shaped tubercles. White areoles bear brown spines (7–12 radials and 1 longer, up-curving central). Diurnal, red or scarlet flowers, 2–3in (5–8cm) long, with orange-yellow throats, and sometimes darker-tipped inner petals, are produced in summer. ↕↔ 3in (8cm). S. Peru, N. Bolivia. ❀ (min. 50°F/10°C)

E. multiplex see *E. oxygona*.

E. oxygona ▣ syn. *E. multiplex*. Clustering cactus with spherical or cylindrical, 12- to 15-ribbed, mid-green stems, to 8in (20cm) thick, offsetting from the base and sides. Large, white-woolly areoles bear yellowish brown spines (10–15 radials and 2–7 longer centrals). In summer, diurnal flowers,

Echinopsis oxygona

to 8in (20cm) long, are produced with dark reddish brown tubes and pink-flushed white outer petals. ↕ 10–12in (25–30cm), ↔ to 12in (30cm). N. Argentina, Uruguay, S. Brazil. ❀ (min. 50°F/10°C)

E. pentlandii ▣ syn. *Lobivia pentlandii*. Clump-forming cactus with spherical to obovoid, mid-green stems, to 6in (15cm) thick, bearing 15 or more warty ribs. Gray areoles produce brown spines (5–15 radials and sometimes 1 central). Diurnal, yellow, orange, pink, red, or purple flowers, 2–3in (5–8cm) long, with white throats, are produced from spring to summer. ↕ to 6in (15cm), ↔ 12in (30cm). S. Peru, N. Bolivia. ❀ (min. 50°F/10°C)

E. rhodotricha. Solitary or clump-forming cactus with spherical, then cylindrical, 8- to 13-ribbed, mid-green stems, 3½in (9cm) thick. White-felted areoles bear brown-tipped, pale yellow spines (4–7 radials and sometimes 1 longer central). Diurnal white flowers, 6in (15cm) long, are produced from spring to summer. ↕ 12in (30cm), ↔ 8in (20cm). Paraguay, N.E. Argentina. ❀ (min. 50°F/10°C)

E. schickendantzii, syn. *Trichocereus shaferi*. Shrub-like cactus with oblong to cylindrical, bright green stems, 2½in (6cm) thick, bearing about 14–18 prominent ribs. White areoles produce about 10 yellow radial spines. White flowers, to 8in (20cm) long, are produced by day or night in summer. ↕ to 12in (30cm), ↔ 5in (13cm). W. Argentina. ❀ (min. 50°F/10°C)

E. spachiana ▣ syn. *Cereus spachianus, Trichocereus spachianus*. Shrub-like

Echinopsis pentlandii

cactus with cylindrical, 10- to 15-ribbed, dark green stems, to 2½in (6cm) thick, branching freely from the base. Areoles are initially yellow, later becoming gray, and bear yellowish brown spines (8–10 radials and often 2 or 3 centrals). Nocturnal flowers, to 8in (20cm) long, are produced in mid-summer, with white inner segments and green outer ones. ↕ 3–6ft (1–2m), ↔ 30in (75cm) or more. Argentina. ❀ (min. 50°F/10°C)

E. spiniflora, syn. *Acanthocalycium violaceum*. Solitary cactus with a spherical to short-cylindrical and decumbent, dull green stem, 6in (15cm) thick, bearing about 15–20 ribs. Gray areoles produce slender, yellowish brown spines (12 or more radials and 3 or 4 longer centrals). Diurnal, erect, pale violet, pink, or white flowers, 1½–2in (4–5cm) long, with green tubes, are borne in summer. ↕ to 24in (60cm), ↔ 5in (13cm). W. Argentina. ❀ (min. 50°F/10°C)

E. thionantha, syn. *Acanthocalycium aurantiacum*. Solitary cactus with spherical to cylindrical, 9- to 16-ribbed, dark grayish green stems, 4–6in (10–15cm) thick. White areoles bear dark, almost blackish brown spines (5–10 radials and occasionally 1 longer central). Diurnal, bright yellow, red, or white flowers, 2in (5cm) long, with yellowish orange inner throats, are borne in summer. ↕↔ 2–5in (5–13cm). N.W. Argentina. ❀ (min. 50°F/10°C)

▷ ***Echinospartum*** see *Genista*

▷ ***Echioides longiflorum*** see *Arnebia pulchra*

Echinopsis spachiana

ECHIUM

BORAGINACEAE

Genus of 40 species of rosette-forming, stiffly hairy annuals and evergreen biennials, perennials (some monocarpic), and shrubs, from stony hillsides, cliffs, open woodland, and grassy steppes in Europe, the Canary Islands, the Mediterranean, Africa, and W. Asia. They are grown for their often one-sided panicles or spikes of roughly funnel-shaped, sometimes bell-shaped, blue, purple, yellow, white, or red flowers, usually ½–¾in (1–2cm) long, borne mainly in summer. The bristly-hairy, usually stalkless leaves are borne in basal rosettes and on the flower stems. Grow echiums in an annual, mixed, or herbaceous border, or in containers. Where not hardy, grow in a cool greenhouse. All parts may cause mild stomach upset if ingested; contact with the foliage may irritate skin.

• **CULTIVATION** Under glass, grow in soil-based potting mix in full light. In the growing season, water freely. Water sparingly in winter. Outdoors, grow in moderately fertile, well-drained soil in full sun. Too-rich soils discourage flower formation. Where marginally hardy, protect perennial species *in situ* with horticultural fleece in winter.

• **PROPAGATION** Sow seed of perennial and biennial species at 55–61°F (13–16°C) in summer, overwintering seedlings at 41–45°F (5–7°C). Sow seed of annuals in spring, either *in situ* or under glass. Root semi-ripe cuttings of shrubby perennials in midsummer.

Echium vulgare

• **PESTS AND DISEASES** Outdoors, slugs may attack young growth. Under glass, whiteflies and spider mites may be problems.

E. bourgaeanum see *E. wildpretii.*

E. candicans ▣ syn. *E. fastuosum* (Pride of Madeira). Open, usually rounded, woody-based biennial with rosetted, lance-shaped, softly white-hairy, prominently veined leaves, 6–10in (15–25cm) long. Bears dense, cylindrical panicles, to 12in (30cm) long, of many narrowly funnel-shaped, white or bluish white flowers, mainly from spring to summer. ↕ 5–8ft (1.5–2.5m), ↔ 5–6ft (1.5–2m). Madeira. ❄ (min. 41–45°F/5–7°C)

Echium candicans

Echium vulgare 'Blue Bedder'

E. fastuosum see *E. candicans.*

E. pininana, syn. *E. pinnifolium.* Rosette-forming biennial or short-lived perennial with elliptic-lance-shaped, densely and roughly silver-hairy leaves, to 3in (8cm) long. In mid- and late summer, each rosette produces a panicle, 5–12ft (1.5–4m) long, of funnel-shaped blue flowers with large bracts. ↕ to 12ft (4m), ↔ 3ft (1m). Canary Islands. ❄ (min. 41°F/5°C)

E. pinnifolium see *E. pininana.*

E. plantagineum. Upright, softly white-hairy annual or biennial with ovate to lance-shaped basal leaves, 5½in (14cm) long, and lance-shaped or oblong stem leaves with nearly heart-shaped bases. Produces cylindrical panicles, to 12in (30cm) long, of funnel-shaped, red to blue-purple flowers, from late spring to summer. ↕ to 24in (60cm), ↔ to 12in (30cm). England, Mediterranean region, Caucasus, Canary Islands. ❄ (min. 41°F/5°C)

E. russicum. Unbranched, upright, bristly hairy biennial with narrowly elliptic to linear-lance-shaped, pointed leaves, to 4in (10cm) long. Bears cylin-drical panicles, to 12in (30cm) long, of narrowly funnel-shaped, softly hairy, dark red flowers. ↕ to 24in (60cm), ↔ 12in (30cm). Europe, W. Asia. ❄ (min. 41°F/5°C)

E. vulgare ▣ (Blueweed, Viper's bugloss). Bushy, upright, bristly biennial with narrowly lance-shaped to linear, toothed, white bristly-hairy leaves, to 6in (15cm) long. In early summer, produces short, dense spikes or cymes, 12in (30cm) long, of broadly bell-shaped flowers, purple in bud, violet-blue (occasionally pink or white) in flower, each bloom with a prominent, hairy green calyx. Suitable for an annual border or wildflower garden. ↕ 24–36in (60–90cm), ↔ to 12in (30cm). Europe. Zone 3. **'Blue Bedder'** ▣ has light blue flowers, aging to bluish pink; ↕ to 12in (30cm). **Dwarf Hybrids** bear flowers in pink, purple, lilac-blue, or white, often with darker streaks; ↕ to 12in (30cm).

E. wildpretii, syn. *E. bourgaeanum.* Woody-stemmed, unbranched biennial or short-lived perennial with a dense rosette of narrowly lance-shaped, silver-hairy, light green leaves, to 8in (20cm) long. From late spring to summer, bears a dense, column-like panicle, 3ft (90cm) or more long, of funnel-shaped red to violet flowers. ↕ to 6ft (2m), ↔ 24in (60cm). Canary Islands. ❄ (min. 45°F/1°C)

Edgeworthia chrysantha

EDGEWORTHIA

Paper bush

THYMELAEACEAE

Genus of 3 species of deciduous or evergreen shrubs with papery bark, found in woodland in the Himalayas and China. The alternate, simple, narrowly oblong or lance-shaped to ovate or oblong, entire, tough, usually hairy leaves are clustered at the branch tips. *E. chrysantha* is valued for its tubular flowers, each with 4 spreading lobes. Where not hardy, grow against a warm wall or in a cool greenhouse; elsewhere, grow in a shrub border or woodland garden.

• **CULTIVATION** Under glass, grow in soil-based potting mix in bright filtered light. When in growth, water freely, applying a balanced liquid fertilizer monthly; water sparingly in winter. Outdoors, grow in moist but well-drained, humus-rich, loamy soil in full sun or light, dappled shade. Pruning group 1.

• **PROPAGATION** Sow seed in containers in a cold frame in autumn. Insert semi-ripe cuttings in summer.

• **PESTS AND DISEASES** Infrequent.

E. chrysantha ▣ syn. *E. papyrifera.* Open, rounded, deciduous shrub with supple shoots and lance-shaped to ovate, dark green leaves, to 6in (15cm) long. Small, fragrant yellow flowers, densely covered with silky white hairs, are borne in spherical heads, 1½–2in (3.5–5cm) across, in late winter and early spring. ↕↔ 5ft (1.5m). China. Zone 7b.

E. papyrifera see *E. chrysantha.*

EDITHCOLEA

ASCLEPIADACEAE

Genus of 1 or 2 species of perennial succulents, closely related to *Caralluma,* from low-lying hills in Yemen, Ethiopia, Somalia, Kenya, and Tanzania. The long, 5-angled stems are very fleshy and may be erect or decumbent. Solitary, colorful, star-shaped flowers, with short-tubed, 5-lobed corollas and fleshy, erect coronas, open during the day from summer to early autumn. Leaves are scale-like and short-lived. Where not hardy, grow in a warm greenhouse. In warm, dry areas, grow outdoors in a desert garden.

• **CULTIVATION** Under glass, grow in equal parts soil-based potting mix and

Edithcolea grandis

grit in full light. From late spring to mid-autumn, water moderately and apply a balanced liquid fertilizer monthly; keep barely moist when dormant. Prone to stem rot if overwatered. Outdoors, grow in sharply drained, moderately fertile soil in full sun. See also pp.48–49.
• **PROPAGATION** Sow seed at 70–75°F (21–24°C) in spring. Root stem cuttings in spring or summer.
• **PESTS AND DISEASES** Infrequent.

E. grandis ■ Variable, decumbent to semi-erect succulent with grayish green stems, 1in (2.5cm) thick, bearing very sharp, thorn-like brown teeth. Stalked, hairy-margined, reddish brown flowers, 4–5in (10–13cm) across, with pale creamy yellow spots and stripes and purple centers, are borne near the stem tips from summer to early autumn. ↕ 12in (30cm), ↔ 5in (13cm). Yemen, Ethiopia, Somalia, Kenya, Tanzania. ⊛ (min. 61°F/16°C)

EDRAIANTHUS

Grassy bells

CAMPANULACEAE

Genus of about 24 species of generally short-lived, herbaceous and evergreen perennials, closely allied to, and sometimes included in *Wahlenbergia*. They occur in well-drained, sunny habitats, sometimes in mountainous areas, from the Mediterranean region to the Caucasus. Delicate, bell-shaped flowers, surrounded by leafy bracts, are produced singly or in terminal heads in summer. The tufted, grass-like leaves usually arise from a central rootstock,

Edraianthus pumilio

and in winter, plants are often reduced to a small, resting bud, which is just visible on each rootstock. Suitable for a rock garden, scree bed, trough, alpine house, or dry wall.
• **CULTIVATION** Grow in light, sharply drained, humus-rich, preferably alkaline soil in full sun. Resting buds are sensitive to excessive winter moisture.
• **PROPAGATION** Sow seed in containers in an open frame in autumn, or take softwood cuttings from sideshoots in early summer.
• **PESTS AND DISEASES** Susceptible to aphids and spider mites under glass, and to slugs and snails outdoors.

E. graminifolius. Tufted, herbaceous or semi-evergreen perennial with rosettes of linear to narrowly spoon-shaped, mid-green leaves, to 1½in (4cm) long, downy and sometimes bristly above. In early and midsummer, erect stems, to 3in (8cm) long, bear spherical heads of upturned, bell-shaped, deep purple flowers, 1in (2.5cm) long, each with a whorl of conspicuous, ovate, long-pointed bracts. ↕↔ to 6in (15cm). Balkans, C. and S. Italy, Sicily. Zone 4.

E. pumilio ■ syn. *Wahlenbergia pumilio.* Cushion-forming, herbaceous perennial with compact tufts of narrowly linear, finely hairy, silvery green leaves, to ½in (1.5cm) long. In early summer, solitary, almost stemless, upturned, bell-shaped, pale to deep violet flowers, ½in (1.5cm) long. ↕ 1in (2.5cm), ↔ to 6in (15cm). S. Croatia (Dalmatia). Zone 4.

E. serpyllifolia, syn. *Wahlenbergia serpyllifolius.* Tight mat-forming, evergreen perennial with tufts of linear-spoon-shaped, dark green leaves, to ¾in (2cm) long, with finely hairy margins. In early summer, spreading leafy stems, 1–5in (2.5–13cm) long, bear solitary, upturned, bell-shaped, deep violet flowers, to ¾in (2cm) long. ↕ to 2in (5cm), ↔ to 6in (15cm). Croatia (Dalmatia), Bosnia & Herzegovina, Albania. Zone 4.

▷ ***Edwardia*** see *Sophora*

EGERIA

HYDROCHARITACEAE

Genus of 2 species of semi-evergreen and evergreen, marginal to deep-water aquatic perennials found in still or slow-moving water in South America. Multi-branched stems bear linear to narrowly oblong leaves in whorls or opposite pairs. Cymes of 2–5 white, 3-parted

Egeria densa

male flowers, and much smaller females, are borne within tubular, translucent spathes in summer. Use to help maintain nutrient balance in the water of a cold-water or tropical aquarium.
• **CULTIVATION** In an aquarium, grow in an inert, sandy medium in full light with a temperature of 41–64°F (5–18°C). Outdoors, grow in full sun in water 1–3ft (30–90cm) deep, rooted into the muddy bottom, or in an aquatic container of soil-based potting mix topped with gravel. Trim regularly to encourage fresh young growth. See also pp.52–53.
• **PROPAGATION** Insert stem cuttings into the pond or aquarium sediment. Allow stems to float just under the water surface; when roots develop, plant in the bottom of a pond or aquarium.
• **PESTS AND DISEASES** Young shoots may be nibbled by snails or fish.

E. densa ■ syn. *Anacharis densa, Elodea densa* (Brazilian waterweed). Submerged, sometimes floating, aquatic perennial with many-branched stems, to 3ft (90cm) long, with numerous whorls of stalkless, linear leaves, to 1in (2.5cm) long, with long, sharp-pointed tips. Tubular spathes, ¾in (2cm) long, of small but showy white male flowers are borne above the water surface in summer. ↔ indefinite. South America. Zone 6b.

EHRETIA

BORAGINACEAE

Genus of about 50 species of deciduous and evergreen trees and shrubs from Africa, Asia, and North and South America, mainly in woodland. They are grown for their spreading habit; ridged or furrowed bark; simple, entire or toothed, alternate leaves; and terminal panicles of small, 5-lobed, tubular to bell-shaped or star-shaped, scented flowers. Ideal for a woodland garden. Where not hardy, grow in a cool or temperate greenhouse.
• **CULTIVATION** Grow in moderately fertile, well-drained soil in full sun or partial shade, sheltered from cold, drying winds. Pruning group 1.
• **PROPAGATION** Sow seed in containers in a cold frame as soon as ripe. Insert softwood cuttings in summer.
• **PESTS AND DISEASES** Infrequent.

E. dicksonii ■ Spreading, deciduous tree with deeply ridged, gray-brown bark and elliptic to oblong-elliptic,

Ehretia dicksonii

glossy, dark green leaves, to 8in (20cm) long, rough-hairy above, velvety-hairy beneath. In late spring and early summer, bears tubular-bell-shaped white flowers in flattish panicles, 2–4in (5–10cm) across. ↕↔ 30ft (10m). China, Taiwan, Japan (Ryukyu Islands). Zone 7b.

EICHHORNIA

Water hyacinth

PONTEDERIACEAE

Genus of 7 species of rhizomatous, marginal to deep-water aquatic perennials, rarely annuals, from lakes, canals, rivers, and streams in subtropical and tropical South America. Submerged leaves are linear to strap-shaped and arranged in 2 ranks; floating and aerial leaves are stalked, mainly obovate, rounded, or heart-shaped, and borne in rosettes. Showy, funnel-shaped flowers are borne in terminal spikes, each within a leafy sheath. Grow in a greenhouse pool, in a tropical aquarium, or outdoors in a decorative pool. Most species multiply rapidly and are highly invasive. They should not be planted near waterways. Classified as noxious weeds in several states, they are banned from interstate commerce. Where not hardy, overwinter under glass.
• **CULTIVATION** Under glass, provide full light with an air temperature of 55–61°F (13–16°C). Aquarium plants need 12–16in (30–40cm) of head space to grow well. Outdoors, grow on open water in full sun. Where not hardy, introduce plants onto the water surface when danger of frost has passed. Overwinter on trays of moist, soilless potting mix, at a minimum of 59°F (15°C) in full light. See also pp.52–53.
• **PROPAGATION** Detach offshoots at any time of year.
• **PESTS AND DISEASES** Infrequent.

E. azurea. Floating or submerged, thick-stemmed aquatic perennial that floats or roots in mud. Bears linear to strap-shaped submerged leaves, 4in (10cm)

E

long, arranged in 2 ranks, and rounded-heart-shaped to diamond-shaped floating leaves, 4in (10cm) long, in rosettes to 8in (20cm) or more across. Pale blue flowers, 2–3in (5–8cm) long, with yellow-spotted, dark purple throats, are borne in spikes 2–6in (5–15cm) long, throughout summer. ↕ 4–5in (10–13cm), ↔ 18in (45cm). Subtropical and tropical South America. ❄ (min. 34°F/1°C)
E. crassipes, syn. *E. speciosa* (Water hyacinth). Floating aquatic perennial with a thick, floating or anchored stem bearing rosettes of rounded to ovate leaves, to 6in (15cm) across, with inflated, shiny, pale green stalks. Long, purplish green roots hang down 12in (30cm) in the water. Pale blue to violet flowers, 1¼in (3cm) across, have yellow markings on the upper petals and are borne in spikes 6in (15cm) tall, in summer. ↕↔ 18in (45cm). Tropical South America. ❄ (min. 34°F/1°C)
E. speciosa see *E. crassipes*.

ELAEAGNUS

ELAEAGNACEAE

Genus of about 45 species of deciduous or evergreen shrubs or trees, mainly from Asia, but a few from S. Europe and North America, growing wild in thickets and dry places. They are cultivated for their often silvery leaves, which are alternate and lance-shaped to ovate or oblong, and for the small, tubular or bell-shaped, sometimes intensely fragrant flowers, produced in clusters from the leaf axils. The flowers are followed by edible, sometimes colorful berries, ½–1in (1–2.5cm) long. Grow in a shrub border or as specimen shrubs; evergreens are also suitable as a hedge.
• **CULTIVATION** Grow in fertile, well-drained soil, ideally in full sun, although evergreens will grow well in partial shade. All tolerate dry soil and coastal winds, but may become chlorotic on shallow, alkaline soil. Pruning group 1 or 2 (deciduous), or 9 (evergreens). Remove nonvariegated reversions.
• **PROPAGATION** Sow seed in a cold frame in autumn. Insert greenwood cuttings in late spring or early summer, or semi-ripe cuttings of deciduous species in midsummer. Insert semi-ripe cuttings of evergreens in summer, or graft in late winter. Remove rooted suckers of deciduous species in autumn.
• **PESTS AND DISEASES** Cankers, dagger nematode, dieback, rust, fungal leaf spots, and root rot occur frequently.

Elaeagnus x *ebbingei* 'Gilt Edge'

E. angustifolia (Oleaster, Russian olive). Deciduous shrub or tree with spreading, red-tinted, sometimes spiny branches, covered with silvery scales, and willow-like, lance-shaped leaves, to 4in (10cm) long, dark green above, silver-scaly beneath. In summer, produces fragrant, yellowish white flowers, to ½in (1.5cm) long, followed in autumn by silver-scaly, edible yellow fruit. ↕↔ 20ft (6m). S. Europe to C. Asia, Himalayas, China. Zone 2b. **'Quicksilver'** ▣ syn. *E.* 'Quicksilver', is a fast-growing, open, pyramidal, suckering shrub with silvery shoots, elliptic to lance-shaped, tapered, very silver-scaly leaves, to 2in (5cm) long, and yellow flowers produced from silvery buds; ↕↔ 12ft (4m). **'Red King'** has bright, rust-red fruit.

E. commutata (Silverberry). Thicket-forming, deciduous shrub, spreading by suckers, with upright, red-brown shoots and broadly elliptic leaves, to 3in (8cm) long, completely covered with silvery scales. Pendent, silver-scaly, fragrant, yellowish white flowers, ½in (1.5cm) long, are borne in late spring, followed in autumn by silver-mealy red fruit. ↕ to 12ft (4m), ↔ 6ft (2m). North America. Zone 2.
***E.* x *ebbingei* cultivars.** Dense, rounded to spreading, evergreen shrubs with elliptic, leathery leaves, to 4in (10cm) long, glossy, dark or metallic sea-green on the upper surfaces, silver-scaly beneath. Silver-scaly, creamy white flowers, ½in (1.5cm) long, are borne in autumn. ↕↔ 12ft (4m). Garden origin. Zone 7. **'Gilt Edge'** ▣ has leaves with dark

Elaeagnus pungens 'Maculata'

green centers and conspicuous, golden yellow margins. **'Limelight'** ▣ has silvery young leaves, which become marked with yellow and pale green in the centers; ↕↔ 10ft (3m).
E. macrophylla. Vigorous, spreading, evergreen shrub with silvery white-scaly branches when young. Broadly ovate to elliptic leaves, to 4in (10cm) long, are very silver-scaly when young, becoming glossy, dark green above. Silver-scaly cream flowers, to ½in (1.5cm) long, are produced in autumn and followed by scaly red fruit. ↕ 10ft (3m), ↔ 15ft (5m). Korea, Japan. Zone 7b.
E. pungens (Thorny elaeagnus). Dense, slightly spiny, evergreen shrub with young branches covered in brown scales. Oblong-elliptic to oblong, lustrous, dark green leaves, to 4in (10cm) long, are often wavy-margined; the undersides are tinged white and brown-scaly. In autumn, bears pendent, fragrant, silvery white flowers, ½in (1.5cm) long, followed by brown fruit that ripen to red. ↕ 12ft (4m), ↔ 15ft (5m). Japan. Zone 7b. **'Argenteovariegata'** see 'Variegata'. **'Aureovariegata'** see 'Maculata'. **'Frederici'** ▣ is slow-growing, and has small, narrow, creamy yellow leaves, 1¼–1½in (3–4cm) long, with narrow, glossy, dark green margins; ↕↔ 6ft (2m). **'Fruitlandii'** bears slightly larger, rounded leaves with wavy margins and silver undersides. **'Maculata'** ▣ syn. 'Aureovariegata', has leaves boldly marked dark yellow in the centers. **'Variegata'**, syn. 'Argenteovariegata', has leaves with narrow, creamy yellow edges.
E. 'Quicksilver' see *E. angustifolia* 'Quicksilver'.

Elaeagnus angustifolia 'Quicksilver'

Elaeagnus x *ebbingei* 'Limelight'

Elaeagnus pungens 'Frederici'

Elaeagnus umbellata

E.* x *reflexa (*E. glabra* x *E. pungens*). Vigorous, semi-scandent, sparsely thorny, evergreen shrub with long shoots and ovate to ovate-lance-shaped, glossy, deep green leaves, to 2½in (6cm) long, intensely brown-scaly beneath. Silvery white flowers, ½in (1.5cm) long, are borne in autumn. Will climb if supported. ↕ 12ft (4m), ↔ 20ft (6m). Garden origin. Zone 7b.
E. umbellata ■ (Autumn olive). Vigorous, frequently wide-spreading, deciduous shrub or small tree with brown-scaly, often spiny shoots. Elliptic to ovate-oblong, wavy-margined leaves, to 4in (10cm) long, are silvery at first, maturing to bright green above. Silvery yellow-white flowers, ½in (1.5cm) long, are borne in late spring and early summer, followed by silvery fruit that turn red in autumn. ↕↔ 15ft (5m). Himalayas, China, Japan. Zone 5.
'Titan' is a dense, upright, branched cultivar, with silver-tinged, olive-green leaves and bright yellow flowers; ↕ 12ft (4m), ↔ 6ft (2m).

ELAEIS
Oil palm
ARECACEAE

Genus of 2 species of single-stemmed, monoecious palms occurring on moist, sandy soils in open forest in tropical regions of America and Africa. Large, pinnate leaves are borne in terminal clusters, the dead ones hanging down like a skirt before falling. The 3-petaled flowers are produced in panicles from the leaf axils. Where not hardy, grow young oil palms in a warm greenhouse; elsewhere, use as lawn specimens.
• **CULTIVATION** Under glass, grow in soil-based potting mix in full light. When in growth, water freely and apply a balanced liquid fertilizer monthly; water sparingly in winter. Pot on or top-dress in spring. Outdoors, grow in fertile, moist but well-drained soil in full sun.
• **PROPAGATION** Soak seed for 7 days and sow at 66–75°F (19–24°C) in spring. Germination is slow.
• **PESTS AND DISEASES** Susceptible to a wide variety of fungal spots and blights, as well as butt rot. Spider mites, mealybugs, and scale insects occur.

E. guineensis (African oil palm, Macaw fat palm). Erect palm bearing a dense crown of arching leaves, 8–15ft (2.5–5m) long, composed of numerous, more or less pendent, crowded, slender, linear, rich green leaflets, held in differing planes along the midribs. Yellow flowers are borne intermittently throughout the year in separate male and female panicles, 12–18in (30–45cm) long. Females develop large, rounded bunches of ovoid fruit, rich in commercially valuable oil. ↕ to 60ft (18m), ↔ 15–28ft (5–9m). Tropical Africa. ❄ (min. 64°F/18°C)

ELAEOCARPUS
ELAEOCARPACEAE

Genus of 60 species of evergreen shrubs and trees occurring in forest and thickets from E. Asia to Indonesia and Malaysia, and from Australasia and the Pacific. They are grown for their axillary racemes of small, 3- to 5-petaled, bell-shaped, fringed, usually fragrant flowers,

Elaeocarpus cyaneus

and for their colorful berries. The mainly alternate leaves are lance-shaped to broad-ovate or oblong, leathery, and entire or toothed. Grow as specimen plants or in a shrub border. Where not hardy, grow in a cool greenhouse. Where marginally hardy, grow against a south-facing wall.
• **CULTIVATION** Under glass, grow in well-drained, soil-based potting mix in full light. From spring to autumn, water freely and apply a balanced liquid fertilizer monthly; water sparingly in winter. Top-dress or pot on in spring. Outdoors, grow in fertile, humus-rich, moist but well-drained, neutral to acidic soil in full sun. Pruning group 1.
• **PROPAGATION** Root semi-ripe cuttings with bottom heat in summer (rooting may be slow).
• **PESTS AND DISEASES** Prone to whiteflies and spider mites under glass.

E. cyaneus ■ syn. *E. reticulatus.* Erect to spreading tree or shrub with oblong-elliptic to oblong-lance-shaped, conspicuously veined and shallowly toothed, shiny, dark green leaves, 4–6in (10–15cm) long. Bears small, fragrant, white or pink flowers in racemes, to 4in (10cm) long, from spring to summer. Long-lasting, lustrous, deep blue berries, ⅜–½in (8–15mm) long, ripen from autumn to winter. ↕ 20–50ft (6–15m), ↔ 6–15ft (2–5m). Queensland to Victoria. ❄ (min. 45°F/7°C)
E. reticulatus see *E. cyaneus.*

ELATOSTEMA syn. PELLIONIA
URTICACEAE

Genus of about 50 species of evergreen perennials and subshrubs, some with succulent or partly woody stems, widely distributed in tropical and subtropical Asia, where they grow in forest clearings. They are cultivated for their decorative leaves, which are alternate, 2-ranked, linear to rounded, entire or toothed, and heavily marked with silver and bronze. The inflorescences are insignificant. Trailing species are ideal for a hanging basket or as a groundcover. Where not hardy, grow as houseplants or in a warm greenhouse; elsewhere, grow in a border or under trees and shrubs.
• **CULTIVATION** Under glass, grow in soilless potting mix in bright indirect light. When in growth, water freely and apply a balanced liquid fertilizer monthly; water moderately (with warm water) in winter. Protect from cold

Elatostema repens

drafts to prevent leaf drop. Outdoors, grow in humus-rich, fertile soil in deep shade. Shorten shoots in spring or summer to maintain shape.
• **PROPAGATION** Root cuttings at any time of year.
• **PESTS AND DISEASES** Infrequent.

E. pulchra, syn. *Pellionia pulchra* (Rainbow vine). Creeping and trailing, evergreen perennial with fleshy, purple-tinged stems. Oblong to broadly elliptic, dark green leaves, ¾–2in (2–5cm) long, are tinged purple beneath, with very dark green midribs and veins above. ↕ 3in (8cm), ↔ 18in (45cm). Vietnam. ❄ (min. 55°F/13°C)
E. repens ■ syn. *Pellionia daveauana, P. repens* (Trailing watermelon begonia). Creeping, evergreen perennial with fleshy, greenish pink stems. Wavy-margined leaves, to 2½in (6cm) long, are oblong, elliptic, or sometimes rounded. They are dark blackish green above, marked gray and paler green, and often bronze-flushed; beneath, they are often tinged pink, with purple margins. ↕ 4in (10cm), ↔ to 24in (60cm). S.E. Asia. ❄ (min. 55°F/13°C)

ELEOCHARIS
Spike rush
CYPERACEAE

Genus of 150 marginal aquatic annuals or perennials from bogs and ponds of the tropics to the arctic. They have leaves reduced to bladeless sheaths, and terminal inflorescences with few- to many-flowered spikelets. Spike rushes are attractive in a bog or water garden, or along a streambed. Where not hardy, grow at the margins of an indoor pool or in an aquarium.
• **CULTIVATION** Under glass, grow in an aquatic planting container in bright filtered light with a water temperature of 60°F (16°C). Outdoors, grow in moderately fertile, wet or moist, slightly acidic soil in full sun to partial shade. See also pp.52–53.
• **PROPAGATION** Sow seed *in situ* as soon as ripe, or divide in spring.
• **PESTS AND DISEASES** Ergot and rust can occur. Storage rot of corms may be a problem; check before planting.

E. dulcis see *E. tuberosa.*
E. montevidensis (Fiber-optic plant). Clump-forming, rhizomatous, emergent aquatic perennial with thin stems and aerial, light green basal leaves reduced to sheaths, 12in (30cm) long. From summer to autumn, bears spikelets, ¼in (6mm) long, of 24–70 insignificant, light brown flowers. Plant to a water depth of 0–2in (0–5cm). ↕ 12–18in (30–45cm), ↔ indefinite. Oregon to S. central US to C. Mexico, S.E. US. Zone 6b.
E. tuberosa, syn. *E. dulcis* (Chinese water chestnut). Emergent to marginal, tuberous aquatic perennial with thin, tubular stems and aerial, light yellow-green leaves reduced to sheaths, to 3ft (1m) long. From summer to autumn, produces spikelets, 1–2in (2.5–5cm) long, of up to 50 insignificant, straw-colored flowers. Plant to a water depth of 0–12in (0–30cm). Used in Asian cooking. ↕ 3ft (1m), ↔ indefinite. Asia. ❄ (min. 41°F/5°C)

ELETTARIA
ZINGIBERACEAE

Genus of 4 species of evergreen, rhizomatous perennials from tropical rainforest in India, Sri Lanka, Malaysia, and Sumatra. The rhizomes produce erect shoots with 2 ranks of linear to lance-shaped leaves. Separate, horizontal flowering shoots, bearing large-bracted spikes of lipped, 3-petaled flowers, are followed by spherical or ellipsoid seed capsules. The only widely cultivated species, *E. cardamomum*, produces aromatic fruit used as a spice. It needs tropical conditions to flower and fruit well, but in temperate regions is still an attractive foliage plant for a warm greenhouse. In frost-free areas, grow in a shady bed or border.
• **CULTIVATION** Under glass, grow in fertile, soil-based potting mix with additional leaf mold or ground bark, in bright filtered light with high humidity. In growth, water freely and apply a balanced liquid fertilizer monthly; water sparingly in winter. Pot on in spring and remove flowered stems. Outdoors, grow in fertile, open, humus-rich soil, in full sun with some midday shade.
• **PROPAGATION** Sow seed at 66–75°F (19–24°C) as soon as ripe. Divide in spring.
• **PESTS AND DISEASES** Susceptible to thrips, cardamom virus, pod rot, and occasionally fungal root rot.

E. cardamomum (Cardamom). Evergreen perennial with thick rhizomes bearing upright shoots with linear-lance-shaped, pointed, dark green leaves, 24in (60cm) long, paler and softly hairy beneath. During summer, its almost prostrate shoots may bear loose panicles, to 24in (60cm) long, of violet-veined white flowers, ¾in (2cm) long, with yellow-margined, or pink-, lilac-, or violet-striped lips, followed by aromatic, pale green capsules, each containing 15–20 seeds. ↕↔ to 10ft (3m) (much smaller in containers). India. ❄ (min. 50°F/10°C)

Eleutherococcus sieboldianus

ELEUTHEROCOCCUS

syn. ACANTHOPANAX

ARALIACEAE

Genus of about 30 species of mainly deciduous trees and shrubs, sometimes climbers, from scrub and woodland in E., S., and S.E. Asia. They have alternate, 3- to 7-palmate leaves, and bear terminal, simple or compound umbels of small, 5-petaled, greenish white flowers from spring to summer, followed by ivy-like, spherical to ellipsoid, black or purple-black fruits. *Eleutherococcus* species are grown for their foliage and autumn fruits. They provide a bold accent when grown as specimens and make a striking addition to a shrub border.

- **CULTIVATION** Grow in well-drained soil, ideally in full sun; *E. sieboldianus* thrives in poor, dry soil and will tolerate shade. Pruning group 1.
- **PROPAGATION** Sow seed in a seedbed in autumn or spring. Insert greenwood cuttings in early summer or take root cuttings in winter. Separate suckers in early spring.
- **PESTS AND DISEASES** Infrequent.

E. pictus see *Kalopanax septemlobus.*
E. sieboldianus ■ syn. *Acanthopanax sieboldianus* (Five-leaf aralia). Spiny, sometimes scandent shrub with slender, arching branches bearing 5- to 7-palmate, bright green leaves, with ovate or obovate, toothed leaflets, to 3½in (9cm) long. Bears solitary umbels of star-shaped, greenish white flowers in late spring and early summer, followed by spherical black fruit, to ⅜in (9mm) across. ↕↔ 8ft (2.5m). E. China. Zone 5. **'Variegatus'** has leaflets margined with creamy white.
E. spinosus. Spiny, scandent shrub with 5- to 7-palmate, bright green leaves, with wedge-shaped, toothed leaflets, to 3½in (9cm) long. Bears umbels of star-shaped, greenish white flowers, in summer, followed by spherical black fruit, to ⅜in (9mm) across. ↕ to 11ft (3.5m), ↔ 8ft (2.5m). Japan. Zone 5.

ELODEA

Pondweed

HYDROCHARITACEAE

Genus of 12 species of submerged aquatic perennials occurring in fresh water from North America to subtropical South America. The erect, spreading stems and lance-shaped to linear or ovate, bright green leaves, borne in whorls of 3, provide excellent cover for fish fry; they are also useful for maintaining nutrient balance. Tiny, solitary flowers are produced within axillary spathes. Grow in a garden pond; the less vigorous species are suitable for an aquarium.

- **CULTIVATION** Outdoors, grow in loamy soil, in an aquatic container in a pond in full sun. See also pp.52–53.
- **PROPAGATION** Take stem cuttings, 6–12in (15–30cm) long, in summer.
- **PESTS AND DISEASES** Infrequent.

E. canadensis (Canadian pondweed). Submerged aquatic perennial with brittle, branching stems, 10–12ft (3–4m) long, bearing lance-shaped to ovate, finely toothed, flat, translucent, bright, dark green leaves, ¼–½in (0.6–1.5cm) long, which curl slightly downward. Floating, petalless, purple-tinged green flowers, ⅜in (9mm) across, borne among the leaves in summer, have long, thread-like stalks. ↔ indefinite. North America. Zone 5.
***E. crispa* of gardens** see *Lagarosiphon major.*
E. densa see *Egeria densa.*

ELSHOLTZIA

LAMIACEAE

Genus of about 35 species of annuals, perennials, and semi-evergreen or deciduous shrubs and subshrubs occurring on dry, open hillsides and roadsides in C. and E. Asia. They are valued for their aromatic foliage and their slender panicles or racemes of 2-lipped, tubular flowers. The leaves are opposite and lance-shaped to ovate-elliptic. Grow in a herbaceous or shrub border. Where not hardy, grow in a cool greenhouse.

- **CULTIVATION** Grow in any well-drained, fertile soil in full sun. Pruning group 6.
- **PROPAGATION** Sow seed at 55°F (13°C) as soon as ripe. Insert softwood cuttings in summer.
- **PESTS AND DISEASES** Infrequent.

E. stauntonii ■ Open, rounded, deciduous subshrub with lance-shaped to ovate-elliptic, toothed, mint-scented, mid-green leaves, to 6in (15cm) long, turning red in autumn. From late summer to autumn, produces terminal racemes or panicles, 4–8in (10–20cm) long, of small, purple-pink flowers. ↕↔ 5ft (1.5m). China. Zone 6.

Elsholtzia stauntonii

ELYMUS

Wild rye

POACEAE

Genus of about 150 species of tufted or rhizomatous, mainly perennial grasses, widely distributed throughout N. and S. temperate regions, and often occurring on sandy soils. They have linear, flat or occasionally rolled leaves, and thick or slender, bristled flower spikes consisting of flattened, stalkless spikelets, arranged alternately along the flower stalks. The genus includes the invasive *E. repens* (quack grass or twitch), but those species described here are not nearly as invasive. Most are useful in a rock garden, or in a mixed or herbaceous border.

- **CULTIVATION** Grow in any moderately fertile, moist but well-drained soil in full sun. *E. canadensis* tolerates damp conditions. Cut back to ground level in late autumn, or leave those species with good winter leaf color until late winter.
- **PROPAGATION** Sow seed *in situ* in autumn or spring. Divide from midspring to early summer.
- **PESTS AND DISEASES** Susceptible to damping off, ergot, cat-tail, powdery mildew, tar spot, rust, smut, brown patch, and other fungal spots and blights.

E. arenarius see *Leymus arenarius.*
E. canadensis (Canadian wild rye). Loosely tufted, perennial grass with erect stems bearing linear, flat or rolled, rough-textured or slightly bristly, green to blue-green leaves, 8–14in (20–35cm) long. In late summer and early autumn, bears dense green flower spikes, 8–10in (20–25cm) long, nodding at the tips; 2- to 5-flowered spikelets, with reddish brown bristles, are arranged alternately in groups of 4 along each spike. ↕ 4–6ft (1.2–1.8m), ↔ 24in (60cm). Temperate North America. Zone 3.
***E. glaucus* of gardens** see *E. hispidus.*
E. hispidus, syn. *E. glaucus* of gardens (Blue wild rye, Intermediate wheatgrass). Loosely tufted, perennial grass with erect or arching, linear, inrolled, bristly, pale silvery blue leaves, 4–8in (10–20cm) long. In early and midsummer, upright stems bear slender, insignificant flower spikes of blunt, 3- to 8-flowered spikelets. ↕ to 30in (75cm), ↔ 16in (40cm). Temperate Eurasia. Zone 7b.
E. magellanicus. Densely tufted, mound-forming, perennial grass with linear, flat or folded, intense blue leaves, to 2in (5cm) long. Lax, almost prostrate flower spikes, 7in (18cm) long, consisting of 2- to 7-flowered spikelets, are borne throughout summer. ↕ 6in (15cm), ↔ 12in (30cm). Temperate S. Chile and S. Argentina. Zone 7b.
E. racemosus see *Leymus racemosus.*

EMBOTHRIUM

Chilean fire bush

PROTEACEAE

Genus of 8 species of evergreen trees and shrubs occurring in forest in the C. and S. Andes of South America. They are cultivated for their showy, tubular, waxy flowers, which split into 4 recurved and coiling, narrow, twisted lobes, and are borne in terminal and axillary racemes. The alternate, simple leaves are lance-shaped to elliptic or oblong, entire, and leathery. Grow in a woodland garden or in a sheltered site. In areas where frosts are light and infrequent, they make good specimen trees.

- **CULTIVATION** Grow in fertile, humus-rich, moist but well-drained, neutral to acidic soil in full sun or partial shade. Shelter from cold, drying winds. Pruning group 1.
- **PROPAGATION** Sow seed at 55–61°F (13–16°C) in spring. Root greenwood cuttings in early summer, or semi-ripe cuttings in mid- or late summer, with bottom heat. Insert root cuttings or remove suckers in late winter.
- **PESTS AND DISEASES** Spider mites may infest plants under glass.

E. coccineum ■ (Chilean fire bush, Flame flower). Upright, freely branching, suckering tree or shrub with oblong to narrowly lance-shaped, mid- to deep green leaves, to 5in (13cm) long. Scarlet, rarely yellow flowers, 1¼–1¾in (3–4.5cm) long, are produced in dense racemes, to 4in (10cm) long, in late spring and early summer. ↕ 30ft (10m) or more, ↔ 15ft (5m) or more. S. Chile. ❀ (min. 35°F/2°C)

Embothrium coccineum

EMILIA syn. CACALIA

Tassel flower

ASTERACEAE

Genus of about 24 species of rosette-forming annuals from disturbed ground or stony slopes, to 11,500ft (3,500m) high, in tropical Africa, India, and Polynesia. The lower leaves are lance-shaped-oblong or pinnatifid, stalkless or with winged stalks; the upper leaves are oblong to ovate, and clasp the stems. In summer, stiff, slender, leafy stems bear upright, tassel-like, red, yellow, purple-red, or orange flowerheads, singly or in corymbs. Grow in an annual border. The flowers are good for drying.

• **CULTIVATION** Grow in well-drained soil in full sun.

• **PROPAGATION** Sow seed at 55–64°F (13–18°C) in midspring, or *in situ*.

• **PESTS AND DISEASES** Infrequent.

E. coccinea, syn. *Cacalia coccinea, C. sagittata, E. flammea, E. javanica* (Flora's paintbrush). Smooth to slightly hairy, rosette-forming annual with mid-green leaves, to 5½in (14cm) long; lower ones stalkless and entire to toothed. In summer, bears fluffy, orange-red or scarlet flowerheads, to ½in (1.5cm) across, singly or in loosely clustered corymbs. ↕ 18–24in (45–60cm), ↔ 12–24in (30–60cm). Tropical Africa.

E. flammea see *E. coccinea*.

E. javanica see *E. coccinea*.

E. sonchifolia, syn. *Cacalia sonchifolia*. Smooth to slightly hairy, rosette-forming annual with toothed, mid- to gray-green leaves, to 4in (10cm) long; the lower leaves have winged stalks, the upper leaves are smaller and almost arrow-shaped. In summer, bears loosely clustered corymbs of fluffy, purple-red flowerheads, to ½in (1.5cm) across. Tropical Africa and Asia. ↕ 18–24in (45–60cm), ↔ 12–24in (30–60cm). **'Lutea'** has yellow flowerheads.

EMMENOPTERYS

RUBIACEAE

Genus of 2 species of deciduous trees from forest in E. Asia. They are valued for their spreading habit and opposite, large, ovate to broadly elliptic, leathery leaves. Terminal panicles of funnel- or bell-shaped white flowers, also a notable feature, are borne on mature trees during prolonged periods of over 75°F (24°C). Grow in woodland or as specimen plants.

Emmenopterys henryi

• **CULTIVATION** Grow in fertile, humus-rich, moist but well-drained soil in full sun. Shelter from cold, drying winds.

• **PROPAGATION** Insert greenwood cuttings in early or midsummer.

• **PESTS AND DISEASES** Infrequent.

E. henryi ▣ Spreading tree with elliptic-oblong to elliptic-ovate leaves, to 8in (20cm) long, dark green above, paler and softly hairy beneath, bronze-purple when young. In summer, bears funnel-shaped white flowers, 1in (2.5cm) across, with 5 spreading lobes, some bearing a large white bract, in panicles to 7in (18cm) long by 10in (25cm) wide. ↕↔ 40ft (12m). W. and C. China, S.E. Asia. Zone 7b.

ENCELIA

ASTERACEAE

Genus of about 15 species of deciduous shrubs and perennials growing in dry, arid landscapes of S.W. US, Mexico, Peru, Chile, and the Galapagos Islands. They have alternate, ovate-oblong or lance-shaped leaves and are grown for their daisy-like, often strongly fragrant, yellow flowerheads. *Encelia* species are ideal in a native or desert garden. Where not hardy, grow in a cool greenhouse.

• **CULTIVATION** Under glass, grow in gravelly, soil-based potting mix, in full light. Water moderately and apply a balanced liquid fertilizer monthly in growth; keep just moist in winter. Pot on or top-dress in spring. Outdoors, grow in moderately fertile, well-drained, sandy soil, in full sun. Pruning group 2.

• **PROPAGATION** Sow seed in containers outdoors in spring. Take softwood cuttings in early summer.

• **PESTS AND DISEASES** Infrequent.

E. farinosa (Brittlebush). Rounded, deciduous shrub with brittle stems and dense clusters of narrowly to broadly ovate, entire or toothed, densely silver-woolly leaves, to 3in (8cm) long. In spring, bears flowerheads, ½in (15mm) across, with yellow or red-brown disks and orange-yellow ray florets, to ½in (15mm) long, solitary or in cymes. ↕ to 3ft (1m), ↔ 30in (75cm). S.W. US. Zone 7b.

ENCEPHALARTOS

ZAMIACEAE

Genus of about 25 species of slow-growing, dioecious cycads, some palm-like, others with a short or buried stem, from open, dry forest and scrub and open, rocky slopes in C. and southern Africa. The pinnate leaves, whorled in terminal crowns, have spiny stalks and hard, leathery, often spiny-toothed leaflets. Cone-like male and female inflorescences ("cones") are borne within the leaf rosettes: male cones are more or less cylindrical; female cones are usually oblong to ovoid. *Encephalartos* species have many uses in the garden because of their varied growth habits. Very woolly-leaved species, or those with fewer pinnae, tolerate lower temperatures, to 40°F (4°C). Where not hardy, grow in a temperate or warm greenhouse; in warmer areas, they make striking accent plants.

• **CULTIVATION** Under glass, grow in deep containers in equal parts loam, coarse sand, and ground bark, with added slow-release fertilizer, in bright filtered light. During the growing season, water freely and apply a balanced liquid fertilizer monthly; water moderately in winter. Pot on or top-dress in spring. Grow *E. horridus* in full light and water sparingly in winter. Outdoors, grow in fertile, humus-rich, well-drained, neutral to slightly acidic soil in partial or light, dappled shade. *E. horridus* needs full sun.

• **PROPAGATION** Sow seed at 75–86°F (24–30°C) in spring, in a very sandy mix. Remove offsets in spring.

• **PESTS AND DISEASES** Sometimes affected by fungal leaf spot, cycad weevil, and scale insects.

E. altensteinii ▣ (Prickly cycad). Palm-like cycad with an erect stem and straight to arching leaves, 6–11ft (2–3.5m) long, composed of numerous narrowly oblong, bright green leaflets, sparsely toothed at the margins. Produces yellow-green flowering cones, usually in summer. ↕↔ 12–22ft (4–7m). South Africa (Eastern Cape). ❄ (min. 61°F/16°C)

E. caffer (Kaffir bread). Cycad with a buried stem, to 16in (40cm) long, only the growing point at or above soil level. Upright then arching leaves, to 3ft (1m) long, are composed of linear-lance-shaped, sometimes sparsely toothed, bright green leaflets. Bears greenish yellow flowering cones, mainly in summer. ↕ to 3ft (1m), ↔ to 6ft (2m). South Africa. ❄ (min. 61°F/16°C)

E. ferox. Palm-like cycad with a short trunk and spreading leaves, 3–6ft

Encephalartos horridus

(1–1.8m) long, composed of narrowly oblong to oblong-ovate, lustrous, deep green leaflets, with spiny teeth. Mature specimens bear flowering cones in summer: male cones are red; females range from pink to bright red. ↕ to 3ft (1m), ↔ 6–10ft (1.8–3m). South Africa. ❄ (min. 55°F/13°C)

E. horridus ▣ (Ferocious blue cycad). Cycad with a stem that is buried at first, then gradually elongates to about 2ft (60cm) tall. Erect, ascending then arching leaves, to 3ft (1m) long, with recurved tips, are composed of numerous lance-shaped, spine-tipped and lobed, rich blue-green leaflets. Produces red-brown flowering cones, usually in summer. ↕ 3–4½ft (1–1.4m), ↔ to 6ft (2m). South Africa. ❄ (min. 61°F/16°C)

Encephalartos altensteinii (inset: cone detail)

E

E

Encephalartos longifolius

E. humilis. Cycad with a buried stem, usually with only the growing tip above ground, or occasionally elongating to 12in (30cm) tall. Strongly arching, twisted leaves, 12–20in (30–50cm) long, with recurved tips, are divided into numerous linear to lance-shaped leaflets, softly hairy at first, then smooth, deep green. Brownish gray flowering cones are produced mainly in summer. ↕4–16in (10–40cm), ↔ 24–36in (60–90cm). South Africa (Eastern Transvaal). ❄ (min. 61°F/16°C)
E. lebomboensis (Lebombo cycad). Palm-like cycad with an erect stem and bright green leaves, 3–10ft (1–3m) long, composed of many overlapping, lance-shaped leaflets, each with a few well-spaced teeth. Produces pink to apricot-yellow flowering cones, usually in summer. ↕10–20ft (3–6m), ↔ 6–20ft (2–6m). South Africa (Northern Transvaal, Eastern Transvaal, KwaZulu/ Natal), Swaziland, Mozambique. ❄ (min. 61°F/16°C)
E. longifolius ■ (Suurberg cycad). Palm-like cycad with a robust, erect trunk and arching, glossy, deep green, occasionally bluish green leaves, 3–6ft (1–2m) long, composed of overlapping, lance-shaped, sometimes sparsely toothed leaflets. Mature specimens bear red-hairy, greenish brown flowering cones in summer. ↕6–12ft (2–4m), ↔ 11ft (3.5m). South Africa (Eastern Cape). ❄ (min. 55°F/13°C)
E. natalensis (Natal cycad). Palm-like cycad with a usually erect stem and deep green leaves, 8–11ft (2.5–3.5m) long, with broadly lance-shaped, entire or sparsely spiny-toothed leaflets. Brown flowering cones, woolly at first, mature to deep yellow, and are borne in summer. ↕to 12ft (4m), occasionally 20ft (6m), ↔ 6–10ft (2–3m). South Africa (Eastern Transvaal, KwaZulu/ Natal). ❄ (min. 61°F/16°C)
E. transvenosus (Modjadji cycad). Palm-like cycad with an erect stem and arching, lustrous, deep green leaves, 5–8ft (1.5–2.5m) long, composed of broadly lance-shaped leaflets, each with a few small teeth. Produces golden brown flowering cones, woolly when young, usually in summer. ↕15–25ft (5–8m), ↔ 10–15ft (3–5m). South Africa (Northern Transvaal, Eastern Transvaal). ❄ (min. 61°F/16°C)
E. villosus ■ Cycad with a buried stem, only the growing point at or above ground level. Arching, deep green leaves, to 10ft (3m) long, are composed of numerous narrowly lance-shaped, entire or sparsely toothed leaflets, more or less hairy beneath. The lowest leaflets are reduced to spines. Yellow flowering cones are produced in summer. ↕5–10ft (1.5–3m), ↔ 10–20ft (3–6m). South Africa (Northern Transvaal, Eastern Transvaal, KwaZulu/Natal, Eastern Cape), Swaziland. ❄ (min. 61°F/16°C)

Encephalartos villosus

ENCYCLIA

ORCHIDACEAE

Genus of approximately 150 species of mainly evergreen, epiphytic orchids found in the US and from Mexico and the West Indies south to tropical N. South America, occurring in forest from sea level to 10,000ft (3,000m). They have fleshy pseudobulbs, which may be rounded or elongated, and usually 2 narrowly oblong to strap-shaped or linear to elliptic, fleshy or leathery leaves. Attractive, variable, often fragrant flowers are produced from the apexes of the pseudobulbs, mainly in late spring or summer but often intermittently throughout the year.

• **CULTIVATION** Cool-growing orchids. Grow in epiphytic orchid potting mix in a slatted basket, in bright filtered light or full light with shade from hot sun. In active growth, water freely and apply fertilizer at every third watering. Keep dry in winter. See also p.46.
• **PROPAGATION** Divide when plants overflow their containers, or remove backbulbs and pot up separately.
• **PESTS AND DISEASES** Susceptible to spider mites, aphids, and mealybugs.

Encyclia cochleata

E. alata. Evergreen orchid with conical to ovoid pseudobulbs and strap-shaped to narrowly elliptic, mid-green leaves, 6in (15cm) long, often flushed red-purple. Fragrant, pale green or yellow-green flowers, 2in (5cm) across, marked purple or red-brown with the lips veined with dark red, are produced in racemes to 5ft (1.5m) long, mostly in summer. ↕5ft (1.5m), ↔ 18in (45cm). S. Mexico to Costa Rica. ❄ (min. 52–54°F/11–12°C; max. 86°F/30°C)
E. brassavolae. Evergreen orchid with elongated, ovoid to spindle-shaped or pear-shaped pseudobulbs and narrowly oblong leaves, 5½–11in (14–28cm) long. Yellow-green to brown flowers, 3in (8cm) across, with purple-tipped white lips, are produced in racemes 6–39in (15–100cm) long, from summer to autumn. ↕24in (60cm), ↔ 18in (45cm). S. Mexico to W. Panama. ❄ (min. 52–54°F/11–12°C; max. 86°F/30°C)
E. citrina. Semi-evergreen orchid with ovoid, conical, or spindle-shaped pseudobulbs and narrowly elliptic, pendent, glaucous gray-green leaves, 7–10in (18–25cm) long. Solitary, occasionally 2, pendent, fleshy, fragrant, bright lemon-yellow flowers, to 3in (8cm) across, are borne from spring to early summer. Requires drier conditions than other species; withhold water when pseudobulbs are fully mature. ↕12in (30cm), ↔ 9in (23cm). Mexico. ❄ (min. 52–54°F/11–12°C; max. 86°F/30°C)
E. cochleata ■ Evergreen orchid with flattened pear-shaped to ellipsoid pseudobulbs and elliptic to lance-shaped leaves, 8–14in (20–35cm) long. Ribbon-like flowers, 4in (10cm) long, with twisted, pale green sepals and petals, dark purple lips flushed yellowish green, and white bases with deep purple veins, are produced in racemes to 20in (50cm) long intermittently throughout the year. ↕↔ 18in (45cm). Florida to Mexico, Colombia, Venezuela. ❄ (min. 52–54°F/11–12°C; max. 86°F/30°C)
E. cordigera. Evergreen orchid with conical to ovoid pseudobulbs and semi-rigid, narrowly elliptic leaves, to 18in (45cm) long. Fragrant, brown, purple-brown, or purple-green flowers, to 2in (5cm) across, with cream lips streaked pink or magenta, are borne in 3- to 15-flowered racemes to 30in (75cm) long, from spring to summer. ↕18in (45cm), ↔ 12in (30cm). S. Mexico, Central America, Colombia, Venezuela. ❄ (min. 52–54°F/11–12°C; max. 86°F/30°C)
E. fragrans. Evergreen orchid with elongated, narrowly ovoid to ellipsoid pseudobulbs, each bearing a single oblong-strap-shaped to elliptic leaf, 14in (35cm) long. Fragrant, cream to greenish white flowers, to 1½in (4cm) across, with red-striped lips held uppermost, are borne in few- to several-flowered racemes to 8in (20cm) long from spring to summer. ↕9in (23cm), ↔ 6in (15cm). S. Mexico, Central America to Brazil, Greater Antilles. ❄ (min. 52–54°F/11–12°C; max. 86°F/30°C)
E. mariae. Evergreen orchid with ovoid, clustered pseudobulbs and narrowly oblong leaves, 5in (13cm) long. In summer, bears racemes, 2–11in (5–28cm) long, of 2–4 pendent, yellow to olive-green flowers, to 2½in (6cm) long, with large, papery white lips, and green veins in the throats. ↕7in (18cm), ↔ 6in (15cm). E. Mexico. ❄ (min. 52–54°F/11–12°C; max. 86°F/30°C)
E. radiata. Evergreen orchid with ellipsoid to ovoid pseudobulbs and elliptic to lance-shaped leaves, to 14in (35cm) long. Fragrant, cream or greenish white flowers, 1½in (4cm)

across, with violet-lined lips held uppermost, are produced in racemes to 8in (20cm) long from autumn to winter. ↕ 10in (25cm), ↔ 12in (30cm). C. and S. Mexico, Guatemala, Honduras, Costa Rica. ❀ (min. 52–54°F/11–12°C; max. 86°F/30°C)

E. vitellina. Evergreen orchid with ovoid to conical pseudobulbs and lance-shaped to elliptic, gray-green leaves, to 9in (23cm) long. Brilliant orange or vermilion flowers, 1½in (4cm) across, with orange- to red-tipped yellow lips, develop in racemes 5–12in (12–30cm) long from spring to summer. ↕ 9in (23cm), ↔ 6in (15cm). S. Mexico, Guatemala. ❀ (min. 52–54°F/11–12°C; max. 86°F/30°C)

▷ ***Endymion*** see *Hyacinthoides*

ENKIANTHUS

ERICACEAE

Genus of about 10 species of mainly deciduous shrubs, occasionally trees, occurring in scrub and woodland from the Himalayas to Japan. They are grown for their terminal umbels or corymb-like racemes of bell- or urn-shaped flowers, usually ¼–⅜in (6–9mm) long, borne from midspring to early summer, and for their simple, lance-shaped to elliptic-obovate, usually toothed, alternate leaves, which turn various shades of orange and red in autumn. Best grown in an open site in a woodland garden.

• **CULTIVATION** Grow in humus-rich, moist but well-drained, acidic to neutral soil in full sun or partial shade. Pruning group 1.

• **PROPAGATION** Sow seed at 64–70°F (18–21°C) in late winter or early spring. Insert semi-ripe cuttings in summer. Layer in autumn.

• **PESTS AND DISEASES** Infrequent.

E. campanulatus ▣ (Redvein enkianthus). Spreading, tree-like, deciduous shrub with whorled branches and obovate-elliptic, toothed, dull green leaves, to 2½in (6cm) long, clustered at the tips of the shoots and turning orange-yellow to red in autumn. Bears pendent, corymb-like racemes of 5–15 bell-shaped, creamy yellow flowers, veined pink to red, in late spring and early summer. ↕↔ 12–15ft (4–5m). Japan. Zone 5b. **f. *albiflorus*** has white flowers. **'Hiraethlyn'** bears cream flowers with dark red veins. **var. *palibinii*** has dark red flowers.

Enkianthus cernuus var. *rubens*

'Red Bells' has red-tipped, red-veined, creamy yellow flowers.

E. cernuus* var. *rubens ▣ Bushy, deciduous shrub with dense clusters of obovate, toothed, bright green leaves, to 2in (5cm) long, tinged purple in summer and turning dark red-purple in autumn. In late spring and early summer, produces slender, pendent racemes of 5–12 broadly bell-shaped, rich red flowers, with finely toothed mouths. ↕↔ 8ft (2.5m). Japan. Zone 6.

E. chinensis. Upright, deciduous shrub with elliptic to elliptic-oblong, toothed, bright green leaves, to 3in (8cm) long, softly hairy along the midribs above, glaucous and hairless beneath, turning orange and red in autumn. Pendent, corymb-like racemes of 12–24 bell-shaped, creamy yellow flowers, with pink veins, are produced in late spring. ↕ to 11ft (3.5m), ↔ 6ft (2m). China, N. Burma. Zone 7b.

E. deflexus ▣ Vigorous, upright, deciduous shrub or small tree with red shoots and oval to obovate, bright green leaves, to 3in (8cm) long, downy beneath, turning orange and red in autumn. Umbels of 8–20 relatively large, broadly bell-shaped, pink-veined cream flowers, ½in (1.5cm) across, are produced in late spring and early summer. ↕ 8–12ft (2.5–4m) sometimes more, ↔ 10ft (3m). Himalayas, W. China. Zone 8.

E. perulatus ▣ Compact, deciduous shrub with red-tinted young branches. Elliptic to obovate, toothed, mid-green leaves, to 2in (5cm) long, clustered at the ends of the shoots, are downy on the

Enkianthus perulatus

midribs beneath and turn brilliant red in autumn. Produces pendent umbels of up to 10 urn-shaped white flowers in midspring. ↕↔ to 6ft (2m). Japan. Zone 7.

ENSETE

MUSACEAE

Genus of 7 species of banana-like, monocarpic, evergreen perennials from lower mountain slopes in tropical Africa and Asia. They have large, paddle-shaped leaves growing from trunk-like pseudostems, which are formed by the bases of the old leaf stalks. Cup-shaped flowers are produced in pendent, terminal inflorescences among large bracts. Fruits are banana-like but dry and unpalatable. Where not hardy, grow in a temperate greenhouse or plunge outdoors during summer to provide subtropical effects in summer bedding. In frost-free climates, grow as specimen plants or in a courtyard.

• **CULTIVATION** Under glass, grow in soil-based potting mix in full light with shade from hot sun. Keep well-ventilated. When in growth, water freely and apply a balanced liquid fertilizer monthly. Outdoors, grow in humus-rich soil in full sun or partial shade. Lift plunged plants before first frosts, cut back long roots, and reduce top-growth to the newest 2 or 3 leaves. Cut the dead leaves no lower than the base of each leaf blade.

• **PROPAGATION** Sow seed at 64–70°F (18–21°C) in spring, after soaking in tepid water for 24 hours. Germination is erratic.

• **PESTS AND DISEASES** Spider mites and aphids may be problems, especially under glass.

E. ventricosum ▣ syn. *Musa arnoldiana, M. ensete* (Abyssinian banana, Ethiopian banana). Fast-growing, banana-like perennial with huge, paddle-shaped, bright olive-green leaves, to 20ft (6m) long, produced from the center of the plant, with thick midribs that are bright red beneath. White flowers, concealed within arching cylinders of bronze-red bracts, are borne in inflorescences 3–4ft (1–1.2m) long in summer. ↕ 20ft (6m) or more, ↔ to 15ft (5m). Ethiopia to Angola. ❀ (min. 50°F/10°C). **'Maurelii'** has leaves tinged red above, especially along the margins, and dark red leaf stalks.

Enkianthus campanulatus

Enkianthus deflexus

Ensete ventricosum

Eomecon chionantha

EOMECON

Snow poppy

PAPAVERACEAE

Genus of one species of rhizomatous perennial occurring on riverbanks in E. China. It has slightly fleshy leaves and nodding, poppy-like flowers. Grow as a groundcover on a moist, shady bank, in a mixed border, or in a woodland garden.
• **CULTIVATION** Grow in humus-rich, moist but well-drained soil in light shade, or in full sun where the soil does not dry out in summer. May spread rapidly in fertile soil.
• **PROPAGATION** Sow seed in containers in a cold frame in spring. Divide, or separate rooted runners, both in spring.
• **PESTS AND DISEASES** Sometimes damaged by slugs and snails.

E. chionantha ■ Vigorous, spreading perennial with heart- to kidney- or arrow-shaped, leathery, dull gray-green leaves, to 4in (10cm) across. Upright, branching stems bear loose panicles of poppy-like, glistening white flowers, to 2in (5cm) across, from late spring to midsummer. ↕ to 16in (40cm), ↔ indefinite. E. China. Zone 7b.

EPACRIS

EPACRIDACEAE

Genus of 35 species of evergreen, heather-like shrubs occurring on heaths, open slopes, and scrub in Australia, New Zealand, and New Caledonia. They are cultivated for their often showy, tubular, cylindrical to bell-shaped, 5-lobed flowers, which are freely produced, usually in leafy, terminal racemes. The linear-lance-shaped to broadly ovate, mid- or dark green leaves are alternate or spiraling, and usually crowded on the stems. Where they are not hardy, grow in a cool greenhouse, where they will flower in winter and provide long-lasting cut flowers. In warmer areas, grow in a border or a large rock garden.
• **CULTIVATION** Under glass, grow in acidic potting mix in full light with shade from hot sun. From spring to autumn, water freely and apply a half-strength, balanced liquid fertilizer monthly. Water moderately in winter. Outdoors, grow in poor to moderately fertile, humus-rich, moist but well-drained, neutral to acidic soil in full sun with some midday shade. Pruning group 10, after flowering.

Epacris longiflora

• **PROPAGATION** Surface-sow seed at 55–61°F (13–16°C) in spring; germination is slow and usually erratic, taking between 3 and 6 months. Root semi-ripe cuttings with bottom heat in summer.
• **PESTS AND DISEASES** Scale insects may infest greenhouse plants.

E. impressa (Common Australian heath). Erect to spreading, often slender, evergreen shrub with narrowly ovate, deep green leaves, to ½in (1.5cm) long, tapering to prickle-like tips. Pendent, cylindrical, red, pink, or white flowers, ¾in (2cm) long, are borne in slender, erect, terminal racemes, 4in (10cm) or more long, from spring to summer. ↕ 1–4ft (30–120cm), occasionally to 6ft (1.8m), ↔ 12–36in (30–90cm). New South Wales to Tasmania. ❀ (min. 41°F/5°C)
E. longiflora ■ Erect or spreading, evergreen shrub, often irregular in habit, with broadly to narrowly ovate, broadly pointed, deep green leaves, to ½in (1.5cm) long. Pendent, cylindrical, white-tipped red flowers, ½–1½in (1–4cm) long, are produced singly from the leaf axils and in raceme-like, terminal spikes, to 1½in (4cm) long, mainly from spring to summer. ↕ 20–60in (0.5–1.5m), ↔ 3–6ft (1–2m). S.W. Australia. ❀ (min. 41°F/5°C). **'White Sport'** produces white flowers.

EPHEDRA

Joint fir

EPHEDRACEAE

Genus of about 40 species of usually dioecious, evergreen shrubs, occasionally climbers, occurring in dry, rocky sites from the Mediterranean to China, and in North and South America. They have green shoots and tiny, scale-like leaves, and are valued for their spherical fruits, which, on female plants, follow the tiny flowers. Grow as a groundcover in a shrub border or rock garden. Where not hardy, grow in a cold greenhouse or alpine house. Some species are used medicinally as stimulants; may be toxic.
• **CULTIVATION** Grow in poor to moderately fertile, sharply drained soil in full sun.
• **PROPAGATION** Sow seed of hardy species in containers in an open frame in autumn; sow seed of tender species at 55–61°F (13–16°C) in spring. Divide in autumn or spring.
• **PESTS AND DISEASES** Rust occurs.

E. distachya. Thicket-forming shrub with straight to arching, jointed, blue-green to dark green shoots. Bears insignificant, yellowish-green flowers in summer. Spherical red fruit, to ¼in (6mm) across, ripen in autumn. ↕ to 3ft (1m), ↔ 10ft (3m). S. Europe to Siberia. Zone 4.
E. gerardiana. Dense, thicket-forming shrub with upright, jointed, deep green shoots. Insignificant, yellowish green flowers are produced in summer. Spherical red fruit, ½in (1.5cm) across, ripen in autumn. ↕ 24in (60cm), ↔ 10ft (3m) or more. Himalayas, China. Zone 6.
E. minima. Narrow, leafless green stems growing from the ground like a coarse broom; spreads underground. The only ephedra commonly in cultivation that sets fruit without another plant of the opposite sex nearby. Tiny red fruit with one or two large black seeds are produced in late summer through autumn. ↕ 4–5in (1½–2cm), ↔ 12–16in (30–40cm). China, Tibet. Zone 5.

EPIDENDRUM

ORCHIDACEAE

Genus of about 750 species of highly varied, evergreen orchids, including epiphytes, lithophytes, and terrestrials. They are widespread in tropical North, Central, and South America, some thriving in montane forest to an altitude of 3,250ft (1,000m). Most produce cylindrical, leafy stems that may be either tall and reed-like or short and fleshy; others have pseudobulbs. The leaves vary greatly. The flowers are produced in usually terminal, umbel-like racemes or panicles, which are a continuation of the leafy stems, or they are occasionally borne from the bases.
• **CULTIVATION** Cool- to intermediate-growing orchids. Grow in containers of epiphytic or terrestrial orchid potting mix; provide support for long, scrambling stems. In summer, provide bright filtered light and high humidity; water freely, applying quarter-strength fertilizer at every third watering, and mist once or twice daily. Provide full light and water sparingly in winter. Keep species with pseudobulbs dry in winter. See also p.46.
• **PROPAGATION** Divide when the plants overflow their containers. Root plantlets of *E. ibaguense* and similar species as soon as they have developed vigorous roots.

Epidendrum difforme

• **PESTS AND DISEASES** Spider mites, mealybugs, whiteflies, and aphids may be problems. Black rot, leaf spots, virus diseases, and rust may occur.

E. ciliare. Epiphytic orchid with leafy, pseudobulb-like stems, and 1 or 2 oblong-elliptic, leathery, mid-green leaves, to 6in (15cm) long. Fragrant, white-lipped, pale yellow-green or pale yellow flowers, 3½in (9cm) across, sometimes with fringed lobes, are produced in terminal racemes, to 12in (30cm) long, mostly in winter. ↕ 20in (50cm), ↔ 12in (30cm). Mexico to N. South America, West Indies. ❀ (min. 55°F/13°C; max. 86°F/30°C)
E. conopseum. Epiphytic orchid with slender, leafy stems and 1–3 narrowly oblong to linear-lance-shaped, rigid, leathery, often purple-flushed, mid-green leaves, 3½in (9cm) long. In summer, bears fragrant, often purple-tinged, light gray-green flowers, ¾in (2cm) across, in terminal sub-umbels, to 6in (15cm) long. ↕ 8in (20cm), ↔ 6in (15cm). Florida to Mexico. ❀ (min. 55°F/13°C; max. 86°F/30°C)
E. difforme ■ Epiphytic orchid with flattened, fleshy, leafy stems and oblong to elliptic-lance-shaped, fleshy to leathery, glossy, yellowish green leaves, to 4½in (11cm) long. Fragrant, pale green, green-yellow, or white, almost translucent flowers, to 1¼in (3cm) across, are produced in clustered racemes, to 6in (15cm) across, in summer. ↕ 20in (50cm), ↔ 12in (30cm). Florida, West Indies, Mexico, Central America, Ecuador, Peru, Brazil. ❀ (min. 55°F/13°C; max. 86°F/30°C)
E. ibaguense, syn. *E. radicans.* Terrestrial orchid with tall, rambling, leafy stems and ovate-oblong to oblong, leathery, yellowish green leaves, 6in (15cm) long. Bright red, occasionally orange or yellow flowers, 1½in (4cm) across, are produced year-round in dense, terminal racemes, to 28in (70cm) long. ↕ 6ft (2m), ↔ 3ft (1m). West Indies, Mexico, Central America, Colombia, Venezuela, Guyana, Peru. ❀ (min. 55°F/13°C; max. 86°F/30°C)
E. nocturnum. Epiphytic orchid with leafy stems and 1 or 2 oblong-lance-shaped to elliptic, leathery, glossy, mid-green leaves, to 6in (15cm) long. Night-scented, white-lipped, pale yellow-green flowers, 2½in (6cm) across, sometimes with fringed lobes, are produced singly or in pairs in succession from summer to

Epidendrum x o'brienianum

autumn. ↕ 24in (60cm), ↔ 12in (30cm). West Indies, Florida, Central America, N. South America. ❀ (min. 55°F/13°C; max. 86°F/30°C)

E.* x *o'brienianum ■ (*E. evectum* x *E. ibaguense*). Epiphytic orchid with tall, rambling, leafy stems and semi-rigid, ovate-oblong to oblong, leathery, yellowish green leaves, 6in (15cm) long. Upright, terminal racemes, 32–36in (80–90cm) long, of long-lasting, bright orange-red or orange flowers, 1½in (4cm) across, are borne in summer and winter. ↕↔ 3ft (1m). Garden origin. ❀ (min. 55°F/13°C; max. 86°F/30°C)

E. pseudepidendrum. Epiphytic orchid with leafy stems and inversely lance-shaped, leathery, glossy, mid-green leaves, to 8in (20cm) long. Distinctive, fleshy green flowers, 2in (5cm) long, with protruding, bright orange lips with finely fringed lobes, are produced in few-flowered, pendent racemes, to 6in (15cm) long, from summer to autumn. ↕ 3ft (1m), ↔ 24in (60cm). Costa Rica, Panama. ❀ (min. 55°F/13°C; max. 86°F/30°C)

E. radicans see *E. ibaguense.*

E. secundum. Epiphytic orchid with leafy stems and ovate-lance-shaped, leathery, mid-green leaves, to 5½in (14cm) long. Rose-pink flowers, 1in (2.5cm) across, with deeply 3-lobed lips marked white and yellowish white, are produced in racemes to 30in (75cm) long throughout summer and autumn. ↕ 24in (60cm), ↔ 12in (30cm). West Indies, tropical South America. ❀ (min. 55°F/13°C; max. 86°F/30°C)

E. stamfordianum. Epiphytic orchid with spindle-shaped, leafy stems and 4–6 linear- to elliptic-oblong, leathery, mid-green leaves, to 7in (18cm) long. In summer, fragrant, white-lipped, yellow-green to pale bronze flowers, 2in (5cm) across, mottled red-brown or purple, are produced in racemes or panicles, to 24in (60cm) long, from the bases of the leafy stems. ↕ 12in (30cm), ↔ 24in (60cm). Guatemala. ❀ (min. 55°F/13°C; max. 86°F/30°C)

EPIGAEA syn. ORPHANIDESIA

ERICACEAE

Genus of 3 species of prostrate, evergreen shrubs and subshrubs from woodland in Turkey, Japan, and North America. They are grown for their short, axillary or terminal clusters or racemes of small, urn-shaped, funnel-shaped, or tubular-bell-shaped flowers, borne in spring, and for their ovate to oblong, entire, tough, prominently veined, dark green leaves, produced from rusty-hairy branches. Grow *Epigaea* species in a shaded niche in a rock garden or woodland garden.

• **CULTIVATION** Grow in humus-rich, moist, acidic soil in deep to light, dappled shade. In an alpine house, *E. gaultherioides* requires acidic potting mix and indirect light.

• **PROPAGATION** Surface-sow seed at 50–55°F (10–13°C) as soon as ripe; keep warm and moist until germination. Water seedlings from below. Separate rooted layers or take greenwood cuttings in early summer.

• **PESTS AND DISEASES** Fungal spots, spider mites, and whiteflies occur.

E. asiatica ■ Creeping, stem-rooting shrub with oblong to elliptic, leathery,

Epigaea asiatica

dark green leaves, 1½–4in (3.5–10cm) long, heart-shaped at the bases and with finely bristly margins. Stems and leaves are clothed in fine brown hairs. In late spring, bears short, pendent, axillary or terminal racemes of slightly fragrant, tubular-bell-shaped, light to mid-pink flowers, ½in (1.5cm) long, often with white tubes. ↕ to 4in (10cm), ↔ to 8in (20cm). Japan. Zone 6.

E. gaultherioides, syn. *Orphanidesia gaultherioides.* Prostrate subshrub with ovate to oblong, leathery, dark green leaves, 3–5in (8–13cm) long, with bristly veins and margins. Produces widely funnel-shaped, shell-pink flowers, to 2in (5cm) across, in axillary clusters in spring. Needs shade. ↕ to 4in (10cm), ↔ to 12in (30cm). N.E. Turkey. Zone 8.

E. repens (Ground laurel, Mayflower, Trailing arbutus). Creeping subshrub with ovate-oblong, sparsely bristly-hairy, glossy, dark green leaves, to 3in (8cm) long, heart-shaped at the bases, borne on hairy, rooting stems. In spring, produces fragrant, urn-shaped white flowers, to ½in (1.5cm) long, sometimes pink-flushed, in dense, raceme-like, terminal clusters. Difficult to transplant and establish; buy from a nursery. ↕ to 3in (8cm), ↔ to 12in (30cm). North America. Zone 4.

EPILOBIUM

syn. CHAMAENERION

Willow herb

ONAGRACEAE

Genus of about 200 species of annuals, biennials, herbaceous and semi-ever-green perennials (some of which are stoloniferous), and semi-evergreen subshrubs. They are widely distributed in temperate regions on waste and disturbed ground, stony slopes, river gravels, and subalpine screes and meadows. They are grown for their 4-petaled, pink or white flowers, borne singly or in leafy racemes from the leaf axils, usually over long periods from summer to autumn. The leaves are linear to broadly ovate. Wind-borne seeds and spreading rhizomes make many species invasive, but those described here are garden worthy. Grow in a rock garden or border. *E. glabellum* of gardens makes a good groundcover.

• **CULTIVATION** Grow in humus-rich, moist but well-drained soil in full sun or partial shade. Alpine species may need some midday shade. Deadhead for repeat flowering and to prevent seeding.

• **PROPAGATION** Sow seed in containers in a cold frame as soon as ripe or in

Epilobium angustifolium f. *album*

spring. Divide in autumn or spring. Take softwood cuttings from sideshoots in spring.

• **PESTS AND DISEASES** Downy mildew, powdery mildew, rust, and fungal spots are common. Snails and slugs sometimes cause problems.

E. angustifolium* f. *album ■ syn. *Chamaenerion angustifolium* f. *album*, *E. angustifolium* var. *leucanthum* (White fireweed). Strongly spreading, rhizomatous perennial with linear-lance-shaped, sometimes wavy, willow-like, pale to mid-green leaves, 1–8in (2.5–20cm) long. From midsummer to early autumn, bears racemes of open saucer-shaped white flowers, to ½in (1.5cm) across, with green sepals. Self-seeds freely. ↕ to 5ft (1.5m), ↔ 3ft (1m) or more. N. Hemisphere. Zone 4.

E. angustifolium* var. *leucanthum see *E. angustifolium* f. *album.*

E. californicum see *Zauschneria californica.*

E. canum see *Zauschneria californica* subsp. *cana.*

E. chlorifolium* var. *kaikourense. Clump-forming, woody-based perennial with ovate to broadly ovate, finely toothed, bronze-green leaves, ½–1¼in (1–3cm) long. In summer, upright, branching stems bear racemes of long-tubed, white or pale pink flowers, ½in (1.5cm) across, with spreading lobes. ↕ to 12in (30cm), ↔ to 6in (15cm). New Zealand. Zone 5.

E. crassum. Prostrate, creeping perennial with narrowly obovate, finely toothed, slightly fleshy, glossy, mid-green leaves, ½–1½in (1–4cm) long, pink-flushed beneath. In summer, bears solitary, open cup-shaped, pink-veined white flowers, ½in (1.5cm) across. Grow in partial shade. ↕ to 4in (10cm), ↔ to 8in (20cm). New Zealand. Zone 5b.

E. dodonaei. Spreading perennial with a woody rootstock and upright stems bearing linear, toothed, bristly-hairy, mid-green leaves, to 1in (2.5cm) long. Throughout summer, produces cup-shaped, deep pinkish purple flowers, to 1½in (4cm) across, in loose, terminal racemes. ↕ 12–36in (30–90cm), ↔ to 8in (20cm). C. and S. Europe to W. Asia. Zone 6.

***E. glabellum* of gardens** ■ Mat- or clump-forming, semi-evergreen perennial with elliptic to ovate, finely

Epilobium glabellum of gardens

E

toothed, bronzed, deep green leaves, to ¾in (2cm) long, on bristly-hairy, often red-tinted stems, 2–16in (5–40cm) long. Outward-facing, cup-shaped, creamy white or pink flowers, 1in (2.5cm) across, are borne singly on slender, branching stems in summer. Prefers cool, damp shade. ↕↔ to 8in (20cm). New Zealand. Zone 5b.
E. latifolium. Spreading, rhizomatous perennial with ovate-elliptic, glaucous, mid-green leaves, ½–3in (1.5–8cm) long. Funnel-shaped, pink or white to pink-purple flowers, to 1¼in (3cm) across, with crimson sepals, are borne in short, leafy racemes from midsummer to early autumn. ↕↔ 18in (45cm). N. Eurasia, North America. Zone 2.
E. septentrionale see *Zauschneria septentrionalis.*

E

EPIMEDIUM

Barrenwort

BERBERIDACEAE

Genus of 30–40 species of evergreen and deciduous, rhizomatous perennials from the Mediterranean to temperate E. Asia, occurring in woodland, scrub, and shady, rocky places. They have mainly basal, 2- or 3-ternate, sometimes pinnate, leathery leaves, the leaflets unequally heart-shaped at the bases and pointed at the tips, with more or less spiny margins. The leaves are sometimes bronze-tinted in spring, and often color well in autumn. Some species are deciduous in autumn; others retain old leaves until the new leaves are produced. Small, mainly saucer- to cup-shaped, yellow, beige, white, pink, red, or purple flowers, often with spurs, are borne in lax racemes, or sometimes in panicles, from spring to early summer. Grow as a groundcover under trees or shrubs, or in a border; the smaller species are suitable for a rock garden.

• **CULTIVATION** Grow in fertile, humus-rich, moist but well-drained soil in partial shade, with shelter from cold, dry winds. *E. perralderianum* tolerates part-day sun where soils remain moist; *E.* x *versicolor* tolerates full sun and slightly drier soils. Except for *E. perralderianum*, most provide the best display of foliage and flowers if the old leaves are clipped back in late winter or early spring, before flower spikes emerge. Provide a deep winter mulch where cold is prolonged or severe.

• **PROPAGATION** Sow seed in containers in a cold frame as soon as ripe. Divide in autumn or after flowering. Root rhizome cuttings under glass in winter; plant out after all danger of frost has passed.

• **PESTS AND DISEASES** Vine weevil and mosaic virus may be a problem.

E. acuminatum ■ Clump-forming, evergreen, rhizomatous perennial with leaves divided into 3 obliquely lance-shaped to narrowly ovate leaflets, 1¼–7in (3–18cm) long, with spiny, marginal teeth, the lower 2 leaflets with very unequally lobed bases. Young leaves are mid-green, marked reddish brown and mauve, becoming glaucous beneath. Long-spurred, usually pale purple to purple-pink flowers, 1¼–1½in (3–4cm) across, are produced from midspring to early summer. ↕ 12in (30cm), ↔ 18in (45cm). W. and C. China. Zone 6.

Epimedium acuminatum

E. alpinum (Alpine barrenwort). Clump-forming, deciduous, rhizomatous perennial with leaves divided into 5–9 ovate, spiny-margined, bright green leaflets, 2–3½in (5–9cm) long, often coloring crimson in winter. Almost spurless flowers, ⅜–½in (0.9–1.5cm) across, with brownish red sepals and yellow petals, are produced in mid- and late spring. ↕ 6–12in (15–30cm), ↔ 12in (30cm). S. Europe. Zone 5.
E.* x *cantabrigiense (*E. alpinum* x *E. pubigerum*). Clump-forming, evergreen, rhizomatous perennial with long-stalked, mid-green leaves, each divided into 7–17 ovate, few-spined leaflets, 2–4in (5–10cm) long, persistently softly hairy beneath and variably colored in autumn. Numerous spurless, pinkish beige and yellow flowers, to ½in (1.5cm) across, are produced well above the foliage in mid- and late spring. ↕ 12–24in (30–60cm), ↔ 24in (60cm). Garden origin. Zone 5b.
E. davidii ■ Clump-forming, evergreen, rhizomatous perennial with leaves divided into 3, occasionally 5, ovate to ovate-lance-shaped leaflets, 1¼–3in (3–8cm) long, copper when young, becoming fresh green later. Pale to deep yellow flowers, ¾–1¼in (2–3cm) across, with curved yellow spurs, are produced from midspring to early summer. ↕ 12in (30cm), ↔ 18in (45cm). W. China. Zone 6.
E. diphyllum. Clump-forming, evergreen or semi-evergreen, rhizomatous perennial bearing leaves divided into 2 broadly ovate to heart-shaped,

Epimedium davidii

Epimedium grandiflorum 'Crimson Beauty'

light green leaflets, ¾–2in (2–5cm) long, with a few marginal spines. Bears spurless, pendent, bell-shaped, pure white flowers, ½in (1.5cm) across, in mid- and late spring. ↕ to 10in (25cm), ↔ 12in (30cm). Japan. Zone 5b.
E. grandiflorum, syn. *E. macranthum* (Bishop's hat, Longspur barrenwort). Clump-forming, deciduous, rhizomatous perennial bearing leaves 12in (30cm) long, with usually 9 ovate-heart-shaped, spiny-margined, light green leaflets, 1¼–2½in (3–6cm) long, flushed bronze when young. Pendent, white, yellow, pink, or purple flowers, 1–1¾in (2.5–4.5cm) across, with spurs 1in (2.5cm) long, are borne in mid- and late spring. ↕ 8–12in (20–30cm), ↔ 12in (30cm). China (S. Manchuria), N. Korea, Japan. Zone 4. **'Crimson Beauty'** ■ has copper markings on young leaves, and produces copper-crimson flowers. **f. *flavescens***, syn. *E. koreanum*, bears pale yellow flowers; Korea. **'Lilac Fairy'** see 'Lilafee'. **'Lilafee'** ■ syn. 'Lilac Fairy', has purple-tinted young leaves and violet-purple flowers; ↕ 8–10in (20–25cm). **'Nanum'** has white flowers; ↕ 3in (8cm). **'Rose Queen'** has dark bronze-purple young leaves, and bears deep rose-pink flowers with long, white-tipped spurs. **f. *violaceum***, syn. 'Violaceum', bears purple-and-white flowers. **'White Queen'** has large, pure white flowers, 1¾in (4.5cm) across.
E. koreanum see *E. grandiflorum* f. *flavescens.*
E. leptorrhizum. Slowly spreading, evergreen, rhizomatous perennial

Epimedium grandiflorum 'Lilafee'

Epimedium x *perralchicum*

bearing 3-ternate, rarely simple, spiny-margined, red-stalked leaves with ovate-lance-shaped, conspicuously veined leaflets, 3–4½in (7–11cm) long, heart-shaped at the bases and with long, pointed tips. Young leaves are bronze-brown with red hairs beneath, especially along the veins, maturing to mid-green and remaining hairy only on the veins beneath. From midspring to early summer, produces white flowers, to 1½in (4cm) across, suffused lilac-pink, with spurs ¾in (2cm) long. ↕ 5–12in (12–30cm), ↔ 18in (45cm). China. Zone 6.
E. macranthum see *E. grandiflorum.*
E.* x *perralchicum ■ (*E. perralderianum* x *E. pinnatum* subsp. *colchicum*). Robust, clump-forming, evergreen, rhizomatous perennial with glossy, deep green leaves, bronze when young; each leaf is divided into 9, occasionally only 3, ovate, spiny-margined leaflets, 3in (8cm) long, often with overlapping lobes at the base. Pendent, bright yellow flowers, to ¾in (2cm) across, with very short brown spurs, are produced in mid- and late spring. ↕ 16in (40cm), ↔ 24in (60cm). Garden origin. Zone 4.

Epimedium pinnatum subsp. *colchicum*

'Fröhnleiten' produces elongated leaflets with more dense marginal spines, and flowers to 1in (2.5cm) across. **'Wisley'** has flowers to 1in (2.5cm) across; ↕ 24in (60cm).
E. perralderianum. Gently spreading, evergreen, rhizomatous perennial forming a bold, dense clump of leaves, each leaf divided into usually 3 ovate, conspicuously toothed leaflets, 2–3in (5–8cm) long, bronze when young, maturing to glossy, dark green. Bright yellow flowers, to ¾in (2cm) across, with short brown spurs, are produced in mid- and late spring. ↕ 12in (30cm), ↔ 24in (60cm). Algeria. Zone 4.
E. pinnatum. Slowly spreading, evergreen, rhizomatous perennial bearing 2-ternate or sometimes pinnate leaves with ovate, spiny-margined, white- or red-hairy, later hairless, dark green leaflets, 2–4in (5–10cm) long. Produces bright yellow flowers, to ¾in (2cm) across, with brownish purple spurs, in late spring and early summer. ↕↔ 8–12in (20–30cm). N. Iran. Zone 5. **subsp. *colchicum*** ■ syn. subsp. *elegans*, is slow-growing, its shorter rhizomes making a denser clump. The leaves are divided into 5, more rounded, less spiny leaflets, 2½–5in (6–13cm) long. Flowers with brown or yellow spurs are borne in spring. ↕ 12–16in (30–40cm), ↔ 10in (25cm). Caucasus to N.E. Turkey.
E. pubigerum ■ Clump-forming, evergreen, rhizomatous perennial producing leaves with up to 9 ovate to rounded, spiny, glossy, mid-green leaflets, 1½–3in (4–8cm) long, heart-shaped at the bases, hairy beneath. Creamy white, sometimes yellowish white flowers, to ½in (1.5cm) across, are borne above the foliage in mid- and late spring. ↕↔ 18in (45cm). Bulgaria, Turkey to Republic of Georgia. Zone 5.
E. x rubrum (*E. alpinum* x *E. grandiflorum*) (Red barrenwort). Slowly spreading, clump-forming, deciduous, rhizomatous perennial. Bears 2-ternate leaves with ovate, pointed, thin, spine-toothed leaflets, 2½–4in (6–10cm) long, flushed red when young, turning red and reddish brown in autumn, and remaining through winter. Crimson and pale yellow flowers, to ¾in (2cm) across, with short spurs, are produced in mid- and late spring. ↕↔ 12in (30cm). Garden origin. Zone 3.
***E. stellulatum* 'Wudang Star'.** Clump-forming, evergreen perennial with a short, creeping rhizome and 2-ternate leaves with ovate, spine-toothed, glossy, mid-green leaflets, 2½–4in (6–10cm) long. In spring, bears panicles of star-shaped white flowers, ½in (1.5cm) across, with prominent yellow stamens. ↕↔ 10–14in (25–35cm). Zone 5b.
E. sutchuenense. Clump-forming, evergreen, rhizomatous perennial with 3-ternate leaves consisting of narrowly ovate, mid-green leaflets, 2–3in (5–8cm) long, heart-shaped at the bases, pointed at the tips, and sparsely gray-hairy above. Long-spurred, rose-pink flowers, ¾in (2cm) across, sometimes purple-tinted, are borne in mid- and late spring. ↕↔ 12in (30cm). China. Zone 6.
E. x versicolor (*E. grandiflorum* x *E. pinnatum* subsp. *colchicum*). Clump-forming, evergreen, rhizomatous perennial with leaves usually divided into 5–15 ovate-heart-shaped, spine-toothed leaflets, 2–3½in (5–9cm) long, copper-red and brown when young, turning mid-green. Bears pink and yellow flowers, ¼–¾in (0.6–2cm) across, with red-tinted spurs, in mid- and late spring. ↕↔ 12in (30cm). Garden origin. Zone 5. **'Cupreum'** has copper-red flowers. **'Neosulfureum'** bears pale yellow flowers and 3–9 leaflets per leaf. **'Sulfureum'** has 5–11 leaflets per leaf, and bears slightly darker yellow flowers and longer spurs than 'Neosulfureum'; ↔ 3ft (1m). **var. *versicolor*** ■ has small flowers, ¼–½in (6–15mm) across, with deep reddish pink sepals and yellow petals.
E. x warleyense ■ (*E. alpinum* x *E. pinnatum* subsp. *colchicum*). Spreading, clump-forming, evergreen, rhizomatous perennial with leaves divided into 5–9 ovate, sparsely spiny, mid-green leaflets, 3–5in (8–13cm) long, hairy beneath, and tinted red in spring and autumn. Produces yellow flowers, ½in (1.5cm) across, with reddish orange sepals, in mid- and late spring. ↕ to 20in (50cm), ↔ 30in (75cm). Garden origin. Zone 5. **'Orangekönigin'** makes a denser clump and has slightly paler orange sepals.
E. x youngianum (*E. diphyllum* x *E. grandiflorum*). Clump-forming, deciduous, rhizomatous perennial with leaves divided into 2–9 leaflets, ¾–3in (2–8cm) long, on red-tinted leaf stalks; leaflets are narrowly ovate, mid-green, thin, wavy-margined, almost spineless, hairy, becoming hairless beneath, with one leaflet distinctly larger. In mid- and late spring, produces greenish white or pale rose-pink flowers, ½–¾in (1.5–2cm) long, sometimes with spurs. ↕ 8–12in (20–30cm), ↔ 12in (30cm). Garden origin. Zone 4. **'Lilacinum'** see 'Roseum'. **'Niveum'** ■ produces pure white flowers, to ½in (1.5cm) across, sometimes spurred, and often has very colorful young foliage. **'Roseum'**, syn. 'Lilacinum', has variable foliage and dusky pink to purple flowers. **'Yenomoto'** has white flowers.

Epimedium pubigerum

Epimedium x *warleyense*

Epimedium x *youngianum* 'Niveum'

Epimedium x *versicolor* var. *versicolor*

EPIPACTIS
Helleborine

ORCHIDACEAE

Genus of 24 species of rhizomatous, terrestrial, herbaceous orchids, mainly found in temperate areas of the N. hemisphere, often occurring in marshes, alpine meadows, rich woodland, or on dunes; a few are tropical species from Africa, Thailand, and Mexico. They usually have ribbed, lance-shaped to ovate leaves, arranged spirally or in 2 ranks. The spurless flowers are borne in loose or dense spikes on twisted stalks. The upper segments of each flower spread or curve inward to form a "helmet," and the 2-parted lower lip unites at the base to form a "cup," with a heart-shaped or triangular lobe beneath. Grow in a damp, shady border, or in a wild or woodland garden.
• **CULTIVATION** Grow in fertile, humus-rich, moist but well-drained soil in partial or deep shade. May spread freely in ideal conditions. See also p.46.
• **PROPAGATION** Divide in early spring, ensuring that each piece of rhizome has at least one growing point.
• **PESTS AND DISEASES** Vulnerable to slugs and snails.

E. gigantea (Giant helleborine). Rhizomatous orchid with upright stems bearing lance-shaped to ovate leaves, to 8in (20cm) long. From spring to early summer, produces loose, terminal spikes of up to 15 nodding, bright greenish yellow flowers, to ¾in (2cm) across, each with a leafy bract beneath; the lips and upper lobes are veined maroon, the widely spreading, yellow lateral lobes are veined brownish purple. ↕ 12–16in (30–40cm), ↔ to 5ft (1.5m). S.W. US. Zone 5.

▷ ***Epiphyllanthus obovatus*** see *Schlumbergera opuntioides*

EPIPHYLLUM

Orchid cactus

CACTACEAE

Genus of about 20 species of mostly epiphytic cacti occurring mainly in rainforest from S. Mexico to Argentina, and also in the West Indies. The strap-shaped, cylindrical, flattened, often deeply toothed, fleshy green stems and branches become 2-ribbed when mature, and bear small, usually spineless areoles. The mainly funnel-shaped flowers, 3–12in (8–30cm) long, are often sweetly scented and last for 2 or more days; many are nocturnal. In areas where temperatures drop below 50°F (10°C), grow as houseplants or in a warm greenhouse. In warmer climates, plant in a shaded courtyard, or in hanging baskets as patio plants.

- **CULTIVATION** Under glass, grow in epiphytic cactus potting mix in bright filtered light, with moderate to high humidity. From midspring to late summer, water freely and apply a high-potash fertilizer every 2 weeks as flower buds form; keep just moist in winter. They require a minimum temperature of 50°F (10°C) for most of the year, but for successful cultivation, the temperature should be increased to 59°F (15°C) in early spring. They will die if exposed to temperatures above 100°F (38°C). Outdoors, grow in fertile, sharply drained soil in light dappled or partial shade. Epiphyllums flower well only if potbound. See also pp.48–49.
- **PROPAGATION** Sow seed at 70°F (21°C) in spring or early summer, but they will not always come true from seed. Take stem cuttings in early summer.
- **PESTS AND DISEASES** Fungal leaf and stem spots, mealybugs, and scale insects occur.

E. ackermannii see *Nopalxochia ackermannii.*

E. anguliger. Erect, bushy, many-branched, epiphytic cactus with partly cylindrical, partly flattened, deeply toothed, mid-green stems, 1½–3in (4–8cm) wide. From late spring to summer, bears diurnal, funnel-shaped, scented flowers, 6in (15cm) long, with narrow, wide-spreading, golden or lemon-yellow outer tepals and white inner tepals. ↕ to 30in (75cm), ↔ 18in (45cm). S. Mexico. ❀ (min. 50–59°F/10–15°C)

E. chrysocardium, syn. *Marniera chrysocardium, Selenicereus chrysocardium.* Erect then semi-pendent, or scandent, epiphytic cactus with very deeply toothed, flattened, mid-green stems, to 12in (30cm) wide, forming lobes 1¼–1½in (3–4cm) wide, the areoles sometimes with 2 or 3 bristles each. In late winter or spring, produces nocturnal, funnel-shaped flowers, 12in (30cm) or more long, that have dull purple outer tepals, white inner tepals, tubes that are pale green below, dull purple above, and golden yellow stamens. ↕ to 6ft (2m), ↔ 30in (75cm). S. Mexico. ❀ (min. 50–59°F/10–15°C)

E. crenatum ▣ Erect, bushy, semi-epiphytic cactus with a cylindrical main stem. Produces leaf-like, grayish green branches, 5in (13cm) wide, the margins wavy and toothed. Diurnal, funnel-shaped, fragrant, creamy white flowers, 8in (20cm) long, with green, pink, or pale yellow outer segments, are produced in summer. ↕↔ to 10ft (3m). S. Mexico to Honduras. ❀ (min. 50–59°F/10–15°C)

E. hookeri, syn. *E. strictum.* Erect, bushy, scandent, epiphytic cactus with flattened, coarsely toothed, bluish green stems, 3in (8cm) wide. Nocturnal, star-shaped, creamy or yellowish white flowers, to 10in (25cm) long, with red-tinged, pale green outer segments, are produced in midsummer. Resembles *E. phyllanthus* but has broader flowers. ↕ 6ft (2m), ↔ 20in (50cm). S. Mexico to Costa Rica, Trinidad. ❀ (min. 50–59°F/10–15°C)

E. laui. Erect, bushy, epiphytic cactus with flattened, frequently red-tinged, glossy, mid-green stems, 4in (10cm) wide, sometimes 4-angled or cylindrical, with slightly toothed margins. Nocturnal or diurnal, funnel-shaped, scented white flowers, 7in (18cm) long, are produced in early summer. ↕ 12in (30cm), ↔ to 20in (50cm). S. Mexico. ❀ (min. 50–59°F/10–15°C)

E. macdougallii see *Nopalxochia macdougallii.*

E. oxypetalum (Dutchman's pipe cactus). Erect or semi-erect, many-branched, epiphytic cactus with cylindrical, mid-green stems and thin, leaf-like, elliptic, sharp-pointed, scalloped branches, 5in (13cm) wide. Nocturnal, funnel-shaped white flowers, 10–12in (25–30cm) long, with long, curved, arching tubes and very pale purplish white outer segments, are produced from late spring to summer. ↕ 10ft (3m), ↔ 3ft (1m). Mexico, Guatemala, Venezuela, Brazil. ❀ (min. 50–59°F/10–15°C)

E. phyllanthus. Semi-erect, bushy, semi-epiphytic cactus with cylindrical stems and leaf-like, linear, blunt or pointed, stiff, scalloped, mid-green branches, 3in (8cm) wide, with prominent midribs and purple-shaded margins. In summer, bears nocturnal, funnel-shaped, glistening white or pale yellowish white flowers, 10–12in (25–30cm) long, with green- or red-tinged outer tepals and slender green tubes. ↕ 6ft (2m), ↔ 24in (60cm). Panama, Colombia, Ecuador, Peru, Brazil. ❀ (min. 50–59°F/10–15°C)

E. pumilum. Semi-erect or pendent, epiphytic cactus with long, leaf-like, mid-green stems, 1¼–3in (3–8cm) wide, often tapering to a point. In summer, produces nocturnal, funnel-shaped, scented, creamy white flowers, 3–5in (8–13cm) long, with red outer tepals, white inner tepals, and green tubes. ↕↔ 20in (50cm) or more. Guatemala. ❀ (min. 50–59°F/10–15°C)

E. strictum see *E. hookeri.*

Epiphyllum crenatum

EPIPREMNUM

ARACEAE

Genus of 8 species of evergreen, root-clinging climbers, with juvenile and adult phases, found in forest from S.E. Asia to the W. Pacific. They are grown for their attractive, alternate leaves, which may be entire to pinnate, sometimes on the same plant. Spikes of tiny, petalless flowers are enclosed in spathes. Where not hardy, grow in a temperate or warm greenhouse, or as houseplants. In warmer areas, grow against a wall, over a pergola, or through trees. All parts may cause severe discomfort if ingested, and contact with the sap of *E. aureum* may irritate skin.

Epipremnum aureum 'Marble Queen'

- **CULTIVATION** Under glass, grow in soil-based potting mix in full or bright filtered light. In growth, water freely and apply a balanced liquid fertilizer monthly; water lightly to moderately in winter. Provide the support of a moss pole if climbing. Outdoors, grow in fertile, moist but well-drained soil in full sun or partial shade. Pruning group 11, in early spring. Tip-prune in spring to promote branching.
- **PROPAGATION** Root leaf-bud or stem-tip cuttings with bottom heat in summer. Layer in spring or summer.
- **PESTS AND DISEASES** Prone to leaf spot, blights, and root rot caused by a variety of fungi and bacteria. Spider mites and scale insects can sometimes be problems.

E. aureum, syn. *Scindapsus aureus* (Devil's ivy, Golden pothos). Strong-growing climber that, when young, has ovate, entire, glossy, bright green leaves, 4–12in (10–30cm) long, heart-shaped at the bases, and dashed or striped white, cream, or yellow. Mature plants have deeply lobed leaves, to 32in (80cm) long, and bear green flowering spathes, 6in (15cm) long, in summer. ↕ 25–40ft (8–12m). Solomon Islands. ❀ (min. 59°F/15°C). **'Exotica'** has lance-shaped, matte, dark green leaves, to 8in (20cm) long, slanted at the bases, and mottled with silver. **'Marble Queen'** ▣ produces mainly white

Epipremnum pictum 'Argyraeum'

leaves, heavily flecked and splashed with yellow, cream, and green; ↕ 3–10ft (1–3m).

***E. pictum* 'Argyraeum'** ▣ syn. *Scindapsus pictus* 'Argyraeus'. Slow-growing climber cultivated in its juvenile phase, when it has ovate, entire leaves, 3–4in (7–10cm) long, heart-shaped at the bases, satin-textured and deep green above, with irregular silver spots, paler and unspotted beneath. ↕ 18–36in (45–90cm) if trained on a support, 3–6ft (1–2m) or more if grown against a wall or through a tree. ❄ (min. 59°F/15°C)

EPISCIA

Flame violet

GESNERIACEAE

Genus of 6 species of creeping, stoloniferous, mat-forming, epiphytic or terrestrial, evergreen perennials found in tropical forest and rocky habitats from Mexico to South America. They and the hundreds of cultivars are grown for their soft, colorful foliage and salverform, 5-lobed flowers, which are borne singly or in small racemes from the leaf axils, from spring to autumn. Opposite, oblong to oblong-elliptic, hairy, often puckered leaves are produced in rosettes or whorls. Where not hardy, grow as houseplants, in a conservatory or terrarium, or in hanging baskets; elsewhere, use as a groundcover.

• **CULTIVATION** Under glass, grow in soilless potting mix with added perlite or vermiculite, in bright filtered light, with high humidity. During the growing season, water moderately, applying a quarter-strength, balanced liquid fertilizer at each watering. Keep just moist in winter. Outdoors, grow in fertile, humus-rich, moist but sharply drained soil in partial shade.

• **PROPAGATION** Surface-sow seed at about 68–77°F (20–25°C) as soon as ripe or in early spring. Divide, separate plantlets, or root stem cuttings or runners with bottom heat.

• **PESTS AND DISEASES** Susceptible to fungal spots and aerial blights, mealybugs, and aphids.

***E.* 'Cleopatra'** ▣ Mat-forming, terrestrial perennial with reddish green stolons and ovate, light green leaves, to 4in (10cm) long, suffused and marked creamy white, and with down-turned, broad pink margins. Axillary racemes of 3–5 orange-red flowers, to 2in (5cm)

Episcia cupreata

long, are produced from spring to autumn. ↕ 7in (18cm), ↔ 16in (40cm). ❄ (min. 59°F/15°C)

E. cupreata ▣ Variable, mat-forming, terrestrial perennial with elliptic, toothed, deep copper-green leaves, to 3½in (9cm) long, purple beneath. Red and yellow flowers, to 2½in (6cm) long, sometimes spotted purple in the throats, are borne in axillary racemes of 3 or 4 from spring to autumn. ↕ 6in (15cm), ↔ indefinite. Colombia, Venezuela, Brazil. ❄ (min. 59°F/15°C). **'Acajou'** has dark tan leaves netted with silvery green, and freely produces orange-red flowers. **'Metallica'** has copper leaves, each with a central silver band and metallic-pink margins, and produces flame-red flowers. **'Tropical Topaz'** produces pale green leaves and bright yellow flowers.

***E.* 'Cygnet'** see *Alsobia* 'Cygnet'.

E. dianthiflora see *Alsobia dianthiflora*.

***E.* 'Fire 'N' Ice'.** Mat-forming, terrestrial perennial bearing ovate, mid-green leaves, 3–4in (8–10cm) long, with silver markings. From spring to autumn, produces orange-red flowers, to 2in (5cm) across, in axillary racemes of up to 5. ↕ 4–6in (10–15cm), ↔ indefinite. ❄ (min. 59°F/15°C)

***E. lilacina*.** Variable, mat-forming, epiphytic or terrestrial perennial bearing ovate, scalloped, copper-green leaves, 2in (5cm) long, with fresh green midribs and veins, and purple undersides. From spring to autumn, white flowers, to 1¾in (4.5cm) long, with lavender-blue throats, are borne in axillary racemes of up to 4. ↕ 6in (15cm), ↔ 16in (40cm). Costa Rica. ❄ (min. 59°F/15°C). **'Cuprea'** has deep copper leaves, with narrow silver markings around the midribs, and white-centered, lavender-blue flowers.

***E.* 'Moonlight Valley'** ▣ Mat-forming, terrestrial perennial with oval, variably multi-colored leaves, to 4in (10cm) long. Bears orange-red flowers, to 2in (5cm) across, in axillary racemes, intermittently throughout the year. ↕ to 2in (5cm), ↔ indefinite. ❄ (min. 59°F/15°C)

***E.* 'Moss Agate'.** Mat-forming, terrestrial perennial with ovate, bright mid-green leaves, 2–3in (5–8cm) long, etched in silver. From spring to autumn, scarlet flowers, to 2in (5cm) across, are produced in axillary racemes of 4–5. ↕ 4–6in (10–15cm), ↔ indefinite. ❄ (min. 59°F/15°C)

***E.* 'Pink Panther'.** Mat-forming, terrestrial perennial with ovate, lime-green leaves, to 5in (13cm) long. Axillary racemes of 3–5 rose-pink flowers, to 2½in (6cm) long, are borne from spring to autumn. ↕ 7in (18cm), ↔ 18in (45cm). ❄ (min. 59°F/15°C)

***E.* 'Pink Ric Rac'.** Mat-forming, terrestrial perennial with ovate, dark bronze leaves, 3–4in (8–10cm) long, etched with pink. From spring to autumn, produces axillary racemes of up to 5 red flowers, to 2in (5cm) across. ↕ 4–6in (10–15cm), ↔ indefinite. ❄ (min. 59°F/15°C)

***E.* 'Silver Skies'.** Mat-forming, terrestrial perennial bearing ovate leaves, to 1¼in (3cm) long, with silvery green centers and broad, mid-green margins. Axillary racemes of 2–5 red flowers, 2in (5cm) long, are produced from spring to autumn. ↕ 7in (18cm), ↔ 14in (35cm). ❄ (min. 59°F/15°C)

EPITHELANTHA

CACTACEAE

Genus of one species of cactus occurring in S. US and Mexico, mainly on calcareous soils. The stems are thickly covered with rows of small tubercles. Small, tufted areoles bear numerous white spines; the apical areoles produce small, funnel-shaped, white or pale orange to pink flowers. Where not hardy, grow in a warm greenhouse; in warm, dry climates, grow in a desert garden or on a raised bed.

• **CULTIVATION** Under glass, grow in standard cactus potting mix, with added limestone chips, in full light. In growth, water moderately and apply low-nitrogen fertilizer monthly; keep completely dry when dormant. Outdoors, grow in poor to moderately fertile, sharply drained soil in full sun. See also pp.48–49.

• **PROPAGATION** Sow seed at 70°F (21°C) in early spring, or graft onto species of *Cereus*.

• **PESTS AND DISEASES** Vulnerable to root mealybugs under glass.

E. micromeris* var. *unguispina see *E. unguispina*.

E. unguispina ▣ syn. *E. micromeris* var. *unguispina*. Solitary or clump-forming, spherical to obovoid, grayish green cactus with diurnal, funnel-shaped, white or pale orange to pink flowers, ½in (1.5cm) across, borne in groups of 2 or 3 or more in summer. ↕ 1½in (4cm), ↔ 1½–3in (4–8cm). S. US, Mexico. ❄ (min. 50°F/10°C), but established plants withstand periods to 20°F (-7°C).

E

Episcia 'Cleopatra'

Episcia 'Moonlight Valley'

Epithelantha unguispina

E

Equisetum hyemale

EQUISETUM

Horsetail

EQUISETACEAE

Genus of 25 species of spreading, rhizomatous, flowerless, often marginal aquatic perennials from pond margins and dry land, primarily in the N. hemisphere. The stems are spreading, branching, jointed, and black-tinged, and the leaves are tiny and brown-tinged, joined to form sheaths. Horsetails are useful in a water garden, although often invasive. Where not hardy, grow at the margins of an indoor pool. All parts may cause severe discomfort if ingested.

• **CULTIVATION** Since *Equisetum* species are very invasive, grow in containers sunk into the ground, with the lip kept above ground level. Grow dry-land species in soil-based potting mix in full sun. Water moderately in the growing season. Grow aquatic species in soilless potting mix in full sun at a water depth of 0–6in (0–15cm). See also pp.52–53.

• **PROPAGATION** Divide in spring or autumn and replant immediately.

• **PESTS AND DISEASES** Sometimes affected by root rot or blight.

E. hyemale ▣ Emergent or marginal evergreen perennial with thin, jointed, rush-like, black-green stems. Leaves are joined to become black-banded, green sheaths, to ½in (1.5cm) long. Bears tiny, light brown strobili at the stem tips, from summer to autumn. ↕ to 4ft (1.2m), ↔ indefinite. Eurasia, North America. Zone 3.

E. scirpoides (Dwarf horsetail). Clumping, emergent or marginal evergreen perennial producing thin, wiry, deep green stems with distinctive nodes. Leaves are joined to become tiny sheaths, ⅛in (3mm) long. From summer to autumn, bears tiny, light brown strobili at the stem tips. Good as a low, grassy groundcover. ↕ to 6–8in (15–20cm), ↔ indefinite. North America. Zone 5b.

ERAGROSTIS

Love grass

POACEAE

Genus of approximately 250 species of clump-forming, annual and perennial grasses widely distributed throughout tropical and temperate regions of the world. They occur on cultivated or disturbed ground, often on sandy soils. The narrowly linear leaves are flat or rolled. Dense or open, sparsely to many-branched panicles of small, flattened, closely overlapping spikelets are borne on slender, upright stems from summer to autumn. Grow as specimen plants, in a mixed or herbaceous border, or in a rock garden. Where not hardy, grow in a cool greenhouse. The inflorescences are useful for fresh or dried flower arrangements.

• **CULTIVATION** Grow in medium to light, poor to moderately fertile, well-drained soil in a warm, sunny site. In late winter or early spring, before new growth begins, cut back any stems and foliage left for winter interest.

• **PROPAGATION** Sow seed in containers in a cold frame in spring, or divide between midspring and early summer.

• **PESTS AND DISEASES** Sterility disease, tar spot, smut, rust, and leaf spots occur.

E. curvula. Densely tufted, mound-forming, perennial grass with arching, narrowly linear, rolled or slightly open, rough-textured, dark green leaves, to 12in (30cm) long. In late summer and early autumn, bears erect or nodding, open panicles, to 12in (30cm) long, consisting of closely overlapping, 3- to 18-flowered, dark olive-gray spikelets, to ½in (1.5cm) long, which persist through winter. ↕↔ 4ft (1.2m). Southern Africa, India. ❄ (min. 35°F/2°C); tolerates brief periods to 14°F (-10°C).

ERANTHEMUM

ACANTHACEAE

Genus of approximately 30 species of woody-based perennials and evergreen shrubs occurring in forest and scrub in tropical Asia. They are cultivated for their tubular, 5-lobed flowers, which are produced in terminal or axillary spikes or panicles in winter. The leaves are opposite, lance-shaped to broadly ovate, simple, entire or toothed, and often prominently veined. Where not hardy, grow in a warm greenhouse or conservatory, or as houseplants. In humid, subtropical climates, they may be grown outdoors and are particularly useful in a lightly shaded border.

• **CULTIVATION** Under glass, grow in soil-based potting mix in bright filtered light. From spring to autumn, water moderately and apply a balanced liquid fertilizer every month; water sparingly in winter. Top-dress or pot on in spring. Outdoors, grow in fertile, moist but well-drained soil in full sun. Pruning group 8; may need restrictive pruning under glass.

Eranthemum pulchellum

• **PROPAGATION** Root softwood cuttings with bottom heat in late spring or early summer.

• **PESTS AND DISEASES** Whiteflies may be troublesome under glass, and leaf spots sometimes occur.

E. atropurpureum see *Pseuderanthemum atropurpureum.*

E. nervosum see *E. pulchellum.*

E. pulchellum ▣ syn. *E. nervosum* (Blue sage). Open shrub with elliptic, slender-pointed, occasionally toothed, boldly veined, lustrous, deep green leaves, 4–8in (10–20cm) long. In winter, rich blue flowers, 1¼in (3cm) long, are produced in spikes to 3in (8cm) long, or sometimes clustered into panicles. ↕ 3–4ft (90–120cm), ↔ 24–36in (60–90cm). India. ❄ (min. 55°F/13°C)

ERANTHIS

Winter aconite

RANUNCULACEAE

Genus of about 7 species of small, clump-forming perennials with knobbly tubers, occurring in damp woodland and shady places in Eurasia. They are grown for their cup-shaped flowers, borne in late winter and early spring. Stem leaves, ¼–½in (0.5–1.5cm) or more long, often finely dissected, form ruffs immediately below the flowers; basal leaves, ½–1¼in (1.5–3cm) or more long, are palmately lobed or pinnate. Most species are best grown around deciduous shrubs or trees, where they will form carpets of flowers and may naturalize in grass; *E. pinnatifida* is best grown in an alpine house or shel-tered woodland garden. All parts may cause mild stomach upset if ingested; contact with the sap may irritate skin.

• **CULTIVATION** Grow in fertile, humus-rich soil that does not dry out in summer, in full sun or light, dappled shade. Plant tubers 2in (5cm) deep in autumn. Overdried tubers are difficult to establish.

• **PROPAGATION** Sow seed in containers in a cold frame in late spring. Separate tubers in spring after flowering.

• **PESTS AND DISEASES** Prone to smuts. Slugs may eat the foliage.

E. cilicica. Clump-forming, tuberous perennial with bright yellow flowers, ¾–1½in (2–4cm) across, produced above ruffs of finely dissected, glossy, bronze-tinged, mid-green leaves in early spring. Similar to *E. hyemalis* but with more numerous leaf lobes and slightly larger flowers. ↕ 2–3in (5–8cm), PD2in (5cm). Turkey to Afghanistan. Zone 5.

E. hyemalis ▣ (Winter aconite). Clump-forming, tuberous perennial producing bright yellow flowers, ¾–1¼in (2–3cm) across, each above a ruff of dissected, bright green leaves, in late winter and early spring. Quickly forms large colonies, particularly in high-alkaline soils. ↕ 2–3in (5–8cm), PD2in (5cm). S. France to Bulgaria. Zone 4.

E. keiskei see *E. pinnatifida.*

E. pinnatifida, syn. *E. keiskei.* Clump-forming, tuberous perennial with white

Eranthis hyemalis

flowers, ¾in (2cm) across, above ruffs of pinnate leaves,which are produced in early spring. ↕PD2in (5cm). Japan. Zone 5.
***E.* x *tubergenii* 'Guinea Gold'** (*E. cilicica* x *E. hyemalis*). Vigorous, clump-forming, sterile, tuberous perennial with golden flowers, ¾–1¼in (2–3cm) across, each above a ruff of dissected, bronze-green leaves, in late winter. ↕3–4in (8–10cm), PD2in (5cm). Zone 4.

EREMOCHLOA

Centipede grass

GRAMINEAE

Genus of 10 species of grasses native to China and parts of Southeast Asia. It was introduced to the US in 1916, and is now found in South America, the West Indies, and parts of Africa. Centipede grasses are used as lawns in the warmest regions of the subtropical zones, and are well-adapted to medium- or coarse-textured soils. They grow actively from spring through autumn and, in the Southern US, remain green thoughout the year.

• **CULTIVATION** Minimum maintenance requeired, and can grow in poor acid soils with a pH of 5.0–7.5. Requires 3½ft (1.1m) of rainfall to flourish.
• **PROPAGATION** Spreads slowly by sprig, plug, or sod.
• **PESTS AND DISEASES** Low susceptibility to diseases, but nematodes may be a problem.

E. ophiuroides. A slow-growing grass that does not require frequent mowing; it should be mowed at a height of 1–2in (2.5–5cm). The grass has a finer texture than *Stenotaphrum secundatum* (St. Augustine grass), and is a popular grass in the Lower South. Produces spikelike clumps of white, yellow, or green flowers 4in (10cm) high. S.E. Asia. ❄ (min. 41°F/5°C)

▷ ***Erdisia*** see *Corryocactus*

EREMOPHILA

Emu bush

MYOPORACEAE

Genus of about 180 species of evergreen perennials, shrubs, and trees occurring on open slopes and in scrub and light woodland in Australia. They are grown for their tubular-based, 2-lipped flowers, produced singly from the uppermost leaf axils, giving the appearance of leafy racemes in some species. Leaves are simple, entire, and linear to rounded, and may be alternate or opposite, or occasionally whorled. Where not hardy, grow in a temperate or cool greenhouse. In warmer, drier areas, plant in a courtyard garden, in a border, or at the base of a warm, sunny wall.

• **CULTIVATION** Under glass, grow in soil-based potting mix in full light. When in growth, water freely and apply a balanced liquid fertilizer monthly. At other times, water sparingly. Top-dress or pot on in spring. Outdoors, grow in moderately fertile, sharply drained soil in full sun. Pruning group 8; may need restrictive pruning under glass.
• **PROPAGATION** Sow seed at 55–61°F (13–16°C) in spring, first soaking for several days; germination may take

Eremophila maculata 'Aurea'

2 weeks to 2 years or more. Root semi-ripe cuttings in a shaded cold frame in summer.
• **PESTS AND DISEASES** Scale insects may be a problem under glass.

E. alternifolia. Rounded shrub with alternate, very narrow, cylindrical, recurved, mid-green leaves, to 1½in (4cm) long. Solitary pink flowers, 1¼–1½in (3–4cm) long, with darker spots, are produced on slender stalks from spring to summer. ↕↔ 10ft (3m). Australia (except Tasmania). ❄ (min. 45°F/7°C)
E. glabra (Common emu bush, Fuchsia bush). Prostrate or erect to spreading shrub with alternate, elliptic to narrowly lance-shaped, densely hairy or hairless, mid-green leaves, ¾–2in (2–5cm) long. Solitary, red, orange, yellow, or green flowers, 1¼in (3cm) long, are borne mainly from early spring to autumn. ↕to 5ft (1.5m), ↔ 3–10ft (1–3m). Australia (except Tasmania). ❄ (min. 45°F/7°C). **'Murchison River'** has silvery foliage and bright red flowers.
E. maculata (Spotted emu bush). Dense shrub with alternate, linear-lance-shaped to ovate-lance-shaped, mid- to gray-green leaves, to 2in (5cm) long, which are hairless when mature. Solitary, red to purple, pink, or almost white flowers, ¾–1½in (2–4cm) long, often spotted with cream or yellow, are produced from winter to late spring or early summer. ↕1¾–8ft (0.5–2.5m), ↔ 3–6ft (1–2m). Australia (except Tasmania). ❄ (min. 45°F/7°C).
'Aurea' ▣ has light to mid-green leaves and produces yellow flowers.

EREMURUS

Desert candle, Foxtail lily

LILIACEAE

Genus of about 40–50 species of clump-forming, fleshy-rooted perennials found in dry grassland and semi-desert in W. and C. Asia. Leafless flowering stems, usually one per crown, each produce a dense raceme of star-shaped, usually pink, white, or yellow flowers, with conspicuous stamens. Tufted rosettes of folded, linear to lance-shaped, basal leaves die back to the conical crown after flowering. Grow in a border; need winter cold to induce flowering.

• **CULTIVATION** Grow in fertile, sandy, well-drained loam in full sun, with shelter from wind. Mulch with compost in autumn. Protect young growth with a dry mulch. Provide support in exposed, windy sites.
• **PROPAGATION** Sow seed in containers in a cold frame in autumn, or at 59°F (15°C) in late winter. Carefully divide the brittle roots after flowering.
• **PESTS AND DISEASES** Susceptible to slug damage.

E. aitchisonii. Tufted perennial with narrowly lance-shaped, rough-margined, glossy, grass-green leaves, 12–24in (30–60cm) long. Pale pink flowers, to 1¼in (3cm) across, are borne in racemes 12in (30cm) long in early summer. ↕3–6ft (1–2m), PD3ft (1m). Tajikistan, Afghanistan. Zone 5.
E. aurantiacus see *E. stenophyllus* subsp. *aurantiacus.*
E. bungei see *E. stenophyllus* subsp. *stenophyllus.*
E. himalaicus ▣ (Himalayan foxtail lily). Tufted perennial with strap-shaped, bright green leaves, 12in (30cm) long. Produces white flowers, 1in (2.5cm) across, in racemes to 3ft (1m) long in late spring and early summer. ↕4–6ft (1.2–2m), PD24in (60cm). Kashmir, N.W. Himalayas. Zone 5.
***E.* 'Himrob'.** Tufted perennial with lance-shaped, blue-green leaves, 24–36in (60–90cm) long. In early and midsummer, produces very pale pink flowers, ¾–1¼in (2–3cm) across, in racemes to 24in (60cm) long. ↕to 4ft (1.2m), PD3ft (1m). Zone 5.
***E.* x *isabellinus* cultivars** (*E. olgae* x *E. stenophyllus*). Robust, tufted perennials with lance-shaped, mid-green leaves, 6–12in (15–30cm) long. In early summer, variously colored flowers, ¾–1½in (2–4cm) across, are borne in racemes 8–20in (20–50cm) long. ↕to 8ft (2.5m), PD3ft (1m). Zone 5. **'Feuerfackel'**, syn. 'Fire Torch', has orange-red flowers. **'Fire Torch'** see 'Feuerfackel'. **'Moonlight'** has pale yellow flowers. **Ruiter Hybrids** bear brightly colored flowers, ½in (1.5cm) across, in early summer; ↕to 6ft (2m).

Eremurus himalaicus

Eremurus robustus

Ruiter Hybrids 'Cleopatra' has orange flowers; **Ruiter Hybrids 'Fatamorgana'** bears white to cream flowers; **Ruiter Hybrids 'Image'** produces clear yellow flowers; **Ruiter Hybrids 'Sahara'** has sandy-copper flowers. **'Schneelanze'**, syn. 'Snow Lance', has greenish white flowers. **Shelford Hybrids** bear numerous yellow, orange, and cream flowers, ½in (15mm) across; ↕PD4ft (1.2m). **Shelford Hybrids 'Isobel'** bears rose-pink flowers tinged with orange; **Shelford Hybrids 'Rosalind'** bears bright pink flowers. **'Snow Lance'** see 'Schneelanze'.
E. robustus ▣ Tufted perennial with strap-shaped, rough-margined, bluish green leaves, to 4ft (1.2m) long. In early and midsummer, bears pale pink flowers, to 1½in (4cm) across, with brown marks at the bases and yellow stamens, in racemes 30–48in (75–120cm) long. ↕to 10ft (3m), PD4ft (1.2m). Tien Shan and Pamir Mountains. Zone 5.
E. spectabilis. Tufted perennial with strap-shaped, often rough-margined, grayish green leaves, 12–16in (30–40cm) long. In midsummer, bears racemes, to 3ft (1m) long, of sulfur-yellow flowers, ¾in (2cm) across, with orange-red stamens. ↕4–6ft (1.2–2m), PD24in (60cm). Turkey, Lebanon, Iraq, Iran, W. Pakistan. Zone 7b.
E. stenophyllus. Tufted perennial with narrowly linear, rough-margined, sometimes softly hairy, grayish green leaves, 10in (25cm) long. In early and midsummer, bears racemes, 6–12in (15–30cm) long, of dark yellow flowers, to ¾in (2cm) across, fading to orange-brown. ↕3ft (1m), PD24in (60cm). C. Asia, Iran, W. Pakistan. Zone 6. **subsp. *aurantiacus***, syn. *E. aurantiacus*, has hairy flower stems; Tajikistan, Afghanistan, Pakistan. **subsp. *stenophyllus***, syn. *E. bungei*, has leaves to 14in (35cm) long, and brighter yellow flowers; ↕to 5ft (1.5m), PD30in (75cm); C. Asia, Iran.

▷ ***Erianthus*** see *Saccharum*

ERICA

Heath, Heather

ERICACEAE

Genus of over 700 species of prostrate to tree-like, evergreen shrubs occurring in a variety of habitats from wet moorland to dry heathland in Europe, temperate Africa (mainly confined to S. of the Limpopo River in South Africa), and temperate W. and C. Asia. The whorled, rarely opposite, mainly linear leaves are tightly curled back and usually ⅛–½in (3–15mm) long, although in some of the larger species they may be ¾in (2cm) long. The usually bell- to urn-shaped flowers, 1⁄16–1½in (0.2–4cm) long, develop in terminal racemes (sometimes leafy, and often spike-like), umbels, or panicle-like heads, or in 2- to 5-flowered, axillary clusters or whorls, on short, lateral branches produced on the previous year's growth. The flowers may be distinguished from those of callunas by the prominent corollas and usually green calyces.

Hardy species are widely grown as a groundcover, either on their own or with other ericaceous plants or dwarf conifers, and provide color throughout the year. Tree-like species are excellent specimen plants. Where not hardy, grow in a cool or cold greenhouse; in warmer climates, grow in a heather or rock garden, among other shrubs.

• **CULTIVATION** Grow in well-drained, acidic soil in an open site in full sun; most winter- and spring-flowering European species, and the summer-flowering *E. manipuliflora*, *E. terminalis*, *E. vagans*, and *E.* x *williamsii*, will tolerate alkaline soil. Under glass, grow in acidic potting mix with added sharp sand, in full light and with good ventilation at all times. In the growing season, water freely and apply a half-strength balanced liquid fertilizer every 4 weeks; water moderately when not in flower. Pruning group 10, after flowering; group 8 for tree-like species.

• **PROPAGATION** Root semi-ripe cuttings in mid- or late summer. Mound-layer in spring.

• **PESTS AND DISEASES** Rust, *Verticillium* wilt, root rot, and powdery mildew occasionally occur.

E. annectens. Upright, spreading shrub with finely hairy young branches and recurved, linear, mid-green leaves, ¼–¾in (6–9mm) long, in whorls of 4–6. In summer, bears clusters of 2–6 tubular, orange-red flowers, to ¾in (2cm) long. ↕ to 36in (90cm), ↔ to 24in (60cm). South Africa (Western Cape). ❀ (min. 35°F/2°C)

E. arborea (Tree heath). Upright shrub with needle-like, dark green leaves, grooved beneath. In spring, bears bell-shaped, honey-scented, grayish white flowers, ⅛in (3mm) long, in pyramidal, leafy racemes, 8–16in (20–40cm) long. ↕ to 20ft (6m), ↔ 10ft (3m). S.W. Europe, Mediterranean, N. Africa, mountains of central E. Africa. Zone 7b. **'Albert's Gold'** has golden foliage but seldom bears flowers; ↕ 6ft (2m), ↔ 32in (80cm). **var. *alpina*** ▣ produces white flowers in dense, cylindrical racemes; ↕ 6ft (2m), ↔ 34in (85cm). **'Estrella Gold'** bears white flowers above compact, lime-green foliage tipped

Erica arborea var. *alpina*

bright yellow; ↕ 4ft (1.2m), ↔ 30in (75cm).

E. australis ▣ (Spanish heath). Erect, open shrub with linear, dark green leaves, channeled beneath. From midspring to early summer, bears tubular to bell-shaped, purplish pink flowers, to ⅜in (9mm) long, in umbel-like racemes, 8in (20cm) long. Prone to damage by wind or snow. ↕ to 6ft (2m), ↔ to 3ft (1m). Portugal, W. Spain, Tangier. Zone 7b. **'Mr. Robert'** produces white flowers. **'Riverslea'** bears lilac-pink flowers.

E. baccans. Robust, erect, many-branched shrub with linear, sea-green leaves. From winter to spring, bears axillary whorls, 1in (2.5cm) long, each with 4 almost spherical, deep pink flowers, ¼in (6mm) across, with constricted throats and keeled, dark pink sepals. ↕ to 8ft (2.5m), ↔ to 3ft (1m). South Africa (Western Cape). ❀ (min. 45°F/7°C)

E. blenna. Thick, upright shrub with linear-lance-shaped, mid-green leaves, grooved beneath. Urn-shaped to ovoid-conical, sticky, bright orange flowers, ⅜–½in (0.9–1.5cm) long, constricted at the mouths, with green throats and lobes, are borne on axillary shoots, to 1¼in (3cm) long, mainly from winter to spring. ↕ to 4ft (1.2m), ↔ to 32in (80cm). South Africa (Western Cape). ❀ (min. 45°F/7°C)

E. canaliculata ▣ Erect shrub with linear leaves, mid-green above, paler with fine hairs beneath. From winter to early spring, produces panicle-like whorls, to 12in (30cm) long, of cup-shaped, pale pink to near-white flowers, ⅛in (3mm) across, with white sepals and very dark brown anthers. ↕ to 6ft (2m), ↔ to 4ft (1.2m). South Africa (Western Cape, Eastern Cape). ❀ (min. 41°F/5°C)

Erica australis

E. carnea, syn. *E. herbacea* (Spring heath, Winter heath). Low, spreading shrub with linear, dark green leaves. Bears one-sided racemes, 3in (8cm) long, of narrowly urn-shaped, purple-pink flowers, ¼–⅜in (6–9mm) long, in late winter and early spring. Tolerates mildly alkaline soil and some shade. ↕ 8–10in (20–25cm), ↔ to 22in (55cm). C. Alps, N.W. Italy, N.W. Balkans, E. Europe. Zone 4. Unless otherwise stated, the following cultivars have mid- to dark green foliage, and bear purplish pink flowers from winter to midspring; ↕ 6in (15cm), ↔ 18in (45cm). **'Adrienne Duncan'** has bronze-hued foliage, and flowers from midwinter to midspring; ↔ 14in (35cm). **'Altadena'** has yellow foliage tipped pink and bronze, and bears lilac-pink flowers, deepening to purplish pink; ↔ 14in (35cm). **'Ann Sparkes'** ▣ has dark golden foliage with bright bronze tips in spring, and rose-pink flowers, darkening to purplish pink; ↔ 10in (25cm). **'Barry Sellers'** has yellow foliage, turning orange in cold weather, and produces deep pink flowers, aging to magenta; ↔ 12in (30cm). **'Challenger'** has bold magenta flowers. **'December Red'** ▣ bears flowers that open pink and deepen to purplish pink. **'Eileen Porter'** ▣ bears magenta flowers with cream sepals; ↕↔ 8in (20cm). **'Foxhollow'** ▣ has bronze-tipped yellow foliage, deepening to orange-red in very cold weather; ↔ 16in (40cm). **'Golden Starlet'** bears white flowers, and lime-green foliage that turns glowing yellow in summer; ↔ 16in (40cm). **'King George'** produces deep pink flowers, and is one of the first to bloom in early winter; ↔ 10in (25cm). **'Lesley Sparkes'** ▣ has mid-green foliage tipped with salmon-pink and gold, particularly in spring; ↔ 10in (25cm). **'March Seedling'** flowers until late spring; ↔ 20in (50cm). **'Myretoun Ruby'** has pink flowers that deepen to crimson with age. **'R.B. Cooke'** produces masses of pink flowers, aging to mauve. **'Springwood Pink'** is trailing, and bears pink flowers that turn deeper pink with age; ↔ 16in (40cm). **'Springwood White'** ▣ is vigorous and trailing, with masses of white flowers above bright green foliage. **'Vivellii'** ▣ has bronze leaves and purplish pink flowers that darken to magenta; ↔ 14in (35cm). **'Westwood Yellow'** is more upright than other yellow-foliaged cultivars, and bears shell-pink flowers; ↔ 12in (30cm). **'White Perfection'** see *E.* x *darleyensis* 'White Perfection'.

E. cerinthoides ▣ (Fire heath). Erect shrub with linear, gray-green leaves, which are variably softly hairy and usually glandular. Tubular, bright red, sometimes pale pink or white flowers, ¾–1½in (2–4cm) long, with slightly constricted throats and inflated bases, are borne in umbels, ¾–1½in (2–4cm) across, from winter to spring, and occasionally throughout the year. ↕ to 5ft (1.5m), ↔ to 3ft (1m). South Africa, Swaziland. ❀ (min. 45°F/7°C)

E. ciliaris (Dorset heath). Spreading shrub with ovate to lance-shaped,

Erica canaliculata

Erica carnea 'Ann Sparkes'

Erica carnea 'December Red'

Erica carnea 'Eileen Porter'

Erica carnea 'Foxhollow'

Erica carnea 'Lesley Sparkes'

Erica carnea 'Springwood White'

Erica carnea 'Vivellii'

Erica cerinthoides

Erica ciliaris 'Corfe Castle'

Erica ciliaris 'David McClintock'

Erica ciliaris 'White Wings'

Erica cinerea 'C.D. Eason'

Erica cinerea 'Eden Valley'

Erica cinerea 'Fiddler's Gold'

Erica cinerea 'Hookstone White'

Erica cinerea 'Purple Beauty'

Erica cinerea 'Yvonne'

usually glandular leaves, gray-green or dark green above, white beneath. From midsummer to midautumn, produces racemes, 3in (8cm) long, of urn-shaped, usually lilac-pink flowers, to ½in (1.5cm) long, sharply constricted at the mouths. Will be damaged in severe winters. ↕ 14–24in (35–60cm), ↔ to 20in (50cm). Europe. Zone 6. **'Aurea'** has straw-yellow foliage in summer, deepening in winter; ↕ 10in (25cm). **'Corfe Castle'** ■ has mid-green foliage that turns bronze-green in winter, and distinctive, rose-pink flowers; ↕ 9in (22cm), ↔ 14in (35cm). **'David McClintock'** ■ bears flowers with white bases and purplish pink mouths; ↕ to 16in (40cm), ↔ 18in (45cm). **'White Wings'** ■ bears white flowers; ↕ 6in (15cm), ↔ 18in (45cm).

E. cinerea (Bell heather). Compact shrub with usually linear, strongly rolled-back, dark bottle-green leaves. Urn-shaped, white, pink, or purple flowers, to ¼in (6mm) long, are borne in racemes, 2in (5cm) long, from early summer to early autumn. ↕ 24in (60cm), ↔ to 32in (80cm). Western Europe. Zone 6. **'Alba Major'** bears white flowers and mid-green foliage; ↕ 12in (30cm), ↔ 22in (55cm). **'C.D. Eason'** ■ has bright magenta flowers, and is a good groundcover; ↕ 10in (25cm), ↔ 20in (50cm). **'Contrast'** bears beet-red flowers; ↕ 10in (25cm), ↔ 18in (45cm). **'Eden Valley'** ■ has lavender-pink flowers, shading to white at the bases, and mid-green foliage; ↕ 8in (20cm), ↔ 20in (50cm). **'Fiddler's Gold'** ■ has lilac-pink flowers, and golden yellow foliage that deepens to red; ↕ 10in (25cm), ↔ 18in (45cm). **'Foxhollow Mahogany'** bears ruby-red flowers, and is good for a groundcover; ↕ 8in (20cm), ↔ 20in (50cm). **'Glencairn'** ■ bears magenta flowers, and has dark green foliage with red tips, which are especially pronounced in spring; ↕ 12in (30cm), ↔ 20in (50cm). **'Golden Hue'** produces amethyst flowers and pale yellow foliage tipped orange in winter; ↕ 14in (35cm), ↔ 28in (70cm). **'Hookstone White'** ■ produces white flowers in racemes, 3–5in (8–13cm) long, above mid-green foliage; ↕ 14in (35cm), ↔ 26in (65cm). **'Janet'** bears shell-pink flowers above compact, light green foliage; ↕ 8in (20cm), ↔ 12in (30cm). **'Lime Soda'** bears a profusion of soft lavender-pink flowers above lime-green foliage; ↕ 14in (35cm), ↔ 22in (55cm). **'Peñaz'** bears masses of bright ruby-red flowers; ↕ 10in (25cm), ↔ 16in (40cm). **'Pentreath'** produces a neat carpet of beet-red flowers; ↕ 12in (30cm), ↔ 22in (55cm). **'Pink Ice'** is dwarf and twiggy, with clear rose-pink flowers, and deep green foliage that is bronze when young and in winter; ↕ 8in (20cm), ↔ 14in (35cm). **'Purple Beauty'** ■ bears bright, deep pinkish purple flowers; ↕ 12in (30cm), ↔ 22in (55cm). **'Rock Pool'** has golden yellow foliage turning orange-red in winter, and produces a few short racemes, 1¼in (3cm) long, of mauve flowers; ↕ 6in (15cm), ↔ 12in (30cm). **'Romiley'** ■ bears magenta flowers, and provides a neat groundcover; ↕ 10in (25cm), ↔ 22in (55cm). **'Rosabella'** bears magenta flowers in racemes 3–4in (7–10cm) long, and is a good groundcover; ↕ 12in (30cm), ↔ 24in (60cm). **'Windlebrooke'** ■ bears golden yellow foliage turning orange-red in winter; ↕ 6in (15cm), ↔ 18in (45cm). **'Yvonne'** ■ produces salmon-pink flowers with deeply cut corollas; ↕ 14in (35cm), ↔ 18in (45cm).

E. cruenta (Blood-red heath). Upright, loosely branched shrub with linear, dark green leaves. Terminal, whorled, leafy racemes, 4in (10cm) long, of tubular, blood-red flowers, ¾–1in (2–2.5cm) long, are produced from spring to early autumn. ↕ 3ft (1m), ↔ 28in (70cm). South Africa (Western Cape). ❄ (min. 45°F/7°C)

E. curviflora (Water heath). Erect shrub with linear to linear-lance-shaped, mid-green leaves. Tubular, usually hairy, red, orange, yellow, or pink flowers, ¾–1½in (2–4cm) long, are flared at the mouths. They are usually borne singly, occasionally in terminal clusters of 3 or 4, at any time of year, but most often from winter to spring. Prefers wet soil. ↕ to 5ft (1.5m), ↔ to 3ft (1m). South Africa (Western Cape, Eastern Cape). ❄ (min. 45°F/7°C)

E. x darleyensis (*E. carnea* x *E. erigena*) (Darley Dale heath). Bushy shrub with lance-shaped, mid-green leaves. In late winter and early spring, bears racemes, 4in (10cm) long, of urn-shaped to cylindrical, white to rose-pink flowers, ¼in (6mm) long. Suitable for any well-drained soil. Particularly good as a groundcover. ↕ to 24in (60cm), ↔ to 30in (75cm). Garden origin. Zone 5. The following cultivars are ↕ 12in (30cm), ↔ 24in (60cm), unless

Erica cinerea 'Glencairn'

Erica cinerea 'Romiley'

Erica cinerea 'Windlebrooke'

Erica x *darleyensis* 'Archie Graham'

Erica x *darleyensis* 'Darley Dale'

Erica x *darleyensis* 'Jenny Porter'

Erica x *darleyensis* 'White Glow'

Erica erigena 'Brightness'

Erica erigena 'Golden Lady'

Erica mackaiana 'Plena'

Erica mackaiana 'Shining Light'

Erica mammosa

Erica x *stuartii* 'Irish Lemon'

Erica tetralix 'Alba Mollis'

Erica tetralix 'Pink Star'

Erica vagans 'Lyonesse'

Erica vagans 'Mrs. D.F. Maxwell'

Erica vagans 'Valerie Proudley'

Erica versicolor

Erica x *watsonii* 'Dawn'

Erica x *williamsii* 'P.D. Williams'

otherwise stated. **'Archie Graham'** ▣ has pink flowers, aging to purplish pink; ↕ 20in (50cm). **'Darley Dale'** ▣ has foliage tipped cream in spring, and shell-pink flowers that darken with age; ↔ 22in (55cm). **'Ghost Hills'** has light green foliage, tipped cream in spring; ↔ 32in (80cm). **'Jack H. Brummage'** has yellow-orange leaves and purplish pink flowers. **'Jenny Porter'** ▣ has foliage with pale cream tips in spring, and pinkish white flowers. **'J.W. Porter'** has dark green foliage, tipped red and cream in spring, and purplish pink flowers; ↕ 10in (25cm), ↔ 16in (40cm). **'Kramer's Rote'**, syn. 'Kramer's Red', has bronze-green foliage and magenta flowers. **'Silberschmelze'** has white flowers, and faintly cream-tipped leaves in spring, later deep green, then tinged red in winter; ↕ 14in (35cm), ↔ 32in (80cm). **'White Glow'** ▣ syn. 'White Gown', is compact, with masses of white flowers; ↕ 10in (25cm), ↔ 20in (50cm). **'White Gown'** see 'White Glow'. **'White Perfection'**, syn. *E. carnea* 'White Perfection', has pure white flowers and bright green foliage; ↕ 16in (40cm), ↔ 28in (70cm).

E. erigena, syn. *E. hibernica*, *E. mediterranea* (Irish heath, Mediterranean heath, Spring heath). Upright shrub with brittle stems and linear, dark green leaves. From winter to spring, produces urn-shaped to cylindrical, honey-scented, deep lilac-pink flowers, ¼in (6mm) long, in racemes 1½in (4cm) long. Good for low hedges in areas free from heavy snowfall. ↕ to 8ft (2.5m), ↔ to 3ft (1m). Ireland, S.W. France, Spain, Portugal, Tangier. Zone 7. **'Brightness'** ▣ has purple-green foliage in winter, becoming glaucous green in summer, and lilac-pink flowers in spring; ↕↔ 20in (50cm). **'Golden Lady'** ▣ has bright golden yellow foliage, which may be burned by cold wind; ↕ 12in (30cm), ↔ 16in (40cm). **'Irish Dusk'** has dark gray-green leaves, and rose-pink flowers from autumn to spring; ↕ 24in (60cm), ↔ 18in (45cm). **'Superba'** bears strongly scented, shell-pink flowers, deepening with age, in mid- and late spring. Suitable as a hedge; ↕ 6ft (1.8m), ↔ 20in (50cm). **'W.T. Rackliff'** is compact, with rich green foliage, and produces masses of white flowers in spring; ↕ 30in (75cm), ↔ 22in (55cm).

E. glandulosa. Untidy shrub with overlapping, linear, light green leaves. Gland-tipped hairs on leaves and stems make the plant sticky to the touch. Axillary clusters, ½in (1.5cm) across, of 2–5 tubular flowers, ⅛–½in (3–15mm) long, in shades of pink, are borne mainly from autumn to spring. ↕ to 24in (60cm), ↔ to 36in (90cm). South Africa (Western Cape, Eastern Cape). ❀ (min. 45°F/7°C)

E. glauca (Cup-and-saucer heath). Upright, sparsely branched shrub with upright to spreading, linear, mid-green leaves, ¼–¾in (6–9mm) long, in whorls of 3. In summer, bears saucer-shaped, wine-red flowers, to ¾in (2cm) across, terminally in panicle-like heads. ↕ to 6ft (2m), ↔ to 36in (90cm). South Africa (Western Cape). ❀ (min. 35°F/2°C). **var. *elegans*** (Petticoat heath) is branching and bears drooping, pale pink flowers, in spring.

E. gracilis. Compact shrub with linear, deep green leaves. From autumn to spring, bears whorls, ½in (1.5cm) long, of 4 urn-shaped, pale pink to cerise flowers, ⅛in (3mm) long. ↕↔ 20in (50cm). South Africa (Western Cape, Eastern Cape). ❀ (min. 45°F/7°C)

E. herbacea see *E. carnea.*

E. hibernica see *E. erigena.*

E.* x *hiemalis. Usually upright shrub with linear, light green leaves. From late autumn to winter, bears tubular, pink-suffused white flowers, ½in (1.5cm) long, in dense racemes, 4in (10cm) long. ↕↔ 24in (60cm). Garden origin. ❀ (min. 45°F/7°C)

E. lusitanica (Portuguese heath, Spanish heath). Erect shrub with feathery, linear, mid-green leaves. From winter to spring, tubular to bell-shaped white flowers, ¼in (6mm) long, opening from pink buds, are borne in branched racemes, 10in (25cm) long. Prefers acidic soil. ↕ to 10ft (3m), ↔ to 3ft (1m). S.W. France, Portugal, W. Spain. ❀ (min. 35°F/2°C). **'George Hunt'** has bright yellow leaves; it requires a sheltered site.

E. mackaiana (Mackay's heath). Decumbent to erect shrub with oblong-lance-shaped, hairy-tipped, dark green leaves; sometimes slightly hairy above, white beneath. From summer to early autumn, produces umbels, ½in (1.5cm) across, of urn-shaped, bright pink flowers, to ¼in (6mm) long, with constricted mouths. Needs damp soil. ↕ to 20in (50cm), ↔ to 30in (75cm). Ireland, Spain. Zone 5. **'Dr. Ronald Gray'** has hairless, bright green leaves and pure white flowers; ↕ 6in (15cm), ↔ 14in (35cm). **'Plena'** ▣ produces double magenta flowers. Good as a groundcover; ↕ 6in (15cm), ↔ 16in (40cm). **'Shining Light'** ▣ has gray-green foliage, and bears masses of white flowers, ⅜in (9mm) long; ↕ 10in (25cm), ↔ 22in (55cm).

E. mammosa ▣ Erect shrub with linear to lance-shaped, dark green leaves. From spring to summer, bears tubular, dark red, orange-red, pink, green, or white flowers, ½–1in (1.5–2.5cm) long, in clustered, terminal racemes, 3in (8cm) long. ↕ to 5ft (1.5m), ↔ to 6ft (2m). South Africa (Western Cape). ❀ (min. 45°F/7°C)

E. manipuliflora, syn. *E. verticillata* of gardens (Whorled heath). Erect to spreading shrub with linear, sharply pointed, mid-green leaves. From late summer to autumn, bears irregular racemes, 4in (10cm) long, of cylindrical to bell-shaped, rose-pink flowers, ⅛in (3mm) long. ↕ to 3ft (1m), ↔ to 3½ft (1.1m). E. Mediterranean. ❀ (min. 35°F/2°C). **subsp. *anthura* 'Heaven Scent'** bears sprays of strongly scented, lilac-pink flowers; ↔ 24in (60cm). Zone 7b.

E. mediterranea see *E. erigena.*

E. nana. Dwarf, prostrate, sometimes erect shrub with linear, mid-green leaves. In autumn, bears whorls, to ¾in (2cm) long, of 3 tubular yellow flowers, to ¾in (2cm) long, with spreading, green-tipped lobes. Good in containers. ↕ 8–10in (20–25cm), sometimes to 20in (50cm), ↔ to 3ft (1m). South Africa (Western Cape). ❀ (min. 45°F/7°C)

E. pageana. Erect shrub with linear, mid-green leaves. In late winter and early spring, short branches bear groups of 3 or 4 bell-shaped, rich yellow flowers, ⅜–½in (9–15mm) long, in dense, spike-like racemes, 4in (10cm) long. ↕ to 24in (60cm), ↔ to 12in (30cm). South Africa (Western Cape). ❀ (min. 45°F/7°C)

E. patersonia (Mealie heath). Erect shrub with linear, mid-green leaves. In late winter and early spring, bears dense, spike-like racemes, 3in (8cm) long, of tubular yellow flowers, ½–¾in (1.5–2cm) long, in groups of 4. ↕ to 36in (90cm), ↔ to 24in (60cm). South Africa (Western Cape). ❀ (min. 45°F/7°C)

***E. persoluta* of gardens.** Variable group of upright cultivars of uncertain origin, possibly from *E. gracilis*, with linear, light green leaves, to ¼in (6mm) long. In winter and spring, produce dense racemes of dark pink flowers, to ⅛in (3mm) long. Grown extensively in California for cut flowers and pot plants. ↕ 36in (90cm), ↔ 24in (60cm). Zone 7b, although rarely survive outdoors in cultivation.

E. perspicua ■ (Prince of Wales heath). Variable shrub with overlapping, linear, gray-green leaves. Bears translucent, tubular flowers, ½–¾in (1–2cm) long, in white, pink and white, red and white, purple and white, or red, in loose, spike-like racemes, 3in (8cm) long, mainly from early autumn to winter. Needs damp soil. ↕ to 6ft (2m), ↔ to 3ft (1m). South Africa (Western Cape). ❄ (min. 45°F/7°C)
E. peziza (Kapokkie heath). Upright, many-branched shrub with linear, mid-green leaves. In spring, bears racemes, 2in (5cm) long, of cup-shaped white flowers, ¼in (6mm) across, covered with woolly hairs. ↕↔ 24in (60cm). South Africa (Western Cape). ❄ (min. 45°F/7°C)
E.* x *praegeri see *E.* x *stuartii.*
E. quadrangularis. Compact, well-rounded shrub with linear, mid-green leaves. From late winter to summer, bears whorls, ¾in (2cm) long, of 4 cup-shaped flowers, 1/16–⅛in (2–3mm) long, ranging from white through pink to red. ↕ 24in (60cm), ↔ 18in (45cm). South Africa (Western Cape). ❄ (min. 45°F/7°C)
E. scoparia (Besom heath). Untidy, erect shrub with linear, dark green leaves. In summer, tiny, bell-shaped, greenish brown flowers, to ⅛in (3mm) long, are borne in spike-like racemes, 2½in (6cm) long. ↕ to 6ft (2m), ↔ to 3ft (1m). S.W. France, Spain, N. Africa, Canary Islands. ❄ (min. 35°F/2°C). **'Minima'** is compact in habit, and bears a few brownish green flowers in late spring and early summer; ↕ 10in (25cm), ↔ 32in (80cm).
E. sessiliflora. Upright shrub with erect to spreading, linear, mid-green leaves. Bears congested, spike-like racemes, to 2½in (6cm) long, of tubular, greenish white flowers, ½–1¼in (1.5–3cm) long, from late winter to spring. Sepals eventually turn red, producing tight fruiting heads that remain on the plant for several years. ↕ to 6ft (2m), ↔ to 3ft (1m). South Africa (Western Cape, Eastern Cape). ❄ (min. 45°F/7°C)
E. speciosa. Sturdy, erect, many-branched shrub with linear, mid-green leaves. Spike-like racemes, 3½in (9cm) long, of tubular, pink- or red-based flowers, ¾–1¼in (2–3cm) long, with white, green, or yellow lobes, are borne in whorls of 3, or occasionally singly, from early spring to early autumn. ↕ to 4ft (1.2m), ↔ to 3ft (1m). South Africa (Western Cape, Eastern Cape). ❄ (min. 45°F/7°C)
E. stricta see *E. terminalis.*
E.* x *stuartii (*E. mackaiana* x *E. tetralix*), syn. *E.* x *praegeri.* Spreading shrub with oblong, glandular, gray-green leaves. Throughout summer and autumn, produces umbels of urn-shaped pink flowers, ⅜in (9mm) long, which are contracted at the mouths. Needs moist soil. ↕ 10in (25cm), ↔ 20in (50cm). W. Ireland. Zone 5. **'Connemara'** is dense, with abundant magenta flowers; ↕ to 6in (15cm). **'Irish Lemon'** ■ has brilliant lemon-yellow spring growth, and bears mauve flowers from late spring to summer. **'Irish Orange'** has dark green leaves, orange-tinged in spring, and clear pink flowers.
E. subdivaricata. Spreading shrub with linear, usually hairy, mid-green leaves. Whorls of 4 cup-shaped, honey-scented, occasionally pink-flushed, white flowers, ⅛in (3mm) long, are produced in the leaf axils from early summer to late autumn. Requires damp soil. ↕ 20–32in (50–80cm), ↔ to 3ft (1m). South Africa (Western Cape). ❄ (min. 45°F/7°C)
E. terminalis, syn. *E. stricta* (Corsican heath). Erect shrub with linear, glossy, dark green leaves. Bears umbels of urn-shaped, lilac-pink flowers, ¼in (6mm) long, from midsummer to early autumn. The faded flowers have a russet hue all winter. Good as a hedge or specimen plant. ↕↔ to 3ft (1m). Europe, S.W. Mediterranean. Zone 7b.
E. tetralix (Cross-leaved heath). Dwarf, spreading shrub with lance-shaped to linear-oblong, often glandular, usually gray-green leaves, white beneath, arranged in whorls of 4 to form crosses. From midsummer to midautumn, bears umbels of urn-shaped, pale pink flowers, ⅜in (9mm) long, with constricted mouths. Prefers moist soil. ↕ to 12in (30cm), ↔ 20in (50cm). W. Europe. Zone 5. **'Alba Mollis'** ■ has silvery gray leaves and pure white flowers; ↕ 8in (20cm), ↔ 12in (30cm). **'Con Underwood'** bears magenta flowers; ↕ 10in (25cm). **'Pink Star'** ■ bears lilac-pink flowers in star-like patterns; ↕ 8in (20cm), ↔ 14in (35cm).
E. umbellata (Portuguese heath). Compact shrub with linear, gray-green leaves. In late spring and early summer, bears umbels of bell-shaped to ovoid mauve flowers, ¼in (6mm) long, with conspicuous, dark brown anthers. Grows in any soil. ↕ 18–32in (45–80cm), ↔ 22in (55cm). Portugal, W. Spain, Tangier. Zone 7.
E. vagans (Cornish heath). Vigorous, spreading shrub with decumbent to ascending stems and linear, dark green leaves. From midsummer to mid-autumn, bears cylindrical to bell-shaped, pink, mauve, or white flowers, to ⅛in (3mm) long, in racemes 5½in (14cm) long. Grows in any well-drained soil. ↕ 16–32in (40–80cm), ↔ to 32in (80cm). Ireland, UK (Cornwall), W. France, Spain. Zone 5. **'Birch Glow'** ■ has deep rose-pink flowers; ↕ 12in (30cm), ↔ 20in (50cm). **'French White'** bears masses of off-white flowers; ↕ 16in (40cm), ↔ 24in (60cm). **'Lyonesse'** ■ has bright green leaves and pure white flowers; ↕ 10in (25cm), ↔ 20in (50cm). **'Mrs. D.F. Maxwell'** ■ bears deep rose-pink flowers; ↕ 12in (30cm), ↔ 18in (45cm). **'St. Keverne'** has clear pink flowers; ↕ 16in (40cm), ↔ 18in (45cm). **'Valerie Proudley'** ■ has bright yellow foliage and white flowers; ↕ 6in (15cm), ↔ 12in (30cm).

Erica vagans 'Birch Glow'

Erica x *veitchii* 'Exeter'

Erica perspicua

***E.* 'Valerie Griffiths'.** Spreading shrub with linear, yellow leaves, deepening to golden yellow in winter. Bears racemes, 2–4in (5–10cm) long, of bell-shaped, pale pink flowers, to ⅛in (3mm) long, from summer to early autumn. Tolerates mildly alkaline soil. ↕ 16in (40cm), ↔ 22in (55cm). Zone 6.
E.* x *veitchii (*E. arborea* x *E. lusitanica*) (Veitch's heath). Erect, open shrub with linear, mid-green leaves. From late winter to spring, bears leafy racemes, 12in (30cm) long, of cylindrical-spherical white flowers, to ⅛in (3mm) long. Tolerates mildly alkaline soil. ↕ to 7ft (2.2m), ↔ 26in (65cm). Garden origin. ❄ (min. 35°F/2°C). **'Exeter'** ■ bears masses of scented flowers in spring; ↕ 6ft (1.9m).
E. versicolor ■ Erect shrub with linear, mid-green leaves. Bears dense, spike-like racemes, 1¼in (3cm) long, of tubular flowers, ¼–1¼in (2–3cm) long, in whorls of 3, usually with red tubes and green to white tips; flowers mainly from autumn to early winter. ↕ to 10ft (3m), ↔ 3ft (1m). South Africa (Western Cape). ❄ (min. 45°F/7°C)
***E. verticillata* of gardens** see *E. manipuliflora.*
E. vestita. Erect shrub with densely packed, linear, mid-green leaves. Bears spike-like racemes, 1¼in (3cm) long, of arching, tubular, red to dark pink, or white flowers, ½–1in (1.5–2.5cm) long, from spring to late summer. ↕↔ to 36in (90cm). South Africa (Western Cape). ❄ (min. 45°F/7°C)
E. vulgaris see *Calluna vulgaris.*
E.* x *watsonii (*E. ciliaris* x *E. tetralix*) (Watson's heath). Compact, spreading shrub with linear, grayish green leaves. In summer, produces dense racemes, ½in (1.5cm) long, of urn-shaped pink flowers, to ½in (1.5cm) long, with constricted mouths. ↕ to 16in (40cm), ↔ to 34in (85cm). UK (Cornwall). Zone 5. **'Dawn'** ■ has red spring growth that turns golden, and bears deep pink flowers from midsummer to midautumn; ↕ 8in (20cm).
E.* x *williamsii (*E. tetralix* x *E. vagans*) (Williams' heath). Decumbent to ascending shrub with linear, mid-green leaves, tipped bright yellow in spring. Bears dense racemes, 1½in (4cm) long, of bell-shaped, lilac-pink flowers, to ⅛in (3mm) long, from midsummer to late autumn. ↕ to 30in (75cm), ↔ 18in (45cm). UK (Cornwall). Zone 5. **'P.D. Williams'** ■ has yellow-tipped spring growth that lasts well into summer; ↕ to 12in (30cm).

ERIGERON

Fleabane

ASTERACEAE

Genus of about 200 species of annuals, biennials, and perennials found in dry grassland and mountainous areas, with a very wide distribution, but occurring especially in North America. They range from low-growing alpine species to taller, bushy, clump-forming plants. All have simple, rarely lobed or dissected, usually oblong to lance-shaped or spoon-shaped, mainly basal leaves; the leaves on the stems are usually shorter and narrower. Leaf descriptions below are of basal leaves unless otherwise stated. Fleabanes are grown for their daisy-like, single to semi-double, mainly yellow-centered, white, pink, blue, or purple, sometimes yellow or orange flowerheads, which are borne singly or in corymbs over long periods, mostly in summer. Herbaceous hybrids have leaves 2½–6in (6–15cm) long, and flowerheads that are mostly 1½–2½in (4–6cm) across. Grow erigerons in a mixed or herbaceous border, or in a rock garden. The flowerheads last well as cut flowers if they are picked when fully open.

• **CULTIVATION** Grow in fertile, well-drained soil that does not dry out in summer, in full sun with some mid-day shade. The smaller alpine species need sharp drainage and protection from excessive winter moisture. Most taller species and hybrids need staking. Deadhead to encourage further flowering. Cut back rock-garden types to ground level in autumn to retain neat growth. Divide every 2 or 3 years in late spring, and discard the woody crowns.

• **PROPAGATION** Sow seed in containers in a cold frame in mid- or late spring. Divide, or root basal cuttings, in spring.

• **PESTS AND DISEASES** Bidens mottle virus, downy mildew, powdery mildew, rust, white smut, leaf spots, Southern blight, and rust can be problems.

E. alpinus ■ (Alpine fleabane). Clump-forming perennial with narrowly elliptic to spoon-shaped, hairy leaves, to 3in (8cm) long. In summer, slender stems, to 8in (20cm) long, produce solitary, or groups of 2 or 3, lilac-blue to red-purple flowerheads, to 1½in (4cm) across, with yellow disk florets. ↕ to 10in (25cm), ↔ to 8in (20cm). Mountains of C. and S. Europe. Zone 5.

Erigeron alpinus

Erigeron aureus 'Canary Bird'

E. aurantiacus. Mat- to clump-forming perennial with elliptic to spoon-shaped, velvety leaves, to 4in (10cm) long. Over long periods in summer, thick, leafy stems produce solitary, brilliant orange flowerheads, to 2in (5cm) across, with yellow disk florets. ↕↔ to 12in (30cm). Mountains of Turkestan. Zone 5.

E. aureus. Short-lived, mound-forming perennial with tufts of broadly elliptic to spoon-shaped, hairy, gray-green leaves, to 3in (8cm) long. In summer, solitary, deep golden yellow flowerheads, ¾in (2cm) or more across, are produced on stems 2in (5cm) long. ↕ 2–4in (5–10cm), rarely to 8in (20cm), ↔ to 6in (15cm). Mountains of W. North America. Zone 5. **'Canary Bird'** ■ is a longer-lived perennial, and produces bright canary-yellow flowerheads; ↕ to 4in (10cm).

***E.* 'Azure Fairy'** see *E.* 'Azurfee'.

***E.* 'Azurfee'**, syn. *E.* 'Azure Fairy'. Clump-forming perennial with inversely lance-shaped leaves. Bears corymbs of semi-double, yellow-centered, lavender-blue flowerheads in early and mid-summer. ↕↔ 18in (45cm). Zone 4.

***E.* 'Black Sea'** see *E.* 'Schwarzes Meer'.

***E.* 'Charity'** ■ Clump-forming perennial with lance-shaped leaves. In early and midsummer, semi-double, yellow-centered, light lilac-pink flower-heads are produced singly or in groups of 2 or 3. ↕ 24in (60cm), ↔ 18in (45cm). Zone 4.

E. compositus. Tufted, loose cushion-forming perennial with fan-shaped, 3- or 4-ternate, lobed or dissected, hairy, gray-green leaves, ¾–2½in (2–6cm) long. In summer, bears solitary, yellow-centered, white, pink, or very pale blue flowerheads, to ¾in (2cm) across. May self-seed excessively. ↕ to 6in (15cm), ↔ to 4in (10cm). Greenland, Canada, W. North America. Zone 4.

Erigeron 'Charity'

Erigeron 'Dignity'

***E.* 'Darkest of All'** see *E.* 'Dunkelste Aller'.

***E.* 'Dignity'** ■ Clump-forming perennial with lance-shaped to spoon-shaped leaves. Solitary, yellow-centered, violet-mauve flowerheads are produced in early and midsummer. ↕ 20in (50cm), ↔ 18in (45cm). Zone 4.

***E.* 'Dunkelste Aller'** ■ syn. *E.* 'Darkest of All'. Clump-forming perennial with lance-shaped, grayish green leaves. In early and midsummer, bears corymbs of semi-double, yellow-centered, dark violet flowerheads, with long ray florets. ↕ 24in (60cm), ↔ 18in (45cm). Zone 4.

***E.* 'Foersters Liebling'.** Clump-forming perennial with lance-shaped, grayish green leaves. Corymbs of semi-double, yellow-centered, deep reddish pink flowerheads, with numerous closely packed ray florets, are produced in early and midsummer. ↕ 24in (60cm), ↔ 18in (45cm). Zone 4.

***E.* 'Gaiety'** ■ Clump-forming perennial with lance-shaped leaves. Corymbs of semi-double, yellow-centered, bright pink flowerheads are produced very freely in early and midsummer. ↕ 24in (60cm), ↔ 18in (45cm). Zone 4.

E. glaucus (Beach aster). Tufted perennial with succulent-looking stems and inversely lance-shaped, obovate, or broadly spoon-shaped, more or less glaucous leaves, 5–6in (12–15cm) long, with blunt points. Semi-double flower-heads, 1½–2½in (3.5–6cm) across, with thin, pale mauve ray florets and yellow, later brown disk florets, are solitary or produced on sparsely branched stems, from late spring to midsummer. ↕ 12in (30cm), ↔ 18in (45cm). Oregon, California. Zone 6. **'Albus'** has white flowerheads. **'Elstead Pink'** ■ produces lilac-pink flowerheads.

E. karvinskianus, syn. *E. mucronatus.* Carpeting, rhizomatous, woody-based, vigorously spreading perennial with lax, branching stems and elliptic-lance-shaped, hairy, gray-green leaves, to 1½in (4cm) long. In summer, produces abundant yellow-centered flowerheads, ¾in (2cm) across, either singly or in loose corymbs of 2–5, opening white and fading through pink to purple. Suitable for a wall or paving crevices. ↕ 6–12in (15–30cm), ↔ 3ft (1m) or more. Mexico to Panama. Zone 5b.

Erigeron 'Dunkelste Aller'

'Profusion' ■ is very floriferous, and bears flowerheads with pink or white ray florets. Excellent for a hanging basket, windowbox, or container. ↕ 8–12in (20–30cm), ↔ to 20in (50cm).

E. mucronatus see *E. karvinskianus.*

E. philadelphicus. Biennial or short-lived perennial with inversely lance-shaped to obovate or rounded, scalloped or lobed, softly hairy basal leaves, to 6in (15cm) long. In summer, produces pale red-purple flowerheads, to ½in (1.5cm) across, solitary or in corymbs. ↕ to 32in (80cm), ↔ 18in (45cm). Canada, N. US. Zone 3.

***E.* 'Pink Jewel'** see *E.* 'Rosa Juwel'.

E. pinnatisectus. Tufted perennial with linear, pinnatisect, hairy leaves, to ¾in (2cm) long. In summer, produces solitary, blue to purple flowerheads, 1in (2.5cm) or more across, with bright yellow to orange disk florets. Suitable for a rock garden. ↕ to 8in (20cm), ↔ to 6in (15cm). C. US. Zone 3.

***E.* 'Prosperity'.** Erect, clump-forming perennial with lance-shaped leaves. Corymbs of almost double, yellow-centered, mauve-blue flowerheads are produced in early and midsummer. ↕↔ 18in (45cm). Zone 4.

E. pulchellus (Robin's plantain). Clump-forming biennial or short-lived perennial with spoon-shaped, entire or toothed basal leaves, to 5in (13cm) long, and smaller, oblong-lance-shaped or ovate, entire, stalkless stem leaves. Produces corymbs of 1–6, single, yellow-centered, blue, pink, or rarely white flowerheads, to 1½in (4cm) across, in summer. ↕ to 28in (70cm), ↔ 18in (45cm). S. central to E. US. Zone 4.

Erigeron 'Gaiety'

Erigeron glaucus 'Elstead Pink'

***E.* 'Quakeress'** ▣ Strong-growing, clump-forming perennial with lance-shaped, grayish green leaves. Produces corymbs of single, yellow-centered, pink-flushed white flowerheads in early and midsummer. ↕ 24in (60cm), ↔ 18in (45cm). Zone 4.
***E.* 'Red Sea'** see *E.* 'Rotes Meer'.
***E.* 'Rosa Juwel'**, syn. *E.* 'Pink Jewel'. Clump-forming perennial with lance-shaped leaves. Corymbs of semi-double, yellow-centered, pale but bright pink flowerheads are produced in early and midsummer. ↕ 24in (60cm), ↔ 18in (45cm). Zone 4.
***E.* 'Rotes Meer'**, syn. *E.* 'Red Sea'. Upright, clump-forming perennial with spoon-shaped leaves. Corymbs of semi-double, dark red flowerheads are produced in midsummer. ↕↔ 24in (60cm). Zone 4.
***E.* 'Schwarzes Meer'**, syn. *E.* 'Black Sea'. Clump-forming perennial with lance-shaped leaves. In early and midsummer, bears corymbs of semi-double, yellow-centered, deep violet flowerheads. ↕ 24in (60cm), ↔ 18in (45cm). Zone 4.
***E.* 'Serenity'** ▣ Somewhat lax, clump-forming perennial with lance-shaped leaves. Bears corymbs of semi-double, yellow-centered, violet-mauve flowerheads in early and midsummer. ↕ 30in (75cm), ↔ 18in (45cm). Zone 4.
***E.* 'Shining Sea'** see *E.* 'Strahlenmeer'.
***E.* 'Sommerneuschnee'**, syn. *E.* 'Summer Snow'. Clump-forming perennial with lance-shaped leaves. Bears yellow-centered, double, pink-blushed white flowerheads, solitary or in corymbs, in mid- and late summer. ↕ 20in (50cm), ↔ 18in (45cm). Zone 4.

Erigeron karvinskianus 'Profusion'

Erigeron 'Quakeress'

E. speciosus. Clump-forming perennial with mostly hairless leaves, to 6in (15cm) long, with fringed, hairy margins; the basal leaves are inversely lance-shaped to inversely spoon-shaped, the stem leaves are lance-shaped to ovate. In summer, bears yellow-centered, lavender-blue to lilac flowerheads, 1½in (4cm) across, in corymbs to 4in (10cm) across. ↕↔ 24in (60cm). Canada to N.W. US. Zone 3. **'Double Beauty'** has double violet-blue flowerheads; ↕ 18in (45cm).
***E.* 'Strahlenmeer',** syn. *E.* 'Shining Sea'. Clump-forming perennial with lance-shaped leaves and corymbs of yellow-centered, single, soft blue-violet flowerheads, produced in summer. ↕ 20in (50cm), ↔ 18in (45cm). Zone 4.
***E.* 'Summer Snow'** see *E.* 'Sommerneuschnee'.

Erigeron 'Serenity'

Erinacea anthyllis

ERINACEA

FABACEAE

Genus of one species of dense, compact, evergreen subshrub from exposed, stony habitats in calcareous mountains in S.W. Europe and Morocco. It has stiff, sharp spines, simple or 3-palmate leaves, and axillary, pea-like, 2-lipped flowers. Long-lived and slow-growing, it flowers profusely once established. Grow in a rock garden, scree bed, or raised bed.
• **CULTIVATION** Grow in deep, gritty, sharply drained soil in full sun.
• **PROPAGATION** Sow seed in containers in an open frame in autumn. Root greenwood cuttings in late spring or early summer.
• **PESTS AND DISEASES** May be infested by spider mites under glass.

E. anthyllis ▣ syn. *E. pungens* (Hedgehog broom). Mound-forming subshrub with spine-tipped, intricately branching stems and simple or 3-palmate, dark gray-green leaves, to ½in (1.5cm) long, with inversely lance-shaped leaflets. In late spring and early summer, bears clusters of 2–4 violet-blue flowers, to ¾in (2cm) long, with white-marked standard petals. ↕ to 12in (30cm), ↔ to 3ft (1m). E. Pyrenees to W. Mediterranean, Morocco. Zone 7b.
E. pungens see *E. anthyllis.*

ERINUS

Fairy foxglove

SCROPHULARIACEAE

Genus of 2 species of semi-evergreen perennials with rosettes of inversely lance-shaped to wedge-shaped, toothed leaves and terminal racemes of tubular flowers with 5 spreading lobes. Growing wild in rocky mountains in North Africa and C. and S. Europe, they are ideal for a rock garden, a wall, or paving crevices.
• **CULTIVATION** Grow in light to moderately fertile, well-drained soil in full sun or partial shade.
• **PROPAGATION** Sow seed *in situ* or in containers in an open frame in autumn. Frequently self-seeds. Root rosettes as cuttings in spring.
• **PESTS AND DISEASES** Infrequent.

E. alpinus ▣ (Alpine liverwort). Short-lived, tufted perennial with inversely lance-shaped to wedge-shaped, sticky leaves, ¼–¾in (0.5–2cm) long. Bears short racemes of 2-lipped, pink,

Erinus alpinus

purple, or white flowers, to ½in (1.5cm) across, from late spring to summer. ↕ 3in (8cm), ↔ 4in (10cm). C. and S. Europe. Zone 5. **'Dr. Hähnle'** has deep crimson flowers.

ERIOBOTRYA

ROSACEAE

Genus of about 30 species of evergreen shrubs and trees from woodland in the Himalayas and E. Asia. They have alternate, simple, lance-shaped to broadly elliptic, often toothed, leathery leaves and small, 5-petaled flowers in broad, pyramidal panicles. Where not hardy, grow in a cool greenhouse or against a sunny wall. In warmer areas, grow as specimens. *E. japonica* is also grown commercially for its fruit.
• **CULTIVATION** Under glass, grow in soil-based potting mix in full light, with good ventilation. In growth, water moderately and apply a balanced liquid fertilizer monthly; water sparingly in winter. Outdoors, grow in fertile, well-drained soil in a sheltered site in full sun. Pruning group 1; may need restrictive pruning under glass.
• **PROPAGATION** Sow seed at 55–61°F (13–16°C) in spring. Insert semi-ripe cuttings in summer.
• **PESTS AND DISEASES** Susceptible to fireblight, fungal spots, blights, cankers, and root rots.

E. japonica ▣ (Loquat). Vigorous, spreading shrub or tree with thick shoots and bold, inversely lance-shaped to narrowly obovate, sharp-pointed, strongly veined, dark green leaves, to

Eriobotrya japonica

E

12in (30cm) long, glossy above. Bears large panicles of fragrant white flowers from autumn to winter, followed in spring by spherical to pear-shaped, edible, orange-yellow fruit, 1½in (4cm) across. ↕↔ 25ft (8m). China, Japan. ❄ (min. 50°F/10°C)

▷ ***Eriocactus*** see *Parodia*
▷ ***Eriocereus jusbertii*** see *Harrisia jusbertii*
▷ ***Eriocereus martianus*** see *Aporocactus martianus*
▷ ***Eriocereus pomanensis*** see *Harrisia bonplandii*

E

ERIOGONUM

St. Catherine's lace, Wild buckwheat

POLYGONACEAE

Genus of approximately 150 species of annuals, perennials, and evergreen shrubs and subshrubs, occurring mostly in desert and mountains in W. US. They are cultivated for their beautiful, often white-woolly foliage and their dense heads, umbels, or cymes of small, long-lasting flowers, cupped in involucres of toothed or lobed bracts. They range from compact, cushion-forming plants with linear to ovate or rounded leaves in basal rosettes, to large shrubs with opposite, alternate, or whorled leaves. Grow the smaller, rosette-forming species in a rock garden or alpine house, the larger ones in a shrub border. Where not hardy, grow in a cool greenhouse or conservatory.

• **CULTIVATION** Under glass, grow in equal parts soil-based potting mix and grit, in full light. During the growing season, water moderately and apply a balanced liquid fertilizer monthly; water sparingly at other times. Outdoors, grow in poor to gritty, moderately fertile, sharply drained soil in full sun; protect from winter moisture. Deadhead unless seed is required. In an alpine house, grow in 1 part leaf mold and 2 parts each loam and grit or sharp sand. Pruning group 1.

• **PROPAGATION** Sow seed of hardy species in containers in an open frame in autumn. Sow seed of tender species in spring at 55–61°F (13–16°C). Root individual rosettes of cushion-forming species as cuttings in spring or early summer. Water only from below. Root semi-ripe cuttings of shrubs in summer.

• **PESTS AND DISEASES** Powdery mildew and rust are common, as well as spider mites and aphids, especially under glass.

E. arborescens ■ Domed, loose or open shrub with oblong or linear leaves, ¾–1¼in (2–3cm) long, borne in tufts at the ends of the branches; leaves are smooth and mid- to deep green above, densely white-woolly beneath, with margins rolled under. From early summer to autumn, bears dense, terminal cymes, 2–6in (5–15cm) across, of white to pale pink flowers. ↕↔ 2–5ft (0.6–1.5m). California. ❄ (min. 41°F/5°C)

E. crocatum (Saffron buckwheat). Branching subshrub or woody-based perennial with broadly ovate to elliptic, white-felted, mid-green leaves, to 1½in (4cm) long. In late spring and early summer, bears tiny, bright yellowish green flowers in dense cymes, to 3in (8cm) across. Best in an alpine house.

Eriogonum arborescens

↕ 12–16in (30–40cm), ↔ to 16in (40cm). California. ❄ (min. 41°F/5°C)

E. fasciculatum. Rounded shrub with spreading branches that bear tufts of narrowly oblong to linear-lance-shaped leaves, ¼–½in (0.5–1.5cm) long, deep green above, white-woolly beneath, with inrolled margins. White, sometimes pink-tinted flowers are produced in loose, terminal heads, 1¼–4in (3–10cm) across, in summer. ↕ 12–24in (30–60cm), ↔ 36in (90cm). California, Nevada, Utah. Zone 8.

E. giganteum (St. Catherine's lace). Freely branching, rounded shrub with oblong to oblong-ovate, leathery leaves, 1¼–4in (3–10cm) long, densely white-downy beneath, smoother and gray above, mainly grouped toward the stem tips. In summer, produces heads of small white flowers in dense cymes, 8–12in (20–30cm) across. ↕↔ 3–6ft (1–2m). Santa Catalina and adjacent islands. ❄ (min. 41°F/5°C)

E. gracilipes, syn. *E. kennedyi* subsp. *gracilipes* (Sulfur flower). Woody-based, mat-forming perennial with oval to oval-lance-shaped, white-woolly, greenish gray leaves, to ⅜in (9mm) long, with margins rolled under. In early and midsummer, umbels, to ½in (1.5cm) across, of pink-tinted white flowers that darken with age are borne on stems to 4in (10cm) long. Best in a scree bed or alpine house. ↕ to 3in (8cm), ↔ to 5in (13cm). Sierra Nevada. Zone 5.

E. kennedyi* subsp. *gracilipes see *E. gracilipes.*

E. ovalifolium. Cushion- or mat-forming, woody-based perennial with

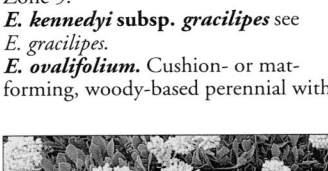

Eriogonum umbellatum

Eriogonum umbellatum var. *torreyanum*

long-stalked, spoon-shaped, silver-hairy leaves, ¼–½in (0.5–1.5cm) long. In summer, stems, to 8in (20cm) long, bear dense, spherical heads, to ¾in (2cm) across, of cream or yellow flowers, sometimes maturing to pink-purple. Suitable for an alpine house. ↕ to 2in (5cm), ↔ to 8in (20cm). Oregon to Nevada. Zone 4.

E. torreyanum see *E. umbellatum* var. *torreyanum.*

E. umbellatum ■ (Sulfur flower). Spreading, mat-forming perennial or subshrub with rosettes of spoon-shaped or ovate leaves, to ¾in (2cm) long, mid-green above, white-woolly beneath. In mid- and late summer, produces umbels, 1¼–2½in (3–6cm) across, of cream to sulfur-yellow flowers that become copper-red-tinted with age, on stems to 10in (25cm) long. Not always free-flowering. ↕ to 12in (30cm), ↔ to 3ft (1m). S.W. Canada to E. Rocky Mountains. Zone 4.

var. *torreyanum* ■ syn. *E. torreyanum,* is a long-lived, upright, domed shrub with hairless, dark green leaves. In mid-summer, produces abundant, noticeably bracted, bright yellow flowerheads on stems 2–4in (5–10cm) long. S. Oregon to N. California.

ERIOPHORUM

Cotton grass

CYPERACEAE

Genus of 20 species of rapidly spreading, evergreen, rhizomatous, bog, marsh, or marginal aquatic perennials found in Europe, southern Africa, and North America. They have slender, needle-like, tough leaves, and produce tufted umbels of many-flowered spikelets in summer. Effective in masses beside a wildlife pool or in a bog garden. Grows best in areas with cooler summers.

• **CULTIVATION** Grow in acidic soil alongside shallow water, or in an aquatic container of peaty soil in a small pool, in full sun and with ample room. Capable of surviving in water to 2in (5cm) deep.

• **PROPAGATION** Divide established clumps in spring.

• **PESTS AND DISEASES** Rust can occur.

E. angustifolium ■ (Common cotton grass). Marginal aquatic perennial with a long rootstock, short, distinctly angled stems, and linear, grooved, mainly basal leaves, 6–12in (15–30cm) long, with long, sharp-pointed tips. In summer, bears umbels of 3–7 pendent, downy,

Eriophorum angustifolium

tufted white spikelets, 1¼–2in (3–5cm) across. ↕ 12–18in (30–45cm), sometimes to 30in (75cm), ↔ indefinite. N. Europe (including Arctic), Russia (Siberia), North America. Zone 4.

E. latifolium (Broad-leaved cotton grass). Marginal aquatic perennial with tufted rhizomes, 3-angled stems, and linear, flat, grooved, mainly basal leaves, 8–16in (20–40cm) long, with long, sharp-pointed tips. In summer, bears umbels of 3–7 pendent, tufted, downy white spikelets, 1¼–2in (3–5cm) across, with purplish green scales. Similar to *E. angustifolium,* but has broader leaves. ↕ 12–18in (30–45cm), ↔ indefinite. Europe, Turkey, Russia (Siberia), North America. Zone 4.

ERIOPHYLLUM

Golden yarrow, Woolly sunflower

ASTERACEAE

Genus of about 12 species of annuals, perennials, and subshrubs occurring mostly in open, sandy scrub, often in mountainous areas, in W. North America. They have alternate, deeply toothed or pinnatifid, white-hairy leaves, and bear cymes or corymbs of daisy-like flowerheads on upright stems, mainly in summer. Grow in a rock garden, at the front of a border, on adry wall, or in paving crevices. *E. lanatum* may overwhelm smaller alpines, and so it should be sited with care.

• **CULTIVATION** Grow in light, poor to moderately fertile, sharply drained soil in full sun. Cut back after flowering to keep compact.

• **PROPAGATION** Sow seed in containers in an open frame in autumn, or divide in spring.

• **PESTS AND DISEASES** Rust and scale insects sometimes occur. Slugs, snails, and mice can attack stems and leaves.

E. lanatum ■ Variable, vigorous, clump-forming perennial with erect or decumbent stems and white-woolly, silvery gray leaves. The basal leaves, to 3in (8cm) long, are spoon-shaped to inversely lance-shaped, and entire or lobed; the smaller stem leaves are pinnatifid, or narrow and entire. Produces a succession of daisy-like, bright yellow flowerheads, ¾–1½in (2–4cm) across, singly or in loose corymbs, over long periods from late spring to summer. Tolerates drought. ↕↔ 8–24in (20–60cm), rarely to 36in

Eriophyllum lanatum

(90cm). British Columbia to N. California and W. Montana. Zone 4.
var. *monoense*, syn. *E. lutescens*, is almost cushion-forming, with spoon-shaped, entire or 3-toothed leaves, to ¾in (2cm) long. Best variant for a rock garden; ↕ to 10in (25cm), ↔ to 3ft (1m). California, Nevada, Wyoming.
E. lutescens see *E. lanatum* var. *monoense*.

ERIOSTEMON
Waxflower
RUTACEAE

Genus of 33 species of evergreen shrubs or small trees from open, rocky slopes, scrub, and open forest in Australia. They are grown mainly for their star-shaped, usually 5-petaled, waxy, white, pink to red, blue, or mauve flowers, which are solitary or borne in terminal or axillary racemes or cymes. The leaves are alternate, flat to cylindrical, linear to rounded, often warty, and strongly aromatic. Where not hardy, grow in a cool greenhouse; elsewhere, plant in a shrub border or against a house wall.
• **CULTIVATION** Under glass, grow in acidic potting mix in full light. During the growing season, water freely and apply a low-phosphate liquid fertilizer monthly; water sparingly in winter. Top-dress or pot on in spring. Outdoors, grow in fertile, moist soil in full sun. Pruning group 1; may need restrictive pruning under glass.
• **PROPAGATION** Sow pre-soaked seed at 50–55°F (10–13°C) in spring. Root semi-ripe cuttings in summer with bottom heat. Germination is often erratic and rooting of cuttings slow.
• **PESTS AND DISEASES** Scale insects may be a problem.

E. australasius (Pink waxflower). Erect, freely branching shrub with angular, minutely hairy stems and narrowly elliptic or oblong to obovate, nearly hairless, glandular, leathery leaves, to 3in (8cm) long. From spring to autumn, bears solitary, pink to mauve-pink, sometimes white flowers, 1½in (4cm) wide, usually in profusion, at the shoot tips. ↕ 3–6ft (1–2m), ↔ 2–5ft (0.6–1.5m). Queensland to New South Wales. ❄ (min. 45°F/7°C)
'Clearview Pink' has red flowerbuds and pink-tinted petals.
E. trachyphyllus ■ Bushy tree or shrub with cylindrical, hairless, warty stems. Elliptic to obovate-oblong leaves, to 2in (5cm) long, are thin, papery, hairless, and finely wrinkled. In winter or early spring, bears solitary white to pink flowers, ½in (1.5cm) across, with fleshy, fringed sepals and long stamens, from the leaf axils. ↕ to 22ft (7m), ↔ 8ft (2.5m). New South Wales, Victoria. ❄ (min. 41°F/5°C)

ERIOSYCE
CACTACEAE

Genus of 35 species of cactus grown in the deep soils of the S.W. US and N. Mexico, through the Andes into Chile. Usually solitary and subglobose, globose, or elongated in shape. Large taproots lead to growth in deep soils. Tubular, yellowish to deep carmine flowers are borne near stem tips, 1 per areole.

Eriostemon trachyphyllus

• **CULTIVATION** Under glass, grow in a mix of 4 parts standard cactus potting mix and 1 part limestone chips, in full light. From spring to summer, water freely and apply a balanced liquid fertilizer every 4–5 weeks. Keep nearly dry at other times. Outdoors, grow in moderately fertile, slightly alkaline, sharply drained, humus-rich soil in full sun. See also pp.48–49.
• **PROPAGATION** Sow seed at 70°F (21°C) in spring or summer.
• **PESTS AND DISEASES** Scale occurs.

E. heinrichiana, syn. *Horridocactus heinrichianus*. Subglobose or globose, sometimes elongated, brownish to blackish green cactus, narrowing adjacent to stems. Slowly clump-forming, rising barely above ground level. Spines are curved to straight, and needle-like, sometimes absent. Young areoles produce creamy yellow to reddish flowers, to 2in (5cm). Bears oval, thin-walled, red fleshy fruit, to ½in (1.5cm). ↔ 1½–4in (4–10cm). Chile. ❄ (min. 50°F/10°C)

E. marksiana. Flattened globose to subglobose gray-green cactus, maturing to an elongated form. Areoles bear varied spines. Numerous funnel- to bell-shaped lemon to reddish yellow flowers, to 1½in (4cm), are borne near sunken, naked stem tips. ↕ to 2in (5cm), ↔ to 9½in (24cm). Chile. ❄ (min. 50°F/10°C)

ERITRICHIUM
Alpine forget-me-not
BORAGINACEAE

Genus of approximately 30 species of low-growing, tufted or cushion-forming perennials found mostly in high-altitude scree and rock crevices in Europe, the Himalayas, and North America. They are grown mainly for their short, axillary or terminal, raceme-like cymes of blue, occasionally white flowers, similar to forget-me-nots (*Myosotis*), which are produced from spring to early summer. The leaves are alternate, usually elliptic to linear, softly hairy, and gray-green. The American cushion-forming species are challenging plants for an alpine house; other species may be grown in a scree bed or trough, or in tufa.
• **CULTIVATION** In an alpine house, grow in a mix of 3 parts grit, 1 part loam, and 1 part leaf mold, with a deep collar of grit or pieces of rock wedged around the neck of the plants. Provide full light and good ventilation. Water freely during the growing season by immersing the containers to their rims in water; avoid wetting the foliage. Keep just moist in winter. Outdoors, grow in poor, sharply drained soil in full sun, with protection from winter moisture.
• **PROPAGATION** Sow seed in containers in an open frame in autumn. Root basal stem cuttings in summer.
• **PESTS AND DISEASES** Prone to aphids and spider mites under glass.

Eritrichium nanum

E. nanum ■ Cushion-forming perennial with rosettes of elliptic or inversely lance-shaped to linear, densely silky-hairy, silvery gray-green leaves, to ½in (1.5cm) long. In late spring and early summer, short-tubed, salverform, yellow-eyed, azure-blue flowers, ¼–⅜in (6–9mm) across, are borne in raceme-like cymes. ↕ 2in (5cm), ↔ 3in (8cm). Alps, Rocky Mountains. Zone 5.

ERODIUM
Heron's bill, Stork's bill
GERANIACEAE

Genus of approximately 60 species of annuals, perennials, and evergreen and deciduous subshrubs occurring in rocky habitats, mainly in the calcareous mountains of Europe and C. Asia, but also in N. Africa, North and South America, and temperate Australia. The leaves are opposite or alternate, and lobed, pinnate, or pinnatisect. In summer, they bear 5-petaled flowers (pink to purple, occasionally yellow or white) singly from the leaf axils or in terminal umbels. Grow in a rock garden, trough, or alpine house; plant the taller, and more robust species at the front of a herbaceous border.
• **CULTIVATION** Grow in gritty, humus-rich, sharply drained, neutral to alkaline soil in full sun. Protect the smallest species from excessive winter moisture. In an alpine house, grow in equal parts loam, leaf mold, and grit.
• **PROPAGATION** Sow seed in containers in an open frame as soon as ripe. Divide in spring. Root basal stem cuttings in late spring or early summer.
• **PESTS AND DISEASES** Leaf galls are common, with some fungal stem rots occurring at times. Aphids and spider mites can cause problems under glass.

E. chamaedryoides see *E. reichardii*.
***E. chamaedryoides* 'Roseum'** see *E.* x *variabile* 'Roseum'.
E. cheilanthifolium ■ syn. *E. petraeum* subsp. *crispum*. Compact, mound-

Erodium cheilanthifolium

E

Erodium chrysanthum

forming perennial with ovate-oblong, 2-pinnatifid, crinkled, grayish green leaves, ¾–2in (2–5cm) long. In summer, bears umbels of up to 5 flat-faced, red-veined, pale pink or white flowers, to 1in (2.5cm) across, stained reddish purple at the bases of the 2 upper petals. ↕ to 8in (20cm), ↔ to 12in (30cm). S. Spain, North Africa. Zone 6.

E. chrysanthum ■ Dense, tufted, mound-forming perennial with ovate, 2-pinnate, finely dissected, silvery green leaves, to 1½in (4cm) long, each with oblong to lance-shaped leaflets. In summer, branching stems bear umbels of 2–7 saucer-shaped, sulfur-yellow, dioecious flowers, to ¾in (2cm) across. ↕ to 6in (15cm), ↔ to 16in (40cm). Greece. Zone 5b.

Erodium corsicum

Erodium glandulosum

Erodium manescaui

E. corsicum ■ Mat-forming perennial with ovate, crumpled, silver-downy, gray-green leaves, ½in (1.5cm) long, with scalloped margins. From late spring to summer, short, branched stems bear umbels of 1–3 saucer-shaped, rose-pink flowers, to ¾in (2cm) across, with darker veins. ↕ 3in (8cm), ↔ to 8in (20cm). Sea cliffs of Corsica and Sardinia. Zone 5.

E. glandulosum ■ syn. *E. macradenum*, *E. petraeum* subsp. *glandulosum*. Compact, tufted perennial bearing ovate-oblong, 2-pinnatifid, silvery, basal leaves, 1½–4in (4–10cm) long, with oblong to lance-shaped divisions. In summer, produces umbels of up to 5 saucer-shaped, lilac-pink flowers, to 1in (2.5cm) across, usually marked dark purple on the 2 upper petals. ↕ 4–8in (10–20cm), ↔ to 8in (20cm). Pyrenees, N. Spain. Zone 5b.

E. macradenum see *E. glandulosum.*

E. manescaui ■ syn. *E. manescavii.* Clump-forming perennial with pinnate, lance-shaped to ovate-lance-shaped, toothed, hairy, mid-green, basal leaves, to 12in (30cm) long, with ovate leaflets. Long-stalked umbels of 5–20 saucer-shaped, magenta-purple flowers, to 1¼in (3cm) across, with darker spots on the upper 2 petals, are profusely borne from early summer to early autumn. Self-seeds freely. ↕ 8–18in (20–45cm), ↔ 8in (20cm). Pyrenees. Zone 4.

E. manescavii see *E. manescaui.*

E. petraeum* subsp. *crispum see *E. cheilanthifolium.*

E. petraeum* subsp. *glandulosum see *E. glandulosum.*

E. reichardii, syn. *E. chamaedryoides.* Mound-forming perennial with heart-shaped, scalloped, slightly downy, dark green leaves, to ½in (1.5cm) long. Bears solitary, saucer-shaped, red-veined white flowers, ⅜in (9mm) across, on very short stems in summer. ↕ 2–3in (5–8cm), ↔ to 6in (15cm). Majorca, Corsica. Zone 5.

E. x variabile (*E. corsicum* x *E. reichardii*). Spreading or cushion-forming perennial with ovate, scalloped or lobed, mid-green leaves, to ¾in (2cm) long, heart-shaped at the bases. In summer, bears solitary, single or double, deep red flowers, to ½in (1.5cm) across, veined maroon. ↕ to 5in (13cm), ↔ to 12in (30cm). Garden origin. Zone 5. **'Flore Pleno'** has narrowly ovate, scalloped, dark to gray-green leaves, and bears rounded, double, deep pink flowers, with darker veining, from spring to autumn. **'Ken Aslet'** has prostrate stems and bears single, deep pink flowers. **'Roseum'**, syn. *E. chamaedryoides* 'Roseum', produces deep pink flowers with darker veining; ↕ to 3in (8cm).

▷ ***Erpetion*** see *Viola*
▷ ***Ervatamia coronaria*** see *Tabernaemontana divaricata*

ERYNGIUM

Eryngo, Sea holly

APIACEAE

Genus of 230 species of hairless annuals, biennials, and deciduous and evergreen perennials. Those that are native to dry, rocky places and coastal areas in Europe, N. Africa, Turkey, C. Asia, China, and Korea usually have taproots, ovate to heart-shaped, often divided leaves, and congested heads of blue or white flowers, with conspicuous bracts. Those that are from often wet and marshy grassland in Mexico, Brazil, Argentina, and warm-temperate regions of North, Central, and South America, usually have fibrous roots, sword-shaped, evergreen foliage, less showy, greenish white (occasionally purplish brown) flowers, and small bracts. Most eryngiums form basal rosettes, the leaves often spiny and with silvery white veins, and bear crowded, hemispherical to cylindrical, thistle-like umbels of stalkless flowers, on branched stems.

• **CULTIVATION** Eryngiums have varying cultivation requirements. For ease of reference, these have been grouped as follows:
1. Grow in dry, well-drained, poor to moderately fertile soil in full sun; protect from excessive winter moisture.
2. Grow in moist, well-drained, fertile soil in full sun.

• **PROPAGATION** Sow seed in containers in a cold frame as soon as ripe. Divide in spring, although they are slow to re-establish. Insert root cuttings of perennials in late winter.

• **PESTS AND DISEASES** Prone to root rot, slugs, snails, and powdery mildew.

E. agavifolium, syn. *E. bromeliifolium* of gardens. Rosette-forming, evergreen perennial with broadly sword-shaped, prominently and sharply toothed, glossy, deep green basal leaves, 16–30in (40–75cm) long. In late summer, lightly branched stems bear cylindrical umbels, 2in (5cm) long, of greenish white flowers, with entire to spiny-toothed bracts, ¼in (6mm) long. Cultivation group 2. ↕ 3–5ft (1–1.5m), ↔ 24in (60cm). Argentina. Zone 6.

E. alpinum ■ (Alpine sea holly). Rosette-forming, taprooted herbaceous perennial with ovate to heart-shaped, spiny-toothed, mid-green basal leaves, 3–6in (8–15cm) long, and palmately 3-lobed stem leaves. From midsummer to early autumn, branched stems, steel-blue near the apex, bear cylindrical umbels, to 1½in (4cm) long, of steel-blue or white flowers, with pinnatifid, softly spiny bracts, to 2½in (6cm) long. Cultivation group 1, but soil should not be too dry. ↕ 28in (70cm), ↔ 18in (45cm). Europe (Jura, Alps, mountains of W. and C. Balkans). Zone 4.

Eryngium alpinum

'Amethyst' has smaller, violet-blue flowerheads, 1in (2.5cm) long. **'Donardt's Blue'** produces conical umbels of blue flowers with feathery blue bracts, in summer; ↕ 30in (75cm). **'Superbum'** is more vigorous than the species.

E. amethystinum (Amethyst sea holly). Clump-forming, taprooted herbaceous perennial with obovate, pinnate, spiny, leathery, mid-green basal leaves, 4–6in (10–15cm) long, with oblong leaflets, and palmately 3-lobed upper leaves. In mid- and late summer, branching, silvery blue stems bear cylindrical umbels, ¾–1¼in (2–3cm) long, of steel-blue to amethyst flowers, with lance-shaped, spiny, silvery green bracts, to 2in (5cm) long. Cultivation group 1. ↕↔ 28in (70cm). Italy, Sicily, Balkans. Zone 4.

E. bourgatii ■ Clump-forming, taprooted herbaceous perennial with rounded, pinnatifid or 2-pinnatifid, spiny, conspicuously silver-veined, dark green basal leaves, to 3in (8cm) long. In mid- and late summer, branching blue stems bear blue or often gray-green flowers in cylindrical umbels, ½–1¼in (1–3cm) long, with lance-shaped, blue-tinged, silver bracts, to 2½in (6cm) long. Cultivation group 1. ↕ 6–18in (15–45cm), ↔ 12in (30cm). Spain (Pyrenees). Zone 4. **'Oxford Blue'** has darker, silvery blue flowerheads.

***E. bromeliifolium* of gardens** see *E. agavifolium.*

E. decaisneanum see *E. pandanifolium.*

E. delaroux see *E. proteiflorum.*

E. eburneum ■ syn. *E. paniculatum.* Clump-forming, evergreen perennial

Eryngium bourgatii

Eryngium eburneum

with narrowly linear, spiny-toothed, mid-green leaves, to 3ft (1m) long. In late summer, arching, branched, pale green stems bear groups of spherical-cylindrical umbels, to ¾in (2cm) long, composed of whitish green flowers, with linear-lance-shaped, spine-tipped bracts. Cultivation group 2. ↕ to 5ft (1.5m), ↔ 24in (60cm). Temperate South America. ❄ (min. 41°F/5°C)

E. giganteum ▣ (Miss Willmott's ghost). Rosette-forming, taprooted biennial with heart-shaped, mid-green basal leaves, 3–6in (8–15cm) long, and ovate, scalloped to toothed, spiny stem leaves. In summer, branched inflorescences consist of cylindrical umbels, to 2½in (6cm) long, of initially pale green, then steel-blue flowers, with ovate, toothed, silvery gray bracts, to 2½in (6cm) long, both prickly. Cultivation group 2. ↕ 36in (90cm), ↔ 12in (30cm). Caucasus, Iran. Zone 4. **'Silver Ghost'** has narrower, very silvery white bracts; ↕ to 24in (60cm).

E.* x *oliverianum ▣ (*E. alpinum* x *E. giganteum*). Clump-forming, taprooted herbaceous perennial with ovate, slightly 3-lobed, spiny-toothed, dark green basal leaves, 3–6in (8–15cm) long, with conspicuous veins and heart-shaped bases,

Eryngium x *oliverianum*

and palmately 4- to 5-lobed stem leaves. From midsummer to early autumn, branched blue stems bear cylindrical umbels, 1½in (4cm) long, of flowers, with linear, spiny bracts, to 2½in (6cm) long, both brilliant blue. Cultivation group 1. ↕ 36in (90cm), ↔ 18in (45cm). Garden origin. Zone 5.

E. pandanifolium, syn. *E. decaisneanum.* Tufted, clump-forming, evergreen perennial with linear to sword-shaped, silvery green leaves, 3–6ft (1–2m) long, with slender marginal spines. Cylindrical umbels, ½in (1.5cm) long, of purplish brown flowers; shorter, ovate bracts, ½in (1.5cm) long, are produced from late summer to midautumn. Cultivation group 2. ↕ to 12ft (4m), ↔ to 6ft (2m). Brazil to Argentina. ❄ (min. 41°F/5°C). **var. *lasseauxii*** has leaves with paired or grouped spines, to ¾in (2cm) long, and greenish white flowerheads, in summer.

E. paniculatum see *E. eburneum.*

E. planum (Flat sea holly). Clump-forming, taprooted, evergreen perennial with oblong to ovate-oblong, toothed, dark green basal leaves, 2–4in (5–10cm) long, with heart-shaped bases, spiny, palmately lobed, blue-tinted stem leaves; both are somewhat leathery. From midsummer to early autumn, strong, branching stems bear numerous spherical-cylindrical umbels, ½–¾in (1–2cm) long, of light blue flowers, with linear, spiky, blue-green bracts, 1in (2.5cm) long. Cultivation group 1. ↕ 36in (90cm), ↔ 18in (45cm). C. and S.E. Europe to C. Asia. Zone 4. **'Azureum'** bears azure-blue flowerheads. **'Blauer Zwerg'**, syn. 'Blue Dwarf', produces intense blue flowers; ↕ to 20in (50cm). **'Blue Diamond'** has a very dwarf, compact habit; ↕ 12–18in (30–45cm). **'Blue Dwarf'** see 'Blauer Zwerg'. **'Blue Ribbon'** has rosettes of heart-shaped leaves and profuse, double, pale blue flowers, in mid- and late summer; ↕ 30–36in (75–90cm). **'Silverstone'** has thistle-like umbels of white flowers, in mid- and late summer; ↕ 24in (60cm).

E. proteiflorum ▣ syn. *E. delaroux.* Rosette-forming, taprooted, evergreen perennial with narrowly linear, spiny-margined, silvery green basal leaves, 4–12in (10–30cm) long, with white midribs. In early and midautumn, branching stems produce cylindrical umbels, 1–3in (2.5–8cm) long, of grayish blue flowers, with linear to lance-shaped, spiny-margined, silvery white bracts, to 4in (10cm) long. Cultivation group 1, or grow in a container. ↕ 36in (90cm), ↔ 24in (60cm). Mexico. ❄ (min. 41°F/5°C)

E.* x *tripartitum ▣ Clump-forming, taprooted herbaceous perennial with narrowly ovate, 3-lobed, toothed, dark green leaves, 2½–5in (6–13cm) long, with a few marginal spines. From midsummer to early autumn, stems bear spherical-cylindrical umbels, to ¾in (2cm) long, of violet-blue flowers, with narrowly lance-shaped, gray-blue bracts, to 1½in (4cm) long. Cultivation group 1. ↕ 24–36in (60–90cm), ↔ 20in (50cm). Mediterranean origin. Zone 4.

E. variifolium ▣ (Moroccan sea holly). Clump-forming, taprooted, evergreen perennial with rosettes of ovate, toothed,

Eryngium x *tripartitum*

spiny, fleshy, dark green leaves, 2in (5cm) long, that have heart-shaped bases; marbled with white veins broadest in the leaf center. In mid- and late summer, stiff, branching stems bear cylindrical umbels, 1¼in (3cm) long, of gray-blue flowers, with longer, sharply pointed, pale blue bracts, to 1½in (4cm) long. Suitable for a rock garden. Cultivation group 1, but soil not too dry. ↕ to 16in (40cm), ↔ 10in (25cm). Morocco. Zone 5.

E. yuccifolium (Rattlesnake-master). Rosetted, taprooted, semi-evergreen perennial with sword-shaped, spiny-margined, blue-gray leaves, 8–39in (20–100cm) long. From midsummer to early autumn, strong, lightly branched stems bear cylindrical umbels, to 1½in (4cm) long, of whitish green to pale blue flowers, with shorter, ovate, gray-green bracts, ⅜in (9mm) long. Cultivation group 2. ↕ 4ft (1.2m), ↔ 24in (60cm). S. and E. US. Zone 5b.

E.* x *zabelii (*E. alpinum* x *E. bourgatii*). Clump-forming, taprooted, semi-evergreen perennial with heart-shaped, spiny-toothed, dark green basal leaves, 3–5in (8–13cm) long. Blue stems bear deeply 3-lobed leaves. In mid- and late summer, bears spherical-cylindrical umbels, ¾–1½in (2–4cm) across, of long-lasting, intense blue or violet flowers, with rigid, spiny-toothed, green-tipped blue bracts, 2½in (6cm) long. Cultivation group 1. ↕ to 18in (45cm), ↔ 12in (30cm). Garden origin. Zone 5. **'Jewel'** is taller and bears rich green leaves and large, finely divided bracts; ↕ to 24in (60cm). **'Violetta'** has umbels, to 2in (5cm) long, of violet-blue flowers and silvery blue bracts.

Eryngium giganteum

Eryngium proteiflorum

Eryngium variifolium

E

ERYSIMUM syn. CHEIRANTHUS

Wallflower

BRASSICACEAE

Genus, now including *Cheiranthus*, of about 80 species of annuals, biennials, and mainly evergreen perennials, often woody based, found mostly on well-drained, calcareous soil from Europe to N. Africa, W. and C. Asia, and N. America. They are cultivated for their often yellow flowers, to 1in (2.5cm) across, each with 4 petals arranged in a cross, borne in dense, usually elongating, corymb-like racemes. Most wallflowers produce inversely lance-shaped, toothed, softly hairy leaves, 1¼–5in (3–13cm) long. Many are ideal for a rock garden or wall, the front of a sunny border, or a raised bed. The biennials are useful as spring bedding plants or in a border.

E

• **CULTIVATION** Grow in poor to moderately fertile, well-drained, neutral or, ideally, alkaline soil in full sun. Trim perennials lightly after flowering to prevent plants from becoming leggy.

• **PROPAGATION** Sow seed of perennials in containers in a cold frame in spring. Take nodal or heeled softwood cuttings from shrubby perennials in spring or summer. Sow seed of biennials in a seedbed from late spring to early summer, grow on in a nursery bed, and transplant to flowering positions in midautumn. Provide protection where frosts are severe or prolonged.

• **PESTS AND DISEASES** White rust, downy mildew, and rust are common; clubroot, mosaic virus, and a few fungal leaf spots sometimes occur. Snails, slugs, and caterpillars also can cause damage.

E.* x *allionii ■ syn. *Cheiranthus* x *allionii* (Siberian wallflower). Tufted, short-lived, evergreen perennial, grown as a biennial, with lance-shaped, coarsely toothed leaves, to 3in (8cm) long. In spring, produces spice-scented, brilliant orange flowers, to ½in (1.5cm) across, in short racemes. ↕ 20–24in (50–60cm), ↔ to 12in (30cm). Garden origin. Zone 4.

E. asperum (Western wallflower). Erect, rarely branched, short-lived, evergreen perennial or biennial with linear to lance-shaped, usually entire leaves, to 5in (13cm) long. From spring to early summer, bears short racemes of open, copper-yellow flowers, to 1in (2.5cm) across. ↕ to 12in (30cm), ↔ to 10in (25cm). British Columbia to Washington, Minnesota, Kansas. Zone 5.

Erysimum 'Bowles' Mauve'

***E.* 'Bowles' Mauve'** ■ syn. *E.* 'E.A. Bowles'. Vigorous, subshrubby, often short-lived evergreen perennial with narrowly lance-shaped, gray-green leaves. Bears mauve flowers, to ½in (1.5cm) across, in long racemes from late winter to summer. ↕ to 30in (75cm), ↔ 24in (60cm). Zone 4.

***E.* 'Bredon'** ■ Sturdy, mound-forming, evergreen perennial with inversely lance-shaped, bluish green leaves. Reddish brown buds open to rich yellow flowers, to ¾in (2cm) across, in long racemes from midspring to early summer. ↕ 12in (30cm), ↔ 18in (45cm). Zone 6.

E. cheiri, syn. *Cheiranthus cheiri* (Wallflower). Subshrubby, short-lived, evergreen perennial, grown as a biennial, forming mounds of lance-shaped to obovate-lance-shaped, dark green leaves, to 9in (23cm) long, the margins entire or with well-spaced teeth. Open, sweet-scented, bright yellow-orange flowers, to 1in (2.5cm) across, are produced in short racemes in spring. ↕ 10–32in (25–80cm), ↔ 12–16in (30–40cm). S. Europe. Zone 4. The cultivars are excellent for bedding, cut flowers, and containers. **Bedder Series** ■ cultivars are dwarf and compact in habit, with flowers in golden yellow, primrose-yellow, orange, or scarlet-red; ↕ to 12in (30cm). **Bedder Series 'Orange Bedder'** freely bears orange flowers; ↕ 9–12in (23–30cm), ↔ 10–12in (25–30cm). **'Blood Red'** ■ bears deep red flowers. **Fair Lady Series** cultivars produce flowers in pale pink, yellow, and creamy white, with some reds. **'Fire King'** bears orange-red flowers. **'Harlequin'** is compact and uniform in habit, and bears flowers in golden yellow, orange, cream, scarlet, crimson, intermediate pastel shades, and bicolors; ↕ to 10in (25cm). **'Harpur Crewe'** see *E.* x *kewense* 'Harpur Crewe'. **'Ivory White'** produces creamy white flowers.

Erysimum cheiri Bedder Series

***E.* 'Constant Cheer'.** Bushy, evergreen perennial with inversely lance-shaped, dark green leaves. Short racemes of dusky orange-red flowers, to ½in (1.5cm) across, becoming purple, are produced from midspring to early summer. ↕ to 12in (30cm), ↔ 24in (60cm). Zone 6.

***E.* 'E.A. Bowles'** see *E.* 'Bowles' Mauve'.

***E.* 'Golden Jubilee'.** Robust, clump-forming, semi-evergreen perennial with narrowly lance-shaped, dark green leaves. From late spring to summer, bears short racemes of soft golden yellow flowers, to ½in (1.5cm) across. ↕ 10in (25cm), ↔ to 16in (40cm). Zone 6.

***E.* 'Jacob's Jacket'.** Bushy, evergreen perennial with inversely lance-shaped, dark green leaves. From early to late spring, bears short racemes of flowers, to ½in (1.5cm) across, that open bronze-tinted, become more orange, and finally turn lilac, with blooms in all shades present at the same time. ↕ 12in (30cm), ↔ 18in (45cm). Zone 6.

***E.* 'John Codrington'** ■ Bushy, evergreen perennial with inversely lance-shaped leaves. Short racemes of pale yellow flowers, to ½in (1.5cm) across, shaded brown and purple, are produced in mid- and late spring. ↕ 10in (25cm), ↔ 12in (30cm). Zone 6.

***E.* 'Jubilee Gold'.** Bushy, evergreen perennial with inversely lance-shaped leaves. Golden yellow flowers, to ½in (1.5cm) across, are produced in short racemes in mid- and late spring. ↕ to 16in (40cm), ↔ 18in (45cm). Zone 6.

E.* x *kewense (*E. bicolor* x *E. cheiri*). Bushy, upright, woody-based, evergreen perennial with branched stems and narrowly lance-shaped or inversely lance-shaped, entire, gray-green leaves, 2–3in (5–8cm) long. From early spring to early summer, bears short racemes of fragrant flowers, 1in (2.5cm) across, initially orange to bronze, turning light purple. ↕ to 16in (40cm), ↔ 12in (30cm). Garden origin. Zone 6.

Erysimum x *allionii*

Erysimum 'Bredon'

Erysimum cheiri 'Blood Red'

Erysimum 'John Codrington'

Erysimum × *kewense* 'Harpur Crewe'

'Harpur Crewe' ▣ syn. *Cheiranthus cheiri* 'Harpur Crewe', *E. cheiri* 'Harpur Crewe', has double yellow flowers; ↕ 12in (30cm), ↔ 24in (60cm). **'Variegatum'** produces leaves irregularly variegated with cream.
E. kotschyanum. Densely tufted, evergreen perennial with crowded clusters of linear, usually toothed, pale green leaves, ½in (1.5cm) long. In summer, produces compact racemes of open, yellow to golden orange flowers, ½in (1cm) across. ↕ 4in (10cm), ↔ to 8in (20cm). Turkey. Zone 5.
E. linifolium. Mat-forming, woody-based, evergreen perennial with narrowly linear-lance-shaped, entire, wavy, grayish green leaves, ¾–3½in (2–9cm) long. From midspring to early autumn, numerous slender, unbranched stems bear long racemes of open, lilac or lavender-blue flowers, ½–¾in (1–2cm) across. Prone to cold damage. ↕ 5–28in (12–70cm), ↔ 10in (25cm). N. Portugal, C. Spain. Zone 6. **'Bicolor'** produces both pinkish violet and white flowers. **'Variegatum'** ▣ syn. *E.* 'Sissinghurst Variegated', is more tufted, with mauve flowers and white-variegated leaves; ↕↔ 18in (45cm).
***E.* 'Moonlight'** ▣ Mat-forming, evergreen perennial with inversely lance-shaped leaves. Short racemes of pale sulfur-yellow flowers, to ½in (1.5cm) across, are produced from early spring to early summer. ↕ 10in (25cm), ↔ 18in (45cm). Zone 6.
E. perofskianum. Rosette-forming biennial or short-lived, evergreen perennial, grown as an annual, with lance-shaped, sometimes finely toothed,

Erysimum linifolium 'Variegatum'

Erysimum 'Moonlight'

grayish green leaves, 2–4in (5–10cm) long. Open, golden orange or red-orange flowers, to ¾in (2cm) across, are borne in long racemes in summer. ↕ 6–16in (15–40cm), ↔ to 10in (25cm). Afghanistan, Pakistan. Zone 6b.
***E.* 'Rufus'.** Bushy, not robust, evergreen perennial with inversely lance-shaped leaves. Bears rich orange-brown flowers, ½–¾in (1.5–2cm) across, in long racemes from early to late spring. ↕ 6in (15cm), ↔ 12in (30cm). Zone 6.
***E.* 'Sissinghurst Variegated'** see *E. linifolium* 'Variegatum'.
***E.* 'Sprite'.** Mat-forming, evergreen perennial with inversely lance-shaped leaves. Pale yellow flowers, to ½in (1.5cm) across, are borne in short racemes from early to late spring. ↕ 8in (20cm), ↔ 18in (45cm). Zone 6.
***E.* 'Wenlock Beauty'.** Bushy, evergreen perennial with inversely lance-shaped leaves. From early to late spring, bears bronze-shaded, mauve and buff-yellow flowers, to ½in (1.5cm) across, in long racemes. ↕↔ 18in (45cm). Zone 6.

▷ ***Erythraea*** see *Centaurium*

ERYTHRINA

Coral tree

FABACEAE

Genus of over 100 species of deciduous, semi-evergreen, or evergreen, usually spiny, trees, shrubs, subshrubs, and woody-based perennials found in woodland and thickets, and on open slopes, in tropical regions worldwide. They are grown for their pea-like, 5-petaled flowers with long standard petals, borne singly or in clusters in the leaf axils, or in axillary or terminal racemes, on often leafless stems. Leaves are alternate and 3-pinnate, with the terminal leaflet larger than the others and sometimes differently shaped. Grow as specimen plants. In cool-temperate areas, grow in a cool or temperate greenhouse.
• **CULTIVATION** Under glass, grow in soil-based potting mix in full light. From spring to autumn, water freely and apply a balanced liquid fertilizer monthly. Outdoors, grow in fertile, moist but well-drained soil in full sun. Pruning group 1; may need restrictive pruning under glass.
• **PROPAGATION** Sow seed at 70–75°F (21–24°C) in spring. Root softwood cuttings in early summer, or semi-ripe cuttings in late summer, both with bottom heat.
• **PESTS AND DISEASES** Fungal root rot and leaf spots can occur. Under glass, spider mites and mealybugs occur.

E.* × *bidwillii ▣ (*E. crista-galli* × *E. herbacea*). Large, deciduous subshrub or shrub in warm regions, woody-based herbaceous perennial in cooler ones. Robust, sparsely branched, spiny stems bear light to mid-green leaves, divided into 3 ovate-oblong leaflets, 8in (20cm) long. In summer, bears dark red flowers, to 2in (5cm) long, in small, axillary clusters of 3, or in terminal racemes, 12–24in (30–60cm) long. ↕ 6–12ft (2–4m), ↔ 5–10ft (1.5–3m). Garden origin. Zones 9–10. ❀ (min. 41°F/5°C)
E. caffra (Cape kaffirboom, Lucky bean tree). Wide-spreading, semi-evergreen tree with sometimes prickly branches, and prickly-stalked leaves divided into 3 broadly ovate leaflets, the longest to 3½in (9cm) long. In spring, bears dense, terminal racemes, to 6in (15cm) long, of orange-scarlet flowers, 2in (5cm) long, with broad, strongly arching standard petals. ↕ 40–60ft (12–18m), ↔ 30–50ft (10–15m). E. South Africa. ❀ (min. 41°F/5°C)
E. crista-galli ▣ (Cock's comb, Common coral tree). Open, deciduous tree in warm regions, woody-based perennial in cooler ones. Branches bear thick spines. Leathery leaves, including the prickly stalks, are 12in (30cm) or more long, with 3 triangular leaflets to 4in (10cm) long; the largest leaflet is ovate-oblong. Deep red flowers, 2–2½in (5–6cm) long, are borne in terminal racemes, 12–24in (30–60cm) or more long, from summer to autumn. ↕ 20–28ft (6–9m), ↔ 10–12ft (3–4m) as a tree; ↕ 5–8ft (1.5–2.5m), ↔ 3–5ft (1–1.5m) as a woody perennial. E. Bolivia to Argentina. ❀ (min. 41°F/5°C)
E. herbacea (Coral bean). Semi-herbaceous, woody-based perennial with a thick, woody rootstock. Leaves are divided into 3 ovate to lance-shaped or arrow-shaped leaflets, 2–4in (5–10cm) long. From midsummer to early autumn, bears deep scarlet flowers, to 2in (5cm) long, with narrow standard petals, in terminal racemes, to 24in (60cm) long. ↕ to 3ft (1m), ↔ 24in (60cm). S.E. US, Mexico. ❀ (min. 35°F/2°C)
E. lysistemon (Lucky bean tree, Transvaal kaffirboom). Open, semi-evergreen tree. Leaves, including the long, sometimes prickly stalks, are to 9in (23cm) long, with 3 ovate, tapering leaflets to 3in (8cm) long. In summer,

Erythrina × *bidwillii*

Erythrina crista-galli

bears compact, terminal racemes, to 8in (20cm) long, of bright scarlet flowers, 2½in (6cm) long. ↕ 22–30ft (7–10m), ↔ 10–15ft (3–5m). South Africa. ❀ (min. 41°F/5°C)
E.* × *sykesii. Open, spreading, deciduous tree with ascending branches and blue-green leaves, divided into 3 ovate to lance-shaped leaflets, 2–4in (5–10cm) long. In late winter and early spring, bears spikes, 6–12in (15–30cm) long, of flame-orange flowers, 2–2½in (5–6cm) across. ↕ 25–30ft (8–10m), ↔ 15–20ft (5–6m). ❀ (min. 41°F/5°C)
E. variegata ▣ Spreading, deciduous tree with many robust branches scattered with prickles. Leaves, including the long stalks, are 10–16in (25–40cm) long, with 3 ovate to broadly diamond-shaped leaflets, 6–8in (15–20cm) long, usually rich green, and often variegated light green and yellow along the main veins. Scarlet or crimson flowers, 2–2½in (5–6cm) long, are produced in dense, terminal racemes, to 8in (20cm) long, in summer. ↕ 60–80ft (18–25m), ↔ 25–50ft (8–15m). E. Africa to India, China, Taiwan, Malaysia, and parts of Polynesia. ❀ (min. 45°F/7°C)

Erythrina variegata

ERYTHRONIUM

Dog's-tooth violet, Trout lily

LILIACEAE

Genus of about 22 species of clump-forming perennials, with long-pointed, tooth-like bulbs. They occur in habitats ranging from deciduous woodland to open mountain meadows in Europe, Asia, and North America. From spring to early summer, slender, upright stems produce 1–10 pendent flowers, usually 1¼–2½in (3–6cm) across, in shades of purple, violet, pink, yellow, or white, each with conspicuous stamens and 6 pointed, recurved tepals. Broadly elliptic to ovate-elliptic, paired, usually semi-erect, basal leaves, 1¼–14in (3–35cm) long, are glossy to glaucous, mid- to dark green, in some species heavily marbled bronze. Grow in clumps under deciduous trees and shrubs, or in a rock garden, or naturalized in thin grass.

• **CULTIVATION** Plant bulbs at least 4in (10cm) deep in autumn, in fertile, humus-rich, well-drained soil that does not dry out, in light, dappled or partial shade. Bulbs must be kept slightly damp during storage and before planting.

• **PROPAGATION** Divide established clumps after flowering.

• **PESTS AND DISEASES** Rust, smuts, and fungal spots can be problems. Slugs can damage plants outdoors.

E. americanum ▣ (Yellow adder's tongue, Yellow trout lily). Stoloniferous, bulbous perennial bearing horizontal, narrowly elliptic, mid- to deep green leaves, to 6in (15cm) long, with purple-

Erythronium americanum

Erythronium californicum 'White Beauty'

brown marbling. Solitary, sulfur-yellow flowers, 1¼–2in (3–5cm) across, with reddish yellow or purple outsides and purple, yellow, or brown anthers, are produced in spring. Often shy to flower. ↕3–6in (8–15cm), ↔4in (10cm). E. North America. Zone 4.

E. californicum ▣ (Fawn lily). Bulbous perennial with elliptic, dark green leaves, 1¼–3in (3–8cm) long, lightly mottled brownish green. In spring, each stem bears 1–3 creamy white flowers, 2–3in (5–8cm) across, with brownish orange central markings, white anthers, and stamens with rounded filaments. ↕6–14in (15–35cm), ↔4in (10cm). California. Zone 4. **'White Beauty'** ▣ syn. *E.* 'White Beauty', is vigorous, with a rust-red basal ring in each flower; it increases well by offsets.

***E.* 'Citronella'.** Vigorous, bulbous perennial with elliptic, bronze-mottled, slightly glossy, mid-green leaves. In spring, each stem bears up to 10 clear yellow flowers with dark yellow anthers. Similar to *E.* 'Pagoda', but flowers slightly later. ↕8–14in (20–35cm), ↔4in (10cm). Zone 5.

E. dens-canis ▣ (European dog's-tooth violet). Bulbous perennial with elliptic-oblong, mid-green leaves, 4–6in (10–15cm) long, marbled purplish brown. In spring, bears solitary, white, pink, or lilac flowers, to 1¼–1½in (3–4cm) across, with purple or blue-purple anthers. ↕4–6in (10–15cm), ↔4in (10cm). Europe, Asia. Zone 4. **'Lilac Wonder'** has rich purple flowers, with a brown basal spot on each petal forming a conspicuous central ring. **'Pink Perfection'** produces clear pink

Erythronium hendersonii

flowers, 1¼–2in (3–5cm) across, in early spring. **'Purple King'** bears rich plum-colored flowers, striped white and brown in the centers. **'Snowflake'** bears pure white flowers. **'White Splendour'** produces white flowers with brown centers, in early spring.

E. grandiflorum. Bulbous perennial with elliptic, bright mid-green leaves, 4–8in (10–20cm) long. In spring, each stem bears 1–3 golden yellow flowers, 2in (5cm) across, with distinctive, 3-lobed stigmas and white, yellow, or red-black anthers. ↕6–12in (15–30cm), ↔4in (10cm). W. US. Zone 5.

E. hartwegii see *E. multiscapoideum*.

E. hendersonii ▣ Bulbous perennial with elliptic, wavy-margined, lightly brown-banded, dark green leaves, 4–8in (10–20cm) long. In spring, each stem bears up to 10 pale lilac flowers, 2in (5cm) across, with purple anthers and deep purple, sometimes yellow centers. Best in partial shade in soil that dries out in summer. ↕6–14in (15–35cm), ↔3in (8cm). S.W. Oregon, N.W. California. Zone 5.

E. japonicum ▣ Bulbous perennial with elliptic, mid- to deep green leaves, 4–6in (10–15cm) long, lightly marbled purplish brown. In spring, bears solitary, pale to rich violet flowers, 1¼–2in (3–5cm) across, with darker centers and purple anthers. ↕4–6in (10–15cm), ↔3in (8cm). Japan. Zone 4.

***E.* 'Joanna'.** Bulbous perennial bearing elliptic, slightly glossy, mid-green leaves, with brown marbling. In spring, each stem produces up to 8 pink-flushed, creamy yellow flowers. ↕10–12in (25–30cm), ↔3in (8cm). Zone 4.

Erythronium oregonum

***E.* 'Kondo'.** Vigorous, bulbous perennial with elliptic, bronze-mottled, mid-green leaves; the mottling fades after flowering. In spring, each stem bears 2–5, sometimes up to 10, scented, green-suffused, lemon-yellow flowers, with red-brown centers and deep yellow anthers. ↕6–14in (15–35cm), ↔4in (10cm). Zone 4.

E. multiscapoideum, syn. *E. hartwegii*, *E. purdyi*. Bulbous perennial with elliptic, lightly brown-mottled, dark green leaves, 1½–4in (3.5–10cm) long. In spring, each branched flower stem produces solitary, red-flushed buds that open into creamy white flowers, 1½–2½in (4–6cm) across, with white anthers and yellow or yellowish green centers. Similar to *E. californicum*, but the flower stem branches at or just below ground. ↕6–14in (15–35cm), ↔4in (10cm). Sierra Nevada. Zone 5.

E. oregonum ▣ Vigorous, bulbous perennial with elliptic, shiny, brown-mottled, mid- to deep green leaves, 5–6in (12–15cm) long. In spring, each stem bears up to 6 creamy white flowers, 1½–3in (4–8cm) across, with yellow centers sometimes surrounded by orange-brown marks, and bright yellow anthers. Similar to *E. californicum*, but stamens have wide, flattened, thread-like filaments. ↕6–14in (15–35cm), ↔4in (10cm). British Columbia to Oregon. Zone 5.

***E.* 'Pagoda'** ▣ Very vigorous, bulbous perennial with elliptic, strongly bronze-mottled, glossy, deep green leaves. In spring, the stems each bear 2–5, sometimes up to 10, sulfur-yellow

Erythronium californicum

Erythronium dens-canis

Erythronium japonicum

Erythronium 'Pagoda'

Erythronium revolutum

flowers, with brown central rings and deep yellow anthers. ↕ 6–14in (15–35cm), ↔ 4in (10cm). Zone 4.
E. purdyi see *E. multiscapoideum*.
E. revolutum ■ (Western trout lily). Bulbous perennial with elliptic, wavy-margined, deep green leaves, 6–8in (15–20cm) long, strongly mottled dark brown. In midspring, each stem bears up to 4 lilac-pink flowers, 1½–3in (4–8cm) across, with yellow central rings and yellow anthers. Sometimes slow to establish, but may self-seed freely once it has. ↕ 8–12in (20–30cm), ↔ 4in (10cm). Vancouver Island, N. California. Zone 6. **var. *johnsonii*** has dark pink flowers. **'Pink Beauty'** bears deep lavender-pink flowers.
E. tuolumnense ■ Vigorous, bulbous perennial with elliptic, often slightly wavy-margined, pale to mid-green leaves, 8–12in (20–30cm) long. In spring, bears up to 4, occasionally up to 7, green-veined, bright yellow flowers, 1¼–2in (3–5cm) across, with yellow anthers, in a cluster toward the top of each stem. ↕ 8–14in (20–35cm), ↔ 3in (8cm). C. California. Zone 4.
***E.* 'White Beauty'** see *E. californicum* 'White Beauty'.

ESCALLONIA

GROSSULARIACEAE

Genus of about 50–60 species of mostly evergreen shrubs or, more rarely, small trees, found in woodland and scrub, and often on mountains, in South America. They are grown for their usually alternate, occasionally whorled, bold, often narrowly to broadly oval, glossy leaves, and for their mainly terminal racemes or panicles of tubular, salver-form, chalice-shaped, or saucer-shaped, 5-petaled, white to pink or red flowers, with spreading or erect lobes. They flower freely over a long period, mainly in summer. Grow in a shrub border, against a wall, or as a hedge, screen, or windbreak, particularly in coastal areas.

• **CULTIVATION** Grow in fertile, well-drained soil in full sun, and shelter from cold, drying winds. Many species and cultivars may survive temperatures below 23°F (-5°C) if planted against a sunny wall. Pruning group 9.

• **PROPAGATION** Take softwood cuttings in early summer, semi-ripe cuttings in late summer, and hardwood cuttings from late autumn to winter.

• **PESTS AND DISEASES** Infrequent.

***E.* 'Apple Blossom'** ■ Compact, bushy, evergreen shrub with elliptic, glossy, dark green leaves, to 2in (5cm) long. In early and midsummer, bears short racemes of chalice-shaped, apple-blossom-pink flowers, ¾–1in (2–2.5cm) across, with white centers. ↕↔ 8ft (2.5m). Zone 7b.
E. bifida ■ syn. *E. montevidensis*. Vigorous, upright, evergreen shrub with narrowly oval to obovate or spoon-shaped, finely toothed, glossy, dark green leaves, to 3in (8cm) long. Bears pure white flowers, to ¾in (2cm) across, with tubular then spreading petals, in panicles, to 6in (15cm) long, from late summer to autumn. Brazil, Uruguay. ↕ 10ft (3m), ↔ 8ft (2.5m). Zone 7b.
***E.* 'C.F. Ball'.** Vigorous, erect, open, evergreen shrub with broadly oval to obovate, deeply toothed, glossy, dark green leaves, to 2½in (6cm) long. Bears tubular, bright rich red flowers, to ¾in (2cm) long, in short racemes throughout summer. ↕↔ 8ft (2.5m). Zone 7b.
***E.* 'Donard Radiance'.** Compact evergreen shrub with obovate, coarsely toothed, glossy, dark green leaves, to 1½in (4cm) long. Chalice-shaped, rich pink flowers, to ¾in (2cm) across, are produced in short racemes in early and midsummer. ↕↔ 8ft (2.5m). Zone 7b.

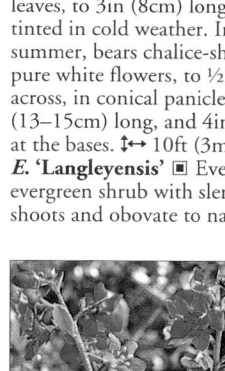

Escallonia bifida (inset: flower detail)

***E.* 'Donard Seedling'** ■ Vigorous, evergreen shrub with arching shoots and obovate to narrowly oval, glossy, dark green leaves, to 1in (2.5cm) long. Produces masses of saucer-shaped, pink-tinted white flowers, ½in (1.5cm) across, opening from pink buds, in short racemes in early and midsummer. ↕↔ 8ft (2.5m). Zone 7b.
***E.* 'Edinensis'.** Evergreen shrub with arching shoots and oblong, glossy, dark green leaves, to ¾in (2cm) long. Short racemes of saucer-shaped, pinkish red flowers, to ½in (1.5cm) across, red in bud, are borne in early and midsummer. ↕ 6ft (2m), ↔ 10ft (3m). Zone 7b.
E. x exoniensis (*E. rosea* x *E. rubra*). Large, upright evergreen shrub with oval, toothed, shiny leaves, ¾in (2cm) long, pale beneath. In summer, bears panicles, to 3in (8cm) long, of white or pink flowers, ½in (1.5cm) across, with spreading petals. ↕ 12–20ft (4–6m), ↔ 10–15ft (3–5m). Garden origin. Zone 7b. **'Frades'** has carmine flowers in terminal clusters.
***E.* 'Iveyi'.** Upright, evergreen shrub with oval to elliptic, glossy, dark green leaves, to 3in (8cm) long, often bronze-tinted in cold weather. In mid- and late summer, bears chalice-shaped, fragrant, pure white flowers, to ½in (1.5cm) across, in conical panicles, 5–6in (13–15cm) long, and 4in (10cm) wide at the bases. ↕↔ 10ft (3m). Zone 7b.
***E.* 'Langleyensis'** ■ Evergreen or semi-evergreen shrub with slender, arching shoots and obovate to narrowly oval,

Erythronium tuolumnense

Escallonia 'Apple Blossom'

Escallonia 'Donard Seedling'

Escallonia 'Langleyensis'

E

Escallonia leucantha

glossy, dark green leaves, to 1in (2.5cm) long. Bears a profusion of saucer-shaped, bright rose-red flowers, to ½in (1.5cm) across, in short racemes in early and midsummer. ↕ 6ft (2m), ↔ 10ft (3m). Zone 7b.

E. leucantha ■ Upright, tree-like, evergreen shrub with narrowly obovate to inversely lance-shaped, toothed, glossy, dark green leaves, to 1in (2.5cm) long. In midsummer, tubular, creamy white flowers, to ½in (1.5cm) long, are borne in panicle-like inflorescences, to 12in (30cm) long, and 3–7in (8–18cm) wide at the bases. ↕ 10ft (3m), ↔ 8ft (2.5m). Chile, Argentina. Zone 8.

E. montevidensis see *E. bifida.*

***E.* 'Peach Blossom'.** Vigorous, bushy, evergreen shrub with arching shoots and elliptic, glossy, dark green leaves, to

Escallonia 'Pride of Donard'

Escallonia rubra 'Woodside'

Escallonia virgata

1½in (4cm) long. In early and midsummer, bears short racemes of chalice-shaped, white-centered, peach-pink flowers, to 1in (2.5cm) across. ↕↔ 8ft (2.5m). Zone 7b.

***E.* 'Pride of Donard'** ■ Erect, compact, evergreen shrub with ovate, glossy, dark green leaves, to 1in (2.5cm) long. Bears chalice-shaped, rich, light red flowers, to 1in (2.5cm) across, in short racemes in early and midsummer. ↕ 5ft (1.5m), ↔ 8ft (2.5m). Zone 7b.

***E.* 'Red Elf'.** Compact, spreading, evergreen shrub with broadly oval to obovate, glossy, dark green leaves, to 1in (2.5cm) long. Bears tubular, dark crimson flowers, to ½in (1.5cm) long, in short racemes in early and midsummer. ↕ 8ft (2.5m), ↔ 12ft (4m). Zone 7b.

E. rubra. Vigorous, variable, evergreen shrub with peeling brown bark and elliptic to broadly ovate or obovate, toothed, glossy, dark green leaves, to 2½in (6cm) long. Bears loose panicles, to 4in (10cm) long, of tubular, dark crimson to pink flowers, ½in (1.5cm) long, in abundance from summer to early autumn. ↕↔ to 15ft (5m). Chile, Argentina. Zone 7b. **'Crimson Spire'** is erect, with deep crimson flowers, to ¾in (2cm) long. **var. *macrantha*** is similar to 'Crimson Spire' but less erect, with broadly oval or obovate leaves, to 3in (8cm) long, and tubular, bright rose-red flowers, to ½in (1.5cm) long; ↕↔ 10ft (3m). **'Pygmaea'** see 'Woodside'. **'Woodside'** ■ syn. 'Pygmaea', is dwarf, compact, and rounded, with crimson flowers. Cut out vigorous shoots when seen; ↕ 30in (75cm), ↔ 5ft (1.5m).

E. virgata ■ Deciduous shrub with arching branches and obovate, finely toothed, glossy, dark green leaves, to ¾in (2cm) long. Axillary racemes, to 2in (5cm) long, of salverform white flowers, to ½in (1.5cm) long, are borne close to the tips of the branches in early and midsummer. ↕ 6ft (2m), ↔ 8ft (2.5m). Chile, Argentina. Zone 7b.

ESCHSCHOLZIA

California poppy

PAPAVERACEAE

Genus of 8–10 species of slender, erect, basally branching annuals and perennials from grassy, open habitats in W. North America. They have finely divided, fern-like, light to blue-green foliage. Solitary, shallowly cupped, paper-thin, 4-petaled (rarely 5- to 8-

Eschscholzia caespitosa

petaled), poppy-like flowers, in red, orange, or yellow, are borne in spring or summer; they close in cloudy weather. Grow in an annual border, or in a gravel or rock garden.

• **CULTIVATION** Grow in poor, well-drained soil in full sun.

• **PROPAGATION** Sow seed *in situ* in midspring or early autumn. Sow in succession for a continuous display.

• **PESTS AND DISEASES** A variety of fungi cause leaf, stem, and root problems.

E. caespitosa ■ Tufted annual with finely divided, almost thread-like leaves, 4–5in (10–13cm) long. In summer, produces numerous scented, single, bright yellow flowers, 1¼–2in (3–5cm) across. ↕↔ to 6in (15cm). C. California. **'Sundew'** bears lemon-yellow flowers.

E. californica ■ (California poppy). Variable, mat-forming, sometimes hairy annual with lance-shaped, finely cut leaves, 6–8in (15–20cm) long. In summer, bears numerous single, predominantly orange, sometimes also red or yellow flowers, to 3in (8cm) across, followed by long, curved seed pods. ↕ to 12in (30cm), ↔ to 6in (15cm). Oregon to coastal California.

Eschscholzia californica

Eschscholzia californica Thai Silk Series

'Apricot Flambeau' bears fluted yellow flowers with coral-orange edges; ↕ 8–10in (20–25cm). **'Ballerina'** has fluted, semi-double or double, red, pink, yellow, or orange flowers. **'Carmine King'** has single, carmine-rose flowers. **'Dali'** is compact, with scarlet flowers; ↕ 10in (25cm). **'Milky-White'** has single, cream flowers with orange centers. **Mission Bells Mix** selections are compact, with single and semi-double scarlet-orange, cream, yellow, and pink flowers, 2in (5cm) across; ↕ 10–12in (25–30cm). **'Monarch Art Shades'** bears semi-double or double, orange, yellow, apricot-yellow, creamy yellow, or red flowers, with frilled petals. **'Orange King'** is taller and has orange flowers; ↕ 12–16in (30–40cm). Cultivars of **Thai Silk Series** ■ are compact, with single or semi-double, fluted, bronze-tinged flowers in red, pink, or orange; ↕ 8–10in (20–25cm).

ESCOBARIA

CACTACEAE

Genus of about 17 species of small, mainly spherical to cylindrical, solitary or clustering cacti from low-lying areas, semi-desert, and arid, uncultivated land in S. Canada, US, N. Mexico, and Cuba. The stems are studded with tubercles (each with a furrow immediately above it) and very spiny, generally white areoles. In summer, diurnal, mostly bell-shaped flowers are produced from the areoles of young tubercles at or around the crowns. Where not hardy, grow escobarias as houseplants or in a temperate greenhouse; in warm, dry areas, grow in a raised bed or desert garden.

• **CULTIVATION** Under glass, grow in standard cactus potting mix in full light. In the growing season, water moderately and apply a low-nitrogen fertilizer every 4–5 weeks; keep dry at other times. Outdoors, grow in poor to moderately fertile, sharply drained soil in full sun. Most tolerate temperatures to 32°F (0°C); *E. vivipara* is hardy to 0°F (-18°C). See also pp.48–49.

• **PROPAGATION** Sow seed at 66–75°F (19–24°C) in spring, or divide offsets in summer.

• **PESTS AND DISEASES** Susceptible to mealybugs.

E. asperispina, syn. *Neobesseya asperispina.* Solitary cactus with a spherical, dull, bluish green stem, 2½in

Escobaria vivipara

(6cm) thick, and conical tubercles. Areoles bear 9 or 10 grayish white radial spines. Bell-shaped flowers, 1¼in (3cm) long, with wide-spreading, whitish yellow petals, each with a pale brown or olive-green mid-stripe, are produced in summer. ↕↔ 2½in (6cm). N. Mexico. ❀ (min. 45°F/7°C)

E. sneedii. Clustering cactus with cylindrical stems, ¾–3in (2–8cm) thick, studded with minute, conical tubercles. Areoles bear 30–60 red radial spines, which turn white. In summer, produces pale pink, pinkish brown, or magenta flowers, to ¾in (2cm) long, with a pink mid-stripe on each petal. ↕ 2½in (6cm), ↔ indefinite. S.W. US. ❀ (min. 45°F/7°C)

E. vivipara ■ syn. *Coryphantha vivipara.* Solitary or clustering cactus with depressed-spherical to short-cylindrical, white-woolly gray stems, 1–2in (2.5–5cm) thick, with cylindrical tubercles. Areoles bear brown spines (12–40 radials and 2–12 centrals). Wide-spreading, almost daisy-like, pink, magenta, purple, or occasionally white flowers, 1½in (4cm) long, are produced in summer. ↕ to 5in (13cm), ↔ indefinite. S. Canada to N. Mexico. ❀ (min. 45°F/7°C)

ESPOSTOA

CACTACEAE

Genus of 10 species of columnar, often tree-like, slow-growing cacti, some of which branch from near their bases to form clumps. They occur in hilly regions of S. Ecuador, Peru, and Bolivia. The straight-ribbed, dark to grayish green stems and branches are covered with areoles bearing numerous spines. As they mature, most species produce a long pseudocephalium that bears cup-shaped to tubular, usually nocturnal flowers in summer. Where not hardy, grow as houseplants or in a temperate greenhouse or conservatory. In warm, dry areas, plant outdoors in a desert garden.

• **CULTIVATION** Under glass, grow in standard cactus potting mix in full light. From spring to summer, water moderately and apply a low-nitrogen fertilizer every 4–5 weeks; keep dry at other times. Outdoors, grow in poor to moderately fertile, sharply drained soil in full sun. See also pp.48–49.

• **PROPAGATION** Sow seed at 70°F (21°C) in early spring.

• **PESTS AND DISEASES** Infrequent.

E. lanata ■ Tree-like or shrubby cactus with a columnar, 20- to 30-ribbed, mid-green stem, 4–6in (10–15cm) thick. The stem is densely covered with white areoles that bear short, usually yellowish white, occasionally red, yellow, brown, or purple spines and long, silky white hairs. Produces cup-shaped, white to purple flowers, 1½–3in (4–8cm) long, in summer. ↕ 5ft (1.5m), ↔ 24in (60cm). S. Ecuador, Peru. ❀ (min. 41–50°F/5–10°C)

E. melanostele. Shrubby, erect cactus with a columnar, 20- to 30-ribbed, grayish green stem, 4in (10cm) thick, with close-set brown areoles and initially yellow, later black spines. In summer, bears tubular white, sometimes yellow or brown flowers, 2in (5cm) long. ↕ 6ft (2m), ↔ 4in (10cm). C. Peru. ❀ (min. 41–50°F/5–10°C)

E. senilis. Shrubby or tree-like cactus with solitary, or occasionally branched, 18- to 25-ribbed, dark green stems, 2–3in (5–8cm) thick. White areoles bear white spines. Solitary, tubular purple flowers, 1¼–1½in (3–4cm) long, are produced in summer. ↕ 6–10ft (2–3m), ↔ 24in (60cm). Peru. ❀ (min. 41–50°F/5–10°C)

Espostoa lanata

ETLINGERA

ZINGIBERACEAE

Genus of 57 species of rhizomatous, evergreen or semi-evergreen perennials occurring in forest margins from Sri Lanka to New Guinea. They have cane-like stems, linear to inversely lance-shaped leaves, and produce torch-like inflorescences at the top of leafless stalks. The inflorescences are composed of overlapping, thick, waxy, usually colorful bracts, with relatively insignificant flowers often concealed in the lower bracts. *E. elatior* is the only widely cultivated species. Where not hardy, grow in a warm greenhouse; in warmer areas, grow in a bed or border.

• **CULTIVATION** Under glass, grow in soil-based potting mix with added bark and leaf mold, preferably in a border, in bright filtered light. In the growing season, water freely and apply a balanced liquid fertilizer monthly. Outdoors, grow in fertile, humus-rich, well-drained soil in full sun or light, dappled shade.

• **PROPAGATION** Sow seed at 68°F (20°C) as soon as ripe. Divide in spring or summer.

• **PESTS AND DISEASES** Infrequent.

E. elatior, syn. *Nicolaia elatior* (Philippine waxflower, Torch ginger). Upright, rhizomatous, evergreen perennial with linear-lance-shaped leaves, to 34in (85cm) long, dark green above, purplish green beneath. In summer, stems 5ft (1.5m) tall bear cone-shaped inflorescences, to 12in (30cm) long, composed of deep pink, sterile bracts, to 5in (13cm) long, and crimson, 3-petaled flowers with white or yellow margins, produced from the smaller, paler, lower bracts. ↕ 20ft (6m), ↔ 10ft (3m). Indonesia (Java, Sulawesi); widely naturalized in the tropics. ❀ (min. 61°F/16°C)

EUCALYPTUS

Gum, Ironbark

MYRTACEAE

Genus of over 500 species of evergreen trees and shrubs found in all but the driest habitats, mainly in Australia, but also in the Philippines, Malaysia, Indonesia, Papua New Guinea, and Melanesia. They are valued for their often aromatic foliage and their attractive bark. Young plants (and sucker shoots) generally have opposite leaves, developing alternate ones as they mature. The petalless flowers, composed of many showy, usually white or creamy yellow, sometimes red stamens, are usually borne in umbels. Most gum trees are best planted as specimens. Where not hardy, grow in a cool greenhouse and place outside for the summer.

• **CULTIVATION** Outdoors, grow in fertile, neutral to slightly acidic soil that does not dry out, in full sun. Under glass, grow in soil-based potting mix with added sharp sand, in full light with good ventilation. In growth, water freely and apply a balanced liquid fertilizer monthly; water sparingly in winter. Pruning group 1 or, for the best display of juvenile foliage, group 7; may need restrictive pruning under glass.

• **PROPAGATION** Sow seed at 55–64°F (13–18°C) in spring or summer.

• **PESTS AND DISEASES** Susceptible to crown gall, gray mold, powdery mildew, collar rot, seedling blights, root rots, and sometimes stem galls. Aphids and scale insects are common.

E. calophylla. Rounded tree with rough, fissured, gray to gray-brown bark. Juvenile leaves are peltate, broadly oval, and dark green; followed by ovate to broadly lance-shaped, adult leaves, to 4–7in (10–18cm) long. Bears terminal, corymb-like panicles of white, red, or rose-pink flowers, intermittently all year. ↕ to 130ft (40m), ↔ 50-100ft (15–30m). W. Australia. ❀ (min. 41°F/5°C)

E. camaldulensis (Murray red gum, Red river gum). Spreading, usually dense tree with a smooth, gray or whitish blue trunk, sometimes streaked or tinted reddish pink. Juvenile leaves are ovate to broadly lance-shaped, and gray-green; adult leaves, to 12in (30cm) long, are lance-shaped to narrowly lance-shaped, and usually mid-green, sometimes gray-green. Bears umbels of 7–11 white flowers, mainly in summer. ↕ 50–160ft (15–50m), ↔ 50–120ft (15–35m). Australia (except Tasmania). ❀ (min. 41°F/5°C)

E. cinerea (Argyle apple). Rounded tree with rough, red-brown bark. Ovate to heart-shaped, stalkless or short-stalked, glaucous mid-green juvenile leaves are followed by broadly lance-shaped, glaucous mid-green adult leaves, 3–4½in (8–11cm) long. Umbels of 3 white flowers are produced in summer. Attractive in cut or dried flower arrangements. ↕ to 50ft (15m), ↔ 30–40ft (10–12m). S.E. Australia. Zone 8.

E. citriodora (Lemon-scented gum). Rounded tree with smooth, powdery white bark, which is sometimes pink, red, or blue-gray. Juvenile leaves are narrow to broadly lance-shaped and mid-green, followed by lance-shaped, strongly lemon-scented, mid-green adult leaves, 3–6in (8–15cm) long. Terminal or axillary, corymb-like panicles of 3 white flowers, are borne in summer. ↕ 80–160ft (25–50m), ↔ 50–100ft (15–30m). Queensland. ❀ (min. 41°F/5°C)

E. coccifera ■ (Mount Wellington peppermint, Tasmanian snow gum). Spreading tree with peeling, white or white-gray bark, which is sometimes yellow or pink when young. Rounded, mid-green juvenile leaves are followed

Eucalyptus coccifera

E

Eucalyptus dalrympleana

by peppermint-scented, elliptic, gray-green adult leaves, to 4in (10cm) long. Bears umbels of 3, sometimes up to 9, white or creamy white flowers in summer. ↕ 60ft (18m), ↔ 22ft (7m). Tasmania. ❄ (min. 41°F/5°C)

E. dalrympleana ■ (Broad-leaved kindling bark, Mountain gum). Vigorous, broadly columnar tree with smooth, creamy white bark. Ovate, light green to blue-green juvenile leaves are followed by narrowly lance-shaped, bright green adult leaves, to 8in (20cm) long. Bears umbels of 3, sometimes up to 7, white flowers from late summer to autumn. Will tolerate alkaline soil. ↕ 70ft (20m), ↔ 25ft (8m). S.E. Australia. Zone 8.

E. delegatensis. Broadly conical tree with peeling bark, rough and gray to brown on the lower half of the trunk, smooth and white above. Juvenile leaves are elliptic to ovate or broadly lance-shaped, and blue-green; adult leaves are lance-shaped, curved, dull, mid-green, and to 8in (20cm) long. Bears umbels of 7–15 white flowers in summer. ↕ 80ft (25m), ↔ 30ft (10m). S.E. Australia. ❄ (min. 41°F/5°C)

E. divaricata see *E. gunnii.*

Eucalyptus ficifolia

Eucalyptus gunnii

E. ficifolia ■ (Red-flowering gum). Dense, spreading tree with rough, dark grayish brown bark. Juvenile leaves are ovate to broadly lance-shaped, mid- to deep green above, and paler beneath; adult leaves, 3–6in (7–15cm) long, are similar to the juvenile leaves. From summer to autumn, bears umbels of 3–7 red, occasionally pink or white flowers. Pendent, woody seed capsules, to 1½in (4cm) long, are urn-shaped. ↕ 20–50ft (6–15m), ↔ 15–70ft (5–20m). Western Australia. ❄ (min. 41°F/5°C)

E. forrestiana (Fuchsia eucalyptus). Large shrub or short-trunked tree with smooth gray to light brown bark. Ovate, mid-green, juvenile leaves are followed by narrow, lance-shaped, pointed, glossy, deep green leaves, 1½–2½in (4–6cm) long. Bears solitary, pendent, red flowers with woody, fuchsia-like flower bases, intermittently all year. ↕ to 12ft (4m), ↔ 10–12ft (3–4m). Western Australia. ❄ (min. 41°F/5°C)

E. glaucescens (Tingiringi gum). Broadly conical tree or shrub with smooth white bark that sheds in red flakes to leave a white surface. Rounded, blue-white juvenile leaves are followed by slender, lance-shaped, blue-gray adult leaves, to 5in (13cm) long. Bears umbels of 3 white flowers in autumn. ↕ 40ft (12m), ↔ 25ft (8m). S.E. Australia. ❄ (min. 41°F/5°C)

E. globulus (Tasmanian blue gum). Spreading, moderately dense tree with smooth, white to cream, yellow, or gray bark that sheds in ribbons to reveal the light green and light brown inner bark. Juvenile plants have square-sectioned or winged stems, and ovate, blue-white, stem-clasping leaves, to 6in (15cm) long. Adult trees have pendent, narrowly lance- to sickle-shaped, mid- to deep green leaves, 4–12in (10–30cm) long, and produce usually solitary, white to cream flowers from spring to summer. Juvenile plants are often employed in summer bedding. ↕ 50–160ft (15–50m), ↔ 30–80ft (10–25m). Victoria, Tasmania. ❄ (min. 41°F/5°C)

E. gregsoniana, syn. *E. pauciflora* var. *nana* (Wolgan snow gum). Spreading shrub with shoots that are glossy red on the exposed side. Elliptic, bluish green to gray-green juvenile leaves are followed by slender, lance-shaped, curved, red-margined, gray-green adult leaves, to 4½in (11cm) long. In late spring and early summer, produces umbels of 5–12 white flowers. ↕ 6–12ft (2–4m), ↔ 15ft (5m). New South Wales. ❄ (min. 41°F/5°C)

E. gunnii ■ syn. *E. divaricata* (Cider gum). Dense, erect then spreading tree with smooth, whitish green bark that is shed annually in late summer to reveal yellowish to grayish green new bark, sometimes flushed pink or orange. Juvenile leaves are ovate to rounded, mid-green, and often glaucous. Adult leaves, 2–3in (5–8cm) long, are elliptic or ovate to broadly lance-shaped, and gray-green. Umbels of 3 white to cream flowers are freely produced in summer or autumn. ↕ 30–80ft (10–25m), ↔ 20–50ft (6–15m). Tasmania. Zone 7b.

E. johnstonii ■ (Tasmanian yellow gum). Vigorous, broadly columnar tree with peeling, reddish brown and creamy white bark. Rounded juvenile leaves are followed by lance-shaped or ovate adult leaves, to 5in (13cm) long; all leaves are glossy and dark green. Umbels of 3 white flowers are produced in summer. ↕ 80ft (25m), ↔ 30ft (10m). Tasmania. ❄ (min. 41°F/5°C)

E. leucoxylon (Blue gum, White ironbark, Yellow gum). Erect to spreading, loose to dense tree with rough, fibrous, gray bark, darker at the base, shedding in late summer to reveal paler, smooth, cream, brown, or bluish gray bark. Broadly lance-shaped to ovate or rounded-heart-shaped, dull, dark green or glaucous juvenile leaves are followed by lance-shaped, matte, mid-green or gray-green adult leaves, to 5in (13cm) long. Umbels of 3 white, pink, or red flowers are produced in summer, and sometimes through to autumn or winter. ↕ 50ft (15m), ↔ 20–70ft (6–20m). S.E. Australia. ❄ (min. 41°F/5°C)

E. macrocarpa (Mottlecah). Wide-spreading, open shrub with white young stems and smooth gray bark that sheds to reveal pinkish red bark beneath. Juvenile and adult leaves, to 5in (13cm) long, are broadly ovate to elliptic, and silvery gray. Solitary flowers open from white buds as a dense brush of bright red stamens with yellow anthers, mainly from spring to summer. Woody, disk-shaped seed pods are 2in (5cm) across. ↕ 6–12ft (2–4m), ↔ 10–40ft (3–12m). Western Australia. ❄ (min. 37–41°F/3–5°C)

E. mannifera* subsp. *maculosa (Brittle gum, Red-spotted gum). Rounded to spreading, moderately dense tree with smooth white bark covered by a powdery bloom. The bark turns pink then red in summer, and flakes from late summer to autumn to reveal a creamy new surface. Juvenile leaves are elliptic to narrowly lance-shaped, and blue-white to blue-green; adult leaves, to 6in (15cm) long, are lance-shaped and gray-green. Bears umbels of up to 7 white flowers from spring to summer. ↕ 30–70ft (10–20m), ↔ 25–50ft (8–15m). New South Wales. ❄ (min. 41°F/5°C)

E. nicholii ■ (Narrow-leaved black peppermint). Wide-spreading, dense tree with a rounded crown and fibrous, gray to reddish brown bark. Narrowly lance-shaped, peppermint-scented leaves, 3–5in (7–13cm) long, are gray- to blue-green on juvenile trees, matte bluish green or light green on adult trees. Bears umbels of 7 white flowers in autumn. ↕ 40–52ft (12–16m), ↔ 15–40ft (5–12m). Queensland, New South Wales. ❄ (min. 41°F/5°C)

Eucalyptus johnstonii (inset: bark detail)

Eucalyptus nicholii

Eucalyptus pauciflora subsp. *niphophila* (inset: bark detail)

E. niphophila see *E. pauciflora* subsp. *niphophila.*
E. parvifolia (Small-leaved gum). Spreading tree with peeling, smooth, gray and white bark. Elliptic, mid-green juvenile leaves are followed by lance-shaped, gray-green adult leaves, to 3in (8cm) long. Bears umbels of 7 white flowers in summer. Tolerates alkaline soil. ↕ 50ft (15m), ↔ 30ft (10m). New South Wales. ❄ (min. 41°F/5°C)
E. pauciflora (Cabbage gum, Weeping gum, White sallee). Usually dense, spreading tree with smooth, whitish gray or pale brown bark that sheds from late summer to autumn to reveal yellow, bronze, or greenish patches; twigs are often yellow or red. Juvenile leaves are ovate to elliptic, and gray-green; adult leaves, to 6in (15cm) long, are lance-shaped to narrowly ovate, pendent, and lustrous, mid- to blue-green. Bears umbels of 7–15 white to cream flowers from late spring to summer. ↕ 25–70ft (8–20m), ↔ 20–50ft (6–15m). South Australia, New South Wales, Victoria, Tasmania. Zone 8. **var. *nana*** see *E. gregsoniana.* **subsp. *niphophila*** ■ syn. *E. niphophila* (Alpine snow gum, Snow gum), is particularly hardy, with twigs covered in a waxy white bloom, glaucous shoots, narrowly lance-shaped leaves, and 3- to 7-flowered umbels; ↕ to 20ft (6m). Zone 8.
E. perriniana ■ (Round-leaved snow gum, Spinning gum). Open to moderately dense, small tree or large shrub, branching from the base, with smooth, flaking, off-white, gray, or green bark. Rounded, bluish green juvenile leaves are joined at the bases around the stem; adult leaves, to 5in (13cm) long, are pendent, lance-shaped, and glaucous. Umbels of 3 white or cream flowers are produced in summer. ↕ 12–30ft (4–10m), ↔ 10–25ft (3–8m). New South Wales, Victoria, Tasmania. ❄ (min. 41°F/5°C)
E. piperita (Sydney peppermint). Open to dense tree with bark that is fibrous and gray at the base, and smooth and gray to white above. Ovate, bluish green juvenile leaves are followed by lance- to sickle-shaped, peppermint-scented, bluish green adult leaves, 3–5½in (8–14cm) long. Bears umbels of 7–15 white flowers in summer. ↕ 40–100ft (12–30m), ↔ 25–70ft (8–20m). New South Wales. ❄ (min. 41°F/5°C). **subsp. *urceolaris*** has larger adult leaves, to 7in (18cm) long.
E. polyanthemos (Red box, Silver dollar gum). Broadly conical tree with sometimes fibrous, red-brown bark. Juvenile leaves are rounded, notched, and silvery green; adult leaves, to 3½in (9cm) long, are ovate to broadly lance-shaped, and gray-green. Umbels of up to 7 white flowers are borne in summer. ↕ to 80ft (25m), ↔ 40ft (12m). New South Wales, Victoria. ❄ (min. 41°F/5°C)
E. pulverulenta (Powdered gum, Silver-leaved mountain gum). Spreading tree with gray to white bark that peels to reveal smooth, gray to bronze or brown bark beneath; twigs are green or white, covered by an intense waxy-white bloom. Heart-shaped, silvery-bloomed juvenile leaves, to 2in (5cm) long, usually persist on mature plants. Umbels of 3 white flowers are produced during winter. ↕ 80ft (25m), ↔ 50ft (15m). New South Wales. ❄ (min. 41°F/5°C)
E. sideroxylon (Mugga, Red ironbark). Tree with a rounded to spreading, open crown and thick, fissured, blackish to reddish brown bark. Linear to lance-shaped, bluish green juvenile leaves are followed by lance-shaped, gray-green adult leaves, to 5½in (14cm) long. Bears umbels of 3–7 red, pink, white, or pale yellow flowers from winter to summer. ↕ 30–100ft (10–30m), ↔ 25–50ft (8–15m). Queensland to Victoria. ❄ (min. 41°F/5°C)
E. viminalis (Manna gum, Ribbon gum, White gum). Erect to spreading, open tree with rough gray bark below, and smooth, gray or whitish yellow bark above, which shreds into ribbons. Juvenile leaves, 1½–2½in (3.5–6cm) long, are lance-shaped to narrowly ovate; adult leaves, to 8in (20cm) long, are lance-shaped or narrowly lance-shaped; all are light green. Bears umbels of 3–7 white flowers from summer to autumn. ↕ 30–160ft (10–50m), ↔ 25–50ft (8–15m). Queensland to Tasmania, South Australia. ❄ (min. 41°F/5°C)

▷ ***Eucharidium*** see *Clarkia*

EUCHARIS

AMARYLLIDACEAE

Genus of 17 species of evergreen, summer-flowering, bulbous perennials occurring in moist, open forest or forest margins in Central and South America. They are cultivated for their umbels of fragrant, daffodil-like white flowers. Each flower has 6 spreading tepals, arranged in two rows (the outer ones longer and narrower than the inner ones), and 6 stamens that fuse to form a cup. The long-stalked, ovate or elliptic to lance-shaped, glossy, basal leaves are often wavy and sometimes folded. Where not hardy, grow in a temperate or warm greenhouse or in a conservatory. In warmer areas, grow outdoors in a bed or border.

- **CULTIVATION** Under glass, grow in soil-based potting mix with added sharp sand and leaf mold, in bright filtered light. When in active growth, water freely and apply a balanced liquid fertilizer weekly; water sparingly in winter. Pot on every 3 or 4 years in spring. Outdoors, grow in moderately fertile, humus-rich, well-drained soil in light, dappled shade.
- **PROPAGATION** Remove offsets in autumn after leaves die down or when repotting, and grow on at 59°F (15°C) until established.
- **PESTS AND DISEASES** Infrequent.

E. amazonica ■ Bulbous perennial producing long-elliptic, wavy, dark green leaves, 16in (40cm) long, that taper to stalks 12in (30cm) long. In late summer, an umbel of up to 8 fragrant, pure white flowers, 3½in (9cm) across, with the stamens protruding ½in (1.5cm), is borne on a leafless stem, 28in (70cm) long. ↕ 28in (70cm), ↔ 6in (15cm). Colombia, N.E. Peru. ❄ (min. 50°F/10°C)
***E. amazonica* of gardens** see *E.* x *grandiflora.*
E.* x *grandiflora, syn. *E. amazonica* of gardens (Amazon lily). Bulbous perennial with semi-erect, elliptic to ovate, wavy, deep green leaves, 12in (30cm) long, on stalks to 1½in (4cm) long. In early summer, a leafless stem, to 20in (50cm) long, produces an umbel of up to 6 fragrant, slightly pendent white flowers, 3in (8cm) across, with long, protruding stamens. ↕ 16–24in (40–60cm), ↔ 12in (30cm). Colombia. ❄ (min. 50°F/10°C)

Eucalyptus perriniana

Eucharis amazonica

E

EUCOMIS

Pineapple flower, Pineapple lily

LILIACEAE

Genus of about 15 species of bulbous perennials found in habitats ranging from rocky screes to seasonally damp meadows in South Africa and tropical southern Africa. They are cultivated for their unusual racemes of flowers borne in late summer and early autumn. Large bulbs each produce a basal rosette of lance-shaped to strap-shaped, glossy, light green (sometimes darker) leaves and a thick stem that bears a tight raceme of star-shaped flowers, to 1in (2.5cm) across, topped by a small tuft of leafy bracts, similar to those of a pineapple. Grow in a sunny, sheltered border or at the base of a warm wall. Where not hardy, grow in a cool greenhouse, or outside during summer in the open ground, or in containers.

• **CULTIVATION** Plant bulbs 6in (15cm) deep. Grow in fertile, well-drained soil in full sun. Under glass, grow in soil-based potting mix with added sharp sand or grit, planted just below the soil surface, in full light. Water freely in active growth. Where not hardy, overwinter dormant bulbs in a frost-free place.

• **PROPAGATION** Sow seed at 61°F (16°C) in autumn or spring, or remove offsets in spring.

• **PESTS AND DISEASES** Infrequent.

E. autumnalis, syn. *E. undulata.* Bulbous perennial bearing semi-erect, broadly strap-shaped, light green leaves, 18in (45cm) long, with wavy margins. In late summer and early autumn, produces racemes, 2–6in (5–15cm) long, of pale greenish white flowers that age to darker green. ↕ 8–12in (20–30cm), PD8in (20cm). South Africa. Zone 7.

E. bicolor ▣ Bulbous perennial that produces semi-erect, strap-shaped, wavy-margined, light green leaves, 12–20in

Eucomis bicolor

Eucomis comosa

(30–50cm) long. In late summer, maroon-flecked stems bear racemes, 6in (15cm) long, of pale green flowers with purple-margined tepals. ↕ 12–24in (30–60cm), PD8in (20cm). South Africa. Zone 7. **'Alba'** has uniformly green-white petals.

E. comosa ▣ syn. *E. punctata.* Bulbous perennial with semi-erect, lance-shaped, wavy-margined, light green leaves, to 28in (70cm) long, with heavy purple spotting beneath. In late summer, purple-striped stems bear racemes, to 12in (30cm) long, of white flowers with conspicuous purple tepal margins and ovaries. ↕ 30in (75cm), PD8in (20cm). South Africa. Zone 7.

E. pallidiflora (Giant pineapple flower). Robust, bulbous perennial with semi-erect, strap-shaped, light green leaves, to 28in (70cm) long, with crinkled margins. In late summer, bears greenish white flowers in racemes 10–18in (24–45cm) long. ↕ 18–30in (45–75cm), PD8in (20cm). South Africa. Zone 7.

E. punctata see *E. comosa.*

E. undulata see *E. autumnalis.*

E. zambesiaca. Compact, bulbous perennial with semi-erect, strap-shaped, light green leaves, to 6in (15cm) long. In late summer, produces white flowers in racemes 4–8in (10–20cm) long. ↕ 6–10in (15–25cm), PD6in (15cm). Malawi. Zone 7.

EUCOMMIA

EUCOMMIACEAE

Genus of one species of dioecious, deciduous tree originally from woodland in C. China. It is cultivated for its habit and foliage, and also for a certain curiosity value: the alternate, ovate to elliptic, prominently veined leaves, if pulled across, will be held together by rubbery fibers. Grow as a specimen tree.

• **CULTIVATION** Grow in fertile, well-drained soil in full sun or partial shade, sheltered from cold, drying winds. Pruning group 1.

• **PROPAGATION** Sow seed in a seedbed in autumn. Insert greenwood cuttings in summer.

• **PESTS AND DISEASES** Infrequent.

E. ulmoides (Hardy rubber tree). Spreading, broadly domed tree with ovate to elliptic, finely toothed, tapered, glossy, dark green leaves, 3–8in (7–20cm) long. Inconspicuous, axillary, petalless green flowers are usually borne singly, sometimes in clusters, before or with the leaves in spring. Female plants bear groups of winged green fruit. ↕ 40ft (12m), ↔ 25ft (8m). C. China. Zone 6.

EUCRYPHIA

EUCRYPHIACEAE

Genus of 5 or 6 mainly evergreen trees and shrubs from moist woodland in Chile and S.E. Australia, which are grown for their habit, foliage, and flowers. They have opposite, simple or pinnate, leathery leaves and produce solitary, occasionally paired, cup-shaped to saucer-shaped, fragrant white flowers from the leaf axils. Effective as specimen plants.

• **CULTIVATION** Grow in fertile, moist but well-drained, neutral to acidic soil (*E. cordifolia* and *E.* x *nymansensis* tolerate alkaline soil). Site so that the roots are shaded and the crown is in full sun. Shelter from cold, drying winds in all but mild, moist areas. Pruning group 1 or 9 for most; group 8 for *E. lucida.*

• **PROPAGATION** Sow seed in containers in a cold frame as soon as ripe or in late winter. Insert semi-ripe cuttings in summer. Overwinter young plants in a cool greenhouse.

• **PESTS AND DISEASES** Infrequent.

E. cordifolia ▣ (Ulmo). Columnar, evergreen tree with simple, oblong, wavy-margined leaves, up to 3in (8cm) long, dark green above, gray-downy beneath. Saucer-shaped white flowers, 2in (5cm) across, are borne from late summer to autumn. ↕ 50ft (15m), ↔ 25ft (8m). Chile. ❀ (min. 35°F/2°C)

E. glutinosa. Upright, deciduous or semi-evergreen tree or shrub with pinnate leaves, to 2½in (6cm) long, composed of 3–5 elliptic–oblong, toothed, glossy, dark green leaflets that turn orange-red in autumn. Produces cup-shaped, sometimes double, white

Eucryphia cordifolia

Eucryphia lucida

Eucryphia x *nymansensis* 'Nymansay'

flowers, 2½in (6cm) across, in mid-and late summer. Considered the hardiest encryphia nd the most tolerant of exposure. ↕ 30ft (10m), ↔ 20ft (6m). Chile. ❀ (min. 35°F/2°C)

***E. x intermedia* 'Rostrevor'.** Upright, evergreen tree with oblong leaves, to 2½in (6cm) long, either simple or with up to 3 oblong leaflets, glossy, dark green above, pale green and sometimes slightly glaucous beneath, with red shoots. Produces shallowly cup-shaped white flowers, 2in (5cm) across, from late summer to autumn. ↕ 30ft (10m), ↔ 20ft (6m). ❀ (min. 41°F/5°C)

E. lucida ▣ Columnar, evergreen tree with simple, narrowly oblong to oblong-lance-shaped, glossy, dark green leaves, to 2in (5cm) long, glaucous beneath. Bears saucer-shaped white flowers, to 2in (5cm) across, in early and mid-summer. ↕ 25ft (8m), ↔ 12ft (4m). Australia (Tasmania). ❀ (min. 45°F/7°C). **'Pink Cloud'** produces pink flowers with crimson centers.

***E. x nymansensis* 'Nymansay'** ▣ Columnar, dense, evergreen tree with elliptic to elliptic-oblong, toothed leaves, to 2½in (6cm) long, dark green above, paler beneath, and simple or composed of 3 oblong leaflets. Bears cup-shaped white flowers, 3in (8cm) or more across, from late summer to autumn. ↕ 50ft (15m), ↔ 15ft (5m). Zone 8.

▷ ***Eugenia aromatica*** see *Syzygium aromaticum*

▷ ***Eugenia australis* of gardens** see *Syzygium paniculatum*

▷ ***Eugenia paniculata*** see *Syzygium paniculatum*

▷ ***Eugenia smithii*** see *Acmena smithii*

▷ ***Eugenia ugni*** see *Ugni molinae*

EULOPHIA

ORCHIDACEAE

Genus of approximately 200 species of deciduous, mainly terrestrial orchids found in grassland and forest from sea level to almost 6,000ft (2,000m) throughout the tropics, especially in Africa. They have pseudobulbs, tuber-like corms, or fleshy roots, and produce usually 2, sometimes several, lance-shaped to linear, folded or leathery leaves. Flowers are borne in upright racemes or, rarely, panicles.
• **CULTIVATION** Intermediate- or warm-growing orchids. Grow in containers of terrestrial orchid potting mix. In summer, water freely, applying fertilizer at every third watering, and provide high humidity and bright filtered light. Admit full light and keep dry during winter. See also p.46.
• **PROPAGATION** Divide when the plants fill and overflow their containers as new growth begins.
• **PESTS AND DISEASES** Leaf spot and cymbidium mosaic virus can occur. Spider mites, aphids, whiteflies, and mealybugs are problems under glass.

E. guineensis. Terrestrial orchid with clustered pseudobulbs and narrowly elliptic leaves, 10in (25cm) long. Purplish green or reddish brown flowers, 2½in (6cm) across, with large, pinkish purple lips streaked and spotted with darker purple, are borne in racemes to 14in (35cm) long, in autumn. ↕↔ 12in (30cm). Gambia to Angola, Uganda. ❀ (min. 61°F/16°C; max. 90°F/32°C)

EULYCHNIA

CACTACEAE

Genus of 5 species of freely branching arborescent cacti, sometimes with distinct trunks. They are found along the coasts, usually below 3,250ft (1,000m), and in the deserts, of Chile and Peru. Their spines are often stout and long, with 9–16 ribs. Small, funnel- to bell-shaped white to pink flowers are borne near the stem tips, opening diurnally or nocturnally. The fleshy globose fruit can be scaly or hairy, occasionally hairy. These plants thrive in landscape or pot culture, in a well-drained soil mix, under bright light conditions.
• **CULTIVATION** Under glass, grow in a mix of 4 parts standard cactus potting mix and 1 part limestone chips, in full light. From spring to summer, water freely and apply a balanced liquid fertilizer every 4-5 weeks. Keep nearly dry at other times. Outdoors, grow in moderately fertile, slightly alkaline, sharply drained, humus-rich soil in full sun. See also pp.48–49.
• **PROPAGATION** Sow seed at 70°F (21°C) in spring or summer
• **PESTS AND DISEASES** Scale occurs.

Eulychnia acida

E. acida ■ Tree-like cactus, usually branched, sometimes with a distinct trunk, with 10–16 ribs. Spines are usually long and needle-like (12 radial, 1–2 central), to 8in (20cm). New spines are brown, changing to gray with age. Areoles produce wool or long hair. White to pink flowers, 2in (5cm) emerge near apex of stems and are open day and night. Juicy fruits are fleshy, scaly, or hairy, globose, and seldom spiny. ↕ to 13ft (4m). Atacama Desert, Chile. ❀ (min. 41°F/2°C)

▷ ***Eunomia*** see *Aethionema*
▷ ***Euodia*** see *Tetradium*

EUONYMUS

Spindle tree

CELASTRACEAE

Genus of 175 species of deciduous, semi-evergreen, and evergreen shrubs, trees, and climbers found mostly in woodland and thickets, mainly in Asia. They are cultivated for their foliage, autumn color, and ornamental, often ribbed, winged, or lobed, spherical or almost spherical fruits, borne from autumn to winter, which split to reveal seeds with often colorful arils. Leaves are opposite (rarely alternate), simple, very variable in shape, and toothed or scalloped. Cymes of 3, sometimes 7–15, small, green or white, occasionally purple-red or red-brown flowers are borne in late spring or summer. Uses range from a shrub border to specimen plantings, and from hedging to groundcover. All parts may cause mild stomach upset if ingested.
• **CULTIVATION** Grow in any well-drained soil in full sun or light shade. If grown in full sun, they need moister soil, although deciduous species and cultivars are more tolerant of dry soil. Shelter evergreens from cold, drying winds. Variegated cultivars need sun to enhance leaf variegation. Pruning group 1 (deciduous) or group 8 (evergreen).
• **PROPAGATION** Sow seed in containers in a cold frame as soon as ripe. Root greenwood cuttings of deciduous species and cultivars, and semi-ripe cuttings of evergreens, in summer.
• **PESTS AND DISEASES** Mites, scale insects, leaf miners, aphids, and mealybugs are common both outside and under glass. Witches' broom, stem dieback, powdery mildew, and fungal spots are frequent problems.

E. alatus ■ (Burning bush, Winged spindle tree). Dense, bushy, deciduous shrub with obovate to ovate-elliptic, toothed, dark green leaves, to 3in (8cm) long, that turn brilliant red in autumn. Shoots are 4-angled, with broad, corky wings. Almost spherical, reddish purple fruit, ⅜in (9mm) across, are 1- to 4-lobed; seeds have orange arils. ↕ 15–20ft (5–6m), ↔ 10ft (3m). China, Japan. Zone 3. **'Compactus'**, syn. 'Ciliodentatus' (Dwarf burning bush) is more compact and dense than the species, and the leaves turn pinkish red in autumn; ↕ 10ft (3m).

Euonymus alatus

E. bungeanus. Graceful, deciduous or semi-evergreen shrub or small tree with arching shoots. Produces oval to ovate, finely toothed, sharp-pointed, pale green leaves, to 4in (10cm) long, that turn yellow and pink in autumn. Spherical, 4-lobed, pink-tinged, yellow-white fruit are ½in (1.5cm) across; seeds have orange arils. ↕ 20ft (6m), ↔ 15ft (5m). China, Korea. Zone 5.
E. europaeus. Broadly conical, deciduous shrub or small tree with spreading, somewhat pendent shoots. Bears oval, scalloped, dark green leaves, to 3in (8cm) long, that turn red in autumn. Spherical, 4-lobed, clustered red fruit are ¾in (2cm) across; seeds have orange arils. ↕ 10ft (3m), ↔ 8ft (2.5m). Europe to W. Asia. Zone 4. **'Red Cascade'** ■ bears abundant fruit.
***E. fortunei* cultivars** (Wintercreeper). Prostrate to mound-forming, evergreen shrubs with oval, toothed, thinly leathery, dark green leaves, usually to 2in (5cm) long, and often variegated gold or white. Spherical white fruit, ¼in (6mm) across, contain seeds with orange arils. The cultivars below are best grown in average soil and full sun; all climb vigorously if supported, and can be trained against a shady wall or through a tree. They may suffer winter burn in cold climates, and best used as a groundcover. ↕ 24in (60cm), or to 15ft (5m) as climbers, ↔ indefinite. Zone 5. **'Coloratus'** (Purple-leaf wintercreeper) has dark green leaves that turn purple-red from late autumn to winter in cold weather.

Euonymus europaeus 'Red Cascade'

Euonymus fortunei 'Emerald 'n Gold'

'Dart's Blanket' has dark green leaves that turn bronze-red in autumn. **'Emerald Cushion'** is compact and mound-forming in habit, with rich green foliage; ↕ 12in (30cm), ↔ 18in (45cm). **'Emerald Gaiety'** is compact and bushy, bearing bright green leaves with white margins that are tinged pink in winter; ↕ 3ft (1m), ↔ 5ft (1.5m). **'Emerald 'n Gold'** ■ is bushy, and bears bright green leaves with broad, bright yellow margins that are tinged pink in winter; ↔ 36in (90cm). **'Golden Prince'**, syn. 'Gold Tip', is small and compact, with deep green leaves that are tipped bright gold when young. **'Gold Tip'** see 'Golden Prince'. **'Kewensis'** forms a dense mat, and bears dark green leaves, to ½in (1.5cm) long, with pale green veins, on slender shoots; ↕ 4in (10cm). **'Longwood'** is more vigorous and larger-leaved than 'Minimus' and 'Kewensis'. **'Minimus'** is similar to 'Kewensis' but has elliptic to rounded leaves, to ¼in (6mm) long. **var. *radicans*** has trailing stems and dark green leaves. **'Sarcoxie'** is vigorous and bushy, with glossy, dark green leaves; ↕↔ 4ft (1.2m). **'Silver Queen'** ■ is bushy and upright, with white-margined, dark green leaves, the margins later tinted pink; ↕ 8ft (2.5m), or 20ft (6m) as a climber, ↔ 5ft (1.5m). **'Vegetus'** (Bigleaf wintercreeper) may be grown as a shrub or a climber and bears dark green, glossy leaves, and fruits prolifically. Often considered the hardiest selection; ↕ 4–5ft (1.2–1.5m) as a shrub, ↕ 15ft (3m) as a climber.
***E. hamiltonianus* subsp. *sieboldianus*,** syn. *E. yedoensis.* Tree-like, deciduous shrub bearing oblong-ovate to elliptic,

Euonymus fortunei 'Silver Queen'

E

Euonymus hamiltonianus subsp. *sieboldianus* 'Red Elf'

scalloped, mid-green leaves, to 5in (13cm) long, sometimes with long, sharp points; they turn yellow, pink, or red in autumn. Almost spherical, 4-lobed pink fruit, ¼–½in (0.7–1.5cm) across, contain blood-red seeds with orange arils. ‡↔ 20ft (6m). Korea, Japan. Zone 5. **'Red Elf'** ▣ is upright, with profusely borne, dark pink fruit, and seeds with red arils; ‡↔ 10ft (3m).

E. japonicus (Japanese spindle tree). Dense, bushy, evergreen shrub or small, erect tree with obovate to narrowly oval, toothed, leathery, glossy, dark green leaves, to 2½in (6cm) long. Spherical fruit, to ⅜in (9mm) long, are pink-tinged white, but are rarely produced; seeds have orange arils. Useful for hedging. ‡ 12ft (4m), ↔ 6ft (2m). China, Japan, Korea. Zone 5b. **'Albomarginatus'** has oval, dark green leaves, 1¼–2in (3–5cm) long, narrowly margined with white. **'Aureovariegatus'** see 'Ovatus Aureus'. **'Aureus'**, syn. 'Aureopictus', 'Luna', has dark green leaves, each with a central golden mark, often reverting to all green or all yellow; ‡ 5ft (1.5m), ↔ 3ft (1m). **'Luna'** see 'Aureus'. **'Macrophyllus'** is vigorous, with leaves to 3½in (9cm)

Euonymus kiautschovicus

Euonymus myrianthus

long. **'Microphyllus'** bears dark green leaves, to 1in (2.5cm) long; ‡ 3ft (1m), ↔ 24in (60cm). **'Microphyllus Aureovariegatus'** has dark green leaves, to ¾in (2cm) long, with narrow yellow margins; ‡↔ 3ft (1m). **'Ovatus Aureus'**, syn. 'Aureovariegatus', has oval, dark green leaves with broad, yellow margins.

E. kiautschovicus ▣ Open, spreading, evergreen or semi-evergreen shrub with oval to obovate, scalloped, bright green leaves, to 3in (8cm) long, that often turn orange-red and pink in autumn. Spherical pink fruit, ½in (1.5cm) across, containing seeds with orange-red arils, ripen in late autumn. ‡ 10ft (3m), ↔ 15ft (5m). China. Zone 6. **'Manhattan'** is a vigorous selection, possibly a hybrid, and less hardy than the species; ‡ 8ft (2.5m), ↔ 12ft (4m).

E. myrianthus ▣ Bushy, upright, evergreen shrub with oval-lance-shaped to oblong-ovate, tapered, sparsely toothed, leathery, dull green leaves, to 4in (10cm) long. Almost spherical, 4-ribbed, bright orange-yellow fruit are ½in (1.5cm) across; seeds have orange-red arils. ‡ 10ft (3m), ↔ 12ft (4m). W. China. Zone 7b.

E. nanus* var. *turkestanicus. Open, upright, deciduous shrub with alternate or opposite, linear to broadly linear, sparsely toothed, dark green leaves, to 2in (5cm) long, that turn bright red to red-bronze in autumn. Red-brown flowers are followed by spherical, 4-lobed pink fruit, ¼–½in (6–15mm) across; seeds have orange arils. ‡↔ 3ft (1m). C. Asia to China. Zone 2.

E. oxyphyllus ▣ Upright, deciduous shrub or tree with ovate to ovate-

Euonymus oxyphyllus

oblong, tapered, finely toothed, dull green leaves, to 3½in (9cm) long, that turn purple-red in autumn. Spherical, dark red fruit, ½in (1.5cm) across, each have 4 or 5 short ribs; seeds have orange-red arils. ‡ 8ft (2.5m) or more, ↔ 8ft (2.5m). Korea, Japan. Zone 6b.

E. planipes, syn. *E. sachalinensis* of gardens. Upright, deciduous shrub with long, pointed leaf-buds opening to elliptic, coarsely toothed, mid-green leaves, to 5in (13cm) long, that turn bright red in autumn. Produces 4- or 5-lobed, almost spherical red fruit, ¾in (2cm) across; seeds have bright orange arils. ‡↔ 10ft (3m). N.E. China, Korea, Japan. Zone 5.

***E. sachalinensis* of gardens** see *E. planipes.*

E. verrucosus. Dense, bushy, rounded, deciduous shrub with rough, warty, dark shoots. Bears ovate to ovate-lance-shaped, tapered, scalloped, mid-green leaves, to 2½in (6cm) long, that turn yellow or red in autumn. Spherical, deeply 4-lobed fruit, ¼in (6mm) across, are red, often tinged with yellow; black seeds have red arils. ‡ 8ft (2.5m), ↔ 10ft (3m). E. Europe, W. Asia. Zone 6.

E. yedoensis see *E. hamiltonianus* subsp. *sieboldianus.*

EUPATORIUM

Hemp agrimony

ASTERACEAE

Genus of 40 species of annuals, herbaceous perennials, subshrubs, and evergreen shrubs. Originally a genus of over 1,000 species, most have now been transferred to other genera, including *Ageratina* and *Bartlettina.* They occur in temperate, subtropical, and tropical regions in Europe, Africa, Asia, and North to South America, in habitats ranging from dry, sandy sites in woodland and thickets to pastureland and swamps. The leaves are opposite, whorled, or alternate, usually toothed and dissected, but sometimes entire. Tubular, bisexual, white, pink, or purple flowerheads are borne in terminal or axillary corymbs or panicles, or occasionally singly. Most eupatorium flowerheads are nectar-rich and attractive to bees and butterflies. Many of the perennials are useful for a border or a wild or woodland garden. The shrubs and subshrubs are suitable for a mixed or shrub border, but need a warm, sunny site in cool climates. Where not hardy, grow in a cool or temperate greenhouse or conservatory.

• **CULTIVATION** Under glass, grow in soil-based potting mix with added grit and humus, in full light. Provide good ventilation. In growth, water freely and apply a balanced liquid fertilizer when the flowerheads appear. After flowering, reduce watering until flower buds reappear. *E. sordidum* grows well in containers and may be forced to flower earlier. Cut back severely in spring to keep plants compact and floriferous. Outdoors, grow in moist soil in full sun or partial shade. Pruning group 8; may require restrictive pruning under glass.

• **PROPAGATION** Sow seed of hardy species in containers in a cold frame, and seed of tender species at 55–61°F (13–16°C), both in spring. Divide hardy species, and root softwood cuttings of tender species, in spring.

• **PESTS AND DISEASES** Rust, powdery mildew, white smut, *Cercospora* and *Septoria* leaf spots, and Southern blight are problems. Whiteflies and spider mites are common under glass, and snails and slugs attack plants outdoors.

E. ageratoides see *E. rugosum.*

E. cannabinum (Hemp agrimony). Robust, clump-forming perennial with erect, red-tinted stems and opposite, palmately lobed, mid- to dark green leaves, 5in (13cm) across, with oblong-lance-shaped, coarsely toothed lobes. From summer to early autumn, bears pink, purple, or white flowerheads in terminal, dense, flat-topped, corymb-like panicles, to 4in (10cm) across. ‡ to 5ft (1.5m), ↔ to 4ft (1.2m). Europe. Zone 4.

E. coelestinum ▣ syn. *Conoclinium coelestinum* (Mistflower, Hardy ageratum). Strongly upright, rhizomatous perennial with softly hairy branches and opposite, ovate to oblong, often wedge-shaped, scalloped, minutely softly hairy leaves, to 4in (10cm) long. Dense, flat-topped corymbs, 2–4in (5–10cm) across, of large, clear blue flowerheads, are borne from late summer to autumn. Good for a wildflower garden or waterside planting. ‡ to 3ft (1m), ↔ 24–36in (60–90cm). New Jersey to Missouri, West Indies. Zone 4.

E. fistulosum (Joe Pye weed). Compact, upright perennial with wine-colored stems and whorls of lance-shaped to ovate-lance-shaped leaves, to 12in (30cm) long. From summer to autumn, bears dense, terminal, domed, corymb-like panicles of dusk-rose flowerheads, 4in (10cm) across. Very attractive to butterflies. ‡ 5ft (1.5m), ↔ 24–36in (60–90cm). E. US. Zone 3. **'Gateway'** ▣ is more compact and sturdy.

E. ligustrinum, syn. *Ageratina ligustrina, E. micranthum, E. weinmannianum.* Densely branched, domed shrub with opposite, elliptic to lance-shaped, toothed, long-pointed, light green leaves, to 4in (10cm) long, dotted with glands beneath. In autumn, bears fragrant, creamy white or pink-tinted flowerheads are produced in clustered, terminal corymbs, to 8in (20cm) across. ‡↔ 6–15ft (2–5m). Mexico to Costa Rica. ❀ (min. 41°F/5°C)

E. maculatum (Joe Pye weed). Robust, upright perennial with whorls of lance-shaped to ovate-lance-shaped, often incised and shallowly toothed, purple-tinted, mid-green leaves, to 10in (25cm) long, on branching stems speckled purple-red. Bears flat-topped, corymb-

Eupatorium coelestinum

Eupatorium fistulosum 'Gateway'

like panicles, 4–6in (10–15cm) across, of light to deep purple flowerheads, from midsummer to early autumn. Prefers alkaline soil. ↕ to 7ft (2.2m), ↔ 3ft (1m). N.E. to S.E. US. Zone 3b. **'Atropurpureum'** has dark purple-red flowerheads. **'Bartered Bride'** bears pure white flowerheads from mid-summer to autumn; ↕ 4–6ft (1.2–2m).

E. micranthum see *E. ligustrinum.*

E. perfoliatum (Boneset, Thoroughwort). Clump-forming perennial with opposite, lance-shaped, toothed, strongly veined, wrinkled, mid-green leaves, to 8in (20cm) long, softly hairy beneath and joined together at the bases. Produces large, corymb-like panicles, 4–6in (10–15cm) across, of often purple-tinged, white flowerheads, from late summer to autumn. ↕ to 5ft (1.5m), ↔ 24–36in (60–90cm). S.E. US. Zone 3.

E. purpureum (Joe Pye weed). Clump-forming perennial with whorls of elliptic-lance-shaped to ovate, finely toothed, sharp-pointed, coarse, purple-tinged, mid-green leaves, to 10in (25cm) long, borne on stiff, upright stems that are variably suffused purple. Bears terminal, domed, corymb-like panicles, 4–6in (10–15cm) across, of pink, pinkish purple, or creamy white flowerheads from midsummer to early autumn. Prefers alkaline soil. ↕ to 7ft (2.2m), ↔ 3ft (1m). E. US. Zone 3.

E. rugosum, syn. *Ageratina altissima, E. ageratoides, E. urticifolium* (White snakeroot). Clump-forming perennial with stiff brown stems bearing opposite, lance-shaped to ovate, nettle-like, gray-green leaves, 1½–5in (4–13cm) long. Long-lasting, pure white flowerheads are produced in terminal corymbs, 2½in (6cm) across, from midsummer to early autumn. Prefers alkaline soil in partial shade. ↕ 5–6ft (1.5–1.8m), ↔ 24in (60cm). E. North America. Zone 4b. **'Braunlaub'** bears brown-flushed young leaves and brown-tinged flowers. **'Chocolate'** has brown leaves.

E. sordidum, syn. *Bartlettina sordida.* Bushy, rounded shrub with young stems covered in red-purple woolly hairs. Opposite, broadly ovate, toothed, deep green leaves, 4in (10cm) long, are red-hairy below. Terminal corymbs, to 5in (13cm) across, of slightly fragrant violet flowerheads, are produced mainly in winter. ↕ 6–10ft (2–3m), ↔ 5–8ft (1.5–2.5m). Mexico. ❄ (min. 45°F/7°C)

E. urticifolium see *E. rugosum.*

E. weinmannianum see *E. ligustrinum.*

EUPHORBIA

Milkweed, Spurge

EUPHORBIACEAE

Very varied genus of about 2,000 species of annuals; biennials; evergreen, semi-evergreen, or herbaceous perennials; deciduous or evergreen subshrubs, shrubs, and trees; and succulents; widely distributed in a range of habitats in temperate, subtropical, and tropical regions. Most have much-reduced, usually male and female floral parts, grouped together into a cyathium; these may be solitary or borne in rounded or pyramidal, terminal or axillary cymes, umbels, or clusters, and are cupped by involucres of long-lasting, yellow, red, purple, brown, or green, fused bracts. Leaves are very variable, and often short-lived. Many herbaceous euphorbias are suitable for a rock garden, a mixed or shrub border, or a woodland garden. Succulent species are suitable for a dry, tropical garden, or a warm or temperate greenhouse where not hardy. All parts cause severe discomfort if ingested; contact with their milky sap may irritate skin.

• **CULTIVATION** Cultivation requirements have been grouped as below. For pruning, apply group 1 to trees, group 6 to non-succulent shrubs.

1. Well-drained, light soil in full sun.
2. Moist, humus-rich soil in light, dappled shade.
3. Permanently moist soil in full sun.
4. Under glass, grow in a mix of 3 parts soil-based potting mix and 1 part grit, in full light in winter and light to deep shade in summer. Ventilate well. When in growth, water sparingly and apply a low-nitrogen liquid fertilizer monthly. Keep nearly dry in winter. Outdoors, apply cultivation group 1. Grow *E. fulgens* and *E. pulcherrima* in soil-based potting mix with added bark and leaf mold, in full light or bright filtered light. In growth, water moderately and apply a balanced liquid fertilizer every 10–14 days. Keep dry after flowering; resume watering as new growth begins. Repot in early summer. *E. pulcherrima* needs 12–14 hours of complete darkness daily for 2 months to initiate flowering. Outdoors, apply cultivation group 2. See also pp.48–49.

Euphorbia balsamifera

• **PROPAGATION** Sow seed of annuals *in situ* in spring. Sow seed of hardy perennials in containers in a cold frame as soon as ripe or in spring. Divide perennials in early spring, or take basal cuttings in spring or early summer; dip cut surfaces in charcoal or lukewarm water to prevent bleeding. Sow seed of frost-tender succulents as soon as ripe at 59–68°F (15–20°C), or root complete stems, or sections of stems, in spring. Root stem-tip cuttings of shrubby and tree species with bottom heat in spring or early summer.

• **PESTS AND DISEASES** Several fungal and bacterial diseases and a few virus problems are relatively common on poinsettias. Nematodes, spider mites, aphids, and mealybugs can also be serious, both outdoors and under glass.

E. amygdaloides (Wood spurge). Bushy, softly hairy, evergreen perennial with reddish green stems and spoon-shaped to obovate, matte, dark green leaves, 1–3in (2.5–8cm) long, red beneath and becoming darker in winter. From midspring to early summer, bears terminal cymes, 8in (20cm) tall, of greenish yellow cyathia and involucres. Cultivation group 2. Remove stems immediately after flowering, to encourage new basal growth. ↕ 30–32in (75–80cm), ↔ 12in (30cm). Europe, Turkey, Caucasus. Zone 6. **'Purpurea'** has dark reddish purple leaves and acid-yellow cymes. **var. *robbiae***, syn. *E. robbiae* (Mrs. Robb's bonnet), may become invasive. Leaves are broader, leathery, shiny, darker green, and more closely set. Cymes are to 7in (18cm) tall and less showy. Cultivation group 2 or 3. N.W. Turkey. ↕ 24in (60cm).

E. balsamifera ▣ Shrubby, evergreen or sometimes periodically deciduous succulent with gnarled, spineless, gray-brown stems, each crowned by a rosette of linear-lance-shaped or oblong-spoon-

EUPHORBIA HABITS

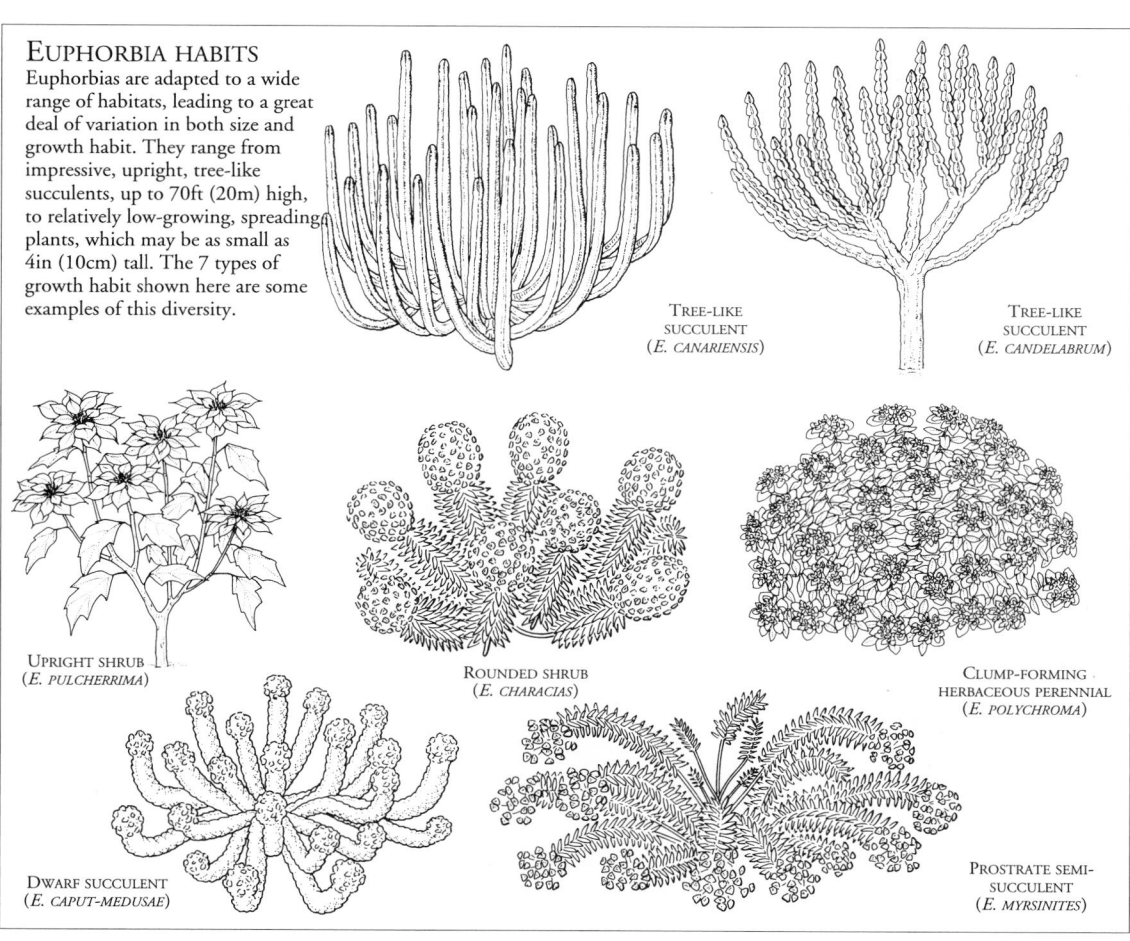

Euphorbias are adapted to a wide range of habitats, leading to a great deal of variation in both size and growth habit. They range from impressive, upright, tree-like succulents, up to 70ft (20m) high, to relatively low-growing, spreading plants, which may be as small as 4in (10cm) tall. The 7 types of growth habit shown here are some examples of this diversity.

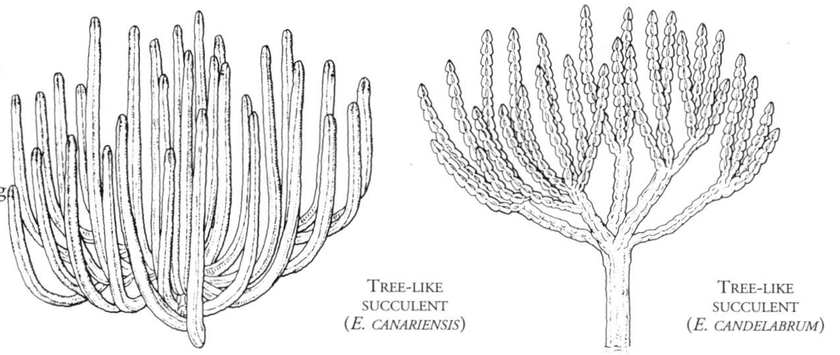

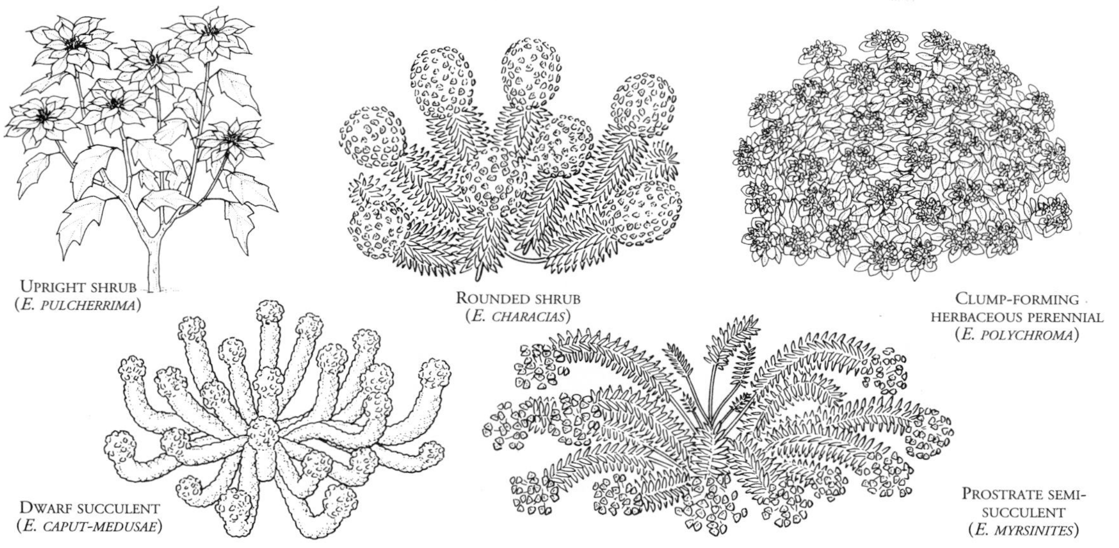

shaped, slightly fleshy, pale green or bluish green leaves, to 1in (2.5cm) long. Solitary, bell-shaped, pale yellowish white cyathia, cupped by pale yellowish white involucres, are borne on short stalks in late spring. Cultivation group 4. ↕ 6ft (2m), ↔ 3ft (1m). Canary Islands. ❀ (min. 50°F/10°C)

E. biglandulosa see *E. rigida.*

E. bupleurifolia. Dwarf, evergreen succulent with a spherical or ovoid, few-branched, scaly caudex with spirally arranged tubercles. Pale green leaves, to 6in (15cm) long, are lance-shaped, tapering, and fleshy. Solitary, pale green cyathia, cupped by green involucres that become red, are borne in late spring and early summer. Cultivation group 4. ↕ to 8in (20cm), ↔ 3in (8cm). South Africa (Eastern Cape, KwaZulu/Natal). ❀ (min. 50°F/10°C)

E. canariensis ▣ Tree-like succulent, branching freely to form large clumps of 4- to 6-angled, fleshy, sharply ridged, toothed, bright green stems. Curved thorns develop in pairs along the angles. Rudimentary leaves soon fall. Solitary, short-stalked, reddish green cyathia, cupped by reddish green involucres, are borne in summer. Cultivation group 4. ↕ 25–40ft (8–12m) or more, ↔ 6ft (2m). Canary Islands. ❀ (min. 54°F/12°C)

E. candelabrum ▣ Freely branching, tree-like succulent with cracked gray bark and 4- or 5-angled, candelabra-like, fleshy, mid- to deep green stems forming a broad, rounded or angular crown. Stems are constricted into oblong segments, to 6in (15cm) long, and have deeply toothed ridges, paired thorns, and short-lived, spear-shaped leaves, ¾–1½in (2–4cm) long. In spring, bears terminal cymes, ¾–2½in (2–6cm) across, of reddish purple cyathia cupped by yellow involucres. Cultivation group 4. ↕ 60ft (20m), ↔ 10ft (3m). Somalia to South Africa. ❀ (min. 54°F/12°C)

E. caput-medusae ▣ (Medusa's head). Freely branching succulent with a caudex-like base, partly subterranean and thickened above. Warty, fleshy, gray-green to blue-green branches are crowned by linear, fleshy, mid-green leaves, to 1in (2.5cm) long. In spring or early summer, bears solitary, fringed cream cyathia cupped by cream involucres. Cultivation group 4. ↕ 12in (30cm), ↔ 3ft (1m). South Africa (Northern Cape, Western Cape, Eastern Cape). ❀ (min. 59°F/15°C)

E. characias. Upright, evergreen shrub with biennial shoots and clumps of

Euphorbia canariensis

Euphorbia candelabrum

erect, densely woolly, purple-tinged stems bearing linear to obovate, gray-green leaves, to 5in (13cm) long. Yellow-green cyathia, with purple-black or purple-brown nectar glands, are cupped by green involucres and borne in dense, cylindrical to spherical, terminal cymes, 4–12in (10–30cm) long, from early spring to early summer. Cut out flowered shoots if seed is not required. Cultivation group 1. ↕↔ 4ft (1.2m). Portugal, W. Mediterranean. Zone 7b. **subsp. *wulfenii*,** syn. *E. veneta*, *E. wulfenii*, has yellow-green cyathia with yellow-green nectar glands; S.E. Europe. **subsp. *wulfenii* 'John Tomlinson'** ▣ has large, nearly spherical cymes, 16in (40cm) long, of bright yellow-green cyathia. **subsp. *wulfenii* 'Lambrook Gold'** has cylindrical cymes of bright golden green cyathia.

E. clavarioides. Dwarf, freely branching succulent with a partly underground caudex and a dense cushion of cylindrical, fleshy stems with thick tips and 4- or 5-sided tubercles. Ovate to lance-shaped, fleshy, mid-green leaves, ¹⁄₁₆ in (2mm) long, are short-lived. In summer, bears solitary green cyathia cupped by green involucres. Cultivation group 4. ↕↔ 12in (30cm) or more. South Africa (except North West Province), Lesotho. ❀ (min. 50°F/10°C)

E. corollata (Wild spurge, Flowering spurge, Tramp's spurge). Upright herbaceous perennial with alternate, elliptic to ovate or linear, entire mid-green leaves, to 2½in (6cm) long. In summer, bears umbel-like cymes, 1¼in (3cm) long, of yellow-green cyathia cupped by hairless, green involucres, and subtended

Euphorbia caput-medusae

Euphorbia characias subsp. *wulfenii* 'John Tomlinson'

by conspicuous white bracts. ↕ to 36in (90cm), ↔ 24in (60cm). Nebraska to Kansas. Zone 5b.

E. cyathophora, syn. *E. heterophylla* of gardens (Annual poinsettia, Fire-on-the-mountain, Painted leaf). Erect, shrubby annual with whorls of linear to ovate or fiddle-shaped, sinuously lobed, dark green leaves, 2–6in (5–15cm) long, becoming red toward the tops of the stems, slightly downy below. In summer, produces terminal, umbel-like cymes, to 4in (10cm) across, of small, crimson-orange cyathia cupped by leafy, scarlet and green involucres. Cultivation group 1. ↕ 28in (70cm) or more, ↔ to 12in (30cm). US, E. Mexico.

E. cyparissias (Cypress spurge). Spreading, rhizomatous herbaceous perennial with slender stems, branching above. Crowded, linear, feathery, bluish green leaves, to 1½in (4cm) long, turn yellow in autumn. From late spring to midsummer, bears yellow-green cyathia and involucres, often turning orange in poor soil, in terminal cymes, ¾–2in (2–5cm) across. Invasive. Cultivation group 1. ↕ 8–16in (20–40cm), ↔ indefinite. W., C., and S. Europe. Zone 4. **'Orange Man'** has cyathia and involucres that are more orange-shaded than the species, and orange-tinted autumn leaves.

E. dulcis. Rhizomatous herbaceous perennial with erect stems and oblong to inversely lance-shaped, dark or bronze-green leaves, to 3in (8cm) long. In early summer, produces terminal cymes, 2–5in (5–13cm) across, of greenish yellow cyathia and involucres. In autumn, stems turn red, and leaves turn red, gold, and orange. Cultivation group 2, but tolerates dry soil. Self-seeds freely. ↕↔ 12in (30cm). W., C., S., and S.E. Europe. Zone 7. **'Chameleon'** ▣ has rich purple leaves and purple-tinted, yellow-green cyathia and involucres.

E. epithymoides see *E. polychroma.*

E. ferox ▣ Clump-forming succulent with 9- to 12-angled, fleshy, partly subterranean, pale green branches armed with thick thorns. Rudimentary leaves soon fall. In spring, bears solitary, pale yellow cyathia, with brown nectar glands, cupped within white-dotted purple involucres. Cultivation group 4. ↕ 6in (15cm), ↔ 20in (50cm). South Africa (Northern Cape, Western Cape, Eastern Cape). ❀ (min. 50°F/10°C)

E. francoisii. Dwarf, variable, many-branched, thorny, evergreen succulent that spreads by means of stolons. Oblong-linear to ovate to irregular, distinctly veined, wavy-margined, fleshy, mid-green leaves, to 2½in (6cm) long, are variegated silvery gray, pink, or white, and often have red midribs and darker undersides. Leaves are arranged in rosettes around the terminal cymes, ¾–2½in (2–6cm) across, of greenish yellow cyathia and involucres borne in summer. Cultivation group 4. ↕ 4in (10cm), ↔ to 12in (30cm). S.E. Madagascar. ❀ (min. 61°F/16°C)

E. fulgens (Scarlet plume). Erect, open, deciduous shrub with slender stems that arch at the tips, and elliptic to lance-shaped, dark green leaves, 2–4in (5–10cm) long. Cyathia contain 5 wide-spreading, petal-like scarlet nectar glands and are produced in cymes, 6–12in

Euphorbia dulcis 'Chameleon'

(15–30cm) across, from the upper leaf axils in winter. Dark-red-leaved and white-flowered forms are available. Cultivation group 4. ↕ to 4ft (1.2m), ↔ 18–30in (45–75cm). Mexico. ❄ (min. 55–59°F/13–15°C)
E. gorgonis. Spherical to inversely conical succulent with a mostly underground caudex and radiating, fleshy, spiralled, dark green, sometimes red branches. Rudimentary leaves soon fall. In late spring, the central stem bears a solitary, dark red or brown cyathium, cupped by a yellow to dull purple involucre. Cultivation group 4. ↕↔ 1¼in (3cm). South Africa (Northern Cape, Western Cape, Eastern Cape). ❄ (min. 54°F/12°C)
E. grandicornis (Cow's horn). Shrub-like succulent with a short, fleshy main stem and prominent, 3-angled, erect or projecting, often tiered branches, the angles curved, with horny margins and prominent, paired, light brown thorns. Rudimentary leaves soon fall. In spring or early summer, bears terminal cymes, to 1½in (4cm) across, of yellow-tinged green cyathia within pale yellow involucres, followed by pale red fruit. Cultivation group 4. ↕ 5ft (1.5m), ↔ 3ft (1m) or more. Kenya to South Africa (KwaZulu/Natal). ❄ (min. 61°F/16°C)
E. griffithii. Rhizomatous, sometimes invasive herbaceous perennial with vigorous, erect stems, reddish green when young. Lance-shaped to linear-oblong, dark green leaves, 3½–6in (9–15cm) long, with red midribs, turn red and yellow in autumn. In early summer, bears terminal cymes, 3–5in (8–13cm) across, of yellow cyathia cupped within orange-red to red involucres. Cultivation group 2. ↕ 36in (90cm), ↔ 24in (60cm). Bhutan, Tibet, S.W. China (Yunnan). Zone 4.
'Dixter' has copper-tinted, very dark green foliage and dusky orange involucres; ↕ 30in (75cm), ↔ 3ft (1m).
'Fireglow' ■ has orange-red involucres; ↕ 30in (75cm), ↔ 3ft (1m).
***E. heterophylla* of gardens** see *E. cyathophora.*
E. lathyris ■ (Caper spurge, Mole plant). Erect, usually unbranched biennial with strap-shaped, leathery, waxy, gray- to blue-green leaves, to 6in (15cm) long. In summer, produces terminal umbels, to 12in (30cm) across, of yellow cyathia cupped by involucres of triangular to lance-shaped, bright green bracts, followed by caper-like fruit. Cultivation group 1; tolerates partial

Euphorbia griffithii 'Fireglow'

shade. ↕ 1–4ft (0.3–1.2m), ↔ to 12in (30cm). Europe, N.W. Africa. Zone 6b.
***E. longifolia* of gardens.** Rhizomatous herbaceous perennial with vigorous, erect stems and oblong to linear-lance-shaped, fresh green leaves, 2½–4½in (6–11cm) long, with white midribs. In early summer, produces flat, terminal cymes, 3–5in (8–13cm) across, of yellow cyathia cupped by yellow involucres. Cultivation group 2. ↕ 3ft (1m), ↔ 24in (60cm). Bhutan. Zone 6b.
E. marginata ■ syn. *E. variegata* (Ghost weed, Snow on the mountain). Erect, initially single-stemmed, later branching annual with ovate to obovate, mid-green leaves, to 3in (8cm) long; the margins of the upper leaves are marked and veined white. From late summer to autumn, produces terminal umbels, to 12in (30cm) across, of greenish white cyathia and involucres, both variegated, margined, or spotted white. Cultivation group 1. Excellent for cutting. ↕ 12–36in (30–90cm), ↔ 12in (30cm). North America.
E. x martinii ■ (*E. amygdaloides* x *E. characias*). Upright, clump-forming, evergreen subshrub. Narrow, inversely lance-shaped, mid-green leaves, to 3in (8cm) long, often tinged purple when young, are borne on red-tinged shoots. From spring to midsummer, produces terminal cymes, 4–5in (10–13cm) across, of yellow-green cyathia with dark red nectar glands; some cyathia are solitary. Cultivation group 1. ↕↔ 3ft (1m). S. France. Zone 7b.
E. mellifera (Honey spurge). Rounded, evergreen shrub with thick shoots and oblong to narrowly lance-shaped, dark

Euphorbia marginata

green leaves, to 8in (20cm) long. In late spring, honey-scented brown cyathia are produced in terminal cymes, 3–4in (8–10cm) across, followed by pea-like, warty fruit from late summer to autumn. Cultivation group 1. ↕ 6ft (2m) or more, ↔ 8ft (2.5m). Madeira. ❄ (min. 41°F/5°C)
E. meloformis. Dwarf, almost spherical succulent with a thick taproot. The usually solitary, furrowed, very fleshy, green to grayish green stem, often cross-banded darker green or red, occasionally banded pale green or purple-brown, has 8–12 usually vertical, sometimes spirally arranged ribs. Rudimentary leaves soon fall. In summer, bears terminal clusters, to 1½in (4cm) across, of green or purple cyathia and involucres. Cultivation group 4. ↕↔ 4in (10cm). South Africa (Northern Cape, Western Cape, Eastern Cape). ❄ (min. 50°F/10°C)
E. milii (Crown of thorns). Bushy, slow-growing, mainly evergreen, semi-succulent shrub with slender, fleshy, thorny stems and branches; the thorns are wider at the bases. Bright green leaves, 1½in (4cm) long, are obovate, pointed, and tough. Yellow cyathia, enclosed by very intense red involucres, are borne in axillary cymes principally in spring or summer. Many flower color and form variants are in cultivation. Cultivation group 4. ↕ 3ft (1m) or more, ↔ 18in (45cm). Madagascar. ❄ (min. 54°F/12°C). **var. *splendens*,** syn. *E. splendens* (Christ's thorn), is semi-prostrate to scrambling; ↕ 12–36in (30–90cm), ↔ 24–39in (60–100cm); ❄ (min. 45–50°F/7–10°C).
var. *tulearensis* ■ has pink cyathia.

Euphorbia milii var. *tulearensis*

E. millottii ■ Compact, slow-growing, mainly evergreen perennial with thick, scarred white stems and lance-shaped, dark green leaves, to 6in (15cm) long, dark red beneath and spiralled around the stems. In spring, bears red-tinged, light green cyathia in axillary cymes. Cultivation group 4. ↕↔ 12in (30cm). Madagascar. ❄ (min. 50°F/10°C)
E. myrsinites ■ (Myrtle spurge). Evergreen perennial with semi-prostrate stems clothed in spirally arranged, obovate to rounded, pointed, succulent, blue-gray leaves, 2–4in (5–10cm) long. In spring, bears terminal umbels, 2–3in (5–8cm) across, of bright greenish yellow cyathia and involucres. Cultivation group 1. ↕ 4in (10cm), ↔ to 12in (30cm). S. and E. Europe to Turkey, C. Asia. Zone 4.

Euphorbia millottii

Euphorbia ferox

Euphorbia lathyris

Euphorbia x *martinii*

Euphorbia myrsinites

E

E

Euphorbia obesa

Euphorbia pulcherrima 'Lilo White'

Euphorbia schillingii

Euphorbia seguieriana

E. nicaeensis. Bushy, evergreen or semi-evergreen perennial with lance-shaped to oblong, leathery, glaucous, gray-green leaves, 3in (8cm) long, borne on upright or procumbent, reddish green stems, arising from a woody rootstock. From late spring to midsummer, produces terminal cymes, to 5in (13cm) across, of long-lasting, greenish yellow cyathia and involucres. Cultivation group 1. ↕32in (80cm), ↔ 18in (45cm). C. and E. Europe, Turkey, Caucasus. Zone 6.
E. obesa ▣ (Living baseball). Succulent with a spherical to squat-cylindrical, 8-ribbed, blunt-toothed, light grayish green stem, checkered reddish brown or faintly banded purple. In summer, bears rounded, terminal cymes, 1½–2½in (4–6cm) across, of yellow cyathia from the crown. Cultivation group 4. ↕6in (15cm), ↔ 5in (13cm). South Africa (Northern Cape, Western Cape, Eastern Cape). ❄ (min. 50°F/10°C)
E. palustris. Robust, clump-forming herbaceous perennial with erect, pale green stems and elliptic to oblong-lance-shaped, bright green leaves, 2½in (6cm) long, turning yellow and orange in autumn. In late spring, bears terminal cymes, to 6in (15cm) across, of large, long-lasting, deep yellow cyathia and involucres. Cultivation group 3. ↕↔ 36in (90cm). S. Scandinavia to Spain to W. Caucasus, W. Asia, Russia (W. Siberia). Zone 6.
E. pilosa (Hairy spurge). Bushy, rhizomatous herbaceous perennial with numerous erect, branching stems, and linear to oblong, softly hairy, mid-green leaves, 1½–4in (4–10cm) long, sometimes less hairy above. From midspring to midsummer, produces terminal cymes, 3–5½in (8–14cm) across, of yellow cyathia and greenish yellow involucres, both becoming greener. Cultivation group 2. ↕24–36in (60–90cm), ↔ 12in (30cm). C. Asia, W. Himalayas. Zone 5b.
E. polychroma ▣ syn. *E. epithymoides* (Cushion spurge). Clump-forming herbaceous perennial with robust, softly hairy stems and obovate to elliptic-oblong, dark green leaves, 1½–2in (3.5–5cm) long, sometimes tinged with purple, and usually turning red, purple, and orange in autumn. Long-lasting yellow cyathia, cupped by showy, bright greenish yellow involucres, are borne in terminal cymes, 1½–3in (4–8cm) across, from midspring to midsummer. Cultivation group 1 or 2. ↕16in (40cm), ↔ 24in (60cm). C. and S. Europe, Turkey. Zone 4. **'Candy'**, syn. 'Purpurea', has dark purple-green stems and leaves, and paler yellow cyathia and involucres. **'Emerald Jade'** has very bright green cyathia and involucres that color well in autumn; ↕14in (35cm), ↔ 18in (45cm). **'Purpurea'** see 'Candy'.
E. pulcherrima (Mexican flame leaf, Poinsettia). Open, erect to spreading, partially deciduous shrub, usually sparsely branched, with ovate to lance-shaped, sometimes lobed or toothed, mid- to deep green leaves, to 6in (15cm) long. In winter, bears dense, terminal cymes, to 12in (30cm) across, of green cyathia ringed by large, leaf-like, bright red involucral bracts. Cultivation group 4. ↕6–12ft (2–4m), ↔ 3–8ft (1–2.5m). Mexico. ❄ (min. 55–59°F/13–15°C). Many cultivars have been produced. **'Ecke's White'** bears ovate, bright green leaves and cream involucres on slender stems. **'Lilo White'** ▣ branches freely and bears olive-green leaves and upright white involucres and cyathia; ↕9in (23cm), ↔ 14in (35cm). **'Menorca'** is vigorous, with dark olive-green leaves, vivid red involucres, and red-and-white cyathia; ↕12in (30cm), ↔ 16in (40cm). **'Paul Mikkelsen'** is freely branching; ↕to 3ft (1m), ↔ 24in (60cm) or more. **'Plenissima'** bears inflorescences formed from a profusion of very narrow involucral bracts, some of them angled upward or erect.
E. reflexa see *E. seguieriana* subsp. *niciciana.*
E. rigida ▣ syn. *E. biglandulosa.* Erect then spreading, evergreen perennial with lance-shaped, stiff, fleshy, gray-green leaves, ¾–3in (2–8cm) long. From early spring to early summer, bears terminal umbels, 2in (5cm) across, of yellow cyathia cupped by yellow involucres that redden with age. Cultivation group 1. ↕12–24in (30–60cm), ↔ to 24in (60cm). Morocco, Mediterranean (Portugal to Turkey), Iran. Zone 7b.
E. robbiae see *E. amygdaloides* var. *robbiae.*
E. schillingii ▣ Robust, clump-forming herbaceous perennial with erect stems and elliptic-oblong to inversely lance-shaped, stalkless, dark green leaves, 5in (13cm) long, with pale green or white veins. Each stem branches near its apex and produces terminal cymes, 3–6in (8–15cm) across, of long-lasting yellow cyathia and rounded, greenish yellow involucral bracts, from midsummer to midautumn. Cultivation group 2. ↕3ft (1m), ↔ 12in (30cm). E. Nepal. Zone 7b.
E. seguieriana ▣ Clump-forming, woody-based, semi-evergreen perennial with linear to oblong-linear, glaucous, bluish green leaves, ½–1½in (1–4cm) long. In late summer and early autumn, thin stems bear terminal cymes, 3–6in (8–15cm) across, of lime-green cyathia and involucres. Cultivation group 1. ↕to 20in (50cm), ↔ 18in (45cm). W. Europe to Russia (Siberia), Caucasus. Zone 8. **subsp. *niciciana***, syn. *E. reflexa,* bears more spreading, narrower, lance-shaped leaves on branched stems, and cyathia with many more yellow-green involucres; Balkans to Pakistan.
E. sikkimensis. Spreading, upright herbaceous perennial with bright pink young shoots. Lance-shaped to linear-oblong, red-marked, deep green leaves, 4–5in (10–13cm) long, become soft green, with red margins and ruby-red veins. In mid- and late summer, bears terminal cymes, 2½–3in (6–8cm) across, of yellow cyathia cupped by pale to greenish yellow

Euphorbia polychroma

Euphorbia rigida

Euphorbia squarrosa

Euphorbia tirucallii

involucres. Cultivation group 2. ↕ 4ft (1.2m), ↔ 18in (45cm). E. Himalayas. Zone 7.
E. splendens see *E. milii* var. *splendens.*
E. squarrosa ■ Dwarf, perennial succulent with a sometimes contorted, subterranean, beige to brown caudex with numerous, 2- to 5-angled, erect or prostrate, usually twisted, dark green branches borne at ground level, margined with pairs of thorns, and minute, deciduous leaves. In spring, bears cymes, to 2in (5cm) across, of 3 bright green cyathia cupped by green involucres with 5 adjoining glands. Cultivation group 4, often grown to reveal the caudex. ↕ to 6in (15cm), ↔ to 4in (10cm). South Africa. ❄ (min. 50°F/10°C)
E. tirucallii ■ Bushy, tree-like succulent with fleshy, segmented, bright green stems, with paler vertical lines, and linear to linear-lance-shaped, short-lived leaves, ½in (1.5cm) long. In spring, produces terminal cymes, to ½in (1.5cm) across, of green cyathia cupped by paler involucres. Cultivation group 4. ↕ to 28ft (9m), ↔ 6ft (2m). Tropical E. and S. Africa. ❄ (min. 50°F/10°C)
E. variegata see *E. marginata.*
E. veneta see *E. characias* subsp. *wulfenii.*
E. villosa. Rhizomatous, semi-evergreen or herbaceous perennial producing numerous pale yellowish green stems with terminal branches, and thin, oblong-lance-shaped to elliptic-oblong, hairless or softly hairy, mid-green leaves, 2½in (6cm) long, which turn yellow in autumn. From midspring to early summer, bears terminal cymes, 2½in (6cm) across, of greenish yellow cyathia cupped within yellow involucres that mature to greenish yellow. Cultivation group 2. ↕ to 4ft (1.2m), ↔ 18in (45cm). Europe (except S.W.) to C. Russia, Caucasus, W. Siberia. Zone 5.
E. wallichii. Clump-forming herbaceous perennial with erect stems and linear to elliptic-oblong, dark green leaves, 2½–4½in (6–11cm) long, with white veins and purple-tinted margins. In early summer, produces cymes, eventually 3–6in (8–15cm) across, of umbel-like, orange-yellow cyathia and bright greenish yellow involucres. Cultivation group 2. ↕ 20in (50cm), ↔ 12in (30cm). W. and C. Himalayas. Zone 6.
E. wulfenii see *E. characias* subsp. *wulfenii.*

EUPTELEA
EUPTELEACEAE

Genus of 2 or 3 species of deciduous trees and shrubs occurring in woodland from the Himalayas to Japan. They are grown mainly for their attractive leaves, which are alternate, simple, rounded to ovate, and often colorful in autumn. The small, petalless, green or reddish green flowers are produced in clusters in spring, before the leaves. Grow in a large shrub border or woodland garden.
• **CULTIVATION** Grow in fertile, moist but well-drained soil in full sun or partial shade. Pruning group 1.
• **PROPAGATION** Sow seed in a seedbed as soon as ripe.
• **PESTS AND DISEASES** Infrequent.

E. polyandra. Spreading, suckering shrub or small tree with broadly ovate to rounded, tapered, deeply toothed, glossy, bright green leaves, to 6in (15cm) long, tinged red when young, turning yellow and red in autumn. Produces clusters, 1–1½in (2.5–4cm) across, of inconspicuous, reddish green flowers in spring, before the leaves emerge. ↕ 25ft (8m), ↔ 20ft (6m). Japan. Zone 7.

EURYA
THEACEAE

Genus of about 70 species of mostly evergreen trees and shrubs from woodland in E. and S.E. Asia and the Pacific islands. They are cultivated for their large, alternate, simple, usually ovate to obovate or elliptic, mid- to dark green leaves with scalloped to toothed margins. The inconspicuous, dioecious flowers are borne singly or in few-flowered clusters from the leaf axils, in spring. Grow in a shrub border or woodland garden. Where not hardy, grow *E. emarginata* in a cool greenhouse.
• **CULTIVATION** Under glass, grow in soil-based potting mix in full light. When in full growth, water freely and apply a balanced liquid fertilizer monthly; water sparingly in winter. Outdoors, grow in moist but well-drained, humus-rich soil in full sun or partial shade, sheltered from cold, drying winds. Pruning group 1.
• **PROPAGATION** Sow seed in containers in a cold frame as soon as ripe. Root semi-ripe cuttings in summer.
• **PESTS AND DISEASES** Infrequent.

E. emarginata. Dense, evergreen shrub or small tree with obovate to oblong-obovate, scalloped, leathery, glossy, dark green leaves, to 1½in (4cm) long, tinged red in winter. Bears yellow-green flowers in spring. Female plants bear almost spherical, purple-black berries, ¼in (6mm) across, in autumn. ↕↔ 5ft (1.5m). S. Japan. ❄ (min. 41°F/5°C)
E. japonica. Dense, evergreen shrub or small tree with elliptic to obovate, toothed, leathery, glossy, dark green leaves, to 3in (8cm) long. In spring, bears greenish white flowers with green or purple-brown sepals. Female plants bear almost spherical black berries, to ¼in (6mm) across, in autumn. ↕↔ 30ft (10m). Korea, Japan, and adjacent islands. ❄ (min. 35°F/2°C)

EURYALE
Fox nuts, Gorgon plant, Prickly waterlily
NYMPHAEACEAE

Genus of one species of deep-water aquatic perennial, often treated as an annual, that occurs in still and slow-moving water in Asia. One of the world's largest aquatic plants, it has large, floating, rounded, thorny leaves, and shuttlecock-like flowers, the stems and calyces covered with stiff prickles. Grow *E. ferox* in a large water garden or warm greenhouse.
• **CULTIVATION** Grow in a large basket of fertile, loamy soil at a water depth of 3ft (1m) in full light (full sun if outdoors). When in growth, apply a balanced liquid fertilizer every 3–6 weeks. See also pp. 52–53.
• **PROPAGATION** Sow seed singly in containers in spring. Submerge in water at 70–73°F (21–23°C), with the tops of the containers just under the surface.
• **PESTS AND DISEASES** Infrequent.

E. ferox. Deep-water aquatic perennial with floating, rounded leaves, 2–5ft (0.6–1.5m) across, that are puckered, sparsely spiny, olive-green above and purple underneath, with prominent, prickly veins. Shuttlecock-like, slightly iridescent, red, purple, or lilac flowers, to 2½in (6cm) across, are produced in summer, followed by many-seeded, prickly berries, 2–3in (5–8cm) across. ↔ 5ft (1.5m). N. India, Bangladesh, China, Taiwan, Japan. ❄ (min. 41°F/5°C)

EURYOPS
ASTERACEAE

Genus of approximately 100 species of evergreen shrubs, subshrubs, herbaceous perennials, and annuals found in rocky areas mainly in southern Africa, with one species in the Arabian Peninsula and Socotra, Yemen. They produce attractive, alternate, simple to pinnatisect, linear, or lance-shaped to broadly ovate leaves and showy, daisy-like flowerheads. Grow in a sheltered shrub border, rock garden, or raised bed, or in containers. Where not hardy, grow in a cool greenhouse, or in an alpine house.

Euryops acraeus

Euryops pectinatus

• **CULTIVATION** Under glass, grow in soil-based potting mix with added sharp sand, in full light. Water freely when in full growth, sparingly in winter. Outdoors, grow in moderately fertile, well-drained soil in full sun. Trim lightly after flowering to restrict growth.
• **PROPAGATION** Sow seed in spring at 50–55°F (10–13°C). Insert softwood cuttings in late spring, or insert semi-ripe cuttings in summer.
• **PESTS AND DISEASES** Infrequent.

E. acraeus ■ syn. *E. evansii* of gardens. Dense, dome-shaped shrub with branching stems clothed in linear, flattened, leathery, silvery gray leaves, to 1¼in (3cm) long, toothed at the tips. In late spring and early summer, bears deep yellow flowerheads, 1in (2.5cm) across, singly or in groups of 2 or 3, on strong stems to 1½in (4cm) long. Requires sharp drainage. ↕↔ to 12in (30cm). South Africa (Drakensberg Mountains, KwaZulu/Natal). ❄ (min. 45°F/7°C)
***E. evansii* of gardens** see *E. acraeus.*
E. pectinatus ■ Vigorous shrub with upright shoots and pinnatifid to pinnatisect, gray-hairy leaves, to 3in (8cm) long, with linear lobes. Bears long-stalked, bright yellow flowerheads, 2in (5cm) across, singly or in small clusters, from early summer to midautumn and, under glass, on through winter. ↕↔ 3ft (1m). South Africa. Zone 8. **'Viridis'** has deep green leaves. Both forms are excellent as standards.

EUSTOMA *syn.* LISIANTHIUS
GENTIANACEAE

Genus of 3 species of erect, taprooted annuals, biennials, and short-lived perennials found in moist prairies and fields from C. and S. US to N. South America. Leaves are opposite, ovate to oblong-lance-shaped, stalkless, and sometimes stem-clasping. In summer, leafy flowering stems produce showy, deeply cup-shaped or bell-shaped, pastel-colored flowers, either singly or in clusters, which gradually open from slender, furled buds. Grow as flowering container plants in a temperate greenhouse or as annuals in a bed or border. Good for cut flowers.
• **CULTIVATION** Under glass, grow in soil-based potting mix in full light, with bright filtered light when in bloom. Ventilate well. In full growth, water freely and apply a balanced liquid fertilizer every 2–3 weeks; water

Eustoma grandiflorum Heidi Series

sparingly in winter. Outdoors, grow in well-drained, neutral to alkaline soil in full sun. Support stems.
• **PROPAGATION** Sow seed at 55–61°F (13–16°C) in autumn or late winter. Seedlings are initially slow-growing.
• **PESTS AND DISEASES** Commonly affected by virus diseases, gray mold, stem cankers, and *Fusarium* wilt.

E. grandiflorum, syn. *E. russellianum*, *Lisianthius russellianus* (Prairie gentian, Texas bluebell). Single-stemmed or branching annual or biennial with slightly fleshy, ovate to oblong, prominently 3- to 5-veined, glaucous, gray-green leaves, to 3in (8cm) long. In summer, broadly bell-shaped, satin-textured, dark-centered, pale purple flowers, to 2in (5cm) across, are produced on long stalks, either singly or in clusters, from the upper leaf axils. ↕ 24–36in (60–90cm), ↔ 12in (30cm). Nebraska, Colorado, Kansas, Texas. ❄ (min. 35°F/2°C). **Echo Series** cultivars have double flowers, 2½–3in (6–8cm)across, in shades and picotees of blue, rose, and white; ↕ 18–24in (45–60cm), ↔ 10–12in (25–30cm). **Flamenco Series** cultivars have longer stems and bloom later than Heidi Series, in shades of purple, pink, and white, and blue picotee. Cultivars of **Heidi Series** ▣ bear flowers in shades of blue, rose-pink, white, and bicolors; ↕ 18in (45cm). **Lisa Series** cultivars are dwarf and compact, and bear blue or white flowers, 2½in (6cm) across; ↕ 8in (20cm). **Mermaid Series** cultivars have pink-, white-, or black-centered blue flowers; ↕ to 6in (15cm). **Yodel Series** cultivars are compact, with flowers in white, salmon-pink, or purple-blue, with dark centers; ↕ 16–18in (40–45cm).
E. russellianum see *E. grandiflorum.*

▷ ***Evodia*** see *Tetradium*

EVOLVULUS

CONVOLVULACEAE

Genus of about 100 species of prostrate to upright annuals, perennials, and evergreen subshrubs found mostly on plains and prairies from N. US to S. Argentina. The leaves are usually simple, mainly narrowly lance-shaped to broadly ovate, and silky-hairy. *Evolvulus* species are grown for their bell- to funnel-shaped, blue, pink, or white flowers, borne singly or in few-flowered, axillary or terminal cymes, usually from spring to autumn. Where not hardy, grow in a warm greenhouse. In dry, frost-free areas, grow in a mixed or shrub border or for bedding.
• **CULTIVATION** Under glass, grow in soil-based potting mix, with added sharp sand, in full light. In the growing season, water moderately and apply a balanced liquid fertilizer monthly; water sparingly in winter, and maintain a dry atmosphere when temperatures are low. Outdoors, grow in poor to moderately fertile, well-drained soil in full sun.
• **PROPAGATION** Sow seed at 55–61°F (13–16°C) in spring, or take softwood cuttings in late spring.
• **PESTS AND DISEASES** *Rhizoctonia* aerial blight, rust, and other fungal spots are common under glass and outdoors in warm climates.

***E. glomeratus* of gardens** see *E. pilosus.*
E. pilosus, syn. *E. glomeratus* of gardens. Slender, trailing, evergreen subshrub or woody-based perennial with spoon-shaped or inversely lance-shaped to ovate-oblong, densely silky-hairy, silvery gray leaves, to ½in (1.5cm) long. In summer, bears solitary, short-tubed, funnel- to bell-shaped, lavender-pink or blue flowers, ½–¾in (1.5–2cm) across. ↕↔ to 20in (50cm). Montana and South Dakota to Arizona and Texas. ❄ (min. 50°F/10°C). **'Blue Daze'** has elliptic-ovate, white-hairy leaves and powder-blue flowers with white eyes.

EXACUM

GENTIANACEAE

Genus of about 25 species of annuals, biennials, and evergreen perennials occurring near streams from Yemen to India. They have erect, often 4-angled, branched stems and stalkless to short-stalked, lance-shaped to elliptic, simple, entire leaves. They are grown for their saucer-shaped, fragrant, violet to blue, occasionally pink or white flowers, with yellow stamens, borne singly or in leafy cymes. Where not hardy, grow in a temperate greenhouse, in a conservatory, or as houseplants. In warmer areas, grow outdoors in a bed or border.
• **CULTIVATION** Under glass, grow in soil-based potting mix, with added sharp sand, in full light. During the growing season, water freely and apply a balanced liquid fertilizer every 2–3 weeks; water sparingly in winter. Outdoors, grow in moderately fertile, well-drained soil in full sun.

Exacum affine

• **PROPAGATION** Sow seed at 64°F (18°C) in early spring.
• **PESTS AND DISEASES** *Botrytis* blight, impatiens necrotic spot virus, canker, and root rot are common.

E. affine ▣ (Persian violet). Bushy annual, or short-lived evergreen perennial usually grown as an annual, with 4-angled stems and ovate to elliptic, shiny leaves, to 1¼in (3cm) long. In summer, bears scented, lavender-blue, rose-pink, or white flowers, to ¾in (2cm) across, with conspicuous yellow stamens. ↕↔ 9–12in (23–30cm). Yemen (Socotra). ❄ (min. 45–50°F/7–10°C). **'Blue Gem'** is compact and bears lavender-blue flowers; ↕ 8in (20cm). **'Blue Midget'** has lavender-blue flowers; ↕ to 5in (13cm). **'White Midget'** has pure white flowers; ↕ to 5in (13cm).

EXOCHORDA

Pearlbush

ROSACEAE

Genus of 4 species of deciduous shrubs occurring in woodland from C. Asia to China and Korea. They are grown for their habit and abundant, showy, cup- or saucer-shaped white flowers, borne in terminal racemes in spring or summer. Leaves are alternate, simple, oblong or obovate, and entire or toothed. Ideal for a shrub border or as isolated specimens.
• **CULTIVATION** Grow in fertile, moist but well-drained soil (most will tolerate all but shallow, alkaline soil) in full sun or light, dappled shade. *E. racemosa* prefers acidic soil. Pruning group 2.
• **PROPAGATION** Sow seed in a seedbed in autumn. Insert softwood cuttings in summer.
• **PESTS AND DISEASES** Infrequent.

E. giraldii (Redbud pearlbush). Arching shrub with obovate leaves, to 3in (8cm) long, pinkish green when young, later pale green with red-tinged veins and red stalks. Upright racemes of 6–8 white

Exochorda x *macrantha* 'The Bride'

flowers, to 1in (2.5cm) across, are borne in late spring. ↕↔ 10ft (3m). N.W. China. Zone 6. **var. *wilsonii*** ▣ is more upright, with green-stalked leaves, to 4in (10cm) long, and flowers to 2in (5cm) across.
E. korolkowii. Upright shrub with upright, softly rust-hairy branches and obovate, tapered, olive to lime-green leaves, to 3½in (9cm) long, gray to yellow-green beneath. In spring, produces erect, 5- to 8-flowered racemes, to 4in (10cm) long, of stalkless white flowers, 1½in (4cm) across. ↕ to 15ft (5m), ↔ 10–12ft (3–4m). C. Asia. Zone 5b.
***E.* x *macrantha* 'The Bride'** ▣ Compact, arching, mound-forming shrub with obovate, light to mid-green leaves, to 3in (8cm) long. Bears racemes of 6–10 white flowers, to 1¼in (3cm) across, in late spring and early summer. ↕ 6ft (2m), ↔ 10ft (3m). Zone 5.
E. racemosa (Common pearlbush). Dense, rounded shrub with arching branches and narrowly obovate leaves, to 3in (8cm) long, light green above, darker beneath. Bears upright racemes of 6–10 pure white flowers, to 1½in (4cm) across, in late spring. ↕↔ 10–12ft (3–4m). N. China. Zone 5b.

Exochorda giraldii var. *wilsonii*

F

FABIANA

SOLANACEAE

Genus of about 25 species of heath-like, evergreen shrubs from dry, upland slopes in temperate regions of South America. They are cultivated for their small, alternate, overlapping, densely arranged, needle-like leaves and solitary, tubular or bell-shaped flowers, borne terminally or opposite the leaves. Grow in a sheltered, mixed or shrub border, in a rock garden, or against a sunny wall.

• **CULTIVATION** Grow in well-drained, poor to moderately fertile, neutral to slightly acidic soil in full sun, sheltered from cold, drying winds. They are lime-tolerant, but may become chlorotic on shallow, alkaline soils. Pruning group 9.

• **PROPAGATION** Sow seed in containers in a cold frame in autumn or spring. In early summer, take greenwood cuttings. Take semi-ripe cuttings in late summer.

• **PESTS AND DISEASES** Infrequent.

F. imbricata. Dense, mound-forming shrub with plume-like branches densely covered with tiny, needle-like, deep green leaves, to ¼in (6mm) long. In early summer, solitary, tubular, white to pale mauve flowers, ½in (1.5cm) long, are borne opposite the leaves. ↕↔ 8ft (2.5m). Chile. ❄ (min. 35°F/2°C). **'Prostrata'** is low-growing, with white flowers; ↕ 3ft (1m), ↔ 6ft (2m). **f. *violacea*** ■ is upright, with branches spreading horizontally, and with lavender-mauve flowers.

Fabiana imbricata f. *violacea*

Fagus grandifolia

FAGUS

Beech

FAGACEAE

Genus of 10 species of deciduous forest trees, widely distributed in temperate regions of the N. hemisphere, valued for their form, foliage, and autumn color. They have alternate, usually ovate to elliptic-oblong, coarsely to finely toothed, mid- or dark green leaves, and usually smooth gray bark. The monoecious flowers appear with the leaves, the males in spherical heads, the females in pairs within 4-lobed bracts, which develop into smooth or spiny, 4-segmented cupules containing the nuts. Grow in a woodland garden or as specimen trees. Use *F. sylvatica* for hedging or pleaching.

• **CULTIVATION** Very tolerant of a wide range of well-drained soils; grow in full sun or partial shade. For best color, position purple-leaved beeches in full sun and yellow-leaved ones in partial shade. Pruning group 1.

• **PROPAGATION** Sow seed in a seedbed in autumn or, after winter stratification, in spring. Graft cultivars in midwinter.

• **PESTS AND DISEASES** Limb canker, powdery mildew, butt and wood rot, and a variety of bracket fungi can be troublesome.

F. americana see *F. grandifolia.*

F. crenata (Japanese beech). Spreading tree with ovate, glossy, mid-green leaves, 3–5in (7–13cm) long, silky when young, turning yellow in autumn. ↕ 30ft (10m), ↔ 25ft (8m). Japan. Zone 5b.

F. grandifolia ■ syn. *F. americana* (American beech). Spreading, often shrubby tree. Oval, dark green leaves, 2½–6in (6–15cm) long, with distinctly toothed margins, silky-haired at first, turn golden brown in autumn. ↕↔ 80ft (25m). E. North America. Zone 4.

F. japonica. Spreading tree with elliptic-ovate to ovate, tapered, blue-green leaves, 2–5in (5–13cm) long, silky-margined, slightly glaucous beneath, turning yellow in autumn. ↕ 30ft (10m), ↔ 25ft (8m). Japan. Zone 5b.

F. orientalis (Oriental beech). Spreading tree with elliptic to obovate, wavy-margined, toothed, dark green leaves, 3–7in (8–18cm) long, turning yellow-brown in autumn. ↕ 70ft (20m), ↔ 50ft (15m). S.E. Europe, N. Iran, Caucasus, S.W. Asia. Zone 5b.

Fagus sylvatica (inset: leaf detail)

Fagus sylvatica 'Dawyck Purple'

F. sylvatica ■ (European beech). Spreading tree with elliptic-ovate, wavy-margined leaves, to 4in (10cm) long, silky-haired and pale green at first, turning glossy dark green, then yellow to orange-brown in autumn. ↕ 80ft (25m), ↔ 50ft (15m). C. Europe to Caucasus. Zone 5b. **'Aspleniifolia'** (Fern-leaved beech) has slender leaves deeply cut into narrow lobes. **'Aurea Pendula'** is narrow, with pendulous branches and bright yellow young foliage, maturing to green; ↕ 30ft (10m), ↔ 5ft (1.5m). **'Dawyck'** is flame-shaped; ↔ 22ft (7m). **'Dawyck Gold'** is compact and columnar, with bright yellow young foliage turning green; ↕ 60ft (18m), ↔ 22ft (7m). **'Dawyck Purple'** ■ is narrowly upright, with deep purple foliage; ↕ 70ft (20m), ↔ 15ft (5m). **f. *laciniata*** has deeply cut leaves. **f. *pendula*** ■ (Weeping beech) has pendulous branches that may reach the ground. **f. *purpurea*** (Copper beech) has purple leaves, coppery in autumn. **'Purpurea Pendula'** is mushroom-headed, with weeping branches and deep blackish purple foliage; ↕↔ 10ft (3m). **'Purpurea Tricolor'**, syn. 'Roseomarginata', 'Tricolor' of gardens, has purple leaves edged and striped pink

Fagus sylvatica f. *pendula*

F

Fagus sylvatica 'Riversii'

and pinkish white. **'Riversii'** ■ has very deep purple leaves. **'Rohanii'** has deeply cut, purple leaves. **'Roseomarginata'** see 'Purpurea Tricolor'. **'Rotundifolia'** is upright when young, later spreading, with small, rounded leaves, to 2in (5cm) long. **'Spaethiana'** has persistent, deep purple foliage with light veins. **'Tricolor' of gardens** see 'Purpurea Tricolor'. **'Zlatia'** has yellow young foliage, maturing to green.

FALLOPIA *syn.* BILDERDYKIA, REYNOUTRIA

POLYGONACEAE

Genus of 7 species of rhizomatous, climbing or scrambling, woody-based perennials found in moist habitats in temperate regions in the N. hemisphere. They have simple, entire, alternate, triangular or narrowly to broadly ovate leaves. In late summer, they produce large panicles of small, funnel-shaped, white, greenish white, or pinkish white flowers. Climbing species are ideal for training on pergolas and deciduous trees and for covering unsightly structures. *F. aubertii* and *F. baldschuanica* are frequently rampant and may be difficult to control. The two species are also often confused and may be represented in gardens by hybrids between them.

• **CULTIVATION** Grow in any poor to moderately fertile, moist but well-drained soil, in full sun or partial shade. Provide strong, durable supports; a vigorous specimen can pull down a small tree or weak support. Pruning group 11, in early spring.

• **PROPAGATION** Sow seed in containers in a cold frame in spring, or as soon as ripe. Take heeled, semi-ripe cuttings in summer, hardwood cuttings in autumn.

• **PESTS AND DISEASES** Leaf miners can be a problem.

F. aubertii, syn. *Bilderdykia aubertii, Polygonum aubertii* (Mile-a-minute plant, Silver flea vine, Silver lace vine). Vigorous, woody, twining, deciduous climber with heart-shaped, mid-green leaves, to 4in (10cm) long, bronze when young. Upright, narrow, minutely hairy, terminal or axillary panicles of tiny, funnel-shaped, white to greenish white flowers, ⅛–¼in (4–6mm) across, are borne laterally on leafy stems in late summer and autumn, followed by small, angled, pinkish white fruit. ↕40ft (12m). China (Gansu, Sichuan, Shaanxi), Tibet. Zone 5b.

Fallopia baldschuanica

F. baldschuanica ■ syn. *Bilderdykia baldschuanica, Polygonum baldschuanicum* (Mile-a-minute plant, Russian vine). Vigorous, woody, twining, deciduous climber with heart-shaped, dark green leaves, to 4in (10cm) long. In late summer and autumn, broad, almost hairless, terminal or axillary panicles of tiny, funnel-shaped, pink-tinged white flowers, ¼–⅜in (6–8mm) across, are produced toward the ends of the shoots, followed by small, angled, pinkish white fruit. ↕40ft (12m). Tajikistan, Afghanistan, W. Pakistan. Zone 5b.

FARFUGIUM

ASTERACEAE

Genus of 2 species of rhizomatous, evergreen perennials, found near streams and seashores in E. Asia, grown mainly for their attractive foliage. The large, leathery leaves are borne on long stalks in basal tufts, and the yellow flowerheads are borne in loose corymbs. Variegated cultivars are excellent foliage and groundcover plants near water, in a border, or in containers.

• **CULTIVATION** Grow in fertile, moist but well-drained soil in partial shade. Shelter from cold, drying winds. Mulch in early winter, particularly where temperatures drop below 23°F (-5°C).

• **PROPAGATION** Sow seed of species in containers in a cold frame in winter or spring. Divide in spring.

• **PESTS AND DISEASES** Prey to slugs.

F. japonicum, syn. *F. tussilagineum, Ligularia tussilaginea.* Loosely clump-forming perennial with kidney-shaped, long-stalked, shiny leaves, 6–12in (15–30cm) across, with entire or short-toothed margins. Bears yellow flowerheads, 1½–2½in (4–6cm) across, in autumn and winter. ↕↔ 24in (60cm). Japan (Honshu, Shikoku, Kyushu). Zone 7b. **'Albovariegatum'** see 'Argenteum'. **'Argenteum'** ■ syn. 'Albovariegatum', 'Variegatum', has variegated leaves with irregular, creamy white margins. **'Aureomaculatum'** has conspicuous, irregular yellow markings on its leaves. **'Variegatum'** see 'Argenteum'.

F. tussilagineum see *F. japonicum.*

Farfugium japonicum 'Argenteum'

FARGESIA

POACEAE

Genus of about 4 species of clump-forming, evergreen bamboos from damp woodland in C. China and the N.E. Himalayas. Some species of *Fargesia* were formerly included in *Arundinaria, Sinarundinaria,* or *Thamnocalamus.* These often vigorous bamboos are grown for their attractive linear to lance-shaped, slightly checkered, bright, mid- or dark green leaves, and erect culms, 6–15ft (2–5m) tall, with yellow, brown, or dark purple-green nodes. The inflorescences are terminal panicles or racemes. Grow as specimen plants; many are suitable for a hedge or screen. Grow *F. nitida* in a wild garden or in a large container.

• **CULTIVATION** Grow in fertile, moisture-retentive soil. *F. nitida* needs partial or light, dappled shade with shelter from cold, dry winds.

• **PROPAGATION** Divide established clumps or take cuttings of sections of young rhizomes in spring.

• **PESTS AND DISEASES** Slugs may attack young shoots.

F. dracocephala. Vigorous bamboo forming a clump of upright, smooth, plum-purple culms, ¾in (2cm) thick, which remain unbranched in the first year. The leaf sheaths are evergreen and beige. The upper portions of the canes produce pendulous branchlets bearing clustered, wide, smooth, linear, deep matte green leaves, 3–4in (8–10cm) long. ↕16ft (5.5m), ↔ 12ft (4m). W. China. Zone 6.

F. murieliae, syn. *Arundinaria murieliae, F. spathacea* of gardens, *Sinarundinaria murieliae, Thamnocalamus spathaceus* of gardens (Umbrella bamboo). Clump-forming bamboo, similar to *F. nitida,* but with white-powdery, yellow-green, then yellow stems, which usually branch in the first year and eventually arch under the weight of lance-shaped, bright green leaves, 2½–6in (6–15cm) long, with long, drawn-out tips. The deciduous leaf sheaths are downy, greenish purple when young, later becoming hairless and pale brown. ↕ to 12ft (4m), ↔ 5ft (1.5m) or more. C. China. Zone 5b.

F. nitida, syn. *Arundinaria nitida, Sinarundinaria nitida* (Fountain bamboo). Slow-growing bamboo forming a dense clump of erect, dark purple-green culms, ⅛–⅜in (4–8mm) thick, lined purple-brown, and white-powdery beneath the nodes; culms remain unbranched in their first year. The deciduous leaf sheaths are pale or purple-brown. The upper portions of the culms produce abundant purple-tinted branchlets bearing cascades of alternate, narrow, lance-shaped, finely tapering, dark green leaves, 1½–4½in (4–11cm) long. ↕ to 15ft (5m), ↔ 5ft (1.5m) or more. C. China. Zone 5. **'Nymphenburg'** is larger than the species and more strongly arching, with very narrow leaves; ↕ 15ft (5m), ↔ 10–12ft (3–4m).

F. utilis. Clump-forming bamboo producing pendulous, arching, smooth, plum-purple culms, ½in (1.5cm) thick, which remain unbranched in the first year and produce profuse, very narrow, small, smooth, matte green leaves, 3in (8cm) long. The leaf sheaths are evergreen, persistent, and beige. ↕ 13ft (4.2m), ↔ 10ft (3m). China (Yunnan). Zone 6.

FASCICULARIA

BROMELIACEAE

Genus of a single species of stemless or short-stemmed, evergreen, xerophytic, terrestrial or epiphytic perennials (bromeliads) from coastal and central areas, to 1,300ft (400m) high, in Chile. They bear linear, widely spreading leaves in dense rosettes forming distinct central cups. An inflorescence appears in the center of each rosette, in summer; it has a very short scape and a spherical, corymb-like flowerhead of tubular blue flowers, and is followed by ovoid, scaly fruits. They are attractive plants for a desert garden, rock garden, or raised bed, and may also be grown at the base of a warm, sunny wall, or in containers. Where temperatures drop below 36–45°F (2–7°C), grow in a cool greenhouse.

• **CULTIVATION** Under glass, grow in terrestrial bromeliad potting mix in full light with good ventilation. In growth, water moderately and apply a nitrogen-based fertilizer monthly; water sparingly in winter. Outdoors, grow in poor, sharply drained soil in full sun. Protect from winter moisture. See also p.47.

• **PROPAGATION** Sow seed at 81°F (27°C) in winter or spring. Divide offsets in spring or summer.

• **PESTS AND DISEASES** Susceptible to aphids while flowering.

F. andina see *F. bicolor.*

F. bicolor, syn. *F. andina.* Rosetted, terrestrial bromeliad with slender, spiny-toothed, rigid, mid- to deep green leaves, 20in (50cm) long, brown-

Fascicularia pitcairniifolia

scaly beneath, the innermost leaves bright crimson at flowering. In summer, each mature rosette bears an inflorescence with dense corymbs of pale blue flowers, 1½in (4cm) long, surrounded by ivory-white bracts. ↕ to 18in (45cm), ↔ 24in (60cm). Chile. ❀ (min. 36°F/2°C)
F. pitcairniifolia ▣ Rosetted, terrestrial bromeliad with glaucous mid-green leaves, to 3ft (1m) long, edged with short, brown, spreading spines. Leaves become hairless as the plant matures, with white-scaly undersides, and conspicuous sheaths grayish white above, sometimes brown-scaly beneath. In summer at flowering time, the inner rosette leaves turn bright red, forming a collar around the inflorescence of blue or bright violet flowers, 1½–2½in (4–6cm long. ↕↔ to 3ft (1m). Chile. ❀ (min. 45°F/7°C)

x FATSHEDERA

ARALIACEAE

Bigeneric hybrid genus of one loose, spreading, evergreen shrub, derived from *Fatsia* and *Hedera*, grown mainly for its foliage. The leaves are palmately 5- or 7-lobed, dark, lustrous green, and 4–10in (10–25cm) long. Umbel-like panicles of small, greenish white flowers are borne in autumn. Tolerant of coastal exposure, atmospheric pollution, shade, and a wide range of soils, x *F. lizei* is suitable for a shrub border, a cool conservatory, or as a houseplant. It can also be trained against a wall or pillar. A good substitute for *Fatsia japonica*, which requires more space and has a less tidy habit. Does not self-cling, but will climb if secured to supporting trellises.
• **CULTIVATION** Outdoors, grow in fertile, moist but well-drained soil in full sun or partial shade. Under glass, grow in soil-based potting mix; most light conditions are acceptable, but variegated cultivars need protection from very strong sunlight. During growth, water moderately and apply

x *Fatshedera lizei*

a balanced liquid fertilizer monthly. Water sparingly in winter. Support container-grown specimens. Pinch young shoots to promote bushiness. Pruning group 1; may need restrictive pruning under glass.
• **PROPAGATION** Root greenwood cuttings in early summer with bottom heat, or heel cuttings at any time of year.
• **PESTS AND DISEASES** Susceptible to fungal and bacterial leaf spots, as well as spider mites, mealybugs, scale insects, and whiteflies.

x *F. lizei* ▣ (Aralia ivy, Botanical wonder, Tree-ivy). Spreading, loosely branched, evergreen shrub with rust-hairy young growth. The palmate, leathery, dark green leaves are divided into 5, sometimes 7 lobes, deeply cut a third to halfway to the base. In autumn, produces umbel-like panicles of sterile, greenish white flowers, to ½in (1.5cm) across. ↕ 4–6ft (1.2–2m) or more, ↔ 10ft (3m). Garden origin. Zone 7b. **'Anna Mikkels'**, syn. 'Lemon and Lime', bears yellow-variegated leaves. **'Lemon and Lime'** see 'Anna Mikkels'. **'Pia'** has very wavy leaves. **'Variegata'** has leaves that are narrowly margined creamy white.

FATSIA

ARALIACEAE

Genus of 2 or 3 species of evergreen shrubs or small trees from E. Asia. They have large, leathery, palmately 7- to 11-lobed leaves, produced mainly at the branch tips, and compound umbels, to 12in (30cm) or more across, of small, creamy white flowers borne in autumn, followed by clusters of usually spherical black fruits. *F. japonica*, the most widely grown species, occurs wild in coastal woodland in Japan and South Korea. It is tolerant of coastal exposure and atmospheric pollution. Valued for its foliage, architectural habit, and late display of flowers in midautumn, *F. japonica* is ideal in a shaded, sheltered courtyard, in a shrub border, or as a container plant in a cool conservatory or greenhouse.
• **CULTIVATION** Outdoors, grow in fertile, moist but well-drained soil in full sun or light, dappled shade, with shelter from cold, drying winds. Variegated cultivars need partial shade. Under glass, grow in soil-based potting mix in bright filtered light. During growth, water moderately and apply a balanced liquid fertilizer monthly. Water sparingly in winter. Pruning group 9.
• **PROPAGATION** Sow seed at 59–70°F (15–21°C) in autumn or spring. Take greenwood cuttings in early or midsummer. Air layer in spring or late summer.
• **PESTS AND DISEASES** Susceptible to fungal and bacterial leaf spots, as well as spider mites, mealybugs, scale insects, and whiteflies.

F. japonica ▣ syn. *Aralia japonica*, *A. sieboldii* (Japanese aralia, Japanese fatsia). Spreading, suckering, rounded, evergreen shrub with thick stems bearing hairless, 7- to 11-lobed, usually toothed, dark green leaves, 6–16in (15–40cm) long. In autumn, 5-petaled, creamy white flowers, ¼in (6mm) across, are produced in branching,

Fatsia japonica

long-stalked umbels, 1–1½in (2.5–4cm) across, forming large compound umbels, followed by small, spherical black fruit. ↕↔ 5–12ft (1.5–4m). South Korea, Japan. Zone 7b. **'Aurea'** is slow-growing, with gold-variegated leaves. **'Marginata'** has deeply lobed, white-margined, gray-green leaves. **'Moseri'** has a compact habit, but with slightly larger leaves. **'Variegata'** bears leaves that are broadly margined with cream at the tips of the lobes.
F. papyrifer see *Tetrapanax papyrifera.*

FAUCARIA

Tiger jaws

AIZOACEAE

Genus of over 30 species of clump-forming, sometimes fleshy-rooted, almost stemless perennial succulents from semi-desert areas in South Africa. The fleshy, spotted leaves are borne 4–8 on each shoot. The leaves, with thick, soft, marginal teeth, often resemble gaping jaws. The large, daisy-like, pink, yellow, or white flowers open in the afternoon from late summer to midautumn. Grow as houseplants or in a temperate greenhouse. In areas where temperatures

Faucaria tigrina

rarely drop below 45°F (7°C), grow in a raised or scree bed, or in a desert garden.
• **CULTIVATION** Under glass, grow in standard cactus potting mix in full light. During growth, water moderately and apply a low-nitrogen fertilizer monthly. Water sparingly in winter. Outdoors, grow in poor soil, with added grit and leaf mold, in full sun. Protect from excessive rain. See also pp.48–49.
• **PROPAGATION** Sow seed at 50–68°F (10–20°C) in autumn or spring. Root stem cuttings in summer in standard cactus potting mix with added sand.
• **PESTS AND DISEASES** Prone to bacterial and fungal rots.

F. albidens. Clump-forming succulent with triangular, glossy, white-spotted, bright green leaves, 1¼in (3cm) long, with white keels and 3–5 pale, pointed teeth. Golden yellow flowers, 1¼–1½in (3–4cm) across, are produced from late summer to autumn. ↕ 3in (8cm), ↔ 8in (20cm). South Africa (Eastern Cape). ❀ (min. 45°F/7°C)
F. felina. Clump-forming succulent with elongated diamond-shaped or 3-angled, long-pointed, white-spotted leaves, 1½–2in (4–5cm) long, which later turn red. Leaves have slender white keels and 3–5 pointed, recurved, fleshy, marginal teeth. Golden yellow flowers, to 2in (5cm) across, open in autumn. ↕ 3in (8cm), ↔ 8in (20cm). South Africa (Eastern Cape, Western Cape). ❀ (min. 45°F/7°C)
F. tigrina ▣ Clump-forming succulent with ovate-diamond-shaped, pointed, grayish green leaves, 1¼–2in (3–5cm) long, with very rounded, white-spotted undersides and up to 10 recurved, hairy-tipped, marginal teeth. Golden yellow, sometimes red-budded flowers, 2in (5cm) across, are borne in autumn. ↕ 4in (10cm), ↔ 8in (20cm). South Africa (Eastern Cape). ❀ (min. 45°F/7°C)

▷ ***Feijoa*** see *Acca*

F

FELICIA *syn.* AGATHAEA

Blue daisy

ASTERACEAE

Genus of about 80 species of annuals, perennials, evergreen subshrubs, and (rarely) shrubs found in open, sunny habitats in the Arabian Peninsula, and tropical and southern Africa. They have alternate or opposite, linear to ovate or obovate leaves, occasionally in basal rosettes. They are grown for their mass of daisy-like, mainly blue flowerheads with yellow disk florets, often borne over long periods in summer. The annuals, and those treated as annuals, are suitable for bedding and containers; the wind-resistant *F. bergeriana* is especially good for a windowbox or balcony. Grow low-growing perennials in a rock garden or raised bed, or at the base of a warm, sunny wall. Blue daisies are attractive container plants for a conservatory or temperate greenhouse.

• **CULTIVATION** Under glass, grow in soil-based potting mix in full light, with low humidity and good ventilation. During growth, water moderately and apply a balanced liquid fertilizer monthly. Water sparingly in winter. Outdoors, grow in poor to moderately fertile, well-drained soil in full sun. Pinch back young shoots a few times to encourage bushiness.

• **PROPAGATION** Sow seed of annuals at 50–64°F (10–18°C) in spring. Root stem-tip cuttings of tender species in late summer and overwinter under glass.

• **PESTS AND DISEASES** Gray mold and root rot can be problems. Aphids and spider mites occur under glass.

F. amelloides, syn. *Aster amelloides, A. capensis, A. coelestis* (Blue daisy). Rounded, bushy subshrub, often grown as an annual, with ovate to obovate, deep green leaves, to 1¼in (3cm) long. Light to deep blue flowerheads, ¾–2in (2–5cm) across, are produced, from summer to autumn. ↕↔ 12–24in (30–60cm). South Africa. ❄ (min. 37–41°F/3–5°C). **'Astrid Thomas'** is more compact than the species; ↕ 10in (25cm), ↔ 10in (25cm). **'Read's Blue'** is compact, with blue flowerheads. **'Read's White'** ■ is compact, with white flowerheads. **'Santa Anita'** ■ bears large, rich blue flowerheads with bright yellow centers. ↕↔ 5ft (1.5m). **'Santa Anita Variegated'** has white-marked leaves.

Felicia amelloides 'Read's White'

Felicia amelloides 'Santa Anita'

F. amoena, syn. *Aster pappei, F. pappei.* Bushy annual or short-lived perennial with linear to elliptic, downy leaves, 1¼in (3cm) long. Solitary, bright blue flowerheads, 1½in (4cm) across, are produced from summer to early autumn. ↕↔ 12–20in (30–50cm). South Africa. ❄ (min. 37–41°F/3–5°C). **'Variegata'** ■ has cream-splashed leaves.

F. bergeriana ■ (Kingfisher daisy). Mat-forming annual with lance-shaped, sometimes toothed, softly hairy, gray-green leaves, to 1½in (4cm) long. Abundant solitary, brilliant clear blue flowerheads, to 1¼in (3cm) across, with yellow centers, are produced in summer. ↕↔ to 10in (25cm). South Africa.

F. heterophylla. Mat-forming annual with inversely lance-shaped, sometimes toothed, gray-green leaves, to 2in (5cm) long. Solitary blue flowerheads, to ¾in (2cm) across, are produced in summer. ↕↔ 20in (50cm). South Africa. **'Snowmass'** bears white flowerheads. **'The Blues'** has pale blue flowerheads; ↕ to 8in (20cm). **'The Rose'** has pink flowerheads.

F. natalensis see *F. rosulata.*

F. pappei see *F. amoena.*

Felicia amoena 'Variegata'

Felicia bergeriana

F. rosulata, syn. *Aster natalensis, F. natalensis.* Rhizomatous, rosette-forming perennial with elliptic to obovate, hairy, dark green basal leaves, 3–4in (7–10cm) long, and smaller, lance-shaped stem leaves. Solitary, mid-blue flowerheads, to 1¼in (3cm) across, with golden yellow disk florets, are produced in summer. ↕ 8in (20cm), ↔ 12in (30cm). South Africa. ❄ (min. 35°F/2°C)

FENESTRARIA

AIZOACEAE

Genus of 1 or 2 species of variable, very dwarf, stemless, cushion-forming, perennial succulents from semi-desert areas of Namibia. They are grown for their daisy-like, bright yellowish orange or white flowers and club-shaped, erect, opposite, hairless, and fleshy leaves, with transparent "windows" in the flattened tips. Grow as a groundcover in an indoor garden or cool greenhouse. Where temperatures remain above 45°F (7°C), grow in a raised bed or desert garden.

• **CULTIVATION** Under glass, grow in standard cactus potting mix in full light with low humidity; ventilate well. During growth, water moderately and apply a low-nitrogen liquid fertilizer monthly. Keep dry in winter. Outdoors, grow in poor, dry, sharply drained soil, with added grit and leaf mold, in full sun, with shelter from excessive rain. They resent root disturbance. See also pp.48–49.

• **PROPAGATION** Sow seed at 59–70°F (15–21°C) in autumn or spring. Separate offsets in spring or summer.

• **PESTS AND DISEASES** Very prone to rot.

F. aurantiaca ■ Succulent that forms dense cushions of club-shaped, erect leaves, ¾–1¼in (2–3cm) long, with "windows" in their slightly flattened tips. Golden yellow flowers, 1¼–3in (3–8cm) across, are produced on stalks 1½–2in (4–5cm) long, from late summer to autumn. ↕ 2in (5cm), ↔ 12in (30cm). Namibia. ❄ (min. 45°F/7°C). **f. *rhopalophylla***, syn. *F. rhopalophylla*, forms less dense cushions and has pure white flowers, to 1¼in (3cm) across; ↔ to 8in (20cm). ❄ (min. 55°F/13°C)

F. rhopalophylla see *F. aurantiaca* f. *rhopalophylla.*

Fenestraria aurantiaca

FEROCACTUS

CACTACEAE

Genus of about 30 species of flattened, spherical to columnar cacti from lowlands and mountainous areas of S. and S.W. US, Mexico, and Guatemala. They are usually solitary but some species form thick clumps. The large, prominent ribs have spiny areoles, some hooked. Large, funnel- or bell-shaped flowers are borne from near the crown in summer, followed by ovoid, fleshy fruits. Only a few *Ferocactus* species flower when young; they are primarily grown for their prominent stems and fierce, often colorful spines. Grow in a desert garden. Where temperatures fall below 50°F (10°C), grow in a temperate greenhouse, although many are hardy to 20°F (-7°C) when established in favorable areas.

• **CULTIVATION** Under glass, grow in standard cactus potting mix with more than 50% grit, in full light with low humidity. During growth, water freely and apply a balanced liquid fertilizer monthly. Keep dry in winter. Mist on warm days in midwinter; keep root zone dry. Outdoors, grow in poor, sharply drained soil in full sun. Protect from excessive rain. See also pp.48–49.

• **PROPAGATION** Sow seed at 50–68°F (10–20°C) in spring.

• **PESTS AND DISEASES** Vulnerable to mealybugs, cactus virus, and a number of fungal rots.

***F. acanthodes* of gardens** see *F. cylindraceus.*

F. bicolor see *Thelocactus bicolor.*

F. chrysacanthus. Solitary cactus with a spherical to cylindrical, dark green stem, and 13–22 warty ribs and areoles (4–6 or more white radials and 4–10 flattened and twisted, yellow or reddish yellow centrals). Bell-shaped, yellow or reddish yellow to orange flowers, 1¾in (4.5cm) long, with outer segments striped red-brown or brownish pink, are borne in summer. ↕ to 3ft (1m), ↔ 16in (40cm). Mexico (Baja California). ❄ (min. 50°F/10°C)

F. crassihamatus see *Sclerocactus uncinatus* var. *crassihamatus.*

F. cylindraceus ■ syn. *F. acanthodes* of gardens. Solitary, sometimes offsetting cactus with an ovoid then cylindrical, glaucous green stem with 13–27 warty ribs and red, orange, or buff-yellow

Ferocactus cylindraceus

spines (9–13 or more radials and 4–7 longer, flat, sometimes hooked, often recurved centrals). Produces bell-shaped, yellow or orange flowers, 1¼–2½in (3–6cm) long, in summer. ↕ 10ft (3m), ↔ 32in (80cm). S.W. US, N.W. Mexico. ❄ (min. 50°F/10°C)
F. fordii. Solitary cactus with a slightly depressed-spherical, grayish green stem and about 21 warty ribs and white spines (about 15 spreading, paler radials and 4–7 flattened, hooked or twisted, red or gray centrals). Funnel-shaped, deep pink to purple flowers, to 1½in (4cm) long, are borne in summer. ↕↔ 16in (40cm). Mexico (Baja California). ❄ (min. 50°F/10°C)
F. hamatacanthus ■ syn. *Hamatocactus hamatacanthus.* Solitary or clustering cactus with a spherical to cylindrical, deep green stem, 13–18 prominent, warty ribs, and brownish red spines (6–20 radials and 4–8 centrals). Bears funnel-shaped yellow flowers, 2½–4in (6–10cm) long, with red throats, in summer. ↕ 24in (60cm), ↔ to 16in (40cm). Texas, N. and N.E. Mexico. ❄ (min. 50°F/10°C)
F. latispinus (Devil's tongue). Usually solitary, depressed-spherical cactus, with 15–23 acute, sometimes spiralled, grayish green ribs, notched with large areoles (6–15 yellow radial spines and 4 red centrals, the lowest flattened and hooked). Bell-shaped, white, red, purple, or yellow flowers, 1½in (4cm) long, develop in summer. ↕ 4–16in (10–40cm), ↔ to 16in (40cm). Central S. Mexico. ❄ (min. 50°F/10°C)
F. setispinus see *Thelocactus setispinus.*
F. wislizenii (Fishhook cactus). Solitary cactus with a spherical then cylindrical, dark green to grayish green stem, with 15–25 ribs and areoles (12–30 grayish yellow radial spines and up to 8 longer, flattened, hooked, yellow, brown, or gray centrals with curved, reddish brown tips). Bell-shaped, yellow, orange, or red flowers, 2–3in (5–8cm) long, with green outer segments, are borne in summer. ↕ 5ft (1.5m), ↔ to 32in (80cm). S.W. US, N.W. Mexico. ❄ (min. 50°F/10°C)

Ferocactus hamatacanthus

FERRARIA

IRIDACEAE

Genus of 10 species of cormous perennials from dry, sandy soils, sometimes near the coast, in tropical Africa and South Africa. They are grown for their few-flowered cymes of unusual, malodorous, patterned, short-lived flowers, 1½–2½in (4–6cm) across, pollinated by flies. The flowers are iris-like with crisped petals, borne in succession on branched stems in late winter and early spring. The basal leaves are lance-shaped; the 2-ranked stem leaves are ovate-lance-shaped. Where not hardy, grow in a temperate greenhouse. Elsewhere, use in a rock garden or raised bed, or against a sunny wall.
• **CULTIVATION** Under glass, plant directly into a greenhouse border or in deep containers of soil-based potting mix, with added grit, in full light. In winter, during growth, water moderately and apply a balanced liquid fertilizer monthly. Keep dry while dormant in summer. Outdoors, plant 6in (15cm) deep in moderately fertile, well-drained soil in autumn.
• **PROPAGATION** Sow seed in summer or autumn at 43–54°F (6–12°C). Separate offsets from dormant parent corms.
• **PESTS AND DISEASES** Infrequent.

F. crispa, syn. *F. undulata.* Cormous perennial with linear-lance-shaped, stem-clasping leaves, 6–12in (15–30cm) long, forming progressively smaller sheaths around the stem. In spring, bears wavy-petaled, green, brown, or yellowish brown, upward-facing flowers, 1in (2.5cm) across, with 3 outer petals and 3 smaller inner petals, lined and spotted yellow and brown. ↕ 8–16in (20–40cm), PD6in (15cm). South Africa. ❄ (min. 45°F/7°C)
F. undulata see *F. crispa.*

FERULA

Giant fennel

APIACEAE

Genus of 170 species of robust, tap-rooted, usually hairless, aromatic, herbaceous perennials found in rough, grassy places, dry slopes, and gravelly roadsides from the Mediterranean to C. Asia. They bear branching or simple stems, with 2- to 5-pinnate, usually basal, light green leaves, to 32in (80cm) long, the ultimate segments linear to obovate. Usually forming a mound of finely divided leaves, they are effective foliage plants when mature. Giant fennels (which should not be confused with the edible fennels, *Foeniculum*) bear white, greenish white, yellow, or purple flowers in terminal, lateral, compound umbels, to 6in (15cm) across, although they may take several years to flower and often die after seeding. Grow at the back of a border or as a specimen plant in a sunny, open site in a wild garden.
• **CULTIVATION** Grow in fertile, well-drained soil in full sun. To enhance foliage, remove flowering stems as soon as they show, or immediately after blooming if seed is not desired. Protect with a dry mulch in winter.
• **PROPAGATION** Sow seed as soon as ripe in containers in a cold frame. Prick out seedlings into deep containers to allow taproot development.
• **PESTS AND DISEASES** Susceptible to aphids, slugs, and mildew.

F. communis ■ Robust perennial with 3- or 4-pinnate leaves, 10–18in (25–45cm) long, subdivided into narrow, linear segments. After a few years, produces thick, ridged, branching stems that bear groups of hemispherical, many-branched umbels, 3in (8cm) across, of small, 5-petaled yellow flowers, in early and midsummer. May die after setting seed. ↕ to 15ft (5m), usually 6–10ft (2–3m), ↔ 24in (60cm). Mediterranean. Zone 7.
F. 'Giant Bronze' see *Foeniculum vulgare* 'Giant Bronze'.

Ferula communis

FESTUCA

Fescue

POACEAE

Genus of 300–400 species of deciduous or evergreen, rhizomatous, often tufted, perennial grasses widely distributed in grassland, woodland edges, and stream margins throughout temperate zones. Many are cultivated as turf or pasture grasses. A few ornamental species have attractive inflorescences, but most are grown for their foliage, which is often blue-green or blue-gray. The 5- to 9-veined, lance-shaped leaves are flat, folded, or rolled. Dense or loose, branched panicles of flattened spikelets, with glaucous or brownish green inflorescences, are borne from spring to summer. Grow fescues singly or in groups in a border or rock garden to provide foliage contrast with alpines.
• **CULTIVATION** Grow in poor to moderately fertile, dry, well-drained soil in full sun. *F. eskia* will not tolerate alkaline soils. Divide and replant every 2 or 3 years to maintain foliage color.
• **PROPAGATION** Sow seed from autumn to spring in containers in a cold frame. Divide in spring.
• **PESTS AND DISEASES** Ergot, powdery mildew, rust, smut, brown patch, *Helminthosporium* leaf spot, net blotch, pink snow mold, anthracnose, eye spot, and summer blight occur.

F. amethystina (Large blue fescue, Tufted fescue). Densely tufted, tussock-forming, evergreen, perennial grass with soft, narrowly linear, gray-green leaves, to 10in (25cm) long, the lower halves inrolled and furrowed. In late spring and early summer, bears lax, flexuous, zigzag panicles, 4–8in (10–20cm) long, with paired branches bearing spikelets of 3–7 violet-tinted, greenish to purple or violet flowers. ↕ to 18in (45cm), ↔ 10in (25cm). C. and E. Europe. Zone 4. **'Aprilgrün'** has olive-green leaves and purple-tinted flowers. **'Bronzeglanz'** has bronze-tinted leaves.
F. elatior (Tall fescue). Clump-forming (tufted), fine-bladed cool-season grass with broad, loose, deep-green spikelets. Mow to 1½–2in (4–5cm). Europe, worldwide. Zone 6.
F. eskia, syn. *F. scoparia.* Compact, rhizomatous, mound- or cushion-forming, evergreen, perennial grass with stiff, narrowly linear, inrolled, rich green leaves, to 8in (20cm) long. In early and midsummer, bears open, pendent, ovoid panicles, to 4in (10cm) long, with spikelets tinted green, orange, or yellow. ↕ to 6in (15cm), ↔ 10in (25cm). Pyrenees. Zone 5b.
F. glacialis (Ice fescue). Densely tufted, hummock-forming, evergreen, perennial grass with erect, narrowly linear, inrolled, gray- to blue-green leaves, to

5in (13cm) long. In mid- and late summer, bears dense, narrow, ovoid, branched panicles, to 1in (2.5cm) long, with spikelets of 3–5 violet flowers. ↕↔ to 4in (10cm). France, Spain, Pyrenees, Alps. Zone 5b.
F. glauca (Blue fescue, Gray fescue). Densely tufted, evergreen, perennial grass with erect or arching, narrowly linear, inrolled, 9-ribbed, smooth, blue-green leaves, 3–8in (7–20cm) long. In early and midsummer, bears dense, obovate, shortly branched panicles, to 4in (10cm) long, with spikelets of 4–7 violet-flushed, blue-green flowers. ↕ to 12in (30cm), ↔ 10in (25cm). N. and S. temperate regions. Zone 3b. **'Blaufink'** (Bluefinch fescue) is compact and fine-textured; ↕ 6–8in (15–20cm). **'Blaufuchs'** ▣ syn. 'Blue Fox', has bright blue leaves. **'Daemling'** (Tom Thumb fescue) is compact, with silver-blue young growth, aging to mid-green. **'Elijah Blue'** has powder-blue leaves; ↕ 8in (20cm). **'Harz'** has purple-tipped, blue-green or dark olive-green leaves. **'Seeigel'**, syn. 'Sea Urchin', has lax, hair-fine, spiky, blue-green leaves in a tight bun, to 6in (15cm) across. **'Soehrenwald'** (Soehrenwald fescue) has olive-green leaves, aging to blue-green; ↕ 8–12in (20–30cm). **'Solling'** (Solling fescue) has blue-gray leaves, turning red-brown in autumn and winter.
F. mairei (Maire's fescue, Atlas fescue, Moroccan fescue). Densely tufted, evergreen, perennial grass with flat, narrowly linear, glossy, pale gray-green leaves, 24–36in (60–90cm) long. In early summer, bears dense, slender, sparsely branched panicles, 2–4in (5–10cm) long, with spikelets of gray-green flowers. Best used for erosion control on a slope or in a highway planting. ↕ 24–36in (60–90cm), ↔ 36in (90cm). Morocco. Zone 6.
F. ovina (Sheep fescue). Clump-forming (tufted) grass with fine blue-green leaves, sometimes used in lawns. ↕ 24in (60cm), ↔ 16in (40cm). Widespread in northern temperate zones. Zone 2.
F. rubra (Red fescue). Fine-textured, low-maintenance grass, with narrow, dark green or glaucous blades, tinged with purple. Produces 3–10 spikelets. Creates a lush effect, on banks and slopes. ↕ 10in (25cm). N. America. Zone 2.
F. rubra commutata (Chewing fescue). Creeping, bunch-type grass, lacking rhizomes. Grows aggressively; a good choice for a low-maintenance turf, in shaded, low-traffic areas of parks and lawns. Mow to 1½–2½in (4–6cm). N.E. and N.W. US, Canada. Zone 2.
F. scoparia see *F. eskia.*
F. valesiaca. Variable, densely tufted, evergreen, sometimes semi-evergreen, perennial grass with narrowly linear, hair-like, flattened, bluish green leaves, 10in (25cm) or more long. In mid- and late summer, bears dense, oblong or ovate-oblong panicles, 2–4in (5–10cm) long, with spikelets of 3–8 white-frosted, pale green flowers, or purple, violet-tinted flowers. ↕ 20in (50cm), ↔ 18in (45cm). C. Europe. Zone 6. **'Silbersee'**, syn. 'Silver Sea', is much more compact, with pale silvery blue leaves; ↕ to 8in (20cm), ↔ 6in (15cm).

Festuca glauca 'Blaufuchs'

FIBIGIA

BRASSICACEAE

Genus of 14 species of perennials growing in warm, dry crevices in rocks and cliffs from Europe to Afghanistan. They are grown for their alternate, simple, gray-, white-, or silver-hairy leaves. Pale yellow or occasionally violet flowers are borne in terminal racemes, followed by compressed, ellipsoid to oblong fruits. The seed pods are attractive in dried arrangements. Useful in a rock garden, a dry border, or a wall planting. Where not hardy, grow in an alpine house.
• **CULTIVATION** Under glass, grow in sandy, soil-based potting mix in full light. Water sparingly when in growth; keep just moist in winter. Outdoors, grow in moderately fertile, sharply drained soil in full sun.
• **PROPAGATION** Sow seed *in situ* as soon as ripe.
• **PESTS AND DISEASES** Infrequent.

F. clypeata. Upright perennial with erect, oblong-lance-shaped, green- or gray-green-woolly leaves, to 6in (15cm) long. In spring, bears racemes, 4–8in (10–20cm) long, of small, yellow flowers, followed by compressed, oblong-ellipsoid, softly short-hairy fruit, ¼–½in (6–15mm) long. ↕ 8in (20cm), ↔ 6in (15cm). S. Europe to Iran. Zone 6.

FICUS

Fig

MORACEAE

Genus of about 800 species of mainly evergreen trees, shrubs, and woody climbers, usually found in moist forest in tropical and subtropical regions worldwide. Some behave as stranglers, outgrowing the host tree and eventually killing it, often becoming massive, free-standing trees themselves. They are usually grown for their foliage, or for their edible fruits (rarely borne on container-grown plants). The alternate leaves are simple, or shallowly to deeply lobed. Minute, petalless flowers are contained in a hollowed-out, inflated stem tip (receptacle) borne in the leaf axils, which enlarges to form the fig fruit, produced sporadically throughout the year. Where not hardy, grow in a temperate greenhouse or as houseplants. In warmer areas, use as specimen or shade trees; train climbers against a wall or tree. The foliage may cause mild stomach upset if ingested; the sap may irritate skin or aggravate allergies. The foliage of *F. carica* can cause photodermatitis; its sap may irritate the eyes.
• **CULTIVATION** Under glass, grow in soil-based potting mix, with added fine bark chips, in full or filtered light. During growth, water moderately and apply a high-nitrogen fertilizer every 4 weeks. Keep moist in winter. Outdoors, grow in humus-rich, leafy, moist but well-drained soil in full sun or partial shade, with shelter from cold, drying winds. Support figs that have long, lax stems. Mulch annually.
• **PROPAGATION** Sow seed at 59–70°F (15–21°C) in spring. Root semi-ripe cuttings or leaf-bud cuttings with bottom heat in spring or summer. Air layer *F. elastica* in spring or late summer.
• **PESTS AND DISEASES** Mealybugs, scale insects, spider mites, root knot nematodes, and thrips occur under most environmental conditions. Fungal and bacterial leaf spots, crown gall, twig dieback, and Southern blight are common. Indoors, *Phomopsis* dieback causes losses of many *F. benjamina* trees.

F. aspera. Small to medium, deciduous or evergreen tree with shaggy, white-hairy branches. Bears 2-ranked, ovate or oblong-ovate to elliptic, coarsely toothed to scalloped or entire, slightly rough, mid-green leaves, to 12in (30cm) long, with prominent lateral veins, raised beneath. Produces axillary, spherical, softly hairy, yellow to orange figs, to 1in (2.5cm) across, ripening to red. ↕ to 70ft (20m), ↔ to 30ft (10m). Melanesia (Vanuatu). ❄ (min. 45°F/7°C). **'Canonii'** has dark bronze-red leaves, wine-purple or red beneath, with bright red leaf stalks and midribs. Bears scarlet figs. **'Parcellii'** (Clown fig, Mosaic fig) has ivory-white-speckled, dark green leaves, and bears pink to purple figs.
F. benghalensis (Banyan, Indian fig). Evergreen tree with spreading, often horizontal branches supported by prop roots. Bears elliptic to broadly ovate, leathery, deep green leaves, 5–10in (13–25cm) long, flushed bronze when young and with a distinct pattern of pale veins when mature. Spherical red figs, to ¾in (2cm) across, are borne in pairs. ↕ 70–100ft (20–30m), ↔ to 700ft (200m). S. Asia. ❄ (min. 59°F/15°C). **'Krishnae'** has basally cup-shaped leaves.
F. benjamina (Weeping fig). Evergreen tree or large shrub, sometimes a strangler, with slender, arching to pendent stems, and ovate-elliptic, thinly leathery, glossy leaves, dark green above, lighter beneath, 2–5in (5–13cm) long, each tapering to a slender, twisted point. Spherical to oblong figs, ½in (1.5cm) long, produced in pairs, mature from green through pink or orange-red to black. ↕ to 100ft (30m) or more, ↔ to 50ft (15m) or more. S. and S.E. Asia, N. Australia, S.W. Pacific. ❄ (min. 59°F/15°C). **'Variegata'** ▣ has white-splashed leaves.
F. carica (Common fig). Deciduous tree or large shrub with a spreading head, and rounded, 3- or 5-lobed leaves, 4–10in (10–25cm) long, heart-shaped at the bases. Pear-shaped receptacles develop into single fruit, to 4in (10cm) long, green when young, maturing to dark green, purple, or dark brown. ↕ 10ft (3m), ↔ 12ft (4m). W. Asia,

Ficus benjamina 'Variegata'

E. Mediterranean. Zone 6b. Many cultivars have been introduced.
F. deltoidea ▣ (Mistletoe fig). Evergreen shrub or small tree, usually bushy, sometimes epiphytic in the wild, with broadly spoon-shaped to obovate, leathery leaves, 1½–3in (4–8cm) long, bright green above and rust-red to olive-brown beneath. Spherical to ellipsoid figs, to ½in (1.5cm) across, ripening from dull yellow to orange and red, are freely produced in pairs. ↕ 15–22ft (5–7m), ↔ 3–10ft (1–3m). S.E. Asia to Borneo, Philippines (Palawan). ❄ (min. 59°F/15°C). **var. *diversifolia***, syn. *F. diversifolia*, has rounded or shallowly notched leaves; ↕ to 6ft (2m).
F. diversifolia see *F. deltoidea* var. *diversifolia.*
F. elastica (India rubber fig, India rubber tree, Rubber plant). Evergreen, many-branched tree with oblong to elliptic, leathery, glossy, dark green, often red-flushed leaves, 12–18in (30–45cm) long. Oblong yellow figs, to ½in (1.5cm) long, develop in pairs or clusters on mature trees in the open. ↕ 100–200ft (30–60m), ↔ 70–200ft (20–60m). E. Himalayas, Assam, Burma, Malaya, Java. ❄ (min. 59°F/15°C). **'Decora'** has

Ficus deltoidea

Ficus elastica 'Doescheri'

Ficus macrophylla

broadly elliptic leaves, red flushed beneath, with creamy white midribs when mature. **'Doescheri'** ■ produces leaves mottled gray-green, creamy yellow, and white, with pink stalks and midribs. **'Foliis aureo-marginata'** has golden-margined leaves, particularly bright in autumn. **'Rubra'** has maroon-red young leaves, maturing to dark green with red midribs. **'Schrijveriana'** produces broad, streaked leaves of green, gray-green, cream-yellow, and white, with red leaf stalks. **'Variegata'** has pale green leaves with white or yellow margins.

F. lyrata ■ (Banjo fig, Fiddle-leaf fig). Open, evergreen tree with leathery, glossy, fiddle-shaped, dark green leaves, 10–18in (25–45cm) long, irregularly corrugated above. Almost spherical figs, to 1¼in (3cm) or more across, which ripen green with white dots, are produced singly or in pairs only on mature trees in the open. ↕ 70–100ft (20–30m) or more, ↔ 30–70ft (10–20m). Tropical W. and C. Africa. ❀ (min. 59°F/15°C)

F. macrophylla ■ (Australian banyan, Moreton Bay fig). Wide-spreading, evergreen tree with aerial roots (some becoming props). Oblong to elliptic or ovate, leathery leaves, mid-green and hairless above, to 10in (25cm) long, are paler beneath, often with rust-red scales. Ovoid figs, to ¾in (2cm) long, ripening from green to purple with yellow-green flecks, are produced only on mature trees in the open, usually in pairs. ↕ 100–180ft (30–55m), ↔ 70–130ft (20–40m). Queensland, New South Wales. ❀ (min. 45–50°F/7–10°C)

F. microcarpa syn. *F. retusa* of gardens (Curtain fig, Indian laurel, Malay banyan). Wide-spreading evergreen tree with curtains of aerial roots (some root upon touching the soil). Bears narrowly to broadly elliptic to obovate, leathery, dark green leaves, 2½–5in (6–13cm) long. Spherical purple figs, ½in (1.5cm) long, are produced in pairs on mature trees, ripening black. ↕ to 80ft (25m), ↔ to 100ft (30m). Japan (Ryukyu Islands), S. China, S. Malaysia, Australia (Queensland), New Caledonia. ❀ (min. 55°F/13°C). **'Hawaii'** has shiny gray-green and white-splashed leaves.

F. palmeri (Desert fig, Anaba). Small to large spreading tree with white to yellow bark. Broadly ovate-triangular, leathery, softly white-hairy young leaves, 5½–7in (14–18cm) long, mature to glaucous green, with prominent veins. Bears pairs of pear-shaped, white figs, to ½in (1.5cm) across, softly hairy when young, becoming hairless. ↕ to 30ft (10m), ↔ to 90ft (25m). Mexico (Baja California). ❀ (min. 41°F/5°C)

F. pumila ■ syn. *F. repens* (Climbing fig, Creeping fig). Root-clinging, evergreen, perennial climber. The leaves of the climbing shoots are asymmetrically ovate, thinly leathery, dark green, to 2in (5cm) long. At the end of its support, leaves on non-climbing stems are oblong to elliptic or ovate, leathery, dark green and very glossy, to 4in (10cm) long. Pear-shaped, mostly solitary, oblong to cylindrical, densely hairy figs, to 2½in (6cm) long, are green with white dots, ripening purple. ↕ 10–15ft (3–5m) or more. China, Vietnam, Japan. ❀ (min. 41–45°F/5–7°C). **'Minima'** has slender stems and juvenile leaves, ½in (1.5cm) long; ↕ to 6ft (2m). **'Oakleaf'** has oak-like, puckered, young leaves to ½in (1.5cm) long; ↕ to 6ft (2m).

F. racemosa (Cluster fig, Red-wooded fig, Country fig, Gular). Small to medium tree, summer- and winter-deciduous, with wide-spreading branches and ovate to ovate-lance-shaped, leathery, stiff, slightly hairy, mid-green leaves, 6–8in (15–20cm) long, with raised veins beneath and a slightly curving midrib. Produces clusters of rounded, minutely densely hairy, white-flecked, green figs, 1¼–1½in (3–4cm) across, ripening to scarlet. ↕ to 70ft (20m), ↔ to 30ft (10m). S and S.E. Asia, N. Australia. ❀ (min. 59°F/15°C)

F. religiosa (Bo tree, Peepul, Sacred fig). Small tree, or taller strangling climber, with wide-spreading branches, semi- or fully deciduous in monsoon climates, and broadly ovate, glossy, leathery, dark green leaves, 5–7in (12–18cm) long, with unusual tail-like tips. Bears pairs of rounded, flat-topped green figs, to ½in (1.5cm) across, ripening to purple with red dots. ↕↔ 25ft (8m). Himalayas, S.W. China, N. Thailand, Vietnam. ❀ (min. 59°F/15°C)

F. repens see *F. pumila.*

***F. retusa* of gardens** see *F. microcarpa.*

F. rubiginosa (Port Jackson fig). Wide-spreading, evergreen tree, sometimes with aerial roots, a few of which become props. Leaves are oblong to elliptic or ovate, 3–7in (8–18cm) long, rust-hairy when young, then smooth, leathery, dark green above, paler beneath. Bears pairs of spherical figs, to ½in (1.5cm) across, ripening to greenish brown with soft, rust-brown hairs. ↕↔ 50ft (15m). Australia (New South Wales). ❀ (min. 50–55°F/10–13°C)

F. virens (Gray fig, Spotted fig, Java willow). Large, spreading, briefly deciduous tree with aerial roots, heavy limbs, and drooping branches. Produces elliptic to ovate, leathery, wavy-margined, green leaves, to 7in (18cm) long, with scarlet or bronze young foliage and prominent veins. Bears pairs of rounded, finely hairy, green figs, ¼–½in (0.6–1.5cm) across, with scarlet dots. ↕ to 50ft (15m), ↔ to 30ft (10m). India to Solomon Islands and N. Australia. ❀ (min. 59°F/15°C)

F. sycomorus (Egyptian sycamore, Mulberry fig, Sycamore, Sycamore fig). Wide-spreading, deciduous tree with broadly ovate, entire to wavy, rough, prominently veined, dark green leaves, to 6in (15cm) long, paler and slightly softly hairy beneath. Produces spherical to obovoid, velvety-woolly, yellow to red figs, to 1½in (4cm) across. ↕ to 90ft (25m), ↔ 40–70ft (12–20m). Africa, Arabian peninsula. ❀ (min. 45°F/7°C)

Ficus lyrata

Ficus pumila

Filipendula palmata 'Rubra'

F

FILIPENDULA

ROSACEAE

Genus of 10 or more species of rhizomatous perennials from damp habitats, such as streamsides and wet ditches, in N. temperate regions, except *F. vulgaris*, which thrives on dry, alkaline grassland. The pinnate, alternate leaves have shallowly or palmately lobed terminal leaflets and smaller lateral leaflets, hairless or softly hairy beneath. Plumes of tiny, fluffy, red, pink, or white flowers are borne from late spring to late summer, mainly in dense, cyme-like corymbs, on single or branched stems well above the foliage. Most are suitable for a moist border or waterside position, or for naturalizing in a damp meadow or woodland garden. Grow *F. vulgaris* in a sunny site in a border.

• **CULTIVATION** Grow all but *F. vulgaris* in moderately fertile, leafy, moist but well-drained soil in full sun or partial shade. *F. rubra* and *F. ulmaria* will also thrive in boggy conditions. Gold-leaved forms color best in partial shade. Grow *F. vulgaris* in drier, alkaline soil in full sun. Mulch in spring.

Filipendula purpurea

Filipendula purpurea f. *albiflora*

• **PROPAGATION** Sow seed in autumn in containers in a cold frame, or in spring at 50–55°F (10–13°C). Divide in autumn or spring. Take root cuttings and place horizontally in seed trays, from late winter to early spring.

• **PESTS AND DISEASES** Powdery mildew, rust, and leaf spot can occur.

F. hexapetala see *F. vulgaris*.

F. kamtschatica. Clump-forming perennial with pinnate, toothed leaves, 6–18in (15–45cm) long, softly hairy beneath. The 3- to 5-lobed terminal leaflets, 6–10in (15–25cm) across, are rounded to obovate, the lateral ones smaller or absent. From midsummer to early autumn, bears corymbs, to 10in (25cm) across, of fragrant, white or pale pink flowers, ¼–⅜in (6–8mm) across, on branched stems. ↕6–10ft (2–3m), ↔ 4ft (1.2m). Russia (Kamchatka), China (Manchuria), Japan. Zone 4.

F. palmata, syn. *Spiraea palmata* (Siberian meadowsweet). Clump-forming perennial with pinnate, sometimes palmate leaves, to 12in (30cm) long, densely white-woolly beneath. The small, toothed lateral leaflets are 2- to 5-lobed, the terminal ones rounded to obovate, 7- to 9-lobed, and 2–4in (5–10cm) across. In midsummer, produces pale to deep pink flowers in feathery corymbs, to 8in (20cm) across, on simple or branching stems. ↕4ft (1.2m), ↔ 24in (60cm). Russia (Kamchatka, Siberia), Mongolia, China, Japan. Zone 3. **f. *alba*** has white flowers. **'Digitata Nana'** see 'Nana'. **'Elegantissima'**, syn. 'Elegans', has deep rose-pink flowers and very small, erect, lance-shaped, bronze-red seed heads; ↕3ft (1m). **'Nana'**, syn. 'Digitata Nana', has fern-like leaves; deep rose-pink flowers become paler as they age; ↕24in (60cm). **'Rubra'** ■ has red-pink flowers.

Filipendula rubra 'Venusta'

F. purpurea ■ (Japanese meadowsweet). Clump-forming perennial bearing pinnate, toothed leaves, with irregularly 5- to 7-lobed, rounded to obovate terminal leaflets, to 10in (25cm) across, and few, if any, small lateral leaflets. In mid- and late summer, branching, crimson-purple stems bear dense corymbs, 2in (5cm) across, of carmine-red flowers, becoming paler as they age. ↕4ft (1.2m), ↔ 24in (60cm). Japan. Zone 3b. **f. *albiflora*** ■ syn. f. *alba*, has white flowers. **'Purpurascens'** has purple-tinted leaves.

F. rubra (Queen of the prairie). Spreading perennial forming large clumps in moist soil. Produces pinnate, irregularly cut leaves, with toothed, 3-lobed, terminal leaflets, to 8in (20cm) across. In early and midsummer, branching red stems bear crowded corymbs, to 6in (15cm) across, of fragrant, deep peach-pink flowers. ↕6–8ft (1.8–2.5m), ↔ 4ft (1.2m). E. US. Zone 3. **'Magnifica'** see 'Venusta'. **'Venusta'** ■ syn. 'Magnifica', 'Venusta Magnifica', has deep rose-pink flowers, becoming paler pink as they age.

F. ulmaria, syn. *Spiraea ulmaria* (Meadowsweet, Queen of the meadow). Clump-forming perennial with leafy stems bearing irregularly pinnate, strongly veined, inversely lance-shaped leaves, white-downy beneath. The terminal leaflets are 2–4in (5–10cm) across. In summer, branching stems bear dense corymbs, to 10in (25cm) across, of creamy white flowers. ↕24–36in (60–90cm), ↔ 24in (60cm). Europe, W. Asia. Zone 3b. **'Aurea'** has warm yellow, then creamy yellow leaves in spring, later becoming pale green. **'Flore Pleno'** has double flowers. **'Variegata'** has leaves striped and marked yellow.

F. vulgaris, syn. *F. hexapetala* (Dropwort). Rosette-forming perennial with swollen rhizomes and pinnate, fern-like, finely divided, toothed, hairless, dark green leaves, each leaflet ¾in (2cm) long. In early and midsummer, slender, branching stems bear loose corymbs, to 6in (15cm) across, of white, often red-tinged flowers. ↕24in (60cm), ↔ 18in (45cm). Europe, N. and C. Asia. Zone 4. **'Flore Pleno'** see 'Multiplex'. **'Multiplex'**, syn. 'Flore Pleno', 'Plena', has bronze buds and double, sometimes pendent, creamy white flowers. **'Plena'** see 'Multiplex'. **'Rosea'** has pink flowers.

FIRMIANA

STERCULIACEAE

Genus of 9 species of deciduous trees and shrubs found in woodland in E. Africa, and E. and S.E. Asia, grown for their handsome foliage. The leaves are alternate, and entire or palmately lobed, and the petalless flowers are unisexual, with bell-shaped, yellow or yellow-green calyces, borne in terminal panicles or racemes. Grow in a woodland garden or as ornamental shade trees. In areas where temperatures fall below 32°F (0°C), give extensive winter protection or overwinter in a cool greenhouse.

Firmiana simplex

• **CULTIVATION** Under glass, grow in soil-based potting mix in full light with shade from the hottest sun, or in bright filtered light. During growth, water freely and apply a balanced liquid fertilizer monthly. Keep just moist in winter. Outdoors, grow in moist but well-drained, moderately fertile soil in full sun or partial shade, sheltered from cold, drying winds. Pruning group 1; needs restrictive pruning under glass.

• **PROPAGATION** Sow seed at 50–55°F (10–13°C) as soon as ripe.

• **PESTS AND DISEASES** Infrequent.

F. platanifolia see *F. simplex*.

F. simplex ■ syn. *F. platanifolia*, *Sterculia platanifolia* (Chinese parasol tree). Rounded tree with smooth green bark and alternate, deeply 3- to 7-lobed, dark green leaves, 10–18in (25–45cm) long, turning yellow in autumn. Bears terminal panicles, 8–12in (20–30cm) long, of small, yellow-green flowers, in summer. In autumn, bears papery fruit, which split open when ripe, revealing the seeds. ↕50ft (15m), ↔ 30ft (10m). Vietnam to Japan (Ryukyu Islands). Zone 7b.

FITTONIA

Nerve plant, Painted net leaf

ACANTHACEAE

Genus of 2 species of evergreen perennials, with freely rooting, mat-forming stems, from tropical rainforest in South America, mainly Peru. The leaves are opposite, with short stems and colorful veins. Thin spikes of insignificant white to reddish white

Fittonia verschaffeltii

Fittonia verschaffeltii var. *argyroneura*

flowers are borne rarely and irregularly. Where temperatures drop below 59°F (15°C), grow in a terrarium or hanging basket indoors or in a warm greenhouse. In tropical or subtropical areas, grow as a groundcover in semi-shaded sites.
• **CULTIVATION** Under glass, grow in soilless potting mix in shallow containers, in indirect light with high humidity. Water moderately, keeping the soil mix just moist; if kept too wet, stem rotting occurs. During growth, apply a balanced liquid fertilizer every 3–4 weeks. Outdoors, grow in humus-rich to leafy, moist but well-drained soil in partial shade.
• **PROPAGATION** Take tip cuttings with 3 or 4 pairs of leaves in spring, or layer stems in spring or summer.
• **PESTS AND DISEASES** Susceptible to bacterial and fungal leaf spots and root rots, and *Bidens* mottle mosaic virus.

F. argyroneura see *F. verschaffeltii* var. *argyroneura*.
F. verschaffeltii ▣ Creeping perennial bearing oval to elliptic, olive-green leaves, 2–4in (6–10cm) long, with slightly sunken, carmine-red veins. ↕ 6in (15cm), ↔ indefinite. Peru. ✾ (min. 59°F/15°C, best at constant temperature of about 64°F/18°C). **var. *argyroneura*** ▣ syn. *F. argyroneura* (Mosaic plant, Silver net leaf) has paler leaves with narrower, silvery white veins. **'Nana'** is compact, with leaves ¾–1½in (2–4cm) long; ↕ to 4in (10cm).

FITZROYA

CUPRESSACEAE

Genus of one species of evergreen, monoecious or dioecious, coniferous tree or shrub found only in limited areas of forest in Chile and Argentina, where it is now rare because of overfelling and habitat loss. Although similar to junipers in general appearance, and in having whorls of 3 short, blunt leaves, the cones of *F. cupressoides* differ in having 3 whorls on each of 3 scales, and the seeds are winged. Grow as a specimen tree or shrub in open woodland.
• **CULTIVATION** Grow in moderately fertile, moist but well-drained soil in full sun, with shelter from cold, dry winds.
• **PROPAGATION** Sow seed *in situ* or in containers in a cold frame in spring. Root semi-ripe cuttings in late summer or autumn, under mist or with gentle bottom heat.
• **PESTS AND DISEASES** Infrequent.

Fitzroya cupressoides

F. cupressoides ▣ syn. *F. patagonica*. Coniferous, conical tree or spreading shrub with red-brown bark that peels in strips, and oblong, dark green leaves, to ¼in (6mm) long. Produces cylindrical male cones and solitary, spherical, terminal, pale brown female cones, ½in (1.5cm) across, which ripen in autumn. ↕ to 50ft (15m), ↔ to 20ft (6m). Chile, S. Argentina. Zone 7.
F. patagonica see *F. cupressoides*.

FOCKEA

ASCLEPIADACEAE

Genus of about 10 species of caudex-forming, mainly deciduous, perennial succulents from open grassland and arid regions of Angola to South Africa (Northern Cape, Eastern Cape, Western Cape), and Zimbabwe. They have thick, fleshy stems, sometimes up to 10ft (3m) wide. Branches are twining or semi-erect, usually with white, milky sap. The leaves are opposite, oblong to oval, sharp-pointed, flat or wavy-edged. In late summer or autumn, starfish-shaped flowers are borne singly, or several in dense clusters, in the leaf axils. Male and female plants are needed to obtain fruits. In areas where temperatures drop below 50°F (10°C), grow in a warm greenhouse. In warmer climates, grow in a desert garden.
• **CULTIVATION** Under glass, grow in standard cactus potting mix in full or bright filtered light with low humidity, in a deep container to accommodate the caudex. When in full leaf, water moderately, allowing soil to dry between waterings, and apply a low-nitrogen liquid fertilizer monthly. Keep dry when dormant. Outdoors, grow in dry, sharply drained, moderately fertile soil, with added leaf mold, in full sun or light, dappled shade. See also pp.48–49.
• **PROPAGATION** Sow seed at 66–75°F (19–24°C) as soon as ripe.
• **PESTS AND DISEASES** Vulnerable to aphids while flowering.

F. capensis see *F. crispa*.
F. crispa ▣ syn. *F. capensis*. Twining or prostrate, deciduous, minutely hairy succulent with a partly subterranean, rough-surfaced, spherical-obovoid caudex bearing many slender branches. Oval, glossy, dark green leaves, ¾–1¼in (2–3cm) long, have wavy margins. Starfish-shaped, greenish gray flowers, 1½in (4cm) across, with small brown marks, are borne in groups of 3–5 in the leaf axils in autumn. ↕ to 3ft (1m), ↔ to 24in (60cm). South Africa (Western Cape). ✾ (min. 50–54°F/10–12°C)

FOENICULUM

Fennel

APIACEAE

Genus of one species of aromatic perennial or biennial, native to rich, well-drained soils in sunny, coastal areas in Europe, especially the Mediterranean. The perennial *F. vulgare* is used to flavor foods; the biennial *F. vulgare* var. *azoricum* is grown for its edible, swollen stem base. Both forms have slender stems and finely cut, anise-flavored leaves. They bear flat umbels of yellow flowers, followed by aromatic seeds. Grow as foliage plants in an herb or wild garden; darker-leaved cultivars provide contrast in a perennial border.
• **CULTIVATION** Grow in fertile, moist but well-drained soil in full sun. Remove stems before they shed seeds.
• **PROPAGATION** In spring, sow seed at 55–64°F (13–18°C), or *in situ*, and thin to space 18–24in (45–60cm) apart.
• **PESTS AND DISEASES** Stem and root rot occur. Susceptible to aphids and slugs.

Fockea crispa

Foeniculum vulgare 'Purpureum'

Larvae of swallowtail butterflies may eat the leaves; fennel is sometimes planted intentionally to attract butterflies.

F. vulgare. Deep-rooting perennial producing airy clumps of triangular, very finely cut, 3- or 4-pinnate, almost hair-like, anise-flavored, mid- to glaucous green leaves, to 12in (30cm) long. Slender, smooth, branching stems bear flat, compound umbels, to 4in (10cm) across, of tiny yellow flowers, in mid- and late summer, followed by aromatic seeds. The leaves and seeds are used in cooking and medicinally. ↕ 6ft (1.8m), ↔ 18in (45cm). S. Europe. Zone 6.
var. *azoricum* (Florence fennel) is biennial, and has swollen, bulb-like leaf bases that are eaten as a vegetable.
var. *azoricum* 'Fino' is shorter but vigorous, with feathery, anise-scented leaves and sturdy, bulb-like bases; ↕ 12in (30cm). **var. *azoricum* 'Romy'** has a bulb-like leaf base free of tough, fibrous, wrapper leaves. **var. *azoricum* 'Rubrum'** has lacy, deep bronze leaves. **'Bronze'** see 'Purpureum'. **'Giant Bronze'**, syn. *Ferula* 'Giant Bronze', has copper foliage, turning dark brownish bronze. **'Purpureum'** ▣ syn. 'Bronze', has bronze-purple foliage when young, becoming glaucous with age.

FONTANESIA

OLEACEAE

Genus of about 2 species of deciduous shrubs from dry, open hillsides in China. Fontanesias are multi-stemmed, privet-like shrubs, grown for their opposite, long, sharp-pointed, bright green leaves. Grow as a large hedge; they are well suited to an urban site.
• **CULTIVATION** Grow in moderately fertile, well-drained soil, in full sun to partial shade. Pruning group 2.
• **PROPAGATION** Sow seed *in situ* in spring. Root cuttings of semi-ripe shoots in late summer in a cold frame, or of hardwood shoots outdoors in autumn.
• **PESTS AND DISEASES** Infrequent.

F. fortunei (Fortune fontanesia). Upright, multi-stemmed shrub with lance-shaped, glossy, bright green leaves, 1–4½in (2.5–11cm) long, that persist into winter. In early summer, bears terminal panicles, 2in (5cm) long, of small white flowers, ¼in (6mm) long. ↕ to 12ft (4m), ↔ 5ft (1.5m). China. Zone 6.

F

FORSYTHIA

OLEACEAE

Genus of about 7 species of mainly deciduous, sometimes semi-evergreen shrubs found in open woodland in E. Asia, with a single species from S.E. Europe. They bear opposite, simple, toothed or entire, sometimes 3-palmate leaves. The 4-petaled yellow flowers are salverform with narrow tubes, and produce long or short styles on different plants. They are borne before the leaves in early and midspring, often profusely, although low or widely fluctuating winter temperatures often kill flower buds. Grow in a shrub border, on a bank, against a wall, or as a specimen plant; they are also useful for hedging.

• **CULTIVATION** Grow in moderately fertile, moist but well-drained soil in full sun or light, dappled shade. Pruning group 2.

• **PROPAGATION** Root greenwood cuttings in late spring or early summer, or semi-ripe cuttings in late summer.

• **PESTS AND DISEASES** *Arabis* mosaic virus, stem gall, dieback, root knot nematode, and leaf spot can occur.

***F.* 'Beatrix Farrand'.** Vigorous, bushy, deciduous shrub with arching shoots bearing oblong, sharply toothed leaves, to 4in (10cm) long. Usually solitary, deep yellow flowers, to 1¼in (3cm) across, are profusely borne in early and midspring. ↕↔ 6ft (2m). Zone 5b.

F. giraldiana ■ Open, deciduous shrub with slender, arching shoots, purple when young, and narrowly ovate leaves, gray-green to mid-green above, slightly downy beneath, 2–5in (5–13cm) long. Produces solitary, pale yellow flowers, 1–1¼in (2.5–3cm) across, in late winter and early spring. ↕↔ 12ft (4m). China (Gansu, Shaanxi, Hubei). Zone 6.

Forsythia giraldiana

Forsythia x *intermedia* 'Arnold Giant'

***F.* 'Golden Nugget'.** Bushy, deciduous shrub with oval to lance-shaped, sharply toothed leaves, to 4in (10cm) long. Golden yellow flowers, ¾–1½in (2–4cm) across, are borne in early and midspring. ↕↔ 5ft (1.5m). Zone 6b.

F.* x *intermedia (*F. suspensa* x *F. viridissima*). Bushy, deciduous shrub bearing ovate to lance-shaped, simple, occasionally 3-lobed leaves, to 4in (10cm) long, with sharp teeth. Deep, bright yellow flowers, 1¼–1½in (2.5–4cm) across, are borne in groups of 2 or 3 in early and midspring. ↕↔ 5ft (1.5m). Garden origin. Zone 6. **'Arnold Giant'** ■ has sparsely borne, deep yellow flowers. **'Karl Sax'** is dense, with deep yellow flowers. Some leaves turn red or purple in autumn; ↕↔ 8ft (2.5m). **'Lynwood'** ■ has rich yellow flowers; ↕↔ 10ft (3m). **'Spectabilis'** is vigorous, and bears deep yellow flowers, ¾–1¼in (2–3cm) across; ↕ 10ft (3m). ↔ 6ft (2m).

***F.* 'Northern Gold'.** Upright, deciduous shrub bearing gray-yellow branches and oval, dark green leaves, 1¾–2in (4.5–5cm) long. Golden yellow flowers, to 1½in (4cm) across, are borne at the tips of the branches in spring. ↕ 6–8ft (2–2.5m), ↔ 5–7ft (1.5–2.2m). Zone 4.

***F.* 'Northern Sun'.** Upright, arching, deciduous shrub with oval, mid-green leaves, 3–5in (8–13cm) long. In spring, bears clear yellow flowers, to ¾in (2cm) across. Very hardy, producing a display of flowers after temperatures of -30°F (-34°C). ↕ 8–10ft (2.5–3m), ↔ 7–9ft (2.2–2.5m). Zone 5.

F. ovata (Early forsythia, Korean forsythia). Bushy, compact, deciduous shrub with broadly ovate, toothed, dark green leaves, to 3½in (9cm) long. Bears bright yellow flowers, ¾in (2cm) across, singly in the leaf axils, in early spring. ↕ 5ft (1.5m), ↔ 10ft (3m). Korea. Zone 4. **'Ottawa'** has flower buds that survive to -25°F (-32°C). **'Tetragold'** bears flowers ¾–1¼in (2–3cm) across, in early spring.

Forsythia suspensa

***F.* 'Spring Glory'.** Upright, deciduous shrub with ovate to lance-shaped leaves, to 5in (13cm) long. In spring, bears pale yellow flowers, 1¼in (3cm) across. ↕ 6ft (2m), ↔ 5–7ft (1.5–2.2m). Zone 6.

F. suspensa ■ (Weeping forsythia). Upright or arching, deciduous shrub with ovate, sometimes 3-palmate, mid- to dark green leaves, to 4in (10cm) long. In early and midspring, produces clusters of up to 6 yellow flowers, 1–1¼in (2–3cm) across, in the leaf axils. ↕↔ 10ft (3m). China. Zone 5b. **f. *atrocaulis*** has purple young shoots and leaves, and pale lemon-yellow flowers, 1½in (4cm) across. **'Nymans'** produces bronze-purple young shoots and soft yellow flowers. **var. *sieboldii*** has slender, pendent shoots and bears nodding flowers.

***F.* 'Vermont Sun'.** Upright, deciduous shrub with oval, deep green leaves, 3–5in (8–13cm) long. Deep yellow flowers, to 1½in (4cm) across, are borne in early spring. Extremely hardy. ↕ 8ft (2.5m), ↔ 6ft (2m). Zone 4.

Forsythia x *intermedia* 'Lynwood' (inset: flower detail)

Forsythia viridissima 'Bronxensis'

F. viridissima (Green-stem forsythia). Erect, deciduous or semi-evergreen shrub with upright shoots, which remain green in the second year, and lance-shaped leaves, to 6in (15cm) long. Bright yellow flowers, 1¼in (3cm) across, are produced singly, or occasionally in pairs or threes, in early and midspring. ↕ 6ft (2m), ↔ 5ft (1.5m). China. Zone 5b. **'Bronxensis'** ■ is spreading, with leaves to 1¾in (4.5cm) long, and primrose-yellow flowers, 1in (2.5cm) across. Used in rock gardens. ↕ 12in (30cm), ↔ 36in (90cm). **var. *koreana* 'Ilgwang'** has yellow-splashed leaves.

FORTUNELLA

Kumquat

RUTACEAE

Genus of about 5 species of sometimes spiny, evergreen shrubs and small trees found in moist woodland from S. China to Malaysia. The simple, leathery, glandular leaves are alternate. Waxy, fragrant, 5-petaled white flowers are borne singly or in few-flowered, axillary clusters, followed by edible, ovoid to spherical, orange-yellow fruits, which resemble miniature oranges. Where not hardy, grow in a conservatory or cool greenhouse. In warmer regions, use in a mixed or shrub border, in a courtyard, or as a specimen plant.

• **CULTIVATION** Under glass, grow in soil-based potting mix in full light. During growth, water freely and apply a balanced liquid fertilizer monthly. Water sparingly in winter. Top-dress or pot on in spring. Outdoors, grow in moderately fertile, moist but well-drained soil in full sun. Pruning group 1; may need restrictive pruning under glass.

• **PROPAGATION** Sow seed at 59–75°F (15–24°C) in spring. Root semi-ripe cuttings in summer with bottom heat.

• **PESTS AND DISEASES** Spider mites, scale insects, and whiteflies can be troublesome under glass. Virus and viroid diseases common to citrus can occur. Foot rot, stem blights, and leaf spot are sometimes problems.

F. japonica (Round kumquat). Large shrub or small tree, usually many-branched, with spines in the leaf axils. Bears lance-shaped, glossy, mid- to light green leaves, to 4in (10cm) long, with distinctive vein patterns. Axillary clusters of fragrant flowers, each ½in (1.5cm) across, are borne from spring to summer, followed by spherical to ovoid, edible, golden yellow fruit, 1¼–1½in (3–4cm) long. ↕ 10–12ft (3–4m), ↔ 5–8ft (1.5–2.5m). S. China, Hong Kong. ❀ (min. 45°F/7°C). **'Sun Stripe'** has variegated, creamy yellow leaves and green-striped yellow fruit.

FOTHERGILLA

HAMAMELIDACEAE

Genus of 2 species of deciduous, low-growing shrubs found in woodland and swamps in S.E. US. They are grown for their bottlebrush-like flowers, borne before the leaves, and attractive autumn color. The leaves are alternate, with coarsely toothed margins. The fragrant, petalless flowers have conspicuously long white stamens and are produced in terminal heads or spikes. Grow in a woodland garden or shrub border.

• **CULTIVATION** Grow in humus-rich or leafy, moist but well-drained acidic soil in full sun or partial shade. (Full sun encourages more flowers and richer autumn color.) Pruning group 1.

• **PROPAGATION** Sow seed in containers in a cold frame, or in a seedbed, in autumn or winter. Root softwood cuttings in summer under mist. Air layer in summer.

• **PESTS AND DISEASES** Infrequent.

F. gardenii ▣ (Dwarf fothergilla). Dense, bushy shrub with alternate, oval to obovate, dark green leaves, to 2½in (6cm) long, with toothed margins, turning bright red, orange, and yellow in autumn. Cylindrical, terminal, fragrant spikes, to 1½in (4cm) long, of small white flowers, with filaments 1in (2.5cm) long, are borne in spring before the leaves. ↕↔ 3ft (1m). S.E. US. Zone 5b. **'Blue Mist'** has blue-green foliage.

F. major ▣ syn. *F. monticola* (Large fothergilla). Upright shrub with obovate to nearly rounded, alternate, glossy, dark green leaves, 3–5in (7–13cm) long, with toothed margins, turning brilliant red, orange, and yellow in autumn. Erect, terminal spikes, 1–2in (2.5–5cm) long, of fragrant, white, occasionally pink-tinged flowers are borne in late spring and early summer, before or as the leaves unfold. ↕ 8ft (2.5m), ↔ 6ft (2m). Allegheny Mountains, Virginia to South Carolina. Zone 5b.

F. monticola see *F. major.*

Fothergilla major

Fothergilla gardenii

FOUQUIERIA

FOUQUIERIACEAE

Genus of about 10 species of mainly bushy or tree-like, deciduous, small, columnar-stemmed succulents and spiny shrubs or trees found in low, arid hill-sides in S.W. US and Mexico. They have grooved, swollen, spiny stems and branches. Showy, bell-shaped or tubular, red, pale purple, creamy yellow, or white flowers are borne in racemes or panicles. The capsule-like fruits contain winged seeds. Grow in a desert garden or as an informal, spiny hedge. Grow in a warm greenhouse in areas where temperatures drop below 59°F (15°C), although when established, many species are hardy to 20°F (-7°C) for short periods.

Fouquieria splendens

• **CULTIVATION** Under glass, grow in standard cactus potting mix in full light with low humidity. From late spring to autumn, water moderately and apply a balanced liquid fertilizer monthly. Keep dry in winter. Outdoors, grow in sharply drained, moderately fertile soil in full sun. See also pp.48–49. Pruning group 1.

• **PROPAGATION** Sow seed at 66–75°F (19–24°C) in spring. Root softwood cuttings in spring or summer.

• **PESTS AND DISEASES** Rust and scale insects can occur.

F. columnaris, syn. *Idria columnaris* (Boojum tree). Spiny tree with a white-barked, caudex-like stem, to 24in (60cm) thick, and simple branches at right angles to the main stem. Bears axillary groups of 2 or 3 elliptic to oval or spoon-shaped leaves, to ½–1½in (1.5–4cm) long. In summer and autumn, bears short racemes of diurnal, narrowly bell-shaped, honey-scented, creamy yellow flowers, to ¼in (6mm) long. ↕ 70ft (20m), ↔ 8ft (2.5m). N.W. Mexico, S.W. California. ❀ (min. 59°F/15°C)

F. splendens ▣ (Ocotillo). Spiny, free-branching shrub with erect, cylindrical, white-striped, dark green stems, 1½–2in (4–5cm) thick, and branches covered with leaf scars and spines. Bears elliptic to inversely lance-shaped leaves, ½–2in (1.5–5cm) long, and shorter, narrowly spoon-shaped leaves, to 1½in (4cm) long. Narrowly bell-shaped, diurnal, bright red flowers, 4–11in (10–28cm) long, are borne from early spring to summer. ↕ 30ft (10m), ↔ 6ft (2m). S. California, Arizona, New Mexico, Texas, N. Mexico (including Baja California). ❀ (min. 59°F/15°C)

FRAGARIA

Strawberry

ROSACEAE

Genus of 12 species of stoloniferous perennials from open woodland, hedgerows, and grassy places in Europe, Asia (as far as S. India), North America, and temperate areas of Chile. The leaves are 3-palmate and radical, with toothed leaflets. The white, sometimes pink flowers have numerous stamens and carpels, usually 5 rounded petals, and are borne in 2- to 10-flowered cymes, followed by succulent strawberries. Strawberries are grown mainly for their edible, fleshy fruit, some species and cultivars are useful as a groundcover. Grow in an herb garden, as border edging, or in a windowbox, container, hanging basket, or specially made "strawberry tower."

• **CULTIVATION** Grow in fertile, moist but well-drained, neutral to alkaline soil in full sun or light, dappled shade. Strawberries tolerate acidic soils, but will thrive in alkaline soils, particularly *F. vesca. F.* 'Pink Panda' may become invasive.

• **PROPAGATION** Sow seed at 55–64°F (13–18°C) in spring. Remove and transplant plantlets.

• **PESTS AND DISEASES** Susceptible to leaf spot, powdery mildew, honey fungus and various fungal wilts, spider mites, aphids, and vine weevil grubs, and eaten by small animals, millipedes, and slugs.

F.* x *ananassa. Among the most successful fruit crops for the gardener; produces edible fruit from early summer on, up to 2in (5cm) long. Grown as a ground cover, in a vegetable garden or container. ↕ 9in (23cm), ↔ indefinite. Temperate N. Hemisphere. Zone 3.

F. indica see *Duchesnea indica.*

***F.* 'Pink Panda'** ▣ Stoloniferous perennial bearing 3-palmate leaves, with broad, ovate, toothed leaflets, 1–1½in (2.5–4cm) long, and reddish green leaf stalks. Cymes of bright pink flowers, to 1in (2.5cm) across, with 5–7 rounded petals, appear from late spring to midautumn. Rarely bears fruit. ↕ 4–6in (10–15cm), ↔ indefinite. Zone 5.

Fragaria 'Pink Panda'

F

FRAILEA

CACTACEAE

Genus of about 10–15 species of dwarf, flattened spherical or columnar, usually offsetting, perennial cacti from scrub and grassland in E. Bolivia, S. Brazil, Paraguay, Uruguay, and N. Argentina. The ribs are divided into tubercles with finely spined areoles. The diurnal, funnel-shaped yellow flowers develop on or close to the crown in summer, and are followed by thin-walled black fruits with numerous small, glossy, black or brown seeds. In areas where temperatures drop below 45°F (7°C), grow as houseplants or in a temperate greenhouse. In warmer climates, grow in a desert garden, at the base of a sunny wall, or in a container on a patio.

• **CULTIVATION** Under glass, grow in standard cactus potting mix (acidic mix) in low humidity with good ventilation, and in full light to ensure that flower buds open. In growth, water moderately and apply a balanced liquid fertilizer monthly. Keep just moist in spring and autumn. Keep dry in winter, watering occasionally to prevent shriveling. Outdoors, grow in sharply drained, moderately fertile, neutral to acidic soil, with added grit and leaf mold, in dappled shade. Protect from excessive winter moisture. See also pp.48–49.

• **PROPAGATION** Sow seed at 59–70°F (15–21°C) in spring.

• **PESTS AND DISEASES** Infrequent.

F. asterioides see *F. castanea*.

F. castanea, syn. *F. asterioides*. Solitary cactus with a flattened spherical, dark reddish brown or chocolate-brown, occasionally bluish green stem with 10–15 shallow, flat to slightly convex ribs. Conspicuous brown or almost white areoles bear about 8 minute brown spines. Pale to golden yellow flowers, 1¼–2in (3–5cm) across, are produced in small groups from the areoles in summer. ↕ ½–¾in (1–2cm), ↔ to 2in (5cm). N.E. Argentina, S. Brazil, N. Uruguay. ❄ (min. 45°F/7°C)

F. pulcherrima see *F. pygmaea*.

F. pygmaea ▣ syn *F. pulcherrima*. Solitary, sometimes offsetting cactus with a spherical to shortly cylindrical, light to dark green or gray-green stem with about 16 shallow ribs. Small gray areoles, with white, gray, or brown wool, each bear 6–9 or more, white, yellow, or pale brown spines. In summer, bears pale yellow flowers, 1¼–2in (3–5cm) across. ↕ ½–¾in (1–2cm), ↔ to 3in (8cm). S. Brazil, Argentina, Uruguay. ❄ (min. 45°F/7°C)

Frailea pygmaea

FRANCOA

Bridal wreath

SAXIFRAGACEAE

Genus of 5 species (or 1 very variable species) of evergreen perennials from semi-shady, rocky crevices in Chile. The leaves are obovate to broadly lance-shaped, wavy-margined, softly hairy, and usually pinnatisect, with several small, often rounded lobes and one large terminal lobe, 2½–5in (6–13cm) long, borne in basal rosettes. Cross-shaped, 4-, occasionally 5-petaled, delicate-looking, white or pink flowers, with darker markings, are borne in long-stalked, terminal, spike-like racemes, some with basal branches. Often cultivated for use in floral arrangements, bridal wreaths can be grown as edging for a border, or in a woodland or courtyard garden. Where not hardy, grow in a cool greenhouse or as short-lived houseplants.

• **CULTIVATION** Outdoors, grow in humus-rich, moist but well-drained soil in full sun or partial shade. Protect from winter moisture. May survive short periods to 14°F (-10°C). Under glass, grow in soilless or soil-based potting mix in full light, with shade from the hottest sun. During growth, water freely and apply a balanced liquid fertilizer every 4 weeks. Water sparingly in winter.

• **PROPAGATION** Sow seed at 59–75°F (15–24°C) in spring. Divide in spring.

• **PESTS AND DISEASES** Infrequent.

F. appendiculata ▣ Rosette-forming perennial with broadly lance-shaped, variably lobed, basal leaves. In midsummer, sparsely branched stems bear wand-like racemes of pale pink flowers, ¾in (2cm) across, with darker pink markings within. ↕ 24–36in (60–90cm), ↔ 12in (30cm). Chile. Zone 7b.

F. glabrata see *F. ramosa*.

F. ramosa, syn. *F. glabrata*. Rosette-forming perennial with stalked, broadly lance-shaped, variably lobed, basal leaves. In summer, branched flowering stems bear spike-like racemes of white flowers, ¾in (2cm) across, with dark pink markings. ↕ 24–36in (60–90cm), ↔ 12in (30cm). Chile. Zone 7b.

Francoa appendiculata

Francoa sonchifolia

F. sonchifolia ▣ Rosette-forming perennial with broadly lance-shaped, variably and deeply lobed, basal leaves. In midsummer, unbranched stems bear compact racemes of pink flowers, ¾in (2cm) across, with darker pink markings, opening from deep pink buds. ↕ 24–36in (60–90cm), ↔ 18in (45cm). Chile. Zone 7b.

FRANKLINIA

THEACEAE

Genus of one species of deciduous tree or shrub, from Georgia, US, which is now thought to be extinct in the wild. Cultivated for its showy, solitary, axillary, camellia-like white flowers and colorful autumn foliage (sometimes occurring with its latest flowers), *F. alatamaha* is suitable for open areas in a woodland garden, or as a specimen tree.

• **CULTIVATION** Grow in humus-rich, moist but well-drained, acidic to neutral soil in full sun. Pruning group 1.

• **PROPAGATION** Sow seed as soon as ripe at 50–64°F (10–18°C). Root softwood cuttings in summer with bottom heat.

• **PESTS AND DISEASES** Japanese beetles may eat the flowers.

Franklinia alatamaha

F. alatamaha ▣ Upright tree bearing alternate, obovate-oblong, sparsely toothed, glossy, mid- to dark green leaves, to 6in (15cm) long, turning red in autumn. Shallowly cup-shaped, fragrant white flowers, to 3in (8cm) across, with yellow stamens, are produced in late summer and early autumn. The fruit are woody, spherical capsules, to ¾in (2cm) across. ↕ 15ft (5m) or more, ↔ 15ft (5m). Georgia. Zone 6.

FRAXINUS

Ash

OLEACEAE

Genus of about 65 species of deciduous, rarely evergreen trees usually found in woodland, mainly in Europe, Asia, and North America. The leaves are opposite and pinnate, light to dark green, 2–20in (5–50cm) long. The flowers are borne in terminal or axillary panicles or racemes, from spring to early summer. Ashes are grown for their habit and foliage. Most have inconspicuous, petalless flowers, although some, including *F. ornus* and *F. sieboldiana*, are grown for their ornamental flowers. *F. americana*, *F. pennsylvanica*, and *F. uhdei* usually produce male and female flowers on separate plants; both are needed to produce the single-seeded, winged fruits. Ashes are excellent specimen trees for woodland or coastal gardens.

• **CULTIVATION** Grow in fertile, moist but well-drained, neutral to alkaline soil in full sun. *F. angustifolia*, *F. ornus,* and *F. texensis* tolerate reasonably dry, acidic to alkaline soils. *F. nigra* 'Fallgold' prefers moist soil. Pruning group 1.

• **PROPAGATION** Stratify seed over winter or chill for 2–3 months in a refrigerator before sowing. Sow seed in autumn or spring in containers in an open frame. Graft cultivars in spring onto seedling stock of the same species.

• **PESTS AND DISEASES** *Mycosphaerella* leaf spot, powdery mildew, rust, brown cubical and white rots, wilt, anthracnose, cankers, and twig diebacks are common problems. Borers, leaf miner, carpenter worm, ash sawfly, fall webworm, and scale insects are problems in many areas.

F. americana (White ash). Fast-growing, broadly columnar, deciduous tree bearing pinnate, dark green leaves, to 14in (35cm) long, each with 5–9 oblong-lance-shaped to ovate, tapered leaflets, turning yellow or purple in autumn. ↕ 80ft (25m), ↔ 50ft (15m). E. North America. Zone 4. **'Autumn Blaze'** has an oval crown and purple autumn foliage; ↕ 60ft (18m), ↔ 30ft (10m). **'Autumn Purple'** is broadly conical, with glossy leaves turning red to red-purple in autumn; ↕ 60ft (18m), ↔ 40ft (12m). **'Champaign County'** is very dense, with glossy leaves and little autumn color; ↕ 46ft (14m), ↔ 30ft (10m). **'Rose Hill'** has dark green leaves turning bronze-red in autumn; ↕ 50ft (15m), ↔ 30ft (10m). **'Skyline'** is oval-headed, with glossy leaves turning orange-red in autumn; ↕ 50ft (15m), ↔ 40ft (12m).

F. angustifolia ▣ syn. *F. oxycarpa* (Narrow-leaved ash). Spreading, deciduous tree bearing pinnate, glossy leaves, dark green above, paler beneath, to 10in (25cm) long, often in whorls

Fraxinus angustifolia (inset: autumn leaf detail)

of 3, each with up to 13 slender, lance-shaped, tapered leaflets, turning yellow-gold in autumn. ↕ 80ft (25m), ↔ 40ft (12m). S.W. Europe, N. Africa. Zone 6b. **'Raywood'** (Claret ash) is very vigorous, with dark green leaves turning reddish purple in autumn; ↕ 70ft (20m).
F. excelsior (European ash). Vigorous, spreading, deciduous tree producing conspicuous black buds in winter. Pinnate, dark green leaves, to 12in (30cm) long, each with 9–13 oval leaflets, turn yellow in autumn. ↕ 100ft (30m), ↔ 70ft (20m). Europe. Zone 4b. **f. *diversifolia*** (One-leaved ash) has leaves with 1, rarely 3 leaflets. **'Hessei'** is extremely vigorous, with simple, prominently toothed, lustrous dark green leaves that remain green into late autumn. Good pest resistance except for borers. **'Jaspidea'** ■ has yellow winter shoots and yellow leaves in spring and autumn. **'Pendula'** ■ (Weeping ash) has branches that weep, often to the ground; ↕ 50ft (15m), ↔ 25–30ft (8–10m). **'Westhof's Glorie'** is narrow, spreading with age. Leaves emerge bronze in late spring then dark green.
F. holotricha. Rounded, deciduous tree bearing velvety shoots and pinnate, gray-green leaves, to 10in (25cm) long, maturing to glossy, dark green, each with 5–13, usually 11, elliptic to lance-shaped leaflets. ↕↔ 40ft (12m). Balkans. Zone 6b. **'Moraine'** is fast-growing and has an even, rounded crown.
F. latifolia, syn. *F. oregona* (Oregon ash). Spreading, deciduous tree bearing pinnate, dark green leaves, 6–12in (15–30cm) long, each with 7–9 oval, tapered leaflets, turning yellow in autumn. ↕ 80ft (25m), ↔ 50ft (15m). W. North America. Zone 6b.
F. mariesii see *F. sieboldiana.*
F. nigra. Upright, deciduous tree bearing pinnate, dark green leaves, to 5in (12cm) long, each with up to 11 oblong, tapered leaflets, turning golden yellow in autumn. ↕ 50ft (15m), ↔ 25ft (8m). N.E. North America. Zone 2b. **'Fallgold'** is vigorous, has long-lasting, golden yellow color in autumn, and bears no fruit.
F. oregona see *F. latifolia.*
F. ornus ■ (Flowering ash, Manna ash). Bushy-headed, rounded, deciduous tree bearing pinnate, dark green leaves, to 8in (20cm) long, each with 5–9 oval leaflets, turning purple-red in autumn. In late spring and early summer, produces large terminal and axillary panicles of fragrant, creamy white flowers. ↕↔ 50ft (15m). S. Europe, S.W. Asia. Zone 7.
F. oxycarpa see *F. angustifolia.*
F. pennsylvanica (Green ash, Red ash). Vigorous, spreading, deciduous tree producing pinnate, olive-green leaves, to 12in (30cm) long, each composed of 7–9, sometimes 5, ovate to lance-shaped, tapered leaflets, turning yellow in autumn. ↕↔ 70ft (20m). North America. Zone 3. **'Emerald'** has a rounded crown and glossy, dark green leaves, and does not bear fruit; ↕ 50ft (15m), ↔ 40ft (12m). **'Marshall's Seedless'** is vigorous and broadly oval, with glossy, dark green leaves. Does not bear fruit; ↕ 50ft (15m), ↔ 40ft (12m). **'Patmore'** has an oval crown and glossy leaves. Disease resistant; does not bear fruit; ↕ 45ft (14m), ↔ 35ft (11m). **'Summit'** ■ is upright, with glossy leaves turning yellow in autumn; ↕ 45ft (14m), ↔ 25ft (8m).
F. sieboldiana ■ syn. *F. mariesii.* Slow-growing, compact, deciduous tree or shrub bearing pinnate, dark green leaves, to 8in (20cm) long, each with up to 7 ovate, tapered leaflets. In late spring and early summer, bears axillary, terminal panicles of small, fragrant, creamy white flowers, followed by winged, purple-tinged fruit. ↕ 20ft (6m), ↔ 15ft (5m). C. China. Zone 7b.
F. texensis. Spreading, deciduous tree bearing pinnate, leathery, dark green leaves, to 8in (20cm) long, each with 5, sometimes 7, ovate leaflets, 1¼–3in (3–8cm) long. ↕↔ 50ft (15m). Texas. Zone 7.
F. uhdei. Upright to rounded, semi-evergreen or evergreen tree producing pinnate, glossy, dark green leaves, to 6in (15cm) long, each with up to 7 oval, tapered leaflets. ↕ 25ft (8m), ↔ 15ft (5m). Central America. Zone 8. **'Tomlinson'** is smaller than the species, with upright branches and leathery leaves; ↕ 10–12ft (3–4m).
F. velutina ■ (Arizona ash, Velvet ash). Spreading, deciduous tree bearing pinnate, leathery, velvety, gray-green leaves, to 6in (15cm) long, each with 3–5, sometimes 7, lance-shaped, tapered leaflets, turning yellow in autumn. ↕↔ 30ft (10m). S.W. US. Zone 7. **'Fan Tex'** is very vigorous, has dark green leaves, and produces no fruit. Heat tolerant.

Fraxinus excelsior 'Jaspidea'

Fraxinus excelsior 'Pendula'

Fraxinus ornus

Fraxinus pennsylvanica 'Summit'

Fraxinus sieboldiana

Fraxinus velutina

F

F

FREESIA

IRIDACEAE

Genus of 6 or more species of cormous perennials from sandy, lowland soils to rocky upland slopes in South Africa. Many cultivars have been developed for use as potted plants and cut flowers. The large, funnel-shaped, usually scented, brightly colored flowers, held erect in dense racemes at the end of arching, frequently branched stems, are produced in late winter and early spring. Narrowly sword-shaped to linear-lance-shaped leaves, 2–16in (5–40cm) long, develop in basal fans. Where not hardy, grow freesias in a cool greenhouse. Specially prepared corms may be grown outdoors for summer flowering.

• **CULTIVATION** Under glass, grow in soil-based potting mix with added grit. Shade from sun and keep moist until established, then grow in full light with good ventilation, and water freely. Keep temperature below 55°F (13°C). After flower buds appear, apply a balanced liquid fertilizer weekly. After flowering, gradually reduce water until dry, then store corms for replanting in containers in late summer or autumn. Outdoors, plant 3in (8cm) deep and 2–3in (5–8cm) apart in moderately fertile, moist but well-drained soil in full sun. Plant in spring for summer flowering; in the mildest parts of British Columbia plant in autumn and apply a deep mulch over winter for spring flowers.

• **PROPAGATION** Sow seed at 55–64°F (13–18°C) in autumn or winter. Remove small offsets in autumn.

Freesia 'Blue Heaven'

Freesia 'Oberon'

• **PESTS AND DISEASES** Prone to spider mites, aphids, root rot, dry rot, and *Fusarium* wilt.

***F. alba* of gardens** see *F. lactea.*
***F.* 'Ballerina'.** Cormous perennial with white flowers, 2in (5cm) long, borne on robust stems. ↕ to 16in (40cm).
***F.* 'Blue Heaven'** ■ Cormous perennial bearing bluish mauve flowers, to 2in (5cm) long, with yellow throats. ↕ to 16in (40cm).
***F.* 'Elan'.** Cormous perennial with semi-double, lilac-purple flowers, 2in (5cm) long, with white throats. ↕ to 16in (40cm).
***F.* 'Golden Melody'.** Vigorous, cormous perennial with yellow flowers, 2in (5cm) long. ↕ to 16in (40cm).
F. lactea, syn. *F. alba* of gardens, *F. refracta* var. *alba.* Cormous perennial with linear leaves, 5–16in (12–40cm) long. Bears strongly scented white flowers, 1–2½in (2.5–6cm) long, occasionally flushed purple outside. ↕ 8–16in (20–40cm). South Africa (Western Cape). ❄ (min. 45°F/7°C)
***F.* 'Oberon'** ■ Cormous perennial with yellow flowers, 1½–2in (4–5cm) long, light blood-red inside; the throats are lemon-yellow with small red veins. ↕ to 16in (40cm).
***F.* 'Red Lion'.** Cormous perennial with yellow-centered, orange-red flowers, 2in (5cm) long. ↕ to 16in (40cm).
F. refracta* var. *alba see *F. lactea.*
***F.* 'Rosalinde'.** Cormous perennial with semi-double, dark rose-pink flowers, to 2in (5cm) long, with yellow throats. ↕ to 16in (40cm).
***F.* 'Uchida'.** Cormous perennial with semi-double, lilac-blue flowers, 1½–2in (4–5cm) long. ↕ to 16in (40cm).

▷ ***Fremontia*** see *Fremontodendron*

FREMONTODENDRON

syn. FREMONTIA

Flannel bush

STERCULIACEAE

Genus of 2 species of evergreen or semi-evergreen shrubs or trees from dry woodland, canyons, and mountain slopes in the US and N. Mexico. They have alternate, rounded, 3-, 5- or 7-lobed, leathery, dark green leaves, softly hairy beneath, and densely hairy young shoots. Large and very showy yellow flowers are produced over a long period, usually in spring and autumn. Grow flannel bushes against a warm, sunny wall, or as specimen plants at the back of a shrub or mixed border. Contact with the foliage and shoots may irritate the skin.

• **CULTIVATION** Grow in poor to moderately fertile, dry but well-drained, neutral to alkaline soil in full sun, with shelter from cold, drying winds. Tolerates occasional periods to 5°F (-15°C) if protected. Pruning group 1, or group 13 if wall-trained.

• **PROPAGATION** Sow seed at 55–64°F (13–18°C) in spring. Root greenwood cuttings in early summer, or semi-ripe cuttings in late summer.

• **PESTS AND DISEASES** Susceptible to root rot and stem rot in containers. Scale insects also occur.

***F.* 'California Glory'** ■ Vigorous, upright then spreading, evergreen shrub with rounded, 5-lobed, dark green leaves, to 3in (8cm) long. From late spring to midautumn, angled buds open to shallowly saucer-shaped, deep yellow flowers, 1½–2½in (4–6cm) across, tinged red outside. ↕ 20ft (6m), ↔ 12ft (4m). Zone 7b.

Fremontodendron 'California Glory'

F. californicum (California flannel bush). Vigorous, upright, evergreen or semi-evergreen shrub with rounded, 3-, 5- or 7-lobed, dark green leaves, 2–4in (5–10cm) long. Shallowly saucer-shaped yellow flowers, to 2½in (6cm) across, are produced from late spring to midautumn. ↕ 20ft (6m), ↔ 12ft (4m). California, Arizona. Zone 8.
***F.* 'Ken Taylor'.** Spreading, evergreen shrub with rounded, 3- or 5-lobed, dark green leaves, to 3in (8cm) long. Shallowly saucer-shaped, orange-yellow flowers, 1½–2½in (4–6cm) across, are borne from spring to autumn. ↕ 6ft (2m), ↔ 10ft (3m). Zone 8.
F. mexicanum (Mexican flannel bush). Upright, vigorous, evergreen or semi-evergreen shrub with rounded, 5- or 7-lobed, dark green leaves, to 3in (8cm) long. From late spring to midautumn, bears shallowly saucer-shaped, deep golden yellow flowers, 2½–3½in (6–9cm) across, tinged red on the exterior. ↕ 20ft (6m), ↔ 12ft (4m). S. California, N. Mexico. ❄ (min. 41°F/5°C)
***F.* 'Pacific Sunset'** ■ Upright, evergreen shrub with rounded, dark green leaves, 2–3in (5–8cm) long, with 3 or 5 angular lobes. In summer, produces saucer-shaped, bright yellow flowers, to 2½in (6cm) across, with long, slender-pointed lobes. Zone 8.

▷ ***Frerea*** see *Caralluma*

Fremontodendron 'Pacific Sunset'

FRITILLARIA

Fritillary

LILIACEAE

Genus of about 100 species of bulbous perennials found in a range of habitats, from woodland to open meadows and high screes, distributed throughout the temperate regions of the N. hemisphere, particularly the Mediterranean, S.W. Asia, and W. North America. Each bulb has 2 or more scales, and sometimes abundant basal bulblets ("rice-grains"). The leaves are usually lance-shaped or linear, with 1, rarely 2, wider basal leaves, and several alternate, opposite, or whorled stem leaves. In some species, there is an involucre of leaf-like bracts above the flowers. The flowers, borne in spring or early summer, are usually pendulous and solitary, or in terminal racemes or umbels, and have 6 tepals. They are bell-shaped, tubular, or saucer-shaped, frequently checkered, and have conspicuous nectaries at the base of the tepals. The fruits are capsules.

Grow in a rock garden, in a raised bed or border, or in a woodland garden, depending on cultivation needs (see below). Smaller species, 2–6in (5–15cm) high, often need the protection of a bulb frame or alpine house.

• **CULTIVATION** Handle the fragile bulbs carefully and plant at 4 times their own depth. Large, hollow-crowned bulbs, such as *F. imperialis*, are very prone to rot and so are best planted on their sides, surrounded by perlite or very sharp sand.

Under glass, grow in soil-based potting mix, with added grit and leaf mold, in full light. Water moderately during growth and keep almost dry when dormant. During the second year, apply a half-strength balanced liquid fertilizer monthly or repot into fresh soil mix.

For ease of reference, the varying cultivation requirements of the different groups have been classified as follows. All except group 3 need a continental climate, or indoor conditions that approximate it: ideally a dry winter and summer, and a damp spring.

1. Toughest, most tolerant species, suitable for a sunny border or rock garden. Need fertile, well-drained soil and full sun.
2. Fairly robust species, but intolerant of rainfall while dormant. Need sharply drained, moderately fertile soil and full sun. Suitable for a rock garden or raised bed; can be grown in a bulb frame or alpine house.
3. Damp meadow or woodland species, needing humus-rich, moisture-retentive soil with added leaf mold, and full sun to light shade. Grow best in areas with cool, damp summers.
4. Species intolerant of excessive moisture. Usually small, needing fertile, well-drained soil and full sun, with shelter from rain. Grow in a bulb frame or cold greenhouse, to keep bulbs almost dry when dormant.

• **PROPAGATION** Sow seed in autumn in a cold frame. Expose to winter cold until germination in spring, then transfer to a cold greenhouse. Small species should be grown on for 2 years in containers. Divide offsets or collect and sow "rice-grain" bulblets in late summer.

• **PESTS AND DISEASES** Rust and leaf spot can occur.

Fritillaria imperialis

F. acmopetala ▣ Bulbous perennial bearing alternate, linear, bluish green leaves, to 8in (20cm) long. In late spring, usually solitary flowers are produced in the uppermost leaf axils, or sometimes in pairs or threes in the lower leaf axils. Flowers are bell-shaped, pendent, pale green, to 1½in (4cm) long, with reflexed tepals; the inner tepals are stained reddish brown. Cultivation group 1. ↕ to 16in (40cm), PD2–3in (5–8cm). Cyprus, S.W. Turkey, Syria, Lebanon. Zone 5.
F. affinis, syn. *F. lanceolata* (Rice-grain fritillary). Bulbous perennial bearing whorls of broadly lance-shaped to linear, blue-green leaves, 1½–6in (4–15cm) long. From early spring to early summer, bears racemes of 3 or 4, occasionally up to 12, cup-shaped, pendent, greenish white flowers, to 1½in (4cm) long, with reddish purple stains or speckles. Cultivation group 2 or 3. ↕ to 24in (60cm), PD5in (12cm). N.W. North America. Zone 5.
F. armena. Bulbous perennial with alternate, stem-clasping, lance-shaped, mid-green lower leaves, 1–4in (2.5–10cm) long, and linear upper leaves. Solitary, narrowly bell-shaped, pendent, checkered, dark purple-brown flowers, to ¾in (2cm) long, with slightly incurved, fringed tepals, are borne in spring. Cultivation group 4. ↕ 3–6in (8–15cm), PD2–3in (5–8cm). N.E. Turkey. Zone 7b.
***F. assyriaca* of gardens** see *F. uva-vulpis.*
F. biflora (Black fritillary, Mission bells). Bulbous perennial with ovate-lance-shaped, very glossy, mid-green leaves, 2–5in (5–12cm) long, usually produced in basal clusters. In early and midspring, bears up to 6, occasionally up to 12, bell-shaped, pendent brown flowers, tinged black to purple, flushed green, to 1½in (4cm) long, with ridges on the inner tepals. Cultivation group 4. ↕ 6–12in (15–30cm), PD2–3in (5–8cm). California. Zone 7. **'Martha Roderick'** ▣ syn. *F. roderickii*, produces deep red-purple flowers; the outer two-thirds of the tepals are white.
F. bucharica. Bulbous perennial with broadly lance-shaped, or lance-shaped to ovate, gray-green leaves, to 3in (8cm) long, the lower ones opposite, the upper ones alternate. Racemes of up to 10 widely cup-shaped, nodding flowers, to ¾in (2cm) long, with pointed, green-based, green-veined white tepals and indented green nectaries, are borne in spring. Cultivation group 4. ↕ to 12in (30cm), PD2in (5cm). Uzbekistan, Turkmenistan, N. Afghanistan, Tajikistan. Zone 6b.
F. camschatcensis ▣ (Black sarana). Variable, bulbous perennial with lance-shaped, glossy, light green leaves, to 5in (12cm) long, the lower ones in whorls, the upper ones alternate. Up to 8 broadly bell- to cup-shaped, pendent, dark black-purple, sometimes green or yellow flowers, to 1¼in (3cm) long, are borne in early summer. Cultivation group 3. ↕ to 18in (45cm), PD3–4in (8–10cm). N.E. Asia, Alaska to N.W. US. Zone 4.
F. chitralensis ▣ Upright, bulbous perennial with loose whorls of ovate, mid- to light green leaves, to 6in (15cm) long. Open umbels of 4 or 5 conical, pendent, bright yellow flowers, 1¼–1½in (3–4cm) long, are borne in early and midspring. Similar to *F. imperialis* and often included under it. Cultivation group 1. ↕ 20–32in (50–80cm), PD4in (10cm). N.E. Afghanistan, Pakistan (Chitral). Zone 7.
F. cirrhosa ▣ Bulbous perennial with whorls of linear, grayish green leaves, to 3in (8cm) long, the uppermost leaves with tendril-like tips. In late spring, produces usually solitary, occasionally 2 or 3 broadly bell-shaped, pendent, pale green, sometimes purple-tinged flowers, to 2in (5cm) long, with brownish purple checkering. Cultivation group 3. ↕ to 18in (45cm), PD2–3in (5–8cm). E. Himalayas, S.W. China. Zone 7.
F. crassifolia. Variable, bulbous perennial with alternate, lance-shaped, gray-green leaves, 1–3in (2.5–8cm) long. In spring, bears 1–3 broadly bell-shaped, pendent, pale green flowers, to 1in (2.5cm) long, usually with faint brown checkering. Cultivation group 2 or 4. ↕ 3–8in (7–20cm) or more, PD2in (5cm). Turkey (Anatolia), Lebanon, Iran. Zone 7.
F. davisii. Bulbous perennial with opposite, broadly lance-shaped, gray-green, mainly basal leaves, 1½–4½in (3.5–11cm) long. In spring, bears 1–3 broadly bell-shaped, pendent green flowers, to 1in (2.5cm) long, often with yellow-margined tepals and brown or black checkering. Cultivation group 4. ↕ to 6in (15cm), PD2in (5cm). S. Greece. Zone 7.
F. delphinensis see *F. tubiformis.*
F. eduardii. Bulbous perennial with whorls of narrowly lance-shaped, glossy, bright mid-green leaves, to 7in (18cm) long. Crowded umbels of broadly bell-shaped, bright orange-red flowers, to 2in (5cm) long, with a tuft of upright, leaf-like bracts above the flowers, are produced in spring. Very similar to *F. imperialis*, but without the distinctive smell. Cultivation group 1. ↕ to 4ft (1.2m), PD to 12in (30cm). Tajikistan. Zone 6.
F. graeca ▣ Variable, bulbous perennial with usually alternate, broadly lance-shaped, glaucous, gray-green leaves, to 4½in (11cm) long, with narrower upper leaves. In late spring and early summer, bears solitary, rarely 2 or 3, broadly bell-shaped, deep green flowers, strongly checkered brownish purple, to 1in (2.5cm) long; each tepal usually has a green central stripe. Cultivation group 2 or 4. ↕ 2–8in (5–20cm), PD2in (5cm). S. Greece (Peloponnese, Crete). Zone 7. **subsp. *thessala***, syn. *F. ionica*, is more robust and easier to grow, with broader, mid-green, not glaucous leaves, and pale greenish brown, lightly checkered flowers, to 1¼–1½in (3–4cm) long; Cultivation group 1. Croatia, Bosnia, Macedonia, S. Albania, N.W. Greece, Corfu.
F. hermonis* subsp. *amana. Very variable, bulbous perennial, usually with alternate, lance-shaped or oblong, very glaucous, sometimes glossy, gray- to mid-green leaves, 1½–3½in (4–9cm) long. In spring, produces broadly bell-shaped, light green, faintly brown- or purple-checkered flowers, to 1½in (4cm) long, with inner tepals margined dark brown-purple, borne singly or in pairs. Cultivation group 2 or 4. ↕ 6–12in (15–30cm), PD3in (8cm). S. Turkey to Lebanon. Zone 7.
F. imperialis ▣ (Crown imperial). Bulbous perennial bearing whorls of lance-shaped, light green leaves, 3–7in (7–18cm) long. Umbels of 3–6, sometimes up to 8, bell-shaped, pendent, orange, yellow, or red flowers, to 2½in (6cm) long, crowned by a cluster of upright, leaf-like bracts, are produced in late spring. The bulbs have a distinctive skunky odor. Cultivation group 1. ↕ to 3ft (1m), PD10–12in (25–30cm). S. Turkey to Kashmir. Zone 5. **'Aureomarginata'** has variegated leaves with deep yellow margins, and orange flowers. **'Crown upon Crown'** see 'Prolifera'. **'Lutea'** has bright yellow flowers. **'Lutea Maxima'** is the hardiest of the yellow cultivars. **'Prolifera'**, syn. 'Crown upon Crown', has orange-red flowers in 2 whorls, one above the other. **'The Premier'** bears yellow-tinted, orange flowers, with purple veins.
F. involucrata. Bulbous perennial bearing opposite, linear-lance-shaped, mid-green leaves, 2–4½in (5–11cm) long. Solitary, broadly bell-shaped, pale green flowers, to 1½in (4cm) long, sometimes faintly checkered purple, topped with an involucre of 3 leaf-like bracts, are produced in spring. Cultivation group 1 or 2. ↕ to 12in (30cm), PD2–3in (5–8cm). S.E. France, N.W. Italy. Zone 7b.
F. ionica see *F. graeca* subsp. *thessala.*
F. lanceolata see *F. affinis.*

Fritillaria acmopetala

Fritillaria biflora 'Martha Roderick'

Fritillaria camschatcensis

Fritillaria chitralensis

Fritillaria cirrhosa

Fritillaria graeca

F

F. latifolia ■ Bulbous perennial with alternate, ovate to lance-shaped, glossy, gray-green leaves, 1½–3in (3.5–8cm) long. In early summer, bears solitary, broadly bell-shaped, dark maroon to purple flowers, to 2in (5cm) long, broad at the shoulders, with yellow checkering within, and slightly glaucous without. (A color variant from S. Caucasus, with greenish cream flowers, has been called *F. lagodechiana*.) Cultivation group 2 or 4. ↕ 4–8in (10–20cm), PD2in (5cm). N.E. Turkey, Caucasus, Iran. Zone 7. **var. *nobilis*** is a Turkish variant of the species, with shorter stems and red-purple flowers, checkered olive-yellow. Cultivation group 4. ↕ to 4in (10cm). Turkish Armenia, Caucasus.

F. meleagris ■ (Checkered lily, Snake's-head fritillary). Bulbous perennial bearing alternate, linear, gray-green leaves, 2½–5in (6–13cm) long. In spring, produces solitary, sometimes paired, broadly bell-shaped, pendent, purple, pinkish purple, or white flowers, to 1¾in (4.5cm) long, with strong, purple-pink checkering. Cultivation group 1 or 3; good for naturalizing in grass. ↕ to 12in (30cm), PD2–3in (5–8cm). S. England to N. Balkans, W. Russia. Zone 4. **f. *alba*** has white flowers. **'Charon'** is a very dark cultivar, bearing light purple flowers with black checkering. **'Orion'** produces dull purple flowers. **'Saturnus'** is one of the brightest colored cultivars, bearing reddish violet flowers.

F. messanensis, syn. *F. oranensis*. Bulbous perennial producing usually opposite, linear, mid-green leaves, 1½–3½in (4–9cm) long. In early spring, bears 1–3 broadly bell-shaped green flowers, to 1½in (4cm) long, checkered brown-purple toward the margins and with a whorl of 3 narrow leaves beneath. Cultivation group 1. ↕ to 12in (30cm), PD2in (5cm). C. Mediterranean. ❀ (min. 41°F/5°C). **subsp. *gracilis***, syn. *F. neglecta*, has purple-brown, obscurely checkered flowers with the tepals incurved at the tips, and without the whorl of 3 leaves below; Croatia, Macedonia, Albania.

F. michailovskyi. Bulbous perennial with mostly alternate, lance-shaped, mid-green leaves, 2–3½in (5–9cm) long. In early summer, bears umbels of 1–4, or rarely up to 7, broadly bell-shaped, pendent, deep brown-purple flowers, to 1¼in (3cm) long, sometimes tinged green on the outside, with distinctive upturned yellow tepal tips. Cultivation group 2 or 4. ↕ 4–8in (10–20cm), PD2in (5cm). N.E. Turkey. Zone 5.

F. neglecta see *F. messanensis* subsp. *gracilis*.

***F. nigra* of gardens** see *F. pyrenaica*.

F. oranensis see *F. messanensis*.

F. pallidiflora ■ Robust, bulbous perennial with opposite or alternate, broadly lance-shaped, glaucous, gray-green leaves, to 6in (15cm) long. In late spring and early summer, bears up to 6, rarely 9 or 10, very broadly bell-shaped, nodding, faintly malodorous, green-based, pale creamy yellow flowers, to 1¾in (4.5cm) long, often with faint red-brown checkering. Cultivation group 1 or 3. ↕ to 16in (40cm), PD2–3in (5–8cm). N.W. China, E. Siberia. Zone 5.

F. persica ■ Robust, bulbous perennial with sturdy, upright stems bearing alternate, lance-shaped, glaucous, gray-green leaves, 4–10in (10–25cm) long. Racemes of up to 30 conical, narrowly bell-shaped, pendent, greenish brown to deep purple flowers, to ¾in (2cm) long, are produced in spring. Cultivation group 1, in a hot site. ↕ to 3ft (1m), PD6in (10cm). S. Turkey. Zone 5. **'Adiyaman'** is taller and more free flowering than the species, with brown-purple flowers; ↕ to 5ft (1.5m).

F. pontica. Bulbous perennial with opposite or subopposite, lance-shaped to ovate-lance-shaped, glaucous, gray-green leaves, 2–4in (5–10cm) long. The highest leaves are in a whorl of 3 above the solitary, sometimes paired, broadly bell-shaped, pendent, pale green flowers, to 1¾in (4.5cm) long, stained maroon at the base, borne in spring. Cultivation group 1 or 2. ↕ 6–8in (15–20cm), PD2in (5cm). N. Greece to N.W. Turkey. Zone 7b.

F. pudica ■ (Yellow fritillary). Bulbous perennial with linear to narrowly lance-shaped, mid-green, sometimes slightly glaucous leaves, 2½–8in (6–20cm) long, the lower ones opposite, the upper ones alternate. In early spring, bears narrowly bell-shaped, pendent, golden to orange-yellow flowers, sometimes tinted red, to 1in (2.5cm) long, singly or in pairs. Cultivation group 4. ↕ to 6in (15cm), PD2in (5cm). W. North America. Zone 3.

Fritillaria latifolia

Fritillaria meleagris

Fritillaria pallidiflora

Fritillaria pudica

Fritillaria raddeana

Fritillaria thunbergii

Fritillaria persica

F. pyrenaica, syn. *F. nigra* of gardens. Bulbous perennial with alternate, lance-shaped, glaucous, gray-green leaves, 1¾–4½in (4.5–11cm) long. In late spring, bears solitary, rarely 2, broadly bell-shaped, deep brownish purple, occasionally yellow flowers, strongly checkered, to 1½in (4cm) long, with recurved tepal tips, yellow-green within. Cultivation group 1. ↕ to 18in (45cm), PD2–3in (5–8cm). Pyrenees. Zone 6.

F. raddeana ■ Robust, bulbous perennial with alternate or whorled, lance-shaped, lustrous, pale green leaves, to 6in (15cm) long. In early spring, bears umbels of 5 or 6, occasionally to 20, broadly bell-shaped, nodding, greenish cream or pale yellow flowers, to 2½in (6cm) long; each umbel is crowned by a tuft of 10–20 leaf-like bracts. Cultivation group 1 or 3. ↕ 24in (60cm), PD3–8in (8–20cm). N.E. Iran, Turkmenistan. Zone 7.

F. recurva (Scarlet fritillary). Bulbous perennial with whorls of linear-lance-shaped, gray-green, often glaucous leaves, 1¼–4in (3–10cm) long. In spring, bears spike-like racemes of 3–12 narrowly bell-shaped, pendent, faintly yellow-checkered, bright orange-red to scarlet flowers, to 1½in (4cm) long, recurved at the mouth. Cultivation group 4. Produces numerous "rice-grain" bulblets that take several years to reach flowering size. ↕ to 24in (60cm), PD3–4in (8–10cm). S. Oregon, California. Zone 7.

F. roderickii see *F. biflora* 'Martha Roderick'.

F. sewerzowii, syn. *Korolkowia sewerzowii*. Variable, thick-stemmed, bulbous perennial with mostly alternate, broadly lance-shaped, gray-green leaves, to 6in (15cm) long, the lowest opposite. In spring, produces elongated racemes of up to 12, rarely solitary, narrowly bell-shaped, nodding, often glaucous, greenish yellow to vivid purple flowers; each flower is yellow to brick-red at the base and within, to 1½in (4cm) long, flared at the mouth, and stained purple at the throat. Cultivation group 2 or 4. ↕ to 12in (30cm), PD3–4in (8–10cm). Uzbekistan, Tajikistan (Pamirs), N.W. China (Tien Shan Mountains). Zone 7b.

F. stenanthera. Bulbous perennial with a pair of opposite, ovate, mid-green basal leaves, and alternate, lance-shaped to linear stem leaves, to 6in (15cm) long. In early spring, bears racemes of 4–8 narrowly bell-shaped, nodding pink flowers, to ¾in (2cm) long, flared at the mouths, with dark purple centers. Cultivation group 4. ↕ to 8in (20cm), PD2in (5cm). Uzbekistan. Zone 7.

F. thunbergii ■ syn. *F. verticillata* var. *thunbergii*. Bulbous perennial with opposite, alternate or whorled, linear, glossy, mid-green leaves, to 6in (15cm) long. In spring, bears loose racemes of 2–6 broadly bell-shaped or cup-shaped, nodding, creamy white flowers, to 1½in (4cm) long, faintly checkered or veined green. Cultivation group 1. ↕ to 24in (60cm), PD4–5in (10–12cm). C. China. Zone 7.

F. tubiformis, syn. *F. delphinensis*. Bulbous perennial with alternate, linear-lance-shaped, glaucous, gray-green leaves, to 2–3½in (5–9cm) long. In late spring, bears solitary, broadly bell-shaped flowers, to 2in (5cm) long, gray-purple externally and white within, with purplish brown checkering. Cultivation group 2 or 4. ↕ to 6in (15cm), PD2in (5cm). French and Italian Alps. Zone 7b. **subsp. *moggridgei*** has bright yellow flowers with black checkering.

F. uva-vulpis, syn. *F. assyriaca* of gardens. Bulbous perennial with alternate, lance-shaped, glossy, mid-green leaves, 2–5in (5–12cm) long. In spring, produces solitary, occasionally 2, narrowly bell-shaped, pendent, glaucous, dark brownish purple flowers, tinged yellow within, to 1in (2.5cm) long, with deep yellow, recurving tepal tips. Cultivation group 2 or 4. ↕ to 8in (20cm), PD2in (5cm). S.E. Turkey, N. Iraq, W. Iran. Zone 5.

F. verticillata* var. *thunbergii see *F. thunbergii*.

FUCHSIA

ONAGRACEAE

Genus of approximately 100 species of deciduous or evergreen trees and shrubs, and a few perennials, from mountainous areas of Central and South America and New Zealand. There are more than 8,000 hybrids and cultivars, which have been developed for their attractive and distinctive flowers, usually borne more or less continuously from summer to autumn. *F. magellanica* is the hardiest species and has been used extensively to produce the modern hardy fuchsias; hybrids of *F. triphylla* have produced the Triphylla Group fuchsias (see panel).

Shrub and bush fuchsias are upright growers, while those referred to as trailers are hanging or prostrate in habit. Fuchsia flowers are axillary and usually pendulous, in terminal clusters, with short to long perianth tubes, each topped by far-spreading, colorful sepals and 4 erect, broad petals forming a cup or bell. In some species, the petals are very small or absent. In the following entries, flowers described as "very small" are ¼–¾in (0.5–2cm) across the sepals; "small" are ¾–1½in (2–4cm) across; "medium" are 1½–2½in (4–6cm) across; and "large" are 2½in (6cm) or more across. Fuchsia leaves are opposite or whorled, rarely alternate, simple, lance-shaped to very broadly ovate, mid-green, ¼–10in (0.5–25cm) long, occasionally to 16in (40cm). They are frequently toothed, grow in pairs (sometimes in whorls of 3), and are deciduous unless stated otherwise below. The fruits are berries, usually with many seeds.

Fuchsias, especially trained forms and pot-grown plants, are usually held to a strict pruning regimen, whether pinched for shape or to force blooming. Heights and spreads given in the entries indicate natural size if not held to a systematic pruning regimen.

Where not hardy, grow fuchsias in a cool greenhouse, placing them outdoors in a protected area for the summer. They do not tolerate high summer heat, drought, and high humidity, preferring cooler, less humid conditions. Plant fuchsias in the open garden in a border. Where hardy, fuchsias can be left outdoors throughout winter if correctly planted and mulched (see below). Outdoors or under glass, grow shrub and bush forms as standards, pillars, espaliers, or fans, while those with a trailing habit may be used as weeping standards or grown in a hanging basket, windowbox, or trough. *F. procumbens* can be grown in a rock garden in frost-free or mild climates.

Fuchsia arborescens

FUCHSIA FLOWERS

Fuchsia flowers are usually tubular and pendent, often bicolored, with a corolla of one hue, and a tube and 4 sepals of another. Single flowers have 4 petals; semi-double flowers 5–7 petals; double flowers 8 or more petals; fully double flowers have more than 8 petals. Triphylla Group fuchsias have long-tubed, single flowers and usually purple-backed foliage. Flowers of *F. procumbens* are erect.

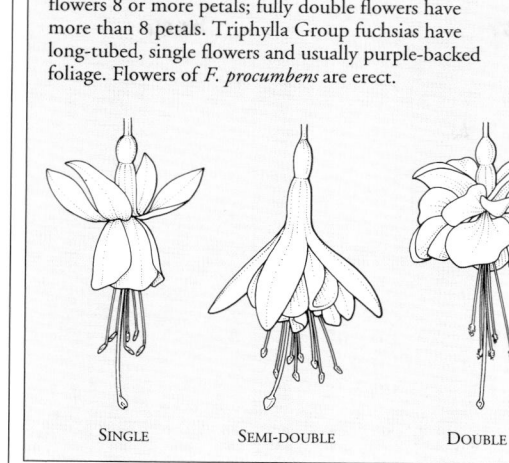

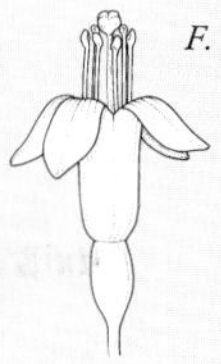

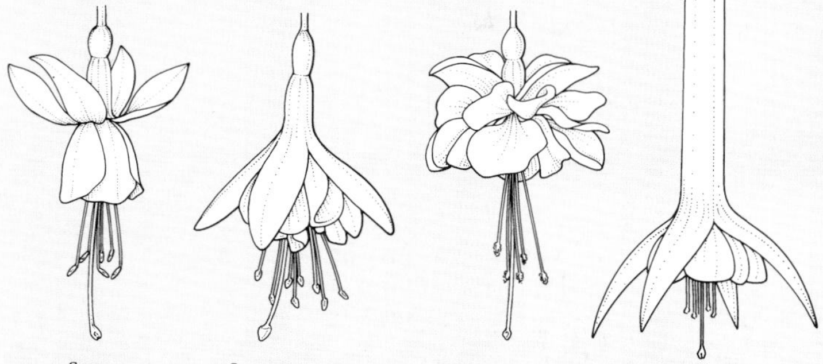

• **HARDINESS** Unless otherwise indicated, fuchsias are tender, with a minimum temperature of 35°F/2°C. Some cultivars may survive outdoors in the mildest parts of Zone 8.

• **CULTIVATION** Outdoors, grow in fertile, moist but well-drained soil in full morning sun to partial afternoon shade. Fertilize monthly. Plant the base of the stem 2in (5cm) below the soil surface and provide a deep winter mulch in colder areas. Shelter from cold, drying winds. Under glass, grow in soil-based potting mix or soilless potting mix, in bright filtered light with moderate humidity; ventilate well. During growth, water freely and apply a balanced liquid fertilizer weekly, especially in soilless mixes. Keep just moist in winter. Pruning group 6, unless specially trained.

• **PROPAGATION** Sow seed at 59–75°F (15–24°C) in spring. Root softwood cuttings in spring, or semi-ripe cuttings in late summer with bottom heat.

• **PESTS AND DISEASES** Prone to spider mites, scale insects, thrips, whiteflies, fuchsia gall mite, aphids, and root-knot nematodes. Rust, gray mold, crown gall, crown and root rots, Southern blight, and *Verticillium* wilt also occur.

***F.* 'Alice Hoffman'.** Free-flowering, upright shrub with densely clustered, purple-tinged, bronze-green leaves. Small, semi-double flowers have rose-pink tubes and sepals, and white corollas veined rose-pink. ↕↔ 18–24in (45–60cm).

***F.* 'Andrew Hadfield'.** Very free-flowering, upright shrub bearing medium, single flowers with carmine-red tubes and sepals, and white-based, pink-veined, bright lilac-blue corollas. ↕ 8–18in (20–45cm), ↔ 8–12in (20–30cm).

***F.* 'Annabel'** ■ Very free-flowering, upright bush with mid- to light green foliage. Medium, fully double flowers have pink-striped white tubes, white sepals with a slight pink flush, and pink-veined white corollas. Flowers bruise easily. ↕↔ 12–24in (30–60cm).

F. arborea see *F. arborescens.*

F. arborescens ■ syn. *F. arborea* (Lilac fuchsia). Erect, evergreen shrub or small tree with opposite or whorled, elliptic to inversely lance-shaped, thin, dark green leaves, 4–8in (10–20cm) long. Erect, corymb-like panicles of very small flowers, to ½in (1.5cm) across, with rose to magenta or purple-pink tubes, rose-purple sepals, and pale mauve corollas, appear in one flush in summer. The purple fruit are almost spherical, to ½in (1.5cm) long. ↕ to 6ft (2m), ↔ to 5½ft (1.7m). Mexico, Central America. ❀ (min. 41°F/5°C)

***F.* 'Auntie Jinks'** ■ Very free-flowering trailer bearing small, single flowers with pink-red tubes, cerise-margined white sepals, and purple corollas. ↕ 6–8in (15–20cm), ↔ 8–16in (20–40cm).

***F.* 'Autumnale'** ■ syn. *F.* 'Burning Bush'. Stiff trailer with green-and-yellow foliage that matures to dark red and salmon with splashes of yellow. Medium, single flowers, with scarlet-rose tubes and sepals, and purple corollas, are produced in late summer. ↕ 6–12in (15–30cm), ↔ 12–24in (30–60cm).

F. x bacillaris ■ (*F. microphylla* x *F. thymifolia*) syn. *F. parviflora* of gardens. Erect or spreading shrub with thin, wiry stems and lance-shaped to ovate, hairy-margined leaves, ¼–1in (0.5–2.5cm) long. Bears very small pink to deep red flowers, ¼–⅜in (5–8mm) across, and almost spherical, glossy, purple-brown fruit. ↕↔ 24–48in (60–120cm). Natural hybrid from Mexico.

Fuchsia 'Auntie Jinks'

***F.* 'Ballet Girl'** ■ Very free-flowering, upright shrub bearing large, double flowers, each with bright cerise tubes and sepals, and white corollas with cerise veins at the bases. ↕ 12–18in (30–45cm), ↔ 18–30in (45–75cm).

***F.* 'Bicentennial'** ■ Free-flowering, lax shrub bearing medium, double flowers with thin white tubes, orange sepals, and double corollas with magenta centers surrounded by orange petals. ↕ 12–18in (30–45cm), ↔ 18–24in (45–60cm).

***F.* 'Billy Green'** ■ Upright Triphylla Group shrub with light olive-green foliage. Bears small flowers, with long, tapering tubes, salmon-pink sepals, and finely pointed, salmon-pink corollas, at each leaf axil on strong stems. ↕ 18–24in (45–60cm), ↔ 12–18in (30–45cm). ❀ (min. 41°F/5°C)

F. boliviana. Shrub or small tree with lax, arching shoots, and opposite or 3-whorled, narrowly elliptic to broadly ovate, finely glandular-toothed, hairless to softly hairy leaves, 8in (20cm) long, sometimes with reddish veins. Bears large, pendent, terminal racemes or panicles, 2in (5cm) long, of small flowers with pale pink to vermilion tubes, reflexed pale pink to red sepals, and scarlet petals. ↕ to 12ft (4m), ↔ 3–4ft (1–1.2m). S. Peru to

Fuchsia 'Annabel'

Fuchsia 'Autumnale'

Fuchsia x *bacillaris*

Fuchsia 'Ballet Girl'

Fuchsia 'Bicentennial'

Fuchsia 'Billy Green'

F

Fuchsia 'Celia Smedley'

Fuchsia 'Display'

N. Argentina. ❄ (min. 41°F/5°C).
var. *alba* ■ syn. var. *luxurians*, has white tubes, and white sepals with light red marks at the bases.
***F.* 'Bon Accorde'.** Free-flowering, upright shrub with strong stems. Bears small, erect, single flowers with waxy, ivory-white tubes and sepals, and pale purple corollas suffused white. ↕ 18–24in (45–60cm), ↔ 12–18in (30–45cm).
***F.* 'Brookwood Belle'.** Lax, bushy shrub with strong, short-jointed stems. Medium, double flowers have deep cerise tubes and sepals, and white corollas flushed pink and veined deep rose-pink. ↕↔ 18–24in (45–60cm).
***F.* 'Burning Bush'** see *F.* 'Autumnale'.
***F.* 'Cascade'.** Free-flowering trailer bearing medium, single flowers with long, thin white tubes and sepals, heavily flushed carmine-red, and deep carmine-red corollas. ↕ 6–12in (15–30cm), ↔ 12–18in (30–45cm).
***F.* 'Celia Smedley'** ■ Very free-flowering, upright shrub bearing large, single flowers with dark pink tubes and sepals, and vivid currant-red corollas. ↕↔ 18–30in (45–75cm).
***F.* 'Charming'.** Free-flowering, upright shrub with strong stems and light yellowish green foliage. Medium, single flowers have carmine-red tubes, strongly reflexed, reddish cerise sepals, and cerise-based, rose-purple corollas. ↕ 18–30in (45–75cm), ↔ 24–30in (60–75cm).
***F.* 'Checkerboard'** ■ Very free-flowering, vigorous, upright shrub with strong stems. Produces medium, single flowers with slightly recurved, long red tubes, red sepals turning white, and white-based, dark red corollas. ↕ 30–36in (75–90cm), ↔ 18–30in (45–75cm).
***F.* 'Coralle'** ■ syn. *F.* 'Koralle'. Upright Triphylla Group shrub with strong stems and velvety, olive-green leaves. Bears terminal clusters of very small flowers with tapering, orange-red tubes, pointed, salmon-pink sepals, and orange-red or salmon-pink corollas. ↕ 18–36in (45–90cm), ↔ 18–24in (45–60cm). ❄ (min. 41°F/5°C)
***F.* 'Dark Eyes'.** Bushy, upright shrub bearing medium, double flowers that hold their shape for a long period. The tubes and upturned sepals are deep red, and the corollas deep violet-blue. ↕ 18–24in (45–60cm), ↔ 24–30in (60–75cm).
***F.* 'Display'** ■ Upright, vigorous, freely branching shrub with strong stems and medium, single flowers with carmine-red sepals and rose-pink corollas. ↕ 24–30in (60–75cm), ↔ 18–24in (45–60cm).
***F.* 'Dollar Princess'**, syn. *F.* 'Princess Dollar'. Vigorous, early-flowering, upright shrub producing abundant small to medium, double flowers with cerise tubes and sepals, and rich purple corollas turning deep pink at the base. ↕ 12–18in (30–45cm), ↔ 12–24in (30–60cm).
***F.* 'Elfriede Ott'.** Lax Triphylla Group shrub with dark green leaves. Very small flowers have long, salmon-pink tubes, pointed, salmon-pink sepals, and deeper salmon-pink corollas with curly, rose-red petal margins. ↕ 18–24in (45–60cm), ↔ 12–18in (30–45cm). ❄ (min. 41°F/5°C)
***F.* 'Estelle Marie'.** Upright shrub with ovate, dark green leaves. Small to medium, semi-erect, single flowers have greenish white tubes, green-tipped, white sepals, and blue-violet corollas that mature to violet with white at the bases. ↕↔ 12–18in (30–45cm).
***F.* 'Flirtation Waltz'.** Vigorous, upright, bushy, freely branching shrub with pale, toothed leaves. Medium, double flowers have pink-flushed, creamy white tubes, wide-spreading, creamy white sepals, and pale pink corollas. ↕ 18–24in (45–60cm), ↔ 12–18in (30–45cm).
F. fulgens ■ Upright shrub with spreading branches and ovate to heart-shaped, pale green leaves, 3½–9in (9–23cm) long, with fine, gland-tipped red teeth, flushed red beneath. Pendent terminal racemes of very small flowers, 1½–2in (4–5cm) long, have pink to dull red tubes, pale red sepals tinged yellow-green toward the margins, and bright red corollas. The fruit are oblong-ellipsoid and deep purple. ↕ 5ft (1.5m) or more, ↔ to 32in (80cm). Mexico. ❄ (min. 41°F/5°C)
***F.* 'Garden News'** ■ Upright shrub with strong stems producing multiple blooms in each leaf axil. Medium, double flowers have short, thick pink tubes, frost-pink sepals, and magenta-rose corollas becoming rose-pink at the petal bases. ↕↔ 18–24in (45–60cm).
***F.* 'Gartenmeister Bonstedt'.** Vigorous, very free-flowering, upright Triphylla Group shrub, similar to *F.* 'Thalia', bearing dark bronze-red leaves with purple undersides and very small, very long-tubed, brick-red flowers. ↕ 24–30in (60–75cm), ↔ 18–24in (45–60cm). ❄ (min. 41°F/5°C)
***F.* 'Genii'** ■ Upright, free-flowering shrub with red shoots and lime-yellow foliage. Small, single flowers have cerise tubes and sepals, and violet to violet-red corollas. ↕↔ 30–36in (75–90cm).
***F.* 'Golden Marinka'** ■ Trailer with variegated leaves of green and yellow. Produces medium, single, rich red flowers with darker red corollas. ↕ 6–12in (15–30cm), ↔ 12–18in (30–45cm).
***F.* 'Gruss aus dem Bodethal'** ■ (Black fuchsia). Freely branching shrub bearing medium, single flowers with crimson tubes and sepals, and very dark purple corollas. ↕ 12–18in (30–45cm), ↔ 18–24in (45–60cm).

Fuchsia fulgens

***F.* 'Heidi Weiss'** see *F.* 'White Ann'.
***F.* 'Herald'.** Vigorous, free-flowering, upright shrub. Medium, single flowers have scarlet tubes and sepals, and deep purple corollas. ↕↔ 24–36in (60–90cm).
***F.* 'Hermiena'.** Trailer bearing small to medium, single blooms with white tubes, narrow white sepals, and violet-purple corollas. ↕ 6–12in (15–30cm), ↔ 12–18in (30–45cm).
***F.* 'Hidcote'** ■ Free-flowering, upright shrub with light green foliage. Medium, single flowers have waxy cream tubes and sepals, and pale salmon-pink corollas shaded light rose-pink. ↕ 18–24in (45–60cm), ↔ 12–24in (30–60cm).
***F.* 'Jack Shahan'** ■ Free-flowering trailer bearing large, single flowers with pale rose-pink tubes and sepals, and rose-pink corollas. ↕ 12–18in (30–45cm), ↔ 18–24in (45–60cm).
***F.* 'Joy Patmore'** ■ Vigorous, upright shrub bearing medium, single flowers with white tubes, waxy white sepals tinged pink on the undersides, and rich carmine-red corollas. ↕ 12–18in (30–45cm), ↔ 18–24in (45–60cm).

Fuchsia boliviana var. *alba*

Fuchsia 'Checkerboard'

Fuchsia 'Coralle'

Fuchsia 'Garden News'

Fuchsia 'Golden Marinka'

Fuchsia 'Gruss aus dem Bodethal'

Fuchsia 'Hidcote'

Fuchsia 'Jack Shahan'

Fuchsia 'Joy Patmore'

Fuchsia 'La Campanella'

Fuchsia 'Lady Thumb'

Fuchsia 'Lena'

Fuchsia 'Genii'

***F.* 'Koralle'** see *F.* 'Coralle'.
***F.* 'La Campanella'** ■ Very free-flowering, self-branching trailer, with sparse growth initially, then rapidly filling out. Small, semi-double flowers have white tubes, white sepals with a slight pink flush, and purple corollas. ↕6–12in (15–30cm), ↔ 12–18in (30–45cm).
***F.* 'Lady Thumb'** ■ Free-flowering, upright shrub bearing small, semi-double flowers with light carmine-red tubes and sepals, and white corollas with slight carmine-red veining. A sport of *F.* 'Tom Thumb'. ↕6–12in (15–30cm), ↔ 12–18in (30–45cm).
***F.* 'Lena'** ■ Vigorous, free-flowering, very hardy trailer bearing toothed, pale to mid-green leaves and medium, single to semi-double flowers with flesh pink, almost white tubes and sepals, the tubes half-reflexed; the rose-magenta corollas are paler pink at the bases. ↕12–24in (30–60cm), ↔ 24–30in (60–75cm).
***F.* 'Leonora'** ■ Vigorous, upright, freely branching shrub with medium, bell-shaped, single, soft pink flowers. ↕24–30in (60–75cm), ↔ 12–24in (30–60cm).
***F.* 'Little Jewel'.** Upright shrub bearing medium, single flowers with carmine-red tubes, star-shaped, carmine-red sepals, and light purple corollas with faint carmine-red markings at the bases. ↕18–24in (45–60cm), ↔ 12–18in (30–45cm).
***F.* 'Love's Reward'** ■ Upright, short-jointed shrub bearing small to medium, single flowers with white to pale pink tubes and sepals, and violet-blue corollas. ↕↔ 12–18in (30–45cm).
***F.* 'Lye's Unique'** ■ Free-flowering, upright shrub with strong stems. Medium, single flowers have waxy white tubes and sepals, and salmon-orange corollas. ↕18–24in (45–60cm), ↔ 12–18in (30–45cm).
***F.* 'Machu Picchu'** ■ Very free-flowering, lax, trailing shrub. Small, single flowers have pale salmon-pink tubes and sepals (with pink undersides to the sepals) and salmon-pink corollas. Heat tolerant. ↕↔ 12–24in (30–60cm).
F. magellanica ■ Erect shrub with ovate-elliptic, scalloped to toothed leaves, ½–2½in (1.5–6cm) long, occasionally with minute stiff hairs, sometimes tinted red beneath. Throughout summer, freely produces small flowers with red tubes, deep red, rarely white or pale pink, wide-spreading sepals, and purple corollas. The fruit are oblong and red-purple. Suitable for hedging in frost-free areas. ↕ to 10ft (3m), ↔ 6–10ft (2–3m). Chile, Argentina. Zone 7 (with extensive protection).
'Riccartonii' see *F.* 'Riccartonii'.
***F.* 'Margaret'.** Very vigorous, upright shrub bearing abundant small, semi-double flowers with carmine-scarlet tubes and sepals, and violet-purple corollas. Suitable for hedging in frost-free areas. ↕↔ to 4ft (1.2m).
***F.* 'Margaret Brown'** ■ Free-flowering, upright shrub with strong stems and light green foliage. Bears small, single, 2-tone pink flowers in summer. ↕↔ 24–36in (60–90cm).
***F.* 'Marinka'** ■ Extremely free-flowering trailer with dark green leaves veined red beneath. Medium, single flowers have red tubes and sepals, and slightly darker red corollas. ↕6–12in (15–30cm), ↔ 18–24in (45–60cm).
***F.* 'Mary'** ■ Upright Triphylla Group shrub bearing elliptic, dark green leaves, veined red-purple. Very small, vivid crimson flowers have long tubes and reflexed sepals. ↕↔ 12–24in (30–60cm). ❀ (min. 41°F/5°C)
***F.* 'Micky Gault'** ■ Free-flowering, upright shrub with light green foliage. Small, semi-erect, single flowers have white tubes flushed pink, white sepals with very pale pink undersides, and pink-purple corollas. ↕12–18in (30–45cm), ↔ 18–24in (45–60cm).

Fuchsia 'Mrs. Lovell Swisher'

***F.* 'Mieke Meursing'.** Upright, bushy, freely branching shrub bearing medium, single or semi-double flowers with red tubes and sepals, and pale pink corollas veined deep pink. ↕↔ 12–24in (30–60cm).
***F.* 'Mrs. Lovell Swisher'** ■ Very vigorous, upright shrub bearing masses of small, single flowers with flesh-pink tubes, pinkish white sepals, and deep rose corollas. ↕18–24in (45–60cm), ↔ 12–24in (30–60cm).
***F.* 'Mrs. Popple'** ■ Upright, bushy, vigorous shrub with deep green leaves. Medium, single flowers have scarlet tubes and sepals, and cerise-centered, purple-violet corollas. ↕↔ 3–3½ft (1–1.1m).
***F.* 'Nellie Nuttall'** ■ Vigorous, very free-flowering, early-blooming, upright shrub bearing small, upward-looking, single flowers with bright red tubes and sepals, and red-veined white corollas. ↕6–18in (15–45cm), ↔ 12–18in (30–45cm).
***F.* 'Neopolitan'.** Upright shrub with wiry stems bearing separate, very small, single flowers of red, pink, or white on the same plant. The sepals of each flower reflex back to the tube, and each corolla opens flat. ↕18–24in (45–60cm), ↔ 24–36in (60–90cm).
***F.* 'Other Fellow'** ■ Very free-flowering, upright shrub bearing small, single flowers with waxy white tubes, green-tipped white sepals, and white-based, coral-pink corollas. ↕↔ 12–18in (30–45cm).
***F.* 'Pacquesa'.** Upright shrub with foliage borne on freely branching, short-jointed stems. Large, single flowers have deep red tubes, reflexed, glowing, deep red sepals, and pure white corollas veined deep red. ↕18–24in (45–60cm), ↔ 12–18in (30–45cm).
***F. parviflora* of gardens** see *F.* x *bacillaris.*
***F.* 'Peppermint Stick'.** Upright shrub bearing medium to large, double flowers with carmine-red tubes and upturned, carmine-red sepals, each with a distinct white stripe down the middle. The corollas have rich, royal-purple petals in the center, and light carmine-rose petals with purple outer margins. ↕↔ 18–30in (45–75cm).
***F.* 'Phyllis'.** Very hardy, vigorous, upright shrub bearing masses of small to medium, semi-double flowers with cerise-flushed, waxy, rose-red tubes and sepals, and rose-cerise corollas. Useful for hedging. ↕3–5ft (1–1.5m), ↔ 30–36in (75–90cm).
***F.* 'Pink Rain'.** Very free-flowering, self-branching trailer bearing small, single flowers with pink tubes, rose sepals, and pinkish purple corollas. ↕6–8in (15–20cm), ↔ 10–14in (25–35cm).
***F.* 'Postiljon'.** Trailer bearing small, single flowers. The tubes are pale-pink-flushed, creamy white; the sepals are creamy white, flushed rose-pink beneath; and the magenta corollas turn dark mauve-purple when mature. ↕↔ 12–18in (30–45cm).
***F.* 'President Margaret Slater'.** Free-flowering trailer bearing medium, single

Fuchsia 'Leonora'

Fuchsia 'Love's Reward'

Fuchsia 'Lye's Unique'

Fuchsia 'Machu Picchu'

Fuchsia magellanica

Fuchsia 'Margaret Brown'

Fuchsia 'Marinka'

Fuchsia 'Mary'

Fuchsia 'Micky Gault'

Fuchsia 'Mrs. Popple'

Fuchsia 'Nellie Nuttall'

Fuchsia 'Other Fellow'

Fuchsia 'Tom Thumb'

flowers with long, thin white tubes and slightly twisted white sepals, flushed salmon-pink on the insides and deep salmon-pink beneath, and mauve-pink corollas. ↕ 12–18in (30–45cm), ↔ 18–30in (45–75cm).
***F.* 'Princess Dollar'** see *F.* 'Dollar Princess'.
F. procumbens ■ (Trailing fuchsia). Prostrate shrub with rounded, heart-shaped leaves, ¼–¾in (6–20mm) long. In summer, bears small, upward-facing flowers, with greenish yellow to pale orange tubes (red-based when mature), and purple-tipped green sepals. There are no corollas, and the stamens bear bright blue pollen. The spherical, glaucous, bright red fruit, to ½in (1.5cm) long, resemble miniature plums. ↕ 4–6in (10–15cm), ↔ 3–4ft (1–1.2m). New Zealand.
***F.* 'R.A.F.'.** Free-flowering trailer or lax bush producing medium, double flowers with bright red tubes and sepals, and rose-pink corollas, splashed and veined cerise. ↕ 6–10in (15–25cm), ↔ 12–18in (30–45cm).
***F.* 'Red Jacket'.** Free-flowering trailer bearing long, showy buds opening to large, double flowers with bright red tubes and sepals, and pure white corollas, opening larger with age and without the usual browning of the petals. ↕ 8–12in (20–30cm), ↔ 12–24in (30–60cm).
***F.* 'Red Spider'.** Vigorous trailer bearing medium, single flowers with deep crimson tubes, narrow, recurved crimson sepals, and deep rose-red corollas. ↕ 6–12in (15–30cm), ↔ 12–24in (30–60cm).
***F.* 'Riccartonii'** ■ syn. *F. magellanica* 'Riccartonii'. Extremely hardy, upright shrub bearing dark green leaves with a slight bronze sheen. Small, single flowers have scarlet tubes and sepals, and dark purple corollas. Suitable for hedging in frost-free areas. ↕ 6–10ft (2–3m), ↔ 3–6ft (1–2m).
***F.* 'Rough Silk'.** Trailer with light green foliage. Large, single flowers have pale carmine-pink tubes, upward-sweeping, pale carmine-pink sepals, and crimson-red corollas, paler at the bases. ↕ 6–12in (15–30cm), ↔ 12–24in (30–60cm).

Fuchsia procumbens

Fuchsia 'Riccartonii'

Fuchsia 'Rufus'

Fuchsia 'Swingtime'

Fuchsia 'Thalia'

Fuchsia 'Tom West'

***F.* 'Royal Velvet'.** Vigorous, very free-flowering, upright shrub. Medium, double flowers have crimson-red tubes, upturned, crimson-red sepals, and deep purple corollas. ↕ 18–30in (45–75cm), ↔ 12–24in (30–60cm).
***F.* 'Rufus'** ■ syn. *F.* 'Rufus the Red'. Vigorous, early-flowering, upright shrub bearing medium, single flowers with bright red tubes, sepals, and corollas. ↕ 18–30in (45–75cm), ↔ 12–24in (30–60cm).
***F.* 'Rufus the Red'** see *F.* 'Rufus'.
***F.* 'Streamliner'.** Free-flowering trailer bearing medium, semi-double flowers, 3in (8cm) long, with crimson tubes and sepals, and rose-red to crimson corollas. ↕ to 8in (20cm), ↔ 12–18in (30–45cm).
***F.* 'Swingtime'** ■ Vigorous, free-flowering, lax, upright shrub bearing red-veined, dark green leaves with finely toothed edges. Large, double blooms have shiny, rich red tubes and sepals, and bright white corollas. May also be grown as a trailer. ↕ 12–24in (30–60cm), ↔ 18–30in (45–75cm).
***F.* 'Tangerine'.** Free-flowering, upright shrub bearing medium, single pink flowers with green-tipped tubes, flesh-pink sepals that do not reflex, and orange corollas, turning rose. ↕↔ 24–36in (60–90cm).
***F.* 'Thalia'** ■ Vigorous, upright Triphylla Group shrub bearing dark olive-green leaves with purple-tinged undersides, and abundant, very small, rich orange-scarlet flowers with very long tubes. ↕↔ 18–36in (45–90cm). ❄ (min. 41°F/5°C)
***F.* 'Tom Thumb'** ■ Extremely free-flowering, early-blooming, upright shrub bearing small, single flowers with carmine-red tubes and sepals, and mauve corollas veined carmine-red. ↕↔ 6–12in (15–30cm).
***F.* 'Tom West'** ■ Rigid trailer with green-and-cream-variegated, cerise-veined foliage that turns pink in sunlight. Small, single flowers have red tubes and sepals, and purple corollas. ↕↔ 12–24in (30–60cm).
***F.* 'Walsingham'.** Lax, upright shrub with toothed, emerald-green leaves. Medium, semi-double flowers have pale pink tubes, upward-sweeping, pale pink sepals, and pale lavender-lilac corollas with very distinctive crimping on the petal margins. ↕ 12–18in (30–45cm), ↔ 18–24in (45–60cm).
***F.* 'White Ann'**, syn. *F.* 'Heidi Weiss'. Vigorous, free-flowering, upright shrub bearing dark green leaves with crimson midribs. Medium, double flowers have crimson-cerise tubes and sepals, and white corollas with scarlet veins. ↕↔ 12–24in (30–60cm).
***F.* 'Winston Churchill'.** Extremely free-flowering, bushy, upright shrub bearing medium, fully double flowers with green-tipped pink tubes, broad, reflexed, green-tipped pink sepals, and lavender-blue corollas, maturing to pale purple. ↕↔ 18–30in (45–75cm).

FURCRAEA

AGAVACEAE

Genus of 12 or more species of perennial succulents from desert-like areas of the West Indies, Central America, and N. South America. Dense clusters of long, fleshy leaves are borne in terminal or basal rosettes. In summer, each rosette produces a large, terminal, pyramidal panicle bearing broadly bell-shaped, pendulous, diurnal flowers. Small, adventitious plantlets often form between the flowers. Where temperatures drop below 50°F (10°C), grow in a temperate greenhouse; in warmer climates, use in a desert garden or as specimen plants.
• **CULTIVATION** Under glass, grow in standard cactus potting mix in full light with low humidity. During growth, water moderately and apply a low-nitrogen fertilizer monthly. Keep just moist in autumn and winter. Outdoors, grow in poor to moderately fertile, sharply drained soil in full sun. Protect from winter moisture. See also pp.48–49.
• **PROPAGATION** Sow seed at 59–75°F (15–24°C) in spring. Divide offsets or pot up plantlets in summer. Root adventitious plantlets in summer.
• **PESTS AND DISEASES** Susceptible to scale insects.

***F. foetida* 'Mediopicta'** ■ syn. *F. foetida* 'Variegata', *F. gigantea* 'Mediopicta'. Succulent, sometimes clump-forming, with a stem 32–36in (80–90cm) long, and terminal rosettes of broadly inversely lance-shaped to lance-shaped, bright, glossy, mid-green leaves, to 8ft (2.5m) long, with creamy white longitudinal lines; the margins are smooth or bear a few hooked spines. In summer, bears inflorescences, 20–40ft (6–12m) high, of strongly scented white flowers, 2–2½in (5–6cm) long, with green outer petals. Produces plantlets freely. ↕ 3–4ft (1–1.2m), ↔ 8ft (2.5m). Probably West Indies, possibly S. Brazil. ❄ (min. 50°F/10°C)
***F. foetida* 'Variegata'** see *F. foetida* 'Mediopicta'.
***F. gigantea* 'Mediopicta'** see *F. foetida* 'Mediopicta'.
F. selloa. Variable succulent, sometimes clump-forming, with stems to 5ft (1.5m) long. Bears spreading terminal rosettes of narrowly lance-shaped to sword-shaped, rough, glossy, mid-green leaves, 4ft (1.2m) or more long, with large, brown, marginal, hooked spines. Lax-branched inflorescences, to 15ft (5m) high, of faintly scented white flowers, 2½–3in (6–8cm) long, with green outer petals, develop in summer. Produces plantlets freely. ↕ 5ft (1.5m), ↔ 6ft (2m). Mexico, Guatemala, Colombia. ❄ (min. 50°F/10°C). **'Marginata'** has pale green-white leaf margins.

Furcraea foetida 'Mediopicta'

G

GAGEA

LILIACEAE

Genus of about 50 species of small, bulbous perennials from Europe, N. Africa, and W. and C. Asia. They are grown for their star-shaped to cup- or funnel-shaped, yellow or white flowers, borne in umbels or racemes, with prominent leaf-like bracts, from spring to early summer. The leaves are basal, long, and linear or linear-lance-shaped. Some species produce bulbils in the axils of basal leaves and in the inflorescences. Most are suitable for a rock garden; in wet climates, *G. graeca* is best grown in an alpine house or bulb frame.

• **CULTIVATION** Plant bulbs 1½in (4cm) deep. Under glass, grow in a mix of equal parts soil-based potting mix and grit in full light. Water freely in growth; keep just moist when dormant. Outdoors, grow in well-drained, humus-rich soil in full sun.

• **PROPAGATION** Sow seed in containers in a cold frame in autumn. Separate bulbs when dormant and pot up bulbils after flowering.

• **PESTS AND DISEASES** Infrequent.

G. arvensis see *G. villosa.*

G. graeca, syn. *Lloydia graeca.* Delicate, bulbous perennial with very narrow, linear leaves, 1½–5in (4–13cm) long. In spring, bears umbels of up to 5 pendent, funnel-shaped, purple-veined white flowers, to ½in (1.5cm) long. Keep dry when dormant. ↕2–4in (5–10cm), PD2in (5cm). Greece (including Crete), S. Turkey. Zone 7b.

G. peduncularis. Bulbous perennial with narrow, linear leaves, 2½–12in (6–30cm) long, taller than the flower stems. Loose racemes of up to 7 funnel-shaped yellow flowers, ½–1¼in (1.5–3cm) across, with central green stripes on the outsides, are borne in spring. ↕2–6in (5–15cm), PD2in (5cm). Balkans, N. Africa. Zone 7.

G. villosa, syn. *G. arvensis.* Bulbous perennial with linear leaves, 6in (15cm) long. In spring, produces loose umbels of up to 15 star-shaped yellow flowers, ¾in (2cm) across. Increases rapidly by bulbils borne from the basal leaf axils. ↕2–4in (5–10cm), PD2in (5cm). Europe, N. Africa, Turkey, Iran. Zone 7.

GAILLARDIA

Blanket flower

ASTERACEAE

Genus of 30 species of annuals, perennials, and biennials found in open, sunny habitats on prairies and hillsides in W., C., and S. North America and South America. They bear entire, toothed, lobed, or pinnatifid, hairy leaves, produced in basal rosettes and alternately on the stems. Red, orange, or yellow, daisy-like flowerheads, with dark purple, brown, red, or yellow disk florets, are borne on long stems. The numerous cultivars are bushy, leafy plants with brightly colored flowerheads and a long flowering period. They are effective in a sunny border and are also good for cutting.

• **CULTIVATION** Grow in fertile, well-drained soil in full sun; poor soil is tolerated. Deadhead regularly. In colder climates, cut perennials back to about 6in (15cm) in late summer to encourage new basal growth, which usually overwinters well.

• **PROPAGATION** Sow seed of annual and perennial species at 55–64°F (13–18°C) in early spring; annual seed may also be sown *in situ* in late spring or early summer. Most perennials flower in their first year from seed. Divide perennials in spring or take root cuttings in winter.

• **PESTS AND DISEASES** Prone to downy mildew, rust, powdery mildew, white smut, bacterial leaf spots, and *Septoria* leaf spot, as well as slugs and snails.

G. aristata ▣ Erect but often spreading perennial with inversely lance-shaped to lance-shaped, entire or toothed, shallowly lobed or pinnatifid, grayish green leaves, to 8in (20cm) long. From summer to autumn, produces flowerheads, to 4in (10cm) across, with yellow ray florets, sometimes tinged red at the base, and reddish orange disk florets. Often requires staking. ↕30in (75cm), ↔24in (60cm). W. British Columbia, Saskatchewan to W. Arizona, New Mexico. Zone 3.

Gaillardia x *grandiflora* 'Dazzler'

G.* x *grandiflora (*G. aristata* x *G. pulchella*). Bushy, often short-lived perennial with inversely lance-shaped, entire or lobed, sometimes pinnatifid, gray to mid-green leaves, to 12in (30cm) long. Flowerheads, 3–5½in (7–14cm) across, with yellow ray florets, touched red at the bases, and yellow-brown disk florets, are produced from early summer to early autumn. ↕to 36in (90cm), ↔18in (45cm). Garden origin. Zone 3. **'Baby Cole'** has flowerheads, to 3in (8cm) across, of maroon disk florets and yellow-tipped, bright red ray florets; ↕8in (20cm), ↔6–8in (15–20cm). **'Burgunder'**, syn. 'Burgundy', has deep wine-red flowerheads; ↕20–24in (50–60cm). **'Dazzler'** ▣ is short-lived and has bright orange-red, yellow-tipped ray florets and maroon disk florets; ↕24–34in (60–85cm). **'Goblin'** see 'Kobold'. **'Golden Goblin'** see 'Goldkobold'. **'Goldkobold'**, syn. 'Golden Goblin', has deep golden yellow ray florets and darker yellow disk florets; ↕10in (25cm). **'Kobold'**, syn. 'Goblin', bears rich red, yellow-tipped ray florets and red disk florets; ↕12in (30cm). **'Wirral Flame'** bears yellow-tipped, deep orange-red flowerheads; ↕to 30in (75cm).

Gaillardia pulchella Plume Series 'Red Plume'

G. pulchella (Blanket flower, Indian blanket). Upright, bushy annual with spoon-shaped to inversely lance-shaped, entire or coarsely toothed, gray-green leaves, to 3in (8cm) long. From summer to autumn, produces red-tipped yellow, or entirely red or yellow flowerheads, to 2in (5cm) across, with dark purple disk florets. ↕18in (45cm), ↔12in (30cm). C. and S. US, Mexico. **Plume Series** cultivars have double, red or yellow flowerheads; ↕12in (30cm); **Plume Series 'Red Plume'** ▣ has rounded, very double flowerheads of vibrant red. **'Portola Giants'** produce bronzed scarlet, gold-tipped flowerheads, to 2½in (6cm) across.

Gaillardia aristata

GALANTHUS

Snowdrop

AMARYLLIDACEAE

Genus of about 19 species of bulbous perennials found from Europe to W. Asia, mostly in upland woodland but also in rocky sites. They bloom mainly from late winter to midspring, each bulb usually producing a single, pendent bloom with an arching flower-stalk on a slender stem, above 2, rarely 3, semi-erect, strap-shaped to inversely lance-shaped, basal leaves. The pear-shaped flowers are white, with 3 small inner tepals variably marked green, and 3 larger, spreading outer tepals. They are sometimes scented. Most snowdrops are vigorous and easily grown; some are suitable for naturalizing in grass or light woodland, and grow well in borders and rock gardens. All parts may cause mild stomach upset if ingested; contact with the bulbs may irritate skin.

• **CULTIVATION** Grow in humus-rich, moist but well-drained soil that does not dry out in summer, in partial shade.

• **PROPAGATION** Sow seed of species as soon as ripe in containers in an open frame; keep shaded in summer. *Galanthus* species hybridize readily in

Galanthus 'Atkinsii'

Galanthus caucasicus of gardens

Galanthus elwesii

Galanthus gracilis

Galanthus ikariae

Galanthus 'John Gray'

Galanthus 'Magnet'

Galanthus nivalis 'Pusey Green Tip'

Galanthus nivalis 'Sandersii'

Galanthus plicatus subsp. *byzantinus*

Galanthus rizehensis

Galanthus 'S. Arnott'

gardens and seed may not come true. Lift and divide clumps of bulbs after flowering but before the leaves begin to die down.
• **PESTS AND DISEASES** Prone to narcissus bulb fly and snowdrop gray mold (*Botrytis galanthina*).

G. allenii. Bulbous perennial with broad, dull, somewhat glaucous leaves, 2½in (6cm) long. In late winter and early spring, bears rounded, almond-scented flowers, ¾in (2cm) long, with a large green mark at the tip of each inner tepal. May be difficult to establish. ↕5in (13cm), PD3in (8cm). Unknown origin; probably hybrid from the Caucasus. Zone 6b.
***G.* 'Arnott's Seedling'** see *G.* 'S. Arnott'.
***G.* 'Atkinsii'** ▣ Vigorous, bulbous perennial with narrow, glaucous leaves, to 4in (10cm) long. In late winter, bears slender, elongated flowers, 1¼in (3cm) long, with a heart-shaped green mark at the tip of each inner tepal. May produce malformed tepals. ↕8in (20cm), PD3in (8cm). Zone 4.
***G.* 'Augustus'.** Robust, bulbous perennial producing broad, pale green leaves, 3–4in (8–10cm) long, each with a glaucous central channel and recurved or folded margins. In late winter and early spring, bears flowers, ½–¾in (1.5–2cm) long, with an H-shaped green mark on each inner tepal. ↕6in (15cm), PD3in (8cm). Zone 5b.

Galanthus nivalis 'Flore Pleno'

***G.* 'Brenda Troyle'.** Vigorous, bulbous perennial with narrow, glaucous, gray-green leaves, 3–6in (8–15cm) long. In late winter, produces flowers ¾–1¼in (2–3cm) long, with an inverted V-shaped green mark at the tip of each inner tepal. ↕8in (20cm), PD3in (8cm). Zone 5b.
***G. caucasicus* of gardens** ▣ Variable, bulbous perennial with broad, glaucous leaves, to 5in (13cm) long, recurving with age. From late autumn to early spring, produces flowers to 1¼in (3cm) long, with a green mark at the tip of each inner tepal. ↕4–6in (10–15cm), PD3in (8cm). Probably Turkey. Zone 5. **'Double'** see *G.* 'Lady Beatrix Stanley'.
G. corcyrensis see *G. reginae-olgae.*
G. elwesii ▣ (Giant snowdrop). Robust, bulbous perennial with broad, sometimes twisted, glaucous leaves, 4–6in (10–15cm) long. In late winter, bears slender, honey-scented flowers, ¾–1¼in (2–3cm) long, with 2 green markings, which sometimes merge, on each inner tepal. ↕5–9in (12–23cm), PD3in (8cm). Balkans, W. Turkey. Zone 4. **var. *minor*** see *G. gracilis.*
G. fosteri. Slender, bulbous perennial with narrow, bright, deep green leaves, 3–5½in (8–14cm) long. In late winter, bears flowers ½–1in (1.5–2.5cm) long, with inner tepals marked green at the bases and apexes. Needs a dry site. Plant bulbs 4in (10cm) deep to minimize development of non-flowering bulbs. ↕to 3–8in (8–20cm), PD2in (5cm). S. Turkey, Lebanon. Zone 5b.
G. gracilis ▣ syn. *G. elwesii* var. *minor, G. graecus* of gardens. Slender, bulbous perennial with linear, twisted, glaucous leaves, 2–6in (5–15cm) long. In late winter and early spring, produces scented flowers, to ½–1in (1.5–2.5cm) long, each with 2 green markings on the flared inner tepals, and with long, pale green ovaries. ↕4in (10cm), PD2in (5cm). Bulgaria, Greece, Turkey. Zone 4.
***G. graecus* of gardens** see *G. gracilis.*
G. ikariae ▣ syn. *G. latifolius* of gardens. Bulbous perennial with broad, glossy, bright green leaves, 2½–6in (6–15cm) long. In late winter and early spring, bears flowers ½–1¼in (1–3cm) long, with a large green mark at the tip of each inner tepal. ↕4–6in (10–15cm), PD2in (5cm). Aegean Islands, Turkey. Zone 4.
***G.* 'Jacquenetta'.** Robust, bulbous perennial producing narrow leaves, 4in (10cm) long, each with a somewhat glaucous central stripe and slightly folded margins. In late winter, bears large, double flowers to 1in (2.5cm) across, occasionally with a few irregular tepals; the inner tepals are strongly marked green at the tips, the outer tepals sometimes each have a faint green mark. ↕8in (20cm), PD3in (8cm). Zone 6b.
***G.* 'John Gray'** ▣ Robust, bulbous perennial with narrow, gray-green leaves, 3–7in (8–18cm) long. Very large flowers, 1¼–1½in (3–4cm) long, are borne on arching stems in early winter, the inner tepals each with an X-shaped, dark green mark. ↕6in (15cm), PD3in (8cm). Zone 5.
***G.* 'Ketton'.** Robust, bulbous perennial with narrow, glaucous leaves, 3–6in (7–15cm) long. In late winter, produces large flowers, 1¼in (3cm) or more long, with a pair of green marks, sometimes joined, at the tip of each inner tepal. ↕7in (18cm), PD3in (8cm). Zone 5.
***G.* 'Lady Beatrix Stanley'**, syn. *G. caucasicus* of gardens 'Double'. Bulbous perennial with glaucous leaves, 3–6in (8–15cm) long, erect then recurved. Bears double flowers, to 1in (2.5cm) across, with a tiny green mark at the tip of each inner tepal, in late winter and early spring. ↕5in (13cm), PD2in (5cm). Zone 5.
***G. latifolius* of gardens** see *G. ikariae.*
***G.* 'Magnet'** ▣ Vigorous, bulbous perennial producing narrow, gray-green leaves, 3–6in (8–15cm) long, with slightly folded margins. In late winter and early spring, bears large flowers, ¾–1in (2–2.5cm) long, on long flower stalks; the inner tepals each have an inverted V-shaped green mark at the tip. ↕8in (20cm), PD3in (8cm). Zone 4.
***G.* 'Merlin'.** Robust, bulbous perennial with narrow, gray-green leaves, 3–6in (8–15cm) or more long. In late winter and early spring, produces large flowers, ¾–1¼in (2–3cm) long, the inner tepals

Galanthus nivalis 'Lady Elphinstone' (inset: flower detail)

mostly covered with deep green marks. ↕7in (18cm), PD3in (8cm). Zone 5.
***G.* 'Mighty Atom'.** Bulbous perennial producing narrow, glaucous leaves, 2–5in (5–13cm) long. In late winter, bears large flowers, 1¼–1½in (3–4cm) long, with an inverted V-shaped, deep green mark at the tip of each inner tepal. ↕5in (13cm), PD3in (8cm). Zone 5.
G. nivalis (Common snowdrop). Bulbous perennial with narrow, glaucous leaves, 2–6in (5–15cm) long. Small flowers, ½–¾in (1.5–2cm) long, with an inverted V-shaped green mark at the tip of each inner tepal, are honey-scented and produced in winter. ↕↔ 4in (10cm). Pyrenees to Ukraine. Zone 3. **'Flore Pleno'** ■ is robust, and produces irregular, double flowers. It is sterile, but will increase rapidly from offsets. **'Howick Yellow'** see 'Sandersii'. **'Lady Elphinstone'** ■ has gray-green leaves and double flowers in late winter and early spring. The inner tepal markings are yellow on established plants; ↕5in (13cm), PD3in (8cm). **'Lutescens'** see 'Sandersii'. **'Pusey Green Tip'** ■ has irregularly double flowers with pale green markings on the outer tepals. **'Sandersii'** ■ syn. 'Howick Yellow', 'Lutescens', is slender with yellow markings on the inner tepals and ovary. **'Scharlokii'**, syn. 'Scharlockii', has slender flowers, with green markings on the outer tepals, overtopped by spathes split in 2. **'Viridapicis'** has a very long spathe, sometimes split in 2, and green marks on the outer tepal tips.
***G.* 'Ophelia'.** Vigorous, bulbous perennial with narrow, glaucous leaves, 4–5½in (10–14cm) long. In late winter, neat, double flowers, to ¾in (2cm) across, the outer tepals marked green, are borne on tall stems. ↕8in (20cm), PD3in (8cm). Zone 5.
G. plicatus. Bulbous perennial producing broad, dull green leaves, 3–7in (8–18cm) long, with glaucous central bands and recurved margins. In late winter and early spring, bears flowers ¾–1¼in (2–3cm) long, with a single green mark at the tip of each inner tepal. ↕to 8in (20cm), PD3in (8cm). Ukraine (Crimea), Romania, N. Turkey. Zone 4. **subsp. *byzantinus*** ■ has green markings at the base and apex of each inner tepal. Turkey (N.W. Anatolia).
G. reginae-olgae, syn. *G. corcyrensis.* Slender, bulbous perennial with narrow, recurving, gray-green leaves, to 2½in (6cm) long, each with a narrow, glaucous central stripe. In autumn, bears faintly scented flowers, to 1in (2.5cm) long, the inner tepal tips marked green. Needs a dry site. ↕4in (10cm), PD2in (5cm). Italy (Sicily), Greece, former Yugoslavia. Zone 7b. **subsp. *vernalis*** blooms in late winter and early spring.
G. rizehensis ■ Slender, bulbous perennial with linear, recurved, deep green leaves, 2½–5in (6–13cm) long. In late winter and early spring, bears small flowers, ½–¾in (1.5–2cm) long, marked with green at the tips of the inner tepals. ↕5in (13cm), PD2in (5cm). N.E. Turkey. Zone 4.
***G.* 'Robin Hood'.** Bulbous perennial with narrow, glaucous leaves, 3–5½in (8–14cm) long. In late winter and early spring, bears slender flowers, 1–1¼in (2.5–3cm) long, with an X-shaped green mark on each inner tepal. ↕6in (15cm), PD3in (8cm). Zone 5.
***G.* 'Sam Arnott'** see *G.* 'S. Arnott'.
***G.* 'S. Arnott'** ■ syn. *G.* 'Arnott's Seedling', *G.* 'Sam Arnott'. Vigorous, bulbous perennial with gray-green leaves, 3–6in (8–15cm) long. In late winter and early spring, bears large, strongly honey-scented, well-rounded flowers, 1–1½in (2.5–4cm) long, with an inverted V-shaped green mark at the tip of each inner tepal. ↕8in (20cm), PD3in (8cm). Zone 4.
***G.* 'Straffan'.** Vigorous, bulbous perennial producing narrow, glaucous leaves, 3–6in (8–15cm) long. In midspring, bears flowers 1in (2.5cm) long, with a small, inverted V-shaped green mark on each inner tepal. Each bulb may produce 2 flower stems. ↕5in (13cm), PD3in (8cm). Zone 5.

GALAX
Wandflower

DIAPENSIACEAE

Genus of one species of tufted, evergreen perennial from open woodland in the mountains of S.E. US. It has a creeping rootstock, rounded leaves, and spike-like racemes of small white flowers. Grown for its flowers and autumn foliage color, *G. urceolata* is suitable for underplanting in a shaded shrub border, for a large rock garden, or as a groundcover in a woodland garden.
• **CULTIVATION** Grow in moist, acidic, humus-rich soil in partial shade; ensure that the roots do not dry out. Mulch annually in spring with pine needles or other acidic organic matter.
• **PROPAGATION** Sow seed in containers of acidic seed-starting mix in an open frame outdoors in autumn. Separate rooted runners in early spring.
• **PESTS AND DISEASES** Anthracnose or sooty mold can occur, as well as slugs and snails.

G. aphylla see *G. urceolata.*
G. urceolata ■ syn. *G. aphylla.* Tufted, evergreen perennial with rounded, toothed, glossy, dark green leaves, to 3in (8cm) across, which are heart-shaped at the bases. The leaves turn red-bronze in autumn. In late spring and early summer, produces narrow, upright, spike-like racemes, to 10in (25cm) long, of tiny, 5-lobed white flowers. ↕to 12in (30cm), ↔ to 3ft (1m). S.E. US. Zone 6.

Galax urceolata

GALEGA
Goat's rue

FABACEAE

Genus of about 6 species of tall, bushy perennials from sunny but damp meadows, slopes, and banks in C. and S. Europe, W. Asia, and the mountains of tropical E. Africa. They have alternate, pinnate, soft green or blue-tinged leaves, 3–8in (8–20cm) long, and produce erect, axillary racemes of pea-like, white, blue, mauve, or bicolored flowers. *Galega* species and cultivars naturalize well, and are effective in a border from midsummer onward; some are also good for cutting.
• **CULTIVATION** Grow in any, preferably moist, soil in full sun or partial shade. They need staking, and may spread rapidly in rich soil. Cut back flowered stems to prevent self-seeding.
• **PROPAGATION** Sow seed of species, soaked overnight, in containers in a cold frame in spring. Divide cultivars between late autumn and spring.
• **PESTS AND DISEASES** Pea and bean weevils may be a problem.

***G.* 'Candida'**, syn. *G.* x *hartlandii* 'Candida'. Erect, clump-forming perennial producing pinnate, soft green leaves, with oval leaflets, 2in (5cm) long. Pure white flowers, the standard petals ½–¾in (1.5–2cm) across, are borne in racemes to 6in (15cm) long, from early summer to early autumn. ↕to 5ft (1.5m), ↔ 36in (90cm). Zone 6.
***G.* x *hartlandii* 'Candida'** see *G.* 'Candida'.
***G.* 'Her Majesty'** see *G.* 'His Majesty'.
***G.* 'His Majesty'** ■ syn. *G.* 'Her Majesty'. Erect, clump-forming perennial with pinnate, soft green leaves consisting of oval leaflets, 2in (5cm) long. Bicolored mauve-pink and white flowers, the standard petals ½–¾in (1.5–2cm) across, are borne in racemes to 6in (15cm) long, from early summer to early autumn. ↕to 5ft (1.5m), ↔ 36in (90cm). Zone 6.
***G.* 'Lady Wilson'.** Erect, clump-forming perennial with pinnate, soft

Galega 'His Majesty'

Galega orientalis

green leaves consisting of oval leaflets, 2in (5cm) long. From early summer to early autumn, produces racemes, to 6in (15cm) long, of bicolored mauve-blue and white flowers, the standard petals ¾in (2cm) across. ↕to 5ft (1.5m), ↔ 36in (90cm). Zone 6.
G. officinalis. Vigorous, clump-forming perennial with lax, sometimes spreading stems and pinnate, soft green leaves, each with 9–17 oblong, elliptic, or lance-shaped, pointed leaflets, ½–2in (1.5–5cm) long. From early summer to early autumn, 30–50 white or mauve, sometimes bicolored flowers, ½in (1.5cm) long, are produced in racemes to 7in (18cm) long. ↕1–5ft (0.3–1.5m), ↔ 36in (90cm). C. and S. Europe, Turkey to Pakistan. Zone 6.
G. orientalis ■ Rhizomatous, upright to somewhat lax perennial with pinnate, soft green leaves composed of 13–25 ovate-lance-shaped leaflets, 2½in (6cm) long, with long, sharp-pointed tips. In late spring and early summer, produces racemes, to 6in (15cm) long, of blue-violet flowers, to ¾in (2cm) long. Spreads rapidly. ↕4ft (1.2m), ↔ 24in (60cm). Caucasus. Zone 6.

▷ ***Galeobdolon*** see *Lamium*

GALIUM
Bedstraw

RUBIACEAE

Genus of about 400 species of annuals and perennials, widely distributed in woodland, hedgerows, meadows, and wasteland, mainly in temperate regions. Most have whorls of linear leaves, produced on weak stems that may be scrambling and rough, with recurved bristles, or shorter and smooth. The flowers are white, pinkish white, or yellow, and are borne singly or in terminal or axillary panicles or cymes; they are tubular, with usually 4 or 5 corolla lobes, which are often recurved. Many *Galium* species are invasive, but a few are good garden plants, including *G. odoratum*, which is useful as a groundcover in woodland and is attractive to bees. Alpine species from dry regions are best grown in a scree bed or alpine house.
• **CULTIVATION** Grow in almost any, preferably moist, humus-rich soil in sun or partial shade.
• **PROPAGATION** Sow seed in containers in a cold frame as soon as ripe. Separate rhizomes in autumn or early spring.

Galium odoratum

• **PESTS AND DISEASES** Prone to downy mildew, powdery mildew, rust, and a variety of fungal leaf spots.

G. odoratum ▣ syn. *Asperula odorata* (Sweet woodruff). Rhizomatous perennial with erect, square, almost hairless stems, and whorls of 6–9 lance-shaped to elliptic, emerald-green leaves, 1–2in (2.5–5cm) long, with tiny, marginal prickles. Bears star-shaped, scented white flowers, ⅛–¼in (4–6mm) across, in umbel-like cymes, 3in (8cm) across, from late spring to midsummer. Leaves may scorch in strong sun. Hay-scented when dried. ↕ 18in (45cm), ↔ indefinite. Europe, N. Africa, Russia (Siberia). Zone 4.

GALTONIA

LILIACEAE

Genus of 4 species of bulbous perennials from moist grassland in South Africa, grown for their cylindrical to conical racemes of pendent or nodding, tubular to trumpet-shaped, green or white flowers. Leaves are basal, semi-erect, broadly to linear-lance-shaped, and fleshy. Good plants for a sunny border, *Galtonia* species are particularly useful because they flower late in summer.
• **CULTIVATION** Grow in fertile, well-drained soil that is reliably moist from spring to summer, in full sun. In areas with hard winters, lift and pot up in late autumn and overwinter in a cool greenhouse, or protect *in situ* with a deep winter mulch.
• **PROPAGATION** Sow seed in containers in a cold frame as soon as ripe, keeping the seedlings frost-free for the first 2 years. Offsets can be removed in spring.
• **PESTS AND DISEASES** Infrequent.

G. candicans ▣ (Summer hyacinth). Bulbous perennial with linear-lance-shaped, gray-green leaves, 20–39in (50–100cm) long. Slender racemes of up to 30 pendent, tubular, slightly fragrant white flowers, to 2in (5cm) long, faintly tinged green at the bases, are produced on long, leafless stems in late summer. ↕ 3–4ft (1–1.2m), PD4in (10cm). South Africa (Northern Transvaal, Eastern Transvaal, Orange Free State, KwaZulu/Natal, Eastern Cape), Lesotho. Zone 6.
G. princeps. Bulbous perennial with basal, linear-lance-shaped, gray-green leaves, 30in (75cm) long, and long, leafless stems. In late summer, bears broad racemes of green-tinged, white flowers, 1in (2.5cm) across. ↕ 3ft (1m), PD4in (10cm). South Africa (KwaZulu/Natal, Eastern Cape). Zone 8.
G. viridiflora. Bulbous perennial producing broad, lance-shaped, gray-green leaves, to 24in (60cm) long. In late summer, arching stems bear compact racemes of 15–30 nodding, trumpet-shaped, pale green flowers, ¾–2in (2–5cm) long. ↕ to 3ft (1m), PD4in (10cm). South Africa (Orange Free State, Eastern Cape), Lesotho. Zone 7b.

Galtonia candicans

GARDENIA

RUBIACEAE

Genus of about 200 species of evergreen trees and shrubs from open woodland or savanna in tropical regions of Africa and Asia. They are grown for their attractive foliage and fragrant, showy flowers, which bloom in succession over a long season. The opposite or whorled leaves are simple and leathery. The terminal or axillary, tubular to funnel-shaped flowers each have 5–12 spreading petal lobes, and are solitary or borne in few-flowered cymes. In cold climates, grow in a temperate or warm greenhouse. In warmer areas, grow in a shrub border.
• **CULTIVATION** Under glass, grow in acidic potting mix in bright filtered light, with moderate humidity. Top-dress or pot on in spring. In growth, water freely and apply a balanced liquid fertilizer every 4 weeks. Keep barely moist in winter. Outdoors, grow in neutral to acidic, fertile, humus-rich, moist but well-drained soil in partial or light, dappled shade. Pruning group 1 for trees; group 8 for early-flowering shrubs; group 9 for late-flowering shrubs. May need restrictive pruning under glass.
• **PROPAGATION** Sow seed at 66–75°F (19–24°C) in spring. Take greenwood cuttings in late spring or early summer, or semi-ripe cuttings in late summer.
• **PESTS AND DISEASES** Powdery mildew, bacterial leaf spot, anthracnose, dieback, fungal leaf spots, and stem cankers, as well as root knot nematode, can be problems. Whiteflies and mealybugs are common indoors; scale insects, aphids, and thrips are common outdoors.

Gardenia augusta 'Veitchii'

Gardenia thunbergia

G. augusta, syn. *G. florida*, *G. grandiflora*, *G. jasminoides* (Cape jasmine, Common gardenia). Medium to large shrub, or sometimes small tree, frequently bushy, with ovate, elliptic, or lance-shaped, glossy, deep green leaves, 4in (10cm) or more long, usually borne in whorls of 3. From summer to autumn, produces 5- to 12-lobed, salverform, strongly fragrant, white to ivory flowers, to 3in (8cm) across, either singly or in few-flowered cymes. Usually grown in its double-flowered variants. ↕ 6–40ft (2–12m), ↔ 3–10ft (1–3m). China, Taiwan, Japan. ❀ (min. 41°F/5°C). **'August Beauty'** is a compact, long-blooming form; ↕ 6ft (2m), ↔ 4ft (1.2m). **'Belmont'**, syn. 'Hadley', is a vigorous, freely branching clone with large leaves, to 6in (15cm) long, and double flowers that age from creamy white to yellow. **'Hadley'** see 'Belmont'. **'Mystery'** is compact, with very deep green leaves, and semi-double flowers; ↕ to 3ft (1m). **'Veitchii'** ▣ syn. 'Veitchiana', is upright in habit and has small green leaves, to 3in (8cm) long, and fully double, pure white flowers.
G. capensis see *Rothmannia capensis.*
G. florida see *G. augusta.*
G. globosa see *Rothmannia globosa.*
G. grandiflora see *G. augusta.*
G. jasminoides see *G. augusta.*
G. rothmannia see *Rothmannia capensis.*
G. thunbergia ▣ (White gardenia). Open, erect shrub or small tree with rigid branches and opposite pairs of elliptic, glossy, dark green leaves, 3–5½in (8–14cm) long, with wavy margins. From winter to spring, bears solitary, tubular, fragrant, white or cream flowers, to 2½in (6cm) across, with 8 spreading petal lobes. ↕ 6–15ft (2–5m), ↔ 5–8ft (1.5–2.5m). South Africa. ❀ (min. 45°F/7°C)

GARRYA

GARRYACEAE

Genus of about 13 species of evergreen shrubs or small trees, found in woodland and scrub from W. US to Central America and the West Indies. They are cultivated for their opposite pairs of narrowly ovate to broadly elliptic, leathery leaves, and for their pendent catkins, consisting of dioecious, petalless flowers. Male and female catkins are borne on separate plants; the males are generally more attractive. Females produce spherical, purple-brown berries. Grow in a shrub border, against a wall, or as a windbreak in coastal areas.
• **CULTIVATION** Grow in moderately fertile, well-drained soil in full sun or partial shade. Shelter from cold winds where not fully hardy. Pruning group 8.
• **PROPAGATION** Sow seed in containers in a cold frame in autumn or spring, or take semi-ripe cuttings in summer.
• **PESTS AND DISEASES** May be attacked by scale insects.

G. elliptica ▣ (Silk-tassel bush). Dense, upright, evergreen shrub or small tree, with ovate to oblong-elliptic, wavy-margined leaves, to 3in (8cm) long, varying from glossy, gray-green to matte, dark green. Pendent, gray-green catkins, the males 6–8in (15–20cm) long, with yellow anthers, are borne from midwinter to early spring. ↕↔ 12ft (4m). W. US. Zone 7b. **'Evie'** is male, with strongly wavy-margined leaves and very long catkins, to 12in (30cm).

Garrya elliptica

Garrya x *issaquahensis* 'Pat Ballard'

'James Roof' is male, with dark sea-green leaves and dense clusters of silver-gray catkins, to 8in (20cm) long.
G. fremontii (Fremont silktassel). Upright evergreen shrub with stiff, bristly-haired shoots and broadly elliptic, smooth-edged, leathery, lustrous yellow-green leaves, to 2½in (6cm) long. Pendent, yellow- or purple-tinged male catkins, to 8in (20cm) long, are borne in spring. ↕ to 8ft (2.5m), ↔ 6ft (2m). Oregon, California. Zone 7.
***G.* x *issaquahensis* 'Pat Ballard'** ▣ Bushy, upright, evergreen shrub with red-purple shoots and ovate, slightly wavy-margined, glossy, mid-green leaves, to 3in (8cm) long. In midwinter, bears pendent, purple-tinged male catkins, to 8in (20cm) long. ↕ 12ft (4m), ↔ 10ft (3m). Zone 8.

GASTERIA

LILIACEAE

Genus of 50–80 species of stemless or very short-stemmed, perennial succulents, usually offsetting freely to form clumps, found in the lowlands, and sometimes hillsides, of Namibia and South Africa. They are grown for their flowers and foliage. The firm, dark or grayish green leaves, occasionally slightly suffused red, have white tubercles, and are frequently arranged in 2 ranks, later often forming rosettes and elongating; the usually pendulous, tubular flowers, swollen at the bases and sometimes green-tipped, are borne in lax racemes or few-branched panicles. Where temperatures drop below 45°F (7°C), grow in a temperate greenhouse, or as houseplants. In warm, dry climates, grow in a desert garden.

• **CULTIVATION** Under glass, grow in standard cactus potting mix in bright filtered light. During growth, water moderately and apply a low-nitrogen liquid fertilizer every 4 or 5 weeks. Keep almost dry when dormant. Outdoors, grow in sharply drained, loamy soil, with added leaf mold, in full sun or dappled shade. See also pp.48–49.
• **PROPAGATION** Sow seed at 66–75°F (19–24°C) in spring or summer. Separate offsets, or take leaf cuttings, during the growing season.
• **PESTS AND DISEASES** Mealybugs sometimes infest the roots or leaves.

G. bicolor* var. *liliputana ▣ syn. *G. liliputana.* Clump-forming succulent with rosettes of lance-shaped to linear, toothed, conspicuously white-spotted, glossy, dark green leaves, to 2½in (6cm) long, rounded and keeled below, with tubercles toward the bases. Racemes of narrow, tubular, orange-green flowers, ½in (1.5cm) long, are produced from spring to summer. ↕ 3in (8cm), ↔ 4in (10cm). South Africa (Western Cape, Eastern Cape). ❄ (min. 45°F/7°C)
G. carinata* var. *verrucosa ▣ syn. *G. verrucosa* (Warty aloe). Clump-forming succulent with 2 ranks of 3-angled, linear-lance-shaped, grayish green leaves, 4–6in (10–15cm) long, grooved above, convex below; they are tapering and flat toward the blunt tips, and have thickened margins and white tubercles. Bears racemes of red-orange flowers, to ½in (1.5cm) long, from late spring to summer. ↕ 6in (15cm), ↔ 12in (30cm). South Africa (Western Cape, Eastern Cape). ❄ (min. 45°F/7°C)
G. liliputana see *G. bicolor* var. *liliputana.*
G. obliqua, syn. *G. pulchra.* Clump-forming succulent with slender, 3-angled, linear, semi-triangular, sometimes sickle-shaped, usually tapering, grayish green leaves, 6–12in (15–30cm) long; they are cross-banded with white marks and have finely toothed, horny white margins. Racemes of red flowers, ¾in (2cm) long, are borne on long, reddish orange stalks from late spring to summer. ↕ 12in (30cm), ↔ 18in (45cm). South Africa (Eastern Cape). ❄ (min. 45°F/7°C)
G. pulchra see *G. obliqua.*
G. verrucosa see *G. carinata* var. *verrucosa.*

Gasteria bicolor var. *liliputana*

▷**x *Gaulnettya*** see *Gaultheria*

GAULTHERIA

syn. x GAULNETTYA, PERNETTYA

ERICACEAE

Genus of approximately 170 species of evergreen shrubs, some rhizomatous, widely distributed in woodland and open, moist, rocky places in the Himalayas, E. Asia, Australasia, and North, Central, and South America. They are grown for their simple, alternate, usually leathery leaves; for their small, bell- or urn-shaped flowers, ⅛–¼in (3–6mm) long, borne singly in the leaf axils or in racemes or panicles; and for their fleshy, usually spherical fruits. Suitable for woodland plantings, gaultherias can also be grown in a rock garden or heather garden, or as a groundcover on a moist, shady hillside. All parts may cause mild stomach upset if ingested, except the fruits, which are edible.

• **CULTIVATION** Grow in acidic to neutral, peaty, moist soil in partial shade; full sun may be tolerated where the soil is permanently moist. Pruning group 8; remove suckers to restrict growth.
• **PROPAGATION** Sow seed in containers outdoors in a cold frame in autumn. Take semi-ripe cuttings in summer or remove rooted suckers (if produced) in spring.
• **PESTS AND DISEASES** Black mildew, powdery mildew, leaf gall, and fungal spots can occur.

G. cuneata. Dwarf, densely branched shrub with pointed, ovate-oblong to obovate, toothed, mid-green leaves, to 1¼in (3cm) long. Produces white flowers in racemes, 1–1½in (2.5–4cm) long, in late spring and early summer, followed by white fruit, to ¼in (6mm) across, in autumn. ↕ to 12in (30cm), ↔ to 3ft (1m). W. China. Zone 5b.
G. forrestii. Spreading, rounded shrub with arching shoots and narrowly ovate to oblong, sharp-pointed, bristly toothed, glossy, dark green leaves, to 3½in (9cm) long. In late spring and early summer, produces broadly urn-shaped, fragrant white flowers in racemes, 1–2in (2.5–5cm) long, followed by black fruit, ¼in (6mm) across. ↕↔ 5ft (1.5m). S.W. China. Zone 7b.
G. miqueliana. Compact, stiff-stemmed shrub with ovate to obovate, rounded to acute, toothed, dark green leaves, net-veined below, to 1½in (4cm) long. Short racemes, 1–2in (2.5–5cm) long, of urn- to bell-shaped white flowers, are produced in late spring and early summer, followed by white, sometimes pink-flushed fruit, to ½in (1.5cm) across, in autumn. ↕ to 12in (30cm), ↔ to 3ft (1m) or more. Japan. Zone 7.
G. mucronata, syn. *Pernettya mucronata.* Compact, bushy, suckering shrub with oval-elliptic to oblong-elliptic, toothed, spine-tipped, glossy, dark green leaves, to ¾in (2cm) long. Produces nodding, urn-shaped, solitary, white, sometimes pink-flushed flowers, in late spring and early summer; they are followed by fruit to ½in (1.5cm) across, variously colored from purple-red to white. Grow male and female plants together to ensure fruiting. ↕↔ 4ft (1.2m). Chile, Argentina. Zone 7.
'Bell's Seedling' has red-tinged young shoots. **'Cherry Ripe'** has bright cerise fruit. **'Edward Balls'** is male, with upright red shoots and broadly oval, bright green leaves. **'Lilian'** has lilac-pink fruit. **'Mother of Pearl'** see 'Parelmoer'. **'Mulberry Wine'** ▣ has magenta fruit, ripening to dark purple. **'Parelmoer'**, syn. 'Mother of Pearl', has light pink fruit. **'Sneeuwwitje'**, syn. 'Snow White', has white fruit slightly spotted with pink. **'Snow White'** see 'Sneeuwwitje'. **'Wintertime'** ▣ has pure white fruit.
G. myrsinoides, syn. *G. prostrata, Pernettya prostrata.* Prostrate, creeping, rhizomatous shrub with elliptic to oblong-elliptic, bristly scalloped, sharp-pointed, dark green leaves, to ¼in (6mm) long. Bears solitary, urn-shaped white flowers in early summer, followed by deep purple fruit, to ½in (1.5cm) across, with persistent, enlarged calyces. ↕ to 8in (20cm), ↔ to 16in (40cm). Costa Rica to C. Chile. Zone 7b. **subsp. *pentlandii*** is more upright in habit than the species, with oblong-ovate leaves, to 1¼in (3cm) long, and paler fruit; ↕↔ to 16in (40cm).
G. nummularioides. Dense, hairy-stemmed, prostrate shrub with rounded, ovate-elliptic, gland-tipped, bristly toothed, dull green leaves, to ½in (1.5cm) long, becoming smaller toward the stem tips. In late spring and early summer, bears solitary, urn-shaped, pink-flushed white or white-tinged red-brown flowers; these are followed by ovoid, purple-black fruit, to ⅜in (9mm) long. ↕ 4in (10cm), ↔ 12in (30cm). Himalayas, China. Zone 7b.

Gasteria carinata var. *verrucosa*

Gaultheria mucronata 'Mulberry Wine'

Gaultheria mucronata 'Wintertime'

Gaultheria procumbens

G. procumbens ■ (Checkerberry, Wintergreen). Creeping, rhizomatous shrublet producing elliptic to elliptic-oblong, pointed or glandular-tipped, scalloped or bristly toothed, glossy, dark green leaves, to 2in (5cm) long. The leaves have a strong fragrance of wintergreen when crushed. In summer, produces urn-shaped, white or pale pink flowers, either singly or in small racemes, ½–1in (1–2.5cm) long; these are followed by aromatic scarlet fruit, ⅜–½in (0.8–1.5cm) across, which frequently persist until spring. ↕ 6in (15cm), ↔ to 3ft (1m) or more. E. North America. Zone 4.
G. prostrata see *G. myrsinoides.*
G. pyroloides. Rhizomatous, groundcovering shrublet with obovate to almost rounded, minutely spine-tipped, toothed, dark green leaves, to 1½in (4cm) long. In late spring, produces short racemes, to 1in (2.5cm) long, of ovoid-urn-shaped, pink-flushed white flowers, which are followed by ellipsoid, blue-black fruit, to ⅜in (9mm) long. ↕ 6in (15cm), ↔ to 20in (50cm). Himalayas. Zone 5b.
G. shallon ■ (Salal, Shallon). Compact, bushy shrub, spreading vigorously by suckers, with red shoots and broadly ovate, sharp-pointed, bristly toothed, glossy, dark green leaves, to 4in (10cm) long. Arching racemes, to 4in (10cm) long, of broadly urn-shaped, pink-suffused white flowers are produced in late spring and early summer; they are followed by purple fruit, to ½in (1.5cm) across. ↕ 4ft (1.2m), ↔ 5ft (1.5m). W. North America. Zone 7.

Gaultheria shallon

Gaultheria tasmanica

G. tasmanica ■ syn. *Pernettya tasmanica.* Mat-forming shrublet with narrowly elliptic to oval, scalloped, lustrous, mid-green leaves, to ⅜in (9mm) long, and axillary, solitary, bell-shaped white flowers borne in spring. Bears bright orange-red, occasionally white or yellow fruit, ¼–⅜in (6–9mm) across. Fruits freely, even in shade. ↕ 3in (8cm), ↔ to 10in (25cm). Australia (Tasmania). ❄ (min. 41°F/5°C)
G. trichophylla. Prostrate, mat-forming, slender-stemmed, suckering shrub with elliptic, bristly toothed, glossy, dark green leaves, to ½in (1.5cm) long. In late spring, bears axillary, solitary, bell-shaped, white or pink flowers, the white sometimes pink-flushed, followed by pale greenish blue fruit, to ½in (1.5cm) across. Attractive in a rock garden. ↕ to 4in (10cm), ↔ to 12in (30cm). Himalayas, W. China. Zone 7.
G. x wisleyensis (*G. mucronata* x *G. shallon*). Upright, suckering shrub with elliptic to elliptic-oblong, dark green leaves, to 1½in (4cm) long. Urn-shaped white flowers are produced in racemes, to 2in (5cm) long, in late spring and early summer, followed by purple-red fruit, ¼in (6mm) across. ↕↔ 3ft (1m). Garden origin. Zone 6b.
'Pink Pixie' ■ syn. x *Gaulnettya* 'Pink Pixie', is dwarf but vigorous, spreading by suckers, and has pink-tinged white flowers, followed by purple-red fruit; ↕ to 12in (30cm), ↔ 18in (45cm).
'Wisley Pearl', syn. x *Gaulnettya* 'Wisley Pearl', has white flowers and dark purple-red fruit.

GAURA

ONAGRACEAE

Genus of about 20 species of annuals, biennials, perennials, and subshrubs from moist places and prairies in North America. They have alternate, simple, rosetted, lance-shaped to elliptic or spoon-shaped, pinnatifid, mainly basal leaves, and airy racemes or panicles of short-lived, flat, irregularly star-shaped, pink or white flowers, usually 4-petaled. They are graceful plants for a border.
• **CULTIVATION** Grow in fertile, moist but well-drained soil in full sun, but drought and partial shade are tolerated.
• **PROPAGATION** Sow seed of annuals *in situ* in spring, and seed of perennials in containers in a cold frame from spring to early summer. Perennials may also be divided in spring, or increased by basal or softwood cuttings in spring or semi-ripe heel cuttings in summer.
• **PESTS AND DISEASES** Prone to rust, *Cercospora* and *Septoria* leaf spots, and sometimes downy and powdery mildews.

G. biennis. Subshrubby, hairy annual or biennial with stem leaves to 5in (13cm) long and basal leaves to 16in (40cm) long; both are narrowly elliptic with irregular margins. Racemes, 4–20in (10–50cm) long, of white flowers, to 1½in (4cm) across, fading to reddish pink, open at dusk in summer. Stems and foliage are flushed coral-red in late summer. ↕ 6ft (1.8m) or more, ↔ to 4ft (1.2m). Texas, Louisiana. Zone 6b.
G. lindheimeri ■ (White Gaura). Bushy, clump-forming perennial with slender stems bearing spoon-shaped to lance-shaped, toothed leaves, 1–3in (2.5–8cm) long. From late spring to early autumn, bears loose panicles, 8–24in (20–60cm) long, of pinkish white buds, opening at dawn to white flowers, 1in (2.5cm) across, fading to pink. ↕ to 5ft (1.5m), ↔ 36in (90cm). Texas, Louisiana. Zone 6. **'Corrie's Gold'** produces gold-margined leaves. **'Whirling Butterflies'** has gray-green leaves, and is very free-flowering, with red sepals; ↕ 24–30in (60–75cm).

Gaultheria x *wisleyensis* 'Pink Pixie'

Gaura lindheimeri

GAYLUSSACIA

Huckleberry

ERICACEAE

Genus of about 40 species of deciduous and evergreen shrubs from woodland and thickets in North and South America, cultivated mainly for their flowers and edible fruits. They have alternate, simple, entire or toothed leaves, and axillary racemes of urn- or bell-shaped flowers in spring. Excellent for a shrub border or open woodland.
• **CULTIVATION** Grow in acidic, peaty, moist but well-drained soil in full sun or partial shade. Pruning group 1 if deciduous; group 8 if evergreen.
• **PROPAGATION** Sow seed in containers in an open frame in autumn, or take softwood cuttings in summer.
• **PESTS AND DISEASES** Leaf gall, powdery mildew, and rusts are common.

G. baccata (Black huckleberry). Upright, deciduous shrub with elliptic-oblong, mid- to dark green leaves, to 2in (5cm) long, sticky when young, turning red in autumn. Small, urn-shaped, dull red flowers, to ¼in (6mm) long, are produced in pendent racemes, to 1½in (4cm) long, in late spring; they are followed by edible, spherical, glossy black fruit, to ⅜in (9mm) across. ↕↔ 3ft (1m). E. North America. Zone 3.

GAZANIA

ASTERACEAE

Genus of about 16 species of low-growing annuals or evergreen perennials from low-altitude sands to alpine meadows in tropical Africa. They have mostly lance-shaped, basal leaves, often covered with gray, felted hairs on one or both surfaces, and varying from deeply lobed to pinnatifid, and from entire to toothed. Large, daisy-like, very brightly colored, dark-centered flowerheads, which close in cloudy or cool weather, are produced over a long period in summer.

Gazania Chansonette Series

Hybrid selections are the most commonly cultivated, and are grown as annuals or half-hardy perennials, with leafy stems bearing spoon-shaped to oblong, often lobed leaves and variously colored flowerheads. They are useful as summer bedding or in patio containers, and tolerate coastal conditions.

• **CULTIVATION** Under glass, grow in soil-based potting mix, with added sharp sand, in full light. Water freely when in growth; keep just moist in winter. Outdoors, grow in light, sandy, well-drained soil in full sun. Deadhead to prolong flowering.

• **PROPAGATION** Sow seed at 64–68°F (18–20°C) in late winter or early spring. Take basal cuttings in late summer or early autumn, to overwinter under glass.

• **PESTS AND DISEASES** Sometimes affected by powdery mildew, bacterial leaf spot, fungal spots, crown rots, and mealybugs.

***G.* Chansonette Series** ■ Vigorous, spreading, evergreen perennials with glossy leaves, to 6in (15cm) long, dark green above, covered with silky white hairs beneath. In summer, bear solitary flowerheads, 3–4in (8–10cm) across, in a mix of bronze, orange, rose-pink, salmon-pink, red-orange, or yellow, zoned in a contrasting color. ↕ to 8in (20cm), ↔ to 10in (25cm). Zone 8.

***G.* Daybreak Series.** Spreading, evergreen perennials with glossy leaves, to 6in (15cm) long, dark green above, with silky white hairs below. In early summer, bear solitary flowerheads, 3–4in (8–10cm) across, in bronze, orange, yellow, bright pink, or white, usually zoned in a contrasting color. ↕ to 8in (20cm), ↔ to 10in (25cm). Zone 8. **'Daybreak Bronze'** is a single-color selection.

***G.* Mini-star Series.** Compact, tuft-forming, evergreen perennials with glossy leaves, to 6in (15cm) long, dark green above, white silky-hairy beneath. In summer, bear solitary, orange, white, yellow, beige, bronze, or bright pink flowerheads, 3–4in (8–10cm) across, some zoned in a contrasting color. ↕ to 8in (20cm), ↔ to 10in (25cm). Zone 8. **'Mini-star Tangerine'** and **'Mini-star Yellow'** are single-color selections.

***G.* Sunshine Giants Mix.** Compact, evergreen perennials with silver-green leaves, to 6in (15cm). In summer, bear large, solitary flowerheads, 3–4in (8–10cm) across, in shades of red, orange, yellow, green, and white, many with contrasting zones. ↕↔ 10in (25cm). Zone 8.

***G.* Talent Series.** Vigorous, evergreen perennials with ornamental, mid-green leaves, to 6in (15cm) long, gray-felted on both surfaces. In summer, produce solitary, yellow, orange, pink, or brown flowerheads, 3–4in (8–10cm) across, on short stems above the leaves. ↕↔ to 10in (25cm). Zone 8. **'Talent Yellow'** ■ has bright yellow flowerheads.

Gazania Talent Series 'Talent Yellow'

GEISSORHIZA

IRIDACEAE

Genus of 60–70 species of erect, cormous perennials from dry lowland sand to moist upland areas in southern Africa. Leaves are basal, lance-shaped, linear, or thread-like, and often curled. Flowers are usually funnel-shaped, and are borne in 1- or 2-sided spikes, with leaf-like bracts, in spring. Where marginally hardy, grow at the base of a warm wall with winter protection, or in a temperate greenhouse. In warmer climates, grow in a bed or border.

• **CULTIVATION** Under glass, grow in soil-based potting mix, with added grit, in full sun. Water freely during the growing season, but keep dry when dormant. Outdoors, grow in well-drained, sandy loam in full sun. Protect from winter moisture.

• **PROPAGATION** Sow seed in containers in a cold frame when ripe; separate offset corms when dormant.

• **PESTS AND DISEASES** Infrequent.

G. radians, syn. *G. rochensis* (Winecups). Upright perennial with thread-like, sometimes 4-angled, basal leaves, to 6in (15cm) long. Funnel-shaped, red-centered, white-ringed purple flowers, ½–¾in (1–2cm) long, are produced in spring. ↕ 6in (15cm), PD2in (5cm). South Africa (Western Cape). ❀ (min. 45°F/7°C)

G. rochensis see *G. radians.*

GELSEMIUM

LOGANIACEAE

Genus of 3 species of evergreen, twining, perennial climbers from S.E. Asia, S. North America, and Central America, usually found in woodland. They are grown for their funnel-shaped, sweetly fragrant flowers, which have 5 petal lobes, borne singly or in small, terminal and axillary clusters. Leaves are simple, entire, and arranged in opposite pairs. Where not hardy, grow in a cool or temperate greenhouse. In warmer climates, train over an arbor, pergola, or arch, or against a wall.

Gelsemium sempervirens

• **CULTIVATION** Under glass, grow in soil-based potting mix in full or bright filtered light. Top-dress or pot on in spring. During the growing season, water freely and apply a balanced liquid fertilizer monthly. Outdoors, grow in moderately fertile, moist but well-drained soil in full sun or partial shade, with shelter from cold, drying winds. Pruning group 12, after flowering.

• **PROPAGATION** Sow seed at 55–64°F (13–18°C) in spring, or take semi-ripe cuttings with bottom heat in summer.

• **PESTS AND DISEASES** Affected by a number of different fungal leaf, stem, and root diseases. Scale insects and whiteflies are common under greenhouse conditions.

G. sempervirens ■ (Carolina jasmine, Carolina yellow jessamine). Vigorous, slender, twining perennial with stems that spiral counterclockwise, and oblong to narrowly ovate, glossy leaves, to 2in (5cm) long. Bears clusters, 2–3in (5–8cm) across, of fragrant, bright, pale to deep yellow flowers, 1¼in (3cm) long, with darker, orange throats, mainly in spring and summer. ↕ 10–20ft (3–6m). S.E. US, Mexico, Guatemala. Zone 7b. **'Pride of Augusta'** has double, more numerous flowers, borne over a longer period.

GENISTA

syn. CHAMAESPARTIUM, ECHINOSPARTUM

Broom

FABACEAE

Genus, similar to *Cytisus*, of about 90 species of mainly deciduous, sometimes spiny shrubs and occasionally trees, found in pasture and moorland to cliffs and rocky places in Europe, the Mediterranean, and W. Asia. They have alternate, simple or 3-palmate leaves, usually ⅛–½in (3–15mm) long, sometimes more, but may be nearly leafless. They are cultivated for their small, pea-like yellow flowers, borne singly or in terminal racemes or dense heads. Grow as specimen plants, or in a shrub border or rock garden. Where not hardy, grow in a cool greenhouse.

• **CULTIVATION** Grow in light, poor to moderately fertile, well-drained soil in full sun. Pruning group 1; group 3 for *G. cinerea.* Do not cut into old wood.

• **PROPAGATION** Sow seed in containers outdoors in a cold frame in autumn, or take semi-ripe cuttings in summer.

• **PESTS AND DISEASES** Dieback, powdery mildew, and scale insects can occur.

G. aetnensis ■ (Mount Etna broom). Upright, deciduous tree or large shrub with weeping branches bearing slender, bright green shoots. Linear leaves are produced on young stems only and soon fall. Fragrant, golden yellow flowers, to ½in (1.5cm) long, are freely borne at the ends of pendent shoots in mid- and late summer. ↕↔ 25ft (8m). Italy (Sardinia, Sicily). Zone 7.

G. cinerea. Erect, deciduous shrub with arching branches, silky when young, and narrow, lance-shaped to elliptic, gray-green leaves. Pairs of fragrant yellow flowers, to ½in (1.5cm) long, are borne profusely in irregular racemes, to 8in (20cm) long, in early and midsummer. ↕ 10ft (3m), ↔ 12ft (4m). S.W. Europe. Zone 7b.

G. decumbens see *Cytisus decumbens.*

G. delphinensis, syn. *Chamaespartium sagittale* subsp. *delphinense*, *G. sagittalis* subsp. *delphinensis.* Low, prostrate, deciduous subshrub with a few lance-shaped, mid-green leaves, softly hairy beneath, and winged green stems that give the plant a leafy, evergreen appearance. Small, golden yellow flowers, to ½in (1.5cm) long, are borne in spike-like, axillary and terminal racemes, to 1½in (4cm) long, in late spring and early summer. ↕ to 6in (15cm), ↔ to 12in (30cm). Pyrenees. Zone 7.

***G. fragrans* of gardens** see *Cytisus* x *spachianus.*

Genista aetnensis

G

Genista hispanica

G. hispanica ■ (Spanish broom). Dense, mound-forming, spiny, deciduous shrub with ovate-oblong, mid-green leaves, hairy or silky beneath, only present on flowering branches. Bears almost terminal racemes, 1in (2.5cm) across, of 2–12 golden yellow flowers, ½in (1.5cm) long, in late spring and early summer. ↕ 30in (75cm), ↔ 5ft (1.5m). S.W. Europe. Zone 7b. **'Compacta'** is of very dense habit.
G. lydia ■ (Lydia woodwaxen). Deciduous, domed shrub bearing slender, arching, prickle-tipped, gray-green branches, with linear-elliptic, blue-green leaves. In early summer, bears yellow flowers, to ½in (1.5cm) long, in short racemes, 2in (5cm) long. ↕ to 24in (60cm), ↔ to 3ft (1m). E. Balkans. Zone 3b.
G. monosperma see *Retama monosperma.*

Genista lydia

Genista pilosa 'Vancouver Gold'

Genista sagittalis

G. pilosa (Silky leaf woadwaxen). Deciduous, prostrate or semi-erect shrub, with downy, ascending branches producing inversely lance-shaped, dark green leaves, to ½in (1.5cm) long, silky-hairy beneath. In late spring and early summer, bears bright yellow flowers, to ½in (1.5cm) long, in racemes to 5½in (14cm) long. ↕ to 16in (40cm), ↔ to 3ft (1m). W. and C. Europe. Zone 5. **'Lemon Spreader'** see 'Yellow Spreader'. **'Vancouver Gold'** ■ is spreading and mound-forming, with profuse golden yellow flowers; ↕ 18in (45cm). **'Yellow Spreader'**, syn. 'Lemon Spreader', is low-growing and spreading, with lemon-yellow flowers; ↕ to 12in (30cm).
G. sagittalis ■ syn. *Chamaespartium sagittale.* Low-growing, deciduous shrub with upright, broadly winged green stems that give the plant an evergreen appearance; they bear a few lance-shaped, mid-green leaves, to ¾in (2cm) long. In early summer, bears dense, spike-like racemes, to 1½in (4cm) long, of yellow flowers, ½in (1.5cm) long. ↕ 6in (15cm), ↔ to 3ft (1m). C. and S. Europe. Zone 5. **subsp. *delphinensis*** see *G. delphinensis.*
G. x spachiana see *Cytisus* x *spachianus.*
G. tinctoria ■ (Dyer's greenweed). Variable, upright, deciduous shrub with narrow, elliptic-lance-shaped or inversely lance-shaped, bright, deep green leaves, to 2in (5cm) long. From spring to early summer, bears golden yellow flowers in upright racemes, 2½in (6cm) long. ↕ 24–36in (60–90cm), ↔ 3ft (1m). Europe, Turkey. Zone 3. **'Royal Gold'** is upright, with flowers in long, conical panicles, to 3in (8cm) long; ↕ 3ft (1m).

Genista tinctoria

GENTIANA

Gentian

GENTIANACEAE

Genus of about 400 species of hardy annuals, biennials, and deciduous, semi-evergreen, and evergreen perennials. They are widely distributed throughout temperate zones, most occurring in alpine habitats, with some, mainly North American and Japanese species, in woodland. They bear large, usually trumpet-shaped, sometimes bell- or almost urn-shaped flowers from spring to autumn, mainly in shades of intense blue, but also in white, yellow, or occasionally red. Leaves are simple and borne along the stems in opposite pairs or whorls, or produced in basal rosettes. Many autumn-flowering species have overwintering rosettes and are classed as semi-evergreen; the flowered stems die back each year to the rosettes.

Small species, to about 6in (15cm) high, are suitable for a rock garden; more robust species are suitable for borders. Woodland natives, like *G. asclepiadea,* thrive in partially shaded sites, associating well with ferns and grasses. *G. sceptrum* is suitable for a bog garden; *G. lutea* is effective beside water. Autumn-flowering gentians go well with small, late-flowering bulbs.

• **CULTIVATION** Grow in light, humus-rich, reliably moist but well-drained soil. Autumn-flowering species, unless otherwise stated, need neutral to acidic soil. Site gentians in full sun only where summers are cool and damp; in areas with warm, dry summers, provide shade from hot sun.

• **PROPAGATION** Sow seed of species in containers in an open frame as soon as ripe. Divide or root offsets in spring.

• **PESTS AND DISEASES** Rust and *Asteromella* and *Cercospora* leaf spots are common. Slugs and snails can cause damage; aphids and spider mites may be problems under glass.

G. acaulis ■ syn. *G. excisa, G. kochiana* (Trumpet gentian). Evergreen, mat-forming perennial with basal rosettes of elliptic to lance-shaped, pointed, glossy, dark green leaves, to 1½in (4cm) long. In late spring and early summer, solitary, trumpet-shaped flowers, to 2in (5cm) long, deep blue and spotted green inside, are produced on short stems. ↕ 3in (8cm), ↔ to 12in (30cm). N.E. Spain, Alps, Italy, former Yugoslavia,

Gentiana acaulis

Gentiana alpina

Carpathians. Zone 3. **'Alba'** bears white flowers, spotted green inside.
G. alba. Thick-stemmed, herbaceous perennial with pairs of ovate to oblong-lance-shaped, yellow-green stem leaves, to 5in (13cm) long. In summer, bears tubular, nearly stalkless, white-tinged, yellow-green flowers, 1¼in (3cm) across, in terminal or axillary clusters. ↕ to 24in (60cm), ↔ 12in (30cm). C. North America. Zone 6.
G. alpina ■ Mat-forming, evergreen perennial with basal rosettes of elliptic to rounded, leathery, mid-green leaves, to ¾in (2cm) long. In early summer, produces solitary, often stalkless, trumpet-shaped flowers, to 1¾in (4.5cm) long, deep blue and spotted green inside. ↕ to 2in (5cm), ↔ to 8in (20cm). Spain (Sierra Nevada), Pyrenees, Alps. Zone 5.
G. andrewsii (Bottle gentian, Closed gentian). Erect, tufted, deciduous perennial producing pairs of lance-shaped to oblong-ovate, deep green, stem leaves, 2–3in (5–8cm) long. In late summer, bears terminal clusters of 5 or more cylindrical to urn-shaped flowers, to 1½in (4cm) long; the flowers are dark blue with white on the lobes, or occasionally pure white. ↕ 12–24in (30–60cm), ↔ 6in (15cm). E. North America. Zone 4.
G. angustifolia ■ Evergreen, clump-forming perennial with basal rosettes of linear-lance-shaped to inversely lance-shaped, dull green leaves, to 2in (5cm) long. In early summer, produces single, short-stalked, trumpet-shaped flowers, to 2in (5cm) long, deep sky-blue outside, paler and spotted green inside. ↕ to 4in (10cm), ↔ to 12in (30cm). Pyrenees, Jura Mountains, S.W. Alps. Zone 6b.
G. asclepiadea ■ (Willow gentian). Clump-forming herbaceous perennial with erect, then arching stems bearing opposite pairs, or whorls of 3, willow-like, lance-shaped to narrowly ovate, pointed, mid-green leaves, 2–3in (5–8cm) long. From mid- or late summer to early autumn, produces axillary clusters of 2 or 3 trumpet-shaped, dark to light blue flowers, to 2in (5cm) long, the throats sometimes all white or, rarely, purple-spotted. ↕ 24–36in (60–90cm), ↔ 18in (45cm). Mountains of C. and S. Europe, Turkey. Zone 4. **var. *alba*** has green-tinged white flowers. **'Knightshayes'** bears white-throated, deep blue flowers; ↕ to 24in (60cm).

Gentiana angustifolia

G. cachemirica, syn. *G. cashmeriana.* Rosette-forming herbaceous perennial with purple-tinged, procumbent stems, narrowly ovate, glaucous, mid-green basal leaves, 1–2in (2.5–5cm) long, and shorter, broader stem leaves. In late summer, bears 1–3 terminal, narrowly trumpet-shaped flowers, to 1½in (4cm) long, bright to pale blue, striped yellow and darker blue. ↕ to 6in (15cm), ↔ to 10in (25cm). Pakistan to India (Kashmir). Zone 7.
G. cashmeriana see *G. cachemirica.*
G. clausa (Closed gentian, Bottle gentian). Erect, herbaceous perennial with paired, lance-shaped to ovate, dark green stem leaves, to 3½in (9cm) long. In summer, bears terminal and upper axillary clusters of 5 or more cylindrical to urn-shaped flowers, to 1½in (4cm) long, white, or dark blue with white on the lobes. ↕ 12–24in (30–60cm), ↔ 6in (15cm). E. North America. Zone 4.
G. clusii (Trumpet gentian). Evergreen, tufted perennial with basal rosettes of elliptic to oblong-lance-shaped, leathery, bright green leaves, to 1in (2.5cm) long. Solitary, trumpet-shaped, deep azure-blue flowers, to 2in (5cm) long, are paler and spotted olive-green inside; they appear in early summer. Lime-tolerant. ↕ to 3in (8cm), ↔ to 12in (30cm). C. and S. Alps. Zone 5.
G. crinita see *Gentianopsis crinita.*
G. cruciata (Cross gentian). Clump-forming, herbaceous perennial with basal rosettes of opposite pairs of lance-shaped, leathery, mid-green leaves, to 4in (10cm) long. From midsummer to autumn, small, fused, bell-shaped, dark blue flowers, to 2in (5cm) long, are borne in terminal or axillary clusters. ↕ 8–16in (20–40cm), ↔ 10in (25cm). Europe, Turkey, Caucasus, Siberia. Zone 5.
G. dahurica. Procumbent, tufted herbaceous perennial, with basal rosettes of lance-shaped, mid-green leaves, 6–8in (15–20cm) long, and thread-like filaments to 8in (20cm) up the stems. The stem leaves are borne in 2 or 3 pairs and are narrowly lance-shaped. In late summer, produces solitary or axillary clusters of tubular, stalkless, deep blue flowers, to 1½in (4cm) long. ↕ 16in (40cm), ↔ 10in (25cm). Turkey to N.W. China. Zone 4.
G. decumbens. Upright, herbaceous perennial with basal rosettes of paired, linear-lance-shaped, mid-green leaves, 6–10in (15–25cm) long. In late summer, bears bell-shaped, stalkless,

Gentiana asclepiadea

deep blue to purple-blue flowers, to 1¼in (3cm) across, solitary or in clusters. ↕ 6–10in (15–25cm), ↔ 6in (15cm). E. Russia, C. and N.E. Asia. Zone 4.
G. dendrologii. Erect or climbing, branched perennial with basal rosettes of lance-shaped to linear mid-green leaves, 4–8in (10–20cm) long, and pairs of broader stem leaves. In summer, cylindrical white flowers, to 1½in (4cm) across, are produced in terminal and axillary clusters. ↕ to 14in (35cm), ↔ 8–10in (20–25cm). W. China. Zone 7.
G. 'Devonhall'. Robust, compact, rosette-forming, semi-evergreen perennial, with linear, mid-green basal leaves, to 1in (2.5cm) long. Stem leaves are smaller and sharply acute. In autumn, produces prostrate stems with solitary, widely trumpet-shaped, pale blue flowers, about 2in (5cm) long, paler at the throats and spotted green inside. ↕ 2in (5cm), ↔ to 8in (20cm). Zone 7.
G. excisa see *G. acaulis.*
G. farreri. Slender, trailing, semi-evergreen perennial with basal rosettes of linear-lance-shaped, bright green leaves,

Gentiana lutea

to 1½in (4cm) long, and paired, recurved stem leaves. In early autumn, bears solitary, narrowly trumpet-shaped, pale blue flowers, to 2½in (6cm) long, the tubes white with greenish blue spots and lines, on prostrate stems. ↕ to 3in (8cm), ↔ to 12in (30cm). N.W. China. Zone 5.
G. gracilipes, syn. *G. purdomii.* Semi-evergreen, rosette-forming perennial with narrowly lance-shaped, dark green basal leaves, to 6in (15cm) long, and decumbent, branching stems with shorter leaves. In summer, produces solitary, long-stalked, narrowly trumpet-shaped, deep purplish blue flowers, to 1½in (4cm) long, stained green outside. Tolerates shade. ↕ 6in (15cm), ↔ 8in (20cm). N.W. China. Zone 7.

Gentiana 'Kingfisher'

Gentiana x *macaulayi* 'Wells's Variety'

G

G. 'Kingfisher' ▣ Rosette-forming, semi-evergreen perennial, similar to *G. sino-ornata* but more compact, with linear-lance-shaped, mid- to dark green, basal leaves, to 1in (2.5cm) long. In autumn, bears solitary, trumpet-shaped, vivid blue flowers, to 1½in (4cm) long, on prostrate stems. ↕ 2in (5cm), ↔ to 12in (30cm). Zone 4.
G. kochiana see *G. acaulis.*
G. lagodechiana see *G. septemfida* var. *lagodechiana.*
G. lutea ▣ (Bitterwort, Yellow gentian). Erect, clump-forming herbaceous perennial with fleshy roots and elliptic to ovate, pleated, strongly ribbed, bluish green basal leaves, to 12in (30cm) long. Stem leaves are in pairs, fused at the base. Terminal and upper axillary clusters of 3–10 star-shaped yellow flowers, 1in (2.5cm) across, with very short tubes, are borne in midsummer. ↕ to 5ft (1.5m), ↔ 24in (60cm). Pyrenees, Alps, Apennines, Carpathians. Zone 5.
G. x macaulayi 'Wells's Variety' ▣ syn. *G.* 'Wellsii'. Semi-evergreen, rosette-forming perennial, with linear-lance-shaped, dark green basal leaves, to 1½in (4cm) long. Solitary, trumpet-shaped, pale blue flowers, to 2in (5cm) long, sometimes mauve-flushed, with pale stripes outside, appear on prostrate stems from late summer to autumn. ↕ 2in (5cm), ↔ to 12in (30cm). Zone 4.
G. makinoi. Erect herbaceous perennial with leafy stems bearing pairs of lance-shaped to narrowly ovate, somewhat bluish green leaves, the upper leaf to 2in (5cm) long, the lower 1in (2.5cm). In late summer, bears terminal and axillary clusters of up to 7 tubular-bell-shaped, pale blue flowers, 1¼–1½in (3–4cm) long, heavily spotted dark blue, with unequal sepals. ↕ to 20in (50cm), ↔ 6in (15cm). Japan. Zone 7.
'Royal Blue' bears bold, blue flowers.
G. menziesii see *G. sceptrum.*
G. purdomii see *G. gracilipes.*
G. scabra. Erect herbaceous perennial with leafy stems bearing paired, ovate to lance-shaped, sharp-pointed, deep green leaves, 1½in (4cm) long. From late summer to autumn, produces stalkless, terminal clusters or axillary pairs of bell-shaped, purple-blue flowers, to 1½in (4cm) long, often spotted white. ↕ to 12in (30cm), ↔ 8in (20cm). N. Asia, Japan. Zone 5.
G. sceptrum, syn. *G. menziesii.* Erect, clump-forming herbaceous perennial

Gentiana septemfida

with paired, ovate to lance-shaped, mid-green basal and stem leaves, 1¼–3in (3–8cm) long. In late summer, broadly trumpet-shaped, green-spotted, bluish purple flowers, 1½–2in (4–5cm) long, with erect corolla lobes, are produced in terminal clusters or in twos or threes from the upper axils. ↕ 18–36in (45–90cm), ↔ 8in (20cm). British Columbia to California. Zone 7.

G. septemfida ▣ (Crested gentian). Spreading herbaceous perennial with prostrate or ascending stems bearing paired, ovate, pointed, mid-green leaves, to 1½in (4cm) long. In late summer, produces terminal clusters of 1–8 narrowly bell-shaped, bright blue or purplish blue flowers, 1½in (4cm) long, with white throats and darker stripes. Best in sun. ↕ 6–8in (15–20cm), ↔ to 12in (30cm). Caucasus, Turkey, Iran to C. Asia. Zone 5. **var. *lagodechiana*,** syn. *G. lagodechiana*, has branched, almost prostrate stems and one flower, rarely 2 or 3, per stem.

G. speciosa, syn. *Crawfurdia speciosa.* Climbing or trailing herbaceous perennial with slender stems bearing elliptic to ovate, pointed, toothed, mid-green leaves, 2–3in (5–8cm) long, in opposite pairs. In late summer, produces axillary clusters of 1–3 narrowly tubular-bell-shaped, deep blue to blue-purple or white flowers, to 2in (5cm) long, green-tinted outside. Prefers acidic soil in shade. ↕ to 3ft (1m). Himalayas, China. Zone 5.

G. stylophora see *Megacodon stylophorus.*

***G.* 'Susan Jane'.** Procumbent, rosette-forming, semi-evergreen perennial with

Gentiana ternifolia

Gentiana triflora

linear-lance-shaped, dark green, basal leaves, to 1¼in (3cm) long. In autumn, bears solitary, trumpet-shaped, bright azure-blue flowers, to 2in (5cm) long, with white throats and notched petals, on prostrate stems. ↕ to 3in (8cm), ↔ to 12in (30cm). Zone 6.

G. ternifolia ▣ Vigorous, trailing, semi-evergreen perennial with loose rosettes of linear-lance-shaped, grayish green basal leaves, to ½in (1.5cm) long; stem leaves are similar, in whorls of 2 or 3. In autumn, solitary, trumpet- to bell-shaped, sky-blue flowers, 1½in (4cm) long, striped darker blue and spotted white and green outside, paler inside, are borne on prostrate stems. ↕ to 3in (8cm), ↔ to 12in (30cm). W. China. Zone 5.

G. triflora ▣ Erect herbaceous perennial with slender, leafy stems bearing paired, narrow, lance-shaped, glossy, mid-green leaves, 2–4in (5–10cm) long. Bears narrowly bell-shaped, deep blue to purple-blue flowers, 1¼–2in (3–5cm) long, with white bands outside, in small, upright, terminal or upper axillary clusters in late summer and early autumn. ↕ 9–24in (22–60cm), ↔ 10in (25cm). Russia (E. Siberia, Sakhalin), China (Manchuria), Japan, Korea. Zone 5.

G. veitchiorum. Trailing, semi-evergreen perennial with many-branched stems, and rosettes of linear-oblong, mid-green basal leaves, to 1½in (4cm) long. Stem leaves are borne in pairs, and are usually fused at the bases. In autumn, bears solitary, dark blue flowers, narrowly trumpet-shaped and to 2in (5cm) long, with very narrow

Gentiana verna

tubes and striped outside with greenish yellow, on prostrate shoots. ↕ 2in (5cm), ↔ to 8in (20cm). W. China. Zone 5.

G. verna ▣ (Spring gentian, Star gentian). Often short-lived, mat-forming, evergreen perennial with basal rosettes of elliptic-lance-shaped, dark green leaves, to 1¼in (3cm) long, and 1–3 pairs of stem leaves. In spring or early summer, bears solitary, short-stemmed, narrowly tubular, usually white-throated, pure sky-blue flowers, to 1¼in (3cm) across, with wide-spreading lobes. ↕ 1½in (4cm), ↔ to 4in (10cm). Mountains in Europe, from Ireland to Russia. Zone 4. **'Angulosa'** forms vigorous, tidy clumps. **subsp. *balcanica*** syn. subsp. *pontica*, subsp. *tergestina*, is more vigorous, with usually ovate leaves and larger flowers, to 1½in (4cm) across; ↕ to 2½in (6cm).

***G.* 'Wellsii'** see *G.* x *macaulayi* 'Wells's Variety'.

GENTIANOPSIS

GENTIANACEAE

Genus of 20–25 species of erect annuals and biennials, sometimes included in the genus *Gentiana*, found in moist grassland throughout North America and Eurasia. They form basal tufts of simple, glossy leaves, and bear tubular-bell-shaped, 4-petaled, fringed blue flowers on long stems from late summer to autumn. They are suitable for a wild garden or a partially shaded border.

- **CULTIVATION** Grow in humus-rich, moist but well-drained soil in a site shaded from hot sun.
- **PROPAGATION** Sow *in situ*, or surface-sow in containers outdoors, in autumn.
- **PESTS AND DISEASES** Slugs and snails may damage young seedlings.

G. crinita, syn. *Gentiana crinita* (Fringed gentian). Tuft-forming annual or biennial with ovate to lance-shaped, glossy, dark green leaves, ¾–1¼in (2–3cm) long. Produces long, branching, hairy stems, terminating in single or clustered, 4-lobed, tubular-bell-shaped, fringed, bright blue flowers, 2in (5cm) long, from late summer to autumn. ↕ 12–36in (30–90cm), ↔ to 9in (23cm). E. North America. Zone 5.

GEOHINTONIA

CACTACEAE

Monotypic genus of cactus, native to the gypsum and limestone cliffs and hills of Sierra Madre Oriental in Nuevo Leon, Mexico. The one species, *G. mexicana*, grows sympatrically with *Aztekium hintonii.*

- **CULTIVATION** Under glass, grow in a mix of 4 parts standard cactus potting mix and 1 part limestone chips, in full light. From spring to summer, water freely and apply a balanced liquid fertilizer every 4-5 weeks. Keep nearly dry at other times. Outdoors, grow in moderately fertile, slightly alkaline, sharply drained, humus-rich soil in full sun. See also pp.48–49.
- **PROPAGATION** Sow seed at 70°F (21°C) in spring or summer.
- **PESTS AND DISEASES** Scale occurs.

G. mexicana ▣ Sometimes columnar, solitary subglobose to globose cactus with 18–20 well-defined blue-green ribs.

Geohintonia mexicana

Oval areoles extending along the rib edges, 1/16–1/8in (2–3mm) apart, bear 3 light-colored, slightly curved spines, to 4¾in (12mm) long, which are shed. Diurnal, funnel-shaped deep pink to magenta flowers emerge apically, ¾–1½in (2–4cm) across. Has no tubercles; initially wooly, becoming naked. The berry-like, naked fruit, hidden in the apical wool, 3½in (9 mm) long, dehisces irregularly. ↕ 4½in (11cm), ↔ 4in (10cm). Sierra Madre Oriental in Nuevo Leon, Mexico. ❄ (min. 50°F/10°C)

GERANIUM

Cranesbill

GERANIACEAE

Genus of about 300 species of annuals, biennials, and herbaceous, semi-evergreen, and evergreen, sometimes tuberous perennials, often confused with the genus *Pelargonium* (which is commonly known as geranium). Cranesbills are found in all except very wet habitats throughout temperate regions. The leaves, usually rounded or 5-pointed, are palmately lobed, the divisions often further lobed and toothed; they are frequently aromatic or interestingly marked, textured, or colored, sometimes also coloring well in autumn. The basal leaves are often arranged in loose, sometimes overwintering or semi-evergreen rosettes; the stem leaves are usually smaller, with fewer lobes. Some bear fragrant foliage. Flowers are white, pink, purple, or blue, usually saucer-shaped, sometimes flat or star-shaped, with petals sometimes reflexed and often contrastingly veined or marked; they are mostly borne in diffuse or dense cymes or umbel- or panicle-like inflorescences.

Cranesbills are generally long-lived, versatile, and undemanding plants. Compact perennials, to about 6in (15cm) tall, are good for a rock garden; trailing, spreading, or mat-forming plants are effective as groundcovers in a woodland or wild garden. Taller, clump-forming species and hybrids are suitable for a border or among shrubs.

- **CULTIVATION** Outdoors, grow larger species and hybrids in any moderately fertile, well-drained soil in full sun or partial shade, but most soils (unless waterlogged), in either sun or shade, are tolerated. Grow small species and hybrids in humus-rich, sharply drained soil in full sun. Under glass, grow tender

Geranium 'Ann Folkard'

species in soil-based potting mix, with added sharp sand, in bright filtered light. During the growing season, water freely and apply a balanced liquid fertilizer in spring and early summer. Water sparingly in winter. For all cranesbills, remove flowered stems and old leaves to encourage the production of fresh leaves and flowers. Many cease flowering during the heat of summer.
• **PROPAGATION** Sow seed of hardy species in containers outdoors as soon as ripe or in spring. Sow seed of marginally hardy species at 55–64°F (13–18°C) in spring. Divide in spring. Increase by basal cuttings, taken in early or mid-spring, and root with bottom heat. Insert root cuttings in a cold frame in midautumn.
• **PESTS AND DISEASES** Prone to bacterial blight, downy mildew, powdery mildew, gray mold (*Botrytis*), and *Cercospora* and *Ramularia* leaf spot in most locations. Leaf miner, slugs, and other pests of pelargoniums can be problems.

G. anemonifolium see *G. palmatum.*
***G.* 'Ann Folkard'** ■ Spreading herbaceous perennial producing many long, procumbent or scrambling stems and numerous 5-lobed, toothed, yellowish green leaves, 2–8in (5–20cm) long, becoming greener with age. Bears a profusion of saucer-shaped magenta flowers, 1½in (4cm) across, with black centers and veins, from midsummer to midautumn. ↕ to 24in (60cm), ↔ 3ft (1m) or more. Zone 4.
G. armenum see *G. psilostemon.*
G. asphodeloides ■ Variable, evergreen perennial, forming a loose mound of 5- to 7-lobed, mid-green, basal leaves, to 3in (8cm) long. Loose cymes of numerous star-shaped, narrow-petaled, pink or white flowers, 1–1½in (2.5–4cm) across, with darker veins, are produced in early summer. ↕ 12–18in (30–45cm), ↔ 12in (30cm). Italy (Sicily) to Turkey, Caucasus, N. Iran. Zone 6b.
***G.* 'Buxton's Blue'** see *G. wallichianum* 'Buxton's Variety'.
***G. candicans* of gardens** see *G. lambertii.*
G. x cantabrigiense ■ (*G. dalmaticum* x *G. macrorrhizum*). Compact, evergreen perennial, spreading slowly by runners, with 7-lobed, toothed, aromatic, glossy, light green, basal leaves, 1¼–3½in (3–9cm) long. In early and midsummer, produces dense cymes of numerous flat, bright purplish pink or white flowers, 1in (2.5cm) across, the petals somewhat reflexed. ↕ 12in (30cm), ↔ 24in (60cm). Garden origin. Zone 4. **'Biokova Karmina'** is low-growing and bears dark pink flowers in early and midsummer. Useful as a groundcover; ↕ 9in (23cm). **'Biokovo'** ■ is compact, with long runners and pink-tinged white flowers; ↔ 30–36in (75–90cm). **'Cambridge'** forms compact mats and bears many pinkish mauve flowers; ↕ 6in (15cm), ↔ 18in (45cm).
G. cinereum. Dwarf, rosette-forming, evergreen perennial with gray-green, basal leaves, to 2in (5cm) across, deeply 5- to 7-lobed, with each division itself usually 3-lobed. In late spring and early summer, produces short-stalked cymes of 1–4 upward-facing, cup-shaped, translucent, white or pale pink flowers, to 1in (2.5cm) across, usually veined purple. Needs good drainage. ↕ to 6in (15cm), ↔ to 12in (30cm). Pyrenees. Zone 4. **'Ballerina'** ■ has grayer leaves and purplish red flowers, dark red-veined, with dark eyes. **'Lawrence Flatman'** resembles 'Ballerina' but is more vigorous, with darker eyes and usually darker petals. **subsp. *subcaulescens*** ■ syn. *G. subcaulescens*, is more vigorous than the species, with darker green leaves, longer stems, and brilliant magenta flowers with black centers; Balkans, N.E. Turkey.
***G.* 'Claridge Druce'** see *G.* x *oxonianum* 'Claridge Druce'.
G. clarkei. Spreading, rhizomatous herbaceous perennial with 7-lobed, mid-green, basal leaves, 1¾–6in (4.5–15cm) long, each lobe deeply cut into narrow, pointed segments. Saucer- to cup-shaped flowers, 1½–2in (4–5cm) across, purple-violet or white with mauve-pink veins, are produced in loose cymes from early to late summer. ↕ to 20in (50cm), ↔ indefinite. India (Kashmir). Zone 4. **'Kashmir Purple'**, syn. *G. pratense* 'Kashmir Purple', has rich lilac-blue flowers with red veins; it spreads rapidly. **'Kashmir White'** ■ syn. *G. pratense* 'Kashmir White', is less vigorous than 'Kashmir Purple' and bears white flowers, 1–1½in (2.5–4cm) across, with pale lilac-pink veins, appearing grayish pink overall; ↕ to 18in (45cm).
G. dalmaticum ■ (Dalmatian cranesbill). Dwarf, rhizomatous, woody-stemmed, creeping perennial, evergreen in all but the severest winters, with rosettes of glossy, light green, basal leaves, to 1½in (4cm) long, each deeply divided into 5–7 segments. In summer, bears long-stalked, umbel-like clusters of pale to bright pink flowers, 1–1½in (2.5–4cm) across, with red anthers and inflated calyces. ↕ to 6in (15cm), ↔ to 20in (50cm) or more. Yugoslavia (Montenegro), Albania. Zone 4.
G. endressii ■ Rhizomatous, hairy, evergreen perennial forming clumps of 5-lobed, toothed, wrinkled, light green, basal leaves, 2–6in (5–15cm) long, each lobe divided into pointed segments. Erect, trumpet-shaped, bright pink flowers, 1¼–1½in (3–4cm) across, with

Geranium asphodeloides

Geranium x *cantabrigiense*

Geranium cinereum 'Ballerina'

Geranium cinereum subsp. *subcaulescens*

Geranium clarkei 'Kashmir White'

Geranium dalmaticum

Geranium endressii

Geranium erianthum

Geranium himalayense

notched petals and a silvery sheen, becoming darker with age, are borne in dense cymes from early summer to early autumn. ↕ 18in (45cm), ↔ 24in (60cm). Pyrenees (mainly France). Zone 4. **'Wargrave Pink'** see *G.* x *oxonianum* 'Wargrave Pink'.
G. erianthum ■ Clump-forming, hairy herbaceous perennial, similar to *G. eriostemon*, with upright stems and 7- to 9-lobed, light green, basal leaves, 2–8in (5–20cm) long, the lobes overlapping and prominently toothed. Bears dense, umbel-like clusters of saucer-shaped to almost flat, violet-blue flowers, 1–1½in (2.5–4cm) across, from late spring to midsummer. Good autumn leaf color. ↕ 18–24in (45–60cm), ↔ 12in (30cm). Russia (E. Siberia, Sakhalin), Japan, North America (Alaska, Aleutian Islands to N. British Columbia). Zone 4.
G. eriostemon, syn. *G. platyanthum.* Clump-forming, hairy herbaceous perennial with upright stems and 5- or 7-lobed, shallowly toothed, basal leaves, 2–8in (5–20cm) long, crinkly above. In late spring and early summer, bears umbel-like clusters of horizontal or nodding, flat, pale violet to violet-pink flowers, 1¼in (3cm) across, shaded darker toward the centers, with small white bases to the petals. Good autumn color. ↕ 12–20in (30–50cm), ↔ 18in (45cm). Russia (E. Siberia), E. Tibet, W. China, Korea, Japan. Zone 4.
G. farreri. Dwarf, taprooted, rosette-forming herbaceous perennial with somewhat spreading or erect red stems and kidney-shaped, red-margined, matte, mid-green, basal leaves, to 2in (5cm) across, each deeply cut into 7 sparsely toothed divisions, which are 3-lobed at the tips. In early summer, bears loose cymes of shallowly cup-shaped, very pale pink, wavy-margined flowers, to 1½in (4cm) wide, with conspicuous black anthers. Best in a scree bed or alpine house. ↕ to 5in (13cm), ↔ to 6in (15cm). W. China. Zone 4.
G. fremontii. Clump-forming herbaceous perennial with 5- to 7-lobed, light green, basal leaves, 2–4in (5–10cm) long, sticky-hairy beneath, the divisions broadly toothed and lobed at the tips. Bears upward-facing, flat, pale to deep pink flowers, to 1½in (4cm) across, in open, branched cymes from early summer to early autumn. ↕ 12–18in (30–45cm), ↔ 18in (45cm). W. Wyoming to Arizona and New Mexico. Zone 5.
G. grandiflorum see *G. himalayense.*
G. grandiflorum* var. *alpinum see *G. himalayense* 'Gravetye'.
G. grevilleanum see *G. lambertii.*
G. himalayense ■ syn. *G. grandiflorum*, *G. himalayense* var. *meeboldii*, *G. meeboldii* (Lilac geranium). Rhizomatous, mat-forming herbaceous perennial bearing 7-lobed, prominently veined, mid-green, basal leaves, 2–8in (5–20cm) long, with broad, blunt-

Geranium x *cantabrigiense* 'Biokovo'

G

toothed lobes, coloring well in autumn. Loose cymes of saucer-shaped, veined, violet-blue to deep mid-blue flowers, 1½–2½in (4–6cm) across, touched with reddish pink, and with white centers, are produced in a main flush in early summer and then sporadically to early autumn. Good as a groundcover, even in full shade. ↕12–18in (30–45cm), ↔24in (60cm). Himalayas. Zone 4. **var. *alpinum*** see 'Gravetye'. **'Birch Double'** see 'Plenum'. **'Gravetye'** ▣ syn. *G. grandiflorum* var. *alpinum*, *G. himalayense* var. *alpinum*, has smaller leaves, 2–5in (5–13cm) long, and larger flowers, to 3in (8cm) across, with more markedly red zones around the white centers; ↕12in (30cm). **'Irish Blue'** produces paler blue flowers, 1½in (4cm) across, with larger, purplish red central zones, and is very free-flowering. **var. *meeboldii*** see *G. himalayense*. **'Plenum'**, syn. 'Birch Double', has smaller leaves, 2–5in (5–13cm) long, and double, purplish pink flowers, 1in (2.5cm) across, shaded blue, with darker veins; ↕10in (25cm).

G. ibericum ▣ Clump-forming, hairy herbaceous perennial with 9- to 11-lobed, basal leaves, 4–8in (10–20cm) long, the lobes toothed and overlapping. Upward-facing, shallowly cup-shaped, violet-blue flowers, 1½–2in (4–5cm) across, with feathered, darker veins, and petals notched at the tips, are borne in dense cymes in early summer. ↕to 20in (50cm), ↔24in (60cm). Caucasus, N.E. Turkey, N. Iran. Zone 5.

G. incanum. Mounded, bushy, evergreen perennial with branching stems and aromatic, filigree, gray-green, basal leaves, to 3in (8cm) long, each deeply cut into 5 segments, which in turn are lobed and toothed. From summer to autumn, bears loose cymes of deep pink flowers, to about 1½in (4cm) across, with dark veins and a V-shaped white mark at the base of each petal. Needs a warm, sunny position. ↕16in (40cm), ↔to 24in (60cm) or more. South Africa. Zone 5b.

***G.* 'Johnson's Blue'.** Rhizomatous, spreading herbaceous perennial, forming a dense mat of 7-lobed, mid-green, basal leaves, 2–8in (5–20cm) long, each lobe itself lobed and toothed. Saucer-shaped, mid- to lavender-blue flowers, 2in (5cm) across, tinged pink at the centers, are produced in loose cymes during summer. ↕12–18in (30–45cm), ↔24–30in (60–75cm). Zone 4.

***G.* 'Kate'**, syn. *G.* 'Kate Folkard'. Dwarf, carpeting, semi-evergreen perennial with rounded, deeply 5- to 7-lobed, dark bronze-green leaves, ½–1½in (1.5–4cm) long, each lobe obovate and further lobed. Bears cymes of funnel-shaped, pale pink flowers, ½in (1.5cm) across, with almost translucent bases and dark veins, from late spring to summer. ↕4–6in (10–15cm), ↔12in (30cm). Zone 4.

***G.* 'Kate Folkard'** see *G.* 'Kate'.

G. kishtvariense. Rhizomatous, rounded, bristly-hairy herbaceous perennial with 5-lobed, finely toothed, wrinkled, bright green, basal leaves, 4–9in (10–23cm) long. Loose cymes of upward-facing, shallowly cup-shaped, deep pinkish purple flowers, 1½in (4cm) across, with purple veins and small white centers, and a white V at each base, are produced throughout summer. ↕12in (30cm), ↔24in (60cm). India (Kashmir). Zone 6b.

G. lambertii, syn. *G. candicans* of gardens, *G. grevilleanum.* Trailing herbaceous perennial with long, procumbent, non-rooting stems bearing rounded or kidney-shaped, wrinkled, mid-green leaves, 4in (10cm) long, each with 5 lobes and a 3-lobed point. In late summer, bears diffuse cymes of nodding, saucer-shaped, pale pink or white flowers, 1¼–1½in (3–4cm) across, marked purple at the bases, and with crimson centers and veins. ↕12–18in (30–45cm), ↔36in (90cm). Himalayas. Zone 5.

G. libani, syn. *G. libanoticum.* Clump-forming perennial, dormant in summer, but with new foliage in autumn, with rounded, deeply 5- or 7-lobed, glossy, mid-green leaves, 4–8in (10–20cm) long, each ovate lobe toothed and further lobed. In spring, violet or violet-blue flowers, with notched, disk-shaped petals, 1¼in (3cm) across, are borne in umbel-like clusters. ↕16in (40cm), ↔18in (45cm). Lebanon, W. Syria, central S. Turkey. Zone 7.

G. libanoticum see *G. libani.*

***G.* x *lindavicum* 'Alanah'**, syn. *G.* x *lindavicum* 'Purpureum'. Dwarf, rosette-forming, evergreen perennial, similar to *G. cinereum*, with deeply 7-lobed, silky, silvery green, basal leaves, to 3in (8cm) long. In late spring and early summer, bears loose cymes of deep crimson-purple flowers, 1¼–2in (3–5cm) across, with a network of darker veins. ↕to 6in (15cm), ↔to 8in (20cm). Zone 5.

***G.* x *lindavicum* 'Purpureum'** see *G.* x *lindavicum* 'Alanah'.

G. macrorrhizum ▣ (Bigroot geranium, Scented cranesbill). Rhizomatous, semi-evergreen perennial with 7-lobed, toothed, sticky, strongly aromatic, light green, basal leaves, 4–8in (10–20cm) long, coloring well in autumn. Umbel-like clusters of erect, flat, pink to purplish pink or white flowers, ¾–1in (2–2.5cm) across, with inflated red calyces, slightly reflexed petals, and protruding stamens and styles, are produced in early summer. Effective as a groundcover in shade. ↕20in (50cm), ↔24in (60cm). S. Europe. Zone 4. **'Album'** produces white flowers with pink stamens in early and midsummer; ↕12in (30cm). **'Bevan's Variety'** has crimson-purple flowers. **'Czakor'** has magenta flowers and purple-tinted foliage in autumn; ↕to 12in (30cm). **'Ingwersen's Variety'** ▣ has glossy, light green leaves and soft pink flowers. **'Spessart'** has dark pink flowers all summer, followed by distinctive seed heads. **'Variegatum'** has grayish green leaves with cream variegation, and produces purplish pink flowers. It is less vigorous than the species, requiring richer soil and more sun; ↕12in (30cm), ↔18in (45cm).

G. maculatum ▣ (Spotted geranium). Erect, clump-forming herbaceous perennial with 5- to 7-lobed, glossy, mid-green, basal leaves, 4–8in (10–20cm) long, with narrow, toothed, widely spaced lobes. Slightly upward-facing, saucer-shaped, lilac-pink to bright pink flowers, 1¼in (3cm) across, usually white near the base of each petal, are produced in loose cymes from late spring to midsummer. Prefers moist soil. ↕24–30in (60–75cm), ↔18in (45cm). E. North America. Zone 4. **f. *albiflorum*** has white flowers and is less vigorous. **'Helen Gallagher'** is bushy, with pure white flowers in late spring; ↕24–36in (60–90cm).

G. maderense ▣ Robust, evergreen perennial, usually short-lived or behaving as a biennial, with short, erect stems bearing rosettes of 5- to 7-lobed, deeply toothed, bright green leaves, to 24in (60cm) long, with long, brownish red stalks. From late winter to late summer, produces a profusion of flat, pinkish magenta flowers, 1½in (4cm) across, with paler pink veins, darkening toward dark magenta centers, and with red anthers; they are borne in imposing,

Geranium ibericum

Geranium maderense

Geranium himalayense 'Gravetye'

Geranium macrorrhizum

Geranium macrorrhizum 'Ingwersen's Variety'

Geranium maculatum

Geranium x *magnificum*

Geranium nodosum

Geranium orientalitibeticum

Geranium x *oxonianum* 'Southcombe Star'

Geranium x *oxonianum* 'Winscombe'

Geranium phaeum

Geranium phaeum f. *album*

Geranium pratense 'Mrs. Kendall Clark'

panicle-like inflorescences, the upper parts of the flower stalks thickly covered with purple, glandular hairs. ↕↔ 4–5ft (1.2–1.5m). Madeira. ❀ (min. 41°F/5°C)
G. x magnificum ■ (*G. ibericum* x *G. platypetalum*) (Showy geranium). Vigorous, clump-forming herbaceous perennial with mid-green, basal leaves, 4–8in (10–20cm) long, that color well in autumn. Each leaf is divided into 9–11 broad lobes, the lobes themselves lobed, toothed, and overlapping. Dense cymes of numerous saucer-shaped, rich violet flowers, 2in (5cm) across, heavily veined in a darker shade, are produced in one burst in midsummer. Prefers a sunny site. ↕↔ 24in (60cm). Garden origin. Zone 4.
G. meeboldii see *G. himalayense.*
G. x monacense (*G. phaeum* x *G. reflexum*) syn. *G. punctatum* of gardens. Clump-forming herbaceous perennial with 5- to 7-lobed, basal leaves, 4–8in (10–20cm) long, usually with brown marks at the lobe bases. In late spring and early summer, bears loose cymes of saucer-shaped, purplish red flowers, ¾in (2cm) across, with white and violet zones at the bases of the reflexed petals. ↕ 18in (45cm), ↔ 24in (60cm). Garden origin. Zone 4. **'Muldoon'** has dark green leaves heavily spotted with purple, and produces flowers with protruding stamens and styles; ↕ 24in (60cm).
G. nodosum ■ Rhizomatous herbaceous perennial forming a clump of 3- or 5-lobed, shallow-toothed, glossy, bright green, basal leaves, 2–8in (5–20cm) long, the stems swollen above the nodes. From late spring to early or midautumn, red-tinted stems bear loose cymes of erect, open funnel-shaped, purplish pink flowers, 1–1¼in (2.5–3cm) across, with paler pink centers, darker veins, and notched petals. Effective as a groundcover in dry soil in full shade. ↕ 12–20in (30–50cm), ↔ 20in (50cm). Pyrenees, C. Italy, Yugoslavia (Serbia). Zone 5.
G. orientalitibeticum ■ syn. *G. stapfianum* var. *roseum* of gardens. Dwarf herbaceous perennial with tuberous, underground runners, and basal leaves, to 4in (10cm) across, cut into narrowly lobed, toothed divisions, marbled dark and pale green. In summer, bears loose cymes of shallowly cup-shaped, deep purplish pink flowers, to 1in (2.5cm) across, the centers white. Spreads rapidly. ↕ to 12in (30cm), ↔ to 3ft (1m) or more. S.W. China. Zone 5.
G. x oxonianum ■ (*G. endressii* x *G. versicolor*). Vigorous, clump-forming, evergreen perennial with 5-lobed, light green, basal leaves, 2–8in (5–20cm) long, each lobe with 5 toothed, wrinkled, conspicuously veined divisions. From late spring to midautumn, bears loose cymes of broadly funnel-shaped pink flowers, to 1½in (4cm) across, with darker veins and notched petals. ↕ to 32in (80cm), ↔ 24in (60cm). Garden origin. Zone 4. **'A.T. Johnson'** has silvery pink flowers and is very free-flowering; ↕ 12in (30cm). **'Claridge Druce'**, syn. *G.* 'Claridge Druce', is very vigorous, forming strong clumps of grayish green, somewhat glossy leaves, with dark-veined, rose-pink flowers, 1½–1¾in (4–4.5cm) across. Self-seeds freely and usually comes true. Good groundcover; ↕ 18–30in (45–75cm). **'Hollywood'** produces pale pink flowers with almost maroon veins; ↕ 18in (45cm). **'Rose Clair'** has red-purple flowers with paler veins and is free-flowering; ↕ 14in (35cm). **'Southcombe Double'** produces usually double, warm pink flowers, ¾in (2cm) across; ↕ 16in (40cm). **'Southcombe Star'** ■ is more spreading, bearing star-shaped, deep purplish pink flowers, ¾–1in (2–2.5cm) across. **'Wargrave Pink'**, syn. *G. endressii* 'Wargrave Pink', is very vigorous and has bright salmon-pink flowers; ↕ 24in (60cm), ↔ 36in (90cm). **'Winscombe'** ■ forms a leafy clump, with very pale pink flowers, becoming bright pink with darker veins, several shades present on the plant at one time; ↕ 18in (45cm).
G. palmatum, syn. *G. anemonifolium.* Taprooted, evergreen, rosetted perennial, sometimes self-seeding as a biennial. Similar to *G. maderense*, it has basal rosettes of 5-lobed, light green leaves, to 14in (35cm) across; each lobe is cut into 6–9 toothed segments, the central segment stalked. Flowering stems with purple glandular hairs bear large, panicle-like inflorescences, to 4ft (1.2m) across, of saucer-shaped, crimson-centered, purple-pink flowers, 1¼–1½in (3–4cm) across, throughout summer. Transplant seedlings while small. ↕↔ to 4ft (1.2m). Madeira. Zone 7b.
G. phaeum ■ (Dusky cranesbill, Mourning widow). Clump-forming herbaceous perennial bearing 7- or 9-lobed, soft green, basal leaves, 4–8in (10–20cm) long, often with purplish brown marks; each lobe is itself shallowly lobed. In late spring and early summer, bears branched, almost one-sided cymes of pendent, white-centered, deep purple-black, deep maroon, violet-blue, light mauve, or white flowers, ¾–1in (2–2.5cm) across, with reflexed petals. Good in damp shade. ↕ 32in (80cm), ↔ 18in (45cm). Mountainous regions from Pyrenees to Balkans, S.E. Germany, Czech Republic, W. Russia. Zone 4. **f. *album*** ■ bears white flowers. **'Langthorn's Blue'** has violet-blue flowers; ↕ 24–36in (60–90cm). **'Lily Lovell'** has large flowers, 1¼–1½in (3–4cm) across, in rich purple-mauve. **var. *lividum*** produces very pale lilac or pink flowers with white bases, and unmarked leaves. **'Variegatum'** produces leaves that are irregularly margined in yellow and splashed reddish pink.

Geranium x *oxonianum*

G. platyanthum see *G. eriostemon.*
G. platypetalum (Broad-petaled geranium). Clump-forming, hairy herbaceous perennial with wrinkled, mid-green, basal leaves, 4–8in (10–20cm) long, each deeply divided into 7 or 9 broadly toothed lobes. During early and midsummer, produces dense cymes of flat, saucer-shaped, deep violet-blue flowers, 1¼–1¾in (3–4.5cm) across, with darker veins. ↕ 12–18in (30–45cm), ↔ 18in (45cm). Caucasus, N.E. Turkey, N.W. Iran. Zone 4.
G. pratense (Meadow cranesbill). Clump-forming herbaceous perennial with hairy stems and 7- to 9-lobed, basal leaves, 8in (20cm) long, the lobes often deeply divided and toothed. Bears erect, saucer-shaped, variously veined, white, blue, or violet flowers, 1½–1¾in (3.5–4.5cm) across, in dense cymes in early and midsummer. ↕ 24–36in (60–90cm), ↔ 24in (60cm). Europe, C. Asia (Altai Mountains), W. China. Zone 4. All except double-flowered cultivars self-seed freely, bearing varying offspring. Double-flowered cultivars have longer-lasting flowers, but require rich soil and regular division, and are more prone to mildew in dry conditions. **f. *albiflorum*** produces white flowers over a long period, sometimes to early autumn; ↕ 3ft (1m). **'Bicolor'** see 'Striatum'. **'Bittersweet'** has purple-tinged leaves and pink-mauve flowers. **'Flore Pleno'** see 'Plenum Violaceum'. **'Galactic'** has dark green leaves and produces milk-white flowers, to 2in (5cm) across; ↕ 30in (75cm). **'Kashmir Purple'** see *G. clarkei* 'Kashmir Purple'. **'Kashmir White'** see *G. clarkei* 'Kashmir White'. **'Mrs. Kendall Clark'** ■ has pearl-gray flowers flushed with pale rose-pink, although plants offered often have violet-blue flowers with white veining. **'Plenum Album'** produces loosely

G

Geranium pratense 'Plenum Caeruleum'

Geranium psilostemon

Geranium pyranaicum

Geranium renardii

Geranium x *riversleaianum* 'Russell Prichard'

Geranium 'Salome'

Geranium sanguineum

Geranium sylvaticum 'Mayflower'

Geranium wallichianum 'Buxton's Variety'

double, violet-tinged white flowers, ¾–1¼in (2–3cm) across. **'Plenum Caeruleum'** ■ produces flowers that are loosely double, lavender-blue, and sometimes tinged pink. **'Plenum Purpureum'** see 'Plenum Violaceum'. **'Plenum Violaceum'**, syn. 'Flore Pleno', 'Plenum Purpureum', bears double, deep violet-blue flowers, purple-blue in the centers. **'Silver Queen'** has white flowers touched with very pale violet; ↕ 4½ft (1.3m). **'Striatum'**, syn. 'Bicolor', has white flowers streaked violet-blue; may come true from seed.
G. procurrens. Spreading herbaceous perennial with procumbent red stems that may root at the nodes. Bears 5-lobed, coarsely toothed, mid-green, basal leaves, 2–4in (5–10cm) long, each division 3-lobed at the tip; leaves are wrinkled above. From midsummer to early autumn, bears loose cymes of somewhat star-shaped, dark purple-pink flowers, 1–1¼in (2.5–3cm) across. Each petal has a V-shaped black mark at the base, and black centers and veins. Ideal in dry soil under shrubs. ↕ 18in (45cm), ↔ 3ft (1m) or more. Himalayas. Zone 7b.
G. psilostemon ■ syn. *G. armenum* (Armenian cranesbill). Upright, clump-forming herbaceous perennial with 7-lobed, toothed, mid-green, basal leaves, 8in (20cm) long, crimson-tinted in spring and red in autumn. From early to late summer, bears loose, upright cymes of numerous erect, shallowly bowl-shaped, brilliant magenta flowers, 1½in (4cm) across, with black centers and veins. ↕ 2–4ft (60–120cm), ↔ 24in (60cm). S.W. Caucasus, N.E. Turkey. Zone 5. **'Bressingham Flair'** has somewhat crumpled, less vivid magenta flowers with a hint of pink.
G. pulchrum. Larger and more solid and bushy form than most other geraniums. Leaves somewhat palmately lobed (about halfway to mid-rib) with a felted upper surface and a densely wooly undersurface, making an interesting contrast of light and dark green. Bears deep pink flowers with purple veining. ↕↔ 3ft (1m). South Africa. ❄ (min. 38°F/3°C)
***G. punctatum* of gardens** see *G.* x *monacense.*
G. pylzowianum. Spreading herbaceous perennial with tuberous, underground runners and dark green, kidney-shaped or semi-circular, basal leaves, to 2in (5cm) across, each deeply cut into 5–7 narrowly lobed, toothed divisions. In early summer, bears cymes of broadly trumpet-shaped, deep rose-pink flowers, 1¼–1¾in (3–4.5cm) wide, white at the bases and with darker veins. Similar to *G. orientalitibeticum*, but less invasive. ↕ 6–10in (15–25cm), ↔ 10in (25cm) or more. W. China. Zone 6.
G. pyrenaicum ■ Clump-forming, hairy, evergreen perennial. Bears scalloped, mid-green, basal leaves, 2–4in (5–10cm) long, with 7 or 9 ill-defined, sometimes toothed lobes. Somewhat star-shaped, violet-pink flowers, ½–¾in (1–2cm) across, white at the bases, with darker veins and notched petals, are borne in loose cymes from spring to autumn. Self-seeds freely. ↕ 12–24in (30–60cm), ↔ 12in (30cm). W. and S. Europe to Caucasus. Zone 5. **f. *albiflorum*** has white flowers. **'Bill Wallis'** has rich purple flowers. Comes true from seed.
G. reflexum. Clump-forming herbaceous perennial, similar to *G. phaeum*, with 7-lobed, mid-green, basal leaves, 4–8in (10–20cm) long, with dark blotches. In late spring and early summer, bears branched, one-sided cymes of bright rose-pink flowers, ½in (1.5cm) across; they have narrow, very reflexed petals with white bases and red-shaded sepals showing behind. ↕ 18–24in (45–60cm), ↔ 24in (60cm). Italy to N. Greece. Zone 6.
G. renardii ■ Clump-forming herbaceous perennial with wrinkled, veined, velvety, gray-green, basal leaves, to 4in (10cm) across, each cut into 5 or 7 broad lobes with scalloped margins. Dense, umbel-like clusters of saucer-shaped, white to pale lavender flowers, 1¼in (3cm) across, with notched petals and bold violet veins, are borne intermittently in early summer. Often shy-flowering, but an effective foliage plant. Best in poor soil. ↕↔ 12in (30cm). Caucasus. Zone 5. **'Whiteknights'** has white flowers, with pale lilac-blue ground color and darker veins.
G. richardsonii. Variable, clump-forming herbaceous perennial with 5- or 7-lobed, broadly toothed, slightly glossy, bright green, basal leaves, 2–4in (5–10cm) long. Bears loose cymes of flat, very lightly veined, pink-tinged white flowers, to 1¼in (3cm) across, from late spring to late summer. Prefers damp soil in sun. ↕ 12–24in (30–60cm), ↔ 12in (30cm). W. North America (British Columbia and Saskatchewan to Mexico). Zone 4.
G.* x *riversleaianum (*G. endressii* x *G. traversii*). Trailing, hairy herbaceous perennial with long, branching stems bearing gray-green leaves, 2–4in (5–10cm) across, each deeply divided into 7 blunt-toothed lobes. In summer, produces loose cymes of erect, broadly funnel-shaped, light pink to dark magenta flowers, to 1½in (4cm) wide, with darker veins. Good groundcover. ↕ to 12in (30cm), ↔ to 3ft (1m). Garden origin. Zone 5. **'Mavis Simpson'** bears clear, light pink flowers with paler centers. **'Russell Prichard'** ■ has more sharply toothed leaves, and produces deep magenta flowers over long periods in summer.
***G.* 'Salome'** ■ Trailing herbaceous perennial with branching stems bearing 5-lobed, toothed, pale green, basal leaves, 2–6in (5–15cm) long. In summer, produces loose cymes of flowers to 1¼in (3cm) wide, with widely spaced, purplish pink petals, veined and basally marked deep violet, with almost black styles and stamens. ↕ 12in (30cm), ↔ to 4ft (1.2m). Zone 6b.
G. sanguineum ■ (Bloody cranesbill). Dense, clump-forming herbaceous perennial with spreading rhizomes. Dark green stem leaves, 2–4in (5–10cm) long, are deeply cut into 5–7 sparsely toothed lobes, each with 3 segments. Has few basal leaves. During summer, bears a profusion of upright, cup-shaped, deep magenta-pink flowers, to 1½in (4cm) wide, with darker veins, white eyes, and usually notched petals, in loose cymes. ↕ 8in (20cm), ↔ to 12in (30cm) or more. Europe, N. Turkey. Zone 4.
'Album' is taller, more lax, with pure white flowers borne over many weeks in summer; ↕ 12in (30cm), ↔ 16in (40cm). **'Alpenglow'** has rounded, finely divided, deep green leaves and carmine-red flowers, in spring and late summer; ↕ 18in (45cm). **'Elsbeth'** has dark green leaves that turn brilliant red in autumn, and bears pink flowers with dark veins, all summer; ↕ 12in (30cm). **'John Elsley'** is prostrate, with dark green leaves and rose-pink flowers all summer; ↕ 3in (8cm). **var. *lancastriense*** see var. *striatum.*
'Max Frei' is mound-forming, with bright carmine-rose flowers, all summer; ↕ 6–9in (15–23cm).
'New Hampshire Purple' has large, dark rose-purple flowers, in summer; ↕ 12in (30cm). **var. *prostratum*** see var. *striatum.*
'Shepherd's Warning' is compact, with rose-pink flowers; ↕↔ 6in (15cm).
'Splendens' see var. *striatum* 'Splendens'. **var. *striatum*** ■ syn. var. *lancastriense*, var. *prostratum*, is compact, with pale flesh-pink flowers, veined darker pink; ↕ 4in (10cm); UK (Walney Island, Cumbria).
var. *striatum* 'Splendens', syn. 'Splendens', is taller, with larger, dark-

Geranium sanguineum var. *striatum*

veined pink flowers, to 1¾in (4.5cm) across; ↕ to 18in (45cm).
***G. sessiliflorum* subsp. *novae-zelandiae* 'Nigrescens'** see *G. sessiliflorum* subsp. *novae-zelandiae* 'Nigricans'.
***G. sessiliflorum* subsp. *novae-zelandiae* 'Nigricans'**, syn. *G. sessiliflorum* subsp. *novae-zelandiae* 'Nigrescens'. Rosette-forming herbaceous perennial with tufts of olive-bronze, basal leaves, ½–1¼in (1.5–3cm) across, divided into 5–7 shallowly 3-lobed segments. In summer, bears loose cymes of erect, funnel-shaped, grayish white flowers, about ¼in (6mm) across. Self-seeds freely. ↕ to 3in (8cm), ↔ to 6in (15cm). Zone 6b.
G. shikokianum. Bushy, clump-forming herbaceous perennial with 5- to 7-lobed, light green, basal leaves, 2–4in (5–10cm) long, gray-marbled above and shiny beneath, each lobe itself divided and toothed. Funnel-shaped pink flowers, 1in (2.5cm) across, with large white centers and netted, red-purple veins, are borne in loose cymes from midsummer to early autumn. Good autumn color. Prefers moist soil in light shade. ↕ 8–18in (20–45cm), ↔ 18in (45cm). Korea, S. Japan. Zone 5.
***G. stapfianum* var. *roseum* of gardens** see *G. orientalitibeticum.*
G. striatum see *G. versicolor.*
G. subcaulescens see *G. cinereum* subsp. *subcaulescens.*
G. sylvaticum (Wood cranesbill). Clump-forming herbaceous perennial with 7-lobed, mid-green, basal leaves, 4–8in (10–20cm) long, the lobes deeply cut and toothed. In late spring and early summer, bears dense cymes of erect or upward-facing, saucer-shaped, white-centered, lightly veined, blue-purple, pinkish purple, pink, or white flowers, ¾–1¼in (2–3cm) across. Best in moist soil. ↕ to 30in (75cm), ↔ 24in (60cm). Europe, N. Turkey. Zone 4. **'Mayflower'** ▣ has larger, rich violet-blue flowers, to 1½in (4cm) across, with smaller white centers. **var. *wanneri*** has purplish pink flowers with red veins.
G. traversii* var. *elegans. Low-growing, clump-forming, evergreen perennial with branching stems bearing silver-hairy, gray-green, basal leaves, to 4in (10cm) across, each deeply cut into 7 lobes, further divided into 3 lobes and with a few teeth. During summer, bears loose cymes of cup-shaped, pale pink flowers, to 1¼in (3cm) across, with dark veins. Needs shelter and well-drained soil to overwinter; usually self-seeds. ↕ to 4in (10cm), ↔ to 12in (30cm). New Zealand (Chatham Islands). ❀ (min. 41°F/5°C)
G. tuberosum. Upright, gently spreading, tuberous perennial, dormant in summer, but with new foliage produced in autumn. The mid-green, basal leaves, 2–4in (5–10cm) long, are deeply cut into 7 narrow, lobed, toothed divisions. Cymes of shallowly cup-shaped flowers, ¾–1¼in (2–3cm) across, with purple-shaded sepals and deeply notched, bright purple-pink petals with darker veins, are borne in midspring. ↕ 8–10in (20–25cm), ↔ 12in (30cm). Mediterranean. ❀ (min. 41°F/5°C)
G. versicolor, syn. *G. striatum.* Clump-forming, semi-evergreen perennial with mounds of 5-lobed, toothed, usually brown-marked, light green, basal leaves, 2–8in (5–20cm) long. Loose cymes of funnel-shaped white flowers, 1–1¼in (2.5–3cm) across, with deeply notched petals and netted magenta veins, are produced in late spring, then sporadically into midautumn. ↕↔ 18in (45cm). Italy (including Sicily), Balkans. Zone 6.
G. wallichianum. Taprooted herbaceous perennial with long, trailing, branching but non-rooting stems, with distinctive pairs of fused stipules and paired, 3- to 5-lobed, toothed, mid-green leaves, 2–6in (5–15cm) long, wrinkled and marbled above. Loose, leafy cymes of upward-facing, saucer-shaped, lilac or deep pinkish purple flowers, 1–1½in (2.5–4cm) across, with darker veins, white centers, and notched petals, are produced from midsummer to midautumn. ↕ 12in (30cm), ↔ 4ft (1.2m). N.E. Afghanistan to N. India (Kashmir). Zone 4. **'Buxton's Variety'** ▣ syn. *G.* 'Buxton's Blue', is dense, compact, and spreading; the flowers, to 1¼in (3cm) across, have sky-blue petals, large, strongly veined white centers, and dark stamens and stigmas. Often comes true from seed. **'Syabru'** has magenta-pink flowers with longer, darker veins than the species and a touch of white at the centers.
G. wlassovianum. Clump-forming, softly hairy herbaceous perennial with 7-lobed, dark green, basal leaves, 2–6in (5–15cm) long, each lobe usually cut into 3 toothed segments, shaded brown and deepening to red in autumn. From midsummer to early autumn, bears loose cymes of long-lasting, broadly funnel-shaped, purple-pink or pink flowers, 1¼in (3cm) across, with darker veins. Prefers moist soil. ↕↔ 24in (60cm). Russia (E. Siberia), Mongolia, N. China. Zone 5.
G. yesoense. Bushy herbaceous perennial with thin, spreading stems and deeply 7-lobed, mid-green, basal leaves, 2–4in (5–10cm) long, each lobe sharply toothed. In mid- and late summer, produces loose cymes of saucer-shaped, pink or white flowers, 1in (2.5cm) across, with darker veins, and green sepals showing between the petals. Needs moist soil. ↕↔ 12–18in (30–45cm). N. and C. Japan (including Kurile Islands). Zone 6b.

GERBERA

ASTERACEAE

Genus of about 40 species of hairy perennials from grassland in temperate and mountainous regions of Africa (except N. Africa), Madagascar, Asia, and Indonesia. Most form spreading, basal rosettes of lobed or pinnate, entire or toothed leaves, and bear long-lasting, solitary, single or double, daisy-like flowerheads in red, pink, purple, orange, or yellow, sometimes with yellow or white centers. Where not hardy, grow in a temperate greenhouse. Elsewhere, grow in a sunny border. Gerberas are also good for cutting.
• **CULTIVATION** Under glass, grow in soil-based potting mix in bright filtered light. During the growing season, water freely and apply a balanced liquid fertilizer every 4 weeks. Keep moist in winter. Pot on annually in spring. Outdoors, grow in moderately fertile, well-drained soil in full sun.

Gerbera jamesonii

• **PROPAGATION** Sow seed at 55–64°F (13–18°C) in autumn or early spring; divide in early spring, or take basal cuttings in summer.
• **PESTS AND DISEASES** Often attacked by gray mold, powdery mildew, anthracnose, bacterial blight, and crown and root rot. Leaf miners, mites, aphids, thrips, and whiteflies are also common.

G. jamesonii ▣ (Barberton daisy, Transvaal daisy). Clump-forming, deep-rooting perennial with inversely lance-shaped, deeply lobed to pinnatifid leaves, 6–18in (15–45cm) long, dark green above, paler and sparsely to densely woolly beneath. Solitary, daisy-like, orange-scarlet flowerheads, 3–5in (8–13cm) across, with yellow centers, appear from late spring to late summer. Resents transplanting. ↕ 12–18in (30–45cm), ↔ 24in (60cm). South Africa (Northern Transvaal, Eastern Transvaal, KwaZulu/Natal), Swaziland. ❀ (min. 41°F/5°C). Seed-raised selections are available in mixed colors. **'Californian Giants'** have single flowers in shades of yellow, apricot, orange, red, and pink; ↕ to 24in (60cm). Cultivars of **Duplex Mix** have flowerheads, 3½in (9cm) across, in a range of colors; ↕ 18in (45cm). **Festival Series** cultivars are compact, with small leaves, and bear flowerheads, 3½in (9cm) across, in white, yellow, salmon, rose, and scarlet; ↕ 10in (25cm). **Pandora Series** cultivars are free-flowering, in shades of cream, apricot, crimson-red, scarlet, pink, or lavender, with mid-green leaves; ↕ 10in (25cm). **Parade Series** cultivars have single or double, yellow, orange, red, or pink flowerheads. **Rainbow Mix** cultivars are compact, with flowerheads, 4–5in (10–13cm) across, in shades of red, rose, pink, yellow, and orange, and white; ↕ 16–18in (40–45cm). Cultivars of **Skipper Mix** are compact and have small leaves; ↕ 8–10in (20–25cm). **Tempo Series** cultivars bloom in shades of red, orange, pink, salmon-pink, cream, and yellow.

GESNERIA

GESNERIACEAE

Genus of about 50 species of mostly tuberous, usually evergreen perennials, subshrubs, and small trees, often epiphytic or rock-dwelling, found in tropical America and the West Indies. Tubular or bell-shaped flowers, usually 5-lobed, are white, red, orange, yellow, green, or brown, and borne singly or in cymes, with bracts at the bases of the flowering stems. The leaves are ovate, elliptic, or heart- or lance-shaped, and borne alternately or in opposite pairs. Where not hardy, grow in a warm greenhouse. Elsewhere, grow in shaded borders or as epiphytes on rocks or trees.
• **CULTIVATION** Under glass, grow in soil-based potting mix, with added sharp sand and leaf mold, in bright filtered or indirect light. During the growing season, maintain at 64°F (18°C), with high humidity, and water freely; keep leaves dry but soil mix always moist. Apply a quarter-strength balanced liquid fertilizer every 4 weeks. Keep dry in winter. Start tubers from late winter onward or grow under lights for continuous bloom throughout the year. Outdoors, grow in moist, humus-rich soil in deep shade.
• **PROPAGATION** Sow seed at 66–75°F (19–24°C) in spring, or take stem or leaf cuttings in late spring.
• **PESTS AND DISEASES** Flower thrips and *Fusarium* wilt may be problems.

G. cuneifolia. Erect or decumbent, woody-based perennial with hairless or slightly hairy, inversely lance-shaped or obovate, scalloped or toothed leaves, ¾–5½in (2–14cm) long, clustered at the branch tips. In summer, bears few-flowered, pendent, arching cymes of tubular, pink or deep red flowers, to 1in (2.5cm) long, and yellow or pink inside. ↕↔ 6in (15cm). Puerto Rico. ❀ (min. 57°F/14°C)
G. zebrina see *Smithiantha zebrina.*

G

GEUM

Avens

ROSACEAE

Genus of about 50 species of rhizomatous, occasionally stoloniferous perennials from mountainous habitats, streamsides, moist meadows, and woodland in arctic and temperate regions of Europe, Asia, New Zealand, North and South America, and Africa. They have unequally pinnate to pinnatisect, wrinkled leaves, the leaflets with toothed or scalloped margins; the leaves are mainly borne in basal rosettes. The erect, open, 5-petaled, saucer- to bowl-shaped, usually upright but occasionally pendent flowers, in shades of cream, yellow, orange, pink, or red, are solitary or borne in cymes, opening from late spring to summer. The stems of *G. chiloense* hybrids tend to be more branched than those of *G. coccineum* hybrids. The smaller geums are suitable for growing in a rock garden; the larger can be grown at the front of a border.

• **CULTIVATION** Grow in fertile, well-drained soil in full sun; *G. rivale* and its cultivars prefer humus-rich, moist soil. Avoid soil that is waterlogged in winter.

• **PROPAGATION** Sow seed in containers in a cold frame, or divide, in autumn or spring. *G.* 'Lady Stratheden' and *G.* 'Mrs. J. Bradshaw' come virtually true from seed, but most of the larger geums hybridize readily in gardens.

• **PESTS AND DISEASES** Prone to downy mildew, fungal leaf spots, powdery mildew, and leaf smut. Various caterpillars may be troublesome.

Geum 'Lady Stratheden'

***G.* x *borisii* of gardens** see *G. coccineum.*

G. chiloense, syn. *G. coccineum* of gardens. Clump-forming, densely woolly perennial. Basal leaves, 4–12in (10–30cm) long, are pinnate; the heart- to kidney-shaped terminal leaflets, 1in (2.5cm) long, are scarcely larger than the lateral leaflets. Stem leaves are deeply 3-lobed and toothed. Branched stems bear cymes of saucer-shaped scarlet flowers, to 1½in (4cm) across, from early to late summer. ↕16–24in (40–60cm), ↔ 24in (60cm). Chile. Zone 5b. **'Dolly North'** produces glowing, deep orange flowers. **'Fire Opal'** produces semi-double, reddish orange flowers on purple stems; ↕ to 30in (75cm).

G. coccineum ▣ syn. *G.* x *borisii* of gardens. Clump-forming perennial with

Geum montanum

upright, pinnate, softly hairy, basal leaves, to 8in (20cm) long, the kidney-shaped terminal leaflets, 2–6in (5–15cm) long, much larger than the lateral leaflets. Stem leaves are deeply toothed but unlobed. From late spring to late summer, brick-red flowers, to 1½in (4cm) across, with spreading petals and conspicuous yellow stamens, are produced in cymes of 2–4. ↕12–20in (30–50cm), ↔ 12in (30cm). Balkans. Zone 5.

***G. coccineum* of gardens** see *G. chiloense.*

***G.* 'Feuerball'** see *G.* 'Mrs. J. Bradshaw'.

***G.* 'Georgenberg'.** *G. chiloense* hybrid with pinnate, bright green leaves, 4–6in (10–15cm) long. The terminal leaflets are kidney-shaped and to 3in (8cm) long; the other leaflets are much smaller. Branched stems bear saucer-shaped, orange-yellow flowers, to 1½in (4cm) across, from late spring to midsummer. ↕10in (25cm), ↔ 12in (30cm). Zone 5b.

***G.* 'Goldball'** see *G.* 'Lady Stratheden'.

***G.* 'Lady Stratheden'** ▣ syn. *G.* 'Goldball'. *G. chiloense* hybrid bearing pinnate, hairy leaves, to 8in (20cm) long, composed of kidney-shaped terminal leaflets, the remainder ovate. Semi-double, rich yellow flowers, 1¾in (4.5cm) across, are produced in cymes of 1–5 throughout summer. ↕16–24in (40–60cm), ↔ 24in (60cm). Zone 5.

G. montanum ▣ Clump-forming perennial with thick, spreading rhizomes and dense clusters of radical, pinnate, dark green leaves, to 4in (10cm) long, each with a large, rounded or kidney-shaped, terminal lobe. From spring to early summer, bears solitary, cup-shaped, deep golden yellow flowers, to 1½in (4cm) across, on short stems, occasionally in cymes of 2 or 3. ↕6in (15cm), ↔ to 12in (30cm). Mountains of C. and S. Europe. Zone 3.

***G.* 'Mrs. Bradshaw'** see *G.* 'Mrs. J. Bradshaw'.

***G.* 'Mrs. J. Bradshaw'**, syn. *G.* 'Feuerball', *G.* 'Mrs. Bradshaw'. Hybrid of *G. chiloense* bearing pinnate, hairy leaves, 6–8in (15–20cm) long, with kidney-shaped terminal leaflets, the remainder ovate. Semi-double scarlet flowers, 1¾in (4.5cm) across, are borne in cymes of 1–5 from early to late summer. ↕16–24in (40–60cm), ↔ 24in (60cm). Zone 5.

***G.* 'Prince of Orange'.** *G. coccineum* hybrid producing pinnate, hairy leaves, to 12in (30cm) long, with kidney-shaped terminal leaflets, the remainder ovate. Bears cymes of 1–4 brilliant orange flowers, 1¾in (4.5cm) across, with slightly cupped petals, in early and midsummer. ↕↔ to 24in (60cm). Zone 5.

***G.* 'Princess Juliana'** see *G.* 'Prinses Juliana'.

***G.* 'Prinses Juliana'**, syn. *G.* 'Princess Juliana'. *G. chiloense* hybrid bearing pinnate, hairy leaves, 4–8in (10–20cm) long, with heart- to kidney-shaped terminal leaflets, the remainder smaller and ovate. Semi-double, red-flushed, bright yellow flowers, 1¾in (4.5cm) across, are borne in cymes of 1–5 in early and midsummer. ↕↔ 16–24in (40–60cm). Zone 5.

***G.* 'Red Wings'** ▣ *G. coccineum* hybrid bearing pinnate, hairy leaves, to 10in

Geum coccineum

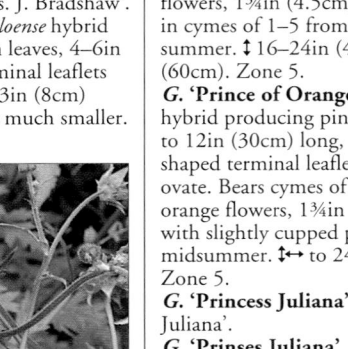

Geum 'Red Wings'

Geum reptans

Geum 'Tangerine'

(25cm) long, with heart- to kidney-shaped terminal leaflets, the remainder smaller and ovate. Bears semi-double, bright scarlet flowers, 1¾in (4.5cm) across, in cymes of 1–3, in early and midsummer. Very free-flowering. ↕ to 24in (60cm), ↔ to 16in (40cm). Zone 5.

G. reptans ■ syn. *Sieversia reptans.* Rhizomatous perennial, spreading by stolons, bearing rosettes of radical, pinnate leaves, to 6in (15cm) long, with deeply toothed, rounded leaflets. Produces usually solitary, shallowly cup-shaped, bright yellow flowers, to 1½in (4cm) across, in early summer. Best grown in a scree bed or alpine house. ↕ to 6in (15cm), ↔ to 8in (20cm). Alps, Carpathians, Balkans. Zone 5.

G. rivale (Indian chocolate, Purple avens). Upright perennial with pinnate, basal leaves, to 6in (15cm) or more long. The terminal and upper pair of leaflets are obovate or wedge-shaped, coarsely scalloped or toothed, and to 2in (5cm) long; the rest are very small. From late spring to midsummer, bears cymes of 2–5 pendent, bell-shaped, dusk-pink to dark orange-red flowers, to ¾in (2cm) across, with conspicuous, red-brown sepals that are almost as long as the petals. ↕↔ 8–24in (20–60cm). Europe. Zone 4. **'Coppertone'**, probably a hybrid of *G. rivale*, has toothed leaves, brown flower stems, and slightly pendent, copper-apricot flowers, to 2in (5cm) across, with wavy petals and reddish brown sepals; ↕↔ to 12in (30cm). **'Lemon Drops'**, probably a hybrid of *G. rivale*, has slender brown stems bearing long-stalked, open, lemon-yellow flowers, pendent at first, with brownish green sepals; ↕↔ to 10in (25cm). **'Leonard's Variety'**, syn. 'Leonardii', is very free-flowering, with pendent, copper-pink, orange-tinged flowers, to 1½in (4cm) across, on mahogany stems, borne in mid- and late summer; ↕ to 18in (45cm). **'Lionel Cox'**, probably a hybrid of *G. rivale*, forms large clumps of soft green leaves, and produces pendent, open bell-shaped, creamy apricot flowers with wavy petals; ↕ 12in (30cm). **'Sigiswang'**, probably a hybrid of *G. rivale*, is mound-forming, bearing bright green leaves, 5–6in (13–15cm) long, with kidney-shaped terminal leaflets, the rest smaller, and cymes of red-shaded orange flowers, 1¼in (3cm) across.

***G.* 'Tangerine'** ■ is a hybrid of *G. rivale*, with similar foliage. Cymes of 1–3 bright orange, slightly nodding, saucer-shaped flowers, to 1in (2.5cm) across, are produced from late spring to midsummer. ↕↔ 12in (30cm). Zone 4.

G. triflorum. Clump-forming, silky-hairy perennial with pinnate, gray-green basal leaves, to 6in (15cm) long, with up to 30 linear to oblong leaflets. Bears cymes of 3 cup-shaped, light maroon to almost yellow flowers, to 1½in (4cm) across, in summer. ↕ to 16in (40cm), ↔ 12in (30cm). N. North America. Zone 2.

GEVUINA

PROTEACEAE

Genus of one species of evergreen tree or shrub found in moist forest in the mountains of Chile. Grown for its attractive, alternate, pinnate or 2-pinnate leaves and its white summer flowers, it thrives outdoors only in relatively mild, moist climates, where it is best planted in sheltered woodland. Elsewhere, grow in a cool greenhouse.

• **CULTIVATION** Under glass, grow in acidic soil mix in bright filtered light. Outdoors, grow in fertile, acidic to neutral, moist but well-drained soil in partial shade; protect from cold, drying winds. Pruning group 1.

• **PROPAGATION** Sow seed in containers in a cold frame in autumn, or root semi-ripe cuttings with bottom heat in late summer.

• **PESTS AND DISEASES** Infrequent.

G. avellana (Chilean hazel, Chile nut). Conical, evergreen tree or large shrub with pinnate or 2-pinnate, glossy, dark green leaves, to 16in (40cm) long, each with up to 30 coarsely toothed, ovate-elliptic, leathery leaflets. In late summer, bears slender racemes, to 5in (13cm) long, of spider-like, white, occasionally red- or green-tinged flowers, 1in (2.5cm) long, sometimes followed by ovoid red fruit, ½in (1.5cm) or more long, ripening black. ↕↔ 30ft (10m). Chile. ❀ (min. 41°F/5°C)

GIBBAEUM

AIZOACEAE

Genus of about 20 species of fleshy, perennial succulents found in semi-desert areas of South Africa. Pairs of thick, fleshy leaves, often of different sizes, unite to form an almost spherical or elongated body. Solitary, daisy-like flowers are borne from early autumn to early winter. The plants offset freely, producing large colonies. Where temperatures drop below 45°F (7°C), grow as houseplants or in a temperate greenhouse. In warm, dry climates, grow in a desert garden or mixed border with other succulents.

• **CULTIVATION** Under glass, grow in standard cactus potting mix in full light. From midautumn (when new growth appears) to early spring, water sparingly and apply a low-nitrogen liquid fertilizer every 6–8 weeks. Keep dry during the rest of the year. Outdoors, grow in poor, sharply drained soil in full sun. See also pp.48–49.

• **PROPAGATION** Sow seed at 66–75°F (19–24°C), or divide offsets, in spring or summer.

• **PESTS AND DISEASES** Prone to rot.

Gibbaeum petrense

G. album. Clump-forming succulent with paired, whitish to pale gray leaves of different sizes, each pair united to form an obliquely ovoid body, to 1in (2.5cm) long, densely covered with tiny white hairs and with a cleft below the tip. Bears white or pink flowers, 1in (2.5cm) across, from early autumn to early winter. ↕ 1in (2.5cm) or more, ↔ 10in (25cm) or more. South Africa (Northern Cape, Western Cape). ❀ (min. 45°F/7°C)

G. gibbosum. Clump-forming succulent producing paired, deep green leaves, to 1½in (4cm) long, of different sizes. The longer leaf is slightly incurved, semi-cylindrical, flattened above and 2-keeled below; the smaller leaf is only one-third the length of the larger leaf. Pink-purple flowers, to ½in (1.5cm) across, are borne from autumn to winter. ↕ 1¼–2½in (3–6cm), ↔ 2½–6in (6–15cm). South Africa (Western Cape). ❀ (min. 45°F/7°C)

G. petrense ■ Mat-forming succulent with fleshy roots and small stems bearing paired, grayish green leaves, ½in (1.5cm) long, keeled above, rounded below, each pair united for one-third of their length. Bears terminal to axillary, magenta to red or pink flowers, ½in (1.5cm) across, from early autumn to early winter. ↕ to 1¼in (3cm), ↔ 6in (15cm) or more. South Africa (Western Cape). ❀ (min. 45°F/7°C)

G. velutinum ■ Mat-forming succulent with small stems bearing paired, slender, differently sized, bluish gray-green leaves, 1½–2½in (4–6cm) long, each pair united toward the base, the longer leaf with an incurved, hooked tip. Bears lilac, pink, or white flowers, 1½–2in (4–5cm) across, from early autumn to early winter. ↕ 3in (8cm), ↔ 12in (30cm). South Africa (Western Cape). ❀ (min. 45°F/7°C)

Gibbaeum velutinum

GILIA

POLEMONIACEAE

Genus of 25–30 species of erect annuals, occasionally perennials, from grassland and chaparral in W. North America and W. and S. South America. The leaves are mostly basal, entire to finely divided, pinnate or 2-pinnate, and often with soft, sticky hairs above. The flowers are small, showy, salverform to tubular-funnel-shaped, violet-blue, pink, or red, produced singly in the leaf axils, in terminal panicles, or in compact clusters borne terminally and in the upper leaf axils, from late spring to late summer. Grow in an annual or mixed border.

• **CULTIVATION** Grow in light, well-drained soil in full sun.

• **PROPAGATION** Sow seed *in situ* in autumn or midspring, or at 50–55°F (10–13°C) in early spring.

• **PESTS AND DISEASES** Prone to rust and powdery mildew.

G. achilleifolia. Erect annual with 2-pinnate leaves, 1½–4in (4–10cm) long, and sickle-shaped leaflets. In summer, bears mid-blue to blue-violet flowers, to 1in (2.5cm) long, in dense, fan-shaped, terminal or axillary cymes, 1¼–3in (3–8cm) across. ↕ to 28in (70cm), ↔ 8–9in (20–23cm). California, Mexico (Baja California).

G. capitata ■ (Queen Anne's thimbles). Erect annual with feathery, 2-pinnate leaves, 1½–4in (4–10cm) long, with linear leaflets. In summer, bears terminal and axillary, pincushion-like heads, ½–1½in (1.5–4cm) across, of many lavender-blue flowers, ¼–⅜in (6–9mm) long, with protruding stamens. ↕ 18–24in (45–60cm), ↔ 8–9in (20–23cm). W. North America.

G. rubra see *Ipomopsis rubra.*

G. tricolor (Bird's eyes). Mound-forming annual with pinnate to 2-pinnate leaves, ½–1½in (1–4cm) long, with very narrow leaflets. From late spring to late summer, bears saucer-shaped, pale to dark violet-blue flowers, ½in (1.5cm) long, with pale violet-blue spots around the orange or yellow centers, are borne on slender, very leafy stalks, either singly or in clusters of 2–5. ↕ 12–18in (30–45cm), ↔ 9in (23cm). California.

Gilia capitata

Gillenia trifoliata

G

GILLENIA

ROSACEAE

Genus of 2 species of rhizomatous perennials from open woodland in C., E., and S.E. North America. They have 3-palmate, bronze-green leaves and loose, few-flowered panicles of white or pink flowers, with slightly unequal, inversely lance-shaped to linear-lance-shaped petals, the sepals enlarging when in fruit. They are graceful plants for light woodland or a shady border, and are good for cutting.

• **CULTIVATION** Grow in fertile, slightly acidic to neutral, moist but well-drained soil in partial shade, or full sun with shade during the hottest part of the day.

• **PROPAGATION** Sow seed in containers in a cold frame, or divide, in spring or autumn.

• **PESTS AND DISEASES** Prone to rust.

G. trifoliata ■ syn. *Porteranthus trifoliata* (Bowman's root, Indian physic). Erect perennial with branched, red-tinted stems and alternate, 3-palmate, coarsely toothed, conspicuously veined, bronze-green leaves, with ovate-oblong leaflets, each 3in (8cm) long. Bears irregularly star-shaped, white to pinkish white flowers, 1–1½in (2.5–4cm) across, with narrow petals and red-tinted calyces, from late spring to late summer. ↕ to 3ft (1m), ↔ 24in (60cm). Ontario to Georgia. Zone 6.

GINKGO

Maidenhair tree

GINKGOACEAE

Genus of one species of deciduous, dioecious tree from S. China, extinct in the wild but preserved and still grown in temple gardens and as a specimen tree. Long shoots bear alternate leaves; woody spur shoots bear densely clustered leaves and flowers. The fan-shaped, divided, mid- to yellow-green leaves turn golden yellow in autumn. The fleshy fruit smell unpleasant as they decay; they contain large, edible "nuts." *G. biloba* tolerates atmospheric pollution and is an excellent landscape tree.

• **CULTIVATION** Grow in any fertile, well-drained soil in full sun. Pruning group 1.

• **PROPAGATION** Sow seed in containers in an open frame as soon as ripe, or take semi-ripe cuttings in summer. Graft in winter.

• **PESTS AND DISEASES** Fungal leaf spots, mealybugs, lesion nematode, and root rots sometimes occur.

G. biloba ■ (Maidenhair tree). Upright tree, columnar then wide-spreading, with furrowed, dull gray bark. Flat, fan-shaped, mid- to yellow-green leaves, to 5in (13cm) across, are tapered into the stalks and usually lobed at the tips. Catkin-like, pendulous, cylindrical yellow male flowers, 3in (8cm) long, are borne in clusters. Round, solitary female flowers produce plum-like, yellow-green fruit, 1¼in (3cm) long, in autumn. ↕ to 100ft (30m), ↔ to 25ft (8m). S. China. Zone 4. **'Autumn Gold'** is broadly conical, very regular in form, and male, and has striking golden yellow autumn color; ↕ 50ft (15m), ↔ 30ft (10m). **'Princeton Sentry'** is narrow, upright, and male.

GLADIOLUS

syn. ACIDANTHERA, HOMOGLOSSUM

IRIDACEAE

Genus of about 180 species of cormous perennials from rocky slopes, seasonally dry grasslands, and marshy areas, mainly in South Africa, but also from the Mediterranean, the Arabian Peninsula, N.W. and E. Africa, Madagascar, and W. Asia. They are grown for their showy spikes of usually open, funnel-shaped flowers, borne mainly from spring to early autumn. The flowers each have 6 tepals: usually 1 central upper tepal, 3 often quite small lower or lip tepals, and 2 side, or wing, tepals. They open from the bottom of the spikes upward, older blooms dying off as new ones develop (the number of buds open at any one time is given in parentheses in each cultivar description below). Erect leaves, borne in basal fans, are narrow, linear or sword-shaped, mid- to dark green, and 10–36in (24–90cm) long.

Plant gladioli in clumps in a mixed border, or in rows for cutting and exhibition. Plant at biweekly intervals for successive bloom. Where not hardy, dig up in autumn and replant in spring, or grow by a sheltered, sunny wall; winter-flowering South African gladioli require a cool greenhouse. In warmer areas, plant in sunny, well-drained sites.

Over 10,000 cultivars have been developed for cutting, exhibition, and garden cultivation. They are classified into three main groups: Grandiflorus, Nanus, and Primulinus (see below). Flowers may be borne either in a formal arrangement, side by side on the stem, so when open there is little or no space visible between them, or, less formally, with one bloom above another, like a stepladder, with visible space.

Grandiflorus Group

Cultivars in this group flower from late spring to early autumn, depending on how early they are planted in spring and on their relative bloom season. Early cultivars bloom the fastest from planting; late cultivars require more time to develop. Each corm normally produces one flower spike, 14–36in (35–90cm) long, with as many as 28 buds, up to 12 open at a time, usually formally arranged. Some cultivars produce multiple flower spikes, especially if grown from large corms. Grandiflorus gladioli are classified into 5 sizes, determined by the diameter of the bottom flower on the spike, as follows:

GIANT	5½in (14cm) or more
LARGE	4½–5½in (11–14cm)
MEDIUM	3½–4½in (9–11cm)
SMALL	2½–3½in (6–9cm)
MINIATURE	under 2½in (6cm)

Miniature cultivars generally grow 36in (90cm) tall; giant cultivars often grow to 5½ft (1.7m), sometimes more. The other classes fall within this range.

Nanus Group

Nanus hybrids and cultivars flower in early summer, and are ideal for cutting and corsages. Each corm produces 2 or 3 slender spikes, 9–14in (22–35cm) long, with loosely arranged flowers, 1½–2in (4–5cm) across. Each spike bears up to 7 buds, 3–5 open at a time.

Primulinus Group

Hybrids and cultivars in this group flower from early to late summer. Each corm produces one thin, whip-like stem, 12–24in (30–60cm) long, which bears as many as 23 buds, up to 7 open at a time, mainly in a semi-formal, step-ladder arrangement. The triangular flowers are usually 1½–3in (3.5–8cm) across. The top central tepal is hooded and held at right angles to the stem, covering the stigma and anthers.

• **HARDINESS** Gladioli are hardy wherever the soil does not freeze deeply in winter (southern Zone 8). Protect with a thick, loose mulch or plant near a warm wall to extend hardiness, in some cases, to Zone 6.

• **CULTIVATION** Grow in fertile, well-drained soil in full sun to partial shade, planting the corms 3–6in (8–15cm) deep, and 3–6in (8–15cm) apart in spring. Make successive plantings to extend the bloom season. For gladioli left in the ground, apply a high-potash liquid fertilizer when the flower spikes reach one-third to half their final height; repeat every 10–14 days until 3 weeks after flowering. Staking is not normally necessary but is recommended for the tallest cultivars, especially when grown for exhibition. Where not hardy, lift them 6 weeks after bloom; cut the stem near the corm, dip in fungicide, and allow to dry for a few weeks. Separate new corms from old, and discard the old. Keep dry and frost-free until planted. Under glass, grow winter-flowering South African gladioli in soil-based potting mix, with additional sharp sand, in full light. Water moderately when in growth.

• **PROPAGATION** Sow seed of hardy species in containers in a cold frame in spring; sow seed of tender species at 59°F (15°C) in spring. Separate cormlets when dormant.

• **PESTS AND DISEASES** Prone to gladiolus corm rot (*Fusarium*), gray mold (*Botrytis*), viruses, aster yellows, spider mites, thrips, and aphids.

Ginkgo biloba (inset: leaf detail)

Gladiolus callianthus

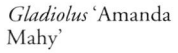

Gladiolus 'Amanda Mahy'

Gladiolus 'Amy Beth'

Gladiolus 'Anna Leorah'

Gladiolus 'Beau Rivage'

Gladiolus 'Billie Lee'

Gladiolus 'Candyman'

Gladiolus 'Charmer'

G. alatus. Short-lived, cormous perennial with linear leaves, 3–16in (8–40cm) long. Bears up to 10 hooded, funnel-shaped, scented flowers, 1¾in (4.5cm) across, from late winter to spring (late spring to summer in cool climates). Upper tepals are salmon-pink to orange or red; lip tepals are lime-green, tipped with salmon-pink to orange or red. Best grown regularly from seed. ↕ 3–14in (8–35cm). South Africa (Northern Cape, Eastern Cape, Western Cape).
***G.* 'Amanda Mahy'** ■ Nanus gladiolus bearing salmon-pink flowers, 2in (5cm) across, with lip tepals flecked violet and white, early in the season. Flower spike is 12in (30cm) long, with 7 buds (3 or 4 open). ↕ 32in (80cm).
***G.* 'Amy Beth'** ■ Small-flowered Grandiflorus gladiolus. In early midseason, bears strongly ruffled, lilac-pink flowers, with cream lip tepals. Flower spike is 22–24in (55–60cm) long, with 22 buds (7 open).
***G.* 'Anitra'.** Primulinus gladiolus producing blood-red flowers, 1½–2½in (4–6cm) across, in midseason. Flower spike is 18in (45cm) long, with 17 buds (6 or 7 open). ↕ 3ft (1m).
***G.* 'Anna Leorah'** ■ Large-flowered Grandiflorus gladiolus producing strongly ruffled, mid-pink flowers, with large white throats, in midseason. Flower spike is 28–32in (70–80cm) long, with 25 buds (10 open).
***G.* 'Antique Rose'.** Medium-flowered Grandiflorus gladiolus. In late midseason, produces slightly ruffled, rose-pink flowers, with lavender-blue throats marked with deep rose-pink flashes. Flower spike is 28–32in (70–80cm) long, with 26 buds (10 open).
***G.* 'Award'.** Large-flowered Grandiflorus gladiolus. In midseason, bears rose-pink flowers, fading to white in the throats, with slightly ruffled tepals. Flower spike is 34in (85cm) long, with 26 buds (8 or 9 open).
***G.* 'Baltica'.** Large-flowered Grandiflorus gladiolus producing pure white flowers, in midseason. Flower spike is 30in (75cm) long, with 25 buds (8 or more open) in formal placement.
***G.* 'Beau Rivage'** ■ Large-flowered Grandiflorus gladiolus producing ruffled, deep coral-pink flowers in midseason. Flower spike is 20in (50cm) long, with 15 buds (5–9 open).
***G.* 'Beverly Ann'.** Large-flowered Grandiflorus gladiolus. Pastel-purple flowers with pure white throats are produced in early midseason. Flower spike is 28in (70cm) long, with 21 buds (6 or 7 open).
***G.* 'Billie Lee'** ■ Medium-flowered Grandiflorus gladiolus producing glistening black-red flowers with a velvety sheen, in midseason. Flower spike is 28in (70cm) long, with 23 buds (6 or 7 open).
G. blandus see *G. carneus.*
G. blandus* var. *carneus see *G. carneus.*
***G.* 'Blue Delight'.** Large-flowered Grandiflorus gladiolus that produces slightly ruffled, mid-blue flowers, with blue-peppered white throats, in early midseason. Flower spike is 28–32in (70–80cm) long, with 25 buds (9 open).
***G.* 'Blue Heaven'.** Large-flowered Grandiflorus gladiolus. In midseason, bears strongly ruffled, mid-blue flowers, with very large, pure white throats. Flower spike is 28–30in (70–75cm) long, with 25 buds (8 open).

Gladiolus cardinalis

***G.* 'Blue Smoke'.** Large-flowered Grandiflorus gladiolus. In midseason, produces heavily ruffled, mulberry-blue flowers with dark salmon throat blotches. Flower spike is 32in (80cm) long, with 21–23 buds (7 or 8 open).
***G.* 'Brown Eyes'.** Medium-flowered Grandiflorus gladiolus. Bears light buff-yellow flowers with brown throats, early in the season. Flower spike is 26in (35cm), with 17–20 buds (6 or 7 open).
G. byzantinus see *G. communis* subsp. *byzantinus.*
G. callianthus ■ syn. *Acidanthera bicolor* var. *murieliae, A. murieliae.* Cormous perennial with linear leaves 6–18in (15–45cm) long. In summer and autumn, bears loose spikes of up to 10 hooded, funnel-shaped, strongly scented, pure white flowers, 2in (5cm) across, each with a prominent purple-red mark in the throat. Blooms curve downward on long, thin tubes. ↕ 28–39in (70–100cm). Eritrea to Mozambique.
***G.* 'Candyman'** ■ Large-flowered Grandiflorus gladiolus with deep cerise-pink flowers, borne in midseason. Flower spike is 28in (70cm) long, with 21 buds (6 or 7 open).
***G.* 'Caravan'.** Large-flowered Grandiflorus gladiolus. In midseason, bears strongly ruffled, chocolate-brown flowers with small cream throats marked with maroon flashes. Flower spike is 28in (70cm) long, with 22–24 buds (9 open).
G. cardinalis ■ Cormous perennial with sword-shaped leaves, 16–36in (40–90cm) long. In summer, arching stems bear up to 12 widely funnel-shaped, bright red flowers, 2in (5cm) across, a white flash on each of the lip tepals. ↕ 24–36in (60–90cm). South Africa (Western Cape).
G. carneus, syn. *G. blandus, G. blandus* var. *carneus.* Slender, cormous perennial with linear or sword-shaped leaves, to 24in (60cm) long. Lax, sometimes branched spikes of 3–12 funnel-shaped flowers, 2in (5cm) across, are produced in late spring and early summer. Flowers are usually cream but may be white or pink; they have a well-defined, usually dark red, sometimes yellow mark on the lip tepals. ↕ 8–39in (20–100cm). South Africa (Western Cape).
***G.* 'Carved Ivory'.** Large-flowered Grandiflorus gladiolus. Produces ruffled, rich cream flowers of heavy substance with deeper cream throats, in midseason. Flower spike is 30–34in (75–85cm) long, with 28 buds (9 or more open) in very formal placement.
G. caryophyllaceus, syn. *G. hirsutus.* Cormous perennial with linear, hairy leaves, 8–24in (20–60cm) long. From late winter to spring, bears one-sided or 2-ranked spikes of 2–8 bell- or funnel-shaped, hawthorn-scented, pink or mauve flowers, ¾–1½in (2–4cm) across, the lip tepals spotted or streaked red or pink. ↕ 20–30in (50–75cm). South Africa (Western Cape).
***G.* 'Charm'** ■ Nanus gladiolus bearing purple-red flowers, 1½in (4cm) across, with ivory throats, in early midseason. Flower spike is 9in (23cm) long, with 7 buds (4 or 5 open). ↕ 28in (70cm).
***G.* 'Charmer'** ■ Large-flowered Grandiflorus gladiolus with strongly ruffled, almost translucent, light pink flowers, produced in midseason. Flower spike is 34in (85cm) long, with 27 buds (10 open).

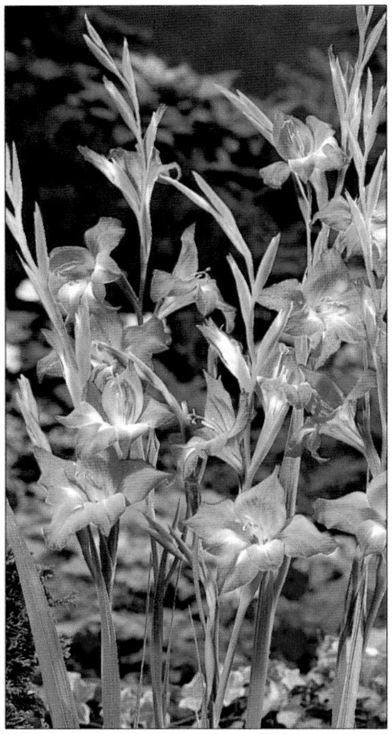
Gladiolus 'Charm'

G

Gladiolus 'Chloe'

Gladiolus 'Côte d'Azur'

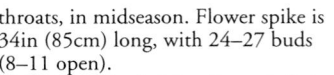

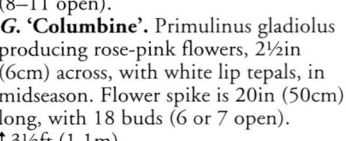

Gladiolus 'Doris Darling'

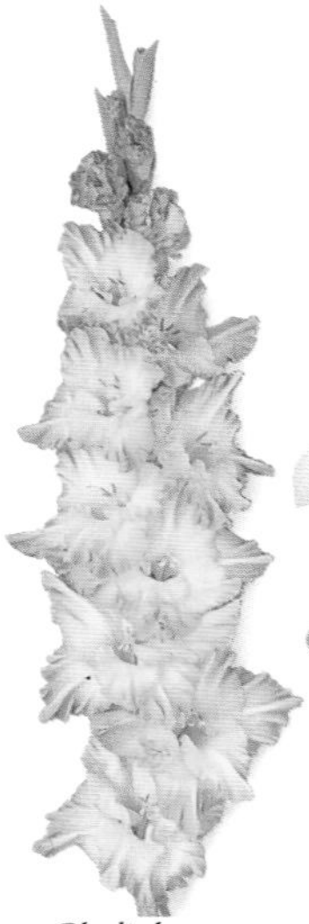

Gladiolus 'Dream's End'

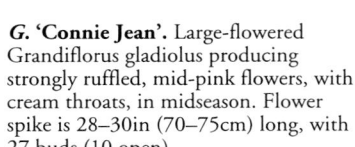

Gladiolus 'Elvira'

Gladiolus 'Firestorm'

Gladiolus 'Florence C'

Gladiolus 'Frank's Perfection'

***G.* 'Chinese Wax'.** Medium-flowered Grandiflorus gladiolus bearing strongly ruffled, deep cream flowers in early midseason. Flower spike is 26–28in (65–70cm) long, with 22 buds (7 open).
***G.* 'Chloe'** ■ Medium-flowered Grandiflorus gladiolus. In early and midseason, produces slightly ruffled, deep orange flowers with lighter throats. Flower spike is 26–30in (65–75cm) long, with 25 buds (9 open).
***G.* 'Chocolate Ripple'.** Large-flowered Grandiflorus gladiolus with chocolate-brown flowers, heavily veined and dusted gold, borne late in the season. Flower spike is 26–30in (65–75cm) long with 22 buds (10 open).
***G.* 'Christabel'.** *G. tristis* hybrid with loose spikes of 6–10 flared, scented, primrose-yellow flowers, 3–4in (8–10cm) across, borne very early in the season. Upper tepals are marked with purple. ↕ 18in (45cm).
***G.* 'Clarence's Choice'.** Large-flowered Grandiflorus gladiolus. Produces rich salmon-pink flowers with large white throats, in midseason. Flower spike is 34in (85cm) long, with 24–27 buds (8–11 open).
***G.* 'Columbine'.** Primulinus gladiolus producing rose-pink flowers, 2½in (6cm) across, with white lip tepals, in midseason. Flower spike is 20in (50cm) long, with 18 buds (6 or 7 open). ↕ 3½ft (1.1m).
***G.* x *colvilei* 'The Bride'** see *G.* 'The Bride'.
***G.* 'Comet'.** Nanus gladiolus bearing cherry-red flowers, 2in (5cm) across, in early midseason. Flower spike is 12in (30cm) long, with 5 buds (3 or 4 open). ↕ 30in (75cm).
G. communis* subsp. *byzantinus ■ syn. *G. byzantinus.* Vigorous perennial producing linear leaves, 4–28in (10–70cm) long. From late spring to early summer, bears spikes of up to 20 funnel-shaped, deep magenta flowers, 2in (5cm) across, with paler marks on the lip tepals. Spreads freely from cormlets. ↕ to 3ft (1m). Spain, N.W. Africa, Sicily. Zone 4b.

Gladiolus communis subsp. *byzantinus*

***G.* 'Connie Jean'.** Large-flowered Grandiflorus gladiolus producing strongly ruffled, mid-pink flowers, with cream throats, in midseason. Flower spike is 28–30in (70–75cm) long, with 27 buds (10 open).
***G.* 'Coral Embers'.** Large-flowered Grandiflorus gladiolus bearing ruffled, soft rose-pink and white flowers, with formal placement, in midseason. Flower spike is 30in (75cm) long, with 25 buds (8 open).
***G.* 'Côte d'Azur'** ■ Giant-flowered Grandiflorus gladiolus producing ruffled, mid-blue flowers, with pale blue throats, in early midseason. Flower spike is 30in (75cm) long, with 23 or 24 buds (9 open).
***G.* 'Crimson Fire'.** Giant-flowered Grandiflorus gladiolus. In midseason, produces strongly ruffled, deep rose-red flowers, with deeper rose-red "thumb prints" on the lip tepals. Flower spike is 36in (90cm) long, with 26 buds (9 open).
G. dalenii, syn. *G. natalensis, G. psittacinus, G. quartinianus.* Robust, cormous perennial, spreading freely by underground runners, with linear or sword-shaped leaves, to 24in (60cm) long. In summer, bears one-sided spikes of few to many hooded, funnel-shaped flowers, 2in (5cm) across, which are red, orange, or yellow, sometimes spotted green or brown. ↕ 3–5ft (1–1.5m), ↔ 3in (8cm). South Africa (Eastern Cape) and through tropical Africa to Ethiopia and W. Arabian Peninsula.
***G.* 'Dark Victory'.** Large-flowered Grandiflorus gladiolus. Bears classically ruffled, black-red flowers in perfect formal placement, during midseason. Flower spike is 30–34in (75–85cm) long with 25–27 buds (8 or more open).
***G.* 'Dave's Memory'.** Small-flowered Grandiflorus gladiolus with ruffled, velvety black-red flowers, slightly white in the throats, with a fine silver picotee around each petal, borne in early and midseason. Flower spike is 26in (65cm) long, with 2 or 3 buds (9 open).
***G.* 'Dawn Jane'.** Miniature-flowered Grandiflorus gladiolus producing very lightly ruffled, pale pink flowers with cream throats, in early midseason. Flower spike is 28in (70cm) long with 26 buds (8 or 9 open).
***G.* 'Déjà Vu'.** Giant-flowered Grandiflorus gladiolus producing ruffled, light pink flowers, with darker margins, in late midseason. Flower spike is 32–34in (80–85cm) long, with 25 buds (9 open).
***G.* 'Dick's Delight'.** Large-flowered Glandiflorus gladiolus bearing wide-open, beautifully ruffled, bright red flowers with large white throats, in midseason. Flower spike is 34in (85cm) long, with 27 buds (8–10 open).
***G.* 'Divinity'.** Giant-flowered Grandiflorus gladiolus. In midseason, bears heavily ruffled, white flowers in formal placement, with heavy substance, and faint lavender feathering in the throats. Stamens are lavender. Flower spike is 34–36in (85–90cm) long, with 27 buds (9 open).
***G.* 'Doris Darling'** ■ Large-flowered Grandiflorus gladiolus producing very soft, rose-pink flowers, very formally placed, in midseason. Flower spike is 32in (80cm) long, with 27 buds (8 or 9 open).
***G.* 'Drama'** ■ Large-flowered Grandiflorus gladiolus bearing slightly ruffled, deep rose-pink flowers, with red-speckled

Gladiolus 'Drama'

Gladiolus 'Georgette'

Gladiolus 'Gold Finch'

Gladiolus 'Green Woodpecker'

Gladiolus 'Halley'

Gladiolus 'Happy Time'

Gladiolus 'Jo Ann'

Gladiolus 'Lady Lucille'

Gladiolus 'Little Darling'

yellow throats, in early midseason. Flower spike is 28–32in (70–80cm) long, with 26 buds (10 open).

***G.* 'Dream's End'** ■ Giant-flowered Grandiflorus gladiolus. Produces light orange flowers, over 5½in (14cm) across, with large yellow centers, in late midseason. Flower spike is up to 3ft (1m) long, with 27 or more buds (9 open).

***G.* 'Dress Parade'.** Large-flowered Grandiflorus gladiolus producing slightly ruffled, deep salmon-pink flowers in late midseason. Flower spike is 32–34in (80–85cm) long, with 26 buds (10 open).

***G.* 'Elvira'** ■ Nanus gladiolus bearing pale pink flowers, 2in (5cm) across, with red marks on the lip tepals, in early midseason. Flower spike is 12in (30cm) long, with 6 buds (3 or 4 open). ↕32in (80cm).

***G.* 'Ermal'.** Giant-flowered Grandiflorus gladiolus. Ruffled, glowing red flowers, with small white throats, are produced late in the season. Flower spike is 32–34in (80–85cm) long, with 27 buds (9 open).

***G.* 'Ermine'.** Medium-flowered Grandiflorus gladiolus producing strongly ruffled white flowers, with creamy throats, in midseason. Flower spike is 28–30in (70–75cm) long, with 25 buds (9 open).

***G.* 'Eternal Beauty'.** Large-flowered Grandiflorus gladiolus. Ruffled, light blue flowers, with chalk-white throats, are produced in midseason. Flower spike is 28–30in (70–75cm) long, with 24 buds (8 open).

***G.* 'Falling Snow'.** Giant-flowered Grandiflorus gladiolus producing ruffled white flowers in midseason. Flower spike is 32–34in (80–85cm) long, with 27 buds (10 open).

***G.* 'Final Touch'.** Giant-flowered Grandiflorus gladiolus producing gently ruffled, salmon-pink flowers, to 7in (18cm) across, with large, snow-white throats, in midseason. Flower spike is 36in (90cm) or more long, with 25–27 buds (7–9 open).

***G.* 'Finesse'.** Large-flowered Grandiflorus gladiolus bearing strongly ruffled, salmon-pink flowers, with yellow throats, in midseason. Flower spike is 32in (80cm) long, with 26 buds (9 open).

***G.* 'Fire and Ice'.** Large-flowered Grandiflorus gladiolus. Late in the season, produces strongly ruffled white flowers, flushed pale pink, with rose-red marks on each tepal. Flower spike is 32–34in (80–85cm) long, with 28 buds (11 open).

***G.* 'Fireball II'.** Large-flowered Grandiflorus gladiolus producing red flowers with yellow-veined throats, in early midseason. Flower spike is 30in (75cm), with 23 buds (8 open), on an exceptionally tall plant. ↕6–7ft (2–2.2m).

***G.* 'Firestorm'** ■ Miniature-flowered Grandiflorus gladiolus producing ruffled, loosely spaced, vivid scarlet flowers, with yellowish white flecks on the outer tepals, very early in the season. Flower spike is 24in (60cm) long, with 22 buds (7 open).

***G.* 'Florence C'** ■ Large-flowered Grandiflorus gladiolus bearing strongly ruffled white flowers in midseason. Flower spike is 30–32in (75–80cm) long, with 26 buds (10 open).

***G.* 'Frank's Perfection'** ■ Primulinus gladiolus producing loosely spaced, bright red flowers, 2in (5cm) across, in early midseason. Flower spike is 24in (60cm) long, with 23 buds (7 open). ↕3½ft (1.1m).

***G.* 'Friendship'.** Large-flowered Grandiflorus gladiolus. Ruffled, pink flowers with white throats are borne early in the season. Flower spike is 26in (65cm) long, with 21 buds (7 open).

***G.* 'Frizzled Coral Lace'.** Medium-flowered Grandiflorus gladiolus with strongly ruffled, coral- to salmon-pink flowers, borne in early midseason. Flower spike is 26in (65cm) long, with 18 buds (7 open).

***G.* 'Georgette'** ■ Small-flowered Grandiflorus gladiolus. In midseason, bears slightly ruffled, yellow-suffused orange flowers with large, lemon-yellow throats. Flower spike is 24in (60cm) long, with 22 buds (10 open).

***G.* 'Globestar'.** Large-flowered Grandiflorus gladiolus bearing ruffled, light orange-buff flowers, with cerise-marked throats, in midseason. Flower spike is 28in (70cm) long, with 21 buds (7 open).

***G.* 'Golden Melody'.** Medium-flowered Grandiflorus gladiolus. Bears ruffled, rich golden yellow flowers in early midseason. Flower spike is 30–32in (75–80cm) long, with 26 buds (9 open).

***G.* 'Gold Finch'** ■ Small-flowered Grandiflorus gladiolus bearing ruffled, deep yellow flowers, in formal placement, early in the season. Tapered flower spike is 24in (60cm) long, with 21–23 buds (7 or 8 open).

***G.* 'Grand Finale'.** Large-flowered Grandiflorus gladiolus bearing strongly ruffled, salmon-pink flowers, with white throats, in midseason. Flower spike is 34in (85cm) long, with 27 buds (9 open).

***G.* 'Green Jeans'.** Small-flowered Grandiflorus gladiolus producing ruffled green flowers, with ivory throats, in late midseason. Flower spike is 24in (60cm) long, with 24 buds (7 open).

***G.* 'Green Woodpecker'** ■ Medium-flowered Grandiflorus gladiolus. In mid- and late season, bears ruffled, greenish yellow flowers with wine-red throat markings. Flower spike is 28–30in (70–75cm) long, with 25 buds (10 open).

***G.* 'Halley'** ■ Nanus gladiolus bearing white-flushed, pale yellow flowers, 2in (5cm) across, with bright red marks in the throats, in early midseason. Flower spike is 14in (35cm) long, with 7 buds (3 or 4 open). ↕3ft (1m).

***G.* 'Happy Time'** ■ Small-flowered Grandiflorus gladiolus. In midseason, produces slightly ruffled, mid-red flowers with ivory throats. Flower spike is 24in (60cm) long, with 21 buds (7 open).

***G.* 'Heavenly Sunshine'.** Giant-flowered Grandiflorus gladiolus. In midseason, bears strongly ruffled, light yellow flowers. Flower spike is 32–34in (80–85cm) long, with 28 buds (9 open).

***G.* 'High Brow'.** Giant-flowered Grandiflorus gladiolus bearing ruffled white flowers, with blush-pink margins, in midseason. Flower spike is 34in (85cm) long, with 27 buds (9 open).

***G.* 'Hi-Lite'.** Large-flowered Grandiflorus gladiolus. Slightly ruffled orange flowers, with small lemon throats, are produced in midseason. Flower spike is 30–32in (75–80cm) long, with 26 buds (9 open).

G. hirsutus see *G. caryophyllaceus.*

G. hygrophilus see *G. imbricatus.*

***G.* 'Ice Cap'.** Large-flowered Grandiflorus gladiolus bearing ruffled white flowers in midseason. Flower spike is 32–34in (80–85cm) long, with 27 buds (9 open).

G. imbricatus, syn. *G. hygrophilus.* Upright, cormous perennial with sword-shaped leaves, 6–14in (15–35cm) long. Bears loose spikes of 4–12 funnel-shaped, pinkish red to reddish purple flowers, 1¼in (3cm) across, in late spring. ↕12–32in (30–80cm). C. and E. Europe, Latvia, Estonia. Zone 5.

***G.* 'Impressive'.** Nanus gladiolus producing rose-pink flowers, 2in (5cm) across, with diamond-shaped, deep rose-pink markings on the lip tepals, in early midseason. Flower spike is 10in (25cm) long, with 7 buds (4 or 5 open). ↕28in (70cm).

G. italicus, syn. *G. segetum.* Slender, cormous perennial with sword-shaped leaves, 2–20in (5–50cm) long. In early summer, bears loose spikes of 5–15 narrowly funnel-shaped, purplish pink to magenta flowers, 1½in (4cm) across, with paler marks on the lip tepals. Best flowers with dry, hot summer dormancy. ↕16–36in (40–90cm). S. Europe.

***G.* 'Jo Ann'** ■ Large-flowered Grandiflorus gladiolus producing slightly ruffled, light salmon-pink flowers, with pale yellow throats, in early midseason. Flower spike is 32–34in (80–85cm) long, with 25 buds (9 open).

***G.* 'Krakatoa'.** Giant-flowered Grandiflorus gladiolus. Bears slightly ruffled, smoky plum-purple flowers, with large white throats, in midseason. Flower spike is 28–30in (70–75cm) long, with 23 buds (8 open).

***G.* 'Kristin'.** Large-flowered Grandiflorus gladiolus bearing strongly ruffled white flowers in midseason. Flower spike is 36in (90cm) long, with 27 buds (10 open).

***G.* 'Lady Lucille'** ■ Medium-flowered Grandiflorus gladiolus producing deep pink flowers, 3½–4½in (9–11cm) across, in very formal placement, with large, pure white throats, in midseason. Flower spike is 32in (80cm) long with 26 or more buds (9 or more open).

***G.* 'Lavender Masterpiece'.** Large-flowered Grandiflorus gladiolus producing ruffled, lavender-pink flowers with deeper rose-pink throats, in formal placement, during midseason. Flower spike is 32in (80cm) or more long with 26 or more buds (9–10 open).

***G.* 'Little Darling'** ■ Primulinus gladiolus producing loosely spaced, salmon- to rose-pink flowers, 1½in (4cm) across, with lemon-yellow lip tepals, in midseason. Flower spike is 16in (40cm) long, with 16 buds (5 or 6 open). ↕3½ft (1.1m).

Gladiolus 'Madison Ave'

Gladiolus 'Midnight Moon'

Gladiolus 'Mi Mi'

Gladiolus 'Mont Blanc'

Gladiolus 'Nymph'

Gladiolus papilio

Gladiolus 'Parade'

Gladiolus 'Peace'

Gladiolus 'Peerless'

G

***G.* 'Madison Ave'** ▣ Large-flowered Grandiflorus gladiolus with deep orange-scarlet flowers, with deeper throats, in midseason. Flower spike is 30in (75cm) long, with 25–27 buds (7 or 8 open).
***G.* 'Magnolia'.** Large-flowered Grandiflorus gladiolus. Ruffled, light lavender-pink to rose-pink flowers, with creamy throats, are produced in midseason. Flower spike is 30in (75cm) long, with 25 buds (9 open).
***G.* 'Major League'.** Large-flowered Grandiflorus gladiolus. Slightly ruffled, deep salmon-pink flowers, with cream throats, are produced in late midseason. Flower spike is 32–34in (80–85cm) long, with 26 buds (9 open).
***G.* 'Margaret Lyall'.** Large-flowered Grandiflorus gladiolus bearing strongly ruffled pink flowers, with small white throats, in midseason. Flower spike is 32in (80cm) long, with 27 buds (8 open).
***G.* 'Memories'.** Large-flowered Grandiflorus gladiolus. In midseason, produces ruffled, clear purple flowers, each petal with a thin silver edging. Flower spike is 30in (75cm) long, with 23 buds (8 open).
***G.* 'Michael B'.** Large-flowered Grandiflorus gladiolus bearing ruffled, deep purple flowers, with darker throats, in midseason. Flower spike is 32in (80cm) long, with 26 buds (9 open).
***G.* 'Midnight Moon'** ▣ Medium-flowered Grandiflorus gladiolus bearing deep blue-violet flowers, with a large, pure white blotch and white-lined, raised midribs, in informal placement and of heavy substance, in midseason. Flower spike is 32in (80cm) long, with 21–24 buds (7 open).

Gladiolus 'Prins Claus'

***G.* 'Mileesh'.** Large-flowered Grandiflorus gladiolus. Bears strongly ruffled, chocolate-tan flowers, with white throats, in midseason. Flower spike is 30in (75cm) long, with 25 buds (9 open).
***G.* 'Mi Mi'** ▣ Small-flowered Grandiflorus gladiolus. In early midseason, bears strongly ruffled, deep lavender-pink flowers with white throats. Flower spike is 26in (65cm) long, with 24 buds (7 or 8 open).
***G.* 'Mont Blanc'** ▣ Large-flowered Grandiflorus gladiolus bearing slightly ruffled white flowers in midseason. Flower spike is 32in (80cm) long, with 28 buds (10 open).
***G.* 'Moon Mirage'.** Giant-flowered Grandiflorus gladiolus with ruffled, canary-yellow flowers, marked deeper yellow on the lip tepals, produced in late midseason. Flower spike is 32–34in (80–85cm) long, with 26 buds (9–11 open).
***G.* 'Moonshadow'.** Medium-flowered Grandiflorus gladiolus bearing ruffled white flowers, with distinctive blue picotee edges, in early midseason. Flower spike is 28in (70cm) long with 21 buds (6 or 7 open).
***G.* 'Mother's Day'.** Large-flowered Grandiflorus gladiolus bearing ruffled, blue-pink flowers, with white throats, in midseason. Flower spike is 32in (80cm) long, with 25 buds (10 open).
G. natalensis see *G. dalenii.*
***G.* 'Norma J'.** Medium-flowered Grandiflorus gladiolus producing heavily ruffled, deep pink flowers in midseason. Flower spike is 30in (75cm) long, with 26 buds (9 or 10 open).
***G.* 'Nymph'** ▣ Nanus gladiolus bearing white flowers, 2in (5cm) across, in early midseason. The lip tepals have creamy white markings edged with cerise-red. Flower spike is 10in (25cm) long, with 6 buds (4 or 5 open). ↕28in (70cm).
***G.* 'Obelisk'.** Primulinus gladiolus producing orange-red flowers, 3in (8cm) across, in midseason. Flower spike is 16in (40cm) long, with 19 buds (6 or 7 open). ↕3½ft (1.1m).
G. papilio ▣ syn. *G. purpureoauratus.* Cormous perennial, spreading freely by underground runners, with sword-shaped leaves, 2–18in (5–45cm) long. From summer to autumn, arching stems each produce 5–10 hooded, funnel- or bell-shaped flowers, to 2in (5cm) long, from bright yellow to yellowish green, heavily suffused purple. The plant illustrated is usually grown as *G. purpureoauratus.* ↕20–36in (50–90cm). South Africa.
***G.* 'Parade'** ▣ Giant-flowered Grandiflorus gladiolus. Late in the season, produces strongly ruffled, deep salmon-pink flowers with cream throats. Flower spike is 32–34in (80–85cm) long, with 27 buds (10 open).
***G.* 'Peace'** ▣ Giant-flowered Grandiflorus gladiolus producing strongly ruffled cream flowers, with pale lemon-yellow throats and pale pink margins, in midseason. Flower spike is 32in (80cm) long, with 26 buds (9 open).
***G.* 'Peerless'** ▣ Large-flowered Grandiflorus gladiolus. In midseason, red flowers are held formally. Flower spike is 32–34in (80–85cm) long, with 25–29 buds (8–10 open).
***G.* 'Phyllis M.'** Large-flowered Grandiflorus gladiolus with strongly ruffled, salmon-pink flowers, of heavy substance, with small, cream throats,

Gladiolus 'Sunsport', 'Shiloh', and 'Sundoro'

Gladiolus 'Pink Flare'

Gladiolus 'Pulchritude'

Gladiolus 'Queen's Blush'

Gladiolus 'Stromboli'

Gladiolus 'Sweet Dreams'

Gladiolus 'Tahiti Sunrise'

Gladiolus 'White Ice'

Gladiolus 'Zephyr'

borne in midseason. Flower spike is 32–34in (80–85cm) long, with 26–29 buds (8 or 9 open).

***G.* 'Pink Flare'** ■ Small-flowered Grandiflorus gladiolus bearing ruffled, mid-pink flowers, with small white throats, in midseason. Flower spike is 26in (65cm) long, with 25 buds (7 or 8 open).

***G.* 'Pink Lady'.** Large-flowered Grandiflorus gladiolus producing deep rose-pink flowers, in formal placement, with large, pure white throats, in midseason. Flower spike is 34in (85cm) long, with 25–27 buds (8 or 9 open).

***G.* 'Piquant'.** Primulinus gladiolus bearing black-red flowers, 2½in (6cm) across, in midseason. Flower spike is 14in (35cm) long, with 16 buds (5 or 6 open). ↕ 3ft (1m).

***G.* 'Prince Indigo'.** Large-flowered Grandiflorus gladiolus. Slightly ruffled purple flowers, are produced in midseason, the white throats marked with wine-red flashes. Flower spike is 34–36in (85–90cm) long, with 26 buds (10 open).

***G.* 'Prins Claus'** ■ Nanus gladiolus bearing pure white flowers, 2in (5cm) across, with cerise markings on the lip tepals, in early midseason. Flower spike is 10in (25cm) long, usually curved and with 6 buds (4 or 5 open). ↕ 28in (70cm).

G. psittacinus see *G. dalenii.*

***G.* 'Pulchritude'** ■ Medium-flowered Grandiflorus gladiolus. Ruffled, light lavender-pink flowers, deepening at the tepal margins and with a magenta-red mark on each lip tepal, are borne in early midseason. Flower spike is 28–30in (70–75cm) long, with 27 buds (9 open).

***G.* 'Puppy Love'.** Miniature-flowered Grandiflorus gladiolus producing ruffled, pure white flowers, with a small, light red blotch, in early and midseason. Flower spike is 18in (45cm) long, with 17–18 buds (7 open).

***G.* 'Purple Star'.** Small-flowered Grandiflorus gladiolus. Slightly ruffled, mid-purple flowers are borne early in the season, inner tepals whorled in a star-like formation. Flower spike is 24in (60cm) long, with 22 buds (6 or 7 open).

G. purpureoauratus see *G. papilio.*

G. quartinianus see *G. dalenii.*

***G.* 'Queen's Blush'** ■ Large-flowered Grandiflorus gladiolus. In midseason, bears slightly ruffled white flowers, pale pink at the margins. Flower spike is 32in (80cm) long, with 26 buds (10 open).

***G.* 'Rajah's Rose'.** Large-flowered Grandiflorus gladiolus producing slightly ruffled, deep rose-red flowers, with small white throats, in early midseason. Flower spike is 32in (80cm) long, with 27 buds (9 open).

***G.* 'Ravenna'.** Giant-flowered Grandiflorus gladiolus producing slightly ruffled, orange-scarlet flowers, with small buff throats, in early midseason. Flower spike is 30in (75cm) long, with 26 buds (10 open).

***G.* 'Rose Elf'.** Small-flowered Grandiflorus gladiolus producing slightly ruffled, light rose-pink flowers, with large, pale cream throats, in midseason. Flower spike is 28in (70cm) long, with 24 buds (8 or 9 open).

***G.* 'Sailor's Delight'.** Large-flowered Grandiflorus gladiolus bearing strongly ruffled, white-throated pink flowers in late midseason. Flower spike is 32–34in (80–85cm) long, with 27 buds (9 open).

G. segetum see *G. italicus.*

***G.* 'Shawna'.** Miniature-flowered Grandiflorus gladiolus bearing wide-open, clear ruby-red flowers, with slightly deeper lip petals, early in the season. Flower spike is 24in (60cm) long, with 21 tiny buds (8 or 9 open).

***G.* 'Shiloh'** ■ Medium-flowered Grandiflorus gladiolus. In early midseason, produces strongly ruffled yellow flowers, each with a bright red mark spreading from the throat. Flower spike is 28–30in (70–75cm) long, with 25 buds (9 open).

Gladiolus tristis

***G.* 'Silent Snow'.** Medium-flowered Grandiflorus gladiolus with beautifully ruffled, pristine white flowers, and light cream throats, in formal placement and of heavy substance, borne in midseason. Flower spike is 30in (75cm) long, with 25–27 buds (8 or 9 open).

***G.* 'Stardust'.** Miniature-flowered Grandiflorus gladiolus. Ruffled, pale yellow flowers, with lighter yellow throats, are produced in midseason. Flower spike is 20in (50cm) long, with 23 buds (8 open).

***G.* 'Stromboli'** ■ Large-flowered Grandiflorus gladiolus. In midseason, bears slightly ruffled, deep red flowers, with paler throats. Flower spike is 30–32in (75–80cm) long, with 25 buds (9 open).

***G.* 'Sumatra'.** Large-flowered Grandiflorus gladiolus. In midseason, produces gently ruffled, light brown flowers, reflexed toward the stem. Flower spike is 30in (75cm) long, with 25 buds (8 open) in a slightly informal arrangement.

***G.* 'Sundoro'** ■ Medium-flowered Grandiflorus gladiolus, a sport of 'Shiloh'. In midseason, produces heavily ruffled, yellow flowers, each petal with a large red blotch and fine red picotee edge, with a waxy substance. Flower spike is 28in (70cm) long, with 23 buds (7 open).

***G.* 'Sunsport'** ■ Medium-flowered Grandiflorus gladiolus, a sport of 'Shiloh'. In early and midseason, bears flowers in ivory and deep yellow, with ruffling and heavy substance. Flower spike is 26–28in (65–70cm) long, with 23–25 buds (7 or 8 open).

***G.* 'Sweet Dreams'** ■ Medium-flowered Grandiflorus gladiolus. In midseason, produces slightly ruffled, creamy white flowers, tinted deep rose-red at the margins and with deep rose-red lip tepals. Flower spike is 30in (75cm) long, with 27 buds (9 open).

***G.* 'Tahiti Sunrise'** ■ Medium-flowered Grandiflorus gladiolus bearing pale buff flowers with dark yellow throats, edged in rose-pink, very early in the season. Flower spike is 26in (65cm) long, with 18–20 buds (6 or 7 open).

***G.* 'Tesoro'.** Medium-flowered Grandiflorus gladiolus bearing slightly ruffled yellow flowers, in midseason. Flower spike is 28–30in (70–75cm) long, with 26 buds (10 open).

***G.* 'The Bride'**, syn. *G.* x *colvilei* 'The Bride'. Slender *G. cardinalis* hybrid producing small spikes of 3–6 white flowers, 2in (5cm) across, marked with yellow on the lower tepals, from very early in the season to early midseason. ↕ to 24in (60cm).

G. tristis ■ Cormous perennial with very narrow leaves, the lower 16–48in (40–120cm) long and often twisted near the tips. In spring, bears spikes of up to 20 open funnel-shaped, pale yellow or creamy white flowers, 2½in (6cm) long, often green-tinged, usually flushed or dotted mauve, red, brown, or purple, on wiry stems. Strongly scented in the evening. ↕ 18–60in (45–150cm). South Africa (Western Cape).

***G.* 'Tropic Sun'.** Large-flowered Grandiflorus gladiolus with wide-open, ruffled, vibrant orange-red flowers, in formal placement, during midseason. Well-tapered flower spike is 32in (80cm) long with 25 buds (8 or 9 open).

***G.* 'True Love'.** Large-flowered Grandiflorus gladiolus. Produces ruffled, satin-sheened, pure pink flowers, with heavy substance, in midseason. Flower spike is 28–32in (70–80cm) long, with 25 buds (8 or 9 open).

***G.* 'Vega'.** Large-flowered Grandiflorus gladiolus, sport of 'True Love'. In midseason, bears precisely ruffled, pure white flowers, with heavy substance. Flower spike is 32in (80cm) long, with 27 buds (8 or 9 open).

***G.* 'White Friendship'.** Large-flowered Grandiflorus gladiolus bearing ruffled, pure white flowers early in the season. Flower spike is 26in (65cm) long with 21 buds (7 open).

***G.* 'White Ice'** ■ Medium-flowered Grandiflorus gladiolus bearing ruffled white flowers in early midseason. Flower spike is 30–32in (75–80cm) long, with 25 buds (10 open). Excellent for exhibition.

***G.* 'Zephyr'** ■ Large-flowered Grandiflorus gladiolus. Ruffled, light lavender-pink flowers, with small ivory throats, are produced in midseason. Flower spike is 30–32in (75–80cm) long, with 26 buds (9 open).

▷ ***Glandularia*** see *Verbena*
▷ ***Glandulicactus*** see *Sclerocactus*

Glaucidium palmatum

Glaucium flavum

GLAUCIDIUM

PAEONIACEAE

Genus of one species of rhizomatous, clump-forming perennial from mountainous woodland in N. Japan. It has palmately lobed leaves and large, peony- or poppy-like flowers. A very effective plant for a woodland garden or border, *G. palmatum* grows best in cool, moist climates.

• **CULTIVATION** Grow in humus-rich, leafy, moist soil in partial to deep shade, sheltered from cold, drying winds.

• **PROPAGATION** Sow seed in containers in an open frame in spring, or divide mature clumps with care in early spring.

• **PESTS AND DISEASES** Susceptible to slug damage.

G. palmatum ■ Slow-growing, rhizomatous perennial, softly hairy when young, with unbranched stems, each bearing 2 or 3 palmately 5- to 11-lobed, many-veined, toothed, light green leaves, 8–12in (20–30cm) long, heart-shaped at the bases, with crinkly leaf surfaces. In late spring and early summer, bears solitary, terminal flowers, 2–3in (5–8cm) across, with 4 soft pinkish lilac or mauve tepals, no petals, and numerous gold stamens. ↕↔ 18in (45cm). N. Japan. Zone 6. **var. *leucanthum***, syn. 'Album', has white flowers.

GLAUCIUM

Horned poppy

PAPAVERACEAE

Genus of 25 species of erect, often rosette-forming annuals, biennials, and short-lived perennials from disturbed or waste ground in Europe, the Middle East, N. Africa, and C. and S.W. Asia. They have pinnatifid, hairless to softly hairy, narrowly ovate to nearly rounded, glaucous leaves with large terminal lobes and orange-yellow sap. Showy, solitary, terminal and axillary, poppy-like, paper-thin flowers, borne mainly in summer, are followed by long, curved, decorative seed heads. Grow in a border, gravel garden, or in seaside plantings. Roots are toxic if ingested.

• **CULTIVATION** Grow in poor to moderately fertile, well-drained soil in full sun. They resent root disturbance.

• **PROPAGATION** Sow seed *in situ* in spring or autumn.

• **PESTS AND DISEASES** Infrequent.

G. corniculatum (Red horned poppy). Rosette-forming, slightly hairy biennial, with pinnatifid, glaucous, silver-gray leaves, 6–12in (15–30cm) long. Crimson-red to orange flowers, to 2in (5cm) across, usually with a black spot at the base of each petal, are produced freely at the tips of the branched stems from summer to early autumn. ↕↔ 12–16in (30–40cm). Europe, S.W. Asia. Zone 6.

G. flavum ■ (Yellow horned poppy). Rosette-forming, slightly hairy, short-lived perennial, usually grown as a biennial, with pinnatifid, glaucous, hairless, rough, blue-green leaves, 6–12in (15–30cm) long, the lobes incised or toothed. Produces branched gray stems of bright golden yellow or orange flowers, to 2in (5cm) across, in summer. ↕ 12–36in (30–90cm), ↔ to 18in (45cm). Europe, Canary Islands, N. Africa, W. Asia. Zone 6.

G. grandiflorum. Rosette-forming perennial with alternate, pinnatifid or pinnatisect, glaucous, bluish green leaves, to 8in (20cm) long, consisting of obovate-oblong segments. Poppy-like, bowl-shaped, dark orange to crimson flowers, to 2½in (6cm) across, each with a dark spot at the base, are freely borne in summer. ↕↔ 12–20in (30–50cm). Greece, N.E. Egypt (Sinai), Turkey, Syria, Caucasus, Iran. Zone 6.

GLEDITSIA

Honeylocust

FABACEAE

Genus of about 14 species of deciduous, usually thorny trees from woodland in Asia, North and South America, and tropical Africa. They are cultivated for their elegant form and pinnate or 2-pinnate, fern-like leaves, which are borne alternately. The inconspicuous racemes of small, greenish white flowers often produce unusual, large, pendent seed pods. The trunks and branches of most species are armed with simple or branched thorns. Grow honeylocusts as specimen trees.

• **CULTIVATION** Grow in any fertile, well-drained soil in full sun. Pruning group 1.

• **PROPAGATION** Sow scarified seed in containers in an open frame in autumn. Bud cultivars in summer, or graft them in late winter.

• **PESTS AND DISEASES** Tar spot, powdery mildew, twig and trunk canker, leaf spot, heart rot, and mushroom root rot can occur. Caterpillars, mites, aphids, borers, webworms, honeylocust pod gall midges, honeylocust plant bugs, scale insects, and plant hoppers can be problems.

Gleditsia triacanthos 'Elegantissima' (inset: leaf detail)

G. caspica (Caspian honeylocust). Spreading, deciduous tree, the trunk armed with branched thorns to 6in (15cm) or more long. Glossy, mid-green leaves, to 10in (25cm) long, turning yellow in autumn, are usually pinnate, occasionally 2-pinnate, with 12–20 ovate to oval leaflets. In autumn, bears pendent, curved, twisted seed pods, to 10in (25cm) long. ↕ 40ft (12m), ↔ 30ft (10m). Caucasus, N. Iran. Zone 7b.

G. japonica. Conical, deciduous tree with a thorny trunk and very thorny shoots, purple when young. Glossy, mid-green leaves, to 12in (30cm) long, turn yellow in autumn. They are either pinnate, with 14–24 ovate to lance-shaped leaflets, or 2-pinnate, with 2–12 leaflets. Bears pendent, curved, twisted seed pods, to 12in (30cm) long, in autumn. ↕ 70ft (20m), ↔ 40ft (12m). Japan. Zone 8.

G. triacanthos (Honeylocust). Spreading, deciduous tree with a thorny trunk (sometimes dangerously so) and shoots, the thorns branched and 3–6in (8–15cm) long. Glossy, dark green leaves, to 10in (25cm) long, turn yellow in autumn, and are pinnate, with 14–24 leaflets, or 2-pinnate, with 4–16 pairs of oblong-lance-shaped leaflets. Pendent, sickle-shaped, twisted seed pods, to 18in (45cm) long, are borne in autumn. ↕ 100ft (30m) or more, ↔ 70ft (20m). The cultivars are generally 30–80ft (10–25m) tall and 25–35ft (8–11m) wide. C. and E. North America. Zone 4. **f. *inermis*** is thornless. All cultivars are essentially selections of this form and are usually thornless: **'Elegantissima'** ■ is dense, shrubby, and slow-growing; ↕ 15–25ft (5–8m), ↔ 15ft (5m). **'Imperial'** is a wide-spreading tree with

Gleditsia triacanthos 'Rubylace'

Gleditsia triacanthos 'Skyline'

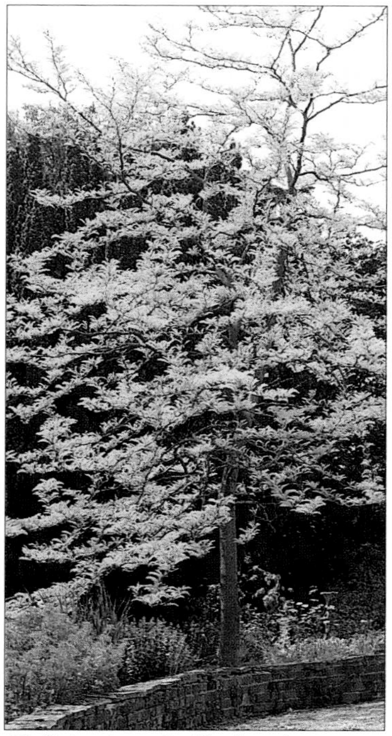
Gleditsia triacanthos 'Sunburst'

rounded, bright green leaves and few seed pods; ↕ to 30ft (10m). **'Moraine'** is graceful and broad, with dark green leaves, turning golden yellow in autumn. Resistant to webworm. **'Rubylace'** ▣ has dark bronze-red young leaves turning dark bronze-green by mid-summer. **'Shademaster'** is strong-growing, with more upright, branches and is nearly podless; ↕ to 45ft (14m). **'Skyline'** ▣ is compact and broadly conical, with ascending upper branches, and dark green leaves, turning golden yellow in autumn; ↕ to 50ft (15m). **'Sunburst'** ▣ is fast-growing and broadly conical, with spreading, thornless branches, and golden yellow young foliage, pale green at maturity, yellow in autumn. Does not fruit; ↕ 40ft (12m), ↔ 30ft (10m).

GLOBBA

ZINGIBERACEAE

Genus of about 70 species of rhizomatous herbaceous perennials from forest in S.E. Asia. Reed-like stems have alternate, 2-ranked, oblong or lance-shaped leaves. They bear 3-petaled, tubular flowers on slender, branched stalks, in terminal, pendent racemes with conspicuous bracts, from autumn to early winter. Among the lower bracts, bulbils may form instead of flowers. Grow as a groundcover in warm climates; elsewhere, grow in a warm greenhouse.

• **CULTIVATION** Under glass, grow in soil-based potting mix in bright filtered or indirect light. During the growing season, maintain high humidity, water freely, and apply a balanced liquid fertilizer every 2 or 3 weeks. Allow to become dormant in late winter and keep just moist. Outdoors, grow in humus-rich, moist but well-drained soil in partial shade.

• **PROPAGATION** Divide in spring, or plant bulbils in summer.

• **PESTS AND DISEASES** Mealybugs may be troublesome.

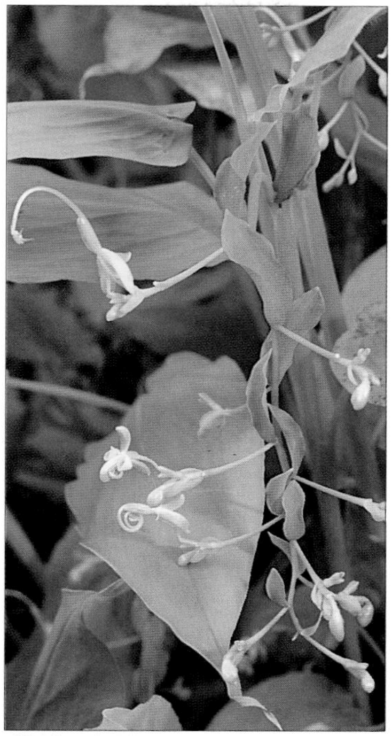
Globba winitii

G. winitii ▣ Rhizomatous perennial with lance-shaped leaves, 8in (20cm) long, heart-shaped at the bases, lower leaves sheathing the stems; leaf stalks are 4in (10cm) long. From autumn to early winter, bears nodding or pendent racemes, 6in (15cm) long, of slender, tubular yellow flowers, to 1½in (4cm) long, with reflexed, pink, mauve, or deep purple bracts. ↕ 3ft (1m), ↔ 24in (60cm). Thailand. ❀ (min. 61°F/16°C)

GLOBULARIA

Globe daisy

GLOBULARIACEAE

Genus of about 20 species of mat- or hummock-forming, mainly evergreen perennials or subshrubs, mostly found in open, rocky habitats around the Mediterranean, often at high altitudes. They produce leathery, simple, entire or sharply toothed leaves and tiny, 2-lipped flowers in dense, spherical heads. Globe daisies are suitable for a rock garden, trough, or alpine house; the more robust species are also useful in wall plantings.

• **CULTIVATION** Grow in neutral to alkaline, sharply drained soil in full sun. Protect from winter moisture.

Globularia meridionalis

• **PROPAGATION** Sow seed in containers in an open frame in autumn. Root individual rosettes, with a bit of woody tissue attached, in spring or summer.

• **PESTS AND DISEASES** Slugs and snails.

G. bellidifolia see *G. meridionalis.*
G. cordifolia. Dwarf, evergreen, mat-forming, woody-based perennial with rooting stems bearing rosettes of spoon-shaped, glossy, dark green leaves to 1in (2.5cm) long, with notched tips. In summer, produces lavender-blue flowers in stemless, spherical heads, to ¾in (2cm) across. ↕ 2in (5cm), ↔ to 8in (20cm). Mountains of C. and S. Europe, W. Turkey. Zone 5. **subsp. *bellidifolia*** see *G. meridionalis.* **subsp. *meridionalis*** see *G. meridionalis.*
G. meridionalis ▣ syn. *G. bellidifolia, G. cordifolia* subsp. *bellidifolia, G. cordifolia* subsp. *meridionalis, G. pygmaea.* Evergreen, dome-shaped, mat-forming subshrub with lance-shaped to inversely lance-shaped, glossy, dark green leaves, ¾–3½in (2–9cm) long. In summer, produces lavender-purple flowers in spherical heads, to ¾in (2cm) across, just above the foliage. More robust than *G. cordifolia.* ↕ to 4in (10cm), ↔ to 12in (30cm). S.E. Alps, C. and S. Apennines, Balkan Peninsula. Zone 6.
G. nana see *G. repens.*
G. pygmaea see *G. meridionalis.*
G. repens, syn. *G. nana.* Very compact, mat-forming, evergreen perennial with folded, spoon-shaped, glossy, dark green leaves, ½–¾in (1–2cm) long. Lavender-blue flowers in stemless or short-stemmed, spherical heads, ½–¾in (1–2cm) across, are borne immediately above the leaves in summer. Similar to *G. cordifolia*, but smaller. Suitable for a trough. ↕ 1in (2.5cm), ↔ to 6in (15cm). Pyrenees, S.W. Alps. Zone 6.

GLORIOSA

LILIACEAE

Genus of one very variable species of climbing, tuberous perennial from woodland and forest, often by rivers, in tropical Africa and India. It is cultivated for its brightly colored flowers, and is effective when scrambling through other plants. Where not hardy, grow in a temperate greenhouse or conservatory, or in pots. Highly toxic if ingested; handling tubers may irritate the skin.

• **CULTIVATION** Plant tubers 3–4in (7–10cm) deep in early spring. Under glass, grow in soil-based potting mix, with added grit, in full light. Water freely when growth begins and apply a balanced liquid fertilizer every 2 weeks. Keep tubers dry in winter. Pot on only when congested, in late winter. Outdoors, grow in fertile, well-drained soil in full sun.

• **PROPAGATION** Sow seed at 66–75°F (19–24°C), or separate the finger-like tubers, in spring.

• **PESTS AND DISEASES** Aphids, viruses, anthracnose, and bulb rots are sometimes problems.

G. carsonii see *G. superba.*
G. minor see *G. superba.*
G. rothschildiana see *G. superba* 'Rothschildiana'.
G. simplex see *G. superba.*

Gloriosa superba 'Rothschildiana'

G. superba, syn. *G. carsonii, G. minor, G. simplex.* Climbing perennial with ovate-lance-shaped to oblong, glossy, bright green leaves, 2–3in (5–8cm) long, which narrow to form terminal tendrils, 1¼–2in (3–5cm) long. From summer to autumn, bears nodding flowers, 2–4in (5–10cm) across, from the upper leaf axils. Flowers have 6 reflexed, wavy-margined, red or purple tepals, often yellow-margined, sometimes entirely yellow, with long, protruding stamens. ↕ to 6ft (2m), ↔ 12in (30cm). Africa, India. ❀ (min. 46–50°F/8–10°C). **'Citrina'** has citrus-yellow flowers, tinted or striped with deep purple-red. **'Rothschildiana'** ▣ syn. *G. rothschildiana*, produces flowers 3–4in (7–10cm) across, with bright red or scarlet tepals fading to ruby or garnet, and yellow near the bases and on the margins.

GLOTTIPHYLLUM

AIZOACEAE

Genus of about 60 species of low-growing, branching, perennial succulents from semi-desert areas of South Africa. They have semi-cylindrical or strap-shaped, fleshy, glossy, bright green or pale green leaves, arranged in opposite pairs or alternately along the stems, with 4 or more leaves on a single shoot. Large, daisy-like, bright yellow, rarely white flowerheads are borne singly in the leaf axils, mainly from summer to late winter. Below 50°F (10°C), grow in a warm greenhouse; in warmer areas, grow in a desert garden.

• **CULTIVATION** Under glass, grow in standard cactus potting mix in full light. Water sparingly from mid-summer to late winter and apply a half-strength low-nitrogen liquid fertilizer once during the growing season. Keep barely moist when dormant. Outdoors, grow in poor, sharply drained soil in full sun. See also pp.48–49.

• **PROPAGATION** Sow seed at 66–75°F (19–24°C), or root basal stem cuttings, in late summer.

• **PESTS AND DISEASES** Infrequent.

G. linguiforme. Succulent, often offsetting, with opposite pairs of strap-shaped, glossy, bright green leaves, 2–2½in (5–6cm) long, which are incurved above and obliquely thickened below, with rounded tips. Produces golden yellow flowerheads, 3in (8cm) across, from autumn to late winter. ↕ 2½in (6cm), ↔ 12in (30cm). South Africa (Northern Cape, Eastern Cape, Western Cape). ❀ (min. 50°F/10°C)

G. nelii. Succulent, forming compact clumps, with thick, strap-shaped, pale green leaves, 1½–2in (4–5cm) long, in uneven, opposite pairs. The shorter leaf of each pair is incurved with rounded margins and tip; the longer is incurved, like a hook, flat above, keeled below, with a rounded tip. Bears bright yellow flowerheads, 1½in (4cm) across, from autumn tolate winter. ↕ 2in (5cm), ↔ 12in (30cm). South Africa (Northern Cape, Eastern Cape, Western Cape). ❀ (min. 50°F/10°C)

G

GLOXINIA

GESNERIACEAE

Genus of 8 species of rhizomatous, soft-stemmed perennials or shrubs from forest in Central and South America. The fleshy, creeping rhizomes give rise to erect stems bearing opposite pairs of ovate to elliptic leaves. Tubular or bell- or funnel-shaped, blue or pink flowers, finely hairy on the outside, are borne singly or in pairs from the leaf axils from summer to midautumn. Where not hardy, grow in a warm greenhouse. Elsewhere, grow in a shady border or woodland setting.

• **CULTIVATION** Under glass, grow in soilless potting mix in bright indirect light and high humidity. During the growing season, water freely and apply a balanced liquid fertilizer every 2 or 3 weeks. Dry off after flowering; resume watering, sparingly at first, in spring. Outdoors, grow in moist, humus-rich soil in dappled shade.

• **PROPAGATION** Sow seed at 66–75°F (19–24°C) in early spring. Divide rhizomes in spring. Root basal cuttings with bottom heat in summer.

• **PESTS AND DISEASES** Scale insects, mites, powdery mildew, and crown rots.

G. perennis ▣ Bushy, rhizomatous perennial bearing toothed, ovate leaves with heart-shaped bases, to 8in (20cm) long, glossy, mid-green above, paler and suffused red below. Bears solitary, bell-shaped, lavender- to purple-blue flowers, 1–1½in (2.5–4cm) long, marked dark violet at the bases, from early summer to midautumn. ↕ 4ft (1.2m), ↔ 3ft (1m). Panama to Peru. ❀ (min. 50°F/10°C)

***G.* 'Red Bird'.** Rhizomatous perennial with ovate, glossy, dark green leaves, to 8in (20cm) long. Produces solitary, tubular, orange-red flowers, to 1½in (4cm) long, with red-spotted, yellow insides, in summer. ↕ 4ft (1.2m), ↔ 3ft (1m). ❀ (min. 55°F/13°C)

G. speciosa see *Sinningia speciosa.*

Gloxinia perennis

GLYCERIA

Manna grass

POACEAE

Genus of 16 species of marsh or marginal, aquatic, perennial grasses, mainly from N. temperate regions, but also found in Australia, New Zealand, and South America. Occurring naturally in water to 30in (75cm) deep, they are vigorous, dense, and spreading plants. Use as cover for a large pool.

• **CULTIVATION** Grow in water to 6in (15cm) deep in full sun; grow in a basket of loamy soil in order to restrict spread. Alternatively, grow in any garden soil that is reliably moist in full sun. Confine to a container to restrict vigorous growth.

• **PROPAGATION** Divide in spring.

• **PESTS AND DISEASES** Affected by ergot, choke, rust, smut, and a variety of other fungal leaf spots.

G. aquatica see *G. maxima.*

G. maxima, syn. *G. aquatica.* Aquatic, rhizomatous, perennial grass, producing narrowly strap-shaped, keeled, deep green leaves, 12–24in (30–60cm) long, flushed pink as they emerge. Panicles of green to purplish green spikelets, to 18in (45cm) long, are borne in mid- and late summer. ↕ 32in (80cm), ↔ indefinite. Temperate Eurasia. Zone 6. **'Variegata'** ▣ is more commonly grown, for its attractive cream-, green-, and white-striped foliage.

Glycyrrhiza glabra

GLYCYRRHIZA

FABACEAE

Genus of about 20 species of perennials from a range of moist or dry habitats in the Mediterranean, tropical Asia, and N. and S. America.They have pinnate, rarely 3-palmate, sticky-glandular leaves, and pea-like flowers borne in axillary racemes or spikes. *G. glabra* is a coarse but interesting plant suitable for a wild garden or informal border; its roots are the source of licorice.

• **CULTIVATION** Grow in deep, fertile, moist soil in full sun. The roots of *G. glabra* are harvested in autumn.

• **PROPAGATION** Sow seed in containers outdoors in spring or autumn. Divide roots, each with one or more growth buds, in early spring.

• **PESTS AND DISEASES** Mildew and rust.

G. glabra ▣ syn. *G. glandulifera* (Licorice, Sweetwood). Taprooted perennial bearing pinnate, sticky-glandular leaves, 2–8in (5–20cm) long, each with 9–17 oblong to elliptic or ovate leaflets. Pea-like, blue or pale violet and white flowers, ½in (1.5cm) long, are borne in loose racemes, usually 2–3in (5–8cm) long, in late summer. ↕ 4ft (1.2m), ↔ 36in (90cm). Mediterranean to S.W. Asia. ❀ (min. 41°F/5°C)

G. glandulifera see *G. glabra.*

G. uralensis. (Chinese licorice). Tall, taprooted perennial with 4–8 pairs of ovoid, dark green leaves, arising on a sturdy, sticky stem. Upright flowers are lavender to white, pea-like, borne in loose racemes. Grown for its licorice-flavored root, the bark and root are also used for flavoring in spice mixes, as a sweetener, and in herbal medicine. Zone 7.

Glyceria maxima 'Variegata'

▷ ***Godetia*** see *Clarkia*

GOMPHOCARPUS

ASCLEPIADACEAE

Genus of 50 species of evergreen and deciduous subshrubs and perennials found in dry, scrubby areas in tropical and southern Africa. Leaves are variable, opposite, alternate, or whorled. Hooded, cup-shaped flowers are borne in terminal or axillary cymes; by seed pods are usually inflated. Where not hardy, they are best grown in a cool greenhouse. In warmer climates, plant in a shrub border. Some species exude a milky sap, which may aggravate skin allergies.

• **CULTIVATION** Under glass, grow in soil-based potting mix, with added leaf mold, in full light or bright filtered light. During the growing season, water freely and apply a balanced liquid fertilizer every 4–6 weeks; keep almost dry in winter. Outdoors, grow in any well-drained soil in full sun or partial shade.

• **PROPAGATION** Sow seed at 55–64°F (13–18°C) in spring, or take softwood cuttings in spring.

• **PESTS AND DISEASES** Infrequent.

G. fruticosus, syn. *Asclepias fruticosa* (Milk bush). Upright, deciduous subshrub with linear-lance-shaped, mid-green leaves, 2–4in (5–10cm) long, borne in opposite pairs. Produces axillary clusters, 2in (5cm) across, of cup-shaped, creamy white flowers, ¼in (6mm) long, in early summer, followed by ovoid, inflated, softly spiny, silver-green fruit, to 3in (8cm) long. ↕ 3–5ft (1–1.5m), ↔ 3ft (1m). Southern Africa. ❀ (min. 45°F/7°C)

G. physocarpus, syn. *Asclepias physocarpa* (Swan plant). Deciduous subshrub, often grown as an annual, with sticky, hairy stems and opposite, sometimes alternate, narrowly lance-shaped, gray-green leaves, to 4in (10cm) long. In summer, bears many-flowered cymes, 2in (5cm) across, of creamy white or greenish white flowers, to ¼in (6mm) across; they are followed by spherical to ovoid, inflated, softly spiny, pale green fruit, to 2½in (6cm) across. ↕ 6ft (2m), ↔ 24in (60cm). South Africa (Eastern Transvaal to Eastern Cape). ❀ (min. 41°F/5°C)

GOMPHRENA

AMARANTHACEAE

Genus of 90 species of erect or prostrate, often many-branched, softly hairy annuals, occasionally perennials, found in a variety of habitats from open, sandy soils to moist woodland, in Australia and tropical Central and South America. Lance-shaped to ovate leaves are borne

Gomphrena 'Strawberry Fields' (inset: flowerhead detail)

in opposite pairs. Upright spikes of clover-like flowerheads, with prominent colorful bracts, are borne from summer to early autumn. Where not hardy, use as summer bedding or in an annual border. The flowerheads are good for cutting and drying.
• **CULTIVATION** Grow in moderately fertile, well-drained soil in full sun.
• **PROPAGATION** Sow seed at 59–64°F (15–18°C) in early spring.
• **PESTS AND DISEASES** Sometimes affected by gray mold and fungal leaf spots.

G. globosa (Globe amaranth). Upright, bushy annual with ovate to oblong leaves, to 6in (15cm) long, densely white-hairy when young, later sparsely hairy. Bears ovoid-oblong flowerheads, to 1½in (4cm) long, of pink, purple, or white flower bracts, from summer to early autumn. ↕ 12–24in (30–60cm), ↔ to 12in (30cm). Guatemala, Panama. **'Buddy'** has vivid, deep purple flowerheads; ↕ 6in (15cm).
***G. haageana* 'Lavender Lady'.** Upright annual with ovate to oblong, mid-green leaves, to 1¼–3in (3–8cm) long. In summer, bears spherical flowerheads, 1½in (4cm) across, of lavender flower bracts. ↕ 24in (60cm), ↔ 12ft (30cm).
***G.* 'Strawberry Fields'** ■ Similar in growth and habit to *G. globosa*, but has brilliant red flowerheads, to 2in (5cm) long. ↕ 30–32in (75–80cm), ↔ to 12in (30cm).

GONIOLIMON

PLUMBAGINACEAE

Genus of about 20 species of perennials found in hot, dry habitats from S.E. Europe to Mongolia, and in N.W. Africa. They are grown for their panicles or spike-like corymbs of tubular-trumpet-shaped, everlasting, white, pink, purple, or red flowers, borne on compressed and flanged, branched stems. Large, smooth, leathery or fleshy leaves are arranged in basal rosettes. They flower best in hot, dry summers or in warm areas. Grow in a perennial or mixed border, or in a cutting garden.
• **CULTIVATION** Grow in sandy, well-drained soil in full sun.
• **PROPAGATION** Sow seed in containers in a cold frame in midspring. Take root cuttings in winter.
• **PESTS AND DISEASES** Infrequent.

G. callicomum. Rosetted perennial with oblong-elliptic to lance-shaped, fleshy, gray-green leaves, 2–4in (5–10cm) long. In early summer, bears upright flowering stems with winged branches, and panicles, ¾–3in (2–8cm) long, of tubular, rose flowers. ↕ 4–20in (10–50cm), ↔ to 12in (30cm). Siberia. Zone 4.
G. tataricum, syn. *Limonium tataricum* (Tatarian statice). Rosetted perennial with oblong to obovate or inversely lance-shaped, pale green leaves, ¾–6in (2–15cm) long, with white spots. Tubular flowers with white sepals and spreading, purple-red to ruby-red petals are borne in wide-spreading panicles, to 5in (13cm) or more long, in mid- and late summer. Excellent for cut or dried arrangements. ↕↔ 12in (30cm). S.E. Europe, Caucasus, steppes of S. Russia. Zone 4b.

GOODYERA

Jewel orchid

ORCHIDACEAE

Genus of about 40 species of evergreen, rarely deciduous, terrestrial, rhizomatous orchids, widely distributed in temperate areas except Africa, occurring in forest leaf litter. They produce basal rosettes of ovate to lance-shaped, veined leaves, usually more attractive than the small white flowers that are borne in erect, narrow spikes or racemes on upright stems, mainly in summer. Grow hardy species in a woodland garden. Tender species can be grown in an alpine house or cool greenhouse.
• **CULTIVATION** Outdoors, grow in sandy, humus-rich, well-drained, acidic soil in a sheltered site in partial shade. See also p.46.
• **PROPAGATION** Divide rhizomes in spring.
• **PESTS AND DISEASES** Aphids, spider mites, and mealybugs can be problems.

G. pubescens. Terrestrial, evergreen orchid with rosettes of ovate to broadly lance-shaped, dark bluish green leaves, to 3½in (9cm) long, with conspicuous white veins. Small white flowers, to ¼in (6mm) long, are produced in dense, cylindrical racemes, 8–16in (20–40cm) tall, from late summer to autumn. ↕ to 16in (40cm) in flower, ↔ 9in (23cm). E. North America. Zone 7.

GORDONIA

THEACEAE

Genus of about 70 species of evergreen trees and shrubs, occurring in moist forest in S.E. Asia, with one species in S.E. US. They are cultivated for their simple, elliptic, oblong or inversely lance-shaped, alternate, leathery, hairless leaves, and for their camellia-like flowers, each with 5–7 petals. Where not hardy, grow in a cool greenhouse. In milder regions, plant in a woodland or as a specimen in a lawn or border.
• **CULTIVATION** Under glass, grow in acidic potting mix in bright filtered light. Water freely when in growth, applying a balanced liquid fertilizer monthly; water sparingly in winter. Outdoors, grow in acidic to neutral, moist but well-drained soil in full sun or dappled shade; shelter from cold, drying winds. Pruning group 1; may need restrictive pruning under glass.
• **PROPAGATION** Sow seed in containers as soon as ripe. Take semi-ripe cuttings in summer.
• **PESTS AND DISEASES** Fungal and bacterial leaf spots; mushroom root rot.

G. axillaris ■ Bushy shrub or tree with elliptic-oblong to inversely lance-shaped, glossy, dark green leaves, to 6in (15cm) long. Large, saucer-shaped white flowers, 3–5in (8–13cm) across, with orange-yellow anthers, are borne from winter to spring. ↕↔ 22–30ft (7–10m). China, Vietnam, Taiwan. ❄ (min. 41°F/5°C)
G. lasianthus (Loblolly bay). Upright tree with narrowly elliptic to inversely lance-shaped, glossy, dark green leaves, to 6in (15cm) long. In summer, produces saucer-shaped, wavy-petaled, fragrant white flowers, 2½–3in (6–8cm) across, with yellow anthers. ↕ 70ft (20m) or more, ↔ 30ft (10m). S.E. US. Zone 8.

Gordonia axillaris

GRAPTOPETALUM

CRASSULACEAE

Genus of about 12 species of rosette-forming, perennial succulents from rocky grasslands to 6,500ft (2,000m) high, in S. US and Mexico. Bell- or star-shaped flowers, each with 5–7 outward-spreading petals, are borne in axillary cymes, mainly in spring or summer. Where temperatures drop below 41°F (5°C), grow in a temperate greenhouse or as houseplants; elsewhere, plant in a desert garden. Most are hardy to 25°F (-4°C) for short periods.
• **CULTIVATION** Under glass, grow in soil-based potting mix, with added grit, in full light or bright filtered light. Water freely in spring and summer and apply a low-nitrogen liquid fertilizer every 6–8 weeks. Keep barely moist in autumn and winter. Outdoors, grow in moderately fertile, sharply drained soil in full sun or partial shade. See also pp.48–49.
• **PROPAGATION** Sow seed at 66–75°F (19–24°C), or take rosette or leaf cuttings, both in spring or summer.
• **PESTS AND DISEASES** Susceptible to mealybugs and, if in containers, root mealybugs.

G. bellum ■ syn. *Tacitus bellus.* Compact, perennial succulent with basal rosettes, 1¼–3in (3–8cm) across, of triangular to oval, abruptly pointed, fleshy gray leaves, ¾–1½in (2–4cm) long. Short-stalked, star-shaped, pink to deep red flowers, ¾–1¼in (2–3cm) across, are produced in cymes from the center of the rosettes from late spring to summer. ↕ 2–3in (5–8cm), ↔ to 6in (15cm). Mexico. ❄ (min. 41°F/5°C)
G. filiferum. Perennial succulent forming clumps of compact, basal rosettes, 2–2½in (5–6cm) across, of wedge- to spoon-shaped, rich green leaves, ½–2in (1–5cm) long. The leaves are white toward the winged margins and have minute papillae near the thin, bristly brown tips. Short-stalked, star-shaped, red-spotted white flowers, ¾in (2cm) across, are produced in 2–5 branched cymes from spring to early summer. ↕ 5in (13cm), ↔ indefinite. N.W. Mexico. ❄ (min. 41°F/5°C)

Graptopetalum bellum

Graptopetalum paraguayense

G. paraguayense ■ syn. *Sedum weinbergii* (Ghost plant, Mother of pearl plant). Prostrate, clump-forming, perennial succulent. Forms basal rosettes, to 6in (15cm) across, of spoon-shaped to obovate-lance-shaped, blunt, pink-tinged, gray-green leaves, ¾–3in (2–8cm) long; the young leaves are pale mauve-gray. Large cymes of star-shaped, red-spotted white flowers, ½–¾in (1–2cm) across, are borne in late winter and early spring. ↕ to 8in (20cm), ↔ indefinite. Mexico. ❄ (min. 41°F/5°C)

GRAPTOPHYLLUM

ACANTHACEAE

Genus of 10 species of evergreen shrubs from Australasia and the S.W. Pacific, often found on rainforest margins, and also on seasonally dry, rocky hillsides or beside rivers. They are cultivated mainly for their foliage: the leaves are simple, usually entire, spotted, mottled, or banded with various colors, and borne in opposite pairs. Tubular, 2-lipped flowers are produced in racemes or panicles at the ends of the shoots. Where temperatures fall below 55°F (13°C), grow in a temperate or warm greenhouse, or as houseplants. In warmer climates, use to brighten shady borders; they are effective with ferns.

• **CULTIVATION** Under glass, grow in soil-based potting mix, with added grit, in full light or bright filtered light. Top-dress or pot on in spring. Water freely from spring to autumn, applying a balanced liquid fertilizer monthly. Water sparingly in winter. Outdoors, grow in fertile, moist but well-drained soil in semi-shade. Pruning group 8; may need restrictive pruning under glass.

• **PROPAGATION** Sow seed at 66–75°F (19–24°C) in spring, root semi-ripe cuttings with bottom heat in summer, or layer in summer.

• **PESTS AND DISEASES** Whiteflies, spider mites, and scale insects may infest greenhouse plants.

Graptophyllum pictum

G. pictum ■ (Caricature plant). Erect shrub, sparsely branched unless regularly pinched out when young. The elliptic-ovate, glossy, deep green leaves, 4–6in (10–15cm) long, are variously veined and marked yellow, or entirely suffused dark purple. In summer, crimson to purple flowers with inflated throats are produced in short racemes, to 3in (8cm) long. ↕ 3–6ft (1–2m), ↔ 24–36in (60–90cm). Probably New Guinea. ❄ (min. 55°F/13°C). **'Tricolor'** has oval, purplish green leaves, mottled yellow and rose-pink, with red stalks and midribs.

x GRAPTOVERIA

CRASSULACEAE

Hybrid genus, produced in cultivation, between *Graptopetalum* and *Echeveria*, of evergreen leaf-succulents, intermediate between the parents in overall appearance, size, and leaf shape, and quite variable in leaf color. They are grown for their rosettes of colorful, oblong-obovate to spoon-shaped leaves. In spring, they bear cymes of inconspicuous, usually urn-shaped, yellow to pink flowers. Graptoverias are appropriate for a container or desert garden. Where not hardy, grow as houseplants or in a cool greenhouse.

• **CULTIVATION** Under glass, grow in soil-based potting mix in full light with low humidity. Water from below, freely in growth; keep just moist in winter. Apply a balanced liquid fertilizer every 2 weeks in the growing season. Outdoors, grow in well-drained, moderately fertile soil in full sun. Container plants may be moved outdoors in summer. Avoid wetting the leaves to discourage rot.

• **PROPAGATION** Take leaf or stem cuttings in spring, and keep shaded until well established.

• **PESTS AND DISEASES** Mealybugs may be a problem.

x *G.* 'Debbi'. Hybrid perennial succulent with rich lavender rosettes, to 4in (10cm) across. Becomes elongated; cut and reroot rosettes to keep a tidy appearance. ↕ to 6in (15cm), ↔ to 8–10in (20–25cm). ❄ (min. 25°F/-4°C)
x *G.* 'Silver Star'. Compact, cluster-forming hybrid perennial succulent with low, dense, gray-green rosettes, to 4in (10cm) across. Larger than the *Graptopetalum* parent and of easier care. ↕ to 6in (15cm), ↔ to 8–10in (20–25cm). ❄ (min. 25°F/-4°C)

GREVILLEA

PROTEACEAE

Genus of at least 250 species of evergreen shrubs and trees, most native to Australia, a few native to Indonesia, New Guinea, and New Caledonia, found in woodland, rainforest, and more open habitats. The alternate leaves vary greatly and may be needle-like or broader; pinnatifid, pinnatisect, or pinnate; and boldly toothed. The petalless flowers, ¼–¾in (0.5–2cm) long, each consist of a colored calyx tube that splits into 4 narrow, rolled-back, petal-like lobes, and long, straight or curved styles. The flowers are produced in simple or branched, terminal racemes or panicles, some one-sided, others cylindrical or feathery. Where not hardy, grow in a cool or temperate greenhouse, or conservatory. Elsewhere, use as specimen plants or in a shrub border. All parts may aggravate skin allergies.

• **CULTIVATION** Under glass, grow in acidic soil mix, with added grit, in full light. Top-dress or pot on in spring. During the growing season, water freely and apply a low-phosphate liquid fertilizer monthly. Water sparingly in winter. Outdoors, grow in acidic to neutral, moderately fertile soil in full sun. Pruning group 1; may need restrictive pruning under glass.

• **PROPAGATION** Sow scarified or pre-soaked seed at 55–64°F (13–18°C) in spring (only *G. robusta* germinates easily). Take semi-ripe cuttings in summer. Graft in winter under glass, or in late summer outdoors.

• **PESTS AND DISEASES** Somewhat prone to root rot and dieback, as well as scale insects and mealybugs.

G. acanthifolia. Sometimes ungainly shrub with wide-spreading, prostrate and ascending branches. The oblong-elliptic, glossy, deep green leaves, to 5in (13cm) long, are pinnatisect, with each segment divided into 3–5 spine-tipped lobes. Purplish pink flowers are borne in one-sided, toothbrush-like racemes, 2–4in (5–10cm) long, mainly from spring to autumn. ↕ 1–10ft (0.3–3m), ↔ 6–15ft (2–5m). New South Wales. ❄ (min. 45°F/7°C)
G. alpestris see *G. alpina.*
G. alpina, syn. *G. alpestris.* Prostrate to erect shrub of open habit, with linear to broadly elliptic leaves, ½–1¼in (1–3cm) long, deep green to gray-green, sometimes glossy above, paler and hairy beneath. The flowers, borne in short, dense racemes, to 1¼in (3cm) long, range from pink, red, orange, or yellow to cream or pale green, and are produced almost all year round. ↕ to 6ft (2m), ↔ 2–6ft (0.6–2m). Mountain slopes and heathland in New South Wales and Victoria. ❄ (min. 41°F/5°C). **'Olympic Flame'** is compact and rounded, with small, sharply pointed, deep green leaves, to ¾in (2cm) long; it produces an abundance of slightly pendulous, dense racemes, 2½in (6cm) long, of bicolored, red-pink and cream flowers; ↕↔ 3–6ft (1–2m).
G. aspleniifolia. Erect to spreading shrub with reddish green young growth, and linear-lance-shaped, usually entire leaves, 7–12in (18–30cm) long, deep green above and greenish white or sometimes fawn-felted beneath. Deep red and green flowers are produced in one-sided, toothbrush-like racemes, 2in (5cm) long, from the upper leaf axils and shoot tips, mainly from late winter to early summer, and again in autumn. ↕ 10–15ft (3–5m), ↔ 20ft (6m). New South Wales. ❄ (min. 45°F/7°C)

Grevillea 'Australflora Canterbury Gold'

***G.* 'Australflora Canterbury Gold'** ■ Prostrate to low-arching or more upright shrub with lance-shaped, divided leaves, 1½–2½in (4–6cm) long, light green above, with dense, silky hairs beneath. Pale yellow flowers in pendent, one-sided racemes, to 2½in (6cm) long, are produced mainly from late winter to late summer. ↕ 2–6ft (0.6–2m), ↔ 6–12ft (2–4m). ❄ (min. 41°F/5°C)
G. banksii ■ Large, open, strongly branched shrub or small tree, sometimes prostrate and mat-forming. Ovate, pinnate, or deeply pinnatifid leaves, 6–10in (15–25cm) long, with long, narrow lobes, are deep green above, silky-hairy or rust-red-hairy beneath. Bears red, pink, or creamy white flowers in erect, cylindrical racemes, 3–7in (8–18cm) long, mostly from late winter to spring, but also at other times. ↕ 3–30ft (1–10m), ↔ 6–15ft (2–5m). Queensland. ❄ (min. 45°F/7°C)
***G.* 'Canberra Gem'** ■ Vigorous, bushy shrub with densely silky-hairy stems, and crowded, linear leaves, 1¼in (3cm) long, each tipped with a hard point, and rich green above, silky-hairy beneath. Produces short, dense racemes, to 2in (5cm) long, of waxy, pinkish red flowers, mainly from late winter to late summer, but also at other times.

Grevillea banksii

Grevillea 'Canberra Gem'

↕ 6–12ft (2–4m), ↔ 6–15ft (2–5m). ❄ (min. 41°F/5°C)
***G.* 'Clearview David'.** Fast-growing, bushy shrub with densely borne, often clustered, linear leaves, 1¼in (3cm) long, each tipped with a hard point, and deep green above, silky-hairy below. Throughout the year, bears large, spider-like racemes, to 3in (8cm) long, of deep red flowers at the tips of all short lateral shoots. ↕ 6–10ft (2–3m), ↔ 6–12ft (2–4m). ❄ (min. 41°F/5°C)
G. juniperina ■ Prostrate to upright-branched, dense, rounded shrub with crowded, often clustered, narrowly lance-shaped to narrowly linear, mid-green to gray-green leaves, ½–¾in (1–2cm) long. Greenish yellow to red flowers are borne in pendent racemes, to 2½in (6cm) long, from late spring to midsummer. ↕ 6ft (2m), ↔ 3ft (1m). New South Wales. ❄ (min. 41°F/5°C). **'Molonglo'** has apricot flowers, and is vigorous and low-spreading in habit; ↕ to 3ft (1m). **'Prostrate Yellow'** is mat-forming, producing very dark foliage and lemon-yellow flowers; ↕ 12–24in (30–60m), ↔ 10–15ft (3–5m). **f. *sulphurea*** ■ syn. *G. sulphurea*, has many-branched, arching stems, and yellow flowers; ↕ 5–6ft (1.5–2m), ↔ 6–10ft (2–3m).
***G.* 'Kentlyn'** see *G.* 'Mason's Hybrid'.
G. lanigera. Usually dwarf to medium-sized, many-branched, rounded shrub, sometimes mat-forming. Bears crowded, linear to narrowly oblong, hairy, mid-green to grayish green leaves, ½–1¼in (1–3cm) long, with margins rolled under. Produces umbel-like, semi-erect racemes, to 2½in (6cm) wide, of light

Grevillea juniperina

Grevillea juniperina f. *sulphurea*

red and cream or green and cream flowers from autumn to summer. ↕ prostrate to 10ft (3m), ↔ 5–15ft (1.5–5m). New South Wales, Victoria. ❄ (min. 41°F/5°C). **'Clearview John'** has lime-green and cream flowers; ↕ 24–36in (60–90cm), ↔ 3–5ft (0.9–1.5m). **'Compacta'**, syn. 'Mt. Tamboritha', 'Prostrate', is spreading, dwarf, and bushy, with pinkish red and cream flowers; ↕ 24–39in (60–100cm). **'Mt. Tamboritha'** see 'Compacta'. **'Prostrate'** see 'Compacta'.
G. lavandulacea. Very variable, sometimes suckering, many-branched, spreading to erect or arching to cascading shrub. Linear to elliptic, sometimes clustered, mid-green to gray-green leaves, to 1½in (4cm) long, are prickle-tipped, with recurved margins. Bears many umbel-like racemes, to 2½in (6cm) long, of red to pale pink, red and cream, pink and cream or, more rarely, entirely cream flowers; they appear from late winter to early summer and late summer to autumn. ↕ prostrate to 6ft (2m), ↔ 3–10ft (1–3m). New South Wales, Victoria. ❄ (min. 41°F/5°C). **'Adelaide Hills'** is dwarf, with elliptic leaves and light red flowers; ↕ to 4ft (1.2m). **'Tanunda'** is low and spreading, with grayish green leaves and bright reddish pink flowers; ↕ 24–39in (60–100cm).
***G.* 'Mason's Hybrid'**, syn. *G.* 'Kentlyn', *G.* 'Ned Kelly'. Spreading shrub, tending to open out from the center, with 2-pinnate, stiffly arching leaves, 5–7in (12–18cm) long, deep green and semi-lustrous above, paler and matte beneath. Bears cylindrical to almost one-sided racemes, 5–6in (12–15cm) long, of orange-red flowers, becoming pink-tinged with age, with deep pink styles and yellow stigmas, intermittently through the year. ↕ 2–6ft (1–2m), ↔ 20–60in (50–150cm). ❄ (min. 41°F/5°C)
***G.* 'Ned Kelly'** see *G.* 'Mason's Hybrid'.
***G.* 'Noelii'.** Dense, mound-forming shrub with narrow, glossy, linear, mid-green leaves, 1in (2.5cm) long. Bears terminal racemes, to 3in (8cm) long, of long, slender, curved, pink and white flowers, in spring. ↕ to 4ft (1.2m), ↔ 4–5ft (1.2–1.5m). ❄ (min. 41°F/5°C)
***G.* 'Poorinda Constance'** ■ Erect to spreading, bushy shrub bearing oblong to elliptic, sharp-tipped leaves, 1¼in (3cm) long, deep green above, paler and silky-hairy beneath, the margins rolled under. Short, dense, spider-like racemes, to 3in (8cm) long, of bright orange-red flowers with darker styles, are produced mainly from late autumn to summer. ↕ 6–10ft (2–3m), ↔ 6–15ft (2–5m). ❄ (min. 41°F/5°C)
***G.* 'Poorinda Golden Lyre'.** Bushy, slow-growing shrub with silky-hairy shoots. Produces narrowly oblong to elliptic leaves, 1¼in (3cm) long, glossy, deep green above, paler and silky-hairy beneath, with margins rolled under. Red, orange, or yellow flowers are borne in pendent, spider-like racemes, to 1½in (4cm) across, from autumn to summer. ↕↔ 3–6ft (1–2m). ❄ (min. 45°F/7°C)
***G.* 'Poorinda Queen'.** Freely branching shrub, the stems ascending to spreading. The elliptic leaves, 1¼–1½in (3–4cm) long, with firm, pointed tips, are glossy, deep green above, densely silky-hairy beneath. Bears pendent, congested racemes, 3in (8cm) across, of apricot-pink flowers with deep pink styles, mainly from late summer to late autumn. ↕ 10–12ft (3–4m), ↔ 10–15ft (3–5m). ❄ (min. 45°F/7°C)
G. robusta (Silk oak). Fast-growing, upright to conical tree, usually developing an open, elongated crown, but sometimes becoming more spreading. The fern-like leaves, 6–12in (15–30cm) long, are ovate and deeply pinnate or 2-pinnate, and bronze to deep green above, paler with silky hairs beneath. Erect, bright orange-yellow or golden yellow flowers are produced in horizontal, one-sided racemes, 4–6in (10–15cm) long, from late spring to summer. ↕ 50–120ft (15–35m), ↔ 15–70ft (5–20m). Queensland, New South Wales. ❄ (min. 41°F/5°C)

Grevillea rosmarinifolia

***G.* 'Robyn Gordon'.** Many-branched, spreading shrub, thinning out from the center with age. Stiffly arching, 2-pinnate leaves, 6–8in (15–20cm) long, are deep green and semi-lustrous above, paler and matte beneath. Cylindrical to almost one-sided racemes, 4–5in (10–13cm) long, of rich reddish pink flowers, aging to a lighter pink, with bright red styles and stigmas, are produced intermittently throughout the year. Foliage may cause skin rashes. ↕ 3–5ft (1–1.5m), ↔ 20–60in (50–150cm). ❄ (min. 45°F/7°C)
G. rosmarinifolia ■ Many-branched shrub with ascending to spreading, sometimes arching stems, and silky-hairy young growth. Crowded or clustered leaves, ½–1½in (1–4cm) long, are linear to narrowly elliptic or lance-shaped, with margins rolled under, often prickle-tipped, and grayish green to deep green above, paler and silky-downy beneath. Bears spider-like racemes, 1½–3in (4–8cm) long, of pink to light red or cream flowers, mainly from late autumn to early summer. Good for hedging. ↕ 20–120in (0.5–3m), ↔ 3–15ft (1–5m). New South Wales, Victoria. ❄ (min. 41°F/5°C)

Grevillea 'Poorinda Constance' (inset: flower detail)

***G.* 'Sandra Gordon'.** Large shrub or small tree, becoming spreading and open unless pruned regularly. The pinnate, ovate leaves, 6–10in (16–25cm) long, with linear leaflets, to 3in (8cm) long, are bronze to silvery when young, maturing to deep green above, silver-hairy beneath. Bright yellow flowers are borne in one-sided to almost cylindrical racemes, 3–5½in (8–14cm) long, all year. ↕ 10–20ft (3–6m), ↔ 6–11ft (2–3.5m). ❀ (min. 45°F/7°C)
G. sulphurea see *G. juniperina* f. *sulphurea*.
G. thelemanniana. Variable prostrate to low-growing shrub with variable, pinnate, long-haired, gray-green to green leaves, to 2in (5cm) long, with narrowly linear segments. In late winter and spring, bears one-sided terminal racemes, to 1in (2.5cm) long, of green-tipped, pink flowers. ↕ to 5ft (1.5m), ↔ to 6ft (2m). Western Australia. ❀ (min. 45°F/7°C)
***G.* 'White Wings'.** Strong-growing, dense shrub with spreading to ascending branches. Bears broadly ovate, pinnate, light green leaves, 1½in (4cm) long, with numerous slender, linear leaflets with recurved margins and spines. Produces terminal and axillary, erect, loose racemes, to 1in (2.5cm) long, of fragrant white flowers, intermittently throughout the year. ↕ 6–11ft (2–3.5m), ↔ 10–15ft (3–5m). ❀ (min. 45°F/7°C)

GREWIA

TILIACEAE

Genus of approximately 150 species of deciduous and evergreen trees, shrubs, and climbers from Africa, S. and E. Asia, and Australia, found in habitats ranging from tropical woodland to dry, open savanna. The alternate leaves are simple and entire or toothed, with persistent stipules. The small, 5-petaled flowers have central bosses of many stamens, and may be borne singly or in small, terminal or axillary cymes. Where not hardy, grow in a temperate greenhouse. In warmer climates, grow as specimens or in shrub plantings.
• **CULTIVATION** Under glass, grow in soil-based potting mix in full light. Top-dress or pot on in spring. Water freely from spring to autumn, applying a balanced liquid fertilizer monthly. Water sparingly in winter. Outdoors, grow in fertile, moist but well-drained soil in full sun. Pruning group 1; may need restrictive pruning under glass.
• **PROPAGATION** Sow seed at 61–64°F (16–18°C), or layer, in spring.
• **PESTS AND DISEASES** Whiteflies and spider mites may infest plants under glass.

G. occidentalis (Four corners). Evergreen shrub, scandent climber, or small tree with slender, erect to spreading branches and shoots covered with soft, star-like hairs. The leaves are ovate-diamond-shaped to lance-shaped, ¾–3in (2–8cm) long, with rounded teeth, and hairless or softly hairy. In summer, bears small, stalked, axillary cymes of flowers, 1¼in (3cm) across, with pink sepals and mauve to purple or white petals; they are followed by fleshy, 4-lobed, yellowish orange, then purple fruit, 1in (2.5cm) across. ↕ 6–20ft (2–6m), ↔ 5–12ft (1.5–4m). Southern Africa. ❀ (min. 45°F/7°C)

Greyia sutherlandii

GREYIA

GREYIACEAE

Genus of 3 species of evergreen shrubs or small trees from South Africa, found in habitats ranging from slopes and rocky places to savanna. They are grown for their showy, 5-petaled flowers, which are borne in terminal racemes. The simple leaves are broadly ovate to rounded, alternate or spiraling, and generally clustered at the stem tips. Where not hardy, grow in a cool greenhouse. In warm climates, plant at the base of a house wall or in a shrub or mixed border.
• **CULTIVATION** Under glass, grow in soil-based potting mix, with added sharp sand, in full light. Top-dress or pot on in spring. Water freely from spring to autumn, applying a balanced liquid fertilizer monthly. Water sparingly in winter. Outdoors, grow in fertile, moist but well-drained soil in full sun. Pruning group 8; may need restrictive pruning under glass.
• **PROPAGATION** Sow seed at 55–61°F (13–16°C), or air layer, in spring.
• **PESTS AND DISEASES** Spider mites may be troublesome under glass.

G. sutherlandii ▣ (Natal bottlebrush). Evergreen, large shrub or small tree of open, stiff habit, with rounded to heart-shaped, irregularly toothed, leathery, mid-green leaves, 2–4in (5–10cm) long. Old leaves often turn bright red before falling. Tubular-bell-shaped, crimson to brick-red flowers, ¾in (2cm) long, with long stamens, are borne in racemes, 4–6in (10–15cm) long, in spring, just before or with the newly expanding leaves. ↕ 6–15ft (2–5m), ↔ 5–10ft (1.5–3m). South Africa (KwaZulu–Natal). ❀ (min. 45°F/7°C)

GRINDELIA

Gum plant, Rosinweed, Tarweed

ASTERACEAE

Genus of about 60 species of annuals, evergreen, frequently woody-based perennials, and some subshrubs from sunny, dry, often rocky habitats in North, Central, and South America. They are cultivated for their daisy-like, bright yellow flowerheads, borne singly or in corymbs, which often glisten with sticky white resin in bud. The stems and the simple, alternate, entire or toothed, sometimes stalkless leaves are also usually sticky. Suitable for a sunny border, wild garden, or hot, dry bank.

Grindelia chiloensis

• **CULTIVATION** Grow in full sun in poor to moderately fertile, well-drained soil. Remove frost-damaged growth in spring.
• **PROPAGATION** Sow seed in containers in a cold frame in spring. Root semi-ripe cuttings in summer.
• **PESTS AND DISEASES** Somewhat prone to root rot and dieback, as well as scale insects and mealybugs.

G. chiloensis ▣ syn. *G. speciosa*. Bushy, evergreen subshrub with thick, upright shoots and mostly basal, inversely lance-shaped to obovate, entire or toothed, grayish green leaves, to 5in (13cm) long. Bears large, bright yellow flowerheads, 3in (8cm) across, singly on long stalks, throughout summer. ↕↔ 3ft (1m). Argentina, Chile. ❀ (min. 41°F/5°C)
G. humilis (Marsh grindelia). Bushy perennial with wedge-shaped to oblong-lance-shaped, toothed, leathery, mid-green leaves, ¾–3in (2–8cm) long. From summer to autumn, bears solitary yellow flowerheads, 1¼–2in (3–5cm) across. ↕ to 5ft (1.5m), ↔ to 3ft (1m). California. Zone 7b.
G. integrifolia. Erect, woody-based perennial producing several stems with stalkless, lance-shaped to inversely lance-shaped, usually toothed leaves, 14in (35cm) long. Bright yellow flowerheads, 1–1½in (2.5–4cm) across, are borne singly or in corymbs to 5in (13cm) across, from midsummer to early autumn. ↕ to 32in (80cm), ↔ 24in (60cm). W. North America. Zone 7b.
G. maritima. Upright, loosely branched perennial with narrowly oblong-lance-shaped, mid-green leaves, to 7in (18cm) long. In late summer and early autumn, bears terminal, solitary yellow flowerheads, 1½in (4cm) across. ↕ to 32in (80cm), ↔ 12in (30cm). California. Zone 7b.
G. robusta. Erect, woody-based perennial with thick, branched stems and oblong-lance-shaped, entire or sharply toothed, basal leaves, to 7in (18cm) long, and smaller, ovate-lance-shaped to linear-oblong stem leaves. Bears solitary, yellow flowerheads, to 2in (5cm) across, from spring to autumn. ↕ to 4ft (1.2m), ↔ 24in (60cm). California, Baja California. Zone 7b.
G. speciosa see *G. chiloensis*.
G. stricta (Pacific grindelia). Clump-forming perennial with both decumbent and upright stems, producing oblong to inversely lance-shaped, entire or minutely toothed leaves, to 10in (25cm) long. Bears solitary, bright yellow flowerheads, to 2in (5cm) across, from midsummer to early autumn. ↕ to 36in (90cm), ↔ 24in (60cm). W. North America. Zone 7b.

GRISELINIA

CORNACEAE

Genus of 6 species of dioecious, evergreen shrubs and trees from forest and coastline of New Zealand and South America. Grown for their handsome, simple, alternate, leathery leaves, they also bear inconspicuous, yellow-green flowers in late spring. In autumn, they produce purple fruits if plants of both sexes are present. Grow as specimen plants for a shrub border, or as hedging; ideal as windbreaks in coastal regions. Where not hardy, grow in a cool greenhouse.
• **CULTIVATION** Under glass, grow in soil-based potting mix, with added sharp sand, in full light. When in growth, water moderately and apply a balanced liquid fertilizer monthly; water sparingly in winter. Outdoors, grow in light, fertile, well-drained soil in full sun, with shelter from cold, drying winds. Pruning group 9; may need restrictive pruning under glass.
• **PROPAGATION** Sow seed at 55–64°F (13–18°C) in spring. Take semi-ripe cuttings in summer.
• **PESTS AND DISEASES** Susceptible to fungal leaf spot.

G. littoralis (Broadleaf). Vigorous, dense, upright shrub (or tree in very mild areas) with broadly ovate to ovate-oblong, glossy, leathery, bright apple-green leaves, to 4in (10cm) long. ↕ to 25ft (8m), ↔ 15ft (5m). New Zealand. Zone 8. **'Dixon's Cream'** ▣ bears leaves boldly marked in the center with creamy white; ↕ 10ft (3m), ↔ 6ft (2m). **'Variegata'** ▣ has leaves irregularly margined creamy white and streaked gray-green; ↕ 10ft (3m), ↔ 6ft (2m).

Griselinia littoralis 'Dixon's Cream'

Griselinia littoralis 'Variegata'

G. lucida. Vigorous, upright shrub with broadly ovate, leathery, glossy, mid-green leaves, very unequal at the bases, to 7in (18cm) long. ↕ 20ft (6m), ↔ 15ft (5m). New Zealand. ❄ (min. 50°F/10°C)

GRUSONIA

CACTACEAE

Genus of 17 species of cacti native to the deserts of S.W. US, Baja California, and parts of N. Mexico, bearing small, cylindrical, early deciduous leaves. The diurnal flowers, in pink, purple, yellow, or white, are borne laterally or almost apically. The fruit produced can be dry or fleshy and is sometimes dehiscent, often sterile. These cacti can be landscaped, generally to the exclusion of children or pets, as the spines of some species are extremely sharp.

• **CULTIVATION** Under glass, grow in standard cactus potting mix in full light or bright filtered light. Large species are best planted directly into a greenhouse border. From early spring to midautumn, water only when approaching dryness and apply a balanced liquid fertilizer 3 or 4 times; this should be diluted from ¼ to ½ strength. Keep reasonably dry at other times. Outdoors, grow in moderately fertile, sharply well drained, gritty, humus-rich soil infull sun. See also pp.48–49.

• **PROPAGATION** Sow pre-soaked seed at 70°F (21°C) in spring. Separate, detach and root stem segments. Handle plants using folded newspaper; dispose after use.

• **PESTS AND DISEASES** Cladode rots, zonate leaf spot, and black spot, as well as mealybugs and scale insects, are common. Bacterial soft rot and several viruses also occur.

G. bradtiana. ▣ Low-branching cactus forming dense, impenetrable mats on desert flats and hills. Green stem segments produce early deciduous leaves, which are linear, fleshy, and green. Bears white areoles, ⅛–⅕in (3–5mm), with 8–10 low and tuberculate ribs, to 3in (8cm), and yellow flowers, 1¼–1½in (3–4cm) long. Fruit is ellipsoidal and strongly umbilicate. ↕ 2–6in (5–15cm) high, ↔ 1½–2½in (4–6cm). Coahuila, Mexico. ❄ (min. 50°F/10°C)

Grusonia bradtiana

G. clavata. Low-spreading grasslands cactus, with widely formed mats. Stem segments are short, club-shaped, and narrowing basally with ovate tubercles. Round areoles with white to gray wool produce 7–15 spines, mostly at distal ends; flochids are yellowish white, to ⅕in (5mm) long, producing bright yellow flowers, to 1in (2.5cm). Barrel-shaped to ellipsoidal fruit is yellow and fleshy, 1¼–1¾in (3–4.5cm) long and half as wide. ↕ 2in–6in(5–15cm),↔ 1½–1¼in (1.5–3cm). Great Plains of US into N. Mexico. ❄ (min. 50°F/10°C)

G. invicta ▣ Small, low-growing, many-stemmed cactus, forming dense clustered masses, and conferring a ferocious appearance. Stem segments are widely obovate to club-shaped, 3–4in (8–10cm) long and 1½–2½in (4–6cm) wide, bearing 10–25 very rigid spines, gray with dark tips, often bent downward, flattened, and 4-angled. Bears yellow flowers, 1½–2in (4–5cm) across, with rather spiny pericarpels, and ovoid, moderately fleshy fruit covered with spines. ↕ 8–18in (20–45cm), ↔ 6ft (2m). C. Baja California Peninsula, Mexico. ❄ (min. 50°F/10°C)

▷ ***Guillauminia albiflora*** see *Aloe albiflora*

Gunnera magellanica

Gunnera manicata

GUNNERA

GUNNERACEAE

Genus of about 45 species of summer-flowering, rhizomatous, herbaceous or evergreen perennials from moist areas in southern Africa, Australasia, and South America. Gunneras vary in size from diminutive and mat-forming to extremely large and clump-forming with massive to ovate, often heart-shaped, lobed, and usually toothed leaves. They are cultivated primarily for their handsome foliage, although in some species the flower spikes and fruits are also attractive. The tiny, usually greenish yellow flowers are borne in dense, upright, brush-like spikes or panicles. Large species are excellent architectural plants for the edge of a pond or stream, or a bog garden, while smaller ones are suitable for a rock garden or an alpine house.

• **CULTIVATION** Grow in deep, permanently moist, humus-rich soil in sun or partial shade. Large species need shelter from cold, drying winds. Small species prefer partial shade, but are best in full sun in areas with cool summers. Where not hardy, protect the crowns of large species in winter with a dry mulch. Most are unsuitable in areas with high heat and humidity.

• **PROPAGATION** Sow seed in containers as soon as ripe, and keep cool but frost-free through the winter; germination is slow. Seed quickly loses viability. Large species may also be increased by taking cuttings of leafy, basal buds in spring. Divide small species in spring.

• **PESTS AND DISEASES** Prone to slug and snail damage outdoors; under glass, may be susceptible to aphids and whiteflies.

G. brasiliensis see *G. manicata.*

G. magellanica ▣ Mat-forming herbaceous perennial with cupped, kidney-shaped, scalloped, dark green leaves, 2–3½in (5–9cm) across, borne on upright stalks, 3–6in (8–15cm) long. In summer, bears compact panicles, ½–5in (1.5–13cm) long, of tiny green flowers, followed by ovoid to spherical, orange-red fruit, ¼in (6mm) across. ↕ 6in (15cm), ↔ 12in (30cm) or more. S. South America, Falkland Islands. Zone 8.

G. manicata ▣ syn. *G. brasiliensis.* Very large, clump-forming herbaceous perennial with rounded to kidney-shaped, palmately lobed, prominently veined, sharply toothed, deep green leaves, to 6ft (2m) long, borne on prickly stalks, to 8ft (2.5m) long. In early summer, branches 6in (15cm) long bear numerous tiny, greenish red flowers in conical, branched panicles, to 3ft (1m) or more tall; these are followed by spherical, red-green fruit, to ⅛in (3mm) long. ↕ 8ft (2.5m), ↔ 10–12ft (3–4m) or more. Colombia to Brazil. Zone 6.

GUZMANIA

BROMELIACEAE

Genus of over 180 species of virtually stemless, evergreen, mainly epiphytic perennials (bromeliads), found in S. Florida, Central America, the West Indies, and N. and W. South America. They occur mainly in the Andean rainforest, to 11,500ft (3,500m) high. Lance-shaped leaves form funnel-shaped rosettes, above or within which flowerheads of tubular, white or yellow flowers, usually ringed by colorful floral bracts, are borne on conspicuous, yellow, orange, or bright red stems, in summer. Where temperatures drop below 59°F (15°C), grow in a warm greenhouse or as houseplants. In warmer areas, grow in shady, humid, moist areas of the garden.

• **CULTIVATION** Under glass, grow in epiphytic bromeliad potting mix in bright filtered or indirect light, or grow epiphytically on artificial tree branches. When in growth, mist daily, preferably in the early morning. In winter, keep barely moist and do not mist. Outdoors, attach to the branches of trees in partial shade. See also p.47.

• **PROPAGATION** Sow seed at 81°F (27°C), or remove offsets, in midspring.

• **PESTS AND DISEASES** Often attacked by mealybugs and fungi causing leaf spots.

G

Guzmania lingulata var. *minor*

Guzmania monostachia

Guzmania sanguinea

Gymnocalycium andreae

G. lingulata. Variable, epiphytic bromeliad with rosettes of narrowly lance-shaped, sometimes red-violet-striped, deep green leaves, 18in (45cm) long, with sheaths brown-scaly beneath. In summer, erect stems bear overlapping, bright red, orange, or pink bracts, around loose corymbs of tubular, yellow-white flowers, 1¾in (4.5cm) long. ↕↔ 12–18in (30–45cm). N. Central America, West Indies to Brazil. ❄ (min. 59°F/15°C) **var. *cardinalis*** has bright red bracts; Colombia, Ecuador. **var. *minor*** ▣ produces dark green sheaths and few-flowered inflorescences with bright red bracts; ↕↔ 9–12in (23–30cm); Central America (Guatemala), N. South America (Colombia to N.E. Brazil). **var. *splendens*** has leaves with longitudinal maroon stripes, maroon beneath, and bears many-flowered inflorescences with purple, red, or pink bracts and strongly hooded floral bracts; West Indies, Guyana.

G. monostachia ▣ syn. *G. monostachya, G. tricolor.* Stemless, epiphytic bromeliad with dense rosettes of lance-shaped to strap-shaped, pale green or yellowish green leaves, to 16in (40cm) long. In summer, produces cylindrical inflorescences, to 6in (15cm) long, with pale green stem bracts and brown-black-striped, green basal bracts. Tubular white flowers, 1–1¼in (2.5–3cm) long, are surrounded by bright red or white bracts. ↕↔ to 16in (40cm). Florida, Central America, West Indies, W. and N. South America. ❄ (min. 59°F/15°C). **'Variegata'** produces green- and white-striped leaves.

G. monostachya see *G. monostachia.*

G. musaica ▣ Stemless, epiphytic bromeliad with rosettes of broadly linear, outward-spreading, brown-sheathed, dark green leaves, to 28in (70cm) long; thinly banded with pale green, deep green, or reddish brown, and often flushed purple beneath. In summer, erect stems with overlapping, bright red or pink bracts produce almost spherical heads of rose-pink floral bracts and white or yellow flowers, to 1¾in (4.5cm) long, with yellow sepals and yellowish white petals. ↕ to 20in (50cm), ↔ 28in (70cm). Panama, Colombia. ❄ (min. 59°F/15°C)

G. sanguinea. Stemless, epiphytic bromeliad with almost flat rosettes of broadly lance-shaped, arching leaves, to 16in (40cm) long, sometimes spotted dark green, becoming suffused with yellow, red, and orange at flowering time. In summer, corymbs of tubular, yellow, greenish yellow, or white flowers, to 3in (8cm) long, with spreading petals and surrounded by red bracts, are borne within the leaf rosettes. Offsets freely. ↕ 8in (20cm), ↔ to 14in (35cm). Costa Rica, Trinidad, Tobago, Venezuela, Colombia, Ecuador. ❄ (min. 59°F/15°C)

G. sprucei. Stemless, stoloniferous, epiphytic bromeliad with rosettes of lance-shaped, mid-green leaves, 12–36in (30–90cm) long, with red-striped, pale green sheaths with dark brown bases. In summer, erect inflorescences of 7–15 flowers, to 1¼–1½in (3–4cm) long, with bright yellow sepals fused to form a tube, and flared white petals, are borne on short stems among overlapping, bright red bracts. ↕↔ to 36in (90cm). Costa Rica, Panama, Colombia. ❄ (min. 59°F/15°C)

G. tricolor see *G. monostachia.*

G. vittata. Stemless, epiphytic bromeliad with loose rosettes of erect, lance-shaped, deep green leaves, 16–24in (40–60cm) long, cross-banded with paler green and sometimes banded purple beneath. In summer, erect stems with overlapping, purple-spotted, pale green basal bracts produce compact, ovoid, branched inflorescences with short spikes of tubular white flowers, ¾in (2cm) or more long. ↕↔ 14–24in (35–60cm). S. and E. Colombia, N.W. Brazil. ❄ (min. 59°F/15°C)

Guzmania lingulata

GYMNOCALYCIUM

CACTACEAE

Genus of 50 or more species of spherical to cylindrical cacti from rocky scrub, hillsides, and grassland in Brazil, Bolivia, Paraguay, Argentina, and Uruguay. Most have prominently rounded, sometimes spiraling ribs, separated by diagonal grooves. Diurnal, funnel- to bell-shaped, often metallic-colored flowers are produced when still young, in early summer, usually from near the crowns or from the side areoles. Where temperatures drop below 50°F (10°C), grow as houseplants or in a warm greenhouse. In warmer climates, grow in a desert garden.

• **CULTIVATION** Under glass, grow in standard cactus potting mix in full light with shade from hot sun, or growth may be stunted or scorched. Water freely in spring and summer, applying a low-nitrogen liquid fertilizer every 4 or 5 weeks. Keep dry in winter. Outdoors, grow in poor, sharply drained soil in full sun or partial shade. See also pp.48–49.

• **PROPAGATION** Sow seed at 66–75°F (19–24°C) in late winter or early spring. Remove offsets in spring.

• **PESTS AND DISEASES** Soft rots caused by fungi and bacteria occur. Mealybugs and scale insects also cause problems.

G. andreae ▣ Clustering cactus with spherical, glossy, dark blue-green or black-green stems, each with about 8 nearly flat, warty ribs. Tubercles are rounded, with a central areole bearing 7 thin, straight, spreading, brown-based white radial spines and 1–3 curved, dark brown centrals. Broadly funnel-shaped, bright yellow flowers, 1¾in (4.5cm) across, with yellow-green, darker-striped outer tepals, are borne in early summer. ↕ to 2½in (6cm), ↔ to 6in (15cm). N. Argentina. ❄ (min. 50°F/10°C); withstands brief periods to 20°F (-7°C).

G. bruchii. Clustering cactus with almost spherical, dark green stems, each with 12 low ribs and rounded, indistinct tubercles. Areoles each produce 10–17 white radial spines, sometimes brown at the base, and 1, occasionally 3, longer white to brown central spines. In early summer, bears funnel-shaped, sometimes faintly scented, pale pink flowers, to 1¾in (4.5cm) across, with dark pink mid-stripes outside. ↕ to 1½in (4cm), ↔ to 4in (10cm). N. Argentina. ❄ (min. 50°F/10°C); withstands brief periods to 10°F (-12°C).

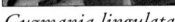

Gymnocalycium mihanovichii 'Red Head'

Gymnocalycium saglionis

G. gibbosum. Simple or offsetting cactus with spherical, later cylindrical, dark bluish green or brownish green stems, each with 12–19 rounded, notched ribs, small, prominent tubercles, and areoles bearing palebrown, later gray spines (7–14 radials and up to 3 centrals). Funnel-shaped flowers, to 3in (8cm) across, pure white or with pale pink mid-stripes on the outsides of the outer tepals, are borne in early summer. ↕ 8in (20cm), ↔ 6in (15cm). Argentina. ❀ (min. 50°F/10°C); withstands brief periods to25°F (-4°C).
***G. mihanovichii* 'Red Head'** ▣ syn. *G. mihanovichii* 'Hibotan', *G. mihanovichii* 'Red Cap'. Cactus bear spherical, flat-topped red stems, each with about 8 prominent, scarcely warty ribs. Areoles bear curved, pinkish white spines (3–5 radials and no centrals). Funnel-shaped pink flowers, to 2in (5cm) across, are borne in early summer. ↕ to 5in (13cm) (grafted), ↔ 2½in (6cm). ❀ (min. 50°F/10°C); endures periods to 28°F (-2°C).
G. quehlianum. Variable cactus with flat-topped, spherical, grayish green stems, bronzing in sun, each with 8–15 ribs divided into prominent, rounded tubercles. Areoles bear pale brown spines (2–5 or more radials and no centrals). Funnel-shaped white flowers, 1¼–2in (3–5cm) across, often pinkish red in the throats, are borne in early summer. ↕ 2in (5cm), ↔ 3in (8cm). N. Argentina. ❀ (min. 50°F/10°C); withstands brief periods to 20°F (-7°C).
G. saglionis ▣ Cactus with flat-topped, spherical, green or bluish green stems, with 10–30 or more ribs bearing prominent, rounded tubercles. Areoles produce red-brown to yellow spines (7–15 radials and about 3 centrals). Broadly funnel-shaped flowers, ¾in (2cm) across, with pinkish white inner tepals and pale green, pink-flushed outer tepals, are borne in early summer. ↕ 4in (10cm), ↔ to 12in (30cm). N.W. Argentina. ❀ (min. 50°F/10°C); withstands brief periods to 20°F (-7°C).
G. schickendantzii. Flat-topped, spherical cactus with 7- to 14-ribbed, dark green stems, bronzing in full sun. Areoles bear gray-red to pale brown, often darker-tipped spines (5–7 radials and no centrals). Funnel-shaped, white to red flowers, to ¾in (2cm) across, with olive-green, often red-tinged outer tepals, are borne in early summer. ↕↔ 4in (10cm). N. Argentina. ❀ (min. 50°F/10°C); withstands brief periods to 28°F (-2°C).

GYMNOCARPIUM

DRYOPTERIDACEAE

Genus of about 5 species of deciduous, rhizomatous, terrestrial ferns found in moist woodland throughout the N. hemisphere. Fronds, arising singly from long, creeping rhizomes in spring, are triangular and 2-pinnate or pinnatifid, with leaf blades that tilt at right angles to the light. Small, rounded sori on undersides of fronds, without protective indusia. Ideal groundcover or rock garden plant in moist, shady places.
• **CULTIVATION** Grow in preferably neutral to acidic, leafy, moist soil, enriched with compost before planting, in light to deep shade.
• **PROPAGATION** Sow spores at 59°F (15°C) when ripe, or divide in spring. See also p.51.
• **PESTS AND DISEASES** Infrequent.

G. dryopteris (Oak fern). Deciduous fern bearing triangular, 2-pinnate fronds, each with a leaf blade 4–7in (10–18cm) long and across, on a stem 4in (10cm) long. Pinnae are triangular, divided into oblong to ovate, toothed and scalloped segments. Pale yellowish green when young, the fronds darken to vivid rich green. ↕ 8in (20cm), ↔ indefinite. Europe, Turkey, N. Asia, China, Japan, Canada, US. Zone 4.
G. robertianum (Limestone polypody). Rhizomatous, deciduous, spreading fern with dull, dark green, broadly triangular, 2- or 3-pinnatifid fronds, to 14in (35cm) long, on stems to 6in (15cm) long. Pinnae are oblong to narrowly triangular, divided into oblong, entire or finely toothed segments. ↕ to 14in (35cm), ↔ indefinite. Eurasia, North America. Zone 4.

GYMNOCLADUS

FABACEAE

Genus of 4 species of dioecious, deciduous trees from rich woodland in E. Asia and North America. They are cultivated for their attractive habit and for their large, 2-pinnate leaves, borne alternately. The small, greenish white flowers are borne in terminal panicles. They are best grown as specimen trees.
• **CULTIVATION** Grow in deep, fertile, moist but well-drained soil in full sun. Pruning group 1.
• **PROPAGATION** Sow seed in containers in a cold frame in autumn, after nicking or soaking. Take root cuttings in winter.
• **PESTS AND DISEASES** Infrequent.

G. dioica (Kentucky coffee tree). Spreading, deciduous tree with large, 2-pinnate leaves, to 3ft (1m) long, each leaflet further divided into 8–14 ovate, softly hairy, dark green leaflets, pink-tinged when young, yellow in autumn. Large panicles of small, star-shaped, greenish white or creamy white flowers, to 12in (30cm) long on female trees, 4–5in (10–13cm) long on males, are borne in early summer, followed on female plants by pendent pods, to 10in (25cm) long. Seeds are toxic if ingested. ↕ 70ft (20m) or more, ↔ 50ft (15m). C. and E. North America. Zone 5.

▷ ***Gymnogramma triangularis*** see *Pityrogramma triangularis*

Gynandriris sisyrinchium

GYNANDRIRIS

IRIDACEAE

Genus of 9 species of small, cormous perennials occurring in garigue, grassy pastures, and stony slopes in South Africa and from the Mediterranean to Pakistan. In spring, they bear narrow, channeled, basal leaves and a succession of small, short-lived, iris-like flowers, each with 3 large, pendent outer petals and 3 usually smaller inner petals. Plant on a warm, sunny bank or by a warm wall. Where marginally hardy, grow in an alpine house or bulb frame.
• **CULTIVATION** Grow in moderately fertile, well-drained soil that is moist in winter and spring but dries out in summer, in full sun. Where not hardy, grow in soil-based potting mix, with added sharp sand, in a bulb frame or alpine house.
• **PROPAGATION** Sow seed in containers in a cold frame as soon as ripe, and overwinter seedlings in frost-free conditions. Remove offsets in summer.
• **PESTS AND DISEASES** Infrequent.

G. sisyrinchium ▣ syn. *Iris sisyrinchium.* Cormous perennial with 1 or 2 semi-erect or prostrate, narrow, basal leaves, ¾–3in (2–8cm) long. In spring, bears a succession of small, iris-like flowers, ¾–1½in (2–4cm) across; opening in the afternoon, they vary from pale lavender-blue to violet-blue, with a white, yellow, or orange mark on the 3 larger petals. ↕ 4–8in (10–20cm), PD2in (5cm). Mediterranean to S.W. Asia. ❀ (min. 41°F/5°C)

GYNURA

ASTERACEAE

Genus of about 50 species of evergreen perennials and subshrubs, some scandent and trailing, from tropical woodland in Africa and Asia. The toothed leaves are alternate, simple, and pinnate or pinnatifid. The flowerheads, usually borne singly or in corymbs at the tips of the branches, lack ray florets; they resemble groundsel (*Senecio*) flowerheads, but are larger and more colorful. Where temperatures fall below 55°F (13°C), grow as houseplants or in a temperate or warm greenhouse. Elsewhere, use in a shady, moist border.
• **CULTIVATION** Under glass, grow in soil-based potting mix in bright filtered light. Pot on or top-dress in spring.

Gynura aurantiaca

During the growing season, water freely and apply a balanced liquid fertilizer monthly. Provide scandent species with light support. Pinch out tips to stop plants from becoming too leggy and to encourage young shoots. Outdoors, grow in fertile, moist but well-drained soil in partial shade.
• **PROPAGATION** Root softwood cuttings in late spring or semi-ripe cuttings in summer, both with bottom heat.
• **PESTS AND DISEASES** Aphids and spider mites may be troublesome under glass.

G. aurantiaca ▣ (Purple velvet plant). Woody-based perennial or subshrub, erect at first, then semi-scandent, densely covered in velvety, violet-purple hairs. Simple, ovate to broadly elliptic leaves, 4–8in (10–20cm) long, are coarsely toothed, semi-lustrous, deep green, and overlaid with purple hairs. Orange-yellow flowerheads, ½–¾in (1.5–2cm) across, tinted purple with age, are borne in loose, terminal corymbs, to 1¼in (3cm) across, mainly in winter. ↕ to 24in (60cm), or 6–10ft (2–3m) with support; ↔ 18–48in (45–120cm). Indonesia (Java). ❀ (min. 55°F/13°C). **'Purple Passion'** syn. *G. sarmentosa* of gardens, is trailing or semi-twining, with purple-haired stems and lance-shaped, lobed leaves, 2½–5½in (6–14cm) long, densely covered with red-purple hairs beneath, more lightly above; ↕ 3–10ft (1–3m), ↔ 3ft (1m) or more.
***G. sarmentosa* of gardens** see *G. aurantiaca* 'Purple Passion'.

GYPSOPHILA

CARYOPHYLLACEAE

Genus of over 100 species of annuals and herbaceous, semi-evergreen, or evergreen perennials, sometimes woody-based, some cushion- or mat-forming. They occur in alpine habitats, dry, stony slopes, or sandy steppes, usually on alkaline soils, from the E. Mediterranean to the Caucasus, C. Asia, and N.W. China. They are valued particularly for their small, 5-petaled, star-shaped to shallowly trumpet-shaped, white or pink flowers, which are either borne singly or in spreading panicles. They usually have lance-shaped to linear-lance-shaped, glaucous leaves, borne in opposite pairs. Larger species are useful annual or border plants, and provide good cut flowers. Alpine species are ideal for a raised bed, dry-stone wall, scree bed, or rock garden.

Gypsophila cerastioides

Gypsophila elegans 'Rosea'

Gypsophila repens 'Dorothy Teacher'

G

• **CULTIVATION** Grow in deep, light, preferably alkaline, sharply drained soil in full sun. Most dislike winter moisture, although *G.* 'Rosenschleier' tolerates moist soil.
• **PROPAGATION** Sow seed of annuals *in situ* in spring. Sow seed of perennials at 55–64°F (13–18°C) in winter, or in a cold frame in spring. Perennials may also be increased by root cuttings (species only), or by grafting (for named cultivars), both in late winter.
• **PESTS AND DISEASES** Crown gall, bacterial soft rot, and crown and stem rot are common.

G. acutifolia. Deep-rooting, many-branched herbaceous perennial with stems bearing lance-shaped, pointed, grayish green leaves, ¾–3in (2–8cm) long. Spreading panicles, 2in (5cm) across, of star-shaped, pale pink flowers, to ¾in (2cm) across, are borne from midsummer to early fall. ↕3ft (1m), ↔ 5ft (1.5m). N. Caucasus, S. Russia. Zone 5.
G. aretioides. Very dense, hard, cushion-forming, evergreen perennial with tiny, oblong, fleshy, gray-green leaves, 1⁄16–¼in (2–6mm) long. Bears small, usually solitary, stemless, star-shaped white flowers in summer. Ideal for an alpine house or scree bed. ↕2in (5cm), ↔ to 6in (15cm). Caucasus, mountains of N. Iran. Zone 5b.
G. cerastioides ■ Loose, mat-forming, semi-evergreen perennial with tufts of gray-hairy leaves, ¼–½in (6–15mm) long, that are long-stalked and spoon-shaped, or almost stalkless and broadly obovate. Loose panicles of shallowly trumpet-shaped white flowers, to ½in (1.5cm) across, veined and faintly tinged pink, are borne over long periods from late spring to summer. ↕2in (5cm), ↔ to 6in (15cm). Himalayas. Zone 5.
G. elegans ■ (Annual baby's breath). Erect, branching annual with narrow, oblong-lance-shaped to linear-lance-shaped, gray-green leaves, ¾–1½in (2–4cm) long. Loosely branched panicles, to 4in (10cm) or more across, of 4-petaled, star-shaped, white or carmine-pink, sometimes pink- or purple-veined flowers, to ½in (1.5cm) across, are produced on long, slender stalks in summer. Good for cut flowers. ↕ to 24in (60cm), ↔ 12in (30cm). S. Ukraine, Turkey. **'Bright Rose'** produces bright rose-pink flowers. **'Bristol Fairy'** has large, double white flowers, to ½in (1.5cm) across, but is less robust. **'Carminea'** has deep carmine-pink flowers. **'Compacta Plena'** has double, soft pink to white flowers; ↕8–12in (20–30cm), ↔ to 24in (60cm). **'Covent Garden'** bears large, white flowers, to ½in (1.5cm) across. **'Flamingo'** is less robust than the species, with larger, double, pale pink flowers, to ½in (1.5cm) across; ↕30–36in (75–90cm), ↔ 36in (90cm). **'Giant White'** has large white flowers, to ¾in (2cm) across. **'Red Cloud'** flowers very profusely, bearing deep carmine-pink blooms. **'Rosea'** ■ produces pale rose-pink flowers.
***G. muralis* 'Garden Bride'** ■ Dense, mounded annual with lance-shaped, mid-green leaves, to ½in (1.5cm) long. Bears loose, open panicles of star-shaped, pale pink to white flowers, ⅛–¼in (3–6mm) across, in summer. Useful in a border or hanging basket. ↕10–12in (25–30cm), ↔ 12in (30cm).
G. paniculata (Baby's breath). Tap-rooted herbaceous perennial with branching stems forming an airy mound of linear-lance-shaped, usually hairless, glaucous leaves, 2–3in (5–8cm) long. In mid- and late summer, bears numerous loose, many-flowered panicles of shallowly trumpet-shaped white flowers, to ⅜in (9mm) across, forming mounds to 18in (45cm) or more across. ↕↔ to 4ft (1.2m). C. and E. Europe. Zone 4. **'Early Snowball'** has mostly double, white flowers; ↕36in (90cm). **'Festival'** is vigorous, erect, and compact, and has double white, sometimes pink-blushed flowers; ↕24in (60cm). **'Perfecta'** has large, double white flowers twice the size of *G. elegans* 'Bristol Fairy'; ↕3–4ft (1–1.2m). **'Pink Star'** has thread-like stems and masses of large, double, pale pink flowers all summer; ↕18in (45cm). **'Snowflake'** blooms earlier, has double white flowers, and is heat resistant; ↕36in (90cm). **'Viette's Dwarf'** is compact, with double pink flowers; ↕12–16in(30–40cm).
G. repens. Mat-forming, semi-evergreen perennial with linear, often sickle-shaped, mid- or slightly bluish green leaves, ½–1¼in (1.5–3cm) long. Over long periods in summer, bears loose, corymb-like panicles, 1½–3in (4–8cm) across, of star-shaped, white, pink, or pink-purple flowers, to ½in (1.5cm) across. ↕8in (20cm), ↔ 12–20in (30–50cm). Mountains of C. and S. Europe. Zone 4. **'Alba'** has creeping foliage and white flowers; ↕4in (10cm). **'Dorothy Teacher'** ■ has a neat habit, blue-green leaves, and bears pale pink flowers that darken with age; ↕2in (5cm), ↔ to 16in (40cm). **'Fratensis'** has gray-green leaves and pale pink flowers; ↕2–3in (5–8cm),↔ to 12in (30cm).
***G.* 'Rosenschleier'** ■ syn. *G.* 'Rosy Veil'. Vigorous, dense, mound-forming, semi-evergreen perennial with branching stems that bear linear-lance-shaped, usually hairless, bluish green leaves, 1–1½in (2.5–4cm) long. In mid- and late summer, bears numerous loose, many-flowered panicles of double flowers, ½in (1.5cm) across, opening white and becoming very pale pink; they form dense clouds of blooms, 18in (45cm) wide. ↕16–20in (40–50cm), ↔ 3ft (1m). Zone 3.
***G.* 'Rosy Veil'** see *G.*'Rosenschleier'.

Gypsophila elegans

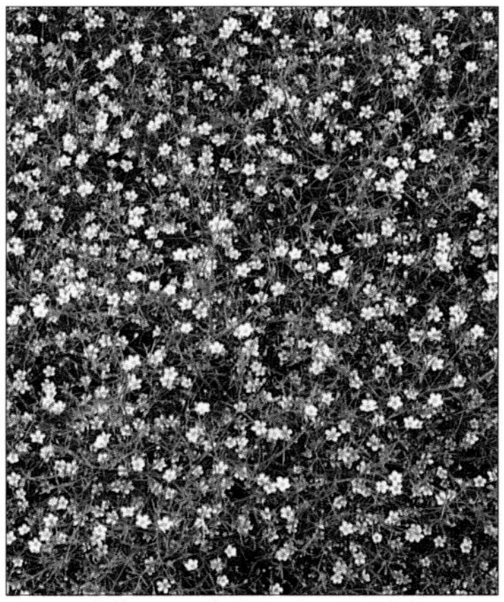
Gypsophila muralis 'Garden Bride'

Gypsophila 'Rosenschleier'

H

HAAGEOCEREUS

CACTACEAE

Genus of 20 species (some authorities accept only 5–10) of shrubby or tree-like, columnar, solitary or clump-forming cacti from dry coastal to mountainous areas, to 8,000ft (2,500m) high, in Peru and Chile. They have ribbed, densely spiny stems and, in summer, bear tubular-funnel-shaped flowers near the tops of the stems; these open from late afternoon until well into the following morning. The green, yellow, or reddish pink fruits, 1¼–1½in (3–4cm) long, are spherical to ovoid, sparsely scaly, hairy, and fleshy. In temperate regions, grow in a temperate greenhouse. In warmer climates, use in a desert garden.

• **CULTIVATION** Under glass, grow in standard cactus potting mix in full light. Provide low humidity and good ventilation. In the growing season, water moderately and apply a low-nitrogen liquid fertilizer monthly; keep completely dry in winter. Outdoors, grow in poor, sharply drained soil in full sun. Protect from excessive winter moisture. See also pp.48–49.

• **PROPAGATION** Sow seed at 66–75°F (19–24°C) in spring, or root stem cuttings in spring or summer.

• **PESTS AND DISEASES** Susceptible to aphids while flowering and prone to rot.

H. acranthus ▣ Columnar cactus with sparsely branched curving or upright stems, and 12–14 ribs forming tubercles. Closely set yellow to dark brown areoles bear 1 or more downward-pointing central spines, to 1½in (4cm), 20–30 yellowish radial spines, to ⅜in (1cm). Flowers are greenish white; fruit is green and round. ↕ 3–6ft (1–2m), ↔ 3in (8cm). Peru. ❀ (min. 52°F/11°C)

H. versicolor ▣ Erect, clump-forming cactus, often branching from the base,

Haageocereus acranthus

Haageocereus versicolor

with 16- to 22-ribbed, dark green stems. Brown-felted areoles bear yellow to reddish brown spines, composed of 25–30 radials and 1–4 longer centrals. White flowers, 2½–3in (6–8cm) long, with pinkish green outer segments and light green tubes, are borne in summer. ↕ 6ft (2m), ↔ 3ft (1m). N. Peru. ❀ (min. 52°F/11°C)

HAASTIA

Vegetable sheep

ASTERACEAE

Genus of 3 species of cushion-forming or clump-forming, occasionally trailing perennials or subshrubs from high-altitude scree and rocky sites, to 6,500ft (2,000m), in the mountains of New Zealand. They have variably shaped, small, usually densely hairy, overlapping leaves, ½–1½in (1.5–4cm) long, and tiny, daisy-like flowerheads. Vegetable sheep are fascinating foliage plants but difficult to cultivate. Grow in an alpine house, because they must have protection from winter moisture.

• **CULTIVATION** In an alpine house, grow in soil-based potting mix with 1 part added leaf mold and 2 parts grit; apply a top-dressing of grit and wedges of small stones to keep the cushion of leaves clear of the soil surface. Provide moderate humidity and good ventilation. When in growth, water moderately but avoid wetting the foliage; keep just moist in winter.

• **PROPAGATION** Sow seed in containers in an open frame as soon as ripe; water seedlings from below. Root rosette cuttings in early summer.

• **PESTS AND DISEASES** Prone to aphids and spider mites in dry conditions.

H. pulvinaris (Vegetable sheep). Extremely dense, cushion-forming perennial with tightly packed branches concealed by rosetted, overlapping, broadly wedge-shaped, gray, tawny-hairy leaves, to ½in (1.5cm) long. In summer, produces insignificant white flowerheads, which are hidden within the cushions. ↕ 2in (5cm), ↔ to 4in (10cm) or more. New Zealand. Zone 7.

HABENARIA

ORCHIDACEAE

Genus of 500–600 species of evergreen and deciduous, terrestrial orchids found in grassland in both tropical and temperate regions, especially in tropical South America, temperate North America, Africa, and Asia. They have fleshy, underground tubers and produce basal tufts of smooth, dark green leaves. Smaller, sheathing leaves are produced on leafy stems, which bear terminal racemes, 5–9in (13–23cm) long, of mostly green or white, hooded flowers with brightly colored lips. Grow hardy species in humus-rich soil in a woodland.

• **CULTIVATION** Cool- to intermediate-growing orchids. Grow in terrestrial orchid potting mix in bright filtered light. Pot on in spring. During the growing season, water freely and apply a dilute balanced liquid fertilizer at every third watering; keep just moist in winter. See also p.46.

• **PROPAGATION** Divide tubers when the foliage has died down.

• **PESTS AND DISEASES** Spider mites, aphids, whiteflies, mealybugs, and rust.

H. rhodocheila. Deciduous, terrestrial orchid with fleshy tubers and an erect stem bearing 4–6 linear to lance-shaped, dark green leaves, 2½–5in (6–13cm) long. Upright racemes of green flowers, 1in (2.5cm) across, with deeply 3-lobed, bold, scarlet, orange, or yellow lips, are borne in summer. ↕ 12in (30cm), ↔ 8in (20cm). S. China to Malaysia and the Philippines. ❀ (min. 55–61°F/13–16°C; max. 86°F/30°C)

HABERLEA

GESNERIACEAE

Genus of 2 species of stemless, evergreen perennials from shaded, rocky habitats in the Balkans. They have basal rosettes of obovate, scalloped, dark green leaves, and loose umbels of up to 6 nodding, trumpet-shaped, 2-lipped flowers, borne from spring to early summer. They are attractive plants for a wall, rock crevice, rock garden, or alpine house.

Haberlea ferdinandi-coburgii

Haberlea rhodopensis 'Virginalis'

• **CULTIVATION** In an alpine house, grow in soil-based potting mix with added grit or sharp sand and leaf mold, in bright indirect light. In the growing season, water freely and apply a half-strength balanced liquid fertilizer monthly. Outdoors, grow in moist but well-drained, acidic to neutral, gritty, humus-rich soil in full or partial shade, planted on their sides in vertical rock crevices to avoid an accumulation of moisture in the foliage rosettes. Protect from excessive winter moisture and cold, drying winds, and avoid root disturbance.

• **PROPAGATION** Sow seed at 55–64°F (13–18°C) in spring. Divide, or root leaf cuttings, in early summer.

• **PESTS AND DISEASES** Slugs and snails.

H. ferdinandi-coburgii ▣ syn. *H. rhodopensis* var. *ferdinandi-coburgii.* Dense, rosette-forming perennial with obovate to oblong-ovate, coarsely scalloped leaves, 1¼–3in (3–8cm) long, smooth and almost hairless above, finely hairy beneath. Umbels of pale lavender flowers, ½–1in (1.5–2.5cm) across, darker lavender and yellow-spotted at the throats, are borne from spring to early summer. ↕ to 6in (15cm), ↔ to 10in (25cm). Bulgaria. Zone 5b.

H. rhodopensis. Dense, rosette-forming perennial with obovate to ovate-oblong, coarsely scalloped leaves, 1¼–3in (3–8cm) long, softly hairy above and beneath. Umbels of pale blue-violet flowers, to 1in (2.5cm) across, are borne from spring to early summer. ↕ to 6in (15cm), ↔ to 10in (25cm). Bulgaria, N.E. Greece. Zone 5.

var. *ferdinandi-coburgii* see *H. ferdinandi-coburgii.* **'Virginalis'** ▣ has pure white flowers.

HABRANTHUS

AMARYLLIDACEAE

Genus of 10 species of bulbous perennials from dry, upland slopes in temperate South America. They have semi-erect, narrow, linear, basal leaves, evergreen in some species, deciduous or developing after the flowers in others. Solitary, funnel-shaped flowers, held at an angle to the stems, are borne from summer to autumn. They are followed by seed capsules, which quickly ripen and open to reveal conspicuous black seeds; the seed capsules are sometimes produced at the same time as the

Habranthus robustus

flowers. Grow in a cool greenhouse, or, where marginally hardy, at the base of a warm, sunny wall. In frost-free regions, grow at the front of a bed or border.

• **CULTIVATION** Under glass, plant bulbs 3–4in (7–10cm) deep, in soil-based potting mix with added grit and leaf mold, in full light. Water moderately as growth begins, freely in leaf; reduce water as foliage dies back, and keep barely moist when dormant. Apply a balanced liquid fertilizer weekly when in bud. Outdoors, plant bulbs in spring with the necks above the soil surface. Grow in fertile, well-drained, neutral to alkaline soil in full sun. Protect from excessive winter moisture.

• **PROPAGATION** Sow seed at 61°F (16°C) as soon as ripe. Remove offsets in winter and pot up separately.

• **PESTS AND DISEASES** Infrequent.

H. andersonii see *H. tubispathus.*

H. robustus ■ syn. *Zephyranthes robusta.* Robust, bulbous perennial with deep green, basal leaves, 6–8in (15–20cm) long, emerging in summer at the same time as, or just before, leafless stems bear solitary, open funnel-shaped, pale pink flowers, 2½in (6cm) across. ↕ 8–12in (20–30cm), PD2in (5cm). Brazil. ❄ (min. 41°F/5°C)

H. texanus see *H. tubispathus.*

H. tubispathus, syn. *H. andersonii, H. texanus, Zephyranthes andersonii.* Upright, bulbous perennial producing a succession of solitary flowering stems, each bearing a small, funnel-shaped, coppery red, orange, or yellow flower, 1in (2.5cm) across, in summer. The deep green, basal leaves, 5–6in (13–15cm) long, emerge after the flowers. ↕ 4–6in (10–15cm), PD1in (2.5cm). Texas, S. Brazil, Uruguay, E. Argentina, S. Chile. ❄ (min. 45°F/7°C)

HACQUETIA *syn.* DONDIA

APIACEAE

Genus of a single species of small, clump-forming, rhizomatous perennial found in lowland and upland woodland in Europe. Grown for its foliage and early, long-lasting, tiny yellow flowers surrounded by bright green bracts, it is suitable for moist, shady sites, such as a rock or woodland garden.

• **CULTIVATION** Grow in humus-rich, moist but well-drained, neutral to acidic soil in partial shade.

• **PROPAGATION** Sow seed in containers in a cold frame as soon as ripe, or in

Hacquetia epipactis

autumn. Divide in spring. Insert root cuttings in winter.

• **PESTS AND DISEASES** Slugs and snails may damage young growth in spring.

H. epipactis ■ syn. *Dondia epipactis.* Rhizomatous, clump-forming perennial with glossy, emerald-green leaves that develop fully only after flowering. The leaves, to 3in (8cm) long, are rounded, with 3 wedge-shaped, toothed lobes. Tiny yellow flowers, surrounded by bright green bracts, are borne in dense umbels, to 1½in (4cm) across, in late winter and early spring. ↕ 2in (5cm), to 6in (15cm) after flowering, ↔ 6–12in (15–30cm). Europe. Zone 6.

HAEMANTHUS

Blood lily

AMARYLLIDACEAE

Genus of 21 species of bulbous perennials, some of them evergreen, from grassy, rocky hillsides in South Africa. From summer to autumn, and occasionally in winter, they bear small flowers in showy umbels that resemble shaving brushes. These are borne above erect, or semi-erect to spreading, strap-shaped to lance-shaped, broadly elliptic, or rounded, mid- to dark green, basal leaves. Where not hardy, grow in a temperate greenhouse or as houseplants. In frost-free areas, grow in semi-shaded or sunny sites between shrubs. All parts of blood lilies may cause mild stomach upset if ingested; contact with the sap may irritate skin.

• **CULTIVATION** Plant bulbs with the necks just above the soil surface, in autumn or winter. Under glass, grow in soil-based potting mix with added leaf mold and grit, in full light. Provide bright filtered light when buds open, to prolong flowering. When in growth, water freely and apply a dilute, balanced liquid fertilizer monthly; keep evergreen species just moist when dormant, and deciduous species dry after flowering. Blood lilies flower best when pot-bound and may remain in the same container for many years; if necessary, pot on as growth begins. Outdoors, grow in well-drained, moderately fertile, neutral to alkaline soil in sun or dappled shade.

• **PROPAGATION** Sow seed at 61–64°F (16–18°C) as soon as ripe. Remove and pot up offsets in early spring.

• **PESTS AND DISEASES** Soft rot, anthracnose, and mealybugs may be troublesome.

H. albiflos (Shaving brush plant, White paintbrush). Evergreen, bulbous perennial producing pairs of semi-erect then spreading, broadly strap-shaped, mid-green leaves, to 16in (40cm) long, sometimes spotted white, with hairy margins. From autumn to winter, thick stems bear brush-like heads, to 1¼–3in (3–8cm) across, of up to 50 small white flowers with protruding stamens; these are followed by ovoid, fleshy, white to red fruit. ↕ 8–12in (20–30cm), PD6in (15cm). South Africa (Eastern Cape, Western Cape). ❄ (min. 50°F/10°C)

H. coccineus ■ (Cape tulip). Deciduous, bulbous perennial with 2, occasionally 3, semi-erect to prostrate, elliptic to strap-shaped, mid-green, sometimes purple-marked leaves, to 18in (45cm) long, developing soon after flowering. From summer to autumn, leafless, dark red-streaked stems bear up to 100 small red flowers, with prominent yellow stamens, surrounded by large scarlet bracts, in umbels to 2–4in (5–10cm) across. Flowers are followed by ovoid, fleshy, white to pink fruit. ↕ to 14in (35cm), PD6in (15cm). South Africa (Eastern Cape, Northern Cape, Western Cape). ❄ (min. 50°F/10°C)

H. humilis. Deciduous, bulbous perennial with 2 or 3, prostrate to erect, elliptic to lance-shaped, softly hairy, mid-green leaves, to 12in (30cm) long. In summer, softly hairy, pale green to maroon stems bear loose to compact umbels, to 5in (13cm) across, of up to 120 white to pink flowers with protruding stamens. Flowers are followed by ovoid, fleshy, green-white to

Haemanthus coccineus

orange fruit. ↕ to 12in (30cm), PD6in (15cm). Namibia, South Africa (Western Cape). ❄ (min. 50°F/10°C).
subsp. *humilis* has loose umbels of white to pink flowers with stamens equal to the tepals or protruding by ⅜in (9mm).

H. katherinae see *Scadoxus multiflorus* subsp. *katherinae.*

H. magnificus see *Scadoxus puniceus.*

H. multiflorus see *Scadoxus multiflorus.*

H. natalensis see *Scadoxus puniceus.*

H. puniceus see *Scadoxus puniceus.*

H. sanguineus. Deciduous, bulbous perennial with pairs of prostrate, broadly elliptic to oblong, dark green leaves, to 16in (40cm) long, hairy beneath, developing soon after flowering. From summer to autumn, leafless, dark red stems bear dense umbels, to 1¼–3in (3–8cm) across, of up to 100 small, red, salmon-pink, or pale pink flowers, with white markings and prominent stamens, followed by spherical to ovoid, fleshy, cream to dark red fruit. ↕ 12in (30cm), PD6in (15cm). South Africa (Eastern Cape, Northern Cape, Western Cape). ❄ (min. 50°F/10°C)

HAKEA

PROTEACEAE

Genus of at least 130 species of evergreen trees and shrubs found in acidic soils from coastal to mountainous areas in Australia, where they grow in woodland, on hillsides, and on heathland. The alternate, leathery leaves are often linear and needle-like, but vary greatly within the genus, and may be toothed or lobed. Small, tubular flowers, borne in short, axillary racemes, have prominent, often brightly colored styles, and are followed by woody seed pods, ¾–1¼in (2–3cm) long, each containing only 1 or 2 seeds. Where not hardy, grow in a cool or temperate greenhouse. Outdoors, grow hakeas at the base of a sunny wall, in a shrub border, as specimens, or as informal hedging. Long, hot summers are needed for good flowering.

• **CULTIVATION** Under glass, grow in a mix of equal parts loam, peat or leaf mold, and sharp sand, in full light. In growth, water moderately, applying a phosphate-free liquid fertilizer monthly; keep just moist in winter. Pot on or top-dress in spring. Outdoors, grow in fertile, well-drained, sandy, slightly acidic soil in full sun, although partial shade is tolerated. Pruning group 1; plants under glass may need restrictive pruning.

• **PROPAGATION** Sow seed at 61–64°F (16–18°C) as soon as ripe; sow seed singly in containers to avoid root disturbance. Root semi-ripe cuttings with bottom heat in summer.

• **PESTS AND DISEASES** *Phytophthora* root rot may be a problem in moist soil.

H. lissosperma ■ syn. *H. sericea* of gardens (Mountain hakea). Erect, open to bushy shrub or small tree with linear, stiffly leathery, often upward-curving, gray-green leaves, to 6in (15cm) long, with prickly tips. From spring to summer, bears small white flowers in axillary racemes, 1in (2.5cm) long, from the upper leaf axils; they are followed by ovoid, smooth or warty, dark brown seed pods. ↕ 10–20ft (3–6m), ↔ 3–12ft (1–4m). New South Wales, Victoria,

Hakea lissosperma

Tasmania. ❄ (min. 35°F/2°C); will tolerate short spells of 23°F (-5°C).
H. salicifolia, syn. *H. saligna* (Willow-leaved hakea). Large shrub or small tree with spreading to pendent branches and narrowly lance-shaped to oblong-elliptic leaves, 4–6in (10–15cm) long. Thin, leathery leaves are purple when young and dark green when mature. In spring, bears axillary racemes, ¾in (2cm) long, of 4–9 tiny, creamy white flowers, sometimes followed by ovoid, warty, dark brown seed pods. ↕ 10–25ft (3–8m), ↔ 3–20ft (1–6m). Queensland, New South Wales. ❄ (min. 41–45°F/5–7°C).
'Gold Medal' has pinkish green young leaves, yellow-variegated when mature.
H. saligna see *H. salicifolia.*
***H. sericea* of gardens** see *H. lissosperma.*

HAKONECHLOA

POACEAE

Genus of one species of deciduous, rhizomatous, clump-forming, perennial grass occurring in wooded and often mountainous areas of Japan. *H. macra* has smooth leaves and loose, nodding panicles of 3- to 5-flowered spikelets. Its variegated cultivars, among the most attractive of ornamental grasses, are useful in a woodland or rock garden, or at the front of a mixed or herbaceous border. They are also ideal for containers or a courtyard garden.
• **CULTIVATION** Grow in fertile, humus-rich, moist but well-drained soil in full sun or partial shade. Variegated cultivars produce best leaf color in partial shade.
• **PROPAGATION** Divide in spring.
• **PESTS AND DISEASES** Infrequent.

Hakonechloa macra 'Aureola'

***H. macra* 'Aureola'** ■ Perennial grass, spreading slowly to form mounds of arching, linear leaves, to 10in (25cm) long. Leaves are bright yellow with narrow green stripes, becoming red-flushed in autumn, the color often persisting into winter. From late summer to midautumn, bears needle-like, pale green spikelets in open panicles, to 7in (18cm) long. ↕ 14in (35cm), ↔ 16in (40cm). Zone 5.

HALESIA

Silverbell, Snowdrop tree

STYRACACEAE

Genus of 5 species of deciduous trees and shrubs found in woodland, at woodland margins, and on riverbanks in E. China and S.E. US. They have alternate, ovate to elliptic, or oblong leaves, and are cultivated for their pendent, bell-shaped flowers, curious winged fruits, and autumn color. Ideal as specimen plants, for the back of a shrub border, or in a woodland garden.
• **CULTIVATION** Grow in fertile, humus-rich, moist but well-drained, neutral to acidic soil in sun or partial shade; shelter from wind. Pruning group 1.
• **PROPAGATION** Sow seed at 57–77°F (14–25°C) in autumn, moving the containers to a cold frame after 60 days. Root softwood cuttings in summer, or layer in spring.
• **PESTS AND DISEASES** Root and wood rot, as well as scale insects, can occur.

H. carolina, syn. *H. tetraptera* (Carolina silverbell). Spreading tree or shrub with ovate to elliptic, minutely toothed, mid-green leaves, to 6in (15cm) long, turning yellow in autumn. Axillary clusters of 2–6 pendent, bell-shaped white flowers, to ¾in (2cm) long, hang in profusion from the branches in late spring, just before the leaves emerge. They are followed by 4-winged green fruit. ↕ 25ft (8m), ↔ 30ft (10m). S.E. US. Zone 6.
H. diptera (Two-winged silverbell). Spreading shrub or small tree with elliptic to obovate, mid-green leaves, to 5½in (14cm) long, turning yellow in autumn. Axillary clusters or short racemes of 3–6, deeply 4-lobed white flowers, to ¾in (2cm) long, are borne in early summer, after the leaves; they are followed by 2-winged green fruit. ↕ 20ft (6m), ↔ 30ft (10m). S.E. US. Zone 5b.
var. *magniflora* ■ has larger flowers, to 1¼in (3cm) long.

Halesia diptera var. *magniflora*

Halesia monticola (inset: flower detail)

H. monticola ■ (Mountain silverbell). Vigorous, usually conical tree with ovate, tapered, downy, mid-green leaves, to 8in (20cm) long, becoming hairless with age, and turning yellow in autumn. Axillary clusters of 2–5 wide, bell-shaped white flowers, to 1in (2.5cm) long, are borne in late spring, before or with the leaves; flowers are followed by 4-winged green fruit. ↕ 40ft (12m), ↔ 25ft (8m). N. Carolina, Arkansas. Zone 6.
f. *rosea* bears pink-tinged white flowers.
f. *vestita* has hairless leaves and larger, white, occasionally pink-tinged flowers.
H. tetraptera see *H. carolina.*

x HALIMIOCISTUS

CISTACEAE

Hybrid genus of evergreen shrubs derived from crosses between *Cistus* and *Halimium*, some of which are found in hot, dry soils from Portugal to France (Cevennes), where the parent species overlap. They have opposite, linear-lance-shaped to elliptic-lance-shaped or ovate leaves, and are cultivated for their flowers, which resemble rock roses (*Cistus* and *Helianthemum*). Grow at the front of a shrub or mixed border, at the base of a sunny wall, or in a raised bed or large rock garden.
• **CULTIVATION** Grow in well-drained, sandy, poor to moderately fertile soil in full sun; they are less hardy if grown in shade or very fertile soil. Shelter from cold, drying winds. Pruning group 9; pruning is rarely needed.
• **PROPAGATION** Root semi-ripe cuttings in late summer.
• **PESTS AND DISEASES** Infrequent.

x *H.* 'Ingwersenii', syn. *Cistus ingwerseniana*, x *H. ingwersenii.* Dense, spreading shrub with linear-lance-shaped, dark green leaves, to 1½in (4cm) long. From late spring to late summer, bears umbel-like cymes of saucer-shaped white flowers, ¾–1in (2–2.5cm) across. ↕ 18in (45cm), ↔ 36in (90cm). ❄ (min. 35°F/2°C)

x *H. revolii* (*Cistus salviifolius* x *Halimium alyssoides*). Dense, spreading shrub with softly white-hairy stems and elliptic to broadly elliptic, mid-green leaves, ¼–¾in (0.6–2cm) long. From early to late summer, bears umbel-like cymes of saucer-shaped, white to pale yellow flowers, to 2in (5cm) across, with pale to deep yellow centers. ↕ to 20in (50cm), ↔ 36in (90cm). S. France. ❄ (min. 35°F/2°C)
x *H. sahucii* ■ (*Cistus salviifolius* x *Halimium umbellatum*) syn. *Cistus revolii* of gardens. Compact, mound-forming or spreading shrub with linear to inversely lance-shaped, dark green leaves, to 1½in (4cm) long. Umbel-like cymes of saucer-shaped white flowers, 1¼in (3cm) across, are borne in summer. ↕ 18in (45cm), ↔ 36in (90cm). S. France. ❄ (min. 35°F/2°C)
x *H. wintonensis* (*Cistus salviifolius* x *Halimium ocymoides*) syn. *Cistus wintonensis, Halimium wintonense.* Spreading shrub with ovate or elliptic-lance-shaped, white-woolly, gray-green leaves, to 2in (5cm) long. In late spring and early summer, bears umbel-like cymes of saucer-shaped white flowers, 2in (5cm) across, with yellow stamens

x *Halimiocistus sahucii*

x *Halimiocistus wintonensis* 'Merrist Wood Cream'

and dark crimson-maroon bands. ↕ 24in (60cm), ↔ 36in (90cm). Garden origin. Zone 8. **'Merrist Wood Cream'** ■ has creamy yellow, red-banded flowers, with yellow centers.

HALIMIUM

CISTACEAE

Genus of 9–12 species of evergreen shrubs found in thickets, rocky and sandy places, and dry woodland in the Mediterranean, Turkey, and N. Africa. They have opposite, variably shaped, light to gray-green leaves and are grown for their showy, saucer-shaped flowers, which resemble rock roses (*Cistus* and *Helianthemum*). Grow at the front of a mixed or shrub border, in a large rock garden, or in containers. They flower best in regions with long, hot summers.

• **CULTIVATION** Grow in well-drained, moderately fertile, sandy soil in full sun, with shelter from cold, drying winds. Established plants dislike transplanting. Pruning group 9.

• **PROPAGATION** Sow seed at 66–75°F (19–24°C) in spring, or root semi-ripe cuttings in late summer.

• **PESTS AND DISEASES** Infrequent.

H. atriplicifolium. Upright shrub with elliptic to broadly elliptic, silver-scaly leaves, to 2in (5cm) long. Bright yellow flowers, 1½–1¾in (4–4.5cm) across, unmarked or with a dark red-brown spot at the base of each petal, are borne in panicle-like cymes in late spring and early summer. ↕ 5ft (1.5m), ↔ 3ft (1m). Spain, Morocco. ❀ (min. 41°F/5°C)

Halimium lasianthum subsp. *formosum*

Halimium 'Susan'

H. formosum see *H. lasianthum.*
H. halimifolium. Upright shrub with narrowly obovate to elliptic leaves, to 1¾in (4.5cm) long, whitish and hairy at first, later gray-green. Yellow flowers, 1¼–1½in (3–4cm) across, sometimes with a dark red-brown spot at the base of each petal, open in panicle-like cymes in late spring and early summer. ↕↔ 3ft (1m). S.W. Europe, N. Africa. ❀ (min. 41°F/5°C)
H. lasianthum, syn. *H. formosum.* Spreading, bushy shrub with ovate to oblong, gray-green leaves, 1½in (4cm) long. Axillary clusters of golden yellow flowers, to 1¼in (3cm) across, with or without a brownish red mark at the base of each petal, open in late spring and early summer. ↕ 3ft (1m), ↔ 5ft (1.5m). S. Portugal, S. Spain. ❀ (min. 41°F/5°C). **subsp. *formosum*** ■ has flowers to 1½in (4cm) across, with bold brownish red marks at the bases of the petals; S. Portugal.
H. ocymoides, syn. *Cistus algarvensis.* Bushy, usually erect shrub with obovate to inversely lance-shaped, white-downy, gray-green leaves, to 1¼in (3cm) long. In early summer, golden yellow flowers, to 1¼in (3cm) across, with black-purple centers, are borne in erect, terminal panicles. ↕ 24in (60cm), ↔ 3ft (1m). Portugal, Spain. ❀ (min. 41°F/5°C)
***H.* 'Susan'** ■ Spreading shrub with oval, gray-green leaves, to 1½in (4cm) long. In summer, bears terminal panicles of bright yellow, often semi-double flowers, ¾–1in (2–2.5cm) across, with bold red-purple centers. ↕ 18in (45cm), ↔ 24in (60cm). ❀ (min. 41°F/5°C)

Halimium umbellatum

H. umbellatum ■ syn. *Helianthemum umbellatum.* Upright shrub with linear, glossy, dark green leaves, to 1¼in (3cm) long, white-hairy beneath. Terminal racemes of up to 8 white flowers, to ¾in (2cm) across, each petal stained yellow at the base, open from red buds in early summer. ↕ 18in (45cm), ↔ 24in (60cm). S.W. Europe. ❀ (min. 41°F/5°C)
H. wintonense see x *Halimiocistus wintonensis.*

HALIMODENDRON

FABACEAE

Genus of one species of deciduous, spiny shrub found on salt-rich flood plains from the Ukraine to N. and E. Asia. Valued for its silvery foliage and pea-like flowers, it is useful for a shrub border, and is ideal for coastal areas, where it is an effective windbreak.

• **CULTIVATION** Grow in poor, sharply drained, neutral to alkaline soil in full sun. Will tolerate salty soil, but not winter moisture. Pruning group 1.

• **PROPAGATION** Sow seed in containers in a cold frame in autumn or spring. Take root cuttings in winter, or layer in summer or autumn. Seedlings grown on their own roots are prone to rot in wet soils or humid climates; graft them onto *Caragana* or *Laburnum* in late winter.

• **PESTS AND DISEASES** Infrequent.

H. halodendron (Salt tree). Open-branched, spiny shrub with alternate, pinnate, silver-gray leaves, ¾–1½in (2–4cm) long, each ending in a spine and having 1 or 2 pairs of inversely lance-shaped leaflets. Axillary racemes, to 1½in (4cm) long, of pea-like, violet to purple-pink flowers, to ¾in (2cm) long, are borne in early and mid-summer. ↕↔ 6ft (2m). Ukraine, Republic of Georgia, N.E. Turkey, Iran, C. and E. Asia, and Russia (S.E. Russia, Siberia). Zone 3.

HAMAMELIS

Witch hazel

HAMAMELIDACEAE

Genus of 5 or 6 species of deciduous shrubs occurring in woodland, at woodland margins, and on riverbanks in E. Asia and North America. They have alternate, broadly ovate to obovate leaves, and are grown for their autumn color and their cold-resistant, fragrant, spider-shaped flowers. The flowers, ¾–1¼in (2–3cm) across, with 4 narrow

Hamamelis x *intermedia* 'Arnold Promise'

Hamamelis x *intermedia* 'Diane'

petals, are borne in dense, axillary clusters, mainly from winter to autumn. Witch hazels are good specimen plants, and are also effective planted in groups in a shrub border or woodland garden.

• **CULTIVATION** Grow in moderately fertile, moist but well-drained, acidic to neutral soil in full sun or partial shade, in an open but not exposed site. Witch hazels also grow in deep, humus-rich, alkaline soils. Pruning group 1.

• **PROPAGATION** Sow seed in containers in a cold frame as soon as ripe. Graft cultivars in late winter, or bud in late summer.

• **PESTS AND DISEASES** Gall aphids, leaf roller, and scale insects, powdery mildew, leaf spots, and wood rot .

H.* x *intermedia (*H. japonica* x *H. mollis*). Vase-shaped shrub with ascending branches and broadly oval to obovate, bright green leaves, to 6in (15cm) long, turning yellow in autumn. In early and midwinter, bears fragrant, yellow, dark red, or orange flowers, with crimped petals, on the bare branches. ↕↔ 12ft (4m). Garden origin. Zone 6b. **'Advent'** has bright yellow flowers in early winter. **'Allgold'** has small, dark yellow flowers in mid- and late winter. **'Arnold Promise'** ■ produces large yellow flowers in mid- and late winter. **'Diane'** ■ has dark red flowers in mid- and late winter, and orange to yellow and red autumn foliage. **'Jelena'** ■ bears large, coppery orange flowers in early and midwinter, and has orange and red autumn foliage. **'Moonlight'** bears large, pale yellow flowers in mid- and

Hamamelis x *intermedia* 'Jelena'

Hamamelis x *intermedia* 'Pallida' (inset: flower detail)

late winter. **'Pallida'** ■ syn. *H. mollis* 'Pallida', has clusters of large, sulfur-yellow flowers in mid- and late winter. **'Sunburst'** is narrowly upright, with large, pale yellow flowers in mid- and late winter; ↔ 8ft (2.5m). **'Vezna'** ■ has large, dark orange-yellow flowers with pendent petals, flushed red at the bases, in mid- and late winter.

H. japonica (Japanese witch hazel). Upright, open-branched shrub with broadly oval to obovate, glossy mid-green leaves, to 4in (10cm) long, which turn yellow in autumn. Yellow flowers, with crimped petals, are produced on bare branches in mid- and late winter. ↕↔ 12ft (4m). Japan. Zone 6b. **'Sulphurea'** ■ bears a profusion of small, pale sulfur-yellow flowers in mid- and late winter. **'Zuccariniana'** bears pale lemon-yellow flowers in late winter and early spring, and has orange-yellow autumn foliage.

H. mollis (Chinese witch hazel). Erect shrub with broadly oval to obovate, softly hairy, mid-green leaves, to 6in (15cm) long, turning yellow in autumn. Very fragrant, golden yellow flowers are borne on bare branches in mid- and late winter. ↕↔ 12ft (4m). W. and W. central China. Zone 6b. **'Brevipetala'** ■ has dense clusters of short-petaled, golden yellow flowers, to ½in (1.5cm) across, marked dark red in the centers; it is possibly of hybrid origin. **'Coombe Wood'** is spreading, and produces large, strongly scented flowers; ↕ 12ft (4m), ↔ 15ft (5m). **'Goldcrest'** bears large flowers, flushed red at the bases of the petals, from midwinter to spring. **'Pallida'** see *H.* x *intermedia* 'Pallida'.

H. vernalis (Vernal witch hazel). Erect shrub with obovate, mid-green leaves, to 5in (13cm) long, turning yellow in autumn. Bears small, yellow to orange, sometimes red-tinged flowers on bare shoots in late winter and early spring. ↕↔ 15ft (5m). S. central US. Zone 5b. **'Lombart's Weeping'** has spreading, pendent branches; ↕ 6ft (2m), ↔ 10ft (3m). **'Red Imp'** has claret petal bases, which become copper at the apexes. **'Sandra'** has purple young leaves, turning yellow, orange, red, and purple in autumn, and dark yellow flowers.

H. virginiana (Common witch hazel). Erect shrub with broadly oval, obovate, or nearly rounded leaves, to 6in (15cm) long, turning yellow in autumn. Small yellow flowers are borne in autumn, before the leaves begin to fall. ↕↔ 12ft (4m). E. North America. Zone 4.

Hamamelis x *intermedia* 'Vezna'

Hamamelis japonica 'Sulphurea'

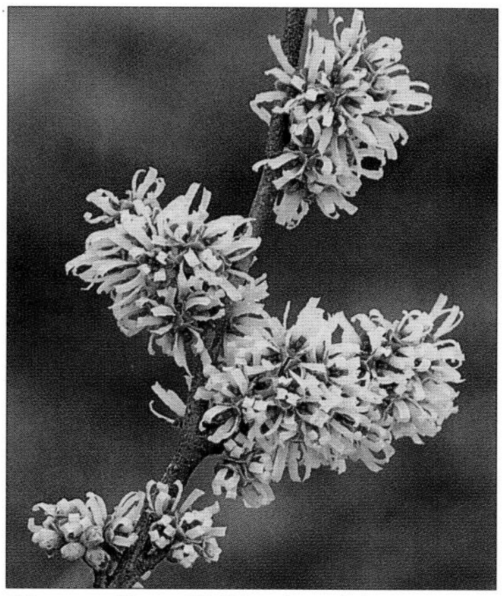

Hamamelis mollis 'Brevipetala'

▷ ***Hamatocactus crassihamatus*** see *Sclerocactus uncinatus* var. *crassihamatus*

▷ ***Hamatocactus hamatacanthus*** see *Ferocactus hamatacanthus*

▷ ***Hamatocactus setispinus*** see *Thelocactus setispinus*

▷ ***Hamatocactus uncinatus*** see *Sclerocactus uncinatus*

HAPLOPAPPUS

ASTERACEAE

Genus of 160 species of annuals, perennials, subshrubs, and shrubs found in open, sunny habitats in North and South America. Cultivated for their usually opposite, entire or lobed leaves, and yellow, sometimes purple, daisy-like flowerheads, they are suitable for a rock garden, trough, or raised bed.

• **CULTIVATION** Grow in neutral to slightly alkaline, poor to moderately fertile, sharply drained soil in full sun; protect from excessive winter moisture. Trim back untidy plants after flowering.

• **PROPAGATION** Sow seed in containers in a cold frame as soon as ripe or in spring. Root softwood cuttings in spring.

• **PESTS AND DISEASES** Rust, powdery mildew, and smut occur.

H. acaulis see *Stenotus acaulis*.

H. coronopifolius see *H. glutinosus*.

H. glutinosus, syn. *H. coronopifolius*. Tufted, evergreen perennial, usually forming dense cushions of spreading or erect stems clothed in oblong or elliptic, lobed or pinnatisect, sticky leaves, to 1½in (4cm) long. Solitary, daisy-like yellow flowerheads, to 1in (2.5cm) across, are borne in summer. ↕ 6in (15cm), ↔ to 12in (30cm). Chile, Argentina. ❄ (min. 41°F/5°C)

HARDENBERGIA

Coral pea

FABACEAE

Genus of 3 species of evergreen, twining or trailing climbers occurring in Australia in a diverse range of habitats, from coastal plains to rocky scree in mountainous areas. They have alternate, ovate to lance-shaped leaves, which may be 3-palmate (rarely 5-palmate) or may consist of only 1 leaflet, with the 2 lateral leaflets suppressed. Colorful, small, pea-like flowers are borne, often in profusion, in axillary racemes or occasionally in panicles. Where not hardy, grow in a temperate greenhouse or conservatory. In milder climates, use to cover an arbor, pergola, or wall, or grow through large shrubs or small trees.

Hardenbergia comptoniana

• **CULTIVATION** Under glass, grow in a mix of equal parts soil-based potting mix, sharp sand, and leaf mold, in full light with shade from hot sun; provide low to moderate humidity. During the growing season, water moderately and apply a balanced liquid fertilizer monthly; keep just moist in winter. Pot on or top-dress in spring. Provide support. Outdoors, grow in moderately fertile, moist but well-drained, acidic to neutral soil in full sun or partial shade. Pruning group 11, after flowering.

• **PROPAGATION** Sow seed at 68°F (20°C) in spring; pre-soak for 24 hours to aid germination. Root softwood cuttings in spring.

• **PESTS AND DISEASES** Sometimes affected by bacterial and fungal leaf spots, as well as spider mites and aphids.

H. comptoniana ■ Vigorous climber with 3-palmate, occasionally 5-palmate, dark green leaves, composed of narrowly lance-shaped to broadly ovate leaflets, to 6in (15cm) long. From early spring to midsummer, bears pendent racemes, to 5in (13cm) long, of mauve to purple-blue flowers, to ½in (1.5cm) across, the standards with green-spotted white marks at the bases. ↕ 10ft (3m) or more. Western Australia. ❄ (min. 37–41°F/3–5°C); may survive short periods to 32°F (0°C)

H. monophylla see *H. violacea*.

H. violacea, syn. *H. monophylla* (Purple coral pea). Strong-growing climber, sometimes trailing in habit. Each leaf has 1 ovate to lance-shaped, leathery, rich green leaflet, to 5in (13cm) long; the other 2 leaflets are suppressed. Purple to violet, sometimes white, pink, or lilac flowers, ½in (1.5cm) across, the standards spotted yellow or green, are borne in pendent racemes, 4–5in (10–13cm) long, from late winter to early summer. ↕ 6ft (2m) or more. South Australia, Queensland to Tasmania. ❄ (min. 45°F/7°C). **'Alba'** see 'White Crystal'. **'Happy Wanderer'** is very vigorous, bearing panicles of purple-blue flowers. **'Pink Cascade'** bears pink flowers. **'White Crystal'**, syn. 'Alba', produces pure white flowers in late winter.

HARRISIA

CACTACEAE

Genus of 10–20 species of tree-like cacti closely allied to *Eriocereus*, with which they are often confused. They are found in hilly and low mountainous areas of S.E. US, the Bahamas, the West Indies, and South America. The slender, erect or spreading, occasionally decumbent stems usually have 9–11 rounded ribs. The large, narrowly or widely funnel-shaped flowers open at night in summer. Where not hardy, grow in a warm greenhouse or conservatory. In warm, dry climates, use *Harrisia* species in a desert garden.

• **CULTIVATION** Under glass, grow in standard cactus potting mix in full light, with shade from hot sun. During the growing season, water moderately and apply a low-nitrogen liquid fertilizer monthly; keep dry in winter. Provide good ventilation but keep clear of drafts. Outdoors, grow in poor, sharply drained, acidic to neutral soil in full sun. Protect from excessive winter moisture. See also pp.48–49.

• **PROPAGATION** Sow seed at 70–75°F (21–24°C) in spring. Root stem cuttings, or remove and pot up offsets, in spring or summer.

• **PESTS AND DISEASES** Prone to scale insects, especially on young growth.

H. bonplandii, syn. *Eriocereus pomanensis, H. pomanensis.* Erect to prostrate cactus with bluish green stems bearing 4 or 5 obtuse or rounded ribs with low, broad grooves between. Gray areoles bear white- or pink-tinged, later black-tipped spines (6–8 radials and 1 longer central). White flowers, 6in (15cm) or more long, with green outer segments, are borne in summer. ↕↔ 6ft (2m). S. Brazil, Paraguay, N. and W. Argentina. ❀ (min. 55°F/13°C)

H. gracilis. Spreading or erect, tree-like cactus producing branching, dark green stems with 8–12 ribs, white areoles, and black-tipped white spines (10–16 radials and 1 central). In summer, bears white flowers, 8in (20cm) long, with toothed inner tepals and pale brown outer segments. ↕ to 15ft (5m) or more, ↔ 6ft (2m). S. Florida, Jamaica. ❀ (min. 55°F/13°C)

H. jusbertii ■ syn. *Eriocereus jusbertii.* Erect, occasionally branching cactus producing dark green stems with 4–6 broad ribs, yellowish gray areoles, and brown or black spines (about 7 radials and 1–4 slightly longer centrals). In summer, bears flowers to 7in (18cm) long, with white inner tepals and brownish green outer segments. Origin unknown. ↕↔ 3ft (1m) or ❀ (min. 55°F/13°C)

H. pomanensis see *H. bonplandii.*

Harrisia jusbertii

HATIORA syn. RHIPSALIDOPSIS

CACTACEAE

Genus of about 6 species of epiphytic or terrestrial, freely branching cacti, now incorporating the Easter cacti (*Rhipsalidopsis*), from forest or rocky areas in Brazil. They have slender, generally segmented, erect or pendent stems. New growth and the trumpet- to funnel-shaped, diurnal flowers are produced only from the areoles, which form at the apex of each segment. The flowers are followed by spherical to obovoid, white or yellow fruits, ⅛–¼in (3–6mm) across. Where temperatures fall below 55°F (13°C), grow as house-plants, or in a warm greenhouse, in containers or hanging baskets, or with air plants (*Tillandsia* species) on a bromeliad "tree." In warmer climates, grow in containers on a patio or in a courtyard garden.

• **CULTIVATION** Under glass, grow epiphytically or in epiphytic cactus potting mix, in bright filtered or indirect light, with high humidity. In the growing season, water moderately, mist daily, and apply a half-strength, low-nitrogen liquid fertilizer monthly. Keep just moist in winter until buds develop, then increase water slightly. Outdoors, grow in containers or in poor, humus-rich, moist but well-drained, acidic to neutral soil in dappled shade. Sensitive to temperatures above 100°F (38°C). See also pp.48–49.

• **PROPAGATION** Sow seed at 70–75°F (21–24°C) in spring. Root cuttings in spring or summer.

• **PESTS AND DISEASES** Susceptible to mealybugs.

Hatiora epiphylloides

Hatiora gaertneri

H. epiphylloides ■ syn. *Pseudozygocactus epiphylloides.* Pendent cactus producing stems with cylindrical to wedge-shaped, fleshy, bright green segments, to 1in (2.5cm) long, and minute, spineless areoles. In early spring, bears funnel-shaped yellow flowers, ½in (1.5cm) long. ↕ 18in (45cm), ↔ 8in (20cm). Brazil. ❀ (min. 55°F/13°C)

H. gaertneri ■ syn. *Rhipsalidopsis gaertneri.* Bushy, semi-pendent cactus producing stems with flat, oblong or elliptic, shallowly scalloped, mid-green segments, 1½–3in (4–8cm) long. Each segment has 3–5 tubercles, with areoles on each side bearing 1 or 2 yellow-brown bristles. Funnel-shaped scarlet flowers, 1½–3in (4–8cm) long, are produced from the newer segments in spring. ↕ 6in (15cm), ↔ 10in (25cm). E. Brazil. ❀ (min. 55°F/13°C)

H. rosea ■ syn. *Rhipsalidopsis rosea* (Easter cactus). Shrubby, pendent or erect cactus producing stems with flat, sometimes 3- to 5-angled, mid-green segments, ¾–1½in (2–4cm) long, usually with thin red margins and minute areoles bearing a few hairy, pale brown bristles. In early spring, trumpet-shaped, rose-pink flowers,

Hatiora salicornioides

1¼–1½in (3–4cm) long, are produced on longer areoles at the tops of the segments. ↕↔ to 6in (15cm). S.E. Brazil. ❀ (min. 55°F/13°C)

H. salicornioides ■ (Drunkard's dream). Bushy, erect or pendent cactus producing stems with club-shaped, mid-green to bronze-green segments, ½–2in (1–5cm) long, usually arranged in whorls of 2–5. In spring, bears funnel-shaped, golden yellow or orange flowers, ½in (1.5cm) long, from the areoles of new segments. ↕↔ 16in (40cm). S.E. Brazil. ❀ (min. 55°F/13°C)

HAWORTHIA

LILIACEAE

Genus of about 100 species of dwarf, basal-rosetted, more or less stemless, perennial succulents from lowland and sometimes hillsides of Namibia, Swaziland, Mozambique, and South Africa. They generally offset to form clumps. The linear to broadly ovate or triangular, fleshy, variably colored leaves are often covered with minute, bright tubercles, which are sometimes almost transparent. The small, tubular to funnel-shaped flowers are borne in

Hatiora rosea

Haworthia arachnoidea

loose racemes from spring to autumn. Where not hardy, grow as foliage plants in a temperate or warm greenhouse or conservatory. In warmer regions, grow haworthias in a trough or raised bed, or in containers outdoors.

• **CULTIVATION** Under glass, grow in standard cactus potting mix in bright filtered light, with low humidity and good ventilation. In the growing season, water moderately and apply a low-nitrogen liquid fertilizer monthly; keep dry in winter. Pot on in spring. Outdoors, grow in poor, sharply drained, neutral to slightly alkaline soil in sun or partial shade; protect from excessive winter moisture.

• **PROPAGATION** Sow seed at 70–75°F (21–24°C) in spring. Pot up offsets or divide in spring. Root leaf cuttings from soft-leaved species in spring or summer.

• **PESTS AND DISEASES** Susceptible to mealybugs, scale insects, and soft rot caused by both fungi and bacteria.

H. arachnoidea ▣ syn. *Aprica arachnoidea, H. setata.* Clump-forming succulent with oblong or lance-shaped, dark green leaves, ¾–3in (2–8cm) long, margined and tipped with white to pale brown teeth; leaf surfaces are transparent, with continuous darker lines. In spring, stems to 12in (30cm) tall bear tubular to funnel-shaped white flowers, to ½in (1.5cm) long, in racemes 3in (8cm) long. ↕ to 2in (5cm), ↔ 4in (10cm). South Africa (Northern Cape, Western Cape, Eastern Cape). ❀ (min. 50°F/10°C)

H. attenuata ▣ Extremely variable, clump-forming succulent, which is

Haworthia attenuata

Haworthia cymbiformis

either stemless or has a short stem. Narrowly triangular, dark green leaves, 1¼–3in (3–8cm) long, are dotted with white tubercles above, and transverse bands of white tubercles beneath. In summer, stems to 16in (40cm) long bear tubular to funnel-shaped, green-keeled white flowers, to ½in (1.5cm) long, in racemes to 7in (18cm) long. ↕↔ to 5in (13cm). South Africa (Northern Cape, Eastern Cape). ❀ (min. 50°F/10°C). **f. *clariperla*** has triangular leaves, to 2½in (6cm) long, the upper surfaces covered with small white tubercles, the undersides with rows of larger tubercles.

H. cymbiformis ▣ syn. *H. planifolia.* Variable, clump-forming succulent with obovate to ovate, tapering, smooth or finely toothed leaves, 1¼–2in (3–5cm) long. They are bright pale green, sometimes flushed pink, concave above, convex beneath, and have translucent tips with thin, longitudinal white stripes. In spring, stems to 8in (20cm) long bear funnel-shaped, pinkish white flowers, to ½in (1.5cm) long, with brownish green keels, in racemes to 4in (10cm) long. ↕ 3in (8cm), ↔ 10in (25cm). South Africa (Eastern Cape). ❀ (min. 50°F/10°C)

H. fasciata ▣ (Zebra haworthia). Very variable, clump-forming, stemless succulent producing triangular-lance-shaped, dark green leaves, to 3in (8cm) long, smooth above, convex and cross-banded with white tubercles beneath. In summer, stems to 16in (40cm) long bear tubular to funnel-shaped white flowers, to ½in (1.5cm) long, with red-brown keels, in racemes 4½in (11cm)

Haworthia fasciata

Haworthia tessellata

long. Often considered synonymous with *H. attenuata.* ↕ to 4in (10cm), ↔ 12in (30cm). South Africa (Eastern Cape). ❀ (min. 50°F/10°C)

H. glauca. Variable, clump-forming succulent with spirally arranged, narrowly triangular to oblong-lance-shaped, gray to blue-green leaves, 1–2in (2.5–5cm) long, with faint dark lines in longitudinal rows, few or no tubercles, and sharp tips. In summer, stems to 2–8in (5–20cm) long bear tubular to funnel-shaped, white flowers, to ½in (1.5cm) long, in racemes, to 5in (13cm) long. ↕ to 3in (8cm), ↔ 12in (30cm). South Africa (Eastern Cape), Orange Free State. ❀ (min. 50°F/10°C)

H. maughanii. Clustering succulent with erect, conical to cylindrical, blunt-tipped, thick, rough, grayish green to reddish brown leaves, to 1in (2.5cm) long; most of the plant is below soil level, with only the flat, translucent, window-like tip of each leaf exposed. From autumn to winter, stems to 8in (20cm) long bear brown-keeled white flowers, to ½in (1.5cm) long, in racemes to 3in (8cm) long. ↕ ¾in (2cm), ↔ 4in (10cm). South Africa (Western Cape). ❀ (min. 50°F/10°C)

Haworthia truncata

H. planifolia see *H. cymbiformis.*

H. pumila (Pearl plant). Very variable, clump-forming succulent with incurved to erect, triangular-ovate, dark green or purple-green leaves, to 3in (8cm) long, with showy, silver tubercles on both surfaces and sharp, red-brown tips. In summer, produces branched stems, to 16in (40cm) long, which bear racemes, 5½in (14cm) long, of tubular to funnel-shaped, brownish or yellowish green flowers, to ½in (1.5cm) long. ↕ to 5in (13cm), ↔ 18in (45cm). South Africa (Western Cape). ❀ (min. 50°F/10°C)

H. reinwardtii. Variable, freely off-setting succulent with dense rosettes of spirally arranged, ovate to lance-shaped, dark green to yellow-green leaves, ¾–2in (2–5cm) long. The leaves have small, green or white tubercles in 1–3 longitudinal rows above; the undersides have tubercles in longitudinal rows or cross-bands. In spring, produces stems to 14in (35cm) long, bearing lax racemes, 3½–7in (9–18cm) long, of tubular, pinkish white flowers, ¾in (2cm) long, with greenish brown keels. ↕ 8in (20cm), ↔ indefinite. South Africa (Western Cape, Eastern Cape). ❀ (min. 50°F/10°C)

H. retusa. Variable, clump-forming succulent with ovate-triangular leaves, 1¼–3in (3–8cm) long, recurved horizontally on the upper surfaces, with rounded, sometimes rough or almost translucent tips. The leaves are pale or deep green, and often have minute tubercles, pale lines, and sometimes numerous isolated soft teeth. In late winter and early spring, stems to 28in (70cm) long bear narrowly tubular, green-keeled white flowers, to ½in (1.5cm) long, in racemes to 20in (50cm) long. ↕ 2½in (6cm), ↔ 8in (20cm). South Africa (Western Cape, Eastern Cape). ❀ (min. 50°F/10°C)

H. setata see *H. arachnoidea.*

H. tessellata ▣ syn. *H. venosa* subsp. *tessellata.* Mat-forming succulent spreading by subterranean branches. The triangular-ovate, tapering, usually recurved, bluish gray-green leaves, 2–3in (5–8cm) long, are convex above, roughly warty beneath and on the margins; the upper surfaces are checkered with pale lines. In spring, produces stems to 20in (50cm) long, which bear tubular, greenish white flowers, to ¾in (2cm) long, in racemes to 6in (15cm) long. ↕ 4in (10cm), ↔ 12in (30cm). Namibia, South Africa (Western Cape). ❀ (min. 50°F/10°C)

H. truncata ▣ Clustering succulent producing rows of erect, incurved, oblong, thick, bluish gray leaves, ¾in (2cm) long, with gray lines, rough, warty surfaces, and very blunt tips forming flat ends, which are slightly translucent when young. In the wild, the plant body is below soil level, with only the window-like tip of each leaf exposed; in cultivation, all or most of the leaf surface is exposed. From summer to autumn, stems 9in (23cm) long bear tubular, green-keeled white flowers, to ½in (1.5cm) long, in racemes to 3in (8cm) long. ↕ ¾in (2cm), ↔ 4in (10cm) in the wild; ↕ 8in (20cm), ↔ 10in (25cm) in cultivation. South Africa (Western Cape). ❀ (min. 50°F/10°C)

H. venosa* subsp. *tessellata see *H. tessellata.*

HEBE

SCROPHULARIACEAE

Genus of about 100 species of evergreen shrubs, rarely trees, from a wide variety of habitats, ranging from rocky sites and cliffs to scrub and grassland; they are found from coastal areas to mountain regions, mainly in New Zealand, but also in S.E. Australia, New Guinea, and South America. The dense, opposite, sometimes 2- or 4-ranked leaves are scale-like to lance-shaped, rounded or ovate. Tubular flowers, expanding into 4 spreading lobes, are borne in terminal or axillary racemes, spikes, or small heads; they vary in color from white to pink, blue, purple, or red, and often lighten with age. Most flowers range in size from ⅛–½in (2–15mm), and are described below as: small, ⅛–¼in (2–6mm) across; medium, ¼–⅜in (6–9mm) across; and large, ⅜–½in (9–15mm) across.

Hebes are suitable for a wide range of sites, including a mixed or shrub border, or a rock garden. In mild areas, particularly along coastal regions, they are useful as hedging and as ground-covers. Grow the less hardy species in an alpine house or cool greenhouse. Hebes are also good container plants and will tolerate some pollution. Those with small, scale-like leaves lying flat against the stems are known as "whip-cord hebes," and are excellent rock garden plants.

• **CULTIVATION** Under glass, grow in soil-based potting mix in full light, with shade from hot sun. Provide low to moderate humidity and good ventilation. In the growing season, water moderately and apply a balanced liquid fertilizer monthly; water more sparingly in winter. Outdoors, grow in poor or moderately fertile, moist but well-drained, neutral to slightly alkaline soil in sun or partial shade, with shelter from cold, drying winds. Pruning group 9; most hebes need little or no pruning.

• **PROPAGATION** Sow seed in containers in a cold frame as soon as ripe. Hebes hybridize freely, so may not come true from seed. Root semi-ripe cuttings with bottom heat in late summer or autumn.

• **PESTS AND DISEASES** Leaf spot, *Phytophthora* root rot, downy mildew, and aphids may be a problem.

Hebe 'Bowles' Variety'

Hebe canterburiensis

Hebe albicans

Hebe 'Autumn Glory'

Hebe brachysiphon 'White Gem'

H. albicans ■ Compact, mound-forming, spreading shrub with ovate, gray-green leaves, to 1¼in (3cm) long. In early and midsummer, bears medium-sized white flowers in short, terminal racemes, 1¼–2½in (3–6cm) long. ↕ 24in (60cm), ↔ 36in (90cm). New Zealand (South Island). Zone 8. **'Pewter Dome'** see *H.* 'Pewter Dome'. **'Red Edge'** see *H.* 'Red Edge'.

***H.* 'Alicia Amherst'**, syn. *H.* 'Veitchii'. Vigorous, upright shrub producing elliptic to elliptic-ovate, glossy, dark green leaves, to 4½in (11cm) long. Medium-sized, dark violet-purple flowers are borne in axillary spikes, 3–3½in (7–9cm) long, from late summer to autumn. ↕↔ 4ft (1.2m). ❄ (min. 41°F/5°C)

***H.* 'Amy'**, syn. *H.* 'Lady Ardilaun', *H.* 'Purple Queen'. Rounded, evergreen shrub with elliptic, dark green leaves, to 3in (8cm) long, dark bronze-purple when young and in winter. In late summer, bears large, violet-purple flowers in short, axillary spikes, to 2in (5cm) long. ↕↔ 5ft (1.5m). ❄ (min. 41°F/5°C)

***H. x andersonii* 'Argenteovariegata'** see *H.* x *andersonii* 'Variegata'.

***H. x andersonii* 'Variegata'**, syn. *H.* x *andersonii* 'Argenteovariegata'. Bushy shrub with elliptic to inversely lance-shaped, dark green leaves, to 4in (10cm) long, streaked with gray-green in the centers and margined creamy white. From midsummer to autumn, bears medium-sized, pale violet flowers in axillary spikes, 2½–3½in (6–9cm) long. ↕↔ 6ft (2m). ❄ (min. 45°F/7°C)

H. anomala see *H. odora.*

H. armstrongii, syn. *H. lycopodioides* 'Aurea'. Rounded, whipcord hebe with broadly ovate, yellow-green leaves, 1/16in (2mm) long, turning light green in winter. Small white flowers are borne in terminal spikes, ½–¾in (1–2cm) long, in late spring and early summer. ↕↔ 36in (90cm). New Zealand (South Island). ❄ (min. 41°F/5°C)

***H.* 'Autumn Glory'** ■ Erect then spreading shrub with bronze shoots and broadly elliptic to obovate, dark green leaves, to 1in (2.5cm) long, with red margins. Small, dark purple-blue flowers, with white tubes, open in dense, axillary and terminal, sometimes branched racemes, 1¼–1¾in (3–4.5cm) long, from midsummer to early winter. ↕ 24in (60cm), ↔ 36in (90cm). ❄ (min. 41°F/5°C)

***H.* 'Bowles' Hybrid'.** Rounded shrub with elliptic, slightly glossy, pale green leaves, to 1in (2.5cm) long. Medium-sized, lavender-purple flowers are borne in axillary racemes, 3–4in (8–10cm) long, from midsummer to autumn. ↕ 20in (50cm), ↔ 24in (60cm). ❄ (min. 45°F/7°C)

***H.* 'Bowles' Variety'** ■ Compact shrub with ovate-oblong, slightly glossy, mid-green leaves, to 1½in (4cm) long. In summer, bears medium-sized, mauve-blue flowers in compact, tapered, terminal racemes, to 3in (8cm) long. ↕ 18in (45cm), ↔ 24in (60cm). ❄ (min. 41°F/5°C)

H. brachysiphon. Dense, rounded shrub with elliptic to lance-shaped, mid- to dark green leaves, to 1in (2.5cm) long. In midsummer, bears small white flowers in dense, axillary racemes, to 1in (2.5cm) long. ↕↔ 6ft (2m). New Zealand (South Island). ❄ (min. 35°F/2°C). **'White Gem'** ■ is a compact hybrid of *H. brachysiphon*, producing flowers in early and midsummer; ↕ 30–39in (75–100cm), ↔ 3ft (1m).

H. buchananii. Compact, much-branched, spreading shrub with broadly ovate, leathery, dark green leaves, to ¼in (6mm) long. In summer, small white flowers are borne in erect, axillary spikes, to ¾in (2cm) long, mainly toward the shoot tips. ↕ 8in (20cm), ↔ to 36in (90cm). New Zealand (Canterbury Alps, South Island). ❄ (min. 41°F/5°C). **'Minor'** is more compact in habit, with smaller leaves, and is suitable for a trough; ↕ to 4in (10cm), ↔ to 6in (15cm).

***H. buxifolia* of gardens** see *H. odora.*

H. canterburiensis ■ syn. *H.* 'Tom Marshall'. Spreading shrub with oval to obovate, dark green leaves, to ½in (1.5cm) long, loosely overlapping and in 2 ranks. In summer, bears a profusion of medium-sized white flowers, to ⅜in (9mm) across, in dense, axillary racemes, to 1in (2.5cm) long. ↕ 24in (60cm), ↔ to 36in (90cm). New Zealand. ❄ (min. 41°F/5°C). **'Prostrata'** is procumbent and lower-growing; ↕ 12in (30cm).

***H.* 'Carl Teschner'** see *H.* 'Youngii'.

H. carnosula. Low or nearly prostrate, spreading shrub with broadly obovate, slightly convex, glaucous, grayish green leaves, to ½in (1.5cm) long. Medium-sized white flowers, purplish pink in bud, are borne in dense, subterminal racemes, ½in (1.5cm) long, in early summer. ↕ 6–12in (15–30cm), ↔ 12in (30cm) or more. New Zealand (South Island). ❄ (min. 41°F/5°C)

H. chathamica ■ Prostrate shrub with elliptic to ovate-oblong, fleshy, glossy, mid- to deep green leaves, to 1¼in (3cm) long. In early summer, bears medium-sized white flowers, tinged violet at first, in dense, axillary racemes, to 1½in (4cm) long. Good as a groundcover in mild areas. ↕ 6in (15cm), ↔ 36in (90cm). New Zealand (Chatham Islands). ❄ (min. 41°F/5°C)

***H.* 'County Park'.** Wide-spreading, decumbent shrub with ovate, red-margined, gray-green leaves, to ½in (1.5cm) long. Small violet flowers are produced in short, axillary spikes, 1in (2.5cm) long, in early and midsummer. Suitable as a groundcover. ↕ 8in (20cm), ↔ 18in (45cm). ❄ (min. 41°F/5°C)

H. cupressoides ■ Dense, upright, whipcord hebe with cypress-like branches of scale-like, narrowly ovate to triangular, glaucous, mid-green leaves, to ½in (1.5cm) long. In early and midsummer,

Hebe chathamica

Hebe cupressoides

mature plants bear masses of small, pale lilac-blue flowers in axillary racemes, to 1in (2.5cm) long. ↕↔ 4ft (1.2m). New Zealand (South Island). Zone 8. **'Boughton Dome'** ■ is a dwarf, domed shrub with congested, slender, gray-green branchlets bearing scale-like, pale green leaves, to ¼in (6mm) long, pressed close to the stems but not hiding them. It seldom flowers. Suitable for a rock garden; ↕ 12in (30cm), ↔ 24in (60cm). **'Nana'** is compact in habit.
***H.* 'Edinensis'.** Low, spreading shrub with ascending branches and whipcord-like, narrowly lance-shaped to oblong-ovate, glossy, mid-green leaves, to ¼in (6mm) long. Occasionally bears small, bluish white flowers in summer, but blooms infrequently. ↕ 12in (30cm), ↔ 30in (75cm). Zone 8.
***H. elliptica* 'Variegata'** see *H.* x *franciscana* 'Variegata'.
H. epacridea. Mat-forming shrub with prostrate and ascending branches clothed in dense, ovate, rigid, dull mid-green leaves, ¼–⅜in (6–9mm) long. Small, fragrant white flowers open in ovoid, terminal heads, to ½in (1.5cm) long, in late spring. ↕ 18in (45cm), ↔ 24in (60cm). New Zealand (South Island). ❄ (min. 35°F/2°C)
***H.* 'Eveline'** see *H.* 'Gauntlettii'.
***H.* 'Fairfieldii'.** Upright shrub with broadly ovate, coarsely toothed, glossy, mid- to dark green, red-margined leaves, ¾–1¼in (2–3cm) long. Medium-sized, lavender-violet flowers are borne in large, open, freely branched, terminal panicles, to 9in (23cm) long, in late spring and early summer. Deadhead after flowering. ↕↔ 24in (60cm). ❄ (min. 41°F/5°C)

Hebe cupressoides 'Boughton Dome'

Hebe x *franciscana* 'Variegata'

H.* x *franciscana (*H. elliptica* x *H. speciosa*). Dense, rounded shrub with 4-ranked, obovate to elliptic, fleshy, dull dark green leaves, 1½–2½in (4–6cm) long. From summer to autumn, pink-tinged purple flowers, to ½in (1.5cm) across, are borne in dense, axillary racemes, 2–3in (5–8cm) long. ↕↔ 2–4ft (60–120cm). Garden origin. ❄ (min. 41°F/5°C). **'Blue Gem'**, syn. *H. latifolia*, is spreading, with elliptic to inversely lance-shaped, light to mid-green leaves, 1–3in (2.5–8cm) long, and light mauve flowers; ↕↔ 4½ft (1.3m). **'Variegata'** ■ syn. *H. elliptica* 'Variegata', has leaves broadly margined creamy white.
***H.* 'Gauntlettii'** ■ syn. *H.* 'Eveline'. Upright, bushy shrub with elliptic to inversely lance-shaped, glossy, rich green leaves, to 3in (8cm) or more long. Medium-sized pink flowers, 6in (15cm) across, with purple tubes, are borne in pendent, axillary racemes, 5–6in (12–15cm) long, from late summer to late autumn. ↕↔ 3ft (1m). ❄ (min. 45°F/7°C)
***H. glaucophylla* 'Variegata'.** Rounded shrub (probably of hybrid origin) with slender shoots and lance-shaped, cream-margined, gray-green leaves, ⅜–½in (9–15mm) long. In summer, bears large, pale lilac-blue flowers in short, terminal racemes, ¾–1¼in (2–3cm) long. ↕↔ 3ft (1m). ❄ (min. 35°F/2°C)
***H.* 'Great Orme'** ■ Open, rounded shrub with dark purple shoots and oblong to lance-shaped, glossy, mid-green leaves, to 2½in (6cm) long. Large, bright pink flowers, fading to white, are borne in dense, slender, axillary spikes, 2–4in (5–10cm) long, over a long period from midsummer to midautumn. ↕↔ 4ft (1.2m). ❄ (min. 41°F/5°C)
***H.* 'Hagley Park'** ■ Erect to slightly spreading shrub with upright shoots and oblong-elliptic to obovate, blunt-toothed, glossy, mid-green leaves, to 2in (5cm) long, margined with red. Medium-sized, rose-purple flowers are produced in large, terminal panicles, to 6in (15cm) or more long, in summer. ↕ 18in (45cm), ↔ 24in (60cm). ❄ (min. 41°F/5°C)
H. hulkeana. Open, upright shrub producing oblong-elliptic to broadly ovate, toothed, glossy, mid-green leaves, to 1½in (4cm) long, with red margins. Bears large, lavender-blue, lilac, or white flowers in terminal panicles, 8–12in (20–30cm) long, in late spring and early summer. ↕↔ 24in (60cm). New Zealand. ❄ (min. 41°F/5°C). **'Lilac Hint'** ■ has pale green leaves without red margins, and produces pale lilac flowers.

Hebe 'Gauntlettii'

***H.* 'Lady Ardilaun'** see *H.* 'Amy'.
***H.* 'La Séduisante'**, syn. *H. speciosa* 'Ruddigore'. Upright shrub with purple-tinged shoots and broadly elliptic, glossy, dark green leaves, to 4in (10cm) long, purple beneath when young. From late summer to autumn, produces medium-sized, dark purple-red flowers in axillary racemes, 3in (8cm) long. ↕↔ 3ft (1m). ❄ (min. 41°F/5°C)
H. latifolia see *H.* x *franciscana* 'Blue Gem'.
***H.* 'Loganioides'**, syn. *H. selaginoides* of gardens. Whipcord hebe with slender, yellow-green shoots and tiny, ovate to lance-shaped, finely hairy, bright green leaves, ¼in (6mm) long. Small white flowers are borne in axillary or terminal racemes, 1–2in (2.5–5cm) long, in summer. ↕↔ 10in (25cm). ❄ (min. 35°F/2°C)
H. lycopodioides. Whipcord hebe with rigid, angled, yellow-green shoots and triangular to rounded, yellow-margined, mid-green leaves, to ¹⁄₁₆in (2mm) long. Small white flowers are borne in small, terminal racemes, ½–¾in (1–2cm) long, in summer. ↕ 24in (60cm), ↔ 36in (90cm). New Zealand (South Island). ❄ (min. 35°F/2°C). **'Aurea'** see *H. armstrongii.*

Hebe 'Great Orme'

Hebe 'Hagley Park'

H. macrantha ■ Erect, open-branched, then spreading shrub with obovate to elliptic, blunt-toothed, leathery, bright green leaves, to 1in (2.5cm) long. Large white flowers, to ¾in (2cm) across, are produced in clusters of 3 from the upper leaf axils in early summer. ↕ 24in (60cm), ↔ 36in (90cm). New Zealand (South Island). ❄ (min. 41°F/5°C)
***H.* 'Marjorie'.** Compact, rounded shrub with elliptic, glossy, mid-green leaves, to 2in (5cm) long. From midsummer to early autumn, bears axillary racemes, to 5in (13cm) long, of medium-sized, mauve-blue flowers, fading to white. ↕ 4ft (1.2m), ↔ 5ft (1.5m). ❄ (min. 41°F/5°C)
***H.* 'Midsummer Beauty'.** Upright, rounded shrub with purplish brown stems and oblong to lance-shaped, bright green leaves, 3½–4½in (9–11cm)

Hebe hulkeana 'Lilac Hint'

Hebe macrantha

H

Hebe ochracea 'James Stirling' (inset: flower detail)

long, flushed red-purple beneath when young. Medium-sized, lilac-purple flowers, fading to white, are borne in axillary racemes, 5–6in (12–15cm) long, from midsummer to late autumn. ↕ 6ft (2m), ↔ 5ft (1.5m). ❄ (min. 41°F/5°C)

***H.* 'Mrs. Winder'**, syn. *H.* 'Waikiki', *H.* 'Warleyensis'. Compact, rounded shrub with purplish brown shoots and oblong-elliptic, dark green leaves, dark red-purple when young, to 1½in (4cm) long, with brown-purple midribs. In late summer, bears medium-sized, violet-blue flowers in axillary racemes, 2½–3in (6–8cm) long. ↕ 3ft (1m), ↔ 4ft (1.2m). ❄ (min. 41°F/5°C)

***H. ochracea* 'James Stirling'** ▣ Compact, erect then arching, whipcord hebe with triangular, rich ochre-yellow leaves, to 1⁄16–⅛in (2–3mm) long, particularly attractive in winter. Bears small to medium-sized white flowers in small, axillary racemes, ½–¾in (1–2cm) long, in late spring and early summer. ↕ 18in (45cm), ↔ 24in (60cm). ❄ (min. 35°F/2°C)

H. odora, syn. *H. anomala, H. buxifolia* of gardens. Bushy shrub with upright shoots and elliptic-ovate, glossy, dark green leaves, ½–¾in (1–2cm) long. In early and midsummer, bears small to medium-sized white flowers in dense, terminal racemes, ½–¾in (1–2cm) long. ↕ 3ft (1m), ↔ 5ft (1.5m). New Zealand. ❄ (min. 35°F/2°C)

***H.* 'Patty's Purple'.** Spreading, mound-forming shrub with wine-red stems and densely ranked, elliptic, dark green leaves, ½in (1.5cm) long. In spring and summer, bears terminal racemes, to 2in (5cm) across, of small purple flowers, fading to near white. ↕↔ 24in (60cm). ❄ (min. 35°F/2°C)

***H.* 'Pewter Dome'** ▣ syn. *H. albicans* 'Pewter Dome'. Dense, dome-shaped shrub producing ovate, gray-green leaves, to ¾in (2cm) long. In late spring and early summer, bears small white flowers in dense, axillary racemes, 1in (2.5cm) long. ↕ 16in (40cm), ↔ 24in (60cm). ❄ (min. 41°F/5°C)

H. pimeleoides. Rounded shrub with upright, purple-tinged shoots and ovate to narrowly lance-shaped, leathery, glaucous, gray-green leaves, to ½in (1.5cm) long, with narrow red margins. Small, purple-blue flowers are produced in axillary spikes, ½in (1.5cm) long, in summer. ↕ 18in (45cm), ↔ 24in (60cm). New Zealand (South Island). ❄ (min. 41°F/5°C). **'County Park'** is decumbent in habit, with red-margined, gray-green leaves, flushed red-purple in cold weather; ↕ to 8in (20cm), ↔ 20in (50cm). **var. *glaucocaerulea*** produces very glaucous foliage. **'Quicksilver'** is spreading in habit, with small, silver-gray leaves and pale lilac-blue flowers; ↕ 12in (30cm).

Hebe 'Pewter Dome'

Hebe pinguifolia 'Pagei'

***H. pinguifolia* 'Pagei'** ▣ Erect then semi-prostrate shrub with 4-ranked, obovate-elliptic, leathery, blue-green leaves, to ½in (1.5cm) long, borne on purple stems. In late spring and early summer, bears a profusion of medium-sized white flowers, to ⅜in (9mm) across, in dense, axillary spikes, to 1in (2.5cm) long. Good groundcover. ↕ 12in (30cm), ↔ 36in (90cm). Zone 7.

***H.* 'Purple Queen'** see *H.* 'Amy'.

***H.* 'Purple Tips' of gardens** see *H. speciosa* 'Tricolor'.

H. rakaiensis ▣ Rounded shrub with dense, elliptic to obovate, glossy, bright green leaves, to ¾in (2cm) long. Bears large white flowers in axillary racemes, to 1½in (4cm) long, in early and midsummer. ↕ 3ft (1m), ↔ 4ft (1.2m). New Zealand (South Island). ❄ (min. 35°F/2°C)

H. recurva. Compact, spreading shrub with slender, narrowly lance-shaped, curved, blue-gray leaves, to 2in (5cm) long. Small to medium-sized white flowers are borne in narrow, axillary spikes, to 2½in (6cm) long, in summer. ↕ 24in (60cm), ↔ 30in (75cm). New Zealand (South Island). ❄ (min. 41°F/5°C)

***H.* 'Red Edge'**, syn. *H. albicans* 'Red Edge'. Spreading shrub producing ovate, gray-green leaves, to ¾in (2cm) long, narrowly margined and veined red when young. Bears medium-sized, lilac-blue flowers, fading to white, in terminal spikes, to 1¼in (3cm) long, in summer. ↕ 18in (45cm), ↔ 24in (60cm). ❄ (min. 41°F/5°C)

H. salicifolia. Erect to spreading shrub with narrow, pointed, willow-like, lance-shaped to oblong-lance-shaped, mid-green leaves, to 5in (13cm) or more long. Small, white or pale lilac-blue flowers are produced in slender, axillary, often pendent racemes, to 8in (20cm) long, in summer. ↕↔ 8ft (2.5m). New Zealand (South Island). ❄ (min. 41°F/5°C)

***H. selaginoides* of gardens** see *H.* 'Loganioides'.

***H.* 'Simon Delaux'.** Rounded shrub with ovate, dark green leaves, to 2in (5cm) long, conspicuously flushed dark red-purple when young. Medium-sized crimson flowers are borne in dense, axillary spikes, to 4in (10cm) long, in summer. ↕↔ 4ft (1.2m). ❄ (min. 45°F/7°C)

***H. speciosa* 'Ruddigore'** see *H.* 'La Séduisante'.

***H. speciosa* 'Tricolor'**, syn. *H.* 'Purple Tips' of gardens. Rounded shrub with upright shoots and elliptic, gray-green leaves, to 2in (5cm) long, margined creamy white and flushed purple beneath, particularly when young and in winter. In summer, bears medium-sized, violet-purple flowers in axillary spikes, to 3in (8cm) long. ↕↔ 4ft (1.2m). ❄ (min. 45°F/7°C)

H. tetragona. Whipcord hebe with thick, upright, 4-angled shoots and tiny, densely set, triangular to awl-shaped, leathery, glossy, yellow-green leaves, 1⁄16in (2mm) long. In early summer, produces terminal spikes, 1½in (4cm) long, of small to medium-sized white flowers. ↕ 18in (45cm), ↔ 24in (60cm). New Zealand (North Island). ❄ (min. 35°F/2°C)

Hebe rakaiensis

H. tetrasticha. Dwarf, whipcord hebe with procumbent then erect, tetragonal stems covered with triangular, scale-like, dark green leaves, to 1⁄16in (2mm) long. In summer, produces 1–3 pairs of large white flowers from the leaf axils at the stem tips. Seldom blooms in cultivation. Needs cool conditions and humus-rich, gritty soil. ↕ 4in (10cm), ↔ 8in (20cm). New Zealand (Canterbury Alps, South Island). ❄ (min. 35°F/2°C)

***H.* 'Tom Marshall'** see *H. canterburiensis.*

H. topiaria. Dense, dome-shaped shrub with broadly elliptic to obovate, glossy, gray-green leaves, to ½in (1.5cm) long. Bears medium-sized white flowers in short, dense, terminal racemes, ½–¾in (1–2cm) long, in summer. ↕ 24in (60cm), ↔ 32–36in (80–90cm). New Zealand (South Island). ❄ (min. 35°F/2°C)

***H.* 'Veitchii'** see *H.* 'Alicia Amherst'.

H. vernicosa. Compact, rounded shrub with dense, elliptic, glossy, dark green leaves, to ½in (1.5cm) long. Medium-sized white flowers, sometimes pale lilac-blue at first, are borne in axillary racemes, to 2in (5cm) long, in early and midsummer. ↕ 24in (60cm), ↔ 4ft (1.2m). New Zealand (South Island). ❄ (min. 41°F/5°C)

***H.* 'Waikiki'** see *H.* 'Mrs. Winder'.

***H.* 'Warleyensis'** see *H.* 'Mrs. Winder'.

***H.* 'Wingletye'.** Low, spreading shrub with obovate, glaucous, gray-green leaves, to ½in (1.5cm) long. Bears small, lilac-blue flowers in axillary racemes, 1in (2.5cm) long, in summer. ↕ 6in (15cm), ↔ 12in (30cm). ❄ (min. 41°F/5°C)

***H.* 'Youngii'**, syn. *H.* 'Carl Teschner'. Compact, mat-forming, dark-stemmed shrub with elliptic to broadly obovate, dark green leaves, to ¼in (6mm) long, sometimes red-margined. Large violet flowers with white throats are borne in axillary racemes, to 1¼in (3cm) long, in summer. ↕ 8in (20cm), ↔ to 24in (60cm). ❄ (min. 35°F/2°C)

HECHTIA

BROMELIACEAE

Genus of over 50 species of short-stemmed or stemless, dioecious, evergreen, terrestrial perennials (bromeliads) found in rocky terrain and forest, up to altitudes of 6,500ft (2,000m), in S.W. US, Mexico, Guatemala, Honduras, and Nicaragua. They have dense rosettes of narrowly triangular, fleshy, coarsely spiny leaves. In summer, inconspicuous, funnel-shaped, green, yellow, or white flowers are produced in long, branching racemes or panicles among the foliage rosettes. Plants of both sexes are needed in order to obtain fruits. Where not hardy, grow in a temperate greenhouse or conservatory. In frost-free regions, grow outdoors in a desert garden.

• **CULTIVATION** Under glass, grow in terrestrial bromeliad or succulent potting mix in full light. During the growing season, water moderately and apply a half-strength, low-nitrogen liquid fertilizer monthly; keep plants completely dry in winter. Outdoors, grow in sharply drained, poor to moderately fertile soil in full sun. Provide protection from winter moisture. *Hechtia* is one of the hardiest genera of bromeliads, tolerating bright sun and brief periods near freezing. See also p.47.

• **PROPAGATION** Sow seed at 70–75°F (21–24°C) as soon as ripe. Remove and pot up offsets in spring.

• **PESTS AND DISEASES** Susceptible to mealybugs and scale insects.

H. argentea ■ syn. *Dyckia argentea.* Rosetted perennial with about 100 narrowly triangular-linear, densely scaly, silvery green leaves, to 24in (60cm) long, with jagged, marginal spines. Lax panicles of white flowers, with brown bracts and white-hairy sepals, are produced from the rosettes in summer. ‡↔ 3ft (1m) or more. Mexico. (min. 41°F/5°C)

H. glomerata. Rosetted perennial producing about 40 narrowly triangular, spreading, often red-tipped, mid-green leaves, 10–16in (25–40cm) long, covered on the undersides with fine, white or brown scales. Narrowly ovoid white flowers, with brown bracts and sepals, are borne in branched, lateral racemes, to 20in (50cm) long, in summer. ‡↔ 16in (40cm) or more. Texas, Mexico, Guatemala. (min. 41°F/5°C)

Hechtia argentea

HEDERA

Ivy

ARALIACEAE

Genus of 8–12 species of evergreen, woody-stemmed, trailing or self-clinging climbers. They are found in light woodland or on trees or rocks in N. Africa, the Canary Islands, the Azores, and Madeira, and from W. Europe to the Himalayas, China, Korea, and Japan. They have alternate, 3- to 5-lobed or entire leaves, which are sometimes attractively variegated. Ivies show 2 distinct stages of growth. In the creeping or climbing juvenile stage, ivies have adventitious rootlets, lobed leaves, and minutely hairy young shoots. In the adult stage, they produce aerial "bushes," often high in the tops of trees, with entire, usually broadly ovate leaves and, in autumn, spherical umbels of tiny, 5-lobed, yellowish green, bisexual flowers; these are followed by spherical, black, sometimes blue, orange, or yellow fruits, ⅛–⅜in (4–9mm) across.

The American Ivy Society categorizes ivies by leaf characteristics as described in the panel at right, also including the following four types: **Miniatures** (M) include all ivies with leaves less than 1in (2.5cm) long, and are delicate in appearance. **Oddities** (O) have unusual traits, such as upright or non-vining habits; flattened, compacted stems; or fasciated, asymmetrical, or distorted leaves. **Variegateds** (V) have leaves of more than one color, or of a single color other than green. **Arborescent** (A) ivies are mature plants with stiff stems, no longer capable of vining; their leaves are generally unlobed, and they bear flowers and fruit. The category symbols appear in parentheses after every cultivar entry.

If temperatures drop below 40°F (4°C), many all-green ivies take on shades of red or purple; the edges of marginally variegated ivies turn pink; and yellow-leaved cultivars become streaked with maroon. Ivies vary greatly in size and vigor, due to seasonal and regional climate variations, growing conditions, and their tendency to sport (mutate) readily. Seasonal variability affects the length of the leaf stalks, the length and width of the lobes, and the prominence of the veins, being most noticeable in the bird's foot ivies. Ivies grown on walls, fences, or trees will bear more widely spaced leaves and produce leaves with more pronounced or narrower lobes than plants grown as groundcovers. Similarly, the same cultivar grown as both a houseplant and a landscape plant may show considerable differences. When grown vertically, a typically unlobed ivy will form lobes.

Generally speaking, ivies trail along the ground and will climb if given the support of a tree, wall, or similar surface. Because they do not twine, they must be fastened to trellises or chain-link fences. Non-branching ivies make the most vigorous groundcovers, and ivies with widely spaced leaves make the best wall covers. Self-branching ivies are more compact and refined in their growth habits, and make good specimen plants or neat groundcovers. Use miniatures or variegateds in a rock garden or as edging plants. Oddities are suitable in a rock garden or as specimens. Ivy is not a parasite and does not damage trees, nor does it damage walls if they are sound. Under glass, ivies may be used as houseplants or in baskets and other containers, and as topiary (on a frame) or bonsai. All parts of ivy may cause severe discomfort if ingested; contact with the sap or airborne hairs may aggravate allergies or irritate skin.

• **CULTIVATION** Under glass, grow in soil-based or soilless potting mix in bright indirect to low light. Water freely when in growth, applying a balanced liquid fertilizer monthly; keep moist in winter. Outdoors, ivies tolerate a range of conditions but grow best in fertile, humus-rich, moist but well-drained soil. Green-leaved ivies are shade-tolerant. Variegated cultivars prefer more light, with protection from strong summer sun. Where marginally hardy, protect all ivies from winter sun and wind. To encourage rapid establishment, break off the lowest 2–4 leaves of young plants and bury up to the lowest leaf axil. Pruning group 11, at any time.

• **PROPAGATION** Root 4–6in (10–15cm) semi-ripe cuttings of juvenile growth from spring to autumn; variegateds and those with poorly developed root systems take longer. Use 7- to 9-month-old adult growth to obtain plants with a bushy, "tree-ivy" habit, but they root very slowly, if at all. If standards are required, graft small-leaved ivies onto single-stemmed x *Fatshedera lizei.*

• **PESTS AND DISEASES** Susceptible to bacterial spot, stem rot, and fungal leaf spots, as well as spider mites, aphids, mealybugs, and scale insects. Deer may eat the foliage.

IVY LEAF SHAPES

The American Ivy Society uses the Pierot Classification System to categorize ivy leaf shapes: **Ivy** (I) ivies have "typical," almost flat, palmately 5-lobed leaves. **Heart-shape** (H) ivies have heart-shaped or triangular, 3-lobed leaves. **Fan** (F) ivies have broad, fan-shaped leaves, with lobes of equal length or forward-pointing, prominently veined lobes. **Bird's Foot** (BF) ivies have narrowly lobed or willow-like, unlobed leaves. **Curly** (C) ivies have ruffled, rippled, or pleated leaves or leaf margins.

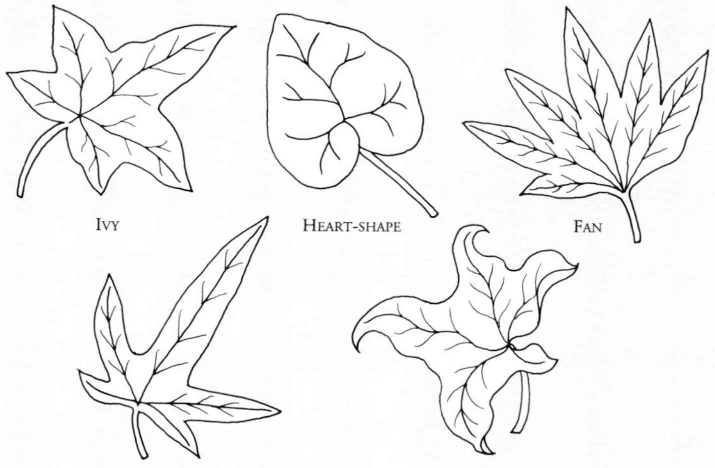

H. azorica (F) syn. *H. canariensis* of gardens 'Azorica' (Azores ivy). Vigorous climber with white-hairy new growth, and large, fan-shaped, matte, light green leaves, to 3in (8cm) long, each with 5–7 nearly equal lobes. Azores. Zone 6b.

***H. canariensis* of gardens** (I) (Canary Island ivy, North African ivy). Vigorous climber with heart-shaped or 3-lobed, glossy, emerald-green leaves, 4–8in (10–20cm) long, borne on long, maroon leaf stalks. Algeria, Tunisia. Zone 7; variegated cultivars are generally hardy in Zone 7b. **'Gloire de Marengo'** ■ (V, H) has leaves with wide, white to cream margins and gray-streaked centers. May sport to 'Striata'. **'Margino-Maculata'** (V, H) has creamy white leaves speckled with green or gray, or gray-streaked centers with speckles in the creamy white margins. Often sports to 'Striata'. **'Striata'** (V, H) is vigorous, with lustrous, mid-green leaves, splashed yellow to chartreuse in the centers.

Hedera canariensis 'Gloire de Marengo'

Hedera helix 'Congesta'

H

H. colchica (H) (Colchis ivy, Persian ivy). Vigorous climber with heart-shaped, leathery, dark green leaves, 3–8in (8–20cm) long, aromatic when crushed. Suitable for a groundcover or for a large wall. Caucasus, N. Iran. Zone 7. **'Dentata'** (H) has arching, dark green leaves, 4–6in (10–15cm) long, slightly toothed at the margins, with purple-flushed stems and leaf stalks. Good for a groundcover or for a large wall. **'Dentata Variegata'** (V, H) has light green leaves, 3–6in (8–15cm) long, streaked gray-green, and broadly margined creamy white. Suitable for a wall or as a groundcover; Zone 7. **'Sulphur Heart'** ■ (V, H) syn. 'Paddy's Pride', is similar to 'Dentata Variegata' but grows faster and has more elongated, mid-green leaves, with gold to chartreuse centers and white main veins. Good for a wall.

H. cypria (syn. *Hedera pastuchovii* var. *cypria*) (BF). A slow-growing ivy that will climb. Its unlobed to 3-lobed thick, leathery leaves are dark blackish green with silver veins. The stems and petioles are purple-green. Use in a rock garden. Cyprus, Troodos Mountains. ❄ (min. 35°F/2°C)

H. helix (I) (English ivy). Vigorous, variable, self-clinging climber or trailing perennial with 3- to 5-lobed, broadly ovate to triangular, glossy, dark green leaves, 1½–2½in (4–6cm) long. Europe. Zone 5b. *H. helix* has given rise to many attractive variants and cultivars. In the descriptions below, leaf sizes have been grouped as follows: small, to 1in (2.5cm) long; medium, 1–2½in (2.5–6cm) long; large, 2½in (6cm) or more long. **'Angularis Aurea'** ■ (V, I) has medium, slightly angular, shallowly lobed, glossy, mid-green leaves; young leaves are suffused and variegated with yellow. Moderately vígorous; ideal for a wall. **'Anita'** ■ (M, BF) is a miniature version of 'Ritterkreuz' and a presumed sport of 'Needlepoint'. The medium green leaves of this very compact ivy are just 1½in (4cm) long and self-branching; they are 5-lobed, with the terminal lobes twice as long as the lateral lobes. It makes a nice houseplant, in a hanging basket or topiary; it is also suitable in a rock garden. **'Anne Marie'** (V, I) has medium, mid-gray-green leaves with heart-shaped bases and 5 rounded, cream-variegated lobes. Use as a houseplant or on a sheltered wall. **'Asterisk'** (BF) is a winter-hardy short-jointed climber or trailer, with small, deeply and narrowly lobed, light green leaves. Use as a houseplant or in a hanging basket. **'Baltica'** (I) closely resembles the species except for its more heart-shaped leaves and conspicuous white veins. Zone 4. **'Boskoop'** (C, F) is similar to 'Green Ripple', with small, 3-lobed, glossy, mid-green leaves, but the leaves are more curled and have less distinctive veining. **'Buttercup'** ■ (V, I) has medium, 3- to 5-lobed leaves (the unlobed adult form is pictured) that are pale green when grown in shade but bright yellow in full sun. Ideal for a wall. Will burn in bright sunlight in Zone 6 south. **'Caecilia'** (V, C) has medium, nearly round, 5-lobed, frilled, light green leaves, occasionally with gray blotches and creamy white edges. Usually grown as a houseplant. **'Calico'** ■ (V, C) is slow-growing, and is usually grown as a houseplant. It has small, 3-lobed, mid-green leaves with white variegation,

Hedera helix 'Eva'

mostly confined to the center of each leaf. **'California'** ■ (C) is self-branching with medium, broadly 5-lobed, curly leaves, with heart-shaped bases and slightly raised veins. Good for indoor and outdoor use. **'California Fan'** (C, F) has medium-sized, light green leaves with 5–7 boldly veined lobes and wedge-shaped bases. Good houseplant. **'Ceridwen'** ■ (V, I) has small, pointed, 3- to 5-lobed, gray-green leaves with broad yellow margins. A popular basket plant. **'Chester'** (V, I) has small, almost triangular, 3-lobed leaves, variegated lime-green and cream with dark green central blotches. Grow on a low wall or as a houseplant. **'Congesta'** ■ (O) is non-climbing, forming a neat bush with spire-like shoots. It has small, 3-lobed, dark green leaves borne in 2 opposite ranks along the stems. Use in a rock garden. **'Conglomerata'** (O) is non-vining, with medium, entire or shallowly 3-lobed, thick, dark green leaves with wavy margins. Use in a rock garden or as a houseplant. **'Curly Locks'** (C) has large, entire, ovate to almost rounded, mid- to dark green leaves with tightly grooved margins. **'Diana'** (H) is trailing, and has variable, medium, 3-lobed, dark green leaves, with the apex of each lobe drawn out to a wisp. Good in a hanging basket. **'Dragon Claw'** (C) syn. 'Curley-Q', is a vigorous, climbing ivy with large, 3- to 5-lobed, strongly curled, dark green leaves. **'Duckfoot'** ■ (M, BF), usually grown as a houseplant, has small, light green leaves with 3 shallow lobes and wedge-shaped bases; each leaf resembles a duck's foot. Good as a bonsai. **'Eva'** ■ (V, BF) is a 'Variegated Needlepoint'. Its medium-size leaves have 3 forward-pointing lobes, with the terminal lobe up to twice the length of laterals. It needs good light to display its best variegation–an irregular gray-green center, with a creamy white margin. As a house plant, it can be used in a topiary; it may also be used as protected ground cover. **'Fan'** (F) has broad, medium, conspicuously veined, apple-green leaves, each with 3–5 shallow, rounded, forward-pointing, downward-cupped lobes. **'Flamenco'** (O, C) has variable, small, dark green, glossy, frilly leaves, usually 5-lobed but often entire, with flattened leaf stalks. Use as a houseplant. A fasciated sport of 'Ivalace'. **'Fluffy Ruffles'** ■ (C) is usually grown as a houseplant and has small, wavy, 5-lobed, mid-green leaves with frilled margins. **'Garland'** (H) has medium to large, broadly heart-shaped, glossy, rich green leaves. **'Glacier'** ■ (V, I) has medium, almost triangular, 3- to 5-lobed, mid-green leaves, with silver-gray variegations and white margins. Use on a wall, as a groundcover, or as a houseplant. Zone 5. **'Gold Child'** (V, I) syn. 'Gold Harald', has medium, 3- to 5-lobed, gray-green leaves with broad yellow margins. Ideal as a houseplant or on a low wall. **'Gold Dust'** ■ (V, I)

Hedera colchica 'Sulphur Heart'

Hedera helix 'Angularis Aurea'

Hedera helix 'Anita'

Hedera helix 'Buttercup'

Hedera helix 'Calico'

Hedera helix 'California'

Hedera helix 'Ceridwen'

Hedera helix 'Duckfoot'

Hedera helix 'Fluffy Ruffles'

Hedera helix 'Gold Dust'

Hedera helix 'Golden Ingot'

Hedera helix 'Gold Heart'

Hedera helix 'Glacier'

has medium, 5-lobed, gold leaves, splashed with green or occasionally gray. Useful on a contrasting wall or as a groundcover. **'Golden Ingot'** ■ (V, I) syn. 'Golden Inge', has medium, 5-lobed, curly or flat, bright yellow leaves, with irregular, mid-green margins and yellow-splashed centers. **'Gold Heart'** ■ (V, H) syn. 'Jubiläum Goldherz', 'Jubilee Goldheart', 'Oro di Bogliasco', has small, 3-lobed, dark green leaves, each with a central splash of bright yellow. An excellent wall ivy, slow to establish but then fast-growing. **'Green Feather'** (M, BF) has small, closely spaced, dark green leaves, each with 3–5, deeply cut, folded, long-tapering, narrow lobes. Densely self-branching; good as a groundcover. **'Green Finger'** (BF) has small, unlobed or 3-lobed, mid-green leaves, each with one basal "ear" or short, rounded lobe at right angles to the midrib. **'Green Ripple'** ■ (F) has medium, mid-green leaves with 3 to 5, jagged, forward-pointing, prominently veined lobes; may not climb well. **'Harrison'** ■ (I) has large, triangular, white-veined, dark green leaves that may turn purple in winter. Zone 5. **'Helena'** (V, BF) has medium-size, star-like, 3- to 5-lobed, mid-green leaves with creamy white margins and gray-splashed centers. Each leaf has a central lobe, twice as long as the lateral lobes, that is curved to one side. Makes a good houseplant. ↕18in (45cm). **'Ingobert'** (V, I) syn. 'Bruder Ingobert', has medium, irregularly shaped, 3- to 5-lobed, gray-green leaves with dark green markings, with a dark green margin, a white inner border, and the center splashed with shades of gray and white. A good houseplant. **'Irish Lace'** (BF) has medium, star-like, flat, dark green leaves with 5 almost linear lobes and margins rolled under. **'Ivalace'** ■ (C) has small, 5-lobed, lustrous, dark green leaves with wavy, curled, and crimped margins. Excellent, all-around ivy for a low wall, as a groundcover, or as a houseplant. **'Jubilee'** (M, V) is a compact, variable, slow-growing ivy with small, entire or 3- to 5-lobed, gray-green leaves, marked darker green, and margined with cream. Use as a houseplant, edging, or annual where not hardy. **'Kolibri'** (V, I) has small, neat, mid-green- to gray-variegated, creamy white leaves, with 3 forward-pointing lobes. Very variable, but a good houseplant. **'Lady Frances'** (V, M, BF) is a miniature ivy with 3–5 irregular sharply pointed lobes. It has gray and white constant variegation that will not fade in low light. No 2 leaves quite the same. It is strongly self-branching and compact and makes a lovely houseplant, suitable in baskets, as a topiary, and as protected groundcover. **'Lalla Rookh'** ■ (C) is trailing, with large, light green leaves; the 5 irregularly toothed lobes are cut almost to the central veins. Use on a tree or a wall. **'Little Diamond'** ■ (M, V) is compact, self-branching, and slow-growing, with small, entire, diamond-shaped, gray-green leaves, margined creamy white. Use as a houseplant or in a rock garden. **'Manda Crested'** ■ (C) has large, curled, 5-lobed, mid-green leaves with downward-pointing tips. The leaves are shiny when young, and become copper-tinted in cold weather. Good for a wall and as a groundcover. **'Maple Leaf'** ■ (BF) has large, star-like, 5-lobed, mid-green leaves with irregularly toothed margins. Suitable for a wall, tree, or hanging basket. **'Midas Touch'** (V, H) syn. 'Golden Kolibri', has medium, ovate, shallowly 3-lobed or entire, dark green leaves with irregular, bright yellow variegation. Use as a houseplant or on a low wall. **'Midget'** ■ (M, BF) has small, flat, star-like, mid-green leaves, with 3–5 narrow lobes. A smaller version of 'Needlepoint', with the leaves arranged in flat sprays. **'Misty'** (M, V, BF) syn. 'Silver Lace', is a neat, self-branching, houseplant ivy, with small, 3-lobed, gray-streaked, mid-green leaves, narrowly white-margined, and with arching central lobes. **'Mrs. Pollock'** (VF) has medium, mid-green leaves with 5–7 forward-pointing lobes, suffused with yellow. A good climber for a wall. **'Needlepoint'** ■ (M, BF) is bushy and self branching, with small, flat, 3-lobed, or inconspicuously 5-lobed, mid-green leaves. **'Parsley Crested'** (C) syn. 'Cristata', has medium, entire, ovate to almost rounded, mid- to dark green leaves with waved and crested margins. Use on a wall. **'Pedata'** (BF) syn. 'Caenwoodiana' (Bird's foot ivy), is an excellent wall ivy, with medium, 5-lobed, gray-green leaves. Each leaf has an elongated central lobe and backward-pointing lateral lobes, resembling the shape of a bird's foot. **'Perkeo'** ■ (H) is a short-jointed ivy, with medium, heart-shaped, thickened, dark green leaves, streaked mid-green, with purple-tinted veins. New leaves are greenish yellow. Leaves turn reddish in wool weather. **'Pin Oak'** (BF) has small, 3-lobed, light green leaves, with rounded tips and the central lobes twice the length of the lateral lobes. Usually grown as a houseplant. ↕3ft (1m). **'Pittsburgh'** (I) is the name for a collection of clones with small to medium, mid-green leaves, heart-shaped at the bases, with 5 pointed lobes. **'Pixie'** (M, BF) syn. 'Holly', has small, grass green to dark green leaves with 5–7 forward-pointing lobes, and a prominent, pale green vein bisecting each. The terminal lobe is twice the length of the laterals. The leaves are closely spaced, with the leaf margin slightly rolled under. Its small, dense, self-branching habit and noninvasiveness make for good ground and wall cover. **'Plume d'Or'** ■ (BF) is a vigorous wall ivy producing large, mid-green leaves with 5 narrow, elongated lobes; the central lobes are often twice as long as the lateral lobes. **f. *poetarum*** ■ (I) syn. 'Poetica Arborea' (Italian ivy, Poet's ivy), has large, 5-lobed to entire, shiny mid-green leaves. It is often grown as a bush ivy, since it bears distinctive, orange-yellow fruit, even on fairly young plants. Good when

Hedera helix f. *poetarum*

grown on a wall. **'Ritterkreuz'** (BF) has 5-lobed leaves, with asymmetric terminal and lateral lobes, which are broadest at the middle and constricted at the base. A sport of 'Needlepoint', from Germany, its name means Knight's Cross or Maltese Cross. Use for a border, groundcover, and wall cover; also a good houseplant. **'Romanze'** (V, C) has large, 5-lobed, gold-variegated, light green leaves, with wavy and curled margins. **'Schaefer Three'** (V, I) syn. 'Schäfer Three', is a short-jointed houseplant ivy with small, entire or shallowly 3-lobed leaves with highly variable coloring. Leaves are dark green; they may be marked gray-green with creamy white variegation, or have white centers and irregular green margins. Often misidentified as 'Kolibri'. **'Shamrock'** (M, BF) (Cloverleaf ivy) has small, dark green leaves with 3 round-tipped lobes; the lateral lobes are cut almost to the central veins. Use for topiary, on a low wall, or in a hanging basket. **'Spectre'** ■ (V, BF) has medium, 3- to 5-lobed, mid-green, cream- and gray-streaked leaves; each lobe is curled and twisted, with pointed, downward-curling tips. **'Spetchley'** (M, BF) syn. 'Gnome', grows in flat sprays and has stiff, maroon, young stems. The leaves are variable, tiny, shiny, and dark green, ¼–½in (5–15mm) long, usually 3-lobed, but often with a single elliptic or triangular lobe. Ideal for a small topiary, on a wall, or in a rock garden.

H

Hedera helix 'Green Ripple'

Hedera helix 'Harrison'

Hedera helix 'Ivalace'

Hedera helix 'Lalla Rookh'

Hedera helix 'Little Diamond'

Hedera helix 'Manda Crested'

Hedera helix 'Maple Leaf'

Hedera helix 'Midget'

Hedera helix 'Needlepoint'

Hedera helix 'Perkeo'

Hedera helix 'Plume d'Or'

Hedera helix 'Spectre'

Hedera helix 'Teardrop'

'Teardrop' ■ (H) has mostly unlobed, teardrop-shaped leaves, but occasionally 1 or 2 basal lobes can be found with a heart-shaped base. The leaf tip is elongated to a point. Slow-growing and stiffly-pointed branches, a good outdoor ivy. **'Telecurl'** ■ (C) is an elegant houseplant ivy with small, 5-lobed, slightly folded, bright dark green leaves, with leaf blades that curl between the lobes. **'Thorndale'** (I) syn. 'Sub-Zero', has large, widely spaced, heart-shaped, irregularly 5-lobed, dark green leaves that are slightly wider than long. The upper veins are pale green to white in winter. Zone 5. **'Tobler'** (BF) syn. 'Professor Friedrich Tobler', has small, 3- to 5-lobed, mid-green leaves; the lobes are sometimes cut almost to the central veins, giving the impression of separate leaflets. Excellent for a hanging basket. **'Treetop'** ■ (A) is an adult, erect shrub with ovate, bright green, glossy young foliage, maturing to dark green; roots easily. **'Walthamensis'** (I) has 3-lobed leaves with shallow sinuses. Dark green, with lighter veins, the winter color is blackish green, with white veins. It is very winter hardy with good coverage despite its small leaves.
H. hibernica (I) syn. *H. helix* subsp. *hibernica* (Atlantic ivy). Vigorous climber producing broadly ovate to triangular, mid- to dark green leaves, 2–3in (5–8cm) long, with 5 triangular lobes and light green veins. Useful for a wall or as a groundcover. W. Europe. Zone 5b. **'Deltoidea'** ■ (H) syn. *H. helix* 'Deltoidea' (Sweetheart ivy), is slow-growing, producing small to medium-sized, neat, densely arranged, entire or very shallowly 3-lobed, dark green leaves, 2½–4in (6–10cm) long. The basal lobes sometimes overlap, giving each leaf a heart shape. **'Rona'** (V, I) has gold leaves with green freckles. **'Variegata'** (V, I) produces leaves with sharply defined, yellow-cream variegation with green blotches. It sometimes has totally green leaves.
H. maderensis (I) (Madeira ivy) has 3-lobed, medium-size, dark matte-green leaves as wide as long, and burgundy stems and petioles. Good groundcover in warmer climates. ❀ (min. 41°F/5°C)
H. maroccana (I) (Moroccan ivy) 3–5-lobed, dark green leaves with red stems and petioles. New growth comes in light green. The leaf base is cuneate to barely heart-shaped. A vigorous grower that does well in a container or as a groundcover. Atlas Mountains. ❀ (min. 45°F/7°C). **'Spanish Canary'** (I) Large 3–5 star-shaped lobes are pointed, with a terminal lobe twice as long as the lateral; small protrusions on basal lobes. Shiny; new growth is pea-green, darkening with age.
H. nepalensis (H) (Nepal ivy). Weak-growing, self-clinging climber with usually entire, elliptic, olive-green leaves, 2½–4in (6–10cm) long; the leaves may have 3–6 toothed, projecting lobes. An interesting climber for a sheltered wall. Himalayas. Zone 6. **'Marbled Dragon'** ■ (H) has triangular to 3-lobed, loosely spaced, dull, gray-white-veined, dark gray-green leaves on long leaf stalks. Ideal on a tree or wall. Zone 7b. **'Suzanne'** ■ (BF) has star-shaped, 5-lobed, white-veined, grayish green leaves with backward-pointing basal lobes. Zone 7b.
H. rhombea (I) (Japanese ivy). Self-clinging climber producing unlobed, ovate to triangular, mid-green leaves, ¾–1½in (2–4cm) long. Korea, Japan. Zone 7. **'Pierot'** (H) is delicate, with small, widely spaced, 3-lobed, ivy-like to heart-shaped, dark green leaves. Grow in a protected site on a wall or tree, or as a groundcover in a small area. **'Variegata'** ■ (V, I) is slower-growing, and has leaves with attractive creamy white margins.

Hedera helix 'Telecurl'

Hedera helix 'Treetop'

Hedera hibernica 'Deltoidea'

Hedera nepalensis 'Marbled Dragon'

Hedera nepalensis 'Suzanne'

Hedera rhombea 'Variegata'

HEDYCHIUM
syn. BRACHYCHILUM
Garland lily, Ginger lily

ZINGIBERACEAE

Genus of about 40 species of rhizomatous perennials from moist, lightly wooded areas of Asia. They have thick, fleshy rhizomes and usually lance-shaped leaves, borne in 2 parallel ranks on unbranched, reed-like stems. Hedychiums are grown for their foliage and for their exotic, 2-lipped, tubular or almost trumpet-shaped, often fragrant, white, yellow, or orange-red flowers, with large bracts, borne in congested, spike-like racemes. The flowers are followed by ovoid, capsular fruits with sometimes colorful seeds. Hedychiums are most effective when planted in groups next to still water, or in a mixed or herbaceous border. Where not hardy, grow in large containers in a warm greenhouse (marginally hardy species in a cool or cold one); in summer, they may be placed outdoors or planted out.

• **CULTIVATION** Under glass, grow in soil-based potting mix in bright indirect light. Provide moderate to high humidity and good ventilation. In the growing season, water freely and apply a balanced liquid fertilizer monthly. In winter, keep just moist and remove old stems as they deteriorate. Outdoors, grow in humus-rich, moist but well-drained soil in sun or partial shade, with shelter from wind. Marginally hardy hedychiums may survive if grown against a warm wall and given a deep winter mulch.

• **PROPAGATION** Sow seed at 70–75°F (21–24°C) as soon as ripe. Divide rhizomes in spring. Sow bulbils of *H. greenei* when mature.

• **PESTS AND DISEASES** Spider mites, aphids, root rot, and leaf spot can occur.

H. coccineum (Red ginger lily, Scarlet ginger lily). Erect, rhizomatous perennial with long, sharp-pointed, lance-shaped, mid-green leaves, 12–20in (30–50cm) long. Tubular, scented, pale to deep red, orange, pink, or white flowers, with prominent red stamens, are borne in terminal, cylindrical racemes, to 10in (25cm) long, from late summer to autumn. ↕ to 10ft (3m), ↔ 3ft (1m). Himalayas. Zone 8. **'Tara'** has orange flowers with slightly redder stamens and styles.
H. coronarium (Garland flower, White ginger lily). Upright, rhizomatous perennial. Long, sharp-pointed, lance-shaped, mid-green leaves, 24in (60cm) long, downy beneath. Bears very fragrant, butterfly-like white flowers, with yellow basal marks, in terminal, elliptic racemes, 8in (20cm) long, in mid- and late summer. ↕ to 10ft (3m), ↔ 3ft (1m) or more. India. ❀ (min. 41°F/5°C)
H. densiflorum ■ Clump-forming perennial with oblong to lance-shaped, pointed, glossy, mid-green leaves, 12–16in (30–40cm) long. In late summer, bears tubular, fragrant, orange or yellow flowers in dense, terminal, cylindrical racemes, 8in (20cm) long. ↕ to 15ft (5m), ↔ 6ft (2m) or more. Himalayas. Zone 8. **'Assam Orange'** bears deep orange flowers in very dense, bottlebrush-like racemes. **'Stephen'** ■ has larger, laxer racemes of flowers, with more protruding, pale orange yellow corolla lobes and deep orange stamens.
H. forrestii. Rhizomatous perennial with leafy stems bearing narrow, lance-shaped, strongly veined, mid-green leaves, 12–20in (30–50cm) long. In late summer and early autumn, bears narrow-lobed white flowers in dense, cylindrical racemes, to 20in (50cm) long. ↕ to 5ft (1.5m), ↔ 24in (60cm). China (Yunnan). ❀ (min. 35°F/2°C)
H. gardnerianum ■ (Kahili ginger). Upright, rhizomatous perennial with lance-shaped, grayish green leaves, 10–16in (25–40cm) long. Butterfly-like, fragrant, lemon-yellow flowers, with bright red stamens, are borne in dense, broadly cylindrical, terminal racemes, 10–14in (25–35cm) long, in late summer and early autumn. ↕ to 6–7ft (2–2.2m) or more, ↔ to 3ft (1m). N. India, Himalayas. Zone 8.

Hedychium densiflorum

Hedychium densiflorum 'Stephen'

H

Hedychium gardnerianum

H. greenei. Rhizomatous, clump-forming perennial with long, oblong, sharp-pointed, mid-green leaves, 8–10in (20–25cm) long. Butterfly-like, bright red flowers are borne in terminal, cylindrical racemes, 5in (13cm) long, in summer. Sometimes produces bulbils from which it can be propagated. ↕ to 6ft (2m), ↔ 24in (60cm) or more. W. Bhutan. ❄ (min. 41°F/5°C)

H. horsfieldii, syn. *Brachychilum horsfieldii.* Slender-stemmed perennial with stalkless, lance-shaped to linear, leathery, glossy, mid-green leaves, 12in (30cm) long. From summer to autumn, bears showy, tubular, greenish white flowers in terminal racemes, 2½–7in (6–18cm) long. ↕ 3–5ft (1–1.5m), ↔ 3ft (1m). Indonesia (Java). ❄ (min. 61°F/16°C)

HEDYOTIS

Bluets

RUBIACEAE

Genus of about 50 species of upright or prostrate, often stem-rooting perennials, from moist habitats in North America. They are attractive, sometimes short-lived plants, valued for their 4-petaled, salverform or funnel-shaped, blue or white flowers, borne in profusion from spring to summer. The small, shiny, ovate or oval leaves, ¼–2in (0.5–5cm) long, are opposite or occasionally clustered. Grow in a woodland or rock garden, ideally in shady rock crevices.

• **Cultivation** Grow in humus-rich, moist but well-drained, preferably acidic soil in dappled to full shade. Mulch with pine needles in autumn and spring.

Hedyotis michauxii

• **Propagation** Sow seed in containers in a cold frame in spring. Divide in spring or autumn. Root stem-tip cuttings in early summer.

• **Pests and diseases** Can be attacked by rust, snails, and slugs.

H. caerulea, syn. *Houstonia caerulea* (Bluets, Quaker ladies). Small, clump-forming perennial with upright, sparsely branched, slender stems and oblong to ovate-spoon-shaped, softly hairy leaves, ¼–¾in (6–9mm) long. In spring, bears solitary, pale blue, almost white, flowers, ½in (1.5cm) across, with yellow eyes. Requires acidic soil. ↕ 2–6in (5–15cm), ↔ indefinite. N. America. Zone 4.

H. michauxii ▣ syn. *Houstonia serpyllifolia* (Creeping bluets). Mat-forming perennial with rooting stems and rounded, ovate or oval, glossy, mid-green leaves, to ¼in (6mm) long. In late spring and early summer, short, erect stems bear usually solitary, axillary and terminal, salverform, light blue flowers, to ½in (1.5cm) across, with white eyes. ↕ 3in (8cm), ↔ to 12in (30cm). Virginia, S. Carolina to W. Tennessee. Zone 5b.

HEDYSARUM

FABACEAE

Genus of 100 species of perennials and subshrubs widespread in mountains and prairies throughout the N. hemisphere. They have alternate, pinnate, mid-green leaves and bear axillary racemes of pea-like flowers in violet, purple, red, or pink, occasionally white or yellow. They are attractive to bees. Tall species, such as *H. coronarium,* are suitable for the back of a mixed or herbaceous border, and provide sweet-smelling cut flowers. Small species are ideal for a rock garden.

• **Cultivation** Grow in well-drained, preferably stony or sandy, poor to moderately fertile, alkaline soil in full sun.

• **Propagation** Sow seed in containers in a cold frame as soon as ripe or in spring. Divide with care in spring, since the roots resent disturbance.

• **Pests and diseases** Sometimes affected by rust.

H. coronarium ▣ (French honeysuckle). Upright, bushy perennial, sometimes biennial, with pinnate leaves consisting of 7–15 paired, elliptic to obovate or rounded, entire leaflets, 1½in (4cm) long. Racemes of very fragrant, pea-like, deep red flowers, to ¾in (2cm) long, are borne on erect, angular stems throughout spring. ↕ to 3ft (1m), ↔ 24in (60cm). W. Mediterranean to Italy (Sicily). Zone 5b. **'Album'** produces white flowers.

Hedysarum coronarium

H. hedysaroides. Rhizomatous, hairless perennial forming spreading clumps of erect, angular, unbranched stems. The numerous pinnate leaves have 7–21 obovate leaflets, 1in (2.5cm) long. Loose, conical racemes of pea-like, red-violet or white flowers, to 1in (2.5cm) long, are borne in mid- and late summer. ↕ to 24in (60cm), ↔ 36in (90cm). Arctic Russia to S. central Europe. Zone 5.

HEDYSCEPE

Umbrella palm

ARECACEAE

Genus of one species of single-stemmed palm from the upper mountain slopes of Lord Howe Island. Pinnate leaves with up to 80 leaflets in terminal tufts above a distinct crown-shaft. Panicles of bowl-shaped, 3-petaled flowers are produced one at a time, just below the leaves. If temperatures fall below 59°F (15°C), grow in a warm conservatory or greenhouse. In tropical areas, use as specimen trees, either singly or in small groups.

• **Cultivation** Under glass, grow in soil-based potting mix with added leaf mold in bright filtered or indirect light. Provide moderate to high humidity and good ventilation. In growth, water moderately and apply a balanced liquid fertilizer monthly; keep just moist in winter. Outdoors, grow in fertile, humus-rich, moist but well-drained soil in full sun or partial shade, sheltered from wind.

• **Propagation** Sow seed at 70–75°F (21–24°C) in spring.

• **Pests and diseases** Infrequent.

H. canterburyana, syn. *Kentia canterburyana.* Small to medium-sized palm with a slender stem topped by a prominent crownshaft, tinted silvery blue-white. Rigidly curved leaves, to 5ft (1.5m) long, have 40–80 lance-shaped, erect to ascending, rich green leaflets, smooth above, downy beneath. In summer, bears deep yellow to orange-yellow flowers, to ½in (1.5cm) across, in horizontal panicles, to 18in (45cm) across. ↕ to 30ft (10m), ↔ to 15ft (5m). Australia. ❄ (min. 59°F/15°C)

▷ ***Heeria*** see *Heterocentron*
▷ ***Heimerliodendron*** see *Pisonia*

HELENIUM

Sneezeweed

ASTERACEAE

Genus of about 40 species of annuals, biennials, and perennials found in damp meadows or at woodland margins in North and Central America. They are mostly clump-forming plants with sturdy, branching stems and ovate to inversely lance-shaped, mid-green leaves, 6–8in (15–20cm) long. The daisy-like flowerheads have prominent yellow or brown disk florets, and ray florets in yellow, bronze, orange, or red. Heleniums flower over a long period and are suitable for a sunny, mixed or herbaceous border. The flowerheads are useful for cutting and are attractive to bees. All parts may cause severe discomfort if ingested; contact with the foliage may aggravate skin allergies.

• **Cultivation** Grow in any fertile, moist but well-drained soil in full sun. Provide support for taller species and cultivars. Deadhead to prolong flowering, and divide every 2 or 3 years.

• **Propagation** Sow seed of species, or root basal cuttings of cultivars, in containers in a cold frame in spring. Divide in autumn or spring.

• **Pests and diseases** Powdery mildew, rust, leaf smut, and fungal spots occur.

H. autumnale (Sneezeweed). Upright, clump-forming perennial with branched, winged stems and ovate to lance-shaped, toothed leaves, 4–6in (10–15cm) long. From late summer to midautumn, bears flowerheads, to 2in (5cm) long, with yellow ray florets that reflex as the brown disk florets open. ↕ to 5ft (1.5m), ↔ 18in (45cm). Canada, E. US. Zone 3b.

***H.* 'Baudirektor Linne'.** Clump-forming perennial bearing large, long-lasting flowerheads, to 3in (8cm) across, with velvety, brownish red ray florets and brown disk florets, in late summer and early autumn. ↕ 4ft (1.2m), ↔ 24in (60cm). Zone 3b.

H. bigelovii. Clump-forming perennial with sparsely branched stems and lance-shaped to inversely lance-shaped leaves, 6–9in (15–23cm) long. In early and midsummer, bears flowerheads, 2½in (6cm) across, with brownish yellow disk florets, and yellow ray florets that reflex as the disk florets open. ↕ 24in (60cm), ↔ 12in (30cm). California to Oregon. Zone 7b. **'Aurantiacum'** has golden yellow flowerheads.

***H.* 'Bressingham Gold'.** Vigorous perennial bearing flowerheads 2½–3½in (6–9cm) across, with deep gold ray florets, shaded crimson, and brown disk florets, in mid- and late summer. ↕ 36in (90cm), ↔ 24in (60cm). Zone 3b.

***H.* 'Bruno'** ▣ Erect perennial bearing flowerheads 2½–3½in (6–9cm) across, with deep crimson or reddish brown ray florets and brown disk florets, in late summer and early autumn. ↕ 4ft (1.2m), ↔ 24in (60cm). Zone 3b.

Helenium 'Bruno'

H

Helenium 'Butterpat'

Helenium 'Moerheim Beauty'

Helenium 'Pumilum Magnificum'

H

***H.* 'Butterpat'** ■ Upright perennial bearing flowerheads 2–3in (5–8cm) across, with rich yellow ray florets and yellow-brown disk florets, from midsummer to early autumn. ↕ 36in (90cm), ↔ 24in (60cm). Zone 3b.
***H.* 'Coppelia'.** Erect perennial bearing flowerheads 2–3in (5–8cm) across, with warm copper-orange ray florets and brown disk florets, from midsummer to early autumn. ↕ 36in (90cm), ↔ 24in (60cm). Zone 3b.
***H.* 'Crimson Beauty'.** Upright perennial bearing flowerheads to 3in (8cm) across, with bronze-carmine ray florets and brown disk florets, from early to late summer. ↕ 30in (75cm), ↔ 24in (60cm). Zone 3b.
***H.* 'Dark Beauty'** see *H.* 'Dunkelpracht'.
***H.* 'Dunkelpracht'**, syn. *H.* 'Dark Beauty'. Erect perennial bearing dark bronze-red flowerheads to 3in (8cm) across, with brown disk florets, from midsummer to early autumn. ↕ 4½ft (1.4m), ↔ 24in (60cm). Zone 3b.
***H.* 'Feuersiegel'.** Upright perennial bearing flowerheads 2–3in (5–8cm) across, with golden brown to red ray florets and brown disk florets, in late summer and early autumn. ↕ 5ft (1.5m), ↔ 24in (60cm). Zone 3b.
***H.* 'Garden Sun'.** Upright perennial producing flowerheads, 2–3in (5–8cm) across, with clear yellow ray florets and brown disk florets, from midsummer to early autumn. ↕ 4ft (1.2m), ↔ 24in (60cm). Zone 3b.
***H.* 'Gold Ball'** see *H.* 'Goldkogel'.
***H.* 'Goldene Jugend'**, syn. *H.* 'Golden Youth'. Upright perennial producing flowerheads to 3in (8cm) across, with golden yellow ray florets and yellow disk florets, in early and midsummer. ↕ 32in (80cm), ↔ 24in (60cm). Zone 3b.
***H.* 'Golden Youth'** see *H.* 'Goldene Jugend'.
***H.* 'Gold Fox'.** Erect perennial bearing flowerheads to 3in (8cm) across, with tawny-orange ray florets and brown disk florets, from midsummer to early autumn. ↕ 36in (90cm), ↔ 24in (60cm). Zone 3b.
***H.* 'Goldkogel'**, syn. *H.* 'Gold Ball'. Upright perennial bearing flowerheads to 3in (8cm) across, with clear yellow ray florets and dark brown disk florets, from midsummer to early autumn. ↕ 4ft (1.2m), ↔ 24in (60cm). Zone 3b.
***H.* 'Goldrausch'.** Upright perennial bearing flowerheads to 3in (8cm) across, with golden yellow, brown-marked ray florets and brown disk florets, in late summer and early autumn. ↕ to 5ft (1.5m), ↔ 24in (60cm). Zone 3b.
H. hoopesii. Erect, clump-forming perennial with basal rosettes of inversely lance-shaped, grayish green leaves, 10–12in (25–30cm) long, becoming smaller toward the tops of the stems. In early summer, bears branched, lax, terminal corymbs of 3–8 flowerheads to 3in (8cm) across, the bright yellow to orange ray florets reflexing as the yellow-brown disk florets open. Tolerates dry soil. ↕ to 3ft (1m), ↔ 18in (45cm). Mountains of California to Oregon, Wyoming, New Mexico. Zone 3.
***H.* 'Kugelsonne'**, syn. *H.* 'Sunball'. Erect perennial bearing lemon-yellow flowerheads, to 3in (8cm) across, with chartreuse disk florets, in late summer and early autumn. ↕ 5ft (1.5m), ↔ 24in (60cm). Zone 3b.
***H.* 'Kupferzwerg'.** Upright perennial bearing flowerheads 2–3in (5–8cm) across, with brownish red ray florets and brown disk florets, in mid- and late summer. ↕ 28in (70cm), ↔ 24in (60cm). Zone 3b.
***H.* 'Margot'.** Upright perennial producing flowerheads 2–3in (5–8cm) across, with brownish red, yellow-tipped ray florets and brown disk florets, from midsummer to early autumn. ↕ 36in (90cm), ↔ 24in (60cm). Zone 3b.
***H.* 'Moerheim Beauty'** ■ Upright perennial bearing flowerheads 2–3in (5–8cm) across, with dark copper-red ray florets and dark brown disk florets, from early to late summer. ↕ 36in (90cm), ↔ 24in (60cm). Zone 3b.

Helenium 'Septemberfuchs'

Helenium 'Wyndley'

***H.* 'Pumilum Magnificum'** ■ Erect perennial producing flowerheads to 3in (8cm) across, with golden yellow ray florets and yellow-brown disk florets, from late summer to midautumn. ↕ 36in (90cm), ↔ 24in (60cm). Zone 3b.
***H.* 'Red and Gold'** see *H.* 'Rotgold'.
***H.* 'Riverton Beauty'.** Upright perennial bearing flowerheads to 3in (8cm) across, with golden yellow ray florets and reddish bronze disk florets, in late summer and early autumn. ↕ 5ft (1.5m), ↔ 24in (60cm). Zone 3b.
***H.* 'Riverton Gem'.** Upright perennial producing flowerheads 2–3in (5–8cm) across, with deep crimson, yellow-streaked ray florets and brown disk florets, in late summer and early autumn. ↕ 4ft (1.2m), ↔ 24in (60cm). Zone 3b.
***H.* 'Rotgold'**, syn. *H.* 'Red and Gold'. Upright perennial bearing flowerheads to 3in (8cm) across, with ray florets in varying shades or combinations of red and yellow, and brown disk florets, in late summer and early autumn. ↕ 4ft (1.2m), ↔ 24in (60cm). Zone 3b.
***H.* 'Septemberfuchs'** ■ Upright perennial bearing flowerheads 2–3in (5–8cm) across, with bright orange-brown ray florets, suffused yellow, and brown disk florets, from late summer to midautumn. ↕ 5ft (1.5m), ↔ 24in (60cm). Zone 3b.
***H.* 'Sonnenwunder'.** Erect perennial bearing flowerheads 2–3in (5–8cm) across, with yellow ray florets and green, then pale brownish yellow disk florets, from late summer to midautumn. ↕ 5ft (1.5m), ↔ 24in (60cm). Zone 3b.
***H.* 'Sunball'** see *H.* 'Kugelsonne'.
***H.* 'Waldtraut'.** Upright, sturdy perennial bearing flowerheads 2–3in (5–8cm) across, with golden brown ray florets and brown disk florets, in late summer and early autumn. ↕ 32–39in (80–100cm), ↔ 24in (60cm). Zone 3b.
***H.* 'Wyndley'** ■ Erect perennial bearing flowerheads 2–3in (5–8cm) across, with yellow ray florets, overlaid dark orange, and with darker orange-brown disk florets, from midsummer to early autumn. ↕ 32in (80cm), ↔ 24in (60cm). Zone 3b.
***H.* 'Zimbelstern'.** Upright perennial producing flowerheads 2–3in (5–8cm) across, with golden brown, wavy-margined ray florets and brown disk florets, in mid- and late summer. ↕ to 4ft (1.2m), ↔ 24in (60cm). Zone 3b.

Helianthemum apenninum

HELIANTHEMUM

Rock rose, Sun rose

CISTACEAE

Genus of about 110 species of evergreen or semi-evergreen shrubs occurring in alpine meadows or open scrub in North and South America, Asia, Europe, and North Africa, particularly around the Mediterranean. They have opposite, oblong to linear, silver- to gray-green or light to mid-green leaves, and are grown for their raceme-like cymes of saucer-shaped, 5-petaled, brightly colored flowers, which are borne over a long period from late spring to midsummer. They are ideal for a rock garden, a raised bed, or the front of a herbaceous or mixed border, or as groundcovers on a sunny bank. The hybrids most often grown are crosses involving *H. apenninum*, *H. nummularium*, and *H. croceum*; those described below are evergreen shrubs of similar habit and appearance to *H. apenninum*, with silver, mid-green, or gray-green leaves and saucer-shaped flowers.

- **CULTIVATION** Grow in moderately fertile, well-drained, neutral to alkaline soil in full sun. Pruning group 10, after flowering.
- **PROPAGATION** Sow seed of species in containers in a cold frame as soon as ripe or in spring. Root softwood cuttings in late spring or early summer.
- **PESTS AND DISEASES** Infrequent.

H. apenninum ■ Spreading, loosely mat-forming, evergreen shrub with elliptic-oblong to linear, downy, gray-green leaves, to 1¼in (3cm) long, on branching, downy stems. From late spring to midsummer, bears few-flowered cymes of white flowers, 1in (2.5cm) across, with conspicuous, deep yellow anthers. ↕ to 16in (40cm), ↔ to 24in (60cm). Europe, Turkey. Zone 7. **var. *roseum*** has hairless, mid-green leaves and bears pink flowers; N.W. Italy; Zone 6.

Helianthemum lunulatum

***H.* 'Ben Hope'.** Spreading shrub with downy, pale gray-green leaves, ½–1½in (1–4cm) long. Bears carmine-red flowers, to 1in (2.5cm) across, with deep orange centers. ↕ 8–12in (20–30cm), ↔ 12in (30cm). Zone 6.
***H.* 'Ben Nevis'.** Spreading shrub, more compact than *H. apenninum*, with dark green leaves, ½–1½in (1–4cm) long. Produces rich orange-yellow flowers, to 1in (2.5cm) across, with bronze-crimson centers. ↕↔ to 8in (20cm). Zone 6.
***H.* 'Brunette'.** Spreading shrub with mid-green leaves, ½–1½in (1–4cm) long. Bears rust-orange flowers, to 1in (2.5cm) across. ↕ to 10in (25cm), ↔ 12in (30cm). Zone 6.
***H.* 'Buttercup'.** Spreading shrub with mid-green leaves, ½–1½in (1–4cm) long. Produces rich, butter-yellow flowers, to 1in (2.5cm) across. ↕↔ 8–12in (20–30cm). Zone 6.
***H.* 'Chocolate Blotch'.** Spreading shrub producing gray-green leaves, ½–1½in (1–4cm) long, and buff-colored flowers, to 1in (2.5cm) across, marked chocolate-brown at the petal bases. ↕ 8–12in (20–30cm), ↔ 12in (30cm). Zone 6.
***H.* 'Fire Dragon'** ■ syn. *H.* 'Mrs. Clay'. Spreading shrub with gray-green leaves, ½–1½in (1–4cm) long. Produces vivid orange-red flowers, to 1in (2.5cm) across. ↕ 8–12in (20–30cm), ↔ 12in (30cm). Zone 6.
H. guttatum see *Tuberaria guttata.*
***H.* 'Henfield Brilliant'.** Spreading shrub producing gray-green leaves, ½–1½in (1–4cm) long, and brick-red flowers, 1in (2.5cm) across. ↕ 8–12in (20–30cm), ↔ 12in (30cm). Zone 6.
H. lunulatum ■ Dwarf, initially erect then spreading, evergreen shrub with elliptic to lance-shaped, hairy, gray-green leaves, to ½in (1.5cm) long. In late spring and early summer, bears clear yellow flowers, to ½in (1.5cm) across, with prominent, orange-yellow anthers, singly or in cymes. ↕ 6in (15cm), ↔ 10in (25cm). S. Europe. Zone 6.

Helianthemum 'Wisley White'

H. 'Mrs. Clay' see *H.* 'Fire Dragon'.
***H. nummularium* 'Amy Baring'.** Dwarf shrub producing erect then procumbent branches and ovate or lance-shaped to elliptic, gray-green leaves, ¼–2in (0.5–5cm) long. Bears deep yellow flowers, to 1in (2.5cm) across, with orange centers. ↕ 6in (15cm), ↔ to 8in (20cm). Zone 6.
***H. oelandicum* subsp. *alpestre*.** Neat, mat-forming shrub with lance-shaped, downy, gray-green leaves, to ¾in (2cm) long. Terminal cymes of up to 5 yellow flowers, each to ½in (1.5cm) across, are borne from late spring to midsummer. ↕ 5in (13cm), ↔ to 8in (20cm). S. Europe. Zone 6.
***H.* 'Orange Surprise'.** Prostrate, spreading shrub with mid-green leaves, ½–1½in (1–4cm) long. Produces light orange flowers, to 1in (2.5cm) across, with burnt orange centers. ↕ 4in (10cm), ↔ 12in (30cm). Zone 6.
***H.* 'Raspberry Ripple'** ■ Spreading shrub with dark grayish green leaves, ½–1½in (1–4cm) long. Bears white flowers, to 1in (2.5cm) across, with purplish pink centers, the color spreading irregularly into the petal margins. ↕ 8in (20cm), ↔ to 12in (30cm). Zone 6.
***H.* 'Rhodanthe Carneum'** ■ syn. *H.* 'Wisley Pink'. Long-flowering, spreading shrub, more robust than *H. apenninum.* It has silver-gray leaves, 1–1½in (2.5–4cm) long, and produces pale pink flowers, to 1in (2.5cm) across, flushed yellow at the centers. ↕ to 12in (30cm), ↔ to 18in (45cm). Zone 6.
***H.* 'Stoplight'.** Spreading shrub with olive-gray leaves, ½–1½in (1–4cm) long. Bears rose-red flowers, to 1in (2.5cm) across. ↕↔ 8–12in (20–30cm). Zone 6.
H. tuberaria see *Tuberaria lignosa.*
H. umbellatum see *Halimium umbellatum.*
***H.* 'Wisley Pink'** see *H.* 'Rhodanthe Carneum'.
***H.* 'Wisley Primrose'.** Spreading shrub with gray-green leaves, to 1½in (4cm) long. Bears pale primrose-yellow flowers, ¾–1in (2–2.5cm) across, with deep golden yellow centers. ↕ to 12in (30cm), ↔ to 18in (45cm). Zone 6.
***H.* 'Wisley White'** ■ Spreading shrub with gray leaves, to 1½in (4cm) long. Bears creamy white flowers, ¾–1in (2–2.5cm) across, with mid- to deep yellow centers and yellow stamens. ↕ to 12in (30cm), ↔ to 18in (45cm). Zone 6.

Helianthemum 'Fire Dragon'

Helianthemum 'Raspberry Ripple'

Helianthemum 'Rhodanthe Carneum'

HELIANTHUS

Sunflower

ASTERACEAE

Genus of about 70–80 species of annuals and perennials, some occurring in dry woodland and prairies, others in damp, swampy habitats, in North America, Central America, Peru, and Chile. Usually tall, coarse plants, they have creeping or tuberous roots and large, simple, bristly, alternate or opposite leaves. The showy, daisy-like flowerheads, with sterile ray florets, are usually 2–4in (5–10cm) across, but 12in (30cm) or more in the giant annuals; they are borne singly or in loose corymbs and have yellow, occasionally red, or very rarely violet, ray florets, and yellow, brown, or purple disk florets.

Sunflowers are effective in an annual, herbaceous, or mixed border. The taller, spreading species and hybrids, such as *H.* x *laetiflorus* and *H. salicifolius*, are suitable for a wild garden; small annuals, such as *H. annuus* 'Teddy Bear', are ideal for containers. Sunflowers provide good cut flowers, and many are attractive to bees and birds. Contact with the foliage of sunflowers may aggravate skin allergies.

• **CULTIVATION** Grow in moderately fertile, humus-rich, moist but well-drained, neutral to alkaline soil in full sun. Sunflowers need long, hot summers to flower well. Most will tolerate dry soil; *H. pauciflorus* and *H. salicifolius* prefer it. *H. decapetalus*, *H.* x *laetiflorus*, and *H.* x *multiflorus* thrive in moist soil, particularly near water. Tall species and cultivars require support. Top-dress perennials annually with compost or well-rotted manure, and divide every 2–4 years to maintain vigor.

• **PROPAGATION** Sow seed of perennials in containers in a cold frame in spring; sow annuals at 61°F (16°C) in late winter or *in situ* in spring. Cultivars may not come true from seed, and hybridize freely. Divide perennials in spring or autumn. Root basal cuttings in spring.

• **PESTS AND DISEASES** Downy mildew, powdery mildew, canker, rust, and many fungal leaf spots are common. Caterpillars, cutworms, beetles, and weevils may attack plants.

H. angustifolius ■ (Swamp sunflower). Upright perennial with rough, hairy stems and narrowly lance-shaped, mid-green leaves, to 8in (20cm) long.

Helianthus angustifolius

Helianthus annuus 'Music Box'

In early autumn, bears daisy-like flowerheads, 3in (8cm) across, with yellow ray florets and purple disk florets. ↕ 5–7ft (1.5–2.2m), ↔ 4ft (1.2m). E. US. Zone 6.

H. annuus (Sunflower). Fast-growing, tall, branched to unbranched, hairy-stemmed annual with broadly oval to heart-shaped, toothed, roughly hairy, mid- to dark green leaves, 4–16in (10–40cm) long. In summer, bears large, daisy-like flowerheads, to 12in (30cm) wide, with yellow ray florets and brown or purple disk florets, sometimes tinged red or purple. Many cultivars have been selected. ↕ to 15ft (5m), ↔ to 24in (60cm). US to Central America. **'Autumn Beauty'** has flowerheads to 6in (15cm) across, with dark mahogany-red, lemon-yellow, golden yellow, or bronze-red ray florets, sometimes zoned with additional shades; ↕ 5ft (1.5m) or more. **'Big Smile'** bears flowerheads to 4in (10cm) across, with yellow ray florets and darker yellow disk florets; ↕ 16in (40cm). **'Mammoth Russian'** has large, bright, golden yellow flowerheads, to 10in (25cm) across; ↕ 6–7ft (2–2.2m). **'Music Box'** ■ is free-flowering and many-branched; it bears flowerheads 4–5in (10–13cm) across, with ray florets in colors ranging from creamy yellow to dark red, including some bicolors, and black disk florets; ↕ 28in (70cm). **'Russian Giant'** is tall, with large yellow flowerheads, 10in (25cm) or more across; ↕ 11ft (3.5m). **'Sunspot'** has large yellow flowerheads, 10in (25cm) or more across; ↕ 24in (60cm). **'Teddy Bear'** ■ is compact, bearing double, deep yellow flowerheads, to 5in (13cm) across; ↕ 36in (90cm). **'Valentine'** is tall and uniform, bearing lemon-yellow flowerheads, 6in (15cm) across, with dark brown disk florets. ↕ 5ft (1.5m).

Helianthus annuus 'Teddy Bear'

H. atrorubens, syn. *H. sparsifolius* (Dark-eyed sunflower). Clump-forming perennial with hairy, purple-green stems and ovate to lance-shaped, toothed to scalloped, hairy, mid-green, mainly basal leaves, 8–12in (20–30cm) long. In late summer, bears flowerheads 2–3½in (5–9cm) across, with deep yellow ray florets and purplish maroon disk florets. ↕ to 5ft (1.5m), ↔ 4ft (1.2m). S.E. US. Zone 5b. **'Gullick's Variety'** is vigorous, wide-spreading, and free-blooming; it produces narrow, pointed leaves, and from late summer to mid-autumn, bears flowerheads with yellow ray florets and brownish purple disk florets; ↕ 4–5½ft (1.2–1.7m). **'Monarch'** ■ is vigorous, bearing semi-double flowerheads, to 6in (15cm) across when disbudded, with yellow-brown disk florets, in early and mid-autumn; ↕ to 6ft (2m).

H. cucumerifolius see *H. debilis* subsp. *cucumerifolius*.

H. debilis. Tall, smooth to hairy annual with thick, strongly branched stems, occasionally mottled purple, and ovate to lance-shaped, sometimes toothed, glossy, mid-green leaves, 2–5½in (5–14cm) long. Slightly nodding flowerheads, 2½in (6cm) or more across, with bright yellow, sometimes red-flushed ray florets and deep purple-red disk florets, are borne in summer. ↕ 6ft (2m), ↔ 18–24in (45–60cm). Florida, Texas. **subsp. *cucumerifolius***, syn. *H. cucumerifolius*, is shorter, with purple-mottled stems; coarsely hairy, sharply toothed leaves, to 4in (10cm) long; and larger flowerheads, to 6in (15cm) across, from summer to autumn. ↕ 3ft (1m). S.E. Texas. **subsp. *cucumerifolius* 'Italian White'** ■ produces flowerheads to 4in (10cm) across, with creamy white to pale primrose-yellow ray florets and black disk florets; ↕ 5ft (1.5m).

H. decapetalus (Thin-leaved sunflower). Rhizomatous perennial with tall stems, hairless at the bases and bristly toward the flowerheads. Thin, lance-shaped to broadly ovate, mid-green leaves, to 8in (20cm) long, are smooth above and rough-hairy beneath. Flowerheads 2–3in (5–8cm) across, with yellow ray florets and yellow-brown disk florets, are borne from late summer to midautumn. ↕ 5ft (1.5m), ↔ 3½ft (1.1m). C. and S.E. US. Zone 5b.

Helianthus atrorubens 'Monarch'

Helianthus debilis subsp. *cucumerifolius* 'Italian White'

H.* x *laetiflorus (*H. pauciflorus* x *H. tuberosus*). Spreading, rhizomatous perennial with rough stems and thin, ovate, coarsely toothed, dark green leaves, to 12in (30cm) long. Flowerheads 4–5in (10–13cm) across, with bright yellow ray florets and yellow disk florets, open from late summer to mid-autumn. ↕ 5–7ft (1.5–2.2m), ↔ 4ft (1.2m) or more. Garden origin. Zone 5. **'Miss Mellish'** spreads vigorously, and bears semi-double flowerheads with orange-yellow ray florets. **'Morning Sun'** ■ bears large, semi-double flowerheads with golden yellow ray florets and quilled disk florets, from midsummer to autumn; ↕ 4ft (1.2m), ↔ 24in (60cm).

H. maximilliani (Maximillian sunflower). Tall, upright perennial with lance-shaped, mid-green leaves, to 12in

Helianthus x *laetiflorus* 'Morning Sun'

Helianthus x *multiflorus* 'Loddon Gold'

(30cm) long. Bears daisy-like flowerheads, 3in (8cm) across, with bright yellow ray florets and dark brown disk florets, in late summer and autumn. ↕ 10ft (3m), ↔ 3ft (1m). North America. Zone 4.
H. mollis (Ashy sunflower). Rhizomatous perennial producing stems covered with sharp, stiff hairs, and ovate to lance-shaped or oblong, slightly toothed, densely hairy, mid-green leaves, to 6in (15cm) long, softly gray-hairy beneath. In late summer and early autumn, bears flowerheads, 4in (10cm) across, with yellow ray florets and yellow disk florets. ↕ to 6ft (2m), ↔ 3ft (1m). Maine to Georgia to Texas. Zone 5.
H. x multiflorus (*H. annuus* x *H. decapetalus*). Clump-forming perennial with lance-shaped to ovate, slightly hairy, dark green leaves, to 8in (20cm) long. Flowerheads to 5in (13cm) across, with domed, yellow-brown disk florets, and golden yellow ray florets, open from late summer to midautumn. ↕ to 6ft (2m), ↔ 36in (90cm). Garden origin. Zone 5. **'Capenoch Star'** has single flowerheads with lemon-yellow ray florets and quilled, slightly darker yellow disk florets; ↕ to 5ft (1.5m). **'Flore Pleno'** has double, bright yellow flowerheads from midsummer to early autumn; ↕ 6ft (2m). **'Loddon Gold'** ■ has double, rich yellow flowerheads; ↕ to 5ft (1.5m). **'Soleil d'Or'** ■ has large, double yellow flowerheads. **'Triomphe de Gand'** bears large flowerheads with deep golden yellow ray florets and quilled disk florets; ↔ 4ft (1.2m).
H. occidentalis. Rhizomatous perennial with slender, simple or branched stems

Helianthus x *multiflorus* 'Soleil d'Or'

and oblong-lance-shaped to ovate, sparsely toothed, mid-green, mainly basal leaves, to 8in (20cm) long. The upper leaves are much smaller and bract-like. From summer to autumn, bears flowerheads, 2½in (6cm) across, with orange-yellow ray florets and yellow disk florets. ↕ to 6ft (2m), ↔ 3ft (1m). Minnesota to Ohio, Texas, Florida. Zone 4b.
H. orgyalis see *H. salicifolius.*
H. pauciflorus, syn. *H. rigidus.* Vigorous, rhizomatous perennial with roughly hairy stems and coarsely hairy, broadly lance-shaped to narrowly ovate, entire or toothed, dark green leaves, to 10in (25cm) long. Flowerheads 3in (8cm) across, with yellow ray florets and reddish purple disk florets, are borne in late summer. ↕ to 6ft (2m), ↔ 24in (60cm). W. to C. US. Zone 6.
H. rigidus see *H. pauciflorus.*
H. salicifolius, syn. *H. orgyalis* (Willow-leaved sunflower). Rhizomatous, clump-forming perennial with linear to lance-shaped, slightly hairy, dark green leaves, to 8in (20cm) long, arching outward from thick stems. Flowerheads 2–3in (5–8cm) across, with golden yellow ray florets and brown disk florets, open in early and midautumn. ↕ 8ft (2.5m), ↔ 36in (90cm). S. central US. Zone 6.
H. sparsifolius see *H. atrorubens.*
H. strumosus. Rhizomatous perennial with hairless, glaucous green stems and linear-lance-shaped to ovate, toothed or entire, roughly hairy, mid-green leaves, to 7in (18cm) long, with stiff, bristly hairs or hairless beneath. From summer to early autumn, bears flowerheads, to 4½in (11cm) across, with deep yellow ray florets and yellow disk florets. ↕ to 6ft (2m), ↔ 3ft (1m). North America. Zone 4.
H. tuberosus (Jerusalem artichoke). Rhizomatous, vigorous perennial with thick, coarsely hairy stems and oblong-lance-shaped to ovate, roughly hairy, toothed, mid-green leaves, to 12in (30cm) long, covered with sharp, stiff hairs beneath. In autumn, bears flowerheads, to 4in (10cm) across, with deep yellow ray florets and yellow disk florets. May be difficult to eradicate. ↕ to 10ft (3m), ↔ 3ft (90cm). Canada, S.E. US. Zone 3.

HELICHRYSUM

ASTERACEAE

Genus of about 500 species of annuals, herbaceous or evergreen perennials, and evergreen shrubs and subshrubs, widely distributed in Europe, Asia, Africa, and particularly in Australasia and South Africa, where they usually occur in dry, sunny sites. They have woolly or hairy stems and alternate leaves, sometimes opposite or in basal rosettes, which are aromatic in some species. The flowerheads are daisy-like or shaving-brush-like, either borne singly or in corymbs, and everlasting when dried. Grow small, prostrate, or cushion-forming helichrysums in a rock garden, scree bed, or alpine house; taller perennials and subshrubs are suitable for a mixed or herbaceous border. Where not hardy, tender species, such as *H. petiolare*, are excellent in hanging baskets or large containers; or, use as annuals in borders or beds.

Helichrysum italicum

• **CULTIVATION** Grow in well-drained, poor to moderately fertile, neutral to alkaline soil in full sun. Low-growing alpines need gritty, sharply drained soil. Protect from excessive winter moisture and cold, drying winds. Pruning group 10, in spring, for larger subshrubs and shrubs, including *H. italicum*, *H. splendidum*, and *H. stoechas.*
• **PROPAGATION** Sow seed at 55–61°F (13–16°C), or in containers in a cold frame, in spring; sow seed of alpines in containers in an open frame as soon as ripe or in spring. Divide perennials in spring. Root heel or semi-ripe cuttings of shrubby species in summer and overwinter in frost-free conditions.
• **PESTS AND DISEASES** Powdery mildew and rust can occur, and caterpillars may attack foliage.

H. alveolatum see *H. splendidum.*
H. angustifolium see *H. italicum.*
***H. argyrophyllum* 'Moe's Gold'.** Creeping, evergreen perennial with hairless stems and obovate to spoon-shaped, satiny, silver-felted leaves, to 1¼in (3cm) long. From summer to autumn, produces solitary or loose corymbs of lemon-yellow flowerheads, ½–1¼in (1.5–3cm) across, with outer bracts of golden brown. ↕ 4–6in (10–15cm), ↔ indefinite. Zone 7b.
H. arwae. Prostrate to low mound-forming, evergreen subshrub producing branched, woody stems and alternate, crowded, oblong to lance-shaped, silvery gray leaves, to ½in (1.5cm) long. Solitary, daisy-like white flowerheads, ½–1¼in (1.5–3cm) across, with incurving white bracts, are borne in summer. ↕ 2in (5cm), ↔ to 12in (30cm). Yemen. ❄ (min. 35°F/2°C)
H. bellidioides. Mat-forming, evergreen perennial with white-hairy stems when young, later smooth and reddish brown. The obovate to narrowly obovate leaves, ¼–½in (6–15mm) long, are mid-green above and white-felted beneath. From late spring to summer, erect, leafy stems bear solitary, papery, daisy-like white flowerheads, ½–1¼in (1.5–3cm) across. ↕ 6in (15cm) in flower, ↔ 24in (60cm). New Zealand. Zone 7b.
H. bracteatum see *Bracteantha bracteata.*
H. coralloides see *Ozothamnus coralloides.*
H. italicum ■ syn. *H. angustifolium.* Bushy, evergreen subshrub with woolly stems and linear, aromatic, silver-gray to yellowish green leaves, to 1¼in (3cm) long. Dark yellow flowerheads, 1/16–1/8in (2–3mm) across, are borne in corymbs to 3in (8cm) across, from summer to autumn. ↕ 24in (60cm), ↔ 3ft (1m). S. Europe. Zone 7. **subsp. *serotinum***, syn. *H. serotinum* (Curry plant), is compact, with leaves to 1½in (4cm) long; the foliage is intensely aromatic; ↕ 16in (40cm), ↔ 30in (75cm).
H. lanatum see *H. thianschanicum.*
H. ledifolium see *Ozothamnus ledifolius.*
***H. marginatum* of gardens** see *H. milfordiae.*
H. milfordiae, syn. *H. marginatum* of gardens. Cushion-forming, evergreen perennial with rosettes of alternate, obovate to oblong, densely silvery hairy, mid-green leaves, to ½in (1.5cm) long. Solitary, everlasting, daisy-like white flowerheads, 1–1¼in (2.5–3cm) across, with glossy, white, crimson-backed bracts, are borne in spring. ↕ 2–4in (5–10cm) in flower, ↔ 6–12in (15–30cm). South Africa (KwaZulu/Natal), Lesotho, at 10,000ft (3,000m) and above. Zone 8.
H. milliganii. Clump-forming, evergreen subshrub or herbaceous perennial with tufted, often woolly stems and ovate-oblong to narrowly spoon-shaped, fleshy, mid-green leaves, to 1in (2.5cm) long. In summer, white-downy stems bear solitary, papery flowerheads, 1½in (4cm) across, white inside and yellowish white or red on the reverse of the bracts. ↕ 6–8in (15–20cm), ↔ 8in (20cm). Australia (Tasmania). ❄ (min. 41°F/5°C)
H. orientale. Subshrubby, bushy, evergreen perennial with white-woolly, leafy stems and oblong-spoon-shaped, white-woolly leaves, ¾–2½in (2–6cm) long, becoming narrower and shorter higher up the stems. Hemispherical, shiny, light yellow flowerheads, ¼–½in (6–15mm) across, are borne in terminal corymbs, to 3in (8cm) across, in midsummer. ↕ 8–12in (20–30cm), ↔ 12in (30cm). E. Mediterranean (including Greece and the Aegean Islands). ❄ (min. 35°F/2°C)
H. petiolare ■ syn. *H. petiolatum* of gardens (Licorice plant). Mound-forming or trailing, evergreen shrub, often grown as an annual, with branching stems and broadly ovate to heart-shaped leaves, 1½in (4cm) long, densely gray-woolly above, lighter beneath. In late summer and autumn, bears hemispherical, off-white flowerheads, to ½in (1.5cm) across, in loose, terminal corymbs, 1–2in

Helichrysum petiolare

Helichrysum petiolare 'Limelight'

(2.5–5cm) across. ↕ to 20in (50cm), ↔ 6ft (2m) or more. South Africa. ❄ (min. 45°F/7°C). **'Aurea'** see 'Limelight'. **'Limelight'** ■ syn. 'Aurea', has bright lime-green leaves. Protect from strong light and heat to maintain leaf color. **'Roundabout'** is a miniature sport of 'Variegatum', and occasionally reverts; ↕ 6in (15cm), ↔ 12in (30cm). **'Sky Net'** has pink-flushed, creamy white flower-heads in corymbs to ¾in (2cm) across, in summer; ↕ 3ft (1m). **'Variegatum'** ■ has gray leaves, variegated cream.

***H. petiolatum* of gardens** see *H. petiolare.*

H. rosmarinifolium see *Ozothamnus rosmarinifolius.*

***H.* 'Schweffellicht'** ■ syn. *H.* 'Sulfur Light'. Clump-forming herbaceous perennial with erect to spreading, white-woolly stems and narrow, lance-shaped, woolly, silvery white leaves, to 4in (10cm) long. Fluffy, hemispherical, sulfur-yellow flowerheads, ⅜–½in (8–15mm) across, becoming orange-yellow with age, are borne in tight, branched corymbs, to 2–3in (5–8cm) across, in late summer. ↕ 16in (40cm), ↔ 12in (30cm). ❄ (min. 41°F/5°C)

H. selago see *Ozothamnus selago.*

H. serotinum see *H. italicum* subsp. *serotinum.*

H. sibthorpii ■ syn. *H. virgineum.* Cushion-forming, evergreen perennial producing densely white-woolly stems and alternate, oblong, strongly 3-veined, white-woolly, mid-green leaves, ½–2½in (1.5–6cm) long. In summer, bears hemispherical yellow flowerheads, to ½in (1.5cm) across, with white

Helichrysum petiolare 'Variegatum'

Helichrysum 'Schweffellicht'

bracts, singly or in corymbs of 2 or 3. ↕ to 4in (10cm), ↔ 8in (20cm). N.E. Greece. ❄ (min. 41°F/5°C)

H. siculum see *H. stoechas* subsp. *barrelieri.*

H. splendidum ■ syn. *H. alveolatum, H. trilineatum.* Compact, bushy, evergreen shrub with white-woolly stems and linear-oblong, strongly 3-veined, silver-gray leaves, ¾–1½in (2–4cm) long. Ovoid-oblong, dark yellow flowerheads, ⅛–¼in (4–6mm) across, are produced in hemispherical corymbs, 1¼in (3cm) across, from late summer to autumn. ↕↔ 4ft (1.2m). South Africa. ❄ (min. 41°F/5°C)

H. stoechas. Bushy, evergreen subshrub or woody-based, aromatic perennial producing branched or unbranched, white-woolly stems and alternate, linear to linear-spoon-shaped, white-woolly, gray-green leaves, ¾–1¼in (2–3cm) long. In late spring, bears spherical to ovoid yellow flowerheads, ⅛–¼in (4–6mm) across, in corymbs 1¼in (3cm) or more across. ↕ 8–20in (20–50cm), ↔ 3ft (1m). W. and S. Europe to Balkans. ❄ (min. 41°F/5°C). **subsp. *barrelieri*,** syn. *H. siculum*, is shorter-growing, and has broadly linear, non-aromatic leaves, to ¾in (2cm) long; it bears small clusters of ovoid yellow flowerheads in summer; ↕ 6–12in (15–30cm); Italy, Greece, Balkans, Turkey, Lebanon, N.W. North Africa. **'White Barn'** has densely white-felted leaves, and bears sulfur-yellow flowerheads.

***H.* 'Sulfur Light'** see *H.* 'Schweffellicht'.

H. thianschanicum, syn. *H. lanatum.* Mound-forming, woolly-hairy herbaceous perennial with erect stems,

Helichrysum sibthorpii

Helichrysum splendidum

lance-shaped, silvery gray basal leaves, to 4in (10cm) long, and stalkless, linear stem leaves. Hemispherical to ovoid yellow flowerheads, to ½in (1.5cm) across, are borne in dense, lateral or terminal corymbs, to 3in (8cm) across, in early and midsummer. ↕↔ to 16in (40cm). C. Asia. ❄ (min. 45°F/7°C). **'Goldkind'**, syn. 'Golden Baby', bears papery, golden yellow flowerheads with a lovage-like scent; ↕ 12in (30cm).

H. thyrsoideum see *Ozothamnus thyrsoideus.*

H. trilineatum see *H. splendidum.*

H. virgineum see *H. sibthorpii.*

HELICONIA

HELICONIACEAE

Genus of about 100 species of evergreen perennials found in habitats ranging from tropical forest to open scrub in tropical and subtropical Central and South America, and the S.W. Pacific. They have short rhizomes and long-stalked, paddle- or spoon-shaped, mid- to dark green leaves, to 6ft (2m) long, similar to those of the closely related banana (*Musa*) and *Strelitzia.* From spring to summer, they produce large, erect or pendent flower spikes, made up of brilliantly colored bracts, arranged spirally or in 2 opposite rows. The bracts enclose the true flowers, which have 3 petals and 3 showy sepals, often in contrasting colors. Where not hardy, grow in a warm greenhouse or conservatory; in warmer regions, use as specimen plants for borders or containers outdoors. All heliconicas last well as cut flowers.

Heliconia aurantiaca

- **CULTIVATION** Under glass, grow in a mix of equal parts pulverized pine bark, peat moss, and coarse sand or grit, in bright filtered to indirect light. During the growing season, water freely and apply a balanced liquid fertilizer monthly; water moderately in winter. Outdoors, grow in humus-rich, moist but well-drained, neutral to slightly acidic soil, enriched with compost, in partial shade. Shelter from strong winds, which will damage foliage.
- **PROPAGATION** Sow seed at 66–75°F (19–24°C) in spring. Divide rhizomes in spring.
- **PESTS AND DISEASES** Leaf spot, spider mites, slugs, and snails occur.

H. acuminata. Rhizomatous perennial with elliptic to narrowly elliptic or oblong, smooth, leathery, dark green leaf blades, 6–28in (15–70cm) long. Erect inflorescences, 20–36in (50–90cm) long, each bear 2 ranks of 4–6 slender, clustered, red, orange, or yellow, green-tipped bracts. The red-, orange-, or yellow-stalked flowers have white to orange-yellow sepals with dark green-banded tips. ↕ 2–10ft (0.6–3m), ↔ indefinite. Brazil to S.E. Peru. ❄ (min. 59°F/15°C)

H. angusta. Rhizomatous perennial with elliptic or oblong, mid- to deep green leaf blades, 10–36in (25–90cm) long, usually brown-woolly beneath. Erect inflorescences, 28in (70cm) long, each bear 4–8 red or yellow bracts in 2 ranks, and flowers with white sepals. ↕ 24–48in (60–120cm), ↔ indefinite. ❄ (min. 59°F/15°C)

H. aurantiaca ■ Rhizomatous perennial with oblong or narrowly elliptic, dark green leaf blades, 7–16in (17–40cm) long. Produces erect, dense inflorescences, to 8in (20cm) long, each with 3–5 broad, clustered, red or yellow, green-tipped bracts arranged in 2 ranks. Flowers have pale yellow to orange sepals, often with paler tips, becoming dark green with age. ↕ 2–6ft (0.6–2m), ↔ indefinite. S. Mexico to Costa Rica. ❄ (min. 59°F/15°C)

H. bihai, syn. *H. humilis* (Firebird). Variable, rhizomatous perennial with oblong or oblong-oval, dark green leaf blades, to 6ft (2m) long, with pale midribs. Erect inflorescences, to 3½ft (1.1m) long, each have 3–15 broad red bracts in 2 ranks, with yellow keels and green margins. Flowers have green-tipped white sepals. ↕ 2–15ft (0.6–5m), ↔ indefinite. Central America, West

Heliconia psittacorum

H

Heliconia schiedeana

Indies (Dominica to Grenada). ❄ (min. 59°F/15°C). **'Aurea'** has inflorescences of 6–12 red-centered bracts with broad, golden yellow margins and green tips; flowers have green and white sepals; ↕ 10–20ft (3–6m). **'Chocolate Dancer'** has inflorescences of 6–9 brown-red bracts, with gold-edged upper margins, and flowers with green and white sepals; ↕ 6–10ft (2–3m). **'Purple Throat'** has maroon leaf stalks, and inflorescences of 7–10 deep red bracts with purple bases and green upper margins; flowers have green sepals; ↕ 15–20ft (5–6m). **'Yellow Dancer'** has inflorescences of 5–12 green-tipped yellow bracts and flowers with green and white sepals; ↕ 5–15ft (1.5–5m).
***H. caribaea* 'Chartreuse'.** Rhizomatous perennial with oblong, glaucous, mid-green leaf blades, 2–4½ft (0.6–1.3m) long. Erect inflorescences, 8–16in (20–40cm) long, have 11 or 12 bright lime-green bracts, arranged in 2 ranks, with yellow bases; the flowers have green and white sepals. ↕ 12–20ft (4–6m), ↔ indefinite. ❄ (min. 59°F/15°C)
H. humilis see *H. bihai.*
***H. humilis* of gardens** see *H. stricta* 'Dwarf Jamaican'.
H. nutans. Rhizomatous perennial producing oblong, dark green leaf blades, 20–36in (50–90cm) long. Pendent inflorescences, 24–39in (60–100cm) long, each have 3–12 spirally arranged or 2-ranked, orange-red bracts; flowers have yellow sepals. ↕ 3–6ft (1–2m), ↔ indefinite. Costa Rica, Panama. ❄ (min. 59°F/15°C)
H. pendula. Rhizomatous perennial with oblong to spoon-shaped, mid-green leaf blades, 2–3ft (60–90cm) long, waxy and glaucous beneath. Bears pendent, waxy white-mealy inflorescences, 3–12in (8–30cm) long, each with 6–9 spirally arranged, reflexed, pink-red bracts; the flowers have white sepals. ↕ to 6ft (2m), ↔ indefinite. Guatemala to Peru. ❄ (min. 59°F/15°C). **'Red Waxy'** has very waxy leaves beneath and 5–11 glowing red bracts.
H. psittacorum ■ (Parrot flower, Parrot's plantain). Variable, rhizomatous perennial with elliptic or oblong to linear, leathery, rich dark green leaf blades, 4–20in (10–50cm) long, on red leaf stalks. Bears erect inflorescences, 5–28in (12–70cm) long, of 2–7 slender, upcurved, orange-red bracts in 2 ranks; flowers have orange-red sepals with green-banded tips. ↕ 2–6ft (0.6–2m), ↔ indefinite. Lesser Antilles to E. Brazil. ❄ (min. 59°F/15°C)
H. rostrata. Rhizomatous perennial producing ovate-oblong, mid-green leaf blades, 24–48in (60–120cm) long. Pendent inflorescences, 12–24in (30–60cm) long, each have 4–35 red bracts, in 2 ranks, with yellow-green tips and green margins; the flowers have yellowish white sepals. ↕ 3–20ft (1–6m), ↔ indefinite. Ecuador, Peru. ❄ (min. 59°F/15°C)
H. schiedeana ■ Upright, rhizomatous perennial with opposite, oblong, mid-green leaf blades, to 5ft (1.5m) long. Produces erect, sparsely to densely hairy inflorescences, 12–28in (30–70cm) long, of 7–10 spirally arranged, slender red bracts, and flowers with yellow sepals. ↕ 3–10ft (1–3m), ↔ 3ft (1m). S. Mexico. ❄ (min. 59°F/15°C)
H. stricta. Variable, rhizomatous perennial with maroon leaf stalks and oblong, mid- to dark green leaf blades, 16–66in (40–150cm) long. Erect inflorescences, 8–12in (20–30cm) long, each have 2 ranks of 3–10 red or orange, green-tipped bracts, with yellow upper margins and keels. Flowers have white-tipped green sepals. ↕ 2–12ft (0.6–4m), ↔ indefinite. Venezuela, Surinam, Ecuador, Bolivia. ❄ (min. 59°F/15°C). **'Bucky'** has inflorescences of 3–6 bright red bracts with narrow green margins; ↕ 3–6ft (1–2m). **'Dorado Gold'** produces inflorescences of 5 or 6 peach-yellow bracts with small, elongated, central pink marks; ↕ 3–6ft (1–2m). **'Dwarf Jamaican'**, syn. *H. humilis* of gardens, has inflorescences bearing 3–5 peach-red bracts with narrow green upper margins; ↕ 1–3ft (30–100cm). **'Fire Bird'** has leaves with maroon midribs and leaf stalks, and produces inflorescences with 6 or 7 dark red bracts with narrow green margins; ↕ 3–5ft (1–1.5m).

HELICTOTRICHON

POACEAE

Genus of about 50 species of tussock-forming, deciduous and evergreen, perennial grasses from rocky slopes, wasteland, or field margins in temperate Europe, W. Asia, and North America. The linear, mid- to light green, or gray-blue leaves are flat, ribbed, or folded, or have rolled margins. Oblong, flattened, glistening spikelets are borne in erect or nodding panicles. Use in a herbaceous or mixed border, or for gravel plantings, where they associate well with purple- or silver-leaved plants.
• **CULTIVATION** Grow in well-drained, poor to moderately fertile, preferably alkaline soil in full sun. Remove dead leaves and old flowering stems in spring.
• **PROPAGATION** Sow seed in containers in a cold frame in spring, or divide in spring.
• **PESTS AND DISEASES** Rust may be a problem.

Helictotrichon sempervirens

H. sempervirens ■ syn. *Avena candida, A. sempervirens* (Blue oat grass). Densely tufted, evergreen, perennial grass, forming a hemispherical mound of flat or tightly rolled, linear, gray-blue leaves, to 9in (23cm) long. In early and midsummer, stiff, upright stems bear glistening, straw-colored, purple-marked spikelets in open panicles, to 7in (18cm) long, nodding at the tips. ↕ to 4½ft (1.4m), ↔ 24in (60cm). C. and S.W. Europe. Zone 4b.

HELIOCEREUS

CACTACEAE

Genus, closely related to *Disocactus*, of about 6 species of epiphytic or terrestrial, free-flowering cacti found in a range of shaded habitats in the lowlands of Mexico, Guatemala, and El Salvador. They produce succulent, sometimes spreading, angular-ribbed stems, which bear spiny, white or pale yellow areoles, later becoming brown. Long-lasting, large, trumpet-shaped, colorful flowers open in early summer. Some species have been cross-pollinated with *Epiphyllum* to produce many outstanding cultivars. Where not hardy, grow as houseplants or in a warm greenhouse. In humid, tropical gardens, use in a shady border, or in containers on a patio.
• **CULTIVATION** Under glass, grow in epiphytic cactus potting mix in bright filtered light, shaded from hot sun; provide high humidity. During the growing season, water freely and apply a half-strength, balanced liquid fertilizer monthly; keep just moist in winter. Outdoors, grow in poor to moderately fertile, sharply drained, acidic soil in partial shade. See also pp.48–49.
• **PROPAGATION** Sow seed at 66–70°F (19–21°C) in spring. Root cuttings of stem segments in spring or summer.
• **PESTS AND DISEASES** Susceptible to mealybugs.

Heliocereus speciosus var. *amecamensis*

H. cinnabarinus. Trailing cactus with 3-ribbed, toothed, dark green stems, 3- or 4-angled above, 5- or 6-angled beneath, bearing short, bristly, white or yellowish brown spines. Trumpet-shaped, glossy red flowers, 5–6in (12–15cm) long, with greenish yellow outer segments, often yellow toward the bases, are produced in early summer. ↕ 24in (60cm), ↔ 18in (45cm). Mexico, Guatemala, El Salvador. ❄ (min. 55°F/13°C)
H. speciosus. Semi-pendent to erect cactus producing cylindrical, unevenly toothed, mid-green stems. The stems have 3–5 prominent, acute ribs, and areoles and spines that are yellow at first, later becoming pale brown. Trumpet-shaped red flowers, 4½–7in (11–18cm) long, with purple-tinged sepals, are borne in early summer. ↕↔ to 18in (45cm). Mexico. ❄ (min. 55°F/13°C). **var. *amecamensis*** ■ produces pure white flowers. **var. *superbus*** has 3- to 7-ribbed stems with yellowish brown spines that often fall quickly; the flowers are rich, glossy, purplish red, with red outer segments.

HELIOPHILA

BRASSICACEAE

Genus of about 75 species of erect, spreading, or occasionally climbing annuals, biennials, perennials, and subshrubs found in a range of habitats, including rocky sites, sandy soils, and coastal areas, in South Africa. The leaves are entire, lobed, or finely divided. Heliophilas are grown for their loose racemes of cross-shaped, 4-petaled, often scented flowers in white, blue, or pink, borne from spring to summer. For short-lived summer color, grow in an annual or mixed border; alternatively, use in a cool greenhouse or conservatory to flower in late winter and spring. The long, pendent, chain-like seed pods of *H. leptophylla* are useful for dried flower arrangements.
• **CULTIVATION** Under glass, grow in soil-based potting mix in bright filtered light. Water plants moderately at all times. Outdoors, grow in fertile, well-drained soil in full sun, providing shelter from strong winds.
• **PROPAGATION** Sow seed *in situ* in spring or, for winter-flowering container plants, at 61–66°F (16–19°C) in early spring or in autumn. Sow seed in succession to obtain a long display of flowers.
• **PESTS AND DISEASES** Infrequent.

Heliophila coronopifolia

H. coronopifolia ▣ syn. *H. longifolia.* Slender-stemmed, many-branched, occasionally hairy annual producing simple or pinnate, mid-green leaves, 2½–6in (6–15cm) long, with linear leaflets. From spring to summer, bears pale to bright blue or blue-violet, occasionally pink or white, sometimes purple-spotted flowers, to ½in (1.5cm) across, with green-yellow centers. ↕ 4in (10cm), ↔ to 12in (30cm). South Africa (Western Cape). **'Atlantis'** produces bright blue flowers with white eyes, which are followed by attractive seed pods in autumn.

H. leptophylla. Slender-stemmed, basally branching annual with pinnate, blue-green leaves, 1–2in (2.5–5cm) long, composed of narrow leaflets. Slightly pendent spikes of clear blue flowers, to ½in (1.5cm) across, with a yellow base to each petal, are borne from spring to summer. ↕ 18in (45cm), ↔ 9in (23cm). South Africa (Western Cape).

H. longifolia see *H. coronopifolia.*

HELIOPSIS

Ox eye

ASTERACEAE

Genus of 12 or 13 species of perennials found in dry prairies and open woodland in North America. They have stiff, branching stems with opposite, ovate to lance-shaped, toothed, 3-veined, mid- or dark green leaves. The solitary, terminal, sunflower-like flowerheads are usually yellow and to 3in (8cm) across. Unlike the ray florets of sunflowers (*Helianthus*), those of *Heliopsis* are fertile. Use in a herbaceous or mixed border, or in informal plantings. Ox eyes also provide long-lasting cut flowers.

Heliopsis helianthoides 'Incomparabilis'

Heliopsis helianthoides subsp. *scabra* 'Sommersonne'

• **CULTIVATION** Grow in moderately fertile, humus-rich, moist but well-drained soil in full sun. Divide every 2–3 years to maintain vigor. Taller species and cultivars may need support.

• **PROPAGATION** Sow seed in containers in a cold frame in spring. Divide in spring or autumn. Root basal cuttings in spring.

• **PESTS AND DISEASES** Prone to powdery mildew and rust.

H. helianthoides. Clump-forming perennial with ovate to lance-shaped, toothed, almost hairless, 3-veined, mid-green leaves, to 6in (15cm) long. Numerous long-stalked, single to double flowerheads, 1½–3in (4–8cm) across, with yellow ray florets and disk florets, are borne on branched stems from mid-summer to early autumn. ↕ 3–6ft (1–1.8m), ↔ 24in (60cm). Ontario to Florida and Missouri. Zone 4. **'Ballerina'** has semi-double flowerheads with golden yellow ray florets and slightly darker disk florets; ↕ 3ft (1m). **'Concave Mirror'** see 'Hohlspiegel'. **'Gigantea'** has large, semi-double, golden yellow flowerheads; ↕ to 4ft (1.2m). **'Goldranunkel'** is dense and bushy, and has large yellow flowerheads, from midsummer to early autumn; ↕ 3½ft (1.1m). **'Hohlspiegel',** syn. 'Concave Mirror', has dark foliage and semi-double, concave, dark orange flowerheads, in midsummer and early autumn; ↕ 4ft (1.2m). **'Karat'** has very large, single, clear yellow flowerheads, from midsummer to early autumn; ↕ 4ft (1.2m). **'Incomparabilis'** ▣ has double, zinnia-like, orange-yellow flowerheads, to 3in (8cm) across; ↕ 36in (90cm). **'Mars'** has large, single, yellow-orange flowerheads; ↕ to 5ft (1.5m). **'Patula'** has large, flattish, semi-double, golden yellow flowerheads, with 3 rows of frilled or toothed ray florets; ↕ to 4ft (1.2m). **subsp. *scabra*** has coarsely hairy leaves and bears only 1–4 yellow flowerheads; ↕ to 3ft (1m); New Jersey to Arkansas, Mexico. **subsp. *scabra* 'Goldgefieder'**, syn. subsp. *scabra* 'Golden Plume', bears double flowerheads with golden yellow ray florets and green disk florets; ↕ to 4½ft (1.4m). **subsp. *scabra* 'Goldgrünherz'**, syn. subsp. *scabra* 'Goldgreenheart', has double, lemon-yellow flowerheads, shaded green in the centers until fully open; ↕ 36in (90cm). **subsp. *scabra* 'Light of Loddon'** has dark green leaves, to 8in (20cm) long, and bears double, bright yellow flowerheads; ↕ to 3½ft (1.1m). **subsp. *scabra* 'Sommersonne'** ▣ syn. subsp. *scabra* 'Summer Sun', bears single, occasionally semi-double flowerheads with deep golden yellow ray florets, sometimes flushed orange-yellow, and brownish yellow disk florets; ↕ 36in (90cm). **'Spitzentanzerin'**, syn. 'Toe Dancer', bears semi-double, deep golden yellow flowerheads, with fine ray florets, each having 2 twisted tips, from midsummer to early autumn; ↕ 4ft (1.2m). **'Toe Dancer'** see 'Spitzentanzerin'.

▷ ***Heliosperma alpestris*** see *Silene alpestris*

HELIOTROPIUM

Heliotrope

BORAGINACEAE

Genus of about 250 species of erect, bushy annuals, perennials, subshrubs, and shrubs from dry, open, and sandy habitats, including scrub, in S.W. and E. US, Mexico, South America, Hawaii, Pacific islands, and the Canary Islands. They have simple, mostly entire, roughly hairy, and usually alternate leaves. Heliotropes are cultivated mainly for their tiny, sweetly scented, tubular flowers, which are produced in summer in clusters of coiled cymes, each forming a slightly domed or flattened flowerhead. They are attractive to butterflies. Contact with the foliage may irritate both skin and eyes. Where not hardy, grow in a cool or temperate greenhouse, or use as summer bedding or in containers or windowboxes. In warmer regions, grow heliotropes at the front of a border or in containers outdoors.

Heliotropium arborescens 'Marine'

• **CULTIVATION** Under glass, grow in soilless or soil-based potting mix, in full light with shade from hot sun; provide moderate humidity. In the growing season, water moderately and apply a balanced liquid fertilizer monthly; keep just moist in winter. Outdoors, grow in any fertile, moist but well-drained soil in full sun.

• **PROPAGATION** Sow seed at 61–64°F (16–18°C) in spring. Root stem-tip cuttings or semi-ripe cuttings of selections and named cultivars in summer.

• **PESTS AND DISEASES** Susceptible to whiteflies, rust, and leaf spot.

H. arborescens, syn. *H. peruvianum* (Cherry pie, Heliotrope). Bushy, short-lived shrub, often grown as an annual, with broadly oval to lance-shaped, wrinkled, mid- to dark green, sometimes purple-tinged leaves, to 3in (8cm) long. Deep violet-blue or lavender-blue flowers are borne in dense flowerheads, 3–4in (8–10cm) across, in summer. ↕ 4ft (1.2m) in open ground, to 18in (45cm) in containers, ↔ 12–18in (30–45cm). Peru. ❄ (min. 50°F/10°C). Numerous named cultivars and unnamed selections of *H. arborescens* are used for summer bedding: **'Alba'** bears vanilla-scented white flowers. **'Iowa'** is compact, with deep green, blue-tinged leaves and dark purple flowerheads. **'Lord Roberts'** is compact, bearing light violet-blue flowerheads. **'Marine'** ▣ is compact, with deep violet-blue flowerheads, to 6in (15cm) across; ↕ to 18in (45cm). **'Mini Marine'** is dwarf, and produces deep violet-blue flowerheads; ↕ to 16in (40cm). **'Princess Marina'** is compact, bearing deep violet-blue, highly scented flowerheads; ↕ to 12in (30cm). **'Regal Dwarf'** is very compact, and has large, fragrant, dark blue flowerheads. **'White Lady'** is compact, producing white flowerheads tinged pink in bud; ↕ to 12in (30cm).

H. peruvianum see *H. arborescens.*

▷ ***Helipterum humboldtianum*** see *Pteropogon humboldtianus*

▷ ***Helipterum manglesii*** see *Rhodanthe manglesii*

▷ ***Helipterum roseum*** see *Rhodanthe chlorocephala* subsp. *rosea*

HELLEBORUS

Hellebore

RANUNCULACEAE

Genus of 15 species of perennials found in scrub, woodland, and grassy and rocky sites, usually on chalky or limestone soils, from C., E., and S. Europe to W. Asia. They are rhizomatous, and either clump-forming with deciduous, basal leaves, or almost shrub-like, with leafy, biennial stems. The leaves are lobed or fully divided into leaflets, and often pedate (the lateral leaflets or lobes further subdivided or lobed); they are generally toothed, leathery, and light to dark green. The loose, usually few-flowered cymes, to 18in (45cm) tall in most species, have leafy bracts and are borne from late winter to midspring. The often very long-lasting flowers are white, cream, pink, purple, or green, sometimes spotted, and are pendent or outward-facing, saucer- to cup-shaped, or tubular-bell-shaped. Each has 5 tepals, numerous stamens, and 2–10 free carpels. Hellebores are effective when grown in groups in a mixed or shrub border, or naturalized in a woodland garden. Smaller species are ideal for a rock garden. All parts may cause severe discomfort if ingested, and the sap may irritate skin on contact.

• **CULTIVATION** Hellebores tolerate a range of moist, fertile, humus-rich soils, but have varying "ideal" cultivation requirements. For ease of reference, these have been grouped as follows:
1. Neutral to alkaline soil in dappled shade.
2. Neutral to alkaline soil in full sun or dappled shade.
3. Any soil, but preferably acidic, in partial shade.
Incorporate leaf mold or organic matter at planting, and mulch annually in autumn, especially *H. argutifolius* and *H. orientalis*. For all groups, avoid dry or waterlogged soils, and provide shelter from strong, cold winds.

• **PROPAGATION** Sow seed in containers in a cold frame as soon as ripe; named cultivars do not come true from seed. Divide all species and named cultivars after flowering, in early spring or late summer. *H. foetidus* and *H. argutifolius* are best raised from seed, since they are not suitable for division.

• **PESTS AND DISEASES** Susceptible to slugs, snails, aphids, leaf spot, and black rot.

Helleborus argutifolius

H. argutifolius ■ syn. *H. corsicus*, *H. lividus* subsp. *corsicus* (Corsican hellebore). Hairless perennial producing overwintering, leafy, biennial flowering stems and leathery, dark green leaves, 3–9in (8–23cm) long, consisting of 3 elliptic to broadly elliptic, spiny-toothed leaflets, paler green beneath. Pendent, shallow bowl-shaped, pale green flowers, 1–2in (2.5–5cm) across, open in many-flowered, terminal cymes in late winter and early spring. Cultivation group 1 or 2. ↕ to 4ft (1.2m), ↔ 36in (90cm). Corsica, Sardinia. Zone 6.

H. atrorubens. Hairless perennial with deciduous, pedate, dark green, basal leaves, to 10in (25cm) long, composed of 7–11 leaflets; the 2 lateral leaflets each have 3–5 narrowly elliptic, toothed lobes. Stems and leaves may be suffused purple. Cymes of 2 or 3 outward-facing, saucer-shaped, deep purple flowers, 1½–2in (4–5cm) across, green-shaded within, open before the leaves, from late winter to spring. Cultivation group 1. ↕ 12in (30cm), ↔ 18in (45cm). N.W. Balkans. Zone 5b.

***H. atrorubens* of gardens** see *H. orientalis* subsp. *abchasicus*.

H. x ballardiae (*H. lividus* x *H. niger*). Clump-forming perennial with short, overwintering, leafy, biennial stems. The pedate, deep bluish green leaves, to 10in (25cm) long, each have 3–5 elliptic to inversely lance-shaped-oblong, toothed leaflets, boldly veined silvery cream. From midwinter to early spring, bears cymes of 3 or 4 saucer-shaped white flowers, 2–3½in (5–9cm) across, flushed pink inside, becoming purplish pink with age. Cultivation group 1. ↕ to 14in (35cm), ↔ 12in (30cm). Garden origin. Zone 6. **'December Dawn'** ■ has saucer-shaped white flowers, 2½–3in (6–8cm) across, flushed pinkish purple, maturing to a dull metallic purple.

H. corsicus see *H. argutifolius*.

H. cyclophyllus ■ Deciduous perennial with pedate, toothed, pale green, basal leaves, to 12in (30cm) long, hairy beneath with bold veins; each central leaflet is divided or entire, the 2 lateral leaflets deeply 5- to 7-lobed. From midwinter to early spring, bears cymes of up to 7 outward-facing or pendent, saucer-shaped, scented, yellowish green flowers, 2–3in (5–8cm) across. Cultivation group 1. ↕ to 16in (40cm), ↔ 18in (45cm). S. Balkans. Zone 6.

H. foetidus ■ (Bear's foot, Dungwort, Stinking hellebore, Stinkwort). Erect perennial with hairless, leafy, biennial stems. The pedate, dark green leaves, 9in (23cm) long, smell unpleasant when crushed, and each has 7–10 narrowly lance-shaped or elliptic, coarsely toothed or nearly entire lobes. From midwinter to midspring, bears many-flowered cymes of pendent, bell-shaped green flowers, ½–1in (1.5–2.5cm) across, often purple-margined and sometimes pleasantly scented, above large, pale green bracts. Cultivation group 1 or 2. ↕ to 32in (80cm), ↔ 18in (45cm). W. and C. Europe. Zone 6. **'Wester Flisk'** has reddish green stems, leaf stalks, and flower stalks, the color diffusing into the leaf bases; the leaves are dark gray-green. Comes true from seed if isolated from other variants of the species.

H. x hybridus. Group of variable, clump-forming, perennial hybrids of *H. orientalis* and other species. The

Helleborus x *ballardiae* 'December Dawn'

deciduous or overwintering, pedate, leathery, mid- to dark green leaves, to 16in (40cm) long, each have 7–11 elliptic to inversely lance-shaped, toothed lobes or leaflets. From midwinter to midspring, thick stems produce loose cymes of up to 4 pendent to outward-facing, saucer-shaped flowers, 2–3in (5–8cm) across, in a range of colors, including white, purple, yellow, green, and pink. Cultivation group 1, but tolerant of all but very poorly drained or dry soils. ↕↔ to 18in (45cm). Garden origin. Zone 6. **'Citron'** ■ produces bowl-shaped, primrose-yellow flowers. **'Peggy Ballard'** ■ bears large flowers, to 3in (8cm) across, deep reddish pink outside, dusky purple-pink with darker veins inside. **'Philip Ballard'** has dark blue-black flowers. **'Pluto'** ■ bears small flowers that are purple outside, green-shaded purple within, with purple nectaries. **'Yellow Button'** bears small, deep yellow flowers that are initially cup-shaped, becoming saucer-shaped.

H. lividus. Erect or spreading perennial with overwintering, hairless, biennial stems. The leathery, glossy, dark green or bluish green leaves, to 9in (23cm) long, each have 3 elliptic or oblong-elliptic leaflets, entire or with a few shallow teeth; they have creamy silver veins, and pinkish purple leaf stalks and main veins beneath. From midwinter to early spring, long, purplish green stalks bear cymes of up to 10 bowl-shaped, creamy green flowers, 1¼–2in (3–5cm) across, suffused pinkish purple. Cultivation group 1. Where marginally hardy, best grown in a cold greenhouse. ↕ to 18in (45cm), ↔ 12in (30cm). Majorca. ❄ (min. 35°F/2°C). **subsp. *corsicus*** see *H. argutifolius*.

H. multifidus* subsp. *hercegovinus ■ Erect, clump-forming perennial producing deciduous, pedate, mid-green, basal leaves, to 9in (23cm) long, each with 45–70 linear, toothed, prominently veined segments, hairy beneath, often brown-tinted when young. Cymes of 3–8 pendent, conical

Helleborus cyclophyllus

Helleborus foetidus

Helleborus x *hybridus* 'Citron'

Helleborus x *hybridus* 'Peggy Ballard'

Helleborus x *hybridus* 'Pluto'

Helleborus multifidus subsp. *hercegovinus*

H

Helleborus niger 'Potter's Wheel'

Helleborus orientalis subsp. *guttatus*

to cup-shaped green flowers, 1½–2in (4–5cm) across, are borne in late winter and early spring. Cultivation group 1 or 2. ↕ to 12in (30cm), ↔ 18in (45cm). Bosnia and Herzegovina (Adriatic coastal mountains). Zone 7b.

H. niger ■ (Christmas rose). Clump-forming, hairless perennial with overwintering, pedate, leathery, dark green, basal leaves, 2–8in (5–20cm) long, consisting of 7–9 oblong to inversely lance-shaped leaflets, toothed toward the apexes. From early winter to early spring, thick, purple-marked stems produce shallowly saucer-shaped flowers, 1¾–3in (4.5–8cm) across, singly, or occasionally in cymes of 2 or 3 blooms; the flowers are white, sometimes strongly pink-flushed, with greenish white centers, aging to pinkish white. Cultivation group 1. ↕ to 12in (30cm), ↔ 18in (45cm). Germany, Austria, Switzerland, Italy, Slovenia. Zone 4. **subsp. *macranthus*** has spiny-toothed, bluish or gray-green leaves with broadly lance-shaped lobes, and white flowers, 3–4½in (8–11cm) across; Italy, Slovenia. **'Potter's Wheel'** ■ has large, bowl-shaped white flowers with green eyes.

H. × nigercors (*H. argutifolius* × *H. niger*). Clump-forming perennial with short, overwintering, leafy, biennial stems. Variable, pedate, mid-green basal and stem leaves, 4–12in (10–30cm) long, have 3–5 coarsely toothed lobes. From midwinter to early spring, short stems bear clustered cymes of numerous flattish, white, sometimes pink-flushed flowers, 3–4in (7–10cm) across. Cultivation group 1. ↕ 12in (30cm), ↔ 36in (90cm). Garden origin. Zone 5. **'Alabaster'** is very vigorous, and bears creamy white flowers, 2½–3in (6–8cm) across, with green shading.

H. odorus. Clump-forming perennial with overwintering, pedate, leathery, deep green, basal leaves, 16in (40cm) long, hairy beneath. Each central leaflet is entire; the lateral leaflets are divided into 3–5 elliptic to inversely lance-shaped, toothed lobes. Cymes of 3–5 saucer-shaped, outward-facing, fragrant green flowers, 2–3in (5–8cm) across, open from midwinter to early spring. Cultivation group 1 or 2. ↕↔ 12–20in (30–50cm). S. Hungary, N. Balkans (including Romania). Zone 6.

H. orientalis (Lenten rose). Hairless or slightly hairy perennial producing overwintering, pedate, leathery, deep green, basal leaves, to 16in (40cm) long, each with 7–9 elliptic or inversely lance-shaped leaflets. From midwinter to midspring, thick, usually branched stems bear pendent or almost outward-facing, saucer-shaped, white or greenish cream flowers, 2–3in (5–8cm) across, becoming pinker with age. Cultivation group 1, but tolerant of most garden conditions. ↕↔ to 18in (45cm). N.E. Greece, N. Turkey, C. and W. Caucasus. Zone 4. **subsp. *abchasicus***, syn. *H. atrorubens* of gardens, has pale green flowers, deeply tinted reddish purple outside, sometimes almost masking the green, and occasionally with deeper purple spots. W. Caucasus. **subsp. *guttatus*** ■ bears creamy white flowers, variably spotted maroon within, with green centers; W. Caucasus. **Millet Hybrids** have large, cup-shaped flowers, 2–3in (5–8cm) across, in shades of white, pink, and red.

H. purpurascens ■ Clump-forming perennial producing deciduous, leathery, mid-green, basal leaves, to 11in (28cm) long, hairy beneath, usually composed of 5 leaflets, each with 2–6 lance-shaped, toothed lobes. Cymes of 2–4 pendent, cup-shaped flowers, 1½–3in (4–8cm) across, are borne before the leaves, from midwinter to early or midspring. The flowers are purplish or slate gray, often pink- or purple-flushed, light green within. Cultivation group 2 or 3. ↕ 2–12in (5–30cm), ↔ 12in (30cm). S.E. Poland, W. Ukraine, Slovakia, C. and N. Hungary, Romania. Zone 5.

H. × sternii ■ (*H. argutifolius* × *H. lividus*). Clump-forming hybrid perennial, sometimes resembling one parent more than the other, with overwintering, leafy, biennial stems. Entire to spiny leaves, 4–11in (10–28cm) long, have 3 broadly elliptic leaflets or lobes, creamy veins, and pinkish purple leaf stalks and main veins. Many-flowered cymes of creamy green flowers, 1–2in (2.5–5cm) across, suffused pinkish purple, are borne from late winter to midspring. Cultivation group 2. ↕ 12–14in (30–35cm), ↔ 12in (30cm). Garden origin. Zone 6. **'Blackthorn'**, syn. Blackthorn Group, has purple stems and boldy veined, grayish green leaves. Bears purplish or pink-stained green flowers. **'Boughton Beauty'** ■ has purple-pink stems and veined, mid-green leaves. The flowers are pinkish purple outside, greener within; ↕ 20–24in (50–60cm).

H. torquatus. Very variable, clump-forming perennial producing pedate, deciduous, mid-green leaves, to 18in (45cm) long, each with 10–30 tapered, lance-shaped, toothed lobes, hairy beneath. Outward-facing to pendent, saucer-shaped, violet-purple flowers, often green within, with dark veins, are produced before the leaves, from midwinter to early spring; they are 1¼–2½in (3–6cm) across, and borne singly or in cymes of 2–5 (occasionally up to 7) flowers. Cultivation group 1 or 2. ↕ 8–16in (20–40cm), ↔ 12in (30cm). Montenegro, Bosnia and Herzegovina, W. Serbia, Croatia. Zone 6b. **'Dido'** ■ produces semi-double flowers, 1½–2in (4–5cm) across, suffused brown or purple-brown on the outsides, green within, with green margins; ↕ 10–12in (25–30cm).

H. viridis ■ (Green hellebore). Clump-forming perennial with deciduous, pedate, slightly hairy or hairless, dark green, basal leaves, to 12in (30cm) long, each with 7–13 narrowly oblong to lance-shaped or elliptic, toothed lobes. In late winter and early spring, bears cymes of 2–4 pendent, saucer-shaped green flowers, 1¼–2in (3–5cm) across. Cultivation group 1. ↕ 8–16in (20–40cm), ↔ 18in (45cm). Spain, UK to Austria, Germany. Zone 5b.

Helleborus niger

Helleborus purpurascens

Helleborus × *sternii*

Helleborus × *sternii* 'Boughton Beauty'

Helleborus torquatus 'Dido'

Helleborus viridis

HELONIAS

LILIACEAE

Genus of one species of evergreen, rhizomatous perennial found in bogs and swampland in the US. It has rosettes of strap-shaped leaves, and is grown for its dense racemes of many fragrant, star-shaped, pinkish purple flowers, borne in spring. Ideal for a bog garden or for growing beside a pond or stream. May also be grown in a cold greenhouse for early flowering.

- **CULTIVATION** Grow in moderately fertile, humus-rich, moist, preferably acid soil in sun or dappled shade.
- **PROPAGATION** Sow seed in containers in an open frame in autumn, or divide in spring.
- **PESTS AND DISEASES** Infrequent.

H. bullata (Swamp pink). Clump-forming, rhizomatous perennial with basal rosettes of strap-shaped, glossy, bright green leaves, 6–18in (15–45cm) long. In spring, 25–30 tiny, fragrant, 6-tepaled, pinkish purple flowers are borne in dense, terminal, conical racemes, 1¼–4in (3–10cm) long, on erect stems above the leaves. ↕ 14–18in (35–45cm), ↔ 12in (30cm). New York to North Carolina. Zone 5b.

HELONIOPSIS

LILIACEAE

Genus of 4 species of rhizomatous, evergreen, rosette-forming perennials found in scrub, woodland, and meadows in the mountains of Japan, Korea, Taiwan, and Sakhalin, Russia. They have oblong or lance-shaped, pale to mid-green leaves. From late spring to summer, erect stems bear one-sided racemes of nodding, funnel-shaped flowers, each with 6 spreading tepals. Grow in a shady rock garden or woodland garden; best suited to areas with cool, damp summers.

• **CULTIVATION** Grow in humus-rich, neutral to slightly acidic, moist but well-drained soil in partial shade. Provide shelter from wind.

• **PROPAGATION** Sow seed in containers in a cold frame in autumn or spring, or divide after flowering in spring.

• **PESTS AND DISEASES** Young growth is prone to slug and snail damage.

H. breviscapa see *H. orientalis* var. *breviscapa*.

H. grandiflora see *H. orientalis* var. *breviscapa*.

H. orientalis ▣ Rosetted perennial with broadly lance-shaped, leathery, pale green leaves, 3–6in (7–15cm) long. In late spring and early summer, dark red stems produce dense, umbel-like racemes of 3–10 nodding, narrowly funnel-shaped, rose-pink flowers, ½in (1.5cm) across, with protruding styles and stamens. The stems usually elongate after flowering. ↕↔ 6–8in (15–20cm). Japan, Korea, Russia (Sakhalin). Zone 7b. **var. *breviscapa***, syn. *H. breviscapa*, *H. grandiflora*, has sharp-pointed, leathery, mid-green leaves, 3–4in (8–10cm) long; it produces smaller, but more widely funnel-shaped, white or very pale pink flowers, on shorter flower stems.

▷ ***Helxine*** see *Soleirolia*

Heloniopsis orientalis

HEMEROCALLIS

Daylily

LILIACEAE

Genus of about 13–15 species of evergreen, semi-evergreen, and herbaceous perennials, from which over 50,000 named cultivars have been raised. Daylilies are found at forest margins, in mountainous areas, marshy river valleys, and meadowland in China, Korea, and Japan. They are mostly clump-forming, and occasionally rhizomatous, with arching, strap-shaped, dark green leaves, usually 30–48in (75–120cm) long, but often only 9–14in (23–35cm) long in dwarf or compact species and cultivars. Flowers, in a variety of forms (see panel at right), are borne on erect, sometimes branching scapes over a long period, mainly from late spring to late summer. Many daylilies are remontant, flowering repeatedly during the season. The flowers range in color from almost white through yellow and orange to dark purple and deepest red-black. Most flowers last for only one day; in nocturnal daylilies, the flowers open in late afternoon and last throughout the night. The flowers of extended-blooming daylilies remain open for at least 16 hours.

Grow daylilies in a mixed or herbaceous border; some are effective planted in drifts in a wild garden. Dwarf daylilies are ideal for a small garden or for containers.

• **HARDINESS** Generally, daylilies are hardy in Zone 3b. However, some dormants do not survive in the mildest parts of British Columbia, and some evergreens are tissue-damaged in very cold regions.

• **CULTIVATION** Grow in fertile, moist but well-drained soil; all those described here prefer full sun, unless otherwise stated. Mulch in late autumn or spring. From spring until buds develop, water freely and apply a balanced liquid fertilizer every 2–3 weeks. Dry conditions and excessive shade will reduce flowering; some red- and purple-flowered cultivars are intolerant of heavy rainfall and hot sun. Divide every 3–5 years, or when the number of flower buds and the size of bloom begin to decline. Plant evergreen species and cultivars in spring rather than autumn.

• **PROPAGATION** Sow seed in containers in a cold frame in autumn or spring; seed from hybrids and cultivars do not come true. Divide dormant daylilies in spring or autumn; divide all evergreen daylilies in spring.

• **PESTS AND DISEASES** Susceptible to rust, hemerocallis gall midge, aphids, spider mites, and thrips. Slugs and snails may damage young leaves. Crown rot is usually a problem only in high humidity and temperatures over 90°F (32°C). In climates with alternating winter freezes and thaws, bacterial leaf and stem rot (spring sickness) may be a problem.

HEMEROCALLIS FLOWER FORMS

Daylilies produce shallowly to deeply trumpet-shaped flowers in a variety of forms. The species and older cultivars bear flowers with tapered tepals, while modern hybrids and newer cultivars usually have flowers with thicker, rounded, ruffled-margined, clearer-colored tepals. The flowers may be **triangular**, with triangular to rounded, flat or ruffled-margined tepals; **circular**, with mostly rounded, flat or sometimes recurved, ruffled-margined tepals; **double**, with rounded or tapered, flat or ruffled-margined outer tepals, with extra tepals in the center of the flower; **star-shaped**, with tapered or sometimes rounded, flat or ruffled-margined tepals; or **spider-shaped**, with mostly narrow, tapered tepals. Hot weather, in particular, may cause some daylilies to bear flowers with extra petals and stamens.

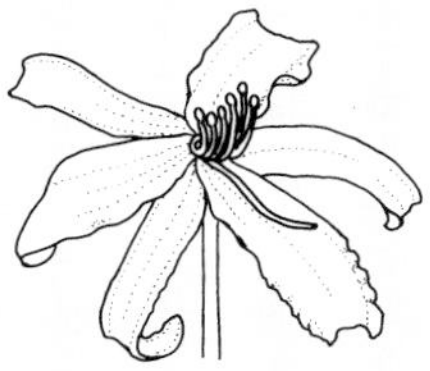

SPIDER-SHAPED

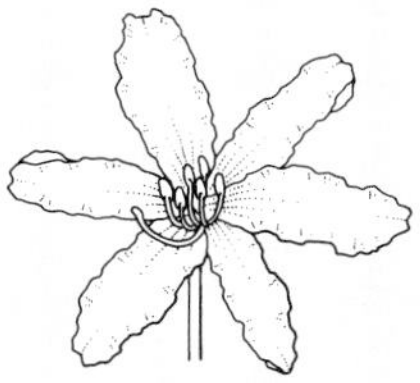

STAR-SHAPED

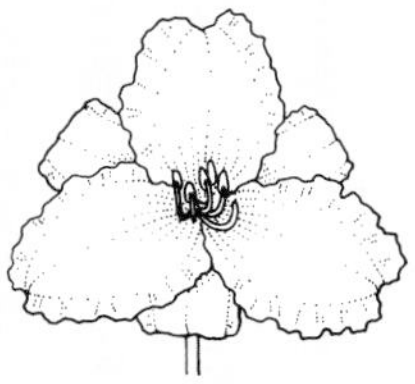

TRIANGULAR

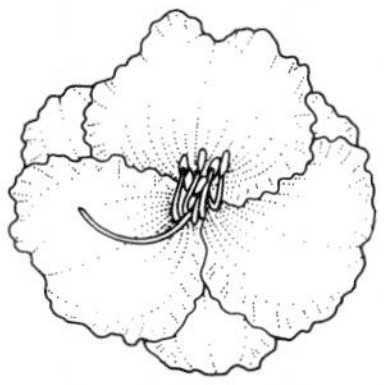

CIRCULAR

DOUBLE

***H.* 'Alexandra'.** Semi-evergreen tetraploid with sturdy, well-branched scapes. Remontant, circular, peach-pink flowers, 5½in (14cm) across, with flat, rounded, very ruffled tepals and green throats, are borne in early and mid-season. ↕ 24in (60cm).

***H.* 'Always Afternoon'.** Semi-evergreen tetraploid with sturdy, well-branched scapes. Early in the season, bears remontant, circular, buff-edged, mauve flowers, 5½in (14cm) across, with flat, rounded, slightly recurved tepals, purple eyezones, and green throats. ↕ 22in (55cm).

***H.* 'American Revolution'.** Free-flowering, dormant diploid with narrow leaves and slender scapes. In early and midseason, black-red buds open to remontant, star-shaped, velvety black to deep red flowers, 4in (10cm) across, with recurved tepals and green throats. ↕ 28in (70cm).

***H.* 'Anastasia'.** Evergreen tetraploid with strong scapes. In midseason, bears circular yellow flowers, 7in (18cm) across, with ruffled tepals and lime-green throats. ↕ 20in (50cm).

***H.* 'Ann Kelley'.** Semi-evergreen diploid with sturdy, branched scapes. Bears upward-facing, circular, deep rose-pink flowers, 5½in (14cm) across, with lighter pink midribs and black anthers, in midseason. ↕ 26in (65cm).

***H.* 'Apple Court Champagne'.** Very free-flowering, semi-evergreen diploid with well-branched scapes. In mid- and late season, bears circular, glistening, creamy lemon flowers, 7in (18cm) across, with recurved, ruffled-margined tepals, ivory-pink midribs, and green throats. ↕ 28in (70cm).

***H.* 'Apple Tart'** ▣ Semi-evergreen tetraploid with sturdy scapes, flowering in mid- and late season. Bears nocturnal, triangular to star-shaped, bright red flowers, 6in (15cm) across, with

Hemerocallis 'Apple Tart'

H

rounded tepals, prominent yellow midribs, and yellow throats. ↕28in (70cm).
***H.* 'Aquamarine'.** Dormant diploid with slender scapes bearing spider- to star-shaped, lavender-blue flowers, 7in (18cm) across, early in the season. ↕28in (70cm).
***H.* 'Atlanta Full House'.** Dormant tetraploid. In midseason, branched scapes bear circular yellow flowers, 6in (15cm) across, with flat, ruffled-margined tepals, recurved at the tips. ↕26in (65cm).
***H.* 'Barbara Mitchell'** ■ Dormant diploid with sturdy, well-branched scapes. In midseason, bears remontant pink flowers, 6in (15cm) across, with rounded, recurved tepals and green throats. ↕20in (50cm).
***H.* 'Bathsheba'.** Evergreen tetraploid with sturdy, well-branched scapes. In early and midseason, bears circular, very ruffled, pink flowers, 6in (15cm) across, of heavy substance, with slightly recurved tepals and green throats. ↕to 26in (65cm).
***H.* 'Beauty To Behold'.** Vigorous, extended-blooming, free-flowering, semi-evergreen diploid with abundant foliage. Nocturnal, circular, glistening, lemon-yellow flowers, 5½in (14cm) across, are borne on sturdy scapes in mid- and late season. ↕24in (60cm).
***H.* 'Ben Adams'.** Semi-evergreen tetraploid with strong, well-branched scapes. Bears remontant, circular, heavily ruffled, flat, pale ivory-cream flowers, 5½in (14cm) across, with green throats, in midseason. ↕26in (65cm).
***H.* 'Bertie Ferris'** ■ Extended-blooming, compact, dormant diploid. Early in the season, star-shaped, peach-orange flowers, 2½in (6cm) across, with rounded tepals, are borne on slender scapes. ↕20in (50cm).
***H.* 'Betty Warren Woods'.** Evergreen tetraploid with strong, well-branched scapes. In early and midseason, bears remontant, fragrant, cream-yellow flowers, 4½in (11cm) across, with flat, rounded tepals and green throats. ↕24in (60cm).
***H.* 'Betty Woods'** ■ Evergreen diploid with well-branched scapes. From midseason to very late in the season, bears nocturnal, remontant, double, deep yellow flowers, 5½in (14cm) across, with rounded, ruffled-margined tepals and green throats. ↕26in (65cm).
***H.* 'Bibbity Bobbity Boo'.** Semi-evergreen tetraploid with sturdy, well-branched scapes. In early and mid-season, bears remontant, lavender flowers, 2½in (6cm) across, with rounded, recurved, ruffled tepals and dark, grape-purple eyezones above green throats. ↕18in (45cm).
***H.* 'Bill Norris'.** Semi-evergreen tetraploid with strong, well-branched scapes. In midseason, bears remontant, fragrant, brilliant, yellow-gold flowers, 5in (13cm) across, with rounded, wide-ruffled tepals. ↕30in (75cm).
***H.* 'Blackberry Candy'.** Dormant tetraploid with sturdy scapes. In midseason, bears remontant, fragrant, gold flowers, 4in (10cm) across, with flat, rounded tepals and dark purple eyezones. ↕26in (65cm).

Hemerocallis 'Barbara Mitchell'

***H.* 'Brocaded Gown'** ■ Extended-blooming, semi-evergreen diploid with branched scapes. In midseason, bears nocturnal, circular, glistening, creamy yellow flowers, 6in (15cm) across, with green throats and recurved, crepe-textured tepals. ↕26in (65cm).
***H.* 'Calypso Bay'.** Semi-evergreen tetraploid with sturdy, well-branched scapes. In early and midseason, bears remontant, yellow-cerise-orange polychrome flowers, 6in (15cm) across, with flat, rounded, ruffled tepals and green throats. ↕28in (70cm).
***H.* 'Camden Gold Dollar'.** Compact, semi-evergreen diploid with narrow, mid- to dark green leaves. Slender scapes bear remontant, circular, deep golden yellow flowers, 3in (8cm) across, with very ruffled-margined tepals, from midseason to very late in the season. ↕↔18in (45cm).
***H.* 'Cat's Cradle'** ■ Evergreen diploid with narrow leaves and slender, well-branched scapes. In midseason, bears nocturnal, spider-shaped, bright yellow flowers, 8in (20cm) across. ↕36in (90cm).
***H.* 'Chance Encounter'.** Fragrant, extended-blooming evergreen tetraploid. In early midseason, bears remontant raspberry rose flowers, 6in (15cm) across, with gold edge and green throat. ↕ 25in (62.5cm).
***H.* 'Charles Johnston'.** Free-flowering, semi-evergreen tetraploid with sturdy scapes bearing circular, bright cherry-red to bluish red flowers, 6in (15cm) across, with green throats, in early and mid-season. ↕24in (60cm).
***H.* 'Charlie Pierce Memorial'.** Semi-evergreen diploid with strong, well-branched scapes. In early and mid-season, bears remontant, semi-triangular, lavender flowers, 6in (15cm) across, with flat, fully recurved, ruffled tepals; wine-purple eyezones; and green throats. ↕24in (60cm).
***H.* 'Chestnut Lane'.** Free-flowering, evergreen tetraploid with sturdy scapes bearing circular, light golden brown flowers, 6in (15cm) across, with fluted tepals, chestnut-brown eyes, and yellow throats, in midseason. ↕30in (75cm).
***H.* 'Chestnut Mountain'.** Evergreen tetraploid with very sturdy, well-branched scapes. In midseason, bears remontant flowers, 5½in (14cm) across, in blends of chestnut-copper- and orange-yellow, with flat, rounded, ruffled tepals and green throats. ↕24in (60cm).
***H.* 'Chicago Apache'.** Vigorous, free-flowering, dormant tetraploid with masses of stiff leaves. In late season, sturdy scapes bear circular, velvety, rich scarlet flowers, 5in (13cm) across, the tepals with ruffled, deeper red margins and white midribs. ↕28in (70cm).
***H.* 'Chorus Line'** ■ Semi-evergreen diploid with stiff, wide-branching scapes. Bears remontant, slightly fragrant, bright pink flowers, 3½in (9cm) across, with pink- and yellow-marked tepals and dark green throats, in early and late season. ↕20in (50cm).
H. citrina ■ Herbaceous perennial with coarse, recurved leaves, 28–32in (70–80cm) long. In midseason, stiff scapes bear nocturnal, star-shaped, fragrant, greenish yellow to pale lemon-yellow flowers, 3½–5in (9–13cm) across, with brown-tipped sepals. China. ↕4ft (1.2m), ↔30in (75cm).
***H.* 'Codie Wedgeworth'.** Evergreen diploid with sturdy scapes bearing remontant, pastel-pink flowers, 6in (15cm) across, with rounded, recurved, ruffled tepals and green throats, early in the season. ↕26in (65cm).
***H.* 'Condilla'.** Slow-growing, dormant diploid with erect scapes bearing double, deep yellow flowers, 4½in (11cm) across, with broad tepals, in early and midseason. ↕20in (50cm).
***H.* 'Corky'.** Compact, free-flowering, dormant diploid with narrow leaves. Slender, wiry scapes bear reddish brown buds that open to star-shaped, clear yellow flowers, 2½in (6cm) across, with reddish brown sepals, in midseason. Prefers a sunny site, but tolerates some shade. ↕28in (70cm).
***H.* 'Court Magician'.** Evergreen tetraploid with sturdy, well-branched scapes. In early and midseason, bears remontant, purple flowers, 5in (13cm) across, with rounded, reflexed, slightly ruffled tepals; very distinctive, chalky-lilac eyezones; and yellow-green throats. ↕26in (65cm).
***H.* 'Custard Candy'.** Dormant tetraploid with sturdy, well-branched scapes. In early and midseason, bears remontant, cream-yellow flowers, 4½in (11cm) across, with rounded, reflexed tepals, maroon eyezones, and green throats. ↕24in (60cm).
***H.* 'Daring Dilemma'.** Semi-evergreen tetraploid with very well-branched scapes. In midseason, bears fragrant, cream-tinted, pink flowers, 5in (13cm) across, with, flat, rounded, very heavily ruffled tepals and distinctive plum picotee edges and eyezones above yellow-green throats. ↕24in (60cm).

Hemerocallis 'Bertie Ferris'

***H.* 'Designer Rhythm'.** Dormant tetraploid with sturdy, well-branched scapes. Light mauve flowers, 6in (15cm) across, with rounded, reflexed, ruffled tepals, large, deep lavender eyezones, and green throats, are borne in midseason. ↕26in (65cm).
***H.* 'Dominic'.** Vigorous, evergreen tetraploid with sturdy scapes bearing circular, very dark black-red flowers, 5½in (14cm) across, in early and mid-season. ↕↔30in (75cm).
***H.* 'Dragon's Eye'.** Semi-evergreen diploid. In late midseason, bears remontant pastel pink flowers, 4in (10cm) across, with rose red eyezone above green throat. ↕24in (60cm).
***H.* 'Druid's Chant'.** Semi-evergreen tetraploid with strong scapes. In early and midseason, bears remontant, triangular, deep lavender flowers, 6in (15cm) across, with wide ruffled tepals, purple eyezones and picotee edges, silver edges outside the picotees, and green throats. ↕24in (60cm).
***H. dumortieri*.** Compact, herbaceous perennial with early-produced, stiff, narrow leaves, to 14in (35cm) long. Slender, arching, reddish brown scapes bear star-shaped, orange-yellow flowers, 2–3in (5–8cm) across, which open from reddish brown buds early in the season. Grow in full sun or partial shade. ↕20in (50cm), ↔18in (45cm). Korea, E. Russia, Japan.
***H.* 'Ed Brown'.** Semi-evergreen tetraploid. In early midseason, bears remontant flowers, 5½in (14cm) across, with pink self and gold edge and green throat. ↕28in (70cm).
***H.* 'Eenie Weenie'.** Compact, free-flowering, dormant diploid with neat, mounded foliage. Erect scapes bear remontant, circular yellow flowers, 2in (5cm) across, with tapered tepals in early and midseason. ↕10in (25cm).
***H.* 'Elizabeth Salter'.** Semi-evergreen tetraploid with very sturdy, well-branched scapes. Bears remontant, pink flowers of excellent substance, 5½in (14cm) across, with flat, rounded, ruffled tepals and green throats, in midseason. ↕22in (55cm).
***H.* 'Ever So Ruffled'.** Semi-evergreen tetraploid with well-branched scapes bearing deep yellow flowers, 5in (13cm) across, with flat, rounded, very ruffled tepals and green throats, in midseason. ↕26in (65cm).
***H.* 'Fairy Tale Pink'.** Semi-evergreen diploid with narrow, wispy, mid-green leaves hidden by profuse blooms. In midsummer, erect scapes bear circular, glistening, pale orange-pink to beige-pink flowers, 5½in (14cm) across, with ruffled-margined tepals. ↕24in (60cm).
H. flava see *H. lilioasphodelus*.
***H.* 'Francis Joiner'** ■ Evergreen diploid with sturdy, well-branched scapes. Bears remontant, double, pink-orange flowers, 5½in (14cm) across, with rounded tepals and greenish yellow throats, in midseason. ↕↔24in (60cm).
***H.* 'Frank Gladney'.** Semi-evergreen tetraploid. Erect scapes bear circular, coral-pink flowers, 7in (18cm) across, with recurved tepals and gold throats,

Hemerocallis 'Betty Woods'

Hemerocallis 'Brocaded Gown'

Hemerocallis 'Cat's Cradle'

Hemerocallis 'Chorus Line'

Hemerocallis citrina

Hemerocallis 'Francis Joiner'

Hemerocallis fulva 'Flore Pleno'

Hemerocallis 'Janice Brown'

Hemerocallis 'Jason Salter'

Hemerocallis 'Jolyene Nichole'

Hemerocallis 'Lavender Tonic'

Hemerocallis lilioasphodelus

from early season to very late in the season. ↕ 26in (65cm).

H. fulva. Semi-evergreen, spreading perennial with wide, dark bluish green leaves, 12–36in (30–90cm) long. Branched scapes bear trumpet-shaped, orange-brown flowers, 2½–4in (6–10cm) across, with recurved tepals, in mid- and late season. ↕ to 3ft (1m), ↔ 4ft (1.2m). China or Japan. **'Europa'** is a robust cultivar bearing tawny-orange flowers with yellow tepal bases. **'Flore Pleno'** ■ has strong, erect scapes bearing double flowers with dark red eyes; ↕ 30in (75cm). **'Kwanzo Variegata'** is similar to 'Flore Pleno', with strong, erect scapes bearing double, red-eyed flowers, 5in (13cm) across, but it has narrow, white-margined leaves; ↕ 30in (75cm).

***H.* 'Gentle Shepherd'.** Semi-evergreen diploid with wispy leaves. Circular, ivory-white flowers, 5½in (14cm) across, with oval tepals and green throats, are borne on slender scapes in midseason. ↕ 26in (65cm).

***H.* 'Ginger Bread Man'.** Semi-evergreen diploid with sturdy scapes bearing remontant, circular, orange-brown flowers, 7in (18cm) across, with dark red-brown eyes, early in the season. ↕ 28in (70cm).

***H.* 'Gleber's Top Cream'.** Semi-evergreen diploid with sturdy scapes. Bears circular ivory flowers, 6in (15cm) across, with recurved, pale peach-tinted tepals and green throats, in midseason. ↕ 18in (45cm).

***H.* 'Golden Chimes'.** Dormant diploid with slender, well-branched, reddish brown scapes. Bears star-shaped, deep yellow flowers, 2in (5cm) across, reddish brown beneath, early in the season. ↕ 36in (90cm).

***H.* 'Golden Scroll'.** Dormant diploid with sturdy, top-branched scapes. Bears remontant, circular, rippled, very ruffled, tangerine-orange flowers, 5½in (14cm) across, early in the season. ↕ to 20in (50cm).

***H.* 'Good Morning America'.** Semi-evergreen tetraploid with strong, well-branched scapes. In midseason, bears remontant, circular, overlapping, heavily ruffled, pink-toned, pale apricot flowers, 6in (15cm) across. ↕ 28in (70cm).

***H.* 'Grape Velvet'.** Dormant diploid with erect scapes. In midseason, bears triangular, deep purple flowers, 4½in (11cm) across, with lighter purple midribs, green throats, and recurved tepals. ↕ 24in (60cm).

***H.* 'Great Northern'.** Evergreen diploid with very strong, low scapes. In early and midseason, bears off-white flowers, 7in (18cm) across, just above the foliage, with flat, rounded, ruffled tepals and green throats. ↕ 16in (40cm).

***H.* 'Green Flutter'.** Extended-blooming, free-flowering, semi-evergreen diploid with narrow leaves. In midseason, slender scapes bear nocturnal, triangular to star-shaped, light yellow flowers, 3½in (9cm) across, with thick, rounded, slightly ruffled-margined tepals and green-tinted throats. ↕ 20in (50cm).

***H.* 'Green Widow'.** Evergreen diploid with wiry, well-branched scapes bearing spider-shaped yellow-green flowers, 7in (18cm) across, with very green throats, early in the season. ↕ 26in (65cm).

***H.* 'Guiniver's Gift'.** Evergreen tetraploid with strong, well-branched scapes. In early and midseason, bears remontant, cream-yellow-blended flowers, 3½in (9cm) across, with flat, rounded, ruffled tepals and green throats. ↕ 18in (45cm).

***H.* 'Happy Returns'.** Free-flowering, dormant diploid with narrow leaves. In early season, erect scapes bear nocturnal, remontant, circular, light yellow flowers, 2½in (6cm) across. Good for containers. ↕ 16in (40cm).

***H.* 'Hope Diamond'.** Evergreen diploid with erect scapes. Nocturnal, triangular to circular, cream to very pale yellow flowers, 4½in (11cm) across, with rounded, crinkly, slightly ruffled-margined tepals, are borne in midseason. ↕ 28in (55cm).

***H.* 'Hyperion'.** Dormant diploid with narrow leaves. Nocturnal, triangular to star-shaped, fragrant, lemon-yellow flowers, 4in (10cm) across, are borne in midseason, on slender scapes. ↕ 36in (90cm).

***H.* 'Ice Castles'.** Vigorous, semi-evergreen diploid with erect scapes bearing circular, pale ivory flowers, 2½in (6cm) across, with yellow-suffused throats, in midseason. ↕ 18in (45cm).

***H.* 'Ida's Magic'.** Everblooming, evergreen tetraploid with strong, well-branched scapes. Bears flowers, 6in (15cm) across, in blends of amber, rose, and lavender, with flat, rounded, ruffled, gold-edged tepals, in early and midseason. ↕ 28in (70cm).

***H.* 'Irving Schulman'.** Semi-evergreen tetraploid with very sturdy, well-branched scapes. In midseason, bears remontant, triangular, ruffled, deep clear lavender flowers, 5½in (14cm) across, with cream edges and eyes, and green throats. ↕ 24in (60cm).

***H.* 'Janice Brown'** ■ Dormant diploid with well-branched scapes. In midseason, bears circular flowers, 4½in (11cm) across, with flat tepals, strongly recurved at the tips. Flowers are light pink, with wide, rose-pink eyes and green throats. ↕ 22in (55cm).

***H.* 'Jason Salter'** ■ Semi-evergreen diploid with erect scapes bearing triangular flowers, 2½in (6cm) across, with flat tepals, recurved at the tips, in midseason. Flowers are deep yellow with deep purple-red eyes, and lime-green throats. ↕↔ 18in (45cm).

***H.* 'Joan Senior'.** Vigorous, free-flowering, semi-evergreen diploid with erect scapes. In mid- and late season, bears circular, off-white, pink-flushed flowers, 6in (15cm) across, with recurved tepals and yellowish green throats. ↕ 24in (60cm).

***H.* 'Joe Marinello'.** Dormant tetraploid with strong, well-branched scapes. Early in the season, bears remontant, cream flowers, 5in (13cm) across, with flat, rounded, ruffled tepals, wine-purple eyezones, and green throats. ↕ 22in (55cm).

***H.* 'Jolyene Nichole'** ■ Vigorous, evergreen diploid with abundant blue-green leaves. Sturdy scapes bear nocturnal, circular, rose-pink flowers, 5½in (14cm) across, the tepals veined deep pink, in midseason. ↕ 18in (45cm).

***H.* 'Journey's End'.** Semi-evergreen diploid. Erect scapes bear circular, off-white flowers, 5in (13cm) across, with crepe-textured tepals and lemon-yellow throats, in midseason. ↕ 16in (40cm).

***H.* 'Judah'.** Dormant tetraploid with sturdy scapes. In midseason, bears circular, deep gold flowers, 6in (15cm) across, with yellow throats and rounded, bronze-margined tepals. ↕ 30in (75cm).

***H.* 'Kathleen Salter'.** Semi-evergreen tetraploid with very well-branched scapes. Bears remontant, yellow flowers, 6in (15cm) across, of excellent substance, with flat, rounded, ruffled tepals and green throats, in early and midseason. ↕ 28in (70cm).

***H.* 'Kindly Light'.** Dormant diploid with narrow leaves. In midseason, slender scapes bear nocturnal, spider-shaped, bright yellow flowers, 9in (23cm) across, with – in cool conditions – faint salmon-pink eyes. ↕ 28in (70cm).

***H.* 'Lady Fingers'.** Dormant diploid with narrow leaves. In midseason, slender scapes bear spider-shaped, pale yellow-green flowers with green throats, 6in (15cm) across, with spoon-shaped tepals. ↕ 32in (80cm).

***H.* 'Lavender Memories'.** Semi-evergreen, very hardy tetraploid with very strong, well-branched scapes. In early and midseason, bears fragrant, clear lavender flowers, 5½in (14cm) across, with flat, rounded, ruffled tepals and green throats. ↕ 24in (60cm).

***H.* 'Lavender Tonic'** ■ Semi-evergreen diploid with sturdy, well-branched scapes bearing circular, soft lavender-pink flowers, 5in (13cm) across, with yellow throats, in midseason. ↕↔ 18in (45cm).

***H.* 'Leonard Bernstein'.** Evergreen tetraploid with well-branched scapes. In early and midseason, bears remontant, bright red flowers, 5½in (14cm) across, with flat, rounded, some recurved, ruffled tepals and green throats. Holds color well in hot weather. ↕ 24in (60cm).

H. lilioasphodelus ■ syn. *H. flava.* Rhizomatous, extended-blooming, semi-evergreen perennial with narrow leaves, 20–26in (50–65cm) long. In early season, slender scapes bear nocturnal, star-shaped, fragrant, clear bright lemon-yellow flowers, to 3½in (9cm) across. ↕↔ 3ft (1m). China.

***H.* 'Little Business'.** Compact, free-flowering, semi-evergreen diploid with abundant mounded leaves. Sturdy scapes bear remontant, triangular, strawberry-crimson flowers, 3in (8cm) across, with velvety tepals and yellow-green throats, in mid- and late season. ↕ 16in (40cm).

H. 'Little Rainbow' ■ Dormant diploid with slender scapes. In mid-season, bears multicolored, creamy yellow, beige-pink, and mauve-pink flowers, 3½in (9cm) across, with rounded tepals and orange throats. ↕ 24in (60cm).
H. 'Love Goddess'. Dormant tetraploid with well-branched scapes. Early in the season, bears remontant, clear pink flowers, 5in (13cm) across, with flat, rounded, slightly recurved, ruffled tepals, amber edges, and green throats. ↕ 26in (65cm).
H. 'Lullaby Baby'. Semi-evergreen diploid with branched scapes. In mid- and late season, bears nocturnal, circular, ice pink flowers, 3½in (9cm) wide, with green throats. ↕ 18in (45cm).
H. 'Lusty Lealand'. Dormant tetraploid with bluish green leaves and sturdy scapes. Nocturnal, scarlet flowers, 5in (13cm) across, with velvety, yellow-backed, star-shaped tepals and yellow throats, are borne in midseason. ↕ 28in (70cm).
H. 'Magic Filigree'. Evergreen tetraploid with well-branched scapes. In midseason, bears remontant, modified triangular, light to mid-lavender flowers, 5½in (14cm) across, with flat, ruffled tepals and very pronounced golden yellow edges. ↕ 24in (60cm).
H. 'Marble Faun'. Evergreen diploid with sturdy scapes bearing remontant, lemon-yellow-marbled, cream flowers, 5in (13cm) across, with flat, ruffled tepals and green throats, early in the season. ↕ 20in (50cm).
H. 'Marion Vaughn'. Free-flowering, evergreen diploid with narrow leaves. Nocturnal, star-shaped, very fragrant, clear lemon-yellow flowers, 4in (10cm) across, are borne on slender scapes in mid- and late season. ↕ 42in (85cm).
H. 'Martha Adams' ■ Extended-blooming, evergreen diploid with erect scapes bearing circular, pale pink, beige-tinted flowers, 7in (18cm) across, with yellow-green throats, early in the season. ↕ 18in (45cm).
H. 'Mary's Gold'. Dormant tetraploid with well-branched scapes. In mid-season,

Hemerocallis 'Little Rainbow'

Hemerocallis 'Midnight Magic'

bears triangular, brilliant golden orange flowers, 7in (18cm) across, with flat, slightly ruffled tepals and green throats. ↕ 34in (85cm).
H. 'Mauna Loa' ■ Dormant tetraploid with sturdy scapes. Bears circular, very bright tangerine-orange flowers, 5in (13cm) across, with crimped tepals, green throats, and black anthers, from early to late season. ↕ 22in (55cm).
H. 'Meadow Sprite'. Free-flowering, vigorous, compact, evergreen diploid with neatly mounded leaves. In early and midseason, bears nocturnal, circular, magenta-lilac flowers, 3½in (9cm) across, with purple eyes, bright green throats, and black anthers, on erect scapes. ↕ 14in (35cm).
H. middendorffii. Semi-evergreen perennial with narrow, stiff leaves, to 12in (30cm) long. Early in the season, slender, reddish brown scapes bear ridged, reddish brown buds that open to star-shaped, deep orange flowers, 2½–3in (6–8cm) across. ↕ 36in (90cm), ↔ 18in (45cm). E. Russia, N. China, Korea, Japan.
H. 'Midnight Magic' ■ Hardy, evergreen tetraploid with very strong, well-branched scapes. In early and mid-season, bears black-red flowers, 5½in (14cm) across, with flat, rounded, recurved, ruffled tepals and green throats. ↕ 28in (70cm).
H. 'Millie Schlumpf' ■ Evergreen diploid with erect scapes bearing nocturnal, remontant, glistening, pale pink flowers, 5in (13cm) across, with darker pink eyes and bright, light green throats, in midseason. Flowers withstand inclement weather. ↕ 20in (50cm).
H. 'Moonlight Mist' ■ Evergreen diploid with erect scapes. Bears green-throated, pale ivory to creamy pink flowers, 3in (8cm) across, with round, ruffled tepals, in midseason. ↕ 18in (45cm).
H. 'Mort's Magic'. Dormant tetraploid bearing purple-edged, wine-violet flowers, 5½in (14cm) across in early and midseason. The tepals are flat, rounded, and ruffled, with darker halos, and white flecks on the edges. ↕ 26in (65cm).
H. 'Mountain Top Experience'. Evergreen diploid with strong, well-branched scapes. Remontant, spider-shaped, green-and-yellow bicolor flowers, 8in (20cm) across, with green throats, are borne early in the season. ↕ 30in (75cm).
H. 'My Darling Clementine'. Everblooming, evergreen tetraploid with low, dark green foliage. Strong, low, well-branched scapes bear very full, creamy yellow flowers, 4½in (11cm) across, with flat, rounded, ruffled tepals and lime-green throats, early in the season. ↕ 22in (55cm).
H. 'Neal Berrey' ■ Semi-evergreen diploid with sturdy, well-branched scapes. Bears flowers in blends of rose and pink, 5in (13cm) across, with flat, rounded, ruffled tepals and green throats, in midseason. ↕ 18in (45cm).
H. 'Nebuchadnezzar's Furnace'. Evergreen diploid with very strong, well-branched scapes bearing double, fiery-red flowers, 5in (13cm) across, with black eyezones and green throats, in midseason. ↕ 22in (55cm).
H. 'Night Raider'. Vigorous, free-flowering, dormant tetraploid with well-branched scapes. Nocturnal, circular, bright to dark red flowers, 5½in (14cm) across, with slightly recurved tepals and yellow throats, are borne in midseason. ↕ 28in (70cm).
H. 'Nile Plum'. Evergreen tetraploid with sturdy scapes. Late in the season, bears nocturnal, circular, rich purple flowers, 5in (13cm) across, with recurved tepals and large, lemon-ivory eyes. ↕ 22in (55cm).
H. 'Nosferatu'. Semi-evergreen tetraploid with sturdy, well-branched scapes. In midseason, bears purple flowers, 6in (15cm) across, with flat, rounded, ruffled tepals, pale green throats, and white-flecked edges. ↕ 26in (65cm).
H. 'Olive Bailey Langdon'. Free-flowering, semi-evergreen tetraploid. Sturdy scapes bear remontant, circular, violet-purple flowers, 5in (13cm) across, with yellow-green throats, in early and midseason. ↕ 28in (70cm).
H. 'Outrageous'. Dormant tetraploid with sturdy scapes. In midseason, bears circular, light copper-orange flowers, 4½in (11cm) across, with large, dark brownish red eyes. ↕ 22in (55cm).
H. 'Pandora's Box'. Free-flowering, vigorous, compact, evergreen diploid with narrow leaves. In midseason, erect scapes bear remontant, star-shaped, pale cream flowers, 4½in (11cm) across, with bright purple eyes and green throats. ↕ 20in (50cm).
H. 'Paper Butterfly' ■ Semi-evergreen tetraploid with sturdy, well-branched scapes. Bears remontant, triangular, cream-, peach-, and violet-blended flowers, 6in (15cm) across, with flat, ruffled petals, feathered, blue-violet eyezones, and green throats, early in the season. ↕ 24in (60cm).

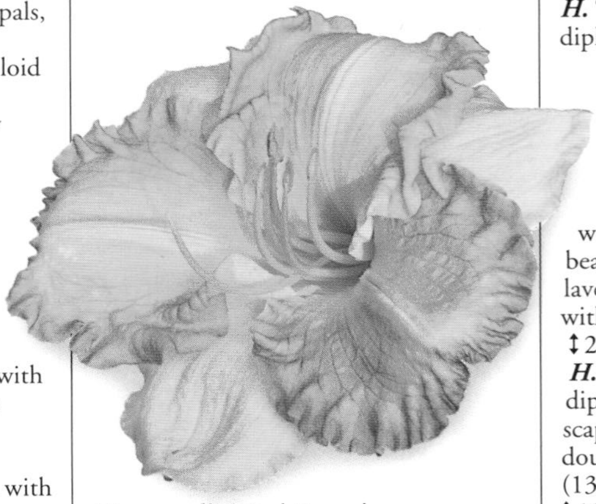

Hemerocallis 'Neal Berrey'

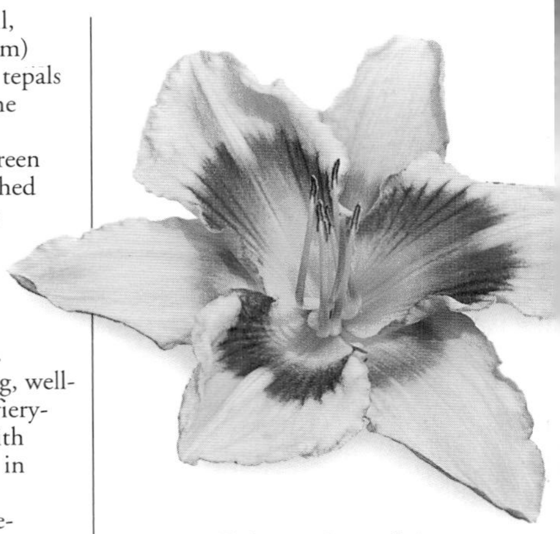

Hemerocallis 'Paper Butterfly'

H. 'Pardon Me'. Free-flowering, compact, dormant diploid producing narrow leaves. Slender, well-branched, stiff scapes bear remontant, circular, rich red flowers, 2½in (6cm) across, with green throats, in midseason. ↕↔ 18in (45cm).
H. 'Peggy Jeffcoat'. Dormant diploid, double extended. Bears remontant flowers 6½in (16.5cm), with a yellow self and light green throat, in late midseason. ↕ 18in (45cm).
H. 'Penny's Worth'. Compact, dormant diploid with arching, grass-like leaves. Early in the season, slender scapes bear circular, pale yellow flowers, 1½in (4cm) across. ↕ 10in (25cm).
H. 'Pink Flirt' ■ Semi-evergreen diploid with strong, well-branched scapes. Early in the season, bears remontant, bright pink flowers, 6in (15cm) across, with flat, rounded, somewhat ruffled tepals and green throats. ↕ 20in (50cm).
H. 'Pirate Treasure'. Semi-evergreen tetraploid with strong, well-branched scapes. Bears circular, very ruffled, deep gold flowers, 7in (18cm) across, with green throats, in mid- and late season. ↕ 26in (65cm).
H. 'Prairie Blue Eyes'. Free-flowering, semi-evergreen diploid with narrow leaves. In midseason, slender scapes bear star-shaped, lavender-blue flowers, 5in (13cm) across, with wide, bluish purple eyes. ↕ 28in (70cm).
H. 'Prince of Midnight'. Semi-evergreen tetraploid with sturdy, well-branched scapes. Bears remontant, circular, ruffled, black-purple flowers, 5½in (14cm) across, with yellow-green throats, in early midseason. ↕ 28in (70cm).
H. 'Priscilla's Rainbow' ■ Evergreen diploid with sturdy, well-branched scapes. In midseason, bears overlapped, triangular, pink-lavender flowers, 6in (15cm) across, each with ruffled tepals and a multicolored eye. ↕ 22in (55cm).
H. 'Prissy Frills'. Dormant diploid with sturdy, well-branched scapes bearing remontant, spider-shaped, lavender flowers, 7in (18cm) across, with green throats, in midseason. ↕ 28in (70cm).
H. 'Rachael My Love'. Evergreen diploid with very strong, well-branched scapes bearing remontant, very fragrant, double, golden yellow flowers, 5in (13cm) across, in early and midseason. ↕ 18in (45cm).

Hemerocallis 'Martha Adams'

Hemerocallis 'Mauna Loa'

Hemerocallis 'Millie Schlumpf'

Hemerocallis 'Moonlight Mist'

Hemerocallis 'Real Wind'

Hemerocallis 'Red Joy'

Hemerocallis 'Red Rum'

Hemerocallis 'Scarlet Orbit'

Hemerocallis 'Siloam Double Classic'

Hemerocallis 'Siloam Merle Kent'

Hemerocallis 'Siloam Virginia Henson'

Hemerocallis 'Solano Bulls Eye'

***H.* 'Real Wind'** ■ Free-flowering, dormant tetraploid with dense foliage. In mid- and late season, sturdy scapes bear triangular, pale salmon-pink flowers, 7in (18cm) across, with recurved tepals and large, rose-pink eyes. ↕26in (65cm).
***H.* 'Red Joy'** ■ Semi-evergreen tetraploid with erect scapes bearing triangular, bright red flowers, 6in (15cm) across, with velvety tepals and wide, yellow-green throats, in midseason. ↕34in (85cm).
***H.* 'Red Rum'** ■ Semi-evergreen diploid with erect, bright green leaves. In midseason, slender scapes bear remontant, star-shaped, deep brick-red flowers, 4½in (11cm) across, with thick, crepe-textured tepals and yellow-green throats. ↕16in (40cm).
***H.* 'Red Suspenders'.** Dormant tetraploid with wiry, sturdy scapes. Bears spider-shaped, bright red flowers, 11in (28cm) across, with green-tinged throats, in midseason. ↕32in (80cm).
***H.* 'Red Volunteer'.** Dormant tetraploid blooms in midseason. Bears flowers, 7in (18cm) across, with a clear candle red self and a gold yellow throat. ↕30in (75cm).
***H.* 'Ruffled Apricot'.** Slow-growing, dormant tetraploid with dense foliage and slender scapes. Bears star-shaped, rich apricot flowers, 7in (18cm) across, in early and midseason. ↕28in (70cm).
***H.* 'Ruffled Perfection'.** Semi-evergreen diploid, an early midseason bloomer, extended. Fragrant flower, 5½in (14cm) across, with lemon yellow self and green throat, ↕24in (60cm).
***H.* 'Ruffled Royalty'.** Dormant tetraploid with very sturdy scapes and excellent branching. Bears remontant, circular, heavily ruffled, rich, royal purple flowers, 5½in (14cm) across, with green throats, in midseason. ↕26in (65cm).
***H.* 'Scarlet Orbit'** ■ Free-flowering, evergreen tetraploid with sturdy scapes bearing nocturnal, circular, bright red flowers, 6in (15cm) across, with yellow-green throats, in midseason. ↕20in (50cm).
***H.* 'Seductor'.** Evergreen tetraploid with abundant foliage and erect scapes. Remontant, circular, cranberry-red flowers, 6in (15cm) across, with ruffled-margined, overlapping tepals and lime-green throats, are borne in early and midseason. ↕↔18in (45cm).
***H.* 'Selma Timmons'.** Semi-evergreen tetraploid. In midseason, well-branched scapes bear circular, orange-pink flowers, 4½in (11cm) across, highlighted deeper pink; they have thick, very ruffled-margined tepals and tiny, rounded, greenish gold throats. ↕18in (45cm).
***H.* 'Seminole Wind'.** Semi-evergreen tetraploid with sturdy, well-branched scapes. In early and midseason, bears remontant, pink flowers, 7in (18cm) across, with flat, rounded, reflexed, ruffled tepals and green throats. ↕24in (60cm).
***H.* 'Siloam Amazing Grace'.** Dormant diploid, extended. Bears fragrant flowers 5½in (14cm) across, with yellow self and green throat, in early midseason. ↕24in (60cm).
***H.* 'Siloam David Kirchhoff'.** Dormant diploid with excellent, well-branched scapes. In early and midseason, bears orchid flowers, 3½in (9cm) across, with flat, rounded, reflexed, ruffled tepals, cerise-penciled eyezones, and green throats. ↕16in (40cm).
***H.* 'Siloam Double Classic'** ■ Dormant diploid with erect scapes bearing double, peach-pink flowers, 4½in (11cm) across, with rounded, recurved, ruffled-margined tepals, in early and midseason. ↕20in (50cm).
***H.* 'Siloam Ethel Smith'.** Compact, dormant diploid, free-flowering once established. Circular, creamy beige flowers, 3½in (9cm) across, with flat tepals, recurved at the tips, and large, triangular, red, yellow, and olive-green eyes, are produced on erect scapes in midseason. ↕20in (50cm).
***H.* 'Siloam Grace Stamile'.** Compact, dormant diploid. In midseason, erect scapes bear circular, deep red flowers, 2½in (6cm) across, with deeper red eyes and green throats. ↕↔16in (40cm).
***H.* 'Siloam Leo Sharp'.** Dormant diploid with excellent, well-branched scapes. In midseason, bears blue-orchid flowers, 3in (8cm) across, with flat, rounded, reflexed, ruffled tepals, smoky-gray eyezones, and green throats. ↕18in (45cm).
***H.* 'Siloam Merle Kent'** ■ Compact, dormant diploid with erect scapes. In midseason, bears circular, bright mauve-pink flowers, 3½in (9cm) across, with deep purple eyes and green throats. ↕↔18in (45cm).
***H.* 'Siloam Olin Frazier'.** Dormant diploid, extended. Double flowers are 5½in (14cm) across, with a hot rose self. Blooms early in the season. ↕22in (55cm).
***H.* 'Siloam Paul Watts'.** Dormant diploid with superior branching and bud count, bearing red flowers, 4½in (11cm) across, with flat, rounded, very ruffled tepals and green throats, in midseason. ↕18in (45cm).
***H.* 'Siloam Royal Prince'.** Dormant diploid with excellent, well-branched scapes. Bears red-purple flowers, 4in (10cm) across, with flat, rounded, ruffled tepals and green throats, in midseason. ↕20in (50cm).
***H.* 'Siloam Ury Winniford'.** Vigorous, free-flowering, compact, dormant diploid with well-branched scapes. In early and midseason, bears remontant, circular to triangular, deep cream flowers, 4in (10cm) across, with red-purple or rich purple eyes and green throats. ↕20in (50cm).
***H.* 'Siloam Virginia Henson'** ■ Free-flowering, compact, dormant diploid with well-branched scapes. In early and midseason, bears remontant, circular, pink-tinted cream flowers, 4in (10cm) across, with flat tepals, recurved at the tips, and ruby-red eyes. ↕↔16in (40cm).
***H.* 'Smoky Mountain Autumn'.** Free-flowering, dormant diploid with narrow leaves. Circular, copper-pink flowers, 5½in (14cm) across, with recurved tepals, lavender-pink halos, and yellow-green throats, are borne on slender scapes in midseason. ↕18in (45cm).
***H.* 'Solano Bulls Eye'** ■ Evergreen evergreen diploid with erect scapes bearing bright yellow flowers, 6in (15cm) across, with yellow tepals and deep brownish purple eyes, in early and midseason. ↕20in (50cm).
***H.* 'Spacecoast Discovery'.** Semi-evergreen tetraploid bears remontant creamy yellow flowers, 6in (15cm), across, with gold edge and yellow throat. Blooms in midseason. ↕30in (75cm).
***H.* 'Spacecoast Tiny Perfection'.** Semi-evergreen tetraploid with remontant flowers, 28in (70cm) across. The flesh pink self has a gold edge and green throat, and full and overlapping flower segments. Blooms early in the season. ↕18in (45cm).
***H.* 'Spider Man'.** Dormant tetraploid with sturdy scapes and good branching and bud count. Remontant, spider-shaped, bright red flowers, 7in (18cm) across, with chartreuse throats, are borne in early and midseason. ↕24in (60cm).
***H.* 'Spindazzle'.** Semi-evergreen diploid with strong, well-branched scapes. In midseason, bears spider-shaped, golden copper flowers, 6in (15cm) across, with swirled, red-tipped, red-veined tepals and green throats. ↕26in (65cm).

Hemerocallis 'Pink Flirt'

Hemerocallis 'Priscilla's Rainbow'

Hemerocallis 'Stella de Oro'

Hemerocallis 'Strawberry Candy'

Hemerocallis 'Super Purple'

Hemerocallis 'Taffy Tot'

Hemerocallis 'Texas Sunlight'

Hemerocallis 'Yellow Lollipop'

***H.* 'Stafford'.** Free-flowering, dormant diploid with narrow leaves. In midseason, slender scapes bear star-shaped scarlet flowers, 4in (10cm) across, with yellow midribs and throats. ↕ 28in (70cm).
***H.* 'Stella de Oro'** ■ Vigorous, free-flowering, dormant diploid bearing remontant, circular, bright yellow flowers, 2½in (6cm) across, on slender scapes in early season. ↕ 12in (30cm), ↔ 18in (45cm).
***H.* 'Strawberry Candy'** ■ Semi-evergreen tetraploid with sturdy, branched scapes. In early and mid-season, bears remontant, strawberry-pink-blended flowers, 4½in (11cm) across, with flat, rounded, reflexed, very ruffled tepals, rose-red eyezones, and yellow-green throats. ↕ 26in (65cm).
***H.* 'Street Urchin'.** Evergreen tetraploid with strong, well-branched scapes. Remontant, bright red flowers, 5½in (14cm) across, with wide, distinctive almond edges and green to yellow throats, are borne in midseason. ↕ 25in (63cm).
***H.* 'Strutter's Ball'.** Free-flowering, dormant tetraploid with dense foliage. Erect scapes bear triangular, rich deep blue-purple flowers, 6in (15cm) across, in midseason. ↕ 28in (70cm).
***H.* 'Sugar Cookie'.** Evergreen diploid with erect scapes bearing circular, ivory flowers, 3½in (9cm) across, with recurved tepals and green throats, in mid-season. ↕ 20in (50cm).

Hemerocallis 'White Temptation'

***H.* 'Super Purple'** ■ Semi-evergreen, extended-blooming diploid. In mid-season, erect scapes bear circular, deep purple flowers, 5½in (14cm) across, with lime-green and yellow throats. ↕ 26in (65cm).
***H.* 'Taffy Tot'** ■ Evergreen diploid with erect scapes bearing tan-buff flowers, 3in (8cm) across, with brown eyes and green throats, in midseason. ↕ 18in (45cm).
***H.* 'Texas Sunlight'** ■ Dormant diploid with sturdy, well-branched scapes bearing full, slightly triangular-shaped, gold flowers, 2½in (6cm) across, with slight ruffling, in midseason. ↕ 28in (70cm).
H. thunbergii, syn. *H. vespertina.* Semi-evergreen, robust diploid with narrow leaves and well-branched, slender, scapes. In late season, bears nocturnal, star-shaped, fragrant, lemon-yellow flowers, 3½–4½in (9–11cm) across, with green throats and green-backed outer tepals. ↕ 3½ft (1.1m), ↔ 3ft (1m). China, Korea.
***H.* 'Tiger Kitten'.** Dormant tetraploid with sturdy, very well-branched scapes bearing light orange flowers, 3½in (9cm) across, with bright, bold, red eyezones and green throats, in midseason. ↕ 22in (55cm).
***H.* 'Tonya Gay'.** Free-flowering, evergreen diploid, vigorous once established, with erect sccapes. In midseason, bears triangular, glistening, light pink flowers, 5½in (14cm) across, with light yellow and green throats. ↕ 16in (40cm).
***H.* 'Unique Style'.** Dormant diploid with erect scapes. In midseason, bears circular, amber-margined, greenish yellow flowers, 3½in (9cm) across, with rounded, ruffled yellow tepals. ↕ 22in (55cm).
H. vespertina see *H. thunbergii.*
***H.* 'White Temptation'** ■ Semi-evergreen diploid with slender scapes bearing circular, off-white flowers, 5in (13cm) across, with green throats and lightly ruffled-margined tepals, in mid-season. ↕ 32in (80cm).
***H.* 'Yellow Lollipop'** ■ Compact, free-flowering, dormant diploid with very narrow leaves. Remontant, circular, bright yellow flowers, 2½in (6cm) across, are borne on erect scapes early in the season. ↕ 11in (28cm).

HEMIGRAPHIS

ACANTHACEAE

Genus of 90 species of low-growing, slender-stemmed annuals, perennials, and subshrubs from woodland margins in tropical Asia. They are grown mainly for their colorful, opposite, toothed or scalloped leaves, which are useful as a groundcover. From spring to summer, small, tubular, 5-lobed, usually white flowers are borne in terminal spikes. Where not hardy, grow in a temperate greenhouse or conservatory; some species are suitable for use in hanging baskets. In warmer climates, grow in a border or as edging.
• **CULTIVATION** Under glass, grow in soilless or soil-based potting mix in bright filtered light, with moderate to high humidity. In growth, water freely and apply a balanced liquid fertilizer monthly; keep moist in winter. Outdoors, grow in any fertile, moist but well-drained soil in partial shade. Shelter from strong winds. Cut back established plants in spring.
• **PROPAGATION** Root softwood or stem-tip cuttings in summer or autumn. Separate rooted stems in spring.
• **PESTS AND DISEASES** Whiteflies may be a problem.

H. alternata, syn. *H. colorata* (Red flame ivy). Slightly hairy, evergreen perennial with prostrate stems that root freely. The heart-shaped to ovate, scalloped leaves, 3½in (9cm) long, are silver-gray above and purple beneath. White flowers, ½in (1.5cm) across, are produced in terminal spikes, 1in (2.5cm) long, from spring to summer. ↕ 6in (15cm), ↔ 18in (45cm). India, Indonesia (Java). ❄ (min. 50°F/10°C)
H. colorata see *H. alternata.*
***H.* 'Exotica'** (Purple waffle plant). Compact, evergreen perennial producing ovate, hairless, purplish green leaves, 3½in (9cm) long, puckered between the veins, with a purple sheen and deep red beneath. White flowers, ½in (1.5cm) across, are borne in terminal spikes, 2½in (6cm) long, from spring to summer. ↕ 9in (23cm), ↔ 20in (50cm). ❄ (min. 50°F/10°C)
H. repanda ■ Creeping, evergreen perennial with slender, maroon or red stems that root freely. The narrowly lance-shaped, toothed leaves, to 2in (5cm) long, are red-flushed grayish green, shading to purple above, and darker purple beneath. White flowers, ½in (1.5cm) across, are borne in dense spikes, 2in (5cm) long, from spring to summer. ↕ 9in (23cm), ↔ 18in (45cm). Malaysia. ❄ (min. 50°F/10°C)

Hemigraphis repanda

HEPATICA

RANUNCULACEAE

Genus, allied to *Anemone*, of about 10 species of spring-flowering perennials from woodland in N. temperate regions. They have usually kidney-shaped, 3- to 5-lobed, simple or toothed, dark green, basal leaves, often purple beneath, and sometimes marbled silver or white. The solitary, bowl- to star-shaped flowers usually open before the leaves have fully developed. They have brightly colored, petal-like sepals with an involucre of 3 leaf-like bracts immediately beneath them. Suitable for a shady site in a rock or woodland garden.
• **CULTIVATION** Grow in humus-rich, moist but well-drained, neutral to alkaline soil in partial shade; hepaticas thrive in heavy soils. Top-dress each year with leaf mold or compost in autumn, or in late spring after flowering. Hepaticas do not transplant easily.
• **PROPAGATION** Sow seed in an open frame as soon as ripe. Divide in spring; divisions are slow to re-establish.
• **PESTS AND DISEASES** Rust and leaf smut may occur. Young growth is susceptible to snail and slug damage.

H. acutiloba (Sharp-leaved hepatica). Slow-growing perennial with rounded or kidney-shaped, 3- to 7-lobed, mid-green leaves, 1½–3in (4–8cm) long, the lobes deeply cut and sharply pointed. In early spring, bears cup-shaped, blue, pink, or white flowers, ½–1in (1–2.5cm) across. ↕ 3in (8cm), ↔ to 6in (15cm). E. US. Zone 4.
H. americana. Slow-growing perennial with heart-shaped, 3-lobed, pointed, mid-green leaves, 1¼–3in (3–8cm) long, purple-tinged beneath. Cup-shaped, pale blue-purple, sometimes

Hepatica nobilis

white or pink flowers, to ¾in (2cm) across, are produced in spring. ↕ to 6in (15cm), ↔ 12in (30cm). Minnesota to Nova Scotia, south to Missouri and Florida. Zone 3.
H. angulosa see *H. transsilvanica.*
H. nobilis ■ syn. *Anemone hepatica, H. triloba.* Slow-growing, semi-evergreen, dome-shaped perennial producing rounded or kidney-shaped, mid-green leaves, 1¼–2½in (3–6cm) long, with 3 ovate, entire lobes, silky-hairy and purple-tinted beneath. Open bowl-shaped, white, pink, blue, or blue-purple flowers, to 1in (2.5cm) across, each with 6 or 7 sepals, are borne in early spring, mainly before the leaves. ↕ 4in (10cm), ↔ 6in (15cm). Europe. Zone 5b. **var. *japonica*** is smaller, bearing dark green leaves with pointed lobes, and flowers that are more star-shaped, each with 6–9 white, pink, or blue tepals; ↕ to 3in (8cm); Japan. Many cultivars have been selected in Japan.
H. transsilvanica, syn. *H. angulosa.* Semi-evergreen, slow-spreading perennial producing hairy, pale green leaves, 2½–4in (6–10cm) long, with 3 ovate, scalloped lobes. In early spring, bears many-petaled, open bowl-shaped, blue, white, or very pale pink flowers, to 1½in (4cm) across. ↕ to 6in (15cm), ↔ to 8in (20cm). Romania. Zone 6.
H. triloba see *H. nobilis.*

HEPTACODIUM

Seven-son flower

CAPRIFOLIACEAE

Genus of 1 or 2 species of vigorous, deciduous shrubs or small trees from mountains at elevations of 2,000ft (600m) of China. They have opposite, pointed, rounded or heart-shaped leaves with wavy margins, and bear inflorescences of single, fragrant, creamy white flowers. These are followed by spherical purple fruits, which fall, leaving the particularly prominent, persistent calyces. Heptacodiums are ideal for an urban garden, since they have good drought and salt tolerance. Where not hardy, grow in a warm greenhouse or conservatory.
• **CULTIVATION** Under glass, grow in soil-based potting mix in full light. Water moderately during the growing season and apply a balanced liquid fertilizer monthly. Water sparingly in winter. Outdoors, grow in moderately fertile, well-drained soil in full sun to light, dappled shade. Pruning group 1.

Heptacodium miconioides

• **PROPAGATION** Sow seed under glass as soon as ripe. Take softwood cuttings in spring.
• **PESTS AND DISEASES** Infrequent.

H. miconioides ■ (Seven-son flower). Vigorous, multi-stemmed shrub or small tree with attractive, peeling, light tan to brown bark. The ovate, wavy-margined, prominently veined, light to mid-green young leaves are 3–4in (8–10cm) long, maturing to dark green, often becoming purple-tinged in autumn. From late summer to late autumn, produces inflorescences to 1¼in (3cm) across, of small, fragrant, creamy white flowers, followed by clusters of spherical purple fruit, ½–¾in (1.5–2cm) long, becoming tan with age. These drop, leaving behind prominent, persistent calyces. ↕ 20ft (6m), ↔ 8–10ft (2.5–3m). China (Jiangsu, Zhejiang). Zone 5b.

HERACLEUM

Cow-parsnip

APIACEAE

Genus of about 60 species of statuesque, herbaceous biennials or perennials from mountains of the N. temperate zone, the Himalayas, S. India, and Ethiopia. They have alternate, simple, palmately lobed, pinnate or 2-pinnate, mid-green leaves, and large, compound flower umbels. Grow heracleums in a herbaceous border or a wild garden. All parts of *H. mantegazzianum* may cause severe discomfort if ingested. Contact with the sap may cause photodermatitis.
• **CULTIVATION** Grow in moderately fertile, moist but well-drained soil in full sun to light, dappled shade. Apply a balanced liquid fertilizer monthly when in growth. After blooming, remove old flower stalks on perennial species to maintain vigor.
• **PROPAGATION** Sow seed *in situ* as soon as ripe; divide perennial species in spring or summer.
• **PESTS AND DISEASES** Leaf spots and stem rot can be problems.

H. mantegazzianum ■ (Giant hog-weed). Short-lived, very large biennial or perennial with hollow, ridged, purple-blotched stems and 3-palmate leaves, 3ft (1m) long, with coarsely hairy, deeply lobed, irregularly toothed, mid-green leaflets. In summer, bears huge umbels, to 2ft (60cm) across, of white flowers. ↕ 8–10ft (2.5–3m), ↔ 3ft (1m). S.W. Asia. Zone 4.

Heracleum mantegazzianum

Herbertia lahue

HERBERTIA

IRIDACEAE

Genus of 6 species of cormous perennials from dry slopes and rocky areas of temperate South America. They have lance-shaped, pleated, mid- to deep green, basal leaves. A succession of short-lived, iris-like flowers, ¾–1½in (2–4cm) across, is borne for several weeks from winter to spring. Where not hardy, grow in a cool greenhouse; elsewhere, grow at the front of a border or in a sheltered site in a rock garden.
• **CULTIVATION** Plant corms 4in (10cm) deep in autumn for spring flowering, or in spring for summer flowering. Under glass, grow in soil-based potting mix with additional sharp sand and leaf mold, in full light. When in leaf, water freely and apply a balanced liquid fertilizer monthly; keep plants dry when dormant. Outdoors, grow in well-drained, humus-rich soil in full sun. Protect from excessive summer and winter moisture; apply a winter mulch where marginally hardy.
• **PROPAGATION** Sow seed in containers in a cold frame as soon as ripe. Remove offsets in late summer or autumn.
• **PESTS AND DISEASES** Infrequent.

H. lahue ■ syn. *Alophia lahue.* Bulbous perennial with erect, linear, basal leaves, 2–8in (5–20cm) long. In spring, bears a succession of pale blue and violet flowers, ¾–1¼in (2–3cm) across, each with a reflexed, cup-like center. ↕ 6in (15cm), PD2in (5cm). Chile, Argentina. ❄ (min. 45°F/7°C)
H. pulchella. Bulbous perennial with erect, linear, basal leaves, to 8in (20cm) long. In spring, bears a succession of blue or lilac flowers, 2–2¼in (5–5.5cm) across, often streaked deep purple; each flower has a white central stripe, and a partially reflexed, bowl-like center. ↕ 4–6in (10–15cm), ↔ 2in (5cm). S. Brazil, Chile. ❄ (min. 45°F/7°C)

HEREROA

AIZOACEAE

Genus of about 30 species of dwarf, short-stemmed, mat-forming, perennial succulents, mostly from low, dry, hilly terrain in Namibia and South Africa. The opposite, fleshy leaves are joined at the bases, and are wedge-shaped and expanded toward the tips. The scented, daisy-like, usually yellow flowers open mainly by day, in summer. Where not hardy, grow as houseplants or in a warm greenhouse. In warmer regions, use in a raised bed, in containers, or in a rock garden or desert garden.
• **CULTIVATION** Under glass, grow in standard cactus potting mix in full light. When in growth, water moderately and apply a low-nitrogen liquid fertilizer monthly; keep almost dry in winter. Outdoors, grow in poor to moderately fertile, sharply drained, neutral to slightly alkaline soil in full sun. Protect from excessive winter and summer moisture. See also pp.48–49.
• **PROPAGATION** Sow seed in spring at 70–75°F (21–24°C). Divide, or separate offsets, in spring or summer.
• **PESTS AND DISEASES** Prone to aphids.

H. dyeri. Compact succulent with short stems bearing cylindrical, bluish green leaves, 2in (5cm) long, keeled beneath, tapering toward the hatchet-shaped tips, and marked with raised dots. In summer, bears open bowl-shaped, golden yellow flowers, 1in (2.5cm) across. ↕ 3in (8cm), ↔ indefinite. South Africa (Eastern Cape, Western Cape, KwaZulu/Natal). ❄ (min. 50°F/10°C)

HERMANNIA

STERCULIACEAE

Genus of at least 100 species of evergreen perennials, subshrubs, and shrubs from open, sandy sites in Africa. The leaves are alternate, and may be simple and entire, or toothed, incised, or lobed, usually with soft, star-shaped hairs. Bell-shaped flowers, each with 5 often overlapping and spirally twisted petals, are borne singly or in terminal or axillary cymes. Where not hardy, grow in a cool or temperate conservatory or greenhouse. In warmer areas, grow at the base of a warm wall or in a border.
• **CULTIVATION** Under glass, grow in soil-based potting mix with additional sharp sand, in full light shaded from hot sun; provide low to moderate humidity. When in growth, water moderately and apply a balanced liquid fertilizer monthly; keep just moist in winter. Pot on or top-dress in spring. Outdoors, grow in fertile, moist but well-drained soil in full sun, shaded from midday sun. Protect from excessive winter moisture. Pinch out the growing tips of young plants to promote bushiness. Pruning group 8; plants under glass may need restrictive pruning.
• **PROPAGATION** Sow seed at 61–66°F (16–19°C) in spring. Root semi-ripe cuttings in summer.
• **PESTS AND DISEASES** Prone to white-flies and spider mites under glass.

H. candicans see *H. incana.*
H. incana, syn. *H. candicans.* Bushy shrub or subshrub, becoming untidy with age unless regularly pruned. Ovate-oblong to oblong, mid-green leaves, to 1½in (4cm) long, have scalloped, wavy margins, and gray-white undersides covered in star-shaped, soft white hairs. From spring to summer, pendent yellow flowers, ½in (1.5cm) long, are borne in terminal cymes, 3–6in (8–15cm) long, or sometimes singly from the leaf axils. ↕ 3ft (1m) (more if unpruned), ↔ 18–36in (45–90cm). South Africa (Western Cape). ❄ (min. 45°F/7°C)

Hermodactylus tuberosus

H

HERMODACTYLUS

IRIDACEAE

Genus of one species of tuberous perennial found on dry slopes and in rocky areas from S. Europe to N. Africa, Israel, and Turkey. It has irregularly shaped, long, finger-like tubers and linear leaves. Grown for its solitary, iris-like, fragrant flowers borne in spring, *H. tuberosus* will thrive in a dry, sunny, mixed or herbaceous border, and is good for naturalizing in grass. It is also suitable for the base of a warm, sunny wall, or as an early-flowering container plant. Where not hardy, grow in an alpine house or bulb frame.

• **CULTIVATION** Plant tubers 4in (10cm) deep in autumn, in moderately fertile, sharply drained, alkaline soil in full sun. Protect from excessive summer rain; needs dry summers to flower well.

• **PROPAGATION** Divide as soon as the leaves have died back in early summer.

• **PESTS AND DISEASES** Slugs and snails may be problems.

H. tuberosus ▣ syn. *Iris tuberosa* (Snake's-head iris, Widow iris). Tuberous perennial with linear, bluish green or grayish green leaves, to 20in (50cm) long, and square in cross-section. In spring, bears solitary, scented, greenish yellow flowers, 2in (5cm) across, with velvety, blackish brown outer segments. ↕ 8–16in (20–40cm), PD2in (5cm). S.E. France to N. Africa, Israel, and Turkey. Zone 7b.

HESPERALOE

AGAVACEAE

Genus of about 3 species of perennial succulents, closely related to *Yucca*, although the flowers are more similar to those of *Aloe*. They occur in semi-arid regions of Texas and N. Mexico. Short, fleshy stems bear basal rosettes of tough, elongating, linear leaves with fibrous margins. The tall inflorescences of tubular-bell-shaped flowers are often curved and branching. Where not hardy, grow in a temperate greenhouse or conservatory. In warmer climates, grow in a desert garden or in containers.

• **CULTIVATION** Under glass, grow in standard cactus potting mix in full light. During the growing season, water moderately and apply a low-nitrogen liquid fertilizer monthly; keep almost

Hesperaloe parviflora

dry in winter. Outdoors, grow in poor to moderately fertile, sharply drained, neutral to acidic soil in full sun. Protect from excessive winter moisture. See also pp.48–49.

• **PROPAGATION** Sow seed at 61–64°F (16–18°C), or pot up offsets, in spring.

• **PESTS AND DISEASES** Prone to scale insects and, while flowering, aphids.

H. parviflora ▣ syn. *Yucca parviflora.* Clump-forming succulent with arching, linear, leathery, bright dark green leaves, 24–36in (60–90cm) long, often with peeling, fibrous margins. In summer, the upper part of the panicle-like inflorescence, 3ft (1m) or more long, bears crowded, pendent, dark to bright red flowers, to 1½in (4cm) long, with golden yellow throats. ↕ 3ft (1m), ↔ 6ft (2m). S.W. Texas. Zone 8.

HESPERANTHA

IRIDACEAE

Genus of 55 species of cormous perennials from rocky and sandy areas in Africa. Those in cultivation have linear to lance-shaped, mostly mid-green, basal leaves, and bear spikes or racemes of cup- or star-shaped flowers on wiry stems in spring. Where not hardy, grow in a cold greenhouse. In warmer regions, grow at the front of a border, in a rock garden or trough, or at the base of a warm, sunny wall.

• **CULTIVATION** Plant corms 4–6in (10–15cm) deep in autumn. Under glass, grow in soil-based potting mix with added leaf mold and grit, in full light. Provide moderate humidity and good ventilation. Water sparingly until flowering, then freely. After flowering, reduce water; keep plants dry while dormant. Outdoors, grow in fertile, well-drained soil in full sun. Protect with a dry mulch in winter.

• **PROPAGATION** Sow seed at 61–64°F (16–18°C) in autumn or spring. Separate offsets when dormant.

• **PESTS AND DISEASES** Infrequent.

H. buhrii see *H. cucullata.*

H. cucullata, syn. *H. buhrii.* Cormous perennial with 3 linear leaves, 5½–8in (14–20cm) long. Single or branched stems of up to 10 star-shaped, scented, white, pink-backed flowers, 1½in (4cm) across, are borne in spring. Flowers open during the afternoon. ↕ to 12in (30cm), PD2in (5cm). South Africa. ❀ (min. 45°F/7°C)

H. falcata, syn. *H. lutea.* Cormous perennial with 2–4 linear leaves, 1½–3in (4–8cm) long. In spring, branched stems bear up to 10 star-shaped flowers, ¾in (2cm) across. Flowers are usually white with red-flushed backs, but yellow variants are also known; the white flowers are scented and open at night, the yellow variants are unscented and open during the day. ↕ to 12in (30cm), PD3in (8cm). South Africa. ❀ (min. 45°F/7°C)

H. inflexa see *H. vaginata.*

H. lutea see *H. falcata.*

H. vaginata, syn. *H. inflexa.* Cormous perennial with 3 linear leaves, 9in (23cm) long. In spring, bears single or branched stems of up to 4 cup-shaped, clear yellow or purple-striped yellow flowers, 2½in (6cm) across, opening in the late afternoon. ↕ to 7in (18cm), PD3in (8cm). South Africa. ❀ (min. 45°F/7°C)

HESPERIS

BRASSICACEAE

Genus of about 30 species of biennials and perennials found in stony sites, wasteland, and woodland from Europe to China and Siberia. Most have ovate to spoon-shaped, entire to pinnatifid, pale to mid-green leaves. They are cultivated for their loose racemes or panicles of cross-shaped, 4-petaled, fragrant, purple, yellowish white, or white flowers. Cultivars with double flowers are particularly good for cutting. Use in a mixed or herbaceous border, or in a wild garden.

• **CULTIVATION** Grow in fertile, moist but well-drained, neutral to alkaline soil in sun or partial shade. Add leaf mold or organic matter when planting double-flowered cultivars. Replace them every 2 or 3 years, since flowering diminishes with age.

• **PROPAGATION** Sow seed *in situ* in spring. Root basal cuttings in spring.

• **PESTS AND DISEASES** Viruses, mildew, slugs, snails, flea beetles, and caterpillars may be problems.

Hesperis matronalis var. *albiflora*

H. matronalis (Dame's violet, Sweet rocket, Wild phlox). Rosette-forming biennial or short-lived perennial with leafy stems and ovate to elliptic or oblong, toothed, hairy, dark green leaves, 4–8in (10–20cm) long. From late spring to midsummer, bears racemes or panicles of usually lilac or purple, sometimes white or very pale lilac flowers, 1¼–1½in (3–4cm) across. Very attractive to insects. ↕ to 36in (90cm), ↔ 18in (45cm). S. Europe, Russia (Siberia), W. and C. Asia. Zone 4. **var. *albiflora*** ▣ has white flowers, and comes true from seed if it is isolated from other color variants. **var. *albiflora* 'Alba Plena'** bears double white flowers. **subsp. *candida*** has hairless leaves and white flowers. **'Lilacina Flore Pleno'** bears double lilac flowers. **'Purpurea Plena'** has double, dark lilac or purple flowers with neatly arranged petals.

HESPEROCALLIS

LILIACEAE

Genus of one species of bulbous perennial occurring in desert areas in the S.W. US. It has linear, wavy-margined, bluish green leaves, and is valued for its terminal racemes of funnel-shaped, fragrant white flowers borne from spring to summer. Where not hardy, grow in a cool greenhouse. In dry, nearly frost-free areas, use in a desert garden or at the base of a warm, sunny wall.

• **CULTIVATION** Plant in autumn with the necks of the bulbs at the soil surface. Under glass, grow in standard cactus potting mix in full light. In the growing season, water sparingly and apply a balanced liquid fertilizer monthly; keep completely dry in winter. Outdoors, grow in gritty, dry, neutral to slightly alkaline soil in full sun. Protect from excessive winter or summer moisture.

• **PROPAGATION** Sow seed at 61–64°F (16–18°C), or remove offsets, in spring.

• **PESTS AND DISEASES** Infrequent.

H. undulata (Desert lily). Bulbous perennial with a basal cluster of linear, wavy-margined, blue-green leaves, to 12in (30cm) long. From spring to summer, produces terminal racemes of upward-facing, funnel-shaped, 6-lobed white flowers, to 3in (8cm) long, with a green central stripe on the outside of each tepal. ↕ to 12in (30cm), PD6in (15cm). S.W. US. ❀ (min. 41°F/5°C)

▷ ***Hesperoyucca*** see *Yucca*

HETEROCENTRON

syn. HEERIA

MELASTOMATACEAE

Genus of 27 species of herbaceous perennials and low-growing, evergreen shrubs or subshrubs from open bush in Mexico and Central and South America. They have heart-shaped to lance-shaped, pale to dark green leaves, and bear open funnel-shaped, 4-petaled, white, pink, or mauve flowers, singly or in panicles, from summer into autumn and winter. Where not hardy, grow as houseplants or in a temperate greenhouse; elsewhere, use as groundcovers on a sunny bank or in a rock garden.

• **CULTIVATION** Under glass, grow in soil-based potting mix in full light. In growth, water freely and apply a

Heterocentron elegans

balanced liquid fertilizer every month; keep moist in winter. Outdoors, grow in moderately fertile, well-drained soil in full sun. Pinch out the growing tips to encourage a bushy habit.
• **PROPAGATION** Sow seed at 66–75°F (19–24°C) in spring. Divide in spring, or root softwood cuttings in spring or early summer.
• **PESTS AND DISEASES** Infrequent.

H. elegans ▣ (Spanish shawl). Carpet-forming, evergreen subshrub with dense, ovate to oblong-ovate, bristly to downy, mid-green leaves, to 1in (2.5cm) long. From summer to autumn, bears solitary, open funnel-shaped magenta flowers, to 2in (5cm) across. ↕4in (10cm), ↔ 18in (45cm). Mexico, Guatemala, Honduras. ❀ (min. 45°F/7°C)

▷ ***Heteromeles*** see *Photinia*

HETEROTHECA

syn. CHRYSOPSIS

ASTERACEAE

Genus of about 20 species of clump-forming, erect annuals and perennials from dry, sunny sites, usually in well-drained, sandy soil, in North America. The alternate, simple, ovate to inversely lance-shaped leaves are toothed or entire, sometimes softly silver-hairy, and usually mid-green. Branched stems bear corymbs of daisy-like yellow flowerheads. Grow in a mixed or herbaceous border or in a large rock garden.
• **CULTIVATION** Grow in well-drained, poor to moderately fertile soil in full sun. Protect from excessive winter moisture.
• **PROPAGATION** Sow seed in containers in a cold frame in spring; if sown early, perennials may flower the same year. Divide perennials in spring.
• **PESTS AND DISEASES** Infrequent.

H. mariana, syn. *Chrysopsis mariana.* Softly gray-hairy perennial with short stolons and both decumbent and erect stems. Basal leaves are spoon-shaped to inversely lance-shaped, shallowly toothed, and to 8in (20cm) long; stem leaves are rounded to elliptic-oblong, entire, and to 1¼in (3cm) long. From midsummer to early autumn, bears corymbs of yellow flowerheads, each 1¾in (4.5cm) across. ↕ to 36in (90cm), ↔ 20in (50cm). New York to Florida and Texas. Zone 5.

H. villosa, syn. *Chrysopsis villosa* (Hairy golden aster). Softly gray-hairy, sometimes rhizomatous perennial with erect to decumbent stems. Basal leaves are oblong-elliptic to lance-shaped, usually entire, occasionally toothed, and ¾–1½in (2–4cm) long; stem leaves are linear-lance-shaped and ½–1¼in (1–3cm) long. From midsummer to early autumn, bears corymbs of yellow flowerheads, each ¾–1½in (2–4cm) across. Needs a very well-drained, sunny site. ↕8–32in (20–80cm), ↔ 8in (20cm). W. and S. central US. Zone 5.

▷ ***Heterotropa*** see *Asarum*

HEUCHERA

Coral flower

SAXIFRAGACEAE

Genus of about 55 species of evergreen and semi-evergreen perennials from woodland and rocky sites in North America, chiefly the Rocky Mountains, with a few from Mexico. They have woody rootstocks and form clumps or mounds of rounded to heart-shaped, lobed, and often toothed, long-stalked, boldly veined leaves. Those with darker or paler shading or variegation are excellent foliage plants. Hybrids of *H. cylindrica*, *H. micrantha,* and *H. sanguinea* share their parents' habits and leaf characteristics to varying degrees. The taxonomy and nomenclature of this genus are not completely clear and are likely to change. The small, sometimes petalless, tubular flowers, 1⁄16–¼in (2–6mm) long, occasionally to ½in (15mm), have conspicuous, colorful calyces, and are borne in narrow, loose racemes or panicles. Use as groundcovers or in a herbaceous, mixed, or shrub border; the flowers are good for cutting and are attractive to bees and hummingbirds.
• **CULTIVATION** Grow in fertile, moist but well-drained, neutral soil in sun or partial shade; full shade may be tolerated in a moist site. The woody rootstock tends to grow upward, so mulch annually; eventually lift and replant in late summer or early autumn, with just the crown above the soil surface, or replace with new plants.
• **PROPAGATION** Sow seed of species in containers in a cold frame in spring. Divide species and cultivars in autumn.
• **PESTS AND DISEASES** Foliar nematodes, powdery mildew, rust, and leaf spots may occur.

H. americana. Mound-forming perennial with rosettes of broadly ovate to heart-shaped, 5- to 9-lobed, glossy, leathery leaves, 2–5½in (5–14cm) long. Young foliage is marbled and veined brown, maturing to deep green with copper-green shading. In early summer, bears panicles of brownish green flowers, 12in (30cm) or more long. ↕18in (45cm), ↔ 12in (30cm). C. and E. North America. Zone 4. A number of selections have been made, including the following: **'Chocolate Veil'** has chocolate-purple leaves with lighter purple and silver between the veins and maroon beneath. Bears panicles of lime-green-tinged purple flowers. **'Dale's Variety'** has silver-mottled leaves with greenish white flowers; ↕30in (75cm). **'Emerald Veil'** has silver-tinged, dark emerald-green leaves and chartreuse flowers; ↕20–24in (50–60cm). **'Garnet'** has mid-green leaves with deep purple-red veins; ↕18–20in (45–50cm). **'Persian Carpet'** has rose-burgundy leaves with dark purple edges, silver highlights, and dark purple veins; ↕20–22in (50–55cm). **'Pewter Veil'** has silver leaves with purple undertones and charcoal-gray veins. Bears tiny blush-white flowers, tinged purple and green, in midsummer; ↕22in (55cm). **'Purpurea'** has leaves marbled purple-brown beneath. **'Ruby Ruffles'** has ruffled red leaves with metallic shading; ↕30in (75cm). **'Ruby Veil'** has deep green leaves with slate-gray veins and zones of metallic-ruby shading; ↕24in (60cm). **'Velvet Night'** has very dark, slate-black leaves with metallic-purple shading; ↕30in (75cm).

***H.* x *brizoides* Hybrids.** Mound-forming perennial group with *H. americana*, *H. micrantha*, or *H. sanguinea* as part of the parentage. They have rounded, 5- to 9-lobed, dark green leaves, to 4in (10cm) long, with scalloped margins. In late spring and early summer, bear panicles, to 7in (18cm) long, of red, pink, or white flowers, to ⅜in (9mm) across. ↕12–30in (30–75cm), ↔ 12–18in (30–45cm). Zone 4. A number of selections have been made, including the following: **'Chatterbox'** has airy panicles of bright rose-pink flowers; ↕1½ft (45cm). **'Firefly'** ▣ syn. 'Leuchtkäfer', has fragrant vermilion flowers, borne in short-branched panicles; ↕30in (75cm). **'Freedom'** bears profuse rose-pink flowers from early to late summer; ↕24–30in (60–75cm). **'Green Ivory'** is clump-forming, with strong, erect stems that bear short-branched panicles of numerous green and white flowers in early summer; ↕↔ 30in (75cm). **'Huntsman'** has panicles of bright red flowers from early to late summer; ↕↔ 12–18in (30–45cm). **'June Bride'** produces large, pure white flowers, ½in (1.5cm) across; ↕18in (45cm). **'Leuchtkäfer'** see 'Firefly'.

Heuchera x *brizoides* 'Firefly'

Heuchera cylindrica 'Greenfinch'

'Matin Bells' has bright red flowers from early to late summer; ↕18in (45cm). **'Mt. St. Helens'** bears large, cardinal-red flowers in early and midsummer; ↕12–14in (30–35cm). **'Oakington Jewel'** has bronze leaves and red flowers from late spring to midsummer; ↕24–36in (60–90cm). **'Pretty Polly'** bears pale pink flowers from early to late summer; ↕10–12in (25–30cm). **'Queen of Hearts'** produces bright red flowers from early to late summer; ↕18in (45cm). **'Raspberry Regal'** has marbled leaves and large, raspberry-red flowers from late spring to late summer; ↕28–42in (70–110cm). **'Rosamundi'** bears coral-pink flowers from early to late summer; ↕18–24in (45–60cm). **'Torch'** has dark scarlet-red flowers in early and mid-summer; ↕28in (70cm).

H. cylindrica. Mound-forming perennial with rounded to broadly ovate, deeply round-lobed, often hairy, dark green leaves, 1–3in (2.5–8cm) long; they have scalloped margins and metallic, paler green mottling. From midspring to midsummer, leafless stems bear yellowish green or cream flowers in very short-branched, spike-like panicles, to 6in (15cm) long. Good foliage plant. ↕12–20in (30–50cm), ↔ 12in (30cm). N.W. North America. Zone 4. A number of selections have been made, including the following: **'Chartreuse'** has pink buds opening to large, lime-green flowers in early summer. **'Greenfinch'** ▣ bears green flowers in tall, stiff, very short-branched panicles; ↕ to 36in (90cm), ↔ 24in (60cm). **'Siskiyou Mts.'** is dwarf and bears racemes, 4in (10cm) long, of cream flowers; ↕8in (20cm).

H. grossulariifolia. Clump-forming perennial producing rounded to kidney-shaped, toothed, mid-green leaves, to 2½in (6cm) long. In early summer, bears bell-shaped, pure white flowers in panicles ½–2½in (1–6cm) long. ↕4in (10cm), ↔ to 6in (15cm). W. US. Zone 4.

H

Heuchera micrantha var. *diversifolia* 'Palace Purple'

H

H. micrantha Mound- or clump-forming perennial with ovate to heart-shaped, shallowly 5- to 7-lobed, hairy, gray-marbled leaves, ¾–3in (2–8cm) long. In early summer, bears loose panicles, to 12in (30cm) or more long, of numerous tiny, tubular, pink-flushed white flowers with red anthers. ↕ 36in (90cm), ↔ 18in (45cm). British Columbia to Sierra Nevada. Zone 4. A number of selections have been made, including the following: **Bressingham Hybrids** bear a profusion of flowers, in pink and red; ↕ 18–20in (45–50cm). **'Chocolate Ruffles'** bears wide, very ruffled, cocoa-brown leaves, burgundy-colored beneath, with panicles of small white flowers on purple spikes; ↕ 28–30in (70–75cm). **var. *diversifolia* 'Palace Purple'** ■ has large, jagged, glistening, almost metallic, bronze-red leaves, to 6in (15cm) long. Bears loose panicles of numerous greenish cream flowers with red anthers, which give them a salmon-pink appearance; flowers are followed by rose-pink seed heads. Many seed-raised plants do not retain the deep bronze-red leaf color; ↕↔ 18–24in (45–60cm). **'Lace Ruffles'** has ruffled leaves with white variegation; ↕ 16–18in (40–45cm). **'Montrose Ruby'** has maple-shaped, maroon leaves with silver marbling, and cream-white flowers in summer; ↕ 18in (45cm). **'Pewter Moon'** ■ bears panicles of large, pale pink flowers; ↕ to 16in (40cm), ↔ 12in (30cm). **'Ruffles'** has very ruffled leaves and stiff white flowers; ↕ 18–24in (45–60cm).

H. richardsonii. Mound-forming perennial with rounded, shallowly lobed, mid-green leaves, 1¼–2½in (3–6cm) long, softly gray-white-hairy beneath. In summer, leafless stems bear panicles, to 8in (20cm) long, of green flowers with clawed petals and numerous stamens. ↕ to 28in (70cm), ↔ 24in (60cm). British Columbia to Colorado to Wisconsin and Indiana. Zone 5.

H. rubescens. Clump-forming, tufted perennial with rounded to broadly ovate, deeply 3- to 7-lobed, sharp-toothed, mid-green leaves, to 2in (5cm) long. In summer, bears loose, spike-like panicles, to 6in (15cm) long, of bell-shaped, white to pale pink flowers, becoming reddish pink with age. ↕↔ to 6in (15cm). W. US. Zone 5.

H. sanguinea (Coral bells). Mat- or clump-forming perennial with rounded to kidney-shaped, shallowly lobed, toothed, glandular-hairy, dark green leaves, ¾–3in (2–8cm) long, marbled with pale green. In summer, bears large, tubular, red, rarely pink or white flowers in open panicles, to 6in (15cm) long. ↕↔ 12in (30cm). S.W. US. Zone 3. A number of selections have been made; except where noted, those that follow are clump-forming and bear flowers in early summer. **'Apple Blossom'** bears short-branched panicles of pale pink flowers opening from rose-pink buds; ↕ 24in (60cm), ↔ 12–18in (30–45cm). **'Brandon Pink'** has bright coral-pink flowers; ↕ 16–18in (40–45cm). **'Cherry Splash'** has green leaves splashed with white and gold, and bears rose-red flowers; ↕ 16in (40cm). **'Coral Cloud'** has crinkled, glistening leaves and wide panicles of coral-red flowers; ↕ 30in (75cm). **'Dennis Davidson'** see 'Huntsman'. **'Fairy Cups'** has cupped leaves and cerise flowers; ↕ 16–18in (40–45cm). **'Feuerregen'** see 'Pluie de Feu'. **'Firesprite'** bears panicles of bright, rose-red flowers on stiff stems; ↕ 20in (50cm). **'Frosty'** has silver-variegated leaves and bright red flowers; ↕ 20in (50cm). **'Huntsman'** ■ syn. 'Dennis Davidson', bears short-branched panicles of bright red flowers; ↕↔ 12–18in (30–45cm). **'Mother of Pearl'** has panicles of pink-flushed white flowers; ↕ 24in (60cm). **'Northern Fire'** bears silver-mottled leaves and scarlet-red flowers; ↕ 16–18in (40–45cm). **'Pearl Drops'** bears dainty, arching panicles of pink-tinged white flowers; ↕ 24in (60cm). **'Pluie de Feu'** ■ syn. 'Feuerregen', 'Rain of Fire', bears narrow panicles of bright red flowers from early to late summer; ↕ 20in (50cm). **'Rain of Fire'** see 'Pluie de Feu'. **'Red Spangles'** bears short-branched, open panicles of large, scarlet-crimson flowers throughout summer; ↕ 20in (50cm), ↔ 10in (25cm). **'Schneewittchen'** produces short-branched panicles of white flowers in early and midsummer; ↕ 20in (50cm), ↔ 10in (25cm). **'Scintillation'** has panicles of deep pink, coral-pink-rimmed flowers; ↕ 24in (60cm). **'Snow Storm'** is clump- or mound-forming, with leaves marbled silvery white, and panicles of cerise-red flowers. **'Splendens'** has bright scarlet-red flowers from late spring to midsummer; ↕ 28in (70cm). **'Splish Splash'** has splashed, variegated leaves and bright rose-pink flowers; ↕ 16–18in (40–45cm). **'Taff's Joy'** has leaves variegated cream and tinged pink, and panicles of pink flowers; ↕ 10–12in (25–30cm), ↔ 8in (20cm). **'White Cloud'** has green leaves with silver-white mottling, and bears profuse white flowers in late spring; ↕ 18in (45cm). **'Winfield Pink'** has bright green leaves and bears neon-pink flowers; ↕ 16in (40cm).

Heuchera micrantha 'Pewter Moon'

Heuchera sanguinea 'Huntsman'

Heuchera sanguinea 'Pluie de Feu'

H. versicolor. Clump-forming perennial with nearly rounded, 5- to 7-lobed, thin, mid-green leaves, 1¼–1¾in (3–4.5cm) long, slightly hairy beneath and finely hairy on the margins. In summer, leafless stems bear panicles, 3–4in (8–10cm) long, of pink to rose-red flowers, petalless or with very small petals and very small stamens. ↕↔ 6–8in (15–20cm). New Mexico. Zone 8.

H. villosa. Mound-forming perennial with triangular, shallowly 7- to 9-lobed, softly hairy, mid-green leaves, 1¼–5in (3–13cm) long, with scalloped margins. In summer, bears panicles, 3½–18in (9–45cm) long, of green-tipped, white or (rarely) pink flowers, with broadly lance-shaped petals. ↕ to 18in (45cm), ↔ 12in (30cm). Appalachian Mountains, Kentucky, Tennessee, Arkansas. Zone 6.

x *Heucherella tiarelloides*

x HEUCHERELLA

SAXIFRAGACEAE

Hybrid genus, resulting from crosses between *Heuchera* and *Tiarella*, of evergreen, mat- or clump-forming, occasionally stoloniferous perennials. They have heart-shaped or broadly ovate, lobed, boldy veined, sometimes hairy leaves, shaded brown when young and turning reddish brown in autumn. Short, loose panicles of tubular-bell-shaped, pink or white flowers, to ¼in (6mm) long, are borne over a long period from spring to autumn. They are excellent as a groundcover or edging in a herbaceous, mixed, or shrub border, or for a woodland garden.

• **CULTIVATION** Grow in light, fertile, moist but well-drained, neutral to slightly acidic soil; sun or partial shade is best, but full shade is tolerated.

• **PROPAGATION** Divide in autumn or spring. Separate plantlets from rooted stolons in autumn.

• **PESTS AND DISEASES** Infrequent.

x *H. alba* 'Bridget Bloom'. Clump-forming perennial, lacking stolons, with broadly ovate, shallowly 7- to 9-lobed, toothed, mid-green leaves, 1½–4in (4–10cm) long, heart-shaped at the bases and marked brown along the veins. From late spring to midautumn, produces erect panicles of tiny white flowers, ⅛–¼in (3–6mm) long, with pink calyces. ↕ to 16in (40cm), ↔ 12in (30cm). Zone 5.

x *H.* 'Pink Frost'. Clump-forming perennial with ovate, shallowly 7- to 9-lobed, frosted, mid-green leaves, 1½–4in (4–10cm) long. From spring to autumn, produces panicles of pink flowers, ⅛–¼in (3–6mm) long. ↕ to 24in (60cm), ↔ 12in (30cm). Zone 5.

x *H. tiarelloides* ■ (*Heuchera* x *brizoides* x *Tiarella cordifolia*). Stoloniferous, hairless perennial with rounded, shallowly lobed, toothed, light green leaves, 3–3½in (7–9cm) long, heart-shaped at the bases, and often with brown markings when young. Brownish red stems bear narrow, short-branched panicles of tiny pink flowers, to ⅛in (3mm) long, from midspring to early summer. May flower again in autumn. ↕↔ 18in (45cm). Zone 5.

▷ ***Hexastylis*** see *Asarum*
▷ ***Heyderia*** see *Calocedrus*

Hibbertia cuneiformis

HIBBERTIA syn. CANDOLLEA

DILLENIACEAE

Genus of about 120 species of evergreen trees, shrubs, and climbers mainly from scrub, heathland, and sandy areas of Australia, but also found in Madagascar, New Guinea, New Caledonia, and Fiji. The alternate, simple, variably shaped, sometimes stem-clasping leaves have entire, wavy, or toothed margins. The saucer- to bowl-shaped, yellow, occasionally pink or white flowers each have 5 spreading, shallowly to deeply notched petals and are borne singly or in terminal or axillary, raceme-like cymes. Where not hardy, grow in a cool greenhouse. Elsewhere, use the shrubs in a shrub border or at the base of a warm, sunny wall; train the climbers over a pergola, arch, or arbor.

• **CULTIVATION** Under glass, grow in soil-based potting mix in bright filtered light, with moderate humidity. In growth, water freely and apply a balanced liquid fertilizer monthly; keep moist in winter. Provide support for climbers. Outdoors, grow in fertile, moist but well-drained soil in partial shade, or in sun with midday shade. Pruning group 8 for shrubs; group 11 for climbers, after flowering.

• **PROPAGATION** Sow seed at 66–75°F (19–24°C) in spring. Root semi-ripe cuttings in late summer.

• **PESTS AND DISEASES** In winter, hairy species are susceptible to gray mold (*Botrytis*). Vulnerable to scale insects under glass.

H. cuneiformis ■ syn. *Candollea cuneiformis*. Erect, freely branching, sometimes spreading and twining shrub with oblong to narrowly obovate, bright green leaves, 1–2in (2.5–5cm) long, often toothed at the tips. From late winter to spring, short, lateral shoots bear solitary, rich yellow flowers, ½–1¾in (1.5–4.5cm) across, with shallowly notched petals. Tolerates full shade and desert conditions. ↕ 3–6ft (1–2m), ↔ 3–5ft (1–1.5m). Coast of Western Australia. ❄ (min. 41°F/5°C)

H. dentata. Trailing or twining shrub or subshrub with red-flushed green stems. Elliptic-oblong to oblong, sparsely toothed, sometimes wavy-margined leaves, 2–3½in (5–9cm) long, are bronze-red or purple-tinted when young, becoming glossy, deep green when mature. From late winter to summer, bears solitary, terminal flowers, 1¼–2in (3–5cm) across, with shallowly notched, bright yellow petals. Good for a hanging basket. ↕↔ 3–6ft (1–2m). New South Wales, Victoria. ❄ (min. 37–41°F/3–5°C)

H. scandens ■ syn. *H. volubilis.* Vigorous shrub with procumbent or twining, reddish brown stems and silky-hairy shoots. Elliptic or oblong-elliptic to obovate, leathery leaves, to 4in (10cm) long, are entire or shallowly toothed near the tips; they are usually glossy, rich green above, paler and silky-hairy beneath. Solitary, terminal, pale to bright yellow flowers, 2–3in (5–8cm) across, with slightly notched petals, are borne mainly in summer. Suitable as a groundcover. Thrives in coastal sites. ↕ 10–20ft (3–6m), ↔ 5–8ft (1.5–2.5m). Often coastal areas of Northern Territory, Queensland, New South Wales, often coastal. ❄ (min. 41°F/5°C)

H. sericea. Dwarf to small shrub, usually erect but sometimes spreading with age, producing gray, silky hairy young shoots. Narrowly linear-lance-shaped to broadly lance-shaped leaves, to ½in (1.5cm) long, are softly hairy and gray- to mid-green, the upper surfaces rough, and the margins rolled under. Pale to rich yellow flowers, ½–1¼in (1.5–3cm) across, with deeply notched, wavy-margined petals, are borne singly or in small, terminal clusters from late winter to summer. ↕ 12–48in (30–120cm), ↔ 12–36in (30–90cm). New South Wales, Victoria, Tasmania. ❄ (min. 41°F/5°C)

H. volubilis see *H. scandens.*

Hibbertia scandens (inset: flower detail)

HIBISCUS

MALVACEAE

Genus of more than 200 species of deciduous and evergreen shrubs, trees, annuals, and herbaceous perennials, widely distributed in warm-temperate, subtropical, and tropical regions, where they occur in a variety of habitats, including streamsides, moist woodland, and dry, rocky sites. They have alternate, entire or shallowly to palmately lobed, sometimes toothed leaves, and are grown for their showy, mainly funnel-shaped, solitary or clustered flowers, borne over a long period from spring to autumn. The flowers are red, pink, purple, blue, yellow, or white, and sometimes have contrasting marks at the bases of the petals, and prominent, colorful stamens. Grow in a sunny mixed, herbaceous, or shrub border; where not hardy, grow in a temperate or warm greenhouse. Some perennials may be grown as annuals.

• **CULTIVATION** Under glass, grow in soilless or soil-based potting mix in bright filtered light. Provide moderate humidity and good ventilation. In the growing season, water freely and apply a balanced liquid fertilizer monthly; water sparingly in winter. Outdoors, grow in humus-rich, moist but well-drained, neutral to slightly alkaline soil in full sun. Hibiscus need long, hot summers to flower well. Many will regenerate from the woody base if cut back by cold. Pruning group 1 for deciduous hibiscus, group 9 for evergreens; however, little or no pruning is usually necessary.

• **PROPAGATION** Sow seed at 55–64°F (13–18°C) in spring. Divide perennials in spring. Root greenwood cuttings of shrubs in late spring, or semi-ripe cuttings in summer. Layer in spring or summer.

• **PESTS AND DISEASES** Prone to rust, fungal leaf spots, bacterial blight, *Verticillium* wilt, viruses, and stem and root rots. Whiteflies, aphids, mealybugs, scale insects, mites, Japanese beetles, and caterpillars can be problems.

H. abelmoschus see *Abelmoschus moschatus.*

H. acetosella, syn. *H. eetveldeanus.* Upright, bushy, fast-growing annual or short-lived, woody-based perennial producing long-stalked, broadly ovate, unlobed or 3- to 5-lobed, often red-flushed, mid-green leaves, to 12in (30cm) long. Solitary, axillary, funnel-shaped, yellow or purple-red flowers, 2½–4in (6–10cm) across, with deep purple centers, are borne from late summer to autumn. ↕ 2–5ft (0.6–1.5m), ↔ to 3ft (1m). C. and E. Africa. ❄ (min. 45°F/7°C). **'Coppertone'** ■ syn. *H.* 'Red Shield', produces iridescent maroon-purple leaves; grow as a summer accent or bedding plant.

H. arnottianus. Rounded, usually fairly open, evergreen, large shrub or small tree with ovate, entire or toothed, leathery, dark green leaves, to 10in (25cm) long. Solitary, lightly scented, funnel-shaped white flowers, 4–7in (10–18cm) across, with pink veins and central sheaves of red stamens, are produced from the leaf axils in summer. ↕ 10–25ft (3–8m), ↔ 6–20ft (2–6m). Hawaii. ❄ (min. 59°F/15°C). **'Wilder's White'** has pure white flowers.

H. calyphyllus. Woody-based, evergreen perennial or shrub producing leaves and young shoots covered with soft, star-shaped hairs. The broadly ovate, entire or shallowly 3-lobed, occasionally 5-lobed, rich green leaves, to 5in (13cm) long, have pointed to rounded teeth. Axillary, solitary, funnel-shaped, sulfur-yellow flowers, 3–5in (7–13cm) across, with maroon or brownish red eyes, are produced from spring to autumn. ↕ to 10ft (3m), ↔ 5–6ft (1.5–2m). Tropical to southern Africa, Madagascar, Mascarene Islands. ❄ (min. 59°F/15°C)

H. cannabinus (Indian hemp, Kenaf). Erect, almost unbranched, fast-growing, minutely spiny-stemmed annual or short-lived, woody-based perennial. Long-stalked, ovate, dark green upper leaves, to 6in (15cm) long, are palmately 3- to 7-lobed; leaves lower down the stems are unlobed. Axillary, funnel-shaped, pale yellow, occasionally purple-red flowers, 3–6in (8–15cm) across, with crimson-red centers, are borne singly or in few-flowered racemes from summer to autumn. ↕ 3–11ft (1–3.5m), ↔ to 5ft (1.5m). Origin uncertain, possibly Indonesia. ❄ (min. 45°F/7°C)

Hibiscus acetosella 'Coppertone'

H

Hibiscus moscheutos 'Southern Belle'

H. coccineus ■ Tall, woody-based perennial with linear-lance-shaped, palmately 3-, 5-, or 7-lobed, mid-green leaves, 4–8in (10–20cm) long. In summer and early autumn, bears solitary, spreading, deep red flowers, to 6in (8cm) across, in the upper leaf axils. ↕ to 10ft (3m), ↔ 4ft (1.2m). Georgia to Florida. Zone 6b.
H. eetveldeanus see *H. acetosella.*
H. huegelii see *Alyogyne huegelii.*
H. moscheutos (Common rose mallow, Swamp rose mallow). Strong-growing, woody-based perennial with erect stems. Produces broadly ovate to lance-shaped, unlobed or shallowly 3- to 5-lobed, toothed, mid-green leaves, 3–9in (8–23cm) long, white-hairy beneath. Widely funnel-shaped flowers, to 8in (20cm) across, with spreading petals, are white, pink, or crimson, sometimes with crimson petal bases, and borne singly from the leaf axils in summer. ↕ 8ft (2.5m), ↔ 3ft (1m). S. US. Zone 6. Many selections have been made, including: **'Anne Arundel'** has deeply lobed, maple-like leaves and saucer-shaped, deep rose-pink flowers, 9in (23cm) across, with bright strawberry-pink eyes; ↕ 4ft (1.2m). **'Blue River II'** is vigorous and has blue-tinged, deep green leaves, and flat, snow-white flowers, 10in (25cm) across; ↕ 4ft (1.2m). **Disco Belle Series** cultivars are compact perennials, often grown as annuals, with red, pink, or white flowers, to 9in (23cm) across; ↕ to 20in (50cm). **'Lady Baltimore'** has glowing pink flowers, 6–8in (15–20cm) across, with red eyes, from midsummer to autumn; ↕ 4ft (1.2m).**'Lord Baltimore'** ■ bears many brilliant red flowers, 10in (25cm) across, with ruffled, overlapping petals, from midsummer to autumn; ↕ 4ft (1.2m). **'Southern Belle'** ■ has toothed leaves and bears deep rose, red, pink, or white flowers, 10in (25cm) across; ↕ to 4ft (1.2m).
H. mutabilis (Confederate rose mallow, Cotton rose). Erect to spreading, usually freely branching, evergreen, large shrub or small tree with stems covered in soft, star-shaped hairs. Broadly ovate to rounded, palmately 3- to 7-lobed, toothed leaves, to 7in (18cm) long, are rich green above, and covered with star-shaped hairs beneath. Funnel-shaped, white or pink flowers, 3–5in (8–13cm) across, sometimes with darker pink bases, are produced singly or in few-flowered, terminal clusters from the leaf axils from spring to autumn. ↕ 6–15ft (2–5m), ↔ 5–8ft (1.5–2.5m). China. ❀ (min. 55°F/13°C)
***H.* 'Red Shield'** see *H. acetosella* 'Coppertone'.
H. rosa-sinensis (Chinese hibiscus, Hawaiian hibiscus, Rose of China). Rounded, bushy, evergreen, large shrub or small tree with hairless or slightly hairy shoots and ovate to broadly lance-shaped, glossy, dark green leaves, to 6in (15cm) long, with toothed margins. Solitary, 5-petaled, bright crimson flowers, 4in (10cm) across, with yellow-anthered red stamens, are produced from the leaf axils from summer to autumn. Flower color is very variable in cultivation, ranging from crimson to orange, yellow, or white. ↕ 8–15ft (2.5m–5m), ↔ 5–10ft (1.5m–3m). Origin unknown, probably tropical Asia. ❀ (min. 50–55°F/10–13°C). Numerous cultivars have been raised, some with semi-double or double flowers. **'Agnes Galt'** ■ is upright, bushy, and very free-flowering; it bears pink flowers, 5–7in (12–18cm) across, lighter red on the petal margins, with deep rose-pink veins and stamens, and yellow anthers. **'Cooperi'** is compact, with lance-shaped leaves marbled olive-green and white, sometimes tinted pink, and bearing red flowers; ↕ 3–6ft (1–2m). **'Crown of Bohemia'** has double, gold-yellow flowers, flushed bright red-dish orange in the centers, with reddish orange stamens. **'Dainty Pink'** see 'Fantasia'. **'Dainty White'**, syn. *H.* 'Swan Lake', *H.* 'White La France', has white flowers, 4in (10cm) across, with petals margined creamy pale yellow, and white stamens. **'Fantasia'**, syn. 'Dainty Pink', 'Pink La France', is free-flowering, bearing strongly veined, reddish pink flowers, 4in (10cm) across, with pink or white stamens; the outer petals are slightly fringed, margined white, and have creamy-white central zones. **'Fiesta'** bears large, deep apricot-orange flowers, 7in (18cm) across, with finely waved petals, bright red and white centers, and cream stamens. **'Full Moon'** see 'Mrs. James E. Hendry'. **'Kinchen's Yellow'** ■ bears yellow flowers, 5–6in (12–15cm) across, with white centers and yellow stamens. **'Mrs. James E. Hendry'**, syn. 'Full Moon', has double, lemon-yellow flowers, 6in (15cm) across, with white eyes and white veins, and deep yellow stigmas. **'Pink La France'** see 'Fantasia'. **'Scarlet Giant'** ■ produces scarlet flowers, 5–7in (12–18cm) across, with red- and yellow-anthered stamens. **'The President'** ■ is erect and bushy, bearing slightly ruffled, rich red flowers, 6–7in (16–18cm) across, with darker red centers, stamens, and veins; the petals have cream markings at the bases.
H. schizopetalus ■ (Japanese lantern). Tall, slender, evergreen shrub with arching or pendent branches and ovate, toothed, mid- to deep green leaves, to 5in (13cm) long. Long-stalked, pendent, pink or red flowers, to 3in (8cm) across, each with a long staminal column, pink stamens, and deeply and irregularly fringed, reflexed petals, are produced singly from the upper leaf axils in summer. ↕ to 10ft (3m) or more, ↔ 3–5ft (1–1.5m). Kenya, Tanzania, Mozambique. ❀ (min. 55°F/13°C)
H. sinosyriacus. Spreading, deciduous shrub of open habit with broadly ovate, shallowly 3-lobed, mid-green leaves, to 4in (10cm) long. From late summer to midautumn, bears solitary, trumpet-shaped white flowers, 3–3½in (8–9cm) across, with red centers and yellow-anthered white stamens. ↕ 8ft (2.5m), ↔ 10ft (3m). C. China. Zone 7. **'Autumn Surprise'** has white flowers with petal bases feathered cherry-pink. **'Lilac Queen'** ■ bears pale lilac-mauve flowers with red centers.
***H.* 'Swan Lake'** see *H. rosa-sinensis* 'Dainty White'.
H. syriacus (Rose of Sharon). Erect, deciduous shrub with ovate to diamond-shaped, shallowly to palmately 3-lobed, coarsely toothed, dark green leaves, to 4in (10cm) long. Large, trumpet-shaped, dark pink flowers, to 2½in (6cm) across, with dark red centers and yellow-anthered white stamens, are produced singly or in pairs from the leaf axils, from late summer to midautumn. ↕ 10ft (3m), ↔ 6ft (2m). China to India. Zone 5b. **'Aphrodite'** produces deep rose-pink flowers, each with a dark red eye. **'Blue Bird'** ■ syn. 'Oiseau Bleu', has bright blue flowers, to 3in (8cm) across, with small red centers. **'Diana'** ■ bears very large white flowers, to 5in (13cm) across, with wavy-margined petals. **'Elegantissimus'** see 'Lady Stanley'. **'Helene'** bears white flowers with bases flushed reddish purple. **'Lady Stanley'**, syn. 'Elegantissimus', has double white flowers, flushed pink and dark red in the centers. **'Meehanii'**, syn. 'Variegatus', has leaves margined creamy white, and lilac-mauve, maroon-centered flowers. **'Minerva'** is low-branched, bearing many pink-tinged, lavender flowers, 4–5in (10–13cm) across, with dark red centers, from summer to autumn; ↕ 8ft (2.5m), ↔ 7ft (2.2m). **'Oiseau Bleu'** see 'Blue Bird'.

Hibiscus coccineus

Hibiscus moscheutos 'Lord Baltimore'

Hibiscus rosa-sinensis 'Agnes Galt'

Hibiscus rosa-sinensis 'Kinchen's Yellow'

Hibiscus rosa-sinensis 'Scarlet Giant'

Hibiscus rosa-sinensis 'The President'

Hibiscus sinosyriacus 'Lilac Queen'

Hibiscus syriacus 'Blue Bird'

Hibiscus syriacus 'Diana'

Hibiscus syriacus 'Red Heart'

Hibiscus syriacus 'Woodbridge'

Hibiscus trionum

Hibiscus schizopetalus

'Pink Giant' has large, clear pink flowers with dark red eyes. **'Red Heart'** ■ produces white flowers with dark red centers. **'Variegatus'** see 'Meehanii'. **'William R. Smith'** bears large white flowers, to 4in (10cm) across. **'Woodbridge'** ■ bears large, rich pink flowers, to 4in (10cm) across, with dark pink centers.
H. trionum ■ (Flower-of-an-hour). Fast-growing, erect to spreading, hairy annual or short-lived perennial with ovate, palmately 3- to 5-lobed, toothed, dark green leaves, to 3in (8cm) long, the central lobes longest; leaves lower down the stems are unlobed. From summer to early autumn, trumpet-shaped, creamy yellow flowers, to 3in (8cm) across, with brown centers and dark purple stamens, are produced singly from the leaf axils; they are followed by inflated, bladder-like seed capsules. ↕ 30in (75cm), ↔ to 24in (60cm). Origin uncertain. ❄ (min. 45°F/7°C)
H. waimeae. Evergreen, spreading, small tree with shoots clothed in soft, star-shaped hairs. Broadly ovate to rounded, toothed leaves, to 7in (18cm) long, are rich green above, gray-downy beneath. From late spring to late summer, produces solitary, richly fragrant, funnel-shaped flowers, 5–8in (12–20cm) across, opening white, then fading to pink, with crimson stamens. ↕ 10–15ft (3–5m), ↔ 6–10ft (2–3m). ❄ (min. 59°F/15°C)
H. 'White La France' see *H. rosa-sinensis* 'Dainty White'.

HIERACIUM

Hawkweed

ASTERACEAE

Genus of 250–260 species (often subdivided into about 10,000 microspecies) of perennials, many of which are weeds. They are widespread over the N. hemisphere, occurring in diverse habitats, including grassland, dry, stony slopes, cultivated fields, and alpine meadows. They have basal rosettes of lance-shaped to linear or obovate, entire to deeply toothed, pale to dark green leaves, and dandelion-like flowerheads with strap-shaped ray florets. Those described below are grown mainly for their downy foliage and loose panicles of yellow flowerheads borne in summer. They are suitable for a large rock garden or wild garden, but may self-seed freely.
• **CULTIVATION** Grow in poor, well-drained soil in full sun. The flowerheads may be removed for best foliage effects, but if retained, should be deadheaded to prevent excessive self-seeding.
• **PROPAGATION** Sow seed in containers in an open frame in autumn or spring. Divide in spring.
• **PESTS AND DISEASES** Caterpillars, slugs, and snails may be problems. Powdery mildew, rust, and smut may be troublesome.

H. aurantiacum see *Pilosella aurantiaca.*
H. brunneocroceum see *Pilosella aurantiaca.*
H. lanatum ■ syn. *H. welwitschii.* Clump-forming perennial with lance-shaped to ovate, gray-green, white-margined leaves, to 4in (10cm) long, densely clothed in long white hairs. Loose panicles of 3–7 deep yellow flowerheads, to 1in (2.5cm) across, are borne on wiry, branching stems in summer. ↕ 18in (45cm), ↔ 8in (20cm). S. Europe. Zone 5b.
H. maculatum. Clump-forming perennial with red-violet or deep purple stems and ovate to narrowly lance-shaped, toothed, brown-purple-marked, mid-green leaves, to ½in (1.5cm) long. Bears one to many deep yellow flowerheads, to 1in (2.5cm) across, often in corymbs. ↕ 8–32in (20–80cm), ↔ 8–12in (20–30cm). W. and C. Europe. Zone 5.
H. umbellatum (Leafy hawkweed). Variable, softly hairy perennial with linear to lance-shaped, slightly toothed, dark green leaves, ½in (1.5cm) long. Lax panicles of up to 10 yellow flowerheads, ¾–1¼in (2–3cm) across, with black-brown bracts, are borne on robust stems in summer. ↕ 16–24in (40–60cm), ↔ 10–16in (25–40cm). Europe, W. Asia. Zone 4.
H. villosum (Shaggy hawkweed). Clump-forming perennial with oblong to lance-shaped, gray-green basal leaves, to 4in (10cm) long, densely clothed in long white hairs. In summer, clear, pale yellow flowerheads, 1½–2in (4–5cm) across, are borne singly or in 2- to 4-flowered panicles on wiry, hairy stems. ↕ to 16in (40cm), ↔ to 8in (20cm). Mountains of Europe. Zone 4.
H. welwitschii see *H. lanatum.*

Hieracium lanatum

HIMALAYACALAMUS

POACEAE

Genus of 15 species of perennial bamboos from cool forest in India and the Himalayas. They are valued for their dense clumps of hollow, glossy culms, sometimes attractively striped or stained, and their linear, bluish green leaves. They thrive in areas with cool, damp summers, but are intolerant of winter moisture and temperatures below 21°F (-6°C). Where not hardy, grow in a cool greenhouse. In warmer areas, grow as specimen plants in a woodland or wild garden, or in containers.
• **CULTIVATION** Under glass, grow in soil-based potting mix with added leaf mold and sharp sand or grit, in bright filtered light. Provide moderate to high humidity. When in growth, water moderately and apply a balanced liquid fertilizer monthly; water sparingly in winter. Outdoors, grow in moist but well-drained, humus-rich soil in sun or dappled shade, with protection from excessive winter moisture.
• **PROPAGATION** Divide in early spring.
• **PESTS AND DISEASES** Infrequent.

H. falconeri, syn. *Arundinaria falconeri, Drepanostachyum falconeri, Thamnocalamus falconeri* (Noble bamboo). Dense, clump-forming bamboo with smooth, olive-green culms, stained purple at the nodes, and linear, blue-green leaves, to 6in (15cm) long. Inner culms are stiffly erect; outer ones arch gently to form a distinctive and graceful clump. ↕ to 28ft (9m) (much smaller in containers), ↔ 10ft (3m). C. Himalayas, India. ❄ (min. 45°F/7°C)

HIPPEASTRUM

Amaryllis

AMARYLLIDACEAE

Genus of about 80 species of bulbous perennials found in Central and South America, in habitats ranging from streambanks to rocky hillsides, from sea level to subalpine regions. Umbels of showy, funnel-shaped flowers are borne on leafless stems, mainly from winter to spring. Semi-erect, strap-shaped, light to mid-green or gray-green, basal leaves develop with or just after the flowers, or are evergreen. Many large-flowered hybrids have been bred for cultivation in containers. These usually produce one or multiple stems bearing 4–6 bold, open funnel-shaped flowers, 4–6in (10–15cm) or more across, and strap-shaped, deep green leaves, 18in (45cm) long. Smaller hybrids are also available. Where not hardy, grow as houseplants or in a warm greenhouse or conservatory. In warmer areas, grow in a border or in containers outdoors. All parts may cause mild stomach upset if ingested.
• **CULTIVATION** Plant bulbs with the neck and shoulders above the soil surface, in autumn. Under glass, grow in soil-based potting mix in a pot 2in (5cm) larger than the diameter of the bulb, at a minimum of 55°F (13°C). Provide bottom heat while the roots are developing. Place in full to bright filtered light and water sparingly until rapid growth begins. Delay and prolong flowering by keeping at minimum temperature, away from full light.
After flowering, remove flower stems and apply a balanced liquid fertilizer every 2 weeks for 3–5 months while foliage grows. As the foliage matures in midsummer, water less. From late summer to autumn, keep just moist (evergreens) or completely dry, allowing the bulbs to go dormant for at least 8 weeks. (If bulbs are watered freely, the leaves will stay green, and the bulbs may not go fully dormant, reducing the possibility of flowering.) Top-dress or repot, and start into growth again. Allow 4–8 weeks to bloom. Amaryllis resent root disturbance; pot on every 3–5 years, in autumn. Remove offsets to encourage large, single bulbs; left attached, large clumps will eventually form. The species and smaller hybrids are especially attractive when grown in clumps.
Outdoors, grow in fertile, well-drained soil in full sun to light, dappled shade. Where marginally hardy, protect with a dry winter mulch.
• **PROPAGATION** Sow seed at 61–64°F (16–18°C) as soon as ripe; keep seedlings growing without a dormant period to encourage early flowering. Remove offsets in autumn.
• **PESTS AND DISEASES** Susceptible to bacterial and fungal rots and leaf spots, as well as viruses. Narcissus bulb fly may occur if grown in shade.

H. × acramannii (*H. aulicum* × *H. psittacinum*). Bulbous perennial with bright green leaves, 12–24in (30–60cm) long, emerging with or just after the flowers. In winter or spring, bears an umbel of up to 3 funnel-shaped scarlet flowers, 6in (15cm) long, with white petal margins and green-and-white centers. ↕ 24in (60cm), PD12in (30cm). ❄ (min. 45°F/7°C)
H. advenum see *Rhodophiala advena.*
H. aulicum ■ syn. *H. morelianum* (Lily of the palace). Bulbous perennial with mid-green leaves, 12–20in (30–50cm) long, produced with the flowers. In winter or spring, a thick stem bears 2 funnel-shaped crimson flowers, 6in (15cm) across, with green throats. ↕ 12–20in (30–50cm), PD12in (30cm). Brazil, Paraguay. ❄ (min. 55°F/13°C)
H. bifidum see *Rhodophiala bifida.*

Hippeastrum aulicum

H

Hippeastrum Large-flowered Hybrid 'Apple Blossom'

H

H. calyptratum. Bulbous, epiphytic perennial with channeled, dark green leaves, to 24in (60cm) long, sharply keeled beneath. In summer, produces umbels of 2 or (rarely) 3 funnel-shaped mid-green flowers, to 5in (13cm) across, with pale pink stamens. ↕ to 24in (60cm), PD12in (30cm). Brazil. ❀ (min. 55°F/13°C)
***H.* Large-flowered Hybrids.** Bulbous perennial cultivars with flowers 4–6in (10–15cm) across, produced in winter. Usually grown deciduously. ↕ 12–20in (30–50cm), PD12in (30cm). ❀ (min. 55°F/13°C). **'Apple Blossom'** ▣ is robust and produces white flowers with pink-tinged petal edges. **'Christmas Gift'** is early-flowering, bearing pure white flowers in early winter. **'Lady Jane'** has double, deep apricot-rose flowers with faint white stripes. **'Liberty'** produces deep red flowers. **'Minerva'** bears white-centered red flowers. **'Orange Sovereign'** has orange-red flowers. **'Picotee'** ▣ produces red-margined white flowers. **'Red Lion'** ▣ bears scarlet flowers. **'Rilona'** produces salmon flowers. **'Star of Holland'** has very large red

Hippeastrum Large-flowered Hybrid 'Red Lion'

flowers, each with a star-shaped white mark in the throat.
***H.* Miniature-flowered Hybrids.** Bulbous perennial cultivars with flowers 3–4in (8–10cm) across, borne in winter. Usually grown deciduously. ↕ 12in (30cm), PD8in (20cm). ❀ (min. 55°F/13°C). **'Pamela'** produces slightly ruffled, orange-red flowers. **'Scarlet Baby'** has brilliant red flowers.
H. morelianum see *H. aulicum.*
H. papilio ▣ (Butterfly amaryllis). Evergreen bulbous perennial with dark green leaves, 12–20in (30–50cm) long. In late winter to early spring, produces umbels of 2 or 3 pinched, funnel-shaped, white flowers, 3½in (9cm) across, with maroon stripes and green throats. ↕ 2ft (60cm), PD12in (30cm). ❀ (min. 55°F/13°C)
H. pratense see *Rhodophiala pratensis.*
H. procerum see *Worsleya rayneri.*
H. puniceum (Barbados lily). Bulbous perennial with mid-green leaves, to 1½in (4cm) long, appearing after the flowers. Umbels of funnel-shaped, bright red, scarlet, or pink flowers, 4in (10cm) across, with green-yellow throats, are produced in summer.

Hippeastrum Large-flowered Hybrid 'Picotee'

Hippeastrum papilio

↕ to 20in (50cm), PD12in (30cm). Mexico south to Chile and Brazil, West Indies. ❀ (min. 55°F/13°C)
H. reginae (Mexican lily). Bulbous perennial with mid-green leaves, to 24in (60cm) long, produced after the flowers. In summer, thick stems bear umbels of 2–4 nodding, funnel-shaped scarlet flowers, 4–6in (10–15cm) across, each with a star-shaped green mark in the throat. ↕ 20in (50cm), PD12in (30cm). Mexico, West Indies, Brazil, Peru. ❀ (min. 55°F/13°C)
H. reticulatum* var. *striatifolium ▣ Upright, bulbous perennial producing dark green leaves, 8–12in (20–30cm) long, with prominent white midribs. In summer, bears an umbel of up to 5 funnel-shaped, rose-pink flowers, 3–4in (8–10cm) across, veined darker pink inside. ↕ 10–14in (25–35cm), PD12in (30cm). ❀ (min. 55°F/13°C)
H. rutilum see *H. striatum.*
H. striatum, syn. *H. rutilum.* Bulbous perennial with bright green leaves, 12–20in (30–50cm) long, emerging with the flowers. In winter and sometimes again in summer, a thick stem bears an umbel of up to 4 funnel-shaped, coral-red to bright orange flowers, 4–6in (10–15cm) across, each petal with a central green stripe. ↕ and PD12in (30cm). Brazil. ❀ (min. 55°F/13°C)
H. stylosum (Long-styled knight's star lily). Bulbous perennial with 4–6 bright green leaves, 10–20in (30–50cm) long, produced at the same time as the flowers. In summer, bears umbels of 3–8 light red or pink flowers, to 4in (10cm) across, with darker speckles,

Hippeastrum reticulatum var. *striatifolium*

green throats, pink-brown veins, and prominent styles. ↕ to 20in (50cm), PD12in (30cm). Guyana, Brazil. ❀ (min. 55°F/13°C)
H. vittatum (St. Joseph's lily). Robust, bulbous perennial producing thick stems with umbels of 3–6 funnel-shaped, red-striped white flowers, 5in (13cm) across, in spring. Bright green leaves, to 24in (60cm) long, develop after the flowers. ↕ to 36in (90cm), PD12in (30cm). Peru. ❀ (min. 55°F/13°C)

HIPPOCREPIS

Horseshoe vetch, Vetch

FABACEAE

Genus of about 20 species of annuals and perennials from Europe, N. Africa, and W. Asia, occurring in scree, among alpine rocks, and in short turf on chalky downland. They usually have woody, creeping stems; alternate, pinnate, light to mid-green leaves; and small, pea-like flowers in raceme-like heads, which are attractive to butterflies. Some may be invasive, but others are suitable for a wild garden or rock garden, scree bed, trough, or raised bed. *H. comosa* 'E.R. Janes' is excellent for crevices in a wall, rock, or paving.
- **CULTIVATION** Grow in poor, well-drained, alkaline soil in full sun.
- **PROPAGATION** Sow scarified seed in containers in a cold frame in spring or autumn. Root cuttings of non-flowering shoots in summer.
- **PESTS AND DISEASES** Infrequent.

H. comosa. Vigorous, creeping, woody-based perennial with mid-green leaves, 1¼–4in (3–10cm) long, each divided into 3–8 pairs of linear to obovate leaflets. Bears raceme-like heads of up to 12 lemon-yellow flowers, ½in (1.5cm) across, from late spring to late summer. ↕↔ to 16in (40cm). C. and S. Europe, N. Africa. Zone 6. **'E.R. Janes'** is compact and spreads less vigorously; ↕ to 3in (8cm), ↔ indefinite.
H. emerus see *Coronilla emerus.*

HIPPOPHAE

ELAEAGNACEAE

Genus of 3 species of deciduous, dioecious shrubs and trees from Europe and Asia, occurring on coastal dunes, and in screes and on riverbanks in the mountains. They are cultivated for their linear or linear-oblong, silvery, gray-green or mid-green leaves, and for their

Hippophae rhamnoides

spherical, usually orange fruits. Both male and female plants are needed to produce fruit. Inconspicuous flowers are borne in racemes in spring. Grow in a mixed or shrub border, in a wild garden, or as specimen plants. In coastal areas, *H. rhamnoides* is used for windbreaks, hedging, and for stabilizing sand dunes.

• **CULTIVATION** Grow in full sun in moist but well-drained, neutral to alkaline, preferably sandy soil. Pruning group 1, in late summer; pruning is seldom necessary.

• **PROPAGATION** Sow seed in containers in an open frame as soon as ripe or in spring. Stratify spring-sown seed for 3 months at 39°F (4°C). Root semi-ripe cuttings in summer, hardwood cuttings in late autumn. Layer in autumn.

• **PESTS AND DISEASES** Infrequent.

H. rhamnoides ■ (Sea buckthorn). Bushy, deciduous, large shrub or small tree with spiny shoots bearing linear, gray-green leaves, to 2½in (6cm) long, silver-scaly to bronze-scaly on both surfaces. Tiny, yellow-green flowers are borne in racemes to ¾in (2cm) long, in spring. On female plants, flowers are followed by persistent, spherical, bright orange fruit, to ⅜in (9mm) across. ↕↔ 20ft (6m). Europe, Asia. Zone 2b.

HOHENBERGIA

BROMELIACEAE

Genus of over 50 species of stemless, evergreen, terrestrial or epiphytic perennials from scrub, rainforest, and rocky terrain up to altitudes of 5,000ft (1,600m) in South America and the West Indies. They produce rosettes of mainly triangular or strap-shaped leaves with spiny tips and margins, and unusually large sheaths. In summer, prominent scapes bear compound spikes of tubular flowers. Where temperatures fall below 59°F (15°C), grow as houseplants or in a warm green-house. In warmer regions, grow in a humid, moist area of the garden, or in containers or a raised bed.

• **CULTIVATION** Under glass, grow in terrestrial bromeliad potting mix in bright indirect to moderate light. Keep just moist at all times. Apply a half-strength, low-nitrogen fertilizer monthly from spring to autumn. Outdoors, grow in fertile, moist but very well-drained soil in partial shade; use terrestrial bromeliad potting mix for container-grown plants outdoors. Protect from strong winds. See also p.47.

• **PROPAGATION** Sow seed at 75°F (24°C) as soon as ripe. Divide offsets in spring or summer.

• **PESTS AND DISEASES** Young growth is susceptible to scale insects.

H. edmundoi. Rosette-forming, terrestrial perennial producing strap-shaped, gray-scaly, mid-green to bronze leaves, to 18in (45cm) long, the rounded tips with sharp brown spines. Branched, spike-like inflorescences, to 28in (70cm) long, have broadly ovate, white-woolly stem bracts, each with 2–4 tiny purple flowers. ↕↔ 18–20in (45–50cm). E. Brazil. ❀ (min. 59°F/15°C)

H. rosea. Rosette-forming, terrestrial perennial producing strap-shaped, white-scaly, mid-green leaves, to 18in (45cm) long, the tips and margins with dark spines. Branched, spike-like inflorescences have pink-woolly stem bracts and blue or pale violet flowers. ↕ to 20in (50cm), ↔ 16in (40cm). Brazil. ❀ (min. 59°F/15°C)

H. stellata. Rosette-forming, terrestrial or epiphytic perennial producing strap-shaped, silver-scaly, dark green leaves, 24–36in (60–90cm) long, the tips and margins with brown spines. Branched, spike-like inflorescences have white-woolly, red or yellow stem bracts and 2–8 bright blue or purple flowers, each surrounded by triangular, red or purple bracts. ↕↔ 3ft (1m). Trinidad, Tobago, Venezuela, N.E. Brazil. ❀ (min. 59°F/15°C)

HOHENBERGIOPSIS

BROMELIACEAE

Genus of a single species of evergreen, epiphytic perennial, closely related to *Hohenbergia*, from rainforest at altitudes up to 6,000ft (1,800m) in Guatemala. It produces rosettes of strap-shaped, spiny-toothed leaves, and thick, woolly scapes bearing cylindrical, densely flowered inflorescences in summer. Where temperatures fall below 64°F (18°C), grow as a houseplant or in a warm greenhouse. In warmer areas, grow in containers, or in a raised bed in a humid, moist area of the garden.

• **CULTIVATION** Under glass, grow in epiphytic bromeliad potting mix in bright filtered light, away from all drafts. Provide moderate to high humidity. Keep just moist and mist daily at all times. Apply a half-strength, low-nitrogen fertilizer monthly from spring to autumn. Outdoors, grow in fertile, moist but well-drained soil in partial shade; use terrestrial bromeliad potting mix for container-grown plants. Protect from cold, drying winds.

• **PROPAGATION** Sow seed at 75°F (24°C) as soon as ripe. Remove offsets in spring.

• **PESTS AND DISEASES** Scale insects may be a problem.

H. guatemalensis. Epiphytic perennial producing strap-shaped, mid-green leaves, 20–24in (50–60cm) long, each tipped with a spine ½in (1.5cm) long. In summer, bears a 2- or 3-branched, cylindrical inflorescence, 8in (20cm) long, with brown floral bracts and deep purple flowers, to ⅜in (9mm) long. ↕↔ 3ft (1m) or more. Guatemala. ❀ (min. 64°F/18°C)

HOHERIA

MALVACEAE

Genus of 5 species of deciduous and evergreen trees and shrubs from New Zealand, where they occur from the coast to the mountains, in forest, at forest margins, and on streambanks. The alternate leaves are lance-shaped to broadly ovate, toothed, sometimes hairy, and gray- to dark green when mature. Juvenile foliage, present for several years, may be lobed and have a metallic cast. Hoherias are grown mainly for their graceful habit and their cup-shaped, fragrant white flowers, attractive to butterflies, borne singly or in cymes. They prefer maritime climates. Grow in a shrub border, in a woodland garden, as specimen plants, or against a sunny wall.

• **CULTIVATION** Grow in moderately fertile, well-drained, neutral to alkaline soil in full sun or partial shade, sheltered from cold, drying winds. The deciduous species are more reliably hardy than the evergreens and may regenerate from their woody bases if cut back by cold in winter; protect the roots of evergreens with a winter mulch. Pruning group 1, in spring or after flowering; pruning is seldom necessary.

• **PROPAGATION** Sow seed in containers in a cold frame in autumn. Root semi-ripe cuttings in late summer or autumn.

• **PESTS AND DISEASES** Prone to coral spot, particularly in damp, shady sites.

H. angustifolia, syn. *H. microphylla.* Columnar, evergreen tree with oblong to inversely lance-shaped, toothed, glossy, dark green leaves, to 1¼in (3cm) long. In mid- and late summer, bears white flowers, to ¾in (2cm) across, often singly from the leaf axils. ↕ 22ft (7m), ↔ 10ft (3m). New Zealand. ❀ (min. 41°F/5°C)

H. glabrata ■ Deciduous, spreading tree with hairless, broadly ovate, tapered, dark green leaves, to 4in (10cm) long, turning yellow in autumn. In midsummer, bears small cymes of white flowers, to 1½in (4cm) across, with purple anthers. Often confused with *H. lyallii.* ↕↔ 22ft (7m). New Zealand (South Island). ❀ (min. 41°F/5°C)

***H.* 'Glory of Amlwch'.** Spreading, semi-evergreen tree with narrowly ovate, toothed, glossy, bright green leaves, to 4in (10cm) long. Cymes of large white flowers, to 1½in (4cm) across, are borne in mid- and late summer. ↕ 22ft (7m), ↔ 20ft (6m). ❀ (min. 41°F/5°C)

Hoheria sexstylosa

H. lyallii, syn. *Plagianthus lyallii.* Spreading, deciduous tree with ovate, deeply toothed, densely hairy, gray-green leaves, to 4in (10cm) long. Cymes of white flowers, to 1¼in (3cm) across, with purple anthers, are borne in mid-summer. Often confused with *H. glabrata.* ↕↔ 22ft (7m). New Zealand (South Island). ❀ (min. 41°F/5°C)

H. microphylla see *H. angustifolia.*

H. populnea (Lace-bark). Spreading, evergreen tree, often with flaky, pale brown and white bark when mature. The elliptic to broadly ovate, toothed leaves, to 6in (15cm) long, are glossy, dark green. Dense cymes of pure white flowers, 1¼in (3cm) across, are borne in late summer and early autumn. ↕ 40ft (12m), ↔ 30ft (10m). New Zealand (North Island). ❀ (min. 41°F/5°C).

var. *lanceolata* see *H. sexstylosa.*

H. sexstylosa ■ syn. *H. populnea* var. *lanceolata* (Ribbonwood). Upright, evergreen tree or shrub with lance-shaped, tapered, toothed, glossy, mid-green leaves, to 3½in (9cm) long. Cymes of pure white flowers, to 1in (2.5cm) across, are borne in mid- and late summer. ↕ 25ft (8m), ↔ 20ft (6m). New Zealand. ❀ (min. 41°F/5°C)

Hoheria glabrata (inset: flower detail)

H

Holboellia coriacea

HOLBOELLIA

LARDIZABALACEAE

Genus of 5 species of twining, evergreen climbers from thickets and shady woodland in the Himalayas and China. They are cultivated mainly for their alternate, 3- to 9-palmate, dark green leaves. Small male and female flowers, to ½in (1.5cm) long, are borne in axillary corymbs or racemes, separately on the same plant; fruits are produced only irregularly. Train on a support, grow through a small tree, or use to clothe a pergola, arch, or trellis.

• **CULTIVATION** Grow in well-drained, moderately fertile, humus-rich soil in full sun or partial shade, sheltered from cold, drying winds. Pruning group 11, in spring.

• **PROPAGATION** Sow seed in containers in a cold frame in spring. Root semi-ripe cuttings in late summer or autumn. Layer in autumn.

• **PESTS AND DISEASES** Infrequent.

H. coriacea ▣ Vigorous climber with dark green leaves, to 6in (15cm) long, composed of 3 oblong leaflets. In spring, bears small, mauve male flowers and purple-tinged, greenish white female flowers in dense corymbs, to 6in (15cm) across. Flowers are sometimes followed by sausage-shaped purple fruit, to 2½in (6cm) long. ↕ 22ft (7m). C. China. ❀ (min. 45°F/7°C)

H. latifolia. Vigorous climber with dark green leaves, to 5in (13cm) long, composed of 3–7 oblong leaflets. Small, greenish white male flowers and purple female flowers are produced in racemes to 5in (13cm) across, in spring. Flowers are sometimes followed by sausage-shaped, red to purple fruit, to 4in (10cm) long. ↕ 15ft (5m). Himalayas. ❀ (min. 45°F/7°C)

HOLCUS

POACEAE

Genus of 8 species of often invasive, annual or perennial grasses from woodland and grassland in Europe, N. Africa, and W. Asia. They have linear, flat or folded, mid-green or bluish green leaves, and dense or open, spike-like panicles of flattened, 2-flowered spikelets borne in summer. Only *H. mollis* 'Albovariegatus' is usually cultivated; it is an attractive carpeting plant for the front of a herbaceous border or rock garden.

Holcus mollis 'Albovariegatus'

• **CULTIVATION** Grow in any moist but well-drained, poor to moderately fertile soil in sun or partial shade; avoid full sun on poor, dry soil. Trim *H. mollis* 'Albovariegatus' lightly after flowering and deadhead to avoid self-seeding, since offspring will be green-leaved and invasive. Avoid planting too close to less vigorous plants.

• **PROPAGATION** Divide *H. mollis* 'Albovariegatus' in spring; it will not come true from seed.

• **PESTS AND DISEASES** Prone to rust, leaf spots, and smut.

***H. mollis* 'Albovariegatus'** ▣ Loosely tufted, mat-forming, perennial grass producing linear, flat, soft, blue-green leaves, 6–18in (15–45cm) long, with wide, creamy white margins. In summer, erect stems bear pale green spikelets in relatively few, narrowly oblong to ovate panicles, to 5in (13cm) long. ↕ to 12in (30cm), ↔ 18in (45cm) or more. Zone 5.

HOLMSKIOLDIA

VERBENACEAE

Genus of 10 species of evergreen shrubs or scandent climbers from tropical woodland in Africa, Madagascar, and the Himalayas. They are valued for their terminal panicles or axillary racemes of tubular to salverform or trumpet-shaped flowers with conspicuous, saucer-shaped, brightly colored calyces. The opposite leaves are simple and usually ovate to obovate. Where temperatures fall below 61°F (16°C), grow in a warm greenhouse or conservatory. In tropical climates, use as specimen plants or grow in a border.

• **CULTIVATION** Under glass, grow in soil-based potting mix in full light, with shade from hot sun. Top-dress in late winter or early spring, and pot on in spring. In summer, water freely and apply a balanced liquid fertilizer monthly; keep moist in winter. Outdoors, grow in moist but well-drained, moderately fertile soil in full sun, with some midday shade and shelter from strong winds. Established plants are drought tolerant and useful in poor, sandy soils. Provide support for climbers. Pruning group 9 for shrubs; group 11 for climbers, after flowering.

• **PROPAGATION** Sow seed at 66–75°F (19–24°C) in spring. Root semi-ripe cuttings with bottom heat in mid- to late summer.

Holmskioldia sanguinea

• **PESTS AND DISEASES** Whiteflies, spider mites, and mealybugs may be problems under glass.

H. sanguinea ▣ (Chinese-hat plant). Erect, then scandent shrub with ovate or ovate-elliptic, slender-pointed, slightly toothed leaves, 2–4in (5–10cm) long. From summer to autumn, bears curved, narrowly trumpet-shaped flowers, to 1in (2.5cm) long, with crimson petals and orange-red calyces, 1in (2.5cm) across, in racemes to 5in (13cm) long. ↕ 10–30ft (3–10m), ↔ 5–10ft (1.5–3m). Himalayas. ❀ (min. 59°F/15°C). **var. *citrina*** bears yellow flowers.

HOLODISCUS

ROSACEAE

Genus of 8 species of deciduous shrubs found in dry woodland from W. North America to N. South America. They produce alternate, oblong to rounded, lobed to pinnatifid, usually softly hairy leaves, and are valued for their attractive, airy panicles of numerous small, cup-shaped flowers. Suitable for a mixed or shrub border, or for growing in light woodland, or as specimen plants.

Holodiscus discolor

• **CULTIVATION** Grow in moist but well-drained, fertile, humus-rich soil in sun or partial shade. Pruning group 1 or 2; remove only a few older shoots each year, after flowering.

• **PROPAGATION** Sow seed in containers in an open frame as soon as ripe. Root semi-ripe cuttings in summer. Layer in summer or autumn.

• **PESTS AND DISEASES** Sometimes affected by powdery mildew and various leaf spots.

H. discolor ▣ (Ocean spray). Vigorous, upright shrub with arching branches and broadly ovate, shallowly to deeply 4- to 8-lobed, gray-green leaves, to 3in (8cm) long, white-hairy beneath. Tiny, cup-shaped, creamy-white flowers are borne in large, pendent, plume-like panicles, to 12in (30cm) long, in midsummer. ↕↔ 12ft (4m). W. North America. Zone 5.

▷ ***Homalocephala texensis*** see *Echinocactus texensis*

HOMALOCLADIUM

Ribbon bush

POLYGONACEAE

Genus of one species of evergreen shrub from tropical forest in the Solomon Islands. It is grown for its ornamental, flattened, jointed green stems with alternate, lance- or arrow-shaped leaves, which are usually short-lived or may be absent. The small, petalless, whitish green flowers have 5-lobed calyces that later turn red or red-purple, enlarging and becoming fleshy as the seeds form. Where not hardy, grow in a warm greenhouse or as a houseplant (plants in containers rarely flower or fruit). In warmer regions, grow in a shrub border or courtyard garden, or at the base of a warm, sunny wall.

• **CULTIVATION** Under glass, grow in soil-based potting mix in bright filtered or full light. Water moderately in growth, more sparingly in winter. Apply

a balanced liquid fertilizer once in spring. Pot on or top-dress in spring. Outdoors, grow in moist but well-drained, fertile, humus-rich soil in full sun; partial shade is tolerated. Pruning group 8, if necessary, in spring.
• **PROPAGATION** Sow seed at 61–64°F (16–18°C) in spring. Root stem-section cuttings with bottom heat in summer.
• **PESTS AND DISEASES** Can be affected by powdery mildew, crown gall, and scale insects.

H. platycladum, syn. *Muehlenbeckia platyclados.* Spreading, erect shrub or scrambling climber producing ribbon-like, jointed, glossy, mid-green stems, to ¾in (2cm) wide, with raised veins running lengthwise. Compact flower clusters, to ½in (1.5cm) across, and usually short-lived, lance-shaped, bright green leaves, ½–2½in (1.5–6cm) long, are borne on the margins or at the joints of the stems in spring. ↕24–48in (60–120cm), ↔ 18–36in (45–90cm) in a container or greenhouse border; ↕to 10ft (3m), ↔ 6ft (2m) outdoors in warm climates. Solomon Islands. ❀ (min. 41–45°F/5–7°C)

HOMERIA

IRIDACEAE

Genus of 31 species of cormous perennials, often found on sandy slopes from low to high altitudes in South Africa. They are cultivated for their scented, showy flowers, borne several in succession from pairs of bracts on branched stems, from spring to summer. They have erect, linear to strap-shaped basal leaves, and 1 or 2 narrow leaves on the lower part of the flowering stems. Where marginally hardy, grow in a sheltered site, at the base of a warm, sunny wall, or in a cool greenhouse. In warmer areas, grow at the front of a border. *H. collina* is toxic to livestock.
• **CULTIVATION** Plant corms 4in (10cm) deep in autumn or spring. Under glass, grow in soil-based potting mix with equal parts additional sand and leaf mold, in full light, with good ventilation. Water freely in growth; reduce water gradually as the flowers fade, and keep completely dry when dormant. Store corms in a cool, dry place until autumn planting. Outdoors, grow in well-drained, fertile, humus-rich soil in full sun. Where temperatures regularly fall below 23°F (-5°C), provide a deep mulch or grow under glass.

Homeria collina

• **PROPAGATION** Sow seed at 61–64°F (16–18°C) in autumn. Separate offsets when dormant.
• **PESTS AND DISEASES** Infrequent.

H. collina ■ Cormous perennial with wiry, unbranched or rarely branched stems and linear, mid-green leaves, to 22in (55cm) long. Cup-shaped, scented, yellow, peach, or pink flowers, to 3in (8cm) across, are borne in succession from spring to summer. ↕6–16in (16–40cm), PD2in (5cm). South Africa. ❀ (min. 41°F/5°C)
H. ochroleuca. Upright, cormous perennial with branched stems and erect, linear, mid-green leaves, to 12in (30cm) long. Cup-shaped, musk-scented, pale yellow flowers, to 3in (8cm) across, sometimes with orange central stains, are borne from spring to summer. ↕16–24in (40–60cm), PD3in (8cm). South Africa. ❀ (min. 41°F/5°C)

▷ ***Homoglossum*** see *Gladiolus*

HOODIA

ASCLEPIADACEAE

Genus, closely related to *Trichocaulon*, of about 20 species of branching, leafless, perennial succulents found in periodically very dry areas of Angola, Namibia, Botswana, and South Africa. The many-angled, fleshy, grayish green stems have hard, thorn-like tubercles, and produce large, saucer- to cup-shaped or shallowly trumpet-shaped, unpleasantly scented flowers in the stem grooves toward the tips. Where temperatures fall below 50°F (10°C), grow in a warm greenhouse; in warm, dry areas, grow in a desert garden, trough, or raised bed.
• **CULTIVATION** Under glass, grow in standard cactus potting mix with additional leaf mold in full light; shade from hot sun, and provide low humidity. From spring to summer, water moderately and apply a low-nitrogen liquid fertilizer monthly; keep just moist in winter. Outdoors, grow in moderately fertile, sharply drained soil with additional leaf mold and sharp sand, in full sun with some midday shade. Protect from excessive winter moisture. See also pp.48–49.
• **PROPAGATION** Sow seed at 66–75°F (19–24°C) in spring.
• **PESTS AND DISEASES** Mealybugs may be a problem.

H. bainii ■ Erect succulent with fleshy stems branching from or near the base, with 12–15 angular ribs, each bearing tubercles with a brown spine. From summer to early autumn, cup-shaped to shallowly trumpet-shaped, beige-pink to dull yellow flowers, ¾–3in (2–8cm) across, with dark red-brown coronas, are borne singly, occasionally in clusters of 2 or 3. The 5 shallow petal lobes have outward-curved margins and small red dots at the centers. ↕8in (20cm), ↔ 4in (10cm). Namibia, South Africa (Western Cape, Northern Cape, Eastern Cape). ❀ (min. 50°F/10°C)
H. currorii. Erect succulent with thick, pale grayish green stems branching freely from the base. The stems have 15–25 angular ribs, each bearing tubercles with sharp, downward-pointing spines. From summer to early autumn, bears cup-

Hoodia bainii

shaped or shallowly trumpet-shaped, thick-stalked flowers, to 5in (13cm) across, singly or in clusters of up to 5. The flowers are green to ivory or pink, later becoming yellowish pink, and each has 5 rounded, violet-hairy lobes and a hairy, pale orange-red corolla. ↕24in (60cm), ↔ 8in (20cm). S.W. Angola, N.W. Namibia. ❀ (min. 50°F/10°C)
H. gordonii. Clump-forming succulent with erect stems branching from the base, each with 12–14 longitudinal ribs and short tubercles tipped with woody spines. Saucer-shaped flowers, 3–4in (7–10cm) across, are borne singly or in clusters of up to 3 blooms, from summer to early autumn. The flowers are pale brownish pink to maroon, with coronas of the same color, and each has 5 shallow petal lobes with outward-curved margins and small red dots at the centers. ↕18in (45cm) or more, ↔ 12in (30cm). S. Namibia, South Africa (Western Cape). ❀ (min. 50°F/10°C)

HORDEUM

Barley

POACEAE

Genus of about 20 species of annual and perennial grasses (including the cereal crop, barley) from disturbed ground in the temperate regions of both hemispheres. They have linear, flat or rolled, light to mid-green or blue-green leaves. Dense, narrow, cylindrical, occasionally flattened, spike-like panicles, with long-bristled spikelets, are borne in 2 ranks. The flowerheads of many species are useful for dried flower arrangements. Use in an annual, mixed, or herbaceous border, or in a wild garden.
• **CULTIVATION** Grow in well-drained, moderately fertile soil in full sun. Cut flowerheads for drying before fully mature.
• **PROPAGATION** Sow seed *in situ* in spring or autumn.
• **PESTS AND DISEASES** Many fungal and bacterial diseases may occur.

H. hystrix (Mediterranean barley). Densely tufted or solitary, annual grass with erect or arching, linear, flat, downy, mid-green leaves, to 3in (8cm) long. In early and midsummer, bears panicles, to 2½in (6cm) long, of stiff, gray-green spikelets, often flushed with purple. ↕to 16in (40cm), ↔ 12in (30cm). Mediterranean, C. Asia.
H. jubatum ■ (Squirrel-tail grass). Densely tufted, annual or perennial

Hordeum jubatum

grass with erect or arching, linear, light green leaves, to 6in (15cm) long. In early and midsummer, erect stems bear dense, broad, nodding panicles, to 5in (13cm) long, of silky, long-bristled, pale green spikelets, flushed red or purple, which turn beige with age. ↕20in (50cm), ↔ 12in (30cm). N.E. Asia, North America. Zones 5.

HORMINUM

LAMIACEAE

Genus of one species of low-growing, rhizomatous perennial from rocks, screes, and meadows in subalpine areas of the Pyrenees and European Alps. It has basal rosettes of dark green leaves, and is grown for its spikes of tubular-bell-shaped, usually violet flowers, borne in summer. Grow at the front of a herbaceous border or in a rock garden.
• **CULTIVATION** Grow in moderately fertile, well-drained soil in full sun.
• **PROPAGATION** Sow seed in autumn in containers in an open frame. Divide in spring.
• **PESTS AND DISEASES** Prone to slug and snail damage.

H. pyrenaicum ■ (Dragon's mouth, Pyrenean dead nettle). Perennial with rosettes of ovate, toothed, glossy, dark green leaves, to 3in (8cm) long. In summer, bears a succession of tubular-bell-shaped, 2-lipped flowers, to ¾in (2cm) long, in axillary whorls. The flowers have prominent stamens, and are usually dark violet-blue, occasionally pink or white. ↕8in (20cm), ↔ to 12in (30cm). Pyrenees, Alps. Zone 6b.

Horminum pyrenaicum

HOSTA

Plantain lily

LILIACEAE

Genus of about 70 species of mostly clump-forming, occasionally rhizomatous or stoloniferous perennials from sun-baked cliffs, rocky streamsides, woodland, and alpine meadows in China, Korea, Japan, and E. Russia. Numerous hybrids have also been raised, mainly in the US. Hostas are grown primarily for their bold foliage, produced in dense mounds of overlapping, ovate to heart-shaped or lance-shaped leaves (see panel below). The leaves may be green, yellow, gray-blue, or variegated, and are often glaucous. One-sided racemes of bell-, funnel-, or spider-shaped flowers, to 1¼in (3cm) long, are borne on usually leafless, sometimes leafy scapes, mainly in summer. They are followed by oblong, green, later pale brown seed capsules. Plant heights given in the descriptions below refer to the mounds of foliage; flower (scape) heights are given separately.

Hostas may be grown as accent plants or as groundcovers under deep-rooted, deciduous trees, in a mixed or herbaceous border, or near water. Smaller hostas are excellent for a rock garden, a peat bed, or containers.

• **HARDINESS** Hostas are very hardy, surviving temperatures to -40°F (-40°C). Zone 4 but some may survive in Zone 3b.

• **CULTIVATION** Grow in fertile, moist but well-drained soil. Hostas are shade tolerant and grow best with full morning sun in northern climates, and filtered shade in S. North America. Chinese species require full sun to bloom properly. Hostas will tolerate drought, although a summer mulch to retain moisture is usually beneficial.

• **PROPAGATION** Sow seed in containers in a cold frame in spring. Divide in late summer or early spring. Many new hostas are propagated through tissue culture.

• **PESTS AND DISEASES** Particularly susceptible to damage from slugs and snails. Container-grown plants are vulnerable to vine weevil. Viruses and foliar nematodes may also be problems.

***H.* 'Abba Dabba Do'.** Vigorous, clump-forming perennial with ovate to heart-shaped, dark green leaves, 12in (30cm) long, with bright yellow margins. Funnel-shaped, closely spaced, pale lavender flowers are produced on leaning, leafy scapes, to 3½ft (1.1m) long, in summer. ↕ 2ft (60cm), ↔ 4½ft (1.4m).

***H.* 'Abiqua Drinking Gourd'** ▣ Slow-growing, clump-forming perennial with deeply cupped, corrugated, blue-green, leaves, 11in (28cm) long. A large specimen producing tubular, near-white flowers, early in the season. ↕ 20in (50cm). ↔ 3½ft (1.1m).

H. albomarginata see *H. sieboldii.*

***H.* 'Alex Summers'** Clump-forming perennial, a sport of *H.* 'Gold Regal', has heart-shaped, green leaves, 9in (3½cm) long, marked with distinctive, irregular, bright gold margins. Large, upright plant, bearing bell-shaped lavender flowers in midseason. ↕ 22in (9cm), ↔ 3½ft (1.1m).

***H.* 'Allan P. McConnell'** ▣ Clump-forming perennial producing broadly to narrowly ovate, olive-green leaves, 3in (8cm) long, with narrow white margins. In midsummer, bears bell-shaped purple flowers on ridged scapes, 14–16in (35–40cm) long. ↕ 6–8in (15–20cm), ↔ 12–18in (30–45cm).

***H.* 'Allegan Fog'.** Clump-forming perennial with white-centered, slightly twisted leaves, 8in (20cm) long, splashed with flecks of green misting, surrounded by wide green margins. Bears pale tubular lavender flowers in midseason. ↕ 18in (45cm), ↔ 3½ft (1.1m).

***H.* 'Antioch'** ▣ Robust, clump-forming perennial with broadly ovate, tapered, arching, matte, dark green leaves, 10in (25cm) long, irregularly margined gray-green and creamy yellow, fading to white. In midsummer, arching, leafy scapes, 36in (90cm) long, bear funnel-shaped, lavender-blue flowers. ↕ 20in (50cm), ↔ 36in (90cm).

***H.* 'August Moon'.** Vigorous, clump-forming perennial with rounded to heart-shaped, cupped, puckered, pale green leaves, 6in (15cm) long, becoming golden yellow with a faint glaucous bloom. In summer, glaucous scapes, 28in (70cm) long, bear bell-shaped, grayish white flowers. ↕ 20in (50cm), ↔ 30in (75cm).

***H.* 'Aurora Borealis'** ▣ Clump-forming perennial with large, round, heavily puckered, blue-green leaves, 8in (20cm) long, with gold margins. In midsummer, bears bell-shaped, pale lavender flowers on glaucous scapes, 26in (65cm) long. ↕ 24in (60cm), ↔ 36in (90cm).

***H.* 'Baby Bunting'.** Clump-forming perennial produces a small, compact mound of rounded, blue-green leaves, 2½in (6cm). Tubular purple flowers are borne in midseason. ↕ 10in (25cm), ↔ 24in (60cm).

Hosta 'Dick Ward'

***H.* 'Big Daddy'.** Clump-forming perennial with rounded to heart-shaped, cupped, deeply puckered, glaucous, gray-blue leaves, 11in (28cm) long. In early summer, bears bell-shaped, grayish white flowers on leafy, glaucous scapes, 32in (80cm) long. ↕ 24in (60cm), ↔ 36in (90cm).

***H.* 'Birchwood Parky's Gold'.** Vigorous, clump-forming perennial with heart-shaped, matte, yellow-green leaves, 5in (13cm) long, becoming rich yellow with age. In midsummer, scapes 28in (70cm) long bear bell-shaped, pale lavender-blue flowers. ↕ 14–16in (35–40cm), ↔ 30in (75cm).

***H.* 'Blue Angel'.** Slow-growing, clump-forming perennial with ovate to heart-shaped, wavy, glaucous, bluish gray leaves, 16in (40cm) long. In mid-summer, bears bell-shaped white flowers on glaucous scapes, 36in (90cm) long. ↕ 36in (90cm), ↔ 4ft (1.2m).

***H.* 'Blue Blush'.** Clump-forming perennial with lance-shaped, glaucous, deep blue-green leaves, 4in (10cm) long. Bell-shaped, lavender-blue flowers are borne on glaucous scapes, 10in (25cm) long, in midsummer. ↕ 8in (20cm), ↔ 14–16in (35–40cm).

***H.* 'Blue Dimples'.** Clump-forming perennial with ovate to heart-shaped, thick, glaucous, blue-green leaves, 7in (18cm) long, becoming dimpled with wavy margins when mature. In midsummer, bell-shaped, lilac flowers are produced on glaucous scapes, 20in (50cm) long. ↕ 14in (35cm), ↔ 20in (50cm).

***H.* 'Blue Moon'** ▣ Slow-growing, clump-forming perennial producing broadly heart-shaped, pointed, glaucous, deep blue-green leaves, 3in (8cm) long, becoming slightly puckered with age. In midsummer, glaucous scapes, 12in (30cm) long, bear dense racemes of bell-shaped, pale mauve-gray flowers. ↕ 4in (10cm), ↔ 12in (30cm).

***H.* 'Blue Skies'.** Clump-forming perennial with heart-shaped, pointed, flat, smooth, glaucous, blue-green leaves, 5in (13cm) long. In midsummer, bears bell-shaped, lavender-blue flowers on glaucous scapes, 16in (40cm) long. ↕ 8in (20cm), ↔ 16in (40cm).

***H.* 'Blue Wedgwood'.** Clump-forming perennial with ovate to lance-shaped, pointed, wavy, glaucous, gray-blue leaves, 6in (15cm) long, dimpled when mature. Bell-shaped, pale lavender-blue flowers are borne on glaucous scapes, 16in (40cm) long, in midsummer. ↕ 10in (25cm), ↔ 22in (55cm).

***H.* 'Bobbie Sue'.** Clump-forming perennial bearing attractive shiny, dark green leaves, 10in (25cm) long, with wide, creamy white, slightly rippled margins. Flowers are tubular, lavender, produced in midseason. ↕ 26in (65cm), ↔ 4½ft (1.4m).

***H.* 'Bright Lights'** ▣ Slow-growing, clump-forming perennial with rounded, cupped, heavily puckered, green-yellow leaves, 8–12in (20–30cm) long, with irregular, blue-green margins and centers splashed with blue-green. Bears bell-shaped white flowers on leafy, glaucous scapes, 16in (40cm) long, in early summer. ↕ 14in (35cm), ↔ 24in (60cm).

***H.* 'Candy Hearts'.** Vigorous, clump-forming perennial with heart-shaped, pointed, greenish gray-blue leaves, 6in (15cm) long. Bell-shaped, pale lavender-blue to off-white flowers are borne on

HOSTA LEAF SHAPES

Hostas are grown for their bold leaves, which may be ovate, lance-shaped, rounded, or heart-shaped.

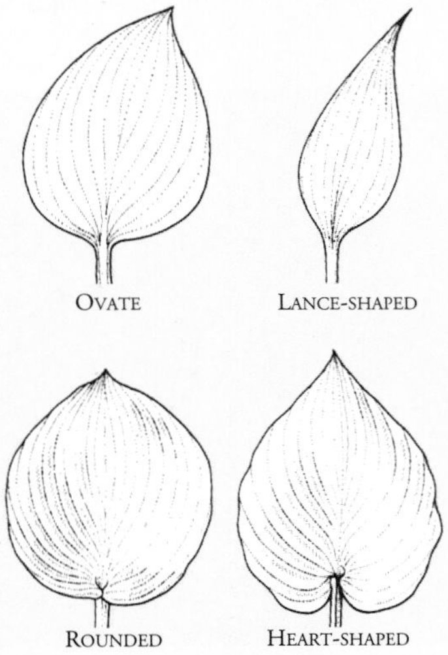

HOSTA LEAF VARIEGATION

Many hostas have attractively variegated foliage. The leaves may be widely or narrowly margined in a paler color, or have a wide, pale, central marking and darker margins.

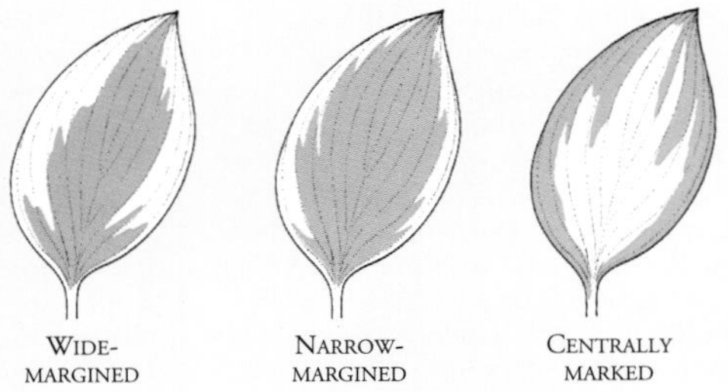

scapes 20in (50cm) long, in summer. ↕ 14–16in (35–40cm), ↔ 22in (55cm).
H. capitata. Clump-forming perennial producing ovate to heart-shaped, thin, ruffled leaves, to 5in (13cm) long, with wavy margins. They are deep olive-green with sunken veins, glossy beneath. In midsummer, bell-shaped purple flowers with darker purple veins, open from spherical buds on straight, ridged, leafy scapes, 12–16in (30–40cm) long. Well-established plants are sometimes remontant. ↕ 7in (18cm), ↔ 18in (45cm). Korea, Japan.
***H.* 'Captain Kirk'.** Fast-growing, clump-forming perennial, a sport of *H.* 'Gold Standard', has heart-shaped leaves, 8in (20cm) long, divided into 3 equal parts: one-third green margin, one-third bright gold center, one-third green margin. Bears pale lavender flowers in midseason. ↕ 23in (58cm). ↔ 3½ft (1.1m).
***H.* 'Choko Nishiki'** see *H.* 'On Stage'.
***H.* 'Christmas Tree'.** Clump-forming perennial with heart-shaped, deeply puckered, glaucous, mid- to dark green leaves, 8in (20cm) long, having irregular, creamy white margins. In midsummer, bears funnel-shaped, very pale lavender-white flowers on arching, leafy scapes, 24in (60cm) long. ↕ 18in (45cm), ↔ 36in (90cm).
H. clausa. Stoloniferous perennial with ovate to lance-shaped, pointed, flat, shiny, mid-green leaves, 5in (13cm) long. In early summer, non-opening, deep lavender buds are borne on erect scapes, 16in (40cm) long. ↕ 10in (25cm), ↔ 24in (60cm). China, Korea.
***H.* 'Delta Dawn'.** Slow-growing, clump-forming perennial produces an attractive mound of chartreuse leaves, 8in (20cm) long, with irregular, creamy white margins. Bell-shaped, near-white flowers appear in midseason. ↕ 20in (50cm), ↔ 4ft (1.2m).
***H.* 'Diamond Tiara'.** Vigorous perennial forming a compact mound of ovate to heart-shaped, slightly wavy-margined, thin, pale olive-green leaves, 4in (10cm) long, irregularly margined cream to white and splashed gray-green. In midsummer, bears bell-shaped, sometimes remontant violet flowers on scapes 28in (70cm) long. ↕ 14in (35cm), ↔ 26in (65cm).
***H.* 'Diana Remembered'** ■ Fast-growing, clump-forming perennial has shiny green leaves, 7in (18cm) long, with attractive, wide, creamy white margins. Produces very large, 3in (8cm), fragrant, tubular, near-white flowers, late in the season. Tolerant of direct sun. ↕ 15in (37cm), ↔ 24in (60cm).
***H.* 'Dick Ward'** ■ Slow-growing, clump-forming perennial, a sport of *H.* 'Zounds', has nearly round, heavily corrugated, bright gold leaves, 11in (28cm) long, with green margins. Produces tubular, pale lavender flowers in summer. ↕ 24in (60cm), ↔ 4ft (1.2m).
***H.* 'Dorset Blue'.** Slow-growing, clump-forming perennial with ovate to heart-shaped, slightly cupped, puckered, thick, dark blue-green leaves, 3in (8cm) long, very glaucous beneath. In midsummer, bears bell-shaped, lavender-white flowers on thick, leafy, glaucous, grayish mauve scapes, 10in (25cm) long. ↕ 8in (20cm), ↔ 18in (45cm).
***H.* 'Dream Weaver'** ■ Slow-growing, clump-forming perennial, with nearly round, corrugated, blue-green leaves, 9in (23cm) long, with narrow white leaf center. Early in the season, produces a bell-shaped near-white flower. It is a sport of *H.* 'Great Expectations', but its wider blue-green margined leaves make it more vigorous. ↕ 18in (45cm), ↔ 30in (75cm).
***H.* 'Dress Blues'.** Clump-forming perennial produces a uniform mound of pointed, blue-green leaves, 7in (18cm) long, with yellow margin, turning creamy white later in the season, when tubular, pale lavender flowers are borne. ↕ 24in (60cm), ↔ 36in (90cm).
***H.* 'Earth Angel'** ■ Slow-growing, clump-forming perennial, a sport of *H.* 'Blue Angel', has heart-shaped, blue-green leaves, 12in (30cm) long, with irregular, creamy white margins. Bell-shaped, pale lavender flowers appear in summer. ↕ 16in (40cm), ↔ 3ft (90cm).
***H.* 'Emerald Tiara'.** Vigorous perennial forming a compact mound of broadly lance-shaped to ovate or heart-shaped, slightly wavy, bright green leaves, 4in (10cm) long. Bell-shaped violet flowers, sometimes remontant, are borne on scapes 28in (70cm) long, in midsummer. ↕ 14in (35cm), ↔ 26in (65cm).
***H.* 'First Frost'** ■ Slow-growing, clump-forming perennial, a sport of *H.* 'Halcyon'. In spring, produces an attractive combination of heart-shaped, powdery blue-green leaves, 7in (18cm) long, with irregular white margins, later becoming dark green with creamy white margins. The flowers are tubular and pale lavender. ↕ 14in (35cm), ↔ 36in (90cm).
***H. fluctuans* 'Sagae'** see *H.* 'Sagae'.
***H. fluctuans* 'Variegated'** see *H.* 'Sagae'.
***H.* 'Fortunei.'** Vigorous, clump-forming perennial with ovate, pointed, matte, dark green leaves, 8–12in (20–30cm) long. In midsummer, leafy scapes, 32in (80cm) long, bear funnel-shaped mauve flowers. ↕ 22in (55cm), ↔ 32in (80cm). **'Fortunei Albomarginata'** has large, dull, mid- to deep green leaves, to 12in (30cm) long, the irregular cream margins turning white with age. The amount of variegation may vary from year to year. **'Fortunei Albopicta'**, syn. *H.* 'Aureomaculata', produces narrowly heart-shaped, thin, creamy yellow leaves, 8–10in (20–25cm) long, irregularly margined dark green, fading slowly to dull mid-green; ↔ 36in (90cm). **'Fortunei Aureomarginata'.** syn. *H.* 'Obscura Marginata', has ovate to heart-shaped, leathery, distinctly veined, deep olive-green leaves, 8–10in (20–25cm) long, irregularly margined yellow. The flowers are borne freely on scapes 34in (85cm) long, in summer. Tolerates sun or partial shade; ↔ 36in (90cm). **'Fortunei Gloriosa'** is slow-growing, producing narrowly elliptic, cupped, slightly puckered, glossy, dark olive-green leaves, 6in (15cm) long, with regular, very narrow white margins. In summer, lavender-blue flowers are borne on scapes 36in (90cm) long; ↕ 18in (45cm), ↔ 24in (60cm). **'Fortunei Hyacinthina'**, syn. *H.* 'Hyacinthina', produces ovate to heart-shaped, wavy, slightly puckered, thick, glaucous, gray-green leaves, finely margined white and blue-gray beneath. In summer, violet flowers are borne freely on slightly arching, glaucous scapes, 36in (90cm) long; ↕ 24in (60cm), ↔ 36in (90cm).

Hosta 'First Frost'

***H.* 'Fragrant Bouquet'.** Clump-forming perennial producing ovate to heart-shaped, slightly wavy-margined, glossy, pale green leaves, 8in (20cm) long, with irregular, creamy yellow margins. In late summer, funnel-shaped, fragrant, mauvish white flowers are borne on scapes 36in (90cm) long. Tolerates sun or partial shade. ↕ 18in (45cm), ↔ 26in (65cm).
***H.* 'Francee'** ■ Vigorous, clump-forming perennial producing ovate to heart-shaped, slightly cupped, puckered, olive-green leaves, 7in (18cm) long, with irregular white margins. Arching, leafy scapes, 30in (75cm) long, bear funnel-shaped, lavender-blue flowers in summer. ↕ 22in (55cm), ↔ 36in (90cm).
***H.* 'Frances Williams'** ■ syn. *H.* 'Golden Circles', *H. sieboldiana* 'Frances Williams', *H. sieboldiana* 'Yellow Edge'. Clump-forming perennial producing heart-shaped, cupped, very puckered, thick, glaucous, blue-green leaves, 8in (20cm) long, with wide, irregular, green-yellow margins. In early summer, bears bell-shaped, grayish white flowers

Hosta 'Abiqua Drinking Gourd'

Hosta 'Allan P. McConnell'

Hosta 'Antioch'

Hosta 'Aurora Borealis'

Hosta 'Blue Moon'

Hosta 'Bright Lights'

Hosta 'Diana Remembered'

Hosta 'Dream Weaver'

Hosta 'Earth Angel'

H

on glaucous scapes, 26in (65cm) long. ↕ 24in (60cm), ↔ 36in (90cm).

***H.* 'Frosted Jade'** ■ Clump-forming perennial with ovate, pointed, glaucous, dark green leaves, 12in (30cm) long, with narrow white margins and splashed gray-green, giving the appearance of frosting. Funnel-shaped, very pale lavender-blue, almost white flowers are borne on arching, leafy scapes, to 3½ft (1.1m) long, in early summer. ↕ 32in (80cm), ↔ 36in (90cm).

***H.* 'Ginko Craig'.** Clump-forming perennial with lance-shaped, flat, dark green leaves, 3in (8cm) long, margined clear white. Mature plants (after about 4 years if not divided) have broader leaves with wider margins. In summer, bare scapes, 18in (45cm) long, bear funnel-shaped, deep purple to violet flowers. ↕ 10in (25cm), ↔ 18in (45cm).

***H.* 'Golden Sculpture'** ■ Clump-forming perennial produces very large, heart-shaped, corrugated, golden yellow leaves, 16in (40cm) long, from a substantial mound. Flowers are bell-shaped and near-white, borne in summer. ↕ 33in (82cm), ↔ 6ft (2m).

***H.* 'Golden Tiara'** ■ Vigorous perennial forming a mound of ovate to heart-shaped, mid-green leaves, 4in (10cm) long, irregularly margined with yellow. In summer, scapes 24in (60cm) long bear bell-shaped, deep purple, sometimes remontant flowers, striped lavender-purple. ↕ 12in (30cm), ↔ 20in (50cm).

***H.* 'Gold Regal'.** Clump-forming perennial with erect leaf stalks bearing ovate, slightly concave, erect, thick, pale green-yellow leaves, 7in (18cm) long; they only color well in full sun. Dense racemes of bell-shaped, grayish purple flowers, 1–3in (2.5–8cm) long, are borne on glaucous scapes, 28in (70cm) long, in summer. ↕ 24in (60cm), ↔ 36in (90cm).

***H.* 'Gold Standard'** ■ Clump-forming perennial with ovate to heart-shaped, green-yellow leaves, 7in (18cm) long, fading through yellow to cream, and narrowly and irregularly margined dark green. In midsummer, funnel-shaped, lavender-blue flowers are borne on scapes to 3½ft (1.1m) long. ↕ 26in (65cm), ↔ 36in (90cm).

H. gracillima. Clump-forming perennial with lance-shaped, wavy-margined leaves, ¾–2½in (2–6cm) long, glossy, deep green above, paler beneath. From summer to autumn, arching, leafless, purple-dotted scapes, 8–10in (20–25cm) long, bear widely funnel-shaped, lavender-blue flowers, purple-striped inside. ↕ 2in (5cm), ↔ 7in (18cm). Japan.

Hosta 'Guacamole'

***H.* 'Great Expectations'** ■ Clump-forming perennial with green-margined white leaf stalks bearing heart-shaped, stiff, puckered, thick leaves, 6in (15cm) long; they are glaucous yellow, fading to white with age, with irregular, wide, blue-green margins. In early summer, bears bell-shaped, grayish white flowers on leafy scapes, 34in (85cm) long. ↕ 22in (55cm), ↔ 34in (85cm).

***H.* 'Green Fountain'.** Clump-forming perennial with red-dotted leaf stalks bearing lance-shaped, tapering, arching, wavy-margined, glossy, mid-green leaves, 10in (25cm) long. In summer, bears funnel-shaped, widely spaced, pale mauve flowers on arching, leafy, red-dotted scapes, 24in (60cm) long. ↕ 18in (45cm), ↔ 36in (90cm).

***H.* 'Green Piecrust'.** Clump-forming perennial with heart-shaped, deeply veined, mid-green leaves, 14in (35cm) long, with ruffled margins. Funnel-shaped white flowers are produced on leaning scapes, 3½ft (1.1m) long, in late spring or early summer. ↕ 28in (70cm), ↔ 4ft (1.2m).

***H.* 'Ground Master'.** Vigorous, stoloniferous, prostrate perennial with ovate to lance-shaped, matte, olive-green leaves, 5in (13cm) long, with wavy, irregular cream margins, fading to white. Mature plants (after about 4 years if not divided) have broader leaves with wider margins. In summer, produces funnel-shaped purple flowers on straight, leafy scapes, 20in (50cm) long. ↕ 10in (25cm), ↔ 22in (55cm).

***H.* 'Guacamole'** ■ Fast-growing, clump-forming perennial, a sport of *H.* 'Fragrant Bouquet'. Shiny leaves, 11in (28cm) long, emerge chartreuse and become brighter gold, later in the season; margins are wide and dark green. Fragrant, attractive flowers, borne late in the season, are trumpet-shaped and near-white. Tolerant of direct sun. ↕ 24in (60cm), ↔ 4½ft (1.4m).

***H.* 'Guardian Angel'** ■ Clump-forming perennial, a sport of *H.* 'Blue Angel', with showy spring display of misted green and white leaves, 13in (37cm) long, bordered with blue-green coloration; later in the season, the slightly folded, twisted leaves turn completely blue-green, and tubular, near-white flowers appear. ↕ 28in (70cm), ↔ 4½ft (1.4m).

***H.* 'Gypsy Rose'** ■ Fast-growing, clump-forming perennial, a sport of *H.* 'Striptease'. Its pointed, oval, heart-shaped leaves, 6in (15cm) long, have an unusual white stripe separating the yellow-green center from wide, dark green margins. Produces its funnel-shaped, pale lavender flowers in summer. ↕ 16in (40cm), ↔ 3½ft (1.1m).

***H.* 'Hadspen Blue'** ■ Slow-growing, clump-forming perennial with ovate to heart-shaped, thick, glaucous, close-veined, gray-blue leaves, 5in (13cm) long. In summer, purple-dotted scapes, 14in (35cm) long, bear dense racemes of bell-shaped, pale gray-mauve flowers. ↕ 10in (25cm), ↔ 24in (60cm).

***H.* 'Hadspen Heron'.** Clump-forming perennial with narrowly lance-shaped, slightly wavy-margined, glaucous, gray-blue leaves, 4in (10cm) long. In summer, bears bell-shaped, gray-mauve flowers on scapes 12in (30cm) long. ↕ 9in (23cm), ↔ 22in (55cm).

Hosta 'Guardian Angel'

***H.* 'Halcyon'** ■ Clump-forming perennial with heart-shaped, smooth, thick, glaucous, bright gray-blue leaves, 8in (20cm) long. In summer, bears dense racemes of bell-shaped, lavender-gray flowers on scapes 18in (45cm) long. ↕ 14–16in (35–40cm), ↔ 28in (70cm).

***H.* 'Honeybells'.** Vigorous perennial forming a lax, open mound of ovate to heart-shaped, slightly wavy-margined, strongly veined, lustrous, pale green leaves, 11in (28cm) long. Fragrant, bell-shaped, white, sometimes lavender-blue-striped flowers are borne on leafy scapes, 36in (90cm) long, in late summer. ↕ 30in (75cm), ↔ 4ft (1.2m).

***H.* 'Hyacinthina'** see *H.* 'Fortunei Hyacinthina'.

H. hypoleuca. Clump-forming perennial with broadly ovate to heart-shaped, slightly wavy-margined, glaucous, pale green leaves, 10–18in (25–45cm) long, intensely white-coated beneath. In summer, bears bell-shaped, very pale lavender-blue flowers on arching, leafy, glaucous, red-dotted scapes, 14in (35cm) long. Thrives in sun or partial shade. ↕ 18in (45cm), ↔ 36in (90cm). Japan.

***H.* 'Invincible'** ■ Vigorous, clump-forming perennial with ovate-oblong to lance-shaped, tapered, wavy-margined, thick, glossy, dark olive-green leaves, 5in (13cm) long. In late summer, funnel-shaped, fragrant, pale lavender-blue to white flowers are borne on arching, leafy scapes, 20in (50cm) long. Grow in sun or partial shade. ↕ 12in (30cm), ↔ 24in (60cm).

***H.* 'Jewel of the Nile'** ■ Clump-forming perennial, a sport of *H.* 'Dee's Golden Jewel'. Produces leaves, 11in (28cm) long, that display a blue-green center with wide, irregular gold margins. Tubular, near-white flowers are borne in summer. ↕ 22in (55cm), ↔ 4ft (1.2m).

***H.* 'June'.** Clump-forming perennial, a variegated sport of *H.* 'Halcyon', with heart-shaped, smooth, glaucous, gray-blue leaves, 8in (20cm) long, centrally and irregularly variegated yellow and yellow-green. In summer, bears racemes of bell-shaped, lavender-gray flowers on glaucous scapes, 18in (45cm) long. ↕ 14–16in (35–40cm), ↔ 28in (70cm).

***H.* 'Kabitan'** ■ syn. *H. sieboldii* 'Kabitan'. Clump-forming perennial producing lance-shaped, thin, bright yellow leaves, 10in (25cm) long, with rippled, dark green margins. In late summer, bears narrow, later flaring, funnel-shaped, deep violet flowers on leafy scapes, 12in (30cm) long. ↕ 8in (20cm), ↔ 10in (25cm).

H. kikutii. Clump-forming perennial with ovate to lance-shaped or elliptic, tapered, prominently veined, arching, glossy, dark green leaves, 7–9in (18–23cm) long, lustrous beneath. In summer, bears dense racemes of funnel-shaped, white, sometimes faintly purple-flushed flowers on arching, leafy, red-dotted scapes, 24in (60cm) long. ↕ 16in (40cm), ↔ 24in (60cm). Japan.

***H.* 'Krossa Regal'.** Clump-forming perennial with semi-erect, ovate to

Hosta 'On Stage'

lance-shaped, deeply veined, glaucous, bluish green leaves, 9in (23cm) long. In summer, glaucous scapes, 4½ft (1.4m) long, bear bell-shaped, pale lilac flowers. ↕28in (70cm), ↔30in (75cm).
***H.* 'Lancifolia'.** Perennial forming a dense mound of arching, narrowly lance-shaped, thin, glossy, dark green leaves, 4–7in (10–18cm) long. In late summer, slender, very leafy, red-dotted scapes, 26in (65cm) long, bear narrowly funnel-shaped, deep purple flowers. ↕18in (45cm), ↔30in (75cm).
***H.* 'Lemon Lime'** ▣ Vigorous, clump-forming perennial with lance-shaped, wavy, thin, yellow-green to yellow leaves, 3in (8cm) long. In summer, bears remontant, bell-shaped, purple-striped flowers on scapes 12in (30cm) long. ↕6in (15cm), ↔18in (45cm).
***H.* 'Liberty'** ▣ Slow-growing, clump-forming perennial, a tetraploid sport of *H.* 'Sagae'. Produces very showy, upright-held leaves, 12in (30cm) long, with yellow margins that fade to creamy white later in the season. Bears tubular, pale lavender flowers in summer. ↕39in (100cm), ↔40in (102cm).
H. longipes. Vigorous, clump-forming perennial with ovate to heart-shaped, sometimes rounded, slightly wavy-margined, mid- to deep green leaves, 3½–5in (9–13cm) long, glossy beneath, and spotted purple at the bases of the midribs and on the leaf stalks. In late summer and autumn, leafy, purple-dotted scapes, 16in (40cm) long, bear bell-shaped, wide-tubed, pale purple to chalky white flowers. ↕12in (30cm), ↔20in (50cm). Korea, Japan.
H. longissima ▣ Moisture-loving, upright, clump-forming perennial with narrowly lance-shaped, erect to arching, dark green leaves, 6–8in (15–20cm) long, glossy beneath. In late summer, bears long racemes of funnel-shaped, purple-striped mauve flowers on leafy scapes, 22in (55cm) long. ↕10in (25cm), ↔20in (50cm). Japan.
***H.* 'Love Pat'** ▣ Slow-growing, clump-forming perennial with upright, heart-shaped, cupped, very puckered, thick, glaucous, deep blue-gray leaves, 6in (15cm) long. In midsummer, bell-shaped, off-white flowers are borne on scapes 22in (55cm) long. ↕18in (45cm), ↔36in (90cm).
***H.* 'Mediovariegata'** see *H.* 'Undulata'.
H. montana. Clump-forming perennial with ovate to heart-shaped, thick, boldly veined leaves, 8–12in (20–30cm) long, varying from shiny, mid- to dark green

Hosta 'Patriot'

to glaucous, pale green, with rough undersides. Leafy, purple-dotted scapes, 36in (90cm) long, bear funnel-shaped, gray-mauve to white flowers in early summer. ↕30in (75cm), ↔36in (90cm). Japan. **'Aureomarginata'** has narrower, tapering, wavy-margined, glossy, dark green leaves, 12in (30cm) long, with irregular yellow margins, turning cream; the leaves emerge early in spring. Scapes are 36in (90cm) long; ↕28in (70cm), ↔36in (90cm).
***H.* 'Moonlight'.** Clump-forming perennial with ovate to heart-shaped, cupped, olive-green leaves, 7in (18cm) long, fading to yellow, and irregularly margined white. In midsummer, bears funnel-shaped, lavender-blue flowers on straight, leafy scapes, 26in (65cm) long. ↕20in (50cm), ↔28in (70cm).
***H.* 'Neat Splash Rim'.** Stoloniferous perennial with broadly lance-shaped, olive-green leaves, 7in (18cm) long, boldly margined with cream, fading to white. Bears funnel-shaped purple flowers on leafy scapes, 20in (50cm) long, in late summer. ↕14in (35cm), ↔24in (60cm).
H. nigrescens ▣ Clump-forming perennial with ovate-heart-shaped, concave, partly wrinkled, glaucous, gray-green leaves, 10–18in (25–45cm) long. In late summer, leafy, glaucous scapes, 4½ft (1.4m) long, bear funnel-shaped white flowers. ↕28in (70cm), ↔26in (65cm). Japan.
***H.* 'On Stage'** ▣ syn. *H.* 'Choko Nishiki'. Clump-forming perennial with ovate to heart-shaped, tapered, light yellow leaves, 8in (20cm) long, irregularly margined and splashed dark and light green. In early summer, bears funnel-shaped, pale lavender-blue flowers on scapes 20in (50cm) long. ↕14in (35cm), ↔24in (60cm).
***H.* 'Orange Marmalade'** ▣ Clump-forming perennial, a sport of *H.* 'Paul's Glory'. In spring, leaves emerge a very bright gold, 7½in (19cm) long, then begin turning lighter, to parchment white, as the season progresses. Margins are blue-green. In summer, tubular, pale lavender flowers appear. ↕20in (50cm), ↔4ft (1.2m).
***H.* 'Patriot'** ▣ Vigorous, clump-forming perennial with ovate to heart-shaped, slightly cupped, puckered, olive-green leaves, 8in (20cm) long, widely and irregularly margined white, and with gray-green splashes. In summer, bears funnel-shaped, lavender-blue flowers on leafy scapes, 30in (75cm) long. ↕22in (55cm), ↔36in (90cm).
***H.* 'Paul's Glory'** ▣ Clump-forming perennial with heart-shaped, puckered yellow leaves, 6in (15cm) long, irregularly margined glaucous, gray-blue and yellow-green. In midsummer, leafy, arching, glaucous scapes, 24in (60cm) long, bear bell-shaped, lavender-gray flowers. ↕20in (50cm), ↔36in (90cm).
***H.* 'Piedmont Gold'** ▣ Robust, clump-forming perennial with narrowly heart-shaped, wavy-margined, matte, glaucous yellow leaves, 11in (28cm) long. In summer, bears funnel-shaped, grayish white flowers on scapes 26in (65cm) long. ↕20in (50cm), ↔36in (90cm).
***H.* 'Pizzazz'.** Clump-forming perennial producing ovate to heart-shaped, puckered, glaucous, mid-green leaves, 7in (18cm) long, splashed blue-green and irregularly margined cream. Bell-

Hosta 'Francee'

Hosta 'Frances Williams'

Hosta 'Frosted Jade'

Hosta 'Golden Sculpture'

Hosta 'Golden Tiara'

Hosta 'Gold Standard'

Hosta 'Great Expectations'

Hosta 'Gypsy Rose'

Hosta 'Hadspen Blue'

Hosta 'Halcyon'

Hosta 'Invincible'

Hosta 'Jewel of the Nile'

Hosta 'Kabitan'

Hosta 'Lemon Lime'

Hosta 'Liberty'

Hosta longissima

Hosta 'Love Pat'

Hosta nigrescens

Hosta 'Orange Marmalade'

Hosta 'Paul's Glory'

Hosta 'Piedmont Gold'

shaped, pale lavender-blue flowers are freely borne on leafy, glaucous scapes, 18in (45cm) long, in summer. ↕ 14in (35cm), ↔ 24in (60cm).

H. plantaginea. Clump-forming perennial with ovate to heart-shaped, slightly wavy, glossy, light green leaves, 6–11in (16–28cm) long, with prominent, widely spaced, raised veins. Trumpet-shaped, long-tubed, very fragrant white flowers, 4in (10cm) long, are borne on leafy, bright green scapes, 26–30in (65–75cm) long, in late summer and early autumn. Prefers a sunny site. ↕ 24in (60cm), ↔ 36in (90cm). China. **'Aphrodite'** bears double flowers that hardly ever open. **'Venus'** has ovate, wavy leaves, 9in (23cm) long, and bears double flowers, 4in (10cm) long.

H. pycnophylla. Slow-growing, clump-forming perennial with ovate to heart-shaped, very wavy-margined, glaucous, dull, light green leaves, 8–10in (20–25cm) long, coated white beneath. In late summer, bears funnel-shaped, purple to dark purple flowers on arching, leafy, glaucous, purple-dotted scapes, 14in (35cm) long. ↕ 12in (30cm), ↔ 28in (70cm). Japan.

***H.* 'Rainforest Sunrise'.** Fast-growing, clump-forming perennial, a sport of *H.* 'Maui Buttercups'. Produces round, cupped, corrugated, bright yellow leaves, 5in (13cm) long, with emerald green margins. Bell-shaped, violet flowers are borne in summer. ↕ 10in (25cm), ↔ 18in (45cm).

H. rectifolia. Sturdy, clump-forming perennial with ovate, shallowly cupped, dull to dark green leaves, to 12in (30cm) long. In late summer, bears widely spaced racemes of bell-shaped, deep-purple-striped purple flowers on thick, leafy scapes, 24–30in (60–75cm) long. ↕ 18in (45cm), ↔ 30in (75cm). Japan, Russia (Kurile Islands).

***H.* 'Regal Splendor'** ▣ Clump-forming perennial with long, arching leaf stalks bearing ovate to lance-shaped, semi-erect, deeply veined, thick, glaucous, gray-green leaves, 12in (30cm) long, irregularly margined white to yellow. In summer, bears bell-shaped, grayish pink flowers on glaucous scapes, 4½ft (1.4m) long. ↕ 30in (75cm), ↔ 36in (90cm).

***H.* 'Robusta'** see *H. sieboldiana* var. *elegans.*

***H.* 'Royal Standard'** ▣ Vigorous, clump-forming perennial with ovate to heart-shaped, ribbed, glossy, bright pale green leaves, 8in (20cm) long. Funnel-shaped, fragrant white flowers, 1–3in (2.5–8cm) long, are borne on leafy scapes, 36in (90cm) long, in late summer. Tolerates sun or partial shade. ↕ 24in (60cm), ↔ 4ft (1.2m).

H. rupifraga. Clump-forming perennial with broadly ovate-heart-shaped, wavy-margined, smooth, thick, glossy, dark green leaves, 5–6in (12–15cm) long, mid-green beneath. In early autumn, arching, leafy, glaucous, purple-dotted scapes, 12–16in (30–40cm) long, bear dense racemes of bell-shaped, light mauve flowers. ↕ 8in (20cm), ↔ 24in (60cm). Japan.

***H.* 'Ryan's Big One'** ▣ Clump-forming perennial with rounded to heart-shaped, deeply puckered, thick, glaucous, grayish blue leaves, 18in (45cm) long, light glaucous gray beneath. Bell-shaped, white flowers are borne on glaucous gray scapes, 34in (85cm) long, just barely above the leaf mound, in late spring. ↕ 34in (85cm), ↕ 5ft (1.5m).

Hosta 'Stained Glass'

***H.* 'Sagae'**, syn. *H. fluctuans* 'Sagae', *H. fluctuans* 'Variegated'. Clump-forming perennial with erect leaf stalks bearing ovate to lance-shaped, horizontal, wavy-margined leaves, 8–12in (20–30cm) long, glaucous, dull olive-green above, glaucous, mid-green beneath, and boldly margined creamy yellow. In mid- and late summer, thick, semi-erect, leafy, glaucous scapes, 4ft (1.2m) long, bear long racemes of bell-shaped white flowers, 2–2½in (5–6cm) long, suffused violet to pale purple. ↕↔ 36in (90cm).

***H.* 'Saishu Jima'.** Vigorous perennial with narrowly lance-shaped, wavy-margined, dark green leaves, 4in (10cm) long. In mid- and late summer, bears bell-shaped, dark purple-striped purple flowers on scapes 9in (23cm) long. ↕ 8in (20cm), ↔ 14–16in (35–40cm).

***H.* 'Sea Drift'.** Slow-growing, clump-forming perennial with heart-shaped, pointed, wavy-margined, dark green leaves, 14in (35cm) long. In summer, funnel-shaped, lavender-blue flowers are borne on scapes 28in (70cm) long. ↕ 24in (60cm), ↔ 36in (90cm).

***H.* 'Sea Octopus'.** Slow-growing, clump-forming perennial with heart-shaped, pointed, very wavy-margined, dark green leaves, 6in (15cm) long. In summer, funnel-shaped, lavender-blue flowers are produced on scapes 28in (70cm) long. ↕ 8in (20cm), ↔ 36in (90cm).

***H.* 'September Sun'** ▣ Vigorous, clump-forming perennial with ovate to heart-shaped, flat, lime-green to yellow leaves, 6in (15cm) long, irregularly margined dark green, the variegation developing as the leaves mature. In summer, scapes 30in (75cm) long bear bell-shaped, very pale lavender-blue flowers. Thrives in sun or partial shade. ↕ 26in (65cm), ↔ 36in (90cm).

***H.* 'Shade Fanfare'** ▣ Clump-forming perennial with heart-shaped, wavy-margined, light to mid-green leaves, 7in (18cm) long, irregularly margined cream, turning white with age. Bears many funnel-shaped, lavender-blue flowers on leafy scapes, 24in (60cm) long, in summer. ↕ 18in (45cm), ↕ 24in (60cm).

***H.* 'Shining Tot'.** Clump-forming perennial with heart-shaped, flat, thick, glossy, dark green leaves, 1¼in (3cm) long. Funnel-shaped, lavender-blue flowers are borne on arching, bare scapes, 6in (15cm) long, in summer. ↕ 2in (5cm), ↔ 8in (20cm).

H. sieboldiana, syn. *H.* 'Sieboldiana'. Imposing, clump-forming perennial with ovate-heart-shaped to rounded, cupped, puckered, thick leaves, 10–20in (25–50cm) long, glaucous, gray-green to blue above, paler, sometimes glaucous beneath. In early summer, leafy, glaucous scapes, 36in (90cm) long, bear bell-shaped, pale lilac-gray flowers, fading to lilac-tinted white or pure white. ↕ 36in (90cm), ↔ 4ft (1.2m). **var. *elegans*** ▣ syn. 'Elegans', *H.* 'Robusta', has rounded-heart-shaped, heavily and deeply puckered, very thickly glaucous gray-blue leaves, 8–12in (20–30cm) long. **'Frances Williams'** see *H.* 'Frances Williams'. **'Yellow Edge'** see *H.* 'Frances Williams'.

H. sieboldii, syn. *H. albomarginata*, *H.* 'Paxton's Original'. Vigorous, clump-forming perennial with broadly lance-shaped, blunt-tipped, flat, matte, olive-green leaves, 4–6in (10–15cm) long, narrowly and irregularly margined white. Racemes of funnel-shaped, deep violet flowers, purple-and-white-striped within, are borne on leafy scapes, 20in (50cm) long, in late summer and early autumn. ↕ 12in (30cm), ↔ 24in (60cm). Japan. **'Alba'**, syn. *H. minor* f. *alba* of gardens, has mid-green leaves and white flowers. **'Kabitan'** see *H.* 'Kabitan'.

***H.* 'Silk Komono'.** Clump-forming perennial with upright growth habit. Slightly rippled, medium green leaves, 13in (32cm) long, have creamy white margins; gray-green coloration appears where margins overlap leaf center. Produces tubular, pale lavender striped, flowers in summer. ↕ 18in (45cm), ↔ 5ft (1.5m).

***H.* 'Snow Cap'.** Clump-forming perennial with heart-shaped, slightly cupped, puckered, glaucous, blue-green leaves, 8in (20cm) long, irregularly margined creamy white. In summer, bears large, fragrant, funnel-shaped, purple-striped white flowers on scapes 22in (55cm) long. ↕ 16in (40cm), ↔ 24in (60cm).

***H.* 'Snowden'** ▣ Slow-growing, clump-forming perennial with ovate to heart-shaped, pointed, flat, thick, glaucous, gray-green leaves, 14in (35cm) long. Funnel-shaped, grayish white flowers are borne on thick scapes, 36in (90cm) long, in midsummer. ↕↔ 36in (90cm).

***H.* 'So Sweet'** ▣ Clump-forming perennial with ovate to lance-shaped, flat, glossy, mid-green leaves, 7in (18cm) long, margined creamy white. In mid- and late summer, lavender-blue buds open to funnel-shaped, fragrant, purple-striped white flowers on scapes 24in (60cm) long. ↕ 14in (35cm), ↔ 22in (55cm).

***H.* 'Spilt Milk'.** Slow-growing, clump-forming perennial whose corrugated, blue-green leaves, 9in (23cm) long, have unique white speckling and irregular white streaking. Near-white, tubular flowers complete the picture in midseason. ↕ 20in (60cm), ↔ 36in (90cm).

***H.* 'Stained Glass'** ▣ Fast-growing, clump-forming perennial, a sport of *H.* 'Guacamole'. All season, it retains its shiny, bright yellow leaves, 9in (23cm) long, which are clearly delineated with dark green margins. Large, fragrant, tubular, near-white flowers are borne late in the season. Tolerates direct sun. ↕ 20in (60cm), ↔ 4ft (1.2m).

***H.* 'Stiletto'.** Vigorous, erect, clump-forming perennial with lance-shaped, rippled, mid-green leaves, 7in (18cm) long, margined creamy white. Funnel-shaped, purple-striped, lavender-blue flowers are borne on leafy scapes, 12in (30cm) long, in summer. ↕ 6in (15cm), ↔ 8in (20cm).

***H.* 'Striptease'.** Clump-forming perennial with ovate to heart-shaped leaves, 7in (18cm) long, emerging mid-green with narrow white centers, becoming dark green with chartreuse, then bright gold, centers. Funnel-shaped, lavender-blue flowers are borne on erect, leafless scapes, to 3½ft (1.1m) long, in midsummer. ↕ 26in (65cm), ↔ 36in (90cm).

***H.* 'Sugar and Cream'.** Vigorous perennial forming a lax, open mound of ovate to heart-shaped, mid-green leaves, 10in (25cm) long, with slightly wavy, irregular cream margins. Fragrant, bell-shaped white flowers, striped lavender-blue, are borne on leafy scapes, 36in (90cm) long, in late summer. Thrives in sun or partial shade. ↕↔ 30in (75cm).

***H.* 'Sultana'.** Vigorous, clump-forming perennial with heart-shaped, slightly cupped, thick, dark green leaves, 5in (13cm) long, with chartreuse margins, varying in width. In late spring, bell-shaped, off-white flowers are produced on erect, leafless scapes, 10in (25cm) long. ↕ 10in (25cm), ↔ 16in (40cm).

***H.* 'Sum and Substance'** ▣ Clump-forming perennial with heart-shaped, flat, glossy, yellow-green to yellow leaves, 20in (50cm) long, glaucous beneath, becoming puckered when mature. In mid- and late summer, bears dense racemes of bell-shaped, very pale lilac flowers on leaning, glaucous scapes, 36in (90cm) long. Thrives in sun or partial shade. ↕30in (75cm), ↔4ft (1.2m).

***H.* 'Summer Fragrance'.** Clump-forming perennial with ovate to heart-shaped, pointed, flat, mid-green leaves, 8in (20cm) long, irregularly and narrowly margined creamy white. Bell-shaped, fragrant, deep lavender-purple flowers are borne on leafy scapes, 34in (85cm) long, in late summer. ↕24in (60cm), ↔5ft (1.5m).

***H.* 'Sun Power'.** Clump-forming perennial with ovate to heart-shaped, wavy, yellow-green to bright yellow leaves, 10in (25cm) long. Funnel-shaped, pale lavender-blue to white flowers are borne on arching, leafy scapes, to 4ft (1.2m) long, in summer. ↕24in (60cm), ↔36in (90cm).

***H.* 'Tardiflora'** ■ Clump-forming perennial producing lance-shaped, thick, glossy, dark green leaves, 3–6in (8–15cm) long, matte, dark green beneath. Funnel-shaped mauve flowers are borne on slightly arching, leafy, glaucous, purple-tinted scapes, to 14in (35cm) long, in autumn. ↕10in (25cm), ↔24in (60cm).

***H.* 'Tiny Tears'.** Clump-forming perennial with narrowly heart-shaped, flat, dark green leaves, ½in (1.5cm) long. In summer, dense racemes of bell-shaped purple flowers are borne on scapes 10in (25cm) long. ↕3in (8cm), ↔6in (15cm).

***H.* 'Tokudama'.** Slow-growing, clump-forming perennial with heart-shaped to rounded, cupped, puckered, vividly glaucous, deep blue-green leaves, 8–12in (20–30cm) long. From early to late summer, widely bell-shaped, grayish white flowers are produced on leafy, glaucous scapes, 16in (40cm) long. ↕14in (35cm), ↔36in (90cm). **'Tokudama Aureonebulosa'** ■ syn. f. *aureonebulosa*, has green-yellow leaves, 8–10in (20–25cm) long, irregularly margined and splashed deep blue-green; **'Tokudama Flavocircinalis'** ■ syn. f. *flavocircinalis*, produces ovate to heart-shaped blue leaves, irregularly margined creamy yellow; it bears flowers on scapes 18in (45cm) long, in midsummer; ↕16in (40cm), ↔30in (75cm).

***H.* 'Touch of Class'** ■ Slow-growing, clump-forming perennial, a tetraploid sport of *H.* 'June'. Heart-shaped leaves, 5½in (14cm) long, have narrow yellow center and very wide, intensely blue-green margins. Bell-shaped, lavender flowers are produced late in the season. ↕7in (18cm), ↔16in (40cm).

***H.* 'True Blue'.** Clump-forming perennial with ovate to heart-shaped, pointed, puckered, thick, glaucous, gray-blue leaves, 12in (30cm) long. In midsummer, bell-shaped, off-white flowers are borne on scapes 28in (70cm) long. ↕24in (60cm), ↔36in (90cm).

***H.* 'Undulata'**, syn. *H.* 'Argentea Variegata', *H.* 'Mediovariegata'. Clump-forming perennial with twisted, lance-shaped to elliptic or narrowly ovate, slightly pointed, mid-green leaves, 5–7in (13–18cm) long; they are thin and strongly wavy-margined, with central white or pale yellow-white markings. Arching, leafy white scapes, 20–32in (50–80cm) long, bear funnel-shaped mauve flowers in early and midsummer. ↕to 36in (90cm), ↔18in (45m). **'Undulata Albomarginata'** ■ produces broadly ovate, flat or only slightly wavy-margined leaves, dark green with irregular cream or pale yellow margins; ↕22in (55cm), ↔24in (60cm). **'Undulata Erromena'** is vigorous, and has broadly ovate, tapering, mid-green leaves, 5–9in (13–23cm) long. **'Undulata Univittata'** ■ has ovate, twisted, matte, olive-green leaves, 5–7in (13–18cm) long, each with a central cream zone; ↕18in (45cm), ↔28in (70cm).

***H.* 'Vanilla Cream'.** Clump-forming perennial with slightly red-dotted leaf stalks bearing ovate to heart-shaped, cupped, slightly puckered, thick, creamy yellow-green leaves, 3in (8cm) long. Funnel-shaped, pale lavender-blue flowers are produced on scapes 12in (30cm) long, in midsummer. ↕5in (13cm), ↔10in (25cm).

H. ventricosa ■ Clump-forming perennial with broadly ovate to heart-shaped, slightly wavy, wide-veined, thin, glossy, dark green leaves, 8–12in (20–30cm) long. In late summer, bears tubular-bell-shaped, deep purple flowers, white-striped within, on leafy, leaning scapes, 32–39in (80–100cm) long. ↕20in (50cm), ↔36in (90cm). China, N. Korea. **'Aureomaculata'** is slow-growing, and has leaves centrally splashed yellow, fading to yellow-green; **'Aureomarginata'** ■ has leaves irregularly margined with yellow, turning creamy white.

H. venusta ■ Clump-forming perennial producing ovate to heart-shaped, flat, wavy-margined, dark green leaves, 1–1½in (2.5–4cm) long, glossy beneath. Trumpet-shaped violet flowers are borne freely on ridged, leafy scapes, 10–14in (25–35cm) long, from mid-summer to midautumn. ↕1½in (4cm), ↔10in (25cm). Korea.

***H.* 'Victory'.** Vigorous, clump-forming perennial, a sport of *H. nigrescens* 'Elatior'. Very large, upright-growing mound of variegated, shiny green leaves, 12in (30cm) long, with creamy white margins. Bell-shaped, near-white flowers are borne on very tall scapes, to 5ft (1.5m) high, in midseason. ↕30in (75cm), ↔6ft (2m).

***H.* 'Wide Brim'** ■ Clump-forming perennial with heart-shaped, slightly cupped, heavily puckered, glaucous, dark green leaves, 7in (18cm) long, irregularly and widely margined cream, fading to white. Funnel-shaped, pale lavender-blue flowers are produced on scapes 22in (55cm) long in summer. ↕18in (45cm), ↔36in (90cm).

***H.* 'Yellow River'** ■ Clump-forming perennial with ovate to heart-shaped, pointed, thick, dark green leaves, 14in (35cm) long, irregularly margined yellow. Leafy scapes, 36in (90cm) long, bear funnel-shaped, very pale lavender-blue flowers in early summer. ↕22in (55cm), ↔36in (90cm).

***H.* 'Zounds'** ■ Clump-forming perennial with heart-shaped, puckered, thick yellow leaves, 11in (28cm) long, with a metallic sheen. In summer, leafy scapes, 24in (60cm) long, bear funnel-shaped, pale lavender-blue flowers. ↕22in (55cm), ↔36in (90cm).

Hosta 'Regal Splendor'

Hosta 'Royal Standard'

Hosta 'Ryan's Big One'

Hosta 'September Sun'

Hosta 'Shade Fanfare'

Hosta sieboldiana var. *elegans*

Hosta 'Snowden'

Hosta 'So Sweet'

Hosta 'Sum and Substance'

Hosta 'Tardiflora'

Hosta 'Tokudama Aureonebulosa'

Hosta 'Tokudama Flavocircinalis'

Hosta 'Touch of Class'

Hosta 'Undulata Albomarginata'

Hosta 'Undulata Univittata'

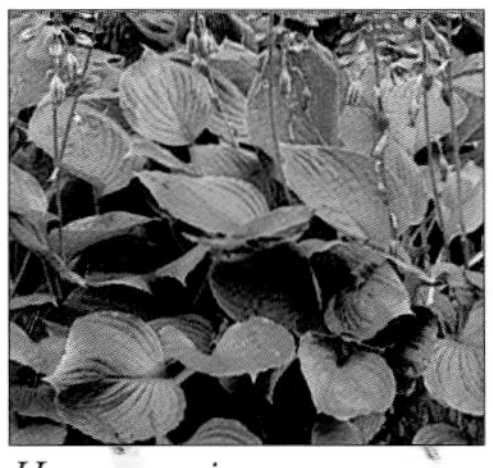
Hosta ventricosa

Hosta ventricosa 'Aureomarginata'

Hosta venusta

Hosta 'Wide Brim'

Hosta 'Yellow River'

Hosta 'Zounds'

H

HOTTONIA

PRIMULACEAE

Genus of 2 species of submerged aquatic perennials, widely distributed in temperate Eurasia and E. US, usually found in slow-moving water in ditches and in shallow water where silting has occurred. They have delicate, primrose-like, white to lilac flowers, borne in terminal racemes, and attractive, whorled or alternate, feathery, pinnate, light green leaves. Hottonias are good oxygenators, and are suitable for a small decorative pool or a larger wildlife pool.

• **CULTIVATION** Grow in the muddy bottom of a shallow pond in clear, still water in full sun. Hottonias may be difficult to establish, particularly in a recently constructed pool. Winter-resting buds will sink to the bottom of the pond, usually rising again and producing new growth in spring. See also pp.52–53.

• **PROPAGATION** Sow seed in trays submerged to their rims in water in spring. Divide, or take cuttings of established plants, in spring, and either throw into the water or plant into the submerged, muddy margins of a pond.

• **PESTS AND DISEASES** Filamentous algae may smother the delicate foliage.

H. inflata (American featherfoil). Submerged perennial with branched, spongy stems bearing whorls of stalkless, pinnate or 2-pinnate, oblong, light green leaves, ½–2in (1–5cm) long, composed of linear leaflets. Salverform white flowers, ¼–⅜in (6–9mm) across, are borne in 2- to 10-flowered racemes, 6–8in (15–20cm) tall, above the water in spring. ↕ 24in (60cm), ↔ 18in (45cm). E. US. Zone 6.

H. palustris (Water violet). Submerged perennial with spreading and erect stems bearing whorled or alternate, pinnate or 2-pinnate, comb-like, light green leaves, ¾–5in (2–13cm) long, with linear leaflets. In spring, produces salverform, pale violet, lilac, or white flowers, ¾–1in (2–2.5cm) across, with yellow throats; they are borne above the water in 3–9 whorls on flower stalks 12–16in (30–40cm) tall. ↕ 12–36in (30–90cm), ↔ indefinite. Eurasia. Zone 6.

▷ ***Houstonia*** see *Hedyotis*

HOUTTUYNIA

SAURURACEAE

Genus of one species of perennial found in damp, shady sites in woodland, scrub, and marshy habitats in E. Asia. It has widely spreading rhizomes and is grown mainly for its foliage. Use as a groundcover in a damp, mixed or herbaceous border, at a pond- or streamside, or for plantings in shallow water. *H. cordata* is invasive, especially in moist soils; cultivars are generally only slightly less vigorous.

• **CULTIVATION** Grow in moderately fertile, humus-rich, moist soil in full sun or dappled shade; variegated cultivars produce greener leaves in shade. On wet soils where marginally hardy, apply a loose but deep winter mulch to protect the roots. At the water's edge, grow in 3–4in (8–10cm) of water; in shallow ponds, the spread

Houttuynia cordata

may be limited by planting in a large container.

• **PROPAGATION** Sow seed in containers in a cold frame as soon as ripe. Divide rhizomes in spring. Root softwood cuttings in late spring.

• **PESTS AND DISEASES** Slugs and snails may be problems.

H. cordata ■ Rapidly spreading perennial with simple, ovate to heart-shaped, dull bluish or grayish green leaves, 1¼–3½in (3–9cm) long, with red-tinted margins. The leaves have an unusual, orange-like scent when bruised. In summer, bears dense spikes, to 1¼in (3cm) long, of tiny, yellowish green flowers, surrounded at the bases by 4–6 green-white, later pure white, obovate, petal-like bracts, ¼–½in (6–15mm) across. ↕ to 6–12in (15–30cm) or more, ↔ indefinite. China, Japan. Zone 5b. **'Chameleon'** ■ syn. 'Tricolor', has brightly variegated leaves in shades of green, pale yellow, and red, and is less spreading than the species. The small flowers of **'Flore Pleno'**, syn. 'Plena', are surrounded by 8 or more pure white bracts. **'Plena'** see 'Flore Pleno'. **'Tricolor'** see 'Chameleon'.

Houttuynia cordata 'Chameleon'

HOVEA

FABACEAE

Genus of about 20 species of evergreen, sometimes spiny shrubs from Australia, found in sheltered woodland, moist gullies, on exposed rocky outcrops, and on heathland, from sea level to above the snow line. They produce usually showy, pea-like flowers from the leaf axils, in either short racemes or clusters. The alternate, linear, lance-shaped, oblong-elliptic, or ovate leaves are simple and entire or toothed. Where not hardy, grow in a cool or temperate greenhouse; elsewhere, grow at the base of a warm, sunny wall, in a shrub border, or in a courtyard garden.

• **CULTIVATION** Under glass, grow in soil-based potting mix in bright filtered or full light, with good ventilation and moderate humidity. Water moderately in growth, applying a balanced liquid fertilizer monthly; keep just moist in winter. Outdoors, grow in well-drained, humus-rich, moderately fertile soil in full sun; woodland species will tolerate dappled shade. Chlorosis may occur in low-nitrogen soils. Shelter from cold, drying winds. Pruning group 8; plants under glass may need restrictive pruning.

• **PROPAGATION** Sow scarified or pre-soaked seed at 55–64°F (13–18°C) in spring. Root semi-ripe cuttings with bottom heat in summer.

• **PESTS AND DISEASES** Infrequent.

H. chorizemifolia (Holly-leaved hovea). Open, upright shrub, often with rust-red-hairy stems. The lance-shaped to ovate, prickle-toothed leaves, 1–3in (2.5–8cm) long, are matte, dark green, and with prominent veins. In spring, bears short racemes or clusters of 2–8 pea-like flowers, ½in (1.5cm) across; they are light blue-purple to violet, and have broad standard petals, each with a white patch at the base. ↕ 20–60in (50–150cm), ↔ 12–32in (30–80cm). Western Australia. ❀ (min. 41°F/5°C)

H. longifolia* var. *montana see *H. montana.*

H. montana ■ syn. *H. longifolia* var. *montana, H. purpurea* var. *montana.* Dwarf, spreading shrub with rust-red-hairy stems. Oblong to linear leaves, ½–1¼in (1–3cm) long, are glossy, deep green above, red-brown-hairy beneath. In spring, bears axillary clusters of 2 or 3 pea-like, deep purple to bluish purple flowers, ⅜–½in (9–15mm) across, with a white patch at the base of each standard petal. ↕ 8–16in (20–40cm), sometimes more, ↔ 20–39in (50–100cm). New South Wales, Victoria, Tasmania. ❀ (min. 35°F/2°C)

H. purpurea* var. *montana see *H. montana.*

Hovea montana

HOVENIA

RHAMNACEAE

Genus of 2 species of deciduous trees found in woodland or forest, cultivated and naturalized in E. and S.E. Asia (their exact country of origin is unknown). The leaves are alternate, heart-shaped to oval, and toothed. They are grown mainly for their fragrant flowers and small, spherical fruits. The shallowly cup-shaped, yellow or greenish yellow flowers, to ¼in (6mm) across, are produced in terminal and axillary, forked cymes. Hovenias are attractive specimen trees and will thrive in regions with long, hot summers. In areas with cool summers, flowers and fruits are not always freely borne.

• **CULTIVATION** Grow in moderately fertile, humus-rich, neutral to slightly alkaline soil in full sun, with shelter from cold, drying winds. Pruning group 1.

• **PROPAGATION** Sow seed in containers in a cold frame in autumn, or scarify seed and sow in spring. Root greenwood cuttings in early summer, and take hardwood cuttings in late autumn.

• **PESTS AND DISEASES** Prone to coral spot.

H. dulcis ■ (Raisin tree). Upright then spreading tree with heart-shaped to oval, toothed, glossy, dark green leaves, 4–8in (10–20cm) long, downy beneath. In summer, bears cymes 2–3in (5–8cm) across of tiny, greenish yellow flowers. After flowering, the flower stalks swell, becoming red, fleshy, sweet, and edible; they later bear spherical black fruit, to ¼in (6mm) across. ↕ 40ft (12m), ↔ 30ft (10m). E. and S.E. Asia. Zone 5b.

Hovenia dulcis

Howea forsteriana

HOWEA

Sentry palm

ARECACEAE

Genus of 2 species of single-stemmed palms found at low altitudes, to 1,000ft (300m), usually on basalt soils, on Lord Howe Island, Australia. The long-stalked, pinnate leaves are arranged in terminal clusters with no crownshaft, and star-shaped, 3-petaled flowers are borne on long spikes between them. Howeas are highly tolerant of adverse growing conditions such as those found in a home: reduced light, fluctuating and low temperatures, lack of humidity, and general neglect.Where not hardy, grow young specimens as houseplants, or in a conservatory or warm greenhouse. In warmer areas, use as free-standing specimens on a lawn or in a courtyard garden.

• **CULTIVATION** Under glass, grow in soil-based potting mix with equal parts added pulverized bark and leaf mold, in full light. Shade from hot sun and provide moderate humidity. In growth, water moderately and apply a balanced liquid fertilizer monthly; water sparingly in winter. Top-dress or pot on in spring; howeas are slow-growing and need repotting infrequently. Outdoors, grow in fertile, moist but well-drained soil in full sun, although they will tolerate dappled shade. Shelter from strong, drying winds.

• **PROPAGATION** Sow seed at 79°F (26°C) as soon as ripe.

• **PESTS AND DISEASES** Susceptible to numerous fungal leaf spots, root rot, lethal yellowing, and manganese deficiency. Prone to scale insects and spider mites under glass.

H. forsteriana ■ syn. *Kentia forsteriana* (Kentia palm, Thatch leaf palm). Moderately slow-growing palm with a slender stem, ringed with old leaf scars. Long-stalked, pinnate, mid- to dark green leaves, 6–10ft (2–3m) long, are borne almost horizontally. The leaves are composed of numerous, narrowly lance-shaped, semi-lustrous leaflets with pendent tips. In summer, bears star-shaped, green female and pale brown male flowers, in erect, later pendent, axillary clusters of spikes to 3ft (1m) long. They are followed by ellipsoid, orange-red fruit, to ¾in (2cm) long. ↕ to 60ft (18m), ↔ to 20ft (6m). Lord Howe Island. ❀ (min. 59°F/15°C)

HOYA

Wax flower

ASCLEPIADACEAE

Genus of over 200 species of evergreen, climbing and shrubby perennials, some epiphytic, from coastal bluffs, stream margins, escarpments, and rainforest in the warmer regions of Asia, Australia, and the Pacific islands. They produce opposite pairs of simple, often fleshy or succulent, sometimes leathery, variably shaped leaves. The often colorful and fragrant flowers are borne in stalked umbels or cymes from the upper leaf axils. They each have 5 waxy, usually fleshy, spreading petals, and a central crown or corona of hooded, white, pale yellow, red, pink, or purple stamens. Flowers may be followed by long, cylindrical pods containing seeds with tufts of hair. Do not remove old flower stalks, because new inflorescences develop on them. Where not hardy, a warm greenhouse is best for all hoyas except *H. carnosa*, which should be grown in a temperate greenhouse or as a houseplant. In warmer areas, grow climbing hoyas through shrubs or trees, or over an arch, arbor, or pergola. Shrubby species may be grown epiphytically on large shrubs or trees, or in hanging baskets.

• **CULTIVATION** Under glass, grow in soil-based potting mix with equal parts added leaf mold, sharp sand, ground bark, and charcoal, in indirect or bright filtered light. Maintain moderate to high humidity. Keep below 100°F (38°C). In growth, water freely and apply a balanced liquid fertilizer monthly; keep just moist in winter. Provide support for climbers. Outdoors, grow in fertile, moist, well-drained soil in full sun, with some shade. Shelter from strong wind. Pruning group 9 for shrubs; group 11 for climbers, after flowering.

• **PROPAGATION** Sow seed at 66–75°F (19–24°C) in spring. Root semi-ripe cuttings with bottom heat in late summer. Layer in spring or summer.

• **PESTS AND DISEASES** Mealybugs and scale insects may occur under glass.

H. australis, syn. *H. darwinii* of gardens. Vigorous, twining, succulent climber with broadly ovate to elliptic or obovate, fleshy, dark green leaves, to 5in (13cm) long, smooth above and densely hairy beneath. In summer, bears umbels, 2½in (6cm) across, of 12–40 star-shaped, fragrant white flowers,

Hoya carnosa

Hoya linearis

to 1½in (4cm) across, with a red spot at the base of each petal, and red-purple coronas. ↕ 12–30ft (4–10m). Queensland, New South Wales. ❀ (min. 50°F/10°C)

H. bella see *H. lanceolata* subsp. *bella*.

H. carnosa ■ (Wax plant). Vigorous, stem-rooting, succulent, often epiphytic climber with ovate, rigid, very fleshy leaves, to 3in (8cm) long, usually smooth and dark green. From late spring to autumn, bears dense, convex umbels, to 2½in (6cm) across, of up to 20 star-shaped, waxy, night-scented, pure white flowers, ½in (1.5cm) across, with red coronas; sometimes produces 2 or more umbels per stem. ↕ to 20ft (6m) or more. India, S. China, Burma. ❀ (min. 41–45°F/5–7°C). **'Exotica'** has yellow-flushed, pink-variegated foliage. **'Green Curls'** see 'Krinkle Kurl'. **'Krinkle Kurl'**, syn. 'Green Curls' (Hindu rope) has contorted, crowded leaves, folded along their lengths. **'Picta'** has leaves with creamy white margins.

H. coronaria. Slow-growing, thick-stemmed climber with broadly oval to oblong, leathery, fleshy, mid-green leaves, to 4in (10cm) long, downy beneath, with prominent midribs. From summer to autumn, bears umbels, 3–4in (8–10cm) across, of up to 10 shallowly bell-shaped, night-scented, creamy yellow to greenish white flowers, to 1in (2.5cm) across; they have a red spot at the base of each petal and crimson-spotted coronas. ↕ to 10ft (3m). Thailand, Philippines, Malaysia, Indonesia, New Guinea. ❀ (min. 50°F/10°C)

***H. darwinii* of gardens** see *H. australis*.

H. imperialis. Strong-growing, twining climber producing thickly downy stems and narrowly oblong to elliptic, leathery, fleshy, mid-green leaves, 6–9in (15–23cm) long, with wavy margins. Umbels, to 8in (20cm) across, of 7–12 star-shaped, reddish brown to purple-brown flowers, to 3in (8cm) across, with white coronas, are borne mainly in summer. ↕ 20ft (6m) or more. Malaysia, Indonesia. ❀ (min. 50°F/10°C)

H. lanceolata* subsp. *bella, syn. *H. bella*. Spreading to pendent, epiphytic shrub with arching, densely downy, soft stems and narrowly ovate or ovate to lance-shaped, fleshy, rich green leaves, to 1¼in (3cm) long. Bears umbels, 1¼–1½in (3–4cm) across, of 7–9 star-shaped, very sweetly scented white flowers, ½in (1.5cm) across; they have red-violet coronas and are borne mainly in summer. ↕↔ to 18in (45cm). Himalayas to N. Burma. ❀ (min. 50°F/10°C)

H. linearis ■ Pendent, epiphytic, succulent perennial with slender, soft, grayish green stems bearing linear, hairy, dark green leaves, 1–2in (2.5–5cm) long, deeply grooved beneath. From late summer to autumn, produces lax umbels, to 1¼–1½in (3–4cm) across, of 10–13 star-shaped, scented, pure white flowers, to ½in (1.5cm) across, with pink-tinged, yellowish white coronas. ↕↔ 24–36in (60–90cm). Himalayas. ❀ (min. 55°F/13°C)

H. longifolia. Vigorous, epiphytic, succulent climber with thin stems and linear-lance-shaped, sharp-pointed, fleshy, pendent, dark green leaves, 2½–6in (6–15cm) long. In early summer, bears few-flowered umbels, 2in (5cm) across, of fragrant, star-shaped, pink-flushed, white flowers, ½–1½in (1–4cm) across, with rose-pink or red coronas. ↕ to 15ft (5m). Himalayas to S. Thailand and Malaysia. ❀ (min. 35°F/2°C)

H. macgillivrayi ■ Strong-growing, twining climber with thick stems and ovate to broadly ovate, rigid, thickly fleshy, lustrous, dark green leaves, 3–8in (7–20cm) long, tinted red-purple when young. From spring to summer, bears umbels, 8–10in (20–25cm) across, of 5–15 cup-shaped, red, red-purple, purple, or brownish red flowers, each 1½–3in (4–8cm) across, with dark red, occasionally white-centered coronas. ↕ 15–25ft (5–8m). Queensland. ❀ (min. 45°F/7°C)

H. nepalensis see *H. polyneura*.

H. polyneura, syn. *H. nepalensis*. Pendent, epiphytic shrub with short-stalked, ovate to lance-shaped, fleshy, glossy, dark green leaves, 2½–4in (6–10cm) long, with slightly pointed tips, and paler green veins. Bears up to 15 star-shaped, waxy, white to cream flowers, ½in (1.5cm) across, with purplish brown or bronze-red coronas, in umbels to 1½–2in (4–5cm) across, in summer. ↕↔ to 3ft (1m). Himalayas to S. China. ❀ (min. 55°F/13°C)

Hoya macgillivrayi

HUERNIA

ASCLEPIADACEAE

Genus of about 60–70 species of low-growing, perennial succulents from South Africa to Ethiopia and the Arabian Peninsula (with one species from W. Africa), occurring in hilly, semi-desert areas. They branch freely from the bases and often form large clumps of short, angled, fleshy stems; the prominent margins have grayish green or red teeth. The leaves are reduced to scales and are lost soon after they develop. Tubular or cup-shaped to shallowly saucer-shaped, warty, fleshy, unpleasantly scented flowers, with 5 pointed lobes, are borne in short-stalked umbels from summer to early autumn. Where temperatures fall below 52°F (11°C), grow in a warm greenhouse. In warmer areas, grow in a trough, raised bed, or desert garden.

• **CULTIVATION** Under glass, grow in standard cactus potting mix with added leaf mold in bright filtered or indirect light; provide low humidity. During the growing season, water moderately and apply a half-strength, low-nitrogen liquid fertilizer monthly. Keep almost dry in winter; overwatering may cause black rot. Outdoors, grow in poor to moderately fertile, preferably sandy, sharply drained soil; incorporate sharp sand and leaf mold at planting. Grow in dappled shade or in full sun with midday shade. Protect from excessive winter moisture.

• **PROPAGATION** Sow seed at 66–75°F (19–24°C) in spring. Root cuttings of stem sections in spring or summer.

• **PESTS AND DISEASES** Black rot and mealybugs may be problems.

H. macrocarpa* var. *arabica ▣ Clump-forming succulent producing slender, 4-angled, glossy, mid-green stems with slightly toothed tubercles. Short-lobed, fleshy, white-hairy flowers, ½in (1.5cm) across, are borne in early autumn; the lobes are pale yellow with concentric purple bands, or unmarked and purple-crimson outside, roughly warty inside. ↕↔ 4in (10cm). South Yemen. ❀ (min. 52°F/11°C)

H. pillansii ▣ Variable succulent with almost spherical, then finger-like, gray-green stems bearing dense, bristly, hairy-tipped tubercles in longitudinal, spiraling rows. Fleshy, densely red-warty and red-spotted, cream to red or pink flowers, 1¼–1½in (3–4cm) across, pale yellow inside with crimson spots, are borne from the base of new growth from summer to early autumn. ↕ 1½in (4cm), ↔ 4in (10cm). South Africa (Western Cape). ❀ (min. 52°F/11°C)

H. primulina see *H. thuretii* var. *primulina*.

H. procumbens. Prostrate or semi-pendent succulent with 5- or 6-angled, dull purplish green stems. In late summer, bears fleshy, pale yellowish brown flowers, to 1¼in (3cm) across, margined with brownish red; the narrowly lance-shaped white lobes are covered with short, dark purple-red hairs. ↕↔ to 6in (15cm). South Africa (Northern Transvaal, Eastern Transvaal). ❀ (min. 52°F/11°C)

H. quinta ▣ Clump-forming succulent producing 4-angled, grayish purple stems with horned teeth. In summer, produces shallowly 5-lobed, fleshy, white or yellow flowers, to 1¼in (3cm) across, the cup-shaped tubes banded dark red, with papillae at the mouths. ↕↔ to 3in (8cm). South Africa (Northern Transvaal, Eastern Transvaal). ❀ (min. 52°F/11°C)

H. thuretii. Clump-forming succulent with 4- or 5-angled, prominently toothed, grayish green stems. From summer to early autumn, bears 5-lobed, fleshy, red-spotted yellow flowers, to 1in (2.5cm) across, with red-banded tubes. ↕ 2in (5cm), ↔ indefinite. South Africa (Eastern Cape). ❀ (min. 52°F/11°C). **var. *primulina*** ▣ syn. *H. primulina*, has tufts of acutely angled, grayish green stems, and bears waxy, fleshy, pale red flowers, creamy yellow with red spots on the lobes, and with blackish brown coronas; ↕↔ 3in (8cm).

H. zebrina (Owl's eyes). Variable, clump-forming succulent producing 4- or 5-angled, grayish green stems with thick, conical teeth. From summer to early autumn, bears fleshy, creamy yellow flowers, 1¼–1½in (3–4cm) across, with shallow, maroon-purple tubes, and 5 triangular lobes strongly cross-banded and heavily suffused maroon-purple. ↕ 2½–3in (6–8cm), ↔ 6in (15cm) or more. Namibia, Botswana, South Africa (Northern Transvaal, Eastern Transvaal, KwaZulu/Natal), Swaziland, Zimbabwe. ❀ (min. 52°F/11°C)

Huernia pillansii

Huernia thuretii var. *primulina*

▷ ***Humea*** see *Calomeria*

HUMULUS

Hops

CANNABIDACEAE

Genus of 2 species of herbaceous perennials, with twining stems, widely distributed and naturalized in woodland and hedgerows in N. temperate regions (their exact country of origin is unknown). The cultivars are grown for their brightly colored foliage, which may be golden or attractively variegated. The leaves are opposite and palmately 3- to 7-lobed, with large, broadly ovate to rounded lobes. Small male and female flowers are borne on separate plants in mid- and late summer: the males in axillary panicles, the females in cone-like spikes. The female inflorescences of *H. lupulus* ("hops") are used in brewing. Train over a fence or trellis, or into a large shrub or small tree. The flowers are useful for dried flower arrangements.

• **CULTIVATION** Grow in moist but well-drained, moderately fertile, humus-rich soil in sun or partial shade. For best leaf color, grow *H. lupulus* 'Aureus' in a sunny position.

• **PROPAGATION** Sow seed at 59–64°F (15–18°C) in spring; seed of *H. japonicus* and its cultivars may be sown *in situ* in late spring. Variegated and golden-leaved cultivars other than *H. japonicus* 'Variegatus' rarely come true from seed. Root softwood cuttings in spring, or greenwood and leaf-bud cuttings with bottom heat in summer.

• **PESTS AND DISEASES** Prone to downy mildew, powdery mildew, anthracnose, ringspot virus, and *Verticillium* wilt.

***H. japonicus* 'Variegatus'.** Twining perennial, usually grown as an annual, with roughly hairy shoots and deeply 5- to 7-lobed, sharply toothed, dark green leaves, to 5–6in (13–15cm) long, heavily mottled and streaked with white. Ovoid spikes of green female flowers, to ¾in (2cm) long, are borne in mid- and late summer. ↕ 10ft (3m). Zone 4.

H. lupulus (Hops). Rhizomatous, twining perennial with roughly hairy shoots and deeply 3- to 5-lobed, coarsely toothed, light green leaves, to 6in (15cm) long. In summer, bears broadly ovoid, fragrant, green, then straw-colored spikes of female flowers, to ¾in (2cm) long. ↕ 20ft (6m). Europe, W. Asia, North America. Zone 4. **'Aureus'** ▣ has golden yellow foliage.

Humulus lupulus 'Aureus'

HUNNEMANNIA

PAPAVERACEAE

Genus of one species of perennial, closely related to *Eschscholzia*, from rocky and stony areas in the highlands of Mexico. It has deeply divided leaves, with 3 narrow lobes, and glossy, saucer- to cup-shaped flowers that are good for cutting. Grow at the base of a warm, sunny wall, or in a herbaceous or mixed border. Where not hardy, grow as an annual or, for winter flowers, in a temperate greenhouse or conservatory.

• **CULTIVATION** Under glass, grow in soil-based potting mix in full light with low humidity. In growth, water moderately and apply a dilute, balanced liquid fertilizer monthly. Outdoors, grow in moderately fertile, well-drained soil in full sun, with protection from winter moisture. Avoid disturbing the roots.

Huernia macrocarpa var. *arabica*

Huernia quinta

Hunnemannia fumariifolia

• **PROPAGATION** Sow seed *in situ* in early spring, or in autumn in frost-free areas. For winter-flowering container plants, sow seed at 55–61°F (13–16°C) in autumn.
• **PESTS AND DISEASES** Susceptible to slugs, snails, and aphids.

H. fumariifolia ■ (Mexican tulip poppy). Woody-based, hairless perennial producing glaucous, blue-green leaves, 2–4in (5–10cm) long, with 3 linear lobes. From midsummer to late autumn, bears poppy-like, solitary, glossy, golden yellow flowers, to 2–3in (5–8cm) across, with 4 rounded, overlapping petals, later spreading to reveal deeper yellow stamens. ↕24–36in (60–90cm), ↔ 10in (25cm). Mexico. ❀ (min. 45°F/7°C). **'Sunlite'** is fast-growing and grown mostly as an annual; it has lax stems and clear yellow flowers; ↕ to 24in (60cm), ↔ 8in (20cm).

HUNTLEYA

ORCHIDACEAE

Genus of about 10 species of evergreen, rhizomatous, epiphytic orchids, without pseudobulbs, from Central and South America, and Trinidad. *H. meleagris*, the only species generally cultivated, grows in cloud forest up to 4,000ft (1,200m). The folded, lance-shaped to ovate, soft-textured leaves are arranged in 2 ranks in a broad fan shape. In summer, scapes arising between the lower leaves bear solitary, star-shaped, waxy flowers with prominent lips.
• **CULTIVATION** Intermediate-growing orchids. Grow in containers of epiphytic orchid potting mix or on slabs of bark in bright indirect light, with high humidity. Water freely during the growing season, and apply fertilizer monthly; water sparingly in winter. See also p.46.
• **PROPAGATION** Pot up offset rhizomes in spring.
• **PESTS AND DISEASES** Prone to spider mites, aphids, and mealybugs.

H. burtii see *H. meleagris*.
H. heteroclita. Epiphytic orchid with a fan of lance-shaped, light green leaves, to 18in (45cm) long. In summer, bears erect inflorescences of star-shaped, waxy, purple-brown-shaded, dull yellow flowers, 3–5in (8–13cm) across. ↕↔ 12in (30cm). Peru. ❀ (min. 55°F/13°C; max. 86°F/30°C)
H. meleagris ■ syn. *H. burtii.* Epiphytic orchid with a fan of tufted, lance-shaped to ovate, pale green leaves, 8–16in (20–40cm) long; new growth develops from the base on extending rhizomes. In summer, scapes to 7in (18cm) long bear solitary, star-shaped, waxy, very glossy, chestnut-brown flowers, 3–5in (8–13cm) across, with white or cream centers, often flecked with yellow. ↕↔ 12in (30cm). Trinidad, Central America, N.W. South America. ❀ (min. 55°F/13°C; max. 86°F/30°C)

Huntleya meleagris

HYACINTHELLA

LILIACEAE

Genus, closely related to *Muscari*, of about 16 species of small, bulbous perennials from E. and S.E. Europe to W. Asia, found on scree and stony, often limestone hillsides and in open pine forest. They have linear to elliptic-ovate, mostly mid-green, basal leaves and are cultivated for their racemes of bell-shaped flowers, ¼–½in (6–15mm) long, borne in spring. In regions with wet summers, they are best grown in an alpine house or bulb frame. In climates with low summer rainfall, grow in a trough, raised bed, or rock garden, or at the base of a warm, sunny wall.
• **CULTIVATION** Plant bulbs 2–3in (5–8cm) deep in autumn. Under glass, grow in soil-based potting mix with added grit, in full light. Maintain low humidity and good ventilation. Water moderately from autumn to spring; keep dry in summer. Apply a high-potash liquid fertilizer once after flowering. Outdoors, grow in moderately fertile, well-drained soil in full sun; protect from summer rain.
• **PROPAGATION** Sow seed in containers in a cold frame in autumn. Remove offsets in summer, when dormant.
• **PESTS AND DISEASES** Infrequent.

Hyacinthella glabrescens

H. dalmatica see *H. pallens.*
H. glabrescens ■ Bulbous perennial with 2 wide, strap-shaped leaves, to 5in (13cm) long. In spring, bears loose, erect racemes, 2–6in (5–15cm) long, of 10–25 tubular-bell-shaped, violet-blue flowers. ↕2–6in (5–15cm), PD3in (8cm). Turkey (S. Anatolia). Zone 7b.
H. pallens, syn. *H. dalmatica.* Bulbous perennial with narrow, linear leaves, to 3in (8cm) long. Dense racemes, to 4in (10cm) long, of 6–20 narrowly bell-shaped, mid-blue flowers are borne in spring. ↕4in (10cm), PD2in (5cm). Croatia (Dalmatia). Zone 7.

HYACINTHOIDES

syn. ENDYMION
Bluebell

LILIACEAE

Genus, closely related to *Scilla*, of 3 or 4 species of vigorous, bulbous perennials from deciduous woodland and moist meadows in W. Europe and N. Africa. They have strap-shaped to lance-shaped or linear, basal leaves, and bear racemes of bell- or tubular-bell-shaped, blue or white, sometimes pink flowers in spring. Bluebells are ideal for naturalizing in grass, for a wild or woodland garden, or for underplanting in a shrub border. All parts may irritate skin on contact, and may cause severe discomfort if ingested.
• **CULTIVATION** Plant bulbs 3in (8cm) deep in autumn, in moderately fertile, humus-rich, moist but well-drained soil in dappled shade. *H. hispanica* tolerates a wide range of soils. Remove flowers as they fade to prevent self-seeding, except in wild plantings.
• **PROPAGATION** Sow seed in containers in a cold frame as soon as ripe; keep shaded and do not allow to dry out. Remove offsets in summer.
• **PESTS AND DISEASES** Infrequent.

Hyacinthoides hispanica 'Excelsior'

Hyacinthoides hispanica 'La Grandesse'

H. hispanica syn. *Endymion hispanicus, Scilla campanulata, S. hispanica* (Spanish bluebell). Robust, bulbous perennial, quickly forming large clumps of erect, strap-shaped, glossy, dark green leaves, 8–24in (20–60cm) long. In spring, bears racemes of up to 15 upright, bell-shaped, unscented blue flowers, ¾in (2cm) long, with reflexed tips and blue anthers. ↕16in (40cm), PD4in (10cm). Portugal, Spain, N. Africa. Zone 4. Most cultivars offered are hybrids with *H. non-scripta.* **'Excelsior'** ■ produces violet-blue flowers, striped paler blue; ↕20–22in (50–55cm). **'La Grandesse'** ■ bears nodding, pure white flowers, 1in (2.5cm) long. **'Rosabella'** has racemes of violet-pink flowers.
H. italica. Bulbous perennial with semi-erect, linear to lance-shaped, dull, dark green leaves, 4–10in (10–25cm) long. Dense racemes of 6–30 upward-facing, bell-shaped, mid-blue flowers, ½in (1.5cm) long, are borne in spring. ↕4–8in (10–20cm), PD2in (5cm). Portugal, Spain, S.E. France, N.W. Italy. Zone 5.
H. non-scripta ■ syn. *Endymion non-scriptus, Scilla non-scripta, S. nutans* (English bluebell). Vigorous, clump-forming, bulbous perennial with spreading, linear to lance-shaped, glossy, dark green leaves, 8–18in (20–45cm) long. In spring, bears 6–12 pendent, narrowly bell-shaped, scented, mid-blue, sometimes white flowers, ½–¾in (1.5–2cm) long, with cream anthers, in a one-sided raceme that bends over at the top. ↕8–16in (20–40cm), ↔ 3in (8cm). W. Europe. Zone 6.

Hyacinthoides non-scripta

HYACINTHUS

Hyacinth

LILIACEAE

Genus of 3 species of bulbous perennials from rocky limestone slopes and cliffs, to 8,200ft (2,600m) high, in W. and C. Asia. They are cultivated for their loose to dense racemes of strongly fragrant flowers, borne in spring. The semi-erect, basal leaves, 6–14in (15–35cm) long, are strap-shaped, channeled, and glossy, dark green. All cultivars are derived from *H. orientalis*, and usually have racemes to 8in (20cm) long, closely packed with tubular-bell-shaped, single or double flowers, ¾–1½in (2–4cm) long. Closer in character to the wild species are the Multiflora and Roman cultivars, which produce several smaller, loosely flowered racemes, to 5in (13cm) long. They are now rarely grown.

Hyacinths are excellent for spring bedding displays in an annual, mixed, or herbaceous border, or for forcing in containers; some are available specially prepared for early flowering indoors. All parts may cause stomach upset if ingested; contact with the bulbs may aggravate skin allergies.

• **CULTIVATION** Outdoors, plant bulbs 4in (10cm) deep, a minimum of 3in (8cm) apart, in autumn. At the northern limits of their hardiness, plant 6–8in (15–20cm) deep. Grow in any well-drained, moderately fertile soil in sun or partial shade. Protect container-grown plants from excessive winter moisture.

Bulbs may be forced into early growth for indoor display in winter. Plant them with the tips just showing, in soil-based potting mix in containers with drainage holes; use bulb fiber if planting in bowls. Keep in a dark place at a temperature above freezing but no higher than 45°F (7°C), for at least 10 weeks to allow roots to develop. When the shoots are about 1in (2.5cm) long, increase light and temperature gradually. Water carefully, avoiding wetting the shoots or waterlogging the soil mix; damp conditions and poor drainage may encourage diseases. After flowering, forced hyacinths may be planted in the garden, where they will flower in subsequent years.

• **PROPAGATION** Remove offsets when dormant in summer.

• **PESTS AND DISEASES** Prone to gray mold *(Botrytis)* and bulb rot.

Hyacinthus orientalis 'Blue Jacket'

Hyacinthus orientalis 'Carnegie'

Hyacinthus orientalis 'City of Haarlem'

Hyacinthus orientalis 'Distinction'

Hyacinthus orientalis 'Jan Bos'

Hyacinthus orientalis 'Lady Derby'

Hyacinthus orientalis 'Princess Maria Christina'

Hyacinthus orientalis 'Queen of the Pinks'

H. amethystinus see *Brimeura amethystina.*

H. azureus see *Muscari azureum.*

H. orientalis. Bulbous perennial with linear to lance-shaped, channeled, bright green leaves, 6–14in (15–35cm) long. In early spring, bears erect racemes of up to 40 tubular-bell-shaped, waxy, very fragrant, single flowers, ¾–1½in (2–4cm) long, pale violet-blue at the bases and almost white above, with spreading, then recurved lobes. ↕ 8–12in (20–30cm), PD3in (8cm). C. and S. Turkey, N.W. Syria, Lebanon. Zone 4b. **'Amethyst'** bears strongly scented, single, violet-lilac flowers. **'Amsterdam'** bears single, bright rose-red flowers. **'Anna Liza'** produces single, pale purple flowers with darker veins. **'Anna Marie'** bears racemes of single, pale pink flowers. **'Attila'** has single, violet flowers with amethyst-edged petals. **'Ben Nevis'** bears compact racemes of double, ivory-white flowers. **'Blue Jacket'** ■ produces racemes of single, navy-blue flowers with purple veins. **'Borah'** (Multiflora group) bears spikes of single, light to mid-blue flowers. **'Carnegie'** ■ bears compact racemes of single, pure white flowers. **'City of Haarlem'** ■ bears racemes of single, soft primrose-yellow flowers. **'Delft Blue'** produces single, soft blue flowers. **'Distinction'** ■ bears slender, open racemes of single, beet-purple flowers. **'Gipsy Queen'** bears single, salmon-orange flowers. **'Hollyhock'** produces double, bright crimson-red flowers. **'Innocence'** bears single, pure white flowers. **'Jan Bos'** ■ produces racemes of single, cerise-red flowers. **'Lady Derby'** ■ has single, rose-pink flowers. **'La Victoire'** produces single, red flowers. **'Ostara'** ■ has single flowers in violet-blue. **'Pink Pearl'** bears single, deep pink flowers with paler edges. **'Princess Maria Christina'** ■ has single apricot flowers. **'Queen of the Pinks'** ■ bears single, deep pink flowers. **'Sheila'** produces single, pale pink flowers. **'Violet Pearl'** bears spikes of single, violet-purple flowers. **'White Pearl'** bears single, pure white flowers. **'Yellow Hammer'** has single, soft yellow flowers.

H. romanus see *Bellevalia romana.*

Hyacinthus orientalis 'Ostara'

HYDRANGEA

HYDRANGEACEAE

Genus of 80 or more species of deciduous and evergreen shrubs and climbers, rarely trees, found in woodland in E. Asia and North and South America. Grown mainly for their large, showy flowerheads, many hydrangeas also have ornamental, flaky, peeling bark when mature, and attractive foliage with good autumn color. The leaves are broadly to narrowly ovate, or lance-shaped, toothed, and either opposite or in whorls of 3. The flat, domed, or conical, terminal flowerheads consist of corymbs or panicles of both tiny fertile flowers and larger sterile flowers with showy, petal-like sepals.

Cultivars of *H. macrophylla* are divided into 2 groups: Lacecaps have flattened flowerheads with small fertile flowers in the centers, surrounded by larger sterile flowers; Hortensias (mophead hydrangeas) have nearly spherical flowerheads of large sterile flowers.

Flower color is affected by the relative availability of aluminum ions in the soil. Acidic soils containing aluminum produce blue flowers; soils with a pH greater than 6.0 produce pink flowers. White flowers are not affected by pH.

Hydrangeas are useful for a range of garden sites: they are excellent as specimen plants or in group plantings, in a shrub border, or in containers. Use climbers to clothe a shaded wall or fence, or grow up tree trunks. The flowerheads may be dried for use in arrangements. All parts of hydrangeas may cause mild stomach upset if ingested; contact with the foliage may aggravate skin allergies.

• **CULTIVATION** Grow in moist but well-drained, moderately fertile, humus-rich soil in sun or partial shade; provide shelter from cold, drying winds. Most hydrangeas become chlorotic in alkaline soil. Reblooming/Remontant *H. macrophylla* produce flowers on current season's wood so bloom is less likely to be lost to incorrect pruning or cold. Pruning group 1 for most species; group 4 for *H. macrophylla*, *H.* 'Preziosa', and *H. serrata*; group 1 or 6 for *H. paniculata*; and group 11 for climbers, after flowering.

• **PROPAGATION** Sow seed in containers in a cold frame in spring. Root softwood cuttings of deciduous hydrangeas in early summer, or hardwood cuttings in winter. Root semi-hardwood cuttings of non-flowering shoots of evergreens with bottom heat in summer.

• **PESTS AND DISEASES** Gray mold, slugs, powdery mildew, rust, ringspot virus, and leaf spots are common.

H. anomala* subsp. *petiolaris see *H. petiolaris.*

H. arborescens (wild or smooth hydrangea). Rounded, deciduous shrub with long-stalked, broadly ovate leaves, to 7in (18cm) long, dark green above and paler beneath. Domed or flattened corymbs, to 6in (15cm) across, of crowded, dull white, mainly fertile flowers are borne in summer. ↕↔ 3–5ft (1–1.7m). E. US. Zone 3b. **'Annabelle'** ■ is more compact, and bears early, large, spherical flowerheads, 12in (30cm) across, consisting of mainly sterile flowers. **'Grandiflora'** ('Hills of

Hydrangea arborescens 'Annabelle'

Hydrangea aspera

Hydrangea involucrata 'Hortensis'

Hydrangea macrophylla 'Ayesha'

Hydrangea macrophylla 'Endless Summer'

Hydrangea macrophylla 'Lanarth White'

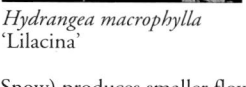

Hydrangea macrophylla 'Lilacina'

Hydrangea macrophylla 'Nikko Blue'

Hydrangea macrophylla 'Penny Mac'

Hydrangea macrophylla 'Veitchii'

Hydrangea paniculata 'Brussels Lace'

Hydrangea paniculata 'Floribunda'

Snow) produces smaller flowerheads than 'Annabelle', but larger sterile flowers. **subsp. *radiata* 'Samantha'** bears mostly white sterile florets in the flowerhead with silvery white backs to the leaves.

H. aspera ■ is an upright, deciduous shrub with large, lance-shaped to narrowly ovate, dark green leaves, to 10in (25cm) long, downy beneath. From late summer to autumn, bears flattened corymbs, to 10in (25cm) across, of blue to purple fertile flowers, surrounded by white, sometimes pink- to light purple sterile flowers. ↕↔ 10ft (3m). E. Asia. Zone 6. **subsp. *sargentiana*** see *H. sargentiana.* **subsp. *strigosa*** has narrower leaves, with short, stiff hairs beneath, and often flowers late in summer. C. China. **Villosa Group** see *H. villosa.*

H. integerrima see *H. serratifolia.*

H. involucrata. Spreading, deciduous shrub with broadly ovate-oblong, bristly, dark green leaves, to 6in (15cm) long. In late summer, bears domed corymbs, to 5in (13cm) across, of small, blue fertile flowers, surrounded by white to pale blue or pink sterile flowers. ↕ 3ft (1m), ↔ 6ft (2m). Japan, Taiwan. Zone 7b. **'Hortensis'** ■ produces flowerheads of double, pinkish white sterile flowers.

Hydrangea macrophylla 'Blue Wave'

H. macrophylla (Bigleaf hydrangea, Florist's hydrangea) is a rounded, deciduous shrub with broadly ovate, coarsely toothed, glossy, dark green leaves, to 8in (20cm) long. In mid- and late summer, produces flattened corymbs, 6–8in (15–20cm) across, of a few pink sterile flowers and numerous blue or pink fertile flowers. ↕ 6ft (2m), ↔ 8ft (2.5m). Japan. Zone 6. Cultivars of *H. macrophylla* are divided into 2 groups: Lacecaps and Hortensias (see introduction).

'All Summer Beauty' (Hortensia) has profuse, dark blue flowers, pinker on soil near neutral; ↕ 3–4ft (1–1.2m).

'Ami Pasquier' (Hortensia) is slow-growing, with dark crimson or blue-purple flowers; may be grown as a houseplant when young; ↕ 5ft (1.5m), ↔ 6ft (2m). **'Ayesha'** ■ (Hortensia) has unusual, lilac-like flowers with small, cupped, light pink to light blue sepals; ↕ 5ft (1.5m), ↔ 6ft (2m). **'Blue Billow'** (Lacecap) has copious amounts of violet-blue flowers. **'Blue Wave'** ■ syn. 'Mariesii Perfecta' (Lacecap), produces rich blue to mauve, or lilac-blue to pink sterile flowers, and darker fertile flowers.

'David Ramsey' (Hortensia) is a prolific bloomer, bearing medium to large flowerheads, from 6–8in (15cm–20 cm) across when the plant becomes established. Blooms change from medium blue in acid soils through aquamarine to mauve as they mature.

'Domotoi' (Hortensia) producess conical flowerheads of large, light blue to mauve or pink flowers with sharply toothed sepals; ↕ 3ft (1m), ↔ 5ft (1.5m). **'Endless Summer** ■ (Hortensia) A hardy, prolific bloomer, ↕ 4–6ft (1.2–2m), with medium to large flowerheads, ↔ 6–8in (15cm–20 cm), that vary in color from blue in acid soils to pink in alkaline soils.

'Enziandom', syn. 'Gentian Dome' (Hortensia), bears deep pink to dark gentian-blue flowers. **'Générale Vicomtesse de Vibraye'** ■ (Hortensia) has pale blue or pink flowers in large flowerheads; may be used as a houseplant when young. **'Gentian Dome'** see 'Enziandom'. **'Geoffrey Chadbund'** (Lacecap) has dark brick-red flowers. **'Goliath'** (Hortensia) is vigorous, with large flowerheads of soft pink or pale blue flowers. **'Kluis Superba'** (Hortensia) has flowerheads of dark purple-blue to dark pink flowers.

'Lanarth White' ■ (Lacecap) produces pale pink to blue fertile flowers surrounded by pure white sterile flowers; ↕↔ 5ft (1.5m). **'Lilacina'** ■ (Lacecap) has mauve-pink to blue fertile and sterile flowers; reblooming. **'Maréchal Foch'** (Hortensia) produces rich pink to purple, or dark vivid blue flowers; may be grown as a houseplant when young.

'Mariesii' (Lacecap) has domed flowerheads of numerous pale pink to pale blue sterile flowers; ↕↔ 4ft (1.2m).

'Mariesii Perfecta' see 'Blue Wave'.

'Mariesii Variegata' (Lacecap) has creamy white-edged leaves and bears pink to mauve-pink flowers, light blue on acidic soil; ↕ 3ft (1m).

'Masja' (Hortensia) is compact, producing dense flowerheads of vivid red flowers against very dark green foliage; ↕ 3ft (1m), ↔ 5ft (1.5m).

'Mme. Emile Mouillère' (Hortensia) produces white flowers becoming pink-tinged with age; use as a houseplant when young. **'Nikko Blue'** ■ (Hortensia) is vigorous, with large, rounded blue flowers; ↕ 6ft (2m).

'Otaksa' (Hortensia) has red leaf stalks and heavy, pink to blue flowers on weak, bending stems; ↕ 3ft (1m). **'Penny Mac'** ■ (Hortensia) bears pink (alkaline soil) or blue (acid soil) flowers on current season's growth; ↕ 3–5ft (1–1.5m). **'Pia'** , syn. 'Pink Elf' (Hortensia), is compact, bearing bright red-pink flowers with white centers; ↕ 24in (60cm), ↔ 3ft (1m). **'Pink Elf'** see 'Pia'. **'Preziosa'** see *H.* 'Preziosa'.

'Quadricolor' (Lacecap) has leaves boldly variegated with pale and dark green, cream, and yellow, and has pale pink flowers; often confused with 'Tricolor', which is weaker-growing; ↕ 5ft (1.5m), ↔ 4ft (1.2m). **subsp. *serrata*** see *H. serrata.* **'Variegata'** (Lacecap) is mound-forming, with creamy white-edged leaves, bearing blue flowers in acid soil; ↕ 4–5ft (1.2–1.5m), ↔ 5–6ft (1.5–2m). **'Veitchii'** ■ (Lacecap) has large flowerheads with white sterile flowers turning pink to red with age.

H. paniculata. Vigorous, spreading to upright, deciduous shrub with ovate, pointed, toothed, mid- to dark green leaves, 3–6in (7–15cm) long. Large, conical panicles, 3–8in (7–20cm) tall, of creamy white fertile flowers and large, white, later pink-tinged sterile flowers are borne in late summer and early autumn. To obtain larger flowerheads on cultivars, cut back previous season's shoots to within a few buds of the woody framework in spring. Excellent for low-water gardening. ↕ 10–22ft (3–7m), ↔ 8ft (2.5m). Russia (Sakhalin), China, Japan. Zone 3b.

'Brussels Lace' ■ bears profuse, small panicles of mainly fertile flowers and a few sterile flowers. **'Floribunda'** ■ produces large flowerheads of white sterile flowers, becoming pink-tinged as they age. **'Grandiflora'** (PeeGee hydrangea) has large flowerheads, 8–12in (20–30cm) tall, sometimes more, of mainly sterile white flowers that turn pinkish white with age.

'Kyushu', an erect plant, with glossy, dark green leaves, produces green-tinged panicles that turn lacey and white as the blooms mature.

'Pee Wee', a dwarf, has a compact and arching habit, bearing abundant white flowerheads; ↕↔ to 5ft (1.5m).

Hydrangea macrophylla 'Générale Vicomtesse de Vibraye'

H

Hydrangea paniculata 'Pink Diamond'

Hydrangea 'Preziosa'

Hydrangea quercifolia 'Little Honey'

Hydrangea serrata 'Bluebird'

Hydrangea serrata 'Rosalba'

Hydrangea villosa

H

'Pink Diamond' ■ has broad, open panicles, to 12in (30cm) tall, of fertile and sterile flowers, creamy white at first, becoming deep pink with a red reverse to the petals as they age. **'Tardiva'** is late-flowering, in early and midautumn. **'Unique'** ■ is similar to 'Grandiflora' but more vigorous, with large sterile flowers in flowerheads 8in (20cm) across. **'White Moth'** produces spherical flowerheads with large sterile flowers, attractive over a long period in the fall.
H. petiolaris ■ syn. *H. anomala* subsp. *petiolaris* (Climbing hydrangea). Vigorous, woody, deciduous climber, clinging by aerial roots. Ovate-rounded leaves, to 4½in (11cm) long, have heart-shaped bases and are dark green, sometimes turning yellow in autumn. In summer, bears domed corymbs, to 10in (25cm) across, of white fertile and sterile flowers. ↕ 50ft (15m). Russia (Sakhalin), Korea, Taiwan, Japan. Zone 5.
***H.* 'Preziosa'** ■ syn. *H. macrophylla* 'Preziosa', *H. serrata* 'Preziosa'. Upright, deciduous shrub with broadly ovate, glossy, mid-green leaves, to 6in (15cm) long. Small, spherical corymbs of white sterile flowers, 4–5in (10–13cm) across, turning to rich red, blue, or mauve on acidic soil, are borne on dark stems in late summer. ↕↔ 5ft (1.5m). Zone 5b.
H. quercifolia (Oakleaf hydrangea). Deciduous, mound-forming shrub with attractively peeling, orange-brown bark and deeply 5- to 7-lobed, mid-green leaves, to 8in (20cm) long, turning bronze-purple in autumn. From midsummer to autumn, bears conical panicles, to 10in (25cm) tall, of white fertile and sterile flowers; the sterile flowers become pink-tinged with age. ↕ 6ft (2m), ↔ 8ft (2.5m). S.E. US. Zone 5b. **'Alice'** is a tall, ↕ 10ft (3m), fast growing plant with abundant 12in (30cm) panicles have delicate white flowerheads; foliage turns deep carmine in the fall. **'Harmony'** has large panicles, 12in (30cm) long and 8in (20cm) wide, with heavy, white blooms. **'Little Honey'** ■ has golden to butter-yellow foliage in spring and throughout the growing season before becoming tinged with scarlet in the fall. **'Pee Wee',** a dwarf, ↕ 4ft (1.2m), bears plentiful white flower panicles in early to mid summer with deep claret fall foliage. **'Snowflake'** has arching panicles of long-lasting, sterile, double white flowers, later turning pink. **'Snow Queen'** ■ has profuse, large sterile flowers in dense, upright flowerheads.
H. sargentiana, syn. *H. aspera* subsp. *sargentiana*. Upright, deciduous shrub with thick, bristly shoots and large, broadly ovate, very bristly, dark green leaves, to 10in (25cm) long. Flattened corymbs, to 9in (23cm) across, of blue to purple fertile flowers, surrounded by white sterile flowers, sometimes tinged purple, are produced from late summer to autumn. ↕ 10ft (3m) or more, ↔ 7–8ft (2.2–2.5m). China. Zone 6.
H. seemannii. Woody, evergreen climber, clinging by aerial roots, with elliptic to lance-shaped, leathery, mid-green leaves, to 6in (15cm) long. In summer, bears greenish white fertile flowers surrounded by white sterile flowers, in domed corymbs, to 6in (15cm) across. ↕ 30ft (10m). Mexico. ❀ (min. 35°F/2°C)
H. serrata, syn. *H. macrophylla* subsp. *serrata* (mountain hydrangea). Compact, erect, deciduous shrub with narrowly ovate, pointed, mid-green leaves, to 6in (15cm) long. Flattened corymbs, 2–4in (5–10cm) across, with a few pink or blue sterile flowers and numerous blue or pink fertile flowers, open from summer to autumn. Some *H. serrata* cultivars are also described as Lacecaps (see introduction). ↕↔ 4ft (1.2m). Korea, Japan. Zone 6. **'Acuminata'** see 'Bluebird'. **'Bluebird'** ■ syn. 'Acuminata' (Lacecap), bears rich blue fertile flowers surrounded by pale blue sterile flowers over a very long period. Leaves turn red in autumn.
'Grayswood' (Lacecap) is vigorous, bearing broad flowerheads of small, mauve fertile flowers; the white sterile flowers turn dark red as they age; ↕↔ 6ft (2m). **'Preziosa'** see *H.* 'Preziosa'. **'Rosalba'** ■ (Lacecap) has flowerheads with small, pink fertile flowers and white sterile flowers, becoming red-marked with age.
H. serratifolia, syn. *H. integerrima*. Vigorous, woody, evergreen climber, similar to *H. seemannii*, but with elliptic, leathery, dark green leaves, to 6in (15cm) long, sharply toothed on young plants. In summer, clustered, corymb-like flowerheads, to 6in (15cm) across, with white fertile flowers and usually no sterile flowers, open from large, spherical buds. ↕ 50ft (15m). Chile, Argentina. ❀ (min. 35°F/2°C)
H. villosa ■ syn. *H. aspera* Villosa Group. Spreading to erect, deciduous shrub or small tree with lance-shaped to narrowly ovate, velvety, dark green leaves, 3½–10in (9–25cm) long. In late summer, bears flattened corymbs, 6in (15cm) across (often more), of blue-purple or rich blue fertile flowers and lilac-white or rose-lilac sterile flowers. ↕↔ 4–12ft (1–4m). Tibet, China, Burma, Taiwan. Zone 7b.

HYDRASTIS

Goldenseal

RANUNCULACEAE

Genus of 2 species of rhizomatous perennials, occurring in woodland in N.E. North America and Japan. They have palmately lobed, dark green basal leaves and 2 alternate stem leaves. They are valued for the small, petalless, greenish white flowers, borne in late spring and summer, followed by a rounded cluster of red berries. Grow as a groundcover in a woodland or shady rock garden; they thrive in areas with cool, damp summers.
• **CULTIVATION** Grow in humus-rich, light, sandy, moist but well-drained, acidic to neutral soil in partial shade; add leaf mold at planting, and do not allow to dry out.
• **PROPAGATION** Sow seed in autumn in containers in a cold frame. Divide in autumn or spring.
• **PESTS AND DISEASES** Infrequent.

Hydrangea paniculata 'Unique'

Hydrangea petiolaris

Hydrangea quercifolia 'Snow Queen'

H. canadensis (Goldenseal, Orange root). Perennial with thick yellow rhizomes and stems to 12in (30cm) long. Leaves are rounded to heart-shaped, palmately 5- to 9-lobed, toothed, to 8in (20cm) long, and dark green; they are composed of a solitary basal leaf and 2 stem leaves, borne just below the flower. In late spring and early summer, bears solitary, greenish white flowers, to ½in (1.5cm) across, with petal-like greenish or pinkish white sepals and yellow-green stamens and stigmas. These are followed by inedible, closely bunched, spherical red berries, to ½in (1.5cm) across. Employed in herbal medicine as an astringent, antibacterial remedy for the mucous membranes. ↕ 12in (30cm), ↔ to 8in (20cm). N.E. North America. Zone 4.

HYDROCHARIS

Frogbit

HYDROCHARITACEAE

Genus of 2 species of submerged or floating aquatic perennials, inhabiting shallow water and marshes in Europe, Asia, and Africa. They have short, stolon-like stems that form mats just below the water surface or root into the mud. Resembling small water lilies, frogbits are cultivated for their foliage and their attractive, 3-petaled white flowers; the male flowers are borne in clusters of up to 4 blooms, the females are solitary. The small, basal leaves are stalked, kidney-shaped to rounded, and mid- to dark green. Use as surface cover for a large wildlife pool.

• **CULTIVATION** Grow in still, alkaline, preferably shallow water in full sun. Strongest growth occurs in water shallow enough for the leaves to float and the stolons to root into the mud at the bottom of the pool; in deep water, the plants float on the surface and are less vigorous. Winter water levels must be sufficient to prevent freezing at the bottom of the pool, since this is where the overwintering buds hibernate; they rise to the surface and produce new growth in spring. See also pp.52–53.

• **PROPAGATION** Sow seed in shallow trays of water as soon as ripe, or separate stolons and place them on the water surface in spring.

• **PESTS AND DISEASES** Leaves may be eaten or disfigured by water snails and larvae of the brown china-mark moth.

H. morsus-ranae (Frogbit). Floating perennial with horizontal, floating stolons, which form new plants at their tips, and with rosettes of rounded, glossy, mid-green leaves, 1¼–2in (3–5cm) long. Bowl-shaped flowers, ¾in (2cm) across, with 3 broadly ovate, papery white petals, each with a yellow spot at the base, are produced in summer. ↔ indefinite. Europe, W. Asia, N. Africa. Zone 4.

HYDROCLEYS

LIMNOCHARITACEAE

Genus of 9 species of stoloniferous, evergreen and deciduous, submerged aquatic annuals or perennials, found in slow-moving or still water in South America. They are cultivated for their attractive, bowl-shaped flowers, borne singly or sometimes in umbels, and their

Hydrocleys nymphoides

waterlily-like, ovate to rounded, mid- to dark green leaves. Where not hardy, grow at the margins of a pond in a cool greenhouse. In warmer climates, grow in submerged containers, or rooted in the mud at the margins of a sunny pond outdoors.

• **CULTIVATION** Grow in acidic water to 9in (23cm) deep. Under glass, grow in aquatic containers at the pool margins, in bright filtered light. Provide a water temperature of up to 77°F (25°C). Outdoors, grow in containers or at pond margins, in full sun. *H. nymphoides* hibernates below 64°F (18°C). See also pp.52–53.

• **PROPAGATION** Sow seed in pans at 68°F (20°C) as soon as ripe; cover the seed with sand, and place the pans in water up to the rims. On germination, immerse so that the surfaces of the pans are covered by ½in (1.5cm) of water. Divide young plantlets in spring.

• **PESTS AND DISEASES** Infrequent.

H. nymphoides ■ (Water poppy). Deciduous, submerged perennial with prostrate, stoloniferous shoots and long-stalked, thick, broadly-ovate to rounded, floating leaves, 2–3in (5–8cm) long, heart-shaped at the bases. Short-lived, solitary, 3-petaled yellow flowers, 2–3in (5–8cm) across, with purple centers, are borne just above the water surface in summer. ↔ indefinite. Tropical S. America. ❀ (min. 34°F/1°C)

HYDROCOTYLE

Pennywort

APIACEAE

Genus of 75 species of moisture-loving herbaceous perennials and marginal aquatic perennials from Eurasia, North America, and New Zealand, found at stream or lake margins, in swamps, or in moist woodland. They have a low, creeping habit; rounded, light to dark green leaves; and inconspicuous, rounded flowers in small umbels. Grow as a groundcover in a bog garden, in damp sites, or at pond margins. Where not hardy, grow at the margins of an indoor pool or in an aquarium.

• **CULTIVATION** Grow in moderately fertile, humus-rich, moist soil in sun or partial shade. To grow pennyworts as marginal aquatics, plant in the muddy margins of a pond, or in containers of loamy soil to confine their spread. In an aquarium, grow in an inert medium in bright filtered light or full light, with a water temperature of 41–75°F (5–24°C). See also pp.52–53.

• **PROPAGATION** Sow seed in containers in a cold frame from autumn to spring. Divide in spring.

• **PESTS AND DISEASES** Infrequent.

H. americana, syn. *H. ranunculoides.* Creeping, marginal aquatic perennial with rounded, mid-green leaves, to 2in (5cm) long, borne on leaf stalks ½–4½in (1–11cm) long. Stalkless umbels of 3–5 inconspicuous, rounded, greenish white flowers are produced in summer. ↔ indefinite. North and South America, New Zealand. ❀ (min. 35°F/2°C)

H. ranunculoides see *H. americana.*

HYGROPHILA

ACANTHACEAE

Genus of 100 species of evergreen and deciduous, marginal and submerged aquatic perennials found in lakes, rivers, streams, bogs, and marshes in tropical regions, particularly in Africa and S.E. Asia. They have opposite, entire to finely pinnatifid or pinnate, ovate or lance-shaped leaves, and produce tight racemes or panicles of whorled, tubular, 2-lipped flowers from the leaf axils in summer. In tropical areas, they are attractive foliage plants for growing at pond margins; elsewhere, grow in a pond in a warm greenhouse, or in an aquarium.

• **CULTIVATION** Outdoors, grow either at pond margins or in the mud at the base of a pond, in full light. Under glass, grow either in containers at the margins of a pool or submerged in an aquarium, in bright filtered light and with a water temperature of 68–75°F (20–24°C). See also pp.52–53.

• **PROPAGATION** Divide in summer. Root stem-tip or softwood cuttings in summer. Detached floating leaves will also form roots.

• **PESTS AND DISEASES** Soft young growth may be damaged by water snails.

H. difformis (Water wisteria). Evergreen, marginal or submerged aquatic perennial with slender, soft stems, to 24in (60cm) long, clothed in pinnate, pinnatifid, or comb-like, mid-green, submerged leaves, to 4in (10cm) long. In summer, whorls of tubular, lilac to violet flowers, to ½in (15mm) long, streaked red-violet within, are produced in leafy racemes, to 18in (45cm) long, from the axils of the thicker, lance-shaped, scalloped, dark green aerial leaves. India to Thailand. ❀ (min. 68°F/20°C)

HYLOCEREUS

CACTACEAE

Genus of about 20 species of robust, climbing, sometimes scrambling, epiphytic cacti from forest in S. Mexico, the West Indies, and Central and tropical South America. They have prominent aerial roots and 3-ribbed stems, which may grow to 15ft (5m) long. The stems often have scalloped ribs with areoles bearing a few short spines or bristles. Large, funnel-shaped flowers open by night in summer; they are followed by spherical to ovoid, scaly red fruits, to 4in (10cm) across, containing kidney-shaped black seeds. Where temperatures fall below 59°F (15°C), grow in a warm greenhouse. In warmer areas, grow against a wall, or over a fence or tree trunk.

• **CULTIVATION** Under glass, grow in soilless, epiphytic cactus potting mix in bright indirect light; provide high humidity. In the growing season, water freely and apply a half-strength, balanced liquid fertilizer monthly; keep moist in winter. Outdoors, grow in sharply drained, poor to moderately fertile, acidic soil in partial or dappled shade. See also pp.48–49.

• **PROPAGATION** Sow seed at 66–75°F (19–24°C) in spring. Root cuttings of stem segments in spring or summer.

• **PESTS AND DISEASES** May be susceptible to scale insects, basal rot, and cactus virus X.

H. calcaratus. Semi-epiphytic cactus with ribbed, bright green stems, 1½–3in (4–8cm) thick. Rib margins are divided into prominent, rounded lobes with small areoles, either spineless or bearing 2–4 white bristles. In summer, bears very fragrant, white or creamy white flowers, 8–12in (20–30cm) across, with long, greenish white outer segments. ↕↔ 6ft (2m) or more. Costa Rica. ❀ (min. 59°F/15°C)

H. ocamponis. Climbing cactus with slightly wavy, glaucous, blue-green stems, 2½in (6cm) thick, and areoles bearing 3–8 yellow spines. Fragrant flowers, to 12in (30cm) across, with wide, pure white inner petals and narrower, pale yellowish green outer segments, are produced in summer. ↕↔ 6ft (2m) or more. S. Mexico. ❀ (min. 59°F/15°C)

H. polyrhizus. Scrambling, epiphytic cactus with slender, low-ribbed, greenish white stems, 1¼–1½in (3–4cm) thick, soon becoming green; the areoles bear 2–4 brown spines. In summer, purple buds open to fragrant flowers, 10–12in (25–30cm) across, with off-white inner petals and red outer segments. ↕ 12ft (4m), ↔ 24in (60cm). Panama to Ecuador. ❀ (min. 59°F/15°C)

H. undatus ■ (Queen of the night). Fast-growing, free-branching, epiphytic or climbing cactus with jointed, scalloped, horny stems, 2–3in (5–8cm) thick, and areoles bearing up to 3 conical, dark brown or gray-brown spines. Fragrant white flowers, 12in (30cm) across, with yellowish green outer segments, are borne in summer. ↕↔ 6–12ft (2–4m). West Indies; widely naturalized in tropical America. ❀ (min. 59°F/15°C)

Hylocereus undatus

Hylomecon japonica

HYLOMECON

PAPAVERACEAE

Genus of one species of rhizomatous herbaceous perennial from woodland in E. Asia. It has mostly basal, pinnate leaves, and is grown for its poppy-like flowers, produced over long periods from late spring to summer. Excellent as a woodland or wild garden plant, or for shady pockets, but may spread quickly and smother small plants nearby.

• **CULTIVATION** Grow in moist but well-drained, moderately fertile, humus-rich, neutral to slightly acidic soil in partial to deep shade.

• **PROPAGATION** Sow seed in containers in a cold frame as soon as ripe or in autumn. Divide in spring.

• **PESTS AND DISEASES** Prone to damage by slugs and snails, especially in spring.

H. japonica ▣ (Wood poppy). Clump-forming perennial with pinnate, pale green leaves, to 8in (20cm) long, consisting of 5- to 7-toothed, ovate or obovate leaflets. Solitary, saucer- to cup-shaped, 4-petaled, deep yellow flowers, to 2in (5cm) across, are borne from late spring to summer. ↕12in (30cm), ↔ 12in (30cm) or more. E. China, Korea, Japan. Zone 6.

▷ ***Hylotelephium roseum*** see *Sedum erythrostictum*

▷ ***Hymenanthera*** see *Melicytus*

HYMENOCALLIS

syn. ISMENE

Spider lily

AMARYLLIDACEAE

Genus of about 40 species of bulbous perennials, some evergreen, found in grassland and rocky habitats from S. US to South America. In spring, summer, or winter, they bear terminal umbels of fragrant flowers resembling spidery daffodils (*Narcissus*), each with 6 narrow petals (tepals), and a large cup, formed from the fused lower parts of the stamens. The anthers are attached to the cup and face inward. The leaves are basal, strap-shaped or oblong, and mid- to dark green. Where not hardy, grow in a warm greenhouse (except for *H. narcissiflora*, which is best in a cool greenhouse); in warmer areas, grow in a bed or border, at the base of a warm, sunny wall, or in containers.

Hymenocallis x *festalis*

• **CULTIVATION** Plant bulbs in autumn with the neck and shoulders above soil level. Under glass, grow in soil-based potting mix with added leaf mold and grit, in bright filtered or full light. Provide low humidity for deciduous species and moderate to high humidity for evergreens. Water freely during the growing season, and apply a dilute, balanced liquid fertilizer every 2 or 3 weeks. Keep deciduous species dry and evergreens just moist when dormant. Outdoors, grow in moderately fertile, moist but well-drained soil in sun or partial shade; when dormant, protect from excessive moisture. Where not hardy, plant in spring and lift for winter.

• **PROPAGATION** Sow seed at 66–75°F (19–24°C) as soon as ripe. Remove offsets in spring.

• **PESTS AND DISEASES** Red leaf spot and mosaic virus can occur.

H. amancaes. Bulbous perennial with semi-erect, strap-shaped, dark green, basal leaves, to 18in (45cm) long, fused at their bases to form a false stem around the bottom of the flower stems. In summer, these bear loose umbels of 2–6 scented, deep yellow flowers, 3½in (9cm) across. ↕12in (30cm), PD10in (25cm). Peru. ❀ (min. 59°F/15°C)

H. calathina see *H. narcissiflora.*

H. caribaea. Evergreen, bulbous perennial with semi-erect, strap-shaped, glossy, mid-green, basal leaves, to 24in (60cm) long. From summer to autumn, bears umbels of 8–10 scented white flowers, 6in (15cm) across. ↕to 24in (60cm), PD12in (30cm). West Indies. ❀ (min. 59°F/15°C)

H. caroliniana. Bulbous perennial with up to 12 strap-shaped, mid-green, basal leaves, to 18in (45cm) long. From spring to summer, bears umbels of 5–10 fragrant white flowers, to 5in (13cm) across. ↕to 24in (60cm), PD12in (30cm). Indiana to Louisiana and Georgia. Zone 7.

H.* x *festalis ▣ (*H. longipetala* x *H. narcissiflora*). Evergreen, bulbous perennial with semi-erect, oblong, mid-green, basal leaves, to 36in (90cm) long. From spring to summer, bears umbels of 2–5 scented white flowers, 3–5in (8–13cm) across, with long, narrow petals, and wide cups; the upper 3 stamens of each flower curve downward, the lower 3 are straight. ↕32in (80cm), PD12in (30cm). Garden origin. ❀ (min. 59°F/15°C)

H. liriosme (Spider lily). Evergreen perennial with strap-shaped, glossy, light green basal leaves, 24in (60cm) long. In spring, bears umbels of 8–10 lemon-scented, white flowers, to 8in (20cm) across. ↕24in (60cm), PD12in (30cm). Louisiana, Texas, Arkansas. Zone 8.

H.* x *macrostephana (*H. narcissiflora* x *H. speciosa*). Bulbous perennial with semi-erect, inversely lance-shaped, bright mid-green, basal leaves, 20–36in (50–90cm) long. Umbels of up to 10 fragrant flowers, 6in (15cm) across, varying from white to cream or greenish yellow, are borne in spring or summer. ↕32in (80cm), PD12in (30cm). Garden origin. ❀ (min. 59°F/15°C)

H. narcissiflora, syn. *H. calathina*, *Ismene calathina* (Peruvian daffodil). Bulbous perennial with strap-shaped, semi-erect, dark green, basal leaves, to 24in (60cm) long, sheathing at the bases to form a false stem. In summer, bears umbels of up to 5 strongly scented white flowers, 4in (10cm) across, sometimes with green-striped tubes; all the stamens curve upward across the cup. ↕24in (60cm), PD12in (30cm). Peruvian Andes. ❀ (min. 41°F/5°C); may withstand short spells around 32°F (0°C).

H. speciosa. Evergreen, bulbous perennial producing semi-erect, broadly elliptic to oblong, mid-green, basal leaves, to 26in (65cm) long. Umbels of up to 12 scented, greenish white flowers, 9in (23cm) across, are produced from autumn to winter. ↕to 18in (45cm), PD12in (30cm). West Indies. ❀ (min. 59°F/15°C)

***H.* 'Sulfur Queen'.** Bulbous perennial with semi-erect, strap-shaped, dark green, basal leaves, 10–24in (25–60cm) long. Umbels of up to 6 scented, soft sulfur-yellow flowers, 6in (15cm) across, with green-striped, paler yellow tubes, are produced from spring to summer. ↕24in (60cm), PD12in (30cm). ❀ (min. 59°F/15°C)

HYMENOSPORUM

Australian frangipani

PITTOSPORACEAE

Genus of one species of evergreen, flowering shrub or tree from rainforest or temperate forest in E. Australia and New Guinea. It is valued for its showy, umbel-like panicles of tubular flowers, with 5 spreading lobes, and its alternate, lance-shaped to obovate or oval-oblong, glossy leaves. Where not hardy, grow in a conservatory or temperate green-house; in warmer regions, grow as a handsome specimen tree.

• **CULTIVATION** Under glass, grow in soil-based potting mix in full light, with shade from hot sun and low to moderate humidity. During the growing season, water moderately and apply a balanced liquid fertilizer monthly; keep moist in winter. Outdoors, grow in humus-rich, moist but well-drained soil in full sun. Pruning group 1 or 8; hard pruning is tolerated.

• **PROPAGATION** Sow seed at 61–64°F (16–18°C) in spring. Root semi-ripe cuttings with bottom heat in summer. Layer, or air layer, in spring or autumn.

• **PESTS AND DISEASES** Infrequent.

H. flavum (Australian frangipani). Large shrub or small to medium-sized tree, usually with a single main stem and well-spaced but bushy branches. Lance-shaped to obovate or oval-oblong leaves, 2½–6in (6–15cm) long, are glossy, dark green above, paler green beneath. From spring to summer, bears loose, umbel-like panicles, to 8in (20cm) across, of tubular, fragrant flowers, 1¼in (3cm) across, with 5 spreading lobes; they open pale cream and rapidly age to orange-yellow. ↕12–70ft (4–20m),

↔ 10–22ft (3–7m). Queensland, New South Wales, New Guinea. ❀ (min. 41°F/5°C); may survive short spells around 32°F (0°C).

▷ ***Hymenoxys acaulis*** see *Tetraneuris acaulis*

HYOPHORBE

Bottle palm

ARECACEAE

Genus of 5 species of single-stemmed palms from volcanic or limestone soils in forest, from sea level to 2,300ft (700m), on the Mascarene Islands, E. of Madagascar. They have erect trunks, swollen at the base or middle, topped by a cluster of pinnate leaves above a prominent crownshaft. Bowl-shaped, 3-petaled flowers are borne in solitary panicles beneath the lowest leaf. Where not hardy, grow in a warm greenhouse or conservatory; elsewhere, use in a courtyard garden or as lawn specimens.

• **CULTIVATION** Under glass, grow in soil-based potting mix in full light, shaded from hot sun, with moderate humidity. Water moderately all year. Apply a dilute, balanced liquid fertilizer monthly in growth. Outdoors, grow in moderately fertile, moist but well-drained soil in sun or partial shade.

• **PROPAGATION** Sow seed at 81°F (27°C) in spring.

• **PESTS AND DISEASES** Root rot, leaf spots, lethal yellowing, and spider mites may be problems.

H. lagenicaulis ■ syn. *Mascarena lagenicaulis* (Bottle palm). Small palm with a flask-shaped gray trunk, swollen at ground level, with vertical fissures in the bark. The narrowly ovate, pinnate leaves, 4½–6ft (1.3–1.8m) long, have many linear, mid- to deep green leaflets. In summer, bears tiny, green to cream flowers in panicles to 32in (80cm) long. ↕ to 20ft (6m), ↔ to 10ft (3m). Mascarene Islands (Round Island). ❀ (min. 59–61°F/15–16°C)

HYOSCYAMUS

Henbane

SOLANACEAE

Genus of 15 species of taprooted, often strong-smelling, hairy, sticky annuals, biennials, and perennials found on banks, cliffs, wasteland, and pebble beaches in Europe, N. Africa, and Asia. They have lance-shaped to rounded, thick, coarse, felted, usually toothed leaves, and bear branching, leafy racemes of funnel- to bell-shaped flowers from late spring to autumn. They are grown, normally as annuals, for their unusual flowers and interesting seed heads, which are useful in dried flower arrangements. Grow in poor stony soils, on a dry bank, or in wall crevices. Henbanes will tolerate coastal conditions. All parts of henbanes are highly toxic if ingested, and may irritate the skin on contact.

• **CULTIVATION** Grow in well-drained, preferably alkaline soil in full sun.

• **PROPAGATION** Sow seed *in situ* in spring; henbanes often self-seed freely.

• **PESTS AND DISEASES** Infrequent.

H. albus. Erect annual or biennial with broadly ovate, sticky, pale mid-green leaves, to 4in (10cm) long. In spring, bears long racemes of unevenly lobed, 2-lipped, veined, pale yellow-green flowers, 1¼in (3cm) long. ↕ 12–36in (30–90cm), ↔ to 18in (45cm). S. Europe. ❀ (min. 45°F/7°C)

H. niger (Black henbane, Henbane, Stinking nightshade). Sticky, strong-smelling annual or biennial producing oval to lance-shaped, entire or toothed, thickly felted, gray-green leaves, to 8in (20cm) long, mostly in basal rosettes. From summer to autumn, 5-lobed flowers, to 1in (2.5cm) across, dull yellow with purple centers and narrow purple veins, are borne singly or in pairs at the tips of forked, arching racemes. ↕ 2–4ft (0.6–1.2m), ↔ to 3ft (1m). Europe, W. Asia. ❀ (min. 45°F/7°C)

Hyophorbe lagenicaulis

HYPERICUM

St. John's wort

CLUSIACEAE

Genus of more than 400 species of deciduous, evergreen, and semi-evergreen shrubs and trees, annuals, and herbaceous perennials, occurring worldwide in a wide range of habitats, from woodland and scrub to mountains and cliffs. They have variably shaped, opposite, or occasionally whorled leaves, some with attractive autumn color. Showy yellow flowers with prominent stamens are borne singly in terminal, occasionally axillary cymes, usually over a long period. The fruits, ornamental in a few species, are usually 3- to 5-valved capsules, or occasionally berry-like. Depending on size, hypericums are suitable for a variety of situations, from a shrub or mixed border to a rock garden; *H. elodes* grows well in boggy ground or as a marginal aquatic. Grow tender species in a cool or temperate greenhouse where not hardy, and in a shrub border in warmer regions.

• **CULTIVATION** Grow in moderately fertile, moist but well-drained soil: the larger species in sun or partial shade, the dwarf species in full sun and in sharply drained soil. *H. androsaemum* and *H. calycinum* thrive in partial to deep shade. Grow *H. elodes* along the margins of a muddy-bottomed pool, in no more than 1in (2.5cm) of water, in dappled shade. Protect small rock garden species from excessive winter moisture; shelter evergreen hypericums from cold, drying winds. Pruning group 1; or group 6 for deciduous species, and group 8 for evergreens. Cut *H. calycinum* to ground level in spring.

• **PROPAGATION** Sow seed in containers in a cold frame in autumn (species may hybridize). Divide perennials in spring or autumn (*H. elodes* in spring only). Root softwood cuttings of perennials in late spring; root greenwood or semi-ripe cuttings of shrubs in summer.

• **PESTS AND DISEASES** Prone to thrips, scale, anthracnose, rust, and leaf spots.

H. acmosepalum. Upright, bushy, semi-evergreen shrub with arching branches and oblong to elliptic-oblong, dark green leaves, to 2½in (6cm) long, bluish green or glaucous beneath, turning orange and red in autumn. In summer, bears terminal cymes of up to 6 star-shaped, deep yellow, sometimes red-tinged flowers, to 2in (5cm) across, followed by conical red capsules. ↕↔ 3–6ft (1–2m). China (Yunnan, Sichuan, Guizhou, Guangxi). Zone 7b.

H. aegypticum. Low-growing, spreading, evergreen shrub with densely arranged, oblong, glaucous, mid-green leaves, to ½in (1.5cm) long. From late spring to summer, bears small, solitary, star-shaped, pale yellow flowers, to ½in (1.5cm) across, clustered at the ends of leafy shoots. ↕ 20in (50cm), ↔ 36in (90cm). Mediterranean. Zone 8.

H. androsaemum (Tutsan). Bushy, deciduous shrub with erect branches and broadly ovate to oblong, mid-green leaves, to 6in (15cm) long, paler green beneath. In midsummer, bears cymes of up to 11 star-shaped or cupped, yellow flowers, to ¾in (2cm) across, followed by spherical red, berry-like fruit that

Hypericum androsaemum 'Albury Purple'

ripen to black. ↕ 30in (75cm), ↔ 36in (90cm). W. Europe, Mediterranean to N. Iran. Zone 4. **'Albury Purple'** ■ produces purple-flushed leaves, and is often considered to be a cultivar of *H.* x *inodorum.*

H. augustinii. Upright, sparsely branched, evergreen to semi-evergreen shrub with broadly ovate to oblong-lance-shaped, leathery, pale green leaves, to 3in (8cm) long. Bears cymes of 3–13 saucer-shaped, pale to golden yellow flowers, to 2½in (6cm) across, from late summer to autumn. ↕↔ 4ft (1.2m). S.W. China (Yunnan). Zone 7b.

H. balearicum. Densely branched, evergreen shrub producing ovate-oblong, leathery, dark green leaves, to ½in (1.5cm) long, with wavy margins and warty glands. From early to late summer, bears solitary, star-shaped, bright yellow flowers, to 1½in (4cm) across. Needs well-drained soil; ideal for a rock garden. ↕↔ to 10in (25cm). Spain (Balearic Islands). Zone 7.

***H. beanii* 'Gold Cup'** see *H.* x *cyathiflorum* 'Gold Cup'.

H. bellum. Bushy, erect to arching, deciduous shrub producing oblong-lance-shaped to broadly ovate, mid-green leaves, to 3in (8cm) long, with wavy margins. In summer, bears cymes of up to 7 cup-shaped, pale to golden yellow flowers, to 1–2½in (2.5–6cm) across. ↕↔ 3ft (1m). W. and S.W. China, Himalayas, N. India, Burma. Zone 6.

H. calycinum ■ (Aaron's beard, Rose of Sharon). Dwarf, evergreen or semi-evergreen shrub, spreading by runners, with oblong to elliptic or narrowly

Hypericum calycinum

Hypericum cerastioides

ovate, dark green leaves, to 4in (10cm) long, paler green beneath. From midsummer to midautumn, saucer-shaped, bright yellow flowers, to 4in (10cm) across, are borne singly, or occasionally in small cymes of 2 or 3. Good as a groundcover in shade. ↕24in (60cm), ↔ indefinite. S.E. Bulgaria, N.W. and N.E. Turkey. Zone 5b.

H. cerastioides ▣ syn. *H. rhodoppeum.* Perennial with upright and arching stems bearing ovate, oblong, or elliptic, downy, gray-green leaves, to 1¼in (3cm) long. Cymes of up to 5 star-shaped, deep yellow flowers, ¾–1¾in (2–4.5cm) across, are produced in profusion in late spring and early summer. ↕6in (15cm), ↔ 16in (40cm) or more. S. Bulgaria, N.E. Greece, N.W. Turkey. Zone 6.

H. coris. Dome-shaped, evergreen subshrub or herbaceous perennial with erect, wiry stems bearing whorls of linear, mid-green leaves, to ½in (1.5cm) long, glaucous beneath. In summer, bears an abundance of pyramidal cymes of up to 20 shallowly cup-shaped, golden yellow, sometimes red-veined flowers, ½–¾in (1.5–2cm) across, with conspicuous stamens. ↕8in (20cm), ↔ to 12in (30cm). S.E. France, Switzerland, Italy. Zone 7.

Hypericum elodes

H. cuneatum see *H. pallens.*

***H.* x *cyathiflorum* 'Gold Cup'**, syn. *H. beanii* 'Gold Cup'. Bushy, deciduous shrub with arching branches and lance-shaped, mid-green leaves, to 3in (8cm) long. Pyramidal cymes of up to 9 cup-shaped, golden yellow flowers, 2in (5cm) across, are produced in summer. ↕5ft (1.5m), ↔ 6ft (2m). Zone 8.

***H.* 'Eastleigh Gold'.** Semi-evergreen shrub with arching branches and elliptic-oblong to lance-shaped, mid-green leaves, to 2in (5cm) long. In summer, bears cymes of up to 4 large, shallowly cup-shaped, golden yellow flowers, to 2½in (6cm) across. ↕3ft (1m), ↔ 5ft (1.5m). Zone 7b.

H. elodes ▣ (Marsh hypericum). Marsh or submerged aquatic perennial with creeping stolons, 4–12in (10–30cm) long, and broadly ovate to elliptic, soft, densely woolly, gray-green leaves, to ½in (1.5cm) long. Saucer-shaped, bright yellow flowers, to ½in (1.5cm) across, are borne singly or in cymes of 3–10 in summer. ↕3–6in (7–15cm), ↔ indefinite. W. Europe. Zone 7.

H. empetrifolium. Dwarf, evergreen, stiffly erect to decumbent and cushion-forming shrub producing linear, mid-green leaves, to ½in (1.5cm) long, usually in whorls of 3. In summer, bears cylindrical to narrowly pyramidal cymes of up to 40 star-shaped, golden yellow flowers, to ¾in (2cm) across. ↕18in (45cm), ↔ 36in (90cm). S.E. Europe, S.W. Asia. Zone 5. **subsp. *oliganthum*,** syn. var. *prostratum* of gardens, is prostrate, with branching stems clothed in whorls of stalkless, linear, or sometimes narrowly elliptic, dark green leaves, to ¼in (6mm) long, with rolled margins. Cymes of 4–7 deep yellow flowers are produced in summer. Suitable for a sunny wall or rock garden; needs good drainage; ↕2in (5cm), ↔ to 12in (30cm); Greece (Crete); Zone 7b. **var. *prostratum* of gardens** see subsp. *oliganthum.*

H. forrestii, syn. *H. patulum* var. *forrestii.* Upright, spreading, deciduous shrub with triangular-ovate to broadly ovate or lance-shaped, mid-green leaves, to 2½in (6cm) long, turning red in late autumn and early winter. Cymes of up to 20 large, cup- to saucer-shaped, golden yellow flowers, to 2½in (6cm) across, are borne from summer to autumn. ↕4ft (1.2m), ↔ 5ft (1.5m). China (Yunnan, Sichuan), N.E. Burma. Zone 7.

H. frondosum ▣ Erect, deciduous shrub with thick, flaking stems and oblong, bluish green leaves, to 2½in (6cm) long. In mid- and late summer, produces cymes of up to 7 saucer-shaped, golden yellow flowers, to 1¾in (4.5cm) across, with prominent, central bosses of yellow stamens. ↕↔ 2–4ft (60–120cm). S.E. US. Zone 5. **'Sunburst'** has reddish brown, exfoliating bark and bears golden yellow flowers, 1–2in (2.5–5cm) across, with long, thick stamens, from midsummer to early autumn.

H. henryi. Variable, bushy, deciduous shrub with upright to arching branches clothed in narrowly elliptic or lance-shaped to ovate, mid-green leaves, to 1½in (4cm) long, glaucous beneath. Cymes of up to 5, occasionally 7, cup-shaped, golden yellow flowers, to 2in (5cm) across, are produced from late summer to autumn. ↕↔ 6ft (2m). S.W. China, E. Burma, North Vietnam, Indonesia. Zone 6.

***H.* 'Hidcote'** ▣ Dense, bushy, evergreen or semi-evergreen shrub with lance-shaped, dark green leaves, to 2½in (6cm) long. From midsummer to early autumn, bears corymb-like cymes of up to 6, sometimes more, large, cup-shaped, golden yellow flowers, to 2½in (6cm) across. ↕4ft (1.2m), ↔ 5ft (1.5m). Zone 6.

H.* x *inodorum (*H. androsaemum* x *H. hircinum*). Upright, bushy, deciduous or semi-evergreen shrub with oblong-lance-shaped to broadly ovate, aromatic, dark green leaves, to 4½in (11cm) long. Cymes of 3–23 small, star-shaped yellow flowers, ½–1¼in (1.5–3cm) across, are produced from midsummer to midautumn, followed by dark cerise, conical capsules. ↕↔ 4ft (1.2m). Garden origin. Zone 7. **'Elstead'** ▣ bears large fruit, which flush pinkish red on ripening. **'Ysella'** produces golden yellow leaves.

H. kalmianum. Erect, bushy, evergreen shrub producing narrowly oblong to

Hypericum frondosum

Hypericum 'Hidcote'

inversely lance-shaped, bluish green leaves, to 2in (5cm) long. In mid- and late summer, bears cymes of up to 7 saucer-shaped, golden yellow flowers, to 1½in (4cm) across. ↕↔ 30in (75cm). E. North America (Great Lakes region). Zone 4.

H. kouytchense, syn. *H. patulum* var. *grandiflorum*, *H.* 'Sungold'. Rounded, bushy, semi-evergreen shrub with arching shoots and elliptic to ovate or lance-shaped, dark bluish green leaves, to 2½in (6cm) long, paler beneath. Cymes of up to 11 star-shaped, golden yellow flowers, to 2½in (6cm) across, with partially reflexed petals, are borne from summer to autumn, followed by conical, bright red fruit. ↕3ft (1m), ↔ 5ft (1.5m). China (Guizhou). Zone 6.

H. lancasteri ▣ Spreading, deciduous shrub with triangular-lance-shaped to oblong leaves, to 2½in (6cm) long, bronze when young, maturing to mid-green, glaucous beneath. In summer, bears cymes of up to 11 star-shaped to shallowly cup-shaped, golden yellow flowers, to 2½in (6cm) across, with star-shaped calyces with red-margined sepals, conspicuous before they open. ↕↔ 3ft (1m). China (N. Yunnan, S. Sichuan). Zone 5b.

***H.* x *moserianum* 'Tricolor'**, syn. *H.* 'Variegatum'. Spreading, semi-evergreen shrub with arching, red-flushed shoots and ovate, mid-green leaves, to 2½in (6cm) long, attractively variegated with cream, pink, and green. From summer to autumn, bears cymes of up to 8 cup-shaped yellow flowers, to 2in (5cm) across. Needs a sheltered position. ↕12in (30cm), ↔ 24in (60cm). Zone 6.

H. olympicum. Deciduous shrub with erect stems clothed in oblong, elliptic, or linear-lance-shaped, pointed, gray-green leaves, to 1½in (4cm) long, glaucous beneath. In summer, bears cymes of up to 5 star-shaped, deep yellow flowers, each to 2½in (6cm) across. ↕10in (25cm), ↔ 12in (30cm). N. Greece, N.W. Turkey. Zone 5b. **f. *uniflorum* 'Citrinum'**, syn. 'Citrinum', produces broadly elliptic to obovate leaves, to ¾–1¼in (2–3cm) long, and pale lemon-yellow flowers; ideal for a rock garden.

H. orientale. Erect or decumbent perennial with elliptic, oblong, linear, or inversely lance-shaped, dark green leaves, ½–1½in (1–4cm) long. Dense cymes of up to 17 star-shaped, deep golden

H

Hypericum x *inodorum* 'Elstead'

yellow flowers, to 1¼in (3cm) across, are borne in summer. ↕ 12in (30cm), ↔ to 12in (30cm). Turkey, Republic of Georgia, Azerbaijan. Zone 7b.

H. pallens, syn. *H. cuneatum*. Dwarf, evergreen shrub with stalkless, elliptic, oblong, inversely lance-shaped, or obovate, mid-green leaves, to 1in (2.5cm) long, borne on brittle, branching, red-tinted stems. Cymes of up to 3 star-shaped, pale yellow flowers, ½–1in (1.5–2.5cm) across, open from red-tipped buds in summer. Excellent for a rock garden or alpine house; requires good drainage. ↕ 6in (15cm), ↔ to 8in (20cm). S. Turkey, W. Syria. Zone 7.

H. patulum. Bushy, evergreen or semi-evergreen shrub with spreading branches and lance-shaped to oblong-lance-shaped or oblong-ovate, dark green leaves, to 2½in (6cm) long. Cymes of up to 15 cup-shaped, golden yellow flowers, to 1½in (4cm) across, are borne from summer to early autumn. ↕ 4ft (1.2m), ↔ 5ft (1.5m). China (Guizhou, Sichuan). Zone 7b. **var. *forrestii*** see *H. forrestii*. **var. *grandiflorum*** see *H. kouytchense*. **var. *henryi* of gardens** see *H. pseudohenryi*.

H. perforatum (Perforate St. John's wort). Tufted perennial with stiff, 2-ridged stems bearing opposite, ovate to elliptic-oblong or linear, mid-green leaves, 1¼in (3cm) long, with large, translucent dots. Bears numerous star-shaped, bright yellow flowers, ½–1½in (1.5–3cm) across, in cylindrical cymes in summer. Ideal for a wild garden. ↕ 24–42in (60–110cm), ↔ to 24in (60cm). Europe, W. Asia. Zone 4.

Hypericum lancasteri

var. *angustifolium* has narrow leaves and bears smaller flowers, ½in (1.5cm) across. **var. *latifolium*** has broad leaves and larger flowers, to 1½in (4cm) across. **var. *microphyllum*** produces small leaves and bears small flowers, ½in (1.5cm) across.

H. pseudohenryi, syn. *H. patulum* var. *henryi* of gardens. Bushy, semi-evergreen shrub with erect shoots and ovate-oblong to lance-shaped, dark green leaves, to 3in (8cm) long. In summer, bears cymes of up to 7, sometimes up to 25, shallowly cup-shaped to star-shaped, golden yellow flowers, to 2½in (6cm) across, followed by conical, red-tinged green fruit. ↕ 5½ft (1.7m), ↔ 6ft (2m). China (Yunnan, Sichuan). Zone 6.

H. reptans ■ Deciduous, prostrate, mat-forming shrub with rooting stems and elliptic, leathery, mid-green leaves, ¼–¾in (0.7–2cm) long, turning red or yellow in autumn. Bears solitary, deeply cup-shaped, crimson-flushed, golden yellow flowers, to 1¼in (3cm) across, in summer. Good in a rock garden. ↕ 2in (5cm), ↔ to 8in (20cm). Himalayas (Nepal to Yunnan). Zone 7b.

H. rhodoppeum see *H. cerastioides*.

***H.* 'Rowallane'.** Semi-evergreen shrub with upright, arching branches and oblong-ovate to oblong-lance-shaped, dark green leaves, to 3in (8cm) long. Cymes of up to 3 shallowly cupped, dark golden yellow flowers, to 3in (8cm) across, are borne from late summer to autumn. ↕ to 6ft (1.8m), ↔ to 3ft (1m). Zone 7.

***H.* 'Sungold'** see *H. kouytchense*.

H. tetrapterum. Upright perennial with pendent branches and ovate to elliptic-oblong or rounded, stalkless, papery, mid-green leaves, ¾–1½in (2–4cm) long. In summer, bears cymes of numerous, star-shaped, bright yellow flowers, ¼–½in (1–1.5cm) across, sometimes with 1 or 2 black dots on each sepal and 1–4 black dots on each petal. ↕ 4–42in (10–100cm), ↔ to 36in (90cm). Europe. Zone 5.

H. trichocaulon. Deciduous subshrub or herbaceous perennial with prostrate branches and ovate-oblong to elliptic or linear, pale gray-green leaves, to ½in (1.5cm) long. In summer, red-tinged buds open to 2 or 3 star-shaped, golden yellow flowers, to 1in (2.5cm) across, borne singly or in cymes. Suitable for an alpine house. ↕ 4in (10cm), ↔ to 8in (20cm). Greece (Crete). Zone 7.

***H.* 'Variegatum'** see. *H.* x *moserianum* 'Tricolor'.

Hypericum reptans

Hyphaene thebaica

HYPHAENE

Doum palm

ARECACEAE

Genus of about 10 species of palms from Africa, Madagascar, the Arabian Peninsula, India, and Sri Lanka, occurring on poor or exhausted soils, often poorly drained, usually in hot, dry areas. Some doum palms are stemless, some have creeping stems; others are tree-like with branching trunks. The leaves are fan-shaped, and tiny, bowl-shaped, 3-petaled flowers are borne in panicles between them. Where not hardy, grow doum palms in a warm greenhouse (they require very dry heat to thrive under glass). In dry, frost-free regions, grow the creeping and stemless species as groundcovers and the tree-like ones as specimen trees.

• **CULTIVATION** Under glass, grow in soil-based potting mix with additional grit, in full light. Provide low humidity. Water sparingly at all times. Apply a balanced liquid fertilizer every 6–8 weeks when in growth. Outdoors, grow in poor to moderately fertile, sharply drained soil in full sun. Protect from winter and summer moisture.

• **PROPAGATION** Sow seed at 66–75°F (19–24°C) in spring; seed may be difficult to germinate.

• **PESTS AND DISEASES** Spider mites may be a problem under glass.

H. coriacea (Doum palm). Small palm with a single stem, or sometimes suckering to form a clump. Each stem forks several times to form a head of branches all on one plane. Long-stalked, waxy, fan-shaped leaves have many fan-shaped blades, 12–32in (30–80cm) long, gray- to blue-green with scale-like black hairs. Tiny, bowl-shaped, green to white flowers are borne in panicles, to 3ft (1m) long, mainly in summer. ↕ to 15ft (5m), ↔ 4–12ft (1.2–4m). E. Africa, South Africa, Madagascar. ❄ (min. 55–59°F/13–15°C)

H. thebaica ■ (Gingerbread palm). Medium-sized palm with a single stem that forks at regular intervals. The fan-shaped, gray-green leaves have long, spiny stalks and numerous rounded leaf blades, 24–30in (60–75cm) long. Tiny, bowl-shaped yellow flowers are borne in panicles, to 3ft (1m) long, usually in summer. ↕ 20–30ft (6–10m), ↔ 10–20ft (3–6m). N. Africa. ❄ (min. 55–59°F/13–15°C)

HYPOCALYMMA

MYRTACEAE

Genus, related to *Leptospermum*, of 13 species of evergreen shrubs found on sandy or gravelly soils from sea level to 3,000ft (900m) in Australia. They have opposite, simple, linear to broadly ovate, gray-green to light or dark green leaves, with entire or fringed margins. Cup-shaped, 5-petaled, many-stamened flowers are produced singly, in pairs, or occasionally in small clusters from the leaf axils. Where temperatures fall below 45°F (7°C), grow in a cool greenhouse. In warmer regions, grow at the base of a warm, sunny wall, in a shrub border, in a courtyard garden, or as a hedge.

• **CULTIVATION** Under glass, grow in soil-based potting mix with additional sharp sand, in full light or bright filtered light; provide low humidity. During the growing season, water freely and apply a balanced liquid fertilizer monthly; keep just moist in winter. Outdoors, grow in moderately fertile, moist but well-drained, light, sandy, neutral to slightly alkaline soil in full sun or dappled shade. Pruning group 8; plants grown under glass may need restrictive pruning.

• **PROPAGATION** Surface-sow seed onto permanently moist seed starting mix at 61–64°F (16–18°C) in spring. Root semi-ripe cuttings with bottom heat in late summer.

• **PESTS AND DISEASES** Prone to gray mold (*Botrytis*) under glass, and to *Phytophthora* root rot outdoors.

Hypocalymma cordifolium 'Golden Veil'

***H. cordifolium* 'Golden Veil'** ■ Dwarf to small shrub with branching, 4-angled or 4-winged stems, often bunched or twisted together. Broadly ovate, bright green, cream-variegated leaves, to ½in (1.5cm) long, have heart-shaped bases and recurved, wavy, fringed margins. From early spring to midsummer, white flowers, to ½in (1.5cm) across, are borne singly or in twos or threes from the leaf axils. ↕ 1–5ft (0.3–1.5m), ↔ 1–8ft (0.3–2.5m). ❄ (min. 45°F/7°C)

▷ ***Hypocyrta*** see *Nematanthus*

HYPOESTES

Polka-dot plant

ACANTHACEAE

Genus of 40 species of woody-based, evergreen perennials, subshrubs, and shrubs from open woodland in South Africa, Madagascar, and S.E. Asia. Some polka-dot plants are grown for their foliage and some for their flowers. The leaves are opposite, usually ovate, entire or toothed, and smooth or slightly velvety. Terminal or lateral racemes of solitary or clustered, tubular, 2-lipped flowers, with twisted corolla tubes, are borne from late summer to winter. Where not hardy, grow in a warm greenhouse. *H. phyllostachya* and its cultivars are good houseplants; they may also be grown as annuals and used as bedding or in patio containers. In warmer regions, grow in a shrub border or in containers.

• **CULTIVATION** Under glass, grow in soil-based potting mix in bright filtered light, with moderate to high humidity. Water freely in growth, sparingly in winter. Apply a balanced liquid fertilizer every 2–3 weeks in summer. Outdoors, grow in moist but well-drained, moderately fertile, humus-rich soil in partial shade, sheltered from cold winds. Pinch out the growing tips to promote a bushy habit.

• **PROPAGATION** Sow seed at 59–64°F (15–18°C) in spring. Root softwood or tip cuttings in late spring, or semi-ripe cuttings in summer.

• **PESTS AND DISEASES** Powdery mildew may be a problem.

H. aristata (Ribbon bush). Erect, evergreen, woody-based perennial with ovate, entire, dull mid-green leaves, to 3in (8cm) long, with velvety surfaces. Racemes of pale magenta to purple flowers, 1¼in (3cm) long, sometimes

Hypoestes phyllostachya

spotted or lined with white or mauve within, are produced from the leaf axils over a long period from summer to winter. ↕ 4ft (1.2m), ↔ 18in (45cm). South Africa. ❄ (min. 55°F/13°C)
H. phyllostachya ■ syn. *H. sanguinolenta* of gardens (Freckle face, Polka-dot plant). Subshrub with ovate, downy, dark green leaves, 2in (5cm) long, spotted with reddish or bluish pink. From late summer to winter, bears terminal, spike-like racemes, 6in (15cm) long, of tiny, magenta to lilac flowers. ↕ 12in (30cm), ↔ 9in (23cm). Madagascar. ❄ (min. 50°F/10°C). **'Carmina'** has bright red foliage. **'Purpuriana'** has purple leaves. **'Splash'** has showy leaves splashed with pink.
***H. sanguinolenta* of gardens** see *H. phyllostachya.*

HYPOXIS

Starflower

HYPOXIDACEAE

Genus of about 150 species of cormous perennials widespread in woodland in Africa, S.E. Asia, Australia, and North, Central, and South America. Species in cultivation have linear to lance-shaped, light to mid-green, basal leaves, and bear small, star-shaped flowers from spring to summer. Where not hardy, grow in an alpine house or cool greenhouse. In warmer climates, grow in a sheltered rock garden.

• **CULTIVATION** Plant corms 1¼in (3cm) deep when dormant. Under glass, grow in soil-based potting mix with added sharp sand and leaf mold; move from a shaded position at planting to full light or bright filtered light as shoots appear. When in growth, water moderately and apply a balanced liquid fertilizer monthly; dry off after flowering and keep dry in winter. Outdoors, grow in humus-rich, moist but well-drained soil in full sun with midday shade, or in dappled shade. Protect from excessive winter and summer moisture, and shelter from cold, drying winds. Starflowers resent transplanting once established.

• **PROPAGATION** Sow seed at 55–61°F (13–16°C) in spring. Remove offsets in summer or autumn.

• **PESTS AND DISEASES** Rust and leaf spots may occur.

H. angustifolia ■ Small, cormous perennial with erect, grass-like, linear to lance-shaped, hairy, mid-green, basal

Hypoxis angustifolia

leaves, 4–6in (10–15cm) long. In summer, bears stems of up to 7 upward-facing yellow flowers, to ½in (1.5cm) across. ↕ 4–8in (10–20cm), PD2in (5cm). Widespread in South Africa. ❄ (min. 41°F/5°C)
H. capensis, syn. *H. stellata, Spiloxene capensis.* Cormous perennial with erect, narrowly linear, finely toothed, folded, mid-green, basal leaves, 4–12in (10–30cm) long. In spring, bears solitary, upward-facing, white or yellow flowers, ¾–2½in (2–6cm) across, with bright purple or green basal spots. ↕ 4–8in (10–20cm), PD2in (5cm). South Africa (Western Cape, Northern Cape, Eastern Cape). ❄ (min. 41°F/5°C)
H. hemerocallidea, syn. *H. rooperi.* Cormous perennial with arching, lance-shaped, hairy, mid-green, basal leaves 12–18in (30–45cm) long. Branched stems of up to 8 yellow, green-backed flowers, 1¼–1½in (3–4cm) across, are produced from spring to summer. ↕ 6–8in (15–20cm), PD2in (5cm). Widespread in South Africa. Zone 7b.
H. hirsuta. Cormous perennial with semi-erect, narrowly linear, ribbed, hairy, mid-green, basal leaves, to 12in (30cm) long. From spring to summer, bears stems of up to 7 upward-facing, yellow, green-backed flowers, to 1in (2.5cm) across. ↕ 4–8in (10–20cm), PD2in (5cm). E. North America. Zone 6.
H. nitida. Cormous perennial with upright, narrowly linear, shiny, mid-green, basal leaves, 7–9in (8–23cm) long, with fine white hairs on the margins and midribs. In spring, bears racemes of up to 12 yellow, green-backed flowers, 1¼–2in (3–5cm) across. ↕ 4–8in (10–20cm), PD2in (5cm). South Africa. Zone 7b.
H. rooperi see *H. hemerocallidea.*
H. stellata see *H. capensis.*

HYPSELA

CAMPANULACEAE

Genus of 4 species of prostrate perennials found in moist sites at mid- to high altitudes in Australia, New Zealand, and South America. They are cultivated for their alternate, variably shaped, entire or toothed, mid- to dark green leaves, and their tubular, 5-lobed flowers. They are suitable for a large rock garden, but are too invasive for a small area.

• **CULTIVATION** Grow in gritty, humus-rich, moist but well-drained soil in sun or shade. Hypselas spread freely in moist soils and warm conditions.

• **PROPAGATION** Sow seed at 43–54°F (6–12°C), or divide, in spring.

• **PESTS AND DISEASES** Slugs and snails may be problems.

H. longiflora see *H. reniformis.*
H. reniformis, syn. *H. longiflora.* Vigorous, creeping perennial with rooting stems and elliptic or rounded to kidney-shaped, fleshy, bright mid-green leaves, to ½in (1.5cm) long. Solitary, almost stemless, white to pale pink flowers, to ⅜in (9mm) long, with crimson veins, open from late spring to summer. ↕ ¾in (2cm), ↔ indefinite. South America. Zone 7b.

HYSSOPUS

Hyssop

LAMIACEAE

Genus of about 5 often variable species of aromatic herbaceous perennials and evergreen or semi-evergreen shrubs, occurring in dry, sandy, and rocky sites from the Mediterranean to C. Asia. The linear to lance-shaped, ovate, or oblong leaves are mid- or blue-green. Tubular, violet-blue to pink flowers are borne in whorls on narrow, spike-like, terminal inflorescences. *H. officinalis* and its cultivars are grown for their aromatic foliage and flowers, and are excellent for a rock garden or herb garden. They are also suitable for low hedging, and for growing at the base of a warm, sunny wall or in containers. The flowers are attractive to bees and butterflies; the foliage has culinary and medicinal uses.

• **CULTIVATION** Grow in fertile, well-drained, neutral to alkaline soil in full sun. Pruning group 10, in midspring.

• **PROPAGATION** Sow seed in containers in a cold frame in autumn. Root softwood cuttings in summer.

• **PESTS AND DISEASES** Infrequent.

H. officinalis ■ (Hyssop). Dwarf, semi-evergreen, aromatic shrub with erect shoots and linear to narrowly lance-shaped, or oblong, mid-green leaves, to 2in (5cm) long. Slender spikes of whorled, funnel-shaped, 2-lipped, dark blue flowers, ½in (1.5cm) long, are produced from midsummer to early autumn. ↕ 24in (60cm), ↔ 3ft (1m). S. Europe. Zone 6. **f. *albus*** has white flowers. **subsp. *aristatus*** has a dense, upright habit, and bright green leaves. **f. *roseus*** bears pink flowers.

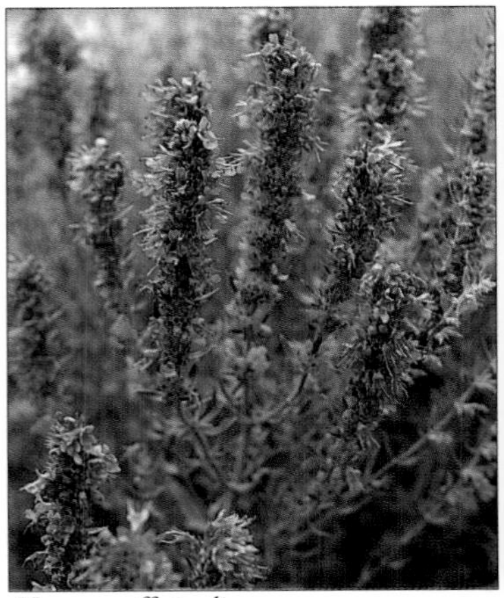

Hyssopus officinalis

I

IBERIS

Candytuft

BRASSICACEAE

Genus of about 40 species of annuals, perennials, and evergreen subshrubs from open sites in free-draining, calcareous soil in Crimea, S. Europe, N. Africa, Cyprus, Syria, N. Iraq, Turkey, and the Caucasus. They have alternate, linear to obovate, and entire to pinnatisect leaves. The inflorescences are corymbs or racemes of sometimes fragrant, white, occasionally purple, pink, or red flowers, ½in (1.5cm) across, each with 4 petals, one pair usually larger than the other. Grow perennials and subshrubs, which may be short-lived, in a rock garden or in walls. Grow annual candytufts as bedding, at the front of borders, or in containers.

• **CULTIVATION** Grow in poor to moderately fertile, moist but well-drained, neutral to alkaline soil in full sun. *I. pruitii* requires sharply drained soil. Pruning group 10, after flowering. Trim perennials and subshrubs lightly after flowering to maintain compactness.

• **PROPAGATION** Sow seed of annuals *in situ* in spring or autumn. Sow seed of perennials and subshrubs in containers in a cold frame in autumn. Root softwood cuttings in late spring or semi-ripe cuttings in summer.

• **PESTS AND DISEASES** Clubroot, damping off, gray mold, and a few fungal spots occur rarely. May be attacked by snails, slugs, and caterpillars.

I. amara (Rocket candytuft). Variable, erect, branched annual with lance-shaped to spoon-shaped leaves, to 3in (8cm) long, toothed toward the tips. Small, lightly scented, purplish white or white flowers are borne in large, domed racemes, 4–6in (10–15cm) long, in summer. ↕ 6–18in (15–45cm), ↔ to 6in (15cm). W. Europe. **'Giant Hyacinth-flowered'** bears large racemes of white

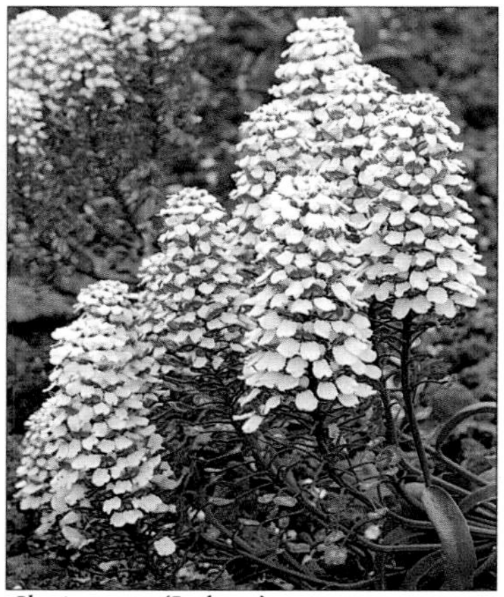

Iberis amara 'Iceberg'

Iberis saxatilis

flowers. **'Iceberg'** ■ produces pure white flowers. **'Pinnacle'** has very fragrant, pure white flowers.

I. candolleana see *I. pruitii*.

I. commutata see *I. sempervirens*.

I. jordanii see *I. pruitii*.

I. pruitii, syn. *I. candolleana*, *I. jordanii*. Short-lived, evergreen, procumbent to erect annual or perennial with rosettes of spoon-shaped, fleshy, dark green leaves, to ¾in (2cm) long. In summer, bears dense corymbs, to 1½in (4cm) across, of white, occasionally lilac flowers. ↕ to 6in (15cm), ↔ to 8in (20cm). Spain, France, Italy, Greece. Zone 6.

I. saxatilis ■ (Perennial candytuft). Evergreen subshrub with linear, almost cylindrical, fleshy, dark green leaves, to ¾in (2cm) long, on upright stems. From late spring to summer, bears flattened corymbs, 1¼–1½in (3–4cm) across, of small white flowers, often purple-tinged with age. Leaves on flowering shoots are flat, linear, and acute. ↕ to 6in (15cm), ↔ to 12in (30cm). Spain, France, Italy, Greece, Romania, Crimea. Zone 6b.

I. semperflorens. Evergreen subshrub with broadly spoon-shaped, slightly fleshy, dark green leaves, ¾–2½in (2–6cm) long. Produces fragrant white flowers borne in crowded corymbs, to 2in (5cm) across, from winter to early spring. ↕ to 12in (30cm), ↔ 24in (60cm) or more. S. Italy (including Sicily). Zone 8.

I. sempervirens ■ syn. *I. commutata*. Spreading, evergreen subshrub with oblong-spoon-shaped, dark green leaves, 1–1½in (2.5–4cm) long. In late spring and early summer, bears corymb-like

Iberis sempervirens

Iberis umbellata Fairy Series

racemes, to 2in (5cm) across, of small white flowers, occasionally flushed lilac. ↕ to 12in (30cm), ↔ to 16in (40cm). S. Europe. Zone 3. **'Autumn Snow'** has white flowers in spring and autumn. **'Climax'** bears more spoon-shaped, deep green leaves, to 2½in (6cm) long; ↕ to 8in (20cm). **'Little Gem'** see 'Weisser Zwerg'. **'Nana'** has an upright habit and narrow, lance-shaped leaves; ↕ to 6in (15cm). **'Purity'** has white flowers over a long season. **'Schneeflocke'**, syn. 'Snowflake', is mound-forming, with dense, corymb-like racemes of snow-white flowers; ↕ to 10in (25cm), ↔ to 24in (60cm). **'Weisser Zwerg'**, syn. 'Little Gem', is a very compact cultivar, with short, linear leaves, to ½in (1.5cm) long. Produces abundant white flowers in spring; ↕ 6in (15cm), ↔ to 10in (25cm).

I. umbellata (Globe candytuft). Bushy, mound-forming annual with linear-lance-shaped leaves, to 4in (10cm) long, the lower leaves toothed. The abundant small, scented flowers are white, pink, lavender, purple, crimson, or bicolored, and are borne in flattened corymbs, to 2in (5cm) across, from spring to summer; ↕ 6–12in (15–30cm), ↔ to 9in (23cm). S. Europe. **Fairy Series** ■ cultivars have white, pink, lilac-purple, or red-pink flowers. **Flash Series** cultivars have vibrant pink, purple, or carmine-red flowers.

IBERVILLEA

CUCURBITACEAE

Genus of 3 or 4 species of climbing, perennial, dioecious succulents from semi-desert regions of Texas and Arizona, and N. Mexico. They have swollen, caudex-like stems that are partly underground, and very slender branches bearing ovate to kidney-shaped, deeply 3- to 5-lobed leaves with simple tendrils. In summer, bell-shaped, usually hairy flowers, with pointed lobes, are borne in racemes or clusters on male plants, or singly on female plants. Where temperatures drop below 35°F (2°C), grow in a warm greenhouse. In warmer climates, grow in a desert garden, or on a trellis in a dry, sunny position.

• **CULTIVATION** Under glass, grow in soil-based potting mix, with added sharp sand or grit in full light, with low humidity. During the growing season, water moderately and apply a balanced liquid fertilizer monthly. Keep totally dry at other times. Outdoors, grow in moderately fertile, sharply drained soil in full sun, and mulch with a layer of limestone chips, 2in (5cm) deep. Protect from excessive winter moisture. See also pp.48–49.

• **PROPAGATION** Sow seed at 68°F (20°C) in early spring. Root softwood cuttings in late spring and early summer with gentle bottom heat.

• **PESTS AND DISEASES** Vulnerable to scale insects.

I. sonorae. Climbing, free-branching succulent with a bottle-shaped caudex and fissured, corky, grayish white bark. Produces bluish green tendrils and fan-shaped, deeply 3-lobed, bluish green leaves, 1½–5in (4–13cm) long, often with rough hairs beneath. Small, hairy, greenish yellow flowers, ½in (1.5cm) across, are borne in summer. ↕ 6–10ft (2–3m), ↔ 12in (30cm). N. Mexico. ❀ (min. 45°F/7°C)

IDESIA

FLACOURTIACEAE

Genus of one species of deciduous tree from woodland in China, Korea, Japan, and Taiwan. Leaves are alternate and slightly toothed. Male and female flowers are borne on separate plants; both are needed to produce fruit. Grown for its bold foliage and clusters of red berries, it is a fine specimen tree or is suitable for a woodland garden.

• **CULTIVATION** Grow in moderately fertile, moist but well-drained, neutral to acidic soil in full sun or light shade, with shelter from other trees. Pruning group 1.

• **PROPAGATION** Sow seed in containers in a cold frame in autumn. Root greenwood cuttings in late spring or semi-ripe cuttings in midsummer.

• **PESTS AND DISEASES** Infrequent.

I. polycarpa ■ Spreading, deciduous tree with open, tiered branches and ovate-heart-shaped, sharply pointed, glossy, mid- to dark green leaves, to 8in (20cm) long, often purple-tinged when young. Large, pendulous panicles, to 12in (30cm) long, of small, fragrant, yellow-green flowers, lacking petals, are borne in midsummer, followed by showy, spherical red berries on female plants. ↕↔ 40ft (12m). China (Sichuan), Korea, Japan, Taiwan. Zone 6b.

▷ ***Idria*** see *Fouquieria*

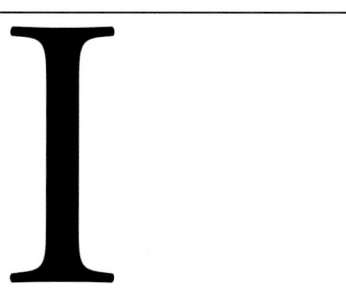

Idesia polycarpa

ILEX

Holly

AQUIFOLIACEAE

Genus of over 400 species of evergreen and deciduous trees, shrubs, and climbers from woodland in tropical, subtropical, and temperate regions, grown for their foliage and berries. The leaves may have entire, spine-toothed, spiny, or rarely scalloped margins, and are usually simple and alternate, sometimes in opposite pairs. Flowers, borne from spring to early summer, are produced singly or in clusters or cymes in the leaf axils. They are small, cup-shaped, up to ⅜in (9mm) across, each with 3–8 petals, usually white or cream, but may be pink, green, or lavender-blue. Male and female flowers are usually borne on separate plants; both sexes are needed to obtain fruits. In temperate climates, hollies bear fruits in autumn. The red or black, occasionally white, orange, or yellow berries are spherical, sometimes ellipsoid, and may cause mild stomach upset if ingested.

Grow hollies in a woodland garden, or as specimen trees; some make good hedges or windbreaks, particularly *I. aquifolium* and *I.* x *meserveae* cultivars; several *I. crenata* cultivars are useful in a rock garden. In cold areas, grow frost-tender species in a cool greenhouse.

• **CULTIVATION** Grow in moist but well-drained, moderately fertile, humus-rich soil in full sun (which produces the best leaf color in variegated hollies) or in partial shade. Planting or transplanting is best done in early spring. Pruning group 1. Prune free-standing specimens to shape in the early years only; clip formally grown plants in summer; trim hedges in spring. Older specimens of *I. opaca* may be cut back severely.

• **PROPAGATION** Sow seed in containers in a cold frame in autumn. Germination may take 2 or 3 years. Take semi-ripe cuttings in summer or early autumn.

• **PESTS AND DISEASES** Young shoots are susceptible to aphids; scale insects and leaf miners may be problems on evergreen species. Sometimes suffer from *Phytophthora* root rot.

***I.* 'Accent'.** Narrowly conical, evergreen male tree, spindly when mature, with brittle branches. Bears elliptic, dark green leaves, ¾–1½in (2–4cm) long. Sometimes short-lived. Pollinating male for *I.* 'Elegance'. ↕ 20ft (6m), ↔ 10ft (3m). Zone 6b.

I. altaclarensis see *I.* x *altaclerensis.*

I.* x *altaclerensis (*I. aquifolium* x *I. perado*) syn. *I. altaclarensis.* Vigorous, evergreen tree or shrub of variable habit, with gray bark. Leaves are elliptic, elliptic-lance-shaped, or broadly ovate, glossy, dark green, 2½–5in (6–13cm) long, with spine-toothed or entire margins. Berries are red and ¼–⅜in (6–9mm) across. Similar to *I. aquifolium* but more vigorous, and usually with less spiny, broader, larger leaves. Tolerates pollution and coastal exposure. Excellent for tall hedges and windbreaks. ↕ to 70ft (20m), ↔ 40–50ft (12–15m). Garden origin. Zone 6. **'Belgica Aurea'**, syn. 'Silver Sentinel', *I. perado* 'Aurea', is an erect female shrub with yellow-streaked green stems, bearing elliptic-lance-shaped, sparsely

ILEX LEAVES

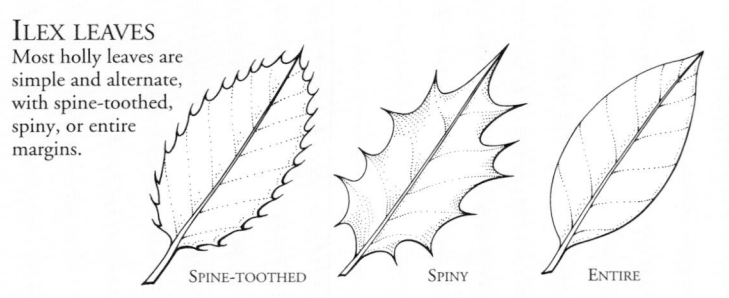

Most holly leaves are simple and alternate, with spine-toothed, spiny, or entire margins.

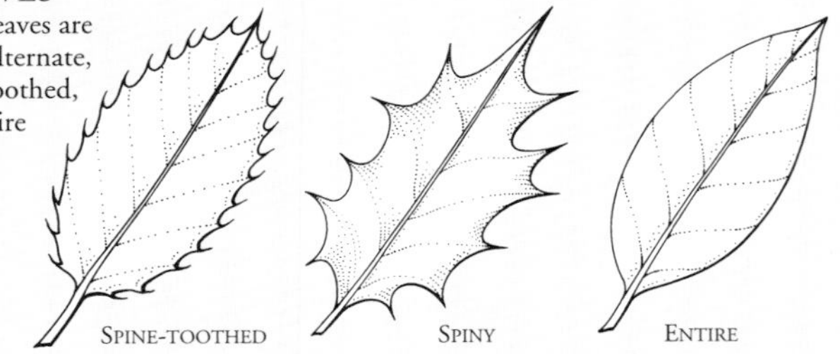

spine-toothed leaves, to 4½in (11cm) long, mottled gray-green in the center and with irregular, golden yellow margins. Produces few berries. ↕ 40ft (12m), ↔ 15ft (5m). **'Camelliifolia'** ■ is a large, conical female shrub with purple-tinged stems, elliptic-oblong, usually entire, deep green leaves, to 5in (13cm) long, and scarlet berries. ↕ 46ft (14m). **'Golden King'** is a compact female shrub, a sport of 'Hendersonii', with oblong to ovate, spine-toothed or entire leaves, to 4in (10cm) long, mottled gray-green in the center, with broad, bright gold margins. Reddish brown berries, ripening to red, are sparsely produced. ↕ 20ft (6m). **'Hendersonii'** is a compact female tree with oblong-elliptic, dull green leaves, to 4½in (11cm) long. Long-lasting, brown-red berries, ripening to red, are sparsely produced. ↕ to 50ft (15m), ↔ to 12ft (4m). **'Hodginsii'** is a magnificent, robust male tree bearing dark purple stems and broadly ovate, glossy, black-green leaves, 2–3in (5–8cm) long, spine-toothed when young. ↕ 46ft (14m), ↔ 30ft (10m). **'Lawsoniana'** is a compact female shrub, a sport of 'Hendersonii'. Yellow-streaked green stems bear oblong to ovate leaves, to 4½in (11cm) long, irregularly splashed gold and light green in the centers. Bears reddish brown berries, ripening to red. ↕ to 20ft (6m). **'Silver Sentinel'** see 'Belgica Aurea'. **'Wilsonii'** is a vigorous, dense, oblong female tree, well-furnished to the base with purple-green branches. Bears broadly ovate, glossy, bright green, spiny leaves, to 4in (10cm) long, with prominent veins. Large scarlet fruit are produced in abundance. ↕ 25ft (8m).

I. aquifolium (English holly). Usually erect, dense, pyramidal or oblong, evergreen shrub or tree with gray bark. Bears elliptic or ovate, glossy, dark green leaves, 2–4in (5–10cm) long, with entire, wavy, spine-toothed, or spiny margins, and long-lasting, red or rarely yellow or orange berries, ⅛–¼in (4–6mm) across. ↕ to 80ft (25m), ↔ 25ft (8m). W. and S. Europe, North Africa, W. Asia. Zone 7. **'Amber'** is a female tree with mid-green stems. Bears elliptic, usually entire, bright green leaves, to 3in (8cm) long, and abundant amber-yellow fruit. ↕ to 20ft (6m), ↔ 8ft (2.5m). **'Argentea Marginata'**, syn. 'Argentea Variegata', is a columnar female tree with cream-streaked green stems and large, broadly ovate, spiny leaves, to 3in (8cm) long, with wide white margins. Leaves are purplish pink when young. Bears abundant bright red berries. ↕ to 50ft (15m), ↔ 12ft (4m). **'Argentea Marginata Pendula'** ■ syn. 'Argentea Pendula', is a weeping female tree with purple stems and elliptic, spiny, cream-margined leaves, to 3in (8cm) long, purple-pink when young. Sparsely produces red fruit. ↕ to 12ft (4m), ↔ 10ft (3m). **'Argentea Pendula'** see 'Argentea Marginata Pendula'. **'Argentea Variegata'** see 'Argentea Marginata'. **'Aurea Regina'** see 'Golden Queen'. **'Bacciflava'** is a female tree with ovate, spiny, dark green leaves, to 3in (8cm) long. Bears yellow berries. ↕ to 50ft (15m), ↔ 12ft (4m). **'Ferox'** (Hedgehog holly) is a large, upright male shrub with purple stems and ovate, thick, leathery leaves, 1¼–1½in (3–4cm) long, covered in spines. ↕ to 50ft (15m). **'Ferox Argentea'** ■ is a sport of 'Ferox', also male but slower-growing, with cream-margined leaves, 1¼–1½in (3–4cm) long, covered in spines. ↕ to 25ft (8m), ↔ 12ft (4m). **'Golden Milkboy'** ■ is a dense, upright male shrub with purplish green stems. Bears elliptic, spiny leaves, 2½–3in (6–8cm) long, with irregular gold central markings. ↕ 20ft (6m), ↔ 12ft (4m). **'Golden Queen'**, syn. 'Aurea Regina', is a male tree bearing cream-streaked green stems and large, broadly ovate, spine-toothed leaves, 2½–3in (6–8cm) long, broadly margined with gold. ↕ 30ft (10m), ↔ 20ft (6m). **'Golden van Tol'** is a broad, upright female shrub bearing purple branches and ovate, puckered, dull green leaves, 1¼–3in (3–8cm) long, with golden yellow margins and few marginal spiny teeth. Sparsely produces red fruit. ↕ 12ft (4m), ↔ 10ft (3m). **'Handsworth New Silver'** ■ is a dense, columnar female shrub with dark purple stems bearing oblong-elliptic, mid-green, spiny leaves, 2½–3½in (6–9cm) long, with creamy margins. Produces bright red berries. ↕ 25ft (8m), ↔ 15ft (5m). **'J.C. van Tol'** ■ is a broad female tree with dark purple stems and elliptic, puckered, almost entire, dark green leaves, to 3in (8cm) long. Bears abundant bright red berries. Self-fertile. ↕ 20ft (6m), ↔ 12ft (4m). **'Pyramidalis'** is a narrowly conical, upright female shrub or small tree with yellow-green stems bearing narrowly elliptic, entire to few-spined, bright green leaves, 2½–3in (6–8cm) long. Produces abundant bright red berries. Self-fertile. ↕ 20ft (6m), ↔ 15ft (5m). **'Silver King'** see 'Silver Queen'. **'Silver Milkboy'** is a dense male shrub bearing greenish yellow stems and elliptic, spiny, mid-green leaves, 2–2½in (5–6cm) long, with irregular silver central markings. Shy flowering, but when it does bear fruit, produces abundant scarlet berries. ↕ 20ft (6m), ↔ 12ft (4m). **'Silver Milkmaid'** ■ is similar to 'Silver Milkboy', with an open habit, spreading when mature. Produces elliptic-ovate, sharply spined, dark green leaves, 1½–2in (3.5–5cm) long, with irregular, silvery white markings in the centers. Bears abundant scarlet berries. ↕ 20ft (6m), ↔ 12ft (4m). **'Silver Queen'**, syn. 'Silver King', is a dense, upright, slow-growing male tree with purple stems. Bears broadly ovate, spiny leaves, 1¾–3in (4.5–8cm) long, with broad, creamy white margins. ↕ 30ft (10m), ↔ 12ft (4m).

Ilex x *attenuata* 'Sunny Foster'

I.* x *aquipernyi (*I. aquifolium* x *I. pernyi*). Conical, evergreen shrub or small tree with diamond-shaped to oblong, spiny, glossy, dark green leaves, to 1½in (4cm) long, with long tips. Bears red fruit, ¼–⅜in (6–9mm) across. ↕ 20ft (6m), ↔ 12ft (4m). Garden origin. Zone 7. **'San Jose'** is a female tree bearing abundant bright red berries.

I.* x *attenuata (*I. cassine* x *I. opaca*) (Topel holly). Conical, evergreen shrub with obovate-lance-shaped, light green leaves, 1¼–3in (3–8cm) long, spine-toothed near the tips. Produces dark red berries, ¼in (6mm) across. ↕ 12ft (4m), ↔ 6ft (2m). Natural hybrid from S. US. Zone 7. **'East Palatka'** ■ is a narrowly pyramidal female tree with a looser habit and larger, spineless leaves. **'Foster #2'** (Foster's holly) is a narrowly pyramidal female tree with narrow, elliptic to oblong leaves. Produces abundant bright red berries. ↕ 20–30ft (6–10m), ↔ 10–15ft (3–5m). **'Sunny Foster'** ■ has yellow-splashed leaves.

I. cassine (Dahoon holly). Rounded, pyramidal, densely branched, evergreen tree with oblong to oblong-lance-shaped, narrow, shiny, entire, mid-green leaves, to 2in (5cm) long. Bears

I

Ilex x *altaclerensis* 'Camelliifolia'

Ilex aquifolium 'Argentea Marginata Pendula'

Ilex aquifolium 'Ferox Argentea'

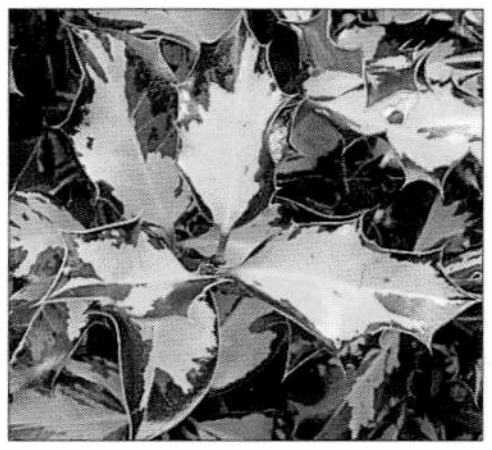

Ilex aquifolium 'Golden Milkboy'

Ilex aquifolium 'Handsworth New Silver'

Ilex aquifolium 'J.C. van Tol'

Ilex aquifolium 'Silver Milkmaid'

Ilex x *attenuata* 'East Palatka'

Ilex ciliospinosa

Ilex cornuta

Ilex cornuta 'Burfordii'

Ilex crenata f. *latifolia*

abundant red to orange-yellow berries, ¼in (6mm) across. Adaptable to wet conditions. ↕ 20–30ft (6–10m), ↔ 8–15ft (2.5–5m). S.E. US. Zone 8.
***I.* 'China Girl'** ■ (*I. cornuta* x *I. rugosa*). Compact, rounded, evergreen female shrub with elliptic-ovate, glossy mid-green leaves, 2in (5cm) long, with slightly downward-cupped teeth. Produces abundant, rich red fruit, ⅓in (9mm) across. ↕↔ 10ft (3m). Zone 5. **'China Boy'** is the male counterpart.
***I. chinensis* of gardens** see *I. purpurea.*
I. ciliospinosa ■ Upright, usually multi-stemmed, evergreen shrub bearing elliptic-ovate, dull, dark green leaves, 1½–2½in (4–6cm) long, with short, fine spines. Produces red fruit, ¼in (6mm) across. ↕ 20ft (6m), ↔ 12ft (4m). W. China. Zone 6.
***I.* 'Clusterberry'.** Upright, evergreen female shrub with oblong or obovate-oblong, few-spined, glossy, dark green leaves, 3–6in (9–15cm) long. Produces large red berries, ⅜–½in (9–15mm) across. ↕ to 15ft (5m), ↔ to 8ft (2.5m). Zone 7b.
I. cornuta ■ (Chinese holly). Dense, rounded, evergreen shrub with rectangular, glossy, dark green leaves, 2–3in (5–8cm) long, usually with prominent spines. Bears long-lasting, large red berries, ½in (15mm) across. ↕↔ to 15ft (5m). China, Korea. Zone 7b. **'Burfordii'** ■ has leaves with a single spine at the apex, and produces red berries very freely. ↔ 12–15ft (4–5m). **'Dwarf Burford'** has a dense, compact habit and produces dark red berries. ↕↔ to 8ft (2.5m). **'Rotunda'** is a female shrub with rounded leaves. Bears dull red berries, ¼–⅓in (6–9mm) across. ↕ 3–4ft (1–1.2m), ↔ 6–8ft (2–2.5m). Zone 7b.
I. crenata (Japanese holly). Evergreen, very variable shrub or small tree, usually with ovate to elliptic, minutely scalloped, glossy, dark green leaves, ¾–1¼in (2–3cm) long, often pitted beneath. Produces glossy black, sometimes white or yellow fruit, ¼in (6mm) across. ↕ 15ft (5m), ↔ 12ft (4m). Russia (Sakhalin), Japan, Korea. Zone 6. **'Aureovariegata'** see 'Variegata'. **'Bee Hive'** is an oval, mounded, male shrub with elliptic, slightly toothed leaves, ½–¾in (1.5–2cm) long. Useful for hedging. ↕ 24–36in (60–90cm), ↔ 24in (60cm). **'Bruns'** is a compact male shrub with grayish green leaves. ↕ 3ft (1m), ↔ 5ft (1.5m). **'Bullata'** see 'Convexa'. **'Convexa'**, syn. 'Bullata', is a dense, broad female shrub with purple-green stems bearing elliptic, curled, glossy, mid- to dark green leaves, ½–¾in (1–2cm) long. Produces abundant glossy black fruit. ↕ to 8ft (2.5m), ↔ 6ft (2m). **'Dwarf Pagoda'** is an upright, dwarf, female shrub with irregular branching and tiny leaves, ¼–½in (3–15mm) long. Produces black berries. Valuable as an accent plant, in a rock garden, or as a bonsai. ↕↔ 12in (30cm). Zone 7b. **'Fukarin'** see 'Shiro-Fukurin'. **'Golden Gem'** is a compact, low-growing, shy-flowering female shrub with golden yellow leaves, ½–¾in (1–2cm) long, turning yellow-green in summer. Bears black berries. Best grown in full sun. ↕ 3½ft (1.1m), ↔ 4–5ft (1.2–1.5m). **'Ivory Tower'** is a fast-growing, upright female shrub with late-ripening, ivory-white fruit. ↕ 12ft (4m), ↔ 10ft (3m). **f. *latifolia*** ■ syn. 'Latifolia', is a shrub or small tree with oval, minutely scalloped leaves, ¾–1½in (2–4cm) long; female plants produce black berries. ↕ to 5ft (1.5m). **'Luteovariegata'** see 'Variegata'. **'Mariesii'**, syn. var. *nummularioides*, *I. mariesii*, is a very slow-growing, erect female shrub with tiny, broadly ovate to rounded, entire, dark green leaves, to ½in (1.5cm) long. Produces black fruit. ↕ 24–36in (60–90cm) after many years. **var. *nummularioides*** see 'Mariesii'. **'Shiro-Fukurin'**, syn. 'Fukarin', *I.* 'Snow Flake', is an upright female shrub bearing ovate, gray-green leaves with cream markings. Produces black fruit. ↕↔ 12ft (4m). **'Variegata'**, syn. 'Aureovariegata', 'Luteovariegata', is a shy-flowering male shrub with elliptic leaves, spotted or marked yellow. Frequently reverts to green-leaved form. ↕ to 12ft (4m).
I. decidua (Possumhaw). Upright, deciduous shrub, late to come into leaf in spring. Oval or narrowly obovate, scalloped, bright green leaves, 1–1½in (2.5–4cm) long, are crowded on short lateral spurs. Bears red or orange, occasionally yellow fruit, ⅛–⅜in (4–9mm) across. ↕↔ 6–20ft (2–6m). C. and S.E. US. Zone 6. **'Warren Red'** is more upright and bears lustrous dark green leaves and abundant, long-persistent, glossy, bright red fruit, ¼in (6mm) across. ↕ 20ft (6m), ↔ 15ft (5m). Zone 5b.
I. dimorphophylla. Evergreen, rounded shrub with ovate, entire, spine-tipped, glossy, dark green leaves, ¾–1¼in (2–3cm) long, elliptic and very spiny when young. Bears small red fruit, ⅛in (3mm) across. ↕ 5ft (1.5m), ↔ 3ft (1m). Japan (Liukiu Islands). Zone 8.
I. dipyrena (Himalayan holly). Dense, upright, evergreen tree bearing oblong or elliptic, leathery, dull green leaves, 2–4½in (5–11cm) long, with abundant spines when young, fewer when mature. Bears red fruit, ¼–⅜in (6–9mm) across. ↕ 50ft (15m), ↔ 40ft (12m). E. Himalayas, W. China. Zone 7b.
***I.* x 'Doctor Kassab'** (*I. cornuta* x *I. pernyi*). Broadly pyramidal, evergreen, female tree with upturned branch ends. Produces elliptic to ovate, lightly toothed, glossy, dark green leaves, 2in (5cm) long. Bears abundant, bright red fruit, ¼–⅜in (6–9mm) across. ↕ 20ft (6m), ↔ 15ft (5m). Zone 7.
***I.* 'Elegance'.** Narrowly conical, evergreen, female tree, sometimes spindly when mature, with brittle branches and elliptic, spiny, dark green leaves, ¾–2in (2–5cm) long. Bears red fruit, to ½in (15mm) across. May be short-lived. *I.* 'Accent' is the pollinating male. ↕ 20ft (6m), ↔ 10ft (3m). Zone 6b.
I. fargesii. Broadly conical, evergreen shrub or tree with oblong to linear-lance-shaped, leathery, dull, dark green leaves, 2½–5in (6–13cm) long. Bears scarlet fruit, ⅛–¼in (3–6mm) across. ↕ 40ft (12m), ↔ 20ft (6m). Tibet, China (Hubei, Sichuan, Yunnan), Myanmar. Zone 7.
I. glabra (Gallberry, Inkberry). Erect, evergreen shrub with narrowly obovate to inversely lance-shaped, glossy, dark green leaves, ¾–2in (2–5cm) long, pitted beneath. Bears black, occasionally white fruit, ⅛–⅜in (3–9mm) across. ↕↔ 10ft (3m). E. North America. Zone 5b. **'Compacta'** ■ is more compact and rounded than the species. ↕↔ 4–6ft (1.2–2m).
***I.* 'Harvest Red'** (*I. verticillata* x *I. serrata*). Vigorous, irregularly rounded, deciduous female shrub with dark branches and narrowly oval to ovate, toothed, lustrous, dark green leaves, 1½–4in (4–10cm) long, turning red-purple in fall. Bears abundant, persistent, bright red berries, ¼in (6mm) across. ↕ 10ft (3m), ↔ 10–12ft (3–4m). Zone 6.
***I.* 'Indian Chief'** (*I. cornuta* x *I. pernyi*). Compact, upright, evergreen female shrub with almost stalkless, diamond-shaped to nearly rectangular, glossy, dark green leaves, to 4in (10cm) long, with 5 prominent spines. Bears red fruit, ¾in (9mm) across. ↕ 6–10ft (2–3m), ↔ 5–8ft (1.5–2.5m). Zone 6.
I. insignis see *I. kingiana.*

Ilex 'China Girl'

Ilex glabra 'Compacta'

Ilex 'John T. Morris'

Ilex x *koehneana* 'Chestnut Leaf'

Ilex latifolia

Ilex x *meserveae* 'Blue Princess'

Ilex pedunculosa

Ilex vomitoria

***I.* 'John T. Morris'** ▣ (*I. cornuta* x *I. pernyi*). Dense, conical, evergreen male shrub. Bears almost stalkless, diamond-shaped to nearly rectangular, glossy, dark green leaves, 1½–2½in (4–6cm) long, with 5 spines. Pollinating male for *I.* 'Lydia Morris'. ↕ 22ft (7m), ↔ 15ft (5m). Zone 7.

I. kingiana, syn. *I. insignis.* Upright, evergreen tree with thick, silvery gray branches. Bears elliptic-lance-shaped to ovate, leathery, glossy, mid- to dark green leaves, 6–8in (15–20cm) long, very spiny when young, slightly toothed or entire when mature. Young seedlings have waxy leaves, ¼–⅜in (6–9mm) long, with marginal spines pointing in all directions. Bears large clusters of bright red berries, ¼in (6mm) across. ↕ 15ft (5m), ↔ 12ft (4m). E. Himalayas, China (Yunnan). Zone 7b.

I.* x *koehneana (*I. aquifolium* x *I. latifolia*). Narrowly conical, evergreen shrub with olive-green twigs. Large, glossy, mid-green leaves are oblong to elliptic, 3–5in (8–13cm) long, with large marginal spines. Produces red fruit, ⅜in (9mm) across. ↕ 22ft (7m), ↔ 15ft (5m). Garden origin. Zone 7b. **'Chestnut Leaf'** ▣ is female, with light or yellowish green leaves and red berries. **'Wirt L. Winn'** is distinctly pyramidal, with oblong, glossy, spiny-margined, dark green leaves and abundant red fruit.

I. latifolia ▣ Narrowly conical, evergreen shrub with thick, olive-green twigs and oblong or oblong-ovate, entire or spine-toothed, leathery, glossy, dark green leaves, 3–7in (8–18cm) long. Yellowish green flowers are borne in late spring and early summer, followed by abundant orange-red berries, ¼in (6mm) across. ↕ 22ft (7m), ↔ 15ft (5m). China, Japan. Zone 7b.

***I.* 'Lydia Morris'** (*I. cornuta* x *I. pernyi*). Dense, conical, evergreen female shrub with almost stalkless, diamond-shaped to nearly rectangular, glossy, black-green leaves, 1½–3in (4–8cm) long, with 5 spines. Produces red fruit, ⅜in (9mm) across, which is often hidden by the foliage. *I.* 'John T. Morris' is the pollinating male. ↕ 22ft (7m), ↔ 15ft (5m). Zone 7.

I. macrocarpa. Rounded to broadly spreading, deciduous tree with spur-like branchlets and elliptic or ovate-elliptic, shallowly toothed, bright green leaves, 3–4½in (7–11cm) long. In late spring, bears greenish white flowers, followed by large, flattened, spherical, mid-green berries, maturing to black, ½–¾in (1.5–2cm). ↕ 56ft (17m), ↔ 40ft (12m). S. and S.W. China. Zone 7b.

I. mariesii see *I. crenata* 'Mariesii'.

I.* x *meserveae (*I. rugosa* x *I. aquifolium*) (Blue holly). Dense, vigorous, erect to spreading, evergreen shrub, resembling *I. aquifolium.* Bears usually small, elliptic to ovate, spiny, glossy, bluish green leaves, ¾–2in (2–5cm) long. White to pinkish white flowers appear in late spring, followed on female plants by glossy red fruit, to ¼in (6mm) across. ↕ 15ft (5m), ↔ 10ft (3m). Garden origin. Zone 5. **'Blue Angel'** is a slow-growing, compact female shrub with dark purple stems and elliptic, glossy, dark bluish green leaves, 1¾in (4.5cm) long. Least hardy of the blue hollies; ↕ 12ft (4m), ↔ 6ft (2m). **'Blue Boy'** is a spreading male shrub with purplish green stems and ovate, glossy, dark greenish blue leaves, 1½–1¾in (4–4.5cm) long. ↕ 10ft (3m). **'Blue Girl'** is the female counterpart of 'Blue Boy', with abundant red berries. ↕ 10ft (3m). **'Blue Maid'** is a dense female shrub producing an abundance of fruit. Probably the hardiest of the blue hollies. ↔ 12ft (4m). **'Blue Prince'** is similar to 'Blue Boy', with purplish green stems bearing glossy, bright green leaves. ↔ 12ft (4m). **'Blue Princess'** ▣ is similar to 'Blue Girl' with larger, glossier leaves, 1¾–2½in (4.5–6cm) long, and more abundant fruit. ↕ 10ft (3m).

***I.* 'Nellie R. Stevens'** (*I. cornuta* x *I. aquifolium*). Vigorous, conical, evergreen female tree with oblong-ovate, sparsely spiny, highly glossy, dark green leaves, 2–3in (5–8cm) long. Produces abundant shiny scarlet fruit, ⅜–½in (9–15mm) across. ↕ 22ft (7m), ↔ 12ft (4m). Zone 7b.

I. opaca ▣ (American holly). Erect, evergreen, large shrub or tree with oblong-elliptic, spine-toothed or entire, leathery, matte, dark green leaves, 2–4in (5–10cm) long. Bears crimson, or occasionally yellow or orange fruit, ¼in (6mm) across. ↕ 40–50ft (12–15m), ↔ 20–40ft (6–12m). C. and E. US. Zone 6. **'Canary'** has light green leaves with small spines and abundant yellow berries. Zone 6. **'Farage'** has large, deeply-spined, dark green leaves and abundant red fruit. **'Jersey Knight'** is a male tree with shiny, dark green leaves; excellent male pollinator for American holly. **'Miss Helen'** is a dense, conical tree with elliptic, spiny, dark green leaves, 3in (8cm) long, and abundant dark red fruit, which ripens early and is borne at a young age. Performs well in C. US. **'Morgan Gold'** is compact and free fruiting, with bright yellow berries. **'Old Heavy Berry'** is vigorous, with elliptic to oval, lustrous, dark green leaves and abundant red fruit.

I. pedunculosa ▣ (Longstalk holly). Upright, evergreen tree or shrub with elliptic to ovate, spineless, glossy, dark green leaves, 1½–3in (4–8cm) long, bronze-tinted when young. Bears bright red fruit, ⅜in (9mm) across, on long stalks. ↕ 30ft (10m), ↔ 22ft (7m). China, Taiwan, Japan. Zone 7.

I. perado. Upright, evergreen shrub or small tree with ovate to oblong or lance-shaped, toothed or entire, leathery, thorny, glossy, dark green leaves, 2½–4in (6–10cm) long. Bears red fruit, ⅜in (9mm) across. ↕ 20–30ft (6–10m), ↔ 22ft (7m). Canary Islands (Gomera, Tenerife), Azores. Zone 8. **'Aurea'** see *I.* x *altaclerensis* 'Belgica Aurea'. **subsp. *platyphylla*,** syn. *I. platyphylla*, has broadly ovate leaves, 4–6in (10–15cm) long.

I. pernyi. Upright, evergreen shrub with almost stalkless, diamond-shaped to nearly rectangular, glossy, dark green leaves, ¾–1¼in (2–3cm) long, with 5 spines. Bears yellowish flowers in late spring, followed by bright red fruit, ¼–⅜in (6–9mm) across. ↕ 28ft (9m), ↔ 10ft (3m). W. and C. China (Gansu, Hubei). Zone 7. **var. *veitchii*** has larger and broader leaves, 1½–2in (4–5cm) long, with 3–5 spines on each side. China (Hubei).

I. platyphylla see *I. perado* subsp. *platyphylla.*

I. purpurea, syn. *I. chinensis* of gardens. Conical, evergreen tree with elliptic-lance-shaped, occasionally ovate, mid- to dark green leaves, 2–4½in (5–11cm) long, purplish green when young. Bears ellipsoid, glossy red fruit, to ½in (12mm) across. ↕ to 43ft (13m), ↔ 12ft (4m). China, Japan. Zone 7b.

***I.* 'September Gem'** (*I.* x *aquipernyi* x *I. ciliospinosa*). Conical, evergreen female shrub bearing ovate, glossy, dark green leaves, 1½–2in (4–5cm) long, with insignificant spiny teeth. Bears bright red berries, ¼–⅜in (6–9mm) across. ↕ 10ft (3m), ↔ 6ft (2m). Zone 6.

I. serrata (Japanese winterberry). Deciduous, bushy shrub with slender, purple twigs and elliptic, finely toothed, dull green leaves, 1½–3in (4–8cm) long, downy on both surfaces. Bears white flowers, followed by bright red, sometimes yellow or white fruit, ⅛–¼in (3–6mm) across. ↕ to 15ft (5m), ↔ 10ft (3m). China (Sichuan), Japan. Zone 6.

***I.* 'Snow Flake'** see *I. crenata* 'Shiro-Fukurin'.

***I.* 'Sparkleberry'** ▣ (*I. serrata* x *I. verticillata*). Vigorous (especially when young), deciduous, upright female shrub or small tree. Bears ovate, toothed, dark green leaves, 1½–4in

Ilex opaca (inset: leaf and fruit detail)

Ilex 'Sparkleberry'

(4–10cm) long, which persist until early winter. Produces glossy red berries, ¼in (6mm) across. *I.* 'Apollo' is the male pollinator. ↕ 15ft (5m), ↔ 12ft (4m). Zone 5.

I. verticillata (Black alder, Winterberry). Suckering shrub or, sometimes, a small tree. Leaves are obovate or lance-shaped, toothed, bright green, 1½–4in (4–10cm) long, with long, sharp-pointed tips, softly hairy beneath. In midspring, produces white flowers, followed by stalkless, spherical, dark red to scarlet, sometimes orange or yellow fruit, ⅛–¼in (3–6mm) across. ↕↔ 15ft (5m). E. North America. Zone 4. Dwarf male selections are available for pollinating cultivars that flower early, as are late-flowering male selections. **'Nana'**, syn. 'Red Sprite', is a small, rounded female shrub with ovate, mid-green leaves, 1¼–2½in (3–6cm) long. Produces abundant large, bright red fruit, to ½in (12mm) across. ↕ 2–4ft (60–120cm), ↔ 3–5ft (1–1.5m). **'Red Sprite'** see 'Nana'. **'Winter Red'** is a robust, broad female shrub with dark green leaves. Produces long-lasting, intensely red berries, ⅜in (9mm) across, which persist until spring. ↕ 8–10ft (2.5–3m). ↔ 10ft (3m).

I. vomitoria ■ (Yaupon holly). Upright, irregularly branched, evergreen shrub or small tree with gray branches, white to gray bark, and narrowly oval to ovate, shallowly toothed, lustrous, dark green leaves, ½–1½in (1.5–4cm) long, tapering at the bases. Bears abundant, persistent, translucent, scarlet-red fruit, ¼in (6mm) across. Useful as a screen or hedge in swampy areas. ↕ 15–20ft (5–6m), ↔ 10–15ft (3–5m). S.E. Virginia to Texas and Florida. ❄ (min. 35°F/2°C). **'Nana'** is dwarf, compact, and mounded. ↕ 5ft (1.5m), ↔ 8ft (2.5m). **'Pendula'** is weeping. ↕ 20ft (6m).

***I.* 'Washington'** (*I. ciliospinosa* x *I. cornuta*). Erect, conical, evergreen female shrub with ovate to oblong, spiny, glossy, light green leaves, 1½–2in (4–5cm) long. Bears red fruit. ↕ 12ft (4m), ↔ 6ft (2m). Zone 6.

I. yunnanensis. Evergreen, upright to rounded shrub with downy branchlets and ovate or ovate-lance-shaped, scalloped to toothed, glossy, dark green leaves, ¾–1½in (2–4cm) long. Bears red fruit, ¼in (6mm) across. ↕↔ 12ft (4m). N. Burma, China (Sichuan, Hubei). Zone 6.

▷ ***Iliamna*** see *Sphaeralcea*

ILLICIUM

ILLICIACEAE

Genus of about 40 species of aromatic, evergreen shrubs and trees from woodland in S.E. Asia, S.E. US, and the West Indies. They are cultivated for their thick, glossy leaves, borne alternately or in near-whorls; their unusual flowers, which are composed of numerous tepals; and their woody, star-shaped fruits. Where temperatures fall below 23°F (-5°C), grow in a cool greenhouse. Elsewhere, grow in a woodland garden or shrub border. Seeds of *I. anisatum* are toxic if ingested.

- **CULTIVATION** Under glass, grow in acidic potting mix in full light, shaded from the hottest sun, or in bright filtered light. During growth, water moderately and apply a balanced liquid fertilizer monthly. Water sparingly in winter. Outdoors, grow in moist but well-drained, humus-rich, acidic soil, in full sun or partial shade. Shelter from cold, drying winds. Pruning group 1.
- **PROPAGATION** Take semi-ripe cuttings in summer. Layer in summer.
- **PESTS AND DISEASES** Prone to bacterial spot, anthracnose, stem canker, and root and crown rots.

I. anisatum ■ syn. *I. religiosum* (Chinese anise). Conical, evergreen shrub or small tree bearing oval to lance-shaped, blunt-tipped, glossy, dark green leaves, to 5in (13cm) long. Star-shaped, fragrant, yellow-green, later creamy white flowers, to 1in (2.5cm) across, are produced in midspring. ↕ to 25ft (8m), ↔ 20ft (6m). China, Japan, Taiwan. Zone 7.

I. floridanum (Purple anise). Bushy, evergreen shrub with narrowly oval to lance-shaped, glossy, dark green leaves, to 4in (10cm) long. Nodding, star-shaped, fragrant, red to red-purple flowers, to 2in (5cm) across, are borne in late spring and early summer. ↕↔ 8ft (2.5m). S.E. US. Zone 7.

I. religiosum see *I. anisatum.*

I. verum (Chinese anise, Star anise). Small, rounded, evergreen tree with inversely lance-shaped to narrowly elliptic, sharply tapered, glossy, dark green leaves, to 6in (15cm) long. Star-shaped flowers, ½in (1.5cm) across, with pink- or red-flushed yellow tepals, are borne in early summer, followed by glossy, red-brown fruit. ↕ 60ft (18m), ↔ 20ft (6m). China, Vietnam. Zone 7.

Illicium anisatum

IMPATIENS

Balsam, Busy Lizzie

BALSAMINACEAE

Genus of about 850 species of erect annuals, and evergreen perennials and subshrubs, found in a great variety of often damp habitats, near streams, lakes, or in woodland, throughout tropical and warm-temperate regions (except Australia, New Zealand, and South America). All have brittle, almost succulent stems and lush, fleshy, semi-translucent foliage; leaves vary from alternate to opposite or whorled. Flowers are asymmetrical, spurred and sometimes hooded, 5-petaled, borne singly or in clusters or racemes, and are followed by explosive seed capsules. Most are excellent as houseplants and summer bedding plants, particularly in light shade, and provide long-lasting summer color in a windowbox or container on a patio. *I. walleriana* cultivars and *I. balsamina* are free-flowering and grow well in shade. Many, including some New Guinea Group hybrids, are also grown for their bronze- or yellow-flushed or variegated foliage. Grow hardy perennials in a woodland garden. Where not hardy, grow in a temperate or warm greenhouse, or as houseplants. All will self-seed in favorable conditions.

- **CULTIVATION** Under glass, grow in soilless or soil-based potting mix in full to bright filtered light, with moderate to high humidity. During growth, water moderately and apply a balanced liquid fertilizer monthly. Water sparingly in winter. Outdoors, grow in humus-rich, moist but well-drained soil in partial shade, with shelter from wind.
- **PROPAGATION** Sow seed at 61–64°F (16–18°C) in early spring. For hardy species, sow seed *in situ* in late spring. Root softwood cuttings of *I. walleriana* and New Guinea Group cultivars in spring or early summer.
- **PESTS AND DISEASES** Spider mites, flower thrips, root knot nematode, white-flies, and aphids are problems, especially under glass, caterpillars are more of a problem outdoors. Gray mold, impatiens necrotic spot virus, fungal leaf spots, *Rhizoctonia* stem rot, *Pseudomonas* leaf spot, and *Verticillium* wilt occur.

I. balsamina (Rose balsam, Touch-me-not). Sparsely branched, slightly hairy annual with alternate, narrowly lance-shaped to narrowly elliptic, deeply toothed, pale green leaves, 1–3½in (2.5–9cm) long. From summer to early autumn, produces cup-shaped, hooded, pink, red, purple, or white flowers, 1–2in (2.5–5cm) across, either singly in the leaf axils or in small clusters of 2 or 3. ↕ to 30in (75cm), ↔ 18in (45cm). India, China, Malaysia. ❄ (min. 41°F/5°C). **'Blackberry Ice'** has abundant, white-splashed, double purple flowers; ↕ to 28in (70cm). **Camellia-flowered Series** ■ cultivars have large, double, white-mottled, pink or red flowers; ↕ to 28in (70cm). Cultivars of **Tom Thumb Series** ■ are dwarf, with large, double, pink, scarlet, violet, or white flowers, 2–2½in (5–6cm) across; ↕ to 12in (30cm).

***I.* New Guinea Group.** Subshrubby, hybrid perennials, usually grown as annuals, valued for their foliage, brightly colored flowers, and suitability for sunny sites. Many cutting-propagated selections have been made; the following two are seed-raised: **'Spectra'** bears opposite or whorled, lance-shaped, toothed, mid-green leaves, 3–6in (8–15cm) long. From summer to autumn, bears abundant flattened, deep rose-pink, scarlet-red, salmon-pink, lavender, or white flowers, with some bicolors, to 2½in (6cm) across. ↕ 14in (35cm), ↔ 12in (30cm). **'Tango'** ■ is a seed-raised cultivar with opposite or whorled, lance-shaped, toothed, dark bronze-green leaves, 3–6in (8–15cm) long. Bears abundant flattened, 5-petaled, tangerine-orange flowers, to 2in (5cm) across, from summer to autumn. ↕ 14in (35cm), ↔ 12in (30cm).

Impatiens balsamina Camellia-flowered Series

Impatiens balsamina Tom Thumb Series

Impatiens New Guinea Group 'Tango'

Impatiens niamniamensis 'Congo Cockatoo'

Impatiens walleriana 'Starbright'

Impatiens walleriana Swirl Series

Impatiens walleriana Tempo Series 'Tempo Lavender'

I

***I. niamniamensis* 'Congo Cockatoo'** ■ Erect, short-lived perennial with spirally arranged, ovate or elliptic, scalloped, dark green leaves, 2–9in (5–23cm) long. Narrow, hooded, bright red and yellow flowers, 1½in (4cm) long, each with a distinctive hooked spur, are borne singly or in small clusters of 2–8 in the leaf axils at any time of year, but more prolifically in summer. ↕ 36in (90cm), ↔ 14in (35cm). ❀ (min. 59°F/15°C)

I. oliveri see *I. sodenii.*

I. repens. Creeping or trailing perennial with alternate, kidney-shaped, scalloped leaves, to 1in (2.5cm) long. Solitary, hooded, clear yellow flowers, 1½in (4cm) long, are produced in the leaf axils from summer to autumn. Good for hanging baskets. ↕ 7in (18cm), ↔ 12in (30cm). India, Sri Lanka. ❀ (min. 55°F/13°C)

I. sodenii, syn. *I. oliveri.* Erect, shrubby perennial with whorls of 6–8 inversely lance-shaped, toothed leaves, 8in (20cm) long, with pale green midribs. Long-stalked, pale lilac, pink, or sometimes white flowers, 2½in (6cm) across, are borne mainly in summer. ↕ 10ft (3m), ↔ 4½ft (1.4m). E. tropical Africa. ❀ (min. 50°F/10°C)

I. tinctoria. Vigorous, erect, tuberous perennial with spirally arranged, oblong, ovate, or oblong-lance-shaped, scalloped or toothed leaves, 3–9in (8–23cm) long. Bears racemes of long-stalked, scented white flowers, 2½in (6cm) across, the throats marked with pink or magenta, and each with a slender spur, from summer to autumn. ↕ 7ft (2.2m), ↔ 3ft (1m). E. Africa. ❀ (min. 55°F/13°C)

I. walleriana (Busy Lizzie, Patience plant). Variable, subshrubby perennial, usually grown as an annual, with light green to red-flushed stems and spirally arranged, elliptic to lance-shaped, slightly toothed, scalloped, light to bronze-green or red-flushed leaves, to 5in (13cm) long. In summer, the many cultivars from the species produce flattened, slender-spurred flowers, 1–2½in (2.5–6cm) across, in white, many shades of orange, pink, scarlet, red, crimson, violet, purple, and lavender-blue, as well as bicolors. ↕↔ to 24in (60cm). ❀ (min. 50°F/10°C). Cultivars of **Accent Series** are compact, with flowers in white and a very wide range of colors, some with central stars; ↕ to 8in (20cm). Cultivars of **Blitz 2000 Series** are tall and many-branched, with dark green foliage, and flowers to 2in (5cm) across, in white and shades of orange, pink, red, and violet; ↕ to 14in (35cm). Cultivars of **Confection Series** bear mostly double and semi-double flowers in shades of orange, pink, and red, and have deep green foliage. Cultivars of **Deco Series** have dark green leaves, and flowers in shades of orange, pink, red, and violet; ↕ to 8in (20cm). **Deco Series 'Deco Pink'** ■ has mid-pink flowers, each with a deep pink eye. **Expo Series** cultivars are compact and uniform, with flowers to 2½in (6cm) across, in white and shades of orange, pink, red, and violet, including bicolors; ↕ to 8in (20cm). **Florette Star Series** cultivars are low-growing, and have flowers in shades of orange, pink, red, and violet, or mixtures, each with a central white star; ↕ 6–8in (15–20cm). **Futura Series** cultivars are free-flowering, compact, and pendulous, with flowers in shades of bright pink, red, white, and purple; ↕ 8–12in (20–30cm). **Impulse Series** cultivars are in a wide color range, including pastel colors and shades of violet, lilac, orange, pink, and red, and some bicolors. **'Mega Orange Star'** has orange flowers, to 2½in (6cm) across, each with a central white star; ↕ 8–10in (20–25cm). **Novette Star Series** cultivars are orange, pink, red, and violet, and have white star markings. **Rosette Series** cultivars bear single, semi-double, and fully double flowers in shades of orange, red, pink, and white, and a red-and-white bicolor; ↕ 18–20in (45–50cm). **'Starbright'** ■ has flowers to 2½in (6cm) across, in rose-pink, red, orange, and violet-blue, each with a central white star; ↕ to 8in (20cm). **Super Elfin Series** ■ cultivars are spreading and flat, with a wide color range, including pastel colors and shades of violet, orange, pink and red; ↕ to 10in (25cm). **Swirl Series** ■ cultivars have pink-and-orange flowers margined in rose-red; ↕ 6–8in (15–20cm). Cultivars of **Tempo Series** have a wide color range, including violet, lavender-blue, orange, pink, and red, as well as bicolors and picotees; ↕ to 9in (23cm). **Tempo Series 'Tempo Lavender'** ■ produces lavender-pink flowers. Cultivars of **Tiara Series** have large flowers in seven separate colors, including a rose picotee; tolerates wet and dry conditions; ↕ 10–12in (25–30cm).

Impatiens walleriana Deco Series 'Deco Pink'

Impatiens walleriana Super Elfin Series

IMPERATA

POACEAE

Genus of 6 species of slender-stemmed, rhizomatous, perennial grasses from tropical and warm-temperate, open grassland in Japan. They have flat, linear, pointed leaves and erect, spike-like panicles of short, silvery spikelets, borne in summer. Variegated cultivars are grown

Imperata cylindrica 'Rubra'

for their striking foliage. Grow at the front of a mixed or herbaceous border, in a light woodland garden, or in containers. All need long, hot summers to flower well.

• **CULTIVATION** Grow in moist but well-drained, humus-rich soil in full sun or light, dappled shade. In cold climates, provide a winter mulch, especially when plants are young.

• **PROPAGATION** Divide in spring or early summer.

• **PESTS AND DISEASES** Infrequent.

***I. cylindrica* 'Rubra'** ■ syn. *I. cylindrica* 'Red Baron' (Japanese blood grass). Slowly spreading, perennial grass forming loose clumps of flat, linear, mid-green leaves, to 20in (50cm) long, which quickly turn deep blood-red from the tips almost to the bases. Narrow, spike-like panicles, to 8in (20cm) long, of fluffy, silvery white spikelets, to 1¾in (4.5cm) long, are produced in late summer. ↕ 16in (40cm), ↔ 12in (30cm) or more. Zone 5.

INCARVILLEA

syn. AMPHICOME

BIGNONIACEAE

Genus of 14 species of annuals and taprooted perennials from mountainous areas, some species in rocky sites, others in open grassland, in C. and E. Asia. They are cultivated for their exotic terminal racemes or panicles of tubular, trumpet-shaped, 2-lipped flowers, with 5 spreading petals. The flowers are supported on strong stems above the usually alternate, pinnate or pinnatisect leaves. Grow in a mixed or herbaceous border, or smaller species in a rock garden or alpine house.

• **CULTIVATION** Grow in fertile, moist but well-drained soil in full sun, with some shade in summer. Does not tolerate excessive winter moisture. Plant crowns 3–4in (8–10cm) deep; mulch in areas where the ground remains frozen for long periods. Avoid damaging the thick, fleshy roots.

• **PROPAGATION** Sow seed in containers in a cold frame in spring or autumn. Keep autumn-sown seedlings frost-free over winter. Seedlings generally take 3 years to flower. In spring, root basal stem cuttings of perennials, or divide with care; established plants dislike root disturbance.

• **PESTS AND DISEASES** May be attacked by slugs.

Incarvillea arguta

Incarvillea delavayi

I. arguta ■ Erect, woody-based perennial, often grown as an annual, with pinnate, dark green leaves, 2–8in (5–20cm) long, some basal and some arranged alternately on red-tinted stems; the leaflets, in 2–6 opposite pairs, are ovate, lance-shaped, or elliptic, and coarsely toothed. Racemes of 5–20 pendent, tubular, pink or white flowers, to 1½in (4cm) long, are produced in early and midsummer. ↕ to 36in (90cm), ↔ 12in (30cm). W. Himalayas to W. China. Zone 7b.

I. delavayi ■ Taprooted perennial with basal rosettes of pinnate, mid-green leaves, to 12in (30cm) long, divided into 6–11 pairs of oblong-lance-shaped, coarsely toothed leaflets, the terminal segment larger. Racemes of up to 10 tubular, widely trumpet-shaped, yellow-throated, deep rose-pink to purple flowers, to 3in (8cm) across, are borne in early and midsummer. ↕ 24in (60cm), ↔ 12in (30cm). China (Yunnan). Zone 6. **'Bee's Pink'** has pale pink flowers, to 4in (10cm) across; ↕ 12–18in (30–45cm), ↔ 8in (20cm).

I. mairei ■ (Garden gloxinia). Taprooted perennial with basal rosettes of pinnate, wrinkled, dark green leaves, 5–10in (12–25cm) long, composed of 4–7 pairs of ovate to oblong, finely toothed or scalloped leaflets, the terminal segment larger. In early summer, bears few-flowered racemes of widely trumpet-shaped, yellow-throated, purple-crimson flowers, 1½–2½in (4–6cm) across, with white-striped purple marks on the lower lobes. ↕ 6–20in (15–50cm), ↔ 12in (30cm). Himalayas to W. Nepal, S.W. China. Zone 5b. **'Frank Ludlow'** has crimson-pink flowers; ↕ 4in (10cm), ↔ 6in (15cm). **var. *grandiflora*** has leaves with only 1 or 2 pairs of leaflets. Flowers are usually solitary but slightly larger than the species and deeper crimson-pink; ↕ 4–6in (10–15cm), ↔ 8in (20cm). **'Nyoto Sama'** has smooth leaves and bears large, bright pink flowers, 3in (8cm) across, in late spring; ↔ 6in (15cm).

Incarvillea mairei

I. olgae. Tap-rooted, woody-based, subshrubby perennial, with several sparsely branched stems bearing opposite, pinnate, mid-green leaves, 2–6in (5–15cm) long, with 3 or 4 pairs of elliptic, slightly toothed leaflets. Loose racemes of 3–10 tubular, rose-pink or pale pink, sometimes white flowers, to 1½in (4cm) across, are produced in early and midsummer. ↕ to 4ft (1.2m), ↔ 12in (30cm). Turkestan, Afghanistan. Zone 7.

INDIGOFERA

FABACEAE

Genus of 700 or more species of evergreen or deciduous trees and shrubs, annuals, and herbaceous perennials, widely distributed in mainly tropical and subtropical regions worldwide, in a variety of habitats. They are grown for their small, pea-like flowers and elegant foliage. The flowers are rarely solitary, often borne in loose or dense, terminal or axillary racemes or spikes. The usually pinnate leaves are arranged alternately. Grow in a shrub border or train against a warm, sunny wall; low-growing species are useful in rock gardens.

• **CULTIVATION** Grow in moderately fertile, moist but well-drained soil in full sun. Pruning group 1, or 13 if wall-trained; pruning group 6 or 7 in areas with severe winters.

• **PROPAGATION** Sow seed in containers in a cold frame in autumn. Root basal cuttings in spring, greenwood cuttings in late spring, and semi-ripe cuttings in early or midsummer.

• **PESTS AND DISEASES** Rust, root rot, and stem rot may occur.

I. amblyantha ■ Deciduous shrub bearing pinnate leaves, to 6in (15cm) long, divided into 7–11 narrowly ovate, bright green leaflets. Produces slender, upright racemes, to 4½in (11cm) long, of small, pea-like pink flowers, to ¼in (6mm) across, from summer to early autumn. ↕ 6ft (2m), ↔ 8ft (2.5m). China. Zone 7.

Indigofera amblyantha

Indigofera decora

I. decora ■ Spreading deciduous shrub with arching branches bearing pinnate leaves, to 8in (20cm) long, each with 7–13 narrowly oblong, glossy, dark green leaflets. Erect racemes, to 8in (20cm) long, of pea-like white flowers, to ¾in (2cm) across, heavily suffused pale crimson, are produced in mid- and late summer. Suitable for a rock garden. ↕ to 24in (60cm), ↔ 36in (90cm). China, Japan. Zone 7b.

I. dielsiana. Upright, open shrub with pinnate, dark green leaves, to 5in (13cm) long, each with 7–11 pairs of oval leaflets. Erect racemes, to 6in (15cm) long, of pea-like, pale pink flowers, ½in (1.5cm) across, are produced from early summer to early autumn. ↕↔ 5ft (1.5m). S.W. China. Zone 7.

I. gerardiana see *I. heterantha.*

I. hebepetala. Upright shrub with pinnate, mid-green leaves, 6–8in (15–20cm) long, each with 7–13 elliptic, elliptic-oblong, or rarely ovate leaflets, softly hairy beneath. In late summer and early autumn, produces racemes, 3–8in (7–20cm) long, of pea-like, dark carmine-red flowers, ½in (1.5cm) across. ↕ 6ft (1.8m), ↕ 3ft (1m). Himalayas. Zone 7b.

I. heterantha ■ syn. *I. gerardiana.* Spreading shrub with arching branches and pinnate, gray-green leaves, to 4in (10cm) long, each composed of up to 21 obovate to oval leaflets. From early summer to early autumn, bears dense, erect racemes, to 6in (15cm) long, of pea-like, purple-pink flowers, ½in (1.5cm) across. ↕↔ 6–10ft (2–3m). N.W. Himalayas. Zone 7b.

Indigofera heterantha

I. kirilowii. Spreading shrub or subshrub with upright shoots and pinnate, bright green leaves, to 6in (15cm) long, composed of up to 11 broadly ovate to almost diamond-shaped leaflets. In early and midsummer, produces pea-like, rose-pink flowers, to ¾in (2cm) across, in dense, upright racemes, to 5in (13cm) long. ↕ 30in (75cm), ↔ 3ft (1m). N. China, Korea, S. Japan. Zone 7.

I. potaninii. Spreading shrub bearing pinnate leaves, to 3in (8cm) long, with 5–9 elliptic-oblong, gray-green leaflets. Produces slender, upright racemes, to 5in (13cm) long, of small, pea-like pink flowers, to ½in (1.5cm) across, from summer to early autumn. ↕ 6ft (2m), ↔ 8ft (2.5m). S.W. China. Zone 7.

***I. tinctoria* 'Rose Carpet'.** Spreading shrub with pinnate leaves, to 3in (8cm) long, each with 8–14 obovate, mid-green leaflets. Bears erect racemes, to 3½in (9cm) long, of pea-like, rose-pink flowers, to ½in (1.5cm) across, in midsummer. Useful as a groundcover or in a rock wall. ↕↔ 24in (60cm). Zone 6.

INULA

ASTERACEAE

Genus of approximately 100 species of herbaceous perennials, some subshrubby, and a few annuals and biennials, from Europe and temperate and subtropical Africa and Asia. They are found in a wide range of habitats, from dry, rocky, montane sites to moist, shady, lowland areas; most grow in well-drained, sunny places. Inulas usually have large basal leaves and progressively smaller stem leaves, arranged alternately. The daisy-like flowerheads are flat, with numerous narrow yellow ray florets and tubular disk florets; they are solitary or borne in small panicles or corymbs. Low-growing forms, such as *I. ensifolia* 'Compacta', are suitable for a rock garden. Tall, robust species, such as *I. magnifica* and *I. racemosa*, are ideal for a wild garden. Grow *I. helenium* in an herb garden. Rhizomatous species may become invasive.

• **CULTIVATION** Grow most species in deep, fertile, moist but well-drained soil in full sun. *I. magnifica* will grow in boggy conditions, *I. helenium* tolerates partial shade, and *I. hookeri* prefers partial shade. Taller species may need support.

• **PROPAGATION** Sow seed in containers in a cold frame in spring or autumn. Divide perennials in spring or autumn.

• **PESTS AND DISEASES** Powdery mildew may be a problem if growing conditions are too dry.

***I. afghanica* of gardens** see *I. magnifica.*

I. ensifolia ▣ Dense, bushy, slender-stemmed, rhizomatous perennial. Bears stalkless, linear-lance-shaped or lance-shaped, entire, mid-green leaves, to 3½in (9cm) long, with finely hairy margins. In mid- and late summer, abundant golden yellow flowerheads, ¾–1¼in (2–3cm) or more across, are produced singly or in small corymbs. ↕ 10–24in (25–60cm), ↔ 12in (30cm). Caucasus. Zone 4. **'Compacta'** is a dwarf cultivar with deep golden yellow flowerheads; suitable for a rock garden; ↕ to 6in (15cm). **'Mediterranean Sun'** has narrow leaves and yellow flowerheads, in late summer; ↕ to 8in (20cm).

Inula ensifolia

I. glandulosa see *I. orientalis.*

I. helenium (Elecampane). Robust, rhizomatous perennial with thick, furrowed, downy stems bearing basal rosettes of ovate or ovate-elliptic, toothed, mid-green leaves, to 32in (80cm) long, densely woolly beneath and with wavy margins. Bright yellow flowerheads, to 3in (8cm) across, are produced singly or in lax corymbs in mid- and late summer. Roots are used medicinally as an expectorant. ↕ 3–6ft (0.9–2m), ↔ 36in (90cm). Europe to W. Asia. Zone 5.

I. hookeri ▣ Clump-forming perennial with creeping roots and numerous willowy, softly hairy stems bearing ovate to oblong-lance-shaped, minutely toothed, hairy, mid-green leaves, 3–6in (8–15cm) long. Pale yellow flowerheads, 1½–3in (4–8cm) across, are borne singly or in clusters of 2 or 3, with narrow ray florets, brownish yellow disk florets, and broad, very hairy involucral bracts, from late summer to mid-autumn. ↕ 24–30in (60–75cm), ↔ 24in (60cm) or more. Himalayas. Zone 4.

***I. macrocephala* of gardens** see *I. royleana.*

I. magnifica, syn. *I. afghanica* of gardens. Robust, clump-forming perennial bearing hairy stems, with dark purple streaks along their lengths, and elliptic-ovate, dark green leaves, to 10in (25cm) long, softly hairy beneath. In late summer, bears corymbs of 8–20 bright golden yellow flowerheads, to 6in (15cm) across. ↕ to 6ft (1.8m), ↔ 3ft (1m). E. Caucasus. Zone 5.

Inula hookeri

Inula royleana

I. oculis-christi. Rhizomatous perennial with erect, hairy stems bearing inversely lance-shaped, entire or toothed, downy, mid-green leaves, to 6in (15cm) long. In mid- and late summer, produces corymbs of usually 3–5 bright golden yellow flowerheads, to 3in (8cm) across, with very downy involucres. ↕ to 20in (50cm), ↔ 24in (60cm). E. Europe, Turkey, Caucasus, N. Iraq, Iran. Zone 5.

I. orientalis, syn. *I. glandulosa.* Rhizomatous perennial producing erect stems, with yellowish brown glandular hairs, bearing ovate-elliptic or inversely lance-shaped, toothed, hairy, mid-green leaves, 5in (13cm) long. Solitary, orange-yellow flowerheads, 3½in (9cm) across, with very woolly buds and wavy ray florets, are produced in summer. ↕ 24–36in (60–90cm), ↔ 24in (60cm). Caucasus. Zone 5.

I. racemosa. Robust, clump-forming perennial with red-marked stems and rough, elliptic-lance-shaped to lance-shaped, toothed, mid-green basal leaves, 18in (45cm) or more long, and deeply lobed at the bases. The progressively smaller stem leaves are densely woolly beneath and stalkless near each apex. From late summer to midautumn, bears long racemes of usually solitary, light yellow flowerheads, 1½–2½in (3.5–6cm) across, with narrow ray florets and darker yellow disk florets. Roots are used medicinally. ↕ to 8ft (2.5m), ↔ 5ft (1.5m). W. Himalayas. Zone 6b.

I. royleana ▣ syn. *I. macrocephala* of gardens. Upright, clump-forming perennial with dark green stems and ovate, prominently veined, slightly toothed, hairy, mid-green leaves, 10in (25cm) long, with winged stalks. Solitary, orange-yellow flowerheads, 4–5in (10–13cm) across, with slightly darker orange disk florets, are borne from midsummer to early autumn, opening from black-brown buds. ↕ 18–24in (45–60cm), ↔ 18in (45cm). W. Himalayas. Zone 5.

IOCHROMA

SOLANACEAE

Genus of 20 species of evergreen or deciduous shrubs and small trees from moist forest areas, particularly clearings and margins, in tropical Central and South America. Leaves are alternate, simple, and entire. They are grown for their nodding to pendent, trumpet-shaped to tubular, purple, blue, red, white, or yellow flowers, produced in clusters or pairs. The fruits are pulpy berries; each one is enclosed by an enlarged calyx. Where not hardy, grow in a temperate greenhouse. In warmer climates, grow in a shrub border or as free-standing specimens.

• **CULTIVATION** Under glass, grow in soil-based potting mix in bright to moderate filtered light. During growth, water moderately and apply a balanced liquid fertilizer every month. Keep just moist in winter. Pinch young plants to encourage bushiness. Top-dress mature plants with fresh soil mix annually in spring. Outdoors, grow in fertile, moist but well-drained soil in full sun or partial shade, with shelter from cold, drying winds. Pruning group 9; group 12 for scandent shrubs, after flowering; plants under glass may need restrictive pruning in late winter.

• **PROPAGATION** Sow seed at 55–64°F (13–18°C) in spring. Root greenwood cuttings in late spring, or root semi-ripe cuttings in summer.

• **PESTS AND DISEASES** Spider mites and whiteflies may be problems under glass.

I. coccinea. Lax shrub with downy stems and ovate to oblong, sharp-pointed, prominently veined, lustrous, rich green leaves, 3–5in (8–13cm) long. Bears clusters of up to 8 tubular scarlet flowers, 1½–2in (4–5cm) long, with light yellow throats, in summer. ↕ to 10ft (3m), ↔ 5–6ft (1.5–2m). Central America. ❀ (min. 45°F/7°C)

I. cyanea ▣ syn. *I. tubulosa.* Erect to spreading shrub with downy shoots and narrowly ovate to oblong-lance-shaped or elliptic, softly hairy, gray-green leaves, 3–6in (8–15cm) long. Umbel-like clusters of up to 20 tubular, deep purple-blue flowers, 2in (5cm) long, with partly reflexed petal tips, are produced mainly in summer. ↕ to 10ft (3m), ↔ 5–6ft (1.5–2m). Colombia, Ecuador, Peru. ❀ (min. 45°F/7°C)

I. tubulosa see *I. cyanea.*

Iochroma cyanea

IPHEION

LILIACEAE

Genus of 10 species of small, bulbous perennials from upland meadows and rocky sites in South America. They are grown for their star-shaped, usually strongly honey-scented flowers, borne in spring, singly or in pairs. Most other parts smell of onions when crushed. The grass-like, basal leaves are linear-strap-shaped. They are useful in a rock garden and for underplanting herbaceous plants such as peonies or hostas. Where not hardy, grow in a cold greenhouse or alpine house.

• **CULTIVATION** Under glass, grow in soil-based potting mix, with added leaf mold and grit, in bright filtered or indirect light. During growth in spring and early summer, water moderately and apply a balanced liquid fertilizer monthly. Keep just moist while dormant. Outdoors, grow in moderately fertile, humus-rich, moist but well-drained soil in full sun. Provide a protective mulch in winter where temperatures regularly fall below 14°F (-10°C). Plant bulbs 3in (8cm) deep, in autumn.

• **PROPAGATION** Sow seed in containers in a cold frame when ripe or in spring. Divide in summer when dormant.

• **PESTS AND DISEASES** Slugs and snails can be problems.

***I.* 'Rolf Fiedler'**, syn. *Tristagma* 'Rolf Fiedler'. Clump-forming, bulbous perennial with short, narrowly strap-shaped, blunt-tipped, light blue-green leaves, to 6in (15cm) long. In spring, produces solitary, occasionally 2, outward-facing, star-shaped, scented, vivid mid-blue flowers, 1¼in (3cm) across. ↕ 4–5in (10–13cm), PD2in (5cm). Zone 6.

I. uniflorum, syn. *Tristagma uniflorum* (Spring starflower). Vigorous, clump-forming, bulbous perennial. In late autumn, produces semi-erect, narrowly strap-shaped, light blue-green leaves, to 10in (25cm) long. Flowers are solitary, upward-facing, star-shaped, scented, pale silvery blue, 1½in (4cm) across, frequently with darker midribs, borne mainly in spring. ↕ 6–8in (15–20cm), PD2in (5cm). Argentina, Uruguay. Zone 5. **'Album'** has pure white flowers. **'Froyle Mill'** produces dusky violet flowers. **'Wisley Blue'** ■ bears lilac-blue flowers.

Ipomoea batatas 'Blackie'

IPOMOEA *syn.* MINA, PHARBITIS

Morning glory

CONVOLVULACEAE

Genus of about 500 species of annuals and perennials, many of them trailers or twining climbers, and a few evergreen shrubs and trees, native to warm regions worldwide. They are found in a great diversity of habitats, from open scrub to dense woodland, seashores, and cliffs. Leaves are alternate, and may be simple and entire, or toothed, lobed, or more finely dissected. The funnel-shaped or tubular flowers are solitary or borne in axillary or terminal cymes, racemes, or panicles. Grow annuals in a sunny, sheltered site. Where temperatures drop below 45°F (7°C), grow perennial or shrubby species in a temperate or warm greenhouse. In warmer areas, train climbers over a pergola or arch, or use them as dense groundcover. Seeds are highly toxic if ingested.

• **CULTIVATION** Under glass, grow in soil-based potting mix in full light, with shade from the hottest sun. During growth, water freely, and apply a balanced liquid fertilizer monthly. Water sparingly in winter. Support climbers and trailing species. Outdoors, grow in moderately fertile, well-drained soil in full sun. Shelter from cold, drying winds. Pruning group 11 for climbing species, in spring.

• **PROPAGATION** Sow seed singly at 64°F (18°C) in spring. Chip seeds or soak for 24 hours before sowing. For perennials and subshrubs, root softwood cuttings

Ipomoea indica

in spring or summer, or semi-ripe cuttings in summer.

• **PESTS AND DISEASES** White blister, rust, fungal leaf spots, stem rot, thread blight, charcoal rot, and wilt occur.

I. acuminata see *I. indica.*

I. alba, syn. *Calonyction aculeatum, I. bona-nox,* (Belle de nuit, Moonflower). Twining perennial, usually grown as an annual, with evergreen, ovate to rounded, sometimes 3-lobed, mid- to deep green leaves, 4–8in (10–20cm) long. Cymes of 1–8 wide-spreading, trumpet-shaped, white flowers, 5–5½in (12–14cm) across, tinted green outside, open at dusk from early summer to autumn. ↕ to 15ft (5m), to 70ft (20m) when grown as a perennial. Tropical regions worldwide. ❄ (min. 45°F/7°C). **'Giant White'** has large white flowers, to 6in (15cm) across.

I. batatas (Sweet potato). Tuberous perennial climber with fleshy, purple stems and heart-shaped to ovate, entire, toothed, or 3-lobed leaves, 2–4in (5–10cm) long. In summer, bears trumpet-shaped, lavender to pale purple flowers, to 1in (2.5cm) across, with the base of the tubes darker or sometimes white. Chartreuse-leaved selections exist. ↕ to 20ft (6m) or more. Pantropical. ❄ (min. 41°F/5°C). **'Blackie'** ■ has lobed, near-black foliage.

I. bona-nox see *I. alba.*

I. coccinea ■ syn. *Quamoclit coccinea* (Red morning glory, Star morning glory). Annual twining climber with entire or boldly toothed, ovate, mid- to deep green leaves, 3–5½in (7–14cm) long. Bears racemes of 3–8 scarlet flowers, to ¾in (2cm) across, with yellow throats, in summer. ↕ 6–12ft (2–4m). S.E. US.

I. hederacea, syn. *Pharbitis hederacea.* Annual twining climber with slender, densely hairy stems and ovate to rounded, usually 3-lobed, mid- to deep green leaves, 2–5in (5–13cm) long, with tapering points. In summer, bears cymes of 2–5 funnel-shaped, blue, sometimes purple flowers, ¾–1½in (2–4cm) across, with white tubes and prominent, long-tailed, green sepals. Often confused with *I. nil*, which has very narrowly triangular sepals. ↕ 6–10ft (2–3m). S. US to Argentina.

I. imperialis see *I. nil.*

I. indica ■ syn. *I. acuminata, I. learii* (Blue dawn flower). Vigorous, perennial climber, bearing evergreen, heart-shaped or 3-lobed, slender-pointed, mid-green leaves, 2½–7in (6–18cm) long. Produces abundant funnel-shaped, rich purple-blue to blue flowers, 2½–3½in (6–8cm) across, often maturing to purplish red, in cymes of 3–5, from late spring to autumn. ↕ 20ft (6m) or more. Tropical regions worldwide. ❄ (min. 45°F/7°C)

I. learii see *I. indica.*

I. lobata ■ syn. *I. versicolor, Quamoclit lobata* (Spanish flag). Perennial climber, grown as an annual, with crimson-flushed stems and stalks. Bears toothed, mid- to deep green leaves, to 4in (10cm) long, with 3 prominent, finger-like lobes and 2–4 smaller basal lobes. Dense, erect, one-sided racemes, to 12in (30cm) long, of slightly curved, narrow, tubular, scarlet flowers, ½–¾in (1.5–2cm) long, maturing to orange and yellow, then white, with very long stamens and styles, appear from summer to autumn, or throughout the year in warm climates. ↕ 6–15ft (2–5m). Mexico, Central to South America. ❄ (min. 50°F/10°C)

I.* x *multifida (*I. coccinea* x *I. quamoclit*), syn. *I.* x *sloteri* (Cardinal climber). Slender, twining annual with broadly triangular-ovate, deeply and narrowly 3- to 7-lobed, mid-green leaves, 1½–5in (4–13cm) long, divided into 7–15 narrowly lance-shaped lobes. In summer, bears salverform crimson flowers, to 1in (2.5cm) across, with white throats. ↕ 3–6ft (1–2m). Garden origin.

I. nil, syn. *I. imperialis.* Vigorous annual or, in tropical climates, woody-based, short-lived, perennial climber, with bristly yellow-hairy stems. Bears broadly ovate, usually entire, sometimes 3-lobed, mid-green leaves, 2–5½in (5–14cm)

I

Ipheion uniflorum 'Wisley Blue'

Ipomoea coccinea

Ipomoea lobata

Ipomoea tricolor 'Heavenly Blue'

long. From summer to autumn, bears solitary, funnel-shaped, white-tubed flowers, 2in (5cm) across, with pale to deep blue, sometimes purple or red petal lobes. ↕ to 15ft (5m) or more. Tropical regions worldwide. ❄ (min. 45°F/7°C). **'Chocolate'** has reddish chocolate-brown flowers, 3in (8cm) across. **'Early Call'** produces white-tubed flowers with scarlet lobes, to 3in (8cm) across. **Platycodon Series** cultivars have single and semi-double, red, purple, or white flowers. **'Scarlet Star'** bears many cerise flowers with central white stars. **'Scarlett O'Hara'** has bright red flowers.

I. purpurea, syn. *Convolvulus purpureus, Pharbitis purpurea* (Common morning glory). Annual twining climber with slender, hairy, and bristly stems. Leaves are broadly ovate, entire or 3-lobed, mid-green, 1½–4in (4–10cm) long. Trumpet-shaped flowers, to 2½in (6cm) across, in pink, purple-blue, magenta, or white (or stripes of these colors on white), with white tubes, are produced in cymes of 3–7, or singly, mainly in summer. ↕ 6–10ft (2–3m). Probably Mexico.

I. quamoclit, syn. *Quamoclit pennata* (Star glory). Annual twining climber with hairless stems and elliptic to broadly ovate, deeply pinnatisect, deep green leaves, 1¼–3½in (3–9cm) long, composed of 9–19 pairs of linear lobes. Slender-tubed, scarlet, sometimes white flowers, to ¾in (2cm) across, with 5 distinct and spreading lobes, are produced in cymes of 2–5, mainly in summer, or for most of the year in the tropics. ↕ 6–20ft (2–6m). Tropical South America.

I. rubrocaerulea see *I. tricolor*.

I. x sloteri see *I.* x *multifida*.

I. tricolor, syn. *I. rubrocaerulea* (Morning glory). Fast-growing, twining annual or short-lived perennial with ovate-heart-shaped, slender-tipped, light to mid-green leaves, 1½–4in (4–10cm) long. Funnel-shaped, bright sky-blue to purple flowers, to 3in (8cm) across, with white tubes, golden yellow inside at the bases, appear singly or in 3- to 5-flowered cymes in summer and throughout the year in the tropics. Tropical Central and South America. ↕ 10–12ft (3–4m). ❄ (min. 45°F/7°C). **'Crimson Rambler'** has red flowers with white throats. **'Flying Saucers'** has variably marbled, white and purple-blue flowers. **'Heavenly Blue'** ■ produces rich azure flowers with white throats. **'Roman Candy'** has cerise and white flowers, and white-variegated leaves.

I. tuberosa see *Merremia tuberosa*.

I. versicolor see *I. lobata*.

IPOMOPSIS

POLEMONIACEAE

Genus of 24 species of erect annuals, biennials, and short-lived perennials from dry and desert habitats of W. and S. US. The leaves are alternate and entire to pinnatifid. They are grown for their tubular flowers, in red, pink, yellow, white, or violet. *I. rubra* is a striking addition to a mixed border; where not hardy, grow in a conservatory or cool greenhouse.

• **CULTIVATION** Under glass, grow in soil-based potting mix in full light. Water moderately in the growing season, sparingly in winter. Apply a balanced liquid fertilizer when in growth. Outdoors, grow in moderately fertile, well-drained soil in full sun.

• **PROPAGATION** Sow seed of perennial types *in situ* in spring or early autumn; sow biennials *in situ* in late summer.

• **PESTS AND DISEASES** Occasionally affected by root rot.

I. rubra, syn. *Gilia rubra.* Erect, unbranched biennial or perennial with basal rosettes of pinnatisect, oblong leaves, to 1in (2.5cm) long composed of linear, dark green leaflets. In summer, bears scarlet flowers, 1in (2.5cm) across, yellow and red-spotted inside, in terminal, narrow panicles. ↕ to 6ft (2m), ↔ 36in (90cm). Texas to Florida, South Carolina. Zone 6b.

IRESINE

AMARANTHACEAE

Genus of about 80 species of evergreen, erect or climbing perennials, annuals, and subshrubs from dry, open areas in South America and Australia. They are cultivated for their striking, colorful foliage and are often grown to provide contrast with flowering plants. The leaves are opposite, simple, and entire. The insignificant white or green flowers are borne in terminal or axillary spikes. Where not hardy, grow as tender perennials for summer bedding, and overwinter in a warm greenhouse. In warmer climates, grow as edging in a bed or mixed border, in a windowbox, or in a container on a patio.

• **CULTIVATION** Under glass, grow in soil-based potting mix in full light, with shade from the hottest sun. During the growing season, water freely and apply a balanced liquid fertilizer every 4 weeks. Water sparingly in winter. Outdoors, grow in fertile, moist but well-drained soil, in full sun for best leaf color. Pinch back young plants in spring to encourage bushiness. Cut back mature plants hard in early spring, or propagate each year to maintain bushy specimens,

Iresine herbstii 'Aureoreticulata'

and plant out after all danger of frost has passed.

• **PROPAGATION** Take stem-tip cuttings at any time. Where not hardy, take stem-tip cuttings of bedding plants in late summer. Overwinter in a warm greenhouse and pinch out 2 or 3 times to produce strong stock plants, which will provide softwood cuttings in late winter and early spring.

• **PESTS AND DISEASES** Prone to powdery mildew. Susceptible to aphids and spider mites, particularly under glass.

I. herbstii (Beefsteak plant, Chicken gizzard). Erect, bushy annual or short-lived perennial with broadly ovate to rounded, waxy, variegated, mid-green, yellow, very deep red, or orange leaves, to 3in (8cm) long, often with vividly contrasting veins and golden hairs beneath, and with notches at the tips. Stems and branches are bright green, purple, or red, and almost translucent when young. ↕ to 5ft (1.5m), ↔ to 36in (90cm). Brazil. ❄ (min. 50°F/10°C). **'Aureoreticulata'** ■ produces mid-green leaves with yellow veins. **'Brilliantissima'** ■ has rich crimson leaves. **'Wallisii'** is dwarf, with purple-black leaves; ↕ to 24in (60cm), ↔ to 20in (50cm).

I. lindenii (Blood leaf). Erect, bushy, compact perennial with blood-red stems bearing ovate or oblong-lance-shaped, pointed, glossy, deep blood-red leaves, 2–4in (5–10cm) long, with prominent deep or light red veins. ↕↔ to 3ft (1m). Ecuador. ❄ (min. 50°F/10°C). **'Formosa'** has yellow leaves with crimson veins.

Iresine herbstii 'Brilliantissima'

IRIS

IRIDACEAE

Genus of about 300 species of upright, rhizomatous or bulbous, sometimes fleshy-rooted perennials found in a wide range of habitats in the N. hemisphere. Irises are grown mainly for their colorful, often spectacular flowers. A few are evergreen, but most are deciduous, dying back completely or to a fan of short leaves. Some are dormant in summer. The distinctive iris flowers are illustrated and described in the accompanying panel (see opposite). The seed pods are 3- to 6-angled, either ribbed or smooth, with large seeds.

Most irises flower in spring or summer. Some, mostly bearded hybrids, are remontant, flowering again in the same year. Taller irises are suitable for a mixed or herbaceous border. Smaller species and cultivars, and those requiring very free-draining conditions, can be grown in a rock garden, raised bed, or trough. Those requiring a totally dry dormancy period should be grown in a bulb frame or alpine house in moist climates. A few are slightly tender and require glass protection in most areas. All parts may cause severe discomfort if ingested; contact with the sap may irritate the skin.

Botanically, irises are divided into several subgenera and sections. In horticulture, these are often simplified as below and in the table opposite.

Rhizomatous irises

These have rhizomes as rootstocks, close to or on the surface, or just below ground level, which produce linear to strap-shaped, sometimes curved leaves, nearly always in basal fans. Each active rhizome produces one to several new growths every year, and this spread can continue indefinitely into large clumps. Rhizomatous irises fall into 3 main groups:

Bearded irises – have thick surface rhizomes, giving rise to fans of sword-shaped, usually broad leaves, and simple or branched flower stems. Most bear multiple flowers per stem. The flowers, produced in a large range of colors, have well-developed standards and falls, with a prominent "beard" of white or colored hairs in the center of each fall petal. Bearded hybrids are the most widely grown group in horticulture. They are classified for garden use or exhibition according to the bloom season and the height of the flower stem, as follows. *Miniature dwarf bearded*: ↕ to 8in (20cm); flowers 1–3in (2.5–8cm) across. The first bearded irises to bloom. *Standard dwarf bearded*: ↕ 8–16in (20–40cm); flowers 3–4in (8–10cm) across. Bloom after the miniature dwarfs. *Intermediate bearded*: ↕ 16–27in (40–68cm); flowers 4–5in (10–13cm) across. Bloom after the standard dwarfs and before the tall beardeds. *Miniature tall bearded*: ↕ 16–27in (40–68cm) (with slender, flexuous stems); flowers not more than 6in (15cm) combined height and width. These irises and the border beardeds bloom with the tall beardeds. *Border bearded*: ↕ 16–27in (40–68cm); flowers 4–5in (10–13cm) across. *Tall bearded*: ↕ 27in (68cm) or more; flowers 4–8in (10–20cm) across.

Aril irises are so called because of the white protrusion, or aril, on each seed. They become dormant in summer after flowering, and should be kept dry during this period. The main groups are the Oncocyclus and the closely related Regelia irises, and their cultivars and hybrids. **Oncocyclus** irises bear large, brightly colored flowers with bearded falls. **Regelia** irises have bearded falls and standards. **Regeliocyclus** irises are hybrids between Oncocyclus and Regelia irises. **Arilbred** irises are hybrids between Oncocyclus or Regelia irises and other bearded irises.

Beardless irises **(Limniris)** – also have rhizomes, but these are normally just below ground. The fall petals on the flowers are smooth. Beardless irises include the following widely differing groups: **Pacific Coast** irises produce flowers in a large range of colors, most with attractive veining. Leaves are usually evergreen. **Siberian** irises bear blue, purple, white, yellow, pink, or deep red flowers and are suitable for an open border. Leaves are usually deciduous. **Spuria** irises, among the tallest-growing in the genus, produce flowers in a wide range of colors. **Laevigatae** irises, also known as water irises, thrive in damp places. The group includes *I. laevigata* and *I. pseudacorus*, the common yellow flag iris. Stems are simple or branched, and bear blue, pink, red, purple, white, or yellow flowers. Also included in Laevigatae irises are the numerous cultivars of *I. ensata* (syn. *I. kaempferi*), known as Japanese irises, which flourish at the margins of ponds or streams, or in moist borders. Japanese irises bear large, often flattened, sometimes double flowers, in shades of blue, white, purple, pink, sometimes yellow, or deep red, often in combination. **Louisiana** irises also thrive in damp conditions, often have zigzag stems, and bear flowers in a large range of colors. **Unguiculares** irises are markedly different from other beardless irises: they develop a mass of rhizomes above ground, are evergreen, and bloom from autumn to spring, bearing blue, violet, lavender-pink, or white, almost stemless flowers with long perianth tubes.

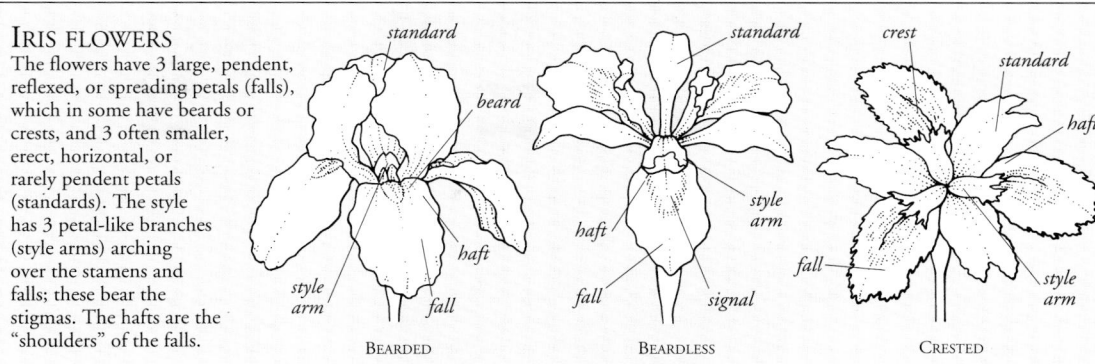

Crested irises **(Lophiris)** – also known as Evansia irises. They spread freely by rhizomes and produce relatively flat flowers in shades of blue, violet, or white. They have a crest or ridge on each fall instead of a beard. Flowers and leaves, which are deciduous to evergreen, may be borne on bamboo-like stems, which vary greatly in height.

IRIS FLOWERS

The flowers have 3 large, pendent, reflexed, or spreading petals (falls), which in some have beards or crests, and 3 often smaller, erect, horizontal, or rarely pendent petals (standards). The style has 3 petal-like branches (style arms) arching over the stamens and falls; these bear the stigmas. The hafts are the "shoulders" of the falls.

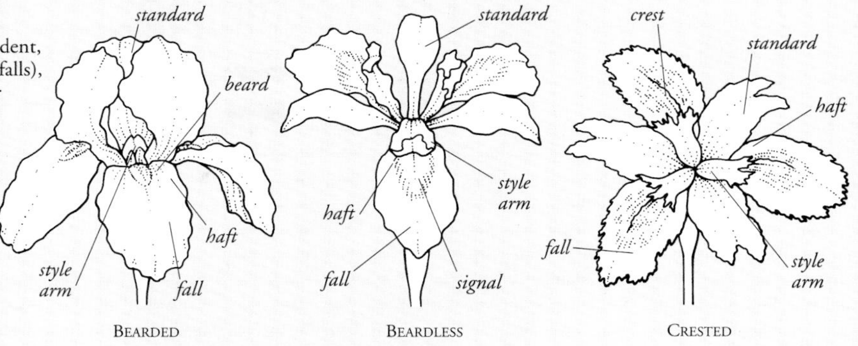

Bulbous irises

These have bulbs as storage organs; Juno irises also have fleshy roots. Leaves are deciduous, and either channeled or quadrangular to almost cylindrical in cross-section. Flowers are beardless and appear from late winter to midsummer. All are summer dormant. Bulbous irises fall into 3 groups. **Reticulata** (Hermodactyloides) irises have netted tunics that cover the bulbs, which produce 1 or 2 long, square-sectioned or cylindrical leaves. The leaf length at flowering is very variable; after flowering, the leaves lengthen to 12in (30cm) or more. Flowers are yellow, blue, white, or reddish violet. **Juno** (Scorpiris) irises have bulbs with fleshy roots and flat or channeled leaves. The flowers have large, brightly colored fall petals and very small standards. Some species, such as *I. bucharica*, are good rock garden plants; others, such as *I. magnifica*, do well in a sunny, open border. Many are challenging to grow. **Xiphium** irises include the Dutch, English, and Spanish groups, with channeled, linear leaves and blue, lavender-blue, yellow, or white flowers. The English irises prefer moist soil. Xiphium irises are popular garden plants, widely used as cut flowers; most are easy to grow but may not persist. Some N. African species are frost tender.

• **CULTIVATION** General cultivation information for irises is outlined here; more specific group requirements are given in the panel below. All irises are best planted from midsummer to early autumn. Outdoors, grow in well-drained, moderately fertile, neutral or slightly acidic or alkaline soil in full sun to light, dappled shade. Grow irises that require protection from rain or cold under glass.

IRIS GROUPS				HEIGHT in/cm	HARDINESS	FLOWER SIZE in/cm	FLOWERING TIME	GENERAL CULTIVATION REQUIREMENTS
RHIZOMATOUS	BEARDED		Species and cultivars	3–48+ (8–120+)	Zone 3	1–8 (2.5–20)	early spring to early summer	Outdoors, grow in well-drained, fertile, neutral to slightly acidic soil in full sun to light shade. Avoid high-nitrogen fertilizer. Keep all types moist during active growth. Increase water and fertilizer for remontants. Mulches may be used if kept away from leaves and rhizomes. Taller cultivars may require staking, especially when grown for exhibition. To grow arils under glass, grow in containers of soil-based potting mix with added grit, in full light. Water moderately when in growth, and keep completely dry during dormancy.
		ARIL	Oncocyclus	4–24 (10–60)	Zone 7b	2–8 (5–20)	mid- and late spring	
			Regelia & Regeliocyclus	4–24 (10–60)	Zone 7b	2–4 (5–10)	mid- and late spring	
			Arilbred	10–36 (25–90)	Zone 7	2–4 (5–10)	midspring to early summer	
	BEARDLESS		Pacific Coast	6–36 (15–90)	Zone 7	2–4 (5–10)	mid- and late spring	Generally, beardless irises prefer well-drained, neutral to slightly acidic soil in full sun or partial shade. Pacific Coast irises grow best in mild areas with winter rain and dry summers; they transplant and grow poorly, if at all, in much of North America. Siberians are highly adaptable to most garden conditions and are good choices for herbaceous or mixed borders and low-maintenance gardens. Most Spurias require a dry summer dormancy, alkaline soil, and high levels of fertility. Most Laevigatae irises require moist to wet, acidic soils, and many of the species require standing water to grow well. Japanese irises may be grown in large containers for convenient display when in bloom. Louisianas thrive in moist soil in areas with hot summers; many "run" (spread widely) through the soil. Grow Unguiculares irises in sharply drained, neutral to alkaline soil in full sun; they are ideal for the base of a sunny wall.
			Siberian	18–48 (45–120)	Zone 4	3–5 (7–13)	midspring to early summer	
			Spuria	48–72 (120–200)	Zone 5	3–6 (7–15)	late spring to midsummer	
			Laevigatae (including Japanese)	24–60 (60–150)	Zone 3	2½–10 (6–25)	late spring and early summer	
			Louisiana	18–60 (45–150)	Zone 6	3–8 (7–20)	midspring to early summer	
			Unguiculares	15–18 (38–45)	Zone 7	2–3 (5–8)	autumn to spring	
	CRESTED			2–72+ (5–200+)	Zone 4	1¼–4 (3–10)	mid- and late spring	Outdoors, grow in moist, humus-rich soil in full sun or partial shade. Under glass, grow in soil-based potting mix with added grit and leaf mold. Provide bright filtered light and moderate humidity. Ventilate freely whenever temperatures rise above freezing. Water moderately when in growth. Keep just moist during dormancy.
BULBOUS	Reticulata			2–6 (5–15)	Zone 5	1–2 (2.5–5)	late winter and early spring	Outdoors, grow in well-drained, neutral or slightly alkaline soil in full sun. Under glass, grow in deep containers of soil-based potting mix with added grit. Provide full light and low humidity. Ventilate freely whenever temperatures rise above freezing. Water moderately when in growth and keep just moist during dormancy. Reticulata irises force well for winter bloom. When planting or transplanting, take care not to damage the fleshy roots of Juno irises.
	Juno			6–24 (15–60)	Zone 5	2–4 (5–10)	early and midspring	
	Xiphium			10–36 (25–90)	Zone 5b	3–3½ (7–9)	midspring to midsummer	

Iris bucharica

Rhizomatous irises – Bearded irises have surface rhizomes that should be partially exposed, or thinly covered with soil in hot climates. Plant rhizomes singly or in groups of 3 with the fans outermost, 3–24in (8–60cm) apart, depending on size. They must not be shaded by other plants; many do best in a special bed on their own. When planting, top-dress with a low-nitrogen fertilizer, and again in early spring. Avoid applying high-nitrogen fertilizers to the surface or carelessly mulching with organic matter, which may encourage rhizome rot. After 2–5 years, when clumps become congested or lose vitality, divide and replant sound rhizomes in fresh soil.

Beardless irises normally have rhizomes below the surface of the soil and benefit from shallow mulching in spring; otherwise, follow the feeding instructions for bearded irises. Plant small divisions of beardless and crested rhizomes 3–24in (8–60cm) apart, depending on size.

Bulbous irises – Plant Xiphium and Juno bulbs 4–6in (10–15cm) apart, depending on the size. Plant Reticulata bulbs 2–4in (5–10cm) apart. Plant all bulbs at a depth at least twice the height of the bulb. After flowering, feed with a high-phosphorous fertilizer to encourage large bulbs to form. Lift and separate bulbs in early autumn.

• **PROPAGATION** Sow seed in containers in a cold frame in autumn. Lift and divide clumps, or separate bulb offsets, and plant within a few weeks (bearded) or immediately (beardless) in the flowering site, usually from midsummer (bearded) to early autumn (beardless).

• **PESTS AND DISEASES** Iris borer, verbena bud moth, whiteflies, iris weevil, thrips, slugs and snails, aphids, and nematodes may be troublesome. Bacterial leaf blight and soft rot, crown rot, rhizome rot, leaf spot, rust, viruses, and scorch occur. Ink spot fungus can kill Reticulata bulbs.

Iris chrysographes

***I.* 'Aachen Elf'** ■ Miniature tall bearded iris, flowering in midseason. Bears flowers with yellow standards and beards, and lavender falls with yellow edges. ↕ 20in (50cm).

***I.* 'Acadian Miss'.** Louisiana iris, flowering in mid- and late season. Produces ruffled, white flowers with yellow-green signals and green style arms. ↕ 30in (75cm).

***I.* 'Ada Perry'.** Spuria iris with dark violet standards, dark red-violet falls, and yellow signals, borne in midseason. ↕ 4ft (1.2m).

***I.* 'Adobe Sunset'** ■ Spuria iris with deep orange-yellow flowers, veined and bordered dark brown, borne late in the season. ↕ 5ft (1.5m).

I. afghanica ■ Regelia iris with curved leaves, 10in (25cm) long. In late spring, each unbranched stem produces 1 or 2 flowers, 3in (8cm) across, with pointed petals. Standards are pale yellow with green beards; falls are cream, veined purple-brown, with purple patches and dark brown beards. ↕ 6–16in (15–40cm). N.E. Afghanistan, Pakistan. Zone 7b.

***I.* 'Alpine Lake'.** Miniature dwarf bearded iris. In mid- and late season, bears flowers with blue-tinted, white standards, light blue falls, and pale blue beards. ↕ 6in (15cm).

***I.* 'Ancilla'.** Regeliocyclus iris. Blooms, early in the season. Standards are white with soft blueveins; falls are netted gray-brown with deep purple patches and beards. ↕ 10in (25cm).

***I.* 'Ann Chowning'.** Louisiana iris. Bears currant-red flowers with gold signals, early in season. ↕ 36in (90cm).

***I.* 'Ann Dasch'.** Siberian iris. Bears mottled, light blue-purple flowers with solid, deeper blue-purple margins, and falls with yellow haft marks, in mid- and late season. ↕ 36in (90cm).

I. aphylla. Bearded iris with broadly lance-shaped, gray-green leaves, to 6in (15cm) long, the outer ones curved, the others erect. In midspring, each branched stem produces 1–5 purple or blue-violet flowers, 2½in (6cm) across, with yellow-tipped white beards. ↕ 6–12in (15–30cm). Central and Eastern Europe to Western Russia, Ukraine, Moldavia, Caucasus. Zone 5.

***I.* 'Apollo'** ■ Dutch iris. In late spring and early summer, bears flowers with creamy white standards and primrose-yellow falls. ↕ 26in (65cm).

***I.* 'Apricot Frosty'** ■ Border bearded iris bearing flowers with white standards, deep apricot falls, and apricot beards, in midseason. ↕ 22in (55cm).

***I.* 'Archie Owen'.** Spuria iris with bright yellow flowers, borne in midseason. ↕ 36in (90cm).

***I.* 'Ask Alma'.** Very vigorous intermediate bearded iris. In midseason, produces coral-orange-pink flowers with tangerine-tipped, white beards. ↕ 22in (55cm).

***I.* 'Baby Blessed'.** Remontant standard dwarf bearded iris. Bears light yellow blooms, with a small white spot and cream beard on each fall, early in the season and, in favorable conditions, again in early autumn. ↕ 10in (25cm).

***I.* 'Batik'** ■ Border bearded iris. In midseason, bears white-striped and splashed, purple flowers with white-tipped, yellow beards. ↕ 26in (65cm).

***I.* 'Bedford Lass'.** Siberian iris producing ruffled, light blue-violet flowers with white and gold signals and lighter style arms, in midseason. ↕ 34in (85cm).

***I.* 'Before the Storm'.** Tall bearded iris. Bears fragrant, near-black flowers and bronze-tipped, black beards, in midseason. ↕ 36in (90cm).

***I.* 'Betty Cooper'.** Spuria iris. Bears flowers with light yellow-streaked, light violet standards and orange-centered, light violet falls with brownish purple veining, in midseason. ↕ 4ft (1.2m).

***I.* 'Beverly Sills'.** Tall bearded iris with laced, coral-pink flowers and tangerine beards, in midseason. ↕ 36in (90cm).

***I.* 'Blue Eyed Blonde'.** Intermediate bearded iris producing mid-yellow flowers with blue-tipped, violet beards, in mid- and late season. ↕ 26in (65cm).

***I.* 'Blue Lassie'.** Spuria iris producing blue flowers with white patches on the falls and yellow signals, in midseason. ↕ 3½ft (1.1m).

I. brevicaulis, syn. *I. foliosa*. Louisiana iris with branched, zigzag stems and large leaves or bracts, to 18in (45cm) long, overtopping the flowers. In early summer, bears terminal and axillary, bright blue-violet flowers, 3–4in (7–10cm) across, with small, spreading standards and broad, ovate falls. ↕ 16–20in (40–50cm). Mississippi Valley. Zone 5b.

***I.* 'Big Money'** ■ Hardy, standard dwarf bearded iris. Dominant color is yellow. Thrive on the edge of woodland clearings. ↕ 12in (30cm). Zone 3.

***I.* 'Bromyard'.** Standard dwarf bearded iris. Early in the season, bears flowers with blue-gray standards, blue-purple and ochre falls, and blue-gray beards. ↕ 11in (28cm).

***I.* 'Brownberry'.** Border bearded iris flowering late in the season. Bears cream standards, heavily marked brownish red-violet. The falls are white, bordered brownish red-violet, and the yellow beards are tipped red-violet. ↕ 22in (55cm).

***I.* 'Brown Lasso'** ■ Border bearded iris flowering in early and midseason. Standards are deep butterscotch-yellow; falls are light violet with brown edging and yellow beards. ↕ 22in (55cm). Zone 3.

I. bucharica ■ Vigorous Juno iris with glossy leaves, to 8in (20cm) long. Bears up to 6 flowers, 1½–2½in (4–6cm) across, in the upper leaf axils in spring. Flowers vary from golden yellow to white, with a yellow mark on each fall. The white and yellow form is more commonly grown commercially. ↕ 8–16in (20–40cm). N.E. Afghanistan, C. Asia. Zone 5.

Iris cristata

Iris danfordiae

I. bulleyana ■ Siberian iris with linear leaves, to 18in (45cm) long, glossy mid-green above, glaucous beneath. In early summer, hollow, unbranched stems bear 1 or 2 flowers, 2½–3in (6–8cm) across, with violet standards, and spreading white falls streaked violet. ↕14–18in (35–45cm). China (Sichuan, Yunnan). Zone 5.
***I.* 'Bumblebee Deelite'.** Miniature tall bearded iris, flowering in early and midseason. Bears flowers with yellow standards, yellow-edged, maroon falls, and orange beards. ↕18in (45cm).
***I.* 'Butter and Sugar'** ■ Siberian iris flowering in midseason. Standards are white; falls are yellow; both have greenish yellow veins. ↕28in (70cm).
***I.* 'Butter Pecan'.** Intermediate bearded iris flowering in early and midseason. Standards are pecan-brown over yellow; falls are yellow, stitched and bordered in deep pecan-brown, with yellow beards. ↕22in (55cm).
***I.* 'Calico Cat'.** Border bearded iris. Produces flowers with soft yellow standards, and lavender-violet falls with wine-red hafts and yellow beards, in mid- and late season. ↕20in (50cm).
***I.* 'Cambridge'.** Siberian iris flowering in midseason. Standards and falls are turquoise-blue, with white and yellow markings on the hafts. ↕36in (90cm).
***I.* 'Canyon Snow'.** Pacific Coast iris. In early and midseason, bears white flowers with yellow patches. ↕18in (45cm).
***I.* 'Caprician Butterfly'.** Japanese iris, flowering in midseason. Bears dark purple standards with fringed, white edges, white falls with dark purple veining, and gold signals. ↕36in (90cm).
***I.* 'Carolyn Rose'.** Miniature tall bearded iris, flowering in midseason. Bears flowers with white standards heavily marked rose-pink, white falls lightly marked rose-pink, and bright yellow beards. ↕24in (60cm).
***I.* 'Cascade Crest'** ■ Tall bearded Japanese iris with a white ground and a soft blue ¾(2cm) band on petal edges. Stylearms are upright and accented in dark blue. ↕36in (91cm). Zone 3.
***I.* 'Cee Jay'.** Intermediate bearded iris with deep violet-edged, white flowers and violet beards, borne early in the season. ↕24in (60cm).
***I.* 'Celebration Song'** ■ Tall bearded iris. From early to late season, bears apricot-pink standards, blue-lavender falls, and tangerine beards. ↕36in (90cm).
I. chamaeiris see *I. lutescens.*
***I.* 'Champagne Elegance'.** Tall bearded iris, flowering in midseason. Bears flowers with pale lavender-pink standards, apricot falls, and amber beards. Remontant in warmer areas. ↕34in (85cm).
***I.* 'Chapter'.** Border bearded iris. In midseason, bears flowers with bronze-tan standards, bronze-tan-edged, silver-lavender falls, and yellow-tipped, bronze beards. ↕24in (60cm).
***I.* 'Chickasaw Sue'.** Border bearded iris, flowering in midseason. Bears standards in blends of orange, red, and violet; white falls edged orange, red, and brown; and bright orange beards. ↕26in (65cm).
I. chrysographes ■ Siberian iris with flat, linear, gray-green leaves, 20in (50cm) long. In early summer, each unbranched stem bears 2 fragrant, dark red-violet flowers, 2½–3in (6–8cm) across, with gold streaks on the falls. ↕16–20in (40–50cm). China (Sichuan, Yunnan). Zone 6. **'Black Knight'** has very dark violet flowers.
***I.* 'Chubby Cheeks'.** Standard dwarf bearded iris, flowering early in the season. Bears ruffled, scented, light violet-edged, gray-chartreuse-banded, white flowers, with tangerine-tipped, pale violet beards. ↕12in (30cm).
***I.* 'Chubby Cherub'.** Miniature dwarf bearded iris. Bears pale yellow standards, yellow-marked white falls, and violet beards, mid- and late season. ↕4in (10cm).
***I.* 'Clyde Redmond'.** Louisiana iris. In midseason, bears cornflower-blue flowers with yellow patches. ↕30in (75cm).
I. colchica see *I. graminea.*
***I.* 'Colorific'.** Louisiana iris, flowering in midseason. Bears white standards with lavender flush and midribs. The falls are mid-red-purple with dark purple veining, and the style arms are greenish white with small yellow signals. ↕36in (90cm).
I. confusa ■ Crested iris with erect, bamboo-like stems, topped by fans of broad, evergreen leaves, 8–16in (20–40cm) long. In midspring, flower stems bear up to 30 short-lived blooms in succession. Flowers are white with yellow or purple spots around the yellow crests, 1½–2in (4–5cm) across. ↕36in (90cm). China (Yunnan). Zone 8.
***I.* 'Conjuration'.** Tall bearded iris. In mid- and late season, bears white standards infused with pale violet-blue. The white falls have light violet edges and tangerine-tipped, white beards ending in fuzzy white horns. ↕36in (90cm).
***I.* 'Continuing Pleasure'.** Japanese iris flowering from mid- to late season. Bears deep violet-blue flowers with white lines, yellow signals, and violet-tipped, white style arms. ↕36in (90cm).
***I.* 'Corn Harvest'.** Remontant tall bearded iris. Yellow flowers with ruffled falls and yellow beards are borne early in the season and, in many areas, again in late summer and early autumn. ↕30in (75cm).
***I.* 'Coronation Anthem'** ■ Siberian iris. Deep blue with yellow signal blending to white. ↕32in (81cm). Zone 3.
***I.* 'Cotton Blossom'.** Standard dwarf bearded iris with ruffled, creamy white flowers, produced in midseason. ↕12in (30cm).
I. cristata ■ Crested iris with lance-shaped, bright green leaves, to 6in (15cm) long at flowering. Bears 1 or 2 stemless blooms, 1½in (4cm) across, on long perianth tubes, 2in (5cm) tall, in late spring. Petals are usually blue-lilac, each with a white patch, and a yellow or orange crest on each fall. ↕4in (10cm). E. US. Zone 4. **f. *alba*** has white flowers.
***I.* 'Cup Race'.** Tall bearded iris. Bears white flowers with a slight blue cast, in midseason. ↕36in (90cm).
***I.* 'Crystal Ruffles'.** Miniature tall bearded iris. In midseason, bears ruffled flowers with white standards, lightly marked orchid at the hafts, and white to light orange beards. ↕24in (60cm).
***I.* 'Custom Design'.** Spuria iris bears deep red-brown flowers with bright yellow signals, in midseason. ↕3½ft (1.1m).
***I.* 'Dancing Nanou'.** Siberian iris, flowering in mid- and late season. Bears ruffled flowers having violet-blue standards with darker edges, mid-purple falls with navy-blue lines, and brown and green hafts. ↕32in (80cm).
I. danfordiae ■ Reticulata iris with 2 erect, narrow, square-sectioned leaves, 4–6in (10–15cm) long at flowering. In late winter, bears a solitary yellow flower, to 2in (5cm) across, with tiny standards and greenish yellow markings on the falls. ↕3–6in (8–15cm). Turkey. Zone 5.
***I.* 'Dark Vader'.** Standard dwarf bearded iris. In midseason, bears ruffled flowers with dark blue-violet standards and black falls with violet beards. ↕11in (28cm).
***I.* 'Delta Star'.** Louisiana iris bearing deep purple flowers, with a yellow signal on each petal, in midseason. ↕36in (90cm).
***I.* 'Dorothea K. Williamson'.** Louisiana iris with zigzag stems bearing violet flowers in midseason. ↕18–32in (45–80cm).
I. douglasiana ■ Vigorous Pacific Coast iris bearing evergreen, stiff, glossy, dark green leaves, to 36in (90cm) long, often bright red at the bases. Red-purple, lavender-blue, blue, cream, or white flowers, 3–4in (7–10cm) across,

Iris 'Aachen Elf'

Iris 'Adobe Sunset'

Iris afghanica

Iris 'Apollo'

Iris 'Apricot Frosty'

Iris 'Batik'

Iris 'Big Money'

Iris 'Brown Lasso'

Iris bulleyana

Iris 'Butter and Sugar'

Iris 'Cascade Crest'

Iris 'Celebration Song'

Iris confusa

Iris 'Coronation Anthem'

Iris douglasiana

Iris 'Early Light'

Iris 'Electric Glow'

Iris 'Fairy Rings'

Iris foetidissima var. *citrina*

Iris forrestii

Iris 'Frosted Intrigue'

Iris 'Frosted Velvet'

Iris x *fulvala*

Iris 'George'

Iris 'Golden Harvest'

Iris graminea

Iris 'Hello Darkness'

Iris histrioides 'Major'

Iris 'Honky Tonk Blues'

Iris hoogiana

Iris 'Howard Brooks'

Iris iberica

Iris japonica

Iris 'Jeweler's Art'

Iris 'Judean Gem'

Iris 'Katharine Hodgkin'

are produced on branched stems, 2 or 3 per branch, in late spring and early summer. ↕6–28in (15–70cm). W. US. Zone 7.

***I.* 'Dover Beach'.** Tall bearded iris. From early to late season, bears flowers with white standards, light blue falls, and lemon-yellow-tipped, white beards. ↕3½ft (1.1m).

***I.* 'Dress Circle'.** Spuria iris, flowering in mid- and late season. Standards are blue-violet with white veins; falls have yellow patches surrounded by white and violet edging. ↕36in (90cm).

***I.* 'Duke of Earl'.** Remontant tall bearded iris. In early and midseason and again in autumn, bears heavily ruffled flowers with red-violet-dotted, white standards. The white falls have narrow, red-violet-dotted edges, and the beards are cream. ↕34in (85cm).

***I.* 'Dusky Challenger'** ■ Tall bearded iris. Bears silky, ruffled, rich purple flowers with deep violet beards in mid- and late season. ↕36in (90cm).

***I.* 'Early Light'** ■ Tall bearded iris. In midseason, bears flowers with lemon-flushed cream standards, slightly darker falls, and yellow beards. ↕39in (100cm).

***I.* 'Edith Wolford'.** Tall bearded iris. Ruffled flowers with clear canary-yellow standards, blue-violet falls, and orange-tipped blue beards appear in midseason. ↕36in (90cm).

***I.* 'Electric Glow'** ■ Japanese iris, blue violet with lighter veins and a ½in(1.5cm) band of solid blue-violet at the edge of the petals. Flowers mid-to late season. ↕38in (97cm). Zone 3.

I. ensata, syn. *I. kaempferi.* Laevigatae (Japanese) iris with single, occasionally branched stems. Leaves are 24–36in (60–90cm) long, with prominent midribs. In early summer, each stem bears 3 or 4 purple or red-purple flowers, 6–12in (15–30cm) across. Standards are erect and much smaller than the falls. ↕36in (90cm). N. China, Japan, E. Russia. Zone 5.

***I.* 'Eolian'.** Louisiana iris bearing ruffled blue flowers with small yellow signals, in midseason. ↕3½ft (1.1m).

***I.* 'Esther the Queen'.** Arilbred iris, flowering in early and midseason. Bears wisteria-blue standards with deep green veining at the bases, light green falls with red dots and a black spot, and black beards. ↕36in (90cm).

***I.* 'Everything Plus'.** Tall bearded iris with pale blue standards, dark purple-edged, white falls, and bronze-tipped, purple beards, in early and midseason. ↕34in (85cm).

***I.* 'Fairy Rings'** ■ Standard dwarf bearded iris. Standards and falls are white with purple ruffles. ↕12in (30cm). Zone 3.

***I.* 'Feed Back'.** Remontant tall bearded iris. Bears sweetly fragrant, blue-violet blooms with yellow beards, early in the season and, in many areas, again in early autumn. ↕36in (90cm).

I. foetidissima (Stinking gladwyn, Stinking iris). Vigorous, beardless iris with tufts of tough, evergreen, dark green leaves, to 30in (75cm) long, unpleasantly scented when crushed. In early summer, each branched stem bears up to 5 dull purple flowers, tinged with yellow, 2–3in (5–8cm) across. Large seed capsules split open in autumn, displaying scarlet seeds. ↕12–36in (30–90cm). S. and W. Europe, Azores, Canary Islands, N. Africa. Zone 6. **var. *citrina*** ■ has yellow flowers.

I. foliosa see *I. brevicaulis.*

I. forrestii ■ Siberian iris with linear leaves, to 10in (25cm) long, glossy, mid-green above, gray-green beneath. In early summer, bears 1 or 2 yellow flowers, 2–2½in (5–6cm) across, with brown lines on the falls. ↕14–16in (35–40cm). China (S. Sichuan, Yunnan), N. Myanmar. Zone 5.

***I.* 'Forty Carats'.** Spuria iris producing deep yellow flowers in mid- and late season. ↕4½ft (1.4m).

***I.* 'Frank Chowning'.** Louisiana iris. In mid- and late season, bears currant-red flowers, with a prominent yellow signal patch on each fall. ↕34in (85cm).

***I.* 'Freckled Geisha'.** Japanese iris. Bears ruffled white flowers with deep maroon edges and mauve to wine spots in early and midseason ↕36in (90cm).

***I.* 'Fringe Benefits'.** Tall bearded iris. Bears heavily laced, intense orange flowers with bright tangerine beards, in midseason. ↕30in (75cm).

***I.* 'Frosted Intrigue'** ■ Japanese iris. Bears flowers with dark blue-violet petals with a narrow white rim in mid season. Style arms are white with feathered violet crests. ↕36in (90cm). Zone 3.

***I.* 'Frosted Velvet'** ■ Miniature tall bearded iris. In midseason, bears white standards, royal-purple falls with a precise white edge, and light cream-white beards. ↕22in (55cm).

I.* x *fulvala ■ (*I. brevicaulis* x *I. fulva*). Robust Louisiana iris. In early summer, bears purple-red flowers, 2–2½in (5–6cm) across. ↕18–32in (45–80cm). Garden origin. Zone 6.

***I.* 'Funny Face'.** Miniature dwarf bearded iris, flowering in midseason. Bears bright yellow standards and bright yellow-edged, cream-white falls with yellow to white beards. ↕6in (15cm).

***I.* 'George'** ■ Reticulata iris bearing well-rounded, sturdy, rich purple flowers, in early spring. ↕5in (13cm).

***I.* 'Golden Harvest'** ■ Dutch iris. In late spring and early summer, bears rich golden yellow flowers. ↕to 28in (70cm).

***I.* 'Golden Icon'.** Vigorous, floriferous tall bearded iris producing ruffled, bright golden yellow flowers, in early and midseason. ↕36in (90cm).

I. gracilipes. Crested iris with grass-like leaves, to 12in (30cm) long. In late spring and early summer, each stem produces several blue-lilac flowers, 1¼–1½in (3–4cm) across. Each fall has a violet-veined white patch and a yellow-tipped white crest. ↕4–6in (10–15cm). Japan, China. Zone 5b.

I. graeberiana. Robust Juno iris producing glossy, bright green leaves, to 6in (15cm) long, with narrow white margins. In early spring, bears up to 6 blue flowers, 3in (8cm) or more across, with white and deeper blue markings. ↕8–16in (20–40cm). C. Asia (Kazakhstan to Tajikistan). Zone 6b.

I. graminea ■ syn. *I. colchica.* Spuria iris with flat, linear, bright green leaves, to 12in (30cm) long. In late spring and early summer, bears 1 or 2 purple-violet flowers, 3in (8cm) across. Falls have violet-veined white tips. ↕8–16in (20–40cm). N.E. Spain to W. Russia, N.and W. Caucasus. Zone 5.

Iris 'Dusky Challenger'

***I.* 'Harmony'** ▣ Reticulata iris. In early spring, bears royal-blue flowes with a yellow central mark on each fall. ↕4–6in (10–15cm) at flowering.
***I.* 'Heart Stealer'.** Arilbred iris. In early and midseason, bears pink flowers, overlaid lavender, and deep brown beards with lavender signals. ↕24in (60cm).
***I.* 'Hegira'.** Japanese iris. In midseason bears lightly spice-scented, white flowers with deep blue stripes and gold signals. ↕36in (90cm).
***I.* 'Helga's Hat'.** Intermediate bearded iris. From early to late season, bears ruffled flowers with white standards, white falls with yellow hafts, and white horns. ↕26in (65cm).
***I.* 'Hellcat'.** Intermediate bearded iris flowering in mid- and late season. Bears light blue-lavender standards, flushed darker at the midribs, and dark blue-purple falls with dark blue-lavender beards. ↕16in (40cm).
***I.* 'Hello Darkness'** ▣ Tall bearded iris bearing ruffled, purple-black flowers with black beards, in early and midseason. ↕36in (90cm).
***I.* 'High Wire'.** Standard dwarf bearded iris, flowering early in the season. Bears pale lavender standards and white-edged, red-purple falls, darker around the purple beards. ↕10in (25cm).
I. histrioides. Reticulata iris with erect, square-sectioned leaves, ½–4in (1.5–10cm) long at flowering. In early spring, bears 1 or 2 mid- to dark blue flowers, 2½–3in (6–8cm) across. Each fall is usually spotted deeper blue in the center with a yellow central ridge. Similar to *I. histrio* but more vigorous. ↕4–6in (10–15cm). Turkey. Zone 5. **'Major'** ▣ is vigorous and bears deep blue flowers.
***I.* 'Honey Glazed'.** Intermediate bearded iris bearing cream standards, amber falls, and gold beards, in midseason. ↕24in (60cm).
***I.* 'Honky Tonk Blues'** ▣ Tall bearded iris. In midseason, bears ruffled, mid-blue flowers, streaked and edged white to gray on the falls, with mid-blue beards. ↕36in (90cm).
I. hoogiana ▣ Regelia iris with erect, purple-tinged, mid-green leaves, to 20in (50cm) long. In early summer, each unbranched stem produces 2 or 3 fragrant, silky, pale to mid-blue flowers, 3–4in (7–10cm) across, with yellow beards. ↕16–24in (40–60cm). Tajikistan (Pamir Mountains). Zone 7.
f. *alba* produces white flowers, faintly overlaid pale lavender-blue.
***I.* 'Hot Fudge'.** Intermediate bearded iris. In midseason, bears dark brown standards with a yellow glow, and dark-brown-edged, yellow falls with blue-tipped, yellow beards. ↕24in (60cm).
***I.* 'Hot Spice'.** Intermediate bearded iris. In midseason, bears flowers with chocolate-brown standards, chocolate-brown-edged, bright yellow falls with white centers, and ochre beards. ↕26in (65cm).
***I.* 'Howard Brooks'** ▣ Japanese iris. Rich deep violet with light white veins. White stylearms are tipped in violet. ↕36in (90cm). Zone 3.
***I.* 'Hue and Cry'** ▣ Japanese iris bears red-veined, plum-red flowers with a white area around the yellow signals, in mid- and late season. ↕36in (90cm).

Iris 'Harmony'

I. iberica ▣ Oncocyclus iris with strongly curved, narrow, gray-green leaves, 6in (15cm) long. In mid- and late spring, each stem produces a solitary, brown-veined, cream or white flower, to 3in (8cm) across. Falls are more heavily veined than the standards, and have black patches and brown-purple beards. ↕6–8in (15–20cm). Caucasus. Zone 7.
subsp. *elegantissima* is taller, with larger flowers, 4in (10cm) across; ↕8–12in (20–30cm). N.E. Turkey, N.W. Iran, Armenia.
***I.* 'Immortality'.** Remontant tall bearded iris with pure white flowers, borne in midseason and again in summer and autumn. ↕30in (75cm).
I. innominata ▣ Pacific Coast iris with evergreen, very narrow, deep green leaves, to 12in (30cm) long, purple at the bases. In early summer, each unbranched stem bears 1 or 2 rounded flowers, 3in (8cm) across, ranging from bright yellow to cream, and from purple to pale lavender-blue. ↕6–10in (15–25cm). S.W. Oregon, N.W. California. Zone 7.
***I.* 'In The Money'.** Pacific Coast iris with bright, deep gold flowers, borne in mid- and late season. ↕10in (25cm).
***I.* 'Jamaican Velvet'.** Siberian iris with velvety deep red flowers, produced in midseason. ↕30in (75cm).
***I.* 'Japanese Pinwheel'.** Japanese iris. From early to late season, produces mid-wine-red flowers with distinctive thin white edges on the falls and mid-yellow signals. Remontant in some areas. ↕to 3½ft (1.1m).
I. japonica ▣ Crested iris, which spreads by surface rhizomes, with fans of strap-shaped, evergreen, glossy, dark green leaves, to 18in (45cm) long. In late spring, each branched stem bears 3 or 4 flattened and frilly, white or pale lavender-blue flowers, 1½–2in (4–5cm) across. Falls have purple patches and orange crests. ↕18in (45cm). C. China, Japan. Zone 7. **'Ledger's Variety'** is hardier, with larger blooms.
***I.* 'Jennifer Rebecca'.** Remontant tall bearded iris bearing ruffled and laced rose-pink flowers with tangerine-pink beards, in midseason and again in autumn. ↕36in (90cm).
***I.* 'Jesse's Song'.** Tall bearded iris, flowering in early and midseason. Bears reddish violet-edged, white flowers with blue-white-tipped, lemon-yellow beards. ↕36in (90cm).
***I.* 'Jewel Baby'.** Standard dwarf bearded iris. From early to late season, bears remontant, dark purple flowers with mid-violet beards. ↕12in (30cm).

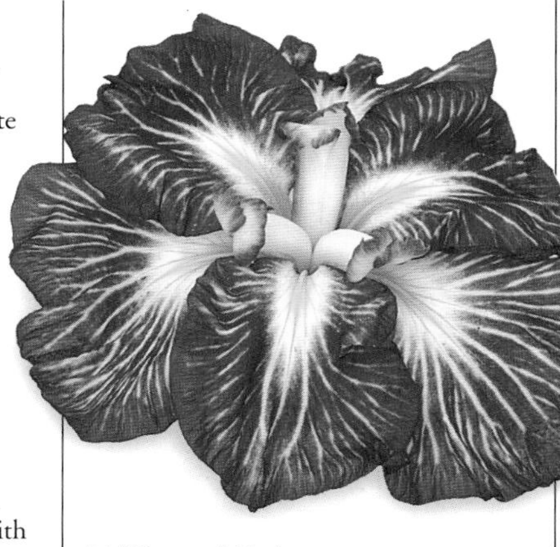

Iris 'Hue and Cry'

***I.* 'Jeweled Veil'.** Arilbred iris. In midseason, produces lavender standards with deeper veining and maroon-veined, light copper-tan falls with bronze beards and black-purple signals. ↕32in (80cm).
***I.* 'Jeweler's Art'** ▣ Standard dwarf bearded iris. Bears violet standards and red falls midseason. Amethyst beards. 12in (30cm). Zone 3.
***I.* 'Jewelled Crown'.** Siberian iris with deep wine-red flowers and distinctive gold and white spots on the falls, borne in midseason. ↕24in (60cm).
***I.* 'Jewel of Omar'.** Arilbred iris. In midseason, produces flowers with purple-based, mid-blue standards. The lime-yellow falls are marked maroon-brown around purple beards, and the style arms are greenish yellow. ↕18in (45cm).
***I.* 'Jitterbug'.** Tall bearded iris. Bears bright yellow flowers with orange-brown-washed falls and yellow beards, in early and midseason. ↕36in (90cm).
***I.* 'Joyce'.** Reticulata iris producing deep sky-blue flowers in early spring. ↕5in (13cm).
***I.* 'Judean Gem'** ▣ Arilbred iris. Early in the season, bears white standards and yellow falls with orange-red signals and yellow beards. ↕9in (23cm).
I. kaempferi see *I. ensata.*
***I.* 'Katharine Hodgkin'** ▣ Reticulata iris. In late winter, produces delicately patterned blue flowers with yellow and blue marks on the falls. ↕5in (13cm) at flowering.

Iris innominata

Iris kerneriana

Iris 'Laced Cotton'

Iris lacustris

Iris 'Lady Mohr'

Iris laevigata

Iris laevigata 'Variegata'

Iris 'Lovely Señorita'

Iris lutescens

Iris magnifica

Iris 'Minidragon'

Iris missouriensis

Iris 'Natascha'

Iris 'Night Game'

Iris 'Opposing Forces'

Iris 'President Hedley'

Iris prismatica

Iris 'Professor Blaauw'

Iris pumila

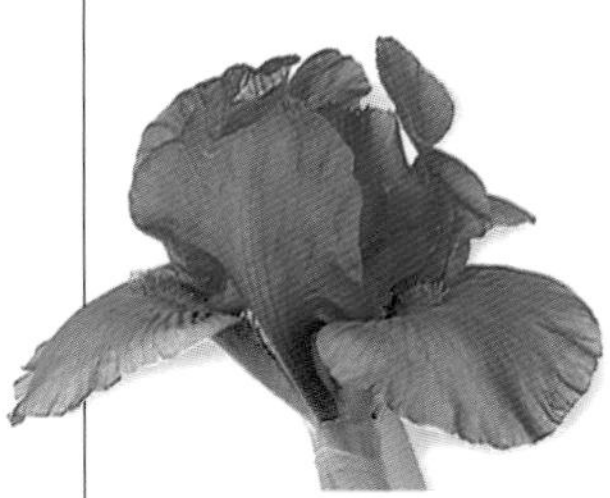
Iris 'Rain Dance'

Iris 'Redwood Supreme'

Iris 'Regimen'

I

I. kerneriana ■ Spuria iris with narrow, linear leaves, to 16in (40cm) long. Each erect stem bears 2–4 lemon-yellow flowers, 3–4in (7–10cm) across, in early summer. ↕ 12–20in (30–50cm). N. Turkey. Zone 6.

***I.* 'Khyber Pass'.** Arilbred iris bearing flowers with dark-veined, light lavender standards, early in the season. The tan falls have maroon dots and veins and dark maroon signals, and the beards are brown. ↕ 34in (85cm).

I. korolkowii. Regelia iris with linear leaves, to 16in (40cm) long. In late spring and early summer, each unbranched stem bears 2 or 3 flowers, 3in (8cm) across, with erect standards and pointed falls. All petals are cream with dark maroon veining; beards are small and dark brown. ↕ 16–24in (40–60cm). N.E. Afghanistan, C. Asia. Zone 8. **f. *violacea*** has violet petals and darker veins.

***I.* 'Laced Cotton'** ■ Tall bearded iris bearing ruffled, laced, pure white flowers with pale yellow to white beards, in mid- and late season. ↕ 36in (90cm).

I. lacustris ■ Crested iris with fans of narrow leaves, to 4in (10cm) long. In late spring, bears small, purple-blue to sky-blue flowers, ¾in (2cm) across, with a gold crest and a white patch on each fall. Often confused with *I. cristata*, but has narrower leaves and much shorter perianth tubes. ↕ 2in (5cm). N. Great Lakes area. Zone 4.

***I.* 'Lady Mohr'** ■ Arilbred iris flowering early in the season. Standards are pearly white; falls are pale yellow, veined and spotted brownish purple around the chrome-yellow beards. ↕ 30in (75cm).

***I.* 'Lady Vanessa'.** Siberian iris flowering in midseason. Standards are light wine-red; falls are darker and ruffled. ↕ 36in (90cm).

I. laevigata ■ Laevigatae iris with broad leaves, to 16in (40cm) long. In early and midsummer, unbranched stems bear 2–4 purple-blue flowers, 3–4in (8–10cm) across, the standards much shorter than the falls. Thrives on pond margins and other wet places. ↕ 32in (80cm). C. Russia to N. China, Korea, Japan. Zone 4. **f. *alba*** bears white flowers. **'Variegata'** ■ has white- and green-striped leaves and paler purple-blue flowers.

I. latifolia, syn. *I. xiphioides* (English iris). Xiphium iris with narrowly lance-shaped leaves, to 26in (65cm) long. Bears 1 or 2 broad, blue, violet, or white flowers, 3–4in (8–10cm) across, in early summer. May be naturalized in grass. ↕ 10–24in (25–60cm). N. Spain. Zone 7.

***I.* 'Lemon Mist'.** Tall bearded iris with light lemon-yellow flowers, slightly lighter at the centers, produced in early and midseason. ↕ 30in (75cm).

***I.* 'Lemon Pop'.** Intermediate bearded iris bearing lemon-yellow flowers with yellow-tipped, white beards, early in the season. ↕ 16in (40cm).

***I.* 'Lenora Pearl'.** Remontant border bearded iris bearing ruffled, salmon-pink flowers with bright orange beards, from early to late season, and again in autumn. ↕ 26in (65cm).

***I.* 'Libation'.** Miniature dwarf bearded iris. In mid- and late season, bears wine-red flowers with a darker spot on the falls, and yellow beards. ↕ 5in (13cm).

***I.* 'Little Showoff'.** Standard dwarf bearded iris. In early and midseason, bears pale blue flowers with bright lavender-blue beards. May be remontant in some areas. ↕ 11in (28cm).

I. lortetii. Oncocyclus iris with straight, linear leaves, to 10in (25cm) long. In late spring, each stem produces a solitary white flower, 3½in (9cm) across. Standards have fine pink veins; each fall has pink or maroon spots, one large deep maroon mark, and a reddish brown beard. ↕ 12–20in (30–50cm). Lebanon. Zone 8.

***I.* 'Lovely Señorita'** ■ Tall bearded iris producing orange standards and brown-orange falls with bright orange beards, from mid- to late season. ↕ to 3½ft (1.1m). Zone 3.

***I.* 'Lullaby of Spring'.** Tall bearded iris bearing light yellow standards, light mauve falls, and straw-yellow beards, in early and midseason. ↕ to 3½ft (1.1m).

I. lutescens ■ syn. *I. chamaeiris.* Very variable bearded iris with nearly straight leaves, 12in (30cm) long. In early and midspring, each stem bears 1 or 2 violet, yellow, bicolored, or rarely white flowers, 2½–3in (6–8cm) across, with yellow beards. ↕ 2–12in (5–30cm). N.E. Spain, S. France, Italy. Zone 7b.

***I.* 'Mabel Coday'.** Siberian iris bearing ruffled, mid-blue flowers with white signals, in early and midseason. ↕ 30in (75cm).

***I.* 'Maid of Orange'.** Border bearded iris producing creamy orange flowers with orange beards, from early to late season. ↕ 24in (60cm).

I. magnifica ■ Robust Juno iris with arching, glossy, mid-green leaves, to 7in (18cm) long. In mid- and late spring, produces up to 7 pale lilac flowers, to 3in (8cm) across, with a pale yellow and white central area on each fall. ↕ 12–24in (30–60cm). Mountains in C. Asia. Zone 6. **f. *alba*** produces white flowers.

***I.* 'Margaret Hunter'.** Louisiana iris with ruffled, light violet flowers, produced early in the season. ↕ 36in (90cm).

***I.* 'Mary Frances'.** Tall bearded iris. In midseason, produces ruffled, light bluish orchid flowers with yellow-tipped, white beards. Flowers lighten with age. ↕ to 3½ft (1.1m).

***I.* 'Maui Moonlight'.** Intermediate bearded iris producing light lemon-

Iris orientalis

Iris 'Oyez'

yellow flowers with light yellow beards, in midseason. ↕22in (55cm).
***I.* 'Maui Surf'.** Border bearded iris bearing light blue-violet flowers with heavily ruffled falls, in mid- and late season. ↕26in (65cm).
***I.* 'Minidragon'** ■ Standard dwarf bearded iris with a bright orange beard. Black-burgundy standards and falls. ↕13in (33cm). Zone 3.
I. missouriensis ■ syn. *I. tolmeiana.* Variable, beardless iris with narrow leaves, to 20in (50cm) long, overtopping the flowers. In summer, each branched stem produces 2–4 blooms , 2½–3in (6–8cm) across. Short pale to deep blue or lilac-purple standards; falls are larger, with deep purple veining. ↕8–20in (20–50cm). W. and C. North America. Zone 4.
***I.* 'Mohr Pretender'.** Arilbred iris. Bears pale blue flowers with purple marks at the base of the blue-tipped, brown beards, in midseason. ↕34in (85cm).
***I.* 'Mystique'.** Tall bearded iris. In early and midseason, bears light blue standards with purple-blue midribs, and deep purple falls with blue beards. ↕30in (75cm).
***I.* 'Natascha'** ■ Delicate Reticulata iris with very pale blue flowers, appearing gray-white in early spring. ↕5in (13cm).
***I.* 'Night Editor'.** Pacific Coast iris bearing purple flowers with a black sheen on the falls, in mid- and late season. ↕10in (25cm).
***I.* 'Night Game'** ■ Tall bearded iris; eggplant-black with bright orange beard. ↕42in (107cm). Zone 3.
I. ochroleuca see *I. orientalis.*

Iris pallida 'Variegata'

***I.* 'Olympiad'.** Tall bearded iris bearing pale blue standards with dark blue centers, light blue falls tinged mid-blue in the centers; light blue beards from early to late season. ↕3½ft (1.1m).
***I.* 'Omar's Torch'.** Arilbred iris bearing flowers with mid-purple standards and darker midribs, in midseason. Falls are plum-purple, with darker centers and lighter edges, and the beards are bright yellow. ↕18in (45cm).
***I.* 'Opposing Forces** ■ Tall bearded iris. Standards and style arms are warm pinkish-violet; falls are pinkish cream with amber hafts. Beard is ocher orange. ↕36in (45cm). Zone 3.
***I.* 'Orange Slices'.** Tall bearded iris. In midseason flowers are bright pinkish with orange beards. ↕34in (91cm).
***I.* 'Orange Tiger'.** Standard dwarf bearded iris bearing mid-orange flowers with deeper orange beards, in midseason. ↕11in (28cm).
I. orientalis ■ syn. *I. ochroleuca.* Robust, rhizomatous Spuria iris with leaves to 36in (90cm) long. In late spring, each stem, to 36in (90cm) long, usually with one branch, produces 3–5 blooms, 3–4in (8–10cm) across. Standards. are white and erect; falls are white with yellow centers. ↕ to 36in (90cm). N.E. Greece, W. Turkey. Zone 7.
***I.* 'Oyez'** ■ Arilbred iris bearing white flowers with dark purple lines on standards and falls. ↕24in (60cm).
I. pallida, syn. *I. pallida* var. *dalmatica.* Bearded iris with sometimes evergreen, gray-green leaves, 8–24in (20–60cm) long, much shorter than the flower stems, and distinctive, very silvery, papery bracts. In late spring and early summer, each branched stem produces 2–6 large, scented, soft blue flowers, 4in (10cm) across, with yellow beards. Ground rhizomes are used as a fixative for potpourri. ↕to 4ft (1.2m). Croatia. Zone 4. **'Argentea Variegata'** is less vigorous than the species, and has pale green leaves with silver-white stripes.
'Aurea Variegata' see 'Variegata'.
var. *dalmatica* see *I. pallida.*
'Variegata' ■ syn. 'Aurea Variegata', has bright green leaves with light golden yellow stripes.
***I.* 'Peccadillo'.** Border bearded iris flowering in early and midseason. Produces flowers with peach-pink standards, peach-pink falls with purple hafts and edges, and rust-orange beards. ↕26in (65cm).
***I.* 'Persian Padishah'.** Arilbred iris bearing mid-rose-purple flowers with purple-black signals and beards, early in the season. ↕22in (55cm).
***I.* 'Petite Monet'.** Miniature tall bearded iris producing sweetly fragrant, creamy white flowers, marked blue-violet, and yellow beards, in midseason. ↕18in (45cm).
***I.* 'Pink Bubbles'.** Border bearded iris, flowering in early and midseason. Produces light pink flowers with pale tangerine beards. ↕20in (50cm).
***I.* 'Pink Haze'** ■ Siberian iris. Bears medium lavender-pink flowers with red-violet haft markings and lines on the falls, in midseason. ↕30in (75cm).
***I.* 'Prairie Twilight'.** Japanese iris. Early in the season, produces lavender-blue flowers with darker blue veining, violet-blue edges, and yellow signals. ↕36in (90cm).

Iris 'Pink Haze'

***I.* 'President Hedley'** ■ Louisiana iris flowering early in the season. Bears dark yellow flowers, with brown shading on the falls, and yellow-orange signals. ↕34in (85cm).
I. prismatica ■ Beardless iris with thin, widely spreading rhizomes, forming large clumps of grass-like leaves, to 30in (75cm) long. In early and midsummer, bears clusters of 2 or 3 violet-blue flowers, 2–3in (5–8cm) across, on slender, angled stems. ↕16–32in (40–80cm). Nova Scotia to South Carolina. Zone 5.
***I.* 'Professor Jim'.** Louisiana iris. In early and midseason, bears mid-red flowers with red-violet veins and yellow signals. ↕3½ft (1.1m).
***I.* 'Professor Blaauw'** ■ Dutch iris flowering in late spring and early summer. Produces violet-blue flowers with a yellow mark on each fall. ↕to 24in (60cm).
I. pseudacorus ■ (Yellow flag). Extremely vigorous Laevigatae iris with ribbed, gray-green leaves, 36in (90cm) long. In mid- and late summer, each branched stem produces 4–12 flowers, 3–4in in (7–10cm) across. Petals are yellow with brown or violet markings and a darker yellow zone on each fall. Suitable for margins of large ponds or lakes, or other wet places, but may become invasive. ↕to 3–5ft (1–1.5m). Europe to W. Siberia, Caucasus, Turkey, Iran, N. Africa. Zone 4.
'Alba' has pale cream flowers.
var. *bastardii* produces clear sulfur-yellow flowers.
I. pumila ■ Variable, miniature dwarf bearded iris with gray-green leaves, to 6in (15cm) long. In midspring, unbranched stems bear usually solitary, scented, blue, purple, or yellow flowers, 2in (5cm) across, with yellow or blue beards. ↕4–6in (10–15cm). E. Europe to Urals. Zone 4. **'Atroviolacea'** bears purple flowers. **'Aurea'** produces yellow blooms.
***I.* 'Puppet Baby'.** Miniature dwarf bearded iris with blue-lavender flowers and plum-brown hafts, borne early in the season. ↕7in (18cm).
***I.* 'Purple Parasol'.** Japanese iris with velvety purple flowers and yellow signals, borne in midseason. ↕4ft (1.2m).
***I.* 'Rain Dance'** ■ Standard dwarf bearded iris. Bears violet-blue flowers with matching beards in mid- and late spring. ↕10in (25cm).
***I.* 'Raspberry Rimmed'.** Japanese iris with extended bloom season; produces white standards with a narrow raspberry rim. Falls are white with a 1in (2.5cm) band of raspberry at the rim. ↕36in (90cm).
***I.* 'Redwood Supreme'** ■ Spuria iris. Bears flowers with dark brown standards, and orange falls with dark brown margins, in midseason. ↕36in (90cm).
***I.* 'Red Zinger'.** Intermediate bearded iris. In mid- and late season, bears mid-burgundy-red standards, deeper red falls, each with a darker spot in the center, and gold beards. ↕26in (65cm).
***I.* 'Regimen'** ■ Tall beared iris. Red chocolate standards and falls. Blue blaze on falls. Burnt organge beard. Lace texture on all petals. ↕31in (79cm). Zone 3.
I. reticulata. Reticulata iris with square-sectioned leaves, ½–4in (1–10cm) long at flowering. In late winter and early

Iris pseudacorus

Iris reticulata 'Cantab'

Iris reticulata 'J.S. Dijt'

Iris ruthenica

Iris 'Santa'

Iris setosa

Iris 'Shirley Pope'

Iris 'Silverado'

Iris 'Somebody Loves Me'

Iris 'Tanzanian Tangerine'

Iris tectorum

Iris 'Telepathy'

Iris tenax

Iris 'Toots'

Iris unguicularis 'Mary Barnard'

Iris variegata

Iris versicolor

Iris warleyensis

Iris 'Whispering Spirits'

Iris 'White Swirl'

Iris 'White Wedgwood'

Iris winogradowii

I

spring, bears a solitary, fragrant flower, 2½–3in (6–8cm) across, varying from pale to deep violet-blue or reddish purple, with a yellow central ridge on each fall. Bulbs frequently split after blooming and may take some years to reach flowering size again. ↕4–6in (10–15cm). Caucasus, N. and E. Turkey, N.E. Iraq, N. Iran. Zone 5. **'Cantab'** ■ bears pale blue flowers withdeeper blue falls, each with a yellow crest. **'J.S. Dijt'** ■ produces reddish purple flowers with a central orange mark on each fall.
***I.* 'Roaring Jelly'.** Siberian iris, flowering in midseason. Produces red-purple-veined, lavender-gray standards, and red-purple-mottled falls with blue-flushed style arms, and white signals. ↕36in (90cm).
***I.* 'Rosemary's Dream'.** Miniature tall bearded iris. In midseason, bears deep rose standards with small white centers, white falls with rose borders, and deep orange beards. ↕24in (60cm).
***I.* 'Roy Davidson'.** Beardless hybrid iris (probably between *I. foetidissima* and *I. pseudacorus*) producing yellow flowers with brown veins and signals in early and midseason. ↕34in (85cm).
I. ruthenica ■ Beardless iris with creeping, branched rhizomes and fans of grass-like, glossy, bright green leaves to 12in (30cm) long. In late spring, each stem, 1¼–6in (3–15cm) tall, produces 1 or 2 fragrant flowers, 1½in (4cm) across. Erect standards are violet or lavender-blue; falls are white with dark violet markings. ↕to 8in (20cm). E. Europe to China, Korea. Zone 5.
***I.* 'Santa'** ■ Bearded iris with creamy yellow standards. Falls are warm white with salmom hafts. Beard is red. ↕28in (70cm). Zone 3.
***I.* 'Serenity Prayer'.** Standard dwarf bearded iris. Flowers in mid- and late season. Bears creamy white standards marked yellow on the midribs, and creamy white falls with yellow on the hafts. The deep blue beards are lighter blue-tipped. ↕14in (35cm).
I. setosa ■ Very variable, beardless iris with linear, mid-green leaves, to 20in (50cm) long, often red-tinted at the bases. In late spring and early summer, each stem produces 2–12 flowers, 2–3½in (5–9cm) across, with blue or purple-blue falls and bristle-like standards. ↕6–36in(15–90cm). E. Russia (including Sakhalin, Kurile Islands), Korea, Japan, Alaska (including Aleutian Islands), N.E. North America. Zone 3.
***I.* 'Shaker's Prayer'.** Siberian iris. Bears violet standards, and white falls with lilac veining, yellow hafts, violet edges, and red-violet styles, from early to late season. ↕36in (90cm).
***I.* 'Shelford Giant'** ■ Spuria iris flowering in mid- and late season. Bears large, lemon-white flowers with a central yellow patch on each fall. ↕6ft (1.8m).
***I.* 'Shirley Pope'** ■ Siberian iris bears dark red-purple flowers in mid-late season; falls are velvety with white patches. ↕34in (85cm).
I. sibirica. Siberian iris with narrow, grass-like leaves, to 18in (45cm) long. In early summer, each branched stem bears up to 5 flowers, to 3in (8cm) across, well above the foliage. All petals are blue-violet; falls have dark veining, the background color changing to white near the hafts. ↕20–48in (50–120cm). C. and E. Europe, N.E. Turkey, Russia. Zone 4. **f. *alba*** bears white flowers.
***I.* 'Silverado'** ■ Tall bearded iris with ruffled, silvery, light lavender-blue flowers and beards, are produced in midseason. ↕to 3½ft (1.1m).
I. sisyrinchium see *Gynandriris sisyrinchium.*
***I.* 'Sky Hooks'.** Tall bearded iris. In midseason, bears soft yellow flowers, lighter in the center of the falls, with gold beards ending in light violet horns. ↕to 3½ft (1.1m).
***I.* 'Social Circle'.** Spuria iris. Lacy-edged, white flowers and bright yellow signals, produced midseason. ↕to 3½ft (1.1m).
***I.* 'Soft Spoken'.** Border bearded iris with light lilac flowers and coral-tipped, white beards, borne in midseason. ↕20in (50cm).
***I.* 'Somebody Loves Me'** ■ Siberian iris. Ruffled medium blue-violet; style arms light blue. Large white blaze on falls. Blooms early-midseason. ↕32in (81cm). Zone 3.
***I.* 'Sonjah's Selah'.** Border bearded iris with white standards and light orange-red falls and beards, borne in mid- and late season. ↕24in (60cm).
***I.* 'Soquel Cove'.** Pacific Coast iris bearing white flowers with a turquoise wash on the falls, early in the season. ↕14in (35cm).
***I.* 'Stepping Out'.** Tall bearded iris. Bears white flowers with sharply patterned, blue-violet margins and paler blue-violet beards, in early and midseason. ↕36in (90cm).
***I.* 'Strawberry Fair'** ■ Siberian iris. Strawberry-pink flowers with small white signals and light blue style arms are borne late in the season. ↕28in (70cm).
I. stylosa see *I. unguicularis.*
***I.* 'Sun Doll'.** Standard dwarf bearded iris with mid-yellow flowers, borne in midseason. ↕14in (35cm).
***I.* 'Super Ego'.** Siberian iris. In mid- and late season, bears pale blue standards with darker blue falls, grading to white edges. ↕30in (75cm).

Iris 'Shelford Giant'

Iris 'Strawberry Fair'

I. susiana (Mourning iris). Oncocyclus iris with slightly curved leaves, 4–6in (10–15cm) long. In late spring, each stem bears a large, solitary flower, 4–6in (10–15cm) across. Petals are gray with deep purple veins, black patches, and purple beards. ‡ 12–16in (30–40cm). Probably Lebanon. Zone 7.
***I.* 'Tanzanian Tangerine'** ■ Tall bearded iris. Orange ground standards. Strippled red wine overlay on the falls, early to mid-season Light orange beard. ‡ 38in (97cm). Zone 3.
I. tectorum ■ (Roof iris). Crested iris with fans of broad, ribbed, glossy, dark green leaves, to 12in (30cm) long. In early summer, each occasionally branched stem bears 2 or 3 lilac flowers, 1¼–4in (3–10cm) across, with darker veins and a white crest on each fall. ‡ 10–16in (25–40cm). C., S. and S.W. China. Zone 5b. **f. *alba*** has white flowers with yellow veins on the crests and falls. **'Variegata'** has green leaves with white stripes.
***I.* 'Telepathy'** ■ Bearded iris with lavender-orchid standards. Darker falls have white luminata patches. ‡ 28in (70cm). Zone 3.
I. tenax ■ Pacific Coast iris with narrow, deep green leaves, to 12in (30cm) long, tinged red at the bases. From midspring to early summer, each stem produces 1 or 2 blue, lavender-blue, yellow, cream, or white flowers, 3–3½in (7–9cm) across. ‡ 8–14in (20–35cm). Washington, Oregon. Zone 7.
***I.* 'Thornbird'.** Tall bearded iris, flowering in midseason. Bears lightly ruffled flowers with pale ecru standards and greenish tan falls with violet lines radiating from mustard yellow-tipped, violet beards, ending in horns. ‡ 36in (90cm).
I. tolmeiana see *I. missouriensis.*
***I.* 'Toots'** ■ Standard dwarf bearded iris. In midseason, bears velvety, wine-red flowers with yellow beards. ‡ 12in (30cm).
I. tuberosa see *Hermodactylus tuberosus.*
I. unguicularis, syn. *I. stylosa.* Unguiculares iris with tough, grass-like, evergreen leaves, to 24in (60cm) long. Flowers are large, fragrant, 2–3in (5–8cm) across, pale lavender to deep violet with contrasting veins, and have a central band of yellow on the falls, and perianth tubes 2½–8in (6–20cm) long. They are produced singly on very short stems arising from a branching rhizome in late winter and early spring, occasionally in late autumn. ‡ 12in (30cm). Greece, W. and S. Turkey, W. Syria, Tunisia, Algeria. Zone 6. **'Mary Barnard'** ■ produces bright violet flowers in midwinter.
I. variegata ■ Bearded iris with curved, strongly ribbed, deep green leaves, to 12in (30cm) long. In late spring, each branched stem produces 3–6 flowers, 2–3in (5–8cm) across. Standards are bright yellow; falls are white with brown or violet veins and yellow beards. Many color variants are available. ‡ 8–20in (20–45cm). C. and E. Europe. Zone 5.
I. versicolor ■ (Blue flag). Laevigatae iris with erect or slightly arched leaves, 14–24in (35–60cm) long. In early and midsummer, each branched stem produces 3–5 violet, purple, or lavender-blue flowers, 2½–3in (6–8cm) across, with a white-veined purple area on each fall. ‡ 8–32in (20–80cm). E. North America. Zone 3. **'Kermesina'** bears red-purple flowers. **'Mint Fresh'** bears white flowers with purple-red stripes in midseason. ‡ 28in (70cm). **'Rosea'** bears pale red-violet flowers.
I. warleyensis ■ Juno iris with curved, glossy leaves, to 8in (20cm) long. In spring, bears up to 5 pale to deep violet or purplish blue flowers, 2–3in (5–8cm) across. Each narrow fall has a white rim, a toothed, cream to yellow crest, and a deep violet patch at the tip. ‡ 8–18in (20–45cm). C. Asia (Altai to Pamir Mountains). Zone 6.
***I.* 'Wedgwood'.** Dutch iris. Clear blue flowers are borne in late spring and early summer. ‡ 24–28in (60–70cm).
***I.* 'Whispering Spirits'** ■ Tall bearded iris, flowering mid- to late season. Bears white standards with yellow gilt edge; styles are white with yellow crests. Falls are on a white ground overlaid with a sanding of violet and magenta, and with a ¼in (6mm) band of yellow at petal edges. ‡ 35in (89cm). Zone 3.
***I.* 'White Swirl'** ■ Siberian iris. In midsummer, bears pure white flowers, yellow at the bases, with rounded, flaring petals. ‡ 36in (90cm).
***I.* 'White Wedgwood'** ■ Dutch iris, flowering in late spring and early summer. Produces creamy white flowers with a prominent yellow mark on each fall. ‡ 26in (65cm).
I. winogradowii ■ Reticulata iris with erect, square-sectioned leaves, ½–4in (1–10cm) long at flowering. In early spring, produces solitary, primrose-yellow flowers, 2½–3in (6–8cm) across, spotted green on the falls. Unlike many other bulbous Reticulata irises, the bulbs do not split up after flowering. ‡ 2½–4in (6–10cm). Caucasus. Zone 6.
I. xiphioides see *I. latifolia.*
***I.* 'Yaemomiji'** ■ Japanese iris. In early and midseason, red-violet flowers, streaked and dotted with white, with green, yellow, and white signals, are produced. Extra white petaloids are marked with red-violet. ‡ 36in (90cm).
***I.* 'Yaquina Blue'.** Tall bearded iris producing light to mid-blue flowers with white-tipped, yellow beards, in mid-season. ‡ 36in (90cm).

Iris 'Yaemomiji'

Isatis tinctoria

ISATIS

BRASSICACEAE

Genus of about 30 species of annuals, biennials, and perennials, growing on waste ground or rocky sites in dry places in C. and S. Europe, and in W. and C. Asia. They have ovate to ovate-oblong, entire or pinnately lobed, stalked basal leaves and smaller, arrow-shaped, stalkless stem leaves. Small, 4-petaled, usually yellow flowers are borne in racemes or panicles, and are attractive to bees. They are ideal for a wild garden; *I. tinctoria* is suitable for an herb garden.
• **CULTIVATION** Grow in moderately fertile, moist but well-drained soil in full sun.
• **PROPAGATION** Sow seed in autumn in containers in a cold frame, or in spring at 55–64°F (13–18°C). Divide in spring.
• **PESTS AND DISEASES** Infrequent.

I. glauca. Upright, clump-forming, almost hairless perennial with glaucous, blue-green leaves: the stalked basal leaves are lance-shaped, to 12in (30cm) long; the smaller, stalkless stem leaves are arrow-shaped, to 5in (13cm) long. Bears abundant 4-petaled yellow flowers, ¼in (6mm) across, in large panicles, 5–12in (12–30cm) across, in early summer. ‡ 2–4ft (60–120cm), ↔ 18in (45cm). Turkey, Iran. Zone 4.
I. tinctoria ■ (Woad). Taprooted, hairless or slightly hairy, short-lived perennial or biennial. Produces basal rosettes of oblong-lance-shaped, gray-green stalked leaves, to 4in (10cm) long, and leafy flowering stems bearing arrow-shaped, gray-green stalkless leaves, to 2in (5cm) long. Branched panicles, 1¼–3in (3–8cm) across, of 4-petaled yellow flowers, ⅜in (9mm) across, are borne in early summer. Leaves produce a blue pigment. ‡ 2–4ft (60–120cm), ↔ 18in (45cm). S. Europe. Zone 4.

▷ ***Ismene calathina*** see *Hymenocallis narcissiflor*

ISOLATOCEREUS

CACTACEAE

Monotypic genus of very tall, arboreal (tree-like) cactus, up to 50ft (15m) high. Isolated individual plants are found on the sides of hills and cliffs and in the mountainous deserts of Oaxaca, Hidalgo, Morelos, Guerrero, Puebla, and Michoacan, Mexico. The single species of this genus, *I dumorteiri,* can be grown from stem cuttings or seeds. It requires very little to moderate water and full sun.
• **CULTIVATION** Under glass, grow in a mix of 4 parts standard cactus potting mix and 1 part limestone chips, in full light. From spring to summer, water freely and apply a balanced liquid fertilizer every 4–5 weeks. Keep nearly dry at other times. Outdoors, grow in moderately fertile, slightly alkaline, sharply drained, humus-rich soil in full sun. See also pp.48–49.
• **PROPAGATION** Sow seed at 70°F (21°C) in spring or summer.
• **PESTS AND DISEASES:** Scale occurs.

I. dumorteiri (Candelabra). Large, arboreal cactus with erect and slightly inward-curved, highly constricted, blue-green stems, to 30ft (10m) long, and 5–8 ribs. Areoles, becoming confluent with age, produce 1–4 yellowish white central spines, to 2in (5cm). Flowers emerge from apical areoles, opening nocturnally, but lasting until midday. Ovate red fruit, 1–1⅜in (2.5–3.5cm) long, have dehiscent floral tubes. ↕ 15–50ft (5–15m), ↔ 2–6in (5-15cm). Mountainous deserts of C. Mexico. ❄ (min. 59°F/15°C)

ISOPLEXIS

SCROPHULARIACEAE

Genus of 3 species of evergreen subshrubs or shrubs, related to *Digitalis,* found in laurel and tree heather forest up to (4,900ft) (1,500m) in Madeira and the Canary Islands. Grown for their tubular, 5-lobed, colorful flowers, which are produced in terminal racemes. Leaves are alternate, narrow, and simple, with toothed margins. Where temperatures fall below 41°F (5°C), grow in a temperate greenhouse. In milder climates, grow in a shrub border, in a small courtyard garden, or as specimen plants.
• **CULTIVATION** Under glass, grow in soil-based potting mix in full or bright filtered light, with low to moderate humidity. During growth water moderately; apply a balanced liquid fertilizer monthly. Water sparingly in winter. Outdoors, grow in fertile, moist but well-drained soil in full sun or partial shade. Shelter from cold, drying winds. Pruning group 9.
• **PROPAGATION** Sow seed at 65–75°F (18–24°C) in spring. Root softwood cuttings in spring, or semi-ripe cuttings in summer with bottom heat.
• **PESTS AND DISEASES** Whiteflies and spider mites may occur, especially under glass.

I. canariensis ■ Erect, bushy shrub when young, spreading with age. Lance-shaped to narrowly ovate, sharply toothed, almost leathery, deep green leaves, to 6in (15cm) long, softly hairy beneath, are borne close together. Produces dense racemes, 12in (30cm) long, of tubular, bright orange-yellow, brownish orange, or yellow-brown flowers, to 1¼in (3cm) long, each with a 2-lobed upper lip, mainly in summer. ↕ to 5ft (1.5m), ↔ to 3ft (1m). Canary Islands (Tenerife). ❄ (min. 41°F/5°C)

Isoplexis canariensis

ISOPOGON

Cone bush, Drumsticks

PROTEACEAE

Genus of more than 35 species of small, evergreen shrubs from Australia, most commonly found in heathland, heath woodland, and sclerophyll forest, from sea level to subalpine zones. The alternate or spiraling, leathery leaves are usually pinnately or ternately divided, sometimes simple. They are grown for their firm, cone-like, spherical flowerheads, composed of many bracts and slender florets radiating outward. Where temperatures regularly fall to 32°F (0°C), grow in a temperate greenhouse; in warm, dry climates grow in a shrub border. Natives of S.W. Western Australia are accustomed to warm, dry summers; eastern species like more humidity. Larger species make unusual specimen plants.
• **CULTIVATION** Under glass, grow in an equal mix of soil-based potting mix, grit, and leaf mold or peat, in full or bright filtered light and low humidity. In the growing season, water sparingly and apply a half-strength, phosphate-free liquid fertilizer monthly. Keep just moist in winter. Outdoors, grow in neutral to acidic, poor to moderately fertile soil in full sun, with shelter from cold, drying winds. Pruning group 1.
• **PROPAGATION** In spring, surface-sow seed at 66–75°F (19–24°C) and cover with a fine layer of vermiculite or grit; before sowing, soak seed for 24 hours. Root semi-ripe cuttings in late summer with bottom heat.
• **PESTS AND DISEASES** *Phytophthora* root rot may kill plants in humid conditions. Scale insects may occur under glass.

I. anemonifolius ■ (Broad-leaf drumsticks). Dense, rounded to spreading shrub with hairy, often red-tinted, young shoots. Mid-green leaves, to 4in (10cm) long, vary from simple to 2- or 3-lobed; each slender lobe is deeply cut at the tips into narrow segments. Bears abundant yellow and cream flowerheads, 1½in (4cm) across, each surrounded by a ruff of dissected leaves, from spring to midsummer. ↕ 2–6ft (0.6–2m), ↔ 3–6ft (1–2m). Australia (New South Wales). ❄ (min. 41°F/5°C)

Isopogon anemonifolius

ISOPYRUM

False rue anemone

RANUNCULACEAE

Genus of 30 species of spring-flowering, rhizomatous, tufted perennials, which grow wild in damp woodland in temperate regions of Europe. They have delicate, deeply divided, ternate to 3-ternate leaves and anemone-like, usually white flowers with 5 petal-like sepals; petals are tiny or absent. Suitable for a woodland or rock garden.
• **CULTIVATION** Grow in humus-rich, neutral to acidic, moist but well-drained soil in partial shade. Shelter from cold, drying winds.
• **PROPAGATION** Sow seed as soon as ripe in containers in an open frame. Divide in autumn.
• **PESTS AND DISEASES** May be badly damaged by slugs and snails.

I. thalictroides. Clump-forming perennial with bluish green leaves, to 2in (5cm) long, each divided into 3 ovate, 3-lobed leaflets. Produces loose, open panicles, to 1½in (4cm) long, of nodding, anemone-like white flowers, to ¾in (2cm) across, from spring to early summer. ↕ 8in (20cm), ↔ 6in (15cm). W. and C. Europe. Zone 6.

▷ ***Isotoma*** see *Solenopsis*

ITEA

GROSSULARIACEAE

Genus of about 10 species of evergreen and deciduous shrubs and trees from woodlands and swamps in E. Asia and E. North America. Grown for their holly-like leaves, attractive autumn color, and small, white, cream, or green-white flowers, the leaves are toothed and arranged alternately. Flowers are borne in axillary or terminal, catkin-like, many-flowered racemes or panicles. Grow evergreen species in a sheltered spot in a shrub border; *I. ilicifolia* and *I. yunnanensis* are suitable for growing against a warm, sunny wall; *I. virginica* prefers more moisture and is best grown in a shrub or mixed border.
• **CULTIVATION** Grow evergreen species in fertile, moist but well-drained soil in full sun. Grow *I. virginica* in moist, slightly acidic soil in partial shade to full sun. Tie in long shoots of wall-trained, evergreen species. Pruning group 9 for evergreens; group 2 for deciduous species; group 13 if wall-trained.
• **PROPAGATION** Sow seed when ripe in containers in an open frame. Root greenwood cuttings in spring, or semi-ripe cuttings in summer.
• **PESTS AND DISEASES** Infrequent.

Itea ilicifolia

I. ilicifolia ■ (Hollyleaf sweetspire). Erect, then spreading, evergreen shrub with arching shoots and oval to elliptic, spiny-toothed, glossy, dark green leaves, to 4in (10cm) long. Small, greenish white flowers, ¼in (6mm) across, are borne in pendent, catkin-like racemes, to 12in (30cm) long, from midsummer to early autumn. ↕ 10–15ft (3–5m), ↔ 10ft (3m). W. China. Zone 7b.

I. virginica ■ (Virginia sweetspire). Upright, then arching, deciduous shrub with narrowly elliptic to oblong, finely toothed, dark green leaves, to 4in (10cm) long, turning red to purple in fall. Bears fragrant, creamy white flowers, ⅜in (9mm) across, in dense, erect racemes, to 6in (15cm) long, in summer. ↕ 5–10ft (1.5–3m), ↔ 5ft (1.5m). E. US. Zone 6. **'Henry's Garnet'** has larger flowers and brilliant red-purple fall color. ↕ 3–4ft (1–1.2m), ↔ 6ft (2m).

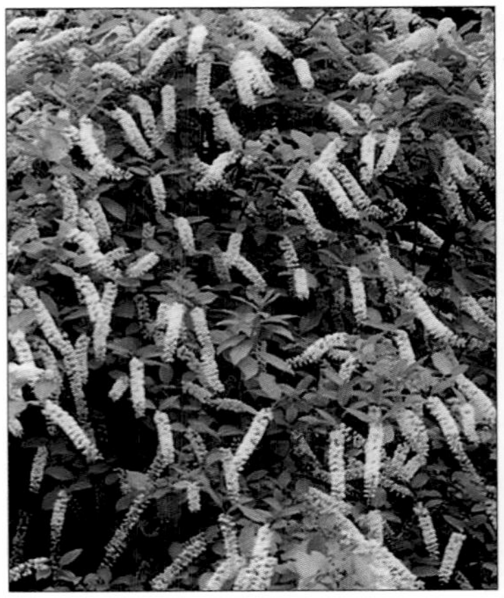

Itea virginica

IXIA

Corn lily

IRIDACEAE

Genus of 40–50 species of cormous perennials found in grassland and sandy, sometimes marshy slopes from low to high altitudes in South Africa. They are grown for their open, star-shaped, brightly colored flowers, which often have conspicuous dark centers, and are borne on wiry stems from early spring to summer. Narrowly linear, usually mid-green leaves are produced from the base of the plant, with shorter leaves on the slender, wiry stems. A large range of cultivars has been developed, with narrow, often branched stems bearing lax or dense spikes of few to many flowers, 1¼–3in (3–8cm) across. Grow in a container on a patio, or at the base of a warm, sunny wall. Where not hardy, grow in a cool greenhouse, or at the front of a border for summer flowering.

• **CULTIVATION** Under glass, plant corms 4–6in (10–15cm) deep, 2–3in (5–8cm) apart, in autumn. Grow in soil-based potting mix, with added leaf mold and sharp sand, in full light, with low to moderate humidity. Water sparingly until flower spikes appear, then water freely and apply a high-potash liquid fertilizer every 2 or 3 weeks until foliage begins to die back. Lift corms in fall and store in dry, frost-free conditions while dormant. Outdoors, grow in moderately fertile, well-drained soil in full sun.

• **PROPAGATION** Sow seed when ripe in containers in a cold frame. Separate offsets when dormant in late summer.

• **PESTS AND DISEASES** Infrequent.

***I.* 'Blue Bird'**, syn. 'Blauwe Vogel'. Cormous perennial with dark purple-centered, white flowers; each outer petal has a broad violet streak and a dark purple tip. ↕16in (40cm). ❀ (min. 45°F/7°C)

***I.* 'Hogarth'.** Cormous perennial bearing purple-centered, creamy white flowers. ↕16in (40cm). ❀ (min. 45°F/7°C)

***I.* 'Hubert'.** Cormous perennial bearing brownish red flowers with black centers. ↕16in (40cm). ❀ (min. 45°F/7°C)

***I.* 'Mabel'** ■ Cormous perennial bearing deep pink flowers, paler inside; the outer petals are brownish red. ↕16in (40cm). ❀ (min. 45°F/7°C)

I. maculata. Cormous perennial with erect, lance-shaped or awl-shaped, usually

Ixia 'Mabel'

Ixia paniculata

twisted leaves, 4–14in (10–35cm) long. From spring to early summer, bears spikes of few to many orange or yellow flowers, 2½in (6cm) across, with dark purple or black centers. ↕7–20in (18–50cm). S. Africa. ❀ (min. 45°F/7°C)

***I.* 'Marquette'.** Cormous perennial bearing purple-tipped yellow flowers with dark purple centers. ↕16in (40cm). ❀ (min. 45°F/7°C)

I. monadelpha. Cormous perennial with erect, lance-shaped or sword-shaped, twisted leaves, 3–11in (8–28cm) long. From spring to early summer, bears compact spikes of 4–12 blue, purple, pink, or white flowers, 1½in (4cm) across, each with a green or brown central mark usually edged with another color. ↕to 12in (30cm). South Africa (Western Cape). ❀ (min. 45°F/7°C)

I. paniculata ■ syn. *Tritonia longiflora.* Cormous perennial with erect, lance-shaped or linear leaves, 6–24in (15–60cm) long. From spring to early summer, branched stems bear spikes of 5–18 pink-suffused, cream or pale yellow flowers, 1½–3in (4–8cm) across, often tinged pink or red on the outside. ↕12–36in (30–90cm). South Africa. ❀ (min. 45°F/7°C)

Ixia viridiflora

I. polystachya. Cormous perennial with erect, grass-like leaves, 6–20in (15–50cm) long, and often branched stems. From spring to early summer, bears spikes or panicles of few to many, lightly fragrant, white, mauve, or blue flowers, 1½–2in (4–5cm) across, often with mauve or purple central marks. ↕12–36in (30–90cm). South Africa. ❀ (min. 45°F/7°C)

***I.* 'Rose Emperor'.** Cormous perennial bearing spikes of pink flowers with dark carmine-red centers. ↕16in (40cm). ❀ (min. 45°F/7°C)

***I.* 'Uranus'.** Cormous perennial bearing dark lemon-yellow flowers with dark red-black centers. ↕16in (40cm). ❀ (min. 45°F/7°C)

***I.* 'Venus'.** Cormous perennial with large, dark-centered magenta flowers, 2–3in (5–8cm) across. ↕16in (40cm). ❀ (min. 45°F/7°C)

I. viridiflora ■ Cormous perennial with erect, linear leaves, 16–22in (40–55cm) long. From spring to early summer, bears spikes of 12 or more pale bluish green flowers, 2in (5cm) across, with conspicuous, red-rimmed, black centers. ↕12–24in (30–60cm). South Africa. ❀ (min. 45°F/7°C)

IXIOLIRION

AMARYLLIDACEAE

Genus of 4 species of bulbous perennials from roadsides and grassy places in S.W. and C. Asia. They are cultivated for their racemes or umbels of funnel-shaped, usually deep blue or violet flowers. Linear-lance-shaped leaves are in basal rosettes. They flower best after hot, dry dormant periods in summer. Grow at the base of a sunny wall, or in a raised bed, alpine house, or bulb frame.

• **CULTIVATION** Plant bulbs 6in (15cm) deep in autumn. Outdoors, grow in humus-rich, well-drained soil in full sun. Mulch to protect from winter moisture. Under glass, grow in soil-based potting mix in full light. During growth, water freely. Keep just moist in autumn and winter, and completely dry when dormant in summer.

• **PROPAGATION** Sow seed in containers in a cold frame as soon as ripe or in autumn. Separate offsets after flowering.

• **PESTS AND DISEASES** Infrequent.

I. montanum see *I. tataricum.*

I. pallasii see *I. tataricum.*

I. tataricum, syn. *I. montanum, I. pallasii* (Tatar lily). Bulbous perennial with erect, linear-lance-shaped, basal leaves, to 24in (60cm) or more long. From spring to early summer, produces loose umbels of up to 10 funnel-shaped, blue or violet-blue flowers, 1¼–2in (3–5cm) long, with a darker central stripe on each petal. ↕10–16in (24–40cm), PD2in (5cm). Israel to N. Iran, S.W. and C. Asia to Kashmir and Tien Shan. ❀ (min. 45°F/7°C)

IXORA

RUBIACEAE

Genus of 400 species of evergreen shrubs and trees from tropical woodland and mountains up to 10,000ft (3,000m) worldwide. They are grown for their large, vibrantly colored, scented, 4-petaled, salverform flowers, produced in terminal panicles or corymb-like cymes. The opposite, occasionally whorled leaves are simple and entire. They grow best in warm, humid climates in a shrub border, or as free-standing specimens. Where temperatures drop below 59°F (15°C), grow as houseplants or in a warm greenhouse.

• **CULTIVATION** Under glass, grow in soilless potting mix with added leaf mold and grit, in bright filtered or indirect light, with moderate to high humidity. Water freely during growth and sparingly in winter. Top-dress annually in spring with fresh soil mix and a balanced, slow-release fertilizer. Outdoors, grow in fertile, moist but well-drained soil, with shade from the hottest sun and shelter from strong winds. Pruning group 9; may need restrictive pruning under glass.

• **PROPAGATION** Root semi-ripe cuttings in summer with bottom heat.

• **PESTS AND DISEASES** Aphids and scale insects may be problems. Iron deficiency, *Xanthomonas* spot, and fungal leaf spots occur outdoors.

I. chinensis. Bushy, rounded shrub with elliptic, ovate, or obovate, semi-lustrous, mid- to deep green leaves, to 2½in (6cm) long. Produces dense, flattened corymb-like cymes, 2–4in (5–10cm) across, of red, orange, pink, or occasionally white flowers, 1½in (4cm) long, mainly in summer. ↕6ft (2m) or more, ↔3–6ft (1–2m). S. China, Taiwan. ❀ (min. 59°F/15°C)

I. coccinea ■ (Flame of the woods, Jungle flame, Jungle geranium). Bushy, gently rounded shrub with oblong or obovate to elliptic, glossy, mid- to deep green leaves, 2–4in (5–10cm) long. Freely produces loose, corymb-like cymes, 2–5in (5–13cm) across, of red, orange, pink, or yellow flowers, 1–1½in (2.5–4cm) long, from late spring or early summer to autumn. ↕8ft (2.5m) or more, ↔5–6ft (1.5–2m). India, Sri Lanka. ❀ (min. 59°F/15°C). **'Angela Busman'** is compact, with shrimp-pink blooms; ↕5ft (1.5m). **'Frances Perry'** bears large clusters of deep yellow flowers. **'Fraseri'** bears bright salmon-pink flowers. **'Gillette's Yellow'** produces pale yellow flowers. **'Henry Morat'** has fragrant pink flowers. **'Herrera's White'** bears well-formed white flowers. **f. *lutea*** has yellow blooms. **'Orange King'** is compact, and has glowing orange flowers; ↕5ft (1.5m). **'Superkings'** is compact, with red flowers; ↕3ft (1m).

Ixora coccinea

J

JABOROSA

SOLANACEAE

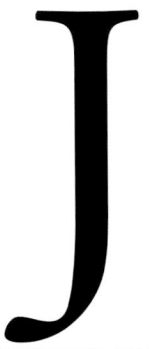

Genus of 20 species of perennials with basal, entire to pinnatifid leaves and axillary, 5- or 6-lobed, tubular or bell-shaped flowers, which are solitary or borne in few-flowered cymes. Most species occur in arid areas of South America. *J. integrifolia*, the only species commonly seen in cultivation, is suitable for a warm, dry site.

• **CULTIVATION** Grow in moderately fertile, light, well-drained soil in a sunny, sheltered spot. *J. integrifolia* is invasive. Provide a dry winter mulch where marginally hardy.

• **PROPAGATION** Divide, or sow seed at 55–61°F (13–16°C), in spring.

• **PESTS AND DISEASES** May be damaged by slugs and snails.

J. integrifolia. Rhizomatous, stemless perennial with basal clusters of oval to elliptic, fleshy, entire, dark green leaves, 8in (20cm) or more long. Bears solitary, tubular, night-scented, greenish white flowers, to 2½in (6cm) across, with star-shaped lobes, in summer. ↕ 6in (15cm), ↔ indefinite. S. Brazil, Uruguay, Argentina. ❄ (min. 35°F/2°C)

JACARANDA

BIGNONIACEAE

Genus of 30–45 species of deciduous and evergreen trees from wet rainforest of tropical America. They have opposite, pinnate or 2-pinnate, often elegant, fern-like leaves and terminal panicles of tubular, narrowly bell-shaped, 5-lobed, foxglove-like flowers. Where not hardy, grow in a cool greenhouse, mainly as foliage plants, although some flowers may form on container-grown specimens, 6ft (2m) or more tall; young plants of *J. mimosifolia* are suitable for summer bedding. In warmer climates, jacarandas are popular as specimen plants and street trees.

• **CULTIVATION** Under glass, grow in soil-based potting mix in full light with good ventilation. In the growing season, water freely and apply a balanced liquid fertilizer every month; water sparingly in winter. Outdoors, grow in fertile, moist, but well-drained soil in full sun. Pruning group 1; plants under glass need restrictive pruning in late winter.

• **PROPAGATION** Sow seed at 61–70°F (16–21°C) in spring. Root semi-ripe cuttings with bottom heat in summer.

• **PESTS AND DISEASES** Whiteflies and spider mites may be troublesome under glass. Occasionally affected outdoors by thornbugs, crown gall, mushroom root rot, and leaf spots.

Jacaranda mimosifolia

***J. acutifolia* of gardens** see *J. mimosifolia.*

J. jasminoides. Small, spreading, deciduous tree with pinnate leaves, 5–10in (13–25cm) long, white beneath, with 2–10 stalkless, ovate to ovate-elliptic, olive-green leaflets, to 2½in (6cm) long. From spring to early summer, bears panicles, 4–8in (10–20cm) long, of dark purple flowers, 1½–2in (3.5–5cm) long, followed by oblong-elliptic, brown to black seed pods. ↕ 6–12ft (2–4m), ↔ 4–8ft (1.2–2.5m). Mexico, Brazil. ❄ (min. 41–45°F/5–7°C)

J. mimosifolia ▣ syn. *J. acutifolia* of gardens, *J. ovalifolia, J. ovatifolia.* Spreading, deciduous tree, with broad, 2-pinnate leaves, 10–18in (25–45cm) long, composed of many small, narrowly elliptic, softly hairy, bright mid-green leaflets. From spring to early summer, broadly pyramidal panicles, 8–12in (20–30cm) long, of white-throated, glowing purple-blue flowers, 1½–2in (3.5–5cm) long, are borne on leafless branches or with young foliage. The flowers are followed by woody, disk-shaped seed pods. ↕ to 50ft (15m), ↔ 22–30ft (7–10m). Bolivia, Argentina. ❄ (min. 41–45°F/5–7°C)

J. ovalifolia see *J. mimosifolia.*

J. ovatifolia see *J. mimosifolia.*

▷ ***Jacobinia carnea*** see *Justicia carnea*

▷ ***Jacobinia coccinea*** see *Pachystachys coccinea*

▷ ***Jacobinia pauciflora*** see *Justicia rizzinii*

▷ ***Jacobinia pohliana*** see *Justicia carnea*

▷ ***Jacobinia spicigera*** see *Justicia spicigera*

▷ ***Jacobinia suberecta*** see *Dicliptera suberecta*

▷ ***Jacobinia velutina*** see *Justicia carnea*

JACQUEMONTIA

CONVOLVULACEAE

Genus of 120 species of evergreen perennials and shrubs, many of them scandent or twining climbers, closely related to *Ipomoea* and *Convolvulus.* Most are found in tropical woodland in Central and South America, with a few elsewhere in the tropics. They are grown for their funnel- to bell-shaped flowers, borne in cymes or panicles, and have alternate leaves, which are usually simple and entire, but may be toothed or lobed. Where temperatures drop below 55–61°F (13–16°C), grow in a warm greenhouse. In tropical areas, grow on a trellis or allow to scramble through other, more vigorous shrubs; they are excellent for a coastal garden.

• **CULTIVATION** Under glass, grow in soil-based potting mix in full light with shade from hot sun. In the growing season, water moderately and apply a balanced liquid fertilizer every month; water sparingly in winter. Outdoors, grow in moderately fertile, moist but well-drained soil in full sun. Pruning group 11.

• **PROPAGATION** Sow seed at 64°F (18°C) in spring. Root softwood cuttings with bottom heat in summer.

• **PESTS AND DISEASES** Whiteflies and spider mites may be troublesome under glass.

J. pentantha, syn. *J. violacea.* Fast-growing, twining climber, branching freely from the base, with heart-shaped to ovate, mid- to bright green leaves, 2in (5cm) long, which taper to a slender point. Long-stalked cymes of up to 12 funnel-shaped, white-eyed, violet-blue to blue flowers, ¾–1½in (2–4cm) wide, are produced mainly from summer to late autumn. ↕ 6–8ft (1.8–2.5m). Tropical America. ❄ (min. 55°F/13°C)

J. violacea see *J. pentantha.*

JAMESIA

HYDRANGEACEAE

Genus of one species of deciduous shrub from mountainous, rocky areas in W. US. It has papery bark and simple, toothed, rough-textured leaves, borne in opposite pairs. Jamesia is cultivated for its 5-petaled, star-shaped white flowers, produced in small, terminal panicles in late spring and early summer. *J. americana* is suitable for a shrub border or large rock garden.

• **CULTIVATION** Grow in fertile, well-drained soil in full sun. Pruning group 1 or 2.

• **PROPAGATION** Take softwood or semi-ripe cuttings in summer.

• **PESTS AND DISEASES** Infrequent.

J. americana (Cliffbush, Waxflower). Small, spreading, deciduous shrub with peeling, papery bark and ovate, toothed, rough-textured, velvety gray-green leaves, to 3in (8cm) long, sometimes turning red in autumn. Small panicles, to 2½in (6cm) long, of star-shaped, slightly fragrant white flowers, ½in (1.5cm) across, are produced in late spring and early summer. ↕ 5ft (1.5m), ↔ 6ft (2m). W. US. Zone 6.

JANCAEA syn. JANKAEA

GESNERIACEAE

Genus of one species of evergreen, rosette-forming perennial, from shady cliffs of Mount Olympus, Greece. It is grown for its white-hairy, silver-green foliage and bell-shaped, pale lavender-blue flowers. *J. heldreichii* is best grown in an alpine house, rock garden, or tufa.

• **CULTIVATION** In an alpine house, grow in a mix of equal parts loam, leaf mold, and sharp grit, with additional limestone chips, in bright filtered light. Place a collar of grit at the neck of the plant. In the growing season, water moderately, avoiding water on the foliage, and maintain a humid but well-ventilated atmosphere; water sparingly in winter. Outdoors, plant in a vertical cleft, and give overhead protection in winter.

Jancaea heldreichii

• **PROPAGATION** Sow seed in containers in a cold frame in autumn; pot on when seedlings have formed small rosettes. Take leaf cuttings in spring.
• **PESTS AND DISEASES** Susceptible to aphids and spider mites under glass.

J. heldreichii ■ Evergreen perennial with neat rosettes of thick, corrugated, obovate, densely white-hairy, silver-green leaves, to 1½in (4cm) long. In late spring bears clusters of 1 or 2, broadly bell-shaped, pale lavender-blue flowers, ¾in (2cm) long, with 4 or 5, spreading lobes. ↕ to 2in (5cm), ↔ to 4in (10cm). N.E. Greece. Zone 6.

▷***Jankaea*** see *Jancaea*

JASIONE

Sheep's bit

CAMPANULACEAE

Genus of about 20 species of summer-flowering annuals, biennials, and perennials with alternate, simple leaves and terminal, pincushion-like heads of usually blue flowers. Most species grow in dry, open grassland in temperate Europe and around the Mediterranean. Grow in a rock garden or at the front of a border.
• **CULTIVATION** Grow in moderately fertile, well-drained, preferably sandy soil in full sun.
• **PROPAGATION** Sow seed in containers in a cold frame as soon as ripe or in autumn. Alternatively, divide in spring.
• **PESTS AND DISEASES** Slugs and snails may damage young growth in spring.

J. laevis ■ syn. *J. perennis* (Sheep's bit scabious, Shepherd's scabious). Densely tufted perennial with basal rosettes of entire, narrowly oblong to narrowly obovate or inversely lance-shaped leaves, to 4in (10cm) long. In summer upright, unbranched stems bear spiky, almost spherical, blue flowerheads, to 1–1½in (2.5–4cm) across. ↕ 8–12in (20–30cm), ↔ to 8in (20cm). W. and S. Europe. Zone 6.
J. perennis see *J. laevis.*

JASMINOCEREUS

CACTACEAE (CACTOIDEAE, BROWNINGIEAE)

Monotypic erect, columnar, freely branching, tree-like genus, native to the Galápagos Islands. Like all Galápagos endemics, these plants are protected and difficult to obtain.
• **CULTIVATION** Under glass, grow in a mix of 4 parts standard cactus potting mix and 1 part limestone chips, in full light. From spring to summer, water freely and apply a balanced liquid fertilizer every 4–5 weeks. Keep nearly dry at other times. Outdoors, grow in moderately fertile, slightly alkaline, sharply drained, humus-rich soil in full sun. See also pp.48–49.
• **PROPAGATION** Sow seed at 70°F (21°C) in spring or summer.
• **PESTS AND DISEASES** Scale occurs.

J. thouarsii. Erect, columnar, freely branching, tree-like, cactus whose jasmine-like salviform flowers are diurnal. Areoles are 1/16in (2mm) wide, spaced ¼–⅜in (6–9mm) apart. Bears about 40 unequal, stiff to somewhat flexible radiating spines, to 1¾in (4.5cm) long, in a yellowish hue, that darkens with age. Produces globose to oblong, greenish to reddish purple, nearly naked, fleshy fruit that hardens with maturity. ↕ 10–22ft (3–7m), ↔ 1¼–2in (3–5cm). Coahuila, Mexico. ❀ (min. 50°F/10°C)

JASMINUM

Jasmine, Jessamine

OLEACEAE

Genus of 200 or more species of deciduous and evergreen shrubs and climbers from woodland, scrub, and rocky places in tropical and temperate regions, mainly in Europe, Asia, and Africa. They are cultivated for their

Jasione laevis

Jasminum angulare

terminal or axillary, sometimes umbel- or panicle-like cymes of salverform, often fragrant flowers with broad or narrow, star-shaped segments, and for their opposite or alternate, simple to pinnate leaves (in some species reduced to only one leaflet). Most species have black berries. Climbing jasmines will twine over any suitable support, such as a trellis, fence, arch, or large shrub. Scandent, shrubby jasmines may be trained against a wall, and dwarf species are suitable for a rock garden. In cool areas, grow jasmines in a sheltered position; grow half-hardy species as houseplants in a conservatory or cool greenhouse, and tender species in a warm or temperate greenhouse.
• **CULTIVATION** Outdoors, grow in fertile, well-drained soil in full sun or partial shade. Under glass, grow in soil-based potting mix in bright filtered light or full light with shade from hot sun. In growth, water freely and apply a low-nitrogen liquid fertilizer monthly; water sparingly in winter. Prune *J. mesnyi*, *J. nudiflorum*, and *J. humile* as for shrubs in pruning group 2. Thin old, flowered, and overcrowded shoots of *J. officinale* after flowering. Remaining species need little regular pruning, other than to thin overcrowded growth after flowering.
• **PROPAGATION** Take semi-ripe cuttings in summer, or layer in autumn.
• **PESTS AND DISEASES** Root rot, fungal and bacterial leaf spots, and a variety of viruses are common. Aphids, scale insects, and mealybugs may be problems.

J. angulare ■ syn. *J. capense.* Scrambling to semi-twining, evergreen climber, usually freely branching when mature, with ridged or angled stems. Leaves are opposite, pinnate, and rich, deep green, with 3, sometimes 5, ovate to lance-shaped, lustrous leaflets, ¾–1½in (2–4cm) long. Bears axillary cymes of 3 salverform, very sweetly scented flowers, to 1¼in (3cm) across, greenish or pale pink then white, from late summer to autumn. ↕ 10–20ft (3–6m). South Africa. ❀ (min. 45°F/7°C)
J. beesianum. Twining, woody, evergreen climber, deciduous in cool areas, with opposite, simple, ovate to lance-shaped, dark green leaves, to 2in (5cm) long. Cymes of 3 small, salverform, fragrant, pinkish red flowers, ½in (1.5cm) across, are produced in early and midsummer. ↕ 15ft (5m). S.W. China. ❀ (min. 45°F/7°C)
J. capense see *J. angulare.*

Jasminum humile

J

J. dichotomum. Bushy, evergreen scrambler or twining climber with whorls of thick, lustrous, mid-green leaves, each reduced to one ovate to elliptic, boldly veined leaflet, 2–4in (5–10cm) long, with an abrupt, sharp point. Produces loosely branched cymes of up to 60 salverform, sweetly scented white flowers, to ¾in (2cm) across, opening from red-purple or red-tinted buds, intermittently all year. ↕ to 10ft (3m) or more. Tropical W., C., and E. Africa. ❀ (min. 50–55°F/10–13°C)
J. fruticans. Dense, upright, evergreen or semi-evergreen shrub with alternate, pinnate, dark green leaves, each having 3 narrow-oblong or linear-obovate leaflets, to ¾in (2cm) long. Terminal cymes of up to 5 small, salverform, slightly fragrant yellow flowers, ½in (1.5cm) across, are produced in summer. ↕↔ 5ft (1.5m). Portugal, North Africa to Jordan, Turkey to Turkmenistan. ❀ (min. 41°F/5°C)
***J. grandiflorum* of gardens** see *J. officinale* f. *affine.*
J. humile ■ (Yellow jasmine). Semi-evergreen or evergreen, erect or arching, bushy shrub with alternate, pinnate, bright green leaves composed of 5–9, occasionally 13, ovate to lance-shaped leaflets, to 2in (5cm) long. Cymes of usually 6, occasionally more, salverform, sometimes fragrant, bright yellow flowers, ½in (1.5cm) or more across, are produced from late spring to early autumn. ↕ 8ft (2.5m), sometimes to 12ft (4m), ↔ 10ft (3m). Afghanistan to Himalayas and S.W. China. Zone 7. **'Revolutum'** (Italian jasmine), syn. *J. reevesii* of gardens, is semi-evergreen, with stout shoots, larger leaves, with 5–7 long-pointed leaflets to ½in (1.5cm) long, and up to 12 fragrant flowers, to 1in (2.5cm) across. **f. *wallichianum*** has leaves with 7–13 leaflets and pendulous, 3- to 5-flowered cymes; India, Nepal.
J. mesnyi, syn. *J. primulinum* (Primrose jasmine). Tall, open, slender-stemmed, evergreen shrub which acts like a climber when grown against a support.

Jasminum nudiflorum

Opposite, pinnate, glossy, deep green leaves have 3 oblong to lance-shaped leaflets, 1¼–3in (3–8cm) long. Salverform, usually semi-double, bright yellow flowers, 1¼–1¾in (3–4.5cm) across, are produced singly or in few-flowered clusters in spring and summer. ↕ to 10ft (3m) or more, ↔ 3–6ft (1–2m). S.W. China. ❄ (min. 35°F/2°C)

J. nudiflorum ▣ (Winter jasmine, Hardy jasmine). Slender, deciduous shrub with arching to scandent green shoots and opposite, pinnate, dark green leaves, each divided into 3 oval-oblong leaflets, to 1¼in (3cm) long. Solitary, salverform, bright yellow flowers, ½–¾in (1–2cm) across, are produced in the leaf axils, before the leaves, in winter and early spring. ↕↔ 10ft (3m). W. China. Zone 7.

J. officinale (Common jasmine, Poet's jasmine). Vigorous, twining, woody, deciduous, occasionally semi-deciduous climber with opposite, pinnate, mid-green leaves composed of 5–9 elliptic leaflets, to 2½in (6cm) long, with long, sharp points. Terminal, umbel-like cymes of up to 5-flowered clusters of salverform, very fragrant white flowers, ¾in (2cm) across, are produced from summer to early autumn. ↕ 40ft (12m). Caucasus, N. Iran, Afghanistan, Himalayas, W. China. Zone 7.
f. *affine*, syn. *J. grandiflorum* of gardens, has pink-tinged white flowers, to 1½in (4cm) across. **'Argenteovariegatum'** ▣ syn. 'Variegatum', has leaves that are gray-green with creamy white margins. **'Aureovariegatum'**, syn. 'Aureum', has leaves with conspicuous yellow margins.

J. polyanthum ▣ Vigorous, twining, evergreen climber with opposite, pinnate, deep green leaves made up of 5–7 lance-shaped leaflets, the terminal ones largest, to 3in (8cm) long, with slender points. Bears an abundance of salverform, strongly fragrant, pink-budded white flowers, to ¾in (2cm) wide, in many-flowered, panicle-like cymes, to 4in (10cm) long. Flowers in late winter or early spring in a warm or temperate greenhouse, from spring to summer in warm climates. ↕ to 10ft (3m) or more. W. and S.W. China. ❄ (min. 41°F/5°C)

Jasminum officinale 'Argenteovariegatum'

J. primulinum see *J. mesnyi.*

***J. reevesii* of gardens** see *J. humile* 'Revolutum'.

J. rex. Vigorous, twining, evergreen climber with opposite, dark green leaves, each reduced to one broadly ovate leaflet, 5–8in (12–20cm) long. Produces axillary cymes of 2 or 3 salverform, unscented white flowers, 2in (5cm) or more across, mainly in summer. ↕ 10ft (3m) or more. Thailand. ❄ (min. 55°F/13°C)

J. sambac (Arabian jasmine, Pikake). Evergreen, twining climber or scrambler with angular stems and bushy growth. Lustrous, dark green leaves, some in whorls of 3, others opposite, are reduced to one broadly ovate leaflet, to 3in (8cm) long. Bears small cymes of 3–12 salverform, strongly scented white flowers, 1in (2.5cm) across, fading to pink, mainly in summer, but often irregularly throughout the year. ↕ 6–10ft (2–3m). Probably tropical Asia. ❄ (min. 55–59°F/13–15°C). **'Grand Duke of Tuscany'**, syn. 'Flore Pleno', bears double flowers resembling miniature gardenias.

Jasminum polyanthum

J. × stephanense (*J. beesianum* × *J. officinale*). Vigorous, twining, woody, deciduous climber with opposite, dull green, sometimes cream-flushed leaves, which may be simple, ovate-lance-shaped, to 2in (5cm) long, or pinnate, with 5 ovate-elliptic leaflets, to 2in (5cm) long. Loose cymes of 5 or 6 or more, salverform, fragrant, pale pink flowers, to ½in (1.5cm) across, appear in early and midsummer. S.W. China (Yunnan). ↕ 15ft (5m). ❄ (min. 35°F/2°C)

JATROPHA

EUPHORBIACEAE

Genus of about 170 species of succulent perennials and evergreen shrubs, rarely trees, from dry or semi-moist areas of South Africa, Madagascar, tropical North, Central, and South America, and the West Indies. Many are very succulent, often forming a caudex; other species have tuberous rootstocks. Leaves are alternate and simple, palmately lobed, or finely divided. In summer, diurnal flowers with prominent petals appear singly or in flat-topped cymes. Where temperatures drop below 50°F (10°C), grow in a warm greenhouse or conservatory; in warmer climates, plant in a shrub border or use as hedging. All parts contain a milky or watery latex, contact with which may irritate skin.

• **CULTIVATION** Under glass, grow in a mix of 2 parts soil-based potting mix with 1 part each leaf mold and grit. Provide full light with shade from hot sun. In spring and summer, water moderately and apply a balanced liquid fertilizer monthly; keep completely dry in autumn and winter. Outdoors, grow in moderately fertile, humus-rich, gritty, sharply drained soil in full sun. Pruning group 1 or 6 for *J. integerrima.* See also pp.48–49.

• **PROPAGATION** Sow seed in spring or summer at 75°F (24°C).

• **PESTS AND DISEASES** Mushroom root rot, rust, and several fungal leaf spots may occur. Vulnerable to scale insects and mealybugs.

J. integerrima ▣ (Peregrina, Spicy jatropha). Evergreen tree with an erect, branching, woody stem and ovate to oblong, palmately 1- to 3-lobed, sharp-pointed, dark green leaves, 3–5in (8–13cm) long, bronze-red when young and green-brown beneath. Bears terminal clusters of star-shaped, bright coral-red flowers, 1–1¼in (2.5–3cm) across. Suitable for containers or a summer border. ↕ 20ft (6m), ↔ 12ft (4m). Cuba, West Indies. ❄ (min. 45°F/7°C)

J. multifida (Coral plant). Tree-like, evergreen, semi-succulent shrub with rounded, 7- to 15-lobed, finely divided leaves, 1½–3in (4–8cm) across. Numerous long-stalked, small scarlet flowers, ¼in (6mm) across, are borne in terminal cymes in summer. ↕ to 22ft (7m), ↔ 12ft (4m). Mexico to Brazil, West Indies. ❄ (min. 50°F/10°C)

J. podagrica ▣ (Bottle plant). Branching, succulent perennial with a short, swollen, caudex-like gray trunk and gray stems covered with spine-like stipules. At the tips, produces rounded-ovate, 3- to 5-lobed leaves, 7–12in (18–30cm) across, dark green above, glaucous white beneath. Terminal, branched cymes of numerous unisexual, small, brilliant scarlet to coral-red flowers, ½in (1.5cm) across, are borne on long, green, sometimes red-tinted stalks from winter to summer. ↕ to 20in (50cm) or more, ↔ 10in (25cm). Central America, West Indies. ❄ (min. 50°F/10°C)

Jatropha integerrima

Jatropha podagrica (inset: inflorescence detail)

JEFFERSONIA

syn. PLAGIORHEGMA
Twinleaf
BERBERIDACEAE

Genus of 2 species of perennials native to damp woodland and forest in N.E. Asia and North America. They have rounded to kidney-shaped, 2-lobed leaves. Jeffersonias are grown for their short-lived, solitary, cup-shaped flowers, with 5–8 petals, borne on long, slender stalks, in late spring or early summer. They are excellent plants for a shaded rock garden or woodland garden.
• **CULTIVATION** Grow in moist, humus-rich soil in partial or full shade. Top-dress with leaf mold or other humus-rich material in autumn.

Jeffersonia dubia

• **PROPAGATION** Sow seed in containers in an open frame as soon as ripe. Divide established plants in spring.
• **PESTS AND DISEASES** Prey to slugs and snails, especially in spring.

J. diphylla (Twinleaf). Tuft-forming perennial with kidney-shaped, deeply cleft leaves, to 6in (15cm) across, pale gray-green above, and glaucous, pale green beneath. In late spring or early summer, solitary, cup-shaped white flowers, 1in (2.5cm) wide, are produced on slender stalks. ↕ 8in (20cm), often taller after flowering, ↔ to 6in (15cm). Ontario to Tennessee. Zone 6.
J. dubia ■ syn. *Plagiorhegma dubia.* Delicate, tufted perennial with kidney-shaped or rounded, 2-lobed, blue-green leaves, to 4in (10cm) across, often purple-tinted, especially when unfolding. In late spring or early summer, bears solitary, cup-shaped, clear lavender-blue, occasionally white flowers, 1¼in (3cm) across, on slender, dark stalks. ↕ 8in (20cm), ↔ to 6in (15cm). N.E. Asia. Zone 6.

JOVELLANA

SCROPHULARIACEAE

Genus of 6 species of herbaceous perennials and semi-evergreen subshrubs, from streambanks and forest margins in New Zealand and Chile. They have simple, toothed or lobed leaves, borne in opposite pairs, and showy, 2-lipped flowers. Grow in a sheltered border or against a wall. Where not hardy, grow or overwinter in a cool greenhouse.

Jovellana violacea

• **CULTIVATION** Under glass, grow in soilless potting mix in full light, with shade from hot sun and good ventilation. In the growing season, water moderately and apply a balanced liquid fertilizer every month; water sparingly in winter. Outdoors, grow in fertile, well-drained soil in full sun. Where marginally hardy, protect with a dry winter mulch. Pruning group 10.
• **PROPAGATION** Take heel cuttings of sideshoots in late summer.
• **PESTS AND DISEASES** Infrequent.

J. sinclairii. Woody-based herbaceous perennial with upright shoots and ovate to ovate-oblong, double-toothed or lobed leaves, to 2in (5cm) long. Terminal panicles, 6in (15cm) long, of 2-lipped, purple-spotted, lilac to white flowers, ⅜in (8mm) across, are borne in summer. ↕ 20in (50cm), ↔ 24in (60cm). New Zealand (North Island). ❄ (min. 41°F/5°C)
J. violacea ■ Upright, suckering, semi-evergreen subshrub with ovate, coarsely toothed or lobed, deep green leaves, ¾–1¼in (2–3cm) long. In summer, bears panicles, 1½–3in (4–8cm) across, of 2-lipped, pale violet-purple flowers, to ½in (1.5cm) across, with purple spots within and yellow throats. ↕ 24in (60cm), ↔ 3ft (1m). Chile. ❄ (min. 41°F/5°C)

JOVIBARBA

CRASSULACEAE

Genus of 6 species of mat-forming, usually stoloniferous, evergreen perennials, very similar to *Sempervivum*, from the mountains of Europe. They are grown for their symmetrical rosettes of fleshy leaves and terminal cymes of small, 6-petaled, bell-shaped flowers, borne on leafy stems in summer. After flowering, the rosettes are replaced by numerous offsets. Easily cultivated, they are suitable for a rock garden, trough, wall, or alpine house.
• **CULTIVATION** Grow in poor, gritty, well-drained soil in full sun. Remove old rosettes after flowering. In an alpine house, grow in equal parts soil-based potting mix and grit.
• **PROPAGATION** Root offsets in spring or early summer.
• **PESTS AND DISEASES** Infrequent.

J. allionii see *J. hirta* subsp. *allionii.*
J. globifera see *J. sobolifera.*
J. globifera* subsp. *allionii see *J. hirta* subsp. *allionii.*

Jovibarba hirta

J. globifera* subsp. *hirta see *J. hirta.*
J. heuffelii, syn. *Sempervivum patens.* Evergreen perennial lacking stolons, with rosettes, 2–3in (5–8cm) across, of lance-shaped, finely hairy or glaucous leaves, to ⅜in (8mm) long. Bears bell-shaped, pale yellow flowers in dense, flat heads, to 2in (5cm) across, in summer. ↕ to 8in (20cm), ↔ to 12in (30cm). E. Carpathians, Balkans. Zone 5.
J. hirta ■ syn. *J. globifera* subsp. *hirta, Sempervivum hirtum.* Evergreen perennial with rosettes, 1–3in (2.5–8cm) across, of lance-shaped to inversely lance-shaped, hairy-margined leaves, to ½in (1.5cm) long, tipped brownish purple and often red-tinted. Bears branching heads, to 3in (8cm) across, of bell-shaped, pale yellowish brown flowers in summer. ↕ 6in (15cm), ↔ to 12in (30cm). C. and S.E. Europe. Zone 5. **subsp. *allionii***, syn. *J. allionii, J. globifera* subsp. *allionii*, has smaller rosettes with glandular-hairy, red-tipped leaves; S.W. and S.E. Alps.
J. sobolifera, syn. *J. globifera, Sempervivum soboliferum.* Evergreen perennial with rosettes, to 2in (5cm) across, of obovate to oblong, glossy, bright green leaves, to ½in (1.5cm) long, with fringed margins, and tips that flush red with age. In summer, bears bell-shaped, greenish yellow flowers in clusters, to 3in (8cm) across. ↕ 8in (20cm), ↔ to 12in (30cm). S.W., C., and S.E. Europe, N.W. and C. Russia. Zone 5.

JUANULLOA

SOLANACEAE

Genus of 10 species of epiphytic and terrestrial, scandent, evergreen shrubs from the rainforest of Central America to Peru. They are grown for their 5-lobed, tubular flowers, each with a bell-shaped, deeply ridged calyx, borne in short racemes or panicles. Leaves are alternate, simple, entire, and leathery. Where temperatures fall below about 55°F (13°C), grow in a warm or

Juanulloa mexicana

temperate greenhouse. In tropical or subtropical climates, use to clothe an arch or pillar, or train through a tree.

• **CULTIVATION** Under glass, grow in soil-based potting mix in full light with shade from hot sun, and moderate to low humidity. In spring and summer, water moderately and apply a balanced liquid fertilizer every month; water sparingly in winter. Outdoors, grow in moderately fertile, humus-rich, moist but well-drained soil in full sun with some midday shade. Pruning group 9, with restrictive pruning under glass; tip-prune young plants.

• **PROPAGATION** Sow seed at 64°F (18°C) in spring. Root semi-ripe cuttings with bottom heat in spring.

• **PESTS AND DISEASES** Prey to mealybugs and spider mites.

J. aurantiaca see *J. mexicana.*

J. mexicana ▣ syn. *J. aurantiaca.* Epiphytic shrub, becoming scandent with age, with elliptic to oblong, mid- to deep green leaves, 3–8in (8–20cm) long, usually densely woolly beneath. Produces short racemes of semi-pendent, tubular, bright orange or orange-yellow flowers, 1½–2in (4–5cm) long, with paler calyces, mainly in summer. ↕ to 6ft (2m) or more, ↔ 24–39in (60–100cm). S. Mexico to Colombia, Peru. ❀ (min. 55°F/13°C)

JUBAEA
Chilean wine palm

ARECACEAE

Genus of one species of single-stemmed palm from the warm-temperate coastal valleys of Chile. Spreading to arching, pinnate leaves form a dense, terminal, rounded head, and 3-petaled flowers appear in panicles between them. Where not hardy, grow as a houseplant or in a cool greenhouse or conservatory. In warm, dry regions, grow as a majestic specimen or street tree.

• **CULTIVATION** Under glass, grow in soil-based potting mix in full light. In the growing season, water moderately and apply a balanced liquid fertilizer every month; water sparingly in winter. Outdoors, grow in fertile, moist but well-drained soil in full sun.

• **PROPAGATION** Sow seed at 77°F (25°C) in spring; germination may take 3–6 months.

• **PESTS AND DISEASES** Spider mites and scale insects may be troublesome under glass.

Jubaea chilensis

J. chilensis ▣ syn. *J. spectabilis* (Coquito palm, Honey palm). Slow-growing palm with a robust, erect, scarred and cracked gray trunk, occasionally swollen in the middle. Pinnate, oblong-ovate leaves, to 15ft (5m) long, consist of many linear, rigid, folded, yellow-green to deep green leaflets. Small, bowl-shaped, dull purple or maroon and yellow flowers are produced in panicles, to 5ft (1.5m) long, in summer, followed by woody, ovoid yellow fruit, to 2in (5cm) long. ↕ to 80ft (25m), ↔ to 28ft (9m). Chile. ❀ (min. 35°F/2°C)

J. spectabilis see *J. chilensis.*

JUGLANS
Walnut

JUGLANDACEAE

Genus of about 15 species of deciduous trees, sometimes shrubs, found in woodland in S.E. Europe, Asia, North America, and N. South America. They have furrowed bark and alternate, pinnate leaves, usually with toothed leaflets. Greenish yellow male and female flowers are borne separately on the same plant in late spring and early summer: males in pendulous catkins and females inconspicuous. Fruits are ovoid or spherical, initially green, ripening to brown, and contain edible nuts with hard, thin or thick, furrowed shells. Cultivated for their habit, foliage, and nuts, walnuts are fine specimen trees.

• **CULTIVATION** Grow in deep, fertile, well-drained soil, preferably in full sun. Avoid frost pockets. Plant out as seedlings or young grafted plants when no more than 12–24in (30–60cm) tall. Pruning group 1; formative pruning and removal of damaged branches should be carried out in late summer to prevent bleeding.

• **PROPAGATION** Sow seed in a seedbed as soon as ripe, or stratify and then sow in spring. Named cultivars of *J. regia* and *J. nigra* are usually grafted onto seedling stocks.

• **PESTS AND DISEASES** Borers, mites, caterpillars (including fall webworm), leaf rollers, aphids, scale insects, nematodes, anthracnose, dieback and canker, mushroom root rot, white mold, and bacterial blight are common.

J. ailantifolia ▣ syn. *J. sieboldiana* (Japanese walnut). Spreading tree with thick shoots and pinnate leaves, to 24in (60cm), each with 11–17 oblong to elliptic, glossy, bright green leaflets and sticky, ovoid fruit, to 2in (5cm) long. ↕↔ 40ft (15m). Japan. Zone 4b. **var. *cordiformis***, syn. *J. cordiformis,* (Heartnut) has narrower leaflets.

J. californica (Californian walnut). Spreading tree or shrub bears pinnate leaves, to 8in (20cm) long, each with 11–15 oblong-lance-shaped leaflets and spherical fruit, to ½in (1.5cm) long. ↕↔ 30ft (10m). S. California. Zone 8.

J. cinerea (Butternut). Vigorous, spreading tree with pinnate leaves, to 20in (50cm) long, each with 7–19 oblong-lance-shaped, aromatic, bright green leaflets. Grown for its sweet, edible nuts, contained within large, clustered, ovoid fruit, to 2½in (6cm) long. ↕ 80ft (25m), ↔ 70ft (20m). E. North America. Zone 3.

J. cordiformis see *J. ailantifolia* var. *cordiformis.*

J. mandshurica (Manchurian walnut). Spreading, suckering tree bears stout shoots and pinnate leaves, to 24in (60cm) long, each with 9–17 oblong, glossy leaflets and sticky, ovoid fruit, to 2in (5cm) long. ↕↔ 70ft (20m). N.E. China, Korea. Zone 3b.

J. microcarpa, syn. *J. rupestris* (Little walnut, River walnut). Bushy-headed, spreading tree or shrub with pinnate, aromatic leaves, to 12in (30cm) long, each with 15–23 slender, glossy leaflets, yellow in autumn, and small, spherical fruit, to 1in (2.5cm) long. ↕↔ 30ft (10m). S.W. US, N. Mexico. Zone 6.

Juglans nigra

J. nigra ▣ (Black walnut). Vigorous, spreading tree with pinnate, aromatic leaves, to 24in (60cm) long, each with 11–23 ovate-oblong, glossy, dark green leaflets. Grown for its edible nuts, contained within spherical fruit, to 2in (5cm) long. Chemicals produced by this species may inhibit the growth of other plants growing under or near it. ↕ 100ft (30m), ↔ 70ft (20m). E. US. Zone 3b.

J. regia ▣ (English walnut). Spreading tree with pinnate, aromatic leaves, to 12in (30cm) or more long, each with 5–9 elliptic to ovate, entire or serrate,

Juglans ailantifolia (inset: leaf and flower detail)

Juglans regia

glossy leaflets, bronze-purple when young. Grown for its edible nuts, contained within spherical fruit, to 2in (5cm) long. ↕ 100ft (30m), ↔ 50ft (15m). S.E. Europe to Himalayas, S.W. China, C. Russia. Zone 4.
J. rupestris see *J. microcarpa*.
J. sieboldiana see *J. ailantifolia*.

JUNCUS
Rush

JUNCACEAE

Genus of about 300 species of grass-like, hairless, evergreen or deciduous, rhizomatous perennials, widely distributed throughout the world, but mostly occurring in cool-temperate regions, particularly in heavy, wet, acidic soil. The stems are cylindrical, nodeless, and usually solid, and the leaves, when present, are small and narrow, often reduced to basal sheaths. Unlike grasses and sedges, rushes produce small green or brown flowers with 6 tepals, borne in cymes in midsummer. Ornamental forms include cultivars with twisted or variegated stems. Rushes are suitable for a pond side or bog garden; some thrive in moist garden soil, or in containers.
• **CULTIVATION** Grow in permanently moist, acidic soil in sun or partial shade. *J. effusus* and *J. inflexus* may also be grown in up to 3in (8cm) of water or in boggy soil. *J. inflexus* thrives in heavy, alkaline soil.
• **PROPAGATION** Sow seed at 43–54°F (6–12°C) in spring, or divide from midspring to early summer.
• **PESTS AND DISEASES** Rusts, fungal leaf spots, and stem rots are common.

Juncus effusus 'Spiralis'

J. articulatus (Jointed rush). Variable, tufted or creeping perennial with slender rhizomes and cylindrical stems bearing alternate, flat, often curved or semi-prostrate, faintly jointed, deep green leaves, 32in (80cm) long. Compound cymes of 5–20 clusters of dark brown flowers, ⅛in (3mm) long, are produced from summer to early autumn. ↕ to 32in (80cm). ↔ to 24in (60cm). W. and S. Europe, Asia, North America. Zone 6.
***J. effusus* 'Spiralis'** ■ syn. *J. effusus* f. *spiralis*, *Scirpus lacustris* 'Spiralis' (Corkscrew rush). Densely tufted, leafless perennial with spiralled, shiny, dark green stems, giving a curious, corkscrew effect and forming a rather tangled mass. Small brown flowers, to ⅛in (3mm) long, are produced in loose cymes, to 2in (5cm) long, along the stems throughout summer. Most effective when grown in a container. Excellent for fresh and dried floral arrangements. ↕ 18in (45cm), ↔ 24in (60cm). Zone 6b.
***J. inflexus* 'Afro'** (Hard rush). Densely tufted, leafless perennial, similar to *J. effusus* 'Spiralis', but with spiralled, matte, blue-green stems, and brown flowers, to ⅛in (4mm) long, produced in small, loose cymes toward the ends of the stems from late spring to midsummer. ↕↔ 24in (60cm). Zone 5.

JUNIPERUS syn. SABINA
Juniper

CUPRESSACEAE

Genus of 50–60 species of evergreen, coniferous shrubs and tall trees from dry forest and hillsides throughout the N. hemisphere. Juvenile leaves are usually needle-like or narrowly wedge-shaped, and ¼–½in (0.5–1.5cm) long. Adult leaves are usually scale-like and overlapping, either lying flat along the shoots or spreading, and 1⁄16–¼in (2–6mm) long. In most cases, male and female cones are borne on separate plants: male cones are spherical to ovoid, yellow, and to ¼in (6mm) across; females develop into usually spherical, fleshy, berry-like fruits, ⅛–½in (3–15mm) across, with 1–10 seeds, and are persistent, generally ripening over 2 to 3 years. Junipers tolerate a wide range of soils and conditions, and are useful for hot, sunny sites. Use as specimen plants: the smallest species in a rock garden and the prostrate species as a groundcover. Contact with the foliage may aggravate skin allergies.
• **CULTIVATION** Grow in any well-drained soil, including dry, chalky, or sandy soils, preferably in full sun or in light, dappled shade. Junipers need little, if any, pruning.
• **PROPAGATION** Difficult to propagate from seed; germination may take up to 5 years. Take ripe cuttings in late autumn through winter and root in a humid cold frame, or take softwood cuttings in summer under mist with bottom heat.
• **PESTS AND DISEASES** Leaf miners, bark beetles, scale insects, aphids, mites, and caterpillars, especially bagworms, are common. *Phomopsis* twig blight, *Gymnosporangium* (cedar-apple) rust, dieback and canker, lesion nematodes, brown felt blight, and a variety of heart and wood rots are very common.

J. ashei (Ashe juniper). Shrub or spreading tree with an irregular crown, light ash-gray bark, peeling in strips, and triangular-ovate, scale-like, glaucous, blue-gray leaves in pairs or threes. Produces bluish black fruit with soft, resinous, juicy pulp. ↕↔ to 20ft (6m). S.E. US. Zone 7b.
J. chinensis (Chinese juniper). Ovoid-conical tree to spreading shrub with brown bark, peeling in long strips, and dark green foliage. Narrowly wedge-shaped juvenile leaves have long, sharp points and are borne in pairs or threes; diamond-shaped, scale-like adult leaves are mainly in 4 ranks, lying flat along the stems. Foliage is pungently scented. Bears violet to brown fruit, marked with the outlines of scales. ↕ to 70ft (20m), ↔ to 20ft (6m). China, Mongolia, Japan. Zone 4. **'Aurea'** is a columnar tree with golden yellow leaves, and produces numerous cones in midspring; ↕ to 35ft (11m), ↔ 15ft (5m). **'Blaauw'**, syn. *J.* x *pfitzeriana* 'Blaauw', is a dense, upright shrub with spreading, long-pointed, diamond-shaped, blue-gray leaves; ↕ 4ft (1.2m), ↔ 3ft (1m). **'Hetzii Glauca'** is a semi-erect shrub with light blue leaves; ↕↔ 5–7ft (1.5–2.2m). **'Kaizuka'** is a spreading shrub with dense, irregular growth, bright green leaves, and many glaucous berries; ↕ 20ft (6m), ↔ 10–12ft (3–4m). **'Keteleeri'** is a narrowly conical, dense, regular tree with diamond-shaped, scale-like, dark gray-green leaves; ↕ to 30ft (10m), ↔ 6ft (2m). **'Kuriwao Gold'** is a rounded shrub with bright gold leaves. Requires a site in full sun; ↕↔ 6ft (2m). **'Maney'** is a rounded, semi-erect shrub with linear, glaucous bluish green leaves, well adapted to cold climates; ↕↔ 6ft (2m). **'Mountbatten'** is a dense, narrow, pyramidal shrub with linear, grayish green leaves; ↕ to 12ft (4m). **'Obelisk'** ■ is a slender, erect shrub with long, glaucous, bluish green juvenile leaves, to ½in (1.5cm) long; ↕ to 8ft (2.5m), ↔ 24in (60cm). **'Old Gold'** has bronze-gold leaves, all year; ↕ 3ft (1m), ↔ 4ft (1.2m). **'Pfitzeriana Compacta'** is a bushy, compact shrub with a gray-green tinge; ↕ 24–36in (60–90cm), ↔ to 6ft (2m). **'Robusta Green'** see *J. virginiana* 'Robusta Green'. **'San José'** is a creeping shrub with scale- and needle-like, sage-green foliage; ↕ 12–18in (30–45cm), ↔ 6–8ft (2–2.5m). **'Sea Green'** is a compact, vase-shaped, arching shrub with mint-green leaves;

Juniperus chinensis 'Obelisk'

Juniperus communis 'Compressa'

↕ 4–6ft (1.2–2m), ↔ 6–8ft (2–2.5m). **'Spartan'** is a rapid-growing, tall, dense pyramidal shrub with rich green leaves; ↕ to 20ft (6m), ↔ 5ft (1.5m). Zone 5.
J. communis (Common juniper). Spreading shrub to small, ovoid or columnar tree. Linear, sharply pointed leaves, deep green to blue-green, with single, glaucous white bands on the inner faces, are borne in threes. Ovoid or spherical fruit, green when first produced, ripen to glaucous blue then black over 3 years. ↕ 1½–20ft (0.5–6m) or more, ↔ 3–20ft (1–6m). N. hemisphere. Zone 3. **'Berkshire'** is a dwarf, mound-forming shrub with very sharp, blue-striated, dark green foliage, silver-striped beneath, plum-colored in winter; ↕ 9–12in (23–30cm), ↔ 12–15in (30–38cm). **'Compressa'** ■ is a dwarf, spindle-shaped shrub, which grows very slowly, at ¾–1¼in (2–3cm) per year. Suitable for growing in a trough; ↕ to 32in (80cm), ↔ 18in (45cm). **subsp. *depressa*** is prostrate with upturned shoot tips and leaves with narrow white bands; ↕ to 24in (60cm), ↔ 5ft (1.5m). North America, Greenland. Zone 3. **'Depressa Aurea'** ■ is a spreading shrub with semi-erect branches and golden yellow leaves in late spring, becoming bronze and almost green over winter; ↕ 24in (60cm), ↔ 5ft (1.5m). **'Gold Cone'** is a slow-growing shrub with a narrow column and pale yellow needles; ↕ 3–5ft (1–1.5m), ↔ 1–2ft (30–60cm). **'Prostrata'** is a very vigorous, prostrate, mat-forming shrub with green foliage; ↕ 8–12in (20–30cm), ↔ 5–6ft (1.5–2m).

Juniperus communis 'Depressa Aurea'

J

'Repanda' is a low-growing, rounded shrub with coarse-textured, medium green leaves; ↕ to 15in (38cm), ↔ 6–8ft (2–2.5m). **'Sentinel'** is an upright, spindle-shaped shrub, similar to 'Compressa' but more vigorous; ↕ to 5ft (1.5m), ↔ to 24in (60cm).
J. conferta (Shore juniper). Prostrate shrub with dense, sharply pointed, needle-like, bright green or gray-green leaves, borne in groups of 3. The black fruit have a glaucous bloom. ↕ to 12in (30cm), ↔ indefinite. Japan, Sakhalin. Zone 5. **'Blue Pacific'** ■ is a trailing, prostrate shrub with blue-green leaves; ↕ to 12in (30cm). **'Emerald Sea'** is a wide-spreading, dense, mat-forming shrub with erect stems and emerald-green foliage. Very salt tolerant; ↕ 10in (25cm). **'Silver Mist'** is a spreading, irregularly mounded shrub with thick main branches and short, bluish green sprays of wide, linear leaves, banded silver-white. New growth is tinged red-brown. Salt tolerant; ↕ 12in (30cm).
J. deppeana (Alligator juniper). Broadly conical tree with thick, grooved, gray bark divided into small, square scales. Needle-like, oval-diamond-shaped, blue-green leaves, to ¼in (6mm) long, lie flat along the branches. Spherical to broadly ellipsoid, red-brown fruit, ½in (1.2cm) across, are produced in summer, ripening in the second year. ↕ to 70ft (20m), ↔ to 12ft (4m). S.W. US, Mexico. Zone 7b. **'Silver Spire'** is a narrowly columnar shrub or tree with ash-gray bark and bright silver foliage. Juvenile leaves are borne in whorls of 2 or 3; diamond-shaped adult leaves lie flat along the stems in 4 ranks. Bears

J

Juniperus conferta 'Blue Pacific'

Juniperus drupacea

reddish brown fruit with dry, fibrous pulp; ↕ to 30ft (10m), rarely 70ft (20m), ↔ 10–15ft (3–5m).
J. drupacea ■ (Syrian juniper). Usually columnar tree with orange-brown bark peeling in strips. Narrowly wedge-shaped leaves, ½–1in (1–2.5cm) long, with long, sharp points, are gray-green with 2 white bands, and borne in whorls of 3. Produces ovoid or spherical green fruit maturing to dark blue, then brown, ¾–1in (2–2.5cm) across. ↕ to 50ft (15m), ↔ to 10ft (3m). S. Greece, Turkey, Syria. Zone 7b.
***J.* 'Grey Owl'**, syn. *J. virginiana* 'Grey Owl'. Large, spreading shrub with horizontal branches and arching, oval-diamond-shaped, scale-like, soft, silver-gray leaves. Bears ovoid, glaucous, brownish violet fruit, which ripen in the first autumn. ↕ 6–10ft (2–3m), ↔ 10–12ft (3–4m). Zone 2b.
***J.* 'Hetz'** see *J. virginiana* 'Hetzii'.
J. horizontalis (Creeping juniper). Prostrate, creeping shrub with gray-green foliage. Needle-like juvenile leaves, with long, sharp points, are borne in pairs or in threes; elliptic, scale-like adult leaves, each with a prominent gland on the back, lie flat along the shoots in 4 rows. Bears ovoid, dark blue fruit. ↕ to 12in (30cm), ↔ indefinite. North America. Zone 2. **'Andorra'** see 'Plumosa'. **'Bar Harbor'** has gray-green leaves, which become mauve-purple in winter. **'Blue Chip'** has very blue summer foliage, tipped purple in winter; ↕ 8–10in (20–25cm), ↔ 8–10ft (2.5–3m). **'Douglasii'** (Waukegan juniper) has a flat, mat-like habit with ascending side branches and glaucous,

Juniperus x *pfitzeriana* 'Aurea'

Juniperus x *pfitzeriana* 'Blue and Gold'

bright green leaves, purple-bronzed in winter. **'Emerald Spreader'** is a very flat shrub with emerald-green juvenile leaves. **'Hughes'** has silvery blue leaves; ↕ 12in (30cm), ↔ 9ft (2.5m). **'Plumosa'**, syn. 'Andorra', has blue- to gray-green leaves. Very susceptible to blight; ↕ 24in (60cm), ↔ 10ft (3m). **'Prince of Wales'** has scale-like, bright green leaves with a blue, waxy bloom, purple in winter; ↕ 4–6in (10–15cm), ↔ 8–10ft (2.5–3m). **'Turquoise Spreader'** is a flat shrub with greenish blue juvenile leaves. **'Wiltonii'** (Blue rug juniper) is glaucous with bright blue-green leaves.
J.* x *media see *J.* x *pfitzeriana.*
***J.* x *media* 'Hetzii'** see *J. virginiana* 'Hetzii'.
J. occidentalis (Western juniper). Spreading shrub or small tree with grooved, peeling, rust-brown bark, and horizontal to pendulous branches. Scale-like, diamond-shaped, pointed, glaucous green leaves, are borne in pairs or threes, and lie flat along the shoots. Rounded, glaucous, dark blue fruit, to ½in (1.5cm) across, are borne singly and ripen in two years. ↕ to 40ft (12m), ↔ 3–10ft (1–3m). S.E. Washington to N.E. California. Zone 6.
J.* x *pfitzeriana, syn. *J.* x *media.* Spreading, male shrub with branches ascending at an angle of 45°, gradually forming a flat-topped bush with tiered foliage. Diamond-shaped, scale-like, gray-green leaves, with free tips, lie flat along the shoots. The spherical fruit are initially dark purple, becoming paler later. ↕ 4ft (1.2m), ↔ 10ft (3m). Garden origin. Zone 4. **'Armstrongii'** has soft, yellow-green leaves; ↕↔ to 3ft (1m).

Juniperus procumbens

Juniperus recurva

'Aurea' ■ has golden yellow leaves which become yellowish green over winter; ↕ 36in (90cm), ↔ 6ft (2m). **'Blaauw'** see *J. chinensis* 'Blaauw'. **'Blue and Gold'** ■ has patches of blue-green foliage intermingled with bright yellow; ↕ 5ft (1.5m), ↔ 6–10ft (2–3m). **'Glauca'** has prickly, silver to grayish blue leaves; ↕ 36in (90cm), ↔ 6ft (2m). **'Gold Coast'** is compact with deep chrome-yellow leaves which retain their color in winter; ↕↔ 36in (90cm). **'Golden Saucer'** has bright golden yellow leaves, especially in winter; ↕ 3–5ft (1–1.5m), ↔ 12in (30cm).
J. procumbens ■ (Bonin Island juniper). Spreading, procumbent shrub with mostly linear, needle-like, sharply pointed, yellow-green leaves in threes. Bears brown or black fruit. ↕ to 30in (75cm), ↔ to 6ft (2m). S. Japan. Zone 4. **'Nana'** (Japanese garden juniper) is dwarf, compact, and mat-forming with layered sprays of branches and leaves that become slightly purple in winter; ↕ 12in (30cm), ↔ 6ft (2m).
J. recurva ■ (Himalayan weeping juniper). Conical or broadly columnar tree with smooth, orange-brown bark, which peels in strips and is fissured in old trees. Narrowly wedge-shaped, gray-green leaves, ⅛–¼in (3–6mm) long, produced in threes and pointing forward along the shoots, are borne in pendulous sprays. Bears spherical or ovoid, greenish brown to black fruit, each with a single seed. ↕ to 30ft (10m), ↔ to 15ft (5m). Himalayas to W. China. Zone 7.
var. *coxii* (Coffin juniper) has longer and more widely spaced, rich, dark green leaves, ¼–⅜in (6–8mm) long. Burma.

Juniperus rigida

'Densa', syn. 'Nana', is a dwarf, conical, low-growing, spreading shrub with ascending branch tips and dark green leaves. ↕ 24in (60cm), ↔ 4ft (1.2m). **'Nana'** see 'Densa'.
J. rigida ▣ (Needle juniper). Spreading tree or large shrub with peeling brown to yellow-brown bark and an open crown of pendulous branches bearing groups of 3 needle-like, sharply pointed, bright green leaves, glaucous on the inner face, and ½–1in (1.5–2.5cm) long. Bears purplish black fruit. ↕ to 25ft (8m) or more, ↔ to 20ft (6m). N. China, Korea, Japan. Zone 4b.
J. sabina (Savin juniper). Spreading, occasionally erect shrub with flaking, red-brown bark and slender, 4-sided shoots. Mainly adult leaves, borne in pairs lying flat along the stems, are ovate, scale-like, and dark green to gray-green, each with a small gland on the back, and a fetid odor when crushed. Flattened, spherical fruit, bluish black with white blooms, ripen over the first winter. ↕ 6–15ft (2–5m), ↔ to 20ft (6m). C. Europe to N. China. Zone 2. **'Arcadia'** is dense and layered, with scale-like, green leaves. Resistant to juniper blight; ↕ 12–18in (30–45cm), ↔ 4ft (1.2m). **'Blaue Donau'**, syn. 'Blue Danube', is very hardy, with shoots erect at the tips and light grayish blue leaves; ↕ 24in (60cm), ↔ 6ft (2m). **'Blue Danube'** see 'Blaue Donau'. **'Broadmoor'** has horizontally aligned main branches and short, ascending branchlet sprays with grayish green leaves. Resistant to juniper blight; ↕ 24–36in (60–90cm), ↔ 10ft (3m). **'Buffalo'** has feathery branches and

Juniperus scopulorum 'Skyrocket'

bright green foliage. Retains good color in winter; ↕ 12in (30cm), ↔ 8ft (2.5m). **'Calgary Carpet'** is lower and more spreading, with soft green leaves; ↕ 6–9in (15–23cm), ↔ to 10ft (3m). **'Skandia'** is compact and densely layered with mostly linear, pale grayish green foliage. Resistant to juniper blight; ↕ 12–18in (30–45cm), ↔ 10ft (3m).
var. *tamariscifolia* ▣ (Tamarisk juniper) is low-growing, with horizontal tiers of spreading, short, sharply pointed, mainly juvenile, bright green or bluish green leaves borne in pairs or threes. ↕ to 3–6ft (1–2m), ↔ 5–6ft (1.5–2m).
J. sargentii (Sargent juniper). Creeping shrub with prostrate, flexuous stems, short branchlets, and mostly ovate, camphor-scented, scale-like, bluish green leaves. Other, dark blue-green leaves are borne in pairs and lie flat to the branches. Juvenile leaves are needle-like, in whorls of 3. Bears dark blue or black fruit. ↕ to 12in (30cm), ↔ indefinite. N.E. China, N.E. Asia, Japan, Sakhalin. Zone 3.
J. scopulorum (Rocky Mountain juniper). Rounded or spreading tree or shrub with red-brown bark, furrowed into strips or square flakes. Paired, ovate,

Juniperus squamata 'Blue Star'

sharp-pointed, scale-like, yellow-green to dark green leaves lie flat to the branches. Bears blue-black fruit. ↕ to 50ft (15m), ↔ to 20ft (6m). Rocky Mountains. Zone 3. **'Blue Heaven'** is a shrub of conical habit and blue-green leaves; ↕ 6ft (2m), ↔ to 24in (60cm). **'Skyrocket'** ▣ syn. *J. virginiana* 'Skyrocket', is a narrow, pencil-shaped tree with glaucous, gray-green leaves; ↕ to 20ft (6m), ↔ 20–24in (50–60cm). **'Springbank'** is a narrow, conical tree with pendent branch tips and intensely silver-blue leaves; ↕ to 6ft (2m), ↔ to 24in (60cm). **'Table Top'** is a spreading shrub with blue leaves and many berries; ↕ to 6ft (2m), ↔ 15ft (5m). **'Tolleson's Blue Weeping'** is a grafted, tree-like shrub with arching branches and pendent, string-like silver-blue foliage; ↕ 20ft (6m), ↔ 10ft (3m).

'Wichita Blue' is a broadly conical tree with bright blue-gray leaves; ↕ to 6ft (2m), ↔ 32in (80cm).
J. squamata (Singleseed juniper). Prostrate shrub, spreading bush, or small upright tree with flaky, rust-brown bark. Spreading, narrowly wedge-shaped, sharply pointed, entirely juvenile leaves, dark gray-green to silvery blue-green, each with a bright blue-white band, are borne in whorls of 3. Bears ovoid, glossy black fruit. ↕ to 30ft (10m), ↔ 3–25ft (1–8m). Mountains of N.E. Afghanistan, Himalayas, W. and C. China. Zone 5. **'Blue Carpet'** is a prostrate shrub with bluish gray-green leaves; ↕ 8–12in (20–30cm), ↔ 4–5ft (1.2–1.5m). **'Blue Star'** ▣ is a compact, rounded bush, with silvery blue leaves; ↕ to 16in (40cm), ↔ to 36in (90cm). **'Holger'** is a spreading shrub with sulfur-yellow new growth contrasting with steel-blue older leaves; ↕↔ 6ft (2m). **'Meyeri'** ▣ is a spreading shrub with arching and nodding shoot tips and glaucous blue leaves. Dead foliage often persists, marring its appearance; ↕ 12–30ft (4–10m), ↔ 20–25ft (6–8m).
J. virginiana (Pencil cedar, Red cedar). Variable, columnar to broad-spreading tree producing brown bark with narrow, spiral ridges, peeling in shreds. Both the narrowly wedge-shaped, sharply pointed juvenile leaves and the diamond-shaped, scale-like adult leaves are gray-green, borne in pairs on the same shoots, and lie flat along the branches. Ovoid, glaucous, brown-violet fruit ripen in the first autumn. ↕ 50–100ft (15–30m), ↔ 15–25ft (5–8m). E. and C. North America. Zone 3.

Juniperus sabina var. *tamariscifolia*

Juniperus squamata 'Meyeri' (inset: leaf detail)

'Burkii' is a dense, upright tree with blue-gray leaves, which become purple-tinged over winter; ↕ to 20ft (6m), ↔ 36in (1m). **'Grey Owl'** see *J.* 'Grey Owl'. **'Hetzii'**, syn. 'Hetz', *J.* 'Hetz', *J.* x *media* 'Hetzii', is an open shrub with tiers of spreading, blue-green leaves on ascending branches. Produces spherical, blue-purple to brown fruit; ↕ 12–15ft (4–5m), ↔ to 10–15ft (3–5m). **'Robusta Green'**, syn. *J. chinensis* 'Robusta Green', is a narrow, columnar tree with blue-green leaves; ↕ to 10ft (3m), ↔ 24in (60cm). **'Skyrocket'** see *J. scopulorum* 'Skyrocket'.

▷ ***Jussiaea longifolia*** see *Ludwigia longifolia*

▷ ***Jussiaea repens*** see *Ludwigia peploides*

JUSTICIA *syn.* BELOPERONE, DREJERELLA, DUVERNOIA, LIBONIA

ACANTHACEAE

J

Genus of about 420 species of evergreen perennials, shrubs, and subshrubs from a wide range of habitats in tropical and subtropical regions worldwide and from temperate North America. The opposite, usually simple leaves are ovate to elliptic and often boldly veined. Justicias are grown mainly for their slender, tubular flowers, which have narrow, arching lips and are produced with conspicuous bracts, in terminal or axillary racemes, cymes, or panicles. Where temperatures fall below 45°F (7°C), grow in a temperate greenhouse or as houseplants. In milder climates, plant in a mixed border.

• **CULTIVATION** Under glass, grow in draft-free conditions in soil-based potting mix with bright filtered light, or full light with shade from hot sun. Provide high humidity, although *J. brandegeeana* and *J. rizzinii* tolerate lower humidity. In the growing season, water freely and apply a balanced liquid fertilizer every 4 weeks; keep just moist in winter. Pot on in spring. Outdoors, grow in fertile, moist but well-drained soil in partial shade. Pruning group 9; tip-prune young plants to promote bushiness. Plants under glass need hard restrictive pruning in late winter; replace when they become leggy.

• **PROPAGATION** Sow seed at 61°F (16°C) in spring. Root softwood or semi-ripe cuttings with bottom heat from late spring to midsummer.

• **PESTS AND DISEASES** Whiteflies and spider mites may be problems under glass. Bacterial and fungal leaf spots and rust may occur.

Justicia adhatoda (inset: flower detail)

J. adhatoda ■ syn. *Adhatoda duvernoia, Duvernoia adhatodoides.* Usually erect and sparsely branched, evergreen shrub, spreading with age, with ovate-elliptic, mid- to deep green leaves, 4–8in (10–20cm) long. Terminal and axillary spikes, 2in (5cm) or more long, of 2-lipped white flowers, 1¼in (3cm) long, appear mainly in summer. The lower lips are veined red or rose-purple. ↕ 6–10ft (2–3m), ↔ 3–5ft (1–1.5m). India, Sri Lanka. ❀ (min. 45°F/7°C)

J. brandegeeana ■ syn. *Beloperone guttata, Drejerella guttata, Justicia guttata* (False hop, Shrimp bush, Shrimp plant). Moderately bushy, soft, evergreen shrub, of rounded habit if regularly tip-pruned, with downy stems and ovate or elliptic leaves, 1–3in (2.5–8cm) long, lustrous mid-green above, downy beneath. Elongated, hop-like, arching to pendent, terminal and axillary spikes, 4in (10cm) or more long, with overlapping, shrimp-pink bracts and slender, tongue-like white flowers, 1¼in (3cm) long, are borne throughout the year. The lower lips are marked with purple or red. ↕ to 36in (90cm), ↔ 24–36in (60–90cm). Mexico. ❀ (min. 45°F/7°C). **'Chartreuse'** has bright, lime-green bracts. **var. *lutea*** see 'Yellow Queen'. **'Yellow Queen'**, syn. var. *lutea*, has glowing yellow bracts.

J. californica (Chuparosa honeysuckle, California beloperone). Arching, deciduous subshrub with brittle, green-white hairy branches, leafless or with ovate, entire, softly hairy, gray-green leaves, ¼in (6mm) long. In early spring, produces axillary spikes, to 2in (5cm) long, with inconspicuous, awl-shaped bracts and tubular red flowers, 1½in (4cm) long. Very drought tolerant. ↕ to 5ft (1.5m), ↔ 4ft (1.2m). Desert areas of Arizona, S. California, Baja California. Zone 6b.

J. carnea ■ syn. *Jacobinia carnea, J. pohliana, J. velutina, Justicia pohliana* (Brazilian plume, King's crown). Erect, sparsely branched, evergreen shrub with robust, 4-angled or 4-ridged stems, and oblong to ovate, mid-green leaves, to 10in (25cm) long, sometimes with short, velvety hairs. Dense, terminal and axillary spikes, 4–6in (10–15cm) long, of overlapping green bracts, largely obscured by tubular, 2-lipped, pink to rose- or purple-pink flowers, 2in (5cm)

Justicia rizzinii

long, are produced during summer and autumn. ↕ to 6ft (2m), ↔ to 3ft (1m). N. South America. ❀ (min. 45°F/7°C)

J. coccinea see *Pachystachys coccinea.*

J. floribunda see *J. rizzinii.*

***J. ghiesbreghtiana* of gardens** see *J. spicigera.*

J. guttata see *J. brandegeeana.*

J. pauciflora see *J. rizzinii.*

J. pohliana see *J. carnea.*

J. rizzinii ■ syn. *Jacobinia pauciflora, Justicia floribunda, J. pauciflora, Libonia floribunda.* Dwarf, soft, evergreen shrub of rounded habit, with downy stems bearing oblong to broadly obovate, mid-green leaves, to ¾in (2cm) long. One of each pair of leaves is smaller than the other. Small, nodding axillary racemes, 1¼in (3cm) wide, of tubular yellow and scarlet flowers, ¾in (2cm) long, are produced from autumn to late spring. ↕↔ 12–24in (30–60cm). Brazil. ❀ (min. 45°F/7°C)

J. spicigera ■ syn. *Jacobinia spicigera, Justicia ghiesbreghtiana* of gardens. Freely branching, rounded, softly hairy, evergreen shrub, with 4-angled stems and oblong-lance-shaped to ovate, arching, sometimes shallowly toothed, matte green leaves, 3–7in (8–18cm) long. Tubular crimson to orange flowers, 1¼–1½in (3–4cm) long, are borne in small, forking, one-sided, terminal and axillary racemes, to 5in (13cm) long, from autumn to spring. The lower lips of the flowers are recurved or coiled. ↕ 3–6ft (1–1.8m), ↔ 2½–4ft (75–120cm). Mexico, Central America to Colombia. ❀ (min. 45°F/7°C)

J. suberecta see *Dicliptera suberecta.*

Justicia brandegeeana

Justicia carnea

Justicia spicigera

K

KADSURA

SCHISANDRACEAE

Genus of about 20 species of woody, twining, evergreen climbers from forest in E. and S.E. Asia. They are grown for their fleshy fruits and attractive, simple, glossy leaves, arranged alternately. Solitary, cup-shaped flowers are usually produced in the leaf axils; both male and female flowers, borne on separate plants, are required to produce the fruits. *K. japonica*, the only species commonly cultivated, is best grown in a sheltered position where it can be trained against a wall or pillar, or through a large shrub.

• **CULTIVATION** Grow in fertile, moist but well-drained soil in full sun or partial shade. Pruning group 12, in winter.

• **PROPAGATION** Take semi-ripe cuttings in summer.

• **PESTS AND DISEASES** Infrequent.

K. japonica. Vigorous, evergreen climber with twining shoots and elliptic to ovate-lance-shaped, slightly toothed, glossy, dark green leaves, to 4in (10cm) long. Small, solitary, cup-shaped, yellowish white flowers, ¾in (2cm) across, are produced from summer to autumn, followed on female plants by red, blackberry-like fruit, 1¼in (3cm) across. ↕ 12ft (4m). China, Korea, Taiwan, Japan. Zone 7b. **'Variegata'** has leaves that are broadly margined with creamy yellow and tinged pink, becoming creamy white in winter.

KAEMPFERIA

ZINGIBERACEAE

Genus of about 40 species of aromatic, rhizomatous perennials from forest in tropical Asia. The leaves are simple and either 2-ranked on short stems or in basal clusters. White, pink, or lilac, 3-petaled flowers, each with a deeply 2-lobed lip, are borne in terminal spikes on short, leafy or scaly stems and are often fragrant. Where not hardy, grow in a warm greenhouse; in tropical and subtropical regions, use outdoors as a groundcover.

• **CULTIVATION** Under glass, grow in soil-based potting mix in bright filtered light. In growth, maintain moderate humidity and water freely, applying a balanced liquid fertilizer every 2 or 3 weeks. Keep completely dry in winter. Outdoors, grow in well-drained, humus-rich soil in partial shade.

• **PROPAGATION** Sow seed at 68°F (20°C) as soon as ripe, or divide rhizomes in spring.

• **PESTS AND DISEASES** Infrequent.

K. pulchra ■ Low-growing, rhizomatous perennial with broadly elliptic, dark green leaves, about 6in (15cm) long, sometimes with silver

Kaempferia pulchra

markings. In summer, produces short spikes, to 2in (5cm) long, of 3-petaled, lilac or lilac-pink flowers, 1½in (4cm) across, amid the foliage. ↕ 6in (15cm), ↔ 12in (30cm). Thailand, Malaysia. ❄ (min. 50°F/10°C)

K. roscoeana (Dwarf ginger lily, Peacock lily). Low-growing, rhizomatous perennial with usually 2 rounded leaves, 4in (10cm) across, deep green with lighter green markings above, mid-green, tinged red beneath. From summer to autumn, bears short spikes, 2in (5cm) long, of 3-petaled white flowers, 1–2in (2.5–5cm) across, amid the foliage. ↕ 6in (15cm), ↔ 8in (20cm). Burma. ❄ (min. 50°F/10°C)

K. rotunda (Resurrection lily). Erect, rhizomatous perennial with lance-shaped leaves, to 16in (40cm) long, with long, sharp points, silver-green and unmarked above, purple beneath. In summer, produces spikes, 3in (8cm) long, of up to 6 lilac-lipped, 3-petaled white flowers, 2in (5cm) across, above the foliage. ↕ 6in (15cm), ↔ 18in (45cm). S.E. Asia. ❄ (min. 50°F/10°C)

KALANCHOE

syn. BRYOPHYLLUM

CRASSULACEAE

Genus of about 130 species of annual, biennial, and perennial succulents, shrubs, climbers, and small trees, occurring in semi-desert or shady areas of Saudi Arabia, Yemen (including Socotra), C. Africa, South Africa, Madagascar, Asia, Australia, and tropical America. Some are tree-like or shrubby; others are more spreading in habit. All have fleshy stems bearing simple to 2-pinnatisect, rarely pinnate, toothed or scalloped, fleshy leaves, arranged in opposite pairs, rarely alternate or whorled. Diurnal, showy, bell-shaped, urn-shaped, or tubular, 4-lobed flowers, often swollen in the middle or at the bases, are borne in terminal, occasionally lateral, cyme-like or corymb-like panicles. Where temperatures drop below 54°F (12°C), grow as houseplants or in a temperate or warm greenhouse; some spreading species, such as *K. pumila* and *K. uniflora*, are particularly effective in a hanging basket. In warmer climates, grow outdoors in a shrub border or in beds.

• **CULTIVATION** Under glass, grow in soil-based potting mix with additional grit, in bright filtered light. During the growing season, water moderately and

Kalanchoe beharensis

apply a balanced liquid fertilizer 3 or 4 times; keep just moist in winter. Outdoors, grow in well-drained, humus-rich, moderately fertile soil in partial shade. See also pp.48–49.

• **PROPAGATION** Sow seed at 70°F (21°C) in early spring. Remove offsets and plantlets from leaves or inflorescences, or take stem cuttings, in spring or summer.

• **PESTS AND DISEASES** Prone to mealybugs and aphids. Susceptible to powdery mildew, leaf spots, crown and root rots, a variety of virus diseases, bacterial soft rot, and fasciation.

K. beharensis ■ (Felt bush, Velvet leaf). Bushy, often tree-like, perennial succulent with broadly triangular to lance-shaped, slightly toothed, long-stalked leaves, to 14in (35cm) long, usually concave and brown above, convex and silvery beneath, and covered with minute, fine, silver or golden hairs. In late winter, mature plants produce many lateral, cyme-like panicles of urn-shaped, green-yellow flowers, ¼in (6mm) long, which are violet-veined inside. ↕↔ 3ft (1m) or more. Madagascar. ❄ (min. 50°F/10°C)

Kalanchoe daigremontiana

K. blossfeldiana ■ Bushy, perennial succulent with oval to oblong-ovate, softly toothed, glossy, dark green leaves, 3in (8cm) long, on long stalks. Tubular scarlet flowers, ½in (1.5cm) long, are borne in early spring, mostly in crowded, corymb-like panicles. ↕↔ to 16in (40cm). Madagascar. ❄ (min. 54°F/12°C). Many cultivars have been developed, with flowers in white, yellow, pink, and other colors.

K. daigremontiana ■ syn. *Bryophyllum daigremontianum* (Devil's backbone, Mexican hat plant). Erect, perennial succulent with lance-shaped leaves, 6–8in (15–20cm) long, usually spotted reddish brown, that produce adventitious plantlets on the toothed margins. Pendent, broadly tubular, grayish violet flowers, to ¾in (2cm) long, are produced in cyme-like panicles in winter. ↕ 3ft (1m), ↔ 12in (30cm). S.W. Madagascar. ❄ (min. 50°F/10°C)

K. delagoensis, syn. *Bryophyllum tubiflorum, Kalanchoe tubiflora* (Chandelier plant). Erect, sparsely branched, perennial succulent with almost cylindrical leaves, to 6in (15cm) long, gray-green, spotted reddish brown; leaves have notched tips that produce

Kalanchoe blossfeldiana

K

Kalanchoe fedtschenkoi 'Variegata'

adventitious plantlets. In late winter and early spring, bears cyme-like panicles of pendent, tubular-bell-shaped, purple-gray to pale orange-yellow flowers, to ¾in (2cm) or more long. ↕ 3ft (1m) or more, ↔ 12in (30cm) or more. Madagascar. ❀ (min. 50°F/10°C)
K. eriophylla. Bushy, perennial succulent with slender stems covered with white hairs, except at the bases. Bears ovate-oblong, very thick, white-woolly, mid-green leaves, 1¼in (3cm) long. Young leaves may have red tips. In spring, bears narrowly bell-shaped, blue-violet flowers, 2½in (6cm) long, in more or less erect, corymb-like panicles. ↕↔ 8in (20cm). Madagascar. ❀ (min. 59°F/15°C)
K. fedtschenkoi. Upright to decumbent, perennial succulent bearing hairless, obovate to oblong, blue-green leaves, ½–2½in (1–6cm) long, each with 2–8 prominent teeth. Pendent, bell-shaped, dull red or purple flowers, to ¾in (2cm) long, are produced in small, loose, corymb-like panicles in summer. ↕ 20in (50cm), ↔ 10in (25cm). Madagascar. ❀ (min. 54°F/12°C). **'Variegata'** ■ is bushy or semi-erect, with scalloped leaves margined creamy white and often flushed pink and mottled yellow. ↕↔ 20in (50cm).
K. grandiflora. Erect, perennial succulent with ovate to obovate, weakly scalloped, glaucous, mid-green leaves, 1½–4in (4–10cm) long. Tubular, bright yellow flowers, ½in (1.5cm) long, are borne in compact, cyme-like panicles in summer. ↕ 32in (80cm), ↔ 16in (40cm). S. India. ❀ (min. 50°F/10°C)
K. laciniata, syn. *K. schweinfurthii.* Erect, perennial succulent with pinnatisect, occasionally pinnate, hairless, mid-green leaves, to 8in (20cm) long, each with 3–5 entire or lobed, ovate to elliptic segments. In summer, produces corymb-like panicles of tubular, greenish white to pale orange flowers, ⅜–½in (0.8–1.5cm) long. ↕ 4ft (1.2m), ↔ 24in (60cm). Namibia to Ethiopia, S. India, Thailand. ❀ (min. 50°F/10°C)
K. manginii. Semi-erect then pendent, free-branching, perennial succulent with obovate to ovate-spoon-shaped, entire or notched, mid-green leaves, 1¼in (3cm) long, minutely hairy when young. In spring, bears few-flowered, cyme-like panicles of tubular, urn-shaped, bright red flowers, ¾–1¼in (2–3cm) or more long. ↕↔ 12in (30cm). Madagascar. ❀ (min. 54°F/12°C)
K. marmorata, syn. *K. somaliensis.* (Pen-wiper). Erect or decumbent, perennial succulent, branching from the base, bearing obovate, toothed, gray-frosted leaves, 2½–8in (6–20cm) long, with large, purple-brown marks. In spring, bears cyme-like panicles of narrowly tubular, erect, white, sometimes pink- or yellow-tinged flowers, 2½–3in (6–8cm) long. ↕↔ to 16in (40cm). Sudan to Zaire, Ethiopia, Somalia. ❀ (min. 54°F/12°C)
K. pumila. Semi-pendent, spreading, succulent subshrub with ovate to obovate, chalky, white-frosted, mid-green leaves, to 1½in (4cm) long, narrowing toward the bases, and with toothed margins at the tips. Urn-shaped flowers, ½in (1.5cm) long, pink with purple lines, are borne in few-flowered, corymb-like panicles in spring. ↕ 8in (20cm), ↔ to 18in (45cm). Madagascar. ❀ (min. 54°F/12°C)
K. schweinfurthii see *K. laciniata.*
K. somaliensis see *K. marmorata.*
***K.* 'Tessa'** ■ Pendent, perennial succulent bearing narrowly oval, mid-green leaves, 1¼in (3cm) long, with red margins. In late winter and early spring, produces cyme-like panicles of pendent, tubular, orange-red flowers, ¾in (2cm) long. ↕ 12in (30cm), ↔ 24in (60cm). ❀ (min. 54°F/12°C)
K. thyrsiflora. Bushy, white-frosted, perennial succulent, increasing by offsets. It is densely covered with oval to inversely lance-shaped, red-margined, pale green leaves, 4–6in (10–15cm) long, with blunt, rounded tips and leaf pairs united at the bases. In spring, bears cyme-like panicles of erect to spreading, tubular to urn-shaped, fragrant yellow flowers, ½–¾in (1–2cm) long. ↕ 24in (60cm), ↔ 12in (30cm). South Africa (Northern Cape, Western Cape, Eastern Cape). ❀ (min. 54°F/12°C)
K. tomentosa (Panda plant, Plush plant, Pussy ears). Erect, bushy, densely white-felted, perennial succulent with thick, oblong, entire gray leaves, ¾–3½in (2–9cm) long, coarsely toothed at the

Kalanchoe 'Tessa'

Kalanchoe 'Wendy'

tips, grooved above, and often finely margined reddish brown with furry silver hairs. Bell-shaped, green-yellow flowers, ½in (1.5cm) long, with red glandular hairs and lobes tinged purple, are borne in cyme-like panicles in early spring. ↕ to 3ft (1m), ↔ 8in (20cm). Madagascar. ❀ (min. 54°F/12°C)
K. tubiflora see *K. delagoensis.*
K. uniflora, syn. *Bryophyllum uniflorum.* Prostrate, perennial succulent with rounded, mid-green leaves, ⅛–½in (4–15mm) long, convex on both sides, and with a few uneven, rounded teeth. Pendent, urn-shaped, red to purple flowers, ½–¾in (1–2cm) long, are borne in few-flowered, corymb-like panicles in summer. ↕ 6in (15cm), ↔ 24in (60cm). Madagascar. ❀ (min. 50°F/10°C)
***K.* 'Wendy'** ■ Pendent to semi-erect, perennial succulent with ovate to oblong-ovate, slightly scalloped, glossy, mid-green leaves, to 3in (8cm) long. Corymb-like panicles of bell-shaped, orange- to yellow-tipped, purple-red flowers, 1¼in (3cm) long, are borne in late winter and early spring. ↕↔ 12in (30cm). ❀ (min. 50°F/10°C)

KALIMERIS

ASTERACEAE

Genus of 10 species of upright, leafy perennials from damp habitats of E. Asia. They have alternate, linear-ovate to elliptic, sometimes toothed or pinnatifid leaves, and are grown for their panicles of white, or sometimes violet- or pink-tinged flowerheads. They are best suited to a wild or informal border.
• **CULTIVATION** Grow in moderately fertile, moist soil in sun or partial shade; stake when grown in exposed sites.
• **PROPAGATION** Sow seed *in situ* when ripe; divide in spring or summer to maintain vigor.
• **PESTS AND DISEASES** Infrequent.

K. mongolica. Upright perennial with oblong, deeply pinnatifid, mid-green lower leaves, to 16in (40cm) long, and linear, entire, stalkless upper leaves, to 1in (2.5cm) long. In summer, produces panicles of purple-tinged, white flowerheads, 1in (2.5cm) across, with yellow disk florets. ↕ to 36in (90cm), ↔ 18in (45cm). Mongolia. Zone 6.
***K. pinnatifida* 'Hortensia'.** Upright, bushy perennial with oblong to ovate-oblong, pinnatifid, softly hairy, mid-green lower leaves, to 3in (8cm) long, with linear-lance-shaped, entire upper leaves, to 1in (2.5cm) long. From midsummer to autumn, bears panicles of semi-double white flowerheads, 1in (2.5cm) across, with yellow disk florets. ↕↔ 24in (60cm). Zone 6.

KALMIA

ERICACEAE

Genus of 7 species of evergreen shrubs found in woodland, swamps, and meadows in North America and Cuba. They have leathery leaves, which may be alternate, in opposite pairs, or in whorls, and showy, bowl-, cup-, or saucer-shaped flowers borne in corymbs or racemes. They are useful for a shrub border or woodland garden; the dwarf species and cultivars are suitable for a large rock garden. All parts may cause severe discomfort if ingested.
• **CULTIVATION** Grow in moist, humus-rich, acidic soil in partial shade, or in sun where soils remain reliably moist. Mulch annually in spring with leaf mold or pine needles. Pruning group 8. *K. angustifolia* tolerates hard pruning; renovate all other species over several seasons.
• **PROPAGATION** Sow seed at 43–54°F (6–12°C) in spring. Take greenwood cuttings in late spring, and take semi-ripe cuttings in midsummer. Layer in late summer.
• **PESTS AND DISEASES** Fungal leaf spots and blights, leaf gall, powdery mildew, weevils, scale insects, lace bugs, and borers sometimes cause problems.

K. angustifolia ■ (Lambkill, Sheep laurel, Wicky). Mound-forming shrub with oblong to elliptic, dark green leaves, to 2½in (6cm) long, in opposite pairs or whorls of 3. Small, bowl- or cup-shaped, pale to deep red, occasionally white flowers, to ½in (1.5cm) across, are produced in corymbs, 2in (5cm) across, in early summer. ↕ 24in (60cm), ↔ 5ft (1.5m). E. North America. Zone 3. **'Candida'** bears white flowers. **f. *rubra*** produces deep red flowers.
K. latifolia ■ (Calico bush, Moun-tain laurel). Dense, bushy shrub with alternate, oval to elliptic-lance-shaped, glossy, dark green leaves, to 5in (13cm) long. From late spring to midsummer, large corymbs, 3–4in (8–10cm) or more across, of bowl- or cup-shaped, pale to deep pink, or occasionally white flowers, ¾–1in (2–2.5cm) across, are produced from distinctively crimped, often dark

Kalmia angustifolia

Kalmia latifolia (inset: flower detail)

pink or red buds. May take several years to recover from hard pruning. ‡↔ 10ft (3m). E. US. Zone 5b. **'Bullseye'** has white flowers heavily banded red-purple within. **'Carousel'** has white flowers conspicuously banded red and intricately patterned red or white within. **'Clementine Churchill'** has rich pink flowers opening from dark pink buds. **'Elf'** is compact, with small leaves, 1¼in (3cm) long, and white flowers opening from pale pink buds; ‡↔ 3ft (1m). **'Freckles'** has pale pink flowers ringed with small, red-purple spots just inside the rim. **f. *fuscata*** ■ has a conspicuous deep maroon, purple, or cinnamon ring inside each of the white flowers. **'Minuet'** is dwarf, with narrow, glossy, dark green leaves and light pink buds opening to white flowers, each with a broad maroon ring inside. **f. *myrtifolia*** is dense, with small leaves, to 2in (5cm) long, and pale pink flowers; ‡↔ 4ft (1.2m) or more. **'Nipmuck'** has pale green leaves and nearly white flowers opening from dark red buds. **'Olympic Fire'** has wavy-margined leaves and large pink flowers, 1in (2.5cm) across, opening from red buds. **'Ostbo Red'** ■ has pale pink flowers opening from bright red buds. **'Pink Charm'** has deep red-pink buds, opening to rich pink flowers, each with a narrow, deep red ring on the inside, near the base of the flower. **'Pinwheel'** has white-edged dark maroon flowers with white centers and scalloped edges. **'Sarah'** produces bright pink-red flowers, opening from vivid red buds. **'Shooting Star'** has unusual white

Kalmia latifolia f. *fuscata*

Kalmia latifolia 'Ostbo Red'

Kalmia polifolia

flowers, each deeply cut into 5 lobes that reflex after the blooms open. **'Silver Dollar'** produces very large white flowers, to 1½in (4cm) long. **'Yankee Doodle'** has yellow-green leaves and red buds, opening to large, white-throated flowers, each with an irregular maroon ring on the inside.
K. microphylla, syn. *K. polifolia* var. *microphylla* (Western laurel). Sparsely branched, dwarf shrub with opposite, leathery, flat, ovate to oval leaves, ¼–1½in (0.6–4cm) long. Bears terminal racemes of saucer-shaped, pink to rose-purple flowers, to 1¼in (3cm) across, in late spring and early summer. ‡ to 6in (15cm), occasionally to 24in (60cm) in very wet, boggy conditions, ↔ 6–12in (15–30cm). Alaska to California. Zone 4.
K. polifolia ■ (Eastern bog laurel). Small, sparsely branched shrub with linear to oblong, glossy, dark green leaves, to 1½in (4cm) long, in opposite pairs or whorls of 3, with rolled-back margins and glandular hairs beneath. Racemes, 1–1½in (2.5–4cm) across, of up to 12 saucer-shaped, purple-pink flowers, ½–¾in (1–2cm) across, are produced in mid- and late spring. Requires moist soil. ‡ 24in (60cm), ↔ 36in (90cm). Canada, N.E. US. Zone 2. **var. *microphylla*** see *K. microphylla.*

KALMIOPSIS

ERICACEAE

Genus of one species of evergreen shrub from Oregon, where it grows on rocky ledges on mountain cliffs. It has simple leaves, arranged alternately, and is cultivated for its terminal racemes of small, cup-shaped flowers. Suitable for a cool position in a woodland garden.
• **CULTIVATION** Grow in moist but well-drained, humus-rich, acidic soil, in full sun (provided that the soil remains cool and moist) or in partial shade. Pruning group 8.
• **PROPAGATION** Sow seed at 43–54°F (6–12°C) in spring, or take semi-ripe cuttings in summer.
• **PESTS AND DISEASES** Infrequent.

K. leachiana. Dwarf, evergreen shrub with oval to obovate, bright deep green leaves, to 1¼in (3cm) long, glandular beneath. Cup-shaped, rose-red to purple-pink flowers, to ¾in (2cm) across, are produced in terminal racemes, 1–2in (2.5–5cm) long, from

Kalmiopsis leachiana 'La Piniec'

early to late spring. ‡↔ 12in (30cm). Oregon. Zone 7. **'La Piniec'** ■ has glossy, dark green leaves, to ¾in (2cm) long. **'Umpqua Valley'** is compact, vigorous, and free-flowering.

KALOPANAX

ARALIACEAE

Genus of one species of deciduous tree from forest in E. Asia. It has a spreading habit and large, variably shaped, palmately lobed leaves, which are arranged alternately and vary from hairless to very hairy beneath. Large, terminal, umbel-like panicles of usually white, 4- or 5-petaled flowers, are borne in late summer, and are followed by spherical, blue-black fruit. It is a fine specimen tree.
• **CULTIVATION** Grow in fertile, moist but well-drained soil in full sun or partial shade, preferably sheltered by other trees and shrubs. Pruning group 1.
• **PROPAGATION** Sow seed in containers in a cold frame in autumn, or take greenwood cuttings in early summer.
• **PESTS AND DISEASES** Infrequent.

K. pictus see *K. septemlobus.*
K. ricinifolius see *K. septemlobus.*
K. septemlobus ■ syn. *Acanthopanax ricinifolius, Eleutherococcus pictus, Kalopanax pictus, K. ricinifolius* (Castor aralia). Spreading, deciduous tree with spines on the trunk and shoots, and variably shaped, shallowly to deeply 5- to 7-lobed, dark green leaves, to 14in (35cm) or more across, which vary from hairless to very hairy beneath. Large, umbel-like panicles, 8–12in (20–30cm)

Kalopanax septemlobus

K

long, of small, 4- or 5-petaled white flowers, 1/16in (2mm) across, are borne in late summer, followed by spherical, blue-black fruit, 1/8in (3mm) across. ↕↔ 30ft (10m). China, Korea, Russia (S. Kurile Islands, Sakhalin), Japan (Ryukyu Islands). Zone 5.
var. *magnificus* has ovate leaves that are shallowly lobed and densely hairy on the lower leaf sides; W. China.
var. *maximowiczii* is similar to var. *magnificus*, but has deeply lobed, lance-shaped leaves.

KELSEYA

ROSACEAE

Genus of one species of evergreen, cushion-forming subshrub found in rock crevices and scree in the Rocky Mountains. Cultivated for its neat rosettes of silvery green foliage, it also has solitary, star-shaped flowers, produced in early summer. It resents winter moisture, and is best grown in an alpine house, although it may be grown outdoors in a scree bed, trough, or vertical rock crevice.
• **CULTIVATION** In an alpine house, grow in a mix of 3 parts grit and 1 part each of loam and leaf mold. Outdoors, grow in very gritty, humus-rich, moist but sharply drained, preferably alkaline soil, in full sun; provide overhead protection from rain in winter.
• **PROPAGATION** Sow seed in containers in an open frame in autumn, or take soft-tip cuttings in spring.
• **PESTS AND DISEASES** Susceptible to aphids and spider mites under glass, and to gray mold (*Botrytis*).

K. uniflora. Slow-growing, cushion-forming subshrub with tight rosettes of overlapping, ovate, leathery, dark green leaves, to 1/8in (3mm) long, clothed in silky silver hairs. Solitary, stemless, star-shaped, white or pink-flushed flowers, 3/8in (9mm) across, are produced from pink buds just above the leaf rosettes in early summer. Does not always flower freely. ↕ to 3in (8cm), ↔ to 6in (15cm). Rocky Mountains. Zone 6.

KENNEDIA *syn.* KENNEDYA

FABACEAE

Genus of 16 species of herbaceous and woody-stemmed climbing and trailing perennials from a variety of habitats, including rainforest, open forest, shrubland, heathland, and semi-desert, in Australia and New Guinea. They are grown for their long-keeled, pea-like flowers, produced singly, in pairs, umbels, or racemes in the leaf axils. The leaves, arranged alternately, each have 3 leaflets and a pair of distinctive stipules at the base of the stalk. Where not hardy, grow in a cool or temperate greenhouse. In milder regions, train over a pergola or arch. The trailers are also good as groundcovers on a bank or between shrubs.
• **CULTIVATION** Under glass, grow in soil-based potting mix with added sharp sand, in bright filtered light. In the growing season, water moderately and apply a balanced liquid fertilizer monthly; water sparingly in winter. Provide support for the climbing stems. Outdoors, grow in fertile, moist, but well-drained soil in partial shade.

Kennedia rubicunda

Pruning group 12, after flowering or in late winter.
• **PROPAGATION** Sow seed at 64–70°F (18–21°C) in spring, ideally after soaking in freshly boiled water for 12 hours.
• **PESTS AND DISEASES** Prone to spider mites and whiteflies under glass.

K. coccinea (Common coral vine). Woody-stemmed, twining climber or trailer, with leaves 1¼–4in (3–10cm) long, each divided into 3 broadly oblong to linear-wedge-shaped, occasionally lobed, slightly leathery, deep green leaflets. From spring to early summer, produces axillary and terminal, umbel-like racemes, 4in (10cm) long, of 4–20 coral-red flowers, ½in (1.5cm) wide, the standard petals marked with yellow and purple-margined at the bases, opening from buds covered with soft red hairs. Tolerates coastal sites and alkaline soil. ↕ 6ft (2m). Western Australia. ❄ (min. 41–45°F/5–7°C)
K. macrophylla. Woody-stemmed, twining climber or trailer with leaves to 6in (15cm) long, each divided into 3 broadly obovate–rounded, dark green leaflets, mid-green beneath and heart-shaped at the bases. In summer, pea-like, reddish brown or red flowers, to 1in (2cm) long, the standard petals reflexed and boldly splashed yellow, are borne in loose axillary racemes, 3–5in (8–13cm) or more long. Thrives in poor, sandy soil; tolerates coastal sites. ↕ to 15ft (5m). Western Australia. ❄ (min. 41–45°F/5–7°C)
K. nigricans (Black coral pea). Vigorous, woody, twining climber with leaves 2–6in (5–15cm) long, each divided into 3 ovate, leathery, rich green leaflets, heart-shaped at the bases. From late winter to late spring or early summer, produces one-sided, axillary racemes, 6in (15cm) long, of elongated, velvety, purple-black flowers, to 1¼in (3cm) long, the standard petals reflexed and boldly splashed yellow. Thrives in poor, sandy soil; tolerates coastal sites. ↕ 12–20ft (4–6m). Australia (Western Australia). ❄ (min. 41–45°F/5–7°C)
K. prostrata (Running postman, Scarlet runner). Prostrate to mat-forming trailer, with numerous, often sparsely branched, densely softly hairy stems radiating from a woody rootstock. The leaves, to 4in (10cm) long, are each composed of 3 ovate-rounded to rounded, wavy-margined, bright green leaflets. From spring to summer, sometimes also in autumn, scarlet flowers, to 1in (2.5cm) long, the standard petals each with a small, greenish yellow mark at the base, are borne in loose racemes, to 3in (8cm) long. ↔ to 5ft (1.5m). Western Australia. ❄ (min. 41°F/5°C)
K. rubicunda ◼ (Dusky coral pea). Twining climber or mat-forming perennial with slender, hairy stems, becoming dense and tangled with age. The leaves, to 6in (15cm) long, are each composed of 3 ovate, hairy, mid-green leaflets. From spring to summer, dark red flowers, 1¼–1½in (3–4cm) long, with pointed keel petals and swept-back standards marked pale tan at the bases, are produced in loose, axillary racemes, to 3in (8cm) long. ↕ to 10ft (3m) or more. New South Wales, Victoria. ❄ (min. 41–45°F/5–7°C)

▷ ***Kennedya*** see *Kennedia*
▷ ***Kentia acuminata*** see *Carpentaria acuminata*
▷ ***Kentia canterburyana*** see *Hedyscepe canterburyana*
▷ ***Kentia forsteriana*** see *Howea forsteriana*

KERRIA

ROSACEAE

Genus of one species of deciduous shrub, found in thickets and woodland in China and Japan. It has alternate, simple leaves, and solitary, cup- or saucer-shaped yellow flowers. Kerrias are grown for their foliage and flowers, and are suitable for a shrub border or an open position in a woodland garden.
• **CULTIVATION** Grow in fertile, well-drained soil in full sun or partial shade. Pruning group 3.
• **PROPAGATION** Take greenwood cuttings in summer. Divide in autumn.
• **PESTS AND DISEASES** Coral spot, fireblight, leaf and twig blight, and canker can occur.

K. japonica. Suckering shrub with arching green shoots and ovate, pointed, sharply toothed, bright green leaves, to 4in (10cm) long. In mid- and late spring, produces solitary, single or double, golden yellow flowers, 1¼–2in (3–5cm) across. ↕ 6ft (2m), ↔ 8ft (2.5m). China, Japan. Zone 5. **'Albiflora'** bears single, pale yellow flowers. **'Golden Guinea'** ◼ produces very large, single flowers, 2–2½in (5–6cm) across. **'Picta'**, syn. 'Variegata', has gray-green leaves margined creamy white; ↕ 5ft (1.5m), ↔ 6ft (2m). **'Pleniflora'** is very vigorous and upright in habit, bearing large, pompon-like, double flowers, 1¼in (3cm) across. Slightly less hardy than the species; ↕↔ 10ft (3m). **'Variegata'** see 'Picta'.

KIGELIA

Sausage tree

BIGNONIACEAE

Genus of one species of variable, evergreen tree from tropical woodland and more open areas in Africa. It has large, pinnate leaves, borne in opposite pairs, and loose, pendent panicles, 3–6ft (1–2m) long, of open, trumpet-shaped flowers, followed by long, woody pods. Where temperatures drop below 61°F (16°C), grow in a warm greenhouse, mainly for its foliage, although flowers may form on specimens reaching 10ft (3m) or more high. In tropical areas, it is an attractive specimen or shade tree.
• **CULTIVATION** Under glass, grow in soil-based potting mix in full light but screened from the hottest summer sun, at least during the early years. In the growing season, water moderately and apply a balanced liquid fertilizer monthly; water sparingly in winter. Outdoors, grow in fertile, well-drained soil in full sun. Pruning group 1; plants under glass need restrictive pruning in late winter or after flowering.
• **PROPAGATION** Sow seed at 70–73°F (21–23°C) in spring.
• **PESTS AND DISEASES** Whiteflies, spider mites, and mealybugs are sometimes problems under glass. Leaf spots can occur outdoors.

Kerria japonica 'Golden Guinea' (inset: flower detail)

Kigelia pinnata

K. pinnata ▣ Rounded to broadly columnar, usually freely branching tree with robust stems. Bears pinnate leaves, to 20in (50cm) long, each composed of 7–11 oblong to obovate, leathery, mid- to deep green leaflets, sometimes notched at the tips. Loose, pendent panicles of bat-pollinated flowers, each 4in (10cm) across, are produced in summer. Yellowish green in bud, they open to rich brownish red at night, when they have an unpleasant smell that is attractive to bats. The cylindrical, woody fruit, to 14–24in (35–60cm) or more long, may weigh 11–15lb (5–7kg), and are pale brown when ripe. They remain on the thickened flowering stems for many months. ↕ 50ft (15m) or more, ↔ 15–30ft (5–10m). Tropical Africa. ❀ (min. 61°F/16°C)

KIRENGESHOMA

HYDRANGEACEAE

Genus of 2 species of clump-forming perennials, with short rhizomes, from woodland in Korea and Japan. They have broadly tubular, waxy, pale or bright yellow flowers, borne on slender stalks in nodding, terminal cymes above pairs of elegant, maple-like leaves. They are suitable for a shady border or woodland garden.

• **CULTIVATION** Grow in moist, acidic soil, enriched with leaf mold, in partial shade sheltered from wind.

• **PROPAGATION** Sow seed in containers in a cold frame as soon as ripe or in spring. Divide as growth begins in spring, taking care not to damage tender young shoots.

• **PESTS AND DISEASES** Slugs and snails may attack young growth and leaves.

K. palmata ▣ (Yellow wax-bells). Clump-forming perennial with short rhizomes and arching, smooth, reddish purple stems. These bear broadly ovate, palmately lobed, slightly hairy, pale green leaves, 4–8in (10–20cm) long, becoming smaller, simple, and almost

Kirengeshoma palmata

stalkless toward the stem tips. Nodding, terminal cymes of 3 broadly tubular, pale yellow flowers, to 1½in (4cm) long, with slightly recurved lobes and fleshy petals that overlap at the bases, are borne in late summer and early autumn. ↕ 24–48in (60–120cm), ↔ 30in (75cm). Japan. Zone 5.

KITAIBELA *syn.* KITAIBELIA

MALVACEAE

Genus of 2 species of imposing, often short-lived herbaceous perennials found in damp meadows and scrub from Slovenia to Macedonia. They have palmately lobed, vine-like leaves and showy, mallow-like flowers, produced singly or in axillary cymes. They are suitable for a wild or meadow garden.

• **CULTIVATION** Grow in deep, moderately fertile, moist but well-drained soil in full sun or partial shade.

• **PROPAGATION** Sow seed in containers in a cold frame in spring or autumn. Root basal or softwood cuttings in spring.

• **PESTS AND DISEASES** Infrequent.

K. vitifolia ▣ Clump-forming, woody-based, softly white-hairy perennial with erect stems bearing 5- to 7-lobed, coarsely toothed leaves, to 7in (18cm) long. Mallow-like, open cup-shaped, 5-petaled, white to rose-red flowers, 1¾in (4.5cm) across, are produced singly or in few-flowered, axillary cymes from midsummer to early autumn. ↕ to 8ft (2.5m), ↔ 15ft (5m). Slovenia to Macedonia. Zone 6b.

▷ ***Kitaibelia*** see *Kitaibela*

Kitaibela vitifolia

KLEINIA

ASTERACEAE

Genus of 40 species of succulent perennials, closely related to *Senecio,* from lowlands and mountains in tropical Africa, N.W. Africa, the Canary Islands, southern Africa, Madagascar, and the Arabian Peninsula. Many species have tuberous roots and prostrate to upright, cylindrical to angular stems, with flat or cylindrical, succulent, usually entire leaves. Colorful, thistle-like flowerheads appear singly or in branched, terminal or axillary corymbs in summer. Where temperatures drop below 50°F (10°C), grow as houseplants or in a warm greenhouse. In warmer climates, grow in a desert garden.

• **CULTIVATION** Under glass, grow in a mix of 2 parts leaf mold and 1 part each loam and coarse sand, in full light. In growth, water moderately and apply a balanced liquid fertilizer 2 or 3 times. Keep dry when dormant. Outdoors, grow in sharply drained, gritty, humus-rich soil in full sun. See also pp.48–49.

• **PROPAGATION** Sow seed at 68°F (20°C), or take cuttings, in spring or summer.

• **PESTS AND DISEASES** Susceptible to scale insects.

K. repens see *Senecio serpens.*
K. rowleyana see *Senecio rowleyanus.*
K. stapeliiformis ▣ syn. *Senecio stapeliiformis.* Erect succulent branching from the base, with new shoots growing underground at first. Thick, fleshy, 5- to 7-angled branches, glaucous green with purple staining, bear very slender, oblong, thread-like, fleshy, gray-green leaves, often flushed purple with dark green lines along their lengths. The leaves, ¼in (6mm) long, become thorny as they age. Solitary, thistle-like, red or orange-red flowerheads, to 1½in (4cm) long, are produced in summer. ↕↔ 8–12in (20–30cm). E. South Africa (KwaZulu/Natal). ❀ (min. 50°F/10°C)

Kleinia stapeliiformis

KNAUTIA

DIPSACACEAE

Genus of 40 or more species of *Scabiosa*-like annuals and perennials from limestone grassland, scrub, and woodland in Europe, Caucasus, Russia (Siberia), and N. Africa. They have overwintering rosettes of simple to pinnatifid basal leaves, and opposite pairs of stem leaves, which are pinnatifid or simple. Tall stems bear cup-shaped involucres of bracts, surrounding dense, bluish lilac or reddish purple flowerheads. They are attractive to bees. Grow in a herbaceous border, cottage garden, or wild garden.

• **CULTIVATION** Grow in moderately fertile, well-drained, preferably alkaline soil in full sun.

• **PROPAGATION** Sow seed in containers in a cold frame in spring, or take basal cuttings in spring.

• **PESTS AND DISEASES** Prone to aphids.

K. arvensis, syn. *Scabiosa arvensis* (Blue buttons). Clump-forming, deeply taprooted perennial with erect but often lax, hairless stems, the lower parts bristly. Produces simple to pinnatifid, hairy, dull green leaves, 2–10in (5–25cm) long, simple or pinnatifid higher up the stem. Flat-topped, bluish lilac flowerheads, 1¼–1½in (3–4cm) across, with softly bristly, involucral bracts, are borne from midsummer to early autumn. ↕ to 5ft (1.5m), ↔ 12in (30cm). Europe, Caucasus, Iran to C. Asia, Russia (Siberia). Zone 5.
K. macedonica ▣ syn. *Scabiosa rumelica.* Clump-forming perennial with slender, branched stems; pinnatifid basal leaves, 3in (8cm) long, each with a large, terminal lobe; and simple or pinnatifid stem leaves, ¾–6in (2–15cm) long. Numerous long-lasting, purple-red flowerheads, ½–1¼in (1.5–3cm) across, with softly bristly, involucral bracts, are produced in mid- and late summer. ↕ 24–32in (60–80cm), ↔ 18in (45cm). C. Balkans into Romania. Zone 5.
K. tatarica. Clump-forming biennial with hairy lower stems and pinnatifid, toothed, mid-green leaves, to 10in (25cm) long, with oblong-elliptic lobes. Bears flat-topped, long-lasting, bright yellow flowerheads, to 1½in (4cm) across, with softly bristly, involucral bracts, from midsummer to early autumn. ↕ to 6ft (2m), ↔ 36in (90cm). E. Russia (Siberia). Zone 5.

Knautia macedonica

KNIGHTIA

PROTEACEAE

Genus of 3 species of evergreen trees or shrubs from lowland to low mountain forest, 1 from New Zealand, 2 from New Caledonia. The leathery, entire or toothed leaves are arranged alternately and vary in shape with age: young plants have long, thin leaves; adults have shorter, thicker ones. Tubular flowers, with 4 petal-like tepals that roll up like springs, are borne in dense racemes. Where not hardy, grow in a cool or temperate greenhouse. In milder climates, use as a specimen tree.

• **CULTIVATION** Under glass, grow in soil-based potting mix in full light, with shade from hot sun and with good ventilation. When in growth, water moderately and apply a balanced liquid fertilizer every month; water sparingly in winter. Outdoors, grow in fertile, well-drained, neutral to acidic soil, in full sun or partial shade, with shelter from cold winds. Pruning group 1.

• **PROPAGATION** Sow seed at 55–61°F (13–16°C) in spring. Root semi-ripe cuttings with bottom heat in summer (rooting may be slow).

• **PESTS AND DISEASES** Spider mites may be a problem under glass.

K. excelsa (New Zealand honeysuckle, Rewarewa). Tall, usually columnar tree, with many short, lateral branches. Adult leaves are narrowly oblong to obovate-oblong, 4–6in (10–15cm) long, blunt-toothed and stiff. From spring to summer, produces few to many tubular red flowers, 1–1½in (2.5–4cm) long, in racemes 4in (10cm) long, covered with short, velvety, red-brown hairs, followed by narrow seed pods, which split open down one side only. ↕ to 100ft (30m), ↔ 22–30ft (7–10m). New Zealand. ❀ (min. 45°F/7°C)

KNIPHOFIA

Red-hot poker, Torch flower

LILIACEAE

Genus of about 70 species of evergreen or deciduous, rhizomatous perennials from mountainous or upland areas, often in moist places in rough grass or along streamsides, in southern and tropical Africa. Most are clump-forming, with arching, tufted, linear to strap-shaped, light to mid-green or blue-green leaves. In deciduous species and hybrids, these leaves are usually thin, grass-like, and 4–39in (10–100cm) long; in evergreens, they are broader, keeled or strap-shaped, and to 5ft (1.5m) long. Erect, usually dense, spike-like racemes, 2–16in (5–40cm) long, of numerous pendent, occasionally erect, tubular or cylindrical flowers, ⅛–2in (0.3–5cm) long, are borne well above the foliage. They are attractive to bees. The flowers are red, orange, yellow, white, or greenish white; some open red, then turn to yellow, making striking, 2-colored racemes. Numerous cultivars have been raised, ranging in size from dwarf plants, 20in (50cm) high, to tall plants, to 6ft (1.8m) high. Grow in a herbaceous border; where not hardy, grow in a cool or temperate greenhouse.

• **CULTIVATION** Grow in deep, fertile, humus-rich, moist but well-drained, preferably sandy soil, in full sun or partial shade. Mulch young plants with straw or leaves for the first winter.

Kniphofia 'Bees' Sunset'

• **PROPAGATION** Sow seed in containers in a cold frame in spring (although cultivars seldom come true from seed). Divide established clumps in late spring. Stimulate offshoots from slow-growing, woody-based, evergreen red-hot pokers by cutting off crowns; leave offshoots in place to develop for 2 years before separating from parent plants, or use new shoots as basal cuttings.

• **PESTS AND DISEASES** Sometimes affected by stem or crown rot. Thrips may cause mottling.

***K.* 'Ada'.** Deciduous perennial with tawny orange-yellow flowers borne in late summer and early autumn. ↕ 36in (90cm), ↔ 24in (60cm). Zone 6b.

***K.* 'Alcazar'.** Deciduous perennial with clear salmon flowers in early summer. ↕ 3½ft (1.1m), ↔ 24in (60cm). Zone 6.

***K.* 'Atlanta'.** Evergreen perennial with gray-green leaves, and orange-red flowers, fading to pale yellow, borne in late spring and early summer. ↕ 4ft (1.2m), ↔ 30in (75cm). Zone 6.

***K.* 'Bees' Lemon'.** Deciduous perennial with toothed leaves, and lemon-yellow flowers, green in bud, borne in late summer and early autumn. ↕ 36in (90cm), ↔ 24in (60cm). Zone 6.

***K.* 'Bees' Sunset'** ■ Deciduous perennial with toothed leaves, and soft yellowish orange flowers borne from early to late summer. ↕ 36in (90cm), ↔ 24in (60cm). Zone 6.

***K.* 'Border Ballet'.** Deciduous perennial with cream to pink flowers borne in late summer and early autumn. ↕↔ 24in (60cm). Zone 6.

***K.* 'Bressingham Comet'.** Deciduous perennial with red-tipped orange flowers, yellow at the bases, borne in early and midautumn. ↕ 18in (45cm), ↔ 9in (23cm). Zone 6.

***K.* 'Buttercup'** Deciduous perennial with green buds, opening to clear yellow flowers in early summer. ↕↔ 30in (75cm). Zone 6.

K. caulescens ■ Evergreen perennial with short, thick, woody-based stems and arching, linear, keeled, finely toothed, glaucous leaves, to 36in (90cm) long, purple at the bases. Coral-red flowers, 1in (2.5cm) long, fading to pale yellow, with protruding stamens, are borne in short, oblong-cylindrical racemes from late summer to midautumn. ↕ to 4ft (1.2m), ↔ 24in (60cm). South Africa (N. Eastern Cape, Orange Free State, KwaZulu/Natal), Lesotho. Zone 7.

***K.* 'C.M. Prichard' of gardens** see *K. rooperi.*

***K.* 'Corallina'.** Deciduous perennial with deep green leaves, and coral-red flowers borne in early summer. ↕ 36in (90cm), ↔ 24in (60cm). Zone 6.

***K.* 'Earliest of All'.** Deciduous perennial with coral-rose flowers, in late spring or early summer; very hardy. ↕ 24–30in (60–75cm), ↔ 24in (60cm). Zone 6.

***K.* 'Early Buttercup'.** Deciduous perennial with yellow flowers borne in late spring and early summer. ↕ 36in (90cm), ↔ 24in (60cm). Zone 6.

Kniphofia caulescens

Kniphofia 'Erecta'

***K.* Early Hybrids.** Deciduous perennials with flowers in shades of red and orange, borne in early and midsummer. ↕ 30in (75cm), ↔ 24in (60cm). Zone 6.

K. ensifolia. Robust, evergreen perennial forming clumps of arching, narrowly elliptic, finely toothed, glaucous leaves, to 6in (15cm) long. Bears greenish white flowers, ½–¾in (1.5–2cm) long, often red in bud, in dense, cylindrical racemes from late summer to midautumn. ↕ 4ft (1.2m) or more, ↔ 24in (60cm). South Africa (Western Cape, Eastern Cape, KwaZulu/Natal, Eastern Transvaal, Northern Transvaal). Zone 6.

***K.* 'Erecta'** ■ Deciduous perennial with bright coral-red flowers, turning upward after opening, borne in late summer and early autumn. ↕ 36in (90cm), ↔ 24in (60cm). Zone 6b.

***K.* 'Fiery Fred'.** Deciduous perennial with orange-red flowers borne from early to late summer. ↕ to 4ft (1.2m), ↔ 24in (60cm). Zone 6.

***K. galpinii* of gardens** see *K. triangularis.*

***K.* 'Glow'.** Deciduous perennial with pastel, coral-red flowers, overlaid with deep rose, in early and midsummer. ↕ 30in (75cm), ↔ 24in (60cm). Zone 6.

***K.* 'Goldelse'.** Deciduous perennial with grass-like leaves, and yellow flowers borne in racemes in early summer. ↕ 30in (75cm), ↔ 12in (30cm). Zone 6.

***K.* 'Gold Mine'.** Deciduous perennial with golden amber flowers from mid-summer to late autumn. ↕ 36in (90cm), ↔ 24in (60cm). Zone 6.

***K.* 'Green Jade'** ■ Robust, evergreen perennial with keeled leaves, and green flowers, becoming cream and then white, borne in racemes in late summer and early autumn. ↕ to 5ft (1.5m), ↔ 24–30in (60–75cm). Zone 6.

K. hirsuta. Evergreen perennial with linear, spreading, hairy, dark green leaves, 16–24in (40–60cm) long, red at

the bases. Pinkish red flowers, ¾–1¼in (2–3cm) long, becoming yellow, are produced in conical racemes in midspring. ↕ 16in (40cm), ↔ 18in (45cm). Lesotho. Zone 7.
***K.* 'Ice Queen'** ▣ Robust, deciduous perennial bearing green-budded flowers opening to pale primrose yellow, fading to ivory, in early and midautumn. ↕ to 5ft (1.5m), ↔ 30in (75cm). Zone 6.
***K.* 'Jenny Bloom'.** Deciduous perennial with pink flowers, shading to cream and coral-pink, borne from late summer to midautumn. ↕ 36in (90cm), ↔ 12in (30cm). Zone 6.
***K.* 'Lemon Ice'.** Deciduous perennial with long-lasting, near-white flowers, lemon-yellow in bud, borne in mid- and late summer. ↕ to 36in (90cm), ↔ 18in (45cm). Zone 6.
***K.* 'Limelight'.** Deciduous perennial with grass-like foliage, and canary-yellow flowers, greenish yellow in bud, borne in early autumn. ↕ 36in (90cm), ↔ 18in (45cm). Zone 6.
***K.* 'Little Maid'** ▣ Deciduous perennial with grass-like leaves, and racemes of flowers, pale green in bud, opening to buff-tinted pale yellow and aging to ivory, borne in late summer and early autumn. ↕ 24in (60cm), ↔ 18in (45cm). Zone 6.
K. macowanii see *K. triangularis.*
***K.* 'Maid of Orleans'.** Deciduous perennial bearing long-lasting flowers, pale primrose in bud, opening to deeper yellow, and maturing to ivory, in mid- and late summer. ↕ to 4ft (1.2m), ↔ 18in (45cm). Zone 6.
***K.* 'Modesta'.** Dwarf, deciduous perennial with cream and coral flowers in mid- and late summer. ↕ to 24in (60cm), ↔ 18in (45cm). Zone 6.
***K.* 'Mount Etna'.** Deciduous perennial with broad racemes of pale greenish yellow flowers, scarlet in bud, borne in late summer and early autumn. ↕ to 4ft (1.2m), ↔ 36in (90cm). Zone 6.
K. nelsonii see *K. triangularis.*
K. northiae. Evergreen perennial forming thick-stemmed, solitary plants,

Kniphofia 'Ice Queen'

not clumps, with arching, linear, broad, unkeeled, glaucous leaves, to 5ft (1.5m) long. Pale yellow flowers, 1–1¼in (2.5–3cm) long, opening from red buds, are produced in oblong, very dense racemes from early to late summer. ↕ 5ft (1.5m), ↔ 36in (90cm). South Africa (Eastern Cape, KwaZulu/Natal), Lesotho. Zone 7.
***K.* 'Parmentier'.** Deciduous perennial with large salmon flowers in mid- or late summer; very hardy. ↕ 36in (90cm), ↔ 24in (60cm). Zone 6.
***K.* 'Percy's Pride'** ▣ Deciduous perennial with keeled leaves, and canary-yellow flowers, green-tinted yellow in bud, opening to cream, borne in late summer and early autumn. ↕ 4ft (1.2m), ↔ 24in (60cm). Zone 6.
***K.* 'Pfitzeri'** see *K.* 'Wayside Flame'.
***K.* 'Primrose Beauty'.** Deciduous perennial with primrose-yellow flowers, produced from early summer to autumn. ↕ 36in (90cm), ↔ 24in (60cm). Zone 6.
***K.* 'Primrose Mascotte'.** Deciduous perennial bearing primrose-yellow flowers with amber undertones, in early and midsummer. ↕ 30in (75cm), ↔ 24in (60cm). Zone 6.

Kniphofia 'Percy's Pride'

***K.* 'Prince Igor'** ▣ Deciduous perennial with glowing, deep orange-red flowers borne in racemes in early and midautumn. ↕ 6ft (1.8m), ↔ 36in (90cm). Zone 6.
K. pumila. Deciduous perennial with arching, linear, glaucous leaves, to 24in (60cm) long, with rough margins. In summer, bears funnel-shaped, narrow racemes of orange-red flowers, ½in (1.5cm) long. ↕↔ to 24in (60cm). South Africa. Zone 7.
K. rooperi ▣ syn. *K.* 'C.M. Prichard' of gardens. Robust, evergreen perennial with arching, broad, linear, acutely pointed, deeply keeled, dark green leaves. Orange-red flowers, 1½–1¾in (3.5–4.5cm) long, becoming orange-yellow, are borne in broadly ellipsoid,

Kniphofia rooperi

shiny racemes from early to late autumn. ↕ 4ft (1.2m), ↔ 24in (60cm). South Africa (Eastern Cape). Zone 7.
***K.* 'Royal Standard'** ▣ Deciduous perennial with bright yellow flowers, scarlet in bud, borne on thick stems in mid- and late summer. ↕ 36–39in (90–100cm), ↔ 24in (60cm). Zone 6.
***K.* 'Samuel's Sensation'.** Deciduous perennial with bright scarlet flowers, tinged with yellow as they fade, borne in racemes in late summer and early autumn. ↕ 5ft (1.5m), ↔ 24–30in (60–75cm). Zone 6.
***K.* 'Shenandoah'.** Deciduous perennial with yellow flowers, orange in bud, in late spring and early summer; very hardy. ↕ 3½ft (1.1m), ↔ 24in (60cm). Zone 6.
***K.* 'Shining Sceptre'.** Deciduous perennial with clear yellow flowers, becoming ivory, borne in midsummer. ↕ 4ft (1.2m), ↔ 24in (60cm). Zone 6.
***K. snowdenii* of gardens** see *K. thompsonii* var. *snowdenii.*
***K.* 'Springtime'.** Deciduous perennial with creamy ivory flowers, coral-red in bud, borne in midsummer. ↕ 36in (90cm), ↔ 24in (60cm). Zone 6.

K

Kniphofia 'Green Jade'

Kniphofia 'Little Maid'

Kniphofia 'Prince Igor'

Kniphofia 'Royal Standard'

Kniphofia 'Strawberries and Cream'

***K.* 'Strawberries and Cream'** ▣ Deciduous perennial with cream flowers, coral-pink in bud, borne in late summer and early autumn. ↕ 24in (60cm), ↔ 12in (30cm). Zone 6.
***K. thompsonii* var. *snowdenii*,** syn. *K. snowdenii* of gardens. Gently spreading, deciduous, rhizomatous perennial forming tufts of upright, linear leaves, to 24in (60cm) long. From midsummer to late autumn, bears a succession of open racemes of few, curved, yellowish orange or coral-pink flowers, to 1½in (4cm) long. ↕ to 36in (90cm), ↔ 18in (45cm). Uganda, Kenya. Zone 7.
K. triangularis ▣ syn. *K. galpinii* of gardens, *K. macowanii*, *K. nelsonii.* Variable, deciduous perennial with arching, linear, grass-like leaves. Wiry stems, freely borne in moist conditions, produce dense racemes of reddish orange flowers, 1–1½in (2.5–4cm) long, becoming slightly yellower around the mouths, in early and midautumn. ↕ 24–36in (60–90cm), ↔ 18in (45cm). South Africa (Eastern Cape, Orange Free State, KwaZulu/Natal), Lesotho. Zone 5b.
K. tuckii. Deciduous perennial with arching, strap-shaped, finely toothed, rough-margined leaves, to 24in (60cm) long. In summer, bears sulfur-yellow flowers, to ½in (1.5cm) long, red-tinged when young, in dense racemes, to 6in (15cm) long. ↕ to 5ft (1.5m), ↔ 24in (60cm). South Africa. Zone 7b.
K. uvaria. Evergreen perennial with lax, linear, keeled, finely toothed, coarse leaves, to 24in (60cm) long. Flowers, 1¼–1½in (3–4cm) long, red in bud, opening to orange, and fading to yellow,

Kniphofia triangularis

Kniphofia 'Wrexham Buttercup'

are borne in slender, oblong-ovoid racemes in early autumn. ↕ 4ft (1.2m), ↔ 24in (60cm). South Africa (S. Western Cape). Zone 7. **'Nobilis'** has longer racemes of rich orange-red flowers, borne from midsummer to early autumn; ↕ 5–6ft (1.5–2m), ↔ 36in (90cm). **'Rosea Superba'** has rose-red flowers, fading to white, from midsummer to early autumn; ↕ 30–36in (75–90cm). **Royal Castle Hybrids** cultivars bear yellow and orange flowers in summer; ↕ 30–36in (75–90cm).
***K.* 'Vanilla'.** Deciduous perennial with cream-white flowers, borne in early summer. ↕ 30in (75cm), ↔ 24in (60cm). Zone 6.
***K.* 'Wayside Flame',** syn. *K.* 'Pfitzeri'. Deciduous perennial with bright, orange-red flowers from late summer to autumn. ↕ 3ft (90cm), ↔ 24in (60cm). Zone 6.
***K.* 'White Fairy'.** Deciduous perennial producing large, creamy white flowers in early summer. ↕ 3ft (90cm), ↔ 24in (60cm). Zone 6.
***K.* 'Wrexham Buttercup'** ▣ Deciduous perennial with clear, bright yellow flowers, borne in dense racemes in midsummer. ↕ 4ft (1.2m), ↔ 24in (60cm). Zone 6.

▷ ***Kochia trichophylla*** see *Bassia scoparia* f. *trichophylla*

KOELERIA

POACEAE

Genus of about 30 species of annual and perennial grasses from chalky and sandy grassland in N. and S. temperate zones and in tropical Africa. Several species are cultivated for their ornamental leaves and narrow panicles of silvery green or blue-green spikelets. They are suitable for a rock garden or the front of a border, either individually or in groups.
• **CULTIVATION** Grow in medium to light, not too fertile, well-drained soil in full sun or light, dappled shade. Koelerias thrive in alkaline and shallow, chalky soil. Cut back flowering stems either before seeding or in autumn.
• **PROPAGATION** Sow seed *in situ* in spring or autumn, or divide from midspring to early summer.
• **PESTS AND DISEASES** Ergot, choke, rust, smut, leaf spots, and blights occur.

K. glauca (Glaucous hair grass). Densely tufted, semi-evergreen, perennial grass, forming a compact mound of narrowly linear, glaucous gray-green leaves, to 8in (20cm) long, with inrolled margins. In early and midsummer, produces numerous erect stems bearing cylindrical panicles, to 4in (10cm) long, of shining, silver-green spikelets, which age to buff. ↕ to 16in (40cm) or more, ↔ 12in (30cm). W. and C. Europe to Russia (Siberia). Zone 6b.

KOELREUTERIA

SAPINDACEAE

Genus of 3 species of deciduous trees or shrubs from dry valley woodlands in China, Korea, and Taiwan. They have alternate, pinnate or 2-pinnate leaves, and large, pyramidal panicles, 4–14in (10–35cm) long, of shallowly bowl-shaped flowers, followed by unusual, inflated fruit capsules. They are fine specimen trees, flowering best in areas with hot summers.
• **CULTIVATION** Grow in fertile, well-drained soil in full sun. Pruning group 1; prune only to remove damaged or dead wood when dormant in winter.
• **PROPAGATION** Sow seed in containers in a cold frame in autumn. Take root cuttings in late winter.
• **PESTS AND DISEASES** Dieback, canker, mushroom root rot, and wilt sometimes occur.

K. bipinnata Spreading tree with large, 2-pinnate, mid-green leaves, to 20in (50cm) long, consisting of numerous oval-oblong, finely toothed leaflets. Red-spotted yellow flowers, ½in (1.5cm) across, are borne in large panicles, to 12in (30cm) long, from summer to autumn, followed by bladder-like fruit capsules, to 2in (5cm) long, red-brown when ripe. ↕ 30ft (10m), ↔ 25ft (8m). S.W. China. Zone 7b.
K. paniculata ▣ (Golden-rain tree, Pride of India, Varnish tree). Spreading tree with pinnate leaves, to 18in (45cm) long, each consisting of 7–15 or more, ovate-oblong, scalloped leaflets. Emerging leaves are pink-red, becoming mid-green, and turning butter-yellow in autumn. Small yellow flowers, ½in (1.5cm) across, are produced in large, pyramidal panicles, to 12in (30cm) long, in mid- and late summer; they are followed by bladder-like, pink- or red-flushed fruit capsules, to 2in (5cm) long. ↕↔ 30ft (10m) or more. China, Korea. Zone 7. **var. *apiculata*** has 2-pinnate leaves and light yellow flowers.

Koelreuteria paniculata

KOHLERIA

GESNERIACEAE

Genus of about 50 species of usually erect, rhizomatous perennials and subshrubs from rainforest of tropical regions of North America, Central America, and South America. They are grown for their foxglove-like flowers, which are bell-shaped or tubular, flaring out into 5 rounded lobes, usually produced from the leaf axils singly, in pairs, or in pendent, umbel-like racemes. Elliptic-lance-shaped to ovate leaves, opposite or in whorls of 3, are usually dark green, sometimes with silver markings, and have toothed or scalloped margins. All parts are hairy, including the flowers. Where not hardy, grow taller species in a warm greenhouse or conservatory; use compact species and cultivars as houseplants. In humid, tropical areas, grow in shaded sites in beds or borders.
• **CULTIVATION** Under glass, start into growth at 70°F (21°C) in early spring. Grow in soilless potting mix in bright filtered light, with high humidity. Water moderately at first, then freely when in full growth. When flower buds appear, apply a high-potash fertilizer every 2 weeks. In autumn, remove dying top growth, then keep dry while dormant. Outdoors, grow in moist, well-drained, humus-rich soil in partial shade.
• **PROPAGATION** Divide in early spring.
• **PESTS AND DISEASES** The growing tips may be infested by aphids, and the flowers may be damaged by thrips. Rhizome rot may occur in winter if conditions are too moist.

K. amabilis. Erect to prostrate, rhizomatous perennial with ovate, scalloped leaves, 4in (10cm) long, veined silver and purple-brown. In summer, bell-shaped, deep pink flowers, 1in (2.5cm) long, with purple and brick-red bars and stripes on the lobes and throats, are borne singly or in few-flowered, umbel-like racemes. May need support. ↕↔ 24in (60cm). Colombia. ❀ (min. 59°F/15°C)
K. bogotensis. Erect, rhizomatous perennial with ovate, toothed, velvety, dark green leaves, 3in (8cm) long, marked paler green or white above. Bell-shaped, red-and-yellow flowers, 1in (2.5cm) long, with mouths spotted red, are borne singly or in pairs, from autumn to early winter. ↕ 24in

Kohleria digitaliflora

Kohleria eriantha

(60cm), ↕↔ 18in (45cm). Colombia. ❀ (min. 59°F/15°C)
***K.* 'Connecticut Belle'.** Erect, compact, rhizomatous perennial with lance-shaped, toothed leaves, 3in (8cm) long, red beneath. Bell-shaped flowers, 1in (2.5cm) long, with bright red tubes, purple upper lobes, and purple-spotted, bright pink lower lobes, are borne singly or in pairs in summer. ↕ 16in (40cm), ↔ 8in (20cm). ❀ (min. 59°F/15°C)
K. digitaliflora ▣ Erect to spreading, rhizomatous perennial with lance-shaped or elliptic-lance-shaped to ovate, scalloped leaves, 8in (20cm) long, marked paler green. From summer to autumn, produces umbel-like racemes of up to 6, occasionally solitary, tubular, purple-pink flowers, 1–1¼in (2.5–3cm) long, white on the inside of the tubes, and with lobes spotted with dark, purplish green. ↕ 24in (60cm), ↔ 16in (40cm). Colombia. ❀ (min. 59°F/15°C)
K. eriantha ▣ Robust, bushy, rhizomatous perennial with ovate to ovate-lance-shaped, scalloped leaves, 3–5in (7–13cm) long. The leaves have prominent red hairs on the margins, and undersides that are paler and red-veined. In summer, produces tubular, orange-red flowers, 1in (2.5cm) long, with yellow-spotted lower lobes, either singly or in umbel-like racemes. ↕ to 4ft (1.2m), ↔ 12in (30cm) or more. Colombia. ❀ (min. 59°F/15°C)
***K.* 'Strawberry Fields'.** Erect to spreading, compact, rhizomatous perennial with ovate to ovate-lance-shaped, scalloped, softly white-hairy, dark gray-green leaves, to 2in (5cm) long. From spring to summer, produces racemes of tubular, pink-red flowers, 1in (2.5cm) long, with darker red spots on the tubes and lobes. ↕ 16in (40cm), ↔ 8in (20cm). ❀ (min. 59°F/15°C)

KOLKWITZIA

Beautybush

CAPRIFOLIACEAE

Genus of one species of deciduous shrub from rocky, mountainous areas of Hubei, China. It has simple leaves, borne in opposite pairs, and is cultivated for its profusion of bell-shaped flowers borne in dense corymbs. Beautybush is excellent for a shrub border or as a specimen plant.
• **CULTIVATION** Grow in fertile, well-drained soil, preferably in full sun, although some shade is tolerated. Pruning group 2.

Kolkwitzia amabilis 'Pink Cloud' (inset: flower detail)

• **PROPAGATION** Take greenwood cuttings in late spring or early summer, or remove suckers in spring.
• **PESTS AND DISEASES** Infrequent.

K. amabilis. Deciduous, suckering shrub with long, arching shoots and broadly ovate, tapered, dark green leaves, to 3in (8cm) long. Masses of bell-shaped, pale to deep pink flowers, to ½in (1.5cm) across, with yellow-flushed throats, are borne in terminal corymbs, 2–3in (5–8cm) across, in late spring and early summer. ↕ 10ft (3m), ↔ 12ft (4m). China (Hubei). Zone 5. **'Pink Cloud'** ▣ has bright, deep pink flowers.

▷ ***Korolkowia sewerzowii*** see *Fritillaria sewerzowii*

KOSTELETZKYA

Fen rose, Seashore mallow

MALVACEAE

Genus of 30 species of upright perennials and subshrubs from coastal areas of tropical Africa, South Africa, Madagascar, and North America. The leaves are often alternate, spear-shaped, and simple or palmately lobed. Three-petaled, tubular flowers with stamens united in a column are borne singly or in terminal racemes or panicles. Where not hardy, grow in a warm greenhouse. In tropical and subtropical climates, use in a wild garden.
• **CULTIVATION** Under glass, grow in soil-based potting mix in full light. In the growing season, water freely and apply a balanced liquid fertilizer every 2 weeks. Keep just moist in winter. Outdoors, grow in moderately fertile, moist soil in full sun. Pruning group 7.
• **PROPAGATION** Sow seed *in situ* in spring, or root greenwood or semi-ripe cuttings in summer.
• **PESTS AND DISEASES** Infrequent.

K. virginica (Salt marsh mallow). Erect perennial or subshrub with rough stems and triangular-spear-shaped, 3- to 5-lobed, toothed, coarsely hairy, mid-green leaves, 2–6in (5–15cm) long. In summer, bears pink or red flowers, to 3in (8cm) across, singly or in panicles. ↕ to 4ft (1.2m), ↔ 24in (60cm). New York to Florida and Louisiana. Zone 6b.

▷ ***Krainzia guelzowiana*** see *Mammillaria guelzowiana*

KUNZEA

MYRTACEAE

Genus of 25 species of evergreen shrubs and small trees from sands or sandy loam areas of mostly coastal habitats in Australia. They have small, often crowded, simple, entire, leathery leaves, and bear terminal "bottlebrush" spikes or heads of flowers. Each flower is composed of 5 small petals and a crown of conspicuous stamens, which in some species give the flowerheads their main color. Where not hardy, grow in a cool greenhouse, moving plants in containers outdoors during the summer. In milder climates, grow at the base of a house wall or in a shrub border.
• **CULTIVATION** Under glass, grow in acidic potting mix in full light, with good ventilation. When in growth, water moderately and apply a balanced liquid fertilizer every month; water sparingly in winter. Outdoors, grow in moderately fertile, neutral to acidic, well-drained, sandy soil in full sun; shelter from strong and dry winds. Pruning group 1; under glass, may need restrictive pruning after flowering.
• **PROPAGATION** Surface-sow seed at 61°F (16°C) in spring, or root semi-ripe cuttings with bottom heat from late spring to midsummer.
• **PESTS AND DISEASES** Infrequent.

K. baxteri ▣ Freely branching shrub, erect at first then spreading to a domed or rounded outline. Produces narrowly oblong, spreading, mid- to deep green leaves, ¾in (2cm) long, with white margins. Scarlet flowers, 1in (2.5cm) across, with long red stamens and yellow anthers, are borne in many short, dense spikes, to 4in (10cm) long, from spring to early summer. Thrives in seaside gardens. ↕↔ 3–6ft (1–2m) or more. Western Australia. ❀ (min. 41°F/5°C)
K. capitata. Bushy, rounded, freely branching shrub, erect at first but soon spreading, with upright, narrowly obovate to elliptic, mid-green leaves, ¼–½in (6–15mm) long, with arching tips. From spring to early summer, produces many small, rounded heads, ¾in (2cm) across, of deep mauve-pink flowers, ½in (1.5cm) long, with long stamens of the same color, tipped with cream anthers. ↕↔ 3–5ft (1–1.5m). New South Wales, Queensland. ❀ (min. 41°F/5°C)

Kunzea baxteri (inset: flower detail)

L

LABLAB *syn.* DOLICHOS

FABACEAE

Genus of one species of short-lived, herbaceous, perennial climber found in scrub in tropical Africa. Twining stems bear alternate, 3-palmate leaves and short, axillary racemes of fragrant, pea-like flowers. *L. purpureus* is extensively cultivated in Asia and North Africa for its edible fruit pods. Where not hardy, grow as a tender annual, or in a cool or temperate greenhouse. In warmer areas, train over a pergola or wall.

• **CULTIVATION** Under glass, grow in soil-based potting mix in full light. When in growth, water freely and apply a balanced liquid fertilizer every 10–14 days until flowering; water sparingly in winter. Outdoors, grow in any well-drained soil in full sun (for the best crop of beans, water and fertilize as for plants under glass). Provide support of netting or a trellis. Pruning group 11, in spring.

• **PROPAGATION** In cool climates, sow seed at 66–75°F (19–24°C) in spring. In warm climates, sow *in situ* when warm enough: 66–75°F (19–24°C).

• **PESTS AND DISEASES** Occasionally affected by leaf spot.

L. purpureus ■ syn. *Dolichos lablab, D. niger, D. purpureus* (Egyptian bean, Hyacinth bean, Indian bean, Lablab). Fast-growing, twining, perennial climber bearing 3-palmate, mid- to dark green leaves, composed of ovate to triangular leaflets, 4–6in (10–15cm) long. Bears fragrant, purple or white flowers, ½–1in (1–2.5cm) long, in racemes 8–16in (20–40cm) long, mainly in summer and autumn. Nearly flat, edible pods, 4–6in (10–15cm) long, are flushed or entirely purple, and contain 3–6 white to buff, reddish brown, brown, or black beans. ↕ 6–20ft (2–6m). Tropical Africa. ❀ (min. 45°F/7°C)

+ LABURNOCYTISUS

FABACEAE

Deciduous tree, a graft hybrid, grown for its colorful, pea-like flowers borne in late spring and early summer. The leaves are alternate and 3-palmate. A curious specimen tree, + *L. adamii* is also effective planted in small groups.

• **CULTIVATION** Grow in moderately fertile, moist but well-drained soil in full sun. Pruning group 1; remove any suckers that arise from the rootstock.

• **PROPAGATION** Graft onto *Laburnum* seedlings in winter.

• **PESTS AND DISEASES** Infrequent.

+ *L. adamii* ■ (*Chamaecytisus purpureus* + *Laburnum anagyroides*). Spreading, deciduous tree with 3-palmate, dark green leaves, consisting of oval leaflets, to 2½in (6cm) long. Pea-like flowers occur in 3 colors, each borne in separate racemes in late spring and early summer: 2 are single colors, yellow and purple, true to each parent; the third is purple-pink with a yellow flush. ↕ 25ft (8m), ↔ 20ft (6m). Garden origin. Zone 7.

Lablab purpureus

+ *Laburnocytisus adamii*

LABURNUM

Golden chain tree

FABACEAE

Genus of 2 species of deciduous trees from woodland and thickets in the mountains of S. central Europe, S.E. Europe, and W. Asia. They are grown for their profuse, pendent, usually axillary racemes of pea-like yellow flowers, produced in late spring and early summer. The leaves are alternate and 3-palmate. Useful in a small garden as specimen trees or to form a pergola. All parts are highly toxic if ingested.

• **CULTIVATION** Grow in moderately fertile, well-drained soil in full sun. Pruning group 1.

• **PROPAGATION** Sow seed (species only) in containers in a cold frame in autumn. Graft in late winter, or bud in summer.

• **PESTS AND DISEASES** May be affected by leaf spot, canker, twig blight, and tip dieback, as well as aphids and mealybugs.

L. anagyroides, syn. *L. vulgare* (Common laburnum). Spreading tree with hairy, gray-green young shoots, and dark green leaves composed of 3 elliptic-obovate leaflets, to 3in (8cm) long, hairy beneath. In late spring and early summer, produces bright yellow flowers in dense racemes, 4–12in (10–30cm) long. ↕↔ 25ft (8m). E. France to Italy, S. central Europe, Slovenia, Croatia. Zone 6.
L. vulgare see *L. anagyroides*.
L. x watereri (*L. alpinum* x *L. anagyroides*). Spreading tree with virtually hairless young shoots, and dark green leaves composed of 3 elliptic-obovate leaflets, to 3in (8cm) long. Produces yellow flowers in dense racemes, to 20in (50cm) long, in late spring and early summer. ↕↔ 25ft (8m). Garden origin (also occurs in the wild where parents grow together). Zone 6. **'Alford's Weeping'** is a small tree with a widely spreading crown and pendulous branches. **'Vossii'** ■ has hairy young shoots, and produces racemes, to 24in (60cm) long, of golden yellow flowers.

Laburnum x *watereri* 'Vossii'

LACCOSPADIX

ARECACEAE

Genus of one species of single- or cluster-stemmed palm from rainforest in N.E. Australia. Arching, pinnate leaves are borne in a terminal cluster and die *in situ*, forming a skirt-like mass below the living crown. Spikes of bowl-shaped, 3-petaled flowers are borne between the leaves. Where not hardy, grow in a temperate or warm greenhouse; in warmer areas, grow as a specimen tree.

• **CULTIVATION** Under glass, grow in soil-based potting mix in full light. In growth, water freely and apply a balanced liquid fertilizer monthly; water sparingly in winter. Pot on or top-dress in spring. Outdoors, grow in moderately fertile, moist, well-drained soil in full sun.

• **PROPAGATION** Sow seed at 81°F (27°C) in spring.

• **PESTS AND DISEASES** Spider mites may be troublesome under glass.

L. australasica. Slow-growing palm, usually with a single stem but sometimes with small clusters of stems, ringed with conspicuous leaf scars. Long-stalked, pinnate leaves, 6–10ft (2–3m) long, consist of many narrowly linear-lance-shaped, sparsely scaly, mid- to deep green leaflets. Yellow flowers are borne in spikes, 3ft (1m) or more long, usually in summer. ↕ 20ft (6m) occasionally more, ↔ 10–15ft (3–5m). Queensland. ❀ (min. 55°F/13°C)

LACHENALIA

Cape cowslip

LILIACEAE

Genus of 90 species of bulbous perennials from grassland or rocky sites, on often seasonally moist ground, in South Africa. They are grown for their spikes or racemes of showy, tubular, bell-shaped, or cylindrical flowers, borne on often mottled stems from autumn to spring. Leaves are basal, variably shaped, and frequently attractively spotted. Where not hardy, grow in a cool greenhouse or a conservatory. In frost-free areas, grow in a rock garden or in an open site among low shrubs.

• **CULTIVATION** Plant bulbs 1in (2.5cm) deep. Under glass, grow in soil-based potting mix in full light. Water moderately until in full growth, then water freely, adding a balanced liquid fertilizer every 10–14 days. Reduce watering as the leaves fade, then keep dry until fresh growth starts in autumn. Outdoors, grow in light, well-drained soil in full sun.

• **PROPAGATION** Sow seed at 55–64°F (13–18°C) as soon as ripe, or remove bulblets in summer or autumn just before replanting or repotting.

• **PESTS AND DISEASES** Infrequent.

L. aloides ▣ syn. *L. tricolor*. Bulbous perennial with semi-erect, broadly lance- to strap-shaped, purple-spotted, slightly glaucous, mid-green leaves, 8in (20cm) long. In winter or early spring, produces racemes of up to 20 pendent, tubular yellow flowers, 1–1½in (2.5–4cm) long, that shade to scarlet at the tips. ↕6–11in (15–28cm), PD2in (5cm). South Africa (Western Cape). ❀ (min. 41°F/5°C). **'Nelsonii'** ▣ has golden yellow flowers and unspotted leaves. **'Pearsonii'** is robust, with semi-erect, strap-shaped, mid-green leaves, to 10in (25cm) long, mottled with brown, and produces apricot flowers, to 1¼in (3cm) long, with the inner tepals tipped red to maroon; ↕12–16in (30–40cm). **var. *quadricolor*** has reddish orange buds opening to reddish orange-based, yellow-and-green flowers, with purple-maroon tips to the inner segments.
L. angustifolia see *L. contaminata*.
L. bulbifera, syn. *L. pendula*. Robust, bulbous perennial with semi-erect, ovate, lance-shaped, or strap-shaped, mid-green leaves, to 12in (30cm) long, usually heavily spotted brown-purple. In winter or spring, produces loose racemes of few to many pendent, cylindrical, red

Lachenalia aloides

Lachenalia aloides 'Nelsonii'

or orange flowers, 1¼–1½in (3–4cm) long, with green and purple tips. ↕12in (30cm), PD2in (5cm). South Africa (Western Cape). ❀ (min. 41°F/5°C)
L. contaminata, syn. *L. angustifolia*. Bulbous perennial with erect or semi-erect, narrow, grass-like, unmarked, mid- to deep green leaves, to 8in (20cm) long. In spring, bears racemes or spikes of few to many, open bell-shaped, slightly scented white flowers, ¼–⅜in (6–9mm) long, with maroon tips and stripes, held at right angles to the stems. ↕2½–10in (6–25cm), PD2in (5cm). South Africa (Western Cape). ❀ (min. 41°F/5°C)
L. glaucina see *L. orchioides* var. *glaucina*.
L. glaucina* var. *pallida see *L. orchioides*.
L. mutabilis. Bulbous perennial with usually one semi-erect, lance-shaped, sometimes glaucous, mid-green leaf, to 8in (20cm) long, occasionally faintly spotted maroon. In winter or spring, produces dense spikes of up to 25 horizontal, stalkless, urn- to bell-shaped flowers, ½in (1.5cm) long, pale blue and white, with dark yellow inner tepals and dark tips, or rarely entirely greenish white. ↕4–18in (10–45cm), PD2in (5cm). South Africa (Northern Cape, Western Cape). ❀ (min. 41°F/5°C)
L. orchioides, syn. *L. glaucina* var. *pallida*. Bulbous perennial with 1 or 2 semi-erect, lance- or strap-shaped, mid-green leaves, to 11in (28cm) long, sometimes spotted brown. In late winter or spring, produces dense spikes of many semi-erect, oblong-cylindrical, fragrant, white, greenish yellow, or creamy yellow flowers, ½in (1.5cm) long, with flared tepals, fading to dull red as they mature. ↕6–16in (15–40cm), PD2in (5cm). South Africa (Western Cape). ❀ (min. 41°F/5°C). **var. *glaucina***, syn. *L. glaucina*, has blue- or purple-shaded flowers with a fainter scent.
L. pendula see *L. bulbifera*.
L. rubida. Bulbous perennial with semi-erect, lance- to strap-shaped, mid- to deep green leaves, to 5½in (14cm) long, mottled deep purple. In autumn or early winter, produces racemes of few to many pendent, cylindrical, bright pink or ruby-red flowers, ¾–1¼in (2–3cm) long, shading to purple at the tips. ↕2½–10in (6–25cm), PD2in (5cm). South Africa (Western Cape, Eastern Cape). ❀ (min. 41°F/5°C)
L. tricolor see *L. aloides*.
L. unicolor. Very variable, bulbous perennial with lance- to strap-shaped, pale to dark green leaves, to 6in (15cm) long, usually with maroon warts above. In spring, bears racemes of many oblong-bell-shaped flowers, ¼–⅜in (6–9mm) long, that vary from cream with green tips, to pink, lilac-pink, magenta, blue, or purple, with darker tips. ↕3–12in (8–30cm), PD2in (5cm). South Africa (Western Cape). ❀ (min. 41°F/5°C)

LACTUCA

COMPOSITAE

Genus of about 100 species of widely variable, leafy, cool-season annuals, native to the Northern Hemisphere. The edible leaves are hairless, growing in a basal rosette and maturing into tightly or loosely folded leaves in a great variety of colors and forms. The tiny, yellow ray flowers are borne in dense clusters.

• **CULTIVATION** Grow in highly organic, garden soil, full sun, or under glass in shallow forms. Sow as soon as all danger of hard frosts is over.

• **PROPAGATION** Sow seeds in situ in rows in early spring, barely cover with soil. Transplant to 4in (10cm) apart.

• **PESTS AND DISEASES** Aphids, slugs, cutworms, mosaic virus, downy mildew.

L. sativa (Iceberg, Romaine, Boston, Bibb, and others). Lettuce is hardy and can be grown in cool conditions throughout the year. Fast-growing, 26–45 days. ↕3–4ft (91–121cm) ↔6in (15cm). ❀ (min. 35°F/2°C)

LAELIA

ORCHIDACEAE

Genus of about 50 species of evergreen, epiphytic or terrestrial orchids occurring in coastal regions up to altitudes of 8,300ft (2,600m), often in oak forests, from Mexico to Brazil and Argentina. They have robust or slender, elongated pseudobulbs, each with 1 or 2 (rarely 3) semi-rigid, narrowly oval, club-shaped, oblong, strap-shaped, or linear leaves. Brightly colored flowers are borne in racemes from the apex of the pseudobulb. Many inter-generic hybrids derived from crosses with *Cattleya* and other related genera are also available.

• **CULTIVATION** Cool-growing orchids. Grow large species in epiphytic orchid potting mix in a slatted basket, and small ones epiphytically on a slab of bark. In summer, provide moist, shady conditions; water freely, adding fertilizer at every third watering, and mist once or twice daily. In winter, provide full light and water sparingly. See also p.46.

• **PROPAGATION** Divide when the plants overflow their containers. Remove backbulbs of the Mexican species and pot up each one separately.

• **PESTS AND DISEASES** Scale insects, spider mites, whiteflies, and mealybugs sometimes are problems. Prone to *Cercospora* leaf spot and black rot.

L. anceps ▣ Epiphytic or lithophytic orchid with ovate-oblong pseudobulbs, each with 1, or occasionally 2, lance-shaped, leathery, light green leaves, 6in (15cm) long. In winter, bears racemes, to 24in (60cm) long, of 2–5 light rose-pink flowers, 2½in (6cm) across, with reddish purple lips and yellow throats with purple veining. ↕6–9in (15–23cm), ↔1¼–1½in (3–4cm). C. Mexico. ❀ (min. 50°F/10°C; max. 86°F/30°C)

Laelia anceps

L. autumnalis. Epiphytic orchid with ovate-oblong pseudobulbs, each with 2 or 3 oblong to lance-shaped, leathery leaves, 5–8in (12–20cm) long. In winter, bears long-stemmed racemes, 12–39in (30–100cm) long, of 4–10 rose-pink flowers, 2½in (6cm) across, with white throats and rose-purple lips. ↕12–39in (30–100cm), ↔12in (30cm). Mexico. ❀ (min. 50°F/10°C; max. 86°F/30°C)
L. cinnabarina ▣ Epiphytic orchid with cylindrical, stem-like pseudobulbs, swollen at the bases, each with 1 or 2 linear to oblong, dark green leaves, 4–10in (10–25cm) long. Bears racemes, to 16in (40cm) long, of 5–15 brilliant cinnabar-red flowers, 2½in (6cm) across, in winter. ↕16in (40cm), ↔6in (15cm). S.E. Brazil. ❀ (min. 55°F/13°C; max. 86°F/30°C)
L. crispa. Epiphytic orchid with slender, compressed pseudobulbs, each with one oblong to strap-shaped, leathery leaf, 6–12in (15–30cm) long. In summer, bears racemes, 4–10in (10–25cm) long, of 2 or 3 white flowers, 4in (10cm) across, with deep magenta veining on frilly lips. ↕16in (40cm), ↔12in (30cm). 86°F/30°C)
L. flava. Epiphytic orchid with cylindrical, stem-like pseudobulbs, each with one lance-shaped to oblong, dark green leaf, 3–6in (8–15cm) long. In spring, bears upright racemes, 12–18in (30–45cm) long, of 5–10 yellow flowers, 1¼–1¾in (3–4.5cm) across. ↕12–18in (30–45cm), ↔6in (15cm). S.E. Brazil. ❀ (min. 55°F/13°C; max. 86°F/30°C)
L. pumila. Epiphytic orchid with ovoid pseudobulbs, each with one linear to oblong leaf, 3–5in (8–13cm) long. In autumn, lilac-rose flowers, 2½in (6cm)

Laelia cinnabarina

across, with rose-purple on the lips, are borne singly, or rarely in twos, on stems 1½–4in (4–10cm) tall, at the apex of each pseudobulb. ↕ 8in (20cm), ↔ 9in (23cm). S.E. Brazil. ❀ (min. 55°F/13°C; max. 86°F/30°C)

L. purpurata. Epiphytic orchid with slender pseudobulbs, each with one oblong, leathery leaf, 8–12in (20–30cm) long. In early summer, bears racemes, to 12in (30cm) long, of 2–7 white to pink flowers, 6in (15cm) across, with purple in the lip centers. ↕ 18in (45cm), ↔ 12in (30cm). Brazil. ❀ (min. 55°F/13°C; max. 86°F/30°C)

L. speciosa, syn. *L. majalis.* Epiphytic orchid with thick, ovoid pseudobulbs, each with one oblong to lance-shaped, stiff leaf, 4–6in (10–15cm) long. In early summer, pale rose-lilac to rich magenta flowers, 3½in (9cm) across, are borne singly or in twos, on slender stems, 4–8in (10–20cm) tall, from the apex of each pseudobulb. ↕↔ 6–8in (15–20cm). C. Mexico. ❀ (min. 50°F/10°C; max. 86°F/30°C)

L. xanthina. Epiphytic orchid with club-shaped pseudobulbs, each with one strap-shaped, fleshy, blue-green leaf, 12in (30cm) long. In spring and summer, bears racemes, 10in (25cm) long, of 2–6 yellow flowers, 4in (10cm) across, with purple-streaked white lips,↕ 20in (50cm), ↔ 12in (30cm). Brazil. ❀ (min. 55°F/13°C; max. 86°F/30°C)

L

x LAELIOCATTLEYA

ORCHIDACEAE

Bigeneric hybrid genus of evergreen orchids, derived from crosses between *Laelia* and *Cattleya.* Racemes of large, showy flowers, in a range of bright colors, are borne at the tips of the pseudobulbs, above the foliage. They mostly produce a single, lance-shaped, leathery leaf, but may also bear 2 on each elongated pseudobulb, depending on the parentage of the hybrid. Often referred to colloquially as cattleyas.

• **CULTIVATION** Cool-growing orchids. Grow in epiphytic orchid potting mix in a slatted basket. In summer, provide high humidity and bright filtered light; water freely, adding fertilizer at every third watering, and mist once or twice daily. In winter, provide full light and water more sparingly. See also p.46.

• **PROPAGATION** Divide when the plants overflow their containers, or remove backbulbs and pot up separately.

• **PESTS AND DISEASES** As for *Laelia.*

x *L.* Trick or Treat 'Orange Princess' ▣ (x *L.* Icarus x x *L.* Chit Chat). Evergreen orchid with cylindrical

x *Laeliocattleya* Trick or Treat 'Orange Princess'

Lagarosiphon major

pseudobulbs and 2 narrowly oval leaves, 4in (10cm) long. Bears star-shaped, bright orange flowers, 1½in (4cm) across, in short racemes in spring. ↕↔ 12in (30cm). ❀ (min. 55°F/13°C; max. 86°F/30°C)

LAGAROSIPHON

Curly water thyme

HYDROCHARITACEAE

Genus of 9 species of semi-evergreen, submerged aquatic perennials occurring in still or slow-moving water in Africa. Used extensively as oxygenators in aquaria and in outdoor pools, they form dense, submerged masses of branched stems that support numerous linear-lance-shaped, recurved, often spirally arranged leaves and very small, white or pink flowers. Where not hardy, grow in a cold-water aquarium.

• **CULTIVATION** In an aquarium, admit full light, but do not provide additional heat; plants tend to become leggy in temperatures above 68°F (20°C). In an outdoor pond, grow in a submerged basket of loamy soil in full sun. Cut back regularly to restrict spread, and remove dead stems to prevent them from decomposing in the water.

• **PROPAGATION** Take stem-tip cuttings in spring or summer.

• **PESTS AND DISEASES** Infrequent.

L. major ▣ syn. *Elodea crispa* of gardens. Submerged aquatic perennial with branched, fragile stems, to 3ft (1m) long, covered in linear to lance-shaped, recurved, dark green leaves, ¼–1in (0.6–2.5cm) long. Tubular, pink-tinged green flowers, ⅛in (3mm) long, develop inside translucent spathes in summer. May become invasive; considered a noxious weed in some areas. ↔ indefinite. Southern Africa. ❀ (min. 35°F/2°C)

LAGENOPHORA

ASTERACEAE

Genus of about 15 species of low-growing, herbaceous perennials found mostly in open sites in scrub, grassland, and at forest margins, from lowland to subalpine altitudes, in Asia, Australasia, and Central and South America. They are cultivated for their solitary, daisy-like, white to purple flowerheads, borne over long periods in summer. The mostly basal leaves are oblong to broadly ovate, and may be entire or toothed to pinnatifid. Grow lagenophoras in a rock garden, on a sunny bank, or at the front of a border.

• **CULTIVATION** Grow in well-drained soil in full sun. Propagate regularly, since they are often short-lived.

• **PROPAGATION** Sow seed in containers in a cold frame as soon as ripe.

• **PESTS AND DISEASES** Slugs and snails may be probems.

L. pinnatifida. Mat-forming herbaceous perennial with rosettes of obovate to oblong, pinnatifid, sometimes toothed or further lobed, hairy, bronze-tinted, mid-green leaves, to 2½in (6cm) long. In summer, bears solitary, off-white flowerheads, to ½in (1.5cm) across, on stems 2–4in (5–10cm) long, sometimes to 10in (25cm) long. ↕ to 4in (10cm), ↔ to 6in (15cm). Mountain grassland in New Zealand. Zone 7b.

LAGERSTROEMIA

LYTHRACEAE

Genus of approximately 50 species of deciduous or evergreen shrubs and trees occurring in deciduous woodland, often near rivers, in warm-temperate and tropical regions from Asia to Australia. They are cultivated for their conical, brightly colored panicles of flowers, with characteristic crinkled petals, and for their often peeling bark. The leaves vary greatly in shape within the genus, but are usually opposite. Where marginally hardy, grow against a warm, sunny wall, or overwinter in a cool or temperate greenhouse. In warmer climates, grow as specimens, in group plantings, or as a hedge or screen.

• **CULTIVATION** Under glass, grow in soil-based potting mix in full light. During the growing season, water freely and apply a balanced liquid fertilizer every 6–8 weeks; water sparingly at other times. Outdoors, grow in moderately fertile, well-drained soil in full sun. Pruning group 1; will withstand hard pruning if renovation is required.

• **PROPAGATION** Sow seed at 50–55°F (10–13°C) in spring. Root softwood cuttings in late spring, or semi-ripe cuttings with bottom heat in summer.

• **PESTS AND DISEASES** Dieback and powdery mildew, as well as aphids, scale insects, mealybugs, and whiteflies, can occur.

Lagerstroemia fauriei

Lagerstroemia indica 'Catawba'

L. fauriei ▣ Upright, many-stemmed, deciduous tree with peeling, red-brown bark and oblong, dark green leaves, to 4in (10cm) long. In summer, white flowers, ½in (1.5cm) across, are produced in panicles 2–4in (5–10cm) long. ↕↔ 25ft (8m). Japan. Zone 7b. **'Fantasy'** is vigorous and hardier than the species. Zone 7.

L. indica (Crape myrtle). Upright, deciduous tree or large shrub with peeling, gray-and-brown bark and obovate to oblong, dark green leaves, to 3in (8cm) long, bronze when young. From summer to autumn, white, pink, red, or purple flowers, ¾–1in (2–2.5cm) across, are produced in panicles to 8in (20cm) long. ↕↔ 25ft (8m). China. Zone 7b. Many of the following are hybrids of *L. indica* and *L. fauriei* and show resistance to powdery mildew. **'Catawba'** ▣ produces purple flowers and orange-red autumn leaves; ↕↔ to 10ft (3m). **'Cherokee'** is an open-branched shrub with brilliant red flowers. **'Dallas Red'** is particularly hardy and fast-growing, and produces dark red flowers. **'Lavender Dwarf'** is a spreading shrub, bearing a profusion of light lavender-purple flowers; ↕↔ to 6ft (2m). **'Miami'** ▣ bears dark pink flowers from mid-summer to early autumn; ↕ 15ft (5m), ↔ 8ft (2.5m). **'Muskogee'** is a vigorous tree with mid-lavender flowers.

Lagerstroemia indica 'Miami'

agerstroemia indica 'Natchez'

Natchez' ■ is a vigorous cultivar with vhite flowers; ↕↔ to 20ft (6m). **'Near ast'** produces pale pink flowers; ↕↔ 15ft 5m). **'Seminole'** ■ is compact, and roduces mid-pink flowers from mid-ummer to early autumn; ↕↔ 7–8ft 2.2–2.5m). **'Sioux'** bears very large pink owers, 2in (5cm) across; ↕↔ to 12ft 4m). **'Tuscarora'** is a fast-growing tree vith dark coral-pink flowers. **'Tuskegee'** as spreading branches and produces large anicles, to 14in (35cm) long, of dark ink flowers; ↕↔ 15ft (5m). **'White Dwarf'** is a low mound-forming shrub, nd freely bears white blooms; ↕↔ 3ft 1m). **'Wichita'** is vase-shaped, ometimes forming a small tree; it bears avender flowers from summer to late utumn; ↕↔ 11ft (3.5m).

. speciosa (Giant crape myrtle, Pride of ndia, Queen's crape myrtle). Spreading, eely branching, evergreen tree with eeling, light brown bark. Ovate to lliptic-oblong leaves, 3–8in (8–20cm) ong, are gray-green above, sepia-flushed eneath. From spring to autumn, roduces erect, open panicles, to 16in 40cm) long, of many pink, mauve, urple, or white flowers, to 3in (5cm) vide. ↕ 30–78ft (10–24m), ↔ 15–30ft (5–10m). Tropical Asia. ❀ (min. 41°F/5°C)

agerstroemia indica 'Seminole' (inset: flower detail)

LAGUNARIA

Norfolk Island hibiscus

MALVACEAE

Genus, allied to *Hibiscus*, of one species of evergreen tree from coastal woodland in E. Australia. It is grown for its habit; its alternate, simple, entire, leathery leaves; and its solitary, 5-petaled, hibiscus-like flowers, produced from the upper leaf axils. Where not hardy, grow in a cool greenhouse. In warmer areas, grow as a specimen tree, or as a windbreak in a coastal garden. Contact with the needle-like spikes of the seed pods can be very irritating to the skin and mucous membranes, causing intense sneezing.

• **CULTIVATION** Under glass, grow in soil-based potting mix in full light. When in full growth, water freely and apply a balanced liquid fertilizer monthly; water sparingly at other times. Outdoors, grow in moderately fertile, well-drained soil in full sun. Pruning group 1; may need restrictive pruning under glass.

• **PROPAGATION** Sow seed at 61°F (16°C) in spring, or root greenwood cuttings with bottom heat in summer.

• **PESTS AND DISEASES** Scale insects may be a problem under glass.

L. patersonii (Cow itch tree, Queensland pyramid tree). Pyramidal to columnar tree, loosely branched when young, denser when mature, with ovate to broadly lance-shaped, blunt-tipped leaves, 2–4in (5–10cm) long, matte, almost olive-green above, densely whitish gray-scaled beneath. Bears a succession of cup- to trumpet-shaped, pink to rose-pink flowers, 1½–2½in (4–6cm) across, mainly in summer, followed by ovoid seed capsules, 1in (2.5cm) long. More than one plant is needed to produce seed. ↕ to 50ft (15m), ↔ 25–40ft (8–12m). E. Australia (including Lord Howe Island, Norfolk Island). ❀ (min. 37–41°F/3–5°C)

Lagurus ovatus

LAGURUS

Hare's tail

POACEAE

Genus of one species of annual grass occurring on maritime sands on the Mediterranean coast of S. Europe and, more rarely, on dry wasteland inland. Valued for the effect of its ornamental flowerheads in summer, it is attractive in groups in a herbaceous or mixed border. The flowerheads are also useful in fresh or dried arrangements; pick them before fully mature for drying.

• **CULTIVATION** Grow in light, ideally sandy, moderately fertile, well-drained soil in full sun.

• **PROPAGATION** Sow seed *in situ* in spring, or in containers in a cold frame in autumn.

• **PESTS AND DISEASES** Infrequent.

L. ovatus ■ (Hare's tail). Tufted grass with arching, linear to narrowly lance-shaped, flat, pale green leaves, to 8in (20cm) long. Throughout summer, bears dense, ovoid to oblong-cylindrical, spike-like panicles, to 2½in (6cm) long, of softly hairy, often purple-tinged, pale green spikelets, which mature to pale creamy buff. ↕ to 20in (50cm), ↔ 12in (30cm). Mediterranean. **'Nanus'** is much more compact; ↕ to 5in (13cm).

LAMARCKIA

POACEAE

Genus of one species of annual grass occurring in open habitats in the Mediterranean region. It has twisted, linear leaves and one-sided panicles of attractively colored spikelets. Grow in a herbaceous, mixed, or annual border for its distinctive inflorescences, which are useful in both fresh and dried flower arrangements.

• **CULTIVATION** Grow in light, sandy, well-drained soil in full sun.

Lamarckia aurea

• **PROPAGATION** Make successive sowings *in situ* from early to late spring. Alternatively, sow in containers in a cold frame in late spring and transfer to the flowering site, to replace earlier sown plants after they have flowered. Plants from early sowings are usually past their best by midsummer.

• **PESTS AND DISEASES** Infrequent.

L. aurea ■ (Golden top, Toothbrush grass). Loosely tufted grass with wiry stems and flat, twisted, broadly linear, pale green leaves, to 5in (13cm) long. From midspring to summer, produces one-sided, oblong panicles, to 3in (8cm) long, of densely packed, downswept, bristled spikelets, shimmering golden yellow or whitish green, becoming silvery, and often purple flushed when mature. ↕ 12in (30cm), ↔ 10in (25cm). Mediterranean.

LAMBERTIA

PROTEACEAE

Genus of 9 or 10 species of evergreen shrubs found on sandy or gravelly soils in heathland and woodland in Australia. They are cultivated for their slender, tubular flowers, which are solitary or borne in terminal clusters of 2–7, and surrounded by often colorful bracts; each flower has 4 narrow tepals that roll back like watch springs on opening. Leaves are usually narrow, simple, and entire, and are borne in pairs or whorls of 3. Where not hardy, grow in a cool or temperate greenhouse. In warmer climates, grow outdoors in a border.

• **CULTIVATION** Under glass, grow in a mix of 1 part loam and 3 parts each grit (or perlite) and peat, in full light. From spring to summer, water freely and apply a phosphate-free liquid fertilizer monthly; water sparingly in winter. Outdoors, grow in poor to moderately fertile, sharply drained, neutral to acidic soil in full sun. Pruning group 1; may need restrictive pruning under glass.

• **PROPAGATION** Sow seed at 64°F (18°C) in spring, ideally singly in small containers. Root softwood cuttings in spring, or semi-ripe cuttings with bottom heat in summer; rooting may be slow and unreliable.

• **PESTS AND DISEASES** *Phytophthora* root rot may be a problem in moist soil.

L. ericifolia. Upright shrub with linear to lance-shaped, wavy-margined, mid-green leaves, ½in (1.5cm) long, borne in

Lambertia formosa

pairs. Bears clusters of up to 7 cream, orange, or pink flowers, 1½–2in (3–5cm) long, surrounded by green floral bracts, shorter than the flowers, throughout the year. ↕ 6–10ft (2–3m), ↔ to 5ft (1.5m). W. Australia. ❄ (min. 45°F/7°C)

L. formosa ▣ (Mountain devil). Erect shrub of open habit, spreading with age, and growing from a thickened, underground rootstock. Linear, sharp-tipped leaves, to 2in (5cm) long, usually borne in whorls of 3, are glossy, mid- to deep green above, white downy beneath. Bears clusters of up to 7 red flowers, 1¼–2in (3–5cm) long, surrounded by narrow, spreading, pink-flushed green bracts, some shorter than the flowers, some much longer, mainly from spring to summer, but often at other times of the year. ↕ to 6ft (2m), ↔ to 5ft (1.5m). New South Wales. ❄ (min. 45°F/7°C)

▷ ***Lamiastrum*** see *Lamium*

LAMIUM

syn. GALEOBDOLON, LAMIASTRUM
Deadnettle
LAMIACEAE

Genus of about 50 species of annuals and usually rhizomatous perennials, occurring in habitats ranging from dry, open scrub to moist woodland, from Europe to Asia, and widespread in the Mediterranean and N. Africa. They have square stems and opposite, mainly ovate or kidney-shaped, coarsely toothed, wrinkled leaves, sometimes with colored markings. The 2-lipped flowers are solitary, or borne in whorls in dense, leafy, spike-like inflorescences ("spikes"),

Lamium maculatum

mainly from late spring to summer. Grown mainly for their foliage, they provide a good groundcover among shrubs or robust perennials. The larger species can be very invasive in moist, moderately fertile soils, but are less vigorous in poor soils; they may also be used in a border or in light woodland. Grow smaller, non-invasive species in a scree bed, rock garden, or alpine house.

• **CULTIVATION** Grow the vigorous, ground-covering species in moist but well-drained soil in deep or partial shade. Site away from other small plants, and dig out rhizomes when necessary to confine spread. Grow *L. armenum* and *L. garganicum* subsp. *striatum* in sharply drained soil in full sun or partial shade. Protect *L. armenum* from excessive winter moisture.

• **PROPAGATION** Sow seed in containers in a cold frame in autumn or spring. Divide in autumn or early spring. For small species, take stem-tip cuttings of non-flowering shoots in early summer.

• **PESTS AND DISEASES** Downy mildew, powdery mildew, leaf spot, slugs, and snails are common problems.

L. armenum. Slow-growing, non-invasive, mat-forming or tufted perennial with obovate to diamond-shaped, scalloped, sometimes palmately lobed, mid-green leaves, ½in (1.5cm) long. In summer, produces solitary, long-tubed and hooded, pale pink to white flowers, to 2in (5cm) long, from the upper leaf axils. ↕ 2in (5cm), ↔ to 4in (10cm). Turkey (Anatolia). Zone 4.

L. galeobdolon, syn. *Galeobdolon luteum*, *Lamiastrum galeobdolon*

Lamium maculatum 'Beacon Silver'

(Yellow archangel). Very invasive, rhizomatous and often stoloniferous perennial with erect or creeping stems bearing very broadly ovate or diamond-shaped, sometimes heart-shaped, toothed, mid-green leaves, to 2½in (6cm) long, often marked silver. Spikes of whorled, brown-spotted yellow flowers, to ¾in (2cm) long, are produced in summer. ↕ 24in (60cm), ↔ indefinite. Europe to W. Asia. Zone 3. The following cultivars are less invasive, but still require careful siting. **'Florentinum'**, syn. 'Variegatum', has creeping stems and silver-centered leaves with green edges. **'Hermann's Pride'** ▣ forms a dense mat of small, ovate, heavily silver-streaked leaves, 1¼in (3cm) long. **'Silver Angel'** is more prostrate, with silver leaves; ↕ to 20in (50cm). **'Variegatum'** see 'Florentinum'.

L. garganicum. Mat- to clump-forming perennial with upright stems that bear heart-shaped, broadly ovate, toothed, mid-green leaves, to 3in (8cm) long. Produces upright spikes of whorled, pale pink flowers, to 1¼in (3cm) long, from the upper leaf axils in early summer. ↕ 18in (45cm), ↔ 20in (50cm). Italy, Greece to Turkey and Iraq. Zone 4. **'Golden Carpet'** has mid-green leaves variegated with gold, and produces pink-and-white striped flowers. **subsp. *striatum*** is compact, with abundant spikes of pink flowers, heavily spotted and streaked dark purple; ↕ to 6in (15cm), ↔ to 8in (20cm).

L. maculatum ▣ (Spotted deadnettle). Low-growing, rhizomatous and stoloniferous perennial with prostrate and ascending stems bearing triangular-ovate, toothed, matte, mid-green leaves, ¾–3in (2–8cm) long, heart-shaped at the bases, and often mottled or zoned silvery white or pink. In summer, bears spikes of whorled, red-purple, sometimes white or pink flowers, to ¾in (2cm) long. Excellent as a groundcover. ↕ 8in (20cm), ↔ 3ft (1m). Europe and North Africa to W. Asia. Zone 3. **f. *album*** ▣ is mat-forming, with matte, mid-green leaves, zoned silvery white; it produces white flowers from midspring to midsummer; ↕ 6in (15cm), ↔ 24in (60cm); Europe. **'Aureum'**, syn. 'Gold Leaf', has yellow leaves with paler white centers, and produces pink flowers. **'Beacon Silver'** ▣ has silver leaves, narrowly margined green, and clear pale pink flowers. **'Beedham's White'** has chartreuse leaves and pure white flowers. **'Chequers'** has silver-centered green leaves and deep mauve-pink flowers; ↕ 6–12in (15–30cm). **'Gold Leaf'** see 'Aureum'. **'Pink Pewter'** has greenish gray-edged, silver-gray leaves, and clear pink flowers from late spring to midsummer. **'White Nancy'** bears pure white flowers above silver leaves that are narrowly margined green; ↕ to 6in (15cm), ↔ to 3ft (1m) or more.

L. orvala ▣ Non-invasive, clump-forming perennial with broadly ovate to triangular, toothed, softly hairy, dark green leaves, 4–6in (10–15cm) long. Produces spikes of whorled, pinkish purple flowers, 1¼–1½in (3–4cm) long, from late spring to summer. ↕ to 24in (60cm), usually less, ↔ 12in (30cm). Central S. Europe. Zone 5.

LAMPRANTHUS

AIZOACEAE

Genus of 180 or more species of erect or prostrate, perennial succulents from semi-desert areas of South Africa, especially the coastal belt. The opposite, cylindrical or 3-angled leaves often redden in full sun. Daisy-like flowers are profusely borne from summer to early autumn. Where not hardy, grow in a temperate greenhouse; they may also be used for summer bedding, especially in arid conditions. All species tolerate light frost for short periods. In warmer areas, grow in a desert garden or in a border with other succulents.

• **CULTIVATION** Under glass, grow in standard cactus potting mix in full light. From late spring to late summer, water

Lamium galeobdolon 'Hermann's Pride'

Lamium maculatum f. *album*

Lamium orvala

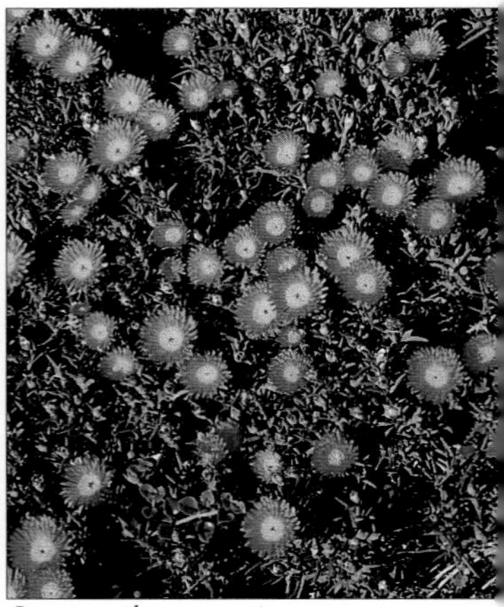

Lampranthus aurantiacus

Lampranthus deltoides

moderately and apply low-nitrogen fertilizer every 4–6 weeks; water very sparingly at other times. Outdoors, grow in poor, sharply drained soil in full sun. Where not hardy, lift in autumn and overwinter under glass. See also pp.48–49.
• **PROPAGATION** Sow seed at 66–75°F (19–24°C) in spring. Root sections of stem in spring and summer.
• **PESTS AND DISEASES** Susceptible to mealybugs and, in flower, aphids.

L. aurantiacus ■ Spreading, shrubby, sparsely branched succulent with semi-cylindrical, tapering, minutely spotted, gray-frosted, mid-green leaves, ¾–1¼in (2–3cm) long. Orange flowers, 1¼–2in (4–5cm) across, open in full sun from summer to early autumn. ↕ to 18in (45cm), ↔ indefinite. South Africa (Western Cape, Eastern Cape). ❄ (min. 45°F/7°C)
L. deltoides ■ syn. *Oscularia deltoides.* Spreading succulent with a mass of short stems bearing 3-angled, toothed, bluish gray leaves, ½in (1.5cm) long. From summer to early autumn, produces sometimes fragrant, pink to red flowers, ½–¾in (1.5–2cm) across. ↕ to 12in (30cm), ↔ indefinite. South Africa (Western Cape). ❄ (min. 45°F/7°C)
L. falcatus. Spreading, prostrate succulent with a mass of slender, tangled stems and 3-angled, curved, spotted, grayish green leaves, ¼in (6mm) long. Fragrant, purplish pink flowers, to ½in (1.5cm) across, are borne from summer to early autumn. ↕ to 12in (30cm), ↔ indefinite. South Africa (Western Cape). ❄ (min. 45°F/7°C)

Lampranthus purpureus

L. haworthii ■ Trailing or semi-erect, freely branching succulent with semi-cylindrical, tapering, densely gray-frosted, pale green leaves, 1–1½in (2.5–4cm) long. Bright purplish pink flowers, to 3in (8cm) across, are borne from summer to early autumn. ↕ to 20in (50cm), ↔ indefinite. South Africa (Western Cape, Eastern Cape). ❄ (min. 45°F/7°C)
L. purpureus ■ Trailing or semi-erect succulent with slender stems and branches bearing rounded, rough, bluish green leaves, to 1½in (4cm) long, shortly tapered at the tips. From summer to early autumn, bears pinkish purple flowers, to 1¼in (3cm) across. ↕ to 16in (40cm), ↔ indefinite. South Africa (Western Cape). ❄ (min. 45°F/7°C)
L. roseus, syn. *Mesembryanthemum multiradiatum.* Creeping or semi-erect succulent with 3-angled, mid-green to glaucous, gray-green leaves, 1¼in (3cm) long, covered with prominent, translucent dots. Bears pale rose-pink flowers, 1½in (4cm) across, from summer to early autumn. ↕ to 20in (50cm), ↔ indefinite. South Africa (Western Cape, Eastern Cape). ❄ (min. 45°F/7°C)

L. spectabilis ■ Variable, spreading, prostrate succulent with narrowly 3-angled to cylindrical, keeled, mid-green leaves, 2–3in (5–8cm) long, partly tinged red. Produces reddish purple or, occasionally, white flowers, 2–3in (5–8cm) across, from summer to early autumn. ↕ to 12in (30cm), ↔ indefinite. South Africa. ❄ (min. 45°F/7°C)

LANTANA

Shrub verbena

VERBENACEAE

Genus of 150 species of evergreen shrubs and perennials from tropical North, Central, and South America, and South Africa, usually occurring in pine woodland and on disturbed ground. They are grown for their small, 5-lobed, salverform flowers, grouped tightly into rounded, flattened, or domed, terminal heads. Leaves are simple and toothed, often wrinkled, and borne in opposite pairs or whorls of 3. Where not hardy, grow in a temperate greenhouse, or use as summer bedding. In warmer areas, grow in a border; low, spreading species are good groundcovers on a bank or between shrubs. All parts may cause

Lantana camara 'Radiation'

severe discomfort if ingested, and contact with foliage may irritate skin.
• **CULTIVATION** Under glass, grow in soil-based potting mix in full light. During the growing season, water freely and apply a balanced liquid fertilizer monthly; keep just moist in winter. Outdoors, grow in fertile, moist but well-drained soil in full sun. Pruning group 9; may need restrictive pruning in late winter under glass.
• **PROPAGATION** Sow seed at 61–64°F (16–18°C) in spring, or root semi-ripe cuttings with bottom heat in summer.
• **PESTS AND DISEASES** Whiteflies, spider mites, rust, virus disease, root knot nematode, stem rot, and leaf spot occur.

L. aculeata* f. *varia see *L. camara* f. *varia.*
***L. camara* cultivars.** Variable, often prickly-stemmed shrubs with ovate, finely wrinkled, strongly scented, slightly toothed, deep green leaves, 2–4in (5–10cm) long. Flowerheads 1–2in (2.5–5cm) across, in colors ranging from white to yellow and salmon-pink to red or purple, often in combinations, are borne from late spring to late autumn. ↕↔ 3–6ft (1–2m). ❄ (min. 50°F/10°C). **'Cream Carpet'** is low and spreading, with creamy white flowers; ↕ 12in (30cm), ↔ 30in (75cm). **'Fabiola'** bears bicolored, salmon-pink and yellow flowers. **'Feston Rose'** ■ produces bicolored, pink and yellow flowers. **'Goldmine'** see 'Mine d'Or'. **'Mine d'Or'**, syn. 'Goldmine', has golden yellow flowers. **'Radiation'** ■ bears bicolored, orange and red flowers. **'Schloss Ortenburg'** bears bicolored,

Lampranthus haworthii

Lampranthus spectabilis

Lantana camara 'Feston Rose'

Lantana camara 'Snow White'

Lantana montevidensis

brick-red and orange-yellow flowers. **'Snow White'** ■ bears white flowers. **'Spreading Sunset'** produces orange-yellow flowers that take on reddish pink tints with age. ***f. varia***, syn. *L. aculeata* f. *varia*, bears yellow flowers turning purple on the outside, orange inside.
L. delicatissima see *L. montevidensis.*
L. montevidensis ■ syn. *L. delicatissima, L. sellowiana* (Weeping lantana). Spreading shrub, often forming a dense mat, with slender, flexible stems, usually covered with coarse, short hairs. Ovate to oblong or lance-shaped, coarsely toothed, mid- to deep green leaves are 1–1½in (2.5–4cm) long. Bears long-stalked, domed flowerheads, ¾–1¼in (2–3cm) wide, of yellow-eyed, lilac-pink to violet flowers, to ½in (1.5cm) across, mainly in summer. ↕ 8–39in (20–100cm), ↔ 2–4ft (60–120cm). Tropical South America. ❄ (min. 50°F/10°C)
L. sellowiana see *L. montevidensis.*
***L.* 'Tangerine'** ■ Low, spreading, often prickly stemmed shrub, probably a cultivar of *L. camara*, with ovate to ovate-oblong, finely wrinkled, slightly toothed, deep green leaves, 2–4in (5–10cm) long. Bears orange flowerheads, 1–2in (2.5–5cm) across, from late spring to late autumn. ↕↔ 3–6ft (1–2m). ❄ (min. 50°F/10°C)
L. tiliifolia. Coarsely hairy shrub with broadly ovate to elliptic or rounded, wrinkled, scalloped or toothed, mid-green leaves, 4in (10cm) long. Yellow or orange flowers, to ½in (1.5cm) across, aging to brick red, are produced in short-stalked, domed flowerheads, to 2½in (6cm) wide, mainly in summer. ↕↔ 5ft (1.5m). Brazil. ❄ (min. 50°F/10°C)

Lantana 'Tangerine'

Lapageria rosea

LAPAGERIA

LILIACEAE

Genus of one species of woody, twining, evergreen climber occurring in moist forest habitats in Chile. It is grown for its very showy, pendent, oblong-bell-shaped flowers. The leaves are alternate and ovate. Where not hardy, grow in a cool greenhouse; elsewhere, it is best grown against a shady wall.
• **CULTIVATION** Under glass, grow in acidic potting mix with added sharp sand, in bright filtered light. During the growing season, water moderately and apply a balanced liquid fertilizer monthly; water sparingly in winter. Outdoors, grow in humus-rich, moist but well-drained, neutral to acidic soil in partial shade. Provide support. Pruning group 11, after flowering.
• **PROPAGATION** Sow seed at 55–64°F (13–18°C) in spring. Take semi-ripe cuttings in summer, or layer in autumn.
• **PESTS AND DISEASES** Aphids, mealybugs, scale insects, and thrips occur.

L. rosea ■ (Chilean bellflower). Twining climber, spreading slowly by suckers, with ovate, dark green leaves, to 5in (13cm) long. From summer to late autumn, oblong-bell-shaped, fleshy, pink to red flowers, to 3½in (9cm) long, are borne singly or in twos or threes in the upper leaf axils. ↕ 15ft (5m). Chile. ❄ (min. 45°F/7°C). **var. *albiflora*** ■ bears white flowers. **'Nash Court'** has soft pink flowers with deeper mottling.

▷ ***Lapeirousia*** see *Anomatheca*

Lapageria rosea var. *albiflora*

LARDIZABALA

LARDIZABALACEAE

Genus of 2 species of monoecious, woody, twining, evergreen climbers from woodland in Chile. They are grown mainly for their ternate to 3-ternate, dark green leaves and striking flowers with 6 fleshy tepals. Train on a pergola or trellis, or against a wall.
• **CULTIVATION** Grow in moderately fertile, well-drained soil in full sun or partial shade. Where not hardy, shelter from cold, drying winds. Pruning group 11, after flowering.
• **PROPAGATION** Sow seed in containers in a cold frame in spring, or take semi-ripe cuttings in late summer or autumn.
• **PESTS AND DISEASES** Infrequent.

L. biternata. Monoecious, sometimes dioecious climber. Ternate to 3-ternate, dark green leaves are composed of up to 9 ovate, rigid leaflets, 2–4in (5–10cm) long. From late autumn to winter, bears reflexed, 6-tepaled, purple-brown and white flowers, ¾–1in (2–2.5cm) across. Male flowers are borne in pendent racemes, 3–4in (8–10cm) long; female flowers are borne singly from the leaf axils. Edible, sausage-shaped purple berries are 2–3in (5–8cm) long. ↕ 10–12ft (3–4m). Chile. ❄ (min. 41°F/5°C)

LARIX

Larch

PINACEAE

Genus of 10–14 species of upright, deciduous, monoecious, coniferous trees from coniferous forest of the N. hemisphere. They have attractive young foliage and normally brilliant, yellow to red autumn color. The needle-shaped leaves are borne in loose spirals on the long shoots, and near-whorls on the short shoots. Terminal, erect, cylindrical or ovoid to conical, usually purple female cones are produced in spring, and turn woody and brown in the first season, usually persisting on the tree. Male cones are spherical to ovoid, and pink or yellow. Larches are useful as specimen trees, and are tolerant of a wide range of conditions.
• **CULTIVATION** Grow in any deep, well-drained soil in full sun.
• **PROPAGATION** Sow seed in a seedbed in early spring, graft in winter, or root semi-ripe cuttings in summer under mist; cuttings are difficult to root.
• **PESTS AND DISEASES** Caterpillars, sawflies, and aphids are problems. Prone to needle blight, needle cast, and rust, as well as cankers.

L. decidua ■ syn. *L. europaea* (European larch). Conical, coniferous tree, often with a large, spreading crown when old, and with smooth, scaly gray bark, ridged on old trees. Linear, soft, pale green leaves, to 1½in (4cm) long, are borne on hairless shoots, which are straw-yellow during the first winter. Cylindrical to conical female cones, to 1½in (4cm) long, have 40–50 scales, and protruding bracts. ↕ 100ft (30m) or more, ↔ 12–20ft (4–6m). Mountains of continental Europe. Zone 3b. **'Corley'** is a dwarf, spreading or rounded shrub. Suitable for a rock garden; ↕↔ 3ft (1m). **'Pendula'** is

Larix decidua

weeping in habit. **'Tortuosa'** has twisted branches.
L.* x *eurolepis see *L.* x *marschlinsii.*
L. europaea see *L. decidua.*
L. kaempferi, syn. *L. leptolepis* (Japanese larch). Conical, coniferous tree with fissured and scaly, rust-brown to gray bark. Very similar to *L. decidua*, but with purplish red winter shoots covered in a waxy bloom. Hairless shoots bear linear, gray-green or bluish green leaves, to 1½in (4cm) long. Conical female cones, to 1¼in (3cm) long, have reflexed scales and concealed bracts. ↕ 100ft (30m) or more, ↔ 12–20ft (4–6m). Japan. Zone 2b. **'Blue Haze'** has brighter foliage than the species.
L. leptolepis see *L. kaempferi.*
L.* x *marschlinsii (*L. decidua* x *L. kaempferi*) syn. *L.* x *eurolepis* (Dunkeld larch, Hybrid larch). Fast-growing, conical, coniferous tree with bloomed, slightly hairy yellow shoots, and linear, gray-green leaves, to 1½in (4cm) long. Conical female cones, to 1¼in (3cm) long, have slightly reflexed scales and only a few visible bract scales. ↕ to 100ft (30m), ↔ to 20ft (6m). Garden origin. Zone 5b.

Larix occidentalis

L. occidentalis ■ (Western larch). Coniferous tree with a narrowly conical crown and scaly, red-brown to brown bark, becoming furrowed and fissured with age. Pointed, linear, blue-green to gray-green leaves, 1–1½in (2.5–4cm) long, each with 2 white bands beneath, are held on thick, orange-brown shoots, which are hairy when young. Female cones, 1–1¾in (2.5–4.5cm) long, are cylindrical to ovoid, with protruding bracts. ↕ to 80ft (25m) or more, ↔ to 15ft (5m). W. North America. Zone 5.
L. russica see *L. sibirica*.
L. sibirica, syn. *L. russica* (Siberian larch). Conical, coniferous tree with scaly, rust-brown bark and bright yellow or yellowish gray shoots, which are hairy when young. Narrowly linear leaves, ¾–1½in (2–4cm) long, are bright green, each with 2 white bands beneath. Ovoid female cones, 1¼–1½in (3–4cm) long, have hairy scales. ↕ 30–100ft (10–30m), ↔ to 15ft (5m). N.E. Europe to Russia (Siberia) and China. Zone 2.

LARREA
Creosote bush

ZYGOPHYLLACEAE

Genus of 5 species of evergreen, xerophytic shrubs growing in the deserts of the S.W. US and N. Mexico. The leaves are alternate and lobed or pinnate, and have a gummy secretion and a distinctive, creosote-like odor, particularly after rainfall. The yellow flowers are solitary, axillary or terminal, with 5 oblong-spoon-shaped petals, followed by rounded, softly hairy fruits. *Larrea* species make good hedging for wind or privacy. Where not hardy, grow in a warm greenhouse.
• **CULTIVATION** Under glass, grow in soil-based potting mix with added sand in full light. Water moderately in the growing season, sparingly in winter. Apply a balanced liquid fertilizer when in growth. Outdoors, grow in moderately fertile, moist soil in full sun or light shade. Pruning group 10.
• **PROPAGATION** Sow seed *in situ* in spring. Take softwood cuttings in mid- or late spring and root in sand in a closed case with bottom heat.
• **PESTS AND DISEASES** *Verticillium* wilt may occur.

L. tridentata (Creosote bush). Upright shrub with dark gray to black bark and pinnate leaves with 2–14 sickle-shaped, leathery, shiny, aromatic, yellow-green to dark green leaflets, ⅜in (9mm) long. Bears solitary, axillary yellow flowers, to ¾in (2cm) across, intermittently throughout the year, followed by rounded, shiny, densely white- or rust-hairy fruit. ↕ 4–8ft (1.2–2.5m), ↔ 4–6ft (1.2–2m). S.W. US to N. Mexico. ❄ (min. 35°F/2°C)

LATANIA
Latan palm

ARECACEAE

Genus of 3 species of single-stemmed palms from seasonally dry areas, often near the coast, in the Mascarene Islands. Fan-shaped, gray- to light green leaves are produced in terminal clusters, with bowl-shaped, 3-petaled flowers borne on separate male and female panicles

Latania lontaroides

between them. *Latania* species prefer a site with only seasonal rainfall and cool, dry winter weather. They are nearly extinct in the wild. Where temperatures fall below 61°F (16°C), grow in a warm greenhouse; in warmer climates, grow as specimen plants.
• **CULTIVATION** Under glass, grow in soil-based potting mix with added leaf mold and sharp sand, in full light with shade from the hottest sun. In growth, water freely and apply a balanced liquid fertilizer monthly; water sparingly in winter. Pot on or top-dress in spring. Outdoors, grow in moderately fertile, well-drained soil in full sun.
• **PROPAGATION** Sow seed at 81°F (27°C) in spring.
• **PESTS AND DISEASES** *Ganoderma* butt rot, leaf spot, lethal yellowing, spider mites, and scale insects may be troublesome.

L. loddigesii. Small to medium-sized palm with blue-green leaf blades, to 5ft (1.5m) across, deeply divided into many narrow lobes. Pale green or greenish white flowers are produced in panicles to 5ft (1.5m) long, usually in summer. ↕ 30–52ft (10–16m), ↔ 10–11ft (3–3.5m). Mascarene Islands (Mauritius). ❄ (min. 61°F/16°C)
L. lontaroides ■ Small to medium-sized palm with deeply lobed, gray-green leaf blades, to 5ft (1.5m) across, with red-purple-flushed bases and leaf stalks. Greenish white to cream flowers are borne in panicles to 5ft (1.5m) long, usually in summer. ↕ 30–52ft (10–16m), ↔ 10–11ft (3–3.5m). Mascarene Islands (Réunion). ❄ (min. 61°F/16°C)
L. verschaffeltii. Small to medium-sized palm with yellow-margined, light green leaf blades, to 4ft (1.2m) across, deeply divided into many slender lobes. Greenish white to cream flowers are usually borne in summer; male panicles are up to 10ft (3m) long, females to 5½ft (1.7m) long. ↕ 40–52ft (12–16m), ↔ 12ft (4m). Mascarene Islands (Rodrigues). ❄ (min. 61°F/16°C)

Lathraea clandestina

LATHRAEA

SCROPHULARIACEAE

Genus of 7 species of leafless, mainly subterranean, parasitic perennials from damp woodland in temperate Europe and Asia. Branching rhizomes bear usually rounded, scale-like, fleshy, ivory to mauve leaves. They are cultivated for their unusual, tubular, 2-lipped, white to mauve flowers, borne in raceme-like inflorescences at ground level in spring. Grow at the base of a host tree or shrub. *L. clandestina* is parasitic on willow (*Salix*), poplar (*Populus*), and alder (*Alnus*). Other species parasitize other trees and are usually host-specific.
• **CULTIVATION** Grow in moist but well-drained soil in partial shade. Mulch with leaf mold in autumn.
• **PROPAGATION** Scatter seed at the base of a suitable host plant as soon as ripe.
• **PESTS AND DISEASES** Infrequent.

L. clandestina ■ (Purple toothwort). Parasitic, rhizomatous perennial with opposite, kidney-shaped, stem-clasping, scale-like white leaves, ¼in (6mm) long. Racemes of 4–8 tubular, 2-lipped mauve flowers, to 1¼in (3cm) long, are borne just above the ground in early and midspring. ↕ ¾in (2cm), ↔ indefinite. W. Europe. Zone 6.

LATHYRUS

FABACEAE

Genus of 150 species of annuals and herbaceous or evergreen perennials from sunny, sandy or pebbly banks, grassy slopes, wasteland, or open woodland in N. temperate regions, N. and E. Africa, and temperate South America. They are grown for their showy, pea-like, often scented flowers, in many colors, which are produced from the leaf axils, either singly or in racemes. Stems are usually winged, and bear alternate, pinnate leaves. Many are climbers (with tendrils); others are clump-forming. The climbers are useful for growing through shrubs or over a bank. Sweet peas (*L. odoratus*) are suitable for a trellis or arch, or an annual border for cut flowers. Clump-forming species and cultivars are suitable for a rock garden, woodland garden, or herbaceous border. Seeds may cause mild stomach upset if ingested.
• **CULTIVATION** Grow in fertile, humus-rich, well-drained soil in full sun or light, dappled shade. Climbers need support. For the best flowers from *L. odoratus*, incorporate well-rotted organic matter in the season before planting, and apply a balanced liquid fertilizer every 2 weeks while in growth. Deadhead regularly. Sweet peas are usually grown on bamboo pyramids or a trellis. Long-stemmed, florist-quality blooms are grown as cordons in beds prepared in autumn. Bush sweet peas are dwarf, largely self-supporting, non-climbing cultivars.
• **PROPAGATION** Soak seed and sow in containers in a cold frame in early spring; seed of annuals may also be sown *in situ* in midspring. Sweet peas may also be sown in autumn: pre-soak or chip seed and sow *in situ* in mild areas, or in containers in a cold frame where winters are severe. Divide perennials in early spring, although they sometimes resent disturbance.
• **PESTS AND DISEASES** Slugs and snails attack young growth. *Pythium* root rot, powdery mildew, rust, gray mold, and various leaf spots are common.

L. aureus, syn. *L. luteus* of gardens, *L. vernus* var. *aurantiacus*, *Orobus aureus*. Clump-forming herbaceous perennial with upright, unwinged stems, and dark green leaves divided into 3–5 pairs of elliptic leaflets, 1½–2in (4–5cm) long. Bears one-sided racemes of 8–25 yellow-orange flowers, ½–¾in (1.5–2cm) long, from late spring to early summer. ↕ to 24in (60cm), ↔ 12in (30cm). Ukraine (Crimea), Caucasus, N. Turkey. Zone 6.
L. chloranthus. Erect or scrambling, sparsely branched, annual climber with slender, winged stems, and mid-green leaves composed of one pair of elliptic leaflets, ¾–2½in (2–6cm) long. Sulfur- to bright yellow flowers, ½–1in (1.5–2.5cm) long, are produced singly or in pairs in summer. ↕ to 28in (70cm), sometimes more. C. and E. Turkey, N. Iraq, Iran, Armenia.
L. gmelinii, syn. *L. luteus*. Clump-forming herbaceous perennial, similar to *L. aureus*, with upright, unwinged stems, and mid-green leaves divided into 3–6 pairs of oval leaflets, to 4in (10cm) long. Produces one-sided racemes of 4–15 brown-striped, orange-yellow flowers, 1–1¼in (2.5–3cm) long, from late spring to midsummer. ↕ to 36in (90cm), ↔ 12in (30cm). C. and S. Urals, mountains of C. Asia. Zone 6b.
L. grandiflorus ■ (Everlasting pea). Herbaceous, perennial climber,

Lathyrus grandiflorus

L

Lathyrus latifolius

spreading by suckers, with unwinged stems. Mid-green leaves usually consist of one pair of ovate to elliptic leaflets, to 2in (5cm) long. Racemes of 1 or 2 (sometimes up to 4) pink-purple and red flowers, to 1¼in (3cm) long, are produced in summer. ↕5ft (1.5m). Italy (including Sicily), Slovenia to Albania, Bulgaria. Zone 6.

L. latifolius ■ (Everlasting pea, Perennial pea). Herbaceous, perennial climber with winged stems. Blue-green leaves consist of one pair of oblong-elliptic leaflets, 3–4½in (8–11cm) long, with 2 broad stipules. Racemes of 6–11 pink to purple flowers, ½–1¼in (1.5–3cm) long, are produced from summer to early autumn. ↕6ft (2m) or more. S. Europe. Zone 5.
'Blushing Bride' produces pink-flushed, white flowers. **'White Pearl'** bears pure white flowers.

L. linifolius* var. *montanus, syn. *L. montanus* (Bitter vetch). Tufted herbaceous perennial with upright, winged stems, and blue-green leaves divided into 1–4 pairs of oval to linear leaflets, to 2in (5cm) long. From spring to early summer, produces long-stalked racemes of 2–6 reddish purple flowers, ½in (1.5cm) long. Suitable for a wild garden. ↕12–16in (30–40cm), ↔8–16in (20–40cm). W. and C. Europe, Asia. Zone 6.

L. luteus see *L. gmelinii.*

***L. luteus* of gardens** see *L. aureus.*

***L. magellanicus* of gardens** see *L. nervosus.*

L. montanus see *L. linifolius* var. *montanus.*

L. nervosus ■ syn. *L. magellanicus* of gardens (Blue pea). Herbaceous, perennial climber with unwinged stems. Prominently veined, leathery, gray-green leaves consist of one pair of ovate leaflets, to 1½in (4cm) long, with prominent stipules. Long-stalked racemes of 3 fragrant, purplish blue flowers, to ¾in (2cm) long, are produced in summer. ↕15ft (5m). South America. Zone 4.

L. odoratus (Sweet pea). Annual climber with winged stems, and mid- to dark green leaves consisting of one pair of ovate-elliptic leaflets, 2–2½in (5–6cm) long. From summer to early autumn, produces racemes of 2–4 fragrant flowers, to 1½in (4cm) long, with wine-red standard petals and purple wings and keels. ↕to 6ft (2m). Italy (including Sicily). Many cultivars have been developed. "Old-fashioned"

Lathyrus nervosus

sweet peas were the earliest, selected mainly for their scent and intense colors; they have prominent stipules, and produce racemes of up to 4 small, highly scented flowers in single or mixed shades of white, red, pink, and blue. They are suitable for growing as a bush and for cutting. ↕6–8ft (2–2.5m). Newer developments, of which by far the most widely grown are the Spencer cultivars, have led to greater variety in the color of the blooms, which occur in most colors except yellow. Spencer cultivars are vigorous, with prominent stipules, and bear racemes of 4 or 5 variably scented flowers, which may be single colors, bicolored, picotee, or variably marked in contrasting colors, with upright standards and spreading wing petals, both waved. They are excellent for cut flowers. ↕6–8ft (2–2.5m), much more when trained as cordons.

Cultivars of **Bijou Group** ■ are bushy, with prominent stipules; they bear racemes of up to 4 slightly scented flowers, to 1½in (4cm) long, with small, wavy petals, in shades of pink, blue, red, or white. Require only limited support. ↕↔to 18in (45cm). Cultivars of **Continental Group** are semi-climbing and vigorous, with prominent stipules, and bear racemes of up to 5 flowers in shades of red, blue, pink, or white, with flat standards and slightly waved, spreading wing petals. Suitable as a bush and for cutting. Require support. ↕3–3½ft (1–1.1m).
Early Multiflora cultivars are vigorous, with prominent stipules, and bear racemes of 5–8 waved, lightly scented flowers in deep rose-pink, salmon-pink, lavender-blue, mid-blue, scarlet, or white. Suitable as a bush and ideal for cutting. Best in a cool greenhouse. ↕6–8ft (2–2.5m). **Explorer Group** cultivars have prominent stipules, and produce racemes of up to 4 waved flowers in mid-blue, navy blue, crimson, scarlet, rose-pink, light pink, purple, or white. Deadhead to prolong flowering. Grow as a bush, for cut flowers, or as a groundcover if sown in autumn and pinched twice. ↕24in (60cm), ↔to 3ft (1m). Cultivars of **Galaxy Group** are vigorous, with prominent stipules, and bear racemes of up to 8 waved flowers in rose-pink, salmon-pink, scarlet, white, or lavender-blue. Grow as a bush (with support); ideal for cutting. ↕6–8ft (2–2.5m). **'Jayne Amanda'** ■ (Spencer cultivar) bears racemes of usually 4,

Lathyrus odoratus Bijou Group

Lathyrus odoratus 'Jayne Amanda'

rarely 5, rose-pink flowers. Suitable as a cordon or bush. Cultivars of **Jet Set Group** are bushy, with prominent stipules, and bear racemes of up to 5 flowers in shades of red, blue, pink, and white; the upright standards and spreading wing petals are both slightly waved. Grow as a bush, or in rows for cutting (with support). ↕3–4ft (1–1.2m). Cultivars of **Knee-hi Group** are bushy, with prominent stipules, and bear racemes of up to 4 flowers in shades of red, blue, pink, and white, with the upright standards and spreading wing petals both slightly waved. Suitable as a bush with support. ↕to 3ft (1m).
'Lady Fairbairn' (Spencer cultivar) produces racemes of usually 4 lilac-pink flowers. Suitable as a cordon or bush. ↕6–8ft (2–2.5m). **'Mrs. Bernard Jones'** (Spencer cultivar) bears racemes of usually 4, occasionally 5, white-flushed, almond-pink flowers. Suitable as a cordon or bush. **Multiflora** cultivars are vigorous, with prominent stipules, and bear racemes of 5–8 waved, lightly scented flowers in mid-blue, lavender-blue, deep rose-pink, salmon-pink, scarlet, or white. Suitable as a bush and excellent for cutting. Best in a cool greenhouse. ↕6–8ft (2–2.5m).
'Noel Sutton' ■ (Spencer cultivar) bears racemes of usually 4, sometimes 5, heavily scented, mid-blue flowers. Grow as a cordon or bush. **'Pink Cupid'** has prominent stipules, and bears racemes of 3–6 small, plain, strongly scented flowers, with pink standards and whitish pink wing petals. Ideal for growing in a barrel, trough, or hanging basket. ↕6in (15cm), ↔18in (45cm). **'Quito'** (Old-

Lathyrus odoratus 'Noel Sutton'

Lathyrus odoratus 'White Supreme'

fashioned) has prominent stipules, and bears racemes of up to 4 small, plain, strongly scented flowers, with maroon standards and variably colored wing petals. **Snoopea Group** cultivars lack tendrils, have prominent stipules, and bear racemes of up to 4 waved flowers in shades of red, blue, pink, and white. Deadhead to prolong flowering. Grow as a bush, or as a groundcover if sown in autumn and pinched twice. ↕ 24in (60cm), ↔ to 3ft (1m). Cultivars of **Supersnoop Group** are similar to Snoopea Group, but slightly stronger-growing. **'White Supreme'** ■ (Spencer cultivar) is vigorous, and bears racemes of usually 4, rarely 5, lightly scented white flowers. Grow as a cordon or bush; ideal for cutting.
L. pratensis (Meadow vetchling, Yellow vetchling). Variable, herbaceous, perennial climber with unwinged stems. Bluish green leaves are composed of one pair of linear-lance-shaped to elliptic leaflets, to 1½in (4cm) long. From late spring to summer, bears long-stalked racemes of 2–12 yellow flowers, to ½in (1.5cm) long. Suitable for a wildflower garden. ↕ 28–48in (70–120cm), ↔ to 6ft (2m). Europe, N. Africa to W. Asia. Zone 4.
L. pubescens ■ Herbaceous, perennial climber with unwinged stems. Mid- to dark green leaves are composed of 1 pair (sometimes 2) of elliptic to lance-shaped leaflets, to 3in (8cm) long, with prominent stipules. In summer, bears long-stalked racemes of 6–16 pale to deep lilac-blue flowers, ⅜–½in (0.8–1.5cm) long. ↕ 10ft (3m). Chile, Argentina. ❄ (min. 41°F/5°C)

Lathyrus pubescens

Lathyrus vernus

L. rotundifolius (Persian everlasting pea). Herbaceous, perennial climber with winged stems. Mid-green leaves consist of one pair of ovate to elliptic leaflets, 1¼–1¾in (3–4.5cm) long. Small racemes of 4–11 dark purplish pink to brownish red flowers, ½–¾in (1.5–2cm) long, are borne in summer. ↕ 3ft (1m). Ukraine (Crimea), Caucasus, E. Turkey, Iraq, Iran. Zone 6.
L. sativus (Chickling pea). Scrambling, annual climber with angular, winged stems, and mid-green leaves divided into 2 or 3 pairs of narrowly elliptic, pointed leaflets, 1½–2½in (4–6cm) long. In summer, produces solitary, dainty blue flowers, to ½in (1.5cm) long, that fade to white and sometimes have pink veins. Mostly grown for animal fodder, but suitable for a mixed or herbaceous border. ↕ to 3ft (1m), ↔ to 18in (45cm). C. and S. Europe, N. Africa, S.W. Asia.
L. sylvestris (Perennial pea). Herbaceous, perennial climber with winged stems. Mid-green leaves consist of one pair of slender, linear-elliptic leaflets, 2–6in (5–15cm) long, with one pair of narrow stipules. Long-stalked racemes of 3–8 pink flowers, to ¾in (2cm) long, with purplish pink wing petals, are produced from summer to early autumn. ↕ 6ft (2m). Europe, N.W. Africa, Caucasus. Zone 6b.
L. tingitanus. Annual tendril climber with slender, winged stems, and mid- to deep green leaves divided into one pair of narrowly elliptic to oblong-elliptic or linear-elliptic leaflets, 1½–3in (4–8cm) long. Pale pink or crimson-magenta flowers, ¾–1¼in (2–3cm) long, are produced singly or in twos or threes, in summer. ↕ to 5ft (1.5m). Spain, Portugal, Azores, Canary Islands, Morocco, Algeria, Sardinia.
L. vernus ■ syn. *Orobus vernus* (Spring vetchling). Dense, clump-forming herbaceous perennial with unwinged, upright stems, and mid- to dark green leaves divided into 2–4 pairs of ovate to elliptic, sharp-pointed leaflets, 1¼–3in (3–8cm) long. In spring, bears one-sided racemes of 3–6 purplish blue flowers, to ¾in (2cm) long, that become almost greenish blue. ↕ 8–18in (20–45cm), ↔ 18in (45cm). Continental Europe, Turkey, Caucasus, Russia (Siberia). Zone 4b. **'Alboroseus'** ■ bears pink-and-white flowers. **f. *albus*** bears white flowers. **var. *aurantiacus*** see *L. aureus.* **'Rose Fairy'** bears racemes, 3–4in (8–10cm) long, of crimson-magenta flowers; ↕ 8in (20cm).

Lathyrus vernus 'Alboroseus'

LAURELIA

MONIMIACEAE

Genus of 3 species of evergreen shrubs and trees occurring in forest and on streambanks in New Zealand, Chile, and Argentina. They are cultivated for their opposite, elliptic, entire or toothed, leathery, aromatic leaves. In summer, inconspicuous, often dioecious flowers are borne in axillary panicles or racemes. Grow in a shrub border, in a woodland garden, or against a warm, sunny wall.
• **CULTIVATION** Grow in moist but well-drained, moderately fertile soil in full sun or partial shade, in a site that is sheltered from cold, drying winds. Pruning group 1.
• **PROPAGATION** Take semi-ripe cuttings in summer.
• **PESTS AND DISEASES** Infrequent.

L. sempervirens, syn. *L. serrata* of gardens. Dense, conical shrub or tree with narrowly elliptic to elliptic, very aromatic, bright green leaves, to 4in (10cm) long, with toothed margins, except near the bases. Axillary panicles of tiny, cup-shaped green flowers are produced in early summer. ↕ 50ft (15m), ↔ 30ft (10m), usually less. Chile, Argentina. ❄ (min. 41°F/5°C)
***L. serrata* of gardens** see *L. sempervirens.*

▷ ***Laurentia axillaris*** see *Solenopsis axillaris*

LAURUS

LAURACEAE

Genus of 2 species of evergreen shrubs and trees from woodland, scrub, and rocky places in the Azores, the Canary Islands, and the Mediterranean. They are valued for their aromatic, alternate, ovate, glossy, dark green leaves. Small, greenish yellow male and female flowers are borne on separate plants. Where not hardy, grow in a container and move into a cool greenhouse during winter and early spring. In warmer areas, grow as specimen trees, in a woodland garden, against a warm, sunny wall, or as a windbreak. They are excellent as a topiary, since they tolerate clipping well.
• **CULTIVATION** Grow in fertile, moist but well-drained soil in full sun or partial shade, sheltered from cold, drying winds. Pruning group 1; clip topiary specimens twice during summer.

Laurus nobilis

• **PROPAGATION** Sow seed in containers in a cold frame in autumn, or take semi-ripe cuttings in summer.
• **PESTS AND DISEASES** Scale insects, mealybugs, powdery mildew, and anthracnose may be troublesome.

L. azorica (Canary laurel). Vigorous, conical tree with aromatic, elliptic-lance-shaped to rounded, long-pointed leaves, 2–4in (5–10cm) long, softly hairy beneath. Clusters of green-yellow flowers, to ⅜in (9mm) across, are produced in spring, followed on female plants by ovoid black berries, to ½in (1.5cm) long. ↕ to 30ft (10m), ↔ 20ft (6m). Azores, Canary Islands. Zone 8.
L. nobilis ■ (Bay laurel, Sweet bay). Conical tree or large shrub with aromatic, narrowly ovate leaves, to 4in (10cm) long. In spring, bears clusters of greenish yellow flowers, ¼in (6mm) across, followed on female plants by broadly ovoid black berries, to ½in (1.5cm) long. Leaves are often used as a flavoring in cooking. Contact with foliage may aggravate skin allergies. ↕ 40ft (12m), ↔ 30ft (10m). Mediterranean. Zone 7. **'Aurea'** ■ has golden yellow foliage.

Laurus nobilis 'Aurea'

LAVANDULA

Lavender

LAMIACEAE

Genus of about 25 species of aromatic, evergreen shrubs and subshrubs occurring in dry, sunny, exposed, rocky habitats from the Canary Islands, the Mediterranean, and N.E. Africa to S.W. Asia and India. The leaves are opposite, and may be simple and entire, or toothed to pinnatifid, pinnate, or 2-pinnate, with the margins usually rolled under. They are cultivated for their mainly long-stalked spikes of fragrant, tubular, 2-lipped flowers, which, in many species, have a very high nectar content, making them particularly attractive to bees. In warm areas, lavenders are suitable for a variety of situations, from a shrub border to a rock garden, and are useful for edging and as a low hedge. Where marginally hardy, grow at the base of a warm, sunny wall, or in a container that can be over-wintered in a cool greenhouse. The leaves and flowerheads are often dried for use in sachets or potpourri. If grown for drying, cut the flowerheads before they are fully open.

- **CULTIVATION** Grow in moderately fertile, well-drained soil in full sun. Pruning group 10, in early spring, then lightly after flowering.
- **PROPAGATION** Sow seed in containers in a cold frame in spring, or layer or take semi-ripe cuttings in summer.
- **PESTS AND DISEASES** *Fusarium* root rot and leaf spot can occur.

L. angustifolia (English lavender). Compact, bushy shrub with linear, gray-green leaves, to 2in (5cm) long. In mid- and late summer, long, unbranched stalks produce fragrant, pale to deep purple flowers in dense spikes, to 3in (8cm) long. ↕ 3ft (1m), ↔ 4ft (1.2m). W. Mediterranean. Zone 6. **'Hidcote'** ■ is more compact, and produces silvery gray leaves and dark purple flowers; ↕ 24in (60cm), ↔ 30in (75cm). **'Jean Davis'** produces pale pink flowers. **'Loddon Pink'** ■ is more compact, and produces soft pink flowers; ↕ 18in (45cm), ↔ 24in (60cm). **'Munstead'** produces blue-purple flowers; ↕ 18in (45cm), ↔ 24in (60cm). Zone 5. **'Nana Alba'** is very compact, and produces spikes of white flowers; ↕↔ 12in (30cm). **'Twickel Purple'** ■ has narrowly oblong leaves, to 2in (5cm) long, and bears purple flowers in midsummer; ↕ 24in (60cm), ↔ 3ft (1m).

Lavandula angustifolia 'Hidcote'

Lavandula angustifolia 'Loddon Pink'

L. dentata ■ (Fringed lavender). Spreading, bushy shrub with linear-oblong, scalloped, dark green leaves, to 1½in (4cm) long. In mid- and late summer, long, unbranched stalks produce dense spikes, to 2in (5cm) long, of slightly fragrant, purple-blue flowers, tipped with purple bracts. ↕ 3ft (1m), ↔ 5ft (1.5m). Atlantic islands, W. Mediterranean, Arabian Peninsula. Zone 8.

L. x intermedia (*L. angustifolia* x *L. latifolia*) (Lavandin). Rounded shrub with branching stems bearing oblong to lance-shaped to almost spoon-shaped, aromatic, gray-green leaves, 1½–2½in (4–6cm) long, covered in fine, silvery gray hairs. In summer, bears spikes, 4–8in (10–20cm) long, of light blue to violet flowers. ↕↔ 12–20in (30–50cm). Garden origin. Zone 6. **'Alba'** has gray foliage and white flowers. **'Dutch'** has violet-tinged, green buds and dark violet flowers. **'Grappenhall'** has narrowly oblong leaves, to 2½in (6cm) long, and bears spikes, to 3in (8cm) long, of slightly fragrant, blue-purple flowers; ↕ 3ft (1m), ↔ 5ft (1.5m). **'Grosso'** has very large, dark violet flowers. Highly disease resistant; ↕ 30in (75cm). **'Provence'** has dark violet flowers. **'Seal'** bears pale purple flowers.

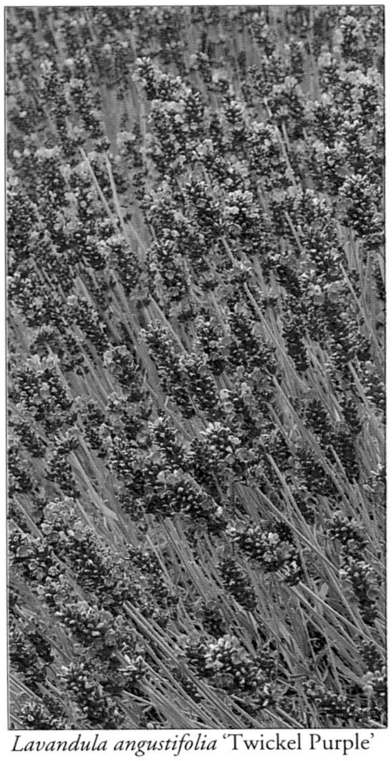

Lavandula angustifolia 'Twickel Purple'

Lavandula dentata

L. lanata. Rounded, bushy shrub with linear to inversely lance-shaped, densely white-woolly leaves, to 2in (5cm) long. Dense spikes, to 4in (10cm) long, of fragrant, dark purple flowers are produced on long, unbranched stalks in late summer. ↕ 30in (75cm), ↔ 36in (90cm). S. Spain. ❄ (min. 35°F/2°C)

L. latifolia (Spike lavender). Upright, bushy shrub or subshrub with slender, elliptic or spoon-shaped to oblong-lance-shaped, gray-green leaves, to 2½in (6cm) long. In mid- and late summer, long, branched stalks produce fragrant, mauve-blue flowers in narrow, branching spikes, to 8in (20cm) long. ↕ 3ft (1m), ↔ 4ft (1.2m). W. Mediterranean. Zone 7.

L. pinnata. Spreading, bushy shrub with pinnate, white-hairy, gray-green leaves, to 3in (8cm) long, consisting of numerous oblong leaflets. In summer, long, unbranched stalks bear fragrant, blue-purple flowers in spikes to 3½in (9cm) long. ↕↔ 3ft (1m). Canary Islands. ❄ (min. 41°F/5°C)

L. stoechas ■ (French lavender). Compact, bushy shrub with linear, gray-green leaves, to 1½in (4cm) long. Dense, ovoid-oblong spikes, to 1¼in (3cm) long, of fragrant, dark purple flowers, topped by conspicuous, purple bracts, are borne on very short, unbranched stalks from late spring to summer. ↕↔ 24in (60cm). Mediterranean. Zone 8. **subsp. *pedunculata*** (Spanish lavender) has flower spikes borne on conspicuously long stalks well above the foliage; Portugal, Spain.

Lavandula stoechas

L. viridis. Upright, bushy shrub with oblong, pale green leaves, to 2in (5cm) long. In mid- and late summer, small white flowers emerge from short-stemmed, unbranched, dense spikes, ¾–1¼in (2–3cm) long, each with a cluster of green bracts at the tip. ↕ 24in (60cm), ↔ 30in (75cm). Portugal, Spain, Madeira. ❄ (min. 41°F/5°C)

LAVATERA

Mallow

MALVACEAE

Genus of approximately 25 species of annuals, biennials, herbaceous, semi-evergreen, or evergreen perennials, and deciduous, semi-evergreen, or evergreen subshrubs and shrubs. They have a wide distribution, occurring from the Azores, Canary Islands, W. Europe, and the Mediterranean to C. Asia, Russia (E. Siberia), Australia, and California, and usually grow in dry, rocky places, often near coasts. They are cultivated for their showy, 5-petaled, saucer- or funnel-shaped flowers (similar to those of *Malva*), borne singly or in racemes, mainly in summer. Leaves are alternate, variably shaped, long-stalked, and usually palmately lobed. The annual, biennial, and short-lived perennial species are suitable for a herbaceous border or for summer bedding; shrubby lavateras are best grown in a shrub border or, where marginally hardy, against a warm, sunny wall.

- **CULTIVATION** Grow in ideally light, moderately fertile, well-drained soil in full sun. Shelter from cold, drying winds. Pruning group 6.
- **PROPAGATION** Sow seed of annuals *in situ* in mid- to late spring, or under glass in midspring. Sow seed of biennials in a cold frame in midsummer. Take softwood and greenwood cuttings of perennials in spring, and of subshrubs and shrubs in early summer. Propagate

Lavatera arborea 'Variegata'

Lavatera 'Barnsley'

regularly, since shrubs and perennials are often short-lived.

• **PESTS AND DISEASES** Scale insects, root rot, rust, and leaf spot are occasionally problems.

L. arborea (Tree mallow). Tree-like, woody-stemmed annual, biennial, or short-lived, evergreen perennial with thick stems and rounded, palmately 5- to 7-lobed, mid-green leaves, to 8in (20cm) long. Racemes of 2–7 funnel-shaped, purple-pink flowers, to 2½in (6cm) across, with darker veins, are profusely borne throughout summer. May be grown as a windbreak in a coastal garden. ↕ 10ft (3m), ↔ 5ft (1.5m). W. Europe, Mediterranean. Zone 8. **'Variegata'** ■ has conspicuously white-marked leaves, fading to green in warm weather.
L. assurgentiflora. Deciduous or semi-evergreen shrub with twisted shoots and palmately 5- to 7-lobed, mid-green leaves, to 6in (15cm) long, with heart-shaped bases and white-hairy lower surfaces. In midsummer, produces funnel-shaped, dark cerise-pink flowers, to 3in (8cm) across, with darker veins, singly or in racemes of 2–4. A good windbreak in coastal gardens. ↕ 6ft (2m), ↔ 5ft (1.5m). California, Santa Catalina Island. ❀ (min. 41°F/5°C)
***L.* 'Barnsley'** ■ Vigorous, semi-evergreen subshrub with palmately 3- to 5-lobed, gray-green leaves, to 5in (13cm) long. Throughout summer, bears profuse racemes of open funnel-shaped, red-eyed white flowers, to 3in (8cm) across, aging to soft pink, with deeply notched petals. ↕↔ 6ft (2m). Zone 5.

Lavatera 'Bredon Springs'

Lavatera cachemiriana

L. bicolor see *L. maritima.*
***L.* 'Bredon Springs'** ■ Vigorous, semi-evergreen subshrub with palmately 3- to 5-lobed, gray-green leaves, to 5in (13cm) long. Funnel-shaped, mauve-flushed, dusky pink flowers, to 3in (8cm) across, are borne in profuse racemes throughout summer. ↕↔ 6ft (2m). Zone 6.
***L.* 'Bressingham Pink'.** Upright, shrubby, semi-evergreen perennial with rounded-heart-shaped, shallowly lobed, hairy, pale gray-green leaves, 3½in (9cm) long. From midsummer to early autumn, produces racemes of many saucer-shaped, pale pink flowers, 2–4in (5–10cm) across. ↕ 6ft (1.8m), ↔ 4ft (1.2m). Zone 5.
***L.* 'Burgundy Wine'.** Vigorous, semi-evergreen subshrub with palmately 3- to 5-lobed, gray-green leaves, to 5in (13cm) long. Profuse racemes of funnel-shaped, rich dark pink flowers, to 3in (8cm) across, with darker veins, are produced throughout summer. ↕↔ 6ft (2m). Zone 6.
L. cachemiriana ■ syn. *L. cachemirica.* Annual, or short-lived, woody-based, semi-evergreen perennial, with rounded to heart-shaped, palmately 3- to

Lavatera 'Kew Rose'

Lavatera trimestris 'Mont Blanc'

5-lobed, blunt-toothed leaves, 3–6in (7–15cm) long, mid-green above, downy beneath. Racemes of many open funnel-shaped, silky-textured, clear rose-pink flowers, to 3in (8cm) across, are borne in summer. ↕ to 8ft (2.5m), ↔ to 4ft (1.2m). India (Kashmir). Zone 8.
L. cachemirica see *L. cachemiriana.*
***L.* 'Candy Floss'.** Vigorous, semi-evergreen subshrub with palmately 3- to 5-lobed, gray-green leaves, to 5in (13cm) long. Profuse racemes of funnel-shaped, pale pink flowers, to 3in (8cm) across, are borne throughout summer. ↕↔ 6ft (2m). Zone 5.
***L.* 'Kew Rose'** ■ Vigorous, semi-evergreen subshrub with purplish green shoots and palmately 3- to 5-lobed, gray-green leaves, to 5in (13cm) long. Profuse racemes of funnel-shaped, bright pink flowers, to 3in (8cm) across, with darker veins, are borne throughout summer. ↕↔ 6ft (2m). Zone 6.
L. maritima, syn. *L. bicolor*, *L. maritima* var. *bicolor.* Upright, shrubby, evergreen perennial that bears almost rounded, shallowly lobed, toothed, hairy, gray-green leaves, to 2½in (6cm) long. From late summer to midautumn, produces solitary, axillary, saucer-shaped, pink, lilac-pink, or white flowers, 1½–3in (4–8cm) across, with magenta veins, each petal notched and with a magenta basal mark. ↕ 5ft (1.5m), ↔ 3ft (1m). W. Mediterranean. Zone 6. **var. *bicolor*** see *L. maritima.*
L. mauritanica. Downy annual with rounded to heart-shaped, shallowly 5- to 7-lobed, toothed, mid-green leaves, 1¼–2in (3–5cm) long. Racemes of many funnel-shaped purple flowers, to 1¼in (3cm) across, are produced in summer. ↕ 32in (80cm), ↔ to 12in (30cm). Algeria, Morocco. ❀ (min. 35°F/2°C)
***L. olbia* 'Rosea'** see *L.* 'Rosea'.
***L.* 'Peppermint Ice'** see *L. thuringiaca* 'Ice Cool'.
***L.* 'Rosea'**, syn. *L. olbia* 'Rosea'. Vigorous, semi-evergreen subshrub with palmately 3- to 5-lobed, gray-green leaves, to 5in (13cm) long. Produces racemes of many funnel-shaped, dark pink flowers, to 3in (8cm) across, throughout summer. ↕↔ 6ft (2m). Zone 8.
***L.* 'Shorty'.** Semi-erect, semi-evergreen perennial with heart-shaped, lobed, hairy, pale green leaves, 2–3in (5–8cm) long. Bears racemes of many saucer-shaped, white or rose-pink flowers, to

Lavatera trimestris 'Pink Beauty'

Lavatera trimestris 'Silver Cup'

2in (5cm) across, from midsummer to early autumn. ↕↔ to 3ft (1m). Zone 5.
L. thuringiaca (Tree lavatera). Upright herbaceous perennial with finely gray-hairy stems. Mid-green leaves, 3½in (9cm) long, are rounded with heart-shaped bases; basal leaves are unlobed, stem leaves are palmately 3- to 5-lobed. In summer, bears open funnel-shaped, long-stalked, purple-pink flowers, to 3in (8cm) across, either singly in the leaf axils or in loose racemes. ↕ to 6ft (2m), ↔ 6ft (1.8m). C. and S.E. Europe. Zone 5. **'Ice Cool'**, syn. *L.* 'Peppermint Ice', produces pure white flowers; ↕↔ 5ft (1.5m).
***L. trimestris* cultivars.** Softly hairy annuals bearing rounded, shallowly 3-, 5-, or 7-lobed, mid- to dark green leaves, 1¼–2½in (3–6cm) long, with heart-shaped bases. Open funnel-shaped, pink, reddish pink, or white flowers, 3–4in (7–10cm) across, are produced singly from the upper leaf axils in summer. They provide good cut flowers. ↕ to 4ft (1.2m), ↔ to 18in (45cm). Mediterranean. **'Loveliness'** produces deep rose-pink flowers; ↕ 3–4ft (0.9–1.2m). **'Mont Blanc'** ■ is compact, with very dark green foliage and white flowers; ↕ 20in (50cm). **'Mont Rose'** has a neater habit than 'Mont Blanc' and bears rose-pink flowers. **'Pink Beauty'** ■ bears purple-centered, very pale pink flowers, with purple veining; ↕ to 24in (60cm). **'Ruby Regis'** bears deep reddish pink flowers; ↕ to 24in (60cm). **'Silver Cup'** ■ produces bright rose-pink flowers, to 5in (13cm) across, with darker veining; ↕ to 30in (75cm).

LAWSONIA

Henna tree, Mignonette tree

LYTHRACEAE

Genus of one species of evergreen shrub or small tree occurring in tropical forest from N. Africa to S.W. Asia and N. Australia. It has opposite, simple, entire leaves and large, terminal panicles of small, 4-petaled, fragrant flowers. Grow *L. inermis* in a shrub border or grow as a hedge. Where not hardy, grow in a temperate or warm greenhouse. Widely cultivated in the tropics and subtropics, it is a source of the orange-red dye, henna.

• **CULTIVATION** Under glass, grow in soil-based potting mix with added sharp sand, in full light. When in full growth, water moderately and apply a balanced liquid fertilizer monthly; water sparingly in winter. Outdoors, grow in moderately fertile, well-drained soil in full sun. Pruning group 1; may need restrictive pruning under glass. Clip hedges in early summer.

• **PROPAGATION** Sow seed at 64–70°F (18–21°C) in spring. Take softwood cuttings in spring or hardwood cuttings in autumn.

• **PESTS AND DISEASES** Whiteflies and spider mites may be troublesome.

L. alba see *L. inermis.*

L. inermis, syn. *L. alba.* Often spiny, large shrub, or sometimes small tree, with an open habit. Elliptic to narrowly obovate or broadly lance-shaped, slender-pointed, mid- to dark green leaves are ¾–2in (2–5cm) long. Many tiny, fragrant flowers, with 4 crumpled, clawed, broadly ovate or spoon-shaped, white, pink, or cinnabar-red petals, are borne in pyramidal panicles, 8–16in (20–40cm) long, mainly in summer. ↕ 10–20ft (3–6m), ↔ 6–12ft (2–4m). N. Africa to S.W. Asia, N. Australia. ❀ (min. 55°F/13°C)

LAYIA

ASTERACEAE

Genus of 15 species of erect to spreading, well-branched annuals, usually found in moist, grassy meadows, but also on sandy and gravelly soils in woodland or in stream washes, in W. US. They are cultivated for their daisy-like, single, terminal flowerheads, which are composed of white, yellow, or white-tipped yellow ray florets (each 3-toothed at the tip), and yellow disk florets, and are profusely borne, mainly in summer. The alternate leaves are narrowly linear to oblong, and entire to finely divided or pinnatifid. Grow in a herbaceous or mixed border or bed, or on a bank. They provide long-lasting cut flowers.

• **CULTIVATION** Grow in moist but well-drained, ideally light, sandy, moderately fertile to poor soil in full sun. Very fertile soil encourages lax growth.

• **PROPAGATION** Sow seed *in situ* in early spring or autumn. Where marginally hardy, protect autumn sowings.

• **PESTS AND DISEASES** Infrequent.

L. elegans see *L. platyglossa.*

L. platyglossa, syn. *L. elegans* (Tidy tips). Almost succulent-stemmed annual with usually linear to narrowly lance-shaped, toothed to pinnatifid, softly hairy, gray-green leaves, to 1¼in (3cm) long. From summer to autumn, bears flowerheads, to 2in (5cm) across, with white-tipped yellow ray florets and deep golden yellow disk florets. ↕ 12–18in (30–45cm), ↔ 10–12in (24–30cm). California.

▷ ***Lechenaultia*** see *Leschenaultia*

LEDEBOURIA

LILIACEAE

Genus of 16 species of semi-evergreen or evergreen, bulbous perennials occurring in seasonally dry, open areas or river valleys in South Africa. They are cultivated for their attractively marked leaves and their racemes of small, bell- or urn-shaped flowers, reminiscent of lily-of-the-valley (*Convallaria*); the flowers are produced in spring or summer. In areas where temperatures drop below 45°F (7°C), they are best grown in a conservatory or cool greenhouse. In warmer areas, grow in open sites in a rock or desert garden.

• **CULTIVATION** Plant bulbs with the necks above soil level. Under glass, grow in soil-based potting mix, with added sharp sand, in full light. In growth, water freely and apply a high-potash fertilizer every 4 weeks; keep just moist in winter. Outdoors, grow in moderately fertile, well-drained soil in full sun.

• **PROPAGATION** Sow seed under glass in spring or autumn. Remove offsets in spring.

• **PESTS AND DISEASES** Infrequent.

L. cooperi, syn. *Scilla adlamii, S. cooperi.* Very variable, semi-evergreen, bulbous perennial producing semi-erect, ovate to ovate-oblong or linear, mid- to dark green, basal leaves, 2–10in (5–25cm) long, with bold purple stripes. In summer, produces racemes of up to 50 bell-shaped, purple-pink flowers, ¼in (6mm) long, tipped or striped green. ↕ 2–4in (5–10cm), PD2in (5cm). South Africa. ❀ (min. 41°F/5°C)

L. hypoxidioides. Evergreen bulbous perennial with 2–4, semi-erect, oblong-lance-shaped to oblong-obovate, stiff, mid-green leaves, to 6in (15cm) long, thickly covered with silky hairs. In summer, produces semi-erect racemes of 75–150 bell-shaped, green or gray flowers, ¼in (6mm) long, sometimes pink-marked. ↕ 2–4in (5–10cm), ↔ 2in (5cm). South Africa. ❀ (min. 41°F/5°C)

L. ovalifolia. Evergreen, bulbous perennial with a lax, solitary, ovate, maroon-marked, mid-green leaf, to 1½in (4cm) long. In summer, bears racemes of 20 or so bell-shaped, pink-striped, green flowers, to ¼in (6mm) long. ↕ to 4in (10cm), PD2in (5cm). South Africa. ❀ (min. 41°F/5°C)

L. socialis ▣ syn. *Scilla socialis, S. violacea.* Evergreen, bulbous perennial bearing erect, broadly lance-shaped, fleshy, pale silvery green, basal leaves, to 4in (10cm) long, with large, dark green marks above, purple beneath. Racemes of up to 25 bell-shaped, purplish green flowers, ¼in (6mm) long, are borne in spring and summer. ↕ 2–4in (5–10cm), PD2in (5cm). South Africa (Northern Cape, Western Cape). ❀ (min. 41°F/5°C)

Ledebouria socialis

x LEDODENDRON

ERICACEAE

Bigeneric hybrid genus of one evergreen shrub, a cross between *Rhododendron trichostomum* and *Ledum glandulosum* var. *columbianum*, with characteristics intermediate between those of its parents. It is grown for its lance-shaped, dark green leaves and large, terminal corymbs of tubular flowers. Grow in a woodland garden, or at the front of a shrub border; associates well with dwarf rhododendrons.

• **CULTIVATION** Grow in humus-rich, moist but well-drained, acidic soil in partial shade. Pinch out the stem tips on young plants to encourage a bushy habit. Pruning group 8.

• **PROPAGATION** Take semi-ripe cuttings in early summer.

• **PESTS AND DISEASES** Infrequent.

x *L.* 'Arctic Tern', syn. *Rhododendron* 'Arctic Tern'. Upright to spreading shrub with lance-shaped, hairy, dark green leaves, to 2in (5cm) long. Bears rounded corymbs of tubular, 5-lobed, pure white flowers, to ¾in (2cm) long, in late spring and early summer. ↕↔ to 24in (60cm). Zone 8.

Ledum groenlandicum

LEDUM

ERICACEAE

Genus of approximately 4 species of evergreen shrubs widely distributed in bogs, marshes, and moist, often coniferous woodland in cool-temperate regions of the N. hemisphere. They are cultivated for their compact habit, their aromatic leaves (which are alternate, and may be linear, ovate, oval, or oblong), and their dense, terminal, umbel-like corymbs of small, 5-petaled white flowers, produced in spring or early summer. Suitable for a cool position in a rock or heather garden.

• **CULTIVATION** Grow in humus-rich, moist but well-drained, acidic to neutral soil in full sun or partial shade. Pruning group 8.

• **PROPAGATION** Surface-sow seed in containers under glass in spring or autumn. Take semi-ripe cuttings in late summer. Layer in autumn.

• **PESTS AND DISEASES** Leaf gall, rust, spot anthracnose, and leaf spots occur.

L. glandulosum. Bushy, rounded shrub with smooth shoots and ovate to oval leaves, to 2in (5cm) long, deeply veined and dark green above, white scaly beneath. In late spring, produces white flowers, to ½in (1.5cm) across, in rounded, terminal corymbs, 2in (5cm) across. ↕ 36in (90cm), ↔ 4ft (1.2m). W. North America. Zone 7b.

L. groenlandicum ▣ (Labrador tea). Bushy, rounded shrub with rust-woolly shoots and narrowly oval to elliptic-oblong leaves, to 2in (5cm) long, dark green above, densely rust-felted beneath, with recurved margins. White flowers, ½–¾in (1–2cm) across, are borne in rounded, terminal corymbs, 2in (5cm) across, in late spring. ↕ 36in (90cm), ↔ 4ft (1.2m). Greenland, Alaska, Canada south to N. US. Zone 2.

L. palustre (Wild rosemary). Bushy, erect to spreading, usually rounded shrub with rust-hairy shoots and narrowly oblong to linear leaves, ½–2in (1–5cm) long, dark green above, rust-hairy beneath, with recurved margins. In late spring, bears white flowers, to ½in (1.5cm) across, in rounded, terminal corymbs, 2in (5cm) across. ↕ 1–4ft (0.3–1.2m), ↔ to 30in (75cm). N. Europe, N. Asia, North America. Zone 2. **f. *decumbens*** is more or less mat-forming, with linear leaves, to ¾in (2cm) long; ↕ 8in (20cm), ↔ 3ft (1m).

LEEA

LEEACEAE

Genus of about 40 species of evergreen shrubs and small trees found in humid forest in tropical Africa, Madagascar, and from India to Malaysia. The alternate or opposite, often velvety leaves are simple to 3-pinnate, and are often flushed red to bronze when young. Small flowers, with tubular bases and 5, sometimes only 4, petal lobes, are borne in flattened, axillary or terminal cymes. Where temperatures drop below 61°F (16°C), grow mainly for their foliage, as houseplants or in a warm greenhouse. In warmer areas, they are distinctive specimens for a small lawn, and are also useful for hedging.

• **CULTIVATION** Under glass, grow in soil-based potting mix in bright filtered light and moderate humidity. When in full growth, water freely and apply a balanced liquid fertilizer monthly; water sparingly in winter. Outdoors, grow in moderately fertile, moist but well-drained soil in partial or dappled shade. Pruning group 9; need restrictive pruning under glass. Prune hedges in spring.

• **PROPAGATION** Sow seed at 64°F (18°C) in spring, take semi-ripe cuttings in summer, or air layer in spring or early autumn.

• **PESTS AND DISEASES** *Phytophthora* blight, bacterial leaf spot, root rot, collar rot, mealybugs, and spider mites are problems.

L. coccinea (West Indian holly). Open shrub, becoming denser with age, bearing 2- or 3-pinnate leaves, to 24in (60cm) long, with numerous, oblong-lance-shaped to elliptic or obovate, slender-pointed, toothed leaflets, bronzed when young, maturing to glossy, deep green. Even when young, bears terminal cymes, 3–5in (8–13cm) across, of rounded scarlet buds opening to small pink flowers with yellow anthers, mainly in summer. ↕ 5–8ft (1.5–2.5m), ↔ 3–5ft (1–1.5m). Burma. ❀ (min. 61°F/16°C)

LEGOUSIA

CAMPANULACEAE

Genus of about 15 species of small, erect or spreading, unbranched or bushy annuals occurring on arable or stony ground in N. Africa, from Spain to Greece, and in the Caucasus, Turkey, Cyprus, Syria, Iraq, and Iran. They have ovate, oblong, or lance-shaped, wavy-margined, light to mid-green leaves, and produce small, 5-lobed, saucer- to bell-shaped flowers, singly or in delicate panicles or corymbs. Suitable for an annual border or wildflower garden. They provide unusual cut flowers.

• **CULTIVATION** Grow in light, well-drained soil in full sun or partial shade.

• **PROPAGATION** Sow seed *in situ* in autumn or midspring.

• **PESTS AND DISEASES** Infrequent.

L. pentagonia. Erect, bushy, bristly-haired annual with obovate to oblong, mid-green leaves, to 2in (5cm) long. From early summer to autumn, bell-shaped, blue to violet flowers, to ¾in (2cm) across, with white bases, are produced singly or in corymbs of 2 or 3, at the tips of the branching stems. ↕ to 12in (30cm), ↔ 4in (10cm). E. Mediterranean, Balkans.

L. speculum-veneris, syn. *Specularia speculum-veneris* (Venus's looking glass). Erect, bushy annual with oblong to inversely lance-shaped, toothed leaves, ½–2in (1.5–5cm) long. From early summer to autumn, saucer-shaped, white-centered, violet-blue, occasionally white or pale purple flowers, to ¾in (2cm) across, with prominent, reflexed sepals, are borne, either singly or in corymbs of 2 or 3, at the tips of branching stems. ↕ to 12in (30cm), ↔ 4in (10cm). C. and S. Europe, N. Africa, Cyprus, W. Syria, N. Iraq, Caucasus.

LEIOPHYLLUM

ERICACEAE

Genus of one species of upright to mat-forming, suckering, evergreen shrub from acidic woodland in E. US. It is grown for its glossy foliage and star-shaped white flowers borne in terminal, umbel-like corymbs. Grow in a rock garden, shrub border, or woodland.

• **CULTIVATION** Grow in humus-rich, moist but well-drained, acidic soil in full sun to partial or deep shade. Where not hardy, protect from cold, drying winds. Pruning group 8.

• **PROPAGATION** Surface-sow seed in containers outdoors in spring, take softwood cuttings in early summer, or pot up rooted suckers in spring.

• **PESTS AND DISEASES** Infrequent.

L. buxifolium ▣ (Sand myrtle). Bushy, usually suckering shrub with upright and spreading stems. Oblong or ovate, glossy, dark green leaves, to ½in (1.5cm) long, are tinted bronze in winter. In late spring and early summer, bears pink-budded white flowers, ¼in (6mm) across, in dense corymbs, to 1in (2.5cm) across. ↕ 12–24in (30–60cm), ↔ 4–5ft (1.2–1.5m) or more. New Jersey to Florida. Zone 7. **'Nanum'** is compact, with pink flowers; ↕ 2–4in (5–10cm), ↔ 12in (30cm) or more.

Leiophyllum buxifolium (inset: flower detail)

LEIPOLDTIA

AIZOACEAE

Genus of about 20 species of erect or prostrate, shrubby, perennial succulents from periodically very dry areas of Namibia and South Africa. Leaves are opposite, often laterally compressed, thicker than wide, and often marked with raised spots. Daisy-like, pink or reddish purple flowers are borne singly or in cymes of 2–5 in summer, followed by ovoid green capsules with rough, papillose seeds. Where not hardy, grow in a warm greenhouse. In frost-free climates, grow in a desert garden.

• **CULTIVATION** Under glass, grow in standard cactus potting mix in full light. When in full growth, water sparingly and apply low-nitrogen fertilizer every 4–6 weeks; keep dry when dormant. Outdoors, grow in poor, sharply drained soil in full sun. Protect from winter moisture. See also pp.48–49.

• **PROPAGATION** Sow seed at 66–75°F (19–24°C) in spring, or take cuttings of stem sections in late spring.

• **PESTS AND DISEASES** Vulnerable to aphids while flowering.

L. weigangiana. Erect, perennial succulent with woody stems, ⅛in (3mm) thick, and yellowish white bark. Boat-shaped, 3-angled, spotted, bluish green leaves are ½in (1.5cm) long by ¼in (6mm) thick. Produces solitary, violet to pink flowers, ¾in (2cm) across, in summer. ↕ to 20in (50cm), ↔ 10in (25cm). Namibia. ❀ (min. 50°F/10°C)

LEITNERIA

LEITNERIACEAE

Genus of one species of small deciduous tree or suckering shrub from damp habitats in E. US. It has alternate, elliptic, and entire leaves. Leitneria is cultivated commercially for its extremely lightweight wood. Grow *L. floridana* in a damp shrub border.

• **CULTIVATION** Grow in moist, acidic, humus-rich soil in full sun.

• **PROPAGATION** Sow seed *in situ* as soon as ripe or remove suckers in spring. Pruning group 5.

• **PESTS AND DISEASES** Infrequent.

L. floridana (Corkwood). Colony-forming, large deciduous shrub or small tree with downy branches becoming thick-barked. Produces elliptic-oblong to lance-shaped mid-green leaves, to 6in (15cm) long, crowded at the tips of the branches, silky hairy beneath. Bears erect, axillary male catkins, to 1½in (4cm) long, and smaller, woolly female catkins, before the leaves in spring, followed by ellipsoid, hairless, dark brown fruit, to ½in (1.5cm) long. ↕ to 25ft (8m), ↔ indefinite. Missouri to Texas to S. Florida. Zone 6.

▷ ***Lemaireocereus euphorbioides*** see *Neobuxbaumia euphorbioides*
▷ ***Lemaireocereus thurberi*** see *Stenocereus thurberi*

LEMBOGLOSSUM

ORCHIDACEAE

Genus of about 14 species of evergreen, mostly epiphytic, rhizomatous orchids (often included within the genus *Odontoglossum*) occurring in humid forest at altitudes of 4,300–10,000ft (1,300–3,000m) in Mexico and Central and South America. They have broadly ovoid to oblong-ovoid, clustered pseudobulbs, each producing up to 3 linear, lance-shaped, ovate, or elliptic leaves. Flowers are produced in racemes from the bases of the pseudobulbs.

• **CULTIVATION** Cool- to intermediate-growing orchids. Grow in fine-grade epiphytic orchid potting mix in a container that constricts the roots, or mount on slabs. In summer, provide high humidity and bright filtered light, water freely, apply fertilizer at every third watering, and mist once or twice daily. In winter, provide full light and water sparingly. See also p.46.

• **PROPAGATION** Divide when the plants fill and overflow their containers.

• **PESTS AND DISEASES** Susceptible to spider mites, aphids, and mealybugs.

L. bictoniense ▣ syn. *Odontoglossum bictoniense.* Epiphytic orchid with ovoid, compressed pseudobulbs, each with 2 or

Lemboglossum bictoniense

Lemboglossum rossii

L

3 elliptic-oblong to linear leaves, 4–8in (10–20cm) long. Light green (occasionally white or yellow) flowers, 1in (2.5cm) across, heavily barred with brown, with heart-shaped, white or pink lips, are borne in tall, upright racemes from winter to spring. ↕ 24in (60cm), ↔ 12in (30cm). Mexico, Guatemala, El Salvador. ❀ (min. 50°F/10°C; max. 75°F/24°C)

L. cervantesii, syn. *Odontoglossum cervantesii.* Epiphytic orchid with ovoid pseudobulbs, each with one ovate-lance-shaped to elliptic-oblong leaf, 1½–12in (4–30cm) long. From winter to spring, produces short, arching racemes of white to pink flowers, 1½–2½in (4–6cm) across, with narrow, central red spots and bands. ↕↔ 6in (15cm). S. Mexico, Guatemala. ❀ (min. 50°F/10°C; max. 75°F/24°C)

L. cordatum, syn. *Odontoglossum cordatum.* Epiphytic orchid with oblong, compressed, furrowed pseudobulbs, each with one narrowly elliptic, leathery leaf, 3½–12in (9–30cm) long. Brown-marked, green, white, or yellow flowers, to 2½in (6cm) across, are borne in erect racemes in late summer. ↕ 8in (20cm), ↔ 6in (15cm). Central America, Venezuela. ❀ (min. 50°F/10°C; max. 75°F/24°C)

L. rossii ■ syn. *Odontoglossum rossii.* Epiphytic orchid with ovoid pseudobulbs, each with one elliptic or elliptic-lance-shaped leaf, 2–8in (5–20cm) long. White, pink, or sometimes yellow flowers, 2–3in (5–8cm) across, with brown to pink-brown bars or spots on the sepals and petal bases, are produced in short, arching racemes from late winter to spring. ↕↔ 6in (15cm). Mexico, Guatemala, Honduras, Nicaragua. ❀ (min. 50°F/10°C; max. 75°F/24°C)

L. stellatum, syn. *Odontoglossum stellatum.* Epiphytic orchid with narrowly oblong pseudobulbs, each with one ovate to elliptic or inversely lance-shaped leaf, 2½–6in (6–15cm) long. From winter to spring, produces short, arching racemes of yellowish white flowers, 1½in (4cm) across, barred with brown (or sometimes entirely brown), with large, pink or white lips spotted deep pink. ↕↔ 6in (15cm). Mexico, Guatemala, El Salvador. ❀ (min. 50°F/10°C; max. 75°F/24°C)

▷ ***Lembotropis nigricans*** see *Cytisus nigricans*

LENOPHYLLUM

CRASSULACEAE

Genus of about 6 species of clustering, perennial succulents, considered by some to be members of the genus *Crassula*, from low-lying, often scrub or woodland areas of California, Texas, New Mexico, and Mexico. Very variably shaped, fleshy leaves are borne mainly in opposite pairs, forming loose, basal rosettes. Sparsely leafy flowering stems produce small, 5-petaled flowers, borne singly or in terminal racemes or panicles, from summer to winter. In areas where temperatures drop below 41°F (5°C), they may be grown outdoors in summer, but need to be protected in a temperate greenhouse at other times. In warmer climates, grow permanently outdoors in a shrub border or a desert garden.

• **CULTIVATION** Under glass, grow in standard cactus potting mix in full light. From spring to late summer, water freely and apply a balanced liquid fertilizer every 6–8 weeks. Water moderately in autumn and keep just moist in winter. Outdoors, grow in moderately fertile, sharply drained soil in full sun. See also pp.48–49.

• **PROPAGATION** Sow seed at 66–75°F (19–24°C), or divide offsets, in spring or early summer. Root leaf cuttings in summer.

• **PESTS AND DISEASES** Prone to aphids while flowering.

L. guttatum. Rosetted, perennial succulent with ovate-elliptic to diamond-shaped, blunt-tipped, gray-green leaves, ¾–1½in (2–4cm) long, with purple-black spots, the upper surfaces broadly grooved. Cup-shaped, thick-sepaled, pale yellow flowers, to ½in (1.5cm) across, later tinged red, are produced in open, sparsely branched panicles from summer to autumn. ↕↔ 4–5in (10–13cm). N.E. Mexico. ❀ (min. 41°F/5°C)

LEOCEREUS

CACTACEAE

Monotypic genus of an erect to some what sprawling cactus, native to Brazil.

• **CULTIVATION** Under glass, grow in a mix of 4 parts standard cactus potting mix and 1 part limestone chips, in full light. From spring to summer, water freely and apply a balanced liquid fertilizer every 4-5 weeks. Keep nearly dry at other times. Outdoors, grow in moderately fertile, slightly alkaline, sharply drained, humus-rich soil in full sun.

• **PROPAGATION** Sow seed at 70°F (21°C) in spring or summer

• **PESTS AND DISEASES** Scale occurs.

L. bahiensis. Erect to somewhat sprawling cactus with 1 or more stems arising from an enlarged, woody rootstock. Woody stems are cylindrical and lack mucilage; 10–19 ribs are rounded to obtuse. Circular areoles, ⅕–¼in (4–7mm) apart, bears 8–16 spines (central and radials alike). Tubular white flowers, borne near stem tips, 1½–2½in (4–6cm) long, open at night. Red globose to ovoid fruit, 1–1¼in (2.5–3cm) long and ¾–1¼in (2–3cm) around, bear deciduous spines. ↕ 10ft (3m), ↔ ⅜–1in (1–2.5cm). ❀ (min. 50°F/10°C)

LEONOTIS

LAMIACEAE

Genus of about 30 species of aromatic annuals, perennials, and evergreen to semi-evergreen subshrubs and shrubs (deciduous in cold climates) from upland grassland and rocky areas, mainly in South Africa, with one species widely distributed in tropical regions. They have square stems and opposite, lance-shaped to ovate leaves, and are cultivated for their showy whorls of 2-lipped flowers, produced in terminal, leafy, raceme-like inflorescences. Where not hardy, they may be treated as tender perennials and grown in a cool greenhouse, or planted outdoors once frost danger has passed. They also make excellent subjects for growing in large containers for seasonal display. In warmer areas, grow outdoors in a border or against a warm wall.

• **CULTIVATION** Under glass, grow in soil-based potting mix in full light. When in full growth, water freely and apply a balanced liquid fertilizer every 6–8 weeks; water sparingly in winter. Outdoors, grow in moderately fertile, well-drained soil in full sun. Pruning group 10, in spring, if grown permanently outdoors; if grown under glass or as tender perennials, cut back severely in early spring.

Leonotis leonurus

• **PROPAGATION** Sow seed at 55–64°F (13–18°C) in spring, or take greenwood cuttings in late spring or summer.

• **PESTS AND DISEASES** Susceptible to gray mold (*Botrytis*), spider mites, and whiteflies under glass.

L. leonurus ■ (Lion's ear). Upright, semi-evergreen or deciduous shrub or subshrub with lance-shaped to inversely lance-shaped, entire or scalloped, mid- to deep green leaves, 2½–5in (6–13cm) long. From autumn to early winter, bears whorls of tubular, 2-lipped, orange-red to scarlet flowers, 2½in (6cm) long. ↕ 6ft (2m) or more, ↔ 3ft (1m) or more. South Africa. ❀ (min. 45°F/7°C). **'Harrismith White'** produces white flowers.

L. ocymifolia. Woody-based, herbaceous perennial with ovate, toothed or scalloped, mid-green leaves, to 3in (8cm) long, with very hairy undersides. From late summer to autumn, produces dense whorls of tubular, 2-lipped, velvety-haired orange flowers, to 1½in (4cm) long, with the upper lip twice as long as the lower. ↕ to 10ft (3m), ↔ 3ft (1m). South Africa. ❀ (min. 45°F/7°C)

LEONTOPODIUM

Edelweiss

ASTERACEAE

Genus of approximately 35 species of perennials found in grassland and stony habitats in the mountains of Europe and Asia. They have simple, entire, hairy, mainly basal leaves. Upright stems bear compact, terminal cymes of small flowerheads consisting only of yellowish white disk florets, surrounded by leaf-like, usually white-felted bracts. Most species are suitable for a rock garden, raised bed, or alpine house.

• **CULTIVATION** Grow in sharply drained, neutral to alkaline soil in full sun. Protect from excessive winter moisture. In an alpine house, grow in soil-based potting mix with added grit or sharp sand.

• **PROPAGATION** Sow seed in containers in an open frame as soon as ripe. Divide in early spring, although divisions are slow to establish.

• **PESTS AND DISEASES** Susceptible to slugs and snails outdoors, and to aphids and spider mites under glass.

L. aloysiodorum see *L. haplophylloides.*

L. alpinum ■ (Edelweiss). Clump-forming perennial with linear to oblong-lance-shaped, gray-green, basal leaves, to 1½in (4cm) long. In spring or early summer, bears conspicuous heads of yellowish white flowers surrounded by stars of flannel-textured, gray-white bracts, 1¼–4in (3–10cm) across. ↕ 8in (20cm) ↔ 4in (10cm). Mountains of Europe. Zone 4. **subsp. *nivale***, syn. *L. nivale*, has densely white-hairy leaves, and bears woolly, pure white flowerheads and bracts, on short stems; ↕↔ to 6in (15cm); C. Apennines, mountains of Bulgaria and former Yugoslavia.

L. haplophylloides, syn. *L. aloysiodorum.* Upright, clump-forming or tufted perennial with linear-lance-shaped,

Leontopodium alpinum

Lepidozamia hopei

lemon-scented, hairy, gray-green leaves, 2–3in (5–8cm) long, spotted black beneath. In early summer, bears yellowish white flowers surrounded by stars of many white-hairy, gray-green bracts, 2in (5cm) across. More tolerant of winter moisture than *L. alpinum*. ↕ 12in (30cm), ↔ to 8in (20cm). Mountains of C. and S.W. China. Zone 6.
L. nivale see *L. alpinum* subsp. *nivale*.
L. stracheyi. Mound-forming perennial with ovate-lance-shaped to linear leaves, to 1¾in (4.5cm) long, sparsely gray-hairy above, gray-downy beneath. In spring, bears short-stemmed heads of glistening, yellowish white flowers surrounded by many white-felted bracts, to 2½in (6cm) across. ↕ to 20in (50cm), ↔ to 12in (30cm). Himalayas, mountains of India (Uttar Pradesh) to S.W. China. Zone 5.

▷ ***Leopoldia comosa*** see *Muscari comosum*
▷ ***Lepachys*** see *Ratibida*

LEPIDOZAMIA

ZAMIACEAE

Genus of 2 species of palm-like, dioecious cycads from slopes, gullies, and rainforest in E. Australia. The erect trunks are clad in old leaf bases, with the pinnate, light or deep green leaves borne in terminal whorls. Narrow, cone-like, green to brown, male or female flowerheads ("cones") are borne in the centers of the leaf rosettes. Where not hardy, grow in a temperate or warm greenhouse or as houseplants. In frost-free climates, grow as specimen plants.
• **CULTIVATION** Under glass, grow in a mix of equal parts compost, loam, and coarse bark, with added slow-release fertilizer, grit, and charcoal, in bright filtered light. Water moderately when in growth, sparingly in winter. Outdoors, site in moderately fertile, moist but well-drained soil in full sun or partial shade.
• **PROPAGATION** Sow seed at 75°F (24°C) in spring.
• **PESTS AND DISEASES** Spider mites, mealybugs, and scale insects may be troublesome under glass.

L. hopei ■ Medium-sized to tall cycad with ascending to arching, pinnate, light green leaves, to 10ft (3m) long, each consisting of many lance-shaped, curved, lustrous leaflets. Green to brown flowering cones are usually borne in summer: the ovoid females to 24in (60cm) long, the cylindrical males to 32in (80cm) long. ↕ to 70ft (20m), ↔ to 20ft (6m). N.E. Queensland. ❀ (min. 55–59°F/13–15°C)
L. peroffskyana. Medium-sized to tall cycad with pinnate, deep green leaves, to 10ft (3m) long, composed of linear to lance-shaped, lustrous leaflets, each with a yellow basal gland. Green to brown flowering cones are borne in summer: the ovoid females to 24in (60cm) long, the cylindrical males to 32in (80cm) long. ↕ to 70ft (20m), ↔ to 20ft (6m). Queensland, New South Wales. ❀ (min. 55–59°F/13–15°C)

LEPTINELLA

ASTERACEAE

Genus of approximately 30 species of annuals and creeping, tufted, or mat-forming perennials from subalpine grassland and rocky areas in Australasia and South America. They form low carpets of pinnatifid, pinnatisect, or pinnate, often aromatic leaves, and bear solitary, button-like flowerheads on short stalks from late spring to summer. Effective as a low groundcover and tolerant of some foot traffic, they are suitable for paving crevices or gravel gardens, but are mostly too invasive for a rock garden. *L. atrata* is suitable for a scree bed or alpine house.
• **CULTIVATION** Grow in moderately fertile, sharply drained soil in full sun.
• **PROPAGATION** Sow seed in containers in an open frame as soon as ripe. Divide in spring.
• **PESTS AND DISEASES** Infrequent.

Leptinella atrata

L. atrata ■ syn. *Cotula atrata*. Creeping, tufted perennial with fern-like, broadly elliptic, 2-pinnatifid, purple-tinged, gray-green leaves, to 3in (8cm) long. In late spring and early summer, bears hemispherical, purplish black flowerheads, to ½in (1.5cm) across, with yellow anthers that become prominent as the flowers mature. ↕ to 6in (15cm), ↔ to 8in (20cm). New Zealand. ❀ (min. 35°F/2°C). **subsp. *luteola*** has less deeply divided leaves, and bears conical flowerheads with dark red-brown centers and very prominent, creamy white stigmas.
L. pectinata. Tufted or mat-forming perennial with narrowly oblong, hairy or hairless, sometimes toothed, pinnatifid to pinnate leaves, 1½in (4cm) long, with linear to lance-shaped leaflets or lobes. Produces white or pale yellow-red flowerheads, to ⅜in (9mm) across, in late spring and early summer. ↕ to 6in (15cm), ↔ to 18in (45cm). New Zealand. ❀ (min. 35°F/2°C)
L. squalida, syn. *Cotula squalida*. Creeping perennial with elliptic to obovate, pinnatifid, hairless or softly hairy, bright green leaves, to 4in (10cm) long. Yellow-green flowerheads, to ¼in (6mm) across, are borne in late spring and early summer. ↕ to 6in (15cm), ↔ indefinite. New Zealand. Zone 6.

LEPTODACTYLON

POLEMONIACEAE

Genus of 12 species of deciduous perennials, subshrubs, and shrubs from deserts and dry areas of W. North America. The leaves are alternate or opposite, palmately or pinnately divided into linear, spine-tipped leaflets. They are grown for their terminal cymes of salverform or funnel-shaped flowers. *L. californicum* is ideal in a desert garden.
• **CULTIVATION** Grow in moderately fertile, well-drained soil in full sun. Pruning group 1.
• **PROPAGATION** Sow seed *in situ* in spring or early autumn.
• **PESTS AND DISEASES** Rust can occur.

L. californicum (Prickly phlox). Upright, branching shrub with 5- to 9-palmate leaves, to 1in (2.5cm) long, with linear, hairless, mid-green leaflets, ⅛–½in (3–15mm) long. Bears cymes of salverform, lavender-pink to rose-pink flowers, ½in (1.5cm) across, from late winter to summer. ↕ to 3ft (1m), ↔ to 24in (60cm). California. Zone 7b.

LEPTOSPERMUM

Tea tree

MYRTACEAE

Genus of about 80 species of evergreen shrubs and trees occurring in rainforest and semi-arid areas mainly in Australia, but also from S.E. Asia to New Zealand. They are cultivated for their usually aromatic, neat foliage and their small, sometimes profusely borne flowers. The variably shaped leaves are alternate, entire, and hairless to densely silky-hairy. The flowers are produced from the leaf axils, either singly or in clusters of 2 or 3, and are shallowly cup-shaped to star-shaped, each with 5 white, red, or pink, clawed, usually broadly ovate petals. Where marginally hardy, grow against a warm, sunny wall; grow frost-tender species in a cool greenhouse or conservatory. A few are also suitable for an alpine house. In warmer areas, grow in a shrub border.
• **CULTIVATION** Under glass, grow in soil-based potting mix in full light or bright filtered light. When in active growth, water freely and apply a balanced liquid fertilizer every 4 weeks; water sparingly in winter. Outdoors, grow in moderately fertile, well-drained soil in full sun or partial shade. Pruning group 8; may need restrictive pruning under glass.
• **PROPAGATION** Sow seed at 55–61°F (13–16°C) in autumn or spring, or root semi-ripe cuttings with bottom heat in summer.
• **PESTS AND DISEASES** Infrequent.

L. flavescens see *L. polygalifolium*.
L. grandiflorum, syn. *L. rodwayanum*. Upright shrub with white-hairy stems and ovate to elliptic, aromatic, silky-hairy, gray-green leaves, to ½in (1.5cm) long. Solitary, saucer-shaped, white or, rarely, pale pink flowers, to ¾in (2cm) across, are produced in mid- and late summer. ↕ 12ft (4m), ↔ 6ft (2m). Tasmania. ❀ (min. 41°F/5°C)
L. humifusum see *L. rupestre*.
L. lanigerum ■ syn. *L. pubescens* (Woolly tea tree). Freely branching, erect shrub or tree with softly hairy and often red-flushed green stems. Crowded, more or less spreading, obovate-oblong to oval, aromatic leaves, ¼–½in (0.5–1.5cm) long, often have recurved points, and are usually gray silky-hairy, at least beneath. From late spring to summer, bears solitary, shallowly cup-

Leptospermum lanigerum

Leptospermum rupestre

shaped white flowers, to ½in (1.5cm) across, with prominent red-brown calyces. ↕ 10–15ft (3–5m), ↔ 5–10ft (1.5–3m). New South Wales, Victoria, Tasmania. ❄ (min. 41°F/5°C)
L. polygalifolium, syn. *L. flavescens.* Erect to spreading, freely branching shrub or tree. Crowded, spreading or occasionally reflexed, mid- to deep green leaves, ¼–¾in (0.5–2cm) long, are linear to inversely lance-shaped-elliptic, with conspicuous oil glands, sometimes lightly aromatic. From late spring to summer, bears solitary, cup-shaped, white or cream, sometimes green- or pink-tinted flowers, ½in (1.5cm) across. ↕ 6–22ft (2–7m), ↔ 3–10ft (1–3m). Queensland, New South Wales, Lord Howe Island. ❄ (min. 41°F/5°C)
L. prostratum see *L. rupestre.*

L

Leptospermum scoparium 'Gaiety Girl'

L. pubescens see *L. lanigerum.*
L. rodwayanum see *L. grandiflorum.*
L. rupestre ■ syn. *L. humifusum, L. prostratum, L. scoparium* var. *prostratum.* Prostrate shrub, sometimes mounded and bushy, with dense foliage. Broadly to narrowly elliptic or obovate, glossy, deep green leaves, ¼–¾in (0.7–2cm) long, are spreading and aromatic. Star-shaped white flowers, to ½in (1.5cm) across, are borne singly or in pairs from late spring to summer. ↕ 1–5ft (0.3–1.5m), ↔ 3–5ft (0.9–1.5m). Tasmania. ❄ (min. 41°F/5°C)
L. scoparium ■ (Manuka, New Zealand tea tree). Compact shrub, rarely tree-like, with arching shoots and ascending to widely spreading, elliptic, broadly lance-shaped, or inversely lance-shaped, aromatic, mid- to dark green

Leptospermum scoparium

Leptospermum scoparium 'Kiwi'

leaves, ¼–¾in (0.7–2cm) long, often silver-hairy when young. Solitary, shallowly cup- to saucer-shaped, white or pink-tinged white flowers, ½in (1.5cm) across, are profusely borne in late spring and early summer. ↕↔ 10ft (3m). S.E. Australia, New Zealand. ❄ (min. 41°F/5°C). **'Apple Blossom'** has white flowers overlaid with pink. **'Gaiety Girl'** ■ bears semi-double flowers, deep pink outside, paler within. **'Helene Strybing'** has rather large, deep pink flowers, and gray-green foliage. **'Huia'** is compact, with dark pink flowers. Suitable for a rock garden or alpine house; ↕ 12in (30cm), ↔ 18in (45cm). **'Keatleyi'** has pale pink flowers, 1in (2.5cm) across. **'Kiwi'** ■ has purple-tinged young foliage and dark crimson flowers. Suitable for a rock garden or alpine house; ↕↔ 3ft (1m). **'Nicholsii'** has purple-tinged foliage and crimson flowers. **'Pink Cascade'** has a weeping habit and produces pink flowers. **var. *prostratum*** see *L. rupestre.* **'Red Damask'** has dark green leaves, and bears double, dark red flowers. **'Ruby Glow'** is compact and upright, with dark red leaves and profuse, double burgundy-red flowers, ¾in (2cm) across; ↕ 6–8ft (2–2.5m). **'Snow Flurry'** has double white flowers.

LESCHENAULTIA

syn. LECHENAULTIA

GOODENIACEAE

Genus of about 20 species of evergreen shrubs, subshrubs, and perennials from semi-arid or arid areas of Australia. The usually linear leaves are entire, stalkless, and alternate or spiraling on the wiry stems. The showy, terminal flowers are solitary or borne in corymbs; they each have 5 free, often centrally "winged," white, yellow to red, or blue petals, 2 small and 3 large, which form a basal tube. Where not hardy, grow in a cool or temperate greenhouse. In frost-free climates, grow in a shrub border or as a groundcover.
• **CULTIVATION** Under glass, grow in a mix of 1 part soil-based potting mix and 3 parts each grit (or perlite) and peat, in full light with shade from hot sun and with good ventilation. In growth, water moderately and apply a phosphate-free liquid fertilizer monthly; water sparingly in winter. Outdoors, grow in sharply drained soil that is low in nitrates and phosphates, in full sun with some mid-day shade. Pruning group 8 for shrubs.

Leschenaultia formosa

• **PROPAGATION** Sow seed at 55–64°F (13–18°C) in spring, or root softwood cuttings in spring with bottom heat.
• **PESTS AND DISEASES** Under glass, spider mites may be troublesome, and poor ventilation in winter will encourage gray mold (*Botrytis*).

L. biloba. Open shrub with linear, soft, mid-green to gray-green leaves, ½in (1.5cm) long. Bright blue, sometimes white flowers, 1¼in (3cm) across, are borne in leafy corymbs, to 3in (8cm) across, in late spring and early summer. Each petal lobe is roughly the shape of a fish tail, the "fins" having sharp to blunt points. ↕↔ 12–24in (30–60cm). Western Australia. ❄ (min. 41–45°F/5–7°C)
L. floribunda. Erect, shrubby, woody-based perennial or short-lived shrub, with alternate, narrowly oblong to linear, mid-green leaves, ⅛–⅜in (3–9mm) long. Blue or white flowers, ½in (1.5cm) across, are produced in loose corymbs, to 4in (10cm) across, from late spring to midsummer. ↕ 18in (45cm), ↔ 14in (35cm). Western Australia. ❄ (min. 41–45°F/5–7°C)
L. formosa ■ Suckering, many-branched, spreading shrub with linear, blunt-tipped or pointed, light to gray-green leaves, to ½in (1.5cm) long. In late spring and early summer, produces solitary flowers, ¾in (2cm) across, in shades of bright red, orange, or orange-yellow. Usually short-lived, especially under glass. ↕↔ 12–24in (30–60cm). Western Australia. ❄ (min. 41–45°F/5–7°C)

LESPEDEZA

Bush clover

FABACEAE

Genus of about 40 species of annuals, perennials, and deciduous subshrubs and shrubs found in meadows, grassland, and rocky places in E. Asia, Australia, and North America. They are cultivated for their small, pea-like flowers, profusely borne in axillary or terminal racemes. Leaves are alternate and 3-palmate. Excellent late-flowering plants for a mixed or shrub border.
• **CULTIVATION** Grow in light, moderately fertile, well-drained soil in full sun. Pruning group 6 for shrubs; treat as perennials in very cold areas, where shrubby species may die to the ground in winter.
• **PROPAGATION** Sow seed in containers outdoors in spring, or take greenwood

Lespedeza thunbergii

cuttings in early summer. *L. thunbergii* may also be divided in spring.
• **PESTS AND DISEASES** Powdery mildew, tar spot, rust, stem rot, and leafhoppers can be problems.

L. bicolor. Upright shrub with arching shoots and 3-palmate, mid- to dark green leaves consisting of broadly oval to obovate leaflets, to 2in (5cm) long. In mid- and late summer, purple-pink flowers, to ½in (1.5cm) long, are borne in slender racemes, 2–5in (5–13cm) or more long, from the upper leaf axils. ↕↔ 6ft (2m). E. Asia. Zone 4.
L. thunbergii ■ Woody-based perennial or subshrub with long, arching shoots and 3-palmate, blue-green leaves consisting of oval or oval-lance-shaped leaflets, to 2in (5cm) long. In late summer, purple-pink flowers, to ½in (1.5cm) long, are profusely borne in pendent, terminal racemes, to 6in (15cm) long. ↕ 6ft (2m), ↔ 10ft (3m). N. China, Japan. Zone 5. **'Gibraltar'** is shorter and bears rose-pink flowers; ↕ to 5ft (1.5m).

LEUCADENDRON

PROTEACEAE

Genus of 80 species of small, dioecious, evergreen shrubs and trees from varied habitats, ranging from sea plains to mountain slopes in dry or moist sites, in South Africa. They are grown mainly for their dense, cone-like, terminal clusters of small, tubular flowers, surrounded by large, leaf-like, often colored or tinted bracts. Leaves are alternate or spiraling, stalkless, entire, leathery, and variably shaped. Both male and female plants are needed for fruiting cones to develop. Where temperatures fall below 41°F (5°C), grow in a cool or temperate greenhouse, although they seldom bear flowers or fruits in the former. In warm, dry areas, grow in a courtyard garden or against a sunny wall; the larger species are spectacular specimen plants.
• **CULTIVATION** Under glass, grow in a mix of 1 part acidic potting mix and 3 parts each grit (or perlite) and peat, in full light and low humidity. During the growing season, water moderately and apply magnesium sulfate and urea at half the recommended strength in spring and autumn; water sparingly in winter. Outdoors, grow in poor, well-drained, neutral to acidic soil in full sun. May become chlorotic in magnesium-deficient soil. Pruning group 1.
• **PROPAGATION** Stratify seed below 41°F (5°C), then sow at 55–61°F (13–16°C) in a mix of equal parts peat and grit in spring. Root semi-ripe cuttings with bottom heat in summer.
• **PESTS AND DISEASES** Spider mites may be a problem under glass.

L. argenteum (Silver tree). Erect, pyramidal to columnar tree with robust stems densely covered with lance-shaped, sharp-pointed, brilliant, silvery-hairy leaves, 4–6in (10–15cm) long. From spring to summer, produces spherical flowerheads, to 1½in (4cm) across, yellowish green on male trees, greenish silver on females, surrounded by leaf-like but broader and more lustrous bracts, to ¾in (2cm) long. The silvery cones often persist on the tree for several years. ↕ 20–30ft (6–10m), ↔ 6–12ft (2–4m). South Africa (Cape Peninsula). ❄ (min. 41–45°F/5–7°C)
L. discolor. Erect, open shrub with grooved, often purple-red stems and inversely lance-shaped, rigid, leathery, densely short-hairy, grayish green leaves, 1–1½in (2.5–4cm) long, often tipped and margined purple. From spring to early summer, bears ovoid to spherical flowerheads, 1¼in (3cm) across, purple-red to red on male shrubs, whitish green on females, surrounded by ivory to creamy white bracts, 1½–2in (4–5cm) long, with purple-red tips or margins (usually more boldly colored in males). Cones are brown. ↕ 5–8ft (1.5–2.5m), ↔ 3–6ft (1–2m). South Africa (Northern Cape, Western Cape, Eastern Cape). ❄ (min. 41–45°F/5–7°C)
***L.* 'Safari Sunset'** ■ Vigorous, erect, freely branching shrub with narrowly oblong leaves, to 3½in (9cm) long, deep green flushed purple-red, more colorful when young. From summer to autumn, produces ovoid, sterile, yellowish green female flowerheads, 1½in (4cm) across, surrounded by light red bracts, 4–8in (10–20cm) long, maturing to purple-red and fading to golden yellow. ↕ to 8ft (2.5m), ↔ to 6ft (1.8m) or more. ❄ (min. 41–45°F/5–7°C)
L. tinctum. Spreading, freely branching shrub with robust stems, bent toward their bases, and oblong, dark green leaves, 3in (8cm) long, increasing in size toward the stem tips. From spring to summer, bears ovoid, greenish yellow flowerheads, to 1¼in (3cm) across, surrounded by glossy yellow bracts, 3in (8cm) long, which reflex after the flowers have faded. Cones have a sweet, spicy aroma. ↕↔ to 4ft (1.2m). South Africa (Northern Cape, Western Cape, Eastern Cape). ❄ (min. 41–45°F/5–7°C)

LEUCANTHEMELLA

ASTERACEAE

Genus of 2 species of hairy perennials found in wet meadows or marshy places, one species in S.E. Europe, the other in E. Asia. They have tall stems, which bear numerous alternate, lance-shaped to broadly elliptic or oblong, entire to sharply toothed leaves. They are grown mainly for their chrysanthemum-like flowerheads, borne singly or in 2- to 8-flowered corymbs in autumn. Grow in a mixed or herbaceous border. Also good for cutting.

Leucadendron 'Safari Sunset' (inset: flowerhead detail)

Leucanthemella serotina

• **CULTIVATION** Grow in any reliably moist but well-drained soil in full sun or partial shade.
• **PROPAGATION** Divide, or take basal cuttings in spring.
• **PESTS AND DISEASES** Susceptible to slugs; thrips may damage leaves.

L. serotina ■ syn. *Chrysanthemum serotinum, C. uliginosum.* Strong-growing, erect perennial with simple, lance-shaped to broadly elliptic or oblong, toothed leaves, 2½–5in (6–13cm) long. From early to late autumn, chrysanthemum-like white flowerheads, to 3in (8cm) across, with greenish yellow centers, are produced singly or in lax corymbs of 2–8. ↕ to 5ft (1.5m), ↔ 36in (90cm). S.E. Europe. Zone 5.

LEUCANTHEMOPSIS

ASTERACEAE

Genus of 6 species of dwarf, tufted, clump- or mat-forming perennials from mountain habitats in Europe and North Africa. They are grown for their solitary, daisy-like, white or yellow flowerheads, borne in summer. The leaves are pinnatisect, pinnatifid, or palmately lobed. Frequently short-lived, they are suitable for a rock garden, scree bed, or alpine house.
• **CULTIVATION** Grow in any sharply drained soil in full sun. In an alpine house, grow in equal parts loam, leaf mold, and grit.
• **PROPAGATION** Sow seed in containers in an open frame as soon as ripe. Divide, or take basal cuttings, in spring.
• **PESTS AND DISEASES** Susceptible to aphids and spider mites under glass.

L. alpina, syn. *Chrysanthemum alpinum* (Alpine chrysanthemum). Mat-forming, rhizomatous perennial with variable, ovate to spoon-shaped, pinnatisect, deeply pinnatifid, or palmately lobed, silvery gray leaves, to 1½in (4cm) long. In mid- and late summer, produces short-stemmed flowerheads, to 1½in (4cm) across, with white ray florets, sometimes turning pink with age, and orange-yellow disk florets. Best grown in a scree bed. ↕ 4in (10cm), ↔ to 8in (20cm). Pyrenees, Alps, Apennines, Carpathians. Zone 6. **subsp. *tomentosa*** is very dwarf in habit and produces ovate, palmately lobed leaves with with 5–7 closely aligned lobes; ↕ 2in (5cm).

Leucanthemopsis pectinata

Leucanthemum x *superbum* 'Horace Read'

Leucanthemum x *superbum* 'Wirral Pride'

L. pectinata ■ syn. *Chrysanthemum pectinata, L. radicans, Pyrethrum radicans.* Densely tufted perennial, spreading by runners, with pinnatifid, gray-green to silvery green leaves, 3–6in (7–14cm) long, with 5–9 lobes. In summer, bears flowerheads to ¾in (2cm) across, with yellow-orange disk florets, and golden yellow ray florets that turn orange-red. ↕ 6in (15cm), ↔ to 12in (30cm). S. Spain. ❄ (min. 35°F/2°C)
L. radicans see *L. pectinata.*

LEUCANTHEMUM

ASTERACEAE

Genus of 26 species of annuals and perennials from rocky alpine slopes and moist meadows, grassland, and wasteland in Europe and temperate Asia. They have alternate, entire, deeply pinnatifid, toothed, scalloped, or lobed leaves, and solitary, daisy-like, terminal flowerheads, which are usually white with yellow disk florets. Grow alpine species in a scree bed or rock garden, taller perennials in a wild garden. Some hybrids and cultivars are useful in a herbaceous border and for cut flowers.

• **CULTIVATION** Grow in moderately fertile, moist but well-drained soil in full sun or partial shade. Alpine species need sharply drained soil in full sun. Many of the taller plants need support.
• **PROPAGATION** Sow seed of annuals *in situ* in spring. Sow seed of perennials in containers in a cold frame in autumn or spring. Divide perennials in early spring or late summer.
• **PESTS AND DISEASES** Aphids, slugs, earwigs, chrysanthemum nematode, and leaf spots may be troublesome.

L. atratum, syn. *Chrysanthemum atratum.* Variable, clump- or mat-forming perennial with spoon-shaped, scalloped or lobed, dark green basal leaves, to 2in (5cm) long, and shorter, oblong to linear, deeply toothed to pinnatifid stem leaves, with toothed tips. In summer, upright stems bear solitary flowerheads, to 2in (5cm) across, with yellow disk florets and white ray florets. ↕↔ to 12in (30cm). Alps, Apennines, mountains of Slovenia, Bosnia and Herzegovina, and Yugoslavia (Serbia and Montenegro). Zone 6.
L. hosmariense see *Rhodanthemum hosmariense.*
L. paludosum, syn. *Chrysanthemum paludosum, Melampodium paludosum.* Hairless, bushy annual with obovate, spoon-shaped, gray-green basal leaves, to 5in (13cm) long, and shorter, oblong-wedge-shaped stem leaves; all leaves are toothed to pinnatifid. In summer, produces solitary flowerheads, ¾–1¼in (2–3cm) across, with yellow or yellowish white ray florets and deeper yellow disk florets. ↕ 2–6in (5–15cm), ↔ 8in (20cm). S. Portugal, S. and S.E. Spain, Balearic Islands. **'Show Star'** ■ has wavy-margined, toothed, mid-green leaves and bright yellow flowerheads.
L. x superbum (*L. lacustre* x *L. maximum*) syn. *Chrysanthemum maximum* of gardens, *C.* x *superbum* (Shasta daisy). Robust, clump-forming perennial with inversely lance-shaped, toothed, glossy, almost fleshy, dark green basal leaves, to 12in (30cm) long, and shorter, lance-shaped, stalkless stem leaves. From early summer to early autumn, bears solitary, single or double white flowerheads, 4–5in (10–13cm) across, with yellow disk florets. Good for cutting. ↕ 36in (90cm), ↔ 24in (60cm). Garden origin. Zone 5. **'Aglaia'** produces fringed, semi-double flowerheads; ↕ 24in (60cm). **'Alaska'** bears single, white flowerheads, 2in (5cm) across. **'Cobham Gold'** ■ bears double flowerheads; ↕ 24in (60cm). **'Esther Read'** produces double, pure white flowerheads; ↕↔ 20–24in (50–60cm). **'Everest'** see 'Mount Everest'. **'Horace Read'** ■ has double white flowerheads with incurved disk florets; ↕ 24in (60cm). **'Little Silver Princess'** see 'Silberprinzesschen'. **'Marconi'** has fully double, white flowerheads, 4in (10cm) across. ↕ 36in (90cm). **'Mount Everest'**, syn. 'Everest', bears single flowerheads, to 4in (10cm) across. **'Nordlicht'**, syn. 'Northern Light' bears many single white flowerheads. ↕ 28in (70cm). **'Northern Light'** see 'Nordlicht'. **'Phyllis Smith'** has single flowerheads with twisted, recurved ray florets. **'Polaris'** has single white flowerheads. ↕ 3ft (90cm). **'Silberprinzesschen'**, syn. 'Little Silver Princess', has single flowerheads; ↕↔ 12in (30cm). **'Snowcap'** very freely bears single flowerheads, to 4in (10cm) across; ↕↔ 18in (45cm). **'Snow Lady'** ■ is a fast-growing, erect, bushy perennial that blooms the first year from seed, with oval to lance-shaped, deeply toothed leaves; produces single white flowerheads in summer; ↕ 10–18in (25–45cm), ↔ 12in (30cm). **'Starburst'** has huge, single white flowerheads, 5½–6in (14–15cm) across. ↕ to 3½ft (1.1m). **'T.E. Killin'** produces double flowerheads, to 4in (10cm) across, with yellow anemone centers. **'White Knight'** is broad and bears many single white flowerheads. ↕ to 22in (55cm), ↔ to 20in (50cm). **'Wirral Pride'** ■ has double flowerheads with anemone centers; ↔ 30in (75cm). **'Wirral Supreme'** has dense, double flowerheads with slightly shorter center ray florets; ↔ 30in (75cm).
L. vulgare, syn. *Chrysanthemum leucanthemum* (Marguerite, Ox-eye daisy). Extremely variable, rhizomatous perennial with obovate-spoon-shaped, toothed, smooth, dark green basal leaves, ¾–4in (2–10cm) long, and shorter, sometimes pinnatifid stem leaves. Solitary flowerheads, 1–2in (2.5–5cm) across, with bright yellow disk florets and white ray florets, are borne in late spring and early summer. ↕ 12–36in (30–90cm), ↔ 24in (60cm). Most of Europe, temperate Asia. Zone 4.

Leucanthemum paludosum 'Show Star'

Leucanthemum x *superbum* 'Cobham Gold'

Leucanthemum x *superbum* 'Snow Lady'

Leuchtenbergia principis

LEUCHTENBERGIA

CACTACEAE

Genus of one species of cactus with a thick, forked, tuberous rootstock, sometimes branching from the base, from hilly regions in central N. Mexico. The plant is covered with narrowly triangular, spirally arranged tubercles, each tipped by an areole bearing papery, twisted spines. The areoles on young tubercles produce fragrant flowers by day from summer to autumn. Where temperatures drop below 50°F (10°C), grow in a warm greenhouse; in warmer climates, grow in a desert garden.

• **CULTIVATION** Under glass, grow in standard cactus potting mix in full light. From midspring to early autumn, water moderately and apply a balanced liquid fertilizer every 6–8 weeks; keep completely dry from midautumn to early spring. Outdoors, grow in moderately fertile, sharply drained, ideally alkaline soil, in full sun. Protect from winter moisture. See also pp.48–49.

• **PROPAGATION** Sow seed at 66–75°F (19–24°C) in spring.

• **PESTS AND DISEASES** Susceptible to scale insects when in growth.

L. principis ■ (Agave cactus). Solitary or branching cactus with a thick, cylindrical, fleshy root, appearing woody when mature, and spherical to short cylindrical stems. Narrowly triangular, glaucous, bluish green tubercles, 4–5in (10–13cm) long, cover the stems. Large gray areoles bear 8–14 radial spines, to 2in (5cm) long, and 1 or 2 centrals, to 6in (15cm) long. Bears funnel-shaped, bright yellow flowers, to 3in (8cm) long, from summer to autumn. ↕ 12–24in (30–60cm), ↔ 12in (30cm). Central N. Mexico. ❀ (min. 50°F/10°C), although will tolerate brief periods to 18°F (-8°C) if kept dry.

LEUCOCORYNE

LILIACEAE

Genus of 12 species of garlic-scented, bulbous perennials from dry scrub and rocky hillsides in Chile. They are grown for their umbels of large, open funnel-shaped, scented, blue, white, or purple flowers, borne in spring. Each bulb produces 2–5 linear, often channeled, basal leaves, smelling of garlic. Where not hardy, grow in a cool greenhouse; in warmer areas, grow in a rock garden.

Leucocoryne ixioides

• **CULTIVATION** Plant bulbs 4in (10cm) deep. Under glass, grow in soil-based potting mix with added sharp sand, in full light with good ventilation. When in growth, water moderately and apply a balanced liquid fertilizer monthly when in leaf. Reduce water after flowering and keep almost dry when dormant in summer. Pot on every 2 years in autumn. Outdoors, grow in moderately fertile, sharply drained soil in full sun.

• **PROPAGATION** Sow seed at 66–75°F (19–24°C) as soon as ripe, or remove offsets in autumn before repotting.

• **PESTS AND DISEASES** Infrequent.

L. ixioides ■ (Glory of the sun). Bulbous perennial with narrow, grass-like, basal leaves, to 18in (45cm) long, which wither as the flowers open. In spring, produces umbels of up to 12 outward-facing, open funnel-shaped, scented flowers, ¾in (2cm) across, white with purple veins, or lilac-blue with white throats. ↕ 18in (45cm), PD3in (8cm). Chile. ❀ (min. 41–45°F/5–7°C)

L. purpurea. Bulbous perennial with narrow, grass-like, basal leaves, to 12in (30cm) long, which wither as the flowers open. In spring, produces umbels of 2–7 open funnel-shaped, scented, pale lilac flowers, 1in (2.5cm) across, with broad, red-purple centers. ↕ 18in (45cm), PD3in (8cm). Chile. ❀ (min. 41–45°F/5–7°C)

LEUCOGENES

New Zealand edelweiss

ASTERACEAE

Genus of 3 or 4 species of dwarf, hummock-, mat-, or clump-forming perennials from screes or rocky fields in the mountains of New Zealand. They have obovate-wedge-shaped or linear to lance-shaped, closely overlapping, intensely silver-hairy leaves and, in summer, bear small, flat yellow flowerheads surrounded by collars of white-woolly bracts. Effective in a rock garden or alpine house, but difficult to grow in dry climates.

• **CULTIVATION** Grow in gritty, humus-rich, moist but sharply drained soil in full sun. They grow best in cool, moist climates and resent a dry atmosphere in summer. Protect from winter moisture. In an alpine house, grow in a mix of equal parts loam, leaf mold, and coarse sand.

• **PROPAGATION** Sow seed in containers in an open frame as soon as ripe. Take stem-tip cuttings in late summer.

Leucogenes grandiceps

• **PESTS AND DISEASES** Susceptible to spider mites under glass; may be damaged by slugs and snails outdoors.

L. grandiceps ■ (South Island edelweiss). Mat-forming perennial with closely overlapping, obovate-wedge-shaped, silver-downy leaves, to ½in (1.5cm) long, that obscure the stems. In early summer, produces yellow flowerheads, ⅜–½in (0.9–1.5cm) across, near the shoot tips, each surrounded by a collar, ½in (1.5cm) across, of densely white-woolly bracts. ↕↔ 4–6in (10–15cm). New Zealand (South Island). Zone 7b.

L. leontopodium, syn. *Raoulia leontopodium* (North Island edelweiss). Hummock-forming perennial with linear to lance-shaped-oblong leaves, to ¾in (2cm) long, clothed in yellowish or grayish silver or silvery white down. In early summer, bears yellow flowerheads, to 1in (2.5cm) across, near the shoot tips, each surrounded by a collar, to ½in (1.5cm) across, of white-woolly bracts. ↕↔ 4–6in (10–15cm). New Zealand. Zone 7b.

LEUCOJUM

Snowflake

AMARYLLIDACEAE

Genus of about 10 species of mainly spring- or autumn-flowering, bulbous perennials from a variety of habitats, including woodland, shaded hillsides, wet sites, dunes, rocky grassland, and scrub, from W. Europe to the Middle East and N. Africa. They are similar to snowdrops (*Galanthus*), with usually 1 or 2, occasionally up to 8 flowers per stem, but the nodding or pendent, bell-shaped, usually white, sometimes pink flowers have 6 equal segments. Leaves are basal and strap-shaped to linear, or occasionally narrowly cylindrical. Small species are suitable for a rock garden, alpine house, or bulb frame, while larger species such as *L. aestivum* and *L. vernum* are excellent in a border, near water, or naturalized in grass.

• **CULTIVATION** Plant bulbs 3–4in (8–10cm) deep in autumn. Grow *Leucojum* species and cultivars in any moist but well-drained soil in full sun, apart from *L. aestivum* and *L. vernum*, which need reliably moist, humus-rich soil; *L. aestivum* grows well in areas with bright light but little direct sun. In an alpine house, grow in equal parts loam, leaf mold, and sharp sand.

Leucojum aestivum 'Gravetye Giant'

• **PROPAGATION** Sow seed in containers in a cold frame in autumn, or remove offsets once the leaves have died down.

• **PESTS AND DISEASES** Prone to slugs and narcissus bulb fly.

L. aestivum (Summer snowflake). Robust, bulbous perennial with erect, strap-shaped, glossy, dark green leaves, to 16in (40cm) long. In spring, leafless stems bear up to 8 bell-shaped, faintly chocolate-scented white flowers, ¾in (2cm) long, with green tips. ↕ 18–24in (45–60cm), PD3in (8cm). Ireland, UK, Belgium, France, C. and E. Europe, N. Turkey, Ukraine (Crimea), Caucasus, N. and N.W. Iran. Zone 4.

'Gravetye Giant' ■ is more robust; ↕ 36in (90cm), especially when grown near water.

L. autumnale ■ Slender, bulbous perennial with erect, narrow, grass-like leaves, to 6in (15cm) long, produced with or just after the flowers. In late summer and early autumn, each bulb produces up to 4 leafless stems, each with 2–4 bell-shaped white flowers, ½in (1.5cm) long, with red-tinged bases. ↕ 4–6in (10–15cm), PD2in (5cm). S.W. Europe, N. Africa. Zone 5b.

Leucojum autumnale

Leucojum vernum var. *vagneri*

L. hiemale see *L. nicaeense.*
L. nicaeense, syn. *L. hiemale.* Bulbous perennial with 2–4 almost prostrate, curled, narrowly linear leaves, to 12in (30cm) long. In early spring, leafless stems produce 1 or 2 bell-shaped, waxy white flowers, ½in (1.5cm) long. Survives outside in a sunny, sheltered site, but is best grown in an alpine house. ↕4in (10cm), PD2in (5cm). S.E. France. Zone 7b.
L. roseum. Bulbous perennial with leafless stems bearing 1 or 2 bell-shaped, pale pink flowers, ½in (1.5cm) long, in late summer or autumn. Erect, narrowly linear leaves, to 4in (10cm) long, appear after the flowers. Best in an alpine house. ↕4in (10cm), PD2in (5cm). Corsica, Sardinia. Zone 7.
L. trichophyllum. Bulbous perennial with 3 linear leaves, 2–8in (5–20cm) long, that appear before or with the flowers. From winter to spring, slender, leafless stems bear 2–4 bell-shaped white flowers, to ¾in (2cm) long, sometimes flushed pink or purple. Best in an alpine house. ↕4–12in (10–30cm), PD2in (5cm). S. Portugal, S.W. Spain, Morocco. Zone 7b.
L. valentinum. Bulbous perennial with narrowly linear, gray-green leaves, to 10in (25cm) long, produced after the flowers. In autumn, leafless stems bear 1–3 bell-shaped white flowers, ½in (1.5cm) long. ↕6in (15cm), PD1¼–2in (3–5cm). C. Spain, N.W. Greece, Ionian Islands. Zone 7.
L. vernum (Spring snowflake). Bulbous perennial with erect, strap-shaped, glossy, dark green leaves, to 10in (25cm) long. In early spring, produces thick, leafless stems with usually 1, occasionally 2, bell-shaped, green-tipped white flowers, 1in (2.5cm) long. ↕8–12in (20–30cm), PD3in (8cm). S. and E. Europe. Zone 5. **var. *carpathicum*** produces 1 or 2 flowers per stem, each with yellow-tipped tepals. **var. *vagneri*** ■ is robust, and flowers in late winter and early spring, bearing 2 flowers per stem; ↕8in (20cm).

L

Leucophyllum frutescens

Leucophyta brownii

x *Leucoraoulia loganii*

LEUCOPHYLLUM

SCROPHULARIACEAE

Genus of about 12 species of low-growing, spreading evergreen shrubs from sandy soil of S.W. US and Mexico. They are grown for their axillary, solitary, bell- to funnel-shaped, 2-lipped, 5-lobed flowers. Plant *Leucophyllum* species as hedging and in seaside plantings for their salt tolerance. Where not hardy, grow in a warm greenhouse.
• **CULTIVATION** Under glass, grow in sandy, soil-based potting mix in full light. Water moderately throughout the year. Apply a balanced liquid fertilizer when in growth. Outdoors, grow in poor, sandy soil in full sun. Pruning group 10.
• **PROPAGATION** Sow seed *in situ* in spring or take greenwood cuttings in early summer.
• **PESTS AND DISEASES** Stem rot, galls, powdery mildew, scale insects, and a variety of root rots can occur under wet conditions.

L. frutescens ■ (Silverleaf, Texas sage). Compact, arching shrub with elliptic to obovate, densely silvery gray-woolly leaves, ½–1in (1.5–2.5cm) long. Bears solitary, bell-shaped, rose-purple flowers, 1in (1.5cm) across, in summer. ↕5–8ft (1.5–2.5m), ↔4–6ft (1.2–2m). Texas, Mexico. ❄ (min. 35°F/2°C).
'Compactum' is dense and has orchid-pink flowers.

LEUCOPHYTA

syn. CALOCEPHALUS
Cushion bush
ASTERACEAE

Genus of 18 species of annuals and evergreen perennials and small shrubs from rocky coastal habitats, often exposed to salt spray, in Australia. They are cultivated for their alternate, very narrow, entire, often white-woolly leaves and spherical, rayless flowerheads, which are clustered into terminal corymbs. Where not hardy, grow in a cool greenhouse, or as summer bedding or edging foliage plants. In warmer climates, they are useful for adding a silver edging to a shrub border.
• **CULTIVATION** Under glass, grow in soil-based potting mix with added grit, in full light. Pot on or top-dress in spring, or plant outside in early summer. When in growth, water moderately and apply a balanced liquid fertilizer monthly; water sparingly in winter. Outdoors, grow in sharply drained, moderately fertile soil in full sun. Pinch out stem tips of young plants to promote bushiness. Pruning group 10, in spring.
• **PROPAGATION** Root semi-ripe cuttings in summer.
• **PESTS AND DISEASES** Prone to gray mold (*Botrytis*) in damp conditions.

L. brownii ■ syn. *Calocephalus brownii.* Bushy shrub with intricately branched, slender, silvery white-downy stems. Scale-like, silvery gray leaves, ¼in (6mm) long, are pressed closely against the stems, so that the bush appears leafless. In summer, produces small, rounded, terminal corymbs of creamy white, rarely purple flowerheads, ½in (1.5cm) across. ↕16–30in (40–75cm), ↔16–36in (40–90cm). Western Australia to New South Wales, Tasmania. ❄ (min. 41–45°F/5–7°C)

LEUCOPOGON

EPACRIDACEAE

Genus of about 150 species of erect or spreading, evergreen shrubs and small trees from heathland and forest in S. Asia and Australasia. They have variably shaped, entire leaves, and bear tubular flowers, with reflexed lobes, either singly or in spikes, followed by small, fleshy, berry-like fruits. Grow in a rock garden. Where not hardy, grow in a cool greenhouse.
• **CULTIVATION** Grow in humus-rich, moist but well-drained, acidic soil in full sun or partial shade. Pruning group 8 or 9.
• **PROPAGATION** Sow seed in containers outdoors as soon as ripe, or take greenwood cuttings in early summer.
• **PESTS AND DISEASES** Infrequent.

L. colensoi see *Cyathodes colensoi.*
L. fraseri, syn. *Cyathodes fraseri* (Orago heath). Creeping subshrub with densely overlapping, heath-like, obovate, short-stalked, bristly-margined, glossy, dark green leaves, ¼–½in (5–10mm) long, often tinted red in autumn. Bears axillary, solitary, 5-lobed, fragrant white flowers, ¼–½in (5–10mm) across, toward the tips of upright shoots in summer. In autumn, produces edible, sweet-tasting, spherical, fleshy, pale orange fruit, ¼–⅜in (6–9mm) across. ↕4–6in (10–15cm), ↔ to 12in (30cm). New Zealand. ❄ (min. 41°F/5°C)

x LEUCORAOULIA

ASTERACEAE

Bigeneric hybrid genus between *Leucogenes leontopodium* and *Raoulia rubra*, from the Tararua Mountains of New Zealand. Grown for its cushions of silvery, rosetted foliage, it is best grown in a scree bed or alpine house.
• **CULTIVATION** Grow in gritty, sharply drained soil in full sun. Protect from winter moisture. Under glass, grow in a mix of equal parts loam, leaf mold, and grit; top-dress with grit. Water freely from spring to summer; resents a hot, dry atmosphere in summer, so mist in hot weather. Keep just moist in winter.
• **PROPAGATION** Detach individual rosettes and root as cuttings in spring.
• **PESTS AND DISEASES** Susceptible to mildew, especially in dry conditions.

x *L. loganii* ■ syn. *Raoulia* x *loganii.* Dense, cushion-forming perennial with neat, symmetrical, almost columnar rosettes of tiny, overlapping, densely hairy, silvery white leaves, to ¹⁄₁₆in (2mm) long. Produces insignificant pink flowerheads in summer in the wild, but very seldom in cultivation. ↕3in (8cm), ↔4in (10cm). New Zealand. Zone 7b.

LEUCOSPERMUM

Pincushion
PROTEACEAE

Genus of 47 species of evergreen shrubs and small trees from varied habitats, including scrub, subtropical coastal dune forest, evergreen temperate forest, and mountain slopes, in Zimbabwe and South Africa. The alternate, leathery, simple, entire or toothed leaves may be linear to elliptic, inversely lance-shaped, oval, ovate, obovate, oblong, or spoon-shaped. Dense, cone-like, clustered or solitary, terminal flowerheads are borne on short axillary shoots and have very prominent, red, orange, pink, yellow, or white styles. Where temperatures fall below 41°F (5°C), grow in a cool or temperate greenhouse. In warmer, dry areas, plant in a shrub border. The larger species are good specimen plants.
• **CULTIVATION** Under glass, grow in a mix of 1 part soil-based potting mix and 3 parts each grit (or perlite) and peat, in full light. In active growth, water moderately and apply magnesium sulfate and urea at half the recommended strength in spring and autumn; water

Leucospermum cordifolium

sparingly in winter, never allowing the soil mix to dry out. Outdoors, grow in well-drained, neutral to acidic soil, with low levels of phosphates and nitrates, in full sun. Magnesium deficiency may lead to chlorosis. Pruning group 1; may need restrictive pruning under glass.
• **PROPAGATION** Stratify ripe seed below 41°F (5°C), then sow at 55–61°F (13–16°C) in spring. Root semi-ripe cuttings in summer with bottom heat.
• **PESTS AND DISEASES** Root rot, dieback, and gray mold can be problems.

L. catherinae (Catherine's pincushion). Densely bushy, erect shrub with a short, thick trunk. Crowded, inversely lance-shaped to elliptic, stalked, hairless leaves, 3½–5½in (9–14cm) long, each with 3 or 4 teeth at the tip, are usually mid- to deep green, tinted yellow or gray, with often red-flushed tips and margins. From spring to early summer, bears solitary, conical flowerheads, 4–6in (10–15cm) across, with erect, then arching styles that are light orange, tipped mauve-pink, aging to deep reddish gold. ↕↔ 8ft (2.5m). South Africa (Western Cape). ❀ (min. 41°F/5°C)
L. cordifolium ■ syn. *L. nutans.* Rounded, spreading shrub with ovate to oblong, entire, stalkless, mid-green leaves, to 3in (8cm) long, heart-shaped at the bases, sometimes with 3–6 teeth at the tips, and initially downy, later almost smooth. From early spring to midsummer, horizontal to downward-arching stems, which bend sharply upward at their tips, produce solitary, spherical flowerheads, 4–5in (10–13cm) wide, with numerous forward-arching, usually orange, but also crimson or yellow styles. ↕ to 6ft (2m), ↔ 5–11ft (1.5–4m). South Africa (Northern Cape, Western Cape, Eastern Cape, on acidic soils). ❀ (min. 41°F/5°C)
L. nutans see *L. cordifolium.*
L. reflexum (Rocket pincushion). Rounded, moderately open shrub, thickening with age. Oblong-elliptic to inversely lance-shaped, hairy, gray-green leaves, ¾–2½in (2–6cm) long, sometimes have 2 or 3 teeth at the tips. From early spring to early summer, erect shoots bear solitary or paired, ovoid to spherical flowerheads, 1¾–2½in (4.5–6cm) across, composed of initially outward- and upward-curving orange styles, later strongly reflexed and deep crimson. ↕ to 10ft (3m), ↔ 6–12ft (2–4m). South Africa (Cedar Berg Mountains in Western Cape). ❀ (min. 41°F/5°C)

LEUCOTHOE

ERICACEAE

Genus of about 50 species of deciduous, semi-evergreen, or evergreen shrubs from woodland, thickets, swamps, and streambanks in Madagascar, the Himalayas, E. Asia, and North and South America. They are cultivated for their handsome leaves, which are alternate, very variably shaped, simple, often glossy, and dark green, and for their cylindrical to urn-shaped, usually white flowers, borne in terminal or axillary racemes or panicles. Effective in a woodland garden.
• **CULTIVATION** Grow in humus-rich, reliably moist, acidic soil in deep or partial shade. Pruning group 1.
• **PROPAGATION** Sow seed in containers in a cold frame in spring. Root semi-ripe cuttings with bottom heat in summer. Divide suckering species in spring.
• **PESTS AND DISEASES** Anthracnose spot, tar spot, powdery mildew, leaf gall, lace bugs, and scale insects occur.

L. axillaris. Upright, evergreen shrub with ovate to ovate-oblong, leathery, short-pointed, toothed, lustrous, dark green leaves, 2–4½ (5–11cm) long, paler green and sparsely bristly hairy beneath. From spring to early summer, bears urn-shaped to cylindrical, white flowers, ¼in (6mm) across, in axillary racemes, ¾–3in (2–8cm) long. ↕↔ 5ft (1.5m). S.E. US. Zone 6.
***L. catesbaei* of gardens** see *L. fontanesiana.*
L. davisiae (Sierra laurel). Upright, suckering, evergreen shrub with ovate-oblong, glossy, dark green leaves, to 3in (8cm) long. Urn-shaped white flowers, ¼in (6mm) long, are produced in erect, axillary racemes, 2–6in (5–15cm) long, in early summer. ↕ 3ft (1m), ↔ 5ft (1.5m). California, Oregon. Zone 8.
L. fontanesiana, syn. *L. catesbaei* of gardens, *L. walteri* (Drooping leucothoe, Fetterbush). Upright, evergreen shrub with arching branches and oblong-lance-shaped to ovate-lance-shaped, toothed, leathery, hairless leaves, 2½–6in (6–15cm) long, dark green and glossy above, paler below. In spring, produces almost cylindrical white flowers, ¼in (6mm) long, in axillary racemes, 1½–2½in (4–6cm) long. ↕ 3–6ft (1–2m), ↔ 10ft (3m). S.E. US. Zone 6. **'Rainbow'** ■ is thicket-forming, with lance-shaped, dark green leaves, heavily

Leucothoe fontanesiana 'Rainbow'

Leucothoe fontanesiana 'Scarletta'

mottled cream and pink; ↕ 5ft (1.5m), ↔ 6ft (2m). **'Scarletta'** ■ has dark red-purple young foliage, which turns dark green, then bronze in winter. Probably hybrid origin.
L. keiskei. Clump-forming, evergreen shrub with upright to prostrate shoots and narrowly ovate to ovate-lance-shaped, slenderly tapered, glossy, dark green leaves, to 3½in (9cm) long, red when young. Urn-shaped white flowers, to ½in (1.5cm) long, are borne in nodding racemes, to 2in (5cm) long, at or near the ends of young shoots in midsummer. ↕↔ 24in (60cm). Japan. Zone 6.
L. racemosa (Fetterbush, Sweetbells). Bushy, suckering, deciduous or semi-evergreen shrub with upright shoots and oblong to ovate or elliptic, pointed, glossy, dark green leaves, to 2½in (6cm) long. In early summer, urn-shaped white flowers, ¼in (6mm) long, are profusely borne in upright to spreading, usually terminal racemes, to 4in (10cm) long. ↕↔ 5ft (1.5m). E. US. Zone 6.
L. walteri see *L. fontanesiana.*

▷ ***Leuzea centauroides*** see *Centaurea* 'Pulchra Major'

LEWISIA

PORTULACACEAE

Genus of approximately 20 species of deciduous or evergreen perennials from W. North America, with fleshy rootstocks, and rosettes or tufts of fleshy leaves that vary greatly in shape. The deciduous species occur in open, stony meadows or grassland, and die down after flowering; evergreens are more commonly found in partial shade among rocks or in crevices. The funnel-shaped to open funnel-shaped flowers, each with 5–9, sometimes up to 19 petals, are produced in shades of pink, magenta, purple, orange, yellow, or white. They are usually borne in cymes or panicles, occasionally singly or in racemes or corymbs, in spring and summer, often over long periods. Grow in an alpine house or rock garden, or in the crevices of a retaining wall.
• **CULTIVATION** Grow in moderately fertile, humus-rich, sharply drained, neutral to acidic soil: deciduous species and hybrids in full sun, evergreens in light shade. Protect all from winter moisture; protect deciduous lewisias from rain in summer, when dormant. In an alpine house, grow in equal parts loam, leaf mold, and sharp sand.
• **PROPAGATION** Sow seed in containers in a cold frame in autumn, or remove offsets (evergreen species only) in early summer.
• **PESTS AND DISEASES** Rust, stem rot, snails, slugs, aphids, and mealybugs sometimes occur.

L. brachycalyx ■ Dwarf, tufted, deciduous perennial with a basal rosette of inversely lance-shaped, dark green leaves, 1¼–3in (3–8cm) long. In late spring and early summer, numerous solitary, funnel-shaped, white, sometimes pale pink flowers, 1–2in (2.5–5cm) across, are borne on scapes to 2½in (6cm) long. ↕↔ to 3in (8cm). S. California, Arizona. Zone 6.

Lewisia brachycalyx

L

Lewisia Cotyledon Hybrids

L. columbiana. Variable, evergreen perennial with compact, symmetrical or irregular rosettes of inversely lance-shaped or linear, dark green leaves, ¾–4in (2–10cm) long. From spring to summer, bears panicles of many open funnel-shaped, usually deep magenta-pink flowers, to 1in (2.5cm) across, sometimes pale pink with darker veins. ↕↔ to 6in (15cm). British Columbia, Oregon. Zone 5.

L. cotyledon. Evergreen perennial with flat rosettes of spoon-shaped or inversely lance-shaped or obovate, slightly glaucous, dark green leaves, 1¼–5½in (3–14cm) long. From spring to summer, produces compact panicles of many open funnel-shaped, paler and darker striped, usually pinkish purple, sometimes white, cream, yellow, or apricot flowers, to 1in (2.5cm) across. ↕ 12in (30cm), ↔ to 10in (25cm). N.W. California. Zone 3b. **var. *howellii*** has leaves with wavy, toothed margins; pale pink flowers with darker veining.

L. Cotyledon Hybrids ▣ Clump-forming, evergreen perennials that produce rosettes of thick, variably shaped, mid- to dark green leaves, 1¼–5½in (3–14cm) long, with toothed or wavy margins. From late spring to summer, funnel-shaped flowers, ¾–1½in (2–4cm) across, in shades of pink, deep magenta, yellow, and orange, are borne in compact panicles. ↕ 6–12in (15–30cm), ↔ 8–16in (20–40cm). Zone 3b.

L

L. 'George Henley' ▣ Clump-forming, evergreen perennial with rosettes of narrowly spoon-shaped, fleshy, dark green leaves, to 3in (8cm) long. From late spring to late summer, bears many-flowered cymes of funnel-shaped, purplish pink flowers, to 1in (2.5cm) across, with magenta veins. ↕ 4in (10cm) or more, ↔ 4in (10cm). Zone 3b.

Lewisia 'George Henley'

Lewisia tweedyi

L. longipetala, syn. *L. pygmaea* subsp. *longipetala.* Deciduous perennial with basal tufts of narrowly linear or linear-inversely lance-shaped, dark green leaves, ¾–2in (2–5cm) long. In late spring or early summer, produces several scapes, 1¼–2½in (3–6cm) long, bearing cymes of 1–3 open funnel-shaped, star-like, pure white or pink-flushed white flowers, 1–1½in (2.5–4cm) across, with red-tinted sepals. Similar to, but easier to grow than *L. brachycalyx.* ↕↔ to 4in (10cm). California. Zone 4.

L. nevadensis. Deciduous perennial with loose, basal rosettes of narrowly linear, suberect, dark green leaves, 1½–6in (4–15cm) long. From late spring to summer, bears solitary, broadly funnel-shaped, star-like, white, rarely pink flowers, to 1½in (4cm) across, on scapes 4–6in (10–15cm) long. ↕↔ to 4in (10cm). W. US. Zone 4.

L. pygmaea. Deciduous perennial with tufts of linear or linear-inversely lance-shaped, erect, dark green leaves, 1¼–3½in (3–9cm) long. In summer, prostrate or semi-erect scapes, ½–2½in (1–6cm) long, bear cymes of 1–7 funnel-shaped, deep purplish pink, occasionally white or pale pink flowers, ½–¾in (1.5–2cm) across. ↕↔ to 3in (8cm). Canada, Alaska to New Mexico. Zone 4. **subsp. *longipetala*** see *L. longipetala.*

L. rediviva (Bitterroot). Deciduous perennial with tufts of linear or club-shaped, dark green leaves, ½–2in (1.5–5cm) long, dying back rapidly at or after flowering. From early spring to summer, bears several solitary, broadly funnel-shaped, pink or white flowers, 2in (5cm) across, with 12–19 narrow petals, on scapes ½–1¼in (1–3cm) long. ↕ 2in (5cm), ↔ 4in (10cm). British Columbia, California, Nevada, Utah. Zone 4.

L. tweedyi ▣ Rosette-forming, evergreen perennial with broad, inversely lance-shaped or obovate, purple-tinted, mid-green leaves, to 4in (10cm) long. From spring to early summer, scapes, 4–8in (10–20cm) long, bear open funnel-shaped, white to peach-pink flowers, to 2½in (6cm) across, singly or in cymes of up to 4. ↕ 8in (20cm), ↔ 12in (30cm). N.W. US. Zone 5. **f. *alba*** has pure white to ivory flowers.

LEYCESTERIA

CAPRIFOLIACEAE

Genus of about 6 species of suckering, deciduous shrubs, with hollow, cane-like stems, from cliffs and mountain woodland in India, the Himalayas, China, and Burma. They are cultivated for their terminal or axillary racemes or spikes of whorled, tubular, 5-lobed flowers; *L. formosa* also has long-persistent, claret-red bracts below the blooms. The leaves are opposite, narrowly ovate to ovate, and long-pointed, with entire or toothed margins. Grow in a woodland garden or shrub border. Where not hardy, grow in a cool greenhouse.

• **CULTIVATION** Grow in moderately fertile, well-drained soil in full sun or partial shade. Protect from cold, drying winds and mulch deeply in autumn where marginally hardy. Pruning group 3 or 6.

• **PROPAGATION** Sow seed in containers in a cold frame in autumn, or take softwood cuttings in summer.

• **PESTS AND DISEASES** Infrequent.

L. crocothyrsos. Upright shrub with arching shoots and ovate, tapered leaves, to 6in (15cm) long. Golden yellow flowers, to ¾in (2cm) long, with wide-spreading lobes, are produced in arching, terminal racemes, 5–7in (13–18cm) long, from late spring to late summer, followed by small, spherical green berries. ↕↔ 6ft (2m). India (Assam), N. Burma. ❄ (min. 45°F/7°C)

L. formosa ▣ (Himalayan honeysuckle). Upright, thicket-forming shrub with attractive, bamboo-like, blue-green first-year shoots, and ovate, tapered, dark green leaves, to 7in (18cm) long. Pendent spikes, to 4in (10cm) long, of white flowers among dark purple-red bracts, are borne terminally or from the upper leaf axils, from summer to early autumn. Flowers are followed by spherical, red-purple berries. ↕↔ 6ft (2m). Himalayas, W. China. ❄ (min. 41°F/5°C)

Leymus arenarius

LEYMUS

POACEAE

Genus of approximately 40 species of rhizomatous, perennial grasses, formerly included in *Elymus.* They occur mainly in grassland in N. temperate regions, with one species from Argentina. They have linear, flat or rolled, stiff, glaucous leaves, and bear narrowly linear racemes of usually paired, sometimes solitary spikelets in summer. The ornamental species are grown for the architectural value of their blue-green leaves; although invasive, they are also suitable for a mixed or herbaceous border.

• **CULTIVATION** Grow in moderately fertile but not heavy, well-drained soil in full sun. Cut down in autumn.

• **PROPAGATION** Divide from midspring to early autumn.

• **PESTS AND DISEASES** Ergot, root rot, and leaf spots can occur.

L. arenarius ▣ syn. *Elymus arenarius.* Densely tufted grass with long rhizomes, forming loose, spreading clumps of arching, broadly linear, flat, pale blue-gray leaves, to 24in (60cm) long.

Leycesteria formosa (inset: flower detail)

Throughout summer, stiff, erect stems bear spike-like racemes, to 14in (35cm) long, of paired, blue-gray, then buff spikelets. ↕ to 5ft (1.5cm), ↔ indefinite. N. and W. Europe, Eurasia. Zone 4.
L. giganteus see *L. racemosus*.
L. racemosus, syn. *Elymus racemosus, L. giganteus.* Rhizomatous grass with arching, broadly linear, flat, blue-green leaves, to 12in (30cm) long, rough textured above, smooth beneath. Throughout summer, stiff, upright stems produce spike-like racemes, to 14in (35cm) long, of flattened, softly hairy, initially bluish green, later buff spikelets, in clusters of 6. ↕ to 4ft (1.2m), ↔ 30in (75cm) or more. N. Europe, Eurasia. Zone 4. **'Glaucus'** is less invasive, and has erect or arching, clear, pale blue-green leaves; ↕ 30in (75cm).

LIATRIS

Blazing star, Gayfeather

ASTERACEAE

Genus of approximately 40 species of perennials with tuber- or corm-like, swollen, flattened stems. They occur mainly in prairie or open woodland, on dry, stony ground (although *L. spicata* grows in damper sites), in E. and C. North America. Linear to ovate-lance-shaped leaves are borne in basal tufts, and arranged alternately on the stiff stems. The numerous button-like flowerheads, produced in corymb-like spikes or racemes, are composed of dense clusters of tubular, pinkish purple or white disk florets, and are unusual in that they open from the top of the inflorescence downward. Suitable for a mixed or herbaceous border and also good for cutting. The flowerheads are attractive to bees and butterflies.

- **CULTIVATION** Grow in light, moderately fertile, moist but well-drained soil in full sun; *L. spicata* needs reliably moist soil. Liable to rot in wet winters in heavy soils.
- **PROPAGATION** Sow seed in containers in a cold frame in autumn. Divide in spring.
- **PESTS AND DISEASES** Stem rot, rust, and leaf spots commonly occur, as well as slug and snail damage.

L. aspera (Rough gayfeather). Tuberous, clump-forming perennial with densely clustered, linear, rough leaves, to 16in (40cm) long, stalkless on the upper stems. Dense spikes, to 18in (45cm), of lavender-purple flowerheads, ½in (1.5cm) across, in late summer and early autumn. ↕ 6ft (2m), ↔ 18in (45cm). N. America. Zone 4.
***L. callilepis* of gardens** see *L. spicata.*
L. punctata (Snakeroot). Tuberous perennial with linear, hairless, stiff leaves, to ½in (1.5cm) long. Bears dense spikes, to 12in (30cm) long, of purple flowerheads, ½in (1.5cm) across, in autumn. ↕ to 32in (80cm), ↔ 24in (60cm). E. Canada to New Mexico and S.E. US. Zone 3.
L. pycnostachya (Kansas gayfeather). Perennial with densely clustered, linear basal leaves, 4–12in (10–30cm) long, which reduce in size up the robust, hairy stems. Bears dense spikes, 18in (45cm) long, of bright purple flowerheads, ½in (1.5cm) across, from midsummer to early autumn. ↕ to 5ft (1.5m), ↔ 18in (45cm). C. and S.E. US. Zone 4.

Liatris pycnostachya 'Alexander'

Liatris spicata

'Alexander' ▣ is sturdier and stouter than the species, with dark green leaves, thick spikes and dark purple flowerheads; rarely needs staking.
L. scariosa. Perennial with densely clustered, lance-shaped to narrowly ovate or obovate, rough basal leaves, to 10in (25cm) long, reducing in size and inversely lance-shaped on the robust, hairy stems. Similar to *L. pycnostachya*, but with less dense spikes, 18in (45cm) long, of reddish purple flowerheads, 1in (2.5cm) across, in early autumn. ↕ 2–4ft (0.6–1.2m), ↔ 18in (45cm). N.E. and S.E. US. Zone 8. **'September Glory'** has deep purple flowerheads; ↕ 4½ft (1.3m). **'White Spires'** has large white flowerheads on branched stems.
L. spicata ▣ syn. *L. callilepis* of gardens (Blazing star, Gayfeather). Perennial with hairless stems and linear or linear-lance-shaped basal leaves, 12–16in (30–40cm) long; stem leaves are smaller and linear. Long-lasting, pink-purple or white flowerheads, to ½in (1.5cm) across, are borne in dense spikes, 18–28in (45–70cm) long, in late summer and early autumn. ↕ to 5ft (1.5m), ↔ 18in (45cm). E. and S. US. Zone 4. **'Blue Bird'** has blue-purple flowerheads. **'Floristan Weiss'** has white flowerheads; ↕ to 36in (90cm). **'Goblin'** see 'Kobold'. **'Kobold'**, syn. 'Goblin', produces deep purple flowerheads; ↕ 16–20in (40–50cm). **'Snow Queen'** bears white flowerheads; ↕ 30in (75cm).

LIBERTIA

IRIDACEAE

Genus of 20 species of fibrous-rooted, clump-forming, rhizomatous, evergreen perennials occurring in moist, grassy areas and scrub in New Caledonia, New Zealand, and temperate North and South America. They have linear, leathery, 2-ranked, overlapping, mainly basal leaves; leaves on the stiff flowering stems are sparse and smaller. They are cultivated for their saucer-shaped, white or blue flowers, each usually with 3 small outer tepals, 3 broad inner tepals, and sheathing bracts, produced in panicles and followed by glossy, light brown seed heads. Grow the larger libertias in a herbaceous or mixed border, or in a gravel garden; the smaller species are suitable for a rock garden.

- **CULTIVATION** Grow in moderately fertile, humus-rich, moist but well-drained soil in full sun. Where marginally hardy, protect in winter with a dry mulch.
- **PROPAGATION** Sow seed in containers outdoors as soon as ripe, or divide in spring.
- **PESTS AND DISEASES** Infrequent.

L. caerulescens. Clump-forming, rhizomatous perennial with linear, rigid, leathery leaves, 12–18in (30–45cm) long. In late spring, flowering stems bear 1 or 2 short leaves, and terminal, short-branched panicles consisting of umbel-like clusters of many pale blue flowers, ½in (1.5cm) across. ↕ to 24in (60cm), ↔ 12in (30cm). Chile. ❄ (min. 41°F/5°C)
L. chilensis see *L. formosa.*
L. formosa, syn. *L. chilensis* (Showy libertia). Rhizomatous perennial forming large clumps of linear, stiff, leathery, deep green leaves, 6–18in (15–45cm) long. Dense panicles composed of umbel-like clusters of 3–8 white or pale yellow-white flowers, 1½in (4cm) across, are borne in long succession from late spring to mid-summer. ↕ 36in (90cm), ↔ 24in (60cm). Chile. ❄ (min. 35°F/2°C)
L. grandiflora ▣ Rhizomatous perennial forming dense clumps of linear, leathery leaves, 12–30in (30–75cm) long. In late spring and early summer, bears long panicles composed of dense, umbel-like clusters of 3–6 white flowers, 1¼in (3cm) across, the outer tepals with olive or bronze keels. ↕ to 36in (90cm), ↔ 24in (60cm). New Zealand. ❄ (min. 35°F/2°C)
L. ixioides. Rhizomatous perennial, similar to *L. grandiflora*, forming dense clumps of linear, leathery leaves, 8–12in (20–30cm) long. Leaves of some variants turn orange-brown in winter. In late spring and early summer, produces dense panicles composed of umbel-like clusters of usually 2–10 white flowers, ¼–⅜in (6–9mm) across, the outer tepals tinted brown or green. ↕↔ 24in (60cm). New Zealand (including Chatham Island). ❄ (min. 35°F/2°C)

Libertia grandiflora

L

LIBOCEDRUS

CUPRESSACEAE

Genus of 6 species of conical, monoecious, evergreen, coniferous trees and shrubs from forest in New Zealand, New Caledonia, and South America. In the past, species of *Austrocedrus* and *Calocedrus* were included in the genus *Libocedrus*. The linear juvenile leaves and usually scale-like adult leaves are arranged in sets of 2 pairs, one on either side of the shoot (spreading pair), and one above and below (facial pair), forming 4 rows. Female cones are solitary, ovoid, and usually 4-scaled, with 2 pairs of enlarged, bract-like leaves at the bases; male cones are small, oblong, and borne at the tips of short shoots. Grow as specimen trees. Where not hardy, grow in a sheltered site or in a cool greenhouse.

• **CULTIVATION** Grow in any deep, moist but well-drained soil in full sun.
• **PROPAGATION** Sow seed in containers in a cold frame in spring, or take semi-ripe cuttings in summer.
• **PESTS AND DISEASES** Infrequent.

L. bidwillii. Conical, coniferous tree at lower elevations, reduced to a shrub at altitudes above 3,200ft (1,000m). It has fibrous bark and scale-like, glossy, yellow-green adult leaves, to 1/16in (2mm) long, lying flat along the shoots. Ovoid female cones, ½in (1.5cm) long, have a green terminal spine on each scale. ↕ to 50ft (15m), ↔ to 10ft (3m). New Zealand. ❄ (min. 35°F/2°C)
L. chilensis see *Austrocedrus chilensis.*
L. decurrens see *Calocedrus decurrens.*
L. plumosa (Kawaka). Conical, coniferous tree with fibrous bark and unequal pairs of scale-like, glossy, bright green adult leaves; the spreading pair, ⅛–¼in (3–6mm) long, is larger than the facial pair. Ovoid female cones are ½–¾in (1–2cm) long. ↕ to 50ft (15m), ↔ to 10ft (3m). New Zealand. ❄ (min. 35°F/2°C)

▷ ***Libonia*** see *Justicia*

LICUALA

ARECACEAE

Genus of approximately 100 species of single- or cluster-stemmed palms found in rainforest and swamps, in low-lying areas from S.E. Asia to Malaysia, the New Hebrides, and Australia. Rounded, fan-like or palmately lobed leaves are arranged spirally along the upper parts of the stems; fibrous leaf bases remain on the stems after the leaves have withered. Spikes of cup-shaped, 3-petaled flowers are produced from the leaf axils. Where temperatures fall below 59–61°F (15–16°C), grow in a warm greenhouse. In warmer areas, grow the shrubby, suckering species in a border or in plantings against a wall, and the larger, single-stemmed species as lawn specimens or in a courtyard garden.

• **CULTIVATION** Under glass, grow in soil-based potting mix, with added peat or leaf mold and sharp sand, in bright filtered light and high humidity. During the growing season, water freely and apply a balanced liquid fertilizer monthly. Mist twice a day in summer. Water moderately in winter. Pot on or top-dress in spring. Outdoors, grow in moderately fertile, moist but well-drained soil in partial shade.

Licuala grandis

• **PROPAGATION** In spring, sow seed at 75°F (24°C), or remove suckers.
• **PESTS AND DISEASES** Fungal leaf spots sometimes occur. Spider mites, scale insects, and mealybugs can be problems under glass.

L. grandis ▣ Small palm with a single, slender, erect trunk clad in fibrous leaf bases. Long-stalked, rounded leaf blades, 3ft (1m) across, are glossy, mid- to pale green with notched margins, and are occasionally divided into 3 broadly wedge-shaped to rounded, wavy-margined segments. Bears green to greenish white flowers, ½in (1.5cm) across, in pendent spikes, longer than the leaves, usually in summer. Flowers are followed by spherical, glossy red fruit. ↕ to 10ft (3m), ↔ 5–8ft (1.5–2.5m). New Hebrides. ❄ (min. 59–61°F/15–16°C)
L. muelleri see *L. ramsayi.*
L. ramsayi, syn. *L. muelleri.* Medium-sized palm with a single, erect stem, the upper part clad with fibrous leaf bases, the lower part smooth. Long, spiny leaf stalks bear rounded leaf blades, to 3ft (1m) across, divided into many wedge-shaped, radiating, rich green segments, some of which may be joined at the tips. Cream flowers, ½in (1.5cm) across, borne in spikes, as long as, or longer than the leaves, usually in summer, followed by spherical, orange-red fruit. ↕ to 40ft (12m), ↔ 10–15ft (3–5m). Australia (N.E. Queensland). ❄ (min. 59–61°F/15–16°C)
L. spinosa. Small, cluster-stemmed palm forming clumps of cane-like stems. These bear spirals of leaves, and are clad with fibrous leaf bases in the upper parts. Long, spiny-stalked, rounded leaf blades, to 5ft (1.5m) across, are divided into 12–20 narrow, deep green, wedge-shaped segments with squared-off tips. Greenish white flowers, ½in (1.5cm) across, are borne in branched spikes, to 6ft (2m) long, mainly in summer, and are followed by ovoid red fruit. ↕↔ to 15ft (5m). Thailand, Malaysian peninsula, Indonesia, Philippines. ❄ (min. 59–61°F/15–16°C)

LIGULARIA

ASTERACEAE

Genus of about 150 species of large, robust, often coarse perennials, mostly from C. and E. Asia, with a few from Europe, found in moist or wet grassland, open, wet scrub and woodland, by mountain streams, and in ditches. They have, ovate-oblong or elliptic to kidney-shaped or rounded, sometimes palmately lobed, often toothed basal leaves, borne on long leaf stalks, and smaller, alternate stem leaves. Erect stems bear terminal corymbs or racemes of few to many, showy, daisy-like, yellow or orange flowerheads, with yellow or brown disk florets. Grow in a mixed or herbaceous border, or naturalize in moist soil; they are also imposing waterside plants.

• **CULTIVATION** Grow in moderately fertile, deep, reliably moist soil, in full

Ligularia dentata 'Desdemona'

sun with some midday shade. Shelter from strong winds.
• **PROPAGATION** Sow seed of species in containers outdoors in autumn or spring, or divide species and cultivars in spring or after flowering. When seed-raised, *L. dentata* 'Desdemona' and *L. dentata* 'Othello' will often produce similar seedlings.
• **PESTS AND DISEASES** Slugs and snails may damage emerging leaves in spring.

L. clivorum see *L. dentata.*
L. dentata, syn. *L. clivorum, Senecio clivorum* (Golden groundsel). Clump-forming perennial with kidney-shaped to rounded, toothed, mid-green leaves, to 12in (30cm) long, deeply heart-shaped at the bases; the basal leaves have red leaf stalks. From summer to early autumn, bears flat corymbs of many red-stalked, brown-centered, orange-yellow flowerheads, 4in (10cm) across. ↕ 3–5ft (1–1.5m), ↔ 3ft (1m). China, Japan. Zone 4. **'Desdemona'** ▣ has deep orange flowerheads and rounded, brownish green leaves that are deep maroon-purple beneath; ↕ 3ft (1m). **'Othello'** is similar to 'Desdemona', but with deep purplish green leaves, purple-red beneath; ↕ 3ft (1m).
L. 'Gregynog Gold' ▣ Clump-forming perennial with rounded, toothed leaves, to 14in (35cm) long, heart shaped at the bases. In late summer and early autumn, bears tall, pyramidal racemes of many brown-centered, golden orange flowerheads, to 4in (10cm) across. ↕ to 6ft (1.8m), ↔ 3ft (1m). Zone 5b.
L. hodgsonii. Clump-forming perennial with kidney-shaped, toothed leaves, to

Ligularia 'Gregynog Gold'

Ligularia przewalskii

5in (13cm) across, heart-shaped at the ›ases. In mid- and late summer, bears :orymbs of many yellow-orange flower- ıeads, 2in (5cm) across, with reddish ›rown centers, on stems often marked ›urple toward the bases. ↕ 36in (90cm), ↔ 24in (60cm). Japan. Zone 4.
L. przewalskii ■ syn. *Senecio przewalskii.* Clump-forming perennial with palmately lobed leaves, to 12in 30cm) long, deeply cut and irregularly obed and toothed. In mid- and late summer, dark purple-green stems bear slender, dense racemes of yellow flower- ıeads, ¾in (2cm) across. ↕ to 6ft (2m), ↔ 3ft (1m). N. China. Zone 4.
L. stenocephala. Clump-forming ›erennial with triangular, pointed, oothed leaves, to 14in (35cm) long, with heart-shaped bases. In early and ate summer, tall, slender racemes of ıumerous yellow flowerheads, to 1½in 4cm) across, with orange-yellow centers, are borne on black-green stems. ↕ 5ft 1.5m), ↔ 3ft (1m). N. China, Taiwan, apan. Zone 4. **'The Rocket'**, of hybrid ›rigin, has tall black flower stems and ›oldly toothed leaves; ↕ 6ft (1.8m).
L. tangutica see *Senecio tanguticus.*
L. tussilaginea see *Farfugium japonicum.*
L. veitchiana. Clump-forming ›erennial bearing triangular to heart- shaped leaves, 12–14in (30–35cm) long, with wavy, toothed margins. Pyramidal acemes of numerous brown-centered yellow flowerheads, to 3in (8cm) across, are borne in mid- and late summer, ollowed by conspicuous, fluffy, purple- ›rown fruit. ↕ 6ft (1.8m), ↔ 4ft (1.2m). W. China. Zone 5.

LIGUSTRUM

Privet

OLEACEAE

Genus of about 50 species of deciduous, semi-evergreen, or evergreen shrubs and trees found in woodland and thickets in Europe, N. Africa, the Himalayas, S.W. and E. Asia, and Australia. They bear opposite, variably shaped, often glossy leaves, and terminal panicles of small, tubular, 4-lobed, scented white flowers, followed by spherical or ovoid fruit. Grown for their foliage and flowers, they are good for a shrub border or as specimen plants; most species may be used for hedging. All parts may cause severe discomfort if ingested.

• **CULTIVATION** Grow in well-drained soil in full sun or partial shade; variegated privets color better in sun. Pruning group 1; clip hedges twice in summer.

• **PROPAGATION** Sow seed in containers in a cold frame in autumn or spring. Take semi-ripe cuttings in summer or hardwood cuttings in winter.

• **PESTS AND DISEASES** Aphids, scale insects, Japanese beetles, weevils, mites, thrips, leaf spots, blights, cankers, crown gall, and root rot may be problems.

L. amurense (Amur privet). Dense, upright, deciduous or semi-evergreen shrub with elliptic, mid-green leaves, to 2in (5cm) long. White flowers are produced in panicles, 1½–2in (4–5cm) long, in late spring and early summer, followed by small, ovoid black fruit. ↕↔ 15ft (5m). N. China. Zone 5.

L. chenaultii. Vigorous, broadly conical, semi-evergreen tree with lance-shaped, occasionally notched, dark green leaves, 6in (15cm) or more long. White flowers are borne in panicles, 6–7in (15–18cm) long, in midsummer, followed by small, spherical black fruit. ↕ 30ft (10m), ↔ 25ft (8m). S.W. China. Zone 7b.

L. delavayanum. Compact, spreading, evergreen shrub with ovate, oval, or oblong, dark green leaves, to 1¼in (3cm) long. White flowers are produced in panicles, to 2in (5cm) long, in early summer, followed by spherical to ovoid, blue-black fruit. Useful for hedging. ↕ 6ft (2m), ↔ 10ft (3m). W. China (Sichuan, Yunnan). Zone 8.

L. x ibolium (*L. obtusifolium* x *L. ovalifolium*). Upright, deciduous to semi-evergreen shrub with oval, glossy,

Ligustrum japonicum 'Rotundifolium'

Ligustrum lucidum

mid-green leaves, to 2½in (6cm) long. White flowers are produced in panicles, 2–3in (5–8cm) long, in midsummer. Useful for hedging. ↕↔ 10ft (3m). Garden origin. Zone 5b.

L. japonicum (Japanese privet). Upright, dense, evergreen shrub with ovate, glossy, very dark green leaves, to 4in (10cm) long. White flowers are produced in panicles, to 6in (15cm) long, from midsummer to early autumn, and are followed by ovoid-oblong black fruit. ↕ 10ft (3m), ↔ 8ft (2.5m). N. China, Korea, Japan. Zone 7b. **'Rotundifolium'** ■ is slow-growing and stiffly branched, with rounded, very leathery leaves, to 2½in (6cm) long; ↕ 5ft (1.5m), ↔ 3ft (1m). **'Variegatum'** has white-margined, white-blotched leaves.

L. lucidum ■ (Chinese privet). Conical, evergreen tree or shrub with ovate or oval, tapered, glossy, dark green leaves, to 6in (15cm) long. White flowers are produced in panicles, to 8in (20cm) long, in late summer and early autumn, followed by ovoid-oblong, blue-black fruit. ↕↔ 30ft (10m). China. Korea, Japan. Zone 8. **'Excelsum Superbum'** ■ has yellow-margined, bright green leaves. **'Tricolor'** has narrow, green and gray-green leaves with white margins (pink when young).

L. obtusifolium (Border privet). Graceful, spreading, deciduous shrub with oval, dark green leaves, to 2in (5cm) long, often tinged purple in autumn. White flowers are produced in nodding panicles, to 2in (5cm) long, in midsummer, followed by spherical, blue-black fruit. Useful for hedging.

Ligustrum lucidum 'Excelsum Superbum'

Ligustrum sinense

↕ 10ft (3m), ↔ 12ft (4m). Japan. Zone 5b. **var. *regelianum*** (Regel privet) is spreading, with 2-ranked, obovate leaves, 2–3in (5–8cm) long, softly hairy beneath.

L. ovalifolium (California privet). Vigorous, upright, evergreen or semi-evergreen shrub with oval, rich green leaves, to 2½in (6cm) long. White flowers are borne in dense panicles, to 4in (10cm) long, in midsummer, followed by spherical, shiny black fruit. Useful for hedging. ↕↔ 12ft (4m). Japan. Zone 6. **'Argenteum'** has leaves margined creamy white. **'Aureum'**, syn. 'Aureomarginatum' (Golden privet), has leaves with broad, bright yellow margins.

L. quihoui. Upright then rounded, deciduous shrub with slender, arching branches and narrowly oval to obovate, glossy, mid-green leaves, to 2in (5cm) long. Fragrant white flowers are produced in open panicles, 8in (20cm) or more long, in late summer and early autumn, followed by ovoid, glossy, black-purple fruit. Useful for hedging. ↕↔ 15ft (5m). China. Zone 5b.

L. sinense ■ (Chinese privet). Vigorous, bushy, tree-like, deciduous or semi-evergreen shrub with arching branches and elliptic-oblong or lance-shaped, pale green leaves, to 3in (8cm) long. White flowers are profusely borne in panicles, to 4in (10cm) long, in midsummer, and are followed by spherical, purple-black fruit. Useful for hedging; can become weedy. ↕↔ 12ft (4m). China. Zone 7b. **'Variegatum'** has white-margined, pale green leaves. **'Wimbei'** is compact and slow-growing, with upright leaves, to ½in (1.5cm) long. Rarely flowers; ↕ 5ft (1.5m), ↔ 4ft (1.2m).

L. 'Vicaryi'. Dense, bushy, semi-evergreen shrub with broadly oval, golden yellow leaves, to 3½in (9cm) long. White flowers are produced in panicles, to 3in (8cm) long, in mid-summer, followed by spherical, blue-black fruit. ↕↔ 10ft (3m). Zone 6.

L. vulgare (Common privet). Bushy, deciduous or semi-evergreen shrub with narrowly oval to lance-shaped, dark green leaves, to 2½in (6cm) long. White flowers are produced in panicles, to 2in (5cm) long, in early and midsummer, followed by spherical to ovoid black fruit. Useful for hedging. ↕↔ 10ft (3m). Europe, N. Africa, S.W. Asia. Zone 5b. **'Aureum'** has golden yellow foliage; ↕↔ 6ft (2m).

LILIUM

Lily

LILIACEAE

Genus of approximately 100 species of bulbous perennials, mainly from wooded habitats and scrub in Europe, Asia south to the Philippines, and North America; there are also innumerable garden hybrids. The bulbs are composed of overlapping, fleshy scales and are sometimes stoloniferous. The stems are unbranched and usually erect; in most lilies, roots develop on the stems just above the bulb. Numerous elliptic to lance-shaped or linear, glossy, mid- to dark green leaves are arranged in whorls or spirals, or are scattered alternately up the stems. Lilies grow from 1½–10ft (0.45–3m) tall and are usually less than 18in (45cm) wide, although some multiply into broad-spreading clumps.

The showy, sometimes very fragrant flowers are solitary or borne in racemes, panicles, or umbels, and are followed by 3-parted capsules containing flat, papery seeds. The flowers may be upward-facing, horizontal or outward-facing, pendent, or nodding. They may be cup- to bowl- or bell-shaped, trumpet-shaped, funnel-shaped, flat-faced, recurved (also called turkscap, in which the blooms have strongly swept-back tepals), or occasionally star-shaped; each with 6 stamens and 6 tepals (see panel above). The tepals, occurring in most colors except blue, may be plain or marked with spots, lines, brushmarks, or papillae. Three approximate categories of flower size – small, medium, and large – are used in the descriptions below. Small flowers are less than 3in (8cm) across; medium flowers are 3–4in (8–10cm) across; large flowers are over 4in (10cm) across.

Lilies bloom from spring through autumn. Spring-bloomers are designated as early season; those that bloom from early to midsummer are midseason; those blooming from late summer onward are late season.

Lilies may be grown in many sites, including woodland and wild gardens and among shrubs or herbaceous plants in borders. They are often grown for exhibition and provide excellent cut flowers. A few species are suitable for a rock garden. Many also grow well in a large container on a patio. Where not hardy, grow lilies in a cool greenhouse; some may be forced.

Lilies are classified into 9 divisions. Each division may be further subdivided according to flowrer orientation and flower form. Orientation subdivisions are: (a) upfacing, (b) outward-facing, and (c) pendant flowers. In addition, flower form descriptions that follow orientation descriptions are (a) trumpet-shaped, (b) bowl-shaped, (c) flat-faced, and (d) distinctly recurved. Thus, an outfacing, flat-faced flower from division I would be classified as I(b,c), and a pendant, trumpet-shaped division VI flower would be VI(c,a).

LILY FLOWERS

Lilies are valued for their very showy, often fragrant flowers. The 6 plain or strikingly marked tepals ("petals") are variably curved, giving rise to the different shapes shown here, and to forms intermediate between them.

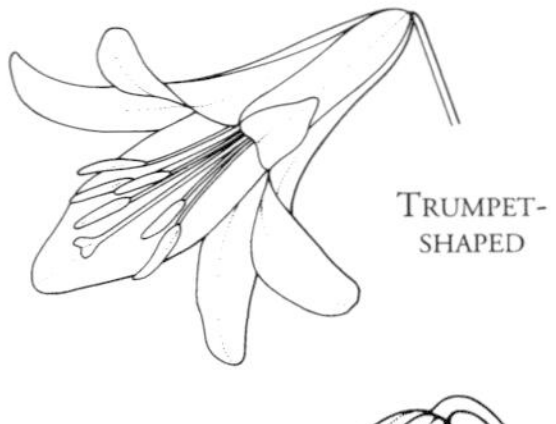

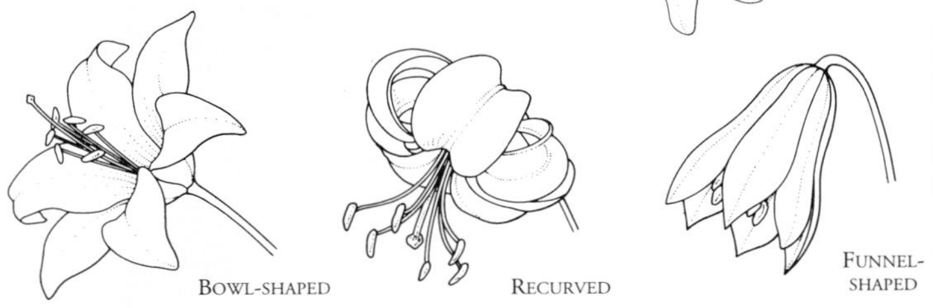

Division I (Asiatic hybrids)
These lilies are derived from various Asiatic species, including *L. bulbiferum*, *L. cernuum*, *L. concolor*, *L. davidii*, *L. lancifolium*, and *L. maculatum*. The flowers are borne in racemes or umbels, and are usually unscented. The leaves are narrowly ovate and arranged alternately.

Division II (Martagon hybrids)
Derived primarily from *L. martagon*, these lilies produce racemes of recurved, sometimes unpleasantly scented flowers, and have whorls of elliptic leaves.

Division III (Candidum hybrids)
Derived from *L. candidum* and other European species, except *L. martagon*, these lilies produce sometimes scented, mostly recurved flowers, singly or in umbels or racemes. Leaves are elliptic, and spirally arranged or scattered.

Division IV (American hybrids)
Derived from American species, these lilies bear racemes of sometimes scented, mostly recurved, but occasionally funnel-shaped flowers, and have whorls of lance-shaped to elliptic leaves.

Division V (Longiflorum hybrids)
Derived from *L. formosanum* and *L. longiflorum*, these lilies bear racemes or umbels of large, often sweetly scented, trumpet- or funnel-shaped flowers, sometimes only 2 or 3 per stem. Leaves are linear to narrowly lance-shaped, and scattered.

Division VI (Trumpet and Aurelian hybrids)
Derived from Asiatic species, including *L. regale*, *L. henryi*, and *L. sargentiae*, these lilies bear racemes or umbels of usually scented flowers. Leaves are elliptic to linear, and alternate or spirally arranged.

Division VII (Oriental hybrids)
These lilies are derived from E. Asian species, such as *L. auratum*, *L. japonicum*, and *L. speciosum*, as well as their hybrids with *L. henryi*. Flowers are produced in racemes or panicles, and are often highly scented. Leaves are lance-shaped and alternate.

Division VIII (Other hybrids)
These lilies include interdivisional hybrids, such as LA (*L. longiflorum* x Asiatic hybrids) and Orienpets (Oriental x trumpet hybrids).

Division IX (All true species)

• **HARDINESS** Lilies require a cold dormant period and are well suited to gardens in all but the coldest parts of Canada. Most Division I, II, and VIII lilies grow in Zone 3. Lilies from other divisions may be more tender or more tolerant of warmer winters.

• **CULTIVATION** Grow in well-drained soil enriched with leaf mold or well-rotted organic matter. Most prefer acidic to neutral soil, but some are lime-tolerant or prefer alkaline soils. The majority like a position in full sun, with the base of the plant in shade; a few prefer partial shade in light woodland. Under glass, grow in soil-based potting mix, with added grit and leaf mold, in full light with shade from hot sun. In active growth, water freely and apply a high-potash liquid fertilizer every 2 weeks. Keep moist in winter. Plant bulbs in autumn, at a depth of 2–3 times their height, and with a distance between them equivalent to 3 times the diameter of the bulb. Plant *L. candidum* and *L.* x *testaceum* no more than 1in (2.5cm) deep; they tolerate drier soil than other lilies, and require alkaline soil.

• **PROPAGATION** Sow seed as soon as ripe in containers in a cold frame, or germinate indoors under lights at 65–70°F (18–21°C) in spring. Remove scales, offsets, or bulblets from dormant bulbs as soon as the foliage dies down, or detach stem bulbils (where these are produced) in late summer.

• **PESTS AND DISEASES** Gray mold (*Botrytis*) is sometimes a problem, especially in a wet, cool spring or summer. Viruses, spread by aphids, may be troublesome, although some cultivars are virus-tolerant and grow well despite infection. Red lily beetles, slugs, and snails, may occur. Deer, rabbits, voles, and groundhogs may eat entire plants; birds sometimes peck holes in the buds.

***L.* 'African Queen'** ■ Vigorous Division VI trumpet-shaped lily with erect stems. In late midseason, large, fragrant, outward-facing to nodding, trumpet-shaped flowers, brownish purple outside, yellow or orange-apricot inside, are borne in pyramid-shaped racemes. ↕ 5–6ft (1.5–2m). Zone 4.

***L.* 'Anastasia'**. Vigorous, second-generation Division VIII (Orienpet) lily. Blooms very late in the season, bearing large racemes of fragrant flat-faced, pendent, recurved flowers with rose-pink centers. ↕ to 6ft (2m). Zone 3.

***L.* 'Angela North'.** Clump-forming, moderately vigorous Division I(c) lily. In midseason, bears racemes of medium-sized, faintly scented, recurved, pendent deep wine-red flowers, with some darker spotting. ↕ 28–48in (70–120cm). Zone 3.

***L.* 'Apricot Supreme'.** Vigorous Division VIII lily. In early and midseason, bears racemes of large, flat-faced, apricot flowers with brown-black spots near the centers, recurved tepals, and brown anthers. ↕ 3–4ft (1–1.2m). Zone 4.

***L.* 'Ariadne'** ■ Division I lily. In midseason, bears racemes of small, fragrant, recurved, pendent buff-rose flowers with purple-flushed tips and lines, and reddish brown anthers. ↕ 4–6ft (1.2–2m). Zone 3.

L. auratum (Golden-rayed lily). Vigorous Division IX lily with stiff stems bearing scattered, lance-shaped, deep green leaves, 9in (23cm) long. Late in the season, produces racemes of usually up to 12, sometimes up to 30, sweetly fragrant, open bowl-shaped flowers, to 12in (30cm) across; the white tepals are recurved toward the tips, have a prominent central gold band, and are often crimson-speckled. Susceptible to virus. ↕ 2–5ft (0.6–1.5m). Japan. Zone 5. **'Crimson Beauty'**

Lilium bulbiferum var. *croceum*

Lilium 'African Queen'

Lilium 'Ariadne'

Lilium auratum var. *platyphyllum*

Lilium 'Avignon'

Lilium Bellingham Hybrids

Lilium 'Black Beauty'

Lilium 'Bright Star'

Lilium canadense

Lilium candidum

Lilium 'Casa Blanca'

Lilium chalcedonicum

Lilium 'Connecticut King'

produces flowers with a crimson band along the center of each tepal; ↕ to 3ft (1m). **var. *platyphyllum*** ▣ has broadly lance-shaped leaves, and bears flowers with a yellow band along each tepal but few spots; ↕ to 5ft (1.5m).

***L.* 'Avignon'** ▣ Vigorous, upright Division I(a) lily. In early and midseason, bears racemes of large, bowl-shaped, upward-facing vivid red flowers. ↕ 3–4ft (1–1.2m). Zone 3.

***L.* Bellingham Hybrids** ▣ (*L. humboldtii* x *L. pardalinum* x *L. parryi*). Vigorous Division IV lilies with rhizomatous bulbs. In midseason, bear racemes of medium-sized, unscented, recurved flowers, ranging from yellow to orange and red, spotted with brown or deep red. They increase rapidly but require acidic soil and partial shade. ↕ 6–7ft (1.8–2.2m). Zone 3.

***L.* 'Black Beauty'** ▣ Vigorous Division VIII lily. In midseason, bears racemes of medium-sized, scented, recurved, dark blackish red flowers, with green centers and white tepal margins. ↕ 4½–6ft (1.4–2m). Zone 4.

***L.* 'Blackbird'.** Division I lily with bowl-shaped, upward-facing deep red flowers, borne early in the season. ↕ 18in (45cm). Zone 2.

***L.* 'Black Dragon'.** Division VI lily producing thick racemes of large, scented, outward-facing, trumpet-shaped flowers, dark purplish red outside, white within, in midseason. ↕ 5ft (1.5m). Zone 4.

***L.* 'Black Jack'.** Division I(a) lily flowering in midseason. Bowl-shaped, upward-facing lily with petals an intense nonfading dark red with an almost black reverse. ↕ 3ft (1m). Zone 3.

***L.* 'Bright Star'** ▣ Division VI lily bearing racemes of large, scented, outward-facing, ivory-white flowers in late midseason; spreading tepals are recurved at the tips, and each has an orange central band, producing a star-like effect. Lime-tolerant. ↕ 3–5ft (1–1.5m). Zone 4.

***L.* 'Brushmarks'.** Division I lily producing racemes of large, upward-facing, cup-shaped orange flowers, with deep red marks and green throats, in midseason. ↕ to 3ft (1m). Zone 3.

***L.* 'Brush Stroke'.** Very vigorous Division I lily. Upward-facing white flowers with plum brush marks are produced in midseason. ↕ 4–5ft (1.2–1.5m). Zone 2.

L. bulbiferum (Orange lily). Vigorous Division IX lily producing scattered, narrowly to broadly lance-shaped leaves, 2–6in (5–15cm) long, with marginal hairs; bulbils are borne in the upper leaf axils. In midseason, bears usually 1- to 5-flowered umbels (sometimes many-flowered, dense racemes) of unscented, erect, bowl-shaped, bright orange-red flowers, 4–6in (10–15cm) across; the tepals are broad, with black or maroon spots and darker bases and tips. Grows well in acidic or alkaline soil. ↕ 16–60in (40–150cm). S. Europe. Zone 3. **var. *croceum*** ▣ has orange flowers and does not produce bulbils.

***L.* 'Cadense'.** Division II lily, *L. martagon* hybrid blooms early in the season. Produces racemes of slightly recurved flowers, yellow inside with dark yellow reverse. Blooms face out and downward. ↕ 4ft (1.2m). Zone 3.

L. canadense ▣ (Meadow lily). Division IX lily with rhizomatous bulbs and whorls of lance-shaped to inversely lance-shaped leaves, 6in (15cm) long, each with 5–7 parallel veins. In late midseason, produces umbels, or occasionally racemes, of up to 30 faintly scented, narrowly to broadly trumpet-shaped yellow flowers, 2–3in (5–8cm) long, with recurved tips and maroon spots in the centers. ↕ 3–5½ft (1–1.6m). E. North America. Zone 3. **var. *coccineum***, syn. var. *rubrum*, bears bright red flowers with yellow throats. **var. *editorum*** has broader leaves and red flowers. **var. *rubrum*** see var. *coccineum*.

L. candidum ▣ (Madonna lily). Division IX lily with broad, inversely lance-shaped, shiny, bright green basal leaves, 9in (23cm) long, appearing in autumn. Stiffly erect stems bear smaller, scattered or spirally arranged, often somewhat twisted, lance-shaped leaves, to 3in (8cm) long. In midseason, produces a raceme of 5–20 sweetly fragrant, broadly trumpet-shaped, pure white flowers, 2–3in (5–8cm) long, with yellowish bases and bright yellow anthers. Produces overwintering basal leaves (the only lily with this character). Requires neutral to alkaline soil. Very susceptible to gray mold (*Botrytis*). ↕ 3–6ft (1–1.8m). S.E. Europe to E. Mediterranean. Zone 6.

***L.* 'Caravan'.** Large, outward-facing Division VIII hybrid (Orienpet) with brilliant red centers. Fragrant blooms are produced late in the season. ↕ 4–5ft (1.2–1.5m). Zone 3.

***L.* 'Casa Blanca'** ▣ Division VII lily, derived from *L. auratum*, with thick, stiff stems. In late midseason, large, sweetly fragrant, bowl-shaped, pure white flowers, with widely spreading tepals that are recurved near the tips, are produced in umbels; they have white papillae near the bases inside, and orange-red anthers. ↕ 3–4ft (1–1.2m). Zone 4.

***L.* 'Casa Rosa'.** Vigorous Division VIII lily. In midseason, bears racemes of large, trumpet-shaped, fragrant pink flowers with pale pink tips and recurved tepals. ↕ 3–4ft (1–1.2m). Zone 4.

L. cernuum (Nodding lily). Small, stem-rooting Division IX lily. Scattered, linear leaves, 3–7in (8–18cm) long, are mostly concentrated in the middle third of the slender stem. In midseason, bears racemes of usually up to 6 (occasionally up to 15) fragrant, recurved, pale lilac, pink, or purple flowers, 1¼–2in (3–5cm) across. Lime-tolerant, but prefers moist, peaty soil. ↕ 16–24in (40–60cm). Russia (N.E. Siberia) to Korea. Zone 2.

L. chalcedonicum ▣ syn. *L. heldreichii* (Scarlet turkscap lily). Relatively small, stem-rooting Division IX lily with spirally arranged, lance-shaped, deep green leaves, 5in (13cm) long, with silver-hairy margins; the lower leaves are spreading, the upper ones erect. In midseason, produces racemes of up to 12 small, unpleasantly scented, recurved, sealing-wax-red flowers, 3in (8cm) across, unspotted, but with self-colored papillae at the bases. Grow in any soil, in full sun or partial shade. ↕ 2–5ft (0.6–1.5m). N. Greece, Albania. Zone 7b.

***L.* 'China Express'.** Division VIII lily (Asiapet). Long panicles of large, pendent, peach flowers, with darker apricot throats, are borne in midseason. ↕ 4–5ft (1.2–1.5m). Zone 2.

***L.* 'Chinook'.** Moderately vigorous Division I(a) lily. In midseason, bears umbels of medium-sized, unscented, bowl-shaped, upward-facing pale apricot-buff flowers. ↕ 3–4ft (1–1.2m). Zone 3.

***L.* 'Citronella'** ▣ Vigorous Division I lily. In midseason, bears racemes or panicles of up to 30 medium-sized, recurved, pendent bright yellow to lemon-yellow flowers, speckled with faint black or reddish spots inside. ↕ 4–5ft (1.2–1.5m). Zone 3.

***L.* 'Classic'.** Vigorous Division I lily. In early and midseason, bears racemes of medium-sized, recurved, pendent lemon-yellow flowers with bronze-pink reverses. ↕ 4–5ft (1.2–1.5m). Zone 3.

***L.* 'Claude Shride'.** Vigorous Division II lily, flowering early in the season. Produces racemes of small, recurved, slightly ruffled, gray-purple flowers with yellow-orange spots. ↕ 5–6ft (1.5–2m). Zone 2.

L. concolor (Morning star lily). Stem-rooting Division IX lily with reddish green stems bearing scattered, linear to linear-lance-shaped leaves, to 3½in (9cm) long, slightly hairy on the margins and beneath. In midseason, produces racemes or umbels of up to 10 fragrant, upward-facing, star-shaped, glossy scarlet flowers, 1¼–1½in (3–4cm) across. ↕ 12–36in (30–90cm). W. China. Zone 3.

***L.* 'Connecticut King'** ▣ Vigorous Division I lily. In midseason, produces racemes of medium-sized, unscented, long-lasting, star-shaped, upward-facing, rich deep yellow flowers, paling slightly toward the tips of the spreading, somewhat recurved tepals. ↕ 3ft (1m). Zone 3.

Lilium 'Citronella'

Lilium x *dalhansonii*

Lilium duchartrei

Lilium 'Enchantment'

Lilium 'Fangio'

Lilium formosanum var. *pricei*

Lilium grayi

Lilium 'Green Dragon'

Lilium hansonii

Lilium henryi

Lilium 'Iowa Rose'

Lilium 'La Center'

Lilium lancifolium

Lilium 'Lativa'

Lilium 'Lime Frost'

Lilium longiflorum

Lilium mackliniae

Lilium martagon

Lilium martagon var. *album*

***L.* 'Copper King'.** Vigorous Division VI(a) lily. In midseason, bears racemes of large, trumpet-shaped, fragrant, orange-apricot-blended flowers with slightly recurved tepals. ↕ 4½–6ft (1.4–2m). Zone 3.
L. cordatum see *Cardiocrinum cordatum.*
***L.* 'Cranberry Dancer'.** Division II, L. martagon hybrid. Blooms early in the season, bearing racemes of slightly recurved yellow flowers, partially overlaid with cranberry spots, with a plum reverse. ↕ 5ft (1.6m). Zone 3.
L.* x *dalhansonii ■ (*L. martagon* var. *cattaniae* x *L. hansonii*). Division VIII lily bearing whorls of inversely lance-shaped leaves, 6–7in (15–18cm) long. In midseason, bears racemes of numerous small, unpleasantly scented, recurved, maroon flowers, 1¼–2in (3–5cm) across, spotted and suffused orange in the centers. ↕ 3–5ft (1–1.5m). Garden origin. Zone 3.
L. dauricum. Stem-rooting Division IX lily with rhizomatous bulbs and brown-spotted green stems. Lance-shaped to linear, hairy-margined leaves, 2in (5cm) long, are scattered, with the uppermost set in a whorl below the flowers. In midseason, produces umbels of up to 6 medium-sized, unscented, upward-facing, bowl-shaped, deep orange-scarlet flowers, to 4in (10cm) across, with yellowish orange centers, brownish red or purple spots, and hairy stalks. Best in acidic soil, in full sun or partial shade. ↕ 20–28in (50–70cm). N.E. Asia. Zone 3.
L. davidii. Division IX lily, sometimes rhizomatous, with brown-spotted green stems bearing scattered, linear, finely toothed, dark green leaves, 2½–4in (6–10cm) long, hairy beneath. In midseason, produces racemes of 10–20 unscented, long-stalked, recurved, vermilion-red flowers, to 3in (8cm) across, with purple-black spots. ↕ 3–4ft (1–1.2m). W. China. Zone 3. **var. *willmottiae*** has rhizomatous bulbs, tall, arching stems with leaves that are broader than those of the species, and up to 40 flowers per raceme; ↕ to 6ft (2m); China. Zone 4.
L. duchartrei ■ Stem-rooting Division IX lily with rhizomatous bulbs and ribbed, brown-flushed green stems bearing scattered, lance-shaped, stalkless leaves, to 4in (10cm) long, with rough margins. In midseason, produces umbels of up to 12 scented, long-stalked, nodding, recurved white flowers, 2½–3in (6–8cm) across, deep purple-spotted inside, and purple-flushed, aging to red outside. ↕ 24–39in (60–100cm). China (Gansu, Sichuan, Yunnan). Zone 7.
***L.* 'Enchantment'** ■ Very vigorous, clump-forming Division I lily, flowering in midseason. Produces umbels of medium-sized, unscented, cup-shaped, upward-facing, rich bright orange flowers with black spots inside. Easy to grow; multiplies quickly. ↕ 24–39in (60–100cm). Zone 3.
***L.* 'Fangio'** ■ Enormous inflorescence of up-facing dark plum bowl-shaped flowers are produced early in the season on this Division VIII lily. ↕ 3ft (1m). Zone 3.
L. formosanum. Elegant, stem-rooting Division IX lily with rhizomatous bulbs, and green stems that are purplish brown toward the bases. Numerous dark green, linear to narrowly oblong-lance-shaped leaves, 3–8in (8–20cm) long, are scattered, and sparse toward the stem tops. Slender, very fragrant, trumpet-shaped white flowers, 5–8in (12–20cm) long, flushed reddish purple outside, and with flared and somewhat recurved tepal tips, are borne singly, in pairs, or in umbels of up to 10, late in the season. Requires moist, acidic soil. Suitable for a conservatory. ↕ 2–5ft (0.6–1.5m). Taiwan. Zone 7.
var. *pricei* ■ produces flowers that are more strongly flushed purple on the outside, borne singly or in clusters of up to 3, earlier in the summer; ↕ 4–12in (10–30cm).
L. giganteum see *Cardiocrinum giganteum.*
***L.* 'Gold Eagle'.** Upright Division VI lily. In mid- and late season, bears racemes of large, strongly fragrant, flat-faced, deep lemon-yellow flowers with gray-orange reverses and gently recurved tepal tips; the green throats have cinnamon-red papillae. ↕ 4½–7ft (1.4–2.2m). Zone 3.
***L.* Golden Splendor Group** ■ Vigorous, variable Division VI lilies. In midseason, strong, sturdy stems produce umbels of large, scented, outward-facing, shallowly trumpet-shaped, almost bowl-shaped flowers, in shades of yellow with dark burgundy-red bands outside. ↕ 4–6ft (1.2–2m). Zone 4.
L. grayi ■ Division IX lily with rhizomatous bulbs. Stems bear whorls of lance-shaped to oblong-lance-shaped leaves, 2–4in (5–10cm) long. In mid-

Lilium Golden Splendor Group

season, produces tiered umbels of up to 12 scented, tubular-funnel-shaped, nodding flowers, 2½in (6cm) long, red outside, paler inside, with yellowish centers and purple spots. Requires moist, acidic soil. ↕3–5½ft (1–1.7m). E. US. Zone 4.
***L.* 'Green Dragon'** ■ Thick Division VI lily, derived from the Olympic Hybrids, flowering in midseason. Produces short racemes of large, fragrant, trumpet-shaped white flowers flushed greenish brown outside and stained yellow in the centers. ↕5–7ft (1.5–2.2m). Zone 4.
L. hansonii ■ Vigorous, stem-rooting Division IX lily. Inversely lance-shaped to elliptic, pale green leaves, to 7in (18cm) long, are borne in dense whorls of 12–20. In midseason, produces racemes of up to 12 small, fragrant, nodding, recurved, brilliant orange-yellow flowers, 1¼–1½in (3–4cm) across, with thick, recurved tepals spotted purplish brown near the bases. Grow in well-drained soil in partial shade. ↕3–5ft (1–1.5m). Russia (E. Siberia), Korea, Japan. Zone 3.
L. heldreichii see *L. chalcedonicum*.
L. henryi ■ Vigorous, stem-rooting, clump-forming Division IX lily with purple-marked green stems. Ovate-lance-shaped to lance-shaped leaves, 3–6in (8–15cm) long, are scattered; the lower leaves have short stalks, the upper ones are crowded below the flowers. Late in the season, produces racemes of up to 10 (occasionally up to 20) faintly scented, recurved, deep orange flowers, 2½–3in (6–8cm) across, spotted black, with deep red anthers. Easy to grow in neutral to alkaline soil in partial shade. ↕3–10ft (1–3m). C. China. Zone 3. **var. *citrinum*** bears soft yellow flowers with chocolate-brown spots; ↕4–7ft (1.2–2.2m).
***L.* 'Herald Angel Yellow'.** Vigorous, upright Division VI lily. In mid- and late season, bears racemes of large, fragrant, trumpet-shaped, dark yellow flowers with darker throats, often with maroon reverses. ↕3–5ft (1–1.5m). Zone 4.
***L.* 'Hornback's Gold'.** Division I lily bearing few-flowered umbels of large, unscented, cup-shaped, pendent pale yellow flowers with light brown spots, in mid-season. ↕3–4ft (1–1.2m). Zone 3.
***L.* 'Imperial Gold'.** Division VII lily bearing racemes, late in the season, of large, fragrant, star-shaped, flat-faced, glistening white flowers, each tepal with recurved tips and a yellow stripe down the center. ↕6ft (1.8–2m). Zone 4.
***L.* 'Indian Summer'.** Elegant Division VIII lily. Clear yellow pendant recurved flowers contrast with dark stem. Lat season. 4 ft (1.4m). Zone 3.
***L.* 'Iowa Rose'** ■ Vigorous Division I lily. In midseason, bears racemes of large, flat-bowl-shaped, outward-facing vivid pink flowers with pale orange-yellow throats, dark pink ribs, recurved tepals, and brown anthers. ↕3½–4ft (1.1–1.2m). Zone 3.
***L.* 'Jamboree'.** Division VII lily. Late in the season, bears racemes of large, fragrant, recurved crimson flowers with silver-white edges and crimson spots. ↕3–6ft (1–2m). Zone 4.
***L.* 'Journey's End'** ■ Thick Division VII lily producing racemes of large, unscented, broad, recurved flowers late

Lilium 'Journey's End'

in the season; the spreading tepals are deep pink, with maroon spots and white margins and tips. ↕3–6ft (1–2m). Zone 4.
***L.* 'Katinka'.** Division I lily, flowering in early and midseason. Produces racemes of medium, loosely recurved, salmon-peach flowers with brownish ink reverses, heavily spotted inner tepals, and dark brown anthers. ↕4–4½ft (1.2–1.4m). Zone 3.
***L.* 'King Pete'.** Vigorous, clump-forming Division I lily. In midseason, produces umbels of medium-sized, unscented, broad, bowl-shaped, outward-facing cream flowers, marked and spotted orange and with orange-red anthers. Long-lasting in flower and good for cutting. ↕3ft (1m). Zone 3.
***L.* 'La Center'** ■ Division I lily. Upfacing intense yelow flowers with large red blush toward center. Dark buds and stem. Early season. ↕4ft (1.2m). Zone 2.
L. lancifolium ■syn. *L. tigrinum* (Tiger lily). Robust, stem-rooting, clump-forming Division IX lily with dark purple, often white-hairy stems. Scattered, narrowly lance-shaped leaves, 5–8in (12–20cm) long, have rough margins; the upper ones produce dark purplish black bulbils in the axils. Up to 40 unscented, nodding, recurved, orange-red flowers, 5in (13cm) across, with dark purple spots and papillae, are produced in racemes, late in the season. Prefers moist, acidic soil, but tolerates some lime. ↕2–5ft (0.6–1.5m). E. China, Korea, Japan. Zone 2. **'Flore Pleno'** bears double flowers with 24–36 tepals and no stamens. **'Yellow Tiger'** is a selection from var. *flaviflorum*, with purple-spotted, bright yellow flowers.
***L.* 'Latvia'** ■ Division I lily. Upward-facing pale yellow flowers, with intense dark purple spreckling ('Tango' pattern) in the center, bloom in midseason. ↕3ft (1m). Zone 2.
***L. leichtlinii* var. *maximowiczii*.** Vigorous, stem-rooting, upright Division IX lily with erect stems and linear-lance-shaped leaves, to 6in (15cm) long. In mid- and late season, bears racemes of 1–12, nodding, recurved, brilliant orange-red to brown-red flowers, 2–3in (5–8cm) across, with profuse, purplish brown spots and reddish anthers. ↕24–96in (60–250cm). Korea, Japan. Zone 3.
***L.* 'Leslie Woodruff'.** Vigorous Division VIII lily. Late in the season, bears racemes of large, slightly fragrant, flat-faced, dark red flowers with white-tipped, slightly recurved tepals; they have star-like, yellow-edged green nectaries and numerous dark papillae. ↕5–7ft (1.5–2.2m). Zone 5.
***L. leucanthum*.** Huge, fragrant, white Division IX lily; trumpets with dark chocolate raspberry reverse are produced in mid-season. Stems grow taller year after year. ↕4–8ft (1.2–2.4m). China. Zone 5.
***L.* 'Lime Frost'** ■ Vigorous, upright Division I lily, flowering in early and midseason. Bears racemes of large, slightly recurved, bowl-shaped green flowers with greenish yellow insides, fading to yellowish white; they have green nectaries, inner tepals with green midribs, and golden orange anthers. ↕4½ft (1.4m). Zone 3.
L. longiflorum ■(Easter lily). Vigorous, stem-rooting Division IX lily with scattered, lance-shaped to oblong-lance-shaped, shiny, deep green leaves, to 7in (18cm) long. In midseason, produces short racemes of 1–6 very fragrant, trumpet-shaped, horizontally placed, pure white flowers, to 7in (18cm) long, with yellow anthers. Widely grown for cut flowers; excellent in a container. Lime-tolerant. Grow in partial shade. ↕16–39in (40–100cm). S. Japan, Taiwan. Zone 6.
***L.* 'Luminaries'.** Orienpet Division VIII lily. Huge tricolor flowers of white and pink with gold throats. Late season. ↕4–6ft (1.2–1.8m). Zone 3.
L. mackliniae ■ Small, stem-rooting Division IX lily with slender green stems, sometimes tinged purple, and linear-lance-shaped to narrowly elliptic, deep green leaves, 1¼–2½in (3–6cm) long, scattered or whorled near the tops of the stems. In midseason, bears racemes of up to 6 unscented, semi-pendent, bowl-shaped, purple-flushed, rose-pink flowers, 2in (5cm) across, with purple anthers. ↕12–24in (30–60cm). N.E. India (Assam). Zone 7b.
***L.* 'Magic Pink'** ■ Clump-forming Division VII lily. In midseason, produces short racemes of large, slightly scented, half-nodding, bowl-shaped, soft pink flowers, with a darker center to each tepal. ↕4ft (1.2m). Zone 4.
***L.* 'Malta',** syn. *L.* 'Ikaria'. Vigorous, upright Division I lily, flowering in midseason. Produces racemes of large, slightly bowl-shaped, upward-facing light purplish pink flowers; the slightly recurved tepals have brownish red midribs, red throats, and red edges. Anthers are red. ↕3ft (1m). Zone 3.
L. martagon ■(Common turkscap lily). Vigorous, clump-forming, stem-rooting Division IX lily producing stiff, purple- or red-flushed green stems. Elliptic to inversely lance-shaped leaves, to 6in (15cm) long, often hairy on the undersides, are mostly borne in dense whorls. In midseason, produces narrow racemes of up to 50 small, somewhat unpleasant-smelling, pendent or nodding, glossy, recurved, pink to purplish red flowers, to 2in (5cm) across, with some darker-colored spotting or flecking. Grow in almost any well-drained soil in full sun or partial shade. ↕3–6ft (0.9–2m). Europe to Mongolia. Zone 3. **var. *album*** ■ has bright green stems bearing small white flowers, to 1½in (4cm) across.
***L. michiganense*.** Upright, stoloniferous Division IX lily producing long, erect stems and elliptic leaves, 4½in (11cm) long, with minutely hairy margins, borne in whorls of 4–8. In midseason, produces racemes of 2–12, nodding, recurved, orange-red flowers, 2–3in (5–8cm) across, with maroon spots toward the bases, yellow filaments, and rust-yellow anthers. ↕2–5ft (60–150m). E. North America. Zone 2.
***L.* 'Mirage'.** Vigorous Division I lily. In early midseason, bears racemes of medium-sized to large, bowl-shaped flowers, red near the bases of the tepals and yellow on the upper parts, and with slightly recurved tips. ↕24–36in (60–90in). Zone 3.

Lilium 'Magic Pink'

Lilium monadelphum

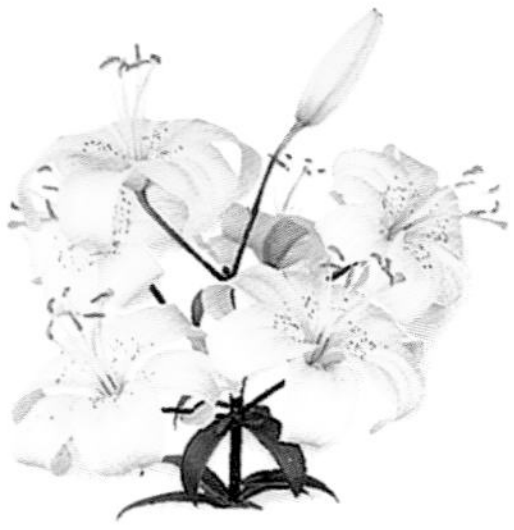
Lilium 'Mont Blanc'

Lilium nepalense

Lilium 'Northern Carillon'

Lilium oxypetalum

Lilium pardalinum

Lilium Pink Perfection Group

Lilium pomponium

Lilium pumilum

Lilium pyrenaicum

Lilium pyrenaicum subsp. *carniolicum* var. *albanicum*

Lilium 'Red Night'

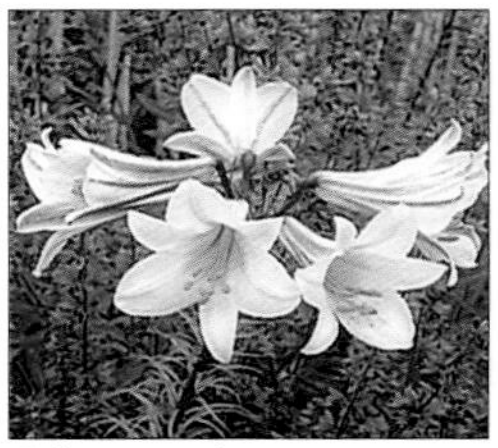
Lilium regale

Lilium rubellum

Lilium speciosum var. *rubrum*

Lilium 'Star Gazer'

Lilium 'Tom Pounce'

Lilium tsingtauense

L

L. monadelphum ■ syn. *L. szovitsianum.* Thick, clump-forming, sparsely stem-rooting Division IX lily with stiff stems and scattered, lance-shaped to inversely lance-shaped or ovate, bright green leaves, to 5½in (14cm) long. In midseason, bears racemes of up to 30 large, nodding, fragrant, broadly trumpet-shaped yellow flowers, to 4in (10cm) across, flecked and spotted maroon or purple inside, flushed purplish brown outside. Tepals are moderately to prominently recurved. Lime-tolerant. Thrives in fairly heavy soil, and survives in drier, sunnier conditions than most lilies. ↕3–5ft (1–1.5m). N.E. Turkey, Caucasus. Zone 5.
***L.* 'Mont Blanc'** ■ Short Division I lily producing umbels of large, unscented, wide, bowl-shaped, upward-facing white flowers, slightly brown-spotted in the centers, in midseason. ↕24–28in (60–70cm). Zone 3.
***L.* 'Montreux'.** Short Division I lily bearing umbels, in midseason, of medium-sized, unscented, cup-shaped, upward-facing pink flowers, with brown dots in the centers and buff-yellow anthers. ↕32–39in (80–100cm). Zone 3.
L. nanum ■ syn. *Nomocharis nana.* Small Division IX lily with slender stems and scattered, linear leaves, to 5in (13cm) long. Bears solitary, scented, bell-shaped, pale pink to rose-purple flowers, ½–1½in (1–4cm) long, often with darker markings or spots, in midseason. Requires cool, moist, acidic soil and partial shade. ↕2½–12in (6–30cm). Himalayas, W. China. Zone 7. **var. *flavidum*** bears pale yellow flowers.
L. nepalense ■ Stem-rooting Division IX lily with rhizomatous bulbs, erect or arching, smooth stems, and scattered, lance-shaped to oblong-lance-shaped, deep green leaves, to 6in (15cm) long. In midseason, produces unscented or unpleasantly scented, funnel-shaped, yellow, greenish yellow, or greenish white flowers, singly or occasionally in groups of 2 or 3 in the upper leaf axils. The tepals later reflex, and are either flecked and spotted reddish purple, or are entirely reddish purple or maroon in the centers. Needs cool, acidic soil and partial shade. ↕24–39in (60–100cm). N. India to Nepal and Bhutan (Himalayas). Zone 7b.
***L.* 'Northern Carillon'** ■ syn. *L.* 'Silk Road'. Huge, fragrant, white trumpet-shaped flowers with dark chocolate raspberry reverse. Stems grow taller year after year. ↕4–8ft (1.2–2.4m). Late midseason. China. Zone 3.
***L.* 'Nutmegger'.** Vigorous, upright, Division I lily. Late in the season, bears racemes of medium-sized, recurved, pendent yellow flowers with brown spots. ↕5½ft (1.7m). Zone 3.
***L.* 'Omega'.** Division VII lily with short stems producing short racemes, late in the season, of large, rose-pink flowers, with yellowish centers and sparse red spotting; the tepals are spreading and slightly recurved. ↕24–32in (60–80cm). Zone 4.
L. oxypetalum ■ syn. *Nomocharis oxypetala.* Small Division IX lily with slender stems and scattered, linear to linear-lance-shaped leaves, to 3in (8cm) long, sometimes whorled below the flowers. In midseason, each slender stem produces 1 or 2 small, unscented, semi-pendent, shallowly bowl-shaped yellow flowers, to 2in (5cm) across, usually with some purple dots in the centers. Needs cool, moist, acidic soil and partial shade. ↕8–12in (20–30cm). N.W. Himalayas. Zone 7b. **var. *insigne*** produces purple flowers.
L. pardalinum ■ Vigorous, clump-forming, rhizomatous Division IX lily. Strong stems bear dense whorls of elliptic to inversely lance-shaped, dull, deep green leaves, to 7in (18cm) long. In midseason, produces racemes of up to 10 unscented, nodding, recurved, orange-red to crimson flowers, 3½in (9cm) across, paler toward the bases and with large maroon spots, some spots encircled with yellow. Prefers moist soil in full sun or partial shade; lime-tolerant, but not in dry soil. ↕5–8ft (1.5–2.5m). W. US. Zone 5. **var. *giganteum*** is particularly vigorous, with as many as 30 flowers per stem; they are crimson, and yellow toward the bases with crimson spots; ↕to 10ft (3m).
L. philadelphicum (Red lily, Wild orange lily, Wood lily). Upright, short-stoloniferous Division IX lily with short, erect stems and narrowly elliptic to lance-shaped leaves, 4in (10cm) long, in whorls of 4–8. In midseason, bears racemes of 1–3 bowl-shaped, orange-scarlet flowers, 3–4in (8–10cm) across, orange on the lower tepals, with dark maroon spots and slightly recurved tepals. ↕18–36in (45–90cm). Quebec to North Carolina. Zone 3.
***L.* 'Pink Flourishes'.** Multipetaled, pollenless Division I lily. Upward-facing peach flowers bloom in early midseason. ↕3ft (1m). Zone 2.
***L.* Pink Perfection Group** ■ Division VI(a) lilies with thick stems. In midseason, bear short racemes or umbels of large, scented, slightly nodding, trumpet-shaped flowers, which are deep purplish red or purple-pink, with bright orange anthers. ↕5–6ft (1.5–2m). Zone 4.
L. pomponium ■ Slender, stem-rooting Division IX lily with green stems that are spotted purple on the lower halves. Scattered, linear leaves, to 6in (15cm) long, have silver-hairy margins. In midseason, bears racemes of up to 6 (rarely up to 10) unpleasantly scented, pendent, recurved, sealing-wax-red flowers, 2in (5cm) across, generally with black spots and streaks in the throats. Prefers alkaline soil in full sun or partial shade. ↕3ft (1m). French and Italian Alps. Zone 6.
L. pumilum ■ syn. *L. tenuifolium.* Stem-rooting Division IX lily with

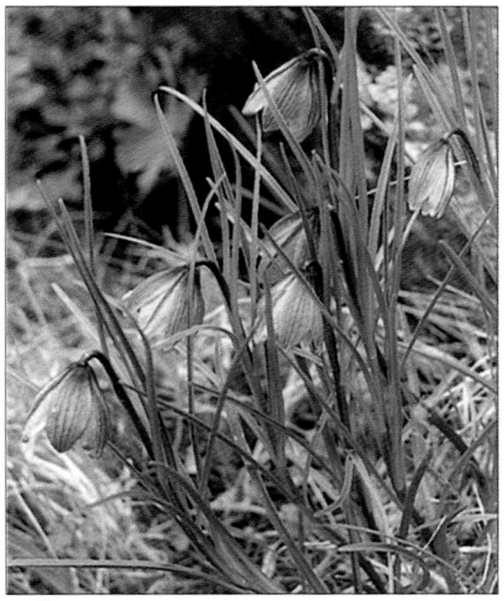
Lilium nanum

Lilium 'Sterling Star'

slender stems bearing numerous scattered, linear leaves, to 4in (10cm) long. In midseason, bears racemes of up to 30 fragrant, nodding to pendent, recurved, scarlet flowers, 2in (5cm) across, unspotted or with a few black spots in the centers. Requires acidic soil and full sun or partial shade. ↕6–18in (15–45cm). Russia (Siberia) to Mongolia, N. China, and N. Korea. Zone 3.

L. pyrenaicum ■ Stem-rooting, clump-forming Division IX lily with green stems, sometimes spotted purple, and numerous scattered, linear to linear-lance-shaped, bright green leaves, 6in (15cm) long, often with silver-hairy margins. In midseason, bears racemes of up to 12 unpleasant-smelling, pendent, recurved, yellow or greenish yellow flowers, 2in (5cm) across, flecked and spotted dark maroon in the throats. Needs neutral to alkaline soil and full sun or partial shade. ↕12–39in (30–100cm). Pyrenees. Zone 4. **subsp. *carniolicum* var. *albanicum*** ■ has leaves that are hairless beneath, and bears plain yellow flowers; ↕ rarely more than 16in (40cm); N. Greece, Albania.

***L.* 'Red Night'** ■ syn. *L.* 'Roter Cardinal'. Division I lily. In midseason, bears umbels of medium-sized, unscented, cup-shaped red flowers, lighter on the tepal lobes, spotted black in the centers. ↕28–39in (70–100cm). Zone 3.

***L.* 'Red Velvet'.** Vigorous, erect Division I lily. In mid- and late season, bears racemes of medium to large, flat-bowl-shaped, outward-facing, almost spotless, deep red flowers with slightly recurved tepal tips. ↕4½ft (1.4m). Zone 3.

L. regale ■ (Regal lily). Vigorous, stem-rooting Division IX lily with erect or arching, purple-flushed, gray-green stems and numerous scattered, linear, shiny, deep green leaves, 2–5in (5–13cm) long. In midseason, produces umbels of up to 25 very fragrant, broadly trumpet-shaped white flowers, 5–6in (12–15cm) long, flushed purple or purple-brown outside, with yellow centers and gold anthers. Grow in most well-drained soils, except very alkaline; prefers a site in full sun. ↕2–6ft (0.6–2m). W. China. Zone 4.

***L.* 'Roter Cardinal'** see *L.* 'Red Night'.

L. rubellum ■ Stem-rooting Division IX lily with scattered, narrowly elliptic or narrowly ovate to lance-shaped leaves, 4in (10cm) long. In midseason, bears up to 9, but usually 1–4, fragrant, funnel-shaped pink flowers, 3in (8cm) long, often spotted maroon in the centers, from the upper leaf axils. Requires moist, acidic soil and partial shade. ↕12–32in (30–80cm). Japan. Zone 3.

***L.* 'Sally'.** Vigorous Division I lily. In midseason, bears racemes of medium, recurved, pendent, orange-pink flowers, burnt orange and heavily spotted in the centers, with maroon bands on the reverses. ↕ to 6ft (2m). Zone 3.

L. sargentiae. White Division IX lily; trumpet-shaped flowers with bulbils in the axils of the upper leaves, produced in late season. Fragrant. ↕1½–5ft (0.5–1.6m). Zone 6.

***L.* 'Scarlet Delight'.** Vigorous Division VIII lily. Late in the season, bears racemes of large, outward-facing, flat to

Lilium superbum

bowl-shaped, ruffled, black-spotted, rich red flowers with white edges and tips, yellowish white nectaries, orange anthers, and slightly recurved tepals. ↕4½ft (1.4m). Zone 5.

***L.* 'Scheherazade'.** Vigorous Division VIII lily. Late in the season, bears racemes of large, flat-faced, gold-bordered, deep red flowers, with white margins and recurved tips. ↕ to 8ft (2.5m). Zone 5.

***L.* 'Screech Owl'.** Vigorous Division I lily. Early in the season, bears racemes of medium, bowl-shaped, upward-facing red flowers with vivid yellow throats, red nectaries, strongly recurved tepals, and orange anthers. ↕3ft (1m). Zone 3.

***L.* 'Shuksan'.** Stem-rooting Division IV lily with thick stems bearing racemes, in midseason, of medium-sized, slightly scented, recurved, orange-yellow flowers, with large black or reddish brown spots. Good in partial shade, especially in acidic soil. ↕4½–6ft (1.4–2m). Zone 4.

***L.* 'Silk Road'** see *L.* 'Northern Carillon'.

***L.* 'Silver Angel'.** Vigorous, upright Division VI lily. In mid- and late season, bears racemes of large, heavily fragrant, trumpet-shaped, creamy white flowers, sometimes with dark pink reverses. ↕5–7ft (1.5–2.2m). Zone 5.

***L.* 'Sinfonia'.** Very large Division VI tetraploid lily. Fragrant white trumpet-shaped flowers edged in rosy pink with pink reverse are produced in late midseason. ↕3–4ft (1–1.2m). Zone 3.

L. speciosum. Vigorous, stem-rooting Division IX lily with erect to ascending, purple-flushed green stems. Short-stalked leaves, to 7in (18cm) long, are scattered and broadly lance-shaped to almost ovate. Late in the season, produces racemes of usually up to 12, sometimes more, large, fragrant, pendent or outward-facing, recurved, pale pink or white flowers, to 7in (18cm) across, flushed deeper pink in the centers, and with papillae and pink or crimson spots. Needs moist, acidic soil and partial shade. ↕3–5½ft (1–1.7m). E. China, Japan, Taiwan. Zone 4. **var. *album*** has purple stems and white flowers. **var. *gloriosides*** Huge, fragrant lily. Extremely late-blooming, white, slightly recurved, pendent tepals are punctuated with prominent dark red center spots. China. ↕3–4ft (1–1.2m). Zone 6. **var. *rubrum*** ■ produces purple-brown stems and deep carmine-red flowers. **'Uchida'** bears crimson-red flowers with delicate, darker red spotting.

***L.* 'Starburst Sensation'.** Vigorous, upright Division VIII lily flowering in midseason. Bears racemes of large, slightly fragrant, outward-facing, slightly pendent, flat-bowl-shaped, deep red flowers with purplish red insides and yellowish white tips; the flowers also have papillae on the bases of the tepals, light yellow-green nectaries, grayish brown anthers, orange stigmas, and somewhat recurved tepals. ↕3ft (1m). Zone 4.

***L.* 'Star Gazer'** ■ Vigorous Division VII lily. In midseason, bears racemes of large, unscented, star-shaped red flowers with spreading tepals, recurved at the tips and marked with darker spots.

Lilium x *testaceum*

Good in a container and for forcing. ↕3–5ft (1–1.5m). Zone 4.

***L.* 'Sterling Star'** ■ Vigorous Division I lily. In midseason, bears short racemes of large, faintly scented, cup-shaped, upward-facing, off-white flowers, flushed cream and speckled brown. ↕3–4ft (1–1.2m). Zone 3.

***L.* 'Sun Ray'.** Division I lily producing umbels of medium-sized, unscented, bowl-shaped yellow flowers, with a sparse scattering of brown dots, in midseason. ↕3ft (1m). Zone 3.

L. superbum ■ (American turkscap lily). Vigorous, stem-rooting Division IX lily with rhizomatous bulbs, purple-mottled green stems, and linear-lance-shaped to elliptic leaves, 1½–4½in (3.5–11cm) long, mostly produced in dense whorls. Late in the season, bears long racemes of up to 40 unscented, pendent, recurved flowers, to 3in (8cm) across; tepals are red-flushed orange, with maroon spots, and green toward the bases. Prefers moist, acidic soil, and full sun or partial shade. ↕5–10ft (1.5–3m). E. US. Zone 4.

L. szovitsianum see *L. monadelphum.*

L. tenuifolium see *L. pumilum.*

L.* x *testaceum ■ (*L. candidum* x *L. chalcedonicum*) (Nankeen lily). Division III lily with alternate, somewhat twisted, lance-shaped leaves. In midseason, produces racemes of up to 12 scented, nodding, recurved, pale apricot-orange flowers, to 3in (8cm) across, with faint red markings in the centers and red anthers. Lime-tolerant; grow in full sun or partial shade. ↕3–5ft (1–1.5m). Garden origin. Zone 6.

***L.* 'Thunderbolt'.** Vigorous Division VI lily. In mid- and late season, bears racemes of large, fragrant, flat-faced, melon-orange flowers with darker centers and recurved tips. ↕6ft (2m). Zone 4.

***L.* 'Tiger Babies'.** Vigorous Division I lily. In early and midseason, bears racemes of medium, loosely recurved, pendent salmon-peach flowers with brownish pink reverses, heavily spotted inner tepals, and dark brown anthers. ↕3–3½ft (1–1.1m). Zone 3.

L. tigrinum see *L. lancifolium.*

***L.* 'Tinkerbell'.** Delicate Division I lily. In early midseason, bears racemes of very small, recurved, pendent lavender-pink flowers with cinnamon-red anthers. ↕24–48in (60–120cm). Zone 3.

***L.* 'Tom Pounce'** ■ Very large, flat-faced Division VII lily (Oriental). Late-season fragrant, bowl-shaped flowers are luminous clear pink, with glowing yellow midribs. ↕3-4ft (1–1.2m). Zone 3.

L. tsingtauense ■ Stem-rooting Division IX lily with hollow stems and inversely lance-shaped, hairless leaves, to 5in (13cm) long, mostly in 2 whorls. In midseason, bears loose umbels of up to 6 (sometimes up to 15) unscented, upright, shallowly trumpet-shaped, maroon-spotted, orange or orange-red flowers, 2–3in (5–8cm) across, with narrow tepals. Lime-tolerant, but best in moist, acidic soil; grow in full sun or partial shade. ↕28–39in (70–100cm). E. China, Korea. Zone 4.

***L.* 'Unique'.** Vigorous, upright Division I lily. In midseason, bears racemes of medium to large, flat-bowl-shaped, upward-facing white flowers with purple-pink tips, purplish red throats,

purplish pink outsides, and slightly recurved tepals. ↕ 3–3½ft (1–1.1m). Zone 3.
L. 'Viva'. Delicate, upright Division I lily, flowering in midseason. Produces racemes of small, recurved, red-orange flowers. ↕ 5–7ft (1.5–2.2m). Zone 3.
L. wallichianum. Stem-rooting Division IX lily with stiff green stems tinged purple and bear numerous scattered, linear to lance-shaped, deep green leaves, to 10in (25cm) long. Late in the season, bears umbels of up to 4 large, horizontal, very fragrant, trumpet-shaped, white or cream flowers, tinged yellow or green, to 8in (20cm) across. Prefers moist, acidic soil. ↕ 3–6ft (1–2m). Himalayas. Zone 7.
L. 'White Henryi'. Vigorous, upright Division VI lily. Late in the season, bears racemes of large, fragrant, flat-faced, white flowers with recurved tepal tips. May need staking. ↕ to 8ft (2.5m). Zone 4.
L. wigginsii. Stem-rooting Division IX lily with hairless stems and linear-lance-shaped leaves, to 9in (23cm) long, that are scattered and in 2–4 whorls roughly halfway up the stems. In midsummer, produces few-flowered racemes of unscented, pendent, recurved, deep yellow flowers, 3in (8cm) across, with purple spots. Needs moist, acidic soil and partial shade. ↕ 3–4ft (0.9–1.2m). W. US. Zone 6.
L. 'Yellow Blaze'. Moderately vigorous Division I lily producing umbels of medium-sized, unscented, bowl-shaped, upward-facing, bright yellow flowers with red-brown spots, in late midseason. ↕ 4–5ft (1.2–1.5m). Zone 3.

▷ ***Limnanthemum nymphoides*** see *Nymphoides peltata*

LIMNANTHES

Poached-egg plant

LIMNANTHACEAE

Genus of about 17 species of low-growing annuals from moist habitats in W. US. They have 2-pinnatifid, bright green leaves, and produce cup-shaped, 5-petaled flowers from summer to autumn. *L. douglasii*, the only species usually cultivated, is suitable for a rock garden and as path edging. It self-seeds freely. The nectar-rich flowers are attractive to bees and hoverflies.
• **CULTIVATION** Grow in fertile, moist but well-drained soil in full sun.
• **PROPAGATION** Sow seed *in situ* in spring or autumn. Protect autumn sowings with a loose, dry winter mulch where marginally hardy.
• **PESTS AND DISEASES** Infrequent.

Limnanthes douglasii

L. douglasii ■ (Meadow foam, Poached-egg plant). Slender-stemmed, erect to spreading annual with 2-pinnatifid, finely toothed, fleshy, glossy, bright yellow-green leaves, 2–5in (5–13cm) long. Numerous shallowly cup-shaped, fragrant, yellow-centered white flowers, to 1in (2.5cm) across, are produced from summer to autumn. ↕↔ to 6in (15cm) or more. Oregon, California.

LIMNOCHARIS

LIMNOCHARITACEAE

Genus of 2 species of evergreen and deciduous aquatic annuals and perennials, found in the shallow margins of tropical pools in S.E. Asia, South America, and the West Indies. They produce rosettes of lance-shaped to ovate leaves, and umbels of saucer-shaped yellow flowers. In areas where temperatures fall below 50°F (10°C), grow in an indoor pool. In mild, temperate areas, use for temporary summer planting around an outdoor pool; in warmer climates, grow permanently outdoors. They self-seed freely, the stems that bear the seed capsules bending over to water level, where each produces another shoot.
• **CULTIVATION** Under glass, grow in containers of heavy loam at the margins of a pool, in slightly acidic water, at 68–77°F (20–25°C), in bright filtered light. Outdoors, grow in deep, acidic, permanently wet soil in full sun. See also pp.52–53.
• **PROPAGATION** Scatter seed on the water surface as soon as ripe. Divide in summer.
• **PESTS AND DISEASES** Infrequent.

L. flava (Velvet leaf). Evergreen, marginal aquatic perennial with upright, long-stalked, lance-shaped to ovate leaves, to 8in (20cm) long, with heart-shaped bases. Umbels of 2–12 saucer-shaped yellow flowers, 1in (2.5cm) across, with off-white margins, are borne sporadically during summer. ↕↔ 24in (60cm). Tropical South America, West Indies. ❄ (min. 50°F/10°C)

LIMONIUM

Sea lavender, Statice

PLUMBAGINACEAE

Genus of 150 species of annuals, biennials, and deciduous and evergreen perennials and subshrubs from coasts, salt marshes, and deserts worldwide. Simple, entire or pinnatifid, tapering leaves, often appearing almost stalkless, are mostly borne in basal rosettes. Spikelets composed of small, stalkless, papery flowers and bracts are borne in more or less one-sided, corymb-like panicles in summer and autumn; the calyces are tubular, and the corollas have 5-lobed petals joined only at the bases. The calyces are usually a different color from the corollas, and persist after the petals have fallen. Long-flowering plants, they are suitable for a sunny herbaceous or annual border and for naturalizing. They are also good for cutting and drying. The larger perennials grow well in coastal sites; the dwarf species are effective in a trough or rock garden, the less hardy ones being suitable for an alpine house.
• **CULTIVATION** Outdoors, grow in preferably sandy, well-drained soil in full sun. Large perennials tolerate dry, stony soil. Protect dwarf species from winter moisture. In an alpine house, grow in a mix composed of equal parts soil-based potting mix and grit.
• **PROPAGATION** Sow seed in early spring: sow perennials in containers outdoors and annuals at 55–64°F (13–18°C). Divide perennials in spring.
• **PESTS AND DISEASES** Rust, leaf and flower spots, gray mold, Southern blight, and crown rot are common.

***L. aureum* 'Supernova'.** Erect perennial, often grown as an annual, with narrowly spoon- to lance-shaped, mostly basal, gray-green leaves, ½–2in (1–5cm) long, tapering gradually to leaf stalks. In summer, stiff, branched stems bear panicles of small, terminal spikelets, each with tiny, funnel-shaped, orange-yellow flowers, to ¼in (6mm) long, enclosed in hairy white, papery calyces. Good for cut flowers. ↕ to 12in (30cm), ↔ to 9in (23cm). Zone 4.
L. bellidifolium, syn. *L. reticulata, Statice bellidifolia.* Compact, dome-forming, evergreen, woody-based perennial with spoon-shaped, dark green leaves, to 2in (5cm) long. Open panicles of dense spikelets that consist of tiny, trumpet-shaped, pale violet or blue-violet flowers, ¼in (6mm) long, with white, papery calyces, are borne on wiry, branched stems in early summer. Suitable for a rock garden, trough, or alpine house. ↕↔ to 6in (15cm). Coasts from E. England to the Mediterranean and the Black Sea. Zone 7.
L. latifolium ■ syn. *L. platyphyllum* (Sea lavender). Rosette-forming perennial with elliptic to spoon-shaped, mid- to dark green leaves, usually to 12in (30cm) long, occasionally to 24in (60cm). In late summer, branched, wiry stems bear panicles of spikelets that consist of shortly tubular, deep lavender-blue flowers, ¼in (6mm) long, with white calyces. ↕ 24in (60cm) or more, ↔ 18in (45cm). E. Bulgaria to S.E. Russia. Zone 4. **'Blue Cloud'** bears mauve flowers, ¼in (6mm) across. **'Violetta'** produces deep violet flowers.
L. minutum, syn. *Statice minuta.* Woody-based, evergreen perennial with cushion-like rosettes of spoon-shaped, dark green leaves, to ½in (1.5cm) long, with incurved margins. In early summer, short, slightly woody, branched stems bear panicles of spikelets with 1–4 tiny purple flowers, ¼in (6mm) long. ↕ 4in (10cm), ↔ 6in (15cm). S.E. France. Zone 8.
L. platyphyllum see. *L. latifolium.*
L. reticulata see. *L. bellidifolium.*
L. sinuatum (Statice). Erect, densely hairy perennial, usually grown as an annual, with basal rosettes of oblong to lance-shaped, deeply lobed, wavy-margined, dark green leaves, 6in (15cm) long. In summer and early autumn, stiff, branched, winged, slightly leafy, bright green stems bear

Limonium sinuatum California Series 'Iceberg'

Limonium latifolium

Limonium sinuatum Forever Series 'Forever Gold'

panicles of clustered spikelets that consist of tiny, funnel-shaped, pink, white, or blue flowers, ⅜–½in (0.9–1.5cm) long, enclosed in hairy, white or pale violet calyces. Good for fresh and dried cut flowers. ↕ to 16in (40cm), ↔ 12in (30cm). Mediterranean. Zone 8. **'Art Shades'** produces flowers in orange, salmon-pink, yellow, rose-pink, red, carmine-red, blue, creamy white, or lavender-blue. **California Series** cultivars have 8 strongly toned color forms, each coming true from seed, from the clear white flowers of **'Iceberg'** ■ to the rich, deep rose flowers of **'American Beauty'**. **Compindi Series** cultivars bear dense flowerheads on strong stems in shades of deep and light blue and rose; ↕ 20in (50cm). Cultivars of **Forever Series** produce large, tightly packed flower spikes in a mixture of 6 or 7 colors, including blue, pink, and yellow; **'Forever Gold'** ■ has yellow flowers; ↕ to 24in (60cm). **Fortress Series** ■ cultivars are freely branched, and bear flowers in about 6 vivid shades, including bright blues, pastels, and unusual apricot-yellows; ↕ to 24in (60cm). Cultivars of **Petite Bouquet Series** are very dwarf, with tightly bunched spikelets in blue, purple, deep salmon-pink, pure white, creamy white, lemon-yellow, or golden yellow; ↕ to 12in (30cm). **'Soireé Series'** cultivars have strong stems and bear richly colored flowers in yellow and blue; ↕ to 30in (75cm). **Sunburst Series** cultivars have flowers in warm colors, including orange-peach, apricot-yellow, and rose-red; good for cutting; ↕ to 30in (75cm).

L. spicatum see *Psylliostachys spicata.*

L. suworowii see *Psylliostachys suworowii.*

L. tataricum see *Goniolimon tataricum.*

L. tetragonum. Erect biennial with basal rosettes of narrowly spoon-shaped to oblong, leathery leaves, 3–6in (8–15cm) long. In autumn, stiff, branched stems bear panicles of small, terminal spikelets that consist of tiny, funnel-shaped pink flowers, ⅛–¼in (4–6mm) long, with white-hairy calyces. Good for cut flowers. ↕ 18in (45cm), ↔ 12in (30cm). China, Korea, Japan. Zone 7b. **'Confetti'** produces lemon-yellow flowers. **'Stardust'** is very tolerant of adverse weather, and bears up to 30 flowering stems per plant; ↕ to 24in (60cm).

Limonium sinuatum Fortress Series

LINANTHUS

POLEMONIACEAE

Genus of about 35 species of annuals and perennials, usually found in sandy and gravelly sites in grassland or scrub in W. US, Mexico, and Chile. They have branched stems with alternate or opposite leaves, which are sometimes simple, but usually pinnately or palmately lobed, or fully divided, with linear segments. Bell- or funnel-shaped, white, blue, lilac, pink, or yellow flowers are borne singly or in loose cymes or dense heads, from spring to summer. Grow the perennial species in a rock garden; the annuals are suitable for an annual border or a wild garden.

• **CULTIVATION** Grow in any light, well-drained soil in full sun.

• **PROPAGATION** Sow seed *in situ*: perennial species in autumn, annuals in spring. Take stem-tip cuttings of *L. nuttallii* in early summer.

• **PESTS AND DISEASES** Rust and leaf spot sometimes occur.

L. dianthiflorus (Ground pink). Erect, slender, branching, downy annual with mostly opposite, narrowly linear leaves, ½–¾in (1–2cm) long. Funnel-shaped then spreading, yellow-throated, white, pink, or lilac-blue flowers, to 1in (2.5cm) across, the petals lobed, toothed, and spotted at the bases, are borne singly or in short, few-flowered, leafy cymes from spring to summer. ↕ 2–5in (5–13cm), ↔ to 2in (5cm). S. California to Mexico (Baja California).

L. grandiflorus (Mountain phlox). Erect, slender, branching, downy to almost smooth annual with alternate or opposite, palmately lobed leaves, to 4in (10cm) long, with 5–11 linear lobes, ½–1¼in (1–3cm) long. From spring to summer, bears dense heads of funnel-shaped then spreading, lavender-pink, lilac, or white flowers, to 1¼in (3cm) across, the petals lobed, toothed, and flecked with white. Good for cut flowers. ↕ 12–20in (30–50cm), ↔ to 9in (23cm). S. California.

L. nuttallii. Compact, bushy perennial with opposite, palmately lobed, pale green leaves, to 3in (8cm) long, with 5–9 pointed, linear lobes, to ½in (1.5cm) long, on densely branched stems. In early summer, bears abundant cymes of funnel-shaped to salverform white flowers, to ½in (1.5cm) across, with spreading lobes. ↕ to 6in (15cm), ↔ to 8in (20cm). Washington to California. ❀ (min. 41°F/5°C)

LINARIA

Toadflax

SCROPHULARIACEAE

Genus of approximately 100 species of annuals, biennials, and herbaceous perennials from dry, sunny habitats, including scree, in temperate regions of the N. hemisphere, especially the Mediterranean. They have erect, sometimes trailing, branched stems, with simple, ovate or linear to lance-shaped, stalkless, often gray-green leaves, the lower ones usually whorled or opposite, the upper more or less alternate. They are grown for their irregular, 2-lipped, spurred, white, pink, red, purple, orange, or yellow flowers, resembling snapdragons (*Antirrhinum*), which are borne in terminal racemes from spring to autumn. The taller toadflaxes are useful for a herbaceous border, or for naturalizing in stony soil or a gravel garden. The smaller, alpine species are suitable for a rock garden, scree bed, or wall crevice. Where not hardy, grow in a cool greenhouse.

• **CULTIVATION** Grow in moderately fertile, light, well-drained, preferably sandy soil, in full sun.

• **PROPAGATION** Sow seed of annuals *in situ* in early spring; they self-seed freely. Sow seed of perennials in containers in a cold frame in early spring and plant out with care. Divide perennials, or take basal softwood cuttings, in spring.

• **PESTS AND DISEASES** Aphids, flea beetles, downy mildew, white smut, and anthracnose occur.

L. alpina ■ (Alpine toadflax). Trailing, short-lived perennial with linear-lance-shaped, blue-green leaves, ¼–½in (0.5–1.5cm) long, the lower leaves whorled, the upper ones alternate. Throughout summer, produces 3- to 15-flowered racemes of 2-lipped, bi-colored, violet and deep yellow flowers, ½–1in (1.5–2.5cm) long, sometimes entirely violet, pink, or yellowish white, with spurs ⅜–½in (8–10mm) long. ↕ 3in (8cm), ↔ to 6in (15cm). C. and S. Europe. Zone 4. **'Alba'** has white flowers. **'Rosea'** bears rose-pink flowers with orange-yellow lower lips.

L. dalmatica see *L. genistifolia* subsp. *dalmatica.*

L. × dominii (*L. purpurea* × *L. repens*). Erect to spreading, branching perennial with opposite, simple, linear or linear-lance-shaped, mid-green leaves, ½–2in (1–5cm) long, the upper leaves sometimes whorled. From early summer to midautumn, produces branching flowerheads of tubular, 2-lipped, pale lilac to purplish violet flowers, ⅜–½in (0.8–1.5cm) long, with spurs to ¼in (6mm) long. ↕ to 3ft (1m), ↔ 24in (60cm). Europe. Zone 6. **'Yuppie Surprise'** produces pink-lilac flowers; ↕ to 3ft (1m).

L. genistifolia. Upright, branching perennial with alternate, semi-erect, linear to ovate, pointed, mid-green leaves, 3½–7in (9–18cm) long. In summer, bears racemes of 2-lipped, lemon-yellow to orange flowers, ½–¾in (1.5–2cm) long, with spurs to 1in (2.5cm) long. ↕ 3ft (1m), ↔ 24in (60cm). Italy to Russia, Turkey. Zone 6.

Linaria alpina

subsp. *dalmatica* ■ syn. *L. dalmatica*, has shorter, ovate to lance-shaped, glaucous leaves and bears yellow flowers, ¾–2in (2–5cm) long, in loose racemes; S. Italy, Balkan Peninsula, Romania.
L. glareosum see *Chaenorhinum glareosum*.
L. maroccana. Erect, sticky-hairy annual with alternate, narrowly linear, light green leaves, to 1½in (4cm) long. In summer, bears slender, slightly lax racemes of tiny, 2-lipped, violet-purple, occasionally pink or white flowers, to ½in (1.5cm) long, the lower lips marked orange to yellow, paler at the centers. ↕ 9–18in (23–45cm), ↔ to 6in (15cm). Morocco. **'Fairy Bouquet'** freely produces flowers, to ¾in (2cm) long, in yellow, rose-pink, salmon-pink, orange, carmine, lavender, and white; ↕ to 9in (23cm). **'Northern Lights'** ■ occurs in the same colors as 'Fairy Bouquet' but is longer-flowering; ↕ to 24in (60cm). **'White Pearl'** has pure white flowers, to ¾in (2cm) long; ↕ to 9in (23cm).
L. purpurea. Erect, slender perennial with linear, mid-green leaves, ¾–2½in (2–6cm) long, the lower whorled, the upper alternate. From early summer to early autumn, 2-lipped, violet-purple flowers, ½in (1.5cm) long, with curved spurs to ¼in (6mm) long, are produced in long, slender, dense racemes. Self-seeds freely. ↕ to 36in (90cm), ↔ 12in (30cm). S. Europe. Zone 5. **'Canon J. Went'** ■ syn. 'Canon Went', bears pale pink flowers. Self-seeds true if isolated from the species. **'Springside White'**, syn. 'Radcliffe Innocence', has white flowers.
L. reticulata (Purple-net toadflax). Erect annual with whorls of linear, blue-green leaves, to ½in (1.5cm) long, deeply channeled at the centers. In late spring and summer, bears short, dense, tapering racemes of 2-lipped, downy, deep purple flowers, to ½in (1.5cm) long, finely veined yellow, each with a large, purple-veined, copper-orange or yellow mark on the lower lip, and a spur ¼–⅜in (5–8mm) long. Often confused with *L. aeruginea* in gardens. ↕ 24–48in (0.6–1.2m), ↔ to 9in (23cm). N. Africa. **'Aureo-purpurea'** has dark, rich purple flowers, each with a purple-veined, orange or yellow mark on the lower lip. **'Crown Jewels'** has maroon-red, orange, red, or golden yellow flowers; ↕ to 9in (23cm). **'Flamenco'** has purple, maroon-red, red, golden yellow, or orange, often bicolored flowers, covered in a fine network of dark purple veins; good for cut flowers.
L. triornithophora (Three birds flying). Erect perennial bearing whorls of lance-shaped to ovate-lance-shaped, mid-green leaves, 1–3in (2.5–8cm) long. From early or midsummer to early autumn, produces loose racemes of 2-lipped, purple-and-yellow flowers, 2–3in (5–8cm) long, usually in whorls of 3, with brownish purple spurs, ½–1in (1.5–2.5cm) long. ↕ 36in (90cm) or more, ↔ 24in (60cm). N. and C. Portugal, W. Spain. Zone 7b.
***L. tristis* 'Toubkal'.** Mound-forming perennial with decumbent stems bearing linear to oblong-lance-shaped, blue-green leaves, ½–1½in (1–4cm) long, the lower leaves in whorls, the upper alternate. In summer, bears racemes of 2-lipped, yellow-green flowers, 1in (2.5cm) long, each with a brown-purple mark on the lower lip and a spur ½in (1.5cm) long. Self-sterile. ↕ 3in (8cm), ↔ to 6in (15cm). Zone 8.
L. vulgaris (Butter and eggs, Toadflax). Erect perennial, spreading by runners, with stiff, branched or unbranched stems bearing linear to narrowly elliptic, pale green leaves, ¾–2½in (2–6cm) long. From late spring to midautumn, bears pale yellow flowers, to 1¾in (4.5cm) long, with spurs ½in (1.5cm) long, in dense racemes. Self-seeds freely. ↕ 12–36in (30–90cm), ↔ 12in (30cm). Europe; widely naturalized in North America. Zone 4.

Linaria maroccana 'Northern Lights'

Linaria genistifolia subsp. *dalmatica*

Linaria purpurea 'Canon J. Went'

LINDELOFIA

BORAGINACEAE

Genus of about 12 species of clump-forming, hairy perennials, sometimes with short rhizomes, found on dry, stony slopes or in scrub from C. Asia to the Himalayas. They have lance-shaped, long-stalked basal leaves and alternate, ovate to oblong-lance-shaped, stalkless stem leaves. From spring to autumn, tubular, 2-lipped, brilliant blue to purple flowers, with 5 spreading lobes, are borne in terminal or axillary, one-sided cymes. Suitable for a sunny herbaceous border, or for naturalizing on a dry bank.
• **CULTIVATION** Grow in moderately fertile, well-drained soil in full sun.
• **PROPAGATION** Sow seed in containers outdoors in spring, or divide in spring.
• **PESTS AND DISEASES** Powdery mildew may be a problem.

***L. anchusiflora* of gardens** see *L. longiflora*.
L. longiflora, syn. *Cynoglossum longiflorum*, *L. anchusiflora* of gardens, *L. spectabilis*. Clump-forming, branched perennial with short rhizomes and long-stalked, lance-shaped, mid-green basal leaves, 3–10in (7–25cm) long; stem leaves are shorter, and clasp the stems. In late spring and early summer, bears deep blue, sometimes purple flowers, to ½in (1.5cm) long, with protruding stamens, in one-sided, terminal cymes. ↕↔ 24in (60cm). W. Himalayas. Zone 7b. **'Hartington White'** has gray-green leaves and bears white flowers; ↕↔ to 12in (30cm).
L. spectabilis see *L. longiflora*.

LINDERA

LAURACEAE

Genus of about 80 species of deciduous and evergreen, dioecious trees and shrubs occurring in woodland and on riverbanks in E. Asia and North America. They are cultivated for their aromatic, alternate, entire or 3-lobed leaves, which often color well in autumn on deciduous species; for their star-shaped flowers, borne in axillary umbels, rarely singly, early in the year; and for their showy fruits, which are attractive to wildlife. Grow in a woodland garden. Grow marginally hardy species in a cool greenhouse or against a warm wall. Both sexes need to be planted together in order to bear fruits.
• **CULTIVATION** Grow in fertile, moist but well-drained, acidic soil in partial shade. Pruning group 1.

Lindera benzoin

Lindera obtusiloba

• **PROPAGATION** Sow seed in containers in a cold frame in autumn. Take greenwood cuttings in early summer.
• **PESTS AND DISEASES** Anthracnose, dieback, and rust are occasional problems.

L. benzoin ■ (Spice bush). Rounded, deciduous shrub with upright branches and obovate, aromatic, bright green leaves, to 5in (13cm) long, turning yellow in autumn. Umbels of tiny, star-shaped, greenish yellow flowers, ⅛in (3mm) across, are borne in midspring, followed by ovoid red berries on female plants. ↕↔ 10ft (3m). S.E. Canada, E. US. Zone 6.
L. obtusiloba ■ (Japanese spicebush). Spreading, deciduous shrub or small tree with ovate to rounded, entire or 3-lobed, aromatic, glossy, dark green leaves, to 5in (13cm) long, turning yellow and brownish yellow in autumn. Bears umbels of tiny, star-shaped, dark yellow flowers, ⅛in (3mm) across, in early and midspring, before the leaves, followed by spherical, glossy, red-brown berries on female plants. ↕↔ 20ft (6m). China, Korea, Japan. Zone 6b.

LINDHEIMERA
Star daisy
ASTERACEAE

Genus of 1, possibly 2 species of erect, branched, roughly hairy annuals from dry, limestone prairies in Texas. They are grown for their small, daisy-like yellow flowerheads, profusely borne in lax, long-stalked corymbs. They have alternate, ovate-lance-shaped, entire to coarsely pinnatifid leaves, which are smaller and finer on the flowering stems. Persistent bright green, bract-like leaves surround the seed heads. Grow in an informal mixed or annual border.
• **CULTIVATION** Grow in moderately fertile, light, well-drained soil in full sun.
• **PROPAGATION** Sow seed in containers in a cold frame in early spring, or *in situ* in midspring.
• **PESTS AND DISEASES** Infrequent.

L. texana ■ (Star daisy). Tall, erect annual with branching red stems. Bears ovate-lance-shaped, pinnatifid, often toothed basal leaves, 1½in (4cm) long, and smaller, entire leaves on the upper stems and flower stalks. Lax corymbs of broad-petaled, yellow-centered, golden yellow to creamy yellow flowerheads, to 1in (2.5cm) across, are borne in late spring and summer. ↕ to 24in (60cm), ↔ to 12in (30cm). Texas.

Lindheimera texana

LINNAEA
Twinflower
CAPRIFOLIACEAE

Genus of one species of slender, prostrate, mat-forming, evergreen shrub, with stems that root where they touch the soil. It is native to woodland, heaths, and tundra in N. Eurasia and North America. Cultivated for its neat foliage and bell-shaped flowers, it is suitable as a groundcover in a woodland garden or large rock garden.
• **CULTIVATION** Grow in moderately fertile, humus-rich, reliably moist, acidic soil in partial shade.

Linnaea borealis var. *americana*

• **PROPAGATION** Sow seed in containers outdoors in autumn. Take softwood cuttings in early summer. Remove rooted runners between autumn and spring and keep in pots until established.
• **PESTS AND DISEASES** Infrequent.

L. borealis. Prostrate, mat-forming shrub with opposite, oval to rounded, scalloped leaves, to ½in (1.5cm) long, glossy, dark green above, buff to pale green beneath. In summer, bears pairs of nodding, narrowly bell- or funnel-shaped, pale pink flowers, to ½in (1.5cm) long, on stalks 2in (5cm) long, from the tips of leafy sideshoots. ↕ to 3in (8cm), ↔ to 3ft (1m) or more. N. Eurasia, North America. Zone 2. **var. *americana*** ■ has rounded, lobed, mid-green leaves, 1in (2.5cm) long, and bears funnel-shaped, white or pale pink flowers, to ½in (1.5cm) long, in late spring; ↕ 4in (10cm), ↔ to 12in (30cm); North America.

LINOSPADIX
ARECACEAE

Genus of about 11 species of slender, single- or cluster-stemmed palms from rainforest and upland or coastal sands in New Guinea and Australia. Pinnate leaves are loosely clustered at the tops of the stems, and axillary, 3-petaled flowers are borne in slim, erect spikes. Where temperatures drop below 55°F (13°C), grow in a warm greenhouse. In tropical areas, grow as specimen plants.
• **CULTIVATION** Under glass, grow in soil-based potting mix in bright filtered light. Pot on or top-dress in spring. In growth, water freely and apply a balanced liquid fertilizer every month. Water moderately in winter. Outdoors, grow in moderately fertile, humus-rich, moist but well-drained, acidic soil in partial shade.
• **PROPAGATION** Sow seed at 75°F (24°C) in spring.
• **PESTS AND DISEASES** Spider mites may be troublesome under glass.

L. monostachya (Walking stick palm). Small palm with a slender, erect stem and spreading to arching, pinnate, lustrous, mid- to deep green leaves, to 3ft (1m) long, with irregularly shaped leaflets. Greenish yellow flowers are produced in initially erect, then pendent, catkin-like spikes, to 3ft (1m) long, from spring to summer. ↕ 6–10ft (2–3m), ↔ 3–6ft (1–2m). Queensland, New South Wales. ❄ (min. 55–59°F/13–15°C)

LINUM
Flax
LINACEAE

Genus of about 200 species of annuals, biennials, and semi-evergreen, evergreen, and deciduous perennials, shrubs, and subshrubs, mainly from grassland, scrub, and dry slopes in temperate areas of the N. hemisphere. They are cultivated for their terminal or axillary racemes, panicles, cymes, or corymbs of colorful, 5-petaled, funnel- to saucer-shaped flowers, which are usually blue, yellow, or white, sometimes pink or red, and are borne over long periods. The simple, mainly alternate, sometimes opposite leaves are usually hairless, and deciduous unless otherwise stated. The smaller species are suitable for a rock garden, the larger ones for a border. Grow annuals in an annual border or as fillers in a herbaceous border.
• **CULTIVATION** Grow in light, moderately fertile, humus-rich, well-drained soil (sharply drained for alpines) in full sun. Protect from winter moisture.
• **PROPAGATION** Sow seed in spring or autumn: sow annuals *in situ*, perennials and shrubs in containers in a cold frame. Take stem-tip cuttings of perennials in early summer, and semi-ripe cuttings of subshrubs and shrubs in summer.
• **PESTS AND DISEASES** Stem rot, rust, wilt, anthracnose, damping off, slugs, snails, and aphids can cause problems.

L. arboreum. Dwarf, evergreen shrub with elliptic or spoon-shaped, thick, glaucous, bluish green leaves, ¾–1½in (2–4cm) long, often in crowded rosettes. Compact, few-flowered, terminal cymes of funnel-shaped, deep yellow flowers, ¾–1¼in (2–3cm) across, are produced in succession in late spring and summer. ↕↔ to 12in (30cm). Greece (S. Aegean to Crete), W. Turkey. Zone 6b.
L. capitatum. Sturdy, rhizomatous perennial, sometimes confused with *L. flavum*, with rosettes of oblong-spoon-shaped basal leaves, and lance-shaped stem leaves, all dark green and ¾–1½in (2–4cm) long. During summer, produces compact, terminal cymes of upward-facing, funnel-shaped yellow flowers, to 1in (2.5cm) across. ↕ 16in (40cm), ↔ 10in (25cm). Balkan Peninsula, S. Italy. Zone 7.
L. flavum (Golden flax, Yellow flax). Upright, woody-based perennial with spoon- to lance-shaped, dark green leaves, ¾–1½in (2–4cm) long. Bears dense, many-branched, terminal cymes of upward-facing, funnel-shaped, golden yellow flowers, to 1in (2.5cm) across, which open in sunshine in summer. ↕ 12in (30cm), ↔ to 8in (20cm). C. and S. Europe. Zone 5. **'Compactum'** ■ is more compact, and produces bright yellow flowers; ↕↔ 6in (15cm).

Linum flavum 'Compactum'

Linum grandiflorum 'Rubrum'

***L.* 'Gemmell's Hybrid'.** Semi-evergreen, dome-forming perennial that has a woody rootstock and bears ovate, glaucous, bluish green leaves, to 2in (5cm) long. Short-stalked, broadly funnel-shaped, chrome-yellow flowers, 1¼in (3cm) across, are profusely borne in terminal cymes over long periods in summer. ↕ 6in (15cm), ↔ to 8in (20cm). Zone 6.

L. grandiflorum (Flowering flax). Erect, slender, basally branching, slightly downy annual with narrowly lance-shaped to ovate-lance-shaped, gray-green leaves, to 1¼in (3cm) long. Bears saucer-shaped, clear rose-pink flowers, to 1½in (4cm) across, with darker eyes, in loose, terminal panicles in summer. ↕ 16–30in (40–75cm), ↔ 6in (15cm). N. Africa. **'Bright Eyes'** produces ivory-white flowers, to 2in (5cm) across, with brownish red eyes; ↕ to 18in (45cm). **'Caeruleum'** produces blue-purple flowers. **'Rubrum'** ▣ produces brilliant crimson-red flowers; ↕ to 18in (45cm).

L. narbonense. Clump-forming, short-lived perennial with wiry stems that bear erect, narrowly lance-shaped, pointed, glaucous, mid-green leaves, to ¾in (2cm) long. Few-flowered, terminal cymes of saucer-shaped, white-eyed, rich blue flowers, 1¼–1½in (3–4cm) across, individually fading by afternoon, are produced continuously in early and midsummer. ↕ 12–24in (30–60cm), ↔ 18in (45cm). W. and C. Mediterranean. Zone 7b. **'Heavenly Blue'** bears marine-blue flowers with white eyes, continuously throughout summer; ↕ 18in (45cm).

Linum perenne

L. perenne ▣ (Perennial flax). Variable, clump-forming perennial, similar to *L. narbonense*, with slender stems bearing narrow, linear to lance-shaped, glaucous, bluish green leaves, to 1in (2.5cm) long. Terminal panicles of wide, funnel-shaped, clear blue flowers, ¾–1¼in (2–3cm) across, individually fading by afternoon, are produced continuously in early and midsummer. ↕ 4–24in (10–60cm), ↔ 12in (30cm). Europe to C. Asia. Zone 5. **'Blau Saphir'**, syn. 'Blue Sapphire', bears sky-blue flowers; ↕ to 12in (30cm).

L. salsoloides see *L. suffruticosum* subsp. *salsoloides*.

***L. suffruticosum* subsp. *salsoloides*,** syn. *L. salsoloides*. Low-cushion-forming, woody-based perennial with branching stems bearing narrowly linear, grayish green leaves, to 1¾in (4.5cm) long. Loose, terminal cymes of saucer-shaped, pearl-white flowers, 1¼in (3cm) across, sometimes faintly veined purple, are produced in succession during summer. ↕ 4in (10cm), ↔ to 6in (15cm). Spain to N. Italy. Zone 7b.

▷ ***Lippia citriodora*** see *Aloysia triphylla*

LIQUIDAMBAR

Sweetgum

HAMAMELIDACEAE

Genus of 4 species of deciduous, monoecious trees occurring in moist woodland in E. and S.W. Asia, North America, and Mexico. They are cultivated particularly for their attractive foliage, which colors well in autumn, and for their upright but open habit. The maple-like leaves are alternate and palmately 3- to 7-lobed. Inconspicuous, yellow-green flowers are produced in rounded heads in late spring; the female flowers are followed by spiky, spherical fruit clusters. Sweetgums are excellent as part of a woodland planting, as street trees, or as specimen trees.

• **CULTIVATION** Grow in moderately fertile, preferably acidic or neutral, moist but well-drained soil, in full sun for best autumn color, or partial shade. Tolerates alkaline soil. Pruning group 1.

• **PROPAGATION** Sow seed in containers in a cold frame in autumn. Take greenwood cuttings in summer.

• **PESTS AND DISEASES** Leaf spot, bleeding canker, butt rot, wood rot, webworm, tent caterpillar, weevils, and borers can be problems.

Liquidambar orientalis

Liquidambar styraciflua (inset: leaf and fruit detail)

***L. formosana*,** syn. *L. formosana* var. *monticola*. Broadly conical tree with palmately 3-lobed leaves, to 5in (13cm) across, purple when young, turning dark green, then orange, red, and purple in autumn. ↕ 40ft (12m), ↔ 30ft (10m). China, Taiwan. Zone 7b.

L. orientalis ▣ (Oriental sweetgum). Small, slow-growing, bushy tree with palmately 5-lobed, mid-green leaves, to 3–4in (7–10cm) across, turning yellow and orange in autumn. ↕ 20ft (6m), ↔ 12ft (4m). S.W. Asia. Zone 7b.

L. styraciflua ▣ (Sweetgum). Broadly conical tree with young shoots that often have corky wings. Palmately 5- or 7-lobed, glossy, mid-green leaves, to 6in (15cm) across, turn orange, red, and purple in autumn. ↕ 80ft (25m), ↔ 40ft (12m). E. US, Mexico. Zone 6. **'Burgundy'** has dark red-purple autumn color. **'Festival'** is more narrow than the species, and turns a wider range of colors in autumn, including pink and peach; ↕ 60ft (18m). **'Golden Treasure'** ▣ is slow-growing, with mid-green leaves margined dark yellow, becoming yellow-margined red-purple in autumn; ↕ 30ft (10m), ↔ 20ft (6m). **'Gumball'** is a rounded, dense shrub; ↕ 10–15ft (3–5m). **'Moonbeam'** is slow-growing, with creamy yellow leaves turning red, yellow, and purple in autumn; ↕ 30ft (10m), ↔ 20ft (6m). **'Palo Alto'** has orange-red autumn color. **'Rotundiloba'** is narrowly pyramidal, with rounded-lobed, shiny, dark green leaves that turn yellow to dark burgundy in autumn. Does not bear fruit. **'Variegata'** has leaves striped and mottled yellow; ↕ 50ft (15m), ↔ 25ft (8m). **'Worplesdon'** produces deeply lobed leaves that turn orange and yellow in autumn.

Liquidambar styraciflua 'Golden Treasure'

LIRIODENDRON

Tulip tree

MAGNOLIACEAE

Genus of 2 species of deciduous trees from woodland in China, Vietnam, and North America. They are cultivated for their stately habit and curiously shaped, alternate leaves, which turn yellow in autumn. The solitary, cup-shaped flowers, inconspicuous from a distance, add interest in summer, but are not produced on young plants; they are followed by cone-like fruits. Excellent grown as specimen trees.

Liriodendron tulipifera

• **CULTIVATION** Grow in moderately fertile, preferably slightly acidic, moist but well-drained soil in full sun or partial shade. Pruning group 1.
• **PROPAGATION** Sow seed in containers in a cold frame in autumn. Graft in early spring, or bud in late summer.
• **PESTS AND DISEASES** Prone to borers, weevils, leaf miners, scale insects, aphids, sooty mold, and mealybugs. Powdery mildew, anthracnose, butt rot, dieback, lesion nematode, and wilt also occur.

L. chinense (Chinese tulip tree). Vigorous, broadly columnar, deciduous tree with saddle-shaped, dark green leaves, to 6in (15cm) long; the leaves are squarish, and indistinctly lobed at the tips, hollowed at the bases, with a pointed lobe at each side. Bears cup-shaped green flowers, 1½in (4cm) long, with yellow veins, in early summer. ↕ 80ft (25m), ↔ 40ft (12m). China, Vietnam. Zone 7b.
L. tulipifera ▣ (Tulip tree). Vigorous, broadly columnar to conical, deciduous tree with saddle-shaped, bright green leaves, to 6in (15cm) long; the leaves are squarish, and lobed at the tips, hollowed at the bases, with a pointed lobe at each side. Cup-shaped, pale green flowers, 2½in (6cm) long, orange-marked at the bases, are produced in early summer. ↕ 100ft (30m), ↔ 50ft (15m). E. North America. Zone 5b. **'Aureomarginatum'** ▣ has leaves with broad, golden yellow margins; ↕ 70ft (20m), ↔ 30ft (10m). **'Fastigiatum'** is narrowly conical, with upright branches; ↕ 70ft (20m), ↔ 25ft (8m).

Liriodendron tulipifera 'Aureomarginatum'

LIRIOPE

Lilyturf

LILIACEAE

Genus of 5 or 6 species of tufted, rhizomatous and tuberous, evergreen and semi-evergreen perennials, found in usually acidic woodland habitats in China, Vietnam, Taiwan, and Japan. They have arching, linear, grass-like, radical leaves, forming dense clumps or mats. Small, ovoid to spherical flowers, opening only slightly, are clustered in short, dense spikes or racemes, and are followed by black berries. Grow in a border or as a groundcover.
• **CULTIVATION** Grow in light, moderately fertile, preferably acidic, moist but well-drained soil in sun to partial or full shade, sheltered from cold, drying winds. Tolerant of drought.
• **PROPAGATION** Sow seed in containers outdoors, or divide, both in spring.
• **PESTS AND DISEASES** Anthracnose, leaf spot, root rot, and slugs occur.

***L. exiliflora* 'Ariaka-janshige'**, syn. *L. exiliflora* 'Silvery Sunproof'. Clump-forming, evergreen, rhizomatous perennial with linear, mid-green leaves, to 16in (40cm) long, striped white and gold. Lax racemes of pale violet-purple flowers, to ¼in (6mm) across, are borne on violet-brown stems in late summer. ↕ 9–12in (22–30cm), ↔ 12in (30cm). Zone 7b.
***L. exiliflora* 'Silvery Sunproof'** see *L. exiliflora* 'Ariaka-janshige'.
L. graminifolia* var. *densiflora see *L. muscari*.
L. muscari, syn. *L. graminifolia* var. *densiflora*, *L. platyphylla* (Big blue lilyturf). Thick, tufted, evergreen, tuberous perennial with dense clumps of linear to strap-shaped, dark green leaves, 10–18in (25–45cm) long. From early to late autumn, purple-green stems bear dense spikes of bright violet-mauve flowers, ¼–⅜in (5–8mm) across. ↕ 12in (30cm), ↔ 18in (45cm). China, Taiwan, Japan. Zone 6. **'Big Blue'** bears violet-blue flowers; ↕ 8–10in (20–25cm). **'John Burch'** has gold-variegated foliage, and bears tall spikes of large flowers. **'Lilac Beauty'** has dark green leaves and produces late-blooming racemes of deep lilac flowers, held well above the foliage. **'Majestic'** has narrower leaves than the species, and produces tall, sometimes fused and flattened spikes of rich lavender-blue flowers. **'Monroe White'** ▣ produces numerous green-stalked racemes of white flowers, to ⅜in (9mm) across, and bears purple fruit. **'Silver Dragon'** has silver and white leaves. **'Variegata'** has cream-yellow-edged, green leaves and produces violet flowers.
L. platyphylla see *L. muscari*.
L. spicata, syn. *Ophiopogon spicatus*. Rhizomatous, semi-evergreen perennial forming a dense mat of grassy, dark green leaves, 8–16in (20–40cm) long, with tiny marginal teeth. Violet-brown stems bear racemes of pale violet to white flowers, ¼–⅜in (7–8mm) across, in late summer. ↕ 10in (25cm), ↔ 18in (45cm). China, Vietnam, Japan. Zone 6.

Liriope muscari 'Monroe White'

▷ ***Lisianthius*** see *Eustoma*

LITHOCARPUS

FAGACEAE

Genus of about 300 species of oak-like, evergreen trees and shrubs from forest and mountain slopes, mainly in E. and S.E. Asia, with one species in the W. US. Leaves are alternate, leathery, and mostly entire, but occasionally toothed. Cylindrical male and female flowers (either unisexual or bisexual) are borne in erect spikes at or near the ends of the branches, and are followed by clusters of acorns, usually closely packed on the spikes. Cultivated for their handsome foliage, they are effective both as specimen trees and in an open site in a woodland garden.
• **CULTIVATION** Grow in moderately fertile, acidic to neutral, moist but well-drained soil in full sun or partial shade. Where not hardy, shelter from cold, drying winds. Pruning group 1.
• **PROPAGATION** Sow seed in containers in a cold frame in autumn.
• **PESTS AND DISEASES** Oak wilt and powdery mildew sometimes occur.

L. densiflorus (Tanbark oak). Spreading, evergreen tree with oblong, toothed, prominently veined, leathery, dark green leaves, to 5in (13cm) long, downy at first, becoming hairless and glossy with age. In summer, produces tiny, cylindrical white flowers in upright spikes, to 4in (10cm) long, sometimes followed by solitary or paired acorns, to 1in (2.5cm) long, in autumn. ↕↔ 30ft (10m). Oregon, California. ❀ (min. 35°F/2°C)
L. henryi ▣ Slow-growing, broadly conical, evergreen tree with narrowly oblong to elliptic-oblong, tapered, entire, leathery leaves, to 10in (25cm) long, pale green at first, later dark green. Tiny white flowers are borne in upright spikes, to 6in (15cm) long, in autumn or winter. Bears clustered acorns, to 1in (2.5cm) long, in upright spikes in winter. ↕↔ 30ft (10m). China. ❀ (min. 35°F/2°C)

Lithocarpus henryi (inset: leaf detail)

L

Lithodora diffusa 'Heavenly Blue'

LITHODORA

BORAGINACEAE

Genus of about 7 species of low-growing, spreading or upright, evergreen shrubs and subshrubs, found in scrub, thickets, and woodland margins, and on mountains, from S.W. Europe to S. Greece, Turkey, and Algeria. They are cultivated for their 5-lobed, funnel-shaped, blue or white flowers, produced in leafy, terminal cymes, mainly in summer. The flowers, especially those of *L.* 'Grace Ward' and *L. rosmarinifolia*, are among the most pure and intense blues in the Boraginaceae. Leaves are linear, lance-shaped, elliptic, or obovate, and hairy. The hardier species are ideal for an open position in a rock garden or raised bed. Where temperatures fall below 23°F (-5°C), grow *Lithodora* species and cultivars in an alpine house.

- **CULTIVATION** Grow most species in well-drained, ideally alkaline to neutral soil, in full sun; *L. diffusa* 'Heavenly Blue' needs acidic, humus-rich soil. In an alpine house, grow in a mix of equal parts loam, leaf mold, and sharp sand. Pruning group 8; or 10, after flowering.
- **PROPAGATION** Take semi-ripe cuttings in summer. Remove rooted suckers of *L. oleifolia* in spring.
- **PESTS AND DISEASES** Prone to aphids and spider mites under glass.

***L. diffusa* 'Heavenly Blue'** ■ syn. *Lithospermum diffusum* 'Heavenly Blue'. Prostrate, spreading, many-branched, evergreen shrub with elliptic to narrowly oblong, deep green leaves, ½–1½in (1.5–4cm) long, hairy above and beneath. In late spring and summer, deep azure-blue flowers, ½in (1.5cm) across, are produced in terminal cymes. ↕ 6in (15cm), ↔ to 24in (60cm) or more. Zone 7.

***L.* 'Grace Ward'.** Low, trailing, many-branched, evergreen shrub with narrowly oblong, hairy, dark green leaves, ½–1½in (1.5–4cm) long. In late spring and summer, bears abundant, long-lasting, azure-blue flowers, ½in (1.5cm) across, in terminal cymes. ↕ to 3in (8cm), ↔ to 24in (60cm). Zone 7.

L. graminifolia see *Moltkia suffruticosa*.

L. x intermedia see *Moltkia* x *intermedia*.

L. oleifolia ■ syn. *Lithospermum oleifolium*. Semi-upright, loosely branched, suckering, evergreen shrub with obovate to oblong, dull, dark green leaves, ½in (1.5cm) long, silky-hairy beneath. Bears loose, terminal cymes of 3–7 sky-blue flowers, ⅜in (9mm) across, opening from pink-tinted buds in early summer. ↕ 8in (20cm), ↔ 12in (30cm) or more. E. Pyrenees. Zone 7b. **'Barker's Form'** is more vigorous, has a spreading habit, and produces pale sky-blue flowers; ↕ to 5in (13cm).

L. rosmarinifolia, syn. *Lithospermum rosmarinifolium*. Domed, tufted, evergreen subshrub with upright, branching stems and lance-shaped to linear, dark green leaves, 1–2½in (2.5–6cm) long, gray-bristly beneath. Produces loose, open, terminal cymes of gentian-blue flowers, ¾in (2cm) across, in summer. ↕ 12in (30cm), ↔ 16in (40cm). S. Italy, Algeria. ❀ (min. 35°F/2°C)

L. zahnii, syn. *Lithospermum zahnii*. Upright, many-branched, evergreen shrub with linear or narrowly oblong, leathery, dark gray-green leaves, to 1½in (4cm) long, gray-bristly beneath. Produces few-flowered, terminal cymes of blue or white flowers, ½in (1.5cm) across, in succession during summer, then intermittently until midautumn. ↕ 12in (30cm), ↔ 16in (40cm). S. Greece. ❀ (min. 35°F/2°C)

Lithodora oleifolia

Lithophragma parviflorum

LITHOPHRAGMA

Woodland star

SAXIFRAGACEAE

Genus of about 9 species of rosette-forming perennials from woodland in W. North America. They have fibrous rootstocks with basal bulbils, and kidney-shaped to rounded, palmately 3- to 5-lobed leaves, the lobes often toothed or further lobed. Simple or branched, upright stems bear racemes of small, 5-petaled flowers in late spring. Grow in a woodland or rock garden.

- **CULTIVATION** Grow in moderately fertile, humus-rich, sharply drained soil in partial or deep shade.
- **PROPAGATION** Sow seed in containers outdoors in autumn. Divide, or separate bulbils, in spring or autumn.
- **PESTS AND DISEASES** Downy mildew and rust sometimes occur.

L. parviflorum ■ (Woodland star). Clump-forming perennial producing basal bulbils and rounded, palmately 3- to 5-lobed, hairy, dark green, basal leaves, ½–1¼in (1–3cm) long. In late spring, unbranched stems produce open racemes of 4–14 nodding, white or pale pink flowers, 1¼in (3cm) across, with 3-lobed petals. ↕ 6in (15cm), ↔ to 12in (30cm). California. Zone 5.

LITHOPS

Living stones, Stone plant

AIZOACEAE

Genus of about 40 species of dwarf, almost stemless, succulent perennials occurring among rocks and pebbles in semi-desert regions of Namibia and South Africa. They have thick, soft rootstocks that produce usually inversely cone-shaped "bodies," each composed of a pair of very fleshy leaves, ¾–1¼in (2–3cm) across, with a fissure usually running along much of their lengths. On the upper surface of each leaf is a window-like, translucent panel of dots, lines, or patches. Solitary, occasionally 2 or 3, daisy-like flowers, usually ¾–1¼in (2–3cm) across, sometimes larger, emerge from each fissure, mainly from midsummer to midautumn. They are followed by small, ovoid, fleshy capsules, containing tiny seeds. In areas where temperatures drop below 54°F (12°C), grow in a warm greenhouse or as houseplants; in warmer climates, grow in a desert garden.

- **CULTIVATION** Under glass, grow in standard cactus potting mix with added leaf mold, in full light. From early summer to late autumn, water freely and apply a half-strength balanced liquid fertilizer monthly. Keep dry at other times. Outdoors, grow in moderately fertile, sharply drained soil in full sun. See also pp.48–49.
- **PROPAGATION** Sow seed at 66–75°F (19–24°C) in spring or early summer, or remove offsets in early summer.
- **PESTS AND DISEASES** Prone to soft rot.

L. aucampiae. Clump-forming succulent with pairs of reddish to sandy brown or ochre leaves forming inversely cone-shaped bodies, with darker marks on the flat upper surfaces. Yellow flowers are produced from late summer to midautumn. ↕ 1¼in (3cm), ↔ to 4in (10cm). South Africa (Northern Cape, Northern Transvaal, Eastern Transvaal). ❀ (min. 54°F/12°C)

L. bella see *L. karasmontana* subsp. *bella*.

L. dinteri ■ Clustering succulent with pairs of reddish or grayish yellow leaves forming inversely cone-shaped bodies with convex upper surfaces. Each leaf has a conspicuous panel with 5–15 red spots. Bears yellow flowers from late summer to midautumn. ↕ 1¼in (3cm), ↔ 4in (10cm). Namibia, South Africa (Northern Cape, Western Cape). ❀ (min. 54°F/12°C)

L. dorotheae ■ Clustering succulent with pairs of unequally sized, beige or buff leaves forming inversely cone-shaped bodies with almost flat or convex upper surfaces. Each leaf has a translucent gray-green or olive panel marked with red lines and dots. Yellow flowers are produced in late summer. ↕ ¾–1¼in (2–3cm), ↔ 4in (10cm). South Africa (Northern Cape). ❀ (min. 54°F/12°C)

L. hookeri see *L. turbiniformis*.

L. insularis. Solitary or clump-forming succulent with pairs of greenish brown leaves united into ovoid bodies with flat to concave upper surfaces. Each leaf has a translucent, dark green panel pitted with large red dots or lines. Bears yellow flowers, to 1½in (4cm) across, from late summer to midautumn. ↕ ½in (1.5cm), ↔ 1¼–3in (3–8cm) or more. South Africa (Western Cape, Eastern Cape). ❀ (min. 54°F/12°C)

L. julii. Variable, clump-forming succulent producing pairs of faintly red-tinged, whitish gray to dark gray leaves; they form spherical bodies with flat to slightly concave, furrowed upper surfaces and brown-marked fissures. Each leaf has dark brown to pale green panels with broad markings and red dots. White flowers are borne from late summer to midautumn. ↕ 1¼in (3cm), ↔ indefinite. Namibia, South Africa (Northern Cape, Western Cape). ❀ (min. 54°F/12°C)

L. karasmontana ■ Variable, clump-forming succulent with pairs of pale red-brown leaves forming inversely cone-shaped bodies, with dark brown markings and wrinkles on the flat to convex upper surfaces. White flowers, 1–1½in (2.5–4cm) across, are borne from late summer to midautumn. ↕ to 1½in (4cm), ↔ indefinite. Namibia, South Africa (Northern Cape, Western Cape). ❀ (min. 54°F/12°C). **subsp. *bella***, syn. *L. bella*, has yellowish brown leaves, with dull olive-green

Lithops dinteri

Lithops dorotheae

Lithops karasmontana

Lithops lesliei var. *hornii*

Lithops pseudotruncatella var. *pulmonuncula*

Lithops schwantesii

marks on the convex, uneven upper surfaces; ↕ to 1¼in (3cm).

L. kuibisensis see *L. schwantesii.*

L. lesliei. Clump-forming succulent with pairs of gray-green to buff to pale terracotta leaves, that form inversely cone-shaped bodies with convex upper surfaces. Each leaf has a pale to dark olive-green panel, with transparent dots. Yellow, rarely white flowers are borne from late summer to midautumn. ↕ to ½in (1.5cm), ↔ to 1½in (4cm). South Africa (Northern Cape, Orange Free State, Northern Transvaal, Eastern Transvaal). ❄ (min. 54°F/12°C). **var. *hornii*** ■ has light to dark brown or greenish brown leaves, the upper surfaces with tiny panels and irregular channels of opaque, dark grayish brown to reddish brown. Flowers are yellow and up to 1½in (4cm) across; ↕ to 1½in (4cm), ↔ 1½in (4cm); South Africa (Northern Cape). **var. *rubrobrunnea*** has reddish brown bodies, with greenish brown panels on flat to slightly convex upper surfaces; ↕ 1¼in (3cm), ↔ 2½–3in (6–8cm); South Africa (Northern Transvaal, Eastern Transvaal).

L. marmorata ■ Mainly solitary succulent with a pair of pale gray or beige, sometimes gray-green or lilac leaves forming an inversely cone-shaped body, with grayish green lines on the slightly convex, deeply fissured upper surface. Scented white flowers are produced from late summer to mid-autumn. ↕ 1¼in (3cm), ↔ 2in (5cm) or more. South Africa (Northern Cape). ❄ (min. 54°F/12°C)

Lithops marmorata

L. optica. Mat-forming succulent with pairs of sometimes uneven, grayish purple to gray-green leaves forming ovoid bodies, with convex, deeply fissured upper surfaces and greenish white panels. From late summer to midautumn, bears white, often pink-tipped flowers. ↕ 1¼in (3cm), ↔ indefinite. Namibia, South Africa (Northern Cape, Western Cape). ❄ (min. 54°F/12°C)

L. otzeniana. Clump-forming succulent. Pairs of grayish violet leaves form inversely cone-shaped bodies, with pale green to violet panels on the convex, deep-fissured upper surfaces. From late summer to midautumn, bears bright yellow flowers, ¾in (2cm) across. ↕ 1¼in (3cm), ↔ indefinite. South Africa (Northern Cape). ❄ (min. 54°F/12°C)

L. pseudotruncatella* var. *pulmonuncula ■ Usually solitary succulent producing a pair of unequal, brownish gray leaves that form an inversely cone-shaped body, with an indistinct panel lined and dotted with brownish green. From late summer to midautumn, produces golden yellow flowers, to 1½in (4cm) across. ↕↔ to 1¼in (3cm). Namibia, South Africa (Northern Cape, Western Cape). ❄ (min. 54°F/12°C)

L. schwantesii ■ syn. *L. kuibisensis, L. schwantesii* var. *kuibisensis.* Very variable, mat-forming succulent with pairs of leaves forming inversely cone-shaped bodies, varying from light to dark gray, to yellowish green, orange, or reddish brown, with pink margins and dark green or pinkish red dots on the flat to slightly convex, often blue-tinged upper surfaces. Bright yellow flowers are borne from late summer to midautumn. The typical form of the species (pictured) has silvery blue-gray bodies, with red or blue-gray marks on the flat upper surfaces. ↕ 1½in (4cm), ↔ 6in (15cm). Namibia, South Africa (Northern Cape, Western Cape). ❄ (min. 54°F/12°C). **var. *kuibisensis*** see *L. schwantesii.*

L. turbiniformis, syn. *L. hookeri.* Variable, clump-forming succulent bearing pairs of brown, buff, or gray leaves forming ovoid bodies with warty, flat or convex upper surfaces, each with a deeply grooved, rich brown panel. Red-tipped, straw-colored flowers, 1¼–1½in (3–4.5cm) across, are borne from late summer to midautumn. ↕ to 1in (2.5cm), ↔ 6in (15cm) or more. South Africa (Northern Cape, Eastern Cape). ❄ (min. 54°F/12°C)

L. vallis-mariae. Clump-forming succulent bearing pairs of yellowish green to bluish white leaves forming inversely cone-shaped bodies, with slightly convex or flat upper surfaces marked with a network of gray lines or dots. Produces yellow flowers, 1–1½in (2.5–4cm) across, in summer. ↕ to ¾–1½in (2–4cm), ↔ 2–4in (5–10cm). Namibia. ❄ (min. 54°F/12°C)

▷ ***Lithospermum diffusum* 'Heavenly Blue'** see *Lithodora diffusa* 'Heavenly Blue'

▷ ***Lithospermum doerfleri*** see *Moltkia doerfleri*

▷ ***Lithospermum graminifolium*** see *Moltkia suffruticosa*

▷ ***Lithospermum oleifolium*** see *Lithodora oleifolia*

▷ ***Lithospermum purpureocaeruleum*** see *Buglossoides purpurocaerulea*

▷ ***Lithospermum rosmarinifolium*** see *Lithodora rosmarinifolia*

▷ ***Lithospermum zahnii*** see *Lithodora zahnii*

▷ ***Litocarpus cordifolia*** see *Aptenia cordifolia*

▷ ***Litsea glauca*** see *Neolitsea sericea*

LITTONIA

LILIACEAE

Genus of 8 species of tuberous, perennial, tendril climbers occurring in scrub and sandy, often coastal areas in Senegal, South Africa, and the Arabian Peninsula. They are cultivated for their pendent, bell-shaped flowers, which are borne in summer. Ovate-lance-shaped to linear leaves are alternate or opposite on the upper parts of the stems, and often almost whorled on the lower parts; they taper to tendrils at the tips. Where not hardy, grow in a temperate greenhouse or conservatory. In warmer areas, grow among low shrubs.

• **CULTIVATION** Plant tubers 4–6in (10–15cm) deep in autumn or early spring. Under glass, grow in soil-based potting mix with added grit, in full light. As growth begins, water freely, then apply a half-strength balanced liquid fertilizer every 3–4 weeks. Reduce watering as the leaves fade, then keep just moist in winter. The brittle tubers resent disturbance, so pot on only when necessary. Outdoors, grow in moderately fertile, humus-rich, well-drained soil in full sun. Stems require support.

• **PROPAGATION** Sow seed at 66–75°F (19–24°C) in spring, or divide tubers with care when dormant.

• **PESTS AND DISEASES** Infrequent.

L. modesta ■ Tuberous tendril climber with slender stems bearing whorled or alternate, linear to ovate-lance-shaped, mid-green leaves, to 6in (15cm) long, with tendrils at their tips. Pendent, bell-shaped orange flowers, to 2in (5cm) long, are produced singly from the leaf axils in summer. ↕ 3–6ft (1–2m). South Africa (Northern Transvaal, Eastern Transvaal, KwaZulu/Natal, Orange Free State). ❄ (min. 46°F/8°C)

Littonia modesta

L

LIVISTONA

ARECACEAE

Genus of about 28 species of single-stemmed palms, found in habitats ranging from streambanks and swamps to woodland, rainforest, and inland gorges, in the warmer parts of Asia and Australasia. Fan-shaped leaves are borne in often dense, terminal heads, and bowl-shaped, 3-petaled flowers are produced in panicles between them. Where not hardy, grow in a cool or warm greenhouse, or as houseplants. In warmer areas, grow as specimen plants.

• **CULTIVATION** Under glass, grow in soil-based potting mix in full or bright indirect light. In the growing season, water freely and apply a balanced liquid fertilizer every month. Water sparingly in winter. Outdoors, grow in fertile, moist but well-drained soil in full sun or partial shade.

• **PROPAGATION** Sow seed at 73°F (23°C) in spring.

• **PESTS AND DISEASES** Tar spot, butt rot, and bud rot occur. Scale insects and spider mites can be problems, especially on young plants.

L. australis ■ (Australian fan palm, Cabbage palm). Large palm with an erect, robust trunk that is initially covered with a skirt of dead leaves and rough or almost prickly fibers. Long, spiny leaf stalks support longer, lustrous, deep green blades, to 5½ft (1.7m) long, divided for two-thirds of their length into many linear lobes, often arching at the tips. From spring to summer, cream flowers are borne in panicles as long as, or shorter than the leaves; they are followed by spherical, brownish red to black fruit, ¾in (2cm) across. ↕ to 80ft (25m), ↔ to 15ft (5m). Coastal forest in E. Australia. ❀ (min. 37–41°F/3–5°C)

L. chinensis ■ (Chinese fan palm). Medium-sized palm with an erect, robust trunk swollen at the base, the upper part covered with fibrous leaf bases, at least at first. Glossy, rich green leaves, to 6ft (2m) long, with shorter, spiny leaf stalks, are divided for up to two-thirds of their length into many linear, pendent segments. Cream flowers are borne in panicles to 3ft (1m) or more long, usually in summer, followed by ovoid to spherical, glossy, blue-green to gray-pink fruit, ¾–1in (2–2.5cm) across. ↕ to 40ft (12m), ↔ to 15ft (5m). S. Japan (including Ryukyu and Bonin Islands) to S. Taiwan. ❀ (min. 37–41°F/3–5°C)

L. mariae (Red fan palm). Tall palm with a slim trunk, swollen at the base, and bearing old leaf bases, at least in the upper part. Spiny leaf stalks, 6ft (2m) long, support prominently ribbed blades, 6ft (2m) long, divided to about half their length into linear, pendent lobes, initially flushed red to bronze-red, maturing to bluish green. In spring and summer, bears cream to pale yellow flowers in erect panicles, shorter than the leaves, followed by spherical, glossy black fruit, ¾in (2cm) across. ↕ to 100ft (30m), ↔ to 25ft (8m). C. Australia. ❀ (min. 55–59°F/13–15°C)

L. rotundifolia. Medium-sized to large palm with a slim trunk bearing prominent leaf scars. Spiny leaf stalks,

Livistona australis

Livistona chinensis

6ft (2m) long, support shorter, rounded, lustrous, deep green blades, divided for about two-thirds of their length into many linear, rigid, shallowly notched lobes. Cream flowers are produced in panicles shorter than the leaves, usually in summer, and are followed by spherical, scarlet fruit, ¾in (2cm) across, which ripen to black. ↕ to 80ft (25m), ↔ to 25ft (8m). Philippines, Malaysia (Sabah), Indonesia (Sulawesi, Moluccas). ❀ (min. 55–59°F/13–15°C)

LLOYDIA

LILIACEAE

Genus of approximately 12 species of bulbous perennials from damp upland meadows and screes in temperate and arctic areas of the N. hemisphere. They have narrowly linear leaves and solitary or paired, bell-shaped flowers borne in spring or summer. Grow in an alpine house, bulb frame, or open rock garden.

• **CULTIVATION** Plant bulbs 3in (8cm) deep in autumn. Grow in poor, peaty, humus-rich, moist but sharply drained soil in partial shade. In an alpine house, use a mix of 1 part loam, 1 part leaf mold or peat, and 2 parts grit.

• **PROPAGATION** Sow seed in containers in an open frame in spring.

• **PESTS AND DISEASES** Infrequent.

L. graeca see *Gagea graeca.*

L. serotina (Alp lily). Bulbous perennial with erect, thread-like, mid-green leaves, to 8in (20cm) long. In late spring and early summer, upright stems bear solitary or paired, upward-facing, bell-shaped white flowers, to ½in (1.5cm) long, with purple-red veins and pale yellow bases. ↕ 2–6in (5–15cm), PD2in (5cm). Arctic and European mountains, Himalayas, S.W. China, Rocky Mountains. Zone 4.

LOASA

LOASACEAE

Genus of about 100 species of usually bushy, occasionally spreading or twining annuals, biennials, perennials, and subshrubs from open habitats, often by roads or on gravelly slopes, in Mexico and temperate South America. They have opposite or alternate, entire to palmately lobed, sometimes 3-palmate leaves, and bear nodding, yellow, white, or red flowers, singly or in racemes. Each flower has 5 boat-shaped petals, which are inflated in appearance, and nectar scales banded in contrasting colors. Some species are covered in stinging hairs. Best grown in containers; grow alpine species in an alpine house.

• **CULTIVATION** Grow in fertile, reliably moist but well-drained soil in full sun.

• **PROPAGATION** Sow seed at 55–64°F (13–18°C) in midspring or *in situ* in late spring.

• **PESTS AND DISEASES** Infrequent.

L. triphylla* var. *volcanica. Erect, bushy to loosely twining, densely glandular-hairy annual, with shallowly to deeply 3- to 5-lobed, coarsely toothed leaves, 3–6in (7–15cm) across, becoming less lobed on the upper parts of the stems. In summer, bears open, leafy racemes of nodding, hooded white flowers, to 2in (5cm) across, each with golden yellow nectar scales, crossbanded red and white, that form a central disk with concentric rings. Covered in stinging hairs. ↕ 24–36in (60–90cm), ↔ to 12in (30cm). Ecuador.

▷ ***Lobeira macdougallii*** see *Nopalxochia macdougallii*

LOBELIA

CAMPANULACEAE

Genus of about 370 species of annuals, perennials (including some aquatics), and shrubs, found in tropical and temperate areas worldwide, especially in North, Central, and South America. Their habitats range from marshes, wet meadows, and riverbanks, to woodland, well-drained hilly and mountainous slopes, and deserts. Valued for their often brightly colored flowers, lobelias vary enormously, but all have simple, alternate, often stalkless leaves and 2-lipped, tubular flowers, each with 5 lobes, the upper 2 lobes often erect, the lower 3 often spreading and fan-like; the calyx tubes are sometimes swollen. The flowers are usually borne in terminal racemes or panicles, but may also be solitary. The Bowden Hybrids, sometimes grouped under *L.* x *speciosa*, are perennials with ovate-lance-shaped, pointed leaves, 4–6in (10–15cm) long, which are sometimes red-purple with matching stems. Their flowers, 1–1½in (2.5–4cm) across, are borne in terminal racemes, 6–8in (15–20cm) long, from midsummer to early autumn.

Perennials are effective beside water, or in a mixed or herbaceous border. Annuals are suitable for edging, or for a

Lobelia 'Bees' Flame'

Lobelia cardinalis

Lobelia erinus 'Crystal Palace'

Lobelia erinus 'Lilac Fountain'

Lobelia erinus 'Sapphire'

hanging basket or windowbox. Aquatic species are useful in a wildlife pool. The shrubby and tree-like species are seldom grown. Contact with the milky sap may irritate skin.

• CULTIVATION Grow in deep, fertile, reliably moist soil in full sun or partial shade. To improve the flowering performance of annuals, apply a balanced liquid fertilizer every 2 weeks in spring and early summer, then a nitrogen-free fertilizer every 2 weeks from midsummer onward. Protect marginally hardy perennials with a dry winter mulch. Grow aquatics in containers of acidic soil at the margins of a pool or stream.

• PROPAGATION Sow seed at 55–64°F (13–18°C): sow seed of annuals in late winter, of perennials as soon as ripe. Divide border perennials in spring, aquatics in summer. Take bud cuttings of *L. cardinalis* in midsummer.

• PESTS AND DISEASES Rust, smut, leaf spots, and slugs may be problems.

L. angulata see *Pratia angulata*.

***L.* 'Bees' Flame'** ■ Clump-forming, slightly hairy perennial with reddish purple stems and linear-lance-shaped, reddish purple leaves, to 6in (15cm) long. In mid- and late summer, bears racemes, to 18in (45cm) long, of tubular, 2-lipped, bright crimson flowers, 1½–1¾in (3.5–4.5cm) across. ↕ 30in (75cm), ↔ 12in (30cm). Zone 5.

***L.* 'Brightness'.** Bowden Hybrid with mid-green leaves, and blood-red flowers produced from midsummer to early autumn. ↕ 36in (90cm), ↔ 12in (30cm). Zone 5.

L. cardinalis ■ (Cardinal flower). Short-lived, clump-forming, semi-aquatic perennial, with short rhizomes, often reddish purple stems, and narrowly ovate to oblong-lance-shaped, toothed, often glossy, bronze-tinged, bright green leaves, to 4in (10cm) long. In summer and early autumn, bears racemes, 14in (35cm) long, of tubular, 2-lipped, brilliant scarlet-red flowers, 2in (5cm) long, with reddish purple bracts. ↕ 36in (90cm), ↔ 12in (30cm). New Brunswick to Michigan to Texas and Florida. Zone 4. **f. *alba*** has white flowers. **'Angel Song'** has salmon and cream flowers. **f. *rosea*** has pink flowers. **'Ruby Slippers'** bears dark ruby-red flowers. **'Twilight Zone'** has soft pink flowers.

Lobelia erinus Cascade Series

***L.* 'Cherry Ripe'.** Bowden Hybrid with mid-green leaves, often suffused maroon. Produces tubular, 2-lipped, cherry-red flowers in mid- and late summer. ↕ 36in (90cm), ↔ 12in (30cm). Zone 5.

***L.* 'Dark Crusader'.** Bowden Hybrid with maroon stems and leaves. Bears tubular, 2-lipped, velvety, red flowers in mid- and late summer. ↕ 24–36in (60–90cm), ↔ 12in (30cm). Zone 5.

L. dortmanna (Water lobelia). Partly submerged aquatic perennial producing hollow, almost leafless stems and a mat of rosette-forming, oblong, dark green leaves, 1¼–3in (3–8cm) long. Pendent, tubular, 2-lipped, pale blue to pale violet flowers, to ¾in (2cm) long, are borne in loose racemes, 2in (5cm) long, above the water in summer. ↕ 24in (60cm), ↔ 12in (30cm). W. Europe, North America. Zone 4.

***L. erinus* cultivars.** Low-growing, bushy, or trailing perennials, grown as annuals, with ovate to narrowly linear, or linear-obovate, toothed, mid- to dark green or bronze-flushed leaves, ½in (1.5cm) long. From summer to autumn, they bear small, loose racemes, 2in (5cm) long, of tubular, 2-lipped, blue, violet, white, pink, red, or purple flowers, to ½in (1.5cm) across, with white or yellow eyes and broad, fan-shaped lower lips. ↕ 4–9in (10–23cm), ↔ 4–6in (10–15cm). **'Alba'** is compact and has white flowers. **'Blue Moon'** is compact and produces dark violet-blue flowers. **'Cambridge Blue'** is compact and bears clear, sky-blue flowers. **Cascade Series** ■ cultivars are trailing, with carmine-red, violet-blue, blue, pink, or white flowers; ↕ 6in (15cm). **'Cobalt Blue'** is compact, with early, intensely mid-blue flowers; ↕ to 5in (13cm). **'Crystal Palace'** ■ is compact, and has dark blue flowers and dark green foliage; ↕ to 4in (10cm). **'Lilac Fountain'** ■ is trailing, and profusely bears lilac-pink flowers; ↕ 6in (15cm). **Moon Series** cultivars are early-flowering, with white, blue-and-white, or deep blue flowers. **'Mrs. Clibran'** is compact, with brilliant blue, white-eyed flowers; ↕ 4–6in (10–15cm). Cultivars of **Palace Series** have neat, blue to dark blue or white flowers, some with white eyes; ↕ to 5in (13cm). **'Pink Flamingo'** is upright and branching, with bright pink flowers. **Regatta Series** cultivars are trailing, and bear blue, pink, crimson, or white flowers over a very long season. They bloom early; ↕ to 8in (20cm). **Riviera Series** cultivars bear very early flowers in lilac-blue, sky-blue, or a mottled blue with picotee margins; ↕ 4–6in (10–15cm). **'Rosamund'** is compact, and produces white-eyed, cherry-red flowers; ↕ 4–6in (10–15cm). **'Sapphire'** ■ is trailing, with bright blue, white-eyed flowers; ↕ to 6in (15cm). **'Waverly Blue'** is compact, with sky-blue flowers. **'White Cascade'** is trailing, with pure white flowers.

L. fulgens see *L. splendens*.

***L.* x *gerardii* 'Vedrariensis'** ■ Clump-forming perennial with short rhizomes and basal rosettes of broadly lance-shaped to elliptic, dark green leaves, to 4in (10cm) long, often suffused red. Throughout summer, thick stems bear many-flowered racemes, to 18in (45cm) long, of tubular, 2-lipped, violet-purple flowers, ¾–1½in (2–4cm) across. ↕ 30–48in (75–120cm), ↔ 12in (30cm). Zone 8.

***L.* 'Illumination'.** Clump-forming perennial with short rhizomes, downy, dark red stems, and linear-lance-shaped, dark green leaves, to 6in (15cm) long. In summer, bears tubular, 2-lipped scarlet flowers, 1–1¼in (2.5–3cm) across, in one-sided racemes, to 14in (35cm) long. ↕ 36in (90cm), ↔ 12in (30cm). ❀ (min. 41°F/5°C)

L. inflata (Indian tobacco). Spreading annual with oblong, softly hairy, scalloped to toothed, mid-green leaves, to 2½in (6cm) long. From summer to autumn, bears loose racemes, to 18in (45cm) long, of tubular, 2-lipped, blue, purple, or pink-tinged flowers, to 1in (2.5cm) across. ↕ to 36in (90cm), ↔ 12in (30cm). North America.

Lobelia x *gerardii* 'Vedrariensis'

Lobelia laxiflora var. *angustifolia*

Lobelia tupa

L. laxiflora. Spreading, hairy, sub-shrubby, rhizomatous perennial with arching, red-tinted stems bearing linear-lance-shaped to elliptic, finely toothed, light green leaves, to 3in (8cm) long, with long, sharp points. In late spring and summer, bears semi-pendent, tubular, 2-lipped, red and yellow flowers, 1½in (4cm) long, usually singly, from the upper leaf axils. ↕ to 36in (90cm), ↔ 6ft (2m) or more. Mexico, Central America. ❀ (min. 41°F/5°C). **var. *angustifolia*** ■ bears linear leaves, to 3in (8cm) long; ↕ to 24in (60cm), ↔ 18in (45cm); Arizona.
L. paludosa (Swamp lobelia). Marginal aquatic perennial bearing inversely lance-shaped, bright mid-green leaves, 6–9in (15–23cm) long. In summer, bears tubular, 2-lipped, pale blue flowers, to ½in (1.5cm) long, in racemes to 12in (30cm) long. ↕ 12–48in (30–120cm), ↔ 36in (90cm). Georgia, Florida. Zone 6.
L. pedunculata see *Pratia pedunculata.*
L. perpusilla see *Pratia perpusilla.*
***L.* 'Queen Victoria'.** Clump-forming, short-lived perennial with deep purple-red stems and lance-shaped, deep purple-red leaves, 4–6in (10–15cm) long. From late summer to midautumn, produces tubular, 2-lipped scarlet flowers, 1–1½in (2.5–4cm) long, in slightly one-sided racemes, to 18in (45cm) long. ↕ 36in (90cm), ↔ 12in (30cm). Zone 4.
L. richardsonii. Bushy then trailing, evergreen perennial with pendent shoots clothed with narrowly elliptic, sparsely toothed, mid- to dark green leaves, to 2in (5cm) long. In summer and autumn, bears numerous long-stalked, tubular, 2-lipped, white-throated, bright lilac-blue flowers, to ¾in (2cm) long, singly in the leaf axils. ↕ 4in (10cm), ↔ 12in (30cm). Origin unknown. Zone 5.
L. siphilitica ■ (Blue cardinal flower). Clump-forming perennial with erect, leafy stems and ovate, oblong, or broadly lance-shaped, irregularly toothed, softly hairy, light green leaves, 4–6in (10–15cm) long. From late summer to midautumn, long-lasting, tubular, 2-lipped, bright blue flowers, 1–1½in (2.5–4cm) across, with leafy green bracts, are borne in dense racemes, 4–20in (10–50cm) long. ↕ 24–48in (60–120cm), ↔ 12in (30cm). E. US. Zone 5. **f. *albiflora*** produces white flowers.
***L. × speciosa* cultivars.** Clump-forming, slightly hairy perennials, often grown as annuals or biennials, with basal rosettes of oval to oblong-obovate, pointed, mid-green to red-flushed or ruby-red leaves, to 5in (13cm) long. From summer to autumn, they bear tubular, 2-lipped, red, pink, or mauve-blue flowers, 1¼–1½in (3–4cm) across, in erect, dense, leafy racemes, to 14in (35cm) long. ↕ 4ft (1.2m), ↔ 12in (30cm). Zone 4. Cultivars of **Compliment Series** have dark green foliage and long-stemmed, loose racemes of scarlet, deep red, or blue-purple flowers; ↕ 30in (75cm) or more, ↔ to 9in (23cm). **Fan Series** cultivars have bronze-green or dark green leaves and compact, dense racemes, branching at the bases, of narrow-petaled flowers, to 1in (2.5cm) long, in pink, deep carmine-pink, scarlet, or deep red; ↕ 20–24in (50–60cm), ↔ to 9in (23cm). **Fan Series 'Fan Scarlet'** bears scarlet-red flowers.
L. splendens, syn. *L. fulgens* (Scarlet lobelia). Clump-forming, rhizomatous perennial with narrowly lance-shaped to linear-lance-shaped, mid-green leaves, to 6in (15cm) long, sometimes flushed red-purple, on downy, dark red stems. In late summer, bears tubular, 2-lipped scarlet flowers, ¾–1½in (2–4cm) long, in one-sided racemes, to 16in (40cm) long. ↕ 36in (90cm), ↔ 12in (30cm). California, Texas, Mexico. Zone 8.
L. tupa ■ Robust, upright, clump-forming perennial with red-purple stems and ovate-lance-shaped to lance-shaped, downy, light gray-green leaves, to 12in (30cm) long. Narrowly tubular, 2-lipped, brick-red to orange-red flowers, 2½in (6cm) long, with red-purple calyces, are borne in racemes, to 18in (45cm) long, from mid- or late summer to midautumn. ↕ to 6ft (2m), ↔ 36in (90cm). Chile. ❀ (min. 35°F/2°C)
***L.* 'Will Scarlet'** ■ Bowden Hybrid with mid-green leaves, suffused maroon and tubular, 2-lipped, bright blood-red flowers, borne from midsummer to early autumn. ↕ 36in (90cm), ↔ 12in (30cm). Zone 5.

Lobelia siphilitica

Lobelia 'Will Scarlet'

▷ ***Lobivia*** see *Echinopsis*

LOBULARIA

Sweet alyssum

BRASSICACEAE

Genus of 5 species of low, mound-forming or spreading, hairy annuals and perennials from seashores, disturbed ground, and stony slopes in the Canary Islands and Mediterranean. They have narrow, linear-lance-shaped to oblong, light to mid-green leaves. In summer and early autumn, they produce cross-shaped, 4-petaled, often scented white flowers in compact, sometimes corymb-like, terminal racemes that elongate in fruit. Grown for their flowers, they are useful for the edges of a gravel drive or to fill paving cracks, and are very tolerant of maritime conditions. *L. maritima* cultivars are particularly good summer bedding plants.
• **CULTIVATION** Grow in light, moderately fertile, well-drained soil in full sun. Clip after the first flush of bloom to encourage further flowering.
• **PROPAGATION** Sow seed *in situ* in late spring. They reseed prolifically.
• **PESTS AND DISEASES** Downy mildew, slugs, flea beetles, clubroot, and white blister may be troublesome.

Lobularia maritima Easter Bonnet Series

L. maritima, syn. *Alyssum maritimum*. Freely branching, usually compact, low-growing annual with linear-lance-shaped, slightly hairy, gray-green leaves, 1¼in (3cm) long. In summer, produces tiny, cross-shaped, slightly cupped, scented, white, occasionally pale purple-pink flowers in rounded, corymb-like racemes, 1–3in (2.5–8cm) across. ↕ 2–12in (5–30cm), ↔ 8–12in (20–30cm). Mediterranean, Canary Islands. **Alice Series** cultivars are compact, with white, purple, or rose-pink flowers; ↕ 3in (8cm).
Basket Series cultivars are vigorous and spreading, in a range of rose-red, violet-blue, white, and peach-apricot; cultivated for hanging baskets or borders; ↕ 4in (10cm). **Basket Series 'Easter Basket Blend'** is a formula color mix of the Basket Series.
'Carpet of Snow' is loosely branched and ground-hugging, with white flowers; ↕ to 4in (10cm). Cultivars of **Easter Bonnet Series** ■ are very compact, bearing early, white, reddish purple, or pink flowers; ↕ 3–4in (8–10cm). **'Little Dorrit'** is loosely branched and spreading, with white flowers; ↕ to 4in (10cm). **'Navy Blue'** is very compact, with deep purple flowers; ↕ to 4in (10cm). **'New Purple'** is very compact and long-flowering, with purple flowers, shading to a lighter tone at the petal margins; ↕ to 4in (10cm). **'Rosario'** is vigorous and compact, with rose-pink flowers; ↕ 4in (10cm). **'Rosie O'Day'** is wide-spreading with rose-pink flowers. **'Royal Carpet'** has rich violet flowers. **'Snowcloth'** is spreading in habit, with white flowers. **Snow Crystals'** ■ is mound-forming and compact, and bears white flowers; ↕ to 10in (25cm). **'Wonderland Rose'** is less densely branched and more compact than 'Snowcloth', and bears rose-pink flowers; ↕ to 6in (15cm).

Lobularia maritima 'Snow Crystals'

L

LOLIUM

POACEAE

Genus of about 10 species of hermaphroditic, annual ryegrass, grown for the narrow, flat leaves. Inconspicuous yellow flowers are hidden in the foliage. These cool- to warm-season annuals and perennials are grown for lawn cover as well as for playing fields. If allowed to grow, some species can be used for pastures, hay, and for erosion control.
- **CULTIVATION** Grow in moderately fertile, well-drained, rich soil in full sun.
- **PROPAGATION** Broadcast seed. Germinates quickly in 2–4 days, for a fairly uniform lawn in about 2 weeks.
- **PESTS AND DISEASES** Red thread, brown patch. New cultivars are disease-resistant.

L. multiflorum (Italian ryegrass). Quick-sprouting, cool-season annual, forms a medium coarse-textured lawn with moderate wear resistance. Plants die in summer heat; mix seed with other species of grass for better lawn cover. Mow to ↕ 2½in (6cm). Eurasia, N. Africa. Zone 4.
L. perenne (Perennial ryegrass). Quick-sprouting, cool-season grass, grows in heavy, moist soils. Produces a fine-textured lawn with high wear tolerance, and is grown mainly for playing fields and home lawns. Eurasia. N. Africa. Zone 4.

LOISELEURIA

Alpine azalea, Trailing azalea

ERICACEAE

Genus of one species of mat-forming, evergreen shrub from high alpine and subarctic regions in Europe, Japan, and North America; cultivated for its foliage and flowers, which are borne on the stem tips. It is suitable for a rock garden or alpine house, but is difficult to grow in dry climates. It flowers sporadically when grown in containers.
- **CULTIVATION** Grow in moderately fertile, humus-rich, moist but well-drained, acidic soil in full sun. In an alpine house, use a mix of 4 parts peat or leaf mold and 1 part sharp sand.
- **PROPAGATION** Root softwood cuttings in early summer, or semi-ripe cuttings in midsummer. Layer in spring.
- **PESTS AND DISEASES** Infrequent.

L. procumbens. Prostrate shrub forming tight mats of crowded, oval to oblong, glossy, dark green leaves, to ½in (1.5cm) long. Terminal, upturned, broadly cup-shaped, rose-pink to white flowers, ¼in (6mm) across, are borne singly or in small umbels in early summer. ↕ 3in (8cm), ↔ to 12in (30cm). Europe, Japan, North America. Zone 3.

LOMANDRA

Mat rush

LOMANDRACEAE

Genus of over 50 species of tuft- or tussock-forming, rhizomatous perennials that are found in a wide range of habitats in Australia, Papua New Guinea, and New Caledonia. Mat rushes have linear, flat or cylindrical, hairy or hairless leaves. The male and female flowers, borne in spikes, racemes, or panicles, are often inconspicuous and not long-lasting. Some species are aromatic, while others have an overpowering smell. Grow for mass planting or as individual accent plants. Where they are not hardy, mat rushes can be grown in a cool greenhouse or conservatory.
- **CULTIVATION** Outdoors, grow mat rushes in any well-drained soil in full sun, or in partial shade in very hot regions. Rejuvenate old clumps by shearing or burning off the foliage. Under glass, grow in well-drained soil-based potting mix in full light. Water moderately during the growing season, sparingly in winter.
- **PROPAGATION** Sow seed at 55–64°F (13–18°C) as soon as ripe. Divide in spring.
- **PESTS AND DISEASES** Infrequent.

L. glauca (Pale mat rush). Tussock-forming perennial with linear, mainly flat, mid-green leaves, 3–8in (8–20cm) long. Cylindrical or tubular, purple-flushed yellow flowers, ¼in (6mm) long, are produced in summer. The male flowers are clustered in spikes 4–6in (10–15cm) long, and the female flowers are borne in spherical heads ½in (1.5cm) across. ↕ 8in (20cm), ↔ 14in (35cm). Australia (New South Wales). ❀ (min. 45°F/7°C)
L. longifolia ■ (Spiny-headed mat rush). Dense, tussock-forming perennial, grown for ornamentation or soil stabilization,with linear, flat or nearly flat, yellow-green to dark green leaves, 3ft (1m) long. In summer, produces cylindrical, often fragrant, yellow or cream, male and female flowers, ⅛in (3mm) long, in racemes or panicles 12–36in (30–90cm) long. ↕ 3ft (1m), ↔ 6ft (2m). E. South Australia, New South Wales, E. Tasmania. ❀ (min. 45°F/7°C)

▷ ***Lomaria gibba*** see *Blechnum gibbum*

Lomandra longifolia

LOMATIA

PROTEACEAE

Genus of approximately 12 species of evergreen trees and shrubs from moist woodland and rain forests of Australasia and South America. They have opposite or alternate, entire to pinnatifid, or pinnate to 3-pinnate leaves, and racemes of initially tubular, later star-shaped flowers, with 4 narrow, twisted lobes and prominent, curved styles. The genus name is derived from "loma," meaning fringe, because the winged seeds give a fringed appearance to the leathery fruit. Grow these plants in a woodland garden or shrub border.
- **CULTIVATION** Grow in poor to moderately fertile, moist but well-drained, acidic to neutral soil in full sun or partial shade. Shelter from cold winds. Pruning group 1.
- **PROPAGATION** Take softwood cuttings in early summer, or take semi-ripe cuttings in midsummer.
- **PESTS AND DISEASES** Infrequent.

L. ferruginea ■ Upright, bushy shrub or small tree with felted brown shoots and oblong to oval, 2-pinnate, dark green leaves, to 20in (50cm) long, the ovate-lance-shaped leaflets sometimes deeply lobed and fawn-felted beneath. In midsummer, yellow-and-red flowers, ½in (1.5cm) long, are produced in axillary racemes to 2in (5cm) long. ↕ 30ft (10m), ↔ 15ft (5m). Rainforests of Chile, Argentina. ❀ (min. 45°F/7°C)
L. silaifolia ■ Bushy shrub with upright branches bear 2- or 3-pinnate, dark green leaves, to 12in (30cm) long, composed of lance-shaped leaflets with margins rolled under. In mid- and late summer, fragrant, creamy white flowers, ½in (1.5cm) long, are produced in erect racemes or panicles, to 12in (30cm) long. ↕↔ 6ft (2m). S.E. Australia (New South Wales). ❀ (min. 45°F/7°C)
L. tinctoria (Guitar plant). Small, bushy, often suckering shrub with ovate to triangular, pinnate or 2-pinnate (rarely simple), dark green leaves, to 3in (8cm) long, deeply and finely cut into linear-lance-shaped leaflets. Fragrant, creamy white flowers, ½in (1.5cm) long, are produced in racemes to 4in (10cm) or more long, in midsummer. ↕ 3ft (1m), ↔ 5ft (1.5m). Tasmania. ❀ (min. 45°F/7°C)

Lomatia silaifolia

Lomatia ferruginea (inset: flower detail)

LOMATIUM

APIACEAE

Genus of approximately 60 species of taprooted herbaceous perennials from open areas and rock crevices in W. North America. Cultivated for their foliage and flowers, they have finely divided, pinnate to 4-pinnate, fern-like leaves, and produce compound umbels of tiny, yellow, green, purple, or white flowers in spring and summer. Suitable for a rock garden, raised bed, or for naturalizing in a wildflower garden.
• **CULTIVATION** Grow in moderately fertile, sharply drained soil in full sun.
• **PROPAGATION** Sow seed in containers in a cold frame as soon as ripe.
• **PESTS AND DISEASES** Downy mildew, rust, and a few leaf spots may be troublesome.

L. dissectum. Low-growing perennial with triangular, 2- to 4-pinnate, fresh mid-green leaves, to 6–14in (15–35cm) long, composed of oblong leaflets. Bright yellow or purple flowers are borne in rounded, compound umbels, 1¼–5in (3–13cm) across, very early in spring, as the leaves develop. ↕ 6in (15cm) in flower, to 16in (40cm) or more later, ↔ to 8in (20cm). Rocky Mountains. Zone 7b. **var. *multifidum*** has flower pedicels that are longer than the sterile flowers.

L

LOMATOPHYLLUM

LILIACEAE

Genus of about 11 species of mainly stemless, succulent perennials occurring on low, hilly terrain in Madagascar and Mauritius. They have fleshy leaves forming loose rosettes, similar to those of many *Aloe* species, and bear racemes or panicles of diurnal, bell-shaped or tubular flowers in summer. Where temperatures drop below 54°F (12°C), grow as houseplants or in a warm greenhouse; in warmer climates, grow in a shrub border or desert garden.
• **CULTIVATION** Under glass, grow in soil-based potting mix with added leaf mold and grit, in full light. From early spring to early autumn, water freely and apply a half-strength balanced liquid fertilizer every 6–8 weeks. Keep barely moist at other times. Outdoors, grow in moderately fertile, sharply drained soil in full sun. See also pp.48–49.
• **PROPAGATION** Sow seed at 66–75°F (19–24°C), or detach offsets, in spring.
• **PESTS AND DISEASES** Susceptible to scale insects.

L. citreum see *L. occidentale* var. *citreum.*
L. occidentale. Stemless or short-stemmed, succulent perennial forming rosettes of 15–20 stiff, spreading, lance-shaped, mid-green leaves, 32–39in (80–100cm) long, with recurved, toothed or sparsely spiny margins. In summer, produces dense panicles of 50 or more tubular, deep pink flowers, ¾–1¼in (2–3cm) long. ↕ to 3ft (1m), ↔ to 5ft (1.5m). W. Madagascar. ❀ (min. 54°F/12°C). **var. *citreum,*** syn. *L. citreum,* has a short stem, dark green leaves, 12in (30cm) long, and yellowish green flowers; ↕ 18–20in (45–50cm), ↔ 24in (60cm).

LONICERA

Honeysuckle

CAPRIFOLIACEAE

Genus of about 180 species of deciduous and evergreen shrubs and twining climbers, widely distributed in the N. hemisphere, where they grow in varied habitats ranging from woodland and thickets to rocky places. They are cultivated mainly for their tubular or funnel- to bell-shaped, often fragrant flowers, which are usually 2-lipped or have 5 small, spreading lobes. The leaves are borne in opposite pairs and are usually simple. Honeysuckles may be grown in a variety of situations: train climbers on a wall or fence, or into a large shrub or small tree; grow shrubs in a shrub border, or use for hedging or as a groundcover. Some species may become invasive. Where not hardy, grow in a cool greenhouse. The berries may cause mild stomach upset if ingested.
• **CULTIVATION** Grow shrubs in any well-drained soil in full sun or partial shade; grow climbers in fertile, humus-rich, moist but well-drained soil. Under glass, grow in soil-based potting mix in bright filtered light. When in growth, water freely and apply a balanced liquid fertilizer monthly; water sparingly in winter. Pruning group 2 for shrubs; group 11 for climbers (those flowering on the previous year's shoots, such as *L. periclymenum,* are best pruned back to strong young growth immediately after flowering each year). Trim hedges twice during summer.
• **PROPAGATION** Sow seed of hardy species in containers in a cold frame as soon as ripe; sow *L. hildebrandiana* at 55–64°F (13–18°C) in spring. Take semi-ripe cuttings of evergreens in summer, and greenwood or hardwood cuttings of deciduous honeysuckles in summer or autumn respectively.
• **PESTS AND DISEASES** Aphids, leaf roller, scale insects, dieback, powdery mildew, leaf spots, and blights are common.

L. × americana ▣ Vigorous, woody, deciduous, twining climber with paired, oval, dark green leaves, to 3in (8cm) long, the upper pairs united. Large whorls of tubular, 2-lipped, very fragrant yellow flowers, to 2in (5cm) long, strongly flushed red-purple, are produced in the leaf axils in summer and early autumn, followed by red berries. ↕ 22ft (7m). Garden origin. Zone 6.
L. × bella. Upright, deciduous shrub with paired, ovate, pointed, mid-green leaves, to 2in (5cm) long. Axillary pairs of tubular, 5-lobed, pink or red flowers, ½–1¼in (1.5–3cm) long, becoming yellow, are produced in summer, and are followed by red berries. ↕ 8ft (2.5m), ↔ 10ft (3m). Garden origin. Zone 2. **'Atrorosea'** produces dark pink flowers with paler margins, in late spring. **'Candida'** bears white flowers.
L. × brownii (*L. hirsuta* × *L. sempervirens*) (Scarlet trumpet honeysuckle). Deciduous or semi-evergreen, twining climber with paired, ovate, blue-green leaves, to 3in (8cm) long. Bears terminal whorls of tubular, 2-lipped, slightly fragrant, orange to red flowers, 1½in (4cm) long, in summer, sometimes followed by red berries. ↕ 12ft (4m). Garden origin. Zone 2b. **'Dropmore Scarlet'** ▣ bears long, trumpet-shaped, bright scarlet flowers over a long period. **'Fuchsioides'** has orange-scarlet flowers.
L. caprifolium (Italian woodbine). Woody, deciduous, twining climber with paired, oval to obovate, gray-green leaves, to 4in (10cm) long, the upper pairs united. Whorls of tubular, 2-lipped, very fragrant, pink-flushed, creamy white to yellow flowers, to 2in (5cm) long, are borne from the leaf axils in summer, and are followed by orange-red berries. ↕ 20ft (6m). Europe, W. Asia. Zone 6. **'Praecox'** bears creamy white flowers in late spring; they are often tinted light red, and turn yellow.
L. chaetocarpa. Upright, deciduous shrub with bristly shoots and paired, ovate to oblong, bristly, mid-green leaves, to 3in (8cm) long. In early summer, paired, sometimes solitary, funnel-shaped, 5-lobed, primrose-yellow flowers, to 1¼in (3cm) long, with large, leafy, pale green bracts, are borne in the leaf axils; the berries are red and cupped by the persistent, now red-tinted bracts. ↕↔ 6ft (2m). W. China. Zone 6.

Lonicera × *americana* (inset: flower detail)

Lonicera × *brownii* 'Dropmore Scarlet'

L. etrusca (Etruscan honeysuckle). Vigorous, woody, twining, deciduous or semi-evergreen climber with paired, oval or obovate, mid-green leaves, to 4in (10cm) long, blue-green beneath, the upper pairs united. Tubular, 2-lipped, fragrant yellow flowers, 2in (5cm) long, flushed red and darkening with age, are produced in terminal and axillary whorls from midsummer to autumn, and are followed by red berries. Grows best in full sun. ↕ 12ft (4m). Mediterranean. Zone 7b. **'Donald Waterer'** bears flowers that are red outside, becoming orange-yellow, and white inside. **'Superba'** ▣ is vigorous, and produces large clusters of cream flowers that turn orange.
L. flava (Yellow honeysuckle). Weakly twining deciduous climber with broadly elliptic, bright green leaves, 1¾–3in (4.5–8cm) long, bluish green beneath. From spring to summer, bears terminal whorls of 1–3 tubular, 2-lipped, orange-yellow flowers, 1¼in (3cm) across, followed by orange berries. ↕ to 8ft (2.5m). Oklahoma to North Carolina. Zone 5.
L. fragrantissima. Bushy, spreading, deciduous or semi-evergreen shrub with

Lonicera etrusca 'Superba'

Lonicera x *heckrottii*

paired, oval leaves, to 3in (8cm) long, dull, dark green above, blue-green beneath, with bristly margins when young. Tubular, 2-lipped, very fragrant, creamy white flowers, ½in (1.5cm) long, are produced in pairs from the leaf axils in winter and early spring. Berries are dull red. ↕ 6ft (2m), ↔ 10ft (3m). China. Zone 7b.

***L.* 'Gold Flame'** see *L.* x *heckrottii* 'Gold Flame'.

L.* x *heckrottii ■ (*L.* x *americana* x *L. sempervirens*). Deciduous or semi-evergreen, twining climber with paired, oblong to oval or elliptic, dark green leaves, to 2½in (6cm) long, blue-green beneath, with the upper pairs united. Tubular, 2-lipped, fragrant flowers, 1½in (4cm) long, pink outside, orange-yellow inside, are borne in terminal whorls during summer, and are sometimes followed by red berries. ↕ 15ft (5m). Garden origin. Zone 5. **'Gold Flame'**, syn. *L.* 'Gold Flame', is more vigorous than the species, with brighter colored flowers.

L. henryi. Vigorous, woody, evergreen, twining climber with paired, oblong-lance-shaped to oblong-ovate, tapered, glossy, dark green leaves, to 4in (10cm) long. Terminal or axillary whorls of tubular, 2-lipped, yellow-throated, purplish red flowers, to ¾in (2cm) long, are produced in early and midsummer, followed by purple-black berries. ↕ 30ft (10m). W. China. Zone 6.

L. hildebrandiana ■ (Giant Burmese honeysuckle). Very vigorous, evergreen or semi-evergreen, twining climber with paired, broadly ovate or oval, dark green leaves, to 6in (15cm) long. Tubular, 2-lipped, very fragrant, creamy white flowers, to 3–6in (8–15cm) long, aging to orange, are borne in pairs in terminal and axillary racemes in summer, and are followed by red berries. ↕ 30ft (10m) or more. China, S.E. Asia. Zone 6b.

L. involucrata (Twinberry). Dense, bushy, deciduous shrub with thick shoots and paired, ovate to oblong or lance-shaped, bright mid-green leaves, to 5in (13cm) long. Tubular, dark yellow, often red-suffused flowers, ½in (1.5cm) long, each with 5 short lobes, are borne in pairs from the leaf axils in late spring; they are surrounded by large green bracts that soon turn red, and are followed by glossy black berries. ↕ 6ft (2m), ↔ 10ft (3m). W. North America, Mexico. Zone 6b.

L. japonica (Japanese honeysuckle). Vigorous, woody, evergreen or semi-evergreen, twining climber with paired, broadly elliptic to ovate, sometimes deeply lobed, dark green leaves, to 3in (8cm) long. Tubular, 2-lipped, very fragrant, often purple-flushed, white flowers, to 1½in (4cm) long, aging to yellow, are borne in pairs from the leaf axils over a long period from spring to late summer, followed by blue-black berries. ↕ 30ft (10m). E. Asia. Zone 6. **'Aureoreticulata'** has leaves attractively veined yellow; ↕ 20ft (6m). **'Dart's World'** is a particularly hardy evergreen cultivar of bushy, spreading habit, with dark green leaves and very fragrant, strongly red-flushed white flowers that turn yellow. **'Halliana'** ■ is very vigorous (often invasive), with pure white flowers that age to dark yellow. **var. *repens*** has purple-tinged foliage, and bears white flowers heavily flushed red-purple. **var. *repens* 'Red Coral'** see 'Superba'. **'Superba'**, syn. var. *repens* 'Red Coral', has mid-green leaves, 2in (5cm) long, and bears scarlet flowers, 1½–2in (4–5cm) long.

L. korolkowii ■ Open, spreading, deciduous shrub with arching shoots and paired, ovate or oval leaves, to 1¼in (3cm) long, with long, sharp points, glaucous pale green above, glaucous blue-green beneath. In early summer, bears tubular, 2-lipped, pale rose-pink flowers, ½in (1.5cm) long, in pairs along the shoots, followed by bright red berries. ↕ 10ft (3m), ↔ 15ft (5m). Mountains of C. Asia, Afghanistan, Pakistan. Zone 2b. **var. *zabelii***, syn. *L. tatarica* 'Zabelii', has bright pink flowers.

L. ledebourii ■ Dense, bushy, deciduous shrub with thick shoots and

Lonicera korolkowii

paired, ovate-oblong, dark green leaves, to 5in (13cm) long. Funnel-shaped, 5-lobed, red-flushed, deep orange-yellow flowers, to ¾in (2cm) long, each with 2 large, persistent red bracts, are borne from the leaf axils in late spring and early summer, followed by glossy black berries. ↕ 10ft (3m), ↔ 12ft (4m). California. Zone 6.

L. maackii. Vigorous, upright, often tree-like, deciduous shrub with paired, oval-lance-shaped, tapered, dark green leaves, to 3in (8cm) long. Tubular, 2-lipped, fragrant white flowers, to ¾in (2cm) long, aging to yellow, are borne in axillary pairs along the shoots in early summer, followed by dark red berries. May become invasive. ↕↔ 15ft (5m). China, Korea, Japan. Zone 2b.

L. morrowii. Spreading, deciduous shrub with arching branches and paired, oblong or ovate to elliptic, dull mid-green leaves, to 2½in (6cm) long, purple-tinged when young. Pairs of tubular, creamy white flowers, ½in (1.5cm) long, aging to yellow, each with 5 short lobes, are borne along the shoots in late spring and early summer, followed by red berries. ↕ 6ft (2m), ↔ 10ft (3m). Japan. Zone 4.

Lonicera periclymenum 'Graham Thomas'

L. nitida (Boxleaf honeysuckle). Bushy, evergreen shrub with paired, ovate to broadly ovate leaves, to ½in (1.5cm) long, glossy, dark green above, lighter beneath. Produces pairs of tubular, creamy white flowers, to ½in (1.5cm) long, from the leaf axils in spring, followed by glossy, blue-purple berries. Good for hedging. ↕ to 11ft (3.5m), ↔ 10ft (3m). S.W. China. Zone 7. **'Baggesen's Gold'** has long, arching shoots and ovate, bright yellow leaves that burn in strong sunlight. Best in partial shade, where the foliage is chartreuse; ↕↔ 5ft (1.5m). **'Ernest Wilson'** is vigorous and spreading, with tiny, ovate, dark green leaves, ⅛–¼in (3–6mm) long; ↕ 6ft (2m). **'Yunnan'** is broad and upright, with larger leaves, ¾in (2cm) long, and with abundant flowers and berries; ↕↔ 6ft (2m).

L. periclymenum (Common honeysuckle, Woodbine). Vigorous, woody, deciduous, twining climber with paired, ovate, oval, or obovate, mid-green leaves, to 2½in (6cm) long, glaucous beneath. Bears terminal whorls of tubular, 2-lipped, very fragrant, white to yellow, often red-flushed flowers, to 2in (5cm) long, in mid- and late summer, followed by bright red berries. ↕ 22ft (7m). Europe, North Africa, Turkey, Caucasus. Zone 4b. **'Belgica'** (Early Dutch honeysuckle) has white flowers that turn yellow, and are richly streaked red outside. **'Graham Thomas'** ■ bears white flowers turning yellow, over a long period. **'Serotina'** ■ (Late Dutch honeysuckle) produces creamy white flowers streaked dark red-purple.

Lonicera hildebrandiana

Lonicera japonica 'Halliana'

Lonicera ledebourii

Lonicera periclymenum 'Serotina'

L. pileata. Dense, spreading, evergreen shrub with paired, ovate-oblong to oblong-lance-shaped, glossy, dark green leaves, to 1¼in (3cm) long. Funnel-shaped, 5-lobed, creamy white flowers, to ⅜in (9mm) long, are produced in pairs from the leaf axils in late spring, followed by violet-purple berries. Good as a groundcover. ↕ 24in (60cm), ↔ 8ft (2.5m). China. Zone 7.
***L.* x *purpusii* 'Winter Beauty'.** Rounded, deciduous or semi-evergreen shrub with red-purple shoots and paired, ovate, dark green leaves, to 3in (8cm) long. Tubular, 2-lipped, very fragrant white flowers, ¾in (2cm) long, with conspicuous yellow anthers, are borne in small, axillary clusters in winter and early spring. Berries are rarely produced. ↕ 6ft (2m), ↔ 8ft (2.5m). Zone 5.
L. rupicola* var. *syringantha see *L. syringantha.*
L. sempervirens ▣ (Coral honeysuckle, Trumpet honeysuckle). Woody, deciduous or evergreen, twining climber with paired, oval or obovate leaves, to 3in (8cm) long, dark green above, blue-green beneath, the upper pairs united. Tubular flowers, to 2in (5cm) long, with 2 short lips, rich scarlet-orange outside, yellowish orange inside, are produced in terminal whorls in summer and autumn, and are followed by bright red berries. ↕ 12ft (4m). E. and S. US. Zone 5. **f. *sulfurea*** bears yellow flowers.
L. standishii. Upright, deciduous or semi-evergreen shrub with paired, oblong-lance-shaped, bristly, dark green leaves, to 4in (10cm) long, with long, slender points. Tubular, 2-lipped, fragrant, creamy white flowers, 1¼in (3cm) long, sometimes tinged very pale pink, are produced in axillary pairs along the shoots from late autumn to

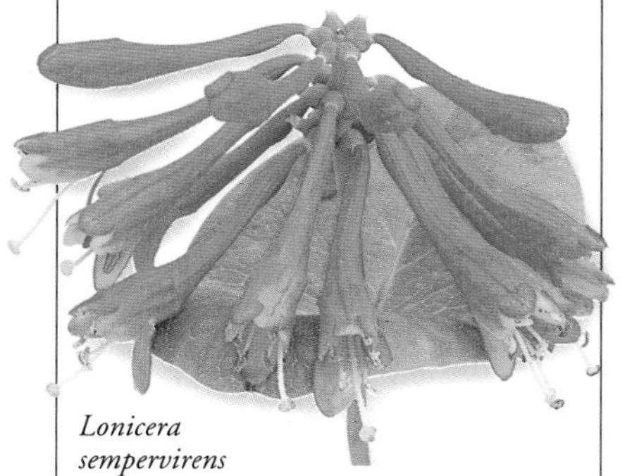
Lonicera sempervirens

Lonicera tatarica

Lonicera x *tellmanniana*

early spring, followed by red berries. ↕↔ 6ft (2m). China. Zone 6.
L. syringantha, syn. *L. rupicola* var. *syringantha.* Graceful, rounded, deciduous shrub with oblong-ovate, gray-green leaves, to 1in (2.5cm) long, usually paired, sometimes in threes. Small, tubular-bell-shaped, 5-lobed, very fragrant, lilac-pink flowers, to ½in (1.5cm) across, are produced in pairs from the leaf axils in late spring and early summer, followed by red berries. ↕ 6–10ft (2–3m), ↔ 6ft (2m). W. China, Tibet. Zone 6.
L. tatarica ▣ (Tatarian honeysuckle). Upright, bushy, deciduous shrub with paired, oblong-ovate to lance-shaped, dark green leaves, to 2½in (6cm) long, glaucous beneath. Axillary pairs of tubular, 5-lobed, white to pink or red flowers, to 1in (2.5cm) long, are profusely borne along the shoots in late spring and early summer, followed by scarlet to yellow-orange berries. May become invasive. ↕ 12ft (4m), ↔ 8ft (2.5m). S. Russia to C. Asia. Zone 2. **'Arnold Pink'** produces dark rose-pink flowers. **'Hack's Red'** bears very dark purplish red flowers. **'Zabelii'** see *L. korolkowii* var. *zabelii.*
L.* x *tellmanniana ▣ (*L. sempervirens* 'Superba' x *L. tragophylla*). Woody, deciduous, twining climber with paired, elliptic-ovate to oblong, deep green leaves, to 4in (10cm) long, blue-white beneath, the upper pairs united. Terminal whorls of tubular, 2-lipped, bright copper-orange flowers, to 2in (5cm) long, are produced from late spring to midsummer. ↕ 15ft (5m). Garden origin. Zone 4b.
L. tragophylla. Woody, deciduous, twining climber with paired, oval to oblong, mid-green leaves, to 5in (13cm) long, blue-white beneath, the upper pairs united. In mid- and late summer, long-tubed, 2-lipped, bright yellow or orange-yellow flowers, to 3in (8cm) long, red-tinted above, are produced in large, terminal whorls , followed by red berries. ↕ 20ft (6m). C. China. Zone 6b.
***L.* x *xylosteoides* 'Clavey's Dwarf'.** Slow-growing, dense, upright, rounded, deciduous shrub with paired, oval to obovate, gray-green leaves, to 2½in (6cm) long. Pairs of small, tubular, 2-lipped white flowers, ½in (1.5cm) long, are produced from the leaf axils in late spring and early summer, followed by red berries. Suitable for hedging. ↕ 5ft (1.5m), ↔ 3ft (1m). Zone 3.

Lonicera xylosteum

L. xylosteum ▣ (Fly honeysuckle). Dense, bushy, deciduous shrub with paired, ovate to obovate or oblong, gray-green leaves, to 2½in (6cm) long. Tubular, 2-lipped, creamy white flowers, to ½in (1.5cm) long, are produced in pairs along the shoots in late spring and early summer, followed by showy red, rarely yellow berries. ↕↔ 10ft (3m). Europe, Caucasus, Russia (Siberia). Zone 2.

LOPEZIA

ONAGRACEAE

Genus of 21 annuals and perennials that are native to the open fields of Central America. These plants are cultivated for their many purple-red to lilac or white, mosquito-like flowers. Use in a wild garden or, where they are not hardy, grow as houseplants or in a warm greenhouse.
• **CULTIVATION** Under glass, grow in soil-based potting mix in full light. During the growing season, water moderately and apply a balanced liquid fertilizer monthly; water sparingly in winter. Outdoors, grow in well-drained, moderately fertile soil in full sun or partial shade.
• **PROPAGATION** Sow seed *in situ* in spring or take cuttings in spring.
• **PESTS AND DISEASES** Infrequent.

L. racemosa. Variable annual or perennial with upright or ascending stems and ovate to lance-shaped, toothed or slightly toothed lower leaves, ½–3in (1.5–8cm) long, and ovate to narrowly lance-shaped, toothed or entire, mid-green upper leaves, ¼–2in (0.6–5cm) long. In summer, bears terminal racemes of numerous mosquito-like, white to lilac-tinted white, purple, or pink to red flowers, 1in (2.5cm) across, over a long period. ↕ to 5ft (1.5m), ↔ 3ft (1m). Mexico, El Salvador. ❄ (min. 45°F/7°C)

▷ ***Lophocereus schottii*** see *Pachycereus schottii*

LOPHOMYRTUS

MYRTACEAE

Genus of 2 species of evergreen shrubs or small trees, closely related to the genus *Myrtus,* occurring in coastal and lowland forest in New Zealand. They are cultivated for their flowers, foliage, and fruits. The leaves are opposite, simple, and leathery. They bear 4-petaled flowers, each with a boss of prominent stamens, singly from the upper leaf axils, followed by many-seeded, purple-black to red berries. Where marginally hardy, grow in a cool greenhouse or against a warm wall. In milder areas, plant in a shrub border.
• **CULTIVATION** Under glass, grow in soil-based potting mix in bright filtered light. During the growing season, water freely and apply a balanced liquid fertilizer monthly. Water sparingly in winter. Outdoors, grow in fertile, humus-rich, moist but well-drained soil in partial shade. Pruning group 1; may need restrictive pruning under glass.
• **PROPAGATION** Sow seed at 55–64°F (13–18°C) as soon as ripe. Root semi-

Lophomyrtus x *ralphii* 'Variegata' (inset: leaf detail)

ripe cuttings, with heels, in summer with bottom heat.
• **PESTS AND DISEASES** Spider mites may be a problem under glass.

L. bullata, syn. *Myrtus bullata.* Rounded, moderately bushy or open, large shrub or small tree with downy stems. Broadly ovate to rounded leaves, ½–1¼in (1.5–3cm) long, sometimes more, are strongly puckered or blistered between the veins, and bronze- to red-tinted when young, maturing to glossy, dark green. In summer, produces open cup-shaped white flowers, ½in (1.5cm) wide, usually followed by broadly ovoid, deep black-red berries, ¼–½in (7–10mm) long. ↕ 10–25ft (3–8m), ↔ 3–10ft (1–3m). New Zealand. ❄ (min. 45°F/7°C)
L. x ralphii (*L. bullata* x *L. obcordata*). Large, rounded, vigorous shrub or small tree, of open habit. Broadly oblong-ovate, dark green leaves, usually ½–1in (1.5–2.5cm) long, are flat or slightly blistered between the veins. Mature plants produce open cup-shaped white flowers, ½in (1.5cm) wide, in summer, followed by dark black-red berries, ⅛–⅜in (3–9mm) long. ↕ 6–15ft (2–5m), ↔ 5–8ft (1.5–2.5m). Garden origin. ❄ (min. 45°F/7°C). **'Gloriosa'** see 'Variegata'. **'Indian Chief'** has rounded, lustrous, reddish green leaves, to ½in (1.5cm) long. **'Kathryn'** has blistered leaves, flushed rich purple. **'Purpurea'** has slightly blistered, bronze-purple to deep purple-red leaves. **'Sundae'**, syn. 'Tricolor', has almost flat, rich green- and yellow-variegated leaves, with pink or bronze-red overtones, especially in sunny sites. **'Tricolor'** see 'Sundae'. **'Variegata'** ▣ syn. 'Gloriosa', *Myrtus bullata* 'Gloriosa', *Myrtus* x *ralphii* 'Variegata', has rounded, lustrous, deep green leaves, barely ½in (1.5cm) long, with creamy yellow variegation.

LOPHOSPERMUM

SCROPHULARIACEAE

Genus of 8 species of deciduous and evergreen, perennial climbers and shrubs from rocky slopes in North and Central America. They have entire or toothed, triangular to rounded leaves, and bear solitary, axillary, tubular to funnel- or trumpet-shaped, white to purple flowers. In temperate areas, grow in a cool greenhouse. In warmer areas, grow through a shrub or small tree.
• **CULTIVATION** Under glass, grow in soil-based potting mix with added sharp sand, in full light. When in growth, water moderately and apply a balanced liquid fertilizer monthly. In summer, provide ventilation and shade from full sunlight. Water sparingly in winter. Outdoors, grow in moderately fertile, ideally sandy, moist but well-drained soil in full sun.
• **PROPAGATION** Sow seed at 66–75°F (19–24°C) in spring. Root semi-ripe cuttings in late summer.
• **PESTS AND DISEASES** Infrequent.

L. erubescens ▣ syn. *Asarina erubescens, Maurandya erubescens* (Creeping gloxinia). Scandent, evergreen, perennial climber (deciduous in cool areas), often grown as an annual, with soft, woody-based stems and triangular, toothed, downy, gray-green leaves, to 3in (8cm) long, with twining leaf stalks. Bears trumpet-shaped, rose-pink flowers, 3in (8cm) long, in summer and autumn. ↕ 10ft (3m) or more. Mexico. ❄ (min. 37–41°F/3–5°C)

Lophospermum erubescens

LOPHOSTEMON

MYRTACEAE

Genus of 4–6 species of evergreen trees or tall shrubs. They occur in heavy, moist soil, frequently in rainforest or along the borders of streams, in N. and E. Australia and S. New Guinea. Leaves are simple, usually entire, and borne alternately or in whorls, often more densely toward the stem tips. The flowers have 5 spreading petals and many stamens fused into 5 separate bundles, and are produced in axillary cymes; they are followed by small, woody, cup- or top-shaped, 3-celled seed capsules. Where not hardy, grow as foliage plants in a cool or warm greenhouse. In milder areas, they are good specimen and shade trees, and are effective as a windbreak or hedge.
• **CULTIVATION** Under glass, grow in acidic potting mix with added sharp sand, in full or bright filtered light. During the growing season, water freely and apply a half-strength, balanced liquid fertilizer every month; water sparingly in winter. Outdoors, grow in poor to moderately fertile, neutral to acidic, moist but well-drained soil in full sun or partial shade. Pruning group 1; trim hedges in late summer.
• **PROPAGATION** Sow seed at 55–64°F (13–18°C) in spring. Root semi-ripe cuttings in summer with bottom heat.
• **PESTS AND DISEASES** Spider mites may be a problem under glass.

L. confertus ▣ syn. *Tristania conferta* (Brush box). Bushy, round-headed tree with lance-shaped to ovate, smooth, bright green leaves, 3–6in (7–15cm) long, usually in whorls of 3–5. Bears cymes of 3–7 star-shaped white flowers, 1–1½in (2.5–4cm) across, in spring and summer, followed by top-shaped seed capsules, ½in (1.5cm) across. ↕ 30–50ft (10–15m), or to 130ft (40m) in moist, warm climates, ↔ 10–30ft (3–10m) or more. Queensland, New South Wales. ❄ (min. 45°F/7°C)
L. lactifluus. Round-headed tree with elliptic to ovate-lance-shaped, hairless, mid-green leaves, to 6in (15cm) long, in whorls of 2 or 3. In spring and summer, bears abyndant cymes of 3–7 star-shaped white flowers, to ½in (1.5cm) across, followed by top-shaped seed capsules, ⅛–½in (3–16mm) across. ↕ to 50ft (15m), ↔ to 10ft (3m). Northern Territory. ❄ (min. 41°F/5°C)

▷ ***Lorinsaria areolata*** see *Woodwardia areolata*

Lophostemon confertus (inset: flower detail)

Loropetalum chinense 'Razzleberri'

LOROPETALUM

HAMAMELIDACEAE

Genus of 1, possibly up to 3 species of rounded, evergreen shrubs or small trees found in woodland in the Himalayas, China, and Japan. The alternate leaves are ovate or oval, mid-green and rough above, paler beneath. Clusters of fragrant, spider-like white flowers, with 4 narrow, strap-shaped petals, are borne in terminal cymes in late winter and early spring. Grow in a woodland garden or shrub border.
• **CULTIVATION** Grow in fertile, humus-rich, moist but well-drained soil in partial shade. Pruning group 8.
• **PROPAGATION** Sow seed in containers in an open frame as soon as ripe. Root semi-ripe cuttings in summer with bottom heat.
• **PESTS AND DISEASES** Infrequent.

L. chinense. Bushy shrub with ovate or oval leaves, 1–2½in (2.5–6cm) long. In late winter or early spring, bears sweetly scented, spider-like white flowers, ¾in (2cm) across, in small, crowded cymes of 3–6. ↕↔ 6ft (2m). China, Burma, Japan. Zone 8. **'Razzleberri'** ▣ has copper-burgundy foliage, maturing to olive-green, and bears red-violet spider-like flowers intermittently through the year; ↕ 4–6ft (1.2–2m), ↔ 4–5ft (1.2–1.5m). Many similar selections are available, including **'Burgundy'**, **'Roseum'**, and **'Rubra'**.

LOTUS syn. DORYCNIUM

FABACEAE

Diverse genus of about 150 species of annuals, short-lived perennials, and deciduous, semi-evergreen, or evergreen subshrubs, found throughout most of the world, some in pasture, others in dry, rocky areas. The alternate leaves are simple, palmate, or pinnate. Pea-like flowers, in a range of colors, occur either singly from the leaf axils or in terminal or axillary clusters. Suitable for a variety of sites, including a wild garden, rock garden, or shrub border; trailing species are useful for a hanging basket. Where not hardy, grow in a cool greenhouse.
• **CULTIVATION** Under glass, grow in soil-based potting mix with added grit, in full light. In growth, water freely and apply a balanced liquid fertilizer monthly; water sparingly in winter. Outdoors, grow in moderately fertile,

well-drained soil in full sun. Pruning group 9 for shrubs (although most do not need pruning); may need restrictive pruning under glass.
• **PROPAGATION** Sow seed of hardy species in containers outdoors in spring or autumn. Sow seed of frost-tender species at 66–75°F (19–24°C) in spring. Take semi-ripe cuttings of shrubs in summer.
• **PESTS AND DISEASES** Mealybugs, aphids, and spider mites can occur under glass. Downy mildew, powdery mildew, root rot, wilt, canker, and blights also occur.

L. berthelotii ■ (Coral gem, Parrot's beak, Pelican's beak). Prostrate or trailing, evergreen subshrub with long stems densely clothed with palmate, silver-gray leaves, each with 3–5 linear leaflets, ½–¾in (1–2cm) long. In spring and early summer, freely bears solitary or paired, orange-red to scarlet, black-centered flowers, 1¼–1½in (3–4cm) long, resembling lobster claws. ↕ 8in (20cm), ↔ indefinite. Canary Islands, Cape Verde Islands. ❄ (min. 34°F/1°C)
***L. corniculatus* 'Plenus'** (Double bird's foot trefoil). Spreading perennial with upright or prostrate stems bearing pinnate, mid- to bluish green leaves, each with 5 obovate to rounded leaflets, ¼–½in (0.5–1.5cm) long, the upper 3 separated from the lower 2 by a short stalk. In spring and early summer, produces axillary, umbel-like racemes of 3–8 pea-like, double yellow flowers, ½in (1.5cm) long, orange in bud, often reddening with age. Less vigorous than the species, which may be invasive. Suitable for a rock garden. ↕ 8–12in (20–30cm), ↔ to 12in (30cm) or more. Zone 4.
L. hirsutus, syn. *Dorycnium hirsutum* (Hairy canary clover). Rounded to spreading, evergreen or semi-evergreen, silver-hairy subshrub with pinnate, densely hairy, gray-green leaves, each consisting of 5 elliptic to narrowly obovate leaflets, to ¾in (2cm) long.

Lotus berthelotii

In summer and early autumn, produces axillary and terminal umbels of 4–10 pea-like, pink-flushed, creamy white flowers, ¾in (2cm) long, followed by reddish brown seed pods. Dislikes wet soil in winter. ↕ to 24in (60cm), ↔ to 36in (90cm). S. Portugal, Mediterranean. Zone 7.
L. jacobaeus. Erect perennial with gray-hairy, sometimes pendent stems. Bears pinnate, mid-green leaves, each composed of 5 linear to narrowly obovate leaflets, 1½in (4cm) long, the upper 3 separated from the lower 2 by a short stalk. Pea-like, chocolate- to purple-brown flowers, to ½in (1.5cm) long, with brown-streaked yellow standard petals, are borne in axillary clusters of up to 6, on stalks longer than the leaves, from spring to autumn, but mainly in summer. ↕ 36in (90cm), ↔ 20in (50cm). Cape Verde Islands. ❄ (min. 41°F/5°C)
L. maculatus. Trailing perennial, similar to *L. berthelotii,* with palmate, mid-green leaves, each consisting of 3–5 linear leaflets, ½–¾in (1–2cm) long. In spring and early summer, red- or orange-tipped yellow flowers, 1in (2.5cm) long and shaped like lobster claws, are borne singly or in clusters of 2–5 from the leaf axils. ↕ 8in (20cm), ↔ indefinite. Canary Islands (Tenerife). ❄ (min. 41°F/5°C)
***L. mascaensis* of gardens** see *L. sessilifolius.*
L. sessilifolius, syn. *L. mascaensis* of gardens. Low-growing, spreading, shrub-by perennial with stalkless, 5-palmate, silver-gray leaves, each with oblong-lance-shaped leaflets, ¼–½in (5–10mm) long. Bears pea-like, vivid yellow flowers, ¼in (6mm) long, in terminal and axillary clusters of 3–5 for several weeks in spring. ↕ to 24in (60cm), ↔ to 5ft (1.5m). Canary Islands. ❄ (min. 41°F/5°C)

LUCULIA

RUBIACEAE

Genus of 5 species of deciduous and evergreen shrubs and small trees from E. Asia, found mostly in upland scrub and woodland and forest margins. They have large, prominently veined leaves, borne in opposite pairs, and terminal panicles or corymbs of salverform, waxy, fragrant flowers with 5 spreading lobes. Where not hardy, grow in a cool or temperate greenhouse. In milder climates, grow in a shrub border.
• **CULTIVATION** Under glass, grow in soil-based potting mix in full light. In spring, pot on or top-dress, and water moderately as growth begins. From summer to autumn, mist daily and water freely, applying a balanced liquid fertilizer monthly; keep just moist in winter. Outdoors, grow in moderately fertile, moist but well-drained soil in full sun. Pruning group 8 or 9; may need restrictive pruning under glass.
• **PROPAGATION** Sow seed at 55–64°F (13–18°C) in spring. Root greenwood cuttings in summer with bottom heat.
• **PESTS AND DISEASES** Spider mites, whiteflies, and mealybugs may be troublesome under glass.

L. grandifolia. Erect to spreading, bushy, deciduous, large shrub or small tree. Ovate to elliptic, mid-green leaves, 8–14in (20–35cm) long, have red to brownish red stalks, veins, and margins, coloring richly in autumn. In summer, bears fragrant, salverform, greenish white to pure white flowers, 2½–3in (6–8cm) long, in corymbs 4–8in (10–20cm) wide. ↕ 12–20ft (4–6m), ↔ 6–12ft (2–4m). Bhutan. ❄ (min. 41–45°F/5–7°C)
L. gratissima. Erect then spreading, semi-evergreen or evergreen, large shrub or sometimes small tree, with downy, red-flushed green stems. Lance-shaped to ovate-oblong, long-pointed, prominently veined, mid- to deep green leaves are 4–8in (10–20cm) long, and downy beneath. Fragrant, salverform pink flowers, 1–1½in (2.5–4cm) long, with very slender tubes, are borne in corymbs, 4–8in (10–20cm) wide, from autumn to winter. ↕ 10–20ft (3–6m), ↔ 5–10ft (1.5–3m). Himalayas. ❄ (min. 41–45°F/5–7°C)

LUDWIGIA

ONAGRACEAE

Genus of 75 species of marginal and submerged aquatic perennials and shrubs, occurring throughout the world, but mainly in warmer regions of North America. They have usually alternate, rarely opposite, simple, mainly stalkless leaves, borne on horizontal or upright, often floating stems. Small, sometimes showy, yellow or white flowers are produced singly from the leaf axils or in terminal clusters. In warm-temperate areas, grow at the margins of a wildlife pool. In cooler climates, grow tender species in an indoor pool or aquarium; *L. peploides* is particularly effective in an aquarium, where it may develop vertical, spongy, white, respiratory roots.
• **CULTIVATION** Grow in mud at the margins of a pool, in containers of heavy loam in water 6–12in (15–30cm) deep, or in fertile soil in a bog garden, in full sun or dappled shade. In an aquarium, grow in bunches in an inert medium, at about 68°F (20°C), in full light. See also pp.52–53.
• **PROPAGATION** Divide in early spring. Take softwood cuttings in spring.
• **PESTS AND DISEASES** Rust and a variety of leaf spots commonly occur.

L. longifolia, syn. *Jussiaea longifolia.* Upright, marginal aquatic perennial with narrowly winged stems sparsely covered with lance-shaped, mid-green leaves, 4–8in (10–20cm) long. Bears solitary, bell-shaped, pale yellow flowers, 1¼–2in (3–5cm) across, from the upper leaf axils in summer. ↕ 6ft (2m), ↔ 3ft (1m). Brazil to Argentina. ❄ (min. 55°F/13°C)
L. palustris (Water purslane). Marginal aquatic perennial with weak stems: either floating, to 20in (50cm) long, in water; or branched, creeping, and mat-forming on mud. Lance-shaped to elliptic-ovate leaves, ¾–2in (2–5cm) long, shiny, bright green above, dark olive-green to red-purple beneath, have long, sharp points. Axillary, paired, bell-shaped, yellowish green flowers, ¹⁄₁₆in (2mm) across, are borne in summer. ↕ 20in (50cm), ↔ indefinite. Europe, Asia, North and South America. ❄ (min. 45°F/7°C)
L. peploides ■ syn. *Jussiaea repens.* Scrambling, marginal aquatic perennial with horizontal shoots, to 24in (60cm) long, that root at the nodes or float.

Ludwigia peploides

Elliptic, mid-green leaves, to 2½in (6cm) long, occasionally have vertical, spongy respiratory roots. In summer, bears axillary, solitary, cup-shaped, bright golden yellow flowers, 2in (5cm) across, with darker yellow spots at the bases. ↕ 24in (60cm), ↔ indefinite. North and South America. ❄ (min. 45°F/7°C)
L. peruviana. Creeping aquatic shrub, completely covered with long hairs, producing lance-shaped to broadly lance-shaped, long-pointed, mid-green leaves, 1½–5in (5–13cm) long. In summer, bears solitary, bell-shaped, bright yellow flowers, ½–¾in (1.5–2cm) across, from the leaf axils. ↕ 1½–10ft (0.5–3m), ↔ 3ft (1m). S.E. US to South America. ❄ (min. 45°F/7°C)
L. sedioides (Mosaic plant). Marginal aquatic perennial, grown as a annual, with thin, branching red stems, 2–18in (5–45cm) long, and floating, diamond-shaped, yellow-green leaves, to 3in (8cm) across, red beneath. The leaves are arranged in a geometric leaf pattern that contracts at night and expands during the day. Floating, solitary, cup-shaped, bright yellow flowers, 1–2in (2.5–5cm) across, are borne in late summer and autumn. ↕ 2–18in (5–45cm), ↔ indefinite. Venezuela, Brazil. ❄ (min. 50°F/10°C)

LUMA

MYRTACEAE

Genus of 4 species of evergreen shrubs and small trees from woodland in Chile and Argentina. They are mainly grown for their aromatic, leathery leaves, borne in opposite pairs, and their axillary,

Luma apiculata

4- or 5-petaled, cup-shaped white flowers; *L. apiculata* is also grown for its peeling bark. Grow as lawn specimens or in a small group; where marginally hardy, grow in a sheltered border or against a wall. They may also be used for hedging.

• **CULTIVATION** Grow in fertile, ideally humus-rich, well-drained soil in full sun or partial shade. Pruning group 1.

• **PROPAGATION** Sow seed in containers in a cold frame in spring. *L. apiculata* may self-seed. Take semi-ripe cuttings in late summer.

• **PESTS AND DISEASES** Infrequent.

L. apiculata ▣ syn. *Myrtus luma*. Vigorous, upright, bushy shrub or tree with peeling, cinnamon-brown and creamy white bark, and broadly elliptic, aromatic, glossy, dark green leaves, to 1in (2.5cm) long. Cup-shaped, 5-petaled white flowers, ¾in (2cm) long, are produced singly or in few-flowered cymes from midsummer to midautumn, followed by spherical purple berries. ↕↔ 30–50ft (10–15m) or more. Chile, Argentina. ❀ (min. 41°F/5°C). **'Glanleam Gold'** is less vigorous, and has leaves with creamy yellow margins, pink-tinged when young; ↕↔ 10ft (3m). **'Penwith'** has red-tinged leaves with yellow to cream stripes, and produces white flowers.

L. chequen, syn. *Myrtus chequen*. Upright shrub or small tree with broadly elliptic or broadly ovate, wavy-margined, aromatic, dark green leaves, to 1in (2.5cm) long. Cup-shaped, 4- or 5-petaled white flowers, ½in (1.5cm) across, are produced singly or in 3-flowered cymes in late summer and early autumn, followed by spherical black berries. ↕ 20ft (6m), ↔ 15ft (5m). Chile. ❀ (min. 41°F/5°C)

Lunaria annua 'Variegata'

LUNARIA

Honesty

BRASSICACEAE

Genus of 3 species of erect, branching annuals, biennials, and perennials occurring on disturbed ground and in uncultivated fields in Europe and W. Asia. They have alternate, ovate to triangular-heart-shaped, toothed leaves, and bear tall, open, terminal racemes of many 4-petaled, cross-shaped, violet-blue to white flowers in late spring and summer. Valued for their flowers, they may be naturalized in a shrub border, in woodland, or in a wild garden, where they self-seed. *L. annua* and *L. rediviva* have translucent seed pods that are excellent for dried flower arrangements: pick when seed pods turn brown, hang in a cool, dry place, and let valves and seed fall naturally.

• **CULTIVATION** Grow in fertile, moist but well-drained soil in full sun or partial shade.

• **PROPAGATION** Direct sow *L. rediviva* in autumn or spring, *L. annua* in early summer. Divide *L. rediviva* in spring.

• **PESTS AND DISEASES** Clubroot, white blister, viruses, and leaf spot can occur.

L. annua ▣ syn. *L. biennis* (Honesty, Money plant, Silver dollars). Annual or biennial with ovate to heart-shaped, coarsely toothed, light to mid-green leaves, to 6in (15cm) long. In late spring, cross-shaped, white to light purple flowers, to ½in (1.5cm) across, are borne in broad, leafy racemes, to 7in (18cm) long. Flat seed pods, 1–3in (2.5–8cm) long, are rounded and brown; the outer walls must fall off or be removed to reveal the silvery inner walls. ↕ to 36in (90cm), ↔ to 12in (30cm). Europe. Zone 4. **'Alba Variegata'** has leaves variegated and margined creamy white, and bears white flowers. **var. *albiflora*** has white flowers. **'Munstead Purple'** has deep reddish purple flowers. **'Variegata'** ▣ has leaves variegated and margined creamy white, and produces purple or red-purple flowers.

L. biennis see *L. annua*.

L. rediviva ▣ (Perennial honesty). Clump-forming perennial with triangular-heart-shaped, finely toothed, dark green leaves, to 8in (20cm) long. Leafy stems bear loose racemes, to 7in (18cm) long, of fragrant, lilac-white flowers, 1in (2.5cm) across, in late spring and early summer, followed by flat, elliptic seed pods, to 2–3in (5–8cm) long, ripening to beige. ↕ 24–36in (60–90cm), ↔ 12in (30cm). Europe, Russia (W. Siberia). Zone 6.

Lunaria annua

Lunaria rediviva

LUPINUS

Lupine

FABACEAE

Genus of about 200 species of annuals, perennials, and semi-evergreen and evergreen subshrubs or shrubs, mostly from the Mediterranean, North Africa, and North, Central, and South America; they are found in dry, hilly grassland and open woodland, on coastal sands or cliffs, and on riverbanks. Most have short-stemmed, palmate, often softly hairy, mid-green, mainly basal leaves, with lance-shaped leaflets; some alpines have silvery green leaves. Long, terminal racemes or spikes of pea-like flowers in many colors, including bicolors, are borne mainly in summer. There are numerous hybrid perennials (including the popular Russell lupines), which form dense clumps of palmate leaves and bear colorful flowers, 1in (2.5cm) long, in racemes or spikes 8–24in (20–60cm) long. Grow larger lupines in a border or wild garden, smaller species in a rock garden or scree bed; where winters are wet, grow the densely silver-hairy species in an alpine house. The seeds may cause severe discomfort if ingested.

• **CULTIVATION** Grow lupines in moderately fertile, light and slightly acidic, well-drained, sandy soil in full sun or partial shade. Most grow best where summers are cool. In an alpine house, grow in equal parts loam, leaf mold, and grit.

• **PROPAGATION** Sow seed in spring or autumn: for annuals and larger species, nick or soak for 24 hours and sow in a seedbed; for alpines and smaller species, sow in containers in a cold frame. Will self-seed. Take basal cuttings of cultivars in midspring.

• **PESTS AND DISEASES** Fungal and bacterial spots, downy mildew, powdery mildew, rust, stem rot, damping off, and Southern blight are common.

L. albifrons ▣ Erect to semi-erect, evergreen subshrub with 7- to 10-palmate, silver silky-hairy leaves, composed of inversely lance-shaped to spoon-shaped leaflets, to 1¼in (3cm) long. In summer, pea-like, pale blue to red-purple flowers, ⅜–½in (0.9–1.5cm) across, with white-marked wing petals, are borne in racemes 4–12in (10–30cm) long. ↕↔ to 30in (75cm) or more. California. Zone 8 (but needs excellent drainage and full sun). **var. *collinus*** is lower-growing and much more compact; ↕↔ 4in (10cm).

Lupinus albifrons

L. arboreus ■ (Tree lupine). Bushy, vigorous, evergreen or semi-evergreen shrub or subshrub, with silky shoots and 5- to 12-palmate, gray-green leaves, composed of obovate-oblong leaflets, to 2½in (6cm) long, silky-hairy beneath. Bears pea-like, fragrant, yellow, or rarely blue flowers, to ½in (1.5cm) long, in dense to lax, upright racemes, to 12in (30cm) long, in late spring and summer. ↕↔ 6ft (2m). California. Zone 8. **'Mauve Queen'** has lilac flowers. **'Snow Queen'** bears white flowers.
***L.* 'Band of Nobles'.** Clump-forming perennial bearing racemes of flowers in white, yellow, pink, red, blue, or bicolors (usually white or yellow in combination with another color), in early and midsummer. ↕ to 5ft (1.5m), ↔ 30in (75cm). Zone 5.
***L.* 'Beryl, Viscountess Cowdray'.** Clump-forming perennial bearing dense racemes of bicolored, rich pink and red flowers in early and midsummer. ↕ 36in (90cm), ↔ 30in (75cm). Zone 5.
***L.* 'Blushing Bride'.** Clump-forming perennial bearing dense racemes of pink-tinged, ivory-white flowers in early and midsummer. ↕ 36in (90cm), ↔ 30in (75cm). Zone 5.
L. breweri. Tufted, mat-forming, short-lived, woody-based perennial with 7- to 10-palmate, densely silky-hairy, silver-green leaves, consisting of inversely lance-shaped leaflets, to ¾in (2cm) long. In summer, produces dense racemes, to 2in (5cm) long, of pea-like, white-throated, violet-blue flowers, ¼–⅜in (6–9mm) long. ↕ 4in (10cm), ↔ to 8in (20cm). Stony meadows in W. US. Zone 6.
***L.* 'Catherine of York'.** Clump-forming perennial bearing racemes of bicolored, pure salmon-orange and yellow flowers in early and midsummer. ↕ 36in (90cm), ↔ 30in (75cm). Zone 5.
***L.* 'Chandelier'** ■ Clump-forming perennial producing racemes of yellow flowers in early and midsummer. ↕ 36in (90cm), ↔ 30in (75cm). Zone 3.
L. cruckshankii see *L. mutabilis.*

L

L. densiflorus* var. *aureus. Simple or branched annual with 7- to 9-palmate, hairless, mid-green leaves, composed of lance-shaped leaflets, to ¾in (2cm) long, softly hairy beneath. From spring to summer, bears spikes, 8in (20cm) or more long, of pea-like, pale yellow flowers, ½in (1–5cm) long, sometimes bordered with red. ↕ to 16in (40cm), ↔ 12in (30cm). California.
***L.* Gallery Hybrids.** Dwarf perennials bearing spikes of pea-like flowers in a range of blue, red, rose, yellow, and white, in early and midsummer. ↕ 16–20in (40–50cm), ↔ 12–16in (30–40cm). Zone 4.
***L.* 'Garden Gnome'.** Dwarf perennial producing spikes of pea-like flowers in a range of blue, red, pink, yellow, white, and bicolors, in early and midsummer. ↕ 24in (60cm), ↔ 12–16in (30–40cm). Zone 4.
L. hartwegii. Tufted, many-branched annual with 7- to 9-palmate, densely hairy, mid-green leaves, composed of oblong to oblong-lance-shaped leaflets, 1¼in (4cm) long. Dense spikes, to 8in (20cm) long, of pea-like, pale blue flowers, ½in (1.5cm) long, are borne from summer to autumn. ↕ to 36in (90cm), ↔ 30in (75cm). Mexico.
***L.* 'Lady Fayre'.** Clump-forming perennial producing racemes of deep rose-pink flowers in early and midsummer. ↕ 36in (90cm), ↔ 30in (75cm). Zone 5.
***L. lepidus* var. *lobbii*,** syn. *L. lyallii.* Semi-prostrate to mat-forming, short-lived perennial with 5- to 7-palmate, silky-hairy, silver-green leaves, consisting of inversely lance-shaped leaflets, to ½in (1.5cm) long. Pea-like, bright blue flowers, ½in (1.5cm) long, the standard petals each with a white spot, are borne in dense racemes, to 2in (5cm) long, in late summer. ↕ 4in (10cm), ↔ to 8in (20cm). Washington to California. ❀ (min. 41°F/5°C)
***L. luteus* 'Yellow Javelin'.** Erect, bushy annual with densely hairy stems and 7- to 11-palmate leaves, each with

Lupinus arboreus

Lupinus 'Chandelier'

obovate-oblong, round-tipped, softly hairy, mid-green leaflets, 1¼–2½in (3–6cm) long. In summer, pea-like, bright golden yellow flowers, to ¾in (2cm) long, are borne in tall racemes, to 10in (25cm) long. ↕ to 24in (60cm), ↔ 12in (30cm).
L. lyallii see *L. lepidus* var. *lobbii.*
***L.* 'Magnificence'.** Clump-forming perennial bearing racemes of lavender-pink flowers, in early and midsummer. ↕ 36in (90cm), ↔ 30in (75cm). Zone 5.
***L.* 'Minarette'.** Dwarf perennial bearing early-blooming spikes of pea-like flowers in a wide range of blue, red, pink, yellow, white, and bicolors, in early and midsummer. ↕ 20in (50cm), ↔ 12–16in (30–40cm). Zone 3.
***L.* 'Moonraker'.** Clump-forming perennial with racemes of lemon-yellow flowers in early and midsummer. ↕ 36in (90cm), ↔ 30in (75cm). Zone 5.
***L. mutabilis*,** syn. *L. cruckshankii.* Erect, bushy annual, with 7- to 9-palmate leaves, each with inversely lance-shaped to spoon-shaped, round-tipped, blue-green leaflets, to 2–2½in (5–6cm) long, softly hairy beneath. In summer, produces racemes, 4–8in (10–20cm) long, of pea-like flowers, ¾–1¼in

Lupinus nanus 'Pixie Delight'

Lupinus 'The Chatelaine'

(2–3cm) long, with pale purple-blue keel petals, yellow standard petals, and deep blue wing petals. ↕ 3–3½ft (1–1.1m), ↔ 18–24in (45–60cm).
***L.* 'My Castle'.** Clump-forming perennial producing racemes of deep rose-pink flowers in early and midsummer. ↕ 36in (90cm), ↔ 30in (75cm). Zone 3.
***L. nanus* 'Pixie Delight'** ■ Erect, single-stemmed to bushy annual with 5- to 7-palmate leaves, composed of linear-lance-shaped, pointed, softly hairy, mid-green leaflets, to 1¼in (3cm) long. In summer, bears racemes, to 8in (20cm) long, of pea-like, pink, blue, lavender-blue, white, or bicolored flowers, ½in (1.5cm) across, the standard petals often with purple-dotted white marks or yellow spots. ↕ 20in (50cm), ↔ to 9in (23cm).
***L.* 'Noble Maiden'.** Clump-forming perennial bearing racemes of creamy white flowers in early and midsummer. ↕ 36in (90cm), ↔ 30in (75cm). Zone 3.
L. perennis (Wild lupine). Erect, softly hairy perennial with 7- to 11-palmate leaves, each with oblong-lance-shaped, mid-green leaflets, 1–2in (2.5–5cm) long. In early summer, bears spikes, 12in (30cm) long, of pea-like, blue (or occasionally pink or white) flowers, to ½in (16mm) long. ↕ 24in (60cm), ↔ 18in (45cm). Maine to Florida. Zone 5b.
L. polyphyllus. Erect perennial with 13- to 15-palmate leaves, composed of lance-shaped, hairless, mid-green leaflets, to 6in (15cm) long, softly hairy beneath. In summer, bears spikes, to 20in (50cm) long, of pea-like, lilac-blue flowers, to ½in (1.5cm) long. ↕ to 4ft (1.2m), ↔ 24–30in (60–75cm). W. North America. Zone 7b. **'Albus'** bears white flowers. **var. *burkei*** has hairless to softly white-hairy leaflets; ↕ 24in (60cm). **'Roseus'** produces rose-pink flowers.
***L.* Popsicle Hybrids.** Dwarf perennials bearing sturdy spikes of pea-like flowers

Lupinus 'The Page'

in a range of blue, red, pink, yellow, and white, in early and midsummer. ↕ 18–24in (45–60cm), ↔ 12–16in (30–40cm). Zone 3.
***L.* Russell Hybrids.** Dwarf perennials producing spikes of large, pea-like flowers in a range of blue, red, pink, yellow, and white, in early and midsummer. ↕ 30–36in (75–90cm), ↔ 12–16in (30–40cm). Zone 3.
L. succulentus. Erect annual with succulent stems and 7- to 9-palmate leaves, composed of wedge-shaped to wedge-shaped-obovate, hairless, deep green leaflets, to 3in (8cm) long, with tiny, stiff hairs beneath. In early spring, bears spikes, to 12in (30cm) long, of pea-like, yellow-centered, deep violet flowers, to ½in (1.5cm) long. ↕ to 3ft (1m), ↔ 30in (75cm). California, Mexico (Baja California).
L. texensis (Texas bluebonnet). Erect to spreading, bushy annual with softly hairy stems and 5-palmate, mid-green leaves, each with lance-shaped, pointed leaflets, to 1¼in (3cm) long, hairy beneath. In summer, pea-like, deep blue to blue-purple flowers, ½in (1.5cm) across, are borne in compact, crowded racemes, to 3in (8cm) long. ↕ 10–12in (25–30cm), ↔ to 9in (23cm). Texas.
***L.* 'The Chatelaine'** ▣ Clump-forming perennial producing racemes of bicolored, pink and white flowers in early and midsummer. ↕ 36in (90cm), ↔ 30in (75cm). Zone 3.
***L.* 'The Governor'.** Clump-forming perennial bearing racemes of bicolored, deep blue and white flowers in early and midsummer. ↕ 36in (90cm), ↔ 30in (75cm). Zone 3.
***L.* 'The Page'** ▣ Clump-forming perennial producing racemes of rich carmine-red flowers in early and midsummer. ↕ 36in (90cm), ↔ 30in (75cm). Zone 3.
***L.* 'Thundercloud'.** Clump-forming perennial bearing racemes of deep violet-blue flowers in early and midsummer. ↕ 36in (90cm), ↔ 30in (75cm). Zone 5.

LUZULA

Woodrush

JUNCACEAE

Genus of approximately 80 species of mostly evergreen, tufted, grass-like perennials (rarely annuals), sometimes with short rhizomes or stolons. Woodrushes are widely distributed on heaths and moors, in fens and bogs, and in scrub, woodland, and mountain grassland throughout the temperate regions of the world. Broadly linear basal and stem leaves are flat or grooved along their lengths, and have fringes of zigzagged white hairs at the margins, which distinguish them from rushes (*Juncus*). Tiny flowers are produced in terminal, panicle-, corymb-, or cyme-like clusters, in spring or summer. Valued for their shade tolerance, woodrushes provide useful groundcover in damp shade, either in a mixed border or in a woodland garden. *L. ulophylla* is also suitable for a trough or rock garden.
• **CULTIVATION** Grow in poor to moderately fertile, humus-rich, moist but well-drained soil in partial or deep shade (or in full sun where the soil is reliably moist). *L. nivea* prefers full sun.
• **PROPAGATION** Sow seed in containers outdoors in spring or autumn. Divide between midspring and early summer.
• **PESTS AND DISEASES** Rust and *Septoria* leaf spot are common.

L. maxima see *L. sylvatica.*
L. nivea ▣ (Snowy woodrush). Slowly spreading, loosely tufted, evergreen perennial forming loose clumps of flat, linear, deep green basal leaves, to 12in (30cm) long; stem leaves are to 8in (20cm) long. In early and midsummer, bears lax panicles, to 2in (5cm) long, of shiny, pure white flowers in tight clusters of up to 20. May be dried. ↕ to 24in (60cm), ↔ 18in (45cm). Spain, France, Italy, Slovenia, C. Europe. Zone 4.
L. sylvatica, syn. *L. maxima* (Greater woodrush). Densely tufted, tussock-forming, evergreen perennial with linear, channeled, glossy, dark green leaves, to 12in (30cm) long. Groups of 2–5 small, chestnut-brown flowers are produced in open panicles, to 3in (8cm) long, from mid-spring to early summer. ↕ to 28–32in (70–80cm), ↔ 18in (45cm). S., W., and C. Europe, S.W. Asia. Zone 5. The following cultivars provide a useful, dense

Luzula nivea

Luzula sylvatica 'Aurea'

groundcover. **'Aurea'** ▣ syn. *L. maxima* 'Aurea', has broad leaves that are bright, shiny yellow in winter, yellow-green in summer. **'Aureomarginata'** see 'Marginata'. **'Marginata'**, syn. 'Aureomarginata', has a dense habit, rich green leaves with neat cream margins, and pendent, brown and gold spikelets.
L. ulophylla. Dwarf, densely tufted, evergreen perennial forming a low mound of linear, deep green leaves, to 1¼–3in (3–8cm) long, V-shaped in cross-section, with conspicuous silvery hairs beneath and on the margins. In early summer, very dark brown flowers, the tepals with white membranous margins, are produced in short, stubby clusters, to ¾in (2cm) long. ↕ to 6in (15cm), ↔ 12in (30cm). New Zealand. ❄ (min. 35°F/2°C)

LYCASTE

ORCHIDACEAE

Genus of about 45 species of deciduous, epiphytic or terrestrial orchids found in cloud forest at altitudes of 2,000–7,700ft (600–2,200m) in Mexico, Central and South America, and the West Indies. They produce robust, ovoid or ellipsoid, compressed pseudobulbs, and a number of broad, lance-shaped to oblong-elliptic, often soft, folded, light green leaves. Large, waxy, fragrant flowers, produced singly on leafless stems from the bases, are typically triangular in shape, with the sepals framing the smaller, cupped petals and 3-lobed lips.
• **CULTIVATION** Cool-growing orchids. Grow in containers of crushed bark or soilless potting mix, or grow epiphytically on bark slabs. In summer, provide high humidity and water freely (keeping the foliage dry); apply a balanced liquid fertilizer at every third watering. In winter, provide bright filtered light and keep dry. See also p.46.
• **PROPAGATION** Divide when plants overflow their containers, or remove and pot up backbulbs.

Lycaste cruenta

• **PESTS AND DISEASES** Spider mites, aphids, whiteflies, and mealybugs may be troublesome.

L. aromatica. Epiphytic orchid with lance-shaped leaves, to 12–16in (30–40cm) long. Cinnamon-scented flowers, 1½–2½in (4–6cm) across, with deep golden to orange-yellow petals, yellowish green sepals, and lips with orange dots, are produced in abundance from winter to spring. ↕↔ 12in (30cm). Mexico, Guatemala, Belize, Honduras. ❄ (min. 52–54°F/11–12°C; max. 86°F/30°C)
L. brevispatha, syn. *L. candida.* Epiphytic orchid with lance-shaped leaves, to 20in (50cm) long. From winter to spring, produces an abundance of flowers, to 4in (10cm) across, with light green sepals with reddish brown spots, brown-spotted white petals, and white lips suffused and spotted pink. ↕↔ 12in (30cm). Guatemala, Nicaragua, Costa Rica, Panama. ❄ (min. 52–54°F/11–12°C; max. 86°F/30°C)
L. candida see *L. brevispatha.*
L. cruenta ▣ Epiphytic orchid with lance-shaped leaves, to 18in (35cm) long. From spring to summer, produces an abundance of faintly cinnamon-scented flowers, to 3in (8cm) across, with greenish yellow sepals, yellowish orange petals with red spots near the bases, and orange lips with red spots and red triangular patches at the bases. ↕↔ 18in (45cm). Mexico, Guatemala, El Salvador, Costa Rica. ❄ (min. 52–54°F/11–12°C; max. 86°F/30°C)
L. deppei ▣ Epiphytic orchid with lance-shaped leaves, 12–20in (30–50cm) long. From spring to summer, produces abundant flowers, 3½in (9cm) across, with green sepals spotted red-brown,

Lycaste deppei

white petals flecked red-brown at the bases, and red-spotted, deep yellow lips, striped and dotted red at the bases. ↕↔ 12in (30cm). Mexico, Guatemala. ❄ (min. 52–54°F/11–12°C; max. 86°F/30°C)
L. gigantea see *L. longipetala.*
L. longipetala, syn. *L. gigantea.* Epiphytic orchid with lance-shaped leaves, to 24in (60cm) long. In summer, bears large, fleshy flowers, to 6in (15cm) across, with pale green sepals suffused brown, darker green petals, and red-brown lips with light orange margins; the flowers do not open fully. ↕↔ 18in (45cm). Venezuela, Colombia, Ecuador, Peru. ❄ (min. 52–54°F/11–12°C; max. 86°F/30°C)
L. skinneri, syn. *L. virginalis* (Nun orchid). Epiphytic orchid with lance-shaped leaves, 20–24in (50–60cm) long. From winter to spring, produces flowers 5–6in (12–15cm) across, with cream sepals shaded white through lavender-pink to pink, reddish purple petals, and pink lips sometimes mottled purple. ↕↔ 12in (30cm). Mexico, Guatemala, Honduras, El Salvador. ❄ (min. 52–54°F/11–12°C; max. 86°F/30°C)
L. virginalis see *L. skinneri.*
***L.* Wyldfire** (*L.* Balliae x *L.* Wyld Court). Robust, epiphytic orchid with lance-shaped leaves, 16in (40cm) long. In spring, produces an abundance of deep wine-red flowers, 5in (13cm) across, with darker lips. ↕↔ 18in (45cm). ❄ (min. 52–54°F/11–12°C; max. 86°F/30°C)

L

LYCHNIS *syn.* VISCARIA
Campion, Catchfly
CARYOPHYLLACEAE

Genus of 15–20 species of biennials and perennials found in sites ranging from damp meadows and woodland to alpine habitats, in N. temperate and arctic regions. They have erect, usually branched stems, and simple, often hairy leaves borne in opposite pairs. The 5-petaled, salverform to tubular or star-shaped flowers occur in scarlet, purple, pink, or white, and are either solitary or borne in terminal cymes or occasionally panicles. Grow the larger perennials in a sunny border or a wild garden, the smaller, alpine species in a rock garden, and the biennials in an annual or herbaceous border.
• **CULTIVATION** Grow in any moderately fertile, well-drained soil in full sun or partial shade. *L. chalcedonica, L.* x *haageana,* and *L. viscaria* prefer moist, fertile soil; gray-leaved species

Lychnis alpina

Lychnis x *arkwrightii* 'Vesuvius'

produce their best leaf color in dry soil in full sun. Deadhead to prolong flowering.
• **PROPAGATION** Sow seed in containers in a cold frame as soon as ripe or in spring; *L.* x *arkwrightii* 'Vesuvius' and *L.* x *haageana* will flower the same year and may be treated as annuals. Divide or take basal cuttings in early spring.
• **PESTS AND DISEASES** Anther smut and leaf spots sometimes occur.

L. alpina ▣ (Alpine campion, Alpine catchfly). Dwarf, tufted perennial with rosettes of oblong-lance-shaped to elliptic-lance-shaped, dark green leaves, to 1½in (4cm) long. In summer, bears dense, rounded, terminal cymes of 6–20 salverform, purplish pink flowers, to ¾in (2cm) across, with frilled, 2-lobed petals. ↕↔ to 6in (15cm). Mountains of N. hemisphere, subarctic regions. Zone 4.
***L.* x *arkwrightii* 'Vesuvius'** ▣ Short-lived, clump-forming perennial with ovate-lance-shaped, hairy, dark brownish green leaves, 3in (8cm) long. In early and midsummer, bears terminal cymes of 5–10 star-shaped, orange-scarlet flowers, 1¼–1½in (3–4cm) across, with notched petals. ↕ 18in (45cm), ↔ 12in (30cm). Zone 4.
L. chalcedonica ▣ (Jerusalem cross, Maltese cross). Erect, stiff perennial with ovate, mid-green basal leaves, and unbranched, hairy stems bearing clasping, ovate leaves, 2–3in (5–8cm) long, with heart-shaped bases. In early and midsummer, produces terminal, rounded, umbel-like cymes of 10–30 star-shaped scarlet flowers, ½in (1.5cm) across, the petals each with 2 deep notches. Requires support. Self-seeds freely. ↕ 3–4ft (0.9–1.2m), ↔ 12in (30cm). European Russia. Zone 4. **'Rosea'** has rose-pink flowers.
L. coeli-rosa see *Silene coeli-rosa.*
L. coronaria ▣ (Dusty miller, Rose campion). Erect, woolly, silver-gray biennial or short-lived perennial with ovate-lance-shaped, silver-gray leaves: the basal leaves up to 7in (18cm) long, the stem leaves up to 4in (10cm). In late summer, long-stalked, salverform, rounded, purple-red or pale purple flowers, 1¼in (3cm) across, with slightly reflexed, shallowly 2-lobed petals, are borne in few-flowered, terminal cymes; they open singly, but in long succession. Self-seeds freely. ↕ 32in (80cm), ↔ 18in (45cm). S.E. Europe. Zone 3b. **'Alba'** produces white flowers. **'Angel's Blush'** has white flowers with cerise eyes.

Lychnis chalcedonica

L. coronata* var. *sieboldii see *L. sieboldii.*
L. flos-cuculi (Ragged robin). Slender, upright or spreading, sparsely hairy perennial with inversely lance-shaped, mid- to bluish green basal leaves, to 5in (13cm) long, and smaller, oblong-lance-shaped stem-clasping leaves. In late spring and early summer, produces loose, few-flowered, branched, terminal cymes of star-shaped, pale to bright purplish pink, sometimes white flowers, to 1½in (4cm) across, with petals deeply cut into 4 linear segments. Suitable for a wild garden. ↕ to 30in (75cm), ↔ to 32in (80cm). Damp places in Europe, Caucasus, and Russia (Siberia). Zone 5.
L. flos-jovis ▣ (Flower of Jove, Flower of Jupiter). Mat-forming perennial with usually unbranched, erect, white-hairy stems, and lance- to spoon-shaped basal and stem-clasping leaves, to 4in (10cm) long. From early to late summer, bears loosely rounded cymes of 4–10 rounded, pink, white, or scarlet flowers, 1in (2.5cm) across, with slightly reflexed, notched petals. ↕ 8–24in (20–60cm) or more, ↔ 18in (45cm). C. Alps. Zone 4. **'Hort's Variety'** has rose-pink flowers; ↕ 12in (30cm).
L.* x *haageana (*L. fulgens* x *L. sieboldii*). Short-lived, clump-forming, hairy perennial with lance-shaped, mid-green leaves, 1½–3in (4–8cm) long. In mid- and late summer, salverform, brilliant red or orange flowers, 2in (5cm) across, with notched petals, are borne in few-flowered, loose, terminal cymes. ↕ 18–24in (45–60cm), ↔ 12in (30cm). Garden origin. Zone 5.

Lychnis coronaria

Lychnis flos-jovis

L. sieboldii, syn. *L. coronata* var. *sieboldii.* Clump-forming, hairy perennial bearing inversely lance-shaped to elliptic, mid-green leaves, 2–3in (5–8cm) long. Clustered, terminal cymes of many flat, rounded, deep red flowers, 2in (5cm) across, the petals with shallowly toothed lobes, are produced in summer and early autumn. ↕ 24in (60cm), ↔ 12in (30cm). Japan. Zone 5.
L. viscaria ▣ syn. *Viscaria vulgaris* (German catchfly). Mat-forming to tufted perennial with elliptic-lance-shaped to oblong-lance-shaped, hairless, dark green basal leaves, to 3in (8cm) long. The usually unbranched stems are sticky, with a few lance-shaped leaves. In early and midsummer, bears narrow, spike-like panicles of numerous salverform, purplish pink flowers, ¾in (2cm) across, with notched petals. ↕↔ 18in (45cm). Europe to W. Asia. Zone 4. **'Alba'** has white flowers; ↕ 12in (30cm). **'Flore Pleno'** see 'Splendens Plena'. **'Fire'** see 'Feuer'. **'Fontaine'** produces large, double, pale red flowers, 1in (2.5cm) across. **'Feuer'**, syn. 'Fire' has red flowers, some double. **'Snow'** produces white flowers, some double.

Lychnis viscaria

'Snowbird' bears white flowers.
'Splendens Plena', syn. 'Flore Pleno', bears double, bright pinkish magenta flowers, 1in (2.5cm) across.

▷ ***Lycianthes rantonnetii*** *see Solanum rantonnetii*

LYCIUM

SOLANACEAE

Genus of about 100 species of sometimes spiny, deciduous and evergreen, often scandent shrubs, occurring throughout temperate and subtropical regions, usually in dry soil. Leaves are entire and alternate, and funnel-shaped or tubular flowers are borne singly or in clusters of up to 4 from the leaf axils. Cultivated for their habit, flowers, and fruits, they are useful for a shrub border or for covering a dry bank; they are particularly effective as a windbreak or hedge in a coastal garden. Grow tender species in a cool or temperate greenhouse.
• **CULTIVATION** Grow in moderately fertile, well-drained soil in full sun. Pruning group 1, or, for scandent species, group 11, in winter or early spring. Cut back hedges hard in spring; trim in early summer.
• **PROPAGATION** Sow seed in containers outdoors in autumn. Take hardwood cuttings in winter, or softwood cuttings in early summer.
• **PESTS AND DISEASES** Powdery midlew and rust sometimes are problems.

L. barbarum, syn. *L. halimifolium* (Chinese box thorn). Variable, vigorous, erect or wide-spreading, sometimes scandent, often spiny, deciduous shrub. Long, arching branches bear narrowly oblong-lance-shaped, elliptic, or ovate, mid-green to gray-green leaves, to 2½in (6cm) long. Small clusters of 1–4 funnel-shaped, purple, lilac, or pink flowers, ⅜in (9mm) long, are produced in late spring and summer, followed by ovoid, orange-red or yellow berries, to ¾in (2cm) long. ↕ 11ft (3.5m) or more, ↔ 15ft (5m). China. Zone 6.
L. halimifolium see *L. barbarum.*

LYCOPERSICON

Tomato

AMARYLLIDACEAE

Genus of 7 species of tropical perennials, often grown in temperate climates as warm-season, frost-tender annuals native to Central America. Tomatoes are either determinate (smaller fruit, bushy type, and with only one fruiting event) or indeterminate (larger fruit, generally needs support, and continues to grow and produce fruit).
• **CULTIVATION** Grow in moderately fertile soil in full sun. Tomatoes will not germinate at temperatures below 50°F (10°C).
• **PROPAGATION** Sow seed indoors in any moist potting mix. Transplant to well-drained, moderately fertile soil when seedlings are 3–6in (8–15cm) tall, or at 5–8 weeks of age.
• **PESTS AND DISEASES** Cutworms, early blight may occur.

L. lycopersicum. Leaves are compound, dark green, deeply toothed, on sturdy, slightly sticky stalks. Flowers are simple, pale to medium yellow, followed by fruits

Lycopodium phlegmaria

of various sizes and colors. Small grape or cherry tomatoes, to ↕↔ ½in (15mm) long, are sweet; large beefsteak varieties can be 6in (15cm) in diameter.
❄ (min. 35°F/2°C)

LYCOPODIUM

Club moss

LYCOPODIACEAE

Genus of 100 or more species of rhizomatous, evergreen, terrestrial or epiphytic, moss-like perennials, found in most parts of the world in a very wide range of habitats, but mainly in tropical or temperate rainforest or cloud forest. They have erect, pendent, or creeping stems, which are usually repeatedly forked, and bear small, simple, linear-lance-shaped to ovate-triangular leaves, overlapping or in whorls. Spores are produced in the leaf axils, or sometimes in terminal cones on the smaller leaves. Only the epiphytic species are cultivated. Where not hardy, grow in a temperate or warm greenhouse. In frost-free climates, grow as epiphytes in shaded, damp sites.
• **CULTIVATION** Under glass, grow in slatted wooden baskets in equal parts peat, roughly chopped sphagnum moss, charcoal, and broken pots, in bright indirect light. In the growing season, water moderately (avoiding the foliage), mist daily in summer, and apply a half-strength, seaweed-based liquid fertilizer as a foliar spray every month. Reduce watering in winter but do not allow the soil mix to dry out. Outdoors, grow epiphytically in a permanently damp niche on a tree, in partial shade.
• **PROPAGATION** Layer tips of fertile leaves at any time of year. See also p.51.
• **PESTS AND DISEASES** Slugs, snails, or mites may eat the soft, tender tips of growing stems. Fern scale may be a serious problem.

L. phlegmaria ▣ Epiphytic perennial with initially upright, later pendent stems, to 3ft (1m) long, forked several times. Produces often upright, broadly ovate-triangular, yellow- to olive-green leaves, to ¾in (2cm) long. Spores are formed in branched, terminal cones, to ½in (1.5cm) across, on small leaves. Probably an aggregate of several species. ↕↔ 36in (90cm). Asia, Australia, Pacific islands. ❄ (min. 50°F/10°C)

LYCORIS

AMARYLLIDACEAE

Genus of 10–12 species of bulbous perennials from wooded hills or rocky sites in low mountains, and the margins of cultivated fields, in China and Japan. They are grown for their showy umbels of tubular-funnel-shaped flowers, with narrow, spreading, sometimes reflexed tepal lobes, borne on leafless stems from spring to early autumn. The leaves are linear or strap-shaped. In areas with hot summers, grow in a sunny border or rock garden. Where summers are cool, they are best grown as container plants in a conservatory or cool greenhouse, but do not always flower regularly.
• **CULTIVATION** Plant in autumn with the necks of the bulbs at the surface. Under glass, grow in soil-based potting

Lycoris aurea

Lycoris radiata

mix in full light. Top-dress when growth begins, then water freely and apply a balanced liquid fertilizer monthly until the leaves die down. Keep dry in summer when dormant. Outdoors, grow in fertile, well-drained soil in full sun. Where marginally hardy, protect with a dry winter mulch.
• **PROPAGATION** Sow seed at 45–54°F (6–12°C) as soon as ripe. Remove offsets after flowering.
• **PESTS AND DISEASES** Infrequent.

L. aurea ▣ (Golden spider lily). Bulbous perennial producing umbels, from spring to summer, of 5 or 6 tubular-funnel-shaped, wavy-margined yellow flowers, 4in (10cm) across, with the tepals reflexed at the tips, and protruding stamens. Semi-erect, strap-shaped, fleshy, glaucous, mid-green leaves, to 24in (60cm) long, appear after the flowers. ↕ to 24in (60cm), PD8in (20cm). China, Japan. Zone 8.
L. radiata ▣ (Red spider lily). Bulbous perennial with wavy-margined, rose-red or deep red flowers, 1½–2in (4–5cm) long, with strongly reflexed tepals and conspicuous, protruding stamens, borne in umbels of 4–6 in late summer and early autumn. Semi-erect, strap-shaped, dark green leaves, 12–24in (30–60cm) long, appear after the flowers. ↕ 12–20in (30–50cm), PD8in (20cm). Japan. Zone 8.
L. squamigera (Resurrection lily). Bulbous perennial with tubular-funnel-shaped, slightly wavy, fragrant, pale rose-red flowers, 3½–4in (9–10cm) across, flushed or veined blue or purple, the tepals with reflexed tips, borne in umbels of up to 8 in summer. Semi-erect, strap-shaped, mid-green leaves, 12in (30cm) long, are produced the following spring. ↕ 18–28in (45–70cm), PD12in (30cm). Japan. Zone 5.

LYGODIUM

Climbing fern

SCHIZAEACEAE

Genus of 40 species of semi-evergreen and deciduous, scrambling or climbing ferns from tropical and subtropical forest worldwide. A single, palmately lobed or pinnate frond arises from the creeping, branching rhizomes. The long-twining midrib of the frond continues to grow, producing new pinnae in distant pairs; each pinna has a long, often forked stalk and a varying number of leaf-like segments. Spores are produced in small

Lygodium japonicum

spikes at the segment margins. Where not hardy, grow in a warm greenhouse. In warmer areas, grow in moist woodland.
• **CULTIVATION** Under glass, grow in a mix of equal parts coarse leaf mold or peat, soil-based potting mix, chopped sphagnum moss, and charcoal, in bright filtered light. Support on wires and provide plenty of space to climb. In growth, water freely, apply a balanced liquid fertilizer monthly, and mist daily. Reduce watering in winter, but do not allow the soil mix to dry out. Outdoors, grow in moderately fertile, moist, peaty soil in deep or partial shade.
L. palmatum needs acidic soil.
• **PROPAGATION** Sow spores at 70°F (21°C) as soon as ripe. Divide plants before the leaves develop. See also p.51.
• **PESTS AND DISEASES** Infrequent.

L. japonicum ■ (Japanese climbing fern). Deciduous, climbing fern producing 2- or 3-pinnate, very finely divided fronds. Sterile pinnae, 2–5in (5–13cm) long, are irregularly and deeply lobed to pinnate; fertile pinnae are similar, or more finely divided. ↕ 6–10ft (2–3m) or more. India, China, Korea, Japan. ❄ (min. 32°F/0°C)
L. palmatum (Hartford fern). Deciduous, climbing fern with palmately 3- to 7-lobed fronds, to 1½in (4cm) long. Fertile pinnae are much more finely divided than sterile ones. ↕ to 6ft (2m) or more. North Carolina to Florida. Zone 7b.

LYONIA

ERICACEAE

Genus of approximately 35 species of deciduous and evergreen shrubs, sometimes small trees, from the Himalayas, E. Asia, US, Mexico, and the Antilles, generally occurring in woodland. They have simple, glossy, leathery leaves, borne alternately, and are cultivated for their dense, axillary racemes or clusters of often urn-shaped, sometimes bell-shaped, ovoid, or cylindrical flowers, borne on the previous year's shoots. Suitable for a woodland garden.
• **CULTIVATION** Grow in acidic to neutral, moderately fertile, humus-rich, moist but well-drained soil in partial or deep shade. Pruning group 1 or 8.
• **PROPAGATION** Sow seed in containers outdoors in autumn. Take semi-ripe cuttings in summer. Layer in spring.
• **PESTS AND DISEASES** Tar spot, rust, and leaf gall occur.

Lyonia mariana

L. ferruginea (Rusty lyonia). Spreading, bushy, evergreen shrub or small tree with elliptic to ovate or obovate, leathery, dark green leaves, to 3½in (9cm) long, usually with the margins rolled under. The shoots and undersides of the leaves are covered with red-brown scales. Pendent clusters of up to 10 urn-shaped white flowers, ⅛in (3mm) long, are produced in late winter or spring. ↕ 15ft (5m), usually less, ↔ 6ft (2m). S.E. US. Zone 8.
L. mariana ■ (Stagger-bush). Rounded, deciduous shrub with oblong, elliptic, or narrowly obovate, leathery, dark green leaves, to 3in (8cm) long, red in autumn, dotted with brown glands beneath. Pendent, ovoid-cylindrical, white to pale pink flowers, ⅜–½in (0.8–1.5cm) long, are borne in many-flowered, umbel-like racemes in late spring and early summer. ↕ to 6ft (2m), ↔ 4ft (1.2m). E. US. Zone 6.

LYONOTHAMNUS

ROSACEAE

Genus of one species of evergreen tree, growing wild in canyons and on dry slopes in California. Cultivated mainly for its habit, attractive bark, and simple to pinnate, thick, glossy leaves, borne in opposite pairs, it is effective as a specimen tree or in woodland.
• **CULTIVATION** Grow in fertile, moist but well-drained soil in full sun or partial shade. Shelter from cold, drying winds where marginally hardy, and protect with a thick, dry mulch in winter. Pruning group 1.
• **PROPAGATION** Sow seed in containers outdoors in autumn, or take greenwood cuttings in summer; propagation may be slow or difficult.
• **PESTS AND DISEASES** Infrequent.

L. floribundus (Catalina ironwood). Conical, evergreen tree with peeling, red-brown bark and oblong to lance-shaped, glossy, deep green leaves, to 8in (20cm) long, gray beneath; leaves are simple, or sometimes partially or fully pinnate on the same tree. From spring to summer, bears large, terminal, corymb-like panicles, to 8in (20cm) across, of small, 5-petaled, star-shaped creamy white flowers. ↕ 40ft (12m), ↔ 20ft (6m). California, Santa Catalina Island. ❄ (min. 41°F/5°C). **var. *aspleniifolius*** has pinnate or 2-pinnate leaves, often with pinnatifid leaflets; islands off the coast of California.

Lysichiton americanus

LYSICHITON

Skunk cabbage

ARACEAE

Genus of 2 species of robust, marginal aquatic perennials, with short rhizomes, from N.E. Asia and W. North America. They are grown for their basal clusters of large, ovate-oblong, glossy, mid- to dark green leaves, and yellow or white spathes that surround spadices bearing small, bisexual green flowers. They have a musky smell. Grow beside a stream or pool.
• **CULTIVATION** Grow in fertile, humus-rich soil at the margins of a stream or pool, in full sun or partial shade. See also pp.52–53.
• **PROPAGATION** Sow seed on a tray of wet soil in a cold frame as soon as ripe. Remove offsets in spring or summer.
• **PESTS AND DISEASES** Infrequent.

L. americanus ■ (Yellow skunk cabbage). Marginal aquatic perennial with rosettes of ovate-oblong, strongly veined, leathery, glossy, mid- to dark green leaves, 20–48in (50–120cm) long. Ovate to narrowly ovate, bright yellow spathes, to 16in (40cm) long, are borne in early spring. ↕ 3ft (1m), ↔ 4ft (1.2m). W. North America. Zone 7.
L. camtschatcensis ■ (White skunk cabbage). Marginal aquatic perennial with rosettes of ovate-oblong, strongly veined, leathery, glossy, mid- to dark green leaves, 20–39in (50–100cm) long. In early spring, produces ovate to broadly lance-shaped, usually pointed white spathes, to 16in (40cm) long. ↕↔ 30in (75cm). N.E. Asia. Zone 7.

Lysichiton camtschatcensis

LYSILOMA

FABACEAE

Genus of 30 species of shrubs and trees from valleys, lakesides, and thinly wooded, dry, rocky slopes of tropical and subtropical America. They are grown for their attractive foliage and flowers, with funnel-shaped corollas and wavy-toothed calyces, borne in heads or spikes. Lysilomas are useful at the back of an informal shrub border or in a transition planting between garden and desert.
• **CULTIVATION** Grow in moderately fertile soil in full sun. Pruning group 1.
• **PROPAGATION** Sow seed *in situ* as soon as ripe.
• **PESTS AND DISEASES** Rust, stem galls, root rot, and scale insects can occur.

L. thornberi (Feather bush, Fern-of-the-desert). Evergreen or deciduous, shrub or small tree, with 2-pinnate, bright green leaves, 6in (15cm) long, with 30–40 oblong, paired leaflets, to ⅜in (9mm) long. In early summer, bears tiny, white flowers, in heads to ½in (1.5cm) across, followed by flat, oblong-linear, ridged, glaucous-green seed pods, 4–8in (10–20cm) long. ↕ to 12ft (4m), ↔ 6–8ft (2–2.5m). Arizona (Rincon Mountains). ❄ (min. 41°F/5°C)

LYSIMACHIA

Loosestrife

PRIMULACEAE

Genus of about 150 species of herbaceous and evergreen perennials and shrubs, mainly growing in damp grassland and woodland or by water, in subtropical regions, including South Africa, and N. temperate regions. They have opposite, alternate, or whorled, simple, entire or sometimes toothed or scalloped, often hairy leaves. The 5-petaled flowers vary from star-shaped to saucer- or cup-shaped, and are usually white or yellow, sometimes pink or purple, and either solitary and axillary or borne in terminal racemes or panicles. Larger species are suitable for a moist herbaceous border, bog garden, or pond margin, or for naturalizing in a wild or woodland garden. Low-growing species make a good groundcover. Where not hardy, grow in a cool greenhouse.
• **CULTIVATION** Grow in humus-rich, preferably moist but well-drained soil

Lysimachia ciliata 'Purpurea'

Lysimachia clethroides

that does not dry out in summer, in full sun or partial shade. Tall species may need support.
• **PROPAGATION** Sow seed in containers outdoors in spring. Divide in spring or autumn.
• **PESTS AND DISEASES** Rust and leaf spot can occur.

L. barystachys. Erect herbaceous perennial with softly hairy stems and alternate, rarely opposite, linear-oblong to lance-shaped, hairy, mid-green leaves, to 3in (8cm) long, glaucous beneath. Bears dense, pendent then erect, terminal racemes, to 12in (30cm) long, of star-shaped white flowers, ¼–½in (7–10mm) across, in mid- and late summer. ↕ 24in (60cm), ↔ 18in (45cm). E. Russia, China, Korea, Japan. Zone 6.
L. ciliata, syn. *Steironema ciliata.* Erect, vigorous, rhizomatous herbaceous perennial with opposite or whorled, ovate-lance-shaped to ovate, hairy, mid-green leaves, to 6in (15cm) long, with hairy leaf stalks. In midsummer, bears solitary or paired, slightly pendent, star-shaped yellow flowers, 1in (2.5cm) across, with small, reddish brown centers, on slender stalks from the upper leaf axils. ↕ 4ft (1.2m), ↔ 24in (60cm). North America. Zone 4. **'Purpurea'** ■ has purple-brown leaves that emerge almost black; ↕ 24–32in (60–80cm).
L. clethroides ■ (Gooseneck loosestrife). Fast-spreading, softly hairy, rhizomatous herbaceous perennial with erect stems bearing alternate, narrowly ovate-lance-shaped, pointed leaves, to 5in (13cm) long, mid-green above, pale green beneath. In mid- and late

Lysimachia ephemerum

Lysimachia nummularia 'Aurea'

summer, saucer-shaped white flowers, ½in (1.5cm) across, are produced in dense, tapering, terminal racemes, 4–8in (10–20cm) long, which are pendent before the flowers open but become upright with arching tips as they mature. ↕ 36in (90cm), ↔ 24in (60cm). China, Korea, Japan. Zone 4.
L. congestiflora (Dense-flowered loosestrife). Mat-forming herbaceous perennial with opposite to whorled, ovate to ovate-lance-shaped, mid-green leaves, to 2in (5cm) long. Upturned, cup-shaped, golden yellow flowers, ½–¾in (1.5–2cm) across, are borne in leafy terminal panicles, from spring to summer. ↕ 4in (10cm), ↔ 12in (30cm). China. Zone 6. **'Eco Dark Satin'** has dark green leaves and red-throated, yellow flowers, from spring to autumn; ↔ 6in (15cm). **'Outback Sunset'** has red-tinged, yellow-variegated, mid-green leaves and yellow flowers with red centers, in spring and summer.
L. ephemerum ■ Clump-forming herbaceous perennial with erect stems and opposite, linear-lance-shaped to linear-spoon-shaped, hairless, glaucous, gray-green, stem-clasping leaves, 6in (15cm) long. Saucer-shaped white

Lysimachia punctata

flowers, ½in (1.5cm) across, are borne in slender, upright, dense, terminal racemes, to 16in (40cm) long, in early and midsummer. ↕ 3ft (1m), ↔ 12in (30cm). W. Portugal, S., C., and E. Spain, Pyrenees. Zone 6.
L. longifolia. Upright herbaceous perennial with erect, opposite, linear, wavy-margined, mid-green leaves, to 1½in (4cm) long. In summer, bears solitary, axillary, cup-shaped, golden yellow flowers, to ½in (1.5cm) across. ↕ to 24in (60cm), ↔ 12in (30cm). N. US. Zone 4.
***L. japonica* 'Minutissima'.** Prostrate, rhizomatous perennial with opposite, rounded-ovate, softly hairy, lime-green leaves, 1in (2.5cm) long. In summer, bears solitary, upturned, cup-shaped, gold-yellow flowers, ½in (1.5cm) across. Ideal for a rock garden. ↕ 2in (5cm), ↔ indefinite. Eurasia. Zone 6.
***L. nummularia* 'Aurea'** ■ (Golden creeping Jenny). Rampant, prostrate, stem-rooting, evergreen perennial with opposite, broadly ovate to rounded, golden yellow leaves, to ¾in (2cm) long, heart-shaped at the bases. During summer, produces usually solitary, upturned, cup-shaped, bright yellow flowers, to ¾in (2cm) across. ↕ to 2in (5cm), ↔ indefinite. Zone 4.
L. punctata ■ (Whorled loosestrife). Erect, rhizomatous, softly hairy herbaceous perennial with opposite or whorled, elliptic to lance-shaped, dark green leaves, 3in (8cm) long. Whorls of cup-shaped yellow flowers, 1in (2.5cm) across, are borne on short stalks from the leaf axils in mid- and late summer. May be invasive. ↕ to 3ft (1m), ↔ 24in (60cm). C. and S. Europe to Turkey. Zone 4.
L. vulgaris (Yellow loosestrife). Stoloniferous, softly hairy herbaceous perennial with erect stems bearing opposite or whorled, ovate to lance-shaped, mid- to bright green leaves, to 3½in (9cm) long. In summer, cupped yellow flowers, to ½in (1.5cm) across, are borne in leafy, terminal panicles, 4–12in (10–30cm) long. ↕ to 4ft (1.2m), ↔ to 3ft (1m). Europe, W. Asia. Zone 5.

LYTHRUM
Loosestrife

LYTHRACEAE

Genus of 38 species of annuals and perennials found in moist meadows and scrub, and in ditches and riversides, in N. temperate regions. They have 4-angled stems and usually opposite, ovate to lance-shaped or linear, stalkless leaves, which are occasionally softly hairy. Small, star-shaped or shallowly funnel-shaped, purple, pink, or rarely white flowers are produced singly or in groups from the leaf axils, sometimes forming spike-like racemes. Loosestrifes are long-flowering, and effective in a border or bog garden. Some provide attractive autumn color. A few species have become noxious weeds in wetlands throughout much of North America, and their sale has been banned in some areas. They should not be planted where they could escape into natural wetlands.
• **CULTIVATION** Grow in any (preferably fertile) moist soil in full sun. Remove flowered stems to prevent self-seeding.
• **PROPAGATION** Sow seed at 55–64°F (13–18°C), or divide, in spring. Take basal cuttings in spring or early summer.

Lythrum virgatum 'The Rocket'

• **PESTS AND DISEASES** Slugs and snails may damage young shoots, and Japanese beetles may eat the flowers.

***L.* 'Morden Pink'.** Clump-forming perennial with erect, branched stems and linear-lance-shaped, hairless leaves, 4in (10cm) long. In summer, bears star-shaped, clear pink flowers, ½in (1.5cm) across, in spike-like racemes, to 18in (45cm) long. ↕ to 32in (80cm), ↔ 18in (45cm). Zone 4.
L. salicaria (Purple loosestrife). Clump-forming perennial with erect, stiff, branched stems bearing lance-shaped, downy leaves, 4in (10cm) long. From midsummer to early autumn, bears star-shaped, bright purple-red to purple-pink flowers, ¾in (2cm) across, in spike-like racemes, to 18in (45cm) long. ↕ 4ft (1.2m), ↔ 18in (45cm). Europe, temperate Asia. Zone 4. **'Feuerkerze'**, syn. 'Firecandle', bears intense rose-red flowers in slender racemes; ↕ to 36in (90cm). **'Firecandle'** see 'Feuerkerze'. **'Flash Fire'** see 'Stichflamme'. **'Gypsy Blood'** see 'Zigeunerblut'. **'Happy'** has dark pink flowers; ↕ 18in (45cm). **'Robert'** produces bright pink flowers; ↕ 36in (90cm). **'Stichflamme'**, syn. 'Flash Fire' produces hot pink flowers; ↕ 4–5ft (1.2–1.5m). **'Zigeunerblut',** syn. 'Gypsy Blood' bears purple-red flowers; ↕ 4–5ft (1.2–1.5m).
L. virgatum. Clump-forming perennial with erect, branched stems and linear-lance-shaped, hairless leaves, 4in (10cm) long. In summer, star-shaped, purple-red flowers, ½in (1.5cm) across, are borne in slender, spike-like racemes, to 12in (30cm) long. ↕ 36in (90cm), ↔ 18in (45cm). E. Europe, W. and C. Asia, N.W. China. Zone 4. **'Dropmore Purple'** has linear, gray-green leaves with purple flowers; ↕ 4–5ft (1.2–1.5m). **'Morden's Gleam'** has rose-pink flowers; ↕ to 4½ft (1.4m). **'Rose Queen'** produces bright rose-pink flowers, purple in bud; ↕ 24in (60cm). **'The Rocket'** ■ produces deep pink flowers; ↕ 32in (80cm).

L

M

MAACKIA

FABACEAE

Genus of about 8 species of deciduous trees or shrubs occurring in woodland in E. Asia. Maackias are cultivated for their foliage, flowers, and exfoliating, copper bark. The leaves are alternate and pinnate, each with up to 17 pairs of leaflets and a single terminal one. The small, pea-like flowers, blooming even on very young trees, are produced in dense, terminal racemes or panicles in summer. These are followed by compressed, linear-oblong seed pods. Maackias make unusual specimen trees.

• **CULTIVATION** Grow in moderately fertile, well-drained, neutral to acidic soil in full sun. Pruning group 1.

• **PROPAGATION** Sow seed outdoors in containers or in a seedbed, in autumn. Insert greenwood cuttings in early or midsummer.

• **PESTS AND DISEASES** Infrequent.

M. amurensis ■ Open, spreading tree with pinnate, dark green leaves, 8–12in (20–30cm) long, with 7–11 ovate leaflets. In mid- and late summer, white flowers, to ½in (1.5cm) long, are produced in upright racemes, 4–6in (10–15cm) long, followed by flattened seed pods, to 2in (5cm) long, with ridged seams. ↕ to 50ft (15m), ↔ to 30ft (10m). N.E. China. Zone 3b.

M. chinensis. Rounded, sometimes flat-topped tree with smooth, dark greenish brown bark. Pinnate, dark green leaves, to 8in (20cm) long, each have 9–13 oblong to elliptic leaflets, silvery gray-blue when they unfold. In mid- and late summer, short-lived white flowers, to ½in (1.5cm) long, are produced in upright panicles, 6–8in (15–20cm) long, followed by oblong to elliptic seed pods, to 3in (8cm) long. ↕↔ 30ft (10m). China (Hubei, Sichuan). Zone 6.

MACFADYENA

syn. DOXANTHA

Cat's claw vine

BIGNONIACEAE

Genus of 3 or 4 species of evergreen climbers found in tropical forest and dry woodland from Mexico and the West Indies to Uruguay and Argentina. The leaves are borne in opposite pairs, each with 2 spreading leaflets and a short, 3-clawed tendril. Tubular-bell-shaped flowers, with 5 spreading lobes, are solitary or produced in axillary cymes from spring to summer. Where not hardy, grow these attractive climbers in a temperate greenhouse. In warm areas, grow over a fence, pergola, arch, or trellis, grow through a large tree, or use as a groundcover. They are also useful for erosion control.

• **CULTIVATION** Under glass, grow in soil-based potting mix in bright filtered light, or full light with shade from hot sun. During the growing season, water freely and apply a balanced liquid fertilizer monthly; water sparingly in winter. Outdoors, grow in moderately fertile, moist but well-drained, slightly acidic to slightly alkaline soil in full sun. Provide shelter from cold, drying winds. Stems may require tying in to their supports. Pruning group 11, after flowering.

• **PROPAGATION** Sow seed at 61–70°F (16–21°C) as soon as ripe or in spring. Root semi-ripe cuttings with bottom heat in summer. Layer in spring.

• **PESTS AND DISEASES** Spider mites, whiteflies, and mealybugs may prove troublesome under glass.

Maackia amurensis

Macfadyena unguis-cati

M. unguis-cati ■ syn. *Bignonia unguis-cati, Doxantha unguis-cati* (Common cat's claw vine). Slender-stemmed, vigorous climber with lance-shaped to ovate leaflets, 2–4in (5–10cm) or more long. Tubular, bright yellow flowers, 4in (10cm) across, usually with orange lines in the throats, are borne from spring to summer. They are followed by slender, bean-like seed pods, 10–36in (25–90cm) long. ↕ 20–30ft (6–10m). Mexico and West Indies to Argentina. ❄ (min. 45°F/7°C)

▷ ***Machaerocereus eruca*** see *Stenocereus eruca*

MACHAERANTHERA

ASTERACEAE

Genus of 26 species of branching annuals and perennials from plains, prairies, and dry hills of W. North America. The leaves are alternate, linear-oblong to oblong-lance-shaped, entire to pinnatisect, and occasionally spiny-toothed. They are grown for their blue to purple or white flowerheads, borne solitary or in panicles or cymes. Grow in a native or wildflower garden, or a rock garden. Where not hardy, grow in a cool greenhouse.

• **CULTIVATION** Under glass, grow in soil-based potting mix in full light. When in growth, water freely and apply a balanced liquid fertilizer monthly; water sparingly in winter. Outdoors, grow in moderately fertile, well-drained, but moisture-retentive soil in full sun.

• **PROPAGATION** For annuals, sow seed under glass as soon as ripe. Divide perennials in spring or summer.

• **PESTS AND DISEASES** Powdery mildew, rust, and leaf spots can occur.

M. bigelovii. Branching biennial or perennial with linear-oblong to inversely lance-shaped, entire or toothed, hairless leaves, 3in (8cm) long. In spring, bears cymes of pink or purple flowerheads, to 2½in (6cm) across. ↕ to 14in (35cm), ↔ to 12in (30cm). W. US. Zone 7b.

Mackaya bella

MACKAYA *syn.* ASYSTASIA

ACANTHACEAE

Genus of one species of evergreen shrub occurring in dry, open, mixed forest in southern Africa. *M. bella* is cultivated for its opposite, slender-pointed, elliptic leaves and its arching, terminal racemes of tubular-funnel-shaped flowers, each with 5 large, flared lobes, usually borne from spring to autumn. Where not hardy, grow in a temperate or warm greenhouse. In warmer climates, grow in a shrub border or as a specimen plant.

• **CULTIVATION** Under glass, grow in soil-based potting mix in bright filtered light, or full light with shade from hot sun. In growth, water freely and apply a balanced liquid fertilizer monthly; water sparingly in winter. Outdoors, grow in moderately fertile, moist but well-drained, neutral to slightly acidic or alkaline soil in full sun or light, dappled shade. Pruning group 9; plants under glass need restrictive pruning in winter.

• **PROPAGATION** Sow seed at 61°F (16°C) in spring. Root semi-ripe cuttings with bottom heat in summer.

• **PESTS AND DISEASES** Spider mites and whiteflies may occur under glass.

M. bella ■ syn. *Asystasia bella.* Erect then spreading shrub, with elliptic, slender-pointed, wavy-margined, lustrous, deep green leaves, 3–5in (8–13cm) long, with prominent veins. Terminal racemes of narrowly funnel-shaped flowers, to 2in (5cm) across, with large, pale lilac petal lobes finely veined dark purple, are mainly produced from spring to autumn. ↕ 3–6ft (1–2m), ↔ 3–5ft (1–1.5m). South Africa (Northern Transvaal, Eastern Transvaal, E. Northern Cape, KwaZulu/Natal), Swaziland. ❄ (min. 50°F/10°C)

MACLEANIA

ERICACEAE

Genus of 40 species of evergreen shrubs and climbers, some scrambling or semi-scandent, and sometimes epiphytic, occurring in tropical forest in Central and South America. They are cultivated for their waxy, tubular flowers, each with 5 short petal lobes, which are produced in pendent racemes from the upper leaf axils. The simple, leathery leaves are arranged alternately. In areas where temperatures fall below 50°F (10°C), grow in a temperate or warm

greenhouse. In frost-free climates, train over an arch or pergola, or grow against a wall.
• **CULTIVATION** Under glass, grow in acidic potting mix in bright filtered light. In growth, water moderately and apply a balanced liquid fertilizer monthly; water sparingly in winter. Outdoors, grow in moderately fertile, humus-rich, moist but well-drained, acidic soil in partial shade. Pruning group 11 for climbers, immediately after flowering; group 8 for shrubs.
• **PROPAGATION** Surface-sow seed at 55–61°F (13–16°C) in spring. Root semi-ripe cuttings with bottom heat in early summer. Air layer in spring.
• **PESTS AND DISEASES** Scale insects may be a problem under glass.

M. insignis. Semi-scandent, sparsely branched shrub with a woody, tuberous base, often epiphytic in the wild. Ovate to elliptic leaves, 2–4in (5–10cm) long, are red-tinted when young, maturing to deep green. Orange to deep scarlet flowers, 1–1½in (2.5–4cm) long, with small, triangular petal lobes and softly hairy mouths, are produced in short, leafy racemes, mainly in summer. ↕6–12ft (2–4m), ↔ 3–5ft (1–1.5m). S. Mexico, Honduras, Guatemala. ❀ (min. 50°F/10°C)

MACLEAYA syn. BOCCONIA
Plume poppy

PAPAVERACEAE

Genus of 2 or 3 species of rhizomatous perennials from grassy meadows, scrub, and woodland in China and Japan. They are cultivated for their foliage and graceful inflorescences. Erect, glaucous stems bear alternate, heart-shaped, palmately lobed, glaucous, gray-green to olive-green leaves, to 10in (25cm) long, with rounded, toothed lobes and prominent veins. Numerous petalless, tubular flowers, to ½in (1.5cm) long, with 2 or 4 sepals and a cluster of

Macleaya microcarpa 'Kelway's Coral Plume'

stamens, are borne in airy, plume-like panicles. The stems and leaf stalks produce a yellowish orange latex. Grow in a mixed or herbaceous border or as free-standing specimens; they may also be grown among large shrubs or used to form a temporary tall screen. They can be invasive, spreading rapidly and widely by underground suckers.
• **CULTIVATION** Grow in moderately fertile, moist but well-drained soil in full sun, although they will tolerate most soils and partial shade. Provide shelter from cold, drying winds.
• **PROPAGATION** Sow seed in containers in a cold frame in spring. Divide in late autumn or spring. Separate and transplant rooted rhizomes when dormant. Insert root cuttings in winter.
• **PESTS AND DISEASES** Slugs may attack young growth.

M. cordata, syn. *Bocconia cordata* (Plume poppy). Rhizomatous perennial with 5- to 7-lobed, gray- to olive-green leaves, white-downy beneath. In mid- and late summer, produces large, plume-like panicles of pendent, buff-white flowers, each with 25–40 stamens, on gray-green stems. ↕ to 8ft (2.5m), ↔ 3ft (1m). China, Japan. Zone 3. **'Alba'** has white flowers.
M. x kewensis (*M. cordata* x *M. microcarpa*). Rhizomatous perennial with 5- to 9-lobed, gray-green leaves. Creamy buff flowers, each with 12–18 stamens, are produced in loose, terminal panicles in early and late summer. ↕ 8ft (2.5m), ↔ 3ft (1m) or more. Garden origin. Zone 4. **'Flamingo'** has pink buds and buff-pink flowers.
***M. microcarpa* 'Kelway's Coral Plume'** ■ Rhizomatous perennial with 5- to 7-lobed, gray- to olive-green leaves, white-downy beneath. Large, loose panicles of pendent, deep buff- to coral-pink flowers, each with 8–15 stamens, open from pink buds in early and midsummer. ↕ 7ft (2.2m), ↔ 3ft (1m) or more. Zone 4.

MACLURA syn. CUDRANIA

MORACEAE

Genus of 15 species of usually thorny, evergreen or deciduous, dioecious trees, shrubs, or climbers, the branches often reduced to spines, found in woodland and clearings, and by roadsides, from E. Asia to Australia, and from S. central US to South America. The alternate or spiraling leaves are obovate or narrowly to broadly ovate. Racemes or clusters of small, spherical or cup-shaped, usually green flowers are followed by fleshy, spherical fruits, surrounded by enlarged bracts. Grow in a shrub border, as a windbreak, or as specimens.
• **CULTIVATION** Grow in moderately fertile, well-drained soil in full sun. Pruning group 1.
• **PROPAGATION** Sow seed in containers in an open frame as soon as ripe. Root semi-ripe cuttings with bottom heat in summer, or take root cuttings in winter.
• **PESTS AND DISEASES** Dieback, gray mold, rust, wilt, and scale insects occur.

M. aurantiaca see *M. pomifera.*
M. pomifera, syn. *M. aurantiaca* (Osage orange). Rounded, deciduous tree, thorny when young, becoming less so with age, with ovate, pointed, dark green leaves, to 4in (10cm) long, turning yellow in autumn. Tiny, cup-shaped, yellow-green flowers – the females in short racemes, the males in dense, spherical clusters – are borne in early summer, followed on female trees by large, wrinkled, fragrant, yellow-green fruit, to 5in (13cm) across. ↕ 50ft (15m), ↔ 40ft (12m). S. central US. Zone 6. **'Double O'** is male and upright. **'Inermis'** has thornless branches. **'Pulverulenta'** has powdery white leaves. **'Wichita'** is one of several male and nearly thornless cultivars.
M. tricuspidata, syn. *Cudrania tricuspidata.* Compact, rounded, deciduous shrub or small tree with ovate or obovate, dark green leaves, to 4in (10cm) long, sometimes 3-lobed at the apexes. In summer, spherical clusters of tiny green flowers are produced singly or in pairs from the leaf axils of the current year's growth, followed on female trees by glossy, edible, orange-red fruit, ¾–2in (2–5cm) across. ↕ 22ft (7m), ↔ 20ft (6m). C. China, Korea. Zone 6b.

MACROPIDIA

HAEMODORACEAE

Genus of one species of evergreen, rhizomatous perennial from Australia, found in open ground at the edges of scrub. It has fans of sword-shaped, basal leaves, and produces panicles of woolly, swollen, tubular flowers, with sharply reflexed segments often likened to a kangaroo's foot. Where not hardy, grow in a cool or temperate greenhouse. In warmer climates, it is an unusual and effective border plant.
• **CULTIVATION** Under glass, grow in soil-based potting mix, with added grit, in bright filtered light, or full light with shade from hot sun, with low humidity. When in growth, water moderately and apply a balanced liquid fertilizer monthly; water sparingly in winter. Outdoors, grow in moderately fertile, well-drained, neutral to slightly acidic soil in full sun, with shade from midday sun. Protect from excessive winter moisture.
• **PROPAGATION** Sow seed at 50°F (10°C) as soon as ripe or in spring. Divide as growth starts in spring.
• **PESTS AND DISEASES** Infrequent.

M. fuliginosa (Black kangaroo paw). Perennial with short rhizomes and fan-shaped tufts of linear to narrowly strap-shaped, bluish green leaves, to 12in (30cm) long. Panicles of yellow flowers, 1¾in (4.5cm) long, covered in plume-like black hairs, are borne on thick, branched stems, to 4ft (1.2m) long, in summer. ↕ 4ft (1.2m), ↔ 24in (60cm). S.W. Australia. ❀ (min. 45°F/7°C)

▷ ***Macrotomia echioides*** see *Arnebia pulchra*

MACROZAMIA

ZAMIACEAE

Genus of 12 species of dioecious cycads from well-drained sites in open forest in Australia. Some species have a palm-like stem; in others, the stem is short and completely or partly buried. Evergreen, pinnate leaves, with linear to lance-shaped, leathery, light to mid-green leaflets, are borne in terminal whorls or

Macrozamia communis

rosettes. Male or female inflorescences ("cones") are borne among the leaves. Where not hardy, grow macrozamias in a temperate or warm greenhouse. In warmer climates, grow in a tub or as a specimen in the landscape where a palm-like focal point is needed.
• **CULTIVATION** Under glass, grow in soil-based potting mix, with added grit, in full light with shade from hot sun, and with low to moderate humidity. Pot on or top-dress in spring. During the growing season, water moderately and apply a balanced liquid fertilizer monthly; water sparingly in winter. Outdoors, grow in poor to moderately fertile, well-drained, neutral to slightly acidic soil in full sun, with shade from midday sun.
• **PROPAGATION** Sow seed at 70–86°F (21–30°C) as soon as ripe or in spring.
• **PESTS AND DISEASES** Infrequent.

M. communis ■ (Burrawong). Cycad with a robust stem, buried at first then slowly elongating. Whorled leaves, to 6ft (2m) long, have linear, sharply pointed, lustrous, rich green leaflets. Cylindrical, green to brown flowering cones usually appear in summer: male cones are 8–18in (20–45cm) long, females to 18in (45cm) long. They are followed by ovoid fruit containing large, fleshy red seeds. ↕ 6–10ft (2–3m), ↔ to 12ft (4m). New South Wales. ❀ (min. 50°F/10°C)
M. corallipes see *M. spiralis.*
M. moorei. Palm-like cycad with a thick, columnar trunk and whorled leaves, to 10ft (3m) long, with narrowly lance-shaped, deep green, often bluish green leaflets. Bears cylindrical, usually green flowering cones in summer: the males to 12in (30cm) long, the females to 36in (90cm) long. Flowers are followed by ovoid fruit with bright red seeds. ↕ to 28ft (9m), ↔ to 20ft (6m). New South Wales, Queensland. ❀ (min. 50°F/10°C)
M. spiralis, syn. *M. corallipes.* Small cycad with a largely underground stem, with only the growing point above the surface. Leaves, to 3ft (90cm) or more long, have stalks with pink, red, or orange bases, and consist of many linear, matte, deep green leaflets that spiral longitudinally, at least when young. Cylindrical to ellipsoid green flowering cones, 6–8in (15–20cm) long, appear in summer, followed by ovoid fruit with orange to scarlet seeds. ↕ 3ft (1m) or more, ↔ to 6ft (2m). New South Wales. ❀ (min. 50°F/10°C)

MAGNOLIA

MAGNOLIACEAE

Genus of about 125 species of deciduous and evergreen trees and shrubs, occurring in woodland, in scrub, and on riverbanks from the Himalayas to E. and S.E. Asia, and from E. North America to tropical North and South America. They are grown for their showy, solitary, fragrant, usually erect, sometimes pendent or horizontal, cup-, saucer-, goblet-, or star-shaped flowers (see panel opposite), often borne before the leaves. The flowers have usually 6–9 petals; colors include pure white, white flushed or stained pink or purple, pink, rich purple, creamy yellow, greenish yellow, glaucous green, and light to mid-yellow. The alternate leaves are usually obovate to ovate, oblong, or elliptic; in a few species, the foliage turns yellow in autumn. Cone-like fruits, often pink or red with red- or orange-coated seeds, are attractive in autumn.

Grow magnolias as specimens or among other trees and shrubs. Where not hardy, grow smaller species in a cool or temperate greenhouse. Some species take many years to flower: up to 30 years for *M. campbellii* when grown from seed and about 15 years for grafted or budded plants. *M. grandiflora* and *M.* x *soulangeana* may be wall-trained.

• **CULTIVATION** Grow in moist, well-drained, humus-rich, preferably acidic to neutral soil in sun or partial shade. *M. delavayi* and *M. grandiflora* will tolerate dry, alkaline soil; *M. kobus*, *M.* x *loebneri*, *M. sieboldii*, *M. stellata*, and *M. wilsonii* will grow in moist, alkaline soils. Flowers, and sometimes young foliage, of early-flowering magnolias are often damaged by late frosts. Mulch with manure and leaf mold in early spring, particularly on dry soils. Pruning group 1 for trees and deciduous shrubs; group 9 for evergreen shrubs; group 13 if wall-trained.

• **PROPAGATION** Sow seed in a seedbed in autumn. Stratified seeds germinate freely. For deciduous magnolias, root greenwood cuttings in early summer, or semi-ripe cuttings in late summer. For evergreens, root semi-ripe cuttings from late summer to early autumn. Graft in winter. Bud in summer. Layer in early spring.

• **PESTS AND DISEASES** Bacterial leaf spot, spot anthracnose, canker, dieback, butt rot, powdery mildew, anthracnose, fungal spots, snails, weevils, scale insects, planthoppers, and thrips are common.

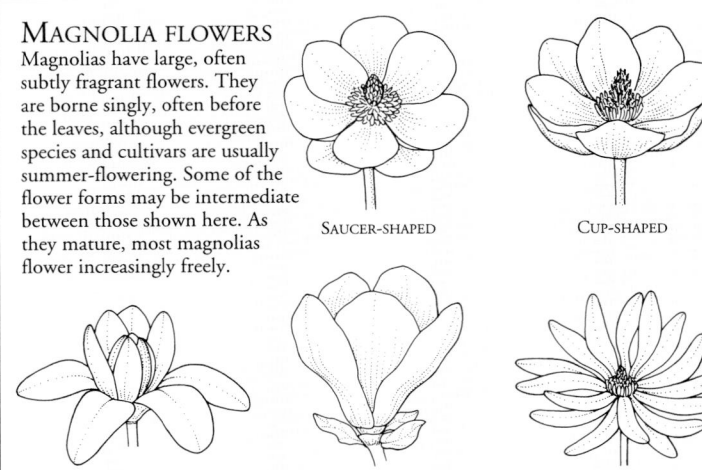

MAGNOLIA FLOWERS

Magnolias have large, often subtly fragrant flowers. They are borne singly, often before the leaves, although evergreen species and cultivars are usually summer-flowering. Some of the flower forms may be intermediate between those shown here. As they mature, most magnolias flower increasingly freely.

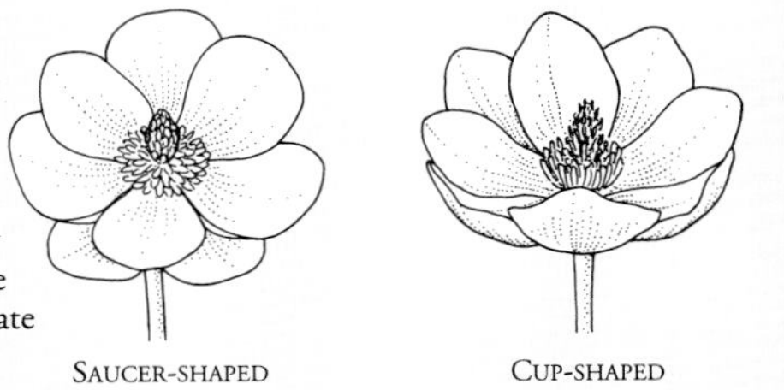

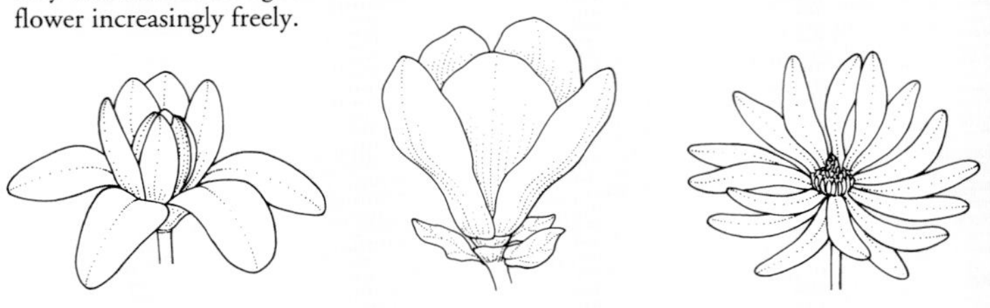

M. acuminata ■ (Cucumber tree). Vigorous, conical, deciduous tree with ovate to elliptic or oblong-ovate leaves, dark green above, lighter and softly hairy beneath, to 10in (25cm) long. In late spring and early summer, produces small, cup-shaped, yellow-green or glaucous green flowers, to 3½in (9cm) across, among the leaves, followed by red or brown fruit. ↕70ft (20m), ↔30ft (10m). E. North America. Zone 5. **'Golden Glow'** has yellow flowers. **var. *subcordata***, syn. *M. cordata* (Yellow cucumber tree) has smaller leaves, to 6in (15cm) long, and pale yellow to yellow-green flowers; ↕25ft (8m), ↔20ft (6m); S.E. US.

Magnolia acuminata (inset: flower detail)

***M.* 'Ann'.** Open, deciduous, shrub with obovate to elliptic-ovate, dark green leaves, 4–7in (10–18cm) long, softly hairy above. Goblet-shaped, deep purple-red flowers, 5in (13cm) across, with 7–9 petals, are produced in midspring. ↕8–10ft (2.5–3m), ↔10ft (3m). Zone 5.

M. ashei ■ syn. *M. macrophylla* subsp. *ashei*. Spreading, deciduous shrub or small tree with thick shoots and large, obovate leaves, glossy, light green above and glaucous beneath, to 24in (60cm) long. In early summer, produces saucer-shaped white flowers, 8–10in (20–25cm) across, the petals stained maroon at the bases. ↕30–70ft (10–20m), ↔25–50ft (8–15m). N.W. Florida. Zone 7b.

***M.* 'Betty'.** Vigorous, rounded, deciduous shrub with broadly ovate, mid-green leaves, to 6in (15cm) long. In midspring, bears large, cup-shaped flowers, to 8in (20cm) across, with up to 19 petals, purple-red outside and white inside. ↕↔12ft (4m). Zone 5b.

***M.* x *brooklynensis* 'Woodsman'.** Conical, later spreading, deciduous tree with ovate, mid-green leaves, to 10in (25cm) long. In late spring and early summer, bears narrowly cup-shaped flowers, to 5in (13cm) across, the outer 3 petals green, the middle 3 green-flushed purple, and the central 3 pale pink. ↕30ft (10m), ↔20ft (6m). Zone 6.

***M.* 'Butterflies'.** Conical, deciduous tree with obovate to elliptic-ovate, sparsely hairy, mid- to dark green leaves, 8in (20cm) long. Numerous cup-shaped, 10–15 petaled, light yellow flowers, 4–5in (10–13cm) across, with red stamens, are borne in midspring. ↕15ft (5m), ↔11ft (3.5m). Zone 5.

M. campbellii ■ Vigorous, conical then spreading deciduous tree with elliptic-ovate to oblong-elliptic, mid-green leaves, to 10in (25cm) long. Cup-and-saucer-shaped, white or crimson to rose-pink flowers, to 12in (30cm) across, with up to 16 petals, are borne from late winter to spring, before the leaves. ↕50ft (15m), ↔30ft (10m). Nepal, India (Sikkim), Bhutan. Zone 7. **var. *alba*** has white flowers. **'Charles Raffill'** ■ has purple-pink flowers. **'Darjeeling'** ■ produces very dark pink flowers. **'Kew's Surprise'** has dark purple-pink flowers. **'Lanarth'** has rich lilac-purple flowers. **'Maharajah'** has large white flowers with purple bases. **subsp. *mollicomata*** ■ bears pink to purple-pink flowers at an earlier age and slightly later in the year; S.W. Tibet, N. Burma, China (Yunnan). **'Strybing White'** has large white flowers.

***M.* 'Charles Coates'** ■ Vigorous, open, spreading, deciduous shrub with ovate leaves, clustered at the shoot tips, dark green above and slightly glaucous green beneath, to 10in (25cm) long. In late spring and early summer, produces erect or horizontal, fragrant, saucer-shaped, creamy white flowers, to 4in (10cm) across, with red anthers and 9–12 petals. ↕30ft (10m), ↔20ft (6m). Zone 6.

M. cordata see *M. acuminata* var. *subcordata*.

M. cylindrica ■ Deciduous small, spreading tree with obovate leaves, to 6in (15cm) long, dark green above and pale green beneath. Cup-shaped, creamy white or yellowish white flowers, to 4in (10cm) long, are borne in spring, before and with the young leaves. ↕↔20ft (6m). E. China. Zone 7.

M. dawsoniana. Broadly oval-headed, deciduous tree, occasionally a large shrub, with obovate, dark green leaves, to 6in (15cm) long, slightly glaucous beneath. Large, horizontal to pendent, saucer-shaped, pale lilac-pink flowers, to 5in (13cm) across, are borne in early spring, before the leaves. ↕50ft (15m), ↔30ft (10m). China. Zone 6b. **'Chyverton'** ■ has deep purplish pink petals, white or very pale pink at the tips and within, and crimson anthers.

M. delavayi ■ Dense, rounded, evergreen shrub or tree with ovate to oblong, dark green leaves, to 12in (30cm) long. Short-lived, cup-shaped, creamy or yellowish white flowers, to 8in (20cm) across, are borne in late summer. Grows well against a wall. ↕↔30ft (10m). China. Zone 7b.

M. denudata ■ syn. *M. heptapeta* (Lily tree, Yulan). Spreading tree with obovate, mid-green leaves, to 6in (15cm) long. Cup-shaped white flowers, to 6in (15cm) across, tinged pale yellow-green when opening, are borne in spring, before the leaves. ↕↔30ft (10m). China. Zone 5b.

***M.* 'Elizabeth'** ■ Conical to rounded, deciduous tree with obovate leaves, to 8in (20cm) long, bronze when young, maturing to dark green. Bears cup-shaped, soft yellow flowers, to 6in

M

(15cm) across, in mid- and late spring, before and with the young leaves. ↕30ft (10m), ↔ 20ft (6m). Zone 5.
M. fraseri ■ (Ear-leaved umbrella tree). Open, spreading, deciduous tree with obovate leaves, usually to 10in (25cm) long, but occasionally much larger, with distinct auricles, bronze when young, maturing to mid-green. Bears narrowly cup- or goblet-shaped, green-flushed, creamy white flowers, 6–8in (15–20cm) across, in late spring and early summer. ↕↔ 30ft (10m). S.E. US. Zone 5b.
***M.* 'Galaxy'.** Fast-growing, broadly conical, deciduous tree with obovate, mid-green leaves, to 8in (20cm) long. Large, goblet-shaped, rich purple-pink flowers, to 5in (13cm) across, are borne in midspring, before the leaves. Flowers when young. ↕40ft (12m), ↔ 25ft (8m). Zone 6.
M. glauca see *M. virginiana.*
M. grandiflora ■ (Bull bay, Southern magnolia). Dense, broadly conical, evergreen tree with narrowly elliptic to broadly ovate, leathery, glossy, dark green leaves, to 8in (20cm) long, with paler green and often rust-hairy undersides. Large, cup-shaped, fragrant, creamy white flowers, to 10in (25cm) across, with 9–12 petals, are produced from midsummer to autumn. ↕20–60ft (6–18m), ↔ to 50ft (15m). S.E. US. Zone 7. Many cultivars have been selected. **'Bracken's Brown Beauty'** is dense and compact, with small, wavy leaves, 6in (15cm) long, small flowers, 5–6in (13–15cm) across; ↕30ft (10m). **'Edith Bogue'** has a conical habit, and is among the hardiest selections; ↕30ft (10m), ↔ 15ft (5m). **'Ferruginea'** ■ has dark green leaves, rust-hairy beneath. **'Goliath'** ■ has broad, slightly twisted leaves and very large flowers, 8–12in (20–30cm) across. **'Little Gem'** is compact and upright, with elliptic to

Magnolia kobus

oval, dark green leaves, to 5in (13cm) long, rust-hairy beneath, and small flowers; ↕20ft (6m), ↔ 10ft (3m). **'Samuel Sommer'** has glossy, dark green leaves, rust-hairy beneath, and very large flowers, to 14in (35cm) across.
***M.* 'Heaven Scent'.** Spreading, deciduous tree or large shrub with broadly elliptic, glossy, mid-green leaves, to 8in (20cm) long. Bears goblet-shaped, fragrant flowers, to 5in (13cm) long, with 9–12 petals, pink outside and white inside, from midspring to early summer. ↕↔ 30ft (10m). Zone 4b.
M. heptapeta see *M. denudata.*
M. hypoleuca ■ syn. *M. obovata* (Japanese big-leaf magnolia, Whitebark magnolia). Vigorous, conical, deciduous tree with large, obovate, mid-green leaves, to 16in (40cm) long, clustered at the ends of the shoots. Large, cup-shaped, very fragrant, creamy white flowers, to 8in (20cm) across, with 9–12 petals and crimson stamens, are produced in late spring and early summer, after the leaves. ↕50ft (15m), ↔ 30ft (10m). Japan. Zone 6.
M. insignis see *Manglietia insignis.*
***M.* 'Iolanthe'.** Vigorous, upright, deciduous tree with obovate, mid-green leaves, to 10in (25cm) long. From an early age, very large, cup-shaped flowers, to 10in (25cm) across, rose-pink outside and creamy white inside, are borne in midspring. ↕40ft (12m), ↔ 25ft (8m). Zone 6b.
***M.* 'Jane'.** Upright, deciduous shrub with ovate, glossy, mid-green leaves, to 6in (15cm) long. Cup-shaped, very fragrant flowers, to 4in (10cm) across, with 10 petals, red-purple outside and white inside, are produced from slender, erect, red-purple buds in late spring. ↕12ft (4m), ↔ 10ft (3m). Zone 5b.
M.* x *kewensis (*M. kobus* x *M. salicifolia*). Deciduous tree or shrub, conical when young, later spreading, with elliptic, mid-green leaves, bluish green below, to 5in (13cm) long. Bears open cup-shaped white flowers, smelling of orange blossoms, to 5in (13cm) across, in midspring, before the leaves. ↕40ft (12m), ↔ 25ft (8m). Garden origin. Zone 6.
M. kobus ■ Broadly conical, deciduous tree with narrowly obovate, often puckered, aromatic, mid-green leaves, to 8in (20cm) long. Goblet- to saucer-shaped, fragrant white flowers, to 4in (10cm) across, occasionally flushed pink at the bases, are borne profusely in midspring. ↕40ft (12m), ↔ 30ft (10m). Japan. Zone 5.
M. liliiflora, syn. *M. quinquepeta* (Lily-flowered magnolia). Bushy, deciduous shrub with elliptic to obovate, dark green leaves, to 8in (20cm) long. Goblet-shaped, purplish pink flowers, to 3in (8cm) across, are borne in midspring and often again in midsummer. ↕10ft (3m), ↔ 12ft (4m). China. Zone 6.

Magnolia x *loebneri* 'Merrill'

'Nigra' ■ is compact and flowers when young, bearing very dark purple-red flowers in early summer and intermittently into autumn; ↔ 8ft (2.5m).
M.* x *loebneri (*M. kobus* x *M. stellata*). Small, slender-branched, upright, deciduous tree or large shrub, with narrowly obovate, mid-green leaves, 4–6in (10–15cm) long. Star-shaped, fragrant flowers, 3–5in (8–13cm) across, with 10–14 slender white petals, sometimes suffused lilac-purple outside and pale pink inside, are produced before the leaves in midspring. ↕30ft (10m), ↔ 22ft (7m). Garden origin. Zone 5. **'Ballerina'** has very fragrant, pure white flowers with pinkish centers, and up to 30 petals; slightly later than many other *M. stellata* selections; ↕15–20ft (5–6m). **'Leonard Messel'** ■ is more rounded, and has abundant, 12-petaled, pale lilac-pink flowers in midspring; ↕25ft (8m), ↔ 20ft (6m). **'Merrill'** ■ is vigorous, erect, and compact, with broader leaves; flowers

M

Magnolia ashei

Magnolia campbellii

Magnolia campbellii 'Charles Raffill'

Magnolia campbellii 'Darjeeling'

Magnolia campbellii subsp. *mollicomata*

Magnolia 'Charles Coates'

Magnolia cylindrica

Magnolia dawsoniana 'Chyverton'

Magnolia delavayi

Magnolia denudata

Magnolia 'Elizabeth'

Magnolia fraseri

Magnolia grandiflora

Magnolia grandiflora 'Ferruginea'

Magnolia grandiflora 'Goliath'

Magnolia hypoleuca

Magnolia liliiflora 'Nigra'

Magnolia x *loebneri* 'Leonard Messel'

Magnolia 'Ricki' (inset: flower detail)

are initially goblet-shaped then star-shaped, with 15 broad white petals; ↔ 25ft (8m). **'Spring Snow'** has pure white flowers with 15 petals; ↕ 28ft (9m).

M. macrophylla (Large-leaved cucumber tree, Umbrella tree). Broadly upright, later rounded, deciduous tree with thick, blue-gray shoots and very large, obovate leaves, to 3ft (1m) long, light green above, silvery gray beneath. In early summer, produces open-cup-shaped, fragrant, creamy white flowers, to 12in (30cm) or more across, with 6 petals, the inner 3 marked maroon at the bases. ↕↔ 30ft (10m). S.E. US. Zone 7. **subsp. *ashei*** see *M. ashei.*

***M.* 'Manchu Fan'** ■ Spreading, deciduous tree or shrub with obovate, mid-green leaves, to 8in (20cm) long. In late spring, bears large, goblet-shaped, creamy white flowers, to 5in (13cm) across, each with 9 petals, the inner ones flushed purple-pink at the bases. ↕ 20ft (6m), ↔ 15ft (5m). Zone 6b.

***M.* 'Maryland'.** Broadly conical, evergreen shrub or tree with oblong, slightly wavy-margined, glossy, mid-green leaves, to 9in (23cm) long. Bears cup-shaped, strongly fragrant white flowers, to 6in (15cm) across, in late summer. Flowers when young. ↕ 20ft (6m) or more, ↔ 15ft (5m). Zone 6b.

***M.* 'Norman Gould'** ■ Small, open, spreading, deciduous tree with obovate, mid-green leaves, to 5in (13cm) long. Goblet-shaped white flowers, to 5in (13cm) across, with 9–12 broad petals, faintly streaked pink on the outside, are borne horizontally in early and mid-spring. ↕↔ 15ft (5m). Zone 6b.

M. obovata see *M. hypoleuca.*

M. parviflora see *M. sieboldii.*

***M.* 'Peppermint Stick'.** Conical, deciduous tree or large shrub, with obovate, mid-green leaves, to 8in (20cm) long. From midspring to early summer, large, cup-and-saucer-shaped flowers, to 4½in (11cm) across, with creamy white petals, flushed dark purple-pink at the bases, are produced from long, slender buds. ↕ 30ft (10m), ↔ 20ft (6m). Zone 6b.

M. x proctoriana (*M. salicifolia* x *M. stellata*). Conical, deciduous tree with oval, aromatic leaves, to 5in (13cm) long, mid-green above and pale green beneath. Erect or horizontal, star-shaped white flowers, to 4in (10cm) across, with up to 12 petals, are borne in midspring. ↕ 25ft (8m), ↔ 20ft (6m). Garden origin. Zone 6.

M. quinquepeta see *M. liliiflora.*

***M.* 'Randy'.** Upright, almost columnar, free-flowering, deciduous shrub with broadly ovate, mid-green leaves, to 6in (15cm) long. The flowers, to 5in (13cm) across, produced from dark purple-red buds in midspring, are initially goblet-shaped, then star-shaped when fully open; each has 10 petals, purple-pink outside and white inside. ↕ 12ft (4m), ↔ 8ft (2.5m). Zone 5b.

***M.* 'Ricki'** ■ Upright, deciduous shrub with broadly ovate, mid-green leaves, to 6in (15cm) long. Goblet-shaped flowers, to 6in (15cm) across, with 15 twisted petals, pink to dark purple-pink at the bases, are produced from dark purple-pink buds in midspring. ↕↔ 12ft (4m). Zone 5b.

M. salicifolia ■ (Anise magnolia, Willow-leaved magnolia). Conical, deciduous tree with narrowly elliptic to lance-shaped, scented leaves, dull green above and gray-white beneath, to 6in (15cm) long. Abundant star-shaped, fragrant, pure white flowers, to 4in (10cm) across, are borne in midspring, before the leaves. ↕ 30ft (10m), ↔ 20ft (6m). Japan. Zone 6. **'Jermyns'** is shrubby and spreading in habit, with flowers to 5in (13cm) across, and broad leaves; ↕ 15ft (5m).

M. sargentiana. Broadly conical, deciduous tree with obovate, light to mid-green leaves, to 7in (18cm) long. Large, horizontal to nodding, goblet- to cup-shaped, 12- to 14-petaled flowers, to 8in (20cm) across, white inside and purple-pink outside, are borne in mid- and late spring, before the leaves. ↕ 50ft (15m), ↔ 30ft (10m). W. China. Zone 7b. **var. *robusta*** is more spreading, with oblong-obovate leaves and large flowers, 9–12in (22–30cm) across.

***M.* 'Sayonara'.** Spreading, deciduous tree or shrub with obovate, mid-green leaves, to 8in (20cm) long. Large, broadly goblet-shaped, creamy white flowers, to 5in (13cm) across, the inner petals faintly flushed purple-pink at the bases, are borne in mid- and late spring. ↕ 20ft (6m), ↔ 15ft (5m). Zone 6.

Magnolia x *soulangeana*

M. sieboldii, syn. *M. parviflora* (Oyama magnolia). Spreading, deciduous shrub with oblong to ovate-elliptic leaves, to 6in (15cm) long, dark green above, gray-green and downy beneath. From late spring to late summer, bears cup-shaped, slightly nodding, fragrant white flowers, to 4in (10cm) across, with 12 petals and crimson anthers. ↕ 25ft (8m), ↔ 40ft (12m). China, Korea, Japan. Zone 6b. **subsp. *sinensis***, syn. *M. sinensis*, produces slightly larger, fully pendent flowers and more rounded, oval leaves; W. China.

M. sinensis see *M. sieboldii* subsp. *sinensis.*

M. x soulangeana ■ (*M. denudata* x *M. liliiflora*) (Saucer magnolia). Variable, deciduous shrub or spreading tree with obovate, dark green leaves, to 8in (20cm) long. Large, goblet-shaped, fragrant flowers, 3–6in (8–30cm) across, varying from deep rose-pink to violet-purple or pure white, are borne in mid- and late spring, before and with the young leaves. ↕↔ 20ft (6m). Garden origin. Zone 5b. **'Alba Superba'**, syn. 'Alba', is upright in habit, and bears large, fragrant white flowers, slightly purple-flushed at the bases; ↕ 22ft (7m), ↔ 15ft (5m). **'Alexandrina'** is upright, with deeply saucer-shaped white flowers, to 4in (10cm) across, purple-flushed outside, giving an overall rose-pink

M

Magnolia 'Manchu Fan'

Magnolia 'Norman Gould'

Magnolia salicifolia

Magnolia x *soulangeana* 'Lennei Alba'

Magnolia x *soulangeana* 'Rustica Rubra'

Magnolia sprengeri

Magnolia stellata 'Royal Star'

Magnolia 'Susan'

Magnolia x *veitchii* 'Peter Veitch'

Magnolia virginiana

Magnolia x *wieseneri*

Magnolia wilsonii

Magnolia stellata

effect. **'Andre LeRoy'** bears cup-shaped flowers, dark pink to purple-pink outside, with white inner petals. **'Brozzoni'** is tree-like, bearing white flowers, to 5in (13cm) across, faintly purple-flushed outside, later than most; ↕25ft (8m). **'Burgundy'** bears profuse deep purple-pink flowers, 4in (10cm) across. **'Grace McDade'** bears white flowers with pink at the petal bases. **'Lennei'** has dark purple-pink flowers, to 8in (20cm) across, white within. **'Lennei Alba'** ▣ bears ivory-white flowers, 4in (10cm) across. **'Lombardy Rose'** is upright, with abundant white flowers, dark rose on the lower surfaces of the petals. **'Picture'** is compact and upright, with flowers, 4–5in (10–13cm) across, richly streaked dark reddish purple, white within, and flowering when only 3ft (1m) high; ↕25ft (8m). **'Rubra'** see 'Rustica Rubra'. **'Rustica Rubra'** ▣ syn. 'Rubra', has deeply goblet-shaped, dark purplish red flowers, 4–5in (10–13cm) across, milky white within. **'San José'** bears creamy white flowers, 4–5in (10–13cm) across, flushed dark pink outside. **'Speciosa'** bears late, slightly reflexed white flowers, purple-flushed at the bases of the petals.

M. sprengeri ▣ Spreading, deciduous tree with obovate, dark green leaves, to 6in (15cm) long. Bears large, cup-shaped, white to pink flowers, to 6in (15cm) across, with 12–15 petals, in midspring, before the leaves. ↕50ft (15m), ↔30ft (10m). China. Zone 7b. **var. *diva*** has rich deep pink flowers, streaked with white and pink inside. **'Wakehurst'** has dark purple-pink flowers, rich pink inside.

M. stellata ▣ (Star magnolia). Compact, bushy then spreading, deciduous shrub with obovate-oblong to inversely lance-shaped, mid-green leaves, to 4in (10cm) long. Silky buds open to star-shaped, mostly erect, fragrant, pure white, sometimes faintly pink-flushed flowers, 5in (13cm) across, with up to 15 petals; flowers are borne profusely in early and midspring, before the leaves. ↕10ft (3m), ↔12ft (4m). Japan. Zone 5. **'Centennial'** bears white flowers, to 5½in (14cm) across, with 28–32 petals. **'Dawn'** has white flowers with 25 petals, each with a longitudinal pink stripe. **'King Rose'** has a spreading, dense habit and bears flowers with blush pink outsides, pink in bud, and 22–25 petals. **'Rosea'** has pink buds, opening white. **'Royal Star'** ▣ has faintly pink buds and white flowers, 5in (13cm) across, with 25–30 petals. **'Rubra'** has dark pink flowers, to 5in (13cm) across. **'Waterlily'** has white flowers, to 5in (13cm) across, with up to 32 petals; it is similar to 'Centennial' but has slightly smaller flowers.

***M.* 'Susan'** ▣ Upright, deciduous shrub bearing ovate, mid-green leaves, to 6in (15cm) long. In midspring, narrowly goblet-shaped, fragrant flowers, to 6in (15cm) across, with usually slightly twisted petals, purple-red outside and paler inside, are produced from slender, dark red-purple buds. ↕12ft (4m), ↔10ft (3m). Zone 5b.

M. tripetala (Umbrella tree). Broadly conical, deciduous tree with obovate to inversely lance-shaped, dark green leaves, to 24in (60cm) long, clustered at the ends of the shoots. Cup-shaped, unpleasantly scented, creamy white flowers, to 6in (15cm) across, with 9–16 petals, are produced in late spring and early summer, followed by showy, fuchsia-pink fruits with orange seeds, in autumn. ↕↔30ft (10m). E. US. Zone 5b.

M.* x *veitchii (*M. campbellii* x *M. denudata*). Large, upright, deciduous tree with purple-green juvenile foliage and branches. Leaves are obovate or oblong, 6–12in (15–30cm) long, mostly rounded at the bases and pointed at the tips, and dark green when mature. Bears goblet-shaped, pink to white flowers, 6in (15cm) long, on bare branches in midspring. ↕100ft (30m), ↔10–30ft (3–10m). Garden origin. Zone 7. **'Isca'** has obovate leaves and satin-textured white flowers, faintly pink-tinged at the petal bases; ↕80ft (25m), ↔50ft (15m). **'Peter Veitch'** ▣ bears pale pink flowers, shading to white at the petal tips.

M. virginiana ▣ syn. *M. glauca* (Swamp magnolia, Sweet bay). Conical to irregularly spreading, deciduous or semi-evergreen shrub or small tree with elliptic to ovate, glossy, bright green leaves, to 6in (15cm) long, glaucous beneath. From early summer to early autumn, produces almost spherical, deeply cup-shaped, strongly lemon- and rose-scented flowers, to 2½in (6cm) across, with 6–9 creamy white petals, fading to yellow with age. ↕28ft (9m), ↔20ft (6m). E. US. Zone 6. **var. *australis* 'Henry Hicks'** remains evergreen to -17°F (-27°C).

***M.* 'Wada's Memory'.** Compact, broadly conical, deciduous tree with narrowly ovate, dark green leaves, to 7in (18cm) long, bronze when young. Abundant cup-shaped white flowers, to 6in (15cm) across, are produced in mid- and late spring, before the leaves. ↕28ft (9m), ↔22ft (7m). Zone 6.

M.* x *watsonii see *M.* x *wieseneri.*

M.* x *wieseneri ▣ (*M. hypoleuca* x *M. sieboldii*), syn. *M.* x *watsonii.* Spreading, deciduous shrub or tree with obovate, leathery, bright green leaves, to 8in (20cm) long, glaucous beneath. In early and midsummer, spherical white buds open to deeply cup-shaped, strongly fragrant flowers, 6in (15cm) across, with 6–9 ivory-white inner petals, 3 smaller, pink-flushed outer petals, and rose-crimson anthers. ↕20ft (6m), ↔15ft (5m). Garden origin. Zone 6.

M. wilsonii ▣ Spreading, deciduous shrub or small tree with red-purple shoots and elliptic or ovate to lance-shaped, dark green leaves, to 6in (15cm) long, felted red-brown beneath. In late spring and early summer, bears pendent, cup-shaped white flowers, to 4in (10cm) across, with crimson stamens. ↕↔20ft (6m). W. China. Zone 7b.

***M.* 'Yellow Bird'.** Conical, later spreading, deciduous tree with ovate, mid-green leaves, to 10in (25cm) long. Deeply cup-shaped, pure yellow flowers, to 5in (13cm) across, are borne in late spring and early summer. ↕30ft (10m), ↔20ft (6m). Zone 5.

MAHONIA

BERBERIDACEAE

Genus of about 70 species of evergreen shrubs occurring in rocky places and woodland in the Himalayas, E. Asia, and North and Central America. They are grown for their handsome foliage, fragrant flowers, decorative fruits, and, in tall species and cultivars, for their deeply fissured bark. The alternate, pinnate or occasionally 3-palmate, usually spiny-margined leaves are light gray-green to dark green, and sometimes purplish red or orange-red when young. Racemes or panicles of cup-shaped, usually yellow flowers, ⅜–½in (0.8–1.5cm) across, are followed by spherical or ovoid, mainly purple to black berries. Mahonias are useful for a variety of situations: use low-growing species and cultivars as a groundcover, and taller ones as specimens in a shrub border or woodland garden.

• **CULTIVATION** Grow in moderately fertile, humus-rich, moist but well-drained soil. Most mahonias prefer full or partial shade, but will tolerate sun if the soil is not too dry. *M. fremontii* and *M. nevinii* require very well-drained soil and full sun. Provide shelter from cold, drying winds. Pruning group 8.

• **PROPAGATION** Sow seed outdoors in a seedbed or containers, in autumn or as soon as ripe. Stratified seeds germinate freely. Root semi-ripe or leaf-bud cuttings from late summer to autumn.

• **PESTS AND DISEASES** Rust, leaf spots, galls, scale insects, and whiteflies can be problems.

M. acanthifolia see *M. napaulensis.*

M. aquifolium (Oregon grapeholly). Open, suckering shrub with pinnate, bright green leaves, to 12in (30cm) long, with up to 9 obliquely ovate, spiny-toothed leaflets, often turning red-purple in winter. Yellow flowers are borne in densely clustered racemes, to 3in (8cm) long, in spring, followed by spherical blue-black berries. ↕3ft (1m), ↔5ft (1.5m). W. North America. Zone 5. **'Apollo'** is a low-growing ground cover with golden orange flowers; ↕to 24in (60cm). **'Atropurpurea'** has leaves that dependably turn dark red-purple in winter. **'Compactum'** is dwarf, with bronze winter color; ↕2–3ft (60–90cm).

Mahonia aquifolium 'Smaragd'

'Golden Abundance' is vigorous, with an upright, dense habit, and bright green leaves; bears heavy, yellow flowers, followed by abundant blue berries. **'King's Ransom'** is upright in habit, with dark green to blue-green leaves, turning bronze-red-purple in winter. **'Mayhan Strain'** is dwarf in habit, with fewer and more closely aligned leaflets; ↕30–42in (75–110cm). **'Moseri'** has red to rich orange new leaves, which age to bright green, and finally dark green. **'Orange Flame'** has rust-orange young foliage, turning red in winter; ↕24in (60cm), ↔3ft (1m). **'Smaragd'** ▣ is compact, and has bronze-purple winter foliage. Bears bright yellow flowers in large clusters, to 4in (10cm) long; ↕to 24in (60cm), ↔to 3ft (1m).

M. bealei see *M. japonica* 'Bealei'.

M. fortunei (Chinese mahonia). Upright shrub with pinnate, dark green leaves, to 8in (20cm) long, with up to 13 slender, sharply toothed, elliptic-lance-shaped leaflets. Bright yellow flowers are borne in dense, upright racemes, to 3in (8cm) long, in early and midautumn; they are followed by ovoid to spherical, white-frosted, dark blue berries. ↕4ft (1.2m), ↔3ft (1m). China. Zone 7.

M. fremontii. Upright, stiffly branched shrub bearing pinnate leaves, to 4in (10cm) long, with 3–7 wavy-margined, sharply toothed, oblong-lance-shaped, glaucous, gray-green leaflets. In summer, produces densely clustered racemes, to 2in (5cm) long, of yellow flowers, followed by ovoid, white-frosted, dark blue berries. ↕↔6ft (2m). S.W. US, Mexico. ❀ (min. 41°F/5°C)

***M.* 'Heterophylla'.** Upright shrub with red-purple shoots and pinnate, glossy, bright green leaves, to 12in (30cm) long, with up to 7 slender, ovate or lance-shaped to narrowly oblong-ovate, twisted leaflets, turning red-purple in winter. Yellow flowers are produced in clustered racemes, to 3in (8cm) long, in spring. Seldom produces fruit. ↕3ft (1m), ↔5ft (1.5m). ❀ (min. 41°F/5°C)

M. japonica. Erect shrub with thick, upright branches and pinnate, dark green leaves, to 18in (45cm) long, with up to 19 sharply toothed, ovate-oblong to lance-shaped leaflets. Fragrant, pale yellow flowers are produced in arching, then spreading racemes, to 10in (25cm) long, from late autumn to early spring, followed by ovoid, blue-purple berries. ↕6ft (2m), ↔10ft (3m). China. Zone 7b.

Mahonia japonica 'Bealei'

'Bealei' ■ syn. *M. bealei* (Leatherleaf mahonia) has blue-green leaves divided into broad leaflets, and less fragrant, later-blooming flowers in shorter, upright racemes, to 4in (10cm) long.
***M.* x *lindsayae* 'Cantab'.** Stoutly branched shrub bearing large, arching, pinnate, glossy, rich, deep green leaves, to 24in (60cm) long, with up to 15 ovate-oblong, sharply toothed leaflets, some turning red in winter. Fragrant, lemon-yellow flowers are produced in spreading racemes, to 12in (30cm) long, in late autumn and early winter. ↕↔ 8ft (2.5m). ❀ (min. 35°F/2°C)
M. lomariifolia. Erect shrub with thick, upright shoots bearing pinnate, dark green leaves, to 24in (60cm) long, with up to 41 oblong-ovate to oblong-lance-shaped, sharply toothed leaflets. Bears fragrant yellow flowers in densely clustered, upright racemes, 8in (20cm) long, from late autumn to winter, followed by ovoid, blue-black berries. ↕ 10ft (3m), ↔ 6ft (2m). W. China (S. Sichuan, Yunnan). ❀ (min. 35°F/2°C)
M.* x *media (*M. japonica* x *M. lomariifolia*). Erect shrub with pinnate leaves, to 18in (45cm) long, with 17–21 ovate to lance-shaped, sharply toothed, dark green leaflets. Bright yellow to lemon-yellow flowers are borne in erect then spreading racemes, 10–14in (25–35cm) long, from late autumn to late winter. ↕ to 15ft (5m), ↔ to 12ft (4m). Garden origin. ❀ (min. 35°F/2°C). **'Arthur Menzies'** produces lemon-yellow flowers in upright, later spreading racemes, to 10in (25cm) long, in late autumn and early winter; ↕ 12ft (4m).
'Buckland' ■ bears bright yellow flowers in arching racemes, to 18in (45cm) long. **'Charity'** ■ has densely clustered, upright then spreading racemes. **'Lionel Fortescue'** bears bright yellow flowers in upright racemes, to 16in (40cm) long. **'Winter Sun'** bears bright yellow flowers in densely clustered, arching racemes.
M. napaulensis, syn. *M. acanthifolia.* Open, upright shrub with pinnate, glossy, dark green leaves, to 20in (50cm) long, with up to 15 lance-shaped to narrowly ovate, sharply toothed leaflets. In early and midspring, bears yellow flowers in spreading racemes, to 8in (20cm) long, followed by ovoid, white-frosted, blue-black berries. ↕ 8ft (2.5m), ↔ 10ft (3m). Himalayas. ❀ (min. 35°F/2°C)
M. nervosa (Cascades mahonia). Dwarf, suckering shrub with pinnate, glossy, dark green leaves, to 24in (60cm) long, with up to 23 ovate-oblong to lance-shaped leaflets, often red-purple in winter. Bears yellow flowers in dense racemes, to 8in (20cm) long, in late spring and early summer, followed by spherical, blue-black berries. ↕ 18in (45cm), ↔ 3ft (1m). W. North America. Zone 7.
M. nevinii. Upright shrub with purplish green shoots and pinnate leaves, gray-green to blue-green above, grayish white beneath, to 4in (10cm) long, with 5 lance-shaped, sharply toothed leaflets. Bright yellow flowers are produced in small, dense racemes, to 2in (5cm) long, in early and midspring, followed by spherical, dark red berries. ↕↔ 6ft (2m). S. California. ❀ (min. 41°F/5°C)

Mahonia repens 'Rotundifolia' (inset: flower detail)

M. pumila. Low, dense, suckering shrub bearing pinnate, gray-green leaves, to 6in (15cm) long, with up to 9 ovate-oblong, sharply toothed leaflets, wedge-shaped at the bases, with long, pointed tips. Dark yellow flowers are produced in densely clustered racemes, to 2in (5cm) long, in spring, and are followed by ellipsoid, blue-black berries. ↕ 12in (30cm), ↔ 3ft (1m). California, Oregon. Zone 8.
M. repens (Creeping mahonia). Upright, suckering shrub bearing pinnate, matte green leaves, to 10in (25cm) long, with up to 7 pointed, ovate, wavy-margined, sharply toothed leaflets. Dark yellow flowers are borne in dense, upright racemes, to 3in (8cm) long, in mid- and late spring, followed by spherical, blue-black berries. ↕ 12in (30cm), ↔ 3ft (1m). W. North America. Zone 3. **'Rotundifolia'** ■ is taller, with broadly ovate, almost entire, rounded leaflets; ↕ 5ft (1.5m), ↔ 6ft (2m).
M.* x *wagneri (*M. aquifolium* x *M. pinnata*). Upright shrub bearing pinnate leaves, to 8in (20cm) long, with 7–11 ovate, sharply toothed, dull to dark green leaflets. Yellow flowers are borne in dense racemes, to 3in (8cm) long, in spring, followed by spherical, white-frosted, blue-black berries. ↕ 32in (80cm), ↔ 3ft (1m). Garden origin. Zone 6. **'Moseri'** has pale green leaves, flushed pink or red. **'Pinnacle'** ■ is upright and taller than the species, with bronze juvenile leaves, maturing to bright green; ↕↔ 5ft (1.5m). **'Undulata'** has leaves with glossy, dark green, wavy-margined leaflets, turning red-purple in winter, and bears rich yellow flowers; ↕↔ 6ft (2m).

MAIANTHEMUM

May lily

LILIACEAE

Genus of 3 species of creeping, rhizomatous perennials from woodland in the N. hemisphere. They are grown for their dense, terminal racemes of tiny, fluffy, star-shaped, 4-tepaled white flowers, followed by red berries, and for their alternate, heart-shaped leaves, borne on upright stems. May lilies are useful as a groundcover in a wild or woodland garden.
• **CULTIVATION** Grow in humus-rich, leafy, moist but well-drained, neutral to acidic soil in light dappled or deep shade.

M

Mahonia x *media* 'Buckland'

Mahonia x *media* 'Charity'

Mahonia x *wagneri* 'Pinnacle'

Maianthemum bifolium

• **PROPAGATION** Sow seed in containers in a cold frame as soon as ripe. Separate rooted runners in spring.
• **PESTS AND DISEASES** Occasionally affected by rust or leaf spots; snails and slugs may attack young growth.

M. bifolium ■ (False lily-of-the-valley). Spreading perennial with 2 broadly heart-shaped to ovate, thin, glossy, dark green leaves, to 3in (8cm) across. In early summer, produces slender-stemmed racemes of 8–20 white flowers, followed by small, spherical berries. ↕ 6in (15cm), ↔ indefinite. W. Europe to Japan. Zone 4.
M. racemosum see *Smilacina racemosa.*

MAIHUENIA

CACTACEAE

Genus of 3–5 species of dwarf, clustering cacti that are found at high altitudes in the Andes of S. Chile and S. Argentina. Cylindrical or spherical, fleshy, jointed stems bear small, ovate, slender, evergreen leaves. Diurnal, cup-shaped flowers are produced from the near-terminal areoles in summer, followed by soft berries, to 2in (5cm) across, containing numerous black-coated seeds. Where temperatures fall below 32°F (0°C), grow in a cool or temperate greenhouse. In warmer areas, grow in a rock or desert garden.
• **CULTIVATION** Under glass, grow in standard cactus potting mix in bright filtered light, or full light with shade from hot sun, with low humidity. From spring to summer, water moderately and apply a dilute fertilizer monthly; at other times, keep almost dry. Outdoors, grow in moderately fertile, sharply drained soil in dappled shade, or full sun with shade from midday sun. Protect from excessive winter moisture. See also pp.48–49.
• **PROPAGATION** Sow seed at 66–75°F (19–24°C) in spring. Root stem cuttings in spring and summer.
• **PESTS AND DISEASES** Mealybugs may cause problems.

M. poeppigii ■ Clustering cactus with many short, cylindrical stems and fleshy, evergreen leaves, ¼in (6mm) long. Areoles bear 3 or 4 slender, generally short, stiff spines, one of which grows to ¾in (2cm) long. Bright yellow flowers, 1¼–1¾in (3–4.5cm) long, are produced in summer. ↕ 2½in (6cm), ↔ 12in (30cm). S. Chile, S. Argentina. ❄ (min. 41°F/5°C)

Maihuenia poeppigii

MAIHUENIOPSIS

CACTACEAE

Genus of 17 species of cushion-forming, densely branched cactus, native to Peru, Bolivia, Chile, and Argentina. The stems of this genus are indistinctly segmented. They produce yellow flowers, and the pericarpels have fewer than 30 areoles. The greenish or yellowish fruit is fleshy and indehiscent.
• **CULTIVATION** Under glass, grow in standard cactus potting mix in full light or bright filtered light. Large species are best planted directly into a greenhouse border. From early spring to mid-autumn, water only when approaching dryness and apply a balanced liquid fertilizer 3 or 4 times; this should be diluted from ¼ to ½ strength. Keep reasonably dry at other times. Outdoors, grow in moderately fertile, sharply well drained, gritty, humus-rich soil in full sun. See also pp.48–49.
• **PROPAGATION** Sow pre-soaked seed at 70°F (21°C) in spring. Separate and detach rootstem segments. Handle plants with folded newspaper.
• **PESTS AND DISEASES** Cladode rots, zonate leaf spot, black spot, mealybugs, and scale insects, are common. Bacterial soft rot and several viruses also occur.

Maihueniopsis clavarioides

M. clavarioides ■ syn. *Opuntia clavarioides, Puna clavarioides* (Fairy castles, Sea coral). Semi-prostrate, tuberous-rooted, many-branched cactus with stems divided into cylindrical, inversely conical, flat, or fan-shaped, grayish brown segments, ¾in (2cm) or more long. Whitish gray areoles bear leaf-like, deciduous red scales, to ¹⁄₁₆in (2mm) long, and each areole has 4–10 minute, fine white spines, but no glochids. In late spring and summer, produces funnel-shaped, brownish green flowers, 2½in (6cm) across, followed by ellipsoid, spineless, grayish brown fruit, ½in (1.5cm) long. ↕↔ to 4in (10cm). Argentina. ❄ (min. 45–50°F/7–10°C)

▷ ***Majorana onites*** see *Origanum onites*

MALCOLMIA

BRASSICACEAE

Genus of 35 species of bushy, sometimes prostrate annuals and perennials found on rocky slopes and as wild species in cultivated and disturbed ground, from the Mediterranean region to Afghanistan. They are grown for their short racemes of narrow, cross-shaped, 4-petaled, white, purple, or red flowers, borne from spring to autumn; they self-seed freely. Leaves are linear-oblong to ovate, spoon-shaped, or pinnatisect with lance-shaped lobes. Suitable for the front of an annual or mixed border, and for paving crevices, edging, or a gravel path; they thrive in coastal gardens.
• **CULTIVATION** Grow in moderately fertile, well-drained soil in full sun, with shade from midday sun. Flowering is poor in regions with hot, humid summers, unless seed is sown early.
• **PROPAGATION** Sow seed thinly *in situ* from late spring. For a succession of flowers, repeat at intervals of 4–6 weeks.
• **PESTS AND DISEASES** Downy mildew may be troublesome.

M. maritima (Virginian stock). Low-growing, erect to spreading, basally branching annual, with oval to elliptic, hairy-toothed or entire, blunt-tipped, gray-green leaves, to 2in (5cm) long. From spring to autumn, produces open, many-flowered, slender-stemmed spikes of sweetly fragrant, red or purple flowers, to ½in (1.5cm) across, each

Malcolmia maritima Compacta Series

Malephora crocea

petal notched at the apex. ↕ 8–16in (20–40cm), ↔ 4–6in (10–15cm). Mediterranean. **Compacta Series** ■ cultivars have white, pink, red, purple, or green flowers; ↕ 16in (40cm).

MALEPHORA

AIZOACEAE

Genus of about 15 species of bushy, prostrate to erect, woody-based, perennial succulents from dry, hilly areas of southern Africa. The stems have prominent internodes. The opposite, semi-cylindrical or bluntly 3-angled, soft, fleshy, pale to mid-green leaves are united at the bases and coated with blue or white wax. Short-stalked, star-shaped, terminal or axillary flowers open in daytime from late summer to autumn. Where not hardy, grow in a cool or temperate greenhouse, and place them outdoors in summer. In warmer areas, grow in a rock garden or desert garden.
• **CULTIVATION** Under glass, grow in standard cactus potting mix in full light with shade from hot sun, and with low humidity. From late spring to early autumn, water freely and apply a balanced liquid fertilizer monthly. Keep just moist at other times. Outdoors, grow in poor or moderately fertile soil in full sun. Provide protection from excessive winter moisture. See also pp.48–49.
• **PROPAGATION** Sow seed at 66–75°F (19–24°C) in spring. Root leaf cuttings or stem segments in spring or summer.
• **PESTS AND DISEASES** Mealybugs.

M. crocea ■ Semi-prostrate or erect, woody-based succulent with a thick, gnarled stem and grayish brown branches. Bears clusters of blunt-tipped, white-frosted, mealy, pale green leaves, to 1¾in (4.5cm) long, on short shoots. Solitary yellow flowers, 1¼in (3cm) across, with red-backed petals, borne in late summer. ↕ 8in (20cm), ↔ indefinite. South Africa. ❄ (min. 45°F/7°C)

MALOPE
Annual mallow

MALVACEAE

Genus of 4 species of tall, bushy to almost unbranched annuals and perennials found on rocky limestone slopes, in thickets of prickly shrubs, and growing wild in arable fields, from the Mediterranean to W. Asia. The ovate leaves are entire or lobed, and the

Malope trifida 'Vulcan'

showy, axillary flowers are long-stalked, broadly trumpet-shaped, and paper thin, ranging from pink or violet-blue to white, often veined in a deeper shade. Grow at the front or middle of an annual or mixed border, where they self-seed freely and provide long-lasting cut flowers. They thrive in coastal gardens, but do poorly in hot, humid summer conditions.

• **CULTIVATION** Grow in moderately fertile, moist but well-drained soil in full sun, although partial shade is tolerated. Deadhead to prolong flowering. Give brushwood support in exposed sites. In cooler climates, repeat seed sowings for successive bloom.

• **PROPAGATION** Sow seed at 55–64°F (13–18°C) in early spring, or *in situ* in midspring.

• **PESTS AND DISEASES** Aphids and rust.

M. trifida (Annual mallow). Erect, branching to almost unbranched, thick-stemmed annual with hairy stems and leaves. Ovate, mid-green leaves, to 4in (10cm) long, are entire near the stem bases but 3- to 5-lobed higher up. From summer to autumn, produces broadly trumpet-shaped, pale to dark purple-red flowers, 2–3in (5–8cm) across, heavily veined dark purple, the petals narrowing at the bases to reveal bright green sepals below. ↕ to 36in (90cm), ↔ 9in (23cm). W. Mediterranean. **'Rosea'** has rose-red flowers. **'Vulcan'** ▣ produces abundant bright magenta-pink flowers, to 3in (8cm) across. **'White Queen'** has pure white flowers, 2in (5cm) across.

MALPIGHIA

MALPIGHIACEAE

Genus of approximately 45 species of evergreen shrubs and small trees that are found in dry woodland in tropical North, Central, and South America, especially the Caribbean. These plants are grown for their opposite, simple, often toothed and leathery leaves, and their star-shaped to shallowly trumpet-shaped flowers, each with 5 unequally sized, clawed petals, often with waved tips or margins. Flowers are borne singly or in corymbs, followed by colorful, edible fruits. Where temperatures fall below 61°F (16°C), grow in a temperate or warm greenhouse. Elsewhere, use them as specimen trees, in a shrub border, or for hedging.

• **CULTIVATION** Under glass, grow in soil-based potting mix in full light, with shade from hot sun. In spring and summer, water moderately and apply a balanced liquid fertilizer every month. Water sparingly in winter. Outdoors, they should be grown in moderately fertile, moist but well-drained soil in full sun with shade from midday sun. Pruning group 9.

• **PROPAGATION** Sow seed at 64–75°F (18–24°C) in spring. Root semi-ripe cuttings with bottom heat in summer.

• **PESTS AND DISEASES** Rarely affected by leaf spot and root rot, as well as tea scale.

M. coccigera (Miniature holly, Singapore holly). Small, bushy shrub, often prostrate unless regularly trimmed. Elliptic to obovate or rounded leaves, ½–¾in (1–2cm) long, are wavy-margined, spiny-toothed, and lustrous, deep green. Shallowly trumpet-shaped, pink or lilac-pink flowers, ½in (1.5cm) across, are produced singly or in pairs from all the upper leaf axils in summer, and usually followed by broadly ovoid red berries, ¼–½in (0.5–1.5cm) across. ↕ 1–5ft (30–150cm), ↔ 3–6ft (1–2m) or more. West Indies. ❀ (min. 61°F/16°C)
M. glabra (Barbados cherry). Upright, bushy shrub with ovate to elliptic-lance-shaped, entire, lustrous, dark green leaves, 1–3in (2.5–8cm) long. In summer, star-shaped pink flowers, ½in (1.5cm) across, with fringed margins, are produced in axillary or terminal corymbs of 3–8 flowers, followed by spherical red berries, ½in (1.5cm) across. ↕ 10ft (3m), ↔ 5ft (1.5m). Texas to West Indies and N. South America. ❀ (min. 61°F/16°C)

MALUS

Apple, Crabapple

ROSACEAE

Genus of about 35 species of deciduous trees and shrubs from woodland and thickets in Europe, Asia, and North America. They are grown for their often fragrant flowers, mostly ¾–2in (2–5cm) across, borne singly or in umbel-like corymbs; for their attractive, spherical to ovoid, edible fruits (although most are unpalatable if uncooked); and sometimes for their purple foliage and autumn color. The flowers are usually shallowly cup-shaped and 5-petaled; in some cultivars, they may be semi-double or double. The leaves are alternate, oval to ovate or elliptic, mostly toothed, rarely entire, and occasionally lobed. Crabapples are ideal specimen trees, many of them suitable for small gardens. Apples of commerce, *Malus* x *domestica* and its cultivars, are not described here.

• **CULTIVATION** Grow in moderately fertile, moist but well-drained soil in full sun, although partial shade is tolerated. Purple-leaved forms color best in full sun. Pruning group 1.

• **PROPAGATION** Sow seed in a seedbed in autumn. Bud in late summer. Graft in midwinter.

• **PESTS AND DISEASES** Apple scab, cedar-apple rust, fireblight, crown and fruit rot, brown rot of fruit, *Nectria* and other cankers, heart rot, mushroom root rot, and many other diseases occur. Japanese beetle, caterpillars, fruit worms, skeletonizers, leaf rollers, scale insects, aphids, and wood borers may attack. *Malus* species and cultivars show a wide range of susceptibility to diseases, especially to the first three listed. Many modern cultivars possess superior resistance and are generally better garden choices than the older, more disease-prone selections.

***M.* 'Adams'.** Dense, rounded tree with oval, mid-green leaves, to 3in (8cm) long. Single, carmine-budded, dull pink flowers are produced in midspring, followed by persistent, red fruit, ½in (1.5cm) across. ↕ to 25ft (8m), ↔ to 20ft (6m). Zone 4.
***M.* 'Anna'** ▣ Upright to semi-spreading tree with leathery, elliptical leaves. In spring bears white flowers up to 2in (5cm) across, followed by large sweet, crisp, slightly acidic red fruit, to 2½in (6cm) across. ↕ to 20ft (6m), ↔ to15ft (5m). Zone 7.
M. x atrosanguinea (*M. halliana* x *M. sieboldii*). Spreading tree with oval or slightly lobed, glossy, dark green leaves, to 3in (8cm) long. Rich pink flowers are produced from red buds in midspring, followed by long-stalked, yellow-flushed red fruit, to ½in (1.5cm) across. ↕↔ 20ft (6m). Garden origin. Zone 4.
M. baccata (Siberian crabapple). Vigorous, rounded tree with oval, dark green leaves, paler beneath, to 3½in (9cm) long. Bears abundant, fragrant white flowers, pink in bud, in mid- and late spring, followed by long-stalked, red or yellow fruit, ½in (1.5cm) across. ↕↔ 50ft (15m). E. Asia. Zone 3. **var. *mandschurica*** ▣ (Manchurian crabapple) has more sparsely toothed leaves, downy beneath.

Malus 'Anna'

***M.* 'Baskatong'.** Small, rounded tree with oval, dark green leaves, to 3in (8cm) long. Purple-red flowers, with paler centers, are produced from darker buds in late spring, followed by dark purple-red fruit, to 1in (2.5cm) across. ↕↔ 25ft (8m). Zone 2b.
***M.* 'Beverly'.** Dense, rounded tree with oval, mid-green leaves, to 3in (8cm) long. In midspring, bears single white flowers, opening from red buds, followed by bright red fruit, ½–¾in (1.5–2cm) across. ↕ 15–25ft (5–8m), ↔ to 20ft (6m). Zone 4.
***M.* 'Butterball'** ▣ Spreading tree with broadly ovate to heart-shaped, bright green leaves, to 3in (8cm) long, gray-green when young. Pink-flushed white flowers are borne in late spring, followed by striking, orange-yellow fruit, red-flushed at first, 1¼in (3cm) across. ↕↔ 25ft (8m). Zone 4.
***M.* 'Callaway'.** Rounded tree with oval, mid-green leaves, to 3in (8cm) long. In midspring, bears single white flowers, opening from pink buds, followed by large, persistent, dark red fruit, ¾–1¼in (2–3cm) across, 1 or 2 weeks later than other rose-colored cultivars. A good choice for warmer areas. ↕ 15–25ft (5–8m), ↔ 20ft (6m). Zone 5.
***M.* 'Candied Apple'**, syn. *M.* 'Weeping Candied Apple'. Small, spreading tree with weeping branches and ovate, red-flushed, dark green leaves, to 3in (8cm) long. In late spring, bears pink flowers, red in bud, followed by long-lasting, bright red fruit, ½in (1.5cm) across. ↕↔ 15ft (5m). Zone 5b.
***M.* 'Centurion'** ▣ Narrowly upright tree, developing an oval head with age.

Malus baccata var. *mandschurica*

Malus 'Butterball' (inset: fruit detail)

Ovate, bronze-green leaves, to 4in (10cm) long, are red when young. Produces rose-red flowers in late spring, followed by long-lasting cerise fruit, to ½in (1.5cm) across. ↕ 25ft (8m), ↔ 20ft (6m). Zone 5.

***M.* 'Chilko'.** Spreading tree with oval, dark green leaves, 3–3½in (8–9cm) long, red-purple when young. Dark rose-pink flowers are produced in midspring, followed by bright crimson fruit, 2in (5cm) across. ↕↔ 25ft (8m). Zone 3.

***M.* 'Coralburst'.** Dwarf, rounded shrub or standard-grafted tree with small, dark green leaves, to 2in (5cm) long. In midspring, bears coral-pink buds opening to double, rose-pink flowers, followed by few, reddish orange fruit, ½in (1.5cm) across. Makes an attractive informal hedge. ↕↔ 8–10ft (2.5–3m). Zone 3.

***M.* 'Coralene'.** Semi-weeping tree with ovate, mid-green leaves, to 3in (8cm) long. In midspring, bears single white flowers opening from red-pink buds, followed by persistent, early-coloring, coral-pink to copper fruit, to ½in (1.5cm) across. ↕ 12ft (4m), ↔ 8ft (2.5m). Zone 4.

***M.* 'Cowichan'** ■ Spreading tree with oval, glossy, dark green leaves, to 4½in (11cm) long, red-purple when young. Rose-pink flowers are produced in midspring, later becoming almost white. These are followed by bright red-purple fruit, 1½in (4cm) across. ↕↔ 25ft (8m). Zone 2b.

***M.* 'David'.** Rounded tree with dense, ovate, mid-green leaves, to 3in (8cm) long. Single white flowers are produced from pink buds in midspring, followed by red fruit, ½in (1.5cm) across. ↕ 15–20ft (5–6m), ↔ 10–12ft (3–4m). Zone 4.

***M.* 'Dolgo'.** Vigorous, spreading tree with ovate, dark green leaves, to 3in (8cm) long. Fragrant white flowers are produced from pink buds in late spring, followed by ovoid-spherical, bright red-purple fruit, 2in (5cm) long. ↕ 35ft (11m), ↔ 30ft (10m). Zone 2b.

***M.* 'Donald Wyman'** ■ Large, spreading tree with glossy, dark green leaves, 3in (8cm) long. In midspring, produces single white flowers, 1¾in (4.5cm) across, opening from red to pink buds, followed by abundant, persistent, lustrous, bright red fruit, ½in (15mm) across. ↕ 20ft (6m), ↔ 25ft (8m). Zone 5.

Malus 'Donald Wyman'

***M.* 'Dorset Gold'.** Upright to semi-spreading tree with leathery, elliptical leaves. Bears firm, golden fruit that is often seedless, to 2in (5cm) across. ↕ to 22ft (7m), to15ft (5m). Zone 7.

***M.* 'Doubloons'.** Rounded tree with ovate, mid-green leaves, to 3in (8cm) long. In midspring, bright red buds open to double white flowers, followed by yellow-gold fruit, ⅜in (9mm) across. ↕ 10–12ft (3–4m), ↔ 8–10ft (2.5–3m). Zone 4.

***M.* 'Echtermeyer'**, syn. *M.* 'Okonomierat Echtermeyer'. Weeping tree with oval, sometimes slightly lobed, bronze-green leaves, 3–4in (8–10cm) long, bronze-purple when young. Dark red-purple flowers are produced in late spring, followed by ovoid-spherical, purple-red fruit, 1in (2.5cm) long. ↕↔ 15ft (5m). Zone 3.

***M.* 'Fiesta'.** Semi-weeping tree with ovate, dark green leaves, to 3in (8cm) long. In late spring, bears single white flowers that open from red buds, followed by persistent, firm, bright brown-coral to orange-gold fruit, ⅜in (9mm) long. ↕ 15ft (5m), ↔ 8–10ft (2.5–3m). Zone 4.

M. floribunda ■ (Japanese flowering crabapple, Showy crabapple). Dense, spreading tree with ovate, sometimes lobed, dark green leaves, to 3in (8cm) long. Pale pink flowers are produced in mid- and late spring, from red buds, followed by small, pea-like yellow fruit, ¾in (2cm) across. ↕↔ 30ft (10m). Japan. Zone 5b.

***M.* 'Golden Dream'.** Rounded tree with ovate, bright green leaves, 3–4in (8–10cm) long. In late spring, single

Malus hupehensis

white flowers open from red buds, followed by persistent, firm, spherical, bright yellow-gold fruit, ¼in (6mm) long. ↕ 12ft (4m), ↔ 8–10ft (2.5–3m). Zone 5.

***M. halliana* var. *parkmanii*.** Upright, vase-shaped, densely branched tree with ovate, leathery, glossy, dark green leaves, to 3in (8cm) long. In midspring, bears double, shell-pink flowers, opening from rose buds, followed by obovoid, dull red fruit, ¼in (3mm) across. ↕ 15–20ft (5–6m), ↔ 10–12ft (3–4m). Zone 6.

***M.* 'Harvest Gold'.** Columnar tree with ovate, mid-green leaves, to 3in (8cm) long. In midspring, bears single white flowers, pink in bud, opening a week later than most crabapples, followed by persistent, ovoid, gold fruit, ½in (1.5cm) across. ↕ 30ft (10m), ↔ 15ft (5m). Zone 5.

M. hupehensis ■ (Tea crabapple). Vigorous, spreading tree, initially vase-shaped, with elliptic to ovate, dark green leaves, to 4in (10cm) long. In mid- and late spring, produces fragrant white flowers that open from pink buds, followed by cherry-like red fruit, ½in (1.5cm) across. ↕↔ 40ft (12m). China. Zone 4b.

***M.* 'Jewelberry'** ■ Dense, rounded tree or shrub with ovate, dark green leaves, 3–3½in (7–9cm) long. White flowers open from pink buds in late spring, followed by glossy red fruit, ½in (1.5cm) across, profusely borne, even on young trees. ↕↔ 15ft (5m). Zone 5.

M

Malus 'Centurion'

Malus 'Cowichan'

Malus floribunda

Malus 'Jewelberry'

Malus 'Jonathan'

Malus 'Lemoinei'

Malus 'Liset'

Malus 'Professor Sprenger'

***M.* 'Jonathan'** ■ Upright to semi-spreading tree with grayish-green, coarse leaves. Bears white to light pink flowers, followed by tender, juicy fruit, to 2½in (6cm) across, that is bright red in sunny climates, and yellow with red stripes in cooler climates. ↕↔ to 25ft (8m). Zone 6.
***M.* 'Katherine'** ■ Open, rounded tree with oval, dark green leaves, to 3in (8cm) long. Large, double, pale pink flowers, maturing to white, are produced in mid- and late spring, followed by very small, pea-like, red-flushed yellow fruit, ½in (1.5cm) across. ↕↔ 20ft (6m). Zone 5b.
***M.* 'Lemoinei'** ■ Spreading tree with ovate or slightly lobed, dark red-purple leaves, to 3in (8cm) long, turning purple-green. Dark wine-red flowers are borne in late spring, followed by cherry-like, dark red-purple fruit, ½in (1.5cm) across. ↕↔ 25ft (8m). Zone 5.
***M.* 'Liset'** ■ Rounded tree with ovate, often lobed, bronze-green leaves, to 3in (8cm) long, reddish purple when young. Dark purple-pink flowers open from dark red buds in late spring, followed by dark purple-red fruit, ½in (1.5cm) across. ↕↔ 20ft (6m). Zone 5.
***M.* 'Mary Potter'.** Mound-forming, low-branching, spreading tree with ovate, lustrous, dark green leaves, to 3in (8cm) long. In midspring, bears single white flowers, opening from pink buds, followed by red fruit, ½in (1.5cm) across. ↕ 10–15ft (3–5m), ↔ 15–20ft (5–6m). Zone 4b.
***M.* 'Molten Lava'.** Weeping tree with yellowish green winter bark and ovate, dark green leaves, 2½–4in (6–10cm) long. White flowers, opening from dark red buds, are produced in late spring, followed by orange-red fruit, ½in (1.5cm) across. ↕ 15ft (5m), ↔ 12ft (4m). Zone 5b.
***M.* 'Narragansett'.** Broad, spreading tree with ovate, mid-green leaves, to 3in (8cm) long. In midspring, produces pink-tinged, white flowers, opening from red buds, followed by cherry-red fruit, ½in (1.5cm) across, with light orange undersides. ↕ 15ft (5m), ↔ 10–12ft (3–4m). Zone 5.
M. niedzwetskyana ■ syn. *M. pumila* var. *niedzwetskyana.* Spreading tree with oval, purple-green leaves, red when young, to 5in (13cm) long. Dark red-purple flowers are produced in late spring, followed by conical, red-purple fruit, to 2in (5cm) long. ↕ 20ft (6m), ↔ 25ft (8m). C. Asia. Zone 4.
***M.* 'Okonomierat Echtermeyer'** see *M.* 'Echtermeyer'.
***M.* 'Pink Spires'.** Narrowly upright tree with ovate, red-purple young leaves, 2½–5in (6–13cm) long, maturing to bronze-green in summer. In mid- and late spring, lavender-pink flowers are produced from darker buds, followed by long-lasting, purple-red fruit, ½in (1.5cm) across. ↕ 20ft (6m), ↔ 12ft (4m). Zone 5.
***M.* 'Prairifire'.** Upright tree, becoming rounded with age, with ovate, reddish maroon leaves, to 3in (8cm) long, maturing to dark green. In midspring, red buds open to dark pinkish red flowers, followed by persistent, dark red-purple fruit, ⅜in (9mm) across. ↕↔ 20ft (6m). Zone 4.
***M.* 'Professor Sprenger'** ■ Dense, rounded tree with broadly ovate, glossy, bright green leaves, to 3in (8cm) long, turning yellow in late autumn. In mid- and late spring, pink buds open to very fragrant white flowers, followed by long-lasting, orange-red fruit, to ½in (1.5cm) across. ↕↔ 22ft (7m). Zone 5.
***M.* 'Profusion'.** Spreading tree with elliptic, bronze-green leaves, to 3in (8cm) long, purple-red when young. Dark purple-pink flowers are freely borne in late spring, followed by cherry-like, reddish purple fruit, ½in (1.5cm) across. ↕↔ 30ft (10m). Zone 4.
M. prunifolia ■ (Chinese crabapple). Spreading tree with elliptic to ovate, dark green leaves, to 4in (10cm) long. Fragrant white flowers open from pink buds in midspring, followed by long-lasting, spherical to ovoid, red or sometimes yellow fruit, 1in (2.5cm) across. ↕↔ 28ft (9m). Probably China. Zone 4.
M. pumila* var. *niedzwetskyana see *M. niedzwetskyana.*
M.* x *purpurea (*M. atrosanguinea* x *M. niedzwetskyana*). Erect, open tree with broadly ovate, sometimes lobed, dark green leaves, to 4in (10cm) long. The young wood and spring foliage are both purplish red. Purplish pink flowers open from ruby-red buds in midspring, followed by dark red fruit, ¾–1in (2–2.5cm) across. Highly susceptible to apple scab and fireblight. ↕ 12–22ft (4–7m), ↔ 6–12ft (2–4m). Garden origin. Zone 3.
***M.* 'Red Baron'.** Broadly upright tree with ovate, bronze-green leaves, 2½–4in (6–10cm) long, purple when young.

M

Malus 'Katherine' (inset: flower detail)

Malus niedzwetskyana

Malus prunifolia

Malus 'Red Jade' (inset: fruit detail)

Dark pink flowers open from dark red buds in late spring, followed by glossy, dark red fruit, ½in (1.5cm) across. ↕↔ 20ft (6m). Zone 4.
***M.* 'Red Jade'** ▣ Weeping tree with ovate, tapered, glossy, mid-green leaves, to 3½in (9cm) long. White or pink-flushed flowers are borne from red buds in late spring, followed by ovoid, glossy, bright red fruit, to ½in (1.5cm) long. ↕ 12ft (4m), ↔ 20ft (6m). Zone 3.
***M.* 'Red Sentinel'** ▣ Broadly upright tree with ovate, dark green leaves, to 3in (8cm) long. White flowers are produced in late spring, followed by long-lasting, yellow-flushed red, later glossy, dark red fruit, 1in (2.5cm) across. ↕↔ 22ft (7m). Zone 4.
***M.* 'Red Siberian'** see *M.* x *robusta* 'Red Siberian'.
***M.* 'Red Snow'.** Graceful, arching tree with narrowly ovate, leathery, mid-green leaves, to 3in (8cm) long, gold in autumn. In midspring, orange-red buds open to pinkish white flowers, followed by narrowly ovoid, bright red fruit, ⅜in (9mm) across. ↕ 8–10ft (2.5–3m), ↔ 6–8ft (2–2.5m). Zone 4.
***M.* x *robusta* 'Red Siberian'**, syn. *M.* 'Red Siberian'. Vigorous, spreading tree with oval, dark green leaves, to 4in (10cm) long. In mid- and late spring, produces abundant pink-tinged white flowers, followed by long-lasting red fruit, ¾in (2cm) across. ↕ 40ft (12m), ↔ 30ft (10m). Zone 4. **'Yellow Siberian'**, syn. *M.* 'Yellow Siberian', bears yellow fruit.
***M.* 'Royal Beauty'.** Small, weeping tree with elliptic, reddish purple leaves, to 2½in (6cm) long, turning dark green, purple beneath. Dark red-purple flowers are produced in late spring, followed by dark red fruit, ½in (1.5cm) across. ↕ 6ft (2m), ↔ 8ft (2.5m). Zone 5.
***M.* 'Royalty'** ▣ Spreading tree with ovate, dark red-purple leaves, to 4in (10cm) long, retaining color well and turning red in autumn, the larger leaves often slightly lobed. Bears crimson-purple flowers in mid- and late spring, followed by dark red fruit, ½in (1.5cm) across. ↕↔ 25ft (8m). Zone 2b.
***M.* 'Rudolph'.** Upright tree with ovate, glossy, dark green leaves, to 3in (8cm) long, reddish purple when young. Rose-red flowers open from darker red buds in late spring, followed by long-lasting, orange-yellow fruit, ½in (1.5cm) long. ↕ 22ft (7m), ↔ 12ft (4m). Zone 3.
***M. sargentii*,** syn. *M. toringo* subsp. *sargentii*. Spreading shrub or small tree with ovate or 3-lobed, dark green leaves, to 3in (8cm) long. Abundant white flowers, opening from red buds, are produced in late spring, followed by long-lasting, dark red fruit, ⅜in (9mm) across. ↕ 6–10ft (2–3m), ↔ 8–15ft (2.5–5m). Japan. Zone 5. **'Tina'** is a dwarf form, often grafted onto a standard; ↕ 5ft (1.5m), ↔ 10ft (3m).
***M.* 'Sentinel'.** Columnar tree with ovate, mid-green leaves, to 3in (8cm) long. Bears single, pale pink flowers, in midspring, followed by persistent, red fruit, ½in (1.5cm) across. ↕ 15–20ft (5–6m), ↔ to 10ft (3m). Zone 6.
M. sieboldii ▣ syn. *M. toringo* (Toringo crabapple). Spreading shrub with arching branches and ovate to deeply 3- to 5-lobed leaves, to 2½in (6cm) long. Fragrant white flowers open from pink buds in midspring, followed by slender-stalked, red or yellow fruit, ½in (1.5cm) across. ↕ 8ft (2.5m), ↔ 10ft (3m). Japan. Zone 5. **'Calocarpa'** see *M.* x *zumi* 'Calocarpa'.
***M.* 'Snowdrift'** ▣ Dense, rounded tree with elliptic to ovate, glossy, dark green leaves, to 4in (10cm) long. Abundant white flowers open from pink buds in late spring, followed by long-lasting, glossy, orange-red fruit, ½in (1.5cm) across. ↕↔ 20ft (6m). Zone 4.
M. spectabilis (Chinese flowering crabapple). Rounded tree with oval, glossy, dark green leaves, to 3½in (9cm) long. Blush-pink flowers are produced from rose-red buds in mid- and late spring, followed by yellow fruit, to 1in (2.5cm) across. ↕↔ 30ft (10m). Probably China. Zone 5.
***M.* 'Spring Snow'.** Dense, upright tree with oval, bright green leaves, 1¼–3in (3–8cm) long. Abundant fragrant white flowers are borne in late spring. Fruit are seldom produced. ↕ 25ft (8m), ↔ 20ft (6m). Zone 5.
***M.* 'Strawberry Parfait'.** Vase-shaped tree with ovate, purple-tinged young leaves, to 3in (8cm) long, aging to leathery, dark green. In midspring, bears red-margined, pink flowers, opening from red buds, followed by red-blushed, yellow fruit, ½in (1.5cm) across. ↕ 20ft (6m), ↔ 25ft (8m). Zone 5.
***M.* 'Sugar Tyme'.** Vigorous, upright, oval-shaped tree with ovate, mid-green leaves, to 3in (8cm) long. In midspring, bears pale pink buds that open to fragrant white flowers, followed by abundant, persistent red fruit, ½in (1.5cm) across. ↕ 20ft (6m), ↔ 15ft (5m). Zone 4.
***M. sylvestris*.** Rounded, sometimes thorny tree with ovate, mid-green leaves, 1½–3in (4–8cm) long. Pink-flushed white flowers are borne in late spring, followed by greenish yellow, red-flushed fruit, to 1in (2.5cm) across. ↕ 28ft (9m), ↔ 22ft(7m). Europe. Zone 5.
M. toringo see *M. sieboldii*.
***M. toringoides*.** Spreading tree with ovate to lance-shaped, usually deeply 3- to 7-lobed, mid-green leaves, to 3½in (9cm) long. Slightly fragrant, creamy white flowers are produced in late spring, followed by spherical to ovoid, yellow fruit, to ½in (1.5cm) long. ↕ 25ft (8m), ↔ 30ft (10m). W. China. Zone 5.

Malus sieboldii

Malus 'Snowdrift'

Malus 'Red Sentinel'

Malus 'Royalty' (inset: flower detail)

M

Malus transitoria

M. toringo* subsp. *sargentii see *M. sargentii*.
M. transitoria ■ Elegant, spreading tree with oblong to deeply 3-lobed, bright green leaves, ¾–1¼in (2–3cm) long, turning yellow in autumn. In late spring, white flowers open from pink buds, followed by very small, pea-like yellow fruit, ⅜in (9mm) long, on slender red stalks. ↕25ft (8m), ↔ 30ft (10m). N.W. China. Zone 5.
M. trilobata. Conical tree with maple-like, 3-lobed, glossy, bright green leaves, to 3½in (9cm) long, the lobes sometimes further lobed, turning yellow, red, and purple in autumn. White flowers are produced in early summer, followed by ellipsoid, red-flushed green fruit, ¾in (2cm) long. ↕50ft (15m), ↔ 22ft (7m). Greece, Syria, Lebanon, Israel. Zone 6.
M. tschonoskii ■ Erect tree with broadly ovate, glossy, mid-green leaves (new foliage is gray-green), to 5in (13cm) long, turning brilliant orange, red, and purple in autumn. In late spring, bears pink-flushed white flowers, followed by red-flushed, yellow-green fruit, 1¼in (3cm) across. ↕40ft (12m), ↔ 22ft (7m). Japan. Zone 6.

Malus tschonoskii

***M.* 'Weeping Candied Apple'** see *M.* 'Candied Apple'.
***M.* 'White Angel'.** Rounded but irregular tree due to heavy fruiting, with ovate, lustrous, dark green leaves, to 3in (8cm) long. Bears single white flowers with pink buds, followed by glossy red fruit, ½–¾in (1.5–2cm) across. ↕↔ 20ft (6m). Zone 5.
***M.* 'White Cascade'.** Weeping tree with ovate, dark green leaves, 2½–4in (6–10cm) long. Bears abundant white flowers, opening from pink buds in late spring, followed by small, greenish yellow fruit, ½in (1.5cm) across. ↕↔ 15ft (5m). Zone 5.
***M.* 'Wildfire'.** Semi-weeping tree with ovate, dark reddish green leaves, to 3in (8cm) long. Bears single pink flowers, opening from bright red buds, followed by long-lasting, firm, brilliant red fruit, ¼–½in (6–15mm) across. ↕15ft (5m), ↔ 8–10ft (2.5–3m). Zone 4.
***M.* 'Winter Gold'.** Rounded tree with elliptic, often slightly lobed leaves, to 3in (8cm) long, bronze-tinged when young. Bears white flowers, pink in bud, in mid- and late spring, followed by long-lasting, lemon-yellow fruit, ½in (1.5cm) across. ↕↔ 20ft (6m). Zone 4.
***M.* 'Woven Gold'.** Semi-weeping tree with ovate, dark green leaves, to 3in (8cm) long. Bears single white flowers opening from carmine-red buds, followed by clusters of long-lasting, firm, yellow-gold fruit, to ½in (1.5cm) across. ↕12ft (4m), ↔ 6–8ft (2–2.5m). Zone 5.
***M.* 'Yellow Siberian'** see *M.* x *robusta* 'Yellow Siberian'.
M. yunnanensis. Broadly upright tree with ovate, sometimes shallowly lobed, pale green leaves, to 5in (13cm) long, with pale brown, felted hairs beneath, turning orange, red, and purple in autumn. White, sometimes pink-tinged, flowers are borne in late spring, followed by speckled red fruit, ½in (1.5cm) across. ↕20–40ft (6–12m), ↔ 20ft (6m). S.W. China. Zone 6b.
***M.* x *zumi* 'Calocarpa'**, syn. *M. sieboldii* 'Calocarpa'. Upright, pyramidal to rounded tree, sometimes irregularly mound-shaped, with ovate, frequently deeply lobed, dark green leaves, to 3½in (9cm) long. Bears white flowers, pink in bud, in late spring, followed by long-lasting, cherry-like, bright red fruit, ½in (1.5cm) across. ↕28ft (9m), ↔ 25ft (8m). Zone 4.

MALVA

Mallow

MALVACEAE

Genus of about 30 species of annuals, biennials, and perennials, sometimes woody-based, occurring in dry, open habitats, waste ground, roadsides, and hedge banks in Europe, N. Africa, and temperate Asia, and widely naturalized elsewhere. The alternate, rounded or heart- or kidney-shaped leaves are entire, toothed, or shallowly 3- to 9-lobed, sometimes pinnatisect. The 5-petaled, shallowly funnel-shaped, or saucer- to cup-shaped, purple, blue, pink, or white flowers are produced singly, in clusters from the leaf axils, or sometimes in leafy, terminal racemes. An involucre of 1–3 distinct bracts is usually produced below the flowers (distinguishing *Malva* species and cultivars from those of the

Malva moschata

genus *Lavatera*, which have 3–9 joined bracts). Mallows are easily grown and produce long-lasting, often showy flowers; they are suitable for an annual, herbaceous, mixed, or shrub border, or for a wild garden.
• **CULTIVATION** Grow in moderately fertile, moist but well-drained soil in full sun. Provide support, especially in rich soils. Perennials are often short-lived, but will self-seed.
• **PROPAGATION** Sow seed *in situ* or in containers in early spring or early summer. Root basal cuttings of perennials in spring.
• **PESTS AND DISEASES** Rust and *Cercospora* leaf spot are common.

M. alcea (Hollyhock mallow). Erect, bushy, hairy, woody-based perennial with heart-shaped, scalloped, light green lower leaves, to 12in (30cm) long, and deeply pinnatisect upper leaves, to 6in (15cm) long. From early summer to early autumn, open funnel-shaped, purplish pink flowers, 2–3in (5–8cm) across, the petals slightly notched, are produced in terminal racemes and axillary clusters. ↕4ft (1.2m), ↔ 24in (60cm). S. Europe. Zone 4b. **var. *fastigiata*** is narrow and upright, bearing deep pink flowers well into autumn; ↕to 32in (80cm).
M. moschata ■ (Musk mallow). Erect, bushy, woody-based perennial with slightly musk-scented leaves, to 4in (10cm) long, the lower ones heart-shaped and the upper ones pinnatisect. From early summer to early autumn, bears saucer-shaped, pale pink or white flowers, 1½–2½in (4–6cm) across, in

Malva sylvestris 'Primley Blue'

axillary clusters. ↕36in (90cm), ↔ 24in (60cm). Europe, N.W. Africa. Zone 4. **'Alba'** has large, open cups of cool white flowers, 2in (5cm) across.
M. nicaeensis. Erect, slightly hairy annual or biennial with semi-circular, shallowly 3- to 7-lobed, blunt-toothed leaves, to 4in (10cm) long, the leaf stalks often considerably longer than the leaf blades. In summer, saucer-shaped pink or lilac-pink flowers, to 1½in (4cm) across, with hairy petal bases, are borne singly or in clusters from the upper leaf axils. ↕to 20in (50cm), ↔ 9in (23cm). Mediterranean, Arabian Peninsula to Iran, S. Russia. Zone 7b.
M. sylvestris (Cheeses). Erect to spreading, bushy, hairy, woody-based perennial, occasionally biennial. Broadly heart-shaped to rounded, shallowly 3- to 7-lobed leaves are dark green, to 4in (10cm) long. From late spring to midautumn, produces axillary clusters of open funnel-shaped, pinkish purple flowers, to 2½in (6cm) across, with notched petals and darker purple veins. ↕to 4ft (1.2m), ↔ 24in (60cm). N. Europe, N. Africa, S.W. Asia. Zone 4. **f. *alba*** has white flowers; ↕to 32in (80cm). **'Bibor Fehlor'** has glossy, rose-purple flowers, veined royal purple. **'Brave Heart'** is upright, with large purple flowers, to 3in (8cm) across, with strong veins and dark purple centers; ↕to 36in (90cm). **'Cottenham Blue'** is early-flowering, and has pale blue flowers, veined darker blue; ↕to 30in (75cm). **'Primley Blue'** ■ is prostrate, and produces pale blue-violet flowers, veined darker blue; ↕to 8in (20cm), ↔ 12–24in (30–60cm). **'Zebrina'** has pink or white flowers with purple stripes; ↕36–48in (1–1.2m).

MALVASTRUM

MALVACEAE

Genus of about 30 species of spreading to erect, evergreen, sometimes semi-evergreen perennials and shrubs, found on rock outcrops, rocky areas of prairies, and alluvial soils in arid and semi-arid areas of North and South America. The alternate, entire or lobed leaves are lance-shaped to rounded, 1–4½in (2.5–11cm) long, often with toothed margins. They are usually cultivated for their attractive, funnel- or cup-shaped, yellow, orange, pink, or red flowers, either solitary and axillary, or borne in terminal or axillary racemes or spikes. Grow in a sunny border or on a bank. Where not hardy, grow in a cool greenhouse.
• **CULTIVATION** Grow in well-drained soil in full sun. Trim back any excess growth or dead shoots in spring.
• **PROPAGATION** Sow seed in containers in spring. Insert softwood cuttings in late spring or summer.
• **PESTS AND DISEASES** Infrequent.

M. capensis see *Anisodontea capensis*.
M. coccineum see *Sphaeralcea coccinea*.
M. lateritium. Prostrate perennial with alternate, rounded leaves, 3in (8cm) long, with 3–5 wedge-shaped to oblong lobes. Solitary, cup-shaped, peach-colored flowers, 2in (5cm) across, with yellow anthers and deep yellow centers surrounded by deep rose-pink bands, are produced from late spring to summer. ↕8in (20cm), ↔ 5ft (1.5m). Argentina, Uruguay. Zone 7b.

MALVAVISCUS

Sleepy mallow

MALVACEAE

Genus of 3 species of evergreen shrubs found in thickets, often in coastal areas, in tropical North and South America. They have alternate, simple to palmately lobed, toothed, pale to mid-green leaves, and solitary, axillary or terminal racemes of long-stemmed, pendent, red, pink, or white flowers. The flowers are similar to those of *Hibiscus*, although the long petals only partially unfurl, producing a narrowly funnel-shaped outline and explaining the common name. Where not hardy, grow in a temperate or warm greenhouse or in a summer border. In warmer areas, grow in a shrub border or as an informal hedge.

• **CULTIVATION** Under glass, grow in soil-based potting mix in bright filtered light, or full light with shade from hot sun. In the growing season, water freely, applying a balanced liquid fertilizer monthly; water sparingly in winter. Outdoors, grow in moderately fertile, moist but well-drained soil in full sun; tolerates partial shade. Pruning group 8.

• **PROPAGATION** Sow seed at 59–70°F (15–21°C) in spring. Root softwood cuttings with bottom heat in spring, or semi-ripe cuttings in summer.

• **PESTS AND DISEASES** Susceptible to spider mites, whiteflies, and mealybugs under glass.

M. arboreus ▣ syn. *M. mollis* (Wax mallow). Large, erect to spreading, usually freely branching shrub with densely velvety, downy stems and leaves. Bright green leaves are broadly ovate to heart-shaped, 2½–5in (6–13cm) long, and sometimes 3-lobed. Mainly in late summer and early autumn, bears axillary, bright red flowers, to 2in (5cm) long. ↕ to 12ft (4m) or more, ↔ 5–10ft (1.5–3m). S.E. US, Mexico to Colombia, Peru, Brazil. ❄ (min. 50°F/10°C)
M. candidus. Erect, freely branching shrub with hairy stems. Hairy, mid-green leaves, to 7in (18cm) long, are broadly ovate to rounded, with 5-lobed, heart-shaped bases. Red flowers, 1¼in (3cm) long, are produced in terminal racemes in summer. ↕ to 12ft (4m), ↔ to 6ft (2m). Mexico. ❄ (min. 46°F/8°C)
M. mollis see *M. arboreus.*

▷ ***Mamillopsis senilis*** see *Mammillaria senilis*

Malvaviscus arboreus

MAMMILLARIA

CACTACEAE

Genus of about 150 species of spherical to cylindrical or columnar cacti from semi-desert regions, mainly in Mexico, but also in S. US, the West Indies, Central America, Colombia, and Venezuela. Most offset freely to form clusters. Conical, cylindrical, or somewhat flattened tubercles encircle spined stems. The funnel-shaped, diurnal, white to yellow, orange, red, pink, or purple flowers are mostly borne in a ring around the crown. The berry-like fruits are oblong-ovoid to club-shaped. Where not hardy, grow in a temperate greenhouse or as houseplants. In warmer areas, grow in a desert garden.

• **CULTIVATION** Under glass, grow in standard cactus potting mix in full light with shade from hot sun. Provide low humidity. From midspring to autumn, water freely, applying a balanced liquid fertilizer monthly in late spring and summer; water sparingly in winter. Outdoors, grow in poor or moderately fertile, sharply drained soil in full sun. See also pp.48–49.

• **PROPAGATION** Sow seed at 66–75°F (19–24°C) in late winter or early spring. Remove offsets in early spring.

• **PESTS AND DISEASES** Soft rot, stem spots, scale insects, root mealybugs, and mealybugs are common.

M. armillata. Clustering or solitary cactus with narrowly columnar, dull green stems, 1¾in (4.5cm) thick, and brown or brown-yellow spines (9–15 radials, one or more hooked, and 1–4 centrals). Pale pink, creamy white, or pale yellow flowers, ¾in (2cm) long, are borne in summer. ↕ to 12in (30cm), ↔ indefinite. N.W. Mexico. ❄ (min. 45–50°F/7–10°C)
M. baumii, syn. *Dolichothele baumii.* Clustering cactus with spherical to ovoid, mid-green stems, 1¼–2½in (3–6cm) thick. The areoles produce 30–35 thread-like white radial spines and 5 or 6 longer, pale yellow centrals. Bright yellow flowers, 1¼in (3cm) long, are produced in summer. ↕ 3in (8cm), ↔ 5in (13cm). N.E. Mexico. ❄ (min. 45–50°F/7–10°C)
M. blossfeldiana, syn. *M. shurliana.* Solitary or clustering cactus with spherical to short, cylindrical, dark green stems, 1½in (4cm) thick, bearing close-set areoles with 15–20 black-tipped

Mammillaria bocasana

Mammillaria bombycina

yellow radial spines and 3 or 4 black centrals, one of which is hooked. In summer, bears pale pink flowers, 1½in (4cm) long, with deep carmine-red median lines. ↕↔ 1½in (4cm). N.W. Mexico. ❄ (min. 45–50°F/7–10°C)
M. bocasana ▣ (Snowball cactus). Clump-forming cactus with spherical, white-hairy, bluish green stems, to 2in (5cm) thick. Close-set areoles bear 25–50 spreading white radial spines and 1–5 red or brown-yellow centrals. From spring to summer, bears yellowish white flowers, ½in (1.5cm) long, with red or pink median lines. ↕ 2in (5cm), ↔ indefinite. C. Mexico. ❄ (min. 45–50°F/7–10°C); will tolerate brief periods to 25°F (-4°C).
M. bombycina ▣ Densely clustering cactus with spherical to cylindrical, mid-green stems, 2–3in (5–8cm) thick, densely white-woolly in the axils. Areoles bear 30–40 white radial spines and 2–4 longer, white to yellow or red-brown centrals, one of which is hooked and twice as long as the other centrals. Produces reddish purple flowers, ½in (1.5cm) long, from spring to summer. ↕ 8in (20cm), ↔ indefinite. W. central Mexico. ❄ (min. 45–50°F/7–10°C); will tolerate brief periods to 28°F (-2°C).
M. camptotricha ▣ syn. *Dolichothele camptotricha.* (Bird's-nest cactus). Freely clustering cactus with spherical, deep green stems, 3in (8cm) thick, the areoles with 2–8 pale yellow radial spines, but no centrals. Scented white flowers, to ¾in (2cm) long, each with a green median line, are produced from summer to autumn. ↕ to 3in

Mammillaria camptotricha

M

(8cm), ↔ 8in (20cm). E. central Mexico. ❄ (min. 45–50°F/7–10°C); will tolerate brief periods to 28°F (-2°C).

M. carmenae ■ Clustering cactus with spherical to ovoid, mid-green stems, 1¼–1½in (3–4cm) thick, with white wool and long white bristles in the axils. The areoles bear 100 or more white or cream radial spines but no centrals. Pink- or cream-flushed white flowers, ½in (1.5cm) long, are produced from spring to summer. ↕ to 3in (8cm), ↔ 6in (15cm). E. central Mexico. ❄ (min. 45–50°F/7–10°C); will tolerate brief periods to 25°F (-4°C).

M. centricirrha see *M. magnimamma.*

M. conoidea see *Neolloydia conoidea.*

M. crucigera. Clustering, branching cactus with depressed spherical or cylindrical to obovoid, dark brownish green stems, 1¼–2in (3–5cm) thick, with white-woolly axils and areoles. The areoles bear 24 or more needle-like white radial spines and usually 4 longer, thicker, waxy-yellow, brown- or black-tipped centrals. Pinkish purple flowers, ½in (1.5cm) long, are produced in summer. ↕ to 6in (15cm), ↔ indefinite. S. Mexico. ❄ (min. 45–50°F/7–10°C); will tolerate brief periods to 20°F (-7°C).

M. dealbata see *M. haageana.*

M. densispina. Solitary cactus with spherical or cylindrical, dark green stems, to 4in (10cm) thick, and white-woolly areoles bearing about 25 yellow or pale brown radial spines and 5 or 6 longer, reddish brown, black-tipped centrals. Produces sulfur-yellow flowers, ¾in (2cm) long, often with red-flushed outer petals, from spring to summer. ↕↔ 4in (10cm). C. Mexico. ❄ (min. 45–50°F/7–10°C); will tolerate brief periods to 35°F (2°C).

M. dixanthocentron. Solitary cactus with cylindrical, mid-green stems, 3in (8cm) thick, and areoles bearing about 20 yellow radial spines and 2–4 shorter centrals. Yellowish-pink flowers, ⅜in (9mm) long, are produced in spring. ↕ 8in (20cm), ↔ 3in (8cm). Mexico (Oaxaca). ❄ (min. 45–50°F/7–10°C); will tolerate brief periods to 28°F (-2°C).

M. elongata (Gold lace cactus). Variable, densely clustering cactus with cylindrical, mid-green stems, ½–1¼in (1–3cm) thick, and white, yellow, or dark reddish brown spines (15–20 radials and up to 3 centrals, although the centrals may be absent). Bears white or yellow, sometimes faintly pink-striped flowers, to ½in (1.5cm) long, in summer. ↕ 6in (15cm), ↔ 12in (30cm).

Mammillaria carmenae

Mammillaria geminispina

C. Mexico. ❄ (min. 45–50°F/7–10°C); will tolerate brief periods to 28°F (-2°C).

M. geminispina ■ Solitary cactus, later offsetting and forming mounds, that produces spherical, mid-green stems, 3in (8cm) thick, becoming cylindrical. The white-woolly areoles bear white spines (16–20 radials and 2–4 longer, often brown-tipped centrals). White to creamy white flowers, ½in (1.5cm) or more long, with carmine-red stripes, are produced from summer to autumn. ↕ 10in (25cm), ↔ 20in (50cm). C. Mexico. ❄ (min. 45–50°F/7–10°C); will tolerate brief periods to 18°F (-8°C).

M. gracilis. Freely clustering cactus producing cylindrical, fresh green stems, 1¼–1¾in (3–4.5cm) thick, and slightly woolly areoles with 3–5 brown central spines and 12–17 shorter, yellowish white

Mammillaria magnimamma

radials. From spring to summer, bears yellowish white flowers, ½in (1.5cm) long, with pink or white median lines. Offsets fall away at the slightest touch. ↕ 2in (5cm), ↔ 8in (20cm). E. central Mexico. ❄ (min. 45–50°F/7–10°C). **var. *fragilis*** has 2 brown-tipped white central spines per areole; ↕ to 1½in (4cm), ↔ to 5in (13cm).

M. guelzowiana, syn. *Krainzia guelzowiana.* Clustering cactus with spherical, light green stems, to 3in (8cm) thick. Areoles bear 60–80 soft, hairlike, white radials and 1–3 shorter, hooked, red to brown centrals. In summer, this cactus produces large, spicy-scented, hot pink flowers, 2in (5cm) long, with dark pink centers. Rot-prone; water from below. ↕ 3in (8cm), ↔ 6in (15cm). Mexico (Durango). ❄ (min. 45–50°F/7–10°C); will tolerate brief periods to 20°F (-7°C).

Mammillaria hahniana

Mammillaria microhelia

M. haageana, syn. *M. dealbata.* Cactus offsetting from the base and sides, with spherical or cylindrical, mid-green stems, 4in (10cm) thick, with slightly woolly axils. Areoles bear 18–20 thin white radial spines and 1 or 2 longer, black-tipped, red-brown centrals. Bears carmine-red flowers, ½in (1.5cm) long, from spring to summer. ↕ 6in (15cm), ↔ 10in (25cm). C. and S.E. Mexico. ❄ (min. 45–50°F/7–10°C); will tolerate brief periods to 20°F (-7°C).

M. hahniana ■ (Old lady cactus). Solitary cactus, forming groups when mature, with spherical, mid-green stems, 5in (13cm) thick, coated with long white hairs, bristles, and spines (20–30 fine, hair-like radials and 1–3 or more shorter, dark-tipped centrals). Purplish red flowers, to ½in (1.5cm) long, are produced from spring to summer. ↕ to 8in (20cm), ↔ to 16in (40cm). C. Mexico. ❄ (min. 45–50°F/7–10°C); will tolerate brief periods to 20°F (-7°C).

M. herrerae. Solitary or clustering cactus with spherical, mid-green stems, ¾–1¼in (2–3cm) thick, occasionally elongating slightly with age, and densely coated with about 100 near-white radial spines but no centrals. Pale pink to reddish violet flowers, 1in (2.5cm) long, are produced from spring to summer. ↕↔ 1¼–1½in (3–4cm). C. Mexico. ❄ (min. 45–50°F/7–10°C); will tolerate brief periods to 35°F (2°C). **var. *albiflora*** has pure white flowers.

M. magnimamma ■ syn. *M. centricirrha.* Extremely variable, freely clustering cactus with spherical, grayish green stems, 4–6in (10–15cm) thick, and white-woolly axils and areoles, the latter with 3–6 brown-tipped, yellowish white radial spines of unequal length, but no centrals. From spring to summer, bears purple-red to pink or brownish yellow flowers, 1in (2.5cm) long. ↕ to 12in (30cm), ↔ to 24in (60cm). C. Mexico. ❄ (min. 45–50°F/7–10°C); will tolerate brief periods to 15°F (-9°C).

M. microhelia ■ Solitary or clustering cactus with cylindrical, grayish green stems, 1½–2in (3.5–5cm) thick, densely covered with spines (up to 50 golden yellow to pale brown-white radials and up to 8, shorter, dark red-brown centrals, although these may be absent). Bears pink, rarely white flowers, to ½in (1.5cm) long, from spring to summer. ↕↔ 6in (15cm). C. Mexico. ❄ (min. 45–50°F/7–10°C); will tolerate brief periods to 35°F (2°C).

M. mystax. Clustering or solitary cactus with spherical to cylindrical, gray-green

M

Mammillaria plumosa

stems, 4in (10cm) thick, with white wool and bristles in the axils. The areoles bear 5–10 brown-tipped white radial spines and 3 or 4 longer, purplish gray centrals. From spring to summer, bears purplish pink flowers, 1in (2.5cm) long. ↕ to 6in (15cm), ↔ 10in (25cm). S. Mexico. ❀ (min. 45–50°F/7–10°C); will tolerate brief periods to 18°F (-8°C).
M. nejapensis. Branching cactus with ovoid to cylindrical dark green stems, 2–3in (5–8cm) thick, with yellowish-white axillary wool and bristles. The areoles bear 3–5 smooth, white radials, and shorter, brown-tipped, white centrals. From spring to early summer, produces red- to red-brown-striped, white flowers, ¾in (2cm) long. ↕ 6in (15cm), ↔ 10in (25cm). Mexico (Oaxaca). ❀ (min. 45–50°F/7–10°C); will tolerate brief periods to 25°F (-4°C).
M. pennispinasa. Short, solitary or clustering, tuberous-rooted cactus with flattened, spherical, mid-green stems, 1½in (4cm) thick. The areoles bear 1–3 yellow radial spines and 1 hooked, brownish-red central. In spring, produces pink-striped, white flowers, ½in (1.5cm) long. Rot-prone; water from below. ↕ ¾in (2cm), ↔ 1½in (4cm). Mexico (Oaxaca). ❀ (min. 45–50°F/7–10°C); will tolerate brief periods to 20°F (-7°C).
M. plumosa ■ (Feather cactus). Clustering cactus with spherical, mid-green stems, 3in (8cm) thick, and white-woolly axils. The areoles bear about 40 feathery white radial spines but no centrals. Greenish white or pale yellow flowers, ½in (1.5cm) long, with reddish brown median lines, are borne in late summer. ↕ 5in (13cm), ↔ 16in (40cm). N.E. Mexico.

Mammillaria zeilmanniana

❀ (min. 45–50°F/7–10°C); will tolerate brief periods to 18°F (-8°C).
M. rhodantha. Solitary cactus with mostly spherical to cylindrical, mid-green stems, 4–5in (10–13cm) thick, and white-woolly axils. The areoles bear 16–24 straight, glossy, white to yellow radial spines and 4–7 longer, often curved, red-brown, occasionally straw-colored or golden yellow centrals. Purplish pink flowers, ¾in (2cm) long, are borne in summer. ↕↔ 16in (40cm). C. Mexico. ❀ (min. 45–50°F/7–10°C); will tolerate brief periods to 20°F (-7°C).
M. schiedeana. Solitary or clustering cactus with slightly depressed spherical, mid-green stems, 1½–2½in (4–6cm) thick, with long, woolly hairs in the axils. The areoles bear 70–80 yellow to white radial spines but no centrals. Cream flowers, ¾in (2cm) long, are produced from summer to autumn. ↕ 4in (10cm), ↔ 12in (30cm). C. Mexico. ❀ (min. 45–50°F/7–10°C); will tolerate brief periods to 18°F (-8°C).
M. sempervivi. Solitary to clump-forming cactus with depressed spherical to short, cylindrical, dark green stems, to 4in (10cm) thick, often elongating, and densely woolly in the axils. The areoles bear 3–7 white radial spines and 2–4 slightly longer, yellow-brown or red centrals. White or yellowish pink flowers, ½in (1.5cm) long, with red median lines, are borne from spring to summer. ↕↔ 3in (8cm). C. Mexico. ❀ (min. 45–50°F/7–10°C); will tolerate brief periods to 18°F (-8°C).
M. senilis, syn. *Mamillopsis senilis.* Slow-growing, solitary cactus, eventually clustering, with spherical to cylindrical, pale green stems, 2½–4in (6–10cm) thick; white-woolly, bristly axils; and white spines (30–40 radials and 4–6 longer centrals, 1 or 2 of which are hooked). Violet-red flowers, 2½in (6cm) long, with slender tubes, are produced from spring to summer. ↕ 6in (15cm), ↔ to 16in (40cm). N.W. Mexico. ❀ (min. 45–50°F/7–10°C); will tolerate brief periods to 18°F (-8°C).
M. shurliana see *M. blossfeldiana.*
M. tayloriorum. Clustering cactus with spherical, light gray-green stems, 3in (8cm) thick, with white-woolly axils. The areoles bear smooth white spines with light brown tips, 18–24 radials and 4–6 longer centrals. In spring, produces purplish pink flowers, to ½in (1.5cm) long. ↕ 4in (10cm), ↔ 3–8in (8–20cm). Mexico (Oaxaca). ❀ (min. 45–50°F/7–10°C); will tolerate brief periods to 28°F (-2°C).
M. zeilmanniana ■ Clustering cactus with spherical, dark green stems, 1¾in (4.5cm) thick, with bare axils. The areoles bear 15–18 hair-like white radial spines and 4 shorter, reddish brown centrals, 1 of which is hooked. Reddish violet, pink, or white flowers, to ¾in (2cm) long, are produced in summer. ↕ 6in (15cm), ↔ 12in (30cm). C. Mexico. ❀ (min. 45–50°F/7–10°C); will tolerate brief periods to 20°F (-7°C).

MAMMILLOYDIA

syn. OREOCEREUS

CACTACEAE

Monotypic genus of spherical, generally solitary, cactus from semi-desert regions in Mexico, including Coahila, Nuevo Laredo, San Luis Potosi, and Guanajuato. The short spines of this cactus appear through a mass of fine white hair, inspiring the species name, *candida,* which means "bright white."
• **CULTIVATION** Under glass, grow in a mix of 4 parts standard cactus potting mix and 1 part limestone chips, in full light. From spring to summer, water freely and apply a balanced liquid fertilizer every 4–5 weeks. Keep nearly dry at other times. Outdoors, grow in moderately fertile, slightly alkaline, sharply drained, humus-rich soil in full sun. See also pp.48–49.
• **PROPAGATION** Sow seed at 70°F (21°C) in spring or summer.
• **PESTS AND DISEASES** Scale occurs.

M. candida (Snowball cushion cactus). Slow-growing, solitary or clustering cactus with spherical to cylindrical, mid-green stems, 2½–5in (6–13cm) thick, with 4–7 white bristles in each axil. White-felted areoles bear white, often brown- or pink-tipped spines (50 radials and 8–12 centrals). From spring to summer, bears rose-pink flowers, ¾in (2cm) long, with white margins. ↕↔ 6in (15cm). N.E. Mexico. ❀ (min. 45°F/7°C)

MANDEVILLA

syn. DIPLADENIA

APOCYNACEAE

Genus of about 120 species of mainly tuberous-rooted, woody-stemmed, twining climbers, with some perennials, from tropical woodland in Central and South America. Opposite, simple leaves are borne on stems containing a milky latex. They have often showy, funnel-shaped to tubular-salverform flowers, each with 5 broad, spreading petal lobes, borne mainly in axillary racemes. Use to clothe a pergola, arch, or trellis, or grow as a screen. Where not hardy, grow in a temperate or warm greenhouse. Contact with the sap may cause skin irritation, and all parts may cause mild stomach upset if ingested.
• **CULTIVATION** Under glass, grow in soil-based potting mix in full light with shade from hot sun. In the growing season, water moderately and apply a balanced liquid fertilizer monthly; water sparingly in winter. Outdoors, grow in moderately fertile, moist but well-drained soil in full sun with some midday shade. Pruning group 12, in late winter or early spring.
• **PROPAGATION** Sow seed at 64–73°F (18–23°C) in spring. Root softwood cuttings in late spring or semi-ripe cuttings with bottom heat in summer.

Mandevilla x *amoena* 'Alice du Pont'

Mandevilla splendens

• **PESTS AND DISEASES** Leaf spots, gray mold, root rot, whiteflies, spider mites, and mealybugs occur.

***M.* x *amoena* 'Alice du Pont'** ■ syn. *M.* x *amabilis* 'Alice du Pont'. Woody-stemmed, twining climber bearing elliptic-oblong to ovate-oblong, slightly wrinkled, mid- to deep green leaves, 3½–7in (9–18cm) long, with short points. Racemes of up to 20 narrowly funnel-shaped, glowing pink flowers, 3–4in (8–10cm) across, are freely produced in summer. ↕ to 22ft (7m). ❀ (min. 50–59°F/10–15°C)
M. boliviensis, syn. *Dipladenia boliviensis.* Slender-stemmed, usually freely branching, woody, twining climber with elliptic to oblong or elliptic-obovate, slender-pointed, shiny, mid-green leaves, 2–4in (5–10cm) long. Racemes of 3–7 white flowers, 2–3in (5–8cm) across, with yellow eyes and angular petal lobes, are produced in mid- and late summer. ↕ 10–12ft (3–4m). Ecuador, Bolivia. ❀ (min. 50–59°F/10–15°C)
M. laxa, syn. *M. suaveolens, M. tweediana* (Chilean jasmine). Vigorous, freely branching, woody-stemmed, twining climber. Ovate to oblong leaves, 2–4in (5–10cm) long, have heart-shaped bases and slender-pointed tips, and are lustrous, rich green above and purple or gray-green beneath. From summer to early autumn, produces racemes of 5–15 tubular, strongly fragrant, pure white or creamy white flowers, 2–3½in (5–9cm) across, with broad, rounded, often crimped petal lobes. ↕ 10–15ft (3–5m). Peru, Bolivia, Argentina. ❀ (min. 41°F/5°C); will tolerate brief periods to 32°F (0°C).
M. splendens ■ syn. *Dipladenia splendens.* Vigorous, moderately to freely branching, woody-stemmed, twining climber with downy young stems and broadly elliptic, lustrous, mid-green leaves, 4–8in (10–20cm) long, with heart-shaped bases and slender-pointed tips. During summer, produces racemes of 3–5 narrowly funnel-shaped flowers, to 4in (10cm) across, with rounded, rose-pink petal lobes and white-and-yellow throats. ↕ 10–20ft (3–6m). S.E. Brazil. ❀ (min. 50–59°F/10–15°C).
'Rosacea' produces rose-pink flowers, margined and flushed deep purplish pink, with the tops of the throats ringed brighter pink.
M. suaveolens see *M. laxa.*
M. tweediana see *M. laxa.*

MANDRAGORA

Mandrake

SOLANACEAE

Genus of 6 species of perennials, with fleshy taproots, found in dry, stony areas from the Mediterranean region to the Himalayas. They produce large basal rosettes of ovate to lance-shaped leaves, and are cultivated for their stemless or short-stemmed, tubular to bell-shaped flowers, with triangular lobes, borne singly or in basal clusters from autumn to early spring. The fleshy fruits are spherical or ellipsoid. Much lore surrounds the vaguely anthropomorphic roots of certain mandrakes. The narcotic and hallucinogenic properties of *M. officinarum* have been employed for various purposes, including surgery and witchcraft in medieval times. Grow in a rock garden or at the base of a warm, sunny wall. Alkaloids in the plant may be harmful if ingested.

• **CULTIVATION** Grow in deep, moderately fertile, well-drained soil in full sun. Shelter from cold, drying winds and protect from excessive winter moisture. Avoid disturbance once established.

• **PROPAGATION** Sow seed in containers in an open frame as soon as ripe or in autumn. Insert root cuttings in winter.

• **PESTS AND DISEASES** Slugs and snails may damage leaves and fruits.

M. autumnalis (Autumn mandrake). Perennial with rosettes of oblong to lance-shaped, dark green leaves, to 10in (25cm) long. From autumn to winter, produces basal clusters of tubular-bell-shaped, violet or white flowers, to 1¼in (3cm) across, often with green or white streaks, followed by ellipsoid, orange or yellow fruit, to 1¼in (3cm) long. ↕ 6in (15cm), ↔ to 12in (30cm). Portugal, Spain, E. Mediterranean. Zone 6.

M. officinarum ▣ (Common mandrake, Devil's apples, Love apple). Perennial with rosettes of ovate to lance-shaped, wavy-margined, dark green leaves, to 12in (30cm) long, upright at first, then lying flat on the ground. In spring, bears basal clusters of upward-facing, tubular-bell-shaped, greenish white flowers, to 1in (2.5cm) across, sometimes stained purple, followed by spherical yellow fruit, to 1¼in (3cm) across. ↕ 6in (15cm), ↔ to 12in (30cm). N. Italy, W. Balkans, Greece, W. Turkey. Zone 6.

Mandragora officinarum

MANETTIA

RUBIACEAE

Genus of about 80 species of evergreen perennials and woody-stemmed, twining climbers from moist woodland or rainforest in tropical North and South America, and the West Indies. They produce opposite pairs of usually simple, sometimes toothed leaves. Tubular to funnel-shaped, often brightly colored flowers, each with 4 short lobes, are borne singly or in small, axillary panicles or cymes. Where not hardy, grow in a cool or temperate greenhouse. In warmer areas, use to clothe an arch, or grow on a wall or through small trees.

• **CULTIVATION** Under glass, grow in soil-based potting mix in full light or bright filtered light. In the growing season, water moderately and apply a balanced liquid fertilizer every 3–4 weeks; water sparingly in winter. Outdoors, grow in moderately fertile, moist but well-drained soil in full sun, although they will tolerate partial shade. Pruning group 12, in late winter or early spring.

• **PROPAGATION** Sow seed at 55–64°F (13–18°C) in spring. Root softwood stem-tip cuttings in late spring or summer.

• **PESTS AND DISEASES** Whiteflies may be a problem under glass.

M. bicolor see *M. luteorubra.*

M. cordifolia (Firecracker vine). Vigorous climber with thin, oblong to lance-shaped, ovate, or heart-shaped leaves, to 3in (8cm) long, lustrous, bright green above, paler and downy or hairless beneath. From late winter to summer, tubular, brilliant red to deep orange flowers, 1¼–2in (3–5cm) long, sometimes yellow-flushed on the lobes, are borne singly or in crowded, leafy panicles. ↕ 6–12ft (2–4m). Peru, Bolivia, Argentina. ❀ (min. 45°F/7°C)

M. inflata see *M. luteorubra.*

M. luteorubra ▣ syn. *M. bicolor, M. inflata* (Brazilian firecracker). Fast-growing climber with angular, slightly sticky, hairy stems bearing ovate to lance-shaped, light to dark green leaves, 1½–6in (3.5–15cm) long, semi-leathery when mature. Solitary, occasionally paired, tubular, bright red, yellow-lobed flowers, 1–2in (2.5–5cm) long, inflated at the bases and with dense velvety hairs, are borne in summer. ↕ 6–12ft (2–4m). Paraguay, Uruguay. ❀ (min. 45°F/7°C)

Manettia luteorubra

MANGLIETIA

MAGNOLIACEAE

Genus of 25 species of upright to spreading, evergreen trees and shrubs found in mountain woodland from the Himalayas to S. and W. China and Malaysia. The alternate, mostly oblong-ovate to elliptic or inversely lance-shaped leaves are glossy, light or dark green. *Manglietia* species are usually cultivated for their magnolia-like flowers, borne singly at the tips of the branches. They are followed by cone-like heads containing oblong to ovoid, fleshy-coated seeds. Grow as specimen plants. Where not hardy, grow in a cool or temperate greenhouse.

• **CULTIVATION** Under glass, grow in soil-based potting mix in bright filtered or indirect light. When in growth, water moderately and apply a balanced liquid fertilizer monthly; water sparingly in winter. Outdoors, grow in humus-rich, moist but well-drained soil in partial shade, or in full sun in humid conditions. Pruning group 1; need restrictive pruning under glass, after flowering.

• **PROPAGATION** Sow seed at 41–48°F (5–9°C) as soon as ripe. Root softwood cuttings with bottom heat in spring. Layer or air layer one-year-old stems in spring.

• **PESTS AND DISEASES** Scale insects may be a problem under glass.

M. insignis, syn. *Magnolia insignis.* Erect then spreading, many-branched tree with gray-downy young shoots. The narrowly oval to inversely lance-shaped, leathery leaves, 4–8in (10–20cm) long, are glossy, rich green above and slightly glaucous beneath. Erect, cup-shaped, cream-tinted, pink to rose-pink or carmine-red flowers, 3in (8cm) across, with 9–12 tepals, are produced from spring to early summer, sometimes followed by elongated, oblong-ovoid purple fruit, 2–4in (5–10cm) long. ↕ 25–40ft (8–12m), ↔ 10–15ft (3–5m). C. Himalayas to N. Vietnam and W. China. ❀ (min. 41°F/5°C); may survive short periods near 32°F (0°C).

MARANTA

MARANTACEAE

Genus of about 20 species of evergreen, rhizomatous perennials from rainforest in tropical Central and South America. They are cultivated for their crowded clumps of often intricately patterned, blunt-ended, elliptic leaves, spreading by day and raised to an erect position in the evening. Small, tubular, often insignificant, 2-lipped white flowers are produced in pairs in loose racemes. Where they are not hardy, grow as houseplants or in a warm greenhouse, in shallow pots or hanging baskets, or trained up moss poles. In warmer climates, use as a groundcover among shrubs in shade.

Maranta leuconeura 'Erythroneura'

• **CULTIVATION** Under glass, grow in soilless or soil-based potting mix in bright filtered or bright indirect light, in half-pots or pans to accommodate the shallow root system. Provide high humidity at all times. In the growing season, water moderately and apply a balanced liquid fertilizer monthly; water sparingly in winter. Outdoors, grow in humus-rich, moist but well-drained soil in deep or partial shade.

• **PROPAGATION** Sow seed at 55–64°F (13–18°C) as soon as ripe. Divide in spring. Take basal cuttings, 3–4in (7–10cm) long, and root with bottom heat in spring.

• **PESTS AND DISEASES** Bud mites, spider mites, mealybugs, leaf spots, and cucumber mosaic virus are common.

M. kerchoveana see *M. leuconeura* 'Kerchoveana'.

M. leuconeura (Prayer plant). Very variable, clump-forming perennial with elliptic to obovate, dark green leaves, 5in (13cm) long, with silver lines that fan from the midribs to the margins; the undersides are deep purple or gray-green. ↕↔ 12in (30cm). Brazil. ❀ (min. 59°F/15°C). **'Erythroneura'** ▣ syn. 'Erythrophylla' (Herringbone plant), bears oblong-obovate to obovate, velvety, olive- and black-green leaves with bright red midribs and veins, and jagged, light yellow-green markings around the midribs; the undersides are deep red. **'Kerchoveana'** ▣ syn. *M. kerchoveana* (Rabbit's foot, Rabbit's tracks), bears broadly oblong-elliptic, light gray-green leaves with roughly square brown marks, turning green

Maranta leuconeura 'Kerchoveana'

M

with age, on either side of the pale green mid-ribs; the undersides are pale blue-gray. **'Massangeana'**, syn. var. *massangeana*, produces broadly elliptic, blackish green leaves with silver-gray feathering along the midribs and veins; the undersides are purple.
M. makoyana see *Calathea makoyana.*

▷ ***Marginatocereus marginatus*** see *Stenocereus marginatus*

MARGYRICARPUS

ROSACEAE

Genus of one species of dwarf, evergreen shrub from dry, open sites in northern mountains and southern lowlands of the Chilean Andes. It produces pinnate leaves and insignificant flowers, and is valued for its attractive, long-lasting fruit. Suitable for a scree bed, a rock garden, or an alpine house.
• **CULTIVATION** Grow in moderately fertile, acidic, moist but well-drained soil in full sun with some midday shade. In an alpine house, grow in acidic soil mix. Shelter from cold, drying winds and protect from excessive winter moisture. Pruning group 1.
• **PROPAGATION** Sow seed in containers in a cold frame in autumn or as soon as ripe. Layer or root softwood cuttings in late spring or early summer.
• **PESTS AND DISEASES** Susceptible to aphids and whiteflies under glass.

M. pinnatus, syn. *M. setosus* (Pearl berry, Pearl fruit). Spreading, densely branched shrub bearing sharply pointed, pinnate leaves, to ¾in (2cm) long, with linear, dark green leaflets with inrolled, silky-hairy margins. In early summer, bears axillary clusters of 1–3 tiny green flowers, followed by spherical, leathery, purple-tinted white fruit, to ¼in (6mm) across. ↕ to 12in (30cm), ↔ to 18in (45cm). Andes. ❀ (min. 35°F/2°C)
M. setosus see *M. pinnatus.*

▷ ***Marniera chrysocardium*** see *Epiphyllum chrysocardium*

MARRUBIUM

Horehound

LAMIACEAE

Genus of about 40 species of woolly perennials from Mediterranean Europe and temperate Asia, mainly found in sunny, dry, stony wasteland. They have square stems and alternate, opposite pairs of usually ovate or ovate-oblong leaves, which are often malodorous. Tubular, 2-lipped flowers are borne in axillary whorls. Grow in a large rock garden or a mixed border; they are especially effective in a Mediterranean-style garden.
• **CULTIVATION** Grow in poor, well-drained soil in full sun. Provide shelter from cold, drying winds and protection from excessive winter moisture.
• **PROPAGATION** Sow seed in containers in a cold frame in late spring, although germination is erratic. Root softwood cuttings in spring or summer.
• **PESTS AND DISEASES** Infrequent.

***M. candidissimum* of gardens** see *M. incanum.*
M. cylleneum. Spreading, densely woolly perennial with long-haired stems and obovate, scalloped, mid-green leaves, to 2in (5cm) long. Tight whorls of yellow flowers, to ½in (1.5cm) across, are produced in summer. ↕ to 20in (50cm), ↔ 12–18in (30–45cm). Greece, Albania. Zone 6b.
M. incanum, syn. *M. candidissimum* of gardens. Spreading, silky-hairy perennial with many erect, densely white-hairy shoots bearing oblong-ovate, scalloped or toothed, gray-green leaves, to 2in (5cm) long, white-felted beneath. In early summer, bears congested whorls of very pale lilac, almost white flowers, to ½in (1.5cm) long, within gray-woolly calyces. ↕ 8–20in (20–50cm), ↔ 24in (60cm). Italy, Sicily, Balkan Peninsula. Zone 4.
M. vulgare (Common horehound, White horehound). Coarse, upright, silky white-hairy perennial with rounded to ovate, scalloped-margined, downy to nearly hairless, wormwood-scented, gray leaves, to 2in (5cm) long, densely woolly beneath. In summer, white flowers, to ½in (1.5cm) across, are borne within white calyces, in rounded whorls. ↕ to 18in (45cm), ↔ 12–18in (30–45cm). Europe, Canary Islands, N. Africa, Asia. Zone 4.

MARSILEA

Pepperwort, Water clover

MARSILEACEAE

Genus of 65 species of rhizomatous, terrestrial, amphibious, and aquatic perennial ferns from warm-temperate Europe, Ghana, N. Asia, Australia, and E. US. They grow in large numbers, mainly beside rivers, but also in lakes, where the elongated rhizomes grow upward, producing a canopy of surface leaves that develop a terrestrial form if the water recedes. Triangular to ovate, 4-lobed leaves each bear a spore case at the base, and close up at night when submerged. Grow at the margins of a pool. Where not hardy, grow in an indoor pool in a warm greenhouse or conservatory, or in a tropical aquarium; *M. quadrifolia* is suitable for a cold-water aquarium or large container.

Marsilea quadrifolia

• **CULTIVATION** Outdoors, grow in the muddy margins of a pool, or in aquatic planting containers filled with water, in full sun, at a depth of 6in (15cm). Under glass, grow in containers of fertile soil at the pool margins, in water at 68–79°F (20–26°C), in full light. In an aquarium, provide high light and root in containers of fine sand or peat; feed with a commercial aquatic fertilizer. See also pp.52–53.
• **PROPAGATION** Cut the rhizomes into sections and anchor to the substrate in shallow water.
• **PESTS AND DISEASES** Infrequent.

M. drummondii ▣ (Common water clover). Creeping, terrestrial or aquatic, perennial fern with fan-shaped leaves, ½–1½in (1–4cm) across, with 4 leaflets, and upright stems, to 12in (30cm) long, produced singly from the rhizomes. ↕ to 6in (15cm), ↔ indefinite. Australia. ❀ (min. 41°F/5°C)
M. mutica. Creeping, aquatic, perennial fern with stems to 24in (60cm) long, depending on water depth, and light green leaves, 3in (8cm) long, with brown markings and 4 triangular leaflets that float on the surface, supported by thread-like leaf stalks. Invasive in earthen ponds, but suitable for containers in lined water gardens. ↕↔ indefinite. Australia. ❀ (min. 41°F/5°C)
M. quadrifolia ▣ (Water clover). Creeping, aquatic, perennial fern with long rhizomes, and leaves to 1¼in (3cm) across, with 4 soft, triangular, sometimes overlapping leaflets, downy when young; when submerged, they float on the surface, on stalks to 6in (15cm) long. ↕ to 6in (15cm), ↔ indefinite. Europe, N. Asia, E. US. ❀ (min. 41°F/5°C)

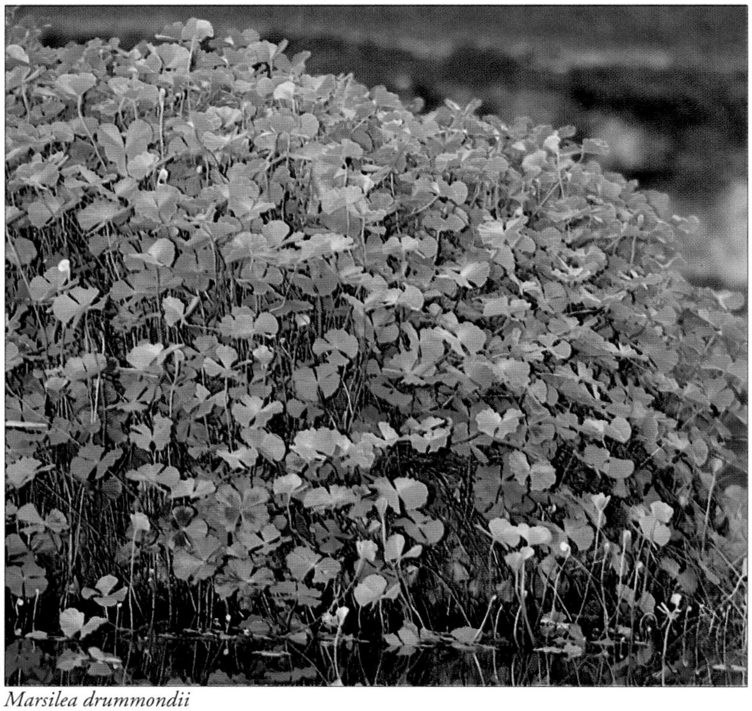
Marsilea drummondii

▷ ***Martynia*** see *Proboscidea*
▷ ***Mascarena lagenicaulis*** see *Hyophorbe lagenicaulis*

MASDEVALLIA

ORCHIDACEAE

Genus of about 340 species of evergreen, epiphytic, terrestrial, or lithophytic orchids, mainly found in cloud forest at 2,600–13,700ft (800–4,200m), from Mexico to Central and South America. They lack pseudobulbs but have short, erect stems, each supporting a single, oblong to ovate or linear to lance-shaped, curved or upright, rigid, fleshy leaf. Flowers are borne singly or in racemes, among or usually above the foliage, mostly from spring to summer; some bloom continuously. Enlarged, often long-tailed sepals surround the minute petals and lips, giving the flowers a triangular shape.
• **CULTIVATION** Medium- to cool-growing orchids. Grow in small pots of epiphytic orchid potting mix made with fine-grade bark. Provide full light and ample ventilation. In summer, provide moist shade, water freely, feed at every third watering, and mist once or twice daily. In winter, water more sparingly, but do not allow to dry out. See also p.46.
• **PROPAGATION** Cuttings or offshoots may be rooted successfully.
• **PESTS AND DISEASES** Spider mites, aphids, mealybugs, and yellow bean virus may be troublesome.

***M.* Angel Frost** ▣ (*M. strobelii* x *M. veitchiana*). Epiphytic orchid with upright, oblong to narrowly ovate leaves, 6in (15cm) long. Bears racemes of orange flowers, 3in (8cm) long, in spring. ↕ 9in (23cm), ↔ 6in (15cm). ❀ (min. 52°F/11°C; max. 75°F/24°C)
***M.* Angel Heart** (*M. infracta* x *M. militaris*). Epiphytic orchid with

Masdevallia Angel Frost

Masdevallia coccinea

upright, linear to lance-shaped leaves, 6in (15cm) long. Red flowers, 3in (8cm) long, are borne singly or in racemes, in spring. ↕ 9in (23cm), ↔ 6in (15cm). ❀ (min. 52°F/11°C; max. 75°F/24°C)
M. coccinea ▣ Terrestrial orchid with upright, oblong to lance-shaped leaves, 6–8in (15–20cm) long. In summer, bears solitary flowers, 2½–4in (6–10cm) long, with purple-pink, crimson, red-orange, yellow, or white sepals, and white petals. ↕ 16in (40cm), ↔ 12in (30cm). Colombia, Peru. ❀ (min. 52°F/11°C; max. 75°F/24°C)
M. elephanticeps* var. *pachysepala see *M. mooreana.*
***M.* Hugh Rogers** ▣ (*M. amabilis* x *M. yungasensis*). Epiphytic orchid with upright, oblong to lance-shaped leaves, 6in (15cm) long. In spring, bears racemes of orange or red flowers, 3in (8cm) long, with darker veins in the same color. ↕ 9in (23cm), ↔ 6in (15cm). ❀ (min. 52°F/11°C; max. 75°F/24°C)
M. ignea see *M. militaris.*
M. infracta ▣ Epiphytic orchid with upright, oblong to lance-shaped leaves, 3–5½in (8–14cm). Bears short racemes of cupped, yellow-flushed, dull red to purplish pink flowers, 4–6in (10–15cm) long, with long, pale yellow tails, in summer. ↕↔ 6in (15cm). Peru, Brazil. ❀ (min. 52°F/11°C; max. 75°F/24°C)
***M.* Measuresiana** (*M. amabilis* x *M. tovarensis*). Epiphytic orchid with upright, oblong to lance-shaped leaves, 4–6in (10–15cm) long. Bears racemes of long-tailed white flowers, 3in (8cm)

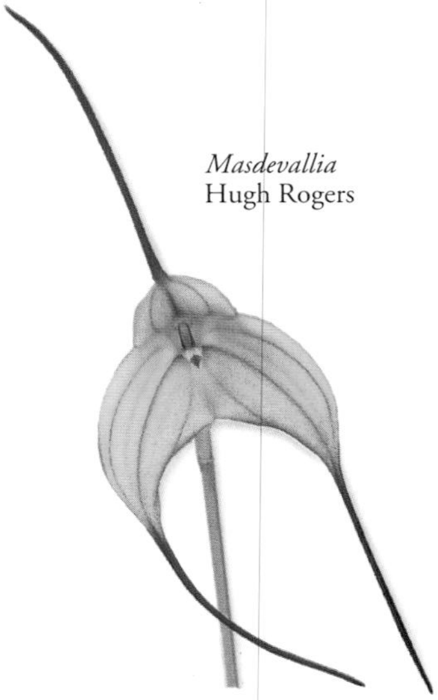

Masdevallia Hugh Rogers

M

Masdevallia infracta

long, flushed pale pink, in succession in winter. ↕ 9in (23cm), ↔ 6in (15cm). ❀ (min. 52°F/11°C; max. 75°F/24°C)
M. militaris, syn. *M. ignea.* Lithophytic orchid with upright, oblong to lance-shaped leaves, to 6in (15cm) long. Orange-scarlet to red-brown flowers, 1¾in (4.5cm) long, are produced singly in summer. ↕ 12in (30cm), ↔ 9in (23cm). Venezuela, Colombia. ❀ (min. 52°F/11°C; max. 75°F/24°C)
M. mooreana, syn. *M. elephanticeps* var. *pachysepala.* Epiphytic orchid with upright, linear-oblong leaves, to 8in (20cm) long. Greenish yellow flowers, to 3½in (9cm) across, spotted dull purple, with bright yellow tails, are produced singly in summer. ↕↔ 6in (15cm). Venezuela, Colombia. ❀ (min. 52°F/11°C; max. 75°F/24°C)
M. rolfeana. Epiphytic orchid with upright, obovate to elliptic leaves, 4½–5½in (11–14cm) long. Dark reddish purple flowers, 2½in (6cm) long, with short yellow tails, are produced singly from spring to summer. ↕↔ 6in (15cm). Costa Rica. ❀ (min. 52°F/11°C; max. 75°F/24°C)
M. tovarensis ▣ Epiphytic orchid with upright, obovate to lance-shaped leaves, to 6in (15cm) long. Milk-white flowers, 3in (8cm) long, with short tails, are produced in short racemes in winter. ↕↔ 6in (15cm). Venezuela. ❀ (min. 52°F/11°C; max. 75°F/24°C)
M. veitchiana. Lithophytic orchid with upright, oblong to narrowly obovate leaves, 6–10in (15–25cm) long. Bright orange-red, purple-hairy flowers, 4–6in (10–15cm) long, shot with crimson, with short tails, are borne singly from spring to summer. ↕ 12in (30cm), ↔ 9in (23cm). Peru. ❀ (min. 52°F/11°C; max. 75°F/24°C)

Masdevallia tovarensis

▷ ***Matricaria parthenium*** see *Tanacetum parthenium*

MATTEUCCIA

DRYOPTERIDACEAE

Genus of 3 or 4 species of deciduous, terrestrial ferns, commonly occurring in moist, deciduous woodland in Europe, E. Asia, and North America. In spring, the erect or creeping rhizomes produce lance-shaped, pinnate to 2-pinnatifid sterile fronds in regular shuttlecocks. The sterile fronds are followed in mid- and late summer by distinctive, densely contracted, smaller, more erect, darker, and longer-stalked fertile fronds, which persist over winter. These ferns should be grown in moist shade in a woodland garden, in a damp border, or at the edge of a pond.
• **CULTIVATION** Grow in humus-rich, moist but well-drained, neutral to slightly acidic soil in partial shade.
• **PROPAGATION** Sow spores at 59°F (15°C) as soon as ripe. Divide established clumps in early spring.
• **PESTS AND DISEASES** Infrequent.

M. pennsylvanica see *M. struthiopteris.*
M. struthiopteris ▣ syn. *M. pennsylvanica* (Ostrich fern). Rhizomatous fern with erect shuttlecocks of broadly lance-shaped, pinnate, pale green sterile fronds, 4ft (1.2m) or more long, with narrowly lance-shaped, pinnatifid pinnae. Shorter, contracted, lance-shaped, dark brown fertile fronds, 12in (30cm) or more long, which appear in late summer, have linear pinnae with very thick, strongly inrolled margins. Vigorously spreads by horizontal rhizomes, producing offset plants 4–8in (10–20cm) from the parent plant. ↕ 5½ft (1.7m), ↔ to 3ft (1m). Europe, E. Asia, E. North America. Zone 3.

Matteuccia struthiopteris

MATTHIOLA

Stock

BRASSICACEAE

Genus of 55 species of bushy, erect annuals and perennials, occasionally subshrubs, from scrub and hilly areas in W. Europe, South Africa, and C. and S.W. Asia. The leaves are simple, usually lance-shaped, sometimes pinnatifid or shallowly lobed, and gray-green to mid-green. *Matthiola* species and cultivars are grown for their usually sweetly scented, pastel pink, purple, or white flowers. The flowers are cross-shaped (double in some cultivar selections), and borne in terminal, spike-like racemes or panicles. Grow in a mixed or annual border.

Cultivars of *M. incana* are useful spring and summer bedding plants, and provide attractive cut flowers. They are often divided by horticulturists into the following 4 groups: **Brompton stocks**, grown as biennials, bear tall panicles of single or double flowers. **East Lothian stocks** may be grown as biennials or spring-sown annuals; more compact and smaller-flowered than Brompton Group stocks, they produce spike-like racemes of single or double flowers. **Ten Week stocks** are grown as annuals, and may be dwarf or tall; dwarf cultivars, suitable for bedding or containers, bear single or double flowers, usually in panicles. Tall cultivars bear mostly double flowers in dense, usually unbranched, spike-like racemes. **Column stocks** are generally grown under glass for cut flowers, and produce long, dense, upright, spike-like racemes of mainly double flowers.
• **CULTIVATION** Grow in moderately fertile, moist but well-drained, preferably neutral to slightly alkaline soil in a sheltered position in full sun. Give support to tall cultivars.
• **PROPAGATION** Sow seed of *M. longipetala* subsp. *bicornis in situ* in spring, and repeat for a succession of flowers. For bedding, sow seed of *M. incana* Cinderella Series, Midget Series, and Ten Week Mixed at 50–64°F (10–18°C) in early spring. Sow seed of *M. incana* Legacy Series, Sentinel Series, and Excelsior Mammoth Column Series in a seedbed or in containers in a cold frame in mid-summer; overwinter in a cold frame in cold climates and plant out in spring. Sow seed of perennials in containers in a cold frame in spring or summer; overwinter in a cold frame and plant out in the following spring.
• **PESTS AND DISEASES** Damping off, crown rot, gray mold, wilt, and leaf spot occur at times. Aphids, flea beetles, cucumber mosaic virus, and club root also occur.

M. bicornis see *M. longipetala* subsp. *bicornis.*
M. fruticulosa. Dwarf, lax or tufted, woody-based, hairy to densely white-woolly perennial with simple or pinnatifid, linear to oblong, gray-green leaves, to 5in (13cm) long. In summer, bears long, upright, spike-like racemes of flowers, ½–1¼in (1.5–3cm) across, from yellow to purplish violet. ↕ to 24in (60cm), ↔ to 8in (20cm). C. and S. Europe, Turkey (in Europe only), Cyprus, Lebanon, N.W. Africa. Zone 7.
subsp. *valesiaca* is tufted, spreads by

Matthiola incana Cinderella Series

underground runners, and bears dense racemes of mauve-purple to red-purple flowers; prefers acidic soil; ↕ 10in (25cm), ↔ 12in (30cm); N. and E. Spain, Pyrenees, S. Alps, Balkans.
M. incana (Stock). Woody-based perennial or subshrub, sometimes short-lived, with entire, occasionally pinnatifid or lobed, inversely lance-shaped to linear-lance-shaped, gray-green to white-hairy leaves, 2–4in (5–10cm) long. Upright racemes of clove-scented, mauve, purple, violet, pink, or white flowers, to 1in (2.5cm) across, are borne from late spring to summer. ↕ to 32in (80cm), ↔ to 16in (40cm). Coastal S. and W. Europe, from Spain to W. Turkey, Cyprus, Arabian Peninsula, Egypt. Zone 7b. The many cultivars of *M. incana*, sometimes resulting from crosses with *M. sinuata*, are grown as annuals or biennials, and produce single or fully double, almost rosette-like, scented flowers in dense, spike-like racemes or panicles, 6–18in (15–45cm) tall, in summer, or earlier when grown under glass. Cultivars of **Cinderella Series** ▣ bear double, dark blue-purple, lavender-blue, red, rose-pink, silvery blue, or white flowers in racemes, 6in (15cm) long; ↕ 8–10in (20–25cm), ↔ to 10in (25cm). **Ten Week Mixed** ▣ bears mainly double flowers in shades of crimson, pink, lavender-pink, purple, and white, in racemes 6in (15cm) long; ↕ 12in (30cm), ↔ to 10in (25cm).

Matthiola incana Ten Week Mixed

MATUCANA
syn. OREOCEREUS

CACTACEAE

Genus of 17 or 19 species of low-growing cactus found at high elevations in the Peruvian Andes. Most are solitary and basal-branching. The areoles of these cacti produce both hairs and spines. Diurnal funnel-shaped to narrowly tubular funnel-shaped, bilaterally symmetrical yellow, orange to pink to bright red flowers are borne subapically. The spherical to oblong fruits are semi-fleshy, hollow, and longitudinally dehiscent.
• **CULTIVATION** Under glass, grow in a mix of 4 parts standard cactus potting mix and 1 part limestone chips, in full light. From spring to summer, water freely and apply a balanced liquid fertilizer every 4–5 weeks. Keep nearly dry at other times. Outdoors, grow in moderately fertile, slightly alkaline, sharply drained, humus-rich soil in full sun. See also pp.48–49.
• **PROPAGATION** Sow seed at 70°F (21°C) in spring or summer.
• **PESTS AND DISEASES** Scale occurs.

M. madisoniorum ▣ Usually solitary cactus that sometimes branches at the base with flattened spherical to broad columnar, dull gray-green stems. Ribs (7–12) are broad and flat with transverse grooves; spines (up to 5) are readily detachable. Produces narrow funnel-shaped, orange-red flowers, 3–4in (8–10cm) long, 1½–2¼in (4–5.5cm) across, and hairy, spherical fruit, to 2½in (6cm). Found at high elevations, 1,300–3,300ft (400–1,000m). ↕ to 6in (15cm), ↔ to 4in (10cm). Andes of Peru. ❄ (min. 50°F/10°C)

Matucana madisoniorum

MAURANDELLA

SCROPHULARIACEAE

Genus of one species of twining, herbaceous, perennial climber from dry desert riverbeds, subject to flooding, in limestone areas of S.W. US and Mexico. It has hairless, slender, many-branched stems, to 7ft (2.2m) long. Tubular flowers are borne singly from the leaf axils throughout summer and autumn. Where not hardy, grow as an annual or in a cool greenhouse. In warmer areas, use on a pergola, arch, trellis, or wall.
• **CULTIVATION** Under glass and when grown as an annual, grow in soil-based potting mix in full light with shade from hot sun. In growth, water moderately and apply a balanced liquid fertilizer monthly; water sparingly in winter. Outdoors, grow in moderately fertile, moist but well-drained soil in full sun with some midday shade or in light, dappled shade. Provide shelter from cold, drying winds.
• **PROPAGATION** Sow seed at 55–64°F (13–18°C) in spring. Root softwood cuttings with bottom heat in late spring.
• **PESTS AND DISEASES** Infrequent.

M. antirrhiniflora ▣ syn. *Asarina antirrhiniflora* (Violet twining snapdragon). Wiry-stemmed climber with ovate-triangular, shallowly lobed, bright to mid-green leaves, 1–4in (2.5–10cm) or more long. Throughout summer and autumn, bears snapdragon-like flowers, to 1¾in (4.5cm) long, with white tubes and usually violet or purple, occasionally pink lobes. ↕ 3–6ft (1–2m). S.W. US, Mexico. ❄ (min. 41°F/5°C)

Maurandella antirrhiniflora

MAURANDYA

SCROPHULARIACEAE

Genus of 2 species of twining, woody-based, herbaceous, perennial climbers found in rocky areas and woodland in Mexico and Central America. The leaves are triangular to broadly ovate, sometimes heart-shaped at the bases and occasionally 5-lobed. Solitary, trumpet-shaped blooms are borne in the leaf axils throughout summer and autumn. Use to clothe a trellis, or grow against a wall. Where not hardy, grow in a cool greenhouse or outdoors as annuals.
• **CULTIVATION** Under glass, grow in soil-based potting mix in full light with shade from hot sun, or in bright filtered light. In growth, water freely; apply a balanced liquid fertilizer monthly. Keep just moist in winter. Outdoors, grow in moderately fertile, moist but well-drained soil in full sun. Remove dead top growth in autumn.
• **PROPAGATION** Sow seed at 55–64°F (13–18°C) in spring. Root softwood cuttings with bottom heat in late spring.
• **PESTS AND DISEASES** Infrequent.

M. barclayana ▣ syn. *Asarina barclayana*. Medium-sized, erect, free-flowering climber with angular to shallowly lobed, ovate, mid- to light green leaves, 1–1¾in (2.5–4.5cm) long, with heart-shaped bases. From summer to autumn, produces flowers, 1½–3in (4–8cm) long, with white or green-tinted white tubes and white, pink, or deep purple lobes. ↕ 6–15ft (2–5m). Mexico. ❄ (min. 41°F/5°C)
M. erubescens see *Lophospermum erubescens*.
M. purpusii, syn. *Asarina purpusii*. Tuberous climber with triangular-ovate, softly hairy, mid-green leaves, 1½–3in (4–8cm) long, sometimes coarsely toothed. Produces purplish pink flowers, 1½in (4cm) long, throughout summer and autumn. ↕ 24in (60cm). Mexico. ❄ (min. 41°F/5°C)

Maurandya barclayana

MAXILLARIA

ORCHIDACEAE

Genus of about 250 species of evergreen, rhizomatous, epiphytic or terrestrial orchids from tropical and subtropical Central and South America, found from sea level to over 10,000ft (3,000m), sometimes in cloud forest. Solitary or clustered, usually laterally compressed, ovoid to spherical, sometimes oblong pseudobulbs produce 1 or 2 thin to leathery, grass-like or broadly oblong, usually mid-green leaves. Flowers are borne singly or in clusters on scapes produced from long or short rhizomes. They range from white to dark red or yellow, and usually appear intermittently throughout summer.

• **CULTIVATION** Cool- or intermediate-growing orchids. Grow in epiphytic orchid potting mix in pots or slatted baskets, or epiphytically on slabs of bark. In summer, grow in moist partial shade, water freely, feed at every third watering, and mist once or twice daily. Admit full light in winter; keep moist throughout the year. See also p.46.

• **PROPAGATION** Divide when plants fill the containers and flow over the sides.

• **PESTS AND DISEASES** Susceptible to spider mites, aphids, and mealybugs.

M. cucullata, syn. *M. meleagris*. Very variable, terrestrial, lithophytic, or epiphytic orchid with small, ovoid pseudobulbs producing 1, occasionally 2, strap-shaped leaves, to 12in (30cm) long. From summer to autumn, bears several deep red, occasionally yellow, pink, or black-maroon flowers with yellow to white lips, heavily spotted and striped dark red, on scapes 5–6in (13–15cm) long. ↕↔ 6in (15cm). Mexico, Guatemala, Panama. ❀ (min. 50°F/10°C; max. 86°F/30°C)

M. grandiflora. Epiphytic orchid with compressed, ovoid pseudobulbs and one strap-shaped, apical leaf, 10–20in (25–50cm) long. White flowers, 2½in (6cm) across, with white or yellow, pink- or purple-margined lips, are borne on scapes 4–12in (10–30cm) long, from spring to early summer. ↕↔ 12in (30cm). N.W. South America. ❀ (min. 50°F/10°C; max. 86°F/30°C)

M. meleagris see *M. cucullata.*

M. picta. Epiphytic orchid with conical pseudobulbs and one narrowly oblong leaf, to 12in (30cm) long. Fragrant, deep yellow to white flowers, spotted purple, dark red, or brown, to 1½in (4cm) across, are borne on scapes 6in (15cm) long, from spring to summer. ↕↔ 9in (23cm). Colombia, Brazil. ❀ (min. 50°F/10°C; max. 86°F/30°C)

Maxillaria porphyrostele

M. porphyrostele ■ Epiphytic orchid with ovoid pseudobulbs and 2 lance-shaped, apical leaves, 8in (20cm) long. From winter to spring, slightly fragrant, light yellow flowers, 1in (2.5cm) across, with purple-striped throats, are borne on scapes 3in (8cm) long. ↕↔ 6in (15cm). Brazil. ❀ (min. 50°F/10°C; max. 86°F/30°C)

M. sanderiana. Robust, epiphytic or terrestrial orchid with compressed, ovoid pseudobulbs, with one narrowly oblong leaf, to 16in (40cm) long. Bears fragrant white flowers, 5in (13cm) across, with heavy red basal spotting, on short, horizontal or erect scapes, to 10in (25cm) long, from summer to early autumn. ↕↔ 18in (45cm). Ecuador, Peru. ❀ (min. 50°F/10°C; max. 86°F/30°C)

MAYTENUS

CELASTRACEAE

Genus of about 225 species of evergreen, mainly dioecious trees and shrubs from forest in North and South America and tropical Africa. The variably shaped, alternate leaves are entire or toothed. Tiny, star-shaped to tubular flowers are produced in axillary cymes, racemes, or panicles, or sometimes singly. Grow as specimen trees or in woodland. Where not hardy, grow in a cool or temperate greenhouse.

• **CULTIVATION** Grow in moderately fertile, moist but well-drained soil in full sun with midday shade. Shelter from cold, drying winds. Pruning group 1.

• **PROPAGATION** Sow seed under glass in autumn. Remove suckers, which may appear at some distance from the parent plant, in spring. Root semi-ripe cuttings with bottom heat in summer.

• **PESTS AND DISEASES** Sometimes affected by scale insects.

M. boaria, syn. *M. chilensis* (Mayten). Tree or shrub, of variable habit, with pendent or upright branches, and narrowly elliptic to lance-shaped, glossy, dark green, finely toothed leaves, to 2in (5cm) long. Bears small clusters of tiny, tubular, pale green flowers, the males with yellow anthers, in mid- and late spring; on the same plant, female flowers have orange-red capsules, which open to release red seeds. ↕ 70ft (20m), ↔ to 30ft (10m). Chile. ❀ (min. 41°F/5°C)

M. chilensis see *M. boaria.*

MAZUS

SCROPHULARIACEAE

Genus of about 30 species of annuals and creeping, usually mat-forming, prostrate perennials, rooting at the nodes, found in wet habitats from lowland to mountainous regions of the Himalayas, India, Pakistan, China, Taiwan, Japan, S.E. Asia, and Australasia. The leaves, ½–2in (1–5cm) long, borne in opposite pairs, are mostly linear to spoon-shaped or obovate, toothed, and usually mid-green. Narrowly tubular flowers, with erect upper lips and large, spreading, 3-lobed lower lips, are produced singly or in few-flowered racemes from the leaf axils.

Mazus reptans

Mazus species are suitable as a groundcover in a rock garden or in paving crevices, or as pan plants in an alpine house.

• **CULTIVATION** Grow in moderately fertile, moist but well-drained soil in a sheltered site in full sun. In an alpine house, grow in shallow containers of soil-based potting mix.

• **PROPAGATION** Sow seed in containers in a cold frame in spring or autumn. Divide in spring.

• **PESTS AND DISEASES** Slugs and snails may be a problem.

M. reptans ■ Mat-forming perennial with lance-shaped to elliptic or obovate, coarsely toothed leaves, ½–1¼in (1–3cm) long. From late spring to summer, produces 2- to 5-flowered racemes of purple-blue flowers, ½–¾in (1.5–2cm) long, with yellow- and red-spotted white lower lips. ↕ to 2in (5cm), ↔ to 12in (30cm) or more. Himalayas. Zone 5. **'Albus'** has white flowers.

MECONOPSIS

PAPAVERACEAE

Genus of about 45 species of annuals, biennials, and deciduous or evergreen, often short-lived or monocarpic perennials. They occur in moist, shady mountainous areas, alpine meadows, woodland, scrub, scree, and rocky slopes in the Himalayas, Burma, and China, with one species from W. Europe. Usually hairy or bristly, they produce basal rosettes of pinnate or simple leaves, which may be entire, toothed, lobed, or pinnatisect. The lower leaves are long-

Meconopsis betonicifolia

stalked, the upper ones short-stalked or stalkless. The flowering stems, usually one per leaf rosette, are either leafless and unbranched, each bearing a solitary flower, or leafy and branched near the top, bearing flowers singly or in short racemes or panicles, the top flower opening first. The flowers are generally pendent, saucer- to cup-shaped, poppy-like, and silky, with numerous stamens and usually 4, but sometimes up to 9 petals. The flower stalks lengthen after flowering as the fruits develop.

Meconopsis species grow best in areas with cool, damp summers, and are difficult to grow where summers are long and hot. Most are suitable for growing in large groups in a moist, cool woodland garden. *M. cambrica* will grow under a wide range of conditions, except in very dry soils.

• **CULTIVATION** Grow in humus-rich, leafy, moist but well-drained, neutral to slightly acidic soil, open enough to prevent stagnation and rot in winter; site in partial shade with shelter from cold, drying winds. Mulch generously, and water in dry spells in summer. Short-lived perennials, e.g. *M. betonicifolia*, are less likely to be monocarpic in moist conditions, and if flowering is prevented until several crowns have been formed.

• **PROPAGATION** Sow seed in containers in a cold frame, preferably as soon as ripe or in spring. Use soilless seed starting mix, sow thinly, and keep moist; light is needed for germination. Over winter, keep young plants produced from autumn sowings in a cold greenhouse or frame. Divide after flowering. Root vegetative buds of *M. chelidoniifolia* when they appear in the upper leaf axils.

• **PESTS AND DISEASES** Susceptible to downy mildew and damping off, and to damage caused by slugs and snails.

M. betonicifolia ■ (Himalayan blue poppy, Tibetan blue poppy). Deciduous perennial, sometimes short-lived, with loose rosettes of oblong to ovate, toothed, light bluish green leaves, 6–12in (15–30cm) long, heart-shaped or truncate at the bases and covered with rust-colored hairs. In early summer, pendent to horizontal, saucer-shaped, bright blue, sometimes purple-blue or white flowers, 3–4in (8–10cm) across, with yellow stamens, are borne singly on bristly stalks, to 8in (20cm) long, sometimes clustered toward the tops of the stems. ↕ 4ft (1.2m),

Meconopsis cambrica

occasionally more, ↔ 18in (45cm). Tibet, S.W. China, Burma. Zone 4.

M. cambrica ■ (Welsh poppy). Taprooted, deciduous perennial with elliptic, pinnatisect to pinnatifid or irregularly lobed, pale to bluish green, hairless to hairy leaves, to 8in (20cm) long, borne on branched stems and in basal tufts. From midspring to mid-autumn, solitary, shallowly cup-shaped, lemon-yellow flowers, 2–2½in (5–6cm) across, are produced on slender stalks, to 10in (25cm) long, from the upper leaf axils. ↕ 18in (45cm) occasionally more, ↔ 10in (25cm). W. Europe. Zone 4.
var. *aurantiaca* has orange flowers.
'Flore Pleno' has double yellow flowers.

M. chelidoniifolia ■ Deciduous perennial, spreading by offset buds to form clumps of slender, semi-scandent, leafy, branched stems. The hairy, pale green leaves, to 16in (40cm) long at the base and 1¼–5in (3–13cm) on the stems, are pinnatisect with pinnatifid lobes. In mid- and late summer, nodding, saucer-shaped, pale yellow flowers, 1–1½in (2.5–4cm) across, are borne from the upper leaf axils, on stalks 1½–2in (4–5cm) long. ↕ 3ft (1m), ↔ 24in (60cm). China (W. Sichuan). Zone 6.

M. dhwojii. Monocarpic, evergreen perennial forming basal rosettes of pinnatisect leaves, to 12in (30cm) long, with elliptic-oblong or inversely lance-shaped, lobed segments, covered with bristly, black-based yellow hairs. Branched, leafy stems, to 24in (60cm) long, bear numerous nodding, shallowly cup-shaped, pale yellow flowers, 1½–2in (4–5cm) across, with stalks to 6in (15cm) long, in early summer. The upper flowers are solitary; those on the lower branches are in short racemes of up to 5 flowers. ↕ to 36in (90cm), ↔ 12in (30cm). E. Nepal. Zone 8.

Meconopsis chelidoniifolia

Meconopsis grandis

M. grandis ■ (Himalayan blue poppy). Clump-forming, deciduous perennial with erect, elliptic, irregularly toothed leaves, 6–10in (15–25cm) long, tapered at the bases. The leaves are borne in basal rosettes and on branched stems, the uppermost forming a whorl below the flowers; they are mid- to dark green, with red-brown or rust-colored hairs. In early summer, nodding, shallowly cup-shaped, rich blue to purplish red flowers, 5–6in (12–15cm) across, each with up to 9 petals and clusters of yellow anthers, are produced singly from the upper leaf axils on stalks to 16in (40cm) long. Monocarpic in dry conditions. ↕ 3–4ft (1–1.2m), ↔ 24in (60cm). E. Tibet, E. Nepal to India (Sikkim) and Bhutan. Zone 5.

M. horridula ■ Monocarpic, deciduous perennial with loose rosettes of simple, entire, elliptic to narrowly inversely lance-shaped, wavy-margined, mid- to gray-green leaves, to 10in (25cm) long, covered with yellow to purple spines. In early and midsummer, branched, leafless, spiny stems bear numerous semi-pendent, cup-shaped, pale to deep blue or reddish blue (rarely white) flowers, 2–3in (5–8cm) across, usually in racemes, on stalks to 6in (15cm) long. ↕ 8–36in (20–90cm), ↔ 18in (45cm). W. Nepal to S.E. Tibet and China (Gansu, Sichuan, Yunnan). Zone 5.

M. integrifolia ■ (Yellow Chinese poppy). Monocarpic, deciduous perennial covered in downy, red-brown or yellow hairs, and forming rosettes of entire, inversely lance-shaped to obovate or linear, pale green, strongly 3-veined leaves, 14in (35cm) long, yellow-hairy when young, almost hairless when mature. From late spring to midsummer, thick, sometimes branched stems bear leaves in a loose whorl below 2–10 erect flowers. The shallowly cup-shaped, 6- to 8-petaled flowers, to 9in (23cm) across, are pale to rich lemon-yellow with dark yellow or orange stamens, and produced on stalks to 18in (45cm) long. ↕ to 36in (90cm), ↔ 18–24in (45–60cm). N.E. Tibet, China (Gansu, Sichuan, Yunnan). Zone 7.

M. napaulensis ■ (Satin poppy). Monocarpic, rosetted, evergreen perennial of pinnatisect, yellow-green, red-bristly basal leaves, to 20in (50cm) long, with oblong, lobed segments; the upper stem leaves are pinnatifid or simple. From late spring to midsummer, branching stems bear semi-pendent, bowl-shaped, pink, red, or purple flowers, 2½–3in (6–8cm) across; they are borne on stalks to 3in (8cm) long, in racemes of up to 17 on lower branches but singly near the tops. ↕ 8ft (2.5m), ↔ 24–36in (60–90cm). C. Nepal to China (W. Sichuan). Zone 8.

Meconopsis horridula

Meconopsis integrifolia

M. paniculata. Monocarpic, evergreen perennial with rosettes of pinnatisect or pinnatifid, grayish green leaves, to 24in (60cm) long, covered with rough yellow hairs. From late spring to midsummer, tall, branched stems bear shallowly lobed leaves and many-flowered racemes or panicle-like cymes of pendent, shallowly cup-shaped, pale yellow flowers, 2–3½in (5–9cm) across. ↕ to 6ft (2m), ↔ 24in (60cm). E. Nepal to India (Assam). Zone 8.

M. punicea. Taprooted, deciduous perennial with crowded rosettes of entire, inversely lance-shaped, densely gray-hairy, mid-green, basal leaves, 6–14in (15–35cm) long. From midsummer to early autumn, unbranched scapes, to 18in (45cm) long, up to 6 per rosette, produce solitary, pendent, narrowly funnel-shaped, vivid crimson flowers, to 4in (10cm) long, with 4–6 long, somewhat flared petals. Monocarpic in dry conditions. ↕ to 30in (75cm), ↔ 12in (30cm). N.E. Tibet, W. China. Zone 7.

M. quintuplinervia (Harebell poppy). Slowly clump-forming, deciduous

Meconopsis napaulensis

perennial forming rosettes of entire, obovate to narrowly inversely lance-shaped or lance-shaped, mid- to dark green, basal leaves, to 10in (25cm) long, with dense golden to rust-colored bristles. From early to late summer, pendent, cup-shaped, pale lavender-blue or purplish blue, rarely white flowers, 1½in (4cm) across, are borne singly (or rarely in twos or threes), on unbranched, slender scapes, to 14in (35cm) long. ↕18in (45cm), ↔ 12in (30cm). N.E. Tibet, W. China (Gansu, N.W. Sichuan to C. Shaanxi). Zone 7.
M. regia ■ Monocarpic, evergreen perennial with branched, leafy, hairy stems, and rosettes of simple, narrowly elliptic, finely but deeply toothed, densely silver- or gold-hairy leaves, to 24in (60cm) long. From late spring to midsummer, bears numerous outward-facing, cup-shaped, soft yellow or red flowers, 3½–5in (9–13cm) across, with 4 (occasionally 6) overlapping, rounded petals. Upper flowers are solitary; the lower ones are grouped on lateral branches in the upper leaf axils. ↕ to 6ft (2m), ↔ 3ft (1m). C. Nepal. Zone 8.
M.* x *sarsonsii (*M. betonicifolia* x *M. integrifolia*). Deciduous, sometimes monocarpic, fertile perennial with ovate, toothed, mid-green leaves, to 6in (15cm) long, covered with rust-colored hairs and arranged in loose rosettes. In early summer, branched stems produce solitary, pendent to erect, saucer-shaped, pale creamy yellow flowers, 3–4in (7–10cm) across, on stalks to 16in (40cm) long, produced from the axils of loose whorls of stem leaves. ↕4ft (1.2m), ↔ 3ft (90cm). Garden origin. Zone 7.
M.* x *sheldonii (*M. betonicifolia* x *M. grandis*). Rosette-forming, hairy perennial with elliptic-oblong to lance-shaped, toothed, dark green basal and stem leaves, 6–12in (15–30cm) long. In late spring and early summer, shallowly cup-shaped, deep rich to pale blue flowers, 2½–4in (6–10cm) across, are borne singly in the upper leaf axils of the branched stems, on stalks 8–20in (20–50cm) long. ↕4–5ft (1.2–1.5m), ↔ 24in (60cm). Garden origin. Zone 7. **'Branklyn'** has coarsely toothed leaves and produces vivid blue flowers, to 5in (13cm) across; ↕ to 6ft (1.8m). **'Ormswell'** has pure, light blue flowers; ↕ to 3ft (1m). **'Slieve Donard'** is vigorous and free-flowering, with entire leaves and brilliant, rich blue flowers with long, pointed petals; ↕ to 3ft (1m).
M. villosa, syn. *Cathcartia villosa.* Rosette-forming, evergreen perennial with ovate to rounded, hairy, light green basal and stem leaves, to 5in (13cm) long, palmately 3- to 5-lobed and sparsely toothed. In late spring and early summer, semi-pendent, saucer-shaped yellow flowers, 1½–2in (4–5cm) across, on stalks to 5in (13cm) long, are produced singly from the upper leaf axils of hairy, branched stems. ↕24in (60cm), ↔ 12in (30cm). E. Nepal to Bhutan. Zone 7.

Meconopsis regia

MEDICAGO
Alfalfa, Medick

FABACEAE

Genus of 50–60 species of annuals, perennials, and small shrubs from dry, sunny grassland in Europe and W. and S.W. Asia. They have 3-palmate, light or yellow-green to mid-green or bluish green leaves, sometimes with red spots, and bear short, axillary racemes of pea-like flowers. Grow annuals and perennials in a wild or meadow garden; the shrubby species tolerate coastal conditions and are best grown in a sunny, open border or against a warm wall. *M. sativa* is grown as a crop plant as fodder for animals, as sprouted seeds for salads, and as a "green manure." Some *Medicago* species seed prolifically and can become weeds, especially in prairies and similar plantings. The flowers attract bees and butterflies.
• **CULTIVATION** Grow in poor to moderately fertile, well-drained soil in full sun. Pruning group 1; remove dead wood in spring.
• **PROPAGATION** Sow seed of perennials *in situ* in spring or autumn. Sow seed of shrubs in containers in a cold frame in spring or autumn. Root greenwood cuttings in early summer.
• **PESTS AND DISEASES** Infrequent.

M. arborea (Moon trefoil). Dense, bushy, evergreen shrub with dark green leaves with obovate leaflets, ¼–¾in (0.6–2cm) long, silky-hairy when young. From late spring to early autumn, bears dense racemes of 4–8 yellow flowers, ½–¾in (1.5–2cm) long, followed by flattened, spiraled, green, later brown seed pods. ↕↔ 6ft (2m). Canary Islands, S. Europe and Mediterranean to S.W. Asia. Zone 7b.
M. sativa (Alfalfa, Lucerne). Erect or spreading, hairy, slender-stemmed perennial producing bluish green leaves with obovate to linear leaflets, to 1¼in (3cm) long. From summer to early autumn, bears long-stalked racemes of mauve to violet flowers, to ½in (1.5cm) long, followed by small, spiraled or sickle-shaped, deep brown seed pods. ↕ to 32in (80cm), ↔ 12–32in (30–80cm). Europe, W. Asia. Zone 5.

MEDINILLA

MELASTOMATACEAE

Genus of about 150 species of evergreen shrubs and scandent climbers, some epiphytic, from rainforest in tropical Africa, S.E. Asia, and the Pacific. They have simple, entire, boldly veined leaves, borne in whorls or opposite pairs. Small, star- to bowl-shaped, 4- to 6-petaled flowers, often with large, colored bracts, are borne in pendent or upright panicles or cymes. Where temperatures fall below 59°F (15°C), grow in a warm greenhouse. In moist, tropical areas, grow climbing species over an arch or pergola; the shrubs are suitable for a border.
• **CULTIVATION** Under glass, grow in soil-based potting mix in bright filtered light, or full light with shade from hot sun; provide high humidity. In the growing season, water moderately and apply a balanced liquid fertilizer monthly; water sparingly in winter. Outdoors, grow in moderately fertile, moist but well-drained soil in dappled shade, or full sun with some midday shade. Pruning group 11 for climbers, after flowering; group 8 for shrubs.
• **PROPAGATION** Sow seed at 66–75°F (19–24°C) in spring. Root softwood cuttings in spring or semi-ripe cuttings in summer. Air layer in spring.
• **PESTS AND DISEASES** Scale insects may be troublesome under glass.

M. magnifica ■ Erect, sparsely branched, epiphytic shrub with robust, ribbed to strongly winged stems bearing broadly ovate to obovate, leathery, lustrous, deep green leaves, 8–12in (20–30cm) long, with prominent, pale green veins. From spring to summer, yellow-stamened pink to coral-red flowers, to 1in (2.5cm) across, are borne in dense, pendent panicles, 10–16in (25–40cm) long, with several pairs of large, cupped pink basal bracts. ↕3–6ft (1–2m), ↔ 2–5ft (0.6–1.5m). Philippines. ❀ (min. 59°F/15°C)

Medinilla magnifica

Meehania urticifolia

MEEHANIA

LAMIACEAE

Genus of 6 species of stoloniferous, clump-forming perennials found in moist, deciduous woodland in Asia and North America. Square stems bear opposite pairs of ovate to heart-shaped, finely hairy leaves. Tubular, 2-lipped, violet or blue flowers are produced from the leaf axils from late spring to summer. Grow in a shady border or as a groundcover in a woodland garden.
• **CULTIVATION** Grow in humus-rich, moist but well-drained soil in full to light, dappled shade.
• **PROPAGATION** Sow seed in containers in a cold frame in spring. Separate stolons in early spring or autumn. Root stem-tip cuttings in spring.
• **PESTS AND DISEASES** Susceptible to damage by slugs.

M. urticifolia ■ Stoloniferous, clump-forming perennial, spreading widely, with broadly ovate to heart-shaped, wrinkled, softly hairy leaves, 1¼–2½in (3–6cm) long, with scalloped margins. One-sided spikes of 3–12 deep violet flowers, 1½–2in (4–5cm) long, sometimes with white lines and the lower lips spotted dark purple, are produced in late spring and early summer. ↕12–18in (30–45cm), ↔ to 8ft (2.5m). Japan. Zone 6.

MEGACODON

GENTIANACEAE

Genus of one species of clump-forming perennial found in damp pastures and streamsides from C. Nepal to S.W. China. It has basal rosettes of elliptic to broadly elliptic leaves, and bears smaller leaves on thick, erect stems. Broadly bell-shaped flowers are produced in summer. Grow in a woodland or bog garden, or plant near pools and streams.
• **CULTIVATION** Grow in humus-rich, moist but well-drained soil in partial or light, dappled shade. Where marginally hardy, provide a dry winter mulch and shelter from cold, drying winds.
• **PROPAGATION** Sow seed in containers in a cold frame as soon as ripe. Basal shoots can be rooted in spring, although seldom successfully. Like the large herbaceous gentians (*Gentiana*), *M. stylophorus* does not transplant readily.
• **PESTS AND DISEASES** Susceptible to damage by slugs.

M. stylophorus, syn. *Gentiana stylophora.* Upright, clump-forming perennial with basal rosettes of elliptic to broadly elliptic, glossy, dark green leaves, 12in (30cm) long, and pairs of smaller leaves, 4–6in (10–15cm) long, joined at their bases around the stems. In mid- and late summer, pale to mid-yellow flowers, 2½–3in (6–8cm) long, with green lines inside, are borne in pairs from the upper leaf axils. ↕ to 6ft (2m), ↔ 24in (60cm). C. Nepal to China (Yunnan). Zone 7b.

▷ ***Megalonium*** see *Aeonium*
▷ ***Megasea*** see *Bergenia*

MEGASKEPASMA

ACANTHACEAE

Genus of one species of evergreen shrub from tropical woodland in Venezuela. It has opposite, simple, entire leaves, and is grown for its colorful, terminal, spike-like cymes of 2-lipped, tubular flowers surrounded by crimson bracts. Where temperatures fall below 59°F (15°C), grow in a temperate or warm greenhouse; in warmer areas, grow in a courtyard garden or a shrub border.
• **CULTIVATION** Under glass, grow in soil-based potting mix in full light, with high humidity. In the growing season, water freely and apply a balanced liquid fertilizer monthly; water sparingly in winter. Outdoors, grow in moderately fertile, moist, well-drained soil in full sun. Pruning group 8; withstands restrictive pruning and renovation well.
• **PROPAGATION** Sow seed at 64–70°F (18–21°C) in spring. Root greenwood cuttings in early summer, or semi-ripe cuttings with bottom heat in late summer.
• **PESTS AND DISEASES** Spider mites, whiteflies, and mealybugs may be troublesome under glass.

M. erythrochlamys ▣ (Brazilian red cloak, Red justicia). Erect, robust-stemmed shrub, sparsely branched unless regularly pruned, with ovate to broadly elliptic or lance-shaped, boldly veined, mid-green leaves, 5–12in (12–30cm) long. From early autumn to winter, terminal, columnar to narrowly pyramidal, spike-like cymes, 8–12in (20–30cm) long, of tubular, 2-lipped, white or pink flowers, to 3in (8cm) long, are produced from the axils of broadly ovate crimson bracts, to 1½in (4cm) long. ↕ 3–10ft (1–3m), ↔ 3–6ft (1–2m). Venezuela. ❄ (min. 59°F/15°C)

Megaskepasma erythrochlamys

MELALEUCA

Paperbark

MYRTACEAE

Genus of at least 150 species of evergreen shrubs and trees, allied to *Callistemon*, found in habitats ranging from rainforest to semi-arid areas in tropical to cool-temperate zones, mainly in Australia but also in New Caledonia, New Guinea, and Malaysia. Many species have several layers of paper-thin, corky bark, which is shed continuously. The small, flat or cylindrical, often leathery leaves are mainly alternate, or sometimes opposite or whorled. Small flowers, each with 5 short petals and numerous conspicuous, colored stamens, arranged in 5 fused bundles, are borne in dense, axillary spikes, resembling those of bottlebrushes. Where not hardy, grow in a cool or temperate greenhouse. Elsewhere, grow in a shrub border or as specimen trees. Some species have become weedy pests in warmer regions.

Melaleuca elliptica

• **CULTIVATION** Under glass, grow in soil-based potting mix, with added leaf mold, in full light with shade from hot sun. During the growing season, water moderately and apply a balanced liquid fertilizer monthly; water sparingly in winter. Outdoors, grow in moderately fertile, well-drained soil in full sun with some midday shade. Shelter from cold, drying winds. Pruning group 1; plants under glass need restrictive pruning after flowering.
• **PROPAGATION** Sow seed at 55–75°F (13–24°C) in spring. Root semi-ripe cuttings with bottom heat in summer.
• **PESTS AND DISEASES** Prone to scale insects, spider mites, mushroom root rot, dieback, and cankers.

M. elliptica ▣ (Granite bottlebrush). Many-branched shrub, erect at first then spreading or rounded, with furrowed, peeling bark. The opposite, broadly elliptic to elliptic-oblong leaves, ¼–¾in (0.5–1.5cm) long, are mid- to deep green above and paler beneath. From spring to early summer, small, bright pink to crimson flowers, with stamens of the same color, are produced in abundant short, dense spikes, to 1½in (4cm) or more long. ↕↔ 3–10ft (1–3m). Western Australia. ❄ (min. 41–45°F/5–7°C)
M. leucadendra (River teatree, Weeping teatree). Spreading tree with layered, papery bark and sparsely borne, alternate, narrowly ovate to elliptic, acute, thinly leathery, mid-green leaves, 3–9in (8–23cm) long. Produces white flowers, in axillary or terminal spikes, to 1½in (4cm) long, in threes, from spring to early summer. ↕ to 100ft (30m), ↔ 50ft (15m). N. Australia, Melanesia. ❄ (min. 41–45°F/5–7°C)
M. nesophila ▣ syn. *M. nesophylla* (Western tea myrtle). Erect to spreading, large shrub or small tree with freely branching stems and spongy, peeling bark. Alternate, mid- to deep green leaves are narrowly obovate, ¾–1¼in (2–3cm) long, with 1–3 faint veins. From spring to summer, bears lavender-pink to rose-pink flowers in dense, spherical spikes, to 1in (2.5cm) or more across. ↕ 10–22ft (3–7m), ↔ 6–12ft (2–4m). Western Australia. ❄ (min. 41–45°F/5–7°C)

Melaleuca nesophila

M. nesophylla see *M. nesophila.*

▷ ***Melampodium paludosum*** see *Leucanthemum paludosum*
▷ ***Melandrium elisabethae*** see *Silene elisabethae*

MELASPHAERULA

IRIDACEAE

Genus of one species of spring-flowering, cormous perennial from shaded woodland in South Africa. It has narrow, grass-like leaves, and produces spikes of star-shaped flowers. Where not hardy, grow in a cool greenhouse or in a bulb frame. In warmer climates, grow at the base of a warm, sunny wall.
• **CULTIVATION** Plant 4–6in (10–15cm) deep. Under glass, grow in soil-based potting mix, with additional sharp sand, in full light. Water sparingly until the flower spikes appear, then water moderately; apply a balanced liquid fertilizer every 6–8 weeks in the growing season; keep just moist in winter. Outdoors, grow in moderately fertile, well-drained soil in full sun. In mild areas, plant in autumn, providing a dry winter mulch; in areas with prolonged cold, plant in early spring and lift in autumn, after the leaves die down. Protect from excessive winter moisture.
• **PROPAGATION** Sow seed at 43–54°F (6–12°C) in autumn. Remove offsets when dormant in autumn.
• **PESTS AND DISEASES** Infrequent.

M. graminea see *M. ramosa.*
M. ramosa, syn. *M. graminea.* Cormous perennial with spreading, branched stems bearing erect, grass-like leaves, 2–10in (5–25cm) long. Spikes of up to 7 star-shaped, creamy white or yellowish flowers, ¾–1¼in (2–3cm) across, often veined purple, are produced in spring. ↕ 8–20in (20–50cm), PD3in (8cm). South Africa (S. Western Cape). ❄ (min. 41°F/5°C)

Melastoma

MELASTOMATACEAE

Genus of up to 70 species of evergreen shrubs, small trees, and a few herbaceous perennials from moist woodland, often in hilly areas, in India, S.E. Asia, and adjacent Pacific islands. The opposite leaves are lance-shaped to oblong or elliptic, mostly dark green, and often leathery. Usually 5-petaled, open bowl- to saucer-shaped, purple, red, pink, or white flowers are produced in terminal cymes of 3–7 or, rarely, are borne singly; the flowers are followed by fleshy berries. Where not hardy, grow in a warm greenhouse. In warmer regions, grow as free-standing specimen plants or among other shrubs.

• **Cultivation** Under glass, grow in soil-based potting mix in full light with shade from hot sun. Provide moderate humidity. In growth, water moderately and apply a balanced liquid fertilizer monthly; water sparingly in winter. Outdoors, grow in moderately fertile, moist but well-drained soil in full sun with some midday shade. Shelter from cold, drying winds. Pruning group 1 or 8; need restrictive pruning under glass.

• **Propagation** Sow seed at 43–54°F (6–12°C) in spring. Root semi-ripe cuttings with bottom heat in summer.

• **Pests and diseases** Scale insects and spider mites may occur under glass.

M. malabathricum (Indian rhododendron). Many-branched, spreading shrub with densely scaly-hairy stems and ovate to broadly lance-shaped, coarsely hairy, dark green leaves, 3–4in (7–10cm) long, with prominent veins. Produces shallowly bowl-shaped purple flowers, 1¼in (3cm) across, singly or in cymes of 2–5, from spring to summer, sometimes followed by spherical, red-purpled berries, ⅜in (9mm) across. ↕ 6–10ft (2–3m), ↔ 5–8ft (1.5–2.5m). India, S.E. Asia. ❀ (min. 55°F/13°C)

Melia

MELIACEAE

Genus of 3–5 species of deciduous or semi-evergreen trees and shrubs from India to China, S.E. Asia, and N. Australia. They have alternate, pinnate or 2-pinnate leaves, and bear small, star-shaped flowers in large, axillary panicles. Each flower has 5 or 6 spreading petals and 10–12 stamens, the filaments of which are fused into a tube, with the anthers arranged around the rim. The attractive, bead-like, spherical, single-seeded berries are poisonous. Where not hardy, grow in a temperate greenhouse mainly for their foliage, although plants in large containers may flower when 6–10ft (2–3m) tall. In warmer areas, grow as specimen or shade trees.

Melia azedarach

• **Cultivation** Under glass, grow in soil-based potting mix in full light. In the growing season, water freely and apply a balanced liquid fertilizer monthly; water sparingly in winter. Outdoors, grow in moderately fertile, well-drained soil in full sun. Provide shelter from cold, drying winds. Pruning group 1; plants under glass may need restrictive pruning.

• **Propagation** Sow seed at 55–64°F (13–18°C) in spring. Root softwood cuttings with bottom heat in summer.

• **Pests and diseases** Canker, dieback, anthracnose, powdery mildew, mushroom root rot, spider mites, and scale insects sometimes occur.

M. azedarach ▣ (Bead-tree, Chinaberry, Persian lilac, Pride of India). Fast-growing, many-branched, spreading, round-headed, deciduous tree with fissured gray bark. Pinnate or 2-pinnate leaves, 12–24in (30–60cm) long, have many ovate to elliptic, sharply toothed, sometimes lobed, mid- to bright green leaflets. Produces a profusion of star-shaped, fragrant lilac flowers, ¾in (2cm) across, in arching to pendent panicles, 4–8in (10–20cm) long, from spring to early summer; they are followed by spherical to broadly ovoid yellow fruit, ½in (1.5cm) long. Seeds are used as beads in Asia. Has become weedy in S.E. US. ↕ 30–50ft (10–15m), ↔ 15–25ft (5–8m). N. India, China. ❀ (min. 45°F/7°C). **'Umbraculiformis'** (Texas umbrella tree) produces upward-growing branches arising from the same point, much like an inside-out umbrella; ↕ 20–25ft (6–8m).

Melianthus

MELIANTHACEAE

Genus of 6 species of evergreen shrubs from grassland in hilly areas of southern Africa. The alternate, pinnate, light green, gray-green, or blue-green leaves have prominent stipules. Small flowers, producing profuse quantities of nectar, are borne in erect, terminal and axillary racemes; each has 5 irregular sepals and petals, the upper ones often forming a hood or tube, and the lower ones making a short spur. Grow in a border or as specimen plants; they are particularly well suited to a coastal garden. Where these shrubs are not hardy, grow as foliage plants in a cold greenhouse, and stand or plant outside in summer. Alternatively, treat them as herbaceous perennials; where temperatures do not fall much below 23°F (-5°C), they will usually resprout annually from the base.

• **Cultivation** Under glass, grow in soil-based potting mix in full light. Provide low humidity. In growth, water freely and apply a balanced liquid fertilizer monthly; water sparingly in winter. Outdoors, grow in moderately fertile, moist but well-drained soil in full sun. Provide a dry winter mulch and protect from excessive winter moisture. Shelter from cold, drying winds. Pruning group 7 or 8.

Melianthus major

• **Propagation** Sow seed at 55–64°F (13–18°C) in spring. Root basal or softwood cuttings in late spring or early summer. Remove any rooted suckers in spring.

• **Pests and diseases** Susceptible to spider mites and whiteflies under glass.

M. major ▣ (Honey bush). Tall, erect to spreading shrub with robust, hollow stems, most of them near ground level and branching sparingly. Spreading, pinnate leaves, 12–20in (30–50cm) long, have 9–17 closely set, ovate, sharply and boldly toothed, gray-green to bright blue-gray leaflets. From late spring to midsummer, produces spike-like racemes, 12–32in (30–80cm) long, of oddly scented, brownish crimson to deep brick-red flowers, 1in (2.5cm) long. ↕ 6–10ft (2–3m), ↔ 3–10ft (1–3m). South Africa (Northern Cape, Western Cape, Eastern Cape). Zone 7b.

Melica

Melick

POACEAE

Genus of about 75 species of deciduous, rhizomatous, clump-forming, perennial grasses occurring in grasslands of most temperate regions, except Australia. In summer, panicles of laterally compressed spikelets are borne on erect stems among clumps of linear, flat or inrolled, arching leaves. Grow in a mixed or herbaceous border or in a woodland garden.

• **Cultivation** Grow in moderately fertile, moist but well-drained soil. *M. altissima* thrives in full sun or light, dappled shade; *M. nutans* prefers light shade; *M. uniflora* will tolerate full shade and drier conditions. Protect from excessive winter moisture.

• **Propagation** Sow seed *in situ* in spring or as soon as ripe. Divide as growth starts in early or midspring.

• **Pests and diseases** Rust, smut, leaf streak, anthracnose, and other leaf spots occur.

M. altissima (Siberian melick). Tufted, perennial grass with creeping rhizomes and pointed, linear, pale to mid-green leaves, 4–9in (10–23cm) long, with rough surfaces. In summer, green spikelets are produced in erect, one-sided panicles, 4–10in (10–25cm) long, with densely flowered tips. ↕ 2–5ft (0.6–1.5m), ↔ 16–32in (40–80cm). Europe. Zone 5b. **'Alba'** has pale green leaves, and bears conspicuous, pale greenish white spikelets from late spring to late summer. **'Atropurpurea'** ▣ has lustrous, deep purple spikelets that become paler with age. Good for drying.

M. nutans (Mountain melick, Wood melick). Slowly creeping, perennial grass forming loose clumps of shiny, fresh green leaves, to 8in (20cm) long. Gracefully arching stems bear one-sided panicles, to 6in (15cm) long, of bead-like, brown and cream spikelets from late spring to midsummer. ↕ 18in (45cm), ↔ 12in (30cm) or more. Europe, N. and S.W. Asia. Zone 6.

Melica altissima 'Atropurpurea'

M. uniflora. Perennial grass with slender, creeping rhizomes forming loose tufts of linear, pointed, bright green leaves, 2–8in (5–20cm) long, with hairy upper surfaces. Purple or brown spikelets are borne in sparsely branched, erect or nodding panicles, 1–8in (2.5–20cm) long, in summer. ↕ 8–24in (20–60cm), ↔ to 24in (60cm). Europe, S.W. Asia. Zone 7. **'Variegata'** has fresh green leaves with creamy white central stripes and purple-flushed bases, and bears dark purplish brown spikelets from late spring to midsummer.

MELICYTUS

syn. HYMENANTHERA

VIOLACEAE

Genus of about 7 species of evergreen or semi-evergreen shrubs from Australasia, found in rocky sites from mountains to woodland, dry riverbeds, and coasts. They have alternate, lance-shaped to broadly ovate, elliptic, or oblong, sweetly fragrant leaves. Small male and female flowers, with 5 spreading petals, are usually borne on separate plants. *M. crassifolius* and *M. dentatus* are grown for their attractive habits and their decorative fruits. Grow in an open, sunny site in a shrub border. Where not hardy, grow in a cool greenhouse. Need long, hot summers to flower and fruit well.

• **CULTIVATION** Grow in moderately fertile, moist but well-drained soil in full sun. Protect from cold, drying winds. Pruning group 8 or 9.

• **PROPAGATION** Sow seed in containers in a cold frame in spring. Root semi-ripe cuttings in summer.

• **PESTS AND DISEASES** Infrequent.

M. crassifolius, syn. *Hymenanthera crassifolia.* Densely branched, twiggy, and often slightly spiny shrub with obovate to oblong-elliptic, leathery, dark green leaves, to ¾in (2cm) long. In late spring and early summer, bears tiny yellow flowers, followed by ovoid purple berries, ¼in (6mm) across. ↕↔ 4ft (1.2m). New Zealand. ❄ (min. 41°F/5°C)

M. dentatus, syn. *Hymenanthera dentata.* Dense shrub with oblong, leathery, dark green leaves, to 1½in (4cm) long. Tiny, yellow to greenish white flowers are borne in late spring, followed by spherical purple berries, ¼in (6mm) across. ↕ 5ft (1.5m), ↔ 6ft (2m) or more. S.E. Australia. ❄ (min. 41°F/5°C)

MELINIS *syn.* RHYNCHELYTRUM

POACEAE

Genus of about 15 species of clump-forming, annual or perennial grasses from savanna grasslands of tropical Africa and S.E. Asia. They have flat, linear to thread-like leaves, and produce compact or open panicles of spikelets from summer to autumn. *M. repens,* the only species in general cultivation, is grown for its brightly colored flower-heads, which may be cut for fresh flowers. Grow at the front of a border; where not hardy, treat as an annual, or lift and keep frost-free in winter.

• **CULTIVATION** Grow in moderately fertile, light, well-drained soil in full sun. Where marginally hardy, provide a deep, dry winter mulch. In colder areas, lift in autumn and pot up in a soil-based potting mix; keep barely moist and frost-free in winter, and plant out in spring when danger of frost has passed.

• **PROPAGATION** Sow seed at 55–64°F (13–18°C) in late winter, harden off, and plant out after all danger of frost has passed. Divide in spring.

• **PESTS AND DISEASES** Infrequent.

M. repens, syn. *Rhynchelytrum repens, R. roseum* (Natal grass). Loosely tufted, annual or short-lived, perennial grass. Upright, ascending stems bear flat, linear, long-pointed leaves, to 12in (30cm) long. From midsummer to early autumn, bears cylindrical to ovoid panicles, to 8in (20cm) long, of keeled, flattened spikelets, densely clothed in silky white hairs and strongly tinted bright purple to rose-red. ↕ 18–48in (45–120cm), ↔ 24–39in (60–100cm). Tropical Africa. ❄ (min. 41°F/5°C)

MELIOSMA

SABIACEAE

Genus of 20–25 species of evergreen and deciduous trees and shrubs occurring in forest from India and Sri Lanka to Japan, and in Mexico, Central America, and tropical South America. The alternate leaves are simple, sometimes pinnate, and mid- to dark green. Large panicles of tiny, cup- and saucer-shaped, 5-petaled, fragrant flowers are borne in spring or summer. Grow as specimen plants in a shrub border or woodland garden, or against a warm, sunny wall.

• **CULTIVATION** Grow in moderately fertile, moist but well-drained, neutral to slightly acidic soil, in full sun with some midday shade. Shelter from cold, drying winds. Pruning group 1, or 13 if grown as a wall specimen.

• **PROPAGATION** Sow seed in containers in a cold frame in autumn. Root greenwood cuttings in early summer.

• **PESTS AND DISEASES** Infrequent.

M. dilleniifolia. Spreading, deciduous shrub or tree with softly hairy stems and obovate to oblong, toothed, rough, mid-green leaves, 1¼–10in (3–25cm) long, softly hairy beneath. In late spring and early summer, bears upright or nodding, terminal panicles, 4–20in (10–50cm) long, of white flowers, followed by spherical red-black fruit, to ¼in (6mm) across. ↕ 30–50ft (10–15m), ↔ 10–20ft (3–6m). Himalayas, China, Japan. ❄ (min. 41°F/5°C). **subsp. *cuneifolia*** bears very fragrant, yellow-white flowers, turning white with age, in erect panicles, to 20in (50cm) long, in summer; these are followed by spherical black fruit; W. China.

M. oldhamii see *M. pinnata* var. *oldhamii.*

M. pinnata* var. *oldhamii, syn. *M. oldhamii.* Stoutly branched, deciduous tree, upright when young, later spreading, with pinnate, dark green leaves, to 14in (35cm) long, with up to 13 broadly ovate to obovate leaflets. White flowers are borne in panicles, to 12in (30cm) long, in early summer, followed by small, black or dark red fruit, ¼in (6mm) across. ↕ 30ft (10m), ↔ 20ft (6m). China, Korea. ❄ (min. 41°F/5°C)

M. veitchiorum ▣ Slow-growing, deciduous tree, upright when young, later spreading, with pinnate, dark green leaves, to 30in (75cm) long, with up to 11 ovate or oblong leaflets and red stalks. Creamy white flowers are borne in dense panicles, to 18in (45cm) long, in late spring, followed by spherical violet fruit, to ⅜in (9mm) across. ↕ 30ft (10m), ↔ 25ft (8m). W. China. ❄ (min. 41°F/5°C)

Meliosma veitchiorum

MELISSA

Balm

LAMIACEAE

Genus of 3 species of herbaceous perennials occurring from Europe to C. Asia on damp wasteland, from sea level to mountains. Toothed, ovate, pale or mid-green leaves, which smell strongly of lemons when bruised, are borne in opposite pairs on square, branching stems. Leafy, whorled spikes of tubular, 2-lipped, pale yellow or white flowers are borne in summer. *M. officinalis* is a decorative, drought-tolerant plant, useful for a herbaceous or mixed border, or an herb garden. The flowers attract bees and other insects, and the leaves may be used in potpourri or for herb tea.

• **CULTIVATION** Grow in poor, well-drained soil in full sun, with protection from excessive winter moisture. In early summer, cut back variegated forms to encourage strongly colored growth.

• **PROPAGATION** Sow seed in containers in a cold frame in spring. Divide as growth starts in spring, or in autumn.

• **PESTS AND DISEASES** Infrequent.

M. officinalis (Lemon balm). Bushy, upright perennial with hairy, glandular stems and wrinkled, ovate, light green leaves, to 3in (8cm) long. Throughout summer, produces irregular spikes of pale yellow flowers, becoming white or lilac-tinted white, to ½in (1.5cm) long. ↕ 2–4ft (60–120cm), ↔ 12–18in (30–45cm). S. Europe. Zone 3. **'All Gold'** has golden yellow leaves and white flowers, tinted pale lilac. **'Aurea'** ▣ syn. 'Variegata' of gardens, has dark green leaves, heavily splashed gold at the margins.

MELITTIS

Bastard balm

LAMIACEAE

Genus of one species of clump-forming perennial occurring in light woodland throughout Europe, except the extreme north, as far as the Ukraine. It has leafy, square stems, bearing opposite pairs of leaves, and produces 2-lipped flowers in

Melissa officinalis 'Aurea'

Melittis melissophyllum

white, pink, or purple, or white with pink or purple lips, in whorls from the upper leaf axils. Grow *M. melissophyllum* in a shady, mixed or herbaceous border, or in a woodland garden. The flowers are attractive to bees.
• **CULTIVATION** Grow in moderately fertile, moist but well-drained soil in partial shade; avoid excessively dry soil.
• **PROPAGATION** Sow seed in containers in a cold frame as soon as ripe or in spring. Divide as growth starts in spring.
• **PESTS AND DISEASES** Infrequent.

M. melissophyllum ■ Herbaceous perennial with erect, hairy or glandular stems. The oval, scalloped, aromatic, honey-scented leaves, to 3in (8cm) long, are hairy and wrinkled, with prominent veins. In late spring and early summer, produces whorls of 2–6 tubular, 2-lipped flowers, 1½in (4cm) long, in pink, purple, or white, or creamy white with pink or purple lips and spots. ↕ 8–28in (20–70cm), ↔ 20in (50cm). Europe to Ukraine. Zone 7.

M

MELOCACTUS
Turk's cap cactus
CACTACEAE

Genus of 20 or more species of spherical, rarely elongated, solitary, occasionally clustering cacti from coastal areas of Central and South America, Cuba, and the West Indies. They have prominently spined ribs. As plants mature, a cephalium, consisting of a mass of wool and bristles, which in some species gradually elongates to over 3ft (1m) tall, forms on the crown of each stem. The plant body essentially does not develop further once the cephalium appears. Spreading, funnel-shaped, diurnal flowers are borne on the cephalium in growth, followed by berry-like fruits with glossy, black-coated seeds. Where temperatures fall below 61°F (16°C), grow in a warm greenhouse. Elsewhere, grow in a desert garden.
• **CULTIVATION** Under glass, grow in standard cactus potting mix in full light and away from drafts. Water seedlings freely and fertilize monthly in growth. Mature plants are prone to root rot if overwatered or will rot if too cold. Water very sparingly in winter. *Melocactus* species have a shallow, fibrous root system, making deep pots undesirable. Outdoors, grow in moderately fertile, gritty, sharply drained soil in full sun. See also pp.48–49.
• **PROPAGATION** Sow seed at 66–75°F (19–24°C) in spring.
• **PESTS AND DISEASES** Prone to mealybugs and soft rot.

M. actinacanthus see *M. matanzanus.*
M. azureus. Cactus with a spherical to cylindrical, mid- to gray-green, often glaucous stem with 9–12 ribs bearing white spines (1–3 centrals and 7–11 radials). The white-woolly cephalium bears conspicuous red bristles. Pink flowers, ½–¾in (1.5–2cm) across, are borne in summer, followed by white to pale pink fruit. ↕ 5½–12in (14–30cm), ↔ 5½–8in (14–20cm). E. Brazil. ❄ (min. 61°F/16°C)
M. communis see *M. intortus.*
M. curvispinus, syn. *M. oaxacensis.* Cactus with a spherical or ovoid, dull green stem bearing 10–15 furrowed ribs and reddish brown spines (8–12 radials and 1 or 2 longer centrals). The low-set cephalium has dense brown bristles and a white-woolly top. Dark rose-pink flowers, ¾–1½in (2–4cm) across, are produced in summer. ↕↔ 6in (15cm). S. and E. Mexico, Guatemala. ❄ (min. 61°F/16°C)
M. intortus, syn. *M. communis.* Cactus with a flattened-spherical, dark green stem, elongating with age, bearing 12–24 ribs and yellow-brown spines (10–14 radials and 1–3 centrals). Rose-pink flowers, ½–¾in (1.5–2cm) across, are borne from the cylindrical, brown-bristly cephalium in summer. ↕ 3ft (1m) or more, ↔ 10in (25cm). West Indies. ❄ (min. 61°F/16°C)
M. macrodiscus see *M. zehntneri.*
M. matanzanus ■ syn. *M. actinacanthus.* Cactus with a spherical, dark green stem bearing 8–13 straight ribs and brownish white or gray spines (5–9 radials and 1 longer central). The low-set cephalium has dense, orange-red bristles. Pink to purple flowers, ½–¾in (1.5–2cm) across, are borne in summer. ↕ 3in (8cm), ↔ 3½in (9cm). N. Cuba. ❄ (min. 61°F/16°C)
M. oaxacensis see *M. curvispinus.*
M. zehntneri, syn. *M. macrodiscus.* Cactus with a spherical, bluish green stem with 10 ribs and pale brown spines (6–10 radials and 1 central, although the central one may be absent). The low-set, white-woolly cephalium is often slow to develop. Rose-red flowers, ½–1in (1.5–2.5cm) across, are borne in summer, followed by reddish violet fruit. ↕ 5½in (14cm), ↔ 7in (18cm). E. Brazil. ❄ (min. 61°F/16°C)

Melocactus matanzanus

MENISPERMUM
Moonseed
MENISPERMACEAE

Genus of 2 species of twining, suckering, semi-woody, sometimes herbaceous, deciduous, dioecious climbers from woodland in E. Asia and E. North America. They are grown for their long racemes or panicles of grape-like, glossy black fruits. The alternate, peltate leaves are ovate-heart-shaped to almost rounded. Inconspicuous, bowl-shaped, male and female flowers are borne in racemes or panicles. Grow on a trellis, against a wall, or through small trees. The fruits may cause severe discomfort if ingested.
• **CULTIVATION** Grow in moderately fertile, moist but well-drained soil in full sun or dappled shade. Provide support. Pruning group 11, in early spring.
• **PROPAGATION** Sow seed in containers outdoors in autumn. Transplant suckers in autumn or spring.
• **PESTS AND DISEASES** Powdery mildew, leaf smut, and a few other leaf spots may occur.

M. canadense (Canada moonseed, Yellow parilla). Usually semi-woody, suckering climber with slender shoots and long-stalked, ovate-heart-shaped to rounded, 3- to 7-angled leaves, 3–6in (8–15cm) long. In summer, produces tiny, yellow-green flowers in axillary racemes or panicles, followed on female plants by grape-like, glossy black fruit, to ½in (1.5cm) long. ↕ 15ft (5m). E. North America. Zone 2b.

MENTHA
Mint
LAMIACEAE

Genus of 25 species of aromatic, rhizomatous perennials, rarely annuals, widely distributed in Europe, Africa, and Asia, often found in shallow water or wet or moist soil. Erect, branching stems bear lance-shaped to rounded, light to dark green, purple-, blue-, or gray-green leaves. The tubular to bell-shaped flowers are weakly 2-lipped, each with 4 spreading lobes and leafy bracts. They are borne in summer, in spikes of whorl-like clusters, or occasionally in a single, terminal cluster. Mints are widely used as culinary, fragrant, medicinal, and industrial herbs.

Grow in an herb or vegetable garden; the less invasive species are also suitable for a herbaceous border. *M. aquatica* is useful for stabilizing the muddy edges of a pool; *M. pulegium* can be used as a low groundcover; and *M. requienii* is useful for a moist, shady rock garden. All attract bees; most dry well for use in herbal teas and potpourri.
• **CULTIVATION** Grow in rich, moist soil in full sun. Restrict spread of invasive species by planting in deep containers and plunging into the soil (leaving an inch of the rim above soil level), or by growing in small, confined beds to restrict root run. *M. aquatica* can be grown in containers submerged in water up to 6in (15cm) deep.
• **PROPAGATION** Sow seed in containers in a cold frame in spring. Divide in spring or autumn. Portions of rhizome will root at any time during the growing season; pot up until established. Root tip cuttings in spring or summer.
• **PESTS AND DISEASES** Powdery mildew, rust, leaf spot, anthracnose, and stem canker can be troublesome.

Mentha aquatica

M. aquatica ■ (Watermint). Marginal aquatic or semi-aquatic perennial with long, thin, segmented rhizomes, often reddish purple stems, and ovate to ovate-lance-shaped, toothed, aromatic, sometimes hairy, dark green leaves, to 2½in (6cm) long, occasionally to 3½in (9cm). In summer, produces whorls of tubular lilac flowers, to ¼in (6mm) long, in dense, spherical, terminal clusters. ↕ 6–36in (15–90cm), ↔ 3ft (1m) or more. Eurasia. Zone 6.
M. corsica see *M. requienii.*
***M. x gentilis* 'Aurea'** see *M.* x *gracilis* 'Variegata'.
***M. x gentilis* 'Variegata'** see *M.* x *gracilis* 'Variegata'.
***M. x gracilis* 'Variegata'** (*M. arvensis* x *M. spicata*), syn. *M.* x *gentilis* 'Aurea', *M.* x *gentilis* 'Variegata' (Ginger mint, Red mint). Spreading perennial with erect, often red-tinted stems and short-stalked, ovate-lance-shaped to elliptic-oblong leaves, 1¼–3in (3–8cm) long, striped and flecked gold, and strongly aromatic and ginger-flavored. In summer, bears dense, whorled clusters of tubular lilac flowers, to ⅛in (3mm) long, widely spaced on upright stems. ↕ 12in (30cm) or more, ↔ to 3ft (1m) or more. Zone 5.
M. longifolia, syn. *M. sylvestris* (Horsemint). Vigorous, creeping perennial with gray-hairy stems and oblong-elliptic, toothed, strongly

Mentha x *smithiana*

Mentha suaveolens 'Variegata'

aromatic, musty-scented, green to silver-gray leaves, 2½–3½in (6–9cm) long, with unbranched hairs. In summer, tubular, lilac or white flowers, to ¼in (6mm) long, are borne in dense whorls in terminal, tapering spikes. ↕ to 4ft (1.2m), ↔ 3ft (1m) or more. Europe, Turkey, Caucasus, N.W. Iran. Zone 6b.

M. odorata see *M.* x *piperita* f. *citrata.*

M.* x *piperita (*M. aquatica* x *M. spicata*) (Peppermint). Vigorous perennial with hairy, red-purple-tinged stems and ovate-lance-shaped to lance-shaped, aromatic, toothed, mid-green leaves, 1½–3½in (4–9cm) long. In summer, bears terminal whorls of tubular, lilac-pink flowers, ⅛in (3mm) long. ↕ 12–36in (30–90cm), ↔ 36in (90cm). Europe. Zone 4. **f. *citrata*,** syn. *M. odorata, M. piperita* var. *citriodora* (Eau de Cologne mint, Lemon mint) has hairless stems and thin, ovate, eau-de-Cologne-scented leaves. Garden origin.

M. piperita* var. *citriodora see *M.* x *piperita* f. *citrata.*

M. pulegium (Pennyroyal). Spreading perennial with upright and procumbent stems bearing short-stalked, narrowly elliptic to rounded, sharply aromatic, bright green leaves, to 1¼in (3cm) long, hairy beneath. Widely spaced, leafy whorls of tubular lilac flowers, ⅛–¼in (4–6mm) long, are borne in spikes in summer. ↕ 4–16in (10–40cm), ↔ to 20in (50cm). S.W. and C. Europe, Mediterranean to Iran. Zone 5. **'Cunningham Mint'** is lower-growing.

M. requienii, syn. *M. corsica* (Corsican mint). Procumbent, mat-forming, hairy or hairless perennial with slender, creeping, rooting stems bearing broadly ovate to rounded, peppermint-scented, bright green leaves, to ¼in (6mm) across. In summer, bears whorls of tiny, tubular lilac flowers, 1/16in (2mm) long, in short spikes. Prefers shade. ↕ to ½in (1.5cm), ↔ indefinite. France (Corsica), Italy (including Sardinia). Zone 5.

***M. rotundifolia* of gardens** see *M. suaveolens.*

M. rubra* var. *raripila see *M.* x *smithiana.*

M.* x *smithiana ■ (*M. aquatica* x *M. arvensis* x *M. spicata*), syn. *M. rubra* var. *raripila* (Red raripila). Vigorous, spreading perennial with ovate, toothed, sweet-smelling, sparsely hairy, dark green, red-tinted leaves, 1¼–3½in (3–9cm) long. In summer, produces spikes of dense whorls of tubular lilac flowers, to ¼in (6mm) long, usually well spaced, sometimes clustered at the stem tips. ↕ to 3ft (1m), ↔ 4ft (1.2m) or more. N. and C. Europe. Zone 6.

M. spicata, syn. *M. viridis* (Spearmint). Spreading perennial with stalkless, lance-shaped to oblong-ovate, toothed, aromatic (usually sweet-smelling but sometimes pungent), bright green leaves, 2–3½in (5–9cm) long, hairless or with branched and unbranched hairs beneath. Bears dense, cylindrical spikes of usually separated whorls of tubular to bell-shaped, pink, lilac, or white flowers, to ⅛in (3mm) long, in summer. ↕ to 3ft (1m), ↔ indefinite. W. and C. Europe, Mediterranean. Zone 4.

M. suaveolens, syn. *M. rotundifolia* of gardens (Apple mint). Vigorous, spreading, apple-scented perennial with often white-hairy stems and toothed, oblong-ovate to rounded, irregularly wrinkled and softly hairy, grayish green leaves, to 1¼in (3cm) long, the margins sometimes rolled under and wavy. In summer, bears tubular, pink or white flowers, to 1/16 in (2mm) long, in dense whorls in terminal, often branched spikes. ↕ to 3ft (1m), ↔ indefinite. W. and S. Europe, Mediterranean. Zone 5. **'Variegata'** ■ (Pineapple mint) has leaves with broad cream streaks and margins, and a rich, fruity fragrance.

M. sylvestris see *M. longifolia.*

M.* x *villosa* f. *alopecuroides (*M. spicata* x *M. suaveolens*) (Bowles' mint). Variable, spreading perennial with softly hairy, broadly ovate or rounded, aromatic, toothed, bright green leaves, 1½–3in (4–8cm) long. In summer, whorls of tubular pink flowers, 1/16–⅛in (2–3mm) long, are produced in large, leafy spikes. ↕ 12–36in (30–90cm), ↔ indefinite. Garden origin. Zone 5.

M. viridis see *M. spicata.*

MENTZELIA

Starflower

LOASACEAE

Genus of 60 species of spreading to erect, freely branching, densely stiff-haired annuals, biennials, perennials, and subshrubs, mostly from dry, sandy, or rocky scrub in S.W. US, Mexico, and the West Indies. Alternate, mainly lance-shaped, coarsely toothed, light to mid-green leaves may be simple, lobed, or pinnatifid. The poppy-like, 5- to 10-petaled, bright orange, yellow, or white flowers, often night-scented or opening only in strong sunlight, are borne singly or in loose cymes in summer. Grow in an annual or mixed border, or a wild garden; they need long, hot summers to flower well. Where not hardy, grow in a cool greenhouse.

• **CULTIVATION** Grow in moderately fertile, well-drained soil in a warm, sheltered site in full sun. Water freely in the growing season for repeat flowering. After the first flush of bloom, cut annuals back to 2in (5cm).

• **PROPAGATION** Sow seed of annuals *in situ* in spring.

• **PESTS AND DISEASES** Infrequent.

M. lindleyi ■ syn. *Bartonia aurea* (Blazing star). Erect, freely branching annual with lance-shaped to oval, pinnatifid, mid-green to gray leaves, to 6in (15cm) long, the lobes sometimes toothed. In summer, 5-petaled, very

Mentzelia lindleyi

fragrant, night-scented, golden yellow blooms, 2–3½in (5–9cm) across, are borne singly from the leaf axils or in 2- or 3-flowered cymes at the stem tips; petals are flushed orange-red at the bases. ↕ 6–28in (15–70cm), ↔ to 9in (23cm). California.

MENYANTHES

MENYANTHACEAE

Genus of one species of rhizomatous, aquatic or semi-aquatic perennial from the N. hemisphere, especially in Europe. It forms large, spreading, floating mats that extend over the shallow, still or slow-moving water of lakes or ponds, and sometimes across the muddy margins. *M. trifoliata* has 3-palmate leaves and bears racemes of star-shaped flowers. It is a decorative plant for ponds and for the margins of a wildlife pool, and is useful for disguising hard edges.

• **CULTIVATION** In a large pool, grow in an aquatic container, at a depth of 6–9in (15–23cm), or in muddy pond margins. Provide a site in full sun to encourage production of the short-lived flowers. See also p.52–53.

• **PROPAGATION** Sow seed in winter in containers standing in water. In summer, divide young rhizomes into pieces, 9–12in (23–30cm) long, and place them horizontally on soft mud in an aquatic container or in shallow water; push in and peg down.

• **PESTS AND DISEASES** Prone to leaf gall.

M. trifoliata ■ (Bogbean, Marsh trefoil). Aquatic perennial with extensive, creeping rhizomes, to 4ft (1.2m) long, and 3-palmate leaves with elliptic to ovate or obovate leaflets, to 2½in (6cm) long. In summer, bears erect racemes of 10–20 white flowers, 1in (2.5cm) across, pink outside and in bud, with very finely fringed and bearded petals. ↕ 8–12in (20–30cm), ↔ indefinite. Europe, N. Asia, N.W. India, North America. Zone 3.

MENZIESIA

ERICACEAE

Genus of about 7 species of freely branching, spreading to upright, deciduous shrubs, found in woodland in E. Asia and North America. The ovate to elliptic or oblong leaves are arranged alternately and often clustered at the shoot tips. Small, nodding, urn- to bell-shaped, 4- or 5-lobed flowers are borne in umbels in late spring and early summer. Grow *Menziesia* species in a woodland garden; they grow best in areas with cool, damp summers.

• **CULTIVATION** Grow in moist but well-drained, humus-rich, acidic soil in partial shade. Shelter from cold, drying winds. Pruning group 8.

Menyanthes trifoliata

Menziesia ciliicalyx var. *purpurea*

• **PROPAGATION** Sow seed in containers in spring at 55°F (13°C), or in a cold frame outdoors in autumn. Root greenwood cuttings in early summer.
• **PESTS AND DISEASES** Leaf and bud galls and tar spot are common.

M

M. ciliicalyx* var. *lasiophylla see *M. ciliicalyx* var. *purpurea.*
M. ciliicalyx* var. *purpurea ■ syn. *M. ciliicalyx* var. *lasiophylla.* Slow-growing, bushy shrub with clustered, obovate to oval, bright green leaves, to 3in (8cm) long. In late spring and early summer, bears umbels of 3–8 urn-shaped, dark purple-pink flowers, ½in (1.5cm) long. ↕↔ 3ft (1m). Japan. Zone 6b.
M. ferruginea (Fool's huckleberry, Rusty leaf). Upright, twiggy shrub with clustered, obovate to elliptic, mid-green leaves, to 2½in (6cm) long, covered in soft, rust-brown hairs and turning red in autumn. From late spring to summer, bears umbels of 2–5 urn-shaped, red-flushed yellow flowers, ¼in (6mm) long. ↕6ft (2m), ↔ 5ft (1.5m). Alaska to N. California. Zone 6.

MERENDERA

LILIACEAE

Genus of about 10 species of bulbous perennials from subalpine meadows and dry sites in open woodland in the Mediterranean region, N. Africa, the Middle East, and W. Asia. They have semi-erect, basal leaves that are linear to linear-lance-shaped, strap-shaped, or inversely lance-shaped, that elongate after flowering. Small, funnel-shaped flowers, with separate, often narrow, star-shaped tepals, are borne at ground level, with or before the leaves in spring or autumn. Grow in a raised bed, alpine house, or bulb frame; *M. montana* is suitable for a sunny rock garden.
• **CULTIVATION** Plant 2–3in (5–8cm) deep in late summer. Outdoors, grow in moist but well-drained soil in full sun. In a bulb frame, grow in soil-based potting mix with added sharp sand. Water moderately in the growing season. *Merendera* species require a hot, dry period of summer dormancy. Repot annually in summer.
• **PROPAGATION** Sow seed in containers in a cold frame: sow in spring for autumn-flowering species, in autumn for spring-flowering species. Remove offsets during summer dormancy.
• **PESTS AND DISEASES** Infrequent.

M. bulbocodium see *M. montana.*
M. caucasica see *M. trigyna.*
M. montana ■ syn. *M. bulbocodium, M. pyrenaica.* Cormous perennial with 3 or 4 linear, channeled leaves, to 9in (23cm) long, borne just with or after the flowers. In autumn, bears 1 or 2 upright, funnel-shaped, purple to red-purple flowers, to 3in (8cm) long, sometimes with white bases. ↕and PD2in (5cm). Pyrenees, Iberian peninsula. Zone 7.
M. pyrenaica see *M. montana.*
M. raddeana see *M. trigyna.*
M. robusta. Cormous perennial with 3–6 linear to lance-shaped leaves, to 10in (25cm) long, with the flowers. Produces 1–4 upright, funnel-shaped, deep pink to lilac or white flowers, ¾–1½in (2–4cm) long, in spring. ↕3in (8cm), PD2in (5cm). Iran, Afghanistan, Turkmenistan, N. India. Zone 7b.
M. trigyna, syn. *M. caucasica, M. raddeana.* Bulbous perennial with linear to linear-lance-shaped leaves, to 7in (18cm) long, borne with the flowers. In spring, bears 1–3 funnel-shaped, purple-pink to white flowers, ¾–1¼in (2–3cm) long, with narrow, inversely lance-shaped tepals. ↕and PD 2in (5cm). Turkey, Caucasus, Iran. Zone 7b.

Merendera montana

MERREMIA

CONVOLVULACEAE

Genus of at least 70 species of woody, evergreen and herbaceous, mainly twining climbers found in tropical regions in diverse habitats, including mudflats, grassland, and woodland. The alternate or spiraling leaves are entire or palmately lobed or divided. Funnel- to bell-shaped flowers are borne singly or in small clusters from the upper leaf axils. Where not hardy, grow in a temperate greenhouse, or treat as tender annuals and grow outdoors. Elsewhere, grow over a pergola, arch, or trellis.
• **CULTIVATION** Under glass, grow in soil-based potting mix, in full light with shade from hot sun. In growth, water moderately and apply a balanced liquid fertilizer monthly; water sparingly in winter. Outdoors, grow in moderately fertile, moist but well-drained soil in full sun with some midday shade. Shelter from cold, drying winds. Pruning group 11, in late winter or early spring.
• **PROPAGATION** Sow seed at 64–75°F (18–24°C) in spring.
• **PESTS AND DISEASES** Susceptible to spider mites and whiteflies under glass.

M. tuberosa, syn. *Ipomoea tuberosa, Operculina tuberosa* (Spanish morning glory, Wood rose, Yellow morning glory). Vigorous, woody-stemmed, evergreen twining climber. Palmately 5- to 7-lobed, bright to mid-green leaves have oblong-lance-shaped lobes, to 6in (15cm) long. Bears funnel-shaped yellow flowers, 2–2½in (5–6cm) across, usually in stalked clusters of 3–9, but sometimes also singly, mainly in summer. Spherical fruit, to 1½in (4cm) across, develop from the woody sepals. ↕30–70ft (10–20m). Mexico to tropical South America. ❀ (min. 45–50°F/7–10°C)

MERTENSIA

BORAGINACEAE

Genus of about 50 species of clump-forming, mound-forming, or prostrate perennials from wet meadows, woodland, and coasts in Europe, Asia, North America, and Greenland. The alternate, lance-shaped to rounded leaves, sometimes with heart-shaped bases, are light to dark green or grayish or bluish green. Pendent, tubular or bell-shaped, 5-lobed blue flowers, with flared, funnel-shaped mouths, are borne in terminal or axillary cymes. Grow the smaller species in a gravel bed, rock garden, or alpine house, the larger ones in a herbaceous border or woodland garden.
• **CULTIVATION** Grow in moist but well-drained, humus-rich soil in light, dappled shade. Alpine species, such as *M. echioides,* require humus-rich, gritty soil; *M. maritima* and *M. simplicissima* prefer low-fertility, sharply drained, very gritty or sandy soil. All prefer full sun with some midday shade.

Mertensia ciliata

• **PROPAGATION** Sow seed in containers in a cold frame in autumn; keep young plants shaded and do not allow the soil to dry out. Divide clumps carefully as new growth commences in spring. Take root cuttings of *M. pulmonarioides* when dormant, in autumn or early winter.
• **PESTS AND DISEASES** Slugs and snails feed on young growth. Powdery mildew, rust, and leaf smut can be common.

M. asiatica see *M. simplicissima.*
M. ciliata ■ Upright perennial with stemless, ovate, lance-shaped, or oblong, bluish green basal leaves, to 6in (15cm) long, and ovate to lance-shaped stem leaves. Axillary cymes of bell-shaped, clear blue flowers, to ⅜in (9mm) long, are borne in summer. ↕to 24in (60cm), ↔ to 12in (30cm). W. US. Zone 5.
M. echioides. Clump-forming perennial with spoon-shaped or ovate to lance-shaped or oblong, dark green leaves, to 3½in (9cm) long. Many-flowered, curving cymes, to 5in (13cm) long, of funnel-shaped, deep blue flowers, to ¼in (6mm) long, are borne on upright stems in summer. ↕6in (15cm), ↔ to 4in (10cm). Himalayas. Zone 7.
M. maritima (Oyster plant). Spreading, prostrate perennial with fleshy, spoon-shaped to oblong-ovate, very glaucous, blue-green leaves, to 4in (10cm) long. Bell-shaped, bright blue flowers, to ⅜in (9mm) across, open from pink buds in branching, terminal cymes in early summer. ↕4in (10cm), ↔ to 12in (30cm). Coasts of E. North America, Greenland, and N. Europe. Zone 4.

Mertensia simplicissima

M. pterocarpa see *M. sibirica.*
M. pulmonarioides, syn. *M. virginica* (Virginia bluebells, Virginia cowslip). Clump-forming perennial with erect, branching stems bearing elliptic to ovate, soft, hairless, bluish green leaves, to 6in (15cm) long. Terminal cymes of flared, long-tubed, sky-blue to purple-blue flowers, ¾–1in (2–2.5cm) long, opening from pink buds, are borne in mid- and late spring. ↕ 18in (45cm), ↔ 10in (25cm). North America. Zone 3. **'Alba'** has white flowers.
M. sibirica, syn. *M. pterocarpa*. Clump-forming perennial with broadly elliptic, broadly ovate, or heart-shaped, light green basal leaves, 2–4in (5–10cm) long. The erect, unbranched, hairless, light green stems bear more oval, pointed leaves. From late spring to midsummer, terminal cymes of flared, tubular, deep blue or purple-blue flowers, to ½in (1.5cm) long, are borne on long, axillary flower stalks. ↕ 24in (60cm), ↔ 12in (30cm). E. Siberia, E. Asia. Zone 4.
M. simplicissima ▣ syn. *M. asiatica*. Prostrate perennial with procumbent, leafy shoots and rosettes of obovate to broadly ovate, glaucous, blue-green leaves, 1¼–3in (3–8cm) long. From late spring to early autumn, terminal cymes of flared, tubular, turquoise-blue flowers, ½in (1.5cm) long, are borne on spreading stems. ↕ to 36in (90cm), ↔ 12in (30cm). Russia (Sakhalin), Korea, Japan. Zone 6.
M. virginica see *M. pulmonarioides.*

▷ ***Mesembryanthemum cordifolium*** see *Aptenia cordifolia*
▷ ***Mesembryanthemum criniflorum*** see *Dorotheanthus bellidiformis*
▷ ***Mesembryanthemum derenbergianum*** see *Ebracteola derenbergiana*
▷ ***Mesembryanthemum multiradiatum*** see *Lampranthus roseus*
▷ ***Mesembryanthemum tricolor*** see *Dorotheanthus gramineus*

MESPILUS

ROSACEAE

Genus of one species of deciduous tree or large shrub found in woodland and thickets in mountainous regions of S.E. Europe and S.W. Asia. It is grown for its attractive, spreading habit, its colorful autumn foliage, its bowl-shaped flowers, borne singly at the ends of short shoots, and its flattened, apple-like fruit, which have prominent, persistent calyces. Grow as a specimen tree. The fruit are edible following the first hard frost in late autumn, when they are extremely well-ripened ("bletted").
• **CULTIVATION** Grow in moderately fertile, moist but well-drained soil in full sun or light shade. Pruning group 1.
• **PROPAGATION** Sow seed in a seedbed in autumn. Bud in late summer.
• **PESTS AND DISEASES** Fireblight, powdery mildew, rust, brown rot, aphids, and caterpillars can be problems.

M. germanica ▣ (Medlar). Spreading tree or large shrub with alternate, lance-shaped to oblong-oval, dark green leaves, to 6in (15cm) long, turning yellow-brown in autumn. Bears white, sometimes pink-tinged flowers, to 2in (5cm) across, in late spring and early summer. Almost spherical, fleshy brown

Mespilus germanica

fruit grow up to 2in (5cm) or more across. ↕ 20ft (6m), ↔ 25ft (8m). S.E. Europe, S.W. Asia. Zone 7. **'Dutch'** has russet-brown fruit. **'Nottingham'** has brown fruit, 1½in (4cm) across.

METASEQUOIA

TAXODIACEAE

Genus of one species of deciduous, monoecious, coniferous tree from valley forests of C. China. It has 2-ranked, linear leaves that turn gold to red-brown in autumn. The shoots, leaves, and cone scales grow in opposite pairs. Tolerant of waterlogged soils, it makes a fine specimen or street tree.
• **CULTIVATION** Grow in humus-rich, moist but well-drained soil in full sun. Initial growth is fast, but on dry sites is slower after plants reach 30ft (10m) tall.
• **PROPAGATION** Sow seed in a seedbed in autumn. Root hardwood cuttings in winter, or semi-ripe cuttings with bottom heat in midsummer.
• **PESTS AND DISEASES** Infrequent.

M. glyptostroboides ▣ (Dawn redwood). Conical tree with ascending branches and fibrous, orange-brown

Metasequoia glyptostroboides

bark, and often deeply fluted, "buttressed" trunks. Soft, spreading leaves are bright fresh green, to ½in (1.5cm) long on mature trees, ¾in (2cm) or more on seedlings, with 2 light green bands beneath. Deciduous shoots are green, without growth buds; permanent shoots, bearing growth buds, are pink-brown, later brown. Produces ovoid, light brown female cones, ¾in (2cm) long, on stalks ¾–1½in (2–4cm) long, and pendent, spherical brown male cones, ¼–½in (0.5–1.5cm) long, with 15–20 scales, in the upper crown. ↕ 70–130ft (20–40m), ↔ 15ft (5m) or more. China (N.W. Hubei). Zone 5b. **'Gold Rush'** has a conical habit with bright, golden yellow foliage. ↕ 44ft (14m), ↔ 25ft (8m).

METROSIDEROS

Pohutakawa, Rata

MYRTACEAE

Genus of 50 species of dwarf to tall, upright, evergreen shrubs, trees, and climbers found in rainforest, dry river valleys, and subalpine areas from South Africa to Malaysia, Australasia, and the Pacific islands (including Hawaii). The simple, mostly entire, leathery leaves are borne in opposite pairs. Small, trumpet-shaped flowers, with insignificant petals and conspicuous, brush-like tufts of stamens with colored filaments, are borne in terminal or axillary cymes or racemes. Where not hardy, grow in a cool greenhouse. Elsewhere, grow as specimens, or as a hedge or screen.
• **CULTIVATION** Under glass, grow in soil-based potting mix in full light, with shade from hot sun. In growth, water freely and apply a balanced liquid fertilizer monthly; water sparingly in winter. Outdoors, grow in humus-rich, moderately fertile, moist but well-drained, neutral to acidic soil, in full sun. Shelter from cold, drying winds. Pruning group 1; plants under glass need restrictive pruning.
• **PROPAGATION** Surface-sow seed at 55–59°F (13–15°C) in spring. Root semi-ripe cuttings with bottom heat in summer. Air layer in spring.
• **PESTS AND DISEASES** Scale insects may be a problem under glass.

M. excelsus ▣ syn. *M. tomentosus* (Christmas tree, Common pohutakawa). Erect, freely branching tree, spreading with age, with elliptic to oblong leaves, 2–4in (5–10cm) long, semi-glossy, dark green above, densely white-felted beneath. Broad, compact, many-flowered, terminal cymes of flowers, 1¼–1½in (3–4cm) long, with crimson filaments and golden anthers, are borne in summer. ↕ to 70ft (20m), ↔ 30–70ft (10–20m). New Zealand (North Island). ❄ (min. 45°F/7°C). **'Aureus'** has rich yellow filaments.
M. kermadecensis. Bushy, rounded to spreading tree with broadly ovate to oblong-elliptic leaves, 1–2in (2.5–5cm) long, with recurved margins, dark green above and densely white-felted beneath. In summer, produces abundant dense, terminal cymes of flowers, ¾in (2cm) long, with crimson filaments and yellow anthers. ↕ to 70ft (20m), ↔ 25–40ft (8–12m). New Zealand, including Raoul Island. ❄ (min. 45°F/7°C). **'Sunninghill'** has variegated leaves,

Metrosideros excelsus

irregularly splashed creamy yellow. **'Variegatus'** has leaves marbled dark green and gray-green, with broad, irregular, creamy white margins.
M. robustus (New Zealand Christmas tree, Northern rata, Rata). Erect, freely branching tree, often epiphytic when young, spreading with age. Elliptic to ovate-oblong leaves, 1–2in (2.5–5cm) long, are semi-glossy, dark green above and hairless and paler beneath. In summer, flowers 1¼in (3cm) long, with matte crimson filaments and yellow anthers, are borne in dense, terminal cymes on 4-angled stems. ↕ to 100ft (30m), ↔ to 40ft (12m). New Zealand. ❄ (min. 45°F/7°C)
M. tomentosus see *M. excelsus.*

MEUM

APIACEAE

Genus of one species of clump-forming perennial from mountain slopes, poor grassland, and roadsides in W. and C. Europe. The hairless, aromatic, mainly basal leaves are pinnate, with whorled, hair-like segments. Small, star-shaped flowers are borne in compound umbels in summer. Grow as a foliage plant in a mixed or herbaceous border.
• **CULTIVATION** Grow in moderately fertile, well-drained, preferably alkaline soil in full sun.
• **PROPAGATION** Sow seed in containers in a cold frame as soon as ripe. Divide in spring; pot up until established.
• **PESTS AND DISEASES** Slugs and snails may damage young growth. Aphids may also be a problem.

M. athamanticum (Baldmoney, Spignel). Perennial with oblong, 3- or 4-pinnate, light to mid-green leaves, with finely cut leaflets, ¼in (6mm) long. In early and midsummer, bears tiny, white or purple-tinged white flowers in small umbels, 1¼–2½in (3–6cm) across, grouped into larger, compound umbels. ↕ 8–24in (20–60cm), ↔ 12in (30cm). W. and C. Europe. Zone 7b.

MEXICOA

ORCHIDACEAE

Genus of one species of deciduous, epiphytic orchid found in oak forest at 6,600 feet (2,000m) in the Oaxaca region of Mexico. It produces ovoid to conical pseudobulbs, and one or two slightly leathery, lance-shaped leaves. Flowers, borne in erect or arching racemes, are off-white to yellow, and longitudinally purple-striped, with prominent yellow lips.

• **CULTIVATION** Cool- to intermediate-growing orchids. Grow in epiphytic orchid potting mix. In summer, provide moist conditions in full light, water freely, feed at every third watering, and mist daily. In winter, grow in drier conditions in full light, and mist lightly. See also p.46.

• **PROPAGATION** Divide when the plant fills the pot and flows over the sides.

• **PESTS AND DISEASES** Prone to aphids, spider mites, and mealybugs.

M. ghiebrechtiana, syn. *Oncidium ghiebrechtiana.* Deciduous, epiphytic orchid with ovoid to conical, grooved pseudobulbs, and 2 lance-shaped, thinly leathery, mid-green leaves, 3–5½in (8–14cm) long. In winter, bears erect to arching racemes, to 8in (20cm) long, of 3–6 widely spaced, off-white to yellow flowers, ¾in (2cm) across, with longitudinal purple stripes and prominent yellow lips. ↕ 7in (18cm), ↔ 2in (5cm). Mexico (Oaxaca). ❀ (min. 54–59°F/12–15°C; max. 85°F/24°C)

M

MICHAUXIA

CAMPANULACEAE

Genus of 7 species of imposing biennials or short-lived, monocarpic perennials from sunny, well-drained, stony sites in the E. Mediterranean region and S.W. Asia. The toothed, hairy, rosette-forming leaves are pinnatisect or pinnatifid, each leaf with a single large, terminal lobe. Racemes or panicles of white or blue flowers, with spreading or reflexed corollas consisting of many narrow petals, are produced on thick, leafy stems. Grow in a mixed border.

• **CULTIVATION** Grow in moderately fertile, well-drained, alkaline soil in full sun. Provide a dry winter mulch.

• **PROPAGATION** Sow seed *in situ* in spring. May also self-seed.

• **PESTS AND DISEASES** Infrequent.

Michauxia tchihatchewii

M. campanuloides. Perennial with robust, branched stems and lance-shaped, pinnatifid leaves, to 8in (20cm) long. Pendent, purple-tinged white flowers, ¾–1½in (2–4cm) across, with narrow, reflexed corolla lobes and protruding, tubular, hairy styles, are produced in panicles in early summer. ↕ to 5ft (1.5m), ↔ 18in (45cm). E. Mediterranean (Turkey, Syria). Zone 8.

M. tchihatchewii ■ Perennial with long-stalked, oblong to broadly lance-shaped, coarsely toothed leaves, 6–8in (15–20cm) long. In midsummer, robust, stiff, branching stems, one per rosette, bear dense, spike-like racemes of nodding, initially broadly bell-shaped, white or blue flowers, to 1¼in (3cm) across, with mildly reflexed corollas, the lobes divided only to one-third of their length. ↕ 5ft (1.5m) or more, ↔ 18in (45cm). Turkey. Zone 8.

MICHELIA

MAGNOLIACEAE

Genus of 45 species of deciduous and evergreen, rounded, spreading shrubs and upright trees from broad-leaved woodland in India and Sri Lanka, and from the Himalayas to China and S.E. Asia. They are grown for their usually fragrant, magnolia-like flowers, borne singly from the leaf axils in spring or summer. The oblong, oval-oblong, or elliptic, leathery leaves are alternate or spiraling. Where not hardy, grow in a cool greenhouse or conservatory. Elsewhere, grow the shrubs in a border or small courtyard garden, and the trees in a woodland garden or as specimens.

• **CULTIVATION** Under glass, grow in soil-based potting mix, with added peat or composted bark, in full light with shade from hot sun, and low or moderate humidity. In growth, water moderately and apply a balanced liquid fertilizer monthly; water sparingly in winter. Outdoors, grow in humus-rich, moist but well-drained, neutral to acidic soil, in full sun with some midday shade, or in partial shade. Shelter from cold, drying winds. Pruning group 1.

• **PROPAGATION** Sow seed in containers in a cold frame or under glass either in autumn or as soon as ripe. Root greenwood cuttings in early summer or semi-ripe cuttings in mid- or late summer. Layer in spring.

• **PESTS AND DISEASES** Prone to scale insects, spider mites, and algal leaf spot.

Michelia doltsopa

Michelia figo

M. doltsopa ■ Small, evergreen tree, sometimes shrubby, that is erect, bushy, and pyramidal when young, with slightly warty stems, spreading with age. Leaves are oval-oblong to lance-shaped, 3–7in (8–18cm) long, lustrous, dark green above, silky, gray-hairy beneath. Bowl-shaped, fragrant, white to very pale yellow flowers, 3–4in (7–10cm) across, are borne from spring to early summer. ↕ 25–50ft (8–15m), ↔ 15–30ft (5–10m). E. Himalayas, Tibet, W. and S.W. China. ❀ (min. 41°F/5°C)

M. figo ■ (Banana shrub). Rounded, bushy, freely branching, evergreen shrub with downy, yellowish brown stems and elliptic-oblong to slightly obovate or oval leaves, 2–4in (5–10cm) long, lustrous, dark green above, paler beneath. From spring to summer, bears cup-shaped, banana-scented, yellowish green to ivory-white flowers, 1¼in (3cm) across, with dark red or maroon petal margins. Flowers are initially enclosed in woolly brown bracts. ↕ 10–20ft (3–6m), ↔ 5–11ft (1.5–3.5m). China. ❀ (min. 41°F/5°C)

MICRANTHOCEREUS

CACTACEAE

Genus of 9 species of shrubby to tall, upright, columnar cacti, sometimes branching basally, from the hillsides of C. and E. Brazil. They are densely spiny and have 10–30 or more narrow ribs. Close-set areoles are often covered with long wool and spines. Flowers are borne in clusters, diurnally or nocturnally, from lateral cephalia, with shapes varying from tubular to bell-like to broad funnel forms. Blooms can be bright lilac-pink or orange-pink to white. The fruit is small, fleshy, naked, and indehiscent; color varies from red to light blue.

• **CULTIVATION** Under glass, grow in a mix of 4 parts standard cactus potting mix and 1 part limestone chips, in full light. From spring to summer, water freely and apply a balanced liquid fertilizer every 4–5 weeks. Keep nearly dry at other times. Outdoors, grow in moderately fertile, slightly alkaline, sharply drained, humus-rich soil in full sun. See also p.48–49.

• **PROPAGATION** Sow seed at 70°F (21°C) in spring or summer.

• **PESTS AND DISEASES** Scale occurs.

M. auriazureus ■ Columnar, basal-branching, cluster-forming cactus with glaucous blue stems. Tubercles emerge

Micranthocereus auriazureus

from 15–18 ribs with rounded, vertical, wavy furrows, bearing areoles with dark golden yellow spines. Cephalia blend with abundant wool. Nocturnal, cylindrical flowers are bright pink, to 1in (2.5cm) long. Bears pale pink, berry-like fruit. ↕ 3½ft (1.1m), ↔ 2½–3in (6–8cm). Brazil. ❀ (min. 50°F/10°C)

M. dolichospermaticus. Columnar, nonbranching cactus with bluish stems and 30 somewhat tuberculate ribs, to ½in (1.5cm) high. Oval areoles with bright brown wool produce 6–8 straight, erect, yellow central spines that later turn gray. Cephalia, to 14in (35cm) long and 2½in (6cm) wide, are covered with cream-colored wool, to 1½in (4cm) long, and bright to dark red bristles. Bears nocturnal, tubular to almost bell-shaped white flowers, to 1½in (4cm) long, and cup-shaped, brownish fruit. ↕ to 6ft (2m), ↔ to 3in (8cm). Brazil. ❀ (min. 50°F/10°C)

M. estevesii. Columnar, rarely branching cactus, with bluish green stems and 37–42 narrow ribs. Round areoles have yellowish white wool and hairs with light brown spines. Cephalia, to 3in (8cm) wide, are covered with white to cream woolly hairs, and red bristles. Bears broad, funnel-shaped, white flowers, to 1½in (4cm) long, and light blue fruit. ↕ to 20ft (6m), ↔ to 6in (15cm). Brazil. ❀ (min. 50°F/10°C)

MICROBIOTA

CUPRESSACEAE

Genus of one species of prostrate to low mound-forming, evergreen, dioecious or monoecious, coniferous shrub from open slopes in S.E. Siberia. It has scale-like, broadly triangular, pointed, bright green leaves that turn bronze-purple over winter. The minute, ovoid cones have leathery scales, each one opening to release a single seed. Grow in a shrub border or as a groundcover.

• **CULTIVATION** Grow in moderately fertile, moist but well-drained soil in

Microbiota decussata

full sun to partial shade. Pruning is rarely required, and then only to remove stray growth.

- **PROPAGATION** Sow seed in a seedbed in autumn. Root semi-ripe cuttings in summer.
- **PESTS AND DISEASES** Infrequent.

M. decussata ▣ Spreading coniferous shrub with green shoots, later turning red-brown, and flat sprays of bright mid-green leaves, to ⅛in (3mm) long, paler below, in symmetrical pairs. Female cones, ⅛in (3mm) long, each have 2–4 scales, one of which is fertile; male cones, 1/16–⅛in (2–3mm) long, are pale yellow. ↕ to 3ft (1m), ↔ indefinite. Russia (S.E. Siberia). Zone 3.

MICROCACHRYS

PODOCARPACEAE

Genus of one species of monoecious, evergreen, spreading, coniferous shrub, found on 2 mountain summits in W. Tasmania. It is cultivated for its small, scale-like, triangular leaves, borne on procumbent, snake-like branches, and, to a lesser extent, for its small, mulberry-like cones. *M. tetragona* is suitable for a shrub border or rock garden, or as a groundcover; it may also be grown as a bonsai.

- **CULTIVATION** Grow in humus-rich, moist but well-drained, neutral to slightly acidic soil in full sun, with some midday shade. It grows best in areas with high humidity.
- **PROPAGATION** Sow seed as soon as ripe in a seedbed, or in containers in a cold frame. Root semi-ripe cuttings with bottom heat in summer.
- **PESTS AND DISEASES** Infrequent.

M. tetragona ▣ Spreading, coniferous shrub with overlapping, dark green leaves, 1/16–⅛in (2–3mm) long, arranged spirally in 4 rows on the shoots. Ovoid female cones, ½in (1.5cm) long, have whorls of 4 rounded scales, becoming fleshy and translucent red, each with a single seed; oblong male cones, ⅛in (3mm) long, are borne at the ends of the shoots. ↕ to 20in (50cm), ↔ 3ft (1m). Australia (W. Tasmania). ❄ (min. 35°F/2°C)

Microcachrys tetragona

MICROLEPIA

DENNSTAEDTIACEAE

Genus of about 45 species of terrestrial, evergreen ferns from tropical regions worldwide, mainly found at forest margins. Long-creeping rhizomes produce soft, usually dark green fronds. These are pinnate to 3-pinnate, the pinnae sometimes shallowly to deeply lobed. The round sori are formed within the margins of the leaf blade. Where not hardy, grow in a temperate greenhouse. In warmer climates, *Microlepia* species and cultivars are suitable for a woodland garden.

- **CULTIVATION** Under glass, grow in 1 part coarse leaf mold (or peat) and charcoal, and 2 parts soil-based potting mix, in bright indirect light with high humidity. In the growing season, water freely and apply a balanced liquid fertilizer monthly. Keep almost wet while in active growth. Water sparingly in winter. Outdoors, grow in humus-rich, moist but well-drained soil in light dappled or partial shade. The plants should not be disturbed once established. See also p.51.
- **PROPAGATION** Sow spores in containers at 68°F (20°C) as soon as ripe. Divide rhizomes of well-established plants in spring, before growth begins.
- **PESTS AND DISEASES** Infrequent.

M. speluncae ▣ Large, terrestrial, clump-forming fern bears long-stalked, triangular, 2- or 3-pinnate, dark green fronds, 32–60in (0.8–1.5m) long, which consist of triangular or lance-shaped to oblong pinnae without raised veins. ↕ to 5ft (1.5m), ↔ to 10ft (3m). S.E. Asia to Australia. ❄ (min. 41–50°F/5–10°C). **'Corymbifera'** syn. *M. pyramidata,* has tasseled blade tips and pinnae. ❄ (min. 45°F/7°C)

Microlepia speluncae

MICROMERIA

LAMIACEAE

Genus of about 70 species of annuals, perennials, and dwarf, evergreen shrubs (which at one time included species now placed in the genus *Acinos*). They occur in dry, rocky sites in the Mediterranean region, the Caucasus, and S.W. China. The ovate, linear, or lance-shaped, often aromatic, light to dark green leaves are arranged in opposite pairs. Spike-like racemes of small, tubular, 2-lipped, white to purple flowers are produced in short-stalked whorls in summer. They are suitable for a rock garden, or at the front of a mixed border.

- **CULTIVATION** Grow in moderately fertile, well-drained soil in full sun, with protection from excessive winter moisture. Pruning group 10, in early spring or after flowering.
- **PROPAGATION** Sow seed of perennials in containers in a cold frame in spring; sow seed of annuals *in situ* in late spring. Divide perennials in spring. Root softwood cuttings in late spring, or semi-ripe heel cuttings in early summer.
- **PESTS AND DISEASES** Aphids and spider mites may occur.

M. juliana. Rounded, evergreen, downy shrub with stalkless, ovate to linear or lance-shaped, aromatic, dark green leaves, ¼–½in (6–15mm) long. In summer, whorls of up to 20 purplish pink flowers, to ⅛in (3mm) long, are borne in upright, spike-like racemes, at the stem tips. ↕↔ 4–16in (10–40cm). Mediterranean. Zone 7b.

MIKANIA

ASTERACEAE

Genus of about 300 species of woody-stemmed and herbaceous, deciduous or evergreen, twining or scandent climbers, allied to *Eupatorium*. They occur in tropical to warm-temperate regions worldwide in a broad range of habitats, from prairies and grassland to deciduous and tropical woodland. The usually opposite leaves are simple, and may be entire, toothed, or shallowly to palmately lobed. Hemispherical flowerheads, similar to those of groundsel (*Senecio*), lack ray florets, and are borne in spikes, racemes, corymbs, or panicles. Where not hardy, grow in a temperate greenhouse. In warmer climates, grow in a woodland garden, use to clothe an arch or pergola, or allow to scramble through shrubs.

- **CULTIVATION** Under glass, grow in soil-based potting mix in bright filtered light. In the growing season, water freely and apply a balanced liquid fertilizer monthly; water sparingly in winter. Outdoors, grow in moderately fertile, moist but well-drained soil in light, dappled shade. Pruning group 11, in early spring.
- **PROPAGATION** Sow seed at 55–59°F (13–15°C) in spring. Insert softwood cuttings in late spring.
- **PESTS AND DISEASES** Spider mites, whiteflies, and rust can be problems.

M. scandens (Climbing hempweed, Hemp vine). Twining climber, often semi- or fully evergreen in tropical areas, with triangular to heart-shaped, glossy, mid- to bright green leaves, 2–4in (5–10cm) long, with entire or irregularly toothed margins. From late summer to late autumn, small but dense corymbs, ¾–2in (2–5cm) long, of vanilla-scented, usually white to pale flesh-pink, sometimes lilac to purple or yellow-tinted white flowerheads are produced from the upper leaf axils. ↕ 6–15ft (2–5m). Tropical North and South America. ❄ (min. 41°F/5°C)

MILLA

LILIACEAE

Genus of about 6 species of bulbous perennials, related to *Brodiaea*, often found on dry slopes in S. US, Mexico, and Central America. They have cylindrical or flat, linear leaves. Umbels of erect, tubular, scented flowers, each with 6 spreading tepals, are produced from summer to autumn. Where not hardy, lift and overwinter in frost-free conditions, or grow in a cool greenhouse or alpine house. In warmer climates, grow in a sheltered bed beside a wall, or in a herbaceous border.

- **CULTIVATION** Under glass, grow in a mix of equal parts loam, leaf mold, and sharp sand, in full light. Water sparingly until shoots appear, then

M

apply a balanced liquid fertilizer every 4–6 weeks and water moderately. Reduce water as leaves wither, and keep dry in winter. In frost-free areas, plant 4in (10cm) deep in autumn, in a well-drained site in full sun. Where not hardy, plant 3in (8cm) deep in well-drained soil in spring. Provide a sheltered site in full sun. Lift after flowering, and keep above freezing during winter.

• **PROPAGATION** Sow seed at 55–64°F (13–18°C) in spring. Remove offsets when dormant.

• **PESTS AND DISEASES** Infrequent.

M. biflora (Mexican star). Bulbous perennial with semi-erect, narrowly linear, glaucous, mid-green, basal leaves, 4–20in (10–50cm) long. In summer, bears umbels of 1–6, occasionally 8, white or white-flushed lilac or pink flowers, ½–1½in (1.5–4cm) long, with green central veins on the flat, spreading, reflexed tepals. ↕ 12in (30cm), PD2in (5cm). S.W. US, Mexico, Central America. ❀ (min. 41°F/5°C)

MILLETTIA

FABACEAE

Genus of about 120 species of deciduous and evergreen trees, shrubs, and woody-stemmed climbers from deciduous and evergreen woodland in Africa, Madagascar, India, and E. Asia. They have pinnate leaves, with lance-shaped to broadly ovate leaflets, borne alternately or in opposite pairs. Pea-like flowers are produced in terminal and lateral racemes or panicles, similar to those of wisterias. Where not hardy, grow in a cool or temperate greenhouse. In milder areas, grow as specimen trees or shrubs, and use climbers to clothe a fence, arch, pergola, or trellis.

• **CULTIVATION** Under glass, grow in soil-based potting mix in full light, with shade from hot sun. When in growth, water freely and apply a balanced liquid fertilizer monthly; water sparingly in winter. Outdoors, grow in moderately fertile, well-drained soil in full sun. Pruning group 1 for trees and shrubs; group 11 for climbers, after flowering; group 13 for wall-trained plants.

• **PROPAGATION** Sow seed at 43–54°F (6–12°C) as soon as ripe. Root semi-ripe cuttings with bottom heat in summer.

• **PESTS AND DISEASES** Whiteflies, aphids, and spider mites may be troublesome under glass.

M. reticulata. Twining, woody climber or scandent shrub bearing pinnate leaves with 5–9 lance-shaped to elliptic, semi-leathery leaflets, 1¼–3½in (3–9cm) long. In summer, produces pea-like, rose-pink, red, or blue flowers, to ½in (1.5cm) long, in dense racemes or panicles, 6–8in (15–20cm) long. ↕ 15ft (5m) or more, ↔ 3–6ft (1–2m). S. China, Taiwan. ❀ (min. 41°F/5°C)

MILTONIA

ORCHIDACEAE

Genus of about 15 species of evergreen, epiphytic orchids (which at one time included species now in *Miltoniopsis*), occurring mainly in warm, moist forest in Brazil. They produce ovoid to cylindrical, compressed pseudobulbs, each with 2 linear, oblong, oblong-linear, or oblong-lance-shaped, apical leaves; these are slightly leathery, thin, hairless, and pale to dark green. Often star-shaped, sometimes fragrant flowers are produced in usually erect racemes from the bases of the pseudobulbs, at various times of the year.

• **CULTIVATION** Intermediate-growing orchids. Grow in containers of epiphytic soil mix, epiphytically on bark, or in slatted baskets. In summer, provide humid conditions with partial shade, water freely, feed at every third watering, and mist once or twice daily. In winter, admit full light and water moderately. See also p.46.

• **PROPAGATION** Divide when the plant fills the pot and flows over the sides.

• **PESTS AND DISEASES** Prone to aphids, spider mites, and mealybugs. Bacterial soft rot and brown rot, cymbidium mosaic virus, basal stem rot, and leaf rot are common.

***M.* 'Bluntii'** (*M. clowesii* x *M. spectabilis*). Naturally occurring, epiphytic hybrid orchid with elongated pseudobulbs and linear leaves, 6in (15cm) long. In autumn, produces racemes of 3–7 star-shaped, fragrant, light yellow flowers, 3in (8cm) long, with red-brown markings, white lips, and purplish crimson bases. ↕↔ 9in (23cm). Brazil. ❀ (min. 55°F/13°C; max. 86°F/30°C)

M. candida, syn. *Anneliesia candida.* Epiphytic orchid with oblong-ovoid pseudobulbs and linear-lance-shaped leaves, 12in (30cm) long. In autumn, produces racemes of 2–8 star-shaped, greenish yellow flowers, 3in (8cm) across, spotted chestnut-brown and yellow, with lips sometimes flushed white or pink. ↕↔ 9in (23cm). Brazil. ❀ (min. 55°F/13°C; max. 86°F/30°C)

M. clowesii ▣ Epiphytic orchid with narrowly ovoid pseudobulbs and linear leaves, 12in (30cm) long. In autumn, bears long racemes of 3–7 star-shaped, greenish yellow flowers, 2in (5cm) across, each barred chestnut-brown, with white lips tinted violet-purple at the bases. ↕↔ 9in (23cm). Brazil. ❀ (min. 55°F/13°C; max. 86°F/30°C)

Miltonia clowesii

M. phalaenopsis see *Miltoniopsis phalaenopsis.*

M. roezlii see *Miltoniopsis roezlii.*

M. spectabilis. Epiphytic orchid producing elongated pseudobulbs and linear-oblong leaves, 6in (15cm) long. Throughout summer, white, red, or purple flowers, 3in (8cm) across, with red or purple lips, each with 3 yellow ridges at the base, are borne singly or occasionally in pairs. ↕↔ 9in (23cm). Brazil. ❀ (min. 55°F/13°C; max. 86°F/30°C). **var. *moreliana*** bears deep plum-purple flowers with deeply veined, rose-streaked and shaded lips.

MILTONIOPSIS

Pansy orchid

ORCHIDACEAE

Genus of 5 species of evergreen, epiphytic or lithophytic orchids (often included in *Miltonia*) from Central and South America, found in mountainous regions from 1,000ft (300m) to over 7,000ft (2,000m). The fleshy, ovoid pseudobulbs are partially covered by soft-textured, linear, gray-green, basal leaves. Decorative, fragrant flowers, with large, flat lips, are produced in racemes from the bases of the pseudobulbs. There are many colorful hybrids, often blooming twice a year, with up to 6 flowers in a raceme.

• **CULTIVATION** Cool-growing orchids. Grow in containers of epiphytic orchid potting mix. In summer, provide humid, shady conditions with plenty of fresh air, water freely, and feed at every third watering; water sparingly in winter and keep light levels low. Do not spray the foliage, since it may become spotted. See also p.46.

• **PROPAGATION** Divide when the plant fills the pot and flows over the sides.

• **PESTS AND DISEASES** Spider mites, aphids, and mealybugs occur.

***M.* Anjou 'St. Patrick'** ▣ (*M.* Hoggar x *M.* Piccadilly). Epiphytic orchid with ovoid pseudobulbs and linear leaves, 8in (20cm) long. Deep red flowers, 3in (8cm) across, with white and orange-red marks at the bases of the lips, are borne in racemes, mostly in summer. ↕↔ 9in (23cm). ❀ (min. 52°F/11°C; max. 75°F/24°C)

***M.* Emotion 'Redbreast'** (*M.* Emoi x *M.* Nyasa). Epiphytic orchid with ovoid pseudobulbs and linear leaves, 8in (20cm) long. Bears racemes of bright cream flowers, 3in (8cm) across, with attractive brownish red flushing on the lips, mostly in summer. ↕↔ 9in (23cm). ❀ (min. 52°F/11°C; max. 75°F/24°C)

Miltoniopsis Anjou 'St. Patrick'

Miltoniopsis Robert Strauss 'Ardingly'

***M.* Jersey** (*M.* Hamburg x *M.* Hannover). Epiphytic orchid with ovoid pseudobulbs and linear leaves, 8in (20cm) long. Produces racemes of dark red flowers, 3in (8cm) across, with red lips, mostly in summer. ↕↔ 9in (23cm). ❀ (min. 52°F/11°C; max. 75°F/24°C)

M. phalaenopsis, syn. *Miltonia phalaenopsis.* Epiphytic orchid with compressed, ovoid pseudobulbs and narrowly linear leaves, 6–9in (15–23cm) long. Racemes of 2–4 white flowers, 2in (5cm) across, with bold, red-purple splashes on the lips, are produced in autumn. ↕↔ 6in (15cm). Colombia. ❀ (min. 52°F/11°C; max. 75°F/24°C)

***M.* Robert Strauss 'Ardingly'** ▣ (*M.* Augusta x *M.* Gattonensis). Epiphytic orchid with ovoid pseudobulbs and linear leaves, 8in (20cm) long. Bears white flowers, 3in (8cm) across, highlighted with yellow, with red or pink petal bases, and flushed orange at the bases of the lips, in racemes, mostly in summer. ↕↔ 9in (23cm). ❀ (min. 52°F/11°C; max. 75°F/24°C)

M. roezlii, syn. *Miltonia roezlii.* Epiphytic orchid with ovoid pseudobulbs. Linear leaves, 6–10in (15–25cm) long, have dark green longitudinal lines beneath. In autumn and winter, bears 4- to 6-flowered racemes of white flowers, 2½in (6cm) across, with purple or red-mauve patches at the bases of the petals. ↕↔ 6in (15cm). Colombia. ❀ (min. 52°F/11°C; max. 75°F/24°C)

MIMETES

PROTEACEAE

Genus of 11 species of upright, evergreen shrubs or subshrubs from heath and scrub, often exposed, in South Africa. Alternate or spiraling, narrowly to broadly ovate, oblong, or lance-shaped, mid- to blue-green or silvery leaves are usually crowded and overlap to varying degrees. Tubular flowers enclosed in overlapping, leaf-like bracts, often with protruding perianth segments and styles, are borne terminally or in the upper leaf axils. Where not hardy, grow in a cool or temperate greenhouse. Elsewhere, grow in a shrub border.

• **CULTIVATION** Under glass, grow in a mix of equal parts loam, leaf mold, and grit or perlite, with added charcoal, in full light and with good ventilation. Water moderately in growth, sparingly in winter. In spring and early autumn, apply a liquid fertilizer of magnesium sulfate and urea. Outdoors, grow in moist but well-drained, neutral to slightly acidic, poor or moderately fertile soil with low levels of phosphates and nitrates, in full sun. Pruning group 1.

• **PROPAGATION** Sow seed at 43–54°F (6–12°C) as soon as ripe, in equal parts of grit and peat. Prick out seedlings into individual containers as soon as possible.

• **PESTS AND DISEASES** Spider mites may be a problem under glass.

M. cucullatus ■ syn. *M. lyrigera* (Rooistompie). Usually erect, sometimes decumbent shrub with densely downy stems that branch from near the base. Spiraling, narrowly oblong, slightly glaucous, mid-green leaves, 1–3in (3–8cm) long, have rounded, irregularly notched, orange-brown tips. In summer, bears axillary, or sometimes terminal flowerheads, 2–3in (5–8cm) long, which consist of overlapping, red and yellow leaf-like bracts and flowers with perianth segments in the same colors but with protruding, feathery, silver-white tips and red styles. Grows on stony slopes. ↕↔ to 5ft (1.5m). South Africa (Western Cape). ❀ (min. 41°F/5°C)

M. hirtus. Erect shrub with stems that branch near the base and spiraling, ovate, very hairy, mid-green leaves, ½–2½in (1–6cm) long, often pinkish brown when young. In summer, bears terminal or axillary flowerheads, 2in (5cm) long, consisting of overlapping, green leaf-like bracts, and flowers with prominent, silvery white and red-tipped, bright yellow perianth segments and red styles. Grows in marshy ground. ↕↔ to 5ft (1.5m). South Africa (Western Cape). ❀ (min. 50°F/10°C)

M. lyrigera see *M. cucullatus.*

Mimetes cucullatus

MIMOSA

FABACEAE

Genus of about 400 species of annuals, evergreen perennials, shrubs (which are sometimes scandent or trailing), and small trees, found in habitats ranging from forest to dry savanna in tropical regions worldwide. The often spiny stems bear alternate, 2-pinnate leaves, which in some species are sensitive to touch. Tiny, pea-like flowers, each with 4 or 5 petals and up to 10 long stamens, are lightly clustered in spherical heads, which are borne singly, or in spikes or panicles. The seed pods are sometimes twisted, curled, or spiny. In climates where temperatures fall below 55–61°F (13–16°C), grow in a warm greenhouse or as houseplants; grow *M. pudica* as an annual. In warmer areas, grow the annuals and perennials as a groundcover, the shrubs in a border, and the trees as specimen plants.

Mimosa pudica

• **CULTIVATION** Under glass, grow in soil-based potting mix in full light, with shade from hot sun. In the growing season, water moderately and apply a balanced liquid fertilizer monthly; water sparingly in winter. Outdoors, grow in moderately fertile, well-drained soil in full sun, although they will tolerate light, dappled shade. Pruning group 1.

• **PROPAGATION** Sow seed at 64–75°F (18–24°C) in spring. Alternatively, root softwood cuttings with bottom heat in early summer.

• **PESTS AND DISEASES** Prone to rust, spider mites, bagworm, webworm, thorn-bug, dieback, canker, butt rot, and wilt.

M. pudica ■ (Humble plant, Sensitive plant). Bushy, mat-forming annual or short-lived, evergreen perennial with slender, prickly, branching stems. Bright green to grayish green leaves, 2–4in (5–10cm) long, each have 4 radiating linear leaflets divided into 10–25 pairs of narrow, oblong segments that fold up at night and when touched. Spherical, light pink to lilac flowerheads, ½–¾in (1–2cm) across, are produced mainly in summer. ↕ 12–30in (30–75cm), ↔ 16–36in (40–90cm). Tropical North and South America. ❀ (min. 55°F/13°C)

MIMULUS syn. DIPLACUS

Monkey flower

SCROPHULARIACEAE

Genus of about 150 species of annuals, perennials, and evergreen shrubs found in southern Africa, Asia, Australia, and North, Central, and South America, usually occurring in damp areas but sometimes found in chaparral or deserts. The opposite, entire or toothed leaves are linear to nearly rounded, and mostly pale to dark green. Snapdragon-like, 5-lobed, 2-lipped, tubular or trumpet- or funnel-shaped flowers, often heavily spotted in contrasting colors, are borne from spring to autumn on upright stems, either in the axils or in spike-like racemes. The smaller species and cultivars are suitable for a damp pocket in a rock garden; grow most of the larger ones in a damp border or bog garden. Use the shrubs in a warm border. Where not hardy, grow the tender perennials in a cold greenhouse or as bedding annuals, and the tender shrubs in a cool greenhouse or conservatory.

Mimulus 'Andean Nymph'

• **CULTIVATION** Outdoors, grow most species in fertile, humus-rich, very moist soil in full sun or light, dappled shade. *M. aurantiacus*, *M. longiflorus*, and *M. puniceus* need well-drained soil and full sun; *M. cardinalis* and *M. lewisii* tolerate drier soils. *M. luteus* can be grown in water to 3in (8cm) deep, *M. ringens* to 6in (15cm). Under glass, grow in soil-based potting mix in full light, with shade from hot sun and good ventilation. Many grow best where summers are cool and moist. In the growing season, water freely and apply a balanced liquid fertilizer monthly; keep moist in winter. Monkey flowers are often short-lived, so propagate regularly. Pruning group 9 for shrubs.

• **PROPAGATION** Sow seed of hardy species and variants in containers in a cold frame in autumn or early spring; sow seed of tender ones at 43–54°F (6–12°C) in spring; plant out after danger of frost has passed. Divide perennials in spring. Root softwood cuttings in early summer, and semi-ripe shrub cuttings in midsummer.

• **PESTS AND DISEASES** Downy mildew, aster yellows, powdery mildew, gray mold, whiteflies, spider mites, and aphids are common.

M. alsiloides. (Chickweed monkey flower). Branched, decumbent annual with ovate to oblong, tiny-toothed, mid-green leaves, ½–1in (1–2.5cm) long. From spring to early summer, bears narrowly bell-shaped, yellow flowers, to 1in (2.5cm) long, each with a dark purple or red blotch at the bases of the lower lips. ↕ 4–6in (10–15cm), ↔ 2–10in (5–25cm). Vancouver Island to California.

M. 'Andean Nymph' ■ Spreading perennial with branching rhizomes and narrowly ovate to triangular-ovate, hairy, sparsely toothed, pale green leaves, to 1¼in (3cm) long. Leafy racemes of trumpet-shaped, white to cream flowers, to ¾in (2cm) across, the lobes heavily stained pink-purple, and with pink-spotted cream throats and lower lips, are borne over a long period in summer. ↕ to 8in (20cm), ↔ to 12in (30cm). Andes. ❀ (min. 41°F/5°C)

Mimulus aurantiacus

M. aurantiacus ■ syn. *Diplacus glutinosus, M. glutinosus.* Erect, often laxly branched shrub with lance-shaped to oblong, toothed, sticky, glossy, rich green leaves, to 3in (8cm) long. Open trumpet-shaped, orange, yellow, or dark red flowers, to 1¾in (4.5cm) long, with wavy petal margins, are produced in leafy racemes from late summer to autumn. ↕↔ 3ft (1m). Oregon, California. Zone 7b.
M.* x *bartonianus (*M. cardinalis* x *M. lewisii*). Upright perennial with elliptic, lobed, toothed, softly hairy, sticky, mid-green leaves, to 3in (8cm) long. From early summer to early autumn, produces solitary, axillary, tubular, bright clear pink to rose-red flowers, to 1¼in (3cm) long, with wide lips and with red-brown spots on the yellow throats. ↕ 24in (60cm), ↔ 18in (45cm). Garden origin. Zone 8.
M. cardinalis ■ (Scarlet monkey flower). Creeping perennial with erect, branching, hairy stems bearing ovate to oblong-elliptic, sharply toothed, downy, light green leaves, to 4in (10cm) long. Throughout summer, produces solitary, axillary, tubular scarlet flowers, 1½–2in (4–5cm) long, sometimes with yellow throat markings; the lips are wide open, but the tubular throats are pinched. ↕ 36in (90cm), ↔ 24in (60cm). W. US to Mexico. Zone 6b.
***M. cupreus* 'Whitecroft Scarlet'** see *M.* 'Whitecroft Scarlet'.
M. glutinosus see *M. aurantiacus.*
M. glutinosus* var. *puniceus see *M. puniceus.*

Mimulus x *hybridus* Magic Series

M. guttatus, syn. *M. langsdorfii* (Common large monkey flower). Upright to spreading, vigorous perennial, producing stolons that root at the nodes. Broadly ovate to oval, mid-green leaves, ½–3in (1–8cm) long, are coarsely or sometimes deeply toothed. In summer, racemes of funnel-shaped yellow flowers, ½–1in (1.5–2.5cm) long, are produced. The flowers are often tinged or strongly spotted or marked red at the throats. ↕ to 12in (30cm), ↔ 20–48in (50–120cm). Alaska to California. Zone 7.
***M.* 'Highland Yellow'.** Upright perennial with branching rhizomes and narrowly ovate, sparsely toothed, hairy, pale green leaves, 1¼–3in (3–8cm) long. Trumpet-shaped, pale creamy yellow flowers, 2 per axil, each to 1in (2.5cm) across, usually with few spots, are produced over a long period in summer. ↕ to 8in (20cm), ↔ to 12in (30cm). Zone 8.
***M.* x *hybridus* cultivars** (*M. guttatus* x *M. luteus*). Erect, basally branching, bushy, tender perennials, often grown as annuals, with oval to elliptic, toothed, mid- to dark green leaves, 1¼–3in (3–8cm) long. In summer, they bear axillary, solitary, tubular then flaring, open-mouthed, brightly colored, usually spotted flowers, to 2in (5cm) across. The upper lips of the flowers are 2-lobed, the lower ones 3-lobed. ↕ 5–12in (12–30cm), ↔ to 12in (30cm). Zone 7. **'Calypso'** is available as a mixture, and produces self-colored, bicolored, and spotted flowers in a wide color range, including mixtures of orange, yellow, burgundy-

Mimulus luteus

red, and pink; ↕ 5–9in (13–23cm). Cultivars of **Magic Series** ■ are early-flowering, producing small flowers in a broad range of colors, including bright oranges, yellows, and reds, as well as more unusual pastel shades and bicolors; ↕ 6–8in (15–20cm). **Malibu Series** cultivars are compact, trailing, and floriferous, with self-colored, bicolored, and spotted flowers in mixtures of yellow, orange, and red; useful in hanging baskets; ↕ 6–8in (15–20cm). **Mystic Series** cultivars are compact and early-flowering, producing wine-red or bright red, ivory-white, yellow, rose-pink, or orange flowers, almost entirely without marking or spotting; ↕ 5–9in (13–23cm). **'Viva'** is large and vigorous, bearing large, bright yellow flowers, with a broad red mark on each lobe; ↕ 8–12in (20–30cm).
M. langsdorfii see *M. guttatus.*
***M.* 'Leopard'.** Spreading perennial with branching rhizomes and narrowly ovate, sparsely toothed, hairy, pale green leaves, 1¼–3in (3–8cm) long. Solitary, axillary, trumpet-shaped yellow flowers, 1in (2.5cm) across, spotted reddish brown, are produced over long periods in summer. ↕ to 8in (20cm), ↔ to 12in (30cm). Zone 8.

M. lewisii ■ Upright perennial with oblong-elliptic, minutely toothed, stalkless, softly hairy, glandular, sticky, mid-green leaves, to 3in (8cm) long. Solitary, axillary, tubular, purple-pink to deep rose-pink, sometimes white flowers, 1¼–2in (3–5cm) long, with yellowish white throats, are produced throughout summer. ↕ 24in (60cm), ↔ 18in (45cm). Alaska to California. Zone 6.
M. longiflorus. Variable, erect-branched shrub with lance-shaped to oblong, toothed, sticky, pale green leaves, to 3in (8cm) long, with impressed veins. From spring to summer, bears trumpet-shaped, orange, lemon-yellow to cream, or dark red flowers, to 2½in (6cm) long, with dark orange bands at the mouths, in leafy racemes. ↕↔ 3ft (1m). California, N.W. Mexico. ❀ (min. 41°F/5°C)
M. luteus ■ (Monkey musk, Yellow monkey flower). Vigorous, spreading perennial with decumbent or upright stems and toothed, broadly ovate to oblong, mid-green leaves, ¾–1¼in (2–3cm) long. Yellow flowers, ¾–2in (2–5cm) long, 2 per axil, with dark red or purple-red spots on the petal lobes and throats, are produced from late spring to summer. Self-seeds freely. ↕ 12in (30cm), ↔ to 24in (60cm). Chile. Zone 7.
M. primuloides. Rhizomatous, mat-forming perennial with hairy, oblong to obovate, entire or toothed, light to mid-green leaves, ½–1½in (1–4cm) long. Trumpet-shaped yellow flowers, to ¾in (2cm) long, with red-spotted throats, are produced on short stems, usually 2 per axil, in summer. ↕ to 4in (10cm), ↔ to 8in (20cm). W. US. Zone 5.
M. puniceus, syn. *M. glutinosus* var. *puniceus.* Erect-branched shrub with narrowly lance-shaped, toothed, sticky, dark green leaves, to 3in (8cm) long. Funnel-shaped, brick-red to orange-red flowers, 2in (5cm) long, are produced in leafy racemes from spring to late summer. ↕ 5ft (1.5m). California, N.W. Mexico. ❀ (min. 41°F/5°C)

Mimulus cardinalis

Mimulus lewisii

Mimulus 'Whitecroft Scarlet'

M

M. ringens (Allegheny monkey flower). Erect, hairless perennial with square, branching stems and semi-clasping, lance-shaped to narrowly oblong or inversely lance-shaped, toothed, mid-green leaves, 2–4in (5–10cm) long. Solitary, axillary, tubular, violet, violet-blue, white, or rarely pink flowers, 1¼in (3cm) long, with narrow throats, are produced from early to late summer. ↕ to 36in (90cm), ↔ 12in (30cm). E. North America. Zone 4.
***M.* 'Whitecroft Scarlet'** ■ syn. *M. cupreus* 'Whitecroft Scarlet'. Short-lived, spreading perennial bearing ovate, mid-green leaves, ¾–3in (2–8cm) long, with toothed margins. Many trumpet-shaped, deep scarlet flowers, ¾in (2cm) across, are produced in racemes from early to late summer. ↕ to 4in (10cm), ↔ to 6in (15cm). Zone 8.

▷ ***Mina*** see *Ipomoea*

MIRABILIS

NYCTAGINACEAE

Genus of about 50 species of annuals and tuberous perennials occurring in dry, open habitats in S.W. US and Central and South America. Branched stems bear opposite, ovate leaves. Large, trumpet-shaped, often fragrant flowers, are borne in axillary corymbs or panicles over a long period in summer. Where not hardy, grow most perennial species as annuals, or lift after flowering and overwinter in frost-free conditions. In warmer climates, grow in a border.

• **CULTIVATION** Outdoors, grow in moderately fertile, well-drained soil in full sun, watering freely while in growth. Provide protection from excessive winter moisture. Where marginally hardy, protect perennials with a mulch or lift tubers and store in frost-free conditions over winter, and then plant out in late spring. Under glass, grow in soil-based potting mix, with added grit, in full light. In the growing season, water freely and apply a balanced liquid fertilizer monthly; keep dry in winter.

• **PROPAGATION** Sow seed at 55–64°F (13–18°C) in early spring, or *in situ* after danger of frost has passed. Divide tubers in spring.

• **PESTS AND DISEASES** Prone to white rust, brown rust, and leaf spot.

M. jalapa ■ (Four o'clocks, Marvel of Peru). Bushy perennial with ovate leaves, 2–4in (5–10cm) long. Fragrant, red, pink, magenta, yellow, or white flowers, to 2in (5cm) long, some striped, and often with several colors present on the same plant, are borne from early to late summer. Flowers open in late afternoon and die by morning. ↕↔ 24in (60cm) or more. Peru, tropical North and South America. ❀ (min. 45°F/7°C)

Mirabilis jalapa

MISCANTHUS

POACEAE

Genus of 17–20 species of deciduous or evergreen, tufted or rhizomatous, perennial grasses occurring in moist meadows and marshland from Africa to E. Asia. The reed-like stems bear linear or narrowly lance-shaped, folded, arching, light or mid-green, or blue- or purplish green leaves. Dense, terminal, arching panicles of silky-hairy spikelets are borne in late summer and autumn; flowerheads are more numerous following long, hot summers. In many cases, the dying growth provides russet autumn colors, and is attractive in winter, along with the dried, beige or silvery flowerheads. Grow *Miscanthus* species and cultivars as free-standing specimens, or in a mixed or herbaceous border. They may also be used for a waterside planting or as temporary summer screening. The flowerheads may be used for cutting; they may also be dried.

• **CULTIVATION** Tolerant of most conditions but best in moderately fertile, moist but well-drained soil in full sun. Protect from excessive winter moisture. Where withered stems are left for winter effect, they should be cut to the ground by early spring; however, *M. floridulus* may lose dead foliage in strong winds.

• **PROPAGATION** Sow seed in containers in a cold frame in early spring. Divide as new growth commences in spring; old clumps become woody and difficult to divide. May be slow to establish; pot on divisions or grow in a cold frame or cold or cool greenhouse until established.

• **PESTS AND DISEASES** Infrequent.

Miscanthus sinensis 'Cabaret'

M. floridulus (Amur silvergrass). Deciduous or evergreen, slowly spreading, clump-forming, perennial grass with sturdy, upright stems and downward-arching, linear, glaucous, pale green leaves, to 36in (90cm) long, with silver midribs. Erect, pyramidal panicles, to 20in (50cm) long, of silvery spikelets, are produced in autumn, although these are rarely borne in cooler regions. Often confused with *M. sacchariflorus*. ↕ 9ft (2.5m), ↔ 5ft (1.5m) or more. S.E. Asia. Zone 6b.
M. sacchariflorus (Silver banner grass). Deciduous, robust, clump-forming, perennial grass bearing stiff, flat, linear, blue-green leaves, to 36in (90cm) long, with pale, silver-green midribs. In late summer and early autumn, produces finely hairy, pyramidal or fan-shaped panicles, to 16in (40cm) long, of numerous silky-hairy, silvery white spikelets. ↕ 5–7ft (1.5–2.2m), ↔ 4½ft (1.4m). S.E. Asia. Zone 4.
M. sinensis (Eulalia grass). Deciduous, clump-forming, perennial grass with erect stems and mostly basal, flat, erect or arching, linear, blue-green leaves, to 4ft (1.2m) long. Pyramidal panicles, to 16in (40cm) long, of silky-hairy, pale gray spikelets, tinted maroon or purple-brown, are produced in autumn. ↕ to 12ft (4m), ↔ 4ft (1.2m). S.E. Asia. Zone 4. **'Cabaret'** ■ has broad, mid-green leaves with conspicuous white stripes; ↕ to 6ft (1.8m). **'Cosmopolitan'** is vigorous, with wider and sturdier white-striped leaves. **'Gracillimus'** (Maiden grass) has very narrow, curved leaves with white mid-ribs, becoming bronzed in autumn; ↕ 4½ft (1.3m). **'Kleine Silberspinne'** is lower-growing, bearing open, spidery, white-tinged red panicles, fading to shining white, from late summer to autumn; ↕ 4ft (1.2m). **'Morning Light'** resembles 'Gracillimus' but has narrow white leaf margins, giving a silvery effect; ↕ 4ft (1.2m). **'Pünktchen'** is stiffly upright, with creamy yellow horizontal bands on the leaves; ↕ 4ft (1.2m). **var. *purpurascens*** has leaves that turn purplish green, with pink midribs, in summer, and develop red and orange tones in autumn; ↕ 4ft (1.2m). **'Rotsilber'** bears rich red-tinted silvery panicles in late summer and early autumn, above narrow leaves with prominent silver midribs; ↕ 4ft (1.2m). **'Silberfeder'** ■ syn. 'Silver Feather', is free-flowering, bearing silvery to pale pinkish brown panicles in early and midautumn, remaining through winter; ↕ to 8ft (2.5m). **'Silver Feather'** see 'Silberfeder'. **'Variegatus'** has leaves with creamy white and pale green longitudinal bands; ↕ 6ft (1.8m). **'Zebrinus'** ■ (Zebra grass) is broadly arching, with creamy white or pale yellow horizontal bands on the leaves; ↕ to 4ft (1.2m).
M. yakushimensis. Dense, clump-forming, deciduous, perennial grass with narrowly linear leaves, to 24in (60cm) long; leaves are light green, with silvery pink midribs, and turn yellow in autumn. Slender, open, conical or fan-shaped silvery panicles, to 20in (50cm) long, are produced in late summer and early autumn. ↕ 24–30in (60–75cm), ↔ 30in (75cm). Japan. Zone 6.

Miscanthus sinensis 'Zebrinus'

Miscanthus sinensis 'Silberfeder'

Mitchella repens

MITCHELLA

Partridge berry

RUBIACEAE

Genus of 2 species of trailing, evergreen perennials found in woodland in North America and Japan. The trailing stems root at the nodes and bear opposite, broadly ovate to lance-shaped leaves. Small, funnel-shaped, fragrant white flowers, borne in pairs in summer, are followed by ornamental red berries. Grow in a rock garden or woodland garden as a groundcover.

• **CULTIVATION** Grow in moist but well-drained, humus-rich, acidic soil in light dappled or partial shade.

• **PROPAGATION** Sow seed in containers in a cold frame in autumn. Separate rooted runners in spring.

• **PESTS AND DISEASES** Infrequent.

M. repens ■ (Partridge berry, Running box). Prostrate, mat-forming perennial with broadly ovate, glossy, dark green, white-veined leaves, to ¾in (2cm) long. White, often pink-flushed flowers, ½in (1.5cm) long, are borne in early summer, followed by spherical, bright red berries, to ½in (1.5cm) across. ↕ 2in (5cm), ↔ to 12in (30cm). North America. Zone 4. **f. *leucocarpa*** has white fruit.

MITELLA

Bishop's cap, Miterwort

SAXIFRAGACEAE

Genus of 20 species of clump-forming, rhizomatous perennials occurring in woodland in E. Asia and North America. The long-stalked, lobed, ovate, glossy, mid- or dark green, basal leaves are heart-shaped at the bases. Slender, often one-sided, occasionally leafy racemes of tiny, pendent or horizontal, bell-shaped flowers, each with 5 fringed petals, are borne in summer. Use as a groundcover in a woodland garden.

• **CULTIVATION** Grow in moist but well-drained, leafy, acidic soil in partial or dappled shade. They self-seed freely.

• **PROPAGATION** Sow seed in containers in autumn. Divide in spring.

• **PESTS AND DISEASES** Prone to rust and leaf spot, as well as snails and slugs.

M. breweri ■ (Miterwort). Perennial with hairy, indistinctly lobed, broadly ovate, mid-green leaves, 2–4in (5–10cm) long. In late spring and summer, bears racemes of 20–40

Mitella breweri

yellowish green flowers, 1/16in (2mm) long, with fringed, comb-like petals, on stems to 6in (15cm) tall. ↕ 6in (15cm), ↔ to 8in (20cm). W. to C. North America. Zone 6.

M. stauropetala. Vigorous perennial with broadly ovate, slightly lobed, often purple-tinged, mid-green leaves, 1½–4in (4–10cm) long. In summer, bears racemes of 10–35 white or purple flowers, to ⅛in (3mm) long, with deeply cut and fringed petals, on stems to 20in (50cm) tall. ↕ to 20in (50cm), ↔ to 12in (30cm). North America (Rocky Mountains). Zone 5.

MITRARIA

GESNERIACEAE

Genus of one species of woody, evergreen, scandent or spreading shrub from moist woodland in Chile and Argentina. The leaves are opposite and ovate, and the showy flowers are tubular. *M. coccinea* prefers cool, humid climates. Grow in a woodland garden or sheltered shrub border. Where not hardy, grow in a cool greenhouse.

• **CULTIVATION** Under glass, grow in acidic potting mix in bright filtered light, with moderate to high humidity. In growth, water freely and apply a balanced liquid fertilizer monthly; water sparingly in winter but do not allow to dry out. Outdoors, grow in moist but well-drained, humus-rich, acidic soil in light, dappled shade. Shelter from cold, drying winds. Keep roots cool and shaded, but allow the top to grow into sunlight. Pruning group 9.

Mitraria coccinea

• **PROPAGATION** Sow seed in containers in a cold frame in spring. Root semi-ripe cuttings with bottom heat in summer.

• **PESTS AND DISEASES** Infrequent.

M. coccinea ■ Weakly scandent shrub with opposite, ovate, toothed, leathery, glossy, dark green leaves, to 1in (2.5cm) long. Scarlet flowers, 1¼in (3cm) long, each with 5 small lobes, are borne singly from the leaf axils over a long period from late spring to autumn. ↕ to 6ft (2m). Chile, Argentina. ❀ (min. 45°F/7°C)

▷ ***Modecca digitata*** see *Adenia digitata*

MOLINIA

POACEAE

Genus of 2 species of loosely or densely tufted, perennial grasses found in damp moorland in Europe and N. and S.W. Asia. They are grown for their attractive habit, autumn foliage, and graceful, dense to open panicles of compressed spikelets, each with 4 florets, held well above the foliage. Grow in a mixed or herbaceous border, or woodland garden.

• **CULTIVATION** Grow in any moist but well-drained, preferably acidic to neutral soil, in full sun or partial shade.

• **PROPAGATION** Sow seed of species in containers in a cold frame in spring. Divide species and cultivars in spring, and pot up until established.

• **PESTS AND DISEASES** Infrequent.

M. caerulea (Purple moor grass). Tufted perennial with dense clumps of flat, linear-oblong, mid-green leaves, to 18in (45cm) long, with purple bases. From spring to autumn, bears dense, narrow panicles, 16in (40cm) long, of purple spikelets on yellow-tinted stems. ↕ to 5ft (1.5m), ↔ 6in (40cm). Europe, N. and S.W. Asia. Zone 4. **subsp. *arundinacea* 'Karl Foerster'** ■ has leaves to 32in (80cm) long, and open panicles of purple spikelets on arching stems. **subsp. *arundinacea* 'Sky Racer'** has leaves, to 3ft (1m) long, that turn clear gold in autumn; ↕ to 7ft (2.2m). **'Moorhexe'** is very upright, with dark purple spikelets held tightly against erect stems; ↕ 18in (45cm). **'Variegata'** is tufted and compact, with dark green, cream-striped leaves, ochre stems, and purple spikelets; ↕ 18–24in (45–60cm).

MOLTKIA

BORAGINACEAE

Genus of about 6 species of perennials or shrubs, some evergreen, found in alkaline soils in rock crevices or on open hillsides from N. Italy and Greece to S.W. Asia. They have alternate, oblong or linear to lance-shaped or inversely lance-shaped, hairy, mid- or dark green leaves. Tubular or funnel-shaped, blue, purple, or yellow flowers are borne in short, one-sided, terminal cymes from

Molinia caerulea subsp. *arundinacea* 'Karl Foerster'

Moltkia doerfleri

late spring to summer. Grow in a rock garden, or at the front of a mixed or shrub border.

• **CULTIVATION** Grow in poor, well-drained, preferably alkaline soil in full sun. Protect from excessive winter moisture and shelter from cold, drying winds. Pruning group 10, after flowering, if required.

• **PROPAGATION** Sow seed under glass or in containers in a cold frame in autumn. Root softwood cuttings in early summer. Layer woody species in spring.

• **PESTS AND DISEASES** Susceptible to aphids and whiteflies under glass.

M. doerfleri ■ syn. *Lithospermum doerfleri*. Rhizomatous, woody-based perennial with wiry, upright stems and lance-shaped, mid-green leaves, to 2in (5cm) long. Bears cymes of pendent, narrowly tubular, deep purple flowers, to 1in (2.5cm) long, from late spring to midsummer. ↕↔ 12–20in (30–50cm). N.E. Albania. Zone 7b.

M. x intermedia (*M. petraea* x *M. suffruticosa*), syn. *Lithodora* x *intermedia*. Evergreen, dome-shaped subshrub with linear or narrowly oblong, dark green leaves, to 4in (10cm) long. In early summer, bears compact cymes of open funnel-shaped, bright blue flowers, ½in (1.5cm) long, often pink-tinged in bud. ↕ 6–12in (15–30cm), ↔ to 12in (30cm). Garden origin. Zone 7b.

M. petraea. Semi-evergreen, dwarf shrub with oblong-lance-shaped to linear, inrolled leaves, to 2in (5cm) long, dark green above and white beneath. In summer, pink-purple buds open to funnel-shaped, deep blue or violet-blue flowers, to ⅜in (9mm) long, with prominent stamens, produced in compact cymes. ↕↔ 8–16in (20–40cm). Former Yugoslavia, Albania, Greece. Zone 7b.

M. suffruticosa ■ syn. *Lithodora graminifolia, Lithospermum graminifolium*. Deciduous, upright, loosely branched shrub with narrowly linear, bristly, dark green leaves, to 6in (15cm) long. In summer, tubular, bright blue to purple-blue flowers, to ½in (1.5cm) long, are borne in dense, clustered cymes. ↕↔ to 12in (30cm). N. Italy. Zone 7b.

MOLUCCELLA

LAMIACEAE

Genus of 4 species of erect, branching annuals and short-lived perennials found in fallow fields and on stony slopes from the Mediterranean to N.W. India. The 4-sided stems bear opposite, simple, rounded to ovate, incised or scalloped, mid- to pale green leaves. From summer to autumn, small, tubular, 2-lipped, hooded flowers, with expanded, bell-shaped calyces, are borne in whorls from the upper leaf axils. Grow in a mixed or annual border; the unusual flower spikes are useful for dried flower arrangements.

• **CULTIVATION** Grow in moderately fertile, moist but well-drained soil in full sun.

• **PROPAGATION** Sow seed at 55–64°F (13–18°C) in early or midspring, or *in situ* in late spring.

• **PESTS AND DISEASES** Infrequent.

Moltkia suffruticosa

Moluccella laevis

M. laevis ■ (Bells of Ireland, Shell flower). Annual with very broadly ovate, deeply scalloped, pale green leaves, to 2½in (6cm) long. In late summer, bears whorls of 6–8 fragrant, white to pale purplish pink flowers in spikes 9–12in (23–30cm) tall; each flower is cupped in a pale green calyx, which becomes white-veined and papery in fruit. ↕ 24–36in (60–90cm), ↔ 9in (23cm). Caucasus, Turkey, Syria, Iraq.

MONADENIUM

EUPHORBIACEAE

Genus of about 50 species of bushy, tree-like, or trailing, monoecious, perennial succulents from low to high altitudes in tropical E. Africa, Angola, Namibia, South Africa, and Zimbabwe. Some species produce annual growth from a subterranean, thickened tuber or caudex; others retain fleshy stems all year. The fleshy or scaly leaves may fall quickly. In summer, unusual, small, petalless, diurnal flowers are borne in cup-like bracts within yellow, green, or brown-orange involucres. Where not hardy, grow monadeniums in a warm greenhouse. Elsewhere, grow in a desert garden.

• **CULTIVATION** Under glass, grow in standard cactus potting mix in full light, with low humidity. From spring to summer, water moderately and apply a low-nitrogen liquid fertilizer monthly; keep dry in winter. Outdoors, grow in poor to moderately fertile, sharply drained soil in full sun. Protect from excessive winter moisture. See also pp.48–49.

• **PROPAGATION** Sow seed at 66–75°F (19–24°C) in spring. Root cuttings of stem sections in spring and summer.

• **PESTS AND DISEASES** Infrequent.

M. ellenbeckii. Bushy succulent with thick, fleshy, cylindrical stems, and pitted branches, to 1in (2.5cm) thick, produced at or near the base. A few oval, stiff, fleshy, hairy, mid-green leaves, ½in (1.5cm) long, are produced at the branch tips and soon fall. Yellow-green involucres, with bract-cups ½in (1.5cm) across, form in summer. ↕ 3ft (1m), ↔ 18in (45cm). Ethiopia, Kenya. ❀ (min. 64°F/18°C)

M. lugardiae ■ Erect succulent with a caudiciform base and a spineless stem, to 1¼in (3cm) thick, branching freely at or near the base. Thick, obovate, scalloped to toothed, fleshy leaves, to 3½in (9cm)

Monadenium lugardiae

long, form at the branch tips. Pale green involucres, yellow or orange-brown within, with bract-cups ¼in (6mm) across, are produced in summer. ↕ 24in (60cm), ↔ 18in (45cm). Namibia, South Africa (Northern Transvaal, Eastern Transvaal, KwaZulu/Natal), Zimbabwe. ❀ (min. 64°F/18°C)

***M. montanum* var. *rubellum*.** Low-growing, bushy succulent with twisted, white stems, to ¾in (2cm) thick, branching freely at or near the base. Lance-shaped, dark green leaves, 1in (2.5cm) long, form at the branch tips. Pink involucres with bract-cups, ⅛in (3mm) across, are produced in spring and summer. ↕ 12in (30cm) or more, ↔ to 2½in (6cm). C. Kenya. ❀ (min. 41°F/5°C)

MONANTHES

CRASSULACEAE

Genus of about 12 species of mat-forming or shrubby, perennial or annual succulents from rocky, upland areas in N. Africa and the Canary Islands. Rosettes of fleshy, often warty leaves are crowded at the ends of thick, fleshy branches. Small, star-shaped, diurnal flowers, often in compact racemes or branched cymes, are borne from spring to summer. Where temperatures fall below 45°F (7°C), grow in a temperate greenhouse throughout the year, or use for outdoor bedding from spring to summer. In warmer climates, grow in a rock or desert garden.

• **CULTIVATION** Under glass, grow in standard cactus potting mix in full light. From spring to autumn, water moderately and apply a low-nitrogen liquid fertilizer monthly; keep dry in winter. Outdoors, grow in poor, sharply drained soil in full sun. Protect from excessive winter moisture. See also pp.48–49.

• **PROPAGATION** Sow seed at 66–75°F (19–24°C) in spring. Root stem-tip or leaf cuttings in spring or summer.

• **PESTS AND DISEASES** Infrequent.

M. dasyphylla. Semi-prostrate succulent with thick, inversely lance-shaped, softly hairy, reddish green to dark green leaves, to ¾in (2cm) long, with purple stripes and spots, the inner leaves shorter and incurved. Sub-erect racemes of 2–5 yellow, red-striped flowers, to ¼in (6mm) across, are produced in summer. ↕ to 2in (5cm), ↔ 6in (15cm). Canary Islands (Tenerife). ❀ (min. 45°F/7°C)

Monanthes muralis

M. laxiflora. Shrubby, slightly pendent succulent with opposite, ovate, wrinkled, dark green leaves, to ½in (1.5cm) long. Suberect racemes of 6–10 yellow, sometimes purple flowers, to ½in (1.5cm) across, with minute red spots, are produced from spring to summer. ↕↔ 4in (10cm) or more. Canary Islands. ❄ (min. 45°F/7°C)

M. muralis ▣ Shrubby succulent with dense rosettes of obovate, warty leaves, to ½in (1.5cm) long, marked deep grayish purple or red. From spring to summer, bears racemes of 3–7 yellowish white flowers, ½in (1.5cm) across, with red tufted stamens. ↕ 4in (10cm), ↔ 6in (15cm) or more. Canary Islands (Hierro, Gomera). ❄ (min. 45°F/7°C)

M. polyphylla. Mat- or cushion-forming succulent with cylindrical to club-shaped, pale green leaves, to ½in (1.5cm) long. From spring to summer, produces erect racemes, usually with 1–4 red flowers, ½in (1.5cm) across, with white-hairy stalks and calyces. ↕ to 5in (13cm), ↔ indefinite. Canary Islands. ❄ (min. 45°F/7°C)

MONARDA

Bee balm

LAMIACEAE

Genus of about 15 species of annuals and clump-forming, rhizomatous herbaceous perennials occurring in dry scrub, prairies, and woodland in North America. Simple or sparsely branching, square stems bear alternate, opposite, lance-shaped to oval, usually toothed but sometimes entire, aromatic, mid- to dark green or purple-green leaves with conspicuous veins. From midsummer to early autumn, tubular, sage-like, white, pink, red, or violet flowers, often with colored bracts, are produced in terminal whorls. Each flower has 2 lips, the upper one hooded and erect, the lower one 3-lobed and more spreading. A number of cultivars and hybrids (with *M. fistulosa*) have been selected from *M. didyma.* They have ovate, toothed, usually dark

Monarda 'Beauty of Cobham'

green leaves, to 5½in (14cm) long, sometimes softly hairy beneath. Flowers, to 2in (5cm) long, are produced in whorls, with usually red-tinged bracts. Monardas are long flowering and suitable for the middle of a mixed or herbaceous border. They are also attractive to bees and hummingbirds.

• **CULTIVATION** Grow in moderately fertile, humus-rich, moist but well-drained soil in full sun or dappled shade. Protect from excessive winter moisture; do not allow to dry out in summer.

• **PROPAGATION** Sow seed in containers in a cold frame in spring or autumn. Divide clumps in spring, before new growth commences. Root basal cuttings in spring.

• **PESTS AND DISEASES** Prone to powdery mildew, rust, and leaf spot.

***M.* 'Adam'.** Clump-forming perennial bearing cherry-red flowers from midsummer to early autumn. ↕ 36in (90cm), ↔ 18in (45cm). Zone 4.

***M.* 'Beauty of Cobham'** ▣ Clump-forming perennial with purplish green leaves. Pale pink flowers, with purple-pink bracts, are produced from midsummer to early autumn. ↕ 36in (90cm), ↔ 18in (45cm). Zone 3b.

***M.* 'Blaustrumpf'**, syn. *M.* 'Blue Stocking'. Clump-forming perennial bearing deep violet-purple flowers, with purple bracts, from midsummer to early autumn. ↕ 36in (90cm), ↔ 18in (45cm). Zone 4.

***M.* 'Blue Stocking'** see *M.* 'Blaustrumpf'.

***M.* 'Cambridge Scarlet'** ▣ Clump-forming perennial producing rich scarlet-red flowers, with brownish red calyces, from midsummer to early autumn. ↕ 36in (90cm), ↔ 18in (45cm). Zone 3b.

***M.* 'Croftway Pink'** ▣ Clump-forming perennial producing clear rose-pink flowers, with pink-tinged bracts, from midsummer to early autumn. ↕ 36in (90cm), ↔ 18in (45cm). Zone 3b.

M. didyma (Bee balm, Bergamot, Oswego tea). Bushy, clump-forming perennial with branching, square stems and ovate to ovate-lance-shaped, dull, mid-green leaves, to 5½in (14cm) long, softly hairy beneath. From mid- to late summer, each flowering stem bears 1 or 2 whorls of bright scarlet or pink flowers, 1¼–1¾in (3–4.5cm) long, with red-tinged bracts. ↕ 36in (90cm) or more, ↔ 24in (60cm). E. North America. Zone 4. **'Aquarius'** has bronze-green foliage and light pink-purple flowers; mildew resistant; ↕ 3–4ft (1–1.2m). **'Balance'** bears bright pink flowers; ↕ to 3½ft (1.1m). **'Bowman'** has purple flowers; mildew resistant; ↕ to 4ft (1.2m). **'Capricornus'** produces purple-green foliage and pink flowers; ↕ to 4ft (1.2m). **'Fishes'** has pale pink flowers with green throats; ↕ 4ft (1.2m). **'Gardenview Scarlet'** has very large scarlet flowers; mildew resistant; ↕ 24–36in (60–90cm). **'Marshall's Delight'** has shiny, light green leaves and clear, mid-pink flowers; highly resistant to powdery mildew; ↕ 30–36in (75–90cm). **Panorama Hybrids** cultivars bloom in shades of scarlet, pink, and salmon; ↕ 30in (75cm). **'Purple Crown'** see 'Purpurkrone' **'Purpurkrone',** syn. 'Purple Crown', has purple flowers. **'Squaw'** has clear red flowers; ↕ 4ft (1.2m). **'Twins'** has dark pink flowers; mildew resistant; ↕ 30in (75cm). **'Violet Queen'** has violet-purple flowers; resistant to mildew; ↕ 30–36in (75–90cm).

M. fistulosa (Wild bee balm). Bushy, clump-forming perennial with branching stems, more rounded than *M. didyma.* Bears ovate to ovate-lance-shaped, softly hairy, dull, mid-green leaves, 1½–4in (4–10cm) long. From mid- to late summer or early autumn, bears lilac-purple or pale pink flowers, ¾–1¼in (2–3cm) long, with purple-tinged bracts. ↕ 4ft (1.2m), ↔ 18in (45cm). E. North America. Zone 4.

***M.* 'Loddon Crown'.** Clump-forming perennial bearing rich, dark red-purple flowers, with purplish brown bracts and calyces, from midsummer to early

Monarda 'Cambridge Scarlet'

Monarda 'Croftway Pink'

Monarda 'Mahogany'

Monarda 'Prärienacht'

autumn. ↕ 36in (90cm), ↔ 18in (45cm). Zone 3b.

***M.* 'Mahogany'** ▣ Clump-forming perennial bearing wine-red flowers, with brownish red bracts, from midsummer to early autumn. ↕ 36in (90cm), ↔ 18in (45cm). Zone 3b.

***M.* 'Prairie Night'** see *M.* 'Prärienacht'.

***M.* 'Prärienacht'** ▣ syn. *M.* 'Prairie Night'. Clump-forming perennial bearing purple-lilac flowers, with green, slightly red-tinged bracts, from midsummer to early autumn. ↕ 3–4ft (1–1.2m), ↔ 18in (45cm). Zone 4.

M. punctata (Spotted bee-balm). Highly variable annual, biennial, or perennial with softly hairy to bristled, branching stems and lance-shaped to oblong, toothed, often softly hairy leaves, ½–3½in (1.5–9cm) long. Bears whorled, purple-spotted, yellow or pink flowers, ½–1in (1.5–2.5cm) across, with pink to lavender bracts, from midsummer to early autumn. ↕ 12–36in (30–90cm), ↔ 10–18in (25–45cm). Coastal E. US. Zone 4. **subsp. *corryi*** is a perennial and has unspotted, pink flowers; Texas. **subsp. *punctata*** is a perennial or biennial with unbristled, softly hairy stems and sparsely hairy leaves. Coastal E. US.

MONARDELLA

LAMIACEAE

Genus of about 20 species of annuals and herbaceous perennials, often with creeping stems, occurring mainly on dry, stony slopes in W. North America. The small, opposite, aromatic, entire or toothed leaves are linear to diamond-lance-shaped, oblong, ovate, or elliptic. Terminal, spherical whorls of 2-lipped, tubular flowers (the upper lip 2-lobed and the lower one 3-lobed), often with purplish red, leaf-like bracts, are produced in summer. Suitable for a rock garden, the front of a mixed border, or an alpine house.

• **CULTIVATION** Grow in poor, sharply drained soil in full sun. Protect from excessive winter moisture, and shelter from cold, drying winds. In an alpine house, grow in shallow containers in a mix of equal parts soil-based potting mix and grit.

• **PROPAGATION** Sow seed under glass in autumn. Divide, or root basal or softwood cuttings in spring, both with bottom heat.

• **PESTS AND DISEASES** Prone to rust, aphids, and whiteflies.

M. macrantha. Deciduous, decumbent, woody-based perennial producing spreading branches and ovate to elliptic, toothed, hairy, slightly leathery, mid-green leaves, to 1¼in (3cm) long. In mid- and late summer, tubular scarlet flowers, ½in (1.5cm) long, are borne in whorls, 1¼–1½in (3–4cm) across, surrounded by purplish red bracts. ↕ 6in (15cm), ↔ to 8in (20cm). California. ❀ (min. 41°F/5°C)

MONSTERA

ARACEAE

Genus of 22 species of evergreen, often epiphytic root climbers found in rainforest in tropical North, Central, and South America. The alternate leaves usually differ in size and shape on young and mature plants, but are mainly ovate and entire, lobed, or deeply pinnatifid. On mature plants, arum-like spathes, enclosing tiny, star-shaped, petalless flowers, are produced singly from the leaf axils. Where temperatures fall below 59°F (15°C), grow in a warm greenhouse or as houseplants. In warmer climates, grow up palm trees or on an arch or pergola. The fruit of *M. deliciosa* taste of pineapple when fully ripe. Other parts may cause mild stomach upset if ingested, and contact with the fruit may irritate skin.

• **CULTIVATION** Under glass, grow in soil-based potting mix, in bright indirect light with moderate to high humidity. In the growing season, water freely and apply a balanced liquid fertilizer monthly; water sparingly in winter. Outdoors, grow in humus-rich, moist but well-drained soil in partial shade. Pruning group 11, in spring; plants grown under glass may require restrictive pruning.

• **PROPAGATION** Sow seed at 64–75°F (18–24°C) as soon as ripe. Root tip or leaf cuttings with bottom heat in summer. Layer in autumn.

• **PESTS AND DISEASES** Prone to scale insects, spider mites, bacterial soft rot and leaf spots, and a few fungal spots.

M. deliciosa ▣ (Ceriman, Mexican breadfruit, Swiss cheese plant, Windowleaf). Robust, strong-growing climber with thick, sparingly branched stems. Mature plants produce broadly ovate to heart-shaped, long-stalked, leathery, glossy, mid- to deep green leaves, 12–36in (30–90cm) long. Each leaf is pinnatifid and often perforated

Monstera deliciosa

with elliptic to oblong holes between the main lateral veins. Juvenile leaves are shorter-stalked, much smaller, and entire. Creamy white spathes, 8–12in (20–30cm) long, are borne usually from spring to summer; they are sometimes followed by edible, cone-shaped cream fruit, to 10in (25cm) long. ↕ 30–70ft (10–20m). S. Mexico to Panama. ❀ (min. 59°F/15°C). **'Albovariegata'** produces leaves with irregular, creamy white patches. **'Variegata'** produces leaves splashed and marbled yellowish cream; very likely to revert to green.

***M. latevaginata* of gardens** see *Rhaphidophora celatocaulis.*

▷ ***Montbretia*** see *Crocosmia*

MORAEA

IRIDACEAE

Genus of about 120 species of deciduous or semi-deciduous, cormous perennials, occurring in seasonally moist grassland throughout Africa. The linear or lance-shaped, flat or rolled, often channeled, light to mid-green leaves may be basal or borne on the stems. From spring to summer, a succession of short-lived, colorful, iris-like flowers are produced in clusters within pairs of large bracts. In frost-free climates, some species, such as *M. angusta, M. moggii,* and *M. spathulata,* are evergreen. Where not hardy, grow in a cool greenhouse. In warmer climates, moreas are attractive in a mixed border or a rock garden; where marginally hardy, grow at the base of a warm, sunny wall and provide a deep, dry, winter mulch.

• **CULTIVATION** Plant 3in (8cm) deep in spring or autumn. Outdoors, grow in well-drained, humus-rich, moderately fertile soil in full sun with some midday shade. Provide protection from excessive winter moisture. Under glass, grow in soil-based potting mix, with additional sharp sand, in full light. Water sparingly as growth begins, then freely when in full growth. Dry off as leaves wither, in order to ensure a dry dormancy from midsummer to autumn.

• **PROPAGATION** Sow seed in a cold frame in spring or autumn. Separate offsets when dormant.

• **PESTS AND DISEASES** Prone to rust.

M. angusta. Cormous perennial producing a solitary, erect, linear, rolled, stem leaf, to 24in (60cm) long. Bears brown- or gray-tinged yellow flowers, 2½–3in (6–8cm) across, in spring. ↕ 8–16in (20–40cm), PD3in (8cm). South Africa (S. Western Cape). ❀ (min. 41°F/5°C)

M. aristata, syn. *M. glaucopis.* Cormous perennial producing a solitary, erect, narrowly linear, flat, basal leaf, to 18in (45cm) long. White flowers, 2–3in (5–8cm) across, with conspicuous, green, blue, or violet central eyes on the outer tepals, are produced on occasionally branched stems in late spring. ↕ 10–14in (25–35cm), PD3in (8cm). South Africa. ❀ (min. 41°F/5°C)

M. glaucopis see *M. aristata.*

M. huttonii ▣ Cormous perennial with a solitary, semi-erect, narrowly linear, flat or channeled, basal leaf, to 3ft (1m) long. Scented, golden yellow flowers, to 3in (8cm) across, with brown marks and deeper yellow eyes toward the centers,

Moraea huttonii

are produced on occasionally branched stems from spring to early summer. Similar to *M. spathulata,* but with purple-brown marks on the styles. ↕ 28–36in (70–90cm), PD3in (8cm). South Africa (KwaZulu/Natal), Lesotho. ❀ (min. 41°F/5°C)

M. moggii. Robust, cormous perennial with a solitary, erect, narrowly linear, basal leaf, to 24in (60cm) long, channeled at the base and rolled at the tip. Yellow, sometimes cream or white flowers, to 2in (5cm) across, with bright yellow and purple veins on the outer tepals, are produced in late summer. One of the easier species to grow. ↕ 28in (70cm), PD3in (8cm). South Africa (KwaZulu/Natal), Swaziland. ❀ (min. 41°F/5°C)

M. natalensis. Cormous perennial with a solitary, narrowly linear, channeled leaf, to 8in (20cm) long, borne near the top of the stem. In summer, produces lilac or violet-blue flowers, 1–1¼in (2.5–3cm) across, with a conspicuous yellow central mark, ringed dark mauve, on each of the outer tepals. ↕ to 18in (45cm), PD3in (8cm). Zaire, Zambia, Malawi, Zimbabwe, Mozambique, South Africa (KwaZulu/Natal, Eastern Transvaal). ❀ (min. 41°F/5°C)

M. polystachya ▣ Cormous perennial bearing 3–5 erect but later spreading, linear, channeled to almost flat leaves, to 32in (80cm) long, on branching stems. In summer, bears violet to pale blue flowers, 2½–3in (6–8cm) across, with a conspicuous, white-margined yellow mark at the center of each outer tepal. ↕ to 32in (80cm), PD3in (8cm). Namibia, Botswana, South Africa (Northern

Moraea polystachya

Moraea ramosissima

Cape, Eastern Cape, W. Northern Transvaal). ❀ (min. 41°F/5°C)
M. ramosissima ▣ Cormous perennial with numerous semi-erect, narrowly linear, channeled, basal leaves, 12–20in (30–50cm) long. Produces yellow flowers, 1½–2½in (4–6cm) across, with deeper yellow centers, on many-branched stems from spring to early summer. Produces offset corms. ↕ 20–48in (50–120cm), PD4in (10cm). South Africa. ❀ (min. 41°F/5°C)
M. spathacea see *M. spathulata*.
M. spathulata, syn. *M. spathacea*. Robust, cormous perennial with a solitary, semi-erect, narrowly linear, flat or channeled, basal leaf, to 32in (80cm) long. Golden yellow flowers, to 3½in (9cm) across, are produced in early and midsummer. The outer tepals each have a deep yellow to orange-yellow central mark and purple-brown margins. Similar to *M. huttonii* but more robust and with larger flowers. ↕ 20–36in (50–90cm), PD3in (8cm). Zimbabwe, Mozambique, Swaziland, Lesotho, South Africa (KwaZulu/Natal, Northern Transvaal, Eastern Transvaal, Eastern Cape). ❀ (min. 41°F/5°C)
M. tripetala. Cormous perennial with a solitary (occasionally 2), trailing, linear or lance-shaped, channeled, basal leaf, 8–24in (20–60cm) long. In spring, pale or deep blue, purple, pink, or sometimes yellow flowers, 1½–2in (4–5cm) across, are produced on occasionally branched stems; the 3 large outer tepals each have a white or yellow central mark. ↕ 4–20in (10–50cm), PD3in (8cm). South Africa (Northern Cape, Western Cape, Eastern Cape). ❀ (min. 41°F/5°C)
M. villosa. Very variable, cormous perennial with a solitary, trailing, narrowly linear, channeled, basal leaf, 8–20in (20–50cm) long. In early spring, branched stems bear white, cream, pink, orange, vivid blue, lilac, or purple flowers, 2–3in (5–8cm) across. The outer tepals each have a yellow central mark, surrounded by 1 or 2 darker yellow, purple, or black bands. ↕ 6–16in (15–40cm), PD2in (5cm). South Africa (Northern Cape, Western Cape, Eastern Cape). ❀ (min. 41°F/5°C). **subsp. *elandsmontana*** has usually unbranched stems bearing orange flowers with dark blue-edged nectar guides; occasionally produces white flowers with brown nectar guides. **subsp. *villosa*** bears flowers in pink, blue, or purple, sometimes cream or green, usually on branched stems.

MORINA *syn.* ACANTHOCALYX

MORINACEAE

Genus of 4 or 5 species of evergreen perennials found on open, rocky and grassy slopes and in open woodland in E. Europe, Turkey to C. Asia, the Himalayas, and S.W. China. They have rosettes of lance-shaped, glossy, mid- to dark green leaves with spiny-toothed, wavy margins; the leaves become smaller near the tops of the stems. Whorled, spiny bracts are held immediately below spikes of tubular, red, pink, white, or yellow flowers, borne in whorled clusters. Each flower has a long perianth tube and a wide, 2-lipped mouth. Grow in a mixed or herbaceous border; *M. persica* is suitable for a rock garden. The seed heads are useful for dried flower arrangements.

• **CULTIVATION** Grow in poor or moderately fertile, sharply drained soil in full sun. Protect from winter moisture.
• **PROPAGATION** Sow seed in a cold frame as soon as ripe, with one seed per container of gritty seed-starting mix. *M. persica* is difficult to germinate. Overwinter young plants in a well-ventilated cold frame. Insert root cuttings in winter.
• **PESTS AND DISEASES** Susceptible to slug damage and rot, especially in shade.

M. longifolia ▣ (Whorlflower). Rosette-forming perennial with linear to oblong, pinnatifid, aromatic, glossy, dark green basal leaves, to 10in (25cm) long, with sharp marginal spines. In midsummer, tiered, whorled clusters of waxy white flowers, 1¼in (3cm) long, are produced in spikes; flowers become rose-pink then red after fertilization. ↕ to 36in (90cm) or more, ↔ 12in (30cm). Himalayas. Zone 6.
M. persica. Rosette-forming perennial with linear to elliptic, deeply lobed to pinnatifid, very spiny, dark green basal leaves, to 8in (20cm) long. In mid- and late summer, numerous flowering stems bear dense whorls of bracts below spikes of whorled clusters of scented flowers, 1¼–1½in (3–4cm) long; flowers are white, sometimes with yellow-flushed throats, and become pink or reddish pink after fertilization. ↕ to 5ft (1.5m), ↔ 24in (60cm). S. and E. Balkans, Turkey, Iran. Zone 6.

Morina longifolia

MORISIA

BRASSICACEAE

Genus of one species of compact, rosette-forming, taprooted perennial occurring in sandy areas of Corsica and Sardinia. It produces pinnatifid leaves and almost stemless, cross-shaped flowers. Grow in a rock garden, scree bed, trough, or alpine house.

• **CULTIVATION** Grow in moderately fertile, sharply drained soil in full sun. Protect from excessive winter moisture. In an alpine house, use a mix of equal parts soil-based potting mix and grit.
• **PROPAGATION** Sow seed in containers in a cold frame in spring. Insert root cuttings in a cold frame in winter.
• **PESTS AND DISEASES** Neck rot may be a problem in very damp conditions.

M. hypogaea see *M. monanthos*.
M. monanthos ▣ syn. *M. hypogaea*. Perennial with rosettes of lance-shaped, pinnatifid, slightly fleshy, glossy, dark green leaves, 2–3in (5–8cm) long, with oblong segments. Bears almost stemless, golden yellow flowers, to ½in (1.5cm) across, in late spring and early summer. ↕ 2in (5cm), ↔ to 4in (10cm). Corsica, Sardinia. Zone 7b. **'Fred Hemingway'** has flowers to ¾in (2cm) across.

MORUS

Mulberry

MORACEAE

Genus of about 10 species of upright to rounded, deciduous shrubs and trees found mainly in woodland in Africa, Asia, and North and South America. The alternate, ovate to rounded, toothed leaves, often lobed and heart-shaped at the bases, are light to dark green. In late spring and early summer, tiny, cup-shaped, pale green male and female flowers are borne in separate catkins on the same plant; each female flower cluster develops into a single, spherical to oblong, edible, raspberry-like fruit. Grow most as specimen trees; *M. nigra* and *M. rubra* are the best species for edible fruit, often used in making jam and wine. The leaves of several species are used to feed silkworms.

• **CULTIVATION** Grow in moderately fertile, moist but well-drained soil in full sun. Shelter from cold, drying winds. Pruning group 1, in late autumn or early winter, since trees bleed at other times.
• **PROPAGATION** Sow seed in containers outdoors in autumn. Root semi-ripe cuttings in summer. Root hardwood cuttings in a prepared bed in a cold frame in autumn; thick pieces of 2- to 4-year-old wood, known as "truncheons," will also root if treated as hardwood cuttings. Bud cultivars in summer.
• **PESTS AND DISEASES** Bacterial leaf scorch, coral spot, powdery mildew, butt rot, canker, Southern blight, root rot, borers, scale insects, and mealybugs can occur.

Morisia monanthos

Morus australis 'Unryu'

M. alba, syn. *M. bombycis* (White mulberry). Spreading tree with ovate to heart-shaped, sometimes lobed, glossy, bright green leaves, to 8in (20cm) long, turning yellow in autumn. Ovoid, insipid-tasting white fruit, to 1in (2.5cm) long, ripening to pink and red, are borne in late summer. ↕↔ 30ft (10m). China. Zone 3. **'Laciniata'** has deeply lobed leaves. **'Pendula'** is weeping, and produces pendent shoots; ↕ 10ft (3m), ↔ 15ft (5m).
***M. australis* 'Unryu'** ▣ Spreading shrub or small tree with zigzag and twisted branches, and ovate, glossy, dark green leaves, 6–7in (15–18cm) long, turning bright yellow in autumn. Ovoid white fruit, ½–1in (1.5–2cm) long, ripen to pink- or purple-violet in midsummer. ↕ 20–30ft (6–10m), ↔ 10–15ft (3–5m). Zone 6b.
M. bombycis see *M. alba*.
M. nigra ▣ (Black mulberry). Rounded tree with ovate to heart-shaped, often doubly toothed, mid-green leaves, to 6in (15cm) long, rough-textured above. Ovoid, green fruit, to 1in (2.5cm) long, turn red then dark purple in summer, and have a pleasant, slightly acidic flavor. ↕ 40ft (12m), ↔ 50ft (15m). Origin probably S.W. Asia. Zone 6.
M. rubra (Red mulberry). Rounded tree with broadly ovate, sometimes lobed leaves, usually to 5in (13cm) long but sometimes more, with heart-shaped bases and abruptly pointed tips; they are dark green, turning yellow in autumn. Cylindrical, sweet-tasting fruit, to 1¼in (3cm) long, ripen to dark purple in late summer. ↕ 40ft (12m), ↔ 50ft (15m). S.E. Canada, E. US. Zone 6.

Morus nigra

MUCUNA

FABACEAE

Genus of about 100 species of herbaceous and woody-stemmed, evergreen, twining climbers and shrubs from woodland in tropical regions worldwide. The 3-palmate leaves are alternate or arranged in spirals. *Mucuna* species are grown for their large, pea-like flowers, with prominent, curved and pointed, keeled petals, which are borne in showy, pendent, axillary racemes. Where temperatures fall below the minimum levels given below, grow in a temperate or warm greenhouse. In warmer areas, use to clothe an arch, pergola, or trellis.
• **CULTIVATION** Under glass, grow in soil-based potting mix in bright filtered light. In growth, water freely and apply a balanced liquid fertilizer monthly; water sparingly in winter. Outdoors, grow in moderately fertile, moist but well-drained soil in full sun, with some midday shade. Pruning group 11 or 12 outdoors; group 12 under glass. Prune after flowering.
• **PROPAGATION** Sow seed at 64–75°F (18–24°C) in spring.
• **PESTS AND DISEASES** Root rot, Southern blight, and leaf spot, as well as spider mites and whiteflies, can occur.

M. bennettii ▣ (New Guinea creeper). Fast-growing, woody-stemmed climber with sparingly to moderately branched, wrinkled stems, and dark green leaves with elliptic to oblong leaflets, 4½–5½in (11–14cm) long. Short, dense racemes of scarlet to flame-red flowers, 3–5in (8–13cm) long, with downy orange calyces, are borne mainly in summer. ↕ to 70ft (20m) or more. New Guinea. ❀ (min. 59°F/15°C)
M. pruriens. Semi-woody, annual or short-lived perennial climber bearing branched stems with a rough covering of long, bristly hairs when young, eventually becoming hairless. Leaves are mid-green with elliptic to oblong leaflets, 2–6in (5–15cm) long. From late spring to summer, produces racemes of deep blackish purple to lilac or white flowers, ¾–1½in (2–4cm) long, with downy, pale brown calyces. ↕ 12ft (4m). Tropical Asia, widely naturalized elsewhere. ❀ (min. 45°F/7°C)

Mucuna bennettii

MUEHLENBECKIA

POLYGONACEAE

Genus of 20 species of dioecious, deciduous and evergreen shrubs (sometimes mat-forming with runners) and twining, woody climbers, from rocky areas and woodland in New Guinea, Australia, New Zealand, and South America. They are cultivated for their intricate habit; their minute, alternate, linear to rounded leaves (absent in some species); and their tiny, cup-shaped, sweet-scented flowers, produced singly or in pairs, in axillary clusters or spikes, or in terminal or axillary racemes or panicles. The shrubs are suitable for a border, the climbing species for clothing an arch, pergola, or trellis. *M. complexa* is also useful as a groundcover. Where not hardy, grow in containers in a temperate greenhouse.
• **CULTIVATION** Grow in moderately fertile, moist but well-drained soil in full sun, with some midday shade. Provide shelter from cold, drying winds and suitable support where required. Pruning group 11, after flowering; may need restrictive pruning under glass.
• **PROPAGATION** Sow seed at 66–75°F (19–24°C) as soon as ripe. Root semi-ripe cuttings in summer.
• **PESTS AND DISEASES** Infrequent.

M. adpressa (Climbing lignum, Macquarie vine). Small, deciduous, wiry-stemmed climber with lance-shaped to broadly ovate, glossy, dark green leaves, ½–2½in (1–6cm) long, with crinkly margins and often heart-shaped bases. From spring to summer, whitish green flowers are produced in short, axillary spikes, 1–3in (2.5–8cm) long. ↕ 6ft (2m) or more. Coastal temperate Australia. ❀ (min. 41°F/5°C)
M. axillaris. Small, deciduous, prostrate or spreading, many-branched shrub, often rooting at the nodes, with broadly ovate-oblong to rounded, mid-green leaves, 2–4in (5–10cm) long; used in rock gardens. Cup-shaped, yellowish green flowers are produced singly or in pairs from the leaf axils, from summer to early autumn. ↕ 8in (20cm), ↔ 32in (80cm). S.E. Australia, New Zealand. ❀ (min. 35°F/2°C)
***M. axillaris* of gardens** see *M. complexa*.
M. complexa, syn. *M. axillaris* of gardens (Maidenhair vine). Vigorous, deciduous, creeping shrub or twining climber with slender shoots and rounded to violin-shaped, dark green leaves, ¼–½in (0.5–1.5cm) long. Bears greenish white flowers in terminal and axillary racemes, 1–1¼in (2.5–3cm) long, in summer, followed by fleshy white fruit, ¼in (6mm) across. ↕ 10ft (3m). New Zealand. ❀ (min. 35°F/2°C).
var. *microphylla* has only a few, rounded leaves; ↕ to 24in (60cm).
'Nana' is dwarf, with violin-shaped leaves; ↕ to 6ft (2m). **var. *triloba*** has deeply lobed, violin-shaped leaves, ½–1½in (1.5–4cm) long.
M. platyclados see *Homalocladium platycladum*.

MUKDENIA

syn. ACERIPHYLLUM

SAXIFRAGACEAE

Genus of 2 species of slowly spreading herbaceous perennials from woodland in N.E. Asia. They have short, thick rhizomes and large, long-stalked, palmately 5- to 9-lobed, toothed leaves. Leafless panicles or racemes of small, bell-shaped, 5- to 6-petaled white flowers are borne in spring. *Mukdenia* species are suitable for a woodland garden, and grow best in areas with cool, damp summers.
• **CULTIVATION** Grow in leafy, moist but well-drained soil in light dappled or partial shade.
• **PROPAGATION** Sow seed in containers in a cold frame in autumn. Divide in spring, just before buds expand.
• **PESTS AND DISEASES** Slugs and snails may damage young leaves.

M. rossii, syn. *Aceriphyllum rossii*. Perennial with short, thick rhizomes and palmately 5- to 9-lobed, bronze-tinted, mid-green leaves, 6in (15cm) across. Dense, short-branched panicles of creamy white flowers, to ¼in (6mm) across, are borne above the leaves in spring. ↕ to 14in (35cm), ↔ to 16in (40cm) or more. N. China, Korea. Zone 7b.

▷***Mulgedium*** see *Cicerbita*

MUSA

Banana, Plantain

MUSACEAE

Genus of 40 species of evergreen, palm-like, suckering perennials found in light woodland and at forest margins, in N.E. India and Bangladesh, and from S.E. Asia to Japan and N. Australia. The leaf blades are huge and often paddle-shaped (although the shape may vary), and light to mid-green, or gray-green; the leaf sheaths form false stems. In summer, clusters of tubular flowers are produced from the axils of broad, colorful bracts in erect or pendent spikes. The cylindrical fruits are edible; several different species and cultivars produce the bananas and plantains of commerce. Where not hardy, grow in a temperate greenhouse (in a border or containers), or plant out in a subtropical, summer bedding design. In warmer climates, grow as specimen plants.
• **CULTIVATION** Under glass, grow in soil-based potting mix in full light, with shade from hot sun. From spring to summer, water freely and apply a balanced liquid fertilizer monthly; keep just moist in winter. Repot ornamental species annually or every other year, in spring. For bedding, plant out when danger of frost has passed; lift and pot up in autumn. Outdoors, grow in humus-rich soil in full sun and in a sheltered position, since wind will cause the large leaves to shred, especially on soft new growth.
• **PROPAGATION** Sow seed as soon as ripe at 70–75°F (21–24°C). Pre-soak spring-sown seed for 24 hours. Separate suckers in early spring, removing the older leaves to promote faster establishment. Divide established clumps of smaller species every 3–5 years.

M

• **PESTS AND DISEASES** Spider mites, aphids, mealybugs, burrowing nema-tode, cucumber mosaic virus, black leaf streak, anthracnose, and wilt can occur.

M. acuminata, syn. *M. cavendishii.* Upright, very variable, suckering perennial with false stems and paddle-shaped, glaucous, mid-green leaf blades, 6–10ft (2–3m) long, with brown, papery margins. In summer, pendent, pear-shaped, white, cream, or yellow flowers, ¾–1¼in (2–3cm) long, with dull purple bracts, are produced in 2 rows per bract, followed by edible fruit, 6–8in (15–20cm) long, which are yellow when ripe. ↕ 12–20ft (4–6m), ↔ 6–10ft (2–3m). S.E. Asia to N. Australia. ❀ (min. 45°F/7°C). **'Dwarf Cavendish'**, syn. 'Basrai', *M.* x *paradisiaca* 'Dwarf Cavendish' (Edible banana), has oblong, mid-green leaf blades, to 5ft (1.5m) long. Pendent clusters of yellow flowers, with reddish purple bracts, are produced irregularly throughout the year. Seedless yellow fruit, to 8in (20cm) long, borne in long bunches, have sweet-tasting white pulp. A suitable cultivar for general garden cultivation; should produce fruit annually if a minimum temperature of 59–64°F (15–18°C) is maintained. ↕↔ to 10ft (3m).
M. arnoldiana see *Ensete ventricosum.*
M. basjoo ■ syn. *M. japonica* (Japanese banana). Suckering perennial with slender false stems, green at first, becoming papery with age, and arching, oblong-lance-shaped, bright green leaf blades, to 10ft (3m) long. In summer, produces pale yellow or cream flowers, ¾–1¼in (2–3cm) long, with large brown bracts, in pendent, terminal spikes, followed by unpalatable, yellowish green fruit, 2½in (6cm) long, with black seeds in white pulp. ↕ to 15ft (5m), ↔ to 12ft (4m). Japan (including Ryukyu Islands). ❀ (min. 41°F/5°C)
M. cavendishii see *M. acuminata.*
M. coccinea, syn. *M. uranoscopus* (Scarlet banana). Suckering perennial with reddish green false stems, becoming papery with age. Produces oval to elliptic leaf blades, 3ft (1m) long, glossy, bright green above, paler and waxy beneath. In summer, bears erect spirals of tubular yellow flowers, ¾–1¼in (2–3cm) long, enclosed in bright red bracts,

Musa basjoo

Musa ornata

followed by orange-yellow fruit, 2in (5cm) long, with black seeds. Good for containers and cut flowers. ↕↔ 5ft (1.5m). S.E. Asia (S. China, Vietnam, Laos, Cambodia). ❀ (min. 45°F/7°C)
M. ensete see *Ensete ventricosum.*
M. japonica see *M. basjoo.*
M. ornata ■ (Flowering banana). Suckering perennial with oblong to elliptic, waxy, slightly glaucous, blue-green leaf blades, 6ft (2m) long. Produces yellowish orange flowers, 1¼in (3cm) long, with purplish pink bracts, on short, erect false stems at various times of year, followed by greenish yellow fruit, 2½in (6cm) long, with black seeds. ↕ to 10ft (3m), ↔ to 12ft (4m). Bangladesh. ❀ (min. 45°F/7°C)
***M. x paradisiaca* 'Dwarf Cavendish'** see *M. acuminata* 'Dwarf Cavendish'.
M. uranoscopus see *M. coccinea.*
M. velutina. Upright perennial with a yellow-green to purple-green stem, and oblong, dark green leaf blades, to 3ft (1m) long, paler with red midribs beneath. Irregularly throughout the year, produces erect spikes of white flowers, to 1¼in (3cm) long, with purple-haired bracts, followed by softly hairy, pink fruit, 3½in (9cm) long, with black seeds in white pulp. ↕ to 5ft (1.5m), ↔ 36in (90cm). N.E. India. ❀ (min. 41°F/5°C)

MUSCARI *syn.* MUSCARIMIA
Grape hyacinth
LILIACEAE

Genus of 30 species of bulbous perennials occurring from sea level to subalpine areas, in woodland and on steppes, stony slopes, and screes, in the Mediterranean region and S.W. Asia. Fleshy leaves, arranged in basal clusters, are linear to inversely lance-shaped, or sickle- or spoon-shaped, mostly channeled, and mid-green, or blue- or gray-green. Flowers are borne in terminal racemes on leafless stems in spring or, occasionally, autumn; the lower fertile flowers are sometimes crowned by smaller, paler sterile ones. May be tubular, bell-shaped, or spherical, often with constricted mouths, and are ⅛–⅜in (3–9mm) long, occasionally to ½in (1.5cm) long. Grow in massed displays in a mixed border; also suitable for a deciduous woodland garden, a wild garden, for

Muscari armeniacum

naturalizing in grassland, or for forcing. Use the smaller species in a rock garden.
• **CULTIVATION** Plant 4in (10cm) deep in groups in autumn, in moderately fertile, moist but well-drained soil in full sun. Lift and divide congested clumps to maintain vigor, when dormant in summer and early autumn.
• **PROPAGATION** Sow seed in containers in a cold frame in autumn. Remove offsets in summer.
• **PESTS AND DISEASES** Prone to viruses.

M. armeniacum ■ Vigorous, bulbous perennial producing semi-erect, narrowly linear to linear-inversely-lance-shaped, mid-green leaves, 12in (30cm) long, in autumn. Tubular, bright blue flowers with distinct, constricted white mouths, are borne in dense racemes, ¾–3in (2–8cm) long, in spring. May be invasive. ↕ 8in (20cm), PD2in (5cm). S.E. Europe to Caucasus. Zone 3. **'Argaei'** has bright blue flowers. **'Blue Spike'** ■ has large, densely bunched, double, blue flowers. **'Valerie Finnis'** ■ is noteworthy for its icy-lavender color.

Muscari armeniacum 'Blue Spike'

Muscari armeniacum 'Valerie Finnis'

M. aucheri ■ syn. *M. lingulatum.* Bulbous perennial with erect or semi-erect, narrowly sickle- to narrowly spoon-shaped, mid-green leaves, 2–8in (5–20cm) long. In spring, bears tight racemes, ½–1½in (1–4cm) long, of tubular, bright blue flowers with constricted white mouths, usually crowned with paler blue, sterile flowers. ↕ 4–6in (10–15cm), PD2in (5cm). Turkey. Zone 5. **'Tubergenianum'**, syn. *M. tubergenianum*, is more robust, with a conspicuous crown of sterile flowers; ↕ 8in (20cm).
M. azureum, syn. *Hyacinthus azureus, Pseudomuscari azureum.* Bulbous perennial with erect, narrowly inversely lance-shaped, grayish green leaves, 2½–8in (6–20cm) long. In spring, bears shortly bell-shaped, bright sky-blue flowers with a darker stripe on each lobe and scarcely constricted mouths, in dense, conical to ovoid racemes, ½–1¼in (1–3cm) long. May self-seed freely. ↕ 4in (10cm), PD2in (5cm). Turkey. Zone 4. **f. *album*** has pure white flowers.
M. botryoides (Common grape hyacinth). Slender perennial with semi-erect, narrowly spoon-shaped, mid-green leaves, 2–10in (5–25cm) long. In spring, bears spherical, bright blue flowers with constricted white mouths, in dense racemes ¾–2in (2–5cm) long. ↕ 6–8in (15–20cm), PD2in (5cm). C. and S.E. Europe. Zone 3. **f. *album*** ■ has slender racemes of fragrant white flowers.
M. comosum, syn. *Leopoldia comosa* (Tassel grape hyacinth). Bulbous

Muscari aucheri

Muscari botryoides f. *album*

perennial with spreading, linear, mid-green leaves, to 6in (15cm) long. In spring, produces oblong-urn-shaped, creamy brown flowers with constricted mouths, in racemes 2½–12in (6–30cm) long. Spherical, bright violet, upper, sterile flowers are borne in tassels on long, upright stalks. ↕ 8–24in (20–60cm), PD2in (5cm). S. Europe, Turkey, Iran. Zone 4. **'Plumosum'**, syn. 'Monstrosum', produces featheryheads composed entirely of purple, sterile threads.
M. latifolium. Bulbous perennial with solitary, semi-erect, inversely lance-shaped, mid-green leaves, 3–12in (7–30cm) long. In spring, bears dense racemes, ¾–2½in (2–6cm) long, of oblong-urn-shaped, violet-black flowers, constricted at the mouths, and crowns of paler, sterile flowers. ↕ 8in (20cm), PD2in (5cm). S.W. Asia. Zone 4.
M. lingulatum see *M. aucheri.*
M. macrocarpum ■ syn. *M. moschatum* var. *flavum*, *M. muscarimi* var. *flavum*. Bulbous perennial with thick, fleshy, persistent roots and semi-erect, linear, grayish green leaves, to 12in (30cm) long. In spring, produces tubular, strongly fragrant yellow flowers, with constricted mouths, opening from purplish brown buds, in racemes 1¾–2½in (4–6cm) long. Requires a hot, dry summer dormancy to flower well. ↕ 4–6in (10–15cm), PD3in (8cm). Greece (Aegean islands), W. Turkey. Zone 6.
M. moschatum* var. *flavum see *M. macrocarpum.*
M. muscarimi* var. *flavum see *M. macrocarpum.*

Muscari macrocarpum

M. neglectum, syn. *M. racemosum* (Musk hyacinth). Bulbous perennial with many semi-erect, linear, channeled to almost cylindrical, bright, mid-green leaves, 2½–16in (6–40cm) long, often produced in autumn. In spring, bears blue-black flowers with constricted white mouths, in dense racemes ½–2in (1–5cm) long. Increases rapidly. ↕ 4–8in (10–20cm), PD2in (5cm). Europe, N. Africa, S.W. Asia. Zone 4.
***M. paradoxum* of gardens** see *Bellevalia pycnantha.*
M. pycnantha see *Bellevalia pycnantha.*
M. racemosum see *M. neglectum.*
M. tubergenianum see *M. aucheri* 'Tubergenianum'.

▷ ***Muscarimia*** see *Muscari*

MUSSAENDA

RUBIACEAE

Genus of about 100 species of evergreen perennials, shrubs, subshrubs, and twining climbers found in woodland from tropical Africa and Asia to Malaysia. The opposite or whorled, membranous, lance-shaped to elliptic, or ovate or oblong, usually mid-green leaves are often hairy on the lower surfaces. Tubular or funnel-shaped, yellow, red, pink, or white flowers, each with 5 spreading lobes, are borne in often large, terminal or axillary panicles or cymes. One sepal of each flower is often greatly enlarged and colorful. Where temperatures fall below 59°F (15°C), grow in a warm greenhouse. In warmer areas, grow as free-standing specimens or in a shrub border; use climbers to clothe an arch or pergola.
• **CULTIVATION** Under glass, grow in soil-based potting mix in full light, with shade from hot sun. In growth, water freely and apply a balanced liquid fertilizer monthly; water sparingly in winter. Outdoors, grow in moderately fertile, moist but well-drained soil in full sun, with some midday shade. Pruning group 1 for shrubs; group 12, after flowering, for climbers under glass.
• **PROPAGATION** Sow seed at 66–75°F (19–24°C) in spring. Root semi-ripe cuttings with bottom heat in summer.
• **PESTS AND DISEASES** Susceptible to spider mites and whiteflies under glass.

***M.* 'Aurorae'**, syn. *M. phillippica* 'Aurorae'. Rounded, evergreen shrub with opposite, ovate, prominently veined, downy leaves, 3–6in (8–15cm)

Mussaenda 'Don Leonila'

Mussaenda erythrophylla

long. Narrowly funnel-shaped, deep golden yellow flowers, with pendent, obovate white sepals, to 3in (8cm) long, are produced in terminal cymes, 3in (8cm) long, in summer, or throughout the year in warm regions. ↕↔ 5ft (1.5m). ❄ (min. 54°F/12°C)
***M.* 'Don Leonila'** ■ Rounded, evergreen shrub with opposite, ovate, downy leaves, 3–6in (8–15cm) long, with prominent veins. In summer, bears narrowly funnel-shaped, deep yellow flowers, with obovate, creamy white sepals, to 3in (8cm) long, in terminal cymes, 3in (8cm) long. ↕ 10ft (3m), ↔ 5ft (1.5m). ❄ (min. 54°F/12°C)
M. erythrophylla ■ Twining climber, usually grown as a shrub, with ovate or broadly elliptic to broadly ovate, softly hairy, red-veined, dark green leaves, 4–7in (10–18cm) long. In summer, bears small, creamy white, red-centered flowers, each with one broadly ovate red sepal, 2–4in (5–10cm) long, in large, dense panicles, 1½in (4cm) long. ↕ 6–10ft (2–3m) (when grown as a shrub), 25–30ft (8–10m) (when grown as a climber); ↔ 5–8ft (1.5–2.5m). Tropical Africa. ❄ (min. 59°F/15°C). **'Queen Sirikit'** bears pendent flowers, with numerous large, wavy, deep pink to ivory sepals, on arching branches.
***M. phillippica* 'Aurorae'** see *M.* 'Aurorae'.

MUTISIA

ASTERACEAE

Genus of about 60 species of evergreen shrubs and tendril climbers occurring in woodland and scrub in South America. The leaves are alternate, linear to oblong-ovate, sometimes pinnate, and mid- or dark green. Showy, daisy-like flowerheads are borne singly from the leaf axils from summer to autumn. Grow in a small courtyard garden, through shrubs in a border, or on a fence or trellis. Where not hardy, grow in a cool or temperate greenhouse.
• **CULTIVATION** Under glass, grow in soil-based potting mix in bright filtered light. In growth, water moderately and apply a balanced liquid fertilizer monthly; keep just moist in winter. Outdoors, grow in moderately fertile, moist but well-drained soil in full sun. Protect from excessive winter moisture. Pruning group 11, in spring.
• **PROPAGATION** Sow seed in autumn; under glass at 55–64°F (13–18°C). Can be difficult to germinate. Root stem-tip

Mutisia decurrens

cuttings in late spring or summer. Layer in autumn. Separate suckers in spring.
• **PESTS AND DISEASES** Infrequent.

M. acuminata. Branched shrub with pinnatisect leaves composed of 18–28, elliptic-lance-shaped, long-pointed, hairless, mid-green leaflets, to 1½in (4cm) long. Each leaf ends in a tendril. From summer to autumn, bears long-stalked, bright red flowerheads, to 3in (8cm) across, with yellow centers. ↕ to 36in (90cm), ↔ 18in (45cm). Peru to Bolivia. ❄ (min. 41°F/5°C)
M. decurrens ■ Suckering climber with winged stems and narrowly oblong, entire or toothed, dark green leaves, to 5in (13cm) long, each ending in a 2-lobed tendril. Bright orange flowerheads, to 5in (13cm) across, are produced in summer. Best propagated from suckers. ↕ 10ft (3m). Chile, Argentina. ❄ (min. 35°F/2°C)
M. ilicifolia. Climber with winged shoots and holly-like, ovate to ovate-elliptic, bright green leaves, to 2½in (6cm) long, each ending in a long, unbranched tendril. Short-stalked, pale pink flowerheads, to 3in (8cm) across, with yellow centers, are produced from summer to autumn and often irregularly during the year. ↕ 10ft (3m). Chile. ❄ (min. 41°F/5°C)
M. oligodon ■ Climber with oblong, sharply toothed, glossy, dark green leaves, white woolly beneath, to 1½in (4cm) long, each ending in a long tendril. Long-stalked pink flowerheads, to 3in (8cm) across, with yellow centers, are borne from summer to autumn. ↕ 5ft (1.5m). Chile, Argentina. ❄ (min. 41°F/5°C)

Mutisia oligodon

M

MYOPORUM

MYOPORACEAE

Genus of about 30 species of spreading, prostrate to upright, evergreen shrubs and trees from open, dry areas, from E. Asia to Australia, New Zealand, and Hawaii. The alternate, variably shaped, entire or toothed, light to mid-green leaves are dotted with glands. Small, bell-shaped or tubular-bell-shaped flowers, each with 5 spreading lobes, are borne singly or in short cymes from the leaf axils, followed by small, succulent berries. Where not hardy, grow in a temperate or warm greenhouse. Elsewhere, they are suitable for a shrub border and are ideal as informal hedges and windbreaks.

• **CULTIVATION** Under glass, grow in soil-based potting mix in full light, with shade from hot sun, or in bright filtered light. In growth, water freely; apply a balanced liquid fertilizer monthly. Water sparingly in winter. Outdoors, grow in moderately fertile, moist but well-drained soil in full sun, with midday shade. Pruning group 9.

• **PROPAGATION** Sow seed at 45–54°F (6–12°C) as soon as ripe. Root semi-ripe cuttings with bottom heat in summer.

• **PESTS AND DISEASES** Scale insects may be a problem under glass.

M. laetum (Ngaio). Large shrub or small tree with sticky stem tips and thick, furrowed brown bark when mature. Fleshy, bright green leaves are lance-shaped to oblong or obovate, 1½–4in (4–10cm) long. Bears cymes of 2–6 bell-shaped, purple-spotted white flowers, ½in (1.5cm) across, in summer. Narrowly ovoid berries are pale to deep reddish purple, ¼–⅜in (6–9mm) long. ↕ 15–30ft (5–10m), ↔ 6–15ft (2–5m). New Zealand. ❀ (min. 36°F/2°C). **var. *decumbens*** is spreading, and useful as a groundcover; ↕ to 3ft (1m).

M. parvifolium ■ Small, spreading, bushy shrub with reddish green, sticky stems, and narrowly spoon-shaped to linear, fleshy, bright green leaves, to 1¼in (3cm) long, with prominent glands. In summer, produces bell-shaped, honey-scented, white, occasionally lilac flowers, ½in (1.5cm) across, usually purple-dotted, singly or in twos or threes, followed by broadly ovoid purple berries, ¼in (6mm) long. ↕ to 24in (60cm), ↔ 24–36in (60–90cm). South Australia, Victoria, Tasmania. ❀ (min. 36°F/2°C)

M

Myoporum parvifolium

Myosotidium hortensia

MYOSOTIDIUM

BORAGINACEAE

Genus of one species of evergreen perennial from rocky or sandy coasts on Chatham Island, New Zealand. It has thick, fleshy stems and leaves, the latter large, simple, and glossy, and forget-me-not-like flowers. Grow in a rock garden; it can be difficult to grow, since it needs cool, damp conditions, preferably in a coastal location. Where not hardy, grow in a cool greenhouse.

• **CULTIVATION** Under glass, grow in soil-based potting mix in bright filtered light. In growth, water freely and apply a seaweed-based fertilizer monthly; keep just moist in winter. Outdoors, grow in humus-rich, gritty, moist but well-drained soil with a seaweed mulch, in light, dappled shade. Provide shelter from cold, drying winds.

• **PROPAGATION** Sow seed under glass in autumn or as soon as ripe. Carefully divide in spring.

• **PESTS AND DISEASES** Prone to slugs.

M. hortensia ■ syn. *M. nobile* (Chatham Island forget-me-not). Clump-forming, evergreen perennial with very glossy, ovate to heart-shaped, ribbed, basal leaves, to 12in (30cm) long, with conspicuous veins and wavy margins. In early summer, bears dense, corymb-like cymes of open bell-shaped, pale to dark blue flowers, ½in (1.5cm) across, sometimes with white-margined lobes. ↕↔ to 24in (60cm). New Zealand (Chatham Island). ❀ (min. 35°F/2°C)

M. nobile see *M. hortensia.*

MYOSOTIS

Forget-me-not

BORAGINACEAE

Genus of 50 or more species of annuals, biennials, and clump- or mat-forming perennials found in woods, meadows, swampy soils, and at pond margins in Europe, Asia, Australasia, and North and South America. They produce alternate, variably shaped, hairy leaves, and usually paired cymes of 5-lobed, salverform, occasionally funnel-shaped flowers in blue, yellow, or white, mostly with yellow or white eyes. The dwarf perennials are mainly short-lived but self-seed freely; they are useful for a rock garden, bank, scree bed, or alpine house. Grow *M. scorpioides* at the margins of a pond. *M. sylvatica* is suitable for a mixed

Myosotis alpestris

Myosotis sylvatica 'Music'

or wildflower border; its cultivars are useful for spring bedding.

• **CULTIVATION** Grow in moderately fertile or poor, moist but well-drained soil in full sun, with some midday shade, or in partial shade. Dwarf perennials need soil that is not too fertile since they may become coarse in rich soils; in an alpine house, grow in a mix of equal parts loam, leaf mold, and grit. Grow *M. scorpioides* in wet soil, or in an aquatic container as a shallow-water marginal, at a maximum depth of 4in (10cm); see also pp.52–53.

• **PROPAGATION** Sow seed of annuals and biennials *in situ* in spring or, for spring bedding, in containers in a cold frame or seedbed in early summer. Sow seed of perennials in containers in a cold frame in spring; divide when dormant, and propagate regularly, since they are often short-lived. Sow seed of *M. scorpioides in situ* in mud at pond margins, or in moist soil mix in containers in a cold frame, in spring; divide and replant in mud or in baskets in shallow water.

• **PESTS AND DISEASES** Slugs, snails, rust, powdery and downy mildew, and gray mold occur.

M. alpestris ■ syn. *M. rupicola* (Alpine forget-me-not). Short-lived, clump-forming perennial with oblong-lance-shaped or spoon-shaped, bright green leaves, to 3in (8cm) long. Dense cymes of salverform, bright blue, yellow-eyed flowers, to ⅜in (9mm) across, are borne from spring to early summer. ↕ 8in (20cm), ↔ to 6in (15cm). Europe. Zone 4.

M. explanata. Clump- to hummock-forming perennial with rosettes of obovate to spoon-shaped, white-hairy, gray-green leaves, to 3in (8cm) long. In early summer, spreading stems bear large cymes of salverform to funnel-shaped white flowers, to ½in (1.5cm) across. ↕ to 8in (20cm), ↔ to 6in (15cm). New Zealand (South Island). Zone 8.

M. palustris see *M. scorpioides.*

M. rupicola see *M. alpestris.*

M. scorpioides, syn. *M. palustris* (Water forget-me-not). Marginal aquatic perennial with creeping rhizomes and upright or semi-upright, angular stems. Leaves are narrowly ovate and mid-green, to 4in (10cm) long at the bases, becoming slightly longer up the stem. In early summer, bears open cymes of salverform, bright blue flowers, to ⅜in

Myosotis sylvatica Victoria Series 'Victoria Rose'

(9mm) across, each with a white, pink, or yellow eye. ↕ 6–12in (15–30cm) or more, ↔ 12in (30cm). Europe, Asia, North America. Zone 5. **'Mermaid'** is strong-stemmed and more compact, with dark green leaves, 1½–2½in (4–6cm) long, and bright blue, yellow-eyed flowers; ↕ 6–9in (15–23cm). **'Sapphire'** is compact and bushy, with brilliant, jewel-blue flowers borne in slightly coiled cymes.

M. sylvatica. Tufted, hairy biennial or short-lived perennial, usually grown as a biennial, with ovate to elliptic or lance-shaped, gray-green leaves, to 4½in (11cm) long. From spring to early summer, bears saucer-shaped, yellow-eyed, blue or occasionally white flowers, to ⅜in (9mm) across, in numerous dense cymes. ↕ 5–12in (12–30cm), ↔ to 6in (15cm). Europe. Zone 4. Cultivars of **Ball Series** are ball-shaped and compact; ↕ 6in (15cm); the series includes **'Blue Ball'** with azure flowers, and **'Snowball'** with white flowers. **'Blue Basket'** is tall and erect, with deep azure flowers; ↕ 10–12in (25–30cm). **'Blue Bird'** has bright blue flowers; ↕ 12in (30cm). **'Carmine King'** is upright in habit, and bears rose-carmine flowers. **'Music'** ■ is vigorous and erect, with large, very bright blue flowers; ↕ to 10in (25cm). **'Pinkie'** bears bright pink flowers; ↕ 8in (20cm). **'Pompadour'** is compact and ball-shaped, and bears large, deep rose-pink flowers; ↕ 6–8in (15–20cm). **'Stricta'** has upright, straight branches. **'Ultramarine'** is dwarf and compact, with deep indigo-blue flowers; ↕ to 6in (15cm). **Victoria Series** cultivars are dwarf and compact, with white, blue, or pink flowers; the series includes **'Victoria Rose'** ■ with bright rose-pink flowers; ↕ 4in (10cm).

MYRICA

MYRICACEAE

Genus of about 50 species of dioecious or monoecious, deciduous and evergreen, usually suckering shrubs and erect trees, found in moist ground worldwide. They have alternate, lance-shaped to ovate, usually aromatic, dark green leaves. Many are effective when grown in groups. *M. cerifera* may also be used as a screening plant; *M. gale* is a useful bog plant.

• **CULTIVATION** Grow in humus-rich, moist soil. *M. gale* will also grow in permanently waterlogged, acidic soil. Pruning group 1.

Myrica pensylvanica

• **PROPAGATION** Sow seed in containers outdoors as soon as ripe. Root greenwood cuttings in early or midsummer. Layer in spring.

• **PESTS AND DISEASES** Prone to leaf spots, stem rots, root rots, dieback, and rust.

M. cerifera (Wax myrtle). Rounded, deciduous or evergreen shrub with upright branches and obovate or narrowly inversely lance-shaped, aromatic leaves, to 4in (10cm) long. In spring, bears inconspicuous, yellow-green male catkins, to ¾in (2cm) long. Spherical, waxy, gray-white fruit, ⅛in (3mm) across, are densely clustered along the shoots and persist over winter. ↕↔ 15ft (5m). S.E. US. Zone 7.

M. gale (Bog myrtle, Sweet gale). Thicket-forming, suckering, deciduous shrub with upright branches and inversely lance-shaped, toothed, aromatic leaves, to 2½in (6cm) long. Bears yellow-brown male catkins, to ½in (1.5cm) long, in mid- and late spring, followed by spherical, yellow-brown fruit, to ⅛in (3mm) across, dotted with resin. ↕↔ 5ft (1.5m). Europe, Asia, North America. Zone 2.

M. pensylvanica ■ (Northern bayberry). Large, upright, rounded, dense, suckering, deciduous to semi-evergreen shrub with obovate, shallowly toothed, aromatic, softly hairy, glossy, dark green leaves, 1½–4in (4–10cm) long. Bears yellowish green male catkins, to ½in (1.5cm) long, in spring before the leaves, followed by waxy, grayish white fruit, ¼in (6mm) across, in autumn, persisting through winter. Good for poor soil conditions or a seashore garden. Berries can be used in making candles. ↕ 9ft (2.5m), ↔ 5–12ft (1.5–4m). Newfoundland to North Carolina. Zone 2.

MYRIOPHYLLUM

Milfoil

HALORAGACEAE

Genus of 45 species of submerged or marginal aquatic annuals and perennials occurring in wet ground, ponds, and streams, widely distributed but mainly found in the S. hemisphere. The foliage is highly decorative, with long, sub-merged, delicate stems and alternate, opposite, or whorled leaves. The sub-merged leaves are linear to oblong or rounded, and pinnatifid, with fine, hair-like segments; the emergent leaves are entire or toothed,

Myriophyllum aquaticum

Myriophyllum hippuroides

and lance-shaped to ovate or linear. Milfoils provide refuge from predators, as well as oxygenating the water. Grow in an outdoor pool or in an aquarium.

• **CULTIVATION** In an aquarium, grow in an inert medium in full light, preferably in hard water, at 50–59°F (10–15°C) for *M. hippuroides* and *M. verticillatum*, 64–75°F (18–24°C) for *M. aquaticum.* Outdoors, grow in containers of loamy soil in full sun, at a depth of 6in (15cm) for *M. aquaticum,* 18in (45cm) for *M. hippuroides*, and 3ft (1m) for *M. verticillatum.* Top growth may be damaged by frost, but should re-emerge below the surface in spring. See also pp.52–53.

• **PROPAGATION** Root cuttings (young tips or segments) by inserting in the bottom sand.

• **PESTS AND DISEASES** Young growth may be eaten by fish, and algae may cover the plants.

M. aquaticum ■ syn. *M. brasiliense, M. proserpinacoides* (Diamond milfoil, Parrot feather). Aquatic perennial with rarely branched stems, to 6ft (2m) long, becoming woody at the bases and creeping out of shallow water. Rounded, pinnatifid, bright yellowish green sub-merged leaves, to 1½in (4cm) long, have 4–8 segments and are arranged in whorls of 4 or 5; rounded, bluish green emergent leaves are shorter. In summer, minute, monoecious, bright yellow-green flowers are borne in spikes from the axils of the submerged leaves. Invasive in earthen ponds. ↔ indefinite. Indonesia (Java), Australia, New Zealand, South America. ❀ (min. 41°F/5°C)

M. brasiliense see *M. aquaticum.*

M. elatinoides. Aquatic perennial with thin stems, to 4ft (1.2m) long. Bears ovate-oblong, mid-green emergent leaves, to ⅜in (9mm) long, in whorls of 3–5, and ovate, finely pinnatifid, mid-green submerged leaves, to ¾in (2cm) long. Produces solitary, minute pink flowers in the axils of the emergent leaves, in summer. ↔ indefinite. Australia, New Zealand, Mexico, South America. ❀ (min. 41°F/5°C)

M. hippuroides ■ (Western milfoil). Aquatic perennial with thin stems, to 24in (60cm) long. Bears lance-shaped to ovate, pinnatifid, yellow-green sub-merged leaves, to ¾in (2cm) long, with up to 25 segments. Linear to lance-shaped, finely divided, olive-green to red emergent leaves, 2in (5cm) long, borne in whorls of 4–6, are usually upward-pointing. Bears minute white flowers from the axils of the emergent leaves in summer. ↔ indefinite. S.W. US. Zone 7b.

M. proserpinacoides see *M. aquaticum.*

M. verticillatum (Myriad leaf). Aquatic perennial with stems to 3ft (1m) long. Linear, pinnatifid, tightly packed, bright green submerged leaves, to 1½in (4cm) long, are arranged in whorls of 4–6, with 8–16 pairs of opposite segments. Emergent leaves are pinnatifid and comb-like, to 1in (2.5cm) long. In summer, bears yellowish flowers in a spike, to 6in (15cm) tall, just above the water surface. ↔ indefinite. Europe, Asia, North America. Zone 3.

▷ ***Myrmecophila tibicinis*** see *Schomburgkia tibicinis*

MYRRHIS

Sweet Cicely

APIACEAE

Genus of one species of aromatic herbaceous perennial originally found in mountains of S. Europe, now wide-spread in damp sites in Europe and Asia. It has compound umbels of small white flowers and delicate, fern-like foliage. Grow in a mixed border, or in an herb garden. Self-seeds freely.

• **CULTIVATION** Grow in moderately fertile, moist but well-drained soil in dappled shade. Harvest leaves from early spring to late summer. To improve the flavor and quality of the leaves, remove the flowering stems as they develop.

• **PROPAGATION** Sow seed in containers or *in situ* as soon as ripe. Divide in spring or autumn.

• **PESTS AND DISEASES** Infrequent.

M. odorata ■ (Garden myrrh, Sweet Cicely). Perennial with thick, hairy, hollow stems and soft, 2- or 3-pinnate, bright green leaves, to 18in (45cm) long, composed of deeply toothed, oblong to lance-shaped pinnae. Compound umbels of small, star-shaped white flowers, are produced in early summer, followed by ridged, beaked, shiny brown fruit, to ¾in (2cm) long. Anise-flavored young shoots, leaves, and seeds provide sweetness when cooked with fruit. ↕ 6ft (2m), ↔ 5ft (1.5m). S. Europe. Zone 4.

Myrrhis odorata

MYRSINE

MYRSINACEAE

Genus of about 5 species of dioecious, evergreen, many-branched, upright or rounded shrubs and small trees, found in forest and scrub in Africa, the Azores, the Himalayas, China, and New Zealand. They are cultivated mainly for their alternate, linear or lance-shaped to rounded, usually entire, leathery, sometimes glossy, mid- or dark green leaves. Inconspicuous male and female flowers are produced in umbels on separate plants; both are needed to produce fruit. Grow in a shrub border, against a wall, or in a rock, heather, or woodland garden. Where not hardy, grow in a temperate greenhouse.

- **CULTIVATION** Grow in humus-rich, moist but well-drained soil in full sun or light, dappled shade. Pruning group 1.
- **PROPAGATION** Sow seed in containers in a cold frame in autumn. Root semi-ripe cuttings in summer.
- **PESTS AND DISEASES** Occasionally affected by leaf spot.

M. africana (African boxwood, Cape myrtle). Slow-growing, densely leafy, upright shrub with narrowly obovate to elliptic, aromatic, glossy, dark green leaves, to ¾in (2cm) long. In late spring, produces umbels of 3–6 tiny, yellow-brown flowers. Female plants bear spherical, pale blue fruit, ¼in (6mm) across. ↕ 4ft (1.2m), ↔ 30in (75cm). Azores, E. and S. Africa, Himalayas, China. ❀ (min. 41°F/5°C)

M

MYRTEOLA

MYRTACEAE

Genus of 12 species of dwarf, evergreen, mat-forming to rounded, bushy shrubs or subshrubs from upland slopes and raised bogs in South America. They are grown for their attractive fruits and glossy foliage. Leaves are opposite, ovate to rounded, and mid- to dark green. Cup-shaped, 4- or 5-petaled, pale yellow to white flowers are borne singly from the leaf axils from late spring to summer, followed by spherical, pink to dark red berries in autumn. Grow in a rock or woodland garden.

- **CULTIVATION** Grow in humus-rich, moist but well-drained, acidic soil in full sun, with some midday shade, or in dappled shade. Pruning is not required; trim wayward shoots if necessary.
- **PROPAGATION** Sow seed in containers in an open frame in autumn. Root semi-ripe cuttings, taken with a heel, with bottom heat in summer.
- **PESTS AND DISEASES** Infrequent.

M. nummularia ▣ syn. *Myrtus nummularia*. Mat-forming subshrub with branching stems clothed in tiny, ovate, dark green leaves, to ⅜in (9mm) long. Small white flowers, ⅜in (9mm) across, are produced in early summer, followed in late summer by spherical to ellipsoid pink berries, ¼–½in (6–15mm) long. ↕ 2in (5cm), ↔ 12in (30cm). S. Chile, S. Argentina, Falkland Islands. ❀ (min. 41°F/5°C)

Myrteola nummularia

MYRTILLOCACTUS

CACTACEAE

Genus of 4 species of shrubby or tree-like cacti occurring in semi-arid areas of Mexico and Guatemala. They have short, deep bluish green stems and thick, erect branches with 5–8 ribs and spiny, felted areoles. Open funnel-shaped, short-tubed flowers are borne from the upper lateral areoles in early and midsummer, followed by ovoid, purplish blue fruits. Where temperatures drop below 50°F (10°C), grow in a warm greenhouse. In warmer areas, grow in a rock or desert garden.

- **CULTIVATION** Under glass, grow in standard cactus potting mix in full light with low humidity. From midspring to early autumn, water moderately and apply a low-nitrogen fertilizer monthly. Keep dry from midautumn until early spring, but lightly mist when warm in late winter. Outdoors, grow in poor to moderately fertile, sharply drained soil in full sun. Shade in hot weather. Provide protection from excessive winter moisture. See also pp.48–49.
- **PROPAGATION** Sow seed at 66–75°F (19–24°C) in spring or take stem cuttings in midsummer.
- **PESTS AND DISEASES** Susceptible to damage by mealybugs.

Myrtillocactus geometrizans

M. cochal. Tree-like cactus with mid-green stems, 6in (15cm) or more thick, with 6–8 shallow-grooved ribs and gray or black spines (3–5 radials and sometimes 1 longer central). White or pale yellow flowers, 1in (2.5cm) across, tinged green or purple, are borne both diurnally and nocturnally in early and midsummer. ↕ 3ft (1m), ↔ 18in (45cm). N.W. Mexico. ❀ (min. 35°F/2°C)

M. geometrizans ▣ (Blue candle). Tree-like cactus with bluish green stems, to 4in (10cm) thick, branching from about 12in (30cm) above ground level. Each has 5–6 smooth, acute ribs with 5–9 red-brown then gray radial spines and 1 longer, almost black central spine. White or cream flowers, 1–1½in (2.5–4cm) across, are produced diurnally in early and midsummer. ↕ 12ft (4m), ↔ 6ft (2m). Mexico. ❀ (min. 35°F/2°C)

MYRTUS

Myrtle

MYRTACEAE

Genus of 2 species of upright or rounded, evergreen trees and shrubs from scrub, woodland, and woodland margins in the Mediterranean region, N. Africa, South America, and the Falkland Islands. They are cultivated for their aromatic leaves and their solitary, bowl-shaped, fragrant white flowers, borne from spring to autumn. Myrtles are suitable for a mixed or shrub border, or for growing against a warm, sunny wall. They may also be grown as topiary, as free-standing specimen shrubs, or as an informal hedge.

- **CULTIVATION** Grow in moderately fertile, moist but well-drained soil in full sun. Pruning group 1 for *M. lechleriana*; group 9 for *M. communis*; group 13 if wall-trained.
- **PROPAGATION** Sow seed in containers in a cold frame in autumn. Root semi-ripe cuttings in summer.
- **PESTS AND DISEASES** Prone to scale insects, mushroom root rot, gray mold, leaf spot, and Southern blight.

M. bullata see *Lophomyrtus bullata*.
***M. bullata* 'Gloriosa'** see *Lophomyrtus* x *ralphii* 'Variegata'.
M. chequen see *Luma chequen*.
M. communis ▣ (Common myrtle). Upright, bushy shrub, arching with age, bearing opposite, ovate, glossy, dark green leaves, to 2in (5cm) long. From mid- to late summer or early autumn,

Myrtus communis

Myrtus communis subsp. *tarentina*

produces solitary, 5-petaled flowers, ¾in (2cm) across, with conspicuous central tufts of white stamens; flowers are followed by oblong-ellipsoid, purple-black berries, ½in (1.5cm) long. ↕↔ 10ft (3m). Mediterranean. Zone 8. **'Compacta'** has a dwarf, dense habit. **'Jenny Reitenbach'** see subsp. *tarentina*. **'Microphylla'** see subsp. *tarentina*. **'Nana'** see subsp. *tarentina*. **subsp. *tarentina*** ▣ syn. 'Jenny Reitenbach', 'Microphylla', 'Nana' (Dwarf myrtle), is more compact and rounded in habit than the species, with narrowly elliptic leaves, to ¾in (2cm) long, pink-tinted cream flowers, and white berries. Excellent for container-grown topiary; ↕↔ 5ft (1.5m). **subsp. *tarentina* 'Microphylla Variegata'** is similar to subsp. *tarentina*, but has white-margined leaves. **'Variegata'** produces leaves margined creamy white.
M. lechleriana, syn. *Amomyrtus luma*, *M. luma* of gardens. Upright, bushy shrub or many-stemmed tree with ovate, slightly aromatic, dark green leaves, to 1in (2.5cm) long, coppery-brown when young. Compact, axillary racemes of 4–10 fragrant, 5-petaled, creamy white flowers, ½in (1.5cm) across, are borne in mid- and late spring, followed by edible, spherical, aromatic red berries, ripening to black. ↕ 20ft (6m) or more, ↔ 12ft (4m). Chile. ❀ (min. 41°F/5°C)
M. luma see *Luma apiculata*.
***M. luma* of gardens** see *M. lechleriana*.
M. nummularia see *Myrteola nummularia*.
***M.* x *ralphii* 'Variegata'** see *Lophomyrtus* x *ralphii* 'Variegata'.
M. ugni see *Ugni molinae*.

N

▷ ***Naegelia*** see *Smithiantha*
▷ ***Nananthus*** see *Aloinopsis*

Nandina

BERBERIDACEAE

Genus of one species of evergreen or semi-evergreen shrub, with alternate, pinnate leaves, from mountain valleys in India, China, and Japan. *N. domestica* is grown for its flowers, fruit, and elegant foliage. Grow in a shrub border; use low-growing cultivars as a groundcover.
• **Cultivation** Grow in a sheltered site in moist but well-drained soil, preferably in full sun. Pruning group 9.
• **Propagation** Sow seed in containers in a cold frame as soon as ripe. Root semi-ripe cuttings in summer.
• **Pests and diseases** Leaf spot, root rot, and *Verticillium* wilt occur. Viruses causing reddish coloration, mosaic, and distortions are common.

N. domestica ▣ (Heavenly bamboo). Evergreen or semi-evergreen shrub with upright shoots and pinnate to 3-pinnate leaves, to 36in (90cm) long, with lance-shaped leaflets, red to reddish purple when young and in winter. In midsummer, bears conical panicles, to 16in (40cm) long, of small, star-shaped white flowers, to ½in (1.5cm) across, with large yellow anthers, followed by long-lasting, spherical, bright red fruit, ⅜in (9mm) across. ↕ 6ft (2m), ↔ 5ft (1.5m). India, China, Japan. Zone 7. **'Compacta'** see 'Harbor Dwarf'. **'Firepower'** is dwarf and compact, with bright red leaves; ↕ 18in (45cm), ↔ 24in (60cm). **'Harbor Dwarf'**, syn. 'Compacta', is compact; ↕ 3ft (1m), ↔ 4ft (1.2m). **'Nana'**, syn. 'Pygmaea', is dense and mound-forming, with little fruit production; ↕ 2–4ft (60–120cm). **'Pygmaea'** see 'Nana'. **'Wood's Dwarf'** is compact, with virus-free foliage and good red winter color; ↕↔ 18in (45cm).

Nandina domestica

Narcissus

Daffodil

AMARYLLIDACEAE

Genus of about 50 species of bulbous perennials from a variety of habitats in Europe and N. Africa, usually found in meadows from sea level to subalpine altitudes, and in woodland, river silts, and rock crevices. Many cultivars have been developed. All are grown for their attractive flowers, borne in spring, sometimes autumn or winter. Leafless stems bear between 1 and 20 flowers, each with 6 spreading perianth segments (petals) surrounding an almost flat or long and narrow corona (the cup or trumpet). The flowers are mostly yellow or white, occasionally green; some have red, orange, or pink coronas. The leaves are basal, often strap-shaped or cylindrical, 6–30in (15–75cm) long, depending on the species.

Most daffodils are suitable for planting between shrubs or in a border, or for forcing; many are easily naturalized in grass. They are excellent for cutting. Smaller species, hybrids, and cultivars are good rock garden plants; some can be naturalized in fine, short grass. Contact with the sap of daffodils may irritate skin or aggravate skin allergies in some people.

Except for three species that flower after autumn rains begin, daffodils bloom in late winter and spring. Along the Gulf Coast and in S. California, the less hardy members of Division 8 and some N. African species may begin blooming in early winter.

For horticultural purposes, daffodils are split into 13 divisions. All are of garden origin, except for Division 13 species. The planting distances given for each division are provided as a guide.

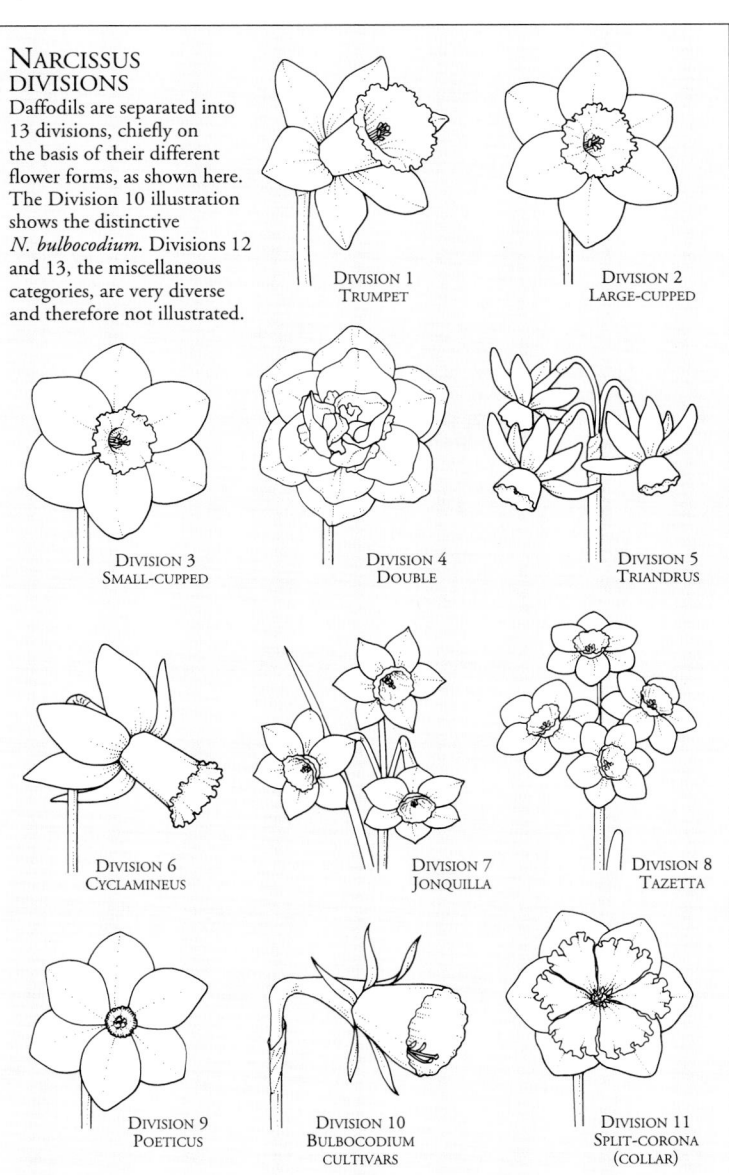

Division 1. Trumpet cultivars
Flowers are solitary, each with a trumpet (corona) as long as, or longer than, the perianth segments. Flowering early in the season. PD3–6in (8–15cm).
Division 2. Large-cupped cultivars
Flowers are solitary, each with a cup (corona) more than one-third the length of, but not as long as, the perianth segments. Usually midseason-flowering. PD6in (15cm).
Division 3. Small-cupped cultivars
Flowers are solitary, each with a cup (corona) up to one-third the length of the perianth segments. Mid- and late-season-flowering. PD6in (15cm).
Division 4. Double cultivars
Each stem has one or more flowers, with doubling of the perianth segments or the corona or both. Some are sweetly scented. Usually mid- and late-season-flowering. PD6in (15cm).
Division 5. Triandrus cultivars
Each stem produces 2–6 nodding flowers, usually with reflexed perianth segments and usually short cups (coronas). Mid- and late-season-flowering. PD2–3in (5–8cm).
Division 6. Cyclamineus cultivars
Flowers are solitary, each acutely angled to the stem, with significantly reflexed perianth segments and usually a long cup or trumpet (corona). Early- and midseason-flowering. PD3in (8cm).
Division 7. Jonquilla cultivars
Each stem produces 1–5 usually scented flowers, with spreading perianth segments and small, shallow cups (coronas). The stems are cylindrical; the dark green leaves are very narrow and almost cylindrical. Mid- and late-season-flowering. PD3in (8cm).
Division 8. Tazetta cultivars
Small-flowered cultivars produce up to 20 flowers per stem; larger-flowered cultivars bear 3 or 4 flowers per stem. They have thick stems, wide leaves, broad perianth segments, and small cups (coronas). They are usually scented, and are good as cut flowers. Some cultivars are less hardy and should be grown in a cool greenhouse. Flowering from late autumn to late in the season. PD3in (8cm).
Division 9. Poeticus cultivars
Flowers are fragrant, usually solitary, with spreading, pure white perianth segments and small, open, red-rimmed cups (coronas). Mid- and late-season-flowering. PD6in (15cm).
Division 10. Bulbocodium cultivars
Includes all wild daffodils and their wild hybrids, such as the tiny hoop-petticoat daffodil, *N. bulbocodium*, the larger, single-flowered *N. pseudonarcissus*, and the multi-headed *N. tazetta.* Some are difficult to grow in an open garden. Autumn- to spring-flowering. PD2–3in (5–8cm), or 6in (15cm) for larger bulbs.
Division 11. Split-corona cultivars
Flowers are usually solitary, each with a corona split for more than half its length. Mid- and late-season-flowering. PD6in (15cm). There are 2 subdivisions: ***Division 11a. Collar*** – The corona segments lie on top of the perianth segments.
Division 11b. Papillon – The flowers have alternating corona segments and perianth segments.
Division 12. Miscellaneous cultivars
Includes daffodils not in other divisions and the twin-headed cyclamineus cultivars, such as *N.* 'Jumblie'. PD2–3in (5–8cm) or 6in (15cm), depending on the size of the bulbs.
Division 13. Daffodils distinguished by botanical name only.
This division is further divided into the following 10 sections: Tapeinanthus, Serotoni, Aurelia, Tazettae, Narcissus, Jonquilla, Abodanthi, Ganymedes, Bulbocodium, and Pseudonarcissus.

• **Hardiness** Daffodils can be grown in most areas of Canada, down to Zone 4 and are worth trying in 3b with good snow cover. Those cultivars that have different hardiness requirements are so noted.

Narcissus Divisions

Daffodils are separated into 13 divisions, chiefly on the basis of their different flower forms, as shown here. The Division 10 illustration shows the distinctive *N. bulbocodium.* Divisions 12 and 13, the miscellaneous categories, are very diverse and therefore not illustrated.

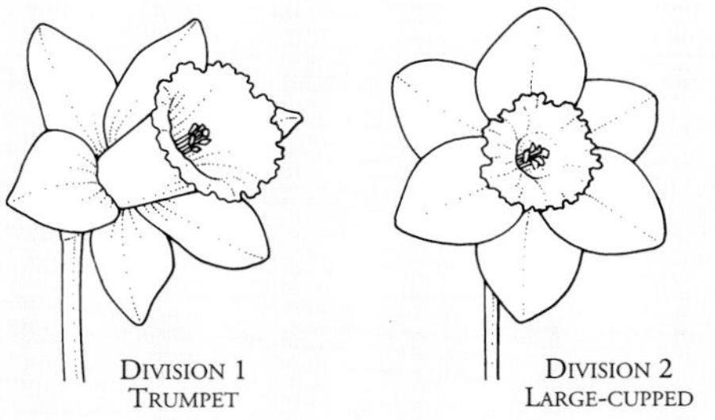

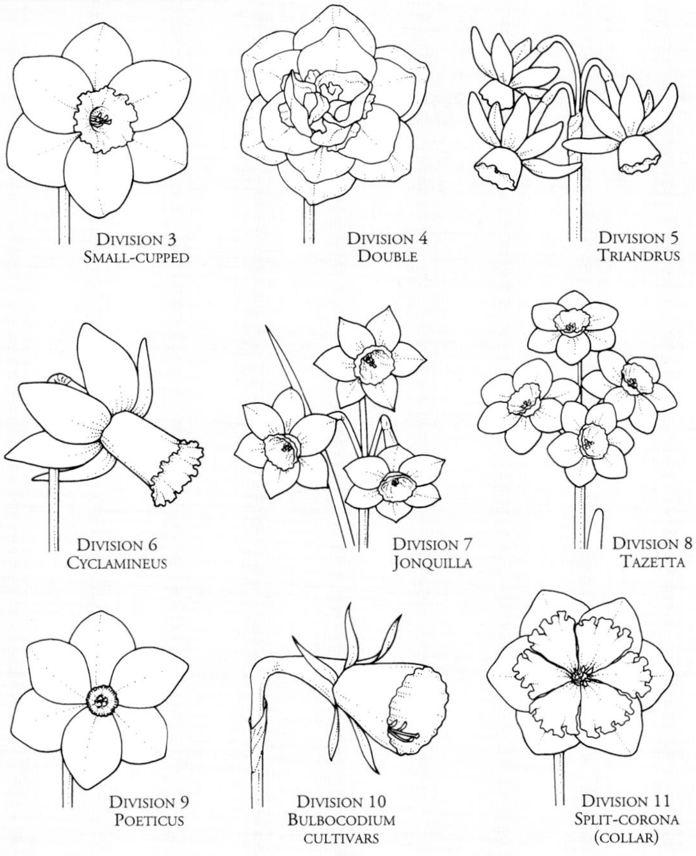

N

Narcissus 'Acropolis'

Narcissus 'Actaea'

Narcissus 'Ambergate'

Narcissus 'Audubon'

Narcissus 'Avalanche'

Narcissus 'Baby Moon'

Narcissus 'Bartley'

Narcissus 'Berlin'

Narcissus 'Beryl'

Narcissus 'Bob Minor'

Narcissus 'Bravoure'

Narcissus 'Bridal Crown'

• **CULTIVATION** Plant bulbs from one-and-a-half to five times their own depth in autumn. Where winters are severe, make sure there is at least 3 inches of soil covering the bulb. Most tolerate a range of soils but grow best in moderately fertile, well-drained soil that is moist during the growing season. *N. bulbocodium*, *N. cyclamineus*, *N. triandrus*, and their cultivars need neutral to acidic soils. *N. jonquilla* and *N. tazetta* prefer slightly alkaline soils. Most daffodils thrive in full sun or dappled part-day shade. Division 6 daffodils like cooler conditions and do well in grass. Division 5, 7, and 8 daffodils flower best in full sun and drier soils. Water late-flowering daffodils in dry spring weather (flowers may abort in dry conditions). Deadhead plants as flowers fade (for neater garden appearance) and allow leaves to remain for at least 6 weeks. Apply a low-nitrogen, high-potash fertilizer after flowering if bulbs are not performing well. Lift and divide clumps when flowering becomes sparse or the clumps congested. If daffodils are naturalized in grass, delay the first cut until 6 weeks after flowers have faded; for species such as *N. bulbocodium*, *N. cyclamineus*, and *N. pseudonarcissus*, delay cutting until seeds have dispersed.

Under glass, grow in a mix of 2 parts soil-based potting mix and 1 part grit. Plunge outdoors in a cool, shady spot and keep dry when dormant.

For forcing indoors, plant bulbs with their necks showing, in bulb pans or azalea pots, in early autumn in soilless or soil-based potting mix. Water well, then plunge in a cold frame or pit outdoors until the roots are well established and shoots appear, usually after 12–16 weeks. Ensure soil mix remains moist throughout the rooting period. Move into a cool greenhouse, first in low light and then increase to full light, and gradually increase the temperature to 50°F (10°C), then to no more than 64°F (18°C) when flowering. After bloom, keep moist and fertilize at least once with a balanced liquid fertilizer. Allow leaves to yellow and die, and plant bulbs in the open garden.

• **PROPAGATION** Sow seed of species as soon as ripe in deep containers, covering seed with ½–1in (1.5–2.5cm) of soil, in a cold frame.

After planting, keep frost-free, cool, and moist. After 2 years, transfer seedlings to a nursery bed and grow on until they reach flowering size, which may take up to 7 years. Alternatively, separate bulbs and replant as leaves fade in early summer, or in early autumn before new roots are produced.

• **PESTS AND DISEASES** The most serious problems include large narcissus bulb fly, bulb scale mite, narcissus nematode, slugs, narcissus basal rot and other fungal infections, and viruses (including narcissus yellow stripe virus).

***N.* 'Abba'** Division 4 daffodil. Double sport of N. 'Cragford', forces with minimal cold period in early to midspring. Flowers, 1–1½in (2.5–4cm) across, growing 3–5 florets per stem, are white with orange-flecked center segments. They have a heavenly fragrance. ↕14–16in (35–40cm).

***N.* 'Accent'.** Strong, vigorous Division 2 daffodil. In midseason, bears flowers 3½in (9cm) across, with flat, white perianth segments and a deep salmon-rose cup. ↕16–18in (40–45cm).

***N.* 'Acropolis'** ▣ Division 4 daffodil bearing well-formed, double flowers, 4½in (11cm) across, in midseason. Numerous snow-white segments are interspersed with bright orange-red ones. ↕18in (45cm).

***N.* 'Actaea'** ▣ Division 9 daffodil producing strongly scented flowers, 3¼in (8.5cm) across, in late season. Open, wavy, pure white perianth segments surround the red ribbon-like margin of the flattened, bowl-shaped yellow corona. ↕18in (45cm).

***N.* 'After All'.** Division 3 daffodil produces flowers, to 3½in (9cm) across, with creamy white petals and a red-rimmed, pale yellow cup. Blooms after almost all other daffodils have finished, in very late spring. ↕14–16in (35–40).

***N.* 'Albus Plenus Odoratus'** see *N. poeticus* 'Plenus'.

***N.* 'Ambergate'** ▣ Division 2 daffodil flowering in midseason. Flowers, 3¾in (9.5cm) across, have soft tangerine perianth segments and an expanded, rich orange cup. ↕16in (40cm).

***N.* 'Arctic Gold'** Division 1 daffodil. In midseason, bears smooth, waxy, rich golden yellow flowers, 3¾in (9.5cm) across, with a widely flanged, deeply notched trumpet. ↕16in (40cm).

***N.* 'Audubon'** ▣ Division 2 daffodil with glistening white flowers 3–3½in (8–9cm) across, set off with a coral-pink banded cup. Petals are rounded, overlapping, and pressed, and are borne in late spring. ↕16–18in (40–45cm).

***N.* 'Avalanche'** ▣ Division 8 daffodil producing 10 or more sweetly scented flowers, 1½in (4cm) across, with pure white perianth segments and a lemon-yellow cup, in midseason. Long-lasting cut flowers. ↕14in (35cm). Zone 6.

***N.* 'Avalon'.** Division 2 daffodil bears flowers, 3–4in (8–10cm) across, in midseason. Yellow petals take on a buffy hue with time; the cup matures to pure white. ↕14–16in (35–40cm).

***N.* 'Baby Moon'** ▣ Division 7 daffodil, a golden yellow, multiflowering clone of *N. jonquilla,* borne in late spring. Sweetly scented flowers are the size of a nickel or quarter, ¾–1in (2–2.5cm) across, and have grass-like foliage. ↕4–8in (10–20cm).

***N.* 'Baccarat'.** Tall-stemmed Division 11a daffodil. In late midseason, bears flowers, 3½in (9cm) across, with flat, rounded, pale yellow perianth segments and a darker corona. ↕20in (50cm).

***N.* 'Bantam'.** Division 2 daffodil with well-shaped flowers, 2¼in (5.5cm) across, on stiff stems, produced in midseason. Short, bright golden yellow perianth segments surround the short, flared, intense orange cup with an orange-red rim. ↕8–10in (20–25cm).

***N.* 'Barrett Browning'.** Division 3 daffodil producing flowers, 3–3½in (8–9cm) across, in early to midspring. White petals are brilliant, almost glowing, and the cup is orange/red. ↕14–16in (35–40cm).

***N.* 'Bartley'** ▣ Division 6 daffodil producing long-lasting, golden yellow flowers, 2½in (6cm) across, with a long, slender, angled trumpet and strongly reflexed perianth segments, borne early in the season. ↕16in (40cm).

***N.* 'Belcanto'.** Division 11a daffodil. Late in the season, bears flowers, 3–5in (8–13cm) across, with a white perianth, almost obscured by the flattened, pale yellow corona. ↕18in (45cm).

***N.* 'Bell Song'.** Division 7 daffodil. In mid- and late season, bears 2 or 3 flower stems, each with 1 or 2 nodding white flowers, 1½in (4cm) across, with a pale pink cup. ↕12in (30cm).

***N.* 'Berlin'** ▣ Division 2 daffodil. Short and sturdy with very large flowers, to 4in (10cm) across, borne in late spring. The flat, red-rimmed, extremely ruffled, Victorian collar-like cup contrasts with medium yellow, rounded perianth segments. ↕12–14in (30–35cm).

***N.* 'Beryl'** ▣ Vigorous Division 6 daffodil flowering early in the season. Flowers, 3in (7.5cm) across, have reflexed perianth segments, opening yellow but quickly fading to creamy white, and a small yellow and orange cup. ↕8in (20cm).

***N.* 'Birma'** Division 3 daffodil. Great perennializer, bearing flowers, 3–3½in (8–9cm) across, in early spring. Its very smooth, bright yellow petals and vivid

Narcissus cantabricus

Narcissus 'Broadway Star'

Narcissus bulbocodium

Narcissus canaliculatus

Narcissus 'Cassata'

Narcissus 'Ceylon'

Narcissus 'Charity May'

Narcissus 'Cheerfulness'

Narcissus 'Curlew'

Narcissus cyclamineus

Narcissus 'Dactyl'

Narcissus 'Delnashangh'

Narcissus 'Dream Light'

red cup prefer partial shade for best color. ↕ 16–18in (40–45cm).

***N.* 'Binkie'.** Robust Division 2 daffodil producing clear lemon-yellow flowers, 4in (10cm) across, in midseason. The long cup gradually fades to cream. ↕ 14in (35cm).

***N.* 'Birthright'.** Division 1 daffodil flowering in midseason. Bears almost square, crystalline, pure white flowers, 4½in (11cm) across, with a narrow, flanged trumpet. ↕ 16in (40cm).

***N.* 'Bittern'.** Division 12 daffodil with 2 to 3 intermediate-size flowers, 1½–2in (4–5cm) across, per stem. Nicely formed, recurved, sulfur yellow petals surrounding a short, demitasse-shaped pumpkin orange cup are produced in early to midspring. ↕ 6–10in (15–25cm).

***N.* 'Bob Minor'** ▣ Division 1 daffodil with stiff stems bearing golden yellow flowers, 2½in (6.5cm) across, in midseason. The perianth segments are twisted, and the long trumpet is slightly flared. ↕ 8in (20cm).

***N.* 'Bossa Nova'.** Free-flowering Division 3 daffodil. In midseason, bears flowers, 4in (10cm) across, with flat, orange-flushed perianth segments and a deep red cup. ↕ 20in (50cm).

***N.* 'Bravoure'** ▣ Division 1 daffodil flowering in midseason. Flowers, 5in (13cm) across, have an unusually long and slender yellow trumpet and overlapping, slightly pointed white perianth segments. ↕ 18in (45cm).

***N.* 'Bridal Crown'** ▣ Division 4 daffodil producing numerous sweetly scented, double flowers, 1½in (4cm) across, in mid- and late season. Flowers are mostly white, highlighted by short, orange-yellow corona segments in central clusters. ↕ 16in (40cm).

***N.* 'Broadway Star'** ▣ Division 11b daffodil with white flowers, 3in (8cm) across, in midseason. The expanded segments of the split corona are flattened against the perianth segments; each has a narrow, orange mid-stripe running lengthwise. ↕ 16in (40cm).

***N.* 'Broomhill'.** Long-lasting Division 2 daffodil. Robust, well-proportioned, smooth, waxy, pure white flowers, 4in (10cm) across, are borne in midseason. ↕ 16in (40cm).

N. bulbocodium ▣ (Hoop-petticoat daffodil). Small Division 10 daffodil with narrow, semi-cylindrical, dark green leaves, 4–16in (10–40cm) long. Funnel-shaped, deep yellow flowers, 1½in (4cm) across, with an expanded trumpet and tiny, pointed perianth segments, are produced in midseason. Can be naturalized in damp grass that dries in summer. ↕ 4–6in (10–15cm). S.W. and W. France, Portugal, Spain, N. Africa.

***N.* 'Burntollet'.** Division 1 daffodil. In midseason, bears smooth, pure white flowers, 4½in (11cm) across, with a long, well-proportioned trumpet, flanged at the mouth. ↕ 16in (40cm).

***N.* 'Camelot'.** Division 2 daffodil, very long-lasting and one of the latest-blooming all-yellow daffodils produced in mid- to late spring. Its flowers are 3½–4in (9–10cm) across, with rounded petals and a nicely formed cup. ↕ 12–14in (30–35cm).

N. campernelli see *N.* x *odorus.*

N. canaliculatus ▣ Division 8 daffodil producing 5–8 little tazetta-type flowers, ¾–1in (2–2.5cm) across, with sweetly fragrant, white petals and golden cups. Forces like a Paper White and prefers to be baked in the warm summer sun. ↕ 4–6in (10–15cm).

N. cantabricus ▣ (White hoop-petticoat daffodil). Division 10 daffodil with narrow, semi-cylindrical, slightly channeled leaves, to 6in (15cm) long. In winter, bears funnel-shaped white flowers, 1½in (4cm) across, with tiny, pointed perianth segments and an expanded trumpet. ↕ 6–8in (15–20cm). S. Spain, N. Africa. Zone 8.

***N.* 'Carlton'.** Division 2 daffodil with flowers, 3½–4in (9–10cm) across. One of the best perennializers, these two-toned yellow blooms, produced in early to midspring, have a vanilla-like fragrance. ↕ 14–16in (35–40cm).

***N.* 'Cassata'** ▣ Division 11a daffodil. In midseason, bears flowers 4in (10cm) across, with pure white perianth segments nearly obscured by the flattened corona segments, which open lemon and become white. ↕ 16in (40cm).

***N.* 'Ceylon'** ▣ Robust, erect Division 2 daffodil. In midseason, bears flowers 4in (10cm) across, with yellow perianth segments and a goblet-shaped, fiery orange cup. ↕ 16in (40cm).

***N.* 'Charity May'** ▣ Division 6 daffodil bearing lemon-yellow flowers, 3½in (9cm) across, with broad, reflexed perianth segments and a long cup, early in the season. ↕ 12in (30cm).

***N.* 'Cheerfulness'** ▣ Division 4 daffodil flowering late in the season. Each stem bears several sweetly scented, double white flowers, 2¼in (5.5cm) across, with a cluster of cream segments in the center. ↕ 16in (40cm).

***N.* 'Cherrygardens'.** Division 2 daffodil flowering in midseason. Flowers, 4¼in (10.5cm) across, have overlapping, sparkling white perianth segments and an intense pink corona, with darker rims and green eyes. ↕ 16in (40cm).

***N.* 'Chiloquin'.** Division 1 daffodil. Strong, vigorous stems bear a solitary greenish yellow flower, 3¼in (8.5cm) across, in midseason. The trumpet fades almost to white. ↕ 16in (40cm).

***N.* 'Chinese Coral'.** Division 1 daffodil with flowers, 3½–4in (9–10cm) across, blooming in midspring. The elegant white, sometimes greenish white, petals and long, coral-pink trumpet, are flared and scalloped at the end; they are eye-catching at the front of a border or pot. ↕ 10–13in (25–32.5cm).

***N.* 'Chit Chat'.** Division 7 daffodil with tiny but prolific flowers, to ¾in (2cm) across. All-yellow flowers are produced in late midspring. ↕ 3–4in (8–10cm).

***N.* 'Chromacolor'.** Division 2 daffodil producing flowers, 3½–4in (9–10cm) across, in mid to late spring. Pure white petals contrast with striking, very deep coral-pink cup, intensifying deeper into the interior. ↕ 14–17in (35–42.5cm).

***N.* 'Colblanc'.** Division 11 daffodil with flowers, 3½–4in (9–10cm) across, produced in midspring. The pure white flower has a "green eye," giving it a tropical appearance. ↕ 14–16in (35–40cm).

***N.* 'Como'.** Division 9 daffodil with scented flowers, 2¼in (5.5cm) across, borne late in the season. The rounded, snow-white perianth segments surround a small, flattened yellow corona with a green throat and bright red margin. ↕ 12in (30cm).

***N.* 'Cotinga'.** Division 6 daffodil. In early midseason, bears flowers, 3½in (9cm) across, with reflexing, ivory-white perianth segments and an apricot-pink trumpet, darker near the margin. ↕ 11in (28cm).

***N.* 'Cragford'.** Division 8 daffodil flowering early in the season. Each stem bears several scented white flowers, 2¼in (5.5cm) across, the corona interspersed with tangerine-orange perianth segments. ↕ 20in (50cm).

***N.* 'Curlew'** ▣ Floriferous hybrid Division 7 with fragrant flowers, 2–2½in (5–6cm) across, borne in late midspring. Long, trumpet-like cup opens creamy yellow and matures to ivory white. ↕ 12–14in (30–35cm).

N. cyclamineus ▣ Robust, vigorous Division 10 daffodil with spreading, narrow, keeled, bright green leaves, 5–12in (12–30cm) long. Produces solitary, nodding, golden yellow flowers, 1¾in (4.5cm) long, early in the season. Narrow perianth segments are completely reflexed from the long, narrow-waisted trumpet. ↕ 6–8in (15–20cm). N.W. Portugal, N.W. Spain.

***N.* 'Dactyl'** ▣ Division 9 daffodil producing flowers, 2½–3in (6–8cm) across, in late spring. Rounded, flat white flower has a contrasting small cup of deep gold, with a green eye and dark red rim. ↕ 12–14in (30–35cm).

***N.* 'Delibes'.** Division 2 daffodil with flowers, 3–4in (8–10cm) across. A great perennializer borne in early to midspring, the buttercup yellow, rounded, overlapping petals have broad, bright orange rim. ↕ 12–16in (30–40cm).

***N.* 'Delnashaugh'** ▣ Division 4 single-flowered daffodil, a double hybrid of 'Romance', with very large, showy flowers, 3–4in (8–10cm) across. White, overlapping, rounded petals surrounding a tight cluster of beautiful apricot-pink inner segments, are produced in late spring. ↕ 16–18in (40–45cm).

***N.* 'Descanso'.** Strong-growing Division 1 daffodil flowering in early and midseason. Flowers, 4½in (11.5cm) across, have triangular, shining white perianth segments and a slender, deep lemon-yellow trumpet, fading to clear lemon-yellow, flanged at the mouth. ↕ 18in (45cm).

***N.* 'Dovekie'.** Free-flowering Division 12 daffodil. In early midseason, each stem bears 1–4 flowers, 2in (5cm) across, with light lemon-yellow perianth segments with darker lobes and a fluted cup. Needs protection in cold areas. ↕ 12in (30cm).

***N.* 'Dreamlight'** ▣ Division 3 daffodil with flowers, 2½–3in (6–8cm) across, is often mistaken as a poeticus because of its form and coloration. Its white petals and a green-eyed, white cup have a

N

Narcissus 'Empress of Ireland'

Narcissus 'February Gold'

Narcissus 'Fortune'

Narcissus 'Geranium'

Narcissus 'Glenfarclas'

Narcissus 'Golden Ducat'

Narcissus 'Golden Quince'

Narcissus 'Grand Soleil d'Or'

Narcissus 'Hawera'

Narcissus 'Honeybird'

Narcissus 'Ice Follies'

Narcissus 'Ice Wings'

pinkish red edge, produced in late spring. ↕ 16–18in (40–45cm).

***N.* 'Dr. Hugh'.** Division 3 daffodil. In midseason, bears flowers, 4½in (11cm) across. The smooth white perianth segments surround a small orange cup with a clear green eye. ↕ 20in (50cm).

***N.* 'Dutch Master'.** Prolific Division 1 daffodil. In midseason, bears golden yellow flowers, 4½in (11cm) across, with broadly ovate perianth segments. The trumpet is expanded at the deeply indented mouth. ↕ 18in (45cm).

***N.* 'Easter Moon'.** Division 2 daffodil with circular, waxy, pure white flowers, 4in (10cm) across, borne in midseason. The short cup has a faintly green-tinted throat. ↕ 16in (40cm).

***N.* 'Erlicheer'** ▣ Division 4 daffodil produces a sweet-smelling bouquet on 1 stem, of little, double flowers, ¾–1¼n (2–3cm) across. White flowers, with honey-yellow segments interspersed, have tazetta blood lines, and are produced in early to midspring. ↕ 10–12in (25–30cm). Zone 4.

***N.* 'Elizabeth Ann'.** Division 6 daffodil blooming in late midseason. Rounded, slightly reflexed, pure white flowers, 2½in (6cm) across, have a cup-shaped trumpet with a narrow rim of rose-pink. ↕ 14in (35cm).

***N.* 'Empress of Ireland'** ▣ Division 1 daffodil flowering in midseason. Produces large white flowers, 4–4½in (10–11cm) across, with very broad, triangular, overlapping perianth segments and a narrow, widely flanged trumpet. Among the largest white trumpet daffodils. ↕ 16in (40cm).

***N.* 'Falconet'.** Division 8 daffodil with musky, sweet-perfumed flowers, 1½in (4cm) across. Three to 5 bright gold and rich orange flowers are produced in midspring. ↕ 12–14in (30–35cm).

***N.* 'February Gold'** ▣ Vigorous Division 6 daffodil flowering in early season. Flowers, 3in (7.5cm) across, have reflexed, golden yellow perianth segments and a long, slightly darker trumpet. ↕ 12in (30cm).

***N.* 'Flower Drift'.** Division 4 daffodil, a sport of 'Flower Record', has flowers, 3–4in (8–10cm) across. Upfacing, single-flowered ivory blooms with yellow/orange, intermingled segments are wonderful for mass plantings. A great perennializer borne in late midspring, it is blast resistant. ↕ 14–16in (35–40cm).

***N.* 'Flower Record'.** Division 2 daffodil with free-flowering blooms, 3–4 (8–9cm) across, produced in late midspring. Its upfacing white petals have a yellow cup that darkens toward the edge, ending with a red rim. ↕ 16–18in (40–45cm).

***N.* 'Fortune'** ▣ Division 2 daffodil. In midseason, bears flowers 4½in (11cm) across, with rich butter-yellow perianth segments and an expanding warm orange cup, becoming darker toward the mouth. ↕ 18in (45cm).

***N.* 'Foundling'.** Division 6 daffodil flowering in late midseason. Flowers, 3in (8cm) across, have broad white perianth segments, reflexed from the short, clear rose cup. ↕ 12in (30cm).

***N.* 'Fragrant Rose'.** Strong, vigorous Division 2 daffodil producing fragrant flowers, 4–4½in (10–11cm) across, with smooth, flat, thick, white perianth segments and a short, goblet-shaped, vivid pink cup, in late midseason. ↕ 18–20in (45–50cm).

***N.* 'Fruit Cup'.** Division 7 hybrid daffodil bearing flowers, 1¾in (4.5cm) across, with sweet, fruity fragrance and foliage of a jonquilla. Flowers are white and pale yellow, produced in late midspring. ↕ 10–12in (25–30cm).

Narcissus 'Erlicheer'

***N.* 'Geranium'** ▣ Division 8 daffodil. Late in the season, bears up to 6 scented, glistening white flowers, 2¼in (5.5cm) across, with a bright orange-red cup. Excellent for cutting. ↕ 14in (35cm).

***N.* 'Gigantic Star'.** Long-lasting Division 2 daffodil with very large flowers, to 4½in (11cm) across. Yellow flowers with a vanilla-like fragrance are produced in early to midspring. ↕ 18–24in (45–60cm).

***N.* 'Glenfarclas'** ▣ Division 1 daffodil with big, bright flowers, 3–4in (8–10cm) across. Produces golden yellow petals with an orange trumpet, in early to midspring. ↕ 12–16in (30–40cm).

***N.* 'Golden Aura'.** Division 2 daffodil producing rich golden yellow flowers, 3¾in (9.5cm) across, in midseason. Flowers have smooth, flat perianth segments and a large, well-proportioned, bell-shaped cup. ↕ 16in (40cm).

***N.* 'Golden Bells'.** Division 12 daffodil producing flowers ¾in (2cm) across, with 4–8 perfect little "hoop petticoats" coming from each bulb. Its rich golden yellow funnel-shaped cup with narrow star-like petals, is borne in midspring. Excellent for pots. ↕ 4–6in (10–15cm).

***N.* 'Golden Dawn'.** Division 8 daffodil. In midseason, each stem bears 1–3 flowers, 1½in (4cm) across, with gold perianth segments and an orange cup. ↕ 14–16in (35–40cm). Zone 5b.

***N.* 'Golden Ducat'** ▣ Division 4 daffodil bearing double, golden yellow flowers, 4½in (11cm) across, with many layers of pointed segments, in midseason. ↕ 14in (35cm).

***N.* 'Golden Quince'** ▣ Division 12 daffodil producing 1–3 soft yellow flowers, 1¼in (3cm) across, with a short, frilled, golden yellow cup, in early and midseason. Each bulb bears a succession of flower stems. ↕ 6in (15cm).

***N.* 'Grand Soleil d'Or'** ▣ Division 8 daffodil with each stem bearing many scented, double gold and tangerine-orange flowers, 1¾in (4.5cm) across, in early season. ↕ 18in (45cm). Zone 8.

***N.* 'Hawera'** ▣ Slender Division 5 daffodil with multiple stems per bulb, each bearing up to 5 canary-yellow flowers, 1¼–2in (3–5cm) across, with slightly reflexed perianth segments, late in the season. ↕ 7in (18cm).

***N.* 'High Society'.** Division 2 daffodil with nicely formed flowers, 3–4in (8–10cm) across, produced in late spring. Ivory white, hooded petals hug a white cup, which has a green eye and a pink rim. ↕ 16–18in (40–45cm).

***N.* 'Hillstar'.** Division 7 daffodil. In late midseason, each stem bears 2 or 3 flowers, 2in (5cm) across, with white-haloed, bright yellow perianth segments and a white-edged, ivory-buff corona. ↕ 16in (40cm).

***N.* 'Honeybird'** ▣ Division 1 daffodil bearing well-proportioned flowers, 4¼in (10.5cm) across, opening greenish yellow, in midseason. The trumpet gradually fades almost to pure white. ↕ 20in (50cm).

***N.* 'Hoopoe'.** Free-flowering Division 8 daffodil. In midseason, each stem produces 2 or 3 very fragrant flowers, 1½in (4cm) across, with rounded, yellow perianth segments and an orange cup. ↕ 18in (45cm).

***N.* 'Ice Follies'** ▣ Division 2 daffodil flowering in midseason. Produces flowers, 3¾in (9.5cm) across, with large, creamy white perianth segments and a wide cup, frilled at the mouth, that opens lemon-yellow and fades almost to white. Superb for forcing. ↕ 16in (40cm).

***N.* 'Ice King'** Division 4 daffodil, a double sport of N. 'Ice Follies', produces flowers, 3–4in (8–10cm) across, in early to midspring. Perianth segments are large and creamy white; the wide cup, frilled at the mouth, opens lemon-yellow and fades almost to white, and gives the appearance of a plate of egg salad. With characteristics similar to those of its cousin, it has a tendency to revert back to the original form. ↕ 16–18in (40–45cm).

***N.* 'Ice Wings'** ▣ Division 5 daffodil. Late in the season, bears 2 or 3 pure white flowers, 1½in (4cm) across, with strongly reflexed perianth segments and a relatively long, straight-sided trumpet. ↕ 14in (35cm).

***N.* 'Intrigue'.** Division 7 daffodil. In late midseason, produces lemon-yellow flowers, 1½in (4cm) across, with a long, frilly cup, which becomes intense white. ↕ 12in (30cm).

***N.* 'Irene Copeland'** ▣ Division 4 daffodil. In midseason, bears double flowers, 3¼in (8.5cm) across, with pure

Narcissus 'Irene Copeland'

Narcissus 'Jack Snipe'

Narcissus 'Jetfire'

Narcissus 'Jumblie'

Narcissus 'Kaydee'

Narcissus 'Lemon Drops'

Narcissus 'Lemon Glow'

Narcissus 'Little Beauty'

Narcissus 'Little Princess'

Narcissus 'Merlin'

Narcissus 'Minnow'

Narcissus 'Mount Hood'

white perianth segments and sulfur-yellow corona segments. ↕ 16in (40cm).
***N.* 'Itzim'.** Long-lasting Division 6 daffodil whose little flower, 2–2½in (5–6cm) across, is borne in early spring. Like a rocket, this yellow flower, with its rich orange cup, often points up with its petals flared back toward the ground. ↕ 10–12in (25–30cm).
***N.* 'Jack Snipe'** ▣ Vigorous Division 6 daffodil. In early and midseason, bears long-lasting flowers, 1½in (4cm) across, with reflexed white perianth segments and a short, lemon-yellow trumpet. Increases rapidly. ↕ 8in (20cm).
***N.* 'Jenny'.** Division 6 daffodil. In early and midseason, bears flowers 2in (5cm) across, with strongly reflexed, pointed, creamy white perianth segments and a long, clear lemon-yellow trumpet that fades to cream. Similar to *N.* 'Dove Wings' but perianth segments are more pointed. ↕ 12in (30cm).
***N.* 'Jetfire'.** ▣ Division 6 daffodil. Early in the season, bears flowers 3in (7.5cm) across, with strongly reflexed, golden yellow perianth segments and a long, bright orange trumpet, which fades in bright sun. ↕ 8in (20cm).
N. jonquilla (Wild jonquil). Division 10 daffodil with erect to spreading, narrow, semi-cylindrical leaves, 16–18in (40–45cm) long. Late in the season, bears heads of up to 5 strongly scented, golden yellow flowers, 1¼in (3cm) across, with small, pointed perianth segments and a tiny, flat cup. ↕ 12in (30cm). Spain. Zone 5.
***N.* 'Jumblie'** ▣ Small Division 12 daffodil. In early spring, bears multiple stems per bulb, each with up to 3 nodding flowers, 1¼in (3cm) across, with strongly reflexed, bright golden yellow perianth segments and a deeper yellow-orange cup. ↕ 7in (18cm).
***N.* 'Kaydee'** ▣ Division 6 medium-size daffodil, producing flowers, 2–2½in (5–6cm) across, in late midspring. The megaphone yellow cup is surrounded by white petals. ↕ 14–16in (35–40cm).
***N.* 'Kinellis'.** Division 10 daffodil. In midspring, produces the pinkest of the pink cyclamineus flowers, 1–1¼in (2.5–3cm) across. White petals enhance a vivid salmon-pink cup. ↕ 10–12in (25–30cm).
***N.* 'Kissproof'** Strong-growing perennial Division 2 daffodil, whose flowers, 3–4in (8–10cm) across, are produced in early to midspring. Flat cup has crimson "lipstick" coloration, surrounded by soft yellow, blushed petals. ↕ 16–18in (40–45cm).
***N.* 'Lark Whistle'.** Floriferous Division 6 daffodil. In midspring, bears long-lasting flowers, 2–2½in (5–6cm) across. Golden blossoms stand well above rosette-type foliage. ↕ 12–14in (30–35cm).
***N.* 'Lemon Beauty'.** Division 11b daffodil flowering in midseason. Flowers, 3½–4in (9–10cm) across, have white perianth segments and a corona with bright yellow stripes down the center. ↕ 16–18in (40–45cm).
***N.* 'Lemon Drops'** ▣ Division 5 daffodil producing large, teardrop-shaped flowers, 2–2½in (5–6cm) across, in midspring. Each stem has 2–3 bowed, two-toned yellow heads. ↕ 12–14in (30–35cm).
***N.* 'Lemon Glow'** ▣ Division 1 daffodil bearing greenish yellow flowers, to 3in (8cm) across, bordering between trumpet and large-cupped, in midseason. The straight corona darkens slightly toward the indented mouth. ↕ 18in (45cm).
***N.* 'Limbo'** Division 2 daffodil bearing flowers, 3–4in (8–10cm) across, in midspring. The bright brick-red cup bleeds into unusual bronzy-orange petals. ↕ 14–16in (35–40cm).
***N.* 'Little Beauty'** ▣ Sturdy, dwarf Division 1 daffodil bearing a well-formed, creamy white perianth, 1¼in (3cm) across, with a yellow trumpet, early in the season. ↕ 5½in (14cm).
***N.* 'Little Gem'.** Dwarf Division 1 daffodil bearing golden yellow flowers, 1¾in (4.5cm) across, early in the season. Similar to *N. minor* and probably a selection from it. ↕ 5in (13cm).
***N.* 'Little Princess'** ▣ Division 6 daffodil with flowers, 2½–3in (6–8cm) across. In mid- to late spring, bears a regal, smooth white perianth and a rich, deep salmon cup. Ideal choice for a window box or pot. ↕ 10–12in (25–30cm).
N. lobularis see *N. pseudonarcissus.*
***N.* 'Lorikeet'.** Division 1 daffodil produces flowers, 3–4in (8–10cm) across, in midspring. Soft yellow petals have a halo at the base, around a long, flaring, salmon-pink trumpet. ↕ 16–20in (40–50cm).
N.* x *mediolutens. Biflorus Division 13 daffodil blooms very late in spring. Usually two per stem, flowers, 1–1¼in (2.5–3cm) across, display a creamy white perianth and a very small, yellow cup. ↕ 10–12in (25–30cm).
***N.* 'Merlin'** ▣ Division 3 daffodil flowering late in the season. Flowers, 3in (7.5cm) across, have rounded, pure white perianth segments and a flattened, pale yellow cup, trimmed with a band of intense red. ↕ 18in (45cm).
***N.* 'Minnow'** ▣ Dwarf Division 8 daffodil. Up to 5 flowers, 1in (2.5cm) across, are produced early in the season, each with a pale yellow cup and yellow perianth segments fading to cream. Increases rapidly but may be shy to flower. ↕ 7in (18cm).
N. minor ▣ syn. *N. nanus* of gardens. Dwarf Division 10 daffodil with erect, narrow, flat or channeled, gray-green leaves, 3–6in (8–15cm) long, and yellow flowers, 1¼in (3cm) across, borne early in the season. Increases well. ↕ 4–6in (10–15cm). France, N. Spain.
subsp. *pumilus* see *N. pumilus.* **subsp. *pumilus* 'Plenus'** see *N.* 'Rip van Winkle'.
***N.* 'Mint Julep'.** Division 3 daffodil with flowers, 2½–3in (6–8cm) across. Very palest yellow, rounded, overlapping perianth segments with a showy, green-eyed cup, are borne in late midspring. ↕ 16–18in (40–45cm).
***N. minor* of gardens** see *N. pumilus.*
***N.* 'Misty Glen'.** Strong, free-flowering Division 2 daffodil. Flower, 3–3½in (8–9cm) across, is produced in late midspring. Opens pure white with satiny smooth perianths and a goblet-shaped cup. ↕ 16–18in (40–45cm).
***N.* 'Mondragon'.** Strong, upright, long-term perennial Division 11 daffodil, bearing flowers, 3–4in (8–10cm) across, in midspring. Bright medium yellow and bold reddish orange coloration with a strong, musky sweet, fragrance hinting of apples. ↕ 13–17in (37.2–42.5cm).
***N.* 'Mount Hood'** ▣ Division 1 daffodil flowering in midseason. Flowers, 4in (10cm) across, have well-formed, broadly overlapping, off-white perianth segments and a creamy white trumpet, soon fading to off-white; the

Narcissus minor

N

Narcissus x *odorus* 'Rugulosus'

Narcissus 'Papillon Blanc'

Narcissus 'Peeping Tom'

Narcissus 'Pencrebar'

Narcissus 'Pipit'

Narcissus poeticus var. *recurvus*

Narcissus 'Polar Ice'

Narcissus 'Precocious'

Narcissus 'Rainbow'

Narcissus 'Rip van Winkle'

Narcissus 'Rockall'

Narcissus romieuxii

trumpet broadens toward the mouth. ↕18in (45cm).
***N. nanus* of gardens** see *N. minor.*
N. obvallaris, syn. *N. pseudonarcissus* subsp. *obvallaris* (Tenby daffodil). Sturdy Division 10 daffodil with erect, glaucous, mid-green leaves, 12in (30cm) long, and stiff stems that bear neat, golden yellow flowers, 1½in (4cm) across, early in the season. Excellent for naturalizing. ↕12in (30cm). UK (S. Wales), W. Europe.
N.* x *odorus (*N. jonquilla* x *N. pseudonarcissus*) syn. *N. campernelli* (Campernelle jonquil). Division 10 daffodil with narrow, strap-shaped, strongly keeled leaves, to 20in (50cm) long. Early in the season, bears 1 or 2 strongly scented, golden yellow flowers, 1½in (4cm) across, with a large cup and narrow perianth segments. ↕10in (25cm). Garden origin. **'Rugulosus'** ■ is more robust, with up to 4 flowers, 2¼in (5.5cm) across; ↕12in (30cm).
***N.* 'Orange Queen'.** Division 7 daffodil with grass-like foliage, whose flowers, 1–1¼in (2.5–3cm) across, are an unusual bronzy gold. Produced in early to midspring. ↕10–12in (25–30cm).
***N.* 'Palmares'.** Division 11 daffodil producing flowers, 3–3½in (8–9cm) across, in mid- to late spring. The clear white perianth and medium-size very ruffled peachy-pink split corona have the appearance of a pink-and-white crinoline petticoat. ↕14–16in (35–40cm).
***N.* 'Paper White'** see *N. papyraceus.*
***N.* 'Paper White Grandiflorus'** see *N. papyraceus.*
***N.* 'Papillon Blanc'** ■ ('White Butterfly'). Division 11 daffodil with flowers, 3–3½in (8–9cm) across, that bloom in mid- to late spring. Smooth, white, overlapping petals have sunbursts of green and yellow in the cup, which mature to pure white. ↕17–18in (42.5–45cm).
N. papyraceus, syn. *N.* 'Paper White', *N.* 'Paper White Grandiflorus' (Paper-white narcissus). Division 8 daffodil with erect, keeled, glaucous, mid-green leaves, 12in (30cm) long. Bears clusters of up to 10 strongly fragrant, glistening white flowers, ½in (1.5cm) across, from winter to early spring. ↕14in (35cm). S. France, S. Spain, N. Africa. Zone 8. **'Ziva'**, syn. *N.* 'Ziva', is one of several clones used for forcing.
***N.* 'Pay Day'.** Division 1 daffodil. Showy recurved flowers are 3–3½in (8–9cm) across. Pressed rich yellow petals have a halo at the base and a yellow trumpet, borne in early to midspring. ↕14–16in (35–40cm).
***N.* 'Peeping Tom'** ■ Division 6 daffodil with a very recurved flower, 2½–3in (6–8cm) across, and the longest "nose" (cup) of the cultivars. All yellow, and produced in midspring. ↕12–16in (30–35cm).
***N.* 'Pencrebar'** ■ Small Division 4 daffodil with circular, fragrant, double, golden yellow flowers, 1¼in (3cm) across, often 2 per stem, borne in midseason. ↕7in (18cm).
***N.* 'Petrel'.** Division 5 daffodil producing clusters of up to 7 nodding, pure white flowers, 1¼in (3cm) across, with slightly reflexed perianth segments, late in the season. ↕10in (25cm).
***N.* 'Pink Angel'.** Division 7 daffodil. Each stem bears 2 or 3 fragrant flowers, 2½in (6cm) across, with flat, milk-white perianth segments and a green-eyed, white cup with a pink rim, in late midseason. ↕14in (35cm).
***N.* 'Pink Charm'.** Division 2 daffodil with elegant flowers, 3–4in (8–10cm) across, often 2 flowers per stem. Pure white petals surround a vivid pink banded cup, produced in late midspring. ↕14–16in (35–40cm).
***N.* 'Pink Paradise'.** Strong, vigorous Division 4 daffodil blooming in late midseason. Double flowers, 4in (10cm) across, have rounded, pure white perianth segments with a rose-pink corona. ↕16–18in (40–45cm).
***N.* 'Pink Pride'.** Division 2 daffodil. Flowers, 3–4in (8–10cm) across, have a sunproof, broad, pink cup, and are borne in midspring. ↕16–18in (40–45cm).
***N.* 'Pinza'.** Division 2 long-lasting daffodil, produced in early to midspring. Flowers, 3–4in (8–10cm) across, have rich golden yellow, spade-shaped petals; the cup is bright orange-red with a vivid golden yellow center. ↕16–18in (40–45cm).
***N.* 'Pipit'** ■ Division 7 daffodil bearing 2 or 3 sweetly scented, lemon-yellow flowers, 2in (5cm) across, in mid- and late season. The cup quickly fades to cream. ↕10in (25cm).
***N.* 'Pistachio'.** Division 1 daffodil produced in midspring. Flowers, 3–4in (8–10cm) across, have very soft yellow petals with a greenish cast, a white halo, and a glowing quality; the cup is white edged with yellow. ↕14–16in (35–40cm).
***N.* 'Pixie's Sister'.** Dwarf Division 7 daffodil producing clusters of up to 5 well-shaped, scented, golden yellow flowers, 1in (2.5cm) across, late in the season. ↕6in (15cm).
N. poeticus, (Poet's narcissus). Robust, variable Division 10 daffodil with erect, narrow, strap-shaped, channeled leaves, to 18in (45cm) long. Late in the season, bears solitary, fragrant flowers, 1¾–3in (4.5–8cm) across, with flat, pure white perianth segments and a tiny, red-rimmed yellow cup. ↕8–20in (20–50cm). France, Switzerland, Italy (widely naturalized in S. Europe). **'Plenus'**, syn. *N.* 'Albus Plenus Odoratus', has strongly fragrant, untidy, double, pure white flowers, 1½in (4cm) across. Occasionally, the remains of the red cup are visible between the perianth segments. Excellent for cutting; ↕16in (40cm). **var. *recurvus*** ■ (Old pheasant's eye) has flowers 1½in (4cm) across, with recurved, glistening white perianth segments; ↕14in (35cm); Switzerland.

Narcissus 'St. Keverne'

***N.* 'Poet's Way'.** Division 9 daffodil. Late in the season, bears scented flowers, 2¼in (5.5cm) across, with broad, smooth, pure white perianth segments and a bright yellow cup with a deep red rim and green eye. ↕16in (40cm).
***N.* 'Polar Ice'** ■ Division 3 all-white daffodil. Flowers, 1½–2½in (4–6cm) across, are produced in late midspring. 14–16in (35–40cm).
***N.* 'Precocious'** ■ Division 2 daffodil with flamboyant flowers, to 3½in (9cm) across, produced in late midspring. Very curly, flat, large cup in shades of bright coral-pink folds back against pristine white petals. ↕14–17in (35–42.5cm).
***N.* 'Primeur'.** Division 1 daffodil. Produces one of the latest-blooming flowers, 3–4in (8–10cm) across, in midspring. The trumpet is a deep rich golden yellow, with enormous substance. ↕14–16in (35–40cm).
***N.* 'Printal'.** Long-lasting Division 11 daffodil that produces flowers, 3–4in (8–10cm) across, in early to midspring. Overlapping white petals circle an almost curly, clear yellow cup. A great forcer. ↕16–18in (40–45cm).
N. pseudonarcissus, syn. *N. lobularis* (Lent lily, Wild daffodil). Very variable Division 10 daffodil with erect, strap-shaped, usually glaucous, mid-green leaves, 3–20in (8–50cm) long. Nodding flowers, 1½–3in (4–8cm) across, with a yellow trumpet and narrow, twisted cream perianth segments, are produced early in the season. Good for naturalizing. ↕6–14in (15–35cm). Europe. **subsp. *obvallaris*** see *N. obvallaris.*
***N.* 'Pueblo'.** Division 7 daffodil. In late spring, produces prolific, fragrant, all-white flowers, 1½–2in (4–5cm) across. ↕12–14in (30–35cm).
N. pumilus, syn. *N. minor* of gardens, *N. minor* subsp. *pumilus.* Small Division 10 daffodil with erect, channeled or flat, gray-green leaves, 3–6in (8–15cm) long. Bears yellow flowers, 1¼in (3cm) across, with a flared, frilled trumpet, early in the season. Similar to *N. minor*, which has a straighter trumpet. ↕4–6in (10–15cm). Possibly garden origin. **'Plenus'** see *N.* 'Rip van Winkle'.
***N.* 'Punchline'.** Division 7 daffodil, borne in midspring. Many fragrant flowers, 1½–2in (4–5cm) across, bloom above the stem. Petals and cup are of the

Narcissus rupicola

Narcissus 'Salome'

Narcissus 'Scarlet Gem'

Narcissus 'Scilly White'

Narcissus 'Shining Light'

Narcissus 'Silver Chimes'

Narcissus 'Sir Winston Churchill'

Narcissus 'Stratosphere'

Narcissus 'Suzy'

Narcissus 'Sweetness'

Narcissus 'Tête-à-Tête'

Narcissus 'Thalia'

palest yellow; the small, broad cup is rimmed in pink. ↕ 14–16in (35–40cm).
***N.* 'Quail'.** Robust Division 7 daffodil. Late in the season, bears 2 or 3 scented, golden yellow flowers, 1½in (4cm) across, with a long cup and neat perianth segments. ↕ 16in (40cm).
***N.* 'Rainbow'** ■ Vigorous Division 2 daffodil flowering in midseason. Bears consistently good-quality flowers, 4in (10cm) across, with fine-textured white perianth segments and a white cup with a broad band of copper-pink at the slightly indented mouth. ↕ 18in (45cm).
***N.* 'Rapture'.** Long-lasting Division 6 daffodil. Early in the season, bears strongly reflexed, pendent, lemon-yellow flowers, 3in (8cm) across, with a very long, narrow trumpet. ↕ 14in (35cm).
***N.* 'Rijnveld's Early Sensation'.** Division 1 daffodil producing yellow flowers, 3½in (9cm) across, in late winter. Very early-flowering and long-lasting. ↕ 10–14in (25–35cm).
***N.* 'Rip van Winkle'** ■ syn. *N. minor* subsp. *pumilus* 'Plenus', *N. pumilus* 'Plenus'. Division 4 daffodil bearing double, greenish yellow flowers, 2in (5cm) across, with irregular, pointed perianth segments, early in the season. ↕ 5½in (14cm).
***N.* 'Rockall'** ■ Division 3 daffodil flowering in late midseason. Flowers, 4½in (11cm) across, have large, overlapping, slightly pointed white perianth segments and a saucer-shaped, finely fluted, rich orange-red corona. ↕ 20in (50cm).
***N.* 'Romance'.** Strong-stemmed Division 2 daffodil, borne in late midspring. Flowers, 3–3½in (8–9cm) across, have clear white perianth segments and pink, teacup-shaped cup, often with a tiny soft pink rim. ↕ 16–18in (40–45cm)
N. romieuxii ■ Small Division 10 daffodil with erect or spreading, narrow, semi-cylindrical, dark green leaves, to 8in (20cm) long. Early in the season, bears funnel-shaped flowers, 1½in (4cm) across, which vary from pale straw-yellow to pale primrose-yellow. Similar to *N. bulbocodium*, which has deeper yellow flowers. ↕ 3–4in (8–10cm). N. Africa. Zone 8.
N. rupicola ■ Division 10 daffodil with erect, thin, cylindrical, keeled, gray-green leaves, 7in (18cm) long. Circular, golden yellow flowers, 1¼in (3cm) across, with a shallow, 6-lobed cup, are produced in midseason. ↕ 6in (15cm). Portugal, Spain.
***N.* 'St. Keverne'** ■ Erect Division 2 daffodil bearing rich golden yellow flowers, 4in (10cm) across, in midseason. The large cup, occasionally trumpet-sized, is indented at the rims and slightly flared. ↕ 18in (45cm).
***N.* 'Salome'** ■ Division 2 daffodil flowering in midseason. Produces consistently good-quality flowers, 3½in (9cm) across, with smooth, waxy, pale cream perianth segments and a large, almost trumpet-shaped, peach pink cup. ↕ 18in (45cm).
***N.* 'Scarlet Gem'** ■ Division 8 daffodil with clusters of many scented yellow flowers, 2in (5cm) across, with a red-orange cup, produced in midseason. Good for cutting. ↕ 14in (35cm).
***N.* 'Scilly White'** ■ Floriferous Division 8 daffodil has fragrant clusters of flowers, 1–1¼in (2.5–3cm) across. Creamy white cups are surrounded by white petals. ↕ 12–16in (30–40cm). Zone 7b.
***N.* 'Segovia'.** Division 3 daffodil producing flowers, to 1½in (4cm) across, in midspring. Pure white, rounded, overlapping petals surround small, light yellow, flat cup. ↕ 5–6in (13–15cm).
***N.* 'Shining Light'** ■ Division 2 daffodil bearing uniform flowers, 3¼in (8.5cm) across, in midseason. They have slightly pointed, smooth, butter-yellow perianth segments and a goblet-shaped, bright orange-red cup, slightly indented at the mouth. ↕ 16in (40cm).
***N.* 'Silent Valley'.** Division 1 daffodil. In midseason, bears snow-white flowers, 4½in (11.5cm) across. Strongly overlapping, broad, pointed, smooth perianth segments surround the trumpet with a striking green eye. ↕ 16in (40cm).
***N.* 'Silver Chimes'** ■ Sturdy Division 8 daffodil. In mid- and late season, bears up to 10 nodding, scented, creamy white flowers, 2in (5cm) across, with a pale primrose cup. ↕ 12in (30cm).
***N.* 'Sir Winston Churchill'** ■ Sturdy Division 4 daffodil, a sport of *N.* 'Geranium', with the same fragrance and perennial habits. Produces 3–5 dollar-size flowers, 1½–2in (4–5cm) across, in late midspring. Creamy white flowers have orange flecks interspersed. ↕ 15–17in (37.5–42.5cm).
***N.* 'Smyrna'.** Division 9 daffodil. In midseason, bears scented flowers, 2½in (6cm) across, with rounded, pure white perianth segments and a small, flattened, bright orange corona. ↕ 16in (40cm).
***N.* 'Sorbet'.** Strong, long-term Division 11 daffodil bearing flowers, 3–3½in (8–9cm) across. A creamy combination of ice white and whipped orange, blooming in late to midspring. ↕ 14–16in (35–40cm).
***N.* 'Space Shuttle'.** Division 11 daffodil, borne in mid- to late spring. Flowers, 3–3½in (8–9cm) across, have a creamy white perianth with a unique orange- and yellow- streaked minimal corona. ↕ 16–18in (40–45cm).
***N.* 'Spellbinder'.** Vigorous Division 1 daffodil bearing greenish yellow flowers, 4–4½in (10–11.5cm) across, in midseason. The corona gradually fades to white, with whitish green at the mouth. ↕ 20in (50cm).
***N.* 'Stratosphere'** ■ Division 7 daffodil. In late midseason, each tall, strong stem bears up to 3 scented

Narcissus 'Tahiti'

blooms, to 2½in (6.5cm) across, with smooth yellow perianth segments and a small, deep gold cup. ↕ 26in (65cm).
***N.* 'Sun Disc'.** Neat, dwarf Division 7 daffodil with stiff stems, each bearing a single, perfectly circular, mid-yellow flower, 2in (5cm) across, late in the season. The perianth segments fade to cream with age. ↕ 7in (18cm).
***N.* 'Suzy'** ■ Division 7 daffodil producing 1 or 2 scented flowers, 2½in (6cm) across, with primrose-yellow perianth segments and a rich orange cup, in midseason. ↕ 16in (40cm).
***N.* 'Sweetness'** ■ Division 7 daffodil. Early in the season, bears solitary, strongly fragrant, golden yellow flowers, 1½in (4cm) across. ↕ 16in (40cm).
***N.* 'Tahiti'** ■ Division 4 daffodil with double flowers, 4½in (11cm) across, borne in midseason. Regular, rounded, rich golden yellow perianth segments surround a cluster of bright red-orange corona segments. ↕ 18in (45cm).
N. tazetta. Very variable Division 10 daffodil with erect, broad, twisted, keeled, glaucous, mid-green leaves, 8–20in (20–50cm) long. In winter or spring, bears up to 20 sweetly scented flowers, 1½in (4cm) across, with white perianth segments and a yellow cup. ↕ 6–20in (15–50cm). Mediterranean region. Widely naturalized in many parts of the world.
***N.* 'Tête-à-Tête'** ■ Vigorous, dwarf Division 12 daffodil. Early in the season, each stem bears 1–3 flowers, 2½in (6.5cm) across, with deep golden yellow perianth segments, slightly reflexed from the deeper yellow cup. Excellent for forcing, naturalizing, or growing in a rock garden. ↕ 6in (15cm).
***N.* 'Thalia'** ■ Division 5 daffodil. In midseason, bears 2 milk-white flowers, 2in (5cm) across, with narrow, twisted, slightly reflexed perianth segments and an open cup. ↕ 14in (35cm).
***N.* 'Tonga'.** Division 4 daffodil bearing well-formed, scented, double flowers, 3in (8cm) across, in midseason. Deep primrose-yellow perianth segments, becoming paler yellow, are intermingled with short, bright red corona segments. ↕ 16in (40cm).
***N.* 'Tracey'.** Division 6 daffodil. Early in the season, bears flowers, 3in (8cm) across, with reflexed white perianth

Narcissus triandrus

Narcissus 'Trousseau'

Narcissus 'Vigil'

Narcissus watieri

Narcissus 'Woodland Star'

Narcissus 'Yellow Cheerfulness'

segments and a trumpet-shaped, pale yellow corona. ↕ 10in (25cm).
N. 'Tresamble'. Robust Division 5 daffodil producing 1–3 well-formed flowers, 3½in (9cm) across, in mid-and late season. Flowers have spreading, milk-white perianth segments and a cream cup. ↕ 16in (40cm).
N. 'Trevithian'. Vigorous Division 7 daffodil bearing 1–3 scented, soft lemon-yellow flowers, 3in (8cm) across, late in the season. The perianth segments are well-rounded; the cup is short and flared. ↕ 18in (45cm).
N. triandrus ■ (Angel's tears). Small Division 10 daffodil with decumbent or erect, narrow, flat or channeled leaves, 8–12in (20–30cm) long. In midseason, bears 1–6 nodding cream flowers, 2½in (6cm) across, with reflexed perianth segments and a rounded cup. ↕ 4–10in (10–25cm). Portugal, Spain.
N. 'Tricollet'. Division 11 daffodil with flowers, 3–3½in (8–9cm) across. Produced in mid- to late spring, it is easily recognized by its white petals and tangerine cup, which has only 3 visible segments. ↕ 14–16in (35–40cm).
N. 'Tripartite'. Division 11a daffodil. Late in the season, produces stems of up to 3 golden yellow flowers, 2–2½in (5–6cm) across. The flowers have an expanded corona, split into 6 segments that lie flat against the perianth segments. ↕ 18in (45cm).
N. 'Trousseau' ■ Division 1 daffodil bearing delicate, satin-like flowers, 5in (13cm) across, in midseason. White perianth segments surround the flanged trumpet, which opens soft yellow and turns beige-pink. ↕ 18in (45cm).
N. 'Tuesday's Child'. Division 5 daffodil. In midseason, bears 1–3 slightly pendent flowers, 2½in (6cm) across. Pointed white perianth segments are swept back from the short, lemon-yellow corona. ↕ 14in (35cm).
N. 'Tutankhamun'. Division 2 daffodil. In midseason, bears trumpet-shaped, intense white flowers, 4¼in (10.5cm) across, with a conspicuous green eye. ↕ 16in (40cm).
N. 'Unique'. Division 4 daffodil producing well-formed, double flowers, 4¼in (10.5cm) across, late in the season. They are circular, with broad, rounded white perianth segments, interleaved with rich yellow corona segments in the center. ↕ 20in (50cm).
N. 'Verona' Division 3 daffodil flowering late in the season. Bears circular flowers, 3¾–4in (9.5–10cm) across, with broadly overlapping white perianth segments. The flattish, fluted cup opens cream and soon fades to white. ↕ 18in (45cm).
N. 'Vigil' ■ Division 1 daffodil. In late midseason, bears pure white flowers, 5in (12.5cm) across, with sharply pointed, finely textured perianth segments and a long, slender trumpet, slightly rolled at the mouth. ↕ 16in (40cm).
N. 'Viking'. Division 1 daffodil. In midseason, bears deep golden yellow flowers, 4½in (11.5cm) across, with broad, pointed perianth segments and a long, slightly expanded trumpet, frilled at the mouth. ↕ 18in (45cm).
N. 'Virginia Sunrise'. Division 2 daffodil bearing flowers, 3½–4in (9–10cm) across, in midspring. Very bright, frilled, large orange cup is offset by a sparkling clear white perianth. ↕ 18–20in (45–50cm).
N. watieri ■ Tiny Division 10 daffodil with erect, narrow, keeled, gray-green leaves, 7in (18cm) long. In midseason, bears solitary flowers, ½in (1.5cm) across, with flat, pure white perianth segments and a widely funnel-shaped corona. ↕ 4in (10cm). N. Africa.
N. 'White Plume'. Strong, sturdy Division 2 daffodil. Produces all-white flowers, 3–3½in (8–9cm) across, in late midspring. ↕ 18–20in (45–50cm).
N. 'Woodland Star' ■ Division 3 daffodil. In late midseason, produces flowers 3¾in (9.5cm) across, with pure white perianth segments contrasting with the small, bowl-shaped, deep orange-red cup. ↕ 20in (50cm).
N. 'W.P. Milner'. Sturdy Division 1 daffodil bearing nodding flowers, 2½in (6cm) across, early in the season. Forward-pointing, cream perianth segments surround the pale, creamy white trumpet. ↕ 9in (23cm).
N. 'Yellow Cheerfulness' ■ Division 4 daffodil producing strong stems of 3 or 4 circular, sweetly scented, double, golden yellow flowers, ¾in (2cm) across, late in the season. ↕ 18in (45cm).
N. 'Ziva' see *N. papyraceus* 'Ziva'.

NAUTILOCALYX

GESNERIACEAE

Genus of 38 species of evergreen perennials, often woody at the bases, from open woodland in the West Indies, Central America, and tropical South America. They are grown for their opposite, prominently veined, glossy leaves and tubular, 5-lobed flowers, borne singly or in clustered cymes in the upper leaf axils, sometimes accompanied by showy, persistent calyces. Where not hardy, grow in a warm greenhouse.
In warmer areas, plant among shrubs or trees.
• **CULTIVATION** Under glass, grow in soilless potting mix in bright filtered light and high humidity. During the growing season, water freely and apply a balanced liquid fertilizer monthly. Water moderately in winter. Outdoors, grow in moist but well-drained, humus-rich soil in light shade.
• **PROPAGATION** Root softwood or stem-tip cuttings in spring or summer.
• **PESTS AND DISEASES** Mealybugs and tarsonemid mites may be troublesome.

N. bullatus, syn. *N. tessellatus*. Erect perennial with elliptic, finely toothed, puckered, dark green leaves, to 9in (23cm) long, purple beneath. From spring to summer, bears cymes of up to 10 hairy, pale yellow flowers, 1¼in (3cm) across. ↕ 24in (60cm), ↔ 14in (35cm). Peru. ❀ (min. 61°F/16°C)
N. lynchii ■ Erect, branched perennial with elliptic-lance-shaped, toothed, very dark green, sometimes red-purple leaves, 5in (13cm) long, red-purple beneath. In summer, bears cymes of 2 or 3 yellow flowers, to 1¼in (3cm) across, with red hairs outside, purple streaks inside, and maroon sepals. ↕ 24in (60cm), ↔ 12in (30cm). Colombia. ❀ (min. 61°F/16°C)
N. pallidus. Upright perennial with ovate-lance-shaped, scalloped to toothed, pale green leaves, to 10in (25cm) long, with sparsely softly woolly veins and recurved apexes. From spring to summer, bears axillary cymes of 3–6 cream-white flowers, to 1¼in (3cm) across, purple-marked inside. ↕ to 20in (50cm), ↔ 12in (30cm). Peru. ❀ (min. 61°F/16°C)
N. tessellatus see *N. bullatus*.

Nautilocalyx lynchii

▷ ***Neanthe bella*** see *Chamaedorea elegans*

NECTAROSCORDUM

LILIACEAE

Genus of 3 species of bulbous perennials, closely allied to *Allium*, from damp or shady woodland, rocky places, and dry mountain slopes of S. Europe and W. Asia. They have linear, deeply channeled or keeled leaves, which smell of garlic. Loose umbels of bell-shaped flowers, ¾–1in (2–2.5cm) long, are borne in summer. Grow in a wild garden or herbaceous border.
• **CULTIVATION** Grow in any moderately fertile, well-drained soil in full sun or partial shade. May self-seed freely.
• **PROPAGATION** Sow seed in containers in a cold frame in autumn or spring. Remove offsets in summer.
• **PESTS AND DISEASES** Infrequent.

N. dioscoridis see *N. siculum* subsp. *bulgaricum*.
N. siculum, syn. *Allium siculum*. Robust, bulbous perennial with linear, sharply keeled, basal leaves, 12–16in (30–40cm) long. In summer, thick stems bear umbels of 10–30 pendulous, open bell-shaped, white or cream flowers, ½–1in (1.5–2.5cm) long, flushed pink or purplish red, and tinted green at the bases. Seed pods become erect as flowers fade. ↕ to 4ft (1.2m), PD4in (10cm). France, Italy. Zone 5.
subsp. *bulgaricum* ■ syn. *Allium bulgaricum*, *N. dioscoridis*, has off-white flowers, flushed green and purple. S.E. Europe, N.W. Turkey, Ukraine (Crimea).

Nectaroscordum siculum subsp. *bulgaricum*

Neillia thibetica

NEILLIA

ROSACEAE

Genus of 10 species of deciduous shrubs and subshrubs, with branching, zigzag stems, found in scrub and at rocky stream margins in the Himalayas and E. Asia. The dark, glossy leaves are alternate, irregularly toothed, each with up to 5, but usually 3 lobes. They are cultivated for their graceful, arching habit and their racemes or panicles of small, bell-shaped or tubular flowers, profusely borne in late spring and early summer. Grow in a shrub border.

• **CULTIVATION** Grow in fertile, well-drained soil in full sun or partial shade. Pruning group 2 or 3, after flowering.

• **PROPAGATION** Take greenwood cuttings in early summer. Remove suckers in autumn.

• **PESTS AND DISEASES** Infrequent.

N. longiracemosa see *N. thibetica.*

N. sinensis. Thicket-forming, suckering shrub with arching shoots and peeling brown bark. Leaves are usually 3-lobed, ovate to oblong, sharply toothed, and long-pointed, to 4in (10cm) long. In late spring and early summer, small, tubular, pinkish white flowers, to ½in (12mm) long, are produced in slender, 12- to 20-flowered racemes, to 2½in (6cm) long. ↕↔ 6ft (2m). C. China. Zone 7.

N. thibetica ■ syn. *N. longiracemosa.* Thicket-forming, suckering shrub with arching shoots and ovate or ovate-oblong, 3-lobed, long-pointed, toothed, bright green leaves, to 4in (10cm) long. In early summer, small, tubular-bell-shaped, rose-pink flowers, to ⅜in (9mm) long, are produced in arching racemes, to 6in (15cm) long. ↕↔ 6ft (2m). W. China. Zone 7.

NELUMBO

Lotus

NELUMBONACEAE

Genus of 2 species of rhizomatous, marginal aquatic perennials from Asia, N. Australia, and E. North America, found at the shallow margins or on the muddy banks of pools. They are widely cultivated and naturalized in subtropical and tropical areas. The handsome, horizontally held, peltate, waxy-bloomed, almost circular leaves are held well above the water. The showy, solitary, fragrant, waterlily-like flowers

Nelumbo lutea

are borne on long stalks, and develop distinctive, flat-topped seed pods that may be dried for use in flower arrangements. They are excellent as specimen plants in an outdoor pool. Where not hardy, grow *N. nucifera* in an indoor tropical pool, or in large, water-filled half-barrels on a patio outdoors.

• **CULTIVATION** In an outdoor pool, grow in large containers in heavy loam enriched with well-rotted manure or soil mix, in full sun. Lotuses require several weeks of sunny weather above 80°F (27°C) to bloom. Fertilize twice monthly during rapid growth with commercial aquatic plant fertilizer tablets. As growth proceeds, gradually lower the containers to increase the water depth to 16–24in (40–60cm), or 6–9in (15–23cm) for smaller cultivars; they will grow satisfactorily with as little as 2–4in (5–10cm) of water over the surface of the container. Remove fading foliage. In very cold areas, reduce the water level gradually in autumn, remove the containers, and overwinter in frost-free conditions, keeping the rhizomes just moist. Alternatively, lower the containers to the bottom of the pool, below the ice line. Under glass, grow in large containers in an indoor pool in full light. See also pp.52–53.

• **PROPAGATION** Sow seed in spring, preferably scarified before sowing, at a minimum temperature of 77°F (25°C), in small containers of loam covered by 2in (5cm) of water. Increase water depth and container size until plants are large enough to plant in the flowering site. Carefully divide the fragile rhizomes, which resent disturbance, in spring.

Nelumbo 'Mrs. Perry D. Slocum'

• **PESTS AND DISEASES** Sometimes affected by leaf spots, caterpillars, spider mites, and whiteflies.

N. lutea ■ (American lotus, Water chinquapin, Yanquapin). Aquatic perennial with radical, concave-circular, bluish green leaves, 20in (50cm) across, prominently veined beneath, held on stalks to 6ft (2m) long. Rose-like yellow flowers, to 10in (25cm) across, are produced in summer. ↕ 6ft (2m), ↔ indefinite. North America. Zone 4.

***N.* 'Mrs. Perry D. Slocum'** ■ Aquatic perennial with rounded, flat or wavy-margined, glaucous, gray-green leaves, 32in (80cm) across, on stalks to 4½ft (1.4m) long. In summer, freely produces deep pink flowers, to 12in (30cm) across, turning yellow over a period of several days. ↕ 4–5ft (1.2–1.5m). ↔ indefinite. Zone 4.

N. nucifera (Sacred lotus). Aquatic perennial with flat or concave-circular, wavy-margined, glaucous, mid-green leaves, 32in (80cm) across, on stalks to 6ft (2m) long. Peony-like, sometimes double, pink or white flowers, to 12in (30cm) across, are produced in summer on long stalks with short, fleshy prickles. ↕ 28–60in (0.7–1.5m), above water level, ↔ indefinite. Asia (Iran to Japan), N. Australia. Zone 6. **'Alba Grandiflora'** has wavy-margined, dark green leaves, and bears white flowers, 9–10in (22–25cm) across, sometimes hidden in the foliage; ↕ 4–6ft (1.2–1.8m). **'Alba Striata'** has white flowers, with jagged red margins. **'Charles Thomas'** has lavender-pink flowers, 6–8in (15–20cm) across. Grow in a barrel or small pool; ↕ 26–36in (60–90cm). **'Chawan Basu'** bears abundant, pink-edged, white flowers. **'Empress'** has crimson-fringed, white flowers. **'Kermesina'** bears fully double, rose-pink to bright red flowers, 6–8in (15–20cm) across, on stiff stems well above the leaves; ↕ 26–36in (60–90cm). **'Momo Botan'** has long-lasting flowers, to 6in (15cm) across, with dark rose-pink petals, yellow toward the bases. Suitable for a small pool or half-barrel; ↕ 2–4ft (60–120cm). **'Rosea Plena'** has double, dark rose-pink flowers, 10–14in (25–35cm) across, yellowish toward the bases; ↕ 4–5ft (1.2–1.5m). **'Speciosum'** bears single, light pink flowers.

NEMATANTHUS

GESNERIACEAE

Genus of about 30 species of scandent or trailing, evergreen, usually epiphytic subshrubs, often becoming woody at the bases, from tropical rainforest in South America. They have opposite, sometimes whorled, elliptic to obovate, entire to toothed, fleshy leaves. The colorful flowers, borne singly or in clustered cymes in the leaf axils, are tubular and pouched. Where not hardy, grow in a warm greenhouse or as houseplants. Elsewhere, grow epiphytically on trees or shrubs, or underplant among them.

• **CULTIVATION** Under glass, grow in soilless potting mix in bright filtered light, or full light with shade from hot sun, with moderate humidity. Water moderately (less in winter), and feed actively growing plants every month with a balanced liquid fertilizer. For

Nematanthus gregarius

sporadic flowering through winter, maintain a minimum temperature of 59–61°F (15–16°C). Tip-prune young plants when young to encourage branching. Outdoors, grow in moist but well-drained, humus-rich soil in partial shade.

• **PROPAGATION** Take stem-tip cuttings in spring.

• **PESTS AND DISEASES** Occasionally affected by leaf spots and aphids.

***N.* 'Cheerio'.** Semi-upright to trailing subshrub with ovate, fleshy, glossy, dark green leaves, ¾–1in (2–2.5cm) long, borne in opposite pairs. Bears solitary, tubular, pouched, bright orange flowers, ¾in (2cm) long, from spring to autumn. ↕ 8in (20cm), ↔ 8–10in (20–25cm). ❀ (min. 50–59°F/10–15°C)

N. gregarius ■ syn. *Hypocyrta radicans, N. radicans.* Trailing to pendent or scandent subshrub with elliptic to obovate, fleshy, glossy, rich green leaves, ¾–1½in (2–4cm) long, borne in opposite pairs or whorls of 3. Clusters of 1–3 tubular, pouched, bright orange flowers, 1in (2.5cm) long, with purple-brown stripes and green, orange-tipped calyces, are borne in summer. ↕ to 32in (80cm), ↔ 36in (90cm) or more. Brazil. ❀ (min. 50–59°F/10–15°C)

N. radicans see *N. gregarius.*

***N.* 'Tropicana'** ■ Erect, freely-branching subshrub with purple stems and opposite, obovate, thick, fleshy, glossy, dark green leaves, 1¼in (3cm) long. Tubular, pouched, glossy, dark yellow flowers, 1in (2.5cm) long, with maroon stripes, enclosed in long-lasting, leafy, bright red calyces, are produced throughout the year. ↕ 12in (30cm), ↔ 18in (45cm). ❀ (min. 55°F/13°C)

Nematanthus 'Tropicana'

NEMESIA

SCROPHULARIACEAE

Genus of 50 or more species of bushy, erect annuals, perennials, and subshrubs from South Africa, where they grow in sandy soils near the coast or in scrubby, often disturbed soil inland. The leaves are opposite, simple, usually linear to lance-shaped, frequently toothed. The showy, almost trumpet-shaped, 2-lipped flowers (the upper lip 4-lobed, the lower lip unlobed or 2-lobed) are borne singly in the upper leaf axils or in short terminal racemes. Annual cultivars are colorful summer bedding plants outdoors, or may be grown as short-lived, early spring-flowering container plants in a cool greenhouse. They are good for cutting. *N. caerulea* is suitable for a raised bed or herbaceous border, and is often used as a container plant.

• **CULTIVATION** Grow in moist but well-drained, moderately fertile, slightly acidic soil in full sun. Water annuals freely in dry weather to maintain flower production. Under glass, grow in soil-based potting mix in full light. Water moderately during growth. Pinch out growing tips to promote bushiness.

• **PROPAGATION** Sow seed at 59°F (15°C) from early to late spring, or in autumn for spring-flowering container plants. Take tip cuttings of unflowered shoots from perennial species in late summer; overwinter young plants in frost-free conditions.

• **PESTS AND DISEASES** Foot rot and root rot may cause problems.

N. caerulea ■ syn. *N. foetens* of gardens, *N. fruticans* of gardens. Woody-based perennial with erect or spreading stems and entire or toothed, linear to lance-shaped leaves, 1½in (4cm) long. Produces terminal racemes of short-tubed, 2-lipped, pink, pale blue, lavender-blue, or white flowers, to ½in (1.5cm) long, with yellow throats, from early summer to autumn. ↕ to 24in (60cm), ↔ 12in (30cm). South

Nemesia strumosa Carnival Series

Africa (Northern Transvaal, Eastern Transvaal, Orange Free State, KwaZulu/Natal), Lesotho. ❄ (min. 41°F/5°C). **'Innocence'** has white flowers. **'Joan Wilder'** has deep lavender-blue flowers.

***N. foetens* of gardens** see *N. caerulea.*
***N. fruticans* of gardens** see *N. caerulea.*
N. strumosa. Basally branching annual with lance-shaped, entire to coarsely toothed, slightly hairy leaves, to 3in (8cm) long. In mid- and late summer, produces terminal racemes of 2-lipped red, yellow, pink, blue, purple, or white flowers, to 1in (2.5cm) across. The flowers may be in single colors, or bicolors with the upper and lower lips in contrasting colors; they often have external purple veins and yellow, "bearded" throats with darker marks. ↕ 7–12in (18–30cm), ↔ 4–6in (10–15cm). South Africa. **'Blue Gem'** bears bright blue flowers. Cultivars of **Carnival Series** ■ are compact and dwarf, bearing purple-veined yellow, red, bronze-yellow, orange, pink, or white flowers; ↕ 7–9in (17–23cm). **'Danish Flag'** has bicolored flowers in red and white. **'Funfair'** bears bright red, dark pink, tangerine-orange, gold, and crimson flowers. **'KLM'** ■ has bicolored flowers in blue and white, with yellow throats. **Mello Series** cultivars have pure white flowers and bicolored maroon and white flowers; ↕ 7–9in (18–23cm). **'National Ensign'** is a bicolored cultivar with deep pink-red and white flowers. **'Prince of Orange'** produces orange flowers with purple veins; ↕ to 8in (20cm). **'Suttonii'** produces white, yellow, rose-pink, orange, crimson, and scarlet flowers. **'Tapestry'** is bushy and upright, and bears purple, red, orange-yellow, pink, and bicolor flowers; ↕ 10in (25cm).

NEMOPANTHUS

Mountain holly

AQUIFOLIACEAE

Genus of one species of deciduous shrub from moist woods and swamps of C. and E. North America. Mountain holly bears alternate, oblong-ovate, entire or slightly toothed leaves, and flowers with 4 or 5 separate petals and much-reduced calyces (distinct from holly). It is grown for its autumn color and attractive rounded, red fruit. Grow *N. mucronatus* in a shrub border or woodland garden.

• **CULTIVATION** Grow in moderately fertile, well-drained soil in full sun to light, dappled shade. Pruning group 1.

• **PROPAGATION** Graft in spring on seedlings of the species or take hardwood cuttings in late summer. (Seed can take 2 or 3 years to germinate.)

• **PESTS AND DISEASES** Powdery mildew and tar spot sometimes occur.

N. mucronatus. Stoloniferous shrub with purplish-green young branches, maturing to ash-gray, and oblong-ovate, bluish green leaves, to 1½in (4cm) long, turning yellow in autumn. Bears green-yellow flowers, to 1½in (4cm) across, in summer, followed by spherical, dark red fruit, to ½in (1.5cm) across. ↕ to 10ft (3m), ↔ to 5ft (1.5m). Minnesota to Newfoundland south to Indiana and Virginia. Zone 6.

Nemophila maculata

NEMOPHILA

HYDROPHYLLACEAE

Genus of 11 species of spreading to erect, slender, fleshy-stemmed annuals found in W. North America, from coastal sands to chaparral and redwood forest. The mid-green or gray-green leaves are opposite, lobed or pinnate, ovate to rounded, spoon-shaped, or oblong, and toothed. Small, saucer- or bell-shaped, blue or white flowers are borne singly in the upper leaf axils in summer. Grow in a border, or in a windowbox or other container.

• **CULTIVATION** Grow in fertile, moist, well-drained soil in full sun or partial shade. Ceases flowering in hot weather.

• **PROPAGATION** Sow seed *in situ* in early spring or autumn; they self-seed freely.

• **PESTS AND DISEASES** Powdery mildew, downy mildew, and aphids can occur.

N. insignis see *N. menziesii.*
N. maculata ■ (Five-spot). Fleshy-stemmed, sometimes slightly downy annual with 5- to 9-pinnate leaves, oblong to oval in outline and ½–1¼in (1–3cm) long. In summer, produces solitary, saucer-shaped white flowers, to 1¾in (4.5cm) across, on long stalks; each petal is tipped with a small, violet-blue mark, and is sometimes faintly veined or tinted mauve-blue. ↕↔ 6–12in (15–30cm). California.
N. menziesii, syn. *N. insignis* (Baby blue-eyes). Fleshy-stemmed, downy annual with 9- to 11-pinnate, toothed, gray-green leaves, oval to oblong in outline, ¾–2in (2–5cm) long. In summer, bears solitary, long-stalked, saucer-shaped, bright blue flowers, to 1½in (4cm) across, with lighter blue centers often stained white or yellow, and with darker blue or deep purple spots on the petals. ↕ 8in (20cm), ↔ 12in (30cm). California. **subsp. *atromaria*** has white flowers, to 1¼in (3cm) across, with black or dark purple spots. **'Coelestis'** has white flowers margined sky-blue. **'Oculata'** has pale blue flowers with deep purple centers. **'Pennie Black'** has deep purple to black flowers with scalloped, silvery white edges. **'Snowstorm'** has white flowers with tiny black spots.

▷ ***Neobesseya asperispina*** see *Escobaria asperispina*
▷ ***Neobesseya macdougallii*** see *Ortegocactus macdougallii*

Nemesia caerulea

Nemesia strumosa 'KLM'

N

NEOBUXBAUMIA

CACTACEAE

Genus of about 8 species of columnar or tree-like cacti from dry to humid areas of Mexico. The ribs usually low-set on the cylindrical stems; the areoles bear numerous bristles and spines. The nocturnal, white, pink, or red flowers, borne in summer, are followed by angular fruits, which open like stars when ripe. In areas where temperatures drop below 59°F (15°C), grow in a warm greenhouse. In warmer climates, grow in a border.

• **CULTIVATION** Under glass, grow in standard cactus potting mix with added grit, in full light with shade from hot sun, and low humidity. From midspring to late summer, water freely and apply a dilute liquid fertilizer monthly. Keep completely dry at other times. Outdoors, grow in sharply drained, gritty, poor to moderately fertile, humus-rich soil in full sun. See also pp.48–49.

• **PROPAGATION** Sow seed at 66–75°F (19–24°C) in spring.

• **PESTS AND DISEASES** Scale insects.

N. euphorbioides ▣ syn. *Cephalocereus euphorbioides, Lemaireocereus euphorbioides, Rooksbya euphorbioides.* Solitary, tree-like cactus with a columnar, grayish green, dark green, or blue-green, sometimes red-tinged stem, 4–6in (10–15cm) thick, with 8–10 acute, straight ribs. White-woolly areoles produce bristly, black to dark gray spines (1–5 radials and sometimes 1 central), becoming white. Funnel-shaped flowers, 3–4in (8–10cm) long, with reddish pink tubes, wine-red outer tepals, and cream throats, are borne in summer. ↕ 3–6ft (1–2m), ↔ 6in (15cm). E. Mexico. ❀ (min. 59°F/15°C)

N. polylopha. Usually solitary, columnar cactus producing a pale green stem, 14in (35cm) or more thick, bearing 20–50 slightly rounded ribs with white-woolly areoles, yellow bristles, and yellow spines (7–9 radials and 1 shorter central). Funnel-shaped, red or pink flowers, to 2–3in (5–8cm) long, with purple-brown tubes, develop in summer. ↕ 6–10ft (2–3m), ↔ 14in (35cm). C. Mexico. ❀ (min. 59°F/15°C); tolerates brief periods to 28°F (-2°C).

N. tetetzo. Columnar, branching cactus, with up to 16 stems, each with 15–20 obtuse, slightly rounded ribs, a single, black central spine, and 8–13 blackish radials. Bell- to funnel-shaped, whitish flowers borne apically, 2–2½in (5–6cm) long. The ovoid fruit, to 1½in (4cm) long, has spiny, green perianth parts. ↕ 50ft (15m) ↔ 28in (70cm). ❀ (min. 59°F/15°C)

Neobuxbaumia euphorbioides

▷ ***Neochilenia chilensis*** see *Neoporteria chilensis*

▷ ***Neochilenia mitis* of gardens** see *Neoporteria napina*

NEOLITSEA

LAURACEAE

Genus of 60 species of evergreen, dioecious shrubs and trees from tropical woodland in E. and S.E. Asia, Malaysia, and Indonesia. Only *N. sericea* is usually cultivated, for its handsome, simple, alternate, leathery leaves. Flowers are insignificant, each having 4 sepals that fall on opening; on female plants these are followed by red or black berries. Where not hardy, grow in a cool greenhouse as foliage plants. In milder climates, grow at the base of a warm, sunny wall, in a woodland garden, or as specimen plants; they also make useful screens or hedges.

• **CULTIVATION** Under glass, grow in soil-based potting mix in full light or bright filtered light. During growth, water moderately and apply a balanced liquid fertilizer monthly. Water sparingly in winter. Outdoors, grow in fertile, moist but well-drained soil in full sun or partial shade, with shelter from cold, dry winds. Pruning group 1; may need restrictive pruning under glass.

• **PROPAGATION** Sow seed in containers in a cool greenhouse as soon as ripe. Root semi-ripe cuttings with bottom heat in summer.

• **PESTS AND DISEASES** Scale insects may be a problem under glass.

N. glauca see *N. sericea.*

N. sericea, syn. *Litsea glauca, N. glauca.* Large shrub or small tree, ovoid to columnar, later spreading, with yellow-brown, silky-hairy shoots. Leaves are ovate to oblong-elliptic, 4–7in (10–18cm) long, with 3 prominent veins; they are softly golden-hairy above when young, becoming deep green above and glaucous beneath. In late summer, produces small, star-shaped yellow flowers in stalkless umbels, followed in autumn by red berries, ½in (1.5cm) long, on female plants. ↕ to 20ft (6m), ↔ to 10ft (3m) or more. China, Taiwan, Korea, Japan. ❀ (min. 41°F/5°C)

NEOLLOYDIA

CACTACEAE

Genus of 10–14 species of spherical or cylindrical cacti found on low hillsides in S.W. Texas, and in E. and N.E. Mexico. They frequently form small clumps by offsetting. The ribs bear spined tubercles, often spirally arranged, sometimes with dense hairs or wool in the axils. The wide-spreading, funnel-shaped, diurnal flowers of this genus are produced from spring to summer. In areas where temperatures drop below 59°F (15°C), grow in a warm greenhouse. In warmer climates, grow in a desert garden.

Neolloydia conoidea

• **CULTIVATION** Under glass, grow in standard cactus potting mix in full light. From midspring to early autumn, water moderately and apply a dilute, balanced liquid fertilizer monthly. Keep dry at other times. Outdoors, grow in sharply drained, humus-rich, moderately fertile soil in full sun. See also pp.48–49.

• **PROPAGATION** Sow seed at 66–75°F (19–24°C) in spring.

• **PESTS AND DISEASES** Susceptible to root mealybugs when grown in containers.

N. conoidea ▣ syn. *Coryphantha conoidea, Mammillaria conoidea.* Often offsetting, variable cactus with spherical to cylindrical, bluish gray or yellow-green stems, to 3in (8cm) thick. Ovoid tubercles have woolly axils and white-woolly areoles (8–28 white to gray radial spines, 0–6 longer black centrals). Reddish violet, magenta, or deep purple flowers, to 2½in (6cm) acros, are produced in summer. ↕ to 4in (10cm), ↔ 6in (15cm) in clusters. S.W. Texas, E. and N.E. Mexico. ❀ (min. 59°F/15°C)

NEOMARICA

IRIDACEAE

Genus of about 15 species of rhizomatous, herbaceous perennials from often mountainous habitats in tropical Central and South America. They are cultivated for their short-lived, iris-like flowers, which are produced in summer on erect stems. The erect, sword-shaped leaves are ribbed or heavily veined, and arranged in basal fans. Where not hardy, grow in a temperate or warm greenhouse. In warmer climates, grow in a border or among shrubs.

• **CULTIVATION** Under glass, grow in soil-based potting mix, with added sharp sand and leaf mold, in bright filtered light, or in full light with shade from the hottest sun. Water moderately in summer, sparingly in winter. Apply a balanced liquid fertilizer monthly when in full growth. Outdoors, grow in well-drained, moderately fertile, humus-rich soil in partial shade.

• **PROPAGATION** Sow seed at 59–64°F (15–18°C) in spring, or divide in spring. Plantlets that appear in the inflorescences may be detached and rooted in water or well-drained rooting medium.

• **PESTS AND DISEASES** Infrequent.

N. caerulea ▣ (Twelve apostles, Walking iris). Rhizomatous perennial with a basal fan of sword-shaped, dark green leaves, to 5½ft (1.6m) long. In summer, bears a succession of flat, scented, mid-blue flowers, 3–4in (8–10cm) across, striped white, yellow, and brown in the centers. ↕↔ 24in (60cm). Brazil. ❀ (min. 50°F/10°C)

Neomarica caerulea

N

NEOPORTERIA

CACTACEAE

Genus of 20–30 species of solitary, sometimes clustering cacti, most from rocky, coastal sites in Chile, a few from S. Peru and W. Argentina. They have spherical to short-cylindrical, ribbed, spiny stems and usually solitary, funnel- or bell-shaped flowers produced from or close to the crowns. Where temperatures drop below 50°F (10°C), grow in a warm greenhouse, although they tolerate brief periods to 28°F (-2°C). Elsewhere, use in a desert garden.

• **CULTIVATION** Under glass, grow in standard cactus potting mix in full light, with low humidity. From midspring to early autumn, water moderately and apply a dilute liquid fertilizer monthly. Keep dry at other times. Outdoors, grow in sharply drained, poor to moderately fertile, humus-rich soil in full sun. See also pp.48–49.

• **PROPAGATION** Sow seed at 66–75°F (19–24°C) in spring or summer.

• **PESTS AND DISEASES** Vulnerable to root mealybugs and mealybugs, especially when container-grown.

N. chilensis, syn. *Echinocactus chilensis, Neochilenia chilensis.* Solitary or clustering cactus with spherical to short-cylindrical, pale green stems, each with about 20 ribs. Areoles each bear about 20 glassy white radial spines and 6–8 longer, yellowish brown centrals. From late spring to early autumn, bears broadly funnel-shaped, white or pink flowers, 2in (5cm) across, with carmine-red outer petals. ↕ 12in (30cm), ↔ 4in (10cm). Chile. ❀ (min. 50°F/10°C)

N. crispa, syn. *Pyrrhocactus crispus.* Solitary cactus with a tuberous rootstock. The spherical, dark green stem has 13–16 ribs, and black or gray spines (6–10 radials, 2–4 longer centrals). Funnel-shaped red flowers, 1½in (4cm) across, with a deeper red mid-stripe to each inner petal, are borne from late summer to autumn. ↕↔ 3in (8cm). Chile. ❀ (min. 50°F/10°C)

N. litoralis see *N. subgibbosa.*

N. mitis see *N. napina.*

N. napina ■ syn. *Neochilenia mitis* of gardens, *Neoporteria mitis.* Variable, solitary cactus with a spherical, brownish green stem, sometimes tinged red, divided into chin-like tubercles, and with dark brownish black spines (3–9 radials, no centrals). From late spring to early autumn, bell- to funnel-shaped, pale yellow, sometimes pink-flushed flowers, 1¼–1½in (3–4cm) across, open from woolly buds. ↕ 1in (2.5cm), ↔ 1½in (4cm). Chile. ❀ (min. 50°F/10°C)

Neoporteria napina

Neoporteria villosa

N. nidus. Solitary cactus with a spherical to short-cylindrical, dark green stem, rarely elongating, bearing 16–18 deeply scalloped ribs hidden by about 30 upward-curved, pale gray, cream, or yellow spines per areole. Tubular-funnel-shaped, red or pink flowers, 1½in (4cm) across, with prominently pointed petals, are produced from late spring to early autumn. ↕ to 12in (30cm), ↔ to 4in (10cm). Chile. ❀ (min. 50°F/10°C)

N. subgibbosa, syn. *N. litoralis.* Variable, solitary cactus producing a spherical, mid-green to gray-green stem, later elongating and often decumbent; the stem bears 16–20 warty ribs and deep orange-yellow, brown, or black spines (16–30 thin radials, 4–8 much thicker centrals). Funnel-shaped, carmine-pink flowers, 1½in (4cm) across, with paler, almost white throats, develop from late spring to early autumn. ↕ to 12in (30cm), ↔ 4in (10cm). Chile. ❀ (min. 50°F/10°C)

N. taltalensis. Solitary cactus with a spherical, dull dark green stem, 10–16 warty ribs, and pale yellowish brown areoles bearing 6–20 curving to twisted, brown, later white radial spines and up to 6 dark grayish brown to black centrals. Bears funnel-shaped, purplish pink, yellow, or white flowers, 1¼in (3cm) across, in summer. ↕↔ 3in (8cm). Chile. ❀ (min. 50°F/10°C)

N. villosa ■ Solitary or clustering cactus with spherical then short-cylindrical, gray-green stems turning black-purple; the stems bear 13–15 ribs covered with upward-curved, hair-like, yellowish gray or pale brown spines (12–16 or more radials, 4 thicker centrals). Funnel-shaped, white-throated pink flowers, to 1¼in (3cm) across, are borne from late spring to summer. ↕ 6in (15cm), ↔ to 4in (10cm). Chile. ❀ (min. 50°F/10°C)

NEOREGELIA syn. AREGELIA

BROMELIACEAE

Genus of over 100 species of evergreen, sometimes rhizomatous or stoloniferous, epiphytic or terrestrial perennials (bromeliads) from coastal scrub, woodland, and rainforest, to 5,000ft (1,600m) high, in South America. Some are grown for the striking coloring of their central leaves and bracts when flowering. The variable, usually spiny-margined leaves are borne in rosettes; large sheaths totally enclose the scape and its bracts. An umbel-like, sometimes raceme- or corymb-like, compact inflorescence nestles in the heart of each leaf rosette and, in summer, bears numerous long-lasting, tubular flowers. Offsets form around the flowering rosettes. Where temperatures drop below 50°F (10°C), grow in a temperate greenhouse, or as houseplants. In warm climates, grow in a shady, moist site.

• **CULTIVATION** Under glass, grow in epiphytic or terrestrial bromeliad potting mix in bright filtered light. When in growth, water freely. Apply a low-nitrogen liquid fertilizer monthly from spring to late autumn. Keep rosette cups filled with water from spring to early autumn. Water sparingly in winter. Sever spent leaf rosettes at the bases. Outdoors, grow in gritty, leafy soil in an open site with partial shade, or grow epiphytically in a tree. See also p.47.

• **PROPAGATION** Sow seed at 81°F (27°C) as soon as ripe. Separate offsets in spring or summer.

• **PESTS AND DISEASES** Susceptible to scale insects and mealybugs. Bacterial soft rot and leaf spot and a variety of fungal leaf spots can occur.

N. ampullacea. Stoloniferous, epiphytic bromeliad with dense, funnel-shaped rosettes of 6–15 tongue-shaped, sometimes red-banded, mid-green leaves, 6–8in (15–20cm) long. Tubular flowers, to 1in (2.5cm) long, with blue, white-based petals and white-margined green sepals, are borne in summer. Stolons appear from beneath the rosettes; at the tips, further rosettes develop. ↕↔ 16in (40cm). Brazil. ❀ (min. 50°F/10°C)

N. carolinae, syn. *Aregelia carolinae, Nidularium carolinae* (Blushing bromeliad). Epiphytic bromeliad with open rosettes of 12–20 strap-shaped, toothed, copper-suffused, mid-green leaves, 16–24in (40–60cm) long; at flowering time, the central leaves turn crimson. Red bracts surround violet-purple to lavender-blue flowers, to 1½in (4cm) long, which are produced in summer. ↕ 8–12in (20–30cm), ↔ 16–24in (40–60cm). Brazil. ❀ (min. 50°F/10°C). **'Tricolor'** ■ syn. f. *tricolor*, has leaves striped ivory-white, green, and rose-red.

Neoregelia carolinae 'Tricolor'

Neoregelia concentrica

N. concentrica ■ Rhizomatous, epiphytic bromeliad with dense rosettes of 7–30 broadly strap-shaped, spreading, glossy, mid- to dark green leaves, 8–16in (20–40cm) long, often marked dark purple at the tips, and with black marginal spines. Yellow-white bracts, suffused violet or purple, turn purple-pink in summer, when the pale blue or white flowers, 1½–2in (4–5cm) long, are produced. ↕ to 12in (30cm), ↔ to 28in (70cm). Brazil. ❀ (min. 50°F/10°C). **var. *plutonis*** ■ syn. 'Plutonis', has spreading rosettes of broad, mid-green, sometimes pale green leaves, which are flushed magenta-red during flowering; the flowers are pale lavender; ↔ 16in (40cm) or more.

N. eleutheropetala. Stoloniferous, epiphytic bromeliad with rosettes of about 30 tongue-shaped, mid-green leaves, 20–28in (50–70cm) long, turning reddish green toward the bases, and with sharp marginal spines and brown sheaths. The innermost, purple-brown leaves surround dense, umbel-like inflorescences of white flowers, to 1½in (4cm) long, borne in summer and interspersed with long, purple-tipped bracts. ↕↔ to 28in (70cm). Venezuela, Colombia, Peru, Amazonian Brazil. ❀ (min. 50°F/10°C)

Neoregelia concentrica var. *plutonis*

N

Neoregelia spectabilis

N. pineliana. Epiphytic bromeliad with a short stem producing ascending stolons, which bear leaves along their lengths. The rosettes have up to 12 narrowly lance-shaped to linear, mid-green leaves, gray-scaly on both surfaces, to 20in (50cm) long, with minute marginal spines and purple sheaths. In summer, the central leaves turn red, and dense umbels of blue, white-based flowers, to 2½in (6cm) long, darkening toward the tips, are produced. ↕↔ 16in (40cm) or more. S.E. Brazil. ❀ (min. 50°F/10°C)

N. princeps. Epiphytic or terrestrial bromeliad with spreading rosettes of 15–20 strap-shaped, pointed, minutely scaly, laxly toothed, mid-green leaves, 20in (50cm) long, with densely gray-scaly sheaths; the inner leaves are smaller and bright red. White flowers, 1¼–1½in (3–4cm) long, with deep blue tips and red sepals, are produced in summer. ↕↔ 30in (75cm). S. Brazil. ❀ (min. 50°F/10°C)

N. spectabilis ■ (Fingernail plant). Terrestrial bromeliad producing broadly funnel-shaped rosettes of 20–30 strap-shaped, arching, red-tipped, gray-scaly, glossy, olive-green leaves, 16–18in (40–45cm) long, with smooth or minutely spiny margins and gray-white cross-banding beneath. Blue flowers, 1½–1¾in (4–4.5cm) long, with red or purple bracts, are borne in summer. ↕ to 16in (40cm), ↔ to 32in (80cm). S. Brazil. ❀ (min. 50°F/10°C)

NEPENTHES

Monkey cup, Tropical pitcher plant

NEPENTHACEAE

Genus of over 70 species and numerous hybrids of dioecious, evergreen, carnivorous, climbing, terrestrial or epiphytic perennials from Madagascar, the Seychelles, S.E. Asia, Borneo, and Queensland. They are found in moist, acidic, organic soils in open grassland or forest, and sometimes grow epiphytically on trees. The usually lance-shaped or strap-shaped leaves, 2–26in (5–65cm) long, each have a prolonged midrib, which acts as a tendril and may be terminated by a hanging, hollow pitcher, 2–14in (5–35cm) long, with 2 vertical ridges, or "wings," at the front. Pitchers vary greatly in shape and color, from pale yellow to green or purplish red, and are frequently mottled; upper and lower pitchers often differ in color on the same plant. The colorful, thickened rim of a pitcher secretes nectar to attract insects, small mammals, and even birds, which become trapped inside. Its apex forms a lid to deflect excess rain. The tiny, petalless male and female flowers, with green or brown sepals, are borne in spike-like racemes. Where they are not hardy, grow in a warm greenhouse or conservatory; in tropical climates, grow climbers through trees, or attach epiphytes to branches. Heights vary greatly according to conditions and support; in cultivation, most are cut back to encourage young foliage and the development of large pitchers.

• **CULTIVATION** Lowland species and hybrids from sea level to 3,300ft (1,000m) need daytime temperatures of 75°F (24°C), and nighttime temperatures of 59°F (15°C) in winter, 70°F (21°C) in summer. Provide ventilation when over 100°F (38°C). Highland species and hybrids from 3,300–9,900ft (1,000–3,000m) need daytime temperatures of 64°F (18°C), and 50°F (10°C) at night. Ventilate when over 70°F (21°C). Under glass, grow in slatted baskets in a mix of 2 parts bark, 2 parts perlite, and 1 part coarse peat or coconut fiber, or in clean, live sphagnum moss. Provide bright filtered light, or full light with shade from hot sun, and high humidity. In summer, apply a high-nitrogen liquid fertilizer weekly. Prune mature plants in spring, reducing stems by two-thirds of their length, to induce vigorous, pitcher-producing shoots. Outdoors, grow in moist, open, leafy soil in partial shade, or as epiphytes.

• **PROPAGATION** Sow seed as soon as it is ripe on the surface of moist peat or fine coconut fiber, and place in a tray of water in a shaded propagator; maintain a temperature of 81°F (27°C). In spring, insert cuttings with 3 or 4 leaves into nepenthes soil mix (described above) and maintain at 70–81°F (21–27°C). Air layer in spring or summer.

• **PESTS AND DISEASES** Mealybugs may be troublesome. Gray mold (*Botrytis*) may affect the leaves.

N. ampullaria. Lowland climber with rounded, squat, deep red or green, sometimes mottled pitchers, to 2in (5cm) long, with round, horizontal mouths and small, narrow, reflexed lids. Wings are broad, spreading, and toothed. Pitchers are produced only from the basal leaves or in clusters from the rhizomes, not from climbing shoots. ↕ to 70ft (20m). Malaysia to New Guinea. ❀ (min. day: 75°F/24°C; night: 59°F/15°C in winter, 70°F/21°C in summer)

N. x coccinea (*N.* x *dominii* x *N. mirabilis*). Lowland climber with yellow-green pitchers, to 6in (15cm) long, mottled purple-red, with inflated bases and oblique mouths. The green lids have red markings. ↕ to 20ft (6m). Garden origin. ❀ (min. day: 75°F/24°C; night: 59°F/15°C in winter, 70°F/21°C in summer)

***N.* 'Director G.T. Moore'** ■ Lowland climber with pear-shaped, light green pitchers, to 5in (13cm) long, with dense purple-red mottling, oblique mouths, and fringed, mottled wings. ↕ 10ft (3m). ❀ (min. day: 75°F/24°C; night: 59°F/15°C in winter, 70°F/21°C in summer)

N. gracilis. Slender, lowland climber with linear to elliptic leaves with numerous pitchers. Lower pitchers are small, cylindrical, light green, sometimes suffused pink or maroon, to 3in (8cm) long, with narrow lips, round lids, and narrow wings. Upper pitchers, to 6in (15cm) long, are dark mahogany-red and narrow in the middle. Even young plants bear inflorescences, 6in (15cm) long, of red-brown flowers. ↕ to 6ft (2m). Philippines to Indonesia. ❀ (min. day: 75°F/24°C; night: 59°F/15°C in winter, 70°F/21°C in summer)

N. x hookeriana (*N. ampullaria* x *N. rafflesiana*). Lowland climber producing ovoid lower pitchers with broad wings and rims, and funnel-shaped upper pitchers. Both are pale green with dark red spots, and have oblique mouths. Upper pitchers grow to 5in (13cm) long, lower to 4¼in (11cm). ↕ 10ft (3m). Malaysia to Borneo. ❀ (min. day: 75°F/24°C; night: 59°F/15°C in winter, 70°F/21°C in summer)

N. mirabilis. Lowland climber or terrestrial perennial with cylindrical pitchers, to 7in (18cm) long, red, or pale green with red blotches; each has an oblique, round mouth and an oval lid. ↕ to 30ft (10m). S. China, S.E. Asia to Australia (N. Queensland). ❀ (min. day: 75°F/24°C; night: 59°F/15°C in winter, 70°F/21°C in summer)

N. rafflesiana ■ Lowland climber with creamy green pitchers, marked chocolate-red, each with a striped rim. Lower pitchers, to 5in (13cm) long, each have a rounded base, an oblique, oval mouth with the rim rising vertically at the back to form a stalk for the lid, and large, toothed wings. Upper pitchers, to 12in (30cm) long, with small wings, are tapered at the bases. ↕ to 28ft (9m). Sumatra to Borneo. ❀ (min. day: 75°F/24°C; night: 59°F/15°C in winter, 70°F/21°C in summer)

N. rajah. Highland climber with large green pitchers, to 14in (35cm) long, mottled red to red-purple, each with an elliptic and oblique mouth, a broad, wavy rim, and a large, oval lid. Lower pitchers are ellipsoid, while upper ones are tapered only at the bases. The pitchers have been known to catch rats. ↕ 6ft (2m). Borneo (Mt. Kinabalu). ❀ (min. day: 64°F/18°C; night: 50°F/10°C)

N. ventricosa. Highland, terrestrial or epiphytic perennial producing numerous cylindrical pitchers, to 7in (18cm) long, each narrower in the middle, with a round to oval mouth and small green lid, suffused red. ↕ 12ft (4m). Philippines. ❀ (min. day: 64°F/18°C; night: 50°F/10°C)

Nepenthes 'Director G.T. Moore'

Nepenthes rafflesiana

NEPETA

Catmint

LAMIACEAE

Genus of approximately 250 species of perennials, rarely annuals, native to a variety of habitats, from cool and moist to hot and dry sites, in scrub, on grassy banks and stony slopes, or in high mountains, in non-tropical parts of the N. hemisphere. Ovate to lance-shaped, entire, scalloped, or toothed, often aromatic leaves are borne in opposite pairs; some are hairy, producing a silvery or grayish green effect. The spike-like cymes (sometimes racemes or panicles) of tubular, irregularly 2-lipped flowers, in white and shades of blue and purple, occasionally yellow, are borne in interrupted axillary whorls along the flower stems, often over long periods. Grow taller catmints in a mixed or herbaceous border, the shorter ones in a rock garden. Some species (especially *N. cataria*) attract cats; most draw bees.

• **CULTIVATION** Grow in any well-drained soil in full sun or partial shade. *N. govaniana* and *N. subsessilis* prefer moist, cool soils. *N. sibirica* likes fairly dry conditions. Grow *N. phyllochlamys* in a hot, dry rock crevice or in a trough. Provide support for taller catmints; trim *N. nervosa* and *N.* x *faassenii* after flowering to keep plants compact and to induce a second flowering.

• **PROPAGATION** Sow seed in a seedbed, or in containers in a cold frame, in autumn; some catmints self-seed freely. Divide in spring or autumn. Take softwood cuttings in early summer.

• **PESTS AND DISEASES** Sometimes affected by leaf spots.

***N.* 'Blue Beauty'** see *N.* 'Souvenir d'André Chaudron'.

N. cataria (Catnip). Erect, branched perennial with softly hairy, gray stems and basally heart-shaped, ovate to lance-shaped, scalloped, aromatic leaves, to 3in (8cm) long, densely gray-woolly beneath. In summer and autumn, produces spike-like inflorescences of purple-spotted, white flowers, ¼–½in (6–15mm) across. ↕ to 36in (90cm), ↔ 18in (45cm). Europe, S.W. and C. Asia. Zone 4.

N.* x *faassenii ■ (*N. nepetella* x *N. racemosa*), syn. *N. mussinii* of gardens. Clump-forming perennial with erect to spreading, branched stems and narrowly ovate to lance-shaped,

Nepeta x *faassenii*

Nepeta govaniana

scalloped, wrinkled, hairy, aromatic, silvery gray-green leaves, to 1¼in (3cm) long. From early summer to early autumn, freely bears spike-like, whorled cymes of pale lavender-blue flowers, to ½in (12mm) long, with darker purple spots. ↕↔ to 18in (45cm). Garden origin. Zone 4. **'Dropmore'** has toothed gray leaves and large lavender-blue flowers; ↕ 18–24in (45–60cm). **'Porzellan'** has narrow gray leaves and light blue flowers. **'Snowflake'** is compact and low-growing, and bears white flowers; ↕ 12–14in (30–35cm). **'Superba'** is spreading, and bears dark blue flowers. **'White Wonder'** has white flowers; ↕ 12in (30cm).

N. govaniana ■ syn. *Dracocephalum govanianum.* Clump-forming perennial bearing erect, branching, hairy stems and ovate to oblong-elliptic, pointed, scalloped, softly hairy, aromatic leaves, to 4in (10cm) long. From midsummer to early autumn, produces long, lax racemes or panicles of light yellow flowers, to 1¼in (3cm) long. ↕ 36in (90cm), ↔ 24in (60cm). W. Himalayas. Zone 6.

N. grandiflora. Clump-forming, softly hairy or hairless perennial with erect,

Nepeta nervosa

Nepeta sibirica

sparsely branched stems and ovate, scalloped, aromatic leaves, 4in (10cm) long. In early summer, produces spike-like, whorled cymes of violet-blue flowers, to ¾in (2cm) long. ↕ 30in (75cm), ↔ 12in (30cm). Caucasus. Zone 4.

N. macrantha see *N. sibirica.*

N. mussinii see *N. racemosa.*

***N. mussinii* of gardens** see *N.* x *faassenii.*

N. nervosa ■ Bushy perennial bearing erect, unbranched stems with narrowly lance-shaped, entire to slightly toothed, conspicuously veined, hairy, faintly aromatic, mid- to gray-green leaves, to 4in (10cm) long. Dense, cylindrical, spike-like, whorled cymes of purplish blue, rarely yellow flowers, to ½in (12mm) long, are borne from mid-summer to early autumn. ↕ 18–24in (45–60cm), ↔ 12in (30cm). India (Kashmir). Zone 5b

N. phyllochlamys. Spreading perennial with decumbent stems and triangular-ovate, scalloped, intensely white-downy, aromatic leaves, to ½in (1.5cm) long. In summer, bears short, spike-like, whorled cymes of lilac-pink flowers, ½in (1.5cm) long, with white-felted bracts. Requires very sharply drained soil. ↕ to 4in (10cm), ↔ to 8in (20cm). Turkey. Zone 8.

N. racemosa, syn. *N. mussinii.* Spreading to upright perennial with opposite, ovate, scalloped, finely hairy, aromatic, mid-green leaves, ½–1¼in (1–3cm) long, with heart-shaped bases. In summer, produces raceme-like, whorled cymes of deep violet- to lilac-blue flowers, ½–¾in (1–2cm) long. ↕ to 12in (30cm), ↔ to 18in (45cm). Caucasus, Turkey, N. and N.W. Iran. Zone 4. **'Little Titch'** has pale lavender-blue flowers; ↕↔ 6in (15cm).

N. sibirica ■ syn. *Dracocephalum sibiricum, N. macrantha.* Erect, leafy perennial with branching stems bearing oblong-lance-shaped, toothed, aromatic, dark green leaves, to 3½in (9cm) long, minutely hairy at the margins. In mid- and late summer, bears long, raceme-like, whorled cymes of blue to lavender-blue flowers, to 1½in (4cm) long. ↕ 36in (90cm), ↔ 18in (45cm). Russia (Siberia), E. Asia. Zone 3.

***N.* 'Six Hills Giant'.** Vigorous, clump-forming perennial with narrowly ovate, toothed, hairy, aromatic, light gray-green leaves, to 1½in (4cm) long. In summer, bears abundant spike-like, whorled cymes of lavender-blue flowers, ¾in (2cm) long. ↕ to 36in (90cm), ↔ 24in (60cm). Zone 4.

***N.* 'Souvenir d'André Chaudron'**, syn. *N.* 'Blue Beauty'. Spreading, clump-forming perennial with oval to lance-shaped, toothed, smooth, aromatic, gray-green leaves, to 3in (8cm) long. Throughout summer, bears spike-like, whorled cymes of large, dark lavender-blue flowers, 1½in (4cm) long. ↕↔ 18in (45cm). Zone 5.

N. subsessilis. Clump-forming perennial with erect, unbranched stems bearing ovate, toothed, hairless, aromatic, dark green leaves, 3–4in (8–10cm) long. Spike-like, whorled cymes of bright blue flowers, 1¼in (3cm) long, are borne from midsummer to early autumn. ↕ to 36in (90cm), ↔ 12in (30cm). Japan. Zone 5.

NEPHROLEPIS

OLEANDRACEAE

Genus of about 30 species of evergreen or semi-evergreen, epiphytic and terrestrial ferns from rainforest or more open habitats in tropical and subtropical regions worldwide. They have short, erect rhizomes, usually with numerous runners. The dense clusters of pinnate fronds may be erect, spreading, or pendent. Pinnae are usually linear and simple, but may be divided, forked, or crisped in cultivars, of which there are many. Where not hardy, grow in a temperate greenhouse or as houseplants; in warmer climates, grow in moist, shady sites among shrubs.

• **CULTIVATION** Under glass, grow in a mix of 1 part loam, 2 parts sharp sand, and 3 parts leaf mold, in bright filtered light, with moderate to high humidity and good ventilation. In the growing season, water moderately and apply a half-strength, balanced liquid fertilizer monthly. Water sparingly in winter. Outdoors, grow in moderately fertile, moist but well-drained, humus-rich soil in partial shade.

• **PROPAGATION** Sow spores at 70°F (21°C) as soon as ripe. Many cultivars are sterile, or do not come true from spores. Separate rooted runners in late winter or early spring. See also p.51.

• **PESTS AND DISEASES** Aerial blight, leaf spots, root rots, spider mites, scale insects, and mealybugs may occur.

N. cordifolia ■ (Ladder fern, Sword fern). Tufted fern bearing erect to arching, lance-shaped to linear fronds,

Nephrolepis cordifolia

Nephrolepis exaltata 'Bostoniensis'

to 32in (80cm) long, with up to 70 pairs of oblong to linear pinnae, sometimes toothed at the tips. ↕ 32in (80cm), ↔ to 5ft (1.5m). Tropical regions. ❀ (min. 41°F/5°C). **'Lemon Buttons'** blades are 10in (25cm) long and 1in (2.5cm) across, with oblong to roundish, reduced pinnae; not symmetrical at the base. **'Plumosa'** is slow-growing, with lobed pinnae.
N. exaltata. Tufted fern with widely arching to erect, linear fronds, to 7ft (2m) long, with shallowly toothed, sickle-shaped pinnae. It is the source of nearly all *Nephrolepis* cultivars. ↕↔ to 7ft (2m). Florida, Mexico, West Indies, Central America, tropical South America, Polynesia, and Africa. ❀ (min. 45°F/7°C). **'Bostoniensis'** ▣ (Boston fern) has broader, lance-shaped fronds, erect at first, then gracefully arching to pendent. A very tolerant houseplant. **'Childsii'** has very broad, 3- or 4-pinnate, closely overlapping fronds. **'Dallas'** has blades bearing oblong pinnae with serrate, rounded tips. ↕ 6–8in (15–20cm), ↔ 2–4in (5–10cm). **'Golden Boston'** ▣ syn. 'Aurea', is similar to 'Bostoniensis' but with golden yellow fronds. **'Verona'** has dense, pendent, 3- or 4-pinnate fronds.
N. falcata. Tufted fern with arching to pendent, lance-shaped, glossy, dark green fronds, 8ft (2.5m) long, divided into close-set, sickle-shaped pinnae. ↕ to 8ft (2.5m), ↔ to 36in (1m). S.E. Asia. ❀ (min. 41°F/5°C). **f. *furcans*** ▣ has pinnae with 1 or 2 forks at the tips.

▷ ***Nephthytis triphylla* of gardens** see *Syngonium podophyllum*

NERINE

AMARYLLIDACEAE

Genus of about 30 species of bulbous perennials, some evergreen, found on mountain screes, on rock ledges, and in other well-drained or arid habitats in southern Africa. They are grown for their spherical umbels of lily-like flowers, with reflexed, often wavy-margined tepals; in herbaceous species, these appear before or with the strap-shaped leaves. Many cultivars with large, colorful flowers have been developed; flowers are borne in umbels, 4–8in (10–20cm) across, of up to 25 flowers, followed by semi-erect, basal leaves. Where hardy, grow in a border or rock garden, or at the base of a sunny wall. All are ideal greenhouse plants, and are good as cut flowers. If ingested, all parts may cause mild stomach upset.

- **CULTIVATION** Under glass, plant in autumn or spring with the tips of the bulbs above the surface of the soil-based potting mix; they flower best when bulbs are congested. Provide full light. Water freely during active growth. Keep warm and dry when dormant in summer. After flowering, apply a low-nitrogen liquid fertilizer. Outdoors, plant in well-drained soil in full sun in early spring. Provide a deep, dry winter mulch where marginally hardy.
- **PROPAGATION** Sow seed at 50–55°F (10–13°C) as soon as ripe. Divide clumps after flowering.
- **PESTS AND DISEASES** Prone to attack by slugs.

***N.* 'Baghdad'.** Bulbous perennial bearing loose umbels of crimson flowers with paler centers in autumn. ↕ 24in (60cm), PD3in (8cm). Zone 8.
***N.* 'Blanchefleur'.** Bulbous perennial bearing glistening white flowers in compact umbels in autumn. ↕ 20in (50cm), PD3in (8cm). Zone 8.
N. bowdenii ▣ Robust, bulbous perennial with broad, strap-shaped leaves, to 12in (30cm) long. In autumn, bears open umbels of up to 7 or more funnel-shaped, faintly scented pink flowers, to 3in (8cm) across, with recurved, wavy-margined tepals. ↕ 18in (45cm), PD3in (8cm). South Africa (Eastern Cape, KwaZulu/Natal, Orange Free State). Zone 8. **f. *alba*** ▣ has white flowers, sometimes flushed pale pink. **'Mark Fenwick'**, syn. 'Fenwick's Variety', has pink flowers on dark stalks.

Nerine bowdenii f. *alba*

***N.* 'Corusca Major'**, syn. *N. sarniensis* var. *corusca* 'Major'. Bulbous perennial bearing compact umbels of scarlet flowers with bold stamens in early autumn. ↕ 24in (60cm), PD3in (8cm). Zone 8.
N. crispa see *N. undulata.*
***N.* 'Early Snow'.** Bulbous perennial with compact umbels of pure white flowers, borne in early autumn. ↕ 24in (60cm), PD3in (8cm). Zone 8.
N. filifolia ▣ Bulbous perennial with narrow, grass-like leaves, 8in (20cm) long. In autumn, produces compact umbels of 5–10 small, bright pink to white flowers, to 1in (2.5cm) across, with wavy-margined tepals. Bears new leaves as old ones fade, so the plant is virtually evergreen. ↕ 12in (30cm), PD2in (5cm). South Africa (Orange Free State). Zone 8.
N. flexuosa. Bulbous perennial with arching, narrow, strap-shaped leaves, to 12in (30cm) long. In late autumn, bears compact umbels of 10–20 dark-veined pink flowers, to 1¼in (3cm) across, with wavy-margined tepals, the upper ones recurved. ↕ 18in (45cm), PD3in (8cm). South Africa (Eastern Cape, KwaZulu/Natal, Orange Free State). Zone 8. **'Alba'** has white flowers.
***N.* 'Fothergillii Major'.** Bulbous perennial bearing large, compact umbels of 10–20 bright orange-red flowers, with wavy-margined tepals, in late summer and early autumn. ↕ 20in (50cm), PD3in (8cm). Zone 8.
N. masoniorum. Slender, bulbous perennial with narrow, grass-like, almost evergreen leaves, to 8in (20cm) long. In autumn, downy stems bear compact

N

Nephrolepis exaltata 'Golden Boston'

Nephrolepis falcata f. *furcans*

Nerine bowdenii

Nerine filifolia

Nerine sarniensis

Nerium oleander

umbels of 4–15 bright pink flowers, to ¾in (2cm) across, with a deep rose-red vein down the center of each wavy-margined petal. ↕ 12in (30cm), PD2in (5cm). South Africa (Eastern Cape). Zone 8.
***N.* 'Radiant Queen'.** Bulbous perennial bearing loose umbels of rose-pink flowers in autumn. ↕ 24in (60cm), PD3in (8cm). Zone 8.
***N.* 'Salmon Supreme'.** Bulbous perennial bearing compact umbels of salmon-pink flowers in autumn. ↕ 24in (60cm), PD3in (8cm). Zone 8.
N. sarniensis ▣ (Guernsey lily). Bulbous perennial with erect, strap-shaped, bright green leaves, to 12in (30cm) long. In early autumn, bears compact umbels of 10–20 crimson to orange-red flowers, 1¼–1½in (3–4cm) across, with wavy-margined tepals and conspicuous stamens. ↕ 18in (45cm), PD3in (8cm). South Africa (Northern Cape, Western Cape). Zone 8. **var. *corusca* 'Major'** see *N.* 'Corusca Major'.
N. undulata, syn. *N. crispa*. Bulbous perennial with strap-shaped leaves, to 18in (45cm) long. In autumn, bears umbels of 8–12 slender, mid-pink flowers, 1½–2in (4–5cm) across, with narrow, crinkled tepals. ↕ 18in (45cm), ↔ 3in (8cm). South Africa (Eastern Cape). Zone 8.

NERIUM
Oleander

APOCYNACEAE

Genus of 1 or 2 species of evergreen shrubs or small trees found in seasonally dry stream beds and margins from the Mediterranean to China. They are grown for their often large, terminal cymes of colorful, narrowly funnel-shaped or salverform flowers, which each have 5 broad, spreading, angular petal lobes, and are followed by forked, elongated, bean-like seed pods. Lance-shaped leaves are narrow, leathery, and borne in opposite pairs or whorls of 3. Numerous cultivars have been raised, both single- and double-flowered, with white, yellow, apricot, pink, red, purple-red, and lilac flowers. Where not hardy, grow *N. oleander* in a cool greenhouse and move outdoors in summer; in warmer areas, use as a specimen plant, or grow in a shrub border or as a hedge. All parts are highly toxic if ingested; contact with foliage may irritate skin.
• **CULTIVATION** Under glass, grow in soil-based potting mix in full light; ventilate well. During growth, water moderately and apply a balanced liquid fertilizer monthly. Water sparingly in winter. Outdoors, grow in fertile, moist but well-drained soil in full sun. Pruning group 9; plants under glass may need restrictive pruning in late winter; will tolerate hard pruning.
• **PROPAGATION** Sow seed at 61°F (16°C) in spring. Root semi-ripe cuttings in summer, with bottom heat. Air layer in spring.
• **PESTS AND DISEASES** Scale insects, spider mites, caterpillars, aphids, bacterial knot (gall), and dieback can be problems.

N. obesum see *Adenium obesum*.
N. oleander ▣ (Oleander, Rose bay). Tall, erect to spreading shrub or small tree with lance-shaped, deep green to grayish green leaves, 2½–8in (6–20cm) long. In summer, bears cymes of up to 80 pink, red, or white flowers, 1½–2in (3–5cm) across. ↕ 6–20ft (2–6m), ↔ 3–10ft (1–3m). E. Mediterranean (possibly to W. China); widely naturalized. ❄ (min. 36–41°F/2–5°C). **'Calypso'** is hardier, with single, cherry-red flowers. **'Casablanca'** ▣ syn. 'Monca', has single white flowers, sometimes suffused pink. **'Double Sister Agnes'** bears very fragrant, double, white, hose-in-hose flowers. **'Eugenia Fowler'** bears double, mid-pink, hose-in-hose flowers. **'Hawaii'** has single yellow flowers. **'Little Red'** has single red flowers. **'Monca'** see 'Casablanca'. **'Monta'** see 'Tangier'. **'Monvis'** see 'Ruby Lace'. **'Mrs. George Roeding'** is dwarf, with double, salmon-pink flowers; ↕ 3–6ft (1–2m), ↔ 24–39in (60–100cm). **'Petite Pink'** is dwarf, with single, pale pink flowers; ↕ 3–6ft (1–2m), ↔ 24–39in (60–100cm). **'Petite Salmon'** ▣ is dwarf, with large, single, salmon-pink flowers; ↕ 3–6ft (1–2m), ↔ 24–39in (60–100cm). **'Red Velvet'** bears very velvety, dark red flowers. **'Ruby Lace'**, syn. 'Monvis', has showy clusters of large, single, deep red flowers, 3in (8cm) across, with fringed lips and wavy edges. **'Tangier'**, syn. 'Monta', bears single, light pink flowers. **'Variegatum'** has leaves with white to pale yellow margins, and double pink flowers.

Nerium oleander 'Petite Salmon' (inset: flower detail)

Nerium oleander 'Casablanca'

NERTERA
RUBIACEAE

Genus of approximately 6 species of mat-forming perennials from moist lowland to mountainous forest, and moist grassland and scrub, in S. China, S.E. Asia to Australasia, the Antarctic, and Mexico to South America. They produce very small, broadly ovate to lance-shaped leaves, tiny funnel- or bell-shaped flowers, and fleshy, spherical to pear-shaped fruits. Where not hardy, grow as houseplants, or in an alpine house or cool greenhouse. Elsewhere, grow as a groundcover in a rock garden.
• **CULTIVATION** Under glass, grow in soilless potting mix in bright filtered light or indirect light. During growth, water freely and apply a balanced liquid fertilizer monthly. Water sparingly in winter. Outdoors, grow in humus-rich, gritty, moist but well-drained soil in partial shade. Protect from excessive winter moisture.
• **PROPAGATION** Sow seed at 55–61°F (13–16°C), or divide, in spring.
• **PESTS AND DISEASES** May be infested by aphids or spider mites.

N. granadensis ▣ (Bead plant). Stem-rooting, moss-like perennial with broadly ovate, bright green leaves, to ⅜in (9mm) long. In summer, bears stemless, bell-shaped, yellowish green flowers, ⅛in (3mm) across, followed by masses of spherical, shiny, orange or red berries, ¼in (6mm) across. ↕ ¾in (2cm), ↔ to 8in (20cm). Mexico, Central America. (Populations from South America, New Zealand, and Australia are sometimes considered a distinct species, *N. depressa*.) ❄ (min. 45°F/7°C)

Nertera granadensis

NICANDRA

Apple of Peru, Shoo-fly

SOLANACEAE

Genus of one species of upright, branching annual from open sites and wasteland in Peru. It has alternate, solitary, oval to elliptic-lance-shaped or ovate, toothed leaves. The short-lived, bell-shaped flowers are followed by brown berries borne in green, lantern-like calyces. Grow in a wild garden or a mixed border. Fruiting branches can be dried for use in winter arrangements.

• **CULTIVATION** Grow in fertile, moist but well-drained soil in full sun.
• **PROPAGATION** Sow seed at 59°F (15°C) in early spring, or *in situ* in midspring; self-seeds freely.
• **PESTS AND DISEASES** Infrequent.

N. physalodes (Apple of Peru, Shoo-fly). Erect, vigorous annual with wavy-margined leaves, to 4in (10cm) or more long. White-throated, light violet-blue flowers, to 1½in (4cm) across, are produced profusely in the upper leaf axils, from summer to autumn, followed by round berries that are enclosed in green calyces, 1¼–1½in (3–4cm) across. Peru. ↕ to 36in (90cm), ↔ 12in (30cm). **'Violacea'** produces flowers with the upper section of each corolla indigo-blue, the lower part white.

▷ ***Nicodemia madagascariensis*** see *Buddleja madagascariensis*
▷ ***Nicolaia elatior*** see *Etlingera elatior*

NICOTIANA

Tobacco plant

SOLANACEAE

Genus of about 67 species of erect, frequently rosette-forming annuals, biennials, perennials, and shrubs from Australia, North America, and tropical South America, where they grow on mountain slopes and valley floors, often in moist soils. They have alternate, linear or oblong-lance-shaped to broadly ovate, glandular-hairy leaves. The flowers are tubular to trumpet-shaped or salverform, occasionally scented, and borne in racemes or panicles, usually over long periods in summer, sometimes in autumn. Flowers usually open only in the early evening and at night; flowers of some cultivars remain open during the day if sited in partial shade. Cultivars derived from *N. alata* and *N.* x *sanderae* are ideal summer bedding annuals, their upward- or horizontally-facing blooms remaining open in full sun. Grow *N. sylvestris* in a mixed border or semi-wild garden. Contact with the foliage may irritate skin.

Nicotiana alata Nicki Series 'Nicki Red'

Nicotiana langsdorffii

• **CULTIVATION** Grow in fertile, moist but well-drained soil in full sun or partial shade. Stake tall plants in open positions. *N. alata* and *N. sylvestris* can be overwintered outdoors where temperatures only occasionally fall to 23°F (-5°C); they will resprout from rootstocks the following spring. Provide a dry winter mulch. Pruning group 6 for shrubs.
• **PROPAGATION** Surface-sow seed at 64°F (18°C) in midspring.
• **PESTS AND DISEASES** Especially susceptible to viruses causing mosaic, vein banding, etch, and ringspots. Stem rot, stalk rot, downy mildew, damping off, and root rot also occur frequently. Aphids, caterpillars, leaf miners, and spider mites can be problems.

N. affinis see *N. alata*.
N. alata, syn. *N. affinis* (Flowering tobacco). Short-lived, rosette-forming perennial, grown as an annual, with spoon-shaped to ovate leaves, to 10in (25cm) long, becoming smaller up the stems. Tubular, greenish yellow flowers, to 4in (10cm) long, with funnel-shaped mouths, white within, are produced in open racemes, and are strongly fragrant at night. ↕ to 5ft (1.5m), ↔ 12in (30cm). S. Brazil, N. Argentina. ❀ (min. 45°F/7°C). **Nicki Series** cultivars are semi-dwarf and bear very fragrant, red, rose, pink, white, and lime-green flowers,

Nicotiana 'Lime Green'

Nicotiana x *sanderae* Domino Series 'Salmon Pink'

in summer; ↕ 16–18in (40–45cm). **Nicki Series 'Nicki Red'** ▣ has red flowers.
N. glauca (Tree tobacco). Fast-growing, gaunt, semi-evergreen shrub with long, arching, smooth, glaucous shoots and ovate, fleshy, blue-gray leaves, 4in (10cm) or more long. Bears tubular, bright yellow flowers, to 1½in (4cm) long. ↕↔ 8–10ft (2.5–3m). S. Bolivia to N. Argentina. ❀ (min. 45°F/7°C)
N. langsdorffii ▣ Sticky annual with a basal rosette of ovate leaves, to 10in (25cm) long. Bears nodding, slender panicles of tubular, apple-green flowers, to 2in (5cm) long, with spreading, 5-lobed mouths, and blue anthers. ↕ to 5ft (1.5m), ↔ to 14in (35cm). Brazil.
***N.* 'Lime Green'** ▣ Upright annual with spoon-shaped leaves, 2–8in (5–20cm) long, the upper leaves oblong-lance-shaped. Produces salverform, lime-green flowers, to 5in (13cm) long, each with an abruptly flattened limb. ↕ 24in (60cm), ↔ 10in (25cm).
N.* x *sanderae (*N. alata* x *N. forgetiana*). Upright, woody-based, sticky annual or short-lived perennial with spoon-shaped to oblong-ovate, wavy-edged basal leaves, 2–10in (5–25cm), the upper

Nicotiana x *sanderae* Starship Series

Nicotiana sylvestris

leaves oblong-lance-shaped. Bears open racemes or panicles of red, occasionally white, rose-pink, or purple, salverform flowers, to 2in (5cm) across. ↕ to 24in (60cm), ↔ 12–16in (30–40cm). Garden origin. ❀ (min. 45°F/7°C). **Domino Series** cultivars have upward-facing flowers in red, white, crimson-pink, lime-green, pink with white eyes, purple, purple with white eyes, salmon-pink, or white with rose-pink margins; ↕ 12–18in (30–45cm). **Domino Series 'Salmon Pink'** ▣ has salmon-pink flowers. **Havana Series** cultivars are compact; colors include pale pink with deep rose-pink reverse, and lime-green with rose-pink reverse; ↕ 12–14in (30–35cm). **Merlin Series** cultivars are dwarf, bred for containers; colors include purple, purple with white eyes, crimson-pink, lime-green, and white; ↕ 9–12in (23–30cm). **Metro Series** cultivars have rose-pink, red, lime-green, white, or lilac-pink flowers; ↕ to 14in (35cm). **Sensation Mix** cultivars stay open all day into the evening and bear fragrant flowers in shades of pink, red, and white; ↕ 2½ft (75cm). **Starship Series** ▣ cultivars have pink, red, rose-pink, white, or lime-green flowers, and good all-weather tolerance; ↕ 12in (30cm).
N. sylvestris ▣ Thick-stemmed annual or short-lived perennial with a basal rosette of dark green, oblong-elliptic to elliptic-ovate leaves, to 36in (90cm) long. Produces short, densely packed panicles of nodding, sweet-scented, long-tubed, trumpet-shaped white flowers, to 3½in (9cm) long, with 5 spreading lobes. Flowers close in full sun. ↕ to 5ft (1.5m), ↔ to 24in (60cm). Argentina. ❀ (min. 45°F/7°C)

NIDULARIUM

Bird's-nest bromeliad

BROMELIACEAE

Genus of about 45 species of rosette-forming, evergreen, epiphytic or terrestrial perennials, sometimes rhizomatous, related to *Neoregelia*, from woodland and rainforest, to 6,500ft (2,000m) high, mainly in Brazil. The toothed leaves are narrow to broadly strap-shaped. The conspicuous leaf sheaths surround tubular flowers, usually borne in summer; they nestle in a cluster of large bracts, resembling a bird's nest. Where temperatures drop below 54°F (12°C), grow in a warm greenhouse or as houseplants; in warmer areas, grow in a moist, shady border.

• **CULTIVATION** Under glass, grow in epiphytic bromeliad potting mix in bright filtered light with moderate to high humidity. During the growing season, water freely. Apply a low-nitrogen liquid fertilizer monthly from spring to late autumn. Keep rosette cups filled with water from spring to early autumn. Keep just moist in winter. Outdoors, grow in an open site, in gritty, moderately fertile, leafy soil in partial shade, or grow epiphytically on a tree. See also p.47.
• **PROPAGATION** Sow seed at 81°F (27°C) as soon as ripe. Separate offsets in spring or summer.
• **PESTS AND DISEASES** Susceptible to scale insects.

N. carolinae see *Neoregelia carolinae.*
N. fulgens (Blushing bromeliad). Epiphytic, rhizomatous bromeliad with spreading rosettes of 15–20 strap-shaped, sparsely and sharply toothed, pointed, bright pale green leaves, to 16in (40cm) long, slightly scaly beneath. Bears clusters of tubular white flowers, 2in (5cm) long, with purple-blue tips and bright red sepals, among the lance-shaped, brilliant red bracts. ↕ 16in (40cm), ↔ to 24in (60cm). S. Brazil. ❀ (min. 54°F/12°C)
N. innocentii. Very variable, epiphytic bromeliad with funnel-shaped rosettes of 30 or more sword- or strap-shaped, minutely toothed, dark green or reddish green leaves, 8–24in (20–60cm) long, widening toward the tips, with dark red undersides. Clusters of tubular, white- or pink-sepaled, green-based white flowers, to 2½in (6cm) long, are produced in rosettes of bright red or green-tipped red bracts. ↕ 8–12in (20–30cm), ↔ 24in (60cm). Brazil. ❀ (min. 54°F/12°C)
N. procerum. Epiphytic bromeliad with erect rosettes of 12–40 sharp-pointed, finely toothed, waxy, copper-suffused, pale green leaves, 16–39in (40–100cm) long. Bears 25–30 or more tubular, blue-tipped vermilion flowers, to 1¼in (3cm) long, among clusters of red floral bracts. ↕ 8–12in (20–30cm), ↔ to 30in (75cm). Brazil. ❀ (min. 54°F/12°C). **var. *kermesianum*** has red-suffused, often narrower, shorter leaves, to 16in (40cm) long; ↔ to 18in (45cm).
N. rutilans ■ Terrestrial or epiphytic bromeliad with tubular rosettes of 12–20 strap-shaped, pointed, toothed, bright green leaves, 14–16in (35–40cm) long, suffused deeper green. Bright red bracts surround clusters of 5–8 tubular red flowers, 1½–2in (4–5cm) long, with purple-tipped white sepals. ↕ 12in (30cm), ↔ 18in (45cm). S. Brazil. ❀ (min. 41°F/5°C)

Nidularium rutilans

NIEREMBERGIA
Cup flower
SOLANACEAE

Genus of over 20 species of annuals, perennials, and shrubs from moist, sunny habitats in temperate South America. Slender, spreading or upright stems bear alternate, entire leaves and colorful, open cup- or bell-shaped, sometimes tubular flowers in summer. Most perennial species are frost tender, but are easily propagated and are often grown as annuals; use as bedding, as border edging, or in containers under glass for early-spring flowers. In warm areas, grow in open sites among shrubs. Grow *N. repens* in a rock garden or in paving crevices; it may become invasive.
• **CULTIVATION** Outdoors, grow in a sheltered site in moist but well-drained soil in full sun. *N. repens* prefers dry, sandy soils. Under glass, grow in soil-based potting mix in full light. During growth, water moderately and apply a balanced liquid fertilizer monthly. Water sparingly in winter. Trim lightly after flowering.
• **PROPAGATION** Sow seed in autumn for spring flowering, or in spring at 59°F (15°C). Take stem-tip cuttings of tender perennials at any time during summer. Divide *N. repens* in spring.
• **PESTS AND DISEASES** Susceptible to aphids and whiteflies under glass, and may be damaged by slugs and snails outdoors. May be affected by viruses, especially tobacco mosaic virus.

N. caerulea, syn. *N. hippomanica.* Upright, branching, downy-stemmed perennial, usually grown as an annual, with narrowly spoon-shaped, pointed leaves, to ⅜in (9mm) long. Cup-shaped, lavender-blue flowers, to ¾in (2cm) across, with yellow throats, are produced over long periods in summer. ↕↔ to 8in (20cm). Argentina. Zone 7b. **'Mont Blanc'** ■ bears white flowers. **'Purple Robe'** has rich violet-blue flowers. **var. *violacea*** has longer leaves, to 1in (2.5cm) long, and deep violet-blue flowers.
N. frutescens see *N. scoparia.*
N. hippomanica see *N. caerulea.*
N. repens, syn. *N. rivularis* (White cup). Creeping, mat-forming, stem-rooting perennial with rounded, spoon-shaped, light green leaves, to 1¼in (3cm) long. Bears open bell-shaped, yellow-centered white flowers, 1–2in (2.5–5cm) across, over long periods in summer. ↕ 2in (5cm), ↔ 24in (60cm) or more. Andes, warm-temperate South America. Zone 7b. **'Violet Queen'** produces rich purple flowers.

Nierembergia caerulea 'Mont Blanc'

N. rivularis see *N. repens.*
N. scoparia, syn. *N. frutescens.* Shrubby perennial with well-branched stems and linear to narrowly spoon-shaped, stalkless leaves, to 2in (5cm) long. Numerous tubular, pale blue flowers, 1in (2.5cm) across, fading to white at the margins, and with wide-spreading mouths, are borne from midsummer to early autumn. ↕ to 18in (45cm) or more, ↔ 12in (30cm). Chile. Zone 7b. **var. *glaberrima*** bears smaller flowers, to ⅜in (9mm) across.

NIGELLA
Devil-in-a-bush, Love-in-a-mist
RANUNCULACEAE

Genus of 20 species of stiffly erect, bushy annuals found on rocky slopes, wasteland, and in fallow fields in the Mediterranean, Eurasia, and N. Africa. Leaves are alternate, feathery, pinnatisect to 3-pinnatisect. The solitary, sometimes paired, terminal or axillary flowers, borne mainly in summer, are pink, blue, yellow, or white, with 5 petal-like sepals and 5–10 smaller, 2-lipped true petals; they sometimes nestle within a showy, ruff-like collar of strongly veined leaves with hair-like, wispy divisions at each tip. The decorative, sometimes inflated capsules with persistent styles can be dried for flower arrangements. Grow in an informal, mixed or annual border; self-seeding usually occurs. They also provide long-lasting cut flowers.
• **CULTIVATION** Grow in any well-drained soil in full sun.
• **PROPAGATION** Sow seed *in situ* in mid-spring or autumn. Provide protection in winter for autumn-sown plants.
• **PESTS AND DISEASES** Infrequent.

N. damascena (Devil-in-a-bush, Love-in-a-mist). Single-stemmed or branching annual with ovate, finely divided, 2- or 3-pinnatisect, bright green leaves, 5in (13cm) long. In summer, bears terminal, saucer-shaped, pale blue flowers, to 1¾in (4.5cm) across, becoming sky-blue with age, surrounded by a ruff of foliage, finely divided at the tips. ↕ to 20in (50cm), ↔ to 9in (23cm). S. Europe, N. Africa. **'Blue Midget'** is dwarf; ↕ 10in (25cm). **'Cambridge Blue'** has long stems and double blue flowers. **'Dwarf Moody Blue'** is dwarf, producing flowers that open violet, fading to sky-blue; ↕ 8in (20cm). Cultivars of **Miss Jekyll Series** ■ produce white, sky-blue, deep blue, and rose flowers; ↕ to 18in (45cm). **'Mulberry Rose'** has large flowers opening creamy pink and deepening to rose-pink; ↕ to 18in (45cm). **'Oxford Blue'** bears double, dark blue flowers. Cultivars of **Persian Jewel Series** ■ have sky-blue, deep violet-blue, rose-pink, deep pink, or white flowers; ↕ to 16in (40cm). **'Red Jewel'** bears deep rose flowers.
***N. hispanica* 'Curiosity'.** Bushy annual bearing broadly ovate, finely divided, 2- or 3-pinnatisect, dark green leaves, to 5½in (14cm) long. Terminal, scented, saucer-shaped, bright blue flowers, to 2½in (6cm) across, with dark eyes and deep maroon-red stamens, are solitary or produced in pairs, in summer. ↕ 24–30in (60–75cm), ↔ to 18in (45cm).
***N. orientalis* 'Transformer'.** Bushy annual with finely divided, 2- or 3-pinnatisect, broadly ovate, bluish green leaves, to 5½in (14cm) long. In late spring and early summer, bears terminal, solitary yellow flowers, to 1¾in (4.5cm) across. The strongly ribbed seed pods resemble inside-out umbrellas, making an unusual addition to dried flower arrangements. ↕ to 18in (45cm), ↔ 9–12in (22–30cm).

Nigella damascena Miss Jekyll Series

Nigella damascena Persian Jewel Series

Nipponanthemum nipponicum

NIPPONANTHEMUM

ASTERACEAE

Genus of one species of herbaceous or subshrubby perennial from sandy, coastal regions of Japan. It has erect or spreading stems bearing alternate leaves crowded together at the ends of the branches. In autumn, it bears solitary, unpleasantly aromatic, daisy-like white flowerheads. Grow *N. nipponicum* in a mixed or herbaceous border.

• **CULTIVATION** Grow in very well-drained, moderately fertile soil in full sun. It performs best when cut back almost to the ground in spring; unpruned plants quickly become leggy and unattractively open-centered.

• **PROPAGATION** Sow seed at 55°F (13°C) in spring. Divide in spring.

• **PESTS AND DISEASES** Slugs and aphids may be troublesome.

N. nipponicum ▣ Subshrubby perennial with erect or spreading, sparsely branched stems and stalkless, narrowly spoon-shaped, irregularly toothed, aromatic, mid- to dark green leaves, to 3½in (9cm) long. In autumn, bears daisy-like white flowerheads, to 2½in (6cm) across, with green disk florets maturing yellow. ↕↔ 24in (60cm). Japan. Zone 7.

NOLANA

SOLANACEAE

Genus of 18 species of often glandular-hairy, erect to spreading annuals, perennials, and subshrubs, usually grown as annuals, found in semi-desert and coastal areas in Peru and Chile. They have simple, alternate or whorled, sometimes succulent leaves. The broadly trumpet-shaped, 5-petaled, blue, pink, or white flowers are borne singly or in clusters in the leaf axils. Grow in a border, or as short-lived container plants in a cool greenhouse. In warm climates, grow perennials in a rock garden.

• **CULTIVATION** Outdoors, grow in any moderately fertile soil in full sun. Under glass, grow in soil-based potting mix in full light. Water moderately during the growing season.

• **PROPAGATION** Sow seed at 55–59°F (13–15°C) in early spring, *in situ* in late spring, or in autumn for spring-flowering container plants.

• **PESTS AND DISEASES** Aphids and leaf miners can be problems.

Nolana paradoxa

***N. humifusa* 'Little Bells'.** Spreading, sticky, glandular-hairy annual, perennial, or subshrub with a basal rosette of stalkless, inversely lance-shaped leaves, to 1in (2.5cm) long, and elliptic stem leaves. Lilac-blue flowers, to 1in (2.5cm) across, with broad white throats, streaked lilac-blue, are produced in summer. ↕ to 6in (15cm), ↔ to 18in (45cm). ❀ (min. 41°F/5°C)

N. paradoxa ▣ Spreading, fleshy, glandular-hairy annual or perennial with a basal rosette of stalkless, inversely lance-shaped leaves, 2in (5cm) long, and ovate to elliptic stem leaves. Bears dark blue to purple-blue flowers, to 2in (5cm) across, with yellow throats and white eyes, in summer; they open only in full sun. ↕ 8–10in (20–25cm), ↔ to 24in (60cm). Peru, Chile. ❀ (min. 41°F/5°C)

▷ ***Nolina*** see *Beaucarnea*

NOMOCHARIS

LILIACEAE

Genus of about 7 species of bulbous perennials from seasonally moist meadows, rocks, and woodland in mountainous areas of W. China, S.E. Tibet, Burma, and N. India. They have linear to lance-shaped or oblong-ovate leaves borne in whorls on the upper halves of the stems, or scattered along them in pairs or threes. In summer, they bear loose racemes of often boldly spotted, saucer-shaped to flat, 6-tepaled flowers, 2–3in (5–8cm) across. They are ideal for a cool woodland garden and are effective grown with rhododendrons.

Nomocharis pardanthina

• **CULTIVATION** Plant 6in (15cm) deep in winter or spring, in humus-rich, acidic soil in partial shade; in cool areas, they may be grown in full sun. They dislike hot, dry conditions; ensure soil is moist in summer but never waterlogged.

• **PROPAGATION** Sow seed at 45–50°F (7–10°C) in autumn or spring. Flowers appear about 4 years after germination.

• **PESTS AND DISEASES** Prone to slug and snail damage.

N. aperta. Bulbous perennial with lance-shaped leaves, 2½–4in (6–10cm) long, in pairs along the stem. In early summer, produces racemes of 5 or 6 nodding, flattish, pale pink flowers, 2–4in (5–10cm) across, spotted deep purple. ↕ 12–32in (30–80cm), PD4in (10cm). W. China. Zone 7b.

N. farreri. Bulbous perennial with linear to lance-shaped leaves, 1½in (4cm) long, in whorls up the stem. In early summer, bears racemes of up to 20 nodding, saucer-shaped, white or pale pink flowers, 2–4½in (5–11cm) across, with heavy reddish purple spotting and dark centers. Similar to *N. pardanthina*, but the petals have smooth margins and the leaves are narrower. ↕ 36in (90cm), PD4in (10cm). N.E. Burma. Zone 7b.

N. mairei see *N. pardanthina.*

N. nana *see Lilium nanum.*

N. oxypetala see *Lilium oxypetalum.*

N. pardanthina ▣ syn. *N. mairei.* Bulbous perennial with elliptic to lance-shaped leaves, 1–4½in (2.5–11cm) long, in whorls up the stem. In early summer, bears racemes of 2–20 nodding, saucer-shaped then flat, white or pale pink flowers, 2–3½in (5–9cm) across; they are heavily spotted reddish purple, and have dark centers and fringed petal margins. ↕ 36in (90cm), PD4in (10cm). W. China. Zone 7b.

N. saluenensis. Bulbous perennial with elliptic leaves, ¾–1½in (2–4cm) long, scattered up the stem. In early summer, bears racemes of 1–6 nodding, saucer-shaped flowers, 2½–3½in (6–9cm) across, that vary from pale to mid-pink or white, with light maroon spotting toward the dark purple centers. ↕ 36in (90cm), PD4in (10cm). W. China, N.E. Burma. Zone 7b.

▷ ***Nopalea cochenillifera*** see *Opuntia cochenillifera*

NOPALXOCHIA

CACTACEAE

Genus of 4 species of freely branching, epiphytic cacti, very closely related to *Epiphyllum*, from forest in S. Mexico and Central America. They have strap-shaped, jointed, spineless stems, often cylindrical at the bases, with notched margins. From late winter to early summer, funnel- to bell- or cup-shaped, diurnal flowers are borne on slender tubes from the marginal areoles. The flowers last for 3 or 4 days and are followed in the species by ovoid red fruits, containing seeds encased in jelly-like pulp. In areas where temperatures drop below 50°F (10°C), grow in a temperate or warm greenhouse, or as houseplants. They do poorly when temperatures exceed 100°F (38°C). In warmer climates, grow in a shady border or in large hanging baskets.

Nopalxochia ackermannii

• **CULTIVATION** Under glass, grow in slightly acidic, epiphytic cactus potting mix in bright filtered light, with moderate humidity, away from drafts. During the growing season, water freely and apply a dilute balanced liquid fertilizer monthly. Keep barely moist when dormant. Outdoors, grow in moist but sharply drained, leafy, gritty soil in a sheltered site in partial shade. See also pp.48–49.

• **PROPAGATION** Sow seed at 66–75°F (19–24°C) in spring. Take cuttings of stem sections after flowering.

• **PESTS AND DISEASES** Vulnerable to mealybugs, especially during early spring.

***N.* 'Achievement'.** Semi-erect cactus producing strap-shaped stems with rounded margins. Bears yellow flowers, 5½in (14cm) across, with frilled petals. ↕ 18in (45cm) or more, ↔ 16in (40cm). ❀ (min. 50°F/10°C)

N. ackermannii ▣ syn. *Epiphyllum ackermannii.* Erect cactus with flat, thin, slightly scalloped, fleshy stems, rarely 3-ribbed. The crimson or orange-red flowers have pale yellow-green tubes, 5in (13cm) long, with short pink styles and white stigma lobes. ↕ 18in (45cm) or more, ↔ 16in (40cm). S. Mexico. ❀ (min. 50°F/10°C)

***N.* 'Alba Superba'.** Erect cactus producing strap-shaped stems with rounded margins. Bears flowers 6–8in (15–20cm) across, with pure white inner petals and pinkish white outer segments. ↕↔ to 20in (50cm). ❀ (min. 50°F/10°C)

***N.* 'Calypso'.** Semi-erect cactus producing strap-shaped stems with rounded margins and lilac-pink flowers, 5in (13cm) or more across. ↕↔ to 12in (30cm). ❀ (min. 50°F/10°C)

***N.* 'Celestine'.** Erect cactus producing strap-shaped stems with rounded margins. Bears ruffled, pale reddish pink flowers, 5in (13cm) across. ↕↔ 14in (35cm). ❀ (min. 50°F/10°C)

***N.* 'Chauncey'.** Erect cactus producing strap-shaped stems with rounded margins. Flowers, 6in (15cm) across, have purple inner petals, each with a red mid-line, and dark red outer segments. ↕ to 24in (60cm), ↔ 18in (45cm). ❀ (min. 50°F/10°C)

***N.* 'Dreamland'.** Erect cactus producing strap-shaped stems with rounded margins. Flowers, 5in (13cm) across, have pinkish orange petals, each with a deeper, almost red mid-line, and rose-red throats. ↕↔ 20in (50cm). ❀ (min. 50°F/10°C)

N

Nopalxochia 'Gloria'

N. 'Gloria' ■ Erect then pendent cactus bearing slender, strap-shaped stems with minutely notched margins. Produces deep, rich reddish pink flowers, paler in the throats, 4in (10cm) across. ↕ 12in (30cm), ↔ 18in (45cm). ❀ (min. 50°F/10°C)
N. 'Helena'. Erect cactus with 3-angled, notched stems and minutely spiny areoles. Red to violet flowers, 5in (13cm) across, with frilled petals are produced. ↕↔ 18in (45cm). ❀ (min. 50°F/10°C)
N. 'Jennifer Ann' ■ Erect then pendent cactus with strap-shaped, strongly notched stems. Bears yellow flowers, paler in the throats, to 6in (15cm) across. ↕ 12in (30cm), ↔ 20in (50cm). ❀ (min. 50°F/10°C)

Nopalxochia 'Jennifer Ann'

Nopalxochia 'Kismet'

Nopalxochia phyllanthoides 'Deutsche Kaiserin'

N. 'King Midas'. Erect cactus with strap-shaped or angular stems. Bears bright yellow flowers, to 8in (20cm) across, each with a deep golden mid-stripe and yellowish orange sepals. ↕ to 3ft (1m), ↔ 20in (50cm) ❀ (min. 50°F/10°C)
N. 'Kismet' ■ Cactus producing wide, strap-shaped stems with rounded margins. Bears widely cup-shaped flowers, 6in (15cm) across, in shades of pale purple in the throats and deepening to dark, rich scarlet in the outer segments. ↕↔ to 16in (40cm). ❀ (min. 50°F/10°C)
N. macdougallii, syn. *Epiphyllum macdougallii, Lobeira macdougallii.* Semi-erect cactus producing flat, 2-winged, scalloped, fleshy stems with inset, marginal areoles. Narrowly trumpet-shaped, lilac-rose flowers, to 3in (8cm) across, have brown-green tubes. ↕ 12in (30cm), ↔ 18in (45cm). S.E. Mexico. ❀ (min. 50°F/10°C)
N. 'M.A. Jeans'. Erect then slightly pendent cactus producing strap-shaped stems with minutely notched margins. Bears deep pink flowers, 3in (8cm) across. ↕ 12in (30cm), ↔ 20in (50cm). ❀ (min. 50°F/10°C)
N. 'Moonlight Sonata'. Erect cactus producing strap-shaped stems with rounded margins. Bears flowers, 7in (18cm) across, with white bases, purple-pink petals, and dark violet sepals. ↕ 18in (45cm), ↔ 12in (30cm). ❀ (min. 50°F/10°C)
***N. phyllanthoides* 'Deutsche Kaiserin'** ■ Semi-erect cactus with strap-shaped, scalloped, fleshy, deep green stems, tapering toward the ends. Bears pink flowers, 3–3½in (7–9cm) across, with white centers. ↕ to 36in (90cm), ↔ 24in (60cm). ❀ (min. 50°F/10°C)
N. 'Queen Anne'. Semi-pendent cactus producing strap-shaped stems with rounded margins. Bears yellow flowers, 4in (10cm) across. ↕ 10in (25cm), ↔ 16in (40cm). ❀ (min. 50°F/10°C)
N. 'Soraya'. Erect cactus producing strap-shaped stems with rounded margins. Bears brilliant deep scarlet flowers, 4½in (11cm) across, with broad, almost oval petals. ↕ 10in (25cm), ↔ 8in (20cm). ❀ (min. 50°F/10°C)
N. 'Tyke'. Erect, untidy cactus producing strap-shaped stems with rounded margins. Reddish orange flowers, 5in (13cm) across, have wide-spreading, twisted petals. ↕ to 20in (50cm), ↔ 18in (45cm). ❀ (min. 50°F/10°C)
N. 'Zoe' ■ Semi-prostrate cactus producing strap-shaped stems with rounded margins. Bears peach-orange flowers, to 5in (13cm) across, each with 3 rows of petals. ↕↔ 16–20in (40–50cm). ❀ (min. 50°F/10°C)

Nopalxochia 'Zoe'

Nothofagus

Southern beech

FAGACEAE

Genus of 20 or more species of evergreen or deciduous trees and shrubs from the S. hemisphere (New Guinea and New Caledonia to Australia, New Zealand, and South America), where they occur as forest trees from sea level to the mountains. Leaves are alternate, simple, entire or toothed, sometimes with wavy margins. Flowers and fruits are inconspicuous. They are grown for their habit and foliage, and, in the case of deciduous species, for their attractive autumn color. Grow as specimen trees in a large garden or woodland garden. In the wild, they often attain much greater heights than in cultivation.

• **Cultivation** Grow in fertile, moist but well-drained, acidic soil in full sun. Shelter evergreen species from strong cold winds, at least when young. Pruning group 1.
• **Propagation** Sow seed in a seedbed in autumn. Seed from garden sources may give rise to hybrids.
• **Pests and diseases** Root rot may be a problem.

***N. alpina* of gardens** see *N. procera.*
N. antarctica ■ (Antarctic beech, Nirre). Broadly conical, often many-stemmed, deciduous tree or shrub bearing ovate to broadly ovate, glossy, dark green leaves, to 1¼in (3cm) long. Leaves are finely toothed and crinkle-margined, and turn yellow in autumn. ↕ 50ft (15m), ↔ 30ft (10m). S. Chile, S. Argentina. Zone 7.
N. betuloides ■ Dense, broadly columnar, evergreen tree with ovate to broadly ovate, blunt-toothed, dark blackish green leaves, to 1in (2.5cm) long, often unequal at the bases, produced on sticky red shoots. ↕ 50ft (15m), ↔ 20ft (6m). Chile, Argentina. Zone 8.
N. cunninghamii (Myrtle beech). Conical, evergreen tree with slender, downy shoots and ovate to triangular-ovate, blunt-toothed, glossy leaves, to ¾in (2cm) long, bronze-red in summer when young. ↕ 40ft (12m), ↔ 25ft (8m). Victoria, Tasmania. ❀ (min. 35°F/2°C)
N. dombeyi ■ Broadly columnar to conical, evergreen tree. Shoots, which are pendulous at the tips, produce narrowly ovate-lance-shaped, finely toothed, dark green leaves, ¾–1½in (2–4cm) long, often unequal at the bases. ↕ 70ft (20m), ↔ 30ft (10m). Chile, Argentina. Zone 8.
N. menziesii (Silver beech). Dense, conical, evergreen tree with silvery white bark when young. Bears broadly ovate to rounded, leathery, dark green leaves, to ¾in (2cm) long, toothed at the margins, pale green when young. ↕ 50ft (15m), ↔ 25ft (8m). New Zealand. ❀ (min. 35°F/2°C)
N. obliqua (Roblé). Fast-growing, narrowly to broadly conical, deciduous tree with arching shoots. Produces oblong or oblong-lance-shaped, dark green leaves, to 3in (8cm) long, blue-

Nothofagus antarctica

Nothofagus betuloides

Nothofagus dombeyi

Nothofagus procera

green beneath, with usually 8–10 pairs of veins and doubly toothed margins that turn yellow to orange or red in autumn. ↕70ft (20m), ↔ 50ft (15m). Chile, Argentina. Zone 7b.
N. procera ▣ syn. *N. alpina* of gardens (Rauli). Fast-growing, broadly conical, deciduous tree. Bears oblong-lance-shaped to elliptic-lance-shaped, slightly scalloped, matte, deep green leaves, to 4in (10cm) or more long, conspicuously marked with 15–18 pairs of veins. Leaves are bronze when young, turning yellow to orange or red in autumn. ↕80ft (25m), ↔ 50ft (15m). Chile, Argentina (Andes). Zone 7b.
N. pumilio ▣ Columnar, sometimes shrubby, often several-stemmed, deciduous tree bearing oblong to obovate, dark green leaves, to 1½in (4cm) long; each has 5–7 pairs of veins with 2 rounded teeth between each vein. ↕50ft (15m), ↔ 30ft (10m). Chile, Argentina (Andes). Zone 8.
N. solandri (Black beech). Broadly conical, evergreen tree with ovate-elliptic to elliptic-oblong, entire, dark blackish green leaves, to ½in (1.5cm) long, gray-hairy beneath, ending in a short point. ↕50ft (15m), ↔ 30ft (10m). New Zealand. Zone 8. **var. *cliffortioides*** (Mountain beech) has ovate, twisted, more sharply pointed leaves.

NOTHOLIRION

LILIACEAE

Genus of 6 species of bulbous perennials, related to *Fritillaria* and *Lilium*, found in open woodland, scrub, and rocky mountains from Afghanistan to W. China. They produce basal tufts of narrowly lance-shaped leaves in winter, followed by racemes of nodding, trumpet- or funnel-shaped flowers in summer. Where marginally hardy, grow in a protected site outdoors, or in a cool greenhouse. They grow best in areas with cool summers.
• **CULTIVATION** Plant 4–6in (10–15cm) deep in autumn. Outdoors, plant in deep, humus-rich, well-drained soil in partial shade. Provide protection during periods of prolonged cold. Under glass, grow in large containers in soilless potting mix with added leaf mold and sharp sand, in bright filtered light. Water freely during the growing season. Keep barely moist when dormant. *Notholirion* bulbs are monocarpic and die after flowering, leaving offsets or a cluster of bulblets that take some time to reach flowering size.
• **PROPAGATION** Sow seed or grow on bulblets in late summer in containers in a cold frame. Remove offsets in autumn.
• **PESTS AND DISEASES** Infrequent.

Nothofagus pumilio (inset: leaf detail)

N. bulbuliferum. Bulbous perennial with narrow, lance-shaped, basal leaves, to 18in (45cm) long. In summer, produces racemes of 10–30 trumpet-shaped, pale lilac flowers, to 1½in (4cm) long, with green tips. ↕to 5ft (1.5m), PD6in (15cm). Nepal to W. China. Zone 7b.
N. campanulatum. Bulbous perennial with narrow, lance-shaped, basal leaves, to 12in (30cm) long. In summer, produces racemes of up to 20 pendent, deep crimson-purple, green-tipped flowers, to 2in (5cm) long. ↕32in (80cm), PD6in (15cm). N. Burma, W. China. Zone 7b.

NOTHOSCORDUM

False garlic

LILIACEAE

Genus of about 20 species of bulbous perennials from rocky hillsides and disturbed ground in North and South America. They have linear, basal leaves and, from spring to summer, bear loose umbels of 6-tepaled, funnel-, bell-, or almost star-shaped flowers, borne on erect, leafless stems. They resemble *Allium* species but without their characteristic smell. Grow in a rock garden or raised bed. *N. gracile* is best in a wild garden, since it increases freely; may become invasive.
• **CULTIVATION** Plant 3in (8cm) deep in any soil in full sun or partial shade in autumn.
• **PROPAGATION** Sow seed as soon as ripe in containers in a cold frame. Remove offsets in autumn.
• **PESTS AND DISEASES** Prone to rust and sometimes anthracnose.

N. fragrans see *N. gracile*.
N. gracile, syn. *N. fragrans*, *N. inodorum* of gardens. Very vigorous, bulbous perennial with narrow, linear, basal leaves, 8–16in (20–40cm) long. Fragrant umbels of 8–15 small, funnel-shaped, brown- or pink-striped, white or occasionally lilac flowers, ⅜–½in (0.9–1.5cm) long, are borne from spring to summer. ↕10–28in (25–70cm), PD2in (5cm). Mexico, South America. Zone 7b.
***N. inodorum* of gardens** see *N. gracile*.
N. neriniflorum see *Caloscordum neriniflorum*.

▷ ***Notocactus*** see *Parodia*

NOTOSPARTIUM

FABACEAE

Genus of 3 species of leafless shrubs or trees found on valley sides and river terraces in South Island, New Zealand. They are grown for their elegant habit, green, leafless branches, and pendulous racemes of colorful, pea-like flowers, borne in summer. Grow *Notospartium* species in a shrub border or at the base of a sunny wall.
• **CULTIVATION** Grow in moist but well-drained soil in full sun; shelter from strong winds. Pruning group 9.

Notospartium glabrescens

• **PROPAGATION** Sow seed in containers in a cold frame in autumn or spring. Take semi-ripe cuttings in summer, with bottom heat.
• **PESTS AND DISEASES** Infrequent.

N. carmichaeliae (Pink broom). Weeping shrub with slender, pendulous, leafless green shoots. Pea-like, purple-veined pink flowers, ⅜in (9mm) long, with broad, standard petals, are produced in dense, slender racemes, to 2in (5cm) long. ↕6–12ft (2–4m), ↔ 5ft (1.5m). New Zealand (South Island). ❀ (min. 35°F/2°C)
N. glabrescens ▣ Upright shrub or small tree with pendulous lower branches and slightly flattened, slender, dark blue-green shoots. Pea-like pink flowers, to ½in (1.5cm) long, flushed and veined purple, are produced in open racemes, to 2in (5cm) long. ↕10ft (3m), ↔ 6ft (2m) or more. New Zealand (South Island). ❀ (min. 35°F/2°C)

NUPHAR

Spatterdock, Yellow pond lily

NYMPHAEACEAE

Genus of 25 species of deciduous, submerged, aquatic perennials, mainly from temperate regions of the N. hemisphere. They have thick, creeping rhizomes, and both leathery floating leaves and membranous submerged leaves. In summer, they bear solitary, almost spherical flowers, which are held above the water surface. The flowers are followed by berry-like, ovoid to flask-shaped fruits. Generally more vigorous than water lilies (*Nymphaea*), they thrive in deeper, cooler water, forming robust groups of foliage on large natural lakes, where they may cover the water surface completely.
• **CULTIVATION** Outdoors, grow vigorous species in water 6ft (2m) deep, anchoring the thick rhizomes in the mud at the bottom. Grow less vigorous species in water about 12in (30cm) deep, providing a free root-run. Grow in

Nuphar japonica

Nuphar lutea

full sun, and divide frequently for optimum flower production.

• **PROPAGATION** Separate pieces of rhizome that have a growing point attached, and transplant.

• **PESTS AND DISEASES** Susceptible to white smut and leaf spot.

N. advena (Common spatterdock). Aquatic perennial with floating or upright, broadly ovate to oblong, thick, tough, leathery leaves, to 12in (30cm) long. In summer, bears red-tinged yellow flowers, 1½in (4cm) across, with coppery-red stamens. ↔ indefinite. C. and E. US. Zone 3.

N. japonica ■ (Japanese pond lily). Aquatic perennial with narrowly ovate to oblong floating leaves, to 16in (40cm) long, arrow-shaped at the bases, and distinctive, narrow, arrow-shaped, wavy-margined submerged leaves, to 12in (30cm) long. Produces yellow, red-tinted flowers, 2in (5cm) across, in summer. ↔ 3ft (1m). Japan. Zone 7.

N. kalmiana. Aquatic perennial with broadly rounded floating leaves, 4in (10cm) long, softly hairy beneath, and distinctive, thin, rounded submerged leaves. In summer, produces orange flowers, ¾in (2cm) across, with yellow margins. ↔ 24–36in (60–90cm). E. US. Zone 6.

N. lutea ■ syn. *N. luteum* (Yellow pond lily). Aquatic perennial with ovate-oblong to rounded, thick, mid- to deep green floating leaves, 16in (40cm) long, and broadly ovate to rounded, wavy-margined, translucent, pale green submerged leaves, each with a deep sinus. In summer, produces yellow flowers, 2½in (6cm) across, with a distinctive, unpleasant smell. ↔ 6ft (2m) or more. Eurasia, N. Africa, E. US, West Indies. Zone 5.

N. luteum see *N. lutea.*

N. polysepala. Aquatic perennial with usually floating, broadly rounded to ovate-oblong, hairless, dull green leaves, to 16in (40cm) long. In summer, bears yellow flowers, to 3in (8cm) across, with green sepals, purple-brown insides, and purple anthers. ↔ to 36in (90cm). N. North America. Zone 4.

N. pumila. Aquatic perennial with broadly ovate floating leaves, 5½in (14cm) long, and broadly ovate to rounded, wavy-margined, translucent, pale green submerged leaves. In summer, bears yellow flowers, to 1¼in (3cm) across. Suitable for a small pool. ↔ 4½ft (1.4m). Europe, Russia (W. Siberia), Japan. Zone 5.

N. sagittifolium. Aquatic perennial with narrowly oblong to oblong-lance-shaped, leathery, mid-green floating leaves, to 11in (28cm) long, and arrow-shaped, wavy-margined, mid-green submerged leaves, to 14in (35cm) long. In summer, bears green-tipped, canary-yellow flowers, to 1¼in (3cm) across, with pale yellow petals and stamens. ↔ to 36in (90cm). S.E. US. Zone 7b.

▷ ***Nuttallia cerasiformis*** see *Oemleria cerasiformis*

▷ ***Nyctocereus serpentinus*** see *Peniocereus serpentinus*

NYMANIA

MELIACEAE

Genus of one species of evergreen shrub from hot, dry areas of South Africa. It is grown for its small, 4-petaled flowers, with 8 long stamens, produced singly from the leaf axils, and its colorful, bladder-like seed pods. The leaves are very narrow and arranged alternately. Where not hardy, grow *N. capensis* in a cool greenhouse or conservatory. In warm, dry climates, grow in a border or as a specimen plant.

• **CULTIVATION** Under glass, grow in soil-based potting mix in full light. During the growing season, water moderately and apply a balanced liquid fertilizer every month. Water sparingly in winter. Outdoors, grow in fertile, well-drained soil in full sun. Pruning group 8; may need restrictive pruning under glass after fruiting.

• **PROPAGATION** Sow seed at 61°F (16°C) in spring. Root semi-ripe cuttings in summer, with bottom heat.

• **PESTS AND DISEASES** Infrequent, although scale insects may be a problem under glass.

N. capensis (Chinese lanterns, Klapperbos). Erect to ascending, large shrub or sometimes small tree, usually very open, with rigid branches. The stems are crowded with linear to narrowly oblong leaves, to 2in (5cm) long. Bears 4-petaled flowers, ½in (1.5cm) long, with erect, carmine-red to rose-pink petals, from late winter to early summer. Inflated seed capsules, 1–1¼in (2.5–3cm) long, are off-white, and heavily mottled and suffused carmine-red. ↕ 6–10ft (2–3m) or more, ↔ 3–6ft (1–2m). South Africa (Eastern Cape). ❄ (min. 41–45°F/5–7°C)

NYMPHAEA

Waterlily

NYMPHAEACEAE

Genus of 50 species of herbaceous, submerged aquatic perennials occurring worldwide, cultivated for their showy, sometimes fragrant flowers and floating leaves. Waterlilies have horizontal or upright rhizomes or stoloniferous tubers, and broadly ovate to rounded, floating leaves, each cleft into 2 lobes, with a basal sinus and a long leaf stalk. The mostly white, yellow, pink, red, or, in the tropical species, blue flowers, borne in summer, each have 4 sepals and numerous narrow petals and stamens. Berry-like fruits, with many seeds, mature under water.

Hardy waterlilies are usually day-blooming and bear floating flowers. Tender, tropical waterlilies are either day-blooming or night-blooming, with larger, often toothed leaves, generally bearing flowers well above the water.

Waterlilies are a decorative addition to any pool; the shade of their leaves is useful in reducing algae growth. Where not hardy, grow tender waterlilies in a conservatory in full sun.

• **HARDINESS** Generally, hardy water-lilies are hardy in Zone 3 but tropical waterlilies are not hardy at all.

• **CULTIVATION** Grow in undisturbed water in full sun. In spring, plant hardy waterlilies in firm, loamy soil; insert the rhizomes just under the surface and cover with washed pea gravel or coarse sand. Submerge freshly planted containers so that 6–10in (15–25cm) of water covers the young crowns, either by temporarily lowering the water level or by raising the containers on brick plinths. For small rhizomes, reduce the depth to 3in (8cm); increase to 20in (50cm) for the largest rhizomes. Once plants are established, gradually increase the water depth above the crowns to twice the initial planting depth. Contain vigorous waterlilies in an aquatic container, or in a specially constructed, permanent planting station, about 3ft (1m) across and 18in (45cm) deep. During active growth, feed container-grown waterlilies with commercial aquatic fertilizer according to the manufacturer's instructions. Remove yellow leaves and deadhead regularly. Divide established plants, whose leaves thrust vertically above the water surface, to maintain flowering.

Nymphaea 'Blue Beauty'

Grow tropical waterlilies year-round in aquatic containers in an indoor pool with a minimum temperature of 50°F (10°C) in winter, and 70°F (21°C) in summer. Alternatively, plant in an outdoor pool in summer, remove the tubers in autumn (after a few hard frosts), air-dry for a few days, and over-winter in water or damp sand at a minimum of 50°F (10°C). Restart young plants in spring when dividing overwintered tubers. See also pp.52–53.

• **PROPAGATION** Surface-sow seed as soon as ripe, and cover with 1in (2.5cm) of water; germinate hardy species at 50–55°F (10–13°C), tropical species at 73–81°F (23–27°C). The seed heads sink as seeds ripen; enclose in a muslin bag to avoid losses. Divide rhizomes of older plants, or separate offsets. Remove young plantlets from viviparous water-lilies in summer, and pot individually in shallow water until established.

• **PESTS AND DISEASES** Susceptible to brown china-mark moth, false leaf-mining midge, waterlily beetle, water-lily aphid (which overwinters on *Prunus* species), and brown spot, crown rot, and waterlily leaf spot.

N. 'Albida' ■ syn. *N.* 'Marliacea Albida'. Hardy waterlily with rounded, dark green leaves, 9in (23cm) across, slightly bronze when young, with open sinuses. The fragrant, cup-shaped white flowers, 5–6in (12–15cm) across, have yellow stamens. ↔ 3–4ft (0.9–1.2m).

N. 'Amabilis'. Hardy waterlily with rounded leaves, 10in (25cm) across, with open sinuses, reddish purple when young, maturing to dark green with red-margined, light green undersides. Produces star-shaped, pink flowers, 6–7in (15–18cm) across, with light pink tips and dark yellow stamens. ↔ 5–7ft (1.5–2.2m).

N. 'American Star' ■ Hardy waterlily bearing rounded leaves, 10–11in (25–28cm) across, with open sinuses, purple-green when young, with red undersides, maturing to light green. Star-shaped flowers, 6–7in (15–18cm) across, with long, salmon-pink petals tipped paler pink, yellow inner stamens, and pinkish orange outer stamens, are borne well above the water surface. ↔ 4–5ft (1.2–1.5m).

N. 'Attraction' ■ Hardy waterlily bearing oval, light bronze leaves, to 10–12in (25–30cm) long, with over-lapping lobes, one of which is distinctly raised. Cup-shaped, later star-shaped flowers, to 9in (23cm) across, have dark garnet-red inner petals, lighter toward the margins, and orange-red stamens. ↔ 4–5ft (1.2–1.5m).

N. 'Aurora' ■ Hardy waterlily producing oval, maroon-mottled, mid-green leaves, to 6in (15cm) long, with open sinuses. Cup-shaped, later flattened flowers, 4in (10cm) across, with orange stamens, change from yellowish apricot-red through orange-red to a slightly flecked burgundy-red. ↔ 3–5ft (0.9–1.5m).

N. 'Blue Beauty' ■ Tropical waterlily producing oval, toothed, wavy-margined, dark green leaves lightly speckled brown above, to 14in (35cm) across, with partly overlapping lobes. Bears day-blooming, star-shaped, fragrant, mid-blue flowers, 8–11in

(20–28cm) across, with dark yellow stamens. ↔ 4–7ft (1.2–2.2m).
***N.* 'Blue Triumph'.** Tropical waterlily with rounded, wavy-margined, bronze-flecked green leaves, 12–18in (30–45cm) across, with rounded sinuses. Star-shaped, very sweetly fragrant flowers, 4–10in (10–25cm) across, have very dark blue petals, bright yellow ovary cups, and dark blue-tipped stamens. ↔ 3–4ft (1–1.2m).
N. caerulea (Blue lotus). Tropical waterlily with ovate, mid-green leaves, 12–16in (30–40cm) long, purple-spotted beneath, with overlapping lobes. Day-blooming, star-shaped, pale blue flowers, 6in (15cm) across, have paler inner petals and yellow stamens. ↔ 8–10ft (2.5–3m). N. and tropical Africa.
N. capensis ■ (Cape blue waterlily). Tropical waterlily with rounded, toothed, wavy-margined, mid-green leaves, 10–16in (25–40cm) across, with slightly overlapping lobes. The young leaves are purple-spotted beneath. Bears day-blooming, star-shaped, fragrant, light blue flowers, 8–10in (21–25cm) across, with dark yellow stamens. ↔ 5–8ft (1.5–2.5m). E. Africa, southern Africa, Madagascar. **'Rosea'** has leaves tinted red beneath and red-flushed, pale pink flowers.
***N.* 'Carnea'**, syn. *N.* 'Marliacea Carnea'. Hardy waterlily with dark green leaves, 7–8in (19–20cm) across, purplish when young, and light pink flowers, 4½–5in (11–13cm) across, with yellow stamens. ↔ 4–5ft (1.2–1.5m).
***N. caroliniana* 'Nivea'.** Hardy waterlily bearing rounded, pale green leaves, 8–10in (20–25cm) across, with slightly open sinuses. Star-shaped, fragrant, ivory-white flowers, 5–6in (12–15cm) across, with yellow stamens. ↔ 4–5ft (1.2–1.5m).
***N.* 'Charlene Strawn'.** Hardy waterlily with rounded leaves, 8–9in (20–23cm) across, red with purple mottling when young, maturing to mid-green, sometimes marked with purple, and with overlapping lobes. Star-shaped, highly fragrant, yellow flowers, 6–8in (15–20cm) across, have yellow stamens. ↔ 3–5ft (0.9–1.5m).
***N.* 'Chromatella'** ■ syn. *N.* 'Marliacea Chromatella'. Hardy waterlily producing olive-green leaves with bronze markings, 6–8in (15–20cm) across, coppery with purple streaks when young. Canary-yellow flowers, 6in (15cm) across, have broad, incurved petals and golden stamens. ↔ 4–5ft (1.2–1.5m).
***N.* 'Colorado'** ■ Hardy waterlily bearing faintly mottled, green leaves, to 10in (25cm) across. Great bloomer, holding its star-shaped salmon-pink flower, 5–6in (13–15cm), above the surface of the water. ↔ 12ft (4m).
***N.* 'Cynthia Ann'** ■ Hardy waterlily bearing green leaves with heavy maroon mottling, to 4–5in (10–13cm) across. Star-shaped, peach flowers are 4–5in (10–13cm) across. ↔ 10ft (3m).
N.* x *daubenyana (*N. caerulea* x *N. micrantha*). Viviparous, tropical waterlily with ovate, olive- to bronze-green leaves, to 12in (30cm) long, with wavy margins and overlapping lobes, many bearing a plantlet. Day-blooming, cup-shaped, fragrant flowers, 4–7in (10–18cm) across, are light blue with dark margins and yellow stamens. Grows well with 3 or 4 hours of sun per day. ↔ 3–4ft (0.9–1.2m). Garden origin.
***N.* 'Ellisiana'.** Hardy waterlily with oval, mid-green leaves, 7–8in (17–20cm) long, with open sinuses; young leaves are dark green, marked purple. Star-shaped, fragrant, bright red flowers, 4–5in (10–13cm) across, have orange-red stamens. ↔ 36in (90cm).
***N.* 'Emily Grant Hutchings'.** Tropical waterlily bearing rounded, wavy-margined leaves, 10–12in (25–30cm) across, bronze-green above, olive-green beneath, with overlapping nodes. Night-blooming, cup-shaped, dark pink flowers, 6–8in (15–20cm) across, have red stamens. ↔ 3–4ft (1–1.2m).
***N.* 'Firecrest'** ■ Hardy waterlily producing rounded, mid-green leaves, 9in (23cm) across, dark purple when young, with open sinuses. Star-shaped, deep pink flowers, 6in (15cm) across, with lavender-pink inner petals, have orange inner stamens and pink outer stamens. ↔ 4ft (1.2m).
N. flava see *N. mexicana.*
***N.* 'Froebelii'** ■ Hardy waterlily with rounded, pale green leaves, 6in (15cm) across, bronzed when young, with open sinuses. Cup-shaped, later star-shaped, burgundy-red flowers, 5in (13cm) across, orange-red stamens. ↔ 36in (90cm).

Nymphaea 'Froebelii'

***N.* 'Fulgens'** ■ syn. *N.* 'Laydekeri Fulgens'. Hardy waterlily producing broadly ovate, dark green leaves, 8in (20cm) long, with overlapping lobes. Young leaves are purplish green and marked dark purple. Cup-shaped, burgundy-red flowers, 5–6in (12–15cm) across, have orange-red stamens. ↔ 4–5ft (1.2–1.5m).
***N.* 'General Pershing'** ■ Tropical waterlily bearing rounded, wavy-margined, olive-green, purple-marked leaves, 9–10in (23–25cm) across, with almost closed sinuses. Day-blooming, cup-shaped, later flat, highly fragrant, lavender-pink flowers, 8–11in (20–28cm) across, have yellow stamens. ↔ 5–6ft (1.5–1.8m).
***N.* 'George L. Thomas'** ■ Hardy waterlily with maroon leaves maturing to green, to 10in (25cm). Produces cup-shaped, vibrant, rosy-red flowers, 5–6in (13–15cm), across. ↔ 12ft (4m).
N. gigantea (Australian waterlily). Tropical waterlily with rounded, toothed, wavy-margined, veined, mid-green leaves, to 24in (60cm) across, tinged pink to purple beneath, with often overlapping lobes. Bears day-blooming, star-shaped, sky-blue to purplish blue flowers, to 12in (30cm) across, with bright yellow stamens. ↔ 6–10ft (2–3m). N. Papua New Guinea, tropical Australia.
***N.* 'Gladstoneana'.** Hardy waterlily with rounded, wavy-margined, dark green leaves, 11–12in (27–30cm) across, with toothed margins along the overlapping lobes, and bronzed when young. Produces star-shaped white flowers, 5–7in (12–18cm) across, with yellow stamens. ↔ 5–8ft (1.5–2.5m).
***N.* 'Gloriosa'.** Hardy waterlily with broadly ovate, bronze-green leaves, 8–9in (20–23cm) long, with open sinuses; young leaves are light purple with darker markings and overlapping lobes. Cup-shaped to star-shaped, bright red flowers, 5in (13cm) across, have orange-red stamens. ↔ 5ft (1.5m).

Nymphaea 'Albida'

Nymphaea 'American Star'

Nymphaea 'Attraction'

Nymphaea 'Aurora'

Nymphaea capensis

Nymphaea 'Chromatella'

Nymphaea 'Colorado'

Nymphaea 'Cynthia Ann'

Nymphaea 'Firecrest'

Nymphaea 'Fulgens'

Nymphaea 'General Pershing'

Nymphaea 'George L. Thomas'

Nymphaea 'Lucida'

***N.* 'Indiana'.** Hardy waterlily with rounded, olive-green leaves, 5in (13cm) long, with open sinuses; young leaves are heavily marked with purplish green. Cup-shaped flowers, gradually flattening to 3½–4in (9–10cm) across, turn from apricot, through apricot-orange, to dark orange-red, and have orange stamens. ↔ 30in (75cm).
***N.* 'James Brydon'** ■ Hardy waterlily with rounded, bronze-green leaves, 7in (18cm) across, with overlapping lobes; young leaves are purplish brown with dark purple markings. Cup-shaped, vivid rose-red flowers, 4–5in (10–13cm) across, have orange-red stamens. ↔ 3–4ft (0.9–1.2m).
***N.* 'Joey Tomocik'** ■ Hardy waterlily with slightly mottled, green leaves, to 10in (25cm), across. Produces the most vibrant yellow flower of all hardy waterlilies, 5–6in (13–15cm) across. ↔ 10ft (3m).
***N.* 'Laydekeri Fulgens'** see *N.* 'Fulgens'.
N. lotus (Egyptian waterlily). Tropical waterlily with rounded, toothed, dark green leaves, to 20in (50cm) across, softly hairy beneath, with wavy margins and overlapping nodes. Bears day- or night-blooming, star-shaped, pink-tinged white flowers, to 10in (25cm) across. ↔ 6–10ft (2–3m). Egypt to tropical and S.E. Africa.
***N.* 'Louise'.** Hardy waterlily with rounded, mid-green leaves, 9–10in (22–25cm) across, with open sinuses; young leaves are slightly bronzed. Cup-shaped, sweetly fragrant, red flowers, 6in (15cm) across, have dark yellow stamens. ↔ 4–5ft (1.2–1.5m).
***N.* 'Lucida'** ■ Hardy waterlily with broadly ovate, mid-green leaves, to 10in (25cm) long, with large purple markings and open sinuses. Star-shaped flowers, 5–6in (12–15cm) across, have red inner petals, pink-veined, whitish pink outer petals, and yellow stamens. ↔ 4–5ft (1.2–1.5m).
***N.* 'Madame Ganna Walska'.** Tropical waterlily with rounded, irregularly wavy-margined, maroon-mottled leaves, 8–12in (20–30cm) across, with rounded sinuses. Star-shaped, fragrant flowers, 3–8in (8–20cm) across, have narrow, pointed, violet-pink petals and bright yellow ovary cups. ↔ 6–12ft (2–4m).
***N.* 'Marliacea Albida'** see *N.* 'Albida'.
***N.* 'Marliacea Carnea'** see *N.* 'Carnea'.
***N.* 'Marliacea Chromatella'** see *N.* 'Chromatella'.
***N.* 'Mayla'.** Hardy waterlily with oval, mid-green leaves, to 12in (30cm) across. Cup-shaped, musk-scented flowers, 4–8in (10–20cm) across, have nearly iridescent, deep pink petals, and yellow stamens. ↔ 5–6ft (1.5–2m).
N. mexicana*, syn. *N. flava (Yellow waterlily). Tropical waterlily producing ovate to rounded, wavy, toothed, leathery, mid-green leaves, to 7in (18cm) across, with brown marks above, purple beneath, and with open sinuses and overlapping lobes. Bears both floating and aerial, pale to bright yellow flowers, to 5in (13cm) across, that are day-blooming, cup-shaped then star-shaped, and slightly fragrant. ↔ 6–10ft (2–3m). S. US, Mexico.
***N.* 'Mme. Wilfon Gonnère'.** Hardy waterlily with rounded leaves, 9–10in (23–25cm) across, with overlapping lobes, slightly bronzed when young, maturing to mid-green; each has a broad yellow stripe in spring that disappears in summer. Peony-like pink flowers, 5in (13cm) across, have light pink outer petals and gold stamens. ↔ 4ft (1.2m).
N. odorata. Hardy waterlily bearing ovate to rounded, leathery, glossy, mid-green leaves, 6–12in (15–30cm) across, with open sinuses. Day-blooming, cup-shaped or later star-shaped, fragrant, white flowers, 4–9in

Nymphaea 'Panama Pacific'

(10–23cm) across, have yellow stamens. ↔ 4–6ft (1.2–1.8m). N.E. US. **'Sulphurea'** has purple-marked, bronze-green leaves, and fragrant yellow flowers, held slightly above the water. ↔ 3–4ft (0.9–1.2m). **'Sulphurea Grandiflora'** ■ is similar to 'Sulphurea', with marbled, dark green leaves and very large, star-shaped, bright rich yellow flowers. **'Turicensis'** has rounded leaves, 5–6in (12–15cm) across, with rounded lobes and open sinuses, and star-shaped, fragrant, soft pink flowers; ↔ 28in (70cm).
***N.* 'Panama Pacific'** ■ Tropical waterlily with rounded, speckled, dark green leaves, 9–10in (23–25cm) across, with overlapping lobes. Star-shaped, fragrant, red-violet flowers, 4–6in (10–15cm) across, have red-violet stamens and yellow centers. Suitable for containers. ↔ 3–6ft (1–2m).
***N.* 'Paul Hariot'.** Hardy waterlily with oval leaves, 6–7in (15–18cm) long, with rounded tips to the lobes and open sinuses; leaves are olive-green and purple-speckled when young, maturing to dark green with irregular purple marks. Cup-shaped flowers, 4–5in (10–13cm) across, are creamy apricot, turning light pink, and have orange stamens. ↔ 3–4ft (1–1.2m).
***N.* 'Perry's Fire Opal'** ■ Hardy waterlily with green leaves, to 10in (25cm) across, maroon when young. Produces cup-shaped, double, multi-petal rich pink flowers, 5–6in (13–15cm), across. ↔ 12ft (4m).
***N.* 'Pink Sensation'** ■ Hardy waterlily with rounded, mid-green leaves, to 10in (25cm) across, with narrow sinuses; young leaves are purple-green. Cup-shaped, later star-shaped, pink flowers, 5–6in (12–15cm) across, have yellow inner stamens and pink outer stamens. ↔ 4ft (1.2m).
N. pygmaea see *N. tetragona.*
***N.* 'Radiant Red'.** Hardy waterlily bearing rounded, mid-green leaves, to 10in (25cm) across, with partly open sinuses. Produces star-shaped, red flowers, 5–6in (12–15cm) across, with long, flecked petals and orange stamens. ↔ 3–4ft (0.9–1.2m).
***N.* 'Red Flare'.** Tropical waterlily with rounded, heavily toothed, reddish bronze leaves, 10–12in (25–30cm) across, with wavy margins and open sinuses. Produces night-blooming, flat, dark red flowers, 7–10in (17–25cm) across, with light pink or yellowish stamens, that are held well above the water. ↔ 5–6ft (1.5–1.8m).
***N.* 'Rembrandt'.** Hardy waterlily with rounded, mid-green leaves, 9–10in (22–25cm) across, with open sinuses; young leaves are purplish green. Bears peony-like red flowers, 6–8in (15–20cm) across, with yellow stamens. ↔ 28in–48in (0.7–1.2m).
***N.* 'René Gérard'.** Hardy waterlily with rounded, mid-green leaves, to 10–11in (25–28cm) across, bronze-tinged when young, with partly open sinuses. Star-shaped, rrose-red flowers, 6–9in (12–23cm) across, have strongly flecked, paler outer petals and yellow stamens. ↔ 5ft (1.5m).
***N.* 'Rose Arey'** ■ Hardy waterlily with rounded, bronze-green leaves, 9in (23cm) across, purple when young, with narrow sinuses. Bears star-shaped, fragrant, deep rose-pink flowers, 7–8in (18–20cm) across, orange-pink toward

Nymphaea 'James Brydon'

Nymphaea 'Joey Tomocik'

Nymphaea odorata 'Sulphurea Grandiflora'

Nymphaea 'Perry's Fire Opal'

Nymphaea 'Pink Sensation'

Nymphaea 'Rose Arey'

Nymphaea 'Sunrise'

Nymphaea tetragona

Nymphaea tetragona 'Helvola'

Nymphaea 'Vésuve'

Nymphaea 'Virginalis'

Nymphaea 'William McLane'

Nymphaea 'White Delight'

the margins, with golden stamens. ↔ 4–5ft (1.2–1.5m).
***N.* 'St. Louis'.** Tropical waterlily with broadly ovate, light green leaves, to 20in (50cm) long, sometimes with wavy margins, purple-marked when young, with open sinuses. Bears day-blooming, star-shaped, fragrant, lemon-yellow flowers, 8–11in (20–28cm) across, with golden yellow stamens. ↔ 8–10ft (2.5–3m).
***N.* 'Sunrise'** ■ Hardy waterlily with broadly ovate, dark green leaves, 11in (28cm) long, with open sinuses; young leaves are purple mottled. Star-shaped, bright yellow flowers, 7–9in (17–23cm) across, have long, narrow petals and yellow stamens. ↔ 4–5ft (1.2–1.5m).
N. tetragona ■ syn. *N. pygmaea.* Hardy waterlily with ovate, dark green, purple-blotched leaves, to 3in (8cm) across, with open sinuses. Produces day-blooming, cup-shaped, slightly fragrant white flowers, 1–2in (2.5–5cm) across, with yellow stamens. ↔ 10–16in (25–40cm). N.E. Europe, N. Asia to Japan, N. America. **'Helvola'** ■ has heavily mottled, purple-marked leaves, 5in (13cm) long. Slightly fragrant, vivid yellow flowers, 2–3in (5–8cm) across, have orange-yellow stamens and become star-shaped.
***N.* 'Texas Shell Pink'.** Tropical waterlily with oval, toothed, red-tinged, mid-green leaves, 12–18in (30–45cm) across. Night-blooming, star-shaped, mint-scented flowers, 6–10in (15–25cm) across, with pale-pink-striped petals and orange-yellow stamens, are borne well above the water surface. ↔ 3–6ft (1–2m).
N. tuberosa. Hardy waterlily with rounded, bright green leaves, 4–16in (10–40cm) across, with open sinuses. Day-blooming, cup-shaped, slightly scented white flowers, 4–9in (10–23cm) across, with yellow stamens, are sometimes held 2–3in (5–8cm) above the water. N.E. US. ↔ to 7ft (2.2m). **'Richardsonii'** has mid-green leaves, 16in (40cm) across, with overlapping lobes. Peony-like white flowers have yellow stamens.
***N.* 'Vésuve'** ■ Hardy waterlily with rounded, mid-green leaves, 9–10in (22–25cm) across, with open sinuses. Star-shaped, fragrant red flowers, 7in (18cm) across, darkening with age, have inward-curving petals and orange-red stamens. ↔ 4ft (1.2m).
***N.* 'Virginalis'** ■ Hardy waterlily with rounded, pale green leaves, 9in (23cm) across, purple or bronze when young, with overlapping lobes. Star-shaped, fragrant white flowers, 4½–5½in (11–14cm) across, have yellow stamens. ↔ 3–4ft (0.9–1.2m).
***N.* 'Virginia'.** Hardy waterlily with ovate, mid-green leaves, 10in (25cm) long, heavily marked with purple, mainly at the margins of older leaves, with open sinuses. Star-shaped, fragrant flowers, 7–8in (17–20cm) across, pale yellow in the centers and off-white toward the outsides, have yellow stamens. ↔ 5–6ft (1.5–1.8m).
***N.* 'White Delight'** ■ Tropical waterlily with rounded, speckled, dark green leaves, 9–10in (23–25cm) across, with open sinuses. Star-shaped, white flowers, 8–11in (20–28cm) across, sometimes with soft pink petal tips, have orange-yellow stamens. ↔ 3–6ft (1–2m).
***N.* 'William Falconer'.** Hardy waterlily with oval, reddish green new leaves, to 12in (30cm) across, maturing to green. Cup-shaped flowers, 4–8in (10–20cm) across, have very dark red petals and yellow stamens. ↔ 3–6ft (1–2m).
***N.* 'William McLane'** ■ Tropical waterlily produces striking green leaves marked with heavy maroon mottling, to 12in (30cm) across. Star-shaped, stunning purple flowers, 5–6in (13–15cm) across. ↔ 12ft (4m).
***N.* 'Wood's White Knight'.** Tropical waterlily bearing rounded, mid-green leaves, 12–16in (30–40cm) across, with scalloped, wavy margins and open sinuses. Produces night-blooming, peony-like, fragrant white flowers, 10–12in (25–30cm) across, with yellow stamens. ↔ 8–10ft (2.5–3m).

NYMPHOIDES

Floating heart

MENYANTHACEAE

Genus of 20 species of rhizomatous, herbaceous, submerged aquatic perennials occurring worldwide. They are often found in shallow, still water in lakes and ponds, where they spread rapidly, the leaves forming a floating carpet. Leaves are rounded with heart-shaped bases, or kidney-shaped, and grow from thin, creeping, branched rhizomes. The yellow or white, fringed flowers, resembling miniature waterlilies (*Nymphaea*), are held above the surface of the water. Grow in a wildlife pool with waterlilies or *Nuphar* species. Where not hardy, grow in a greenhouse pool or aquarium.

• **CULTIVATION** Outdoors, grow hardy species, and tender species in frost-free areas, in water no deeper than 2ft (60cm). In a small pool, contain within an aquatic container; in a larger pool or lake, growth is limited to the shallow margins. Where not hardy, grow tender species in an inert medium in a large aquarium or indoor pool in full light; most are tolerant of a range of water conditions. See also pp.52–53.
• **PROPAGATION** Separate and replant runners during summer.
• **PESTS AND DISEASES** Larvae of the china-mark moth may attack.

N. crenata (Yellow water snowflake). Rhizomatous, aquatic perennial with ovate, green-veined, chestnut-brown leaves, 2–3in (5–8cm) across. Solitary, star-shaped, 5-petaled, bright yellow flowers, ½–¾in (1.5–2cm) across, are borne from early spring to midautumn. ↔ indefinite. Australia. Zone 7b.
N. cristata (Water snowflake). Rhizomatous, aquatic perennial with ovate, reddish brown-marked, yellow-green leaves, 2–3in (5–8cm) across. From early spring to late autumn, bears umbels, ¼–½in (6–15mm) across, of star-shaped, crinkled, fragrant white flowers, ½–¾in (1.5–2cm) across, with yellow stamens and nectar cups. ↔ indefinite. Australia. Zone 7b.
N. humboldtiana. Rhizomatous, aquatic perennial with spreading runners. Produces kidney-shaped, shiny, pale green leaves, 6in (15cm) across, reddish green beneath, on stalks to 3ft (1m) long. Funnel-shaped white flowers, to 1½in (4cm) across, with fringed petals, are produced in summer. ↔ indefinite. Mexico, West Indies, Central America and tropical South America. ❀ (min. 41°F/5°C)
N. indica (Water snowflake). Rhizomatous, aquatic perennial producing rounded, glossy, pale green leaves, 2–8in (5–20cm) across, with heart-shaped bases. In summer, bears funnel-shaped white flowers, to ¾in (2cm) across, with yellow centers, and fringed petals covered with hairy white glands. ↔ indefinite. Tropical regions worldwide. ❀ (min. 41°F/5°C)
N. peltata ■ syn. *Limnanthemum nymphoides, Villarsia nymphoides* (Water fringe, Yellow floating heart). Rhizomatous, aquatic perennial with runners, to 6ft (2m) long, and ovate to rounded, mottled, bright mid-green leaves, 2–4in (5–10cm) across. Funnel-shaped, bright golden yellow flowers, ¾in (2cm) across, are produced on long stalks in summer. ↔ indefinite. Europe, Asia; widely naturalized from Arizona to Texas and New York. Zone 5.

Nymphoides peltata

NYSSA

Tupelo

NYSSACEAE

Genus of about 5 species of deciduous trees from woodland and swampland in E. Asia and E. North America. Leaves are simple and alternate. Small, inconspicuous green flowers, borne in clusters in early summer, are followed by small, ovoid blue fruits, about ½in (1.5cm) long. Tupelos are grown for their attractive foliage and brilliant autumn color. They are ideal as specimen trees or in group plantings, and are also effective near water.
• **CULTIVATION** Grow in fertile, moist but well-drained, neutral to acidic soil in sun or partial shade. Plant as small specimens, to 12in (30cm) tall, from containers; they are difficult to transplant successfully. Pruning group 1; in cool-maritime climates, where it may be difficult to maintain a leader, grow as multi-stemmed trees.
• **PROPAGATION** Sow seed in a seedbed in autumn. Take greenwood cuttings in early summer, or semi-ripe cuttings in midsummer.
• **PESTS AND DISEASES** Dieback, wood rot, canker, wood stain, leaf spots, white rot, scale insects, blister mite gall, leaf miners, and caterpillars occur.

N. sinensis. (Chinese tupelo). Broadly conical, deciduous tree, sometimes with several stems. Oblong to elliptic, entire, slenderly tapered, dark green leaves, to 8in (20cm) long, are sparsely hairy and bronze-red when young, turning brilliant shades of orange, red, and yellow in autumn, and becoming nearly hairless when mature. ↕↔ 30ft (10m). C. China. Zone 7b.
N. sylvatica ■ (Black gum, Sour gum, Tupelo). Broadly conical to columnar, deciduous tree with often drooping lower branches. Bears ovate to obovate, matte or glossy, dark green leaves, to 6in (15cm) long, downy beneath when young, with short, blunt points. Leaves turn vivid orange or red in autumn, and usually a few leaves turn color precociously throughout summer. ↕ 70ft (20m), ↔ 30ft (10m). E. North America. Zone 5b.

Nyssa sylvatica

O

O

OBREGONIA

CACTACEAE

Genus of one species of low-growing, solitary, sometimes clustering cactus, closely related to *Ariocarpus*, found on periodically dry, rocky hillsides in N.E. Mexico. Its stems are covered by leaf-like, spirally arranged tubercles. Funnel-shaped flowers are produced from the woolly, depressed center of each crown during daytime in summer; they are followed by white berries containing pear-shaped, slightly curved seeds. Below 50°F (10°C), grow in a temperate greenhouse; in warm, dry climates, use in a desert garden. Native populations of *O. denegrii* have been badly abused by collectors in the trade, and, as a result, exportation and importation of specimens collected from the wild is illegal, limiting the availability of this species.

• **CULTIVATION** Under glass, grow in standard cactus potting mix in full light with shade from hot sun. From midspring to late summer, water moderately and apply a low-nitrogen liquid fertilizer every 4–5 weeks. In autumn, reduce water gradually, then keep completely dry until early spring. Outdoors, grow these cacti in sharply drained, neutral to slightly alkaline, gritty, poor, humus-rich soil in full sun. Although initially prone to rot as a seedling, by the time it reaches ¾–1¼in (2–3cm) across, the growth quickens and becomes more vigorous. It can be grown to flowering size in 2 or 3 years. See also pp.48–49.

• **PROPAGATION** Sow seed at 70°F (21°C) in spring or summer.

• **PESTS AND DISEASES** Susceptible to aphids, especially while flowering.

O. denegrii ▣ Cactus with a thick, tuberous rootstock and flattened-spherical, grayish green or brownish green stems. Triangular tubercles have woolly hairs in the axils, and areoles at their tips, from which a few bristly spines emerge, but quickly fall. In summer, bears solitary, broadly funnel-shaped, very narrow-petaled, white or pale pink flowers, ¾–1½in (2–4cm) across, with yellow centers. ↕ 3–4in (7–10cm), ↔ 5in (13cm). N.E. Mexico. ❄ (min. 45–50°F/7–10°C); will tolerate brief periods to 25°F (-4°C).

Obregonia denegrii

OCHAGAVIA

BROMELIACEAE

Genus of 3 species of evergreen, terrestrial perennials (bromeliads) found on exposed, coastal rock faces in Chile. They have almost stemless, spreading rosettes of stiff, spiny-toothed leaves. The spherical inflorescences, produced in summer, sit low in the centers of the rosettes and have conspicuous, narrow bracts and tubular, red or pink flowers; these are followed by ovoid green berries containing large, spherical brown seeds. Where temperatures regularly drop below 41°F (5°C), grow these bromeliads in a cool greenhouse or as houseplants; in warmer climates, use outdoors in a desert garden.

• **CULTIVATION** Under glass, grow in terrestrial bromeliad potting mix or succulent mix in full light with low humidity. In growth, water moderately (avoiding the crown), and apply a half-strength, low-nitrogen liquid fertilizer every 3–4 weeks; keep dry when dormant. Outdoors, grow in moderately fertile, humus-rich, gritty, sharply drained soil in full sun. See also p.47.

• **PROPAGATION** Sow seed at 81°F (27°C) as soon as ripe.

• **PESTS AND DISEASES** Susceptible to scale insects.

O. carnea ▣ syn. *O. lindleyana.* Terrestrial bromeliad with wide-spreading, dense rosettes of 30–50 stiff, very narrow, linear-lance-shaped, spiny-toothed leaves, 20in (50cm) long, tapering to pointed tips; they are bright dark green above, sometimes with gray-white scales, and densely covered with gray-white scales beneath. In summer, produces many tubular, rose-pink flowers, to 2in (5cm) long, in congested, short-stalked, spherical inflorescences, each with a collar of white and pink bracts. ↕↔ 24in (60cm). C. Chile. ❄ (min. 41°F/5°C); can sometimes withstand short periods to 32°F (0°C) in a sheltered site.

O. lindleyana see *O. carnea.*

Ochagavia carnea

Ochna serrulata

OCHNA

Bird's eye bush

OCHNACEAE

Genus of over 80 species of deciduous or semi-evergreen trees and shrubs from tropical woodland in Africa and Asia, grown for their flowers and fruits. The leathery, often shiny or lustrous leaves are alternate, simple, and usually minutely toothed. The 5- to 10-petaled, saucer-shaped flowers are solitary, or borne in racemes, panicles, cymes, or umbels. After the petals fall, the calyces and receptacles enlarge and become thick and colorful, contrasting with the unusual, shiny, purplish black or black, usually spherical, one-seeded fruits, borne 3–12 on each receptacle. Where not hardy, grow *Ochna* species in a conservatory or temperate greenhouse. Elsewhere, grow bird's eye bushes in a shrub border, as accent or specimen plants, or as standards in containers.

• **CULTIVATION** Under glass, grow in soil-based potting mix in full light with shade from hot sun. During the growing season, water moderately and apply a balanced liquid fertilizer monthly; water sparingly in winter. Outdoors, grow in fertile, moist but well-drained soil in full sun. Pruning group 8; plants under glass need restrictive pruning after flowering.

• **PROPAGATION** Sow seed at 61°F (16°C) in spring. Root semi-ripe cuttings with bottom heat in summer, or air layer in spring.

• **PESTS AND DISEASES** Spider mites may infest plants under glass.

O. multiflora see *O. serrulata.*

***O. serratifolia* of gardens** see *O. serrulata.*

O. serrulata ▣ syn. *O. multiflora, O. serratifolia* of gardens (Mickey Mouse plant). Bushy, semi-evergreen shrub or small tree, with bronze shoots covered with close-set, raised, corky dots. Shiny, bright green leaves, 2½in (6cm) long, are narrowly elliptic and finely toothed. Saucer-shaped flowers, to ¾in (2cm) across, each with 5 or 6 spreading, bright yellow petals, are borne singly or in small cymes, mainly in late spring and summer; after the petals fall, the receptacle and sepals turn glossy red. Produces clusters of 5 or 6 spherical, lustrous black fruit. ↕ 5–8ft (1.5–2.5m), ↔ 3–6ft (1–2m). South Africa. ❄ (min. 45°F/7°C)

Ocimum basilicum 'Dark Opal'

OCIMUM

LAMIACEAE

Genus of 35 species of aromatic annuals and evergreen perennials and shrubs occurring in hot, dry scrub in tropical Africa and Asia. They have erect, usually branching stems, with linear to almost rounded leaves, borne in opposite pairs. The tubular flowers, usually in whorls of 6, are arranged in loose or dense spikes, and have small to large, occasionally brightly colored bracts. *O. basilicum* (basil) and its cultivars are widely grown as culinary herbs. Grow as annuals in an herb or vegetable garden, or among early-blooming plants in a border.

• **CULTIVATION** Grow in light, fertile, well-drained soil in a warm, sheltered site in full sun. Water freely during dry periods in summer. Pinch out flower-heads as soon as they appear to ensure continued leaf growth.

• **PROPAGATION** Sow seed at 55°F (13°C) in early spring, or sow *in situ* in early summer.

• **PESTS AND DISEASES** Susceptible to aphids and a variety of bacterial and fungal leaf, stem, and root diseases.

Ocimum basilicum 'Mini Purple'

O. basilicum (Basil, Sweet basil). Erect, bushy, aromatic annual or short-lived perennial. Narrowly oval to elliptic leaves, to 2in (5cm) long, are entire or toothed, sometimes slightly hairy, and bright green, occasionally flushed deep purple. In late summer, bears whorls of 6 tubular, 2-lipped, sometimes pink-purple-tinged, white flowers, to ½in (1.5cm) long, in lax, slightly hairy spikes. ↕ 12–24in (30–60cm), ↔ 12in (30cm) if grown as an annual. Tropical and subtropical Asia. ❄ (min. 35°F/2°C). **'Cinnamon Basil'** has purple-flushed stems, strongly spice-scented leaves, and bears pale pink to purple flowers; ↕ to 30in (75cm). **'Citriodorum'**, syn. *O. citriodora* (Lemon basil) has small, pointed, strongly lemon-scented leaves and white flowers. **'Dark Opal'** ▣ has red-purple leaves and pink flowers. **'Minimum'**, syn. *var. minimum* (Greek bush basil) is compact and rounded, with ovate leaves, to ½in (1.5cm) long, and flowers 1/16–⅛in (2–3mm) long; ↕↔ 6–12in (15–30cm). **'Mini Purple'** ▣ is dwarf and has small leaves, ¼–½in long, variably marked green and purple; ↕ 6–8in (15–20cm). **'Purple Ruffles'** has purple leaves, curled and fringed at the margins. **'Siam Queen'** has narrow, fragrant, mid-green leaves, to 4in (10cm) long, with burgundy flowers; ↕ to 30in (75cm). **'Spicy Globe'** is more rounded than 'Minimum', with tiny, richly scented leaves, ¼–½in (0.6–1.5cm) long; ↕ 6in (15cm).

O. citriodora see *O. basilicum* 'Citriodorum'.

O. sanctum see *O. tenuiflorum*.

O. tenuiflorum, syn. *O. sanctum* (Holy basil). Aromatic, annual or short-lived perennial subshrub with upright, branched, basally woody, hairy stems. Produces broadly elliptic, toothed, hairy, gray-green leaves, ½–1¼in (1.5–3cm) long, and lax spikes of tubular, 2-lipped, hairless, pink or white flowers, to ½in (1.5cm) long, in late summer. ↕ to 36in (90cm), ↔ to 24in (60cm). India and Malaysia. ❄ (min. 41°F/5°C)

ODONTIODA

ORCHIDACEAE

Hybrid genus of epiphytic, evergreen orchids derived from crosses between *Odontoglossum* and *Cochlioda*; they are vegetatively indistinguishable from *Odontoglossum*. They have ovoid, compressed pseudobulbs, each with 2 linear, mid-green leaves, 8in (20cm)

Odontioda Mount Bingham

Odontioda Petit Port

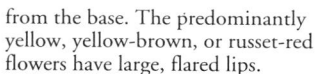

long, at the tip. Erect to arching racemes, 12–18in (30–45cm) tall, of 12 or more rounded to star-shaped flowers, 3in (8cm) across, often with ruffled or crisped margins, arise from the bases of the pseudobulbs at almost any time of the year, most commonly in spring. The flowers range in color from pastel shades to deep reds, and are often spotted or marked red or yellow.

• **CULTIVATION** As for *Odontoglossum*.

• **PROPAGATION** Divide when the plant fills the pot and flows over the sides.

• **PESTS AND DISEASES** Spider mites, mealybugs, aphids, and whiteflies are sometimes problems. Bacterial soft rot, *Cercospora* leaf spot (and others), and a variety of viruses can cause damage.

***O.* City of Birmingham** (*O.* Gold Wood x *Odontoglossum harryanum*). Epiphytic orchid that produces yellow flowers marked purple and bronze. ↕ 18in (45cm), ↔ 12in (30cm). ❄ (min. 50°F/10°C; max. 75°F/24°C)

***O.* Mount Bingham** ▣ (*O.* Ingera x *O.* Marzorka). Epiphytic orchid with flowers patterned in red and lilac. ↕ 18in (45cm), ↔ 12in (30cm). ❄ (min. 50°F/10°C; max. 75°F/24°C)

***O.* Petit Port** ▣ (*O.* Colwell x *O.* Margia). Epiphytic orchid bearing rich red flowers with pink-, yellow-, or brown-patterned lips. ↕ 18in (45cm), ↔ 12in (30cm). ❄ (min. 50°F/10°C; max. 75°F/24°C)

***O.* Red Rum** (*O.* Brocade x *O.* Ingera). Epiphytic orchid with flowers richly patterned in red-mauve and purple. ↕ 18in (45cm), ↔ 12in (30cm). ❄ (min. 50°F/10°C; max. 75°F/24°C)

ODONTOCIDIUM

ORCHIDACEAE

Hybrid genus of epiphytic, evergreen orchids derived from crosses between *Odontoglossum* and *Oncidium*; they are vegetatively indistinguishable from *Odontoglossum*. They have rounded or ovoid to conical pseudobulbs (all those described are rounded and compressed), each with 2 linear, mid-green leaves, 9in (23cm) long, at the tip. Tall, arching racemes or panicles of 12 or more flowers, 3in (8cm) across, arise

Odontocidium Artur Elle 'Columbien'

from the base. The predominantly yellow, yellow-brown, or russet-red flowers have large, flared lips.

• **CULTIVATION** As for *Odontoglossum*.

• **PROPAGATION** Divide when the plants overflow their containers.

• **PESTS AND DISEASES** Spider mites, aphids, whiteflies, mealybugs, *Colletotrichum* leaf spot, and cymbidium mosaic virus are sometimes problems.

***O.* Artur Elle 'Columbien'** ▣ (*Odontoglossum* Hambühren Gold x *Oncidium tigrinum*). Epiphytic orchid bearing yellow flowers, delicately patterned with chestnut-brown, all year round. ↕ 18in (45cm), ↔ 12in (30cm). ❄ (min. 50°F/10°C; max. 75°F/24°C)

***O.* 'Crowborough'** (*Odontoglossum* Golden Guinea x *Oncidium leucochilum*). Epiphytic orchid that produces deep brown and yellow flowers with white lips, mainly in spring. ↕ 18in (45cm), ↔ 12in (30cm). ❄ (min. 50°F/10°C; max. 75°F/24°C)

***O.* 'Purbeck Gold'** (*Odontoglossum* Gold Cup x *Oncidium tigrinum*). Epiphytic orchid that produces deep yellow, brown-spotted flowers, with flared yellow lips, mainly in autumn. ↕ 18in (45cm), ↔ 12in (30cm). ❄ (min. 50°F/10°C; max. 75°F/24°C)

***O.* Tiger Hambühren** ▣ (*Odontoglossum* Goldrausch x *Oncidium tigrinum*). Epiphytic orchid bearing rich

Odontocidium Tiger Hambühren

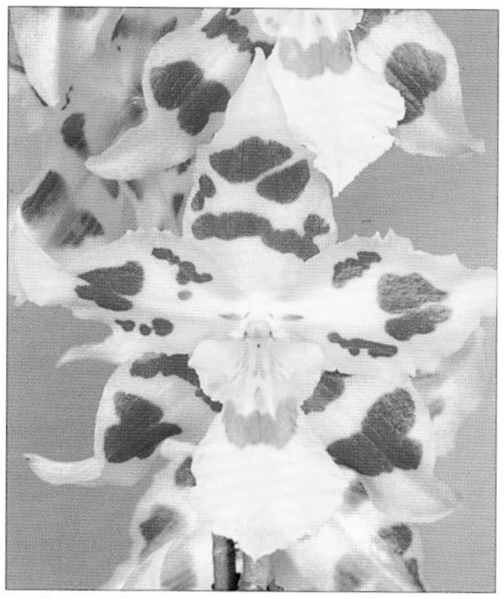

Odontocidium Tigersun 'Orbec'

yellow flowers, heavily spotted and barred with chestnut-brown, mainly in autumn. ↕ 18in (45cm), ↔ 12in (30cm). ❄ (min. 50°F/10°C; max. 75°F/24°C)

***O.* Tigersun 'Orbec'** ▣ (*Odontoglossum* Sunmar x *Oncidium tigrinum*). Epiphytic orchid bearing yellow flowers, lightly marked with chestnut-brown, mainly in autumn. ↕ 18in (45cm), ↔ 12in (30cm). ❄ (min. 50°F/10°C; max. 75°F/24°C)

ODONTOGLOSSUM

ORCHIDACEAE

Genus of about 200 species of evergreen, epiphytic or lithophytic, rhizomatous orchids from mountainous regions, at altitudes of 7,000–10,000ft (2,000–3,000m), in Central and South America. They produce ovoid or oblong-ellipsoid to conical pseudobulbs, each with 1–3 variably shaped, thinly leathery, mid-green leaves at the tip. Flowers are borne in tall or short, erect or arching racemes or panicles that arise from the bases of the pseudobulbs, and are highly variable in color and shape. Many hybrids have been produced that will flower at almost any time of year, with 12 or more flowers in a raceme.

• **CULTIVATION** Cool-growing orchids. Grow in small pots of epiphytic orchid potting mix, preferably made with fine-grade bark to suit the fine root system. In summer, provide bright filtered light and high humidity; water and mist freely, and apply fertilizer at every third watering. In winter, provide full light and water sparingly. See also p.46.

• **PROPAGATION** Divide when the plant fills the pot and flows over the sides. Hybrids are better retained as one plant; pot on in late summer or early spring.

• **PESTS AND DISEASES** Spider mites, mealybugs, aphids, and whiteflies are sometimes problems. Bacterial soft rot, *Cercospora* leaf spot (and others), and a variety of viruses can cause damage.

O. bictoniense see *Lemboglossum bictoniense*.

***O.* Buttercrisp** (*O.* Brimstone Butterfly x *O.* Crispania). Epiphytic orchid with ovoid, compressed pseudobulbs and narrowly oval leaves, 6in (15cm) long. Clear yellow flowers, 2½in (6cm) across, with a few brown spots and brown-spotted, white-margined lips, appear at any time of year. ↕ 12in (30cm), ↔ 10in (25cm). ❄ (min. 50°F/10°C; max. 75°F/24°C)

Odontoglossum crispum

O. cariniferum. Epiphytic orchid with oblong-ellipsoid, compressed, furrowed pseudobulbs and oblong-elliptic leaves, to 12in (30cm) long. In spring, bears yellow-margined brown flowers, 2in (5cm) across, in erect or arching panicles, 2–4ft (0.6–1.2m) long. ↕ to 4ft (1.2m), ↔ 12in (30cm). Costa Rica, Panama, Colombia, Venezuela. ❀ (min. 50°F/10°C; max. 75°F/24°C)
O. cervantesii see *Lemboglossum cervantesii.*
O. cordatum see *Lemboglossum cordatum.*
O. crispum ▣ Epiphytic orchid with ovoid pseudobulbs and linear-elliptic leaves, to 16in (40cm) long. In winter, white flowers, 3in (8cm) across, the lips sometimes yellow and spotted red in the centers, are produced in racemes to 20in (50cm) long. ↕ 20in (50cm), ↔ 10in (25cm). Colombia. ❀ (min. 50°F/10°C; max. 75°F/24°C)
O. grande see *Rossioglossum grande.*
O. harryanum. Epiphytic orchid with slender, ovoid pseudobulbs and elliptic-oblong leaves, to 18in (45cm) long. Flowers, 3in (8cm) across, varying in color from olive-green to buff or chestnut-brown, with lips lined purplish mauve, are produced in racemes to 3–4ft (1–1.2m) long, in winter. ↕ 3–4ft (1–1.2m), ↔ 9in (23cm). Colombia, Peru. ❀ (min. 50°F/10°C; max. 75°F/24°C)
O. odoratum. Epiphytic orchid with ovoid pseudobulbs and narrowly lance-shaped leaves, to 12in (30cm) long. Star-shaped, fragrant flowers, 2½in (6cm) across, pale to deep yellow, dotted and marked dark maroon or red-brown, are borne in panicles to 30in (75cm) long, in spring. ↕ 30in (75cm), ↔ 8in (20cm). Colombia, Venezuela. ❀ (min. 50°F/10°C; max. 75°F/24°C)
O. rossii see *Lemboglossum rossii.*
***O.* Royal Occasion** ▣ (*O.* Ardentissimum x *O.* Pumistor). Epiphytic orchid with ovoid pseudobulbs and narrowly oval leaves, 12in (30cm) long. White flowers, 2½in (6cm) across, with deep yellow markings in the centers of the lips, are produced in early summer. ↕ 12in (30cm), ↔ 10in (25cm). ❀ (min. 50°F/10°C; max. 75°F/24°C)
***O.* Saint Brelade 'Jersey'** (*Lemboglossum rossii* x *O.* Ophyras). Epiphytic orchid with ovoid pseudobulbs and narrowly oval leaves, 6in (15cm) long. Highly decorative, pale mauve flowers, 2½in (6cm) across, with deeper mauve or maroon markings and pale mauve lips marked with white and maroon, are produced in late spring. ↕ 12in (30cm), ↔ 10in (25cm). ❀ (min. 50°F/10°C; max. 75°F/24°C)
O. spectatissimum, syn. *O. triumphans.* Epiphytic orchid producing ovoid pseudobulbs and narrowly elliptic leaves, 16in (40cm) long. In spring, bears erect or arching racemes, to 36in (90cm) long, of golden yellow flowers, heavily barred and spotted chestnut-brown, 4in (10cm) across. ↕ 36in (90cm), ↔ 8in (20cm). Colombia, Venezuela. ❀ (min. 50°F/10°C; max. 75°F/24°C)
O. stellatum see *Lemboglossum stellatum.*
O. triumphans see *O. spectatissimum.*

ODONTONEMA

ACANTHACEAE

Genus of 26 species of evergreen perennials and shrubs from woodland in tropical America. They are grown for their terminal racemes or panicles of tubular, brightly colored flowers, which are 2-lipped or symmetrical. The simple, entire leaves are borne in opposite pairs. Where temperatures fall below 55°F (13°C), grow in a warm greenhouse. In warmer climates, these plants work well in a shrub border.
• **CULTIVATION** Under glass, grow in soil-based potting mix in full light with shade from hot sun, and with moderate humidity. During the growing season, water moderately and apply a balanced liquid fertilizer every month; water sparingly in winter. Outdoors, grow in fertile, moist but well-drained soil in full sun. Pruning group 8; plants under glass need restrictive pruning after flowering.
• **PROPAGATION** Sow seed at 61–64°F (16–18°C) in spring. Root greenwood cuttings in early summer, or semi-ripe cuttings with bottom heat in summer.
• **PESTS AND DISEASES** Prone to whiteflies and spider mites under glass. Heavily saturated soil or high humidity may cause edema.

O. strictum. Erect shrub with robust, sparsely branched, rigid stems and oblong, wavy-margined, glossy, deep green leaves, 4–6in (10–15cm) long, with long, sharp points. In winter and spring, bears tubular, 2-lipped, waxy crimson flowers, 1in (2.5cm) long, in slender, erect, compact panicles, to 12in (30cm) long. ↕ 6ft (2m) or more (if unpruned), ↔ 24–39in (60–100cm). Central America. ❀ (min. 55°F/13°C)

ODONTONIA

ORCHIDACEAE

Hybrid genus of epiphytic, evergreen orchids derived from crosses between *Odontoglossum* and *Miltonia*; they are vegetatively indistinguishable from *Odontoglossum.* They produce ovoid to conical pseudobulbs, each with 2 leaves at the tip. The flowers have large, flat lips and are produced in tall, arching racemes arising from the bases of the pseudobulbs at almost any time of year.
• **CULTIVATION** As for *Odontoglossum*; see p.715.
• **PROPAGATION** Divide when the plants overflow their containers.
• **PESTS AND DISEASES** Spider mites, mealybugs, aphids, whiteflies, and cymbidium mosaic virus may occur.

***O.* Olga** (*Odontoglossum crispum* x *Odontonia* Thisbe). Epiphytic orchid producing ovoid pseudobulbs and narrowly oval leaves, 12in (30cm) long. White flowers, 3in (8cm) across, with lips marked nut-brown, are borne in tall, arching racemes in winter. ↕ 12in (30cm), ↔ 10in (25cm). ❀ (min. 50°F/10°C; max. 75°F/24°C)

OEMLERIA *syn.* NUTTALLIA, OSMARONIA

ROSACEAE

Genus of one species of deciduous shrub found in forests and canyons in W. North America. It is grown for its simple, alternate, glossy leaves, and its pendent racemes of bell-shaped flowers, both of which appear very early in the year (it is one of the first plants to come into leaf, often in late winter). Male and female flowers are borne on separate plants, and both must be grown to bear the small, black, plum-like fruit. Grow in a shrub border or woodland garden.
• **CULTIVATION** Grow in fertile, moist but well-drained soil in sun or partial shade. In moist soil, vigorously growing plants may sucker extensively; remove excess suckers to restrict growth. Pruning group 1 or 2.
• **PROPAGATION** Sow seed in a seedbed as soon as ripe. Take greenwood cuttings in early summer. Transplant suckers in autumn.
• **PESTS AND DISEASES** Powdery mildew and leaf spot occur occasionally.

O. cerasiformis ▣ syn. *Nuttallia cerasiformis, Osmaronia cerasiformis* (Indian plum, Oregon plum, Oso berry). Suckering shrub, forming a thicket of upright, eventually arching shoots. These bear narrowly oblong, or lance-shaped to inversely lance-shaped, glossy, dark green leaves, to 3½in (9cm) long, gray-green and softly hairy beneath. Small, bell-shaped, almond-scented white flowers are produced in pendent racemes, to 4in (10cm) long, in early spring. They are followed on female plants by ovoid, plum-like, purple-black fruit, ¾in (2cm) long. ↕ 8ft (2.5m) or more, ↔ 12ft (4m). British Columbia to California. Zone 7.

OENANTHE

APIACEAE

Genus of about 30 species of moisture-loving, hairless perennials from wet meadows, marshland, and shallow water in the N. Hemisphere, South Africa, and Australia. Most have alternate, pinnate leaves and bear compound umbels of small, star-shaped white flowers, each with 5 notched petals. They are suitable for damp soil in a bog garden, or for planting as a groundcover near a stream or pool. Where not hardy, grow in a cool greenhouse. In some species, all parts may cause severe discomfort if ingested; some species are deadly. *O. javanica* is the exception; it is grown as a leafy vegetable in areas where it grows naturally.
• **CULTIVATION** Grow in any moderately fertile, preferably moist or wet soil, in full sun or partial shade, although quite

Odontoglossum Royal Occasion

Oemleria cerasiformis (inset: flower detail)

Oenanthe javanica 'Flamingo'

dry soil is tolerated, especially in partial shade. Shelter from cold, drying winds. Where marginally hardy, provide a dry winter mulch; take cuttings and overwinter in a cold greenhouse to ensure against losses.
• **PROPAGATION** Divide in late spring, as growth begins. Take stem-tip cuttings in spring.
• **PESTS AND DISEASES** Prone to rust, slug and snail damage, and aphids.

O. japonica see *O. javanica.*
O. javanica, syn. *O. japonica.* Spreading perennial with horizontal, rooting stems and celery-like, triangular, pinnate or 2-pinnate leaves, 3–6in (7–15cm) long, with narrowly ovate, toothed, mid-green segments. Compound umbels of star-shaped white flowers, ⅛in (3mm) long, are produced in late summer. ↕ 8–16in (20–40cm), ↔ 36in (90cm). India to Japan, Malaysia, Australia (Queensland). ❄ (min. 41°F/5°C). **'Flamingo'** ▣ is grown for its attractive foliage, which is variegated pink, cream, and white.

OENOTHERA

Evening primrose, Sundrops

ONAGRACEAE

Genus of about 125 species of annuals, biennials, and perennials, some with taproots or fibrous roots and a few with rhizomes or runners. Mostly from North America, with a few from South America, they grow in well-drained, sunny sites, such as mountain slopes, although some are from deserts. They have upright or decumbent stems with alternate, more or less lance-shaped, simple or pinnatifid, entire or toothed stem leaves, and occasionally basal rosettes of slightly larger leaves. Evening primroses are grown for their flowers, which are mainly produced over long periods in summer; they are often fragrant, white, yellow, or pink and are large, saucer- to cup-shaped, sometimes trumpet-shaped. Each flower has a long tube and 4 petals, and is either solitary and axillary, or borne in terminal racemes. Individual flowers open at dawn or dusk and fade quickly. Taller species are suitable for a sunny, mixed or herbaceous border; low-growing ones are better for border edging. *O. acaulis, O. caespitosa,* and *O. macrocarpa* are excellent for a scree bed or rock garden.
• **CULTIVATION** Grow in poor to moderately fertile, well-drained, even stony soil, in full sun. *O. fruticosa* prefers slightly more fertile soil. Protect rock-garden plants and *O. speciosa* from excessive winter moisture.
• **PROPAGATION** Sow seed in containers in a cold frame: annuals and perennials in early spring, biennials in early summer; or sow annuals and biennials *in situ* in autumn. *O. glazioviana* self-seeds prolifically. Divide in early spring, or take softwood cuttings of unflowered shoots of perennials from late spring to midsummer. To avoid damage to taprooted species, grow seedlings and cuttings individually in pots before planting out.
• **PESTS AND DISEASES** Leaf gall, downy mildew, rust, powdery mildew, and *Septoria* leaf spot are common. Root rot may occur in wet soils.

O. acaulis, syn. *O. taraxacifolia.* Clump-forming, short-lived perennial with rosettes of inversely lance-shaped, irregularly pinnatifid, mid-green leaves, 5–8in (12–20cm) long, and a few decumbent stems, to 12in (30cm) or more long. In summer, bears 2–5 trumpet-shaped white flowers, to 3in (8cm) across, from the leaf axils; they open at sunset, and turn pink the next day. ↕ 6in (15cm), ↔ to 8in (20cm). Chile. Zone 5b.
O. albicaulis. Spreading annual, biennial, or short-lived perennial, usually grown as a biennial, with basal rosettes of spoon-shaped to ovate, gray-green leaves, to 2in (5cm) long, and white-hairy stems bearing lance-shaped, pinnatifid leaves. In summer, produces solitary, bowl-shaped, scented flowers, to 3in (8cm) across, which open in the evening and are initially white, then cream, and finally pale pink. ↕ 6–12in (15–30cm), ↔ to 12in (30cm). Rocky Mountains. Zone 6.
O. berlandieri see *O. speciosa* 'Rosea'.
O. biennis (Evening primrose). Erect, hairy annual or biennial, usually grown as a biennial. Produces large rosettes of oblong to lance-shaped, shallowly toothed, slightly sticky, red-veined, mid-green leaves, 4–12in (10–30cm) long, and lance-shaped stem leaves, to 6in (15cm) long. Bowl-shaped, fragrant flowers, to 2in (5cm) across, initially pale yellow, aging to dark golden yellow, and opening in the evening, are borne in leafy, spike-like racemes from summer to autumn. Seeds are used to produce evening primrose oil. ↕ 3–5ft (1–1.5m), ↔ to 24in (60cm). E. North America; naturalized in many parts of the world. Zone 4.
O. caespitosa. Clump-forming biennial or perennial with numerous rosettes of inversely lance-shaped to diamond- or spoon-shaped, entire or irregularly toothed, gray-green leaves, ¾–10in (2–25cm) long. In summer, produces cup-shaped, fragrant white flowers, to 4in (10cm) across, from the rosette leaf axils, several opening at once at sunset; they turn pink with age. ↕↔ to 8in (20cm). W. US. Zone 5.
O. deltoides (Desert evening primrose). Erect annual or perennial, branching from the base, with triangularly ovate to lance-shaped, entire to pinnatifid, mid-green leaves, 2–4in (5–10cm) long. Often produces decumbent basal branches in addition to erect stems. In summer, bears solitary, bowl-shaped

Oenothera fruticosa 'Fyrverkeri'

flowers, 1½–3in (4–8cm) across, initially white then pink, opening in the morning. Needs sharply drained soil. ↕ to 12in (30cm), ↔ to 8in (20cm). Arizona, Mexico (Baja California). ❄ (min. 41°F/5°C)
O. elata* subsp. *hookeri, syn. *O. hookeri.* Erect perennial or biennial bearing basal rosettes of lance-shaped, slightly toothed, mid-green leaves, 2–5in (5–13cm) long, and hairy, branching stems with smaller leaves. Throughout summer, bears numerous, cup-shaped flowers, 2–3in (5–8cm) across, initially pale yellow becoming orange-red, which open at dusk in terminal spikes. ↕ 36in (90cm), ↔ 12in (30cm). W. North America. Zone 7b.
O. fraseri see *O. fruticosa* subsp. *glauca.*
O. fruticosa, syn. *O. linearis* (Sundrops). Erect perennial or biennial with branched, softly hairy, red-tinged stems bearing lance-shaped to ovate, toothed, mid-green leaves, 1–4½in (2.5–11cm) long, turning dull red after a light frost; the basal leaves inversely lance-shaped to obovate. From late spring to late summer, produces racemes of 3–10 saucer- to cup-shaped, deep yellow flowers, 1–2in (2.5–5cm) across, opening during the day. ↕ 12–36in (30–90cm), ↔ 12in (30cm). E. North America. Zone 4. **'Fireworks'** see 'Fyrverkeri'. **'Fyrverkeri'** ▣ syn. 'Fireworks', has purple-brown-flushed leaves, and yellow flowers opening from red buds. **subsp. *glauca***, syn. *O. fraseri, O. glauca, O. tetragona,* has broader, only sparsely hairy, sometimes glaucous leaves, red-tinted when young, and light yellow flowers; E. US. **'Highlight'** see 'Hoheslicht'. **'Hoheslicht'**, syn. 'Highlight', produces an abundance of bright yellow flowers; ↕ 24in (60cm). **'Sonnenwende'**, syn. 'Summer Solstice', has deep green leaves that turn bright red in summer and burgundy-red in autumn, and produces bright yellow flowers from early summer to early autumn; ↕ 12–16in (30–40cm). **'Summer Solstice'** see 'Sonnenwende'. **'Yellow River'** has red stems and large, canary-yellow flowers, 1½–2½in (4–6cm) across. **'Youngii'** is mat-forming, with leaves turning bright red in autumn. Bears clear yellow flowers, in early and midsummer. Adaptable to almost any soil; ↕ 18in (45cm).
O. glauca see *O. fruticosa* subsp. *glauca.*
O. glazioviana, syn. *O. glazouana.* Erect biennial or short-lived perennial bearing basal rosettes of ovate-lance-shaped, hairy, mid-green leaves, to 8in (20cm) long, with conspicuous white midribs above, red beneath; slightly smaller leaves are borne on the hairy, unbranched, red-spotted stems. In mid- and late summer, produces racemes of bowl-shaped yellow flowers, 2–3in (5–8cm) across, with red-tinged calyces, opening at dusk. ↕ to 5ft (1.5m), ↔ 24in (60cm). N. America. Zone 4.
O. glazouana see *O. glazioviana.*
O. hookeri see *O. elata* subsp. *hookeri.*
O. laciniata. Upright to lax annual or short-lived perennial with simple to many-branched, hairy, green or red-flushed stems. Produces basal rosettes of linear-lance-shaped, deeply lobed or toothed, mid-green leaves, 1½–6in (4–15cm) long, and slightly smaller stem leaves. From early summer to autumn, bears spikes of cup-shaped, red-flushed or -edged, yellow flowers, ½–1¼in (1–4.5cm) across, that open in evening. ↕ to 36in (90cm), ↔ to 24in (60cm). C. and E. US. Zone 4b.
O. linearis see *O. fruticosa.*
O. macrocarpa ▣ syn. *O. missouriensis* (Ozark sundrops). Vigorous perennial with trailing, hairy, often red-tinted stems, branching from a central rootstock. Leaves are lance-shaped to ovate, toothed, pale to mid-green, ¾–3in (2–8cm) long, with white midribs. From late spring to early autumn, produces solitary, cup-shaped, bright golden yellow flowers, to 5in (13cm) across, with red-flecked calyces, remaining open in daytime. May become invasive. ↕ 6in (15cm), ↔ to 20in (50cm). S. Central US. Zone 5.
O. missouriensis see *O. macrocarpa.*
O. pallida. Spreading, rhizomatous, hairless, freely branching perennial with lance-shaped, wavy-edged mid-green leaves, 1–2½in (2.5–6cm) long. From early summer to autumn, produces saucer-shaped, fragrant white flowers, ¾–4in (2–5cm) across, aging to pink, opening at dusk. ↕ 8–20in (20–50cm), ↔ 8–12in (20–30cm). W. North America. Zone 4.

Oenothera macrocarpa

Oenothera perennis

O. perennis ▣ syn. *O. pumila* (Sundrops). Clump-forming perennial with rosettes of spoon-shaped to inversely lance-shaped, mid-green leaves, 1–2in (2.5–5cm) long. Loose, leafy, upright, few-flowered racemes of funnel-shaped yellow flowers, to ¾in (2cm) across, open during the day in summer. ↕↔ to 8in (20cm) or more. E. North America. Zone 5.
O. pumila see *O. perennis.*
O. speciosa. Perennial, spreading by runners, with basal rosettes of oblong-lance-shaped to lance-shaped, toothed or pinnatifid, mid-green leaves, 1–2in (2.5–5cm) long, and arching stems bearing slightly smaller leaves. Solitary, shallowly cup-shaped, fragrant white flowers, 1–2½in (2.5–6cm) across, sometimes aging to pink, are borne from early summer to early autumn, opening during the day. ↕↔ 12in (30cm). S.W. US to Mexico. Zone 6. **'Childsii'** see 'Rosea'. **'Rosea'** ▣ syn. 'Childsii', *O. berlandieri,* has pale pink flowers; ↕ 12in (30cm). **'Siskiyou'** has pink flowers, 2in (5cm) across; ↕ 10in (25cm).
O. taraxacifolia see *O. acaulis.*
O. tetragona see *O. fruticosa* subsp. *glauca.*

OLEA

Olive

OLEACEAE

Genus of about 20 species of evergreen trees and shrubs often found in dry, rocky places in the Mediterranean and Africa to C. Asia and Australasia. They have opposite, leathery leaves, which may be entire or toothed, and produce terminal or axillary panicles of small, 4-lobed, white or off-white flowers; these are followed by edible, ovoid or spherical fruits. Thriving only in areas with a Mediterranean or similar climate, *O. europaea,* the only cultivated species, is of great economic importance for its fruit (olives) and the oil extracted from them. Grow *O. europaea* as a specimen tree or in a border; where not hardy, grow in a cool greenhouse or conservatory, or at the base of a sunny, sheltered wall.

• **CULTIVATION** Under glass, grow in soil-based potting mix with additional sharp sand, in full light. During the growing season, water moderately and apply a balanced liquid fertilizer every month; water sparingly in winter. Outdoors, grow in deep, fertile, sharply drained soil in full sun. Pruning group 1; plants under glass need restrictive pruning in spring.

• **PROPAGATION** Sow seed at 55–59°F (13–15°C) in spring. Take semi-ripe cuttings in summer.

• **PESTS AND DISEASES** Prone to olive knot, *Verticillium* wilt, mushroom root rot, lesion nematode, and Southern blight. Scale insects are especially common.

O. europaea (Olive). Slow-growing, evergreen tree, developing a rounded head, which becomes irregular with age. The opposite, leathery, elliptic to lance-shaped, irregularly toothed leaves, to 3in (8cm) long, are gray-green above, silvery gray-green beneath. Tiny, fragrant, creamy white flowers are borne in axillary panicles, to 2in (5cm) long, in summer, followed by spherical to ovoid green fruit (olives), to 1½in (4cm) long, ripening to black. ↕↔ 30ft (10m). Mediterranean. Zone 8.

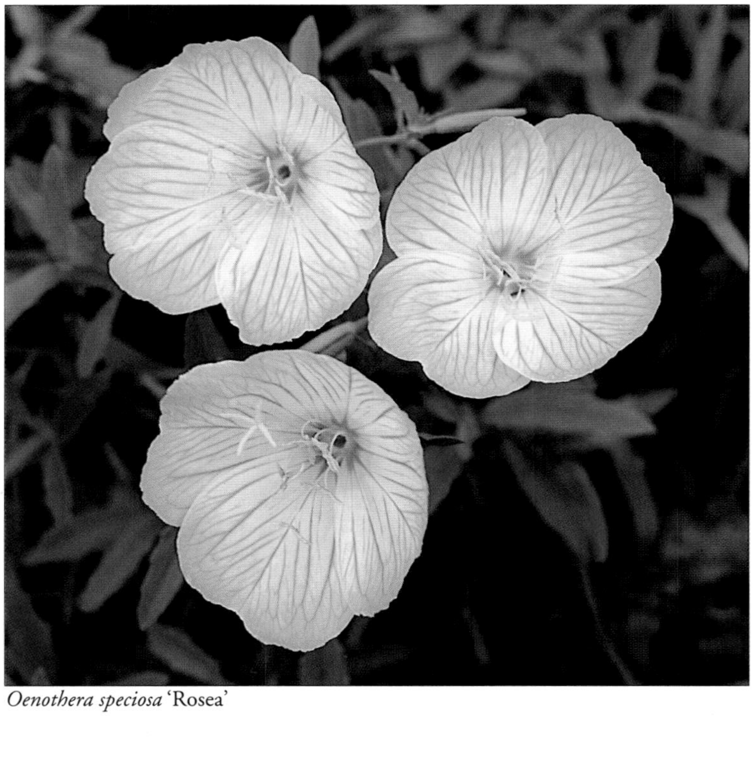

Oenothera speciosa 'Rosea'

OLEARIA

Daisy bush

ASTERACEAE

Genus of about 130 species of evergreen shrubs and small trees, and some herbaceous perennials, from a wide variety of habitats, including coastal areas, bogs, forest, riverbanks, and mountain scrub, in Australia and New Zealand. They have generally alternate, occasionally clustered, simple, usually leathery leaves, and are cultivated for their daisy-like flowerheads, often with colorful ray florets, borne singly, or in corymbs or panicles, in spring or summer. Olearias are suitable for planting in a shrub border, or in a sheltered site if not fully hardy. Some, such as *O.* x *haastii, O. macrodonta,* and *O. traversii,* may be grown as hedges and windbreaks, particularly in coastal areas. Where not hardy, grow in a cool or temperate greenhouse.

• **CULTIVATION** Outdoors, grow in fertile, well-drained soil in full sun, with shelter from cold, drying winds. Under glass, grow in soil-based potting mix in full light. Water moderately and apply a balanced liquid fertilizer monthly during the growing season; water sparingly in winter. Pruning group 8 for early-flowering species, group 9 for late-flowering species; trim lightly to maintain a compact habit. Most species break freely from old wood and tolerate hard pruning.

• **PROPAGATION** Root semi-ripe cuttings in summer, using bottom heat for tender species.

• **PESTS AND DISEASES** Infrequent.

O. albida (Tanguru). Vigorous, upright shrub or small tree with alternate, oblong to ovate-oblong, wavy-margined leaves, to 4in (10cm) long, dark green above, white-felted beneath. Bears small, white flowerheads, to ¼in (6mm) across, each with 1–5 ray florets, in panicles, to 2in (5cm) across, in summer. ↕ 15ft (5m), ↔ 10ft (3m). New Zealand (North Island). ❀ (min. 41°F/5°C)
***O. albida* of gardens** see *O.* 'Talbot de Malahide'.
O. avicenniifolia. Rounded, bushy shrub or small tree with alternate, elliptic to lance-shaped, dark gray-green leaves, to 4in (10cm) long, white- or pale-yellow-felted beneath. Small, fragrant white flowerheads, to ¼in (6mm) across, each with usually 1 or 2 ray florets, are borne in broad corymbs, to 3in (8cm) across, in late summer and early autumn. ↕ 10ft (3m), ↔ 15ft (5m). New Zealand (South Island, Stewart Island). ❀ (min. 41°F/5°C)
O. cheesemanii ▣ syn. *O. rani* of gardens. Upright-branched shrub or small tree with alternate, oblong or elliptic to lance-shaped, slightly toothed, leathery, glossy, dark green leaves, to 3½in (9cm) long, white-felted beneath. White flowerheads, to ⅜in (9mm) across, with yellow centers, are borne in large corymbs, to 8in (20cm) across, in mid- and late spring. ↕ 12ft (4m), ↔ 10ft (3m). New Zealand. ❀ (min. 41°F/5°C)

Olearia cheesemanii

O. ciliata. Upright shrub with rough shoots and clustered, rigid, linear, deep green leaves, to ½in (1.5cm) long, the margins strongly rolled back. Solitary, long-stalked flowerheads, 1in (2.5cm) across, blue or white with yellow centers, are produced in spring. ↕ 12in (30cm), ↔ 8in (20cm). Temperate regions of Australia. ❀ (min. 41°F/5°C)
O. erubescens. Upright shrub with alternate, oblong to lance-shaped, toothed, sometimes lobed, glossy, dark green leaves, to 1½in (4cm) long, sometimes red-tinged when young. In late spring and early summer, yellow-centered white flowerheads, 1in (2.5cm) across, appear singly or in clusters of 2–5, forming leafy panicles to 18in (45cm) long. ↕ 5ft (1.5m), ↔ 24in (60cm). S.E. Australia. ❀ (min. 41°F/5°C)
O. frostii. Spreading shrub with alternate, obovate, entire or wavy-toothed, gray-green leaves, to 1in (2.5cm) long, covered with star-like hairs. In midsummer, bears very showy, yellow-centered mauve flowerheads, to 1½in (4cm) across, singly or in groups of 2 or 3. ↕ 24in (60cm), ↔ 3ft (1m). S.E. Australia. ❀ (min. 45°F/7°C)
O. gunniana see *O. phlogopappa.*
O.* x *haastii ▣ (*O. avicenniifolia* x *O. moschata*). Dense, bushy shrub with alternate, oval or ovate, glossy, dark green leaves, to 1in (2.5cm) long, white-felted beneath. Dense corymbs, to 3in (8cm) across, of yellow-centered white flowerheads, to ⅜in (9mm) across, appear in mid- and late summer. ↕ 6ft (2m), ↔ 10ft (3m) or more. Natural hybrid from New Zealand (South Island). ❀ (min. 35°F/2°C)

Olearia x *haastii*

O

Olearia macrodonta

***O.* 'Henry Travers'**, syn. *O. semidentata* of gardens. Rounded shrub with slender, white-felted shoots and alternate, lance-shaped, leathery, gray-green leaves, to 3in (8cm) long, white-felted beneath. Solitary flowerheads, 2in (5cm) across, with purple centers and numerous lilac ray florets, are produced in early and midsummer. ↕ 8ft (2.5m), ↔ 6ft (2m). Natural hybrid from New Zealand (Chatham Islands). ❀ (min. 45°F/7°C)

O. ilicifolia (Mountain holly). Dense, spreading, bushy shrub or small tree with alternate, stiff and leathery, narrowly oblong, wavy-margined, sharply toothed, gray-green leaves, to 4in (10cm) long. Fragrant white flowerheads, to ½in (1.5cm) across, with yellow centers, are produced in large corymbs, to 4in (10cm) across, in summer. ↕↔ 15ft (5m). New Zealand. Zone 8.

O. insignis see *Pachystegia insignis.*

O. lacunosa. Rounded, strongly branched shrub with densely gray-woolly branchlets. Bears alternate, slender, linear to linear-oblong, sharp-pointed, leathery leaves, 3–7in (8–18cm) long, dark green with yellow midribs above, silver-hairy to pale brown-hairy beneath. Small white flowerheads, ¼in (6mm) across, with yellow centers, are produced in spherical, corymb-like panicles, to 8in (20cm) across, in summer; they are borne more freely in warm, but not dry, climates. ↕ 6–10ft (2–3m), sometimes 12–15ft (4–5m), ↔ 10ft (3m). New Zealand. ❀ (min. 35°F/2°C)

O. macrodonta ▣ (Arorangi). Vigorous, upright shrub or small tree with alternate, holly-like, ovate-oblong, sharply toothed and pointed, glossy, dark green leaves, to 4in (10cm) long, silver-white-felted beneath. In summer, bears large corymbs, to 6in (15cm) across, of fragrant white flowerheads, to ½in (1.5cm) across, with reddish brown centers. ↕ 20ft (6m), ↔ 15ft (5m). New Zealand. ❀ (min. 41°F/5°C)

***O.* x *mollis* 'Zennorensis'**, syn. *O.* 'Zennorensis'. Dense, rounded shrub with alternate, lance-shaped, sharply toothed leaves, to 4in (10cm) long, glossy, dark olive-green above, densely white-woolly beneath. White flowerheads, ½–¾in (1.5–2cm) across, with yellow centers, are produced in spherical corymbs, 6–8in (15–20cm) across, in late spring. ↕↔ 6ft (2m). Zone 7b.

O. moschata (Incense plant). Dense, upright, bushy shrub with alternate, obovate to oblong, leathery, musk-scented, gray-tinged green leaves, to ½in (1.5cm) long, densely white-hairy on both surfaces. Produces dense corymbs of 12–30 yellow-centered white flowerheads, each to ½in (1.5cm) across, in midsummer. ↕ 3–6ft (1–2m), ↔ 3ft (1m). New Zealand (South Island). ❀ (min. 41°F/5°C)

O. nummulariifolia ▣ Dense, rounded, slow-growing shrub with thick, upright shoots. Bears alternate, small, obovate to rounded, very leathery leaves, to ½in (1.5cm) long, the margins rolled back; they are bright green when young, becoming dark green, and densely white-woolly to buff- or yellow-woolly beneath. Fragrant white flowerheads, ¾in (2cm) across, with cream or pale yellow centers, are produced singly or in clusters of 2 or 3 at the shoot tips in midsummer. ↕↔ 6ft (2m). New Zealand. Zone 7b.

Olearia phlogopappa 'Comber's Pink'

O. phlogopappa, syn. *O. gunniana, O. stellulata* of gardens. Compact, upright shrub with alternate, oblong to narrowly obovate, wavy-margined, shallowly toothed leaves, to 2in (5cm) long, gray-green above, densely white-woolly or gray-white-woolly beneath. Usually white, sometimes blue, mauve, or pink flowerheads, 1¼in (3cm) across, with yellow centers, are freely borne in loose, erect corymbs, to 3in (8cm) across, in spring and early summer. ↕↔ 6ft (2m). S.E. Australia. ❀ (min. 35°F/2°C). **'Comber's Blue'** bears blue ray florets. **'Comber's Pink'** ▣ has pink ray florets.

O. ramulosa ▣ Arching, slender-branched shrub bearing alternate, linear to linear-obovate, dark green leaves, to ½in (1.5cm) long, the margins rolled back, and densely hairy beneath. Solitary, white, or sometimes blue, mauve, or pink flowerheads, ½in (1.5cm) across, with white centers, are produced in spring, or in late winter under glass. ↕↔ 5ft (1.5m). Australia. ❀ (min. 41°F/5°C)

Olearia x *scilloniensis*

***O. rani* of gardens** see *O. cheesemanii.*

O.* x *scilloniensis ▣ (*O. lirata* x *O. phlogopappa*). Dense, initially upright then rounded shrub, with alternate, elliptic-oblong, wavy-margined, dark green leaves, to 4in (10cm) long, densely felted and pale green beneath. In late spring, white flowerheads, to 2½in (6cm) across, with yellow centers, are very profusely borne in corymbs to 3in (8cm) across. ↕↔ 6ft (2m). Garden origin. Zone 8. **'Master Michael'** has gray-green foliage and bears blue flowerheads.

***O. semidentata* of gardens** see *O.* 'Henry Travers'.

O. solandri ▣ Dense, upright, bushy shrub or small tree with slender, sticky, yellow-hairy shoots and heather-like, opposite, narrowly spoon-shaped to narrowly obovate or linear, dark green leaves, to ⅜in (9mm) long, densely white- to yellow-felted beneath. Solitary, very strongly fragrant, pale yellow flowerheads, ⅜in (9mm) across, with about 20 tiny florets, are produced from summer to autumn. ↕↔ 6ft (2m). New Zealand. ❀ (min. 35°F/2°C)

***O. stellulata* of gardens** see *O. phlogopappa.*

Olearia nummulariifolia

Olearia ramulosa

Olearia solandri

O

Olearia 'Talbot de Malahide'

O. 'Talbot de Malahide' ■ syn. *O. albida* of gardens. Dense, upright, bushy shrub with alternate, narrowly ovate, glossy, dark green leaves, to 4in (10cm) long, white- or yellowish-white-felted beneath. Small, fragrant white flowerheads, to ½in (1.5cm) across, each with up to 6 ray florets and an inconspicuous, brownish yellow center, are borne in broad corymbs, to 4in (10cm) across, in late summer and early autumn. ↕ 10ft (3m), ↔ 15ft (5m). ❀ (min. 41°F/5°C)
O. traversii. Dense, upright shrub, sometimes a small tree, with thick, angled shoots and opposite, oval to ovate-oblong leaves, to 2½in (6cm) long, glossy, dark green above, white-felted beneath. In early summer, bears relatively inconspicuous, gray-white flowerheads, to ¼in (6mm) across, without ray florets, in panicles to 2in (5cm) long. Useful for coastal hedging. ↕ 15–30ft (5–10m), ↔ 10–15ft (3–5m) or more. New Zealand (Chatham Islands). ❀ (min. 41°F/5°C)
O. virgata ■ Arching shrub with smooth, slender, wiry shoots and opposite, narrowly obovate to linear, dark green leaves, to ¾in (2cm) long, densely white-felted beneath. In summer, small, fragrant, yellowish white flowerheads, ½in (1.5cm) across, each with 3–6 ray florets and an inconspicuous center, are profusely borne in opposite clusters, to 1½in (4cm) across, along the branches. ↕↔ 15ft (5m). New Zealand. Zone 7b. **var. *lineata*** has pendulous, softly hairy branchlets with linear leaves, to 1½in (4cm) long, the margins strongly rolled back, and flowerheads with 8–14 ray florets; ↕ to 6ft (2m); New Zealand (South Island).
***O.* 'Zennorensis'** see *O.* x *mollis* 'Zennorensis'.

Olearia virgata

▷ ***Oliveranthus elegans*** see *Echeveria harmsii*

OLNEYA

FABACEAE

Genus of one species of branched deciduous tree from washes in desert areas of S.W. North America. It is grown for its foliage and racemes of tiny, pea-like flowers. Grow in a wild garden; where not hardy, grow in a cool to warm greenhouse.
• **CULTIVATION** Under glass, grow in soil-based potting mix, with added sand, in full light. Apply a balanced liquid fertilizer monthly and water moderately in the growing season; water sparingly in winter. Outdoors, grow in moderately fertile, well-drained soil in full sun. Cannot withstand extended freezes. Pruning group 1.
• **PROPAGATION** Sow seed as soon as ripe at 55–64°F (13–18°C) or *in situ*.
• **PESTS AND DISEASES** Infrequent.

O. tesota (Desert ironwood). Slow-growing, erect evergreen tree with spreading branches at maturity. Produces alternate, pinnate leaves, with 8–24 oblong-wedge-shaped, gray-green leaflets, ¾in (2cm) long, 2-spined at the bases. In early summer, pinkish lavender flowers, ½in (1.5cm) long, are borne in axillary racemes, followed by thick-walled, mid-green seed pods, 2in (5cm) long, with black seeds. Possesses extremely hard, heavy heartwood. Deciduous in hard frosts. ↕↔ to 25–30ft (8–10m). California, Arizona, N.W. Mexico. ❀ (min. 41°F/5°C)

OLSYNIUM

IRIDACEAE

Genus of about 12 species of fibrous-rooted, clump-forming perennials, often included in *Sisyrinchium*, found in moist grassland from sea level to subalpine regions in North and South America. They have mostly basal, stem-clasping, linear or lance-shaped leaves, and are grown for their nodding, trumpet-shaped to bell-shaped flowers, which are borne in spring. Grow in a shady rock garden or alpine house.
• **CULTIVATION** Grow in moist, humus-rich, moderately fertile soil in partial shade. In an alpine house, use a mix of equal parts loam, leaf mold, and grit.
• **PROPAGATION** Sow seed in containers in a cold frame in autumn. Plants take 2 or 3 years to flower.
• **PESTS AND DISEASES** Infrequent.

O. biflorum, syn. *Phaiophleps biflora, Sisyrinchium odoratissimum.* Slender, clump-forming perennial, with short rhizomes producing upright stems with narrow, rush-like leaves, 1½–9in (4–23cm) long. In late spring or summer, bears cymes of usually 2, occasionally more, trumpet-shaped, fragrant, red-veined, creamy yellow flowers, 1in (2.5cm) long. ↕ 8–14in (20–35cm), ↔ 2in (5cm). Argentina (Patagonia). ❀ (min. 41°F/5°C)

O. douglasii, syn. *Sisyrinchium douglasii, S. grandiflorum.* Clump-forming perennial with upright, slender, rush-like stems sheathed with linear, grayish green leaves, to 4in (10cm) long. In early spring, nodding, bell-shaped, satin-textured, rich purple flowers, to ¾in (2cm) long, are borne in several terminal spathes, each with 1–4 flowers. ↕ 6–12in (15–30cm), ↔ to 4in (10cm). W. North America. ❀ (min. 41°F/5°C) **var. *album*** has white flowers.

OMPHALODES

Navelwort

BORAGINACEAE

Genus of about 28 species of annuals, biennials, and perennials, some of which are evergreen or semi-evergreen, from a wide range of habitats in Europe, N. Africa, and Asia. They have clusters of simple leaves either in basal tufts or arranged alternately on stems. In spring and summer, they produce blue or white flowers, similar to forget-me-nots (*Myosotis*), each with a short tube and 5 spreading lobes, usually in terminal racemes or cymes, sometimes singly from the leaf axils. Most are shade-loving, and are used as a groundcover in a border, or rock or woodland garden. Grow *O. luciliae* in a rock garden, scree bed, tufa, or alpine house; use *O. linifolia* in an annual border or for cut flowers.
• **CULTIVATION** Most of the perennials thrive in moist, moderately fertile, humus-rich soil in partial shade. Grow *O. linifolia* in moderately fertile, well-drained soil in sun. Grow *O. luciliae* in tufa, or in very gritty, alkaline soil, in full sun; in an alpine house, use a mix of equal parts loam, leaf mold, and grit, with added limestone chips.
• **PROPAGATION** Sow seed in spring: sow annuals *in situ*; sow perennials in containers in a cold frame. Carefully divide perennials in early spring, since the roots resent disturbance.
• **PESTS AND DISEASES** Very prone to slug and snail damage.

O. cappadocica ■ (Navelwort). Clump-forming, rhizomatous, evergreen perennial with ovate to heart-shaped, pointed, finely hairy, mid-green, basal leaves, to 4in (10cm) long. Produces loose, terminal racemes, to 10in (25cm) long, of 3–12 white-eyed, azure-blue flowers, each to ¼in (6mm) across, in early spring. ↕ to 10in (25cm), ↔ to 16in (40cm). Woodland in Turkey. Zone 7. **'Cherry Ingram'** ■ is more compact, producing larger, deep blue flowers. **'Starry Eyes'** also has larger flowers than the species, with a central white stripe on each petal.
O. linifolia ■ (Venus's navelwort). Erect annual, branching from the base, with narrowly lance-shaped to spoon-shaped, sparsely white-hairy, glaucous basal leaves, to 4in (10cm) long, and smaller, very narrow, stalkless stem leaves. From spring to summer, produces loose, terminal racemes of 5–15 tiny, slightly scented, white, or very occasionally pale blue flowers, to ½in (1.5cm) across. Self-seeds readily. ↕ 12–16in (30–40cm), ↔ to 6in (15cm). Dry, open sites, often in alkaline soil, in S.W. Europe.
O. luciliae. Clump-forming, semi-evergreen perennial with upright to prostrate stems and ovate to elliptic or oblong, pale gray-blue, basal leaves, to 4in (10cm) long. Loose, terminal cymes of 3–15 clear light blue flowers, to ⅜in (9mm) across, often opening pink, are produced over long periods in summer. May be difficult to establish. ↕ 4in (10cm) or more, ↔ to 6in (15cm).

Omphalodes cappadocica 'Cherry Ingram'

Omphalodes cappadocica

Omphalodes linifolia

Vertical limestone cliffs, generally in shade, in Greece and Turkey. Zone 7b.
O. verna (Blue-eyed Mary, Creeping forget-me-not). Clump-forming, stoloniferous, semi-evergreen perennial with heart-shaped, ovate to ovate-lance-shaped, pointed, hairy, mid-green, basal leaves, to 8in (20cm) long. Terminal racemes of 5–20 white-eyed, deep bright blue flowers, pink-tinted with age, to ½in (1.5cm) across, appear in spring. ↕ to 8in (20cm), ↔ 12in (30cm) or more. Moist woodland in S.E. Alps to N. Apennines and to mountains of Romania. Zone 6. **'Alba'** produces white flowers.

OMPHALOGRAMMA

PRIMULACEAE

Genus of about 15 species of usually rhizomatous perennials, related to *Primula*, from the Himalayas and the mountains or moist, open alpine slopes of China. They are grown for their solitary, horizontally borne, salverform flowers, with long tubes and 6–8 spreading lobes, produced in spring or early summer. The lance-shaped to ovate or elliptic, often white-hairy, primrose-like, mid- to dark green leaves are borne in rosettes, and arise from a large, dormant winter bud surrounded by scales. They grow best in cool, moist climates. Grow *O. vinciflorum* in a shady rock garden or in an alpine house.
• **CULTIVATION** Grow in cool, moist conditions, in open, moderately fertile, humus-rich, well-drained soil in partial shade. In an alpine house, use a mix of equal parts loam, leaf mold, and grit; move plants to a cool, shady site outdoors during summer.
• **PROPAGATION** Sow seed in containers in an open frame as soon as ripe, or divide in spring.
• **PESTS AND DISEASES** Prone to aphids and whiteflies under glass. Young leaves are susceptible to slug and snail damage.

O. vinciflorum ▣ Rosette-forming perennial, lacking a rhizome but with a large, dormant winter bud. Bears obovate-oblong to oblong, entire to scalloped, hairy, mid-green leaves, to 8in (20cm) long. In spring, produces solitary, salverform flowers, spreading to 2in (5cm) across, with deep violet-purple lobes and darker throats. ↕ 8in (20cm), ↔ 4in (10cm). China (Yunnan, Sichuan). Zone 7.

Omphalogramma vinciflorum

ONCIDIUM

ORCHIDACEAE

Genus of over 450 species of evergreen, terrestrial, epiphytic, or lithopythic orchids found in a variety of habitats, from sea level to altitudes of 10,000ft (3,000m), in Mexico, Central America, South America, and the West Indies. Some oncidiums are compact, with fan-like foliage; others have pseudobulbs that bear either 1 large, rigid leaf or 2 smaller, flexible leaves. The flowers are typically yellow, with prominent lips, and are produced in short or tall racemes or panicles from the bases of the plants.
• **CULTIVATION** Cool- to intermediate-growing orchids. Grow compact species in pots of epiphytic orchid potting mix; grow those with large, leathery leaves and elongated habit (e.g., *O. flexuosum*) epiphytically on bark or in baskets. In summer, provide high humidity and bright filtered light; those with leathery leaves prefer full light. During the growing season, mist daily and water freely, applying a half-strength fertilizer at every third watering. Provide full light in winter. Keep oncidiums with large pseudobulbs dry in winter; those with small pseudobulbs, or none, require watering all year. See also p.46.
• **PROPAGATION** Divide when the plants overflow their containers, or remove backbulbs (produced by *O. flexuosum* and *O. tigrinum*) and pot up separately.
• **PESTS AND DISEASES** Prone to many viruses and leaf and bulb rots, as well as gray mold (*Botrytis*) on flowers. Aphids, mealybugs, spider mites, and whiteflies are common.

O. cavendishianum. Epiphytic orchid with very small pseudobulbs (sometimes none), each with one elliptic to broadly lance-shaped, rigid, leathery leaf, 6–18in (15–45cm) long. In spring, fragrant, waxy, red-spotted yellow flowers, 1½in (4cm) across, with deep yellow lips, are borne in panicles, 5ft (1.5m) or more tall. ↕ 24in (60cm), ↔ 12in (30cm). S. Mexico, Guatemala, Honduras. ❀ (min. 55°F/13°C; max. 86°F/30°C)
O. crispum. Epiphytic orchid with ovoid pseudobulbs, each with 2 narrowly lance-shaped, leathery leaves, 8in (20cm) long. From autumn to spring, produces chestnut-brown and yellow-spotted flowers, to 3in (8cm) across, in erect to pendent panicles, to 3½ft (1.1m) long. ↕ 24in (60cm), ↔ 12in (30cm). Brazil. ❀ (min. 55°F/13°C; max. 86°F/30°C)
***O.* Fire Opal** (*O.* Persian Red x *O.* Susan Perreira). Epiphytic orchid with a fan of overlapping, rigid, flattened, linear-oblong leaves, 4in (10cm) long. Highly decorative flowers, 1in (2.5cm) or more across, in shades of rich pink over creamy white, are produced in long racemes several times during the year. ↕ 12in (30cm), ↔ 6in (15cm). ❀ (min. 55°F/13°C; max. 86°F/30°C)
O. flexuosum ▣ (Dancing doll orchid). Epiphytic orchid with ovoid-oblong pseudobulbs, each with 1 or 2 linear, leathery leaves, to 4–8in (10–20cm) long. From autumn to winter, rich canary-yellow flowers, ¾in (2cm) across, with red-brown markings on the sepals and petals, are clustered toward the tips

Oncidium flexuosum

of panicles to 32in (80cm) long. ↕ 24in (60cm), ↔ 12in (30cm). S.E. Brazil, Paraguay, Argentina, Uruguay. ❀ (min. 55°F/13°C; max. 86°F/30°C)
O. ghiebrechtiana see *Mexicoa ghiebrechtiana.*
***O.* Gypsy Beauty** (*O.* Phyllis Hetfield x *O.* Thelma Beaumont). Epiphytic orchid with a fan of overlapping, rigid, flattened, linear-oblong leaves, 4in (10cm) long. Highly decorative white and burgundy-red flowers, 1in (2.5cm) or more across, with raspberry lips, are produced in clusters toward the ends of racemes several times during the year. ↕ 12in (30cm), ↔ 6in (15cm). ❀ (min. 55°F/13°C; max. 86°F/30°C)
O. longipes. Epiphytic orchid with slender, oblong-ovoid pseudobulbs, each with 2 oblong, soft leaves, to 6in (15cm) long. In spring, produces short racemes of 2–6 yellow flowers, 1½in (4cm) across, heavily spotted and streaked red-brown, with yellow lips. ↕ 5in (13cm), ↔ 6in (15cm). S.E. Brazil. ❀ (min. 55°F/13°C; max. 86°F/30°C)
O. macranthum, syn. *Crytochilum macranthum.* Epiphytic orchid with oblong-conical, fleshy pseudobulbs, each with 2 narrowly inversely lance-shaped to oblong leaves, 10–20in (25–50cm) long. Yellow to brown-gold flowers, 3in (8cm) across, with yellowish white lips bordered violet-purple, are produced in lax, spreading panicles, to 10ft (3m) tall, in summer. ↕ 3ft (1m), ↔ 24in (60cm). Colombia, Ecuador, Peru. ❀ (min. 55°F/13°C; max. 86°F/30°C)
O. ornithorrhynchum ▣ Epiphytic orchid producing ovoid or ellipsoid pseudobulbs, each with 2 linear-lance-

Oncidium ornithorrhynchum

Oncidium tigrinum

shaped to linear-elliptic, soft leaves, 4–16in (10–40cm) long. In autumn, fragrant, white, pink, or purple-pink flowers, ¾–1in (2–2.5cm) across, with darker pink or lilac-pink lips, are borne in strongly arching panicles, to 20in (50cm) long. ↕ 6in (15cm), ↔ 9in (23cm). S. Mexico, Guatemala, El Salvador, Costa Rica. ❀ (min. 55°F/13°C; max. 86°F/30°C)
O. papilio see *Psychopsis papilio.*
O. pusillum, syn. *Psygmorchis pusilla.* Epiphytic orchid with a flattened fan of linear-oblong to oblong-elliptic, fleshy leaves, 2½in (6cm) long. Bears axillary racemes, to 2½in (6cm) long, of 1–4 bright yellow flowers, marked rust-red, to 1¼in (3cm) across, intermittently all year. ↕↔ 3in (8cm). Central America, South America, West Indies. ❀ (min. 55°F/13°C; max. 86°F/30°C)
O. sphacelatum. Epiphytic orchid with ribbed, ovoid-ellipsoid pseudobulbs, each with 2 linear-oblong to linear-lance-shaped, semi-leathery leaves, to 3ft (1m) long. In spring, deep yellow flowers, to 1¼in (3cm) across, marked and spotted red-brown, with golden yellow lips, are produced in dense, upright panicles, to 5ft (1.5m) tall. ↕↔ 24in (60cm). Central America, Venezuela. ❀ (min. 55°F/13°C; max. 86°F/30°C)
O. tigrinum ▣ Epiphytic orchid with spherical pseudobulbs, each with 1 or 2 linear-oblong, leathery leaves, 12–20in (30–50cm) long. Fragrant yellow flowers, 2in (5cm) across, with sepals and petals heavily suffused dark red-brown, and with large yellow lips, are produced in long, thick, usually erect panicles, to 5ft (1.5m) tall, in winter. ↕ 18in (45cm), ↔ 12in (30cm). Mexico. ❀ (min. 55°F/13°C; max. 86°F/30°C)

ONOCLEA

DRYOPTERIDACEAE

Genus of one species of deciduous, terrestrial fern found in damp sites in E. Asia and E. North America. In spring, long-stalked, pinnate or deeply pinnatisect sterile fronds are produced singly at short intervals from creeping rhizomes, dying down at the first frost. The fertile fronds are 2-pinnate, with contracted, bead-like black segments that curl in to cover the sori, and are produced in late summer, persisting throughout winter. *O. sensibilis* will thrive at the edge of water, or in a damp, shady border.

Onoclea sensibilis

• **CULTIVATION** Grow in a sheltered site, in moist, fertile, humus-rich, preferably acidic soil, in light, dappled shade (the fronds will scorch if exposed to too much sun).
• **PROPAGATION** Sow spores at 59–60°F (15–16°C) as soon as ripe, or divide in spring. See also p.51.
• **PESTS AND DISEASES** Prone to rust.

O. sensibilis ▣ (Sensitive fern). Deciduous fern, producing upright then arching, broadly lance-shaped or triangular, pinnate to deeply pinnatisect, pale green sterile fronds, to 18in (45cm) long, in spring; these each have 8–12 pairs of pinnae, which are lobed to wavy-margined or entire. Fertile fronds are produced in late summer, and are stiffly erect, lance-shaped, and 2-pinnate, to 24in (60cm) long; the pinnae are reduced to bead-like black lobes that enclose the sori. The emerging fronds may sometimes be pinkish bronze in spring. ↕ 24in (60cm), ↔ indefinite. E. Asia, E. North America. Zone 3b.

ONONIS

Restharrow

FABACEAE

Genus of about 75 species of annuals, perennials, and dwarf shrubs occurring in dry, rocky sites or in grassland, often in alkaline soil, in Europe, the Mediterranean, the Canary Islands, and from N. Africa to Iran. They have alternate, 3-palmate or simple, usually toothed and hairy, clover-like, mostly mid-green leaves, and are grown for their pea-like flowers, borne in panicles, spikes, or racemes in summer. Grow in a rock garden, wall, or sunny bank, or at the front of a mixed or shrub border. *O. repens* is a source of food for the common blue butterfly, and is best sited in a wild garden, due to spreading, underground runners.
• **CULTIVATION** Grow in a warm, sunny position in moderately fertile, well-drained soil. They may be short-lived, so propagate regularly.
• **PROPAGATION** Sow seed in containers in an open frame in autumn or spring. Take greenwood cuttings of shrubby species in early summer.
• **PESTS AND DISEASES** May be infested with spider mites under glass.

O. fruticosa ▣ (Shrubby restharrow). Short-lived, deciduous shrub with 3-palmate, leathery leaves, 1½in (4cm) long, composed of leaflets that are oblong-lance-shaped and unevenly toothed. Nodding clusters, 2–3in (5–8cm) long, of pea-like pink flowers, each to ¾in (2cm) long, with dark central markings and paler wings, are borne over long periods in summer. ↕↔ to 24in (60cm), occasionally to 3ft (1m). S.E. France, C. Pyrenees, C. and E. Spain. Zone 7b.

Ononis fruticosa

O. repens (Common restharrow). Upright or spreading, often stem-rooting, deciduous subshrub, sometimes with soft spines, bearing ovate, simple or 3-palmate leaves, to ¾in (2cm) long, composed of leaflets that are ovate, hairy, and toothed. Open, leafy racemes of pea-like, pink or pink-purple flowers, each to ¾in (2cm) long, are produced throughout summer. ↕ 12–24in (30–60cm), ↔ 20–32in (50–80cm) or more. Europe. Zone 7.
O. rotundifolia. Upright, deciduous or semi-evergreen, dwarf shrub with 3-palmate leaves, 1¼in (3cm) long, consisting of broadly elliptic to rounded, coarsely toothed, hairy leaflets, the terminal leaflet long-stalked. In summer, produces axillary racemes or panicles of pea-like, pale to deep pink or white flowers, to ¾in (2cm) long, striped darker pink. ↕ to 20in (50cm), ↔ to 12in (30cm). S. Europe (S.E. Spain to E. Austria, C. Italy). Zone 7b.

▷ ***Onopordon*** see *Onopordum*

ONOPORDUM

syn. ONOPORDON

Cotton thistle, Scotch thistle

ASTERACEAE

Genus of approximately 40 erect, rosette-forming biennials from steppes, stony slopes, fallow fields, and disturbed ground in Europe, the Mediterranean, and W. Asia. Thistles have simple to pinnatifid or pinnatisect, spiny-toothed leaves covered in cobweb-like, soft gray hair; the leaves are borne alternately on coarse, usually freely branching, mostly white-woolly stems, the leaf bases often continuing down the stems as very conspicuous wings. Large, round flowerheads, typically thistle-like and without ray florets, are produced either singly or in tight clusters at the stem tips in summer. They may be bright purple, blue-violet, rose-pink, or occasionally white, and are attractive to bees and butterflies. They readily self-seed and may be grown in a large border, or in a semi-wild or gravel garden. The seeds are often eaten by goldfinches.

Onopordum acanthium (inset: flowerhead detail)

• **CULTIVATION** Grow in fertile, well-drained, neutral to slightly alkaline soil in full sun.
• **PROPAGATION** Sow seed in containers in a cold frame or *in situ* in autumn or spring.
• **PESTS AND DISEASES** Slugs, snails, and caterpillars may damage the foliage.

O. acanthium ▣ Taprooted, rosette-forming biennial with oblong-ovate to lance-shaped or ovate, pinnatifid, spiny-toothed, gray-green leaves, to 14in (35cm) long, sparsely hairy above. In the second year, produces massive, branching, 2- to 4-winged, spiny, hairy, yellow-green stems; in summer, these produce solitary or clustered, round, thistle-like, pale purple or white flower-heads, 1½–2in (4–5cm) across, encased in spine-tipped bracts. ↕ to 10ft (3m), ↔ 3ft (1m). W. Europe to W. and C. Asia. Zone 5.
O. arabicum see *O. nervosum.*
O. nervosum, syn. *O. arabicum.* Taprooted, rosette-forming biennial with oblong-lance-shaped, pinnatisect, spiny-toothed, silver-gray leaves, to 20in (50cm) long; they have prominent pale veins and are sparsely hairy beneath. In the second year, produces massive, branching, broad-winged, deeply veined, densely hairy, yellow-tinged stems; in summer, these bear clusters of round, thistle-like, bright purple-red to purple-pink flowerheads, to 1½in (4cm) across, encased in spine-tipped bracts. ↕ to 9ft (2.5m), ↔ 3ft (1m). Portugal, Spain. Zone 6.

ONOSMA

BORAGINACEAE

Genus of about 150 species of biennials and often woody-based perennials found in sunny, rocky sites, often rock crevices, from the Mediterranean to Turkey. They are grown for their nodding cymes of narrowly tubular to cylindrical-bell-shaped flowers, mainly yellow, pink, red, or white. The simple, alternate leaves are covered in fine hairs, contact with which may irritate skin. Grow in a scree bed, or in a rock or wall crevice; in wet climates, they grow best in an alpine house or cold greenhouse.
• **CULTIVATION** Outdoors, grow in full sun in a very gritty scree bed, or grow plants on their sides in vertical wall or rock crevices. Protect from excessive rainfall. Under glass, grow in a mix of equal parts loam, leaf mold, and grit; avoid wetting the foliage when watering.
• **PROPAGATION** Sow seed in containers in an open frame in autumn. Take softwood or greenwood cuttings of shrubs in late spring or early summer.
• **PESTS AND DISEASES** May be infested with aphids or whiteflies under glass.

Onosma alborosea

O. alborosea ■ Evergreen, clump-forming perennial with white-hairy, branching stems bearing densely white-bristly-hairy, gray-green leaves, which are spoon- to lance-shaped or obovate to oblong, and to 2½in (6cm) long. In summer, produces congested, terminal cymes of nodding, narrowly tubular-bell-shaped white flowers, to 1¼in (3cm) long; the petal tips quickly darken to pink and sometimes mature to deep purple or violet-blue. ↕↔ 10in (25cm). S.W. Asia. Zone 7b.
O. frutescens. Upright perennial with unbranched stems covered with tiny, soft hairs. The bristly-hairy, grayish green leaves, to 3in (8cm) long, are lance-shaped to oblong-lance-shaped or linear, with margins rolled back. In summer, bears cymes of cylindrical-bell-shaped, bright yellow flowers, to ¾in (2cm) long, maturing to orange-brown or reddish brown. ↕ 10in (25cm), ↔ to 24in (60cm). Greece, Turkey, Syria. Zone 8.

OOPHYTUM

AIZOACEAE

Genus of 2 species of succulent perennials found in dry, hilly areas in Western Cape, South Africa. They have pairs of erect, thick, fleshy leaves, which join to form ovoid, egg-like "bodies" that shrivel during the dormant period. Solitary, daisy-like flowers are produced from a cleft at the top of each body in late summer. In areas where temperatures drop below 45°F (7°C), grow in a temperate greenhouse; in warm, dry climates, grow in a scree bed, raised bed, or desert garden.
• **CULTIVATION** Under glass, grow in a mix of 2 parts loam to 1 part each sharp sand and leaf mold, in full light with shade from hot sun. Water moderately from late summer to early autumn, and sparingly on warm days from mid-autumn to spring. Keep barely moist when semi-dormant from late spring to midsummer. Outdoors, grow in gritty, poor, humus-rich soil, in full sun with some midday shade. See also pp.48–49.
• **PROPAGATION** Sow seed at 68–77°F (20–25°C), or separate and root complete bodies, in spring or summer.
• **PESTS AND DISEASES** Susceptible to greenflies, especially while flowering.

O. oviforme. Clump-forming, succulent perennial with papillose, glossy, olive-green to bright reddish green leaves, united in pairs to form ovoid bodies, ½in (1.5cm) across. In late summer, bears daisy-like white flowers, ¾in (2cm) across, with purplish pink tips. ↕ ¾in (2cm), ↔ 4in (10cm). South Africa (Western Cape). ❀ (min. 45°F/7°C)

▷ ***Operculina tuberosa*** see *Merremia tuberosa*

OPHIOPOGON

Lilyturf

LILIACEAE

Genus of about 50 species of evergreen, rhizomatous or tufted perennials, often with swollen, fleshy roots, sometimes also stoloniferous, from shady scrub or woodland in E. Asia, especially China and Japan. They are grown mainly for their dense tufts of somewhat grass-like

Ophiopogon jaburan 'Vittatus' (inset: flower detail)

leaves. Racemes of numerous small, 6-tepaled, semi-spherical to bell-shaped, pinkish white, lilac, or white flowers are produced on leafless stems in summer, followed by spherical to oblong-ellipsoid, glossy, blue or black fruits. Grow as a grass-like groundcover, for border edging, or in a rock garden. Where not hardy, grow for seasonal bedding, or in a cool or temperate greenhouse.
• **CULTIVATION** Outdoors, grow in moist but well-drained, slightly acidic, fertile, humus-rich soil in full sun or partial shade. Top-dress annually with leaf mold in autumn. Under glass, grow in soil-based potting mix in full light or bright indirect light. In the growing season, water freely and apply a balanced liquid fertilizer monthly; water sparingly in winter.
• **PROPAGATION** Sow seed in containers in a cold frame as soon as ripe. Divide in spring as growth resumes.
• **PESTS AND DISEASES** Sometimes affected by root rots and leaf spot. Slugs and snails may damage new leaves.

O. jaburan (Jaburan lily, White lilyturf). Tufted, stoloniferous perennial with strap-shaped, leathery, dark green leaves, to 24in (60cm) long. Short bell-shaped, white or lilac-tinted flowers, ½in (1.5cm) long, are borne in racemes, to 6in (15cm) long and occasionally curled, in late summer, followed by oblong-ellipsoid, violet-blue fruit, ½in (1.5cm) long. ↕ to 24in (60cm), ↔ to 12in (30cm). Japan. Zone 7b. **'Argenteovittatus'** see 'Vittatus'. **'Javanensis'** see 'Vittatus'. **'Nanus'** (Dwarf mondo grass) is compact, slow-growing, and rarely blooms. Useful between paving stones; ↕ 4–5in (10–13cm). **'Variegatus'** see 'Vittatus'. **'Vittatus'** ■ syn. 'Argenteovittatus', 'Javanensis', 'Variegatus', has pale green leaves, striped and margined cream, yellow, or white. **'White Dragon'** has leaves boldly striped with white, almost obliterating the green.

O. japonicus (Mondo grass). Tuberous-rooted, rhizomatous perennial forming clumps of narrowly linear, curved, rigid, dark green leaves, 8–12in (20–30cm) long. In summer, produces short racemes, 2–3in (5–8cm) long, of small, bell-shaped, white, occasionally lilac-tinged flowers, ¼in (6mm) across, followed by spherical, blue-black berries, ¼in (6mm) across. ↕ 8–12in (20–30cm), ↔ 12in (30cm). Japan. Zone 7b. **'Compactus'** is tiny and dense; ↕ to 2in (5cm). **'Kyoto Dwarf'** is compact in habit; ↕↔ 4in (10cm). **'Silver Dragon'** has white-variegated leaves; ↕ to 12in (30cm), ↔ to 6in (15cm).
O. planiscapus. Clump-forming, spreading, rhizomatous perennial with strap-shaped, curving, dark green leaves, 4–14in (10–35cm) long. Short bell-shaped, pale purplish white flowers, to ¼in (6mm) long, are borne in racemes, 1½–3in (4–8cm) long, in summer, followed by spherical, fleshy, dark blue-black fruit, ⅛–¼in (3–6mm) across. ↕ 8in (20cm), ↔ 12in (30cm). Zone 6. **'Nigrescens'** ■ syn. 'Arabicus', 'Black Dragon', 'Ebony Knight', has almost black leaves.
O. spicatus see *Liriope spicata.*

Ophiopogon planiscapus 'Nigrescens'

OPHRYS

ORCHIDACEAE

Genus of about 30 species of deciduous, tuberous, terrestrial orchids from Europe, Mediterranean islands, N. Africa, and W. Asia, occurring in habitats ranging from marshes and grassland to woodland and mountain-sides. They produce rosettes of oblong-ovate, ovate, or lance-shaped, mid-green leaves. From the rosettes arise erect inflorescences with small, bract-like leaves and racemes of 2–12 flowers; each has 3 spreading sepals, 2 petals, and a large lip, often strikingly colored and resembling the abdomen of a bee or other insect. *Ophrys* species are suitable for a rock garden or for naturalizing in fine grass; in wet, cold climates, they are best grown in an alpine house.
• **CULTIVATION** Outdoors, grow in sharply drained, gritty, leafy, humus-rich soil in partial shade. Plant dormant tubers in autumn, at least 2in (5cm) deep. Where marginally hardy, provide a dry winter mulch. In an alpine house, grow in terrestrial orchid potting mix in bright filtered light. During the growing season, water moderately; keep dry and frost-free when dormant. See also p.46.
• **PROPAGATION** Separate offsets in autumn.
• **PESTS AND DISEASES** Slugs and snails may cause problems.

O. apifera ■ (Bee orchid). Terrestrial orchid with oblong-ovate leaves, 2½in (6cm) long. Produces erect racemes, to 12in (30cm) tall, of 2–11 flowers, 1in (2.5cm) across, each with green or purplish pink sepals and petals, and a lip marked red-purple and yellow, in midspring and early summer. ↕ 12in (30cm), ↔ 6in (15cm). W., S., and C. Europe, N. Africa, W. Asia. Zone 7.
O. aranifera see *O. sphegodes.*
O. fuciflora see *O. holoserica.*
O. fusca (Somber bee orchid). Terrestrial orchid with oblong-ovate or lance-shaped leaves, 2½in (6cm) long. In mid- and late spring, produces erect racemes, to 12in (30cm) tall, of up to 8 variable green or yellow-green flowers, 2in (5cm) across, each with a yellow- or white-margined, bluish, brown, purple, or purplish red lip.

Ophrys apifera

Ophrys fusca subsp. *iricolor*

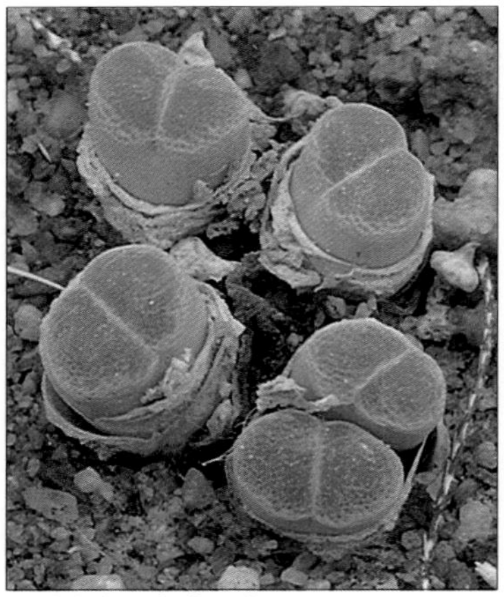

Ophthalmophyllum longum

Oplismenus africanus 'Variegatus'

↕ 12in (30cm), ↔ 6in (15cm). Mediterranean, S.W. Romania. Zone 7b.
subsp. *iricolor* ■ has racemes of up to 4 flowers, each with a longer lip that has 2 elongated, iridescent blue patches.
O. holoserica, syn. *O. fuciflora* (Late spider orchid). Terrestrial orchid with ovate-oblong leaves, 2½in (6cm) long. From midspring to midsummer, produces short, erect racemes, to 12in (30cm) tall, of 2–6 flowers, 1¼in (3cm) across; each has green, bright pink, or white sepals, pink to purple-pink petals, and a dark brown to dark maroon or ochre lip, sometimes with yellow margins. ↕ 12in (30cm), ↔ 6in (15cm). W., S.W., and C. Europe. ❀ (min. 35°F/2°C)
O. lutea. Terrestrial orchid with ovate leaves, 2½in (6cm) long. Erect racemes, to 12in (30cm) tall, of 2–7 yellow-green flowers, 1in (2.5cm) across, each with a bright yellow lip, dark brown or purplish black in the center, are borne from midspring to early summer. ↕ 12in (30cm), ↔ 6in (15cm). Portugal, Mediterranean. ❀ (min. 35°F/2°C)
O. speculum see *O. vernixia.*
O. sphegodes, syn. *O. aranifera* (Early spider orchid). Variable, terrestrial orchid with ovate-lance-shaped leaves, 3in (8cm) long. From late spring to midsummer, bears erect racemes, to 18in (45cm) long or less, of up to 10 flowers, to 1in (2.5cm) across; each has green, occasionally brownish green sepals and petals, and a pale to blackish brown, velvety lip. ↕↔ 6in (15cm). Europe. Zone 7b.
O. vernixia, syn. *O. speculum* (Mirror orchid). Terrestrial orchid with oblong to lance-shaped leaves, 2½in (6cm) long. In late spring and early summer, produces erect racemes, to 12in (30cm) tall, of up to 15 green flowers, 1in (2.5cm) across, with dark brown stripes; the lip is velvety, black- or brown-margined, with glossy, deep blue, yellow-bordered centers. ↕ 12in (30cm), ↔ 6in (15cm). Portugal, N. Africa, Mediterranean. ❀ (min. 35°F/2°C)

OPHTHALMOPHYLLUM

AIZOACEAE

Genus, sometimes considered part of *Conophytum,* of 19 species of perennial succulents growing wild in rock crevices and among lichens in dry, hilly areas of Namibia and South Africa. They bear "bodies" of paired, erect, compressed-cylindrical, very fleshy leaves, united for most of their length, with transparent "windows" on the usually flat tops. Solitary, daisy-like flowers are borne from clefts between the paired lobes, during the day in late summer and autumn. In areas where temperatures drop below 50°F (10°C), grow in a temperate greenhouse; in warm, dry climates, grow in a desert garden or in a scree bed or raised bed.
• **CULTIVATION** Under glass, grow in a mix of 2 parts loam to 1 part each sharp sand and leaf mold, in full light. From late spring to early autumn, water sparingly and apply a dilute, low-nitrogen liquid fertilizer every 4–6 weeks. Reduce water from mid- to late autumn; keep completely dry from winter to midspring. Outdoors, grow in gritty, poor, humus-rich soil in full sun. See also pp.48–49.
• **PROPAGATION** Sow seed at 68–77°F (20–25°C), or separate and root complete bodies, in spring or summer.
• **PESTS AND DISEASES** Infrequent.

O. longum ■ syn. *Conophytum longum.* Clump-forming, perennial succulent with gray-green to brown bodies, ¾in (2cm) across, consisting of rounded lobes with translucent dots above and keeled undersides. Daisy-like, white to pale pink flowers, ¾in (2cm) across, are borne in late summer and autumn. ↕ 1¼in (3cm), ↔ indefinite. Namibia, South Africa. ❀ (min. 41–45°F/5–7°C)
O. maughanii. Clump-forming, perennial succulent producing yellowish green bodies, ¾in (2cm) across, with short, conical lobes. In late summer and autumn, produces daisy-like white flowers, ½in (1.5cm) across. ↕ 1½in (4cm), ↔ indefinite. Namibia, South Africa. ❀ (min. 41–45°F/5–7°C)

OPLISMENUS

POACEAE

Genus of 6 species of trailing, annual or perennial grasses from subtropical and tropical forest of Africa, Asia, Polynesia, and Central and South America. They have slender, rooting, leafy stems with flat, lance-shaped to ovate leaves, and bear one-sided racemes of insignificant flowers. Only *O. africanus* 'Variegatus' is of decorative value: in warm areas, it makes an excellent groundcover, and is also a useful edging plant; where not hardy, grow as an ornamental plant in a hanging basket in a temperate greenhouse or conservatory.
• **CULTIVATION** Under glass, grow in soilless or soil-based potting mix in bright filtered or full light. During the growing season, water freely and apply a balanced liquid fertilizer every 4 weeks. Water sparingly in winter. Outdoors, grow in any moist but well-drained soil in full sun or partial shade.
• **PROPAGATION** Separate rooted stems in spring; pot up and keep in a propagating case until established.
• **PESTS AND DISEASES** Infrequent.

O. africanus, syn. *O. hirtellus* (Basket grass). Evergreen perennial with wiry stems, spreading and rooting at the nodes, bearing narrowly lance-shaped to ovate, softly hairy, mid-green leaves, to 2in (5cm) long, with long points. Small flowers are produced in one-sided racemes, to 6in (15cm) long, from summer to winter. ↕ 6in (15cm), but may form mounds to 36in (90cm), ↔ indefinite. Africa, Polynesia, tropical Central and South America. ❀ (min. 41°F/5°C).
'Variegatus' ■ syn. 'Vittatus', has white-striped leaves, flushed purple-pink.
O. hirtellus see *O. africanus.*

OPUNTIA

CACTACEAE

Genus of about 200 species of cacti, ranging from alpine and groundcover plants to bushy and tree-like species, from often very arid regions in North, Central, and South America, and the West Indies. They have usually pad-like and flattened, or sometimes cylindrical, club-shaped, or spherical, segmented branches, with areoles producing spines and glochids (barbed spines); a few species have leaf-like scales, which soon fall. Funnel- or bowl-shaped flowers are produced singly from the areoles at the tips or sides of the segments; they appear during the day in spring or summer, and are followed by usually spiny, obovoid or spherical fruits (prickly pears). In a few species, these are edible, and contain large, smooth white seeds in pulp.
Where temperatures drop below 50°F (10°C), grow tender species in a cool or temperate greenhouse. In warmer areas, grow opuntias in a desert garden or in a border with other cacti. Contact with the bristles causes intense irritation to skin, and they are difficult to remove.
• **CULTIVATION** Under glass, grow in standard cactus potting mix in full light or bright filtered light. Large species are best planted directly into a greenhouse border. From early spring to mid-autumn, water freely and apply a balanced liquid fertilizer 3 or 4 times. Keep dry at other times. Outdoors, grow in moderately fertile, sharply drained, gritty, humus-rich soil in full sun. See also pp.48–49.
• **PROPAGATION** Sow pre-soaked seed at 70°F (21°C) in spring. Separate and root stem segments. Handle plants using folded newspaper; dispose of it after use.
• **PESTS AND DISEASES** Cladode rots, zonate leaf spot, and black spot, as well as mealybugs and scale insects, are common. Bacterial soft rot and several viruses also occur.

O. basilaris see *Brisiliopuntia braziliensis*
O. chlorotica (Flapjack cactus). Bushy or tree-like cactus with pale bluish green stems composed of flattened, rounded to obovate segments, to 8in (20cm) long. Gray areoles each bear yellow glochids and 1–6 or more pale yellow or brown spines, which blacken with age. Broadly funnel-shaped yellow flowers, 3in (8cm) across, flushed red outside, are produced from spring to summer; they are followed by ovoid purple fruit, 1½in (4cm) long, with short spines that are lost as the fruit mature. ↕ to 6ft (2m), ↔ 30in (75cm). California, Nevada, New Mexico, N. Mexico. ❀ (min. 45–50°F/7–10°C); will tolerate brief periods to 15°F (-9°F).
O. claverioides, see *Maihueniopsis claverioides.*
O. cochenillifera, syn. *Nopalea cochenillifera.* Shrubby or tree-like cactus with stems composed of flattened, elliptic to obovate, glossy, dark green segments, 3–10in (8–25cm) long. Mid-green areoles produce yellow glochids, and sometimes 1–3 yellow spines, usually none. Narrowly funnel-shaped, bright red flowers, to 1½in (4cm) across, appear in late spring and summer, followed by ellipsoid, fleshy, spineless red fruit, 1–1½in (2.5–4cm) long. ↕ to 12ft (4m), ↔ 3ft (1m). Mexico. ❀ (min. 45–50°F/7–10°C)
O. compressa ■ syn. *O. humifusa.* Clump-forming, semi-prostrate cactus with stems divided into flattened, elliptic to obovate or rounded, grayish green segments, 2–5in (5–13cm) long, often tinged purple, and bearing narrowly wedge-shaped leaves, to ¼in (6mm) long. Brown areoles produce brown glochids, and sometimes 1 or 2 black-tipped white spines. Produces broadly funnel-shaped, bright yellow

Opuntia compressa

flowers, 1½–2½in (4–6cm) across, in late spring and summer; they are followed by obovoid, spineless, edible purple or red fruit, 1–1½in (2.5–4cm) long. Plants "deflate" during dormancy. ↕ 4–12in (10–30cm), ↔ to 3ft (1m) or more. C. and E. US. Zone 5.

O. decumbens. Shrubby, prickly pear cactus whose branches sprawl across the ground with tips raised. Green stem segments are purple tinted, either obovate, elliptical, or widely ovate, usually prostrate; spines may be absent, or few, 1–3. Bears plentiful yellow glochids, 1/16–1/5in (2–5mm) long, and reddish-tinted, yellow flowers, 1¾in (4.5cm) long, followed by pear-shaped purplish fruit. ↕ to 20in (50cm) tall. S. Mexico, Guatemala, Honduras, Nicaragua, Costa Rica. ❀ (min. 45°F/7°C)

O. elatior. Tree-like cactus with many branches divided into flattened, narrowly oblong-oval, pale to fresh green segments, 4–10in (10–25cm) long. Gray areoles each have yellow glochids and 2–5 sheathed, yellow then gray spines. From spring to summer, produces funnel-shaped, bright, deep red flowers, to 2½in (6cm) across, followed by ovoid, spiny red fruit, to 1½in (4cm) long. ↕ to 11ft (3.5m), ↔ 3ft (1m). Origin unknown. ❀ (min. 50°F/10°C)

O. engelmannii Shrubby cactus, with more or less ascending branches, forming dense thickets. Green to blue-green stem segments are flattened, oval to round, sometimes elongated, 6–12in (15–30cm) long, with yellowish, awl-shaped, slightly flattened areoles producing yellow glochids that become brown with age. Spines are extremely variable. Produces

Opuntia microdasys var. *albispina*

Opuntia phaeacantha

Opuntia polycantha var. *erinacea* var. *ursina*

yellow, sometimes reddish, flowers, 2–3in (5–8cm) long, and oval to elongated, purple fruit, 1¼–2¾in (3–7cm). ↕ to 11ft (3.5m), ↔ 3ft (1m). Arizona, N. Mexico, Texas, Oklahoma, Louisiana, N. and C. Mexico as far as San Luis Potosi, Tamaulipas, Hidalgo. ❀ (min. 50°F/10°C)

O. falcata, syn. *Consolea falcata.* Tree-like cactus with glossy, dark green stems composed of flattened, oblong to lance-shaped segments, to 14in (35cm) long, marked with small tubercles. White areoles each bear a few brownish white glochids and 2–8 needle-like, rough, pale yellow or yellowish brown spines. Produces bowl-shaped red flowers, 1¼–2in (3–5cm) across, in late spring and summer, followed by ovoid, spineless, dark green fruit, to 1½in (4cm) long. ↕ to 5ft (1.5m), ↔ 30in (75cm). Haiti. ❀ (min. 45–50°F/7–10°C)

O. ficus-indica (Indian fig, Prickly pear). Bushy or tree-like cactus with stems composed of flattened, obovate to oblong, grayish green or mid-green segments, 4–16in (10–40cm) long, with white areoles producing yellow glochids and usually 1 or 2 spines. Bowl-shaped yellow flowers, 4in (10cm) across, are produced in late spring and summer, and are followed by edible, ovoid, spineless purple fruit, to 4in (10cm) long. Some cultivars have yellow, orange, or red fruit. ↕↔ 15ft (5m). Mexico. ❀ (min. 45–50°F/7–10°C); tolerates brief periods to 25°F (-4°C).

O. humifusa see *O. compressa.*

O. histricina see *O. polycantha var histricina.*

O. imbricata syn *Cylindropuntia imbricata* (Chain-link cactus). Variable, many-branched cactus with cylindrical, mid-green to bluish green stem segments, 4–16in (10–40cm) long, with very prominent tubercles, and cylindrical leaves, ½in (1.5cm) long. Large yellow areoles each bear yellow glochids and 8–30 brown-sheathed, reddish yellow or white spines. Broadly funnel-shaped, purple or red flowers, usually 1½–3in (4–8cm) across, are produced in late spring and summer, followed by nearly spherical, spineless yellow fruit, 1¼in (3cm) long. ↕ to 10ft (3m), ↔ 3ft (1m). S.W. US, Mexico. ❀ (min. 45–50°F/7–10°C)

O. macrocentra, syn. *O. violacea* (Purple prickly pear). Clump-forming cactus with bluish green stems composed of oblong to nearly rounded segments, 4–8in (10–20cm) long, purple-tinged on the edges. Dark purple-brown areoles 1 or 2 black or sometimes white spines. In spring and summer, bears cup-shaped, yellow flowers, 3–3½in (8–9cm) across, with red centers, followed by spherical, spineless, red or purple-red fruit, 1–1½in (2.5–4cm) long. The purple coloration is due to the pigment beta cyanin, produced in response to cold temperatures or drought conditions. ↕↔ to 36in (90cm). E. Arizona to W. Texas. ❀ (min. 50°F/10°C)

O. megalacantha. See *O. ficus-indica.*

O. microdasys. Bushy cactus with stems consisting of flattened, oblong, obovate, or almost rounded, velvety, pale to mid-green segments, 2½–6in (6–15cm) long; these are thickly dotted with white areoles bearing minute, yellow, white, or reddish brown glochids and usually no spines. Bowl-shaped, bright yellow flowers, 1½–2in (4–5cm) across, often tinged red on the outside, are produced from spring to summer; they are followed by oblong-ellipsoid, spineless, light purplish red fruit, to 1¾in (4.5cm) long. ↕↔ 16–24in (40–60cm). N. and C. Mexico. ❀ (min. 45–50°F/7–10°C). **var. *albispina*** ■ (Honey bunny, Polka-dot cactus) has dark green stem pads, white glochids, whitish yellow flowers, and darker purple-red fruit. **var. *pallida*** (Bunny ears) has thin, grayish green stem segments, 3–6in (8–15cm) long, with yellow areoles and glochids; ↕↔ 24in (60cm).

O. paraguayensis. Semi-erect cactus with glossy, dark green stems composed of flattened, inversely lance-shaped or narrowly elliptic segments, 7–12in (18–30cm) long, with prominent, yellowish white areoles, tufts of yellow glochids, and usually no spines or one pale yellow spine. Broadly bowl-shaped orange flowers, 3in (8cm) across, are produced in late spring and summer, and are followed by conical, spineless, dark purple fruit, to 3in (8cm) long. ↕ to 6ft (2m), ↔ 5ft (1.5m). Paraguay, Argentina. ❀ (min. 45–50°F/7–10°C)

O. phaeacantha ■ Variable cactus with stems divided into flattened, obovate or rounded, pale to bluish green, sometimes purple-tinged segments, 4–16in (10–40cm) long. Brown areoles each have a tuft of brown glochids and 1–8 sheathed, brown or red-brown spines. Produces broadly funnel-shaped, sulfur-yellow flowers, 2in (5cm) across, sometimes red-tinged inside, in late spring and summer, followed by ovoid, red fruit, to 1½in (4cm) long. ↕ to 5ft (1.5m), ↔ to 6ft (2m). S.W. US, N. Mexico. ❀ (min. 45–50°F/7–10°C); tolerates brief periods to 15°F (-9°C).

O. polycantha. Clump-forming cactus with bluish green stems composed of flattened, rounded to broadly obovate segments, 2–4in (5–10cm) long. Brown or white areoles each have yellow glochids and 9 or more thread-like white spines, to 4in (10cm) long. In summer, produces shallowly bowl-shaped, red, pink, purplish pink, or yellow flowers, 2½in (6cm) across, followed by ovoid by ovoid, light green, very spiny fruit, to ¾in (2cm) long. ↕ 20in (50cm), ↔ 5ft (1.5m). S.W. US. ❀ (min. 50°F/10°C). **var. *erinacea*** ■ syn. *O. histricina* var. *ursina* (Grizzly bear cactus), has oblong-elliptic stem segments with numerous, very long, thread-like, deflexed spines, to 4in (10cm) long,

O

Opuntia tunicata

and orange or pink flowers; ‡↔ to 18in (45cm). California, Nevada, Arizona. **var. *histricina*** syn. *O. histricina*.
O. pycnantha. Bushy, semi-prostrate cactus with stems composed of flattened, rounded, slightly softly hairy, dark green segments, 4–7in (10–18cm) long; they are covered with pale brown areoles, each bearing brownish yellow glochids and 3–12 reflexed, yellow or red-brown spines. From spring to summer, produces broadly funnel-shaped, greenish yellow, often red-tinged flowers, 1¾in (4.5cm) across; they are followed by ovoid, very prickly, spiny, dull green fruit, 1½in (4cm) long. ‡↔ 18in (45cm). Mexico (Baja California). ❄ (min. 45–50°F/7–10°C)
O. robusta. Variable, shrubby or tree-like cactus with stems composed of flat, thick, oval to almost rounded, grayish or bluish green segments, to 16in (40cm) across. Brown areoles bear reddish brown glochids and, in each upper areole, 2–12 sheathed white, pale brown, or yellow spines. Shallowly bowl-shaped yellow flowers, 3in (8cm) across, appear in late spring and summer, followed by spherical to ellipsoid, spineless, deep red fruit, 3in (8cm) long. ‡↔ 6ft (2m) or more.

Opuntia verschaffeltii

Opuntia santa-rita

C. Mexico. ❄ (min. 45–50°F/7–10°C); tolerates brief periods to 25°F (-4°C).
O. santa-rita ■ (Santa Rita prickly pear). Succulent with uniformly purple-green or purple pads and maroon developing segments is taller than the species. Stem segments are round or nearly round, 6–8in (15–20cm) across, with 1–3 needle-like, straight, or slightly curved, flexible spines, light reddish brown to pink or darker, 3–3½in (8–9cm). Bears large, lemon-yellow flowers with bright red bases, 3½in (9cm) across, and large, oblong, purplish edible fruit, 1in high and ½in across. ‡↔ 2–5ft (60cm–1.5m). S. Arizona, S. New Mexico, W. Texas, N. Sonora, Mexico. ❄ (min. 50°F/10°C)
O. subulata (Eve's-pin cactus). Freely branching, tree-like cactus, with cylindrical, unsegmented, dark green stems, 2–3in (5–8cm) in diameter; they are covered with oblong tubercles and, on the upper stems, semi-cylindrical, sharp-pointed, more or less evergreen leaves, 2in (5cm) or more long. Yellow areoles each have yellow glochids and 1 or 2 pale yellow spines. Cup-shaped red flowers, 3in (8cm) across, are produced from spring to summer, followed by persistent, oblong-ellipsoid, spineless, dark green fruit, 2½–4in (6–10cm) long. ‡ to 12ft (4m), ↔ to 5ft (1.5m). S. Peru. ❄ (min. 45–50°F/7–10°C); tolerates brief periods to 28°F (-2°C).
O. tunicata ■ syn. *Cylindropuntia tunicata.* Densely bushy, freely branching cactus with whorls of glaucous green stems divided into cylindrical segments, 2½–6in (6–15cm) long. Prominent white areoles have yellow glochids and 6–10 sheathed, off-white or yellow spines. From spring to summer, bears cup-shaped yellow flowers, 1¼–2in (3–5cm) across, followed by spherical to broadly club-shaped, spineless, glaucous green fruit, to 1¼in (3cm) long. ‡ 24in (60cm), ↔ 3ft (1m). C. Mexico. ❄ (min. 45–50°F/7–10°C)
O. verschaffeltii ■ syn. *Austrocylindropuntia verschaffeltii.* Clump-forming cactus with dull green stems composed of cylindrical segments, 4–8in (10–20cm) or more long, with low tubercles and persistent, cylindrical leaves, to 1¼in (3cm) long. White areoles have yellow glochids and 1–3 or more, hair-like white spines. Cup-shaped, red or orange-red flowers, 1½in (4cm) across, are produced from spring to summer, followed by spherical, spineless red fruit, to 1¼in (3cm) long. ‡ 6in (15cm), ↔ 3ft (1m). Bolivia, N. Argentina. ❄ (min. 45–50°F/7–10°C)

O. vestita syn. *Austrocylindropuntia vestita* (Cotton-pole cactus, Old man cactus). Low-growing cactus with fragile, warty, pale green stems, and cylindrical segments to 8in (20cm) long. Yellow areoles, the upper ones with cylindrical, more or less evergreen leaves, ½in (1.5cm) long, each produce white glochids and 4–8 white spines that are intermingled with many fine white hairs, which envelop the stems. Cup-shaped, dark violet-red flowers, 1½in (4cm) across, are borne in late spring and summer, followed by spherical, spineless red fruit, to ¾in (2cm) long. ‡↔ 3ft (1m). Bolivia. ❄ (min. 45–50°F/7–10°C); tolerates brief periods to 28°F (-2°C).
O. violacea, see *O. macrocentra*

ORBEA

ASCLEPIADACEAE

Genus of about 20 species of dwarf, erect to decumbent, mainly clump-forming, leafless, perennial succulents, closely related to *Stapelia*, from semi-arid, hilly, often rocky terrain in E. Africa and South Africa. They have large, warty teeth along the angled stem margins, and produce funnel-shaped, usually 5-lobed, often unpleasantly scented flowers, which attract bluebottles. The diurnal flowers, borne singly or in few-flowered cymes from summer to autumn, each have a slightly wrinkled, usually flattened corolla, surrounded by a very pronounced, smooth annulus (ring). Where temperatures fall below 52°F (11°C), grow in a warm greenhouse; in warm, dry climates, use in a desert garden.
• **CULTIVATION** Under glass, grow in standard cactus potting mix, top-dressed with grit. Provide low humidity, with bright filtered light in summer, full light in winter. From spring to early autumn, water moderately, applying a low-nitrogen fertilizer every 3–4 weeks. Keep dry at other times, but water sparingly on warm winter days to prevent shriveling. Outdoors, grow in gritty, loamy, moderately fertile, humus-rich soil in partial shade. See also pp.48–49.
• **PROPAGATION** Sow seed at 64–70°F (18–21°C) in spring. Take stem-segment cuttings in spring and summer.
• **PESTS AND DISEASES** Susceptible to mealybugs and root mealybugs, and to black rot if overwatered.

O. ciliata, syn. *Diplocyathus ciliata.* Mat-forming succulent with erect, 4-angled, toothed, mid-green stems, the tips tinged red. In summer, bears solitary, bowl-shaped, pale yellow flowers, to 3in (8cm) across, with dark purple-spotted annuli. ‡ 2in (5cm), ↔ to 6in (15cm). South Africa (Northern Cape, Eastern Cape). ❄ (min. 52°F/11°C)
O. variegata ■ syn. *Stapelia variegata* (Starfish cactus, Toad cactus). Variable, clump-forming succulent with erect, obtusely angled, prominently toothed, grayish green stems, often mottled purple. In summer, produces cymes of up to 5 funnel-shaped, flat, densely wrinkled, dark brownish red flowers, 2–3½in (5–9cm) across, patterned white or yellowish white. ‡ 4in (10cm), ↔ to 12in (30cm). South Africa (Eastern Cape). ❄ (min. 52°F/11°C)

Orbea variegata

ORBEOPSIS

ASCLEPIADACEAE

Genus of about 10 species of leafless, perennial succulents from dry hillsides in Angola, Mozambique, and South Africa. They have angled, freely branching, usually grayish green stems, and bear umbel-like clusters of star-shaped, malodorous flowers during the day in early summer. In areas where temperatures drop below 50°F (10°C), grow in a warm greenhouse; in warm, dry climates, grow in a desert border.

• **CULTIVATION** Under glass, grow in standard cactus potting mix and top-dress with grit. Provide low humidity and full light with shade from hot sun. From spring to early autumn, water moderately and apply a low-nitrogen fertilizer every 4 or 5 weeks. Keep dry at other times, but water sparingly on warm winter days to prevent shriveling. Outdoors, grow in moderately fertile, gritty, loamy, and humus-rich soil, in full sun. See also pp.48–49.

• **PROPAGATION** Sow seed at 64–70°F (18–21°C) in spring. Take stem-segment cuttings in spring and summer.

• **PESTS AND DISEASES** Infrequent.

O. albocastanea, syn. *Caralluma albocastanea.* Semi-erect, succulent perennial that offsets from the base, producing 4-angled, upward-curving, reddish brown stems with pale spots and large, projecting teeth. In early summer, star-shaped flowers, 1–1¼in (2.5–3cm) across, are borne in umbel-like clusters of 3–6; they are green outside with red spots, and cream inside with brownish purple spots, the margins having thick, dark red hairs. They have dark brown coronas. ↕ 3in (8cm), ↔ 7in (18cm). Namibia. ❀ (min. 50°F/10°C)

O. lutea, syn. *Caralluma lutea.* Variable, mat-forming, succulent perennial with 4-angled, coarsely toothed, grayish green stems. In early summer, bears dense, umbel-like clusters of 3–26 star-shaped flowers, 1½–3in (4–8cm) across, ranging in color from reddish brown to maroon or pale lemon-yellow, with yellow-hairy margins and yellow coronas. ↕ 4in (10cm), ↔ 10in (25cm). Southern Africa. ❀ (min. 50°F/10°C)

ORCHIS

ORCHIDACEAE

Genus of about 35 species of deciduous, terrestrial orchids from Europe and Asia, mostly occurring in open, grassy places, frequently in poor, dry soil. They have 2 or 3 spherical or ovoid tubers, and rosettes of linear-lance-shaped to oblong-ovate, sometimes purple-spotted, light to dark green leaves. Dense, erect racemes of delicate purple, red, pink, yellow, green, or white flowers, each with a short spur, and sometimes with a pungent odor, are borne from spring to summer. They are suitable for a rock garden, but are usually grown in an alpine house or very sheltered site outdoors to protect the flowers.

• **CULTIVATION** In an alpine house, grow in terrestrial orchid potting mix in bright filtered light. Water moderately during the growing season; keep dry and frost-free when dormant. Outdoors, grow in fertile, well-drained, gritty,

Orchis morio

humus-rich, slightly acidic soil in partial shade. Plant dormant tubers in autumn, at least 3in (8cm) deep. See also p.46.

• **PROPAGATION** Separate offsets in early or midspring.

• **PESTS AND DISEASES** Slugs and snails may be troublesome.

O. elata *see Dactylorhiza elata.*

O. maderensis see *Dactylorhiza foliosa.*

O. mascula (Early purple orchid). Terrestrial orchid with mid-green, often purple-spotted leaves, 6in (15cm) long. From spring to midsummer, bears light to dark purple flowers, ¾in (2cm) long, in erect racemes, to 12in (30cm) tall. ↕ 12in (30cm), ↔ 6in (15cm). Europe. Zone 5.

O. morio ■ (Green-veined orchid). Terrestrial orchid with pale to mid-green leaves, 2½in (6cm) long. Pale to deep purple flowers, ¾in (2cm) long, with green veins on the cupped sepals, are borne in erect racemes, to 6in (15cm) tall, from spring to midsummer. ↕ 6–12in (15–30cm), ↔ 3in (8cm). Europe to W. Iran. Zone 7.

O. papilionacea (Butterfly orchid). Terrestrial orchid with mid-green leaves, 2½in (6cm) long. In spring and early summer, bears erect racemes, to 6in (15cm) tall, of pale purple to lilac, darker veined flowers, ¾in (2cm) long, with large, pink-veined lips. ↕ 6–12in (15–30cm), ↔ 3in (8cm). S. Europe to S.W. Asia. Zone 6.

OREOCEREUS

syn. BORZICACTUS

CACTACEAE

Genus of about 6 species of mainly columnar cacti from mountainous regions in South America. The thick, cylindrical, many-ribbed stems, usually branching from the bases, have tubercles and spiny areoles and, in some species, are covered in long hairs. Solitary, tubular-funnel-shaped flowers are produced during the day in summer. Below 50°F (10°C), grow as houseplants or in a warm greenhouse; in warm, dry climates, grow in a desert garden.

• **CULTIVATION** Under glass, grow in a mix of 4 parts standard cactus potting mix and 1 part limestone chips, in full light. From spring to summer, water freely and apply a balanced liquid fertilizer every 4–5 weeks. Keep nearly dry at other times. Outdoors, grow in moderately fertile, slightly alkaline, sharply drained, humus-rich soil in full sun. See also pp.48–49.

Oreocereus celsianus

• **PROPAGATION** Sow seed at 70°F (21°C) in spring or summer.

• **PESTS AND DISEASES** Scale occurs.

O. celsianus ■ syn. *Borzicactus celsianus.* Slow-growing, clump-forming cactus with cylindrical, erect stems branching from the bases, each with 10–17 warty ribs. Gray-woolly areoles bear white hairs and yellow to reddish brown spines (7–9 radials and 1–4 much longer centrals). In summer, bears solitary, pale purplish pink flowers, 3–3½in (7–9cm) long, brownish red outside. ↕ 3–10ft (1–3m), ↔ 18in (45cm) or more. Bolivia, N.W.Argentina. ❀ (min. 50°F/10°C)

O. hempelianus, syn. *Arequipa hempeliana, Borzicactus leucotrichus.* Solitary cactus with branching, spherical then short-cylindrical, erect or semi-prostrate, grayish green or glaucous green stems, each with 10–20 warty ribs and yellow wool at the tips. White areoles each bear 11–40 spines (8–30 radials and 3–10 longer centrals). Solitary, bright scarlet to purplish red flowers, to 3in (8cm) long, are borne in summer. ↕ to 16in (40cm), ↔ 4in (10cm). Mountains of S. Peru, N. Chile. ❀ (min. 50°F/10°C)

O. intertexta, syn. *Matucana intertexta.* Clump-forming cactus with erect, spherical to short-cylindrical, shiny, dark green stems, each with 14–18 warty ribs, often spiraled. Elliptic areoles each bear yellow spines, reddish brown beneath (16–18 radials and 3–7 longer centrals). In summer, bears solitary, orange-red flowers, 2–3in (5–8cm) across. ↕↔ to 6in (15cm). Peru. ❀ (min. 50°F/10°C)

O. leucotrichus ■ Thick, cylindrical, shrubby cactus, branching from the

Oreocereus leucotrichus

Oreocereus ritteri

base, forming dense clumps with many upcurved stems and flattened ribs, 10–15, with shallow furrows. Areoles have abundant white to black hairs, 2–4in (5–10cm) long (1–4 slightly curved central, 2–3in (5–8cm) long; 5–10 radial, to 1.5cm long). Carmine red flowers, 3–4in (8–10cm) long, emerge near the stem tips. The fruit is pear-shaped, reddish purple, and pubescent fruit, 1–1½in (2.5–4cm) long. ↕ 65–160ft (20–50m). C. Peru to N. Chile. ❀ (min. 50°F/10°C)

O. peruviana see *Oroya peruviana.*

O. ritteri ■ Cylindrical, shrubby, gray-green to dark green cactus, branching from the base. The 12–14 ribs are notched deeply below areoles covered with dense white hairs and spines, 1–2 erect central, ¾–4in (2–10cm) long, up to 10 radiating radials, whitish with dark tips, to ¾in (2cm) long. Bears oblique, red flowers, to 4½in (11cm) long, and globose, yellowish green fruit, 1¼–2in (3–5cm) long. ↕ 3–5ft (1–1.5m), ↔ 6–12ft (2–4m). Ayacucho, Peru. ❀ (min. 50°F/10°C)

O. trollii ■ Columnar pale green cactus, forming small clusters, with short stems covered with dense wool. Low, strongly tuberculate ribs, 15–25, have areoles bearing white wool, to 3in (8cm). The spines are yellow, reddish, or brown (3–5 dark-tipped, stout, and awl-like centrals, 10–15 bristle-like radials). Bears carmine to pink flowers, to 1½in (4cm) long, and globose fruit. ↕ 20in (50cm), ↔ 2½–4in (6–10cm). S. Bolivia, N. Argentina. ❀ (min. 50°F/10°C)

Oreocereus trollei

ORIGANUM

Marjoram, Oregano

LAMIACEAE

Genus of about 20 species of often rhizomatous, summer-flowering, herbaceous perennials and deciduous and evergreen subshrubs from open habitats, often in mountainous areas of the Mediterranean and S.W. Asia. They have spreading to upright stems bearing simple, aromatic leaves in opposite pairs, and inflorescences in spiked whorls, which are sometimes panicle- or corymb-like. The elongated, tubular or funnel-shaped, 2-lipped flowers are borne amid conspicuous, often brightly colored bracts, which remain attractive for many weeks. Some origanums, including *O. dictamnus*, *O. majorana*, *O. onites*, and *O. vulgare* and their cultivars, are used as culinary herbs. Grow smaller species in a rock garden, scree bed, alpine house, or at the front of a border; grow larger ones in a herbaceous border or herb garden. All attract bees and other insects.

• **CULTIVATION** Outdoors, grow in full sun in poor to moderately fertile, well-drained, preferably alkaline soil. Grow dwarf perennials and subshrubs in free-draining soil. Some resent winter moisture, and are best grown in an alpine house; grow in a mix of equal parts loam, leaf mold, and sharp sand. Cut back old, flowered stems in early spring.

• **PROPAGATION** Sow seed in containers in a cold frame in autumn, or at 50–55°F (10–13°C) in spring. Divide in spring, or take basal cuttings in late spring.

• **PESTS AND DISEASES** Sometimes affected by root and stem rots. May be attacked by aphids and spider mites.

O. amanum ■ Low-spreading, evergreen subshrub with ovate, bright green leaves, to ½in (1.5cm) long, and heart-shaped at the bases. In summer and autumn, curved, funnel-shaped pink flowers, 1½in (4cm) long, with small spreading lobes, are produced in congested, terminal whorls among green bracts, to ¾in (2cm) long, which become flushed purple-pink with age. ↕4–8in (10–20cm), ↔ to 12in (30cm). E. Mediterranean, Turkey. Zone 6.

Origanum 'Kent Beauty'

***O.* 'Barbara Tingey'.** Dense, mound-forming, semi-evergreen subshrub, similar to *O. rotundifolium.* Produces rounded, bluish green leaves, purple beneath, ¾in (2cm) long. From summer to autumn, nodding whorls of tubular pink flowers, ½in (1.5cm) long and flared at the mouths, are borne among green bracts, ¾in (2cm) long, which age to deep purple-pink. ↕4in (10cm), ↔ to 8in (20cm). Zone 7b.

***O.* 'Buckland'.** Upright perennial with rounded, hairy, gray-green leaves, ½in (1.5cm) long. In summer, whorls of tubular pink flowers, ½in (1.5cm) long, are borne among bracts, ¾in (2cm) long, which are pink from an early age. ↕8in (20cm), ↔ to 6in (15cm). Zone 7b.

O. dictamnus (Dittany of Crete, Hop marjoram). Dome-forming, evergreen subshrub with arching, branching stems bearing rounded-ovate to rounded, densely white-felted, mid-green, sometimes purple-mottled leaves, to 1in (2.5cm) long. In mid- and late summer, produces dense, pendent, panicle-like whorls of small, open funnel-shaped pink flowers, ½in (1.5cm) long, among hop-like purple bracts, ⅜–½in (9–15mm) long. In wet climates, grow in an alpine house. ↕6in (15cm), ↔ to 8in (20cm). Crete. Zone 8.

Origanum laevigatum

O. heracleoticum see *O. vulgare* subsp. *hirtum.*

***O.* 'Kent Beauty'** ■ Prostrate, semi-evergreen subshrub with trailing stems clothed in rounded-ovate, bright green leaves, to ¾in (2cm) long. In summer, produces whorls of small, tubular, pale pink to mauve flowers, ½in (1.5cm) long, among deep rose-pink bracts, ¾in (2cm) long. Must be grown in extremely well-drained soil. ↕4in (10cm), ↔ to 8in (20cm). Zone 5.

O. laevigatum ■ Woody-based perennial with erect, wiry, red-purple stems and ovate to elliptic, dark green leaves, ½–¾in (1.5–2cm) long, hairy only along the midribs beneath. Loose, panicle-like whorls of numerous tubular, scarcely 2-lipped, purplish pink flowers, ½in (1.5cm) long, are produced from late spring to autumn. The flowers have darker purple calyces, surrounded by red-purple bracts, ½in (1.5cm) long. ↕ to 20–24in (50–60cm), ↔ 18in (45cm). Turkey, Cyprus. Zone 5. **'Herrenhausen'** ■ has purple-flushed young leaves and winter foliage, and denser whorls of pink flowers; ↕18–30in (45–75cm). **'Hopleys'**, syn. 'Hopley's Purple', bears large, deep pink flowers, ¾in (2cm) long, and large bracts, ½in (1.5cm) long, in narrow whorls over a long period; ↕24–36in (60–90cm).

O. majorana (Knotted marjoram, Sweet marjoram). Upright, evergreen subshrub, often grown as an annual or biennial, with branching stems bearing ovate or elliptic, softly hairy, scented, gray-green leaves, ⅛–1¼in (0.3–3cm) long. Panicles of tubular, white or pink flowers, ⅜in (9mm) long, with gray-green bracts, to ⅛in (3mm) long, appear from early to late summer. ↕ to 32in (80cm), ↔ 18in (45cm). S.W. Europe, Turkey. Zone 7b.

O.* x *majoricum (*O. majorana* x *O. vulgare* subsp. *virens*) (Hardy marjoram, Italian oregano). Clump-forming perennial with rounded, aromatic, mid-green leaves, to 1in (2.5cm) long. Bears whorls of bell-shaped, white flowers, with pink bracts in early summer. Possesses the sweetness and pungency of its respective parents. ↕18–24in (45–60cm), ↔ 12in (30cm). S.W. Europe. Zone 7.

O. microphyllum. Domed, spreading, evergreen subshrub with ovate, downy gray leaves, to ¼in (6mm) long, on slender branches. In summer, bears loose, panicle-like whorls of tubular, pink to purple flowers, ¼in (6mm) long, among purple bracts, to ⅛in (3mm) long. ↕10in (25cm), ↔ to 12in (30cm). Crete. Zone 8.

O. onites, syn. *Majorana onites* (Pot marjoram). Small, mound-forming, semi-evergreen subshrub with red-hairy stems and ovate to elliptic, bright green leaves, to ¾in (2cm) long, rounded to heart-shaped at the bases. In late summer, produces tubular white flowers, to ¼in (6mm) long, in dense, corymb-like whorls, with green bracts, to ⅛in (3mm) long. ↕24in (60cm), ↔ 12in (30cm). E. Mediterranean. Zone 7.

O. rotundifolium. Rhizomatous, woody-based perennial or deciduous, rounded subshrub, with rounded to heart-shaped, blue-gray leaves, to 1in (2.5cm) long. Throughout summer, produces nodding, hop-like whorls of

Origanum amanum

Origanum laevigatum 'Herrenhausen'

Origanum vulgare

Origanum vulgare 'Aureum'

small, tubular, pale pink flowers, to ½in (1.5cm) long, among pale lemon-green bracts, to 1in (2.5cm) long. ↕ 4–12in (10–30cm), ↔ to 12in (30cm). Turkey, Armenia, Republic of Georgia. Zone 7b.
O. vulgare ■ (Oregano). Bushy, rhizomatous, woody-based perennial with upright to spreading stems bearing very aromatic, rounded to ovate, dark green leaves, to 1½in (4cm) long. From midsummer to early autumn, bears loose panicle- or corymb-like whorls of tubular flowers, to ⅛in (3mm) long, varying from deep to pale pink or white, with whorls of leafy, purple-tinted green bracts, to ½in (1.5cm) long. ↕↔ 12–36in (30–90cm). Europe. Zone 3. **'Aureum'** ■ (Golden oregano) has golden leaves and pink flowers, and spreads less vigorously than the species; ↔ to 12in (30cm). **'Aureum Crispum'**, syn. 'Curly Gold', is more spreading than the species, and has curly golden leaves; ↔ 18in (45cm). **'Compactum'** (Compact oregano) is dense, compact, and dome-forming, with smaller leaves, to ¾in (2cm) long; ↕ to 6in (15cm), ↔ to 12in (30cm). **'Curly Gold'** see 'Aureum Crispum'. **'Gold Tip'**, syn. 'Variegatum', is similar to 'Aureum Crispum', but the leaves are yellow only at their tips; ↕ 16in (40cm), ↔ 18in (45cm). **'Heiderose'** is upright and bushy in habit, and bears pink flowers; ↕ to 16in (40cm). **subsp. *hirtum***, syn. *O. heracleoticum* (Greek oregano) has a compact habit, producing hairy leaves, hairy green bracts, and small heads of white flowers; ↕ 12–28in (30–70cm), ↔ 8–18in (20–45cm); Greece, Turkey. **'Variegatum'** see 'Gold Tip'.

ORIXA

RUTACEAE

Genus of one species of deciduous, spreading, dioecious shrub from woodland and thickets in mountainous regions of China, Korea, and Japan. Cultivated for its elegant, aromatic foliage and open habit, it is suitable for a shrub border, mixed border, or woodland garden.
• **CULTIVATION** Grow in fertile, well-drained soil in sun or shade. Tolerant of dry soils and exposed positions. Pruning group 1.
• **PROPAGATION** Sow seed in containers in a cold frame in spring. Take semi-ripe cuttings in midsummer.
• **PESTS AND DISEASES** Infrequent.

O. japonica. Spreading, slender-branched, deciduous shrub with simple, alternate, obovate to inversely lance-shaped, aromatic, dark green leaves, to 5in (13cm) long, pale yellow in autumn. Cup-shaped, 4-petaled green flowers, to ¼in (6mm) across, are borne in the leaf axils as the leaves emerge in spring; the males are borne in small panicles, to 1¼in (3cm) long, the females singly. Female plants bear 4-lobed brown fruit, ¾in (2cm) across. ↕ 8ft (2.5m), ↔ 12ft (4m). China, Korea, Japan. Zone 7.

ORNITHOGALUM

Star-of-Bethlehem

LILIACEAE

Genus of 80 species of bulbous perennials found in a variety of habitats, ranging from dry, rocky hillsides to meadows and woodland, in C. and S. Europe, the Mediterranean, former USSR, W. and S.W. Asia, tropical Africa, and South Africa. They are grown for their sometimes corymb-like racemes of often star-, cup-, or funnel-shaped, occasionally scented flowers; usually white, sometimes yellow or orange, they are borne on leafless stems in spring or summer. The leaves are basal, and vary from linear to obovate, sometimes with a silver stripe down the center. Smaller species are suitable for a rock garden, taller ones for a herbaceous border. In ideal growing conditions, *O. nutans* and *O. umbellatum* may become invasive but, as with *O. montanum*, may be suitable for naturalizing in short turf or beneath shrubs. Where not hardy, grow in a cool greenhouse, or grow outdoors and lift in autumn. All parts may cause severe discomfort if ingested, and the sap may irritate skin.
• **CULTIVATION** Plant bulbs 4in (10cm) deep. Outdoors, plant hardy species in autumn, in moderately fertile, well-drained soil, in a sunny situation. *O. nutans* and *O. umbellatum* tolerate partial shade. Plant tender species in spring for summer flowering; in growth, water freely and lift after flowering; keep frost-free over winter. Under glass, grow in large containers of soil-based potting mix, in full light with shade from hot sun. When in growth, water freely; keep dry when dormant, and repot annually in spring. *O. dubium* and *O. thyrsoides* may be planted under glass in autumn for spring bloom.
• **PROPAGATION** Sow seed in containers in a cold frame in autumn or spring. Remove offsets when dormant.

Ornithogalum dubium

Ornithogalum lanceolatum

• **PESTS AND DISEASES** Sometimes affected by leaf spot and rust.

O. arabicum. Bulbous perennial with basal rosettes of semi-erect, broadly linear, dark green leaves, to 24in (60cm) long. In early summer, bears corymb-like racemes of 6–25 cup-shaped, scented, white or cream flowers, 1¼in (3cm) across, each with a black ovary. ↕ 12–32in (30–80cm), PD3in (8cm). Mediterranean. ❀ (min. 41°F/5°C)
O. balansae, syn. *O. oligophyllum* of gardens. Slender, bulbous perennial with almost prostrate, inversely lance-shaped, glossy, mid-green, basal leaves, to 6in (15cm) long. In early spring, produces corymb-like racemes of 2–5 cup-shaped flowers, 1¼in (3cm) across, glistening white inside, bright green outside. ↕ to 3in (8cm), PD4in (10cm). Balkans, Turkey, Republic of Georgia. Zone 6.
O. caudatum see *O. longibracteatum.*
O. dubium ■ syn. *O. florescens*, *O. triniatum.* Bulbous perennial with almost prostrate, lance-shaped to ovate-lance-shaped, dark green to yellow-green basal leaves, 4in (10cm) long. From winter to spring, bears racemes of up to 25 star- to cup-shaped, yellow, orange, red, or rarely white flowers, 1in (2.5cm) across, with dark, almost black, ovaries. ↕ 8–12in (20–30cm), PD3in (8cm). Southern Africa. Zone 7b.
O. florescens see *O. dubium.*
O. lanceolatum ■ Dwarf, bulbous perennial producing basal rosettes of prostrate, lance-shaped, shiny, mid-green leaves, 4–5in (10–13cm) long. Compact, almost stemless racemes of 5–13 star-shaped white flowers, ¾–1¼in (2–3cm) across, striped green on the outsides, are borne in spring. ↕ 2–4in (5–10cm), PD4in (10cm). Turkey, Syria, Lebanon. Zone 6.
O. longibracteatum, syn. *O. caudatum* (False sea onion). Bulbous perennial with lax, strap-shaped, semi-succulent, pale green, basal leaves, to 24in (60cm) long. In summer, bears tall racemes of up to 300 bell-shaped white flowers, to ½in (1.5cm) across, striped green outside, with bracts extending far beyond the flowers. ↕ 3–5ft (1–1.5m), PD6in (15cm). Tropical Africa, South Africa (Northern Cape, Eastern Cape) ❀ (min. 41°F/5°C)
O. montanum ■ Bulbous perennial producing basal rosettes of prostrate,

Ornithogalum montanum

linear, shiny, pale to grayish green leaves, 4–6in (10–15cm) long. In spring, bears corymb-like racemes of 10–20 star-shaped white flowers, ¾in (2cm) across, striped green on the outsides. ↕ 4–10in (10–25cm), PD4in (10cm). S. Europe, Turkey, Lebanon, Israel. Zone 7.
O. narbonense ■ Bulbous perennial with semi-erect, linear, gray-green, basal leaves, to 24in (60cm) long. Produces upright, narrowly pyramidal racemes of 25–75 star-shaped white flowers, ¾in (2cm) across, in late spring and early summer. ↕ 12–36in (30–90cm), PD2in (5cm). Mediterranean, Turkey, Caucasus, Iran. Zone 7b.
O. nutans. Bulbous perennial with semi-erect, strap-shaped, bright mid-green, basal leaves, 12–16in (30–40cm) long, each with a central silver stripe above. In spring, bears one-sided racemes of up to 20 semi-pendent, funnel-shaped, silvery white flowers, 1¼in (3cm) across, broadly striped green outside. ↕ 8–24in (20–60cm), PD2in (5cm). Europe, S.W. Asia. Zone 5.
***O. oligophyllum* of gardens** see *O. balansae.*

Ornithogalum narbonense

Ornithogalum umbellatum

O. pyramidale. Bulbous perennial with basal clusters of semi-erect, linear, glossy, mid-green leaves, to 24in (60cm) long, which wither as the flowers open. In late spring and early summer, produces stiff racemes of numerous star-shaped white flowers, ½–¾in (1.5–2cm) across, striped green on the outsides. ↕ 12–48in (30–120cm), PD3in (8cm). C. Europe, Balkans. Zone 7.

O. pyrenaicum (Russian asparagus). Bulbous perennial with basal tufts of semi-erect, narrowly linear, gray-green leaves, 8–14in (20–35cm) long, often withering as the flowers open. Long racemes of 25–40 star-shaped, pale yellow flowers, to ½in (1.5cm) across, broadly or narrowly striped green outside, are produced in early summer. ↕ to 3ft (1m), PD4in (10cm). Europe, Turkey, Caucasus. Zone 7.

O. saundersiae (Giant chincherinchee). Robust, bulbous perennial with erect, strap-shaped, dark green, sometimes grayish green, basal leaves, 24in (60cm) long. In winter or spring, produces dense, corymb-like racemes of cup-shaped, white or creamy white flowers, ¾–1¼in (2–3cm) across, with black or greenish black ovaries. ↕ to 3ft (1m), PD4in (10cm). South Africa (Northern Transvaal, Eastern Transvaal, KwaZulu/Natal), Swaziland. ❀ (min. 41°F/5°C)

O. thyrsoides (Chincherinchee). Robust, bulbous perennial with semi-erect, linear to narrowly lance-shaped, mid-green, basal leaves, to 12in (30cm) long, with hairy margins, withering before the flowers open. In spring and early summer, produces dense racemes of many cup-shaped white flowers, ¾in (2cm) across, tinted cream or green at the bases. Excellent for cut flowers. ↕ to 28in (70cm), PD4in (10cm). South Africa (Western Cape). Zone 7b.

O. triniatum see *O. dubium*.

O. umbellatum ▣ (Dove's dung, Star-of-Bethlehem). Bulbous perennial with semi-erect, linear, white-veined, mid-green, basal leaves, to 12in (30cm) long, each with a central silver stripe above; the leaves wither as the flowers open in early summer. Produces corymb-like racemes of 6–20 long-stalked, star-shaped white flowers, ¾in (2cm) across, striped green outside. Increases rapidly and is often invasive in lawns and borders. ↕ 4–12in (10–30cm), PD4in (10cm). Europe, Turkey, Syria, Lebanon, Israel, N. Africa. Zone 4.

ORNITHOPHORA

ORCHIDACEAE

Genus of 1 or possibly 2 species of evergreen, epiphytic orchids from Brazil, occurring in warm, moist, forested areas. These orchids have slender, compressed, ovoid pseudobulbs, each with 2 linear leaves at the tip, and a fine mat of aerial roots. Tiny flowers are borne in slender racemes arising from the bases of the pseudobulbs, and resemble a swarm of insects hovering above the plant.

• **CULTIVATION** Cool- to intermediate-growing orchids. Grow in epiphytic orchid potting mix in shallow pots or slatted baskets, or epiphytically on slabs of bark. Provide high humidity and bright filtered light all year. In summer, mist daily, water freely, and apply a quarter-strength fertilizer at every third watering. Water more sparingly in winter; do not allow to dry out completely. See also p.46.

• **PROPAGATION** Divide when the plant fills the pot and flows over the sides.

• **PESTS AND DISEASES** Susceptible to spider mites, aphids, and mealybugs.

O. radicans, syn. *Sigmatostalix radicans*. Epiphytic orchid with grass-like leaves, 4–7in (10–18cm) long. In autumn, intricately patterned, slightly fragrant, white-green or green-yellow flowers, to ⅜in (9mm) across, with cream lips, are produced in racemes 3–6in (7–15cm) long. ↕ 4in (10cm), ↔ 12in (30cm). Brazil. ❀ (min. 55°F/13°C; max. 86°F/30°C)

▷ ***Orobus*** see *Lathyrus*

Orontium aquaticum

ORONTIUM

Golden club

ARACEAE

Genus of one species of marginal aquatic perennial from E. US. It has large, thick rhizomes producing oblong to narrowly elliptic, submerged, floating, or aerial leaves, and curious, pencil-like spadices that stand well above the water. Ideal for the margins of an informal pool, it associates well with waterside irises and primroses in early summer.

• **CULTIVATION** Grow in deep mud at a pool margin with ample room to spread, or in containers of loamy soil, in water no deeper than 18in (45cm), and in full sun to develop the glaucous leaves. Remove the short-lived flower spikes when they fade. See also pp.52–53.

• **PROPAGATION** Sow seed as soon as ripe in a cold frame in trays of soil-based seed-starting mix, and cover with no more than ½–1¼in (1.5–3cm) of water. Divide the rhizomes in spring.

• **PESTS AND DISEASES** Infrequent.

O. aquaticum ▣ Rhizomatous, marginal aquatic perennial with oblong to narrowly elliptic, submerged, aerial, or floating leaves, to 12in (30cm) long, dark green and glaucous, often purple-tinted beneath. From late spring to midsummer, bears small, bright yellow flowers near the tops of numerous cylindrical white spadices, 7in (18cm) tall. ↕ 12–18in (30–45cm), ↔ 24–30in (60–75cm). E. US. Zone 7.

OROSTACHYS

CRASSULACEAE

Genus of about 10 species of freely offsetting, monocarpic perennials, closely related to *Sedum*, from low to mountainous, rocky areas of Russia, China, North Korea, South Korea, and Japan. They have dense, hemispherical to spherical rosettes of fleshy leaves, and produce erect stems bearing terminal, spike-like racemes or panicles of short-stalked, star-shaped flowers during summer or autumn. The rosettes die after flowering and fruiting. Below 46°F (8°C), grow in a cool greenhouse; in warmer climates, grow in a bed or border with other succulents.

• **CULTIVATION** Under glass, grow in standard cactus potting mix in full light. From spring to autumn, water freely and apply a half-strength, balanced liquid fertilizer every 4 weeks. Keep almost dry in winter. Outdoors, grow in poor, well-drained soil in full sun. See also pp.48–49.

• **PROPAGATION** Sow seed at 55–64°F (13–18°C), or divide offsets, in spring.

• **PESTS AND DISEASES** Susceptible to mealybugs and root rot.

O. chanetii. Clump-forming, perennial succulent with a stoloniferous rootstock and compact, basal rosettes of linear, grayish green leaves, 1½in (4cm) long. Dense, pyramidal, spike-like racemes or panicles, to 8in (20cm) long, of star-shaped white flowers, ½–¾in (1.5–2cm) across, reddish pink outside, are borne in summer and autumn. ↕ to 8in (20cm), sometimes more, ↔ 4in (10cm). China. ❀ (min. 46°F/8°C)

O. iwarenge. Perennial succulent with rosettes of pink-tinged gray leaves. Pyramidal raceme of small white flowers, borne in late summer, can reach 4–5in (10–13cm) before withering, leaving the side rosettes to continue growing outward. ↕ 4–5in (10–13cm), ↔ 12in (30cm). Japan. Zone 5.

OROYA

CACTACEAE

Genus of 2 or 3 species of cacti from dry, stony slopes, screes, and cliffs, at altitudes to 13,000ft (4,000m), in Peru. They have flattened-spherical to very short-cylindrical, rarely offsetting stems with numerous warty ribs and spined areoles. Bell- or funnel-shaped flowers are usually borne in a ring around the crown of each stem in summer, followed by obovoid to ovoid red or yellow berries containing black-coated seeds. Where temperatures drop below 55°F (13°C), grow in a warm greenhouse or as houseplants; in warm, dry climates, use in a desert garden.

• **CULTIVATION** Under glass, grow in standard cactus potting mix in full light. From spring to autumn, water freely and apply a half-strength, balanced liquid fertilizer 3 or 4 times. Keep barely moist in winter. Outdoors, grow in sharply drained, neutral to slightly alkaline, poor, humus-rich soil in full sun. See also pp.48–49.

• **PROPAGATION** Sow seed at 64–70°F (18–21°C) in spring.

• **PESTS AND DISEASES** Susceptible to aphids while flowering.

O. neoperuviana see *O. peruviana*.

O. peruviana ▣ syn. *Oreocereus peruviana, Oroya neoperuviana.* Cactus

Oroya peruviana

O

producing solitary, dull green or bluish green stems, each with up to 35 rounded ribs notched into long tubercles. Linear areoles bear brownish yellow spines (10–30 radials, in comb-like formation, and up to 6 longer centrals). Bell-shaped, pale carmine-red to vermilion, usually yellow-based flowers, ½–1¼in (1.5–3cm) long, are borne in summer. ↕6–8in (15–20cm), occasionally more, ↔ to 6in (15cm). Peru. ❀ (min. 55°F/13°C); tolerates brief periods to 25°F (-4°C).

▷ ***Orphanidesia*** see *Epigaea*

ORTEGOCACTUS

CACTACEAE

Genus of one species of cactus, closely related to *Mammillaria*, from dry areas of S.W. Mexico. It has spherical to short-cylindrical stems, often offsetting to form small clusters, with spirally arranged, warty ribs and spined areoles. Solitary, funnel-shaped yellow flowers are produced in summer, followed by orange-yellow or dull red fruit. In areas where temperatures drop below 59°F (15°C), grow in a warm greenhouse; in warm, dry climates, grow in a border with other cacti, or in a raised bed or desert garden.

• **CULTIVATION** Under glass, grow in standard cactus potting mix in full light. From spring to early autumn, water freely and apply a half-strength, balanced liquid fertilizer every 4 or 5 weeks. Keep dry at other times. Outdoors, grow in moderately fertile, sharply drained, humus-rich, slightly acidic soil in full sun. See also pp.48–49.

• **PROPAGATION** Sow seed at 70°F (21°C) in spring.

• **PESTS AND DISEASES** Vulnerable to mealybugs and root rot.

O. macdougallii ■ syn. *Neobesseya macdougallii.* Clustering cactus with spherical to short-cylindrical, pale grayish green stems, 1¼–1½in (3–4cm) thick, covered with large, diamond-shaped tubercles. White-woolly areoles bear black-tipped, white or totally black spines (7 or 8 radials and 1 shorter central spine). Solitary, funnel-shaped yellow flowers, to 1¼in (3cm) long, the outer tepals tinted purple outside, in summer, followed by spherical-ellipsoid, orange-yellow or dull red fruit with black-coated seeds. ↕ to 2½in (6cm), ↔ 5in (13cm). S.W. Mexico. ❀ (min. 59°F/15°C); tolerates brief periods to 25°F (-4°C).

Ortegocactus macdougallii

ORTHOPHYTUM

BROMELIACEAE

Genus of about 18 species of mat-forming, evergreen, semi-succulent, terrestrial perennials (bromeliads) from dry, rocky slopes, to 4,000ft (1,200m) high, in E. Brazil. They spread by stolons to form wide rosettes of usually stemless, softly spiny leaves. In summer, they produce variably branched inflorescences with leafy bracts and small, dense clusters of slender, tubular, mainly white flowers. In areas where temperatures drop below 59°F (15°C), grow in a warm greenhouse; in warm, dry climates, use in a desert garden.

• **CULTIVATION** Under glass, grow in terrestrial bromeliad potting mix in full light. In the growing season, water moderately, applying a half-strength, balanced liquid fertilizer every 3 or 4 weeks. Keep plants dry in winter. Outdoors, grow in sharply drained, moderately fertile, humus-rich soil in full sun. See also p.47.

• **PROPAGATION** Sow seed at 81°F (27°C) in early spring. Separate offsets in spring.

• **PESTS AND DISEASES** Susceptible to aphids while flowering.

O. navioides, syn. *Cryptanthopsis navioides.* Stemless bromeliad that spreads by stolons to form clustered rosettes of narrowly lance-shaped, finely toothed, sparsely scaly, mid-green leaves, to 12in (30cm) long. In summer, tubular white flowers, to 1¼in (3cm) long, with pale yellowish green sepals and bracts, are produced in few-flowered clusters, sunk in the center of each rosette. The whole plant often turns bright red or red-purple as the flowers mature. ↕ to 8in (20cm), ↔ to 24in (60cm). E. Brazil. ❀ (min. 59°F/15°C)

Orthophytum vagans

O. saxicola. Stemless bromeliad, spreading by stolons to form large clusters of rosettes. Narrowly triangular, toothed, pale bright green leaves, 1¼–2½in (3–6cm) long, are usually thick and fleshy. In summer, bears head-like clusters of thick, fleshy bracts and short-stalked, tubular white flowers, to ¾in (2cm) long, with white-margined green sepals, and petals with 2 basal projections. Both bracts and flowers are almost hidden in the rosettes. ↕3in (8cm), ↔ indefinite. E. Brazil. ❀ (min. 59°F/15°C)

O. vagans ■ Trailing bromeliad with an elongated, branching caudex, the branches rooting down and forming large, spreading groups. Produces loosely rosetted rows of narrowly triangular, deeply channeled, slightly toothed, bright green leaves, to 4in (10cm) long, scaly beneath, turning red-purple with age. In summer, bears stemless inflorescences of red or orange bracts and 15–30 tubular, apple-green flowers, ¾in (2cm) long, with white-woolly sepals, on stalks 2in (5cm) long. ↕ to 8in (20cm), ↔ indefinite. E. Brazil. ❀ (min. 59°F/15°C)

ORTHROSANTHUS

IRIDACEAE

Genus of 7 species of evergreen perennials occurring in sandy soils in Australia and tropical America. They have narrowly strap-shaped or linear, rigid or arching leaves, arising from short, woody rhizomes. They are grown for their bowl-shaped to open saucer-shaped, 6-tepaled blue flowers, borne in loose, terminal panicles on slender, erect stalks. The flowers are short-lived, but open in succession from late spring to summer. Where not hardy, grow in a cool greenhouse; in warmer areas, grow in a warm, sunny border.

• **CULTIVATION** Under glass, grow in soil-based potting mix, with additional sharp sand and leaf mold, in full light. Water moderately during the growing season; keep almost dry when dormant. Repot or top-dress in spring. Outdoors, grow in light, fertile, well-drained, humus-rich soil in full sun.

• **PROPAGATION** Sow seed at 55–64°F (13–18°C), or divide, in spring.

• **PESTS AND DISEASES** Infrequent.

Orthrosanthus multiflorus

O. chimboracensis. Rhizomatous perennial with stiff, leathery, linear, basal leaves, to 16in (40cm) long, rough to the touch. Loose panicles of shallowly bowl-shaped, lavender-blue flowers, 1½in (4cm) across, are produced in summer. ↕12–24in (30–60cm), ↔ 12in (30cm). Mexico to Peru. ❀ (min. 45°F/7°C)

O. multiflorus ■ Rhizomatous perennial with rigid, linear, basal leaves, to 18in (45cm) long, with smooth margins. From late spring to summer, bears narrow panicles of open saucer-shaped, blue-violet flowers, to 1½in (4cm) across. ↕24in (60cm), ↔ 12in (30cm). S.W. Australia. ❀ (min. 45°F/7°C)

ORYCHOPHRAGMUS

BRASSICACEAE

Genus of 2 species of annuals or biennials occurring in fallow fields and on wasteland in C. Asia and China. They have thin, pinnatifid, lower leaves and entire stem-clasping leaves. Cross-shaped flowers, with 4-clawed violet petals, are produced in terminal racemes from late spring to summer. Grow outdoors as an annual or biennial, or, for flowers in winter and spring, grow in a cool or temperate greenhouse.

• **CULTIVATION** Outdoors, grow in fertile, well-drained soil in a warm, sunny site. Under glass, grow in soil-based potting mix in full light. In growth, water moderately.

• **PROPAGATION** Sow seed *in situ* in spring or early summer or, in frost-free climates, in autumn.

• **PESTS AND DISEASES** Infrequent.

O. violaceus. Upright annual or biennial, with moderately fast-growing, branching stems bearing thin, pinnatifid, pale green basal leaves, 5–6in (12–15cm) or more long, and smaller, entire, pale green stem leaves. In late spring and early summer, bears terminal racemes of 5–25 cross-shaped violet flowers, to 1in (2.5cm) across. ↕12–24in (30–60cm), ↔ 12in (30cm). China. ❀ (min. 45°F/7°C)

ORYZA
Rice

POACEAE

Genus of about 20 species of annual or perennial, rhizomatous grasses with flat, linear leaves, and panicles of laterally compressed spikelets producing rice-grain seeds when ripe. They are native to tropical and subtropical Africa and Asia, and are widely cultivated in subtropical and tropical regions. *O. sativa* 'Nigrescens' has unusually colored leaves, and is the only *Oryza* grown for ornamental reasons. Where not hardy, grow in a warm greenhouse or conservatory; in warmer areas, grow as a pond marginal or in a bog garden.
• **CULTIVATION** Under glass, provide full light and use soil-based potting mix in shallow clay pots, or in fiberglass trays with drainage holes. Keep the soil surface submerged to a depth of about 1in (2.5cm), and refresh water regularly; maintain water temperature at 68–86°F (20–30°C). Drain off as flowerheads form, and keep evenly moist. Algal growth on the soil surface is unsightly but not harmful. Outdoors, grow in very moist, fertile, clay-loam soil, or in pots at a pond margin, in full sun.
• **PROPAGATION** Surface-sow seed at 66–75°F (19–24°C) in late winter, in pots standing in containers of water.
• **PESTS AND DISEASES** Sheath rots, brown patch, glume blotch, and other leaf diseases are common.

***O. sativa* 'Nigrescens'.** Loosely tufted annual, rhizomatous grass with strong, erect stems bearing arching, broadly linear, dark brownish purple leaves, to 3ft (1m) long. From midsummer to midautumn, produces spikelets in open, arching panicles, 14in (35cm) long. ↕30in (75cm), ↔ 12in (30cm). S.E. Asia. ❀ (min. 50°F/10°C)

OSBECKIA

MELASTOMATACEAE

Genus of 40–60 species of evergreen perennials, subshrubs, and shrubs from Africa to China, and southward from Japan to Australia, where they thrive in habitats ranging from grassland to woodland. They are grown for their often showy, 4- or 5-petaled flowers, borne in terminal, leafy panicles or cymes, or sometimes singly, and for their simple, opposite, usually entire, somewhat leathery and bristly-hairy, strongly 3- to 7-veined leaves. Where temperatures fall below 55–59°F (13–15°C), grow in a warm greenhouse; in warmer climates, use in a border.
• **CULTIVATION** Under glass, grow in soil-based potting mix in bright filtered light or full light, with shade from hot sun. In growth, water freely and apply a balanced liquid fertilizer monthly; water moderately in winter. Outdoors, grow in fertile, moist but well-drained, humus-rich, neutral to acidic soil in partial shade or with some midday shade. Pruning group 9; plants under glass need restrictive pruning in early spring.
• **PROPAGATION** Sow seed at 64°F (18°C) in spring. Root semi-ripe cuttings with bottom heat in summer.
• **PESTS AND DISEASES** Prone to scale insects and spider mites under glass.

O. stellata. Erect shrub, spreading with age, with moderately branched, finely hairy stems and narrowly ovate, hairy-margined, deep green leaves, 2½–6in (6–15cm) long, with long, sharp points; each leaf has 5–7 prominent veins. Produces loose cymes of 4-petaled, saucer-shaped, blue-purple to reddish lilac, pink, or white flowers, 2in (5cm) across, mainly in summer. ↕4–6ft (1.2–1.8m), ↔ 3–5ft (1–1.5m). India to China. ❀ (min. 55°F/13°C)

▷ ***Oscularia deltoides*** see *Lampranthus deltoides*

OSMANTHUS
syn. × OSMAREA

OLEACEAE

Genus of about 15–20 species of evergreen shrubs and small trees from woodland in Asia, the Pacific islands, and S. US. They are grown for their foliage and flowers. The leaves are lance-shaped to ovate, borne in opposite pairs. The small, tubular, 4-lobed, usually fragrant, white, occasionally yellow or orange flowers are produced in mainly axillary clusters or terminal panicles. The flowers are usually followed by ovoid, blue-black fruits. *Osmanthus* species and cultivars are ideal for a shrub border or woodland garden. *O. delavayi* may be wall-trained; *O.* × *burkwoodii*, *O. delavayi*, and *O. heterophyllus* are very good for hedging and topiary. Where not hardy, grow in a cool or temperate greenhouse.
• **CULTIVATION** Outdoors, grow in fertile, well-drained, neutral to acid soil in sun or partial shade, with shelter from winter sun and wind. *O.* × *burkwoodii*, *O. delavayi*, and *O. yunnanensis* prefer alkaline or chalky soil. Under glass, grow in soil-based potting mix in full light with shade from hot sun. When in growth, water freely and apply a balanced liquid fertilizer monthly; water sparingly in winter. Pruning group 8 for early-flowering species; group 9 for late-flowering species; all tolerate hard pruning. Trim hedges after flowering, or in spring for *O. heterophyllus.*
• **PROPAGATION** Sow seed in containers in a cold frame as soon as ripe. Root semi-ripe cuttings in summer with bottom heat. Layer in autumn or spring.
• **PESTS AND DISEASES** Susceptible to black mildew, anthracnose, olive knot, *Verticillium* wilt, and root rot, as well as scale insects.

Osmanthus × *burkwoodii*

O. armatus. Dense, rounded shrub with oblong-lance-shaped, sharply spine-toothed, leathery, glossy, dark green leaves, to 6in (15cm) long. Broadly tubular, fragrant, creamy white flowers, with spreading lobes, to ¼in (6mm) across, are borne in axillary clusters in autumn, followed by ovoid, dark violet fruit, to ¾in (2cm) long. ↕8–15ft (2.5–5m), ↔ 12ft (4m). W. China. Zone 8.

O.* × *burkwoodii ▣ (*O. decorus* × *O. delavayi*), syn. × *Osmarea* × *burkwoodii.* Dense, rounded shrub with oval to ovate, slightly toothed, leathery, glossy, dark green leaves, to 2in (5cm) long. Tubular, very fragrant white flowers, the lobes to ¼in (6mm) across, are profusely borne in small, axillary clusters in mid- and late spring. Seldom produces fruit. ↕↔ 10ft (3m). Garden origin. Zone 7.

O. decorus, syn. *Phillyrea decora.* Dense, rounded, spreading shrub with narrowly oval to oblong, pointed, leathery, glossy, dark green leaves, to 5in (13cm) long, very rarely with a few teeth. Tubular white flowers, the lobes to ⅜in (9mm) across, are borne in dense, axillary clusters in midspring, followed by ellipsoid, blue-black fruit, to ½in (1.5cm) long. ↕10ft (3m), ↔ 15ft (5m). Republic of Georgia, N.E. Turkey. Zone 7.

O. delavayi ▣ syn. *Siphonosmanthus delavayi.* Rounded, bushy shrub with arching branches and ovate, finely toothed, leathery, glossy, dark green leaves, to 1in (2.5cm) long. Tubular, very fragrant white flowers, the lobes to ½in (1.5cm) across, are borne in axillary and terminal clusters in mid- and late spring, followed by ovoid, blue-black fruit, to ½in (1.5cm) long. ↕6–20ft (2–6m), ↔ 12ft (4m) or more. W. China (Sichuan, Yunnan). Zone 7.

O. forrestii see *O. yunnanensis.*

O.* × *fortunei (*O. fragrans* × *O. heterophyllus*). Upright shrub with holly-like, oval to ovate, leathery, glossy, dark green leaves, to 4in (10cm) long, with spiny margins, but spineless toward the tops of mature plants. Tubular, fragrant white flowers, the lobes to ½in (1.5cm) across, are produced in axillary clusters from late summer to autumn. Seldom produces fruit. ↕to 6ft (2m), sometimes to 20ft (6m), ↔ 15ft (5m). Garden origin. ❀ (min. 41°F/5°C). **'San José'** has narrower, more spiny leaves.

O. fragrans (Fragrant olive, Sweet olive). Vigorous, upright shrub or small tree

Osmanthus delavayi

Osmanthus heterophyllus 'Aureomarginatus'

with oblong to oblong-lance-shaped, leathery, entire or finely toothed, glossy, dark green leaves, 4–5in (10–13cm) long. Tubular, very fragrant white flowers, the lobes to ½in (1.5cm) across, appear singly or in few-flowered, axillary clusters from autumn to spring; they are followed by ovoid, blue-black fruit, to ½in (1.5cm) long. ↕↔ 20ft (6m). Himalayas, China, Japan. ❀ (min. 41°F/5°C). **f. *aurantiacus*** has orange flowers.

O. heterophyllus (False holly). Dense, rounded shrub with holly-like, oval to elliptic-oblong, sharply toothed, leathery, glossy, dark green leaves, to 2½in (6cm) long, often spineless on mature plants. Tubular, fragrant white flowers, the lobes to ¼in (6mm) across, are borne in small, axillary clusters from late summer to autumn, followed by ovoid, blue-black fruit, to ½in (1.5cm) long. ↕↔ 15ft (5m). Japan, Taiwan. Zone 7. **'Aureomarginatus'** ▣ syn. 'Aureus', has yellow-margined leaves. **'Goshiki'** ▣ is compact and mound-forming, with pink-tinged young foliage, creamy yellow-splotched and dark green when mature; ↕3½ft (1.1m), ↔ 3–5ft (1–1.5m). **'Gulftide'** is

Osmanthus heterophyllus 'Goshiki'

Osmanthus heterophyllus 'Purpureus'

compact, with very spiny leaves; ↕ 8ft (2.5m), ↔ 10ft (3m). **'Kembu'** is dwarf in habit, with irregularly shaped, white-variegated, dark green leaves; ↕↔ 24in (60cm). **'Myrtifolius'** has entire, spine-tipped leaves, to 2in (5cm) long; ↕↔ 10ft (3m). **'Ogon'** has bright gold new leaves, fading to gold-green; grow in partial shade. **'Purpureus'** ■ has dark blackish purple young leaves. **'Rotundifolius'** has small, spineless leaves, to 1½in (4cm) long, rounded at the tips; ↕↔ 10ft (3m).
O. yunnanensis, syn. *O. forrestii.* Large shrub or small tree, broadly upright at first, later spreading. The oblong to ovate-lance-shaped, spiny-toothed to entire leaves, to 8in (20cm) long, have long, sharp points and are leathery, glossy, dark green, spotted black beneath. Broadly tubular, very fragrant, creamy white flowers, with lobes to ⅜in (9mm) across, are borne in small, axillary clusters in late winter and early spring; they are followed by ovoid, dark purple fruit, to ½in (1.5cm) long, with a white bloom. ↕↔ 30ft (10m) or more. W. China. Zone 8.

▷ **x *Osmarea*** see *Osmanthus*
▷ ***Osmaronia*** see *Oemleria*

OSMUNDA

OSMUNDACEAE

Genus of about 12 species of deciduous, terrestrial ferns found in damp places and watersides in all continents except Australasia. Broadly lance-shaped to triangular-ovate or ovate, pinnate, 2-pinnate, or 2-pinnatifid sterile fronds arise from large, erect rhizomes and turn yellow or golden brown in autumn. Distinctive, partially or wholly fertile fronds produce branched clusters of spherical greenish sporangia, which turn rust-brown or blackish on reduced pinnae. Grow in a damp border, or at the margins of a pond or stream, where many, especially *O. regalis*, make a striking focal point near a waterside.
• **CULTIVATION** Grow in moist, fertile, humus-rich, preferably acidic soil, in light, dappled shade, although many are perfectly sited in full sun. (*O. regalis* does well in full sun as long as water is plentiful, since it prefers a wetter site.)
• **PROPAGATION** Sow spores at 59–61°F (15–16°C) within 3 days of ripening in summer; they lose viability quickly. Divide clumps from established colonies in autumn or early spring. See also p.51.
• **PESTS AND DISEASES** Prone to rust.

Osmunda regalis

O. cinnamomea (Cinnamon fern). Deciduous fern bearing shuttlecocks of ovate-lance-shaped, pinnate, pale green sterile fronds, 2–5ft (0.6–1.5m) long, with pinnatifid segments, surrounding much narrower, erect fertile fronds, to 3ft (1m) long. The top of each fertile frond is a mass of cinnamon-brown sporangia in spring. ↕ 36in (90cm), ↔ 24in (60cm). E. North America. Zone 4.
O. claytoniana (Interrupted fern). Deciduous fern bearing shuttlecocks of ovate-lance-shaped, pinnate, pale green sterile fronds, to 36in (90cm) long, with pinnatifid segments; they surround taller fertile fronds, similar but with some of the middle pinnae reduced and, in late spring, covered in sporangia, which are initially blackish, later yellow-green, then rust-brown. ↕ 36in (90cm), ↔ 24in (60cm). E. North America. Zone 4.
O. regalis ■ (Flowering fern, Royal fern). Deciduous fern producing dense clumps of broadly triangular-ovate, 2-pinnate, bright green sterile fronds, 3ft (1m) or more long. In summer, partially fertile fronds, to 6ft (2m) long, have tassel-like tips, with brown or rust-colored sporangia covering the much smaller pinnae. The fibrous rootstock is the source of osmunda fiber, used as a potting mix for orchids. ↕ 6ft (2m), ↔ 12ft (4m). Temperate and subtropical regions. Zone 4. **'Cristata'** has pinnae and segments with crested tips; ↕↔ 4ft (1.2m). **'Purpurascens'** bears red-purple-flushed fronds in spring; ↕↔ 4ft (1.2m). **'Undulata'** bears fronds with wavy segments; ↕↔ 4ft (1.2m).

OSTEOMELES

ROSACEAE

Genus of 3 species of deciduous, semi-evergreen, or evergreen shrubs or small trees from river valleys in China, Japan, Hawaii, and New Zealand. They have alternate, finely pinnate leaves and terminal corymbs of small, cup-shaped, 5-petaled white flowers, followed by

Osteomeles schweriniae

spherical to ovoid, red-brown, black, or blue-black fruits, to ⅜in (9mm) across. They are best grown in a sheltered shrub border or against a wall. Where not hardy, grow in a cool greenhouse.
• **CULTIVATION** Outdoors, grow in fertile, well-drained soil in full sun or partial shade, sheltered from strong, cold winds. Under glass, grow in soil-based potting mix in full light. In growth, water freely and apply a balanced liquid fertilizer monthly; water sparingly in winter. Pruning group 8; may need restrictive pruning under glass.
• **PROPAGATION** Sow seed in containers in a cold frame in autumn. Take semi-ripe cuttings in summer.
• **PESTS AND DISEASES** Infrequent.

O. schweriniae ■ Deciduous or semi-evergreen, arching shrub with long, slender shoots and ovate to oblong-ovate, pinnate leaves, to 3in (8cm) long, consisting of 15–31 ovate-oblong leaflets. In early summer, small, cup-shaped white flowers, to ½in (1.5cm) across, are produced in corymbs, to 3in (8cm) across, at the shoot tips; they are followed by spherical, red-brown, later blue-black fruit. ↕↔ 10ft (3m). S.W. China (Yunnan). Zone 7b.

OSTEOSPERMUM

ASTERACEAE

Genus of about 70 species of evergreen subshrubs, perennials, and annuals, mostly from southern Africa, but also from the Arabian Peninsula, mainly found in grassland, on rocky mountains, or at forest margins. The alternate leaves are linear to broadly obovate, with entire, toothed, or lobed margins. Osteospermums are grown for their daisy-like, usually white, pink, or yellow flowerheads, sometimes with disk florets in a contrasting color, borne singly or in open panicles from late spring to autumn. Numerous cultivars have been selected and named; they have ray florets varying from deep magenta through deep or pale pink to white or yellow. Grow in a border; where not hardy, they are best grown as annuals.
• **CULTIVATION** Grow in light, moderately fertile, well-drained soil in a warm, sheltered site in full sun. Deadhead regularly to prolong flowering. Where not hardy, propagate annually and overwinter in frost-free conditions.
• **PROPAGATION** Sow seed at 64°F (18°C) in spring. In late spring, root softwood cuttings; root semi-ripe cuttings in late summer.
• **PESTS AND DISEASES** Prone to aphids, downy mildew, and *Verticillium* wilt.

***O. barberae* of gardens** see *O. jucundum.*
***O.* 'Bodegas Pink'.** Semi-upright subshrub with mostly inversely lance-shaped, toothed, mid-green leaves with pale yellow margins. From late spring to autumn, bears solitary flowerheads, 2in (5cm) across, with mauve-pink ray florets, mauve-purple on the reverse, and dark bluish mauve disk florets. ↕↔ 18in (45cm). ❄ (min. 45°F/7°C)
***O.* 'Buttermilk'** ■ Upright subshrub with mostly inversely lance-shaped, sparsely toothed, mid-green leaves. Solitary flowerheads, 2in (5cm) across, with white-based, primrose-yellow ray florets, bronze-yellow on the reverse, and dark bluish mauve disk florets, are borne from late spring to autumn. ↕↔ 24in (60cm). ❄ (min. 45°F/7°C)
***O.* 'Cannington Roy'.** Densely spreading subshrub with obovate, sparsely toothed, mid-green leaves. From late spring to autumn, bears solitary flowerheads, 2in (5cm) across, with purple-tipped white ray florets that age to mauve-pink, mauve-purple on the reverse, and with purple disk florets. Good as a groundcover. ↕ 6in (15cm), ↔ 24in (60cm). ❄ (min. 45°F/7°C)
O. caulescens, syn. *O. ecklonis* var. *prostratum* of gardens. Prostrate subshrub with inversely lance-shaped, toothed, mid-green leaves, to 4in (10cm) long. From late spring to autumn, bears solitary flowerheads, 2–2½in (5–6cm) across, with white ray florets, flushed purple on the reverse, and blue-gray disk florets. ↕ 4in (10cm), ↔ 24in (60cm). South Africa. ❄ (min. 45°F/7°C)
O. ecklonis, syn. *Dimorphotheca ecklonis.* Variable, erect to almost prostrate subshrub with inversely lance-shaped, toothed, gray-green leaves, to 4in (10cm) long. From late spring to autumn, bears solitary flowerheads, 2–3in (5–8cm) across, with white ray florets, indigo-blue on the reverse, and dark blue disk florets. ↕ 2–5ft (0.6–1.5m), ↔ 24–48in (0.6–1.2m). South Africa (Eastern Cape). ❄ (min. 45°F/7°C). **'Blue Streak'** has slate-blue disk florets and white ray florets, slate-blue on the reverse; ↕↔ 24in (60cm). **var. *prostratum* of gardens** see *O. caulescens.* **'Silver Sparkler'** has leaves edged and marked pale yellow.

Osteospermum 'Buttermilk'

Osteospermum jucundum

O. fruticosum. Woody-based perennial with erect or decumbent stems and obovate to spoon-shaped, slightly fleshy, entire or minutely toothed, mid-green leaves, to 4in (10cm) long, mainly in basal rosettes. Solitary flowerheads, 2½–3in (6–8cm) across, the ray florets white with purple bases, the disk florets purplish violet, are borne from late spring to midautumn. ↕ to 24in (60cm), ↔ 30in (75cm). South Africa (Western Cape, Eastern Cape, KwaZulu/Natal). ❄ (min. 45°F/7°C)

O. jucundum ■ syn. *Dimorphotheca barberae* of gardens, *O. barberae* of gardens. Neat, clump-forming perennial, spreading by surface rhizomes, with linear to inversely lance-shaped, entire or sparsely toothed, grayish green leaves, to 3–4in (8–10cm) long. From late spring to autumn, bears solitary, long-stalked flowerheads, 2in (5cm) across, with mauve-pink to magenta-purple ray florets, bronze-purple to purple-pink on the reverse, and purple disk florets that age to gold. ↕ 4–20in (10–50cm), ↔ 20–36in (50–90cm). South Africa (Northern Transvaal, Orange Free State, KwaZulu/Natal), Swaziland, Lesotho. ❄ (min. 45°F/7°C). **var. *compactum***

Osteospermum 'Whirligig'

forms neat, compact mats; ↕ 4–8in (10–20cm). **var. *compactum* 'Blackthorn'**, syn. var. *compactum* 'Blackthorn Seedling', has dark purple florets.

***O.* 'Nairobi Purple'** ■ syn. *O.* 'Tresco Purple'. Spreading subshrub with broadly obovate to spoon-shaped, sparsely toothed, bright green leaves, and purplish green stems. From late spring to autumn, bears dark purple flowerheads, 2in (5cm) across, with purple ray florets, flushed white on the reverse, and black disk florets. ↕ 6in (15cm), ↔ 36in (90cm). ❄ (min. 45°F/7°C)

***O.* 'Tauranga'** see *O.* 'Whirligig'.

***O.* 'Tresco Purple'** see *O.* 'Nairobi Purple'.

***O.* 'Whirligig'** ■ syn. *O.* 'Tauranga'. Spreading subshrub with inversely lance-shaped, toothed, gray-green leaves. From late spring to autumn, bears solitary flowerheads, 2–3in (5–8cm) across, with crimped and spoon-shaped white ray florets, slate-blue or powder-blue on the reverse, and slate-blue disk florets. ↕↔ 24in (60cm). ❄ (min. 45°F/7°C)

OSTROWSKIA

Giant bellflower

CAMPANULACEAE

Genus of one species of taprooted perennial from well-drained, stony hillsides in Uzbekistan and Tajikistan. It has thick, unbranched stems that produce whorls of ovate, toothed leaves, and is grown mainly for its racemes of outward-facing, bell-shaped, deep to pale milky-blue flowers. Grow in a sunny, herbaceous or mixed border.

• **CULTIVATION** Grow in deep, moderately fertile, moist but well-drained soil in full sun. Dies back soon after flowering; when dormant, protect from moisture, and provide a deep, dry winter mulch.

• **PROPAGATION** Sow seed singly in containers in a cold frame as soon as ripe; only seed leaves are produced in the first year. Take care to avoid root damage when potting on and planting out. May produce flowers in the third or fourth year. Take root cuttings in late autumn; they may be slow to become established.

• **PESTS AND DISEASES** Susceptible to slug damage.

O. magnifica ■ Erect, clump-forming perennial with thick, unbranched stems bearing whorls of 4 or 5 ovate, toothed, hairless, somewhat glaucous leaves, 4–6in (10–15cm) long. In early and midsummer, produces few-flowered racemes of outward-facing, open bell-shaped, silver-sheened, pale to deep milky-blue or pale purple flowers, 5–6in (12–15cm) across, veined and suffused lilac. ↕ to 5ft (1.5m), ↔ 18in (45cm). Uzbekistan, Tajikistan. Zone 7b.

OSTRYA

BETULACEAE

Genus of approximately 10 species of monoecious, deciduous trees occurring in woodland in Europe, Asia, North America, and Central America. They have simple, ovate to ovate-oblong, or ovate-lance-shaped leaves, arranged alternately. The flowers are produced in catkins, males and females on the same tree, but only the males are conspicuous. Female catkins develop into hop-like fruits in late summer. They are excellent specimen trees for a woodland garden.

• **CULTIVATION** Grow in fertile, well-drained soil in sun or partial shade. Pruning group 1.

• **PROPAGATION** Sow seed as soon as ripe in containers in a cold frame or seedbed.

• **PESTS AND DISEASES** Canker, dieback, powdery mildew, leaf curl, leaf spots, and scale insects may occur.

O. carpinifolia (European hop hornbeam). Broadly conical to rounded tree with hairy shoots and ovate, doubly toothed, lustrous, dark green leaves, to 4in (10cm) long, each with 15–20 pairs of veins; the leaves turn yellow in autumn. Pendulous, yellow male catkins, to 3in (8cm) long, are formed in autumn and open in midspring. Hop-like white fruit clusters, 2in (5cm) long, develop in summer and turn brown in autumn. ↕↔ 70ft (20m). S. Europe, Turkey, Syria, Caucasus. Zone 6.

O. virginiana ■ (American hop hornbeam, Ironwood). Conical tree with glandular-hairy shoots and ovate-lance-shaped, sharply, sometimes doubly toothed, dark green leaves, to 5in (13cm) long, each with 11–15 pairs of veins. Pendulous, yellow male catkins, to 2in (5cm) long, are formed in autumn and open in midspring; hop-like white fruit clusters, to 2in (5cm) long, develop in summer and turn brown in autumn. ↕ 50ft (15m), ↔ 40ft (12m). E. North America. Zone 3. **var. *glandulosa*** has shoots and leaves more glandular-hairy than the species.

OTHONNA

ASTERACEAE

Genus of about 150 species of evergreen or deciduous, shrubby, succulent perennials and small shrubs, often arising from caudices or thick, tuberous rootstocks. They are found in dry, hilly areas of Tunisia, Algeria, Namibia, and South Africa. They have entire or dissected, fleshy leaves, which are lobed or toothed, and terminal, daisy-like, usually yellow, rarely white or purple flowerheads, produced singly or in corymbs from summer to winter. In areas where temperatures drop below 50°F (10°C), grow tender species as houseplants or in a temperate green-house; in warm, dry climates, use in a desert border. Grow *O. cheirifolia* in a raised bed or rock garden, or in a sunny border.

• **CULTIVATION** Under glass, grow in standard cactus potting mix in full light. Water moderately during the growing season, more sparingly in winter. Apply a balanced liquid fertilizer 3 or 4 times during summer and autumn. Outdoors, grow in sharply drained, moderately fertile, gritty soil in full sun. See also pp.48–49.

• **PROPAGATION** Sow seed at 64–70°F (18–21°C) in spring. Insert basal or semi-ripe cuttings with bottom heat in late summer. Take basal cuttings of *O. cheirifolia* in early summer.

• **PESTS AND DISEASES** Prone to spider mites and aphids.

Osteospermum 'Nairobi Purple'

Ostrowskia magnifica

Ostrya virginiana

Othonna cheirifolia

Othonna herrei

O. capensis (Little pickles). Evergreen, perennial succulent with cylindrical to cylindrical-obovoid, entire, fleshy, pale green leaves, to 1in (2.5cm) long, often clustered on slender, trailing stems. In summer, bears few-flowered corymbs of yellow flowerheads, ½in (1.5cm) across, which open only in sun. Excellent for a hanging basket. ↕ 8in (20cm), ↔ 3ft (1m). South Africa (Eastern Cape). ❄ (min. 41°F/5°C)
O. cheirifolia ▣ syn. *Othonnopsis cheirifolia*. Spreading, evergreen shrub with branching stems bearing lance- to spoon-shaped, entire, fleshy, pale gray-green leaves, to 3in (8cm) long. In summer, bears solitary, yellow flowerheads, about 1½in (4cm) across. ↕ 12in (30cm), ↔ 24in (60cm). N. Africa. ❄ (min. 35°F/2°C)
O. herrei ▣ Deciduous, perennial succulent with thickened stems and prominent, woody nodules formed from persistent leaf bases. Bears irregularly obovate, wavy-margined, toothed, fleshy, bluish green leaves, 2in (5cm) long, at the tips of short branches. Produces corymbs of yellow flowerheads, ¾in (2cm) across, in late autumn and early winter. ↕↔ 4in (10cm). Namibia, South Africa (Northern Cape). ❄ (min. 45–50°F/7–10°C)

▷ ***Othonnopsis cheirifolia*** see *Othonna cheirifolia*

OURISIA

SCROPHULARIACEAE

Genus of approximately 25 species of low-growing, mainly rhizomatous, evergreen or semi-evergreen perennials occurring in alpine regions of Tasmania, New Zealand, South America, and Antarctica. They have mostly radical leaves, which are usually conspicuously veined, but are cultivated for their usually short-tubed flowers, each with 5 spreading lobes, the 3 lower lobes larger than the upper 2. The flowers are borne singly from the leaf axils, or in whorls or racemes on leafless stems. Ourisias grow best in cool, moist climates, and are suitable for a shady rock garden or wall, or an alpine house.
• **CULTIVATION** Grow in reliably moist, fertile, humus-rich soil in partial shade. Rhizomatous species quickly exhaust soil nutrients, so divide and replant them when they begin to deteriorate. In an alpine house, grow in a mix of 1 part each loam and grit with 2 parts leaf

Ourisia macrophylla

mold, and keep slightly moist in winter; they resent a dry atmosphere.
• **PROPAGATION** Sow seed in containers in a cold frame, as soon as ripe or in early spring. Divide rhizomatous species, or separate rooted sections, in spring. Take stem-tip cuttings of *O. microphylla* in early summer.
• **PESTS AND DISEASES** Often damaged by slugs and snails.

O. caespitosa. Dwarf, mat-forming, evergreen perennial with broadly ovate-spoon-shaped, entire or notched, gray-green leaves, ⅛–⅜in (3–9mm) long. Leafless stems bear up to 5-flowered whorls of tubular, yellow-throated white flowers, to ½in (1.5cm) across, in early summer. ↕ 2in (5cm), ↔ to 8in (20cm). New Zealand. Zone 6. **var. *gracilis*** is more compact, with leaves to ¼in (6mm) long, and solitary flowers; ↕ 1¼in (3cm), ↔ 6in (15cm).
O. coccinea. Mat-forming, evergreen perennial with rosettes of broadly elliptic or oblong, toothed, strongly veined, light green leaves, ⅛–¼in (3–6mm) long. Throughout summer, produces loose, terminal racemes of pendent, long-tubed, noticeably 2-lipped scarlet flowers, to 1½in (4cm) long. May spread widely in cool, moist areas. ↕ 8in (20cm), ↔ 16in (40cm) or more. Chilean Andes. Zone 7b.
***O.* 'Loch Ewe'.** Vigorous, spreading, evergreen perennial, similar to *O. coccinea*, with tight rosettes of broadly oval, leathery, mid-green leaves, 1¼–2½in (3–6cm) long, heart-shaped at the bases. Dense, spike-like racemes of tubular, clear pale pink flowers, 1in (2.5cm) across, are borne in late spring and early summer. ↕ to 8in (20cm), ↔ 12in (30cm). Zone 7b.
O. macrocarpa. Vigorous, upright, evergreen perennial with ovate-oblong to rounded, scalloped, leathery, dark green leaves, to ½in (1.5cm) long. Bears whorls of tubular flowers, ½–1in (1.5–2.5cm) across, sometimes yellow-throated, from spring to summer. ↕ to 24in (60cm), ↔ 12in (30cm). New Zealand. Zone 7.
O. macrophylla ▣ Mat-forming, evergreen, rhizomatous perennial with ovate to rounded-oblong, coarsely veined, bright green leaves, to 9in (23cm) long. Upright stems produce whorled racemes of many yellow-throated white flowers, to ¾in (2cm) across, in summer. ↕ 12in (30cm) or more, ↔ 16in (40cm) or more. New Zealand. Zone 7b.
O. microphylla ▣ Cushion-forming, semi-evergreen perennial with slender, branching stems clothed in heath-like, pale green leaves, 1⁄16in (2mm) long, pressed closely to the stems. In late spring and early summer, produces a profusion of solitary, small, tubular, pale pink flowers, ½in (1.5cm) across, with white centers. ↕ 2in (5cm), ↔ to 6in (15cm). Chile, Argentina. Zone 6.
***O.* 'Snowflake'.** Robust, mat-forming, evergreen perennial, similar to *O. caespitosa*, with obovate, spoon-shaped, glossy, dark green leaves, to ½in (1.5cm) long. Clusters of tubular white flowers, ½–¾in (1.5–2cm) across, are produced in summer. ↕ 4in (10cm), ↔ to 10in (25cm). Zone 7b.

Ourisia microphylla

OXALIS

Shamrock, Sorrel

OXALIDACEAE

Genus of about 500 species of fibrous-rooted, bulbous, rhizomatous, or tuberous annuals and perennials, some of which are very invasive weeds. They occur in open habitats or in woodland, and are widely distributed, with many species from southern Africa and South America. Those grown as ornamentals are valued for their palmate, often clover-like foliage (some have leaves that fold at night), and for their funnel- to cup- or bowl-shaped, 5-petaled flowers; these are furled umbrella-like in bud, are borne singly or in cymes, sometimes umbel-like, and usually open only in sunlight, closing in dull weather or at night. Woodland species, such as *O. acetosella* and *O. oregana*, are suitable for naturalizing in a shady site. Many of the hardy species from southern Africa and South America, as well as various cultivars, are suitable for a rock garden, raised bed, trough, or alpine house. Where not hardy, grow in a temperate or warm greenhouse.
• **CULTIVATION** Grow hardy woodland species in moist, fertile, humus-rich soil in full or partial shade. Other hardy species need full sun and well-drained, moderately fertile, humus-rich soil. Under glass, grow in soil-based potting mix with added grit, in bright filtered light and low humidity. When in growth, water moderately and apply a balanced liquid fertilizer every month. Keep all container-grown plants barely moist when dormant. In an alpine house, grow in a mix of equal parts loam, leaf mold, and grit.
• **PROPAGATION** Sow seed at 55–64°F (13–18°C) in late winter or early spring. Divide in spring; small sections of rhizomatous species root readily with bottom heat.
• **PESTS AND DISEASES** Rust, seed smut, powdery mildew, and fungal leaf spots are common. Leaf miners and spider mites are sometimes problems.

O. acetosella* var. *purpurascens see *O. acetosella* var. *subpurpurascens*.
O. acetosella* var. *rosea see *O. acetosella* var. *subpurpurascens*.
O. acetosella* var. *subpurpurascens ▣ syn. *O. acetosella* var. *purpurascens*, *O. acetosella* var. *rosea* (Irish shamrock). Mat-forming, rhizomatous perennial

Oxalis acetosella var. *subpurpurascens*

Oxalis adenophylla

with clover-like, pale green leaves, each with 3 inversely heart-shaped, sparsely hairy leaflets, to ¾in (2cm) long. Bears solitary, cup-shaped, dark-veined, rose-pink flowers, ¾in (2cm) across, in spring. ↕ 2in (5cm), ↔ indefinite. N. hemisphere. Zone 4.

O. adenophylla ▣ Clump-forming perennial with fiber-covered bulbs that produce gray-green leaves, each consisting of 9–22 narrowly and inversely heart-shaped leaflets, to ¾in (2cm) long. In late spring, bears solitary, widely funnel-shaped, purplish pink flowers, about 1in (2.5cm) across, with darker veins and purple throats. ↕ 4in (10cm), ↔ to 6in (15cm). Andes, Chile, Argentina. Zone 5.

O. bowiei, syn. *O. purpurata* var. *bowiei*. Clump-forming, bulbous perennial with long-stalked, clover-like, leathery leaves, each with 3 rounded to inversely heart-shaped, notched leaflets, ½–1in (1.5–2.5cm) long, mid-green above, hairy and often purple beneath. Bears loose, umbel-like cymes of 3–12 funnel-shaped, deep purplish pink flowers, to 1½in (4cm) across, with yellow-green tubes, in summer. Very similar to *O. purpurata*, which produces runners and may be invasive. ↕ to 10in (25cm), ↔ to 6in (15cm). South Africa (Western Cape, Eastern Cape, KwaZulu/Natal). ❀ (min. 35°F/2°C)

O. carnosa see *O. megalorrhiza*.

O. chrysantha. Fibrous-rooted, mat-forming perennial with creeping and rooting, slender stems and white-hairy, light green leaves, each divided into 3 triangular to inversely heart-shaped leaflets, ⅜in (9mm) long. Produces

Oxalis depressa

Oxalis enneaphylla 'Rosea'

solitary, funnel-shaped, bright yellow flowers, ½–¾in (1.5–2cm) across, with red markings at the mouths, in summer and autumn. ↕ 2in (5cm), ↔ 12in (30cm) or more. Brazil. ❀ (min. 35°F/2°C)

O. deppei see *O. tetraphylla*.

O. depressa ▣ syn. *O. inops*. Clump-forming, bulbous perennial with short runners and short-stalked, sometimes sparsely hairy and dark-spotted, gray-green leaves, each divided into 3 triangular-obovate leaflets, to ½in (1.5cm) long. In summer, bears solitary, widely funnel-shaped, deep rose-pink to purple-pink flowers, to ¾in (2cm) across, with yellow tubes. ↕ 2in (5cm), ↔ to 8in (20cm) or more. Southern Africa. Zone 6.

O. enneaphylla. Clump-forming perennial with scaly, branching rhizomes, producing tufts of umbrella-like, somewhat fleshy, hairy, blue-gray leaves, each consisting of 9–20 narrowly oblong, pleated leaflets, to ¾in (2cm) long. Solitary, widely funnel-shaped, fragrant, white to deep red-pink flowers, ¾–1in (2–2.5cm) across, are produced in late spring and early summer. ↕ 3in (8cm), ↔ to 6in (15cm). Patagonia, Falkland Islands. Zone 7. **'Minutifolia'** has a more compact habit, with much smaller leaflets, to ½in (1.5cm) long, and white flowers; ↕ 2in (5cm), ↔ 4in (10cm). **'Rosea'** ▣ has light purple-pink flowers.

O. hedysaroides. Semi-evergreen subshrub with upright, branching, leafy stems, bearing light green leaves, glaucous beneath, each with 3 broadly ovate leaflets, to 1in (2.5cm) long. Produces axillary cymes of 3–6 widely funnel-shaped yellow flowers, to ½in (1.5cm) across, in summer. Suitable for a cool greenhouse. ↕ to 3ft (1m), ↔ to 18in (45cm). Central America. ❀ (min. 41°F/5°C). **'Rubra'** (Firefern) has red leaves.

O. herrerae, syn. *O. succulenta*. Erect, succulent perennial with short-branched, scaly stems. Bears clusters of broad, hairless, mid-green leaves, each with 3 inversely heart-shaped, fleshy leaflets, to ½in (1.5cm) long, often slightly hairy beneath, on stalks ¾–2in (2–5cm) long. Short-branched cymes of 5–7 bowl-shaped, red-veined yellow flowers, to ½in (1.5cm) across, appear in summer. ↕ to 12in (30cm), ↔ 8in (20cm). Peru, Chile. ❀ (min. 50°F/10°C)

O. hirta. Variable, bulbous perennial with upright or decumbent, leafy stems bearing almost stalkless, hairy, pale green leaves, each with 3 linear to oblong or obovate leaflets, to ½in (1.5cm) long. In autumn and winter, bears solitary, open funnel-shaped, white, red-pink, or purple flowers, ¾in (2cm) across, with yellow throats. Best in a cool greenhouse where not hardy. ↕ 12in (30cm), ↔ 4in (10cm). South Africa (Western Cape). ❀ (min. 41°F/5°C)

O. inops see *O. depressa*.

***O.* 'Ione Hecker'.** Clump-forming, rhizomatous perennial, similar to *O. enneaphylla*, with gray-green leaves, each consisting of 9–15 narrowly oblong leaflets, to ½in (1.5cm) long. In summer, produces solitary, widely funnel-shaped, blue-violet flowers, to 1¼in (3cm) across, conspicuously veined dark purple, and with dark purple throats. ↕ 3in (8cm), ↔ 4in (10cm). ❀ (min. 35°F/2°C)

O. laciniata, syn. *O. squamosoradicosa*. Tuft-forming, rhizomatous perennial, with tiny bulbils, producing tufts of blue-gray, often purple-margined leaves, each with 8–12 inversely heart-shaped, folded, crinkly-margined leaflets, to ½in (1.5cm) long. Solitary, widely funnel-shaped, scented, violet-blue, lilac-blue, red, pink, or white flowers, to 1in (2.5cm) across, with light green throats, are produced in late spring and summer. Prefers cool conditions. ↕ 2–4in (5–10cm), ↔ 4in (10cm). Patagonia. ❀ (min. 35°F/2°C)

O. lobata ▣ syn. *O. perdicaria*. Clump-forming, bulbous perennial with tuberous roots, producing compact clusters of bright green leaves, each with 3 inversely heart-shaped leaflets, ¼in (6mm) long. The leaves, which appear

Oxalis lobata

in spring, die down quickly and reappear in late summer and autumn at the same time as the solitary, funnel-shaped, bright yellow flowers, ½–¾in (1.5–2cm) across, which are often dotted and veined red. ↕↔ to 4in (10cm). Chile. ❀ (min. 35°F/2°C)

O. megalorrhiza, syn. *O. carnosa*. Slow-growing, succulent perennial with fleshy rhizomes and few-branched, fleshy stems, later becoming woody. These produce terminal clusters of fleshy, glossy, mid-green leaves, each with 3 inversely heart-shaped leaflets, ½–¾in (1.5–2cm) long. Umbel-like cymes of 2–5 bowl-shaped yellow flowers, to ¾in (2cm) across, are borne in summer and autumn. ↕ 6in (15cm), to 16in (40cm) with age, ↔ to 8in (20cm). Coastal regions of Galapagos Islands, and Peru, Chile, Bolivia. ❀ (min. 50°F/10°C)

O. obtusa ▣ Slowly spreading, mat-forming, bulbous perennial with runners producing bulbils. It is similar to *O. depressa*, but with shorter-stemmed, hairy, gray-green leaves, each with 3 rounded to triangular-obovate leaflets, ¼–1in (0.5–2.5cm) long. Bears solitary, widely funnel-shaped, rose-pink, brick-red, or yellow flowers, to ¾in (2cm) across, in summer. ↕ 2in (5cm), ↔ 8in (20cm). Namibia, South Africa (Eastern Cape, Southern Cape). ❀ (min. 35°F/2°C)

O. oregana (Redwood sorrel). Creeping, rhizomatous perennial with hairy, mid-green leaves, each divided into 3 inversely heart-shaped leaflets, ½–1¼in (1.5–3cm) long. Solitary, cup-shaped, rose-pink, lilac, occasionally

Oxalis obtusa

Oxalis tetraphylla

white flowers, 1in (2.5cm) across, are produced on slender stems from spring to autumn. ↕ to 8in (20cm), ↔ indefinite. Woodland in W. North America. Zone 7b.
O. perdicaria see *O. lobata.*
O. purpurata* var. *bowiei see *O. bowiei.*
O. purpurea. Variable, bulbous perennial with clusters of silky, white-hairy, dark green leaves, each with 3 diamond-shaped to rounded or broadly obovate leaflets; these are often deep purple beneath, ¾in (2cm) long, and hairy at the margins and on the surfaces. Solitary, widely funnel-shaped, cream, white, pink, or purple flowers, 1¼–2in (3–5cm) across, are produced in autumn and winter. ↕ 4in (10cm), ↔ 6in (15cm). South Africa (Northern Transvaal, Eastern Transvaal, Eastern Cape), Swaziland. ❄ (min. 41°F/5°C). **'Ken Aslet'** has bright, deep yellow flowers.
O. squamosoradicosa see *O. laciniata.*
O. succulenta see *O. herrerae.*
O. tetraphylla ■ syn. *O. deppei* (Good luck plant, Lucky clover). Clump-forming, bulbous perennial with mid-green leaves, each consisting of 4 strap-shaped to inversely triangular, entire or notched leaflets, ¾–3in (2–8cm) long, usually banded purple at the bases. In summer, produces loose, umbel-like cymes of 4–12 widely funnel-shaped, reddish purple flowers, with greenish yellow throats, ¾–1¼in (2–3cm) across. ↕↔ to 6in (15cm). Mexico. ❄ (min. 35°F/2°C)
O. versicolor (Candycane sorrel). Clump-forming, bulbous perennial with mid-green leaves, each divided into 3 wedge-shaped-linear to linear, almost hairless leaflets, ½–¾in (1.5–2cm) long. A profusion of solitary, funnel-shaped white flowers, ¾–1¼in (2–3cm) across, crimson-margined on the reverse and crimson-striped in bud, are produced from late summer to winter. Suitable for an alpine house. ↕ 3in (8cm), ↔ 8in (20cm) or more. Southern Africa. ❄ (min. 41°F/5°C)

OXYDENDRUM

ERICACEAE

Genus of one species of deciduous, large shrub or small tree from woodland and streamsides in E. North America. It has rust-red to gray bark; simple, alternate leaves, which turn vivid red in autumn; and cylindrical to urn-shaped white flowers, borne in large, terminal panicles. Cultivated for the autumn color of its foliage and for its flowers, it

Oxydendrum arboreum

is best grown in an open glade in a woodland garden, or as a specimen.
• **CULTIVATION** Grow in fertile, moist but well-drained, acidic soil, preferably avoiding exposed situations. Pruning group 1.
• **PROPAGATION** Sow seed in containers in a cold frame in autumn. Take semi-ripe cuttings in summer.
• **PESTS AND DISEASES** Leaf spots sometimes occur.

O. arboreum ■ (Sorrel tree, Sourwood). Conical to columnar shrub or tree with elliptic to oblong-lance-shaped, toothed, glossy, dark green leaves, to 8in (20cm) long, turning brilliant shades of red, yellow, and purple in autumn. Cylindrical to urn-shaped white flowers, to ¼in (6mm) long, are produced in large panicles, to 10in (25cm) long, in late summer and early autumn. ↕ 30–50ft (10–15m), ↔ 25ft (8m). E. North America. Zone 6.

▷ ***Oxypetalum*** see *Tweedia*

OXYTROPIS

FABACEAE

Genus of approximately 175 species of subalpine and alpine legumes, some of which are popular for use in rock gardens. They can be grown in dry crevices of rock gardens and also do well in troughs.
• **CULTIVATION** Grow under very well-drained conditions; resents wetness around crowns, especially in winter.
• **PROPAGATION** Seed in spring after scarification; basal cuttings in summer.
• **PESTS AND DISEASES** Infrequent.

Oxytropis purpurea

O. purpurea ■ syn. *O. olympia, O. thessala.* Tightly tufted perennial with silver, shortly tomentose leaflets. Flowers ½in (1.5cm) across, purple oroccasionally white, are borne in compact capitate raceme in summer, followed by small, kidney-shaped beans. ↕ to 6in (15cm), ↔ to 10in (25cm). Mountains of Albania, Greece, Yugoslavia. Zone 3.

OZOTHAMNUS

ASTERACEAE

Genus of about 50 species of evergreen shrubs and woody-based perennials, closely related to *Helichrysum*, from Australia and New Zealand, where they grow in rocky places and on heathland, from the coast to the mountains. They are cultivated for their often aromatic, usually small, heath-like, alternate leaves, and for their solitary or corymb-like flowerheads, displaying white disk florets. Grow larger species in a shrub border; smaller species are good in a trough, rock garden, or alpine house.
• **CULTIVATION** Grow in moderately fertile, well-drained soil in a sheltered site in full sun. *O. coralloides* and *O. selago* need gritty, sharply drained soil; protect from excessive winter moisture. In an alpine house, use a mix of equal parts loam, leaf mold, and grit. Pruning group 8.
• **PROPAGATION** Sow seed in containers in an open frame as soon as ripe. Take semi-ripe cuttings in summer.
• **PESTS AND DISEASES** Infrequent.

O. coralloides ■ syn. *Helichrysum coralloides.* Compact, rounded shrub with diamond-shaped, scale-like, leathery leaves, ¼in (6mm) long, white-woolly beneath, and pressed flat to the cylindrical branches. Solitary, terminal, yellowish white, cylindrical flowerheads, ¼in (6mm) across, are produced in summer. ↕↔ 24in (60cm). New Zealand. ❄ (min. 35°F/2°C)
O. ledifolius ■ syn. *Helichrysum ledifolium* (Kerosene bush). Compact, rounded shrub with yellow-green shoots densely covered with oblong-linear, aromatic, dark green leaves, to ½in (1.5cm) long, yellow-downy beneath, the margins strongly curved under. In early summer, bears white flowerheads, ¼in (6mm) across, in dense, terminal corymbs, 1¼–2in (3–5cm) across. ↕↔ 3ft (1m). Tasmania. ❄ (min. 41°F/5°C)

Ozothamnus coralloides

Ozothamnus ledifolius

O. rosmarinifolius ■ syn. *Helichrysum rosmarinifolium.* Compact, upright shrub with rosemary-like, linear, dark green leaves, to 1½in (4cm) long, woolly beneath, the margins curved under. Fragrant white flowerheads, ⅛in (3mm) across, red in bud, are borne in dense, terminal corymbs, 1½in (4cm) across, in early summer. ↕ 6–10ft (2–3m), ↔ 5ft (1.5m). S.E. Australia. ❄ (min. 35°F/2°C). **'Silver Jubilee'** has silvery gray leaves.
O. selago ■ syn. *Helichrysum selago.* Dense, upright shrub with rigid shoots densely covered in tiny, ovate to triangular, aromatic leaves, ⅛in (3mm) long, pressed flat to the shoots. Terminal, solitary cream flowerheads, ¼in (6mm) across, are produced in summer. ↕ to 16in (40cm), ↔ 10in (25cm). New Zealand (South Island). ❄ (min. 41°F/5°C)

Ozothamnus rosmarinifolius

Ozothamnus selago

O

P

PACHYCEREUS
syn. LOPHOCEREUS

CACTACEAE

Genus of possibly 9 species of columnar, often tree-like, ribbed cacti from semi-desert areas of the US and Mexico. These often massive cacti branch from the bases, and have large, spiny, usually scaly areoles, sometimes woolly or bristly in the axils. The nocturnal or diurnal, funnel- or bell-shaped, or short, tubular flowers are produced only on mature plants. The bristly, spherical, fleshy fruits contain large, black-coated seeds. Where temperatures drop below 50°F (10°C), grow in a temperate or warm greenhouse. In warmer climates, use in a desert garden.

• **CULTIVATION** Under glass, grow in standard cactus potting mix in full light. From spring to summer, water moderately and apply a low-nitrogen liquid fertilizer every 4–5 weeks. Keep dry at other times. Outdoors, grow in moderately fertile, sharply drained soil in full sun. See also pp.48–49.

• **PROPAGATION** Sow seed at 66–75°F (19–24°C) in spring. Take stem-tip cuttings in summer.

• **PESTS AND DISEASES** Vulnerable to scale insects and occasionally mealybugs.

P. marginatus. Erect cactus with sometimes sparsely branched, 4- to 7-ribbed, dark green stems, 3–6in (8–15cm) across, with gray-white areoles bearing brown to gray spines (5–8 radials, 1 or 2 longer centrals). Produces nocturnal and diurnal, tubular, greenish white or pink flowers, 1¼–2in (3–5cm) across, in summer. ↕ to 10–22ft (3–7m), ↔ 3ft (1m). C. and S. Mexico. ❀ (min. 50°F/10°C); tolerates brief periods to 35°F (2°C).

Pachycereus pringlei

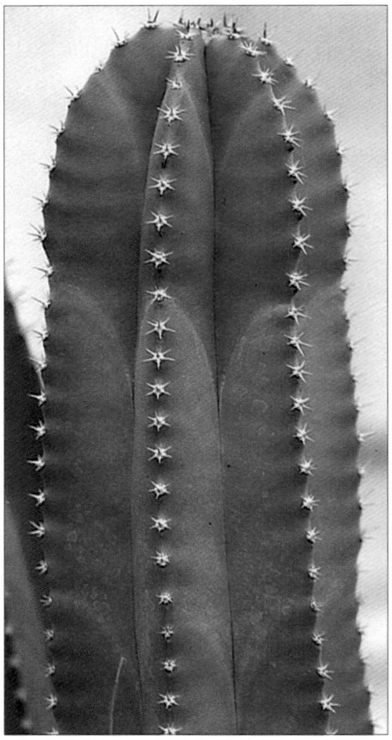
Pachycereus schottii

P. pecten-aboriginum (Hairbrush cactus). Erect, tree-like cactus with branched, dark bluish green stems, 12in (30cm) thick, each with 10 or 11 acute ribs and gray-white areoles bearing stiff brown spines, fading to gray (8 or 9 radials, 1 or 2 longer centrals). In summer, bears nocturnal and diurnal, funnel-shaped white flowers, 2½–3in (6–8cm) across, with greenish red outer petals. ↕ to 25ft (8m), ↔ 10ft (3m). W. Mexico. ❀ (min. 50°F/10°C)

P. pringlei ■ (Giant Mexican cereus). Tree-like cactus with dark blue-green stems, 3ft (1m) or more thick, and erect branches, each with 10–17 rounded ribs. Gray areoles have reddish to dark brown spines, fading to gray (about 20 radials, 1–3 slightly longer centrals). In summer, bears nocturnal, bell- to funnel-shaped white flowers, 3in (8cm) across, with greenish red outer petals. ↕ to 40–50ft (12–15m), ↔ 10ft (3m). N.W. Mexico. ❀ (min. 50°F/10°C)

P. schottii ■ syn. *Lophocereus schottii.* Erect, columnar cactus with dull, dark green stems, to 4–6in (10–15cm) thick, each with 4–9 ribs. Gray-woolly areoles produce almost black spines, fading to gray (4–7 radials, often 1 central). As the plant matures, a spiny, hairy pseudocephalium forms; in summer, it produces nocturnal, slender, funnel-shaped, red, pink, or white flowers, 1¼–1½in (3–4cm) across, green outside, with an unpleasant smell. ↕ 22ft (7m), ↔ 10ft (3m). S. Arizona, N.W. Mexico. ❀ (min. 50°F/10°C); tolerates brief periods to 35°F (2°C). **'Monstrosus'** has misshapen stems, irregular ribs, and spineless areoles; ↕ to 10ft (3m), ↔ 3ft (1m).

P. weberi. Tree-like cactus producing glaucous, blue-green stems, 8in (20cm) or more thick, and erect, 8- to 10-ribbed branches. White-woolly areoles each produce up to 13 spines (6–12 yellowish white, later reddish brown or black radials, 1 longer gray central). In midsummer, bears nocturnal, funnel-shaped white flowers, yellowish white outside, to 4in (10cm) long. ↕ 30ft (10m), ↔ 10ft (3m) or more. S. Mexico. ❀ (min. 50°F/10°C)

PACHYCORMUS
ANACARDIACEAE

Genus of one species of very variable, slow-growing, deciduous, perennial succulent from desert or semi-desert areas of Mexico. Gray- or silver-barked branches bear pinnate, feathery leaves. Dense, terminal racemes of tiny, cup-shaped flowers are produced by day in summer. Where temperatures drop below 59°F (15°C), grow in a warm greenhouse. In warmer climates, use in a desert garden.

• **CULTIVATION** Under glass, grow in soil-based potting mix, with added grit, in full light. From midspring until the leaves fall, water freely and apply a balanced liquid fertilizer every 6–8 weeks. Keep just moist at other times. Outdoors, grow in sharply drained, moderately fertile soil in full sun. See also pp.48–49.

• **PROPAGATION** Sow seed at 66–75°F (19–24°C) in spring.

• **PESTS AND DISEASES** Young growth is vulnerable to spider mites.

P. discolor ■ (Elephant tree). Free-branching succulent. The trunk and branches are very swollen, and both contain sponge-like wood and white latex. Pinnate, mid-green leaves, to 3in (8cm) long, consist of 6–8 oval, slightly toothed or lobed leaflets, hairy toward the tips. In summer, bears lax, dense racemes of cup-shaped, white to yellow or red flowers, to ¼in (6mm) long. ↕ 12ft (4m), ↔ 18in (45cm) or more. N.W. Mexico. ❀ (min. 59°F/15°C)

Pachycormus discolor

PACHYCYMBIUM
ASCLEPIADACEAE

Genus of about 30 species of leafless, perennial succulents, formerly classified under *Caralluma*, from mostly hilly terrain in the Arabian Peninsula, E. Africa, Zimbabwe, and South Africa. They have erect or prostrate, 4-angled or rounded, prominently toothed stems, and produce compact cymes of diurnal, bell- or cup-shaped flowers, usually near the stem tips, in summer. Where temperatures drop below 50°F (10°C), grow in a warm greenhouse. In warmer climates, use in a desert garden.

• **CULTIVATION** Under glass, grow in soil-based potting mix, with added grit or sharp sand, in full light. From midspring to early autumn, water moderately and apply a low-nitrogen liquid fertilizer every 6–8 weeks. Keep just moist at other times. Outdoors, grow in moderately fertile, sharply drained soil in full sun. See also pp.48–49.

• **PROPAGATION** Sow seed at 66–75°F (19–24°C) in spring. Take stem-tip cuttings in spring or early summer.

• **PESTS AND DISEASES** Prone to ant infestation while flowering (ants feed on the nectar).

P. dummeri, syn. *Caralluma dummeri.* Erect, spreading succulent with 4-angled or slightly rounded, grayish green stems, ½in (1.5cm) thick, with dark red stripes. In summer, produces cymes of 1–4, sometimes up to 6, bell-shaped, olive-green to dark green flowers, 1½in (4cm) across, with tapering, spreading lobes, hairy inside, smooth outside. ↕ 4in (10cm), ↔ to 6in (15cm). Uganda, Kenya, Tanzania. ❀ (min. 50°F/10°C)

PACHYPHRAGMA
BRASSICACEAE

Genus of one species of semi-evergreen, rhizomatous perennial found in moist beech woods in N.E. Turkey and the Caucasus. It produces long-stalked, basal leaves, glossy, dark green at first, becoming duller. Broad, terminal corymbs of 4-petaled white flowers appear just as the leaves develop; the stems later elongate so that the flattened fruit are held above the foliage. A slow-growing groundcover plant, *P. macrophyllum* is suitable for siting beneath trees and deciduous shrubs.

Pachyphragma macrophyllum

• **CULTIVATION** Grow in moderately fertile, moist, leafy soil, preferably in partial shade.
• **PROPAGATION** Sow seed in containers in a cold frame in autumn. Divide or take basal stem cuttings in late spring.
• **PESTS AND DISEASES** Slugs may occur.

P. macrophyllum ▣ syn. *Thlaspi macrophyllum.* Semi-evergreen perennial with ovate to rounded, scalloped leaves, 1–4in (2.5–10cm) long, produced in basal clusters that partially persist over winter. Flat corymbs of cross-shaped, 4-petaled, unpleasantly scented white flowers, ¾in (2cm) across, with pale green veins, are borne in early spring, followed by distinctive, flat, inversely heart-shaped fruit. ↕ 8–16in (20–40cm), ↔ 24–36in (60–90cm). Caucasus, N.E. Turkey. Zone 6.

PACHYPHYTUM

CRASSULACEAE

Genus of 12 or more species of rosette-forming, perennial succulents from arid areas of Mexico, closely resembling *Echeveria*, with which it hybridizes. The semi-erect, usually branching, spreading stems become decumbent with age, and bear variably shaped, swollen, fleshy, mid- to dark or gray-green, frequently white-frosted leaves. Racemes of diurnal, bell-shaped flowers are borne on fleshy, sometimes sparsely branched stems, mainly in spring. Where temperatures drop below 45°F (7°C), grow in a temperate greenhouse, although most species tolerate brief periods to 25°F (-4°C). In warmer climates, use in a desert garden.
• **CULTIVATION** Under glass, grow in standard cactus potting mix in full light, with shade from hot sun. In the growing season, water moderately and apply a low-nitrogen liquid fertilizer every 6–8 weeks. Keep almost dry at other times. Outdoors, grow in moderately fertile, sharply drained soil in full sun, with some midday shade. See also pp.48–49.
• **PROPAGATION** Sow seed at 66–75°F (19–24°C) in spring. Take leaf or stem-tip cuttings in spring or summer.
• **PESTS AND DISEASES** Infrequent.

P. compactum (Thick plant). Compact succulent with short-stemmed rosettes of oblong to lance-shaped, white-frosted, dark green leaves, ¾–1¼in (2–3cm) long, sometimes tinged red-

Pachyphytum longifolium

Pachyphytum oviferum

purple, with rounded, angular margins. Racemes of 3–10 pendent, blue-tipped, orange-red flowers, ½in (1.5cm) long, with pink or green calyces, are produced in spring. ↕ 4–6in (10–15cm), ↔ 12in (30cm) or more. Mexico. ❄ (min. 45°F/7°C)
P. hookeri. Clump-forming, long-stemmed succulent with scattered, almost cylindrical, pointed, mid-green leaves, to 2in (5cm) long, with a blue-gray to white bloom; they are slightly flattened on the upper surfaces, with blunt to rounded margins. Racemes of 5–18 yellowish pink flowers, to ½in (1.5cm) long, flushed pale purple-red, with green-tipped pink sepals, are borne in spring. ↕ 24in (60cm), ↔ indefinite. Mexico. ❄ (min. 45°F/7°C)
P. longifolium ▣ Rosette-forming succulent with inversely lance-shaped, gray-green leaves, 2½–4½in (6–11cm) long, with a blue-glaucous bloom, blunt or pointed at the tips, and grooved beneath. Racemes of 10–50 white flowers, ½in (1.5cm) long, strongly suffused red, develop mainly in spring, but also irregularly throughout the year. ↕ 6in (15cm) or more, ↔ 8in (20cm) or more. Mexico. ❄ (min. 45°F/7°C)
P. oviferum ▣ (Moonstones). Clump-forming succulent producing short-stemmed rosettes of obovoid, white-frosted, light green leaves, ¾–2in (2–5cm) long, flushed lavender-blue. Racemes of 10–15 vivid orange-red or greenish red flowers, ½in (1.5cm) long, with pale blue-white calyces, are borne from winter to spring. ↕ 4–5in (10–13cm), ↔ 12in (30cm) or more. Mexico. ❄ (min. 45°F/7°C)

PACHYPODIUM

APOCYNACEAE

Genus of 13 species of shrubby or tree-like, perennial succulents from mostly arid regions of Namibia, South Africa, and Madagascar. Many have swollen, irregularly shaped caudices and very thick, thorny stems. Leaves are simple,

Pachypodium lamerei

entire, and variably shaped; they are usually deciduous but may persist in cultivation. Diurnal, salverform to funnel- or bell-shaped flowers are produced usually in terminal clusters, in summer. Where temperatures drop below 59°F (15°C), grow pachypodiums in a warm greenhouse. In warmer climates, use in a desert garden or as focal points on a lawn.
• **CULTIVATION** Under glass, grow in standard cactus potting mix in full light. From late spring to early autumn, water moderately and apply a low-nitrogen liquid fertilizer every 4–5 weeks. Keep dry at other times. Outdoors, grow in moderately fertile, sharply drained soil in full sun. See also pp.48–49.
• **PROPAGATION** Sow seed at 66–75°F (19–24°C), or take stem-tip cuttings, in late spring.
• **PESTS AND DISEASES** Prone to aphids when flowering. Various leaf spots can be problems.

P. baronii. Tree-like succulent with a massive, thick, thorny caudex and thick, thorny stems bearing obovate to elliptic, tapering, grayish green leaves, to 6in (15cm) long. Salverform, bright red flowers, to 2½in (6cm) across, develop in summer. ↕ 10ft (3m), ↔ to 3ft (1m). N. Madagascar. ❄ (min. 59°F/15°C)
P. bispinosum. Shrubby succulent with a rugged, partly underground caudex and thin, thorny, fleshy branches bearing lance-shaped to narrowly lance-shaped, roughly hairy, mid-green leaves, 1½–3in (4–8cm) long. Broadly bell-shaped, pink to purple flowers, 1¼in (3cm) across, with recurving white lobes, are produced in summer. ↕ 18in (45cm), ↔ 7in (18cm). South Africa (Eastern Cape). ❄ (min. 59°F/15°C)
P. densiflorum. Shrubby, slow-growing succulent with a thorny caudex, short stem, and short, thick, thorny branches. The obovate to oblong-ovate leaves, to 4in (10cm) long, are mid- to dark green, gray-felted beneath. In summer, bears salverform, bright yellow flowers, to 1¼in (3cm) across, each with prominent yellow anthers forming a cone. ↕ to 18in (45cm), ↔ 5in (13cm) or more. Madagascar. ❄ (min. 59°F/15°C)
P. geayi. Tree-like succulent with a thorny caudex, branching near the top with age. Thorny branches bear linear, grayish green leaves, to 16in (40cm) long, silver-gray-hairy beneath. Salverform, pure white flowers, 3in (8cm) across, are produced in summer. ↕ to 25ft (8m), ↔ to 6ft (2m). S.W. Madagascar. ❄ (min. 59°F/15°C)
P. lamerei ▣ Tree-like succulent with a thick caudex branching near the top, with thorns generally in groups of 3. Bears terminal clusters of linear to lance-shaped, shining, dark green leaves, 10–16in (25–40cm) long. Salverform, yellow-throated, creamy white flowers, to 4½in (11cm) across, are borne in summer. ↕ to 20ft (6m), ↔ 6ft (2m). S. and S.W. Madagascar. ❄ (min. 59°F/15°C)
P. namaquanum. Tree-like succulent with a thick, fleshy, thorny, caudex-like trunk, rarely branching, with spirally arranged tubercles, and thorns in groups of 3. Produces terminal rosettes of lance-shaped, slightly hairy, pale green leaves, 5in (13cm) long, with wavy, crisped margins. In summer, bears tubular, yellow-green and purple-red flowers, striped yellow inside, to ¾in (2cm) long. ↕ to 8ft (2.5m), ↔ 5ft (1.5m). S. Namibia, South Africa (Northern Cape). ❄ (min. 59°F/15°C)
P. rosulatum. Variable, shrubby succulent with a spherical or irregularly shaped, thorny caudex, branching stems, and elliptic, mid- to dark green leaves, to 3in (8cm) long, slightly hairy above. Salverform yellow flowers, to ½in (1.5cm) across, with rounded, flat lobes, are produced in summer. ↕ to 5ft (1.5m), ↔ 3ft (1m) or more. Madagascar. ❄ (min. 59°F/15°C).
var. *gracilis* is smaller and has fewer, more slender branches and thinner, red-brown spines; ↔ to 16in (40cm).
var. *horombense* has inflated, bell-shaped flowers.

P

Pachypodium succulentum

P. succulentum ■ Shrubby succulent with a mainly underground caudex. Strong, sturdy branches bear paired thorns and narrowly lance-shaped, minutely hairy, mid- to dark green leaves, to 2½in (6cm) long. Salverform, pink, white, or red flowers, 1½in (4cm) across, sometimes red-striped, with narrow, spreading lobes, develop in summer. ↕↔ 24–36in (60–90cm). South Africa. ❀ (min. 59°F/15°C)

PACHYSANDRA

BUXACEAE

Genus of 4 species of evergreen or semi-evergreen perennials and subshrubs occurring in woodland in China, Japan, and S.E. US. They have often rhizome-like, fleshy green stems and upright branches with alternate, broadly ovate to obovate, entire or coarsely toothed, gray- to dark green leaves clustered at their tips. Terminal or axillary spikes of small, unisexual, petalless flowers are produced in spring or early summer. They are useful as a groundcover in a shrub border or woodland garden.

• **CULTIVATION** Grow in any but very dry soil in full or partial shade.
• **PROPAGATION** Divide in spring. Root softwood cuttings in early summer.
• **PESTS AND DISEASES** Affected by leaf spot, dieback, and stem rot, and may be damaged by slugs and snails.

P. procumbens ■ (Allegheny spurge). Clump-forming, semi-evergreen perennial with very loose whorls of coarsely toothed, ovate to rounded, gray-green to dark green leaves, 2–4in

P

Pachysandra procumbens

Pachysandra terminalis

(5–10cm) long, sometimes brown-green-mottled. Bears spikes, 2–4in (5–10cm) long, of fragrant, white flowers, in spring, generally as the foliage appears. ↕ to 12in (30cm), ↔ indefinite. S.E. US. Zone 5.
P. terminalis ■ (Japanese spurge). Spreading, evergreen perennial with obovate, coarsely toothed, glossy, dark green leaves, to 4in (10cm) long, clustered at the ends of short, smooth stems. Tiny white male flowers are produced in spikes, ¾–1¼in (2–3cm) long, in early summer. ↕ 8in (20cm), ↔ indefinite. N. China, Japan. Zone 4. **'Green Carpet'** is more compact, with smaller, finely toothed leaves, to 3in (8cm) long; ↕ 6in (15cm), ↔ to 24in (60cm). **'Green Sheen'** has glossy, dark green leaves. **'Variegata'** is slower-growing in habit, and bears attractive white-margined leaves; ↕ 10in (25cm), ↔ to 24in (60cm).

PACHYSTACHYS

ACANTHACEAE

Genus of 12 species of evergreen perennials and shrubs, closely allied to *Justicia*, from woodland or rainforest in the West Indies and tropical Central and South America. They are cultivated for their tubular, 2-lipped flowers, borne in erect, terminal spikes with large, overlapping, usually brightly colored bracts. Leaves are opposite and simple, ovate to lance-shaped, and mid- to dark green. Where temperatures drop below 50–59°F (10–15°C), grow in a warm or temperate greenhouse, or as houseplants. In warmer areas, use in a border.

Pachystachys coccinea

Pachystachys lutea

• **CULTIVATION** Under glass, grow in soil-based potting mix in full light, with high humidity. In growth, water freely and apply a balanced liquid fertilizer monthly. Water moderately in winter. Outdoors, grow in fertile, moist, well-drained soil in full sun. Pruning group 8; needs restrictive pruning under glass.
• **PROPAGATION** Root softwood cuttings with bottom heat in summer.
• **PESTS AND DISEASES** Whiteflies, spider mites, leaf spots, and root rot may occur.

P. cardinalis see *P. coccinea*.
P. coccinea ■ syn. *Jacobinia coccinea*, *Justicia coccinea*, *P. cardinalis* (Cardinal's guard). Erect shrub producing robust, simple or sparsely branched stems and ovate-elliptic, strongly veined, lightly wrinkled, dark green leaves, 6–8in (15–20cm) long. In winter, tubular, strongly 2-lipped scarlet flowers, 2in (5cm) long, are borne in terminal spikes, 6in (15cm) long, with 4-ranked, pale green bracts. ↕ to 6ft (2m) or more, ↔ 24–36in (60–90cm). West Indies, N. South America. ❀ (min. 55°F/13°C)
P. lutea ■ (Lollipop plant). Erect shrub with moderately to sparsely branched stems and narrowly ovate, elliptic, or lance-shaped, slender-pointed, strongly veined, mid- to deep green leaves, 3–6in (8–15cm) long. In spring and summer, produces tubular, strongly 2-lipped white flowers, 1½–2in (4–5cm) long, borne in terminal spikes, 4in (10cm) long, with 4-ranked, bright golden yellow bracts. ↕ to 3ft (1m), ↔ 18–30in (45–75cm). Peru. ❀ (min. 55°F/13°C)

PACHYSTEGIA

ASTERACEAE

Genus of one species of evergreen shrub, occurring in rocky places from sea level to mountains in New Zealand. It has alternate, simple leaves, and bears terminal or axillary, solitary flowerheads, to 2½in (6cm) across, with white ray florets and yellow disk florets. It is suitable for a rock garden.

• **CULTIVATION** Grow in fertile, well-drained soil in full sun; shelter from cold, drying winds. Pruning group 1.
• **PROPAGATION** Sow seed in containers in a cold frame in autumn. Take semi-ripe cuttings in summer.
• **PESTS AND DISEASES** Infrequent.

P. insignis, syn. *Olearia insignis* (Marlborough rock daisy). Spreading shrub with thick, white- or brown-felted shoots and oval to obovate, glossy, dark green leaves, to 6in (15cm) long, gray-green when young, and clustered at the tips of the shoots. In summer, bears long-stalked, daisy-like, solitary white flowerheads, to 2½in (6cm) across, with yellow centers. ↕ 36in (90cm), ↔ 4ft (1.2m). New Zealand (South Island). ❀ (min. 41°F/5°C)

▷ ***Pachystima*** see *Paxistima*

x PACHYVERIA

CRASSULACEAE

Hybrid genus of mainly rosetted, sometimes clump-forming, perennial succulents, the result of crosses between *Pachyphytum* and *Echeveria*. They have alternate, fleshy, light to mid- or gray-green leaves in very variable shapes, sometimes forming rosettes. Diurnal, bell- or star-shaped flowers are borne in one-sided cymes, in spring or summer. Where temperatures drop below 45°F (7°C), grow in a temperate greenhouse. In warmer areas, use in a desert garden.

• **CULTIVATION** Under glass, grow in standard cactus potting mix in full light, with shade from hot sun. From mid-spring to late summer, water moderately and apply a low-nitrogen liquid fertilizer every 6–8 weeks. Keep almost dry at other times. Outdoors, grow in moderately fertile, sharply drained soil in full sun, with midday shade. See also pp.48–49.
• **PROPAGATION** Take leaf or stem-tip cuttings in spring or summer.
• **PESTS AND DISEASES** Mealybugs occur.

x *P. glauca* ■ syn. *Echeveria* x *fruticosa*. Rosetted, offsetting succulent with semi-cylindrical, red-tipped, blue-green, white-frosted leaves, to 2½in (6cm) long, with darker markings. Pendent, star-shaped yellow flowers, ½in (1.5cm) long, with recurving red tips, are produced in terminal, one-sided cymes in spring. ↕ 12in (30cm), ↔ indefinite. ❀ (min. 45°F/7°C)

PAEONIA

Peony

PAEONIACEAE

Genus of 30 or more species of clump-forming herbaceous perennials and deciduous, sometimes suckering shrubs or subshrubs (tree peonies) found in meadows, scrub, and rocky places from Europe to E. Asia, and in W. North America. They are grown for their large, brightly colored, sometimes fragrant, showy flowers and bold, dissected leaves. They bear pod-like fruits, each with 2–5 lobes and large, sometimes showy, red or black seeds. Herbaceous peonies, with tuberous rootstocks, include the majority of species and cultivars; most cultivars are derived from *P. lactiflora.* They, and many of the species, bloom in late spring and early summer. Tree peonies have woody stems, often with lax branches, and bloom in mid- and late spring.

Peonies have mid- to dark green, sometimes silver-, bluish, or gray-green leaves; these are 2-ternate or occasionally pinnate, with few to many, usually oval to obovate, sometimes linear, entire or lobed leaflets, occasionally softly hairy, especially on the veins beneath.

Peony flowers are usually erect and solitary, or sometimes borne several to a stem. They are saucer-, cup-, or bowl-shaped, sometimes spherical when first open, and each single flower has 5 green sepals and 5–10 brightly colored petals. Most have a crowded central boss of usually cream or yellow stamens; those with double flowers have either no stamens or a few hidden among the petals. The flowers can be divided into 4 major groups: single, semi-double, double (including the bomb type, with a central mound of petals), and Japanese (see panel). In the descriptions below, flower sizes of herbaceous cultivars are defined as: small, 2–4in (5–10cm) across; medium-sized, 4–6in (10–15cm) across; large, 6–8in (15–20cm) across; or very large, over 8in (20cm) across. Tree peonies have single to double flowers, 2–12in (5–30cm) across.

Peonies are long-lived plants, but they often resent disturbance. They are ideal for a mixed, herbaceous, or shrub border. If ingested, all parts can cause mild stomach upset.

• **HARDINESS** Most herbaceous cultivars are hardy in Zone 2. Tree peonies are generally hardy in Zone 5. The hardiness of other species varies.

• **CULTIVATION** Grow in deep, fertile, humus-rich, moist but well-drained soil in full sun or partial shade. Plant the graft union of tree peonies 5–6in (13–15cm) below the soil surface, and provide shelter from strong winds. Large-flowered, herbaceous cultivars may need support. Pruning group 1 for tree peonies.

• **PROPAGATION** Sow seed in containers outdoors in autumn or early winter (may take 2 or 3 years to germinate). Divide herbaceous peonies in early autumn, and replant so that the new growths (the "eyes") are 2in (5cm) below the soil surface. Take root cuttings in winter. Take semi-ripe cuttings of tree peonies in summer, or graft in winter.

• **PESTS AND DISEASES** Prone to *Verticillium* wilt, ringspot virus, tip blight, stem rot, *Botrytis* blight, leaf blotch, Japanese beetle, and nematodes.

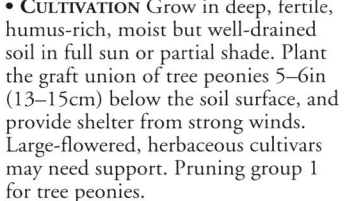

Paeonia 'A la Mode'

Paeonia 'America'

Paeonia 'Angel Cheeks'

Paeonia 'Avant Garde'

Paeonia 'Barrington Belle'

Paeonia 'Bowl of Beauty'

***P.* 'A la Mode'** ▣ Herbaceous perennial with strong stems and deep green leaves, flowering early in the season. Produces large, single, fragrant, white flowers with very prominent gold stamens. ↕↔ 34in (85cm).

P. albiflora see *P. lactiflora.*

***P.* 'Alexander Fleming'** ▣ Herbaceous perennial with glossy mid-green leaves with strong stems. In midseason, bears double, pink, sweetly scented flowers. ↕↔ 32–34in (80–85cm).

***P.* 'America'** ▣ Herbaceous perennial with mid-green leaves. Early in the season, produces large, single, bowl-shaped, deep crimson flowers, with broad, slightly frilled petals. ↕↔ 3–3½ft (0.9–1.1m).

***P.* 'Angel Cheeks'** ▣ Herbaceous perennial with mid-green leaves. In midseason, bears large, double, slightly fragrant, pale pink flowers with red-striped central petals. ↕↔ 26in (65cm).

***P.* 'Angela Cobb Freeborn'.** Herbaceous perennial with glossy dark green leaves. Producing double, coral red flowers in midseason, it is prized for its long flowering period. ↕↔ 36–40in (90–100cm).

***P.* 'Ann Berry Cousins'.** Herbaceous perennial with mid-green leaves. Early in the season, produces large, semi-double, cup-shaped, salmon flowers with yellow stamens, occasionally interspersed with small tufts of salmon petals. ↕↔ 28–30in (70–75cm).

P. anomala. Herbaceous perennial with dark green leaves, gray-green beneath, each with 9 narrow-oblong, pinnatifid leaflets, with bristly veins above. Bears single, cup-shaped, bright reddish purple flowers, 3–4in (7–10cm) across, with rounded, wavy petals and golden yellow stamens. ↕↔ 20–24in (50–60cm). Kyrgyzstan, China (E. Tien Shan Mountains). Zone 4.

P. arietina see *P. mascula* subsp. *arietina.*

***P.* 'Auguste Dessert'.** Herbaceous perennial with deep green leaves, turning crimson in autumn. In midseason, bears large, semi-double to double, carmine-red flowers, flushed salmon-pink, with slightly ruffled, silver margins. ↕↔ 28–32in (70–80cm).

***P.* 'Avant Garde'** ▣ Herbaceous perennial with abundant mid-green leaves. Bears large, single, bowl-shaped, rose-pink, darker-veined flowers, with yellow stamens, very early in the season. ↕↔ 36–39in (90–100cm).

***P.* 'Baroness Schröder'.** Free-flowering herbaceous perennial with deep green leaves. In late midseason, bears large, double, pale pink flowers that fade to white; the outer petals are broad and spreading, the inner ones crowded and incurved, with ruffled margins. ↕↔ 36–39in (90–100cm).

***P.* 'Barrington Belle'** ▣ Herbaceous perennial with strong stems and dark green leaves. Bears large, single cherry-red flowers with Japanese-type centers and pinkish staminodes, in midseason. ↕↔ 32in (80cm).

***P.* 'Best Man'.** Herbaceous perennial with thick stems and sturdy, mid-green leaves. Produces large, double, deep red flowers, late in the season. ↕↔ 34in (85cm).

***P.* 'Bowl of Beauty'** ▣ Herbaceous perennial with mid-green leaves. In midseason, produces very large, Japanese-type, carmine-red, pink-tinted flowers with dense, creamy white centers consisting of many crowded, narrow petaloids. ↕↔ 32–39in (80–100cm).

***P.* 'Bowl of Cream'.** Herbaceous perennial with mid-green leaves. Extremely large, double, bowl-shaped, white flowers with hidden gold stamens, are produced in midseason. ↕↔ 32in (80cm).

P. broteroi. Herbaceous perennial bearing semi-glossy, mid-green leaves, glaucous beneath, each with 9 leaflets, the lower leaves cut into 2 or 3 narrow, pointed lobes, the upper leaves unlobed. Produces single, cup-shaped, pink flowers, 4–5in (10–13cm) across, with oval petals and yellow stamens. ↕↔ 16–20in (40–50cm). Portugal, W. and S. Spain. Zone 7b.

Paeonia 'Alexander Fleming'

PEONY FLOWER FORMS

Peony flowers may be saucer-, cup-, or bowl-shaped, in one of the following forms: **single** – with a whorl of 5–10 broad, overlapping, often slightly incurved petals, and a large, central boss of stamens; **semi-double** – like single peonies, but with 2 or 3 whorls of similar petals; **double** – large, spherical flowers, with narrower, overlapping, often crowded, ruffled petals filling the center, and stamens inconspicuous or absent; or **Japanese** (also known as anemone-form) – single or semi-double flowers, with the stamens replaced by narrow, crowded, petal-like structures, known as petaloids or staminodes.

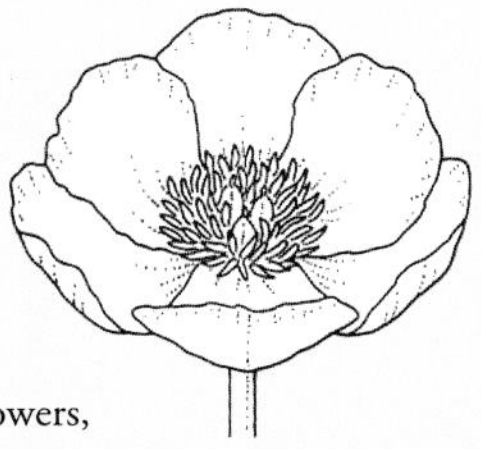
SINGLE

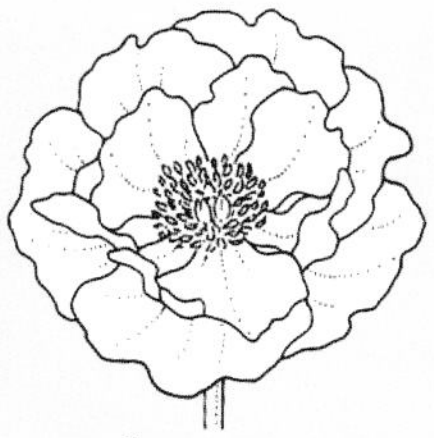
SEMI-DOUBLE

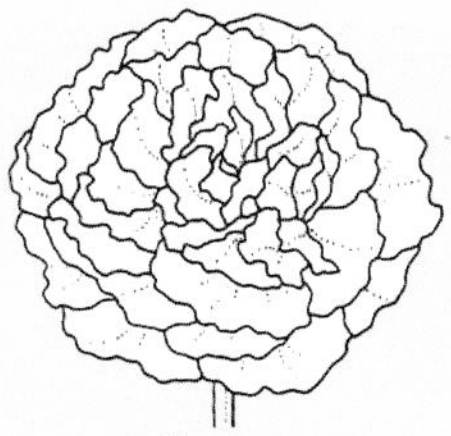
DOUBLE

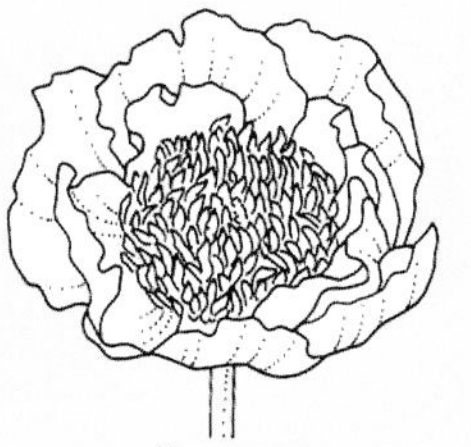
JAPANESE

P

Paeonia cambessedesii

Paeonia 'Charlie S. White'

Paeonia 'Claire de Lune'

Paeonia 'Coral Charm'

Paeonia 'Dawn Pink'

Paeonia 'Duchesse de Nemours'

Paeonia 'Edulis Superba'

Paeonia 'Henry Bockstoce'

Paeonia 'Krinkled White'

Paeonia 'Laura Dessert'

Paeonia lutea var. *ludlowii*

Paeonia 'Mikado'

Paeonia 'Miss America'

Paeonia mlokosewitschii

Paeonia 'Mme. Louis Henri'

Paeonia 'Moonstone'

Paeonia 'Nellie Saylor'

Paeonia 'Nick Shaylor'

Paeonia obovata var. *alba*

Paeonia officinalis 'Rubra Plena'

Paeonia peregrina

***P.* 'Buckeye Belle'.** Herbaceous perennial with strong, mid-green foliage and large, semi-double dark red flowers with narrower inner petals, early in the season. ‡↔ 30in (75cm).
P. cambessedesii ▣ (Majorcan peony). Herbaceous perennial, usually flushed overall with red or purple, especially when young. Purple-veined leaves, dark green above, reddish purple beneath, are each divided into 9 pointed, lance-shaped, elliptic, or ovate leaflets. Produces single, bowl-shaped, deep pink flowers, 2½–4in (6–10cm) across, with wavy-margined petals and yellow stamens with red filaments, in mid- and late spring. ‡↔ 18–22in (45–55cm). Balearic Islands (Majorca). Zone 8.
***P.* 'Charlie S. White'** ▣ Herbaceous perennial with shiny green leaves. Early in the season, produces delicately scented double flowers that are white with yellow tinge. Makes an excellent long-lasting cut flower. ‡↔ 3–4ft (90–120cm).
***P.* 'Cheddar Cheese'.** Herbaceous perennial with mid-green leaves. In midseason, bears large, double flowers with incurving, ivory-white inner petals and shorter, slightly ruffled yellow outer petals. ‡↔ 36–39in (90–100cm).
***P.* 'Claire de Lune'** ▣ syn. *P. mlokosewitschi* 'Mons. Jules Elie'. Herbaceous perennial with dull dark green leaves tinged with red. This very early bloomer bears single, creamy yellow flowers with crinkled petals and prominent yellow stamens. ‡↔ 24–28in (60–70cm).
***P.* 'Coral Charm'** ▣ Herbaceous perennial with dark green leaves. Early in the season, bears large, semi-double, dark coral-pink flowers, which fade somewhat with age. Flowers are very cupped until they age. ‡↔ 28in (70cm).
P. corallina see *P. mascula.*
***P.* 'Crusader'.** Herbaceous perennial with dark green leaves. Flowers are semi-double, deep red, produced early in the season. Blooms are large, with stiff stems. ‡↔ 30–32in (75–80cm).
***P.* 'Dawn Pink'** ▣ Herbaceous perennial with sturdy stems and mid-green leaves. Early in the season, bears large, single, slightly fragrant pink flowers, paler at the petal bases and with bright gold stamens. ‡↔ 34in (85cm).
P. decora see *P. peregrina.*
P. delavayi. Upright, sparsely branched, deciduous shrub (tree peony) with 2-pinnate, dark green leaves, blue-green beneath, the leaflets deeply cut into pointed lobes. Bears horizontal to nodding, single, cup-shaped, rich dark red flowers, 4in (10cm) across. ‡↔ 6ft (2m), ↔ 4ft (1.2m). China. Zone 5b.
var. *ludlowii* see *P. lutea* var. *ludlowii.*
***P.* 'Double Cherry'** see *P. suffruticosa* 'Yae-zakura'.
***P.* 'Duchesse de Nemours'** ▣ syn. *P.* 'Mrs. Gwyn Lewis'. Robust herbaceous perennial with deep green leaves. Early in the season, produces large, fragrant, double, pure white flowers, flushed green in bud, with spreading outer petals and dense, unevenly ruffled, yellow-based inner petals. ‡↔ 28–32in (70–80cm).
***P.* 'Edulis Superba'** ▣ Herbaceous perennial with mid-green leaves. Early in the season, bears very fragrant double, pink flowers with pale outer petals. Introduced in 1824, it is popular and does well on heavy soils. ‡↔ 32in (80cm).
***P.* 'Elsa Sass'.** Herbaceous perennial with mid-green leaves. Late in the season, bears large, double white flowers with slightly pink-blushed centers. ‡↔ 34in (85cm).
P. emodi ▣ (Himalayan peony). Herbaceous perennial with erect to arching stems and dark green leaves, each divided into 9 narrow, sometimes 2- or 3-lobed, elliptic leaflets. Semi-pendent, single, cup-shaped, pure white flowers, 4–7in (10–18cm) across, with golden yellow stamens, are borne several to a stem in late spring. ‡↔ 24–32in (60–80cm). W. Himalayas. Zone 6.
***P.* 'Fancy Nancy'.** Herbaceous perennial with dark green foliage and large, Japanese-type, cerise-pink flowers with lacy, pink staminodes, borne in midseason. ‡↔ 30in (75cm).
***P.* 'Félix Crousse'**, syn. *P.* 'Victor Hugo'. Herbaceous perennial with deep green leaves. In midseason, bears large, fragrant, double, deep crimson-pink flowers, with darker centers and ruffled, silver-margined petals. ‡↔ 28–30in (70–75cm).
***P.* 'Festiva Maxima'.** Herbaceous perennial with strong, erect stems and abundant mid-green foliage. Early in the season, produces very large, fragrant, double white flowers, with loosely arranged, irregularly margined petals, the inner petals with crimson marks at their bases. ‡↔ 36–39in (90–100cm).
***P.* 'Flame'.** Herbaceous perennial with dark green leaves. Bears large, single, bright rose flowers with yellow stamens, early in the season. ‡↔ 26in (65cm).
***P.* 'Flight of Cranes'** see *P. suffruticosa* 'Renkaku'.
***P.* 'Floral Rivalry'** see *P. suffruticosa* 'Hana-kisoi'.
***P.* 'Gay Paree'.** Herbaceous perennial with light green foliage. In midseason, bears large, Japanese-type, deep cerise-pink flowers with shell-pink centers. ‡↔ 30in (75cm).
***P.* 'General MacMahon'.** Herbaceous perennial with shiny mid-green leaves. In midseason, bears slightly perfumed double, red flowers. ‡↔ 36in (90cm).
***P.* 'Henry Bockstoce'** ▣ Upright herbaceous perennial with dark green leaves and strong stems. Flowers are double, dark red with paler center, produced early in the season. ‡↔ 28–30in (70–75cm).
P. humilis, syn. *P. officinalis* subsp. *humilis*, *P. officinalis* subsp. *microcarpa.* Herbaceous perennial with hairy stems and leaf stalks, and mid-green leaves, pale green and densely hairy beneath, each with 9 leaflets deeply cut into narrowly elliptic to oblong lobes. Bears single, bowl- or cup-shaped, purple-red flowers, 4–5in (10–13cm) across, with yellow stamens. ‡↔ 28–32in (70–80cm). S.W. Europe. Zone 4.
***P. japonica* of gardens** see *P. lactiflora.*
***P.* 'Kamada Brocade'** see *P. suffruticosa* 'Kamada-nishiki'.
***P.* 'Kansas'.** Herbaceous perennial with mid-green leaves. Bears large, double, bright red flowers, early in the season. Does not fade in sun. ‡↔ 36in (90cm).

P

P. 'Karl Rosenfield'. Herbaceous perennial with hairy stems and leaf stalks, and mid-green leaves with leaflets deeply cut into narrowly elliptic to oblong lobes. In midseason, bears large, double, bright deep red flowers, 4–5in (10–13cm) across. ↕↔ 28–32in (70–80cm).
P. 'Krinkled White' ■ Herbaceous perennial with mid-green leaves and strong stems. Early in the season, bears large, single, cup-shaped white, occasionally pink-flushed flowers, with slightly ruffled petals and golden yellow stamens. ↕↔ 30–32in (75–80cm).
P. lactiflora, syn. *P. albiflora*, *P. japonica* of gardens (Common garden peony). Herbaceous perennial with erect, red-mottled stems and dark green leaves, each with 9 elliptic or lance-shaped, rough-margined leaflets, paler and slightly hairy beneath. Bears usually solitary, single, cup- or bowl-shaped, fragrant, white to pale pink flowers, 3–4in (7–10cm) across, with pale yellow stamens. ↕↔ 20–28in (50–70cm). Russia (E. Siberia), Mongolia, N. and W. China, Tibet. Zone 4.
P. 'Lady Alexandra Duff'. Herbaceous perennial with abundant, mid-green leaves and strong stems. In midseason, bears double blush-pink flowers in clusters, with good fragrance. Enjoyed for its very free-flowering, large blooms. ↕↔ 34–36in (85–90cm).
P. 'Laura Dessert' ■ Herbaceous perennial with pale to mid-green leaves. In midseason, bears large, fragrant, double flowers with spreading, pink-flushed, creamy white outer petals and pale canary-yellow, incurving inner petals. ↕↔ 28–30in (70–75cm).
P. × lemoinei (*P. lutea* × *P. suffruticosa*). Upright to spreading, sparsely branched, deciduous shrub (tree peony) with dark green leaves, deeply divided into pointed lobes. Single to double, cup-shaped flowers, 6–8in (15–20cm) across, are white to yellow, often with orange, red, or pink marks. ↕↔ 5ft (1.5m). Garden origin. Zone 6. **'Mme. Louis Henri'** see *P.* 'Mme. Louis Henri'.

Paeonia emodi

Paeonia 'Nippon Beauty'

P. lobata see *P. peregrina*.
P. lutea. Upright, sparsely branched, deciduous shrub (tree peony) with dark green leaves, blue-green beneath, each with 9 leaflets, deeply cut into pointed lobes. Bears horizontal to nodding, single, cup-shaped, vivid yellow flowers, 2½in (6cm) across. ↕↔ 5ft (1.5m). S.W. China. Zone 6. **var. *ludlowii*** ■ syn. *P. delavayi* var. *ludlowii* (Tibetan peony) is more widely grown and more vigorous than the species, with bright green foliage and larger flowers, to 5in (13cm) across, borne in late spring; ↕↔ 8ft (2.5m); S.E. Tibet. **'Superba'** has bronze young foliage, and pink-flushed yellow flowers with red filaments and orange anthers.
P. 'Magnificent Flower' see *P. suffruticosa* 'Hana-daigin'.
P. mascula ■ syn. *P. corallina*. Erect herbaceous perennial with leaves divided into 9 broadly ovate, obovate, or elliptic leaflets, bluish green above, paler green beneath. Produces cup- to bowl-shaped, single, deep purplish red flowers, 3–5in (7–13cm) across, with deep yellow stamens. ↕↔ 24–39in (60–100cm). S. Europe. Zone 5b. **subsp. *arietina***, syn. *P. arietina*, has narrower, often lobed leaflets, hairy beneath, and reddish pink flowers; ↕↔ 20–30in (50–75cm). E. Europe, Turkey. **subsp. *arietina* 'Northern Glory'** has gray-green leaves and deep pink-purple flowers; ↕↔ 24–28in (60–70cm).
P. 'Mikado' ■ Herbaceous perennial with dull green leaves. In midseason, bears Japanese-type flowers with cupped petals and central dark crimson staminodes tipped with yellow; unpleasantly scented. ↕↔ 30–34in (75–85cm).
P. 'Miss America' ■ Herbaceous perennial with dark green foliage. Bears large, semi-double white flowers with fluted and crinkled inner petals, early in the season. ↕↔ 36in (90cm).
P. mlokosewitschii ■ (Caucasian peony, Molly the witch). Erect herbaceous perennial with bluish green leaves, each divided into 9 broadly elliptic, ovate, or obovate, blunt, sometimes red-margined leaflets, paler and slightly hairy beneath. In mid- and late spring, bears single, bowl-shaped, lemon-yellow flowers, 4–5in (10–13cm) across, with broad, oval petals and pale yellow stamens. ↕↔ 26–36in (65–90cm). Caucasus. Zone 5.
P. 'Mme. Louis Henri' ■ syn. *P.* × *lemoinei* 'Mme. Louis Henri'. Upright, deciduous shrub (tree peony) with mid-green leaves divided into pointed lobes. Bears semi-double, warm orange-yellow flowers, to 7in (18cm) across, heavily flushed orange-red. ↕↔ 6ft (2m).
P. 'Monsieur Jules Elie'. Herbaceous perennial with deep green leaves. Early in the season, bears very large, rounded, double, deep rose-red flowers with a silver sheen. ↕↔ 36–39in (90–100cm).
P. 'Moonstone' ■ Herbaceous perennial with mid-green leaves. Large, double white flowers with slightly pink-blushed inner petals, are borne in midseason. ↕↔ 36in (90cm).
P. 'Mother's Choice'. Herbaceous perennial with strong, vigorous stems and mid-green leaves. In midseason, bears large, double white flowers, with occasional slight, red edging. ↕↔ 3ft (1m).
P. 'Mrs. F.D. Roosevelt'. Herbaceous perennial with mid-green leaves. In midseason, bears large, double, fragrant, seashell-pink flowers. ↕↔ 34in (85cm).
P. 'Mrs. Gwyn Lewis' see *P.* 'Duchesse de Nemours'.
P. 'Nellie Saylor' ■ Herbaceous perennial with mid-green leaves. Bears large, Japanese-type, very fragrant, wine-red flowers, with cream to pink centers, in mid- and late season. ↕↔ 3ft (1m).
P. 'Nick Shaylor' ■ Herbaceous perennial with dark green leaves. Reliable bloomer, with large double, light pink flowers, with long, stiff stems, late in the season. ↕↔ 34in (85cm).
P. 'Nippon Beauty' ■ Herbaceous perennial with dark green leaves. In late season, produces deep red Japanese-type flowers, with petaloids the same color as petals, but flushed with yellow. ↕↔ 36in (90cm).
P. 'Nymphe'. Herbaceous perennial with dark green leaves. Late in the season, bears fragrant Japanese-type, light pink flowers, with prominent yellow petaloids in the center. ↕↔ 34in (85cm).
P. obovata. Herbaceous perennial with erect stems and large, deep green leaves, each with 9 uneven, broadly elliptic leaflets, pale gray-green and slightly hairy beneath. Bears single, cup-shaped, white to purplish red flowers, 3–4in (7–10cm) across, with yellow anthers and green-white or purple filaments. ↕↔ 24–28in (60–70cm). China. Zone 5. **var. *alba*** ■ has white flowers with purple filaments; ↕↔ 28–36in (70–90cm).
P. officinalis (Common peony). Herbaceous perennial with erect stems, slightly hairy at first, and deep green leaves, each divided into 9 leaflets with elliptic to oblong lobes, paler and sometimes hairy beneath. Bears single, cup-shaped, shiny, deep red or rose-pink flowers, 4–5in (10–13cm) across, with yellow stamens. ↕↔ 24–28in (60–70cm). Europe. Zone 3. **'Alba Plena'** has large, double white flowers, sometimes flushed pink, the slightly ruffled petals spreading to reveal the carpels at the center of each flower; ↕↔ 28–30in (70–75cm). **'China Rose'** has dark green leaves and single, deeply cup-shaped, deep salmon-pink flowers with golden yellow stamens; ↕↔ 18–20in (45–50cm). **subsp. *humilis*** see *P. humilis*. **subsp. *microcarpa*** see *P. humilis*. **'Rosea Superba Plena'** bears large, double, deep rose-pink flowers with slightly ruffled petals. **'Rubra Plena'** ■ has leaves with deep green leaflets, divided into broad, oval segments, and large, double, vivid crimson flowers with satiny, ruffled petals; ↕↔ 28–30in (70–75cm).
P. 'Paula Fay'. Herbaceous perennial with deep green foliage. Bears large, semi-double, dark rose-pink flowers with gold centers, early in the season. ↕↔ to 36in (90cm).
P. peregrina ■ syn. *P. decora*, *P. lobata*. Herbaceous perennial with erect stems and stiff, lustrous, deep green leaves, each with 9 notched or deeply lobed leaflets, bristly on the veins above, usually hairless beneath. Single, bowl-shaped, glistening, deep red flowers, 4–5in (10–13cm) across, with yellow stamens, are borne in late spring and early summer. ↕↔ 20–24in (50–60cm). S. Europe. Zone 6b.

Paeonia mascula

P

Paeonia 'Pillow Talk'

Paeonia 'Pink Hawaiian Coral'

Paeonia 'Pink Lemonade'

Paeonia potaninii var. *trollioides*

Paeonia 'Salmon Surprise'

Paeonia 'Sarah Bernhardt'

Paeonia 'Shirley Temple'

Paeonia suffruticosa 'Cardinal Vaughan'

Paeonia suffruticosa 'Godaishu'

Paeonia suffruticosa 'Reine Elisabeth'

Paeonia suffruticosa subsp. *rockii*

Paeonia 'Sword Dance'

Paeonia tenuifolia

Paeonia veitchii

Paeonia wittmanniana

***P.* 'Pillow Talk'** ▣ Herbaceous perennial with strong stems and dark green foliage. Large, double pink flowers, with darker petals at the bases, are borne in midseason. ↕↔ 30in (75cm).
***P.* 'Pink Hawaiian Coral'** ▣ Herbaceous perennial with mounded, mid-green foliage. Bears large, double, round-petaled, coral-pink flowers, fading to light pink toward the petal edges, with yellow stamens, early in the season. ↕↔ 36in (90cm).
***P.* 'Pink Lemonade'** ▣ Herbaceous perennial with upright stems and dark green foliage. Bears large, semi-double, fragrant, pink flowers, with peach-pink tones in the centers, in midseason. ↕↔ 28in (70cm).
***P.* 'Pink Parfait'.** Herbaceous perennial with dark green leaves. Produced late in the season, the double, light pink flowers have petals edged in silver, and are slightly fragrant. ↕↔ 36–38in (90–95cm).
***P.* 'Pink Princess'** ▣ Herbaceous perennial with mid-green leaves. In midseason, bears large, single, dark-pink-splashed, blush-pink flowers, with yellow stamens. ↕↔ to 3½ft (1.1m).
P. potaninii. Low-growing, deciduous subshrub (tree peony), spreading by suckers, bearing 2-pinnate, dark green leaves with slender lobes. Produces nodding, single, cup- or bowl-shaped, deep maroon-red flowers, 2in (5cm) across, with red filaments. ↕ 24in (60cm), ↔ 5ft (1.5m) or more. W. China. Zone 5. **f. *alba*** bears white flowers with green filaments. **var. *trollioides*** ▣ produces deeply cup-shaped yellow flowers in late spring.
***P.* 'Raspberry Sundae'.** Herbaceous perennial with dark green leaves. In midseason, bears large, double, fragrant, pale pink flowers, with outer petals aging to near white. ↕↔ to 28in (70cm).
***P.* 'Red Charm'.** Herbaceous perennial with dark green leaves. Bears large, double, very ruffled, dark red flowers, early in the season. ↕↔ 30in (75cm).
P. rockii see *P. suffruticosa* subsp. *rockii.*
***P.* 'Salmon Surprise'** ▣ Herbaceous perennial with mid-green leaves. Produces large, single salmon-pink flowers with gold centers, early in the season. ↕↔ 30in (75cm).
***P.* 'Sarah Bernhardt'** ▣ Robust herbaceous perennial with erect stems, mid-green leaves. Late in the season, bears very large, double, fragrant, rose-pink flowers, the inner petals with ruffled and silvered margins. ↕↔ 36–39in (90–100cm).
***P.* 'Scarlett O'Hara'.** Herbaceous perennial with mid-green leaves. Bears large, single scarlet flowers, fading to bright pink, with gold stamens, early in the season. ↕↔ 36in (90cm).
***P.* 'Sea Shell'.** Herbaceous perennial with dark green foliage. Produces large, single, shell-pink flowers with yellow stamens, in midseason. ↕↔ 36in (90cm).
***P.* 'Shirley Temple'** ▣ Herbaceous perennial with deep green leaves. In midseason, bears large, double, rose-pink flowers, fading to buff-white, with whorled petals, the innermost paler, narrower, and loosely arranged. ↕↔ 32–34in (80–85cm).
P.* x *smouthii (*P. lactiflora* x *P. tenuifolia*). Erect herbaceous perennial with bright green leaves, each divided into 9 leaflets with many, very narrow segments. In late spring, bears single, cup-shaped, fragrant, bright red flowers, 3–4in (7–10cm) across, with yellow stamens. A sterile hybrid. ↕↔ 24–32in (60–80cm). Garden origin. Zone 4.
P. suffruticosa (Moutan). Upright, sparsely branched, deciduous shrub (tree peony) with dark green leaves, blue-green beneath, each with 9 elliptic or ovate leaflets, deeply cut into pointed lobes. In late spring and early summer, bears single, cup- to bowl-shaped, sometimes scented, white, pink, red, or purple flowers, 6–12in (15–30cm) across, some with maroon marks at the bases. ↕↔ to 7ft (2.2m). China. Zone 5. **'Banksii'** has double, purple-red flowers with white tips. **'Cardinal Vaughan'** ▣ produces semi-double, ruby-purple flowers. **'Five Continents'** see 'Godaishu'. **'Godaishu'** ▣ syn. 'Five Continents', produces semi-double white flowers. **'Hana-daigin'**, syn. *P.* 'Magnificent Flower', has double, violet-purple flowers. **'Hana-kisoi'**, syn. *P.* 'Floral Rivalry', has semi-double, shell-pink flowers. **'Joseph Rock'** see subsp. *rockii.* **'Kamada-nishiki'**, syn. *P.* 'Kamada Brocade', has double, reddish mauve flowers. **'Mrs. William Kelway'** bears double white flowers. **'Reine Elisabeth'** ▣ has semi-double to double, salmon-pink flowers tinged red, with ruffled margins. **'Renkaku'**, syn. *P.* 'Flight of Cranes', has large, semi-double white flowers with deep yellow stamens. **'Rimpo'** has very large, double, purple-black flowers, with contrasting yellow stamens. **subsp. *rockii*** ▣ syn. 'Joseph Rock', 'Rock's Variety', *P. rockii*, has semi-double white flowers, marked deep maroon at the bases.

Paeonia 'Pink Princess'

'Rock's Variety' see subsp. *rockii.* **'Yae-zakura'**, syn. *P.* 'Double Cherry', has double, soft pink flowers.
***P.* 'Sword Dance'** ▣ Herbaceous perennial with mid-green leaves. Bears Japanese-type, bright red flowers with numerous very striking red and yellow petaloids, in midseason. Heat-tolerant. ↕↔ 34in (85cm).
P. tenuifolia ▣ (Fernleaf peony) Herbaceous perennial with deep green leaves, pale and gray-green beneath, with many pointed, linear segments. In mid- and late spring, bears single, cup-shaped, deep red flowers, 3–3½in (7–9cm) across, with yellow stamens. ↕↔ 20–28in (50–70cm). S.E. Europe to S. Russia. Zone 4. **'Plena'** produces long-lasting, double, rich red flowers.
***P.* 'Top Brass'.** Herbaceous perennial with mid-green leaves. In midseason, bears flowers with large, fragrant, rounded, ivory guard petals surrounding double centers of light pink, canary-yellow, and ivory. ↕↔ 28in (70cm).
P. veitchii ▣ Herbaceous perennial with hairless stems and deep green leaves, each divided into 9 lance-shaped, pointed leaflets, hairy along the veins above, pale gray-green and hairless beneath. Usually solitary, semi-pendent, single, cup-shaped, white or pink to pale magenta-pink flowers, 3–3½in (7–9cm) across, with pale lemon stamens, open widely. ↕↔ 20–24in (50–60cm). W. China. Zone 7. **f. *alba*** produces white flowers with yellow stamens; ↕↔ 28–30in (70–75cm).
***P.* 'Victor Hugo'** see *P.* 'Félix Crousse'.
***P.* 'Walter Faxon'.** Herbaceous perennial with dark green leaves. The vivid color of the double, shell-pink flowers is both distinctive and unusual. It has a slight fragrance and blooms in midseason. ↕↔ 30in (75cm).
***P.* 'Westerner'.** Herbaceous perennial with mid-green leaves. In midseason, bears large, Japanese-type, mid-pink flowers with large centers of bright yellow staminodes. ↕↔ 36in (90cm).
P. wittmanniana ▣ Herbaceous perennial with stiff, hairless stems and shiny, dark green leaves with broadly ovate to broadly elliptic leaflets, paler and downy beneath. In late spring and early summer, bears deeply cup-shaped to almost hemispherical, single, primrose-yellow flowers, 4–5in (10–13cm) across, with yellow anthers and red filaments. ↕↔ 32–42in (80–110cm). N.W. Caucasus. Zone 5.

P

Paliurus spina-christi

PALIURUS

RHAMNACEAE

Genus of about 8 species of spiny, deciduous or evergreen shrubs and trees occurring in dry and rocky places in woodland and at stream margins from S. Europe to E. Asia. The glossy, mid- to dark green leaves are alternate, ovate to broadly ovate, entire or toothed, often with heart-shaped bases. Star-shaped, 5-petaled, yellowish green flowers are produced in small, axillary cymes. The fruits are large, flat, winged disks. *P. spina-christi* is cultivated for its foliage, small flowers, and unusual fruit. Grow in a shrub border or against a wall; can be used for hedging in regions with hot summers.
• **CULTIVATION** Grow in full sun in any well-drained soil. Pruning group 1.
• **PROPAGATION** Sow seed in containers in a cold frame in autumn. Take softwood cuttings in summer.
• **PESTS AND DISEASES** Infrequent.

P. spina-christi ▣ (Christ's thorn, Jerusalem thorn). Bushy, deciduous shrub with slender, thorny shoots and ovate, 3-veined, glossy, bright dark green leaves, to 1½in (4cm) long. Small cymes of tiny, star-shaped yellow flowers are produced in summer, followed by woody fruit, to 1in (2.5cm) across, each with a rounded green wing, turning brown. ↕ 12ft (4m), ↔ 10ft (3m). S. Europe to N. China. Zone 7b.

PAMIANTHE

AMARYLLIDACEAE

Genus of 2 or 3 species of evergreen or deciduous, bulbous perennials from moist, sandy but rocky areas at altitudes of 3,250–7,000ft (1,000–2,000m) in South America. They have false stems formed from the bases of the strap-shaped, keeled leaves, and are grown for their umbels of large, fragrant white spring flowers, resembling daffodils (*Narcissus*), each with 6 spreading outer tepals and an inner cup. Where not hardy, grow in a temperate or warm greenhouse. In warmer regions, grow among small shrubs or in a border.
• **CULTIVATION** Plant in late summer or early autumn, with the neck of each bulb just above soil level. Under glass, grow in soil-based potting mix, with added grit and well-rotted organic matter, in full light. When in growth, water moderately and apply a balanced liquid fertilizer every month. Water sparingly at other times. Outdoors, grow in moderately fertile, moist but sharply drained soil in full sun.
• **PROPAGATION** Sow seed at 61–70°F (16–21°C) when ripe. Remove offsets in autumn.
• **PESTS AND DISEASES** Infrequent.

Pamianthe peruviana

P. peruviana ▣ (Peruvian daffodil). Deciduous, bulbous perennial with a false stem formed by the bases of the semi-erect, strap-shaped, mid-green leaves, 20in (50cm) long, with rounded keels. In spring, produces terminal umbels of 2–4 large, strongly fragrant flowers, 5in (13cm) across, with spreading, creamy white outer petals and bell-shaped, split white cups with green central stripes. ↕ to 4ft (1.2m), ↔ 12in (30cm). Peruvian Andes. ❄ (min. 59°F/15°C)

PANAX

Ginseng

ARALIACEAE

Genus of about 5 species of herbaceous perennials, occurring in moist woodland in S. and E. Asia and E. US. Aromatic, thickened or tuberous rootstocks produce annual stems, each bearing a single whorl of 3 mid- or dull green palmate leaves with 3–7 leaflets, and a single, terminal umbel of tiny, star-shaped, greenish white flowers, followed by fleshy fruit. The roots of ginseng are much prized for their stimulative and restorative properties. It is suitable for growing in an herb garden, and as a groundcover in a woodland garden. Harvest the roots 6 years after sowing.
• **CULTIVATION** Grow in deep, fertile, humus-rich, moist soil in light dappled or partial shade.
• **PROPAGATION** Sow seed in containers outdoors or divide in spring.
• **PESTS AND DISEASES** Rhizome rots, leaf blight, wilt, and gray mold can be problems.

P. ginseng (Korean ginseng). Perennial with a long, cream-colored, carrot-shaped root, and mid-green leaves, to 5in (13cm) long, each with 5 ovate leaflets. In summer, bears 5-petaled, star-shaped greenish white flowers, ⅜in (9mm) long. ↕ 32in (80cm), ↔ 24in (60cm). N.E. China, Korea. Zone 6.
P. quinquefolius (American ginseng, Sang). Perennial with branching, carrot-shaped, aromatic roots and long-stalked, mid-green leaves, to 5in (13cm) long, each with 3–7 ovate to obovate, narrowly pointed, coarsely toothed leaflets. In early summer, bears star-shaped, green-white flowers, ⅜in (9mm) long, followed by bright red fruit. ↕ to 36in (90cm), ↔ 24in (60cm). E. North America. Zone 4.

PANCRATIUM

Sea lily

AMARYLLIDACEAE

Genus of about 16 species of bulbous perennials found in sandy or rocky sites from the Canary Islands, W. Africa to Namibia, and the Mediterranean to tropical Asia. They have 2-ranked, linear to strap-shaped, basal leaves, and produce terminal umbels of showy, fragrant flowers, each with 6 spreading outer petals and a central cup. Grow sea lilies against a warm, sunny wall or, where not hardy, in a cool greenhouse or in containers.
• **CULTIVATION** Plant bulbs 6–8in (15–20cm) deep when dormant. Under glass, grow in soil-based potting mix with added grit, in deep containers or in a greenhouse border, in full light. When in growth, water freely and apply a balanced liquid fertilizer monthly. Keep dry in summer when dormant. Water sparingly in autumn and winter. Outdoors, grow in any sharply drained soil in full sun.
• **PROPAGATION** Sow seed at 55–64°F (13–18°C) when ripe, or remove offsets when dormant.
• **PESTS AND DISEASES** Infrequent.

Pancratium illyricum

P. illyricum ▣ Bulbous perennial with semi-erect, broad, strap-shaped, mid-green, glaucous, basal leaves, to 20in (50cm) long. Bears umbels of 10–15 white flowers, 3in (8cm) across, in late spring and early summer. ↕ 16in (40cm), ↔ 6in (15cm). Corsica, Sardinia. ❄ (min. 35°F/2°C)
P. maritimum (Sea daffodil). Bulbous perennial with long-necked bulbs and semi-erect, narrow, strap-shaped, gray-green, basal leaves, to 20in (50cm) long. In late summer, produces umbels of up to 6 fragrant white flowers, to 4in (10cm) across. ↕↔ 12in (30cm). Coastal S.W. Europe, Mediterranean. ❄ (min. 35°F/2°C)

PANDANUS

Screw pine

PANDANACEAE

Genus of 250 or more species of dioecious, evergreen shrubs and trees occurring in dry and moist sites throughout tropical regions of Africa, India, Asia, Australasia, and the Pacific islands. The sparsely branched stems of mature plants are often supported by stilt roots. Screw pines are grown for their attractive foliage: the linear, light to dark green leaves are tough and usually spiny-toothed, and borne in 3 spiraling ranks forming terminal rosettes. The small and petalless male and female flowers are produced on separate plants, males in slender, often branched spikes, and females in short, dense, cone-like heads, which develop into small fruits, resembling pineapples when fertilized. Where temperatures fall below 55°F (13°C), grow young plants in a warm greenhouse or as houseplants. In warmer regions, use as specimens.
• **CULTIVATION** Under glass, grow in soil-based potting mix, with added leaf mold and charcoal, in full light, with moderate to high humidity. From spring to summer, water moderately and apply a balanced liquid fertilizer every month. Water sparingly in winter. Outdoors, grow in fertile, moist but well-drained soil in full sun. Pruning group 1.
• **PROPAGATION** Sow seed at 64°F (18°C) as soon as ripe or in spring, first soaking them for 24 hours. Remove suckers or offsets in spring.
• **PESTS AND DISEASES** Scale insects and spider mites can cause problems under glass. Basal stem rot, leaf whorl rot, anthracnose, and leaf spots can occur.

P

Pandanus tectorius

P. odoratissimus see *P. tectorius.*
P. sanderi. Slow-growing, suckering shrub that seldom branches and rarely flowers. Bears rosettes of arching, linear, minutely spiny yellow leaves, 18–30in (45–75cm) long, becoming green with pale yellow stripes when mature. ↕ 3ft (1m), ↔ 30–60in (0.75–1.5m). Malaysia, possibly Indonesia. ❄ (min. 55°F/13°C). **'Roehrsianus'** is more robust, and has leaves to 3ft (1m) long.
P. tectorius ▣ syn. *P. odoratissimus* (Thatch screw pine). Many-branched, upright tree with thick stilt roots. Whorls of robust branches bear rosettes of linear, long-pointed, stiffly leathery, bluish green leaves, 3–5ft (1–1.5m) long, with spines along the margins and midribs beneath. Each male flower spike, 8–12in (20–30cm) long, is branched and sheathed in a fragrant white spathe; female flowerheads are small and solitary, about 2in (5cm) across. Flowers are borne mainly in summer, followed by spherical to broadly ovoid fruit, 6–10in (15–25cm) long; they may be yellow or light green flushed red. ↕ 10–20ft (3–6m), ↔ 6–12ft (2–4m). S.E. Asia, Pacific islands. ❄ (min. 55°F/13°C). **var. *bulbosus*** is larger, with fleshier fruit; widely grown in the Pacific; ↕ 12–20ft (4–6m). **var. *laevis*** has spineless leaves.

P

PANDOREA

BIGNONIACEAE

Genus of 6 species of woody-stemmed, evergreen, twining climbers, rarely shrubs, related to *Tecomaria* and *Tecoma*. They are found in rainforest from sea level to 10,000ft (3,000m) in Malaysia, Papua New Guinea, Australia, and New Caledonia, and are grown for their attractive flowers and foliage. Leaves are opposite or whorled, pinnate, and mid- or dark green, each with up to 7 pairs of leaflets. The fragrant, tubular flowers, each with 5 broad, spreading petal lobes, the upper 2 smaller than the lower 3, are borne usually in terminal, cyme-like panicles or racemes. In mild climates, they are suitable for a pergola or arch, and look especially effective cascading from a tree. Where not hardy, grow in a cool greenhouse.
• **CULTIVATION** Under glass, grow in soil-based potting mix in full light. When in growth, water moderately and apply a balanced liquid fertilizer monthly. Water sparingly in winter. Outdoors, grow in fertile, moist but well-drained soil in full sun. Provide support for climbing stems. Pruning group 11, after flowering.
• **PROPAGATION** Sow seed at 55–64°F (13–18°C) in spring. Root greenwood cuttings with bottom heat in summer. Layer in spring.
• **PESTS AND DISEASES** Susceptible to spider mites and aphids under glass.

Pandorea jasminoides

P. jasminoides ▣ syn. *Bignonia jasminoides* (Bower plant). Vigorous, twining climber with wiry, branching stems, and pinnate leaves composed of 5–9 ovate to lance-shaped, glossy, bright green leaflets, 1–2in (2.5–5cm) long. Tubular flowers with spreading lobes, 1½–2in (4–5cm) across, are white, flushed crimson-pink in the throats, and freely produced in small, cyme-like panicles from spring to summer. ↕ 15ft (5m) or more. Queensland, New South Wales. ❄ (min. 41°F/5°C). **'Alba'** has pure white flowers. **'Lady Di'** has white flowers with creamy yellow, sometimes orange-yellow throats. **'Rosea'** bears pink flowers with deeper pink throats. **'Rosea Superba'** produces large pink flowers, to 2½in (6cm) long, with purple-spotted, deep pink throats.
P. lindleyana see *Clytostoma callistegioides.*
P. pandorana, syn. *Bignonia pandorana, Tecoma australis* (Wonga wonga vine). Strong-growing, twining climber with slender, branching stems. Pinnate leaves have usually 6 pairs of ovate to broadly lance-shaped, mid-green leaflets, 1¼–4in (3–10cm) long, deeply and narrowly lobed when young, entire or sometimes scalloped when mature. Tubular, creamy yellow flowers spotted and streaked reddish purple, ½–1¼in (1.5–3cm) across, with spreading lobes, are borne in terminal and axillary cyme-like racemes in winter and spring. ↕ 20ft (6m) or more. E. Australia (including Tasmania), Papua New Guinea, Pacific islands. ❄ (min. 41°F/5°C)
P. ricasoliana see *Podranea ricasoliana.*

PANICUM

POACEAE

Genus of about 470 annual or perennial, deciduous or evergreen grasses occurring in open grassland or wooded areas, often in rocky, moist limestone soil, in tropical regions worldwide, in Europe, and in temperate North America. The leaves are thread-like in bud, usually becoming flat and linear-ovate, and may be light to mid-green, gray-green, or purple. In late summer and autumn, they produce finely branching panicles or racemes of 2-flowered spikelets. Ornamental species are valued mainly for their light, airy flowerheads, suitable for cutting and drying; a number of species, such as millet (*P. miliaceum*), are also valuable fodder crops. Grow in a sunny, mixed or herbaceous border.
• **CULTIVATION** Grow in moderately fertile, well-drained soil in full sun.
• **PROPAGATION** Sow seed at 55–64°F (13–18°C) in spring. Divide perennials between midspring and early summer.
• **PESTS AND DISEASES** Prone to damping off, black ring, tar spot, rust, smut, leaf spots, anthracnose, and sugarcane mosaic virus.

P. capillare (Witch grass). Lax, loosely tufted annual with clumps of flat, linear to narrowly lance-shaped, mid-green leaves, to 12in (30cm) long. In late summer and autumn, produces dense panicles, to 18in (45cm) long, of tiny, greenish brown spikelets on hair-fine branchlets. ↕ 24–39in (60–100cm), ↔ 24in (60cm). North America.
P. miliaceum (Millet). Erect, clump-forming annual with flat, narrow, lance-shaped, mid-green, sometimes purple-flushed leaves, to 16in (40cm) long. Produces rigid, intricately branched panicles, to 12in (30cm) long, of slightly pendent, purple-tinged green flowers, borne in small spikelets, to ¼in (6mm) long, in late summer. ↕ to 36in (90cm), ↔ to 9in (23cm). C., S., and E. Europe. **'Violaceum'**, syn. *P. violaceum*, has purple-violet leaves and spikelets.
P. violaceum see *P. miliaceum* 'Violaceum'.
P. virgatum (Switch grass). Narrowly upright, rhizomatous, deciduous, perennial grass forming clumps of purple to glaucous, mid-green stems that bear upright, flat, linear, mid-green leaves, to 24in (60cm) long. Leaves turn yellow in autumn and light brown in winter. Produces broad, diffuse, weeping panicles, to 20in (50cm) long, of tiny, purple-green spikelets in early autumn. ↕ 3ft (1m), ↔ 30in (75cm). S. Canada, US to Central America. Zone 4. **'Hänse Herms'**, syn. 'Haense Herms', has a fountain-like habit, and rich reddish purple autumn foliage. **'Heavy Metal'** ▣ has stiffer, more erect, metallic blue-gray leaves, yellow in autumn. **'Strictum'** is narrowly upright, with leaves that turn bright yellow in autumn; ↕ 4ft (1.2m), ↔ 24in (60cm).

Panicum virgatum 'Heavy Metal'

PAPAVER

Poppy

PAPAVERACEAE

Genus of 70 species of annuals, biennials, and perennials occurring in a wide range of habitats, from lowlands to high mountains; most are from C. and S. Europe and temperate Asia, a few from South Africa, Australia, W. North America, and subarctic regions. The usually unbranched, wiry, sometimes hairy stems, which exude latex if damaged, produce a few alternate, mostly radical leaves, which may be simple and toothed, or pinnate to 3-pinnate, pinnatifid or pinnatisect, bristly or smooth, and gray-green or light to dark green. The short-lived flowers are wide-spreading, bowl-, cup-, or saucer-shaped, usually 4-petaled, and brightly colored, sometimes with basal marks or spots. They are borne singly or in panicles or racemes, the buds often pendent, and are followed by distinctive "pepper-pot" seed pods (capsules). Most larger species are spectacular plants for a mixed or herbaceous border; several of the smaller poppies are suitable for a rock garden or an annual border.
• **CULTIVATION** Grow in deep, fertile, well-drained soil in full sun, except *P. alpinum* and its cultivars, which require very sharply drained soil. Grow summer-dormant species such as *P. orientale* among later-flowering perennials to fill in gaps left by disappearing foliage.
• **PROPAGATION** Sow seed in spring: for annuals and biennials, sow seed *in situ*; for perennials, sow seed in containers in a cold frame. Divide perennials in spring, or take root cuttings from them in late autumn or early winter.
• **PESTS AND DISEASES** Powdery mildew, leaf smut, gray mold (*Botrytis*), root rot, and damping off occur.

Papaver alpinum

Papaver atlanticum

Papaver fauriei

Papaver 'Fireball'

Papaver orientale 'Allegro'

P. alpinum ■ (Alpine poppy). Tuft-forming, short-lived perennial with variable, 2- or 3-pinnate, sometimes pinnatisect, hairy, gray-green leaves, to 8in (20cm) long, with linear segments. Solitary, cup- to saucer-shaped, white, yellow, orange, or red flowers, to 1½in (4cm) across, are produced in summer. The name *P. alpinum* is often used to include a range of plants that are now considered distinct species. ↕ 6–8in (15–20cm), ↔ 4in (10cm). Europe (Pyrenees, Alps, Carpathian Mountains). Zone 5. **subsp. *burseri*** see *P. burseri.* **subsp. *rhaeticum*** see *P. rhaeticum.*
P. atlanticum ■ Erect, clump-forming, short-lived perennial with oblong to lance-shaped, coarsely toothed, mid-green leaves, to 6in (15cm) long, very hairy, particularly beneath. In summer, bears solitary, saucer-shaped, soft orange flowers, to 2in (5cm) across, with very hairy sepals. ↕ 12in (30cm), ↔ 6in (15cm). Morocco. Zone 5.
P. bracteatum. (Great scarlet poppy). Upright, clump-forming, bristly perennial producing pinnatisect, mid-green leaves, 10–18in (25–45cm) long, with lance-shaped, toothed segments. In early summer, bears solitary, bowl-shaped, blood-red flowers, 4–7in (10–18cm) across, with 4–6 petals, each with a large, elongated, black spot at the base. Similar to *P. orientale* but with taller, stiffer stems, sepal-like bracts below the flowers, and longer spots on the petals. ↕ to 4ft (1.2m), ↔ 36in (90cm). N. Iran. Zone 6.
P. burseri, syn. *P. alpinum* subsp. *burseri.* Tuft-forming, almost hairless, semi-evergreen, short-lived perennial with 2- or 3-pinnate, gray-green leaves, to 8in (20cm) long, consisting of linear to lance-shaped segments. In summer, produces solitary, saucer-shaped white flowers, to 1½in (4cm) across, with yellow stamens. ↕ 6in (15cm), ↔ 4in (10cm). Europe (Alps, Carpathian Mountains). Zone 4.
P. commutatum. Erect, branching annual with oval to oblong, pinnatisect, downy, mid-green leaves, to 6in (15cm) long, with lance-shaped segments. Solitary, bowl-shaped, brilliant red flowers, to 3in (8cm) across, spotted black at the petal bases, are borne on softly gray-hairy stems in summer. ↕ to 18in (45cm), ↔ 6in (15cm). Greece (Crete), Turkey, Caucasus, N. Iran.

Papaver croceum 'Summer Breeze'

P. croceum, syn. *P. nudicaule* of gardens (Arctic poppy, Iceland poppy). Erect, tuft-forming, hairy perennial, usually grown as a biennial, producing oval, pinnatifid to pinnatisect, densely hairy, blue-green leaves, 1¼–6in (3–15cm) long, with oblong segments. Solitary, bowl-shaped, occasionally double, fragrant, yellow or white, sometimes orange or pale red flowers, to 3in (8cm) across, are borne on short, hairy stalks in summer. ↕ to 12in (30cm), ↔ to 6in (15cm). Subarctic regions. Zone 3. **'Champagne Bubbles'** has large flowers, to 5in (13cm) across, in a range of mostly pastel shades, including red, bronze-yellow, apricot-yellow, pink, and yellow; ↕ to 18in (45cm). **'Garden Gnome'** is dwarf, with flowers mainly in bright shades, including orange-red, yellow, pink, salmon-pink, and white. **'Sparkling Bubbles'** has large flowers in pastel shades and bright shades, including yellow, rose, orange, scarlet, and cream-white; ↕ 16in (40cm). **'Summer Breeze'** ■ bears orange, golden yellow, yellow, or white flowers over a very long flowering period; ↕ 12–14in (30–35cm). **'Wonderland'** is dwarf, with large, short-stalked, white, orange, yellow, or red flowers, and is ideal in containers; ↕ to 10in (25cm).
P. dubium (Long-headed poppy). Upright, slender-stemmed, hairy annual with pinnatisect, blue-green leaves, 4–6in (10–15cm) long, with ovate segments. Throughout summer, produces solitary, saucer-shaped, pale scarlet or pinkish red flowers, to 3in (8cm) across, sometimes marked black at the petal bases. ↕ to 24in (60cm), ↔ to 8in (20cm). Europe, W. Asia.
P. fauriei ■ syn. *P. miyabeanum* of gardens. Compact, mound-forming, short-lived perennial, similar to *P. alpinum*, bearing pinnate, gray-green leaves, to 6in (15cm) long, with lance-shaped, deeply lobed leaflets. Solitary, bowl-shaped, pale yellow or greenish yellow flowers, ¾–1¼in (2–3cm) across, are produced in summer. ↕↔ to 4in (10cm). Russia, Japan. Zone 5.
***P.* 'Fireball'** ■ syn. *P.* 'Nanum Flore Pleno'. Upright, densely hairy perennial, spreading freely by runners, bearing lance-shaped, conspicuously toothed, bristly, mid-green leaves, to 8in (20cm) long. Bears solitary, hemispherical, semi-double to double, orange-scarlet flowers, 1¼–1½in (3–4cm) across, with narrow petals, from late spring to midsummer. ↕↔ 12in (30cm). Zone 4.

P. lateritium. Clump-forming, upright perennial with very hairy, oblong, deeply toothed, mid-green leaves, to 8in (20cm) long. Branching stems produce bowl-shaped, deep orange flowers, to 2in (5cm) across, usually solitary but occasionally in pairs, in mid- and late summer. ↕ 16in (40cm), ↔ 12in (30cm). Turkey. Zone 5.
***P. miyabeanum* of gardens** see *P. fauriei.*
***P.* 'Nanum Flore Pleno'** see *P.* 'Fireball'.
***P. nudicaule* of gardens** see *P. croceum.*
P. orientale (Oriental poppy). Clump-forming perennial, spreading by runners, with erect, white-bristly stems and pinnatisect, mid-green leaves, to 12in (30cm) long, with lance-shaped, toothed segments. From late spring to midsummer, bears solitary, cup-shaped, orange-scarlet flowers, 4–6in (10–15cm) across, with no bracts; the 4–6 petals have large, bluish black or white basal spots, broader than they are long. ↕ 18–36in (45–90cm), ↔ 24–36in (60–90cm). Caucasus, N.E. Turkey, N. Iran. Zone 3. Most plants grown in gardens as cultivars of *P. orientale* are hybrids with *P. bracteatum* and the closely related *P. pseudoorientale;* they are listed here for easy reference. **'Allegro'** ■ has bright orange-scarlet flowers with bold, black basal marks. **'Beauty of Livermere'** has large, crimson-scarlet flowers, to 8in (20cm) across, with a black mark at the base of each petal; ↕ 3–4ft (0.9–1.2m), ↔ 36in (90cm). **'Black and White'** ■ produces white flowers with a crimson-black mark at the base of each petal.

Papaver orientale 'Black and White'

Papaver orientale 'Cedric Morris'

'Carnival' has frilled petals, white at the bases and orange-red above. **'Cedric Morris'** ▣ has gray-hairy leaves and very large, soft pink flowers, to 6in (15cm) across, the frilled petals each with a black basal mark. **'Helen Elizabeth'** bears soft, clear, salmon-pink flowers. **'Indian Chief'** has deep mahogany-red flowers without spots. **'Maiden's Blush'** blooms late and has very ruffled white flowers, 6in (15cm) across, with a wide blush-pink edge; ↕ 24–30in (60–75cm). **'May Queen'** produces double, orange-red flowers with slightly quilled, unmarked petals. **'Mrs. Perry'** bears pale salmon-pink flowers with black basal marks. **'Perry's White'** has white flowers with maroon-purple centers. **'Picotée'** produces pure white flowers with creased petals that have broad, frilled, orange-pink margins. **'Pinnacle'** has large, bicolored, white and scarlet flowers; ↕ 30in (75cm). **'Prince of Orange'** produces orange-scarlet flowers; ↕ 30in (75cm). **'Princess Victoria Louise'** bears salmon-pink flowers with a basal black blotch on each petal; ↕ 24–30in (60–75cm).

P. rhaeticum, syn. *P. alpinum* subsp. *rhaeticum*. Tufted perennial, similar to *P. alpinum*, bearing pinnate, finely hairy, gray-green leaves, to 3in (8cm) long, composed of ovate to lance-shaped segments. Bears solitary, bowl-shaped, golden yellow or orange flowers, to 2in (5cm) across, in summer. ↕ 6in (15cm), ↔ 4in (10cm). Pyrenees. Zone 5.

P. rhoeas (Corn poppy, Field poppy, Flanders poppy). Erect, branching, sparsely hairy annual with oblong, pinnatifid to pinnatisect, downy, light green leaves, to 6in (15cm) long, with lance-shaped segments. Solitary, bowl-shaped, brilliant red flowers, to 3in (8cm) across, sometimes marked black at the petal bases, are produced on short, downy stalks in summer. ↕ to 36in (90cm), ↔ to 12in (30cm). Eurasia, N. Africa; also widely naturalized. **'Fairy Wings'** see 'Mother of Pearl'. **'Mother of Pearl'** ▣ syn. 'Fairy Wings', produces dove-gray, soft pink, or lilac-blue flowers, with some paler zoning. **Shirley Series** ▣ cultivars have single, semi-double, or double flowers in yellow, pink, orange, or sometimes red, always unmarked at the bases; they need careful selection to maintain the true stock. **Shirley Series 'Reverend Wilks'** has single and semi-double flowers in red, pink, or white, with some picotees and bicolors.

Papaver rhoeas 'Mother of Pearl'

Papaver rhoeas Shirley Series

P. rupifragum. Erect, clump-forming perennial with obovate, toothed or lobed, mid-green leaves, to 6in (15cm) long. In summer, produces solitary, bowl-shaped, pale brick-red flowers, to 3in (8cm) across. May self-seed freely. ↕ 18in (45cm), ↔ 8in (20cm). Spain. Zone 5.

P. somniferum ▣ (Opium poppy). Erect annual with oblong, deeply lobed, glaucous, blue-green leaves, to 5in (13cm) or more long. In summer, leafy stems bear solitary, bowl-shaped, pink, mauve-purple, red, or white flowers, to 4in (10cm) across, sometimes with dark spots at the petal bases. They are followed by large, blue-green seed pods that are good for dried arrangements. All parts may cause mild stomach upset if ingested. ↕ to 4ft (1.2m), ↔ to 12in (30cm). Origin unknown; very widely cultivated and naturalized. **'Hen and Chickens'** is grown primarily for its seed heads, with very large capsules surrounded by clusters of much smaller ones. **'Peony Flowered'** ▣ has large, double, frilly flowers in red, purple, pink, salmon-pink, maroon-red, or white. **'White Cloud'** produces double white flowers.

Papaver somniferum

Papaver somniferum 'Peony Flowered'

P. triniifolium. Erect, branching, hairless or sparsely hairy biennial. In the first year, forms a basal rosette of 3 or 4 ovate to oblong, pinnatisect, glaucous, blue-green leaves, to 3in (8cm) long, with linear segments covered in short yellow hairs. In the summer of the second year, many-branched, leafy stems produce solitary, cup-shaped, orange-pink flowers, to 2in (5cm) across. ↕ to 12in (30cm), ↔ 6in (15cm). E. and S. Turkey. Zone 6.

PAPHIOPEDILUM

Slipper orchid

ORCHIDACEAE

Genus of about 60 species of evergreen, mainly terrestrial orchids, some epiphytic or lithophytic, occurring at sea level to over 7,000ft (2,000m), from India to China, S.E. Asia, and Papua New Guinea. Slipper orchids are sympodial, lack pseudobulbs, and produce short stems bearing strap-shaped, lance-shaped, or elliptic to ovate, leathery, sometimes mottled, gray to pale, mid-, or dark green leaves. Each shoot ends in a distinctive solitary flower, or a raceme of 2–8 flowers, each with an upright upper sepal, 2 spreading petals, and 2 lateral sepals united under a variably shaped pouch. Many hybrids exist.

• **CULTIVATION** Cool- to intermediate-growing orchids. Grow in terrestrial orchid potting mix, with added crushed bark and dolomitic limestone chips, in pots that constrict the roots. In summer, provide high humidity and bright filtered light, water freely, and apply fertilizer at every third watering. Do not mist. In winter, provide slightly fuller light and water sparingly; do not allow the soil mix to dry out completely between waterings. See also p.46.

• **PROPAGATION** Older clumps often separate naturally when being repotted. Single plants may be separated off when new growth begins.

• **PESTS AND DISEASES** Spider mites, whiteflies, mealybugs, and aphids commonly occur. Prone to gray mold (*Botrytis*), anthracnose, root rot, iron deficiency, cymbidium mosaic virus, and bacterial soft rot.

P. appletonianum ▣ Terrestrial orchid with elliptic, mottled, mid-green and purple leaves, to 8in (20cm) long. Solitary flowers, 5in (13cm) across, with slender green and rose-pink petals, pale green, darker veined upper sepals, and light brown pouches, are produced in winter and spring. ↕ 20in (50cm), ↔ 6in (15cm). Laos, Thailand, Cambodia. ❀ (min. 55°F/13°C; max. 86°F/30°C)

P. argus. Terrestrial orchid with oblong-lance-shaped, pale green leaves with darker mottling, 5–8in (12–20cm) long. In spring, produces solitary flowers, 4in (10cm) across, with dark purple-spotted, off-white petals, pink at the tips; upper sepals have dark green or purple veining; dark green-veined pouches are red above the lips, yellow beneath. ↕ 18in (45cm), ↔ 6in (15cm). Philippines. ❀ (min. 55°F/13°C; max. 86°F/30°C)

P. bellatulum ▣ Terrestrial orchid with rigid, leathery, elliptic to strap-shaped leaves, mottled green and gray, to 8in (20cm) long. Solitary, almost stemless, rounded, white or pale yellow flowers, 3½in (9cm) across, with large, dark red spots, are produced in spring. ↕ 5in (13cm), ↔ 6in (15cm). Burma, Thailand. ❀ (min. 55°F/13°C; max. 86°F/30°C)

***P.* Buckhurst 'Mont Millais'** ▣ (*P.* Greenville x *P.* Spring Vigil). Terrestrial orchid with strap-shaped to ovate, mid-green leaves, 6in (15cm) long. Solitary yellow flowers, 5in (13cm) across, with white upper sepals, are usually produced in winter. ↕ 12in (30cm), ↔ 8in (20cm). ❀ (min. 55°F/13°C; max. 86°F/30°C)

P. callosum ▣ Terrestrial orchid with strap-shaped to elliptic, grayish green leaves, to 10in (25cm) long, with dark green mottling. In spring, produces solitary, maroon and green flowers, 3–3½in (7–9cm) across, with white-striped maroon upper sepals and maroon lips. ↕ 12in (30cm), ↔ 6in (15cm). Thailand, Cambodia, S. Vietnam. ❀ (min. 55°F/13°C; max. 86°F/30°C)

P. delenatii. Terrestrial orchid with rigid, leathery, elliptic to strap-shaped leaves, 4–6in (10–15cm) long, mottled green and gray above, deep purple beneath. In spring, almost stalkless white to pink flowers, 3in (8cm) across, with pink lips, are produced singly or in pairs. ↕ 8in (20cm), ↔ 6in (15cm). C. Vietnam. ❀ (min. 55°F/13°C; max. 86°F/30°C)

P. fairrieanum ▣ Terrestrial orchid with strap-shaped, dark green leaves, 3½–6in (9–15cm) long. In autumn, produces solitary, purple-veined, pale green-white flowers, 2½–3in (6–8cm) across, with recurved petals and greenish yellow lips suffused purple-brown. ↕↔ 6in (15cm). Himalayas, N.E. India (Sikkim), Bhutan. ❀ (min. 50°F/10°C; max. 86°F/30°C)

***P.* Freckles** ▣ (*P.* Burleigh Mohur x *P.* F.C. Puddle). Terrestrial orchid with strap-shaped, mid-green leaves, 6in (15cm) long. In early winter, produces solitary cream flowers, 5in (13cm) across, spotted purple-brown, with pink-flushed lips. ↕ 12in (30cm), ↔ 8in (20cm). ❀ (min. 55°F/13°C; max. 86°F/30°C)

***P.* Goultenianum 'Album'** ▣ (*P. callosum* x *P. curtisii*). Terrestrial orchid with broadly ovate, mottled, gray-green and dark green leaves, 4in

Paphiopedilum fairrieanum

(10cm) long. Solitary, lime-green and white flowers, 4in (10cm) across, with striped upper sepals, are usually produced in spring. ↕ 12in (30cm), ↔ 8in (20cm). ❀ (min. 55°F/13°C; max. 86°F/30°C)

P. haynaldianum ▣ Terrestrial or lithophytic orchid with strap-shaped, light green leaves, to 16in (40cm) long. Produces racemes of up to 6 slender flowers, to 5in (13cm) across, with green petals tipped and spotted rose-pink, and with spotted upper sepals and greenish brown pouches, are borne in spring. ↕ 18in (45cm), ↔ 12in (30cm). Philippines. ❀ (min. 55°F/13°C; max. 86°F/30°C)

P. hirsutissimum. Terrestrial orchid with linear to strap-shaped, mid-green leaves, to 18in (45cm) long. Solitary flowers, to 5½in (14cm) across, with green and rose-mauve petals, green upper sepals, shaded brown, and greenish brown pouches, all dotted with fine brown hairs, are borne in spring. ↕ 6in (15cm), ↔ 8in (20cm). N.E. India, S. China, Thailand. ❀ (min. 50°F/10°C; max. 86°F/30°C)

P. insigne. Terrestrial orchid with linear to lance-shaped, yellowish green leaves, 8–12in (20–30cm) long. Solitary flowers, 3–3½in (7–10cm) across, with yellow-bronze petals and pouches, and pale green-yellow to brown, spotted upper sepals, appear from autumn to spring. ↕ 6in (15cm), ↔ 10in (25cm). E. Himalayas. ❀ (min. 50°F/10°C; max. 86°F/30°C)

***P.* Joanne's Wine** ▣ (*P.* Maudiae x *P.* Vintner's Treasure). Terrestrial orchid with broadly ovate, grayish green leaves, 4in (10cm) long, with dark mottling. In spring, produces solitary flowers, 4in (10cm) across, mostly dark purple and light green. ↕ 9in (23cm), ↔ 8in (20cm). ❀ (min. 55°F/13°C; max. 86°F/30°C)

***P.* Lyric 'Glendora'** ▣ (*P.* Lucid x *P.* Paeony). Terrestrial orchid with strap-shaped to ovate, mid-green leaves, 6in (15cm) long. Solitary, rounded flowers, 5in (13cm) across, with deep red and green petals, and white upper sepals with dark red centers, are usually produced in winter. ↕ 12in (30cm), ↔ 8in (20cm). ❀ (min. 55°F/13°C; max. 86°F/30°C)

***P.* Maudiae** (*P. callosum* x *P. lawrenceanum*). Terrestrial orchid with attractive, ovate leaves, mottled light and dark green, 5in (13cm) long. Solitary, green-and-white-striped flowers, 4in (10cm) across, are borne in spring or summer. ↕ 12in (30cm), ↔ 6in (15cm). ❀ (min. 55°F/13°C; max. 86°F/30°C). **'Coloratum'** ▣ produces wine-red flowers with striped upper sepals and greenish white centers.

***P.* Miller's Daughter** ▣ (*P.* Chantal x *P.* Dusty Miller). Terrestrial orchid with strap-shaped to ovate, mid-green leaves, 6in (15cm) long. Solitary white flowers, 4in (10cm) across, with pink veins and spots, are usually produced in spring. ↕ 9in (23cm), ↔ 8in (20cm). ❀ (min. 55°F/13°C; max. 86°F/30°C)

P. niveum ▣ Terrestrial orchid with rigid, leathery, elliptic to strap-shaped leaves, 4–6in (10–15cm) long, mottled green and gray. Solitary, powder-white flowers, 3in (8cm) across, with small red spots, are borne in summer. ↕↔ 6in (15cm). S. Thailand, N. Malaysia. ❀ (min. 55°F/13°C; max. 86°F/30°C)

P. rothschildianum. Terrestrial orchid with semi-rigid, elliptic to strap-shaped, shiny, mid-green leaves, to 20in (50cm) long. In spring and summer, produces racemes of 2–6 flowers, to 8in (20cm) across, with thin, purple-spotted cream petals, white upper sepals, spotted and striped dark purple, and purplish brown, yellow-rimmed pouches. ↕ 24in (60cm), ↔ 18in (45cm). N. Borneo. ❀ (min. 55°F/13°C; max. 86°F/30°C)

***P.* Silvara 'Jancis'** ▣ (*P.* F.C. Puddle x *P.* Sungrove). Terrestrial orchid with narrowly ovate, mid-green leaves, 6in (15cm) long. Solitary white flowers, 4in (10cm) across, with upper sepals peppered orange-brown, are usually produced in spring. ↕ 9in (23cm), ↔ 8in (20cm). ❀ (min. 55°F/13°C; max. 86°F/30°C)

P. sukhakulii ▣ Terrestrial orchid with narrowly elliptic, mottled, dark gray and mid- and dark green leaves, to 6in (15cm) long. In autumn, bears solitary flowers, 4–5in (10–13cm) across. They produce green petals, heavily spotted purplish black, green-striped white upper sepals, and reddish brown pouches. ↕↔ 6in (15cm). Thailand. ❀ (min. 55°F/13°C; max. 86°F/30°C)

***P.* Vanda M. Pearman** ▣ (*P. bellatum* x *P. delenatii*). Terrestrial orchid with elliptic to strap-shaped leaves, to 10in (25cm) long, mottled gray and dark green above, purple beneath. From spring to summer, white flowers, 3½in (9cm) across, with pink-flushed pouches, are borne singly or in pairs. ↕ 8in (20cm), ↔ 7in (18cm). ❀ (min. 55°F/13°C; max. 86°F/30°C)

P. venustum ▣ Terrestrial orchid with ovate-lance-shaped leaves, to 10in (25cm) long, mottled gray-green and purple. From winter to spring, produces solitary flowers, 3in (8cm) across, with green and rose-red, maroon-spotted petals, green-striped white upper sepals, and yellowish green to reddish brown, prominently veined pouches. ↕↔ 6in (15cm). Himalayas. ❀ (min. 50°F/10°C; max. 86°F/30°C)

P. villosum ▣ Terrestrial orchid with strap-shaped, dull mid-green leaves, 10–16in (25–40cm) long. Solitary, glossy, red-brown flowers, 3in (8cm) across, with green and brown upper sepals and light yellow-bronze to green pouches, appear from winter to spring. ↕↔ 6in (15cm). N.E. India, Burma, Thailand, Laos. ❀ (min. 55°F/13°C; max. 86°F/30°C)

***P.* Vintage Harvest 'Applemint'** ▣ (*P.* Chianti x *P.* Golden Acres). Terrestrial orchid with strap-shaped, dark green leaves, 6in (15cm) long. In winter, bears solitary, green-yellow flowers, 5in (13cm) across, with cream margins on the upper sepals, turning gold. ↕ 12in (30cm), ↔ 8in (20cm). ❀ (min. 55°F/13°C; max. 86°F/30°C)

Paphiopedilum appletonianum

Paphiopedilum bellatulum

Paphiopedilum Buckhurst 'Mont Millais'

Paphiopedilum callosum

Paphiopedilum Freckles

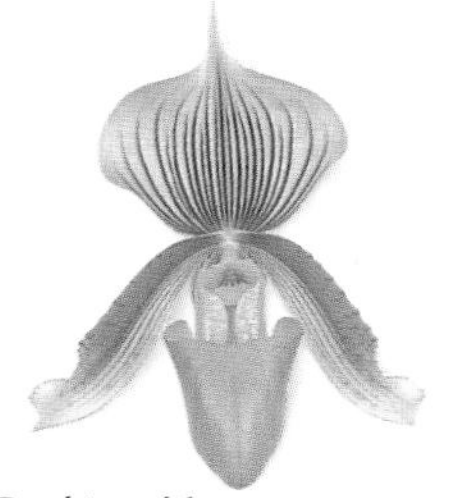
Paphiopedilum Goultenianum 'Album'

Paphiopedilum haynaldianum

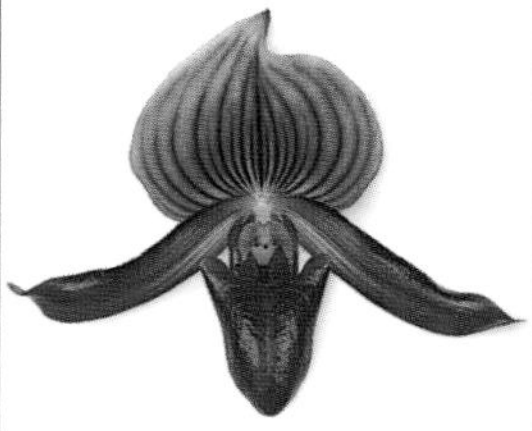
Paphiopedilum Joanne's Wine

Paphiopedilum Lyric 'Glendora'

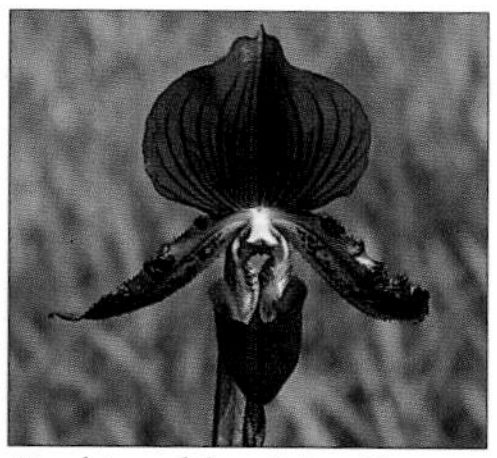
Paphiopedilum Maudiae 'Coloratum'

Paphiopedilum Miller's Daughter

Paphiopedilum niveum

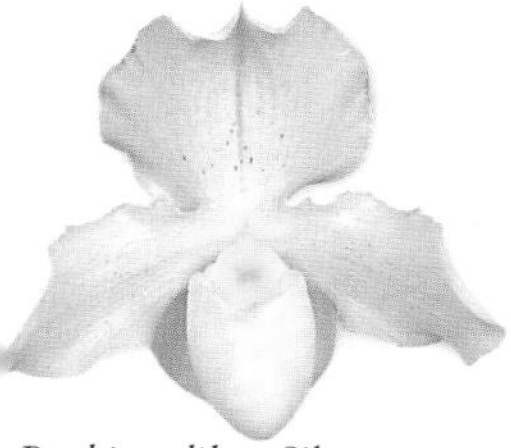
Paphiopedilum Silvara 'Jancis'

Paphiopedilum sukhakulii

Paphiopedilum Vanda M. Pearman

Paphiopedilum venustum

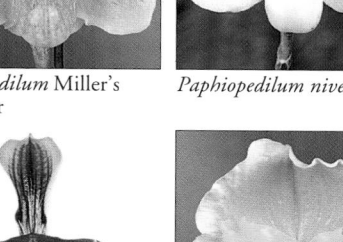

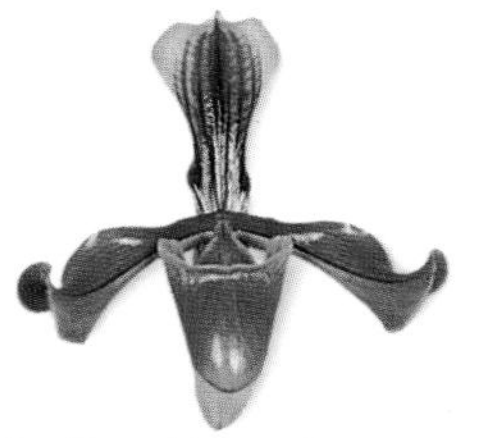
Paphiopedilum villosum

Paphiopedilum Vintage Harvest 'Applemint'

Paradisea liliastrum 'Major'

PARADISEA

Paradise lily, St. Bruno's lily

LILIACEAE

Genus of 2 species of clump-forming perennials occurring in subalpine or damp meadows and woodland in S. Europe. They have short rhizomes with clustered, fleshy roots, and linear, hairless, grayish green, basal leaves. They are cultivated for their loose racemes, borne on slender stems, of trumpet-shaped, 6-tepaled, fragrant flowers, which are good for cutting. Grow in a mixed or herbaceous border.

• **CULTIVATION** Grow in humus-rich, fertile, moist but well-drained soil in full sun or dappled shade.

• **PROPAGATION** Sow seed in containers in a cold frame as soon as ripe or in spring. Divide after flowering, or in early spring.

• **PESTS AND DISEASES** Slugs may occur.

P. liliastrum (St. Bruno's lily). Clump-forming perennial producing short rhizomes and grass-like leaves, 5–10in (12–25cm) long. One-sided racemes of white flowers, 1¼–2½in (3–6cm) long, with conspicuous yellow anthers, are borne in late spring or early summer. ↕ 12–24in (30–60cm), ↔ 12in (30cm). Mountains of S. Europe. Zone 7b. **'Major'** ■ bears larger flowers, 2–2½in (5–6cm) long.

PARAHEBE *syn.* DERWENTIA

SCROPHULARIACEAE

Genus of about 30 species of evergreen or semi-evergreen subshrubs and perennials, often classified under *Hebe* or *Veronica.* Most are from Australia and New Zealand, with a few from Papua New Guinea, occurring mainly in sunny and dry, stony habitats or scree. They have woody-based stems, and produce opposite, usually more or less ovate, toothed, mid- to dark green or blue-green leaves, stalkless or with very short stalks. They are cultivated for their erect, axillary racemes of small, saucer-shaped, usually white, pink, lilac, or blue flowers, frequently with contrasting markings; each flower has 4, rarely 5, often pointed, unequal petals. Often mat-forming or decumbent, parahebes are effective tumbling over walls or large rocks, or growing through shrubs, and are also suitable for a gravel bed.

• **CULTIVATION** Grow in well-drained, poor to moderately fertile soil in full sun. Where not hardy, shelter from cold, drying winds.

• **PROPAGATION** Sow seed in containers in a cold frame as soon as ripe or in spring. Take semi-ripe cuttings in early or midsummer.

• **PESTS AND DISEASES** Slugs may eat young growth.

***P. x bidwillii* 'Kea'.** Prostrate, mat-forming, evergreen subshrub with oblong to obovate, leathery, dark green leaves, to ¼in (6mm) long. Bears short, slender racemes of saucer-shaped, crimson-veined white flowers, to ⅜in (9mm) across, in summer. ↕ 4in (10cm), ↔ 6in (15cm). ❄ (min. 41°F/5°C)
P. canescens. Tiny, prostrate, mat-forming perennial with short-stalked, broadly ovate, slightly hairy, brown-tinged, mid-green leaves, to ⅛in (3mm) long. In summer, bears solitary, or occasionally pairs of, funnel-shaped blue flowers, to ¼in (6mm) across. ↕ to 4in (10cm), ↔ to 8in (20cm). New Zealand (South Island). Zone 8.
P. catarractae ■ Decumbent or upright, evergreen subshrub with ovate to elliptic or lance-shaped, shallowly to sharply toothed, dark green leaves, to 1½in (4cm) long, tinged purple when young. In summer, produces racemes of saucer-shaped, purple-veined white flowers, ½in (1.5cm) across, with red eyes. ↕↔ to 12in (30cm). New Zealand. ❄ (min. 41°F/5°C). **'Alba'** produces white flowers. **'Delight'** is shrubby and bears blue flowers; ↕ to 6in (15cm). **'Diffusa'** bears sprays of tiny, pink-flushed flowers; ↕ to 8in (20cm). **'Porlock'** bears blue and white flowers; ↕ to 10in (25cm). **'Rosea'** produces pink flowers; ↕ to 8in (20cm).

Parahebe perfoliata

P. hookeriana. Mat-forming, evergreen subshrub with crowded, overlapping, broadly ovate to oblong or oval, deeply toothed, leathery, sparsely hairy, mid-green leaves, to ½in (1.5cm) long. Saucer-shaped, white to lavender-blue flowers, to ½in (1.5cm) across, each usually with a crimson eye, are borne in racemes in summer. ↕ 6in (15cm), ↔ 20in (50cm). New Zealand (North Island). ❄ (min. 35°F/2°C)
P. lyallii. Variable, prostrate, stem-rooting, semi-evergreen shrub with rounded to ovate, leathery, toothed to scalloped, dark green leaves, to ½in (1.5cm) long. In early summer, bears dense racemes of saucer-shaped, usually purple-veined, white to pink flowers, ½in (1.5cm) across, with red eyes. ↕ 10in (25cm), ↔ 20in (50cm). New Zealand. ❄ (min. 35°F/2°C)
P. perfoliata ■ syn. *Veronica perfoliata* (Digger's speedwell). Woody-based, evergreen perennial with arching, spreading stems. Produces pairs of broadly ovate, toothed, slightly leathery, glaucous, blue- or gray-green leaves, 2in (5cm) long, overlapping at the bases, each pair arranged at right angles to the next pair. In late summer, bears racemes of saucer-shaped blue flowers, ¼–½in (6–15mm) across. ↕ 24–30in (60–75cm), ↔ 18in (45cm). S.E. Australia. ❄ (min. 41°F/5°C)

Parahebe catarractae

PARAQUILEGIA

RANUNCULACEAE

Genus of 4–6 species of tufted perennials occurring in rock crevices and scree in the Himalayas and mountains of C. Asia and China. They are grown for their solitary, short-stalked, cup-shaped flowers, produced in spring, and for their fern-like, ternate to 3-ternate, often gray or blue-green leaves, arranged alternately. These attractive alpines are suitable for a scree bed, trough, or alpine house, but may be difficult to establish; they grow best in climates with cool summers and cold, dry winters. Site carefully to avoid more invasive plants.

• **CULTIVATION** Outdoors, grow in poor, sharply drained, alkaline soil in full sun. Protect from winter moisture. In an alpine house, grow in a mix of equal parts loam, leaf mold, and grit.

• **PROPAGATION** Sow seed in containers in an open frame in autumn.

• **PESTS AND DISEASES** Susceptible to aphids and spider mites under glass, and prone to damage by slugs and snails.

P. anemonoides ■ syn. *P. grandiflora.* Tufted perennial producing long-stalked, 2- or 3-ternate, blue-green leaves, 1¼in (3cm) long, with many deeply lobed segments. In late spring, produces violet-blue, purple-blue, or pale lilac, occasionally white flowers, 1in (2.5cm) across, with golden nectaries and yellow anthers. ↕↔ to 4in (10cm). C. Asia, Himalayas, W. China. Zone 5.
P. grandiflora see *P. anemonoides.*

▷ ***Paraserianthes*** see *Albizia*

Paraquilegia anemonoides

PARIS syn. DAISWA

LILIACEAE

Genus of about 20 species of rhizomatous perennials occurring in woodland from Europe to the Caucasus, and from the Himalayas to E. Asia. Erect stems each bear a whorl of 4 or more very variable, lance-shaped to ovate, mid- or dark green leaves, just below a solitary, terminal, wheel-shaped, spider-like, or star-shaped flower, with protruding stamens. The flowers are followed by fleshy, capsular fruits with shiny, black or red seeds; these may cause mild stomach upset if ingested. Suitable for a woodland, wild garden, or shady rock garden.

• **CULTIVATION** Grow in moist, fertile, leafy soil in full or partial shade. Leave plants undisturbed to increase.

• **PROPAGATION** Sow seed in containers outdoors in autumn. Divide after the foliage has died down.

• **PESTS AND DISEASES** Slugs may attack rhizomes and young growth.

P. polyphylla, syn. *Daiswa polyphylla*. Slowly spreading perennial with short rhizomes and erect, smooth stems, each bearing a whorl of 6–12 oblong to inversely lance-shaped, mid-green leaves, 3–7in (8–18cm) long, rounded at the bases. Throughout summer, bears solitary, spider-like flowers, each consisting of 4–8 narrow green outer tepals, 1–4in (2.5–10cm) long, and thread-like, yellowish green inner tepals, to 4in (10cm) long, with numerous stamens. Angled, almost spherical green capsules, to ¾in (2cm) across, split to reveal shiny red seeds when ripe. ↕ 24–36in (60–90cm), ↔ 12in (30cm). Himalayas to Burma, Thailand, W. China. Zone 6.

P. quadrifolia. Upright perennial with creeping rhizomes and erect stems, each with a whorl of usually 4, sometimes 5 or 6, ovate, mid-green leaves, 2–6in (5–15cm) long. In late spring, bears solitary, star-shaped flowers, 1½–3in (4–8cm) across, with mid-green outer tepals, white inner tepals, and twice as many stamens as inner tepals; these are followed by blue-black, spherical, berry-like capsules, ½in (1.5cm) across. ↕ 6–16in (15–40cm), ↔ 12in (30cm). Eurasia. Zone 6.

PARKINSONIA

FABACEAE

Genus of more than 12 species of deciduous or evergreen shrubs and trees from dry savanna or scrubland in the drier regions of Africa, S. North America, and Central America. They are grown for their attractive flowers and delicate foliage. The branches have pairs of spines at each node, produce green to silvery young bark, and bear alternate, 2- or 3-pinnate leaves with very small, light to mid- or yellow-green leaflets. The mostly yellow, red-spotted flowers, with spreading, clawed petals, are produced in short, usually axillary racemes from the upper leaf nodes, followed by leathery or woody, pea-like pods. Grow as specimen trees in a lawn, massed in a shrub border, or as a hedge or screen planting. Their open growth habit admits light, dappled shade through their branches, allowing turf to thrive. Where not hardy, grow in a cool or temperate greenhouse.

Parkinsonia aculeata

• **CULTIVATION** Under glass, grow in soil-based potting mix in full light, with low humidity. From spring to summer, water moderately and apply a balanced liquid fertilizer every month. Water sparingly in winter. Outdoors, grow in fertile, well-drained soil in full sun. Pruning group 1; may need restrictive pruning under glass, after flowering.

• **PROPAGATION** Sow seed at 64–70°F (18–21°C) in spring.

• **PESTS AND DISEASES** Galls, spider mites, mushroom root rot, dieback, and some leaf spots can be problems.

P. aculeata ■ (Jerusalem thorn). Small, spreading, often weeping, deciduous tree, or occasionally large shrub, bearing spiny green stems and branchlets. Slender, 2-pinnate, stalkless, mid-green leaves, to 12in (30cm) long, have distinctive flat midribs and many tiny, ovate to oblong leaflets, 1⁄16–¼in (2–6mm) long, often quickly deciduous; they fold up at night. In spring, produces racemes of 2–15 cup-shaped, fragrant, bright yellow flowers, to ¾in (2cm) across, with orange-spotted standard petals and orange-red stamens. ↕ to 30ft (10m), ↔ 15–25ft (5–8m). S. US, Mexico; widely naturalized in tropical and subtropical regions. ❀ (min. 41°F/5°C)

P. florida, syn. *Cercidium floridum* (Blue palo verde, Palo verde). Small, bushy tree, leafless most of the year, with smooth, blue-green bark, and sharp spines. Slender, 2-pinnate, mid-green leaves, 6–8in (15–20cm) long, have 2–8 ovate to obovate, slightly hairy leaflets, to ¼in (6mm) long. In spring, bears corymbs of yellow flowers, to ¾in (2cm) across, with standards blotched red at the bases, followed by oblong, flat, straight or curved fruit, to 3in (8cm) long. ↕ to 25ft (8m), ↔ 15–20ft (5–6m). S. California, Arizona, N.W. Mexico. ❀ (min. 41°F/5°C)

PARNASSIA

Bog star, Grass of Parnassus

SAXIFRAGACEAE

Genus of 15 species of herbaceous perennials found in bogs in temperate regions in the N. hemisphere. They produce basal rosettes of broadly ovate, heart-, or kidney-shaped, mid- to dark green leaves. They are grown for their large, solitary, bowl- or saucer-shaped, white to pale yellow flowers, with yellow, nectar-bearing staminodes, borne on upright stems in spring, summer, or early autumn. Grow in a moist rock garden or bog garden.

• **CULTIVATION** Grow in humus-rich, moderately fertile, wet soil in full sun.

• **PROPAGATION** Sow seed in containers in a cold frame in autumn; keep moist. Divide in autumn or spring.

• **PESTS AND DISEASES** Susceptible to slug and snail damage.

P. fimbriata. Rosette-forming perennial with kidney-shaped, mid-green basal leaves, ¾–2in (2–5cm) long, and long-stalked, broadly ovate stem leaves, ¾in (2cm) long. Solitary, bowl-shaped white flowers, 1¼–1½in (3–4cm) across, are borne in late summer and early autumn. ↕↔ 8–24in (20–60cm). Alaska to California. Zone 7b.

Parnassia palustris

P. palustris ■ (Grass of Parnassus). Rosette-forming perennial with ovate, heart-shaped, pale green leaves, to 1¼in (3cm) long. Slender stems bear solitary, green-veined white flowers, 1in (2.5cm) across, with yellow nectar glands, in late spring and early summer. ↕ 8in (20cm), ↔ 4in (10cm). N. temperate regions. Zone 4.

PAROCHETUS

FABACEAE

Genus of 2 species (often confused in cultivation) of trailing, deciduous or evergreen perennials found in montane habitats in E. Africa, the Himalayas to Sri Lanka, S.W. China, and S.E. Asia. They are grown for their clover-like leaves and bright blue, occasionally white, pea-like flowers. Grow in a rock garden or alpine house. *P. africana* is ideal in a hanging basket.

• **CULTIVATION** Grow in any moist but well-drained soil in partial shade, but protect from winter moisture. Plants may be short-lived, so propagate regularly. In an alpine house, grow in a mix of equal parts soil-based potting mix, leaf mold, and grit.

• **PROPAGATION** Divide in spring, or separate rooted runners when in growth.

• **PESTS AND DISEASES** May be damaged by slugs and snails.

P. africana ■ (Shamrock pea). Prostrate, mat-forming, non-tuberous, evergreen perennial with freely rooting stems. Each leaf has 3 inversely heart-shaped, rich dark green leaflets, to 1¼in (3cm) long, with bold, dark brown horseshoe markings. Solitary or paired, bright blue flowers, 1in (2.5cm) across, are borne mainly from late autumn to late spring. ↕ 4in (10cm), ↔ 24–39in (60–100cm). Mountains of E. Africa. ❀ (min. 35°F/2°C)

Parochetus africana

P. communis. Prostrate, tuberous-rooted, deciduous perennial with trailing stems. Leaves are divided into 3 inversely heart-shaped, mid-green leaflets, to ¾in (2cm) long, with irregular bronze-brown horseshoe markings. Produces a succession of solitary or paired, bright blue flowers, 1in (2.5cm) across, in late summer and autumn. ↕4in (10cm), ↔ 12in (30cm) or more. Himalayas to Sri Lanka, S.W. China, S.E. Asia. ❀ (min. 35°F/2°C)

PARODIA *syn.* ERIOCACTUS, NOTOCACTUS, WIGGINSIA

CACTACEAE

Genus of 35–50 species of solitary or clustering, mainly spherical, many-ribbed, spiny cacti, sometimes becoming columnar and sometimes offsetting from the bases. The genus includes many species transferred from *Eriocactus*, *Notocactus*, and *Wigginsia*. They occur mainly in the highlands of Colombia, Brazil, Bolivia, Paraguay, Argentina, and Uruguay. Solitary, diurnal, bell- to funnel-shaped flowers develop near or at the crowns. Where temperatures drop below 50°F (10°C), grow in a warm greenhouse, although they may tolerate brief periods of lower temperatures (see entries). In warmer climates, use in a desert garden.

• **CULTIVATION** Under glass, grow in standard cactus potting mix in full or bright filtered light. From midspring to late summer, water moderately and apply a low-nitrogen liquid fertilizer every 6–8 weeks. Keep dry at other times, except for light misting on warm days in late winter. Outdoors, grow in sharply drained, moderately fertile soil in full sun, with some midday shade. See pp.48–49.

• **PROPAGATION** Sow seed at 66–75°F (19–24°C) in spring or summer.

• **PESTS AND DISEASES** Vulnerable to mealybugs and, while flowering, aphids.

P. brevihamata ▣ syn. *Notocactus brevihamatus.* Solitary or clustering cactus producing spherical, olive-green stems, each with 20–26 closely set ribs, rounded tubercles, white to yellow areoles, and yellow, later brownish yellow spines (about 16 radials, 1–4 slightly longer centrals). Funnel-shaped, lemon-yellow, sometimes red-tinted flowers, 1½in (4cm) across, are borne in spring. ↕↔ to 2½in (6cm). S. Brazil. ❀ (min. 50°F/10°C)

Parodia chrysacanthion

P. chrysacanthion ▣ Solitary cactus producing a spherical to depressed-spherical, pale green stem with about 24 spirally arranged, warty ribs, and a crown covered with thick yellow wool. Yellowish white areoles bear yellow spines (30–40 fine radials, 1 or more centrals). Funnel-shaped yellow flowers, ¾in (2cm) across, develop in spring. ↕3–5in (8–13cm), ↔ 4in (10cm). N. Argentina. ❀ (min. 50°F/10°C)

P. claviceps, syn. *Notocactus claviceps.* Solitary or clustering cactus producing spherical to short-cylindrical, dark green stems, each with 23–30 ribs. White areoles bear wide-spreading, semi-pendent, yellow spines (5–8 radials, 1–3 centrals). Funnel-shaped, sulfur-yellow flowers, 2in (5cm) across, appear in summer. ↕4–20in (10–50cm), ↔ 5in (13cm). S. Brazil. ❀ (min. 50°F/10°C); tolerates brief periods to 18°F (-8°C).

P. concinna, syn. *Eriocactus apricus, Notocactus apricus, N. concinnus.* Solitary cactus producing a flattened-spherical, 15- to 32-ribbed, dark green stem with a woolly crown, white areoles, and white, pale yellow, brown, or red-brown spines (10–12 radials, 4–6 or more, longer, slightly darker centrals). Funnel-shaped, red-tipped, deep lemon-yellow flowers, 2–3in (5–8cm) across, are produced in spring. ↕ to 2½in (6cm), ↔ 4in (10cm). S. Brazil, Uruguay. ❀ (min. 50°F/10°C)

P. erinacea, syn. *Wigginsia erinacea, W. vorwerkiana.* Freely offsetting cactus with spherical to short-cylindrical, light to dark green stems, 2½–12in (6–30cm) thick, each with 15–30 spiraling ribs, gray areoles, and off-white, gray, or brown spines (2–12 radials, 1 longer central). In summer, bears funnel-shaped, glossy yellow flowers, 1½in (4cm) across. ↕6in (15cm) or more, ↔ 10in (25cm). S. Brazil, Uruguay, N.E. Argentina. ❀ (min. 50°F/10°C); tolerates brief periods to 18°F (-8°C).

Parodia leninghausii

P. graessneri, syn. *Notocactus graessneri.* Solitary cactus producing a spherical, dark green stem with an angled, spiny crown, and 50–60 heavily warty ribs. White areoles bear both pale to golden yellow and pale brown to white spines (about 55 radials, 5 or 6 centrals). In spring, bears funnel-shaped, pale yellow-green flowers, ¾in (2cm) across. ↕4–6in (10–15cm), ↔ 4in (10cm). S. Brazil. ❀ (min. 50°F/10°C)

P. haselbergii ▣ syn. *Notocactus haselbergii* (Scarlet ball cactus). Solitary cactus, with a spherical, grayish green stem, to 6in (15cm) thick, with a woolly crown set at an angle, and 30–60 or more ribs. White-woolly areoles bear yellowish white to yellow spines (25–60 radials, 3–5 slightly longer centrals). Funnel-shaped, bright orange-red or orange-yellow flowers, ½in (1.5cm) across, appear from winter to spring. ↕1½–6in (4–15cm), ↔ 6in (15cm) in clusters. S. Brazil. ❀ (min. 50°F/10°C)

P. leninghausii ▣ syn. *Eriocactus leninghausii.* Solitary or clustering cactus with spherical, later columnar, mid-green stems, each to 4in (10cm) thick, with a woolly crown set at an angle, and 30–35 ribs. White-woolly areoles bear pale yellow, deep yellow, or pale brown spines (15–20 or more radials, 3 or 4 centrals). Funnel-shaped, bright yellow or lemon flowers, 1½–2in (4–5cm) across, are borne in summer. ↕ to 24in (60cm), ↔ 8in (20cm) in clusters. S. Brazil. ❀ (min. 50°F/10°C); tolerates brief periods to 28°F (-2°C).

P. liliputana see *Blossfeldia liliputana.*

P. maassii. Solitary cactus, sometimes clustering, producing a spherical, mid-green stem with 10–21 prominent, straight or spiraled ribs. White-wooly areoles bear variably colored spines (6–18 radials, 1–6 centrals). Funnel-shaped, red to yellow flowers, 1¼–1¾in (3–4.5cm) across, are borne in spring and summer. ↕4–20in (10–50cm), ↔ 3–10in (8–25cm). S. Bolivia, N. Argentina. ❀ (min. 50°F/10°C)

P. magnifica, syn. *Notocactus magnifica.* Solitary, sometimes clustering cactus with spherical, later columnar, 11- to 15-ribbed, bluish green stems, to 6in (15cm) thick. Gray-felted areoles bear yellow or brown spines (12–15 or more radials, up to 12 longer centrals). Funnel-shaped, sulfur-yellow flowers, 2in (5cm) across, develop in summer. ↕3–6in (7–15cm), ↔ to 18in (45cm). S. Brazil. ❀ (min. 50°F/10°C); tolerates brief periods to 28°F (-2°C).

P. mammulosa ▣ syn. *Notocactus mammulosus, N. submammulosus.* Solitary cactus producing a spherical, dark green stem with a woolly crown and 13–21 heavily warty ribs. White areoles bear white, gray, or brown spines (6–25 radials, 2–4 longer centrals). Funnel-shaped, yellow flowers, 1½–2in (3.5–5cm) across, with red stigmas, develop in summer. ↕4–5in (10–13cm), ↔ 2½in (6cm). S. Brazil, Uruguay, N.E. Argentina. ❀ (min. 50°F/10°C); tolerates brief periods to 18°F (-8°C).

P

Parodia brevihamata

Parodia haselbergii

Parodia mammulosa

Parodia nivosa

P. microsperma, syn. *P. mutabilis* var. *sanguiniflora*, *P. sanguiniflora*. Solitary cactus producing a depressed-spherical to spherical, sometimes cylindrical, mid-green stem with 15–21 warty ribs. White areoles bear white and red to brown spines (10–25 radials, 3 or 4 longer centrals). Funnel-shaped, yellow or red flowers, 1½in (4cm) across, are borne from spring to summer. ↕ 8in (20cm), ↔ 4in (10cm). N. Argentina. ❀ (min. 50°F/10°C)
P. mutabilis, syn. *Notocactus mutabilis*. Solitary cactus producing a spherical, glaucous, mid-green stem with a white-woolly, brown-spiny crown and 25 or more, spirally arranged, warty ribs. White-woolly areoles bear white and yellow, reddish brown, or orange-brown spines (20–50 fine, almost hair-like radials, 4–10 strong, sometimes hooked centrals). Funnel-shaped, golden yellow flowers, 1¼–2in (3–5cm) across, are produced from spring to summer. ↕↔ 3in (8cm). N. Argentina. ❀ (min. 50°F/10°C). **var. *sanguiniflora*** see *P. microsperma*.
P. nivosa ■ Solitary cactus producing a spherical to short-cylindrical, dull green stem with a white-woolly crown and 16–20 spirally arranged, warty ribs. White-felted areoles have white spines (15–20 radials, 3–5 longer centrals). Funnel-shaped, brilliant red flowers, 1¼in (3cm) across, develop in spring. ↕ 6in (15cm), ↔ 2½in (6cm). N. Argentina. ❀ (min. 50°F/10°C)
P. ocampoi. Clustering cactus with spherical to short-cylindrical, 13- to 20-ribbed, dark green stems, 2½in (6cm) thick, with gray areoles and pale reddish brown spines (8 or 9 radials, 1 smaller central). Funnel-shaped, golden yellow flowers, 1¼in (3cm) across, are borne from spring to summer. ↕ 3–8in (7–20cm), ↔ 6in (15cm). C. Bolivia. ❀ (min. 50°F/10°C)
P. ottonis, syn. *Notocactus ottonis*. Variable, solitary, later clustering cactus with spherical or cylindrical, 6- to 15-ribbed, light or dark green or bluish or purplish green stems, 2–6in (5–15cm) thick, each with a white-woolly crown. Pale brown-woolly areoles produce off-white to yellow and brown spines (10–18 radials, 3–6 centrals). Funnel-shaped, deep yellow, rarely orange-red flowers, 1½–2½in (4–6cm) across, are borne in summer. ↕ 1¼–6in (3–15cm), ↔ 7in (18cm). S. Brazil, S. Paraguay, N.E. Argentina, Uruguay. ❀ (min. 50°F/10°C)

Parodia rutilans

P. penicillata, syn. *Notocactus penicillata*. Solitary, spherical, later cylindrical cactus producing a mid-green stem with about 17–20 spiraling ribs and close-set tubercles. Brown-woolly areoles bear white, off-white, pale yellow, or pale brown spines (about 40 radials, 10–20 centrals). In summer, bears funnel-shaped, orange-yellow or vermilion-red flowers, 2in (5cm) across. ↕ 12in (30cm), ↔ 5in (13cm). N. Argentina. ❀ (min. 50°F/10°C)
P. rutilans ■ syn. *Notocactus rutilans*. Solitary cactus producing a spherical to cylindrical, bluish dark green stem with a slightly sunken, white-woolly crown and 18–24 spirally arranged ribs. White-woolly areoles produce reddish brown and brown-tipped white spines (14–16 radials, 2 slightly longer centrals). In summer, bears funnel-shaped flowers, 1¼–1½in (3–4cm) across, with pink-tipped petals and yellowish white throats. ↕↔ 2in (5cm). N. Uruguay. ❀ (min. 50°F/10°C)
P. sanguiniflora see *P. microsperma*.
P. schumanniana. Usually solitary cactus producing a spherical to cylindrical, mid-green stem with 21–48 straight, acute ribs. White-woolly areoles bear golden yellow, brown, or reddish brown, later gray spines (about 4 radials, 3 or 4 shorter centrals). Produces funnel-shaped, lemon to golden yellow flowers, 1¾–3in (4.5–8cm) across, in summer. ↕ to 6ft (1.8m), ↔ 12in (30cm). S. Paraguay, N.E. Argentina. ❀ (min. 50°F/10°C)
P. scopa, syn. *Notocactus scopa* (Silver ball cactus). Solitary or clustering cactus with spherical to cylindrical, 25- to 40-ribbed, dark green stems with spiny, woolly crowns. Gray areoles bear white, pale yellow, red, or brown spines (35–40 or more radials, 3 or 4 longer centrals). Funnel-shaped, bright yellow flowers, 1½in (4cm) across, are produced in summer. ↕ 2–20in (5–50cm), ↔ 4in (10cm). S. Brazil, Uruguay. ❀ (min. 50°F/10°C)

PARONYCHIA

Whitlow-wort

CARYOPHYLLACEAE

Genus of about 50 species of annuals and evergreen, mat-forming perennials found mainly in hot, dry habitats around the Mediterranean and in N. Africa, with some in North America. They have linear to lance-shaped, silvery green leaves and dense, axillary cymes of very small, cup-shaped flowers surrounded by conspicuous, translucent silver bracts. Cultivated for their flowers and foliage, they are good carpeting plants for a rock garden.
• **CULTIVATION** Grow in sharply drained, poor to moderately fertile soil in full sun.
• **PROPAGATION** Divide in spring. Take stem-tip cuttings in early summer.
• **PESTS AND DISEASES** Infrequent.

P. capitata, syn. *P. nivea* (Willow wort, Nailwort). Vigorous, mat-forming perennial with linear-lance-shaped to oblong, silvery gray-green leaves, to ¼in (6mm) long. In summer, bears tiny green flowers in cymes, to ½in (1.5cm) across, enclosed by ornamental, ovate, silvery, papery bracts. ↕ 2in (5cm), ↔ to 12in (30cm). Mediterranean. Zone 8.
P. kapela subsp. *serpyllifolia*. Very compact, mat-forming perennial with ovate to lance-shaped or elliptic, silvery bluish green leaves, to ⅛in (3mm) long. In summer, tiny, greenish white flowers are borne in cymes, to ¾in (2cm) across, enclosed by silvery white, papery bracts. ↕ to 2in (5cm), ↔ to 8in (20cm). Mediterranean. Zone 6.
P. nivea see *P. capitata*.

PARROTIA

HAMAMELIDACEAE

Genus of one species of deciduous tree occurring in forests in the Caucasus and N. Iran. *P. persica* is cultivated for its simple, alternate, rich green foliage, attractively colored in autumn; for its peeling bark; and for its petalless flowers with bright red stamens, borne in dense clusters along the branches in late winter or early spring. Grow *P. persica* as a specimen tree or in an open site in a woodland garden.
• **CULTIVATION** Grow in deep, fertile, moist but well-drained soil in full sun or partial shade. Grow in acidic soil for best autumn color. Pruning group 1.
• **PROPAGATION** Sow seed in containers in a cold frame in autumn. Take greenwood cuttings in early summer, or semi-ripe cuttings in mid- and late summer.
• **PESTS AND DISEASES** Infrequent.

P. persica ■ (Persian ironwood). Dense, spreading, short-trunked tree with peeling, gray and fawn bark when mature. Obovate, glossy, rich green leaves, to 5in (13cm) long, turn yellow, orange, and red-purple in autumn. Tiny, spider-like red flowers are produced in spherical clusters, ½in (1.5cm) across, in late winter or early spring, before the leaves. ↕ 25ft (8m), ↔ 30ft (10m). Caucasus, N. Iran. Zone 7. **'Pendula'** is very compact and weeping in habit; ↕ 5ft (1.5m), ↔ 10ft (3m).

PARROTIOPSIS

HAMAMELIDACEAE

Genus of one species of deciduous shrub found in forests in the W. Himalayas. It is cultivated for its showy flowerheads of petalless flowers, each with 20 or more yellow stamens surrounded by large bracts. Leaves are simple and arranged alternately. Grow *P. jacquemontiana* as a specimen shrub.
• **CULTIVATION** Grow in deep, fertile, preferably acidic, moist but well-drained soil in full sun or partial shade. Pruning group 1.
• **PROPAGATION** Sow seed in containers in a cold frame in autumn. Take greenwood cuttings in early summer, or semi-ripe cuttings in late summer.
• **PESTS AND DISEASES** Infrequent.

P. jacquemontiana. Upright shrub, or sometimes small tree, with very broadly ovate to ovate, mid-green leaves, to 4in (10cm) long. From midspring to early summer, bears spider-like flowerheads, to 2in (5cm) across, consisting of yellow-anthered stamens surrounded by conspicuous white bracts. ↕ 20ft (6m), ↔ 12ft (4m). W. Himalayas. Zone 7.

Parrotia persica (inset: leaf detail)

PARTHENOCISSUS

VITACEAE

Genus of about 10 species of deciduous tendril climbers found in forests in the Himalayas, E. Asia, and North America. Some species are twining, but more commonly they cling by disk-like suckers on the tips of tendrils. They are grown for their lobed or fully divided, palmate leaves, usually brightly colored in autumn. Clusters of inconspicuous flowers, with 5, sometimes 4, short, thick green petals, are produced in summer, and may be followed by dark blue or black berries, to 3/8in (9mm) across. Grow through a large tree or use to cover a wall, fence, or stump. The disk-like suckers attach themselves to walls, requiring no support. The foliage of wall-grown plants often harbors a variety of wildlife. The berries may cause mild stomach upset if ingested.

• **CULTIVATION** Grow in any fertile, well-drained soil in shade or sun; *P. henryana* usually colors best in partial shade. Young plants may need support initially. Pruning group 11, in early winter and, if necessary, also in summer.

• **PROPAGATION** Sow seed in containers in a cold frame in autumn. Take softwood cuttings in early summer, greenwood cuttings in midsummer, or hardwood cuttings in winter.

• **PESTS AND DISEASES** Downy mildew, powdery mildew, black rot, bacterial leaf scorch, scab, dieback, canker, and several leaf spots are common. Leaf skeletonizer, Japanese beetle, grape flea beetle, and scale insects also occur.

Parthenocissus henryana

Parthenocissus quinquefolia

Parthenocissus thomsonii

P. henryana ■ syn. *Vitis henryana.* Woody climber with palmate, dark green leaves composed of 3–5 oval, toothed leaflets, to 5in (13cm) long, conspicuously veined white, and sometimes pink in the centers, turning bright red in autumn. ↕ 30ft (10m). China. Zone 6b.

P. quinquefolia ■ syn. *Vitis quinquefolia* (Virginia creeper). Vigorous, woody climber with palmate, dull, mid-green leaves composed of usually 5 oval, sharply toothed leaflets, to 4in (10cm) long, turning brilliant red in autumn. ↕ 50ft (15m) or more. E. North America. Zone 2b.

P. striata see *Cissus striata.*

P. thomsonii ■ syn. *Cayratia thomsonii, Vitis thomsonii.* Woody climber with palmate, dark green leaves consisting of usually 5 oval, sharply toothed leaflets, to 4in (10cm) long, reddish purple when young, turning purple-green in summer and bright red in autumn. ↕ 30ft (10m). China, Himalayas. Zone 5.

P. tricuspidata ■ (Boston ivy). Vigorous, woody climber with variable, broadly ovate, deeply toothed, bright green leaves, to 8in (20cm) long, either 3-lobed or with 3 ovate leaflets, turning brilliant red to purple in autumn. The leaf blades often drop off before the leaf stalks, creating a curious effect. ↕ 70ft (20m). China, Korea, Japan. Zone 5b. **'Beverly Brooks'**, syn. 'Beverley Brook', produces purple-tinged summer foliage, turning brilliant red in autumn. **'Fenway'** has chartreuse to gold leaves. **'Green Showers'** bears bright green leaves, to 10in (25cm) across, turning burgundy-red in autumn. **'Lowii'** ■ has small, deeply 3- to 7-lobed leaves, 4in (10cm) long. **'Purpurea'** has reddish purple leaves, all season. **'Robusta'** is vigorous in habit, with trifoliate, waxy, shiny, mid-green leaves, turning orange to red in autumn. **'Veitchii'**, syn. *Ampelopsis veitchii*, has dark red-purple foliage in autumn.

Parthenocissus tricuspidata 'Lowii'

Parthenocissus tricuspidata

PASPALUM

POACEAE

Genus of about 400 species of warm-season, tall, perennial grasses occurring in seashore areas; generally tolerant of brackish water. Flat to folded, dense, coarse leaf blades, are useful for lawns and erosion control in sandy or saline areas. All species spread by rhizomes and stolons (suckers). Stems are flattened at the base; inflorescences of 1 to many spiky branches, alternate or paired, are forked at the ends of the stems.

• **CULTIVATION** Grow in warm, subtropical to tropical regions, in full sun or partial shade, in moist, sandy to moderately fertile soil. Mow at ¾–1in (2–2.5cm).

• **PROPAGATION** Self-seeds or plant by sprigs or sod.

• **PESTS AND DISEASES** Brown patch, dollar spot, and mole crickets. Most cultivars are drought and disease resistant.

P. notatum (Bahia grass). Warm-season, midgreen, perennial grass, extremely salt and drought tolerant. Spreads by runners, forming a dense mat, which is difficult to mow evenly. Once established in a lawn, Bahia grass forms a thick, low-maintenance turf. Florida, Gulf Coast of N. America. ❄ (min. 35°F/2°C)

P. vaginatum (Seashore paspalum). Robust, warm-season, deep green, saline-tolerant perennial grass with forked pairs of spikelet branches, to 6in (15cm) long, at tip of stems, to 30in (76cm) tall. Inconspicuous flowers, to ½in (1.5cm) across. Finer textured than other salt-tolerant varieties, making it a good choice for lawns in coastal areas. North Carolina to Texas. ❄ (min. 55°F/12°C)

PASSIFLORA

Granadilla, Passionflower

PASSIFLORACEAE

Genus of more than 400 species of mostly evergreen tendril climbers, and a few annuals, perennials, shrubs, and trees. They occur usually in tropical woodland, on rocks, and in grassland, mainly in tropical North, Central, and South America, and also in tropical Asia, Australia, New Zealand, and the Pacific islands. The leaves are usually alternate,

Passiflora 'Amethyst'

P

simple or 2- to 9-lobed (mainly 3- or 5- lobed), elliptic to rounded or broadly ovate, and often with prominent nectar glands on the margins or stalks. The exotic flowers are produced mostly singly, sometimes in racemes, from the upper leaf axils. Each has a wide, tubular base and 10, sometimes 5 tepals that spread out flat, reflex, or form a saucer or bowl shape. A stalk in the center of each flower bears the ovary and stamens, and is surrounded by one or several rings of fleshy filaments (the corona). The ovoid to spherical, edible, usually yellow fruits are very variable in size. They are ideal for covering a wall or trellis. Where not hardy, grow in a cool to warm greenhouse or in large containers. In warmer climates, train over a pergola or arch, or through a tree.

• **CULTIVATION** Under glass, plant in a greenhouse border or in large tubs of soil-based potting mix in full light, with shade from hot sun. Water freely when in growth, sparingly in winter. Top-dress annually in spring. Outdoors, grow in moderately fertile, moist but well-drained soil in full sun or partial shade, with shelter from cold, drying winds. Pruning group 11 or 12, if necessary, in early spring.

• **PROPAGATION** Sow seed at 55–64°F (13–18°C) in spr[illegible] semi-ripe cuttings in [illegible] spring or au[illegible] [illegible]ites, [illegible]r. [illegible]ell as [illegible]ged- [illegible] an[illegible] so[illegible] to light gree[illegible]cm) long. From s[illegible] summer, bears nodding, [illegible]agrant, bowl-shaped, bright carmine-red flowers, 4–5in (10–13cm) across, with curved outer tepals, opening from light crimson buds; coronas have purple, red, and white zones. Bears ovoid to pear-shaped, yellow fruit, 4–6in (10–15cm) long. ↕ to 20ft (6m) or more. Peru to E. Brazil. ❀ (min. 41–45°F/5–7°C)

***P.* 'Amethyst'** ▣ syn. *P. amethystina* of gardens, *P.* 'Lavender Lady', *P. violacea* of gardens. Vigorous climber with smooth, slender stems and deeply 3-lobed, membranous, rich green leaves, 2½–3in (6–8cm) long. In late summer and autumn, bears bowl-shaped, purple to purple-blue flowers, to 4½in (11cm) across, with green anthers, tepals that reflex as the flower fades, and darker corona filaments. Bears ellipsoid orange fruit, to 2½in (6cm) long. ↕ 12ft (4m) or more. Garden origin. ❀ (min. 41°F/5°C)

***P. amethystina* of gardens** see *P.* 'Amethyst'.

P. antioquiensis ▣ syn. *Tacsonia van-volxemii* (Red banana passionflower). Vigorous climber with slender, branched stems and finely toothed, deeply 3-lobed, mid- to deep green leaves, 4–6in (10–15cm) long, downy beneath, each lobe with a slender point; occasionally produces simple, ovate to lance-shaped leaves. Bears long-tubed, bright rose-red, rarely pink flowers, to 5½in (14cm) across, with small violet coronas, mainly in summer. Ellipsoid yellow fruit, to 4in (10cm) long, have a delicate flavor. ↕ 15ft (5m) or more. Colombia. ❀ (min. 41–45°F/5–7°C)

P. caerulea ▣ (Blue passionflower). Fast-growing climber with moderately branching, slender, 4-angled, grooved stems bearing rich green leaves, to 4in (10cm) long, divided almost to the base into 3–9, usually 5, oblong lobes. From summer to autumn, bears bowl-shaped, white, sometimes pink-tinged flowers, 3–4in (8–10cm) across, with purple-, blue-, and white-zoned coronas. Ovoid, orange-yellow fruit, to 2½in (6cm) long, are edible but not flavorful. ↕ 30ft (10m) or more. C. and W. South America. Zone 7. **'Constance Elliott'** ▣ has fragrant white flowers with pale blue or white filaments. **'Grandiflora'** has flowers to 6in (15cm) across.

P.* x *caeruleoracemosa ▣ (*P. caerulea* x *P. racemosa*). Variable, vigorous climber with branching, slender, smooth stems and deeply 3- to 5-lobed, rich green leaves, 5–6in (12–15cm) long. From summer to autumn, bears bowl-shaped, red-purple flowers, 4–5in (10–13cm) wide, with spreading corona filaments, deep purple to black at the bases and white above. Produces ovoid green fruit, to 2½in (6cm) long. ↕ 20ft (6m) or more. Garden origin. ❀ (min. 41°F/5°C). **'Eynsford Gem'** is shrubby, with pink-mauve flowers and white filaments.

P. coccinea ▣ syn. *P. fulgens*, *P. velutina* (Red granadilla). Vigorous climber with very slender, smooth, red to purple stems, and oblong-ovate, mid-green leaves, 2½–5½in (6–14cm) long, with soft, red-brown hairs and large, lobe-like teeth. From midsummer to autumn, produces saucer-shaped scarlet flowers, 3–4in (8–10cm) across; coronas have purple, pale pink, and white zones. Spherical to ovoid, finely white-woolly fruit, 2in (5cm) long, ripen orange or yellow with darker stripes. ↕ 12ft (4m) or more. N.W. South America. ❀ (min. 50–55°F/10–13°C)

P. edulis (Passionfruit, Purple granadilla). Vigorous, woody climber with 3-lobed, toothed, glossy, mid-green leaves, to 8in (20cm) long. In summer, bears bowl-shaped white flowers, 3in (8cm) across, green beneath, with wavy, purple-zoned white coronas and ovoid, yellow to purple fruit, 2in (5cm) long. ↕ 15ft (5m). Brazil. Zone 7. **'Incense'** bears very fragrant, royal purple flowers.

P. fulgens see *P. coccinea.*

***P.* 'Lavender Lady'** see *P.* 'Amethyst'.

P. manicata ▣ (Red passionflower). Robust climber with branching, angular stems bearing glossy, rich green leaves, to 4in (10cm) long, with 3 broad, ovate, sharply toothed lobes, densely woolly beneath. From

Passiflora caerulea

Passiflora x *caeruleoracemosa*

Passiflora antioquiensis

Passiflora caerulea 'Constance Elliott'

Passiflora coccinea

Passiflora manicata

P

Passiflora quadrangularis

spring to autumn, produces saucer-shaped, bright red flowers, 4in (10cm) across, white at the bases, with short, purple-blue and white coronas. Bears ovoid, glossy, deep green fruit, to 2in (5cm) long. ↕ 10ft (3m). N. South America. ❀ (min. 41–45°F/5–7°C)
P. quadrangularis ▣ (Giant granadilla). Strong-growing, tuberous-rooted climber with sparsely branched, 4-angled, winged stems and broadly ovate, rich green leaves, 4–10in (10–25cm) long, with abrupt, slender points. From midsummer to autumn, bears nodding, fragrant, bowl-shaped, pale to deep red flowers, to 5in (13cm) across; they have massive coronas of wavy filaments, 2½in (6cm) long, banded red-purple and white with pink, red, or violet mottling. Greenish yellow to orange, oblong-ovoid fruit, 8–12in (20–30cm) long, have sweetly acidic pulp. ↕ 50ft (15m) or more. Central and South America, West Indies. ❀ (min. 55°F/13°C)
P. racemosa ▣ (Red passionflower). Vigorous, woody climber with slender, angled stems. The leathery, glossy, mid-green leaves, to 4in (10cm) long, are ovate and simple, or with 3 oblong lobes. Bowl-shaped, bright red flowers, 5in (13cm) across, with purple and white coronas, are borne in pendent racemes, to 12in (30cm) long, in summer and autumn. Produces oblong, deep green fruit, to 3in (8cm) long, becoming paler as they ripen. ↕ 15ft (5m). Brazil. ❀ (min. 61°F/16°C)
P. sanguinea see *P. vitifolia.*
P. velutina see *P. coccinea.*
***P. violacea* of gardens** see *P.* 'Amethyst'.
P. vitifolia, syn. *P. sanguinea.* Vigorous climber with moderately branching, slender, downy, reddish brown stems. Glossy, dark green leaves, 3–5½in (8–14cm) long, have 3 ovate, toothed or scalloped lobes, minutely hairy on the veins. From early summer to autumn, bears bowl-shaped, glowing, bright red flowers, 5–7in (13–18cm) across, with coronas of short, pale red or white filaments and longer, dark red or yellow ones. Produces ovoid, downy, yellow-green fruit, 2½in (6cm) long, with white mottling. ↕ 15ft (5m) or more. Nicaragua to Peru. ❀ (min. 55°F/13°C)

Passiflora racemosa

PASTINACA

APIACEAE

Genus of about 14 species of cool-season biennials, usually grown as annuals for food and forage. The long-stemmed, divided, dark to midgreen, carrot-like leaves arise directly from the taproot. If allowed to remain *in situ,* bears tiny, white, umbrella-shaped flowers, which can grow to 3ft (1m) above the leaves. Flavor of the crop is enhanced by moderate frost.
• **CULTIVATION** Grow in light, deeply cultivated, fertile soil, in full sun. Work in organic matter in the fall or apply fertilizer a few times during growth.
• **PROPAGATION** Sow seeds *in situ* in early spring in northern and central areas as soon as soil can be worked (45°F/7°C); in areas with mild winters, sow seed in late summer to mature and germinate over winter. Sow seeds ¾in (2cm) deep in rows 12in (30cm) apart; thin to 3in (7cm) for small, tender roots, or 4in (10cm) apart for longer, larger roots.
• **PESTS AND DISEASES** Gray mold, parsnip canker, bacterial and water soft rot may occur.

P. sativa (Parsnip). Hardy, cool-season crop with long and tapered, or round to oblong taproots, to 1–2in (2.5–5cm) in diameter, and 4–9in (10–23cm) long. Early types are usually small, slender, and tender; the larger types can be stored for later use. Zone 7.

PATERSONIA

IRIDACEAE

Genus of 13–18 species of tufted, evergreen, rhizomatous perennials occurring in dry grassland or scrub in Borneo, New Guinea, and Australia. They are cultivated for their short-lived, iris-like, blue or purple, occasionally yellow or white flowers, with 3 broad, spreading outer tepals and 3 smaller, erect inner tepals, the inner ones sometimes absent. They are produced few to many in each inflorescence, on erect to spreading stems in spring or summer. Fans of linear, mid- to gray-green leaves arise from the bases of the stems. Where not hardy, grow in a cool greenhouse. Elsewhere, grow in a border.
• **CULTIVATION** Under glass, grow in soil-based potting mix, with added grit, in full light. During the growing season, water freely and apply a balanced liquid fertilizer monthly. Water sparingly in winter. Outdoors, grow in light, fertile, well-drained soil in full sun.
• **PROPAGATION** Sow seed at 55–64°F (13–18°C), or divide, in autumn.
• **PESTS AND DISEASES** Infrequent.

P. glabrata. Rhizomatous perennial with very narrow, mid-green leaves, to 12in (30cm) long and purple flowers, to 1½in (4cm) long in summer, on stems 6in (15cm) long. ↕ to 12in (30cm), ↔ 9in (23cm). Victoria, New South Wales, Queensland. ❀ (min. 41°F/5°C)
P. occidentalis. Tuft-forming, rhizomatous perennial with few or many mid-green leaves, to 16in (40cm) long. In spring and summer, purple or deep blue flowers, 1½in (4cm) long, are borne on stems to 20in (50cm) long. ↕ to 20in (50cm), ↔ 12in (30cm). Western Australia. ❀ (min. 41°F/5°C)

Patersonia sericea

P. sericea ▣ Rhizomatous perennial with very rigid, erect, mid-green leaves, 22in (55cm) long. In summer, bears deep purple-blue flowers, to 1½in (4cm) long, on woolly stems, to 20in (50cm) long. ↕ 12in (30cm), ↔ 9in (23cm). Victoria, New South Wales, Queensland. ❀ (min. 41°F/5°C)
P. umbrosa. Rhizomatous perennial with rigid, mid-green leaves, 24–39in (60–100cm) long. In summer, bears blue flowers, to 1½in (4cm) long, on stems 32in (80cm) long. ↕ to 3ft (1m), ↔ 12in (30cm). Western Australia. ❀ (min. 41°F/5°C).
f. *xanthina* has yellow flowers.

PATRINIA

VALERIANACEAE

Genus of about 15 species of clump-forming herbaceous perennials occurring in grassy mountain habitats in Siberia and Japan. They are cultivated for their long-stemmed, sometimes corymb-like panicles of small, 5-lobed, cup-shaped, yellow or white flowers, produced in summer and autumn. The leaves are mainly basal, ovate to rounded, lobed, palmate, or pinnate, rarely entire, and mid- to dark green. Grow in a woodland garden or rock garden, in a mixed or herbaceous border, or as a groundcover.
• **CULTIVATION** Grow in fertile, humus-rich, moist soil in partial or deep shade.
• **PROPAGATION** Sow seed as soon as ripe in containers. Divide in spring.
• **PESTS AND DISEASES** Young leaves may be damaged by slugs and snails.

P. scabiosaefolia ▣ Upright, variable perennial with leafy stems, ovate to oblong, mid-green basal leaves, and pinnatifid, coarsely toothed, hairy, lobed stem leaves, 6in (15cm) long. From late summer to autumn, bears cymes, to 4in (10cm) across, in large panicles of cup-shaped, yellow flowers. ↕ 3–7ft (1–2.2m), ↔ 24in (60cm). E. Asia. Zone 5.
P. triloba. Clump-forming, stoloniferous perennial with palmately 3- to 5-lobed, mid-green leaves, 2½–4in (6–10cm) across, turning yellow in autumn. In mid- and late summer, branching, red-tinted stems produce panicles, to 4in (10cm) across, of small, fragrant, cup-shaped yellow flowers, each with a short tube and 5 spreading lobes. ↕ 8–20in (20–50cm), ↔ 6–12in (15–30cm). Japan. Zone 5. **var. *palmata*** has flowers with short spurs.

Patrinia scabiosaefolia

PAULOWNIA

SCROPHULARIACEAE

Genus of 6 species of deciduous trees occurring in woodland in E. Asia. They produce thick shoots and usually large, hairy, opposite, ovate or 3- to 5-lobed, mid- or yellow-green leaves. The flower buds are formed in autumn, and open, before the leaves appear, to bell- to trumpet-shaped, foxglove-like flowers, borne in terminal panicles. Grown for their showy flowers, they make spectacular specimen trees. They grow and flower best in climates with long, hot summers. They may be grown coppiced or pollarded, which will produce very large, ornamental leaves.

• **CULTIVATION** Grow in fertile, well-drained soil in full sun. Where not hardy, shelter from cold, drying winds. Flower buds will be killed during hard winters. Pruning group 1, or group 7 if larger leaves are desired.

• **PROPAGATION** Sow seed in containers in a cold frame in autumn or spring. Take root cuttings in winter.

• **PESTS AND DISEASES** Canker, dieback, powdery mildew, wood rot, and mushroom root rot can be problems.

P. fortunei. Broadly columnar tree with thick shoots and ovate, mid-green leaves, to 8in (20cm) long, glossy above and densely hairy beneath. Fragrant flowers, 4in (10cm) long, pale purple outside and creamy white with purple spots inside, are produced in upright panicles in late spring. ↕↔ 25ft (8m). China, Taiwan. Zone 7.

P. imperialis see *P. tomentosa.*
P. tomentosa ■ syn. *P. imperialis* (Empress tree, Foxglove tree, Princess tree, Royal paulownia). Fast-growing, broadly columnar to spreading tree with thick shoots and ovate, sometimes shallowly lobed, bright light green leaves, to 12in (30cm) long, hairy above, densely hairy beneath. Fragrant, pinkish lilac flowers, 2in (5cm) long, with purple and yellow marks inside, are borne in large, upright panicles in late spring as the leaves emerge. Very tolerant of atmospheric pollution and poor soil. ↕ 40ft (12m), ↔ 30ft (10m). China; naturalized in E. US. Zone 6b.

▷ ***Paurotis*** see *Acoelorraphe*

PAVONIA

MALVACEAE

Genus of about 150 species of evergreen perennials, subshrubs, and shrubs, often occurring on sandy soils in tropical and subtropical regions of Africa, Asia, the Pacific islands, and North and South America. They are grown for their brightly colored flowers, solitary, axillary, or borne in terminal, spherical clusters or panicles, mainly in summer. Petals spread or form a tube surrounded by a bell- or cup-shaped calyx, with a whorl of hairy bracts beneath; the stamens are often protruding. Most have alternate, linear to broadly ovate or oblong, light to dark green leaves, each with a bract-like stipule at the base of the leaf stalk. In subtropical and tropical gardens, grow in a shrub border. In cooler areas, grow in a warm greenhouse.

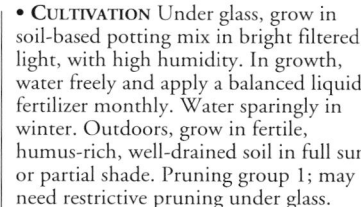

• **CULTIVATION** Under glass, grow in soil-based potting mix in bright filtered light, with high humidity. In growth, water freely and apply a balanced liquid fertilizer monthly. Water sparingly in winter. Outdoors, grow in fertile, humus-rich, well-drained soil in full sun or partial shade. Pruning group 1; may need restrictive pruning under glass.

• **PROPAGATION** Sow seed at 66–75°F (19–24°C) in spring. Root semi-ripe cuttings with bottom heat in summer.

• **PESTS AND DISEASES** Spider mites and whiteflies may be troublesome.

P. x gledhillii (*P. mackoyana* x *P. multiflora*) syn. *P. intermedia* of gardens, *P. multiflora* of gardens. Sparsely branched shrub with pointed, elliptic to lance-shaped, glossy, light green leaves, 4–6in (10–15cm) long, with linear to lance-shaped stipules. In late summer, bears solitary, dark purple flowers, to 1¼in (3cm) long, enclosed in almost cylindrical, hairy calyces with gray-pink teeth, and each with a whorl of red bracts beneath; the stamens have red filaments and chalky, lilac-blue anthers. ↕ to 6ft (2m), ↔ 3ft (1m). Garden origin. ❄ (min. 61–64°F/16–18°C)
***P. intermedia* of gardens** see *P. x gledhillii.*
***P. multiflora* of gardens** see *P. x gledhillii.*

PAXISTIMA *syn.* PACHYSTIMA

CELASTRACEAE

Genus of 2 species of low-growing, evergreen shrubs found in rocky sites on mountains and in coniferous woodland in North America. They are grown for their small, opposite, linear to ovate or oblong, sometimes finely toothed, leathery leaves. Tiny, cross-shaped, 4-petaled, greenish white or white flowers, solitary or in axillary clusters, are borne in summer. Grow as a groundcover in a woodland or rock garden.

• **CULTIVATION** Grow in moderately fertile, humus-rich, moist but well-drained soil in full sun or dappled shade.

• **PROPAGATION** Take semi-ripe cuttings in summer. Remove rooted layers in spring or autumn.

• **PESTS AND DISEASES** Infrequent.

P. canbyi ■ (Cliff green, Ratstripper). Spreading, branching, stem-rooting shrub with stalkless, linear-oblong, sometimes finely toothed, glossy, dark green leaves, to ¾in (2cm) long, with incurved margins. Bears short, pendent clusters of greenish white flowers, ¼in (6mm) across, in summer. ↕ 16in (40cm), ↔ to 3ft (1m). C. North America. Zone 2b.
P. myrsinites see *P. myrtifolia.*
P. myrtifolia, syn. *P. myrsinites* (Mountain lover, Oregon boxwood). Spreading, almost prostrate, very leafy shrub with hairless brown branches and stalkless, ovate, oblong, or oblong-lance-shaped, finely toothed, pointed, glossy, dark green leaves, to 1¼in (3cm) long, paler green beneath. In spring and summer, bears 1–3 greenish white flowers, ¼in (6mm) across, in pendent clusters. ↕ 2in (5cm), ↔ to 3½ft (1.1m). W. North America. Zone 6.

▷ ***Pectinaria pillansii*** see *Stapeliopsis pillansii*

PEDILANTHUS

EUPHORBIACEAE

Genus of about 14 species of variable, bushy, succulent shrubs and small trees occurring mainly in low, rocky terrain in Mexico, Central and South America, the West Indies, and Florida. The fleshy, narrow to broadly ovate, light to mid-green, sometimes white-mottled leaves are usually quickly deciduous. Terminal or axillary cymes of flower-like, tubular bract-cups bloom during the day in summer. Where temperatures drop below 50°F (10°C), grow as houseplants or in a warm greenhouse. In warmer climates, use in a desert garden or shrub border. The stems and leaves contain a milky sap that may cause stomach upset.

• **CULTIVATION** Under glass, grow in soil-based potting mix, with added well-rotted organic matter and sharp sand, in bright filtered light. In spring and summer, water moderately and apply a balanced liquid fertilizer every month. Water sparingly in winter. Outdoors, grow in moderately fertile, sharply drained soil in full sun or partial shade. See also pp.48–49.

• **PROPAGATION** Sow seed at 66–75°F (19–24°C) in spring. Take stem-tip cuttings in summer.

• **PESTS AND DISEASES** Powdery mildew, leaf spots, and stem spots occur.

P. tithymaloides (Devil's backbone, Jacob's ladder). Upright, bushy, clump-forming, succulent shrub with thin, fleshy to woody, zigzagged stems. Evergreen or deciduous, ovate to elliptic,

Paulownia tomentosa (inset: flower detail)

Paxistima canbyi

P

Pedilanthus tithymaloides 'Variegatus'

mid-green leaves, to 3in (8cm) long, are keeled and slightly hairy or powdery beneath. In summer, bears fleshy red bract-cups, to ½in (1.5cm) long, yellow-green at the bases. ↕ 6ft (2m), ↔ to 3ft (1m). Florida to Venezuela, West Indies. ❀ (min. 50°F/10°C). **'Variegatus'** ▣ has variably shaped leaves, to 6in (15cm) long, with white or pink variegation; ↔ to 18in (45cm).

PEDIOCACTUS

CACTACEAE

Genus of about 6 species of clustering, spherical cacti occurring in rocky terrain in W. and S. US. The spiny stems have spiraling, tuberculate ribs. Bell-shaped flowers are produced near or at the stem tips, followed by spherical, pink or greenish yellow fruits. Where temperatures drop below 36°F (2°C), grow pediocacti as houseplants or in a cool greenhouse. In warmer areas, grow in a desert garden.

• **CULTIVATION** Under glass, grow in standard cactus potting mix in full light. From spring to summer, water moderately and apply a low-nitrogen fertilizer every 6–8 weeks. Keep dry at other times. Outdoors, grow in moderately fertile, sharply drained soil in full sun. See also pp.48–49.

• **PROPAGATION** Sow seed at 66–75°F (19–24°C) in spring.

• **PESTS AND DISEASES** Bacterial soft rot and mealybugs can occur.

P. simpsonii (Snowball cactus). Simple or clustering cactus with spherical to ovoid, mid-green stems, each with 12 ribs, and white-woolly areoles bearing fine spines (15–25 white radials and 5–10 slightly longer, reddish brown centrals). In spring, white, pink, magenta, yellow, or yellow-green flowers, ½–1¼in (1–3cm) long, are borne singly or in clusters by day. ↕ 5–6in (12–15cm), ↔ to 6in (15cm). W. US. ❀ (min. 36°F/2°C); tolerates brief periods to 0°F (-18°C).

P

PELARGONIUM

Geranium

GERANIACEAE

Genus of about 280 species of mainly evergreen perennials, succulents, subshrubs, and shrubs, commonly known as geraniums. They occur in a variety of habitats, from mountains to deserts, mostly in South Africa. The many cultivars, derived from about 20 species, are popular garden plants; few species are commonly grown. Leaves are variable, but are usually alternate, palmately lobed or pinnate, sometimes aromatic, often on long stalks. Erect stems bear 5-petaled flowers in terminal, umbel-like clusters (pseudoumbels), referred to in this account as "clusters." The flowers are saucer- or star-shaped, trumpet- or funnel-shaped, or butterfly-shaped (the upper 2 petals larger than the lower 3); they are usually borne from spring to summer, although many will flower throughout the year if kept above 45–50°F (7–10°C).

Where not winter-hardy, use in containers outside in summer or as bedding plants, and overwinter in a cool greenhouse or conservatory. In frost-free areas, grow in a sunny border. For winter flowers, grow in a temperate greenhouse or as houseplants. Contact with the foliage may occasionally aggravate skin allergies.

Most cultivars belong to one of the following 6 horticultural groups:

Angel
Very bushy, evergreen perennials and subshrubs, originally derived from *P. crispum* crossed with a regal geranium. They have rounded, crinkled, sometimes scented, mid-green leaves, ¾–1¼in (2–3cm) long, and bear clusters of small, single flowers of the regal type (see panel), ¾–1½in (2–4cm) across, in shades of pink, purple, mauve, or white. Heights range from 9–36in (23–90cm).

Ivy-leaved
Trailing, evergreen perennials with lobed, sometimes pointed, stiff, fleshy, usually mid-green leaves, 1–5in (2.5–13cm) long, very similar to those of English ivy (*Hedera helix*). Some cultivars have short-jointed stems. Clusters of single to double flowers, to 1½in (4cm) across, are produced in shades of red, pink, mauve, purple, or white. Spreads range from 6–48in (15–120cm).

Regal or Martha Washington
Bushy, evergreen perennials and shrubs, some with short-jointed stems. The leaves are rounded, sometimes lobed or partially toothed, mid-green, and 2–3½in (5–9cm) long. Clusters of single, rarely double flowers, 1½–4in (4–10cm) across, are produced in single or combined shades of red, pink, salmon, burgundy, purple, orange, white, or reddish black. Heights range from 12–48in (30–120cm).

Scented-leaved
Shrubby, evergreen perennials and shrubs grown mainly for their attractive leaves, which release scent when brushed. Leaves are mainly mid-green, sometimes variegated, and are very variable in shape and size, usually ½–5in (1.5–13cm) long, sometimes toothed, lobed, or deeply incised. They bear clusters of small, single flowers, to 1in (2.5cm) across, in shades of red, mauve, pink, purple, or white. Heights range from 12–84in (0.3–2.2m).

Unique
Shrubby, evergreen perennials with rounded or lobed, sometimes incised, mid-green leaves, 2–5½in (5–14cm) across, often with a pungent scent when crushed. They produce clusters of trumpet-shaped, single, white, pink, red, purple, or orange flowers of the regal type (see panel), to 1¼in (3cm) across. Heights range from 24–48in (60–120cm).

Zonal
Erect, bushy, succulent-stemmed, evergreen perennials, some with short-jointed stems, derived mainly from *P. inquinans* and *P. zonale*. The leaves are rounded, 1½–5½in (4–14cm) across, light to deep green, often bicolored or multi-colored, with zones of dark bronze-green or maroon. Flowers are single, semi-double, or double, to 1in (2.5cm) across, in shades of red, scarlet, maroon, purple, lavender

PELARGONIUM GROUPS

Leaves and flower clusters (pseudoumbels) of the 4 main pelargonium groups are shown here. Angel and unique pelargoniums have clusters similar to those of regal pelargoniums.

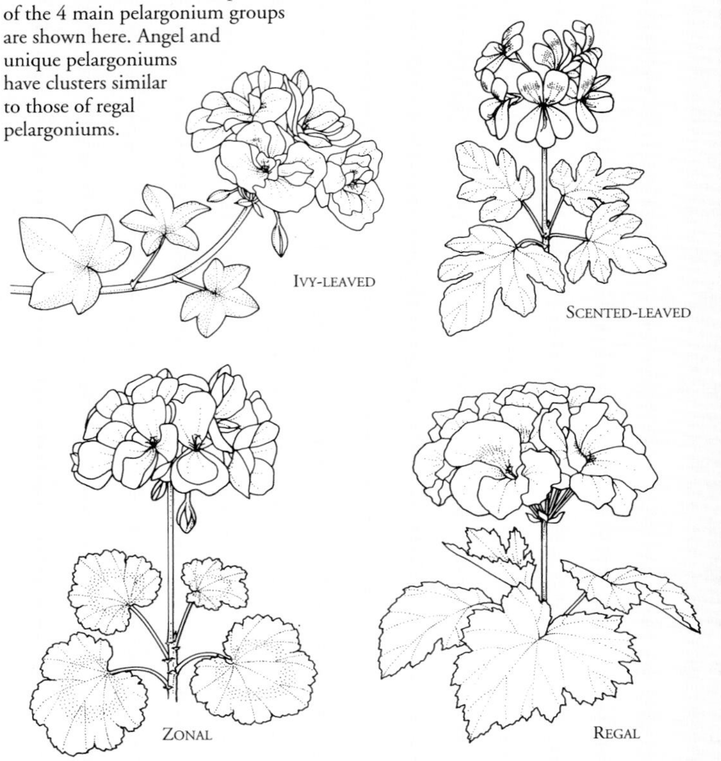

Pelargonium abrotanifolium

Pelargonium 'Apple Blossom Rosebud'

pink, salmon, white, orange, or rarely yellow. Rain may damage the flowers of many cultivars. As bedding plants, most grow to 24in (60cm) tall; dwarf cultivars are 5–8in (12–20cm) tall, miniature cultivars to 5in (13cm) tall.

There are 2 main groups of zonal pelargoniums: the seed-raised bedding types, mainly consisting of the single-flowered F1 hybrids, which flower in the first year and are uniform with respect to color and type when raised from seed; and the large-flowered cultivars propagated from cuttings, which are ideal container plants in a conservatory or as house-plants, or outdoors in frost-free periods.

Zonal pelargoniums can be separated into the following subgroups:

Cactus-flowered – Flowers, resembling those of cactus dahlias, are single or double, the petals twisted into quills.

Double- and semi-double-flowered – Flowers consist of 6 or more petals.

Fancy-leaved – These are grown mainly for their foliage, which may have tricolor combinations of green, white, gold, and other colors; or may be bronze and gold, almost black, or butterfly-leaved with a distinct mark in the leaf center. Flowers may be single, semi-double, or double and occur in most zonal colors.

Formosum hybrids – Flowers are flat, single or double, with narrow petals resembling a daisy. Leaves are deeply cut.

Rosebud – Flowers are double, with rosebud-like centers (the central petals remaining unopened).

Single-flowered – Flowers usually have no more than 5 petals.

Stellar – Flowers are irregularly star-shaped: the bottom 3 petals are wedge-shaped and broad, the top 2 are much narrower and toothed. The leaves have pointed lobes and, often, dark zones.

• **HARDINESS** Geraniums are generally hardy to 36°F (2°C). Some, particularly the scented-leaved types, may overwinter at the base of a warm wall during mild winters in Zone 8, coming back from the roots in spring.

• **CULTIVATION** Under glass, grow in soilless or soil-based potting mix in full light, with shade from hot sun and good ventilation. Water moderately during growth; apply a balanced liquid fertilizer every 10–14 days in spring and early summer, and a high-potash fertilizer when in flower. Water sparingly in winter. If kept at 45–50°F (7–10°C), plants may flower over winter. Otherwise, cut back by up to two-thirds and keep almost dry. Outdoors, grow in fertile, neutral to alkaline, well-drained soil. Most prefer full sun; regal cultivars prefer partial shade and areas with cool summers, and zonals tolerate some shade. Where summers are hot, provide afternoon shade. Lift bedding plants in autumn and overwinter in dry, frost-free conditions; cut back top-growth by one-third and repot in late winter as new growth resumes. Deadhead all pelargoniums regularly.

• **PROPAGATION** Sow seed at 70°F (21°C) from late winter to early spring. Take softwood cuttings in spring, late summer, or early autumn.

• **PESTS AND DISEASES** Thrips, spider mites, mealybugs, caterpillars, gray mold, mildew, black leg, flower break virus, *Xanthomonas* blight, and edema commonly occur.

P. abrotanifolium ■ (Southernwood geranium). Bushy, erect or trailing, woody-stemmed subshrub. Rounded, finely divided, gray-green leaves, to ½in (1.5cm) long, have linear lobes and smell like southernwood (*Artemisia abrotanum*). Star-shaped, white or pink flowers, ½in (1.5cm) across, are produced in clusters of up to 5, to 2in (5cm) across, from spring to autumn. ↕6–12in (15–30cm), ↔ 10–12in (25–30cm) or more. South Africa (Orange Free State, Northern Cape, Western Cape, Eastern Cape).

P. acetosum ■ Erect perennial with succulent stems bearing obovate, toothed, fleshy, gray-green leaves, ¾–2½in (2–6cm) long, sometimes margined red. From spring to summer, star-shaped, light salmon-pink flowers, ¾–1½in (2–4cm) across, with long, narrow petals, are borne in sparse clusters, 2½–3in (6–8cm) across. ↕20–24in (50–60cm), ↔ 8–10in (20–25cm). South Africa (Eastern Cape).

***P.* 'A Happy Thought'** see *P.* 'Happy Thought'.

***P.* 'Alberta'** ■ Single-flowered zonal pelargonium bearing bicolored coral-pink and white flowers in clusters 3½–4in (9–10cm) across. ↕16–20in (40–50cm), ↔ 8–10in (20–25cm).

***P.* 'Alice Crousse'** ■ Short-jointed ivy-leaved pelargonium with double, bright cerise-pink flowers borne in clusters 3½in (9cm) across. ↕10–12in (25–30cm), ↔ 8–10in (20–25cm).

***P.* 'Always'**. Bushy, double-flowered zonal pelargonium with very large, tight clusters, 4in (10cm) across, of creamy-white-flushed, soft salmon-pink flowers, deep salmon-pink in the centers. ↕12–18in (30–45cm), ↔ 10–12in (25–30cm).

***P.* Americana Series.** syn, *P.* 'Americana' **'Lt. Pink Splash II'** ■ Early-flowering, compact, self-branching plant produces a large, semi-double geranium. Flowers are very free-blooming, held above medium to dark green foliage. Petals are pink with a white eye. Excellent heat tolerance. ↕↔ 10–15in (25–37.5cm).

***P.* 'Amethyst'** ■ Vigorous, short-jointed ivy-leaved pelargonium. Semi-double purple flowers are produced in clusters 3½–4in (9–10cm) across; the upper petals are marked with deep purple and white feathering. ↕10–12in (25–30cm), ↔ 8–10in (20–25cm).

***P.* 'Apple Blossom Rosebud'** ■ Rosebud zonal pelargonium bearing greenish white flowers, with each petal margined rose-red, in clusters to 3in (8cm) across. ↕12–16in (30–40cm), ↔ 8–10in (20–25cm).

***P.* 'Apple Scented'** see *P. odoratissimum.*

***P.* 'Apricot Scented'** see *P.* 'Paton's Unique'.

***P.* 'Attar of Roses'.** Scented-leaved pelargonium with 3-lobed, rose-scented leaves. Bears mauve flowers in clusters, 1–1¼in (2.5–3cm) across. ↕20–24in (50–60cm), ↔ 10–12in (25–30cm).

***P.* 'Autumn Festival'** ■ Bushy, short-jointed regal pelargonium bearing

Pelargonium 'Bird Dancer'

clusters, 3½–4in (9–10cm) across, of bicolored salmon-pink and white flowers with mahogany, feather-like markings in the centers. ↕10–12in (25–30cm), ↔ 8–10in (20–25cm).

***P.* 'Beauty of Eastbourne'.** Ivy-leaved pelargonium. Large, light magenta-pink flowers are held above vigorous medium-green foliage.

***P.* 'Belinda Adams'.** Miniature, double-flowered zonal pelargonium bearing clusters, 3in (8cm) across, of white flowers flushed pink. ↕4–5in (10–13cm), ↔ 3–4in (8–10cm).

***P.* 'Ben Franklin'.** Fancy-leaved zonal pelargonium with rounded white leaves. Produces clusters, 3–3½in (8–9cm) across, of double, salmon-pink flowers. ↕12–16in (30–40cm), ↔ 6–8in (15–20cm).

***P.* 'Bird Dancer'** ■ Dwarf, stellar zonal pelargonium with dark-zoned leaves. Produces single flowers, with pale pink lower petals and salmon-pink upper petals, in clusters to 3in (8cm) across. May be trained into a topiary if started

Pelargonium acetosum

Pelargonium 'Alberta'

Pelargonium 'Alice Crousse'

Pelargonium americana 'Lt. Pink Splash II'

Pelargonium 'Amethyst'

Pelargonium 'Autumn Festival'

from an unbranched, young plant. ↕ 6–8in (15–20cm), ↔ 10in (25cm).
P. Black Velvet Series, syn. *P.* x *hortorum* 'Black Magic Series'. Seed-propagated, single-flowered zonal pelargoniums with unique chocolate-colored leaves edged in green. Bears apple blossom, rose, red, and salmon colored flowers in clusters, to 5in (13cm) ↕ 10–14in (25–35cm).
P. 'Blazonry' ■ Fancy-leaved zonal pelargonium producing rounded, deep cream leaves with rose-pink, mid-green, and purple zones. Bears single red flowers in clusters 3in (8cm) across. ↕↔ 12in (30cm).
P. Blizzard Series. Ivy-leaved pelargoniums noted for vigorous growth and heat resistance. Plants produce large to extra-large flowers, in several colors. **'Blue Blizzard'** produces extra-large flowers of a unique blue-lavender shade. **'Fire Blizzard'** is a very heat-resistant plant with bright scarlet flowers.
P. 'Both's Snowflake'. Sprawling, scented-leaved pelargonium with lobed, incised, rose- to lemon-rose-scented, white- and cream-splashed leaves. Bears clusters, to 1½in (4cm) across, of single, light mauve flowers. ↕↔ 12–24in (30–60cm).
P. 'Bravo' ■ Large, spreading zonal pelargonium bears clusters, to 4in (10cm) across, of double, soft orange flowers. ↕ to 24in (60cm), ↔ 12in (30cm).
P. 'Brockbury Scarlet' ■ Cactus-flowered zonal pelargonium. Single scarlet flowers are produced in clusters to 3in (8cm) across. ↕ 10–12in (25–30cm), ↔ 6–8in (15–20cm).
P. 'Brookside Primrose' ■ Miniature, fancy-leaved zonal pelargonium with golden-green leaves, each with a central zone. Double, light pink flowers are borne in clusters 3in (8cm) across. ↕ 4–5in (10–13cm), ↔ 3–4in (8–10cm).
P. 'Butterfly Loreli'. Fancy-leaved zonal pelargonium with yellow butterfly markings in the center of each leaf. Bears double, pale pink flowers in clusters to 3in (8cm) across. ↕ 10–12in (25–30cm), ↔ 6–8in (15–20cm).
P. 'Caligula' ■ Miniature, double-flowered zonal pelargonium with almost black leaves. Bears clusters, 2–2½in (5–6cm) across, of scarlet flowers. ↕ 4–5in (10–13cm), ↔ 3–4in (8–10cm).

Pelargonium carnosum

P. 'Caravan'. Spreading angel pelargonium with clusters, 1in (2.5cm) across, of single, mid-pink flowers. ↕ 6–8in (15–20cm), ↔ to 18in (45cm).
P. 'Carisbrooke' ■ Regal pelargonium with clusters, 4in (10cm) across, of pale rose-pink flowers, feathered and blazed wine-red on the upper petals. ↕ 16–18in (40–45cm), ↔ 8–10in (20–25cm).
P. carnosum ■ Deciduous, perennial succulent with a smooth, swollen stem, 2in (5cm) thick, and fleshy branches, swollen at the joints. Ovate-oblong, pinnate, stalked, slightly hairy, gray-green leaves, 3–5½in (8–14cm) long, have lobed segments with scalloped margins. Clusters, 1½in (4cm) across, of 2–8 star-shaped, white to pale yellow-green flowers with red markings, ½in (1.5cm) across, are borne from spring to summer. ↕ 16in (40cm), ↔ 10in (25cm). Namibia, South Africa (Northern Cape, Western Cape, Eastern Cape).
P. 'Catford Belle'. Angel pelargonium producing single, rose-purple flowers with deep purple feathering on the upper petals, in clusters, 1in (2.5cm) across. ↕↔ 10–12in (25–30cm).
P. 'Charlotte Brontë'. Fancy-leaved zonal pelargonium with rounded, red, golden yellow, and green leaves. Bears single, salmon-pink flowers in clusters 2½–3in (6–8cm) across. ↕ 10–12in (25–30cm), ↔ 8–10in (20–25cm).
P. 'Clorinda' ■ Vigorous, eucalyptus-scented pelargonium with 3-lobed, cedar-scented leaves. Bears rose-pink flowers in clusters 3in (8cm) across. ↕ 18–20in (45–50cm), ↔ 8–10in (20–25cm).
P. 'Coconut Scented' see *P. grossularioides.*
P. 'Coddenham' ■ Miniature, double-flowered zonal pelargonium bears orange-red flowers in clusters 3in (8cm) across. ↕ 4–5in (10–13cm), ↔ 3–4in (8–10cm).
P. Colorcade Series. Vigorous, ivy-leaved pelargoniums noted for their uniform free-branching habit. Bears large bright semi-double to double flowers. **'Colorcade Burgundy'** bears semi-double deep burgundy flowers with deep green foliage.
P. 'Contrast' ■ Fancy-leaved zonal pelargonium producing rounded, golden yellow, green, and red leaves. Bears single scarlet flowers in clusters to 3in (8cm) across. ↕ 10–12in (25–30cm), ↔ 6–8in (15–20cm).
P. 'Copthorne'. Vigorous scented-leaved pelargonium with large-lobed leaves exuding a pungent, cedar-like scent. Bears clusters, 3–3½in (8–9cm) across, of mauve flowers with purple feathering on the upper petals. ↕ 18–20in (45–50cm), ↔ 8–10in (20–25cm).
P. 'Creamery'. Trailing, semi-double zonal pelargonium with sharply lobed, light green leaves. Produces profuse clusters, to 2in (5cm) across, of few, creamy white flowers. Good in a hanging basket. ↕ 8–10in (20–25cm), ↔ 12in (30cm).
P. crispum. Shrubby, stiff, upright, evergreen perennial with rounded, crinkled, lemon-scented, mid-green leaves, ¾–1in (2–2.5cm) long. Single, pale mauve flowers, ½in (1.5cm) across, are produced in clusters, ¾–1in (2–2.5cm) across, from summer to autumn. ↕ 14–18in (35–45cm), ↔ 6–10in (15–25cm). South Africa. **'French Lace'** see 'Variegated Prince Rupert'. **'Variegated Prince Rupert'** ■ syn. 'French Lace', 'Variegatum' (Variegated lemon-scented geranium) produces lemon-scented, cream-margined, mid-green leaves; ↔ 5–6in (12–15cm). **'Variegatum'** see 'Variegated Prince Rupert'.
P. cucullatum ■ Shrubby, evergreen perennial with cup-shaped, softly hairy mid-green leaves, to 3in (8cm) long. From spring to summer, produces abundant, trumpet-shaped, light to deep mauve-purple or white flowers, to 2in (5cm) across, in clusters 3–3½in (8–9cm) across. Flowers range from single to double. ↕ 24–36in (60–90cm), ↔ 8–10in (20–25cm). South Africa (Western Cape).
P. 'Dame Anna Neagle'. Dwarf zonal pelargonium producing rounded, light to mid-green leaves. Double, light pink flowers are borne in clusters 2½–3in (6–8cm) across. ↕↔ 6–8in (15–20cm).
P. 'Davinia'. Miniature, double-flowered zonal pelargonium. Bears clusters, 3in (8cm) across, of salmon-pink flowers, flushed and veined deeper salmon-pink. ↕ 4–5in (10–13cm), ↔ 3–4in (8–10cm).
P. denticulatum see *P.* 'Filicifolium'.
P. 'Dr. Livingston', syn. *P.* 'Skeleton Leaf Rose'. Rangy, scented-leaved pelargonium with very deeply cut, rough-textured, rose-scented leaves. Produces single, light lavender flowers in clusters, to ½in (1.5cm) across. ↕ 18–36in (45–90cm), ↔ 8–12in (20–30cm).
P. 'Dolly Vardon' ■ Fancy-leaved zonal pelargonium with rounded, white, red, and green leaves. Bears single scarlet flowers in clusters 2in (5cm) across. ↕ 10–12in (25–30cm), ↔ 5–6in (12–15cm). Suitable for training as an informal standard.
P. 'Easter Greeting' ■ Low-growing regal pelargonium. Light cerise-pink flowers, with a distinct, wine-red blaze on each petal, are borne in clusters 3–3½in (8–9cm) across. ↕ 10–12in (25–30cm), ↔ 5–7in (13–18cm).
P. echinatum (Cactus geranium). Shrubby, tuberous-rooted, deciduous, perennial succulent with an erect, swollen stem bearing a few gray branches, ½in (1.5cm) thick, covered with spiny stipules. Heart-shaped, scalloped, gray-green leaves, to 1¼in (3cm) long, with 3–5 shallow lobes, are hairy above, more so beneath. From late winter to spring, produces clusters, to 4in (10cm) across, of 3–8 small, star-shaped, white to pink flowers, 1¼in (3cm) across, with dark red marks on the upper petals. ↕ 12in (30cm) or more, ↔ to 12in (30cm). South Africa (Northern Cape).
P. Elegance Series. Vigorous regal pelargoniums noted for traditional 'Martha Washington'-type flowers.

Pelargonium 'Blazonry'

Pelargonium 'Bravo'

Pelargonium 'Brockbury Scarlet'

Pelargonium 'Brookside Primrose'

Pelargonium 'Caligula'

Pelargonium 'Carisbrooke'

Pelargonium 'Clorinda'

Pelargonium 'Coddenham'

Pelargonium 'Contrast'

Pelargonium crispum 'Variegated Prince Rupert'

Pelargonium cucullatum

Pelargonium 'Dolly Vardon'

ᴾelargonium 'Eric Hoskins'

xtra-large flowers come in a wide variety f solid and multicolored combinations nd bloom early to late season. **'Elegance ink Chiffon'** has soft pink flowers with small dark eye; **'Dandy'** is a light red.
. 'Elmsett'. Dwarf, fancy-leaved zonal elargonium with bright gold leaves. ears clusters, 3in (8cm) across, of ouble, white to pale pink flowers with cattered red spots and splashes. ↕ 4–6in 10–15cm), ↔ 4–5in (10–13cm).
. 'Emma Hössle' see *P.* 'Frau Emma Hössle'.
. 'Eric Hoskins' ■ Bushy zonal elargonium producing mid-green eaves, each with a wide, dark brown one. Bears clusters, 3–4in (8–10cm) cross, of double, white to pale salmon owers with deeper salmon centers. 12–16in (30–40cm), ↔ 8–10in 20–25cm).
. 'Fair Ellen' ■ Scented-leaved elargonium with deeply lobed leaves hat have a strong perfume. Bears lusters, 2–2½in (5–6cm) across, of urple-pink flowers with spotted, oothed petals. ↕ 12–16in (30–40cm), → 6–8in (15–20cm).
. 'Fairyland' ■ Miniature, fancy-eaved, zonal pelargonium with tricolor eaves of white with green centers and right red to pink zones. Single red lowers are borne in clusters, ½–¾in 1.5–2cm) across. ↕ 3–4in (8–10cm), → 2–3in (5–8cm).
. 'Fairy Orchid'. Spreading angel elargonium bearing single white flowers with reddish purple bands on the tips of the upper petals, in clusters, 1in (2.5cm) across. ↕ 6–8in (15–20cm), ↔ 10–16in (25–40cm).
***P.* Fantasia Series.** Vigorous plants noted for very large flowers, produced in several colors. Useful in containers or dotting the landscape. ↕↔ 10–15in (25–37.5cm).
***P.* 'Fenton Farm'.** Dwarf, fancy-leaved zonal pelargonium with rounded gold leaves. Single, white-eyed purple flowers are produced in clusters 1¾–2in (4.5–5cm) across. ↕ 6–8in (15–20cm), ↔ 4–5in (10–13cm).
***P.* 'Filicifolium'**, syn. *P. denticulatum.* Scented-leaved pelargonium producing fern-like leaves with a balsam scent. Pale mauve flowers are borne in small clusters, ¾–1in (2–2.5cm) across. ↕ 12–18in (30–45cm) or more, ↔ 6–10in (15–25cm).
***P.* 'Flower of Spring'** ■ Fancy-leaved zonal pelargonium with rounded, white-marked leaves. Single scarlet flowers are borne in clusters 3in (8cm) across. ↕ 18–24in (45–60cm), ↔ 8–10in (20–25cm).
P.* x *fragrans see *P.* 'Fragrans'.
***P.* 'Fragrans'** ■ syn. *P.* x *fragrans, P.* Fragrans Group (Nutmeg geranium). Bushy scented-leaved pelargonium with nutmeg-scented, gray-green foliage. Small white flowers are borne in trailing clusters, 1–1¼in (2.5–3cm) across. ↕ 8–10in (20–25cm), ↔ 10–12in (25–30cm).
***P.* Fragrans Group** see *P.* 'Fragrans'.
***P.* 'Fraicheur Beauty'** ■ Double-flowered zonal pelargonium bearing white flowers in clusters, to 5in (13cm) across; the petals have very fine red margins. ↕ 12–16in (30–40cm), ↔ 6–8in (15–20cm).
***P.* 'Francis Parrett'.** Miniature, double-flowered zonal pelargonium producing purple-pink flowers in clusters 3in (8cm) across. ↕ 4–5in (10–13cm), ↔ 3–4in (8–10cm).
***P.* 'Frank Headley'** ■ Fancy-leaved zonal pelargonium with gray-green and white leaves. Single salmon-colored flowers are borne above the foliage.
***P.* 'Frau Emma Hössle'**, syn. *P.* 'Emma Hössle'. Very bushy, dwarf, double-flowered zonal pelargonium. Bears mid-pink flowers, with white-based upper petals, in clusters 2½–3in (6–8cm)

Pelargonium 'Golden Staph'

across. ↕ 6–8in (15–20cm), ↔ 4–5in (10–13cm).
***P.* 'Freckles'** ■ Seed-raised, single-flowered zonal pelargonium. Produces clusters, 5in (13cm) across, of bright rose-pink flowers, each with a small white eye, and with a darker rose-pink mark at the base of each petal. ↕↔ to 12in (30cm).
***P.* Freestyle Series.** Vigorous ivy-leaved pelargoniums, yet with a compact, well-branched habit. The foliage shows some resistance to edema. Large to extra-large, semi-double flowers are freely produced above the deep green foliage. **'Freestyle Arctic Red'** bears semi-double flowers with unique red-edged white petals. **'Freestyle Burgundy II'** ■ has extra-large, semi-double, deep burgundy flowers held above the foliage.
***P.* 'Friesdorf'.** Dwarf, fancy-leaved zonal pelargonium with rounded, almost black leaves and narrow-petaled, single crimson flowers in clusters 3in (8cm) across. ↕ 6–8in (15–20cm), ↔ 4–5in (10–13cm).
***P.* 'Garnet Rosebud'.** Dwarf, zonal pelargonium bearing clusters, 2½–3in (6–8cm) across, of rosebud-shaped, deep garnet-red flowers. ↕ 4–6in (10–15cm), ↔ 4–5in (10–13cm).
***P.* Global Series.** Ivy-leaved pelargoniums noted for heat tolerance and edema-resistant foliage. The extensive selection of colors includes the trailing **'Global Salmon Rose'** whose large rose flowers have an undertone of salmon, and **'Global Sangria'** ■ with its white-striped burgundy blooms.
***P.* 'Golden Brilliantissimum'.** Fancy-leaved zonal pelargonium producing rounded leaves with orange, mid-green, and dark wine-red zones. Double, cherry-red flowers are borne in clusters to 3in (8cm) across. ↕ 10–12in (25–30cm), ↔ 5–6in (12–15cm).
***P.* 'Golden Staph'** ■ Fancy-leaved, zonal pelargonium with bronze-zoned, gold, sharply lobed leaves. Single, star-shaped, red-orange flowers are borne in clusters to 3in (8cm) across. ↕ 10–16in (25–40cm), ↔ 8–10in (20–25cm).
***P.* 'Gooseberry Leaf'**, syn. *P.* 'Peach'.
***P.* 'Graveolens' of gardens** ■ (Rose geranium). Vigorous, bushy, erect scented-leaved pelargonium with slightly rough, lobed and cut, mid-green leaves, which have a pungent lemon-rose scent. Mauve flowers are borne in clusters 1–1¼in (2.5–3cm) across. ↕ 18–24in (45–60cm), ↔ 8–16in (20–40cm).
P. grossularioides, syn. *P.* 'Coconut Scented'. Spreading to weakly upright perennial with red stems and rounded, lobed, toothed, coconut-scented, mid-green leaves, to 1½in (4cm) long. In spring and summer, bears star-shaped, magenta flowers, ⅜in (9mm) across, marked with darker spots on the upper petals, in clusters, to ½in (1.5cm) across. ↕ 6in (15cm), ↔ 8–12in (20–30cm). Southern and S.E. Africa.
***P.* 'Hallelujah'.** Zonal pelargonium bears single white to very pale salmon flowers, veined and centered with deeper salmon, in clusters to 4in (10cm) across. ↕ 10–16in (25–40cm), ↔ 8–10in (20–25cm).
***P.* 'Happy Thought'** ■ syn. *P.* 'A Happy Thought'. Fancy-leaved zonal pelargonium bearing rounded leaves, each with a greenish yellow butterfly marking in the center. Single, light

ᴾelargonium 'Easter Greeting'

Pelargonium 'Fair Ellen'

Pelargonium 'Fairyland'

Pelargonium 'Flower of Spring'

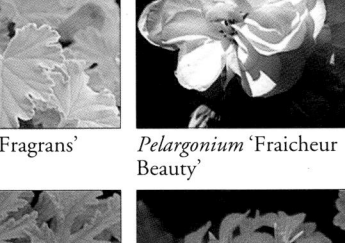

Pelargonium 'Fragrans'

Pelargonium 'Fraicheur Beauty'

ᴾelargonium 'Frank Headley'

Pelargonium 'Freckles'

Pelargonium 'Freestyle Burgundy II'

Pelargonium 'Global Sangria'

Pelargonium 'Graveolens' of gardens

Pelargonium 'Happy Thought'

crimson flowers are produced in clusters 3–3½in (8–9cm) across. ↕ 16–18in (40–45cm), ↔ 8–10in (20–25cm).

***P.* 'Helen Christine'.** Dwarf, bushy, stellar zonal pelargonium with dark green leaves. Produces clusters, 1in (2.5cm) across, of single, intense purple flowers. ↕ 4–6in (10–15cm), ↔ 4–5in (10–13cm).

***P.* 'Honeymoon'.** Zonal pelargonium bearing clusters, 1½in (4cm) across, of large, flat, single, white to very pale salmon flowers with deeper salmon-pink centers. ↕ 12–16in (30–40cm), ↔ 6–8in (15–20cm).

***P.* 'Honeywood Suzanne'.** Dwarf zonal pelargonium with clusters, 2½in (6cm) across, of loose, semi-double white flowers with pink shading. ↕↔ 5–8in (13–20cm).

***P.* Horizon Series** ■ Compact, bushy, seed-raised, single-flowered zonal pelargoniums with strongly zoned foliage. Bear flowers in white or shades of pink or red, in clusters to 5in (13cm) across, early in the season. Good wet-weather tolerance. ↕ to 12in (30cm), ↔ 10in (25cm). **'Horizon Scarlet'** has dark, strongly zoned leaves and scarlet flowers.

***P.* 'Icecrystal'.** Semi-double-flowered zonal pelargonium. Bears clusters, to 5in (13cm) across, of white-eyed, lavender-blue flowers with a purple dot on each petal. ↕ 12–16in (30–40cm), ↔ 8–10in (20–25cm).

***P. inquinans*.** Erect, evergreen perennial producing soft, woody stems and rounded, mid-green leaves, 2–2½in (5–6cm) across. Saucer-shaped scarlet flowers, 1½in (4cm) across, are borne in clusters, 3½in (9cm) across, from spring to summer. One of the original parents of zonal pelargoniums. ↕ 24–36in (60–90cm), ↔ 8–10in (20–25cm). South Africa (Eastern Transvaal, KwaZulu/ Natal, Eastern Cape).

***P.* 'Jazz'** ■ Vigorous, semi-double, zonal pelargonium. Watermelon flowers are held in clusters above dark green zoned foliage.

***P.* 'Just William'.** Miniature, double-flowered zonal pelargonium with bright red flowers in clusters 2½–3in (6–8cm) across. ↕ 4–5in (10–13cm), ↔ 3–4in (8–10cm).

***P.* 'Kardino'.** Vigorous, compact, semi-double, zonal pelargonium. Magenta-violet flowers are produced above dark green zoned leaves.

Pelargonium Horizon Series

***P.* 'Kath Peat'.** Zonal pelargonium producing clusters, 3–4in (8–10cm) across, of very double flowers in mixed shades of white, pink, and light salmon. ↕ 8–16in (20–40cm), ↔ 6–8in (15–20cm).

***P.* 'Lachsball'** ■ Vigorous, semi-double-flowered zonal pelargonium bearing clusters, 4in (10cm) across, of deep salmon-pink flowers with tiny white eyes. ↕ 18–20in (45–50cm), ↔ 6–8in (15–20cm).

***P.* 'Lachskönigin'** ■ Short-jointed ivy-leaved pelargonium with semi-double, rosy salmon-pink flowers that are produced in clusters 4½in (11cm) across. ↕ 10–12in (25–30cm), ↔ 6–8in (15–20cm).

***P.* 'Lady Plymouth'** ■ Scented-leaved pelargonium with eucalyptus-scented, white-margined leaves. Lavender-pink flowers are produced in clusters 1¼–1½in (3–4cm) across. This cultivar is a variant of *P.* 'Graveolens' of gardens. ↕ 12–16in (30–40cm), ↔ 6–8in (15–20cm).

***P.* 'Lavender Sensation'.** Bushy regal pelargonium bearing frilly, lavender-pink flowers, with plum markings, in clusters 4½–5in (11–13cm) across. ↕ 12–16in (30–40cm), ↔ 6–8in (15–20cm).

***P.* 'L'Elégante'** ■ Ivy-leaved pelargonium with gray-green leaves, each with a white edge that turns pink if the plant is kept dry. Bears single white flowers in clusters, to 3in (8cm) across. ↕ 8–10in (20–25cm), ↔ 12–16in (30–40cm).

***P.* 'Leslie Judd'** ■ Regal pelargonium with pale salmon-pink flowers, feathered wine-red on each petal, borne in clusters 3½–4in (9–10cm) across. ↕ 16–18in (40–45cm), ↔ 6–8in (15–20cm).

***P.* 'Lilac Mini Cascade'.** Bushy, dwarf, ivy-leaved pelargonium with single, lilac flowers, borne in clusters ½–¾in (1.5–2cm) across. ↕ 4–5in (10–13cm), ↔ 6–8in (15–20cm).

***P.* 'Lilian Pottinger'.** Scented-leaved pelargonium with irregular, 3-lobed, toothed, gray-green leaves exuding a camphor-pine fragrance. White flowers are produced in clusters 1–1¼in (2.5–3cm) across. ↕ 8–10in (20–25cm), ↔ 5–6in (13–15cm).

***P.* 'Lime'.** Scented-leaved pelargonium with toothed, smooth, lime-scented leaves. Bears clusters, 1½in (4cm) across, of single, pale lavender flowers. ↕ 12–18in (30–45cm), ↔ 8–10in (20–25cm).

***P.* 'Lord Bute'.** Regal pelargonium producing dark reddish black flowers, the petals with dark red margins, in clusters to 4in (10cm) across. ↕ 18in (45cm), ↔ 12in (30cm).

***P.* 'Loverly'.** Bushy, semi-double-flowered zonal pelargonium. Produces clusters, to 3in (8cm) across, of two-toned, salmon-pink flowers. ↕ 8–10in (20–25cm), ↔ 5–6in (12–15cm).

***P.* 'Mabel Grey'** ■ Scented-leaved pelargonium with deeply cut, rough-textured leaves with a very strong lemon scent. Produces purple flowers in clusters 2in (5cm) across. Makes an attractive standard. ↕ 12–14in (30–35cm), ↔ 5–6in (12–15cm).

***P.* 'Magda'.** Double-flowered zonal pelargonium producing clusters, 3in (8cm) across, of pale pink flowers, spotted and streaked scarlet. ↕ 10–12in (25–30cm), ↔ 5–6in (12–15cm).

***P.* 'Magic'** ■ Vigorous, early flowering semi-double zonal pelargonium. The freely branching plant produces large magenta flowers held above dark green zoned leaves.

***P.* Maiden Series.** Regal pelargoniums noted for their free-flowering, compact plants, ideal for pots. Large flowers, in both solid and bicolor combinations, are borne in early to midseason. **'Maiden Deep Orange'** has hot salmon-orange flowers; **'Maiden Petticoat'** ■ is an early-blooming cultivar with purple flowers edged in white.

***P.* 'Mandarin'** ■ Vigorous ivy-leaved pelargonium with semi-double, bright orange flowers. Its fully trailing habit makes this cultivar an excellent choice for hanging baskets.

***P.* 'Mauritania'** ■ Single-flowered zonal pelargonium. White flowers, tinged rose-pink in the centers, are produced in clusters 3½in (9cm) across ↕ 10–12in (25–30cm), ↔ 5–6in (12–15cm).

Pelargonium 'Jazz'

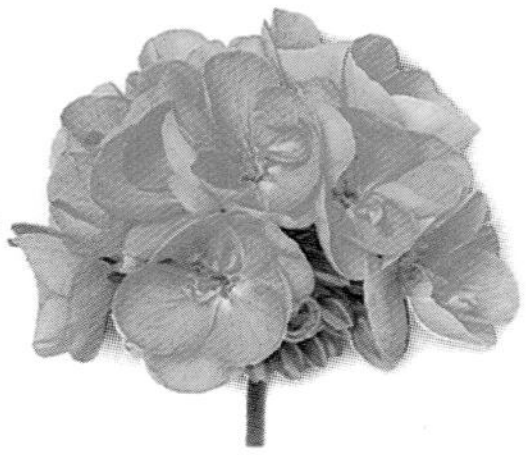

Pelargonium 'Lachsball'

Pelargonium 'Lachskönigin'

Pelargonium 'Lady Plymouth'

Pelargonium 'L'Elégante'

Pelargonium 'Leslie Judd'

Pelargonium 'Mabel Grey'

Pelargonium 'Magic'

Pelargonium 'Maiden Petticoat'

Pelargonium 'Mandarin'

Pelargonium 'Mauritania'

Pelargonium 'Mr. Everaarts'

P

P. 'Mauve Salter Bevis'. Cactus-
lowered zonal pelargonium bearing
ingle, lavender-pink flowers in clusters
o 3in (8cm) across. ↕ 10–12in
25–30cm), ↔ 5–6in (12–15cm).
P. 'Miss Wackles'. Miniature, double-
lowered zonal pelargonium producing
nid-green leaves with dark brown zones.
roduces cerise-red flowers in clusters
¾–2in (4.5–5cm) across. ↕ 4–5in
10–13cm), ↔ 3–4in (8–10cm).
P. 'Mme. Crousse'. Very long-jointed
vy-leaved pelargonium with semi-
ouble, pale pink flowers borne in
lusters to 3in (8cm) across. ↕ 20–24in
50–60cm), ↔ 6–8in (15–20cm).
P. 'Mme. Fournier'. Miniature, single-
lowered zonal pelargonium with
urple-black leaves and stems. Scarlet
lowers are borne in clusters 1¾–2in
4.5–5cm) across. ↕ 4–5in (10–13cm),
↔ 3–4in (8–10cm).
P. 'Mr. Everaarts' ▣ Bushy, dwarf,
ouble-flowered pelargonium with
right rose-pink flowers borne in
lusters 2–2½in (5–6cm) across. ↕ 6–8in
15–20cm), ↔ 4–5in (10–13cm).
P. 'Mr. Henry Cox' ▣ syn. *P.* 'Mrs.
Henry Cox'. Fancy-leaved zonal
elargonium with rounded, golden
ellow leaves marked with mid-green,
ark purple, and red. Single pink flowers,
vith small white eyes, are borne in
lusters 3in (8cm) across. ↕ 10–12in
25–30cm), ↔ 4–5in (10–13cm).
P. 'Mrs. Henry Cox' see *P.* 'Mr. Henry
Cox'.
P. 'Mrs. Pollock' ▣ Fancy-leaved zonal
elargonium with rounded, golden
ellow leaves marked with brownish
urple, pink, and mid-green. Single,
ight red-orange flowers are borne in
lusters 3in (8cm) across. ↕ 10–12in
25–30cm), ↔ 5–6in (12–15cm).
P. 'Mrs. Quilter' ▣ Fancy-leaved zonal
elargonium bearing rounded gold
eaves with wide bronze zones. Single,
ale pink flowers are borne in clusters
in (8cm) across. Leaf color deepens
n full sun. ↕ 12–16in (30–40cm),
↔ 5–6in (12–15cm).
P. 'Mr. Wren'. Bushy, single-flowered
onal pelargonium with white flowers,
verlaid orange, borne in clusters 3in
8cm) across. ↕ 16–18in (40–45cm),
↔ 6–8in (15–20cm).
P. Multibloom Series ▣ Seed-raised,
ingle-flowered zonal pelargoniums with abundant flowers in white or shades of pink or red, some with white eyes, borne in clusters 3–5in (8–13cm) across. Early-flowering over a long period; good wet-weather tolerance. ↕ 10–12in (25–30cm), ↔ 12in (30cm).

***P.* 'New Life'.** Zonal pelargonium bearing single, red- and white-striped flowers with some petals all red or pale salmon, in clusters, 3in (8cm) across. ↕ 8–10in (20–25cm), ↔ 5–6in (13–15cm).

***P.* 'Nicole'.** Ivy-leaved pelargonium noted for its candy-pink flowers and medium green zoned leaves. A white-flowered sport is also available.

P. odoratissimum, syn. *P.* 'Apple Scented' (Apple geranium). Bushy, spreading, evergreen perennial with rounded, light green leaves, 1½–2in (4–5cm) across, with a scent reminiscent of apples. Trailing clusters, 1–1¼in (2.5–3cm) across, of 3–10 star-shaped white flowers, to ¼in (6mm) across, are produced from spring to summer. ↕ 8–10in (20–25cm), ↔ 18–24in (45–60cm). South Africa (KwaZulu/Natal, Northern Transvaal, Eastern Cape, Western Cape).

***P.* 'Old Spice'** ▣ Bushy, erect scented-leaved pelargonium with rounded, spicy-scented leaves. Bears white flowers in trailing clusters 1¼–1½in (3–4cm) across. ↕ 10–12in (25–30cm), ↔ 5–6in (12–15cm).

***P.* 'Orange Appeal'** ▣ Seed-raised, single-flowered zonal pelargonium with clear, bright orange flowers borne in clusters to 3in (8cm) across. ↕ 12–16in (30–40cm), ↔ 12in (30cm).

***P.* Orbit Series.** Very early-flowering, seed-raised, single-flowered zonal pelargoniums that branch from the base and have fine leaf zoning. Produce large clusters, 5–5½in (12–14cm) across, of flowers in white or shades of pink, orange, or red. ↕ to 14in (35cm), ↔ 10in (25cm). **'Cherry Orbit'** is upright in habit, bearing purple-zoned leaves and cherry-red flowers.

***P.* 'Paintbox Mix'.** Vigorous, seed-propagated, single-flowered F2 zonal pelargonium mixture. Compact plants bear flowers in shades of rose, pink, scarlet, salmon, and white, as well as bicolor mixtures. ↕↔ 10–18in (25–45cm).

***P.* 'Palais'.** Vigorous, semi-double-flowered zonal pelargonium bearing pale salmon-pink flowers in clusters 4½in (11cm) across. ↕ 16–18in (40–45cm), ↔ 8–10in (20–25cm).

***P.* 'Paton's Unique'** ▣ syn. *P.* 'Apricot Scented'. Vigorous unique pelargonium bearing coral-red and pale pink flowers, with small white eyes, in clusters 1½–1¾in (4–4.5cm) across. The leaves release a pungent scent when bruised. ↕ 16–18in (40–45cm), ↔ 6–8in (15–20cm).

***P.* 'Patricia Andrea'**, syn. *P.* 'Tulip Flowered'. Vigorous zonal pelargonium with shiny, toothed leaves. Bears clusters, 3–4in (8–10cm) across, of single, deep salmon-pink flowers, which do not fully open, keeping the form of a half-opened tulip. Tolerates rainy weather. ↕ 12–18in (30–45cm), ↔ 6–10in (15–25cm).

***P.* Patriot Series.** Vigorous, semi-double, zonal pelargonium with good heat and weather tolerance. Flowers are borne in clusters 4–5in (10–13cm) across, and are borne in a wide variety of colors. **'Patriot Cranberry Red'** produces unique red-magenta flowers, and **'Patriot Violet'** has large, intense purple flowers with medium green leaves. The mounded, free-branching habit makes it ideal for containers, hanging baskets, and bedding.

***P.* 'Peach'**, syn. *P.* 'Gooseberry Leaf'. Stiff-limbed, scented-leaved pelargonium bearing rounded, ruffled, mid-green leaves with cream- to white-mottled variegation and a citrus scent. Produces clusters, ½in (1.5cm) across, of single pale lilac flowers. ↕ 10–12in (25–30cm), ↔ 5–6in (13–15cm).

***P.* 'Peppermint Lace'.** Strong, scented-leaved pelargonium with deeply incised, velvety, strongly peppermint-scented, gray-green leaves. Single white flowers are produced in clusters, 1½in (4cm) across. ↕ 12–18in (30–45cm), ↔ 8–10in (20–25cm).

***P.* 'Picasso'** ▣ Vigorous, ivy-leaved pelargonium with semi-double flowers. Burgundy and white bicolor flowers cover the medium green leaves.

***P.* Pillar Series** (*P.* 'Pillar Pink,' *P.* 'Pillar Flame,' and *P.* 'Pillar Violet'). Reliably vigorous upright-growing zonal pelargoniums with medium green leaves marked with a distinct dark zone. Plants produce single to semi-double flowers profusely, on free-branching plants. Useful in large containers and for a vertical garden accent. ↕ to 6ft (2m).

***P.* Pinto Series** see *P.* Pulsar Series.

***P.* 'Pixie Rose'** ▣ Stellar zonal pelargonium producing double, rose-red flowers, with white petal reverses and small white eyes, in clusters 3–3½in (8–9cm) across. ↕ 10–12in (25–30cm), ↔ 6–8in (15–20cm).

***P.* 'Platinum'.** Fancy-leaved zonal pelargonium producing gray-green leaves edged in cream. Single salmon flowers are borne above the foliage.

***P.* 'Polka'** ▣ Vigorous unique pelargonium with flower clusters, 4in (10cm) across. Upper petals are rosy orange with dark feathering; the lower petals are salmon-orange. ↕ 18–20in (45–50cm), ↔ 8–10in (20–25cm).

***P.* 'Prince of Orange'.** Erect, thin-stemmed scented-leaved pelargonium with small, rounded, orange-scented leaves. Produces mauve flowers in clusters 1–1¼in (2.5–3cm) across. ↕ 10–12in (25–30cm), ↔ 6–8in (15–20cm).

***P.* Pulsar Series**, syn. *P.* Pinto Series. Seed-raised, single-flowered zonal pelargoniums with strongly zoned foliage. Flowers, in white or shades of pink or red, including bicolors, are borne in clusters 5–5½in (12–14cm) across. ↕ 12–14in (30–35cm), ↔ 12in (30cm). **'Pulsar Scarlet'** ▣ produces deep red flowers.

***P.* 'Purple Emperor'** ▣ Regal pelargonium with clusters, 3½–4in (9–10cm) across, of light purple-pink flowers, blazed and feathered deep wine-red on each petal. ↕ 12–16in (30–40cm), ↔ 6–8in (15–20cm).

***P.* 'Queen of Hearts'.** Stiff-stemmed, ivy-leaved, zonal pelargonium hybrid with large, softly lobed leaves. Double white flowers with red markings on the petals are produced. ↕↔ 10–12in (25–30cm).

P. radens (Crowfoot geranium). Vigorous, upright, bushy subshrub with triangular, deeply 2-pinnatifid, rough, strongly aromatic, gray-green leaves, 2½in (6cm) long, consisting of oblong segments with margins rolled under. Bears star-shaped, pale to purple-pink flowers, ½in (1.5cm) across, in 2- to 6-flowered clusters, to 2½in (6cm)

Pelargonium 'Mr. Henry Cox'

Pelargonium 'Mrs. Pollock'

Pelargonium 'Mrs. Quilter'

Pelargonium Multibloom Series

Pelargonium 'Old Spice'

Pelargonium 'Orange Appeal'

Pelargonium 'Paton's Unique'

Pelargonium 'Picasso'

Pelargonium 'Pixie Rose'

Pelargonium 'Polka'

Pelargonium Pulsar Series 'Pulsar Scarlet'

Pelargonium 'Purple Emperor'

Pelargonium 'Splendide'

across, in late spring and summer. ↕ 12–18in (30–45cm), ↔ 8–12in (20–30cm). South Africa (Western Cape, Eastern Cape).

***P.* 'Rober's Lemon Rose'.** Vigorous, scented-leaved pelargonium with pinnatifid, gray-green leaves, rose-scented with lemon undertones. Produces mauve flowers in clusters 1½–1¾in (4–4.5cm) across. ↕ 18–20in (45–50cm), ↔ 8–10in (20–25cm).

***P.* Rocky Mountain Series.** Large, semi-double flowers are held above vigorous, dark-green foliage, with a spreading habit. Flowers are produced in a wide selection of shades. Good heat tolerance. ↕↔ 10–15in (25–37.5cm).

***P.* 'Rollisson's Unique'** ■ Scented, unique pelargonium with clusters, 3in (8cm) across, of magenta flowers with deep purple and white feathering on the upper petals. The leaves are very curly and mint-scented. ↕ 16–18in (40–45cm), ↔ 6–8in (15–20cm).

***P.* 'Rouletta'** ■ Vigorous, ivy-leaved pelargonium with semi-double, light crimson-and-white-striped flowers borne in clusters 3½in (9cm) across. May temporarily revert to plain crimson in hot weather. ↕ 3–4in (8–10cm), ↔ 18–24in (45–60cm).

***P.* Royalty Series.** Vigorous, long-flowering, medium-size, compact, regal pelargoniums. Plants begin flowering in early to midseason. In midseason, **'Baroness'** produces large, deep-rosy-red flowers, and **'Camelot'** ■ brings forth flowers in a rich purple and light-purple picotee.

***P.* 'Samantha Stamps'.** Dwarf, fancy-leaved zonal pelargonium with rounded, bronze-zoned gold leaves. Produces double, pink-flushed white flowers in clusters 3in (8cm) across. ↕ 8in (20cm), ↔ 6in (15cm).

***P.* 'Schöne Helena'** ■ Semi-double-flowered zonal pelargonium with clusters, 4–4½in (10–11cm) across, of light salmon-pink flowers. ↕ 12–16in (30–40cm), ↔ 8–10in (20–25cm).

***P.* 'Skeleton Leaf Rose'**, syn. *P.* 'Dr. Livingston'.

***P.* 'Snowdrift'.** Short-jointed ivy-leaved pelargonium with double white flowers borne in clusters 3in (8cm) across. ↕ 10–12in (25–30cm), ↔ 6–8in (15–20cm).

***P.* 'Snowflake'.** Scented-leaved pelargonium with large, softly lobed, rose- to lemon-rose-scented, cream- to white-variegated, mid-green leaves. Clusters, 1–2in (2.5–5cm) across, of light mauve flowers are produced. ↕ 12–18in (30–45cm), ↔ 10–12in (25–30cm).

***P.* 'Splendide'** ■ Slow-growing, short-branching species hybrid pelargonium. Butterfly-shaped flowers, ¾–1¼in (2–3cm) across, are borne singly or in clusters, 4–5in (10–13cm) across. Red-violet upper petals each have a black spot at the base; lower petals are white, sometimes stained red. ↕ 10–12in (25–30cm), ↔ 6–8in (15–20cm).

***P.* 'Star of Persia'.** Cactus-flowered pelargonium bearing clusters, 2–3in (5–8cm) across, of double, crimson- and purple-blended flowers with narrow, twisted petals. ↕ 8–10in (20–25cm), ↔ 5–6in (13–15cm).

***P.* Starburst Series.** Large, very free-flowering plants are ideal for planters and hanging baskets. Red or violet rose

Pelargonium 'Starburst Red'

flowers are marked with a white stripe; they come in two colors, which are exemplified by **'Starburst Red'** ■ and **'Starburst Violet Rose'.**

***P.* Stardom Series.** Leaves are similar to those of zonal geraniums on a plant that spreads and mounds like ivy-leaved geraniums. Heavy-flowering with small, very profuse, semi-double to double flowers. **'Natalie'** ■ bears semi-double to double deep lavender flowers with compact, dark green lightly zoned leaves. **'Pink and White'** produces double soft pink-and-white bicolor flowers with compact, dark green leaves. **'Sophia'** has double candy-pink flowers with a white eye on a spreading plant. More heat and drought tolerant than other zonals.

***P.* Summer Showers Series** ■ Vigorous, early-flowering, seed-propagated ivy-leaved pelargoniums. Large single flowers in shades of white and pale-pink to burgundy are produced in clusters 4–5in (10–13cm) across. The deep green ivy leaves are resistant to edema. ↕ 12in (30cm).

***P.* 'Super Nova'.** Stellar zonal pelargonium that produces double, lilac-pink flowers in clusters 3in (8cm) across. ↕ 12–16in (30–40cm), ↔ 8–10in (20–25cm).

***P.* 'Sweet Mimosa'** see *P.* 'Sweet Miriam'.

***P.* 'Sweet Miriam'**, syn. *P.* 'Sweet Mimosa'. Vigorous, pungently scented-leaved pelargonium with

Pelargonium Summer Showers Series

deeply lobed leaves and clusters, 3in (8cm) across, of single, mid-pink flowers. ↕ 18–20in (45–50cm), ↔ 8–10in (20–25cm).

***P.* 'Sybil Holmes'.** Trailing, ivy-leaved pelargonium bearing rosebud-type, very double pink flowers in clusters, 1–1½in (2.5–4cm) across. ↕ 3–4in (8–10cm), ↔ 6–10in (15–25cm).

***P.* 'Tavira'** ■ Slow-growing, short-jointed ivy-leaved pelargonium. Semi-double, light cerise-red flowers, feathered wine-red, are produced in clusters to 3in (8cm) across. ↕ 12–16in (30–40cm), ↔ 8–10in (20–25cm).

***P.* 'The Boar'** ■ Lax, trailing perennial producing rounded, mid-green leaves, 2½in (6cm) long, with dark purple-black centers. From spring to summer, bears masses of single, salmon-pink flowers in long-stalked, loose clusters, 3–3½in (8–9cm) across. ↕ 20–24in (50–60cm), ↔ 8–10in (20–25cm).

***P.* 'Timothy Clifford'** ■ Miniature zonal pelargonium with very dark green, almost black foliage. Bears double, salmon-pink flowers in clusters 1¾–2in (4.5–5cm) across. ↕ 4–5in (10–13cm), ↔ 3–4in (8–10cm).

***P.* 'Tip Top Duet'** ■ Angel pelargonium bearing clusters, 1¾–2in (4.5–5cm) across, of very pale pink flowers, the lower petals veined and margined mauve, the upper petals feathered and blazed red-purple. ↕ 12–16in (30–40cm), ↔ 6–8in (15–20cm).

P

Pelargonium 'Rollisson's Unique'

Pelargonium 'Rouletta'

Pelargonium Royality Series 'Camelot'

Pelargonium 'Schöne Helena'

Pelargonium Stardom Series 'Natalie'

Pelargonium 'Tavira'

Pelargonium 'The Boar'

Pelargonium 'Timothy Clifford'

Pelargonium 'Tip Top Duet'

Pelargonium tomentosum

Pelargonium Tornado Series

Pelargonium 'Voodoo'

ᑭelargonium 'Turkish Delight'

ᑭ. tomentosum ▣ (Peppermint
;eranium). Vigorous perennial that
›roduces heart-shaped, lobed, velvety,
›eppermint-scented, mid-green
eaves, 1½–2½in (4–6cm) long, on
crambling stems. Clusters, 1¾–2in
4.5–5cm) across, of 4–15 butterfly-
haped white flowers, ½in (1.5cm)
.cross, are produced from spring
hrough summer. ↕ 30–36in (75–90cm),
↔ 24–30in (60–75cm). South Africa
Western Cape).
ᑭ. Tornado Series ▣ Neat, compact,
arly-flowering, ivy-leaved pelargoniums
hat are raised from seed. Single lilac
›r white flowers,are produced in
:lusters 4–5in (10–13cm) across, on
railing stems. ↕ to 10in (25cm),
↔ 8in (20cm).
ᑭ. triste. Tuberous-rooted herbaceous
›erennial that produces finely pinnate,
railing, mid-green leaves, 7in (18cm)
›ng. Clusters, 1¼–1½in (3–4cm)
.cross, of 6–20 star-shaped, freesia-
cented, nocturnal-blooming flowers,
¾–1¼in (2–3cm) across, in yellow,
;reen, or pink, either in combination or
vith reddish black, are produced from
pring to summer. ↕ 6–8in (15–20cm),
↔ 18–20in (45–50cm). South Africa
Western Cape, Northern Cape).
ᑭ. 'Tulip Flowered', syn. *P.* 'Patricia
\ndrea'.
ᑭ. 'Turkish Delight' ▣ Fancy-leaved
.onal pelargonium. Each leaf has a
›and of green and gold, separated by
wide zone of bronze-red. Produces
:lusters, 2–3in (5–8cm) across, of
ingle, red-orange flowers. ↕ 8–12in
20–30cm), ↔ 6–8in (15–20cm).
ᑭ. 'Vancouver Centennial'. Stellar
.onal pelargonium that produces
;old leaves that have a brown center
plotch. Single red-orange flowers are
›roduced in clusters 3in (8cm) across.
10–12in (25–30cm), ↔ 6–8in
15–20cm).
ᑭ. 'Variegated Nutmeg'. Bushy
cented-leaved pelargonium that bears
ounded, hairy, spice- and pine-
cented, gray-green leaves with cream
.nd white variegation. Produces
preading clusters, 1–1¼in (2.5–3cm)
.cross, of small white flowers.
: 8–10in (20–25cm), ↔ 6–8in
15–20cm).
ᑭ. 'Voodoo' ▣ Unique pelargonium
›earing clusters, 3in (8cm) across, of
ingle, deep burgundy-red flowers,
›lazed purple-black on each petal.
20–24in (50–60cm), ↔ 8–10in
20–25cm).

Pellaea rotundifolia

PELLAEA

ADIANTACEAE

Genus of about 80 species of deciduous or evergreen, terrestrial ferns occurring usually in sheltered sites in semi-desert regions, mainly in South Africa and South America, but also in Canada, the US, and Australasia. Pinnate or 2-pinnate fronds arise from an erect rhizome in spring. Sori are produced around the segment margins. Grow in a terrace or rock garden. In cool climates, grow in a cool to warm greenhouse.
• **CULTIVATION** Grow in moderately fertile, moist but well-drained soil in full sun, with some midday shade. Where marginally hardy, protect with a dry winter mulch.
• **PROPAGATION** Sow spores at 55–64°F (13–18°C) when ripe. See also p.51.
• **PESTS AND DISEASES** Prone to fungal spots, root rot, and mealybugs.

P. rotundifolia ▣ (Button fern). Evergreen fern producing a tuft of narrowly oblong, pinnate, leathery, dull dark green fronds, 6–12in (15–30cm) long, with red-flushed midribs, and narrowly oblong to rounded pinnae with finely scalloped margins. Prefers moist, acidic soil. ↕ to 12in (30cm), ↔ 16in (40cm). Australia, New Zealand. ❀ (min. 41°F/5°C)

▷ ***Pellionia*** see *Elatostema*

PELTANDRA

Arrow arum

ARACEAE

Genus of 4 species of rhizomatous, monoecious, marginal aquatic perennials from marshland in E. North America. They have decorative, arrow-shaped or spear-shaped, glossy, mid- or dark green leaves. Tiny male and female flowers are produced on spadices, each surrounded by a longer, sometimes wavy-margined, green or white spathe; they are followed by clusters of green or red berries. Grow on the muddy banks of a pond or a bog garden; the rhizomes help to stabilize the soil. May become invasive.
• **CULTIVATION** Grow in full sun, in the margins of a pond or in containers of loamy soil in water to 8in (20cm) deep.
• **PROPAGATION** Divide in spring.
• **PESTS AND DISEASES** Occasionally affected by leaf spot and rust.

P. alba see *P. sagittifolia.*

Peltandra virginica

P. sagittifolia, syn. *P. alba* (White arrow arum). Aquatic perennial producing arrow-shaped, bright green leaves, to 6in (15cm) long, on stalks to 20in (50cm) long. White spathes, 3–4in (8–10cm) long, which open widely, are borne in early summer, followed by red berries. ↕ 18in (45cm), ↔ 24in (60cm). S.E. US. Zone 7b.
P. undulata see *P. virginica.*
P. virginica ▣ syn. *P. undulata* (Green arrow arum, Tuckahoe, Water arum). Aquatic perennial with narrowly arrow-shaped, strongly veined, mid-green leaves, 12in (30cm) long, produced on stalks to 18in (45cm) long. Bears green spathes, 8in (20cm) long, which open only slightly, with wavy, yellow or white margins, in early summer, followed by green berries. ↕ 36in (90cm), ↔ 24in (60cm). E. and S.E. US. Zone 6.

▷ ***Peltiphyllum*** see *Darmera*

PELTOBOYKINIA

SAXIFRAGACEAE

Genus of 2 species of rhizomatous perennials from mountain woodland in S. Japan. They have peltate, lobed or deeply cut, toothed, glossy, olive- to mid-green leaves: the basal leaves have long leaf stalks; the stem leaves become progressively smaller and almost stalkless up the stem. Short-lived, small, open bell-shaped, pale greenish yellow flowers are borne in terminal cymes in summer. Grow as a groundcover or as foliage plants in a moist, shady position, such as bog or streamside plantings.
• **CULTIVATION** Grow in moist, moderately fertile, humus-rich soil in partial shade.
• **PROPAGATION** Sow seed in containers in a cold frame in spring. Divide in autumn or spring.
• **PESTS AND DISEASES** Infrequent.

P. tellimoides, syn. *Boykinia tellimoides.* Clump-forming perennial with rounded to heart-shaped, shallowly lobed, finely toothed, olive- to mid-green leaves, to 12in (30cm) long. Bears pale greenish yellow flowers, to ½in (15mm) across, in early summer. ↕ to 36in (90cm), ↔ 30in (75cm). Japan. Zone 7.

PELTOPHORUM

FABACEAE

Genus of 9 species of evergreen trees, related to *Caesalpinia*, occurring in open savanna and dense woodland in tropical regions worldwide. Cultivated mainly as foliage plants, they have often large, alternate, 2-pinnate leaves. Yellow flowers, each with 5 frilled, spreading petals, are produced in racemes or panicles from the uppermost leaf axils. Where temperatures drop below 45°F (7°C), grow in a temperate greenhouse. In warmer climates, grow as specimen, street, or shade trees.
• **CULTIVATION** Under glass, grow in soil-based potting mix, with added sharp sand, in full light. During the growing season, water moderately and apply a balanced liquid fertilizer monthly. Water sparingly in winter. Outdoors, grow in fertile, moist but well-drained soil in full sun. Pruning group 1; needs restrictive pruning under glass.
• **PROPAGATION** Sow pre-soaked or scarified seed at 64–70°F (18–21°C) in spring.
• **PESTS AND DISEASES** Prone to spider mites and whiteflies under glass.

P. pterocarpum (Flame tree, Yellow flamboyant tree). Vigorous, fast-growing tree, wide-spreading, freely branching, and often with an umbrella-shaped crown, with rust-red-downy stems. Large, 2-pinnate, deep green leaves are composed of 8–20 pairs of elliptic-oblong leaflets, ¾in (2cm) long. In summer, produces ascending racemes, to 18in (45cm) long, of fragrant, bright, translucent yellow flowers, 1½in (4cm) across, with showy orange stamens and obovate, crinkly petals, each with a central brownish red mark. The flowers emerge from tight, bronze-colored buds. Elliptic to oblong, winged, purple-brown seed pods are 3–4in (8–10cm) long. ↕ 50ft (15m), ↔ 25–30ft (8–10m). Sri Lanka to Malaysia and N. Australia (coast). ❀ (min. 45°F/7°C)

PENIOCEREUS

CACTACEAE

Genus (now incorporating the genus *Nyctocereus*) of 20 species of thin-stemmed, climbing or prostrate cacti, sometimes with thick, tuberous roots. They are found in semi-arid areas of S.W. US, Mexico, and Central America. The branching, ribbed stems usually have only a few spines, and bear axillary, sometimes terminal, solitary, trumpet-shaped flowers, with wide-spreading petals, which open at night in summer. Where temperatures drop below 55°F (13°C), grow in a warm greenhouse. In warmer climates, grow in a desert garden or against a wall.
• **CULTIVATION** Under glass, grow in a mix of 4 parts standard cactus potting mix and 1 part well-rotted organic matter, in full light with shade from hot sun. From spring to summer, water freely and apply a low-nitrogen fertilizer every 6–8 weeks. Keep barely moist at

other times. Outdoors, grow in sharply drained, moderately fertile soil in full sun, with some midday shade. Stake tall species. See also pp.48–49.

• **PROPAGATION** Sow seed at 66–75°F (19–24°C) in early spring.

• **PESTS AND DISEASES** Mealybugs and aphids, especially while flowering.

P. serpentinus, syn. *Nyctocereus serpentinus*. Climbing or slightly pendent cactus, sometimes branching from the base. Mid-green stems, 2in (5cm) thick, have 10–17 rounded ribs, with areoles bearing about 12 white or brown spines. White flowers, red outside, 6–8in (15–20cm) long, are borne in summer. ↕ 6–10ft (2–3m), ↔ 3ft (1m) or more. Mexico. ❀ (min. 55°F/13°C)

PENNISETUM

POACEAE

Genus of approximately 120 species of rhizomatous or stoloniferous, clump-forming, annual and perennial grasses found in woodland and savanna in tropical, subtropical, and warm-temperate zones worldwide. They have linear leaves, and are grown for their feathery, spike-like panicles of clustered, oblong to lance-shaped spikelets, borne in summer and autumn, which are useful for both fresh and dried arrangements. Grow in a mixed, herbaceous, or annual border, or rock garden. Some self-seed readily and may become invasive in warmer areas.

• **CULTIVATION** Grow in preferably light, moderately fertile, well-drained soil in full sun. Cut back dead top-growth by early spring. Where not hardy, protect with a dry winter mulch.

• **PROPAGATION** Sow seed at 55–64°F (13–18°C) in early spring. Divide in late spring or early summer.

• **PESTS AND DISEASES** Rust, eye spot, and other leaf spots occur.

P

P. alopecuroides, syn. *P. compressum* (Fountain grass). Clump-forming, densely tufted, evergreen perennial grass with flat, linear, pointed, mid- to dark green leaves, 12–24in (30–60cm) long. In summer and autumn, bears bristly, yellow-green to dark purple spikelets in cylindrical to narrowly oblong panicles, to 8in (20cm) long. ↕ 2–5ft (0.6–1.5m), ↔ 2–4ft (0.6–1.2m). E. Asia to W. Australia. Zone 5. **'Hameln'** ■ is compact in habit, and produces early-flowering, greenish white spikelets, gray-brown when mature, in panicles to 5in (13cm) long. Dark green leaves, to 6in (15cm) long, turn golden yellow in autumn. **'Little Bunny'** is a dwarf form of the species; ↕ 10–11in (25–28cm), ↔ 12in (30cm).

P. compressum see *P. alopecuroides*.

P. longistylum see *P. villosum*.

P. orientale. Mound-forming, densely tufted, deciduous perennial grass with upright or arching, narrowly linear, dark green leaves, to 4in (10cm) long. In mid- and late summer, bears softly long-bristled, pink spikelets in long, narrow panicles, to 5½in (14cm) long, resembling bottle brushes. ↕ 24in (60cm), ↔ 30in (75cm). C. and S.W. Asia to N. India. Zone 7.

P. rueppellii see *P. setaceum*.

P. setaceum, syn. *P. rueppellii* (Fountain grass). Mound-forming, densely tufted, deciduous perennial grass, often grown as an annual, with upright, narrowly linear, flat or rolled, rough-textured, mid-green leaves, to 12in (30cm) long. From mid-summer to early autumn, bears pink to purplish pink spikelets in plumed, long-bristled, upright to nodding, narrow panicles, to 12in (30cm) long. ↕ 3ft (1m), ↔ 18in (45cm). Tropical Africa, S.W. Asia, Arabian Peninsula. ❀ (min. 35°F/2°C). **'Atropurpureum'** see 'Purpureum'. **'Burgundy Giant'** is larger, and is suffused deep burgundy-purple throughout; produces pendulous panicles more than 12in (30cm) long; ↕ 5ft (1.5m), ↔ 24in (60cm). **'Purpureum'** ■ syn. 'Atropurpureum', has dark purple leaves and crimson-shaded flowers.

P. villosum, syn. *P. longistylum* (Feathertop). Loosely tufted, deciduous perennial grass, often grown as an annual, with upright or arching stems bearing flat or folded, narrowly linear, mid-green leaves, to 6in (15cm) long, with long hairs just below the flower-heads. In late summer and early autumn, produces cylindrical to almost spherical, plume-like panicles, to 4½in (11cm) long, with soft, feathery pale green or white bristles, becoming purple when mature. ↕↔ 24in (60cm). Mountains of N.E. tropical Africa. ❀ (min. 41°F/5°C)

Pennisetum alopecuroides 'Hameln'

Pennisetum setaceum 'Purpureum'

PENSTEMON

SCROPHULARIACEAE

Genus of approximately 250 species of deciduous, semi-evergreen, or evergreen perennials and subshrubs occurring in a variety of habitats, from open plains to subalpine and alpine areas, in North and Central America. Leaves are stalked or stalkless, usually linear to lance-shaped, and borne in opposite pairs or whorls, or sometimes alternately on the upper parts of the shoots. They are grown for their racemes or panicles of tubular, tubular-bell-shaped, or tubular-funnel-shaped, 2-lipped flowers; the upper lip is usually 2-lobed, the lower lip 3-lobed.

Numerous bushy, free-flowering cultivars have been developed; most are semi-evergreen with persistent basal growth, and produce racemes or panicles of foxglove-like flowers from early summer to midautumn. Other leaf and flower characteristics are very variable: leaves are defined simply as narrow or large, and flowers as small or large. Narrow leaves are linear-lance-shaped to lance-shaped, to 3in (8cm) long; large leaves are elliptic to narrowly ovate, usually 5in (13cm) or more long. Small flowers are 1–1¼in (2.5–3cm) long; large flowers are 2–3in (5–8cm) long.

Grow larger species and cultivars in a border or as bedding and smaller ones in a rock garden or at the front of a border.

• **CULTIVATION** Grow border perennials in fertile, well-drained soil in full sun or partial shade; grow shrubby and dwarf species in poor to moderately fertile, very gritty, sharply drained soil in full sun. Where marginally hardy, protect with a dry winter mulch. Many cultivars tend to be short-lived.

• **PROPAGATION** Sow seed in late winter or spring: sow seed of rock garden plants in containers in a cold frame; sow seed of border perennials at 55–64°F (13–18°C). Take softwood cuttings in early summer or semi-ripe cuttings in midsummer. Divide in spring.

• **PESTS AND DISEASES** Powdery mildew, rust, leaf spots, and Southern blight occur. Slugs and snails can be troublesome on young plants.

***P.* 'Alice Hindley'** ■ syn. *P.* 'Lady Alice Hindley'. Large-leaved perennial bearing large, tubular-bell-shaped, pale lilac-blue flowers, white inside, tinged mauve-pink outside, from midsummer to early or midautumn. ↕ 36in (90cm), ↔ 18in (45cm). Zone 7.

P. ambiguus (Moth penstemon, Prairie penstemon). Shrublike perennial with basally woody, hairless stems and linear leaves, ½–2in (1.5–5cm) long. From early summer to early autumn, profusely bears flattened, phlox-like, white to rose-pink to flesh-pink flowers, with rose-purple reverses. ↕ to 2ft (60cm), ↕↔ 20in (50cm). California to Texas, Mexico. Zone 5.

***P.* 'Andenken an Friedrich Hahn'** ■ syn. *P.* 'Garnet'. Vigorous, bushy, narrow-leaved perennial bearing small, tubular-bell-shaped, deep wine-red flowers from midsummer to early or midautumn. ↕ 30in (75cm), ↔ 24in (60cm). Zone 8.

***P.* 'Apple Blossom'** ■ Narrow-leaved perennial bearing small, tubular-bell-shaped, pale pink flowers, with white throats, from midsummer to early or midautumn. ↕↔ 18–24in (45–60cm). Zone 5.

P. barbatus, (Beardlip penstemon). Erect perennial with evergreen basal rosettes and deciduous stems bearing lance-shaped to linear, entire, sometime glaucous, mid-green leaves, to 8in (20cm) long. From early summer to early autumn, bears long panicles of pendent, tubular red flowers, tinged pink to carmine-red, 1¼–1½in (3–4cm long, the reflexed lower lips with yellow beards, the upper ones projecting over them. ↕ 6ft (1.8m) or more, ↔ 12–20in

Penstemon 'Alice Hindley'

Penstemon 'Andenken an Friedrich Hahn'

Penstemon 'Apple Blossom'

'enstemon 'Burgundy'

30–50cm). W. US to Mexico. Zone 4. **Elfin Pink'** has clear pink flowers; ↔ 12in (30cm).
'. *barrettiae.* Bushy, clump-forming, emi-evergreen perennial with deciduous tems. Ovate to elliptic-ovate, toothed, eathery, gray-green leaves, 1½–2½in 4–6cm) long, are tinged red. In early ummer, bears dense racemes of tubular-ell-shaped, lilac-purple flowers, 1½in 4cm) long. ↕ 8–16in (20–40cm), ↔ 10in (25cm). N.W. US. Zone 6.
'. 'Burgundy' ▣ Large-leaved erennial bearing large, tubular-bell-haped, wine-red flowers, with white tyles and stigmas and white-marked, ghter red throats, from midsummer to arly or midautumn. ↕ 36in (90cm), ↔ 18in (45cm). Zone 7.
'. *campanulatus.* Upright, semi-vergreen perennial with wiry stems earing narrowly linear to lance-shaped, oothed, dark green leaves, to 4in 10cm) long. Bears loose racemes f tubular-bell-shaped, pinkish urple or violet flowers, to 1¼in 3cm) long, in early summer. A parent f many hybrids. ↕ 12–24in (30–60cm), ↔ 18in (45cm). Mexico, Guatemala. Zone 7b.
'. *cardwellii* ▣ Spreading, sometimes em-rooting, evergreen subshrub with lliptic, finely toothed, mid-green leaves, o 1½in (4cm) long. In early summer, ears few-flowered, raceme-like panicles f slender, tubular-funnel-shaped, deep urple flowers, to 1in (2.5cm) long. 4–8in (10–20cm), ↔ 12in (30cm). Washington, Oregon. Zone 7. **Roseus'** produces rose-pink flowers; ↔ 16in (40cm).

enstemon cardwellii

Penstemon 'Chester Scarlet'

***P.* 'Chester Scarlet'** ▣ Large-leaved perennial bearing large, tubular-bell-shaped scarlet flowers from midsummer to midautumn. ↕ 24in (60cm), ↔ 18in (45cm). Zone 6.
P. clutei. Upright perennial with lance-shaped-ovate to ovate, leathery, serrated, blue-green leaves, to 2in (5cm) long. From summer to autumn, bears dense racemes of tubular, brilliant pink to purple-pink flowers, to 1in (2.5cm) across. ↕ 32in (80cm), ↔ 14in (35cm). Arizona. Zone 5b.
P. cyananthus. Upright, hairless perennial with ovate, glaucous, smooth stem leaves, to 2½in (6cm) across, broadly rounded at the bases. Bears compound panicles of tubular, bright blue flowers, ¾–1in (2–2.5cm) across, in late summer. ↕ 1–2ft (30–60cm), ↔ 6–12in (15–30cm). Montana to Utah and Colorado. Zone 4.
P. davidsonii. Prostrate, evergreen subshrub with rounded-elliptic, leathery, entire, mid-green leaves, to ½in (1.5cm) long. In late spring and early summer, bears panicles of tubular-funnel-shaped, deep pink to purple flowers, to 1½in (4cm) long. ↕ 8in (20cm), ↔ 16in (40cm). Coastal W. US. Zone 5.

Penstemon digitalis 'Husker Red'

Penstemon 'Evelyn'

var. *menziesii,* Creeping, mat-forming, semi-evergreen subshrub with elliptic to rounded, minutely toothed, mid-green leaves, to ½in (1.5cm) long. Bears few-flowered racemes of tubular-funnel-shaped, violet-purple flowers, to 1½in (4cm) long, in summer. ↕ 6in (15cm), ↔ 8in (20cm). W. Canada, N.W. US. Zone 6b.
P. diffusus see *P. serrulatus.*
P. digitalis. Vigorous perennial producing semi-evergreen basal rosettes and deciduous or semi-evergreen stems often marked reddish purple. Leaves are inversely lance-shaped, entire or sparsely toothed, mid-green, and 4–6in (10–15cm) long. Panicles of tubular-bell-shaped white flowers, 1in (2.5cm) long, sometimes flushed very pale violet, with purple lines inside, are borne from early to late summer. Tolerates high heat and humidity. ↕ to 24–48in (60–120cm), ↔ 18in (45cm). E. and S.E. US. Zone 3. **'Husker Red'** ▣ has maroon-red young leaves, becoming red-flushed green, and pink-tinted white flowers; ↕ 20–30in (50–75cm), ↔ 12in (30cm).
P. eatonii (Firecracker penstemon). Upright perennial with lance-shaped-oblong, leathery, mid-green or blue-green leaves, the basal leaves to 6in (15cm) long, the stem leaves shorter. In late summer, bears erect, one-sided panicles of tubular, scarlet flowers, 1in (2.5cm) long. ↕ 12–39in (30–100cm), ↔ 8–14in (20–35cm). California to Nevada and Utah. Zone 4.
P. eriantherus (Crested beard-tongue, Crested-tongued penstemon). Upright, compact perennial with lance-shaped to ovate, entire to slightly toothed, softly hairy, gray-green leaves, 1½–3in (4–8cm) long. In summer, produces compact terminal panicles of tubular, prominently 2-lipped, lilac-purple flowers, ¾–1¼in (20–35mm) across, with maroon-purple lines and enlarged throats. ↕ 4–12in (10–30cm), ↔ 6in (15cm). Alberta to Washington, Nebraska to North Dakota. Zone 4.
***P.* 'Evelyn'** ▣ Bushy, narrow-leaved perennial. Small, tubular, rose-pink flowers, paler inside and marked with darker pink lines, are borne from midsummer to early or midautumn. ↕ 18–24in (45–60cm), ↔ 12in (30cm). Zone 7.
***P.* 'Firebird'** see *P.* 'Schoenholzeri'.
P. fruticosus (Shrubby penstemon). Evergreen, spreading, semi-upright subshrub with lance-shaped to elliptic, toothed, glossy, mid-green leaves, to 2in (5cm) long. Dense racemes of tubular-funnel-shaped, purplish blue flowers, 1–1½in (2.5–4cm) long, are borne in late spring and early summer. ↕↔ to 16in (40cm). N. US. Zone 4. **'Purple Haze'** is an evergreen subshrub with lilac-purple flowers; ↕ 8in (20cm).

Penstemon fruticosus var. *scouleri* 'Albus'

var. ***scouleri*** **'Albus'** ■ bears white flowers; ↕↔ to 12in (30cm).
***P.* 'Garnet'** see *P.* 'Andenken an Friedrich Hahn'.
P. grandiflorus (Large beard-tongue). Upright, hairless perennial with thick, obovate-oblong, gray-green leaves, to ¾–3½in (2–9cm) long. In summer, bears wand-like racemes of tubular, pink to blue-lavender flowers, 1½–1¾in (4–4.5cm) long. ↕ to 3½ft (1.1m), ↔ 10in (25cm). North Dakota to Wyoming, Texas, Illinois. Zone 4. **'Prairie Snow'** has pure white flowers and comes true from seed.
P. heterophyllus ■ (Foothill penstemon). Evergreen subshrub with linear to lance-shaped, entire, mid-green or bluish green leaves, ¾–2in (2–5cm) long, narrowing at the bases. In summer, produces racemes of tubular-funnel-shaped, pinkish blue flowers, 1–1½in (2.5–4cm) long, with blue or lilac lobes. ↕↔ 12–20in (30–50cm). California. Zone 5. **'Blue of Zurich'** bears purple buds that open to gentian-blue throughout summer; ↕ 20in (50cm). **'Heavenly Blue'** has blue flowers. **subsp. *purdyi*** is compact, with loose racemes of sky-blue flowers; ↕↔ to 8in (20cm). **'True Blue'** is more lax, with racemes of pure bright blue flowers; ↕↔ to 16in (40cm).
P. hirsutus. Spreading to upright, evergreen subshrub with lance-shaped, toothed, dark green leaves, to 4in (10cm) long. In summer, produces loose racemes of tubular-funnel-shaped, pale violet flowers, ¾–2in (2–5cm) long, with white throats are produced in summer. ↕ 16–32in (40–80cm), ↔ 12–24in (30–60cm). N.E. North America. Zone 4. **'Purpureus'** bears bright clear purple flowers. **'Pygmaeus'** ■ is compact and mat-forming, with purple-tinted leaves, 3in (8cm) long; ↕↔ 4in (10cm).
P. isophyllus ■ Erect, sometimes spreading, evergreen subshrub with lance-shaped, purple-tinged, mid-green leaves, 1¼–2in (3–5cm) long. From early to late summer, produces tubular-bell-shaped, red to deep pink flowers, 1½in (4cm) long, slightly suffused white, in one-sided racemes, to 12in (30cm) long. ↕ to 28in (70cm), ↔ 18in (45cm). Mexico. ❄ (min. 35°F/2°C)
***P.* 'Lady Alice Hindley'** see *P.* 'Alice Hindley'.
P. linarioides. Spreading, semi-evergreen subshrub with many slender, upright shoots bearing linear, mid-green leaves, to 1in (2.5cm) long. In summer,

P

Penstemon heterophyllus

Penstemon hirsutus 'Pygmaeus'

produces narrow, spike-like racemes of narrowly tubular-funnel-shaped, pale to deep purple flowers, ½–¾in (1.5–2cm) long, with darker streaks in the throats. ↕ 20in (50cm), ↔ 10in (25cm). New Mexico, Arizona. Zone 5.
***P.* 'Maurice Gibbs'** ■ Large-leaved perennial bearing large, tubular-bell-shaped, cerise-red flowers, with white throats, from midsummer to early or midautumn. ↕ 30in (75cm), ↔ 18in (45cm). Zone 7.
***P.* 'Mesa'.** Large-leaved perennial bearing large reddish purple flowers with pale throats and purple markings, in mid- and late summer. ↕ 20in (50cm), ↔ 18in (45cm). Zone 4.
P. montanus* subsp. *idahoensis. Clump-forming perennial with oblong to ovate-lance-shaped, hairless to densely hairy, green-blue to pale blue leaves, to 1in (2.5cm) long. In summer, bears short, dense spikes of lavender flowers, 1in (2.5cm) long. ↕ 6in (15cm), ↔ 9in (23cm). Idaho. Zone 4.
P. newberryi ■ Evergreen, mat-forming subshrub with elliptic to ovate, minutely toothed, leathery, dark green leaves, ½–1½in (1.5–4cm) long. In early summer, produces dense racemes of tubular-funnel-shaped, deep red-pink flowers, to 1¼in (3cm) long. ↕ 10in (25cm), ↔ 12in (30cm). Nevada, California. Zone 6.
P. palmeri (Palmer's penstemon, Scented penstemon). Upright perennial with hairless, glaucous, gray stems and ovate-lance-shaped, irregularly toothed leaves, to 6in (15cm) long. In summer, bears spikes of scented, pink-flushed, pale pink, white, or lilac flowers,

Penstemon isophyllus

Penstemon 'Maurice Gibbs'

1¼–1½in (2.5–3.5cm) long, with conspicuous red lines running from the lower lip to the throat. ↕ 1½–4½ft (45–140cm), ↔ 8–10in (20–25cm). S.W. US. Zone 4.
P. parryi. Upright perennial with oblong-lance-shaped to spoon-shaped basal leaves and oblong, mid-green stem leaves, 2–3in (5–8cm) long. In spring, bears raceme-like panicles of few, funnel-shaped, rose-magenta flowers, ½–¾in (1.5–2cm) long. ↕ 12–24in (30–60cm), ↔ 12in (30cm). S. Arizona. Zone 8.
***P.* 'Pennington Gem'** ■ Narrow-leaved perennial. Bears large, tubular-bell-shaped, mid-pink flowers, with white throats and purple anthers, from midsummer to early or midautumn. ↕ to 30in (75cm), ↔ 18in (45cm). Zone 7.
P. pinifolius. Spreading, evergreen subshrub with crowded, needle-like, pale to mid-green leaves, ½–1in (1–2.5cm) long. In summer, produces loose, terminal, spike-like racemes of narrowly tubular, bright scarlet flowers, each 1in (2.5cm) long. ↕ 16in (40cm), ↔ 10in (25cm). S. US, Mexico. Zone 5. **'Compactum'** has leaves ¼in (6mm) long, and bears red-orange flowers in short racemes; ↕ 6in (15cm), ↔ 14in (35cm). **'Mersea Yellow'** ■ has soft yellow flowers.
***P.* 'Prairie Dusk'.** Upright perennial with racemes of tubular purple flowers, 1in (2.5cm) long, in early summer and intermittently to late summer. ↕↔ 18–24in (45–60cm). Zone 4.
P. pseudospectabilis (Desert penstemon). Upright perennial with

Penstemon newberryi

Penstemon 'Pennington Gem'

ovate, thin, toothed, blue-green leaves, t 5in (13cm) long. In spring and summer, bears spike-like racemes of tubular rose-purple flowers, ¾–1¼in (2–3cm) long, with often yellow-tinged throats. ↕ 2–3ft (60–90cm), ↔ 1½in (4cm). California to Arizona. Zone 5.
P. richardsonii. Upright semi-evergreen perennial with green, smooth, hairless, to canescent leaves and stems. The leaves are toothed or almost pinnate, 3in (7.5cm) long, the inflorescence an open panicle, glandular-pubescent throughout. Blooms mid- to late summer. The flowers are tubular, pink or reddish pink, the upper lobes projecting forward slightly, the lower lobes projecting downward; the interior of the flower is marked with conspicuous darker pink or reddish guidelines. 8–30in (20–75cm). Southern British Columbia to northern Oregon. Zone 7b.
P. rostriflorus, syn. *P.* bridgesii. Upright semi-evergreen perennial, often woody at the base, with green leaves and stem. The narrow leaves are inversely lance-shaped, 2–3in (5–7.5cm) long. Flowers are secund, orange-red or red, tubular, with the upper lobe projecting, the lower lobe strongly reflexed. Flowers late mid to late summer. 12–36in (30–90cm). Western U.S. ❄ (min. 41°F/5°C)
P. rupicola (Rock penstemon). Prostrate, evergreen subshrub producing elliptic to rounded, leathery, toothed, thick, blue-green leaves, to ¾in (2cm) long. In late spring or early summer, bears tubular-funnel-shaped, deep red-pink flowers, 1–1½in (2.5–4cm) long. ↕ to 4in (10cm), ↔ 18in (45cm). Coastal W. US. Zone 4. **'Diamond Lake'** is more robust, wit pink flowers, 1½in (4cm) long. **'Pink Dragon'** is more compact, with pale salmon-pink flowers; ↕ 8in (20cm), ↔ 12in (30cm).
***P.* 'Scarlet Queen'.** Upright perennial with glossy, slightly serrated, pointed,

Penstemon pinifolius 'Mersea Yellow'

deep green leaves, 1–3in (2.5–8cm) long. In midsummer, produces tubular, white-throated, scarlet flowers, to 1½in (4cm) long, on stiff, weak-based stems. ↕ 30–36in (75–90cm), ↔ 24in (60cm). Zone 7.

***P.* 'Schoenholzeri'** ▣ syn. *P.* 'Firebird'. Narrow-leaved perennial bearing large, tubular-bell-shaped scarlet flowers, 3in (8cm) long, from midsummer to early or midautumn. ↕ 30in (75cm), ↔ 24in (60cm). Zone 5.

P. serrulatus ▣ syn. *P. diffusus* (Cascade penstemon). Spreading, semi-evergreen subshrub with ovate to lance-shaped or elliptic, toothed, glossy, dark green leaves, ¾–3½in (2–9cm) long. Broad, dense, one-sided panicles of narrowly tubular-bell-shaped, pinkish purple flowers, to 1in (2.5cm) long, are borne in late summer. ↕ 20in (50cm), ↔ 12in (30cm). Alaska to Oregon. Zone 3.

P. smallii (Small's penstemon). Bushy, long-blooming perennial with lance-shaped to ovate, toothed, mid-green leaves, 2–5in (5–13cm) long. Bears spikes of tubular, rose- to lilac-pink flowers, 1½in (4cm) across, striped white within. ↕ 18–24in (45–60cm), ↔ 12–24in (30–60cm). Tennessee to North Carolina. Zone 5.

***P.* 'Sour Grapes'** ▣ Large-leaved perennial. Large, tubular-bell-shaped, grayish blue flowers, suffused rich purple and tinged green, are produced from midsummer to early or mid-autumn. ↕ 24in (60cm), ↔ 18in (45cm). Zone 7.

Penstemon 'Schoenholzeri'

Penstemon serrulatus

P. spectabilis. Upright perennial with oblong-lance-shaped to ovate, blue-green leaves, 1½–4in (4–10cm) long. In early summer, bears long, slender panicles of 2-lipped, tubular, lavender-purple flowers, 1¼–1½in (3–4cm) long, with white insides. ↕ 30–48in (80–120cm), ↔ 18–24in (45–60cm). California to N. Baja California. Zone 8.

***P.* 'Stapleford Gem'** ▣ Large-leaved perennial. Large, tubular-bell-shaped, lilac-purple flowers are produced from midsummer to midautumn; upper lips are pale pink-lilac; lower lips and throats are white with purple lines. ↕ to 24in (60cm), ↔ 18in (45cm). Zone 7.

P. strictus (Rocky Mountain penstemon, Stiff beard-tongue). Upright perennial with spoon-shaped basal leaves and linear to broadly lance-shaped, hairless stem leaves, 4in (10cm) long. Produces narrow, spike-like racemes of dark blue to violet flowers, ¾–1¼in (2–3cm) long, with expanded throats, in summer. ↕ to 32in (80cm), ↔ 24in (60cm). Wyoming to Arizona, New Mexico. Zone 4.

P. superbus. Upright semi-evergreen perennial, bearing glaucous, inversely lance-shaped to oval-shaped leaves to 4in (10cm) long that taper at the tips. Stem leaves are clasping and are oblong or oval-shaped. Narrow tubular red or orange red flowers have flaring lobes, in racemes. Prefers dry soil. Flowers early to midsummer. 12–48in (30–120cm). Southern New Mexico and Arizona, northern Mexico. ❀ (min. 45°F/7°C)

Penstemon 'Sour Grapes'

Penstemon 'Stapleford Gem'

P. utahensis (Utah bugler). Upright perennial with narrow, lance-shaped, leathery, glaucous, mid-blue leaves, to 3in (8cm) long. In mid-and late spring, bears racemes of brilliant, carmine-pink flowers, to 1in (2.5cm) long. ↕ 12–24in (30–60cm), ↔ 6–12in (15–30cm). S.W. US. Zone 4.

P. venustus. Upright perennial with almost stalkless, lance-shaped to oblong, minutely toothed, bluish green leaves, to 3in (8cm) long. Spike-like panicles of tubular-funnel-shaped, pale to deep violet flowers, ¾in (2cm) long, are borne in early summer. ↕ 16–39in (40–100cm), ↔ 14in (35cm). N.W. US. Zone 4.

P. whippleanus (Whipple's penstemon). Upright perennial with ovate to spoon-shaped basal leaves and lance-shaped to oblong-lance-shaped, entire to tiny-toothed, hairless stem leaves, 1–3in (2.5–8cm) long. In autumn, bears thin stems of whorled, purple, sometimes lavender or cream flowers, ¾–1¼in (2–3cm) long, with the lobes of the lower lips exceeding the lobes of the upper lips. ↕ to 24in (60cm), ↔ 12in (30cm). Idaho to New Mexico. Zone 3.

Penstemon 'White Bedder'

***P.* 'White Bedder'** ▣ Large-leaved perennial producing large, tubular-funnel-shaped white flowers, which become pink-tinged, with brown anthers, from midsummer to early or midautumn. ↕ 24in (60cm), ↔ 18in (45cm). Zone 7.

PENTACHONDRA

EPACRIDACEAE

Genus of 3 species of prostrate, evergreen shrubs occurring in boggy meadows in Australia, Tasmania, and New Zealand. They are grown for their heath-like, linear to ovate or elliptic, mid- or dark green leaves, and for their solitary, axillary, small, tubular flowers; the colorful, berry-like fruits are seldom produced in cultivation. They are suitable for a rock garden and grow best in cool climates with mild winters; they are difficult to cultivate in hot, dry conditions.

- **CULTIVATION** Grow in moderately fertile, humus-rich, moist but well-drained soil in full sun.
- **PROPAGATION** Sow seed at 55–64°F (13–18°C) as soon as ripe. Take semi-ripe cuttings in summer.
- **PESTS AND DISEASES** Infrequent.

P. pumila. Procumbent shrub with crowded, obovate, hairy, purplish green leaves, to ¼in (6mm) long. In early summer, produces white flowers, to ¼in (6mm) long, with recurving lobes, occasionally followed by orange-red fruit. ↕ 3in (8cm), ↔ 12in (30cm). Australia, New Zealand. Zone 7b.

PENTAGLOTTIS

Green alkanet

BORAGINACEAE

Genus of one species of evergreen perennial, related to *Anchusa*, occurring in damp, shady habitats, and in hedgerows and woodland margins, in S.W. Europe. It is valued for its flowers, which resemble forget-me-nots and are produced in spring and early summer. The simple leaves are long-stalked in basal rosettes, and stalkless along the branching, erect or ascending stems. Grow in a wild or woodland garden, or in a wildflower border; may self-seed freely.

- **CULTIVATION** Grow in humus-rich, damp soil in partial or deep shade. Deadhead after flowering to prevent self-seeding.
- **PROPAGATION** Sow seed in containers in a cold frame when ripe or in early spring. Divide in early spring; the roots are brittle, and any pieces left in the soil will sprout freely.
- **PESTS AND DISEASES** Infrequent.

P. sempervirens, syn. *Anchusa sempervirens* (Green alkanet). Bristly, taprooted perennial with erect to ascending stems that arise from a basal rosette of pointed, ovate to ovate-oblong, mid-green leaves, 4–16in (10–40cm) long; stem leaves are smaller. Leafy cymes of bright blue flowers, to ½in (1.5cm) across, each with a short tube and 5 spreading lobes, are produced from spring to early summer. ↕↔ 28–39in (70–100cm). S.W. Europe. Zone 7.

PENTAS

RUBIACEAE

Genus of up to 40 species of mainly evergreen perennials, biennials, and shrubs from forest margins and scrub in the Arabian Peninsula, tropical Africa, and Madagascar. They are grown for their flat or domed corymbs of salverform flowers, each with 5 spreading petals, which last well as cut flowers. Leaves are ovate to elliptic or lance-shaped, mostly mid-green, and opposite or whorled, on prostrate or erect stems, to 6ft (2m) long. Where not hardy, grow in a temperate greenhouse, or in containers outdoors in summer. In warmer areas, grow in a bed or border, or in containers on a patio.

• **CULTIVATION** Under glass, grow in soil-based potting mix, with added leaf mold and sharp sand, in bright filtered light. During growth, water freely and apply a balanced liquid fertilizer every month. Water sparingly in winter. Outdoors, grow in fertile, well-drained soil in full sun. Pruning group 9, in late winter; plants under glass need restrictive pruning.

• **PROPAGATION** Sow seed at 61–64°F (16–18°C) in spring. Take softwood cuttings at any time of year; root with bottom heat, especially in winter.

• **PESTS AND DISEASES** Aphids and spider mites may be troublesome.

***P.* 'California Lavender'.** Dwarf, shrubby perennial with ovate to elliptic or lance-shaped leaves, to 6in (15cm) long. Large, flat corymbs of pale lavender flowers, to ¾in (2cm) across, are borne in summer. ↕ 14in (35cm), ↔ 18in (45cm). ❀ (min. 45°F/7°C)

***P.* 'California Pink'.** Compact herbaceous perennial with elliptic to lance-shaped leaves, 3–6in (8–15cm) long. In summer, bears flat corymbs of pink flowers, to ¾in (2cm) across. ↕↔ 16in (40cm). ❀ (min. 45°F/7°C)

P. carnea see *P. lanceolata.*

P. lanceolata ■ syn. *P. carnea* (Egyptian star cluster, Star cluster). Erect or prostrate, woody-based evergreen perennial or subshrub with ovate to elliptic or lance-shaped, hairy leaves, to 6in (15cm) long. From spring to autumn, bears flat or domed corymbs of long-tubed, pink, magenta, blue, lilac, or white flowers, to ½in (1.5cm) across. ↕ 6ft (2m), ↔ 3ft (1m). Yemen to tropical E. Africa. ❀ (min. 45°F/7°C).

Pentas lanceolata

Pentas lanceolata 'Kermesina'

'Avalanche' has white-variegated leaves, and white flowers. **'Kermesina'** ■ has red-throated, deep pink flowers. **'New Look'** ■ has dark green leaves and light pink flowers. **subsp. *quartiniana*** has short-tubed, pink to red flowers.

***P.* 'Orchid Star'.** Erect, shrubby perennial with elliptic or lance-shaped, light green leaves, 3–6in (8–15cm) long. Bears domed corymbs of lilac flowers, to ¾in (2cm) across, in summer. ↕ 18in (45cm), ↔ 20in (50cm). ❀ (min. 45°F/7°C)

***P.* 'Tu-tone'.** Compact, subshrubby perennial with elliptic or lance-shaped leaves, 3–6in (8–15cm) long. Large, domed corymbs of pink, red-centered flowers, ½–¾in (1–2cm) across, are borne in summer. ↕ 3ft (1m), ↔ 24in (60cm). ❀ (min. 45°F/7°C)

Pentas lanceolata 'New Look'

PEPEROMIA

PIPERACEAE

Genus of 1,000 or more species of evergreen, sometimes succulent, rosette-forming or erect perennials, some with trailing stems. They occur in tropical and subtropical regions worldwide, in habitats varying from high-altitude cloud forest to near-desert conditions. All have small, short-lived root systems, but absorb water from the atmosphere and store it in their leaf cells. They are grown mainly for their fleshy, often long-stalked, elliptic to ovate or heart-shaped, usually alternate leaves, sometimes in whorls or panicles. Small, white or greenish white flowers are produced in upright, sometimes branched and panicle-like spikes. Flowering is erratic but mainly in late summer. Where not hardy, grow in a warm greenhouse or as houseplants; grow trailing species in a hanging basket. In tropical areas, grow as a groundcover or in a border.

• **CULTIVATION** Under glass, grow in soilless or soil-based potting mix, in bright indirect light when in active growth, and in full light in winter. Water moderately in summer, sparingly in winter, preferably with tepid water. From spring to summer, maintain moderate to high humidity, mist twice daily, and apply a balanced liquid fertilizer monthly. Outdoors, grow in humus-rich, moist but well-drained soil in partial shade. Most species tolerate low light, and many of the thicker-leaved species will survive in dry conditions for some time.

Peperomia caperata

• **PROPAGATION** Sow seed at 66–75°F (19–24°C) when ripe. During growth, take softwood, leaf, or leaf-bud cuttings, or remove offsets of rosetted variants.

• **PESTS AND DISEASES** Infrequent.

P. argyreia, syn. *P. sandersii* (Watermelon peperomia). Upright, rosette-forming perennial with heart-shaped, leathery, deep green, silver-striped leaves, 2–3½in (5–9cm) long, with long red stems. Bears small green flowers in spikes 2–3in (5–8cm) long. ↕ 8in (20cm), ↔ 6in (15cm). N. South America. ❀ (min. 59°F/15°C)

P. caperata ■ Mound-forming perennial with rosettes of long-stemmed, deeply corrugated, heart-shaped, dark green leaves, 1–1½in (2.5–4cm) long. Tiny white flowers are borne in spikes 2–3in (5–8cm) long. ↕↔ 8in (20cm). Brazil. ❀ (min. 59°F/15°C). **'Emerald Ripple'** has deep green leaves with darker stripes along the veins. **'Little Fantasy'** is dwarf, with dark green leaves; ↕↔ 3in (8cm). **'Luna Red'** ■ has dark crimson leaves and stems. **'Tricolor'** is slow-growing, and has pale green leaves with wide cream margins and central pink markings.

Peperomia caperata 'Luna Red'

P

'eperomia clusiifolia

'. **clusiifolia** ■ (Red-edge peperomia). tiff, erect perennial with obovate, lightly concave, mid-green leaves, ½–4½in (4–11cm) long, often purple-inged when young. Pale green flowers re borne in spikes 5–7in (13–18cm) ong. ↕ 10in (25cm), ↔ 6in (15cm). 3razil. ❀ (min. 59°F/15°C). **'Variegata'** as red-margined, cream-variegated, nid-green leaves.
'. **dolabriformis** (Prayer peperomia). Robust, erect perennial, becoming voody with age, with succulent, purse-haped, bright green leaves, 1½–2in 4–5cm) long; the 2 halves of each eaf are folded upward and fused along he dark green margins. Leafy stems roduce panicle-like spikes, 1¼–3in 3–8cm) long, of white flowers. ↕ to 0in (25cm), ↔ 8in (20cm). Peru. ❀ (min. 59°F/15°C)
'. **fraseri**, syn. *P. resediflora* (Flowering eperomia). Upright, rosette-forming erennial with stiff, heart-shaped, shiny, ark green leaves, 1–1¾in (2.5–4.5cm) ong, pale green beneath with red eins. Leafy stems produce panicle-like pikes, to 16in (40cm) long, of showy vhite flowers. ↕ 16in (40cm), ↔ 8in 20cm). Ecuador, Colombia. ❀ (min. 9°F/15°C)
'. **glabella** ■ (Wax privet peperomia). preading perennial with trailing stems nd broadly elliptic to slightly obovate, nid-green leaves, 1½–2½in (4–6cm) ong, dotted with black glands. Bears reen flowers in spikes 3–5in (8–13cm) ong. ↕ 6in (15cm), ↔ 12in (30cm). Vest Indies, Central and South America. ❀ (min. 59°F/15°C). **'Variegata'** has eaves with creamy yellow margins.

'eperomia glabella

P. griseoargentea, syn. *P. hederifolia* (Ivy-leaf peperomia). Rosette-forming perennial with heart-shaped, silvery gray leaves, 1¼–2½in (3–6cm) long, tinged copper along the veins. Green flowers are borne in spikes 2–3½in (5–9cm) long. ↕ 8in (20cm), ↔ 6in (15cm). Brazil. ❀ (min. 59°F/15°C)
P. hederifolia see *P. griseoargentea*.
P. incana (Felted peperomia). Stiff, semi-erect perennial, later spreading, with succulent, broadly ovate, gray-green leaves, 1¼–2½in (3–6cm) long, covered in white-woolly hairs. Green flowers with purple anthers are produced in spikes 6–8in (15–20cm) long. ↕↔ 12in (30cm). S.E. Brazil. ❀ (min. 59°F/15°C)
P. maculosa (Radiator plant). Robust, erect perennial, becoming untidy as it grows larger, with ovate, shiny, dark green leaves, 5–6in (12–15cm) long, on long stems. Bears spikes, 8in (20cm) or more long, of dark purple flowers. ↕↔ to 8in (20cm). West Indies, Panama, N. South America. ❀ (min. 59°F/15°C)
P. magnoliifolia see *P. obtusifolia*.
P. marmorata ■ syn. *P. verschaffeltii* (Sweetheart peperomia). Rosette-forming perennial with heart-shaped, dull, mid- or bluish green leaves, 3–5in (8–13cm) long, striped silver-gray, with indented veins. Bears green flowers in spikes to 3½in (9cm) long. ↕↔ to 10in (25cm). S. Brazil. ❀ (min. 59°F/15°C). **'Silver Heart'** has pale green leaves with broad silver stripes.
P. metallica (Red tree). Erect, bushy perennial with elliptic, dark red leaves, ¾–1¼in (2–3cm) long, each with a broad silver band down the center. Bears red flowers in spikes 1¼–1½in (3–4cm) long. ↕ to 8in (20cm), ↔ 6in (15cm). Peru. ❀ (min. 59°F/15°C)
P. nivalis. Variable, creeping or erect, succulent perennial with fleshy stems containing anise-scented sap. Boat-shaped, keeled, fleshy, bright green leaves, ½in (1.5cm) long, white or white-flushed pink beneath, are densely crowded at the tips of the stems. Tiny, dull yellow flowers develop in very compressed spikes, to ½in (1.5cm) long. ↕ 4–6in (10–15cm), ↔ indefinite. Peru. ❀ (min. 46°F/8°C)
P. nummulariifolia see *P. rotundifolia*.
P. obtusifolia, syn. *P. magnoliifolia* (Baby rubber plant, Pepper face). Stiff, upright perennial with elliptic, leathery, dull green leaves, 2–6in (5–15cm) long. White flowers are borne in spikes 3½–5in (9–13cm) long. ↕↔ 10in

Peperomia marmorata

Peperomia obtusifolia 'Variegata'

(25cm). ❀ (min. 59°F/15°C). **'Green and Gold'** has leaves with golden yellow margins. **'Variegata'** ■ has leaves with wide, white or yellow margins.
P. orba, syn. *P.* 'Princess Astrid'. Erect, bushy perennial with ovate, succulent, softly hairy, gray-green leaves, 1½–2in (4–5cm) long, each with a broad silver stripe down the center. Bears green flowers in spikes 3–5in (8–13cm) long. ↕ to 6in (15cm), ↔ 8in (20cm). Origin unknown. ❀ (min. 59°F/15°C). **'Pixie'**, syn. 'Teardrop', is a dwarf cultivar, with leaves ¾–1¼in (2–3cm) long. Propagate from the smaller shoots. It may revert, producing larger leaves; shoots bearing these should be cut out as they appear. ↕ 3in (8cm), ↔ 4in (10cm). **'Teardrop'** see 'Pixie'.
***P.* 'Princess Astrid'** see *P. orba*.
P. resediflora see *P. fraseri*.
P. rotundifolia, syn. *P. nummulariifolia* (Yerba linda). Creeping, usually epiphytic, succulent perennial with slender, fleshy stems, often covered with minute, fine hairs or bristles, and bearing rounded to broadly elliptic, fleshy, bright green leaves, ½in (1.5cm) long. Produces short spikes, ½in (1.5cm) long, of yellowish white flowers. ↕ 1¼in (3cm), ↔ to 10in (25cm). South Africa, West Indies, Central and South America. ❀ (min. 59°F/15°C)
P. rubella. Erect, branching perennial, becoming untidy with age, with whorls of 4 or 5 elliptic, pale-veined, pale to deep green leaves, to ½in (1.5cm) long, red beneath, giving a copper tinge to the foliage. Green flowers are borne in spikes ¾–2in (2–5cm) long. ↕ to 8in (20cm), ↔ 10in (25cm). West Indies. ❀ (min. 59°F/15°C)
P. sandersii see *P. argyreia*.
P. scandens (False philodendron). Trailing perennial with heart-shaped, pale green leaves, 2–3in (5–8cm) long. Green flowers are produced in spikes 5–5½in (12–14cm) long. ↕ to 8in (20cm), ↔ 20in (50cm). Mexico to South America. ❀ (min. 59°F/15°C). **'Variegata'** produces leaves with broad yellow margins; it tends to revert to plain green.
P. velutina. Upright, bushy perennial with broadly elliptic, fleshy, velvety, dark green leaves, ¾–1¾in (2–4.5cm) long, with pale veins, and red beneath. Green flowers are borne in spikes 3½–4in (9–10cm) long. ↕ to 12in (30cm), ↔ 8in (20cm). Ecuador. ❀ (min. 59°F/15°C)
P. verschaffeltii see *P. marmorata*.
P. verticillata. Erect, fleshy perennial with rounded to obovate leaves (variable on the same plant), pale green above, red-pink beneath, ⅜–1¼in (0.8–3cm) long, and borne in whorls of 5 at the nodes. Leaves and the lower parts of stems are softly white-hairy. Green flowers are produced in spikes, ¾–1in (2–2.5cm) long. ↕ to 20in (50cm), ↔ to 18in (45cm). W. Indies. ❀ (min. 50°F/10°C)

PERAPHYLLUM

ROSACEAE

Genus of one species of upright, wide-spreading, deciduous shrub from dry hillsides of W. North America. It has clustered or spirally arranged, lance-shaped, lustrous mid-green leaves. It is cultivated for its inflorescences of white flowers, which are followed by cherry-like yellow fruit. Grow *P. ramosissimum* in a native garden.
• **CULTIVATION** Grow in well-drained, neutral or acidic soil in full sun.
• **PROPAGATION** Sow seed *in situ* when ripe, or layer. Pruning group 4.
• **PESTS AND DISEASES** Generally trouble-free, but sometimes affected by leaf spot and cedar apple rust.

P. ramosissimum. Upright shrub with lance-shaped, softly hairy leaves, ¾–2in (2–5cm) long, becoming shiny green with age. Bears clusters of 2–5, pink-tinged, white flowers, ¾in (2cm) across, with rounded, spreading petals, in late spring, followed by pendent, rounded, yellow fruit, tinged with red-brown. ↕ 5–6ft (1.5–2m), ↔ 4–5ft (1.2–1.7m). Oregon to California to Colorado. Zone 6.

PERESKIA

CACTACEAE

Genus of 16 species of tree-like, scandent, or shrubby cacti occurring in wooded, often hilly regions of Florida, Mexico, Central America, tropical South America to N. Argentina, and the West Indies. They have spiny, slightly fleshy branches; some become woody with age. Some have tuberous roots. The fleshy, lance-shaped to rounded or oblong leaves are usually evergreen (deciduous in species with a dormant period). Bowl-shaped flowers, solitary or borne in axillary or terminal corymbs or panicles, open by day from spring to autumn. Where temperatures drop below 50–59°F (10–15°C), grow in a temperate or warm greenhouse. In warm, dry climates, use in a desert garden or courtyard garden.
• **CULTIVATION** Under glass, grow in standard cactus potting mix in full light, with shade from hot sun. From midspring to late summer, water moderately and apply a low-nitrogen fertilizer every 5 or 6 weeks. Water sparingly in winter; mist lightly when warm in late winter. Provide support for stems of climbing species. Outdoors, grow in moderately fertile, sharply drained soil in light, dappled shade. See also pp.48–49.
• **PROPAGATION** Sow seed at 66–75°F (19–24°C) in spring. From late spring to summer, take cuttings of stem sections.
• **PESTS AND DISEASES** Susceptible to mealybugs and, while flowering, aphids.

P

Pereskia aculeata

P. aculeata ■ (Barbados gooseberry). Vigorous, scandent, deciduous cactus producing spiny, fleshy stems and lance-shaped or elliptic to ovate, soft, dark green leaves, to 4½in (11cm) long. Brown areoles bear 1–3 yellowish brown spines. Panicles of long-lasting, scented, creamy white flowers, to 2in (5cm) across, with orange-red stamens, are produced in autumn. ↕ 25–30ft (8–10m), ↔ indefinite. Florida, West Indies, Paraguay to S. Brazil. ❄ (min. 59°F/15°C)
P. amapola see *P. nemorosa.*
P. argentina see *P. nemorosa.*
P. grandiflorus see *P. grandifolia.*
P. grandifolia ■ syn. *P. grandiflorus, Rhodocactus grandifolius* (Rose cactus). Shrubby, erect, evergreen cactus with thick, spiny stems and narrowly elliptic, ovate, or obovate to lance-shaped leaves, 3½–9in (9–23cm) long. Brown areoles bear up to 8 almost black spines. Corymbs of bright pink to purple-pink flowers, 1¼–2in (3–5cm) across, with white-based petals, are produced from spring to autumn. ↕ to 15ft (5m), ↔ 3ft (1m). Brazil. ❄ (min. 59°F/15°C)
P. nemorosa, syn. *P. amapola, P. argentina, P. sacharosa* of gardens. Shrubby, often tree-like, erect, evergreen cactus with smooth green branches and lance-shaped leaves, to 5in (13cm) long. Grayish white areoles bear 3 or more red spines. From spring to summer, bears corymbs of white or pink flowers, 3in (8cm) across. ↕ 20–25ft (6–8m), ↔ 3ft (1m). S. Brazil, Paraguay, Argentina, Uruguay. ❄ (min. 59°F/15°C)
***P. sacharosa* of gardens** see *P. nemorosa.*

Pereskia grandifolia

P

PERESKIOPSIS

CACTACEAE

Genus of 8–10 species (some authorities accept only 8) of shrubby or tree-like cacti with several irregular branches, often scrambling or rambling. These plants clamber among bushes for support, in Mexico and south into Guatemala. They are quite similar to Pereskia, but with the presence of glochids. Diurnal flowers, in yellow to pink or red, are borne laterally on stems of the previous season, but sometimes terminally. The club-shaped, red or orange fruit is fleshy and indehiscent, with few seeds.

• **CULTIVATION** Under glass, grow in standard cactus potting mix in full light, with shade from hot sun. From midspring to late summer, water moderately and apply a low-nitrogen fertilizer every 5 or 6 weeks. Water sparingly in winter; mist lightly when warm in late winter. Provide support for stems of climbing species. Outdoors, grow in moderately fertile, sharply drained soil in light, dappled shade.

• **PROPAGATION** Sow seed at 66-75° (19-24°C) in spring. From late spring to summer, take cuttings of stem sections.

• **PESTS AND DISEASES** Susceptible to mealybugs and, while flowering, aphids.

P. diguetii. Densely shrubby cactus with poorly developed trunks. Branches are sometimes bending or deciduous, to root and form new growth. Reddish green stems are finely hairy, ⅛–⅜in (3–8mm) thick; areoles are whitish with abundant glochids, to 1/16in (2mm) long, with wool and a few spines (1–5) on stem areoles, more on trunks. Leaves are elliptical to ovate and finely hairy. Produces yellow flowers, 1¼–3in (3–7.5cm) long. Top-shaped to ovoid, hairy fruit is yellow or orange and can turn red. ↕ 3–6ft (1–2m). Guanajuato, Querétaro, Morelos, Oaxaca, Jalisco, Michoacán, Guerrero, Mexico. ❄ (min. 59°F/15°C)
P. gatesii ■ Shrubby cactus with pale green to grayish, woody stems. Areoles are round and dark, with long dark brown glochids, with 1 to several gray to nearly black spines, to 2in (5cm) long. Bears ovate, pointed green leaves, to ⅛in (3mm), which are not hairy. Flowers are bright yellow, ¾–1¼in (2–3cm); deep red fruit are borne, to ¾in (2cm). ↕ 6–10ft (2–3m), ↔ to 5ft (1.5m). Baja California Sur, Mexico. ❄ (min. 59°F/15°C)

Pereskiopsis gatesii

PERICALLIS

ASTERACEAE

Genus of 15 species of perennials and subshrubs, sometimes grown as annuals, occurring in forests and on slopes and rocky outcrops in the Canary Islands, Madeira, and the Azores. They are grown for their daisy-like flowerheads, solitary or borne in corymbs, appearing from winter to early autumn. Stems are upright to spreading, simple or branching. Leaves are simple, rounded to broadly lance-shaped or arrow-shaped, arranged alternately or in basal rosettes. Where not hardy, grow in a cool greenhouse or as houseplants. In warmer climates, grow in a shrub border or use as summer bedding.

• **CULTIVATION** Under glass, grow in soil-based potting mix in full light, with shade from hot sun. During growth, water moderately and apply a balanced liquid fertilizer every 2 weeks. Outdoors, grow in fertile, well-drained soil, in full sun with midday shade, or in partial shade. Discard plants after blooming.

• **PROPAGATION** Sow seed at 55–64°F (13–18°C) from spring to midsummer. Root semi-ripe cuttings in summer.

• **PESTS AND DISEASES** Suceptible to aphids, spider mites, thrips, whiteflies, and chrysanthemum leaf miner.

P. x hybrida, syn. *Cineraria cruentus* of gardens, *C.* x *hybrida, Senecio cruentus, S.* x *hybridus* (Florists' cineraria). Cushion-forming or loosely branched perennial, usually grown as an annual, with alternate, ovate, triangular-heart-shaped, mid- to deep green leaves, 10–12in (25–30cm) long. From winter to spring, produces loose, terminal and axillary corymbs, 1–3in (2.5–8cm) across, of flower-heads in single colors and bicolors, in pink, red, blue, white, magenta, lavender-blue, and copper. ↕ 18–24in (45–60cm), ↔ 10–24in (25–60cm). Garden origin. ❄ (min. 45°F/7°C).
'Spring Glory' ■ is compact and early-flowering, with abundant flower-heads in blue, copper, carmine-red, and pink, as well as bicolors; ↕ 8in (20cm), ↔ 10in (25cm).

Pericallis x *hybrida* 'Spring Glory'

PERILLA

LAMIACEAE

Genus of 6 species of erect, bushy, aromatic annuals, with 4-angled stems, found in variable habitats, usually in woodland, from India to Japan. They are cultivated for their opposite, simple, usually ovate, often fragrant, mid- or dark green leaves, sometimes flushed or variegated red, purple, or bronze. Whorls of insignificant, 2-lipped, 5-lobed, bell-shaped flowers, each encased in a prominent, 2-lipped calyx, are borne in upright spikes in late summer and autumn. *P. frutescens* and its cultivars are the most commonly grown; their decorative, often purple and frilly foliage contrasts well with the flowers of summer bedding plants. They self-seed abundantly and can quickly become invasive.

• **CULTIVATION** Grow in fertile, moist but well-drained soil in full sun or partial shade. Add compost or well-rotted manure for best growth.

• **PROPAGATION** Sow seed at 55–64°F (13–18°C) in spring.

• **PESTS AND DISEASES** Infrequent.

Perilla frutescens var. *crispa*

P. frutescens (Shiso). Vigorous, hairy annual with broadly ovate, pointed, deeply toothed, long-stalked, mid-green, sometimes purple-flecked leaves, to 5in (13cm) long, with a cinnamon-lemon flavor. Whorls of tiny white flowers are borne in spikes, to 6in (15cm) long, in summer. ↕ to 3ft (1m), ↔ to 12in (30cm). Himalayas to E. Asia. **'Atropurpurea'** (Beefsteak plant) produces dark red-purple leaves. **var. *crispa*** ■ syn. var. *nankinensis*, has attractive, dark purple or dark bronze, sometimes dark green leaves with frilly margins. **var. *nankinensis*** see var. *crispa*.

PERIPLOCA

ASCLEPIADACEAE

Genus of 11 species of deciduous or evergreen shrubs and climbers found in woodland, in thickets, and on riverbanks in the Mediterranean, tropical Africa, and E. Asia. They are grown for their attractive, lance-shaped to broadly ovate leaves, borne in opposite pairs. Small, star-shaped flowers are produced in terminal or axillary corymbs or cymes. Train *P. graeca*, the most commonly grown species, on wires against a wall, or grow over a pergola, trellis, or similar support. The fruits and sap may cause stomach upset if ingested.

• **CULTIVATION** Grow in any well-drained soil in a warm, sheltered site in full sun. Support climbing stems. Pruning group 11, in early spring.

• **PROPAGATION** Sow seed at 55–61°F (13–16°C) in spring. Take semi-ripe cuttings in summer.

• **PESTS AND DISEASES** Infrequent.

P. graeca (Silk vine). Twining, deciduous climber with ovate, glossy, dark green leaves, to 4in (10cm) long. Star-shaped, unpleasantly scented, 5-lobed flowers, 1in (2.5cm) across, greenish yellow outside and purple-brown inside, are borne in long-stalked corymbs of up to 12, in mid- and late summer. They are followed by slender seed pods, to 5in (13cm) long, which open to release silky-tufted seeds. ↕ 28ft (9m). S.E. Europe, S.W. Asia. Zone 7.

Pernettya see *Gaultheria*

PEROVSKIA

LAMIACEAE

Genus of 7 species of deciduous subshrubs occurring in rocky sites from C. Asia to the Himalayas, grown for their foliage and flowers. They have opposite, often finely cut and deeply divided, lance-shaped to ovate or oblong, aromatic, gray-green leaves. Terminal panicles of small, tubular, 2-lipped blue flowers are produced in late summer and early autumn. Grow in a mixed or herbaceous border.

• **CULTIVATION** Grow in well-drained, poor to moderately fertile soil in full sun. They tolerate dry, alkaline soil and coastal conditions. Pruning group 6.

• **PROPAGATION** Root softwood cuttings in late spring, or semi-ripe cuttings in summer.

• **PESTS AND DISEASES** Infrequent.

P. atriplicifolia (Russian sage). Upright subshrub with gray-white shoots and ovate, deeply cut and lobed,

Perovskia 'Blue Spire'

silvery-gray-green leaves, to 2in (5cm) long. Small, tubular, violet-blue flowers are borne in tall panicles, to 12in (30cm) long, in late summer and early autumn. ↕ 4ft (1.2m), ↔ 3ft (1m). Afghanistan. Zone 5. **'Filagran'** has finely cut leaves; ↕ 30in (75cm). **'Longin'** is more erect, narrow, and upright in habit, and has less toothed leaves than the species.

***P.* 'Blue Spire'** ■ Upright subshrub with gray-white stems bearing ovate, very deeply divided, silver-gray leaves, to 2in (5cm) long. Tubular, violet-blue flowers, in panicles to 12in (30cm) long, are very profusely borne in late summer and early autumn. ↕ 4ft (1.2m), ↔ 3ft (1m). Zone 5.

***P.* 'Hybrida'.** Upright subshrub with gray-white shoots and ovate, deeply cut, gray-green leaves, to 2in (5cm) long. In late summer and early autumn, bears tubular, dark lavender-blue flowers in tall panicles, to 16in (40cm) long. ↕ 3ft (1m), ↔ 30in (75cm). Zone 5.

PERSEA

LAURACEAE

Genus of 150 species of brittle-branched, evergreen trees and shrubs from well-drained soils to swamps of S.E. Asia, Micronesia, and tropical and subtropical North and South America. They are grown for their alternate, laurel-like, pinnately veined leaves.

• **CULTIVATION** Under glass, grow in soil-based potting mix in full light at a minimum temperature of 55–60°F (13–16°C). In growth, water moderately and apply a balanced liquid fertilizer every 2 weeks. Water sparingly in winter. Outdoors, grow in moderately fertile, well-drained soil in full sun. Protect from strong wind, since the branches are brittle. Pruning group 10.

• **PROPAGATION** Sow seed at 55–60°F (13–16°C) as soon as ripe. Germination may take 5–6 months. Take greenwood cuttings in early summer, and grow in a closed case with bottom heat.

• **PESTS AND DISEASES** Leaf spots, trunk cankers and rot, black mildew, root rot, *Verticillium* wilt, and minor element deficiencies are common. Thrips, mealybugs, nematode infestations of roots, and sun scald also occur.

P. borbonia (Florida mahogany, Red bay, Swamp red bay). Much-branched evergreen tree with lance-shaped to oblong-lance-shaped, hairless, glaucous, fragrant, mid-green leaves, to 6in (15cm) long. Bears panicles, to 6in (15cm) long, of few to several yellow-green flowers, ½in (1.5cm) across, followed by blackish blue fruit, ½in (1.5cm) across. ↕ 30–40ft (10–12m), ↔ 20ft (6m). Delaware to Florida. Zone 8.

PERSICARIA

syn. ACONOGONON, BISTORTA, POLYGONUM, TOVARA

Fleeceflower, Knotweed

POLYGONACEAE

Genus of 50–80 species of annuals, often rhizomatous or stoloniferous perennials, and rarely subshrubs. They may be evergreen, semi-evergreen, or deciduous; some have attractive autumn leaf color. They are found in a variety of habitats worldwide. Often spreading and sometimes invasive, they have usually fleshy stems and simple, entire, variably shaped, often conspicuously veined leaves: basal leaves are long stalked, stem leaves are fewer, smaller, alternate, and stalkless. Spikes or panicles of small, usually long-lasting, funnel-, bell-, or cup-shaped, white, pink, or red flowers are followed by distinctive, usually brownish red, 3-angled or ovoid fruits. Some of the larger perennials are undemanding plants for a border, or as a groundcover, and are suitable for naturalizing in a meadow or woodland garden. Grow smaller species in a large rock garden, or at the front of a border. Contact with all parts may irritate skin; the sap may cause mild stomach upset if ingested.

Persicaria affinis 'Donald Lowndes'

Persicaria affinis 'Superba'

• **CULTIVATION** Grow in any moist soil in full sun or partial shade. *P. bistorta* tolerates dry soil.

• **PROPAGATION** Sow seed in containers in a cold frame in spring. Divide perennials in spring or autumn.

• **PESTS AND DISEASES** Aphids, slugs, and snails may occur.

P. affinis, syn. *Polygonum affine* (Himalayan knotweed). Mat-forming, evergreen perennial with elliptic-lance-shaped, dark green leaves, 2–6in (5–15cm) long, turning red-bronze in autumn. From midsummer to mid-autumn, bears spikes, 2–3in (5–8cm) long, of cup-shaped, bright rose-red flowers, to ¼in (6mm) long, fading to pale pink; flowers turn brown with age, providing color during winter. ↕ to 10in (25cm), ↔ 24in (60cm) or more. Himalayas. Zone 3b. **'Border Jewel'** has pale pink flowers. **'Darjeeling Red'** has large leaves, to 6in (15cm) long, and flowers that open pink and turn red when mature; ↔ 20in (50cm). **'Dimity'** bears dense spikes of light pink flowers; the leaves turn red in autumn; ↕ 4in (10cm), ↔ 18in (45cm). **'Donald Lowndes'** ■ has pointed leaves, and produces dense spikes of pale pink flowers, becoming darker when mature; ↕ to 8in (20cm), ↔ 12in (30cm). **'Superba'** ■ is vigorous, and has pale pink flowers, becoming deep pinkish red, with red calyces; leaves turn rich brown in autumn.

P. amplexicaulis, syn. *Bistorta amplexicaulis, Polygonum amplexicaule* (Bistort, Mountain fleece). Robust, clump-forming, semi-evergreen perennial with ovate-lance-shaped, pointed, mid-green leaves, to 10in (25cm) long; they are slightly puckered and prominently veined above, downy beneath. Bears long-stalked, narrow spikes, to 4in (10cm) long, of narrowly bell-shaped, bright red to purple or white flowers, ¼in (6mm) long, from midsummer to early autumn. ↕↔ to 4ft (1.2m). Himalayas. Zone 4.

Persicaria bistorta 'Superba'

'Arun Gem' is low-growing, and has pendent spikes of dark pink flowers with bronze tips; ↕ 12in (30cm), ↔ 36in (90cm). **'Firetail'** has bright red flowers. **'Inverleith'** forms mounds of dark green leaves, and produces short spikes of dark red flowers; ↕↔ to 18in (45cm).
P. bistorta, syn. *Polygonum bistorta* (Bistort, Snakeweed). Vigorous, clump-forming, leafy, hairless, semi-evergreen perennial with broadly ovate, pointed, boldly veined, mid-green leaves, 4–12in (10–30cm) long. Narrowly bell-shaped, pale pink or white flowers, ¼in (6mm) long, are borne in short, dense, cylindrical spikes, 2–3in (5–8cm) long, from early summer to midautumn. ↕ 30in (75cm), ↔ 36in (90cm). Europe, N. and W. Asia. Zone 4. **subsp. *carnea***, syn. *Polygonum carneum*, has deeper pink flowers borne in more spherical spikes; ↕ 18–28in (45–70cm), ↔ 18in (45cm); Caucasus, N. and E. Turkey. **'Superba'** ■ has dense, spherical spikes of soft pink flowers, freely borne over a long period; ↕ to 36in (90cm).
P. campanulata ■ syn. *Polygonum campanulatum*. Clump-forming, stoloniferous, deciduous or semi-

Persicaria campanulata

Persicaria macrophylla

evergreen perennial with few, lance-shaped to elliptic-ovate basal leaves, to 6in (15cm) long, and numerous stem leaves; all are hairy, with conspicuous veins, and mid-green above, white or light brown beneath. From midsummer to early autumn, slender stems bear loose, short-stalked panicles, 6in (15cm) long, of bell-shaped, fragrant, pink or white flowers, ¼in (6mm) long. ↕↔ 36in (90cm). N. India, N. Burma, S.W. China. Zone 6. **'Southcombe White'** has white flowers.
P. capitata, syn. *Polygonum capitatum*. Branching, stem-rooting, evergreen to deciduous perennial with ovate to elliptic, dark green leaves, to 2in (5cm) long, each with a purple V-shaped band. Bears bell-shaped pink flowers, 1/16–1/8in (2–3mm) long, in dense, rounded, short-stemmed panicles, to ½in (1.5cm) across, in summer. Good groundcover; may be invasive. ↕ 3in (8cm), ↔ 20in (50cm) or more. Himalayas. Zone 8.
P. macrophylla ■ syn. *Polygonum macrophyllum, P. sphaerostachyum*. Rosette-forming, semi-evergreen perennial with woody crowns and lance-shaped, boldly veined, mid-green leaves, to 8in (20cm) long. Dense, cylindrical spikes, ½in (1.5cm) long, of bell-shaped, pink to red flowers, ¼in (6mm) long, are borne from early summer to early autumn. ↕↔ 12in (30cm). Himalayas to S.W. China. Zone 6.
P. milletii ■ syn. *Polygonum milletii*. Clump-forming, erect, semi-evergreen perennial with linear-lance-shaped, pointed, dark green leaves, to 12in (30cm) long, with prominent midribs and long sheaths. From early summer

Persicaria milletii

Persicaria tenuicaulis

to late autumn, bears dense, cylindrical spikes, to 1½in (4cm) long, of bell-shaped crimson flowers, ¼in (6mm) long. Similar to *P. macrophylla*, but longer-flowering. ↕↔ to 24in (60cm). Himalayas to S.W. China. Zone 6.
P. orientale, syn. *Polygonum orientale* (Kiss-me-over-the-garden-gate, Prince's feather, Princess feather). Erect, thick-stemmed, branching, hairy annual with broadly ovate, pointed, mid-green leaves, 4–8in (10–20cm) long, heart-shaped at the bases. Bell-shaped, pink to rose-red or white flowers, to 1/8in (3mm) long, are borne in dense, branching, pendent spikes, ¾–3in (2–8cm) long, in late summer and autumn. ↕ to 4ft (1.2m), ↔ to 24in (60cm). E. and S.E. Asia, Australia.
P. tenuicaulis ■ syn. *Polygonum tenuicaule*. Slow-growing, mat-forming, deciduous or semi-evergreen perennial with ovate-elliptic, dark green leaves, 1¼–3in (3–8cm) long. Bears short, dense spikes, about 1½in (4cm) long, of bell-shaped, fragrant white flowers, 1/8in (3mm) long, in late spring. ↕ 2in (5cm), ↔ 6in (15cm). Japan. Zone 6b.
P. vacciniifolia ■ syn. *Polygonum vacciniifolium*. Creeping, semi-evergreen perennial with branching, red-tinted stems bearing ovate-elliptic, glossy, mid-green leaves, to 1in (2.5cm) long, turning red in autumn. Bell-shaped, deep pink flowers, 1/8–¼in (4–6mm) long, are produced in narrow, upright spikes, to 3in (8cm) long, in late summer and autumn. ↕ 8in (20cm), ↔ 20in (50cm) or more. Himalayas. Zone 7b.

Persicaria vacciniifolia

Persicaria virginiana 'Painter's Palette'

P. virginiana, syn. *Polygonum virginianum, Tovara virginiana*. Upright herbaceous perennial with ovate to elliptic, mid-green leaves with dark green markings, 3–10in (8–25cm) long. In late summer and early autumn, produces slender, very loose, terminal and axillary spikes, 4–12in (10–30cm) long, of cup-shaped green flowers, 1/16–1/8in (2–3mm) across, turning red. Can become invasive. ↕ 16–48in (40–120cm), ↔ 24–56in (60–140cm). Himalayas, Japan, E. North America. Zone 4. **'Painter's Palette'** ■ produces variegated leaves with central V-shaped brown marks, yellow patches, deep pinkish red tints, and red midribs and stalks.

PETASITES

Butterbur, Sweet coltsfoot

ASTERACEAE

Genus of about 15 species of dioecious, rhizomatous perennials from Europe, Asia, and North America, some found in mountainous regions, others in swampy sites, by streams, and in moist woodland. They have long-stalked, heart- to kidney-shaped basal leaves and smaller, short-stalked or stalkless, scale-like stem leaves. Thick stems bear purple, white, or yellow flowerheads, which usually consist of a mixture of disk florets, ray florets, and thread-like florets (some fertile, some sterile); they are borne singly or in dense corymbs, racemes, or panicles. Individual plants are either male or female. Grown for their large leaves, they provide good groundcover beside a stream or pool, or in a wild garden, although they easily become invasive. The flowers provide early nectar for bees.
• **CULTIVATION** Grow in deep, humus-rich, fertile soil that is permanently moist but not stagnant, in partial or full shade. *P. fragrans* tolerates drier soil.
• **PROPAGATION** Divide in spring or autumn.
• **PESTS AND DISEASES** Prone to rust.

P

Petasites japonicus

P. fragrans (Winter heliotrope). Spreading perennial with fleshy rhizomes and kidney-shaped, toothed, basal leaves, to 5in (13cm) across, hairy beneath, borne on stalks to 12in (30cm) long. Short, lax panicles of about 10 strongly vanilla-scented, pale lilac to purple flowerheads, ½in (1.5cm) across, appear with the leaves from midwinter to early spring. ↕ to 12in (30cm), ↔ 5ft (1.5m). C. Mediterranean. Zone 7b.
P. japonicus ▣ (Fuki). Rhizomatous perennial with kidney-shaped, irregularly toothed, basal leaves, to 32in (80cm) across, hairy beneath, borne on stalks 3ft (1m) long. Densely clustered corymbs of yellowish white flowerheads, to ½in (1.5cm) across, with oblong bracts below, are borne before the leaves in late winter and early spring. Normally invasive. ↕ 3½ft (1.1m), ↔ 5ft (1.5m). China, Korea, Japan. Zone 6.
var. *giganteus* 'Variegata' has white-edged, wavy-margined leaves, 24–36in (60–90cm) across, with fragrant flowers.

PETREA

VERBENACEAE

Genus of 30 species of deciduous or semi-evergreen climbers, shrubs, and small trees found in woodland from Mexico to tropical South America. They are grown for their salverform flowers, each with 5 petal lobes, produced in terminal racemes or from the uppermost leaf axils, sometimes forming panicles. Simple, elliptic leaves, with prominent veins, are borne in whorls or opposite pairs. Where temperatures fall below 50–55°F (10–13°C), grow in a warm or temperate greenhouse. In warmer areas, grow in open beds, in borders, or as specimen plants cascading from a tree.
• **CULTIVATION** Under glass, grow in soil-based potting mix in full light. When in growth, water moderately and apply a balanced liquid fertilizer every month. Water sparingly in winter. Outdoors, grow in fertile, moist but well-drained soil in full sun. Support climbing stems. Pruning group 11, in late winter or early spring.
• **PROPAGATION** Root semi-ripe cuttings with bottom heat in summer. Layer or air layer in late winter.
• **PESTS AND DISEASES** Scale insects, mealybugs, and spider mites occur.

P. kohautiana. Woody-stemmed, semi-evergreen climber producing branching, twining stems and stalkless, oblong-elliptic, dark green leaves, 2–8in (5–20cm) long, with heart-shaped bases. Bears erect to nodding panicles, to 24in (60cm) long, of small, salverform, violet to white flowers, from late winter to summer. ↕ to 30ft (10m). West Indies. ❄ (min. 50°F/10°C)
P. volubilis ▣ (Purple wreath, Queen's wreath). Woody-stemmed, semi-evergreen climber with branching, twining stems and short-stalked, oblong-elliptic leaves, 4–8in (10–20cm) long, deep green above, paler beneath. Bears erect to arching panicles, 8–14in (20–35cm) long, of small, salverform, amethyst to deep violet flowers, with lilac calyx lobes, from late winter to summer. ↕ to 40ft (12m). Mexico, Central America, Lesser Antilles. ❄ (min. 50°F/10°C).
'Albiflora' has white flowers.

Petrea volubilis

PETROCOSMEA

GESNERIACEAE

Genus of about 30 species of evergreen perennials occurring on shady rocks in the mountains of Asia. They produce rosettes of variably shaped, usually lance-shaped to nearly rounded, felted leaves, and are grown for their 5-lobed, tubular to bell-shaped flowers, produced singly or in several-flowered, axillary, umbel-like clusters in spring. Where not hardy, grow *Petrocosmea* species in an alpine house or cold greenhouse. In frost-free climates, grow on a shady wall or in a rock crevice.
• **CULTIVATION** Under glass, grow in soil-based potting mix, with added grit and leaf mold, in bright indirect light. When in growth, water moderately and apply a balanced liquid fertilizer every 2 or 3 weeks. Do not overwater, but when in active growth, expose to medium or high humidity. Water sparingly in winter. Outdoors, grow in gritty, moderately fertile, humus-rich soil in partial shade.
• **PROPAGATION** Sow seed at 55–64°F (13–18°C) as soon as ripe. Take leaf cuttings in summer.

Petrocosmea kerrii

• **PESTS AND DISEASES** Susceptible to slugs and snails, aphids, thrips, spider mites, and whiteflies.

P. kerrii ▣ Rosette-forming perennial with downy, ovate-lance-shaped to oblong, rich green leaves, to 4in (10cm) long. In summer, produces short-stemmed, umbel-like clusters of 1–3 short-tubed white flowers, to ½in (1.5cm) across, with 2-lobed upper lips and 3-lobed lower lips, and yellow throats. ↕ 3in (8cm), ↔ 6in (15cm). Thailand. ❄ (min. 45°F/7°C)

PETROPHILE

PROTEACEAE

Genus of about 40 species of evergreen shrubs, allied to *Isopogon*, occurring on heathland, in woodland, and on cliffs, in rocky or sandy soil in Australia. The alternate leaves are linear to broadly triangular; simple, lobed, or pinnate or 2-pinnate; and rigidly leathery. They are cultivated for their unusual flowers, borne in dense spikes or cone-like clusters, surrounded by small bracts, from winter to spring. Each flower is tubular in bud, then splits open to the base into 4 rolled sepals, each with a stamen attached. When the flowers fade, the bracts enlarge and become woody, enclosing the seed pods. Where not hardy, grow in a well-ventilated cool greenhouse. In warmer climates, use in a shrub border.
• **CULTIVATION** Under glass, grow in a mix of equal parts soil-based potting mix, grit or perlite, and peat or coir, in full light. In growth, water moderately and apply a phosphate-free liquid fertilizer every month. Water sparingly in winter. Outdoors, grow in poor, neutral to acidic, well-drained, sandy or gritty soil that is low in phosphates and nitrates. Pruning group 1; may need restrictive pruning under glass.
• **PROPAGATION** Sow seed at 64°F (18°C) in spring. Take semi-ripe cuttings with bottom heat in summer.
• **PESTS AND DISEASES** Prone to *Phytophthora* root rot when grown in moist soil and high humidity.

P. linearis. Moderately bushy shrub with wiry stems bearing sickle-shaped, flat, thick, gray-green leaves, 1¼–3in (3–8cm) long, with rounded margins. In spring, produces terminal, ovoid heads, to 2in (5cm) long, of pink flowers, 1in (2.5cm) long; the flowers open to reveal swollen yellow stigmas that turn orange when mature. ↕ to 3ft (1m), ↔ to 32in (80cm). Western Australia. ❄ (min. 41–45°F/5–7°C)

▷ ***Petrophyton*** see *Petrophytum*

PETROPHYTUM

syn. PETROPHYTON
Rock spirea
ROSACEAE

Genus of 3 species of evergreen subshrubs, related to *Spiraea*, occurring in screes or rock crevices in the mountains of W. North America. They are grown for their short, dense, spike-like racemes of tiny, fluffy, cup-shaped flowers, each with 5 overlapping petals, produced in summer, and for their neat, compact habit. They form dense mats or mounds of short, prostrate, branching shoots with densely packed, entire, inversely lance-shaped to spoon-shaped, leathery, hairy leaves. Grow in crevices in a rock garden or scree planting, or in tufa, in a trough, or in an alpine house (where they often flower more prolifically).
• **CULTIVATION** Grow in poor to moderately fertile, sharply drained, preferably slightly alkaline soil in full sun. In an alpine house, grow in a mix of 1 part each loam and leaf mold and 2 parts grit.
• **PROPAGATION** Sow seed in containers in an open frame in autumn. Take semi-ripe cuttings in early summer. Remove offsets in spring,
• **PESTS AND DISEASES** Aphids and spider mites may be troublesome under glass.

Petrophytum hendersonii

P. caespitosum. Mat-forming subshrub with dense tufts of spoon-shaped, silky-hairy, bluish green leaves, to ½in (1.5cm) long. Tiny, cup-shaped, creamy white flowers, with prominent stamens, are produced in conical, spike-like racemes, to 4in (10cm) long, in summer. ↕2in (5cm), ↔ 12in (30cm). Rocky Mountains. Zone 7.
P. hendersonii ■ Dome-forming subshrub with branched stems bearing hairy, spoon-shaped, blue-green leaves, to ¾in (2cm) long. In summer, tiny, cup-shaped white flowers are borne in dense, conical, spike-like racemes, to 3in (8cm) long. ↕4in (10cm), ↔ 8in (20cm). N.W. US. Zone 7.

PETRORHAGIA

CARYOPHYLLACEAE

Genus of about 30 species of annuals and perennials, occurring in rocky and sandy habitats in S. and C. Europe. They produce wiry stems, swollen at the nodes, and bear linear to lance-shaped or oblong, sometimes keeled leaves. They are cultivated for their terminal panicles or cymes of 5-petaled, salverform, white, sometimes pink or yellow flowers, borne in summer. Grow in a sunny position on a bank, in a rock garden, or against a wall.
• **CULTIVATION** Grow in any poor to moderately fertile, well-drained soil in full sun.
• **PROPAGATION** Sow seed in containers in a cold frame in autumn. Take stem-tip cuttings in early summer.
• **PESTS AND DISEASES** May be damaged by slugs and snails.

P. saxifraga ■ syn. *Tunica saxifraga* (Tunic flower). Mat-forming perennial with linear, pointed, grass-like, rich green leaves, ½in (1.5cm) long. Bears delicate cymes of small, salverform, white or pink flowers, ½in (1.5cm) across, with darker veining, over long periods in summer. ↕4in (10cm), ↔ 8in (20cm). C. and S. Europe. Zone 5. **'Alba'** has white flowers. **'Alba Plena'** produces double white flowers. **'Lady Mary'** has double, soft pink flowers; ↕to 3in (8cm). **'Pleniflora Rosea'** produces double pink flowers. **'Rosea'** has light pink flowers. **'Rosette'** is more compact in habit, and bears double pink flowers; ↕3in (8cm), ↔ 6in (15cm).

Petrorhagia saxifraga

PETROSELINUM

Parsley

APIACEAE

Genus of 6 species of biennials, with thick rootstocks, occurring in fallow fields and on rocky slopes and waste ground in Mediterranean Europe. The solid, ridged stems bear triangular, pinnate to 3-pinnate, mid-green leaves with toothed leaflets. Terminal, compound umbels of tiny, star-shaped, white or greenish yellow flowers, sometimes tinged red, are produced in the second year, followed by small, ovoid fruits. *P. crispum* (parsley) is grown as a culinary flavoring or garnish, and is widely naturalized in temperate regions; many cultivars are available. Parsley is usually grown as an annual, because the leaves become coarser in the second year. The tuberous-rooted Hamburg parsley (*P. crispum* var. *tuberosum*) is used as a root vegetable. Grow as an edging for herb, vegetable, or flower gardens, where the frilly, bright green leaves make an attractive groundcover.
• **CULTIVATION** Grow in fertile, moist but well-drained soil in full sun or partial shade. For best culinary yield, overwinter in a cold greenhouse or provide cloche protection.
• **PROPAGATION** Sow seed *in situ* from spring to late summer, and keep well watered until germinated. (Germination is often slow and erratic.) Where marginally hardy, protect late sowings with cloches or a dry mulch.
• **PESTS AND DISEASES** Stem rot, damping off, and leaf spots can be problems. Carrot fly and celery fly larvae attack plants and may transmit viruses. Parsley is a favorite food of black swallowtail larvae.

Petroselinum crispum 'Afro'

P. crispum (Parsley). Hairless, clump-forming biennial producing triangular, 3-pinnate, shiny, bright green leaves, divided into ovate, toothed segments, each to 1¼in (3cm) long. In summer of the second year, bears tiny, star-shaped, yellow-green flowers in flat-topped, terminal umbels, ½–1½in (1.5–4cm) across. ↕32in (80cm), ↔ 24in (60cm). S. Europe. Zone 4. **'Afro'** ■ is upright, with tightly curled, dark green leaves. **'Champion Moss Curled'** has finely cut, curled, dark green leaves. **'Clivi'** is a compact, dwarf cultivar with dark green leaves; ↕8in (20cm), ↔ 12in (30cm). **'Crispum'** is strongly flavored, with crinkly leaves. **'Dark'** has closely curled, very dark green leaves, and is very tolerant of cold. **'Italian Plain Leaf'** has deeply cut, flat, dark green leaves. **var. *neapolitanum*** (French parsley, Italian parsley) has leaves with flat segments, and a stronger flavor. **'New Dark Green'** is very compact and produces bright, emerald-green leaves. **'Paramount'** is vigorous and bears dense, tightly curled, very dark green leaves. **var. *tuberosum*** (Hamburg parsley) has enlarged, edible roots; ↕to 14in (35cm), ↔ 12in (30cm).

PETTERIA

FABACEAE

Genus of one species of deciduous shrub, related to *Laburnum*, occurring in mountain scrub in the Balkans. It is grown for its dense, erect, terminal racemes of fragrant, yellow, pea-like flowers, produced in late spring and summer. *P. ramentacea* has long-stalked, 3-palmate leaves, arranged alternately. Grow in a mixed or shrub border. The seeds may cause stomach upset if ingested.
• **CULTIVATION** Grow in well-drained, fertile soil in full sun. Pruning group 1.
• **PROPAGATION** Sow seed in containers outdoors in autumn. Take greenwood cuttings in early summer.
• **PESTS AND DISEASES** Infrequent.

P. ramentacea (Dalmatian laburnum). Upright shrub with 3-palmate, dark green leaves, to 3½in (9cm) long, light green beneath, consisting of elliptic to rounded leaflets. Fragrant yellow flowers, to ¾in (2cm) long, are borne in dense, upright racemes, to 3in (8cm) long, in late spring and early summer. ↕6ft (2m), ↔ 3ft (1m). Balkans. Zone 7.

PETUNIA

SOLANACEAE

Genus of about 40 species of spreading to erect, branching, sticky-hairy annuals and perennials from stony slopes, steppes, and disturbed ground in South America. Simple, ovate to lance-shaped, mid- to dark green leaves are mostly alternate; upper leaves may be opposite. Showy, solitary, 5-lobed, fluted, single or double, saucer- or trumpet-shaped flowers are borne in the upper leaf axils.

Many cultivars have been produced, derived primarily from *P. axillaris*, *P. integrifolia*, and *P. violacea*. Although perennials, they are grown as annuals, and are particularly useful in coastal gardens or in poor soil. The flowers, 1¼–5in (3–13cm) across, are borne from late spring to late autumn, in a variety of colors, mainly pink, red, pale yellow, violet-blue, or white. Some have dark veining, central white stars, halos (throats in contrasting colors), or picotee margins. Leaves are usually 2–5in (5–13cm) long.

The cultivars are divided into two groups. **Grandiflora** petunias have very large flowers, generally to 4in (10cm) across. Many are susceptible to rain damage and, where rain is frequent, are best grown in sheltered hanging baskets and containers. **Multiflora** petunias are bushier than Grandiflora petunias, with smaller flowers, to 2in (5cm) across, produced in greater quantity. They are usually more tolerant of wet weather, and are ideal for summer bedding or in a mixed border; individual plants may carpet an area up to 3ft (1m) across.

New *Petunia* cultivars are developed and introduced regularly, often rendering existing cultivars obsolete.
• **HARDINESS** Petunias will withstand several light frosts and may live through the winter in the mildest parts of Zone 8.
• **CULTIVATION** Under glass, grow in soil-based potting mix in full light. When in growth, water freely and apply

Petunia Carpet Series

Petunia 'Purple Wave'

a high-potassium fertilizer every 2 weeks. Outdoors, grow in light, well-drained soil in full sun, with shelter from wind. Deadhead to prolong flowering.
• **Propagation** Sow seed at 55–64°F (13–18°C) about 10–12 weeks before plants are to be set outdoors. Take softwood cuttings in spring or summer; where not hardy, overwinter young plants under glass.
• **Pests and diseases** Aphids, caterpillars, leaf miners, gray mold, bacterial soft rot, a variety of leaf spots, cucumber mosaic virus, and impatiens necrotic spot virus cause problems.

***P.* 'Blue Danube'.** Compact and free-flowering Grandiflora petunia, bearing fully double lavender-blue flowers, 2½in (6cm) across, with darker blue veins. ↕ 10–12in (25–30cm), ↔ 12–36in (30–90cm).
***P.* Carpet Series** ■ Very compact and spreading Multiflora petunias, bearing flowers in a color range that includes strong reds and oranges. Ideal for groundcover. ↕ 8–10in (20–25cm), ↔ 12–36in (30–90cm).
***P.* Celebrity Series.** Compact and mounded Multiflora petunias, bearing flowers, 2½–3in (6–8cm) across, in a wide range of colors. ↕ 9–12in (20–30cm), ↔ 12–36in (30–90cm).
***P.* Cloud Series.** Grandiflora petunias producing very large flowers, 4–5in (10–13cm) across, in a wide range of colors. Excellent in hanging baskets and containers. ↕ 9–12in (23–30cm), ↔ 12–36in (30–90cm).
***P.* Daddy Series.** Early-flowering Grandiflora petunias bearing large, heavily veined flowers in pastel to deep pink, salmon-pink, purple, or lavender-blue. ↕ to 14in (35cm), ↔ 12–36in (30–90cm). **'Sugar Daddy'** ■ has purple flowers with dark veins.
***P.* Duo Series.** Multiflora petunias with double flowers in a color range that includes pink, lavender-pink, red, and burgundy, some with dark veining and some bicolors. Tolerant of wet weather, but best with some protection. ↕ to 12in (30cm), ↔ 12–36in (30–90cm). **'Peppermint'** ■ has pink flowers with darker rose-pink veining.
***P.* Flash Series.** Compact, early-flowering Grandiflora petunias in a range of colors, including rose-pink, salmon-pink, coral-pink, scarlet, red, sky-blue, blue, and white, all with creamy yellow throats; bicolors are also available. ↕ 9–16in (23–40cm), ↔ 12–36in (30–90cm).
***P.* 'Fluffy Ruffles'.** Grandiflora petunia bearing large, ruffled flowers, 6in (15cm) across, often tricolored in shades of rose, violet, and white, with contrasting veining and throats. ↕ 18in (45cm), ↔ 12–36in (30–90cm).
***P.* Horizon Series.** Multiflora petunias with flowers in a range of colors, including white, blue, salmon-pink, and red, as well as halo cultivars, which have throats in white or shades of red or pink. ↕ 10–14in (25–35cm), ↔ 12–36in (30–90cm). **'Horizon Red Halo'** ■ has red flowers with white throats.
***P.* Hula Hoop Series.** Early-flowering Grandiflora petunias with blooms in blue, purple, red, or rose-pink, all with broad, ruffled white margins; also available as a mixture. ↕ 12in (30cm), ↔ 14in (35cm).
P. integrifolia (Violet-flowered petunia). Spreading, branched annual or short-lived shrub with elliptic to lance-shaped mid-green leaves, to 2in (5cm) long. From spring to frost, bears solitary, axillary flowers, to 1½in (4cm) across, dark violet inside and violet to rose-red outside. ↕ to 24in (60cm), ↔ 24–36in (60–90cm). Argentina. ❀ (min. 35°F/2°C)
***P.* Merlin Series.** Very compact Multiflora petunias, remaining dwarf throughout the season, with flowers mainly in red, rose-pink, or blue, with some picotees. ↕ 8–10in (20–25cm), ↔ 12–36in (30–90cm).
***P.* Mirage Series.** Multiflora petunias producing large flowers, to 3in (8cm) across, in white or shades of blue, pink, red, or purple, some with darker veining or with central stars. Good wet-weather tolerance. ↕ to 12in (30cm), ↔ 12–36in (30–90cm). **'Mirage Lavender'** ■ has deep lavender-blue flowers.
***P.* Picotee Series.** Grandiflora petunias bearing flowers in rich blue, purple, red, or rose-pink, all with broad, ruffled white margins. ↕ 9–16in (23–40cm), ↔ 1–3ft (30–90cm). **'Picotee Rose'** ■ is compact, with deep rose-pink, white-margined flowers; ↕ to 8in (20cm), ↔ 18in (45cm).
***P.* Plum Series.** Dwarf, mound-forming Multiflora petunias bearing flowers 2½in (6cm) across, in pink, deep red, purple, blue, and yellow, with prominent veining. Very wet-weather-tolerant. ↕ 9–12in (23–30cm), ↔ 12–36in (30–90cm).
***P.* Polo Series.** Compact Multiflora petunias with flowers in a range of plain, strong colors, some with veining and some bicolors. Extremely tolerant of wet weather. ↕ to 10in (25cm), ↔ 12–36in (30–90cm).
***P.* 'Purple Wave'** ■ Multiflora petunia with a vigorous, spreading habit and vibrant magenta flowers. Use as a groundcover or in hanging baskets. ↕ 18in (45cm), ↔ 12–36in (30–90cm).
***P.* Razzle Dazzle Series.** Grandiflora petunias producing bicolor flowers of white, mixed with shades of red, rose, and deep blue. ↕ 12in (30cm), ↔ 12–36in (30–90cm).

Petunia Daddy Series 'Sugar Daddy'

Petunia Duo Series 'Peppermint'

Petunia Horizon Series 'Horizon Red Halo'

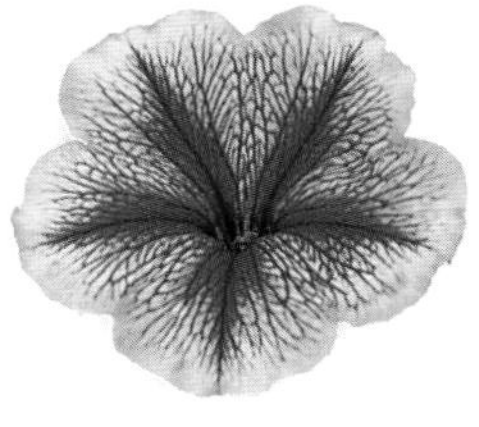
Petunia Mirage Series 'Mirage Lavender'

Petunia Picotee Series 'Picotee Rose'

Petunia Ultra Series 'Rose Star'

***P.* 'Sonata'.** Grandiflora petunia producing huge, deeply fringed, fully double, pure white flowers. ↕ 14in (35cm), ↔ 12–36in (30–90cm).
***P.* 'Summer Sun'.** Mound-forming, Multiflora petunia with deep green leaves. Bears golden yellow flowers, to 2½in (6cm) across, lightening to canary-yellow in warmer temperatures. ↕ 10in (25cm), ↔ 12–36in (30–90cm).
***P.* Supercascade Series.** Grandiflora petunias, very free-flowering over a long period, producing huge flowers, to 5in (13cm) across, in white and blue, lilac-pink, rose-pink, salmon-pink, or deep red. ↕ to 12in (30cm), ↔ 12–36in (30–90cm).
***P.* Supertunia Group.** Robust, free-flowering, cutting-propagated petunias resulting from crosses between various cultivars and *P. integrifolia*. Produce flowers 2–3in (5–8cm) across, in white, rose-magenta, and shades of purple. Excellent for a hanging basket. Weather tolerant. ↕ 8in (20cm), ↔ 30in (75cm).
***P.* Ultra Series.** Compact but spreading, early-flowering Grandiflora petunias, with good wet-weather tolerance. They bear large flowers in a range of colors, including white and shades of blue, pink, and red, some with central stars. ↕ 10–12in (25–30cm), ↔ 12–36in (30–90cm). **'Rose Star'** ■ produces rose-pink flowers, each with a broad, white central star, creating a striped effect.
***P.* 'Valentine'.** Grandiflora petunia with ruffled, fringed, fully double, deep red flowers, 3in (8cm) across. ↕ 10–12in (25–30cm), ↔ 12–36in (30–90cm).

▷ ***Peucedanum graveolens*** see *Anethum graveolens*

PHACELIA

HYDROPHYLLACEAE

Genus of about 150 species of usually erect annuals, biennials, and perennials from variable habitats, including stony slopes, scrub, and woodland, in North and South America. The usually pinnate, sometimes simple leaves are broadly ovate to elliptic or linear, and mostly alternate, the lower ones sometimes opposite. They produce terminal cymes, racemes, or panicles of tubular, bell-shaped, or bowl-shaped, blue, violet, white, or yellow flowers, each with 5 narrow, spreading lobes, and with prominent styles and stamens. The annual species are suitable for a border or a wildlife garden; their nectar-rich flowers attract bees and other insects. Grow *P. sericea* in an alpine house or scree bed; it resents winter moisture. Contact with foliage may aggravate skin allergies.
• **Cultivation** Grow annuals in any fertile, well-drained soil in full sun. Outdoors, grow *P. sericea* in gritty, sharply drained soil in full sun. Protect from winter moisture. In an alpine house, grow in a mix of equal parts loam, leaf mold, and grit.
• **Propagation** Sow seed of annuals *in situ* in spring or early autumn. Sow seed of *P. sericea* in containers in a cold frame in autumn.
• **Pests and diseases** Downy mildew, powdery mildew, rust, and leaf spot can be problems. Aphids and spider mites are sometimes serious under glass.

Phacelia campanularia

P. campanularia ▣ (California bluebell). Erect, compact, intricately branched, glandular-hairy, aromatic annual with simple, ovate to elliptic, coarsely toothed, dark green leaves, to 2in (5cm) long. Lax cymes of upturned, spreading, bell-shaped, dark blue, occasionally white flowers, to 1in (2.5cm) across, are borne in late spring and summer. ↕ 6–12in (15–30cm), ↔ 6in (15cm). S. California.
P. grandiflora. Vigorous, erect, glandular-hairy annual with simple, broadly ovate to elliptic, irregularly toothed, mid-green leaves, to 8in (20cm) long. Produces erect, densely flowered cymes of upturned, spreading, bell-shaped, lilac-blue or white flowers, to ¾in (2cm) across, in summer. ↕ to 36in (90cm), ↔ to 12in (30cm). S. California.
P. sericea. Rosette-forming biennial or short-lived perennial with silvery, silky-hairy, deeply pinnatifid leaves, to 4in (10cm) long, with oblong-lance-shaped lobes. In summer, produces short, dense, panicle-like cymes of bell-shaped, indigo-blue flowers, ¼–⅜in (6–8mm) across, with pale blue anthers and protruding stamens. ↕ to 22in (55cm), ↔ 4in (10cm). Rocky Mountains. Zone 4.
P. tanacetifolia (Fiddleneck). Erect, hairy annual, with pinnatifid to 2-pinnatifid or pinnate, mid-green leaves, to 10in (25cm) long, composed of lance-shaped lobes or pinnae. Dense, curved racemes of spreading, bell-shaped, blue or lavender-blue flowers, to ½in (1.5cm) across, are produced in summer. ↕ to 4ft (1.2m), ↔ to 18in (45cm). California to Mexico.

PHAEDRANASSA

Queen lily

AMARYLLIDACEAE

Genus of about 6 species of bulbous perennials from meadows and rocky slopes at high altitudes in South America. They are grown for their colorful, tubular or narrowly funnel-shaped, pendent flowers with anthers protruding from the rims, borne in terminal umbels of 3–11, from spring to summer. The leaves are basal, lance-shaped to elliptic, and up to 16in (40cm) long, developing with or after the flowers. Where not hardy, grow in a cool or temperate greenhouse. In warmer climates, grow in a warm, sunny position in a border.

Phaedranassa carmioli

• **CULTIVATION** Under glass, grow in soil-based potting mix with added sharp sand and leaf mold, in full light. During the growing season, water moderately and apply a balanced liquid fertilizer every month. Keep just moist when dormant in autumn and winter. Outdoors, grow in moderately fertile, well-drained soil that does not dry out in summer. They withstand temperatures to 32°F (0°C) for short periods.
• **PROPAGATION** Sow seed at 55–64°F (13–18°C) when ripe. Remove offsets in autumn.
• **PESTS AND DISEASES** Infrequent.

P. carmioli ▣ Bulbous perennial producing erect, lance-shaped, mid-green, basal leaves, to 16in (40cm) long, developing with the flowers. From spring to summer, bears umbels of 4–10 pendent, tubular, shiny crimson flowers, 1½–1¾in (3.5–4.5cm) long, with green and yellow tips, and with conspicuous, protruding white anthers. ↕ 20–28in (50–70cm), ↔ 3in (8cm). South America. ❀ (min. 45°F/7°C)
P. dubia. Bulbous perennial producing erect, elliptic, mid-green, basal leaves, to 20in (50cm) long, with the flowers. In summer, produces umbels of 7–9 pendent, tubular, green-tipped, purple-pink flowers, 1¾–2in (4.5–5cm) long, with protruding stamens. ↕ 20–28in (50–70cm), ↔ 3in (8cm). Peru. ❀ (min. 45°F/7°C)
P. tunguraguae. Bulbous perennial with ovoid bulbs and erect, lance-shaped or inversely lance-shaped, glossy, dark green, basal leaves, 12–16in (30–40cm) long, developing after the flowers. Bears umbels of 6–8 pendent, tubular, green-tipped, coral-red flowers, to 1¼in (3cm) long, in summer. ↕ 20–28in (50–70cm), ↔ 3in (8cm). Ecuador. ❀ (min. 45°F/7°C)
P. viridiflora. Bulbous perennial with erect, narrow, bright green, basal leaves, to 16in (40cm) long, appearing with the flowers. Umbels of 3–5 pendent, tubular, yellow and green flowers, 1in (2.5cm) long, are borne in summer. ↕ 24in (60cm), ↔ 3in (8cm). Ecuador, possibly Peru. ❀ (min. 45°F/7°C)

▷ ***Phaedranthus buccinatorius*** see *Distictis buccinatoria*
▷ ***Phaiophleps biflora*** see *Olsynium biflorum*
▷ ***Phaiophleps nigricans*** see *Sisyrinchium striatum*

PHAIUS

ORCHIDACEAE

Genus of about 30 species of deciduous to evergreen, terrestrial and epiphytic orchids from lowland and montane forest in Africa, Madagascar, Asia, Indonesia, N. Australia, and the Pacific islands. They have spherical to ovoid, sometimes stem-like pseudobulbs, each with 3–10 large, folded, lance-shaped to elliptic, mid-green leaves, arranged alternately. Colorful, often spectacular flowers, with entire or lobed lips and spreading petals, are produced in tall, upright, axillary, many-flowered racemes from near the bases of the plants.
• **CULTIVATION** Intermediate-growing orchids. Grow in terrestrial orchid potting mix in deep containers that allow room for the copious root system. In summer, provide high humidity and bright filtered light, and water freely, applying fertilizer at every third watering. Once the leaves are fully developed, mist twice daily. In winter, water sparingly and provide full light. See also p.46.
• **PROPAGATION** Divide when the plants overflow their containers.
• **PESTS AND DISEASES** Scale insects, spider mites, aphids, and mealybugs may be troublesome. Petal blight, bacterial soft rot, pseudobulb rots, cymbidium mosaic, and odontoglossum viruses can cause problems.

P. flavus, syn. *P. maculatus*. Semi-evergreen orchid with conical pseudobulbs and lance-shaped, mid-green leaves, to 24in (60cm) long, with yellow and white spots. Racemes of fragrant yellow flowers, 3in (8cm) across, with red-brown markings on the lips, are produced in spring. ↕ 3ft (1m), ↔ 24in (60cm). India, Thailand, Malaysia, Indonesia (Java). ❀ (min. 59°F/15°C; max. 86°F/30°C)
P. maculatus see *P. flavus*.
P. tankervilleae ▣ (Nun orchid). Semi-evergreen orchid with ovoid pseudobulbs and several elliptic to lance-shaped, pointed, mid-green leaves, to 3ft (1m) long. In summer, produces racemes of nodding, fragrant, red-brown flowers, 3in (8cm) across, with pink to purplish red lips; throats are yellow and purplish red inside, silvery outside. ↕↔ 3ft (1m). C. China, N. India, Sri Lanka through S.E. Asia to Australia. ❀ (min. 59°F/15°C; max. 86°F/30°C)

Phaius tankervilleae

PHALAENOPSIS

Moth orchid

ORCHIDACEAE

Genus of approximately 50 species of mostly evergreen, mainly epiphytic, monopodial orchids occurring from sea level to lowland forest in the Himalayas, S.E. Asia, and N. Australia. They each have a short, upward-growing, stem-like rhizome, lacking pseudobulbs and producing 3–6 broadly obovate or oval, upright or semi-pendent, fleshy, mid- to dark green, sometimes mottled leaves. Flowers, in simple or branched racemes, are produced from the bases of the leaves, often throughout the year, remaining in bloom for many months.
• **CULTIVATION** Warm-growing orchids. Grow epiphytically on slabs of bark, or in epiphytic orchid potting mix in a slatted basket to allow the aerial roots to hang outside. Provide high humidity and bright filtered light all year. From spring to autumn, water freely, mist daily, and apply a balanced fertilizer monthly. In winter, water sparingly, keeping the foliage dry. Support the racemes, and cut back flowered stems to a lower node to encourage production of further flowers. See also p.46.
• **PROPAGATION** Not suitable for division, although cuttings or offshoots may be rooted successfully. Some species produce plantlets on the flower spikes.
• **PESTS AND DISEASES** Petal blight, bacterial soft rot, pseudobulb rots, cymbidium mosaic, odontoglossum viruses, edema, and iron deficiency can cause problems.

Phalaenopsis Allegria

Phalaenopsis cornu-cervi

P

Phalaenopsis Doris

Phalaenopsis Lipperose

Phalaenopsis stuartiana

P. Allegria ▣ (*P.* Alice Gloria x *P.* Wilma Hughes). Epiphytic orchid with semi-pendent, broadly oval leaves, 12in (30cm) or more in length. Numerous large, rounded, heavy, pure white flowers, to 5in (13cm) across, are produced in pendent racemes, 3ft (1m) long, throughout the year. ↕ 3ft (1m), ↔ 18in (45cm). ❀ (min. 64°F/18°C; max. 86°F/30°C)
P. amabilis. Epiphytic orchid with semi-pendent, broadly oval leaves, 6–20in (15–50cm) long. Numerous white flowers, 2½–4in (6–10cm) across, with yellow-margined lips and red throat markings, are produced in pendent, simple or branched racemes, 3ft (1m) long, from autumn to early spring. ↕↔ 12in (30cm). Philippines, Indonesia to N.E. Queensland. ❀ (min. 64°F/18°C; max. 86°F/30°C)
P. cornu-cervi ▣ Epiphytic orchid with oblong-ovate leaves, to 10in (25cm) long. Star-shaped, fragrant, waxy, yellow-green flowers, 2in (5cm) across, overlaid with red-brown, are produced in succession throughout the year, in short, branched or simple racemes, 6in (15cm) long. ↕ 6in (15cm), ↔ 8in (20cm). Burma, S.E. Asia. ❀ (min. 64°F/18°C; max. 86°F/30°C)
P. Doris ▣ (*P.* Elizabethae x *P.* Katherine Siegwart). Epiphytic orchid with semi-pendent, broadly oval, gray-green leaves, 12in (30cm) long. Pink-washed and lined flowers, 3in (8cm) across are produced in arching racemes, 3ft (1m) long, throughout the year. The flowers have purple-red lips marked yellow-orange. ↕↔ 12in (30cm). ❀ (min. 64°F/18°C; max. 86°F/30°C)

P. equestris. Epiphytic orchid with oblong-ovate leaves, to 8in (20cm) long. From spring to winter, bears simple or branched, erect to arching racemes, 14in (35cm) long, of small, rose-pink flowers, ¾in (2cm) across, with deep pink or purple lips, streaked dark red. ↕↔ 8in (20cm). Philippines, Taiwan. ❀ (min. 64°F/18°C; max. 86°F/30°C)
P. Esmé Hennessy (*P.* Anna Queen x *P.* Pekoe). Vigorous epiphytic orchid with semi-pendent, broadly oval leaves, 12in (30cm) or more long. White flowers, 3in (8cm) across, with faint yellow markings and crimson lips, appear in pendent racemes, 3ft (1m) long, mainly in winter. ↕↔ 12in (30cm). ❀ (min. 64°F/18°C; max. 86°F/30°C)
P. Golden Horizon 'Sunrise' ▣ (*P.* Barbara Freed Saltzman x *P.* Golden Buddha). Epiphytic orchid with broadly oval leaves, to 10in (25cm) long. Fleshy, creamy yellow flowers, 2½in (6cm) across, with red-brown stripes and orange-red lips, are borne throughout the year in short racemes, 6in (15cm) long. ↕ 6in (15cm), ↔ 12in (30cm). ❀ (min. 64°F/18°C; max. 86°F/30°C)
P. Henriette Lecoufle 'Boule de Neige' (*P.* Lachésis x *P.* Ramona). Epiphytic orchid with semi-pendent, broadly oval leaves, 12in (30cm) long. Produces large, pure white flowers, 4–5in (10–13cm) across, in pendent racemes, 3ft (1m), long, mainly in winter. ↕ 3ft (1m), ↔ 12in (30cm). ❀ (min. 64°F/18°C; max. 86°F/30°C)
P. Lipperose ▣ (*P.* Ruby Wells x *P.* Zada). Epiphytic orchid with semi-pendent, broadly oval leaves, 12in (30cm) long. Pink flowers, 4in (10cm) across, with red lips, are produced throughout the year in many-flowered, pendent racemes, 3ft (1m) long. ↕ 3ft (1m), ↔ 12in (30cm). ❀ (min. 64°F/18°C; max. 86°F/30°C)
P. lueddemanniana. Epiphytic orchid with oblong-ovate leaves, to 12in (30cm) long. In summer, full, rounded, fragrant, waxy white flowers, 2in (5cm) across, with red-purple bands and pink to purple lips, are produced in succession in short, simple or branched racemes, 6in (15cm) long. ↕ 6in (15cm), ↔ 8in (20cm). Philippines. ❀ (min. 64°F/18°C; max. 86°F/30°C)
P. schilleriana ▣ Epiphytic orchid with semi-pendent, broadly elliptic, fleshy leaves, to 18in (45cm) long, dark green spotted with silver-gray above, purple beneath. Numerous rose-pink flowers, 2in (5cm) or more across, with white or yellow lips spotted reddish purple, appear in branching racemes, 3ft (1m) long, in winter and spring. ↕ 24in (60cm), ↔ 12in (30cm). Philippines. ❀ (min. 64°F/18°C; max. 86°F/30°C)
P. stuartiana ▣ Epiphytic orchid with semi-pendent, broadly oval, mid-green leaves, 14in (35cm) long, mottled gray-green above, purple beneath. In winter, bears branching racemes, 3ft (1m) long, of white flowers, 3in (8cm) across, with yellow marks and brownish red spots on the lower sepals and lips. ↕ 24in (60cm), ↔ 12in (30cm). Philippines. ❀ (min. 64°F/18°C; max. 86°F/30°C)
P. violacea. Epiphytic orchid with broadly oblong leaves, 8–10in (20–25cm) long. In spring and summer, star-shaped, fragrant, waxy, rich violet-purple, yellow, and white flowers, 2½in (6cm) across, with reddish purple lips, are borne in succession in short racemes, 6in (15cm) long. ↕ 6in (15cm), ↔ 12in (30cm). Malaysia, Indonesia (Sumatra), Borneo. ❀ (min. 64°F/18°C; max. 86°F/30°C)
P. Yukimai ▣ (*P.* Grace Palm x *P.* Musashino). Epiphytic orchid with broadly oval leaves, 8in (20cm) long. White flowers, 3in (8cm) across, with yellow-tinted, sometimes purple-red lips, appear in racemes 12in (30cm) long, throughout the year. ↕↔ 12in (30cm). ❀ (min. 64°F/18°C; max. 86°F/30°C)

Phalaenopsis Golden Horizon 'Sunrise'

Phalaenopsis schilleriana

Phalaenopsis Yukimai

PHALARIS

POACEAE

Genus of about 15 species of tufted, annual grasses or spreading rhizomatous, perennial grasses found in extremely variable habitats in temperate regions, from dry slopes to moist lake margins. They produce compact panicles of ovate spikelets, each with 1–3 flowers. Leaves are pale to mid-green, usually broadly linear and flat, with short points. *P. arundinacea* and its cultivars need to be contained if grown in a mixed or herbaceous border, but are good as a groundcover, or planted at the side of a pond or stream.
• **CULTIVATION** Grow in any soil in full sun or partial shade. Cut back dead foliage in early spring. On variegated cultivars, which may otherwise revert to plain green after midsummer, cut back in early summer to encourage fresh growth. Color is best in cooler weather.
• **PROPAGATION** Divide from midspring to midsummer.
• **PESTS AND DISEASES** Ergot, rust, smut, brown patch, and a variety of leaf spots may occur.

P. arundinacea (Reed canary grass, Ribbon grass). Erect, evergreen, rhizomatous, perennial grass with flat, linear, short-pointed, mid-green leaves, to 14in (35cm) long, occasionally striped yellow. In early and midsummer, bears narrow panicles, to 7in (18cm) long, of pale green spikelets, fading to buff with age. ↕ to 5ft (1.5m) in flower, ↔ indefinite. Eurasia, Southern Africa, North America. Zone 3b. **'Feesey'**, syn. 'Mervyn Feesey', is flushed pink at the stem bases, and has light green leaves with broad white stripes, and panicles with a faint purplish flush; less invasive than the species. **'Mervyn Feesey'** see 'Feesey'. **var. *picta*** (Gardeners' garters) has a number of variants with white-striped leaves; it is a notorious spreader and very difficult to eradicate once established; ↕ to 3ft (1m).

▷ ***Phanerophlebia*** see *Cyrtomium*
▷ ***Pharbitis*** see *Ipomoea*
▷ ***Phaseolus caracalla*** see *Vigna caracalla*

PHEBALIUM

RUTACEAE

Genus of 45 species of evergreen trees and shrubs occurring in woodland or open, moist and dry habitats in Australia and New Zealand. They are grown for their foliage and flowers. The simple, alternate, often aromatic, light to dark green leaves are linear to rounded or oblong, sometimes cylindrical. Small,

tubular, star- or bell-shaped, 4- or 5-petaled flowers are usually borne singly or in axillary and terminal, umbel-like clusters. Where temperatures regularly fall below 41°F (5°C), grow in a cool greenhouse. In milder climates, grow at the back of a border, or use as a hedge.
• **CULTIVATION** Under glass, grow in acidic potting mix in full light. During growth, water moderately and apply a balanced liquid fertilizer monthly. Water sparingly in winter. Outdoors, grow in neutral to slightly acidic, moderately fertile, humus-rich, moist but well-drained soil in full sun. Pruning group 1; may need restrictive pruning under glass, after flowering.
• **PROPAGATION** Sow seed at 55–64°F (13–18°C) in spring. Root semi-ripe cuttings with bottom heat in summer.
• **PESTS AND DISEASES** Infrequent.

P. squameum (Bobie-bobie, Satinwood). Large shrub or small tree, erect and lightly to moderately branched if unpruned. Elliptic to oblong-lance-shaped, leathery leaves, 1¼–4in (3–10cm) long, are mid- to deep green above, silver-white scaly with translucent oil glands beneath. In spring or early summer, bears umbel-like clusters of star-shaped white flowers, ⅜–½in (9–15mm) across, with prominent stamens. ↕ 10–20ft (3–6m), ↔ 5–10ft (1.5–3m). Queensland to Tasmania. ❀ (min. 41°F/5°C)

PHEGOPTERIS

Beech fern

THELYPTERIDACEAE

Genus, often considered synonymous in part with *Thelypteris*, of 3 or 4 species of deciduous, terrestrial ferns found on shady banks and rocks in high rainfall areas throughout the N. hemisphere and in S.E. Asia. The pinnate to 2-pinnate or pinnatifid fronds, with pinnatifid or pinnatisect pinnae, arise at random from each erect to creeping rhizome, the fronds turning at right angles to the light. Round sori, without protective indusia, are produced in 2 rows on the undersides of the frond segments. Beech ferns are ideal for growing in a moist, shady border, or among rocks where the soil does not dry out.
• **CULTIVATION** Grow in moderately fertile, humus-rich, reliably moist soil, preferably in deep shade.
• **PROPAGATION** Sow spores at 59°F (15°C) as soon as ripe. Divide in spring. See also p.51.
• **PESTS AND DISEASES** Infrequent.

P. connectilis ▣ syn. *Thelypteris phegopteris* (Narrow beech fern). Deciduous fern bearing long-stalked, arrow-shaped to triangular, pinnate, pale green fronds, 12in (30cm) long, with oblong or linear to lance-shaped, deeply pinnatifid pinnae, composed of oblong segments. The lowest pair of pinnae points forward and downward. ↕ 12in (30cm), ↔ indeterminate. N. hemisphere. Zone 4.
P. decursive-pinnata, syn. *Thelypteris decursive-pinnata*. Deciduous fern producing tufts of narrowly lance-shaped, pinnate or 2-pinnatifid, pale green fronds, to 32in (80cm) long, each tapering gradually to a stalk up to 8in (20cm) long. Pinnae are entire and

Phegopteris connectilis

linear, occasionally pinnatifid. ↕ 32in (80cm), ↔ 16in (40cm). E. Asia. Zone 7b.
P. hexagonoptera, syn. *Thelypteris hexagonoptera* (Broad beech fern). Deciduous fern with long-stalked, triangular, pinnate-pinnatifid fronds, 16in (40cm) long. Similar to *P. connectilis*, but fronds and pinnae are broader, and the lowest pair of pinnae does not point forward or downward. ↕ 16in (40cm), ↔ indeterminate. E. North America. Zone 3b.

PHELLODENDRON

Cork tree

RUTACEAE

Genus of 10 species of deciduous, dioecious trees found in moist stream margins in the mountains of E. Asia. They have opposite, pinnate, dull yellowish green to dark green leaves. Small, cup-shaped green male and female flowers are borne in clusters on separate plants in summer, and both must be grown to produce the dark blue-black, spherical, aromatic fruits, ½in (1.5cm) across. Grown for their habit; deeply furrowed, attractive bark; and aromatic foliage, usually giving fine autumn color; they are best used as specimen trees in a garden large enough to accommodate their spreading habit.
• **CULTIVATION** Grow in deep, fertile, well-drained soil in full sun. Pruning group 1.
• **PROPAGATION** Sow seed in containers outdoors in autumn. Root heeled semi-ripe cuttings in midsummer.
• **PESTS AND DISEASES** Infrequent.

P. amurense ▣ (Amur cork tree). Spreading tree with thick shoots, and with thick, corky, pale gray-brown bark when mature. Bears pinnate leaves, to 14in (35cm) long, with up to 13 ovate to lance-shaped, glossy, dark green leaflets, glaucous beneath, turning yellow in autumn. ↕ to 46ft (14m), ↔ 50ft (15m). N.E. Asia. Zone 3.

Phellodendron amurense

P. chinense (Chinese cork tree). Spreading tree with thick shoots and thin, dark gray-brown bark. Bears pinnate leaves, to 16in (40cm) long, with up to 13 oblong to lance-shaped leaflets, yellow-green above, light green and downy beneath, turning yellow in autumn. ↕ 30ft (10m), ↔ 40ft (12m). C. China. Zone 6.
P. lavallei (Lavalle's cork tree). Spreading tree with thick shoots and slightly corky, pale gray-brown bark when mature. Bears pinnate leaves, to 14in (35cm) long, with up to 11 oval to lance-shaped, tapered, matte, mid-green leaflets, downy on the veins beneath, turning yellow in autumn. ↕ 30ft (10m), ↔ 40ft (12m). Japan. Zone 3.
P. sachalinense (Sakhalin cork tree). Spreading tree with thick shoots and thin, finely channeled, dark brown bark. Pinnate leaves, to 12in (30cm) long, with up to 13 ovate-oblong leaflets, are dull green above, smooth and blue-green beneath, turning yellow in autumn. ↕ 30ft (10m), ↔ 40ft (12m). Russia (Sakhalin), Korea, Japan. Zone 3.

PHILADELPHUS

Mock orange

HYDRANGEACEAE

Genus of about 40 species of mainly deciduous shrubs found in scrub and on rocky hillsides from E. Europe to the Himalayas, E. Asia, and North and Central America. They are cultivated for their usually fragrant, 4-petaled, cup- or bowl-shaped, sometimes cross-shaped, single, semi-double, or double flowers, produced singly or in racemes, panicles, or cymes. The leaves are simple, mostly ovate, and usually mid-green, arranged in opposite pairs. Grow in a shrub border, or as specimen plants in a woodland garden; larger species and cultivars may be used for screening. Grow *P. mexicanus* against a wall; where not hardy, grow in a cool greenhouse.
• **CULTIVATION** Grow in any moderately fertile, well-drained soil in full sun or

Philadelphus 'Beauclerk'

partial shade. *P. microphyllus* needs full sun. Under glass, grow in soil-based potting mix in full light or bright filtered light. During the growing season, water freely and apply a balanced liquid fertilizer monthly. Keep just moist in winter. Pruning group 2.
• **PROPAGATION** Take softwood cuttings in summer, or hardwood cuttings in autumn or winter.
• **PESTS AND DISEASES** Scale insects, rust, gray mold (*Botrytis*), powdery mildew, and fungal spots are common.

***P.* 'Avalanche'.** Upright, spreading, deciduous shrub with arching branches and elliptic, entire leaves, to 1in (2.5cm) long. Racemes of up to 7 single, cup-shaped, fragrant white flowers, 1in (2.5cm) across, are borne profusely in mid- and late summer. ↕ to 5ft (1.5m), ↔ 10ft (3m). Zone 4.
***P.* 'Beauclerk'** ▣ Slightly arching, deciduous shrub with broadly ovate, toothed leaves, to 2½in (6cm) long. Large, single, cup-shaped white flowers, 2in (5cm) across, with slightly pink-flushed centers, are borne singly or in racemes of 3–5, in early and mid-summer. ↕↔ 8ft (2.5m). Zone 3.
***P.* 'Belle Etoile'.** Arching, deciduous shrub with narrowly ovate, tapered, entire leaves, to 3½in (9cm) long. Single, cup-shaped, very fragrant white flowers, 2in (5cm) across, marked pale purple in the centers, are freely borne singly or in 3- to 5-flowered racemes, in late spring and early summer. ↕ 4ft (1.2m), ↔ 8ft (2.5m). Zone 5.
***P.* 'Boule d'Argent'** ▣ Arching, compact, bushy, deciduous shrub with

Philadelphus 'Boule d'Argent'

P

Philadelphus 'Buckley's Quill' (inset: flower detail)

roadly ovate, entire, dark green leaves, o 2½in (6cm) long. In early and mid-ummer, slightly fragrant, semi-double o double, milk-white flowers, 1¾in 4.5cm) across, are profusely borne n racemes of 5–7. ↕↔ 5ft (1.5m). Zone 4.
P. 'Bouquet Blanc'. Upright, deciduous hrub with ovate, nearly entire leaves, to in (5cm) long. Semi-double to double, ragrant white flowers, 1in (2.5cm) cross, are borne singly, in pairs, or in acemes of 3–5, in early or midsummer. 6ft (2m), ↔ 5ft (1.5m). Zone 4.
P. 'Buckley's Quill' ■ Upright, eciduous shrub with ovate, entire, dark reen leaves, to 3in (8cm) long. Double, ragrant white flowers, 1in (2.5cm) cross, each with about 30 quill-like etals, are produced singly or in racemes f 3–5, in early or midsummer. ↕ 6ft 2m), ↔ 4ft (1.2m). Zone 4.
P. 'Burfordensis' ■ Vigorous, upright, eciduous shrub with ovate, toothed, ark green leaves, to 4½in (11cm) long. arge, single, cup-shaped, slightly ragrant white flowers, to 3in (8cm) cross, are profusely borne in racemes f 5–9, in early and midsummer. ↕ 10ft 3m), ↔ 6ft (2m). Zone 5.

Philadelphus 'Burfordensis'

P. coronarius (Mock orange). Broadly upright, deciduous shrub with ovate, shallowly toothed leaves, to 4in (10cm) long. Short, terminal racemes of 5–9 cup-shaped, single, very fragrant, creamy white flowers, 1in (2.5cm) across, are produced in early summer. ↕ 10ft (3m), ↔ 8ft (2.5m). S. Europe, Caucasus. Zone 3. **'Aureus'** produces golden yellow leaves, turning yellow-green in summer; ↕ 8ft (2.5m), ↔ 5ft (1.5m). **'Variegatus'** ■ has leaves with broad white margins, and white flowers; ↕ 8ft (2.5m), ↔ 6ft (2m).
P. 'Dame Blanche' ■ Compact, arching, bushy, deciduous shrub with peeling, dark blackish brown bark and ovate, entire, dark green leaves, to ¾in (2cm) long. Semi-double to nearly

Philadelphus coronarius 'Variegatus'

Philadelphus 'Dame Blanche'

double, fragrant, pure white flowers, to ¾in (2cm) across, are freely borne, usually in pairs or in 3- to 5-flowered racemes, in early or midsummer. ↕↔ 6ft (2m). Zone 4.
P. delavayi. Upright, deciduous shrub with arching branches and ovate, tapered, sometimes toothed, dark green leaves, to 4in (10cm) or more long. In early or midsummer, bears racemes of 5–9 single, cup-shaped, very fragrant, pure white flowers, 1½in (4cm) across, often purple-flushed on the backs of the sepals. ↕ 10ft (3m), ↔ 8ft (2.5m). W. China, S.E. Tibet, N. Burma. Zone 7. **f. *melanocalyx*** ■ syn. *P. purpurascens*, has white flowers with dark purple sepals.
P. 'Girandole'. Upright, deciduous shrub with ovate leaves, to 2in (5cm) long, nearly entire or each with 1–6 teeth on both margins. Dense, double, fragrant, creamy white flowers, to 1½in (4cm) across, are borne in racemes of up to 7, in early and midsummer. ↕↔ 5ft (1.5m). Zone 5.
P. 'Glacier'. Upright, deciduous shrub with small, ovate, toothed leaves, to 1½in (4cm) long. Dense racemes of up to 9 double, fragrant white flowers, 1in

Philadelphus delavayi f. *melanocalyx*

Philadelphus 'Lemoinei'

(2.5cm) across, are borne in mid-summer. ↕↔ 5ft (1.5m). Zone 4.
P. 'Innocence'. Upright, deciduous shrub with arching branches and ovate, entire leaves, to 2in (5cm) long, strongly mottled yellow. Single, or sometimes semi-double, cup-shaped, very fragrant white flowers, 1¼–1½in (3–4cm) across, usually in 3-flowered racemes, are produced in early or midsummer. ↕ 10ft (3m), ↔ 6ft (2m). Zone 4.
P. 'Lemoinei' ■ Upright, deciduous shrub with arching branches and ovate, tapered leaves, to 2in (5cm) long, each with 2 or 3 teeth on both margins. Small, single, cup-shaped, extremely fragrant, pure white flowers, 1in (2.5cm) across, are profusely borne in racemes of 3–5, in early or midsummer. ↕↔ 5ft (1.5m). Zone 5.
P. lewisii. Spreading, deciduous shrub with arching branches and ovate, sometimes finely toothed, bright green leaves, to 4in (10cm) long. Racemes of 5–11 unscented or slightly fragrant, single, cup-shaped, pure white flowers, 1½in (4cm) across, are profusely produced in early or midsummer. ↕↔ 10ft (3m). British Columbia to California. Zone 2b.
P. magdalenae. Spreading, bushy, deciduous shrub with ovate, short-pointed, entire leaves, to 2½in (6cm) long. Bears single, cup-shaped, slightly fragrant, pure white flowers, 1in (2.5cm) across, in racemes of up to 11, in late spring and early summer. ↕↔ 12ft (4m). W. China. Zone 7.
P. 'Manteau d'Hermine' ■ Bushy, compact, deciduous shrub with arching shoots and elliptic, pointed, entire, pale

Philadelphus 'Manteau d'Hermine'

to mid-green leaves, to 1in (2.5cm) long. Produces double, very fragrant, creamy white flowers, 1½in (4cm) across, usually in racemes of 3, in early and midsummer. ↕ 30in (75cm), ↔ 5ft (1.5m). Zone 4.
P. mexicanus. Spreading, evergreen shrub with pendent, bristly shoots and ovate, sometimes sparsely toothed leaves, to 4½in (11cm) long. Single, cup-shaped, strongly rose-scented, creamy white flowers, to 1½in (4cm) across, are borne singly or in racemes of 3, in summer. ↕↔ 6ft (2m) or more. Mexico, Guatemala. ❄ (min. 41°F/5°C). **'Rose Syringa'** has flowers with conspicuous purple-pink markings in the centers.
P. microphyllus ▣ Compact, upright, deciduous shrub with peeling, dark chestnut-brown bark and small, elliptic, entire, glossy, mid-green leaves, to ¾in (2cm) long. Solitary or paired, single, cross-shaped, very fragrant, pure white flowers, 1in (2.5cm) across, are borne in early and midsummer. ↕↔ 3ft (1m). S.W. US. Zone 4.
***P.* 'Mont Blanc'.** Upright, deciduous shrub with ovate, sparsely toothed leaves, to 1¼in (3cm) long. Single, cross-shaped, fragrant, pure white flowers, to 1in (2.5cm) across, are profusely borne singly or in racemes of up to 5, in early summer. ↕↔ 3ft (1m). Zone 5.
P. purpurascens see *P. delavayi* f. *melanocalyx.*
***P.* 'Silberregen'**, syn. *P.* 'Silver Showers'. Rounded, deciduous shrub with upright, arching shoots and ovate, entire leaves, to 1½in (4cm) long. Solitary, single, cup-shaped, strawberry-scented, pure white flowers, 1½in (4cm)

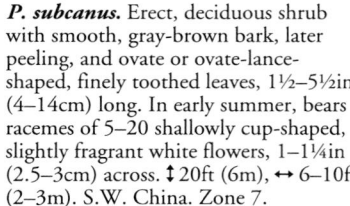

Philadelphus 'Virginal'

across, are profusely borne in early summer. ↕ 4ft (1.2m), ↔ 5ft (1.5m). Zone 4.
***P.* 'Silver Showers'** see *P.* 'Silberregen'.
***P.* 'Snowdwarf'.** Compact, deciduous shrub with upright, arching shoots and ovate, entire, dark green leaves, to 2in (5cm) long. Racemes of 5 cup-shaped, fragrant, pure white flowers, 1½–1¾in (4–4.5cm) across, are borne in summer. ↕ 18–30in (45–75cm), ↔ 18in (45cm). Zone 3.
***P.* 'Snowgoose'.** Free-flowering, deciduous shrub with upright, arching shoots and ovate, entire, dark green leaves, 1½–2½in (4–6cm) long. Cup-shaped, very fragrant, double, pure white flowers, to 2in (5cm) across, are borne in summer. ↕ 4–5ft (1.2–1.5m), ↔ 24–42in (60–110cm). Zone 3.

Philadelphus microphyllus

P. subcanus. Erect, deciduous shrub with smooth, gray-brown bark, later peeling, and ovate or ovate-lance-shaped, finely toothed leaves, 1½–5½in (4–14cm) long. In early summer, bears racemes of 5–20 shallowly cup-shaped, slightly fragrant white flowers, 1–1¼in (2.5–3cm) across. ↕ 20ft (6m), ↔ 6–10ft (2–3m). S.W. China. Zone 7.
***P.* 'Sybille'.** Arching, deciduous shrub with broadly ovate, entire leaves, to 2in (5cm) long. In early or midsummer, single, cup-shaped, very fragrant white flowers, to 2in (5cm) across, with conspicuous purple marks in the centers, are profusely borne singly or in racemes of 3–5. ↕ 4ft (1.2m), ↔ 6ft (2m). Zone 5.
***P.* 'Virginal'** ▣ Vigorous, upright, deciduous shrub with ovate, entire, dark green leaves, to 3in (8cm) or more long. Double, very fragrant, pure white flowers, 2in (5cm) across, are produced in loose racemes of 5–9, in early or midsummer. ↕ 10ft (3m) or more, ↔ 8ft (2.5m). Zone 4b.
***P.* x *virginalis* 'Minnesota Snowflake'.** Upright, heavily branched, deciduous shrub with ovate, mid-green leaves, 1½–4in (4–10cm) long. Double, fragrant white flowers, 2in (5cm) across, in racemes of 5–7, are produced in midsummer. Very cold tolerant. ↕ 8ft (2.5m), ↔ 8–10ft (2.5–3m). Zone 3b.

x PHILAGERIA

LILIACEAE

Hybrid genus of one evergreen shrub, derived from crosses between *Philesia* and *Lapageria.* It is cultivated for its pendent, tubular flowers, produced in summer, and has entire, leathery leaves, arranged alternately. Where not hardy, grow in a cool greenhouse. In warmer areas, grow on a moist, shady bank or against a shaded wall.
• **CULTIVATION** Under glass, grow in acidic soil mix with added sharp sand, in bright indirect light. When in growth, water freely and apply a balanced liquid fertilizer every month. Water sparingly in winter. Outdoors, grow in moderately fertile, humus-rich, reliably moist, acidic soil in partial shade. Support climbing stems. Pruning group 12, in spring.
• **PROPAGATION** Layer in autumn.
• **PESTS AND DISEASES** Infrequent.

x *P. veitchii* (*Lapageria rosea* x *Philesia magellanica*). Twining or scrambling, evergreen shrub producing oblong, 3-veined, glossy, dark green leaves, to 1½in (4cm) long. Pendent, tubular, bright rose-pink flowers, 2in (5cm) long, are borne singly from the leaf axils in summer. ↕ 10–12ft (3–4m). ❄ (min. 35°F/2°C)

PHILESIA

PHILESIACEAE

Genus of one species of evergreen shrub occurring in moist forest in Chile. The alternate leaves are leathery and scale-like. Grown for its showy, trumpet-shaped flowers, produced from the leaf axils in summer and autumn, it is suitable for a moist, shady position.
• **CULTIVATION** Grow in moderately fertile, humus-rich, moist but well-drained, acidic soil in partial shade. Does not tolerate hot, dry conditions. Pruning group 9.
• **PROPAGATION** Take semi-ripe cuttings in summer, or remove suckers in spring.
• **PESTS AND DISEASES** Infrequent.

P. magellanica. Erect, suckering shrub or, in mild, moist areas, root climber, with oblong, rigid, dark green leaves, to 1½in (4cm) long, blue-white beneath. Trumpet-shaped, waxy, crimson-pink flowers, to 2½in (6cm) long, are borne singly in the leaf axils from midsummer to autumn. ↕ 3ft (1m), ↔ 6ft (2m). Chile. Zone 7b.

PHILLYREA

OLEACEAE

Genus of 4 species of evergreen shrubs and trees occurring in woodland and rocky places from the Mediterranean to S.W. Asia. Grown for their habit and foliage, they have opposite, linear to ovate-elliptic, yellow-green to dark green leaves. The 4-lobed, salverform white flowers are borne in axillary cymes, followed by spherical or ovoid, blue-black fruits. Grow in a shrub border or woodland garden, or as specimen plants. Where marginally hardy, grow against a sheltered wall.
• **CULTIVATION** Grow in fertile, well-drained soil, ideally in full sun, with shelter from cold, dry winds. Tolerates partial shade. Pruning group 1 or 8.
• **PROPAGATION** Root semi-ripe cuttings with bottom heat in summer.
• **PESTS AND DISEASES** Whiteflies may be troublesome.

P. angustifolia. Dense, bushy shrub with narrowly linear, dark green leaves, to 2½in (6cm) long. Inconspicuous, fragrant, greenish white flowers are produced in cymes, ½in (1.5cm) across, in late spring and early summer, followed by spherical, blue-black fruit, ¼in (6mm) across. ↕↔ 10ft (3m). Mediterranean. Zone 7b.
P. decora see *Osmanthus decorus.*
P. latifolia ▣ Dense, rounded shrub or small tree with oval, glossy, dark green leaves, to 2½in (6cm) long. Inconspicuous, fragrant, greenish white flowers are borne in cymes, ½in (1.5cm) across, in late spring and early summer, followed by spherical, blue-black fruit, ¼in (6mm) across. ↕↔ to 28ft (9m). Mediterranean, S.W. Asia. Zone 7b. **'Spinosa'** has ovate leaves with very distinct, toothed margins.

Phillyrea latifolia

P

PHILODENDRON

ARACEAE

Genus of up to 500 species of often epiphytic, evergreen shrubs, root climbers, or small trees from variable habitats, usually rainforest, in Florida, Mexico, the West Indies, and Central and tropical South America. They are grown for their leathery, glossy leaves, which may be simple, pinnatifid, or pinnatisect; ovate to oblong, heart-, arrow-, or broadly spear-shaped; and toothed or entire. They are borne alternately, or in tufts or rosettes. Seed-raised species often have a distinct juvenile stage, with leaves quite unlike those of mature plants. Inflorescences, consisting of tiny, petalless flowers borne on spadices and enclosed by spathes, are produced intermittently. Where temperatures fall below 59°F (15°C), grow philodendrons in a warm greenhouse or as houseplants. In warmer areas, train climbing species through a tree or against a wall, and grow large shrubs as specimen plants. Small epiphytes are suitable for a large hanging basket. All parts may cause severe discomfort if ingested; contact with sap may irritate skin.

• **CULTIVATION** Under glass, grow in soilless potting mix in bright filtered or indirect light. In the growing season, water freely and apply a balanced liquid fertilizer every month. In summer, mist twice daily. Water sparingly in winter. Support climbing stems with a moss pole. Outdoors, grow in fertile, humus-rich, moist but well-drained soil in dappled or partial shade. Pruning group 1 for shrubs; group 11 for climbers, in spring; plants under glass may need restrictive pruning.

• **PROPAGATION** Surface-sow seed at 66–75°F (19–24°C) in spring. Take stem-tip or leaf bud cuttings in summer. Layer or air layer in spring.

• **PESTS AND DISEASES** Dasheen mosaic virus, red-edge, mealybugs, scale insects, spider mites, fungal and bacterial leaf spots, and root rot are common.

P. andreanum see *P. melanochrysum.*
P. angustisectum, syn. *P. elegans.* Sparsely branched climber with ovate, pinnatisect, reflexed leaves, 12–24in (30–60cm) long, each with 16–32 slender, finger-like lobes, glossy, deep green above, paler beneath. Green spathes, 6in (15cm) long, are yellow

Philodendron bipinnatifidum

Philodendron melanochrysum

inside, with pink-flushed margins. ↕ 15ft (5m). Colombia. ❄ (min. 59°F/15°C)
***P. auritum* of gardens** see *Syngonium auritum.*
P. bipennifolium, syn. *P. panduriforme* (Fiddleleaf, Panda plant). Sparsely branched climber with ovate to arrow-shaped, reflexed, lustrous, deep green leaves, 12–18in (30–45cm) long, each with 5 broad lobes, the terminal one longest. Bears greenish cream spathes, to 4½in (11cm) long. ↕ to 15ft (5m) or more. S.E. Brazil. ❄ (min. 59°F/15°C)
P. bipinnatifidum ▣ syn. *P. selloum* (Tree philodendron). Tree-like shrub, usually with a single, robust, erect stem, reclining with age. Very long-stalked, reflexed leaves, to 3ft (1m) long, are broadly ovate, heart-shaped at the bases, and deeply pinnatisect, with many narrow, wavy-margined, semi-glossy, rich green lobes. Green to red-purple spathes, 12in (30cm) long, are cream with red margins inside. ↕↔ to 15ft (5m). S.E. Brazil. ❄ (min. 59°F/15°C). **'German Selloum'** has narrower leaf lobes. **'Variegatum'** has leaves splashed yellow to light green.
P. cordatum (Heart leaf). Fast-growing, moderately to sparsely branched,

Philodendron scandens

slender-stemmed climber. The glossy, deep green leaves, 12–18in (30–45cm) long, are ovate-triangular, reflexed, and heart-shaped at the bases, the lower lobes touching or overlapping. Bears green spathes, 4–6in (10–15cm) long. ↕ 10–20ft (3–6m). S.E. Brazil. ❄ (min. 59°F/15°C)
P. domesticum, syn. *P. hastatum* of gardens (Elephant's ear). Usually sparsely branched climber with narrowly triangular to arrow-shaped, reflexed, bright green leaves, 18–24in (45–60cm) long, with wavy margins. Spathes are 5–7in (12–18cm) long, green on the outside, cherry-red inside. ↕ 10–20ft (3–6m). Origin unknown. ❄ (min. 59°F/15°C)
P. elegans see *P. angustisectum.*
P. erubescens (Blushing philodendron, Red-leaf philodendron). Sturdy-stemmed climber with red-purple stems when young. Ovate-triangular, glossy, dark green leaves, 10–16in (25–40cm) long, heart-shaped at the bases, are coppery red-purple beneath, with purple-tinged stalks. Bears red-purple spathes, 6in (15cm) long, crimson inside, with an unusual aroma. ↕ 10–20ft (3–6m). Colombia. ❄ (min. 59°F/15°C). **'Burgundy'** is slower-growing, with smaller, red-flushed leaves, to 12in (30cm) long.
***P. hastatum* of gardens** see *P. domesticum.*
P. imbe, syn. *P. sellowianum.* Robust climber with long aerial roots and red-purple stems bearing ovate-oblong to arrow-shaped, reflexed leaves, to 14in (35cm) long; they have a parchment-like texture and are glossy, mid- to dark green above, often flushed or tinted red beneath. Spathes, 6in (15cm) long, are cream and green. ↕ 10–15ft (3–5m). S.E. Brazil. ❄ (min. 59°F/15°C)
P. laciniatum see *P. pedatum.*
P. melanochrysum ▣ syn. *P. andreanum* (Black gold philodendron, Velour philodendron). Sparsely branched climber. Bears narrowly ovate to oblong-lance-shaped, reflexed to pendent, velvety blackish green leaves, to 3ft (1m) long, with pale green veins; they have short, slender points and heart-shaped bases (the lobes touch or just overlap). Juvenile plants have much smaller, broader, coppery red leaves. Produces green and white spathes, to 8in (20cm) long. ↕ 10–20ft (3–6m). Colombia. ❄ (min. 59°F/15°C)
P. micans see *P. scandens* f. *micans.*
P. oxycardium see *P. scandens* subsp. *oxycardium.*
P. panduriforme see *P. bipennifolium.*
P. pedatum, syn. *P. laciniatum.* Robust, moderately branching climber. Reflexed, pinnatifid, glossy, deep green leaves, to 18in (45cm) long, are ovate to arrow-shaped, with 5–7 narrowly triangular lobes, the 2 basal lobes sometimes lobed and pointing backward. Bears green and white spathes, red-flushed at the bases and cream inside, 4–5in (10–13cm) long. ↕ 10–15ft (3–5m). Venezuela to Brazil. ❄ (min. 59°F/15°C)
P. scandens ▣ (Heart leaf, Sweetheart plant). Fast-growing climber producing sparsely to moderately branching, slender stems. Glossy, deep green leaves, sometimes red-purple beneath, are up to 12in (30cm) long on mature plants, 4–6in (10–15cm) long on juveniles; they are rounded, heart-shaped at the bases, and reflexed, with abruptly tapered, slender-pointed tips. Bears green spathes, 6–8in (15–20cm) long, white inside, sometimes red-tinted at the bases. Good as a houseplant. ↕ 10–20ft (3–6m). Mexico, West Indies, S.E. Brazil. ❄ (min. 59°F/15°C). **f. *micans***, syn. *P. micans*, has bronze leaves, red-tinted beneath, with larger, overlapping basal leaf lobes. **subsp. *oxycardium***, syn. *P. oxycardium* (Parlor ivy) has young leaves flushed bronze-brown; E. Mexico.
P. selloum see *P. bipinnatifidum.*
P. sellowianum see *P. imbe.*
P. trifoliatum see *Syngonium auritum.*

PHLEBODIUM

POLYPODIACEAE

Genus of 10 species of semi-evergreen ferns occurring on trees and rocks in Florida, Mexico, the West Indies, and Central and tropical South America. They have thick, creeping rhizomes, densely covered with golden brown scales, and large, pinnate or pinnatifid, sometimes glaucous fronds. Spores are formed in groups, in one or more rows parallel to the midribs. Where not hardy, grow in a warm greenhouse or as houseplants; they are very effective in hanging baskets. In warmer regions, grow in a warm, sheltered border.

• **CULTIVATION** Under glass, grow in 1 part each loam, medium-grade bark, and charcoal, 2 parts sharp sand, and 3 parts coarse leaf mold. Provide full light or bright filtered light. During growth, water moderately and apply a balanced liquid fertilizer every month. Water sparingly in winter. Outdoors, grow in fertile, well-drained soil in full sun or light, dappled shade.

• **PROPAGATION** Sow spores at 66–75°F (19–24°C) as soon as ripe. Divide rhizomes in spring. See also p.51.

• **PESTS AND DISEASES** Scale insects may be a problem.

P. aureum ▣ syn. *Polypodium aureum* (Golden polypody, Hare's foot fern, Rabbit's foot fern). Large, creeping fern with arching, ovate to oblong or triangular, deeply pinnatifid, glaucous, gray-green fronds, to 5ft (1.5m) long, each with up to 35 narrowly linear to lance-shaped, oblong, or strap-shaped, wavy-margined segments. ↕ 30in (75cm), ↔ to 5ft (1.5m). Florida, Mexico, West Indies, Central and tropical South America. ❄ (min. 41°F/5°C).

Phlebodium aureum

Phlebodium aureum 'Mandaianum'

var. *areolatum*, syn. 'Glaucum', has leathery fronds, 24in (60cm) long, with a more pronounced glaucous bloom.
'Glaucum' see var. *areolatum*.
'Mandaianum' ■ (Blue fern) has slightly lobed fronds with wavy margins.

PHLOMIS

LAMIACEAE

Genus of about 100 species of sage-like herbaceous perennials and evergreen shrubs or subshrubs found in rocky sites in Europe, North Africa, and Asia. Leaves are opposite, lance-shaped to ovate, light to gray-green, often with star-shaped hairs. They are grown for their foliage and showy, tubular, dead-nettle-like, often hooded, white, yellow, or lilac flowers, borne in dense, axillary whorls on tall, erect stems; they are effective massed in a border. Where marginally hardy, grow against a wall. *P. lanata* is suitable for a rock garden. In winter, seed heads of herbaceous species may be left for their ornamental effect.

- **CULTIVATION** Grow in any fertile, well-drained soil in full sun; *P. russeliana* and *P. samia* tolerate some shade. Pruning group 8 or 9.
- **PROPAGATION** Sow seed at 55–64°F (13–18°C) in spring. Divide perennials in spring (preferably) or in autumn. Take softwood cuttings of shrubs in summer.
- **PESTS AND DISEASES** Leafhoppers may be troublesome.

P. bovei* subsp. *maroccana, syn. *P. samia* subsp. *maroccana*. Erect, sticky-hairy perennial with elliptic to oblong, scalloped, gray-green basal leaves, 2½–3in (6–8cm) long, heart-shaped at the bases, and smaller stem leaves. Purple-pink flowers, 1½–1¾in (4–4.5cm) long, with purple spots inside, white-woolly outside, are borne in summer. ↕ to 5ft (1.5m), ↔ 3ft (1m). Mountains in Morocco. ❀ (min. 41°F/5°C)

Phlomis cashmeriana

P. cashmeriana ■ Erect, densely woolly perennial with ovate to lance-shaped basal leaves, 4–10in (10–25cm) long, yellow-gray above, paler beneath, and smaller stem leaves. In midsummer, bears hooded, lilac-purple flowers, 1in (2.5cm) long, from the upper leaf axils. ↕ to 36in (90cm), ↔ 24in (60cm). India (Kashmir), W. Himalayas. Zone 8.
P. chrysophylla (Goldleaf Jerusalem sage). Rounded, evergreen shrub with thick, spreading branches and elliptic to broadly ovate, gray-green leaves, to 2½in (6cm) long, turning golden green in late summer. Golden yellow flowers, 1¼in (3cm) long, are produced in early summer. ↕ 3ft (1m), ↔ 4ft (1.2m). S.W. Asia. Zone 8.
***P.* 'Edward Bowles'.** Upright, evergreen subshrub with large, heart-shaped, wrinkled, gray-green leaves, 6in (15cm) long, woolly beneath. Bears sulfur-yellow flowers, 1¼in (3cm) long, paler on the hoods, in early and midsummer. ↕ 3ft (1m), ↔ 5ft (1.5m). Zone 8.
P. fruticosa ■ (Jerusalem sage). Mound-forming, evergreen shrub with upright shoots and sage-like, ovate-lance-shaped, wrinkled, gray-green leaves, to 4in (10cm) long, woolly beneath. In early and midsummer, bears dark golden yellow flowers, 1¼in (3cm) long. ↕ 3ft (1m), ↔ 5ft (1.5m). E. Mediterranean. Zone 8.
P. italica ■ Upright, evergreen shrub bearing oblong-lance-shaped, gray-woolly leaves, to 2in (5cm) long. Lilac-pink flowers, ¾in (2cm) long, are borne in midsummer. ↕ 12in (30cm), ↔ 24in (60cm). Balearic Islands. ❀ (min. 41°F/5°C)
P. lanata. Compact, mound-forming, evergreen shrub bearing oblong to rounded, deeply veined, scaly, sage-green leaves, to 1in (2.5cm) long.

Phlomis italica

Golden yellow flowers, ¾in (2cm) long, covered with brown hairs, are produced in summer. ↕ 20in (50cm), ↔ 30in (75cm). Greece (Crete). ❀ (min. 35°F/2°C)
P. longifolia. Spreading, evergreen shrub with white-woolly young shoots and lance-shaped, deeply veined, bright green leaves, to 3in (8cm) long, gray-woolly beneath. Dark yellow flowers, to 1½in (4cm) long, with calyx teeth to ⅛in (3mm) long, are produced in summer. ↕ 4ft (1.2m), ↔ 6ft (2m). S.W. Asia. ❀ (min. 35°F/2°C). **var. *bailanica*** has ovate leaves, and flowers with longer calyx teeth, ⅛–¼in (3–6mm) long.
P. purpurea ■ Upright, evergreen shrub with woolly shoots and lance-shaped, leathery, gray-green leaves, to 4in (10cm) long, with star-shaped hairs above, woolly beneath. Purple to pink, occasionally white flowers, 1in (2.5cm) long, are produced in summer. ↕↔ to 24in (60cm). Spain, Portugal. ❀ (min. 35°F/2°C)
P. russeliana ■ syn. *P. samia* of gardens, *P. viscosa* of gardens. (Sticky Jerusalem sage). Erect, hairy perennial with mid-green leaves: basal leaves are ovate, 2½–8in (6–20cm) long, and heart-shaped at the bases; stem leaves are

Phlomis purpurea

smaller and scalloped. Hooded, pale yellow flowers, 1–1½in (2.5–4cm) long, are produced from late spring to early autumn, mainly in early summer. Often confused with *P. samia*. ↕ to 36in (90cm), ↔ 30in (75cm). Turkey, Syria. Zone 5.
P. samia (Greek Jerusalem sage). Erect perennial producing ovate, scalloped, woolly basal leaves, 4–8in (10–20cm) long, heart-shaped at the bases, and mid-green above, gray beneath; stem leaves are smaller. Hooded lilac flowers, 1¼–1½in (3–4cm) long, tinged rose-pink, especially on the lips, are produced from early to late summer. ↕ to 3ft (1m), ↔ 32in (80cm). S.E. Europe, Turkey. Zone 7b. **subsp. *maroccana*** see *P. bovei* subsp. *maroccana*.
***P. samia* of gardens** see *P. russeliana*.
P. tuberosa. Erect, tuberous, perennial with arrow-shaped, oblong-ovate, softly hairy mid-green leaves, to 10in (25cm) long. Bears many false whorls of purple or pink flowers, ¾–1in (2–2.5cm) long, with straight upper lips, in summer. ↕ to 5ft (1.5m), ↔ 3–4ft (1–1.2cm). C. and S.E. Europe to C. Asia. Zone 6.
***P. viscosa* of gardens** see *P. russeliana*.

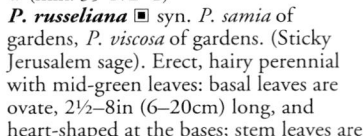

Phlomis fruticosa (inset: flower detail)

Phlomis russeliana

PHLOX

POLEMONIACEAE

Genus of about 70 species of evergreen or herbaceous, low-growing or cushion-forming to erect perennials, as well as a few annuals and shrubs, found mostly in North America (one from Siberia). They are grown for their showy flowers, borne mainly in terminal corymbs or panicle-like cymes, sometimes singly. The flowers are salverform, occasionally funnel-shaped, each with a narrow, tubular base opening to 5 flat, ovate petal lobes, sometimes in a star-shaped arrangement. Leaves are simple, entire, linear to ovate, light to dark green, and often in opposite pairs, the upper leaves sometimes alternate. Mat- and cushion-forming species, from dry, rocky habitats, flower in spring or early summer; grow in a rock garden or alpine house, in a dry wall, or as edging. Woodland species are mainly trailing, and usually flower in spring; grow in shady sites. The taller phlox are mostly from moist riverside habitats, and produce large corymbs of flowers, usually in midsummer, which are good for cutting. Annuals, from dry rocky slopes and coastal sands, flower from late spring to autumn, and are useful for bedding.

• **CULTIVATION** Grow annuals in any fertile, well-drained soil in full sun. Perennials and shrubs have varying needs, which may be grouped as listed below. Cut back all tall herbaceous species to the ground in autumn. Deadhead *P. maculata* and *P. paniculata* to prolong flowering. Stake tall cultivars.
1. Grow in fertile, moist soil in full sun or partial shade.
2. Grow in humus-rich, fertile, moist but well-drained soil in partial shade.
3. Grow in well-drained, fertile soil in full sun, or in dappled shade in low rainfall areas.
4. Grow in gritty, sharply drained, poor to moderately fertile soil in full sun. In an alpine house, grow in a mix of equal parts loam, leaf mold, and sharp sand.

• **PROPAGATION** Sow seed of annuals at 55–64°F (13–18°C) in early spring; sow seed of perennials in containers in a cold frame when ripe or in spring. Divide *P. carolina*, *P. maculata*, and *P. paniculata*, and their cultivars, in autumn or spring. Insert basal cuttings in spring, or take root cuttings in early autumn or winter. Take softwood cuttings of non-flowering stems of cushion-forming perennials in spring. Detach rooted pieces of stem from trailing perennials in spring or early autumn.

• **PESTS AND DISEASES** Powdery mildew, stem canker, rust, Southern blight, stem nematodes, *Cercospora* and *Septoria* leaf spots, leaf miners, and caterpillars occur.

P. adsurgens. Creeping, stem-rooting, semi-evergreen perennial with prostrate to ascending stems bearing stalkless, rounded to narrowly ovate, light to mid-green leaves, to 1in (2.5cm) long. In late spring and early summer, bears open cymes of salverform, broad-petaled, salmon-pink flowers, to 1in (2.5cm) across, with paler centers. Cultivation group 2. ↕↔ 12in (30cm). N.W. US. Zone 4. **'Red Buttes'** has deep pink flowers with large, overlapping petal lobes. **'Wagon Wheel'** ■ has salmon-pink flowers with narrow petal lobes, resembling the spokes of a wheel.

***P. amoena* 'Variegata'** see *P.* x *procumbens* 'Variegata'.

P. bifida ■ (Sand phlox). Mound-forming, evergreen perennial with hairy, needle-like, linear leaves, to 2½in (6cm) long. In spring, bears abundant cymes of salverform, fragrant, deep lavender-blue to white flowers, ¾in (2cm) across, with star-shaped, deeply cleft petal lobes. Cultivation group 3 or 4. ↕ to 8in (20cm), ↔ 6in (15cm). C. US. Zone 4. **'Colvin's White'** produces pure white flowers.

P. bryoides. Cushion-forming, evergreen perennial with overlapping, lance-shaped, hairy leaves, to ¼in (6mm) long. In late spring and early summer, solitary, stalkless, salverform, pure white flowers, ½in (1.5cm) across, are borne toward the shoot tips. May become lax and fail to flower freely in cultivation. Cultivation group 4. ↕ ¾–2in (2–5cm), ↔ 6in (15cm). Oregon, W. Montana to Nevada, W. Nebraska. Zone 4.

P. carolina (Carolina phlox). Upright and spreading herbaceous perennial bearing thick, lance-shaped to ovate-oblong leaves, 5in (13cm) long. In summer, produces cymes of salverform, purple to pink, rarely white flowers, to

Phlox bifida

¾in (2cm) across. Good in hot climates. Cultivation group 1. ↕ 4ft (1.2m), ↔ 18in (45cm). C. and E. US. Zone 5. **'Bill Baker'** ■ has bright green leaves and pink flowers in early summer; ↕ 18in (45cm), ↔ 12in (30cm).

***P.* 'Chattahoochee'** ■ Short-lived, prostrate, branching, semi-evergreen perennial with purple-tinted stems and lance-shaped leaves, ¾–2in (2–5cm) long, purple-flushed when young. Bears cymes of salverform, lavender-blue flowers, ¾–1in (2–2.5cm) across, with conspicuous red-purple eyes, over long periods in summer and early autumn. Cultivation group 2. ↕ 6in (15cm), ↔ 12in (30cm). Zone 4.

P. divaricata (Blue phlox, Wild sweet William, Woodland phlox). Spreading, stem-rooting, semi-evergreen perennial with ovate, hairy leaves, to 2in (5cm) long, narrower on the flowering stems. In spring, bears open cymes of salverform, lavender-blue to pale violet and white flowers, ¾–1¼in (2–3cm) across, with notched or unnotched petal lobes. Cultivation group 2. ↕ to 14in (35cm), ↔ 20in (50cm). Woodland in Canada, E. US. Zone 4. **'Dirigo Ice'** ■ bears clear, pale blue flowers. **'Fuller's White'** is a compact, white-flowered selection; ↕ 8in (20cm). **subsp. *laphamii*** ■ has pale to deep lilac-blue flowers with narrow petal lobes.

P. douglasii. Mound-forming, evergreen perennial densely covered with stiff, narrowly lance-shaped, dark green leaves, to ½in (1.5cm) long. In late spring or early summer, bears salverform, white, lavender-blue, or pink flowers, ½in (1.5cm) across, singly or in twos or threes. Cultivation group 3. ↕ to 8in (20cm), ↔ 12in (30cm). S. Washington to California. Zone 5. **'Boothman's Variety'** ■ produces violet-pink flowers with dark eyes. **'Crackerjack'** ■ is more compact, with reddish magenta flowers; ↕ to 5in (13cm), ↔ to 8in (20cm). **'Iceberg'** has white flowers, sometimes faintly tinged blue. **'Red Admiral'** ■ bears deep crimson flowers. **'Violet Queen'** is compact, with deep purple flowers; ↕ to 4in (10cm), ↔ to 6in (15cm). **'Waterloo'** bears crimson flowers.

P. drummondii (Annual phlox). Erect to spreading, bushy, hairy annual with very variable, narrowly inversely lance-shaped to nearly ovate, almost stalkless, stem-clasping leaves, 1–3in (2.5–8cm) long. In late spring, produces cymes of salverform, hairy, purple, pink, red, lavender-blue, or white flowers, to 1in (2.5cm) across, often pale inside, with contrasting marks at the bases of the petal lobes. ↕ 4–18in (10–45cm), ↔ to 10in (25cm) or more. E. Texas. **'African Sunset'** ■ has dusky to deep red flowers. **'Chanal'** ■ is spreading, but still compact, and bears double, almost rose-like pink flowers. **'Dwarf Beauty'** is early-flowering, with abundant, very large blooms, to 1¼in (3cm) or more across, in a wide range of colors; ↔ 16in (40cm) or more. **Globe Mixed** cultivars are dwarf, compact, and mound-forming, with single, rounded flowers in pastels and solid colors; ↕ 6–8in (15–20cm). **Palona Series** cultivars are dwarf and bushy, forming spherical plants, with flowers in colors including white, light blue, violet, salmon-pink, rose-pink, carmine-red, or crimson, some with contrasting eyes. **Palona Series 'Light Salmon'** ■ has pale salmon-pink flowers. **'Petticoat'** is dwarf, with very small flowers, to ½in (1.5cm) across, available as a mixture of cream and pink shades, including bicolors; flowers late, but over a long season; ↕ to 4in (10cm). **'Promise Pink'** produces semi-double, deep salmon-pink flowers. **'Sternenzauber'** ■ syn. 'Twinkle', has tiny flowers, to ¾in (2cm) across, in shades of pink and red,

Phlox adsurgens 'Wagon Wheel'

Phlox carolina 'Bill Baker'

Phlox 'Chatahoochee'

Phlox divaricata 'Dirigo Ice'

Phlox divaricata subsp. *laphamii*

Phlox douglasii 'Boothman's Variety'

Phlox douglasii 'Crackerjack'

Phlox douglasii 'Red Admiral'

Phlox drummondii 'African Sunset'

Phlox drummondii 'Chanal'

Phlox drummondii Palona Series 'Light Salmon'

Phlox drummondii 'Sternenzauber'

Phlox nana 'Arroyo'

as well as picotees; petal lobes are often fringed and pointed, appearing star-like. **'Twinkle'** see 'Sternenzauber'.
***P.* 'Emerald Cushion'.** Compact, mound-forming, evergreen perennial, similar to *P. subulata*, with linear to elliptic, light green leaves, to ¾in (2cm) long. In late spring and early summer, bears cymes of salverform, pale violet flowers, ¾–1in (2–2.5cm) across, with narrow, notched petal lobes. Cultivation group 3. ↕ 3in (8cm), ↔ 8in (20cm). Zone 3.
P. glaberrima (Smooth phlox). Vigorous, clump-forming perennial with lance-shaped, mid-green basal leaves, to 4in (10cm) long, and smaller, narrower, lance-shaped stem leaves with curled margins. Bears clusters of saucer-shaped, purple-pink flowers, ¾in (2cm) across, in profusion, in late spring and early summer. Cultivation group 3, in acid soil. ↕ 2–3ft (60–90cm), ↔ 18in (45cm). S.E. US. Zone 4.
P. hoodii. Dwarf, tuft-forming, evergreen perennial with hairy, lance-shaped leaves, to ½in (1.5cm) long. Produces solitary, salverform, white to pale violet flowers, ½in (1.5cm) across, in late spring and early summer. Cultivation group 4. ↕ 2in (5cm), ↔ 4in (10cm). Rocky Mountains. Zone 5.
***P.* 'Kelly's Eye'** ■ Vigorous, mound-forming, evergreen perennial, similar to *P. douglasii*, with narrowly lance-shaped, dark green leaves, to ½in (1.5cm) long. In late spring and early summer, bears cymes of salverform, very pale pink flowers, ½in (1.5cm) across, with red-purple eyes. Cultivation group 3. ↕ 4in (10cm), ↔ 12in (30cm) or more. Zone 5b.
P. maculata (Meadow phlox, Wild sweet William). Erect herbaceous perennial with hairy stems, often red-spotted, and linear to ovate, smooth leaves, 2½–5in (6–13cm) long. In early and midsummer, bears narrowly conical, panicle-like cymes of salverform, fragrant, violet, pink, or white flowers, ¾–1in (2–2.5cm) across. Cultivation group 1. ↕ to 36in (90cm), ↔ 18in (45cm). E. US. Zone 3b. **'Alpha'** has lilac-pink flowers. **'Miss Lingard'** bears highly fragrant, pure white flowers in early summer. **'Omega'** ■ has white flowers with lilac-red eyes. **'Rosalinde'** has deep rose-pink flowers all summer.
P. mesoleuca see *P. nana* subsp. *ensifolia*.
***P.* 'Millstream'** see *P.* x *procumbens* 'Millstream'.
P. nana (Santa Fe phlox). Deciduous or semi-evergreen perennial, spreading by runners, with trailing or upright shoots, to 8in (20cm) long, sparsely covered with linear to lance-shaped, downy, gray-green leaves, to 1½in (4cm) long. Produces abundant solitary, salverform, bright pink, purple, or white, rarely pale yellow flowers, to 1in (2.5cm) across, from summer to autumn. Cultivation group 4. ↕ to 8in (20cm), ↔ to 12in (30cm). S.W. US, Mexico. Zone 7b. **'Arroyo'** ■ bears brilliant magenta flowers, with small white eyes, over long periods in summer. **subsp. *ensifolia*,** syn. *P. mesoleuca*, produces white-eyed, soft pink, purple, soft yellow, or white flowers; slower-growing than the species, with shorter shoots, and more difficult to grow. **'Mary Maslin'** ■ has vivid scarlet flowers with yellow eyes. **'Paul Maslin'** has pale yellow flowers with deep purple eyes. **'Tangelo'** has brilliant orange-red flowers with yellow eyes.
P. nivalis ■ (Trailing phlox). Decumbent, evergreen perennial with trailing shoots, to 12in (30cm) long, and hairy, lance-shaped leaves, 1in (2.5cm) long. Cymes of salverform, purple, pink, or white flowers, to ½in (1.5cm) across, are borne in summer. Cultivation group 3. ↕ 8in (20cm), ↔ 12in (30cm). C. US. Zone 5. **'Camla'** has very pale pink, almost white flowers.
P. paniculata (Garden phlox). Erect herbaceous perennial with ovate or lance-shaped to elliptic, toothed, thin leaves, 2–5in (5–13cm) long. Panicle-like cymes of salverform, fragrant, white or pale to dark lilac flowers, ½–1in (1.5–2.5cm) across, are borne from summer to early or midautumn. Cultivation group 1. ↕ 4ft (1.2m), ↔ 24–39in (60–100cm). E. US. Zone 3. **'Aida'** has crimson flowers with purple eyes. **'Amethyst'** produces violet flowers. **'Balmoral'** is vigorous, with large clusters of pink flowers; ↕ 36in (90cm). **'Blue Boy'** is strong-growing, and bears mauve-blue flowers with white eyes; ↕ 36in (90cm). **'Brigadier'** has orange-tinged, pinkish red flowers, and deep green leaves. **'Bright Eyes'** has clear pale pink flowers with red eyes. **'David'** is vigorous and sturdy in habit, bearing white-flowers from midsummer to early autumn. Mildew resistant; ↕ 42in (1.1m). **'Dodo Hanbury Forbes'** bears clear pink flowers with red eyes; ↕ 36in (90cm). **'Eva Cullum'** ■ is very free-blooming, producing bright deep pink flowers with darker pink centers. **'Eventide'** has lavender-blue flowers; ↕ 36in (90cm). **'Franz Schubert'** has dense heads of lilac-pink flowers with darker, star-shaped eyes and pale blue margins. **'Fujiyama'** ■ syn. 'Mt. Fuji', produces white flowers; ↕ to 30in (75cm). **'Graf Zeppelin'** ■ produces

Phlox paniculata 'Starfire'

white flowers with red centers. **'Hampton Court'** has dark green foliage and mauve-blue flowers. **'Harlequin'** has leaves with broad, ivory-white margins, and reddish purple flowers. **'Le Mahdi'** has deep bluish purple flowers with darker eyes; ↕ 3½ft (1.1m). **'Mia Ruys'** bears large white flowers, to 1¼in (3cm) across; ↕ 24in (60cm). **'Mother of Pearl'** ■ has pink-tinted white flowers; ↕ 30in (75cm). **'Mt. Fuji'** see 'Fujiyama'. **'Norah Leigh'** ■ has extensively white-variegated leaves and small, pale lilac flowers, ½in (1.5cm) across, with deeper lilac-pink centers; ↕ 36in (90cm). **'Orange Perfection'** has deep orange flowers. **'Prime Minister'** bears white flowers with red eyes; ↕ 36–42in (1–1.1m). **'Prince of Orange'** has orange-red flowers; ↕ to 32in (80cm). **'Prospero'** has pale lilac flowers with almost white petal margins; ↕ to 36in (90cm). **'Sandra'** bears bright scarlet flowers with a hint of orange; ↕ 20in (50cm). **'Sandringham'** bears pale pink flowers with deeper pink centers and widely spaced petal lobes. **'Sir John Falstaff'** has deep salmon-pink flowers with wine-red eyes. **'Starfire'** ■ bears dark green leaves and deep crimson-red flowers; ↕ 36in (90cm). **'The King'** produces deep blue-purple flowers; ↕ 24–30in (60–75cm). **'White Admiral'** bears white flowers; ↕ 36in (90cm). **'Windsor'** ■ has reddish pink flowers with purple-pink eyes.

Phlox 'Kelly's Eye'

Phlox maculata 'Omega'

Phlox nana 'Mary Maslin'

Phlox nivalis

Phlox paniculata 'Eva Cullum'

Phlox paniculata 'Fujiyama'

Phlox paniculata 'Graf Zeppelin'

Phlox paniculata 'Mother of Pearl'

Phlox paniculata 'Norah Leigh'

Phlox stolonifera 'Ariane'

Phlox subulata 'G.F. Wilson'

Phlox subulata 'Marjorie'

Phlox paniculata 'Windsor'

***P. pilosa* subsp. *ozarkana*.** Vigorous, clump-forming, deciduous perennial with softly hairy stems and oval to ovate, mid-green leaves, to 3in (8cm) long. Bears abundant, saucer-shaped, pink flowers, ¾in (2cm) across, in late spring and summer. Good as a groundcover under shrubs. ↕ 12–18in (30–45cm), ↔ to 18in (45cm). Missouri to E. Oklahoma, south to N. Louisiana. Zone 4.

P.* x *procumbens (*P. stolonifera* x *P. subulata*). Decumbent, mat-forming, semi-evergreen perennial with inversely lance-shaped to elliptic, glossy leaves, 1in (2.5cm) long. Bears open, flat cymes of salverform, bright purple flowers, ¾in (2cm) across, in early summer. Cultivation group 2 or 3. ↕ 4in (10cm), ↔ 12in (30cm). Garden origin. Zone 4. **'Millstream'**, syn. *P.* 'Millstream', bears a profusion of deep lavender-pink flowers, each with a darker eye. **'Rosea'** produces pale pink flowers. **'Variegata'**, syn. *P. amoena* 'Variegata', has leaves with cream margins, and bears deep pink flowers. **'Violacea'** produces mauve-blue flowers. **'Violet Vere'** has violet flowers.

P. stolonifera (Creeping phlox). Stoloniferous, spreading herbaceous perennial with obovate, dark green leaves, to 2in (5cm) long. In spring, upright stems produce open cymes of salverform, pale to deep purple flowers, to 1¼in (3cm) across. Cultivation group 2. ↕ 4–6in (10–15cm), ↔ 12in (30cm) or more. Woodland in C. US. Zone 4. **'Ariane'** ▣ has pale green leaves, and white flowers, 1¼in (3cm) or more across, with star-shaped petal lobes and small yellow eyes. **'Blue Ridge'** bears clear pale blue flowers. **'Bruce's White'** has pure white flowers with yellow eyes. **'Home Fires'** has deep pink flowers. **'Mary Belle Frey'** bears pink flowers. **'Pink Ridge'** produces bright pink flowers. **'Sherwood Purple'** bears purple-blue flowers.

P. subulata (Creeping phlox, Moss phlox). Dense, evergreen perennial forming cushions or mats of hairy, linear to elliptic, bright green leaves, ¼–¾in (0.6–2cm) long. Salverform, purple or red, sometimes violet-purple, lilac, pink, or white flowers, ½–1in (1.5–2.5cm) across, often with star-shaped petal lobes, are produced in few-flowered cymes, rarely singly, in late spring and early summer. Cultivation group 3. ↕ 2–6in (5–15cm), ↔ 20in (50cm) or more. E. to C. US. Zone 3. **'Amazing Grace'** has a lax habit, and bears pale pink flowers with deep pinkish purple eyes. **'Apple Blossom'** bears pale lilac flowers with dark eyes. **subsp. *brittoni*** has pale blue flowers with deeply notched petals. **'Candy Stripe'** has bicolored flowers of white and pink. **'Coral Eye'** produces white flowers, each with a striking coral eye, and blooms intermittently all season. **'Emerald Blue'** has light blue flowers. **'Emerald Pink'** produces soft pink flowers. **'Fort Hill'** bears fragrant, deep pink flowers. **'G.F. Wilson'** ▣ is vigorous and cushion-forming, and bears deep lavender-blue flowers. **'Greencourt Purple'** has mauve flowers with darker eyes. **'Maiden Blush'** has pink flowers with red eyes. **'Maischnee'** see 'May Snow'. **'Marjorie'** ▣ is mat-forming, and bears very large, narrow-petaled, deep pink flowers, 1¼in (3cm) across, each with a darker pink band around a yellow eye. **'May Snow'**, syn. 'Maischnee', bears pure white flowers. **'McDaniel's Cushion'** is vigorous, cushion-forming, and extremely free-flowering, with very large, deep pink flowers, to 1½in (4cm) across. **'Red Wings'** has large crimson flowers with dark red centers. **'Samson'** bears deep rose-pink flowers. **'Scarlet Flame'** is vigorous and mat-forming, with deep scarlet flowers. **'Temiskaming'** is slow-growing and cushion-forming, with small, deep magenta flowers, ½in (1.5cm) across. **'White Delight'** has snow-white flowers.

PHOENIX

ARECACEAE

Genus of 17 species of single- and cluster-stemmed palms occurring in tropical and subtropical forest or low scrub thickets in the Canary Islands, Africa, Crete (Greece), and W. and S. Asia to the Philippines. They have linear to ovate or oblong, pinnate leaves, usually borne in dense, terminal clusters. The bowl-shaped, 3-petaled, cream to yellow flowers are produced in panicles from the lower axils, followed by yellow, orange, red, brown, or black fruits. Where not hardy, grow in a warm greenhouse or as houseplants. In warmer areas, use as specimen plants on a lawn.

• **CULTIVATION** Under glass, grow in soil-based potting mix in full light, with shade from hot sun. Pot on or top-dress in spring. When in growth, water freely and apply a balanced liquid fertilizer monthly. Water sparingly in winter. Outdoors, grow in fertile, moist but well-drained soil in full sun, with some midday shade.

• **PROPAGATION** Sow seed at 66–75°F (19–24°C) in spring.

• **PESTS AND DISEASES** Butt rot, pink rot, false smut, bud rot, various leaf spots, and heart rot occur. Spider mites, mealybugs, scale insects, and thrips may be problems on seedlings and young plants.

P. canariensis (Canary Island date palm). Medium-sized palm with a thick, columnar trunk marked with oblong leaf scars wider than they are long. Spreading to broadly arching leaves, 12–20ft (4–6m) long, consist of many linear, bright mid- to deep green leaflets, set in a single plane. Bowl-shaped, cream to yellow flowers are borne in pendent panicles, 3–4ft (1–1.2m) long, in summer. Fruit are cylindrical to ellipsoid, and red-flushed yellow, ¾in (2cm) long, with edible, sweet, but almost dry flesh. ↕ to 50ft (15m), ↔ 40ft (12m). Canary Islands. ❀ (min. 50–61°F/10–16°C)

P. dactylifera (Date palm). Tall, sometimes suckering palm producing a columnar trunk usually clad with old leaf bases, at least toward the top. Leaves, 12–20ft (4–6m) long, are composed of many linear, grayish green leaflets, the lowest ones reduced to spines, arranged in various planes, giving a 3-dimensional effect. Bowl-shaped cream flowers appear in long-stalked panicles, 5–6ft (1.5–2m) long, in spring or summer. Ellipsoid to cylindrical, edible, sweet, fleshy, yellow to reddish brown fruit, 1–3in (2.5–8cm) long, are very variable both in texture and flavor. ↕ to 100ft (30m), ↔ 20–40ft (6–12m). Probably N. Africa and W. Asia. ❀ (min. 50–61°F/10–16°C)

Phoenix reclinata

P. humilis see *P. loureirii*.

P. loureirii, syn. *P. humilis*. Small palm, often with clustered stems, bearing leaves to 6ft (2m) long or more, composed of linear, glaucous, bright mid-green leaflets, clustered along the midribs. Bowl-shaped cream flowers appear in panicles, to 3ft (1m) long, usually in summer, followed by ovoid, dry-fleshed, red to black fruit, ½–¾in (1.5–2cm) across. ↕ 6–15ft (2–5m), ↔ 6–12ft (2–4m). Sri Lanka, India to S. China. ❀ (min. 50–61°F/10–16°C)

P. reclinata ▣ Small, clustering palm with ascending or leaning, slender stems clad with fibrous, red-brown leaf remains. Leaves, to 8ft (2.5m) long, are composed of many linear, mid- to deep green leaflets, usually arranged in several planes. Bowl-shaped cream flowers are produced in panicles, to 5ft (1.5m) long, usually in summer, followed by cylindrical-ellipsoid, edible but dry, orange-red to black fruit, to ¾in (2cm) across. ↕↔ to 30ft (10m). Tropical Africa. ❀ (min. 50–61°F/10–16°C)

P. roebelenii (Miniature date palm, Pygmy date palm). Small, sometimes clustering palm, often with a narrow skirt of dead leaves. Living leaves, 3–4ft (1–1.2m) long, have many linear, bright deep green leaflets, sometimes with flattened, scale-like hairs beneath. Bowl-shaped cream flowers appear in panicles, to 18in (45cm) long, usually in summer, followed by ellipsoid, edible black fruit, to ½in (1.5cm) long. ↕ 6ft (2m) or more, ↔ to 8ft (2.5m). Laos. ❀ (min. 50–61°F/10–16°C)

PHORMIUM

AGAVACEAE

Genus of 2 species of evergreen perennials found in scrub and swamps, and on hillsides and riverbanks, in areas ranging from coasts to mountains in New Zealand. They form clumps of large, linear, keeled leaves, each folded into a V-shape at the base, and ranging in color from yellow-green to dark green, with many fine stripes. Cultivars often have attractive, colorful or variegated foliage. Abundant small, tubular, 6-tepaled flowers are produced in erect panicles on leafless stems in summer. In milder climates, they

Phormium cookianum subsp. *hookeri* 'Tricolor'

provide a focal point in a border, by a building, or at the edge of a lawn, and are ideal for a coastal garden. Elsewhere, grow in containers for summer display.
• **CULTIVATION** Grow in fertile, moist but well-drained soil in full sun. Where marginally hardy, provide a deep, dry mulch in winter or overwinter indoors in a cold greenhouse.
• **PROPAGATION** Sow seed at 55–64°F (13–18°C) in spring. Divide in spring.
• **PESTS AND DISEASES** Leaf spots sometimes occur.

P. colensoi see *P. cookianum.*
P. cookianum, syn. *P. colensoi* (Mountain flax). Clump-forming perennial with broad, arching, linear, light to yellowish green leaves, to 5ft (1.5m) long. Tubular, yellow-green flowers, to 1½in (4cm) long, are produced in upright panicles, 6ft (2m) long, in summer. ↕ to 6ft (2m), ↔ 10ft (3m). New Zealand. Zone 8. **subsp. *hookeri* 'Cream Delight'** has leaves with broad bands of creamy yellow in the centers and narrower bands toward the margins. **subsp. *hookeri* 'Tricolor'** ■ has leaves conspicuously margined creamy yellow and red. **'Maori Chief'**, a hybrid

Phormium tenax

of *P. cookianum*, has pink- and red-striped bronze leaves. **'Maori Sunrise'**, a hybrid of *P. cookianum*, produces slender, apricot-and-pink-striped leaves with bronze margins. **'Variegatum'** has light green leaves with cream to lime-green stripes and margins.
***P.* 'Sundowner'** ■ Clump-forming perennial with broad, upright, bronze-green leaves, to 5ft (1.5m) long, with dark rose-pink margins. Tubular, yellow-green flowers, to 1½in (4cm) long, in upright panicles, 6ft (2m) long, in summer. ↕↔ to 6ft (2m). Zone 8.
P. tenax ■ (New Zealand flax). Clump-forming perennial with rigid, upright, linear leaves, to 10ft (3m) long, dark green above, blue-green beneath. Thick, red-purple panicles, to 12ft (4m) long,

Phormium 'Sundowner'

Phormium tenax 'Dazzler'

of tubular, dull red flowers, 2in (5cm) long, are borne in summer. ↕ 12ft (4m), ↔ 6ft (2m). New Zealand. Zone 8. **'Aurora'**, a hybrid of *P. tenax*, has arching bronze leaves striped red, salmon-pink, and yellow; ↕↔ 4ft (1.2m). **'Bronze Baby'**, a dwarf hybrid of *P. tenax*, has bronze leaves, pendent at the tips; ↕↔ 24–32in (60–80cm). **'Dazzler'** ■ a hybrid of *P. tenax*, has arching bronze leaves with red, orange, and pink stripes; ↕ 3ft (1m), ↔ 4ft (1.2m). **'Variegatum'** produces leaves with creamy yellow stripes at the margins. **'Veitchianum'** has leaves with broad, creamy white stripes.
***P.* 'Yellow Wave'.** Clump-forming perennial producing broad, arching, yellow-green leaves, to 3ft (1m) long, longitudinally striped mid-green. Tubular, dull red flowers, 2in (5cm) long, in thick, red-purple panicles, to 12ft (4m) long, are borne in summer. ↕ 12ft (4m), ↔ 6ft (2m). Zone 8.

PHOTINIA

syn. HETEROMELES, STRANVAESIA

ROSACEAE

Genus of about 60 species of deciduous or evergreen shrubs and trees found in woodland and thickets from the Himalayas to E. and S.E. Asia. Leaves are alternate, lance-shaped to broadly ovate, and mid- or dark green; evergreen leaves are attractive and glossy, often brightly colored in shades of red when young; deciduous leaves often color well in autumn. The small, 5-petaled flowers are saucer- to cup-shaped, and are produced in dense, terminal and axillary, corymb-like panicles, followed by spherical or ovoid, usually red fruits, ¼–½in (0.6–1.5cm) across. Grow deciduous species in a woodland garden, or as specimens on a lawn; grow evergreens as a hedge, in a shrub border, or among other trees and shrubs. Where marginally hardy, grow evergreen shrubs against a wall or in the shelter of trees.
• **CULTIVATION** Grow in fertile, moist but well-drained soil in full sun or partial shade. *P. beauverdiana* and *P. villosa* need acidic to neutral soil. Pruning group 1.
• **PROPAGATION** Sow seed in containers in a cold frame in autumn. Root semi-ripe cuttings with bottom heat in summer.
• **PESTS AND DISEASES** Crown gall, mushroom root rot, gray mold (*Botrytis*), leaf scorch, and *Entomosporium* leaf spot may be problems.

Photinia davidiana

P. beauverdiana. Spreading, deciduous tree with elliptic to obovate, dark green leaves, to 5in (13cm) long, turning red in autumn. In late spring, bears small white flowers in corymb-like panicles, to 2in (5cm) across, followed by ovoid red fruit. ↕ to 30ft (10m), ↔ 20ft (6m). W. China. Zone 7.
P. davidiana ■ syn. *Stranvaesia davidiana.* Upright, evergreen tree or shrub with elliptic to inversely lance-shaped, tapered, dark green leaves, to 5in (13cm) long; older leaves turn red in autumn. In midsummer, small white flowers are produced in corymb-like panicles, 3in (8cm) across, followed by spherical, bright red fruit. ↕ 25ft (8m), ↔ 20ft (6m). China, Vietnam. Zone 7. **'Palette'** is slow-growing and shrubby, with leaves boldly marked creamy white; ↕ 15ft (5m), ↔ 10ft (3m). **var. *undulata* 'Fructu Luteo'** bears yellow fruit.
P. x fraseri (*P. glabra* x *P. serratifolia*) (Red tip). Upright, evergreen shrub or small tree with inversely lance-shaped to elliptic, leathery, dark green leaves, 4–8in (10–20cm) long, bronze to bright red when young. In mid- and late spring, produces small white flowers in corymb-like panicles, to 6in (15cm) across. ↕↔ 15ft (5m). Garden origin. Zone 8. **'Birmingham'** is bushy-headed, spreading, and often many-stemmed, with oblong to obovate leaves, bright purple-red when young; sometimes bears spherical red fruit. **'Red Robin'** ■ is compact, with bright red young foliage.
P. glabra (Japanese photinia). Dense, rounded, evergreen shrub with elliptic to

Photinia x *fraseri* 'Red Robin'

Photinia glabra 'Rubens'

obovate, dark green leaves, to 3½in (9cm) long, red when young. In early summer, bears flattened, corymb-like panicles, 4in (10cm) across, of small white flowers, followed by spherical red fruit, turning black. ↕↔ 10ft (3m). Japan. Zone 7b. **'Rosea Marginata'** has green-, white-, gray-, and pink-variegated leaves. **'Rubens'** ▣ produces bright red young foliage. **'Variegata'** produces pink leaves, aging to white-edged, green leaves.
P. nussia, syn. *Stranvaesia nussia.* Spreading, often rather spiny, evergreen tree with oblong to obovate, leathery, glossy, dark green leaves, to 4in (10cm) long, paler beneath. In midsummer, bears small white flowers in flattened, corymb-like panicles, to 4in (10cm) across, followed by spherical, downy, orange-red fruit. ↕↔ 20ft (6m). Himalayas to S.E. Asia. ❄ (min. 41°F/5°C)
P. parvifolia. Spreading, deciduous shrub with dark red young shoots and oval to obovate, toothed, dark green leaves, 1¼–2½in (3–6cm) long, pale green beneath. In late spring, bears white flowers in flattened, terminal heads, 1¼in (3cm) across, followed by ovoid, orange-red to bright red fruit, ½in (1.5cm) across. ↕ 6–10ft (2–3m), ↔ 6–8ft (2–2.5m). China. Zone 7.
***P.* 'Redstart'.** Upright, evergreen shrub or small tree bearing oblong to elliptic, dark green leaves, to 4½in (11cm) long, bronze-red when young, on red shoots. Small white flowers, in dense, corymb-like panicles, 4in (10cm) across, appear in early summer before spherical, yellow-flushed, orange-red fruit. ↕ 15ft (5m), ↔ 10ft (3m). Zone 7.

Photinia villosa

P. serratifolia ▣ syn. *P. serrulata.* Spreading, evergreen tree with peeling, gray and red-brown bark when mature. Oblong to inversely lance-shaped, glossy, shallowly but sharply toothed, dark green leaves, to 8in (20cm) long, are red when young. In late spring and early summer, bears small white flowers in flattened, corymb-like panicles, 4–7in (10–18cm) across, followed by spherical red fruit. ↕ 30–40ft (10–12m), ↔ 25ft (8m). China. Zone 7. **'Aculeata'** produces red-tinged young stems and longer leaves.
P. serrulata see *P. serratifolia.*
P. villosa ▣ (Oriental photinia). Spreading, deciduous tree, sometimes shrubby, with elliptic to obovate, dark green leaves, to 3in (8cm) long, bronze when young, turning orange and red in autumn. In late spring, small white flowers are borne in flattened, corymb-like panicles, 1½in (4cm) across, followed by ovoid red fruit. ↕↔ 15ft (5m). China, Korea, Japan. Zone 5b. **var. *laevis*** produces narrower, less hairy leaves than the species.

Photinia serratifolia

Phragmipedium

ORCHIDACEAE

Genus of 15–20 species of large, evergreen, mainly terrestrial, occasionally lithophytic or epiphytic orchids from Mexico and Central and South America, often found in between rocks or near rivers at low altitudes. They have robust, fleshy, clustered shoots with fibrous roots, but lack pseudobulbs. Leaves are leathery, strap-shaped, often mid-green, and arranged in 2 ranks. Upright stems, arising from the center of each shoot, bear one or several often brightly colored flowers in terminal racemes or panicles; some have very long petals, and each has a significant, slipper-shaped lip.

Phragmipedium Sedenii

• **Cultivation** Cool-growing orchids. Grow in epiphytic orchid potting mix in containers that restrict the roots. In summer, provide bright filtered light and high humidity, and apply fertilizer at every third watering. In winter, provide full light, with some midday shade, water sparingly, and apply fertilizer every 6–8 weeks. See also p.46.
• **Propagation** Divide clustered shoots by separating offshoots before growth begins in late winter or early spring.
• **Pests and diseases** Prone to spider mites, aphids, and mealybugs.

P. besseae. Terrestrial or lithophytic orchid with 6–10 strap-shaped, leathery leaves, to 8in (20cm) long. Bright scarlet flowers, 2½in (6cm) across, are produced singly or in short, upright racemes in spring. ↕↔ 6in (15cm). Ecuador, Peru. ❄ (min. 57°F/14°C; max. 86°F/30°C)
P. caudatum. Epiphytic or lithophytic orchid with usually 6–9 strap-shaped, blunt-tipped, leathery, light green leaves, to 24in (60cm) long. In summer, bears upright racemes of very large flowers, 4–6in (10–15cm) across, with very narrow, ribbon-like, dark reddish to greenish brown, pendent petals, 24in (60cm) long; sepals are off-white to yellow-green, veined darker green or orange, and lips are deep pinkish white with pink or brown veins and yellow rims. ↕↔ 24in (60cm). Mexico to Peru. ❄ (min. 57°F/14°C; max. 86°F/30°C)
P. longifolium. Terrestrial orchid with about 6 strap-shaped, leathery leaves, to 3ft (1m) long, with sharp-pointed tips. In autumn, bears racemes of pale yellow-green flowers, 6in (15cm) across, with wavy, purple-margined petals, dark green-veined sepals, and purple-flushed lips. ↕↔ 24in (60cm). Costa Rica, Panama, Colombia, Ecuador. ❄ (min. 57°F/14°C; max. 86°F/30°C)
***P.* Sedenii** ▣ (*P. longifolium* x *P. schlimii*). Terrestrial orchid with strap-shaped leaves, to 12in (30cm) long. Erect racemes of rounded, ivory-white flowers, 2½in (6cm) across, flushed and margined rose-pink, with twisted petals and rose-pink lips, are produced sporadically throughout the year. ↕↔ 24in (60cm). ❄ (min. 57°F/14°C; max. 86°F/30°C)

Phragmites australis 'Variegatus'

Phragmites

Reed

POACEAE

Genus of approximately 4 species of rhizomatous, perennial grasses widely distributed in fen, marsh, and riverside habitats in temperate and tropical zones worldwide. They have robust stems bearing deciduous, flat, linear, mid- or slightly gray-green leaves. From late summer to mid- or late autumn, they produce large, plumed, silky-hairy panicles of 3- to 11-flowered spikelets, which are useful for dried arrangements. *P. australis*, the only species commonly grown, is vigorous and highly invasive, especially in shallow water. Grow in plantings with ample space; where space is limited, grow in large containers sunk in water to restrict growth.
• **Cultivation** Grow in moderately fertile, reliably moist, deep soil in full sun. Cut back dead stems by late winter.
• **Propagation** Divide from early spring to early summer.
• **Pests and diseases** Damping off, seed smut, leaf streak, and eye spot sometimes occur.

P. australis, syn. *P. communis* (Giant reed). Vigorous, rhizomatous reed grass with robust stems bearing flat, linear, long-pointed, grayish green leaves, to 24in (60cm) long, turning golden russet in autumn. From late summer to mid-autumn, bears spikelets in plume-like, silky-hairy, glistening, dark brownish purple panicles, to 18in (45cm) long. ↕ to 10ft (3m) in flower, ↔ indefinite. Tropical and temperate regions worldwide. Zone 5. **'Variegatus'** ▣ is less invasive, and has leaves striped golden yellow, fading almost to white.
P. communis see *P. australis.*

Phuopsis *syn.* Crucianella

RUBIACEAE

Genus of one species of mat-forming, stem-rooting perennial found in open sites on hillsides in the Caucasus Mountains and N.E. Iran. It produces whorls of narrowly elliptic leaves, and is cultivated for its abundant clusters of small, tubular-funnel-shaped, scented flowers, each with 5 spreading petal lobes, borne at the tips of the stems in summer. Grow as a groundcover on a bank, in a rock garden, or at the front of a border.

Phuopsis stylosa

• **CULTIVATION** Grow in moderately fertile, gritty, moist but well-drained soil in full sun or partial shade. Cut back after flowering to maintain a compact shape.
• **PROPAGATION** Sow seed in containers in an open frame in autumn. Divide or take stem-tip cuttings from spring to early summer.
• **PESTS AND DISEASES** Infrequent.

P. stylosa ■ syn. *Crucianella stylosa.* Mat-forming perennial with slender, branching stems bearing whorls of 6–8 pointed, narrowly elliptic, musk-scented, pale green leaves, ½–1in (1.5–2.5cm) long. Produces rounded heads of many tiny, tubular-funnel-shaped pink flowers, ½–¾in (1.5–2cm) long, in summer. ↕ 6in (15cm), ↔ 20in (50cm) or more. Caucasus, N.E. Iran. Zone 6.

PHYGELIUS

SCROPHULARIACEAE

Genus of 2 species of evergreen shrubs or subshrubs found on wet slopes and streambanks in South Africa. They are cultivated for their panicles of showy, tubular flowers, each with 5 recurved lobes, borne over a long period in summer and often into autumn. The ovate to lance-shaped, dark green leaves are mostly in opposite pairs, the upper leaves sometimes alternate. Grow in a shrub border or herbaceous border, or against a wall. Where temperatures regularly drop below 32°F (0°C), treat as herbaceous or tender perennials. They may spread extensively by suckers, given ideal conditions.

Phygelius aequalis

Phygelius aequalis 'Yellow Trumpet'

• **CULTIVATION** Grow in fertile, moist, well-drained soil in full sun. Where marginally hardy, provide a dry winter mulch. If grown as perennials, cut back to the bases in spring; otherwise, pruning group 9.
• **PROPAGATION** Sow seed in containers in a cold frame in spring. Take softwood cuttings in late spring. Remove rooted suckers in spring.
• **PESTS AND DISEASES** Figwort weevils and capsid bugs may be a problem.

P. aequalis ■ Upright, suckering shrub with ovate, dark green leaves, to 4½in (11cm) long. In summer, produces upright panicles, to 10in (25cm) long, of nodding, dusk-pink flowers, to 2½in (6cm) or more long, with crimson lobes and yellow throats. ↕↔ 3ft (1m). South Africa. Zone 8. **'Yellow Trumpet'** ■ has pale green leaves, and bears pale creamy yellow flowers.
P. capensis (Cape figwort, Cape fuchsia). Upright, suckering shrub with ovate, dark green leaves, to 3½in (9cm) long. In summer, bears upright panicles, to 24in (60cm) long, of yellow-throated orange flowers, to 2½in (5cm) long, with orange-red lobes; the flowers turn

Phygelius x *rectus* 'Moonraker'

back toward the stems. ↕ 4ft (1.2m), ↔ 5ft (1.5m). South Africa. Zone 7b. **'Coccineus'** has scarlet flowers.
P.* x *rectus (*P. aequalis* x *P. capensis*). Upright, suckering shrub with ovate, dark green leaves, to 4in (10cm) long. In summer, pale red flowers, to 2½in (6cm) long, are borne in panicles 6–12in (15–30cm) long. ↕↔ to 5ft (1.5m). Garden origin. Zone 7b. **'African Queen'** ■ bears pendent, pale red flowers, with orange-red lobes and yellow mouths, in upright panicles, 12in (30cm) or more long; ↕ 3ft (1m), ↔ 4ft (1.2m). **'Devil's Tears'** has pendent, deep red-pink flowers, turning back toward the stems, with orange-red lobes and yellow throats. **'Moonraker'** ■ has slightly downward-curved, pale creamy

Phygelius x *rectus* 'African Queen'

Phygelius x *rectus* 'Salmon Leap'

yellow flowers. **'Pink Elf'** produces slender, pale pink flowers, with spreading, dark crimson lobes, in panicles to 6in (15cm) long; ↕ 30in (75cm), ↔ 36in (90cm). **'Salmon Leap'** ■ has deeply lobed orange flowers, turning slightly back toward the stems, in panicles to 18in (45cm) long; ↕ 4ft (1.2m), ↔ 5ft (1.5m). **'Winchester Fanfare'** has pendent, dusky, red-pink flowers.

PHYLICA

Cape myrtle

RHAMNACEAE

Genus of about 150 species of heath-like, evergreen shrubs occurring in a range of habitats from seashores to rocky mountain slopes, mainly in South Africa but also in Madagascar and Tristan da Cunha. Leaves are small, alternate, often densely borne, usually narrow, simple, and entire, often with rolled margins. Each tiny flower either has 5 sometimes petal-like sepals and no petals, or has modified petals forming bristles or filaments. Where temperatures fall below 41°F (5°C), grow in a cool greenhouse. In warmer areas, use in a shrub border, or as a hedge or low windbreak.
• **CULTIVATION** Under glass, grow in acidic potting mix in full light; ventilate well. When in growth, water moderately and apply a balanced liquid fertilizer monthly. Keep just moist in winter. Outdoors, grow in moderately fertile, humus-rich, moist but well-drained, ideally neutral to acidic soil in full sun. Pruning group 10, after flowering; clip hedges after flowering or in midsummer.
• **PROPAGATION** Sow seed at 55–64°F (13–18°C) in spring. Take greenwood cuttings in early summer.
• **PESTS AND DISEASES** Infrequent.

P. plumosa, syn. *P. pubescens.* Moderately bushy, downy shrub with wiry stems. Linear to lance-shaped, mid-green leaves, ½–1¼in (1–3cm) long, have rolled margins, and are dotted with glands above, long-hairy beneath. In spring, bears plume-like inflorescences of tiny, cup-shaped, dark brown flowers, surrounded by leaf-like bracts, ¾–1¼in (2–3cm) long, densely clothed in long, brownish white hairs. ↕ 3–6ft (1–2m), ↔ 1½–5ft (0.75–1.5m). South Africa. ❄ (min. 41°F/5°C)
P. pubescens see *P. plumosa.*

▷ ***Phyllanthus nivosus*** see *Breynia disticha*

P

× PHYLLIOPSIS

RICACEAE

Hybrid genus of dwarf, evergreen shrubs, erived from crosses between *Phyllodoce* nd *Kalmiopsis*. They are grown for their ell-shaped flowers, borne in spring. The stems are upright, bearing simple, lternate, glossy leaves. Grow in a shady ite in a rock garden.

CULTIVATION Grow in moderately ertile, humus-rich, acidic, reliably moist oil in deep or partial shade. Pruning roup 10, after flowering.

PROPAGATION Take semi-ripe cuttings n summer.

PESTS AND DISEASES Infrequent.

× ***P. hillieri* 'Pinocchio'.** Upright shrub with branching, hairy shoots. Oblong-bovate, glossy, dark green leaves, ¾in 2cm) long, have margins slightly rolled nder. Produces erect, terminal racemes f 5-lobed, widely bell-shaped, red-urple flowers, ½in (1.5cm) across, in ate spring. ↕ 8in (20cm), ↔ to 12in 30cm). Zone 6.

Phyllitis scolopendrium see *Asplenium scolopendrium*

Phyllocactus see *Disocactus*

PHYLLOCLADUS

Celery pine

PHYLLOCLADACEAE

Genus of 5 species of monoecious or ioecious, evergreen, coniferous trees nd shrubs found in forests in Indonesia, Malaysia, the Philippines, Tasmania Australia), and New Zealand. They ave 2 kinds of shoots: normal shoots hat produce radial, reduced, scale-like, on-functioning leaves; and flattened, nodified shoots that form leaf-like, hotosynthesizing elements called hylloclades, which resemble the leaves f celery. Female cones each bear one to everal seeds within fleshy, cup-like arils, sually on the edges of the phylloclades. Male cones are catkin-like, borne in erminal groups. Celery pines are nusual specimen plants, and are ttractive in spring with their colorful nale cones. Where not hardy, grow in a ool greenhouse.

CULTIVATION Under glass, grow in oil-based potting mix, with added leaf nold, in full light. When in growth, water freely and apply a balanced liquid ertilizer every month. Water sparingly in winter. Outdoors, grow in any well-drained soil in full sun.

• **PROPAGATION** Sow seed at 43–54°F (6–12°C) in spring. Take semi-ripe cuttings in summer.

• **PESTS AND DISEASES** Infrequent.

P. trichomanoides ■ (Tanekaha). Pyramidal tree with smooth, gray-black bark and whorled branches. Pinnate phylloclades, to 12in (30cm) long, each with 7–15 diamond-shaped segments, are reddish brown when young, then mid-green. In spring, produces spherical, dark blue or black female cones, 1in (2cm) long, and catkin-like, cylindrical, purple male cones, ½in (1.5cm) long, ripening red then yellow, borne in clusters of 5–10. ↕ to 40ft (12m) or more, ↔ to 20ft (6m) or more. New Zealand. ❄ (min. 45°F/7°C)

PHYLLODOCE

ERICACEAE

Genus of 8 species of spreading or erect, evergreen shrubs and subshrubs from alpine and arctic habitats in the N. hemisphere. Leaves are alternate, linear, leathery, downy beneath, with rolled, toothed margins. Bell-, urn-, or pitcher-shaped, nodding or horizontally held flowers are borne in terminal racemes or umbel-like clusters, sometimes solitary. Grow in a rock garden.

• **CULTIVATION** Grow in moderately fertile, humus-rich, moist but well-drained, acidic soil in partial shade. Pruning group 10, after flowering.

• **PROPAGATION** Sow seed at 43–54°F (6–12°C) in early spring. Take semi-ripe cuttings in summer. Layer in spring.

• **PESTS AND DISEASES** Spider mites may be a problem under glass.

P. aleutica. Decumbent or scrambling, mat-forming shrub with linear, minutely toothed, bright dark green leaves, ½in (1.5cm) long, softly yellow-downy and with a central white line beneath. In late spring and early summer, bears pendent, umbel-like clusters of urn-shaped, pale yellow-green flowers, to ⅜in (9mm) long. ↕ to 8in (20cm), ↔ 10in (25cm). Japan, Russia (Sakhalin, Kurile Islands, Kamchatka), Alaska. Zone 2. **'Flora Slack'** bears white flowers.

P. caerulea, syn. *P. taxifolia*. Upright shrub with linear, fine-toothed, glossy, dark green leaves, to ½in (1.5cm) long, downy beneath. Pitcher-shaped, purplish pink flowers, ½in (1.5cm)

Phyllodoce x *intermedia* 'Drummondii'

long, are produced singly or in umbel-like clusters, in late spring and summer. ↕ 6–9in (15–23cm), ↔ 12in (30cm). Europe, Asia, US. Zone 2.

P. empetriformis ■ Loose, mat-forming shrub with linear, glossy, bright green leaves, ½in (1.5cm) long, with glandular-toothed margins, downy beneath. Bears umbel-like clusters of long-stalked, bell-shaped, purple-pink to rose-red flowers, ½in (9mm) long, in late spring and early summer. ↕ 12in (30cm), ↔ to 16in (40cm). W. North America. Zone 3.

P.* x *intermedia (*P. aleutica* var. *glanduliflora* x *P. empetriformis*). Bushy, low-spreading subshrub with linear, glossy, fine-toothed, dark green leaves, ½in (1.5cm) long, downy beneath. In midspring, bears umbel-like clusters of pendent, urn-shaped to narrowly bell-shaped, reddish purple to pink flowers, to ¼in (6mm) long, on slender red stalks. ↕ 6–9in (15–23cm), ↔ 14in (35cm). Zone 2. **'Drummondii'** ■ has deep red-purple flowers. **'Fred Stoker'** bears light purple flowers.

P. nipponica. Erect subshrub with linear, dark green leaves, to ½in (1.5cm) long, with white-downy midribs beneath, and minutely glandular-toothed, rolled margins. Loose, umbel-like clusters of pendent, bell-shaped, white, sometimes pink-tinged flowers, ¼in (6mm) long, are produced on upright, red-tinted stalks in late spring and early summer. ↕↔ to 8in (20cm). Japan. Zone 3. **var. *amabilis*** has red calyx lobes, red or pink corolla tips, and short, crimson anthers.

P. taxifolia see *P. caerulea*.

PHYLLOSTACHYS

POACEAE

Genus of about 80 species of medium-sized to large, evergreen bamboos occurring in deciduous woodland and groves in E. Asia and the Himalayas. They have a branching habit and spreading rhizomes, although in cool-temperate climates they usually form compact clumps. The culms are hollow and grooved, and often zigzag from node to node on young plants. Leaves are yellow-green or light to dark green, narrowly lance-shaped, and checkered. Valued for their elegant form and foliage, some also for their subtly colored culms, they are suitable for containers outdoors, as specimen plants, or in groups among shorter shrubs in a border. They thrive in a woodland garden, and may also be used to create a screen.

• **CULTIVATION** Grow in fertile, humus-rich, moist but well-drained soil in full sun or dappled shade. In containers, use soil-based potting mix, and apply a balanced liquid fertilizer monthly. Where not hardy, shelter from cold, drying winds.

• **PROPAGATION** Divide in spring.

• **PESTS AND DISEASES** Rust and stem smut are common. Slugs and snails attack emerging shoots.

P. aurea (Fishpole bamboo, Golden bamboo). Clump-forming, stiffly upright bamboo with grooved culms, bright mid-green at first, becoming brown-yellow when mature; there are cup-shaped swellings beneath each node, and the lower nodes are asymmetrical, distorted, and often densely crowded. Produces narrowly lance-shaped, yellowish to golden green leaves, to 6in (15cm) long. ↕ 6–30ft (2–10m), ↔ indefinite. S.E. China. Zone 7. **'Albo-variegata'** has slender culms and white-striped leaves. **'Holochrysa'** bears yellow-orange culms, occasionally green-striped, and sometimes striped leaves. **'Violascens'** see *P. violascens*.

P. aureosulcata (Yellow-groove bamboo). Clump-forming bamboo producing rough, brownish green culms, often zigzagged at the bases, with yellow grooves and striped sheaths. Leaves are narrowly lance-shaped and mid-green, to 7in (18cm) long. ↕ 10–20ft (3–6m), ↔ indefinite. N.E. China. Zone 7. **var. *aureocaulis*** ■ produces sulfur-yellow culms, occasionally with green

P

Phyllocladus trichomanoides

Phyllodoce empetriformis

Phyllostachys aureosulcata var. *aureocaulis*

Phyllostachys bambusoides

stripes near the bases; C. China. **'Spectabilis'** has thick yellow culms with green grooves.

P. bambusoides ■ (Giant timber bamboo). Clump-forming bamboo that has thick, shiny, deep green culms and large, thick leaf sheaths with kinked bristles. Produces broadly lance-shaped, glossy, dark green leaves, to 8in (20cm) long. ↕ 10–25ft (3–8m), ↔ indefinite. China, possibly also Japan. Zone 7b. **'Allgold'** ■ syn. 'Holochrysa', 'Sulfurea' of gardens, produces rich golden yellow culms, although, in some, the culms are green and the groove is yellow; occasionally has yellow-striped leaves. Young culms may feel waxy. **'Castillon'** (Castillon bamboo) produces yellow culms with green grooves, and has green leaves with yellow stripes. **'Holochrysa'** see 'Allgold'. **'Sulfurea' of gardens** see 'Allgold'. **'Violascens'** see *P. violascens*. **'White Crookstem'** has the characteristic crooked culms with a white powder that covers the older culms.

P. dulcis (Sweetshoot bamboo). Clump-forming bamboo producing upright, mid-green culms. Bears broadly lance-shaped, smooth green leaves, 7in (18cm)

Phyllostachys bambusoides 'Allgold'

Phyllostachys flexuosa

long. ↕ 40ft (12m), ↔ indefinite. China. Zone 7b.

P. flexuosa ■ (Zigzag bamboo). Clump-forming bamboo with slightly ribbed, slender, arching culms, often zigzagged between the nodes, bright green at first, turning yellow-brown to almost black with age, and with a waxy-white bloom below the nodes. Bears narrowly lance-shaped, fresh green leaves, to 6in (15cm) long, which retain their color throughout winter. ↕ 6–30ft (2–10m), ↔ indefinite. China. Zone 7.

P. glauca see *P. violascens*.

***P.* 'Henonis'** see *P. nigra* var. *henonis*.

P. nidularia (Swollen-node bamboo). Clump-forming bamboo that produces upright, smooth green culms with very prominent culm nodes. Bears broadly lance-shaped, smooth green leaves, 6–7in (15–18cm) long. ↕ 35ft (11m), ↔ indefinite. China. Zone 7b.

P. nigra ■ (Black bamboo). Clump-forming bamboo producing arching, slender green culms that turn lustrous black in their second or third year. Bears abundant lance-shaped, dark green leaves, 1½–5in (4–13cm) long. ↕ 10–15ft (3–5m), ↔ 6–10ft (2–3m). E. and C. China. Zone 7. **'Boryana'** has green to yellowish green culms with purple-brown marks. **var. *henonis*** ■ syn. *P.* 'Henonis', has bright green culms, turning yellow-green when mature, and glossy leaves, downy and rough when young. **'Robert Young'** (Sulfur bamboo) has green-striped, gold culms, sulfur-green when young.

P. sulphurea (Ougon-Kou chiku, Robert Ougon-chiku). Clump-forming

Phyllostachys nigra

Phyllostachys nigra var. *henonis*

bamboo with upright yellow culms, which become more yellow with age, sometimes green-striped, with the lower nodes pitted, hairless, and white-powdery. Bears narrowly lance-shaped, occasionally striped, mid-green leaves, 2½–6in (6–15cm) long. ↕ 12–40ft (4–12m), ↔ indefinite. E. China. Zone 7. **var. *viridis*** (Kou-chiku) produces green culms, which remain smaller in cooler climates.

P. violascens, syn. *P. aurea* 'Violascens', *P. bambusoides* 'Violascens', *P. glauca*. Clump-forming then spreading bamboo with swollen green culms, finely striped purple, becoming violet. Produces narrowly lance-shaped, glossy, dark green leaves, to 5in (13cm) long, glaucous beneath. ↕ to 16ft (5m) or more, ↔ 6ft (2m) or more. China. Zone 7b.

P. viridi-glaucescens. Clump-forming bamboo with arching, smooth, hairless green culms, with prominent nodes and waxy white powder below the nodes. Produces broadly lance-shaped, mid-green leaves, 1½–8in (4–20cm) long. ↕ 12–40ft (4–12m), ↔ indefinite. E. China. Zone 7b.

P. vivax. Clump-forming bamboo producing upright, smooth, mid-green culms, with a white powdery band beneath each node. Bears broadly lance-shaped, smooth, green leaves, 8in (20cm) long. ↕ 70ft (20m), ↔ indefinite. China. Zone 7b.

x PHYLLOTHAMNUS

ERICACEAE

Hybrid genus of one upright, evergreen shrub, derived from crosses between *Phyllodoce* and *Rhodothamnus*. This shrub is grown for its heath-like, alternate, linear leaves and its funnel-shaped flowers, produced from late spring through early summer. Grow in a shady rock garden.

- **CULTIVATION** Grow in acidic, humus-rich, moderately fertile, moist but well-drained soil in partial shade. Pruning group 10, after flowering.
- **PROPAGATION** Root semi-ripe cuttings in summer.
- **PESTS AND DISEASES** Spider mites may be troublesome under glass.

x *P. erectus* (*Phyllodoce empetriformis* x *Rhodothamnus chamaecistus*). Evergreen shrub with linear, glossy, dark green leaves, to ½in (1.5cm) long. Produces terminal clusters of 2–10 widely funnel-shaped, deep rose-pink flowers, ½in (1.5cm) across, in late spring and early summer. ↕ 10in (25cm), ↔ to 12in (30cm). Garden origin. Zone 7.

▷ ***Phyodina*** see *Callisia*

PHYSALIS

Ground cherry

SOLANACEAE

Genus of approximately 80 species of upright, bushy, sometimes rhizomatous annuals and perennials found in sunny or lightly shaded, well-drained habitats worldwide, although mostly in the Americas. They have alternate or whorled, entire or pinnatifid, mid-green leaves. Tiny, inconspicuous, bell-shaped flowers, with star-shaped mouths, are produced singly (rarely in small clusters) from the leaf axils; they are followed by spherical, bright red, yellow, or purple, sometimes edible berries, enclosed in decorative, papery, orange to scarlet calyces. In some species, the calyces skeletonize, and persist throughout winter with the berries inside, remaining attractive; they can be used in dried arrangements. Ground cherries are suitable for a border, although they may become invasive. All parts of *P. alkekengi*, except the fully ripe fruit, may cause mild stomach upset if ingested; contact with foliage may irritate skin. P. ixocarpa, however, may be used green for a hotter tasting salsa or relish, or when red for a milder condiment.

- **CULTIVATION** Grow in any well-drained soil in full sun or partial shade. Cut stems for drying as the calyces begin to color.
- **PROPAGATION** Sow seed of perennials in containers in a cold frame in spring; sow seed of annuals *in situ* in midspring. Divide in spring.
- **PESTS AND DISEASES** Rust, white smut, caterpillars, and *Cercospora* leaf spot are common.

P. alkekengi ■ (Chinese lantern, Japanese lantern). Vigorous, spreading, often invasive, rhizomatous perennial with triangular-ovate to diamond-shaped leaves, to 5in (13cm) long. Nodding, bell-shaped cream flowers, ¾in (2cm) long, with star-shaped mouths, are produced from the leaf axil in midsummer, followed by large, bright orange-scarlet berries enclosed in papery red calyces, to 2in (5cm) across.

Physalis alkekengi

↕ 24–30in (60–75cm), ↔ 36in (90cm) or more. C. and S. Europe, W. Asia to Japan. Zone 4. **var. *franchetii*** has broadly ovate leaves, and produces tiny, solitary, creamy white flowers, to ¼in (6mm) long. **'Gigantea'**, syn. 'Monstrosa', produces large berries, to ¾in (2cm) across. **'Monstrosa'** see 'Gigantea'. **'Variegata'** has leaves with cream and yellow-green borders.

P. ixocarpa ■ (Tomatillo). Frost-tender annual with a bushy, sprawling form. The compound leaves are dark to midgreen, on sturdy, somewhat sticky stems. The small flowers are yellow with purple markings, followed in 50–70 days by small, green fruits enclosed in a yellow-purple, bladder-like calyx. Fruits can be harvested from their papery husks when immature for a tart, but slightly sweet taste, useful in salsas and curries, or when ripe for a milder, sweeter taste. Grow in a vegetable garden as for tomatoes, starting indoors and transplanting out after seedings are 4–6in (10–15cm) tall. ↕ 3–5ft (1–1.5m), ↔ to 24in (60cm). Mexico, Central America.

PHYSARIA

Bladderpod

BRASSICACEAE

Genus of 14 species of rosette-forming, often short-lived perennials occurring mainly in the mountains of W. North America, usually in rocky sites and open screes. They are cultivated for their unusual, bladder-like seed pods and their attractive symmetrical rosettes of obovate to lance-shaped, mid-green, often silver-hairy leaves. Raceme-like clusters of 4-petaled, cross-shaped yellow flowers are borne in summer, followed by the inflated seed pods. Grow bladderpods in a scree bed or alpine house; they are intolerant of excessive winter moisture.

- **CULTIVATION** Grow in moderately fertile, gritty, sharply drained soil in full sun. In an alpine house, grow in a mix of equal parts loam, leaf mold, and grit.
- **PROPAGATION** Sow seed in containers in an open frame as soon as ripe.
- **PESTS AND DISEASES** Prone to damage by slugs, snails, aphids, and spider mites.

P. didymocarpa. Rosette-forming perennial with obovate, silver-gray leaves, ½–1½in (1.5–4cm) long, with a suede-like texture. In summer, bears open clusters of cross-shaped, bright yellow flowers, ¾in (2cm) across, followed by large, inflated, gray-hairy seed pods, ½in (1.5cm) long. ↕ 3–4in (8–10cm), ↔ to 6in (15cm). W. North America. Zone 4.

Physalis ixocarpa

PHYSOCARPUS

ROSACEAE

Genus of about 10 species of deciduous shrubs occurring in thickets and on rocky slopes in E. Asia and North America. They have peeling bark and alternate, ovate to rounded or kidney-shaped, palmately lobed, mid- or dark green leaves. They are cultivated for their foliage and dense, terminal corymbs of small, cup-shaped white flowers, borne in early summer. Grow in a shrub border.

- **CULTIVATION** Grow in preferably acidic, fertile, moist but well-drained soil in full sun or partial shade. May become chlorotic if grown in alkaline soil. Pruning group 1 or 2.
- **PROPAGATION** Sow seed in containers outdoors in spring or autumn. Take greenwood cuttings in summer. Remove rooted suckers in autumn or spring.
- **PESTS AND DISEASES** Leaf spots, fireblight, powdery mildew, and witches' broom sometimes occur.

P. monogynus (Mountain ninebark). Upright, compact shrub with rounded to ovate, 3-lobed, doubly toothed, mid-green leaves, ¾–1½in (2–4cm) long. From spring to summer, produces few rosy white flowers, ¼in (6mm) across, in corymbs, 2in (5cm) across, followed by clusters of bladder-like, green-flushed red fruit, ¼in (6mm) long. ↕↔ 24–36in (60–90cm). Wyoming and South Dakota to New Mexico and Texas. Zone 3.

P. opulifolius, syn. *Spiraea opulifolius* (Ninebark). Compact, thicket-forming shrub, spreading by suckers, with arching branches and broadly ovate, 3-lobed, doubly toothed, mid-green leaves, to 3in (8cm) long. Small, cup-shaped, pink-tinged white flowers are produced in dense corymbs, 2in (5cm) across, in early summer, followed by clusters of bladder-like, green-flushed red fruit, ¼in (6mm) long. ↕ 10ft (3m), ↔ 15ft (5m). E. North America. Zone 2b. **'Dart's Gold'** ■ has bright yellow young foliage; ↕ 6ft (2m), ↔ 8ft (2.5m).

Physocarpus opulifolius 'Dart's Gold'

Physoplexis comosa

PHYSOPLEXIS

CAMPANULACEAE

Genus of one species of tuft-forming, deciduous perennial found in rock crevices in the Alps. Clusters of unusual, bottle-shaped flowers arise from basal tufts of ovate to heart-shaped, toothed leaves. Grow in an alpine house, rock crevice, or scree bed.

- **CULTIVATION** Grow in gritty, poor to moderately fertile, sharply drained, alkaline soil in full sun, with some mid-day shade. Protect from winter moisture. In an alpine house, grow in a mix of equal parts loam, leaf mold, and grit.
- **PROPAGATION** Sow seed in containers in an open frame in autumn.
- **PESTS AND DISEASES** Very susceptible to damage by slugs and snails.

P. comosa ■ syn. *Phyteuma comosum.* Tufted, deciduous perennial with ovate to heart-shaped, deeply toothed, mid- to dark green leaves, ¾–2in (2–5cm) long. In late summer, produces terminal clusters of 10–20 bottle-shaped, pale violet flowers, to ¾in (2cm) across, with inflated bases and narrow "necks," and with tapered, deep violet tips. ↕ 3in (8cm), ↔ to 4in (10cm). Europe (Alps). Zone 5.

PHYSOSTEGIA

Obedient plant

LAMIACEAE

Genus of about 12 species of erect, hairless, deciduous, rhizomatous perennials occurring in moist, sunny sites in E. North America. They have square stems and alternate pairs of variable, often toothed leaves. Almost stalkless, tubular, 2-lipped, purple, pink, or white flowers, with flattish upper lips, 3-lobed lower lips, and tubular calyces, are borne in sometimes branched racemes, mainly in summer. The flowers will remain in a new position if they are moved on the stalks, hence the common name. Grow in a border; good for cut flowers.

- **CULTIVATION** Grow in fertile, reliably moist soil in full sun or partial shade.
- **PROPAGATION** Sow seed in containers in a cold frame in autumn. Divide in winter or early spring before new growth.
- **PESTS AND DISEASES** Sometimes affected by rust and slugs.

P. speciosa see *P. virginiana.*

Physostegia virginiana 'Variegata'

P. virginiana, syn. *P. speciosa* (False dragonhead, Obedient plant). Spreading perennial with lance-shaped, elliptic, or spoon-shaped, sharply toothed, mid-green leaves, to 5in (13cm) long. Bears racemes of deep purple or bright lilac-pink, sometimes white flowers, ¾–1¼in (2–3cm) long, with inflated mouths, from midsummer to early autumn. ↕ to 4ft (1.2m), ↔ 24in (60cm) or more. E. North America. Zone 3b. **'Alba'** has pure white flowers from midsummer to early autumn; ↕ 18–24in (45–60cm). **'Bouquet Rose'** has pale, lilac-pink flowers. **'Crown of Snow'** has white flowers on low-growing plants; ↕ 2½ft (75cm). **'Galadriel'** is dwarf, with pale pink-purple flowers; ↕↔ to 18in (45cm). **'Pink Bouquet'** has rose-pink flowers; ↕ 3ft (90cm). **'Rosea'** has pink flowers; ↕ 2ft (60cm). **subsp. *speciosa* 'Variegata'** see 'Variegata'. **'Summer Snow'** bears white flowers with green calyces; ↕↔ to 24in (60cm). **'Variegata'** ■ syn. subsp. *speciosa* 'Variegata', produces grayish green leaves with white margins, and magenta-pink flowers. **'Vivid'** ■ forms dense clumps, and bears bright purple-pink flowers; ↕ 12–24in (30–60cm), ↔ 12in (30cm).

Physostegia virginiana 'Vivid'

PHYTOLACCA

Pokeweed

PHYTOLACCACEAE

Genus of about 25 species of perennials, shrubs, and trees found in open fields or woodland in tropical and subtropical areas of Africa, Asia, and North to South America. They are grown for their attractive autumn foliage color and their decorative fruits. Leaves are alternate, ovate to elliptic, and entire, and most of the perennial species have colored stems. Racemes or panicles of small, shallowly cup-shaped, petalless flowers are followed by spherical, dark red to blackish purple berries. Grow in a large border, light woodland, or a waterside planting. All parts may cause severe discomfort if ingested; the fruit of *P. americana* may be lethal if eaten. Contact with the sap may irritate skin.

• **CULTIVATION** Grow in any fertile, moist soil in full sun or partial shade. Support taller species in open sites.

• **PROPAGATION** Sow seed at 55–64°F (13–18°C) in early spring or autumn. Divide perennial species in summer. Self-sows freely, possibly becoming invasive in certain conditions.

• **PESTS AND DISEASES** Leaf spots and virus mosaic diseases may occur.

P. americana ▣ syn. *P. decandra* (Pigeon berry, Pokeweed, Red ink plant). Erect perennial with branching, red-marked stems and fleshy roots. Ovate to lance-shaped, mid-green leaves, 6–12in (15–30cm) long, are purple-tinged in autumn. From midsummer to early autumn, bears white to pink flowers, 3/8in (9mm) across, in racemes 8in (20cm) long; these elongate to 12in (30cm), and are usually pendent when bearing the blackish maroon berries (highly toxic if ingested). ↕ to 12ft (4m), ↔ 3ft (1m). E. North America to Mexico. Zone 6.

P. clavigera see *P. polyandra.*

P. decandra see *P. americana.*

P. polyandra, syn. *P. clavigera.* Erect, shrubby perennial with stems becoming vivid crimson. Ovate to elliptic, mid-green leaves, to 12in (30cm) long, turn yellow in autumn. In late summer, purplish pink flowers, 3/8in (9mm) across, are produced in erect, compact racemes, to 7in (18cm) long, elongating to 12in (30cm) long when bearing the dense masses of black berries. ↕ 6ft (2m), ↔ 24in (60cm). China. Zone 6b.

Phytolacca americana

Picea abies

PICEA

Spruce

PINACEAE

Genus of 30–40 species of monoecious, evergreen, coniferous trees occurring in forest in cool-temperate regions of the N. hemisphere. They have whorled branches and needle-like leaves set singly around the shoots. The woody, oval to oblong-cylindrical female cones, terminal on main shoots and sideshoots, are erect at flowering, later pendent; they ripen in a season from green or red when young, to purple or brown when mature. Ovoid, yellow to red-purple male cones, 3/4–1 1/4in (2–3cm) long, are borne in spring on the previous year's shoots. Spruces are useful for shelter planting or as specimen trees; many cultivars are dwarf or slow-growing.

• **CULTIVATION** Grow in any deep, moist but well-drained, ideally neutral to acidic soil in full sun. *P. omorika* tolerates alkaline soils.

• **PROPAGATION** Sow seed in containers in a cold frame in spring. Graft cultivars in winter. Take ripewood cuttings of dwarf cultivars in late summer.

Picea abies 'Aurea'

Picea abies 'Ohlendorffii'

• **PESTS AND DISEASES** Gall insects, aphids, caterpillars, sawfly, spider mites, lesion nematode, and scale insects are common. Diseases include butt rot, heart rot (and other wood rots), witches' broom, mistletoe, rust, and needle cast.

P. abies ▣ (Norway spruce). Conical tree when young, columnar when mature, with red-brown bark and orange-brown shoots. Produces blunt, 4-sided, dark green leaves, to 1in (2.5cm) long, pointing forward and upward on the shoots, and cylindrical, deep green, later brown female cones, 4–8in (10–20cm) long. The most commonly cultivated spruce. ↕ 70–130ft (20–40m), ↔ 20ft (6m). S. Scandinavia to C. and S. Europe. Zone 2b. **'Acrocona'** is small, with pendent

Picea breweriana

branches, and produces abundant cones, even on young plants; ↕ 3–10ft (1–3m), ↔ 10–12ft (3–4m). **'Aurea'** ▣ produces bright greenish yellow young foliage, maturing to dark green. **'Clanbrassiliana** (Tolleymore spruce) is very slow-growing and dwarf, and forms a low, flat-topped mound; ↕ to 3ft (1m), ↔ 3–5ft (1–1.5m). **'Gregoryana'** is a bushy, dwarf shrub, with a tight, rounded habit; ↕↔ 32in (80cm). **'Inversa'** has very downward-growing branches with light green leaves. Prostrate unless trained. **'Little Gem'** is slow-growing, very dense, and flat-topped, with tiny leaves. **'Nidiformis'** (Bird's-nest spruce) is a spreading, slow-growing, bushy shrub with a hollow "nest" in the center; ↕ to 5ft (1.5m), ↔ 10–12ft (3–4m). **'Ohlendorffii'** ▣ is

Picea asperata (inset: leaf detail)

Picea glauca var. *albertiana* 'Conica'

a very slow-growing, rounded, bushy shrub, becoming more conical, with short leaves, to ⅜in (9mm) long; ↕ 10ft (3m), ↔ 6–15ft (2–5m). **'Pygmaea'** is an extremely slow-growing form and has thin, wide-spreading gray-green young leaves, maturing to dark green. Requires judicious pruning; ↕ 12in (30cm), ↔ 20in (50cm). **'Reflexa'** is prostrate, unless trained on a stem, when it becomes pendent and weeping; ↕ to 6in (15cm), ↔ indefinite.
P. asperata ■ (Dragon spruce). Conical or columnar tree with scaly, purplish gray bark and thick, ridged, yellow-brown shoots, turning ash-gray. Thick, curved, 4-sided, glaucous, blue-green to dark green leaves, ½–1in (1–2.5cm) long, point upward on the shoots. Cylindrical, green, later light brown female cones are 2–6in (5–15cm) long. ↕ 80ft (25m), ↔ 20ft (6m). W. China. Zone 5.
P. brachytyla (Sargent spruce). Conical tree, becoming domed in old age, with cracked gray bark and slender, white or pale brown shoots. Pendent branchlets bear flattened, glossy, mid-green leaves, white beneath, ½–1in (1–2.5cm) long, spreading at the sides of the shoots. Bears cylindrical, green, later dark brown female cones, 2½–6in (6–15cm) long. ↕ 80ft (25m), ↔ 20–25ft (6–8m). C. to W. China. Zone 6.
P. breweriana ■ (Brewer spruce). Slow-growing, columnar tree with level branches, gray bark, becoming scaly, and pendent side branchlets. Thick, blunt, flattened leaves, glossy, deep green above, whitish green beneath, 1–1½in (2.5–4cm) long, are arranged radially on the shoots. Cylindrical, red-brown female cones are 3–5½in (7–14cm) long. ↕ 30–50ft (10–15m), ↔ 10–12ft (3–4m). N. California, S. Oregon. Zone 5b.
P. engelmannii (Engelmann spruce). Conical tree with short branches, scaly, red-brown bark, and pale brown shoots. Flexible, slender, 4-sided, bluish green to steel-blue leaves, ½–1¼in (1.5–3cm) long, are arranged radially, pointing slightly forward along the shoots. Ovoid to cylindrical, stalkless, light brown female cones, 1–3in (2.5–8cm) long, have flexible scales. ↕ 70–130ft (20–40m), ↔ to 15ft (5m). N. America (Rocky Mountains). Zone 3.
P. glauca (White spruce). Narrowly or broadly conical tree with ash-gray bark, becoming scaly, and buff-white shoots. Four-sided, blue-green leaves, ½–¾in

Picea morrisonicola

(1–2cm) long, are spreading at the sides of the shoots, overlapping above. Ovoid, green, later light brown female cones are 1½–2½in (4–6cm) long. ↕ to 160ft (50m), ↔ 10–20ft (3–6m). Canada, N. US. Zone 2. **var. *albertiana* 'Conica'** ■ syn. 'Albertiana Conica' (Dwarf Alberta spruce) is a neat, cone-shaped, dwarf, bushy shrub; ↕ 6–20ft (2–6m), ↔ 3–8ft (1–2.5m). There are many other selections for color and form.
P. jezoensis (Hondo spruce). Conical tree, becoming sparsely branched in old age, with large, spreading branches, fissured gray bark, and dense, pendent, white or pale brown shoots. Bears flattened, over-lapping, glossy, dark green leaves, ½–¾in (1–2cm) long, bright silver beneath. Cylindrical, green, later pale reddish brown female cones,

Picea omorika

Picea orientalis

1½–2½in (4–6cm) long, have thin, stiff scales. ↕ 100ft (30m), ↔ to 25ft (8m). Japan (Honshu). Zone 4.
P. likiangensis (Lijiang spruce). Broadly conical tree with fissured or scaly gray bark and thick, pale brown shoots. Flattened, bluish green leaves, to ½in (1.5cm) long, overlap above the shoots, and spread below. Cylindrical, bright reddish purple, later brown female cones are 3–6in (7–15cm) long. Flowers early if planted in poor, sandy soil. ↕ 100ft (30m), ↔ 20–28ft (6–9m). S. and W. China, S.E. Tibet. Zone 6b.
P. mariana (Black spruce). Conical tree with scaly, gray-brown bark and brown shoots with reddish brown hairs, the lower shoots often layering to form a skirt. Blunt, 4-sided, bluish green leaves are ¼–¾in (0.5–2cm) long. Ovoid, green, later gray-brown female cones, ¾–1½in (2–4cm) long, persist on the tree for 2 or 3 years. ↕ 30–70ft (10–20m), ↔ 6–10ft (2–3m). Canada, N.E. US. Zone 3. **'Nana'** is a rounded, bushy, dwarf shrub with bluish gray foliage; ↕↔ to 20in (50cm).
P. morrisonicola ■ (Taiwan spruce). Conical tree with pink-brown or gray-brown bark and very slender, ash-gray shoots. Slender, 4-sided, grass-green leaves, to ½in (1.5cm) long, lie flat on top of the shoots and are spreading below. Bears oblong-cylindrical purple female cones, 2–3in (5–8cm) long. ↕ to 70ft (20m), ↔ to 15ft (5m). Taiwan. Zone 7b.
P. omorika ■ (Serbian spruce). Narrow, spire-like tree with pendent branches ascending at the tips, brown bark cracking into square plates, and orange-brown shoots with black hairs. Flattened, dark to blue-green leaves, ½–¾in (1–2cm) long, white beneath, lie flat at the sides of the shoots and are spreading below. Bears ovate-oblong, red-brown, later brown female cones, 1¼–3in (3–8cm) long. ↕ 70ft (20m), ↔ 6–10ft (2–3m). Bosnia, Serbia (Drina River valley). Zone 3b. **'Pendula'** is a very narrow, weeping form with draping branches and striking blue-gray foliage. ↕ to 5ft (1.5m), ↔ 3ft (1m).
'Nana' is compact and slow-growing, dense and spherical when young, pyramidal with age; ↕↔ 3ft (1m).
P. orientalis ■ (Caucasian spruce, Oriental spruce). Broadly columnar tree, conical when young, with smooth, pink-gray bark, becoming cracked with age, and hairy, gray-brown shoots. Very short, blunt, 4-sided, dark green leaves,

Picea orientalis 'Skylands'

¼–⅜in (6–9mm) long, are arranged radially on the shoots. Male cones are deep red. Ovoid-conical, dark purple, later brown female cones are 2½–4in (6–10cm) long. ↕ 100ft (30m), ↔ 20–25ft (6–8m). Caucasus, N.E. Turkey. Zone 5. **'Nigra Compacta'** is a low, flat-topped, spreading form with very dark green foliage. At 15 years, ↕ 30in (75cm), ↔ 4ft (1.2m). **'Skylands'** ■ is similar to 'Aurea', but the creamy gold color lasts all year.
P. pungens (Colorado spruce). Conical to columnar tree with scaly, purplish gray bark and thick, orange-brown shoots. Stiff, thick, sharp-pointed, 4-sided, bluish gray-green leaves, ½–1¼in (1.5–3cm) long, arranged radially on the shoots, curve upward, and are covered in glaucous wax. Cylindrical, green, later pale brown female cones are 3–5in (8–13cm) long, with flexible scales. ↕ 50ft (15m), ↔ to 15ft (5m). S. Rocky Mountains from Wyoming to Colorado. Zone 2.
f. *glauca* (Blue Colorado spruce) is the group or form name for all very glaucous to blue-gray-leaved cultivars. **'Hoopsii'** has glaucous, blue-white foliage. **'Koster'** ■ produces glaucous, silvery blue foliage. **'Moerheimii'** has a strong, erect habit and long, powder-blue leaves, to 1½in (4cm) long. **'Montgomery'** is a slow-growing, dwarf shrub, with silvery-gray-blue leaves and a broad, conical habit; ↕ to 5ft (1.5m), ↔ 3ft (1m). **'Mrs. Cesarini'** is dwarf in habit, with blue-green leaves; ↕ to 6ft (2m), ↔ 5ft (1.5m). **'Thompsen'** is densely branched, and has distinctively blue foliage.

Picea pungens 'Koster'

Picea smithiana

P. purpurea (Purple-cone spruce). Columnar or conical tree with flaky, orange-brown bark and slender, densely hairy, buff-white shoots. Slightly flattened, glossy, mid-green leaves, gray-white beneath, ¼–½in (7–12mm) long, lie flat on top of the shoots and are spreading below. Ovoid, purple, later purple-brown female cones are 1–1½in (2.5–4cm) long. ↕ to 70ft (20m), ↔ to 15ft (5m). N.W. China. Zone 4.
P. rubens (Red spruce). Narrow conical tree with scaly, purple-brown bark, changing to red-brown, and curved branches, upturned at the tips, with buff-colored shoots. Glossy, 4-sided, grass-green leaves, ½–¾in (10–15mm) long, become darker and are overlapping on the upper part of the stems and are spreading below. Ovoid-oblong, shiny, red-brown female cones are ¾–2in (2–5cm) long, with broadly blunt, convex, finely-toothed scales. ↕ to 100ft (30m), ↔ 30–40ft (10–12m). N. North America. Zone 4b. **'Nana'** is dwarf and broadly conical, with spreading, red-tinged young shoots.
P. sitchensis (Sitka spruce). Narrowly conical tree with wide-spreading branches when old, purple-brown bark becoming gray, and white shoots. Produces sharp-pointed, flattened, dark green leaves, white beneath, ¾–1in (2–2.5cm) long, that overlap above the shoots, and spread below. Cylindrical, green, later pale brown female cones are 2–4in (5–10cm) long. ↕ 80–160ft (25–50m), ↔ 20–40ft (6–12m). Coastal W. North America (Alaska to California). Zone 2.
P. smithiana ■ (Himalayan spruce). Conical then columnar tree with spreading branches, pendent branchlets, scaly gray bark, and pale brown shoots. Sparse, incurved, 4-sided, dark green leaves, to 1½in (4cm) long, are arranged radially. Cylindrical, green, later bright brown female cones are 4–8in (10–20cm) long. ↕ 70–100ft (20–30m), ↔ 20–28ft (6–9m). E. Afghanistan to W. Nepal. Zone 7b.

Picrasma quassioides

PICRASMA

SIMAROUBACEAE

Genus of 8 species of deciduous trees occurring in forest in E. and S.E. Asia, the West Indies, Central America, and tropical South America. They have alternate, pinnate leaves, each with a terminal leaflet, and produce axillary, umbel-like panicles of bowl-shaped flowers. *P. quassioides* is valued for its autumn foliage color; grow in an open position in a woodland garden.
• **CULTIVATION** Grow in fertile, well-drained soil in full sun or partial shade. Pruning group 1.
• **PROPAGATION** Sow seed in containers in a cold frame in autumn.
• **PESTS AND DISEASES** Infrequent.

P. ailanthoides see *P. quassioides*.
P. quassioides ■ syn. *P. ailanthoides* (Quassia). Upright tree with pinnate leaves, to 14in (35cm) long, composed of 9–15 ovate, sharply toothed, glossy, mid-green leaflets, turning yellow, orange, and red in autumn. Tiny, bowl-shaped green flowers are produced in umbel-like panicles, to 6in (15cm) long, in early summer. ↕↔ 25ft (8m). N. India, Nepal, Bhutan, China, Korea, Japan. Zone 7.

PIERIS

ERICACEAE

Genus of 7 species of evergreen shrubs occurring in forest and on hillsides in the Himalayas, E. Asia, North America, and the West Indies. They are grown for their alternate or whorled, oblong or lance-shaped to obovate, glossy, mid- to dark green leaves, often attractively colored when young, and their terminal panicles of small, urn-shaped flowers, ¼–⅜in (5–9mm) long, usually borne in spring. Grow in a shrub border or in a woodland garden, or rock garden. Leaves may cause severe discomfort if ingested.
• **CULTIVATION** Grow in moderately fertile, humus-rich, moist but well-drained, acidic soil in full sun or light shade. Pruning group 8.
• **PROPAGATION** Sow seed in containers in a cold frame in spring or autumn. Take greenwood cuttings in early summer, or semi-ripe cuttings in mid- to late summer, with bottom heat.
• **PESTS AND DISEASES** Canker, dieback, *Phytophthora* root rot, lacebug, and nematodes occur.

Pieris floribunda (inset: flower detail)

P. 'Bert Chandler'. Conical shrub with lance-shaped, finely toothed leaves, to 4in (10cm) long, bright pink when young, turning creamy yellow and white, then dark green. Small white flowers are produced only rarely, in pendent panicles to 4in (10cm) long, in spring. ↕ 6ft (2m), ↔ 5ft (1.5m). Zone 7b.
P. 'Brouwer's Beauty'. Dense, erect shrub with obovate to oblong-lance-shaped, lightly toothed, glossy, dark green leaves, 1¼–3in (3–8cm) long. In spring, purplish red buds open to white flowers in semi-erect to pendent, terminal panicles, 2–5in (5–13cm) long. ↕ to 10ft (3m), ↔ to 6ft (2m). Zone 6.
P. floribunda ■ (Fetterbush, Mountain pieris). Compact, rounded shrub with elliptic-ovate, toothed, glossy, dark green leaves, to 3in (8cm) long. White flowers, opening from greenish white buds, are borne in erect, terminal panicles, to 5in (13cm) long, at the shoot tips, in early and midspring. ↕ 6ft (2m), ↔ 10ft (3m). S.E. US. Zone 6.
P. 'Forest Flame'. Compact, upright shrub with slender, inversely lance-shaped, finely toothed, glossy, dark green leaves, to 5in (13cm) long, bright red when young, turning pink, then creamy white, and finally green. White flowers, in erect then pendent, terminal panicles, to 6in (15cm) long, are borne in mid- and late spring. ↕ 12ft (4m), ↔ 6ft (2m). Zone 5b.
P. formosa. Upright, often suckering, large shrub with oblong, finely toothed, glossy, dark green leaves, to 4in (10cm) long, bronze when young. White flowers are produced in large, semi-erect to pendent, terminal panicles, to 6in (15cm) long, in mid- and late spring. Grows best where summers are cool. ↕ 15ft (5m), ↔ 12ft (4m). China, Himalayas. Zone 7. **var. *forrestii* 'Charles Michael'** has red young growth, and produces large flowers, ⅜–½in (9–11mm) long, in large panicles, to 7in (18cm) long. **var. *forrestii* 'Jermyns'** is spreading, with arching branches and dark red young foliage; produces pendent panicles of white flowers opening from dark red buds; ↕↔ 8ft (2.5m). **var. *forrestii* 'Wakehurst'** ■ has brilliant red young foliage. **'Henry Price'** has deeply veined, very dark green leaves, dark bronze-red when young.

Pieris formosa var. *forrestii* 'Wakehurst'

Pieris japonica

Pieris japonica 'Blush'

Pieris japonica 'Flamingo'

P. japonica ■ (Lily-of-the-valley bush). Compact, rounded shrub with narrowly obovate to elliptic, toothed, glossy, mid-green leaves, to 3½in (9cm) long. White flowers are produced in pendent or semi-erect, terminal panicles, to 6in (15cm) long, clustered at the tips of the shoots, in late winter and spring. ↕ 12ft (4m), ↔ 10ft (3m). E. China, Taiwan, Japan. Zone 5b. **'Blush'** ■ has very dark green leaves, and bears pink-flushed white, later all-white flowers, opening from dark pink buds. **'Christmas Cheer'** bears pink flowers with deep rose-red tips. **'Daisen'** has red flowers, opening from dark pink buds, and fading to pink. **'Debutante'** is compact and low-growing, bearing white flowers in dense, erect panicles, to 5in (13cm) long; ↕↔ 3ft (1m).

Pieris japonica 'Scarlett O'Hara'

Pieris japonica 'Variegata'

'Dorothy Wyckoff' produces deeply veined, very dark green leaves, turning bronze in cold weather, and purple-red buds, opening pale pink, later turning white. **'Firecrest'** has deeply veined, dark green leaves, 4in (10cm) long, bright red when young; ↔ 6ft (2m). **'Flamingo'** ■ has dark red buds, opening dark pink. **'Grayswood'** has brownish red new growth, narrow, dark green leaves, and white flowers borne in long, dense panicles, to 7in (18cm) or more long. **'Little Heath'** is dwarf and compact, with leaves to 1¼in (3cm) long, pink-flushed when young, and with silvery white margins; ↕↔ 24in (60cm). **'Mountain Fire'** produces red young leaves, turning glossy chestnut-brown. **'Purity'** is compact, and bears white flowers in upright panicles, and pale green leaves when young; ↕↔ 3ft (1m). **'Scarlett O'Hara'** ■ produces white flowers borne in dense panicles. **'Valley Valentine'** has large panicles of dark dusky red flowers. **'Variegata'** ■ has white-margined leaves and produces white flowers. **'White Cascade'** ■ has white flowers in long panicles, 7in (18cm) or more long, borne over a long period.

P. nana, syn. *Arcterica nana*. Wiry-stemmed, slow-spreading, cushion-forming, dwarf shrub with ovate-elliptic, leathery, toothed, dark green leaves, to ½in (1.5cm) long, in pairs or whorls of 3, tinted red-bronze in winter. In late spring and early summer, produces fragrant white flowers in pendent, terminal panicles, to 2½in (6cm) long. ↕ 3in (8cm), ↔ to 12in (30cm). Russia (Kamtchatka), Japan. Zone 4.

Pieris japonica 'White Cascade'

Pilea cadierei

PILEA

URTICACEAE

Genus of about 600 erect or creeping, semi-succulent annuals and evergreen perennials, sometimes woody at the bases, found in rainforest throughout tropical regions worldwide, except Australia. Stems may be branched or unbranched. They are cultivated for their textured, occasionally fleshy, attractively marked, opposite leaves, which are very variable in shape and color. They also produce wispy, usually insignificant, unisexual, 3- or 4-tepaled flowers, in cymes or panicles, or sometimes singly, from the leaf axils. Where not hardy, grow in a warm greenhouse or as houseplants; use trailing species in a hanging basket. In warmer climates, grow as a groundcover in a damp, shady border.

• **CULTIVATION** Under glass, grow in shallow pots of soilless potting mix in bright indirect light, with high humidity. During the growing season, water moderately, and apply a balanced liquid fertilizer every month. Water sparingly in winter. Outdoors, grow in any reliably moist soil in partial or deep shade.

• **PROPAGATION** Sow seed at 66–75°F (19–24°C) in spring. Divide or detach rosettes in spring. Root stem-tip cuttings with bottom heat in spring.

• **PESTS AND DISEASES** Prone to mealybugs, spider mites, stem rot, and bacterial leaf spot.

P. cadierei ■ (Aluminum plant). Erect perennial with branches becoming basally woody. The obovate to oblong-inversely-lance-shaped, toothed, dark green leaves, 3in (8cm) long, each have 4 rows of raised silver patches on the upper surface. ↕ 12in (30cm), ↔ 6–8in (15–20cm). Vietnam. ❄ (min. 59°F/15°C). **'Minima'** is a compact cultivar; ↕ 6in (15cm).

P. grandifolia. Rounded to upright, shrubby perennial producing ovate, coarsely toothed, glossy, dark or bronze-green leaves, 4–8in (10–20cm) long, with pointed tips, sometimes puckered between the veins. ↕ to 5ft (1.5m), ↔ to 32in (80cm). Jamaica. ❄ (min. 50°F/10°C)

P. involucrata ■ syn. *P. mollis* (Friendship plant, Panamiga). Trailing or creeping perennial producing tight rosettes of virtually stalkless, ovate to obovate, toothed, dark green leaves, 2½in (6cm) long, with bronze-flushed, quilted surfaces, sometimes with paler margins. ↕ 1¼in (3cm), ↔ to 12in (30cm). Central and South America. ❄ (min. 59°F/15°C). **'Moon Valley'** is more upright and open in habit, and produces ovate, toothed, fresh green

Pilea involucrata

P

Pilea microphylla

leaves, to 4in (10cm) long, with deep purple sunken veins; ↕↔ 12in (30cm).
P. microphylla ■ (Artillery plant). Densely branching, succulent annual or short-lived perennial with thick, fleshy, hairless stems; these bear unequal pairs of obovate to rounded, bright green leaves, to ½in (1.5cm) long, with blunt or pointed tips, or rounded leaves, to ⅛in (3mm) long. ↕↔ 12in (30cm). Florida, Mexico, West Indies, South America. ❀ (min. 59°F/15°C)
P. mollis see *P. involucrata.*
P. nummulariifolia ■ (Creeping Charlie). Trailing or creeping perennial with frequently branching stems, rooting at the nodes. Rounded, deeply quilted, light green leaves, ¾in (2cm) long, fold inward slightly at the midribs. ↕ 6in (15cm), ↔ 24in (60cm). West Indies, tropical South America. ❀ (min. 59°F/15°C)
P. peperomioides. Open-bushy, erect, perennial succulent with thick, fleshy stems covered with persistent stipules. Produces spirally arranged, long-stalked, elliptic to almost rounded, succulent, pale green leaves, 3½in (9cm) long. ↕↔ 12in (30cm) or more. China (Yunnan). ❀ (min. 50°F/10°C)

Pilea nummulariifolia

Pileostegia viburnoides

PILEOSTEGIA
HYDRANGEACEAE

Genus of 4 species of woody, evergreen root climbers, occurring on forest trees and cliffs in India and E. Asia. They have opposite, obovate to oblong, mid-green leaves, and produce dense, terminal, corymb-like panicles of small, cup- or star-shaped, 4- or 5-petaled, creamy white flowers, in late summer and autumn. *P. viburnoides* is valued for its foliage and flowers. Grow on a large tree trunk or a wall.
• **CULTIVATION** Grow in fertile, well-drained soil in sun or shade. Pruning group 11, in early spring.
• **PROPAGATION** Root semi-ripe cuttings in summer. Layer in spring.
• **PESTS AND DISEASES** Infrequent.

P. viburnoides ■ syn. *Schizophragma viburnoides.* Evergreen climber with oblong, leathery, dark green leaves, to 6in (15cm) long. In late summer and autumn, small, star-shaped, creamy white flowers, with prominent stamens, are borne in dense panicles, to 6in (15cm) across. ↕ 20ft (6m). India, China, Taiwan. Zone 7.

PILGERODENDROM
CUPRESSACEAE

Genus of 2 conical, monoecious, evergreen, coniferous trees from South America. The linear juvenile leaves and usually scale-like adult leaves are arranged in sets of 2 pairs, one on either side of the shoot (spreading pair), and one above and below (facial pair), forming 4 rows. Female cones are solitary and usually have four scales.
• **CULTIVATION** Prefers a wet site or copious water supply. Where marginally hardy, shelter from cold, driving winds.
• **PROPAGATION** Sow seed in containers in a cold frame in spring, or take semi-ripe cuttings in summer.
• **PESTS AND DISEASES** Infrequent.

P. uviferum. Slow-growing, conical, coniferous shrub or small tree with thin bark, peeling in strips. Green shoots bear narrrowly wedge-shaped leaves, to ¼in (6mm) long, with fine, tapered points, whitish green on the inner side, dark green on the outer. Ovoid female cones are ½in (1.5cm) long. ↕ to 20ft (6m), ↔ to 6ft (2m). S. Chile, S. Argentina. Zone 7b.

Pilosella aurantiaca

PILOSELLA
ASTERACEAE

Genus of about 20 hairy, rhizomatous or stoloniferous herbaceous perennials from a variety of habitats in Eurasia and North Africa, including grassland, sand dunes, dry slopes, and open woodland. The ovate to narrowly lance-shaped or spoon-shaped, entire or toothed leaves are usually in basal rosettes, sometimes with smaller stem leaves. Greenish yellow or yellow to orange-red, rarely white or red, dandelion-like flowerheads are borne singly or in terminal clusters on usually leafless stems in summer. Grow in a wild garden or meadow, or on dry walls and banks.
• **CULTIVATION** Grow in poor to moderately fertile, well-drained or dry soil in full sun or partial shade.
• **PROPAGATION** Sow seed in containers outdoors. Divide in autumn or spring.
• **PESTS AND DISEASES** Infrequent.

P. aurantiaca ■ syn. *Hieracium aurantiacum, H. brunneocroceum* (Fox and cubs, Orange hawkweed). Stoloniferous perennial producing basal rosettes of elliptic to lance-shaped, bluish green leaves, to 8in (20cm) long. In summer, black-hairy stems bear dense clusters of 8–10 orange-red or orange-brown flowerheads, ½in (1.5cm) across. ↕ to 8in (20cm), ↔ 36in (90cm). Grassy places in Europe. Zone 5.

PILOSOCEREUS
CACTACEAE

Genus of 60 species of tree-like or bushy cacti, branching from the stems or the bases, found in warm, humid, moist areas of Mexico, Central and South America, and the West Indies. The many ribs have spiny, generally densely woolly, hairy areoles, sometimes as long as 2in (5cm), the wool forming skeins covering the ribs. In summer, nocturnal, tubular to bell-shaped flowers are produced from pseudocephaliums, from prominent areoles, or at the crowns, followed by fleshy, fig-like fruits. Below 59°F (15°C), grow *Pilosocereus* species in a warm greenhouse. In warmer areas, use as a focal point on a lawn or in a large courtyard.
• **CULTIVATION** Under glass, grow in standard cactus potting mix with added grit (more than 50%) and acidity, in full light. From spring to summer, water freely and apply a balanced liquid fertilizer every 6–8 weeks. Keep just moist at other times. Outdoors, grow in gritty, moderately fertile, sharply drained soil in full sun. See also pp.48–49.
• **PROPAGATION** Sow seed at 66–75°F (19–24°C) in spring.
• **PESTS AND DISEASES** Vulnerable to mealybugs, and to ants if planted out.

P. leucocephalus see *P. palmeri.*
P. palmeri, syn. *P. leucocephalus.* Tree-like cactus with a blue-green stem, 2–4in (5–10cm) thick, with 7–9 rounded ribs. The areoles bear dark brown or grayish black spines (8–12 radials, 1 or 2 longer centrals), pale brown or yellow at first. Some areoles become covered with woolly gray hairs, borne more densely at the crown, forming a pseudocephalium. Pinkish purple flowers, 3in (8cm) long, purple-brown outside, are borne in summer. ↕ to 20ft (6m), ↔ 3ft (1m). E. Mexico, Central America. ❀ (min. 59°F/15°C)

PIMELEA
THYMELAEACEAE

Genus of about 80 species of evergreen shrubs and subshrubs found in scrub, rocky places, and grassland from coastal areas to mountains in Australasia. Those commonly cultivated usually have opposite pairs of ovate to oblong leaves. Tubular, sometimes fragrant flowers, each with 4 spreading lobes, are borne in flat to almost spherical, terminal heads, surrounded by often colorful bracts. They are followed in some species by white, red, green, or black fruits (one-seeded drupes or nuts). Where not hardy, grow in containers outdoors and bring under cover in winter, or grow in a cool greenhouse. In warmer climates, grow in a border or a rock garden.
• **CULTIVATION** Under glass, grow in acidic potting mix with added sharp sand, in full light. During growth, water moderately and apply a balanced liquid fertilizer every month. Water sparingly in winter. Outdoors, grow in fertile, well-drained, neutral to acidic soil in full sun. Pruning group 8.
• **PROPAGATION** Sow seed in containers in a cold frame in spring. Root semi-ripe cuttings with bottom heat in summer.
• **PESTS AND DISEASES** Spider mites may be a problem under glass.

P. ferruginea ■ Bushy, domed shrub, at least when young. Densely borne,

Pimelea ferruginea

Pimelea prostrata

glossy, mid-green leaves, to ½in (1.5cm) long, are ovate to oblong, with rolled margins. In late spring and early summer, has almost spherical heads, to 1½in (4cm) across, of slender-tubed, white-hairy, rose-pink flowers, ⅜in (9mm) across, surrounded by pink to red bracts. ↕ 3–6ft (1–2m), ↔ 3–5ft (1–1.5m). Western Australia. Zone 7b.

P. prostrata ▣ Compact, spreading shrub with dark shoots and densely clustered, ovate, gray-green, often red-margined, leathery leaves, to ¼in (6mm) long. In summer, bears flat heads, to ¾in (2cm) across, of tubular, fragrant white flowers, to ¼in (6mm) across, followed by tiny, fleshy, white or red fruit. ↕ 8in (20cm), ↔ 20in (50cm). New Zealand. ❀ (min. 41°F/5°C)

PIMPINELLA

APIACEAE

Genus of about 150 species of annuals, biennials, and perennials occurring in rough grassland, hedgerows, and woodland in Europe, N. Africa, Asia, and South America. Most have hairy stems, with simple or pinnate leaves, and bear compound umbels of tiny, star-shaped, usually white or yellow, sometimes pink or purple flowers, followed by ovoid-oblong to nearly spherical fruits. Most are suitable for naturalizing in a wild garden; *P. major* 'Rosea' is also effective in a border.

• **CULTIVATION** Grow in any, but preferably fertile, moist soil in full sun or partial shade.

• **PROPAGATION** Sow seed in containers as soon as ripe. Avoid damage to the taproots when transplanting.

• **PESTS AND DISEASES** Aphids, slugs, snails, and leaf spot occur.

Pimpinella major 'Rosea'

P. major (Greater burnet). Erect perennial with triangular to rounded, pinnate, mid-green basal leaves, to 7in (18cm) long, with 7–13 ovate to lance-shaped, lobed or toothed leaflets, ¾–3in (2–8cm) long; stem leaves are smaller. In mid- and late spring, ridged stems bear tiny, white or pink flowers in compound umbels, 2½in (6cm) across. ↕ to 4ft (1.2m), ↔ 24in (60cm). Europe to Caucasus. Zone 5. **'Rosea'** ▣ has both deep pink and pale pink flowers, in early and midsummer.

PINANGA

ARECACEAE

Genus of about 120 species of single- or cluster-stemmed palms of the tropical rainforest undergrowth at low to medium altitudes from the Himalayas to S. China, S.E. Asia, and Papua New Guinea. Simple or pinnate, light to dark green leaves are borne in terminal tufts above distinct crownshafts. Bowl-shaped, 3-petaled flowers are produced in spikes or panicles (erect at first, then pendent) arising from the bases of the crownshafts. Where not hardy, grow *Pinanga* species in a warm greenhouse. In tropical, lowland areas, plant in a shady site near other trees or in a courtyard.

• **CULTIVATION** Under glass, grow in soil-based potting mix, with added peat and sharp sand, in bright filtered to low light. Pot on or top-dress in spring. In the growing season, water freely and apply a balanced liquid fertilizer monthly. Water moderately in winter. Outdoors, grow in fertile, moist but well-drained soil in light, dappled to deep shade.

• **PROPAGATION** Sow seed at 75°F (24°C) in spring.

• **PESTS AND DISEASES** Spider mites and leaf spot can occur, especially on young plants.

Pinanga patula

P. patula ▣ Small, cluster-stemmed palm with erect, smooth, cane-like stems with swollen bases. Irregularly pinnate leaves, to 5ft (1.5m) long, each with 16–36 lance-shaped, bright green leaflets. Bowl-shaped green flowers, turning red with age, are borne in recurved panicles, to ½in (1.5cm) across, usually in summer. ↕↔ to 8ft (2.5m). Indonesia (Sumatra), Borneo. ❀ (min. 61–64°F/16–18°C)

PINCKNEYA

RUBIACEAE

Genus of 1 or 2 species of deciduous shrubs or trees growing in swampy areas in the S.E. US. They are grown for their flowers, usually with enlarged pink or white sepals, and are borne in terminal and axillary corymbs. The leaves are opposite, simple, elliptic to oblong-ovate, and dark green. Grow *P. pubens* as a specimen tree; it is also particularly effective along the edge of a streambed or small pond. Where not hardy, grow in a temperate greenhouse.

• **CULTIVATION** Under glass, grow in soilless potting mix, in full light. In the growing season, water freely and apply a balanced liquid fertilizer monthly; water sparingly in winter, but do not let the potting mix dry out. Outdoors, grow in moist but well-drained soil in partial shade or at the edge of a stream or pond. Pruning group 1.

• **PROPAGATION** Take ripewood cuttings in autumn.

• **PESTS AND DISEASES** Infrequent.

P. pubens (Bitter-bark, Fever tree, Georgia bark, Poinsettia tree). Spreading tree or shrub with opposite, elliptic or ovate, hairy, dark green leaves, 8in (20cm) long, paler beneath. In summer, flowers with enlarged pink sepals are borne in corymbs, to 8in (20cm) across. ↕ to 28ft (9m), ↔ to 15ft (5m). South Carolina to Florida. Zone 8.

PINELLIA

ARACEAE

Genus of about 6 species of vigorously spreading, sometimes highly invasive, tuberous perennials found in deciduous forest, in cultivated fields, and at roadsides in China, Korea, and Japan. The simple, 3-palmate or pedate, basal leaves are rounded to ovate-lance-shaped or heart-shaped. Usually long, fine, black, green, or dark purple spadices, protruding from cylindrical spathes, are produced in summer. Grow in a woodland or rock garden.

• **CULTIVATION** Plant tubers 4–6in (10–15cm) deep in spring. Grow in fertile, humus-rich, well-drained soil in full sun or partial shade.

• **PROPAGATION** Sow seed in containers in a cold frame as soon as ripe. Remove offsets in autumn or early spring, or detach bulbils in late summer.

• **PESTS AND DISEASES** Infrequent.

P. ternata. Tuberous perennial with 3-palmate, mid-green leaves, composed of ovate-elliptic to oblong segments, 1¼–5in (3–13cm) long. Bears slightly hooded green spathes, to 3in (8cm) long, each with a protruding, slender green spadix, in summer. Often highly invasive. ↕ to 8in (20cm), ↔ 2in (5cm). China, Korea, Japan. Zone 7.

Pinguicula moranensis

PINGUICULA

Butterwort

LENTIBULARIACEAE

Genus of about 45 species of spring- or summer-flowering, insectivorous perennials from boggy habitats widely distributed in the N. hemisphere and in South America. They have rosettes of mucilage-secreting, lance-shaped to almost rounded leaves, and leafless stems bearing solitary, spurred, 2-lipped, trumpet-shaped flowers, the upper lip 2-lobed, the lower with 3 widely spreading lobes. Some species die back to resting buds in winter. The sticky leaves trap insects, which are then digested; under glass, butterworts may be used to assist in controlling aphids and whiteflies. Where not hardy, grow butterworts as houseplants or in a temperate greenhouse. Hardy species are suitable for an alpine house or as bog plants.

• **CULTIVATION** Under glass, grow in a mixture of equal parts chopped peat and sphagnum moss, with added broken clay pots, in bright filtered light. During the growing season, water freely and apply a balanced liquid fertilizer every month. Water sparingly in winter. Outdoors, grow in poor, peaty, permanently moist soil in full sun or partial shade. Keep birds or other animals from disturbing dormant buds on hardy species.

• **PROPAGATION** Surface-sow seed on damp sphagnum moss at 55–64°F (13–18°C), as soon as ripe. Divide in late winter.

• **PESTS AND DISEASES** Slugs and snails.

P. grandiflora. Rosette-forming perennial with resting buds in winter. Obovate-oblong, sticky, pale green leaves are 1¼–1¾in (3–4.5cm) long. During summer, trumpet-shaped, spurred, dark blue flowers, 1in (2.5cm) across, with widely spreading lobes and white throats, are borne on slender stems. ↕ 6in (15cm), ↔ 4in (10cm). W. Europe. Zone 3.

P. moranensis ▣ Rosette-forming perennial with ovate, sticky, dull pale green leaves, 2½–4in (6–10cm) long, with inrolled, purple-green margins. Trumpet-shaped, deep carmine-red flowers, to 1¼in (3cm) across, are produced on slender stems in summer. ↕ 6in (15cm), ↔ 4in (10cm). Mexico. ❀ (min. 45°F/7°C)

PINUS

Pine

PINACEAE

Genus of approximately 120 species of monoecious, evergreen, coniferous trees or shrubs, widely distributed in forests of the N. hemisphere, from the Arctic Circle to Central America, Europe, N. Africa, and S.E. Asia. The bark is often fissured, and in some species is divided into irregular, plate-like sections. Pines bear small bundles of 2–5, rarely 1 or 6–8, needle-like, light to dark green or yellow-green to bluish or gray-green leaves, which usually persist for 2–4 years, sometimes for longer. The winter buds are usually cylindrical or ovoid, and often resinous. Female cones take 2, or occasionally 3 years to ripen; the seeds are winged in most species. Male cones are yellow and catkin-like, clustered at the shoot bases. Pines are useful as specimen trees, and for shelter and windbreaks; some cultivars and slow-growing species are suitable for a rock garden or mixed border.

- **CULTIVATION** Grow in any well-drained soil in full sun.
- **PROPAGATION** Sow seed of species in containers in a cold frame in spring. Graft cultivars in late winter.
- **PESTS AND DISEASES** Sawfly, caterpillars, scale insects, mealybugs, miners, and borers are common pests. Diseases include blister rust, butt rot, blights (including *Diplodia* tip blight), pitch canker, cone rust, tar spot, and brown cubical rot.

P. aristata ▣ (Bristlecone pine). Slow-growing, dense, conical tree with upturned branch tips, smooth, dark gray bark, and red-brown shoots with pale hairs and ovoid buds. Bright green leaves, ¾–1½in (2–4cm) long, have flecks of white resin and are borne in fives; young needles have blue-white inner sides. Leaves are retained for up to 20 years. Long-ovoid brown female cones, 1½–4in (4–10cm) long, have a bristle-like prickle on each scale. ↕ to 30ft (10m), ↔ to 20ft (6m). Arizona, New Mexico, Colorado. Zone 3. **var. *longaeva*** see *P. longaeva.*
P. armandii (Armand pine). Broadly conical tree with an open, whorled habit, smooth bark, becoming cracked with age, and olive-green shoots with cylindrical-ovoid buds. Forward-pointing, pendent, shiny, deep green

Pinus aristata

Pinus bungeana

leaves, 4–8in (10–20cm) long, with white inner sides and curved at the bases, are borne in fives. Cylindrical-conical female cones, 5–8in (12–20cm) long, have wingless seeds. ↕ 50–70ft (15–20m), ↔ 20–25ft (6–8m). Tibet, N. Burma, China, Taiwan. Zone 6.
P. attenuata (Knobcone pine). Conical tree with ascending branches, smooth gray bark, becoming fissured and scaly with age, and green-brown shoots with resinous, narrow, spindle-shaped buds. Stiff, slender, gray-green leaves, 3–7in (8–18cm) long, are borne in threes. Ovoid-conical, yellow-brown female cones, swollen on the outer sides, are 3½–8in (9–20cm) long, and may persist for over 20 years. ↕ to 80ft (25m), ↔ to 20–25ft (6–8m). Oregon to Baja California. Zone 7b.
P. ayacahuite (Mexican white pine). Conical to broadly conical tree with smooth gray bark, becoming domed and scaly with age, and finely hairy, pale yellow-brown shoots with resinous, conical buds. Forward-pointing, pendent, shiny green leaves, 4–8in (10–20cm) long, with white bands on the inner sides, appear in fives. Very resinous, cylindrical female cones, 8–18in (20–45cm) long, have conical apexes and reflexed scales. ↕ to 100ft (30m), ↔ 20–25ft (6–8m). S. Mexico, Guatemala, Honduras. Zone 7b.
P. balfouriana (Foxtail pine). Broad, conical tree with ridged gray bark and hairy, orange-brown shoots with ovoid buds. Dark green leaves, ¾–1¼in (2–3cm) long, with faint white bands on the inner sides, are borne in fives, and retained for 10–20 years. Oblong-cylindrical, purple-brown female cones, 3–5½in (8–14cm) long, have a short prickle on each scale. Similar to *P. aristata*, but does not have flecks of resin on its leaves. ↕ 50ft (15m), ↔ 20–25ft (6–8m). California. Zone 6.
P. banksiana (Jack pine). Narrow, conical tree when young, becoming irregular and scruffy with age. It has fissured, red-brown or gray bark, thin, flexible brown shoots, and very resinous, cylindrical buds. Thick, twisted, divergent, yellow-green leaves, ¾–1½in (2–4cm) long, are borne in pairs. Forward-pointing, ovoid-conical, strongly curved, yellow-buff to gray female cones, 1½–2½in (4–6cm) long, are persistent. ↕ 30–70ft (10–20m), ↔ 10–15ft (3–5m). Grows on poor, sandy soils. Yukon Territory to Nova Scotia, south to N.E. US. Zone 1.

P. bungeana ▣ (Lacebark pine). Columnar or bushy-crowned, slow-growing tree with smooth bark, which flakes with age into small, rounded, irregular scales to reveal light green to cream patches that darken to reddish brown and gray-green. Shoots are olive-green with ovoid to ellipsoid buds, and bear hard, shiny, yellow-green leaves, 2–4in (5–10cm) long, in threes. Ovoid female cones, 1½–3in (4–8cm) long, bear seeds with short, brittle wings. ↕ 30–50ft (10–15m), ↔ 15–20ft (5–6m). N. and C. China. Zone 5b.
P. canariensis ▣ (Canary Islands pine). Conical to broadly conical tree, becoming domed with age, with fissured, red-brown bark, yellow shoots, and large, ovate buds. Spreading, grass-green adult leaves, 6–12in (15–30cm) long, are borne in threes. Glaucous blue juvenile leaves are borne singly and are retained for several years. Ellipsoid-ovoid female cones, 3½–8in (9–20cm) long, are borne on long stalks, ¾in (2cm) long. ↕ to 80ft (25m), ↔ 20–28ft (6–9m). Canary Islands. ❄ (min. 41°F/5°C)
P. cembra (Arolla pine, Swiss stone pine). Narrow, columnar tree with smooth, dark gray bark, becoming fissured with age, and densely brown-hairy shoots with ovate, resinous buds. Dark green leaves, bluish white on the inner sides, 3–3½in (7–9cm) long, are borne in fives. Broad, oblong-conical, bluish green female cones, 2½in–3in (6–8cm) long, are resinous, and bear edible, wingless seeds. ↕ 50–70ft (15–20m), ↔ 20–25ft (6–8m). C. Europe. Zone 2. **'Nana'** is uniformly

Pinus canariensis

Pinus coulteri

conical, slow-growing when young, and densely branched to the ground.
P. cembroides (Mexican stone pine). Domed, rounded tree with scaly, silver-gray bark, fissured red-brown, and orange-brown shoots with ellipsoid buds, which have tapered, reflexed scales. Radially arranged, dark green leaves, 1¼–2½in (3–6cm) long, with glaucous inner sides, are borne in threes, occasionally in pairs. Spherical green female cones, 1–1½in (2.5–4cm) across, ripen to brown, and have wingless seeds. ↕ 30–60ft (10–18m), ↔ 20–25ft (6–8m). S.W. US, N. Mexico. Zone 7b.
P. chylla see *P. wallichiana.*
P. contorta (Beach pine, Shore pine). Broadly conical tree when young, becoming domed with age, with scaly, red-brown bark, shiny, greenish brown shoots, and very resinous, cylindrical buds. Dense, forward-pointing, deep green leaves, 1½–2in (4–5cm) long, are borne in pairs. Long-conical, yellow-brown to brown female cones, 1–3in (2.5–8cm) long, have reflexed scales, and are persistent. ↕ to 80ft (25m), ↔ to 25ft (8m). Coastal N.W. North America. Zone 5. **var. *latifolia*** (Lodgepole pine) has a conical habit, flakier bark, and brighter green, spreading leaves, 2½–3½in (6–9cm) long, with ovoid cones, 1½in (4cm) long; Rocky Mountains. Zone 1. **'Spaan's Dwarf'** is dwarf, with a sloping trunk and an open habit, with erect branches; leaves are ½in (1.5cm) long; ↕↔ 30in (75cm).
P. coulteri ▣ (Big-cone pine, Coulter pine). Domed tree with gray bark, becoming black-gray and fissured, and brown, glaucous shoots with long, cylindrical to ovoid buds. Radially arranged, stiff, gray-green or bluish green leaves, 8–12in (20–30cm) long, are borne in threes. Massive, ovoid, yellow-brown female cones, 8–14in (20–35cm) long, have thick, forward-pointing spines and large, wingless seeds. ↕ to 80ft (25m), ↔ 25–30ft (8–10m). California, Mexico (Baja California). ❄ (min. 35°F/2°C)
P. densiflora (Japanese red pine). Broadly conical to rounded tree, becoming flat-topped, with reddish brown bark, flaky in the upper crown, gray and fissured at the base. The whitish pink shoots have slightly resinous, ovoid buds. Slender, bright green leaves, 3–5in (8–13cm) long, are borne in pairs. Bears long-ovoid, yellow-brown female cones, 1¼–2½in (3–6cm

P

Pinus densiflora 'Umbraculifera'

long. ↕ 50–80ft (15–25m), ↔ 15–22ft (5–7m). N.E. Asia, Japan. Zone 5. **'Alice Verkade'** is a globe-shaped, dwarf selection with bright green leaves; it grows only about 3in (8cm) per year; ↕ 20in (50cm) or more, ↔ 3ft (1m). **'Ja-nome'** see 'Oculus Draconis'. **'Oculus Draconis'**, syn. 'Ja-nome', is a large shrub or small tree with two distinctive yellow bands on each leaf. Bears blue-green female cones. **'Tagyosho'** see 'Umbraculifera'. **'Umbraculifera'** ▣ syn. 'Tagyosho' (Tanyosho pine) is a slow-growing, rounded to broadly spreading tree with a domed or umbrella-shaped crown; ↕ 12ft (4m), ↔ 20ft (6m).

P. edulis (Pinyon pine). Compact, irregular, domed tree with silvery gray bark, orange, bloomed shoots, and ovoid buds. The dark green leaves, 1¼–2½in (3–6cm) long, glaucous on the inner sides, are borne mainly in pairs, and persist for 3–9 years. Spherical, pale brown or green-brown female cones are 1¼in (3cm) long, with wingless seeds. The pinyon seeds, or pine kernels, of commerce come mainly from this species. ↕ 20–50ft (6–15m), ↔ 20–25ft (6–8m). S.W. US. Zone 5b.

P. excelsa see *P. wallichiana.*

P. flexilis (Limber pine). Broadly conical tree, later domed at the top, with smooth gray bark, later fissured; very pliant, hairy green shoots have broadly cylindrical to ovoid buds. Dark green leaves, 1½–3½in (4–9cm) long, are produced in tight bundles of five, and persist for 5 or 6 years. Bears long-ovoid, yellow-ochre female cones, 3–6in (7–15cm) long, with wingless

Pinus x *holfordiana*

Pinus jeffreyi

seeds. Male cones are red. ↕ 50–70ft (15–20m), ↔ 20–28ft (6–9m). Rocky Mountains from Alberta to Arizona. Zone 3. **'Vandewolf's Pyramid'** is upright in habit, and produces blue-green foliage; ↕ 20–25ft (6–8m), ↔ 10–20ft (3–6m).

P. griffithii see *P. wallichiana.*

P. halepensis (Aleppo pine). Conical tree, becoming rounded with age, with scaly, red-brown bark, glaucous gray shoots, and ovate buds with reflexed scales. Slender, sparse, bright green leaves, 2½–4½in (6–11cm) long, are borne in pairs. Long-ovoid, red-brown female cones are 2–5in (5–13cm) long. ↕ to 70ft (20m), ↔ to 20ft (6m). Mediterranean. ❀ (min. 41°F/5°C)

P. heldreichii* var. *leucodermis see *P. leucodermis.*

P. × holfordiana ▣ (*P. ayacahuite* × *P. wallichiana*) (Holford pine). Broadly conical tree with gray-brown bark, becoming fissured, and with hairy shoots and cylindrical-conical buds. Blue-green leaves, to 4–8in (10–20cm) long, are borne in fives. Ellipsoid green female cones, 10–12in (25–30cm) long, ripen to buff or yellow-brown. Differs from *P. ayacahuite* in having less reflexed cone scales and smaller seeds, and from *P. wallichiana* in having hairy shoots and wider cones. ↕ to 100ft (30m), ↔ 20–25ft (6–8m). Garden origin. Zone 7.

P. insignis see *P. radiata.*

P. jeffreyi ▣ (Jeffrey pine). Broadly conical tree with smooth, deeply fissured black bark and thick, glaucous, gray-green shoots with long, oblong-conical buds. Gray-green or bluish green leaves, 5–10in (13–25cm) long, are borne in threes. Long-ovoid, yellow-gray female cones, 5–12in (13–30cm) long, have rounded bases. ↕ 80–120ft (25–35m), ↔ 20–25ft (6–8m). Oregon to Baja California. Zone 5.

P. koraiensis ▣ (Korean pine). Broadly conical tree with smooth, dark gray bark, becoming scaly with age, and green shoots with dense, orange-brown hairs and ovoid to cylindrical buds. Shiny, deep green leaves, with silvery white bands on the inner sides, are borne in fives, and are 2½–5in (6–13cm) long. Long-conical, bright green female cones, 3½–6in (9–15cm) long, have large, free-tipped scales and large, wingless seeds. ↕ to 70ft (20m), ↔ to 25ft (8m). Pacific Russia, Korea, N.E. China. Zone 2.

P. leucodermis, syn. *P. heldreichii* var. *leucodermis* (Bosnian pine). Narrow, long-conical tree with scaly, ash-gray bark, glaucous shoots becoming white, and broad, non-resinous, ovoid buds. Dense, forward-pointing, very rigid, dark green leaves, 3–3½in (7–9cm) long, are borne in pairs. Long-conical female cones, 2–4in (5–10cm) long, are cobalt-blue in early summer, ripening to brown. ↕ 50–70ft (15–20m), ↔ 15–20ft (5–6m). Balkans. Zone 5. **'Compact Gem'** is dense, with dark green-black leaves growing 1in (2.5cm) per year.

P. longaeva, syn. *P. aristata* var. *longaeva* (Ancient pine). Small, conical, dense-crowned tree, becoming gnarled in old age, with scaly, dark brown bark, hairy, red-brown shoots, and ovoid-conical buds. Shiny, gray-green leaves, 1–1¼in (2.5–3cm) long, with white inner sides, are borne mainly in fives (some in threes or fours). A few older leaves bear flecks of resin. Ovoid, rust-red female cones, 2½–4in (6–10cm) long, have a small, fragile prickle on each scale. Formerly confused with *P. aristata*; both have living specimens over 4,700 years old. ↕ to 30ft (10m), ↔ to 20ft (6m). White Mountains of California. Zone 5.

P. monophylla (Single-leaf pinyon). Slow-growing shrub or small tree with a domed crown, smooth, brown or gray bark, becoming fissured with age, and orange shoots with cylindrical-conical buds. Long-persistent, gray-green leaves, ¾–2in (2–5cm) long, are mainly produced singly, and are round in section (occasionally set in pairs and then half-moon-shaped in section). Ovoid, yellow-buff female cones, 3in (8cm) long, have large, wingless seeds. ↕ 15–30ft (5–10m), ↔ to 20ft (6m). S.W. US. Zone 7.

P. montezumae ▣ (Rough-barked Mexican pine). Broadly conical tree, becoming domed when old; it has fissured, gray-brown bark, very thick, rough brown shoots, and ovoid-acute buds. Fresh green, pendent leaves, 6–12in (15–30cm) long, are borne in fives, rarely in sixes or sevens. Produces ovoid to ovoid-conical, yellow to rust-brown female cones, 5–8in (13–20cm) long. ↕ 50–100ft (15–30m), ↔ 20–28ft (6–9m). C. and S. Mexico to Guatemala. Zone 7.

P. monticola (Western white pine). Narrowly conical tree when young, becoming columnar with age. It has smooth, dark gray bark, becoming plate-

Pinus koraiensis

Pinus montezumae

like, and brownish green shoots with rust-brown hairs and cylindrical to spherical buds. Pale green leaves, 3–4in (7–10cm) long, with bluish green inner sides, are borne in fives. Narrowly conical female cones, 6–12in (15–30cm) long, are green to purple-green when young, yellow-brown when mature. ↕ 80–130ft (25–40m), ↔ 20–25ft (6–8m). British Columbia to California. Zone 7.

P. mugo (Mountain pine, Mugo pine). Shrub or rounded to broadly spreading tree with thick, ascending or spreading branches, scaly gray bark, green shoots, becoming brown, and very resinous, ovoid-oblong buds. Well-spaced, dark to bright green leaves, 1¼–3in (3–8cm) long, are borne in pairs. Ovoid to long-conical, dark brown female cones are ¾–2½in (2–6cm) long and symmetrical at maturity. ↕ to 11ft (3.5m), ↔ to 15ft (5m). C. Europe. Zone 2b. **'Gnom'** is a squat shrub when young, becoming more rounded. **'Mops'** ▣ is almost spherical, with green leaves, growing approximately 2½in (6cm) per year. **var. *mugo*** is low-growing, but variable due to seed source; ↕ to 8ft (2.5m), ↔ to 15ft (5m). **var. *pumilio*** is dense and prostrate; ↔ to 10ft (3m).

P. muricata (Bishop pine). Conical tree, becoming broadly domed or columnar with age, with fissured, dark gray bark, orange-brown shoots, and conical to cylindrical buds. Stiff, gray-green or blue-green leaves, 4–6in (10–15cm) long, are borne in pairs, occasionally threes. Oblique, ovoid-conical, nut-brown female cones, 3–3½in (7–9cm) long, have thick spines

Pinus mugo 'Mops'

Pinus nigra

on the outer scales and persist for 20–30 years. Northern populations in California have blue-green foliage and are faster-growing in cultivation. ↕ to 70ft (20m) ↔ 20–28ft (6–9m). California. Zone 7b.

P. nigra ■ (Austrian pine, European black pine). Domed tree with dense, spreading branches, plate-like dark brown or black bark, brown shoots, and broadly ovoid, abruptly sharp-pointed buds with papery scales. Dense, straight, rigid, dark green leaves, 3–6in (8–15cm) long, are borne in pairs. Long-ovoid, yellow-brown female cones are 2½–3in (6–8cm) long. Highly susceptible to *Diplodia* tip blight. ↕ to 100ft (30m), ↔ 20–25ft (6–8m). Austria, N. Italy to the Balkans. Zone 4. **subsp. *laricio***, syn. var. *maritima* (Corsican pine), is a narrowly conical tree, becoming columnar with age, with dark gray bark, yellow-brown shoots, and narrowly conical, tapered buds. Flexible, well-spaced, gray-green or green leaves are 4½–7in (11–18cm) long; ↕ to 130ft (40m), ↔ to 30ft (10m). Corsica, S. Italy (including Sicily). **var. *maritima*** see subsp. *laricio*.

P. palustris (Pitch pine, Southern yellow pine). Ovoid-conical tree with deeply ridged, red-brown bark, peeling in thin plates, and thick, ridged, orange-brown shoots and very large, rounded buds. Finely toothed, acute, bright green leaves, 7–18in (18–45cm) long, with silvery white lines on all sides, are borne in threes and persist for 2 years. Rounded to oblong, spreading, dull brown female cones, 6–10in (15–25cm) long, each have a short, reflexed spine, and winged seeds, ½in (15mm) long. ↕ to 130ft (40m), ↔ 40ft (12m). Virginia to Florida. Zone 8.

P. parviflora (Japanese white pine). Conical or columnar tree, often with a spreading crown, with scaly, purplish brown bark, grayish brown shoots, and ovoid buds. Deep green leaves, ¾–2½in (2–6cm) long, with whitish blue inner sides, are borne in fives. Ovoid-oblong, red-brown female cones, 2–3in (5–8cm) long, have short-winged seeds. Salt tolerant. ↕ 30–70ft (10–20m), ↔ 20–25ft (6–8m). Japan. Zone 5b. **'Adcock's Dwarf'** is dense and slow-growing, with short, gray-green leaves, ½–1in (1.5–2.5cm) long. **'Brevifolia'** is upright and narrow. **f. *glauca*** ■ syn. 'Glauca', is the most common variant in cultivation; it is shorter and spreading, with twisted, glaucous leaves.

P. patula ■ (Mexican yellow pine). Rounded to broadly spreading tree with scaly, reddish brown bark, pale green-brown, glaucous shoots, and cylindrical buds. Slender, pendent, shiny, light green leaves, 6–12in (15–30cm) long, are borne in threes, rarely fours or fives. Stalkless, long-conical, yellow to brown female cones are 2½–4in (6–10cm) long. ↕ 50–70ft (15–20m), ↔ 20–30ft (6–10m). C. Mexico. ❀ (min. 35°F/2°C)

P. peuce ■ (Macedonian pine). Conical or columnar tree with smooth, gray-green bark, becoming fissured with age, and green, slightly glaucous shoots with ovoid-conical buds. Stiff, gray-green leaves, 3–3½in (8–9cm) long, are borne in fives. Cylindrical-conical green female cones, ripening brown, are 3–6in (8–15cm) long. Tolerates a wide variety of conditions, including very poor soils and harsh climates. ↕ 80ft (25m), ↔ to 20–25ft (6–8m). S. Balkans to N. Greece. Zone 4.

P. pinea ■ (Stone pine, Umbrella pine). Conical tree when young, becoming domed, with thick, radiating branches, plate-like, orange-brown bark, orange-brown shoots, and ovate buds. Well-spaced, twisted, glossy green adult leaves, 5–6in (12–15cm) long, are borne in pairs. Solitary, glaucous blue juvenile leaves are retained for several years. Ovoid, shining brown female cones, 5in (13cm) long, ripen in the third year and have wingless seeds. ↕ 50–70ft (15–20m), ↔ 20–40ft (6–12m). Mediterranean. ❀ (min. 41°F/5°C)

P. ponderosa (Ponderosa pine, Western yellow pine). Conical tree, becoming columnar, with deeply fissured bark

Pinus patula

with smooth, broad plates, and thick, green-brown shoots with oblong-cylindrical buds. Dense, rigid, gray-green leaves, 4–10in (10–25cm) long, are borne in threes, rarely pairs or fives. Ovoid or long-ovoid purple female cones, 2½–6in (6–15cm) long, age to brown. ↕ 80–120ft (25–35m), ↔ 20–25ft (6–8m). Rocky Mountains from British Columbia to California. Zone 2b.

P. pumila (Dwarf Siberian pine). Spreading, low shrub with branches that are flexible and bend down in cold weather, and hairy, green-brown shoots with cylindrical-conical buds. Dark green leaves, 1½–2½in (4–6cm) long, with bright blue inner sides, are borne in fives. Ovoid female cones, violet-purple when young, becoming red- or yellow-brown, are 1¼–2½in (3–6cm) long, with wingless seeds. Male cones are bright red in spring. ↕↔ 6–20ft (2–6m). Russia (Siberia) to Japan, N.E. China. Zone 2. **'Compacta'** is a rounded bush with very dense, gray-green leaves, 2–3in (5–8cm) long, gray-white beneath; ↕↔ 10ft (2–3m).

P. radiata, syn. *P. insignis* (Monterey pine, Radiata pine). Narrow, conical tree, becoming broadly domed, with heavily ridged black bark, gray-green shoots, and cylindrical buds. Slender, shining, bright green leaves, 4–6in (10–15cm) long, are borne in threes. Very oblique, ovoid, glossy, yellow-brown female cones, 3–6in (8–15cm) long, with 20 swollen outer scales, persist for 20–30 years. Widely planted in forestry throughout the world. ↕ 80–130ft (25–40m), ↔ 25–40ft (8–12m). California. Zone 7b.

P. resinosa ■ (Red pine). Conical tree with upswept branches, flaky red bark in the upper crown, scaly, pink-gray bark at the base, and thick, orange to red-brown shoots with ovoid to narrowly conical buds. Yellow-green leaves, 4–6in (10–15cm) long, are produced in pairs and persist for 4–5 years; they snap if bent. Long-ovoid female cones, 1½–2½in (4–6cm) long, are chestnut-brown. Male cones are purple. ↕ 50–80ft (15–25m), ↔ 20–25ft (6–8m). Nova Scotia to West Virginia. Zone 2b.

P. sabiniana (Digger pine). Conical or domed tree with fissured gray bark, gray-bloomed shoots, and narrow, cylindrical buds. Flexible, sparse, blue-green or gray-green leaves, 6–12in (15–30cm) long, are borne in threes. Ovoid, dark brown female cones, 4–10in (10–25cm) long, each have a hooked spine and wingless seeds. ↕ to 70ft (20m), ↔ 15–20ft (5–6m). California. ❀ (min. 35°F/2°C)

P. strobus (Eastern white pine). Slender, conical tree when young, becoming irregular and flat-topped with age, often losing major branches. It has smooth gray bark, which becomes black and cracked, and slender, olive-brown shoots with ovoid-oblong buds. Slender, gray-green leaves, 3–5½in (8–14cm) long, are borne in fives. Cylindrical, tapered green female cones, ripening to brown, are 3–6in (8–15cm) long. Excellent specimen tree or hedge. ↕ to 120ft (35m), ↔ 20–25ft (6–8m). Newfoundland to Georgia. Zone 2b. **'Contorta'** has twisted blue-green needles on twisted branches. **'Fastigiata'**

Pinus parviflora f. *glauca*

Pinus peuce

Pinus pinea (inset: cone detail)

Pinus sylvestris

Pinus sylvestris 'Gold Coin'

has a narrow, columnar crown of ascending branches. **'Nana'** is compact, rounded or mounded, with light green foliage. **'Pendula'** ■ is vigorous and weeping, with twisted, hanging branches and long, blue-green leaves.
P. sylvestris ■ (Scots pine). Conical to columnar-conical tree, becoming domed, with flaky, red-brown or orange bark in the upper crown, ridged, purple-gray bark at the base, and green-brown shoots with oblong-ovate buds. Twisted, blue-green or yellow-green leaves, 2–3in (5–8cm) long, are borne in pairs. Ovoid-conical green female cones, 1¼–3in (3–8cm) long, ripen to gray or red-brown. ↕ 50–100ft (15–30m), ↔ 20–28ft (6–9m). Europe (excluding the far north), temperate Asia. Zone 2. **'Argentea'** see 'Edwin Hillier'. **'Aurea'** has bright golden yellow foliage in winter, resuming normal color in spring; ↕ 30–50ft (10–15m). **'Beuvronensis'** is a dwarf, rounded bush, to 3ft (1m) high. **'Edwin Hillier'**, syn. 'Argentea', bears bright, silvery blue leaves. **'Fastigiata'** is narrow and has an upright habit, with ascending branches; ↕ to 25ft (8m), ↔ 3–10ft (1–3m). **'Gold Coin'** ■ is a slow-growing shrub with intense golden foliage; ↕↔ to 6ft (2m). **'Nana'** is a slow-growing, small tree with an upright habit; ↕ 12ft (4m), ↔ 22ft (7m). **'Watereri'** is similar to 'Nana' but has a faster growth rate.
P. tabuliformis (Chinese pine). Conical tree when young, becoming flat-topped when old. It has scaly, red-brown bark in the upper crown, fissured gray bark at the base, and yellow-brown shoots with ovoid-conical buds. The leaves, 3½–6in (9–15cm) long, are produced in pairs. Broadly ovoid-conical, dark brown female cones are 1½–3½in (4–9cm) long. ↕ to 50–70ft (15–20m), ↔ 20–30ft (6–10m). N. China. Zone 6.
P. taeda (Loblolly pine). Conical tree becoming ovoid-rounded with age, with scaly, gray bark, deeply furrowed with age, and glaucous, mid-green young shoots and oblong-conical, long-pointed buds. Finely toothed, dark yellowish green leaves, 6–10in (15–25cm) long, with silvery white lines on all sides, are borne in threes or occasionally in pairs, and persist until the second autumn. Ovoid-spherical to narrowly conical, rust-brown female cones, 3–6in (8–15cm) long, have thick, sharp spines and winged seeds. Useful as a quick screen. One of the leading timber species in the US. ↕ 60–90ft (18–25m), ↔ variable. S. New Jersey to Oklahoma, E. Texas, and Florida. Zone 7.
P. thunbergiana see *P. thunbergii.*
P. thunbergii ■ syn. *P. thunbergiana* (Japanese black pine). Conical tree, becoming rounded, with dark purplish gray bark, yellow-brown shoots, and cylindrical-ovoid buds covered with silky white scales. Thick, dark gray-green leaves, 3–6in (7–15cm) long, are borne in pairs. Long-ovoid, green-brown female cones are 1½–3in (4–8cm) long. Tolerates salt spray; often broken by heavy snow loads. ↕ 50–80ft (15–25m), ↔ 20–25ft (6–8m). N.E. China, Japan, Korea. Zone 5. **'Majestic Beauty'** has shiny, dark green foliage and is smog resistant. **'Thunderhead'** is compact and bears distinctively white buds above dense, glossy, dark green foliage.
P. wallichiana, syn. *P. chylla, P. excelsa, P. griffithii* (Bhutan pine, Blue pine, Himalayan pine). Conical tree when young, developing a broad, domed crown. It has smooth gray bark, later scaly and dark brown, and thick, olive-green shoots with cylindrical-conical buds. Arching to pendent, gray-green to glaucous blue leaves are 4½–8in (11–20cm) long, and produced in fives. Ellipsoid green female cones, 4–12in (10–30cm) long, ripening to brown, have forward-pointing scales. ↕ 70–120ft (20–35m), ↔ 20–40ft (6–12m). Himalayas from Afghanistan to N.E. India. Zone 5.

P

Pinus resinosa

Pinus strobus 'Pendula'

Pinus thunbergii

PIPER

Pepper

PIPERACEAE

Genus of more than 1,000 species of shrubs, climbers, and small trees from very variable habitats throughout tropical regions of the world. Many have a pungent aroma, and some, including *P. nigrum*, are grown as spice crops in tropical regions. They bear alternate, asymmetric, very variable, but often narrowly to broadly ovate to rounded green leaves, heart-shaped at the bases, on stems that are swollen at the nodes. Some ornamentals have white-marbled foliage. Cylindrical spikes of small (often unisexual) flowers without petals or sepals are followed by single-seeded fruit. In warm, humid, tropical areas with heavy, well-distributed rainfall, peppers are grown in fertile soils, with the shade and support of trees. Fruits are harvested at different stages of ripeness for different uses: dried, green mature fruit for black pepper; ripening green fruit for pickled pink peppercorns; ripened, red or yellow fruit (soaked to remove the outer layer of skin) for white pepper. In temperate zones, *P. nigrum* is grown in a conservatory or warm greenhouse; it may bear fruit under glass. Grow outdoors only in tropical areas.

• **CULTIVATION** Under glass, grow in soil-based potting mix with added sharp sand, in bright filtered light and with high humidity. In the growing season, water moderately and apply a balanced liquid fertilizer every month; water sparingly in winter. Outdoors, grow in fertile, well-drained soil in dappled shade. Support climbing stems. Pruning group 11, in late winter.

• **PROPAGATION** Sow seed at 20–24°F (66–75°C) in early spring, or take semi-ripe cuttings in summer.

• **PESTS AND DISEASES** Susceptible to fungal root rot, pepper weevil, and pepper flea beetle.

P

P. nigrum ■ (Black pepper, White pepper). Evergreen, woody-stemmed, perennial climber with ovate, heart-shaped, leathery, deeply veined, dark green leaves, to 5in (13cm) long. In summer, bears small white flowers in spikes to 4½in (11cm) long, on the side of the swollen stem joint opposite the leaf, followed by spherical fruit that are red when ripe. ↕↔ 12ft (4m) or more. India, Sri Lanka. ❄ (min. 61°F/16°C)

Piper nigrum

PIPTANTHUS

FABACEAE

Genus of 2 species of deciduous or semi-evergreen shrubs occurring in scrub and woodland in the mountains of China and the Himalayas. They have alternate, 3-palmate, mid- to dark green, sometimes gray- or blue-green leaves, occasionally with white hairs and a gray-green surface. Grown for their foliage and pea-like flowers, they are suitable for a shrub border or for growing against, or training on, a wall.

• **CULTIVATION** Grow in fertile, well-drained soil in sun or partial shade. Shelter from cold, drying winds. Pruning group 1, or group 13 if wall-trained.

• **PROPAGATION** Sow seed in containers in a cold frame in spring or autumn. Take heeled, semi-ripe basal cuttings in summer.

• **PESTS AND DISEASES** Infrequent.

P. laburnifolius see *P. nepalensis*.

P. nepalensis ■ syn. *P. laburnifolius* (Evergreen laburnum). Open, upright, deciduous or semi-evergreen shrub with 3-palmate leaves composed of lance-shaped, dark blue-green leaflets, to 6in (15cm) long, blue-white beneath. Pea-like, bright yellow flowers, 1½in (4cm) long, are borne in upright, terminal racemes in late spring and early summer, followed by pendent green seed pods, to 9in (23cm) long. ↕ 8ft (2.5m), ↔ 6ft (2m). Himalayas, S.W. China. ❄ (min. 41°F/5°C)

P. tomentosus. Open, upright, deciduous or semi-evergreen shrub bearing 3-palmate leaves composed of ovate, gray-green leaflets, to 6in (15cm) long, densely silky-hairy beneath. In late spring and early summer, bears pea-like, lemon-yellow flowers, 1¼in (3cm) long, in upright racemes, followed by pendent, woolly seed pods, to 3in (8cm) long. ↕ 8ft (2.5m), ↔ 6ft (2m). S.W. China. Zone 8.

Piptanthus nepalensis (inset: leaf and flower detail)

PISONIA

syn. HEIMERLIODENDRON

NYCTAGINACEAE

Genus of 50 species of evergreen trees, shrubs, and climbers from chiefly maritime habitats in tropical regions worldwide, but mainly in North and South America. They are cultivated for their attractive leaves, which are simple and entire, and borne alternately, in opposite pairs, or in whorls of 3. They also produce small, funnel-shaped, petalless flowers: the males with tufts of stamens, the females with solitary ovaries that develop into nutlets (achenes). Where not hardy, grow pisonias in a temperate or warm greenhouse, or as houseplants. In warmer climates, grow as specimen trees, as windbreaks, or as a hedge.

• **CULTIVATION** Under glass, grow in soil-based potting mix in full light or bright indirect light. In the growing season, water freely and apply a balanced liquid fertilizer every month; water sparingly in winter. Outdoors, grow in fertile, humus-rich, well-drained soil in full sun or partial shade. Pruning group 1; may need restrictive pruning under glass.

Pisonia umbellifera 'Variegata'

• **PROPAGATION** Sow seed at 59–64°F (15–18°C) in spring. Take greenwood cuttings in early summer, or take semi-ripe cuttings in mid- to late summer. Air layer in spring.

• **PESTS AND DISEASES** Leaf spot, spider mites, and scale insects can occur.

P. brunoniana see *P. umbellifera*.

P. umbellifera, syn. *Heimerliodendron brunonianum*, *P. brunoniana* (Bird-catcher tree, Parapara). Small tree or large shrub, erect at first, then spreading and usually freely branching. Densely borne, opposite or whorled, elliptic to lance-shaped leaves, 4–16in (10–40cm) long, are thinly leathery, glossy, and rich green. Insignificant, funnel-shaped, pink or yellow flowers, about ⅛–¼in (3–6mm) long, are borne in leafy panicles, intermittently throughout the year. Female sepals are sticky-glandular and elongate, enclosing the nutlets. ↕ 15–70ft (5–20m) sometimes more, ↔ 10–15ft (3–5m). Mauritius to Australia, New Zealand, and Japan. ❄ (min. 50°F/10°C). **'Variegata'** ■ has leaves irregularly splashed and margined creamy white, and pink-tinged stalks.

PISTACIA

Pistachio

ANACARDIACEAE

Genus of 11 species of rounded to upright, dioecious, deciduous and evergreen trees and shrubs from dry habitats in the Mediterranean, C. Asia to Japan, Malaysia, Mexico, and S. US. They are grown for their foliage, flowers, and fruit (although *P. vera*, which produces the edible pistachio nut, is not grown ornamentally). The alternate leaves are usually pinnate, occasionally ternate or simple; the small, petalless, mostly mid-green flowers appear in usually axillary racemes or panicles, followed by the peppercorn-like fruits. Grow as specimen trees; they thrive in coastal conditions. Where not hardy, grow in a cool or warm greenhouse.

• **CULTIVATION** Under glass, grow in soil-based potting mix with added sharp sand, in full light. During growth, water freely and apply a balanced liquid fertilizer monthly; water sparingly in winter. Outdoors, grow in moderately fertile, sharply drained soil in full sun. Pruning group 1; may need restrictive pruning under glass.

• **PROPAGATION** Sow seed at 77°F (25°C) in early spring. Take greenwood

Pistacia chinensis

cuttings in late spring or early summer, or semi-ripe cuttings in summer.
• **PESTS AND DISEASES** *Verticillium* wilt, dieback, root rot, and scale insects occur.

P. chinensis ■ (Chinese mastic). Deciduous tree, erect at first, then spreading. Pinnate leaves, to 10in (25cm) long, each with 10–12 oblong-elliptic, toothed, leathery, glossy, dark green leaflets, with no terminal leaflet, turning yellow to red in autumn. Aromatic green to red flowers are produced in mid- and late spring; the males are in crowded panicles, to 4in (10cm) long, the females in looser panicles, 6–10in (15–25cm) long. The flowers are followed by spherical red fruit, ⅛in (3mm) across, maturing blue. Tolerates a wide range of conditions, including drought. ↕ 50–80ft (15–25m), ↔ 22–30ft (7–10m). C. and W. China. Zone 8.
P. terebinthus (Cyprus turpentine, Terebinth). Deciduous, freely branching tree, or sometimes large shrub, with pinnate leaves, 4–8in (10–20cm) long; these each consist of 3–6 pairs of oval, semi-glossy, mid- to rich green leaflets, with a terminal leaflet. In spring or early summer, produces greenish red flowers; the males are in compact panicles, 2½–4in (6–10cm) long, the females in looser panicles, 2–6in (5–15cm) long. The flowers are surrounded by brown bracts, and are followed by obovoid, edible red to purple-brown fruit, to ¼in (6mm) long. The sap yields a fragrant gum, used in cancer treatments. ↕ 20ft (6m) or more, ↔ 6–20ft (2–6m). Portugal to Turkey, Canary Islands, Morocco to Egypt. ❄ (min. 41°F/5°C)

PISTIA

Shell flower, Water lettuce

ARACEAE

Genus of one species of evergreen, floating aquatic perennial distributed worldwide in the tropics and subtropics. It is grown for its rosettes of attractive, wedge-shaped leaves, and for the exquisite coloring of its fine, feathery roots (which turn from white to purple, and finally black). Although regarded as a noxious weed in some areas, where its radiating stolons cover the surface of the water, it is an excellent ornamental plant for a sunny, temperate pool, for a greenhouse pool, or for a large aquarium.
• **CULTIVATION** Grow as a floating aquatic in full sun with some midday shade. Where not hardy, lift before the first frosts and overwinter at a minimum of 50°F (10°C); alternatively, grow under glass on the surface of an indoor pool (or in containers at the pool margins), in full light, with shade from hot sun, maintaining a water temperature of 59–72°F (15–22°C). Growth is more rapid at higher water temperatures. See also pp.52–53.
• **PROPAGATION** Separate plantlets in summer or early autumn.
• **PESTS AND DISEASES** Aphids occur.

P. stratiotes ■ (Shell flower, Water lettuce). Evergreen, floating aquatic perennial with spreading or semi-upright, wedge-shaped, glaucous leaves, to 8in (20cm) long, fluted above and ribbed beneath, borne in floating rosettes. Inconspicuous, tubular flowers are borne in leaf-like spathes in the leaf axils, irregularly throughout the year. ↕ 4in (10cm), ↔ indefinite. Tropics and subtropics worldwide. ❄ (min. 50°F/10°C). **'Rosette'** bears denser clusters of leaves.

PISUM

FABACEAE

Genus of 6 species of cool-season annual legumes, native to the Old World, grown for its edible seeds, pods, and for forage. Grow in a vegetable garden or as a hedge.
• **CULTIVATION** Easily grown from seed as soon as soil can be worked in spring or late winter. Vines should be staked or trained to a trellis. Peas do best in full sun unless daytime temperatures reach 80°F (27°C).
• **PROPAGATION** For successive crops, sow seeds at 14-day intervals.
• **PESTS AND DISEASES** Aphids.

P. sativum (Garden pea, Snow pea, Snap pea) The 1½in (4cm) pea flowers develop into pods 2–5in (10–13cm) long. ↕ 2–3ft (60–90cm), ↔ 3–4in (8–10cm).

PITCAIRNIA

BROMELIACEAE

Genus of over 260 species of very variable, rosette-forming, usually evergreen perennials (bromeliads), mostly terrestrial, a few epiphytic. All but one species occur in rocky, generally dry areas of Mexico, Central America, South America, and many West Indian islands. They are cultivated for their linear, lance-shaped, or strap-shaped leaves, which have smooth or spiny margins, and for their bell-shaped, white, yellow, orange, green, or red flowers, which are produced in spikes, racemes, or panicles on branched or unbranched stems. In areas where temperatures drop below 50°F (10°C), grow in a warm greenhouse; in warmer climates, pitcairnias are suitable for a shrub border.
• **CULTIVATION** Under glass, grow in standard bromeliad potting mix in full or bright filtered light. From midspring to late autumn, water moderately and apply a nitrogen-based fertilizer every 6–8 weeks. Evergreen species require moderate to high humidity; deciduous species require low humidity. When dormant, keep deciduous species dry and evergreen species just moist. Outdoors, grow in moderately fertile,

Pistia stratiotes

Pitcairnia heterophylla

sharply drained soil in sun or partial shade. See also p.47.
• **PROPAGATION** Sow seed at 66–75°F (19–24°C) in spring. Remove offsets in late spring or early summer.
• **PESTS AND DISEASES** Susceptible to scale insects and mealybugs, especially early in the growing season.

P. atrorubens. Rosette-forming, epiphytic or terrestrial, evergreen bromeliad with variable leaves: the outer ones are much reduced, smooth-margined, ovate, and very pointed; the lance-shaped inner ones, 24–36in (60–90cm) long, have smooth margins and spiny black stalks. In summer, up to 20 bell-shaped, pale yellow flowers, surrounded by red-purple to green floral bracts, are produced in spikes, to 12in (30cm) long, on stems with pointed, brownish purple scape-bracts. ↕ to 36in (90cm), ↔ to 24in (60cm). Mexico, Central America, N.W. South America. ❄ (min. 50°F/10°C)
P. bifrons. Rosette-forming, terrestrial, evergreen bromeliad with strap-shaped, smooth-margined leaves, to 28in (70cm) or more long. During summer, 20–30 bell-shaped, red, red-orange, or yellow flowers, with red or yellow floral bracts, are produced in racemes, 7–11in (18–28cm) long, on white-scaly scapes. ↕↔ 28in (70cm). West Indies (Leeward and Westward Islands, St. Kitts, Guadeloupe). ❄ (min. 50°F/10°C)
P. heterophylla ■ Epiphytic or lithephytic bromeliad, evergreen for most of the year, but deciduous for a brief period, with a bulbous-based rosette of linear, viciously barbed, spiny outer leaves, to 28in (20cm) long, sometimes reduced to brown spines. Inner leaves, to 8in (70cm) long, are smooth-margined, linear, and white-woolly beneath. During summer, 3–12 bell-shaped, red-pink or white flowers are produced in spikes, to 6in (15cm) long, among red floral bracts, on very short scapes. ↕ 5in (13cm) or more, ↔ to 12in (30cm). Mexico to Venezuela and Peru. ❄ (min. 50°F/10°C)

PITHECELLOBIUM

FABACEAE

Genus of about 20 species of deciduous shrubs or trees from temperate climates of subtropical and tropical North and South America. They have thorns and 2-pinnate leaves, and are grown for their often fragrant, mimosa-like flowers. Ideal as a

specimen tree; where not hardy, grow in a temperate greenhouse.
• **CULTIVATION** Under glass, grow in soil-based potting mix with equal parts loam and peat, in full light. Water freely and apply a balanced liquid fertilizer monthly in the growing season; water sparingly in autumn, and keep almost dry in winter. Outdoors, grow in well-drained soil, in full sun.
• **PROPAGATION** Sow seed under glass as soon as ripe. Take greenwood cuttings in early summer; put under mist with bottom heat. Pruning group 1.
• **PESTS AND DISEASES** Spider mites and whiteflies sometimes attack under glass.

P. flexicaule (Texas ebony). Spreading tree with black spines, thick branches, and 2-pinnate leaves with thick, elliptic-oblong, lustrous leaflets, ½in (1.5cm) long. In summer, bears panicles, 1½in (4cm) long, of scented, nectar-rich yellow flowers. ↕ to 50ft (15m), ↔ 30ft (10m). Texas, N. Mexico. ❄ (min. 45°F/7°C)

PITTOSPORUM

PITTOSPORACEAE

Genus of about 200 species of usually evergreen shrubs and trees, a few epiphytic, found in habitats ranging from sandy savanna to rainforest, mainly in Australasia, but also in southern Africa, S. and E. Asia, and the Pacific islands. They are grown for their attractive, glossy, often leathery leaves, which are simple, usually entire, and borne alternately or in whorls. The often fragrant, 5-petaled flowers are borne mostly singly in the leaf axils, or in axillary or terminal corymbs, umbels, panicles, or clusters; they are followed by nearly spherical, woody fruits (capsules) that contain usually black seeds embedded in a sticky, brownish yellow mucilage. Where temperatures fall below 32°F (0°C), grow in a cool greenhouse, moving the plants outdoors for the summer. In warmer climates, the trees are fine specimens for a lawn; the shrubs are suitable for a border, and make a good hedge or windbreak, especially in coastal regions.
• **CULTIVATION** Under glass, grow in soil-based potting mix in full light. When in growth, water moderately and apply a balanced liquid fertilizer monthly; water sparingly in winter. Outdoors, grow in fertile, moist but well-drained soil in full sun or partial shade, although those with variegated or purple leaves produce the best leaf effect in full sun. Where not hardy, shelter from cold, drying winds. Pruning group 1; may need restrictive pruning under glass. Trim hedges in spring and midsummer.
• **PROPAGATION** Sow seed ideally as soon as ripe, or in spring in containers in a cold frame. Take semi-ripe cuttings in summer, or layer or air layer in spring.
• **PESTS AND DISEASES** Prone to aphids, spider mites, mealybugs, scale insects, leaf spots, dieback, root knot nematode, galls, and cankers.

Pittosporum crassifolium 'Variegatum'

P. bicolor. Large shrub or small tree, erect and bushy, with downy young stems. Alternate, oblong, leathery leaves, 1–2½in (2.5–6cm) long, have rolled margins, and are deep green above, white- to brown-felted beneath. Bears nodding, bell-shaped, fragrant, maroon-crimson flowers, about ½in (1.5cm) long, singly or in small, axillary clusters, mainly in spring, followed by dark red capsules, ½in (1.5cm) or more across. ↕ 12–15ft (4–5m), occasionally more, ↔ 6–15ft (2–5m). New South Wales, Victoria, Tasmania. ❄ (min. 41°F/5°C)
P. colensoi see *P. tenuifolium* subsp. *colensoi.*
P. crassifolium (Karo). Large, monoecious shrub or small tree, usually bushy and erect. It has erect to ascending stems, white- to buff-felted when young, and alternate, leathery leaves, 2–3in (5–8cm) or more long, which are obovate to elliptic, and dark green above, white- or buff-felted beneath. Tubular-bell-shaped, dark red to purple flowers, to ½in (1.5cm) across, are borne in terminal clusters in early summer: the males in clusters of up to 10, the females in clusters of 5. The flowers are followed by almost spherical brown capsules, to ½in (1.5cm) across. ↕ 15–30ft (5–10m), ↔ 6–15ft (2–5m). New Zealand (North Island). ❄ (min. 41°F/5°C). **'Compactum'** is smaller, denser, and has gray-green leaves, 1¼–2in (3–5cm) long, in tight whorls; ↕ 5ft (1.5m), ↔ 3ft (1m). **'Variegatum'** ■ has gray-green leaves with broad, irregular, creamy white margins; ↕ 8ft (2.5m).
P. dallii. Small, broadly upright tree or sometimes large, rounded shrub, opening out with age, with reddish purple stems. Very deep green leaves, alternate, or whorled at the stem tips, are 2½–4½in (6–11cm) long, elliptic to elliptic-oblong, either coarsely and sharply toothed or virtually entire. In summer, produces small, shallowly cup-

Pittosporum eugenioides 'Variegatum'

Pittosporum 'Garnettii'

shaped, fragrant, yellow-green or white flowers, to ¼–¾in (0.6–2cm) across, in dense, terminal, compound umbels; they are followed by ovoid brown capsules, ½in (1.5cm) long. ↕ to 20ft (6m), ↔ 6–12ft (2–4m). New Zealand (South Island). ❄ (min. 41°F/5°C)
P. eugenioides (Lemonwood, Tarata). Small tree, erect and conical when young, becoming rounded with age. Alternate, elliptic to narrowly ovate, wavy-margined leaves, to 5in (13cm) long, are thinly leathery, glossy, light green, and lemon-scented when crushed. Produces star-shaped, fragrant, light greenish yellow flowers, ⅛in (3mm) across, in dense, terminal, compound umbels in summer, followed by ovoid brown capsules, ¼in (6mm) long. ↕ 15–40ft (5–12m), ↔ 6–15ft (2–5m). New Zealand. ❄ (min. 41°F/5°C). **'Variegatum'** ■ produces leaves with bold, irregular, cream to creamy yellow margins. **'Zita Robinson'** is similar to the species, but is dense and columnar, with wavy leaf margins.
P. 'Garnettii' ■ Large, bushy shrub, erect at first, then spreading. Alternate, oblong to elliptic leaves, 1½–2½in (4–6cm) long, are sparsely hairy below, almost hairless above, grayish green and pink-spotted, with slightly wavy, creamy white margins. In late spring and early summer, bell-shaped, dark purple flowers, about ½in (1.5cm) long, are borne singly from the leaf axils, followed by almost spherical brown capsules, ½in (1.5cm) long. ↕ 10–15ft (3–5m), ↔ 6–12ft (2–4m). ❄ (min. 41°F/5°C)
P. phillyreoides (Desert willow, Weeping pittosporum). Large shrub or small tree of spreading, weeping habit, with softly hairy young stems and alternate, linear-oblong to narrowly lance-shaped, thick leaves, 2–4in (5–10cm) long, mid- to deep green above, paler beneath. In summer, bears bell-shaped, cream to yellow flowers, ½in (1.5cm) long, occasionally singly or more often in axillary, corymb-like clusters. They are followed by almost spherical yellow capsules, ½in (1.5cm) long, which split to reveal sticky, orange-red seeds. ↕ 20–30ft (6–10m), ↔ 10–15ft (3–5m). Dry areas of Australia. ❄ (min. 41°F/5°C)
P. ralphii ■ Fast-growing, large shrub or small tree, erect then spreading, with white- to buff-downy young stems, and alternate, elliptic, sometimes wavy-margined leaves, 3–5in (7–13cm) long, semi-lustrous, deep green above, white

Pittosporum ralphii

to buff-felted beneath. In late spring and early summer, bears tubular-bell-shaped, very dark red flowers, to ½in (1.5cm) long, in loose, terminal, umbel-like clusters, followed by ovoid, hairy, brown capsules, ½in (1.5cm) long. ↕ 10–12ft (3–4m), ↔ 5–8ft (1.5–2.5m). New Zealand (North Island). ❄ (min. 41°F/5°C). **'Variegatum'** has grayish green leaves with irregular, fairly wide, creamy white margins. **'Wheeler's Dwarf'** is smaller, very dense, and slow-growing; ↕ 3ft (1m), ↔ 24in (60cm).
P. revolutum. Large, bushy shrub with brown-downy young stems and alternate, ovate to lance-shaped, semi-lustrous, mid- to deep green leaves, 1¼–4½in (3–11cm) long, pale brown and densely woolly beneath, especially on the midribs. In late spring and early summer, produces bell-shaped yellow flowers, ⅜–½in (9–15mm) long, in small, compact, terminal, few-flowered umbels, sometimes followed by almost spherical orange capsules, ½in (1.5cm) or more long, which split to reveal sticky red seeds. ↕ 6–12ft (2–4m), much taller in a warm climate with high rainfall, ↔ 5–8ft (1.5–2.5m). Queensland, New South Wales. ❄ (min. 41°F/5°C)
P. rhombifolium (Queensland pittosporum). Conical tree, moderately bushy when young, with long-stalked, broadly lance-shaped to diamond-shaped or narrowly oval, lustrous, mid- to deep green leaves, arranged alternately. In summer, produces bell-shaped white flowers, ⅜–½in (9–15mm) long, in axillary or terminal, many-flowered clusters; they are sometimes followed by spherical, bright

Pittosporum tenuifolium

Pittosporum tenuifolium 'Irene Paterson'

orange capsules, ½in (1.5cm) long, which split to reveal the red capsule interior and sticky, glossy black seeds. ↕30–70ft (10–20m), ↔ 10–20ft (3–6m). Queensland. ❄ (min. 41°F/5°C)

P. tenuifolium ■ (Kohuhu). Large, bushy shrub to small tree, erect and fast-growing when young, broader and slower-growing with age. Produces dark gray to black young stems and alternate, oblong-ovate to elliptic-obovate, usually wavy-margined, thinly leathery, glossy, mid-green leaves, 1–2½in (2.5–6cm) long. In late spring and early summer, bears bell-shaped, honey-scented, black-red flowers, ⅜–½in (9–15mm) across, singly or sometimes in small, few-flowered axillary clusters; they are followed by gray-black capsules, ½in (1.5cm) long. ↕12–30ft (4–10m), ↔ 6–15ft (2–5m). New Zealand. Zone 8. **'Abbotsbury Gold'** has yellow leaves with irregular green margins; ↕10ft (3m), ↔ 5ft (1.5m). **subsp. *colensoi***, syn. *P. colensoi*, produces softly hairy young stems and broader, thicker leaves, 2–4in (5–10cm) long; ↕25ft (8m), ↔ 3–12ft (1–4m). **'Deborah'** bears small leaves, 1in (2.5cm) long, with cream and green variegation; ↕6ft (2m), ↔ 3ft (1m). **'Golden King'** is erect, with light golden green leaves; ↕to 10ft (3m), ↔ 3ft (1m). **'Irene Paterson'** ■ grows slowly, and bears white leaves speckled and mottled between the veins; ↕to 4ft (1.2m), ↔ to 24in (60cm). **'Limelight'** bears elliptic, lime-green leaves with dark green, only slightly wavy margins. **'Margaret Turnbull'** is compact, bearing dark green leaves centrally splashed golden yellow; ↕to 6ft (1.8m), ↔ 3ft (1m). **'Nigricans'** produces black twigs and deep bronze-purple mature leaves. **'Purpureum'** is similar to 'Nigricans' but more open in habit, with purple foliage; ↕10ft (3m), ↔ 5ft (1.5m). **'Silver Queen'** is compact in growth, and has gray-green leaves with irregular white margins; ↕3–12ft (1–4m), ↔ 6ft (2m). **'Tom Thumb'** ■ forms a low bush, and bears foliage flushed bronze-purple; ↕to 3ft (1m), ↔ 24in (60cm). **'Warnham Gold'** has golden green leaves that mature golden yellow. **'Wendle Channon'** has light green leaves with cream-colored margins.

P. tobira ■ (Japanese mock orange). Large shrub or small tree, usually rounded and dense, with erect, sturdy stems and alternate, obovate, leathery leaves, 1¼–4in (3–10cm) long, lustrous and deep green above, paler beneath, and with recurved margins. In late spring and early summer, bears large, handsome, terminal, umbel-like clusters of bell-shaped, very sweetly scented, creamy white flowers, to 1in (2.5cm) across, aging yellow; they are followed by spherical, yellow-brown capsules, ½in (1.5cm) long, with red seeds. ↕6–30ft (2–10m), ↔ 5–10ft (1.5–3m). China, Korea, Japan. ❄ (min. 41°F/5°C). **'Variegatum'** has congested stems and smaller leaves, 1¼in (3cm) long, with irregular white margins.

Pittosporum tenuifolium 'Tom Thumb'

Pittosporum tobira

P. undulatum (Australian mock orange, Cheesewood). Dense, rounded tree with alternate, oblong-lance-shaped to narrowly oblong-ovate, wavy-margined leaves, 3–6in (7–15cm) long, glossy, deep green above, paler beneath. From late spring to midsummer, bears bell-shaped, fragrant, creamy white flowers, ½in (1.5cm) across, in terminal, umbel-like clusters; they are sometimes followed by spherical, orange to brown capsules, to ½in (1.5cm) across, which split to reveal sticky, ruby-red seeds. ↕25–50ft (8–15m), sometimes to 80ft (24m), ↔ 10–22ft (3–7m). Queensland to Tasmania. ❄ (min. 41°F/5°C). **'Variegatum'** has leaves with irregular white margins.

P. viridiflorum. (Cape pittosporum). Usually free-branching, large shrub or small tree, bearing hairy young stems and alternate, obovate, leathery leaves, 1¼–4in (3–10cm) long; the leaves are lustrous, deep green above, paler beneath, sometimes with margins rolled under. From late spring to midsummer, produces terminal, corymb-like panicles of small, jasmine-scented, yellow-green flowers, to ¼in (6mm) across; they are short-tubed and open trumpet-shaped, with 5 spreading lobes, and are followed by almost spherical brown capsules, ½in (1.5cm) long. ↕10ft (3m), sometimes to 20ft (6m), ↔ 6–10ft (2–3m). South Africa. ❄ (min. 41°F/5°C)

PITYROGRAMMA

PTERIDACEAE

Genus of about 14 species of evergreen, terrestrial ferns, native to woodland and shady rocks in W. North America and tropical areas of Africa, Central America, and South America. They have creeping rhizomes that produce tufts of attractive, triangular, pinnate to 3-pinnate fronds, with a silvery white, yellow, or rarely pink, mealy powder on the undersides. Elongated sori are produced along the veins, without protective indusia. Where not hardy, grow in a warm greenhouse or as houseplants. In warmer regions, grow in a sheltered, shady border.

• **CULTIVATION** Under glass, grow in 1 part each of loam, medium-grade bark, and charcoal, 2 parts sharp sand, and 3 parts coarse leaf mold, in bright filtered light. When growing, water moderately, avoiding wetting the foliage, and apply a balanced liquid fertilizer every month. Water sparingly in winter. Outdoors, grow in humus-rich, moist but well-drained soil in partial shade.

• **PROPAGATION** Sow spores at 66–75°F (19–24°C) when ripe. Divide in spring. See also p.51.

• **PESTS AND DISEASES** Infrequent.

Pityrogramma argentea

P. argentea ■ Tufted fern bearing long-stalked, arching, broadly triangular, 2- or 3-pinnate fronds, to 24in (60cm) long, with a silvery white or golden yellow bloom beneath. Pinnae are narrowly triangular-ovate, composed of wedge-shaped to broadly oblong-ovate and deeply pinnatifid secondary segments. ↕to 24in (60cm), ↔ 3ft (1m). Africa, Madagascar, Mascarene Islands. ❄ (min. 45°F/7°C)

P. calomelanos (Silver fern). Neat, tufted fern producing triangular-ovate, very regularly 2-pinnate, mid-green fronds, to 32in (80cm) long, usually silvery white, rarely pink-mealy, on the undersides, with narrowly diamond-shaped segments. ↕to 12–36in (30–90cm), ↔ to 3ft (1m). Tropical Central America and South America. ❄ (min. 45°F/7°C). **var. *austroamericana*** has a yellow or orange bloom on the undersides of the fronds.

P. chrysophylla (Gold fern). Tufted fern producing very long-stalked, ovate or triangular-ovate, 2- or 3-pinnate, mid-green fronds, 8–24in (20–60cm) long. Similar to *P. calomelanos*, but the frond undersides are covered with a bright yellow, waxy powder, and the segments are ovate to narrowly diamond-shaped. ↕↔ 4–16in (10–40cm). West Indies, South America. ❄ (min. 45°F/7°C)

P. triangularis, syn. *Gymnogramma triangularis, Pentagramma triangularis* (Goldback fern). Tufted fern bears triangular, 2-pinnate, mid- to yellow-green fronds, to 8in (20cm) long, rarely more, the undersides covered with a gold or silver, waxy powder. Pinnae are divided into narrow, triangular or oblong segments. ↕↔ 4–8in (10–20cm). S.W. US, N.W. Mexico. ❄ (min. 45°F/7°C)

▷ ***Plagianthus lyallii*** see *Hoheria lyallii*
▷ ***Plagiorhegma dubia*** see *Jeffersonia dubia*

PLANTAGO

Plantain

PLANTAGINACEAE

Genus of some 200 species of mostly rosette-forming annuals, biennials, evergreen perennials and shrubs, many of which are invasive, from very variable habitats worldwide. Grown mainly for their attractive basal rosettes of linear to almost rounded leaves, they also bear tiny, tubular flowers with 4 small petal lobes, in long-stemmed, spherical to oblong spikes, in summer. Grow larger

Plantago nivalis

species in a herbaceous border, and smaller, alpine species in a rock garden or alpine house. Where not hardy, grow in a cool greenhouse.

• **CULTIVATION** Under glass, grow in 4 parts peat or leaf mold to 1 part grit or sharp sand. Outdoors, grow in preferably neutral to acidic, moderately fertile, sharply drained soil in full sun. Protect from winter moisture.

• **PROPAGATION** Sow seed in containers in a cold frame in autumn, or divide in spring.

• **PESTS AND DISEASES** Aphids, spider mites, rust, downy mildew, powdery mildew, leaf spots, and spot anthracnose are common.

P. nivalis ▣ Compact perennial with neat rosettes of lance-shaped, very silky-hairy, silver-green leaves, to ½in (1.5cm) long. In summer, leafless stems, 4in (10cm) long, bear spikes, to ½in (1.5cm) across, of tiny, tubular, gray-brown flowers. ↕ 1in (2.5cm), ↔ 3in (8cm). Mountains in S. Spain. Zone 7.

PLATANUS

Plane, Sycamore

PLATANACEAE

Genus of about 6 species of deciduous trees found in valley bottoms and watercourses in North America and Mexico, with one species in S.E. Europe and one in S.E. Asia. They are grown for their imposing stature and open habit; their large, alternate, palmately lobed leaves, which turn golden brown in autumn; and their flaking bark. The flowers are inconspicuous, but spherical clusters of fruits hang from the shoots throughout winter. They are best as street trees or for large gardens or parks. They thrive in urban conditions, with great tolerance for compacted soil and air pollution, but if planted close to buildings, their vigorous roots may damage drains. Contact with the basal tufts of hair on the fruits may irritate the skin and respiratory system.

• **CULTIVATION** Grow in fertile, well-drained soil in full sun. Pruning group 1.

• **PROPAGATION** Sow seed (of species only) in autumn. Take hardwood cuttings in winter or layer.

• **PESTS AND DISEASES** Anthracnose blight, powdery mildew, canker stain, branch canker, and mushroom root rot can occur. Borers, weevils, Japanese beetles, caterpillars, mites, and scale insects may also occur.

Platanus occidentalis

P. x acerifolia see *P.* x *hispanica.*

P. x hispanica (*P. occidentalis* x *P. orientalis*) syn. *P.* x *acerifolia* (London plane). Vigorous, broadly columnar, deciduous tree with flaking brown, gray, and cream bark and very variable but usually sharply 3- to 5-lobed, bright green leaves, to 14in (35cm) long. Green, later brown fruit clusters, 1in (2.5cm) across, are borne in groups of up to 4, and persist during autumn and winter. ↕ 100ft (30m), ↔ 70ft (20m). Garden origin. Zone 6. **'Bloodgood'** is fast-growing, drought-tolerant, and relatively resistant to anthracnose. **'Suttneri'** has leaves marked creamy white; ↕ 70ft (20m), ↔ 50ft (15m).

P. occidentalis ▣ (Buttonwood, Sycamore). Vigorous, wide-spreading and irregular, open-crowned, deciduous tree with attractive, flaking brown, gray, and cream bark and usually 3-lobed, scented, bright green leaves, to 8in (20cm) long. Green, later brown fruit clusters, 1in (2.5cm) across, are produced usually singly, rarely in pairs, and persist during autumn and winter. ↕ 80ft (25m), ↔ 70ft (20m) or more. E. and S. North America. Zone 5.

Platanus orientalis (inset: leaf detail)

P. orientalis ▣ (Oriental sycamore). Vigorous, spreading, deciduous tree with flaking gray, brown, and cream bark and deeply 5-lobed, glossy green leaves, to 10in (25cm) long. Green, later brown fruit clusters, to 1in (2.5cm) across, are borne in groups of up to 6, and persist during autumn and winter. ↕↔ 100ft (30m) or more. S.E. Europe. Zone 7b.

P. racemosa (California sycamore). Vigorous, broadly columnar tree with flaking gray bark and deeply 5-lobed, occasionally 3-lobed, dark green leaves, to 6–12in (15–30cm) long, velvety when young. Green, later brown fruit clusters, 1in (2.5cm) across, are produced in groups of 2–7, and persist during autumn and winter. Tolerant of much heat and wind. ↕ 80ft (25m), ↔ 70ft (20m) or more. S. California, Mexico. ❄ (min. 35°F/2°C)

PLATYCARYA

JUGLANDACEAE

Genus of one species of deciduous, large shrub or small tree from forest in E. Asia. It is cultivated for its long, pinnate leaves that color yellow in autumn, for its upright catkins, and for its long-lasting, cone-like racemes of fruit. The bark is often used for making a black dye. Best grown as a specimen tree in woodland.

• **CULTIVATION** Grow in fertile, moist but well-drained soil in full sun. Pruning group 1.

• **PROPAGATION** Sow seed when ripe or stratified in containers in autumn. Layer or graft onto *Carya* stock.

• **PESTS AND DISEASES** Infrequent.

P. strobilacea. Rounded tree with alternate, pinnate, mid-green leaves, to 12in (30cm) long, composed of 7 to 15 ovate to oblong-lance-shaped, toothed leaflets. In mid- and late summer, tiny flowers are borne in erect, yellow-green catkins: several males, to 4in (10cm) long, surround a single female. Bears small-winged, green, later brown, fruit in cone-like racemes to 1½in (4cm) long, in autumn, that persist until the following year. ↕↔ 50ft (15m). China, Taiwan, Korea, Japan. Zone 7.

PLATYCERIUM

Staghorn fern

POLYPODIACEAE

Genus of 15 or more species of evergreen, epiphytic ferns, with short-creeping rhizomes; most are found in temperate and tropical rainforest in Africa, Asia, and Australia; one occurs in South America. They are grown mainly for their attractive, often elegant foliage, each plant bearing both sterile and fertile fronds. The mid- to deep green sterile fronds are stalkless, rounded to oblong, and entire to irregularly lobed at the upper margins; they become brown and papery, and usually form a persistent mound at the base of the plant. The fertile fronds are spreading or pendent to erect, wedge-shaped at the bases, usually gray-green and leathery, and often repeatedly forked. All fronds are covered on both sides with small, star-shaped hairs. Spores are formed in large patches on the undersides of fertile fronds; in some species, new plants develop from root buds on the sides of established mounds. Where not hardy, grow in a conservatory or cool or temperate greenhouse, or as houseplants, preferably hanging. In warmer regions, grow epiphytically in a tree.

• **CULTIVATION** Under glass, grow epiphytically in long-fiber sphagnum moss, or fastened to a board or thick branch, in bright filtered light. When in growth, water freely, mist daily, and apply a balanced liquid fertilizer every month; water sparingly in winter. Outdoors, grow epiphytically on a tree in partial shade.

• **PROPAGATION** Sow spores at 70°F (21°C) when ripe. Detach plantlets produced from root tips as soon as mounds, 4in (10cm) across, have formed. See also p.51.

• **PESTS AND DISEASES** Scale insects can be a problem.

***P. alcicorne* of gardens** see *P. bifurcatum.*

P. bifurcatum ▣ syn. *P. alcicorne* of gardens (Common staghorn fern). Very variable, epiphytic fern with erect or horizontal, rounded to heart- or kidney-shaped sterile fronds, 5–18in (12–45cm)

Platycerium bifurcatum

Platycerium hillii

long, which are mid- to deep green then brown, and are entire, wavy, or lobed at the upper margins. Gray-green fertile fronds, to 36in (90cm), are erect, spreading, or pendent, and forked 2 or 3 times into strap-shaped, densely hairy segments. A popular plant, from which many cultivars have been derived. ↕ to 36in (90cm), ↔ 32in (80cm). Java to E. Australia. ❄ (min. 41°F/5°C)
P. elephantotis (Cabbage fern, Elephant's ear fern). Epiphytic fern with erect, rounded to oblong, papery, mid- to deep green then brown sterile fronds, to 36in (90cm) long. Fertile fronds are pendent, wedge-shaped, light gray-green, to 30in (75cm) long. Spores form along frond margins. ↕ to 36in (90cm), ↔ 32in (80cm). Tropical Africa. ❄ (min. 45°F/7°C)
P. grande. Epiphytic fern bearing bronze to green sterile fronds, to 3ft (1m) tall, rounded to heart- or kidney-shaped, with deeply lobed upper margins; they are papery, spreading or lying flat on the branches, forming an impressive crown. Gray-green fertile fronds, to 6ft (1.8m) tall, are pendent, wedge-shaped, leathery, and forked into strap-shaped segments. Spores form in 2 large patches on the second forks of fertile fronds. ↕ to 6ft (1.8m), ↔ 4ft (1.2m). Philippines, Malaysia, Australia. ❄ (min. 45°F/7°C)
***P. grande* of gardens** see *P. superbum.*
P. hillii ▣ (Elk's horn). Epiphytic fern with rounded, dark green sterile fronds, to 16in (40cm) long, shallowly lobed at the upper margins, and lying flat on the branches. Leathery, light gray-green fertile fronds are erect or arching, broadly wedge-shaped, irregularly forked or palmately lobed above, and 30in (75cm) or more tall. Sometimes considered a variety of *P. bifurcatum.* ↕ 28in (70cm) or more, ↔ 24in (60cm). N.W. Australia, New Guinea. ❄ (min. 41°F/5°C)
P. superbum, syn. *P. grande* of gardens. Very large, epiphytic fern producing a crown of gray to gray-green sterile fronds, to 5½ft (1.6m) tall, deeply lobed at the spreading upper margins, and lying flat on the branches. Grayish green fertile fronds, to 6ft (2m) long, are spreading to pendent, and forked up to 5 times with often twisted segments. Similar to *P. grande* but has only a single spore patch in the first fork of fertile fronds. ↕ to 6ft (2m), ↔ 5ft (1.5m). Western Australia. ❄ (min. 41°F/5°C)

▷ ***Platycladus orientalis*** see *Thuja orientalis*

Platycodon grandiflorus

PLATYCODON

Balloon flower

CAMPANULACEAE

Genus of one species of perennial, variable in habit and form, from grassy slopes and mountain meadows in E. Asia. Late emerging, it forms a neat clump of hairless stems with simple, ovate to ovate-lance-shaped, toothed, bluish green leaves. It is cultivated mainly for its clusters of bell-shaped, 5-petaled, mid-blue, dark blue, or lilac-purple flowers, which open from large, balloon-like buds. Suitable for a rock garden or the front of a herbaceous border. It is also good for cutting. Established plants resent disturbance.
• **CULTIVATION** Grow in deep, light, fertile, loamy, reliably moist but well-drained soil in full sun or partial shade. Stems may require support.
• **PROPAGATION** Sow seed *in situ* or in containers, in spring. Divide or detach rooted basal shoots, in early summer.
• **PESTS AND DISEASES** Leaf spot, blight, snails, and slugs can occur.

P. grandiflorus ▣ (Balloon flower). Compact, clump-forming perennial with ovate to ovate-lance-shaped, toothed, bluish green leaves, to 2in (5cm) long, borne in whorls on the lower stem, alternately higher up. In late summer, clusters of large, balloon-like buds open to shallow, bell-shaped, 5-petaled, purple-blue flowers, to 2in (5cm) across, with darker blue veins and pointed tips to the petals. Plants with pinkish mauve and variegated flowers sometimes occur from seed. ↕ to 24in (60cm), ↔ 12in (30cm). Russia (E. Siberia), N. China (including Manchuria), Korea, Japan. Zone 3b. **f. *albus*** has white flowers with blue veins. **f. *apoyama*** has deep violet flowers; ↕ 8in (20cm). **'Baby Blue'** is bushy and dense, with blue flowers. **Balloon Series** cultivars are compact, with blue flowers. **'Komachi'** bears blue flowers that hold their balloon shape. ***subsp. mariesii*** is semi-dwarf in habit, and bears single blue flowers; ↕ 12–18in (30–45cm). **'Mother of Pearl'** see 'Perlmutterschale'. **'Park's Double Blue'** produces double, violet-blue flowers. **'Perlmutterschale'**, syn. 'Mother of Pearl', has pale pink flowers. **'Plenum'** bears semi-double, pale blue flowers. **'Shell Pink'** produces very pale pink flowers.

PLATYSTEMON

Creamcups

PAPAVERACEAE

Genus of one very variable species of erect to spreading, basally branching, hairy annual from grassland, desert margins, and chaparral in W. US. It has almost stalkless, stem-clasping, entire leaves, sometimes borne in small whorls. It is grown for its short-lived, poppy-like flowers, each with a central boss of flattened stamen filaments, borne in profusion where the climate is neither too hot nor too humid. Suitable for edging in an annual border and as massed plantings in rock gardens.
• **CULTIVATION** Grow in very light, well-drained soil in full sun.
• **PROPAGATION** Sow seed *in situ* in autumn or spring.
• **PESTS AND DISEASES** Infrequent.

P. californicus (Creamcups). Many-branched, spreading annual bearing linear-oblong to lance-shaped, densely hairy, strongly parallel-veined, gray-green leaves, to 3in (8cm) long. In spring, produces single, slender-stemmed, 6-petaled, creamy yellow flowers, to 1in (2.5cm) across. ↕ 4–12in (10–30cm), ↔ to 9in (23cm). California to Arizona, Utah.

PLECTRANTHUS

LAMIACEAE

Genus of 350 species of annuals, evergreen perennials, semi-succulents, and shrubs from Africa, Madagascar, Asia, Australasia, and Pacific islands. Cultivated for their foliage and flowers, they are often upright at first but become trailing or spreading with growth. The heart-shaped to ovate or rounded leaves have usually scalloped, sometimes toothed or wavy margins; they are mostly soft, often slightly furry, and aromatic. The small, tubular, 2-lipped, whorled flowers are borne in terminal panicles, racemes, or spikes. Where not hardy, grow shrubby species as container plants in a cool or temperate greenhouse or conservatory, or as houseplants. Grow trailing species in hanging baskets, which may be placed outside in summer and autumn. In warmer areas, grow in a sunny border. Many species are fast-growing, developing into filled-out specimens in a few months.
• **CULTIVATION** Under glass, grow in soil-based potting mix in full light, with shade from hot sun. During the growing season, water freely and apply a balanced liquid fertilizer every month; keep just moist during winter. Outdoors, grow in moderately fertile, well-drained soil in dappled shade.
• **PROPAGATION** Sow seed at 66–75°F (19–24°C) when ripe. Divide in mid- or late spring. Take stem-tip cuttings at any time of year. Remove rooted branches of trailing species.
• **PESTS AND DISEASES** Sometimes affected by mealybugs, spider mites, leaf spots, and root rot.

P. amboinicus. Spreading, often decumbent, evergreen perennial with hairy, ovate, aromatic, mid-green leaves, to 1¾in (4.5cm) long, dotted with

Plectranthus forsteri 'Marginatus'

glands, and with finely scalloped margins. In summer, whorled, tubular, 2-lipped, lilac-pink, mauve, or white flowers, 3–3½in (7–9cm) across, are borne in terminal racemes, to 6in (15cm) long. ↕ 12in (30cm), ↔ 3ft (1m). Tropical to Southern Africa. ❄ (min. 50°F/10°C)
P. argentatus. Erect to spreading, evergreen shrub with silver-hairy stems and densely hairy, ovate, light gray-green leaves, 2–4½in (5–11cm) long, with scalloped margins. In summer, whorled, tubular, pale bluish white flowers, ⅜–½in (9–15mm) across, are produced in terminal racemes, to 12in (30cm) long. ↕↔ 3ft (1m). Australia. ❄ (min. 50°F/10°C)
P. australis (Swedish ivy). Upright then trailing, evergreen perennial producing rounded, glossy, dark green leaves, 1–1½in (2.5–4cm) long, with scalloped margins. Intermittently bears terminal racemes, 8in (20cm) long, of whorled, tubular, white or pale mauve flowers. ↕ 24–36in (60–90cm), ↔ to 3ft (1m). Australia. ❄ (min. 50°F/10°C). **'Variegata'** has white-marked leaves.
***P. coleoides* of gardens** see *P. forsteri.*
***P. coleoides* 'Variegatus' of gardens** see *P. madagascariensis* 'Variegated Mintleaf'.
P. forsteri, syn. *P. coleoides* of gardens. Upright then trailing, evergreen perennial producing ovate to broadly ovate, hairy, light green leaves, 2½–4in (6–10cm) long, with scalloped margins. Intermittently bears terminal racemes, 6–8in (15–20cm) long, of whorled, tubular, pale mauve or white flowers, 1¼in (3cm) across. ↕ 10in (25cm), ↔ to 3ft (1m). E. Australia, Fiji, New Caledonia. ❄ (min. 50°F/10°C) **'Marginatus'** ▣ has leaves with broad, creamy white margins.
P. madagascariensis (Mintleaf). Creeping, shrubby, semi-succulent perennial with square brown stems and rounded, scalloped, firm, fleshy leaves, 1¼–1½in (3–4cm) long, sometimes wrinkled, and coated with white bristles; when crushed, they smell of mint. Terminal spikes, 4–6in (10–15cm) long, of whorled, tubular, 2-lipped, pale lavender-blue or white flowers, to ½in (1½cm) across, often dotted with red glands, are borne in early summer. ↕ to 12in (30cm), ↔ indefinite. S.E. Africa, Madagascar. ❄ (min. 59°F/15°C). **'Variegated Mintleaf'**, syn. *P. coleoides* 'Variegatus' of gardens, has variegated white leaves.

Plectranthus oertendahlii

P. oertendahlii ■ (Candle plant). Trailing perennial with freely branching, reddish purple stems bearing ovate to almost rounded, scalloped, bronze-green leaves, 1¼–1½in (3–4cm) long, with pale veins above, and undersides with soft purple felting. Loose, terminal racemes, 8in (20cm) long, of whorled, white or light blue flowers, ¼in (6mm) long, are produced at intervals all year round. ↕ 8in (20cm), ↔ trailing to 3ft (1m) or more. South Africa (KwaZulu/Natal). ❄ (min. 50°F/10°C)

P. thyrsoideus, syn. *Coleus thyrsoideus.* Bushy, branching perennial or subshrub, often grown as an annual or a winter-flowering container plant, with hairy stems and heart-shaped, toothed, hairy, mid-green leaves, to 6in (15cm) long. At various times of the year, bright blue flowers, to ½in (1.5cm) long, are produced in terminal spikes, to 3½in (9cm) long. ↕ to 36in (90cm), ↔ to 24in (60cm). C. Africa. ❄ (min. 39°F/4°C)

P. verticillatus. Mat-forming, semi-succulent perennial with creeping stems rooting at the nodes. Ovate to rounded, coarsely toothed, soft, fleshy leaves, ½–1½in (1.5–4cm) long, have purplish green undersides. Terminal spikes, 6in (15cm) long, of whorled, tubular, 2-lipped, purple-speckled, white or pale mauve flowers, ½–1in (1.5–2.5cm) across, are produced in summer. ↕ 2½–3in (6–8cm), ↔ indefinite. South Africa (Northern Transvaal, Eastern Transvaal, Eastern Cape), Swaziland, Mozambique. ❄ (min. 50°F/10°C)

P

PLEIOBLASTUS

POACEAE

Genus of about 20 upright, evergreen, woody bamboos usually found in woodland and woodland margins in China and Japan. They are cultivated for their leaves, which are linear to lance-shaped, 2–14in (5–35cm) long, often checkered, sometimes variegated, and usually white-bristled on the margins. They generally have vigorously spreading rhizomes, and produce thickets of erect woody culms, round in section, and either hollow or almost solid; on the lower part of each culm there are 1–7 branches per node. Spikes or racemes of spikelets, each containing 5–13 florets, are sometimes produced, but flowering occurs only rarely. They are suitable for growing in open glades in a woodland garden or as large, informal hedges.

Pleioblastus auricomus

• **CULTIVATION** Grow in fertile, humus-rich, moist but well-drained soil in full sun, or in partial shade if not variegated. Some are vigorous, requiring restraint.
• **PROPAGATION** Separate rhizomes in spring; keep divisions moist and shaded until established.
• **PESTS AND DISEASES** Infrequent.

P. auricomus ■ syn. *Arundinaria auricoma, A. viridistriata, P. viridistriatus.* Upright bamboo with short-running rhizomes and hollow, purple-green culms with hairy nodes. The leaves, to 7in (18cm) long, are linear, brilliant yellow with green stripes, and margined with fine bristles. ↕ to 5ft (1.5m), ↔ 5ft (1.5m). Japan. Zone 7b.

***P. chino* 'Variegatus'.** Vigorous, upright bamboo with hollow, smooth, purple culms. The leaves, 5in (13cm) long, are linear, smooth, hairless, and mid-green with white stripes. ↕ 6ft (2m), ↔ 6ft (2m) or more. Japan. Zone 7b.

P. gramineus. Upright, branched bamboo producing hollow, hairless, green culms, with white waxy powder below the nodes. The leaves, 6–12in (15–30cm) long, are linear, long-pointed, hairless, pendent, and

Pleioblastus variegatus

somewhat twisted at the tips. ↕ 6–15ft (2–5m), ↔ 6ft (2m) or more. Japan, E. China. Zone 7b.

P. humilis, syn. *Arundinaria humilis, Sasa humilis.* Upright bamboo with hollow, dark green culms, 1–3 branches per node, and linear, mid-green leaves, to 8in (20cm) long, sometimes downy beneath. Can be very invasive. ↕ 4ft (1.2m), ↔ 6ft (2m) or more. Japan. Zone 7b. **var. *pumilis*** is more vigorous and compact in habit than the species, with conspicuously bearded scars on the upper culm sheaths, and brighter green leaves.

P. pygmaeus, syn. *Arundinaria pygmaea* (Pygmy bamboo). Upright, woody bamboo with usually solid, mid-green culms, flattened above; they are purplish green at the tips, with 1 or 2 branches at each node. The leaves are linear, checkered, downy, mid-green, and 3in (8cm) long. ↕ 16in (40cm), ↔ 3ft (1m). Japan. Zone 7b.
var. *distichus* ■ syn. *Arundinaria disticha, A. pygmaea* var. *disticha, P. pygmaeus* 'Minezuzme', *P. pygmaeus* 'Orishimazasa', *P. pygmaeus* 'Tsuyuzasa', has hollow culms and hairless leaves; ↕ 3ft (1m), ↔ 5ft (1.5m).

Pleioblastus pygmaeus var. *distichus*

***P. shiboyanus* 'Tsuboi'.** Upright bamboo with hollow, smooth green culms. Bears linear, smooth, white-striped, mid-green leaves, 4½in (11cm) long. ↕ 3ft (1m), ↔ 6ft (2m) or more. Japan. Zone 7b.

***P. simonii* 'Variegatus'**, syn. *Arundinaria simonii* 'Variegata', *P. simonii* f. *variegatus.* Upright, woody bamboo with hollow culms, which have a waxy bloom and 3 branches at each white node. Mid-green, linear to lance-shaped leaves, to 8in (20cm) long, are sometimes striped white, and are finely downy beneath. ↕ 10ft (3m), ↔ 6ft (2m) or more. Japan. Zone 7.

P. variegatus ■ syn. *Arundinaria fortunei, A. variegata.* Upright, woody bamboo with hollow, pale green culms; the nodes have a white, waxy bloom beneath, and each bears 1 or 2 branches. Linear leaves, 5½in (14cm) long, are dark green with cream stripes, and have fine white hairs on both sides. ↕ 30in (75cm), ↔ 4ft (1.2m). Japan. Zone 7b.

P. viridistriatus see *P. auricomus.*

PLEIONE

ORCHIDACEAE

Genus of about 16–20 species of small, deciduous, epiphytic, terrestrial, or lithophytic orchids mainly from wet forest or woodland, at altitudes of 3,250–13,000ft (1,000–4,000m) or higher, from N. India to S. China and Taiwan. They produce short-lived, variably shaped pseudobulbs with 1 or 2 folded, lance-shaped to elliptic, mid-green leaves, 6in (15cm) long, which usually fall before flowering. The often solitary flowers, 3in (8cm) across, are borne on short stems, 2–4in (5–10cm) long, from new growth, at various times of the year. Grow in a cool or temperate greenhouse, or alpine house, or as cool-growing houseplants. Where temperatures seldom fall below 23°F (-5°C), they may be grown in a woodland garden or sheltered rock garden.
• **CULTIVATION** Cool-growing orchids. Grow in shallow pans of terrestrial or epiphytic orchid potting mix. Repot annually before flowering. Water freely in spring and summer until the leaves begin to die down, then keep just moist and admit full light. In summer, provide bright filtered light and moderate humidity, mist twice daily, and feed at every third watering. In winter, allow a brief period of rest, reducing the temperature to 32–35°F (0–2°C). Outdoors, grow pleiones in sharply drained, moderately fertile, leafy, humus-rich soil in a sheltered site in partial shade. Plant in midspring. Protect from severe weather and excessive moisture with an open cloche, or provide a thick, dry, winter mulch, from early autumn to spring. See also p.46.
• **PROPAGATION** Divide annually when repotting, discarding old pseudobulbs.
• **PESTS AND DISEASES** Prone to aphids, spider mites, slugs, and mealybugs.

P. bulbocodioides ■ Terrestrial or lithophytic orchid with almost spherical pseudobulbs, each bearing one folded, lance-shaped to elliptic leaf, to 5½in (14cm) long. In spring, bears solitary, rose-lilac flowers, with white to pink lips spotted with pale brown or purplish

'leione bulbocodioides

ink. ↕ 6in (15cm), ↔ 12in (30cm).
ɩurma, China, Taiwan. Zone 8.
'. **Eiger** ▣ (*P. formosana* x *P. humilis*).
'errestrial or lithophytic orchid with
ɩrge, pear-shaped pseudobulbs, each
earing one elliptic leaf, to 7in (18cm)
ɩng. In mid- and late winter, produces
vhite flowers, shaded pink, 1 or 2 per
em, with white lips marked red, or red
nd yellow. ↕ 5in (13cm), ↔ 2in (5cm).
❀ (min. 41°F/5°C)
'. ***formosana*** ▣ Terrestrial or
thophytic orchid with almost spherical
seudobulbs, each bearing one folded,
ınce-shaped to elliptic leaf, to 5½in
14cm) long. In spring, bears solitary,
ale rose-lilac flowers with white lips
ıat have brownish markings, pink
ıargins, and brown or purplish pink
oots. ↕ 6in (15cm), ↔ 12in (30cm).
.. China, Taiwan. ❀ (min. 41°F/5°C)
'. ***forrestii.*** Terrestrial or lithophytic
rchid with conical pseudobulbs, each
earing one folded, lance-shaped leaf,
–6in (10–15cm) long. In winter and
oring, produces solitary yellow flowers
vith red-dotted lips. ↕ 6in (15cm),
↔ 12in (30cm). China. Zone 8.
'. ***hookeriana.*** Epiphytic or lithophytic
rchid with conical to ovoid pseudo-

'leione Eiger

Pleione formosana

bulbs, each bearing one folded, lance-shaped to elliptic leaf, 2–8in (5–20cm) long. In summer, produces very pale pink to pale purple flowers, 2in (5cm) across, with solitary, white to pale pink lips. ↕ 4in (10cm), ↔ 6in (15cm). Tibet, Nepal, N.E. India, Bhutan, Burma, Laos, N. Thailand, China. ❀ (min. 41°F/5°C)
P. humilis. Epiphytic or lithophytic orchid with conical pseudobulbs, each bearing one folded, lance-shaped leaf, 8–12in (20–30cm) long. From winter to spring, produces solitary white flowers with red-streaked lips. ↕ 6in (15cm), ↔ 12in (30cm). Nepal, N.E. India, Burma. ❀ (min. 41°F/5°C)
P. x lagenaria (*P. maculata* x *P. praecox*). Epiphytic or lithophytic orchid with inverted, cone-shaped pseudobulbs, each bearing 2 folded, lance-shaped leaves, to 12in (30cm) long. Fragrant, pink to rose-lilac to purple flowers, with a yellow central area and purple marks around the margins, are borne 1 or 2 per pseudobulb, in autumn. ↕ 6in (15cm), ↔ 12in (30cm). India (Assam), possibly S. China. ❀ (min. 41°F/5°C)
P. limprichtii. Epiphytic or lithophytic orchid with conical, ovoid or pear-shaped pseudobulbs, each bearing one folded, conical to ovoid leaf, to 5½in (14cm) long. In spring, deep pink to pink-magenta flowers, with rose-red spotted lips, are borne 1 or rarely 2 per pseudobulb. ↕ 6in (15cm), ↔ 12in (30cm). S.W. China, possibly N. Burma. Zone 8
P. maculata. Epiphytic or lithophytic orchid with barrel-shaped pseudobulbs, each bearing 2 folded, lance-shaped to elliptic leaves, 6–12in (15–30cm) long. In autumn, produces solitary, white or pale cream flowers, sometimes streaked with pink, the lips white with purple markings and a central yellow patch. ↕ 6in (15cm), ↔ 12in (30cm). N. India, Bhutan, Burma, S.W. China, N. Thailand. ❀ (min. 41°F/5°C)
P. praecox. Epiphytic or lithophytic orchid with bottle-shaped pseudobulbs, each bearing 2 folded, lance-shaped to narrowly elliptic leaves, to 8in (20cm) long. Solitary, bright rose-purple flowers are produced in autumn. ↕ 6in (15cm), ↔ 12in (30cm). Nepal, N. India (Sikkim), Bhutan, Burma, S.W. China, Thailand. ❀ (min. 41°F/5°C)
***P.* Stromboli 'Fireball'** (*P. bulbocodioides* x *P. speciosa*). Epiphytic orchid with conical pseudobulbs, each bearing one folded, lance-shaped to narrowly elliptic leaf, to 10in (25cm) long. In spring, produces solitary, rose-lilac flowers with lips that have reddish pink markings. ↕ 6in (15cm), ↔ 12in (30cm). ❀ (min. 41°F/5°C)

PLEIOSPILOS

Living granite

AIZOACEAE

Genus of about 35 species of solitary or clump-forming, stemless, perennial succulents from arid areas of South Africa. They are grown for their unusual form and attractive flowers. Most have 1 or 2, occasionally 3 pairs of often unequal, erect, very fleshy, grayish or yellowish green or brown to red leaves, often with variably colored dots; they are usually flattened on the upper surfaces, keeled, rounded, or rounded and partly keeled beneath, and united at the bases. The daisy-like, diurnal, yellow or orange flowers, which sometimes have a coconut-like fragrance, open in late summer and early autumn. In areas where temperatures drop below 45°F (7°C), grow as houseplants or in a temperate greenhouse; although most species tolerate brief periods to 28°F (-2°C). In warm, dry climates, grow in a raised bed or succulent border.
• **CULTIVATION** Under glass, grow in standard cactus potting mix in full light. From early summer to late autumn, water sparingly but regularly and apply a low-nitrogen liquid fertilizer every 4–6 weeks. Keep dry at all other times. Outdoors, grow in low-fertility, sharply drained soil in full sun. See also pp.48–49.

Pleiospilos bolusii

Pleiospilos simulans

• **PROPAGATION** Sow seed at 66–75°F (19–24°C), or detach offsets, from late spring to summer.
• **PESTS AND DISEASES** Vulnerable to aphids while flowering.

P. bolusii ▣ (Mimicry plant). Usually solitary, perennial succulent with one pair of ovoid, gray-green leaves, 1½–3in (4–8cm) long, sometimes tinged red and with dark green dots; they are generally broader than long, with the undersides more rounded and partly keeled. Daisy-like, golden yellow flowers, 2½–3in (6–8cm) across, are solitary or produced in cymes of 2–4 in late summer and early autumn. ↕ 3in (8cm), ↔ 6in (15cm). South Africa (Eastern Cape). ❀ (min. 45°F/7°C)
P. nelii (Splitrock). Solitary, perennial succulent with up to 3 pairs of unequal, almost hemispherical, densely dotted, grayish green leaves, 1½–3in (4–8cm) long, with the tips of the very rounded undersides drawn over the flat upper surfaces. In late summer and early autumn, produces solitary, daisy-like, orange-pink flowers, 3in (8cm) across. ↕ 3in (8cm), ↔ 5in (13cm). South Africa (Western Cape, Eastern Cape). ❀ (min. 45°F/7°C)
P. simulans ▣ Clump-forming, perennial succulent bearing one pair of slightly unequal, ovate to 3-angled, spreading, densely dotted, reddish, yellowish, or brownish green leaves, 2–3in (5–8cm) long, the keeled undersides thickening toward the tips. Daisy-like, scented, yellow or orange flowers, 2½in (6cm) across, are solitary or produced in cymes of 1–3 in late summer and early autumn. ↕ 4in (10cm), ↔ to 12in (30cm). South Africa (Eastern Cape). ❀ (min. 45°F/7°C)

▷ ***Pleroma macrantha*** see *Tibouchina urvilleana*

PLEUROTHALLIS

ORCHIDACEAE

Genus of about 900 species of mainly small, evergreen, epiphytic or rarely lithophytic orchids found in tropical North, Central, and South America, from Mexico to Peru and Brazil; they occur in forest, from low altitudes to over 8,000ft (2,500m). Although extremely variable in form and habit, they typically produce slender stems on creeping rhizomes, with a solitary, lance-shaped to almost rounded, leathery,

mid-green leaf at the apex of each stem. One or many flowers, ½–1¼in (1.5–3cm) across, may be produced singly or in racemes from the base of each leaf.
• **CULTIVATION** Cool- to intermediate-growing orchids. Grow epiphytically on bark, or pot tightly into small containers of epiphytic orchid potting mix made with fine-grade bark. In summer, provide bright filtered light and high humidity; water freely, mist twice daily, and apply a balanced liquid fertilizer at every third watering. In winter, admit full light and water more sparingly. See also p.46.
• **PROPAGATION** Divide when the plant fills the pot and flows over the sides.
• **PESTS AND DISEASES** May be infested by spider mites, aphids, and mealybugs.

P. bivalvis. Medium-sized, tufted epiphytic orchid with erect stems bearing spear-shaped, leathery, mid-green leaves, to 16in (40cm) long. In summer, short racemes of pale green-yellow- or brownish yellow-sepaled flowers, 1in (2.5cm) long, with maroon petals, red lips with white bases, and maroon-flushed orange columns, are borne in succession from a brown basal sheath above the foliage. ‡↔ to 12in (30cm). Colombia, Venezuela. ❀ (min. 54–59°F/12–15°C; max 82°F/28°C)
P. glandulosa, syn. *P. vittariaefolia.* Small, densely tufted epiphytic orchid bearing one narrowly ovate, mid-green leaf, ¾–1½in (2–4cm) long, at the apex of the stem. In summer, bears racemes, 1¾in (4.5cm) long, of 1 or 2, reddish yellow or greenish yellow flowers, ½in (1.5cm) across, with glandular margins. ‡↔ ¾–2in (2–5cm). Mexico to Panama. ❀ (min. 54–59°F/12–15°C; max 82°F/28°C)
P. grobyi. Small, epiphytic orchid bearing fleshy, lance-shaped to narrowly ovate leaves, 3in (8cm) long, with blunt or rounded tips. Loose racemes of translucent, pale yellow to green flowers, ½in (1.5cm) long, with scattered purple veins, streaked with brown, are borne above the foliage in summer. ‡ 3in (8cm), ↔ 4in (10cm). Mexico, West Indies, Central and South America. ❀ (min. 50°F/10°C; max 75°F/24°C)
P. tuerkheimii. Upright epiphytic orchid with stout, cylindrical, erect stems, each bearing one oblong-elliptic, mid-green leaf, 1½–10in (4–25cm) long, at the apex. In summer, bears many-flowered racemes, to 14in (35cm) long, subtended by large, compressed sheaths, of reddish brown and white flowers, 1–2in (2.5–5cm) long, with white petals striped with reddish brown dots. ‡ 6–28in (15–70cm), ↔ 6–20in (15–50cm). Mexico to Panama. ❀ (min. 54°F/12°C; max 77°F/25°C)
P. vittariaefolia see *P. glandulosa.*

PLUMBAGO
Leadwort
PLUMBAGINACEAE

Genus of 10–15 species of annuals, perennials, and evergreen shrubs and scandent climbers from tropical woodland and scrub in warm-temperate to tropical regions worldwide. They have alternate, simple, entire leaves, and are grown for their terminal, sometimes corymb-like racemes of attractive, white, red, or blue, salverform flowers, each

Plumbago auriculata

with 5 spreading petal lobes. Where temperatures fall below 45°F (7°C), grow in a cool or temperate greenhouse or conservatory; plants grown in containers can be moved outdoors in summer. In warmer climates, use shrub and perennial species in a mixed or shrub border; train climbers over a pergola or arch.
• **CULTIVATION** Under glass, grow in soil-based potting mix in full light. Top-dress or pot on in spring. During the growing season, water freely and apply a balanced liquid fertilizer every month; water sparingly in winter. Outdoors, grow in fertile, well-drained soil in full sun. Tie stems to supports. Pruning group 12 for climbers, in early spring; group 8 for shrubs. May need restrictive pruning under glass.
• **PROPAGATION** Sow seed at 55–64°F (13–18°C) in spring, or root semi-ripe cuttings in midsummer with bottom heat. Take softwood cuttings from *P. indica* in late spring or early summer, or insert root cuttings in late winter.
• **PESTS AND DISEASES** Spider mites, whiteflies, and mealybugs may be a problem under glass.

P. auriculata ■ syn. *P. capensis* (Cape leadwort). Scandent, evergreen shrub, grown as a climber, with slender, whippy, moderately branching stems. Oblong to oblong-spoon-shaped leaves, 1½–3in (4–8cm) long, are mid- to bright matte green, sometimes with a blue-gray tone. Bears long-tubed, light sky-blue flowers, 1½in (4cm) long, in dense, terminal, corymb-like racemes, 6in (15cm) across, from summer to late autumn. ‡ 10–20ft (3–6m), ↔ 3–10ft (1–3m). South Africa. ❀ (min. 41°F/5°C) **var. *alba*** bears pure white flowers.
P. capensis see *P. auriculata.*
P. indica, syn. *P. rosea* (Scarlet leadwort). Small, evergreen shrub becoming spreading or semi-scandent if not pruned annually. Ovate-elliptic leaves, 2–4½in (5–11cm) long, are mid- to deep green. Long-tubed, red to deep rose-pink flowers, 1in (2.5cm) long, are borne in terminal racemes, 4–12in (10–30cm) long, in winter (earlier if unpruned). ‡ to 6ft (2m), ↔ to 3ft (1m). S.E. Asia. ❀ (min. 45°F/7°C)
P. larpentiae see *Ceratostigma plumbaginoides.*
P. rosea see *P. indica.*

PLUMERIA
Frangipani, Pagoda tree, West Indian jasmine
APOCYNACEAE

Genus of 7 or 8 species of deciduous or semi-evergreen shrubs and small trees, with succulent stems and very thick, fleshy branches, from tropical and subtropical America. The simple, entire leaves, clustered toward the stem tips, are alternately or spirally arranged. The fragrant, salverform flowers, each with 5 broad petal lobes, are produced in showy, terminal clusters or panicles, often on bare stems or with the young leaves. Below 50°F (10°C), it is best to grow in a temperate or warm greenhouse, or as houseplants. In warmer climates, use as specimen plants in a lawn or as a focal point in an island planting. The milky sap may cause mild stomach upset if ingested.
• **CULTIVATION** Under glass, grow in soil-based potting mix with added sharp sand, in full light. During the growing season, water moderately and apply a balanced liquid fertilizer monthly; keep almost dry in winter. Outdoors, grow in moderately fertile, well-drained soil in full sun. Pruning group 1; may need restrictive pruning under glass.

Plumeria rubra

• **PROPAGATION** Sow seed at 64°F (18°C) in spring. Take ripe cuttings of leafless stem tips in early spring; allow these to dry at the bases before inserting.
• **PESTS AND DISEASES** Spider mites may be troublesome under glass.

P. acuminata see *P. rubra* var. *acutifolia.*
P. acutifolia see *P. rubra* var. *acutifolia.*
P. alba ■ (West Indian jasmine). Large, deciduous shrub or small, spreading tree with robust, sparsely branched, very thick stems. Spirally arranged, lance-shaped, slightly wrinkled, rich green leaves, to 12in (30cm) long, are usually finely hairy beneath. Salverform, yellow-eyed white flowers, 2½in (6cm) across, are produced in terminal panicles from

Plumeria alba

summer to autumn. ↕ to 20ft (6m), ↔ to 12ft (4m). Puerto Rico, Lesser Antilles. ❀ (min. 50–55°F/10–13°C)

P. rubra ▣ (Nosegay frangipani). Large, deciduous shrub or small, sparsely branched tree, upright in habit, with very thick stems bearing alternately arranged, broadly elliptic to oblong or inversely lance-shaped, mid-green leaves, 8–16in (20–40cm) long, with paler midribs. Salverform, yellow-eyed flowers, 3–4in (7–10cm) across, usually rose-pink but sometimes yellow or red to bronze, are produced in terminal panicles from summer to autumn. ↕ to 22ft (7m), ↔ to 15ft (5m). Mexico to Panama. ❀ (min. 50–55°F/10–13°C). **var. *acutifolia*,** syn. *P. acuminata*, *P. acutifolia* (Pagoda tree) produces oblong-elliptic, pointed, dark green leaves, to 4in (10cm) long, on long stalks. Terminal panicles of salverform, very fragrant, yellow-centered white flowers, 3–3½in (8–9cm) across, with widely spreading petals, are produced from late summer to autumn. ↕ 12ft (4m), ↔ to 6ft (2m). Mexico to Panama, N. South America, West Indies. **f. *tricolor*** bears pink-margined white flowers with yellow eyes.

POA

Meadow grass, Spear grass

POACEAE

Genus of about 500 species of mainly perennial grasses (some are annuals) found in cool-temperate regions in a wide range of habitats, from seashores to alpine zones. They include a number of important fodder, lawn, and pasture grasses. Of variable habit, they are grown for their narrowly linear, flat to folded leaves, and open or compact, summer-flowering panicles. Most cultivated species (most notably *P. pratensis*, Kentucky bluegrass) are grown as turf grasses or for agricultural purposes. *P. alpina* var. *vivipara* is grown as a curiosity, either in a rock garden or at the front of a border. *P. chaixii* and other ornamental species are suitable for a border, and for naturalizing in woodland and other shady situations.

• **CULTIVATION** Grow in moderately fertile, medium to light, well-drained soil in full sun or partial shade. Remove flowering stems to prevent self-seeding; cut back dead foliage in early spring.

• **PROPAGATION** Sow seed in containers in a cold frame in spring or autumn, or divide between midspring and early summer. Peg down mature flowerheads of *P. alpina* var. *vivipara* to allow plantlets to root.

• **PESTS AND DISEASES** Infrequent.

P. alpina (Alpine meadow grass). Densely tufted perennial with neat mounds of thick, flat, linear, short-pointed, mid-green leaves, 1½–4in (4–10cm) long. From early to late summer, produces dense, ovoid-pyramidal, short-branched, purplish green flowering panicles, to 3in (8cm) long. ↕ 12in (30cm), ↔ 8in (20cm). W. Europe to C. Asia. Zone 6. **var. *vivipara*** has panicles in which lower spikelets have been replaced by tiny plantlets.

P. chaixii. Densely tufted perennial bearing flat or folded, unusually broad, linear, glossy, bright green leaves, to 18in (45cm) long and ½in (1.5cm) wide, each abruptly contracted at the tip to form a hood. In late spring and early summer, bears open, slightly nodding, straight-branched, ovate to ovate-oblong, pale green, often purple-tinted flowering panicles, to 10in (25cm) long, on strong, erect stems held well above the foliage. ↕ 3ft (1m), ↔ 18in (45cm). Europe, S.W. Asia, North America. Zone 5.

P. prantensis (Kentucky bluegrass). Perennial, fine-textured, blue-green grass with vigorous spreading ability. Produces 3–5 crowded, compressed flowers, to ¼in (7mm). ↕ 3in (8cm). N. and N.W. US. Zone 3.

P. trivialis (Rough bluegrass). Soft-bladed, fine-textured, bright green, grass, a shallow-rooted relative of Kentucky bluegrass. Produces oblong panicles; spikelets are 2½in (6cm). ↕ to 3–4ft (1m–1.2m). Eurasia, N. Africa. Zone 5.

PODALYRIA

FABACEAE

Genus of about 25 species of evergreen shrubs from woodland, forest margins, and streamsides in southern Africa. They have simple, usually densely hairy leaves with rolled margins, and are grown for their fragrant, pea-like flowers, borne singly or in pairs from the leaf axils. Where temperatures fall below 45°F (7°C), grow in a cool greenhouse. In warmer areas, grow in a shrub border or at the base of a house wall.

• **CULTIVATION** Under glass, grow in soil-based potting mix in full light. When in growth, water moderately and apply a balanced liquid fertilizer every month; water sparingly in winter. Outdoors, grow in moderately fertile, moist but well-drained soil in full sun. Pruning group 8; may need restrictive pruning under glass.

• **PROPAGATION** Sow seed at 55–64°F (13–18°C) in spring. Root semi-ripe cuttings with bottom heat in summer.

• **PESTS AND DISEASES** Spider mites may be troublesome under glass.

P. sericea. Spreading, densely leafy shrub with obovate leaves, ¾in (2cm) long, thickly covered with silver-silky hairs that age to gold. From autumn to spring, produces solitary, upright, pea-like, fragrant, lavender-blue to lavender-pink flowers, ½in (1.5cm) across, with a purple mark at each petal base. ↕ 18–36in (45–90cm), ↔ 18–39in (45–100cm). South Africa (Northern Cape, Western Cape, Eastern Cape). ❀ (min. 45°F/7°C)

PODOCARPUS

PODOCARPACEAE

Genus of about 100 species of dioecious, occasionally monoecious, evergreen, coniferous trees and shrubs from forest habitats, mainly in warm-temperate to tropical zones. They are grown for their spirally arranged leaves, which are variable in shape and are mainly borne in 2 ranks. Male and female flowers are usually borne on separate trees: the males are yellow or red, solitary or in axillary clusters of up to 5, or, in some species, borne in narrow, catkin-like cones; the females are green and produced in cone-like structures. Male and female plants are both needed to produce the plum-shaped, rounded to oblong, usually single-seeded fruits, which have fleshy, often red arils at the bases.

Podocarpus nivalis (inset: fruit detail)

Grow as specimens or in a woodland garden; *P. alpinus* and *P. nivalis* are also suitable for a shrub border or large rock garden. *P. macrophyllus* needs long, hot, humid summers to achieve tree stature, remaining shrub-like in cooler areas. They make attractive specimens in warm climates, but need temperate or warm greenhouse protection where not hardy.

• **CULTIVATION** Tolerant of a range of soils, but best in fertile, moist but well-drained, humus-rich soil in full sun, with shelter from cold, dry winds. Most species thrive best in humid or high-rainfall climates.

• **PROPAGATION** Sow seed as soon as ripe, or in containers in an open frame in spring; germination may take as long as 12–18 months. Take semi-ripe cuttings from upright leading shoots in late summer.

• **PESTS AND DISEASES** Infrequent.

P. alpinus (Tasmanian podocarp). Spreading, dense, rounded shrub bearing slender green shoots. Linear, dull green leaves, ¼–½in (7mm–1.5cm) long, each with 2 gray bands beneath, are parted on either side of the shoots. Male flowers are produced in yellow, catkin-like cones, female flowers in green cone-like structures. Ovoid, bright red fruit, ¼in long, are borne in autumn on female plants.↕↔ to 6ft (2m). New South Wales, Tasmania. Zone 7b.

P. andinus see *Prumnopitys andina.*

P. macrophyllus (Buddhist pine, Kusamaki, Southern yew). Conical tree, becoming domed, with reddish brown bark and erect or spreading, yellowish green shoots. Lance-shaped, firm, leatherly leaves, 2½–4in (6–10cm) long, are light green becoming dark green above, each with 2 glaucous bands beneath, and are erect or spreading on the shoots. Male flowers are borne in yellow, catkin-like cones, female flowers in green cone-like structures. Ovoid, reddish purple fruit, about ½in (1.5cm) long, are borne on female plants in autumn. ↕ to 50ft (15m), ↔ 20–25ft (6–8m). E. China, Japan. Zone 7b.

P. nivalis ▣ (Alpine totara). Spreading, dense, rounded shrub, very similar to *P. alpinus*, but with more rigid, linear, green-bronze leaves, ½–¾in (1–2cm) long, set radially around the slender, mid-green shoots, unparted on either side. Male flowers are borne in yellow, catkin-like cones, female flowers in green cone-like structures. Oblong, bright red fruit, ¼in (6mm) long, are produced in autumn on female plants. ↕↔ to 6ft (2m). New Zealand. Zone 7b.

P. salignus ▣ (Willowleaf podocarp). Columnar or broadly conical tree with spreading, later pendent branches, fibrous, peeling, red-brown bark, and green shoots that become gray-brown with age. Spreading, linear, often sickle-shaped leaves, 2–4½in (5–11cm) long, are dark bluish green (with a ridge above), and yellow-green beneath; they occur mainly near the shoot tips. The male flowers are produced in yellow, catkin-like cones, female flowers in green cone-like structures. Egg-shaped, green or dark violet fruit, ⅜in (9mm) long, are produced in autumn on female plants. Very graceful as a mature tree. ↕ to 70ft (20m), ↔ 20–28ft (6–9m). Chile. Zone 8.

Podocarpus salignus

PODOPHYLLUM

Mayapple

BERBERIDACEAE

Genus of about 9 species of shade-loving, rhizomatous perennials, cultivated for their foliage and flowers, from scrub and forest in North America and from the Himalayas to China and Taiwan. Each plant has 1 or 2 peltate, palmately lobed, radical leaves, sometimes with purplish brown patches between the conspicuous veins; the leaves are pushed up by the lengthening leaf stalks and emerge looking like tiny, folded umbrellas. Terminal, cup-shaped, pink, white, or red flowers are solitary or produced in small umbels, and are followed by red or yellow fruits, 1–2in (2.5–5cm) long. Mayapples are suitable for a woodland garden or a moist, shady border. All parts of the plants are highly toxic if ingested, except for the fully ripe fruit of some species.

• **CULTIVATION** Grow in humus-rich, leafy, moist soil in full or partial shade (*P. peltatum* tolerates drier soil). In cold areas, protect marginally hardy species with a dry winter mulch.

• **PROPAGATION** Sow seed in containers in an open frame as soon as ripe. Divide in spring or late summer.

• **PESTS AND DISEASES** Susceptible to slug damage in spring as the leaves emerge.

P. emodi see *P. hexandrum.*

P. hexandrum ▣ syn. *P. emodi* (Himalayan mayapple). Rhizomatous perennial bearing long-stalked, 3- to 5-lobed, deeply toothed, mid-green leaves, to 10in (25cm) long, with purplish brown markings; they unfurl after flowering. Solitary, open cup-shaped, usually 6-petaled, white or pale pink flowers, 1–2in (2.5–5cm) across, with prominent yellow anthers, are borne from late spring to midsummer; they are followed by plum-like, ovoid, fleshy red fruit, to 2in (5cm) long. ↕ 18in (45cm), 12in (30cm). N. India (Himalayas) to China. Zone 4.

P. japonicum see *Ranzania japonica.*

P. peltatum ▣ (American mandrake, Mayapple). Creeping, rhizomatous perennial producing long-stalked, 5- to 9-lobed, toothed, sometimes 2-cleft, glossy leaves, to 12in (30cm) long, well-developed at flowering. Solitary, semi-pendent, shallowly cup-shaped, usually 9-petaled, fragrant, waxy white to pale pink flowers, 2in (5cm) across, are produced beneath the leaves in spring, that are followed by edible, ovoid, yellowish green fruit, 1–2in (2.5–5cm) long. ↕ 18in (45cm), ↔ 4ft (1.2m) or more. Ontario and Quebec to Texas and Florida. Zone 4.

Podophyllum hexandrum

Podophyllum peltatum

PODRANEA

BIGNONIACEAE

Genus of 2 species of woody-stemmed, evergreen climbers from open woodland in Zimbabwe and S. Africa. Pinnate leaves, borne in opposite pairs, are grown for their 5-lobed, trumpet-shaped, foxglove-like flowers. Where temperatures regularly fall below 32°F (0°C), grow in a cool or temperate green house.

• **CULTIVATION** Under glass, grow in soil-based potting mix in bright filtered light. In growth, water moderately and apply a balanced liquid fertilizer monthly; water sparingly in winter. Outdoors, grow in fertile, moist but well-drained soil in light, dappled or partial shade. Pruning group 12, immediately after flowering.

• **PROPAGATION** Sow seed at 55–64°F (13–18°C) in spring, take semi-ripe cuttings in summer, or layer in spring.

• **PESTS AND DISEASES** Prone to spider mites and mealybugs under glass.

P. ricasoliana, syn. *Pandorea ricasoliana, Tecoma ricasoliana* (Pink trumpet vine). Scandent, twining climber, becoming bushy with age, with pinnate leaves, to 10in (25cm) long, composed of 5–11 lance-shaped to ovate, unevenly toothed, rich green leaflets with slender points. Produces loose, terminal panicles of about 12 trumpet-shaped pink flowers, to 2½in (6cm) long, with red veins, paler tubes, and wavy-margined, round lobes, from winter to summer, depending on the temperature. ↕ 10–15ft (3–5m). South Africa (Eastern Cape, KwaZulu/Natal). ❀ (min. 50°F/10°C)

▷ ***Poinciana gilliesii*** see *Caesalpinia gilliesii*

▷ ***Poinciana pulcherrima*** see *Caesalpinia pulcherrima*

▷ ***Poinciana regia*** see *Delonix regia*

POLASKIA

CACTACEAE

Genus of 2 species of tree-like, many-branched cactus that form a dense canopy in the mountain slopes of Oaxaca and Puebla, Mexico. The plants have 7–12 ribs, which are sharply triangular in cross section. Diurnal and nocturnal flowers are borne, urn- to bell-shaped, of whitish to yellowish green. They bear an edible fruit, which is globose, red, and juicy, 1/16–⅕in (2–5mm).

• **CULTIVATION** Under glass, grow in a mix of 4 parts standard cactus potting mix and 1 part limestone chips, in full light. From spring to summer, water freely and apply a balanced liquid fertilizer every 4–5 weeks. Keep nearly dry at other times. Outdoors, grow in moderately fertile, slightly alkaline, well drained, humus-rich soil in full sun. See also pp.48–49.

• **PROPAGATION** Sow seed at 70°F (21°C) in spring or summer.

• **PESTS AND DISEASES** Scale occurs.

P. chende ▣ Tree-like cactus, branching terminally, with distinct trunks. Yellowish green stems are straight or slightly curved, 16–20in (40–50cm) long; 7–10 semi-wavy ribs are separated by wide furrows, with round, dark areoles. Most plants have 5 awl-shaped, gray radials, ⅕–½in (5–15mm) long, and no central spines. Solitary white flowers, to ¼in (6.5cm), open in the morning in summer. Clusters of short spines cover globose fruit. 1⅜–1½in (3.5–4cm). ↕ to 12ft (4m), ↔ 15–22ft (5–7m). S.E. Mexico. ❀ (min. 50°F/10°C)

POLEMONIUM

Jacob's ladder

POLEMONIACEAE

Genus of about 25 species of deciduous, clump-forming or occasionally rhizomatous perennials and annuals, found in stony, arctic or alpine soils, often by streams, or in damp meadows, woodland, or scrub, in Europe, Asia, North America, and Central America. Most have basal clumps of unequally pinnate leaves, usually with numerous leaflets, and erect or decumbent stems bearing smaller leaves. They are grown for their spring and summer flowers, which are bell-shaped, saucer-shaped, narrowly tubular, or funnel-shaped and spreading at the mouths; they are usually white or blue, sometimes purple, pink, or yellow, and either solitary or in terminal or axillary cymes. Grow taller species in a border or woodland garden, the smaller, alpine species in a rock garden, scree bed, or alpine house. *P. brandegeei* and *P. pauciflorum* are usually short-lived.

Polaskia chende

Polemonium caeruleum

• **CULTIVATION** Grow tall species in any fertile, well-drained but moist soil, preferably in full sun or partial shade. Grow small species in gritty, sharply drained soil in full sun with some midday shade. Deadhead regularly.

• **PROPAGATION** Sow seed in containers in a cold frame in autumn or spring, or divide in spring.

• **PESTS AND DISEASES** Powdery mildew may be a problem.

P. brandegeei. Clump-forming perennial bearing mainly basal, sticky, pinnate leaves, to 4in (10cm) long, with many lance-shaped leaflets, each to ½in (1.5cm) long. In early summer, upright stems bear short, terminal cymes of long-tubed, funnel-shaped, pale to deep golden yellow, rarely white flowers, to 1in (2.5cm) long. ↕ 8in (20cm), ↔ 6in (15cm). Rocky Mountains. Zone 4. **subsp. *mellitum***, syn. *P. mellitum*, bear looser cymes of white or pale cream flowers in summer.

P. caeruleum ▣ (Greek valerian, Jacob's ladder). Clump-forming perennial, mainly hairless but softly hairy near the inflorescences. Bears 2-pinnate leaves, to 16in (40cm) long, each composed of 19–27 oblong-lance-shaped leaflets, ½–1½in (1.5–4cm) long. Lax, terminal or axillary cymes of open bell-shaped, lavender-blue, rarely white flowers, ½–1in (1–2.5cm) across, are produced on erect, branched stems in early summer. ↕ 12–36in (30–90cm), ↔ 12in (30cm). N. and C. Europe, N. Asia, W. North America. Zone 3b. **'Brise d'Anjou'** has leaflets distinctively edged with pale cream, and less profuse flowers than the species. **var. *lacteum***, syn. var. *album*, has white flowers.

P. confertum see *P. viscosum.*

P. foliosissimum. (Leafy Jacob's ladder) Leafy, clump-forming perennial producing a few erect, softly hairy stems. Pinnate leaves, to 6in (15cm) long, each have 11–25 elliptic-lance-shaped leaflets ½–2in (1–5cm) long. Dense, axillary and terminal cymes of bell-shaped, blue-violet, cream, or white flowers, to ½in (1.5cm) across, are produced in

Polemonium 'Lambrook Mauve'

midsummer. ↕ 30–32in (75–80cm), ↔ 24in (60cm). Central W. US. Zone 4. **var. *flavum*** bears yellow flowers that are shaded orange-red outside; ↕ 16–28in (40–70cm). S. Arizona, New Mexico.

***P.* 'Lambrook Mauve'** ■ syn. *P. reptans* 'Lambrook Manor', *P. reptans* 'Lambrook Mauve'. Clump-forming perennial forming rounded mounds of neat, pinnate leaves, to 10in (25cm) long, each composed of 7–19 ovate or oblong leaflets, 1¼–2in (3–5cm) long. Erect, branched stems very freely bear lax, terminal cymes of bell-shaped, lilac-blue flowers, ½–¾in (1.5–2cm) across, in late spring and early summer. ↕↔ to 18in (45cm). Zone 3b.

P. mellitum see *P. brandegeei* subsp. *mellitum*.

P. pauciflorum ■ Short-lived, clump-forming perennial with spreading to erect, branched, softly hairy stems and mainly pinnate leaves, to 6in (15cm) long, each composed of 11–25 elliptic-lance-shaped leaflets, to 1in (2.5cm) long. From early to late summer, bears horizontal to semi-pendent, narrowly tubular, red-tinted, pale yellow flowers, 1½in (4cm) across, with spreading mouths, either singly or in loose, few-flowered, terminal or axillary cymes. ↕↔ to 20in (50cm). S.E. Arizona, New Mexico. Zone 6.

P. pulcherrimum (Skunkleaf Jacob's ladder). Clump-forming perennial with pinnate leaves, to 5½in (14cm) long, each composed of 11–25 ovate leaflets, to 1½in (4cm) long. Dense, terminal and axillary cymes of bell-shaped, light blue to purple-blue or white flowers, to ½in (1.5cm) across, with short tubes, yellow

Polemonium pauciflorum

within, are borne on erect, branched stems in early summer. ↕↔ 12in (30cm). Alaska to California. Zone 4.

***P. reptans* 'Lambrook Mauve'** see *P.* 'Lambrook Mauve'.

P. viscosum, syn. *P. confertum*. Clump-forming perennial bearing mainly basal, pinnate leaves, to 8in (20cm) long, with whorls of many palmately 3- or 5-lobed leaflets, each to ½in (1.5cm) long. In summer, produces large, terminal cymes of funnel-shaped, deep blue flowers, to ¾–1¼in (2–3cm) across, on upright, branched stems. ↕ 2–20in (5–50cm), ↔ 2–8in (5–20cm). Mountains from Canada to New Mexico. Zone 5.

POLIANTHES

AGAVACEAE

Genus of 13 species of tuberous perennials found in open woodland and at roadsides in sandy areas in Mexico and Texas. Grown for their showy, loose racemes or spikes of tubular flowers, they are borne in summer. Mostly basal leaves are lance-shaped or linear. Where not hardy, grow in a warm greenhouse or summer border; elsewhere, grow in a sheltered border.

• **CULTIVATION** Under glass, grow in soil-based potting mix in full light. In the growing season, water moderately, and apply a balanced liquid fertilizer every 2 weeks. Reduce watering as the leaves die down, and keep dry when dormant. Outdoors, grow in moderately fertile, well-drained soil in full sun. Lift after the first frost and store tubers in sand in frost-free conditions.

• **PROPAGATION** Sow seed at 66–75°F (19–24°C) as soon as ripe. Remove offsets when the plants are dormant.

• **PESTS AND DISEASES** Prone to viruses.

P. geminiflora, syn. *Bravoa geminiflora*. Tuberous perennial with semi-erect, narrow, linear, basal leaves, 12–16in (30–40cm) long. In summer, bears lax racemes of paired, pendent, tubular, light to bright orange-red flowers, 1in (2.5cm) long. ↕ to 28in (70cm), PD3in (8cm). Mexico. ❀ (min. 59°F/15°C)

P. tuberosa ■ (Tuberose). Tuberous perennial with semi-erect, thin, linear-lance-shaped leaves, to 18in (45cm) long, in a basal rosette. Spikes of tubular, intensely fragrant, waxy white flowers, 1¼–2½in (3–6cm) long, are borne from summer to early autumn. ↕ to 4ft (1.2m), PD6in (15cm). Mexico.

Polianthes tuberosa

❀ (min. 59°F/15°C). **'The Pearl'** bears semi-double flowers.

POLIOTHYRSIS

FLACOURTIACEAE

Genus of one species of small, shrub-like deciduous tree from mountain woodland in central China. It is grown for its glossy, dark green, dentate leaves and fragrant, papery greenish white then yellow summer flowers. Male flowers are ↕ ⅕in (5 mm) across; female flowers are bigger, from ¼–⅜in (7–8mm) across, at the end of inflorescence, and produced in 6–8in (15–20cm) terminal panicles. Grow as a specimen or among other trees in a woodland setting. ↕ 30–40ft (10-12m), ↔ 15–25ft (5–8m).

• **CULTIVATION** Grow in fertile, well-drained soil in full sun or partial shade, with shelter from cold, drying winds. Pruning group 1.

• **PROPAGATION** Sow seed in containers in an open frame in autumn, or take greenwood cuttings in summer.

• **PESTS AND DISEASES** Infrequent.

P. sinensis ■ Spreading, deciduous tree with gray bark, which is deeply furrowed in mature trees. Ovate, slender-pointed, glossy, dark green leaves, to 6in (15cm) long, red-tinged when young, are arranged alternately, and are borne on red stalks. In mid- and late summer, white buds open to tiny, cup-shaped, fragrant, papery, greenish white then yellow flowers, produced in conical

Poliothyrsis sinensis (inset: flower detail)

P

panicles, to 10in (25cm) long. ↕ 30ft (10m) or more, ↔ 20ft (6m). C. China. Zone 7b.

POLYGALA

Milkwort, Seneca, Snakeroot

POLYGALACEAE

Genus of about 500 species of annuals and evergreen perennials and shrubs distributed in a wide range of habitats worldwide, except in New Zealand, Polynesia, and arctic regions. They are grown for their terminal or axillary racemes of colorful, pea-like flowers, produced in late spring and summer, or in some species in autumn; each flower has 5 sepals, the inner two forming broad, petal-like "wings," and 5 petals, the lowest forming a keel with a fringed apex. The leaves are alternate, opposite, or whorled, linear to rounded, and usually leathery. Grow hardy species in a woodland, rock garden, or shrub border, or in an alpine house. Where not hardy, grow in a cool greenhouse.

• **CULTIVATION** Under glass, grow in soilless potting mix in full light, with shade from hot sun. In growth, keep well-ventilated, water freely, and apply a balanced liquid fertilizer monthly; water sparingly in winter. Outdoors, grow in moderately fertile, humus-rich, sharply drained soil in full sun or partial shade. Pruning group 9 for *P.* x *dalmaisiana* and *P. myrtifolia.*

• **PROPAGATION** Sow seed of hardy species in containers in an open frame in autumn; sow seed of tender species at not less than 59°F (15°C) in spring. Take softwood cuttings in early summer, or semi-ripe cuttings in mid- to late summer.

• **PESTS AND DISEASES** Aphids and whiteflies may be problems under glass.

P. calcarea ■ (Milkwort). Prostrate, creeping, mat-forming, evergreen perennial with basal rosettes of obovate, leathery, mid-green leaves, ½–1½in (1.5–4cm) long. In late spring and early summer, trailing stems bear deep blue flowers, to ¼in (6mm) long, with white-fringed lips, in terminal racemes, to 1¼in (3cm) long. ↕ 2in (5cm), ↔ to 8in (20cm). W. Europe. Zone 7b. The following cultivars are more robust and free-flowering. **'Bulley's Form'** ■ has larger flowers in a deeper blue. **'Lillet'** has a compact habit and produces brighter blue flowers over a long period.

Polygala calcarea

Polygala calcarea 'Bulley's Form'

P. chamaebuxus. Small, spreading, evergreen shrub with lance-shaped, leathery, dark green leaves, ½–1¼in (1.5–3cm) long. The flowers, ½in (1.5cm) long, have bright yellow lips, white or pale yellow wings, and a bright yellow keel that ages to purple or brownish crimson; the flowers may be solitary or in pairs, and are produced in the upper leaf axils, mainly in late spring and early summer. ↕ 2–6in (5–15cm), ↔ to 12in (30cm). W. central Europe. Zone 7. **var. *grandiflora*** ■ syn. var. *purpurea*, var. *rhodoptera*, produces flowers with deep purplish pink wings and yellow lips; Alps, Carpathians.
var. *purpurea* see var. *grandiflora.*
var. *rhodoptera* see var. *grandiflora.*
P. cowellii. Small to medium, deciduous tree with alternate, elliptic, leathery, yellow-green leaves, 2–5in (5–13cm) long, with many prominent, nearly parallel, lateral veins. Short, axillary racemes of violet flowers, ¾in (2cm) across, are borne from spring to autumn. ↕ 15–40ft (5–12m), ↔ 10–20ft (3–6m). Puerto Rico. ❀ (min. 45°F/7°C)

Polygala chamaebuxus var. *grandiflora*

P.* x *dalmaisiana ■ (*P. myrtifolia* x *P. oppositifolia*) syn. *P. myrtifolia* var. *grandiflora* of gardens. Erect, rounded, evergreen shrub, tending to spread with age. Elliptic, ovate, or lance-shaped, glaucous, mid- to deep green leaves, to 1in (2.5cm) long, can be alternate or opposite on the same plant. Leafy, terminal racemes of purple or rose-magenta flowers, 1in (2.5cm) long, with the bases of the keels white, are borne from midsummer to late autumn. Garden origin. ↕↔ 3–8ft (1–2.5m). ❀ (min. 41–45°F/5–7°C)
P. myrtifolia. Erect, bushy, evergreen shrub, spreading with age, with elliptic-oblong or obovate, leathery, mid- to deep green leaves, 1–2in (2.5–5cm) long. Short, leafy, terminal racemes of purple-veined, greenish white flowers, to ¾in (2cm) long, with crested keel petals, are borne from spring to autumn. ↕ 3–8ft (1–2.5m), ↔ 3–6ft (1–2m). South Africa. ❀ (min. 41–45°F/5–7°C).
var. *grandiflora* of gardens see *P.* x *dalmaisiana.*

Polygala x *dalmaisiana*

POLYGONATUM

Solomon's seal

LILIACEAE

Genus of about 50 species of rhizomatous perennials from woodland in temperate regions of Eurasia and N. America. Cultivated for their foliage and flowers, they have usually arching stems and alternate, opposite, or whorled, linear to broadly elliptic or ovate, parallel-veined leaves that turn yellow in autumn. Mostly pendent, sometimes erect, tubular to bell-shaped, mainly white or cream, occasionally purple-pink flowers, with green markings, are either solitary or borne in small clusters, often along the lower sides of the stems Flowers are usually followed by berry-like, spherical, red or black fruits. Solomon's seals are suitable for a shady mixed or herbaceous border, or for a woodland or rock garden. All parts may cause mild stomach upset if ingested.

• **CULTIVATION** Grow in fertile, humus-rich, moist but well-drained soil in full or partial shade.

• **PROPAGATION** Sow seed in containers in a cold frame in autumn. Divide rhizomes when growth begins in spring, taking care to avoid damaging young, brittle shoots, or divide in autumn.

• **PESTS AND DISEASES** Susceptible to slugs and sawfly larvae.

P. biflorum, syn. *P. canaliculatum*, *P. commutatum, P. giganteum.* (Small Solomon's seal). Rhizomatous perennial with arching, hairless stems bearing alternate, narrowly lance-shaped to broadly elliptic leaves, to 7in (18cm) long, with hairless or minutely hairy undersides that are glaucous along the veins. From late spring to midsummer, usually solitary or 2–4 pendent, tubular, greenish white flowers, ½–1in(1–2.5cm) long, are produced in the leaf axils; they are followed by spherical black fruit, ⅜in (9mm) across. ↕ to 16–72in (0.4–2m), ↔ 24in (60cm). S. central Canada, E. North America. Zone 3.
P. canaliculatum see *P. biflorum.*
P. commutatum see *P. biflorum.*
***P. cyrtonema* of gardens** see *Disporopsis pernyi.*
P. giganteum see *P. biflorum.*

Polygonatum hirtum

P

Polygonatum hookeri

P. hirtum ▣ syn. *P. latifolium.* Rhizomatous perennial producing erect stems with alternate, lance-shaped to ovate leaves, 3–6in (8–15cm) long, slightly hairy beneath. From late spring to midsummer, produces 1–5 pendent, tubular, green-tipped white flowers, ¾in (2cm) long, in the leaf axils; they are followed by spherical black fruit, ¼in (6mm) across. ↕ to 4ft (1.2m), ↔ 24in (60cm). C. and S.E. Europe, Turkey, W. Russia, Caucasus. Zone 4b.
P. hookeri ▣ Creeping, slowly spreading perennial with upright stems bearing alternate, linear to narrowly elliptic leaves, to 1½in (4cm) long, hairless beneath. In late spring and early summer, produces solitary, erect, pale to deep pink, short-tubed flowers, ¾in (2cm) across, with wide-spreading tepals, in the upper leaf axils; they are followed by spherical black fruit, ⅛in (3mm) across. ↕ to 4in (10cm), ↔ to 12in (30cm) or more. E. Himalayas, China. Zone 5.
P. humile. Rhizomatous perennial with upright stems bearing lance-shaped to ovate leaves, 1½–3in (4–8cm) long, arranged alternately, and finely hairy on the lower veins. In late spring, produces solitary or paired, pendent, tubular white flowers, to ¾in (2cm) long, in the upper leaf axils; they are followed by spherical, blue-black fruit, to ¼in (6mm) across. ↕ 8in (20cm), ↔ 20in (50cm) or more. E. Europe, W. Asia. Zone 5.
P. x hybridum (*P. multiflorum* x *P. odoratum*) syn. *P. multiflorum* of gardens (Common Solomon's seal). Rhizomatous perennial with scarcely

Polygonatum odoratum 'Variegatum'

Polygonatum stewartianum

arching, hairless stems bearing alternate, ovate-lance-shaped leaves, to 8in (20cm) long, held horizontally. Pendent, tubular, green-tipped, creamy white flowers, ¾in (2cm) long, slightly constricted around the middle, are produced in late spring, usually 4 per axil; they are followed by spherical, blue-black fruit, to ⅜in (9mm) across. ↕ to 5ft (1.5m), ↔ 12in (30cm). Garden origin. Zone 4. **'Variegatum'** has cream-striped leaves.
P. latifolium see *P. hirtum.*
P. multiflorum. Rhizomatous perennial with arching, hairless stems bearing ovate-lance-shaped leaves, to 2–6in (5–15cm) long, arranged alternately. In late spring, each lower leaf axil produces 2–6 pendent, tubular, green-tipped white flowers, ½in (1.5cm) long; they are followed by spherical black fruit, ⅛–¼in (4–6mm) across. ↕ to 36in (90cm), ↔ 10in (25cm). Europe, temperate Asia. Zone 4. **'Striatum'**, syn. 'Variegatum', produces leaves striped creamy white.
***P. multiflorum* of gardens** see *P.* x *hybridum.*
P. odoratum, syn. *P. officinale* (Fragrant Solomon's seal). Creeping, rhizomatous perennial with arching, angular stems bearing alternate, lance-shaped to ovate, hairless leaves, 2–6in (5–15cm) long, usually in 2 rows. In late spring and early summer, 1 or 2 pendent, tubular, fragrant, green-tipped white flowers, to 1¼in (3cm) long, are borne in the upper leaf axils, followed by spherical black fruit, ¼in (6mm) across. ↕ to 34in (85cm), ↔ 12in (30cm). Europe, Caucasus, Russia (Siberia) to Japan. Zone 4. **'Flore Pleno'** has double flowers with more extensive green markings. **'Gilt Edge'** has leaves with narrow yellow margins. **'Grace Barker'** produces creamy-white-striped leaves, to 6in (15cm) long; ↕ 3½ft (1.1m). **'Variegatum'** ▣ produces white-margined leaves and pendent, creamy white flowers all along the stems.
P. officinale see *P. odoratum.*
P. roseum. Rhizomatous perennial with arching, linear to narrowly lance-shaped, pointed, mid-green leaves, 3–6in (8–15cm) long, the upper leaves opposite or whorled in clusters of 3 at the tips of the stems, somewhat rough beneath. In late spring, bears upright, tubular, rose flowers, to ½in (1.5cm) long, from the leaf axils, solitary or in pairs. They are followed by spherical, blue-black fruit, to ¼in (6mm) across. ↕ to 28in (70cm), ↔ 10in (25cm). W. Siberia, C. Asia. Zone 3.
P. stewartianum ▣ Rhizomatous perennial with short, erect, slightly angular, hairless stems bearing whorled, linear-lance-shaped leaves, to 4in (10cm) long. From late spring to mid-summer, produces small clusters of 1–3 pendent, tubular, purple-pink flowers, to ½in (1.5cm) long, in the leaf axils. The spherical red fruit, to ¼in (6mm) across, are spotted purplish white. ↕ 8–36in (20–90cm), ↔ 10in (25cm). Europe, temperate Asia. Zone 6b.
P. verticillatum (Whorled Solomon's seal). Rhizomatous perennial with erect, slightly angular, hairless stems bearing stalkless, mainly whorled, sometimes opposite, lance-shaped leaves, 2½–6in (6–15cm) long. From late spring to midsummer, produces 1–4 pendent, tubular, greenish white flowers, to ½in (1.5cm) long, in the upper leaf axils; they are followed by spherical red fruit, ¼in (6mm) across. ↕ 8–36in (20–90cm), ↔ 10in (25cm). Europe, Caucasus, Afghanistan. Zone 6.

▷ ***Polygonum*** see *Persicaria*; also:
▷ ***Polygonum aubertii*** see *Fallopia aubertii*
▷ ***Polygonum baldschuanicum*** see *Fallopia baldschuanica*

POLYPODIUM

POLYPODIACEAE

Genus of about 75 species of mostly evergreen, usually epiphytic, sometimes terrestrial ferns, mainly from tropical regions of the US, Central America, and South America, but also from temperate and other tropical regions. They are often found growing on trees, rocks, walls, or well-drained banks and sand dunes. They are cultivated for their sculptural fronds, which are usually lance-shaped, simple to pinnatifid or pinnate, occasionally further divided, and borne at random in 2 rows along creeping, often surface rhizomes. Sori, without indusia, are arranged in rows on each side of the midrib of each frond or pinna. The hardy species are good for a rock garden, mixed border, or bank, especially where winter greenery and groundcover are desired. Grow tender species in a warm greenhouse. Else-where, the tropical species, which are mostly epiphytic, are suitable for growing in trees.
• **CULTIVATION** Under glass, grow in equal parts fine-grade bark, perlite, and charcoal. May be grown epiphytically in bright filtered light; wrap the rhizomes in moss and tie to a suitable rooting medium, such as osmunda fiber, and keep moist until established. Water moderately during the growing season, sparingly in winter. Outdoors, grow in moderately fertile, humus-rich, gritty or stony, well-drained soil (*P. cambricum* requires neutral to alkaline soil) in full sun or dappled shade, with shelter from cold, dry winds.
• **PROPAGATION** Sow spores at 59–61°F (15–16°C) when ripe. Divide in spring or early summer. See also p.51.
• **PESTS AND DISEASES** Infrequent.

P. aureum see *Phlebodium aureum.*
P. australe see *P. cambricum.*
P. californicum. Wintergreen, colonizing fern. Semi-leathery deltate blades are nearly once divided, widest at base. Found on rocky slopes and ledges. ↕ 4–8in (10–20cm). W. California to Baja, California. ❀ (min. 41°F/5°C)
P. x calirhiza, a fertile hybrid of *californicum* x *glycyrrhiza.* Found on rocky slopes and ledges along the Pacific coast of North America.
P. cambricum, syn. *P. australe, P. vulgare* subsp. *serratum* (Southern polypody). Terrestrial, deciduous fern producing broadly lance-shaped to broadly triangular-ovate, pinnate, mid-green fronds, to 24in (60cm) long, with linear or oblong pinnae, the longest usually being the second pair from the base; the pinnae often have toothed margins. New fronds appear in late summer and die back in spring. Sori are conspicuously yellow in winter. ↕ 6–24in (15–60cm), ↔ indefinite. S. and W. Europe. Zone 7. Sterile variants, producing yellow-green fronds with deeply cut margins, are often listed or grown as *P. cambricum.* **'Cristatum'** bears crested frond tips and pinnae. **'Grandiceps'** has much larger crests than 'Cristatum', with the crests at the tips usually wider than the rest of the fronds. **'Omnilacerum Oxford'** has tall, erect, oblong-lance-shaped fronds, to 24in (60cm) long, with lance-shaped pinnae cut irregularly almost to the midribs. **'Willharris'** produces thick-textured, lance-shaped fronds, to 18in (45cm) long, with pinnae deeply divided into long segments.
P. formosanum. Epiphytic, evergreen fern with arching to pendent, ovate to oblong, pinnate, glaucous, pale green fronds, to 20in (50cm) long, composed of spreading, lance-shaped to linear pinnae. The rhizome is conspicuously glaucous, and is very sparsely covered with small scales. ↕↔ to 18in (45cm). China, Taiwan, Japan. ❀ (min. 41°F/5°C)
P. glycyrrhiza ▣ (Licorice fern). Terrestrial, evergreen fern producing lance-shaped, pinnate or very deeply pinnatifid, mid- to dark green fronds, to 14in (35cm) long, composed of sickle-shaped, linear pinnae. Similar to *P. vulgare*, except that the fronds are

Polypodium glycyrrhiza

Polypodium polypodioides

darker green, pinnae tips more pointed, and sori smaller. The rhizome has a very sweet, licorice taste. ↕ 12in (30cm), ↔ indefinite. Alaska to California. Zone 5. **'Longicaudatum'**, syn. *P. vulgare* 'Longicaudatum', has fronds with very long, pointed tips. **Malahatense Group** consists of fertile variants with deeply cut pinnae; they come true from spores.

P. polypodioides ■ (Resurrection fern). Small, semi-evergreen, terrestrial or epiphytic fern with narrowly triangular or oblong, pinnate, fairly leathery, mid-green fronds, to 12in (30cm) tall, covered with scales, and composed of well-spaced, linear or oblong pinnae. Frond margins temporarily roll inward during dry weather. ↕ to 12in (30cm), ↔ indefinite. Southern Africa, tropical regions of America. ❀ (min. 35°F/2°C)

P. scouleri ■ (Leathery polypody). Terrestrial, evergreen fern bearing broadly ovate to triangular, pinnate or very deeply pinnatifid, leathery, thick, rigid, glossy, deep green fronds, 12in (30cm) long. Pinnae are spreading and narrowly oblong. ↕ 12in (30cm), ↔ indefinite. N.W. North America (coastal belt). ❀ (min. 41°F/5°C)

Polypodium scouleri

Polypodium vulgare

P. virginianum (American wall fern, Rockcap fern, Virginia polypody). Terrestrial or epiphytic, evergreen fern, very similar to *P. vulgare*, with arching or pendent, narrowly lance-shaped or triangular to oblong, pinnate or very deeply pinnatifid, leathery to thin, dark green fronds, 10in (25cm) long, composed of lance-shaped to linear or oblong pinnae. ↕ 10in (25cm), ↔ indefinite. E. Asia, North America. Zone 4.

P. vulgare ■ (Wall polypody). Terrestrial or epiphytic, evergreen fern with lance-shaped to oblong, pinnate or very deeply pinnatifid, thin to leathery, dark green fronds, 16in (40cm) long, composed of close, spreading, oblong to linear pinnae. ↕ 12in (30cm), ↔ indefinite. Mostly in northern regions or on higher ground in Europe, Africa, E. Asia. Zone 7. **'Bifidograndiceps'** produces large, flat crests; ↕ 12–20in (30–50cm). **'Cornubiense'** ■ is very vigorous, bears both pinnatifid and 3- or 4-pinnatifid fronds, and is excellent as a groundcover; ↕ 12–16in (30–40cm). **'Longicaudatum'** see *P. glycyrrhiza* 'Longicaudatum'. **subsp. *serratum*** see *P. cambricum.*

Polypodium vulgare 'Cornubiense'

POLYSCIAS

ARALIACEAE

Genus of about 100 species of rounded or upright, evergreen shrubs and small trees from tropical regions of Africa, Asia, and the Pacific. They are cultivated for their alternate or spiraling leaves, which may be simple, 3-palmate, or pinnate to 3-pinnate, and tend to be grouped toward the stem tips. The small, usually whitish green flowers have 4–15 tepals, and are most often produced in panicles composed of small umbels, or in terminal clusters; they are followed by small, usually purple to black berries. Below 61°F (16°C), grow in a warm greenhouse or as houseplants; they are sometimes trained to resemble bonsai. In warmer climates, grow in a shrub border; strong-growing species are also effective for hedging.

• **CULTIVATION** Under glass, grow in soil-based potting mix in full light or bright filtered light. In growth, water freely, mist daily, and apply a balanced liquid fertilizer every month. Water sparingly in winter. Outdoors, grow in fertile, humus-rich, moist but well-drained soil in full sun or partial shade. Pruning group 1; trim hedges in late summer and, if necessary, in late winter or early spring; may need restrictive pruning under glass.

• **PROPAGATION** Sow seed at 66–75°F (19–24°C) in spring. Take greenwood cuttings in early summer, or root semi-ripe or ripe, leafless stem sections with bottom heat in summer.

• **PESTS AND DISEASES** Spider mites, mealybugs, and root-knot nematodes may be troublesome under glass.

P. filicifolia ■ (Chotito, Fern-leaf aralia). Erect, evergreen shrub, sparsely branched (at least when young) unless regularly tip-pruned. Young plants bear arching to semi-pendent, pinnate to 3-pinnate leaves, to 4in (10cm) long, composed of 9–17 narrowly elliptic,

Polyscias filicifolia

Polyscias guilfoylei 'Victoriae'

bright green leaflets, with purple-tinted midribs. Mature plants produce leaves to 36in (90cm) long, composed of leaflets with entire or finely toothed margins. Star-shaped, whitish green flowers are borne in terminal, umbel-like panicles, in summer, followed by black fruit. Flowers and fruit are seldom produced. Probably a hybrid. ↕ to 6–8ft (2–2.5m) or more, ↔ to 3ft (1m) or more. S. Malaysia, Pacific. ❀ (min. 61°F/16°C). **'Marginata'** has leaves with white margins.

P. guilfoylei (Coffee tree, Geranium aralia). Large, erect, evergreen shrub or small tree, generally sparsely branched, with foliage confined to the stem tips. Pinnate leaves, 12–18in (30–45cm) long, are each composed of 5–9 broadly ovate to oblong-elliptic, shallowly lobed, irregularly spiny-toothed, white- to cream-margined, mid-green leaflets. In summer, mature plants produce brown-budded, 5-petaled, star-shaped, yellow-green flowers in large, loose, terminal, umbel-like panicles, to 20in (50cm) long, followed by spherical, black-purple fruit, ¼in (6mm) long. ↕ 12–20ft (4–6m), ↔ 3–8ft (1–2.5m). E. Malaysia, W. Pacific. ❀ (min. 61°F/16°C). **'Laciniata'** has pendent, 2-pinnate leaves composed of lance-shaped leaflets with white margins. **'Victoriae'** ■ (Lace aralia) is compact, with much-dissected, fern-like leaves; each leaflet irregularly toothed and white-margined; ↕ 5ft (1.5m), ↔ 32in (80cm).

POLYSTICHUM

DRYOPTERIDACEAE

Genus of nearly 200 species of usually evergreen, terrestrial ferns found in a range of habitats, from alpine cliffs to tropical forests worldwide. They are cultivated for their often lance-shaped, pinnate to 3-pinnate fronds, which arise from erect or short-creeping rhizomes, usually in shapely, shuttlecock crowns. The pinnae are sometimes lobed, each lobe ending in a sharp point or bristle. Sori are borne on the undersides of the fronds, each usually protected by a rounded indusium. Grow in a rock garden, fernery, or well-drained border, or as a groundcover in woodland settings. Where not hardy, grow in a cool, temperate, or warm greenhouse.

• **CULTIVATION** Grow in fertile, humus-rich, well-drained soil in deep or partial shade. Remove dead fronds before new ones unfurl.

Polystichum acrostichoides

• **PROPAGATION** Sow spores at 59–61°F (15–16°C) when ripe. Divide rhizomes in spring. Detach fronds bearing bulbils in autumn. See also p.51.
• **PESTS AND DISEASES** Infrequent.

P. acrostichoides ■ (Christmas fern). Terrestrial, evergreen fern producing a shuttlecock of narrowly lance-shaped, pinnate, dark green fronds, 24in (60cm) long, with small pinnae. Fertile fronds narrow abruptly toward tips where sori occur. ↕ 18in (45cm), ↔ 36in (90cm). N.E. North America. Zone 4.
P. braunii ■ Evergreen to semi-evergreen, arching fern with elliptic-lanceolate soft-textured bipinnate blades, bearing silvery, scaled new fiddleheads. Found in boreal moist forests. ↕ 24in (60cm). N.America, Europe, Asia. Zone 6.
P. makinoi. Evergreen, arching fern, producing olive-green, satiny, oblong-triangular bipinnate blades. The stipe and rachis have numerous brown scales, with pale margins. ↕ 24in (60cm). Asia. ❄ (min. 35°F/2°C)
P. munitum (Western sword fern). Terrestrial, evergreen fern with narrowly lance-shaped, leathery, pinnate, dark green fronds, 36in (90cm) long or more, forming shuttlecocks. Pinnae are linear and spiny-toothed. Larger than *P. acrostichoides*, its fertile fronds do not narrow at the tips. ↕ 36in (90cm), rarely to 5ft (1.5m), ↔ 4ft (1.2m). N.W. North America. Zone 4.
P. neolobatum ■ (Long-eared holly fern). Evergreen, slightly arching fern, with well-developed "thumb" or acropscopic auricle by the rachis. Stipe

Polystichum setiferum Divisilobum Group

and rachis have abundant, deep brown, papery scales; blades are hard-textured, glossy, and bipinnate-lanceolate. ↕ 24in (60cm). Asia. ❄ (min. 35°F/2°C)
P. polyblepharum (Japanese tassel fern). Terrestrial, evergreen fern bearing shuttlecocks of spreading, lance-shaped, 2-pinnate, shiny, dark green fronds, 12–32in (30–80cm) longcovered with golden hairs when they unfurl. Pinnae lobes are oblong-ovate and have spiny-toothed margins. ↕ 24–32in (60–80cm), ↔ 36in (90cm). South Korea, Japan. Zone 7.
P. rigens. Terrestrial, evergreen fern producing shuttlecocks of narrowly ovate-oblong, 2-pinnate, leathery, harsh-textured, dull green fronds, 12–18in (30–45cm) long. Broad, lance-shaped pinnae are divided into ovate, spiny-toothed lobes. In spring, fronds are yellowish green. ↕ 16in (40cm), ↔ 24in (60cm). Japan. Zone 7.
P. setiferum (Hedge fern). Terrestrial, evergreen fern with soft, lance-shaped, 2-pinnate, dark green fronds, 12–48in (30–120cm) long, arranged in shuttlecocks. Pinnae lobes are ovate, bristle-toothed, stalked, and obtusely angled at the point of attachment to the midribs. ↕ 4ft (1.2m), ↔ 36in (90cm). Europe. Zone 7. **Congestum Group.** Rachis are shortened, so pinnae overlap; they are brittle and grey-green in color. **Divisilobum Group** ■ produces usually spreading, 3-pinnate fronds, consisting of narrowed and leathery segments; bulbils often form along the frond midribs; ↕↔ 20–28in (50–70cm) or more. **Plumoso-divisilobum Group** bears fronds, 4-pinnate at the base, with segments narrowed toward the frond tips; lower pinnae often overlap. **'Plumoso-multilobum'** has overlapping, very leafy pinnae, which give it a moss-like appearance; similar to the Plumoso-divisilobum Group, but the segments are not narrowed. **'Plumosum Bevis'** ■ syn. *P. aculeatum* 'Pulcherrimum', 'Pulcherrimum Bevis', produces elongated pinnae and segments that sweep gracefully toward the tips; it is only very rarely fertile; ↕↔ 24–32in (60–80cm). **'Pulcherrimum Bevis'** see 'Plumosum Bevis'.
P. tsus-simense (Dwarf holly fern, Korean rock fern). Terrestrial, evergreen fern producing shuttlecocks of broadly lance-shaped, 2-pinnate, dark green fronds, 8–16in (20–40cm) long. The narrow, ovate to oblong-ovate, spiny-toothed pinnae are sharply and abruptly pointed. ↕↔ 16in (40cm). East Asia. Zone 7.

PONCIRUS syn. AEGLE

RUTACEAE

Genus of one species of spiny, deciduous shrub or small tree from woodland in China and Korea. It produces alternate, 3-palmate, dark green leaves, and is cultivated for its 5-petaled, fragrant white flowers and orange-like fruit. Grow in a shrub border or against a sunny wall, or as a very thick, spiny hedge. It is sometimes used as a rootstock for *Citrus* cultivars.
• **CULTIVATION** Grow in fertile, well-drained soil in full sun, with shelter from cold, dry winds. Pruning group 1; trim hedges after flowering or fruiting.
• **PROPAGATION** Sow seed in containers in a cold frame in autumn. Take semi-ripe cuttings in summer.
• **PESTS AND DISEASES** Infrequent.

P. trifoliata ■ (Hardy orange, Trifoliate orange). Rounded, bushy, deciduous shrub or tree with rigid greenshoots armed with very sharp spines. Alternate, 3-palmate leaves, 1–2½in (2.5–6cm) long, consist of 3 obovate, dark green leaflets, to 2in (5cm) long, turning yellow in autumn. Solitary, cup-shaped then saucer-shaped, fragrant white flowers, 2in (5cm) across, are borne in late spring and early summer, often again in autumn, followed by orange-like, green then orange fruit, 1½in (4cm) across. ↕↔ 15ft (5m). N. China, Korea. Zone 6b. **'Flying Dragon'** has twisted stems.

Polystichum braunii

Polystichum neolobatum

Polystichum setiferum 'Plumosum Bevis'

Poncirus trifoliata

PONGAMIA

FABACEAE

Genus of one species of wide-spreading, deciduous or semi-evergreen tree from seashores and riverbanks in Malaysia, Indonesia, N. Australia, and Pacific islands. It has pinnate leaves and axillary racemes of pea-like flowers. Where not hardy, grow in a warm greenhouse for its foliage. In tropical areas, it is a fine shade tree, suitable for coastal gardens.

• **CULTIVATION** Under glass, grow in soil-based potting mix with added sharp sand, in full light. In the growing season, water moderately and apply a balanced liquid fertilizer monthly; water sparingly in winter. Outdoors, grow in fertile, well-drained soil in full sun. Pruning group 1; may need restrictive pruning under glass.

• **PROPAGATION** Sow seed at 64–75°F (18–24°C) in spring. Root semi-ripe cuttings in summer with bottom heat.

• **PESTS AND DISEASES** Whiteflies may be a problem under glass.

P. pinnata (Karum oil tree, Poona oil tree). Many-branched, spreading, deciduous or semi-evergreen tree with a domed head and a usually short trunk. The pinnate, glossy, bright green leaves, 6–12in (15–30cm) long, consist of 5–9 ovate to elliptic leaflets, emerging pink-bronze. In summer and autumn, produces racemes, 5in (13cm) long, of pea-like, mauve-pink or cream flowers, strongly scented when crushed; they have rounded, standard petals, to ½in (1.5cm) across, often incurled. ↕ 70–80ft (20–25m), ↔ 50–80ft (15–25m). Malaysia, Indonesia, N. Australia, Pacific islands. ❀ (min. 61°F/16°C)

PONTEDERIA

Pickerel weed

PONTEDERIACEAE

Genus of 5 species of marginal aquatic perennials from freshwater marshes and swamp ditches in North, Central, and South America. They are grown for their neat habit, distinctive foliage, and very colorful flowers. The thick rootstock produces clumps of often linear or lance-shaped leaves. Terminal spikes of tubular, 2-lipped, usually blue flowers are borne in summer and early autumn. Grow at the margins of a pond or in a large, water-filled barrel on a sunny, sheltered patio. Flower spikes may not open fully in cool, wet summers.

• **CULTIVATION** Grow in aquatic containers of fertile, loamy soil at the margins of a pool; grow in no more than 4–5in (10–13cm) of water, in full sun. See also pp.52–53.

• **PROPAGATION** Sow seed in containers outdoors as soon as ripe. Germination is highest after a 30-day dry dormancy period. Divide in late spring when growth starts.

• **PESTS AND DISEASES** Rust and spider mites can occur.

P. cordata ▣ (Pickerel weed). Marginal aquatic perennial with erect, lance-shaped, triangular to ovate, glossy, emergent, floating, or submerged leaves, 8in (20cm) wide, with heart-shaped bases, borne on stalks to 10in (25cm)

Pontederia cordata

long. From late spring to autumn, tubular blue flowers are produced in closely packed spikes, ¾–6in (2–15cm) long, on flowerstalks to 14in (35cm) tall. ↕ 3–4½ft (0.9–1.3m), ↔ 24–30in (60–75cm). E. North America to Caribbean. Zone 4. **var. *lancifolia***, syn. *P. lanceolata,* has narrower leaves, to 5–8in (12–20cm) long, on stalks 24–28in (60–70cm) long; ↕ 4–5ft (1.2–1.5m), ↔ 3ft (1m); E. and S. US, South America; Zone 5b.

P. lanceolata see *P. cordata* var. *lancifolia.*

POPULUS

Aspen, Cottonwood, Poplar

SALICACEAE

Genus of about 35 species of usually dioecious, mainly deciduous trees found in woodland, valley bottoms, riverbanks, and swampland in N. temperate regions. They are cultivated for their very rapid growth as specimen trees, and for their alternate, ovate, triangular-ovate, or diamond-shaped leaves, often aromatic in bud and when unfolding. They have tiny flowers borne in catkins, generally 2–6in (5–15cm) long, mostly in late winter or spring, before the leaves. Male and female flowers are usually borne on separate trees, the females producing copious fluffy white seeds ("cotton"). Most poplars are useful as windbreaks; *P. alba* and *P.* x *canescens* will thrive in coastal sites. The vigorous root systems may damage drains and foundations, so avoid growing poplars within 100ft (30m) of a building.

• **CULTIVATION** Tolerant of any, except constantly waterlogged, soil, although best in deep, fertile, moist but well-drained soil in full sun. *P. alba* and *P.* x *canescens* tolerate dry conditions; Pruning group 1.

• **PROPAGATION** Take hardwood cuttings in winter. Remove suckers in autumn or late winter.

• **PESTS AND DISEASES** Borers, leaf miners, caterpillars, scale insects, and

Populus alba

leaf hoppers may be problems. Canker, butt rot, crown gall, dieback, root rot, leaf blister, white rot, rust, and powdery mildew occur.

P. alba ▣ (White poplar). Spreading, deciduous tree with white-hairy young shoots and broadly ovate to almost rounded, wavy-margined to maple-like, deeply 5-lobed leaves, to 4in (10cm) long, dark green above, thickly white-hairy beneath, and turning yellow in autumn. In early spring, bears pendent red male catkins, 3in (8cm) long, or green females, 2in (5cm) long. ↕ 70–130ft (20–40m), ↔ 50ft (15m). N. Africa, Turkey, C. and S. former USSR (including S.W. Siberia). Zone 2. **f. *pyramidalis*** ▣ is pyramidal in shape; ↔ 15ft (5m). **'Raket'** ▣ syn. 'Rocket', is narrowly conical; ↔ 25ft (8m). **'Richardii'** has leaves that are golden yellow above; ↕ 50ft (15m), ↔ 40ft (12m). **'Rocket'** see 'Raket'.

P. balsamifera (Balsam poplar, Tacamahac). Fast-growing, columnar, deciduous tree producing smooth, hairless shoots, balsam-scented buds, and ovate, glossy leaves, to 5in (13cm) long, dark green above, whitish green

Populus alba 'Raket'

beneath. Pendent green catkins, the males to 2in (5cm) long, the females to 3in (8cm) long, are produced in early spring. ↕ 100ft (30m), ↔ 25ft (8m). North America. Zone 6. **var. *michauxii*** produces downy shoots; N. US.

***P.* 'Balsam Spire'**, syn. *P.* 'TT 32'. Very fast-growing, narrowly columnar, deciduous tree bearing ovate leaves, 2–5in (5–13cm) long, which are obtuse at the rounded bases and hairy beneath. Cylindrical green female catkins, 4–5½in (10–14cm) long, are produced from pleasantly aromatic buds in late winter or spring. ↕ 100ft (30m), ↔ 30ft (10m). Zone 4.

P.* x *canadensis (*P. deltoides* x *P. nigra*). Fast-growing, conical to columnar,

Populus alba f. *pyramidalis*

Populus x *canadensis* 'Robusta'

Populus x *candicans* 'Aurora'

Populus deltoides (inset: leaf detail)

deciduous tree bearing triangular to ovate, scalloped, tapered, glossy, bright green leaves, to 4in (10cm) long, turning yellow in autumn. Red male or green female catkins, each to 4in (10cm) long, are produced in early spring. ↕ 100ft (30m), ↔ 40ft (12m). Garden origin. Zone 3b. **'Aurea'**, syn. 'Serotina Aurea', is columnar and male, producing bronze young leaves in late spring, later turning golden yellow; ↕ 80ft (25m), ↔ 30ft (10m). **'Eugenei'** (Carolina poplar) is columnar, with short, spreading branches. **'Robusta'** ■ (False Lombardy poplar) is narrowly conical and male, producing bronze-red young leaves in midspring. **'Serotina'** is similar to 'Aurea', but is broadly domed, with spreading branches, and produces gray-green foliage in summer. **'Serotina Aurea'** see 'Aurea'. **'Serotina de Selys'**, syn. 'Serotina Erecta', has an upright habit, and produces pale green young leaves and red male catkins.

P.* x *candicans (*P. balsamifera* x *P. deltoides*), syn. *P. gileadensis, P.* x *jackii* (Balm of Gilead). Broadly columnar, deciduous tree bearing broadly ovate leaves, to 6in (15cm) long, heart-shaped at the bases, dark green above, whitish green beneath. Green female catkins, to 6in (15cm) long, are produced in early spring. ↕ 80ft (25m), ↔ 50ft (15m). Garden origin. Zone 4. **'Aurora'** ■ has leaves conspicuously marked white, cream, and pink; ↕ 50ft (15m), ↔ 20ft (6m).

P.* x *canescens ■ (*P. alba* x *P. tremula*) (Gray poplar). Broadly columnar to spreading, deciduous tree bearing glossy, dark green leaves; they may be broadly ovate, gray-woolly beneath, and to 3in (8cm) long, or rounded, almost hairless, and to 2½in (6cm) long. Red male catkins, to 4in (10cm) long, are borne in early spring. Green catkins, ¾–4in (2–10cm) long, are borne on female trees, which are rarely seen. ↕ to 100ft (30m), rarely to 160ft (50m), ↔ 50ft (15m). Europe. Zone 4.

P. deltoides ■ (Eastern cottonwood, Necklace poplar). Fast-growing, short-lived, weak-wooded, spreading, deciduous tree bearing oval to triangular, glossy, bright green leaves, to 5in (13cm) long, strongly balsam-scented when young. Red male or green female catkins, each to 4in (10cm) long, are produced in early spring. Produces copious "cotton," which may become a nuisance. ↕ 100ft (30m), ↔ 70ft (20m). E. North America. Zone 2b. **'Siouxland'** is rust-resistant and male.

P. fremontii. Fast-growing, round-headed, deciduous tree with spreading branches and glossy, yellow-green, broadly triangular leaves, to 3in (8cm) long, which turn yellow in autumn. Pendent red male or green female catkins, both to 4in (10cm) long, open in early spring. ↕ 80ft (25m), ↔ 50ft (15m). W. US. Zone 4.

P. gileadensis see *P.* x *candicans.*

P. glauca see *P. jacquemontii* var. *glauca.*

P. grandidentata (Bigtooth aspen). Spreading, deciduous tree with gray-hairy young shoots and ovate, gray-woolly young leaves, to 5in (13cm) long, dark green when mature and pale green beneath. Red male catkins, to 2½in (6cm) long, or green females, to 4in (10cm) long, are produced in early spring. ↕ 70ft (20m), ↔ 40ft (12m). E. North America. Zone 2b.

P.* x *jackii see *P.* x *candicans.*

***P. jacquemontii* var. *glauca*,** syn. *P. glauca.* Fast-growing, broadly conical, deciduous tree bearing broadly ovate, blue-green leaves, to 7in (18cm) long, on red leaf stalks marked with darker red veins. The leaves emerge bronze in early spring, and turn yellow in autumn. Pendent catkins are produced in late spring, the red males to 5in (13cm) long, the green females to 6in (15cm) long. ↕ 70ft (20m), ↔ 30ft (10m). E. Himalayas. Zone 4.

P. lasiocarpa (Chinese necklace poplar). Broadly conical, later round-headed, deciduous tree bearing thick shoots, hairy when young, and large, heart-shaped, tapered, dark green leaves, to 12in (30cm) long, produced on red stalks. Yellow-green catkins, to 4in (10cm) long, usually containing both male and female flowers, are produced in midspring. ↕ 70ft (20m), ↔ 40ft (12m). C. China. Zone 6b.

P. maximowiczii ■ (Japanese poplar). Fast-growing, conical, deciduous tree with hairy young shoots and ovate-elliptic leaves, to 5in (13cm) long, bright green above, whitish green beneath, with green veins. Red male catkins, to 4in (10cm) long, or green females, to 6in (15cm) long, are borne in early spring. Produces attractive "cotton." ↕ to 100ft (30m) or more, ↔ 30ft (10m). N.E. Asia. Zone 5.

Populus x *canescens*

Populus maximowiczii

Populus nigra var. *italica*

P. nigra (Black poplar). Fast-growing, spreading, deciduous tree with dark bark and triangular to ovate, tapered, glossy, dark green leaves, to 4in (10cm) long, bronze when young, turning yellow in autumn. Red male or green female catkins, both 2in (5cm) long, are borne in early and midspring. ↕ 120ft (35m), ↔ 70ft (20m). Europe, N. Africa, C. Asia (including Kazakhstan), Russia (Siberia). Zone 4. **'Afghanica'** see 'Thevestina'. **var. *italica*** ▣ (Lombardy poplar) is male and narrowly columnar, living fast and dying young; ↕ 100ft (30m), ↔ 15ft (5m). **'Thevestina'**, syn. 'Afghanica', is narrowly columnar and female, with striking white bark; ↕ 100ft (30m), ↔ 15ft (5m).
P. simonii. Columnar, deciduous tree with diamond-shaped-ovate to elliptic,

Populus trichocarpa

tapered, dark green leaves, to 5in (13cm) long, emerging yellow-green and balsam-scented very early in spring. Red male or green female catkins, both to 1¼in (3cm) long, are produced in early spring. Susceptible to damage by late frosts. ↕ 40ft (12m), ↔ 20ft (6m). N. and W. China. Zone 2b. **'Fastigiata'** is narrowly upright; ↔ 10ft (3m).
P. szechuanica. Broadly columnar, deciduous tree with ovate-oblong to broadly lance-shaped, smooth, dark green leaves, to 12in (30cm) long, whitish green beneath, bronze when young. Red male catkins, to 4in (10cm) long, or green females, to 6in (15cm) long, are borne in midspring. ↕ to 130ft (40m), ↔ 30ft (10m). W. China. Zone 5. **var. *tibetica*** has leaves that are downy beneath, with dark red veins and leaf stalks.
P. tremula (European aspen). Vigorous, spreading, deciduous tree or shrub bearing flat-stalked, rounded to ovate, coarsely toothed, dark green leaves, to 3in (8cm) long, bronze when young, turning yellow in autumn; they tremble and rattle in the breeze, hence the botanical name. Gray-red male or green female catkins, both to 3in (8cm) long, are produced in early spring. ↕ 70ft (20m), ↔ 30ft (10m). Temperate Europe and Asia to China and Japan. Zone 2. **'Erecta'** is upright in habit and may be considered an alternative to *P. nigra* var. *italica*. **'Pendula'** ▣ (Weeping aspen) bears long, pendent branches; ↕ 20ft (6m), ↔ 25ft (8m).
P. tremuloides (Quaking aspen). Vigorous, spreading, deciduous tree with flat-stalked, rounded to ovate, finely toothed, glossy, dark green leaves, to 2½in (6cm) long, bronze when young, turning brilliant yellow in autumn; light winds cause quivering and rattling of the leaves. Gray-red male or green female catkins, both to 2½in (6cm) long, are borne in early spring. ↕ 50ft (15m), ↔ 30ft (10m). W. North America. Zone 1.

P. trichocarpa ▣ (Black cottonwood, Western balsam poplar). Fast-growing, conical, deciduous tree with ovate, glossy leaves, to 8in (20cm) long, dark green above, white beneath, turning yellow in autumn, and strongly balsam-scented when young. Red male catkins, 3in (8cm) long, or green females, to 6in (15cm) long, are borne in midspring. ↕ 100ft (30m) or more, ↔ 30ft (10m). W. North America. Zone 6.
***P.* 'TT 32'** see *P.* 'Balsam Spire'.

PORANA

CONVOLVULACEAE

Genus of about 20 species of evergreen, twining climbers or shrubs, closely related to *Ipomoea*, from open or dense woodland in tropical Africa, Asia, and Australia. They have alternate, usually heart-shaped leaves, and are grown for their small, bell- to funnel-shaped, white, blue, or purple flowers, borne singly or in terminal panicles or cymes. Where temperatures drop below 45°F (7°C), grow in a cool or temperate greenhouse. In warmer regions, they are suitable for training over a pergola or arch, or through a shrub.
• **CULTIVATION** Under glass, grow in soil-based potting mix in full light. During the growing season, water moderately and apply a balanced liquid fertilizer every 4 weeks; water sparingly in winter, after flowering. Outdoors, grow in fertile, moist but well-drained soil in full sun. Provide support for the climbing stems. Pruning group 11, in early spring.
• **PROPAGATION** Soak seed and sow at 64°F (18°C) in spring. Root greenwood cuttings in early summer, or semi-ripe cuttings with bottom heat in mid- and late summer.
• **PESTS AND DISEASES** Prone to spider mites and whiteflies under glass.

P. paniculata (Bridal bouquet, Snow in the jungle, White corallita). Strong-growing, twining climber bearing slender-pointed, heart-shaped, mid-green leaves, 3–6in (8–15cm) long, smooth above, white-powdery beneath when young. Produces large, terminal panicles, to 12in (30cm) long, of many funnel-shaped, scented white flowers, ⅜in (9mm) across, from summer to early winter. ↕ to 28ft (9m). N. India, N. Burma. ❀ (min. 45°F/7°C)

PORTEA

BROMELIACEAE

Genus of about 9 species of rosette-forming, evergreen, terrestrial perennials (bromeliads) from Brazil, where they usually grow in coastal shrubland and shaded forest, to 2,000ft (600m) high. They are cultivated for their foliage and flowers: the strap-shaped, spiny-margined, fairly stiff leaves are mostly scaly, especially beneath; the tubular, blue or violet flowers are borne in cylindrical heads on long, slender flower stalks. Where temperatures fall below 59°F (15°C), grow in an indoor garden; in warmer climates, they are suitable for growing outdoors in a desert garden.
• **CULTIVATION** Under glass, grow in terrestrial bromeliad potting mix in full light, with shade from hot sun. Water moderately at all times; overwatering

Portea petropolitana

often causes root rot. During the growing season, apply a low-nitrogen fertilizer every 6–8 weeks. Outdoors, grow in humus-rich, leafy, loamy soil in full sun, with some midday shade. See also p.47.
• **PROPAGATION** Sow seed at 66–75°F (19–24°C) in spring or summer. Remove offsets in late spring.
• **PESTS AND DISEASES** Susceptible to beetles when grown outdoors. Scale insects sometimes attack new growth.

P. petropolitana ▣ Terrestrial perennial bearing a rosette of strap-shaped, minutely scaly, mid- to dark green leaves, to 32in (80cm) long, with black marginal spines. Large-toothed leaf sheaths have dark brown scales. In summer, the thick, reddish brown scapes produce branched, pendent, compound, cylindrical inflorescences, to 16in (40cm) long, with rose-red bracts. The tubular flowers, to 1¼in (3cm) long, have blue-violet petals and red ovaries. ↕ to 3ft (1m), ↔ 16in (40cm). E. Brazil. ❀ (min. 59°F/15°C). **var. *extensa*** has lilac-blue flowers with purple-tipped green ovaries, borne in more open inflorescences, on arching, coral-red scapes.

▷ ***Porteranthus trifoliata*** see *Gillenia trifoliata*

PORTULACA

Purslane, Rose moss

PORTULACACEAE

Genus of 100 semi-succulent, mainly erect to trailing annuals, with a few perennials, found mostly in dry, sandy soils in warm-temperate and tropical regions. They have small, fleshy, alternate to sometimes opposite, flat to cylindrical, almost moss-like leaves, which are very variable in color, often white, green, or red. They are grown for their showy, cup-shaped, rose-like, 4- to 7-petaled, scarlet, carmine, purple, yellow, pink, apricot, or white flowers,

Populus tremula 'Pendula'

ortulaca grandiflora Sundance Hybrids

hich usually have a leafy rosette of
liage below each flowerhead; flowering
best in dry summers. Grow as annuals
a sunny, dry border or bank, or in a
indowbox or other container.
CULTIVATION Outdoors, grow in poor,
ndy, well-drained soil in full sun.
PROPAGATION Sow seed at 55–64°F
3–18°C) in midspring.
PESTS AND DISEASES White rust,
amping off, black stem rot, and aphids
n be problems.

. grandiflora (Moss rose, Rose moss,
un plant). Spreading, red-stemmed
nnual with clusters of cylindrical,
eshy, bright mid- to dark green
aves, to 1in (2.5cm) long. In summer,
roduces single or double, satin-
xtured, rose-pink, red, yellow, or white
owers, to 1in (2.5cm) or more across,
ometimes striped and flecked in a
ontrasting color. They typically open
eir flowers only in bright sunlight.
4–8in (10–20cm), ↔ 6in (15cm).
razil, Argentina, Uruguay. **Calypso
lixed** cultivars have mostly double
owers in a range of bright colors; ↕ 5in
3cm). **Minilaca Hybrids** have a neat,
ompact habit, with large, double
owers, to 2in (5cm) across, in a wide
nge of colors; they are good container
lants; ↕ 4–6in (10–15cm). **Sundance
lybrids** ▣ are semi-trailing in habit,
ith large, semi-double or double
owers, to 2in (5cm) across, in a broad
nge of bright colors; ↕ to 6in (15cm).
undial Series cultivars were bred for
etter flowering in cooler, grayer
imates; they produce double flowers in
broad color range, including an
nusual bicolor: white, striped and
ecked with lavender-blue.

ORTULACARIA

ORTULACACEAE

enus of 1–3 species (often considered
ne variable species) of bushy, perennial,
cculent shrubs from semi-arid, hilly
wland in Namibia, South Africa,
waziland, and Mozambique. Grown
ainly for their foliage, they have fleshy
ems, leaves, and branches, and
conspicuous, cup- or saucer-shaped
owers in cymes or short racemes. In
eas where temperatures fall below
0°F (10°C), grow in a warm green-
ouse; in warm, dry climates, use in a
rub border or desert garden.
CULTIVATION Under glass, grow in
il-based potting mix with added grit,

Portulacaria afra 'Foliisvariegatus'

in full light or bright filtered light. From early spring to early autumn, water freely and apply a low-nitrogen liquid fertilizer every 6–8 weeks; keep almost completely dry at other times. Outdoors, grow in moderately fertile, sharply drained soil in full sun or partial shade. Pruning group 1. See also pp.48–49.
- **PROPAGATION** Root cuttings of stem sections in spring with bottom heat.
- **PESTS AND DISEASES** Susceptible to scale insects.

P. afra. Bushy, succulent shrub with thick, gray-barked stems and jointed, short, twig-like, projecting branches. The obovate, sometimes pointed, opposite, glossy green leaves, to ¾in (2cm) long, are flat above, convex below. Inconspicuous, saucer-shaped, pale pink flowers, 1/16in (2mm) across, are borne in summer. ↕ 6–10ft (2–3m), ↔ 5ft (1.5m). Namibia, South Africa (Northern Cape, Eastern Cape, Northern Transvaal, Eastern Transvaal), Swaziland, Mozambique. ❀ (min. 50°F/10°C) **'Foliisvariegatus'** ▣ produces yellow-mottled leaves.

POSOQUERIA

RUBIACEAE

Genus of 12–16 species of upright to rounded, evergreen shrubs and trees occurring in habitats from forest to moist ravines in tropical regions of North and South America. They are cultivated for their simple, leathery leaves, produced in opposite pairs, and corymbs of tubular, pendent, salver-form, fragrant, white, pink, or red flowers. The flowers each have 5 spreading petal lobes with very long corolla tubes, sometimes as long as 12in (30cm). They are borne in terminal corymbs; pollen is dislodged explosively in some species. They are followed by yellow berries. In areas where temperatures fall below 41–45°F (5–7°C), grow *Posoqueria* species in a cool or temperate greenhouse; elsewhere, they are suitable for a shrub border, or as specimens.
- **CULTIVATION** Under glass, grow in soil-based potting mix with added grit, in full light or bright filtered light. From early spring to early autumn, water freely and apply a balanced liquid fertilizer every 6–8 weeks; keep just moist at other times. Outdoors, grow in moderately fertile, sharply drained soil in full sun or partial shade. Pruning group 8; plants under glass need restrictive pruning.
- **PROPAGATION** Take greenwood cuttings in early summer, or semi-ripe cuttings in mid- or late summer.
- **PESTS AND DISEASES** Susceptible to spider mites, whiteflies, and mealybugs under glass.

P. latifolia. Moderately bushy shrub, or sometimes small, broadly upright tree if unpruned, bearing ovate or oblong to elliptic, prominently veined, rich green leaves, 6–10in (15–25cm) long. In spring, produces dense corymbs of few to many slender-tubed, fragrant white flowers, 2½in (6cm) across, with long, slender tubes, to 6in (15cm) long; they are followed by yellow berries, 1½–3in (4–8cm) across. ↕ 6–45ft (2–14m), ↔ 6–20ft (2–6m). Mexico to Brazil, West Indies. ❀ (min. 45°F/7°C)

POTAMOGETON

POTAMOGETONACEAE

Genus of 80–100 species of marginal to deep-water aquatic perennials, distributed almost throughout the world, flourishing in freshwater ditches, ponds, canals, and waterways. They are cultivated as oxygenators in water gardens and for their decorative effect in aquariums. The branched, creeping rhizomes spread rapidly in muddy pool bottoms, where they support an inter-woven, mat-like network of translucent, linear to lance-shaped submerged leaves, and leathery, opaque, lance-shaped to rounded floating leaves. Inconspicuous flowers are borne in fleshy spikes just above the water.

Grow the hardy species as oxygenators in outdoor pools; *P. crispus* tolerates polluted water better than most other oxygenators, and can also be used in cold-water aquariums. Where not hardy, grow in cool-water aquariums; in warmer climates, they are suitable for outdoor pools.
- **CULTIVATION** In an aquarium, grow in pots of an inert medium in full light. Feed with commercial aquarium plant fertilizer. In an outdoor pool, grow in aquatic containers of sandy loam, or root in a muddy pond bottom at a depth of 6–24in (15–60cm), ideally in full sun, or in partial shade. Cut back frequently and thin to keep in check. *P. crispus* prefers alkaline water. Submerged leaves may become encrusted with mineral deposits. See also pp.52–53.
- **PROPAGATION** Take cuttings of stem sections in late spring or early summer.
- **PESTS AND DISEASES** Rust and stem rot may occur.

P. crispus (Curled pondweed). Marginal to deep-water aquatic perennial with cylindrical, branching stems, to 12ft (4m) long, bearing narrowly oblong, almost translucent submerged leaves, about 1½in (4cm) long, wavy-margined when mature, and stalked, pointed, leathery floating leaves. Spikes of inconspicuous, crimson and creamy white flowers, ¼–½in (0.5–1.5cm) across, are produced just above the water surface in summer. May become an aggressive weed in earth-bottom ponds. ↔ indefinite. Europe, Asia to Australasia. Zone 7.

POTENTILLA *syn.* COMARUM

Cinquefoil

ROSACEAE

Genus of about 500 species of shrubs, herbaceous perennials, and a few annuals and biennials, found throughout the N. hemisphere, in habitats ranging from meadows to mountain screes. They are cultivated for their attractive, usually 5-petaled, saucer- to cup-shaped, occasionally star-shaped, white, yellow, orange, pink, or red flowers; they are produced over long periods from spring to autumn, either singly or, more often, in cymes or terminal panicles. The alternate leaves may be pinnate or 3- to 7-palmate, and are often strongly veined and wrinkled. The shrubby potentillas, mainly derived from *P. fruticosa*, are excellent, long-flowering plants for a mixed or shrub border and for low hedges. Many species are also suitable for rock gardens, raised beds, or mixed borders. Most clump-forming hybrids are valued for their single, semi-double, or double, mainly red or yellow flowers, providing summer and autumn color in herbaceous borders: they have strawberry-like, 5-palmate, mid- to dark green leaves, 2–4in (5–10cm) long, conspicuously veined and toothed.
- **CULTIVATION** Grow in poor to moderately fertile, well-drained soil in full sun. Rock-garden species prefer poor, gritty, sharply drained soil. Pruning group 10, in spring.
- **PROPAGATION** Sow seed in containers in a cold frame in autumn or spring. Divide perennials in autumn or spring. Take greenwood cuttings of shrubs in early summer.
- **PESTS AND DISEASES** Downy mildew, powdery mildew, leaf blister, rust, and a variety of fungal leaf spots occur.

P. alba ▣ Clump-forming perennial with spreading stems, bearing 5-palmate leaves, with oblong to obovate-lance-

Potentilla alba

P

shaped leaflets, ¾–1½in (2–4cm) long, light green above, silver-silky-hairy beneath. In late spring and early summer, bears loose cymes of flat, saucer-shaped white flowers, 1in (2.5cm) across. ↕ 3in (8cm), ↔ to 12in (30cm). C. and S. Europe. Zone 4.
P. arbuscula see *P. fruticosa* var. *arbuscula.*
P. atrosanguinea (Himalayan cinquefoil). Clump-forming, hairy perennial bearing 3-palmate, dark green leaves, 2–3in (5–8cm) long, with ovate to elliptic or obovate, toothed leaflets, gray-silky-hairy to densely white-hairy. From summer to autumn, panicle-like cymes of saucer-shaped, yellow, orange, or pale to deep red flowers, 1¼in (3cm) across, are borne on erect, branching, wiry stems. ↕ 18–36in (45–90cm), ↔ 24in (60cm). Himalayas. Zone 5. **var. *argyrophylla*** has leaves composed of 3–5 leaflets, and yellow or yellow-orange flowers.
P. aurea ■ Mat-forming perennial with 3- or 5-palmate, glossy, mid-green leaves, to 1¼in (3cm) long, composed of oblong leaflets with sharply toothed, silver-hairy margins. Produces cymes of flat, saucer-shaped, deep golden yellow flowers, ¾in (2cm) across, with overlapping petals, from late spring to summer. ↕ 4in (10cm), ↔ 8in (20cm). Pyrenees, Alps. Zone 5.

Potentilla fruticosa 'Goldfinger'

Potentilla fruticosa 'McKay's White'

P. cinerea. Dwarf, clump-forming perennial with procumbent stems and 3-palmate leaves, consisting of 3–5 gray-green, narrowly ovate leaflets, to ¾in (2cm) long, gray beneath. In summer, bears cymes of up to 6 saucer-shaped, pale yellow flowers, ¾in (2cm) across. ↕ to 4in (10cm), ↔ 8in (20cm). C., S., E. Europe. Zone 4.
***P. davurica* var. *mandschurica* of gardens** see *P. fruticosa* 'Manchu'.
***P. davurica* 'Veitchii'** see *P. fruticosa* var. *veitchii.*

Potentilla aurea

Potentilla fruticosa 'Daydawn'

Potentilla fruticosa 'Farrer's White'

Potentilla fruticosa 'Primrose Beauty'

Potentilla fruticosa 'Princess'

Potentilla fruticosa 'Red Ace'

Potentilla fruticosa 'Sunset'

Potentilla megalantha

Potentilla nepalensis 'Miss Willmott'

Potentilla neumanniana 'Goldrausch'

Potentilla recta 'Warrenii'

Potentilla 'William Rollison'

P. erecta, syn. *P. tormentilla* (Tormentil). Low-growing perennial with trailing, non-rooting stems and usually 3-palmate, rarely 4- or 5-palmate leaves consisting of wedge- to lance-shaped, toothed leaflets, to ¾in (2cm) long, dark green above, silver-silky-hairy beneath. Loose, terminal cymes of slender-stemmed, 4-petaled, saucer-shaped yellow flowers, to ½in (1.5cm) across, are borne from late spring to summer. Suitable for a wild garden. ↕ 4–12in (10–30cm), ↔ to 24in (60cm). Europe, Asia. Zone 5b.
P. eriocarpa. Carpet-forming perennial with 3-palmate, bright green leaves, to 1¼in (3cm) long, composed of wedge-shaped, toothed leaflets. Solitary or clustered, short-stalked, cup-shaped, deep yellow flowers, to 1½in (4cm) across, are produced in early summer. ↕ 3in (8cm), ↔ 12in (30cm). Pakistan to China, Himalayas. Zone 6.
***P.* 'Flamenco'.** Clump-forming perennial with deep green leaves, and panicles of single, bright scarlet flowers, 1–1¼in (2.5–3cm) across, borne from late spring to midsummer. ↕ to 18in (45cm), ↔ 24in (60cm). Zone 6.
P. fragiformis see *P. megalantha.*
P. fruticosa (Shrubby cinquefoil). Compact, bushy, deciduous shrub with pinnate leaves, to 1½in (4cm) long, composed of usually 5 or 7 narrowly oblong, dark green leaflets. Saucer-shaped yellow flowers, to 1½in (4cm) across, are borne singly or in cymes of 3 over a long period from late spring to midautumn. ↕ 3ft (1m), ↔ 5ft (1.5m). Europe, N. Asia, North America. Zone 3. **'Abbotswood'** has white flowers and dark blue-green leaves; ↕ 30in (75cm), ↔ 4ft (1.2m). **var. *arbuscula***, syn. *P. arbuscula*, has gray-green to silvery gray foliage and golden yellow flowers, 1¾in (4.5cm) across; ↔ 4ft (1.2m); Himalayas, China. **'Beesii'**, syn. 'Nana Argentea', is slow-growing and compact, with silver-silky-hairy leaves and golden yellow flowers, ¾in (2cm) across; ↕ 24in (60cm), ↔ 4ft (1.2m). **'Blink'** see 'Princess'. **'Boskoop Red'** bears bright green leaves and early-blooming, flame-red flowers, fading to a lighter red. **'Coronation Triumph'** bears profuse bright yellow flowers. **'Dakota Sunrise'** is prostrate when young, becoming dense and rounded, with bright yellow flowers; ↕ 24–36in (60–90cm). **'Daydawn'** ■ has creamy yellow flowers, flushed orange-pink; ↔ 4ft (1.2m). **'Elizabeth'** produces bright yellow flowers, to 1¾in (4.5cm) across. **'Farrer's White'** ■ has profuse white flowers, 1in (2.5cm) across. **'Friedrichsenii'** is vigorous and upright in habit, with gray-green leaves and pale yellow flowers, 1¼in (3cm) across; ↕ 5ft (1.5m), ↔ 4ft (1.2m). **'Gold Drop'**, syn. 'Goldkugel', *P. parvifolia* 'Gold Drop', is upright, with profuse golden flowers, 1in (2.5cm) across; ↕↔ 4ft (1.2m). **'Goldfinger'** ■ produces large, rich yellow flowers, to 2in (5cm) across. **'Goldkugel'** see 'Gold Drop'. **'Jackman's Variety'** has bright yellow flowers, 1¼–1½in (3–4cm) across. **'Katherine Dykes'** has profusely borne, canary-yellow flowers. **'Klondike'** produces bright green leaves and bright yellow flowers. **'Longacre'** is low-growing and spreading, with bright yellow flowers, to 1½in (4cm) or more across; ↕ 24in (60cm). **'Maanelys'**, syn. 'Moonlight', *P.* 'Manelys', has soft yellow flowers, 1¼in (3cm) across, and gray-green foliage; ↕ 4ft (1.2m), ↔ 6ft (2m). **'Manchu'**, syn. *P. davurica* var. *mandschurica* of gardens, is dwarf and mound-forming, with dark pink shoots, silvery gray, silky-hairy leaves, and white flowers, 1in (2.5cm) across; ↕ 12in (30cm), ↔ 30in (75cm). **'McKay's White'** ■ bears creamy white flowers; the foliage remains healthy throughout the season. **'Moonlight'** see 'Maanelys'. **'Nana Argentea'** see 'Beesii'. **'Pretty Polly'** has pale pink flowers, ¾in (2cm) across; ↕ 20in (50cm), ↔ 30in (75cm). **'Primrose Beauty'** ■ has gray-green leaves and pale primrose-yellow flowers, 1½in (4cm) across. **'Princess'** ■ syn. 'Blink', is low-growing, with pale pink flowers, 1in (2.5cm) across, fading to white in full sun; ↕ 24in (60cm), ↔ 3ft (1m). **'Red Ace'** ■ has bright vermilion flowers, yellow on the backs of the petals, fading in full sun and in hot weather. **'Royal Flush'** has rich pink flowers with yellow centers, fading to white in full sun; ↕ 18in (45cm), ↔ 30in (75cm). **'Snowbird'** has double white flowers. **'Sunset'** ■ has dark orange flowers, 1¼in (3cm) across, fading in full sun; ↔ 3ft (1m). **'Sutter's Gold'** has low-growing, arching, silvery-green branches and bright yellow flowers. **'Tangerine'** has yellow flowers, 1¼in (3cm) across, flushed pale orange-red; ↔ 3ft (1m). **'Tilford Cream'** is dense and spreading, with creamy white flowers, 1½in (4cm) across; ↕ 24in (60cm), ↔ 3ft (1m). **var. *veitchii***, syn. *P. davurica* 'Veitchii', has white flowers,

P

ɔtentilla 'Gibson's Scarlet'

.n (2.5cm) across. **'Vilmoriniana'** is ɔright in habit, with silvery gray leaves ıd creamy white flowers, 1½in (4cm) :ross; ↕ 4ft (1.2m), ↔ 3ft (1m). **'ellow Gem'** is low and spreading, ·oducing gray foliage and ruffled, ·ight yellow flowers; ↕ 24in (60cm), · 4ft (1.2m).
. 'Gibson's Scarlet' ▣ Clump-ırming perennial with soft green leaves ıd raceme-like cymes of single, very ·ight scarlet flowers, 1¼in (3cm) across, ɔm early to late summer. ↕ to 18in 5cm), ↔ 24in (60cm). Zone 3b.
. 'Gloire de Nancy', syn. *P.* 'Glory of ancy'. Clump-forming perennial with ırk green leaves, and racemes of ɔuble, reddish orange flowers, 1–1¼in .5–3cm) across, from early to late ımmer. ↕ to 18in (45cm), ↔ 24in 0cm). Zone 6.
. 'Glory of Nancy' see *P.* 'Gloire de ancy'.
. 'Manelys' see *P. fruticosa* 'Maanelys'.
. megalantha ▣ syn. *P. fragiformis.* ɔmpact, clump-forming perennial ·oducing 3-palmate leaves, to 3in cm) long, with broadly elliptic to ɔovate, coarsely scalloped leaflets, mid-een and slightly hairy above, gray-een and more hairy beneath. Erect ·mes of 3–7 saucer-shaped yellow ɔwers, 1¼–1½in (3–4cm) across, are ·oduced in mid- and late summer. 5–12in (15–30cm), ↔ 6in (15cm). Asia, Japan. Zone 4.
'Monsieur Rouillard'. Clump-rming perennial with mid- to deep een leaves and raceme-like cymes of ɔuble, yellow-marked, deep blood-red ɔwers, 1¼in (3cm) across, borne from early to late summer. ↕ to 18in (45cm), ↔ 24in (60cm). Zone 3b.
P. nepalensis. Loose, clump-forming perennial with numerous branching, red-tinged, wiry stems bearing 5-palmate, mid-green leaves, 3–4in (8–10cm) long, composed of large, obovate or elliptic, coarsely toothed, hairy leaflets. In summer, bears loose cymes of saucer-shaped, dark crimson flowers, 1in (2.5cm) across, on long leaf stalks. ↕ 12–36in (30–90cm), ↔ 24in (60cm). W. Himalayas. Zone 4. **'Flammenspiel'** bears red flowers with narrow yellow edges; ↕ 16in (40cm). **'Miss Willmott'** ▣ has cherry-pink flowers suffused yellow, with darker pink centers; ↕ 12–18in (30–45cm). **'Roxana'** has copper-pink flowers with cherry-red centers; ↕ to 18in (45cm).
P. neumanniana, syn. *P. tabernaemontani, P. verna.* Procumbent, mat-forming perennial, similar to *P. eriocarpa*, with 5- or 7-palmate leaves, to 1½in (4cm) long, composed of inversely lance-shaped to obovate, toothed, mid-green leaflets. Loose cymes of up to 12 saucer-shaped yellow flowers, to 1in (2.5cm) across, are borne over long periods from spring onward. ↕ to 4in (10cm), ↔ 12in (30cm). Europe. Zone 5. **'Goldrausch'** ▣ produces loose cymes of up to 10 bright golden yellow flowers from spring to early summer; ↕ 4in (10cm), ↔ 8in (20cm). **'Nana'** is more compact; ↕ 3in (8cm), ↔ 6in (15cm).
P. nitida. Densely tufted perennial with palmate, silver-hairy leaves, to ½in (1.5cm) long, consisting of 3, rarely 4 or 5, inversely lance-shaped to obovate leaflets. In summer, bears solitary or paired, short-stemmed, saucer-shaped, deep pink, rarely white flowers, 1in (2.5cm) or more across. Attractive in a scree bed; not always free-flowering. ↕ to 4in (10cm), ↔ 6in (15cm). S.W. and S.E. Alps, Apennines. Zone 5.
P. palustris, syn. *Comarum palustre* (Marsh cinquefoil). Rhizomatous, woody-based perennial with upright to decumbent stems and pinnate leaves, 1¼–3in (3–8cm) long, composed of 5–7 toothed, oblong, gray-green leaflets, to 2½in (6cm) long. Produces lax cymes of bowl-shaped, purple to maroon flowers, to 1¼in (3cm) across, in early summer. Suitable for the margins of a pond. ↕ to 20in (50cm), ↔ to 32in (80cm) or more. Europe, W. Asia, North America. Zone 4.
***P. parvifolia* 'Gold Drop'** see *P. fruticosa* 'Gold Drop'.
P. recta. Erect, clump-forming, hairy perennial producing 5- or 7-palmate leaves, 4in (10cm) long, with oblong to obovate, toothed, gray-green to mid-green leaflets. Flat cymes of saucer-shaped, pale yellow flowers, to 1in (2.5cm) across, are borne from early to late summer. ↕ 24in (60cm), ↔ 18in (45cm). Europe, Caucasus, Russia (Siberia). Zone 4. **'Citrina'** see var. *pallida.* **'Macrantha'** see 'Warrenii'. **var. *pallida***, syn. 'Citrina', var. *sulphurea*, produces pale yellow to cream flowers; ↕ 18in (45cm). **var. *sulphurea*** see var. *pallida.* **'Warrenii'** ▣ syn. 'Macrantha', produces loose cymes of bright canary-yellow flowers.
P. tabernaemontani see *P. neumanniana.*
P. x tonguei (*P. anglica* x *P. nepalensis*). Clump-forming perennial with long, spreading stems bearing 3- or 5-palmate, dark green leaves, to 2in (5cm) long, composed of obovate leaflets. Over long periods in summer, produces solitary or loose, few-flowered cymes of rather flat, bowl-shaped, apricot-yellow flowers, ½in (1.5cm) across, with deep carmine-red eyes. ↕ 4in (10cm), ↔ to 12in (30cm). Garden origin. Zone 5.
P. tormentilla see *P. erecta.*
P. tridentata. Dwarf, evergreen perennial with a woody base and 3-palmate, basal leaves, to 3in (8cm) long, composed of slightly toothed, wedge-shaped, mid-green leaflets. In early summer, bears compact cymes of saucer-shaped white flowers, ¼in (3mm) across. Useful in a rock garden or on a dry, rocky bank. ↕ 6–12in (15–30cm), ↔ 12in (30cm). Greenland, Wisconsin to Georgia. Zone 2.
P. verna see *P. neumanniana.*
***P.* 'William Rollison'** ▣ Clump-forming perennial with mid-green leaves. Raceme-like cymes of semi-double, yellow- or red-orange flowers, 1–1¼in (2.5–3cm) across, with yellow centers and petal backs, are borne from early to late summer. ↕ to 18in (45cm), ↔ 24in (60cm). Zone 3b.
***P.* 'Yellow Queen'.** Clump-forming perennial with mid-green leaves and raceme-like cymes of double or semi-double, pure yellow flowers, 1–1¼in (2.5–3cm) across, from early to late summer. ↕ 12–18in (30–45cm), ↔ 24in (60cm). Zone 5.

▷ ***Pothos celatocaulis*** see *Rhaphidophora celatocaulis*

x *Potinara* Cherub 'Spring Daffodil'

x POTINARA

ORCHIDACEAE

Quadrigeneric hybrid genus of evergreen orchids derived from crosses between *Brassavola, Cattleya, Laelia,* and *Sophronitis.* They are vegetatively similar to the 4 parent genera, which are loosely referred to as "cattleyas," and have thick to slender pseudobulbs and 1 or 2 mostly broadly oblong, semi-rigid, leathery leaves. The short racemes of flowers, with usually strong and clear colors, often yellow or red, are borne at the bases of the leaves, with or without sheaths.
• **CULTIVATION** Intermediate-growing orchids. Grow in pots of epiphytic orchid potting mix made with coarse bark. When in growth, provide high humidity and bright filtered light, water freely, and feed at every third watering. In winter, admit full light and water sparingly. See also p.46.
• **PROPAGATION** Divide into groups of 3 backbulbs plus attached new growth in spring.
• **PESTS AND DISEASES** Scale insects, spider mites, aphids, and mealybugs may be troublesome.

x *P.* Cherub 'Spring Daffodil' ▣ Epiphytic orchid with elongated pseudobulbs and semi-rigid, broadly oval leaves, 4in (10cm) long. Clear yellow flowers, 2in (5cm) across, are produced in short racemes in spring. ↕ 6in (15cm), ↔ 8in (20cm). ❀ (min. 55°F/13°C; max. 86°F/30°C)

PRATIA

CAMPANULACEAE

Genus of about 20 species of prostrate, spreading, freely rooting, evergreen perennials, mostly from damp, shady habitats in Africa, Asia, Australia, New Zealand, and South America. They produce alternate, usually stalkless, often toothed, ovate to rounded leaves, and are grown for their mass of solitary, 2-lipped, star-shaped, usually white or blue-purple flowers. Good groundcover in damp soil, they are also suitable for a rock garden or paving crevice, but can be invasive. Grow marginally hardy and tender species in an alpine house.
• **CULTIVATION** Grow in fertile, loamy, reliably moist soil in partial or deep shade; *P. pedunculata* tolerates drier soils. In an alpine house, use a mix of equal parts loam, leaf mold, and grit.

Pratia pedunculata

• **PROPAGATION** Divide at any time of year. Keep divisions moist until well-established.
• **PESTS AND DISEASES** Prone to slugs and snails, and to aphids under glass.

P. angulata, syn. *Lobelia angulata.* Mat-forming, evergreen perennial with red-tinted stems that spread and root down freely. The broadly ovate to rounded, coarsely toothed leaves are very variable in size, but usually ¼–½in (6–15mm) long. In late spring and early summer, bears short-stalked, axillary, star-shaped, sometimes purple-streaked white flowers, to ½in (1.5cm) across; they are followed by spherical, red-purple, fleshy fruit, ⅛in (3mm) across. Moderately invasive in moist conditions. ↕ 2in (5cm), ↔ 12–24in (30–60cm). Malaysia, Indonesia, New Zealand. Zone 7b. **'Ohau'** has large white flowers, to 1in (2.5cm) across, and bright red fruit. **'Treadwellii'**, syn. *P. treadwellii*, is larger overall than the species, and may be very invasive; ↕ 2½in (6cm), ↔ 3ft (1m).
P. pedunculata ▣ syn. *Lobelia pedunculata.* Ground-hugging perennial with ovate to rounded leaves, to ⅜in (9mm) long. Short-stalked, star-shaped, pale blue flowers, to ¼in (6mm) across, are borne over long periods in summer. Rather invasive, even in dry conditions. ↕ ½in (1.5cm), ↔ indefinite. Australia. Zone 6. **'County Park'** bears blue flowers. **'Jack's Pass'** has a creeping habit and bears deep red fruit. **'Tom Stone'** is trailing, with pale blue flowers.
P. perpusilla, syn. *Lobelia perpusilla.* Mat-forming perennial bearing tiny, obovate leaves, ⅛–¼in (3–6mm) long, with deeply toothed margins. During summer, bears short-stalked, star-shaped white flowers, ¼–½in (6–15mm) across, with recurving lobes. ↕ to ¾in (2cm), ↔ indefinite. Zone 6. **'Fragrant Carpet'** produces fragrant flowers. **'Summer Meadows'** has bronze-colored leaves and fragrant white flowers.
P. physaloides. Mat-forming perennial with ovate, pointed, toothed, hairless, mid-green leaves, to 7in (18cm) long. In summer, bears 5–15 star-shaped, pale blue flowers, to 2in (5cm) long, in terminal racemes, to 6in (15cm) long, followed by spherical, leathery blue fruit, to ½in (1.5cm) across. ↕ to 6in (15cm), ↔ indefinite. New Zealand. Zone 7.
P. treadwellii see *P. angulata* 'Treadwellii'.

PRIMULA

Primrose

PRIMULACEAE

Genus of about 425 species of mainly herbaceous perennials, some woody-based and evergreen. Occurring in a wide range of habitats, from bogs and marshland to alpine areas, they are widely distributed throughout the N. hemisphere, with almost half the species from the Himalayas; a few are also found in the S. hemisphere. They have linear to broadly ovate or obovate, pale to dark green leaves in basal rosettes, and attractive, often salverform, sometimes tubular, bell-shaped or funnel-shaped flowers, with usually spreading petals joined at the bases into tubes. The flowers may be clustered together among the leaves, or produced on slender to thick flower stalks in umbels, whorls, or spikes. In some primroses, the leaves, flower stems, and calyces are covered with a white or yellow, waxy meal, or "farina." The flowering season extends from late winter to midsummer in temperate regions. Primroses can be used for a variety of garden sites, from bog and waterside plantings to borders, rock gardens, and bedding; they can also be grown in an alpine house. In general, primroses prefer climates with cool summers. Some alpine species need dry conditions during winter months. A few tender species and their cultivars are grown as cool or temperate greenhouse container plants, or as houseplants. Many species and cultivars are well adapted to container culture and are often grown specifically for exhibition.

Primula is a complex genus, divided into many different botanical sections. Numerous hybrids have been developed. The most horticulturally important of these can be grouped into 5 types.

Auricula type
Evergreen primulas, developed from *P. auricula* and *P. hirsuta.* They bear umbels of several large, flat-faced, salverform flowers above smooth, leathery, often white-mealy foliage. There are 3 main subgroups: alpine, show, and garden (or border).
Alpine Auriculas – These have flowers with either a "light" (white or cream) or "gold" (yellow or gold) center. The color of the petals is in sharp contrast to that of the center, with the color shading outward from dark to light. There is no meal on the flowers or the foliage. Grow in an alpine house or rock garden.
Show Auriculas – These have a distinct circle of white meal, or "paste," in the center of each flower. They may be described as "selfs" if the petals consist of one color from the paste to the petal margins. In "edged" auriculas, the paste is surrounded by a ring of black, and the petal margins are green, gray, or white. "Fancies" are similar to edged auriculas, except that the black portion of the petal is replaced by another color. Grow in an alpine house.
Garden (Border) Auriculas – These are generally robust, often fragrant, garden plants available in a wide variety of colors. The foliage may or may not be white-mealy. Grow in a mixed or herbaceous border, or in a rock garden.
Candelabra type
Robust herbaceous perennials with several whorls of flowers arranged in tiers on tall, sturdy stems. They are deciduous, dying back to basal buds, or semi-evergreen, dying back to reduced rosettes. Grow in moist shade or woodland; they are seen at their best in groups by streams or in bog gardens.
Acaulis type
A very diverse group of evergreen or semi-evergreen, early spring-flowering perennial hybrids derived from *P. vulgaris.* They have rosettes of broadly ovate to obovate leaves. Most produce large, solitary, salverform flowers clustered among the basal rosettes. A few may have both solitary and umbel-like inflorescences. They are available in a wide range of colors and are grown as annuals for bedding or containers or as perennials for rock gardens, herbaceous and mixed borders.
Polyanthus type (including Primrose group)
These evergreen or semi-evergreen perennial descendants from *P. vulgaris, P. veris,* and *P. elatior* have rosettes of broadly ovate to obovate leaves and umbels of up to 20 flowers. Some strains are fairly hardy and may be grown as spring-flowering herbaceous perennials. Others are cultivated as annuals for bedding or containers. Propagate both the Acaulis and Polyanthus types by division in spring immediately after flowering or in early autumn. Both can easily be raised by seed.
Juliana type (*P.* x *pruhoniciana*)
P. juliae was crossed with *P. veris* or *P. vulgaris* to yield a diverse group of small, sturdy, semi-evergreen perennials suitable for an herbaceous or mixed border or rock garden. They are hardy and available in a wide variety of colors. In early spring, the flowers are borne singly or in umbels. Propagation is by division in early spring, either before or after flowering, or from seed.

PRIMULA GROUPINGS

The genus *Primula* is classified into many botanical sections. These drawings illustrate 3 of the 5 most important horticultural groups.

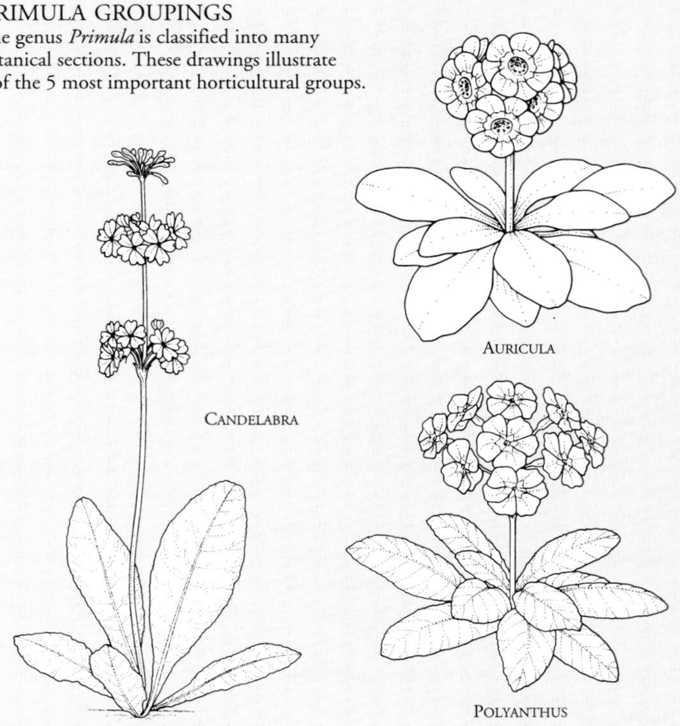

• **CULTIVATION** For ease of reference, cultivation requirements have been set out in groups, as follows:
1. Full sun in mild coastal areas, or partial shade, in moderately fertile, moist but well-drained, humus-rich soil.
2. Partial shade, in deep, humus-rich, moist, neutral to acidic loam, or peaty soil. Tolerates full sun if soil remains moist at all times.
3. Deep or partial shade in peaty, gritty, moist but sharply drained, acidic soil. Protect from excessive winter moisture.
4. Under glass in an alpine house or frame. Use a mix of equal parts soil-based potting mix, leaf mold or peat, and grit. Avoid wetting the foliage of mealy species and hybrids.
5. Full sun with some midday shade, or partial shade, in moist but sharply drained, gritty, humus-rich, slightly alkaline soil.
6. In a cool or temperate greenhouse, or as a houseplant. Use a mix of 4 parts soil-based potting mix and 1 part each grit and leaf mold (or peat), in bright filtered light. In growth, water freely and apply a half-strength balanced liquid fertilizer every week.
• **PROPAGATION** Surface-sow seed of tender species in early spring. Sow seed of hardy species in containers in an open frame, as soon as ripe or in late winter or early spring. Divide in early spring. Root basal cuttings or offsets in autumn or early spring. Take root cuttings when dormant in winter.
• **PESTS AND DISEASES** Aphids, spider mites, weevils, and slugs cause damage. Diseases include gray mold (*Botrytis*), viruses, root rot, rust, and leaf spots.

P. acaulis see *P. vulgaris.*
***P.* 'Adrian'** ▣ Alpine Auricula primrose with oval to rounded, mid-green leaves, to 4in (10cm) long. In midseason,

•roduces salverform, light-centered lowers, 1¼in (3cm) across, with purple-•lue petals, paler at the margins. Cultivation group 1 or 4. ↕↔ 4in 10cm). Zone 5.

?. *allionii* ■ Rosette-forming, ever-;reen perennial with entire, sometimes calloped or finely toothed, glandular-•airy, inversely lance-shaped, gray-green eaves, to 2in (5cm) long. Very early in he season, produces usually solitary, alverform flowers, each to 1¼in (3cm) cross, varying from white to pink to eddish purple. Each corolla has a flat ace and a white eye. Cultivation group (lime-loving). ↕ 3–4in (7–10cm), ↔ to in (20cm). Alpine areas in S. France nd N. Italy. Zone 4. There are several amed cultivars. **'Snowflake'** is igorous, with large white flowers, 1in 2.5cm) across, sometimes flushed pink.

?. *alpicola* ■ Rosette-forming, leciduous perennial with elliptic, oothed or scalloped, mid-green leaves, o 4in (10cm) long. Late in the season, vhite-mealy stems produce umbels of –12 pendent, tubular to funnel-shaped, ragrant, white, yellow, or violet flowers, ½–1in (1–2.5cm) across, with white-nealy eyes. Cultivation group 2. ↕ 20in 50cm), ↔ 12in (30cm). Moist alpine reas in S.E. Tibet. Zone 4.

?. 'American Beauty'. Show Auricula •rimrose with oval to rounded, mid-;reen leaves, to 4in (10cm) long. In arly and midseason, bears umbels of –8 salverform crimson-red flowers, ¼in (3cm) across, with white-mealy enters and yellow tubes. Cultivation roup 4. ↕ 6in (15cm), ↔ 5in (13cm). Zone 5.

?. *amoena*, syn. *P. elatior* subsp. *meyeri.* Rosette-forming, deciduous perennial vith elliptic to spoon-shaped, scalloped r finely toothed leaves, to 7in (18cm) ong, bright green above, usually densely airy beneath. Early in the season, hairy tems bear usually one-sided umbels of –10 flat to shallowly tubular to funnel-haped, red-purple, violet-blue, or ccasionally white flowers, 1in (2.5cm) cross, with yellow eyes. Cultivation roup 2 or 4. ↕↔ 6in (15cm). Peaty anks and rocky hillsides in Caucasus nd N.E. Turkey. Zone 4.

?. *anisodora*, syn. *P. wilsonii* var. *nisodora.* Rosette-forming, semi-vergreen Candelabra primrose with bovate, finely toothed, anise-scented, nid-green leaves, to 10in (25cm) long. Thick stems produce 3–5 whorls of –10 pendent, tubular to bell-shaped, green-eyed, deep purple to black flowers, ½in (1.5cm) across, late in the season. Cultivation group 2. ↕↔ 24in (60cm). Wet meadows in S.W. China. Zone 5.

rimula 'Argus'

P. 'Argus' ■ Very vigorous alpine Auricula primrose with oval to rounded, mid-green leaves, to 5in (13cm) long. In midseason, produces salverform flowers, to 1¼in (3cm) across, with almost white centers, and petals shading from plum-red to beet-red. Cultivation group 1 or 4. ↕↔ 4in (10cm). Zone 5.

P. aureata ■ Rosette-forming, evergreen perennial with spoon-shaped to oblong, toothed, white-mealy, mid-green leaves, to 3in (8cm) long. In early and midseason, very short stems, hidden within the foliage, produce umbels of 2–10 salverform, cream to yellow flowers, 1¼–1½in (3–4cm) across, with large, darker yellow eyes. Cultivation group 3 or 4. ↕ 6in (15cm), ↔ 8in (20cm). Moist cliffs and rocky hillsides in Nepal. Zone 5.

P. auricula. Rosette-forming, evergreen, sometimes white-mealy perennial, with usually obovate-spoon-shaped to rounded, entire to toothed, pale green to gray-green leaves, to 5in (13cm) long. Umbels of 2–30 salverform, fragrant, deep yellow flowers, ½–1in (1.5–2.5cm) across, are produced early in the season. Cultivation group 1, 4, or 5. ↕ 8in (20cm), ↔ 10in (25cm). Alps, Apennines, Carpathians. Zone 4. **var. *albocincta*** ■ bears gray-green leaves with white margins; Dolomites.

P. 'Beatrice Wooster'. Rosette-forming, evergreen perennial with obovate, scalloped or finely toothed, glandular-hairy, gray-green leaves, to 3in (8cm) long. Early in the season, large, shallowly cup-shaped, clear pink flowers, to 1¼in (3cm) across, with white eyes, are produced in umbels of 2–10 on short stems. Cultivation group 4 or 5. ↕ 4in (10cm), ↔ 8in (20cm). Zone 5b.

P. beesiana ■ syn. *P. bulleyana* subsp. *beesiana.* Rosette-forming, deciduous or semi-evergreen Candelabra primrose that dies back to basal buds or reduced rosettes. The leaves are inversely lance-shaped to obovate, toothed, mid-green, and to 9in (23cm) long, with red midribs. In mid- and late season, thick, white-mealy stems each bear 2–8 whorls of 8–16 salverform, yellow-eyed, reddish pink flowers, ¾in (2cm) across. Cultivation group 2. ↕↔ 24in (60cm). Moist mountain meadows in China. Zone 3.

P. x *berninae* (*P. hirsuta* x *P. latifolia*). Small, neat, rosette-forming, semi-evergreen perennial with ovate, toothed, mid-green leaves, to 5in (13cm) long. Early in the season, very short stems produce tubular to cup-shaped purple flowers, ½in (1.5cm) across, singly or in umbels of up to 15. Cultivation group 1 or 4. ↕ 3in (8cm), ↔ 6in (15cm). Garden origin. Zone 5.

P. 'Betty Green'. Vigorous, rosette-forming, semi-evergreen Juliana hybrid with obovate, apple-green leaves, to 6in (15cm) long. Tubular to saucer-shaped, crimson flowers, to 1½in (4cm) across, with yellow eyes, are borne in clusters of 3–25 early in the season. Cultivation group 1 or 2. ↕ 4–6in (10–15cm), ↔ 12–16in (30–40cm). Zone 4.

P. bhutanica. Rosette-forming, deciduous perennial, dying back to a

Primula 'Adrian'

Primula allionii

Primula alpicola

Primula aureata

Primula auricula var. *albocincta*

Primula x *bileckii*

Primula 'Blossom'

Primula 'Buckland Wine'

Primula bulleyana

large bud in winter. The spoon-shaped, finely toothed, slightly white-mealy, crinkled leaves are mid-green, and to 4in (10cm) long. Early in the season, each very short stem bears umbels of 2–10 salverform, yellow-eyed blue flowers, 1in (2.5cm) across. Cultivation group 3. ↕ 6in (15cm), ↔ 8in (20cm). Mixed forest in Tibet, Bhutan, and India (Assam). Zone 5.

P. x *bileckii* ■ (*P. hirsuta* x *P. minima*). Dwarf, rosette-forming, evergreen perennial with wedge-shaped, leathery, toothed, shining dark green leaves, ½–1¼in (0.5–3cm) long, with soft, glandular hairs. Early in the season, bears umbels of 2 or 3 salverform, red-pink flowers, ½–1¼in (0.5–3cm) across, on very short stems. Cultivation group 1 or 4. ↕ 3in (8cm), ↔ 4in (10cm). Ausria (Alps). Zone 5.

P. 'Blairside Yellow' Compact border Auricula primrose, with rounded to oval, pale green leaves, to 5in (13cm) long. Early in the season, produces open funnel-shaped yellow flowers, to 1in (2.5cm) across. Cultivation group 1, 4, or 5. ↕ 4in (10cm), ↔ 8in (20cm). Zone 5.

P. 'Blossom' ■ Vigorous alpine Auricula primrose with oval, dark green leaves, 5in (13cm) long. Bears salver-form, gold-centered flowers, 1in (2.5cm) across, with shaded crimson petals, early in the season. Cultivation group 1 or 4. ↕↔ 4in (10cm). Zone 4.

P. 'Broadwell Gold'. Vigorous border Auricula primrose bearing obovate, mid-green leaves, to 6in (15cm) long. In early and midseason, bears salverform, golden yellow flowers, to 1½in (4cm) across, with white-mealy eyes. Cultivation group 1, 2, or 4. ↕↔ 10in (25cm). Zone 5.

P. 'Buckland Wine' ■ Compact, rosette-forming, semi-evergreen, Juliana hybrid with oval, bronze-green leaves, to 6in (15cm) long. Early in the season, produces solitary, salverform, wine-red flowers, to 1½in (4cm) across. Cultivation group 1 or 2. ↕ 4in (10cm), ↔ 10in (25cm). Zone 4.

P. bulleyana ■ Rosette-forming, semi-evergreen Candelabra primrose with ovate to ovate-lance-shaped, toothed, mid-green leaves, to 12in (30cm) long. In mid- and late season, thick stems bear 5–7 whorls of 5 to many salverform orange flowers, ¾in (2cm) across, red in bud. Cultivation group 2. ↕↔ 24in (60cm). Hillsides in China. Zone 5. **subsp. *beesiana*** see *P. beesiana.*

Primula beesiana

Primula capitata

Primula chungensis

Primula clarkei

Primula clusiana

Primula 'Craddock White'

Primula denticulata var. *alba*

Primula elatior

Primula flaccida

Primula forrestii

P. burmanica. Rosette-forming, deciduous Candelabra primrose with inversely lance-shaped, toothed, deep dull green leaves, to 12in (30cm) long. Thick stems produce up to 6 whorls of 10–18 salverform, yellow-eyed, red-purple flowers, ¾in (2cm) across, in midseason. Cultivation group 2. ↕↔ 24in (60cm). Meadows and forests in China and Burma. Zone 5.

P. capitata ■ Rosette-forming, deciduous, short-lived perennial, with inversely lance-shaped or oblong-lance-shaped, finely toothed, usually mealy, pale green leaves, to 6in (15cm) long, white-mealy beneath. Tubular, dark purple flowers, to ½in (1.5cm) long, with shallowly lobed petals, are borne in flattened, spherical spikes on white-mealy stems, late in the season. Cultivation group 1 or 2. ↕↔ 16in (40cm). Moist alpine regions in Tibet, Bhutan, and India (Sikkim). Zone 4. **subsp. *mooreana*** is vigorous, and larger overall; ↕↔ 24in (60cm).

P. chionantha. Rosette-forming, deciduous perennial with inversely lance-shaped, toothed or almost entire, mid-green leaves, to 10in (25cm) long, covered in yellow or white meal. In midseason, thick stems produce 1–3 many-flowered whorls of tubular to funnel-shaped, fragrant, milk-white flowers, with or without whitish eyes, to 1in (2.5cm) across. Cultivation group 1 or 2. ↕↔ 24in (60cm). Damp, open, alpine meadows in China. Zone 4. **subsp. *melanops*** see *P. melanops.*

***P.* 'Chloe'** ■ Green-edged show Auricula type with oval, dark green leaves, to 5in (13cm) long. Bears salverform, 5- to 7-petaled black flowers, 1in (2.5cm) across, in early and midseason. Cultivation group 4. ↕↔ 4in (10cm). Zone 5.

P. chungensis ■ Vigorous, rosette-forming, deciduous Candelabra primrose with oblong-obovate, toothed and shallowly lobed, mid-green leaves, to 12in (30cm) long. Late in the season, thick stems bear 2–5 whorls of up to 12 salverform, pale orange flowers, ½–¾in (1.5–2cm) across, with red tubes. Cultivation group 2. ↕ 32in (80cm), ↔ 24in (60cm). Wet, open forest in China and S.E. Tibet. Zone 5.

P. clarkei ■ Small, rosette-forming, deciduous perennial with rounded to ovate, toothed, pale green leaves, to 2in (5cm) long. Early in the season, flat, yellow-eyed, rose-pink flowers, to ¾in (2cm) across, are borne singly or sometimes in short-stemmed umbels of 2–6. Cultivation group 1 or 4. ↕ 3in (8cm), ↔ 6in (15cm). Moist hillsides in India (Kashmir). Zone 6.

P. clusiana ■ Small, rosette-forming, evergreen perennial with oblong to ovate, leathery, dark green leaves, to 3in (8cm) long. Early in the season, salverform, white-eyed, rose-pink to lilac flowers, to 1½in (4cm) across, are borne singly or in umbels of up to 4. Cultivation group 4 or 5. ↕ 3in (8cm), ↔ 6in (15cm). Austria (N. calcareous Alps). Zone 5.

P. cockburniana. Rosette-forming, deciduous biennial or short-lived perennial Candelabra primrose with oblong to oblong-obovate, mid-green leaves, to 6in (15cm) long, with small, toothed lobes. Slender stems bear 1–3 whorls of 3–8 salverform, red-tinged orange flowers, ½in (1.5cm) across, late in the season. Cultivation group 1 or 2. ↕↔ 16in (40cm). Marshy, alpine meadows in China (S.W. Sichuan). Zone 5.

P. cortusoides, syn. *P. saxatilis.* Small, rosette-forming, deciduous perennial with ovate-oblong, softly hairy, toothed, mid-green leaves, to 3½in (9cm) long. Umbels of 2–15 salverform, rose-red or pink to red-violet flowers, to ¾in (2cm) across, are borne in midseason. Cultivation group 1 or 2. ↕↔ 12in (30cm). Woodland in Russia (W. Siberia) and Japan. Zone 4.

***P.* 'Craddock White'** ■ Rosette-forming, deciduous or semi-evergreen Juliana hybrid with oval, dark green, bronze-veined leaves, 6in (15cm) long. Early in the season, bears solitary, salverform, scented white flowers, to 1½in (4cm) across, with yellow eyes. Cultivation group 1 or 2. ↕ 5in (13cm), ↔ 10in (25cm). Zone 4.

P. cuneifolia. Rosette-forming, deciduous, short-lived perennial with inversely lance-shaped, obovate, or wedge-shaped, coarsely toothed, pale green leaves, to 3in (8cm) long. In midseason, salverform, pink to rose, yellow-eyed flowers, to ¾in (2cm) across, are borne singly or in umbels of up to 9, on stems ranging from tiny to 12in (30cm) tall. Cultivation group 2 or 4. ↕↔ to 12in (30cm). Russia (Siberia), Japan, E. Alaska to British Columbia, Aleutian Islands. Zone 4.

P. denticulata (Drumstick primrose). Robust, rosette-forming, deciduous perennial with oblong-obovate or spoon-shaped, mid-green leaves, to 10in (25cm) long, finely toothed, and white-mealy beneath. Thick stems bear crowded, spherical umbels of tubular to trumpet- or bell-shaped, yellow-eyed, purple flowers, to ¾in (2cm) across, early in the season. Cultivation group 1 or 2. ↕↔ 18in (45cm). Moist alpine regions from Afghanistan to S.E. Tibet, Burma, and China. Zone 3. **var. *alba*** ■ has white flowers. **'Rubra'** has red-purple flowers.

***P.* 'Dorothy'.** Vigorous, rosette-forming, semi-evergreen, Juliana hybrid with spoon-shaped, mid-green leaves, to 5in (13cm) long. Early in the season, produces tubular, pale yellow flowers, ¾in (2cm) across, in umbels of 8–20. Cultivation group 1 or 2. ↕ 6in (15cm), ↔ 12–16in (30–40cm). Zone 4.

***P.* Dreamer Series.** Rosette-forming, semi-evergreen or evergreen Primrose Group with inversely lance-shaped to obovate, mid-green leaves, 4in (10cm) long. Early in the season, bear salverform flowers, 1½–2in (4–5cm) across, in cream, apricot, pink, or rose-pink; all bicolors have darker eyes and yellow centers. Cultivation group 2 or 6. ↕ 3–4in (8–10cm), ↔ 6–8in (15–20cm). Zone 5.

P. edgeworthii, syn. *P. nana.* Rosette-forming, deciduous perennial with spoon-shaped to triangular-ovate, pale green leaves, to 5in (13cm) long, contracting to a tight rosette or crown in winter. Very early in the season, very short stems bear umbels of flat, blue, lilac, pink, or white flowers, 1½in (4cm) across, with yellow and white eyes. Cultivation group 3 or 4. ↕ 4in (10cm), ↔ 6in (15cm). W. Himalayas. Zone 4.

Primula 'Chloe'

P. egaliksensis. Rosette-forming deciduous perennial with ovate to elliptic entire leaves, to 0.5in (1.5cm) long. Early in the season, bears umbels of 1–3 tiny white or lavender flowers, ⅕–½in (0.5–1.0cm) across. Cultivation group 2. ↕ 2–4in (5–10cm), ↔ 1–2in (2.5–5cm). Wet silty, gravelly, or peaty meadows; limestone barrens in Greenland, Iceland, N. America (Alaska, British Columbia to Quebec, Labrador, Newfoundland, Colorado, Wyoming). Zone 6.

P. elatior ■ (Oxlip). Variable, rosette-forming, evergreen or semi-evergreen perennial with ovate to oblong or elliptic, scalloped, mid-green leaves, to 8in (20cm) long, softly hairy beneath. In early and midseason, one-sided umbels of 2–12 tubular yellow flowers, to 1in (2.5cm) long, are produced on stiff, upright stems. Cultivation group 1, 2, or 5. ↕ 12in (30cm), ↔ 10in (25cm). Moist meadows and open woodland in Europe, Turkey to the Altai Mountains, and Russia (Siberia). Zone 4. **subsp. *meyeri*** see *P. amoena.*

P. ellisiae. Rosette-forming, deciduous perennial with inversely lance-shaped to spoon-shaped, finely toothed, mid-green leaves, to 6in (15cm) long. In midseason, sturdy stems bear umbels of 4–8 saucer-shaped, yellow-eyed, pinkish purple flowers, to 1in (2.5cm) across. Cultivation group 1 or 4. ↕↔ 12in (30cm). Moist crevices and ledges in New Mexico. Zone 6b.

***P.* 'E. R. Janes'.** Vigorous, rosette-forming, semi-evergreen Juliana hybrid with broadly oval, toothed, mid-green leaves, to 6in (15cm) long. Masses of salverform, orange-flushed, salmon-pink flowers, 1½in (4cm) across, are borne in fascicles early in the season, sometimes again in autumn. Cultivation group 1 or 2. ↕ 4–6in (10–15cm), ↔ 12–16in (30–40cm). Zone 4.

P. farinosa (Bird's-eye primrose). Rosette-forming, deciduous perennial with inversely lance-shaped, sometimes toothed, mid-green leaves, to 4in (10cm) long, and white-mealy beneath. Produces compact umbels of 2–20 tubular, white-mealy, yellow-eyed, lilac-pink flowers, ½in (1.5cm) across, early in the season. Cultivation group 1, 2, or 4. ↕↔ to 10in (25cm). Moist meadows in Europe, N. Asia, and N. Pacific. Zone 4.

***P.* Finesse Series.** Rosette-forming, evergreen or semi-evergreen Primrose Group primulas bearing inversely lance-shaped to obovate, mid-green leaves, 4in (10cm) long. Very early in the season, produce salverform flowers, 1¾in (4.5cm) across, in shades of red, blue, and purple; each flower has a thin, "laced" margin in silver or gold. Cultivation group 2 or 6. ↕ 3–4in (8–10cm), ↔ 6–8in (15–20cm). Zone 5.

P. flaccida ■ syn. *P. nutans* of gardens. Rosette-forming, deciduous, short-lived perennial with narrowly elliptic or obovate, downy, finely toothed, pale to mid-green leaves, to 8in (20cm) long. Late in the season, bears conical spikes of 5–15 pendent, broadly tubular to funnel-shaped, fragrant, white-mealy, lavender-blue to violet flowers, 1in (2.5cm) across. Cultivation group 3 or 4. ↕ 20in (50cm), ↔ 12in (30cm). Open forest and alpine meadows in China. Zone 4.

P. florindae ■ (Giant cowslip). Rosette-forming, deciduous perennial with ovate, toothed, mid-green leaves, to 18in (45cm) long, with heart-shaped bases. Umbels of up to 40 pendent, slender, tubular to funnel-shaped, white-mealy, fragrant, sulfur-yellow flowers, ½–¾in (1–2cm) across, are borne on thick stems late in the season. Cultivation group 1 or 2. ↕ to 4ft (1.2m), ↔ 36in (90cm). Marshes and streams in S.E. Tibet. Zone 3.

P. forrestii ■ Rosette-forming, evergreen, perennial subshrub with ovate-elliptic, scalloped to toothed, dark green leaves, to 8in (20cm) long, wrinkled above, white-mealy beneath. In midseason, thick stems bear umbels of 10–25 salverform, orange-eyed, golden yellow flowers, ½–1in (1.5–2.5cm) across. Cultivation group 4 or 5. ↕ 24in (60cm), ↔ 18in (45cm). Dry, shady crevices in cliffs in China. Zone 6.

P. frondosa ■ Rosette-forming, deciduous perennial with spoon-shaped, finely toothed or lobed, mid-green leaves, to 4in (10cm) long, white-mealy beneath. Early in the season, salverform, yellow-eyed, pale pinkish lilac to red-purple flowers, to ½in (1.5cm) across, are borne singly or in loose umbels of up to 30. Cultivation group 2 or 4. ↕ 6in (15cm), ↔ 10in (25cm). Bulgaria (Stara Planina plateau). Zone 4.

***P.* 'Garryarde Guinevere'** ■ Vigorous, rosette-forming, evergreen Polyanthus Group primrose with oval, toothed, deep bronze leaves, 6in (15cm) long, and salverform, yellow-eyed, pale purplish pink flowers, 1½in (4cm) across, borne in umbels of 3–8, early in the season. Cultivation group 2. ↕ 5in (13cm), ↔ 10in (25cm). Zone 4.

P. geraniifolia. Rosette-forming, hairy, deciduous perennial with rounded, 7- to 9-lobed leaves, to 6in (15cm) long, with scalloped margins. Umbels of 2–12 semi-pendent, tubular to bell-shaped, pinkish purple flowers, to ¾in (2cm) across, are produced on slender stems, in midseason. Cultivation group 2. ↕↔ 12in (30cm). Shady hillsides in India (Sikkim), Nepal, Bhutan, Tibet, and China. Zone 4.

P. glutinosa. Rosette-forming, evergreen perennial with narrowly inversely lance-shaped to oblong, leathery, sticky, glandular-hairy leaves, to 2½in (6cm) long, with slightly toothed tips. In midseason, bears cup-shaped, fragrant, blue-violet flowers, to ¾in (2cm) across, singly or in umbels of up to 8. Cultivation group 1, 3, or 4. ↕↔ 4in (10cm). Wet, acidic alpine meadows in E. Alps and C. Balkans. Zone 5.

***P.* Gold Laced Group** ■ Erect, semi-evergreen or evergreen Polyanthus Group primroses with oval, sometimes red-tinged, mid-green leaves, 7in (18cm) long. Early in the season, bear umbels of 3–12 salverform, golden-eyed, very dark mahogany-red or black flowers, to 1¼in (3cm) across, each petal with a narrow gold margin. Cultivation group 1 or 2. ↕ 10in (25cm), ↔ 12in (30cm). Zone 5.

P. gracilipes ■ Rosette-forming, evergreen or semi-evergreen perennial with oblong to spoon-shaped to elliptic, toothed, mid-green leaves, to 6in (15cm) long. Early in the season, umbels of salverform, purple-pink flowers, ½–1in (1.5–2.5cm) across, with white-bordered, orange-yellow eyes, are borne on very short stems hidden within the foliage. Cultivation group 3 or 4. ↕ 4in (10cm), ↔ 8in (20cm). Moist alpine regions in S.E. Tibet and C. Nepal. Zone 5.

P. halleri. Rosette-forming, deciduous perennial with inversely lance-shaped, elliptic to obovate, sometimes finely toothed, white-mealy, mid-green leaves, to 3in (8cm) long. Thick stems bear umbels of up to 20 salverform, yellow-eyed, lilac-pink flowers, to ¾in (2cm) across, early in the season. Cultivation group 2 or 4. ↕ 12in (30cm), ↔ 10in (25cm). Stony alpine meadows in Alps, Carpathians, and Balkans. Zone 5.

Primula florindae

Primula frondosa

Primula 'Garryarde Guinevere'

Primula Gold Laced Group

Primula gracilipes

Primula hirsuta

Primula 'Inverewe'

Primula 'Iris Mainwaring'

Primula japonica 'Miller's Crimson'

Primula japonica 'Postford White'

P. heucherifolia. Rosette-forming, stoloniferous, hairy, deciduous perennial with long-stalked, rounded leaves, to 6in (15cm) long, with 7–11 rounded lobes. Slender stems bear 3–10 pendent, bell-shaped, mauve-pink to rich purple flowers, ½–1in (1–2.5cm) across, in midseason. Cultivation group 2. ↕↔ 12in (30cm). Shady, rocky hillsides in China (Sichuan). Zone 5b.

P. hirsuta ■ syn. *P. rubra.* Rosette-forming, evergreen perennial with spoon-shaped to obovate, toothed, glandular-hairy, mid-green leaves, to 3in (8cm) long. Early in the season, salverform, usually white-eyed, mauve-pink flowers, ½–1in (1.5–2.5cm) across, are borne singly or in umbels of up to 15, on short stems. Cultivation group 1 or 4. ↕ 4in (10cm), ↔ 10in (25cm). Pyrenees, Alps. Zone 4.

P. hongshanensis. Rosette-forming deciduous perennial with toothed to entire, lance-shaped, entire leaves white-mealy underneath, to 8–16in (20–40cm) long. In midseason, produces umbels of 2–5 amethyst-pink flowers ¾–1¼in (2–3cm) across, with a large white-mealy eye. Cultivation group 1 or 2. ↕ 10–20in (25–50cm), ↔ 16–32in (40–80cm). Cool summer areas in N.W. Yunnan, China. Zone 6.

***P.* 'Inverewe'** ■ Vigorous, rosette-forming, semi-evergreen Candelabra primrose with oval to lance-shaped, toothed, coarse, mid-green leaves, to 8in (20cm) long. In mid- and late season, many stems bear several whorls of 5–15 salverform, brilliant red flowers, to 1¼in (3cm) across. Cultivation group 2. ↕ 30in (75cm), ↔ 24in (60cm). Zone 4.

P. involucrata. Rosette-forming, deciduous perennial with ovate to oblong, entire or finely toothed, mid-green leaves, to 6in (15cm) long. In midseason, long, slender stems bear umbels of 2–6 pendent, shallowly tubular to bell-shaped, yellow-eyed white flowers, ½–¾in (1.5–2cm) across. Cultivation group 2. ↕↔ 12in (30cm). Moist alpine meadows from Pakistan to S.W. China. Zone 5.

P. ioessa. Rosette-forming, deciduous perennial with narrowly oblong or inversely lance-shaped to spoon-shaped, deeply toothed, mid-green leaves, to 8in (20cm) long. Late in the season, bears umbels of 2–8 pendent, tubular to funnel-shaped, white-mealy, fragrant, mauve-pink to violet or white flowers, 1in (2.5cm) across. Cultivation group 2, 3, or 4. ↕↔ 12in (30cm). Wet alpine meadows in S.E. Tibet. Zone 5.

***P.* 'Iris Mainwaring'** ■ Compact, rosette-forming, evergreen or semi-evergreen Juliana hybrid with oval, deep green leaves, to 7in (18cm) long. Early in the season, bears solitary, delicate, salverform, mauve flowers, 1½in (4cm) across, with yellow centers. Cultivation group 1, 2, or 4. ↕ 4–6in (10–15cm), ↔ 12–16in (30–40cm). Zone 4.

P. japonica (Japanese primrose). Robust, rosette-forming, deciduous perennial with obovate to oblong, broadly spoon-shaped, finely scalloped or toothed, light green leaves, to 10in (25cm) long. Stems bear 1–6 whorls of 5–25 salverform, red-purple to white flowers, ¾in (2cm) across, in midseason. Cultivation group 2. ↕↔ 18in (45cm). Moist, shady places in Japan. Zone 3. **'Miller's Crimson'** ■ has crimson flowers. **'Postford White'** ■ produces red-eyed, clear white flowers.

P

Primula Joker Series

Primula x *kewensis* 'Mountain Spring'

Primula 'Linda Pope'

Primula 'Linnet'

Primula marginata 'Kesselring's Variety'

Primula 'Mark'

Primula modesta var. *faurieae*

Primula obconica Cantata Series 'Cantata Lavender'

Primula obconica 'Queen of the Market'

P. 'Jay-Jay'. Compact, rosette-forming, semi-evergreen, Juliana hybrid with obovate, deep green leaves, to 6in (15cm) long. Early in the season, salverform, dark red flowers are borne singly above a modified calyx of bract-like leaves. Cultivation group 1 or 2. ↕5in (13cm), ↔ 12–16in (30–40cm). Zone 4.

P. jesoana. Rosette-forming, hairy, deciduous or semi-evergreen perennial with rounded, deeply 7- to 9-lobed, mid-green leaves, to 12in (30cm) long. Slender stems each bear 1–4 umbels of 2–6 shallowly tubular to bell-shaped, yellow-eyed, pinkish purple or white flowers, ¾in (2cm) across, in midseason. Cultivation group 2 or 4. ↕↔ 12in (30cm). Mountain areas in C. Japan. Zone 4.

P. 'Johanna'. Rosette-forming, deciduous perennial bearing inversely lance-shaped, mid-green leaves, to ¾in (2cm) long. Early in the season, bears few-flowered umbels of salverform, yellow-eyed, clear pink flowers, ½in (1.5cm) across. Cultivation group 2 or 4. ↕4in (10cm), ↔ 6in (15cm). Zone 4.

P. Joker Series ▣ Compact, rosette-forming, evergreen or semi-evergreen Primrose Group primulas with small, short-stemmed, inversely lance-shaped to obovate, mid-green leaves, 4in (10cm) long. Bear salverform flowers, 1¾in (4.5cm) across, in a range of colors, including numerous bicolors, with prominent yellow or creamy yellow eyes, early in the season. Cultivation group 2 or 6. ↕3–4in (8–10cm), ↔ 8in (20cm). Zone 5.

P. juliae. Rosette-forming, semi-evergreen or deciduous perennial with rounded, scalloped, dark green leaves, to 2½in (6cm) long, deeply heart-shaped at the bases. Early in the season, produces solitary, long-stalked, saucer-shaped, magenta flowers, to 1in (2.5cm) across, with yellow eyes. Cultivation group 1, 2, or 4. ↕3in (8cm), ↔ 10in (25cm). Rocky mountain forest in E. Caucasus. Zone 4.

P. x kewensis (*P. floribunda* x *P. simensis*). Rosette-forming, evergreen perennial with obovate to spoon-shaped, toothed, sparsely white-mealy, mid-green leaves, 6in (15cm) long. Each stem bears 2–5 whorls of 6–10 long-tubed, salverform, fragrant yellow flowers, to ¾in (2cm) across, early in the season. Cultivation group 6. ↕to 18in (45cm), ↔ 8in (20cm). Garden origin. ❀ (min. 41°F/5°C). **'Mountain Spring'** ▣ is compact, and bears bright golden yellow flowers; ↕to 10in (25cm). **'Thurgold'** has clear lemon-yellow flowers.

P. 'Kinlough Beauty'. Vigorous, evergreen or semi-evergreen Juliana hybrid with oval, dark green leaves, to 6in (15cm) long. Early in the season, salverform, salmon-pink flowers, 1½in (4cm) across, with lighter pink stripes, are produced in umbels of 3–12. Cultivation group 1, 2, or 4. ↕4–6in (10–15cm), ↔ 12–16in (30–40cm). Zone 4.

P. kisoana. Rosette-forming, hairy, deciduous perennial with rounded, shallowly lobed, mid-green leaves, to 6in (15cm) long. In midseason, produces umbels of 2–6 tubular to funnel-shaped, rose to white flowers, to 1¼in (3cm) across. Cultivation group 2 or 3. ↕8in (20cm), ↔ 16in (40cm). Woodland in S.W. Japan. Zone 4.

P. 'Lady Greer'. Dainty, evergreen or semi-evergreen Juliana hybrid with spoon-shaped, bottle-green leaves, to 5in (13cm) long. Early in the season, bears umbels of funnel-shaped, pale yellow flowers, ¾in (2cm) across. Cultivation group 2 or 3. ↕4–6in (10–15cm), ↔ 12–16in (30–40cm). Zone 4.

P. latifolia. Rosette-forming, deciduous perennial with broadly lance-shaped, glandular-hairy, dull green leaves, to 6in (15cm) long, sometimes toothed at the tips. One-sided umbels of 2–25 salverform, sometimes white-mealy, fragrant, red-purple flowers, ½–¾in (1.5–2cm) across, are produced in midseason. Cultivation group 1, 2, or 4. ↕8in (20cm), ↔ 12in (30cm). Moist, shady, acidic cliffs in Pyrenees and Alps. Zone 4.

P. 'Linda Pope' ▣ syn. *P. marginata* 'Linda Pope'. Vigorous, rosette-forming, evergreen or semi-evergreen perennial with oval, toothed, white-mealy, mid-green leaves, 4in (10cm) long. Umbels of 4–16 salverform, mauve-blue flowers, to 1¼in (3cm) across, with white-mealy eyes, are borne early in the season. Cultivation group 4 or 5. ↕6in (15cm), ↔ 12in (30cm). Zone 4.

P. 'Linnet' ▣ Rosette-forming, evergreen perennial with obovate, mid-green leaves, to 3in (8cm) long. Early in the season, bears umbels of salverform, yellow-eyed, rose-pink flowers, 1¼in (3cm) across. Cultivation group 3 or 4. ↕4in (10cm), ↔ 8in (20cm). Zone 5.

P. 'Lismore Yellow'. Rosette-forming, evergreen perennial with ovate, dark green leaves, to 1¼in (3cm) long. In early and midseason, very short stems bear umbels of 2–5 open funnel-shaped, pale yellow flowers, 1in (2.5cm) across. Cultivation group 4 or 5. ↕4in (10cm), ↔ 6in (15cm). Zone 5.

P. 'Lovebird'. Show Auricula primrose with spoon-shaped to ovate, white-mealy, dark green leaves, 5in (13cm) long. In early and midseason, salverform, black flowers, 1in (2.5cm) across, with gray margins, white centers, and yellow tubes, are borne in umbels of 4–8. Cultivation group 4. ↕6in (15cm), ↔ 5in (13cm). Zone 4.

P. luteola. Rosette-forming, deciduous perennial with lance-shaped, sharply double-toothed, mid-green leaves, to 12in (30cm) long. In midseason, robust, white-mealy stems bear symmetrical to spherical umbels of 10–25 salverform yellow flowers, ½in (1.5cm) across. Cultivation group 1 or 2. ↕14in (35cm), ↔ 18in (45cm). Moist meadows in E. Caucasus. Zone 5.

P. macrophylla. Short-lived, rosette-forming, deciduous perennial with lance-shaped to inversely lance-shaped, entire or finely scalloped, mid-green leaves, to 10in (25cm) long, usually white-mealy beneath. Late in the season, white-mealy stems produce umbels of 5–25 salverform purple flowers, ¾in (2cm) across; the eyes are usually darker or tinged yellow. Cultivation group 2 or 4. ↕10in (25cm), ↔ 12in (30cm). Rocky alpine meadows in Himalayas. Zone 4.

P. malacoides (Fairy primrose). Erect, rosette-forming, evergreen perennial, usually grown as an annual, with dainty, oval, slightly frilly-margined, softly downy, pale green leaves, to 4in (10cm) long. Early in the season, flat, single or double, pale lilac-purple, red-pink, or white flowers, to ½in (1.5cm) across, are borne in whorls of decreasing size up slender, softly hairy stems. Cultivation group 6. ↕12–18in (30–45cm), ↔ 8in (20cm). China. ❀ (min. 35°F/2°C)

P. marginata. Rosette-forming, evergreen or semi-evergreen perennial

Primula Polyanthus Group Cowichan Series

with obovate to oblong, toothed, leathery, mid-green leaves, to 4in (10cm) long, white-mealy on the margins. Early in the season, white-mealy stems each bear a symmetrical umbel of 2–20 shallowly tubular to funnel-shaped, faintly fragrant, lavender-blue flowers, to ¾in (2cm) across, with white-mealy eyes. Cultivation group 4 or 5. ↕6in (15cm), ↔ 12in (30cm). Europe (Alps). Zone 4. **'Hyacinthia'** see *P.* 'Hyacinthia'. **'Ivy Agee'** is vigorous in habit, with heavily white-mealy leaves and lilac-blue flowers with cream eyes. **'Kesselring's Variety'** ▣ is moderately vigorous, bearing deep lavender-blue flowers. **'Linda Pope'** see *P.* 'Linda Pope'.

P. 'Mark' ▣ Vigorous alpine Auricula primrose with oval, vibrant green leaves, to 5in (13cm) long. In early and midseason, bears salverform, light-centered, wine-purple to pink flowers, 1in (2.5cm) across. Cultivation group 4. ↕↔ 4in (10cm). Zone 4.

P. 'Marven'. Rosette-forming, evergreen or semi-evergreen *P. marginata* hybrid with white-mealy, ovate or obovate-oblong, light green leaves, to 4in (10cm) long. Early in the season, produces umbels of up to 15 tubular to funnel-shaped, deep violet-blue flowers, ¾in (2cm) across, each with a very dark eye, bordered by a white-mealy zone. Cultivation group 4 or 5. ↕4in (10cm), ↔ 10in (25cm). Zone 4.

P. 'McWatt's Cream'. Rosette-forming, evergreen or semi-evergreen Polyanthus Group primrose with short scapes and spoon-shaped, deep green leaves, 5in (13cm) long. Early in the season, bears 3- to 12-flowered umbels of salverform cream flowers, ¾in (2cm) across. Cultivation group 1, 2, or 4. ↕4–6in (10–15cm), ↔ 12–16in (30–40cm). Zone 5.

P. melanops, syn. *P. chionantha* subsp. *melanops.* Rosette-forming, deciduous perennial with lance-shaped, toothed or scalloped, mid-green leaves, to 10in (25cm) long, white-mealy beneath. In mid- and late season, white-mealy stems each bear 1 or 2 umbels of 5–12, narrowly tubular to bell-shaped, fragrant, black-eyed purple flowers, ¾in (2cm) across. Cultivation group 2. ↕14in (35cm), ↔ 20in (50cm). Alpine meadows in China. Zone 4.

P. minima. Dwarf, rosette-forming, evergreen perennial with wedge-shaped, leathery, sharply toothed, shiny, dark

‑een leaves, to 1¼in (3cm) long.
ı midseason, very short stems each
‑oduce 1, sometimes 2 salverform,
hite-eyed, rose-pink, lilac, or white
owers, to 1¼in (3cm) across.
ultivation group 2 or 4. ↕ 3in (8cm),
‑ 8in (20cm). Alpine meadows in
. Alps and Balkans. Zone 4.
. *modesta.* Rosette-forming, deciduous
‑rennial with elliptic to spoon-shaped,
avy-margined or toothed, mid-green
aves, to 3in (8cm) long, yellow-mealy
‑neath. Early in the season, produces
nbels of 2–15 salverform, purple-pink
owers, ½in (1.5cm) across. Cultivation
oup 1 or 4. ↕↔ 8in (20cm). Moist
pine meadows in Japan. Zone 4.
ır. *faurieae* ■ is smaller, with yellow-
‑ed, pinkish purple flowers, and
oadly ovate, yellow-mealy leaves with
lled-back margins.
. *nana* see *P. edgeworthii.*
. *nutans* of gardens see *P. flaccida.*
. *obconica.* Erect, rosette-forming,
‑ergreen perennial, usually grown as an
ınual, with fairly coarse, oval to heart-
aped, toothed, mid-green leaves, to
n (15cm) long. Very early in the
ason, produces salverform, pink, lilac-
ue, red, or white flowers, 1–2in
.5–5cm) across, sometimes with
ghtly frilled petal margins, in whorls
‑ decreasing size up thick, hairy stems.
he foliage may irritate skin upon
ntact and cause mild stomach upset
ingested. Cultivation group 6.
)–16in (23–40cm), ↔ to 10in (25cm).
hina. ❄ (min. 45°F/7°C). Cultivars of
antata Series are long-blooming, with
owers in carmine-red, pink, rose-pink,
ricot-pink, lavender-blue, or white;
1 0–12in (25–30cm); **'Cantata
avender'** ■ bears lavender-blue
owers. **Juno Series** cultivars are early
ıd free-flowering in a variety of soft
lors; ↕↔ 10in (25cm). ❄ (min.
5°F/7°C). **Libre Series** cultivars are
stel-colored and produce little or no
‑imin, the skin-irritating substance
und in the foliage of other obconicas;
↔ 10in (25cm); ❄ (min. 45°F/7°C).

‑imula pulverulenta 'Bartley Strain'

'Queen of the Market' ■ has red-pink flowers; ↕ to 8in (20cm).
***P.* 'Old Yellow Dusty Miller'.** Vigorous border Auricula primrose with spoon-shaped, white-mealy, mid-green leaves, to 5in (13cm) long. Early in the season, bears salverform yellow flowers, 1¼in (3cm) across, with white-mealy eyes. Cultivation group 1 or 4. ↕ 6in (15cm), ↔ 10in (25cm). Zone 4.
P. palinuri ■ Rosette-forming, evergreen perennial with spoon-shaped to oblong-ovate, sometimes glandular-hairy, more or less toothed, fleshy, mid-green leaves, to 8in (20cm) long. Very early in the season, thick stems bear umbels of 3–40 nodding, narrowly funnel-shaped, scented, white-mealy-eyed yellow flowers, ½in (1.5cm) across. Cultivation group 1 or 4; grows in full sun. ↕↔ 12in (30cm). Coastal cliffs in S. Italy. Zone 6.
***P.* 'Parakeet'.** Show Auricula primrose with broadly ovate, mid-green leaves, to 4in (10cm) long. In early and mid-season, bears umbels of 5–8 salverform, bright yellow and green flowers, 1¼in (3cm) across, with white-mealy centers. Cultivation group 4. ↕ 6in (15cm), ↔ 5in (13cm). Zone 4.
P. parryi. Rosette-forming, deciduous perennial with obovate to inversely lance-shaped, leathery, entire or finely toothed, mid-green leaves, to 14in (35cm) long, covered in short glands. In midseason, thick, erect stems bear one-sided umbels of 3–20 pendent, funnel-shaped, strongly scented, red-purple to magenta flowers, to 1¼in (3cm) across, with yellow eyes. Cultivation group 1 or 2. ↕↔ 18in (45cm). Shady mountain areas in W. US. Zone 4.
***P.* 'Peter Klein'.** Rosette-forming, semi-evergreen or deciduous perennial with rounded to ovate, bright mid-green leaves, to 2½in (6cm) long. Early in the season, thick stems bear umbels of 2–5 salverform, bright, deep pink flowers, 1in (2.5cm) across. Cultivation group 2 or 4. ↕↔ 6in (15cm). Zone 4.
P. petiolaris ■ Rosette-forming, evergreen perennial with spoon-shaped, finely toothed, mid-green leaves, to 4in (10cm) long. Early in the season, salverform, magenta-purple flowers, ¾in (2cm) across, yellow-eyed and with thin white borders, are borne singly on short stalks, ¾–2in (2–5cm) long. Cultivation group 3 or 4. ↕ 4in (10cm), ↔ 8in (20cm). Himalayas. Zone 4.
***P.* Polyanthus Group** (Polyanthus). Rosette-forming, evergreen to semi-evergreen perennials of garden origin, with a complicated parentage believed to include *P. veris, P. elatior,* and *P. vulgaris.* They form sturdy rosettes of oval, heavily veined, dark green leaves, to 7in (18cm) long, almost corrugated in appearance. Large, salverform, mostly yellow-centered, red, blue, orange, yellow, white, or pink flowers, to 2in (5cm) across, are borne in umbels of 3–15 on thick, hairy stems, to 6in (15cm) long, early in the season. Some seed mixtures are available that produce attractive bedding plants. Cultivation group 1, 2, 4, or 6. Zone 5.
Cowichan Series ■ cultivars bear bronze-flushed foliage, and flowers in strong, velvety, yellow, blue, red, maroon, or purple, without central yellow eyes. **Crescendo Series** ■ cultivars bear large, yellow-centered

Primula palinuri

Primula petiolaris

Primula Polyanthus Group Crescendo Series

Primula polyneura

Primula prolifera

Primula Prominent Series

Primula x *pubescens* 'Mrs. J.H. Wilson'

Primula pulverulenta

Primula reidii var. *williamsii*

flowers, 2in (5cm) across, available in a number of separate colors. Cultivars of **Rainbow Series** are short-stemmed, with yellow-centered flowers in blue, creamy yellow, pink, carmine-red, scarlet-red, white, or yellow, as well as some unusual rust-orange shades.
P. polyneura ■ Rosette-forming, deciduous perennial with ovate to rounded, 7- to 11-lobed, mid-green leaves, to 12in (30cm) long. Each stem produces 1–3 umbels, each with 2–12 salverform, yellow-eyed, purplish pink flowers, 1in (2.5cm) across, in midseason. Cultivation group 2. ↕↔ 18in (45cm). Woodland in W. China. Zone 4.
P. prolifera ■ Rosette-forming, evergreen Candelabra primrose with spoon-shaped to diamond-shaped, finely toothed, deep green leaves, to 14in (35cm) long. In mid- and late season, thick stems bear 1–7 whorls of 3–12 salverform, fragrant, white-mealy, pale to golden yellow or occasionally dull violet flowers, 1in (2.5cm) across. Cultivation group 2. ↕↔ 24in (60cm). Moist, shady alpine areas from India (Assam) to S.W. China, N. Burma, and Indonesia (Sumatra, Java). Zone 5.
***P.* Prominent Series** ■ Dwarf, compact, semi-evergreen or evergreen Primrose Group primulas with inversely lance-shaped to obovate, mid-green leaves, 4in (10cm) long. Very early in the season, salverform flowers, 1½–2in (4–5cm) across, are borne in a very wide range of colors, including bicolors. Cultivation group 6. ↕ 3–4in (8–10cm), ↔ 6–8in (15–20cm). Zone 5.
P.* x *pubescens (*P. auricula* x *P. hirsuta*). Vigorous, rosette-forming, evergreen perennial with obovate to broadly spoon-shaped, sometimes entire, white-mealy, usually mid-green leaves, to 4in (10cm) long. Umbels of few to many salverform flowers, ½–1in (1.5–2.5cm) across, in white, yellow, pink, red, purple, or brown, are borne very freely early in the season. Cultivation group 1 or 4. ↕ to 6in (15cm), ↔ 12in (30cm). Garden origin. Zone 4. **'Faldonside'** bears dusky red-pink flowers with white eyes; ↕ 3–4in (7–10cm). **'Harlow Car'** has shallowly toothed leaves and large, creamy white flowers, 1¼in (3cm) across; ↕ 3–4in (7–10cm). **'Mrs. J.H. Wilson'** ■ bears compact rosettes of lance-shaped to obovate, rather thick, gray-green leaves and fragrant, white-eyed purple flowers; ↕ 3in (8cm). **'Rufus'** has shallowly toothed, pale green leaves and umbels of up to 16 large, almost brick-red flowers, to 1¼in (3cm) across, with golden yellow eyes; ↕ 3–4in (8–10cm).
P. pulverulenta ■ Rosette-forming, deciduous Candelabra primrose with obovate or inversely lance-shaped, finely toothed, mid-green leaves, to 12in (30cm) long. In midseason, thick, white-mealy stems each bear several whorls of tubular, deep red or red-purple flowers, 1in (2.5cm) across, with darker red or purple eyes. Cultivation group 2. ↕ to 3ft (1m), ↔ 24in (60cm). Wet hillsides in China (Sichuan). Zone 4. **'Bartley Strain'** ■ has shell-pink flowers with red eyes.
P. reidii. Robust, rosette-forming, deciduous perennial with oblong to oblong-lance-shaped, scalloped or lobed leaves, to 8in (20cm) long. Late in the season, bears compact umbels of 3–10 pendent, bell-shaped, fragrant white flowers, 1in (2.5cm) across, often white-mealy on the outsides. Cultivation group 3 or 4. ↕ 2–6in (5–15cm), ↔ 5–6in (10–15cm). N.E. India to C. Nepal (Himalayas). Zone 5.
var. *williamsii* ■ is more robust, with flowers that are pale blue to white; ↕↔ 6in (15cm); W. and C. Nepal.

P

Primula rosea

Primula rusbyi

Primula scotica

Primula secundiflora

Primula sieboldii 'Wine Lady'

Primula sonchifolia

Primula tschuktschorum

Primula veris

Primula warshenewskiana

***P.* 'Remus'.** Show Auricula primrose with ovate to rounded, mid-green leaves, to 4in (10cm) long. In early and midseason, salverform flowers, 1¼in (3cm) across, with dark blue petals, white centers, and yellow tubes, are borne in umbels of 6–10. Cultivation group 4. ↕ 6in (15cm), ↔ 5in (13cm). Zone 5.

P. rosea ■ Rosette-forming, deciduous perennial bearing obovate to inversely lance-shaped, scalloped or finely toothed, mid-green, often bronze-flushed leaves, to 8in (20cm) long, tinted red-bronze at first, emerging after the flowers. Umbels of 4–12 salverform, yellow-eyed, red-pink flowers, to 1in (2.5cm) across, are produced early in the season. Cultivation group 2. ↕↔ 8in (20cm). Wet meadows from Afghanistan to Nepal. Zone 4. **'Grandiflora'** is vigorous, producing larger flowers, to 1¼in (3cm) across; ↕ to 8in (20cm).

P

Primula vialii

P. rubra see *P. hirsuta.*

P. rusbyi ■ Rosette-forming, deciduous perennial with elliptic to spoon-shaped, entire or toothed, glandular-hairy, mid-green leaves, 1¼–4in (3–10cm) long. One-sided umbels of 4–12 salverform, rose-red to deep purple flowers, 1¼in (3cm) across, are produced in mid-season. Cultivation group 3 or 4. ↕ 8in (20cm), ↔ 14in (35cm). S.E. Arizona, S.W. New Mexico. Zone 4.

P. saxatilis see *P. cortusoides.*

***P.* 'Schneekissen'**, syn. *P.* 'Snow Cushion'. Very compact, rosette-forming, evergreen Juliana hybrid with rounded, pale green leaves, 4in (10cm) long. Short stems bear solitary, salver-form, pure white flowers, 1in (2.5cm) across, early in the season. Cultivation group 1, 2, or 4. ↕ 3–4in (8–10cm), ↔ 8in (20cm). Zone 4.

P. scotica ■ Dwarf rosette-forming plant with oblong to elliptic or spoon-shaped, mealy leaves, to 0.5–2in (1–5cm) long. Short stems bear 1–6 fragrant, violet to bright red-purple, white or yellow-eyed flowers, ⅕–½in (0.5–1.0cm), early to midseason. Often reblooms late in the season. Cultivation group 1, 2, or 4. ↕ to 4in (to 10cm), ↔ 1¼–3in (4–8cm). Sand-dune and limestone turf with wind-blown sand, near the sea on the north coast of Scotland. Zone 5.

P. secundiflora ■ Rosette-forming, evergreen or semi-evergreen perennial with oblong to obovate or inversely lance-shaped, mid-green leaves, to 12in (30cm) long, with scalloped to toothed margins, and yellow-mealy beneath when young. Late in the season, thick stems produce one-sided umbels of 5–20 nodding, tubular to bell-shaped, red-purple or deep rose-red flowers, 1in (2.5cm) across. Cultivation group 1 or 2. ↕ 24–36in (60–90cm), ↔ 24in (60cm). Wet alpine meadows in S.E. Tibet and W. China. Zone 4.

P. sieboldii. Rosette-forming, deciduous perennial with oblong-ovate, lobed, toothed, downy, pale green leaves, to 8in (20cm) long. Early in the season, bears umbels of 2–15 salverform flowers, 1in (2.5cm) across; the flowers are pink to lilac-purple or deep crimson, with white eyes, sometimes pure white. Cultivation group 1 or 2. ↕ 12in (30cm), ↔ 18in (45cm). Moist meadows and woodland in Japan. Zone 4. **'Musashino'** is vigorous, and bears large, pale rose-pink flowers, 1½in (4cm) across, darker beneath. **'Shi-un'** produces fringed flowers that are dark lavender-pink, fading to lavender-blue. **'Snowflake'** is vigorous, producing large white flowers, 1½in (4cm) across, with deeply cut petals. **'Sumina'** bears large, wisteria-blue flowers, 1¼in (3cm) across. **'Wine Lady'** ■ produces white flowers, flushed with purple-red.

P. sikkimensis (Himalayan cowslip). Rosette-forming, deciduous perennial with oblong to lance-shaped, elliptic or oblong to inversely lance-shaped, toothed, shining, pale green leaves, to 12in (30cm) long. Produces umbels of numerous pendent, fragrant, funnel-shaped, white-mealy, yellow or cream flowers, 1in (2.5cm) across, late in the season. Cultivation group 2. ↕ 24–36in (60–90cm), ↔ 24in (60cm). Wet meadows in Himalayas (W. Nepal to S.W. China). Zone 3.

P. sinopurpurea. Rosette-forming, deciduous perennial with oblong-lance-shaped, mid-green leaves, 2–14in (5–35cm) long, yellow-mealy beneath. In midseason, produces nodding, tubular to funnel-shaped, magenta, purple, and violet flowers, to 1¼in (3cm) across, with pale purple eyes, in umbels of 6–12. Cultivation group 1 or 2. ↕ 12–18in (30–45cm), ↔ 12–14in (30–35cm). China. Zone 4.

P. sonchifolia ■ Rosette-forming, deciduous perennial with oblong to obovate, mid-green leaves, to 8in (20cm) long, with small, toothed lobes. Early in the season, very short stems (elongating in fruit) bear umbels of 3–20 salverform, yellow-eyed, white-margined, lavender-blue flowers, 1in (2.5cm) across. Overwinters as large, white-mealy buds. Cultivation group 3 or 4. ↕ 2in (5cm), ↔ 12in (30cm). Open meadows near the snow line in China, S.E. Tibet, and Burma. Zone 5.

***P.* 'Springtime'.** Vigorous, rosette-forming, semi-evergreen Juliana hybrid with inversely lance-shaped to obovate, toothed, bright green leaves, to 8in (20cm) long. Early in the season, salverform, pale pink-lilac flowers, 1–1½in (2.5–4cm) across, are borne singly. Cultivation group 1 or 2. ↕ 7in (18cm), ↔ 12in (30cm). Zone 4.

P. suffrutescens. Mat-forming, evergreen perennial with long rhizomes, and rosettes of wedge-shaped to spoon-shaped, scalloped to toothed, fleshy, dusky green leaves, to 1½in (4cm) long. Late in the season, produces umbels of 2–10 salverform, yellow-eyed, rose-pink to red or purple flowers, ¾in (2cm) across. Cultivation group 1 or 4. ↕ 6in (15cm), ↔ 12in (30cm). California, Sierra Nevada Mountains. Zone 5.

P. tschuktschorum ■ Rosette-forming deciduous perennial, with oblong-linear entire leaves, to ¾–1¼in (2–4cm) long. Umbels of 2–5 tiny, lavender, violet-purple flowers, ½–¾in (1–2cm) across, are produced early to midseason. Cultivation group 2. ↕ ¾–4in (2–10cm), ↔ 1¼–3in (4–8cm). Wet meadows, frost boils, and gravel stream edges in Seward Peninsula Alaska, across the Bering Sea in Russia. Zone 6.

P. veris ■ (Cowslip). Very variable, rosette-forming, evergreen or semi-evergreen perennial with oblong-ovate to ovate, sometimes scalloped, mid-green leaves, to 8in (20cm) long. In early and midseason, produces umbels of 2–16 salverform, nodding, fragrant, deep yellow flowers, ½–1in (1.5–2.5cm) across. Cultivation group 1 or 2. ↕↔ 10in (25cm). Europe to W. Asia. Zone 3.

P. vialii ■ Rosette-forming, deciduous, often short-lived perennial with broadly lance-shaped to oblong, toothed, softly hairy, mid-green leaves, to 12in (30cm) long. Stiff, thick, white-mealy stems produce dense spikes, to 6in (15cm) long, of many pendent, tubular, blue-violet flowers, ½in (1.5cm) across, late in the season. In bud, the calyces are bright crimson. Cultivation group 2. ↕ 12–24in (30–60cm), ↔ 12in (30cm). Moist mountain areas in China (Sichuan, Yunnan). Zone 4.

P. villosa. Rosette-forming, evergreen perennial bearing obovate or spoon-shaped to oblong, toothed, fleshy, glandular-hairy leaves, ¾–6in (2–15cm) long. In midseason, red-hairy stems produce umbels of 4–12 salverform, white-eyed, pink to lilac flowers, to 1in (2.5cm) across. Cultivation group 2, 3, or 4. ↕↔ 6in (15cm). Austria (Tyrol). Zone 4.

P. vulgaris, syn. *P. acaulis* (Common primrose). Rosette-forming, evergreen or semi-evergreen perennial with inversely lance-shaped to obovate, toothed to scalloped, deeply veined, bright green leaves, to 10in (25cm) long, softly hairy beneath. Clusters of 3–25 salverform, often fragrant, usually pale yellow flowers, 1–1½in (2.5–4cm) across, are

Primula vulgaris 'Miss Indigo'

borne early in the season. Cultivation group 2. ↕ 8in (20cm), ↔ 14in (35cm). Open woodland and shady banks in Europe and W. Turkey. Zone 4. Many cultivars have been produced, of which some are hybrids, but with a similar habit to the species, and with double flowers. **'Cottage White'**, syn. 'Double White', is vigorous and free-flowering, with fully double white flowers on long stalks. **'Double Sulphur'** is vigorous, bearing sage-green leaves and double yellow flowers. **'Double White'** see 'Cottage White'. **'Marie Crousse'** is vigorous in habit, with large, scented, double violet flowers, 1¼in (3cm) across, splashed with white. **'Miss Indigo'** is vigorous and bears double, deep rich purple flowers with creamy white tips. **'Quaker's Bonnet'** has double, pale lavender flowers. **subsp. *sibthorpii*** ■ has wedge-shaped leaves, with usually rose-pink, red, lilac, purple, or white flowers; Balkans, Ukraine (Crimea), Caucasus, Turkey, Armenia.

***P.* 'Wanda'.** Very vigorous, long-flowering, rosette-forming, evergreen or semi-evergreen Juliana hybrid with oval, toothed, purplish green leaves, to 5in (13cm) long. Bears clusters of solitary, salverform, dark claret-red flowers, to 1½in (4cm) across, early in the season. Thrives in both sun and shade. Cultivation group 1 or 2. ↕ 4–6in (10–15cm), ↔ 12–16in (30–40cm). Zone 4.

***P.* Wanda Supreme Series** ■ Evergreen or semi-evergreen Primrose Group primulas bearing small, inversely lance-shaped to obovate, bronze to dark

Primula Wanda Supreme Series

green leaves, 3–4in (8–10cm) long. Produce flowers, 1½–2in (4–5cm) across, in a mixture of different shades of blue, yellow, purple, burgundy, red, rose, and pink bicolors, early in the season. Cultivation group 1 or 2. ↕ 3–4in (8–10cm), ↔ 6in (15cm). Zone 4.

P. warshenewskiana ■ Rosette-forming, deciduous perennial with oblong to inversely lance-shaped, finely toothed, dark green leaves, to 3in (8cm) long. Salverform, rose-pink flowers, ½in (1.5cm) across, with white-ringed yellow eyes, are borne singly or in umbels of up to 8, on short stems in midseason. Cultivation group 2 or 4. ↕ 3in (8cm), ↔ 6in (15cm). Streamsides and wet ground from Tajikistan to Pakistan. Zone 4.

Primula vulgaris subsp. *sibthorpii*

P. wilsonii* var. *anisodora see *P. anisodora*.

P. wulfeniana. Rosette-forming, evergreen perennial with lance-shaped or elliptic to inversely lance-shaped or obovate, leathery, glandular-hairy, dark green leaves, ½–1½in (1.5–4cm) long. Bears solitary or paired, salverform, rose-red to lilac flowers, to 1in (2.5cm) across, with deeply notched petal lobes, early in the season. Cultivation group 4 or 5. ↕↔ 3in (8cm). Austrian Alps to S. Carpathians. Zone 4.

PRINSEPIA

ROSACEAE

Genus of 4 species of arching, spiny, deciduous shrubs found in woodland and thickets in the Himalayas and China. They are cultivated for their linear to elliptic or oblong-lance-shaped leaves, which are rich green on opening, later glossy or dull dark green. They are also valued for their fragrant, cup-shaped, white to yellow flowers, and for their cherry-like, spherical or ovoid, purple or red fruits, attractive to birds and other wildlife. Grow prinsepias in a shrub border, against a wall, or as a hedge; the leaves appear early, and are an excellent foil for other early-flowering shrubs.

• **CULTIVATION** Grow in fertile, well-drained but not dry soil in full sun, in an open position with room to spread. Pruning group 1; they may be severely pruned for rejuvenation.

• **PROPAGATION** Sow seed in containers in an open frame in autumn. Take greenwood cuttings in early summer.

• **PESTS AND DISEASES** Infrequent.

P. sinensis (Cherry prinsepia). Loose, spreading, deciduous shrub bearing arching, light gray-brown branches with sharp spines and ovate-lance-shaped to lance-shaped, pointed, entire or slightly toothed, finely hairy, bright green leaves, to 3in (8cm) long. In spring, clusters of up to 8 cup-shaped, bright yellow flowers, ½in (1.5cm) across, are borne along the shoots, followed by ovoid, red to purple fruit, ½in (1.5cm) across. ↕ 6ft (2m), ↔ 6–10ft (2–3m). China (Manchuria). Zone 2.

P. uniflora ■ (Hedge prinsepia). Spreading, deciduous shrub with arching shoots bearing sharp spines and alternate, narrowly oblong to linear-oblong, glossy, rich dark green leaves, to 2½in (6cm) long. From early spring to summer, cup-shaped, fragrant white flowers, ½in (1.5cm) across, are produced singly or in clusters along the shoots; they are followed by cherry-like, red or purple fruit, ½in (1.5cm) across. ↕ 5ft (1.5m), ↔ 8ft (2.5m). China (N.W. China, Inner Mongolia). Zone 3.

Prinsepia uniflora

PRITCHARDIA

ARECACEAE

Genus of about 37 species of single-stemmed palms from upland areas with high rainfall, on moist hillsides, and in rainforest valleys on volcanic soils in Fiji, Hawaii, and adjacent Pacific islands. They are cultivated for their fan-shaped, mid-green or silvery or grayish green leaves, which are borne in terminal tufts. They produce small, bell-shaped, white, yellow, or orange flowers in spikes or panicles between the leaves. Where not hardy, grow these palms in a warm greenhouse. In tropical areas, they are suitable for growing as lawn specimens.

• **CULTIVATION** Under glass, grow in soil-based potting mix with added sharp sand, in bright filtered light. When in growth, water freely and apply a liquid fertilizer every month; water sparingly in winter. Outdoors, grow in fertile, moist, well-drained soil in partial shade.

• **PROPAGATION** Sow seed at 75°F (24°C) in spring.

• **PESTS AND DISEASES** Lethal yellowing, leaf spots, scale insects, and spider mites can occur.

P. gaudichaudii ■ Small palm with an erect, columnar trunk and long-stalked, fan-shaped leaves, 3–4ft (1–1.2m) long, deeply cut into many slender lobes, brown-hairy beneath, rich to silvery green above. Bell-shaped yellow flowers are produced in spikes up to 3ft (1m) long, usually in summer. ↕ 6–15ft (2–5m), ↔ 8–11ft (2.5–3.5m). Hawaii. ❄ (min. 61–64°F/16–18°C)

P. pacifica (Fiji fan palm). Small to medium-sized palm with a smooth, slim, columnar trunk. Long-stalked, fan-shaped leaves, 3ft (1m) or more long, are white-downy when young, then smooth, rich green; they are divided for about one-third of their length into slender, pointed lobes. Bell-shaped, white to yellow flowers are borne in stiff panicles, 3ft (1m) long, in summer. ↕ to 30ft (10m), ↔ 12–15ft (4–5m). Fiji. ❄ (min. 61–64°F/16–18°C)

Pritchardia gaudichaudii

PROBOSCIDEA

syn. MARTYNIA

Unicorn plant

PEDALIACEAE

Genus of about 9 species of erect to spreading, robust, frequently sticky-hairy annuals and perennials found in open plains in tropical North, Central, and South America. They are grown for the tropical effect of their foliage and fruits; the fruits can be dried and used for winter arrangements. The opposite, occasionally alternate, long-stemmed, fairly coarse leaves are rounded to ovate-lance-shaped, entire to palmately or pinnately lobed, and strongly veined. The flowers are borne in racemes, and are funnel- to bell-shaped, 5-lobed, and reddish purple, lavender-pink, creamy white, or orange-yellow, with enclosing calyces split to the bases on one side; they are followed by unusually shaped fruits, which each have a pair of strongly upcurved, slender, horn-like beaks or projections at one end, and a fringed crest along the center of the capsule body. The cultivated species are annuals, and are suitable for a mixed border, but are particularly effective on a fence or trellis or when permitted to sprawl among other plants. They may also be grown as decorative container plants in a cool or temperate greenhouse or conservatory.

• **CULTIVATION** Under glass, grow in soil-based potting mix in full light. During the growing season, water freely and apply a balanced liquid fertilizer every 4 weeks. Discard after fruiting. Outdoors, grow in fertile, moist but well-drained soil in full sun.

• **PROPAGATION** Sow seed at 70–75°F (21–24°C) in spring. Pot on and harden off after danger of frost has passed.

• **PESTS AND DISEASES** Infrequent.

P. fragrans. Spreading, thick-stemmed, softly hairy annual bearing rounded, broadly ovate to broadly triangular, 5-lobed leaves, to 10in (25cm) long. In summer, produces loose racemes of 8–20 funnel-shaped, fragrant, reddish purple to purple flowers, to 2in (5cm) across; the upper lobes are marked dark purple, each with a strong yellow band extending into the throat. The flowers are followed by narrow, canoe-shaped, crested fruit, to 2½in (6cm) long, with beak-like projections, to 7in (18cm) long, at one end. ↕ to 18in (45cm), ↔ to 36in (90cm). Texas to Mexico.

P. jussieui see *P. louisianica.*

P. louisianica, syn. *P. jussieui, P. proboscidea* (Common devil's claw, Common unicorn plant, Ram's horn). Erect to spreading, thick-stemmed, softly hairy annual with rounded to broadly ovate, unlobed, wavy-margined leaves, 2½–8in (6–20cm) long. In summer, bears open racemes of 8–20 funnel-shaped, creamy white to purple flowers, 1½–2in (4–5cm) across, flecked reddish purple and marked yellow within the throats; they are followed by crested, boat-shaped fruit, 4–8in (10–20cm) long, each with a pair of horn-like projections at one end that are longer than the fruit body. ↕ to 18in (45cm), ↔ to 36in (90cm). C. and S.E. US.

P. proboscidea see *P. louisianica.*

Promenaea xanthina

PROMENAEA

ORCHIDACEAE

Genus of about 15 species of small, evergreen, epiphytic orchids from Brazil, occurring in forest areas at an altitude of around 5,000ft (1,500m). They produce oval pseudobulbs with 1–3 soft-textured, ovate-lance-shaped, light green, apical leaves. Usually yellow or white flowers are borne in ones or twos, rarely more, in short racemes from the bases of the pseudobulbs, mostly in summer and autumn.

• **CULTIVATION** Cool-growing orchids. Grow in small pots of epiphytic orchid potting mix made with fine bark, or epiphytically on slabs of bark. During summer, provide high humidity and bright filtered light, water freely (taking care not to overwater), and feed at every third watering. In winter, admit full light and water sparingly. See also p.46.

• **PROPAGATION** Divide when the plant fills the pot and flows over the sides, or remove backbulbs.

• **PESTS AND DISEASES** Prone to spider mites, aphids, and mealybugs.

P. stapeloides. Epiphytic orchid bearing fleshy, oval pseudobulbs, each with 1–3 broadly folded, soft-textured, light green leaves, 3in (8cm) long. In summer, bears 1 or rarely 2 greenish yellow flowers, 2in (5cm) across, densely barred and spotted purple, with almost solid purple lips. ↕ 4in (10cm), ↔ 2in (5cm). Brazil. ❄ (min. 54–59°F/12–15°C; max. 82°F/28°C)

P. xanthina ■ Epiphytic orchid with clustered, oval pseudobulbs, each with 2 broadly oval, soft-textured, light green leaves, 2in (5cm) long. Fragrant, lemon-yellow flowers, 1½in (4cm) across, with red-dotted lips, are borne in summer. ↕ 3in (8cm), ↔ 6in (15cm). Brazil. ❄ (min. 55°F/13°C; max. 86°F/30°C)

▷ ***Prosartes*** see *Disporum*

PROSOPIS

Mesquite

FABACEAE

Genus of 44 species of trees, shrubs, and subshrubs from deserts and semi-deserts of S.W. US and Mexico. They have thorny branches, 2-pinnate leaves with many oblong leaflets, and axillary racemes of pea-like flowers. Mesquites are grown for a variety of commercial purposes: the wood is used in grilling, the flowers to make honey, and the seed pods in cattle feed. Use *Prosopis* species to control erosion or to stabilize dunes, or as a windbreak or screen. Where not hardy, grow in a temperate greenhouse.

• **CULTIVATION** Under glass, grow in soil-based potting mix with added sand, in full light at a minimum winter temperature of 40°F (5°C). Water moderately in growth; keep completely dry in winter. Outdoors, grow in dry, sandy soil in full sun. Mesquites do not transplant well because of deep, extensive root systems, so grow on in containers until planting out in their final site. Pruning group 1.

• **PROPAGATION** Sow seed *in situ* when ripe. Remove suckers or root semi-ripe cuttings in sand in mid- and late summer.

• **PESTS AND DISEASES** Rust, white rots, butt rot, and root rot (especially when young or under wet conditions) can be problems.

P. glandulosa (Honey mesquite). Thorny shrub or tree with 2-pinnate leaves, each having 12–34 linear to oblong, mid-green leaflets, to 3in (8cm) long, prominently veined beneath. In spring, produces many fragrant green to cream-white flowers in racemes, to 5½in (14cm) long, followed by yellow seed pods, to 8in (20cm) long, sometimes violet-tinged. ↕ to 28ft (9m), ↔ to 15ft (5m). S.W. US, Mexico. ❄ (min. 45°F/7°C)

PROSTANTHERA

Mint bush

LAMIACEAE

Genus of 50 species of bushy, evergreen shrubs and small trees from heathland and dry forest to rainforest and seashore (some species at subalpine and alpine level) in Australia. They are grown for their simple, entire or toothed, aromatic leaves, borne in opposite pairs, and for their leafy, terminal racemes or panicles of broadly tubular, cup- or bell-shaped, 2-lipped, 5-lobed, white, blue, or purple, occasionally red, yellow, or green flowers. Where not hardy, grow in a cool greenhouse. In warmer areas, grow in a mixed or shrub border, or at the base of a house wall.

• **CULTIVATION** Under glass, grow in soil-based potting mix in full light. When in growth, water moderately and apply a balanced liquid fertilizer monthly; water sparingly in winter. Outdoors, grow in moderately fertile, moist but well-drained soil in full sun.

Prostanthera cuneata

Prostanthera ovalifolia

Pruning group 8, after flowering; hard pruning may be detrimental or fatal.

• **PROPAGATION** Sow seed at 55–64°F (13–18°C) in spring, or take semi-ripe cuttings in summer.

• **PESTS AND DISEASES** Prone to spider mites and whiteflies under glass.

P. cuneata ■ (Alpine mint bush). Bushy, erect to spreading shrub producing tiny, obovate to rounded, entire, glossy, mid- to dark green leaves, ¼in (6mm) long, with wedge-shaped bases and rolled margins, strongly aromatic when crushed. In summer, bears racemes, 8in (20cm) long, of numerous broadly tubular white flowers, ½in (1.5cm) across, with purple and yellow markings within the wide tubes. ↕↔ 12–36in (30–90cm). Australia (subalpine and alpine levels from New South Wales to Tasmania). ❄ (min. 41°F/5°C)

P. nivea (Snowy mint bush). Moderately bushy shrub, erect at first, then spreading, with slender, square-sectioned stems and entire, narrowly lance-shaped to linear, inrolled, bright green leaves, 1–1½in (2.5–4cm) long. In spring and early summer, bears bell-shaped, pure white, sometimes lavender-blue-tinted flowers, to ¾in (2cm) across in racemes to 6in (15cm) long. ↕ 6–10ft (2–3m), ↔ 5–6ft (1.5–2m). S.E. Australia. ❄ (min. 41°F/5°C) **var. *induta*** has lilac flowers and silvery green leaves.

P. ovalifolia ■ (Oval-leaved mint bush). Bushy shrub with erect stems and lance-shaped to inversely lance-shaped, entire, matte, gray-green leaves,

Prostanthera rotundifolia

to ½in (1.5cm) long. In late spring and early summer, an abundance of cup-shaped purple flowers, ½in (1.5cm) across, sometimes mauve, or white tinged with lilac, are borne in leafy, terminal racemes, 2½–3in (6–8cm) long. ↕ 8–12ft (2.5–4m), ↔ 5–8ft (1.5–2.5m). E. Australia. ❀ (min. 41°F/5°C)
P. rotundifolia ■ (Round-leaved mint bush). Bushy, spreading shrub with slender, hoary stems and rounded to ovate, scarcely toothed leaves, to ½in (1.5cm) long, deep green above, paler beneath. In late spring and early summer, bears bell-shaped, purple to lilac-purple flowers, ½in (1.5cm) across, in numerous short racemes, to 3in (8cm) long. ↕ 6–12ft (2–4m), ↔ 3–10ft (1–3m). S.E. Australia (including Tasmania). ❀ (min. 41°F/5°C).
var. *rosea*, syn. 'Chelsea Girl', produces gray-green leaves and light rose-pink flowers with mauve anthers.

PROTEA

PROTEACEAE

Genus of 115 species of evergreen shrubs and, rarely, small, usually upright trees found on rocky hillsides and dry scrub from tropical Africa to South Africa. The leaves are alternate to spiraling, simple, entire, and leathery. Proteas are cultivated for their usually solitary and terminal, mainly cone-like clusters or flat heads of small flowers surrounded by petal-like, green, white, pink to purple, or yellow bracts, each cluster resembling a single, large flower. Each floret is tubular, splitting into 4 sepals to reveal the long, straight or curved, usually colorful style. Where not hardy, grow in a cool, well-ventilated greenhouse. In warmer areas, use in a mixed or shrub border. Larger species are also fine specimen plants.
• **CULTIVATION** Under glass, grow in a mixture of 1 part loam with added charcoal and 3 parts equal measures of grit (or perlite) and peat, in full light. Water moderately during spring and summer; apply a liquid fertilizer of magnesium sulfate and urea, both at half recommended strength, once in spring and again in early autumn. Water sparingly in winter. Outdoors, grow in poor, neutral to acidic, well-drained soil in full sun. Pruning group 1; may need restrictive pruning under glass.
• **PROPAGATION** Sow seed at 55–64°F (13–18°C) as soon as ripe or in spring, or take semi-ripe cuttings in summer.

Protea cynaroides

Protea eximia

• **PESTS AND DISEASES** Magnesium deficiency, *Phytophthora* blight, and dieback can occur. Dieback and general failure to thrive usually indicate that the growing medium is too rich.

P. barbata see *P. speciosa*.
P. barbigera see *P. magnifica*.
P. compacta. Erect, moderately bushy shrub with oblong to elliptic, stalkless, horny-margined leaves, 2–5in (5–13cm) long. In spring and summer, oblong buds open to obovoid flowerheads, 3–4in (8–10cm) across, with bright pink, rarely white bracts, fringed with white hairs. ↕ 8–11ft (2.5–3.5m), ↔ 5–8ft (1.5–2.5m). South Africa (Western Cape). ❀ (min. 41°F/5°C)
P. cynaroides ■ (King protea). Robust-stemmed, sparsely to moderately branched shrub, often spreading with age. Rounded to elliptic leaves are 3–5½in (8–14cm) long, and are borne on stalks 1½–7in (4–18cm) long. From late spring to summer, produces goblet- or bowl-shaped flowerheads, 5–12in (13–30cm) across, with deep crimson-red to pink or cream bracts. ↕↔ 3–6ft (1–2m). South Africa (Western Cape, Eastern Cape). ❀ (min. 41°F/5°C)
P. eximia ■ Large shrub or small tree, rounded to broadly columnar, with fairly robust, sparsely branched stems. Ovate leaves are purple-flushed, silvery green, and glaucous, 2½–4in (6–10cm) long, sometimes with red margins, and heart-shaped at the bases. In spring and summer, oblong to inversely cone-shaped flowerheads, to 5½in (14cm) across, are produced, with red or red-tinted pink bracts, fringed with white hairs. ↕ 10–15ft (3–5m), ↔ 6–10ft (2–3m). South Africa (Western Cape). ❀ (min. 41°F/5°C)
P. longifolia, syn. *P. minor*. Erect to spreading shrub with linear, ascending, stalkless, mid- to deep green leaves, 3½–8in (9–20cm) long. During summer, produces oblong to inversely conical flowerheads, 4in (10cm) long, with greenish white to pink bracts, the inner ones fringed with hairs. ↕ 6–10ft (2–3m), ↔ 5–8ft (1.5–2.5m). South Africa (Western Cape). ❀ (min. 41°F/5°C)
P. magnifica, syn. *P. barbigera* (Woolly-bearded protea). Erect shrub, often spreading when young, with robust stems and oblong or lance-shaped, wavy-margined, grayish green leaves, 4in (10cm) or more long. From spring to summer, produces densely packed flowerheads, 6in (15cm) across, initially narrowly bell-shaped, opening to cup-shaped, with black-tipped white inner bracts and clear pink outer bracts, fringed with white hairs. ↕↔ 5–8ft (1.5–2.5m). South Africa (Western Cape). ❀ (min. 41°F/5°C)
P. mellifera see *P. repens*.
P. minor see *P. longifolia*.
P. repens ■ syn. *P. mellifera* (Honey flower, Sugarbush). Erect, moderately bushy shrub or sometimes small tree bearing erect, linear to lance-shaped leaves, to 6in (15cm) long. From spring to summer, produces flowerheads, obovoid in bud, goblet-shaped when open, to 3½in (9cm) across, with hairless bracts, uniformly cream-white or tipped with dark red to pink, and coated with a sticky resin. ↕ 6–12ft (2–4m), ↔ 5–10ft (1.5–3m). South Africa (Western Cape, Eastern Cape). ❀ (min. 41°F/5°C)
P. scolymocephala. Rounded shrub with linear to spoon-shaped, tapered, wavy-margined, olive-green leaves, 1½–3½in (4–9cm) long. From late spring to summer, bears bowl-shaped flowerheads, to 2in (5cm) across, with creamy green bracts flushed pink at the tips. ↕ 3–5ft (0.9–1.5m), ↔ 30–48in (75–120cm). South Africa (Western Cape). ❀ (min. 41°F/5°C)
P. speciosa, syn. *P. barbata*. Erect, moderately branched shrub with elliptic, leathery, orange-margined, mid-green leaves, 4½in (11cm) long. From summer to autumn, bears oblong-goblet-shaped flowerheads, 3in (8cm) across, with bearded, bright pink to creamy yellow bracts, fringed with tawny brown hairs. ↕ 3ft (1m), ↔ 32in (80cm). South Africa (Western Cape). ❀ (min. 41°F/5°C)

Protea repens (inset: flower detail)

PRUMNOPITYS

PODOCARPACEAE

Genus of 10 species of dioecious, occasionally monoecious, evergreen, coniferous trees from forest in Puerto Rico through the Andes to southern Argentina, and from Malaysia to New Zealand. They are upright trees with whorled shoots, grown mainly for their yew-like foliage. Male and female cones are borne at various times of the year: ovoid or cylindrical male cones are solitary or borne in groups of 2–20; spherical or ovoid female cones are solitary or borne in groups of up to 8. The fruits are like small, upright plums, and are borne in the axils of short sideshoots. Grow as specimen trees or for hedging. Where not hardy, grow in a cool or temperate greenhouse.
• **CULTIVATION** Grow in moderately fertile, moist but well-drained soil in full sun, with shelter from cold, drying winds. Clip hedges in summer.
• **PROPAGATION** Sow seed in containers outdoors in spring. Take semi-ripe cuttings in late summer.
• **PESTS AND DISEASES** Infrequent.

P. andina, syn. *Podocarpus andinus* (Plum yew). Dioecious, ovoid tree, conical when young, frequently with several stems, with smooth, gray-brown bark and shoots that are green for 3 years. Linear, soft, dull bluish green leaves, ¾–1¼in (2–3cm) long, parted below the shoot, are more upright above; each has 2 white bands beneath. Ovoid, yellow male cones, ½–1in (1.5–2.5cm) long, are borne in racemes of 5–20. Plum-shaped, yellowish white fruit, ¾in (2cm) long, have thin, fleshy, edible layers. ↕ 30–70ft (10–20m), ↔ 20–25ft (6–8m). Chile, Argentina. ❀ (min. 35°F/2°C)
P. taxifolia. Dioecious, rounded tree with upright to pendent branches and exfoliating blue-black or brown-tinged purple bark. Linear to sickle-shaped, dark green leaves, ⅜–½in (9–15mm) long, are bronze-tinged, glaucous-green beneath. Stalkless, cylindrical, yellow-tinged, white male cones, to ¼in (6mm) long, are borne in racemes of 15–30. Bears spherical black fruit, to ⅜in (9mm) long. ↕ to 80ft (25m), ↔ 20–25ft (6–8m). New Zealand. ❀ (min. 35°F/2°C)

PRUNELLA

Selfheal

LAMIACEAE

Genus of 7 species of spreading, semi-evergreen perennials, rooting freely at the nodes, occurring on dry grassland, on sunny banks, and in open woodland in Europe, Asia, North Africa, and North America. They are grown for their dense, upright spikes or heads of tubular, 2-lipped, white, pink, or violet flowers. The leaves are linear-lance-shaped to broadly ovate, simple or deeply lobed, often rounded at the bases, and either basal or in tufts on the stems. Selfheals are useful ground-covering plants for banks, for the front of a border, or in a wild garden, where they attract bees and other beneficial insects. They can be extremely vigorous, and must be sited where they will not crowd out smaller plants.

• **CULTIVATION** Grow in any soil in full sun or partial shade. Deadhead to prevent self-seeding.

• **PROPAGATION** Sow seed at 43–54°F (6–12°C) in spring. Divide in spring or autumn.

• **PESTS AND DISEASES** Sometimes affected by slugs and snails. Leaf spots, tar spot, and powdery mildew can occur.

P. grandiflora ■ (Large selfheal). Vigorous, spreading perennial bearing simple, ovate to ovate-lance-shaped, sparsely toothed, deep green leaves, 4in (10cm) long. In summer, leafy stems produce whorls of purple flowers, to 1¼in (3cm) long, with darker lips, in dense, upright spikes. ↕ 6in (15cm), ↔ 3ft (1m) or more. Europe. Zone 3b. **subsp. *grandiflora*** has leaves that are heart-shaped at the bases, and bears flower spikes, to 2in (5cm) long; Europe except Portugal and S.W. Spain. **subsp. *pyrenaica*** produces spear-shaped leaves. **'Pink Loveliness'** bears clear pink flowers. **'White Loveliness'** produces pure white flowers.

Prunella grandiflora

PRUNUS *syn.* AMYGDALUS

Almond, Cherry, Cherry laurel, Nectarine, Peach, Plum

ROSACEAE

Genus of more than 200 species of deciduous or evergreen, upright, rounded, or occasionally spreading trees or shrubs, widely distributed in N. temperate regions and in the Andes of South America and mountains of S.E. Asia. They occur mainly in woodland, woodland margins, and thickets, but also in a range of other habitats, including coastal sands, rocky places, and cliffs. They have alternate, broadly ovate to lance-shaped, elliptic, oblong, or obovate to almost rounded, usually toothed leaves. Ornamental *Prunus* species and cultivars are grown for their white, or pink or red flowers, which are saucer-, bowl-, or cup-shaped, with 5 petals (more in semi-double or double forms); they are usually followed by fleshy, spherical or ovoid fruits (notably edible in *P. americana*, *P. maritima*, and *P. tomentosa*). Some, such as *P. maackii* and *P. serrula*, are also grown for their shiny, colorful bark; many, including *P. sargentii*, have good autumn leaf color; others, such as *P. cerasifera* and *P.* x *cistena*, have attractive purple foliage. Leaves and fruits of many species may cause severe discomfort if ingested.

They are excellent, although often short-lived, specimen trees and shrubs, many being suitable for a small garden. Dense, bushy species, such as *P. laurocerasus* and *P. lusitanica*, are useful for screening and groundcover. *P. cerasifera*, *P.* x *cistena*, *P. incisa*, *P. spinosa*, and *P. tomentosa* are suitable for hedging. Grow shrubby species and their cultivars, such as *P. glandulosa* and *P. triloba*, against a wall or in a shrub border.

• **CULTIVATION** Grow in any moist but well-drained, moderately fertile soil: deciduous species and cultivars in full sun, evergreens in full sun or partial shade. *P. laurocerasus* may become chlorotic on shallow alkaline soil. Pruning group 1 for trees and most deciduous shrubs; group 5 for *P. glandulosa* and *P. triloba* (group 13 if wall-trained); group 8 or 9 for evergreen shrubs. Trim deciduous hedges after flowering, evergreens in early or midspring.

• **PROPAGATION** Sow seed of species in containers outdoors in autumn. Root greenwood cuttings of deciduous species in early summer, and semi-ripe cuttings of evergreens in midsummer, both with bottom heat. Bud cultivars in summer, or graft in early spring.

• **PESTS AND DISEASES** Caterpillars, borers, scale insects, aphids, leaf hoppers, nematode, and eriophyid mites are common. Crown gall, mushroom root rot, canker, dieback, lesions, fireblight, leaf curl, powdery mildew, mosaic and ringspot viruses, and many other diseases can occur.

***P.* 'Accolade'.** Spreading, deciduous tree with oblong, tapered, dark green leaves, to 4in (10cm) long. Bears clusters of 3 semi-double, pale pink flowers, 1½in (4cm) across, that open from dark pink buds in early spring. ↕↔ 25ft (8m). Zone 7.

Prunus americana

***P.* 'Amanogawa'.** Upright, deciduous tree bearing obovate leaves, to 5in (13cm) long, yellowish bronze in spring while still folded, often red, yellow, and green on the same tree, at the same time, in autumn. In midspring, produces dense clusters of saucer-shaped or semi-double, fragrant, pale pink flowers, 1½in (4cm) across, held vertically on thick stalks. ↕ 25ft (8m), ↔ 12ft (4m). Zone 6.

P. americana ■ (American plum). Spreading, deciduous shrub producing obovate to oblong-ovate, doubly toothed, hairless, dark green leaves, 2–4in (5–10cm) long. Before the leaves in early spring, bears stalkless umbels of 2–5 bowl-shaped, pure white flowers, 1in (2.5cm) across; they are followed by spherical, yellow to red fruit, 1in (2.5cm) across. ↕ 15–25ft (5–8m), ↔ 10–15ft (3–5m). Manitoba to Massachusetts, south to Utah, New Mexico, and Georgia. Zone 2b.

P.* x *amygdalopersica (*P. dulcis* x *P. persica*) syn. *P.* x *persicoides*. Spreading, deciduous tree bearing lance-shaped tapered, mid-green leaves, to 5in (13cm) long, with sharply toothed margins. Solitary, saucer-shaped, light pink flowers, 2in (5cm) across, are borne in early and midspring, followed by spherical, peach-like, dry-fleshed green fruit, 1½in (4cm) across. ↕↔ 22ft (7m). Garden origin. Zone 7. **'Pollardii'** produces large, rich pink flowers in early spring.

P. armeniaca (Apricot). Small, deciduous, round-crown tree with reddish bark, simple heart-shaped, glossy leaves 3–5in (7–12cm) long. Bears cup-shaped white to pinkish flowers, 1in (2.5cm) across, on bare branches, followed by yellow to orange edible drupes, 1½–2 in (3–5 cm) long. Needs long, hot, dry summers and chilly winters with little risk of late frost. ↕↔ 15ft (5m). Japan, China, Korea. Zone 6.

P. avium ■ (Bird cherry, Gean). Spreading, deciduous tree with red-banded bark and ovate-oblong, dark green leaves, to 6in (15cm) long, bronze when young, turning red and yellow in autumn. In midspring, bears umbels of bowl-shaped white flowers, 1¼in (3cm) across, followed by heart-shaped to ovoid red fruit, ½in (1.5cm) across. ↕ 70ft (20m), ↔ 30ft (10m). Europe, N. Africa, S.W. Asia, Russia (W. Siberia). Zone 4b. **'Plena'** ■ has double flowers and red autumn color; ↕↔ 40ft (12m).

Prunus cerasifera 'Nigra' (inset: flower detail)

***P.* x *blireana*.** Spreading, deciduous shrub or small tree bearing ovate, red-purple leaves, to 2½in (6cm) long, turning dark green in summer. Solitary, double pink flowers, 1¼in (3cm) across, are produced before the leaves in early and midspring. ↕↔ 12ft (4m). Garden origin. Zone 6.
P. campanulata (Bell-flowered cherry, Taiwan cherry). Spreading, deciduous tree bearing ovate, tapered mid-green leaves, to 4in (10cm) long. Shallowly bowl-shaped, pink or red flowers, ¾in (2cm) across, in umbels of 2–5, are borne before or with the leaves in early and midspring, followed by ovoid, cherry-like red fruit, to ½in (1.5cm) across. ↕↔ 25ft (8m). S. China, Taiwan, S. Japan. Zone 7b.
P. caroliniana (Carolina cherry laurel). Large, pyramidal-ovoid evergreen shrub or small tree with oblong to lance-shaped, shiny, dark green leaves, 2–3in (5–8cm) long, yellow-green or bronze when young. In spring, bowl-shaped, 5-petaled, fragrant white flowers, ¼in (6mm) across, are produced in dense clusters, 1½–3in (4–8cm) long, followed by ovoid to spherical, cherry-like, lustrous black fruit, ½in (1.5cm) long. Useful for screens and hedging; can become weedy. ↕ 20–30ft (6–10m), ↔ 15–25ft (5–8m). Coastal Virginia to N. Florida and Louisiana. Zone 7b.
P. cerasifera (Cherry plum, Myrobalan). Rounded, deciduous tree with ovate to obovate, dark green leaves, to 2½in (6cm) long. Solitary, bowl-shaped white flowers, 1in (2.5cm) across, are borne along bare shoots in early spring, with the leaves, and are sometimes followed by spherical, plum-like, edible, red or yellow fruit, 1¼in (3cm) across. ↕↔ 30ft (10m). S.E. Europe, S.W. Asia. Zone 4. **'Newport'** has dark purple leaves, light bronze-purple when young, and pale pink to white flowers. **'Nigra'** ▣ syn. 'Pissardii Nigra', produces dark purple leaves, red when young, and pink flowers. **'Pissardii'**, syn. *P. pissardii*, has dark red-purple leaves, and pale pink flowers that fade to white. **'Pissardii Nigra'** see 'Nigra'. **'Thundercloud'** has pink flowers and dark purple foliage.
P. ceresus (Sour cherry). Spreading, deciduous tree with dark green, oval, doubly serrate alternate leaves, 2–3in (5–7cm) long. Cup-shaped, pink or white flowers borne in clusters of 3–5 per cluster; followed by sour, bright red fruit. ¾in (2cm) across, matures June–July. Eurasia. ↕ 20ft (6m) ↔ 12–20ft (4–6m). Zone 4b.

Prunus dulcis 'Roseoplena'

Prunus avium

Prunus avium 'Plena'

Prunus glandulosa 'Alba Plena'

Prunus 'Hokusai'

Prunus incisa

Prunus jamasakura

***P.* 'Cheal's Weeping'**, syn. *P.* 'Kiku-shidare-zakura'. Weeping, deciduous tree bearing lance-shaped, tapered, mid-green leaves, to 4in (10cm) long, bronze when young. Fully double, bright pink flowers, 1½in (4cm) across, are borne in dense clusters, before or with the leaves, in mid- and late spring. ↕↔ 10ft (3m). Zone 6.
***P.* 'Chôshû-hizakura'.** Broadly upright, deciduous tree with elliptic, tapered, dark green leaves, to 6in (15cm) long, bronze-red when young. Bowl-shaped or semi-double, mid-pink flowers, 1¼in (3cm) across, are borne in clusters of 2–4 in midspring. ↕ 22ft (7m), ↔ 20ft (6m). Zone 6.
P.* x *cistena (*P. cerasifera* 'Atropurpurea' x *P. pumila*) (Purpleleaf sand cherry). Slow-growing, upright, deciduous shrub with oval, red-purple leaves, to 2½in (6cm) long, red when young. Solitary, bowl-shaped white flowers, ½in (1.5cm) across, are produced in midspring; they are sometimes followed by spherical, cherry-like, dark purple fruit, ¾in (2cm) across. ↕↔ 5ft (1.5m). Garden origin. Zone 3.
P. domestica (Common plum, European plum). Small to medium, deciduous tree with 4in(10cm) crenate, serrate leaves. 1½–2in (4–5cm) cup-shaped, white flowers, followed by fruit in varied colors from yellow to blue and black, 1–2in (2.5–5cm) across. SW Asia. ↕ 15–18ft (4–5m), ↔ 8ft (2.5m). Zone 4b.

Prunus 'Hally Jolivette'

P. dulcis (Common almond). Upright, spreading, deciduous tree with lance-shaped, finely toothed, tapered, dark green leaves, to 5in (13cm) long. Solitary or paired, bowl-shaped, pink or white flowers, 2in (5cm) across, are produced on bare shoots in early spring, followed by ovoid, velvety green fruit, to 2½in (6cm) long, each containing an edible nut. ↕↔ 25ft (8m). N. Africa, C. and S.W. Asia. Zone 6. **'Roseoplena'** ▣ has double pink flowers.
***P.* 'Fudan-zakura'**, syn. *P. serrulata* f. *semperflorens*. Small, spreading, deciduous tree with ovate, mid-green leaves, 2½–5in (6–13cm) long, rough on the upper surfaces. Intermittently from late autumn to midspring, soft pink buds open to shallowly cup-shaped, single white flowers, 1½in (4cm) across, in short-stalked clusters. ↕↔ 15ft (5m). Zone 6.
***P. glandulosa*.** Rounded, deciduous shrub bearing narrowly ovate or elliptic, finely toothed, pale to mid-green leaves, to 4in (10cm) long. In midspring, bowl-shaped, white to pale pink flowers, to ½in (1.5cm) across, are borne singly or in pairs, densely clustered along the branches; they are followed by spherical, dark red fruit, to ½in (1.5cm) across. ↕↔ 5ft (1.5m). N. and C. China, Japan. Zone 5. **'Alba Plena'** ▣ bears double, pure white flowers. **'Rosea Plena'** see 'Sinensis'. **'Sinensis'**, syn. 'Rosea Plena', has double pink flowers.
***P.* 'Hally Jolivette'** ▣ Rounded, bushy, deciduous tree or shrub with ovate, dark green leaves, to 2in (5cm) long. Double white, dark pink centered flowers, 1¼in (3cm) across, in clusters of up to 5, open from pink buds over an extended period in mid- and late spring. ↕↔ 15ft (5m). Zone 7.
***P.* 'Hillieri'.** Spreading, deciduous tree with elliptic, dark green leaves, to 4in (10cm) long, bronze when young, orange-red in autumn. Many bowl-shaped, soft pink flowers, 1½in (4cm) across, are produced in clusters of up to 4, in midspring. ↕↔ 30ft (10m). Zone 6.
***P.* x *hillieri* 'Spire'** see *P.* 'Spire'.
***P.* 'Hokusai'** ▣ syn. *P.* 'Uzuzakura'. Spreading, deciduous tree with oval, dark green leaves, to 5in (13cm) long, bronze when young, orange and red in autumn. In mid- and late spring, bears double, pale pink flowers, 2in (5cm) across, singly or in dense clusters of up to 6. ↕ 20ft (6m), ↔ 25ft (8m). Zone 6.
***P.* 'Hosokawa'** see *P.* 'Mount Fuji'.
***P.* 'Ichiyo'.** Spreading, deciduous tree with elliptic, dark green leaves, to 4in (10cm) long, bronze when young. Wide-open, double, soft pink flowers, 2in (5cm) across, are borne in long, pendent clusters of 3 or 4 in mid- and late spring. ↕↔ 25ft (8m). Zone 6.
P. incisa ▣ (Fuji cherry). Spreading, deciduous, rounded shrub, rarely tree-like, with ovate to obovate, sharply toothed, dark green leaves, to 2½in (6cm) long, bronze-red when young, turning orange-red in autumn. Saucer-shaped, white or pale pink flowers, ¾in (2cm) across, solitary or in clusters of 2 or 3, are borne before the leaves in early and midspring; they are followed by ovoid, cherry-like, purple-black fruit, to ⅜in (9mm) long. ↕↔ 25ft (8m). S.W. Japan. Zone 7. **'February Pink'** bears pale pink flowers over a long period in winter and early spring. **'Praecox'** has pink buds that open to white flowers in late winter.
P. jamasakura ▣ syn. *P. serrulata* var. *spontanea* (Hill cherry). Spreading, deciduous tree with oblong, dark green leaves, to 5in (13cm) long, bronze-red when young, turning red and yellow in autumn. In mid- and late spring, bears a profusion of cup-shaped white flowers, 1¼in (3cm) across, in clusters of 3–5, followed by ovoid, cherry-like, magenta-red fruit, to ½in (1.5cm) long. ↕↔ 40ft (12m). China, Korea, Japan. Zone 6.
***P.* 'Jo-nioi'.** Spreading, deciduous tree with elliptic, mid-green leaves, to 4in (10cm) long, pale bronze when young. Bowl-shaped, fragrant white flowers, 1½in (4cm) across, in clusters of 3–5, open from pink buds in midspring. ↕↔ 30ft (10m). Zone 6.
***P.* 'Kanzan'** ▣ syn. *P.* 'Kwanzan'. Upright, deciduous tree, vase-shaped when young, spreading wider with age, with ovate, dark green leaves, to 5in (13cm) long, bronze when young. Double, deep pink flowers, 2in (5cm) across, are profusely borne in clusters of 2–5 in mid- and late spring, before and as the leaves emerge. Often grafted onto a high understock. ↕↔ 30ft (10m). Zone 6.
***P.* 'Kiku-shidare-zakura'** see *P.* 'Cheal's Weeping'.
***P.* 'Kursar'.** Spreading, deciduous tree with elliptic, dark green leaves, to 5in (13cm) long, bronze when young.

Prunus 'Kanzan'

Prunus maackii

Saucer-shaped, dark pink flowers, ¾in (2cm) across, are profusely borne in clusters of 3 or 4 in early spring, before the leaves. ↕↔ 25ft (8m). Zone 6.
***P.* 'Kwanzan'** see *P.* 'Kanzan'.
P. laurocerasus ■ (Cherry laurel, English laurel). Dense, bushy, evergreen shrub, becoming spreading and tree-like with age, with oblong, glossy leaves, to 6in (15cm) long, dark green above, pale green beneath. In mid- and late spring, cup-shaped, fragrant white flowers, ⅜in (9mm) across, are produced in upright racemes, 2–5in (5–13cm) long, followed by conical, cherry-like red fruit, ½in (1.5cm) across, ripening to black. ↕ 25ft (8m), ↔ 30ft (10m). E. Europe, S.W. Asia. Zone 7b. **'Camelliifolia'** is upright, with conspicuously twisted leaves; ↔ 12ft (4m). **'Castlewellan'** see 'Marbled White'. **'Green Carpet'** see 'Grünerteppich'. **'Grünerteppich'**, syn. 'Green Carpet', is low and spreading, with leaves to 5in (13cm) long; ↕ 3ft (1m), ↔ 10ft (3m). **'Herbergii'** has a compact habit, with narrow leaves; ↕↔ 10ft (3m). **'Marbled White'**, syn. 'Castlewellan', has leaves conspicuously marked white; ↕↔ 15ft (5m). **'Otto Luyken'** ■ is very compact, with narrow, pointed, dark green leaves, to 4½in (11cm) long; frequently flowers again in autumn; ↕ 3ft (1m), ↔ 5ft (1.5m). **'Rotundifolia'** is vigorous and upright; excellent for hedging; ↕ 15ft (5m), ↔ 12ft (4m). **'Schipkaensis'** is spreading, and flowers profusely; ↕ 6ft (2m), ↔ 10ft (3m). **'Zabeliana'** is low and wide-spreading, with very narrow leaves, and often flowers again in autumn; ↕ 3ft (1m), ↔ 8ft (2.5m).
P. lusitanica (Laurel, Portugal laurel). Dense, bushy, evergreen shrub or tree with red-stalked, ovate to elliptic, glossy, dark green leaves, to 5in (13cm) long. Cup-shaped, fragrant white flowers, ½in (1.5cm) across, are produced in slender, ascending, spreading, or pendent racemes, to 10in (25cm) long, in early summer, followed by ovoid, cherry-like red fruit, ½in (1.5cm) across, ripening to black. ↕↔ to 70ft (20m). S.W. Europe. Zone 7. **subsp. *azorica*** has broader leaves, and racemes to 4in (10cm) long; Azores. **'Variegata'** ■ has leaves narrowly margined with white.
P. maackii ■ (Amur cherry). Conical, deciduous tree or shrub with peeling, yellow-brown bark and ovate, dark green leaves, to 3in (8cm) long, turning yellow in autumn. In midspring, produces dense racemes, 2–3in (5–8cm) long, each with 6–10 bowl-shaped, fragrant white flowers, ½in (1.5cm) across; they are followed by spherical, cherry-like, glossy black fruit, ¼in (6mm) across. ↕ 30ft (10m), ↔ 25ft (8m). N.E. Asia. Zone 2b.
P. mahaleb ■ (Saint Lucie cherry). Spreading, deciduous tree with rounded, glossy, dark green leaves, to 2½in (6cm) long, turning yellow in autumn. In mid- and late spring, bowl-shaped, very fragrant white flowers, ½in (1.5cm) across, are produced in racemes to 2in (5cm) long; they are followed by ovoid, glossy red cherries, ¼in (6mm) long, ripening to black. ↕ 30ft (10m), ↔ 25ft (8m). Europe. Zone 7.

Prunus laurocerasus

Prunus laurocerasus 'Otto Luyken'

Prunus lusitanica 'Variegata'

Prunus mahaleb

Prunus 'Mount Fuji'

Prunus padus 'Colorata'

P. maritima (Beach plum). Rounded, dense, suckering, deciduous shrub with ovate to elliptic, sharply toothed, dull green leaves, 1½–3in (4–8cm) long, pale green and softly hairy beneath. In midspring, bears single or double white flowers, ½in (15mm) across, followed by edible, glaucous-purple fruit, ½–1in (1.5–2.5cm) across, ripening in late summer. Extremely salt tolerant. ↕ 6–8ft (2–2.5m), ↔ indefinite. Coastal Maine to Virginia. Zone 4.
***P.* 'Mount Fuji'** ■ syn. *P.* 'Hosokawa', *P.* 'Shirotae'. Spreading, deciduous tree with slightly arching branches and elliptic, dark green leaves, to 5in (13cm) long, pale green when young, orange and red in autumn. In midspring, bears cup-shaped or semi-double, fragrant white flowers, 2in (5cm) across, in pendent clusters of 2 or 3. ↕ 20ft (6m), ↔ 25ft (8m). Zone 6.
P. mume ■ (Japanese apricot). Spreading, deciduous tree producing green shoots and rounded, tapered, dark green leaves, to 4in (10cm) long. Bears bowl-shaped, fragrant, white to dark pink flowers, 1in (2.5cm) across, singly or in pairs, on bare shoots, in late winter and early spring; they are followed by spherical, softly hairy, apricot-like, sour to bitter, edible yellow fruit, to 1¼in

Prunus mume (inset: flower detail)

Prunus 'Okame' (inset: flower detail)

(3cm) across. ↕↔ 28ft (9m). China, Korea. Zone 6. **'Beni-chidori'**, syn. 'Benishidore', is upright and shrubby, with dark pink flowers; ↕↔ 8ft (2.5m). **'Dawn'** produces double, ruffled pink flowers. **'Omoi-no-mama'**, syn. 'Omoi-no-wac', is upright and shrubby, with semi-double, pink-flushed white flowers; ↕↔ 8ft (2.5m). **'Peggy Clark'** bears double, deep rose flowers with red calyces and very long stamens. **'Pendula'** has weeping branches and pink flowers; ↕↔ 20ft (6m). **'Rosemary Clark'** bears early, double white flowers with red calyces. **'W.B. Clarke'** is weeping, with double pink flowers; ↕↔ 20ft (6m).

P.* var. *nectarina (Nectarine). Spreading, deciduous tree with simple, lanceolate, mid to dark green leaves, 1½–3in (4–8cm) long. Mutation of a peach produces smooth rather than fuzzy fruit. Clustered, cup-shaped pink or white flowers, and smooth-skinned orange-red fruit, 3–5in (7–12cm) across. ↕ 25–30ft (7–9m) ↔ 12–16ft (4–5m). Zone 6b. **var. *nucipersica*** dwarf variety, ↕↔ 15–25ft (5–8m).

***P.* 'Okame'** ■ (*P. campanulata* x *P. incisa*). Bushy, deciduous tree or shrub with narrowly oval, sharply toothed, dark green leaves, to 3in (8cm) long, turning orange and red in autumn. In early spring, profuse, cup-shaped, carmine-red flowers, ¾–1in (2–2.5cm) across, are borne in clusters of 2–5. ↕ 30ft (10m), ↔ 25ft (8m). Zone 6.

P. padus (European bird cherry). Spreading, deciduous tree or shrub, conical when young. Elliptic, dark green leaves, to 4in (10cm) long, turn red or yellow in autumn. Bears pendent racemes, to 6in (15cm) long, of cup-shaped, fragrant white flowers, to ½in (1.5cm) across, in midspring, followed by spherical, pea-like, glossy black fruit, ⅜in (9mm) across. ↕ 50ft (15m), ↔ 30ft (10m). Europe, N. Asia to C. Japan. Zone 2. **'Albertii'** bears abundant flowers in dense racemes. **'Colorata'** ■ has reddish purple young foliage and produces pink flowers. **var. *commutata*** (Mayday tree) flowers much earlier than other bird cherries. **'Plena'** has double flowers. **'Watereri'** ■ has flowers in slender racemes, to 8in (20cm) long.

***P.* 'Pandora'** ■ Spreading, deciduous tree, upright when young, with oval, dark green leaves, to 3in (8cm) long, bronze when young, turning orange and red in autumn. In early spring, masses of solitary, cup-shaped, pale pink flowers, 1¼in (3cm) across, open before the leaves, from dark pink buds. ↕ 30ft (10m), ↔ 25ft (8m). Zone 7.

***P. pendula* 'Pendula Rosea'** see *P.* x *subhirtella* 'Pendula Rosea'.

***P. pendula* 'Pendula Rubra'** see *P.* x *subhirtella* 'Pendula Rubra'.

P. pensylvanica (Pin cherry). Spreading, deciduous tree or shrub with peeling, red-banded bark and ovate to oblong-lance-shaped, bright green leaves, to 4½in (11cm) long, turning yellow and red in autumn. In mid- and late spring, cup-shaped white flowers, ½in (1.5cm) across, are borne before or with the leaves, in stalkless umbels of 3–6, followed by spherical red fruit, ¼in (6mm) across. ↕↔ to 30ft (10m). North America. Zone 1. **'Stockton'** has double flowers and red autumn color.

P. persica (Peach). Spreading, deciduous tree with narrowly elliptic, slender-pointed, glossy, mid- to dark green leaves, to 6in (15cm) long. Bears solitary, bowl-shaped, pink or red flowers, 1½in (4cm) across, in early and midspring, before the leaves, followed (in fertile cultivars) by spherical, downy, edible, red-blushed yellow fruit, 3in (8cm) across. ↕↔ 25ft (8m). China. Zone 6. The following are all non-fruiting cultivars: **'Helen Borchers'** bears semi-double, rose-pink flowers, 2½in (6cm) across. **'Klara Meyer'** ■ produces double, bright pink flowers. **'Peppermint Stick'** bears double white flowers with red stripes. **'Prince Charming'** is upright in habit, and bears double, dark pink flowers; ↕ 12ft (4m), ↔ 5ft (1.5m).

P.* x *persicoides see *P.* x *amygdalopersica*.

***P.* 'Pink Star'** see *P.* x *subhirtella* 'Stellata'.

P. pissardii see *P. cerasifera* 'Pissardii'.

P. sargentii ■ (Sargent cherry). Spreading, deciduous tree with copper-tinted bark, and elliptic, tapered, dark green leaves, to 5in (13cm) long, red when young, turning brilliant orange-red in early autumn. Bowl-shaped, pale pink flowers, 1½in (4cm) across, are produced in umbels of 2–4 in midspring; they are followed by ovoid, cherry-like, glossy crimson fruit, to ½in (1.5cm) long. ↕ to 70ft (20m), ↔ 50ft (15m). Russia (Sakhalin), Korea, Japan. Zone 5b. **'Columnare'** is narrow and upright; ↔ 10ft (3m).

Prunus padus 'Watereri'

Prunus 'Pandora'

Prunus persica 'Klara Meyer'

Prunus sargentii

Prunus 'Shirofugen'

Prunus x *subhirtella* 'Pendula Rosea'

P. serotina (Black cherry, Wild rum cherry). Broadly columnar, deciduous tree with elliptic, glossy, dark green leaves, to 5in (13cm) long, turning yellow or red in autumn. In late spring, bowl-shaped, fragrant white flowers, ½in (1.5cm) across, are borne in racemes to 6in (15cm) long; they are followed by spherical, edible red fruit, ½in (1.5cm) across, ripening to black. ↕ to 60ft (18m), ↔ 30ft (10m). North America. Zone 2b.

P. serrula ■ Rounded, deciduous tree with peeling, glossy, copper-brown bark and lance-shaped, tapered, dark green leaves, to 4in (10cm) long, turning yellow in autumn. Bowl-shaped white flowers, ¾in (2cm) across, solitary or in umbels of 2–4, are borne as the leaves emerge in midspring, followed by ovoid, cherry-like fruit, ½in (1.5cm) long. ↕↔ 30ft (10m). W. China. Zone 7.

P. serrulata* f. *semperflorens see *P.* 'Fudan-zakura'.

P. serrulata* var. *spontanea see *P. jamasakura*.

***P.* 'Shirofugen'** ■ Spreading, deciduous tree bearing oblong, dark green leaves, to 5in (13cm) long, bronze-red when young, turning orange-red in autumn. Clusters of 3–5 double, fragrant white flowers, 2in (5cm) across, open from pink buds in midspring; they turn pink before they fall. ↕ 25ft (8m), ↔ 30ft (10m). Zone 6.

***P.* 'Shirotae'** see *P.* 'Mount Fuji'.

***P.* 'Shôgetsu'.** Rounded, deciduous tree bearing oblong, mid-green leaves, to 5in (13cm) long, bronze when young, turning orange and red in autumn. Frilly-margined, double, pink and white flowers, 2in (5cm) across, in pendent clusters of 3–6, open from pink buds in midspring. ↕ 15ft (5m), ↔ 25ft (8m). Zone 6.

***P.* 'Spire'**, syn. *P.* x *hillieri* 'Spire'. Vase-shaped, deciduous tree, conical when young, with obovate, dark green leaves, to 4in (10cm) long, bronze when young, turning orange and red in autumn. Bowl-shaped, pale pink flowers, 1½in (4cm) across, in clusters of 3–5, are produced as the leaves emerge in midspring. ↕ 30ft (10m), ↔ 20ft (6m). Zone 6.

P.* x *subhirtella (*P. incisa* x *P. pendula*) (Higan cherry, Rosebud cherry). Spreading, deciduous tree with broadly elliptic or ovate, sometimes 3-lobed, sharply toothed, dark green leaves, to 3in (8cm) long, pale bronze when young, turning yellow in autumn. Bowl-shaped, white or pink flowers, ¾in (2cm) across, are borne in clusters of 2–5, sometimes in autumn but mostly in spring, before or with the leaves; they are sometimes followed by ovoid, cherry-like, red, later nearly black fruit, ⅜in (9mm) long. ↕↔ 25ft (8m). Japan. Zone 7. **'Autumnalis'** bears semi-double, pink-tinged white flowers in mild periods in autumn and again in spring. **'Autumnalis Rosea'** is similar to 'Autumnalis' but produces pink flowers. **'Fukubana'** produces semi-double, dark rose-pink flowers. **'Pendula Rosea'** ■ syn. *P. pendula* 'Pendula Rosea', has weeping branches and rose-pink flowers. **'Pendula Rosea Plena'** ■ has weeping

Prunus serrula

Prunus x *subhirtella* 'Pendula Rosea Plena' (inset: flower detail)

P

Prunus x *subhirtella* 'Stellata'

Prunus 'Taihaku'

Prunus tenella

Prunus 'Ukon'

Prunus 'Yae-murasaki'

Prunus x *yedoensis*

branches and semi-double, rose-pink flowers. **'Pendula Rubra'**, syn. *P. pendula* 'Pendula Rubra', has weeping branches and dark pink flowers. **'Stellata'** ■ syn. *P.* 'Pink Star', has pale pink flowers, red in bud, with narrow, pointed petals. **'Yae-shidare-higan'** has pendulous branches that bear longer-lasting, profuse, double pink flowers.
***P.* 'Taihaku'** ■ (Great white cherry). Vigorous, spreading, deciduous tree bearing elliptic, dark green leaves, to 8in (20cm) long, bronze when young. Bowl-shaped white flowers, to 2½in (6cm) across, are produced in clusters of up to 4 in midspring. ↕25ft (8m), ↔ 30ft (10m). Zone 6b.
P. tenella ■ (Dwarf Russian almond). Bushy, deciduous shrub with upright shoots and obovate to inversely lance-shaped, glossy, dark green leaves, to 3in (8cm) long. Bowl-shaped, bright pink flowers, to 1¼in (3cm) across, solitary or in profuse clusters of 2 or 3, are produced with the young leaves in midspring; they are followed by ovoid, almond-like, velvety, gray-yellow fruit, to 1in (2.5cm) long. ↕to 5ft (1.5m), ↔ 5ft (1.5m). C. Europe to Russia (Siberia). Zone 2. **'Fire Hill'** has very dark pink flowers.
P. tomentosa (Manchu cherry, Nanking cherry). Spreading, dense, deciduous shrub, opening with age, producing peeling, shiny, reddish brown bark. Obovate to elliptic, pointed, toothed, softly hairy, dull dark green leaves are ¾–1½in (2–4cm) long. In early spring, bears bowl-shaped, fragrant white flowers, ¾in (2cm) across, pinkish white in bud, followed by spherical, edible, scarlet fruit, to ½in (1.5cm) across. ↕6–10ft (2–3m), ↔ to 15ft (5m). N. and W. China, Japan. Zone 2.
***P.* 'Trailblazer'.** Broadly upright, deciduous tree with oval, red-purple leaves, to 3in (8cm) long. Solitary, bowl-shaped, white or pale pink flowers, ¾in (2cm) across, are borne before the leaves in midspring, and are sometimes followed by plum-like, edible red fruit, 2½in (6cm) across. ↕30ft (10m), ↔ 20ft (6m). Zone 6.
P. triloba (Flowering almond). Densely branched, deciduous shrub or small tree bearing broadly elliptic, often 3-lobed leaves, 1½–3in (4–8cm) long, dark green above, mid-green and softly hairy beneath. Solitary or paired, bowl-shaped pink flowers, ¾–1½in (2–4cm) across, are produced in early and midspring; they are followed by spherical red fruit, ½in (1.5cm) across. ↕↔ 10ft (3m). China. Zone 4. **'Multiplex'** (Double flowering almond) is spreading, bearing oval leaves, to 2½in (6cm) long. Double pink flowers, 1½in (4cm) across, are produced in midspring; ↕↔ 12ft (4m).
***P.* 'Ukon'** ■ Vigorous, spreading, deciduous tree with elliptic, tapered, dark green leaves, to 5in (13cm) long, bronze when young. Clusters of 3–6 double flowers, 1½in (4cm) across, yellowish white on the outsides and slightly pink at the tips, open from pink buds in midspring. ↕25ft (8m), ↔ 30ft (10m). Zone 6.
***P.* 'Umineko'** ■ Upright, deciduous tree with ovate, sharply toothed, dark green leaves, to 3in (8cm) long, pale green when young. Cup-shaped white flowers, 1½in (4cm) across, are borne in clusters of 2 or 3 in midspring, with the young leaves. ↕25ft (8m), ↔ 10ft (3m). Zone 6.
***P.* 'Uzuzakura'** see *P.* 'Hokusai'.
P. virginiana (Choke cherry, Virginia bird cherry). Conical, often suckering, deciduous tree or shrub with broadly obovate to broadly elliptic, glossy, mid- to dark green leaves, to 4in (10cm) long. In late spring, bears cup-shaped white flowers, ½in (1.5cm) across, in dense racemes, to 4in (10cm) long; they are followed by spherical, red to purple fruit, ⅜in (9mm) across. ↕30ft (10m), ↔ 25ft (8m). North America. Zone 2. **'Shubert'** ■ produces leaves that turn dark red-purple in summer.
***P.* 'Yae-murasaki'** ■ Spreading, very slow-growing, deciduous tree with elliptic, tapered, mid-green leaves, to 5in (13cm) long, bronze when young, orange-red in autumn. In mid-spring, bears semi-double, dark pink flowers, 1½in (4cm) across, in clusters of 2–4. ↕15ft (5m), ↔ 25ft (8m). Zone 6.
P.* x *yedoensis ■ (*P. speciosa* x *P.* x *subhirtella*) (Potomac cherry, Yoshino cherry). Spreading, deciduous tree bearing arching branches and elliptic, dark green leaves, to 4½in (11cm) long. In early spring, before the leaves, produces a profusion of racemes of 5 or 6 bowl-shaped, pale pink flowers, 1½in (4cm) across, fading to nearly white. ↕to 50ft (15m), ↔ 30ft (10m). Japan. Zone 7. **'Afterglow'** is upright and spreading in habit, with lustrous bright green foliage turning yellow in autumn; bears pink flowers; ↕↔ 25ft (8m). **'Pink Shell'** bears flowers with shell-pink petals, which fade to lighter pink. **'Shidare-yoshino'**, syn. 'Pendula', 'Perpendens', has weeping branches that arch to the ground; they must be staked to the height of choice and then allowed to weep. **'Snow Fountains'**, syn. 'White Fountain', is semi-weeping in habit, has dark green leaves that turn gold and orange in autumn, and bears snow-white flowers before the leaves in spring; ↕↔ 6–12ft (2–4m).

Prunus 'Umineko' (inset: flower detail)

Prunus virginiana 'Shubert'

PSEUDERANTHEMUM

ACANTHACEAE

Genus of about 60 species of evergreen perennials, subshrubs, and shrubs from woodland habitats in tropical regions worldwide. They are grown primarily for their variegated or colorful leaves, which are opposite, simple, and entire or toothed. The long, tubular, 2-lipped, white, blue, purple, or red flowers, sometimes marked with yellow, are borne in spikes, racemes, or cymes. In areas where temperatures fall below 55°F (13°C), grow as foliage plants in a warm greenhouse. In tropical climates, they are suitable for growing in a shrub border.

- **CULTIVATION** Under glass, grow in soil-based potting mix in bright filtered light, providing high humidity. During the growing season, water moderately and apply a balanced liquid fertilizer every month; water sparingly in winter. Outdoors, grow in fertile, moist, but well-drained soil in full sun with some midday shade, or in partial shade. Pruning group 9; needs restrictive pruning under glass.
- **PROPAGATION** Root semi-ripe cuttings in midsummer with bottom heat.
- **PESTS AND DISEASES** Spider mites and whiteflies under glass.

P. atropurpureum, syn. *Eranthemum atropurpureum.* Erect, open shrub, the stems sparsely branched unless pinched out at intervals when young. Ovate to broadly elliptic leaves, 4–6in (10–15cm) long, are deep purple, sometimes metallic green, spotted yellow, pinkish purple, pink, green, or white. During summer, bears tubular white flowers, spotted rose-red or purple at the bases, 1in (2.5cm) long, in dense, terminal spikes, to 7in (18cm) long. ↕3–5ft

'seuderanthemum atropurpureum
Variegatum'

0.9–1.5m), ↔ 12–30in (30–75cm).
'olynesia. ❀ (min. 55°F/13°C).
Variegatum' ■ syn. 'Tricolor', has
ronze-purple leaves, splashed and
uffused creamy yellow and pink,
nd bears pink flowers.

PSEUDOCYDONIA

:OSACEAE

Genus of one species of deciduous or emi-evergreen shrub or tree from emperate woodland in China. It has imple, dark green leaves, but is grown nainly for its peeling bark, cup-shaped ink flowers, and large, edible yellow ruit. It is best cultivated as a specimen ree, but will achieve tree stature only in egions with long, hot summers; in areas vith cool summers, it remains shrubby nd is best trained against a wall.
CULTIVATION Grow in fertile, well-rained soil in full sun. Pruning group , or group 13 if wall-grown.
PROPAGATION Sow seed in containers utdoors in autumn.
PESTS AND DISEASES Infrequent.

. sinensis ■ syn. *Cydonia sinensis.* preading shrub or small tree with a listinctively fluted trunk, bearing eeling, jigsaw-puzzle-like bark in hades of green and brown, turning gray vith age. Oval, finely toothed, dark reen leaves grow to 4in (10cm) long. olitary, cup-shaped pink flowers, 1½in 4cm) across, are produced in mid- and ate spring, followed by ovoid yellow ruit, 6in (15cm) long. ↕↔ 20ft (6m). China. Zone 7.

'seudocydonia sinensis

▷ ***Pseudofumaria lutea*** see *Corydalis lutea*
▷ ***Pseudogynoxys chenopodioides*** see *Senecio confusus*

PSEUDOLARIX

PINACEAE

Genus of one species of monoecious, deciduous, coniferous tree occurring in forest in China. The leaves are linear and borne in rosettes on short shoots (spurs), or spirally on long lateral or upright shoots (as in *Larix*). It is grown for its attractive branch arrangement and for the golden orange color of its autumn foliage. The female cones have large, triangular green scales and release the seeds by disintegrating; the male cones are catkin-like and clustered on short shoots. *P. amabilis* is an excellent specimen tree, but is initially slow-growing.
• **CULTIVATION** Grow in deep, fertile, acidic to neutral, well-drained soil in a warm, sheltered site in full sun. Pruning group 1.
• **PROPAGATION** Sow seed in containers outdoors in spring. Take greenwood cuttings in early summer.
• **PESTS AND DISEASES** Infrequent.

P. amabilis ■ syn. *P. kaempferi* (Golden larch). Broadly conical or flattened, open-crowned tree with spreading branches, gray bark furrowed with raised, plate-like pieces, and purple, later grayish purple shoots with ovoid buds. Linear, soft, fresh green leaves, ¾–2in (2–5cm) long, turning golden orange in autumn, are borne on both long and short shoots. Erect, ovoid, yellow-green female cones, 2½–3in (6–8cm) long, ripening to brown, are spiky due to the free tips of the scales. ↕ to 50–70ft (15–20m), ↔ 20–40ft (6–12m). S. and E. China. Zone 5b.
P. kaempferi see *P. amabilis.*

▷ ***Pseudomuscari azureum*** see *Muscari azureum*

Pseudolarix amabilis

PSEUDOPANAX

ARALIACEAE

Genus of 12–20 species of evergreen trees and shrubs from forest and scrub in Tasmania (Australia), New Zealand, and Chile. Cultivated for their upright habit, foliage, and fruits, they are valuable architectural or specimen plants. The alternate, simple or palmate, entire or variously toothed leaves may vary greatly in shape, depending on the age of the plant. Inconspicuous, 4- or 5-petaled green flowers are borne mainly in winter, in terminal or, less commonly, lateral umbels, clusters, racemes, or mixtures of these. Male and female flowers usually grow on separate plants; both are required to produce the fruits, which are drupe-like, each with 2–5 stones. Grow in a warm, sheltered shrub border. Where not hardy, grow in a cool greenhouse or conservatory.
• **CULTIVATION** Under glass, grow in soil-based potting mix, with added sharp sand, in full light with shade from hot sun, or bright filtered light. In the growing season, water moderately and apply a balanced liquid fertilizer monthly; water sparingly in winter. Outdoors, grow in fertile, well-drained soil in full sun or partial shade. Where marginally hardy, shelter from wind. Pruning group 1; may need restrictive pruning under glass.
• **PROPAGATION** Sow seed in autumn or spring: seed of tender species at 66–75°F (19–24°C), seed of hardy species in containers in a cold frame. Take semi-ripe cuttings, or air layer, in summer.
• **PESTS AND DISEASES** Infrequent.

P. crassifolius (Lancewood). Evergreen tree, unbranched for many years, with long, slender seedling leaves, to 24in (60cm) long, and downward-pointing, dark green mature leaves, to 3ft (1m) or more long. Seedling leaves are simple, ovate to lance-shaped, membranous, coarsely toothed or lobed; mature leaves

Pseudopanax ferox

Pseudopanax lessonii 'Gold Splash'

are linear, rigid, somewhat variegated, with red midribs and spine-tipped teeth. Mature plants develop a rounded head and narrow, spreading, linear to linear-obovate, 3- or 5-palmate, leathery leaves, with linear or sword-shaped leaflets, 8in (20cm) long. Star-shaped, greenish white flowers are produced in umbels, 3–4in (8–10cm) across, in summer and early autumn; they are followed on female or hermaphrodite flowers by spherical black fruit, ¼in (6mm) across. ↕ to 50ft (15m) ↔ 6ft (2m). New Zealand. ❀ (min. 35°F/2°C)
P. ferox ■ (Toothed lancewood). Upright, dioecious, evergreen tree, later developing a small, rounded head. Young plants produce simple, pendent, narrow, linear, sharply pointed, coarsely and jaggedly toothed, dark bronze-green mature leaves, to 18in (45cm) long, marked white or gray. Mature plants bear spreading, linear, dark green leaves, to 6in (15cm) long. Green flowers are borne in umbel-like panicles, to 4in (10cm) across, in summer and early autumn; they are followed on female plants by ovoid black fruit, ⅜in (9mm) across. ↕ 15ft (5m), ↔ 6ft (2m). New Zealand. ❀ (min. 35°F/2°C)
P. laetus. Rounded, dioecious, evergreen tree or shrub with thick shoots, and 5- or 7-palmate leaves composed of long-stalked, obovate, leathery, dark green leaflets, to 12in (30cm) long. In winter, greenish purple flowers are produced in compound umbels, to 8in (20cm) across, followed on female plants by spherical, purple-black fruit, ¼in (6mm) across. ↕ 20ft (6m), ↔ 10ft (3m). New Zealand (North Island). ❀ (min. 35°F/2°C)
P. lessonii (Houpara). Erect to spreading, evergreen, large shrub or small tree, with thick branches. The deep green leaves are 3- or 5-palmate: on juvenile plants they have 5 lance-shaped, coarsely and irregularly toothed leaflets, to 5in (13cm) long; on mature plants, they consist of 3 smaller, stalkless, obovate, entire to sparsely toothed leaflets, to 4in (10cm) long. Yellowish green flowers are borne in compound umbels, 4in (10cm) across, in summer; they are followed by oblong, purple-black fruit, ¼in (6mm) long. ↕ 10–20ft (3–6m), ↔ 6–12ft (2–4m). New Zealand (North Island, Three Kings Island). ❀ (min. 36°F/2°C). **'Gold Splash'** ■ has yellow-marked leaves. **'Purpureus'** has bronze-purple foliage.

PSEUDORHIPSALIS

CACTACEAE

Genus of 6 species of epiphytic, occasionally lithophytic, shrub-like cacti with arching stems and no spines. They are native to Central America, South America, and the Caribbean. Diurnal funnel-shaped or rotate flowers are produced in shades of white or yellowish white. The berry-like, ovoid to globose fruit is whitish, often tinged with purple.

• **CULTIVATION** Under glass, grow in a mix of equal parts loam, peat (or peat substitute), leaf mold, and gritty sand, in full light. In the growing season, water freely, applying fertilizer monthly, keep just moist in winter. Outdoors, grow in sharply drained, gritty, humus-rich soil in full sun. See also pp.48–49.

• **PROPAGATION** Sow seed at 70-75°F (21-24°C) in spring or summer.

• **PESTS AND DISEASES** Susceptible to scale insects, mealy bugs and sciara fly (fungus gnats).

P. acuminata Spiphytic, occasionally lithophytic cactus, branching profusely. Older stems are flattened and leaf-like, notched marginally, 6in (15cm) or more long, and spineless. Produces pale pink flowers, to 6in (15mm) long, and berry-like, ovoid to globose, pinkish to pale magenta fruit, to ⅜in (8mm). ↕ to 12ft (4m), ↔ 15–22ft (5–7m). Costa Rica. ❄ (min. 45°F/7°C)

PSEUDOTSUGA

PINACEAE

Genus of 6–8 species of tall, evergreen, coniferous trees from forest in China, Taiwan, Japan, W. North America, and Mexico. The linear leaves, arranged radially on the shoots, develop from pointed, many-scaled buds that are unique to the genus. The female cones have protruding, trident-shaped bract scales; the male cones are cylindrical. They are imposing specimen trees.

• **CULTIVATION** Grow in any well-drained, non-alkaline soil, in full sun.

• **PROPAGATION** Sow seed in containers outdoors in spring. Graft cultivars in late winter.

• **PESTS AND DISEASES** Dieback, brown felt blight, canker, butt rot, lesion nematode, needle cast, caterpillars, budworm, bark beetle, aphids, scale insects, and weevils may be problems.

P. douglasii see *P. menziesii*.
P. menziesii, syn. *P. douglasii*, *P. taxifolia* (Douglas fir). Broadly conical tree when young, becoming columnar with spreading branches. The bark is smooth and gray at first, then thick, corky, deeply ridged, and red-brown. Ovoid, sharp-pointed, red-brown buds open to linear, soft, dark green leaves, ½–1¼in (1.5–3cm) long, loosely parted on the shoots, each with 2 white bands beneath. Ovoid-conical female cones, 3–4in (8–10cm) long, with long, erect bracts are produced. ↕ 80–160ft (25–50m), ↔ 20–30ft (6–10m). British Columbia to California. Zone 4. **'Fastigiata'** is very upright, with crowded branching and grayish green leaves. **'Fletcheri'**

Pseudotsuga menziesii 'Fretsii'

is a spreading, flat-topped, dwarf cultivar, producing blue-green leaves; ↕ 6ft (2m), ↔ 6–8ft (2–2.5m). **'Fretsii'** ■ is slow-growing, forming a small, spreading, conical tree, with dull green leaves, ⅜–½in (0.9–1.5cm) long; ↕ to 20ft (6m). **var. *glauca*** ■ (Blue Douglas fir) is a fast-growing, conical conifer that produces smaller cones, 1¾–2½in (4.5–6cm) long, with reflexed three-pronged bracts; the leaves are blue-glaucous, and the gray or black bark is thinner and more scaly. **'Oudemansii'** is slow-growing, with short leaves, ½–¾in (1.5–2cm) long; ↕ 15–30ft (5–10m). **'Pendula'** has very weeping branches and branchlets held closely to the stems, hanging like sheets.
P. taxifolia see *P. menziesii*.

Pseudotsuga menziesii var. *glauca* (inset: cone detail)

PSEUDOWINTERA

WINTERACEAE

Genus of 3 species of aromatic, evergreen trees and shrubs from mountain forest in New Zealand. They are cultivated mainly for their alternate, broadly elliptic, leathery leaves, which have obvious glands. Cup-shaped, greenish yellow to white flowers are produced in axillary clusters, and are followed by spherical, dark red or black fruits. They grow best in a sheltered border or woodland situation. Where marginally hardy, grow in a cool greenhouse.

• **CULTIVATION** Under glass, grow in soil-based potting mix in full light or bright filtered light. During growth, water freely, applying a balanced liquid fertilizer monthly; water sparingly at all other times. Outdoors, grow in humus-rich, preferably neutral to acidic, moist but well-drained soil in full sun or partial shade. Pruning group 8; may need restrictive pruning under glass.

• **PROPAGATION** Sow seed at 55–64°F (13–18°C) in autumn or spring. Root semi-ripe cuttings in midsummer with bottom heat.

• **PESTS AND DISEASES** Infrequent.

P. colorata ■ syn. *Drimys colorata*. Spreading, bushy shrub bearing broadly elliptic, leathery, yellow-green leaves, to 3in (8cm) long, marked pink and margined dark red-purple above, glaucous beneath. In midspring, bears clusters of 2–5 or more, cup-shaped, greenish yellow flowers, ½in (1.5cm)

Pseudowintera colorata

across, followed by spherical red, later black berries, ¼in (6mm) across. ↕ 3ft (1m), ↔ 5ft (1.5m). New Zealand. ❄ (min. 41°F/5°C)

▷ ***Pseudozygocactus epiphylloides*** see *Hatiora epiphylloides*

PSILOTUM

PSILOTACEAE

Genus of 2 species of terrestrial or epiphytic, evergreen, rhizomatous, fern-like perennials from moist tropical and warm-temperate forest or woodland worldwide. They are grown for their upright, spreading, or pendent habit, and for their distinctive, repeatedly forked, triangular or flattened, yellow-green stems, 1/16–⅛in (2–3mm) thick, which may die back in winter. The leaves are very small and inconspicuous, and the stems sometimes bear small, spherical, 3-lobed sporangia in the axils of minute bracts. *P. nudum* is an ancient plant, cultivated in Japan for centuries, and collectors pay high prices for very rare clones. Some cultivars have distinct characteristics, such as dwarfness, weeping habits, yellow or dark green leaves, or production of many yellow sporangia. Where not hardy, grow in a cool or temperate greenhouse, and leave undisturbed for long periods; in warmer areas, grow beneath shrubs or tree ferns

• **CULTIVATION** Under glass, grow in 1 part each of loam, medium-grade bark, and charcoal, 2 parts sharp sand, and 3 parts coarse leaf mold; or grow epiphytically on tree-fern bark. Provide bright filtered light and high humidity. In growth, water and mist freely, and apply a balanced liquid fertilizer every month; water sparingly in winter. Outdoors, grow in moderately fertile, moist but well-drained soil in light, dappled shade.

• **PROPAGATION** Divide established plants in spring. See also p.51.

• **PESTS AND DISEASES** Infrequent.

P. nudum (Whisk fern). Bushy, evergreen, fernlike perennial with upright, spreading, or pendent, branching, yellow-green, triangular stems, to 24in (60cm) long. Dull yellow sporangia, ⅛in (3mm) wide, are produced on the upper parts of the stems. Leaves are sparse and scale-like, 1/16in (2mm) long. ↕↔ 24in (60cm). Tropical to warm-temperate areas worldwide. ❄ (min. 41°F/5°C)

P

Psychopsis papilio

PSYCHOPSIS

Butterfly orchid

ORCHIDACEAE

Genus of about 5 species of small, evergreen, epiphytic orchids from lowland to mountainous forest, at altitudes of up to 3,250ft (1,000m), in Central America, South America, and Trinidad. They have compressed, clustered, oval pseudobulbs, and solitary, semi-rigid, oblong-elliptic leaves, which are mottled dark green and dull purple. Butterfly-like flowers are borne over a long period in long, slender, few-flowered, jointed racemes, occasionally singly, from the base of each pseudobulb.

• **CULTIVATION** Intermediate-growing orchids. Grow epiphytically on slabs of bark or cork; pot culture is not advised. Throughout the year, provide full light and high humidity, and water sparingly. During summer, mist rather than water, and feed every week. See also p.46.

• **PROPAGATION** Divide when the support begins to deteriorate.

• **PESTS AND DISEASES** May be infested by spider mites, aphids, and mealybugs.

P. papilio ▣ syn. *Oncidium papilio*. Epiphytic orchid with spherical pseudobulbs, each producing a single, ovate to elliptic leaf, 5–10in (13–25cm) long. Orange-brown flowers, 6in (15cm) across, are slightly mottled greenish yellow, with 3 erect green and brown segments, 3 yellow and brown segments, and yellow and brown mottled lips. They are borne in few-flowered racemes, to 4ft (1.2m) long, throughout the year. ↕ 24in (60cm), ↔ 12in (30cm). Trinidad, Venezuela, Colombia, Ecuador, Peru. ❀ (min. 60°F/16°C; max. 86°F/30°C)

▷ ***Psygmorchis pusilla*** see *Oncidium pusillum*

PSYLLIOSTACHYS

Statice

PLUMBAGINACEAE

Genus of about 6–8 species of erect, usually rosette-forming annuals found in sandy soils on plains and in foothills from Syria to Iran and C. Asia. They have mostly basal, deeply lobed or occasionally simple and entire, oblong or lance-shaped to obovate, light to mid-green leaves. From spring to autumn, they produce branching or simple spikes of tiny, tubular, pink or

Psylliostachys suworowii

white flowers, each with 5 spreading lobes. Statices are suitable for the front of an annual border, and are tolerant of coastal conditions. They are also excellent for cutting and drying.

• **CULTIVATION** Grow in fertile, moist, well-drained soil in full sun.

• **PROPAGATION** Sow seed at 70°F (21°C) in spring.

• **PESTS AND DISEASES** Prone to gray mold (*Botrytis*) and powdery mildew.

P. spicata, syn. *Limonium spicatum, Statice spicata*. Rosette-forming annual with deeply lobed, inversely lance-shaped leaves, 2–6in (5–15cm) long; the leaf stalks and midribs are densely clothed in long hairs. Rose-pink flowers are borne in terminal spikes, to 3½in (9cm) long, and shorter, lateral spikes, from summer to early autumn. ↕ 12–18in (30–45cm), ↔ to 12in (30cm). Ukraine (Crimea), Caucasus, Iran.

P. suworowii ▣ syn. *Limonium suworowii, Statice suworowii*. Rosette-forming annual bearing simple, basal, inversely lance-shaped to oblong-obovate, wavy-margined to slightly lobed, light green leaves, to 6in (15cm) long. Rose-pink flowers are borne in narrow, cylindrical, branching spikes, to 8in (20cm) long, from summer to early autumn. ↕ 12–18in (30–45cm), ↔ to 12in (30cm). Iran, W. Turkmenistan, N. Afghanistan, C. Asia.

PTELEA

RUTACEAE

Genus of 3 or more species of aromatic, deciduous trees and shrubs found in thickets and on rocky slopes in North America. Cultivated for their 3-palmate, strongly scented leaves, they also bear corymbs of inconspicuous, cup-shaped or star-shaped, sometimes unisexual, greenish white flowers, followed by winged, more or less rounded and flattened fruits. Suitable for growing in a shrub border or as lawn specimens.

Ptelea trifoliata 'Aurea'

• **CULTIVATION** Grow in fertile, well-drained soil in full sun or dappled shade. Pruning group 1.

• **PROPAGATION** Sow seed in containers outdoors in autumn or spring. Take greenwood cuttings in early summer.

• **PESTS AND DISEASES** Tree hoppers, rust, and leaf spot can occur.

P. trifoliata (Hop tree, Stinking ash). Upright, deciduous shrub with aromatic bark and alternate, 3-palmate, scented, dark green leaves, to 5in (13cm) long, with ovate to elliptic leaflets. Corymbs of star-shaped, greenish white flowers are borne in summer, followed by winged, rounded and flattened, pale green fruit, to 1in (2.5cm) across. ↕ 25ft (8m), ↔ 12ft (4m). Ontario to Connecticut, Michigan, Iowa, Florida, Texas, and N. Mexico. Zone 3b. **'Aurea'** ▣ bears bright yellow to yellow-green leaves, turning dark green, then yellow in autumn; ↕ 15ft (5m).

PTERIS

Brake, Table fern

PTERIDACEAE

Genus of approximately 280 species of deciduous, semi-evergreen, and evergreen, terrestrial ferns, found mainly in tropical and subtropical forests throughout the world. The rhizomes are thick and erect to slender and short-creeping. Brakes are cultivated for their closely spaced fronds, which are pinnatisect or pinnate to 4-pinnate, and range from less than 12in (30cm) to 10ft (3m) long. Spores form at the frond margins, which curl under to protect them. Where not hardy, grow the tender species and cultivars in a cool or temperate greenhouse, or as houseplants. In warmer areas, use singly as feature plants, or in mixed foliage plantings.

• **CULTIVATION** Under glass, grow in 1 part each of sharp sand, coarse leaf mold, and charcoal, and 2 parts soil-based potting mix, in bright filtered light and high humidity; *P. cretica* and *P. vittata* prefer slightly alkaline soil, so add limestone chips. In the growing season, water freely, applying a high-nitrogen liquid fertilizer monthly; water sparingly in winter. Outdoors, grow in any moist but well-drained soil (except alkaline soil for most kinds), with added leaf mold, in partial or deep shade, and protect from strong wind.

• **PROPAGATION** Sow spores at 70°F (21°C) when ripe. Divide plants with creeping, branched rhizomes in spring. See also p.51.

• **PESTS AND DISEASES** Scale insects, mealybugs, rust, and leaf spots can occur.

P. argyraea ▣ (Silver brake, Silver fern). Evergreen fern with erect rhizomes bearing erect, pinnate or 2-pinnate fronds, 24–39in (60–100cm) long, each with up to 6 pairs of oblong, dark green pinnae with broad, silvery white stripes down their centers. The pinnatisect pinnae are composed of numerous linear-oblong lobes; the lowest pair is usually forked. Requires shade. ↕↔ to 3ft (1m). Tropics. ❀ (min. 45°F/7°C)

P. biaurita. Evergreen fern with erect rhizomes producing erect, oblong or triangular-oblong, pinnate, light apple-green fronds, to 4½ft (1.3m) long, each with 5–15 pairs of pinnatisect pinnae, the lowest pair usually forked. Similar to *P. argyraea*, but pinnae lack the central white streaks. Thrives in damp shade. ↕ 24–60in (0.6–1.5m), ↔ 16–60in (40–150cm). Tropics. ❀ (min. 45°F/7°C)

P. cretica (Cretan brake). Evergreen fern with a short-creeping, many-branched rhizome. Produces arching,

Pteris argyraea

Pteris cretica 'Albolineata'

crowded, ovate or rounded, pinnate, pale green fronds, 12–28in (30–70cm) long, each with 1–5 pairs of narrowly lance-shaped, simple or forked pinnae. Fertile fronds are taller and have narrower pinnae than sterile fronds. ↕ to 30in (75cm), ↔ 24in (60cm). Europe, Africa, Asia. ❀ (min. 41°F/5°C). **'Albolineata'** ■ has a broad white band along the center of each pinna, and is easier to grow than the species. **'Childsii'** has broader pinnae than the species, with incised margins and small crested tips. Possibly of hybrid origin; ↕ to 20in (50cm), ↔ 12in (30cm). **'Distinction'** is smaller than the species, and produces deeply lobed pinnae with branched tips; ↕↔ 16in (40cm). **'Mayi'** is similar to 'Albolineata', but has crested pinnae tips. **'Wimsettii'** is compact; the margins of the pinnae are deeply and irregularly lobed, with the tips often crested; ↕↔ 18in (45cm).
P. dentata. Evergreen fern that forms clumps of triangular to ovate, very variably divided, 2- or 3-pinnate, bright green fronds, to 5ft (1.5m) long, arising from short-creeping to erect rhizomes. Sterile fronds have pinnae segments with finely toothed margins, but on fertile fronds the margins are entire. ↕ 20–72in (0.5–1.8m), ↔ 24–60in (0.6–1.5m). Tropical Africa, South Africa, Arabian Peninsula. ❀ (min. 45°F/7°C)
P. ensiformis (Sword brake). Evergreen fern with short-creeping, branched rhizomes producing narrow-triangular, 2-pinnate, dark green fronds, often grayish white around the midribs. Fertile fronds, up to 16in (40cm) long, have 4 or 5 pairs of linear pinnae, each with a few toothed segments at the base. Sterile fronds are shorter, and have narrower pinnae with entire margins. ↕↔ 12in (30cm). Himalayas to Japan, Philippines, Polynesia, tropical Australia. ❀ (min. 45°F/7°C). **'Arguta'** has dark green fronds with strongly contrasting silver-white central midribs. **'Victoriae'** has white bands running either side of the midribs.
P. fauriei. Small, neat, evergreen fern with erect rhizomes producing arching, broadly triangular to ovate, mid-green fronds, 8–24in (20–60cm) long, each with 3–5 pairs of oblong, deeply pinnatisect pinnae. ↕ to 18in (45cm), ↔ 24in (60cm). China, Japan. ❀ (min. 45°F/7°C)
P. multifida ■ (Spider brake). Evergreen fern with short-creeping to erect, many-branched rhizomes producing numerous erect, ovate, light green fronds, 8–20in (20–50cm) long. Each frond is 2-pinnate at the base, pinnatisect above, with 3–5 pairs of pinnae. Pinnae are linear, with long, tapering tips, the upper ones decurrent to the stem. ↕ to 18in (45cm), ↔ 9in (23cm). China, Korea, Japan to Taiwan, Indonesia. ❀ (min. 45°F/7°C). **'Corymbifera'** has crested pinnae tips.
P. tremula (Australian brake, Shaking brake, Tender brake). Evergreen fern with an erect rhizome producing ovate, arching, light green fronds, to 6ft (2m) tall, 3- or 4-pinnate at the base, with overlapping pinnae, giving a feathery appearance. Pinnae are narrowly oblong to linear, with finely toothed margins. Fast-growing, and may become invasive.

Pteris vittata

↕ to 5ft (1.5m), ↔ 3ft (1m). New Zealand, Australia, Fiji. ❀ (min. 45°F/7°C)
P. tricolor (Painted brake). Evergreen fern with erect, ovate, pinnate fronds, 16–24in (40–60cm) long, arising from creeping, branched rhizomes. Fertile fronds have 2–5 pairs of pinnatisect, oblong pinnae; they are red-purple when young, aging to mid-green, but stalks and midribs remain purple. ↕ to 24in (60cm), ↔ 24in (60cm). Malacca. ❀ (min. 45°F/7°C)
P. umbrosa (Jungle brake). Evergreen fern with short-creeping, many-branched rhizomes. Triangular-ovate, shining, dark green, erect fronds, to 36in (90cm) tall, are 2-pinnatisect, with 3–7 pairs of narrowly lance-shaped lobes, the lower ones divided into 3 or 5 segments. Similar in appearance to *P. cretica*, but more luxuriant. ↕ to 4ft (1.2m), ↔ 3ft (1m). Australia. ❀ (min. 45°F/7°C)
P. vittata ■ (Ladder brake). Evergreen fern with short-creeping rhizomes covered with golden scales. Fronds are erect, oblong, pinnate, to 36in (90cm) tall, with up to 40 pairs of simple, linear, dark green pinnae. Tolerates alkaline soil and some exposure to sun. ↕ to 3ft (1m), ↔ 24in (60cm). Tropical and warm-temperate regions of Europe, Africa, Asia, Australasia. ❀ (min. 41°F/5°C)

Pteris multifida

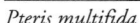

PTEROCACTUS

CACTACEAE

Genus of 9 species of dwarf, shrub-like cacti occurring in hilly regions of Argentina. They arise from tuberous rootstocks, and branch from the bases to produce somewhat club-shaped stems. The areoles bear very fine, almost hair-like spines and minute glochids. Small, white or yellow to reddish brown and coppery, diurnal flowers, without tubes, are produced terminally in early summer. Where not hardy, grow in a cool greenhouse or in a bowl garden; in warmer regions, they are suitable for growing outdoors in a desert garden.
• **CULTIVATION** Under glass, grow in standard cactus potting mix in full light. From spring to summer, water moderately and apply a low-nitrogen liquid fertilizer every 4 or 5 weeks. Keep completely dry at other times. Outdoors, grow in poor, sharply drained soil in full sun. See also pp.48–49.
• **PROPAGATION** Sow seed at 66–75°F (19–24°C) in spring. Take basal cuttings in spring or early summer.
• **PESTS AND DISEASES** Susceptible to mealybugs, and sometimes to aphids when flowering.

P. fischeri. Short-stemmed, shrub-like cactus producing spherical or ovoid, cylindrical, jointed, brown-green stems, ¾in (2cm) thick. White areoles bear about 16 spines (12 yellow radial spines and 4 longer, brownish yellow centrals). White flowers, 1½in (4cm) or more across, are produced in early summer. ↕ 6in (15cm), ↔ to 8in (20cm). S. Argentina. ❀ (min. 36–45°F/2–7°C); tolerates brief periods to 10°F (-12°C) if kept dry.
P. kuntzei ■ syn. *P. tuberosus.* Shrub-like cactus producing cylindrical, brown or green-brown stems, to ⅜–½in (0.8–1.5cm) thick, with a vertical violet line below each areole. The gray areoles bear minute, off-white spines that lie flat on the stems. Pale yellow flowers, 1¼–2in (3–5cm) across, sometimes tinged orange-brown or coppery brown, are produced in early summer. ↕↔ to 16in (40cm). Argentina. ❀ (min. 36–45°F/2–7°C); tolerates brief periods to 10°F (-12°C) if kept dry.
P. tuberosus see *P. kuntzei.*

Pterocactus kuntzei

PTEROCARYA

Wingnut

JUGLANDACEAE

Genus of about 10 species of fast-growing, deciduous trees found in woodland and on riverbanks, mainly in the mountains of Asia, from the Caucasus to Japan. They are cultivated for their attractive, spreading habit; for their large, alternate, more or less oblong, pinnate leaves, composed of 5–27 leaflets, which color yellow in autumn; and for their long, pendent spikes of winged fruit, which are produced over a long period in summer. Inconspicuous green male and female flowers are produced in separate catkins in spring as the leaves emerge. Wingnuts grow to a considerable size; they are best suited to large gardens or parks.

• **CULTIVATION** Grow in deep, fertile, moist but well-drained soil in full sun. Pruning group 1; remove unwanted suckers as they appear.

• **PROPAGATION** Sow seed in containers outdoors in autumn. Remove rooted suckers in autumn.

• **PESTS AND DISEASES** Infrequent.

P. fraxinifolia (Caucasian wingnut). Vigorous, spreading tree bearing pinnate leaves, to 16in (40cm) long, with cylindrical midribs; the leaves are composed of 23 or more, oblong to ovate, glossy, dark green leaflets. Small, winged green fruit are produced in pendent spikes, to 20in (50cm) long, in summer. ↕ 80ft (25m), ↔ 70ft (20m). Caucasus, N. Iran. Zone 6b.

P. x rehderiana (*P. fraxinifolia* x *P. stenoptera*). Very vigorous, spreading, strongly suckering tree bearing pinnate leaves, to 8in (20cm) long, with slightly winged midribs; the leaves are composed of up to 21 oblong to ovate, glossy, dark green leaflets. Small, winged green fruit are produced in pendent spikes, to 18in (45cm) long, in summer. ↕ 80ft (25m), ↔ 70ft (20m). Garden origin. Zone 6b.

P. rhoifolia (Japanese wingnut). Spreading tree with pinnate leaves, to 16in (40cm) long; the leaves are composed of up to 21 ovate-oblong, tapered, glossy, mid-green leaflets. Small, winged green fruit are produced in pendent spikes, to 12in (30cm) long, in summer. ↕ 100ft (30m), ↔ 80ft (25m). Japan. Zone 5b.

P. stenoptera ▣ (Chinese wingnut). Spreading tree with pinnate leaves, to 16in (40cm) long, with winged midribs; the leaves consist of up to 21 oblong, bright green leaflets, the terminal leaflet often absent. Small, winged green fruit are produced in pendent spikes, to 12in (30cm) long, in summer. ↕ 80ft (25m), ↔ 50ft (15m). China. Zone 7b.

PTEROCELTIS

ULMACEAE

Genus of one species of deciduous tree found near streams, in rocky places, and in valleys in the mountains of China. It is cultivated for its habit, peeling bark, bright green foliage, and winged green fruit. Inconspicuous, very small green flowers are produced in spring. *P. tatarinowii* is most effective as a specimen tree; it is exceedingly rare in cultivation. It is possibly urban tolerant, and thus a good street tree candidate.

• **CULTIVATION** Grow in fertile, moist but well-drained soil in full sun. Pruning group 1.

• **PROPAGATION** Sow seed in containers outdoors in autumn.

• **PESTS AND DISEASES** Infrequent.

P. tatarinowii. Spreading tree with arching branches, flaking gray bark, and ovate, tapered, 3-veined, bright green leaves, to 4in (10cm) long, with toothed margins. The tiny, green male flowers are produced in stalkless clusters; the very small, green female flowers are solitary. Both male and female flowers are produced in spring, from the leaf axils; they are followed by round, winged green fruit, ¾in (2cm) across, in autumn. ↕↔ 30ft (10m). N. and C. China. Zone 7.

Pterocarya stenoptera (inset: fruit detail)

PTEROCEPHALUS

DIPSACACEAE

Genus of approximately 25 species of annuals, perennials, and evergreen shrubs, occurring on rocky slopes, roadsides, and waste ground from the Mediterranean and tropical Africa to C. Asia, the Himalayas, and W. China. They have opposite, simple, entire or pinnatifid leaves, sometimes with scalloped margins. They are cultivated for their scabiosa-like, pink or mauve flowerheads, produced on long stems in summer, and the attractive, papery seed heads that follow. *P. perennis*, the only species widely grown, is suitable for a rock garden or the front of a border.

• **CULTIVATION** Grow in any well-drained soil in full sun.

• **PROPAGATION** Sow seed in containers in a cold frame in autumn. Take softwood or semi-ripe cuttings in early or midsummer.

• **PESTS AND DISEASES** Infrequent.

P. perennis ▣ syn. *P. parnassi.* Evergreen, mat-forming perennial bearing opposite, ovate to fiddle-shaped, hairy, gray-green leaves, to 1½in (4cm) long, scalloped at the margins. During summer, long stems, to 3in (8cm) long, bear solitary, dense, flattened heads of tubular, pale pinkish purple flowers, to 1½in (4cm) across; they are followed by papery seed heads. ↕ 3in (8cm), ↔ 8in (20cm). Greece. Zone 6.

P. parnassi see *P. perennis.*

Pterocephalus perennis

PTERODISCUS

PEDALIACEAE

Genus of 18 species of succulent perennials and subshrubs found in semi-desert, rocky regions from tropical E. to S.W. Africa. They have a swollen caudex, tuberous roots, and solitary or branching stems. They are grown for their foliage and flowers: the leaves are very variable, light to dark green, and have entire, toothed, or deeply cut margins; the 5-lobed, funnel- to bell-shaped flowers are slightly 2-lipped, diurnal, usually yellow, orange, red, purple, or white, and are produced singly from the leaf axils in summer. In areas where temperatures fall below 59°F (15°C), grow *Pterodiscus* species as houseplants or in a warm greenhouse; in warm, dry climates, grow in a succulent border.

• **CULTIVATION** Under glass, grow in standard cactus potting mix in full light. From spring to summer, water sparingly and apply a low-nitrogen liquid fertilizer every 4–6 weeks. Keep dry at other times. Outdoors, grow in moderately fertile, sharply drained soil in full sun. Protect from excessive moisture. See also pp.48–49.

• **PROPAGATION** Sow seed in spring at 66–75°F (19–24°C).

• **PESTS AND DISEASES** Infrequent.

P. speciosus. Succulent with a conical to spherical, fleshy caudex, 2½in (6cm) thick toward the base, and stems bearing linear-oblong, dark green leaves, to 2½in (6cm) long, with irregularly toothed margins. Funnel-shaped, pale reddish purple flowers, 1¼in (3cm) long, are produced in summer. ↕ 6in (15cm), ↔ 4in (10cm). South Africa (Northern Transvaal, Eastern Cape). ❀ (min. 59°F/15°C)

PTEROPOGON

ASTERACEAE

Genus of 10 erect to slightly spreading, slender-stemmed, white-woolly annuals, previously part of the genus *Helipterum*, from semi-arid regions of South Africa and Australia. They bear alternate, narrowly lance-shaped, light to mid-green, white-woolly leaves, but are cultivated for their long-stemmed, leafy clusters of small, rounded, papery, daisy-like, usually yellow flowerheads, borne from summer to early autumn. Pteropogons are suitable for an annual or mixed border. The flowerheads are good for drying, the clustered blooms of *P. humboldtianus* turning an attractive metallic green.

• **CULTIVATION** Grow in poor, sharply drained soil in full sun.

• **PROPAGATION** Sow seed *in situ* in late spring.

• **PESTS AND DISEASES** Prone to aphids.

P. humboldtianus, syn. *Helipterum humboldtianum.* Erect, single-stemmed or slightly branching annual with narrowly lance-shaped, white-woolly leaves, to 1¼in (3cm) long. Slightly fragrant, straw-textured yellow flowers are produced in flowerheads to 3in (8cm) across, from summer to early autumn. ↕ to 18in (45cm), ↔ to 6in (15cm). S. Australia.

P

Pterostyrax hispida

PTEROSTYRAX

STYRACACEAE

Genus of 4 species of spreading, deciduous trees or shrubs, with peeling, aromatic bark, occurring in mountain woodland in China and Japan. They are cultivated for their alternate, oblong to ovate, pale green leaves; pendent panicles of fragrant, 5-lobed white flowers; and unusual, ribbed or winged fruits. Grow as shrubs or as single- or multiple-stemmed specimen trees in a lawn or woodland setting.
• **CULTIVATION** Grow in deep, fertile, well-drained, neutral to acidic soil in full sun or partial shade. Pruning group 1.
• **PROPAGATION** Sow seed in containers outdoors in autumn. Take semi-ripe cuttings in summer.
• **PESTS AND DISEASES** Infrequent.

P. hispida ■ (Epaulette tree). Spreading tree or shrub with peeling, aromatic gray bark and oblong to ovate, pale green leaves, to 8in (20cm) long. Bell-shaped, fragrant white flowers, ½in (1.5cm) across, each with 5 lobes divided almost to the base, are borne in pendent panicles, to 8in (20cm) long, in early and midsummer, followed by oblong, 5-ribbed fruit, to ½in (1.5cm) long, covered in yellow-brown bristles. ↕ 50ft (15m), ↔ 40ft (12m). China, Japan. Zone 6.

▷ ***Ptilotrichum spinosum*** see *Alyssum spinosum*

PTILOTUS

AMARANTHACEAE

Genus of about 100 species of annuals, herbaceous perennials, and subshrubs from open scrub in Australia. They are grown for their dense, rounded, ovoid or conical to cylindrical spikes of tiny, 5-tepaled, white, yellow, pink, mauve, purple, or green flowers, often enhanced by long white hairs. The leaves are alternate and usually narrow. Where not hardy, grow in a cool greenhouse or in an alpine house, or as annual summer bedding plants; in warmer areas, grow in a border or rock garden.
• **CULTIVATION** Under glass, grow in soil-based potting mix in full light. During the growing season, water moderately and apply a balanced liquid fertilizer monthly; keep almost dry in winter. Outdoors, grow in fertile, sharply drained soil in full sun; avoid wet conditions.
• **PROPAGATION** Sow seed at 55–61°F (13–16°C) in spring. Take root cuttings in early spring.
• **PESTS AND DISEASES** Infrequent.

P. exaltatus (Pink mulla mulla). Robust, bushy perennial with rosettes of oblong-lance-shaped, thick, wavy-margined, bluish green leaves, to 3in (8cm) long, often tinged red. Very small, white to pink or red flowers, with hairy brown bracts, are borne in conical, later cylindrical spikes, to 6in (15cm) long, from winter to summer. ↕ to 12in (30cm) or more, ↔ 24in (60cm). Australia. ❄ (min. 41°F/5°C)
P. manglesii, syn. *Trichinium manglesii.* Erect or spreading perennial bearing rosettes of narrow to broadly ovate, thick, smooth-margined, white-hairy, mid-green leaves, 1–3in (2.5–8cm) long. The lower leaves are borne on long stalks; the upper leaves are smaller and stalkless. In summer, very small, pink to violet flowers, with dark brown bracts, are produced in round to ovoid, white-hairy spikes, 3–4in (8–10cm) long. ↕↔ 4–16in (10–40cm). Australia. ❄ (min. 41°F/5°C)

PTYCHOSPERMA

ARECACEAE

Genus of about 30 species of single- or cluster-stemmed palms found in moist forest habitats from coastal lowlands to mountain valleys, from Micronesia to Australia, New Guinea, and the Solomon Islands. Pinnate, oblong-elliptic, glossy leaves are composed of linear leaflets. Greenish white or greenish yellow, 3-petaled flowers are produced in panicles below the leaves, followed by spherical to ovoid, red, orange, or purplish black fruits. Where not hardy, grow in a warm greenhouse, or as houseplants. In tropical regions, grow as specimens in a small lawn, or to add height and interest to a shrub border.
• **CULTIVATION** Under glass, grow in soil-based potting mix with added well-rotted organic matter and sharp sand, in bright indirect light. Pot on or top-dress in spring; during the growing season, water freely and apply a balanced liquid fertilizer every month. Water sparingly in winter. Outdoors, grow in fertile, moist, well-drained soil in partial shade.
• **PROPAGATION** Sow seed at 75°F (24°C) in spring.
• **PESTS AND DISEASES** Butt rot, bud rot, and lethal yellowing can occur on large specimens. Young plants may be prone to spider mites and scale insects.

P. alexandrae see *Archontophoenix alexandrae.*
P. elegans, syn. *Seaforthia elegans* (Alexander palm, Solitaire palm). Small to medium-sized palm with a slender, columnar trunk, ringed with old leaf scars. The woolly crownshaft produces pinnate, short-stalked leaves, 3–8ft (1–2.5m) long, composed of many broadly linear, mid-green leaflets with notched or toothed tips. In summer, fragrant, greenish white flowers, each to ⅜in (9mm) across, are produced in nodding panicles, 12–24in (30–60cm) long; they are followed by ovoid, bright red fruit, ¾in (2cm) across. ↕ 25–40ft

Ptychosperma macarthurii

(8–12m), ↔ 6–12ft (2–4m). N.E. Australia. ❄ (min. 61°F/16°C)
P. macarthurii ■ (Macarthur palm). Small, cluster-stemmed palm with slender, ring-scarred trunks. Pinnate, short-stalked leaves, 5ft (1.5m) long, are composed of many linear, bright green leaflets with ragged-toothed tips. Greenish yellow flowers, each to ⅜in (9mm) across, are produced in panicles 12–18in (30–45cm) long, usually in summer; they are followed by ovoid red fruit, ½in (1.5cm) long. ↕ 10–22ft (3–7m), ↔ 6–12ft (2–4m). New Guinea, N.E. Australia (Cape York Peninsula). ❄ (min. 61°F/16°C)

PUERARIA

FABACEAE

Genus of 17 species of mainly woody-stemmed, deciduous or evergreen, twining climbers from thickets and woodland in S.E. Asia and Japan. They are grown for their alternate, 3-palmate or pinnate leaves and for their axillary or terminal racemes of pea-like flowers. *P. lobata*, the only species commonly cultivated, is extremely vigorous and must be sited with care; it has earned its appellation of "the vine that ate the South." It is suitable for growing as a groundcover, for screening an unsightly building, or for covering a tall tree stump. Where not hardy, it may also be grown as an annual.
• **CULTIVATION** Grow in fertile, moist but well-drained soil in full sun or partial shade. Support twining stems. Pruning group 11, in spring.
• **PROPAGATION** Sow seed at 55–64°F (13–18°C) in spring.
• **PESTS AND DISEASES** Leaf spots, blights, and dieback may occur.

P. hirsuta see *P. lobata.*
P. lobata, syn. *P. hirsuta, P. thunbergiana* (Japanese arrowroot, Kudzu vine). Very vigorous, deciduous, twining climber, with a large tuber, sometimes grown as an annual. Bears 3-palmate leaves composed of ovate to diamond-shaped, lobed leaflets, the central one largest, to 7in (18cm) long. In summer and autumn, fragrant, pea-like purple flowers, ¾in (2cm) long, are produced in erect racemes, to 10in (25cm) long. ↕ to 70ft (20m) or more (it may easily reach half this height in one season's growth). China, Japan, Pacific islands. Zone 7b.
P. thunbergiana see *P. lobata.*

PULMONARIA

Lungwort

BORAGINACEAE

Genus of about 14 species of deciduous or evergreen, low-growing perennials, with slowly spreading rhizomes. They are found in Europe and Asia, on acidic to alkaline soils in a wide range of habitats, including mountainous areas, moist, subalpine woodland, and streamsides. They are grown for their early flowers, often among the first perennial blooms, in late winter or spring, and for their simple, ovate to elliptic or oblong, hairy basal leaves, which are often attractively spotted white or silver. The stem leaves are few, smaller, and more or less stalkless. Regular, funnel-shaped flowers, ¼–½in (6–15mm) across, with 5 spreading lobes, are borne in terminal cymes; the flowers may be pink, red, violet, purple, blue, or white; blue, purple, or violet flowers may often be pink in bud. After flowering, new so-called "summer" leaves develop, showing the markings at their best. Lungworts are good groundcover plants for a shady position: grow in woodland, among shrubs, in a wild garden, or at the front of a border. They are attractive to bees.
• **CULTIVATION** Grow in humus-rich, fertile, moist but not waterlogged soil, in full or partial shade; *P. officinalis* will tolerate full sun. Remove old leaves after flowering. Divide every 3–5 years.
• **PROPAGATION** Sow seed in containers outdoors as soon as ripe. Lungworts hybridize freely in cultivation, and plants raised from seed of species in gardens often do not come true. Divide after flowering, or in autumn. Take root cuttings in midwinter.
• **PESTS AND DISEASES** Prone to powdery mildew in dry conditions. Slugs and snails may damage new growth.

P. angustifolia (Blue cowslip, Blue lungwort). Open clump-forming, rhizomatous, usually deciduous perennial with lance-shaped, unspotted, mid- to dark green leaves, 16in (40cm) long. Funnel-shaped, rich blue flowers are borne profusely on erect then spreading stems, from early to late spring. ↕ 10–12in (25–30cm), ↔ 18in (45cm). C., N.E., and E. Europe. Zone 4.
subsp. *azurea* ■ syn. *P. azurea*, has brighter blue flowers, tinted red in bud; ↕ to 10in (25cm). **'Beth's Pink'** see

Pulmonaria angustifolia subsp. *azurea*

ulmonaria 'Lewis Palmer'

. 'Beth's Pink'. **'Blaues Meer'** bears right blue flowers very freely.
. azurea see *P. angustifolia* subsp. *zurea.*
. 'Beth's Pink', syn. *P. angustifolia* 3eth's Pink'. Clump-forming, iizomatous, deciduous perennial with vate, white-spotted, dark green leaves, o 10in (25cm) long, narrowing bruptly to the leaf stalks. In mid- and te spring, bears funnel-shaped, deep oral-pink flowers. ↕ to 12in (30cm), ↔ 18in (45cm). Zone 5.
. 'Blue Ensign'. Clump-forming, iizomatous, deciduous perennial with vate, unspotted, dark green leaves, to 0in (25cm) long, and large, blue-violet owers, borne in spring. ↕ to 14in 35cm), ↔ to 18in (45cm). Zone 5.
. 'Excalibur'. Clump-forming, iizomatous perennial with ovate, shiny, lvery white leaves, to 10in (25cm) ng, with deep green midribs and arrow, deep green margins. In early pring, bears long-blooming, funnel-aped, violet-blue flowers, which age to ink. Mildew resistant. ↕ 10in (25cm), ↔ 18in (45cm). Zone 4.
. 'Lewis Palmer' ■ syn. *P. longifolia* ewis Palmer'. Clump-forming,

ulmonaria 'Mawson's Blue'

Pulmonaria officinalis 'Sissinghurst White'

rhizomatous, deciduous perennial with lance-shaped, softly hairy, dark green basal leaves, to 12in (30cm) long, irregularly splashed and spotted greenish white, and ovate-lance-shaped stem leaves. In early spring, bears funnel-shaped flowers that open pink and become bright blue. ↕ 14in (35cm), ↔ 18in (45cm). Zone 5.
P. longifolia (Longleaf lungwort). Densely clump-forming, rhizomatous, deciduous perennial with narrowly lance-shaped, dark green leaves, to 18in (45cm) long, spotted silvery white. Dense cymes of long-lasting, funnel-shaped, clear blue flowers are borne from late winter to late spring. ↕ to 12in (30cm), ↔ 18in (45cm). W. Europe, including Sweden and Britain. Zone 4. **'Bertram Anderson'** has longer, narrower, more strongly marked leaves, and produces brighter blue flowers. **'Lewis Palmer'** see *P.* 'Lewis Palmer'.
***P.* 'Mawson's Blue'** ■ syn. *P.* 'Mawson's Variety'. Erect to spreading, rhizomatous, deciduous perennial bearing ovate to elliptic, softly hairy, unspotted, dark green leaves, to 12in (30cm) long. Produces dark blue flowers in spring. ↕ to 14in (35cm), ↔ to 18in (45cm). Zone 5.
***P.* 'Mawson's Variety'** see *P.* 'Mawson's Blue'.
P. mollis, syn. *P. montana*. Vigorous, clump-forming, rhizomatous, deciduous perennial bearing elliptic to narrowly ovate, softly hairy, unspotted, mid-green leaves, to 18in (45cm) long. From late winter to midspring, produces funnel-shaped, rich blue flowers, sometimes

Pulmonaria rubra 'Redstart'

Pulmonaria saccharata

pink-tinged fading to purplish blue. ↕ to 18in (45cm), ↔ 24in (60cm). Belgium, N.W. France, W. Germany, W. Switzerland. Zone 6.
P. montana see *P. mollis.*
P. officinalis (Jerusalem cowslip, Soldiers and sailors, Spotted dog). Open clump-forming, rhizomatous, evergreen perennial with ovate, bristly, white-spotted, bright mid-green leaves, 4–5in (10–13cm) long, heart-shaped at the bases. From early to late spring, bears funnel-shaped flowers, opening pink and becoming reddish violet then blue. ↕ 10in (25cm), ↔ 18in (45cm). Europe. Zone 5. **'Cambridge Blue'**, syn. 'Cambridge', bears heart-shaped leaves and abundant pale blue flowers, pink-tinted on opening; ↕ to 12in (30cm). **'Sissinghurst White'** ■ syn. *P. saccharata* 'Sissinghurst White', bears leaves 8–10in (20–25cm) long, with numerous white spots, and pure white flowers opening from pale pink buds; ↕ to 12in (30cm). **'White Wings'** bears pink-eyed white flowers in late spring.
***P.* 'Roy Davidson'.** Clump-forming, rhizomatous perennial with long, narrow, lance-shaped, evenly silver-blotched, mid-green leaves. Funnel-shaped, sky-blue flowers, are borne in early spring. ↕ to 14in (35cm), ↔ to 18in (45cm). Zone 5.
P. rubra (Red lungwort). Loosely clump-forming, rhizomatous, leafy, evergreen perennial with elliptic, almost diamond-shaped, velvety, unspotted, matte, bright green leaves, to 24in (60cm) long. Funnel-shaped, bright brick-red to salmon-red flowers are borne over a long period from late winter to midspring. ↕ to 16in (40cm), ↔ 36in (90cm). S.E. Europe. Zone 4. **var. *alba*** see var. *albocorollata.* **var. *albocorollata***, syn. var. *alba*, has white flowers; ↕ to 12in (30cm). **'Barfield Pink'** has pink-and-white-striped flowers; ↕ to 12in (30cm). **'David Ward'** has strongly white-variegated, sage-green leaves, with cream margins, and coral-red flowers; ↕ to 12in (30cm). **'Redstart'** ■ has coral-red flowers and is often the first pulmonaria to flower, in midwinter.
P. saccharata ■ (Bethlehem sage). Clump-forming, rhizomatous, evergreen perennial with elliptic, white-spotted, mid-green leaves, to 11in (28cm) long, the stem leaves nearly as large as the basal leaves. From late winter to late spring, bears funnel-shaped, red-violet, violet, or white flowers, with dark green calyces. ↕ 12in (30cm), ↔ 24in (60cm). S.E. France, N. and C. Italy. Zone 4. Cultivars in **Argentea Group** have almost completely silver leaves, and flowers opening red, aging to dark violet. **'Bielefeld'** has pink flowers; ↕ 8–12in (20–30cm). **'Dora Bielefeld'** has mid-green, silver-spotted leaves, and profuse, clear pink flowers; ↕ 12in (30cm). **'Frühlingshimmel'** ■ has many-spotted leaves, and light blue flowers with darker blue-purple eyes and calyces; ↕ 10in (25cm). **'Janet Fisk'** has strongly silver-marked leaves and pink flowers, aging to blue; ↕ 12in (30cm). **'Leopard'** has many-spotted, dark green leaves, and red, pink-tinted flowers. **'Mrs. Moon'** has pink buds opening to bluish lilac flowers. **'Pierre's Pure Pink'** has shiny, spotted leaves and produces clear, shell-pink flowers; ↕ 12in (30cm). **'Pink Dawn'** bears deep pink flowers aging to violet. **'Sissinghurst White'** see *P. officinalis* 'Sissinghurst White'.
***P.* 'Spilled Milk'.** Clump-forming, compact, rhizomatous perennial with purple-tinged young leaves and broad, ovate, silvery, mid-green adult leaves, to 10in (25cm) long. In early spring, bears funnel-shaped flowers, which open rose-pink and become blue. ↕ 9in (23cm), ↔ 18in (45cm). Zone 4.
P. vallarsae. Clump-forming, rhizomatous, deciduous perennial with elliptic-oblong, wavy-margined, densely softly hairy, dark green leaves, 8in (20cm) long, narrowing abruptly to the leaf stalks; they have bright green or whitish green spots, in rare cases none. Funnel-shaped violet flowers, becoming more purple with age, are produced on glandular-hairy stems from early to late spring. ↕ 6–12in (15–30cm), ↔ 24in (60cm). Italy. Zone 6. **'Margery Fish'** has bright green leaves, 6in (15cm) long, densely silvered on the upper surfaces, with the midribs and margins spotted. The flowers are coral-pink to red-violet, becoming violet; ↕ 7–11in (18–28cm). Zone 5.

Pulmonaria saccharata 'Frühlingshimmel'

PULSATILLA

RANUNCULACEAE

Genus of about 30 species of clump-forming, deciduous perennials (sometimes with a few overwintering leaves) with a coarsely fibrous rootstock, found mainly in short turf and alpine meadows in Eurasia and N. America. They are cultivated for their finely dissected, fern-like leaves and their solitary, usually silky-hairy, bell- or cup-shaped flowers, produced in spring and early summer. The flowers are followed by spherical seed heads with silver-silky, plume-like styles, borne on stems that often elongate considerably after flowering; heights given below are for plants in flower. Grow in a rock garden, scree bed, or alpine house, where the flowers and fluffy seed heads will make an impact. All parts of the plant may cause mild stomach upset if ingested, and contact with the sap may irritate skin.

• **CULTIVATION** Grow in fertile, very well-drained soil in full sun; *P. vernalis* needs very gritty, moist but sharply drained soil in a scree bed, and requires protection from excessive winter moisture. Pulsatillas resent root disturbance and may be difficult to establish, so plant when small and leave undisturbed. In an alpine house, use a mix of equal parts soil-based potting mix and grit.

• **PROPAGATION** Sow seed as soon as ripe in containers in an open frame. Take root cuttings in winter.

• **PESTS AND DISEASES** Young growth may be attacked by slugs and snails.

Pulsatilla alpina

Pulsatilla halleri

Pulsatilla vernalis

P. alpina ■ (Alpine pasque flower). Clump-forming perennial with finely divided, 2-pinnate, hairy, mid-green leaves, 2½–5in (6–13cm) long, composed of 30–80 toothed leaflets. In spring, bears cup-shaped white flowers, to 2½in (6cm) across, with silky-hairy petals, blue-tinted on the reverse, and yellow stamens, followed by ornamental seed heads. ↕ 6–12in (15–30cm), ↔ 8in (20cm). Mountains in C. Europe. Zone 4. **subsp. *apiifolia***, syn. subsp. *sulfurea*, has pale yellow flowers, and usually occurs in acidic soils.
subsp. *sulfurea* see subsp. *apiifolia.*
P. halleri ■ Tufted perennial, densely clothed in long silver hairs, with pinnate, light green leaves, 2–7in (5–18cm) long, consisting of 3–5 pinnatifid leaflets with oblong-lance-shaped lobes; the terminal leaflet is long-stalked. Erect, silky-hairy, bell-shaped, violet-purple to lavender-blue flowers, to 3½in (9cm) across, are borne with the leaves in late spring. ↕ 8in (20cm), ↔ 6in (15cm). C. and S.E. Europe, Crimea. Zone 3.
subsp. *grandis*, syn. *P. vulgaris* subsp. *grandis*, has silvery golden brown hairs. It bears very finely divided leaves after the shallowly bell-shaped, lavender-blue flowers, which have rounded segments; C. Europe, Ukraine.
P. patens (Eastern pasque flower). Clump-forming perennial with rounded-heart-shaped, roughly hairy, 3- to 7-palmate, mid-green leaves, to 5in (13cm) long; each of the leaflets is divided into 15–80 linear to linear-lance-shaped segments. In late spring, bears erect, broadly cup-shaped, blue-violet, lilac, or occasionally yellowish or yellowish white flowers, 2–3in (5–8cm) across. ↕ 6in (15cm), ↔ 4in (10cm). E. Europe, Russia (Siberia), North America. Zone 4.
P. vernalis ■ Clump-forming perennial (with overwintering basal leaves) bearing clusters of finely cut, very sparsely hairy, pinnate, light green leaves, 2½–5in (6–13cm) long, composed of 3–5 deeply toothed leaflets. In spring, produces pendent buds that open to erect, bell-shaped white flowers, to 2½in (6cm) across, deeply flushed with bluish violet and silky on the outside. ↕↔ to 4in (10cm). Mountains from Spain to Scandinavia, Bulgaria, and Russia (Siberia). Zone 4.
P. vulgaris ■ (Pasque flower). Clump-forming perennial with finely divided, pinnate, light green leaves, 3–8in (8–20cm) long, consisting of 7–9 leaflets, each 2- or 3-pinnatisect; the lobes are linear to linear-lance-shaped, very hairy when young. In spring, bears upright or semi-pendent, bell-shaped or narrowly bell-shaped, silky-hairy flowers, 1½–3½in (4–9cm) across, in shades of deep to pale purple, occasionally white. ↕ 4–8in (10–20cm), ↔ 8in (20cm). UK, W. France to Ukraine. Zone 3. **f. *alba*** ■ bears pure white flowers of variable size.
subsp. *grandis* see *P. halleri* subsp. *grandis.* **'Rode Klokke'** syn. 'Rote Glocke', produces deep red flowers.
var. *rubra* has deep red-violet flowers.

Pulsatilla vulgaris

Pulsatilla vulgaris f. *alba*

PULTENAEA

FABACEAE

Genus of about 120 species of evergreen shrubs from dry forest in Australia. They are cultivated for their usually alternate, occasionally opposite, linear to almost rounded leaves, and for their pea-like flowers. The axillary, usually yellow or pink flowers have notched standard petals, and are produced singly or in clusters, which are often crowded into apparently terminal heads. Where not hardy, grow in a cool greenhouse; in warmer areas, grow in a shrub border, or at the base of a wall.

• **CULTIVATION** Under glass, grow in soilless potting mix with added sharp sand, in full light. In growth, water moderately and apply a balanced liquid fertilizer every month; water sparingly in winter. Outdoors, grow in moderately fertile, well-drained soil in full sun. Pruning group 8; may need restrictive pruning under glass.

• **PROPAGATION** Sow seed at 55–64°F (13–18°C) in autumn or spring. Root semi-ripe cuttings with bottom heat in summer.

• **PESTS AND DISEASES** Gray mold may be a problem in damp conditions.

P. procumbens (Bush pea, Eggs and bacon). Low, spreading to mat-forming shrub with alternate, narrowly elliptic, mid- to deep grayish green leaves, ⅜–½in (9–15mm) long, with upfolded sides and reflexed points. In spring and early summer, bears pea-like, orange-re flowers, ½in (1.5cm) across, shaded orange-yellow, in small, apparently terminal heads. ↕ 6–12in (15–30cm), ↔ 16in (40cm) or more. New South Wales, Victoria. ❀ (min. 50°F/10°C)

▷ ***Puna clavarioides*** see *Maihueniopsis clavarioides*

PUNICA

Pomegranate

PUNICACEAE

Genus of 2 species of rounded, deciduous shrubs or trees found in scru one species occurring from S.E. Europe and S.W. Asia to the Himalayas, the other from Socotra (Yemen). They hav mostly opposite, narrowly oblong, enti leaves, and are grown for their showy, funnel-shaped, bright red flowers and large, spherical, edible fruits. Where no fully hardy, grow in a cool greenhouse or against a sunny wall, either as free-standing shrubs or fan-trained; in warmer areas, use as specimen trees, in a shrub border, or as hedging.

Punica granatum var. *nana*

• **CULTIVATION** Under glass, plant directly in a greenhouse border or in large containers of soil-based potting mix in full sun. When in growth, water freely and apply a balanced liquid fertilizer every month; water sparingly in winter. A temperature of 55–61°F (13–16°C) in autumn is required for fruit to ripen. Outdoors, grow in fertile, well-drained soil in full sun. Pruning group 1, from spring to summer; group 13 if wall-trained. Remove wayward shoots in spring.
• **PROPAGATION** Sow seed at 55–64°F (13–18°C) in spring. Root semi-ripe cuttings with bottom heat in summer.
• **PESTS AND DISEASES** Dieback, powdery mildew, leaf blotch, gray mold, and scale insects occasionally cause problems.

P. granatum (Pomegranate). Upright, spiny shrub or small, rounded tree with opposite, narrowly oblong, glossy, bright green leaves, coppery or red-veined when young, to 3in (8cm) long. Over a long period in summer, bears funnel-shaped, 5-petaled, bright orange-red flowers, to 1½in (4cm) across, singly or in clusters of up to 5, followed by spherical, yellow-brown, edible fruit, to 5in (13cm) across. ↕20ft (6m), ↔ 15ft (5m). S.E. Europe to Himalayas. ❄ (min. 35°F/2°C). **var. *nana*** ▣ is a compact, rounded shrub that bears fruit very freely; ↕↔ 12–39in (30–100cm). **'Wonderful'** Orange fruit. ↕20ft (6m), ↔ 5ft (1.6m). S.E. Europe, S. Asia.

PURSHIA

Antelope bush

ROSACEAE

Genus of 2 species of deciduous shrubs or small trees from hot, dry regions of W. North America.They have alternate, deeply 3-lobed, wavy-margined, gray-green leaves and terminal, solitary, white, cream, or yellow flowers. Grow in a warm, sheltered shrub border or at the base of a warm, sunny wall.
• **CULTIVATION** Grow in well-drained, moderately fertile soil in full sun.
• **PROPAGATION** Sow seed *in situ* when ripe or layer. Pruning group 4.
• **PESTS AND DISEASES** Infrequent.

P. tridentata. Erect, wide-spreading shrub with gray or brown bark, densely woolly branches, and wedge-shaped, softly hairy, gray-green leaves, to 1¼in (3cm) long, densely white-woolly beneath. Solitary, cream-yellow flowers, ½in (1.5cm) across, are borne from spring to summer. ↕ to 10ft (3m), ↔ 8–10ft (2.5–3m). Oregon to New Mexico. Zone 7.

PUSCHKINIA

LILIACEAE

Genus of one species of bulbous perennial, related to *Chionodoxa* and *Scilla*, occurring in the Middle East, in damp grassland. It is cultivated for its small, densely packed racemes of bell-shaped, pale blue flowers with darker blue stripes, borne in spring. The bulbs each have 2 semi-erect, basal leaves. Grow *P. scilloides* in a rock garden or among shrubs.
• **CULTIVATION** Grow in any well-drained soil in full sun or dappled shade.

Puschkinia scilloides

• **PROPAGATION** Sow seed in containers in a cold frame in summer or autumn, or remove offsets in summer.
• **PESTS AND DISEASES** Prone to viruses.

P. libanotica see *P. scilloides* var. *libanotica*.
P. scilloides ▣ (Striped squill). Small, bulbous perennial with 2 semi-erect, linear, basal leaves, 6in (15cm) long. In spring, bears compact racemes of 4–10 open bell-shaped, bluish white flowers, ½in (1.5cm) across, with dark blue stripes. ↕ to 8in (20cm), PD2in (5cm). Caucasus, Turkey, Lebanon, N. Iraq, N. Iran. Zone 4. **var. *libanotica*** ▣ syn. *P. libanotica*, has smaller white flowers, ¼–⅜in (6–9mm) across, rarely striped blue, with long, sharply pointed lobes; Turkey, Lebanon.

Puschkinia scilloides var. *libanotica*

PUTORIA

RUBIACEAE

Genus of 3 species of dwarf, evergreen shrubs occurring in sunny, rocky areas around the Mediterranean. They bear opposite, lance-shaped to obovate or oblong, malodorous, leathery, lustrous, rich, mid-green leaves. Putorias are cultivated for their long-tubed, funnel-shaped, pink to purple flowers, produced singly or in clusters from early to late summer. *P. calabrica*, the only cultivated species, is suitable for growing in a rock garden or at the base of a warm, sunny wall.
• **CULTIVATION** Grow in any well-drained soil in full sun.
• **PROPAGATION** Sow seed in containers in a cold frame in spring. Take softwood cuttings in early summer.
• **PESTS AND DISEASES** Infrequent.

P. calabrica (Stinking madder). Slow-growing, spreading shrub with elliptic-lance-shaped, leathery, mid-green leaves, ¾in (2cm) long, fetid if crushed. Produces dense, terminal clusters of funnel-shaped pink flowers, to ½in (1.5cm) long, from early to late summer. ↕3in (8cm), ↔ to 12in (30cm). Mediterranean. ❄ (min. 35°F/2°C)

PUYA

BROMELIACEAE

Genus of about 170 species of terrestrial, evergreen perennials (bromeliads) from rocky slopes, to 6,500ft (2,000m) high, in Andean South America, Costa Rica, Colombia, Guyana, N. Brazil, and N. central Argentina. They have erect or widely spreading rosettes of linear leaves with coarse marginal spines; young leaf blades are upright, mature ones are outspread. The leaf sheaths are prominent, often forming bulbous bases. The flowers are trumpet- or bell-shaped, in colors from white, greenish yellow, and sea-green to ice-blue, teal-blue, or violet; they are usually produced in erect panicles in a few species, the branches having sterile tips (which act as perches for hummingbird pollinators). Flowers are followed by green fruit capsules containing winged seeds. Puyas tolerate cold more than most bromeliads. Where not hardy, grow in a conservatory or cool greenhouse; in warmer climates, use in a desert or alpine garden, mixed border, or raised bed.
• **CULTIVATION** Under glass, grow in terrestrial bromeliad potting mix in full light. From midspring to late summer, water moderately and apply a low-nitrogen liquid fertilizer every 6–8 weeks; water sparingly at other times. Outdoors, grow in any well-drained soil in full sun. Protect from winter moisture. See also p.47.
• **PROPAGATION** Sow seed at 66–75°F (19–24°C) as soon as ripe.
• **PESTS AND DISEASES** New growth is susceptible to scale insects.

P. berteroniana ▣ Bromeliad with a caudex-like stem bearing spreading, terminal rosettes of lance-shaped, arching, dark green leaves, 24–39in (60–100cm) long, white-scaly beneath. In early summer, produces loose, pyramidal panicles, over 3ft (1m) long,

Puya berteroniana

of funnel-shaped, rich bluish green or deep blue-green flowers, 2in (5cm) long, with bright orange-yellow stamens. ↕ to 6ft (2m), ↔ 10ft (3m). C. Chile. ❄ (min. 41°F/5°C)
P. caerulea see *P. coerulea*.
P. chilensis ▣ Bromeliad with a very woody, caudex-like stem, sometimes branched, bearing spreading, dense, terminal rosettes of lance-shaped, stiff, leathery, mid-green leaves, 3ft (1m) long, with marginal spines. In summer, bears bell- to trumpet-shaped, yellow or green flowers, to 2in (5cm) long, with green sepals, in loosely branched panicles, 5ft (1.5m) long; the upper parts of the panicle branches are covered with reduced bracts. ↕15ft (5m), ↔ 6ft (2m) or more. C. Chile. ❄ (min. 41°F/5°C)

Puya chilensis

Puya mirabilis

P. coerulea, syn. *P. caerulea.* Extremely variable bromeliad producing well-developed, erect, thick stems, each with terminal, spreading rosettes of lance-shaped leaves, to 24in (60cm) long, the leaf blades ash-white, the margins with hooked, reddish brown spines, to ¼in (6mm) long. In summer, produces tubular, erect, stalked, white to dark blue flowers, 2in (5cm) or more long, in racemes or panicles, 16in (40cm) or more long. ↕↔ to 6ft (2m). C. Chile. ❄ (min. 41°F/5°C)
P. mirabilis ▣ Stemless bromeliad bearing terminal, spreading rosettes of loose, linear-lance-shaped, finely toothed, white to brownish green leaves, to 24in (60cm) long. In summer, bears loose, simple racemes, to 20in (50cm) long, of funnel-shaped, yellowish green flowers, 4in (10cm) long. ↕↔ to 24in (60cm). Bolivia, N. Argentina. ❄ (min. 41°F/5°C)
P. raimondii. Bromeliad with a thick, caudex-like stem, to 20in (50cm) across. Produces broadly lance-shaped, often red-suffused, bright green leaves, to 6ft (2m) long, densely scaly beneath, in a dense, globular, terminal rosette. In summer, tubular, greenish white, flowers, 2in (5cm) long, are borne in a cylindrical, compound raceme, to 15ft (5m) long. Monocarpic; may take 20 years or more to reach flowering size in cultivation. ↕ to 6ft (2m), ↔ 3ft (1m). Peru, Bolivia. ❄ (min. 41°F/5°C)

PYCNANTHEMUM

American mountain mint

LAMIACEAE

Genus of 21 species of perennials from open woodland and meadows of the US. *Pycnanthemum* species are grown for their opposite, lance-shaped or ovate, softly hairy, mid-green leaves, which are very aromatic when bruised. They are useful in an herb garden.
• **CULTIVATION** Grow in fertile, well-drained soil in full sun to partial shade.
• **PROPAGATION** Sow seed *in situ* in spring or autumn. Divide established plants in summer.
• **PESTS AND DISEASES** Rust is common.

P. virginianum. Upright perennial with short, leafy branches and lance-shaped to linear-elliptic leaves, to 2½in (6cm) long. In late summer, bears many 2-lipped, pink or white flowers, ⅛–⅜in (3–9cm) across, in compact corymbs. ↕ 30–36in (75–90cm), ↔ 12–18in (30–45cm). E. US. Zone 4.

PYCNOSTACHYS

LAMIACEAE

Genus of 40 species of erect, evergreen perennials or soft-stemmed shrubs occurring in forest margins in tropical and southern Africa and Madagascar. They are cultivated for their dense, terminal spikes of 2-lipped, tubular, deep blue flowers. The leaves are opposite or in whorls; linear, lance-shaped, or ovate; and rather pungent when crushed. Where not hardy, grow in a warm greenhouse or conservatory. In warmer areas, they are suitable for growing in a shrub border.
• **CULTIVATION** Under glass, grow in soil-based potting mix with added sharp sand, in full light. During the growing season, water freely and apply a balanced liquid fertilizer every month; water sparingly in winter. Outdoors, grow in fertile, well-drained soil in full sun.
• **PROPAGATION** Sow seed at 59–64°F (15–18°C) in spring. Take softwood cuttings at any time.
• **PESTS AND DISEASES** Whiteflies occur.

P. dawei ▣ Pyramidal, evergreen perennial bearing opposite, linear, mid-green leaves, to 12in (30cm) long, red beneath, with sharp points and toothed margins. In summer, bears tubular, cobalt-blue flowers, to 1in (2.5cm) long, in dense, terminal spikes, 6in (15cm) long. ↕ 6ft (1.8m), ↔ 36in (90cm). Tropical Africa. ❄ (min. 54°F/12°C)
P. urticifolia. Erect, soft-stemmed, evergreen shrub, becoming somewhat woody at the base and branching freely, with opposite, narrowly ovate, hairless or softly hairy, mid-green leaves, to 5in (13cm) long, often with toothed margins. In winter, tubular, deep blue flowers, ½–¾in (1.5–2cm) long, sometimes white with a blue tinge, are produced in dense, terminal spikes, to 4in (10cm) long. ↕ 8ft (2.5m), ↔ 4ft (1.2m). Tropical Africa and Mozambique. ❄ (min. 54°F/12°C)

Pycnostachys dawei

PYGMAEOCEREUS

CACTACEAE

Genus of 3 species of small, green cacti, many barely rising above ground level, from the coastal areas of Peru. Stems are globose and green, bearing nocturnal, broadly funnel-shaped, white flowers, 3in (8cm) across. They produce globose to pear-shaped fruit.
• **CULTIVATION** Under glass, grow in a mix of 4 parts standard cactus potting mix and 1 part limestone chips, in full light. From spring to summer, water freely and apply a balanced liquid fertilizer every 4-5 weeks. Keep nearly dry at other times. Outdoors, grow in moderately fertile, slightly alkaline, sharply drained, humus-rich soil in full sun. See also pp.48–49.
• **PROPAGATION** Sow seed at 70°F (21°C) in spring or summer.
• **PESTS AND DISEASES** Scale occurs.

P. familiaris. Numerous green stems and 9-14 wavy, tuberculate ribs, 2-3mm high. Sometimes form low clumps, with 4–10 fine to thick, brown to black, central spines; 15–25 white radials. Bear funnel-shaped, white flowers, to 3in (8cm) long. ↕ to ¾in (2cm), ↔ ½–¾in (1.5–2cm). Arequipa, Peru. ❄ (min. 50°F/10°C)

PYRACANTHA

Firethorn

ROSACEAE

Genus of 7 species of spiny, evergreen, spreading to erect shrubs, occasionally trees, found in scrub and woodland margins from S. Europe to S.W. Asia, the Himalayas, China, and Taiwan. They are cultivated for their foliage, flowers, and, in particular, fruits: the variably shaped leaves are alternate and often have toothed margins; the 5-petaled white flowers are hawthorn-like and borne in compound corymbs; the showy, spherical berries that follow them in autumn are yellow, orange, or red. Grow firethorns as free-standing shrubs in a shrub border, or against a wall, or for hedging. The seeds may cause mild stomach upset if ingested.
• **CULTIVATION** Grow in fertile, well-drained soil in full sun or partial shade. Where marginally hardy, shelter from cold, drying winds. Pruning group 1 for free-standing shrubs. Trim hedges in early to midsummer. On wall-trained plants, tie in any shoots needed to extend the framework, and cut back unwanted shoots to the main stem. After flowering, shorten lateral shoots to 2 or 3 leaves from the base to expose the developing berries. In spring, remove old fruit clusters to make way for new growth.
• **PROPAGATION** Sow seed in containers in a cold frame in autumn. Root semi-ripe cuttings with bottom heat in summer.
• **PESTS AND DISEASES** Spider mites, lacebug, caterpillars, scale insects, aphids, fireblight, dieback, scab, and wilt can be problems.

P. angustifolia. Dense, bushy shrub with narrowly oblong or obovate, dark green leaves, to 2in (5cm) long, gray-felted beneath. Small white flowers are produced in corymbs in midsummer; they are followed by orange-yellow

Pyracantha atalantioides 'Aurea'

berries, ⅜in (9mm) across. ↕↔ 10ft (3m). W. China. Zone 7.
P. atalantioides. Vigorous shrub with arching shoots and oblong-elliptic to lance-shaped, glossy, dark green leaves, to 3in (8cm) long. In spring, bears small white flowers in corymbs; they are followed by bright orange-red berries, to ¼in (6mm) across. ↕ to 20ft (6m), ↔ 12ft (4m). C. China. Zone 6b.
'Aurea' ▣ bears yellow berries.
P. coccinea (Scarlet firethorn). Dense, bushy shrub with ovate-lance-shaped, dark green leaves, to ¾–1½in (2–4cm) long. Bears small, creamy white flowers in corymbs in early summer, followed by bright scarlet berries, ¼in (6mm) across. ↕↔ 12ft (4m). S.E. Europe to Caucasus. Zone 6. **'Lalandei'** is upright in habit, with profuse, bright orange-red berries, ¼–⅜in (6–9mm) across; ↕ to 20ft (6m).
***P.* 'Golden Charmer'** ▣ Vigorous, bushy shrub with arching branches and inversely lance-shaped, glossy, bright green leaves, to 2in (5cm) long. Small white flowers are produced in corymbs in early summer, followed by bright orange-yellow berries, ⅜in (9mm) across. ↕↔ 10ft (3m). Zone 7.

Pyracantha 'Golden Charmer'

'yracantha 'Mohave'

Pyracantha 'Rutgers'

'. **'Golden Dome'.** Spreading shrub, ›rming a dense mound of arching ranches bearing oblong, glossy, dark reen leaves, to 2½in (6cm) long. In arly summer, small white flowers are roduced in corymbs; they are followed y an abundance of golden yellow erries, ¼in (6mm) across. ↕ 6ft (2m), › 10ft (3m). Zone 7.
'. **'Harlequin'**, syn. *P.* 'Variegated'. preading shrub with oblong, dark reen leaves, 2in (5cm) long, strikingly arked creamy white, flushed pink hen young. Small white flowers are roduced in corymbs in early summer, ›llowed by red berries, ¼in (6mm) cross. ↕ 5ft (1.5m), ↔ 6ft (2m). one 7.
'. ***koidzumii*** (Formosa firethorn). Erect rub with inversely lance-shaped, ossy, dark green leaves, to 2in (5cm) ›ng. Small white flowers are produced corymbs in early summer, followed y orange-red berries, ¼in (6mm) cross. ↕ 10ft (3m), ↔ 12ft (4m). 'aiwan. Zone 8. **'Low-Dense'** is ound-forming in habit, producing rge, orange-red fruit; ↕ to 6ft (2m), › to 6ft (2m). **'Rosedale'** has arching ranches and bright red berries, ⅜in mm) across.
'. **'Mohave'** ■ Vigorous, bushy shrub ith oval, dark green leaves, to 2½in cm) long. In early summer, small hite flowers are produced in corymbs, ›llowed by long-lasting red berries, ⅜in mm) across. ↕ 12ft (4m), ↔ 15ft (5m). one 6.
'. **'Orange Charmer'.** Vigorous, bushy rub with arching branches and elliptic › obovate, glossy, bright green leaves, to 2in (5cm) long. Small white flowers are produced in corymbs in early summer, followed by dark orange berries, ⅜in (9mm) across. ↕↔ 10ft (3m). Zone 6b.
***P.* 'Orange Glow'** ■ Upright, later spreading, loosely branched shrub with broadly elliptic to obovate, glossy, dark green leaves, ¾–1½in (2–4cm) long. Small white flowers are produced in corymbs in late spring, followed by a profusion of persistent, orange-red to dark orange berries, ¼–⅜in (6–9mm) across. ↕↔ 10ft (3m). Probably a cultivar of *P. fortuneana*. Zone 7.
P. rogersiana. Spreading shrub with arching branches and inversely lance-shaped to narrowly obovate, glossy, bright green leaves, to 1½in (4cm) long. Small white flowers are produced in corymbs in spring, followed by orange-red berries, ⅜in (9mm) across. ↕↔ 12ft (4m). W. China. Zone 8. **f. *flava*** has yellow berries.
***P.* 'Rutgers'** ■ Vigorous, spreading, bushy shrub with oval, glossy, dark green leaves, to 2½in (6cm) long. In early summer, small white flowers are borne in corymbs, followed by abundant, orange-red berries, ⅜in (9mm) across. ↕ 3ft (1m), ↔ 9ft (2.5m). Zone 6.
***P.* 'Santa Cruz'.** Low, compact, spreading shrub with oblong, dark green leaves, to 3in (8cm) long. Small white flowers are produced in corymbs in early summer, followed by small red berries,. ¼–⅜in (6–9mm) across. ↕ 3ft (1m), ↔ 6ft (2m). Zone 7.
***P.* 'Shawnee'.** Spreading shrub with narrowly elliptic, glossy, dark green leaves, to 2in (5cm) long. Small white flowers are borne in corymbs in early summer, followed by slightly flattened, orange-yellow berries, ⅜in (9mm) across. ↕ 10ft (3m), ↔ 12ft (4m). Zone 6b.
***P.* 'Soleil d'Or'** ■ Upright shrub with red-tinged shoots and broadly elliptic, glossy, dark green leaves, 2½in (6cm) long. In early summer, bears small white flowers in corymbs, followed by golden yellow berries, ½in (1.5cm) across. ↕ 10ft (3m), ↔ 8ft (2.5m). Zone 6.
***P.* 'Teton'.** Vigorous, upright shrub with oblong, wavy-margined, glossy, bright green leaves, to 2in (5cm) long. Small white flowers are produced in corymbs in early summer, followed by an abundance of yellow-orange berries, ¼in (6mm) across. ↕ 15ft (5m), ↔ 10ft (3m). Zone 6.
***P.* 'Variegated'** see *P.* 'Harlequin'.
P.* x *watereri ■ (*P. atalantioides* x *P. rogersiana*). Dense, upright shrub with elliptic, dark green leaves, to 2½in (6cm) long. In early summer, small white flowers are produced in corymbs, followed by bright red berries, ⅜in (9mm) across. ↕↔ 8ft (2.5m). Garden origin. Zone 6b.

'yracantha 'Orange Glow'

Pyracantha 'Soleil d'Or'

Pyracantha x *watereri*

▷ ***Pyrethropsis*** see *Rhodanthemum*
▷ ***Pyrethrum*** see *Tanacetum*
P. radicans see *Leucanthemopsis pectinata*

PYROLA

Shinleaf, Wintergreen

PYROLACEAE

Genus of 35 species of creeping, rhizomatous, evergreen perennials from woodland and moorland in the N. hemisphere. They are grown for their basal clusters of alternate, simple, usually rounded to ovate, long-stalked, mid- to dark green leaves, and their upright racemes of cup- to bowl-shaped, usually white, occasionally pink or red flowers, borne in summer. They can be difficult to establish, possibly needing a mycorrhizal association with specific, soil-dwelling fungi. Grow in a woodland garden or rock garden.

• **CULTIVATION** Grow in fertile, acidic, leafy, moist but well-drained soil in partial or dappled shade.

• **PROPAGATION** Surface-sow seed in containers of damp sphagnum moss as soon as ripe. Divide with care in spring; roots resent disturbance.

• **PESTS AND DISEASES** Slugs and snails may attack new growth. Rust is very common.

P. rotundifolia (Round-leaved winter-green, Wild lily-of-the-valley). Creeping perennial with basal clusters of rounded or broadly oval, mid- to dark green leaves, ¾–2½in (2–6cm) long. In summer, produces upright stems bearing loose racemes of up to 20 cup-shaped, pure white, rarely pink-tinged flowers, ⅜–½in (0.8–1.5cm) across, with incurving petals. ↕ 8in (20cm), ↔ 6in (15cm). Europe, North America. Zone 6.

PYROSTEGIA

BIGNONIACEAE

Genus of 3 or 4 species of woody-stemmed, evergreen tendril climbers found in tropical woodland in South America. Leaves, produced in opposite pairs, each have 2 or 3 leaflets and sometimes a terminal, 3-branched tendril. The tubular or bell-shaped, usually orange or red flowers each have a tapered base and club-like tip, with 5 short petal lobes. Where temperatures fall below 50–55°F (10–13°C), grow in a temperate or warm greenhouse. In warmer areas, grow *Pyrostegia* species over a pergola or arch, or allow to cascade from a tree.

• **CULTIVATION** Under glass, grow in soil-based potting mix with added leaf mold and sharp sand, in full light. During the growing season, water moderately and apply a balanced liquid fertilizer monthly; water sparingly in winter. Outdoors, grow in fertile, moist but well-drained soil in full sun. Support climbing stems. Pruning group 11 or 12, after flowering.

• **PROPAGATION** Sow seed at 61°F (16°C) in spring. Root semi-ripe cuttings with bottom heat in summer.

• **PESTS AND DISEASES** Scale insects, whiteflies, aphids, and spider mites occur under glass.

P. ignea see *P. venusta.*

P

Pyrostegia venusta

P. venusta ■ syn. *P. ignea* (Flame vine, Golden shower). Very vigorous climber with numerous slender stems, and opposite leaves composed of ovate to oblong-lance-shaped, rich green leaflets, to 3in (8cm) long. Bears a profusion of curved, tubular, waxy, golden to reddish orange flowers, 2½in (6cm) long, in terminal clusters, mainly in winter. ↕30ft (10m) or more. Bolivia to Brazil, Paraguay, N. Argentina. ❄ (min. 50–55°F/10–13°C)

▷ ***Pyrrhocactus crispus*** see *Neoporteria crispa*

PYRROSIA

Felt fern

POLYPODIACEAE

Genus of about 100 species of epiphytic and terrestrial, evergreen ferns with long-creeping rhizomes, mainly from tropical forest in North and South America, but also found in temperate areas in E. Asia. They are cultivated for their very small to large, mostly simple, linear to almost rounded, sometimes palmately lobed, thick, leathery fronds, the undersides of which are usually densely covered with matted and felt-like, star-shaped, branched hairs. Where not hardy, grow in a container or hanging basket in a temperate greenhouse; elsewhere, grow epiphytically on a tree or on other mossy support, or in a sheltered, shady border.

• **CULTIVATION** Under glass, grow in a mix of 1 part each loam, medium-grade bark, and charcoal, 2 parts sharp sand, and 3 parts coarse leaf mold. Provide bright filtered or indirect light, with high humidity. In growth, water freely and apply a balanced liquid fertilizer monthly; water sparingly in winter. Outdoors, grow in moderately fertile, leafy, well-drained soil in partial shade, or epiphytically on trees or slabs of wood or bark.

• **PROPAGATION** Sow spores at 70°F (21°C) when ripe. Divide in spring. See also p.51.

• **PESTS AND DISEASES** Scale insects may be troublesome.

P. lingua ■ (Japanese felt fern, Tongue fern). Evergreen fern bearing simple, lance-shaped to ovate, leathery, glossy, dark green fronds, to 12in (30cm) long, sparsely hairy above, densely covered with star-shaped hairs beneath. Spores form in patches over a large part of the undersides of the fronds. ↕4–8in (10–20cm), ↔ 12in (30cm). E. Asia, China, Taiwan, Japan (Ryukyu Islands). ❄ (min. 41°F/5°C). **'Cristata'** has fronds repeatedly forked at the tips.

PYRUS

Pear

ROSACEAE

Genus of about 45 species of upright, mainly deciduous trees and shrubs, found in woodland, in rocky places, and on hillsides in Europe, W. to E. Asia, and N. Africa. They are grown for their habit, flowers, and fruits. The leaves are alternate, entire or very rarely lobed, ovate to oblong, elliptic, or oval, the margins often with forward-pointing teeth; some have good autumn color. The 5-petaled, saucer- to bowl-shaped flowers, borne in umbel-like racemes, are white, occasionally pink, and usually have red anthers. The fruits are spherical to typically pear-shaped; numerous cultivars have been bred specifically for the production of culinary and dessert pears. Ornamental pears are best grown as specimen trees on a lawn or as street trees; the smaller ones, such as *P. salicifolia* 'Pendula', and those of narrow habit, such as *P. calleryana* 'Chanticleer', are particularly suitable for growing in a small garden or espaliered on a wall or fence.

• **CULTIVATION** Grow in any fertile, well-drained soil in full sun. Pruning group 1.

• **PROPAGATION** Sow seed in an open frame or in a seedbed in autumn. Bud in summer, or graft in winter.

Pyrus communis

• **PESTS AND DISEASES** Caterpillars, leaf roller, blister mites, aphids (foliar and root), scale insects, anthracnose, dieback, canker, scab, powdery mildew, and fireblight can occur.

P. calleryana. Broadly conical, often very thorny, deciduous tree with ovate to broadly ovate, finely scalloped or toothed, glossy, dark green leaves, to 3in (8cm) long, turning red in late autumn. White flowers, ¾in (2cm) across, are borne in umbel-like racemes of up to 12, in early spring, followed in autumn by spherical brown fruit, ½in (1.5cm) across. ↕↔ 50ft (15m). China. Zone 5b. **'Aristocrat'** has more horizontal branching and wider crotch angles, and shiny, wavy-edged, dark green leaves. **'Autumn Blaze'** has red-purple autumn color. **'Bradford'** is narrowly conical, becoming broader with age, and thornless. Bred for especially narrow branch angles, which can result in major damage to older specimens during severe snow, wind, and ice storms; ↔ 40ft (12m). **'Capital'** is narrowly conical in habit, with copper autumn color; ↕40ft (12m), ↔ 15ft (5m). **'Chanticleer'** ■ is narrowly conical; ↔ 20ft (6m). **'Red Spire'** is pyramidal, with foliage turning yellow in autumn.

P. communis ■ (Common pear). Columnar, occasionally thorny, deciduous tree with ovate to elliptic, glossy, dark green leaves, to 4in (10cm) long, with fine, forward-pointing teeth. White flowers, 1½in (4cm) across, ofte tinged pink in bud, are borne in umbel like racemes of 5–9 in midspring; they are followed by edible, pear-shaped to spherical, green to yellow fruit, to 4in (10cm) long. Parent of numerous fruit-bearing cultivars. ↕50ft (15m), ↔ 30ft (10m). S. Europe, S.W. Asia. Zone 6. **'Beech Hill'** is narrowly conical, with leaves that turn orange and red in autumn; ↕30ft (10m), ↔ 22ft (7m).

P. japonica see *Chaenomeles speciosa.*

P. nivalis (Snow pear). Broadly conica thornless, deciduous tree with elliptic t obovate, entire or shallowly scalloped, silvery gray leaves, to 3in (8cm) long, white-hairy beneath. In midspring, bea white flowers, 1¼in (3cm) across, in umbel-like racemes of 6–9, followed by spherical, yellow-green fruit, 1½in (4cm) across. ↕40ft (12m), ↔ 25ft (8m C. and S.E. Europe. Zone 7.

P. salicifolia (Willow-leaved pear). Spreading, deciduous tree with penden shoots and lance-shaped to narrowly elliptic, willow-like, gray-felted leaves, to 3½in (9cm) long, becoming hairless with age. In spring, creamy white flowers, ¾in (2cm) across, are borne in dense, umbel-like racemes of 6–8, followed by pear-shaped green fruit, 1¼in (3cm) long. ↕25ft (8m), ↔ 20ft (6m). S.E. Europe, Turkey, Iran. Zone 5. **'Pendula'** ■ has stiffly weeping branches; ↕15ft (5m), ↔ 12ft (4m).

P. ussuriensis (Chinese pear). Broadly conical, deciduous tree with broadly oval, glossy, dark green leaves, to 4in (10cm) long. White flowers, 1¼in (3cm) across, are borne in umbel-like racemes of 6–9 in midspring, followed by almost spherical green fruit, 1½in (4cm) across. ↕40ft (12m), ↔ 25ft (8m N.E. Asia. Zone 5.

P

Pyrrosia lingua

Pyrus calleryana 'Chanticleer'

Pyrus salicifolia 'Pendula'

Q

> ***Quamoclit*** see *Ipomoea*

QUAQUA

ASCLEPIADACEAE

Genus of 14 species of perennial succulents, closely related to *Caralluma*, from hilly, often rocky terrain in S. Namibia and South Africa, grown for their prominently to shallowly lobed, bowl-shaped flowers, which are borne singly or in clusters during daytime in early summer. Where temperatures fall below 50°F (10°C), grow in a warm greenhouse; in warm, dry climates, use in a raised bed with other succulents.

• **CULTIVATION** Under glass, grow in a mix of equal parts soil-based potting mix and sharp grit, in full light with shade from hot sun. During growth, water freely and apply a dilute balanced fertilizer 2 or 3 times. Keep barely moist in winter. Outdoors, grow in gritty, sharply drained, moderately fertile soil in full sun with some midday shade. See also pp.48–49.

• **PROPAGATION** Sow seed at 64–70°F (18–21°C) in spring. Take stem cuttings in late summer.

• **PESTS AND DISEASES** Prone to aphids.

Q. pillansii, syn. *Caralluma pillansii*. Erect, freely branching succulent with prominently 4-angled, sturdy, dark gray-green stems, to 1in (2.5cm) thick, spotted red, and bearing compressed brown teeth with spine-like tips. Dense clusters of 4–20 bowl-shaped, purple-brown flowers, to 1in (2.5cm) across, with purple- or red-spotted, grayish green lobes, develop from the stem grooves in early summer. ↕↔ to 12in (30cm). S. Namibia, South Africa (Western Cape). ❅ (min. 50°F/10°C)

QUERCUS

Oak

FAGACEAE

Genus of about 600 species of monoecious, deciduous, semi-evergreen or evergreen trees and shrubs, widely distributed in woodland and scrub in the N. hemisphere, and grown for their habit and foliage. They have usually fissured bark, downy to hairless shoots, and alternate, entire, lobed, or toothed leaves, which in some deciduous species produce excellent autumn color. The tiny male and female flowers are produced separately on the same plant from midspring to early summer; the males are borne in pendent catkins, the females singly, in pairs, or in racemes, followed by usually ovoid brown nuts (acorns) in scaly cups. The acorns are mostly ½–1¼in (1–3cm) long, sometimes more, and solitary or paired, but in some species are borne in racemes. Oaks are best as specimens in a large garden or a park.

• **CULTIVATION** Grow in deep, fertile, well-drained soil in sun or partial shade; evergreen species prefer full sun. They tolerate alkaline soils unless stated otherwise. Pruning group 1.

• **PROPAGATION** Sow seed in containers in a cold frame or seedbed as soon as ripe. Graft in midautumn or late winter.

• **PESTS AND DISEASES** Borers, caterpillars (including gypsy moth larvae), leaf miners, skeletonizers, scale insects, and leaf rollers can be problems. Wilt, anthracnose, twig blight, cankers, powdery mildews, orange hobnail canker, leaf blister (curl or gall), rust, mushroom root rot, white heart rot, and a variety of leaf spots may occur.

Q. acutissima, syn. *Q. serrata* (Sawtooth oak). Rounded, deciduous tree with fissured, corky, ashen-gray to black bark and long-lasting, chestnut-like, oblong-lance-shaped to obovate, glossy, mid-green leaves, to 8in (20cm) long, margined with bristle-tipped teeth. Solitary, ovoid acorns are borne in cups covered with slender, long, hairy scales. ↕↔ 50–70ft (15–20m). Himalayas, China, Korea, Japan. Zone 5.

Q. aegilops see *Q. macrolepis*.

Q. agrifolia ■ (California live oak). Spreading, evergreen tree or shrub with ridged, gray to reddish brown bark and convex, ovate-elliptic to broadly elliptic, spiny-toothed, glossy, dark green leaves, to 3in (8cm) long. Bears solitary, slender, ovoid, pointed acorns, to 1½in (4cm) long. ↕↔ 50–70ft (15–20m). California. ❅ (min. 35°F/2°C)

Q. alba (White oak). Spreading, deciduous tree with peeling, pale gray to brown bark. The obovate, oblong, or elliptic, deeply lobed, bright green leaves, to 9in (23cm) long, often pink-tinged when young, turn purple-red in autumn. Solitary acorns are ovoid-oblong. Grows best in acidic soil. ↕↔ 60–100ft (18–30m). E. North America. Zone 4.

Q. aliena (Oriental white oak). Spreading, deciduous tree with fissured, gray-brown bark, obovate, prominently toothed and veined, glossy, bright green leaves, to 8in (20cm) long, blue-green beneath, and stalked, ovoid acorns. ↕ 80ft (25m), ↔ 40ft (12m). China, Korea, Japan. Zone 6.

Q. bicolor (Swamp white oak). Spreading, deciduous tree with peeling, fissured, gray-brown bark and oblong-obovate or obovate, shallowly lobed, glossy, dark green leaves, to 6in (15cm) long, white-hairy beneath when young, orange to bright red in autumn. Bears long-stalked, oblong-ovoid acorns. ↕ 70ft (20m), ↔ 50ft (15m). S.E. US. Zone 4b.

Q. borealis see *Q. rubra*.

Q. canariensis (Mirbeck's oak). Deciduous or semi-evergreen tree, narrow when young, broadening with age, with rugged, thick black bark. Obovate-oblong to obovate, shallowly lobed, rich green leaves, to 7in (18cm) long, turn yellow-brown in autumn. Ovoid acorns are borne in clusters of up to 4. ↕ 100ft (30m), ↔ 50ft (15m). S.W. Europe, N. Africa. Zone 7b.

Q. castaneifolia ■ (Chestnut-leaved oak). Fast-growing, spreading, deciduous tree with rough, corky brown bark and chestnut-like, elliptic-oblong to oblong-lance-shaped, triangular-toothed, glossy, dark green leaves, to 6in (15cm) long, gray beneath. Ovoid acorns, in long-scaled cups, are solitary or in groups of up to 5. ↕ 80ft (25m), ↔ 70ft (20m). Caucasus, N. Iran. Zone 7b. **'Green Spire'** has upright branches; ↔ 30ft (10m).

Q. cerris (Turkey oak). Fast-growing, spreading, deciduous, very variable tree with gray-white bark, splitting into thick plates, and oblong-elliptic to oblong-lance-shaped, deeply lobed or toothed, dark green leaves, to 5in (13cm) long, pale green beneath, and yellow-brown in autumn. Ellipsoid acorns, 1–1½in (2.5–4cm) long, in cups densely covered with long, slender scales, are solitary or in groups of 2–4. ↕ 100ft (30m), ↔ 80ft (25m). C. and S. Europe. Zone 7b. **'Argenteovariegata'** ■ syn. 'Variegata', produces leaves margined with creamy yellow, later creamy white; ↕ 50ft (15m), ↔ 40ft (12m).

Q. chrysolepis (Canyon oak). Spreading, evergreen tree or shrub with scaly, whitish gray or red-tinted bark and oblong-ovate to elliptic, spiny-toothed, leathery, shining, dark green leaves, to 2½in (6cm) long, gray- or yellow-hairy beneath. Ovoid to oblong-ovoid acorns, 1–2in (2.5–5cm) long, are borne in felted cups. ↕ 70ft (20m), ↔ 30ft (10m). California. Zone 7b.

Q. coccifera (Kermes oak). Bushy, compact, evergreen shrub or tree with smooth gray bark, cracking with age, and holly-like, ovate to oblong-lance-shaped, spiny-margined, glossy, dark green leaves, 1¼–2in (3–5cm) long. Bears solitary, spherical or ovoid acorns in very spiny cups. ↕ to 30ft (10m), ↔ 12–20ft (4–6m). Mediterranean. Zone 7b.

Q. coccinea ■ (Scarlet oak). Rounded, deciduous tree with pale gray-brown bark in scaly plates. Glossy, dark green leaves, to 6in (15cm) long, are elliptic, with deep lobes ending in bristle-tipped teeth, and tufts of hairs in the vein axils beneath; the leaves turn bright red in autumn. Acorns are ovoid to nearly spherical. Requires acidic soil. ↕ 70ft (20m), ↔ 50ft (15m). E. North America. Zone 4. **'Splendens'** is very dark red in autumn.

Q. conferta see *Q. frainetto*.

Q. dentata ■ (Daimyo oak). Rugged, spreading, stoutly branched, deciduous tree with fissured brown bark, splitting into gray, scaly plates. Produces obovate, shallowly lobed to wavy-margined, dark green leaves, to 12in (30cm) or more long. Bears ovoid to nearly spherical, solitary acorns. Requires acidic soil. ↕ 50ft (15m), ↔ 30ft (10m). E. Asia. Zone 6.

Q. douglasii (Blue oak). Spreading, deciduous tree with a rounded, dense, symmetrical crown and white-gray bark with small brown or red scales. The oblong to elliptic, deeply 3–5 lobed, blunt- or round-tipped, mid-green leaves are 2–3in (5–8cm) long and become blue-green. Solitary, stalkless, ovoid acorns are borne in flat, thin cups with softly-hairy, pale green insides. ↕ to 65ft (20m), ↔ 40ft (12m). California. Zone 6b.

Q. dumosa (California scrub oak). Semi-evergreen shrub or small tree with variable, leathery, mid-green leaves, ½–1in (1.5–2.5cm) long, woolly beneath. Thick cups cover half of the stalkless, ovoid acorns. ↕ to 12ft (4m), ↔ 6–8ft (2–2.5m). W. California, Mexico (N. Baja California). Zone 7b.

Q. ellipsoidalis ■ (Northern pin oak). Spreading, deciduous tree with smooth gray bark. Glossy, dark green leaves, to 5in (13cm) long, are elliptic with wedge-shaped bases, and deeply cut into bristle-tipped lobes; they turn red-purple in autumn. Acorns are ellipsoid. Needs acidic soil. ↕ 70ft (20m), ↔ 50ft (15m). Central N. US. Zone 3.

Q. falcata (Southern red oak). Spreading, deciduous tree with fissured, gray-brown bark. Elliptic, dark green leaves, 3½–9in (9–23cm) long, white- or gray-hairy beneath, are deeply cut into bristle-tipped, usually curved lobes, the terminal lobe often long. Bears broadly ellipsoid to spherical acorns. Requires acidic soil. ↕ 50ft (15m), ↔ 40ft (12m). S.E. US. Zone 7.

Q. frainetto, syn. *Q. conferta* (Hungarian oak, Italian oak). Fast-growing, spreading, deciduous tree with rugged, dark gray bark and obovate, dark green leaves, to 8in (20cm) long, cut into numerous rounded lobes and turning yellow-brown in autumn. Ellipsoid to ovoid-oblong acorns are borne in clusters of 2–4. ↕ 100ft (30m), ↔ 70ft (20m). S.E. Europe. Zone 7.

Quercus agrifolia

Quercus castaneifolia

Quercus cerris 'Argenteovariegata'

Quercus coccinea

Quercus dentata

Quercus ellipsoidalis

Quercus ilex

'Hungarian Crown' is compact and upright; ↕ 70ft (20m), ↔ 30ft (10m).
Q. gambellii (Gambel oak). Deciduous shrub or small tree with deeply grooved, often red-brown-tinted, dark gray bark. Obovate, hairless, mid-green leaves, 3–5in (8–13cm) long, have 6–12 deep, irregular lobes. Ovoid, woolly, round-tipped acorns have spherical to top-shaped tops. ↕ to 25ft (8m), ↔ 10–12ft (3–4m). Wyoming, Utah, Colorado, New Mexico. Zone 5.
Q. garryana ■ (Oregon oak). Rounded, deciduous tree with shallowly cracked, pale gray bark and orange-red, hairy young shoots. Glossy, oblong-obovate, dark green leaves, to 6in (15cm) long, have up to 5 deep, entire lobes on each side. The solitary, ovoid acorns are sweet and edible. ↕↔ 30ft (10m). W. North America. Zone 7b.
Q. hemisphaerica (Laurel oak). Pyramidal-rounded deciduous tree with gray-brown bark and lance-shaped-obovate to oblong-obovate, thick, shiny, dark green leaves, 1¼–4in (3–10cm) long. Bears solitary ovoid acorns, ½in (1.5cm) long. ↕ 40–60ft (12–18m), ↔ 30–40ft (10–12m). S. New Jersey to Florida to E. Texas. Zone 7.
Q. x heterophylla ■ (*Q. phellos* x *Q. rubra*) (Bartram oak). Spreading, deciduous tree with smooth, pale gray bark. Oblong-lance-shaped to obovate, entire to shallowly bristle-toothed, glossy, mid-green leaves, are to 6in (15cm) long, turning orange to red in autumn. Ovoid acorns have very shallow cups. Requires acidic soil. ↕ 70ft (20m), ↔ 50ft (15m). E. US. Zone 7.
Q. x hispanica (*Q. cerris* x *Q. suber*), syn. *Q.* x *pseudosuber*. Upright, semi-evergreen tree with corky, gray-brown bark and very variable (often fiddle-shaped, lobed, or oblong-elliptic), glossy, dark green leaves, to 2in (5cm) long, white-hairy beneath. Oblong-ovoid acorns are to 1½in (4cm) long. ↕ 40ft (12m), ↔ 25ft (8m). Portugal to Balkans. Zone 7b. **'Diversifolia'**, syn. *Q.* x *lucombeana* 'Diversifolia', has unusual leaves: in some, the central portions are reduced to narrow strips; others are fiddle- or spoon-shaped; ↔ 12–15ft (4–5m). **'Lucombeana'** ■ syn. *Q.* x *lucombeana*, *Q.* x *lucombeana* 'William Lucombe' (Lucombe oak) has ovate to oblong leaves, to 5in (13cm) long; ↕ 80ft (25m), ↔ 70ft (20m).
Q. ilex ■ (Holly oak, Holm oak). Rounded, evergreen tree with smooth, dark gray bark and very variable, usually oblong-ovate to lance-shaped, entire or toothed, glossy, dark green leaves, to 3in (8cm) long, gray-hairy beneath, and silvery gray when young. Bears oblong-ovoid to nearly rounded acorns, solitary or in groups of 2 or 3. ↕ 80ft (25m), ↔ 70ft (20m). S.W. Europe. Zone 7b. **'Fordii'** has narrowly oblong, wavy-margined leaves.
Q. ilicifolia (Scrub oak). Spreading, deciduous small tree or shrub with smooth gray bark and obovate to elliptic leaves, to 4in (10cm) long, each with usually 5 bristle-tipped, triangular lobes, dark green above and gray-hairy beneath; they turn red or yellow in autumn. Bears paired, ovoid to nearly spherical acorns. ↕ 20ft (6m), ↔ 15ft (5m). E. US. Zone 5.
Q. imbricaria (Shingle oak). Spreading, deciduous tree with smooth, gray-brown bark and oblong to lance-shaped or obovate, entire, glossy, dark green leaves, to 7in (18cm) long, gray-hairy beneath, turning yellow-brown in autumn, and normally drying and persisting until spring. Bears solitary, nearly spherical acorns. ↕ 70ft (20m), ↔ 50ft (15m). C. and E. US. Zone 4b.
Q. kelloggii (California black oak). Rounded, deciduous tree with cracked, dark brown bark and elliptic, deeply lobed, glossy, dark green leaves, 3–9in (8–23cm) long; they each have usually 7 bristle-tipped lobes, and turn yellow-brown in autumn. Produces ovoid-oblong acorns, to 1½in (4cm) long. ↕ 70ft (20m), ↔ 50ft (15m). Oregon, California. Zone 7b.
Q. laurifolia ■ (Laurel oak). Rounded, deciduous tree with fissured, gray-black bark and narrowly oblong to obovate, entire to 3-lobed, smooth, glossy, dark green leaves, to 4in (10cm) long, bronze when young, lasting well into winter. Acorns are spherical-ovoid. Requires acidic soil. ↕↔ 70ft (20m). S.E. US. Zone 7b.
***Q. x libanerris* 'Rotterdam'.** Fast-growing, spreading, deciduous tree with fissured gray bark and oblong, sharply toothed and lobed, glossy, dark green leaves, to 5in (13cm) long, gray-hairy beneath. Acorns are similar to those of *Q. cerris.* ↕ probably 70ft (20m), ↔ 50ft (15m). Recent garden origin. Zone 7.
Q. libani (Lebanon oak). Rounded, deciduous or semi-evergreen tree with smooth, later fissured, gray bark and slender shoots. Chestnut-like, oblong-lance-shaped to oblong, glossy, dark green leaves, to 4in (10cm) long, with numerous bristly marginal teeth, last well into winter. Acorns are ovoid to cylindrical. ↕↔ 50ft (15m). Turkey, Syria, N. Iraq, N. Iran. Zone 7.
Q. lobata (Valley oak). Slow-growing, spreading, deciduous tree with deeply furrowed, gray to brown bark. Obovate, dark green leaves, to 3in (8cm) long, are each deeply divided into 11 rounded lobes, and are finely hairy beneath. Bears ovoid, sweet, edible acorns, to 1½in (4cm) long. ↕ 52ft (16m), ↔ 50ft (15m). California. Zone 7b.
Q. x lucombeana see *Q.* x *hispanica* 'Lucombeana'.
***Q. x lucombeana* 'Diversifolia'** see *Q.* x *hispanica* 'Diversifolia'.
***Q. x lucombeana* 'William Lucombe'** see *Q.* x *hispanica* 'Lucombeana'.
Q. lyrata (Overcup oak). Deciduous tree with a rounded crown and red-brown-tinted, light gray bark, which breaks into large plates. Obovate, dark green leaves, 7–8in (18–20cm) long, softly hairy beneath, have 6–8 lobes, th upper ones more finely divided. Gray-woolly cups cover two-thirds or more o the spherical, chestnut-brown acorns. ↕ to 100ft (30m), ↔ 50–70ft (15–20m) C. and S. US. Zone 5.
Q. macranthera ■ Fast-growing, spreading, deciduous tree with fissured, gray-brown bark and thick, hairy shoot Obovate, mid- to dark green leaves, to 7in (18cm) long, have numerous rounded lobes, cut more deeply toward the bases. Bears solitary, ovoid-ellipsoid acorns. ↕ 70ft (20m), ↔ 50ft (15m). Caucasus, N. Iran. Zone 7.
Q. macrocarpa ■ (Bur oak, Mossycup oak). Slow-growing, spreading, deciduous tree with ridged, dark brown bark and corky, hairy shoots. Glossy, dark green leaves, to 10in (25cm) long, white-hairy beneath, are obovate to oblong-obovate, with deep and irregula lobes. Solitary, ovoid acorns, to 2in (5cm) long, are borne in large, fringed cups. ↕ 50ft (15m), ↔ 30ft (10m). E. North America. Zone 2.
Q. macrolepis ■ syn. *Q. aegilops.* Spreading, deciduous or semi-evergreen often broad-crowned tree with fissured, dark gray bark. Ovate to oblong, gray-green leaves, to 4in (10cm) long, with angular, bristle-tipped lobes, are densel white-hairy or yellowish white-hairy on both surfaces. Bears acorns, to 1¾in

Quercus phellos (inset: autumn leaf color)

Q

(4.5cm) long, singly or in clusters of 2 or 3, in unusually large, scaly cups, to 2½in (6cm) across. ↕50ft (15m), ↔40ft (12m). S.E. Europe, Turkey. Zone 8.

Q. marilandica ▣ (Blackjack oak). Spreading, deciduous small tree with very rough, black-brown bark. Broadly obovate, glossy, dark green leaves, 2½–7in (6–18cm) long, each end in 3 bristle-tipped lobes, and turn yellow, red, or brown in autumn. Produces ovoid acorns. Requires acidic soil. ↕40ft (12m), ↔50ft (15m). S.E. US. Zone 7.

Q. mongolica. Spreading, deciduous tree with rough gray bark and obovate, dark green leaves, to 8in (20cm) or more long, with rounded lobes. Produces ovoid to ellipsoid acorns. ↕70ft (20m), ↔50ft (15m). E. Asia. Zone 3. **var. *grosseserrata*** has leaves with acutely triangular and tooth-like lobes.

Q. muehlenbergii ▣ (Chinkapin oak, Yellow chestnut oak). Rounded, deciduous tree with gray, scaly bark and elliptic to obovate, pointed, glossy, dark green or yellow-green leaves, to 6in (15cm) long, whitish green beneath, triangularly lobed and with numerous curved teeth, turning yellow-brown in autumn. Produces ovoid acorns. ↕50ft (15m), ↔40ft (12m). E. US. Zone 4b.

Q. myrsinifolia (Chinese evergreen oak). Rounded, evergreen tree or shrub with smooth, dark gray bark and lance-shaped, tapered, weakly toothed, glossy, dark green leaves, to 5in (13cm) long, bronze-red when young. Solitary, ovoid-oblong acorns are borne in distinctively

Quercus robur f. *fastigiata*

ringed cups. ↕40ft (12m), ↔30ft (10m). S. China, Laos, Japan. Zone 7b.

Q. nigra ▣ (Water oak). Broadly conical, deciduous tree with smooth, brown then dark gray bark. Variable, dark green leaves, 1½–6in (4–15cm) long, are narrowly obovate or spoon-shaped, rarely elliptic, usually 3-lobed, and retained late on the tree. Acorns are spherical. Needs acidic soil. ↕50ft (15m), ↔40ft (12m). S.E. US. Zone 7b.

Q. palustris ▣ (Pin oak). Fast-growing, broadly conical, deciduous tree with pendent lower branches and smooth gray bark. Elliptic, deeply lobed, glossy, mid-green leaves, to 6in (15cm) long, are broadly tapered at the bases; they have large tufts of hairs in the leaf vein axils beneath, and turn scarlet to red-brown in autumn. Acorns are nearly spherical. ↕70ft (20m), ↔40ft (12m). E. US. Zone 4. **'Sovereign'** has spreading lower branches.

Q. pedunculata see *Q. robur.*

Q. petraea, syn. *Q. sessiliflora* (Durmast oak). Spreading, deciduous tree with ridged gray bark and yellow-stalked, ovate, obovate, or oblong, dark green leaves, 2½–7in (6–18cm) long, margined with rounded lobes. Stalkless, ovoid to oblong-ovoid acorns are borne singly or in clusters of 2–5. ↕100ft (30m), ↔80ft (25m). Europe. Zone 5. **'Columna'** is upright and columnar, with oblong, lobed or entire, bluish green leaves; ↕70ft (20m), ↔20ft (6m).

Q. phellos ▣ syn. *Q. pumila* (Willow oak). Spreading, deciduous tree with smooth gray bark and willow-like, entire or slightly wavy-margined, slender, linear to narrowly oblong, bright dark green leaves, to 5in (13cm) long; in autumn, they turn yellow, then brown. Acorns are spherical. ↕70ft (20m), ↔50ft (15m). E. US. Zone 7.

Q. phillyreoides ▣ (Ubame oak). Spreading, evergreen tree with smooth, brownish gray to dark gray bark and oblong to ovate-oblong, toothed, dark green leaves, to 2½in (6cm) long, often bronze when young. Ovoid acorns are borne in cone-shaped cups. ↕↔30ft (10m). China, S. Japan. Zone 7b.

Q. pontica (Armenian oak). Shrubby or oval-headed, deciduous, small tree with shallowly fissured, pale gray-brown bark and thick reddish shoots. Obovate or elliptic to broadly elliptic, bright mid-green leaves, to 10in (25cm) long, with numerous parallel veins ending in small, pointed teeth, turn yellow-brown in autumn. Ovoid acorns are borne singly or in thick-stalked clusters of 2–5, at the shoot tips. ↕20ft (6m), ↔15ft (5m). N.E. Turkey, Caucasus. Zone 6.

Q. prinus (Basket oak, Chestnut oak). Dense, rounded, deciduous tree with obovate to obovate-oblong, shiny, dark yellowish green leaves, 4–6in (10–15cm) long, slightly densely gray-woolly beneath, turning orange-yellow to yellowish brown in autumn. Bears ovoid acorns, ¾in (2cm) across, singly or in pairs. ↕↔60–70ft (18–20m). S. Maine and Ontario to South Carolina and Alabama. Zone 5.

Q. x pseudosuber see *Q.* x *hispanica.*

Q. pubescens. Spreading, deciduous tree with deeply furrowed, gray to black bark and densely hairy shoots. Oblong-ovate, gray-green leaves, to 4in (10cm) long, hairy beneath, have rounded lobes ending in small, pointed teeth. Ovoid

Quercus garryana

Quercus x *heterophylla*

Quercus x *hispanica* 'Lucombeana'

Quercus laurifolia

Quercus macranthera

Quercus macrocarpa

Quercus macrolepis

Quercus marilandica

Quercus muehlenbergii

Quercus nigra

Quercus palustris

Quercus phillyreoides

Quercus robur 'Concordia'

Quercus rubra

Quercus rubra 'Aurea'

acorns are borne singly or in groups of up to 4. ↕30–70ft (10–20m), ↔50ft (15m). C. and S. Europe, Turkey, Ukraine (Crimea). Zone 6.

Q. pumila see *Q. phellos.*

Q. pyrenaica. Broadly columnar, deciduous tree with furrowed, brown to black bark and often pendent, downy shoots. Obovate, elliptic, or broadly oblong, deeply lobed and toothed, glossy, dark green leaves, to 6in (15cm) long, downy when young, emerge in late spring. The oblong-ovoid acorns are produced in clusters of 2–4. ↕70ft (20m), ↔40ft (12m). France, Spain, Portugal, Morocco. Zone 7b.

Q. robur, syn. *Q. pedunculata* (English oak, Pedunculate oak). Rugged, spreading, deciduous tree with fissured, gray-brown bark. Dark green, very short-stalked leaves, to 5½in (14cm) long, are ovate-oblong, with rounded lobes, each base with two small, ear-like lobes. Ovoid acorns are borne singly or in clusters of 2 or 3. ↕120ft (35m), ↔80ft (25m). Europe. Zone 5. **'Concordia'** ▣ has bright yellow young foliage, turning green; ↕↔30ft (10m). **f. *fastigiata*** ▣ has upright branches; ↕↔50ft (15m). **f. *pendula*** has weeping shoots.

Q. rubra ▣ syn. *Q. borealis* (Northern red oak). Fast-growing, spreading, deciduous tree with smooth, grayish brown or dark gray bark. Elliptic, matte, dark green leaves, to 8in (20cm) long, cut into bristle-tipped lobes, turn yellow- to red-brown in autumn. Acorns are hemispherical. Requires acidic soil. ↕80ft (25m), ↔70ft (20m). E. North America. Zone 3. **'Aurea'** ▣ produces golden yellow leaves in spring, turning green; ↕60–70ft (18–20m), ↔50ft (15m).

Q. serrata see *Q. acutissima.*

Q. sessiliflora see *Q. petraea.*

Quercus suber

Q. shumardii. (Shumard red oak). Broadly columnar, deciduous tree with smooth gray bark. Leaves are glossy, dark green, to 7in (18cm) long, elliptic to elliptic-obovate, truncate, each with up to 9 lobes ending in bristle-tipped teeth, and turn red to red-brown in autumn. Acorns are ovoid. Requires acidic soil. ↕ 70ft (20m), ↔ 40ft (12m). S.E. US. Zone 5.
Q. suber ▣ (Cork oak). Rounded, evergreen tree with thick, corky bark (the cork of commerce). Ovate-oblong, toothed, rigid, dark green leaves, to 3in (8cm) long, are gray-hairy beneath. Bears ovoid-oblong acorns. ↕↔ 70ft (20m). W. Mediterranean, N. Africa. Zone 8.
Q. x turneri (*Q. ilex* x *Q. robur*) (Turner oak). Dense, rounded, semi-evergreen tree with fissured, brownish gray to dark gray bark and obovate, shallowly lobed, dark green leaves, to 5in (13cm) long. Bears ovoid acorns in clusters of 3–7. ↕↔ 70ft (20m). Garden origin. Zone 6b.
Q. velutina (Black oak). Fast-growing, spreading, deciduous tree with ridged, dark brown, almost black bark. Elliptic, glossy, dark green leaves, to 10in (25cm) long, each with up to 7 pointed, deep lobes, turn red-brown in autumn. Acorns are more or less spherical. Requires acidic soil. ↕ 100ft (30m), ↔ 80ft (25m). E. North America. Zone 5.
Q. virginiana ▣ (Live oak). Massive, wide-spreading evergreen tree with shallow-grooved, red-brown bark and elliptic-ovate, leathery, shiny, dark green leaves, 1¼–5in (3–13cm) long, softly woolly beneath. Bears acorns, ¾–1in (2–2.5cm) long, singly or in clusters of 2–5. ↕ 40–80ft (12–25m), ↔ 60–100ft (18–30m). Virginia to Florida to Mexico. ❄ (min. 35°F/2°C)
Q. wislizeni (Interior live oak). Spreading, evergreen tree or shrub with blackish or reddish brown bark and broadly lance-shaped to broadly elliptic, usually spiny-toothed, glossy, dark green leaves, 1–1½in (2.5–4cm) long. Bears solitary, oblong-ellipsoid acorns, to 1½in (4cm) long. ↕ to 70ft (20m), ↔ 40ft (12m). California. Zone 8.

QUESNELIA

BROMELIACEAE

Genus of approximately 16 species of almost stemless, evergreen, terrestrial or epiphytic perennials (bromeliads), some rhizomatous, found in scrub, woodland, or rainforest in E. Brazil, to 6,500ft (2,000m). They are cultivated for their rosetted, lance-shaped, spiny-margined, thick, stiff leaves, which may actually be toothed in the larger species, and their upright or pendent, ellipsoid or cylindrical, dense or lax inflorescences of ovoid or tubular flowers, borne among showy bracts from late spring to summer. The flowers range in color from red, violet, and blue to nearly black. Below 55°F (13°C), grow as houseplants or in a warm greenhouse; elsewhere, grow in a humid, moist part of the garden.

• **CULTIVATION** Under glass, grow in epiphytic or terrestrial bromeliad potting mix in bright filtered light. Water moderately at all times and regularly mist lightly. Apply a nitrogen-based fertilizer monthly during the growing season. Outdoors, grow in open, humus-rich, moist, well-drained soil in partial shade. See also p.47.

• **PROPAGATION** Sow seed at 81°F (27°C) as soon as ripe. Remove offsets in late spring or summer.

• **PESTS AND DISEASES** Young growth is vulnerable to scale insects.

Quercus virginiana

Quesnelia marmorata

Q. arvensis. Terrestrial or epiphytic perennial with spreading rosettes of narrowly lance-shaped, leathery, mid-green leaves, 2ft (60cm) long, with sharply toothed leaf blades and silver bands. In summer, bears erect, cone- or bottlebrush-shaped, short-lived inflorescences, to 8in (20cm) long, of iridescent salmon-pink bracts and half-hidden blue flowers, 1¾in (4.5cm) long, with blue sepals. ↕↔ 2ft (60cm). E. Brazil. ❄ (min. 41°F/5°C)
Q. liboniana. Epiphytic perennial with funnel-shaped rosettes of lance-shaped, stiff, minutely brown-scaly, dark green leaves, 30–32in (75–80cm) long, margined with straight or curved spines. From late spring to summer, bears simple or few-branched inflorescences, 4in (10cm) long, consisting of orange-red bracts and tubular, deep purple-blue flowers, 2in (5cm) long, with yellow sepals, flushed orange-red. ↕↔ 30in (75cm). E. Brazil. ❄ (min. 55°F/13°C)
Q. marmorata ▣ syn. *Aechmea marmorata*. Epiphytic, rhizomatous perennial with tubular rosettes of thick, 2-ranked, lance-shaped, grayish green leaves, 16–24in (40–60cm) long, marked lilac and green, with pinkish gray marginal spines. From late spring to summer, bears pyramid-shaped, terminal inflorescences, 8in (20cm) long, consisting of tiny pink floral bracts and ovoid, blue or purple flowers, 1¼in (3cm) long, with blue-purple sepals. ↕ 24in (60cm), ↔ 12in (30cm) or more. E. Brazil. ❄ (min. 55°F/13°C)

QUISQUALIS

COMBRETACEAE

Genus of about 16 species of woody-stemmed, evergreen climbers or scanden shrubs from tropical forest in Africa, South Africa, Indonesia, and Malaysia. They have been introduced throughout the tropics as an ornamental plant. In nature, quisnalias are propagated by seed and dispersed by water. They are cultivated for their small, tubular, 5-lobed flowers, borne in terminal or axillary racemes or panicles. Leaves are simple and usually produced in opposite pairs. In some areas, their seeds and leaves are used for therapeutic purposes. Where temperatures fall below 55°F (13°C), grow in a warm greenhouse. In tropical climates, use to cover an arch or wall.

• **CULTIVATION** Under glass, grow in soil-based potting mix in full light with shade from hot sun. When in growth, water freely and apply a balanced liquid fertilizer every month. Water sparingly in winter. Outdoors, grow in fertile, moist but well-drained soil in full sun with some midday shade. Pruning group 11, in late winter or early spring.

• **PROPAGATION** Sow seed at 64°F (18°C) in spring. Root softwood cuttings in late spring. Layer in spring.

• **PESTS AND DISEASES** Spider mites and fungal leaf spots sometimes occur.

Q. indica ▣ (Rangoon creeper). Freely branching, perennial climber, shrub-like when young. Mid- to deep green leaves, 3–7in (8–18cm) long, are elliptic-oblong, with rounded to heart-shaped bases, long, sharp tips, and prominent veins. In summer and autumn, bears slender-tubed, fragrant flowers, 1½–3in (4–8cm) long, with 5 spreading lobes, in pendent, terminal racemes, 4in (10cm) long; initially white, becoming pink and purplish red, then bright red over a 3-day period. ↕ to 70ft (20m) or more. Tropical Africa and S.E. Asia. ❄ (min. 55°F/13°C)

Quisqualis indica

Q

R

RAMONDA

GESNERIACEAE

Genus of 3 species of rosette-forming, evergreen perennials from shady rock crevices and cliff faces in N.E. Spain, the Pyrenees, and Balkan Mountains. They are cultivated for their hairy, crinkled leaves, of variable shape and color, and their flat or shallowly cup-shaped, colorful flowers. The flowers are often slightly 2-lipped, with 4 or 5, rarely 6 petals, and are borne singly or in cyme-like panicles on slender, leafless stems, in late spring and early summer. Grow ramondas in a rock garden, in crevices in a stone wall, or in an alpine house.

• **CULTIVATION** In an alpine house, grow in equal parts loam, leaf mold, and grit, in bright filtered light with shade from hot sun. Outdoors, grow in moist but well-drained, humus-rich, moderately fertile soil in partial shade. Plants are best grown on their sides to avoid accumulation of moisture in the rosettes, which may cause rotting in winter. Leaves wither in dry conditions, but recover if watered thoroughly.

• **PROPAGATION** Sow seed very thinly in containers in a cold frame as soon as ripe. Seedlings develop slowly, so do not prick out until they have several leaves. Root rosettes in early summer, or root leaf cuttings in early autumn.

• **PESTS AND DISEASES** Very susceptible to slug and snail damage.

R. myconi ▣ syn. *R. pyrenaica.* Rosette-forming, evergreen perennial with elliptic to very broadly ovate, hairy, slightly crinkled, dark green leaves, to 3in (8cm) long. Cyme-like panicles of outward-facing, flat, 5-petaled flowers, 1in (2.5cm) across, usually deep violet-blue with yellow anthers, are produced in late spring and early summer; pink- and white-flowered variants also occur.

Ramonda myconi

↕4in (10cm), ↔ to 8in (20cm). Pyrenees, N.E. Spain. Zone 4.

R. nathaliae. Rosette-forming, evergreen perennial with elliptic to broadly ovate, hairy, slightly crinkled, glossy, pale green leaves, to 2in (5cm) long, entire or with slightly scalloped margins. In late spring and early summer, bears cyme-like panicles of outward-facing, flattish, 4-petaled, deep mauve-blue flowers, to 1½in (4cm) across, with orange-yellow eyes and yellow anthers. ↕↔ 4in (10cm). Bosnia and Herzegovina, Macedonia, N. Greece. Zone 6.

R. pyrenaica see *R. myconi.*

R. serbica. Rosette-forming, evergreen perennial with narrowly obovate, hairy, crinkled, irregularly scalloped, pale green leaves, to 2in (5cm) long. In late spring and early summer, outward-facing, saucer- to cup-shaped, lilac-blue flowers, 1½in (4cm) across, each with 5, sometimes 6 petals and violet-blue anthers, open singly or in pairs in cyme-like panicles. ↕4in (10cm), ↔ 6in (15cm). Croatia, Yugoslavia, Albania, W. Greece, N.W. Bulgaria. Zone 6.

RANUNCULUS

Buttercup, Crowfoot

RANUNCULACEAE

Genus of about 400 species of annuals, biennials, and mainly deciduous, sometimes evergreen perennials, widely distributed in temperate regions of the world. They are found in a range of habitats, varying from damp woodland to grassland, and from mountain screes and summer-dry sites to bogs or shallow water. They may be rhizomatous, tuberous, fibrous-rooted, or spread by runners. The leaves form basal rosettes or are sometimes stem-clasping; they are very variable in shape, and may be simple and entire, toothed to palmately lobed, or pinnatisect. Buttercups are grown for their bowl-shaped, or cup- to saucer-shaped, usually 5-petaled, mainly yellow, but also white, pink, orange, or red flowers, which are borne singly or in cyme-like panicles in spring, summer, or occasionally in autumn. Buttercups are suitable for a wide range of sites (see cultivation groups below). Contact with the sap may irritate skin.

• **CULTIVATION** Buttercups have a range of cultivation requirements; for ease of reference, they have been divided into groups as follows:

1. Woodland buttercups, best in partial or full shade in moist, humus-rich soil.

2. Buttercups easily grown in sun or partial shade, in fertile, moist, well-drained soil; grow in a border or rock garden.

3. High alpine buttercups, best grown in gritty, humus-rich, sharply drained soil in a scree bed in full sun, or in an alpine house in a mix of equal parts loam, leaf mold, and grit, in full light.

4. Aquatic or bog plants, best grown in mud at a pond margin or streamside. Grow *R. aquatilis* in 6–24in (15–60cm) of still or fast-moving water; grow *R. lingua* and *R. flammula* in 6–9in (15–23cm) of still or slow-moving water.

5. Tuberous buttercups (except *R. ficaria*) that require a dry, dormant period in summer; best in a bulb frame or alpine house in a mix of equal parts loam, leaf mold, and grit, in full light.

• **PROPAGATION** Sow seed of most alpine species in pans in an open frame

Ranunculus aconitifolius

when seed is still slightly green; germination is erratic, and pans should be retained for several years if seeds fail to germinate in the first year. Sow seed of perennials, aquatic perennials, and mat-forming alpines in containers in a cold frame as soon as ripe, or divide in spring or autumn. Divide tuberous species, or detach basal bulbils (where these form), in spring or autumn.

• **PESTS AND DISEASES** Susceptible to viruses, bacterial spots, downy mildew, powdery mildew, rust, leaf smut, and a few fungal spots. Slugs, snails, leaf miners, spider mites, and aphids also cause problems outdoors.

R. aconitifolius ▣ (Bachelor's buttons). Clump-forming, hairy, fibrous-rooted perennial producing palmately 3- to 5-lobed, toothed, glossy, dark green, basal leaves, to 8in (20cm) long. In late spring and early summer, freely branched stems bear numerous red-tinged buds that open to panicles of saucer-shaped white flowers, ½–¾in (1–2cm) across, with red- or purple-backed sepals. Cultivation group 1 or 2. ↕24in (60cm), ↔ 18in (45cm). C. Europe. Zone 5. **'Flore Pleno'** ▣ (Fair maids of France, Fair maids of Kent, White bachelor's buttons) has long-lasting, double white flowers with numerous small petals.

R. acris (Tall buttercup). Erect, hairy, fibrous-rooted perennial, sometimes with short rhizomes. The long-stalked, broadly ovate, palmately 3- to 7-lobed, mid-green, basal leaves, 3in (8cm) long, have toothed lobes, which are sometimes further divided. Many-branched

Ranunculus aconitifolius 'Flore Pleno'

Ranunculus acris 'Flore Pleno'

stems bear panicles of numerous saucer-shaped, glossy, golden yellow flowers, to 1in (2.5cm) across, in early and mid-summer. Cultivation group 1 or 2. ↕8–36in (20–90cm), ↔ 9in (23cm). Europe and W. Asia. Zone 4. **'Farrer's Yellow'** has pale yellow flowers. **'Flore Pleno'** ▣ bears many-petaled yellow flowers.

R. alpestris ▣ Short-lived, tufted, occasionally evergreen perennial with fibrous roots. The kidney-shaped, palmately 3- to 5-lobed, basal leaves, are 1¼–2in (3–5cm) long, round-toothed, glossy and dark green. From late spring to midsummer, bears cup-shaped white flowers, to ¾in (2cm) across, singly or occasionally in clusters of 2 or 3. Cultivation group 3. ↕↔ to 4in (10cm). Mountains of C. and S. Europe. Zone 7b.

R. amplexicaulis. Clump-forming perennial with fibrous roots and ovate-lance-shaped, entire, sometimes sparsely hairy, gray-green basal leaves, to 3in (8cm) long, and smaller leaves clasping the upright, branching stems. In early summer, bears cyme-like panicles of up to 5 cup-shaped white flowers, each ¾–1in (2–2.5cm) across. Cultivation

Ranunculus alpestris

Ranunculus aquatilis

group 2. ↕ to 12in (30cm), ↔ 8in (20cm). Pyrenees, N. and C. Spain. Zone 3.

R. aquatilis ▣ (Water crowfoot). Aquatic annual or usually evergreen perennial with submerged, branched, slender stems and dark green leaves, 1¼–3in (3–8cm) long. The kidney-shaped to rounded, floating leaves are deeply divided into 3–7 lobes; the submerged leaves have many thread-like segments. Solitary, bowl- or saucer-shaped, white-based yellow flowers, ¾in (2cm) across, are borne on the water's surface in midsummer. Cultivation group 4. ↔ indefinite. Europe. Zone 5.

R. asiaticus ▣ (Persian buttercup). Tuberous, fibrous-rooted perennial with long-stalked, broadly ovate to rounded, deeply 3-lobed, hairy, pale to dark green, basal leaves, to 5½in (14cm) long, the lobes further subdivided and toothed. Branching flowering stems bear 1–4 cup-shaped, red, pink, yellow, or white flowers, 1¼–2in (3–5cm) across, with purple-black centers, in late spring and early summer. Cultivation group 5. ↕ 8–18in (20–45cm), ↔ 8in (20cm). E. Mediterranean, N.E. Africa, S.W. Asia. Zone 7b. Cultivars of **Bloomingdale Series** are dwarf, with double flowers, 4in (10cm) across, in shades of red, pink, yellow, pale orange, and white; ↕ 8–10in (20–25cm), ↔ 12–16in (30–40cm). **Tecolote Mixed** cultivars have double and single flowers, 4in (10cm) across, in yellow, orange, pink, and white; ↕↔ 12–16in (30–40cm). **Turban Group** cultivars have double flowers.

R. bulbosus (Bulbous buttercup). Erect, hairy, sometimes semi-evergreen perennial with fibrous roots and a swollen, corm-like stem base. Ovate, 3-lobed, dark green basal and lower stem leaves, to 5in (13cm) long, each have a long-stalked middle segment. In late spring and early summer, bears branched, cyme-like panicles of several saucer-shaped, rich golden yellow flowers, ¾–1¼in (2–3cm) across, with reflexed, paler yellow sepals. Cultivation group 2. ↕ 6–16in (15–40cm), sometimes to 32in (80cm), ↔ 12in (30cm). Europe, N. Africa, Caucasus. Zone 7b. **var. *farreri*** see 'F.M. Burton'. **'F.M. Burton'**, syn. var. *farreri*, bears glossy, pale creamy yellow flowers. **'Speciosus Plenus' of gardens** see *R. constantinopolitanus* 'Plenus'.

R. bullatus. Tuberous perennial with broadly obovate, puckered, glossy, dark green, basal leaves, to 4in (10cm) long, hairy beneath, and often with 3 shallow lobes or teeth at the tips. In autumn, short, unbranched stems each bear 1 or 2 bowl-shaped, violet-scented, shining yellow flowers, 1in (2.5cm) across. Both autumn-flowering and scented. Cultivation group 5. ↕↔ to 4in (10cm). W. to E. Mediterranean (including Spain and Portugal). Zone 7.

R. calandrinioides ▣ Clump-forming perennial with thick, fleshy roots and broadly lance-shaped to ovate-lance-shaped, hairless, blue-green leaves, to 3in (8cm) long, dying down in summer. In late winter and early spring, unbranched stems bear short, cyme-like panicles of up to 3 cup-shaped, usually pink-flushed white flowers, to 2in (5cm) across. Cultivation group 3 or 5. ↕ 8in (20cm), ↔ 6in (15cm). Atlas Mountains. Zone 8.

R. constantinopolitanus. Clump-forming perennial with short rhizomes and deeply 3-lobed, mid-green basal and lower stem leaves, 1¼–4in (3–10cm) long. From midspring to midsummer, branched stems bear cyme-like panicles of 3–8 bowl-shaped, glossy, bright yellow flowers, to 1¼in (3cm) across, with reflexed, pale yellow sepals. Cultivation group 1 or 2. ↕ 12–28in (30–70cm), ↔ 12in (30cm). E. Europe, Balkans, Cyprus, Syria, Iraq, Iran, Caucasus, Ukraine (Crimea). Zone 6. **'Plenus'** ▣ syn. *R. bulbosus* 'Speciosus Plenus' of gardens, *R. gouanii* 'Plenus', *R. speciosus* 'Flore Pleno', produces double yellow flowers; ↕ 12in (30cm), ↔ 6in (15cm).

Ranunculus constantinopolitanus 'Plenus'

R. crenatus. Rosette-forming, semi-evergreen perennial with fibrous roots and rounded, glossy, mid-green leaves, ¼–½in (6–15mm) long, toothed or shallowly 3-lobed at the tips. In summer, flowering stems bear solitary, or occasionally pairs of, shallowly cup-shaped white flowers, 1in (2.5cm) across. Cultivation group 3. ↕↔ to 3in (8cm). E. Alps, C. Apennines, mountains of Balkan peninsula, S. and E. Carpathians. Zone 6.

R. ficaria (Lesser celandine, Pilewort). Very variable, tuberous perennial with long-stalked, broadly heart-shaped, glossy, usually dark green, basal leaves, ¾–2in (2–5cm) long, often with silver or bronze markings and scalloped or toothed margins. In early spring, bears usually solitary, shallowly cup-shaped, brilliant, shining, golden yellow flowers, ¾–1¼in (2–3cm) across, fading to white with age. The leaves die down after flowering. Some variants produce axillary bulbils and are extremely invasive. Cultivation group 1. ↕ 2in (5cm), ↔ to 12in (30cm) or more. Europe, N.W. Africa, S.W. Asia. Zone 5. **f. *albus*** ▣ has very pale yellow flowers, fading to white, and leaves marked dark bronze. **f. *aurantiacus*** ▣ syn. 'Cupreus', has silvery leaves, each with a bronze central mark, and deep coppery orange flowers, darker on the reverse. **'Bowles Double'** has double flowers with green centers, turning pale yellow. **'Brazen Hussy'** has glossy, deep chocolate-brown leaves, and shining, golden yellow flowers with a bronze reverse. Seedlings often have bronze leaves. **'Collarette'** produces leaves with bronze central bands, and double yellow flowers with anemone-form centers. **'Cupreus'** see f. *aurantiacus*. **'Double Bronze'** bears double yellow flowers with a bronze reverse to the petals. **'Double Cream'** see 'Double Mud'. **'Double Mud'**, syn. 'Double Cream', has double cream flowers, with a gray-tinted reverse to the petals. **'Salmon's White'** bears pale green leaves with bronze marks, and cream flowers, tinted blue-purple on the reverse of the petals.

R. flammula (Lesser spearwort). Marginal aquatic perennial with semi-erect, red-tinted green stems bearing broadly ovate to linear-lance-shaped, dark green leaves, ½–1in (1–2.5cm) long. Shallowly cup-shaped, bright yellow flowers, ¾in (2cm) across, are borne in few-flowered, cyme-like panicles, or sometimes singly, in early summer. Cultivation group 4. ↕ 28in (70cm), ↔ 30in (75cm). Europe, Asia. Zone 5.

R. glacialis. Hummock-forming perennial with fibrous roots and very broadly ovate, deeply 3-lobed, slightly fleshy, hairless, dark green leaves, 1¼–3in (3–8cm) long. In late spring and early summer, flowering stems bear solitary, occasionally 2 or 3, shallowly cup-shaped, white or pink flowers, ¾–1¼in (2–3cm) across, flushed deep pink after fertilization. Protect from excessive winter moisture. Cultivation group 3. ↕ 2–10in (5–25cm), ↔ 2in (5cm). Spain (Sierra Nevada), Pyrenees, Alps, Greenland. Zone 3.

***R. gouanii* 'Plenus'** see *R. constantinopolitanus* 'Plenus'.

Ranunculus asiaticus

Ranunculus calandrinioides

Ranunculus ficaria f. *albus*

Ranunculus ficaria f. aurantiacus

R. gramineus ▣ Clump-forming perennial, very variable in size and habit, with basal clusters of grass-like, linear to lance-shaped, very finely hairy, glaucous leaves, to 8in (20cm) long. In late spring and early summer, branched flowering stems bear 1–3 cup-shaped, lemon-yellow flowers, to ¾in (2cm) across. Cultivation group 2. ↕ to 12in (30cm), ↔ to 6in (15cm). S.W. Europe. Zone 4.

R. insignis. Semi-evergreen, clump-forming perennial, similar to *R. lyallii*, with ovate-lance-shaped, leathery, dark green, basal leaves, to 6in (15cm) long, brown-hairy beneath. In summer, bears panicles of 5–20 shallowly cup-shaped, deep yellow flowers, ¾–2in (2–5cm) across. Cultivation group 1 or 2. ↕ to 24in (60cm), ↔ to 12in (30cm). New Zealand. ❀ (min. 35°F/2°C)

R. lingua ▣ (Greater spearwort). Marginal aquatic perennial with erect, hollow stems. Non-flowering stems bear long-stalked, ovate to ovate-oblong, blue-green leaves, to 8in (20cm) long, with heart-shaped bases. In early summer, branched flowering stems, with short-stalked, linear to lance-shaped leaves, bear cup-shaped, golden yellow flowers, 2in (5cm) across, singly or in few-flowered, cyme-like panicles. Cultivation group 4. ↕ 5ft (1.5m), ↔ 6ft (2m). Europe to Siberia. Zone 4.

R. lyallii (Giant buttercup, Mount Cook lily). Semi-evergreen, clump-forming, rhizomatous perennial with peltate, rounded, scalloped, leathery, dark green, basal leaves, to 12in (30cm) long, becoming progressively smaller up the branching stems. Cyme-like panicles

Ranunculus gramineus

Ranunculus lingua

of 5–15 cup-shaped white flowers, 2in (5cm) across, are borne in summer. Requires cool conditions. Cultivation group 1 or 2. ↕ to 3ft (1m), ↔ to 14in (35cm). Rocky areas in New Zealand. Zone 7.

R. montanus 'Molten Gold'. Vigorous, mat-forming, rhizomatous perennial with rounded-obovate, 3- to 5-lobed, glossy, deep green basal leaves, to 1½in (4cm) long, and narrower stem leaves. In early summer, short flowering stems bear 1–3 shallowly cup-shaped, shining, gold-yellow flowers, ¾–1¼in (2–3cm) across. Cultivation group 2. ↕ 4in (10cm), ↔ 12in (30cm). Zone 5.

R. parnassiifolius ▣ Rosette-forming perennial with fibrous roots and broadly lance-shaped to ovate-heart-shaped, hairy, dark green, basal leaves, to 2in (5cm) long. In early summer, stems bear solitary, occasionally 2 or 3, cup-shaped flowers, 1in (2.5cm) across, opening white but often turning pink with age, usually finely pink- or red-veined. Cultivation group 3. ↕ 6in (15cm), ↔ 4in (10cm). High screes in the Alps, Pyrenees, N. Spain. Zone 6.

R. repens 'Pleniflorus', syn. *R. repens* var. *pleniflorus* (Double creeping buttercup). Erect, fast-spreading, hairy, stoloniferous perennial. Long-stalked, triangular-ovate, mid-green basal and lower stem leaves, 3½in (9cm) long, each have 3 lobes, further cut into 3 toothed segments, the middle lobe long-stalked. Branched stems bear cyme-like panicles of double, glossy, bright yellow flowers, ½–¾in (1.5–2cm) across, with tightly packed petals and pale yellow sepals, from late spring to midsummer. Cultivation group 1 or 2. ↕ 12–24in (30–60cm), ↔ 6ft (2m). Zone 4.

R. repens var. pleniflorus see *R. repens* 'Pleniflorus'.

R. speciosus 'Flore Pleno' see *R. constantinopolitanus* 'Plenus'.

Ranunculus parnassiifolius

RANZANIA

BERBERIDACEAE

Genus of one species of herbaceous perennial found in deciduous mountain woodland in S. Japan. It has short rhizomes, and is grown for its attractive foliage and flowers. Smooth stems, with opposite, 3-palmate leaves at their tips, bear pendent, bell-shaped flowers, either singly or in few-flowered cymes, before the leaves have fully developed; the long flower stalks become upright as berries form. Grow in a woodland garden or shady border.

• **CULTIVATION** Grow in moist, leafy, humus-rich soil in partial or deep shade.

• **PROPAGATION** Sow seed in containers in a cold frame in autumn; seedlings will flower in about 4 years. Divide in early spring.

• **PESTS AND DISEASES** Susceptible to slug damage in spring.

R. japonica, syn. *Podophyllum japonicum*. Rhizomatous perennial with smooth stems, each bearing 2 or 3 opposite, broadly triangular leaves, to 3in (8cm) long, composed of 3 broadly ovate to heart-shaped leaflets, mid-green above, bluish green beneath. In mid- and late spring, long flower stalks bear pendent, bowl-shaped, pale mauve-blue flowers, 1–1¼in (2.5–3cm) across, each with 6 large, pointed tepals and 6 small petals that recurve with age. The flowers are followed by elliptic white berries, to ½in (1.5cm) long. ↕ to 12in (30cm), ↔ 8in (20cm). S. Japan (N. Hondo). Zone 6.

RAOULIA

ASTERACEAE

Genus of about 20 species of evergreen perennials or subshrubs from screes and open rocky places at high and low altitudes in New Zealand. They form mats or cushions of dense, overlapping, linear to diamond- or spoon-shaped, silvery leaves. The usually small, disk-shaped flowerheads are borne singly or in few-flowered, terminal clusters. They thrive in regions with cool summers and mild winters, and are excellent foliage plants for a rock garden, raised bed or scree bed, or for an alpine house.

• **CULTIVATION** Under glass, grow in a mix of equal parts loam, leaf mold, and sharp sand, with a top dressing of grit, in bright filtered light. When in growth, water freely (avoiding the foliage); keep just moist in winter. Outdoors, grow in gritty, humus-rich, moist but sharply drained soil in full

Raoulia australis

sun, or in partial shade in warmer areas. Protect from excessive winter moisture.

• **PROPAGATION** Divide or separate rooted stems of mat-forming species in spring. Root new rosettes of cushion-forming species as cuttings in early summer in partial shade; water carefully and moderately until rooted.

• **PESTS AND DISEASES** Prone to spider mites and aphids under glass.

R. australis ▣ syn. *R. lutescens*. Prostrate, mat-forming, gray-silver perennial with branching, rooting stems, densely clothed in overlapping, spoon-shaped, silver-hairy leaves, ⅟₁₆in (2mm) long. In summer, produces sulfur-yellow flowerheads, ¼in (6mm) across. Plants sold under this name are often variants of *R. hookeri*. ↕ ½in (1.5cm), ↔ 12in (30cm) or more. New Zealand. Zone 8.

R. eximia (Vegetable sheep). Extremely dense, cushion-forming perennial with tightly packed rosettes of overlapping, oblong to ovate, gray-hairy leaves, to ⅟₁₆in (2mm) long. Yellowish white flowerheads, to ⅛in (3mm) across, are borne in late spring or summer. Resents winter moisture; best grown in an alpine house. ↕ 2in (5cm), ↔ to 4in (10cm). New Zealand. Zone 7b.

R. haastii ▣ Dense, cushion-forming perennial with loosely overlapping, ovate to linear-oblong, silky-hairy leaves, to ¼in (6mm) long; pale green at first, they darken in summer, becoming brown-tinted in winter. In spring, bears yellow flowerheads, to ¼in (6mm) across. ↕ ½in (1.5cm), ↔ 12in (30cm) or more. New Zealand. Zone 7b.

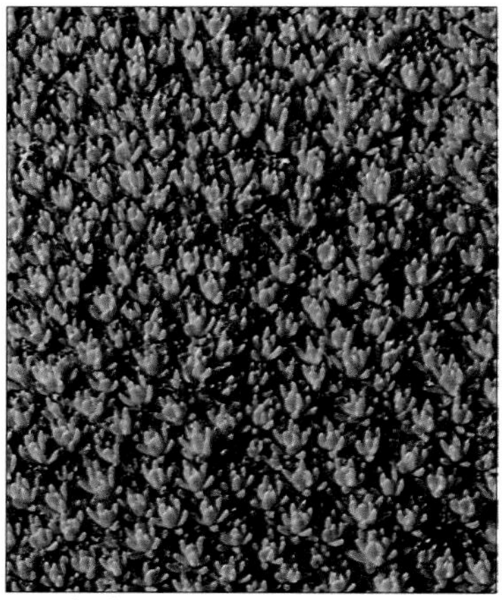

Raoulia haastii

Raoulia hookeri var. *alboserricea*

R. hookeri* var. *alboserricea ■ Mat-forming perennial producing branching, rooting stems clothed in closely overlapping, narrowly obovate-spoon-shaped leaves, 1/16in (2mm) long, covered with white-silky hairs. Silky-hairy, pale green or straw-colored flowerheads, to ¼in (6mm) across, are borne briefly in summer. Similar to, but less tolerant of winter moisture than *R. australis.* ↕ ½in (1.5cm), ↔ to 8in (20cm). New Zealand (North Island). ❁ (min. 35°F/2°C)
R. leontopodium see *Leucogenes leontopodium.*
R.* x *loganii see x *Leucoraoulia loganii.*
R. lutescens see *R. australis.*

RAPHANUS
BRASSICACEAE

Genus of about 10 species of biennial and annual plants, grown for their swollen, various sized roots. Leaves are simple, round, and slightly hairy, and can grow to 5in (13cm). Flowers are small, ranging in color from white to pink and red. Roots range from the large, oriental radishes, to the small (1in/2.5cm in diameter), round, "salad" types. The roots have a spicy, peppery taste. Grow in vegetable gardens.
• **CULTIVATION** Grow in a sunny site, in light, rich, well-drained soil, with adequate moisture. Prepare soil with manure well before planting.
• **PROPAGATION** Broadcast thinly or sow seeds 1/4–1/2in (.6–1cm) deep, 6in (15cm) apart, in rows. Thin to 1–2in (2.5cm) apart. Harvest 26–32 days after planting
• **PESTS AND DISEASES** Root maggots, flea beetles.

R. sativus (Radish). These cool-season, cultivated vegetables are easy to grow in almost any moist. fertile soil, in full sun. For successive crops, reseed every 10–14 days. Europe to E. Asia. Zone 6b.

RAPHIA
Raffia
ARECACEAE

Genus of about 30 species of massive, single- or cluster-stemmed, spreading, monocarpic palms, mainly found in moist, wet, or swampy sites and by streams in Central and South America, Africa, and Madagascar. Some species have short, underground stems (caudices) and appear to be stemless. The pinnate, light to mid-green leaves, with folded linear leaflets, are produced in terminal heads or tufts. Panicles of bowl-shaped, 3-petaled flowers are borne either between the leaves or just beneath the lowest leaf. Where not hardy, grow young specimens as houseplants or in a warm greenhouse or conservatory. In tropical areas, use the stemless species in a border, and those with stems as specimens on a lawn.
• **CULTIVATION** Under glass, grow in soilless potting mix in bright filtered light. In the growing season, water freely and apply a balanced liquid fertilizer monthly; water moderately in winter. Pot on or top-dress in spring. Outdoors, grow in moist, moderately fertile, humus-rich soil in partial shade.
• **PROPAGATION** Sow seed at 81°F (27°C) in spring.
• **PESTS AND DISEASES** Spider mites may be a problem under glass.

R. farinifera (Raffia palm). Large, spreading palm with a sturdy trunk covered in old leaf bases. Erect to arching leaves, to 70ft (20m) long, each have numerous linear leaflets, to 6ft (2m) long; they are waxy, light to mid-green above, and waxy, powdery white beneath. Green flowers, ⅜–½in (8–15mm) across, are borne in panicles to 10ft (3m) long, in summer, followed by ovoid to ellipsoid, scaly orange fruit, 3–4in (7–10cm) long. ↕ to 80ft (25m), ↔ to 70ft (20m) or more. Tropical Africa, Madagascar. ❁ (min. 61°F/16°C)

▷ ***Raphidophora*** see *Rhaphidophora*

RATIBIDA
Mexican hat, Prairie coneflower
ASTERACEAE

Genus of 5 or 6 species of biennials and perennials, mainly found on prairies in North America and Mexico. Woody-based crowns produce erect stems, branching above the middle, that produce alternate, pinnate to pinnatifid leaves and solitary, terminal flowerheads. They are cultivated for their daisy-like flowerheads, which have a few long, yellow or yellow-brown ray florets and prominent, spherical or cone-shaped centers of brown disk florets. Grow in a sunny border, gravel garden, or wildflower meadow. The flowerheads are good for cutting.

Ratibida columnifera

• **CULTIVATION** Grow in dry, well-drained, neutral to slightly alkaline, moderately fertile soil in full sun. Ratibidas are drought-resistant.
• **PROPAGATION** Sow seed in containers in a cold frame in early spring. Divide perennials in spring when young (the roots become woody with age).
• **PESTS AND DISEASES** Sometimes affected by downy mildew, powdery mildew, leaf smut, and fungal spots.

R. columnifera ■ syn. *Lepachys columnifera, Rudbeckia columnifera.* Erect perennial, sometimes grown as a biennial or annual, with pinnate, hairy, grayish green leaves, 1¼–6in (3–15cm) long; the leaflets are usually linear, entire, and often pinnatifid. From early summer to early autumn, long, thin, branching stems bear daisy-like flowerheads, to 3in (8cm) across, with reflexed yellow ray florets and large, columnar centers of green, then brown disk florets. ↕ to 32in (80cm), ↔ 12in (30cm). S.W. Canada, W. and C. US to New Mexico. Zone 4.

RAVENALA
Traveler's tree
STRELITZIACEAE

Genus of one species of small, tree-like, evergreen perennial, occurring in open rainforest or deforested areas in Madagascar, grown for its foliage, spathes, and palm-like habit. The large, alternate, long-stalked, banana-like leaves have expanded leaf bases that accumulate water. Boat-shaped spathes, enclosing cymes of tiny, 3-petaled flowers, are produced from the leaf axils. Where temperatures fall below 61–64°F (16–18°C), grow in a warm greenhouse or conservatory. In tropical regions, use as a distinctive specimen tree.
• **CULTIVATION** Under glass, grow in soil-based potting mix in full light, with high humidity. Water freely in spring and summer, applying a balanced liquid fertilizer monthly; water more sparingly in winter. Outdoors, grow in fertile, moist, but well-drained soil in full sun. Provide shelter from strong winds.
• **PROPAGATION** Sow seed at 68–70°F (20–21°C), or remove rooted suckers, in spring.
• **PESTS AND DISEASES** Spider mites, root rot, and leaf spots occur.

R. madagascariensis. Large, erect tree-like perennial with an unbranched, palm-like stem topped by a distinctive, fan-shaped crown of 2-ranked, paddle-shaped, leathery, lustrous, rich green leaves, normally extensively shredded by the wind. The leaves resemble palm fronds. The oblong leaf blades, 6–12ft (2–4m) long, are borne on thick, grooved stalks, of about the same length, closely overlapping at the bases. On mature plants, tiny, narrow white flowers, each with 6 tepals, emerge from pointed, boat-shaped, greenish white spathes, a few at a time, in summer; they are followed by fruit capsules that contain edible seeds with bright blue arils. ↕ 30–52ft (10–16m), ↔ 10–20ft (3–6m). Madagascar. ❁ (min. 61–64°F/16–18°C)

Rebutia aureiflora

REBUTIA
syn. SULCOREBUTIA, WEINGARTIA
CACTACEAE

Genus of about 40 species of mostly dwarf, clump-forming, solitary or clustering cacti found in mountainous terrain, to 13,000ft (4,000m) high, in Bolivia and N.W. Argentina. They are cultivated for their habit and colorful flowers. The spherical to short-cylindrical, ribbed stems are divided into low tubercles in some species. The areoles have mainly short, bristly spines, and in summer, those near the stem bases produce trumpet-shaped, diurnal flowers. Where not hardy, grow in a temperate green-house or as house-plants. In warm, dry areas, use in a desert garden or a raised bed. Depend-ing on the species, they are hardy to 15–25°F (-17 to -4°C) if kept dry.
• **CULTIVATION** Under glass, grow in standard cactus potting mix in full light, with low humidity. From spring to summer, water moderately and apply a balanced liquid fertilizer 3 or 4 times; keep completely dry at other times. Outdoors, grow in moderately fertile, gritty, sharply drained soil in full sun. See also pp.48–49.
• **PROPAGATION** Sow seed at 70°F (21°C) in early spring, or remove offsets in spring or summer.
• **PESTS AND DISEASES** Prone to scale insects, mealybugs, and fungal stem rot, especially during propagation.

Rebutia fiebrigii

ℛebutia krainziana

ℛ. aureiflora ■ Freely clustering :actus with depressed-spherical to pherical, mid-green to greenish ·iolet, often red-tinged stems, to .½in (4cm) thick. The stems are :overed with prominent, spirally ırranged tubercles set with white areoles .nd grayish white spines (10–16 radials .nd 1–4 longer centrals). White-hroated, yellow or yellowish orange, ometimes orange, red, or purple lowers, 1½in (4cm) across, are ›roduced in summer. ↕ 4in (10cm), → to 8in (20cm). N.W. Argentina. ❄ (min. 41°F/5°C)

ℛ. fiebrigii ■ syn. *R. muscula.* Variable, lustering cactus with spherical to ovoid ›r depressed-spherical, dark green stems, ½in (6cm) thick, with up to 18 ribs. White areoles bear 30–40 white radial pines and 2–5 longer, brownish white entrals. Bears bright yellowish brown ›r bright orange to red flowers, ¾–1½in 2–4cm) across, in summer. ↕ 4in 10cm), ↔ to 6in (15cm). Bolivia, N.W. Argentina. ❄ (min. 41°F/5°C)

ℛ. heliosa. Initially solitary, later lustering cactus producing depressed-pherical to cone-shaped, grayish green tems, to 1in (2.5cm) thick, with 15–40 ›w-tubercled, spirally arranged ribs. Brown-felted areoles have 24–26 tiny, omb-like, undifferentiated white pines. In summer, bears orange or deep ose-red flowers, 1½in (4cm) across; the nner petals often have a central lilac tripe. ↕ 4in (10cm), ↔ 6in (15cm). Bolivia. ❄ (min. 41°F/5°C)

ℛ. krainziana ■ Clustering cactus vith depressed-spherical, warty, bright › dull green stems, 1½in (4cm) thick.

Rebutia neocumingii

The stems have 20 or more, spirally arranged ribs, and close-set white areoles with 8–12 tiny, undifferentiated white spines. Bright red flowers, to 2in (5cm) across, sometimes with a violet sheen and violet throats, are borne in summer. ↕ 2in (5cm), ↔ 8in (20cm). Probably of garden origin. ❄ (min. 41°F/5°C)

R. minuscula ■ syn. *R. violaciflora* (Red crown). Freely clustering cactus with slightly flattened, spherical, dull mid- to dark green stems, 2in (5cm) thick, with 16–20 warty, spirally arranged ribs, and brown areoles bearing 25–30 undifferentiated white spines. Bright pinkish purple flowers, 1¼–1½in (3–4cm) across, are produced in summer. ↕ 2in (5cm), ↔ 5in (13cm). N. Argentina. ❄ (min. 41°F/5°C)

R. muscula see *R. fiebrigii.*

R. neocumingii ■ syn. *Weingartia neocumingii.* Solitary cactus, of variable form and shape, with hemispherical to spherical, bright dark green stems, 4in (10cm) thick. The stems have 16–18 warty ribs, white areoles, and brown-tipped yellow spines (16–20 radials and 3–10 thicker centrals). Orange or yellow flowers, ¾in (2cm) or more across, are borne in summer. ↕ 8in (20cm), ↔ 4in (10cm). Bolivia. ❄ (min. 41°F/5°C)

R. pulchra see *R. rauschii.*

R. pygmaea. Solitary or clustering cactus producing ovoid to short-cylindrical, mid- to dark green stems, ½–¾in (1–2cm) thick, with tubercles arranged in 8–12 spiral rows, and white spines, 1⁄16–⅛in (2–3mm) long (9–11 radials, no centrals).

Rebutia spegazziniana

Solitary, pink-purple flowers, ¾–1in (2–2.5cm) across, are borne on the lower parts of the stems in summer. ↕ 1½in (4cm), ↔ 3in (8cm). N.W. Argentina. ❄ (min. 50°F/10°C)

R. spegazziniana ■ Clustering cactus producing spherical, pale to deep green stems, 2in (5cm) thick, with about 18 prominently warty ribs, white-felted areoles, and white spines (14 radials and 3–6 shorter centrals). Pale vermilion to dark red flowers, 1–1¼in (2.5–3cm) across, are produced in summer. ↕ to 4in (10cm), ↔ to 8in (20cm). N.W. Argentina. ❄ (min. 41–45°F/5–7°C)

R. spinosissima. Freely offsetting cactus producing spherical, bright green stems, 2–2½in (5–6cm) thick, with 15 or more warty, spirally arranged ribs, white-hairy areoles, and white spines (numerous radials and 5 or 6 thicker, brown-tipped centrals). Pale orange to mid-red flowers, 1¼–1½in (3–4cm) across,are borne in summer. ↕ to 4in (10cm), ↔ 6in (15cm). N. Argentina. ❄ (min. 41–45°F/5–7°C)

R. tiraquensis ■ Upright cactus with mid-green stems, solitary at first, but eventually clump-forming, covered in spirally arranged tubercles. Elongated areoles, to ¼in (6mm) long, bear 2–4 reddish brown central spines, 2½–3in (6–8cm) long, and 14–18 glassy white radials. Solitary, funnel-shaped, purple or magenta flowers, 1½in (4cm) across, are borne in summer. ↕ 3½–4in (9–10cm), ↔ 4in (10cm). Bolivia. ❄ (min. 45–50°F/7–10°C)

R. violaciflora see *R. minuscula.*

▷ ***Rechsteineria leucotricha*** see *Sinningia canescens*

REHDERODENDRON

STYRACACEAE

Genus of 9 species of deciduous shrubs and trees from mountain woodland in China and Vietnam. They are valued for their cup-shaped, 5-petaled white flowers, borne in leafless, axillary, cyme-like panicles or racemes, and for their oblong or elliptic, ribbed, woody fruits. The leaves are alternate and finely toothed. *R. macrocarpum,* the only species usually cultivated, is ideal for a woodland garden.

• **CULTIVATION** Grow in fertile, moist but well-drained, neutral to acidic soil in sun or partial shade, sheltered from cold, dry winds. Pruning group 1.

• **PROPAGATION** Sow seed in containers in a cold frame as soon as ripe. Root semi-ripe cuttings in summer.

• **PESTS AND DISEASES** Infrequent.

R. macrocarpum. Small, broadly upright, deciduous tree with red young shoots and elliptic to oblong, glossy, dark green leaves, to 6in (15cm) long. As the leaves emerge in late spring, bears cyme-like racemes of 6–10 cup-shaped, fragrant, creamy white flowers, 2½in (6cm) across. Flowers are followed by pendent, ellipsoid, green, then red fruit, to 3in (8cm) long. ↕ 30ft (10m), ↔ 22ft (7m). W. China. ❄ (min. 35°F/2°C)

ebutia minuscula

Rebutia tiraquensis

R

REHMANNIA

SCROPHULARIACEAE

Genus of 8 or 9 species of perennials, sometimes grown as biennials, from woodland and stony sites in China. They are cultivated for their large, foxglove-like flowers, which are 2-lipped and borne in terminal racemes. The leaves, arranged in basal rosettes, are large, obovate to oblong, shallowly lobed or toothed, conspicuously veined, and hairy. Where hardy, grow at the front of a sunny border; elsewhere, grow or overwinter in a cool greenhouse.

• **CULTIVATION** Under glass, grow in soil-based potting mix in bright filtered light. During the growing season, water freely and apply a balanced liquid fertilizer monthly; keep just moist in winter. Outdoors, grow in well-drained, moderately fertile, humus-rich soil in a sheltered site in full sun. Where not hardy, lift in autumn, pot up, and overwinter in a cool, dry place at 45°F (7°C).

• **PROPAGATION** Sow seed at 55–61°F (13–16°C) in late winter. Take root cuttings in late autumn, or take softwood cuttings from basal shoots before flowering. Separate and pot up runners in spring.

• **PESTS AND DISEASES** Susceptible to slug and snail damage.

***R. angulata* of gardens** see *R. elata.*

R. elata ■ syn. *R. angulata* of gardens (Chinese foxglove). Rosette-forming perennial with obovate, lobed or toothed, conspicuously veined, hairy, mid-green basal leaves, 8–10in (20–25cm) long. Branched stems bear leafy racemes of semi-pendent, tubular flowers, 3–4in (7–10cm) long, from summer to autumn. The flowers have bright, pinkish purple lips and paler tubes; they are red-spotted, especially in the throats. ↕ to 5ft (1.5m), ↔ 20in (50cm). China. ❀ (min. 41°F/5°C)

R. glutinosa. Sticky, purple-hairy perennial with slender runners and rosettes of obovate, scalloped, conspicuously veined basal leaves, to 4in (10cm) long, mid-green above and often red-tinted beneath. From midspring to summer, branched, leafy stems bear few, pendent, tubular flowers, to 2in (5cm) long, in cyme-like racemes, or singly on long flower stalks from the leaf axils. The flowers have reddish brown tubes, marked with darker reddish purple veins, and pale yellow-brown lips. ↕ 6–12in (15–30cm), ↔ to 12in (30cm). N. China. ❀ (min. 41°F/5°C)

REINECKEA

LILIACEAE

Genus of one species of rhizomatous, evergreen perennial from deciduous woodland or sandy, open areas among shrubs in China and Japan. It is grown for its arching, pale green leaves and spikes of tiny, fragrant pink flowers. *R. carnea* makes an attractive, leafy groundcover, but rarely flowers freely or bears its spherical red berries in areas with cool summers.

• **CULTIVATION** Grow in moist but well-drained, humus-rich, neutral or acidic soil in partial shade.

• **PROPAGATION** Sow seed in containers in a cold frame as soon as ripe. Separate rhizomes from the margins of established clumps in spring.

• **PESTS AND DISEASES** Susceptible to damage from slugs and snails.

R. carnea. Evergreen, rhizomatous perennial with tufts of arching, linear-lance-shaped, glossy, mid- to dark green leaves, 6–14in (15–35cm) long, borne in 2 ranks at the ends of the rhizomes. In late spring, bears dense, terminal spikes of shallowly cup-shaped, pale to deep pink flowers, to ½in (1.5cm) across, each with 6 segments, the tips reflexing with age. In areas with warm summers, spherical red berries, ⅜–½in (9–15mm) across, are produced in autumn. ↕ 8in (20cm), ↔ 16in (40cm) or more. China, Japan. Zone 7b.

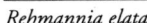

Rehmannia elata

Reinwardtia indica

REINWARDTIA

LINACEAE

Genus of 1 or 2 species of evergreen shrubs or subshrubs, found in mountain woodland from Pakistan to S.W. China and S.E. Asia. They are grown for their funnel-shaped flowers, each with 5 spreading petal lobes, borne in terminal or axillary, cyme-like clusters, or singly. The alternate, elliptic- to oblong-obovate leaves are entire or toothed. Where temperatures fall below 45°F (7°C), grow in a temperate greenhouse. In milder regions, grow at the base of a sunny wall, or in a courtyard garden.

• **CULTIVATION** Under glass, grow in soil-based potting mix in full light, with shade from hot sun and moderate humidity. When in growth, mist regularly, water freely, and apply a balanced liquid fertilizer monthly; water moderately at other times. Winter flowers are borne most freely at a minimum temperature of 55°F (13°C). Outdoors, grow in fertile, moist but well-drained, humus-rich soil in full sun. Pruning group 8; tip-prune young plants to encourage branching.

• **PROPAGATION** Sow seed at 61–64°F (16–18°C) in spring. Root softwood cuttings in early summer.

• **PESTS AND DISEASES** Spider mites may be a problem under glass.

R. indica ■ syn. *R. tetragyna, R. trigyna* (Yellow flax). Open, erect to spreading shrub with elliptic- to oblong-obovate, finely toothed, deep green to grayish green leaves, 1¼–3in (3–8cm) long. From fall to late spring, bears funnel-shaped, bright golden yellow flowers, 1¼–2in (3–5cm) across, singly or in short, cyme-like clusters from the leaf axils. ↕↔ 24–36in (60–90cm). Pakistan, N. India, Burma, S.W. China, S.E. Asia. ❀ (min. 45°F/7°C)

R. tetragyna see *R. indica.*

R. trigyna see *R. indica.*

RESEDA

Mignonette

RESEDACEAE

Genus of 55–60 species of erect to spreading, branching, and occasionally rosette-forming annuals and perennials from stony hillsides, scrub, or field margins, mainly in the Mediterranean and S.W. Asia, but also in E. Africa and N.W. India. They have alternate, small, variably shaped, entire, toothed, or

Reseda odorata

pinnatifid, prominently veined, mostly mid-green leaves. Star-shaped, greenish white or greenish yellow, sometimes red tinged flowers, each with 4–10 narrow petals, are borne in long, unbranched or branching, spike-like racemes from spring to autumn. *R. odorata* has been grown for centuries, mainly for its fragrant flowers, which hold their scent for months even when cut and dried; modern cultivars have larger, more strongly colored flowers, which tend to be less fragrant. All are attractive to bees and are ideal for a mixed or herbaceous border, or for a wild garden.

• **CULTIVATION** Grow in well-drained, moderately fertile, preferably alkaline soil in full sun or partial shade. Deadhead to prolong flowering.

• **PROPAGATION** Sow seed at 55°F (13°C) in late winter, or *in situ* in early spring or autumn. Where temperatures fall below 23°F (-5°C), provide protection for autumn-sown seedlings.

• **PESTS AND DISEASES** Infrequent.

R. odorata ■ (Common mignonette). Erect to slightly spreading, hairless annual with branching, strongly ribbed stems and entire, elliptic to spoon-shaped, sometimes 3-lobed leaves, to 4in (10cm) long. From summer to early autumn, bears loose, conical, raceme-like heads of tiny, star-shaped, highly fragrant, yellowish green or white to reddish green flowers, to ¼in (6mm) across; each flower has 4–7 petals and a central tuft of orange stamens. ↕ 12–24in (30–60cm), ↔ to 9in (23cm). N. Africa.

RETAMA

FABACEAE

Genus, related to *Genista*, of 4 species of deciduous shrubs found on sandy and rocky soils in the Canary Islands, the Mediterranean, and W. Asia. They have willowy, dark green stems with alternate, mid-green leaves that soon fall, and pea-like, yellow or white flowers borne in dense, axillary racemes. *R. monosperma*, the only species usually cultivated, has an elegant, arching habit and fragrant flowers. Where not hardy, grow in a cool greenhouse. In warmer areas, grow in a sheltered border or at the base of a warm, sunny wall.

• **CULTIVATION** Under glass, grow in soil-based potting mix in full light. When in growth, water moderately;

R

keep just moist in winter. Outdoors, grow in moderately fertile, sharply drained soil in full sun, in a sheltered position. Pruning group 3, although pruning is seldom needed; do not cut back into old wood.
• **PROPAGATION** Sow seed in containers in a cold frame in spring. Root semi-ripe cuttings in summer.
• **PESTS AND DISEASES** Infrequent.

R. monosperma, syn. *Genista monosperma.* Graceful, deciduous shrub with slender, arching, silky gray stems and a few linear leaves, to ¾in (2cm) long, which soon fall. In early spring, produces small, very fragrant, pea-like white flowers in dense, axillary racemes, ¾–1½in (2–4cm) long. ↕ to 12ft (4m), ↔ 5ft (1.5m). Portugal, Spain, N. Africa, Canary Islands. ❀ (min. 41°F/5°C)

Reynoutria see *Fallopia*

RHAMNUS

RHAMNACEAE

Genus of 125 or more species of usually thorny, deciduous or evergreen shrubs and trees, widely distributed in N. temperate regions, with a few in the S. hemisphere. They occur in woodland, heathland, scrub, fens, bogs, or rocky places, often on alkaline soils. They are cultivated primarily for their foliage, which has good autumn color in some deciduous species, and for their decorative fruits. The leaves are opposite or alternate. Tiny, hermaphrodite or unisexual, cup-shaped flowers, 1/16–1/8in (2–3mm) across, with 4 or 5 petals, are borne in axillary racemes or umbel-like clusters; they are often fragrant and usually yellowish white, greenish white, or white. Some flowers, particularly those of *R. frangula*, are very attractive to bees. Grow in a shrub border; *R. cathartica* and *R. frangula* may be used as hedging. All parts may cause severe discomfort if ingested.
• **CULTIVATION** Grow in moderately fertile soil in full sun or partial shade. *R. cathartica, R. frangula,* and *R. imeretina* prefer moist soils. *R. alaternus* needs well-drained soil in full sun. Pruning group 1; trim hedges in early spring. Cut out reverting shoots as they appear.
• **PROPAGATION** Sow seed in containers in a cold frame as soon as ripe. Root semi-ripe cuttings of evergreen species in summer. Root greenwood cuttings of deciduous species in early summer, or layer in autumn or spring.
• **PESTS AND DISEASES** Susceptible to scale insects, caterpillars, rust, and *Cercospora* and *Septoria* leaf spots.

R. alaternus (Italian buckthorn). Erect to spreading, evergreen shrub with ovate to oblong, leathery, glossy, dark green leaves, to 3in (8cm) long. Unisexual and hermaphrodite, yellow-green flowers are borne in axillary clusters in late spring and early summer; they are followed by spherical red fruit, ¼in (6mm) across, ripening to black in late summer. ↕ 15ft (5m), ↔ 12ft (4m). Portugal, Morocco, Mediterranean, Ukraine (Crimea). Zone 7b. **'Argenteovariegata'** ▣ syn. 'Variegata', has gray-green leaves with conspicuous white margins.

Rhamnus alaternus 'Argenteovariegata'

Rhamnus frangula 'Asplenifolia'

R. californica (Coffeeberry). Upright, evergreen or semi-evergreen shrub with red shoots and oblong to oval, glossy, mid-green leaves, to 3in (8cm) long. In late spring and early summer, bears axillary clusters of hermaphrodite, yellowish white flowers. Spherical red fruit, ¼in (6mm) across, ripen to purple-black in late summer and autumn. ↕ 12ft (4m), ↔ 10ft (3m). W. US. Zone 7b.
R. cathartica (Common buckthorn). Dense, thicket-forming, spiny, deciduous shrub, sometimes small tree, with oval to ovate or elliptic, glossy, dark green leaves, to 2½in (6cm) long, turning yellow in autumn. Axillary clusters of unisexual, yellowish green flowers are borne in late spring and early summer. In autumn, bears spherical red fruit, to ¼in (6mm) across, ripening to black. Has become a weed in some areas. ↕ 20ft (6m), ↔ 15ft (5m). Europe, N.W. Africa, Asia. Zone 4.
R. frangula (Alder buckthorn). Bushy, spreading, deciduous shrub with oval to obovate, glossy, dark green leaves, to 3in (8cm) long, turning red in autumn. In late spring and early summer, bears axillary clusters of hermaphrodite green flowers, followed by fleshy, spherical red fruit, to ½in (1.5cm) across, ripening to black in autumn. ↕↔ 15ft (5m). Europe, N. Africa, Russia to Altai Mountains. Zone 3b. **'Asplenifolia'** ▣ is slow-growing and has fern-like, linear, irregularly scalloped leaves; ↕ 10–12ft (3–4m), ↔ 6–10ft (2–3m). **'Columnaris'** ▣ (Tallhedge buckthorn) is narrow and upright, and is primarily used as hedging.
R. imeretina. Open, spreading, deciduous shrub with thick shoots and oblong to oval, conspicuously veined, dark green leaves, to 12in (30cm) long, turning bronze-purple in autumn. In early summer, unisexual green flowers are borne in axillary clusters, followed in late summer and autumn by spherical red fruit, ¼in (6mm) across, ripening to black. ↕ 10ft (3m), ↔ 15ft (5m). Republic of Georgia, E. Turkey, Armenia. Zone 7.

RHAPHIDOPHORA

syn. RAPHIDOPHORA

ARACEAE

Genus of 60 species of evergreen root climbers and trailers from woodland in tropical S. and S.E. Asia and the Pacific islands. They are cultivated for their attractive leaves, which are short-stalked and entire on young plants, and long-stalked, larger, and pinnatifid or pinnate on mature specimens. In summer, mature plants grown outdoors produce yellow spadices of tiny, petalless flowers, surrounded by boat-shaped, yellow to green spathes. Where not hardy, grow as houseplants, or in a warm greenhouse or conservatory. In tropical climates, grow through a tree or on a damp, shady wall.
• **CULTIVATION** Under glass, grow in equal parts loam, leaf mold, bark, and sharp sand in bright filtered light. Provide moderate humidity, draft-free conditions, and the support of a moss pole or similar structure. When in full growth, water moderately, mist regularly, and apply a balanced liquid

Rhamnus frangula 'Columnaris'

fertilizer every 2–3 weeks; water sparingly in winter. Outdoors, grow in moist, humus-rich soil in partial shade. Pruning group 11, after flowering; pruning is seldom needed.

- **PROPAGATION** Sow seed at 64–70°F (18–21°C) in spring. Root stem-tip or leaf-bud cuttings, or air layer, in spring or early summer.
- **PESTS AND DISEASES** Prone to scale insects and spider mites under glass.

R. celatocaulis, syn. *Monstera latevaginata* of gardens, *Pothos celatocaulis*, *R. pinnata* (Shingle plant). Erect, sparsely branched climber mostly grown in its juvenile phase, when it has short-stalked, elliptic-ovate, entire, blue-green leaves, to 4in (10cm) long, closely overlapping and lying flat along the stems. Mature leaves are entire, pinnatifid, or pinnatisect, and 8–16in (20–40cm) long, with stalks of the same length. In summer, produces yellow spathes, 4–6in (10–15cm) long, singly from the leaf axils on long stems. ↕ 30ft (10m). Borneo. ❀ (min. 59°F/15°C)

R. decursiva ■ Erect, robust climber usually grown in its adult phase, when it has thick, stiff, sparsely branched, slow-growing stems and oblong, pinnatisect, leathery, lustrous, rich green leaves, 20–36in (50–90cm) long. Juvenile leaves are arranged in 2 ranks and are broadly ovate, entire, and mid-green, to 12in (30cm) long. Fleshy yellow spathes, 5½–7in (14–18cm) long, are borne singly from the leaf axils in summer. ↕ to 30ft (10m). N. Burma, India, Sri Lanka. ❀ (min. 59°F/15°C)

R. pinnata see *R. celatocaulis.*

Rhaphidophora decursiva

RHAPHIOLEPIS

ROSACEAE

Genus of about 3–5, possibly up to 15 species of evergreen shrubs and trees from scrub in S.E. and E. Asia. They are grown for their alternate, often toothed leaves, which are glossy, dark green, and leathery, and for their fragrant, apple-blossom-like, star-shaped flowers, borne in erect, terminal racemes or panicles in spring or summer. Grow in a sheltered border, or at the base of a warm, sunny wall. Where not hardy, grow in a cool greenhouse or in containers.

- **CULTIVATION** Under glass, grow in soil-based potting mix in full light. In the growing season, water moderately and apply a balanced liquid fertilizer monthly; water sparingly in winter. Outdoors, grow in moist but well-drained, moderately fertile soil in full sun, with shelter from cold, drying winds. Pruning group 8.
- **PROPAGATION** Root semi-ripe cuttings in late summer. Layer in autumn.
- **PESTS AND DISEASES** Prone to scale insects, fireblight, *Entomosporium* leaf spot, and web blight.

R. x delacourii (*R. indica* x *R. umbellata*). Dome-shaped, evergreen shrub with broadly obovate to inversely lance-shaped, shallowly toothed, leathery, dark green leaves, to 3in (8cm) long. Star-shaped pink flowers, to ¾in (2cm) across, are produced in erect, broadly conical panicles, to 4in (10cm) long, in spring or summer. ↕ 6ft (2m), ↔ 8ft (2.5m). Garden origin. ❀ (min. 41°F/5°C). **'Coates' Crimson'** bears dark pink flowers. **'Enchantress'** is compact, with rose-pink flowers. **'Indian Princess'** produces light pink flowers fading to white. **'Spring Song'** produces pale pink flowers over an extended period. **'Springtime'** has rich pink flowers, borne from late winter to spring. **'White Enchantress'** is dwarf and compact, bearing pure white flowers.

R. indica (Indian hawthorn). Bushy, spreading, evergreen shrub producing narrowly elliptic to lance-shaped, deeply toothed, leathery, glossy, dark green leaves, to 3–4½in (7–11cm) long. In spring or early summer, bears white flowers, to ½in (1.5cm) across, with pink-flushed centers, in loose racemes or panicles, to 3in (8cm) long. ↕ 5ft (1.5m), ↔ 6ft (2m). China. ❀ (min. 41°F/5°C)

R. japonica see *R. umbellata.*

R. ovata see *R. umbellata.*

R. umbellata ■ syn. *R. japonica, R. ovata.* Bushy, evergreen shrub with oval to obovate or inversely lance-shaped, leathery, dark green, shallowly toothed leaves, to 3½in (9cm) long. White flowers, to ¾in (2cm) across, sometimes tinted rose-pink, are borne in conical racemes, to 4in (10cm) long, in early summer. ↕↔ 5ft (1.5m). Korea, Japan. ❀ (min. 41°F/5°C)

Rhaphiolepis umbellata

RHAPIDOPHYLLUM

Needle palm

ARECACEAE

Genus of one species of almost stemless palm from wooded, swampy areas in coastal S.E. US. It is grown for its fan-shaped, palmately lobed leaves, cut almost to the midribs. The tiny, bowl-shaped, 3-petaled flowers are borne in small panicles among the leaf sheaths. Where not hardy, grow in a cool or temperate greenhouse. In warmer areas, use as a lawn or courtyard specimen.

- **CULTIVATION** Under glass, grow in soil-based potting mix in bright filtered light. In growth, water freely and apply a balanced liquid fertilizer monthly; water more sparingly in winter. Pot on or top-dress in spring. Outdoors, grow in any moderately fertile, moist but well-drained soil in partial shade.
- **PROPAGATION** Sow seed at 61–64°F (16–18°C) in spring. Remove smaller suckers in spring.
- **PESTS AND DISEASES** Spider mites, mealybugs, and scale insects may be a problem under glass.

Rhapidophyllum hystrix

R. hystrix ■ (Blue palmetto, Porcupin palm). Small, slow-growing, clump-forming palm with a short-branching stem system below or at the soil surface Sheaths at the bases of the leaf stalks bear long, erect spines; each smooth, erect leaf stalk bears a deeply lobed leaf blade, to 3ft (1m) long, with 5–12 lobes, bright green above, tinted blue-gray beneath. Tiny, bowl-shaped, purplish red flowers, borne in summer, are hidden by the foliage. ↕ 5–6ft (1.5–2m), ↔ 6–12ft (2–4m). South Carolina to Florida and Mississippi. ❀ (min. 45–50°F/7–10°C)

RHAPIS

Lady palm

ARECACEAE

Genus of 12 species of small, cluster-stemmed palms found in shady tropica and subtropical forest from S. China to S.E. Asia. The light or mid-green leave arranged in spirals or loose tufts at the stem tips, are divided almost to the bases into 2–10 or more lobes. Bears bowl-shaped, 3-petaled flowers in short panicles between the leaves. Where not hardy, grow in a temperate or warm greenhouse, or as houseplants. In frost-free regions, use in a shady border.

- **CULTIVATION** Under glass, grow in soilless potting mix in bright filtered light. In the growing season, water freely and apply a balanced liquid fertilizer monthly; water moderately in winter. Pot on or top-dress in spring. Outdoors, grow in any moderately fertile, moist but well-drained soil in dappled shade.
- **PROPAGATION** Sow seed at 81°F (27°C), or divide, in spring.
- **PESTS AND DISEASES** Prone to *Stigmina* and *Cercospora* leaf spots, spider mites, and scale insects.

R. excelsa ■ syn. *R. flabelliformis* (Miniature fan palm). Small, clump-forming palm with slender, erect, bamboo- or reed-like stems. The long-stalked, deeply lobed, lustrous, dark green leaves, 8–12in (20–30cm) long, each have 3–10 broadly to narrowly lance-shaped, puckered lobes. Tiny, bowl-shaped cream flowers are borne i panicles, to 5in (13cm) long, among th leaves, in summer. ↕↔ 5–15ft (1.5–5m S. China. ❀ (min. 50–55°F/10–13°C). Many cultivars have been selected. **'Variegata'** has leaves with white-strip lobes. **'Zuikonishiki'** has leaves with

Rhapis excelsa

yellow-variegated lobes; ↕ to 24in (60cm), rarely more.
R. flabelliformis see *R. excelsa.*

▷ ***Rhazya orientalis*** see *Amsonia orientalis*

RHEUM

Rhubarb

POLYGONACEAE

Genus of about 50 species of rhizomatous, often tough or woody perennials found in a range of habitats, from marshy meadows and streamsides to scrub and rocky slopes, in E. Europe and C. Asia to the Himalayas and China. Unlike *R.* x *hybridum*, which is grown for its edible leaf stalks, the rhubarbs described below are cultivated for their imposing, large, basal leaves and tall flower panicles. A few species from mountainous regions in Asia are dwarf, with small flower spikes. The rounded, entire to palmately lobed leaves often emerge from bright red buds; they are sometimes crimson-purple when young, usually with coarse teeth and conspicuous veins and midribs. Large panicles of tiny, petalless, star-shaped flowers are borne on hollow, leafless, flowering stems in summer; they have large, colorful, showy bracts in some species. The flowers are followed by small, triangular, winged, usually brown fruits. Grow rhubarbs near water, or in a moist border or woodland garden. The leaves may cause severe discomfort if ingested.

• **CULTIVATION** Grow in deep, moist, humus-rich soil in full sun or partial shade. *R. alexandrae* prefers wet, marshy soil. Mulch annually in early spring with well-rotted organic matter. *R. nobile* may be difficult to establish.

• **PROPAGATION** Sow seed in containers in a cold frame in autumn. Divide in early spring.

• **PESTS AND DISEASES** Root rot, rust, crown rot (sore shin), and Southern blight occur.

***R.* 'Ace of Hearts'** ■ syn. *R.* 'Ace of Spades'. Rhizomatous perennial with elongated, heart-shaped, dark green leaves, to 14in (35cm) long, red-veined above and purple-red beneath. In mid- and late summer, numerous tiny, star-shaped, very pale pink to white flowers open in panicles to 4ft (1.2m) long. ↕ to 4ft (1.2m), ↔ 36in (90cm). Zone 5.

Rheum 'Ace of Hearts'

***R.* 'Ace of Spades'** see *R.* 'Ace of Hearts'.
R. acuminatum (Ornamental rhubarb). Growing in or near water, with heavily veined leaves, rich red petioles and upright, branched and spidery stems, or red flowers to 4ft (1.2m). Red seed pods are borne in summer. Adaptive to full sun or partial shade in rich, humusy soil. After flowering cut back to rejuvenate foliage for the remaining season. Offers excellent autumn tones of red in full sun. Zone 7.
R. alexandrae. Rhizomatous perennial with rosetted, oblong-ovate, entire, glossy, dark green leaves, to 8in (20cm) long, with heart-shaped bases and prominent veins. In early summer, bears narrow, arching, then pendent panicles, 24in (60cm) long, of tiny, star-shaped, yellow-green flowers, which are almost hidden by creamy white or greenish cream bracts, to 4in (10cm) or more long. ↕ to 5ft (1.5m), ↔ 24in (60cm). W. China, Tibet. Zone 7.
R. australe see *R. emodii.*
R. emodii, syn. *R. australe* (Himalayan rhubarb, Red-veined pie plant). Rhizomatous perennial with rounded to broadly ovate, wavy-margined, mid-green leaves, 16–30in (40–75cm) long, hairy beneath. In summer, bears dense panicles, 8–12in (20–30cm) long, of numerous tiny, star-shaped white to wine-red flowers on branching stems. ↕ to 10ft (3m), ↔ 6–8ft (2–2.5m). Himalayas. Zone 6.
R. nobile. Rhizomatous perennial, similar to *R. alexandrae*, with broadly ovate, entire, glossy, dark green leaves, to 12in (30cm) or more long, veined and margined red. In midsummer, bears panicles, 24in (60cm) long, of showy, arching to pendent, overlapping cream bracts, to 6in (15cm) long, which conceal short, erect clusters of tiny, star-shaped green flowers. ↕ to 6ft (2m), ↔ 24in (60cm). Himalayas, Nepal to S.E. Tibet. Zone 7.
R. officinale (Chinese rhubarb/Indian rhubarb). Hardy perennial; rhizome considered medicinal. ↕ to 7ft (2.2m). E. Asia, Tibet. Zone 2b.
R. palmatum (Chinese rhubarb). Rhizomatous perennial with a massive rootstock and thick leaf stalks that bear broadly ovate to rounded, palmately 3- to 9-lobed, coarsely toothed, dark green leaves, to 36in (90cm) long, purple-red or red and softly hairy beneath. In early summer, numerous tiny, star-shaped, creamy green to deep red flowers are borne in panicles, to 6ft (2m) long. ↕ to 8ft (2.5m), ↔ to 6ft (1.8m). N.W. China, N.E. Tibet. Zone 4.
'Atropurpureum' see 'Atrosanguineum'.
'Atrosanguineum' ■ syn. 'Atropurpureum', has leaves that emerge from almost scarlet buds; the leaves are vivid crimson-purple when young, fading gradually to dark green above. Bears clustered panicles of rich cerise-pink flowers. **'Bowles' Crimson'** has darker red flowers, and leaves that are crimson beneath. **'Hadspen Crimson'** has deep red leaves and deep crimson flowers; ↕ to 15ft (5m). **'Irish Bronze'** has broad, deeply lobed leaves and small pink flowers. **var. *tanguticum*** has leaves with jagged leaflets, emerging reddish green and becoming dark green, often purple-tinted, with age. Massive flowering stems bear erect panicles of numerous white, pink, or crimson flowers; ↕ 6ft (2m).
R. rhabarbarum (Rhubarb, Pieplant). Strong perennial, with thick clustered roots and blunt, smooth leaves. Large, thick roots run deep into the ground, and are reddish-brown outside and yellow within. Stems are 2–3ft (60-1m) high, jointed and purplish. The flowers

Rheum palmatum 'Atrosanguineum'

are white. Succulent, red-colored petioles, ↕ to 18in (45cm) long and ½in (1.5cm) in diameter, are edible. Leaf blades are up to 1ft (30cm) or more in width and length and may be toxic if ingested. ↕↔ to 4ft (1.2m). Zone 2b.

▷ ***Rhipsalidopsis*** see *Hatiora*

RHIPSALIS

CACTACEAE

Genus of about 50 species of mostly epiphytic or rock-dwelling cacti from wooded and forested areas of Central and South America and the West Indies, with one species found in tropical Africa, Madagascar, and Sri Lanka. They often have aerial roots and freely branching stems, which vary in shape from cylindrical to winged, or flat and leaf-like, and may be ribbed or angled, some having spines or bristles. Small, funnel-shaped, diurnal flowers are borne singly or in small clusters from the areoles, mainly from spring to summer. These are followed by fleshy, berry-like, usually spherical fruits. Where not hardy, grow as houseplants in containers or hanging baskets, or in a temperate or warm greenhouse. In frost-free regions, grow epiphytically on a tree, or in a sheltered, humid border.

• **CULTIVATION** Under glass, grow in epiphytic cactus potting mix in bright filtered or indirect light with moderate to high humidity. Mist daily in warm weather. In growth, water freely and apply a balanced liquid fertilizer 3 or 4 times; water sparingly at other times. Outdoors, grow in an open site in fertile, humus-rich, moist but sharply drained soil in partial shade. See also pp.48–49.

• **PROPAGATION** Sow seed at 66–75°F (19–24°C), or root cuttings of stem sections, in spring or summer.

• **PESTS AND DISEASES** Susceptible to a variety of fungal stem and leaf spots, scale insects, and mealybugs.

R. baccifera, syn. *R. cassutha* (Mistletoe cactus). Pendent, epiphytic cactus with aerial roots and cylindrical, sparsely branched, mid-green stems, ⅛–¼in (3–6mm) thick. Minute areoles bear clusters of funnel-shaped white flowers, ¼–½in (6–15mm) long, from winter to spring, followed by spherical, pale pink or translucent white fruit, ¼–⅜in (6–9mm) across. ↕ to 12ft (4m), ↔ 24in (60cm). Africa, Madagascar, Sri Lanka, Tropical America. ❀ (min. 45–54°F/7–12°C)

Rhipsalis capilliformis

Rhipsalis cereuscula

R. capilliformis ▣ Pendent, epiphytic cactus bearing cylindrical, jointed, pale green stems with bunches of side branches, 1/16–⅛in (2–3mm) thick. The stems have slightly woolly, bristly areoles and, near the tips of the joints, minute, bristleless areoles bearing clusters of funnel-shaped, glossy, greenish white flowers, to ⅜in (9mm) long, in late spring. These are followed by spherical white fruit, ⅛–¼in (3–6mm) across. ↕ 16in (40cm) or more, ↔ 12in (30cm). E. Brazil. ❀ (min. 45–54°F/7–12°C)

R. cassutha see *R. baccifera.*

R. cereuscula ▣ (Coral cactus). Erect then pendent, epiphytic cactus bearing cylindrical, many-branched, mid-green stems, ⅛in (3mm) thick, with whorls of short, jointed branches. In spring, woolly, few-bristled areoles at the tips of the short branches bear usually solitary, narrowly funnel-shaped white flowers, ½in (1.5cm) long, with pinkish green sepals, followed by obovoid white fruit, ¼in (6mm) across. ↕ to 24in (60cm), ↔ 16in (40cm). Brazil, Paraguay, Argentina. ❀ (min. 45–54°F/7–12°C)

R. crispata. Semi-pendent, epiphytic cactus producing branching, flat, leaf-like, light green stems, ¾–1½in (2–4cm) thick, with elliptic, inversely lance-shaped, or obovate segments, with sometimes 3-winged, scalloped margins. In early summer, minute, spineless areoles bear solitary, funnel-shaped, creamy white flowers, ½in (1.5cm) across, followed by spherical white, sometimes red-flushed fruit, ⅜–½in (9–15mm) across. ↕ 24in (60cm), ↔ indefinite. S.E. Brazil. ❀ (min. 45–54°F/7–12°C)

Rhipsalis floccosa

R. fasciculata. Erect or semi-pendent, epiphytic cactus producing cylindrical, branching, pale bluish green stems, ¼in (6mm) thick, with woolly, few-bristled areoles along the margins. In early summer, the areoles bear funnel-shaped, white or pale greenish white flowers, to ⅜in (9mm) long, singly or in small clusters. They are followed by spherical white fruit, ⅛–¼in (3–6mm) across. ↕ to 24in (60cm), ↔ to 12in (30cm). Brazil. ❀ (min. 45–54°F/7–12°C)

R. floccosa ▣ syn. *R. tucumanensis.* Pendent, epiphytic cactus with aerial roots and cylindrical, branching, mid-green stems, to ½in (1.5cm) thick. Stem segments are arranged in whorls of 2–6, and have slightly woolly, sunken areoles bearing solitary, funnel-shaped, pink-tipped, white or creamy white flowers, ½in (1.5cm) long, from winter to spring. These are followed by spherical white, sometimes pink-tinged fruit, ¼–½in (6–15mm) across. ↕ 18in (45cm), ↔ 10in (25cm). Brazil, Bolivia, N. Paraguay, Argentina. ❀ (min. 45–54°F/7–12°C)

R. paradoxa (Chain cactus). Pendent, epiphytic cactus with aerial roots and branching, mid-green stems, 1¼–2in (3–5cm) thick. Stems have long, 3-angled segments, twisted into shorter segments every ¾–2½in (2–6cm), with white wool at the top of each angle. Funnel-shaped white flowers, ¾in (2cm) across, are borne singly from sunken areoles in late spring. They are followed by spherical red fruit, ⅜in (9mm) across. ↕ 3ft (1m) or more, ↔ indefinite. S.E. Brazil. ❀ (min. 45–54°F/7–12°C)

R. tucumanensis see *R. floccosa.*

RHODANTHE

syn. ACROCLINIUM

Strawflower

ASTERACEAE

Genus of over 40 species of erect, drought-tolerant annuals, perennials, and subshrubs, frequently included in the genera *Acroclinium* and *Helipterum*, occurring in arid areas of Australia. They are cultivated for their solitary or corymb-like clusters of daisy-like, straw-textured, everlasting, single to double, yellow, white, or pink flowerheads, borne mainly in summer. The alternate leaves are entire, linear to oblong or obovate, and mid- to gray-green. Grow in an annual or mixed border; the perennials and subshrubs are usually

Rhodanthe chlorocephala subsp. *rosea*

Rhodanthe manglesii

grown as annuals, even in frost-free areas. The flowerheads are excellent for dried flower arrangements.

• **CULTIVATION** Grow in light, well-drained, preferably poor soil in full sun. Cut for drying before flowerheads are fully open, and hang upside down in a warm, dry, dark place.

• **PROPAGATION** Sow seed at 61°F (16°C) in early spring and plant out when all danger of frost has passed, or sow *in situ* in midspring.

• **PESTS AND DISEASES** Seedlings and young plants are prone to aphids and slug damage.

R. chlorocephala* subsp. *rosea ▣ syn. *Acroclinium roseum, Helipterum roseum.* Fast-growing, erect annual producing linear, pointed, stem-clasping, gray-green leaves, to 1½in (4cm) long. In summer, bears solitary flowerheads, 1–3in (2.5–8cm) across, with yellow disk florets surrounded by spreading, papery, white or rose-pink bracts, often with white bases; they close in cloudy weather. ↕ 12–24in (30–60cm), ↔ 6in (15cm). S.W. Australia.

R. manglesii ▣ syn. *Helipterum manglesii* (Swan River everlasting). Erect, bushy annual with oblong to ovate, pointed, gray-green leaves, to 4in (10cm) long. From summer to early autumn, bears stiff-stemmed clusters of small flowerheads, to 1¼in (3cm) across, with light yellow disk florets surrounded by decorative, spreading, papery, red, pink, or white bracts. ↕ 24in (60cm), ↔ 6in (15cm). W. Australia.

RHODANTHEMUM

syn. CHRYSANTHEMOPSIS, PYRETHROPSIS

ASTERACEAE

Genus of about 10 species of mat-forming, often rhizomatous perennials and subshrubs, previously included in the genera *Chrysanthemum* or *Leucanthemum*, from exposed rocky areas in N. Africa, with one species from Spain. They are cultivated for their solitary, large, daisy-like flowerheads, surrounded by prominent, usually green bracts, borne on erect, branched or unbranched stems, mainly in spring and summer. The deeply or shallowly 3-lobed leaves are hairy and sometimes silvery. Grow in a sunny rock garden, in a raised bed, at the base of a warm, sunny wall, or in an alpine house.

• **CULTIVATION** Under glass, grow in soil-based potting mix in full light. In

Rhodanthemum hosmariense

Rhodiola rosea

the growing season, water freely and apply a balanced liquid fertilizer monthly; water moderately in winter. Outdoors, grow in moderately fertile, very well-drained soil in full sun.
• **PROPAGATION** Sow seed in containers in a cold frame in spring. Root softwood cuttings in early summer.
• **PESTS AND DISEASES** Susceptible to aphids and spider mites under glass.

R. atlanticum, syn. *Chrysanthemum atlanticum, Pyrethropsis atlantica.* Prostrate, rhizomatous perennial with unbranched stems and 3-lobed, hairy, mid-green leaves, to 1½in (4cm) long, the middle lobe divided into 3, the outer lobes finely divided. In summer, bears solitary flowerheads, 1¼in (3cm) across, with white ray florets, flushed pink beneath, and yellow disk florets. ↕ 3in (8cm), ↔ 12in (30cm). Morocco. ❄ (min. 41°F/5°C)
R. catananche, syn. *Chrysanthemum catananche, Pyrethropsis catananche.* Rhizomatous perennial producing unbranched stems and hairy, silver-gray leaves, to 2½in (6cm) long, irregularly cut into 3 toothed lobes.In summer, bears solitary flowerheads, to 2in (5cm) across, with cream ray florets, each with a maroon stripe, surrounding a small center of deep yellow disk florets. ↕ 6in (15cm), ↔ 12in (30cm). Morocco. ❄ (min. 41°F/5°C)
R. gayanum, syn. *Chrysanthemum gayanum, Pyrethropsis gayana.* Semi-erect subshrub with branching stems and deeply 3-lobed, softly hairy, gray-green leaves, 1in (2.5cm) long. Solitary flowerheads, 1–1½in (2.5–4cm) across, with rose-pink or white, pink-backed ray florets and brown disk florets, are borne freely in summer. ↕↔ to 12in (30cm). Morocco, Algeria. ❄ (min. 41°F/5°C)
R. hosmariense ■ syn. *Chrysanthemum hosmariense, Leucanthemum hosmariense, Pyrethropsis hosmariensis.* Spreading, bushy subshrub with stalkless, softly hairy, intensely silver, deeply 3-lobed leaves, to 1½in (4cm) long. From early spring to autumn, bears solitary, short-stemmed flowerheads, to 2in (5cm) across, with white ray florets and wide centers of yellow disk florets; they are surrounded by silvery bracts, the outer ones with distinctive black margins. It is one of the easiest species to grow in an open garden; in an alpine house, it flowers for most of the year if dead-headed. ↕ 4–12in (10–30cm), ↔ 12in (30cm). Atlas Mountains. ❄ (min. 41°F/5°C)

R. maresii, syn. *Chrysanthemum maresii, Pyrethropsis maresii.* Spreading subshrub, similar to *R. hosmariense*, with deeply 3-lobed, softly hairy, silver-green leaves, to 2½in (6cm) long. In summer, bears solitary flowerheads, ¾–1½in (2–4cm) across, with yellow ray florets and yellow disk florets that become increasingly purple-tinged with age. ↕ 4–12in (10–30cm), ↔ 12in (30cm). Algeria. ❄ (min. 41°F/5°C)

RHODIOLA

CRASSULACEAE

Genus of about 50 species of perennials, some dioecious, widely distributed in the N. hemisphere in sunny, rocky habitats. They have thick, fleshy rhizomes producing scaly brown basal leaves, and stiffly erect, unbranched or occasionally branched stems that bear alternate, triangular-ovate to lance-shaped, often toothed, fleshy, gray-green stem leaves. The small, star-shaped, green, yellow, orange, or red flowers, with 8–10 prominent stamens, are borne in dense, rounded, terminal, corymb- or raceme-like heads, and may be unisexual or bisexual. Rhodiolas are cultivated for their foliage and flowers, and are suitable for a rock garden, or the front of a mixed or herbaceous border.
• **CULTIVATION** Grow in moderately fertile soil in full sun.
• **PROPAGATION** Sow seed in containers in a cold frame in spring or autumn. Divide rhizomes in spring or early summer. Root leaf cuttings in summer.
• **PESTS AND DISEASES** Aphids can be a problem.

Rhodiola heterodonta

R. heterodonta ■ syn. *Sedum heterodontum, S. rosea* var. *heterodontum.* Erect, hairless, dioecious, rhizomatous perennial with branching stems of ovate, fleshy, grayish green leaves, 1–1¼in (2.5–3cm) long, either entire or with a few coarse teeth. In late spring and early summer, bears dense, terminal cymes of numerous star-shaped yellow flowers, ⅛in (3mm) across, opening from rounded red buds. Male flowers have red or purple-red anthers that color the whole of the flowerheads; females have purple-tipped carpels. ↕↔ to 16in (40cm). Afghanistan, Pamir Mountains, W. Himalayas, Tibet. Zone 5.
R. rosea ■ syn. *Sedum rosea, S. rhodiola* (Roseroot). Variable, clump-forming, dioecious, rhizomatous perennial with purple stems bearing broadly ovate to narrowly inversely lance-shaped, entire or irregularly toothed, fleshy, glaucous, gray-green leaves, to 1½in (4cm) long, with red-tinted tips. In summer, bears dense, terminal, corymb- or umbel-like heads of numerous male or female, yellow-green flowers, ¼in (6mm) across, opening from slightly pink buds. ↕ 2–12in (5–30cm), ↔ 8in (20cm). Throughout N. hemisphere. Zone 1. **subsp. *integrifolia*** has smaller leaves and red-purple, sometimes green flowers, borne on reddish green stems.
R. wallichiana, syn. *Sedum crassipes, Sedum wallichiana.* Erect, rhizomatous, hairless perennial with linear-lance-shaped, slightly toothed, mid-green leaves, ½–1¼in (1.5–3cm) long. In early summer, bears dense but few-flowered, terminal, corymb-like flowerheads with bisexual, star-shaped, pale yellow to greenish white flowers, ¼–½in (6–15mm) across, sometimes tinged pink. ↕ to 14in (35cm), ↔ 12in (30cm). W. Himalayas, W. China, Tibet. Zone 5.

▷ ***Rhodocactus grandifolius*** see *Pereskia grandifolia*

RHODOCHITON

SCROPHULARIACEAE

Genus of 3 species of deciduous, perennial climbers found in woodland in Mexico. They are cultivated for their flowers, which have pendant, long-tubed corollas, with 5 rounded segments, and inflated calyces. Twining leaf stalks bear alternate, simple, sparsely toothed leaves. Where not hardy, grow rhodochitons as annuals outdoors,or in a cool greenhouse. In frost-free areas, use to cover a pergola or arch. With support, they will climb to as much as 10ft (3m), in open, sunny conditions, and produce a profusion of flowers the first year from seed.
• **CULTIVATION** Under glass, grow in soil-based potting mix in full light with shade from hot sun. When in growth, water freely and apply a balanced liquid fertilizer monthly;keep just moist in winter. Pot on in spring. Outdoors, grow in fertile, humus-rich, moist but well-drained soil in full sun.
• **PROPAGATION** Sow seed at 59–64°F (15–18°C) as soon as ripe or in spring.
• **PESTS AND DISEASES** Prone to spider mites and whiteflies under glass.

R. atrosanguineus ■ syn. *R. volubile.* Slender-stemmed climber bearing heart-shaped, rich green leaves, 1½–3in (4–8cm) long. Long, pendent stalks bear solitary, tubular, black to reddish purple flowers, 1¾in (4.5cm) long, with cup-shaped, rose-pink or mauve calyces, from summer to autumn. ↕ to 10ft (3m), sometimes more. Mexico. ❄ (min. 37–41°F/3–5°C)
R. volubile see *R. atrosanguineus.*

Rhodochiton atrosanguineus

R

RHODODENDRON

syn. AZALEA

ERICACEAE

Genus of 500–900 species of evergreen and deciduous trees and shrubs, sometimes epiphytic, from Europe, Australasia, North America, and Asia, particularly S.W. China, Tibet, Burma, N. India, and New Guinea. They occur in diverse habitats, from dense forest to alpine tundra, and from sea level to high altitudes. They vary greatly in habit, and may reach a height of 80ft (25m) or creep at ground level to form prostrate shrubs.

The leaves are mostly lance-shaped or elliptic, and mid- to dark green, ranging in size from ⅛in (3mm) to 30in (75cm) long. All hybrids described below conform to one of the following leaf length ranges: very large, 18–30in (45–75cm) long; large, 6–18in (15–45cm) long; medium-sized, 2–6in (5–15cm) long; small, ½–2in (1–5cm) long; very small, ⅛–½in (4–10mm) long. Some have leaves and young stems with a dense woolly covering of hairs or scales (indumentum); a few have leaves that are aromatic when crushed.

Rhododendrons are grown mainly for their spectacular, sometimes strongly scented flowers, which are borne singly or in lateral or terminal racemes (known as trusses), usually from late winter to late autumn. The individual flowers vary greatly in size and shape (see panel below), but are usually 5-lobed, and often marked with flares or spots inside, on the upper or lower lobes or in the throats; some also have conspicuous or brightly colored, basal nectar pouches inside. There are thousands of hybrids, encompassing nearly every flower color.

Bloom seasons vary significantly throughout North America. In the milder areas along the Pacific and in the S.E. US, "very early" corresponds to February, with "very late" beginning in late June. In contrast, in C. US, N.E. US, and the lower maritime provinces, "very early" is early April and "very late" runs from late July onward.

Some rhododendrons also have attractive young growth, which ranges in color from red to bronze-brown or metallic blue-green; a few have decorative, exfoliating bark, which may be any color from brown-pink or deep maroon to silvery gray. A number of the deciduous rhododendrons are valued for their autumn color.

Rhododendrons have a wide range of garden uses: dwarf alpine varieties are effective in a rock garden; larger woodland rhododendrons are excellent for brightening shady areas; the "ironclad" rhododendrons are tolerant of more exposed sites and also suitable for hedges or informal screens; and many of the modern compact hybrids are ideal for growing on shaded patios, or in containers or tubs. Where not hardy, tender rhododendrons, including Vireyas, are best grown in a conservatory or cool greenhouse. The nectar of some rhododendron flowers may cause severe discomfort if ingested.

In horticulture, rhododendrons are often divided into 5 main groups: large-leaf (elepidote) evergreen rhododendrons, small-leaf (lepidote) evergreen rhododendrons, Vireya rhododendrons, deciduous azaleas, and evergreen azaleas.

Large-leaf (elepidote) evergreen rhododendrons
These vary in habit from low, mound-forming shrubs to tree types. They have medium-sized to very large leaves, and bear flowers in a variety of shapes, sizes, and colors. Included within this group, among many others, are the so-called "ironclads," derived from *R. catawbiense*, *R. ponticum*, and *R. caucasicum* crosses; the Fortunei hybrids, characterized by tall, vigorous growth and large flowers, often scented; and the Yakushimanum hybrids, which tend to form low, compact shrubs with leaves that often bear indumentum.

Small-leaf (lepidote) evergreen rhododendrons
The growth habit of this group varies from almost prostrate spreaders and dwarf cushions to tall shrubs. Leaf size varies from very small to medium-sized, and flower colors cover the spectrum except for true red. The group includes some of the hardiest of all evergreen rhododen-drons, derived in part from *R. dauricum* and *R. minus*, as well as the tender Maddenii types, with large, often fragrant blossoms.

Vireya rhododendrons
Sometimes known as Malesian rhododendrons, these are evergreen, usually epiphytic shrubs from tropical areas of S.E. Asia, and are frost tender. They have scaly leaves and stems. The flowers are extremely varied in shape, color, and season; a range of plants will give flowers throughout the year. This group tends not to follow a seasonal pattern of flowering. Some flower only in spring, while others may bloom several times a year. The flowering times given below are a general indication of when flowering is most likely to occur. Grow in a cool greenhouse or conservatory. Use containers to restrict the spread of larger plants.

RHODODENDRON FLOWER FORMS

Rhododendron flowers are tubular-, funnel-, trumpet-, or bell-shaped, or may have a form between these shapes. A few have saucer-shaped or hose-in-hose flowers (with 2 flower tubes, one inside the other).

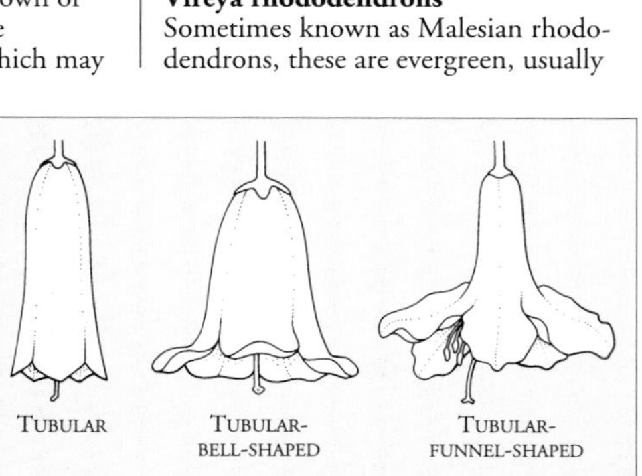

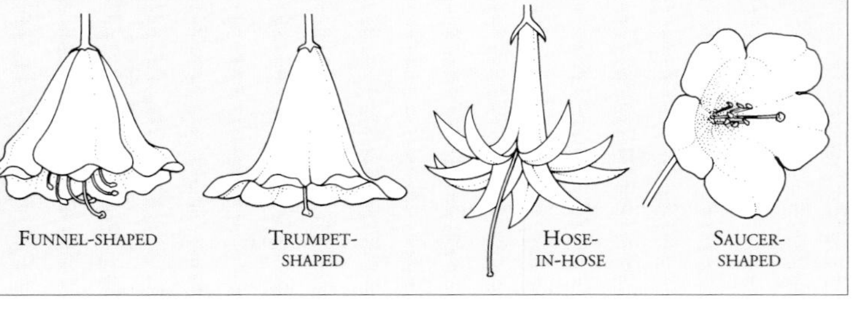

Deciduous and evergreen azaleas
These are small to medium-leaved shrubs belonging to the subgenera *Pentanthera* and *Tsutsusi*, and commonly known to gardeners as azaleas. They bear a profusion of small to large trusses of usually small flowers in a variety of shapes. Azalea hybrids may be further divided into many subgroups, some of which are described below. Azaleas classified into other groups are indicated in the entries as (O).

Deciduous azaleas – **Ghent hybrids** (Gh) are Belgian-raised, resulting from crosses between American azalea species and *R. luteum.* The funnel-shaped, white, yellow, orange, pink, or red flowers, borne in late midseason, are long-tubed, sometimes double, and usually scented. **Knap Hill-Exbury hybrids** (K-E) are English hybrid azaleas with complex origins (American azalea species x *R. molle*), characterized by large trusses of trumpet-shaped, scented or scentless flowers, in a wide range of bright colors, borne from midseason to late midseason. **Mollis hybrids** (M) have Dutch and Belgian origins, and are a result of crossing selections of *R. molle* subsp. *japonicum* and *R. molle.* Funnel-shaped, usually scented flowers, in a wide range of colors, including cream, yellow, pink, orange, or red, are borne before the leaves in late midseason. **Occidentale hybrids** (Oc) are English azaleas, raised by crossing Mollis hybrids with *R. occidentale.* Funnel-shaped, usually scented, pink or white flowers are borne late in the season, later than those of Ghent hybrids.

Evergreen azaleas – **Glenn Dale hybrids** (GD) are varied, complex azaleas raised in Glenn Dale, Maryland. The relatively large, funnel-shaped flowers, usually white or pink to red, are borne from midseason to late midseason. Some are frilled, semi-double, or multicolored. **Indica hybrids** (In) are complex azaleas, mostly of Belgian origin, bred from *R. simsii*, *R. mucronatum*, *R. indicum*, and other species. Very early in the season, they produce large, funnel-shaped, unscented flowers in a wide range of colors, and are popular for growing indoors in containers for winter decoration. They are widely grown outdoors in the S.E. US. **Kaempferi hybrids** (K) are Dutch-raised azaleas bred from *R. kaempferi*, *R.* 'Malvatica', and *R.* 'Maxwelli'. They are taller, hardier, and later-flowering than Kurume hybrids (below), which are also derived from *R. kaempferi.* They bear funnel-shaped, unscented, white, pink, or red flowers in spring, on bushes about 4ft (1.2m) tall. **Kurume hybrids** (Ku) are Japanese-raised dwarf azaleas, originating from crosses between *R. kaempferi*, *R. kiusianum*, and *R. obtusum.* Numerous, very small, funnel-shaped, unscented flowers are borne in a wide range of colors in midseason. They are particularly effective in massed plantings, and they are a traditional choice for bonsai. **North Tisbury hybrids** (NT) are a group bred by Polly Hill on Martha's Vineyard, MA. Most are hardy, evergreen, low-growing or prostrate shrubs, ideal for use as groundcovers. They bear open funnel-shaped flowers in shades of pink and red, in mid- and late midseason. **Robin Hill hybrids** (RH) are the result of crossing Satsuki azaleas with other azaleas to produce hardier evergreen cultivars. They are low-growing, excellent as groundcovers, bearing large, open funnel-shaped flowers, mostly in shades of red, pink, and white, late in the season. **Satsuki hybrids** (S) are Japanese-raised azaleas, originally used for bonsai work. They have been bred using mainly *R. indicum* and *R. simsii.* They have a low, twiggy habit, and bear large, funnel-shaped, unscented flowers in white, pink, red, or purple, late in the season. They have a tendency to sport. **Shammarello hybrids** (Sh) were raised by Shammarello in N. Ohio. They are ideal for growing in cold climates, and are hardy from -15 to -10°F (-26 to -23°C) (Zone 6). Many have been raised by crossing *R.* 'Hino-crimson' with *R. yedoense* var. *poukhanense.* They have small, trumpet-shaped, unscented flowers in a range of colors, borne in late midseason. **Vuyk (Vuykiana) hybrids** (V) were bred by Vuyk van Nes Nurseries in Holland, using a complex cross of *R. kaempferi* and *R. mucronatum*, and probably other species. They bear very showy, medium-sized, funnel-shaped, unscented flowers in a range of colors, in late midseason.

• **CULTIVATION** Under glass, grow tender rhododendrons in acidic potting mix in bright filtered light, with moderate to high humidity. For Vireyas incorporate ground bark, osmunda fiber, or conifer needles to keep the soil mix open; they will tolerate a maximum day temperature of 90°F (32°C). When in growth, water tender rhododendrons freely and apply a balanced liquid fertilizer monthly; keep just moist in winter. Mist Indica hybrids grown as houseplants daily until the flower buds show color; provide a maximum temperature of 55–61°F (13–16°C) when in bloom. Remove spent flowers and repot after flowering, then transfer to a cool greenhouse or windowsill in bright, indirect light. Plunge pots in a shaded, well-ventilated cold frame for the summer months, and keep cool, moist, and humid; protect from autumn frost and bring plants indoors in late autumn.

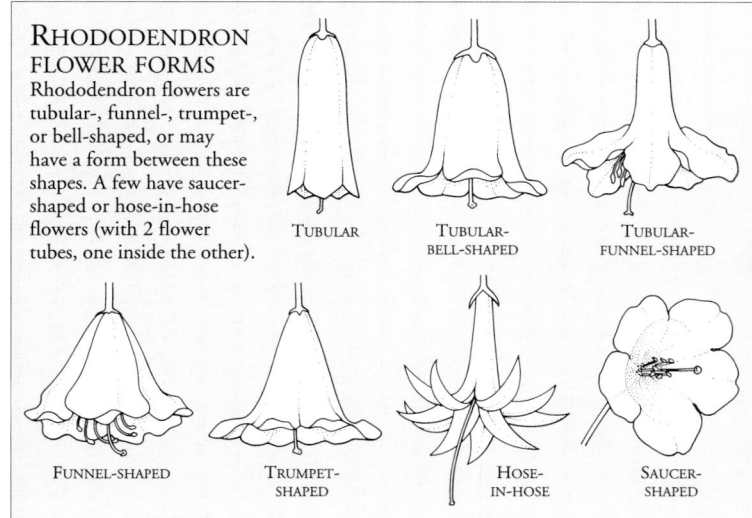

Outdoors, grow in moist but well-drained, leafy, humus-rich, acidic soil (ideally pH4.5–5.5). Shallow planting is essential: all rhododendrons are surface-rooting and will not tolerate deep planting. Most large-leaved species and hybrids require dappled shade in sheltered woodland conditions; avoid the deep shade immediately beneath a tree canopy. Rhododendrons generally perform best in temperate climates with adequate rainfall, such as the Pacific

Rhododendron 'Alexander'

Rhododendron arborescens

Rhododendron atlanticum

Northwest (including British Columbia) and the Atlantic states and provinces from Virginia north. Success is more difficult to achieve in the humid S.E. US (except for azaleas), the arid S.W. US, and the continental climate of the Rockies and Central Plains. In these areas, heat tolerance becomes as important as cold hardiness. For example, a variety that will flourish in Vancouver may not even survive in the climate of Dallas TX, although both have a similar hardiness zone. Proper siting, soil preparation, wind protection, and attention to watering are essential for success in these less favorable areas. Most azaleas and many of the smaller-leaved evergreen rhododendrons, as well as the "ironclad" hybrids, prefer full sun in the N. US and Canada, dappled shade in the S. US. Most dwarf alpine species will tolerate full sun in cooler climates, provided the soil remains moist. Avoid frost pockets to reduce the risk of split bark occurring in winter. To conserve moisture and to protect the shallow roots from extremes of heat and cold, mulch annually with a loose, open material, such as pine needles, bark, or chopped oak leaves. After flowering, deadhead where practical, to promote vegetative growth rather than seed production. When deadheading, be careful not to damage or remove young growth emerging from below the flowers. Pruning group 8.

• **PROPAGATION** Surface-sow seed at 55–64°F (13–18°C) in acidic propagating soil mix or fine peat, as soon as ripe or in early spring. Sow seed of hardy dwarf species and hybrids in containers in a cold frame as soon as ripe. Rhododendrons hybridize freely, so garden-collected seed may not come true; however, seed collected from species in the wild or from hand-pollinated garden plants will generally produce plants that are true to type. Root semi-ripe cuttings in late summer or autumn. Layer in autumn. Graft in late winter or late summer.

• **PESTS AND DISEASES** Susceptible to vine weevil, whiteflies, leafhoppers, lacebugs, scale insects, caterpillars, aphids, powdery mildew, bud blast, rust, leafy gall, petal blight, *Phytophthora* root rot, and lime-induced chlorosis (if the soil is not sufficiently acidic).

***R.* 'A. Bedford'** see *R.* 'Arthur Bedford'.
***R.* 'Aglo'.** Evergreen shrub with small, glossy, bright green leaves, which turn a coppery bronze in winter. Early in the season, bears small trusses of open funnel-shaped, bright pink flowers, 1½in (4cm) across, with rust-red throats. Plant in full sun. ↕↔ 4ft (1.2m). Zone 5.
R. alabamense (Alabama azalea). Compact, suckering, deciduous azalea with oblong-elliptic, obovate, or elliptic, usually hairy, mid-green leaves, 1¼–3in (3–8cm) long, usually densely gray-green-hairy beneath. Trusses of 6–10 funnel-shaped, fragrant, usually yellow-blotched, white flowers, 1½in (4cm) across, are borne with the leaves, in mid-season. ↕ 5–6ft (1.5–2m), ↔ indefinite. Tennessee, Alabama, Georgia, Florida. Zone 7b.
R. albrechtii ▣ Twiggy, deciduous azalea with obovate, finely toothed, dark green leaves, 1½–5in (4–13cm) long, gray-downy beneath. Trusses of 3–5 widely bell-shaped, deep to purplish rose-pink flowers, 1½–2in (4–5cm) across, spotted olive-green inside, are borne early in the season. Tolerates full sun. ↕↔ 8ft (2.5m). Japan. Zone 6.
***R.* 'Alexander'** ▣ Prostrate evergreen azalea (NT) producing small, narrowly elliptic, hairy, olive-green leaves. Trusses of open funnel-shaped, salmon-red flowers, 1½–2in (4–5cm) across, are borne very late in the season. Makes an attractive, medium-height groundcover. ↕ 8in (20cm), ↔ 36in (90cm). Zone 6.
***R.* 'Alison Johnstone'** ▣ Evergreen shrub producing small, elliptic leaves with a metallic luster. In early mid-season, bears loose trusses of pendent, tubular-bell-shaped, pale yellow flowers, 2in (5cm) across, flushed peach-pink inside. Prefers a sunny, sheltered site. ↕↔ 6ft (2m). Zone 7b.
***R.* 'Anna H. Hall'.** Evergreen shrub producing large elliptic leaves. In midseason, bears full trusses of open funnel-shaped, white flowers, 2in (5cm) across, with intense pink buds. ↕ to 6ft (2m), ↔ to 5ft (1.5m). Zone 5b.
***R.* 'Anna Rose Whitney'.** Evergreen shrub with large leaves. In late mid-season, bears loose, rounded trusses of widely funnel-shaped, deep rose-pink flowers, 2½–4in (6–10cm) across, spotted brown inside. ↕↔ 12ft (4m). Zone 7b.
***R.* 'April Gem'.** Broadly upright, compact evergreen shrub with small, elliptic, aromatic mid-green leaves. Early in the season, produces dense trusses of double, broadly funnel-shaped, white flowers, 1½–2in (4–5cm) across, with 3–5 flowers per cluster. ↕ 36in (90cm), ↔ 24in (60cm). Zone 5.
***R.* 'April Song'.** Upright, evergreen shrub with small, elliptic, dark green leaves, which turn yellow and mahogany-red in autumn. Early in the season, produces large trusses of funnel-shaped, frilly, double, light pink flowers, 1½–2in (4–5cm) across, with nearly white inner petals, creating a two-tone effect. ↕ to 5ft (1.5m), ↔ 3–4ft (1–1.2m). Zone 6.
R. arborescens ▣ (Sweet azalea). Upright, deciduous azalea with obovate or sometimes elliptic to oblong-lance-shaped, shiny, dark green leaves, 1¼–3in (3–8cm) long, turning reddish green in autumn. Very late in the season, bears trusses of 3–7 funnel-shaped, clove-scented, white to light pink flowers, 1½–2in (4–5cm) across, often with red stamens. ↕↔ 8–20ft (2.5–6m). S. Pennsylvania to Alabama and Georgia. Zone 6b.
R. arboreum ▣ (Tree rhododendron). Evergreen tree producing inversely lance-shaped, dark green leaves, 3–7in (7–18cm) long, with a silvery, fawn, or cinnamon-brown indumentum beneath. Dense trusses of tubular-bell-shaped, red, pink, or white flowers, 2in (5cm) across, with black nectar pouches and black spots inside, are borne early in the season. ↕ 40ft (12m), ↔ 12ft (4m). China to Thailand, N. India, Bhutan, Sri Lanka. Zone 7b.
***R.* 'Arctic Tern'** see x *Ledodendron* 'Arctic Tern'.
R. argyrophyllum ▣ Evergreen shrub with oblong to lance-shaped, dark green leaves, 2½–6in (6–15cm) long, with gray-white hairs beneath. In early mid-season, bears lax trusses of funnel- to bell-shaped, mid- to pale pink flowers, 1½–2in (4–5cm) across, spotted deep pink inside and with showy red anthers. ↕ 20ft (6m), ↔ 8ft (2.5m). S.W. China. Zone 8.
R. arizelum see *R. rex* subsp. *arizelum*.
***R.* 'Arthur Bedford'**, syn. *R.* 'A. Bedford'. Vigorous, evergreen shrub with large leaves. In late midseason, bears pyramid-shaped trusses of funnel-shaped, light mauve flowers, 2½–3in (6–8cm) across, each with a deep brown-red flare in the throat. Tolerant of sun. ↕↔ 10ft (3m). Zone 7.
R. atlanticum ▣ (Coast azalea). Suckering, deciduous azalea with obovate or oblong-obovate, bluish green leaves, 1½–2in (4–5cm) long, occasionally softly hairy along the midribs. Trusses of 4–13 funnel-shaped, very fragrant, pinkish white flowers, 1½in (4cm) across, are borne with or just before the leaves in midseason. ↕↔ 3–6ft (1–2m). Coastal plains from Delaware to South Carolina. Zone 5.
R. augustinii ▣ Bushy, evergreen shrub producing oblong to lance-shaped, mid- to dark green leaves, 1½–4½in (4–11cm) long. Trusses of 2–5 broadly funnel-shaped, pale to deep blue or lavender-blue flowers, to 3in (8cm) across, spotted greenish brown inside, open in early midseason. Grows in full sun. ↕↔ 7ft (2.2m). China. Zone 7b.
R. austrinum (Florida azalea, Mayflower azalea, Piedmont azalea). Deciduous azalea with elliptic to obovate, softly hairy, mid-green leaves, 2–3½in (5–9cm) long. Dense trusses of 8–15, tubular-funnel-shaped, fragrant, yellow to orange flowers, 1–1½in (2.5–4cm) across, often with red-tinged tubes, are borne early in the season. ↕ 6ft (2m), ↔ 4ft (1.2m). S. Mississippi to S. Georgia to N. Florida. Zone 7b.
***R.* 'Azuma-kagami'** ▣ Compact, evergreen azalea (Ku) with small leaves. In early midseason, bears numerous small trusses of hose-in-hose, bright pink flowers, 1¾in (4.5cm) across. ↕↔ 4ft (1.2m). Zone 7b.

Rhododendron albrechtii

Rhododendron 'Alison Johnstone'

Rhododendron arboreum

Rhododendron argyrophyllum

Rhododendron augustinii

Rhododendron 'Azuma-kagami'

***R.* 'Beauty of Littleworth'** ▣ Vigorous, showy, evergreen shrub with large leaves. In midseason, bears cone-shaped trusses of funnel-shaped, fragrant white flowers, to 5in (13cm) across, spotted crimson inside. Suitable only for dappled shade. ↕↔ 12ft (4m). Zone 7b.
***R.* 'Beethoven'** ▣ Dwarf, evergreen azalea (V) producing small leaves. In midseason, bears lax trusses of funnel-shaped, fringe-petaled, mauve-pink flowers, 2in (5cm) across, each with a deeper mauve mark inside. ↕↔ 4½ft (1.3m). Zone 7.
***R.* 'Betty Anne Voss'.** Dwarf, dense, rounded evergreen azalea (RH) with small, elliptic, dark green leaves. Late in the season, produces trusses of double, hose-in-hose, broadly funnel-shaped, soft pink flowers, 2½–3in (6–8cm) across, with deeper pink centers. ↕ 18in (45cm), ↔ 30in (75cm). Zone 7.
***R.* 'Blue Diamond'** ▣ Dwarf, small-leaved, evergreen shrub with a compact, upright habit. In early midseason, bears trusses of up to 5 funnel-shaped, violet-blue flowers, 2in (5cm) across. ↕↔ 5ft (1.5m). Zone 7.
***R.* 'Blue Peter'** ▣ Large-leaved, evergreen shrub of open habit. In midseason, bears tight, rounded trusses of funnel-shaped, lavender-blue flowers, 2½–3in (6–8cm) long, with frilled petals and purple marks inside. Tolerates full sun. ↕↔ 10ft (3m). Zone 6b.
***R.* 'Boule de Neige'.** Compact, rounded, evergreen shrub producing large, elliptic, shiny, dark green leaves. In midseason, bears large trusses of funnel-shaped, white flowers, 1¾in (4.5cm) across. ↕ 5ft (1.5m), ↔ 8ft (2.5m). Zone 5b.
***R.* 'Bow Bells'.** Free-flowering, compact, evergreen shrub with small to medium-sized, broadly ovate to rounded leaves, reddish bronze when young, mid-green when mature. In early midseason, bears lax trusses of long-stalked, bell-shaped, light pink flowers, 2½in (6cm) across. ↕↔ 6ft (2m). Zone 7.
R. bullatum see *R. edgeworthii.*
R. bureaui see *R. bureavii.*
R. bureavii ▣ syn. *R. bureaui.* Multi-stemmed, evergreen shrub producing ovate to lance-shaped, dark green leaves, 1¾–5in (4.5–13cm) long, initially covered with a light brown indumentum above and a woolly, bright orange-brown indumentum beneath. In midseason, bears neat trusses of tubular-bell-shaped, white or soft pink, crimson-

Rhododendron calendulaceum (inset: yellow color variant)

spotted flowers, to 2½in (6cm) across. ↕↔ 10ft (3m). S.W. China. Zone 7.
R. calendulaceum ▣ (Flame azalea). Robust, deciduous azalea with elliptic-oblong, mid-green leaves, 1½–3½in (3.5–9cm) long, softly hairy on both sides. In late midseason, bears lax trusses of funnel-shaped, bright orange to scarlet flowers, to 2in (5cm) across, usually opening with the leaves, or just after they emerge. Prefers full sun. ↕↔ 8ft (2.5m). E. US. Zone 5.
R. calophytum. Multi-stemmed evergreen shrub or small tree with oblong to inversely lance-shaped, dark green leaves, 5½–12in (14–30cm) long. Early in the season, bears large trusses of broadly bell-shaped, 5- to 7-lobed, fragrant, pale pink flowers, to 3in (8cm) across, with basal, carmine-red marks in the throats. ↕ 30ft (10m), ↔ 20ft (6m). S.W. China, Tibet. Zone 6.
R. calostrotum ▣ Compact, dwarf, evergreen shrub with oblong-ovate to rounded leaves, ½–1¼in (1–3cm) long, scaly and glaucous above, with dense brown scales beneath. In midseason, freely bears solitary or pairs of saucer-shaped, bright rose-purple flowers, 1½–1¾in (4–4.5cm) across, often with purple spots on the upper lobes. Tolerates full sun if kept moist. ↕ 30in (75cm), ↔ 36in (90cm). N.E. India, Tibet, W. China. Zone 6b. **subsp. *keleticum***, syn. *R. keleticum*, is almost prostrate, with glossy, dark green leaves, 1/16–3/8in (2–9mm) long, densely brown-scaly beneath. Bears trusses of up to 3 widely funnel-shaped, purplish crimson flowers, crimson-spotted inside; ↕ 12in (30cm), ↔ 36in (90cm). S.E. Tibet, S.W. China, N.E. Burma. Zone 6.
***R.* 'Calsap'** ▣ Evergreen shrub with large, elliptic leaves. In midseason, produces large, dome-shaped trusses of open funnel-shaped, white flowers, 2½in (6cm) across, with blotches of dark purple. ↕ to 6ft (2m), ↔ 4–5ft (1.2–1.5m). Zone 5.
R. campylocarpum ▣ (Honeybell rhododendron). Robust, evergreen shrub or small tree with neat, elliptic-ovate, dark green leaves, 1¼–4in (3–10cm) long, pale gray-green beneath. Trusses of 3–15 delicate, bell-shaped, pale to mid-yellow flowers, 2½–3in (6–8cm) across, are borne in early midseason. Some variants have deep red basal marks inside. ↕ to 15ft (5m), ↔ 12ft (4m). S.E. Tibet, S.W. China, N.E. Burma. Zone 7b.
R. campylogynum. Dwarf, compact, evergreen shrub with inversely lance-shaped leaves, ½–¾in (1.5–2cm) long, glossy, dark green above, often off-white or silver beneath. In early midseason, bears small trusses of long-stemmed, nodding, broadly bell-shaped flowers, ½–1in (1–2.5cm) across, varying in color from white or pink to purple or purplish black. Suitable for growing in a rock garden. ↕↔ 30in (75cm). E. India (Arunachal Pradesh), Tibet, W. China, N.E. Burma. Zone 6.
R. camtschaticum. Deciduous shrub with an unusual, dwarf, procumbent habit, and obovate, hairy-margined, mid-green leaves, ¾–2in (2–5cm) long, on hairy shoots. Saucer-shaped, reddish purple or pink flowers, 1in (2.5cm) across, each with a leafy calyx, are borne singly or in pairs in late midseason. ↕ to 12in (30cm), ↔ 36in (90cm). E. Asia, Alaska. Zone 5.
R. canescens (Florida pinxter, Hoary azalea, Piedmont azalea). Narrow, deciduous azalea with oblong-obovate to oblong-lance-shaped, sparsely softly hairy, mid-green leaves, ¾–3in (2–8cm) long, densely softly hairy beneath. Trusses of 6–19 funnel-shaped, fragrant white, pink, or deep rose flowers, 1–1½in (2.5–4cm) across, are borne in early midseason. ↕ 10–15ft (3–5m), ↔ 5–6ft (1.5–2m). Texas, Tennessee and North Carolina to N. Florida. Zone 7b.
***R.* 'Carita'** ▣ Neat, evergreen shrub, becoming more open with age, with medium-sized leaves. In midseason, bears flat-topped trusses of funnel-shaped flowers, 3–3½in (8–9cm) across pale pink to pale lemon yellow, each with a small, cerise-red basal flash in the throat. ↕↔ 8ft (2.5m). Zone 8.
R. carolinianum see *R. minus.*
R. catawbiense (Mountain rosebay). Evergreen shrub with oblong-ovate, glossy, dark green leaves, 3–6in (7–15cm) long, paler beneath. Large trusses of funnel-bell-shaped, reddish purple flowers, 1½–2in (4–5cm) across, are produced in late midseason. Thrives in full sun. Parent of many cultivars. ↕↔ 10ft (3m). E. North America. Zone 4.
***R.* 'Catawbiense Album'.** Vigorous, shrubby, evergreen "ironclad" rhododendron with medium-sized leaves. In late midseason, pale lilac buds open to conical trusses of bell-shaped white flowers, to 2½in (6cm) across, with green flashes in the throats. Tolerates sun and wind. ↕↔ 10ft (3m). Zone 5.
***R.* 'Cécile'** ▣ Vigorous, deciduous azalea (K-E) with medium-sized leaves. In midseason, dark salmon-pink buds open to dense, rounded trusses of tubular-funnel-shaped, clear salmon-pink flowers, 2½in (6cm) across, with yellow flares in the throats. ↕↔ 7ft (2.2m). Zone 5.
***R.* 'Chionoides'.** Dense, evergreen shrub with medium-sized leaves. In late midseason, bears dense trusses of funnel-shaped, pure white flowers, 2–2½in (5–6cm) long, each with a conspicuous yellow flare on the inside of the upper lobe. Tolerant of wind, sun, and heat. ↕↔ 6ft (2m). Zone 6.
***R.* Choptank River Hybrids** (*R. atlanticum* x *R. periclymenoides*). Broadly upright, dense, stoloniferous, deciduous azaleas (O) with small, narrowly obovate to elliptic, glaucous, bluish green leaves. In midseason, bear dense trusses of tubular-funnel-shaped, clove-scented, pink-flushed, white flowers, 1¾in (4.5cm) across. There are several named selections, including **'Marydel'** and **'Nacoochee'**. ↕ 5ft (1.5m), ↔ 4ft (1.2m). Zone 6.
***R.* 'Cilpinense'** ▣ Showy, compact, small-leaved, evergreen shrub. Very early in the season, bears profuse trusses of up to 3 funnel-shaped, pale to mid-pink flowers, to 2in (4cm) across. Flowers are vulnerable to early frosts. ↕↔ 3½ft (1.1m). Zone 7b.
R. cinnabarinum ▣ Vigorous, erect, evergreen shrub producing neat, aromatic, elliptic-obovate, hairless, dark green leaves, 1¼–3½in (3–9cm) long, with a metallic gray-green sheen above,

Rhododendron 'Blue Diamond'

R

scaly beneath. Loose trusses of pendent, narrowly tubular-bell-shaped, waxy, red, sometimes yellow, orange, apricot-pink or reddish purple flowers, 1–1½in (2.5–4cm) across, are borne in mid- and late season. ↕ 20ft (6m), ↔ 6ft (2m). Himalayas to N. Burma. Zone 7b. **subsp. *xanthocodon*** ▣ syn. *R. xanthocodon*, bears trusses of 5–10 rich yellow flowers. E. India, Bhutan, China.
***R.* 'Coral Bells'** see *R.* 'Kirin'.
***R.* 'Corneille'** ▣ Deciduous, tall-growing azalea (Gh) of open habit, with small leaves. Domed trusses of open trumpet-shaped, honeysuckle-like, fragrant cream flowers, 1½in (4cm) across, strongly suffused pink on the outside, are borne in late midseason. ↕↔ 5–8ft (1.5–2.5m). Zone 5b.
***R.* 'Cottage Garden's Pride'** see *R.* 'Mrs. G.W. Leak'.
***R.* 'Crest'** ▣ syn. *R.* 'Hawk Crest'. Evergreen shrub of open habit, with medium-sized leaves. In midseason, orange-yellow buds open to trusses of up to 12 long-lasting, broadly funnel-shaped, primrose-yellow flowers, 3–3½in (8–9cm) across. ↕↔ 11ft (3.5m). Zone 6b.
R. cubittii ▣ syn. *R. veitchianum*. Evergreen shrub with purple-brown young shoots and oblong-elliptic, leathery, sparsely scaly, mid- to dark green leaves, to 4in (10cm) long. In midseason, bears funnel-shaped, white to pale pink flowers, to 5in (13cm) across, with brownish or orange-yellow markings. ↕ 5ft (1.5m), ↔ to 3ft (1m). N. Burma. ❀ (min. 41°F/5°C)
R. cumberlandense. Branching, deciduous azalea with elliptic to broadly elliptic or ovate-oblong, softly hairy, mid-green leaves, 1½–3½in (4–9cm) long, often hairless beneath. Trusses of 3–7 funnel-shaped, orange, red, yellow, or sometimes pink flowers, 1¾in (4.5cm) across, are borne after the leaves, very late in the season. ↕ to 10ft (3m), ↔ 5–6ft (1.5–2m). E. Kentucky and W. Virginia to N. Alabama and N. Georgia. Zone 6.
***R.* 'Cunningham's White'.** Compact, evergreen shrub with medium-sized leaves. In late midseason, mauve buds open to lax trusses of funnel-shaped white flowers, 2–2½in (5–6cm) long, with yellow to green-brown markings inside. ↕↔ 7ft (2.2m). Zone 6.
***R.* 'Curlew'.** Dwarf, spreading, small-leaved, evergreen shrub. In early mid-season, bears numerous trusses of 2 or 3 broadly funnel-shaped, bright yellow flowers, 2in (5cm) across, spotted greenish brown inside. ↕↔ 24in (60cm). Zone 7b.
***R.* 'Cynthia'**, syn. *R.* 'Lord Palmerston'. Large, evergreen shrub with large leaves. In midseason, bears pyramidal trusses of funnel-shaped, deep rose-pink to magenta flowers, 3in (8cm) across, with deep crimson markings on the insides of the upper lobes. Grows well in sun. ↕↔ 20ft (6m). Zone 7.
R. dauricum. Deciduous or semi-evergreen shrub with small, elliptic, leathery, glossy, dark green leaves, ½–1½in (1–4cm) long, scaly beneath, turning purple-brown in winter. Very early in the season, bears small trusses of funnel-shaped, vivid rose-purple flowers, 1–2in (2.5–5cm) across. Suitable for an open site. ↕↔ 5ft (1.5m). E. Asia. Zone 4b.
R. davidsonianum. Vigorous, evergreen shrub producing lance-shaped to oblong-lance-shaped, glossy, dark green leaves, 1¼–3in (3–8cm) long, densely brown-scaly beneath. In early mid-season, bears trusses of 2–6 broadly funnel-shaped, pale pink to purplish pink flowers, to 2in (5cm) across, sometimes spotted red inside. Grow in partial shade. ↕ to 12ft (4m), ↔ 10ft (3m). W. China. Zone 6b.
***R.* 'Daviesii'.** Compact, deciduous azalea (Gh) with small leaves. In late midseason, bears lax trusses of tubular to funnel-shaped, fragrant white flowers, to 2in (5cm) across, with yellow flares inside. ↕↔ 5ft (1.5m). Zone 5b.
R. decorum ▣ Large shrub or small tree with rough, fissured bark and oblong-ovate, dark green leaves, 2½–8in (6–20cm) long, glaucous beneath. In early midseason, bears trusses of 7–10 funnel- to bell-shaped, 6- or 7-lobed, strongly scented white flowers, 3½–4½in (9–11cm) across, sometimes faintly tinged pink, often with greenish yellow bases. ↕ 20ft (6m), ↔ 8ft (2.5m). China. Zone 7b.
***R. degronianum* subsp. *heptamerum*,** see *R. metternichii*.
R. degronianum* subsp. *yakushimanum see *R. yakushimanum*.
***R.* 'Delaware Valley White'** ▣ Broad, spreading evergreen azalea (O) with small, ovate to oblong-lance-shaped, hairy, mid-green leaves. In midseason, bears trusses of broadly funnel-shaped, white flowers, 2–2½in (5–6cm) across. ↕ 3ft (1m), ↔ 4ft (1.2m). Zone 7.
***R.* 'Dexter's Champagne'** ▣ Upright, open, evergreen shrub with medium, elliptic, olive-green leaves. In midseason, bears loose trusses of open funnel-shaped, fragrant, cream to pale yellow flowers, 3in (8cm) across, with light pink shading. ↕ 5ft (1.5m), ↔ 3ft (1m). Zone 6.
R. discolor see *R. fortunei* subsp. *discolor*.
***R.* 'Doc'** ▣ Small, compact, evergreen shrub with medium-sized leaves. In midseason, bears rounded trusses of funnel-shaped, wavy-margined, rose-pink flowers, 2in (5cm) across, with deeper pink margins and spots, fading to white. ↕↔ 4ft (1.2m). Zone 5b.
***R.* 'Dora Amateis'** ▣ Reliable, semi-dwarf, compact, evergreen shrub with small leaves. In early midseason, bears abundant, lax trusses of 6–8 broadly funnel-shaped white flowers, 2in (5cm) across, the insides flushed pink, with small green flecks. ↕↔ 24in (60cm). Zone 5.
R. edgeworthii, syn. *R. bullatum*. Evergreen, epiphytic shrub with elliptic to ovate, wrinkled, dark green leaves, 2–4in (5–10cm) long; the shoots and undersides of the leaves have a thick, tawny indumentum. In early midseason, bears trusses of 2 or 3 broadly funnel-shaped, strongly scented flowers, 2½–4in (6–10cm) across, white to pale or mid-pink, flushed deep red outside. ↕↔ 8ft (2.5m). E. Himalayas. Zone 8.
***R.* 'Edmond Amateis'** ▣ Upright, dense evergreen shrub with large, elliptic, glossy leaves. In midseason, bears large trusses of open funnel-shaped, white flowers, 3–3½in (8–9cm) across, with bold red blotches and lines. ↕ 6–8ft (2–2.5m), ↔ to 6ft (2m). Zone 6.

Rhododendron 'Beauty of Littleworth'

Rhododendron 'Beethoven'

Rhododendron 'Blue Peter'

Rhododendron bureavii

Rhododendron calostrotum

Rhododendron 'Calsap'

Rhododendron campylocarpum

Rhododendron 'Carita'

Rhododendron 'Cécile'

Rhododendron 'Cilpinense'

Rhododendron cinnabarinum

Rhododendron cinnabarinum subsp. *xanthocodon*

Rhododendron 'Corneille'

Rhododendron 'Crest'

Rhododendron cubittii

Rhododendron decorum

Rhododendron 'Delaware Valley White'

Rhododendron 'Dexter's Champagne'

Rhododendron 'Doc'

Rhododendron 'Dora Amateis'

Rhododendron 'Edmund Amateis'

R

***R.* 'Elizabeth'** ▣ Compact, dwarf, evergreen shrub with small leaves. In early midseason, bears trusses of up to 5 funnel-shaped, bright red flowers, 3in (8cm) across, in such abundance that they almost hide the foliage. Suitable for sun. ↕↔ 3ft (1m). Zone 7.
***R.* 'Elsie Lee'.** Dwarf, evergreen azalea (Sh) with small leaves. Numerous small trusses of broadly funnel-shaped, semi-double, light reddish purple flowers, 2–2½in (5–6cm) across, are borne in midseason. Suitable for full sun and exposed sites. ↕↔ 3ft (1m). Zone 6b.
***R.* 'Fabia'** ▣ Evergreen shrub with medium-sized leaves. Loose trusses of long-lasting, funnel-shaped, orange-red flowers, to 3in (8cm) across, marked pale brown inside, are borne in midseason. ↕↔ 6ft (2m). Zone 7b.
R. falconeri ▣ Multi-stemmed, evergreen tree with flaking, red-brown bark. Produces broadly elliptic to obovate, dark green leaves, 7–14in (18–35cm) long, with a dense, woolly brown indumentum beneath and on the leaf stalks. In early midseason, bears large trusses of 20–25 widely bell-shaped, fleshy, creamy white or yellow flowers, 2–2½in (5–6cm) long, sometimes pink-tinged, often with purple marks inside. ↕ to 40ft (12m), ↔ 15ft (5m). E. Himalayas. Zone 7b.
***R.* 'Fantastica'.** Rounded, evergreen shrub producing large, elliptic leaves, woolly beneath. In late midseason, bears dense trusses of funnel- to bell-shaped, rose flowers, 2–2½in (5–6cm) across, with white-shaded throats and yellow-green spots. ↕↔ 3ft (1m). Zone 7.
***R.* 'Fastuosum Flore Pleno'** ▣ Dome-shaped, shrubby, "ironclad" rhododendron with medium-sized leaves. Long-lasting trusses of funnel-shaped, wavy-margined, double mauve flowers, 2½in (6cm) across, with brown-crimson flashes inside, are borne in late midseason. ↕↔ 12ft (4m). Zone 5b.
R. ferrugineum (Alpine rose). Compact, evergreen shrub producing narrowly to broadly elliptic, glossy, dark green leaves, 1–1½in (2–4cm) long, the leaf stalks and undersides covered in red-brown scales. In late midseason to late in the season, bears trusses of 6–8 tubular, rose-pink to crimson, occasionally white flowers, ¾–1in (2–2.5cm) across, with spreading lobes. ↕ to 5ft (1.5m), ↔ 4ft (1.2m). C. Europe. Zone 5.
R. fictolacteum see *R. rex* subsp. *fictolacteum*.
***R.* 'Firefly'** see *R.* 'Hexe'.

R

Rhododendron falconeri

***R.* 'Firestorm'.** Mounded evergreen shrub with large, elliptic leaves. In midseason, bears large trusses of broadly funnel-shaped, red flowers, 3in (8cm) across. ↕ to 6ft (2m), ↔ to 12ft (4m). Zone 5.
R. flammeum, syn. *R. speciosum* (Oconee azalea). Broadly upright deciduous azalea with ovate to elliptic, mid-green leaves, 1½–2½in (4–6cm) long. Dense trusses of 6–11 tubular-funnel-shaped, orange to scarlet flowers, 1½in (4cm) across, are borne in midseason. ↕ 5ft (1.5m), ↔ 4ft (1.2m). South Carolina to Georgia. Zone 7.
R. forrestii. Prostrate, creeping, evergreen shrub with neat, broadly obovate to rounded, glossy, dark green leaves, ½–1¼in (1–3cm) long, purple beneath. Tubular to bell-shaped, fleshy scarlet flowers, 1¼–1½in (3–4cm) across, with dark carmine-red nectar pouches, are borne singly or in pairs in early midseason. ↕ 8in (20cm), ↔ 5ft (1.5m). Tibet, China (Yunnan), N.E. Burma. Zone 7b.
R. fortunei. Evergreen shrub or small tree with oblong-elliptic to oblong leaves, 3–7in (8–18cm) long, matte, dark green above, paler green beneath. Trusses of 6–12 broadly funnel-shaped, 7-lobed, fragrant, pink or lilac-pink flowers, 2½–3in (6–8cm) across, are borne in midseason. ↕ 30ft (10m), ↔ 8ft (2.5m). China. Zone 6b.
subsp. *discolor* ▣ syn. *R. discolor*, has a more open habit, and produces trusses of 8–10 funnel- to bell-shaped, white, pink, or rose-pink flowers, to 4in (10cm) across, late in the season. ↕ 20ft (6m), ↔ 10ft (3m).
***R.* 'Fragrantissimum'** ▣ Lax, evergreen shrub with hairy, medium-sized leaves. In early midseason, bears trusses of up to 4 broadly funnel-shaped, nutmeg-scented, white, sometimes pink-flushed flowers, to 4in (10cm) across, with yellow throats. ↕↔ 6ft (2m). ❄ (min. 41°F/5°C)
***R.* 'Frome'** ▣ Deciduous azalea (K-E) of open habit, with medium-sized leaves. In midseason, bears frilled, wavy-margined, broadly funnel-shaped, saffron-yellow flowers, 3in (8cm) across, overlaid red in their throats. Ideal in an open site. ↕↔ 5ft (1.5m). Zone 6.
R. fulgens. Rounded, evergreen shrub with smooth, peeling, pink-gray to red-brown bark. The broadly ovate to obovate, glossy, dark green leaves, 3–4½in (7–11cm) long, have a dense, reddish brown indumentum beneath. Compact trusses of 10–15 tubular to bell-shaped, crimson-scarlet flowers, ¾–1½in (2–4cm) long, with black-red nectar pouches, are borne in early midseason. ↕ 12ft (4m), ↔ 10ft (3m). E. Himalayas, Tibet. Zone 7b.

Rhododendron 'Golden Torch'

R. fulvum ▣ Large, evergreen shrub or small tree with inversely lance-shaped to elliptic leaves, 3–9in (8–22cm) long, glossy, dark green above, with a red-brown to fawn indumentum beneath. Compact trusses of up to 20 tubular-bell-shaped white flowers, to 3in (8cm) across, flushed rose-pink to deep rose-pink, sometimes each with a basal crimson mark, open in early midseason. ↕ 15ft (5m), ↔ 10ft (3m). E. Himalayas, China. Zone 7b.
***R.* 'Furnivall's Daughter'** ▣ Upright, rounded, showy, evergreen shrub with medium-sized leaves. In midseason, bears compact trusses of funnel-shaped, bright pink flowers, 3½in (9cm) across, each with a bold, strawberry-red flare in the throat. ↕↔ 10ft (3m). Zone 6.
***R.* 'George Budgen'.** Vigorous, evergreen, compact Vireya rhododendron with medium-sized leaves. Trusses of up to 5 tubular-funnel-shaped flowers, 3in (8cm) across, bright orange at the petal tips, shading to rich yellow at the centers, are borne intermittently from winter to summer. ↕ 4½ft (1.3m), ↔ 3–4ft (1–1.2m). ❄ (min. 41°F/5°C)
***R.* 'George Reynolds'** ▣ Deciduous, bushy azalea (K-E) with medium-sized leaves. In midseason, bears large trusses of broadly funnel-shaped yellow flowers, 2½in (6cm) across, flushed pink in bud, with or before the leaves. Suitable for full sun. ↕↔ 6ft (2m). Zone 5.
***R.* 'Gibraltar'.** Vigorous, deciduous azalea (K-E) with medium-sized leaves. In midseason, crimson-orange buds open to dense trusses of funnel-shaped, brilliant orange flowers, 2½–3in (6–8cm) across, each with a distinct yellow flash and crinkled petals. Suitable for full sun. ↕↔ 5ft (1.5m). Zone 5.
***R.* 'Ginny Gee'** ▣ Dwarf, evergreen shrub forming dense, cushion-like mats of small, dark green leaves. Multiple trusses of tubular-funnel-shaped, pale purplish pink flowers, 1in (2.5cm) across, fading to white-pink, cover the leaves in early midseason. Suitable for sun. ↕↔ 24–36in (60–90cm). Zone 7.
***R.* 'Glacier'.** Vigorous, broadly upright evergreen shrub with small to medium-sized, elliptic to obovate, dark green leaves. Early in the season, produces trusses of open funnel-shaped, white flowers, 2½–3in (6–8cm) across. ↕↔ 5ft (1.5m). Zone 7.
R. glaucophyllum. Compact, semi-dwarf, evergreen shrub with oblong to elliptic-lance-shaped, aromatic leaves, 1½–2½in (3.5–6cm) long, matte, dark green above, white-glaucous and scaly beneath. In midseason, bears lax trusses of 4–10 bell-shaped, white, rose-pink, or pink-purple flowers, ½–1¼in (1–3cm) long. Suitable for full sun. ↕↔ 5ft (1.5m). E. Himalayas. Zone 7b.
***R.* 'Gloria Mundi'** ▣ Deciduous, twiggy azalea (Gh) with small leaves. In late midseason, bears lax trusses of honeysuckle-like, tubular-funnel-shaped, fragrant orange flowers, 2in (5cm) across, with yellow flares inside and frilled margins. Suitable for full sun. ↕↔ 6ft (2m). Zone 5b.
***R.* 'Glory of Littleworth'** ▣ Semi-evergreen shrub of untidy habit, with medium-sized leaves. Compact trusses of broadly funnel-shaped, creamy white flowers, 2½in (6cm) across, with bright orange-red flashes on the upper petals, open in midseason. ↕↔ 5ft (1.5m). Zone 7b.
***R.* 'Gold Crown'** see *R.* 'Goldkrone'.
***R.* 'Golden Showers'.** Upright, densely branched, deciduous azalea (O) with small, oblong to elliptic, glossy, dark green leaves. Very late in the season, bears dense trusses of tubular-funnel-shaped yellow flowers, 1½in (4cm) across, pale orange in bud. ↕ 36in (90cm), ↔ 24in (60cm). Zone 5b.
***R.* 'Golden Torch'** ▣ Compact, upright, evergreen shrub with medium-sized leaves. In late midseason, salmon-

ink buds open to rounded trusses
f funnel-shaped, soft yellow flowers,
½–3in (6–8cm) across, fading to
ale yellow or cream. ↕↔ 5ft (1.5m).
one 7b.
. **'Goldkrone'** ■ syn *R.* 'Gold Crown'.
ow-growing, compact, evergreen shrub
ith medium-sized leaves. Trusses of
6–18 funnel- to bell-shaped, bright
olden yellow flowers, 2–2½in (5–6cm)
ng, delicately spotted ruby-red inside,
re borne in succession in midseason.
→ 5ft (1.5m). Zone 6.
. **'Goldsworth Orange'.** Upright,
vergreen shrub, of dense, compact
abit, with medium-sized leaves. Late in
e season, bears full trusses of tubular-
nnel-shaped, salmon-pink flowers,
½in (6cm) across, with subtle orange
ading. ↕↔ 6ft (2m). Zone 7b.
. **'Gomer Waterer'.** Compact,
vergreen shrub with medium-sized
aves. In late midseason, lilac-pink buds
pen to hemispherical trusses of funnel-
aped white flowers, to 3–3½in
–9cm) across, flushed mauve-pink at
e margins, each with a bold yellow-
rown flare in the throat. Very tolerant
f sun, heat, and wind. ↕↔ 6ft (2m).
one 7.
. **'Greeting'.** Dwarf, evergreen azalea
GD) with small leaves. Early in the
ason, bears lax trusses of funnel-shaped,
avy-margined, coral flowers, 1¾–2in
.5–5cm) across. Grow in full sun or
artial shade. ↕↔ 3ft (1m). Zone 7.
. ***griersonianum*** ■ Striking, evergreen
rub with bristly, woolly shoots.
lliptic to oblong-lance-shaped, matte,
ive-green leaves, 4–8in (10–20cm)
ng, have a loose brown indumentum
eneath. Late in the season, trusses
f 5–12 tubular-bell-shaped scarlet
owers, 2½–3in (6–8cm) across, open
om buds with long, tapering scales.
→ 10ft (3m). W. China, N.E Burma.
one 8.
. ***griffithianum.*** Evergreen, large
rub or tree with peeling, smooth, red-
rown bark. Oblong-elliptic, pale green
aves, 4–12in (10–30cm) long, are
ightly glaucous beneath. Trusses of
–6 open bell-shaped, fragrant, white
r pale pink flowers, 1¾–3in (4.5–8cm)
ng, spotted green inside, open in
idseason. ↕ 20ft (6m), ↔ 8ft (2.5m).
. and E. Himalayas, Bhutan.
one 7b
. **'Gumpo'**, syn. *R. indicum* var.
iocarpum 'Gumpo'. Late-flowering,
warf, evergreen azalea (S) with small
aves. In late midseason to late in the
ason, bears few-flowered trusses of
nnel-shaped, wavy-petaled, white,
metimes pink or pink-flushed white
owers, 2½–3in (6–8cm) across. Heat-
lerant. ↕↔ 3ft (1m). Zone 7b.
. ***haematodes.*** Slow-growing, compact,
vergreen shrub producing oblong-
bovate, dark green leaves, 1¾–4in
.5–10cm) long, with a dense, reddish
rown indumentum beneath. In early
idseason, bears lax trusses of 6–10
bular-bell-shaped, fleshy crimson
owers, to 2in (5cm) across. ↕↔ 6ft
m). China (Yunnan). Zone 7b.
. **'Halfdan Lem'** ■ Very vigorous, lax,
vergreen shrub with large leaves. In
idseason, bears tight trusses of broadly
nnel-shaped red flowers, 3½in (9cm)
cross, spotted dark red, fading to pink
ith age. ↕↔ 8ft (2.5m). Zone 7b.
. **'Hawk Crest'** see *R.* 'Crest'.

***R.* 'Helen Curtis'** ■ Rounded, semi-dwarf, evergreen azalea (Sh) with small, broadly elliptic, glossy, mid-green leaves. In midseason, bears trusses of semi-double, broadly funnel-shaped, white flowers, 2–2½in (5–6cm) across. ↕ 24in (60cm), ↔ 36in (90cm). Zone 6b.
***R.* 'Hello Dolly'** ■ Rounded, well-branched, evergreen shrub with medium-sized, narrowly elliptic, mid-green leaves, beige-woolly beneath. In early midseason, bears loose trusses of open funnel-shaped flowers, 2½in (6cm) across, in blends of pale orange to yellow, with large calyces. ↕↔ 36in (90cm). Zone 6.
***R.* 'Henry's Red'.** Broad, evergreen shrub with large, elliptic, dark green leaves. In midseason, bears dense trusses of broadly funnel-shaped, deep red flowers, 2in (5cm) across. ↕ 5ft (1.5m), ↔ 5–8ft (1.5–2.5m). Zone 5.
***R.* 'Hexe'**, syn. *R.* 'Firefly'. Dwarf, evergreen azalea (In) of neat habit, with small leaves. Lax trusses of numerous hose-in-hose, glowing crimson flowers, 1¾in (4.5cm) across, are borne in late midseason. ↕↔ 24in (60cm). Zone 7.
***R.* 'Hilda Niblett'.** Low, spreading, evergreen azalea (RH) with small, elliptic to obovate, mid-green leaves. Late in the season, bears trusses of open funnel-shaped, peach-pink flowers, 3in (8cm) across. ↕ 12in (30cm), ↔ 36in (90cm). Zone 7.
***R.* 'Hino-crimson'.** Dwarf, evergreen azalea (Ku) of dense habit, with small leaves. In midseason, bears abundant funnel-shaped, brilliant red flowers, ¼–1in (0.7–2.5cm) long, in rounded trusses. ↕↔ 24in (60cm). Zone 7.
***R.* 'Hinode-giri'** ■ Compact, dwarf, evergreen azalea (Ku) with small leaves. In early midseason, bears domed trusses of numerous broadly funnel-shaped, bright crimson flowers, 1½in (4cm) across. Prefers full sun. ↕↔ 24in (60cm). Zone 7.
***R.* 'Hino-mayo'** ■ Dwarf, small-leaved, evergreen azalea (Ku) of dense, compact habit. In midseason, produces lax trusses of broadly funnel-shaped, clear pink flowers, 1½in (3cm) across. Will tolerate full sun. ↕↔ 24in (60cm). Zone 7b.
R. hippophaeoides ■ Upright, semi-dwarf, evergreen shrub with narrowly lance-shaped, aromatic, scaly, gray-green leaves, ¾–1¼in (2–3cm) long. In early midseason, bears trusses of 6–8 funnel-shaped, lavender-blue or pale lilac flowers, 1in (2.5cm) long. Prefers full sun. ↕ 5ft (1.5m), ↔ 30in (75cm). S.W. China. Zone 5.
***R.* 'Homebush'** ■ Compact, bushy, deciduous azalea (K-E) with medium-sized leaves. In midseason, bears tight, rounded trusses of trumpet-shaped, semi-double, bright pink flowers, 1½in (4cm) across, with paler pink shading. ↕↔ 5ft (1.5m). Zone 5.
***R.* 'Hotei'.** Dense, evergreen shrub with medium-sized leaves. In midseason, bears slightly open trusses of funnel-shaped, deep yellow flowers, to 2½in (6cm) across, each with a prominent calyx. ↕↔ 5–8ft (1.5–2.5m). Zone 7b.
***R.* 'Humming Bird'.** Neat, compact, dome-shaped, evergreen shrub with small, rounded, glossy leaves. In early midseason, bears loose trusses of 4 or more, nodding, widely bell-shaped, cherry-red flowers, 2–2½in (5–6cm) across. ↕↔ 5ft (1.5m). Zone 7b.

Rhododendron 'Elizabeth'

Rhododendron 'Fabia'

Rhododendron 'Fastuosum Flore Pleno'

Rhododendron fortunei subsp. *discolor*

Rhododendron 'Fragrantissimum'

Rhododendron 'Frome'

Rhododendron fulvum

Rhododendron 'Furnivall's Daughter'

Rhododendron 'George Reynolds'

Rhododendron 'Ginny Gee'

Rhododendron 'Gloria Mundi'

Rhododendron 'Glory of Littleworth'

Rhododendron 'Goldkrone'

Rhododendron griersonianum

Rhododendron 'Halfdan Lem'

Rhododendron 'Helen Curtis'

Rhododendron 'Hello Dolly'

Rhododendron 'Hinode-giri'

Rhododendron 'Hino-mayo'

Rhododendron hippophaeoides

Rhododendron 'Homebush'

R

Rhododendron luteum

***R.* 'Hydon Dawn'** ■ Very compact, low-growing, evergreen shrub with medium-sized leaves. Tight trusses of funnel-shaped, frilled, pale pink flowers, 2½–3in (6–8cm) across, fading to white, are borne in midseason. Tolerates full sun. ↕↔ 5ft (1.5m). Zone 7b.
***R.* 'Ilam Cream'** ■ Evergreen shrub producing large leaves. Lax trusses of lilac-pink buds open to funnel-shaped, fragrant, creamy yellow flowers, 4–4½in (10–11cm) across, in midseason. ↕↔ 12ft (4m). Zone 8.
R. impeditum. Compact, dwarf, evergreen shrub with tiny, elliptic-ovate, aromatic, scaly, gray-green leaves, ⅛–½in (4–15mm) long. In early midseason, bears abundant, broadly funnel-shaped, purplish blue flowers, ¾in (2cm) across, singly or in pairs. ↕↔ 24in (60cm). W. China. Zone 5.
***R. indicum* var. *eriocarpum* 'Gumpo'** see *R.* 'Gumpo'.
R. insigne. Compact, dome-shaped, evergreen shrub with elliptic to lance-shaped, stiff leaves, 3–5in (7–13cm) long, glossy, dark green above, copper beneath. In late midseason, bears trusses of 8–15 bell-shaped, pinkish white flowers, to 1½in (4cm) long, the insides striped rose-pink with crimson spots. Tolerates full sun. ↕↔ 12ft (4m). W. China. Zone 7b.
***R.* 'Irene Koster'** ■ Deciduous azalea (Oc) with medium-sized leaves. Bold trusses of delicate, funnel-shaped, fragrant, pink-suffused yellow flowers, 2½in (6cm) across, with orange-yellow flashes inside, appear in late midseason. ↕↔ 6ft (2m). Zone 6b.
***R.* 'Irohayama'** ■ Compact, dwarf evergreen azalea (Ku) producing small leaves. Small trusses of abundant funnel-shaped white flowers, 1½in (4cm) across, margined pale lavender, open in midseason. Grow in sun. ↕↔ 24in (60cm). Zone 7b.
R. irroratum. Evergreen, large shrub or small tree with inversely lance-shaped to elliptic leaves, 2–2½in (5–6cm) across, mid-green above, paler beneath. Trusses of up to 15 tubular-bell-shaped white flowers, 2–2½in (5–6cm) across, sometimes suffused pale pink, and variably crimson-spotted within, open early in the season to early midseason. Grow in sun. ↕ 25ft (8m), ↔ 12ft (4m). China (Yunnan, Sichuan), Vietnam, Indonesia, Laos. Zone 7b.
***R.* 'Jack A. Sand'.** Upright, well-branched, deciduous azalea (O) with medium-sized, narrowly elliptic to oblong-lance-shaped, light green leaves with bronze new growth. In midseason, bears dense trusses of tubular-funnel-shaped, very fragrant double flowers, 1¾–2in (4.5–5cm) across, in blends of pale pink, yellow, and white, with vivid pink edges. ↕ 36in (90cm), ↔ 30in (75cm). Zone 5.
***R.* 'Janet Blair'.** Rounded, well-branched, evergreen shrub with large, elliptic leaves. In late midseason, bears large trusses of open funnel-shaped, frilled, light pink flowers, 3–3½in (8–9cm) across, each with a yellow-green flare on the upper petal. ↕ 6ft (2m), ↔ 4–6ft (1.2–2m). Zone 5b.
R. japonicum see *R. molle* subsp. *japonicum.*
R. jasminiflorum. Evergreen Vireya rhododendron with a lax, untidy habit. Elliptic to lance-shaped or oblong, dark green leaves, 1–2in (2.5–5cm) long, arranged in whorls of 3–5, have small but distinct brown scales beneath. Trusses of 5–12 trumpet-shaped, sweet-scented flowers, ½in (1.5cm) across, often opening pale pink and fading to white, with red flower stalks, are borne intermittently from summer to winter. ↕ 3ft (1m), ↔ 3–6ft (1–2m). W. Malaysia, Philippines, Sumatra. ❄ (min. 41°F/5°C)
***R.* 'Jean Mary Montague'** see *R.* 'The Hon. Jean Marie de Montague'.
***R.* 'Jericho'.** Low, spreading, evergreen shrub with small to medium-sized, elliptic, mid-green leaves. In early midseason, bears loose trusses of open funnel-shaped, cream-white flowers, 1¾–2in (4.5–5cm) across, each with a yellow flare in the center. ↕ 24in (60cm), ↔ 4ft (1.2m). Zone 5.
***R.* 'John Cairns'** ■ Striking, robust, small-leaved, evergreen azalea (K) of compact, upright habit. Flat-headed trusses of abundant funnel-shaped, orange-red flowers, 1½–1¾in (4–4.5cm) across, are borne in midseason. Grow in sun. ↕↔ 5ft (1.5m). Zone 7.
***R.* 'Jonathan Shaw'** ■ Compact, evergreen shrub with large, elliptic, matte green leaves. Late in the season, bears large trusses of open funnel-shaped, wavy-edged, purple-red-centered, vivid violet-purple flowers, 3in (8cm) across, each with a black flare. ↕ 3½ft (1.1m), ↔ 3–4ft (1–1.2m). Zone 5.
R. kaempferi ■ (Torch azalea). Loosely branched, erect, semi-evergreen azalea with glossy, mid-green leaves, 1½–2in (1–5cm) long, ovate to lance-shaped in spring, smaller and elliptic-obovate in summer. In midseason, bears trusses of 2–4 broadly funnel-shaped flowers, 1½–2in (4–5cm) across, in shades of red. ↕ 10ft (3m), ↔ 5ft (1.5m). Korea, Japan. Zone 6b.
R. keiskei ■ Compact, dwarf or semi-dwarf, evergreen shrub with small, oblong-lance-shaped, dark green leaves, 1–3in (2.5–8cm) long, slightly scaly above, densely scaly beneath. Trusses of 2–5 broadly funnel-shaped, pale to lemon-yellow flowers, to 2in (5cm) across, are borne freely in early midseason. ↕ 10–36in (25–90cm), ↔ 4ft (1.2m). S. Japan. Zone 5b. **'Yaku Fairy'** is prostrate; ↕ 6in (15cm).
R. keleticum see *R. calostrotum* subsp. *keleticum.*
***R.* 'Ken Janeck'** see *R. yakushimanum* 'Ken Janeck'.
***R.* 'Kilimanjaro'** ■ Vigorous, evergreen shrub with medium-sized leaves. From late midseason to late in the season, bears very large trusses of funnel-shaped, bright deep red flowers, 3½–4in (9–10cm) across, spotted crimson on the lobes. ↕↔ 7ft (2.2m). Zone 7b.
***R.* 'Kirin'** ■ syn. *R.* 'Coral Bells'. Free-flowering, evergreen, dwarf azalea (Ku) with small leaves. In midseason, bears small trusses of hose-in-hose, deep pink flowers, 1½in (4cm) across, shaded a delicate silvery rose-pink. Suitable for sun. ↕↔ 5ft (1.5m). Zone 7b.
R. kiusianum ■ (Kyushu azalea). Dwarf, semi-evergreen shrub with variable, broadly elliptic to obovate, short-bristled, mid-green leaves, ¼–¾in (0.5–2cm) long, larger in spring than in summer. Trusses of 2 or 3 funnel-shaped, pink or purple, sometimes white flowers, 1–1¼in (2.5–3cm) across, are borne in midseason. Prefers full sun. ↕↔ 4ft (1.2m). Japan. Zone 6.
***R.* 'Klondyke'.** Striking, deciduous azalea (K-E) with medium-sized leaves. In midseason, red-flushed buds open to large trusses of funnel-shaped, glowing orange-gold flowers, 2½–3in (6–8cm) long, tinted red on the reverse of the petals. Grow in full sun. ↕↔ 6ft (2m). Zone 6.
R. konorii. Erect, evergreen Vireya rhododendron producing obovate to broadly elliptic, dull, mid-green leaves, 4½–5½in (11–14cm) long, with small brown scales beneath. From summer to winter, intermittently bears trusses of 4–7 elongated, funnel-shaped, usually 7-lobed, fragrant flowers, 3–4in (8–10cm) across, pale to deep pink, or pink fading to white, with prominent cream stamens. ↕ 6ft (2m), ↔ 5ft (1.5m). New Guinea. ❄ (min. 41°F/5°C)
***R.* 'Kure-no-yuki'** ■ syn. *R.* 'Snowflake'. Compact, dwarf, evergreen azalea (Ku) with small leaves. In midseason, freely bears trusses of 2 or 3 hose-in-hose white flowers, 1–1¼in (2.5–3cm) across. ↕↔ 3ft (1m). Zone 7b.
R.* x *laetevirens (*R. carolinianum* x *R. ferrugineum*) (Wilson rhododendron). Slow-growing, mound-forming, evergreen shrub with small, pointed, narrowly elliptic, lustrous, dark green leaves. Small, dense trusses of tubular, rose-pink to purplish pink flowers, ¾in (2cm) across, are borne in late midseason. Cultivated for its habit and foliage, rather than flowers. Useful in a rock garden or foundation planting. ↕ 24–36in (60–90cm), ↔ 24–72in (60–200cm). Garden origin. Zone 6.
R. laetum ■ Erect, evergreen Vireya rhododendron with elliptic to broadly elliptic, glossy, dark green leaves, 2–3½in (5–9cm) long, with tiny scales beneath. In spring, bears trusses of 5–1[illegible] funnel-shaped, golden yellow flowers, 2½–3in (6–8cm) across, later suffused orange-red, on red flower stalks. ↕↔ 5ft (1.5m). N.W. New Guinea. ❄ (min. 41°F/5°C)
***R.* 'Lavender Girl'** ■ Evergreen, large-leaved shrub with domed trusses of funnel-shaped, fragrant, pink-mauve flowers, 2½–3in (6–8cm) accross, fading to near white in the centers. Blooms open in midseason, earlier than most

Rhododendron 'Martha Hitchcock'

R

other hybrids with lavender-blue or mauve-pink flowers. Grow in an open site. ↕↔ 8ft (2.5m). Zone 7.
***R.* 'Ledifolium'** see *R. mucronatum*.
***R.* 'Lee's Dark Purple'.** Upright, somewhat open, evergreen shrub with medium-sized, elliptic, glossy, dark green leaves. In late midseason, produces dense trusses of open funnel-shaped, purple flowers, 2in (5cm) across. ↕ 6ft (2m), ↔ 5ft (1.5m). Zone 5.
***R.* 'Lem's Cameo'** ■ Evergreen shrub producing medium-sized leaves, brown-bronze when young. In midseason, bears large, domed trusses of funnel-shaped, frilled, pale peach flowers, 3½in (9cm) across, fading to apricot-cream or pink, and marked and spotted red in the throats. ↕↔ 7ft (2.2m). Zone 7b.
R. leucaspis ■ Densely branched, dwarf, evergreen shrub with bristly calyces and shoots, producing broadly elliptic, dark green leaves, 1¼–1¾in (3–4.5cm) long, bristly above, scaly and yellowish green beneath. Trusses of up to 3 saucer-shaped white flowers, 2in (5cm) across, with chocolate-brown anthers, are borne early in the season. ↕ 3ft (1m), ↔ 5ft (1.5m). S.E. Tibet. Zone 8.
***R.* 'Lionel's Triumph'.** Tall, large-leaved evergreen shrub with an open habit. Large trusses of funnel-shaped, creamy yellow flowers, 4in (10cm) long, with crimson-spotted throats and pink-flushed margins, open from pink buds in midseason. Grow in partial shade. ↕↔ 12ft (4m). Zone 7.
***R.* 'Loderi King George'** ■ Large, evergreen shrub of open habit, with large leaves. In midseason, pale pink buds open to huge trusses of funnel-shaped, fragrant, pure white flowers, to 6in (15cm) long, with subtle green markings in the throats. ↕↔ 12ft (4m). Zone 7.
***R.* 'Lord Palmerston'** see *R.* 'Cynthia'.
***R.* 'Louise Dowdle'** ■ Compact, evergreen azalea (GD) with medium-sized leaves. Late in the season, bears compact trusses of funnel-shaped, vivid red-purple flowers, 3in (8cm) long, the throats with bright rose-red marks. Suitable for full sun. ↕↔ 3ft (1m). Zone 7.
R. lutescens ■ Graceful, bushy, erect, semi-evergreen shrub with ovate-oblong to lance-shaped, sparsely scaly leaves, 2–3½in (5–9cm) long, bronze when young, maturing to dull green, and paler green with yellow scales beneath. In early midseason, bears trusses of 3–6 broadly funnel-shaped, primrose-yellow flowers, 1½–2in (4–5cm) across, spotted green inside. ↕↔ 15ft (5m). S.W. China. Zone 7b.
R. luteum ■ (Pontic azalea). Deciduous azalea of open habit, with oblong to lance-shaped, sparsely hairy, mid-green leaves, 2–4in (5–10cm) long. Bears trusses of 7–12 funnel-shaped, strongly scented, sticky yellow flowers, 1½in (4cm) across, in late midseason. Prefers full sun. ↕↔ 12ft (4m). E. Europe to Caucasus. Zone 5.
***R. macabeanum*.** Evergreen shrub or tree with large, oblong-ovate, dark green leaves, 8–12in (20–30cm) long, with a woolly, pale fawn indumentum beneath. Early in the season, bears huge trusses of up to 20 broadly bell-shaped, creamy to deep yellow flowers, 2–2½in (5–6cm) across, with purple marks inside, and purple nectar pouches. ↕ 50ft (15m), ↔ 20ft (6m). India (Manipur). Zone 8.
R. macgregoriae ■ Bushy, evergreen Vireya rhododendron with ovate-lance-shaped to ovate-elliptic, glossy, dark green leaves 1½–3½in (4–9cm) long, minutely scaly beneath. Trusses of up to 25 short, widely funnel- to bell-shaped, usually yellow or orange, occasionally pink flowers, to 1½in (4cm) across, with protruding brown stamens, open in winter. ↕ to 15ft (5m), ↔ 3–6ft (1–2m). New Guinea. ❄ (min. 41°F/5°C)
***R.* 'Macrantha'.** Low-growing, compact, spreading, evergreen azalea (In) with small, narrowly lance-shaped to oblong-lance-shaped, mid-green leaves. Late in the season, bears trusses of open funnel-shaped, reddish orange to deep pink flowers, 2in (5cm) across. ↕ 24in (60cm), ↔ 36in (90cm). Zone 7b.
***R. macrophyllum*.** Large, free-flowering, evergreen shrub with oblong-obovate to elliptic leaves, 3–7in (7–18cm) long, dark green above, paler green beneath. In late midseason, bears compact trusses of 15–20 funnel-shaped, rose-purple to pink, sometimes white flowers, to 2in (5cm) across, with red-brown spots inside. Suitable for sun. ↕↔ to 15ft (5m). W. North America. Zone 6.
***R.* 'Mardi Gras'.** Evergreen shrub with large, elliptic leaves with woolly, cinnamon-brown undersides and buds. In midseason, bears dense, rounded trusses of funnel- to bell-shaped, white flowers, 2½in (6cm) across, opening from bright pink buds. ↕ to 3ft (1m), ↔ to 4ft (1.2m). Zone 6.
***R.* 'Martha Hitchcock'** ■ Spreading evergreen azalea (GD) with small to medium-sized, elliptic to obovate, mid-green leaves. In midseason, bears trusses of open funnel-shaped, white flowers, 3in (8cm) across, with broad, rose-purple margins, often fading in warm weather. ↕↔ 4ft (1.2m). Zone 6.
***R.* 'Mary Belle'.** Evergreen shrub producing large, elliptic leaves. In midseason, bears rounded trusses of open funnel-shaped, peach flowers, 3–3½in (8–9cm) across, turning to peach-gold. ↕ 5ft (1.5m), ↔ 4–6ft (1.2–2m). Zone 6.
***R.* 'Mary Fleming'.** Semi-dwarf, evergreen shrub with medium-sized, mid-green leaves, which may turn bronze in winter in sunny sites. In early midseason, bears small trusses of 2 or 3 funnel-shaped, brownish yellow flowers, 1¼–1½in (3–4cm) across, marked with salmon-pink at the rims. Thrives in full sun. ↕↔ 30in (75cm). Zone 6.
R. maximum (Great laurel, Rosebay rhododendron). Open, evergreen rhododendron with large, elliptic, dark green leaves, 4–8in (10–20cm) long. Trusses of 14–25, bell-shaped. rose, purplish pink, or white flowers, 1½–2in (4–5cm) across, spotted with olive-green to orange, are borne very late in the season. Requires shade. ↕ 4–15ft (1.2–5m), ↔ indefinite. E. Canada to Georgia. Zone 4.
***R.* 'May Day'** ■ Low-growing, spreading, large-leaved evergreen shrub. In early midseason, freely bears loose trusses of funnel-shaped scarlet flowers, to 3in (8cm) across, with petal-like calyces. Tolerates full sun. ↕↔ 5ft (1.5m). Zone 7b.

Rhododendron 'Hydon Dawn'

Rhododendron 'Ilam Cream'

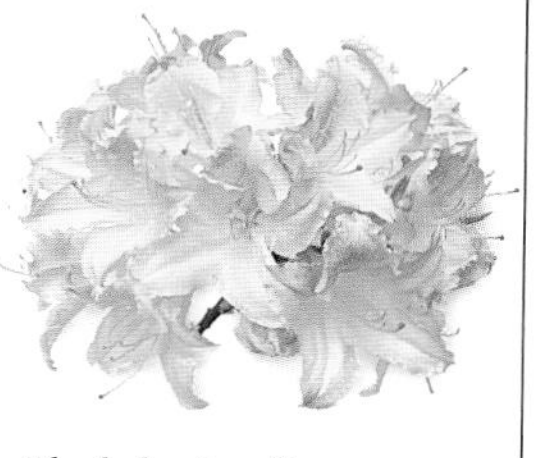
Rhododendron 'Irene Koster'

Rhododendron 'Irohayama'

Rhododendron 'John Cairns'

Rhododendron 'Jonathan Shaw'

Rhododendron kaempferi

Rhododendron keiskei

Rhododendron 'Kilimanjaro'

Rhododendron 'Kirin'

Rhododendron kiusianum

Rhododendron 'Kure-no-yuki'

Rhododendron laetum

Rhododendron 'Lavender Girl'

Rhododendron 'Lem's Cameo'

Rhododendron leucaspis

Rhododendron 'Loderi King George'

Rhododendron 'Louise Dowdle'

Rhododendron lutescens

Rhododendron macgregoriae

Rhododendron 'May Day'

R

Rhododendron 'Patty Bee'

***R.* 'Medway'** ■ Deciduous, open, bushy azalea (K-E) with medium-sized leaves. In late midseason, bears trusses of trumpet-shaped, pale pink flowers, to 2½in (6cm) across, with darker margins, orange-flashed throats, and frilled petals. ↕↔ 5–8ft (1.5–2.5m). Zone 6.

R. metternichii ■ syn *R. degronianum* subsp. *heptamerum.* Evergreen shrub with oblong to inversely lance-shaped leaves, 3–5½in (8–14cm) long, often red when young, maturing to glossy, deep green above, with a thick brown indumentum beneath. In early mid-season, bears trusses of up to 12 funnel- to bell-shaped, 5- to 7-lobed, pale to deep pink flowers, 2½in (6cm) across, sometimes lined deeper pink inside. Will tolerate full sun. ↕↔ 6ft (2m). N. Japan. Zone 7.

***R.* 'Mi Amor'.** Open, somewhat leggy, evergreen shrub with medium-sized to large, elliptic to oblong-elliptic, dark green leaves, gray-green beneath. In midseason, bears loose trusses of bell-shaped, very fragrant, white flowers, 5–6in (13–15cm) across, with yellow throats. ↕ 6ft (2m), ↔ 4ft (1.2m). ❄ (min. 41°F/5°C)

R. minus, syn. *R. carolinianum.* Evergreen shrub with ovate-elliptic to elliptic, dark green leaves, 2–4½in (5–11cm) long, brown-scaly beneath. From early midseason to late midseason, bears trusses of 6–12 funnel- to bell-shaped, pink-purple, pink, or white flowers, 1¼–2in (3–5cm) across, with green-brown spots. Suitable for an open site. ↕↔ 12ft (4m). E. North America. Zone 5.

R. molle* subsp. *japonicum, syn. *R. japonicum* (Japanese azalea). Vigorous, deciduous azalea of upright habit, with obovate, obovate-oblong, or inversely lance-shaped leaves, 2–4in (5–10cm) long, mid-green above, paler bluish green beneath. Trusses of 2–12 widely funnel-shaped, often scented, orange-red, orange, red, yellow, or yellow-orange flowers, 2–2½in (5–6cm) across, softly hairy outside, are borne just as the leaves emerge, in midseason. Tolerates full sun. ↕↔ 7ft (2.2m). C. and E. Japan. Zone 5b.

***R.* 'Moonshine Crescent'.** Evergreen shrub of open, upright habit, with medium-sized leaves. In midseason, dome-shaped trusses of bell-shaped, primrose-yellow flowers, 2–3in (5–8cm) long, open from brightly contrasting, red winter buds. ↕↔ 6–8ft (2–2.5m). Zone 7.

***R.* 'Morgenrot'.** Compact, evergreen shrub with large, elliptic, hairy leaves. In midseason, produces dense trusses of funnel-shaped, bright red flowers, 1¾–2in (4.5–5cm) across, shaded lighter red in the centers. ↕ 4ft (1.2m), ↔ 3–4ft (1–1.2m). Zone 7.

***R.* 'Mrs. Furnival'** ■ Compact, evergreen shrub with medium-sized leaves. From an early age, bears neat trusses of funnel-shaped, light rose-pink flowers, to 3–3½in (8–9cm) across, each with a bold, brownish red flare inside, in late midseason. Suitable for partial shade or full sun. ↕↔ 7ft (2.2m). Zone 7b.

***R.* 'Mrs. G.W. Leak'** ■ syn. *R.* 'Cottage Garden's Pride'. Compact, evergreen shrub with medium-sized leaves. In early midseason, bears upright trusses of funnel-shaped, light rose-pink flowers, to 3in (8cm) across, each with a deep brown and crimson central flare. ↕↔ 12ft (4m). Zone 7b.

***R.* 'Mrs. T.H. Lowinsky'** ■ Free-flowering, vigorous, evergreen shrub with medium-sized leaves. Dense trusses of funnel-shaped, pink-flushed white flowers, to 3in (8cm) across, each with a bright orange-brown flare inside and reflexed lobes, open from lavender-pink buds in early midseason. Grow in sun. ↕↔ 7–10ft (2.2–3m). Zone 7.

R. mucronatum ■ syn. *R.* 'Ledifolium' (Snow azalea). Spreading, semi-evergreen azalea with lance-shaped to ovate- or oblong-lance-shaped, hairy, mid-green leaves, 1¼–2½in (3–6cm) long. In midseason, freely bears trusses of 2 or 3 broadly funnel-shaped, fragrant white, occasionally pink flowers, 2½–3in (6–8cm) across. Grows well in full sun. ↕↔ 4–5ft (1.2–1.5m). Origin uncertain. Zone 7b.

R. mucronulatum. Dwarf to medium-sized, deciduous azalea of erect habit, with lance-shaped, dark green leaves, 1½–2½in (4–6cm) long, scaly beneath. Solitary, funnel-shaped, pinkish purple or occasionally white flowers, 1¼–1¾in (3–4.5cm) across, are produced very early in the season. Grow in full sun. ↕ 1–8ft (0.3–2.5m), ↔ 3ft (1m). E. Russia, N. and C. China, Mongolia. Zone 4. **'Cornell Pink'** ■ has bright pink flowers.

***R.* 'Nancy Evans'.** Floriferous, evergreen shrub with large, elliptic leaves. In midseason, bears full, rounded trusses of open funnel-shaped, orange-flushed, golden flowers, 2½in (6cm) across, opening from orange-red buds. ↕↔ to 3ft (1m). Zone 7.

***R.* 'Nancy of Robinhill'.** Broad, semi-dwarf, evergreen azalea (RH) with small, broadly elliptic, glossy, dark green leaves. Late in the season, bears trusses of double, hose-in-hose, broadly funnel-shaped, light pink flowers, 2½–3in (6–8cm) across. ↕ 24in (60cm), ↔ 36in (90cm). Zone 7.

***R.* 'Naomi'.** Tall, evergreen shrub or small tree with medium-sized leaves. In midseason, produces large trusses of widely funnel-shaped, fragrant, pale lavender-pink flowers, 3½in (9cm) across, shading to greenish yellow in the throats and each with a subtle brown stripe. ↕↔ 15ft (5m). Zone 7.

***R.* 'Narcissiflora'** ■ Compact, vigorous, deciduous azalea (Gh) with medium-sized leaves. In late midseason, bears compact trusses of hose-in-hose, sweetly scented, pale yellow flowers, 1¾in (4.5cm) across, darker yellow toward the centers and on the outsides of the petals. ↕↔ 5–8ft (1.5–2.5m). Zone 5.

***R.* 'Ne Plus Ultra'.** Vigorous, upright, evergreen Vireya rhododendron with medium-sized leaves. Trusses of up to 14 tubular-funnel-shaped, bright red flowers, 2–2½in (5–6cm) across, with purplish pink throats, are produced intermittently from summer to winter. ↕ 5ft (1.5m), ↔ 3ft (1m). ❄ (min. 41°F/5°C)

R. neriiflorum ■ Evergreen shrub producing elliptic to oblong or inversely lance-shaped, dark green leaves, 1½–4½in (4–11cm) long, glaucous beneath. In early midseaosn, bears trusses of 5–12 tubular-bell-shaped, fleshy, bright scarlet to crimson flowers, to 2in (5cm) across. Suitable for full sun. ↕ to 20ft (6m), ↔ 12ft (4m). Tibet, China, Burma. Zone 8.

***R.* Northern Lights Group.** Broad, rounded, deciduous azaleas (O) with medium-sized, oblong-lance-shaped to elliptic, mid- to dark green leaves. In midseason, bears dense trusses of tubular-funnel-shaped flowers, 2–2½in (5–6cm) across, in various colors, including pink, orange, red, yellow, and white. ↕ 5ft (1.5m), ↔ 4ft (1.2m). Zone 3. **'Golden Lights'** bears yellow flowers. **'Rosy Lights'** produces deep pink flowers. **'Spicy Lights'** bears soft orange-red flowers. **'White Lights'** bears creamy white flowers.

***R.* 'Nova Zembla'** ■ Evergreen shrub with medium-sized leaves. Full, rounded trusses of broadly funnel-shaped, deep red flowers, 2–2½in (5–6cm) across, spotted darker red inside, are produced in late midseason. ↕↔ 5–10ft (1.5–3m). Zone 4.

R. nudiflorum see *R. periclymenoides.*

R. obtusum (Hiryu azalea). Spreading, dense evergreen azalea with elliptic, glossy, mid-green leaves, to 1¼in (3cm) long. Trusses of 1–3 funnel-shaped, reddish violet to crimson flowers, 1–1¼in (3cm) across, are borne in midseason. ↕ 18in (45cm), ↔ 36in (90cm). Japan (Kyushu). Zone 7.

R. occidentale ■ (Western azalea). Deciduous shrub with elliptic to oblong-lance-shaped leaves, 1¼–3½in (3–9cm) long, glossy, mid-green above, glaucous beneath. In midseason, bears trusses of 6–12 broadly funnel-shaped, sweetly scented, usually creamy white or pale pink flowers, 2½–3in (6–8cm) across, each with a yellow or yellow-orange mark inside. Grow in sun. ↕↔ 10ft (3m). W. North America. Zone 6b.

***R.* 'Odee Wright'** ■ Compact, sometimes low-growing, dense, evergreen shrub with medium-sized leaves. In midseason, peach-colored buds open to trusses of up to 15 broadly funnel-shaped, greenish yellow flowers, 3½–4in (9–10cm) across, tinted pink, and spotted carmine-red in the throats. ↕↔ 5ft (1.5m). Zone 7b.

***R.* 'Olga Mezzitt'** ■ Vigorous, upright evergreen shrub with small, elliptic, dark green leaves, turning light red in autumn and winter. Early in the season, produces small trusses of open funnel-shaped, bright peach-pink flowers, 1½in (4cm) across. ↕ 4ft (1.2m), ↔ 5–6ft (1.5–2m). Zone 5.

Rhododendron 'Polar Bear' (inset: flower detail)

R

***R.* 'Olive'.** Free-flowering, upright, small to medium-sized, evergreen shrub producing small, ovate-elliptic leaves, mid-green above, paler green beneath. Trusses of 2 or 3 funnel-shaped flowers, 1½–2in (4–5cm) across, mauve-pink with deeper spots inside, are borne very early in the season. ↕ 4ft (1.2m), ↔ 3ft (1m). Zone 7.
R. oreodoxa ▣ Evergreen shrub or small tree with obovate-elliptic, dark green leaves, 2½–3½in (6–9cm) long, pale bluish green and glaucous beneath. In early midseason, bears abundant trusses of 10–12 tubular- to broadly bell-shaped, usually 7-lobed pink flowers, 1½–2in (4–5cm) across, sometimes purple-spotted inside. Tolerates full sun. ↕ 10–15ft (3–5m), ↔ 10ft (3m). W. China. Zone 7.
R. oreotrephes ▣ Evergreen shrub producing oblong-elliptic, mid- or gray-green leaves, ¾–3in (2–8cm) long, usually with purple, red-brown, or gray scales, and glaucous beneath. In early midseason, bears trusses of 3–11 funnel- to bell-shaped, mauve, purple, or rose-pink flowers, to 1½–2in (4–5cm) across, sometimes purple-spotted inside. Thrives in sun. ↕↔ 15ft (5m). Tibet, China, Burma. Zone 7b.
R. pachysanthum ▣ Evergreen, mound-forming shrub. Lance-shaped to oval leaves, 1½–4in (4–10cm) long, have a conspicuous silver-brown indumentum above, and a dense silver indumentum beneath, later becoming rich brown. In early midseason, bears trusses of 11 or more funnel- to bell-shaped, pale rose-pink flowers, to 2in (5cm) across, with variable markings inside. Grow in sun. ↕ 5–8ft (1.5–2.5m), ↔ 8ft (2.5m). Taiwan. Zone 7b.
***R.* 'Palestrina'** ▣ syn. *R.* 'Wilhelmina Vuyk'. Compact, evergreen azalea (V) with small leaves. Trusses of 2 or 3 open funnel-shaped, pure white flowers, 2in (5cm) across, with faint green markings in the throats, are borne freely in mid-season. ↕↔ 4ft (1.2m). Zone 7.
***R.* 'Party Pink'** ▣ Wide-spreading, branching evergreen shrub with large, broadly elliptic leaves. In late midseason, bears large, rounded trusses of open funnel-shaped, soft orchid-pink flowers, 3in (8cm) across, each with a greenish yellow flare on the upper petal. ↕ 5ft (1.5m), ↔ 5–8ft (1.5–2.5m). Zone 6.
***R.* 'Patty Bee'** ▣ Free-flowering, dwarf, evergreen shrub, of compact, rounded habit, with small leaves turning purple-bronze in winter. Compact trusses of broadly funnel-shaped, clear pale yellow flowers, 2in (5cm) across, smother the foliage in early midseason. ↕↔ 30in (75cm). Zone 6.
***R.* 'Percy Wiseman'.** Low-growing, compact, evergreen shrub with medium-sized leaves. In midseason, bears rounded trusses of funnel-shaped, peach-pink and cream flowers, 2–2½in (5–6cm) across, fading to creamy white, with green markings in the throats. ↕↔ 6ft (2m). Zone 6.
R. periclymenoides ▣ syn. *R. nudiflorum* (Pinxterbloom azalea). Low-growing, well-branched, stoloniferous, deciduous azalea with elliptic, bright green leaves, 1¼–3in (3–8cm) long, turning dull yellow in autumn. Trusses of 6–12, narrow, tubular-funnel-shaped, fragrant, white or pale pink to to deep violet flowers, 1½in (4cm) across, are borne in midseason, before the leaves. ↕ 4–6ft (1.2–2m), ↔ 8–10ft (2.5–3m). Massachusetts to Ohio and North Carolina. Zone 5.
***R.* 'Persil'.** Deciduous, bushy azalea (K-E) producing medium-sized leaves. Funnel-shaped, pure white flowers, to 2½in (6cm) across, each with a bold orange-yellow flare inside, open in midseason. ↕↔ 6ft (2m). Zone 5.
***R.* 'Peter Tigerstedt'.** Evergreen shrub with large, elliptic, dark green leaves. In late midseason, bears dense trusses of open funnel-shaped, white flowers, 2–2½in (5–6cm) across, with violet freckles. ↕ 6ft (2m), ↔ 4–5ft (1.2–1.5m). Zone 4.
***R.* 'Pink and Sweet'.** Upright, rounded, deciduous azalea (O) with medium-sized, elliptic to obovate leaves. Very late in the season, bears loose trusses of tubular-funnel-shaped, strongly scented, pink flowers, 1¾in (4.5cm) across. ↕ 4ft (1.2m), ↔ 3ft (1m). Zone 4b.
***R.* 'Pink Pancake'.** Prostrate, evergreen azalea (NT) producing small, narrowly elliptic to oblong-lance-shaped, hairy, mid-green leaves. In late midseason, bears small trusses of open funnel-shaped, bright pink flowers, 2in (5cm) across. ↕ 10in (25cm), ↔ 36in (90cm). Zone 6.
***R.* 'Pink Pearl'** ▣ Vigorous, evergreen shrub of open, erect habit, with large leaves. In midseason, bears abundant trusses of funnel-shaped, soft pink flowers, 2½–3in (6–8cm) across, fading to white. ↕↔ 12ft (4m). Zone 7b.
***R.* 'PJM'.** Dwarf, compact, evergreen shrub with small, ovate, dark green leaves, which turn brownish purple in winter if grown in full sun. Trusses of 4–9 small, broadly funnel-shaped, bright lavender-pink flowers, 1½in (4cm) across, are borne early in the season. ↕↔ 4ft (1.2m). Zone 4.
***R.* 'Polar Bear'** ▣ Late-flowering, vigorous, multi-stemmed, evergreen shrub or small tree with large leaves. Very late in the season, bears large trusses of tubular-funnel-shaped, strongly scented white flowers, 3–3½in (8–9cm) across, with light brown-flecked, pale green throats. ↕ 15ft (5m), ↔ 12ft (4m). Zone 7b.
R. ponticum. Vigorous, evergreen shrub with inversely lance-shaped to broadly elliptic leaves, 2½–7in (6–18cm) long, glossy, dark green above, paler beneath. Late in the season, bears trusses of 10–15 broadly funnel-shaped, reddish purple, occasionally white flowers, to 2in (5cm) across, often spotted yellowish green inside. ↕ 20–25ft (6–8m), ↔ 20ft (6m). Zone 7b.
R.* x *praecox see *R.* 'Praecox'.
***R.* 'Praecox'**, syn. *R.* x *praecox*. Early-flowering, sometimes low-growing, evergreen shrub producing small leaves. Very early in the season and in early midseason, trusses of 2 or 3 widely funnel-shaped, rose-purple flowers, 1½–1¾in (4–4.5cm) across, are borne at the shoot tips. Thrives in full sun. ↕↔ 4½ft (1.3m). Zone 7.
***R.* 'President Roosevelt'** ▣ Evergreen shrub with splashes of bright yellow on medium-sized, glossy, dark green leaves. In early midseason, bears conical trusses of funnel-shaped, bright red flowers, 2½in (6cm) across, fading to white in the centers. ↕↔ 6ft (2m). Zone 7b.

Rhododendron 'Medway'

Rhododendron metternichii

Rhododendron 'Mrs. Furnival'

Rhododendron 'Mrs. G.W. Leak'

Rhododendron 'Mrs. T.H. Lowinsky'

Rhododendron mucronatum

Rhododendron mucronulatum 'Cornell Pink'

Rhododendron 'Narcissiflora'

Rhododendron neriiflorum

Rhododendron 'Nova Zembla'

Rhododendron occidentale

Rhododendron 'Odee Wright'

Rhododendron 'Olga Mezitt'

Rhododendron oreodoxa

Rhododendron oreotrephes

Rhododendron pachysanthum

Rhododendron 'Palestrina'

Rhododendron 'Party Pink'

Rhododendron periclymenoides

Rhododendron 'Pink Pearl'

Rhododendron 'President Roosevelt'

R

Rhododendron prinophyllum (inset: flower detail)

R. prinophyllum ■ syn. *R. roseum* (Roseshell azalea). Deciduous azalea with elliptic to obovate, mid-green leaves, 2–3in (5–8cm) long, softly hairy beneath. Dense trusses of 5–9 tubular-funnel-shaped, strongly clove-scented, rose-pink flowers, 1¼–1½in (3–4cm) across, are borne in midseason. ↕↔ 6ft (2m). Quebec to Oklahoma, Arkansas, and Virginia. Zone 5.
R. prunifolium ■ (Plumleaf azalea). Hairless evergreen azalea with elliptic, mid-green leaves, 1¼–4½in (3–11cm) long. Very late in the season, bears trusses of 4–7 funnel-shaped, orange-red to red flowers, 1½–1¾in (2–2.5cm) across. ↕ 8–10ft (2.5–3m), ↔ 6–8ft (2–2.5m). E. Alabama, S.W. Georgia. Zone 7.
***R.* 'Ptarmigan'** ■ Free-flowering, dwarf, evergreen shrub with a spreading habit and small, dark green leaves. Clustered trusses of funnel-shaped, pure white flowers, 1–1¼in (2.5–3cm) across, appear in early midseason. ↕↔ 18–36in (45–90cm). Zone 7b.
***R.* 'Purple Gem'.** Rounded, dwarf evergreen shrub with small, elliptic, dark green leaves. In early midseason, produces small trusses of open funnel-shaped, small, light purple flowers, 1–1¼in (2.5–3cm) across. Excellent in the front of a border or in a rock garden. ↕ to 24in (60cm), ↔ 3–4ft (1–1.2m). Zone 6.
***R.* 'Purple Splendour'** ■ Evergreen shrub with medium-sized leaves. In late midseason, bears trusses of about 15 striking, frilled, funnel-shaped, deep purple-blue flowers, to 2½–3in (6–8cm) across, each with a purple-black basal mark inside. ↕↔ 10ft (3m). Zone 7.
R. racemosum ■ Stiffly branched, evergreen shrub producing broadly obovate to oblong-elliptic, mid- to dark green leaves, ½–2in (1.5–5cm) long, glaucous beneath. Bears abundant trusses of up to 4 widely funnel-shaped, deep rose-red, pink, or white flowers, to 1¼in (3cm) across, along the stems, in early midseason. ↕↔ 6ft (2m). W. China. Zone 7b.
R. rex. Evergreen, large shrub or small tree producing inversely lance-shaped leaves, 10–18in (25–45cm) long, with a cinnamon-brown indumentum above when young, becoming wrinkled, dark green, with a thick, cinnamon-brown or darker brown indumentum beneath. In early midseason, bears trusses of 12–25 bell-shaped, 7- or 8-lobed, white-tinged pink flowers, 2–2½in (5–6cm) across, each with a crimson basal mark and sometimes heavily spotted crimson. Requires a sheltered site in light woodland. ↕↔ 40ft (12m). China (Sichuan, Yunnan). Zone 7.
subsp. *arizelum* ■ syn. *R. arizelum,* has obovate leaves, 5–9in (13–22cm) long, and usually yellow, sometimes pink, rarely white flowers, with crimson marks in the throats; ↕↔ 25ft (8m); China (W. Yunnan), N.E. Burma.
subsp. *fictolacteum* ■ syn. *R. fictolacteum,* has oblong-ovate to lance-shaped leaves, 4½–12in (11–30cm) long, and bears trusses of 12–25 white, sometimes pink-tinged flowers with crimson throats and sometimes crimson spotting; S.E. Tibet, China (W. Yunnan), N.E. Burma.

Rhododendron prunifolium

***R.* 'Rose Bud'.** Compact, low-growing, evergreen azalea (Ku) with small leaves. In late midseason, bears an abundance of small trusses of rosebud-like, funnel-shaped, rose-pink flowers, 1½in (4.5cm) across. Thrives in sun. ↕↔ 24–36in (60–90cm). Zone 7.
R. roseum see *R. prinophyllum.*
***R.* 'Roseum Elegans'.** Wide evergreen shrub with large, elliptic, olive-green leaves. In late midseason, bears dense trusses of small, open funnel-shaped, pink-shaded lilac flowers, 1¾–2in (4.5–5cm) across, fading to pink. ↕ 6ft (2m), ↔ 6–8ft (2–2.5m). Zone 4.
***R.* 'Roza Harrison'** see *R.* 'Roza Stevenson'.
***R.* 'Roza Stevenson'** ■ syn. *R.* 'Roza Harrison'. Vigorous, open, erect, evergreen shrub with medium-sized leaves. In early midseason, bears abundant loose trusses of 10–12 saucer-shaped, clear lemon-yellow flowers, 4½in (11cm) across. ↕↔ 5–12ft (1.5–4m). Zone 7b.
R. russatum ■ Dwarf, compact, evergreen shrub with narrowly to broadly elliptic or oblong, dark green leaves, to 1½in (4cm) long, brown to red-brown and scaly beneath. In early midseason, bears trusses of 4–6 broadly funnel-shaped, reddish purple to indigo-blue, occasionally white flowers, 1–1¼in (2.5–3cm) across. Prefers full sun. ↕ to 5ft (1.5m), ↔ 4ft (1.2m). S.W. China. Zone 5.
***R.* 'St. Valentine'** ■ syn. *R.* 'Valentine'. Evergreen Vireya rhododendron of spreading habit, with small, elliptic leaves. Trusses of 3–5 pendent, tubular-bell-shaped, bright red flowers, 1½in (4cm) across, are borne in spring. ↕ 5ft (1.5m), ↔ 6ft (2m). ❅ (min. 41°F/5°C)
***R.* 'Sappho'** ■ Free-flowering, tall, evergreen shrub with medium-sized leaves. Funnel-shaped white flowers, 2½–3in (6–8cm) across, attractively flared purple-black in the throats, are borne in high-domed trusses in midseason. Grow in full sun. ↕↔ 10ft (3m). Zone 7.
***R.* 'Satan'.** Free-flowering, deciduous azalea (K-E) with medium-sized leaves. In midseason, produces trusses of funnel-shaped, bright red flowers, 2in (5cm) long. ↕↔ 6ft (2m). Zone 5.
R. schlippenbachii ■ (Royal azalea). Deciduous, densely branched azalea with obovate or broadly ovate leaves, 1–4½in (2.5–11cm) long, dark green above, paler green beneath, borne in whorls of 5 at the branch tips. Produces attractive autumn color if grown in sun and moist soil. Early in the season to early midseason, bears trusses of 3–6 flat or saucer-shaped, pale pink or rose-pink sometimes white flowers, 2–3in (5–8cm) across, spotted reddish pink on the upper lobes. ↕↔ to 15ft (5m). China, Korea. Zone 5.
***R.* 'Scintillation'.** Large-stemmed, strong-growing evergreen shrub with large, waxy, curling, lustrous, dark green leaves. In midseason, bears large trusses of large, open funnel-shaped, light pink flowers, 2½–3in (6–8cm) across, with pink-flared markings in the throats, becoming rich bronze as the flowers age. ↕ 5ft (1.5m), ↔ 4–5ft (1.2–1.5m). Zone 5.
R. serrulatum see *R. viscosum.*
***R.* 'Seta'** ■ Free-flowering, evergreen shrub of open habit, with small leaves. Early in the season, bears upright, clustered trusses of tubular-bell-shaped, light pink flowers, 1½in (4cm) across, striped deep pink on the outsides. ↕↔ 3–5ft (1–1.5m). Zone 7b.
***R.* 'Seven Stars'** ■ Vigorous, upright, evergreen shrub with medium-sized leaves. In midseason, bears rounded trusses of funnel-shaped, pale pinkish white flowers, 2in (5cm) across, flushed deep red-purple on the outsides on opening. ↕↔ 12ft (4m). Zone 7b.
R. sinogrande ■ Evergreen shrub or small tree with very large, oblong to lance-shaped, glossy, dark green leaves, to 30in (75cm) long, with a smooth, silver to buff indumentum beneath. Early in the season, bears trusses of 20–30 widely bell-shaped, pale yellow

Rhodendron schlippenbachii (inset: fall color)

Rhododendron 'Taurus'

to creamy white flowers, 2–2½in (5–6cm) across, marked crimson inside. ↕↔ 30ft (10m). Tibet, China, Burma. Zone 8.

R. smirnowii. Evergreen shrub producing oblong to lance-shaped, dark green leaves, 3–5½in (7–14cm) long, with a thick, woolly, fawn indumentum beneath. Trusses of 10–12 funnel- to bell-shaped, pale to deep rose-purple flowers, to 1¾–2in (4.5–5cm) across, are borne in late midseason. ↕ to 12ft (4m), ↔ 15ft (5m). N.E. Turkey, Republic of Georgia, Caucasus. Zone 6.

***R.* 'Snowflake'** see *R.* 'Kure-no-yuki'.

***R.* 'Solidarity'** ▣ Compact evergreen shrub with large, elliptic, dark green leaves, woolly beneath. In midseason, produces large trusses of open funnel-shaped, deep pink flowers, 3in (8cm) across, opening from red buds. ↕ 3ft (1m), ↔ 3–4ft (1–1.2m). Zone 6.

R. souliei ▣ Evergreen shrub with ovate-rounded leaves, 2½–3in (6–8cm) long, metallic blue-green above when young, becoming mid-green with age, light green and glaucous beneath. In midseason and early summer, bears trusses of 5–8 saucer-shaped, pink or rose-red, occasionally white flowers, 2–3in (5–8cm) across. ↕ to 15ft (5m), ↔ 12ft (4m). W. China. Zone 7b.

R. speciosum see *R. flammeum.*

***R.* 'Spek's Brilliant'** ▣ Deciduous azalea (M) with medium-sized leaves. In late midseason, produces full trusses of funnel-shaped, bright orange-scarlet flowers, 2½in (6cm) across, with deeper orange-scarlet flares inside. Suitable for full sun. ↕↔ 8ft (2.5m). Zone 5b.

***R.* 'Spek's Orange'** ▣ Deciduous, bushy azalea (M) with medium-sized leaves. In late midseason, bears dense trusses of broadly funnel-shaped, bright reddish orange flowers, 2½in (6cm) across. Suitable for full sun. ↕↔ 8ft (2.5m). Zone 5b.

***R.* 'Strawberry Ice'** ▣ Bushy, deciduous azalea (K-E) with medium-sized leaves. Rounded trusses of broadly funnel-shaped, pale flesh-pink flowers, 2½–3in (6–8cm) across, heavily veined and mottled deeper pink at the petal margins, with deep yellow-marked throats, are borne in midseason. Thrives in full sun. ↕↔ 6ft (2m). Zone 5.

R. strigillosum. Large, dome-shaped, evergreen shrub with densely bristly shoots and recurved, oblong to lance-shaped leaves, 3–5½in (7–14cm) long, bright green above, scaly and brown-hairy beneath. Early in the season, bears trusses of 8–12 tubular-bell-shaped, glossy crimson-scarlet flowers, 2½in (6cm) long. ↕↔ 20ft (6m). W. China. Zone 7b.

***R.* 'Susan'** ▣ Vigorous but compact, evergreen shrub with medium-sized leaves. In midseason, bears trusses of 12–16 funnel-shaped, cool mauve-blue flowers, 3–3½in (8–9cm) across, with darker margins, fading to near white. ↕↔ 10ft (3m). Zone 6b.

R. sutchuenense. Spreading, evergreen shrub or small tree with oblong to lance-shaped leaves, 4½–10in (11–25cm) long, matte, mid-green above, paler green beneath. Early in the season, bears trusses of 8–12 broadly bell-shaped, rose-pink or pale lilac flowers, to 3in (8cm) across, often with purple spots inside. ↕↔ 25ft (8m). W. China. Zone 5b.

***R.* 'Swansdown'** ▣ Rounded, well-branched, evergreen shrub with large, elliptic, mid-olive-green leaves. In midseason, produces dense trusses of open funnel-shaped, white flowers, 3in (8cm) across, each with a yellow flare. ↕↔ 5ft (1.5m). Zone 5.

***R.* 'Taurus'** ▣ Vigorous evergreen shrub with large, elliptic, pointed, deep green leaves. In early midseason, deep red buds open to large, rounded trusses of bell-shaped red flowers, 3–3½in (8–9cm) across, each with black speckling on the upper petals. ↕ 6ft (2m), ↔ 6–8ft (2–2.5m). Zone 7b.

***R.* 'Taylori'.** Erect, evergreen Vireya rhododendron with medium-sized, narrowly elliptic leaves. From winter to spring, intermittently bears rounded trusses of up to 15 funnel-shaped pink flowers, 2in (5cm) across. ↕ 5ft (1.5m), ↔ 3ft (1m). ❀ (min. 41°F/5°C)

***R.* 'Teddy Bear'.** Low-growing evergreen shrub with large, elliptic, glossy, dark green leaves, white-woolly beneath, becoming cinnamon-brown with age. In early midseason, bears dome-shaped trusses of large, funnel- to bell-shaped, pale pink flowers, 2½in (6cm) across, with lighter pink centers. ↕ 3ft (1m), ↔ 3–4ft (1–1.2m). Zone 6.

***R.* 'The Hon. Jean Marie de Montague'**, syn. *R.* 'Jean Mary Montague'. Free-flowering, compact, evergreen shrub with medium-sized leaves. Dense trusses of funnel-shaped, scarlet-crimson flowers, 2–3in (5–8cm) across, are borne in midseason. Tolerates heat, sun, and an exposed site. ↕↔ 8ft (2.5m). Zone 7.

R. thomsonii ▣ Evergreen shrub or small tree with smooth, peeling, purple-brown bark and broadly ovate leaves, 1¼–4½in (3–11cm) long, dark green above, glaucous beneath. Pendent trusses of 6–12 bell-shaped, waxy, fleshy, deep blood-red flowers, 1½–2½in (3.5–6cm) long, with large calyces, open in early midseason. ↕↔ 20ft (6m). Himalayas, W. China. Zone 8.

***R.* 'Titian Beauty'** ▣ Low-growing, compact, evergreen shrub producing medium-sized, deep green leaves, with a thin brown indumentum beneath. Lax trusses of tubular-bell-shaped, waxy, rich red flowers, 2½in (6cm) across, are borne on long flower stalks above the foliage, in midseason. Suitable for full sun. ↕↔ 6ft (2m). Zone 7.

Rhododendron 'Ptarmigan'

Rhododendron 'Purple Splendour'

Rhododendron racemosum

Rhododendron rex subsp. *arizelum*

Rhododendron rex subsp. *fictolacteum*

Rhododendron 'Roza Stevenson'

Rhododendron russatum

Rhododendron 'St. Valentine'

Rhododendron 'Sappho'

Rhododendron 'Seta'

Rhododendron 'Seven Stars'

Rhododendron sinogrande

Rhododendron 'Solidarity'

Rhododendron souliei

Rhododendron 'Spek's Brilliant'

Rhododendron 'Spek's Orange'

Rhododendron 'Strawberry Ice'

Rhododendron 'Susan'

Rhododendron 'Swansdown'

Rhododendron thomsonii

Rhododendron 'Titian Beauty'

Rhododendron 'Trude Webster'

Rhododendron vaseyi

Rhododendron wardii

Rhododendron 'Windbeam'

Rhododendron 'Yaku Prince'

Rhododendron yakushimanum

***R.* 'Todmorden'.** Vigorous evergreen shrub with large, elliptic leaves. In midseason, produces dense trusses of open funnel-shaped, brilliant pink and white flowers, to 3½in (9cm) across, each with brownish spotting on the upper petals. ↕ to 6ft (2m), ↔ 5–7ft (1.5–2.2m). Zone 7.
***R.* 'Tow Head'.** Dwarf evergreen shrub with small, elliptic leaves. In early midseason, bears small trusses of narrowly bell-shaped, greenish yellow flowers, 1½in (4cm) across, with orange-yellow spotting. Useful as a rock garden plant. ↕ 12in (30cm), ↔ 24in (60cm). Zone 5.
***R.* 'Trude Webster'** ▣ Compact, upright evergreen shrub with large, broadly elliptic, slightly twisted leaves. In midseason, produces large trusses of broadly funnel-shaped, clear pink flowers, to 5in (13cm) across, each with black spots on the upper petals. ↕ 5ft (1.5m), ↔ 4–5ft (1.2–1.5m). Zone 7b.
***R.* 'Unique'.** Rounded evergreen shrub with large, smooth, dense, oblong, clover-green leaves. In early midseason, dense trusses of open funnel-shaped, light cream-yellow flowers, 2½–3in (6–8cm) across, open from bright pink buds. ↕↔ 4ft (1.2m). Zone 6b.
***R.* 'Valentine'** see *R.* 'St. Valentine'.
R. vaseyi ▣ (Pinkshell azalea). Deciduous azalea with elliptic to elliptic-oblong, hairless, shiny, dark green leaves, 2–5in (5–13cm) long, paler green beneath. In early midseason, trusses of 4–8 broadly funnel-shaped, rose-pink to white flowers, 1½–2in (4–5cm) across, spotted red, are borne before the leaves. Suitable for full sun or in an open woodland garden. ↕↔ 15ft (5m). E. North America. Zone 5.
R. veitchianum see *R. cubittii.*
***R.* 'Vida Brown'.** Slow-growing, evergreen azalea (Ku) of low, compact habit, producing small leaves. Hose-in-hose, rose-pink flowers, 1½in (4cm) long, are borne in small trusses in midseason. ↕ 30in (75cm), ↔ 4ft (1.2m). Zone 7b.
***R.* 'Vinecrest'.** Low-growing, mounded evergreen shrub with large, elliptic, bright green leaves. In midseason, produces medium, rounded trusses of broadly funnel-shaped, slightly fragrant, chartreuse-yellow flowers, 2in (5cm) across. Provide good drainage. ↕ to 4ft (1.2m), ↔ 3–4ft (1–1.2m). Zone 5b.
***R.* 'Virginia Richards'.** Compact evergreen shrub with large, elliptic, glossy, dark green leaves. In midseason, produces large trusses of widely funnel-shaped, pink flowers, to 4½in (11cm) across, turning yellow with a crimson blotch. ↕ 4ft (1.2m), ↔ 3–4ft (1–1.2m). Zone 7b.
***R.* 'Vivacious'.** Free-flowering evergreen shrub with large, narrowly elliptic leaves. In midseason, bears dense, rounded trusses of funnel-shaped red flowers, 2½in (6cm) across. ↕ to 4ft (1.2m), ↔ 3–4ft (1–1.2m). Zone 5b.
R. viscosum, syn. *R. serrulatum* (Swamp azalea, Sweet azalea). Deciduous azalea with hairy shoots and elliptic-obovate to oblong-obovate, dark green leaves, ½–1¼in (1.5–3cm) long, often glaucous beneath. Very late in the season, bears trusses of 4–12 narrowly tubular to funnel-shaped, fragrant, pink-suffused white flowers, 1–1½in (2.5–4cm) across. Thrives in damp soil in sun. ↕↔ 8ft (2.5m). E. North America. Zone 5.
R. wardii ▣ Evergreen shrub or small tree with oblong-elliptic to broadly obovate, hairless, dark green leaves, 2½–4½in (6–11cm) long, paler green beneath. Trusses of 7–14 broadly funnel-shaped flowers, 2–3in (5–8cm) across, in various shades of yellow, sometimes with basal crimson marks inside, are borne in midseason. ↕ 20ft (6m), ↔ 15ft (5m). S.E. Tibet, S.W. China. Zone 7b.
***R.* 'Weston's Pink Diamond'.** Vigorous, upright semi-evergreen shrub with small, elliptic, dark green leaves, turning red, yellow, and orange in autumn. Early in the season, bears loose trusses of saucer-shaped, double pink flowers, 1½in (4cm) across, with silver-toned centers. ↕ 6ft (2m), ↔ 5ft (1.5m). Zone 5.
***R.* 'Wheatley'** ▣ Vigorous, well-branched evergreen shrub with large, elliptic leaves. In midseason, produces dense, rounded trusses of open funnel-shaped, frilled, fragrant, rose-pink flowers, 3in (8cm) across, with yellow-green rays in the throats. ↕ 6ft (2m), ↔ 5–6ft (1.5–2m). Zone 7.
***R.* 'White Peter'.** Mound-forming evergreen shrub with large, broadly elliptic, glossy, dark green leaves. In midseason, produces medium, conical trusses of broadly funnel-shaped, wavy-edged, white flowers, 2½–3in (6–8cm) across, each with a heavily speckled reddish maroon flare. ↕ 4ft (1.2m), ↔ 3–4ft (1–1.2m). Zone 6.
***R.* 'Wigeon'.** Free-flowering, semi-dwarf, evergreen shrub with small leaves. In midseason, bears neat trusses of numerous saucer-shaped, rich lavender-pink flowers, to 1½in (4cm) across, with deeper spotting on the upper lobes inside. ↕↔ 4ft (1.2m). Zone 7.
***R.* 'Wilhelmina Vuyk'** see *R.* 'Palestrina'.
R. williamsianum. Dome-shaped, evergreen shrub with ovate-rounded leaves, ¾–1¾in (2–4.5cm) long, brown when young, bright green above and glaucous beneath when mature. Loose trusses of 2 or 3 bell-shaped flowers, 1½–2in (4–5cm) across, in various shades of pink, occasionally white, are borne in abundance in early midseason. ↕ to 5ft (1.5m), ↔ 4ft (1.2m). W. China. Zone 7b.
***R.* 'Windbeam'** ▣ Semi-dwarf, compact, evergreen shrub with small, elliptic, dark green leaves. In early midseason, produces dense trusses of open funnel-shaped, white flowers, 1–1¼in (2.5–3cm) across, aging to pale pink. ↕↔ 4ft (1.2m). Zone 4b.
***R.* 'Winsome'.** Compact, dense, sometimes low-growing, evergreen shrub with medium-sized, mid-green leaves, bronze when young. Loose trusses of funnel-shaped, cherry-pink flowers, 2½–3in (6–8cm) long, open in early midseason. Suitable for sun or partial shade. ↕↔ 5ft (1.5m). Zone 7.
***R.* 'Wombat'.** Prostrate, vigorous, evergreen azalea (O) with small leaves. Lax trusses of funnel-shaped pink flowers, to 1½in (4cm) across, are borne in abundance late in the season. Excellent groundcover in full sun. ↕ 10in (25cm), ↔ 4ft (1.2m). Zone 7b.
R. xanthocodon see *R. cinnabarinum* subsp. *xanthocodon.*
***R.* 'Yaku Prince'** ▣ Compact, dense evergreen shrub with narrowly elliptic, olive-green leaves, beige-woolly beneath. In midseason, bears dense, rounded trusses of funnel- to bell-shaped, pink flowers, 2½in (6cm) across, with reddish pink edges fading slightly toward the centers. ↕ 36in (90cm), ↔ 24–36in (60–90cm). Zone 5.
***R.* 'Yaku Princess'.** Dense, compact, low-growing, evergreen shrub producing medium-sized, olive-green leaves, with a buff indumentum beneath. Spherical trusses of funnel-shaped, pinkish white flowers, 2½in (6cm) across, each with deeper pink mark and greenish spots inside, are borne in midseason. ↕↔ 5ft (1.5m). Zone 5.

Rhododendron 'Wheatley'

R. yakushimanum ▣ syn. *R. degronianum* subsp. *yakushimanum.* Tightly dome-shaped, evergreen shrub with recurved, linear to lance-shaped, glossy, dark green leaves, 3–5½in (8–14cm) long, with a thick, reddish brown indumentum beneath. Young foliage has a pale cinnamon-brown indumentum on the upper surfaces. In midseason, trusses of 5–10 deep rose-pink buds open to tubular-funnel-shaped flowers, 1½–2in (4–5cm) acros fading to pale pink or white. ↕↔ 3ft (1m). Japan (Yakushima Island). Zone
'Ken Janeck', syn. *R.* 'Ken Janeck', is low-growing, bearing full trusses of funnel-shaped white flowers, 1½–2in (4–5cm) long, lined with pinkish purp and spotted with green; ↕↔ 4ft (1.2m). **'Mist Maiden'** grows taller and wider, and bears denser flower trusses, each with 14–17 flowers, 2½in (6cm) across ↕↔ 4ft (1.2m).
R. yedoense* var. *poukhanense ▣ (Korean azalea). Wide-growing deciduous azalea with elliptic-lance-shaped, dark green leaves, 1¼–3in (3–8cm) long, turning orange to red-purple in autumn. Early in the season, bears trusses of 2 or 3 broadly funnel-shaped, fragrant, rose to lilac-purple flowers, to 2in (5cm) across. ↕ 3–6ft (1–2m), ↔ 6ft (2m). S. and C. Korea. Zone 6.

Rhododendron yedoense var. *poukhanense*

R

RHODOHYPOXIS

HYPOXIDACEAE

Genus of 6 species of small, clump-forming herbaceous perennials, with corm-like rootstocks, from open meadows in areas with heavy summer rainfall in the eastern provinces of South Africa, and Swaziland. The basal leaves are lance-shaped and hairy. Short-stalked, almost flat, white, pink, red, or deep purple flowers are produced over long periods in summer. Each flower has 6 overlapping tepals, arranged in 2 ranks of 3, which are fused at the bases to form a tube; the outer tepals are broader than the inner ones. Grow in a trough, rock garden, or alpine house.

• **CULTIVATION** Under glass, grow in a mix of equal parts acidic potting mix, leaf mold, and sharp sand, in full light. When in growth, water freely and apply a balanced liquid fertilizer monthly; keep just moist in winter. Outdoors, grow in well-drained, moderately fertile, humus-rich soil in full sun, with protection from excessive winter moisture. *R. milloides* thrives in damp conditions, and will tolerate more winter moisture.

• **PROPAGATION** Sow seed at 45–54°F (6–12°C) as soon as ripe or in spring. Divide established clumps, or separate offsets, in late autumn.

• **PESTS AND DISEASES** Susceptible to spider mites and thrips under glass.

R. baurii. Clump-forming perennial with basal clusters of narrowly lance-shaped, keeled, folded leaves, to 4in (10cm) long. The leaves are dull grayish green, and very hairy on both surfaces and at the margins. Solitary, pale to deep reddish pink flowers, to ¾in (2cm) across, are produced on stalks 2–4in (5–10cm) tall, throughout summer. ↕↔ 4in (10cm). South Africa. ❄ (min. 41°F/5°C). The following cultivars, derived mainly from *R. baurii* and *R. baurii* var. *platypetala*, are generally large-flowered and

Rhodohypoxis baurii 'Albrighton'

Rhodohypoxis baurii 'Margaret Rose'

vigorous. **'Albrighton'** ▣ has deep red-pink flowers. **var. *baurii*** has narrower leaves and red to deep pink flowers. **'Harlequin'** has pink-flushed white flowers, to ½in (1.5cm) across, with distinct pink margins. **'Helen'**, syn. *R.* 'Tetra White', has very large white flowers, 1¼in (3cm) or more across. **'Margaret Rose'** ▣ has clear pink flowers. **var. *platypetala*** is more robust than *R. baurii*, with wider, gray-green leaves and bearing white, rarely pink flowers, to 1¼in (3cm) across; ↕ 5in (13cm), ↔ 6in (15cm). **var. *platypetala* 'Great Scott'** has dark carmine flowers. **'Tetra Pink'** and **'Tetra Red'** have large flowers, 1¼in (3cm) or more across, in pink and reddish purple, respectively.

R. milloides. Vigorous, clump-forming perennial with runners, and with erect, hairless or sparsely hairy, linear-lance-shaped, keeled, folded, light green, basal leaves, to 7in (18cm) long. Cerise or dark crimson, occasionally deep pink or white flowers, to 1½in (4cm) across, are produced on hairy flower stalks, to 5in (13cm) or more tall, over long periods in summer. ↕ 6in (15cm), ↔ 8in (20cm). South Africa. ❄ (min. 35°F/2°C)

***R.* 'Tetra White'** see *R. baurii* 'Helen'.

RHODOPHIALA

AMARYLLIDACEAE

Genus, closely related to *Hippeastrum*, of about 35 species of bulbous perennials from coastal sands to rocky, dry sites in the mountains of Uruguay, Argentina, and Chile. They are grown for their funnel-shaped flowers, borne in umbels on leafless stems in summer or autumn. The basal leaves are linear and mid-green. Grow *Rhodophiala* species in an alpine house; in frost-free areas, *R. advena* and *R. pratensis* may be grown outdoors against a warm, sunny wall.

• **CULTIVATION** Under glass, plant bulbs with the necks and shoulders above soil level, in autumn. Grow in soil-based potting mix in full light or bright

Rhodophiala advena

filtered light. Water sparingly until plants are in active growth, then water moderately and apply a half-strength balanced liquid fertilizer every 2–3 weeks. Keep dry when dormant. Avoid root disturbance; pot on only every 3 years. Outdoors, plant bulbs 6–8in (15–20cm) deep in moderately fertile, well-drained soil in full sun. Provide a deep, dry winter mulch where marginally hardy, and grow against a warm wall.

• **PROPAGATION** Sow seed at 61°F (16°C) as soon as ripe. Remove offsets in autumn or winter.

• **PESTS AND DISEASES** Infrequent.

R. advena ▣ syn. *Hippeastrum advenum.* Bulbous perennial producing umbels of 2–6 horizontal, open funnel-shaped, red, yellow, or pink flowers, 2in (5cm) across, in late summer and early autumn, just before the semi-erect, linear, basal leaves, 6–12in (15–30cm) long, emerge. ↕ 12–20in (30–50cm), PD4in (10cm). Chile. ❄ (min. 41°F/5°C)

R. bifida, syn. *Hippeastrum bifidum.* Bulbous perennial producing umbels of up to 5 erect, narrowly funnel-shaped, bright deep red flowers, 2in (5cm) long, in summer; flowers are borne as, or just before, the semi-erect, linear, basal leaves, to 18in (45cm) long, emerge. ↕ to 12in (30cm), PD4in (10cm). Argentina, Uruguay. ❄ (min. 41°F/5°C)

R. pratensis, syn. *Hippeastrum pratense.* Bulbous perennial bearing umbels of 2–8 horizontal, broadly funnel-shaped red flowers, 2–3in (5–8cm) across, in early summer, at the same time as the semi-erect, linear, basal leaves, 12–20in (30–50cm) long. ↕ to 24in (60cm), PD4in (10cm). Chile. ❄ (min. 41°F/5°C)

RHODOTHAMNUS

ERICACEAE

Genus of 2 species of dwarf, evergreen shrubs found in pockets of humus-rich soil, often among limestone rocks, in the eastern Alps and Turkey. They have glossy, dark green foliage, and are grown for their solitary, occasionally clustered, cup-shaped pink flowers, produced in profusion from the leaf axils in early summer. Grow in a rock garden or alpine house. They are not easy to establish.

• **CULTIVATION** Under glass, grow in soil-based potting mix with additional leaf mold, in full light. In the growing season, water freely and apply a balanced liquid fertilizer monthly; water more sparingly in winter. Outdoors, grow in moderately fertile, humus-rich, acidic or alkaline, moist soil with a cool root run. They prefer full sun, but partial shade is tolerated, especially in drier areas. Avoid disturbing the roots.

• **PROPAGATION** Sow seed in containers in an open frame in autumn. Root semi-ripe cuttings in summer.

• **PESTS AND DISEASES** Susceptible to aphids and spider mites under glass.

R. chamaecistus. Semi-prostrate, evergreen shrub with elliptic to inversely lance-shaped, glossy, bright dark green leaves, ¼–½in (6–15mm) long, paler beneath, fringed with bristly white hairs. In late spring and early summer, abundant cup-shaped, 5-petaled, pale clear pink flowers, to 1¼in (3cm) across, with red eyes, are produced singly from the leaf axils or in few-flowered terminal clusters. ↕ 8in (20cm), ↔ 10in (25cm). E. Alps. Zone 7b.

RHODOTYPOS

ROSACEAE

Genus of one species of deciduous shrub occurring in scrub and woodland in China and Japan. It has opposite, ovate, toothed leaves, but is cultivated mainly for its large, papery, 4-petaled white flowers, borne from spring to summer, and for its shiny black berries. Grow in a shrub border or woodland garden.

• **CULTIVATION** Grow in moderately fertile, moist but well-drained soil, preferably in sun, although partial shade is tolerated. Pruning group 1 or 2.

• **PROPAGATION** Sow seed in a seedbed, or in containers in a cold frame, in autumn. Root greenwood cuttings in early summer, or semi-ripe cuttings in late summer.

• **PESTS AND DISEASES** Infrequent.

R. kerrioides see *R. scandens.*

R. scandens ▣ syn. *R. kerrioides* (Jetbead, White kerria). Deciduous shrub with arching shoots and ovate, tapered, sharply toothed, deeply veined, mid-green leaves, to 2½in (6cm) long. In late spring, 4-petaled white flowers, 1½in (4cm) across, are produced singly from the shoot tips; they are followed by spherical, glossy black berries, to ⅜in (9mm) across, usually in groups of 4. ↕↔ 5ft (1.5m). China, Japan. Zone 5b.

▷ ***Rhoeo*** see *Tradescantia*

Rhodotypos scandens

RHOICISSUS

VITACEAE

Genus of 10–12 species of evergreen trees and woody-stemmed tendril climbers or scramblers from understory in forest and woodland in tropical Africa and South Africa. The leaves are alternate, and simple or 3-, occasionally 5-palmate, with entire or toothed leaflets. Tendrils are produced opposite the leaves. Tiny, yellowish green flowers are borne in small cymes that are almost hidden by the leaves; they are followed by red to purple berries. Where temperatures fall below 45°F (7°C), grow in a cool or temperate greenhouse, or as houseplants. Elsewhere, use *R. capensis* to cover a wall, pergola, or arch, or grow through a small tree.

• **CULTIVATION** Under glass, grow in soil-based potting mix in full light. During the growing season, water moderately and apply a balanced liquid fertilizer monthly; water sparingly in winter. Outdoors, grow in fertile, moist but well-drained soil in full sun or partial shade. Pruning group 11, in early spring.

• **PROPAGATION** Sow seed at 55°F (13°C) in spring. Root semi-ripe cuttings with bottom heat in summer. Layer in spring.

• **PESTS AND DISEASES** Spider mites and powdery mildew may be a problem.

R. capensis ■ syn. *Cissus capensis*, *Vitis capensis* (Cape grape). Robust climber with tuberous roots and very long, forked tendrils. Leathery, lustrous, dark green leaves, 4–8in (10–20cm) long, pale claret-red when young, are rounded to kidney-shaped, and bluntly 5-angled, with broad, wavy teeth. Insignificant, yellowish green flowers are produced in spring, and are followed by grape-like, spherical, blackish red berries. ↕ 15ft (5m) or more. South Africa. ❄ (min. 45°F/7°C)

R. rhombifolia see *Cissus rhombifolia*.

Rhoicissus capensis

Rhombophyllum rhomboideum

RHOMBOPHYLLUM

AIZOACEAE

Genus of 3 species of very fleshy, usually compact, mat-forming, perennial succulents occurring on hillsides and often in the lowlands of South Africa. The crowded, fleshy leaves are linear or semi-cylindrical, expanded toward the middle, and opposite or united at the bases; they are mid- to dark grayish green, with white or translucent spots, and margins that are entire or have 1 or 2 short teeth. Attractive, daisy-like, bright golden yellow flowers, which open during the day, are borne singly or in cymes of 3–7 in summer. Where not hardy, grow in a temperate greenhouse. In warm, dry climates, grow outdoors in a raised bed or desert garden.

• **CULTIVATION** Under glass, grow in standard cactus potting mix in full light with low humidity. In spring and summer, water moderately and apply a dilute, low-nitrogen liquid fertilizer monthly; keep completely dry at other times. Outdoors, grow in poor to moderately fertile, sharply drained soil in full sun. See also pp.48–49.

• **PROPAGATION** Sow seed at 66–75°F (19–24°C), or divide offsets, in spring or summer.

• **PESTS AND DISEASES** Prone to aphids while flowering.

R. rhomboideum ■ Clump-forming succulent with 4 or 5 uneven pairs of semi-cylindrical, white-spotted, dark grayish green leaves, 1–2in (2.5–5cm) long; the upper surfaces of the leaves are more or less flat, the undersides are rounded, thickened, and keeled toward the tips, with paler green, occasionally toothed margins. Golden yellow flowers, 1¼in (3cm) across, tinged red on the reverse of the petals, are produced in summer. ↕ 2in (5cm), ↔ 6in (15cm). South Africa (Eastern Cape). ❄ (min. 45°F/7°C)

RHUS syn. TOXICODENDRON

Sumac

ANACARDIACEAE

Genus of about 200 species of deciduous or evergreen shrubs, trees, and woody climbers, widely distributed in temperate and subtropical North America, South Africa, E. Asia, and N.E. Australia. They are found in woodland, thickets, dry sites, bogs, and on

Rhus aromatica

rocky slopes. Sumacs are grown mainly for their alternate, simple, pinnate, or palmate leaves, which in many species and cultivars turn brilliant shades of yellow, red, or orange in autumn; some also produce showy fruit clusters. The inconspicuous flowers, usually 1/16in (2mm) across, are borne in spring or summer in terminal, normally erect, ovoid, or conical to pyramidal panicles. In autumn, they are followed by spherical, usually red fruits, 1/8–1/4in (4–6mm) across. *R. glabra*, *R.* x *pulvinata*, and *R. typhina* usually produce male and female flowers on separate plants; plants of both sexes must be grown together to obtain fruit. Grow in a shrub border or woodland garden, or as specimen plants. Where not hardy, grow in a cool greenhouse. All parts of *R. verniciflua* are highly toxic if ingested; contact with the foliage, and that of a number of related species, including *R. succedanea*, causes dermatitis and may aggravate skin allergies.

• **CULTIVATION** Grow in moist but well-drained, moderately fertile soil, in full sun to obtain best autumn color. Suckering species, such as *R. typhina*, may be invasive. Pruning group 1, or

Rhus glabra

group 7 for *R. typhina*, *R.* x *pulvinata*, and *R. glabra*.

• **PROPAGATION** Sow seed in a seedbed in autumn. Root semi-ripe cuttings in summer, or insert root cuttings in winter. Separate suckers when dormant.

• **PESTS AND DISEASES** Powdery mildew, *Verticillium* wilt, wood rot, leaf spot, blister, canker, and dieback can be troublesome, as well as caterpillars and scale insects.

R. aromatica ■ (Fragrant sumac). Mound-forming, suckering, deciduous shrub with spreading shoots. The 3-palmate, aromatic leaves, to 4in (10cm) long, are softly hairy or almost hairless, with ovate or obovate, sharply toothed, dark green leaflets, turning

Rhus copallina

Rhus trichocarpa

orange to red-purple in autumn. Tiny yellow flowers are borne in small, erect, ovoid panicles, ¾in (2cm) long, in midspring, followed by spherical red fruit. ↕ 3–5ft (1–1.5m), ↔ 5ft (1.5m). E. North America. Zone 3.
'Gro-low' is vigorous, spreading, and low-growing, with dense, glossy green foliage turning red-orange in autumn. Useful as a groundcover. ↕ 2–2½ft (60–75cm), ↔ 6–8ft (2–2.5m).
R. chinensis (Nutgall tree). Upright, deciduous tree with thick, downy shoots bearing pinnate leaves, to 16in (40cm) long, with winged stalks and 7–13 ovate-oblong, mid-green leaflets, turning red in autumn. In late summer, bears yellowish white flowers in erect, conical panicles, to 10in (25cm) long, followed by spherical, orange-red fruit. ↕↔ 20ft (6m). E. Asia. Zone 8.
R. copallina ▣ (Dwarf sumac, Shining sumac). Upright, deciduous, often suckering shrub or tree with long, branching, softly hairy, reddish green shoots. Pinnate leaves, to 14in (35cm) long, have winged stalks, and 9–15 oblong-lance-shaped, glossy, dark green leaflets, turning bright red in autumn. In summer, bears yellow-green flowers in erect, conical panicles, to 6in (15cm) long, followed by spherical red fruit. ↕↔ 10ft (3m) or more. E. North America. Zone 5.
R. cotinoides see *Cotinus obovatus.*
R. cotinus see *Cotinus coggygria.*
R. glabra ▣ (Scarlet sumac, Smooth sumac). Bushy, suckering, deciduous shrub producing smooth, hairless shoots and pinnate leaves, to 18in (45cm) long, with 15–31 oblong-lance-shaped, toothed, glossy, bluish green leaflets, turning rich red in autumn. In summer, bears yellow-green flowers in upright, conical panicles, to 10in (25cm) long; they are followed on female plants by spherical red fruit. ↕↔ 8ft (2.5m) or more. North America, Mexico. Zone 2b.
var. *cismontana* has fewer, lance-shaped leaflets. **'Laciniata' of gardens** see *R.* x *pulvinata* 'Red Autumn Lace'.
'Morden's' is slow-growing, with bright red seed heads; ↕ to 5½ft (1.7m).
R. potaninii. Rounded, deciduous tree with hairless or finely hairy shoots and pinnate leaves, to 14in (35cm) long, composed of 7–11 oblong to oblong-lance-shaped, dark green leaflets, turning red in autumn. Creamy white flowers are borne in pendent, pyramidal panicles, 8in (20cm) long, in summer, followed by spherical, hairy red fruit.

Rhus typhina

↕ 40ft (12m), ↔ 25ft (8m). China. Zone 6.
***R.* x *pulvinata* 'Red Autumn Lace'**, syn. *R. glabra* 'Laciniata' of gardens. Spreading, suckering, deciduous shrub with smooth shoots and pinnate leaves, to 20in (50cm) or more long, composed of 11–13 oblong-lance-shaped, rich green leaflets, turning orange to red-purple in autumn. Yellow-green flowers are borne in erect, conical panicles, to 8in (20cm) long, in summer, followed by spherical, bristly red fruit. ↕ 10ft (3m), ↔ 15ft (5m). Zone 2b.
R. succedanea, syn. *Toxicodendron succedaneum* (Wax tree). Spreading, deciduous tree with softly hairy young shoots. Pinnate leaves, to 12in (30cm) long, have 9–15 ovate-oblong, glossy, dark green leaflets, turning red in autumn. Yellow-green flowers are borne in dense, erect, conical panicles, to 5in (13cm) long, in summer, followed by spherical, waxy, yellow-brown fruit. ↕↔ 30ft (10m). E. Asia. Zone 6.
R. trichocarpa ▣ Spreading, deciduous tree or shrub with softly hairy young shoots, later becoming hairless. Pinnate leaves, to 20in (50cm) long, have 13–17 broadly ovate, usually entire, dark green leaflets, pink-tinged when young, turning red-purple to orange in autumn. In summer, bears yellow flowers in erect, conical panicles, to 4in (10cm) long, followed by spherical, bristly, brownish yellow fruit. ↕↔ 20ft (6m). C. China, Korea, Japan. Zone 7b.
R. trilobata (Skunkbush sumac). Upright, clump-forming shrub with softly hairy young shoots. The 3-palmate leaves are made up of ovate, toothed, dark green leaflets, 3in (8cm) long, malodorous when crushed, turning yellow to red in autumn. Produces panicles, ½in (1.5cm) long, of greenish yellow flowers in spring, followed by spherical red fruit. Useful in a mass planting. ↕ 3–6ft (1–2m), ↔ 6–8ft (2–2.5m). California, Texas, Illinois to Washington. Zone 3b.
R. typhina ▣ (Staghorn sumac, Velvet sumac). Upright, suckering, deciduous shrub or tree with densely velvety red shoots, resembling a stag's horns. Pinnate leaves, to 24in (60cm) long, have 11–31 oblong-lance-shaped, dark green leaflets, turning brilliant orange-red in autumn. Yellow-green flowers are produced in erect, conical panicles, to 8in (20cm) long, in summer; they are followed on female plants by dense clusters of spherical, hairy, deep crimson-red fruit. ↕ 15ft (5m) or more, ↔ 20ft (6m). E. North America. Zone 3.
'Dissecta', syn. 'Laciniata' of gardens, is female, more compact, and gracefully spreading, with finely cut leaflets; ↕ 6ft (2m), ↔ 10ft (3m).
R. verniciflua, syn. *Toxicodendron vernicifluum* (Varnish tree). Spreading, deciduous tree with softly hairy young shoots, later becoming hairless. Pinnate leaves, to 24in (60cm) long, have 7–13 broadly ovate, glossy, bright green leaflets, turning red in autumn. Yellow-green flowers are produced in lax, semi-pendent panicles, to 8in (20cm) long, in summer, followed by spherical, pale yellow fruit. ↕ 50ft (15m), ↔ 30ft (10m). E. Asia. Zone 7.

▷ ***Rhynchelytrum*** see *Melinis*

RHYNCHOSTYLIS

ORCHIDACEAE

Genus of about 6 species of evergreen, monopodial, epiphytic orchids from warm, moist forest in India, Malaysia, Indonesia, the Philippines, Thailand, Laos, Burma, and Sri Lanka. They have thick, rigid, aerial roots, and produce 8–10 pairs of semi-rigid, linear to strap-shaped leaves at the apexes of short, thick stems. Many small flowers are borne in dense, upright or pendent racemes that arise laterally from the bases of the leaves from spring to winter.
• **CULTIVATION** Intermediate-growing orchids. Grow in epiphytic orchid potting mix in half-pots or (preferably) in slatted baskets. Provide high humidity, full light, and shade from hot sun. In summer, water freely, mist daily, and apply a balanced liquid fertilizer at every third watering; water moderately in winter. Disturb as little as possible. See also p.46.
• **PROPAGATION** Divide when the plant fills the container and flows over the sides. Cuttings or offshoots may be rooted successfully.
• **PESTS AND DISEASES** Spider mites, aphids, and mealybugs may be problems.

R. gigantea. Epiphytic orchid with linear, mid-green leaves, 10in (25cm) long. Fragrant, waxy, pale purple-spotted, white or deep violet flowers, to 1½in (4cm) across, are borne in pendent racemes, 8–10in (20–25cm) long, from autumn to winter. ↕↔ 12in (30cm). Burma, Thailand, Laos. ❀ (min. 55–59°F/13–15°C; max. 86°F/30°C)
R. retusa. Epiphytic orchid with linear to oblong, bluish green leaves, 10in (25cm) long. Fragrant, waxy white flowers, to 1¼in (3cm) across, spotted purple or pink, with purple lips, are produced in pendent racemes, to 12in (30cm) long, in summer. ↕ 6in (15cm), ↔ 10in (25cm). India, Burma, Sri Lanka to Malaysia, Philippines. ❀ (min. 55–59°F/13–15°C; max. 86°F/30°C)

RIBES

Flowering currant

GROSSULARIACEAE

Genus of about 150 species of mainly deciduous, occasionally evergreen, sometimes spiny shrubs, widely distributed in woodland, scrub, and rocky places. Most are found in N. temperate regions; some occur in South America. Some species, such as blackcurrant (*R. nigrum*), redcurrant (*R. rubrum*), and gooseberry (*R. uva-crispa*), are grown for their edible fruits. Those described below are cultivated primarily for their flowers. The leaves are alternate and often 3- to 5-lobed. Small, tubular, cup- or bell-shaped flowers, each with small petals and 4, rarely 5, larger, spreading sepals, are borne singly or in pendent racemes, mostly in spring or summer. The berry-like fruits are spherical or ovoid, and vary in color from red or black to green or white. Grow in a shrub border; *R. laurifolium* is best where its late winter flowers can be seen; *R. speciosum* and *R. viburnifolium* are attractive grown against a wall. *R. sanguineum* may be used as informal hedging; *R. alpinum* may be sheared into a formal hedge.

Ribes alpinum 'Aureum'

• **CULTIVATION** Grow in moderately fertile, well-drained soil in full sun. *R. laurifolium* will grow well in partial shade; *R. sanguineum* 'Brocklebankii' should be shaded from hot sun. Pruning group 2; group 13 if wall-grown, in late summer. Trim hedges after flowering.
• **PROPAGATION** Root hardwood cuttings of deciduous flowering currants in winter. Root semi-ripe cuttings of evergreens in summer.
• **PESTS AND DISEASES** Prone to aphids, caterpillars, scale insects, dieback, downy mildew, anthracnose, powdery mildew, rust, white heart rot, and *Septoria* leaf spot.

R. alpinum. Compact, mound-forming, much-branched, deciduous shrub with spineless shoots and broadly ovate, 3- to 5-lobed, mid-green leaves, to 2in (5cm) long, often smaller. In spring, bears bell-shaped, greenish yellow flowers (males and females on separate plants) in erect racemes, to 1½in (4cm) long, followed on female plants by spherical, dark red fruit, ¼in (6mm) long. ↕ 24in (60cm), ↔ 36in (90cm). N. Europe to Russia (Siberia). Zone 2. **'Aureum'** ■ is female, and has bright yellow leaves, becoming paler in summer.
***R. aureum* of gardens** see *R. odoratum.*
R.* x *gordonianum (*R. petraeum* x *R. sanguineum*). Spreading, spineless, deciduous shrub with rounded, 3- to 5-lobed, toothed, aromatic, dark green leaves, to 2in (5cm) long. Tubular, 5-lobed flowers, red outside and yellow within, open in dense, pendent racemes, to 3in (8cm) long, in early summer. It is not known to produce fruit and is

Ribes odoratum

probably sterile. ↕ 6ft (2m), ↔ 8ft (2.5m). Garden origin. Zone 6.
R. laurifolium ■ Spreading, spineless, dioecious, evergreen shrub with ovate-oblong, scalloped, leathery, dark green leaves, 2–4in (5–10cm) long. In late winter and early spring, bears cup-shaped, greenish yellow flowers in pendent racemes, the males to 2in (5cm) long, the females to 1in (2.5cm) long. Female flowers are followed by ovoid fruit, to ½in (1.5cm) long, red at first, ripening to black. ↕ 3ft (1m), ↔ 5ft (1.5m). W. China. Zone 7.
R. odoratum ■ syn. *R. aureum* of gardens (Buffalo currant, Clove currant). Spineless, erect, deciduous shrub with hairy young shoots (hairless in the true *R. aureum*). Broadly ovate, 3- to 5-lobed, toothed, bright green leaves, to 3in (8cm) long, turn red and purple in autumn. In early and mid-spring, bears tubular, clove-scented yellow flowers in pendent racemes, to 2in (5cm) long, followed by spherical black fruit, to ½in (1.5cm) across. ↕↔ 6ft (2m). C. US. Zone 2.
R. sanguineum (Flowering currant). Upright, spineless, deciduous shrub with rounded, 3- to 5-lobed, toothed,

Ribes sanguineum 'Pulborough Scarlet'

aromatic, dark green leaves, 2–4in (5–10cm) long, heart-shaped at the bases, and slightly hairy above, white-hairy beneath. Tubular, deep pinkish red flowers are borne in pendent racemes, 2–4in (5–10cm) long, in spring, followed by spherical, glaucous, blue-black fruit, ¼in (6mm) across. ↕↔ 6ft (2m). W. North America. Zone 6b. **'Brocklebankii'** ■ is slow-growing, with bright yellow leaves, paler in summer, and pale pink flowers; ↕↔ 4ft (1.2m). **'King Edward VII'** is compact and upright, with dark red flowers. **'Pulborough Scarlet'** ■ is vigorous, and bears dark red, white-centered flowers; ↕ 10ft (3m), ↔ 8ft (2.5m). **'Tydeman's White'** produces pure white flowers; ↕↔ 8ft (2.5m).

'White Icicle' bears white flowers in early spring; ↕ 6–8ft (2–2.5m).
R. sativum (Red currant). Upright deciduous shrub with rounded, alternate, toothed dark green leaves, 1–1⅕ (2.5–3cm) wide. Small, greenish yellow to purple flowers are borne in trumpet-shaped, drooping clusters in early spring, followed in summer by shiny red to black fruit. Grows well in full sun or partial shade. Useful in hedges or yard borders; prune in dormant season. May be hosts to white pine blister rust and may be banned. ↕ to 5ft (7m), ↔ 1½ft (45cm). Zone 3.
R. uva-crispa (Gooseberry). Compact, sturdy evergreen shrub with deeply lobed, maple-leaf-shaped, glossy leaves. Tiny, pendulous, purplish to pink flowers; medium small, round, pale green, then pink to red fruit. Remove first-year blooms to help root growth and encourage fruiting on 2–3-year-old wood. Needs full to partial sun, acidic to neutral soil, and adequate water. ↕ to 4ft (1.2m). Zone 3.
R. viburnifolium. Arching, spineless, evergreen shrub with long, pendent or semi-climbing, spineless shoots and broadly ovate to elliptic, aromatic, glossy, dark green leaves, to 1½in (4cm) long. In midspring, bears tiny, bell-shaped pink flowers in small, erect racemes, to 1in (2.5cm) long, followed by ovoid red fruit to ⅜in (9mm) long. ↕↔ 8ft (2.5m). S. California. ❀ (min. 41°F/5°C)

RICHEA

EPACRIDACEAE

Genus of 11 species of evergreen shrubs and small trees found in moist forest in Australia, often at high altitudes. They have crowded branches with spiraling, alternate, narrow leaves, overlapping at the bases. The small, ovoid to conical or bottle-shaped flowers are borne in terminal spikes or panicles; they are open at the bases and almost closed at the tips, quickly losing their petals and leaving the stamens and stigmas exposed. Where not hardy, grow in a cool greenhouse. In frost-free areas, grow the shrubby species at the base of a warm, sunny wall or in a shrub border; use the trees as specimen plants.
• **CULTIVATION** Under glass, grow in acidic potting mix in full light. When in growth, water freely and apply a half-strength balanced liquid fertilizer monthly; water sparingly in winter. Outdoors, grow in moist but well-

Ribes laurifolium

Ribes sanguineum 'Brocklebankii' (inset: leaf and flower detail)

Richea dracophylla

R

drained, poor to moderately fertile, humus-rich, neutral to acidic soil in full sun; shelter from cold, dry winds. Pruning group 9.
• **PROPAGATION** Surface-sow seed in containers outdoors, ideally as soon as ripe, or in spring (germination is unreliable). Root semi-ripe cuttings with bottom heat in late summer.
• **PESTS AND DISEASES** Infrequent.

R. dracophylla ▣ Medium to large shrub or small tree with sparse, erect branches. Spreading, spiraling, flexuous, lance-shaped, dark green leaves, 6–12in (15–30cm) long, with tapering, red-tinged tips, are crowded at the ends of the stems. Small, obovoid white flowers are produced in dense, upright panicles, 6–10in (15–25cm) long, in summer. ↕6–15ft (2–5m), ↔ 2–5ft (0.6–1.5m). Tasmania. ❄ (min. 41°F/5°C)

RICINUS

EUPHORBIACEAE

Genus of one species of erect, very fast-growing, mound-forming, suckering, monoecious, evergreen shrub, widely naturalized in wasteland, at roadsides, and on stony slopes, from N.E. Africa to W. Asia. It is grown mainly for its large, glossy, palmately lobed leaves. Spikes of small, cup-shaped flowers are followed by prickly, ovoid capsules. Grow as an annual in a cool greenhouse or conservatory, or as a specimen plant for summer bedding. In warmer climates, grow in a border. All parts of *R. communis*, particularly the seeds, are highly toxic if ingested; contact with the foliage may aggravate skin allergies.
• **CULTIVATION** Under glass, grow in soil-based potting mix in full light. In growth, water freely and apply a balanced liquid fertilizer monthly; water sparingly in winter. Outdoors, grow in fertile, humus-rich, well-drained soil in full sun. Stake in exposed sites. Plants grown on poor soils tend to produce flowers at the expense of vegetative growth and bear smaller leaves. Pruning group 9; plants grown under glass may need restrictive pruning.
• **PROPAGATION** Soak seed for 24 hours before sowing in late spring; sow singly into 3½in (9cm) pots, at 70°F (21°C). Plant out or pot on into 5in (13cm) pots before they become pot-bound, to prevent premature flower production. Plant out when all danger of frost has passed.

Ricinus communis

Ricinus communis 'Impala'

• **PESTS AND DISEASES** Spider mites, gray mold (*Botrytis*), seedling blight, charcoal rot, bacterial wilt, and bacterial leaf spot can be problems.

R. communis ▣ (Castor bean). Erect, branching shrub, usually grown as an annual, with alternate, very broadly ovate, deeply 5- to 12-lobed, toothed, glossy, mid-green, reddish purple, or bronze-red leaves, 6–18in (15–45cm) long. Greenish yellow flowers, to 1in (2.5cm) long, are borne in ovoid spikes, to 6in (15cm) long, in summer; the female flowers are borne above the males at the tips of the spikes, and each female has a prominent red stigma. The flowers are followed by spherical, reddish brown capsules, covered with soft brown spines. ↕ to 6ft (1.8m) or more, ↔ to 3ft (1m) as an annual; ↕ to 30ft (10m), ↔ to 12ft (4m) as a shrub. N.E. Africa to W. Asia. ❄ (min. 41°F/5°C). Heights given for cultivars are for annual growth. **'Carmencita'** is tall and well-branched, with dark bronze-red foliage and bright red female flowers; ↕6–10ft (2–3m). **'Impala'** ▣ is compact, with reddish purple foliage and yellowish green male flowers; young shoots and leaves are carmine-red; ↕4ft (1.2m). **'Red Spire'** is tall, with red stems and bronze-flushed leaves; ↕6–10ft (2–3m). **'Zanzibarensis'** is tall in habit, producing large, white-veined, mid-green leaves, 20in (50cm) long; ↕6–10ft (2–3m).

RIGIDELLA

IRIDACEAE

Genus, closely related to *Tigridia*, of 4 species of bulbous perennials from dry pine to cloud forest in Central America. They are cultivated for their iris-like, brightly colored flowers, borne in succession in spring or summer. The long, broadly lance-shaped, many-folded leaves are reduced to short, sharp-pointed, leaf-like bracts on the flowering stems. Where not hardy, grow in a cool greenhouse. In warmer areas, grow at the base of a sunny wall or in a warm site where the soil dries out in summer.
• **CULTIVATION** Plant bulbs 4in (10cm) deep in spring. Under glass, grow in deep containers of soil-based potting mix with added sharp sand, in full light. Water moderately in growth; keep completely dry in winter. Pot on in spring. Outdoors, grow in humus-rich, well-drained soil in full sun; where not hardy, lift for frost-free winter storage.
• **PROPAGATION** Sow seed at 55–64°F (13–18°C) in spring.
• **PESTS AND DISEASES** Infrequent.

R. flammea. Bulbous perennial with lance-shaped basal leaves, to 12in (30cm) long, and shorter, sheathing stem leaves. Short-lived, iris-like, semi-pendent, brilliant scarlet flowers, 4in (10cm) across, with striking purple markings at the bases of the petals, are borne in succession before the leaves in spring or early summer. ↕3–5ft (1–1.5m), PD12in (30cm). Mexico. ❄ (min. 41°F/5°C)

ROBINIA

FABACEAE

Genus of about 20 species (or only 4, according to some authorities) of deciduous, sometimes bristly or thorny trees and shrubs found in woodland and thickets in North America. They are cultivated for their alternate, pinnate leaves, and pendent racemes of pea-like flowers, borne in late spring and early summer. Grow the trees as specimen plants; shrubby species and cultivars are suitable for a large shrub border. *R. hispida* is effective grown against a sunny wall. All parts may cause severe discomfort if ingested.
• **CULTIVATION** Grow in full sun in moderately fertile, moist but well-drained soil; they will tolerate poor, dry soils. Shelter from strong winds, because the branches are brittle. Suckers from *R. pseudoacacia* may be a problem. Pruning group 1; *R. pseudoacacia* 'Frisia' also group 7. Prune in late summer or early autumn to prevent bleeding.
• **PROPAGATION** Sow seed in containers in a cold frame in autumn. Insert root cuttings or graft in winter. Remove suckers in autumn.
• **PESTS AND DISEASES** Borers, caterpillars, weevils, scale insects, whiteflies, and leaf miners can be problems, as can leaf spots, wood rot, canker, powdery mildew, *Verticillium* wilt, and heart rot.

R. fertilis see *R. hispida* var. *fertilis.*
R. hispida (Bristly locust, Rose acacia). Upright, suckering shrub with bristly shoots and pinnate, dark green leaves, to 12in (30cm) long, composed of 9–13 ovate to broadly elliptic leaflets. In late spring and early summer, bears light rose-pink flowers, 1¼in (3cm) long, in pendent racemes, to 5in (13cm) long, followed by bristly brown seed pods, 1½–2½in (4–6cm) long. ↕8ft (2.5m), ↔ 10ft (3m). S.E. US. Zone 5. **var. *fertilis***, syn. *R. fertilis*, has dense, spreading bristles on shoots and leaves, and narrow, oblong-ovate to elliptic leaflets; ↕↔ 6ft (2m). **var. *kelseyi***, syn. *R. kelseyi* (Allegheny moss locust) is similar to *R. hispida* but has bristles only on the flower stalks and raceme axes; leaves have oblong to ovate leaflets. It bears bright rose-pink flowers very freely. **'Monument'** is compact and conical, with sparsely bristly shoots and lilac-pink flowers; ↕12ft (4m).
***R.* 'Idaho'** ▣ Open, spreading tree with arching branches and pinnate, mid- to dark green leaves, to 10in (25cm) long, with 15 oval leaflets. In late spring and early summer, produces fragrant, dark

Robinia 'Idaho'

pink flowers, 1in (2.5cm) long, in pendent racemes, to 8in (20cm) long. It is sterile and does not bear seed pods. ↕40ft (12m), ↔ 30ft (10m). Zone 7.
R. kelseyi see *R. hispida* var. *kelseyi.*
R. luxurians see *R. neomexicana.*
R.* x *margaretta see *R.* x *slavinii.*
***R.* x *margaretta* 'Casque Rouge'** see *R.* x *slavinii* 'Casque Rouge'.
***R.* x *margaretta* 'Pink Cascade'** see *R.* x *slavinii* 'Casque Rouge'.
R. neomexicana, syn. *R. luxurians* (New Mexico locust). Upright, thicket-forming, spiny shrub or small tree with pinnate, hairy, blue-green leaves, to 8in (20cm) long, composed of 13–25 lance-shaped, narrowly ovate or oblong leaflets. In early summer, bears pink flowers, 1in (2.5cm) long, in pendent racemes, to 4in (10cm) long, followed by sparsely glandular brown seed pods, to 4in (10cm) long. ↕20ft (6m), ↔ 15ft (5m). New Mexico, Arizona. Zone 6.
R. pseudoacacia ▣ (Black locust). Fast-growing, suckering, broadly columnar tree with usually spiny shoots. Pinnate, dark green leaves, to 12in (30cm) long, have up to 23 lance-shaped or elliptic to ovate, blunt leaflets. In late spring and early summer, fragrant white flowers, ¾in (2cm) long, are borne in pendent racemes, to 8in (20cm) long, followed by smooth brown seed pods, 4in (10cm) long. ↕80ft (25m), ↔ 50ft (15m). E. US. Zone 4. The following selections do not flower freely. **'Appalachia'** is narrowly upright. **'Aurea'** has yellow-green leaves. **'Bessoniana'** is erect when young, later rounded; ↕50ft (15m), ↔ 30ft (10m). **'Crispa'** has smaller, narrow leaves, 8–10in (20–25cm) long.

Robinia pseudoacacia

Robinia pseudoacacia 'Frisia'

'Fastigiata' see 'Pyramidalis'. **'Frisia'** ■ has golden yellow foliage, turning yellow-green in summer, then orange-yellow in autumn; ↕ 50ft (15m), ↔ 25ft (8m). **'Inermis'** see 'Umbraculifera'. **'Pyramidalis'**, syn. 'Fastigiata', is narrowly columnar, with upright, spineless shoots; ↕ 50ft (15m), ↔ 10ft (3m). **'Tortuosa'** is slow-growing, with twisted shoots; ↕ 50ft (15m), ↔ 30ft (10m). **'Umbraculifera'**, syn. 'Inermis', has a rounded crown; ↕↔ 20ft (6m).

R.* x *slavinii (*R. hispida* var. *kelseyi* x *R. pseudoacacia*), syn. *R.* x *margaretta*. Open, rounded, spiny tree or shrub with bristly young branches and pinnate, dark green leaves, to 8in (20cm) long, composed of up to 19 ovate leaflets. Fragrant, lilac-pink to dark pink flowers, ¾in (2cm) long, are borne in pendent racemes, to 6in (15cm) long, in late spring; they are followed by brown, warty seed pods, to 4in (10cm) long. ↕↔ 30ft (10m). Garden origin. Zone 5. **'Casque Rouge'**, syn. *R.* x *margaretta* 'Casque Rouge', *R.* x *margaretta* 'Pink Cascade', has dark purple-pink flowers.

▷ ***Rochea*** see *Crassula*

RODGERSIA

SAXIFRAGACEAE

Genus of 6 species of vigorous, clump-forming, rhizomatous perennials occurring in moist woodland and scrub, and at streamsides, in the mountains of Burma, China, Korea, and Japan. They have large, long-stalked, palmate or pinnate, sometimes bronze-tinted, basal leaves, in some species turning shades of red and brown in autumn. In summer, tall stems bear star-shaped, petalless, white or pink flowers, each ¼–⅜in (6–9mm) across, in large, fluffy, pyramidal panicles; they are followed by dark red or brown, capsular fruits. Grow near water, in a bog garden or moist border, or use for naturalizing at woodland margins.

Rodgersia aesculifolia

• **CULTIVATION** Grow in humus-rich, moist soil in full sun or partial shade. They resent drought, but will tolerate drier conditions with more shade.
• **PROPAGATION** Sow seed in containers in a cold frame in spring. Divide in early spring.
• **PESTS AND DISEASES** Slugs can occur.

R. aesculifolia ■ Clump-forming, rhizomatous perennial producing horse-chestnut-like, palmate, crinkled, mid-green leaves, to 10in (25cm) long. The leaves have densely woolly, red-brown stalks and veins, and usually 7, sometimes 5–9, obovate, toothed leaflets. In midsummer, bears many star-shaped, white or pink flowers in large panicles, to 24in (60cm) long. ↕ to 6ft (2m), ↔ 3ft (1m). N. China. Zone 5.

Rodgersia podophylla

R. japonica see *R. podophylla.*
R. pinnata. Rhizomatous, clump-forming perennial producing pinnate, or partially pinnate or palmate, crinkled, heavily veined, glossy, dark green leaves, to 36in (90cm) long; leaves have reddish green stalks and 5–9 obovate-inversely-lance-shaped leaflets. In mid- and late summer, reddish green stems produce star-shaped, yellowish white, pink, or red flowers in panicles 12–28in (30–70cm) long. ↕ to 4ft (1.2m),↔ 30in (75cm). China (Sichuan, Yunnan). Zone 5. **'Superba'** ■ has purplish bronze young leaves, sometimes with fewer leaflets than the species, and bright pink flowers.
R. podophylla ■ syn. *R. japonica.* Clump-forming, rhizomatous perennial with palmate leaves, to 16in (40cm) long, composed of usually 5 large,

Rodgersia sambucifolia

jagged, obovate, 3- to 5-lobed leaflets, crinkled and bronze when young, becoming smoother, glossy, and mid-green, with brown hairs. The leaves turn bronze-red in autumn. In mid- and late summer, bears star-shaped, creamy green flowers in panicles 12in (30cm) long. ↕ to 5ft (1.5m), ↔ to 6ft (1.8m). Korea, Japan. Zone 5.
R. sambucifolia ■ Clump-forming, rhizomatous perennial with elder-like, pinnate, hairy, dark green leaves, to 30in (75cm) long, with usually 7, sometimes 3–11, oblong-lance-shaped, toothed leaflets. In early and midsummer, bears star-shaped, white or pink flowers in dense panicles, to 18in (45cm) long, arching at the tips. ↕↔ 36in (90cm). W. China. Zone 5.
R. tabularis see *Astilboides tabularis.*

RODRIGUEZIA

ORCHIDACEAE

Genus of about 30 species of evergreen, rhizomatous, epiphytic orchids from warm, moist, forest areas of Central and South America. They have fine, aerial, sometimes mat-forming roots; ovoid pseudobulbs partially enveloped by overlapping leaf sheaths; and narrowly strap-shaped to oblong, leathery, mid-green leaves. They are grown mainly for their fragrant flowers, borne in pendent racemes arising from the bases of the pseudobulbs.
• **CULTIVATION** Intermediate-growing orchids. Grow in small containers of epiphytic orchid potting mix made with fine-grade bark, or grow epiphytically on bark. Provide full light with shade from hot sun, and high humidity. In summer, water freely, mist daily, and apply a balanced liquid fertilizer at every third watering; water more sparingly in winter. See also p.46.
• **PROPAGATION** Divide when the plant fills the pot and flows over the sides.
• **PESTS AND DISEASES** Fungal and bacterial spots, cymbidium mosaic virus, mealybugs, whiteflies, scale insects, and spider mites occur.

R. venusta. Epiphytic orchid with compressed, ovoid pseudobulbs, each producing several narrowly oblong, leathery leaves, 6in (15cm) long. Arching racemes of many very fragrant, pure white flowers, 1¼in (3cm) across, with yellow-marked lips, are borne in autumn. ↕↔ 6in (15cm). E. Brazil. ❄ (min. 55°F/13°C; max. 86°F/30°C)

Rodgersia pinnata 'Superba'

ROHDEA

LILIACEAE

Genus of one species of rhizomatous perennial from woodland in S.W. China and Japan, grown for its basal rosettes of fleshy, dark green leaves, and erect spikes of narrowly bell-shaped flowers, borne in early spring. Grow in a woodland garden or damp, shady border.

• **CULTIVATION** Grow in humus-rich, moist, moderately fertile soil in deep or partial shade.

• **PROPAGATION** Sow seed in containers in a cold frame in autumn. Divide in spring or autumn.

• **PESTS AND DISEASES** Prone to damage by slugs, snails, and vine weevil larvae.

R. japonica (Lily of China). Rosetted, rhizomatous perennial with thick, semi-erect, usually inversely lance-shaped, leathery, dark green leaves, 11–18in (28–45cm) long. In early spring, erect stems bear dense spikes, 1–2in (2.5–5cm) long, of narrowly bell-shaped, greenish white flowers, to ¼in (6mm) across, followed by fleshy red berries. ↕10in (25cm), ↔ 8in (20cm). S.W. China, Japan. Zone 7b.

ROMANZOFFIA

HYDROPHYLLACEAE

Genus of 4 species of low-growing, clump-forming perennials, with tuber-like roots, from shaded, rocky, alpine, or woodland habitats in W. North America and the Aleutian Islands. They produce tufts of rounded or kidney-shaped, lobed or deeply scalloped leaves, which die back after flowering and re-emerge in autumn. The bell- or funnel-shaped flowers, each with 5 rounded petal lobes and conspicuous anthers, are borne in raceme-like cymes in early summer. Suitable for a woodland garden or rock garden, or in an alpine house.

• **CULTIVATION** Grow in moist but well-drained, humus-rich, neutral to acidic soil in deep or partial shade.

• **PROPAGATION** Sow seed in containers as soon as ripe. Divide in early spring.

• **PESTS AND DISEASES** Susceptible to damage by slugs and snails.

R. sitchensis, syn. *R. suksdorfii.* Tufted perennial with swollen roots and kidney-shaped, deeply lobed, glossy, dark green leaves, 1in (2.5cm) long. In early summer, bears small, funnel-shaped white flowers, ⅜in (9mm) long, with yellow petal bases and deep yellow anthers, in branching, terminal, raceme-like cymes, to 6in (15cm) long. ↕12in (30cm), ↔ to 6in (15cm). Alaska to Montana. Zone 6.

R. suksdorfii see *R. sitchensis.*

ROMNEYA

Matilija poppy, Tree poppy

PAPAVERACEAE

Genus of 2 species of suckering, woody-based, subshrubby perennials found in chaparral and sage scrub in S. California and N. Mexico. They are grown for their glaucous foliage and fragrant, showy white flowers. The leaves are alternate, and pinnatifid to pinnatisect. The poppy-like, solitary, terminal, 6-petaled flowers, with bright yellow

Romneya coulteri 'White Cloud'

stamens, are borne in summer. Grow in a border or, where marginally hardy, against a warm, sunny wall.

• **CULTIVATION** Grow in fertile, well-drained soil in full sun, sheltered from strong, cold winds. Provide a deep, dry winter mulch. Tree poppies are sometimes difficult to establish and resent transplanting, but may eventually spread vigorously by suckers. Usually cut back to the base in winter; in warmer areas, pruning group 6.

• **PROPAGATION** Sow seed at 55–61°F (13–16°C) in spring. Root basal cuttings in spring; insert root cuttings in winter.

• **PESTS AND DISEASES** *Verticillium* wilt and caterpillars may be a problem.

R. coulteri. Upright, deciduous subshrub producing ovate to rounded, pinnatifid, intensely glaucous, gray-green leaves, to 5in (13cm) long, with 3–5 lance-shaped to ovate lobes. Solitary, shallowly cup-shaped white flowers, to 5in (13cm) across, with prominent yellow stamens, are borne over a long period in summer. ↕3–8ft (1–2.5m), ↔ indefinite. Zone 7b. **'White Cloud'** ▣ is vigorous and fast-spreading, with very glaucous foliage.

ROMULEA

IRIDACEAE

Genus of about 80 species of small, cormous perennials from a range of habitats, including mountainous areas and coastal cliff tops in Europe, the Mediterranean, N. Africa, and South Africa. They are grown for their colorful, crocus-like flowers, produced

Romulea bulbocodium

Romulea sabulosa

in spring. The flowers often open only at midday, closing in the evening. Each plant produces up to 6 erect, or recurved and arching, thread-like, basal leaves, 2–16in (5–40cm) long. Grow in a sunny rock garden, or in containers in an alpine house or cool greenhouse.

• **CULTIVATION** Plant corms 3in (8cm) deep in autumn. Under glass, grow in soil-based potting mix with additional grit, in full light. In the growing season, water moderately and apply a balanced liquid fertilizer monthly. After flowering, reduce water gradually; keep completely dry when dormant in summer. Outdoors, grow in moderately fertile, well-drained soil in full sun.

• **PROPAGATION** Sow seed at 45–54°F (6–12°C) in autumn, or remove offsets when dormant.

• **PESTS AND DISEASES** Infrequent.

***R. bulbocodioides* of gardens** see *R. flava.*

R. bulbocodium ▣ syn. *R. grandiflora.* Small, cormous perennial with recurved, linear, channeled, mid-green, basal leaves. In spring, stems bear up to 5 upright, funnel-shaped, pale to deep lilac-purple flowers, 1in (2.5cm) long, with white or yellow centers. ↕2–4in (5–10cm), PD2in (5cm). Portugal, N.W. Spain, Bulgaria. (❀ min. 35°F/2°C). **var. *crocea*** has yellow flowers.

R. flava, syn. *R. bulbocodioides* of gardens. Cormous perennial with upright, sheathing, linear, mid-green, basal leaves. In spring, produces up to 4 solitary, funnel-shaped, yellowish green, sometimes white or blue flowers, 1¼–1½in (3–4cm) long, with yellow centers. ↕4in (10cm), PD2in (5cm). South Africa (Western Cape, Northern Cape, Eastern Cape). (❀ min. 41°F/5°C)

R. grandiflora see *R. bulbocodium.*

R. longituba see *R. macowanii* var. *alticola.*

R. macowanii* var. *alticola, syn. *R. longituba.* Cormous perennial with erect or recurved, linear, mid-green, basal leaves. In summer, stems bear up to 3 tubular, bright yellow flowers, 1¼–2½in (3–6cm) long, with orange-yellow centers. ↕3in (8cm), PD2in (5cm). Lesotho (Drakensberg Mountains), South Africa. (❀ min. 41°F/5°C)

R. requienii. Cormous perennial with arching to almost prostrate, linear, mid-green, basal leaves. Stems of up to 3 funnel-shaped violet flowers, 2in (5cm) long, sometimes with darker violet veining and with paler violet or white centers, are borne in spring. ↕↔ 5in (13cm), PD2in (5cm). Mediterranean, France (Corsica), Italy (Sardinia). (❀ min. 41°F/5°C)

R. sabulosa ▣ Showy, cormous perennial with upright or recurved, linear, mid-green, basal leaves. In early spring and summer, stems bear up to 4 funnel-shaped flowers, 2in (5cm) long; the flowers are shiny, bright scarlet to ruby-red, with black centers, sometimes with paler margins, and open wide in the sun. ↕4–8in (10–20cm), PD2in (5cm). South Africa (Western Cape, Eastern Cape). (❀ min. 41°F/5°C)

RONDELETIA

RUBIACEAE

Genus of 125–150 species of evergreen shrubs and trees from tropical woodland in Central and South America. The simple, leathery to paper-thin leaves are borne in opposite pairs or whorls of 3. They are grown for their small, tubular to salverform, sometimes fragrant flowers, each with 4–6 spreading petal lobes, which are borne in large, axillary or terminal panicles, cymes, or corymbs. Where temperatures fall below 54°F (12°C), grow in a temperate or warm greenhouse. In warmer areas, grow in a shrub border.

• **CULTIVATION** Under glass, grow in soil-based potting mix with added leaf mold, in full light with shade from hot sun. Water freely in growth, and apply a balanced liquid fertilizer monthly; water moderately in winter. Outdoors, grow in fertile, moist, well-drained soil in sun or partial shade. Pruning group 9; plants under glass may need restrictive pruning.

• **PROPAGATION** Root semi-ripe cuttings with bottom heat in summer.

• **PESTS AND DISEASES** Prone to spider mites, mealybugs, and whiteflies.

R. amoena ▣ Bushy, rounded shrub or small tree with smooth to downy stems and elliptic or ovate-oblong leaves, 3–6in (8–15cm) long, glossy, mid-green above, brown-hairy or hairless beneath. In summer, bears axillary or terminal cymes or panicles, 2–6in (5–15cm) long, of small, salverform, fragrant, pink or white flowers with bearded yellow throats. ↕5–15ft (1.5–5m) or more, ↔ 5–12ft (1.5–4m). Mexico, Guatemala, Panama. (❀ min. 54°F/12°C)

▷ ***Rooksbya euphorbioides*** see *Neobuxbaumia euphorbioides*

Rondeletia amoena

R

ROSA

Rose

ROSACEAE

Genus of about 150 species of semi-evergreen or deciduous shrubs and perennial climbers, some of which have been in cultivation for many centuries. They are found in a wide variety of habitats in Asia, Europe, N. Africa, and North America. Roses have erect, arching, scrambling, or sometimes trailing, often prickly stems. The alternate leaves range from 1in (2.5cm) long in miniature roses to 7in (18cm) or more long in bush, shrub, and climbing roses; each leaf usually has 3, 5, or 7 sometimes toothed, variably shaped leaflets.

Roses are grown for their attractive and often very fragrant flowers, borne mainly in early summer and autumn, and sometimes also for their fruits, known as hips. The flowers are solitary or borne in corymbs (referred to in this account as clusters), are sometimes remontant, and vary greatly in color, size, and form (see panel below). Roses are suitable for a range of garden situations: as specimen plants or standards, for a shrub or mixed border, as hedges, or as climbers to clothe walls, trees, pillars, pergolas, and arbors. Groups of roses are often grown together in a single bed; a well-chosen mix of cultivars ensures a long display. Miniature roses are suitable for a rock garden, raised bed, or containers. The flowers of roses, especially modern roses, are popular for cutting.

Many modern rose cultivars are known by their trademark names rather than by their registered cultivar names; where this is the case, the plant is listed below under its trademark name, with the cultivar name given as a synonym. For reasons of space, these cultivar names have not been cross-referenced.

Rose species and cultivars are divided into old garden roses, consisting of classes in existence before 1867 and all species, and modern roses, introduced since 1867. The many subgroups of both are described below.

Species, or wild, roses (including interspecific hybrids, which share most of the characteristics of their parent species) are either shrubs or climbers, mostly bearing single, 5-petaled, often fragrant flowers from spring to early summer, usually in one flush on short shoots from second-year wood; the flowers are followed by red or black hips.

Cultivars number many thousands and are very varied in habit. In the subgroup descriptions below, leaflet lengths are defined as small, up to 1½in (4cm); medium-sized, 1½–3in (4–8cm); and large, over 3in (8cm). The flowers, in a range of shapes, are borne mainly in summer, over a longer period than in species roses; they are often remontant. Flowers are either single (having 8 petals or fewer), semi-double (8–20 petals), double (20 petals or more), or fully double (over 30 petals).

ROSE FLOWER FORMS

Flat – Open, usually single or semi-double flowers with petals that are almost flat.
Cupped – Open, single to fully double flowers with petals that curve outward and upward from the centeR.
Rounded – Usually double or fully double flowers with even-sized, overlapping petals forming a bowl shape or more rounded form.
High-centered – Semi-double to fully double flowers with high, tight centers.
Urn-shaped – Semi-double to fully double flowers with inner petals that curve inward to form an urn shape, and outer petals that are flatter and more spreading.
Rosette-shaped – Almost flat, double or fully double flowers with slightly overlapping, often uneven petals.
Quartered-rosette – Almost flat, double or fully double flowers with the petals, often of uneven size, arranged so that the flower appears divided into 4 sections.
Pompon – Small, rounded, double or fully double flowers, usually in clusters, with masses of small petals.

FLAT

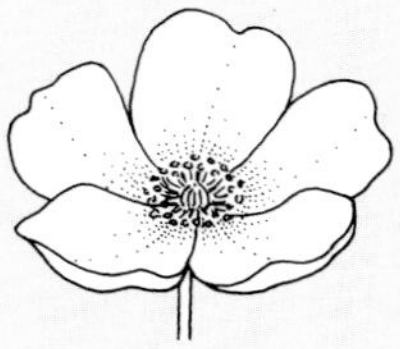
CUPPED

ROUNDED

HIGH-CENTERED

URN-SHAPED

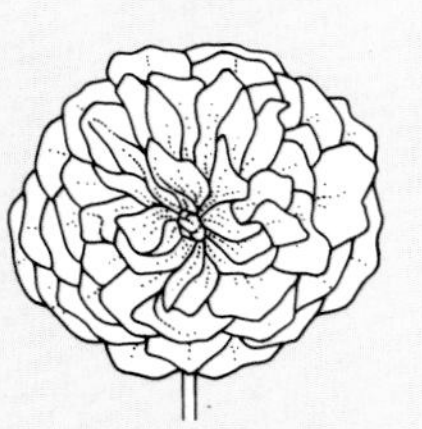
ROSETTE-SHAPED

QUARTERED-ROSETTE

POMPON

Old Garden Roses

Alba – Free-branching shrub roses, varying greatly in size, with only a few prickles on the stems. They have grayish green leaves with medium-sized to large, oval leaflets, and bear clusters of 5–7 semi- to fully double, scented flowers in spring or early summer, on shoots from second-year wood. Very hardy. Most are suitable for a border, as hedges, or as specimen plants.

Bourbon – Large, open, remontant shrub roses, often with long, smooth or prickly stems, which may be trained as climbers. They have often glossy leaves with medium-sized, oval leaflets, and most bear numerous scented, double or fully double flowers, usually in clusters of 3, in flushes in spring or early summer and usually autumn. Flowers are borne on short shoots from second-year wood and on new wood. Ideal for a border, or for training on a fence, wall, or pillar.

Boursault – Climbing roses with long, arching, usually smooth stems, and dark green leaves with medium-sized to large, oval leaflets. They bear semi-double or double, slightly scented flowers, singly or in clusters of 3, in spring or early summer, on short shoots from second-year wood. Grow against a sheltered wall or fence.

Centifolia (commonly called cabbage roses or Provence roses) – Lax, prickly shrub roses producing matte, dark green leaves with small to medium-sized, oval leaflets. Double or fully double, often scented flowers, are borne singly or in clusters of 3 in spring or early summer, on shoots from second-year wood. Grow in a border.

China – Spindly, remontant shrub roses with mostly smooth stems, bearing only a few reddish brown prickles, and glossy leaves consisting of small to medium-sized, lance-shaped leaflets. They bear single to fully double, sometimes scented flowers, singly or in clusters of 3–13, in flushes from spring to autumn. Flowers are borne on short shoots from second-year wood and on new wood. Use in a border or grow against a low wall in a sheltered site in Zone 6.

Damask – Open shrub roses with prickly stems, and downy leaves with medium-sized to large, oval leaflets. They bear semi- to fully double, often very fragrant flowers, singly or in loose clusters of 5–7, mainly in spring or early summer, on shoots from second-year wood; a few also flower on new wood in autumn. Ideal for a border or training on a support.

Eglanteria – Vigorous, free-branching shrub roses with usually prickly stems, and sweetly scented (often apple-scented), dark green leaves composed of small to medium-sized, oval leaflets. In summer, they bear single to double, usually scented flowers, singly or in clusters of up to 7, on short shoots from second-year wood. Use as hedges, as specimen plants, or in a large border.

Gallica – Shrub roses of dense, free-branching habit, with usually prickly stems, and mostly dull, dark green leaves with medium-sized, oval leaflets. In spring or early summer, they bear single to fully double, mostly scented flowers, often in clusters of 3, on shoots from second-year wood. Use in a bed or as hedges.

Hybrid Perpetual – Free-branching, remontant shrub roses with upright, prickly growth, and dark green leaves with medium to large, oval leaflets. They bear often scented, fully double flowers, singly or in clusters of 3, in flushes from spring to autumn, on shoots from second-year wood and on new wood. Ideal for a bed or border.

Hybrid Sempervirens – Vigorous, semi-evergreen climbing or rambler roses with shiny, light green leaves composed of small to medium-sized, lance-shaped leaflets. Arching, prickly stems bear clusters of 3–15 unscented, semi- to fully double flowers in summer, on short stems from second-year wood. Use to clothe a fence or pergola, or in informal, unconfined plantings.

Hybrid Spinosissima – Suckering shrub roses, selections or hybrids of *R. spinosissima*, of low, spreading, rarely upright habit, with prickly stems and dark green leaves consisting of small to medium-sized, oval leaflets. The single to double, occasionally scented flowers are solitary or borne in clusters of 3 or more, on short stems from second-year wood, usually in spring. Suitable for a bed or border.

Moss – Often lax shrub roses with moss-like, furry, fragrant growth on the calyces, and mostly dark green leaves with medium-sized to large, oval leaflets. Semi- to fully double, usually fragrant flowers, often in clusters of 3 or more, are borne on very thorny shoots from second-year wood in spring or early summer. Suitable for a bed or border.

Noisette – Remontant climbing roses with smooth stems, and usually glossy leaves consisting of medium-sized to large, oval or lance-shaped leaflets. They bear large clusters of 3–15 slightly spice-scented, normally double to fully double flowers, in flushes from spring to autumn. Flowers are borne on shoots from second-year wood, occasionally on new wood. Grow against a sheltered wal in Zone 6.

Portland – Upright, compact, remontant shrub roses with prickly stems, and usually dark green leaves composed of medium to large, oval leaflets. Semi- to fully double, usually scented flowers are borne singly or in clusters of 3, in flushes from spring to autumn, mainly on shoots from second-year wood. Grow in a bed or border.

Tea and Climbing Tea – Remontant shrub and climbing roses with smooth to prickly stems, sometimes bearing a few large red prickles, and medium-sized, glossy, light or sometimes dark green leaves with lance-shaped leaflets. Semi- to fully double, spice-scented flowers are borne singly or in clusters of 3, in flushes from spring to autumn, on shoots from second-year wood and on new wood. Grow in a sheltered site in a bed or border, or against a wall in Zone 6.

Modern Roses

Climber – Often vigorous climbing roses with prickly, arching, stiff stems and often dense, glossy, mid- to dark green foliage. They bear often scented flowers in a variety of forms, singly or in clusters of 3–7 or more. Some bloom in spring or early summer only, on short shoots from second-year wood; many are remontant and also flower on new

wood. Train against a wall or fence, or use to cover garden structures. Designations include ***Large-flowered Climber***, Hybrid Wichurana, ***Climbing Floribunda***, ***Climbing Grandiflora***, ***Climbing Hybrid Tea***, and ***Climbing Polyantha Floribunda*** – Everblooming, free-branching shrub roses of upright or bushy habit, usually with prickly stems, and glossy, dark green leaves composed of medium-sized, oval or lance-shaped leaflets. The single to fully double, sometimes scented flowers are usually in clusters of 3–25, rarely solitary, and borne continuously from summer to autumn on shoots from second-year wood and on new wood. Use in a border or as hedges.
Groundcover – Spreading and trailing shrub roses, mostly with prickly stems, producing often glossy leaves with small to medium-sized, lance-shaped leaflets. They bear clusters of numerous single to fully double, sometimes scented flowers; some flower in summer only, on short shoots from second-year wood; some are remontant, and also flower on new wood. Many bear flowers all along the stems. Ideal for a bed, bank, or container, or for trailing over walls.
Hybrid Rugosa – Hardy shrub roses with tough, wrinkled, usually bright green leaves with medium to large, oval or lance-shaped leaflets and prickly stems. Most bear single or semi-double, scented flowers, in clusters of 3–11, throughout summer and autumn, on shoots from second-year wood and on new wood. They are often followed by tomato-like, usually red hips. Use as hedges, for a bed or border, or as specimen plants.
Hybrid Tea and Grandiflora – Remontant, free-branching shrub roses of upright or bushy habit, with usually prickly stems, and glossy or matte, mid- to dark green leaves with medium-sized to large, oval or lance-shaped leaflets. Large, usually double, often scented flowers are solitary or borne in clusters of 3–6 in flushes from summer to autumn, on shoots from second-year wood and on new wood. Use as hedges or in a formal bed, and for cut flowers.
Miniature and Mini-Flora – Remontant shrub roses with very compact, sparsely prickly, short stems, and leaves with very small, usually lance-shaped leaflets. Sprays of 3–11 tiny, single to fully double, rarely scented flowers are borne in flushes from summer to autumn, on very short shoots from second-year wood and on new wood. Mini-Flora plant and its blooms are larger than the Miniature but smaller than the average Floribunda and exhibit the same variety of colors and forms as the miniatures. Both are ideal for edging paths, or for a raised bed, rock garden, or container.
Climbing Miniature – Remontant climbing roses with restrained, sparsely prickly growth, and leaves consisting of very small, lance-shaped leaflets. Clusters of 3–9 tiny, single to fully double, rarely scented flowers are borne in flushes from summer to autumn, on shoots from second-year wood and on new wood. Grow against a low wall, fence, or pillar.
Polyantha – Remontant, compact-growing shrub roses with sparsely prickly stems, and glossy leaves with small, lance-shaped leaflets. Sprays of many small, single to double, rarely scented flowers are borne in flushes from late spring or early summer to autumn, on short shoots from second-year wood and on new wood. Suitable for a bed or border, as hedges, and for containers.
Rambler – This class has been disbanded and its members ave been reclassed as either Large-flowered Climber or Hybrid Wichurana.
Shrub – A very diverse group, including modern hybrids of species, hybrid musks, hybrid kordesii, and English roses. They are usually larger than hybrid tea roses, with often prickly stems, and produce leaves with medium-sized to large, oval or lance-shaped leaflets. The usually scented, single to fully double flowers are borne in few- to many-flowered clusters, sometimes singly, from spring to autumn; some bloom in spring or early summer only, from second-year wood; most are remontant and also flower on new wood. Ideal for a border or bed, or as hedges; some are also excellent specimen plants.

Rosa 'Abraham Darby'

• **HARDINESS** Roses may be grown in all but tropical regions, but cold tolerance varies widely within the genus. In the colder parts of their range, most modern roses and some of the old garden roses require specific planting depths and winter protection regimes, which are beyond the scope of this book. See entries for specific zones.
• **CULTIVATION** Roses tolerate a wide range of conditions, but usually prefer an open site in full sun. They thrive on moderately fertile, humus-rich, moist but well-drained soil. The best time for planting is late autumn or early spring, when the ground is not frozen. For best flowering, apply a balanced fertilizer and mulch in late winter or early spring. In spring and summer, apply a balanced liquid fertilizer every 3 weeks. The height and spread measurements in the descriptions at left are for pruned plants; unpruned, roses grow much larger.
Most roses offered for sale are budded on the rootstock of a wild rose, such as *R. multiflora*, to ensure vigorous growth. The rootstock may produce shoots, known as "suckers," which should be removed at their point of origin as soon as they appear. To identify a sucker, check that it originates from the rootstock itself, and not from above the point where the plant was budded.
• **PROPAGATION** Root softwood cuttings from first flush of bloom to summer; root hardwood cuttings in autumn. Bud in summer. Sow seed in containers in autumn.
• **PESTS AND DISEASES** Susceptible to aphids, leafhoppers, spider mites, scale insects, caterpillars, sawfly larvae, cane borers, Japanese beetles, rose stem girdlers, thrips, rose chafers, rose midges, rose slugs, and leaf-cutting bees; rabbits and deer may cause damage. Prone to black spot, rust, powdery mildew, dieback, canker, crown gall, viruses, and downy mildew.

***R.* 'Abraham Darby'** ▣ English shrub rose with a strong, bushy habit and large, glossy, dark green leaves. Cupped, fully double, fruit-scented, apricot-pink flowers, 4½in (11cm) across, are borne from spring to autumn. ↕↔ 5ft (1.5m). Zone 5b.
***R.* 'Adelaide Hoodless'.** Floriferous shrub rose with glossy, dark green leaves. In spring and autumn, bears cupped, semi-double red flowers, to 3in (8cm) across, in large clusters. ↕↔ 3ft (1m). Zone 2b.

PRUNING REQUIREMENTS

On planting, shorten thick roots to 10in (25cm) and remove damaged ones. Reduce top-growth to 3–5 strong shoots, and cut these back to outward-facing buds: to 3–6in (8–15cm) above ground for large- and cluster-flowered bushes and dwarf variants; to 16in (40cm) for ramblers; to 8–12in (20–30cm) for other groups. For climbers and standards, remove only dead, diseased, damaged, weak, or crossing shoots.

When in growth, remove dead, damaged, and diseased wood, suckers, and blind shoots, and prune as below. Deadhead all roses unless hips are wanted. In autumn, trim long shoots back by 6–12in (15–30cm) to reduce wind rock. Avoid pruning in frosty weather when roses are dormant; delay until early spring in areas with severe winters. Prune in the cooler months in warm climates, to simulate dormancy.

The pruning chart below gives specific advice for individual rose groups. For standard roses, prune according to the type of rose that forms the head; leave weeping standards unpruned on planting and for 2 subsequent years, to develop their form.

GROUP	SEASON	FOR MAINTENANCE	FOR RENEWAL
HYBRID TEA, GRANDIFLORA, TEA, HYBRID PERPETUAL	Late winter or early spring	Cut back main stems to 8–10in (20–25cm) above ground in temperate climates; to 18–24in (45–60cm) in warm climates. Reduce sideshoots to 2 or 3 buds or 4–6in (10–15cm). Remove weak, spindly shoots.	Cut back ⅓ of oldest stems almost to the base; repeat for rest of old stems over next 2 or 3 years.
FLORIBUNDA, MINIATURE, POLYANTHA	Late winter or early spring	Cut back main stems to 10–18in (25–45cm) above ground; reduce sideshoots to 2 or 3 buds. Cut back stems and sideshoots of dwarf cultivars and miniature bushes by ⅓–½.	As above.
CLIMBERS (INC. MINIATURE CULTIVARS), BOURSAULT, NOISETTE, CLIMBING BOURBON, CLIMBING TEA	Late winter or early spring	In the first 2 years, cut out only dead, diseased, or damaged wood; train stems onto wires or other, preferably horizontal supports. From year 3, prune main shoots to within designated area for growth; reduce sideshoots by ⅔, or to 3 or 4 buds.	Cut back 1 or 2 of oldest stems to 12–18in (30–45cm) above ground. Repeat every 1–3 years.
HYBRID SEMPERVIRENS	Summer, after flowering	In the first 2 years, train stems onto support; reduce sideshoots only, by ⅔ or to 2–4 buds. In year 3, reduce sideshoots as before, and begin renewal pruning.	Cut out ¼–⅓ of flowered stems at the base. New shoots arise from base.
GROUNDCOVER	Late winter or early spring	Cut back to outward-facing buds to confine to designated area for growth. Shorten sideshoots if overcrowded.	Cut out ⅕–¼ of oldest flowered stems.
SPECIES, SHRUB, RUGOSA	Summer, after flowering	For non-remontant roses, prune main stems lightly, or cut back by up to ⅓, as necessary; reduce sideshoots by ½–⅔. For remontant roses, see below.	As above.
BOURBON, CHINA, PORTLAND; & remontant roses of group above	Late winter or early spring	As for category above, but during the dormant season.	As above.
ALBA, CENTIFOLIA, DAMASK, MOSS, EGLANTERIA, HYBRID SPINOSISSIMA	Summer	Immediately after flowering, prune main stems lightly or cut back by ¼–⅓, as necessary; reduce sideshoots by ⅔.	Cut out up to ¼ of oldest stems; cut back rest by ⅓.
GALLICA	Summer	Cut back overlong shoots by up to ⅓; reduce sideshoots by ⅔.	Cut out 1 or 2 of oldest stems every 1–3 years.

Rosa 'Agnes'

Rosa 'Alba Maxima'

Rosa 'Albéric Barbier'

Rosa 'Albertine'

Rosa 'Alec's Red'

Rosa 'Alister Stella Gray'

Rosa 'Aloha'

Rosa 'Alpine Sunset'

Rosa 'Amber Queen'

Rosa 'American Pillar'

Rosa 'Angela Rippon'

Rosa 'Anisley Dickson'

***R.* 'Agnes'** ▣ Rugosa rose with upright stems, dark green leaves, and cupped, double, scented, light yellow flowers, 4in (10cm) across, which are produced in spring. ↕ 6ft (2m), ↔ 4ft (1.2m). Zone 3.

***R.* 'Aimée Vibert'**, syn. *R.* 'Bouquet de la Mariée'. Noisette climbing rose with long stems and glossy, dark green leaves. Cupped, fully double, lightly scented white flowers, 3in (8cm) across, are borne in large clusters from spring to autumn. May be grown as a shrub. ↕ 10–15ft (3–5m), ↔ 10ft (3m). Zone 6.

***R.* 'Alba Maxima'** ▣ syn. *R.* x *alba* 'Maxima' (Great double white rose, Jacobite rose, White rose of York). Alba rose of vigorous, upright habit, with grayish green leaves. Flat, double, sweet-scented, creamy white flowers, 3in (8cm) across, are borne in spring or early summer. ↕ 7ft (2.2m), ↔ 5ft (1.5m). Zone 4.

***R.* 'Alba Semiplena'**, syn. *R.* x *alba* 'Semiplena'. Alba rose of vigorous, bushy habit, with grayish green leaves. In spring or early summer, produces flat, semi-double, scented white flowers, 3in (8cm) across. ↕ 7ft (2.2m), ↔ 5ft (1.5m). Zone 4.

***R.* 'Albéric Barbier'** ▣ Vigorous, semi-evergreen rambler with pendent growth and glossy, dark green leaves. Clusters of rosette-shaped, fully double, slightly fragrant, creamy white flowers, 3in (8cm) across, aging to pure white, are produced in spring. ↕ to 15ft (5m), ↔ 10ft (3m). Zone 6.

***R.* 'Albertine'** ▣ Vigorous, rampant, large-flowered climber with arching, prickly, reddish green stems and mid-green leaves. Rounded to cupped, fully double, sweetly scented, light salmon-pink flowers, 3in (8cm) across, are borne freely in early summer. ↕ to 15ft (5m), ↔ 12ft (4m). Zone 6.

***R.* 'Alec's Red'** ▣ Hybrid tea rose with mid-green leaves and high-centered, fully double, strongly fragrant red flowers, 6in (15cm) across, borne from spring to autumn. ↕ 3ft (1m), ↔ 24in (60cm). Zone 6.

***R.* 'Alexander'** ▣ Vigorous hybrid tea rose with shiny, dark green foliage. Urn-shaped, double, bright red flowers, 5in (13cm) across, often with scalloped petals, are borne on long stems from spring to autumn. ↕ to 6ft (2m), ↔ 32in (80cm). Zone 6.

***R.* 'Alister Stella Gray'** ▣ syn. *R.* 'Golden Rambler'. Noisette climbing rose with long, vigorous, arching stems and mid-green foliage. Quartered-rosette, fully double, musk-scented flowers, 2½in (6cm) across, yolk-yellow fading to white, are borne freely from spring to autumn. ↕ to 15ft (5m), ↔ 10ft (3m). Zone 6.

***R.* 'Aloha'** ▣ Strong-stemmed hybrid tea climber with leathery, dark green leaves. Produces rounded, fully double, sweetly scented, rose-pink and salmon-pink flowers, 3½in (9cm) across, from summer to autumn. ↕ to 10ft (3m), ↔ 8ft (2.5m). Zone 6.

***R.* 'Alpine Sunset'** ▣ Hybrid tea rose of neat habit, with glossy, light green leaves. From spring to autumn, produces rounded, fully double, fragrant, light peach-yellow flowers, 7in (18cm) across, edged pink. ↕↔ 3ft (1m). Zone 6.

***R.* 'Altissimo'.** Climber with dark green leaves and cupped, single, bright red flowers, 5in (13cm) across, showing yellow stamens, borne from spring to autumn. ↕ 10ft (3m), ↔ 8ft (2.5m). Zone 6.

***R.* 'Amanda'** see *R.* 'Red Ace'.

***R.* 'Amber Queen'** ▣ syn. *R.* 'Prinz Eugen van Savoyen'. Floribunda rose of neat, spreading habit, with leathery, dark green foliage, reddish green when young. Cupped, fully double, fragrant, amber-yellow flowers, 3in (8cm) across, are produced from spring to autumn. ↕ 3ft (1m), ↔ 24in (60cm). Zone 6.

***R.* 'America'.** Free-branching, large-flowered climber producing mid-green leaves. From spring to autumn, bears cupped, fully double, fragrant, coral- to salmon-pink flowers, 4in (10cm) across. ↕ to 12ft (4m), ↔ 8ft (2.5m). Zone 6.

***R.* 'American Pillar'** ▣ Rampant, large-flowered climber with long stems and leathery, glossy, mid-green foliage. Large clusters of cupped, single, carmine-red flowers, 2in (5cm) across, with white eyes, are borne freely in early summer, followed by spherical red hips. Superb when trained as a pillar. ↕ to 15ft (5m), ↔ 12ft (4m). Zone 6.

***R.* 'Amy Grant'.** Low, upright miniflora, with medium green, glossy foliage, has few prickles, small and slightly hooked downward. Bears lightly fragrant, large, double blooms (17–25 petals), whose light pink color varies by temperature. ↕ 18–24in (45–60cm). Zone 6.

***R.* 'Andeli'** see *R.* 'Double Delight'.

***R.* x *anemonoides* 'Ramona'** see *R.* 'Ramona'.

***R.* 'Angela Rippon'** ▣ syn. *R.* 'Ocarina'. Miniature rose of upright habit, with many dark green leaves. Urn-shaped, fully double, rose- to salmon-pink flowers, 1½in (4cm) across, are borne from spring to autumn. ↕ 18in (45cm), ↔ 12in (30cm). Zone 6.

Rosa 'Alexander'

***R.* 'Angel Face'.** Spreading floribunda rose with leathery, dark green leaves. From spring to autumn, produces cupped, fully double, scented, deep mauve flowers, 4in (10cm) across. ↕ 3ft (1m), ↔ 24in (60cm). Zone 6.

***R.* 'Angelita'** see *R.* 'Snowball'.

***R.* 'Anisley Dickson'** ▣ syn. *R.* 'Dicky'. Vigorous floribunda rose with shiny, dark green leaves and large clusters of high-centered, double, deep reddish salmon-pink flowers, 3in (8cm across, borne from spring to autumn. ↕ 4ft (1.2m), ↔ 30in (75cm). Zone 6.

***R.* 'Anna Ford'** ▣ Miniature rose of compact habit, with dark green leaves. Produces many urn-shaped, semi-double, orange-red flowers, 1½in (4cm across, opening flat, from spring to autumn. ↕ 18in (45cm), ↔ 16in (40cm Zone 6.

***R.* 'Anne Harkness'** ▣ Floribunda rose of vigorous, tall habit, with mid-green foliage. Urn-shaped, double, apricot-yellow flowers, 3in (8cm) across, are borne in spectacular, many-flowered sprays from spring to autumn. ↕ 4ft (1.2m), ↔ 24in (60cm). Zone 6.

***R.* 'Apricot Nectar'.** Floribunda rose with mid-green leaves and rounded, fully double, scented, apricot to apricot pink flowers, 4in (10cm) across, borne in tight clusters from spring to autumn ↕ to 4–5ft (1.2–1.5m), ↔ 26in (65cm). Zone 6.

***R.* 'Arizona'**, syn. *R.* 'Tocade', Grandiflora rose with shiny, dark green leaves. Urn-shaped, double, sweet-scented, orange-yellow flowers, 4in (10cm) across, are borne from spring to autumn. ↕ to 5ft (1.5m), ↔ 30in (75cm). Zone 6.

***R.* 'Arizona Sunset'.** Miniature rose of spreading habit, with mid-green foliage. From spring to autumn, bears cupped, double flowers, 1¾in (4.5cm) across, light yellow, flushed orange-red. ↕↔ 16in (40cm). Zone 6.

***R.* 'Arthur Bell'** ▣ Floribunda rose with shiny, bright green leaves. Cupped, double, fragrant, yellow to cream flowers, 3in (8cm) across, are produced from spring to autumn. ↕ 3ft (1m), ↔ 24in (60cm). Zone 6.

R

osa 'Anna Ford'

Rosa 'Anne Harkness'

Rosa 'Arthur Bell'

Rosa 'Autumn Splendor'

Rosa 'Awakening'

Rosa 'Baby Masquerade'

osa banksiae 'Lutea'

Rosa 'Bantry Bay'

Rosa 'Baronne Edmond de Rothschild'

Rosa 'Belle de Crécy'

Rosa 'Berries 'n Cream'

Rosa 'Betty Boop'

R. 'Autumn Damask' syn. *R. damascena bifera, R. damascena emperflorens, R.* 'Four Seasons Rose', R. 'Quatre Saisons', *R.* 'Rose of Castille', R. 'The Alexandria Rose'. Damask rose vith bluish green, broad, dull leaves. Produces scented, loosely double, cupped nedium pink flowers, 2in (7cm) across, n early summer and autumn. ↕ 4–5ft 1.2–1.5m), ↔ 3–4ft (1–1.2m). Zone 6.
R. 'Autumn Splendor' ▣ Large miniflora with medium green foliage. Bears arge, brilliant yellow, orange, gold, and ed blooms, 2½in (6cm) across, with full etals (30–40) and a slight fragrance. 24–36in (60–90cm). Zone 6.
R. 'Avon', syn. *R.* 'Fairy Lights', R. 'Sunnyside'. Groundcover rose of ompact habit, with dark green leaves. Clusters of flat, semi-double, pale pink o pearl-white flowers, 1¾in (4.5cm) cross, are borne along the stems from pring to autumn. ↕ 14in (35cm), ↔ 3ft (1m). Zone 6.
R. 'Awakening' ▣ syn. *R.* 'Probuzini'. Large-flowered climber with shiny, midgreen leaves. Clusters of cupped, fully double, fragrant, pale pearl-pink flowers, in (8cm) across, are borne from ummer to autumn. Tolerates a partially haded site. Sport of 'New Dawn'. 10ft (3m), ↔ 8ft (2.5m). Zone 6.
R. 'Baby Blanket', syn. *R.* 'Sommermorgen'. Groundcover rose of ow, spreading habit, with small, glossy, dark green leaves. From spring to utumn, bears large clusters of cupped, emi-double, clear pink flowers, 1½–3in 4–8cm) across, with yellow stamens. 30–36in (75–90cm), ↔ 4–5ft 1.2–1.5m). Zone 6.
R. 'Baby Masquerade' ▣ syn. *R.* 'Baby Carnival'. Miniature rose of dense, wiggy habit, with dark green leaves and clusters of many rosette-shaped, double, yellow-pink flowers, 1in (2.5cm) across, borne from summer to autumn. ↕↔ 16in 40cm). Zone 6.
R. 'Bad Nauheim' see *R.* 'National Trust'.
R. 'Ballerina' ▣ Polyantha rose of dense, spreading habit, with mid-green eaves. Spectacular in flower, it bears many shallowly cupped, single, whitecentered, light pink flowers, 1¼in (3cm) cross, in mop-headed clusters, from pring to autumn. ↕ 3–5ft (.9–1.5m), ↔ 3–4ft (1–1.2m). Zone 6.

R. banksiae, syn. *R. banksiae* var. *alba, R. banksiae* 'Alba Plena' (Double white banksian rose). Climbing species rose with long, slender, smooth stems and small, pale green leaves composed of 3–7 oblong-lance-shaped to elliptic-ovate leaflets, 1¼–2½in (3–6cm) long. Clusters of many rosette-shaped, double, violet-scented white flowers, 1in (2.5cm) across, with notched petals, are produced in late spring. Protect from frost for best results. Prune spent wood only. ↕↔ to 20ft (6m). W. and C. China. Zone 6. **var. *alba*** see *R. banksiae*. **'Alba Plena'** see *R. banksiae*. **'Lutea'** ▣ syn. var. *lutea* (Yellow banksian rose) produces fully double yellow flowers, ¾in (2cm) across. Requires a sheltered wall; ↕↔ to 20ft (6m). **'Lutescens'**, syn. f. *lutescens*, produces single, strongly scented yellow flowers. **var. *normalis*** (Single white banksian rose) bears single, fragrant white flowers on prickly stems; ↕↔ to 20ft (6m).
R. 'Bantry Bay' ▣ Large-flowered climber of upright, free-branching habit, with dark green leaves. Clusters of cupped, semi-double, lightly scented, deep pink flowers, 3½in (9cm) across, are borne from spring to autumn. ↕ 12ft (4m), ↔ 8ft (2.5m). Zone 6.
R. 'Baronne Edmond de Rothschild' ▣ Vigorous hybrid tea rose producing leathery, glossy, mid-green foliage. Bears rounded, fully double, fragrant, ruby-red flowers, 5in (13cm) across, with pale pink reverses, from spring to autumn. ↕ 3ft (1m), ↔ 30in (75cm). Zone 6.
R. 'Baronne Prévost'. Erect hybrid perpetual rose with prickly stems and dark green leaves. Quartered-rosette, fully double, scented pink flowers, 4in (10cm) across, are borne from spring to autumn. ↕ to 5ft (1.5m), ↔ 3ft (1m). Zone 5.
R. 'Beauty of Glazenwood' see *R.* x *odorata* 'Pseudindica'.
R. 'Belle Amour'. Alba rose of upright habit, with gray-green foliage. Camellia-like, rounded, semi-double, myrrh-scented, light salmon-pink flowers, 3½in (9cm) across, cupped on opening, are produced in spring or early summer, followed by spherical red hips. ↕ 5–6ft (1.5–2m), ↔ 4ft (1.2m). Zone 4.
R. 'Belle Courtisane' see *R.* 'Königin von Dänemark'.
R. 'Belle de Crécy' ▣ Gallica rose of lax habit, with bristly stems and grayish green leaves. In spring or early summer, produces quartered-rosette, full-petaled, fully double, fragrant, deep pink to purple flowers, 3in (8cm) across, showing green centers as they open. ↕ 4ft (1.2m), ↔ 3ft (1m). Zone 5.
R. 'Belle de Londres' see *R.* 'Compassion'.
R. 'Belle of Portugal' see *R.* 'Belle Portugaise'.
R. 'Belle Portugaise', syn. *R.* 'Belle of Portugal'. Very vigorous, climbing tea rose with glossy, olive-green leaves and high-centered, semi-double, fragrant, light salmon-pink flowers, 5in (13cm) across, borne in spring or early summer. ↕ to 15ft (5m), ↔ 10ft (3m). Zone 8.
R. 'Berkeley' see *R.* 'Tournament of Roses'.
R. 'Berries 'n Cream' ▣ syn. *R.* 'Calypso', *R.* 'Cl. Berries 'n Cream'. Tall, large-flowered climber with large, medium green, glossy foliage and few prickles. Double blooms (26–40 petals), 4–5in (12.5cm) across, are pink striped, and have a moderate apple fragrance. ↕ 10–12ft (3–3.5m). Zone 6.
R. 'Betty Boop' ▣ syn. *R.* 'Centenary of Federation'. Floribunda rose with young, dark red leaves maturing to glossy green. Bears clusters of semi-double, mildly scented, white flowers with red edges, 3–4in (8–10cm) across, from spring to autumn. ↕ 3–5ft (1–1.5m). ↔ 4–5ft (1.2–1.5m). Zone 6.
R. 'Bizarre Triomphant' see *R.* 'Charles de Mills'.
R. 'Black Jade'. Miniature rose of upright habit with semi-glossy, dark green leaves. From spring to autumn, double, high-centered, almost black, deep red flowers, 1½in (4cm) across, are produced singly and in clusters. ↕ 18–24in (45–60cm), ↔ 12in (30cm). Zone 6.
R. 'Blanc Double de Coubert'. Rugosa rose of dense, spreading habit, with

Rosa 'Ballerina'

Rosa 'Blessings'

Rosa 'Bobbie James'

Rosa 'Bonica'

Rosa 'Boule de Neige'

Rosa 'Bourbon Queen'

Rosa 'Breath of Life'

Rosa 'Bridal White'

Rosa 'Brown Velvet'

Rosa 'Buff Beauty'

Rosa 'Camaïeux'

Rosa 'Cardinal de Richelieu'

Rosa 'Carefree Sunshine'

leathery, mid-green foliage. From spring to autumn, produces loose-petaled, cupped to flat, semi-double, fragrant white flowers, 3in (8cm) across, with yellow stamens, followed in some years by spherical red hips. ↕ 5ft (1.5m), ↔ 4ft (1.2m). Zone 2b.

***R.* 'Blanche Moreau'.** Moss rose of lax growth, with dark green leaves. In summer, bears cupped, fully double, fragrant white flowers, 4in (10cm) across, with brownish green mossing on the stems and calyces. ↕ 5ft (1.5m), ↔ 4ft (1.2m). Zone 4.

***R.* 'Blaze'.** Branching, large-flowered climber with mid-green leaves and clusters of cupped, semi-double red flowers, 2½in (6cm) across, borne freely from spring or early summer to autumn. May be mistakenly sold as 'Improved Blaze'. ↕↔ 8ft (2.5m). Zone 5b.

***R.* 'Blessings'** ■ Vigorous hybrid tea rose with dark green leaves. Produces urn-shaped, fully double, scented, salmon-pink flowers, 4in (10cm) across, from spring to autumn. ↕ 3½ft (1.1m), ↔ 30in (75cm). Zone 6.

***R.* 'Bobbie James'** ■ Rampant rambler producing glossy leaves, reddish green when young, maturing mid-green. Large clusters of cupped, semi-double, scented, creamy white flowers, 2in (5cm) across, are produced in early summer. ↕ to 30ft (10m), ↔ 20ft (6m). Zone 6.

***R.* 'Bonica'** ■ syn. *R.* 'Bonica '82'. Vigorous shrub rose of low, spreading habit, with dense, glossy, rich green foliage. Large sprays of cupped, fully double, rose-pink flowers, 3in (8cm) across, are borne from spring to autumn. ↕ 3–4ft (1–1.2m), ↔ 3½ft (1.1m). Zone 5.

***R.* 'Bonica '82'** see *R.* 'Bonica'.

***R.* 'Boule de Neige'** ■ Bourbon rose of vigorous, uneven growth, with glossy, dark green leaves. From spring to autumn, produces cupped to rosette-shaped, fully double, fragrant, pink-touched white flowers, 3in (8cm) across. ↕ 5ft (1.5m), ↔ 4ft (1.2m). Zone 6.

***R.* 'Bouquet de la Mariée'** see *R.* 'Aimée Vibert'.

***R.* 'Bourbon Queen'** ■ syn. *R.* 'Souvenir de la Princesse de Lamballe'. Vigorous bourbon rose with long, leafy stems and mid-green foliage. Clusters of numerous cupped, double, scented, magenta to rose-pink flowers, 3in (8cm) across, are borne mainly in summer. ↕ to 8ft (2.5m), ↔ 5ft (1.5m). Zone 6.

R. bracteata (Chickasaw rose, Macartney rose). Fast-growing, semi-evergreen species rose producing prickly, brownish green stems and glossy, dark green leaves, each with 5–11 obovate to elliptic leaflets, ¾–2in (2–5cm) long. In spring, bears cupped to flat, single, lightly scented white flowers, 3½in (9cm) across, with gold stamens and curling petals, followed by spherical orange hips. ↕↔ to 20ft (6m) as a climber in warmer climates, ↕↔ 5–10ft (1.5–3m) as a shrub. S.E. China, Taiwan. Zone 5.

***R.* 'Breath of Life'** ■ Upright, large-flowered climber with mid-green leaves and rounded, fully double, scented, apricot to apricot-pink flowers, 4in (10cm) across, borne from spring to autumn. ↕ 8ft (2.5m), ↔ 7ft (2.2m). Zone 6.

***R.* 'Bridal White'** ■ syn. *R.* 'Tricia'. Floribunda rose with mid-size, glossy leaves. Bears clusters of ivory-white, scented, double flowers, 4in (10cm) across, from spring to autumn. ↕ 3–4ft (.9–1.2m). ↔ 3ft (90cm). Zone 6.

***R.* 'Brite Lites'** see *R.* 'Princess Alice'.

***R.* 'Broadway'.** Hybrid tea rose with glossy, dark green foliage. From spring to autumn, produces high-centered, fully double, spice-scented, orange-yellow flowers, 4in (10cm) across, the outer petals flushed with pink. ↕ 5ft (1.5m), ↔ 24in (60cm). Zone 6.

***R.* 'Brown Velvet'** ■ syn. *R.* 'Colorbreak'. Floribunda rose with glossy, dark green leaves. Produces fully double, brownish orange flowers, 3in (8cm) across, quartered-rosette on opening, from summer to autumn. ↕ 3ft (1m), ↔ 24in (60cm). Zone 6.

***R.* 'Buffalo Bill'** see *R.* 'Regensberg'.

***R.* 'Buff Beauty'** ■ Hybrid musk shrub rose of rounded habit, with dense, dark green leaves. Freely produces large clusters of remontant, cupped, fully double, lightly fragrant flowers, 3½in (9cm) across, apricot fading to buff, in early summer. ↕↔ 5ft (1.5m), ↕ 6–7ft (2–2.2m) when trained. Zone 6.

***R.* 'Burgund '81'** see *R.* 'Loving Memory'.

***R.* 'Burning Sky'** see *R.* 'Paradise'.

R. californica. Shrubby species rose with bristly shoots and dull, mid-green leaves, each composed of 5–7 ovate to broadly elliptic leaflets, ½–1¼in (1–3cm) long. Clusters of flat, single, scented, lilac-pink flowers, 1½in (4cm) across, are borne freely in spring or early summer, a few later in autumn, before the spherical, orange-red hips. ↕ 5–8ft (1.5–2.5m), ↔ 4–6ft (1.2–2m). S. Oregon to S. California, N.W. Mexico. Zone 7. **'Plena'** see *R. nutkana* 'Plena'.

***R.* 'Calypso'** see *R.* 'Berries 'n Cream'.

***R.* 'Camaïeux'** ■ Gallica rose of dense habit, with mid-green foliage. Cupped, fully double, scented, light pink flowers, 3½in (9cm) across, striped with crimson-purple to lilac-gray, are borne in spring or early summer. ↕ 3–3½ft (1–1.1m), ↔ 30in (75cm). Zone 5.

***R.* 'Camelot'.** Vigorous, grandiflora rose with leathery, dark green leaves. From spring to autumn, bears cupped, fully double, spice-scented, coral-pink flowers, 3½in (9cm) across. ↕ 5ft (1.5m), ↔ 3ft (1m). Zone 6.

***R.* 'Canary Bird'** see *R. xanthina* 'Canary Bird'.

***R.* 'Capitaine John Ingram'.** Vigorous, bushy moss rose with dark green leaves and clusters of peony-like, pompon-shaped, fully double, fragrant, dark crimson to purple flowers, 3in (8cm) across, with a lilac-pink reverse to the petals, borne in spring or early summer. ↕ 4ft (1.2m), ↔ 3ft (1m). Zone 5.

***R.* 'Cardinal de Richelieu'** ■ Gallica rose of vigorous, compact, lax habit, with smooth stems and dense, dark green foliage. Rounded, fully double, fragrant, deep burgundy-purple flowers, 3in (8cm) across, are borne in spring or early summer. ↕ 3ft (1m), ↔ 4ft (1.2m). Zone 4.

***R.* 'Carefree Beauty'**, syn. *R.* 'Audace', *R.* 'Bucbi'. Vigorous, upright, spreading shrub rose with smooth, olive-green leaves. From spring to autumn, bears clusters of cupped, semi-double, fragrant, light mid-pink flowers, 4½in (11cm) across, followed by spherical orange-red hips. ↕ 5ft (1.5m), ↔ 3ft (1m). Zone 4.

***R.* 'Carefree Delight'**, syn. *R.* 'Bingo Meidiland', *R.* 'Bingo Meillandecor'. Bushy shrub rose with small, glossy, dark green leaves. Remontant, flat, single, carmine-pink flowers, 1½–3in (4–8cm) across, with yellow centers, are borne in large clusters in spring or early summer. Excellent disease resistance. ↕↔ 3–4ft (1–1.2m). Zone 6.

***R.* 'Carefree Sunshine'** ■ Shrub rose with mid-green, semi-glossy leaves, bearing clusters of scented, flat, semi-double, medium yellow flowers, 2in (6cm) across, from spring to autumn. ↕ 3ft (1m), ↔ 4ft (1.2m). Zone 6.

***R.* 'Carefree Wonder'.** Free-branching, leafy shrub rose of rounded, upright, bushy habit, with mid-green leaves. From spring to autumn, freely bears clusters of cupped, double pink flowers, 3½in (9cm) across, with a pale pink reverse to the petals. ↕ 4–5ft (1.2–1.5m) ↔ 3ft (1m). Zone 6.

***R.* 'Casino'** ■ syn. *R.* 'Gerbe d'Or', *R.* 'Macca'. Large-flowered climber with sparse, dark green leaves and rounded, fully double, fragrant yellow flowers, 3½in (9cm) across, sometimes opening quartered-rosette, borne from spring to autumn. ↕ 10ft (3m), ↔ 7ft (2.2m). Zone 6.

***R.* 'Cécile Brunner'** ■ syn. *R.* 'Mignon', *R.* 'Sweetheart Rose'. Polyantha rose of upright growth, with sparse, dark green leaves. Perfectly formed, urn-shaped, fully double, light pink flowers, 1½in (4cm) across, are borne from spring to autumn. ↕ 30in (75cm), ↔ 24in (60cm). Zone 6.

***R.* 'Céleste'** see *R.* 'Celestial'.

***R.* 'Celestial'** ■ syn. *R.* 'Celeste'. Vigorous, spreading alba rose with grayish green foliage. Clusters of cupped, double, fragrant, light pink flowers, 3in (8cm) across, are produced in spring or early summer. ↕ 5ft (1.5m), ↔ 4ft (1.2m). Zone 3.

***R.* 'Celine Forestier'** ■ syn. *R.* 'Liesis', *R.* 'Lusiades'. Noisette rose with dark green, glossy leaves. Producing small clusters of spicy-scented, light yellow flowers with a green button eye, 4in (10cm) across, from spring to autumn. ↕ 6–8ft (2–2.5m), ↔ 4ft (1.2m). Zone 6.

R. 'Centenary of Federation' see *R.* 'Betty Boop'.

R.* x *centifolia (Cabbage rose, Provence rose). Vigorous centifolia rose of branching habit, with arching, dull, mid-green leaves consisting of 5–7 broadly ovate leaflets, to 2in (5cm) long. In summer, produces cupped, fully double, very fragrant, deep rose-pink, sometimes red or white flowers, 3½in (9cm) across.

Rosa 'Casino'

Rosa 'Cécile Brunner'

Rosa 'Celestial'

Rosa 'Celine Forestier'

Rosa x *centifolia* 'Muscosa'

Rosa 'Champagne Cocktail'

Rosa 'Cherry Brandy'

Rosa 'Chinatown'

Rosa 'Cider Cup'

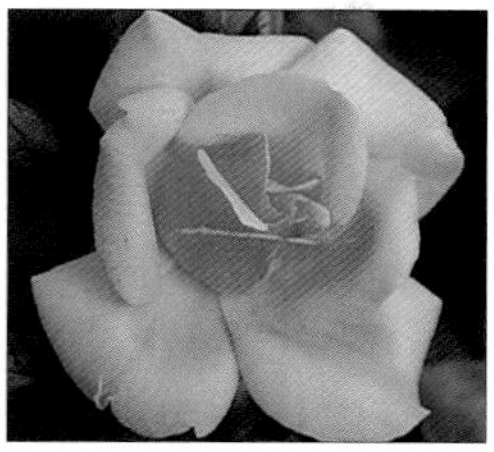
Rosa 'City Girl'

Rosa 'City of London'

Rosa 'City of York'

5ft (1.5m), ↔ 4ft (1.2m). Garden origin. Zone 4. **'Cristata'**, syn. *R.* 'Chapeau de Napoléon', *R.* 'Cristata' (Crested moss) has a lax, branching habit, and double, rose-pink flowers on bowing stems. It has no true moss, but mossy tufts on the calyces. Best grown on a support. **'Muscosa'** ▣ syn. *R.* x *centifolia* 'Communis' (Common moss rose, Old pink moss) is a vigorous, branching moss rose with dull, dark green leaves, and dense moss on the stems and calyces. Rounded to cupped pink flowers are 3in (8cm) across. **var. *pomponia*** see *R.* 'De Meaux'.
***R.* 'C.F. Meyer'** see *R.* 'Conrad Ferdinand Meyer'.

***R.* 'Champagne Cocktail'** ▣ Floribunda rose with dark green leaves. From summer to autumn, bears open clusters of cupped, double, scented, light yellow flowers, 3½in (9cm) across, with pink markings. ↕ 3ft (1m), ↔ 28in (70cm). Zone 6.
***R.* 'Champlain'.** Bushy shrub rose with upright habit and small, dark yellow-green leaves. From spring to autumn, produces cupped, double, velvety, dark red flowers, 2½–3in (6–8cm) across, in clusters. ↕↔ 3ft (1m). Zone 3.
***R.* 'Champneys' Pink Cluster'.** Vigorous noisette climbing rose with arching, smooth stems and shiny, light green leaves. From spring to autumn,

Rosa 'Charles de Mills'

bears large clusters of cupped, double, fragrant pink flowers, 2in (5cm) across. ↕ 8–12ft (2.5–4m), ↔ 8ft (2.5m). Zone 6.
***R.* 'Chapeau de Napoléon'** see *R.* x *centifolia* 'Cristata'.
***R.* 'Charles Albanel'.** Vigorous, low-spreading, hybrid rugosa rose with wrinkled, yellow-green leaves. Bears cupped, double, fragrant mid-red flowers, 2½–3½in (6–9cm) across, in spring or early summer, sporadically to autumn. Good groundcover. ↕ 18in (45cm), ↔ 3ft (1m). Zone 2b.
***R.* 'Charles de Mills'** ▣ syn. *R.* 'Bizarre Triomphant'. Upright, arching gallica rose with smooth stems and mid-green foliage. In spring or early summer, pink buds open to quartered-rosette, fully double, fragrant, magenta-pink flowers, 4in (10cm) across. ↕↔ 4ft (1.2m) or more. Zone 4.
***R.* 'Cheerio'** see *R.* 'Playboy'.
***R.* 'Cherish'**. Floribunda rose of compact habit, with dark green leaves. High-centered, double, light pink flowers, 3in (8cm) across, the petals with white bases inside, open from spring to autumn. ↕ 3–4ft (1–1.2m), ↔ 24in (60cm). Zone 6.
***R.* 'Cherry Brandy'** ▣ Fast-growing, hybrid tea rose of uneven habit, with dense, glossy, bright green leaves. Produces high-centered to cupped, double orange flowers, 3½in (9cm) across, suffused salmon-pink, singly and in open clusters from summer to autumn. ↕ 30in (75cm), ↔ 24in (60cm). Zone 6.
***R.* 'Child's Play'.** Upright, miniature rose has medium growth and medium dark green matte foliage. Produces semi-double flowers with a moderate, sweet fragrance. Blooms are a pink blend with porcelain pink/white flowers with pink edges. ↕ 15–20in (37–50cm). Zone 5b.
***R.* 'China Doll'.** Polyantha rose with leathery, mid-green leaves and cupped, double, china-pink flowers, 1½in (4cm) across, borne from spring to autumn. ↕↔ 18in (45cm). Zone 6.
***R.* 'Chinatown'** ▣ syn. *R.* 'Ville de Chine'. Vigorous floribunda rose with strong, uneven growth and abundant, glossy, dark green leaves. From spring to autumn, produces rounded, double, scented yellow flowers, 4in (10cm) across, flushed pink. ↕ 4ft (1.2m), ↔ 3ft (1m). Zone 6.

R. chinensis* var. *minima see *R.* 'Rouletii'.
***R. chinensis* 'Mutabilis'** see *R.* x *odorata* 'Mutabilis'.
***R. chinensis* 'Semperflorens'** see *R.* x *odorata* 'Semperflorens'.
***R. chinensis* 'Viridiflora'** see *R.* x *odorata* 'Viridiflora'.
***R.* 'Christian IV'** see *R.* 'The Times'.
***R.* 'Chrysler Imperial'.** Hybrid tea rose producing dark green leaves. From spring to autumn, bears high-centered, fully double, very fragrant, deep red flowers, 5in (13cm) across. ↕ 4–5ft (1.2–1.5m), ↔ 24in (60cm). Zone 6.
***R.* 'Cider Cup'** ▣ Miniature rose of neat habit, with dense, glossy, mid-green foliage. From spring to autumn, produces well-spaced clusters of high-centered, double, deep apricot-pink flowers, 1½in (4cm) across. ↕ 18in (45cm), ↔ 12in (30cm). Zone 6.
***R.* 'Cinderella'.** Upright, miniature rose with tiny, glossy, leathery, dark green leaves. From spring to autumn, produces high-centered, fully double, fragrant shell-pink flowers, ¾in (2cm) across. ↕↔ 10–12in (25–30cm). Zone 6.
***R.* 'City Girl'** ▣ Free-branching, large-flowered climber producing glossy, dark green leaves. From spring to autumn, produces clusters of cupped, semi-double, scented, salmon-pink flowers, 4½in (11cm) across. ↕↔ 7ft (2.2m). Zone 6.
***R.* 'City of London'** ▣ Floribunda rose or climbing rose of spreading, uneven habit, with glossy mid-green leaves. Loosely formed, rounded to flat, semi-double to double, fragrant, light pink flowers, 3in (8cm) across, are produced from spring to autumn. ↕ 32in (80cm), ↔ 30in (75cm). Zone 6.
***R.* 'City of York'** ▣ syn. *R.* 'Direktor Benschop'. Large-flowered climber with glossy, bright green foliage. Clusters of cupped, semi-double, scented, creamy white flowers, 2½in (6cm) across, are borne in spring or early summer. ↕ to 12ft (4m), ↔ 10ft (3m). Zone 6.
***R.* 'Class Act'**, syn. *R.* 'First Class', *R.* 'White Magic'. Floribunda rose producing dark green leaves and loosely formed, flat, semi-double white flowers, 3in (8cm) across, from spring to autumn. ↕ 3ft (1m), ↔ 30in (75cm). Zone 6.

R

Rosa 'Climbing Mrs. Sam McGredy'

Rosa 'Compassion'

Rosa 'Complicata'

Rosa 'Congratulations'

Rosa 'Conrad Ferdinand Meyer'

Rosa 'Constance Spry'

Rosa 'Cordon Bleu'

Rosa 'Cornelia'

Rosa 'Crimson Glory'

Rosa 'Crimson Shower'

Rosa x *damascena* var. *semperflorens*

Rosa 'Danse du Feu'

***R.* 'Climbing Cécile Brunner'.** Vigorous climber with strong growth and sparse, dark green leaves composed of lance-shaped leaflets. In early summer, bears exquisitely formed, urn-shaped, double, light pink flowers, 1½in (4cm) across. ↕↔ 12ft (4m). Zone 6.
***R.* 'Climbing Crimson Glory'.** Climber of branching habit, producing fairly sparse, mildew-prone, dark green leaves and prickly stems. Produces cupped, fully double, intensely fragrant, dark crimson flowers, 4½in (11cm) across, on bowing stems from summer to autumn. ↕ to 15ft (5m), ↔ 8ft (2.5m). Zone 6.
***R.* 'Climbing Ena Harkness'.** Climber of branching habit, with mid-green foliage and high-centered, fully double, fragrant, bright crimson flowers, 5in (13cm) across, borne from summer to autumn. ↕ 15ft (5m), ↔ 8ft (2.5m). Zone 6.
***R.* 'Climbing Etoile de Hollande'.** Climber with rampant, open growth, dark green foliage, and cupped, double, very fragrant, dark crimson flowers, 4½in (11cm) across, borne mainly in late spring and summer. ↕ to 20ft (6m), ↔ 15ft (5m). Zone 6.
***R.* 'Climbing Iceberg'** ▣ Climber with strong, well-branched growth and dense, light green foliage. Showy clusters of numerous cupped, double white flowers, 3in (8cm) across, are borne freely from spring to autumn. ↕↔ 10ft (3m). Zone 6.
***R.* 'Climbing Lady Hillingdon'.** Climbing tea rose with stiff, vigorous growth, purplish green wood, and glossy, dark green foliage. From spring to autumn, high-centered to cupped, semi-double to double, fragrant, light apricot-yellow flowers, 3½in (9cm) across, are borne on nodding stems. ↕ to 15ft (5m), ↔ 8ft (2.5m). Zone 6.
***R.* 'Climbing Little White Pet'** see *R.* 'Félicité Perpétue'.
***R.* 'Climbing Mrs. Sam McGredy'** ▣ Vigorous hybrid tea climber with a stiff, branching habit and sparse, dark green foliage. Urn-shaped, fully double, copper-red to salmon-pink flowers, 4½in (11cm) across, are borne mainly in late spring and early summer. ↕↔ 10ft (3m). Zone 6.
***R.* 'Climbing Orange Sunblaze'**, syn. *R.* 'Climbing Orange Meillandina'. Miniature climber with upright, branching growth and many dark green leaves. Cupped, fully double, bright orange-red flowers, 1½in (4cm) across, are borne from summer to autumn. ↕ 5ft (1.5m), ↔ 4ft (1.2m). Zone 6.
***R.* 'Climbing Pompon de Paris'.** Vigorous, miniature China climbing rose with spreading, arching growth producing abundant matte, mid-green foliage. Many-flowered clusters of cupped, fully double, rose-red flowers, 1in (2.5cm) across, are borne in early summer. ↕ to 12ft (4m), ↔ 8ft (2.5m). Zone 6.

Rosa 'Climbing Iceberg'

***R.* 'Climbing Shot Silk'.** Branching climber with shiny, deep green foliage. Urn-shaped to cupped, double, sweet-scented flowers, 4in (10cm) across, salmon-pink suffused yellow, are borne mainly in summer. ↕ 10ft (3m), ↔ 8ft (2.5m). Zone 6.
***R.* 'Colorbreak'** see *R.* 'Brown Velvet'.
***R.* 'Color Magic'.** Hybrid tea rose of branching habit, producing dark green leaves. Cupped, wide-opening, double flowers, 5in (13cm) across, ivory becoming deep pink, are borne freely from summer to autumn. ↕ 3½ft (1.1m), ↔ 30in (75cm). Zone 6.
***R.* 'Commandant Beaurepaire'**, syn. *R.* 'Panachée d'Angers'. Vigorous, bushy, spreading bourbon rose with wavy, pale green leaves. In spring and autumn, bears cupped, double, fragrant pink flowers, 4in (10cm) across, with purple and white stripes. ↕↔ 4ft (1.2m). Zone 6.
***R.* 'Compassion'** ▣ syn. *R.* 'Belle de Londres'. Large-flowered climber with upright, free-branching growth and dark green leaves. Rounded, fully double, fragrant flowers, 4in (10cm) across, salmon-pink suffused with apricot, are borne from spring to autumn. ↕ 10ft (3m), ↔ 8ft (2.5m). Zone 6.
***R.* 'Complicata'** ▣ Very vigorous gallica rose with strong, arching, open growth and grayish green leaves. In spring or early summer, bears clusters of cupped to flat, single pink flowers, 4½in (11cm) across, with paler centers and folded petals. ↕ 7ft (2.2m), ↔ 8ft (2.5m). Zone 4.
***R.* 'Comtesse de Labarthe'** see *R.* 'Duchesse de Brabant'.
***R.* 'Comtesse Ouwaroff'** see *R.* 'Duchesse de Brabant'.
***R.* 'Conundrum'** ▣ Mini-flora with medium upright growth, producing medium, dark green semi-glossy foliage. Lightly fragrant, double blooms (17–25 petals) have yellow petals edged in red at the top, 2–3in (5–6.5cm) across. Zone 6.
***R.* 'Congratulations'** ▣ syn. *R.* 'Sylvia'. Tall, vigorous hybrid tea rose with dark green leaves. Neatly formed, urn-shaped, fully double, rose-pink flowers, 4½in (11cm) across, are borne on long stems from spring to autumn. ↕ 5ft (1.5m), ↔ 3ft (1m). Zone 6.
***R.* 'Conrad Ferdinand Meyer'** ▣ syn. *R.* 'C.F. Meyer'. Strong, vigorous hybrid rugosa rose with prickly, arching stems and coarse, grayish green leaves. Bears cupped, fully double, fragrant, silvery pink flowers, 4in (10cm) across, mainly in spring; some rebloom in summer and autumn. Prone to rust. ↕↔ 8–12ft (2.5–4m). Zone 2b.
***R.* 'Constance Spry'** ▣ English shrub rose of arching habit, which will climb if supported, with dense, grayish green leaves. Rounded, fully double, myrrh-scented pink flowers, 5in (13cm) across, are borne on nodding stems in spring or early summer. ↕ 6ft (2m), ↔ 5ft (1.5m) as a shrub; ↕↔ 10ft (3m) as a climber. Zone 4.
***R.* 'Cordon Bleu'** ▣ Hybrid tea rose with dark green foliage and cupped, double, scented, reddish apricot flowers 4in (10cm) across, borne from spring to autumn. ↕ 3–4ft (1–1.2m), ↔ 24in (60cm). Zone 6.
***R.* 'Cornelia'** ▣ Vigorous, hybrid musk shrub rose of arching, spreading habit, producing dense, dark green leaves with lance-shaped leaflets. From spring to autumn, produces large clusters of many rosette-shaped, double, pink-tinged flowers, 2in (5cm) across, copper at the centers. ↕↔ 5ft (1.5m), ↕ 6–8ft (2–2.5m) when trained. Zone 6.
***R.* 'Corylus'.** Vigorous hybrid nitida shrub rose with small, dense, elongated, shiny, dark green leaves, becoming red-tinged gold in autumn. Flat, single, fragrant pink flowers, 4in (10cm) across are borne in spring or early summer, followed by spherical red hips. ↕↔ 36in (90cm). Zone 4.
***R.* 'Cramoisi Superieur'** syn. *R.* 'Agrippina', *R.* 'Lady Brisbane'. Hybrid China rose with glossy leaves. Bearing large clusters of medium red, small, raspberry-scented, double, cupped flowers 2in (5cm) across, from spring to autumn. ↕ 4–5 ft (1.2–1.5m), ↔ 24–36in (60–90cm). Zone 6.
***R.* 'Crazy for You'** see *R.* 'Fourth of July'.
***R.* 'Crimson Glory'** ▣ Hybrid tea rose of branching habit, with sparse, mildew prone, dark green leaves and prickly stems. Cupped, fully double, intensely fragrant, dark crimson flowers, 4½in (11cm) across, are borne on bowing

›sa 'De la Maître d'Ecole'

Rosa 'Desprez à Fleur Jaune'

Rosa 'Disco Dancer'

Rosa 'Don Juan'

Rosa 'Doris Tysterman'

Rosa 'Dortmund'

›sa 'Double Delight'

Rosa 'Dr. W. Van Fleet'

Rosa 'Dublin Bay'

Rosa 'Duc de Guiche'

Rosa 'Duchesse de Brabant'

Rosa 'Dutch Gold'

ems from spring to autumn. ↕↔ 24in
0cm). Zone 6.
'Crimson Shower' ▣ Rambler with
x stems and many glossy, bright green
aves. Dense clusters of rosette-shaped,
uble crimson flowers, 1¼in (3cm)
ross, are produced from summer to
tumn. ↕ to 8ft (2.5m), ↔ 7ft (2.2m).
ne 6.
'Cristata' see *R.* x *centifolia* 'Cristata'.
'Cuisse de Nymphe' see *R.* 'Great
aiden's Blush'.
'Cupcake'. Vigorous miniature rose
compact, bushy habit, with glossy,
id-green leaves. High-centered, fully
uble, mid-pink flowers, 1½in (4cm)
ross, are borne from spring to
tumn. ↕ 14in (35cm), ↔ 12in (30cm).
one 6.
'Dainty Bess'. Branching hybrid tea
se with leathery, dark green leaves.
at, single, scented, pale pink flowers,
½in (9cm) across, with maroon
amens, are borne from summer to
tumn. ↕ 3ft (1m), ↔ 24in (60cm).
one 6.
x *damascena* (Damask rose).
gorous damask rose with arching,
ickly stems and dull, grayish green
aves, each composed of 5, rarely 7,
ate to elliptic leaflets, to 2½in (6cm)
ng. In summer, produces clusters of
-11 cupped to flat, semi-double,
agrant, pale pink to white flowers, 3in
cm) across. ↕ 6ft (2m), ↔ 5ft (1.5m).
iddle East. Zone 4. **var. *bifera*** see var.
mperflorens. **var. *semperflorens*** ▣

›sa 'Conundrum'

syn. var. *bifera*, *R.* 'Quatre Saisons' (Autumn damask rose, Four seasons rose, Rose of Castille) has an open, arching habit and light green leaves. Loosely formed, rose-pink flowers, 3½in (9cm) across, are produced in lax clusters, mainly in summer and sporadically in autumn. Best in a sunny position; ↕ 5ft (1.5m), ↔ 4ft (1.2m). **'Versicolor'** (York and Lancaster rose) has a twiggy, untidy habit, and produces loosely cupped, double, pink-tinged white flowers, 2½in (6cm) across; ↕ 5ft (1.5m), ↔ 4ft (1.2m).

***R.* 'Danse du Feu'** ▣ syn. *R.* 'Spectacular'. Stiffly branched, large-flowered climber bearing abundant glossy, mid-green leaves. Rounded, double scarlet flowers, 3in (8cm) across, are produced from spring to autumn. ↕↔ 8ft (2.5m). Zone 6.

***R.* 'Darling Flame'**, syn. *R.* 'Minuetto'. Bushy, well-branched miniature rose producing glossy, dark green leaves. Urn-shaped, double, orange-red flowers, 1½in (4cm) across, are borne freely from summer to autumn. ↕ 16in (40cm), ↔ 12in (30cm). Zone 6.

***R.* 'David Thompson'**. Medium-sized hybrid rugosa rose with wrinkled, yellow-green leaves. Freely produces cupped, double, fragrant magenta-red flowers, to 3in (8cm) across, from spring to autumn. ↕↔ 4ft (1.2m). Zone 2b.

***R.* 'Dearest'**. Floribunda rose of neat, spreading habit, with dark green leaves. Large clusters of camellia-like, rounded, double, fragrant, light rose-pink flowers, 3in (8cm) across, are borne from summer to autumn. ↕↔ 24in (60cm). Zone 6.

***R.* 'Deep Secret'**, syn. *R.* 'Mildred Scheel'. Hybrid tea rose with glossy, dark green foliage. Rounded, fully double, scented, deep crimson flowers, 4in (10cm) across, are borne from summer to autumn. ↕ 3ft (1m), ↔ 30in (75cm). Zone 6.

***R.* 'De la Maître d'Ecole'** ▣ syn. *R.* 'Du Maître d'Ecole', *R.* 'Rose Du Maître d'Ecole'. Gallica rose of bushy, spreading habit, with mid-green foliage. Quartered-rosette, fully double, fragrant, carmine-red to light pink flowers, 4in (10cm) across, are borne on bowing stems in summer. ↕ 3ft (1m), ↔ 3½ft (1.1m). Zone 4.

***R.* 'De Meaux'**, syn. *R.* x *centifolia* var. *pomponia*, *R.* 'Rose de Meaux' (Pompon rose). Dwarf centifolia rose of upright habit, with bright green leaves. Clusters of pompon, fully double, scented, rose-pink flowers, 1½in (4cm) across, are borne in summer. ↕ 3ft (1m), ↔ 30in (75cm). Zone 4.

***R.* 'Desprez à Fleur Jaune'** ▣ syn. *R.* 'Jaune Desprez'. Vigorous noisette climbing rose with arching growth and light green leaves. Flat, fully double, scented, pale creamy apricot flowers, 3in (8cm) across, are borne mainly in summer. ↕↔ 15ft (5m). Zone 6.

***R.* 'Dicky'** see *R.* 'Anisley Dickson'.

***R.* 'Direktor Benschop'** see *R.* 'City of York'.

***R.* 'Disco Dancer'** ▣ Free-branching, vigorous floribunda rose with dense, glossy, mid-green foliage. Showy, cupped, double, bright orange-scarlet flowers, 2½in (6cm) across, are produced from summer to autumn. ↕ 3ft (1m), ↔ 24in (60cm). Zone 6.

***R.* 'Dolly Parton'**. Hybrid tea rose with dark green foliage and high-centered, fully double, fragrant, vivid orange-red flowers, 4½in (11cm) across, borne from spring to autumn. ↕ 4–5ft (1.2–1.5m), ↔ 24in (60cm). Zone 6.

***R.* 'Donatella'** see *R.* 'Granada'.

***R.* 'Don Juan'** ▣ Tall, large-flowered climber with dark green, glossy, leathery foliage and intense fragrance. Bears cupped, very double flowers (30–35 petals) in velvety crimson red. ↕ 12–14ft (4–4.3m). Zone 6.

***R.* 'Doris Tysterman'** ▣ Tall hybrid tea rose producing glossy, dark green foliage. High-centered, double, orange-red flowers, 4in (10cm) across, are borne from spring to autumn. ↕ 5ft (1.5m), ↔ 30in (75cm). Zone 6.

***R.* 'Dorothy Perkins'**. Lax rambler with many glossy, dark green leaves. Produces dense clusters of rosette-shaped, double, rose-pink flowers, ¾in (2cm) across, in summer. ↕↔ to 10ft (3m). Zone 6.

***R.* 'Dortmund'** ▣ Upright kordesii shrub grown as a climber, with dense, glossy, dark green leaves. Showy clusters of flat, single red flowers, 4in (10cm) across, each with a white eye, are borne freely from spring to autumn. Deadhead to repeat bloom. ↕ 10ft (3m), ↔ 6ft (2m). Zone 5.

***R.* 'Double Delight'** ▣ Hybrid tea rose of uneven, branching habit, with dull, mid-green foliage. From spring to autumn, bears rounded, fully double, sweet-scented flowers, 5in (13cm) across, pale pink, margined and flushed carmine-red. The flowers spoil in rain. ↕ 4–5ft (1.2–1.5m), ↔ 24in (60cm). Zone 6.

***R.* 'Dr. W. Van Fleet'** ▣ Vigorous large-flowered climber with dark green foliage. Produces pointed buds that mature to double, nonrecurrent, moderately fragrant, large blooms in cameo-pink, fading to flesh-white. ↕ 15–20ft (4.5–6m). Zone 6.

***R.* 'Dublin Bay'** ▣ Free-branching, large-flowered climber, which may be pruned to form a shrub. Bears glossy, dark green leaves and clusters of cupped, double, bright crimson flowers, 4in (10cm) across, from spring to autumn. ↕↔ 7ft (2.2m). Zone 6.

***R.* 'Duc de Guiche'** ▣ Gallica rose of spreading habit, with dark green leaves. Fully double, crimson-purple flowers, 4in (10cm) across, opening flat and quartered-rosetted, are produced in spring or early summer. ↕↔ 4ft (1.2m). Zone 4.

***R.* 'Duchesse de Brabant'** ▣ syn. *R.* 'Comtesse de Labarthe', *R.* 'Comtesse Ouwaroff'. Tea rose of spreading, shrubby habit, with mid- to dark green leaves. Cupped, silky-petaled, double, scented, rose-pink flowers, 4½in (11cm) across, are borne from spring to autumn. ↕ 4–6ft (1.2–2m) or more, ↔ 3ft (1m). Zone 6.

***R.* 'Duchesse d'Istrie'** see *R.* 'William Lobb'.

***R.* 'Duchess of Portland'** see *R.* 'Portlandica'.

***R.* 'Duet'**. Vigorous hybrid tea rose producing leathery, mid-green leaves. High-centered, double flowers, 4in (10cm) across, in two shades of pink, are borne freely from spring to autumn. Good for cut flowers. ↕ 4–5ft (1.2–1.5m), ↔ 24in (60cm). Zone 6.

***R.* 'Dutch Gold'** ▣ Vigorous hybrid tea rose producing large, dark green leaves. Rounded, fully double, scented yellow flowers, 6in (15cm) across, are borne from summer to autumn. ↕ 3½ft (1.1m), ↔ 30in (75cm). Zone 6.

R

Rosa ecae

Rosa eglanteria

Rosa 'Elina'

Rosa 'Elizabeth Harkness'

Rosa 'Emily Gray'

Rosa 'Empereur du Maro

Rosa 'Ena Harkness'

Rosa 'English Garden'

Rosa 'English Miss'

Rosa 'Ernest H. Morse'

Rosa 'Escapade'

Rosa 'Eye Paint'

R. ecae ▣ Erect, wiry, suckering species rose with red stems and small, fern-like, mid-green leaves, each composed of 5–9 broadly elliptic to obovate leaflets, ⅛–⅜in (4–8mm) long. Cupped, single, musk-scented, bright yellow flowers, ¾in (2cm) across, are produced along the stems in late spring. Liable to die-back. ↕ 5ft (1.5m), ↔ 4ft (1.2m). Turkmenistan, Uzbekistan, Tajikistan, N.E. Afghanistan, N.W. Pakistan. Zone 7b.

***R.* 'Eden Climber',** syn. *R.* 'Eden', *R.* 'Eden Rose 88', *R.* 'Pierre de Ronsard'. Vigorous, spreading, large-flowered climber with semi-glossy, light green leaves. Remontant, rounded, fully double, fragrant, light yellow-tinted, creamy white flowers, 4–5in (10–13cm) across, suffused with pink, are borne singly and in nodding clusters, mainly in early summer. ↕↔ 8–10ft (2.5–3m). Zone 6.

R. eglanteria ▣ syn. *R. rubiginosa* (Eglantine rose, Sweet briar). Vigorous, arching, prickly species rose with apple-scented, dark green leaves composed of 5–9 ovate leaflets, 1–1½in (2.5–4cm) long. Cupped, single, rose-pink flowers, 1in (2.5cm) across, are produced in spring or early summer, followed by ovoid to spherical red hips in autumn. ↕↔ to 8ft (2.5m). Europe, N. Africa to W. Asia. Zone 5b.

***R.* 'E.H. Morse'** see *R.* 'Ernest H. Morse'.

***R.* 'Electron'** see *R.* 'Mullard Jubilee'.

***R. elegantula* 'Persetosa'**, syn. *R. elegantula* f. *persetosa*, *R. farreri* f. *persetosa*. Upright species rose with wiry stems, red-bristled when young, and pale gray-green leaves, each composed of 7–11 narrowly ovate to elliptic, fern-like leaflets, ½in (1.5cm) long, reddening in autumn. Shallowly cupped, single, light pink flowers, ¾in (2cm) across, are produced in summer; they are followed by ovoid, orange-red hips. ↕↔ 6ft (2m). N.W. China. Zone 5.

R. elegantula* f. *persetosa see *R. elegantula* 'Persetosa'.

***R.* 'Elina'** ▣ syn. *R.* 'Peaudouce'. Vigorous hybrid tea rose with abundant dark green foliage. Rounded, fully double, scented, ivory-white flowers, 6in (15cm) across, with lemon-yellow centers, are borne freely from spring to autumn. ↕ 5ft (1.5m), ↔ 30in (75cm). Zone 6.

***R.* 'Elizabeth Harkness'** ▣ Hybrid tea rose of neat habit, with dark green leaves. High-centered to rounded, fully double, fragrant, creamy pink flowers, 5in (13cm) across, are produced from spring to autumn. ↕ 4ft (1.2m), ↔ 24in (60cm). Zone 6.

***R.* 'Emily Gray'** ▣ Large-flowered climbler with lax stems covered in lustrous, dark green leaves. In early summer, produces small clusters of loosely formed, rounded, double, scented, butter-yellow flowers, 2in (5cm) across. ↕ to 15ft (5m), ↔ 10ft (3m). Zone 6.

***R.* 'Empereur du Maroc'** ▣ Hybrid perpetual rose of compact, shrubby habit, with mid-green leaves. Quartered-rosette, fully double, fragrant, maroon-crimson flowers, 3in (8cm) across, are borne freely on bowed stems in spring or early summer, sparsely in autumn. ↕ 4ft (1.2m), ↔ 3ft (1m). Zone 6.

***R.* 'Empress Josephine'** syn. *R.* x *francofurtana*. Bushy, wide-spreading gallica rose with smooth stems and grayish green leaves composed of 5–7 broadly ovate leaflets, to 2in (5cm) long. Loosely formed, rounded, semi-double flowers, 3½in (9cm) across, with wavy-margined, bright pink petals and deeper pink veining, open in spring or early summer, followed by inversely cone-shaped red hips. ↕↔ 4ft (1.2m). Garden origin. Zone 5.

***R.* 'Ena Harkness'** ▣ Hybrid tea rose of branching habit, with mid-green leaves. High-centered, double, fragrant, bright crimson flowers, 4in (10cm) across, are borne from spring to autumn. ↕ 3–4ft (1–1.2m), ↔ 24in (60cm). Zone 6.

***R.* 'English Garden'** ▣ Upright English shrub rose with light green leaves and rosette-shaped, double, lightly scented flowers, 4in (10cm) across, buff yellow, paling toward the edges, borne from spring to autumn. ↕ 3ft (1m), ↔ 30in (75cm). Zone 6.

***R.* 'English Miss'** ▣ Spreading floribunda rose with leathery, dark green leaves. Wide clusters of camellia-like, cupped, fully double, fragrant, pale pink flowers, 3in (8cm) across, are borne from spring to autumn. ↕ 30in (75cm), ↔ 24in (60cm). Zone 6.

***R.* 'Ernest H. Morse'** ▣ syn. *R.* 'E.H. Morse'. Hybrid tea rose with semi-glossy, dark green foliage. High-centered, double, very fragrant crimson flowers, 5in (13cm) across, are freely produced from spring to autumn. ↕ 4ft (1.2m), ↔ 24in (60cm). Zone 6.

***R.* 'Escapade'** ▣ Floribunda rose of dense habit, with abundant light green foliage. Showy, cupped, semi-double, scented, pink-violet flowers, 3in (8cm) across, each with a white eye, are borne freely from summer to autumn. ↕ 3–3½ft (1–1.1m), ↔ 24in (60cm). Zone 6.

***R.* 'Esmeralda'** see *R.* 'Keepsake'.

***R.* 'Essex'**, syn. *R.* 'Pink Cover'. Groundcover rose of dense habit, with dark green leaves. From spring to autumn, clusters of many small, cupped, single, light reddish pink flowers, 1in (2.5cm) across, with whitish pink centers, are borne freely along the stems. ↕ 24in (60cm), ↔ 4ft (1.2m). Zone 6.

***R.* 'Evelyn Fison'**, syn. *R.* 'Irish Wonder'. Floribunda rose with sparse, glossy, dark green foliage. Many neatly formed, rounded, double, bright deep red flowers, 2½in (6cm) across, are borne from summer to autumn. ↕ 28in (70cm), ↔ 24in (60cm). Zone 6.

***R.* 'Excelsa'**, syn. *R.* 'Red Dorothy Perkins'. Lax rambler with abundant shiny, mid-green leaves. In early summer, bears dense clusters of rosette-shaped, fully double crimson flowers, ¾in (2cm) across. Prone to mildew. ↕ 12ft (4m), ↔ 10ft (3m). Zone 6.

***R.* 'Eye Paint'** ▣ syn. *R.* 'Tapis Persan'. Vigorous floribunda or shrub rose with dense, dark green foliage. Large clusters of cupped to flat, single scarlet flowers 2in (5cm) across, with white eyes, are borne from summer to autumn. ↕ 3½f (1.1m), ↔ 30in (75cm). Zone 6.

***R.* 'Fairyland'**. Polyantha rose of vigorous, arching, spreading habit, wit small, dark green leaves. Large sprays c many rosette-shaped, double, scented, pale pink flowers, 1½in (4cm) across, are borne from summer to autumn. ↕ 30in (75cm), ↔ 4ft (1.2m). Zone 6.

***R.* 'Fairy Lights'** see *R.* 'Avon'.

***R.* 'Fanny Bias'** see *R.* 'Gloire de France'.

***R.* 'Fantin-Latour'** ▣ Vigorous centifolia rose of open habit, producin broad, dark green leaves. Cupped to fl fully double, fragrant, light pink flowe 4in (10cm) across, each with a green button eye, are borne in early summer. ↕ 5ft (1.5m), ↔ 4ft (1.2m). Zone 3.

R. farreri* f. *persetosa see *R. elegantul* 'Persetosa'.

R. fedtschenkoana. Very vigorous, suckering species rose with arching, bristly stems and pale gray-green leave with 5–9 elliptic to obovate leaflets, 1in (2.5cm) long. Single, flat white flowers, 1¾in (4.5cm) across, with yellow stamens, are borne in clusters of up to 4 blooms, mainly in summer; they are followed by pear-shaped, orange-red hips. ↕↔ 7ft (2.2m). C. Asi Zone 6.

***R.* 'Fée des Neiges'** see *R.* 'Iceberg'.

***R.* 'Felicia'** ▣ Vigorous hybrid musk shrub rose with abundant dark green

Rosa 'Ferdy'

R

Rosa 'Fantin-Latour'

Rosa 'Felicia'

Rosa 'Félicité Parmentier'

Rosa 'Félicité Perpétue'

Rosa 'Fellowship'

Rosa 'Ferdinand Pichard'

Rosa 'Fire Princess'

Rosa 'Flower Carpet'

Rosa foetida

Rosa foetida 'Persiana'

Rosa 'Fragrant Cloud'

Rosa 'François Juranville'

leaves. Large clusters of cupped, double, scented, light pink flowers, 3in (8cm) across, flushed yellow-apricot, are produced from spring to autumn. ↕ 5ft (1.5m), ↔ 7ft (2.2m). Zone 6b.
***R.* 'Félicité et Perpétue'** see *R.* 'Félicité Perpétue'.
***R.* 'Félicité Parmentier'** ■ Vigorous alba rose of upright, compact habit, producing abundant gray-green leaves. In early summer, bears quartered-rosette, fully double, fragrant, cream to pale pink flowers, 2½in (6cm) across. ↕ 4½ft (1.3m), ↔ 4ft (1.2m). Zone 3.
***R.* 'Félicité Perpétue'** ■ syn. *R.* 'Climbing Little White Pet', *R.* 'Félicité et Perpétue'. Hybrid sempervirens rambler rose producing long, slender stems clothed in dense, dark green leaves. Rosette-shaped, fully double, pale pink to white flowers, 1½in (4cm) across, are borne freely in early summer. ↕ to 15ft (5m), ↔ to 12ft (4m). Zone 6.
***R.* 'Fellowship'** ■ syn. *R.* 'Livin' Easy'. Floribunda rose with even growth and abundant glossy, mid-green foliage. Well-spaced clusters of cupped, double, scented, deep orange flowers, 3½in (9cm) across, are borne freely from spring to autumn. ↕ 30in (75cm), ↔ 24in (60cm). Zone 6.
***R.* 'Ferdi'** see *R.* 'Ferdy'.
***R.* 'Ferdinand Pichard'** ■ Upright, compact hybrid perpetual rose with smooth stems and long, light green leaves. Cupped, double, fragrant, pale pink flowers, 3in (8cm) across, with pink and red stripes, are produced from spring to autumn. ↕ 5ft (1.5m), ↔ 4ft (1.2m). Zone 5.
***R.* 'Ferdy'** ■ syn. *R.* 'Ferdi'. Floribunda rose of initially uneven, spiky growth, with fine-cut, mid-green leaves. Unusually abundant, dense clusters of cupped to flat, double, bright pink flowers, 1in (2.5cm) across, wreathe the stems in early summer, sometimes followed by spherical red-orange hips. ↕ 32in (80cm), ↔ 4ft (1.2m). Zone 6.
***R.* 'Festival'**. Compact, dwarf floribunda rose with abundant dark green leaves. From summer to autumn, bears dense clusters of rounded, semi-double, crimson-scarlet flowers, 1¾in (4.5cm) across, with a silvery white reverse to the petals. ↕ 24in (60cm), ↔ 20in (50cm). Zone 6.
***R. filipes* 'Kiftsgate'** ■ Rampant rambler producing abundant glossy, light green leaves, each composed of 5–7 narrowly elliptic to narrowly ovate leaflets, 2–3in (5–8cm) long. Large clusters of cupped, single, fragrant, creamy white flowers, 1in (2.5cm) across, are borne in early summer. ↕ to 30ft (10m), ↔ 20ft (6m). Zone 6.
***R.* 'Fiona'**. Floribunda rose with a wide, spreading habit and shiny, dark green leaves. Large clusters of cupped to flat, double red flowers, 2½in (6cm) across, are borne from summer to autumn. ↕ 32in (80cm), ↔ 4ft (1.2m). Zone 6.
***R.* 'Fire Princess'** ■ Upright miniature rose with glossy, mid-green leaves. Rosette-shaped, fully double scarlet flowers, 1½in (4cm) across, are borne from spring to autumn. ↕ 18in (45cm), ↔ 12in (30cm). Zone 6.
***R.* 'First Class'** see *R.* 'Class Act'.
***R.* 'First Prize'**. Hybrid tea rose of vigorous, spreading habit, with leathery, dark green foliage.

Rosa filipes 'Kiftsgate'

High-centered, double, scented, two-toned pink flowers, 5in (13cm) across, are borne from spring to autumn. ↕ 4–5ft (1.2–1.5m), ↔ 30in (75cm). Zone 6.
***R.* 'Flower Carpet'** ■ syn. *R.* 'Heidetraum'. Vigorous groundcover rose with abundant, shiny, bright green leaves. Showy clusters of cupped, double, deep rose-pink flowers, 2in (5cm) across, are borne freely along the stems from spring to autumn. ↕ 30in (75cm), ↔ 4ft (1.2m). Zone 6.
R. foetida ■ (Austrian briar, Austrian yellow rose). Species rose of upright, open habit, with arching, brownish green stems and pale green leaves, each consisting of 5–7 elliptic to obovate leaflets, ¾–1½in (2–4cm) long. Cupped, single, pungent, bright yellow flowers, 2in (5cm) across, are borne in spring or summer; the flowers are followed by spherical red hips. Susceptible to blackspot. ↕↔ 5ft (1.5m). W. to C. Asia. Zone 3. **'Bicolor'**, syn. *R.* 'Rose Capucine' (Austrian copper rose), a sport of *R. foetida*, has vivid nasturtium-orange flowers with a yellow reverse to the petals. **'Persiana'** ■ syn. var. *R. persiana* (Persian yellow rose) has gaunt, arching growth, small, fern-like leaves, and fully double yellow flowers, 2½in (6cm) across; ↔ 4ft (1.2m).
***R.* 'Fontaine'** see *R.* 'Fountain'.
***R.* 'Fountain'**, syn. *R.* 'Fontaine', *R.* 'Red Prince'. Vigorous hybrid tea rose with strong, upright growth and glossy, dark green leaves. From spring to autumn, bears large clusters of cupped, double, scented, bright crimson flowers, 5in (13cm) across. ↕ 6ft (2m), ↔ 4ft (1.2m). Zone 6.
***R.* 'Fourth of July'** syn. *R.* 'Crazy for You'. Tall climber with deep green foliage produces single flowers (10–16 petals) in large clusters, with a moderate apple fragrance. Large, red-and-white striped petals have ruffled edges. ↕ 10ft (3m). Zone 6.
***R.* 'Fragrant Cloud'** ■ syn. *R.* 'Tanellis'. Hybrid tea rose with branching growth and abundant, dark green leaves. Rounded, double, intensely fragrant, dusky scarlet flowers, 4½in (11cm) across, are produced freely from spring to autumn. ↕ 4–5ft (1.2–1.5m), ↔ 24in (60cm). Zone 6.
***R.* 'Fragrant Delight'**. Hybrid tea bush rose of willowy, uneven habit, with abundant reddish green foliage. Freely bears large sprays of urn-shaped, double, scented, salmon-pink flowers, 3in (8cm) across, from summer to autumn. ↕ 3ft (1m), ↔ 30in (75cm). Zone 6.
***R.* 'Fragrant Surprise'** see *R.* 'Samaritan'.
***R.* 'Francine Austin'**. English shrub rose of arching, open habit, with long, light green leaves. Small sprays of many pompon, double, scented white flowers, 1½in (4cm) across, are borne on bowed stems from spring to autumn. ↕ 3ft (1m), ↔ 4ft (1.2m). Zone 6.
R.* × *francofurtana, see *R.* 'Empress Josephine'.
***R.* 'François Juranville'** ■ Rambler with abundant, shiny, dark green leaves and clusters of rosette-shaped, fully double, apple-scented, light salmon-pink flowers, 3in (8cm) across, borne in early summer. ↕ 20ft (6m), ↔ 15ft (5m). Zone 6.

R

Rosa 'Frau Dagmar Hastrup'

Rosa 'Frau Karl Druschki'

Rosa 'Freedom'

Rosa 'Frühlingsmorgen'

Rosa 'Fulton Mackay'

Rosa gallica var. *officinalis*

Rosa gallica var. *officinalis* 'Versicolor'

Rosa 'Gentle Touch'

Rosa glauca

Rosa 'Glenfiddich'

Rosa 'Gloire de Dijon'

Rosa 'Glowing Amber'

***R.* 'Frau Dagmar Hastrup'** ■ syn. *R.* 'Fru Dagmar Hartopp'. Sturdy hybrid rugosa rose of spreading habit, producing leathery mid-green leaves. Shallowly cupped, single, clove-scented, light pink flowers, 3½in (9cm) across, are borne mainly in spring, with sporadic repeat blooms until autumn, followed by tomato-shaped, dark red hips in autumn. ↕ 3–4ft (1–1.2m), ↔ 4ft (1.2m). Zone 2b.

***R.* 'Frau Karl Druschki'** ■ syn. *R.* 'Reine des Neiges', *R.* 'Snow Queen', *R.* 'White American Beauty'. Vigorous hybrid perpetual rose with strong, arching stems, mid-green leaves, and high-centered, fully double, milk-white flowers, 4½in (11cm) across, borne from spring to autumn. ↕ 5–7ft (2.2m), ↔ 4ft (1.2m). Zone 5.

***R.* 'Freedom'** ■ syn. *R.* 'Dicjem'. Hybrid tea rose of uneven growth, with many shoots and abundant glossy, mid-green foliage. Rounded, double, stiff-petaled, bright yellow flowers, 3½in (9cm) across, are produced freely from spring to autumn. ↕ 3–4ft (1–1.2m), ↔ 24in (60cm). Zone 6.

***R.* 'French Lace'**, syn. *R.* 'Jaclace'. Upright floribunda rose with well-branched growth and mid-green foliage. From summer to autumn, bears high-centered, fully double, scented white flowers, 3½in (9cm) across. ↕ 3ft (1m), ↔ 24in (60cm). Zone 6.

***R.* 'Friesia'** see *R.* 'Sunsprite'.

***R.* 'Fru Dagmar Hastrup'** see *R.* 'Frau Dagmar Hartopp'.

***R.* 'Frühlingsgold'**, syn. *R.* 'Spring Gold'. Vigorous hybrid spinosissima shrub rose with strong, arching branches covered in downy red bristles when young, and toothed, matte, light green leaves. Cupped, semi-double, scented, pale yellow flowers, 4in (10cm) across, with golden stamens, are borne mainly in spring. ↕ 8ft (2.5m), ↔ 7ft (2.2m). Zone 5b.

***R.* 'Frühlingsmorgen'** ■ syn. *R.* 'Spring Morning'. Open, free-branching hybrid spinosissima shrub rose with grayish green leaves. Shallowly cupped, single, hay-scented pink flowers, 5in (13cm) across, with primrose-yellow centers and maroon stamens, are produced in spring. ↕ 6ft (2m), ↔ 5ft (1.5m). Zone 5b.

***R.* 'Fulton Mackay'** ■ Hybrid tea rose with handsome, glossy, mid-green foliage. High-centered, double, scented, golden apricot, pink-flushed flowers, 5in (13cm) across, are borne from spring to autumn. ↕ 3–4ft (1–1.2m), ↔ 24in (60cm). Zone 6.

R. gallica* var. *officinalis ■ syn. *R. officinalis* (Apothecary's rose, Crimson damask rose, Provins rose, Red rose of Lancaster). Species rose of neat, rounded habit, producing rough, dark green leaves with 3–5, rarely 7, broadly elliptic to almost rounded leaflets, 1–3in (2.5–8cm) long. Cupped to flat, semi-double, scented, pinkish red flowers, 3in (8cm) across, are borne singly or in clusters of 2–4 in spring or early summer, followed by spherical to ellipsoid, orange-red hips. ↕ 3–4ft (1–1.2m), ↔ 3ft (1m). Zone 4. **'Versicolor'** ■ (Rosa mundi rose) is compact, with pale pink flowers, striped reddish pink.

***R.* 'Garden Party'.** Vigorous hybrid tea rose with mid-green leaves. From spring to autumn, bears high-centered, double, fragrant white flowers, 5in (13cm) across, margined pale pink. ↕ 4ft (1.2m), ↔ 32in (80cm). Zone 6.

***R.* 'Gentle Touch'** ■ Miniature rose of neat habit, producing dark green leaves. Sprays of urn-shaped, semi-double, pale salmon-pink flowers, 2in (5cm) across, are borne close to the foliage from spring to autumn. ↕ 20in (50cm), ↔ 16in (40cm). Zone 6.

***R.* 'Gerbe d'Or'** see *R.* 'Casino'.

***R.* 'Gertrude Jekyll'**. Lanky large-flowered English shrub rose with grayish green leaves. Cupped, double, fragrant, deep pink flowers, 4in (10cm) across, with infolded petals, are borne from spring to autumn. ↕ 5ft (1.5m), ↔ 3ft (1m). Zone 6.

***R.* 'Gioia'** see *R.* 'Peace'.

***R.* 'Gipsy Boy'** see *R.* 'Zigeunerknabe'.

R. glauca ■ syn. *R. rubrifolia.* Vigorous, arching species rose with reddish green stems and grayish purple leaves, each composed of 5–9 ovate to narrowly elliptic leaflets, 1–1½in (2.5–4cm) long. Flat, single, cerise-pink flowers, 1½in (4cm) across, with paler pink centers and gold stamens, are borne in small clusters in late spring or early summer; they are followed by many spherical orange-red hips in autumn. ↕ 6ft (2m), ↔ 5ft (1.5m). Mountains of C. and S. Europe. Zone 2b.

***R.* 'Glenfiddich'** ■ Floribunda rose with glossy, dark green leaves. Produces clusters of urn-shaped, double, scented, amber to yellow flowers, 4in (10cm) across, from spring to autumn. ↕ 32in (80cm), ↔ 24in (60cm). Zone 6.

***R.* 'Gloire de Dijon'** ■ (Old glory rose). Vigorous, stiffly branching noisette or climbing tea rose with glossy, dark green leaves. Quartered-rosette, fully double, scented, creamy buff flowers, 4in (10cm) across, are borne from summer to autumn. ↕ to 15ft (5m), ↔ 12ft (4m). Zone 6.

***R.* 'Gloire de France'**, syn. *R.* 'Fanny Bias'. Lax gallica rose with crisp, dark green foliage. Quartered-rosette, fully double, fragrant, lilac-pink flowers, 3in (8cm) across, are borne freely in summer. ↕ 3ft (1m), ↔ 4ft (1.2m). Zone 4.

***R.* 'Glowing Amber'** ■ Miniature rose of medium bushy growth and medium dark green glossy foliage, with some prickles. Red-blend, scarlet red rose has a deep yellow reverse and yellow center, double (26–40 petals), 1½–2in (3–5cm) across, and a slight fragrance. ↕ 17–20in (40–50cm). Zone 6.

***R.* 'Golden Cherry'** see *R. laevigata.*

***R.* 'Golden Rambler'** see *R.* 'Alister Stella Gray'.

***R.* 'Golden Showers'** ■ Stiff, upright large-flowered climber with glossy, dark green leaves. Numerous cupped, double, fragrant, clear yellow flowers, 4in (10cm) across, are borne mainly in late spring or early summer, with some repeat flowering to autumn. ↕ to 10ft (3m), ↔ 6ft (2m). Zone 6.

***R.* 'Golden Sunblaze'** see *R.* 'Rise 'n' Shine'.

***R.* 'Golden Wings'** ■ Dense, spreading shrub rose with many prickly stems and light green leaves. Shallowly cupped, single, scented, pale yellow flowers, 5in (13cm) across, are borne in late spring or early summer, with some repeat flowering to autumn. ↕ 3½ft (1.1m), ↔ 4½ft (1.3m). Zone 3.

Rosa 'Golden Wings'

Rosa 'Golden Showers'

Rosa 'Goldfinch'

Rosa 'Graham Thomas'

Rosa 'Grandiflora'

Rosa 'Grandpa Dickson'

Rosa 'Great Maiden's Blush'

Rosa 'Grouse'

Rosa 'Gruss an Aachen'

Rosa 'Handel'

Rosa 'Hannah Gordon'

Rosa 'Harry Wheatcroft'

Rosa 'Heidelberg'

***R.* 'Goldfinch'** ▣ Vigorous, arching rambler producing abundant light green leaves. Masses of rosette-shaped, double, scented flowers, 1½in (4cm) across, deep yellow fading to creamy white, are borne in early summer. ↕ 8ft (2.5m), ↔ 6ft (2m). Zone 6.
***R.* 'Gold Medal'**. Upright, vigorous grandiflora rose with dark green leaves. High-centered, fully double, deep yellow flowers, 3½in (9cm) across, with a light, fruity fragrance, are borne from spring to autumn. ↕ 5–6ft (1.5–2m), ↔ 28in (70cm). Zone 6.
***R.* 'Gold of Ophir'** see *R.* x *odorata* 'Pseudindica'.
***R.* 'Gourmet Popcorn'**. Vigorous, rounded miniature rose with dark green leaves. From spring to autumn, produces clusters of numerous cupped to flat, semi-double, honey-scented white flowers, ¾in (2cm) across. ↕ 18in (45cm), ↔ 24in (60cm). Zone 6.
***R.* 'Graham Thomas'** ▣ Vigorous English shrub rose of lax, arching habit, with bright green leaves. Quartered-rosette to cupped, fully double, scented yellow flowers, 4½in (11cm) across, are produced from spring to autumn. ↕ 5–7ft (1.5–2.2m), ↔ 24in (60cm). Zone 5.
***R.* 'Granada'**, syn. *R.* 'Donatella'. Vigorous hybrid tea rose with leathery, dark green leaves. High-centered, double, slightly fragrant flowers, 4½in (11cm) across, blended rose-pink, red, and lemon-yellow, are borne from spring to autumn. ↕ 4ft (1.2m), ↔ 30in (75cm). Zone 6.
***R.* 'Grandiflora'** ▣ syn *R. spinosissima* var. *altaica*. Vigorous spinosissima rose of upright habit, with twiggy stems and dark green leaves. Cupped to flat, single, scented, creamy white flowers, 2½in (6cm) across, with yellow stamens, are borne in spring or early summer. ↕ to 6ft (2m), ↔ 4ft (1.2m). Zone 2.
***R.* 'Grandpa Dickson'** ▣ syn. *R.* 'Irish Gold'. Hybrid tea rose of neat habit, with glossy, light green leaves. High-centered, fully double, primrose-yellow flowers, 7in (18cm) across, are produced from spring to autumn. ↕ 30in (75cm), ↔ 24in (60cm). Zone 6.
***R.* 'Great Maiden's Blush'** ▣ syn. *R.* 'Cuisse de Nymphe', *R.* 'La Séduisante'. Vigorous alba rose with strong, arching stems and gray-green leaves. Cupped, fully double, very fragrant, pinkish white flowers, 3in (8cm) across, with infolded petals, are borne freely in early summer. ↕ 6ft (2m), ↔ 4½ft (1.3m). Zone 4.
***R.* 'Green Ice'**. Bushy, low-growing, miniature rose with small, glossy, leathery, dark green leaves. From spring to autumn, bears clusters of flat, double white flowers, 1in (2.5cm) across, fading to soft green. ↕ 12in (30cm), ↔ 16in (40cm). Zone 6.
***R.* 'Grouse'** ▣ syn. *R.* 'Immensee'. Very vigorous, trailing groundcover rose with shiny, dark green leaves. Flat, single, scented, light pink to near white flowers, 1½in (4cm) across, are borne close to the stems in early summer. ↕ 24in (60cm), ↔ 10ft (3m). Zone 6.
***R.* 'Gruss an Aachen'** ▣ Erect early floribunda rose with leathery, dark green foliage. Rounded, fully double, scented, pale pink to creamy white flowers, 3in (8cm) across, are borne from spring to autumn. ↕ 24–30in (60–75cm), ↔ 18in (45cm). Zone 6.
***R.* 'Gruss an Heidelberg'** see *R.* 'Heidelberg'.
***R.* 'Guletta'** see *R.* 'Tapis Jaune'.
***R.* 'Hampshire'** ▣ syn. *R.* 'Korhamp'. Groundcover rose producing glossy, mid-green leaves. From spring to autumn, produces clusters of flat, single scarlet flowers, 2in (5cm) across, with yellow centers fading to white. ↕ 12in (30cm), ↔ 30in (75cm). Zone 6.
***R.* 'Handel'** ▣ Large-flowered climber of stiff, erect habit, with glossy, dark green leaves. Open clusters of urn-shaped, double, lightly scented cream flowers, 3in (8cm) across, with pinkish red margins, are borne from spring to autumn. Superb trained on a pillar or pergola, or when grown with *Clematis* cultivars. ↕ 10ft (3m), ↔ 7ft (2.2m). Zone 6.
***R.* 'Hannah Gordon'** ▣ syn. *R.* 'Korweiso', *R.* 'Raspberry Ice'. Floribunda rose of spreading, open habit, with dark green leaves. From spring to autumn, bears sprays of cupped, double, pale pink flowers, 3in (8cm) across, margined reddish pink. ↕ 32in (80cm), ↔ 26in (65cm). Zone 6.

Rosa 'Hampshire'

***R.* 'Harisonii'** see *R.* x *harisonii* 'Harison's Yellow'.
***R.* x *harisonii* 'Harison's Yellow'**, syn. *R.* 'Harisonii', *R.* 'Harison's Yellow.' Suckering spinosissima rose of gaunt habit, with prickly, dark brown stems and small, fern-like, mid-green leaves with 5–7 oval leaflets, ¾in (2cm) long. In spring, produces cupped, semi-double, bright deep yellow flowers, 2in (5cm) across, on short stems, followed by spherical-oblong, blackish red hips. ↕ 6ft (2m), ↔ 4ft (1.2m). Zone 2b. **'Williams' Double Yellow'**, syn. *R.* 'William's Double Yellow', has a suckering, branching habit, and produces loosely double, fragrant flowers.
***R.* 'Harison's Yellow'** see *R.* x *harisonii* 'Harison's Yellow'.
***R.* 'Harry Wheatcroft'** ▣ Vigorous hybrid tea rose with glossy, reddish green leaves. Bears high-centered, double, scarlet-red flowers, 5in (13cm) across, with yellow-striped petals, from spring to autumn. ↕ 3ft (1m), ↔ 24in (60cm). Zone 6.
***R.* 'Heart Throb'** see *R.* 'Paul Shirville'.
***R.* 'Heckenzauber'** see *R.* 'Sexy Rexy'.
***R.* 'Heidekönigin'** see *R.* 'Pheasant'.
***R.* 'Heidelberg'** ▣ syn. *R.* 'Gruss an Heidelberg'. Hybrid musk rose with dark green, semi-glossy, leathery leaves. Clusters of cupped, double, medium red flowers, 4in (10cm) across, are produced from spring to autumn. ↕ 6–8ft (2–2.5m), ↔ 5ft (1.5m). Zone 6.
***R.* 'Heideröslein'** see *R.* 'Nozomi'.
***R.* 'Helen Naudé'** Large hybrid tea with dull, medium green bushy foliage, of medium growth and moderately prickly stems. White blooms, 4¾in (11cm) across, are very double (40–45 petals), flushed with pink, and have a slight fragrance. ↕↔ 3–5ft (1.2–1.5m). Zone 6.
***R.* 'Heidetraum'** see *R.* 'Flower Carpet'.
***R.* 'Hello'**. Miniature rose with dense, mid-green foliage. Numerous cupped to flat, single crimson flowers, 2in (5cm) across, with white eyes, are borne freely from spring to autumn. ↕↔ 18in (45cm). Zone 6.

Rosa 'Henri Martin'

Rosa 'Heritage'

Rosa 'Hermosa'

Rosa 'Hertfordshire'

Rosa 'High Hopes'

Rosa 'High Sheriff'

Rosa 'Hula Girl'

Rosa 'Iceberg'

Rosa 'Iced Ginger'

Rosa 'Ingrid Bergman'

Rosa 'Intrigue'

Rosa 'Jean Kenneally'

***R.* 'Henri Martin'** ▣ (Red moss rose). Vigorous moss rose of arching growth, with rough, dark green leaves. Rounded, double, scented crimson flowers, 3in (8cm) across, with light green moss on the stems and sepals, open in early summer. ↕ to 6ft (2m), ↔ 4ft (1.2m). Zone 5.
***R.* 'Henry Hudson'.** Semi-dwarf, hybrid rugosa rose with wrinkled, dark green leaves. From spring to autumn, freely produces flat, semi-double, pink-tinged white flowers, 2½–3in (6–8cm) across. ↕↔ 10ft (3m). Zone 2b.
***R.* 'Henry Kelsey'.** Hardy kordesii shrub rose with a trailing habit, grown as a climber, and with glossy, dark green leaves. Produces clusters of remontant, cupped, double, fragrant mid-red flowers, 2½–3in (6–8cm) across, mainly in spring or early summer. ↕ 6–8ft (2–2.5m), ↔ 6ft (2m). Zone 3.
***R.* 'Heritage'** ▣ Vigorous English shrub rose with dark green leaves. Open clusters of cupped, fully double, lemon-scented, light pink flowers, 4½in (11cm) across, with infolded petals, are borne from spring to autumn. ↕↔ 4ft (1.2m). Zone 6.
***R.* 'Hermosa'** ▣ syn. *R.* 'Mélanie Lemaire', *R.* 'Mme. Neumann'. Upright, bushy China rose with grayish green leaves, and rounded, double, scented, rose-pink flowers, 3in (8cm) across, borne freely from spring to autumn. ↕ 3ft (1m), ↔ 24in (60cm). Zone 6.
***R.* 'Hertfordshire'** ▣ Groundcover rose of compact, uneven, spiky habit, with dense, bright green leaves. Flat, single, carmine-pink flowers, 1¾in (4.5cm) across, with paler pink centers, are borne freely in large clusters on short stems, from spring to autumn. ↕ 18in (45cm), ↔ 3ft (1m). Zone 6.
***R.* 'Hiawatha'.** Vigorous, spreading rambler with leathery, semi-glossy, dark green foliage. In early summer, produces large clusters of cupped, single crimson flowers, 1½in (4cm) across, with white eyes. ↕ 15ft (5m), ↔ 12ft (4m). Zone 6.
***R.* 'High Hopes'** ▣ syn. *R.* 'Haryup'. Stiff, vigorous, arching, large-flowered climber with glossy, dark green leaves. Urn-shaped to rounded, double, scented, light rose-pink flowers, 3in (8cm) across, are borne freely from summer to autumn. ↕ 12ft (4m), ↔ 8ft (2.5m). Zone 6.
***R.* 'High Sheriff'** ▣ Tall, free-branching, vigorous hybrid tea rose with glossy, mid-green foliage. From spring to autumn, produces high-centered, double, peach-orange flowers, 4in (10cm) across, red on the reverse of the petals. ↕ 4ft (1.2m), ↔ 28in (70cm). Zone 6.
***R.* 'Hotline'.** Fast-growing, compact miniature rose with light mossing and mid-green leaves. High-centered to cupped, semi-double, mid-red flowers, 1½in (4cm) across, are borne from spring to autumn. ↕ 18in (45cm), ↔ 14in (35cm). Zone 6.
***R.* 'Hot Tamale'** syn. *R.* 'Sunbird'. Low, bushy, compact miniature rose with small, dark green, semi-glossy foliage. Bears double blooms (26–40 petals), 1½–2¾in (4–7cm) across, with slight fragrance. Flowers are a yellow-orange blend, changing to yellow-pink, and maturing to pink. ↕ 14in (36cm). Zone 6.
R. hugonis see *R. xanthina* f. *hugonis.*
***R.* 'Hula Girl'** ▣ Miniature rose of neat, upright habit, with semi-glossy, mid-green foliage. Urn-shaped, fully double, lightly scented, pale orange-pink flowers, 1¼in (3cm) across, are borne from spring to autumn. ↕ 20in (50cm), ↔ 12in (30cm). Zone 6.
***R.* 'Iceberg'** ▣ syn. *R.* 'Fée des Neiges', *R.* 'Schneewittchen'. Vigorous floribunda rose of rounded habit, with abundant light green foliage. Large clusters of many cupped, double, creamy to pure white flowers, 3in (8cm) across, are borne freely from spring to autumn. ↕ 4–5ft (1.2–1.5m), ↔ 26in (65cm). Zone 5.
***R.* 'Iced Ginger'** ▣ Floribunda rose of lanky habit, with sparse, light green foliage. High-centered, fully double, buff to copper-pink flowers, 4½in (11cm) across, are borne from spring to autumn. ↕ 3ft (1m), ↔ 28in (70cm). Zone 6.
***R.* 'Immensee'** see *R.* 'Grouse'.
***R.* 'Impatient'.** Vigorous floribunda rose with glossy, light green leaves. Bears flat, semi-double, slightly fragrant, orange-red flowers, 3in (8cm) across, from spring to autumn. ↕ 3½ft (1.1m), ↔ 24in (60cm). Zone 6.
***R.* 'Incarnata'** see *R.* 'Maiden's Blush'.
***R.* 'Ingrid Bergman'** ▣ Hybrid tea rose of branching habit, with leathery, dark green leaves. High-centered, fully double, dark red flowers, 4½in (11cm) across, are borne from spring to autumn. ↕ 4–5ft (1.2–1.5m), ↔ 26in (65cm). Zone 6.
***R.* 'Integrity'** see *R.* 'Savoy Hotel'.
***R.* 'Intrigue'** ▣ syn. *R.* 'Lavaglut'. Vigorous floribunda rose of compact habit, with glossy, purplish green leaves. Rounded, double, dark red flowers, 3in (8cm) across, are borne in large clusters from spring to autumn. ↕ 3–4ft (1–1.2m), ↔ 24in (60cm). Zone 6.
***R.* 'Irish Gold'** see *R.* 'Grandpa Dickson'.
***R.* 'Ispahan'** ▣ syn. *R.* 'Pompon des Princes', *R.* 'Rose d'Isfahan'. Vigorous damask rose with abundant gray-green foliage. Cupped, double, fragrant, clear pink flowers, 3in (8cm) across, are borne in early summer. ↕ 5ft (1.5m), ↔ 4ft (1.2m). Zone 5.
***R.* 'Jack Dayson'** see *R.* 'Perfect Moment'.
***R.* 'Jacques Cartier'** see *R.* 'Marchesa Boccella'.
***R.* 'Jean Kenneally'** ▣ Vigorous miniature rose with upright, bushy growth has medium green, semi-glossy foliage. Generally produces one small bloom per long stem, double (22 petals), in pale to medium apricot rose. ↕ 15–20in (37–50cm). Zone 6.
***R.* 'Jeanne Lajoie'.** Climbing miniature rose of bushy habit, producing glossy, dark green leaves and high-centered, fully double, lavender-pink flowers, 1¾in (4.5cm) across, from summer to autumn. ↕ to 6ft (2m) on a support, ↔ 28in (70cm). Zone 6.
***R.* 'Jeepers Creepers'.** Low-growing, spreading, groundcover rose with semi-glossy, dark green leaves. Flat, semi-double white flowers, 1½–3in (4–8cm) across, are borne in large clusters from spring to autumn. ↕ 24–30in (60–75cm), ↔ 4–5ft (1.2–1.5m). Zone 5.
***R.* 'Jenny Duval'** see *R.* 'Président de Sèze'.
***R.* 'Jen's Munk'.** Hybrid rugosa rose with mid-green, deeply veined leaves. Bears clusters of intensely scented, cupped, double, medium pink flowers, 3in (8cm) across, from spring to autumn. Cold-hardy and disease resistant. ↕ 4–6ft (1.2–2m),. ↔ 1.2–1.5m). Zone 2b.
***R.* 'John Cabot'** ▣ Vigorous kordesii shrub rose producing abundant light green leaves. Clusters of cupped, double, scented magenta flowers, 2½in (6cm) across, are borne in early summer, with repeat flowering to autumn. ↕ 5ft (1.5m), ↔ 4ft (1.2m). ↕ 8–10ft (2.5–3m) when grown as a climber. Zone 2b.
***R.* 'John Davis'.** Hardy kordesii shrub rose with a trailing habit and glossy, dark green leaves. Remontant, rounded, fully double, lightly fragrant, pink flowers, 3–3½in (8–9cm) across, with yellow bases, are borne in large clusters in spring or early summer; use as a pilla*R.* ↕ 6–8ft (2–2.5m), ↔ 6ft (2m). Zone 3.
***R.* 'Joseph's Coat'.** Vigorous, branching, large-flowered climber or shrub rose with dark green leaves. Showy clusters of urn-shaped to cupped, double yellow flowers, 3in (8cm) across, suffused orange-pink and red as the flowers grow older, are borne from spring to autumn. ↕↔ 10ft (3m) as a climber; ↕ to 4ft (1.2m), ↔ 3ft (1m) as a shrub. Zone 6.
***R.* 'Judy Garland'.** Vigorous floribunda rose with semi-glossy, mid-green foliage. Cupped, double, lightly scented yellow flowers, 3in (8cm) across, the petals margined orange-red, are borne freely from spring to autumn. ↕ 30in (75cm), ↔ 26in (65cm). Zone 6.
***R.* 'Julia's Rose'** ▣ Hybrid tea rose with spindly, branching growth and sparse reddish green foliage. High-centered, double, brownish pink to buff flowers, 4in (10cm) across, are borne from spring to autumn. ↕ 30in (75cm), ↔ 18in (45cm). Zone 6.
***R.* 'Just Joey'** ▣ Hybrid tea rose of open, branching habit, with sparse, dark green foliage. Rounded, fully double, fragrant, copper-pink flowers, 5in (13cm) across, with wavy-margined petals, are borne from summer to autumn. ↕ 4–5ft (1.2–1.5m), ↔ 28in (70cm). Zone 6.
***R.* 'Katharina Zeimet'**, syn. *R.* 'White Baby Rambler'. Vigorous polyantha rose producing abundant dark green leaves. From spring to autumn, produces dense clusters of cupped, double white flowers, 1¾in (4.5cm) across. ↕↔ 20in (50cm) or more. Zone 6.

?osa 'Ispahan'

Rosa 'John Cabot'

Rosa 'Julia's Rose'

Rosa 'Just Joey'

Rosa 'Keepsake'

Rosa 'Kent'

?osa 'Knock Out'

Rosa 'Königin von Dänemark'

Rosa 'Korresia'

Rosa 'Lady Mitchell'

Rosa 'Lamarque'

Rosa 'Laughter Lines'

?. 'Kathleen Harrop'. Bourbon rose f arching, lax habit, with dark green eaves. Cupped, double, fragrant, ale pink flowers, 3in (8cm) across, re borne in spring or early summer, vith repeat flowering to autumn. usceptible to mildew. ↕ 8ft (2.5m), ↔ 6ft (2m). Zone 6.
?. 'Keepsake' ▣ syn. *R.* 'Esmeralda'. Hybrid tea rose of uneven habit, vith dark green leaves. From spring to utumn, bears well-formed, high-entered, fully double, lightly cented, deep pink flowers, 5in 13cm) across, with light pink shading. to 5ft (1.5m), ↔ 24in (60cm). one 6.
?. 'Kent' ▣ syn. *R.* 'Pyrenees', . 'White Cover'. Compact, spreading, roundcover shrub rose with shiny, dark reen leaves. Cupped to flat, semi-ouble white flowers, 1¾in (4.5cm) cross, are borne on short stems from pring to autumn. ↕ 18in (45cm), ↔ 3ft m). Zone 6.
?. 'Kew Rambler'. Vigorous rambler ith stiff but pliable growth and ense, gray-green leaves. Clusters of upped, single, scented pink flowers, ½in (4cm) across, each with a white ye and yellow stamens, are borne in arly summer. ↕ 15ft (5m), ↔ 12ft (4m). one 6.
?. 'King's Ransom'. Hybrid tea rose roducing leathery, glossy, dark green aves. Produces urn-shaped to cupped, illy double, lightly scented yellow owers, 5in (13cm) across, on long ems from spring to autumn. 4–5ft (1.2–1.5m), ↔ 24in (60cm). one 6.
?. 'Knock Out' ▣ Shrub rose with id-green, semi-glossy leaves. Bears nall clusters of single-petalled, ghtly scented, flat, cherry-red flowers, –3in (5–8cm) across, from spring autumn. Disease-resistant and lerant of partial shade. ↕↔ 3–4ft 9–1.2m). Zone 6.
?. 'Königin von Dänemark' ▣ syn. . 'Belle Courtisane', *R.* 'Queen of enmark'. Vigorous, lax alba rose with ull, bluish green leaves. In early ummer, bears quartered-rosette, fully ouble, very fragrant, deep to light pink owers, 3½in (9cm) across, with green utton eyes. ↕ 5ft (1.5m), ↔ 4ft (1.2m). one 3.

***R.* 'Königliche Hoheit'** see *R.* 'Royal Highness'.
***R.* 'Kordes Robusta'** see *R.* 'Robusta'.
***R.* 'Korp'**, syn. *R.* 'Prominent'. Grandiflora rose with uneven growth and dark green foliage. Cupped, stiff-petaled, fully double, vivid orange-red flowers, 3½in (9cm) across, are borne on long stems from summer to autumn. ↕ 4–5ft (1.2–1.5m), ↔ 26in (65cm). Zone 6.
***R.* 'Korresia'** ▣ syn. *R.* 'Friesia', *R.* 'Sunsprite'. Compact floribunda rose with light green leaves. Sprays of urn-shaped to cupped, double, fragrant, bright yellow flowers, 3in (8cm) across, with wavy-margined petals, are borne from spring to autumn. ↕ 4ft (1.2m), ↔ 24in (60cm). Zone 6.
***R.* 'Kristin'** syn. *R.* 'Kristen', *R.* 'Pirouette'. Upright, bushy, miniature rose of medium growth, with large, dark green, semi-glossy foliage. Bears bicolored red and white petals, 1½in (3.75cm) across. The unscented, double flower (27–30 petals), does not open beyond half-open stage. Zone 6.
***R.* 'La Belle Sultane'** see *R.* 'Violacea'.
***R.* 'Lady Mitchell'** ▣ Hybrid tea rose with dark green leaves and rounded, fully double, scented, deep pink flowers, 5in (13cm) across, borne from spring to autumn. ↕ 3ft (1m), ↔ 26in (65cm). Zone 6.

Rosa 'Laura Ashley'

***R.* 'Lady Penzance'.** Vigorous, twiggy, free-branching eglanteria rose with apple-scented, shiny, dark green leaves. Cupped, single, copper-pink and yellow flowers, 1½in (4cm) across, are borne briefly in midsummer, followed by ovoid red hips. ↕↔ 6ft (2m). Zone 4b.
R. laevigata, syn. *R.* 'Golden Cherry' (Camellia rose, Cherokee rose). Vigorous species rose with large prickles, arching stems, and attractive, glossy, dark green leaves, each with 3, rarely 5, lance-shaped to elliptic or ovate leaflets, 1¼–2½in (3–6cm) long. Solitary, flat, single, scented white flowers, to 4in (10cm) across, with scalloped petals and gold stamens, are borne in spring; they are followed by pear-shaped, bristly, brownish orange-red hips. Evergreen in mild climates. ↕↔ 6–20ft (2–6m). E. and S. China, Taiwan, S.E. Asia. Naturalized widely in the S.E. US. Zone 7b.
***R.* 'Lamarque'** ▣ Vigorous noisette climbing rose with smooth stems and limp, shiny, bright green foliage. Flat, quartered-rosette, fully double, fragrant, yellowish white flowers, 3½in (9cm) across, are borne on nodding stems from summer to autumn. ↕ to 15ft (5m), ↔ 8ft (2.5m). Zone 6.
***R.* 'Landora'** see *R.* 'Sunblest'.
***R.* 'La Royale'** see *R.* 'Maiden's Blush'.
***R.* 'La Séduisante'** see *R.* 'Great Maiden's Blush'.
***R.* 'Las Vegas'**. Vigorous hybrid tea rose with glossy, mid-green foliage. From summer to autumn, bears urn-shaped, double, deep orange flowers, 4in (10cm) across, with a yellow reverse to the petals. ↕ 3ft (1m), ↔ 26in (65cm). Zone 6.
***R.* 'Laughter Lines'** ▣ Upright floribunda rose with dark green foliage. Cupped, semi-double, rose-pink flowers, 3½in (9cm) across, with red, gold, and white markings, are borne from spring to autumn. ↕ to 3ft (1m), ↔ 24in (60cm). Zone 6.
***R.* 'Laura Ashley'** ▣ Dense, compact groundcover rose producing abundant mid-green leaves. Large clusters of cupped to flat, single, magenta-pink to lilac flowers, 1¼in (3cm) across, with pale yellow centers, cover the plant from spring to autumn. ↕ 24in (60cm), ↔ 4ft (1.2m). Zone 6.

Rosa 'Laura Ford'

Rosa 'Lavender Jewel'

Rosa 'Little Artist'

Rosa 'Little Bo-Peep'

Rosa 'Lovely Lady'

Rosa 'Lovers' Meeting'

Rosa 'Loving Memory'

Rosa 'Maiden's Blush'

Rosa 'Maigold'

Rosa 'Many Happy Returns'

Rosa 'Marchesa Boccella'

Rosa 'Maréchal Niel'

***R.* 'Laura Ford'** ■ Stiff, upright, climbing miniature rose with abundant shiny, light green leaves. From spring to autumn, bears clusters of urn-shaped to flat, semi-double, lightly scented yellow flowers, 1¾in (4.5cm) across, becoming pink-tinged with age. ↕ 7ft (2.2m), ↔ 4ft (1.2m). Zone 6.
***R.* 'Lavaglut'**, syn. *R.* 'Intrigue', *R.* 'Lavaglow'. Bushy, spreading floribunda rose with glossy, purplish green leaves. Bears large clusters of dark red, camellia-shaped, double flowers, 2in (6cm) across, from spring to autumn. ↕ 2ft (60cm), ↔ 3ft (1m). Zone 6.
***R.* 'Lavender Jewel'** ■ Miniature rose of neat, spreading habit, with dark green foliage. Cupped, double, lavender-pink flowers, 1½in (4cm) across, are produced in clusters from spring to autumn. ↕↔ 12in (30cm). Zone 6.
***R.* 'Leda'** (Painted damask rose). Lax damask rose with prickly stems and gray-green leaves. In early summer, bears rosette-shaped, fully double, fragrant, carmine-tipped white flowers, 3in (8cm) across, with button centers, reflexing into a ball. ↕↔ 3ft (1m). Zone 5.
***R.* 'Lemon Pillar'** see *R.* 'Paul's Lemon Pillar'.
***R.* 'Leonard Dudley Braithwaite'**. Open English shrub rose producing grayish green leaves. Loosely formed, rosette-shaped, fully double, scented, bright crimson flowers, 3½in (9cm) across, with infolded petals, are borne from spring to autumn. ↕ 3ft (1m), ↔ 4ft (1.2m). Zone 6.
***R.* 'Little Artist'** ■ syn. *R.* 'Top Gear'. Neat, upright miniature rose with mid-green foliage. Cupped to flat, semi-double red flowers, 1¾in (4.5cm) across, with white markings, are borne on short, stiff stems from spring to autumn. ↕↔ 12in (30cm). Zone 6.
***R.* 'Little Bo-Peep'** ■ syn. *R.* 'Natchez', *R.* 'White Carpet'. Miniature rose of low, spreading habit, with dark green foliage. Dense clusters of many rounded to flat, semi-double, light pink flowers, 1½in (4cm) across, are borne close to the plant from spring to autumn. ↕ 12in (30cm), ↔ 20in (50cm). Zone 6.
***R.* 'Little White Pet'** ■ syn. *R.* 'White Pet'. Vigorous polyantha rose with deep green foliage. From spring to autumn, red buds open to sprays of rosette-shaped, double white flowers, 1½in (4cm) across. ↕ 18in (45cm), ↔ 22in (55cm). Zone 6.
***R.* 'Livin' Easy'**, syn. *R.* 'Beauty Star'. Vigorous hybrid tea rose with glossy, mid-green leaves. From spring to autumn, bears high-centered, fully double, vermilion flowers, 2½–3in (6–8cm) across. ↕ 5–6ft (1.5–2m), ↔ 24–30in (60–75cm). Zone 6.
***R. longicuspis* of gardens** see *R. mulliganii.*
***R.* 'L'Ouche'** see *R.* 'Louise Odier'.
***R.* 'Louise Odier'**, syn. *R.* 'L'Ouche', *R.* 'Mme. de Stella'. Bourbon rose of slender, arching growth, with light gray-green foliage. Camellia-shaped, rosetted, fully double, fragrant pink flowers, 3½in (9cm) across, with lilac tints, are borne in early summer, with repeat flowering to autumn. ↕ 6ft (2m), ↔ 4ft (1.2m). Zone 5.
***R.* 'Louis Jolliet'**. Kordesii shrub rose with trailing habit and semi-glossy, mid-green leaves. From spring or early summer to autumn, bears rounded, fully double, fragrant, pink flowers, to 3in (8cm) across, in clusters. Use as a short climber or pillar. ↕↔ 4ft (1.2m). Zone 3.
***R.* 'Love'**. Vigorous, strongly upright grandiflora rose with semi-glossy, copper-tinged, dark green leaves. From spring to autumn, high-centered, double, crimson-red flowers, 3½in (9cm) across, with striking silver-white reverses, are freely borne singly or in clusters. Recovers quickly from hard pruning. ↕ 5ft (1.5m), ↔ 30in (75cm). Zone 6.
***R.* 'Lovely Lady'** ■ Hybrid tea rose with a vigorous, free-branching habit and abundant glossy, mid-green leaves. Urn-shaped, fully double, scented, salmon-pink flowers, 4in (10cm) across, are borne from spring to autumn. ↕ 4ft (1.2m), ↔ 24in (60cm). Zone 6.
***R.* 'Lovers' Meeting'** ■ Free-branching hybrid tea rose of vigorous, spreading habit, with bronze-green foliage. High-centered, double, reddish orange flowers, 3½in (9cm) across, are borne singly and in wide sprays from spring to autumn. ↕↔ 4ft (1.2m). Zone 6.

Rosa 'Little White Pet'

***R.* 'Loving Memory'** ■ syn. *R.* 'Burgund '81', *R.* 'Korgund'. Robust hybrid tea rose with dull, dark green leaves. High-centered, fully double, lightly scented, dark red flowers, 5in (13cm) across, are borne on strong, stiff stems from spring to autumn. ↕ 4–5ft (1.2–1.5m), ↔ 30in (75cm). Zone 6.
R. lucida see *R. virginiana.*
***R.* 'Lü E'** see *R.* x *odorata* 'Viridiflora'.
***R.* 'Magic Carrousel'.** Miniature rose o neat, bushy habit, with glossy, mid-green leaves. Rosette-shaped, double, pale yellow flowers, 1½in (4cm) across, with crimson edging, are produced fron spring to autumn. ↕ 16in (40cm), ↔ 12in (30cm). Zone 6.
***R.* 'Maiden's Blush'** ■ syn. *R.* 'Incarnata', *R.* 'La Royale'. Vigorous, upright, arching alba rose with matte, bluish green foliage. Cupped, fully double, fragrant, very pale pink flowers, 3in (8cm) across, with irregular centers, are freely borne in early summer. ↕ 4ft (1.2m), ↔ 36in (90cm). Zone 3.
***R.* 'Maigold'** ■ Strong, upright shrub rose, often grown as a climber, with ver prickly, arching stems and leathery, dar green leaves. Cupped, semi-double, scented, bronze-yellow flowers, 4in (10cm) across, are borne in early summer. ↕↔ 8ft (2.5m). Zone 3.
***R.* 'Many Happy Returns'** ■ syn. *R.* 'Prima'. Floribunda rose of shrubby habit, with attractive, shiny, mid-green foliage. Cupped, semi-double, scented, pale pink flowers, 4in (10cm) across, ar borne in dense clusters from spring to autumn. ↕↔ 30in (75cm). Zone 6.
***R.* 'Marchesa Boccella'** ■ syn. *R.* 'Jacques Cartier'. Portland rose of dense habit, with abundant light green foliage Quartered-rosette, fully double, scented rose-pink flowers, 4½in (11cm) across, are borne on short stems in early summer and usually again in early to midautumn. ↕ 4ft (1.2m), ↔ 3ft (1m). Zone 6.
***R.* 'Maréchal le Clerc'** see *R.* 'Touch of Class'.
***R.* 'Maréchal Niel'** ■ Vigorous noisette rose with long, shiny, rich green leaves. High-centered, fully double, scented, clear yellow flowers, 4in (10cm) across, are produced on nodding stems from spring to

R

Rosa 'Margaret Merril'

Rosa 'Marguerite Hilling'

Rosa 'Marion Harkness'

Rosa 'Marmalade Skies'

Rosa 'Mary Rose'

Rosa 'May Queen'

Rosa 'Melody Maker'

Rosa 'Memorial Day'

Rosa 'Mme. Alfred Carrière'

Rosa 'Mme. Ernst Calvat'

Rosa 'Mme. Hardy'

Rosa 'Mme. Isaac Pereire'

autumn. ↕ to 15ft (5m), ↔ 8ft (2.5m). Zone 7b.

***R.* 'Margaret Merril'** ▣ Floribunda rose with crisp, dark green leaves. Bears high-centered to cupped, double, fragrant, pale pink to white flowers, 4in (10cm) across, with maroon stamens, singly or in clusters from spring to autumn. ↕ 36in (80cm), ↔ 24in (60cm). Zone 6.

***R.* 'Marguerite Hilling'** ▣ syn. *R.* 'Pink Nevada'. Vigorous, arching, hybrid moyesii shrub rose with red stems and dense, light green foliage. Flat, semi-double, scented, rose-pink flowers, 4in (10cm) across, with deeper shading, are borne freely in early summer and sparsely in autumn. ↕↔ 7ft (2.2m). Zone 5.

***R.* 'Marion Harkness'** ▣ Hybrid tea rose of well-branched habit, with glossy, dark green leaves. Rounded, double yellow flowers, 3½in (9cm) across, shaded orange-red toward the petal tips, are borne freely from spring to autumn. ↕ 4ft (1.2m), ↔ 24in (60cm). Zone 6.

***R.* 'Marjike Koopman'.** Vigorous, upright, hybrid tea rose with large, leathery, dark green leaves. High-centered, double, rich rose-pink flowers, 5in (13cm) across, with deep pink swirls, are borne singly and in clusters from spring to autumn. ↕ 5–6ft (1.5–2m), ↔ 24in (60cm). Zone 6.

***R.* 'Marjorie Fair'**, syn. *R.* 'Red Ballerina', *R.* 'Red Yesterday'. Dense polyantha rose with glossy, mid-green leaves. Mop-headed clusters of many cupped, single, wine-red flowers, 1¾in (4.5cm) across, each with a white eye, are borne from spring to autumn. ↕↔ 4ft (1.2m). Zone 6.

***R.* 'Marlena'.** Floribunda rose of compact habit, with dark green leaves. Sprays of cupped, double, bright crimson flowers, 2½in (6cm) across, are borne freely from spring to autumn. ↕↔ 30in (75cm). Zone 6.

***R.* 'Marmalade Skies'** ▣ syn. *R.* 'Tangerine Dream'. Bushy floribunda rose with satiny, olive-green, glossy leaves. Bears clusters of tangerine-orange, double, high-centered flowers, 2–3in (6–8cm) across, from spring to autumn. Tolerant of light shade. ↕↔ 36in (90cm). Zone 6.

***R.* 'Mary Rose'** ▣ English shrub rose of upright, uneven growth, with matte, mid-green leaves. Cupped, double, scented, deep rose-pink flowers, 3½in (9cm) across, are borne from spring to autumn. ↕ 4ft (1.2m), ↔ 3ft (1m). Zone 6.

***R.* 'Masquerade'.** Floribunda rose of compact habit, with leathery, dark green leaves. From spring to autumn, bears sprays of cupped to flat, semi-double flowers, to 2½in (6cm) across, changing in color from yellow to pink and dark red. ↕ 36in (90cm), ↔ 24in (60cm). Zone 6.

***R.* 'May Queen'** ▣ Vigorous, arching rambler with abundant glossy, mid-green foliage. In early summer, bears clusters of quartered-rosette, apple-scented, double, clear rose-pink flowers, 3in (8cm) across. ↕ 12ft (4m), ↔ 10ft (3m). Zone 6.

***R.* 'Meg'.** Stiff, vigorous, climbing hybrid tea rose with dark green leaves and open clusters of cupped to flat, semi-double, fragrant, pink-apricot to pink flowers, 5in (13cm) across, with red stamens, borne from spring to autumn. ↕↔ 12ft (4m). Zone 6.

***R.* 'Mélanie Lemaire'** see *R.* 'Hermosa'.

***R.* 'Melody Maker'** ▣ Floribunda rose of dense habit, with abundant dark green foliage. Freely bears rounded, fully double, light scarlet flowers, 3½in (9cm) across, from spring to autumn. ↕ 36in (90cm), ↔ 24in (60cm). Zone 6.

***R.* 'Memorial Day'** ▣ Robust rose with upright growth. Orchid-pink hybrid tea with a soft lavender wash, very double (50 petals), with 6in (15cm) blooms. Has strong damask fragrance. ↕ 5–6ft (1.5–2m). Zone 6.

***R.* 'Mermaid'.** Vigorous, slow-growing hybrid bracteata with climbing growth, stiff, red-brown stems, hooked prickles, and shiny, dark green leaves. From spring to autumn, bears cupped to flat, single, primrose-yellow flowers, 4½in (11cm) across, with sulfur-yellow stamens. Striking when grown against a wall. ↕↔ to 20ft (6m). Zone 6.

***R.* 'Mevrouw Nathalie Nypels'**, syn. *R.* 'Nathalie Nypels'. Polyantha rose of neat habit, with glossy, mid-green leaves. Freely bears cupped, semi-double, rose-pink flowers, 2½in (6cm) across, from spring to autumn. ↕ 30in (75cm), ↔ 24in (60cm). Zone 6.

***R.* 'Michèle Meilland'.** Hybrid tea rose of well-branched, leafy habit, with mid-green foliage. Neatly formed, urn-shaped, double, light pink flowers, 3½in (9cm) across, are borne from spring to autumn. Excellent for flower arrangements. ↕ 4ft (1.2m), ↔ 24in (60cm). Zone 6.

***R.* 'Mignon'** see *R.* 'Cécile Brunner'.

***R.* 'Mischief'.** Hybrid tea rose producing abundant but rust-prone, mid-green leaves. Urn-shaped, double, scented, pink-orange to pink flowers, 4in (10cm) across, are borne from spring to autumn. ↕ 3ft (1m), ↔ 24in (60cm). Zone 6.

***R.* 'Mister Lincoln'.** Stiff-stemmed, hybrid tea rose of upright habit, with leathery, dull, dark green foliage. High-centered to cupped, fully double, fragrant, dark velvety red flowers, 5in (13cm) across, are produced from spring to autumn. ↕ 4–5ft (1.2–1.5m), ↔ 24in (60cm). Zone 6.

***R.* 'Mme. Alfred Carrière'** ▣ Noisette rose with slender, smooth stems and pale green foliage. Rounded, fully double, fragrant, pale pink to white flowers, 2½in (6cm) across, are borne from spring to autumn. ↕ 15ft (5m), ↔ 10ft (3m). Zone 6.

Rosa 'Mme. Grégoire Staechelin'

***R.* 'Mme. A. Meilland'** see *R.* 'Peace'.

***R.* 'Mme. Delaroche-Lambert'.** Upright, arching moss rose with rough, dull, light to mid-green leaves and brownish green moss. Rounded, fully double, scented, purplish pink flowers, 3in (8cm) across, some with button centers, are borne mainly in early summer, sometimes also in autumn. ↕ 4ft (1.2m), ↔ 3ft (1m). Zone 6.

***R.* 'Mme. de Stella'** see *R.* 'Louise Odier'.

***R.* 'Mme. Ernst Calvat'** ▣ Vigorous, arching bourbon rose with dark green leaves, purplish green when young. In early summer and autumn, produces quartered-rosette, fully double, fragrant, rose-pink flowers, 6in (15cm) across. ↕ 6ft (2m), ↔ 4ft (1.2m). Zone 6.

***R.* 'Mme. Grégoire Staechelin'** ▣ syn. *R.* 'Spanish Beauty'. Very vigorous, arching, climbing hybrid tea rose with masses of large, dark green leaves. Rounded, fully double flowers, 5in (13cm) across, with ruffled, red-flushed, clear pink petals, are borne in early summer. Flowers are followed by large, spherical red hips. ↕ to 20ft (6m), ↔ 12ft (4m). Zone 6.

***R.* 'Mme. Hardy'** ▣ Vigorous, upright damask rose with abundant leathery, dark green leaves. Quartered-rosette, fully double, fragrant white flowers, 4in (10cm) across, each with a green button eye, are borne in early summer. ↕ 5ft (1.5m), ↔ 4ft (1.2m). Zone 5.

***R.* 'Mme. Hébert'** see *R.* 'Président de Sèze'.

***R.* 'Mme. Isaac Pereire'** ▣ Vigorous, arching bourbon rose with large, dark green leaves. In early summer and autumn, bears quartered-rosette, fully double, fragrant, deep purplish pink flowers, 6in (15cm) across. Train as a pillar. ↕ 7ft (2.2m), ↔ 6ft (2m). Zone 6.

***R.* 'Mme. Legras de St. Germain'.** Upright alba rose with smooth stems and grayish green leaves. Rosette-shaped, fully double, fragrant, lemon-white flowers, 3½in (9cm) across, are borne in early summer. May be trained on a support. ↕↔ 6ft (2m) as a shrub; ↕ to 15ft (5m) as a climber. Zone 4b.

Rosa 'Mme. Zoetmans'

Rosa 'Moonlight'

Rosa 'Moonstone'

Rosa 'Morning Jewel'

Rosa moschata

Rosa moyesii 'Geranium'

Rosa 'Mrs. John Laing'

Rosa mulliganii

Rosa 'National Trust'

Rosa 'Nevada'

Rosa 'New Dawn'

Rosa 'News'

***R.* 'Mme. Neumann'** see *R.* 'Hermosa'.
***R.* 'Mme. Pierre Oger'.** Lax bourbon rose with slender stems and light green leaves. In early summer and autumn, bears precisely cupped, double, scented, creamy pink flowers, 3in (8cm) across, marked with lilac, resembling Victorian shell flowers. ↕ 6ft (2m), ↔ 4ft (1.2m). Zone 6.
***R.* 'Mme. Plantier'** ■ Vigorous, arching alba shrub or noisette climbing rose with long, smooth, mid-green leaves. In early summer, bears clusters of cupped, fully double, scented white flowers, 3in (8cm) across, reflexing into a ball. ↕ 6ft (2m), ↔ to 20ft (6m) on a support, ↔ 8ft (2.5m) grown as a shrub. Zone 3.
***R.* 'Mme. Zoetmans'** ■ Damask rose with mid-green leaves. Bears small clusters of white, flat, double, richly scented, quartered flowers with a green button eye, 2in (6cm) across, in early summer. ↕ 4ft (1.2m), ↔ 3ft (1m). Zone 6.
***R.* 'Montezuma'.** Tall, strong hybrid tea rose with stiff stems and leathery leaves. High-centered, fully double, salmon-pink to red flowers, 3½in (9cm) across, are borne singly and in large sprays from spring to autumn. ↕ 5½ft (1.7m), ↔ 28in (70cm). Zone 6.
***R.* 'Moonlight'** ■ Hybrid musk rose of dense habit, with stems and leaves both reddish green. Clusters of flat, semi-double, scented, lemon-white flowers, 1¾in (4.5cm) across, are borne freely from spring to autumn. ↕↔ 4ft (1.2m). Zone 6.
***R.* 'Moonstone'** ■ syn. *R.* 'Cadillac DeVille'. Elegant hybrid tea buds open into ivory-white blooms edged in pink, with mild fragrance. Free blooming in hot weather, of exhibition quality. Has upright growth. ↕ 3–4ft (1–1.2m), ↔ 24in (60cm). Zone 6.
***R.* 'Morden Amorette'.** Compact shrub rose with dark green leaves. From spring to autumn, cupped, double, carmine flowers, 2½–3in (6–8cm) across, are borne in clusters. ↕↔ 12–20in (30–50cm). Zone 3.
***R.* 'Morden Blush'.** Everblooming, low-growing shrub rose with matte-green leaves. From spring to autumn, bears clusters of rosette-shaped, fully double, light pink flowers, 2in (5cm) across, that fade to ivory and open flat. ↕↔ 18–36in (45–90cm). Zone 2b.
***R.* 'Morden Cardinette'.** Dwarf, everblooming shrub rose with dark green leaves. Cupped, double, cardinal-red flowers, 3in (8cm) across, are borne in clusters from spring to autumn. ↕↔ 12–20in (30–50cm). Zone 3b.
***R.* 'Morden Centennial'.** Floriferous shrub rose with semi-glossy, dark green leaves. Bears rosette-shaped, fully double, lightly scented pink flowers, 2½–3in (6–8cm) across, in clusters, mainly in spring or summer, and also in autumn. ↕↔ 28–36in (70–90cm). Zone 2.
***R.* 'Morden Fireglow'.** Compact shrub rose with matte-green leaves. From spring to autumn, bears cupped, double, red-orange flowers, 2½–3in (6–8cm) across, with red reverses, in clusters. ↕↔ 18–28in (45–70cm). Zone 2b.
***R.* 'Morden Ruby'.** Vigorous shrub rose with glossy, dark green leaves. Bears rosette-shaped, double, ruby-red flowers, 2½–3in (6–8cm) across, from spring to autumn. ↕↔ 3ft (1m). Zone 3b.
***R.* 'Morning Jewel'** ■ Vigorous, free-branching, large-flowered climber producing glossy, mid-green leaves. Clusters of cupped, double, scented, bright pink flowers, 3½in (9cm) across, are borne from spring to autumn. Tolerates partial shade. ↕ 10ft (3m), ↔ 8ft (2.5m). Zone 6.

Rosa 'Mme. Plantier'

R. moschata ■ (Musk rose). Species rose of tall, lax habit, with dark green stems and purplish green leaves, each consisting of 5–7 broadly ovate to broadly elliptic leaflets, ½–1½in (1.5–4cm) long. Few-flowered, loose clusters of flat, single to semi-double, musk-scented, milk-white flowers, 2in (5cm) across, are borne from summer to autumn; they are followed by spherical to ovoid, orange-red hips. ↕↔ to 10ft (3m). W. Asia. Zone 6.
R. moyesii. Vigorous, arching species rose producing mid- to dark green leaves, each consisting of 7–13 small, broadly elliptic to ovate leaflets, ½–1½in (1–4cm) long. Flat or cupped, single, deep scarlet or pink flowers, 2in (5cm) across, with yellow stamens, are borne singly or in small clusters in spring or early summer; they are followed by large, flask-shaped red hips. ↕ 12ft (4m), ↔ 10ft (3m). W. China. Zone 4. **var. *fargesii*** is less vigorous, and has pink flowers; ↕ 8ft (2.5m), ↔ 5ft (1.5m). **'Geranium'** ■ has a compact habit, and bears brighter, cherry-red flowers with cream stamens, followed by orange-red hips; ↕ 8ft (2.5m), ↔ 5ft (1.5m). **'Highdownensis'** see *R.* 'Highdownensis'.
***R.* 'Mrs. John Laing'** ■ Hybrid perpetual rose with abundant light green foliage. From spring to autumn, bears rounded, fully double, fragrant, silvery pink flowers, 5in (13cm) across. ↕ 3ft (1m), ↔ 30in (75cm). Zone 5.
***R.* 'Mrs. Oakley Fisher'.** Hybrid tea rose with spindly stems and sparse, bronze-green foliage. From spring to autumn, bears cupped to flat, single, scented apricot flowers, 3in (8cm) across, fading to pale buff with age. ↕↔ to 3ft (1m). Zone 6.
***R.* 'Mullard Jubilee'**, syn. *R.* 'Electron'. Vigorous hybrid tea rose producing abundant mid-green leaves. Urn-shaped, fully double, scented, deep rose-pink flowers, 5in (13cm) across, are borne from spring to autumn. ↕ 30in (75cm), ↔ 24in (60cm). Zone 6.
R. mulliganii ■ syn. *R. longicuspis* of gardens. Rampant species rose with large, shiny, grayish green leaves, each consisting of 5–7 elliptic-ovate to oblong-ovate leaflets, to 2½in (6cm) long. Large clusters of many pendent, cupped to flat, single white flowers, to 2½in (6cm) across, are borne on

R

Rosa 'New Zealand'

Rosa 'Noisette Carnée'

Rosa 'Nozomi'

Rosa nutkana 'Plena'

Rosa x *odorata* 'Mutabilis'

Rosa x *odorata* 'Pallida'

Rosa x *odorata* 'Viridiflora'

Rosa 'Old Master'

Rosa 'Ophelia'

Rosa 'Oranges and Lemons'

Rosa 'Orange Sunblaze'

Rosa 'Painted Moon'

slender flower stalks in early summer. ↕ to 20ft (6m), ↔ 10ft (3m). W. China. Zone 6.

R. multiflora. Upright, arching, very vigorous species rose producing masses of dull, light to mid-green leaves, each with 7–9, rarely 5–11, obovate or elliptic leaflets, ½–2in (1.5–5cm) long. Large clusters of cupped to flat, single, fruit-scented white flowers, to 1¼in (3cm) across, fading to red, are borne freely but fleetingly in early summer, followed by ovoid to spherical red hips, to ¼in (6mm) long. Highly invasive; its sale is prohibited or discouraged in many areas. ↕ to 15ft (5m), ↔ 10ft (3m). Japan, Korea. Zone 4.

***R.* 'Mutabilis'** see *R.* x *odorata* 'Mutabilis'.

***R.* 'National Trust'** ■ syn. *R.* 'Bad Nauheim'. Compact hybrid tea rose with abundant dark green foliage. Neatly formed, urn-shaped, fully double, scarlet-crimson flowers, 4in (10cm) across, are borne freely from spring to autumn. ↕↔ 3ft (1m). Zone 6.

***R.* 'Nevada'** ■ Vigorous, arching, hybrid moyesii shrub rose with red stems and dense, light green leaves. Flat, semi-double, scented, creamy white flowers, 4in (10cm) across, are borne freely in early summer and sparsely in autumn. ↕↔ 7ft (2.2m). Zone 2b.

***R.* 'New Dawn'** ■ syn. *R.* 'Everblooming Dr. Van Fleet'. Climber of vigorous, arching habit, with shiny, mid-green leaves. From early summer to autumn, bears clusters of cupped, double, fragrant, pale pearl-pink flowers, 3in (8cm) across. Tolerates a partially shaded site. ↕ 10ft (3m), ↔ 8ft (2.5m). Zone 6.

***R.* 'Newport Fairy',** syn. *R.* 'Newport Rambler'. Hybrid wichurana with small, single, very deep pink rosy, blooms with a white eye and golden stamens.

***R.* 'Newport Rambler'** see *R.* 'Newport Fairy'.

***R.* 'News'** ■ Floribunda rose with dark green foliage. Cupped, wide-opening, double, scented, bright beet-purple flowers, 3in (8cm) across, are borne from spring to autumn. ↕ 3ft (1m), ↔ 20in (60cm). Zone 6.

***R.* 'New Zealand'** ■ syn. *R.* 'Aotearoa', *R.* 'Aotearoa–New Zealand'. Large bloom with medium green foliage, upright, medium growth. Bears double, shell-pink flower (34 petals), 4½–5in (11–13cm), across, with intense honeysuckle fragrance. ↕ 4–5ft (1.2–1.5m). Zone 6.

***R.* 'Noisette Carnée'** ■ syn. *R.* 'Blush Noisette'. Branching noisette climbing rose that can be grown as a shrub, with lax stems and matte, mid-green foliage. Cupped, double, spice-scented, pale pink flowers, 1½in (4cm) across, are produced from early summer to autumn. ↕ 4–8ft (1.2–2.5m), ↔ 4ft (1.2m). Zone 6.

***R.* 'Normandica'** see *R.* 'Petite de Hollande'.

***R.* 'Nozomi'** ■ syn. *R.* 'Heideröslein'. Trailing groundcover rose with shiny, dark green leaves. Clusters of flat, single, pale pink-white flowers, 1in (2.5cm) across, cover the plant in early summer. ↕ 18in (45cm), or to 5ft (1.5m) when trained on a pillar, ↔ 4ft (1.2m). Zone 6.

***R.* 'Nuit d'Orient'** see *R.* 'Big Purple'.

***R.* 'Nuits de Young'** (Old black rose). Erect moss rose with wiry stems, brownish green mossing, and dark green leaves. In early summer, bears flat, double, scented, dark maroon-purple flowers, 2in (5cm) across, showing yellow stamens. ↕ 4ft (1.2m), ↔ 3ft (1m). Zone 5.

R. nutkana (Nutka rose). Robust species rose producing brownish green stems and toothed, mid-green leaves, each with 5–9 ovate to elliptic leaflets, ¾–2in (2–5cm) long. In summer, bears usually solitary, cupped, single, reddish pink flowers, 2–3in (5–8cm) across, followed by spherical, purplish red hips. ↕ to 10ft (3m), ↔ 6ft (2m). Alaska to N. California. Zone 3. **'Plena'** ■ syn. *R. californica* 'Plena', has semi-double pink flowers; ↕ 5–8ft (1.5–2.5m), ↔ 4–6ft (1.2–2m).

***R.* 'Ocarina'** see *R.* 'Angela Rippon'.

R.* x *odorata (*R. chinensis* x *R. gigantea*). Shrubby or climbing China rose with lax, prickly stems and light green leaves consisting of 3–5 narrowly ovate leaflets, 1½–2½in (4–6cm) long. From summer to autumn, bears rounded, double, pale pink flowers, 2–3in (5–8cm) across. ↕↔ 6ft (2m) as a shrub; ↕ 15ft (5m), ↔ 10–12ft (3–4m) as a climber. Zone 6b. **'Mutabilis'** ■ syn. *R. chinensis* 'Mutabilis', *R.* 'Mutabilis', *R.* 'Tipo Ideale', is shrubby, with reddish purple, sparsely prickly stems that will climb if supported, and glossy dark green leaves, flushed purple. Bears cupped, single flowers, 2½in (6cm) across, which change from light yellow to copper-pink and then to deep pink. ↕ 4ft (1.2m), ↔ 3ft (1m) as a shrub; ↕ to 10ft (3m), ↔ 6ft (2m) as a climber. Zone 6. **'Pallida'** ■ (Old blush China rose, Parsons' pink China rose) is bushy, with shiny, mid-green leaves. It freely bears cupped, double pink flowers, 2½in (6cm) across. ↕ 3ft (1m), sometimes to 10ft (3m) in mild climates, ↔ 32in (80cm). Zone 6. **'Pseudindica',** syn. *R.* 'Beauty of Glazenwood', *R.* 'Gold of Ophir', *R.* 'San Rafael' (Fortune's double yellow rose) is a lax climber with glossy, light green leaves. It bears cupped, semi-double, scented, copper-red to yellow flowers, 2in (5cm) across. ↕ 8–15ft (2.5–5m), ↔ 5–10ft (1.5–3m). Zone 8. **'Semperflorens',** syn. *R. chinensis* 'Semperflorens' (Slater's crimson China rose) is open-branched, with dark green leaves and produces semi-double, crimson-red flowers, 2½in (6cm) across. ↕↔ 3ft (1m). Zone 6. **'Viridiflora'** ■ syn. *R. chinensis* 'Viridiflora', *R.* 'Lü E', *R.* 'Viridiflora' (Green rose) is upright, with shiny, dark green leaves and sprays of rosette-shaped, double flowers, 2in (5cm) across, green aging to purplish green, with narrow petals that resemble sepals. ↕ 30in (75cm), ↔ 24in (60cm). Zone 6.

R. officinalis see *R. gallica* var. *officinalis.*

***R.* 'Old Master'** ■ Vigorous floribunda rose with glossy, dark green leaves. Cupped, semi-double flowers, 4½in (11cm) across, shaded and marked carmine-red on a white background, are borne from spring to autumn. ↕ 36in (90cm), ↔ 24in (60cm). Zone 6.

***R.* 'Olympiad'.** Hybrid tea rose with mid-green foliage and high-centered, fully double, velvety, bright red flowers, 4in (10cm) across, borne from spring to autumn. Flowers last well when cut. ↕ 5–6ft (1.5–2m), ↔ 26in (65cm). Zone 6.

R. omeiensis* f. *pteracantha see *R. sericea* subsp. *omeiensis* f. *pteracantha.*

***R.* 'Opa Pötschke'** see *R.* 'Precious Platinum'.

***R.* 'Ophelia'** ■ Hybrid tea rose with stiff growth and sparse, dark green foliage. Neatly formed, urn-shaped to cupped, double, fragrant, creamy pale pink flowers, 3in (8cm) across, are produced from spring to autumn. ↕ 3ft (1m), ↔ 24in (60cm). Zone 6.

***R.* 'Oranges and Lemons'** ■ Vigorous shrub rose with shiny, dark green foliage, reddish green when young. From spring to autumn, bears rounded, fully double flowers, 4in (10cm) across, with stiff, infolded, orange-yellow petals, striped scarlet, fading to pinkish red. ↕ 32in (80cm), ↔ 24in (60cm). Zone 6.

***R.* 'Orange Sensation'.** Vigorous, spreading floribunda rose producing shiny, light green foliage. Rounded, double, scented, bright orange-red flowers, 3in (8cm) across, are borne from spring to autumn. ↕ 36in (90cm), ↔ 24in (60cm). Zone 6.

***R.* 'Orange Sunblaze'** ■ syn. *R.* 'Sunblaze'. Miniature rose of compact habit, with dense, dark green leaves. Cupped, fully double, bright orange-red flowers, 1½in (4cm) across, are borne from spring to autumn. ↕↔ 12in (30cm). Zone 6.

***R.* 'Orange Triumph'.** Stiff, vigorous polyantha rose with glossy, dark green leaves. Full, showy clusters of cupped, double, dull red flowers, 1½in (4cm) across, are borne from spring to autumn. ↕ 3ft (1m), ↔ 30in (75cm). Zone 6.

***R.* 'Paestana'** see *R.* 'Portlandica'.

***R.* 'Painted Moon'** ■ Leafy, spreading hybrid tea rose producing mid-green foliage. Wide sprays of cupped, double flowers, 3½in (9cm) across, light yellow, strongly suffused pink and crimson, are borne from spring to autumn. ↕ 3–4ft (1–1.2m), ↔ 24in (60cm). Zone 6.

***R.* 'Panachée d'Angers'** see *R.* 'Commandant Beaurepaire'.

***R.* 'Papa Meilland'.** Hybrid tea rose with a lanky habit and olive-green leaves. High-centered, fully double, very fragrant, dark velvet-crimson flowers, 5in (13cm) across, are borne on long stems from spring to autumn. Prone to mildew. ↕ 4ft (1.2m), ↔ 24in (60cm). Zone 6.

***R.* 'Parade'.** Vigorous, upright, bushy, climbing rose with large, glossy, dark green leaves. Remontant, cupped, old rose-shaped, double, fragrant, deep rose-pink flowers, 3½in (9cm) across, are borne in nodding clusters in early summer. ↕↔ 10ft (3m). Zone 6.

***R.* 'Paradise',** syn. *R.* 'Burning Sky'. Vigorous hybrid tea rose producing

Rosa 'Paul Neyron'

Rosa 'Paul Shirville'

Rosa 'Paul's Lemon Pillar'

Rosa 'Peace'

Rosa 'Pearl Drift'

Rosa 'Penelope'

Rosa 'Perle d'Or'

Rosa 'Pheasant'

Rosa 'Piccadilly'

Rosa pimpinellifolia 'Plena'

Rosa 'Pink Bells'

Rosa 'Pink Chimo'

glossy, dark green leaves. From spring to autumn, bears high-centered, double, scented, lavender-pink flowers, 4in (10cm) across, edged ruby-red, especially during cool, bright autumn weather. ↕ 5–6ft (1.5–2m), ↔ 28in (70cm). Zone 6.

***R.* 'Parkdirektor Riggers'.** Stiff, vigorous kordesii shrub rose, grown as a climber, with glossy, dark green leaves. Large clusters of cupped, semi-double scarlet flowers, 2½in (6cm) across, with wavy-margined petals, are borne from spring to autumn. ↕ 12ft (4m), ↔ 8ft (2.5m). Zone 6.

***R.* 'Party Girl'.** Bushy, compact miniature rose with dark green leaves. Neatly formed, high-centered, double, scented, apricot-yellow flowers, 1¼in (3cm) across, suffused salmon-pink, are borne from spring to autumn. ↕↔ 14in (35cm). Zone 6.

***R.* 'Pascali'.** Hybrid tea rose with sparse, dark green foliage. Neatly formed, urn-shaped, double white flowers, 3½in (9cm) across, are borne from spring to autumn. ↕ 5ft (1.5m), ↔ 24in (60cm). Zone 6.

***R.* 'Paul Neyron'** ▣ Vigorous, upright hybrid perpetual rose producing olive-green leaves. Rounded, fully double, scented flowers, to 6in (15cm) across, with ruffled, lilac-tinged, deep pink petals, are borne from spring to autumn. ↕ 5ft (1.5m), ↔ 4ft (1.2m). Zone 6.

***R.* 'Paul Ricault'.** Hybrid perpetual rose of open, lax habit, with arching, prickly stems and mid-green leaves. Rounded buds open to flat, quartered-rosette, fully double, fragrant, deep pink flowers, 3in (8cm) across, from spring to autumn. ↕ 5ft (1.5m), ↔ 4ft (1.2m). Zone 6.

***R.* 'Paul's Himalayan Musk'**, syn. *R.* 'Paul's Himalayan Rambler'. Rampant rambler with trailing shoots and arching, dark green leaves. Large clusters of rosette-shaped, double, pale pink flowers, 1½in (4cm) across, are borne freely in early summer. Effective trained on a tree. ↕↔ 30ft (10m). Zone 6.

***R.* 'Paul's Himalayan Rambler'** see *R.* 'Paul's Himalayan Musk'.

***R.* 'Paul Shirville'** ▣ syn. *R.* 'Heart Throb'. Hybrid tea rose of spreading, shrubby habit, with dark reddish green foliage. High-centered, double, fragrant, rose-pink to salmon-pink flowers, 4in (10cm) across, are borne from spring to autumn. ↕ 4ft (1.2m), ↔ 30in (75cm). Zone 6.

***R.* 'Paul's Lemon Pillar'** ▣ syn. *R.* 'Lemon Pillar'. Stiff, upright climbing hybrid tea with dark green leaves and high-centered to rounded, fully double, lemon-scented white flowers, 5in (13cm) across, borne in early summer. ↕ 12ft (4m), ↔ 10ft (3m). Zone 6.

***R.* 'Paul's Scarlet Climber'.** Very vigorous, arching, large-flowered climber with dense, semi-glossy, mid-green foliage. Clusters of many cupped, double, bright red flowers, 3in (8cm) across, are borne freely in early summer. ↕↔ 10ft (3m). Zone 6.

***R.* 'Peace'** ▣ syn. *R.* 'Gioia', *R.* 'Gloria Dei', *R.* 'Mme. A. Meilland'. Vigorous, shrubby hybrid tea rose with glossy, dark green foliage. High-centered to rounded, fully double, scented, pink-tinged yellow flowers, 6in (15cm) across, are produced from spring to autumn. ↕ 5ft (1.5m), ↔ 3ft (1m). Zone 6.

***R.* 'Pearl Drift'** ▣ Vigorous shrub rose of spreading habit, with abundant glossy, dark green leaves. From spring to autumn, bears clusters of cupped, semi-double, scented, pale pink flowers, 4in (10cm) across. ↕ 3ft (1m), ↔ 4ft (1.2m). Zone 6.

***R.* 'Pearl Meidiland'**, syn. *R.* 'Perle Meillandecor'. Low-spreading shrub rose with dark green, glossy leaves. Bears clusters of flat, double, light pink flowers, 2in (6cm) across, from spring to autumn. ↕ 2ft (75cm), ↔ 4–6ft (1.2–2m). Zone 6.

***R.* 'Perle Meillandecor'**.see *R.* 'Perle Meidiland'.

***R.* 'Peaudouce'** see *R.* 'Elina'.

***R.* 'Penelope'** ▣ Bushy, dense, hybrid musk rose with dark green leaves. Large clusters of well-spaced, cupped to flat, semi-double, scented, pale creamy pink flowers, 3in (8cm) across, are borne in summer and autumn. ↕↔ 3½ft (1.1m). Zone 6.

***R.* 'Perfect Moment'**, syn. *R.* 'Jack Dayson'. Vigorous hybrid tea rose with glossy, dark green foliage. Rounded, double flowers, 3½in (9cm) across, orange-red shaded with yellow, are borne on stiff stems from spring to autumn. ↕ 4½ft (1.4m), ↔ 28in (70cm). Zone 6.

***R.* 'Perle d'Or'** ▣ syn. *R.* 'Yellow Cécile Brunner'. Polyantha rose forming a leafy, twiggy shrub with glossy, dark green foliage. From spring to autumn, neatly formed, urn-shaped, fully double, pale apricot flowers, 1½in (4cm) across, are borne in clusters on slender stems. ↕ to 4ft (1.2m), ↔ 3ft (1m). Zone 6.

***R.* 'Perpetual White Moss'** see *R.* 'Quatre Saisons Blanche Mousseuse'.

***R.* 'Petite Lisette'.** Centifolia rose with toothed, grayish green leaves. Well-spaced clusters of pompon, fully double, scented, rose-pink flowers, 1in (2.5cm) across, with infolded center petals, are borne in early summer. ↕↔ 3ft (1m). Zone 5.

***R.* 'Petit Four'** ▣ syn. *R.* 'Interfour'. Compact, leafy, miniature rose with mid-green foliage and many flat, semi-double, pink and white flowers, 1½in (4cm) across, borne from spring to autumn. ↕↔ 16in (40cm). Zone 6.

***R.* 'Pheasant'** ▣ syn. *R.* 'Heidekönigin'. Groundcover rose of creeping habit, producing abundant glossy, mid-green leaves. Cupped, double pink flowers, 2in (5cm) across, showing yellow stamens, are borne in clusters along the stems in summer. ↕ 20in (50cm), ↔ 10ft (3m). Zone 6.

***R.* 'Phyllis Bide'.** Vigorous climbing polyantha rose with many lax shoots and shiny, mid-green leaves with narrow leaflets. Rosette-shaped, double yellow flowers, 2in (5cm) across, flushed pink, are borne in wide clusters from early summer to autumn. ↕ 8ft (2.5m), ↔ 5ft (1.5m). Zone 6.

Rosa 'Petit Four'

Rosa 'Pink Favorite'

Rosa 'Pink Grootendorst'

Rosa 'Pink Perpetue'

Rosa 'Playgirl'

Rosa 'Polar Star'

Rosa 'Portlandica'

Rosa 'Pot o' Gold'

Rosa 'Precious Platinum'

Rosa 'Président de Sèze'

Rosa 'Pretty Polly'

Rosa 'Pride of Maldon'

Rosa 'Prima Donna'

***R.* 'Piccadilly'** ■ Vigorous hybrid tea rose producing abundant glossy, reddish green foliage. From spring to autumn, bears high-centered, double, bicolored, red and yellow flowers, 5in (13cm) across. ↕ 3–4ft (1–1.2m), ↔ 24in (60cm). Zone 6.
R. pimpinellifolia, syn. *R. spinosissima* (Burnet rose, Scotch rose, Scots rose). Dense, spreading, prickly species rose of suckering habit, with small, fern-like, dark green leaves, composed of 7–9, rarely 11, broadly elliptic or broadly obovate to almost rounded leaflets, ¼–¾in (0.5–2cm) long. Solitary, cupped, single, creamy white flowers, 1½in (4cm) across, are borne freely in spring or early summer, followed by spherical, purplish black hips. ↕ to 3ft (1m), ↔ 4ft (1.2m). W. and S. Europe, S.W. and C. Asia to China and Korea. Zone 3. **var. *altaica*** see *R.* 'Grandiflora'. **'Dunwichensis'** see *R.* 'Dunwich Rose'. **'Plena'** ■ has double white flowers.
***R.* 'Pink Bells'** ■ Vigorous, spreading groundcover rose of dense habit, with abundant, mid-green foliage. Pompon, fully double, bright pink flowers, 1in (2.5cm) across, are borne along the stems in summer. ↕ 30in (75cm), ↔ 5ft (1.5m). Zone 6.
***R.* 'Pink Chimo'** ■ syn. *R.* 'Interchimp'. Vigorous groundcover shrub rose with abundant dark green leaves. Cupped to flat, semi-double, deep pink flowers, 2in (5cm) across, are borne freely along the stems from spring to autumn. ↕ 24in (60cm), ↔ 5ft (1.5m). Zone 6.
***R.* 'Pink Cover'** see *R.* 'Essex'.
***R.* 'Pink Favorite'** ■ Branching hybrid tea rose with long, shiny, dark green leaves. High-centered to cupped, double, bright rose-pink flowers, 3½in (9cm) across, deeper in bud, are produced freely from spring to autumn. ↕ 4ft (1.2m), ↔ 24in (60cm). Zone 6.
***R.* 'Pink Grootendorst'** ■ Hybrid rugosa rose of upright, dense habit, with prickly stems and coarse, leathery, dark green leaves. Crowded clusters of rosette-shaped, double, rose-pink flowers, 1½in (4cm) across, with frilled petals, are borne from early summer to autumn. ↕ 4½ft (1.3m), ↔ 3½ft (1.1m). Zone 2b.
***R.* 'Pink Nevada'** see *R.* 'Marguerite Hilling'.
***R.* 'Pink Parfait'.** Floribunda rose of neat habit, producing mid-green foliage. High-centered to cupped, double flowers, 3½in (9cm) across, in shades of light pink, are borne freely from spring to autumn. ↕ 28in (70cm), ↔ 24in (60cm). Zone 6.
***R.* 'Pink Perpetue'** ■ Stiffly branched climber with leathery, dark green leaves. Rounded to cupped, double, scented pink flowers, 3in (8cm) across, with a deeper pink reverse to the petals, are borne from summer to autumn. ↕ to 10ft (3m), ↔ 8ft (2.5m). Zone 6.
***R.* 'Pink Revelation'** Floribunda rose with mid-green leaves. Clusters of cupped, light pink flowers, 3in (8cm) across, are borne from spring to autumn. ↕ 3–4ft (1–1.2m). ↔ 3ft (1m). Zone 6.
***R.* 'Pink Symphony'** see *R.* 'Pretty Polly'.
***R.* 'Playboy'** ■ syn. *R.* 'Cheerio'. Floribunda rose with dense, glossy, dark green foliage. Cupped, semi-double, orange-yellow flowers, 3in (8cm) across, shaded scarlet, with reflexed petals, are produced from summer to autumn. ↕ 30in (75cm), ↔ 26in (65cm). Zone 6.
***R.* 'Playgirl'** ■ Floribunda rose with dark green foliage and sprays of cupped, single, deep rose-pink flowers, 3in (8cm) across, with golden stamens, borne freely from spring to autumn. ↕ 30in (75cm), ↔ 26in (65cm). Zone 6.
***R.* 'Pleasure'.** Floribunda rose with semi-glossy, dark green leaves. From spring to autumn, bears clusters of cupped, fully double coral-pink flowers, 3½in (9cm) across, with lighter reverses. ↕ 36in (90cm), ↔ 24in (60cm). Zone 6.
***R.* 'Poesie'** see *R.* 'Tournament of Roses'.
***R.* 'Polar Star'** ■ syn. *R.* 'Polarstern'. Vigorous, free-branching hybrid tea rose with dark green leaves. High-centered, fully double, creamy white flowers, 4½in (11cm) across, are produced on long, stiff stems, from spring to autumn. ↕ 5–6ft (1.5–2m), ↔ 28in (70cm). Zone 6.
***R.* 'Polarstern'** see *R.* 'Polar Star'.
***R.* 'Pompon de Paris'** see *R.* 'Rouletii'.
***R.* 'Pompon des Dames'** see *R.* 'Petite de Hollande'.
***R.* 'Pompon des Princes'** see *R.* 'Ispahan'.
***R.* 'Popcorn'.** Vigorous miniature rose of compact habit, producing small, glossy, dark green leaves. Clusters of numerous cupped to flat, semi-double, honey-scented white flowers, 1in (2.5cm) across, showing yellow stamens, cover the plant from spring to autumn. ↕↔ 12in (30cm). Zone 5.
***R.* 'Portlandica'** ■ syn. *R.* 'Duchess of Portland', *R.* 'Paestana' (Portland rose). Vigorous portland rose of shrubby habit, with dark green leaves. Cupped, single to semi-double, cerise-red flowers, 3in (8cm) across, with golden stamens, are borne in summer, and again in autumn if deadheaded. ↕↔ 3ft (1m). Zone 6.
***R.* 'Pot o' Gold'** ■ Hybrid tea rose of neat, spreading habit, with abundant, mid-green foliage. Rounded, fully double, fragrant, golden yellow flowers, 3½in (9cm) across, are borne from spring to autumn. ↕ 3–4ft (1–1.2m), ↔ 24in (60cm). Zone 6.
***R.* 'Precious Platinum'** ■ syn. *R.* 'Opa Pötschke'. Vigorous hybrid tea rose of uneven growth, producing glossy, dark green leaves. Rounded, fully double, bright crimson-scarlet flowers, 4in (10cm) across, are borne from spring to autumn. ↕ 5–6ft (1.5–2m), ↔ 26in (65cm). Zone 6.
***R.* 'Preference'** see *R.* 'Princesse de Monaco'.
***R.* 'Président de Sèze'** ■ syn. *R.* 'Jenny Duval', *R.* 'Mme. Hébert'. Vigorous gallica rose of open habit, with grayish green foliage. Quartered-rosette, fully double, fragrant, pale lilac-pink flowers, 4in (10cm) across, with deep magenta margins, are produced in early summer. ↕↔ 4ft (1.2m). Zone 4.
***R.* 'Pretty Polly'** ■ syn. *R.* 'Pink Symphony', *R.* 'Sweet Sunblaze'. Compact, miniature rose with abundant dark green leaves. Many cupped, fully double, rose-pink flowers, 1¾in (4.5cm) across, are borne from spring to autumn. ↕ 16in (40cm), ↔ 18in (45cm). Zone 6.
***R.* 'Pride of Maldon'** ■ Vigorous floribunda rose of dense, leafy growth, with lustrous, dark green leaves. From spring to autumn, bears many showy, cupped, semi-double orange flowers, 3½in (9cm) across, with a yellow reverse to the petals. ↕ 30in (75cm), ↔ 24in (60cm). Zone 6.
***R.* 'Prima'** see *R.* 'Many Happy Returns'.
***R.* 'Prima Ballerina'.** Vigorous hybrid tea rose, often with scaly marks on the stems, producing leathery, mid-green leaves. Urn-shaped, double, fragrant, warm rose-pink flowers, 4in (10cm) across, are borne from spring to autumn. ↕ 4–5ft (1.2–1.5m), ↔ 24in (60cm). Zone 6.
***R.* 'Prima Donna'** ■ syn. *R.* 'Tobone'. Tall grandiflora rose producing mid-green leaves. High-centered, double, deep pink flowers, 4in (10cm) across, are produced on long stems from spring to autumn. ↕ 5–6ft (1.5–2m), ↔ 28in (70cm). Zone 6.

Rosa 'Playboy'

Rosa primula

Rosa 'Princess Michael of Kent'

Rosa 'Pristine'

Rosa 'Queen Elizabeth'

Rosa 'Queen Mother'

Rosa 'Radox Bouquet'

Rosa 'Ramona'

Rosa 'Raubritter'

Rosa 'Red Ace'

Rosa 'Red Blanket'

Rosa 'Regensberg'

Rosa 'Reine des Violettes'

R. primula ▣ (Incense rose). Erect to arching species rose with aromatic, dense, fern-like, mid-green leaves consisting of 9, rarely 7–13, elliptic to obovate or inversely lance-shaped leaflets, to ¾in (2cm) long, on slender, reddish green stems. Solitary, cupped, single, scented, pale primrose-yellow flowers, to 2in (5cm) across, are borne in late spring; they are followed by spherical to inversely cone-shaped, brownish maroon hips. ↕↔ 4–5ft (1.2–1.5m). Asia (Turkmenistan to N. China). Zone 6.

***R.* 'Princess Alice'** ▣ syn. *R.* 'Brite Lites', *R.* 'Zonta Rose'. Floribunda rose of narrow habit, with mid-green leaves consisting of lance-shaped leaflets. Long-stemmed sprays of rounded, double, bright yellow flowers, 2½in (6cm) across, are borne from spring to autumn. ↕ 3½ft (1.1m), ↔ 24in (60cm). Zone 6.

***R.* 'Princesse de Monaco'**, syn. *R.* 'Preference'. Vigorous, branching hybrid tea rose with dark green foliage. High-centered, fully double, fragrant white flowers, 4½in (11cm) across, with pink-margined petals, are borne from spring to autumn. ↕ 4–5ft (1.2–1.5m), ↔ 26in (65cm). Zone 6.

***R.* 'Princess Michael of Kent'** ▣ Neat floribunda rose with glossy, bright green foliage. Rounded, fully double, scented yellow flowers, 3½in (9cm) across, are borne from spring to autumn. ↕ 24in (60cm), ↔ 20in (50cm). Zone 6.

***R.* 'Prinz Eugen van Savoyen'** see *R.* 'Amber Queen'.

***R.* 'Pristine'** ▣ Vigorous hybrid tea rose producing dark green leaves with large leaflets. From spring to autumn, bears high-centered, double, scented ivory flowers, 5in (13cm) across, flushed pale pink, with long, overlapping petals. ↕ 5–6ft (1.5–2m), ↔ 30in (75cm). Zone 6.

***R.* 'Probuzini'** see *R.* 'Awakening'.

***R.* 'Prominent'** see *R.* 'Korp'.

***R.* 'Prosperity'.** Dense, arching, hybrid musk shrub rose with many dark green leaves. In summer and autumn, produces large clusters of rosette-shaped, double, scented, creamy white flowers, 2in (5cm) across, flushed pale pink. ↕ to 8ft (2.5m), ↔ 4ft (1.2m). Zone 6.

***R.* 'Pyrenees'** see *R.* 'Kent'.

***R.* 'Quatre Saisons'** see *R.* x *damascena* var. *semperflorens*.

***R.* 'Quatre Saisons Blanche Mousseuse'**, syn. *R.* 'Perpetual White Moss', *R.* 'Rosier de Thionville'. Open, arching moss rose, a sport of *R.* x *damascena* var. *semperflorens*, with light green leaves, and stems and buds covered with stiff, brownish green moss. Loosely formed, cupped to flat, double, fragrant white flowers, 3½in (9cm) across, are borne in early summer, and sporadically in autumn. ↕ 5ft (1.5m), ↔ 4ft (1.2m). Zone 5.

***R.* 'Queen Elizabeth'** ▣ syn. *R.* 'The Queen Elizabeth'. Vigorous grandiflora rose with leathery, dark green leaves. Rounded, fully double pink flowers, 4in (10cm) across, are borne on long, stiff stems from spring to autumn. ↕ to 7ft (2.2m), ↔ 3ft (1m). Zone 6.

***R.* 'Queen Mother'** ▣ Dwarf floribunda rose of spreading habit, with abundant glossy, mid-green foliage. Many cupped to flat, semi-double, clear pink flowers, 2½in (6cm) across, are borne from spring to autumn. ↕ 36in (90cm), ↔ 24in (60cm). Zone 6.

***R.* 'Queen of Denmark'** see *R.* 'Königin von Dänemark'.

***R.* 'Radox Bouquet'** ▣ syn. *R.* 'Rosika'. Floribunda rose producing shiny, mid-green foliage. Rosette-shaped, fully double, fragrant, rose-pink flowers, 3½in (9cm) across, are borne from spring to autumn. ↕ 3ft (1m), ↔ 24in (60cm). Zone 6.

***R.* 'Rambling Rector'** ▣ Rampant rambler with strong, arching stems and abundant gray-green foliage. Clusters of many cupped to flat, semi-double, scented, creamy white flowers, 1½in (4cm) across, showing golden stamens, are borne in early summer, followed by spherical red hips in autumn. ↕↔ 20ft (6m). Zone 6.

***R.* 'Ramona'** ▣ syn. *R.* x *anemonoides* 'Ramona', *R.* 'Red Cherokee'. Stiff, open, hybrid laevigata climber with sparse, dark green leaves. Flat, single, carmine-red flowers, 4in (10cm) across, with a grayish red reverse to the petals and gold stamens, are borne in spring. ↕ 8ft (2.5m), ↔ 10ft (3m). Zone 6.

***R.* 'Raspberry Ice'** see *R.* 'Hannah Gordon'.

***R.* 'Raubritter'** ▣ Hybrid macrantha shrub rose of lax, spreading habit, with dark grayish green leaves. Clusters of many rounded, semi-double pink flowers, 2in (5cm) across, are borne in early summer. Prone to mildew. ↕ to 3ft (1m), ↔ 6ft (2m). Zone 6.

***R.* 'Red Ace'** ▣ syn. *R.* 'Amanda', *R.* 'Amruda'. Compact miniature rose with mid-green foliage. Clusters of rounded, semi-double, dark crimson flowers, 1½in (4cm) across, are borne from spring to autumn. ↕ 14in (35cm), ↔ 12in (30cm). Zone 6.

***R.* 'Red Ballerina'** see *R.* 'Marjorie Fair'.

***R.* 'Red Blanket'** ▣ syn. *R.* 'Intercell'. Groundcover shrub rose of spreading habit, with abundant dark green leaves. Semi-double flowers, opening flat, to 3in (8cm) across, are rose-red paling to white at the petal bases, and are borne in wide, showy clusters from spring to autumn. ↕ 30in (75cm), ↔ 4ft (1.2m). Zone 6.

***R.* 'Red Cascade'.** Climbing miniature of dense, spreading habit, with dark green leaves. Tight clusters of cupped, fully double, dark red flowers, 1½in (4cm) across, are borne from spring to autumn. ↕↔ to 5ft (1.5m). Zone 6.

***R.* 'Red Cherokee'** see *R.* 'Ramona'.

***R.* 'Red Dorothy Perkins'** see *R.* 'Excelsa'.

***R.* 'Red Fountain'.** Large-flowered climbing rose with leathery, dark green leaves. Cupped, double, fragrant, scarle flowers, 4in (10cm) across, are borne from spring to autumn. ↕ 8–10ft (2.5–3m), ↔ 8ft (2.5m). Zone 6.

***R.* 'Red Prince'** see *R.* 'Fountain'.

***R.* 'Red Ribbons'**, syn. *R.* 'Chilterns', *R* 'Fiery Sensation', *R.* 'Mainaufeuer'. Low-growing, spreading groundcover rose with small, glossy, dark green leaves. From spring to autumn, bears clusters of flat, semi-double, scarlet flowers, 1½–3in (4–8cm) across, with golden stamens. ↕ 30in (75cm), ↔ 4ft (1.2m). Zone 5b.

***R.* 'Red Yesterday'** see *R.* 'Marjorie Fair'.

***R.* 'Regensberg'** ▣ syn. *R.* 'Buffalo Bil *R.* 'Young Mistress'. Floribunda rose of short, dense habit, with glossy, mid-green leaves. Cupped, double flowers, opening to 4½in (11cm) across, deep

Rosa 'Princess Alice'

?osa 'Reine Victoria'

Rosa 'Remember Me'

Rosa 'Rise 'n' Shine'

Rosa 'Robin Redbreast'

Rosa 'Robusta'

Rosa 'Roger Lambelin'

?osa 'Rosemary Harkness'

Rosa 'Roseraie de l'Haÿ'

Rosa 'Rosy Cushion'

Rosa 'Rosy Mantle'

Rosa roxburghii

Rosa 'Royal William'

ink marked with white, are borne in ense clusters from spring to autumn. 30–36in (75–90cm), ↔ 20in (50cm). 'one 6.

. 'Reine des Neiges' see *R.* 'Frau Karl)ruschki'.

. 'Reine des Violettes' ▣ Arching ybrid perpetual rose with smooth tems and grayish green leaves. In early ummer, bears remontant, quartered-osette, fully double, fragrant, violet-urple flowers, 3in (8cm) across. Highly susceptible to blackspot. ↕ 5ft 1.5m), ↔ 4ft (1.2m). Zone 6.

. 'Reine Victoria' ▣ syn. *R.* 'La Reine 'ictoria'. Lax bourbon rose with slender tems and light green leaves. Cupped, ouble, scented, light rose-pink flowers, in (8cm) across, are borne in spring or arly summer and autumn. ↕ 6ft (2m), ↔ 4ft (1.2m). Zone 6.

. 'Remember Me' ▣ Vigorous hybrid ea rose of stiff habit, with abundant lossy, dark green leaves. High-centered, ully double, copper-orange flowers, ½in (9cm) across, are borne singly nd in wide sprays from spring to autumn. ↕ 4ft (1.2m), ↔ 24in (60cm). Zone 6.

***R.* 'Rise 'n' Shine'** ▣ syn. *R.* 'Golden Sunblaze'. Miniature rose of upright habit, with dark green leaves. Urn-shaped, fully double yellow flowers, 1½in (4cm) across, are borne from spring to autumn. ↕ 16in (40cm), ↔ 10in (25cm). Zone 6.

***R.* 'Rhonda'.** Vigorous, large-flowered climber produces medium green, semi-glossy foliage. The large, double, carmine-rose blooms have a slight fragrance. Zone 6.

***R.* 'Robin Redbreast'** ▣ syn. *R.* 'Robin Red Breast'. Dwarf groundcover rose of dense habit, with many shiny, mid-green leaves. Dense clusters of cupped to flat, single, dark red flowers, 1¾in (4.5cm) across, with pale white centers, are produced from spring to autumn. ↕ 18in (45cm), ↔ 24in (60cm). Zone 6.

***R.* 'Robusta'** ▣ syn. *R.* 'Kordes Robusta'. Vigorous, stiff-growing rugosa rose with prickly stems and leathery, dark green leaves. Clusters of cupped, single, wine-red flowers, 2½in (6cm) across, with wavy-margined petals, are produced from spring to autumn. ↕ 5ft (1.5m), ↔ 3ft (1m). Zone 3.

***R.* 'Rock 'n' Roll'** see *R.* 'Tango'.

***R.* 'Roger Lambelin'** ▣ Shrubby hybrid perpetual rose producing dark green leaves. Loosely formed, rounded, double, fragrant flowers, 3in (8cm) across, with maroon, white-margined petals, are borne mainly in early summer. Prone to rust. ↕↔ 3ft (1m). Zone 6.

***R.* 'Rose Capucine'** see *R. foetida* 'Bicolor'.

***R.* 'Rose de Meaux'** see *R.* 'De Meaux'.

***R.* 'Rose de Rescht'.** Compact portland rose with rounded, dull green leaves. Producing single or clusters of richly scented, deep pink, double, semi-pompon flowers, 2in (6cm) across, from spring to autumn. ↕ 3–4ft (.9–1.2m), ↔ 24–36in (60–90cm). Zone 5.

***R.* 'Rose des Maures'** see *R.* 'Sissinghurst Castle'.

***R.* 'Rose d'Isfahan'** see *R.* 'Ispahan'.

***R.* 'Rose-Marie Viaud'.** Vigorous rambler with conspicuously veined, light green leaves. Sprays of rosette-shaped, double, lavender-pink to purple flowers, 1½in (4cm) across, fading to grayish mauve, are produced in summer. ↕ to 15ft (5m), ↔ 8ft (2.5m). Zone 6.

***R.* 'Rosemary Harkness'** ▣ Vigorous hybrid tea rose of shrubby habit, with glossy, dark green foliage. Urn-shaped buds open to rounded, double, fragrant, orange to salmon-pink flowers, 4in (10cm) across, from summer to autumn. ↕↔ 32in (80cm). Zone 6.

***R.* 'Roseraie de l'Haÿ'** ▣ Vigorous, dense rugosa rose with leathery, wrinkled, light green leaves. Cupped to flat, double, strongly scented, rich purple-red flowers, 4½in (11cm) across, are produced from summer to autumn. ↕ 7ft (2.2m), ↔ 6ft (2m). Zone 2b.

***R.* 'Rosette Delizy'.** Vigorous, upright, shrubby tea rose with glossy, dark green leaves. From spring to autumn, produces high-centered, double, tea-scented, pale yellow flowers, 3½in (9cm) across, flushed apricot-pink. ↕ to 4ft (1.2m), ↔ 3ft (1m). Zone 7b.

***R.* 'Rosier de Thionville'** see *R.* 'Quatre Saisons Blanche Mousseuse'.

***R.* 'Rosika'** see *R.* 'Radox Bouquet'.

***R.* 'Rosy Cushion'** ▣ Dense, spreading shrub rose with abundant glossy, dark green leaves. Clusters of cupped, semi-double, scented pink flowers, 2½in (6cm) across, with off-white centers are produced from spring to autumn, . ↕ 3ft (1m), ↔ 4ft (1.2m). Zone 6.

***R.* 'Rosy Mantle'** ▣ Stiff climber of open habit, with sparse, dark green leaves. High-centered, fully double, fragrant, rose- to salmon-pink flowers, 4in (10cm) across, are borne from summer to autumn. ↕ 8ft (2.5m), ↔ 6ft (2m). Zone 6.

***R.* 'Rouletii'**, syn. *R. chinensis* var. *minima*, *R.* 'Pompon de Paris'. Compact miniature China rose with thin stems and mid-green leaves consisting of many lance-shaped leaflets. Cupped, double, deep pink flowers, ¾in (2cm) across, are borne freely from spring to autumn. A supposed parent of many miniature roses. ↕↔ 8in (20cm). Zone 6.

R. roxburghii ▣ syn. *R. roxburghii* 'Plena' (Burr rose, Chestnut rose, Chinquapin rose). Vigorous, stiff-growing species rose with flaky bark and light to mid-green leaves, each consisting of 7, rarely 17–19, narrowly ovate to obovate leaflets, ½–1in (1.5–2.5cm) long. Solitary, neatly formed, rounded, double, lilac-pink flowers, 3in (8cm) across, open from prickly buds in summer. ↕↔ 6ft (2m). E. Asia. Zone 6. **'Plena'** see *R. roxburghii.*

***R.* 'Royal Dane'** see *R.* 'Troika'.

***R.* 'Royal Highness'**, syn. *R.* 'Königliche Hoheit'. Hybrid tea rose producing strong stems and leathery, dark green leaves. High-centered, fully double, fragrant, pearl-pink flowers, 5in (13cm) across, are borne from spring to autumn. ↕ 4–5ft (1.2–1.5m), ↔ 24in (60cm). Zone 6.

***R.* 'Royal William'** ▣ syn. *R.* 'Duftzauber '84'. Vigorous hybrid tea rose with dark green leaves. High-centered, fully double, fragrant, deep crimson flowers, 5in (13cm) across, are produced from spring to autumn. ↕ 4ft (1.2m), ↔ 30in (75cm). Zone 6.

R. rubiginosa see *R. eglanteria.*

R. rubrifolia see *R. glauca.*

'osa 'Rambling Rector'

Rosa rugosa

Rosa 'Rugul'

Rosa 'Salet'

Rosa 'Sally Holmes'

Rosa 'Sanders' White Rambler'

Rosa 'Sandringham Centenary'

Rosa 'Sarah van Fleet'

Rosa 'Savoy Hotel'

Rosa 'Seagull'

Rosa 'Sexy Rexy'

Rosa 'Sheila's Perfume'

Rosa 'Sheri Anne'

R. rugosa ▣ (Hedgehog rose, Japanese rose, Ramanas rose, Sea tomato). Vigorous, dense species rose with very prickly stems and wrinkled, leathery, dark green leaves, each composed of 7–9, rarely up to 11, narrowly oblong leaflets, 1–2in (2.5–5cm) long. Cupped, single, fragrant, violet-carmine-red flowers, 3in (8cm) across, showing yellow stamens, are borne singly or in small clusters from spring to autumn, followed by tomato-shaped, red to orange-red hips. Good as a hedge. ↕↔ 3–8ft (1–2.5m). E. Russia, N. China, Korea, Japan. Zone 2b. **var. *alba*** has white flowers, to 3½in (9cm) across, opening from pale pink buds. **var. *rosea*** ▣ has rose-pink flowers. **var. *rubra***, syn. f. *rubra*, has purplish red flowers. **'Scabrosa'** see *R.* 'Scabrosa'.
***R.* 'Rugul'** ▣ syn. *R.* 'Guletta', *R.* 'Tapis Jaune'. Compact, miniature rose of dense habit, with bright green foliage. Cupped to flat, double yellow flowers, 2in (5cm) across, are produced from spring to autumn. ↕ 12in (30cm), ↔ 14in (35cm). Zone 6.
***R.* 'Salet'** ▣ Upright, arching moss rose with lightly mossed stems and matte, pale green foliage. Bears remontant, rounded, double, fragrant, clear rose-pink flowers, 3in (8cm) across, mainly in summer. ↕ 4ft (1.2m), ↔ 3ft (1m). Zone 5.
***R.* 'Sally Holmes'** ▣ Upright, narrow shrub rose with glossy, dark green leaves. Large clusters of many wide, cupped, single, scented, creamy white flowers, 3½in (9cm) across, are borne on long stems from spring to autumn. ↕ 6ft (2m), ↔ 3ft (1m). Zone 6.
***R.* 'Samaritan'**, syn. *R.* 'Fragrant Surprise'. Hybrid tea rose with abundant glossy, mid-green foliage. From spring to autumn, wide sprays of pointed buds open to quartered-rosette, fully double, scented flowers, 3½in (9cm) across, which age from apricot-pink to orange-red. ↕ 3–4ft (1–1.2m), ↔ 24in (60cm). Zone 6.
***R.* 'Sanders' White Rambler'** ▣ Vigorous, arching rambler of lax growth, with abundant glossy, light green leaves. Sprays of many rosette-shaped, fully double, scented white flowers, 2in (5cm) across, cover the plant in early summer. ↕↔ to 12ft (4m). Zone 6.
***R.* 'Sandringham Centenary'** ▣ Vigorous hybrid tea rose producing dark green leaves. High-centered, double, rose- to salmon-pink flowers, 4½in (11cm) across, are borne from spring to autumn. ↕ 4ft (1.2m), ↔ 30in (75cm). Zone 6.
***R.* 'San Rafael'** see *R.* x *odorata* 'Pseudindica'.
***R.* 'Sarah van Fleet'** ▣ Vigorous, erect to arching hybrid rugosa rose producing large, wrinkled, bronze-green leaves. Cupped, semi-double, fragrant, clear light pink flowers, 3in (8cm) across, showing yellow stamens, are borne from spring to autumn. ↕ 8ft (2.5m), ↔ 5ft (1.5m). Zone 2b.
***R.* 'Savoy Hotel'** ▣ syn. *R.* 'Integrity'. Vigorous hybrid tea rose with strong stems and dark green leaves. From spring to autumn, bears high-centered to rounded, fully double, light pink flowers, 4½in (11cm) across, with a deeper pink reverse to the petals. ↕ 3–4ft (1–1.2m), ↔ 24in (60cm). Zone 6.
***R.* 'Scabrosa'**, syn. *R. rugosa* 'Scabrosa'. Vigorous, dense-growing rugosa rose of rounded habit, with wrinkled, leathery, light green leaves. Cupped, single, fragrant, reddish mauve flowers, 4in (10cm) across, with prominent yellow stamens, are borne from spring to autumn, followed by tomato-shaped red hips. ↕↔ 5½ft (1.7m). Zone 2b.
***R.* 'Scarlet Fire'** see *R.* 'Scharlachglut'.
***R.* 'Scarlet Glow'** see *R.* 'Scharlachglut'.
***R.* 'Scharlachglut'**, syn. *R.* 'Scarlet Fire', *R.* 'Scarlet Glow'. Very vigorous, arching shrub or climbing rose of open habit, with dark green leaves. Showy, cupped, single, bright crimson-scarlet flowers, 5in (13cm) across, with golden stamens, are borne freely in early summer, followed by pear-shaped, bright red hips. ↕ to 10ft (3m), ↔ 6ft (2m). Zone 4.
***R.* 'Schneewittchen'** see *R.* 'Iceberg'.
***R.* 'Schneezwerg'**, syn. *R.* 'Snow Dwarf'. Rugosa rose of dense, bushy, even habit, with wrinkled, mid-green leaves. From summer to autumn, produces flat, semi-double, scented white flowers, 3in (8cm) across, showing yellow stamens; they are followed by tomato-shaped, orange-red hips. ↕ 4ft (1.2m), ↔ 5ft (1.5m). Zone 2b.
***R.* 'Schoolgirl'.** Stiff, lanky, large-flowered climber producing sparse, deep green leaves. High-centered to rounded, fully double, scented, deep apricot flowers, 4in (10cm) across, are borne from spring to autumn. ↕ 10ft (3m), ↔ 8ft (2.5m). Zone 6.
***R.* 'Seagull'** ▣ Rampant rambler of arching habit, with grayish green leaves. Large clusters of numerous cupped to flat, single to semi-double, fragrant white flowers, 1in (2.5cm) across, with golden stamens, cover the plant in early summer. ↕ to 20ft (6m), ↔ 12ft (4m). Zone 6.
***R.* 'Secret'**. Upright hybrid tea rose with leathery, dark green leaves. Spring to autumn, bears high-centered, double, fragrant, deep pink-edged, light pink flowers, 4½in (11cm) across, mostly singly. ↕ 4–5ft (1.2–1.5m), ↔ 24in (60cm). Zone 6.
R. sericea* subsp. *omeiensis* f. *pteracantha, syn. *R. omeiensis* f. *pteracantha* (Winged thorn rose). Stiff, upright, vigorous species rose with large translucent, ornamental red prickles, to 1¼in (3cm) or more wide and ¾in (2cm) tall, on young stems. Small, fern-like, light green leaves each have 11–17 elliptic, oblong, or obovate leaflets, ½–1¼in (1–3cm) long. Solitary, flat, usually 4-petaled white flowers, 1–2½in (2.5–6cm) across, are borne briefly along the stems in spring. ↕ 8ft (2.5m), ↔ 7ft (2.2m). W. China. Zone 6.
***R.* 'Sexy Rexy'** ▣ syn. *R.* 'Heckenzauber'. Floribunda rose producing abundant glossy, dark green foliage. Showy, heavy heads of camellia-like, rounded, fully double, rose-pink flowers, 3in (8cm) across, are borne from spring to autumn. ↕ 3–3½ft (1–1.1m), ↔ 24in (60cm). Zone 6.
***R.* 'Sheila's Perfume'** ▣ Floribunda rose with glossy, dark green leaves. Urn-shaped, double, fragrant yellow flowers, 3½in (9cm) across, strongly marked and veined with red, singly or in open clusters from spring to autumn. ↕ 36in (90cm), ↔ 24in (60cm). Zone 6.
***R.* 'Sheri Anne'** ▣ Miniature rose of neat, upright habit, with glossy, mid-green leaves. From spring to autumn, bears clusters of many urn-shaped, double, light orange-red flowers, 1in (2.5cm) across, the petals with yellow bases. ↕ 14in (35cm), ↔ 12in (30cm). Zone 6.

Rosa rugosa var. *rosea*

Rosa 'Showbiz'

Rosa 'Silver Jubilee'

Rosa 'Simba'

Rosa 'Snowball'

Rosa 'Sonia'

Rosa 'Souvenir de la Malmaison'

Rosa 'Stacey Sue'

Rosa 'Stanwell Perpetual'

Rosa 'Sue Lawley'

Rosa 'Summer Wine'

Rosa 'Sunblest'

Rosa 'Surrey'

***R.* 'Shocking Blue'**. Floribunda rose with dark green leaves. Urn-shaped buds open to rounded, fully double, fragrant, lilac-purple flowers, 4in (10cm) across, borne singly or in clusters from spring to autumn. ↕ 36in (90cm), ↔ 24in (60cm). Zone 6.

***R.* 'Showbiz'** ■ syn. *R.* 'Bernhard Daneke Rose', *R.* Ingrid Weibull'. Very compact floribunda rose with dark green, glossy leaves. Large clusters of medium-red, semi-double, flat, unscented flowers, 3in (8cm) across, are produced from spring to autumn. Disease resistant. ↕ 2–4ft (.6–1.2m), ↔ 2–3ft (60–90cm). Zone 6.

***R.* 'Silver Jubilee'** ■ Dense hybrid tea rose with dark green leaves. High-centered, fully double, rose-pink flowers, to 5in (13cm) across, flushed peach- or salmon-pink, are borne singly or in open clusters on strong stems from spring to autumn. ↕ 4½ft (1.4m), ↔ 24in (60cm). Zone 6.

***R.* 'Silver Moon'.** Vigorous, free-branching, large-flowered climber with long, arching stems and glossy, dark green leaves. In early summer, freely bears clusters of cupped, semi-double, scented, creamy white flowers, 4in (10cm) across. ↕ to 20ft (6m), ↔ 10ft (3m). Zone 6.

***R.* 'Simba'** ■ syn. *R.* 'Helmut Schmidt'. Hybrid tea rose of neat habit, with mid-green leaves. Urn-shaped buds open to well-formed, rounded, fully double yellow flowers, 3½in (9cm) across, borne from spring to autumn. ↕ 4–5ft (1.2–1.5m), ↔ 20in (50cm). Zone 6.

***R.* 'Simon Fraser'.** Upright, low-growing shrub rose with semi-glossy, dark green leaves. Clusters of cupped, single to semi-double, mid-pink flowers, 2in (5cm) across, are produced from spring to autumn. ↕↔ 24in (60cm). Zone 3.

***R.* 'Sissinghurst Castle'**, syn. *R.* 'Rose des Maures'. Gallica rose of upright, free-suckering habit, with slender, firm stems and dark green leaves. Cupped to flat, semi-double, scented, deep maroon-crimson flowers, 2½in (6cm) across, showing yellow stamens, are borne in early summer. ↕↔ 3ft (1m). Zone 4.

***R.* 'Snowball'** ■ syn. *R.* 'Angelita'. Compact miniature rose of spreading habit, with many tiny, bright green leaves. Clusters of pompon, narrow-petaled, fully double white flowers, 1in (2.5cm) across, are borne from spring to autumn. ↕ 8in (20cm), ↔ 12in (30cm). Zone 6.

***R.* 'Snow Carpet'**. Prostrate, creeping miniature groundcover rose with bright green leaves. Pompom, fully double, creamy white flowers, 1¼in (3cm) across, are produced in early summer. Attractive as a ground-cover in containers. ↕ 6in (15cm), ↔ 18in (45cm). Zone 6.

***R.* 'Snow Dwarf'** see *R.* 'Schneezwerg'.

***R.* 'Snow Queen'** see *R.* 'Frau Karl Druschki'.

***R.* 'Sombreuil'**, syn. *R.* 'Mme. Sombreuil'. Climbing tea rose with dark green, glossy leaves. Bearing clusters of flat, double, quartered, scented, creamy white flowers tinged with hints of pink, 3in (9cm) across, from spring to autumn. ↕ 8–13ft (2.5–4.1m), ↔ 5–6ft (1.5–2m). Zone 6.

***R.* 'Sommerwind'** see *R.* 'Surrey'.

***R.* 'Sonia'** ■ syn. *R.* 'Sonia Meilland', *R.* 'Sweet Promise'. Grandiflora of medium growth habit and glossy dark leathery foliage. Long buds open to a pink bloom suffused coral to yellow, double (30 petals) 4–4½in (10–11cm) across, with intense fruity fragrance. Zone 6.

***R.* 'Sonia' Meilland'** see *R.* 'Sonia'.

***R.* 'Souvenir de la Malmaison'** ■ syn. *R.* 'Queen of Beauty & Fragrance'. Dense, spreading bourbon rose with dark green foliage and quartered-rosette, fully double, spice-scented, pale pink to white flowers, 5in (13cm) across, borne from summer to autumn. Rain may spoil flowers. ↕ 24–36in (60–90cm), ↔ 36in (90cm). Zone 6.

***R.* 'Souvenir de la Princesse de Lamballe'** see *R.* 'Bourbon Queen'.

***R.* 'Spanish Beauty'** see *R.* 'Mme. Grégoire Staechelin'.

***R.* 'Spanish Shawl'** see *R.* 'Sue Lawley'.

***R.* 'Spectacular'** see *R.* 'Danse du Feu'.

R. spinosissima see *R. pimpinellifolia.*

***R.* 'Spring Gold'** see *R.* 'Frühlingsgold'.

***R.* 'Spring Morning'** see *R.* 'Frühlingsmorgen'.

***R.* 'Stacey Sue'** ■ Miniature rose of neat, spreading habit, with dark green leaves. Rosette-shaped, fully double, rose-pink flowers, 1in (2.5cm) across, are borne in dense sprays from spring to autumn. ↕ 10in (25cm), ↔ 12in (30cm). Zone 6.

***R.* 'Stanwell Perpetual'** ■ Hybrid spinosissima rose of spreading, twiggy habit, with prickly stems and fern-like, dark grayish green leaves. Loosely formed, cupped, fully double, scented, pale pink flowers, 3in (8cm) across, are borne singly on thin stems from summer to autumn. ↕ 3ft (1m), ↔ 4ft (1.2m). Zone 4.

***R.* 'Starina'**. Neat miniature rose with shiny, dark green leaves. High-centered, fully double, orange-red flowers, 1½in (4cm) across, are borne from spring to autumn. ↕↔ 14in (35cm). Zone 6.

***R.* 'Stars 'n' Stripes'.** Miniature rose of uneven, spreading habit, with small, dark green leaves. From spring to autumn, produces cupped, semi-double flowers, 1¾in (4.5cm) across, pale pink to white, striped strawberry-red. ↕ 12in (30cm), ↔ to 28in (70cm). Zone 6.

R. stellata* var. *mirifica (Sacramento rose). Species rose of suckering habit, with springy, wiry, prickly stems and mid-green leaves, each with 3–5 deeply cut, gooseberry-like, wedge-shaped leaflets, ¼–½in (0.6–1.5cm) long. In summer, produces solitary, wide-opening, cupped to flat, single, scented, pink to deep rose-purple flowers, 1½–2¼in (3.5–6cm) across. ↕ to 3½ft (1.1m), ↔ 4ft (1.2m). New Mexico. Zone 7.

***R.* 'Sterling Silver'.** Hybrid tea rose with sparse, leathery, mid-green foliage. From spring to autumn, bears high-centered to cupped, double, fragrant, lilac-mauve flowers, 3½in (9cm) across. ↕ 36in (90cm), ↔ 24in (60cm). Zone 6.

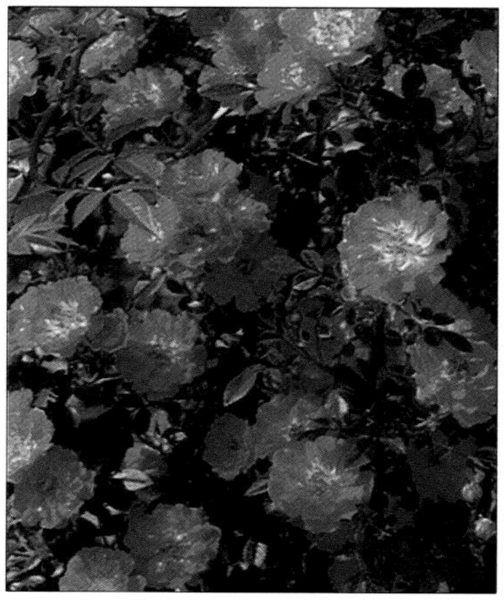
Rosa 'Suma'

***R.* 'Stretch Johnson'** see *R.* 'Tango'.

***R.* 'Sue Lawley'** ■ syn. *R.* 'Spanish Shawl'. Floribunda rose with dark green leaves. From spring to autumn, produces sprays of cupped, wide-opening, double, carmine-red flowers, 3½in (9cm) across, with paler pink or white centers and petal margins. ↕↔ 24in (60cm). Zone 6.

***R.* 'Suma'** ■ Prostrate groundcover shrub rose with shiny, dark green foliage, turning burnished crimson in autumn. Clusters of rosette-shaped, double, ruby-red to deep pink flowers, 1¼in (3cm) across, are borne along the stems from spring to autumn. ↕ 20in (50cm), ↔ 5ft (1.5m). Zone 6.

***R.* 'Summer Wine'** ■ Large-flowered climber with stiff, branching growth and mid-green leaves. Cupped, single, scented, coral-pink flowers, 4in (10cm) across, shaded yellow at the bases and with folded petals, are produced from spring to autumn. ↕ 10ft (3m), ↔ 7ft (2.2m). Zone 6.

***R.* 'Sunbird'** see *R.* 'Hot Tamale'.

***R.* 'Sunblaze'** see *R.* 'Orange Sunblaze'.

***R.* 'Sunblest'** ■ syn. *R.* 'Landora'. Hybrid tea rose producing shiny, mid-green leaves. Pointed buds open to cupped, double yellow flowers, 3½in (9cm) across, borne freely from spring to autumn. ↕ 3–4ft (1–1.2m), ↔ 24in (60cm). Zone 6.

***R.* 'Sun Flare'.** Floribunda rose with small, glossy, disease-resistant leaves. Produces small to medium clusters of medium yellow, flat, double, scented flowers, 4in (10cm) across, from spring to autumn. ↕ ↔ 3–4ft (1–1.2m). Zone 6.

***R.* 'Sunnyside'** see *R.* 'Avon'.

***R.* 'Sunsprite'** see *R.* 'Korresia'.

***R.* 'Super Star'**, syn. *R.* 'Tropicana'. Hybrid tea rose of open, uneven habit, with small, dark green leaves. Rounded, fully double, lightly scented, vermilion to pale scarlet flowers, 4½in (11cm) across, are borne from spring to autumn. Considered among the very best hybrid teas. ↕ 5–6ft (1.5–2m), ↔ 3ft (1m). Zone 6.

***R.* 'Surrey'** ■ syn. *R.* 'Sommerwind'. Vigorous, mounding groundcover shrub rose with abundant dark green foliage. Clusters of cupped, double, rose-pink flowers, 2½in (6cm) across, are borne along the stems from spring to autumn. ↕ 32in (80cm), ↔ 4ft (1.2m). Zone 6.

R

Rosa 'Swany'

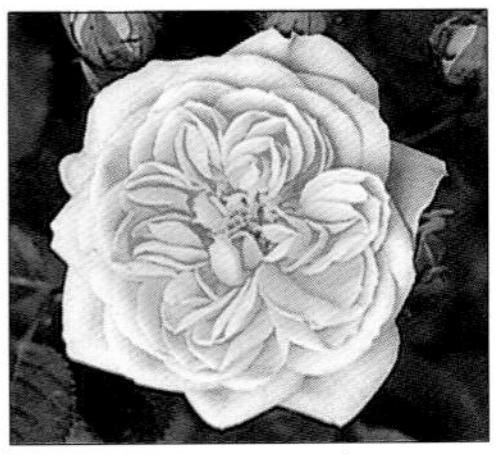
Rosa 'Sweet Dream'

Rosa 'Sweetheart'

Rosa 'Sweet Magic'

Rosa 'Sydonie'

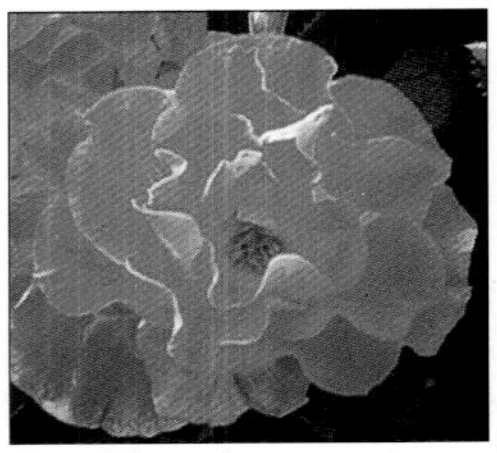
Rosa 'Tango'

Rosa 'Tequila Sunrise'

Rosa 'The Fairy'

Rosa 'Tiffany Lynn'

Rosa 'Tigress'

Rosa 'Tricolore de Flandre'

Rosa 'Troika'

***R.* 'Sutter's Gold'.** Spindly hybrid tea rose with sparse, leathery, dark green foliage. High-centered buds open to loosely formed, high-centered, double, fragrant, golden orange flowers, 4½in (11cm) across, overlaid with red, from spring to autumn. ↕3–4ft (1–1.2m), ↔ 24in (60cm). Zone 6.

***R.* 'Swany'** ▣ Vigorous, dense groundcover shrub rose with shiny, dark green leaves. Profuse clusters of numerous flat, fully double white flowers, 2in (5cm) across, are borne from spring to autumn. ↕ to 30in (75cm), ↔ to 5½ft (1.7m). Zone 4b.

***R.* 'Sweet Dream'** ▣ Miniature rose of neat, leafy habit, with mid-green foliage. Dense clusters of cupped, fully double, peach-apricot flowers, 2½in (6cm) across, are borne on stiff stems from spring to autumn. ↕16in (40cm), ↔ 14in (35cm). Zone 6.

***R.* 'Sweetheart'** ▣ Hybrid tea rose of upright habit, with dense, light green foliage. Rounded, double, fragrant, rose-pink flowers, 4½in (11cm) across, are borne from spring to autumn. ↕3–4ft (1–1.2m), ↔ 24in (60cm). Zone 6.

***R.* 'Sweetheart Rose'** see *R.* 'Cécile Brunner'.

***R.* 'Sweet Juliet'**. Hybrid tea rose of prolific growth, with mid-green leaves. Cupped, fully double, tea-scented, apricot-yellow flowers, 4in (10cm) across, are borne from summer to autumn. ↕4–5ft (1.1m), ↔ 3ft (1m). Zone 6.

***R.* 'Sweet Magic'** ▣ Neat, miniature rose with bright green leaves. From spring to autumn, well-spaced clusters of urn-shaped buds open to cupped, double, apricot-orange and yellow flowers, 1½in (4cm) across. ↕↔ 14in (35cm). Zone 6.

***R.* 'Sweet Promise'** see *R.* 'Sonia'.

***R.* 'Sweet Sunblaze'** see *R.* 'Pretty Polly'.

***R.* 'Sydonie'** ▣ syn. 'Sidonie'. Hybrid perpetual rose with red thorns and mid-green, semi-glossy leaves. Producing clusters of medium pink, flat, quartered, scented flowers, 3–4in (8–10cm) across, from spring to autumn. ↕3–5ft (1–1.5m), ↔ 3–4ft (1–1.2m). Zone 6.

***R.* 'Sylvia'** see *R.* 'Congratulations'.

***R.* 'Sympathie'** ▣ Free-branching, vigorous, large-flowered climber with dense, glossy, dark green foliage. Cupped, fully double, bright deep red flowers, 3in (8cm) across, are borne from summer to autumn, usually in clusters. ↕10ft (3m), ↔ 8ft (2.5m). Zone 6.

***R.* 'Taifun'** see *R.* 'Typhoon'.

***R.* 'Tall Story'**. Groundcover shrub rose with abundant glossy, light green leaves. Graceful sprays of cupped, semi-double, scented, light primrose-yellow flowers, 2½in (6cm) across, are borne on bowed stems from spring to autumn. ↕30in (75cm), ↔ 4ft (1.2m). Zone 6.

***R.* 'Tanellis'** see *R.* 'Fragrant Cloud'.

***R.* 'Tango'** ▣ syn. *R.* 'Rock 'n' Roll', *R.* 'Stretch Johnson'. Floribunda rose with mid-green leaves. From spring to autumn, bears cupped, wide-opening, semi-double, orange-red flowers, 2½in (6cm) across, with petals margined yellowish white, and yellow on the reverse sides. ↕4ft (1.2m), ↔ 24in (60cm). Zone 6.

***R.* 'Tanryrandy'** see *R.* 'Cherry Brandy'.

***R.* 'Tapis d'Orient'** see *R.* 'Yesterday'.

***R.* 'Tapis Jaune'** see *R.* 'Rugul'.

***R.* 'Tapis Persan'** see *R.* 'Eye Paint'.

Rosa 'Sympathie'

***R.* 'Tequila Sunrise'** ▣ Hybrid tea rose of open habit, with glossy, dark green leaves. Wide sprays of rounded, fully double yellow flowers, 4in (10cm) across, with scarlet-margined petals, are borne freely from summer to autumn. ↕4–5ft (1.2–1.5m), ↔ 24in (60cm). Zone 6.

***R.* 'The Fairy'** ▣ Vigorous polyantha rose of dense, cushion-forming habit, with abundant shiny, mid-green leaves. Rosette-shaped, double, light pink flowers, 1in (2.5cm) across, are borne freely from early summer to autumn. ↕↔ 24–36in (60–90cm). Zone 6.

***R.* 'The Queen Elizabeth'** see *R.* 'Queen Elizabeth'.

***R.* 'Tiffany Lynn'** ▣ Upright mini-flora of bushy growth, bearing semi-glossy, medium green foliage with red edges and downward-slanting prickles. Double flowers (21 petals) have light to medium pink edges, blending to white at the center. Zone 6.

***R.* 'Tigress'** ▣ Deep purple grandiflora buds open into purple and white striped, high-centered double blooms. Often borne in clusters. Double (34 petals), 4½–5in (11–13cm). Lush damask and ripe currant fragrance. Foliage large, medium green. Upright. medium growth. ↕4–5 ft (1.2-1.5 m.) Zone 6.

***R.* 'Tipo Ideale'** see *R.* x *odorata* 'Mutabilis'.

***R.* 'Tobone'** see *R.* 'Prima Donna'.

***R.* 'Tocade'** see *R.* 'Arizona'.

***R.* 'Top Gear'** see *R.* 'Little Artist'.

***R.* 'Touch of Class'**, syn. *R.* 'Kricarlo', *R.* 'Maréchal le Clerc'. Hybrid tea rose with dark green leaves. High-centered, double flowers, 5in (13cm) across, pale creamy pink suffused with coral-pink, are borne on long stems from spring to autumn. ↕5–6ft (1.5–2m), ↔ 28in (70cm). Zone 6.

***R.* 'Tournament of Roses'**, syn. *R.* 'Berkeley', *R.* 'Poesie'. Strong-growing grandiflora rose with glossy, dark green leaves. Rounded, double, light rose- to salmon-pink flowers, 4in (10cm) across, are borne from summer to autumn. ↕4–5ft (1.2–1.5m), ↔ 24in (60cm). Zone 6.

***R.* 'Tricolore de Flandre'** ▣ Vigorous gallica rose of bushy, upright habit, with dull, dark green leaves. Cupped to flat, fully double, fragrant, pale pink flowers, 2½in (6cm) across, striped with pink and purple, are borne in early summer. ↕↔ 3ft (1m). Zone 4b.

***R.* 'Troika'** ▣ syn. *R.* 'Royal Dane'. Vigorous, branching hybrid tea rose with abundant semi-glossy, mid-green leaves. High-centered, double, fragrant, reddish orange flowers, 6in (15cm) across, with pink flushes, are produced from summer to autumn. ↕4–5ft (1.2–1.5m), ↔ 30in (75cm). Zone 6.

***R.* 'Tropicana'** see *R.* 'Super Star'.

***R.* 'Trumpeter'** ▣ Floribunda rose of neat habit, with deep green foliage. Showy, cupped, fully double, vivid orange-red flowers, 2½in (6cm) across, are borne from spring to autumn. ↕36in (90cm), ↔ 20in (50cm). Zone 6.

***R.* 'Tuscany Superb'** ▣ (Double velvet rose). Vigorous, rounded gallica rose with dark green leaves. In early summer, erect stems produce cupped to flat, double, scented, deep crimson-maroon to purple flowers, 2in (5cm) across, showing gold stamens. ↕↔ 3ft (1m). Zone 4.

***R.* 'Typhoon'** ▣ syn. *R.* 'Taifun'. Spreading hybrid tea rose with shiny, dark green leaves. Rounded, fully double, fragrant, salmon- to orange-pink flowers, 4in (10cm) across, are borne from spring to autumn. ↕4–5ft (1.2–1.5m), ↔ 26in (65cm). Zone 6.

***R.* 'Valencia'** ▣ Hybrid tea rose of open habit, with leathery, glossy, dark green foliage. From spring to autumn, bears high-centered, fully double, fragrant, amber-yellow flowers, 4in (10cm) across. ↕4–5ft (1.2–1.5m), ↔ 26in (65cm). Zone 6.

***R.* 'Valentine Heart'** ▣ Floribunda rose of open habit, with dark green foliage. From spring to autumn, pale scarlet buds open to cupped, semi-double, scented, pale pink and deeper pink flowers, 3in (8cm) across, with infolded, frilled petals at the centers. ↕36in (90cm), ↔ 20in (50cm). Zone 6.

***R.* 'Variegata di Bologna'.** Willowy, arching, smooth-stemmed bourbon rose with pale green leaves. Remontant, quartered-rosette, fully double, fragrant, pale pink flowers, 3in (8cm) across, stippled with purple-crimson, are borne in early summer. Prone to black spot. ↕7ft (2.2m), ↔ 5ft (1.5m). Zone 6.

***R.* 'Veilchenblau'** ▣ syn. *R.* 'Blue Rambler', *R.* 'Violet Blue'. Vigorous rambler with light green leaves. In early summer, produces large clusters of

Rosa 'Trumpeter'

Rosa 'Tuscany Superb'

Rosa 'Typhoon'

Rosa 'Valencia'

Rosa 'Valentine Heart'

Rosa 'Veilchenblau'

Rosa 'Veteran's Honor'

Rosa 'Westerland'

Rosa 'White Cockade'

Rosa 'William Lobb'

Rosa xanthina 'Canary Bird'

Rosa xanthina f. *hugonis*

many cupped, double, fruit-scented violet flowers, 1¼in (3cm) across, streaked with white. ↕↔ 12ft (4m). Zone 6.

***R.* 'Veteran's Honor'** ■ Dark red buds open into thick, heavy, high-centered large, fragrant, bright red hybrid tea with open blooms, 5in (12cm) across. ↕ 5ft (1.5m). ↔ 24in (60cm). Zone 6.

***R.* 'Ville de Chine'** see *R.* 'Chinatown'.

***R.* 'Violacea'**, syn. *R.* 'La Belle Sultane'. Tall, smooth-stemmed gallica rose with sparse gray-green foliage. Cupped to flat, single, fragrant, violet-purple flowers, 4in (10cm) across, with golden stamens, are produced during early summer. ↕ 7ft (2.2m), ↔ 5ft (1.5m). Zone 4.

***R.* 'Violet Blue'** see *R.* 'Veilchenblau'.

R. virginiana, syn. *R. lucida.* Species rose of erect, suckering habit, with shiny, light to mid-green leaves composed of 5–9 obovate to oblong-elliptic leaflets, 1–2½in (2.5–6cm) long, reddening in autumn. Cupped to flat, single, pale to bright pink flowers, 2–3in (5–8cm) across, are borne singly or in clusters of up to 8 blooms in early summer; they are followed by spherical, ruby-red hips in autumn. ↕ 4ft (1.2m), ↔ 5ft (1.5m). E. North America. Zone 3.

***R.* 'Viridiflora'** see *R.* x *odorata* 'Viridiflora'.

***R.* 'Warm Welcome'**. Stiff, arching, climbing miniature with many dark green leaves. Small clusters of urn-shaped, semi-double, orange-red flowers, 1½in (4cm) across, are borne freely from spring to autumn. ↕↔ 7ft (2.2m). Zone 6.

***R.* 'Wedding Day'.** Rampant rambler producing shiny, mid-green leaves with lance-shaped leaflets. Large clusters of flat, single, fruit-scented, creamy white flowers, 1in (2.5cm) across, aging to pale pink, are borne in early summer. ↕ to 25ft (8m), ↔ 12ft (4m). Zone 6.

***R.* 'Westerland'** ■ Vigorous, stiff-stemmed shrub or climbing rose with bright green leaves. From spring to autumn, bears bold clusters of loosely formed, cupped, double, scented, apricot-orange flowers, 3in (8cm) across, suffused yellow. ↕ 6ft (2m), ↔ 4ft (1.2m) as a shrub; ↕ to 8ft (2.5m) as a climber. Zone 6.

***R.* 'Whisky'** see *R.* 'Whisky Mac'.

***R.* 'Whisky Mac'**, syn. *R.* 'Whisky'. Hybrid tea rose with reddish green stems and glossy, dark green foliage. From spring to autumn, produces rounded, double, fragrant, light amber-yellow flowers, 4in (10cm) across. Prone to mildew. ↕ 4–5ft (1.2–1.5m), ↔ 24in (60cm). Zone 6.

***R.* 'White American Beauty'** see *R.* 'Frau Karl Druschki'.

***R.* 'White Baby Rambler'** see *R.* 'Katharina Zeimet'.

***R.* 'White Cloud'** see *R.* 'Hakuun'.

***R.* 'White Cockade'** ■ Upright, shrubby, large-flowered climber with dark green leaves. From spring to autumn, bears rounded, fully double, milk-white flowers, 3½in (9cm) across. ↕ 7ft (2.2m), ↔ 5ft (1.5m). Zone 6.

***R.* 'White Cover'** see *R.* 'Kent'.

***R.* 'White Magic'** see *R.* 'Class Act'.

***R.* 'White Pet'** see *R.* 'Little White Pet'.

***R.* 'White Wings'.** Hybrid tea rose with dark green leaves. Cupped to flat, single, scented white flowers, 3in (8cm) across, with chocolate-brown stamens, open from spring to autumn. ↕ 3–4ft (1–1.2m), ↔ 24in (60cm). Zone 6.

R. wichuraiana see *R. wichurana.*

R. wichurana, syn. *R. wichuraiana* (Memorial rose). Vigorous, climbing, semi-evergreen species rose, mound-forming as a groundcover, producing numerous small, shiny, dark green leaves consisting of 5–9 elliptic to broadly ovate leaflets, to 1in (2.5cm) long. Cupped to flat, single, clover-scented white flowers, 1¾in (4.5cm) across, with prominent golden yellow stamens, are borne in loose clusters of 6–10 in summer. Ovoid to spherical hips are orange-red to dark red, and to ½in (1.5cm) long. ↕ 6ft (2m), ↔ 20ft (6m). E. China, Korea, Japan, Taiwan. Zone 4.

***R.* 'William Allen Richardson'.** Noisette rose with arching, branching growth and shiny, dark green leaves. From spring to autumn, urn-shaped buds open to quartered-rosette, double, scented, apricot-yellow flowers, 1¾in (4.5cm) across, paler toward the petal margins. ↕ 10ft (3m), ↔ 8ft (2.5m). Zone 7b.

***R.* 'William Baffin'.** Vigorous kordesii shrub rose, usually grown as a climber, with strong, arching canes and glossy, mid-green leaves. Clusters of remontant, cupped, double, deep strawberry-pink flowers, 2½–3in (6–8cm) across, are borne in spring or early summer. ↕ 8–10ft (2.5–3m), ↔ 6ft (2m). Zone 2b.

***R.* 'William Lobb'** ■ syn. *R.* 'Duchesse d'Istrie'. Vigorous moss rose with arching, prickly stems, abundant mossy growth, and mid-green leaves. Cupped, fully double, scented, purple to lavender-gray flowers, 3in (8cm) across, are borne in early summer. Best grown on a support. ↕↔ 6ft (2m). Zone 3.

***R.* 'William III'.** Suckering, spreading hybrid spinosissima with wiry stems and gray-green leaves. In spring, bears cupped, semi-double, scented, magenta-crimson flowers, 1¾in (4.5cm) across, shaded purplish red or lilac, followed by spherical, brownish red hips in autumn. ↕ 20in (50cm), ↔ 32in (80cm). Zone 5.

***R.* 'Winnipeg Parks'.** Dense, bushy shrub rose with matte-green leaves, red-tinged in autumn. Remontant, cupped, double, deep pink flowers, 3in (8cm) across, are borne in clusters in spring or early summer. ↕↔ 16–28in (40–70cm). Zone 2b.

***R.* 'Winter Sunset'**, syn. *R.* 'Fuzzy Navel'. Shrub rose with large, dark green, glossy leaves. High-centered, double, scented clusters of amber-yellow flowers, 3in (9cm) across, are produced from spring to autumn. ↕ 3–4ft (1–1.2cm), ↔ 3ft (1m). Zone 6.

Rosa 'Zéphirine Drouhin'

R. xanthina. Species rose of shrubby, dense growth, with reddish green stems and fern-like, grayish green leaves, each with 7–13 broadly elliptic to obovate leaflets, ½–¾in (1–2cm) long. Loosely formed, cupped to flat, semi-double, scented yellow flowers, 2in (5cm) across, are borne, usually singly, along the stems in late spring. ↕↔ 8ft (2.5m). N. China, Korea. Zone 4b. **'Canary Bird'** ■ syn. *R.* 'Canary Bird', is arching in habit, with cupped, single, musk-scented yellow flowers, borne in spring, sometimes sparsely later; ↕ 10ft (3m), ↔ to 12ft (4m). **f. *hugonis*** ■ syn. *R. hugonis* (Father Hugo's rose, Golden rose of China) produces cupped, single, lightly scented, pale yellow flowers, 1¾in (4.5cm) across, in late spring; ↔ 6ft (2m); W. and C. China. **f. *normalis*** bears single flowers.

***R.* 'Yellow Cécile Brunner'** see *R.* 'Perle d'Or'.

***R.* 'Yesterday'**, syn. *R.* 'Tapis d'Orient'. Polyantha rose of uneven growth, with shiny, mid-green leaves. Sprays of many rosette-shaped, semi-double, scented, lilac-pink to rose-violet flowers, 1in (2.5cm) across, are borne very freely from spring to autumn. ↕↔ 3–5ft (1–1.5m); it may be maintained much shorter through pruning. Zone 6.

***R.* 'Young Mistress'** see *R.* 'Regensberg'.

***R.* 'Yvonne Rabier'.** Compact polyantha rose with abundant bright green leaves. From spring to autumn, bears rounded, fully double, lightly scented, creamy white flowers, 1¾in (4.5cm) across. ↕↔ 16in (40cm). Zone 6.

***R.* 'Zéphirine Drouhin'** ■ (Thornless rose). Bourbon rose with lax, open, prickle-free growth and mid-green leaves. In early summer, freely bears remontant, loosely cupped, double, lightly fragrant, deep pink flowers, 3in (8cm) across. May be easily trained as a climber; good as a hedge. Prone to black spot. ↕ to 10ft (3m), ↔ 6ft (2m). Zone 6.

***R.* 'Zigeunerknabe'**, syn. *R.* 'Gipsy Boy'. Vigorous, lanky bourbon rose with coarse, dark green leaves. Remontant, cupped to flat, double, scented, purplish crimson flowers, 3in (8cm) across, with prominent golden yellow stamens, are borne in early summer. ↕ 6ft (2m), ↔ 4ft (1.2m). Zone 6.

***R.* 'Zonta Rose'** see *R.* 'Princess Alice'.

ROSCOEA

ZINGIBERACEAE

Genus of about 18 species of tuberous perennials from meadows, slopes, and partially forested areas in the Himalayas and China. They are cultivated for their unusual, hooded, orchid-like flowers, which have prominent, entire or 2-lobed lips. The flowers are surrounded by overlapping bracts, and are produced on leafy stems from the leaf axils in summer or autumn. The arching leaves are stem-sheathing and linear, or lance-shaped to oblong-ovate. Roscoeas thrive in cool climates; grow in a woodland garden or damp, shady border.

• **CULTIVATION** Plant tubers 6in (15cm) deep in winter or early spring. Grow in moderately fertile, humus-rich, leafy, moist but well-drained soil, in a cool, sheltered site in partial shade. Where marginally hardy, apply a deep winter mulch.

• **PROPAGATION** Sow seed in containers in a cold frame as soon as ripe. Divide in spring.

• **PESTS AND DISEASES** Slugs and vine weevils may be problems.

Roscoea cautleoides

Roscoea humeana

R. alpina. Tuberous perennial with 1–4 oblong-lance-shaped, mid-green leaves, 4in (10cm) long. In summer, bears condensed spikes of pink or mauve flowers, to 1in (2.5cm) across, hidden in the upper leaf sheaths. ↕ 1ft (30cm), PD6in (15cm). N. India (Kashmir), Nepal. Zone 6b.

R. auriculata. Tuberous perennial with 3–10 linear to broadly lance-shaped, dark green leaves, to 10in (25cm) long. Rich purple flowers, 1½in (4cm) across, are produced from the upper leaf axils in late summer or autumn. ↕ 10–22in (25–55cm), PD6in (15cm). Nepal, India (Sikkim). Zone 7. **'Beesiana'** occasionally bears mauve-streaked yellow flowers.

***R. capitata* of gardens** see *R. scillifolia.*

R. cautleoides ■ Tuberous perennial with 1–4 linear to lance-shaped, deep to mid-green leaves, 16in (40cm) long, usually to 6in (15cm) long at flowering. In midsummer, produces yellow, white, or purple flowers, 1½in (4cm) across, from the upper leaf axils. ↕ to 22in (55cm), PD6in (15cm). China (Sichuan, Yunnan). Zone 7.

R. humeana ■ Sturdy, tuberous perennial bearing a succession of up to 10 rich purple flowers, 1½in (4cm) across, from the upper leaf axils in early summer. The 1 or 2, rarely 3, oblong to ovate, deep green leaves, to 9in (23cm) long, are usually only partially developed at flowering time. ↕ 6–10in (15–25cm), PD6in (15cm). China (Sichuan, Yunnan). Zone 7b.

R. procera see *R. purpurea.*

R. purpurea ■ syn. *R. procera, R. purpurea* var. *procera.* Tuberous perennial with 4–8 lance-shaped to oblong-ovate, deep green leaves, to 10in (25cm) long. Purple, occasionally white or bicolored flowers, 2½in (6cm) across, are produced in succession from the upper leaf axils in early and midsummer. ↕ 10–16in (25–40cm), PD6in (15cm). Himalayas. Zone 7. **var. *procera*** see *R. purpurea.*

R. scillifolia, syn. *R. capitata* of gardens. Slender, tuberous perennial with 1–5 linear to linear-lance-shaped, mid-green leaves, 2½–5in (6–13cm) long. In summer, produces 2–4 blackish pink or purplish pink flowers, ¾in (2cm) across, on leafless stalks above the leaves. May seed freely. ↕ 14in (35cm), PD3in (8cm). China (Yunnan). Zone 8.

▷ ***Roseocactus fissuratus*** see *Ariocarpus fissuratus*

Roscoea purpurea

Rosmarinus officinalis

ROSMARINUS

Rosemary

LAMIACEAE

Genus of 2 species of evergreen shrubs found in rocky sites, woodland, and scrub in the Mediterranean region, and cultivated for their aromatic foliage and flowers. The leaves are opposite and narrowly linear; the 2-lipped, tubular flowers are borne in short, few-flowered, axillary whorls. Grow rosemary in a shrub or mixed border, in an herb garden, against a sunny wall, or as a hedge. Low-growing cultivars, such as *R. officinalis* 'Prostratus', are ideal for a rock garden or the top of a dry wall. The leaves are rich in aromatic oils and are commonly used as a culinary herb.

• **CULTIVATION** Grow in well-drained, poor to moderately fertile soil in full sun. Pruning group 9. Trim hedges after flowering.

• **PROPAGATION** Sow seed in containers in a cold frame in spring. Root semi-ripe cuttings in summer.

• **PESTS AND DISEASES** Prone to aerial blight, bacterial leaf spots, and several root rots.

***R. eriocalyx* of gardens** see *R. officinalis* 'Prostratus'.

***R. lavandulaceus* of gardens** see *R. officinalis* 'Prostratus'.

R. officinalis ■ (Rosemary). Upright to rounded, dense, bushy, aromatic, evergreen shrub with linear, leathery, dark green leaves, to 2in (5cm) long, white-felted beneath. Whorls of tubular, 2-lipped blue flowers, ½in (1.5cm) long, are produced from the upper leaf axils from midspring to early summer, and often again in autumn. ↕↔ 5ft (1.5m). Mediterranean region. Zone 7. **'Arp'** is slightly hardier and more open; Zone 6b. **'Benenden Blue'**, syn. 'Collingwood Ingram', has narrow, dark green leaves and vivid blue flowers. **'Collingwood Ingram'** see 'Benenden Blue'. **'Fastigiatus'** see 'Miss Jessopp's Upright'. **'Golden Rain'** has new foliage edged clear gold; ↕ 18–36in (45–90cm). **'Logee's Blue'** has striking, blue-violet flowers; ↕ 24–30in (60–75cm). **'Miss Jessopp's Upright'**, syn. 'Fastigiatus', 'Pyramidalis', is vigorous and upright; ↕↔ 6ft (2m). **'Prostratus'** ■ syn. *R. eriocalyx* of gardens, *R. lavandulaceus* of gardens, is prostrate in habit and the least hardy variant; ↕ 6in (15cm). **'Pyramidalis'** see 'Miss Jessopp's Upright'. **'Roseus'** has pink flowers. **'Santa Barbara'** is low-growing, with dark blue flowers; ↕ 12in (30cm), ↔ 36in (90cm). **'Severn Sea'** is spreading in habit, with arching branches and bright blue flowers; ↕ 3ft (1m). **'Tuscan Blue'** is upright and fast-growing, bearing dark blue flowers.

ROSSIOGLOSSUM

ORCHIDACEAE

Genus of 6 species of epiphytic, evergreen orchids from rainforest, up to altitudes of 9,000ft (2,700m), in Central America. At its apex, each conical to ovoid, dark gray-green pseudobulb produces 1–3 broadly oval, dark green to gray- or bluish green leaves, marked brown at the bases. Erect or arching, few-flowered racemes of showy, yellow and brown flowers are produced from the base of new growth from autumn to winter. Grow in a cool greenhouse or use as houseplants.

• **CULTIVATION** Cool-growing orchids. Grow in epiphytic orchid potting mix, with added leaf mold and sphagnum, in bright filtered light. In summer, provide good ventilation

Rosmarinus officinalis 'Prostratus'

R

and, as new growth begins, water freely, applying a balanced liquid fertilizer monthly; keep just moist in winter. See also p.46.

- **PROPAGATION** Divide when the plant fills the pot and flows over the sides.
- **PESTS AND DISEASES** Prone to spider mites, aphids, and mealybugs.

R. grande, syn. *Odontoglossum grande* (Clown orchid, Tiger orchid). Epiphytic orchid with elliptic to lance-shaped, leathery, dark or bluish green leaves, 4–8in (10–20cm) long. From autumn to winter, bears erect racemes of 4–8 rich, glossy, chestnut-brown and yellow flowers, 5in (13cm) across, spotted red, brown, or yellow, with white lips. ↕ 14in (35cm), ↔ 8in (20cm). Mexico, Guatemala. ❄ (min. 50°F/10°C; max. 86°F/30°C)

ROTHMANNIA

RUBIACEAE

Genus of 25–30 species of evergreen shrubs and small trees from woodland and open savanna in tropical Africa, the Seychelles, Madagascar, and Asia. The leaves are simple and usually in opposite pairs, but sometimes in threes. They are cultivated for their bell- or funnel-shaped flowers, each with 5 spreading petal lobes, borne singly or in terminal and axillary clusters or cymes. Where temperatures fall below 45–50°F (7–10°C), grow in a cool or temperate greenhouse. In milder climates, grow at the base of a warm, sunny wall or in a shrub border.

- **CULTIVATION** Under glass, grow in soilless or soil-based potting mix in full light, with shade from hot sun. When in growth, water freely and apply a balanced liquid fertilizer monthly; water sparingly in winter. Outdoors, grow in moist but well-drained, fertile, neutral to acidic soil in full sun with midday shade. Pruning group 1; plants under glass may need restrictive pruning.
- **PROPAGATION** Sow seed at 61°F (16°C) in spring. Root semi-ripe cuttings with bottom heat in summer.
- **PESTS AND DISEASES** Whiteflies, stem mealybugs, and root mealybugs may be problems under glass.

R. capensis, syn. *Gardenia capensis, G. rothmannia* (Candlewood). Spreading tree with gray to brown bark. The broadly lance-shaped or elliptic to ovate leaves, 2–4in (5–10cm) long, are lustrous, deep green with conspicuous, sunken veins above, paler green beneath. Solitary, funnel-shaped, fragrant, white, cream, or yellow flowers, to 3in (8cm) long, are borne in summer. ↕ to 46ft (14m), ↔ to 22ft (7m). South Africa. ❄ (min. 45–50°F/7–10°C)

R. globosa, syn. *Gardenia globosa* (September bells). Spreading, large shrub or small tree with dark gray to brown bark. Inversely lance-shaped to lance-shaped or elliptic leaves, 2½–5in (6–13cm) long, are bright green with yellow, pink, or maroon veins, more obvious beneath than above. Narrowly bell-shaped, fragrant, ivory to white, occasionally pink-tinged flowers, to 1½in (4cm) long, with arching to reflexed petal lobes, are produced singly or in small clusters in the leaf axils in summer. ↕ 10–22ft (3–7m), ↔ 6–11ft (2–3.5m). South Africa. ❄ (min. 45–50°F/7–10°C)

ROYSTONEA

Royal palm

ARECACEAE

Genus of about 10 species of single-stemmed palms found in moist, rich soil on the Caribbean islands and adjacent coasts. The trunks may be columnar, or swollen in the middle or at the bases, each topped by a crownshaft and a tuft of pinnate, feather-shaped, bright mid-green leaves. The tiny, cup-shaped, 3-petaled flowers are borne in panicles just below the crownshaft. Where not hardy, grow young plants in a warm greenhouse. In tropical regions, use as lawn specimens or street trees.

- **CULTIVATION** Under glass, grow in soilless potting mix in full light, shaded from hot sun. When in growth, water freely and apply a balanced liquid fertilizer monthly; water moderately in winter. Pot on or top-dress in spring. Outdoors, grow in moderately fertile, moist but well-drained soil in full sun.
- **PROPAGATION** Sow seed at 81°F (27°C) in spring.
- **PESTS AND DISEASES** Scale insects, mealybugs, and spider mites are problems under glass; butt rot, *Stigmina* leaf spot, false smut, bud rot, and anthracnose can be problems in the landscape.

R. borinquena, syn. *R. caribaea.* Medium-sized palm with a spindle-shaped trunk ringed with old leaf scars. The arching leaves, up to 10ft (3m) long, have many narrow, linear, rich green leaflets in 2 double ranks. Cup-shaped cream flowers, with green-purple anthers, are produced in panicles, 3ft (1m) long, usually in summer. ↕ to 60ft (18m), ↔ to 20ft (6m). Puerto Rico (including Vieques), US Virgin Islands (St. Croix). ❄ (min. 59°F/15°C)

R. caribaea see *R. borinquena.*

Roystonea regia

R. regia ■ Tall palm with a sturdy trunk, usually thickened at the base and again in the middle, becoming thinner toward the crownshaft. Leaves, 10–15ft (3–5m) long, have many linear, rich green leaflets arranged in several ranks. Cup-shaped white flowers are borne in panicles, to 3ft (1m) long, usually in summer. ↕ to 80ft (25m), ↔ to 30ft (10m). Cuba. ❄ (min. 59°F/15°C)

RUBUS

ROSACEAE

Genus of 250 or more species of often prickly or bristly, deciduous or evergreen shrubs and climbers, occasionally herbaceous perennials, found worldwide in a range of habitats from coastal sand dunes to thickets, woodland, forest, and mountain slopes. The leaves are alternate and entire, lobed, palmate, or pinnate, each with 3 to many, usually toothed leaflets. The saucer- to cup-shaped, 4- or 5-petaled flowers are borne in racemes or panicles, sometimes singly or in few-flowered clusters, and are pink, white, red, or purple.

Blackberries or brambles (*R. fruticosus*), raspberries (*R. idaeus*), and hybrids between these and other species are grown for their edible fruits. Ornamental species are grown for their flowers, their foliage, and sometimes their attractive winter shoots, and are suitable for a shrub border. Prostrate species make a good groundcover in sun or shade. Vigorous species are best grown in a wild or woodland garden.

- **CULTIVATION** Grow in well-drained, moderately fertile soil. Grow deciduous species cultivated for their winter shoots in full sun; grow evergreen or semi-evergreen species in sun or partial shade. Pruning group 7 for *R. biflorus, R. cockburnianus, R. thibetanus*; group 2 for other deciduous species and cultivars; group 11 for *R. henryi*, after flowering, although pruning is seldom needed.
- **PROPAGATION** Divide *R. odoratus* in autumn. Root greenwood cuttings of deciduous species and cultivars in summer, or hardwood cuttings in early winter. Root semi-ripe cuttings of evergreens in summer. Detach rooted pieces of prostrate evergreens between autumn and spring.
- **PESTS AND DISEASES** Cane blight, canker, anthracnose, powdery mildew, rust, gray mold (*Botrytis*), *Verticillium* wilt, fireblight, scale insects, leafhoppers, and caterpillars can be problems.

R. 'Benenden' ■ Spreading, deciduous shrub with arching, thornless branches, peeling bark, and broadly ovate, shallowly 3- to 5-lobed, dark green leaves, 2½–3in (6–8m) long. Solitary, rose-like, saucer-shaped, pure white flowers, to 3in (8cm) across, are borne profusely in late spring and early summer. ↕↔ 10ft (3m). Zone 6.

R. 'Betty Ashburner '. Prostrate evergreen shrub with erect then arching roots, densely covered in red bristles. Heart-shaped, shallowly 5-lobed, wavy-margined, glossy, mid-green leaves, 2½in (6cm) long, are deeply veined above, glaucous beneath. In summer, produces racemes of saucer-shaped white fowers, ¾in (2cm) across, from the leaf axils. ↕ 12in (30cm), ↔ indefinite. Zone 7.

Rubus 'Benenden'

R. biflorus ■ Erect, prickly, deciduous shrub with chalky-white-bloomed young shoots, particularly conspicuous in winter. Ovate, pinnate leaves, to 10in (25cm) long, each have 3, sometimes 5, ovate to elliptic, dark green leaflets, white-felted beneath. In summer, produces saucer-shaped white flowers, ¾in (2cm) across, singly or in clusters of 2 or 3 from the leaf axils, followed by edible, spherical yellow fruit, to ¾in (2cm) across. ↕↔ 10ft (3m). Himalayas, China. Zone 6b.

var. *quinqueflorus*, the most commonly grown variant, has intensely white stems and bears clusters of 5 or more flowers.

R. calycinoides see *R. pentalobus.*

R. cockburnianus (Ghost bramble). Thicket-forming, deciduous shrub producing arching, prickly shoots with a brilliant white bloom in winter. Ovate, pinnate leaves, to 8in (20cm) long, with 5–7, sometimes 9, diamond-shaped or ovate-lance-shaped leaflets, are dark green above and white-hairy beneath, appearing greenish white overall. In summer, bears terminal racemes of saucer-shaped purple flowers, ½in (1.5cm) across, followed by spherical black, unpalatable fruit, to ½in (1.5cm) across. ↕↔ 8ft (2.5m). China. Zone 6.

Rubus biflorus

R

Rubus odoratus

***R. fockeanus* of gardens** see *R. pentalobus.*
R. idaeus (Red raspberries). Thornless shrub producing red fruit and self-pollinated rose flowers. ↕ 4–6ft (1.2–2m). Eurasia. Zone 3.
R. occidentalis (Black raspberries). Bears small whitish flowers, in dense clusters; leaves have white undersides. ↕ 3–5ft (1–1.5m). Quebec to Colorado, S. to Georgia, Arkansas. Zone 4b.
R. odoratus ■ (Flowering raspberry, Thimbleberry). Fast-growing, thicket-forming, deciduous shrub with spineless shoots and large, broadly ovate, 5-lobed, velvety, dark green leaves, to 10in (25cm) long. From early summer to early autumn, bears panicles of shallowly cup-shaped, fragrant, purple-pink flowers, to 2in (5cm) across; they are followed by tasteless, flattened-hemispherical red fruit, to ¾in (2cm) across. ↕↔ 8ft (2.5m) or more; E. North America; Zone 7b. **'Albus'** has pale green leaves and white flowers.
R. pentalobus, syn. *R. calycinoides, R. fockeanus* of gardens. Prostrate, evergreen shrub with sparsely prickly shoots that root as they creep along the ground. The rounded, shallowly 3- to 5-lobed, glossy, dark green leaves, to 2in (5cm) long, are heart-shaped at the bases, with deeply impressed veins and wrinkled margins. In summer, bears solitary, saucer-shaped white flowers, ¾in (2cm) across, sometimes followed by spherical red fruit, to ½in (15mm) across. ↕ 4in (10cm), ↔ indefinite. Taiwan. Zone 7b.
***R. spectabilis* 'Flore Pleno'** see *R. spectabilis* 'Olympic Double'.

Rubus spectabilis 'Olympic Double'

***R. spectabilis* 'Olympic Double'** ■ syn. *R. spectabilis* 'Flore Pleno'. Thicket-forming, deciduous shrub with upright, slightly prickly shoots and 3-palmate leaves, to 6in (15cm) long, composed of ovate, glossy, mid-green leaflets. Usually solitary, very showy, double, bright purple-pink flowers, 2in (5cm) across, open in midspring. ↕↔ 6ft (2m). Zone 5.
R. thibetanus. Erect, thicket-forming, deciduous shrub with arching, prickly shoots, conspicuously white-bloomed in winter. Triangular, pinnate, dark green leaves, to 9in (23cm) long, have 7–13 lance-shaped to ovate leaflets, densely gray-hairy above, densely white-hairy beneath. In summer, saucer-shaped, red-purple flowers, ½in (1.5cm) across, are borne singly from the upper leaf axils or in few-flowered terminal racemes, followed by spherical black fruit, to ½in (1.5cm) across, with a whitish bloom. ↕↔ 8ft (2.5m). W. China. Zone 7b.
R. tricolor. Prostrate, evergreen shrub with both creeping and arching shoots, covered in conspicuous red bristles. Ovate, entire or very shallowly 3- to 5-lobed, glossy, dark green leaves, to 4in (10cm) long, are heart-shaped at the bases and white-hairy beneath. Saucer-shaped white flowers, 1in (2.5cm) across, open singly or in few-flowered terminal racemes in summer, followed by edible, raspberry-like red fruit, to 1in (2.5cm) across. ↕ 24in (60cm), ↔ indefinite. China (Sichuan, Yunnan). Zone 7b.
***R. ulmifolius* 'Bellidiflorus'.** Fast-growing, deciduous or semi-evergreen shrub of open habit, with long, arching, thorny shoots and 3- to 5-palmate leaves, to 5in (13cm) long, composed of ovate, dark green leaflets. Large panicles of hemispherical, double pink flowers, to ½in (1.5cm) across, are produced in mid- and late summer. ↕ 8ft (2.5m), ↔ 12ft (4m). Zone 7.

RUDBECKIA

Coneflower

ASTERACEAE

Genus of about 20 species of annuals, biennials, and perennials (some of which may be grown as annuals), with short rhizomes, from moist meadows and light woodland in North America. They have branched or unbranched stems, and most have alternate, simple to pinnatifid, occasionally pinnate, prominently veined leaves, toothed toward the tips. Usually solitary, daisy-like flowerheads, often with reflexed yellow ray florets and conical centers consisting of black, brown, or green disk florets, are borne on long stems over a long period from summer to autumn. Most are good for cut flowers. Grow in a border, or naturalize in a meadow or woodland garden. Most cultivars of *R. hirta* are grown as annuals, and are good for bedding or borders.

• **CULTIVATION** Grow in moderately fertile, preferably heavy but well-drained soil that does not dry out, in full sun or partial shade. *R. fulgida* var. *deamii* is more drought-tolerant than other species. On fertile soils, *R. laciniata* 'Golden Glow' may become invasive.

• **PROPAGATION** Sow seed of perennials in containers in a cold frame in early spring, or divide in autumn or spring.

Rudbeckia fulgida var. *sullivantii* 'Goldsturm'

Rudbeckia hirta 'Becky Mixed'

Sow seed of annuals and biennials at 61–64°F (16–18°C) in spring.

• **PESTS AND DISEASES** Slugs and snails feed on young plants. Aphids, powdery mildew, rust, smut, and *Ramularia* and *Septoria* leaf spots occur.

***R.* 'Autumn Sun'** see *R.* 'Herbstsonne'.
R. columnifera see *Ratibida columnifera.*
R. deamii see *R. fulgida* var. *deamii.*
R. fulgida (Black-eyed Susan). Rhizomatous perennial with branched stems, long-stalked, oblong to lance-shaped, entire basal leaves, to 5in (13cm) long, and lance-shaped, toothed stem leaves; both are mid-green and slightly hairy, with prominent veins. Flowerheads, to 3in (8cm) across, with orange-yellow ray florets and conical, blackish brown disk florets, are borne from late summer to midautumn. ↕ to 36in (90cm), ↔ 18in (45cm). E. US. Zone 3b. **var. *deamii***, syn. *R. deamii*, is free-flowering, and has very hairy stems with long-pointed, ovate or oval-ovate, toothed, rough basal and stem leaves; ↕ to 24in (60cm); Indiana. **var. *speciosa***, syn. *R. newmanii, R. speciosa*, has elliptic to lance-shaped, almost sickle-shaped basal leaves and coarsely toothed stem leaves; New Jersey to Alabama and Georgia. **var. *sullivantii***, syn. *R. sullivantii*, has broadly ovate to narrowly ovate-lance-shaped, less hairy, coarsely toothed, dark green basal leaves and stem leaves, which become progressively smaller up the stems. The flowerheads are 3–3½in (8–9cm) across; Michigan to Missouri, Connecticut to West Virginia. **var. *sullivantii* 'Goldsturm'** ■ has large, golden yellow flowerheads, 3½–5in (9–13cm) across, on shorter stems than the species; ↕ to 24in (60cm).
R. gloriosa see *R. hirta.*
***R.* 'Herbstsonne'** ■ syn. *R.* 'Autumn Sun'. Upright, rhizomatous, clump-forming perennial with oval, toothed or slightly lobed, prominently veined, glossy, mid-green leaves, to 6in (15cm) long. From midsummer to early autumn, branching stems bear flowerheads, 4–5in (10–13cm) across, with bright yellow ray florets and high, conical centers of green disk florets, becoming yellowish brown with age. ↕ to 6ft (2m), ↔ 36in (90cm). Zone 3.

Rudbeckia 'Herbstsonne'

Rudbeckia hirta 'Irish Eyes'

R. hirta, syn. *R. gloriosa* (Black-eyed Susan, Gloriosa daisy). Erect, thick-stemmed, branching, bristly biennial or short-lived perennial, often grown as an annual, with mid-green leaves. The basal leaves are ovate to diamond-shaped, sometimes slightly toothed, strongly 3-veined, and to 4in (10cm) long; stem leaves are usually narrower and ovate to lance-shaped. Daisy-like flowerheads, to 3in (8cm) across, with pale to golden yellow ray florets and prominent, conical centers of deep brown-purple disk florets, are borne from summer to early autumn. ↕ 12–36in (30–90cm), ↔ 12–18in (30–45cm). C. US. Zone 3. **'Bambi'** has flowerheads with bronze-brown, chestnut-brown, and golden yellow ray florets; ↕ to 12in (30cm). **'Becky Mixed'** ▣ is very dwarf, and has flowerheads with ray florets in shades of lemon-yellow, golden yellow, and dark red or reddish brown; ↕ to 10in (25cm). **Gloriosa Daisy Mixed** cultivars have large, single flowerheads, 6in (15cm) across, in yellow, mahogany, bronze, and gold, with many bicolors; ↕ 36in (90cm). **'Goldilocks'** has double and semi-double flowerheads with golden-orange ray florets; ↕ to 24in (60cm). **'Green Eyes'** see 'Irish Eyes'. **'Irish Eyes'** ▣ syn. 'Green Eyes', has flowerheads with bright yellow ray florets and green disk florets; ↕ 24–30in (60–75cm). **'Kelvedon Star'** has flowerheads with deep golden yellow ray florets, zoned in brownish red. **'Marmalade'** is bushy and compact, with large flowerheads, sometimes to 5in (13cm) across, with deep golden orange ray florets; ↕ to 18in (45cm). **'Rustic Dwarfs'** ▣ has flowerheads with golden yellow, brownish red, or bronze-orange ray florets, with some bicolors; ↕ to 24in (60cm). **'Sonora'** is compact, bearing flowerheads with bright yellow ray florets; ↕ to 16in (40cm). **'Toto'** is dwarf and compact; ideal for containers or for bedding at the front of a border; ↕ 10in (25cm).

R. laciniata (Coneflower). Rhizomatous, hairless, glaucous perennial, forming loose clumps of tall, wiry stems, branched toward their tips. Basal leaves, to 4in (10cm) long, are pinnate or pinnatisect, each with deeply 3- to 5-lobed, toothed leaflets and prominent veins; stem leaves become less deeply lobed up the stems. Bears flowerheads, 3–6in (7–15cm) across, with reflexed, pale yellow ray florets and hemispherical to conical centers of greenish yellow disk florets, from midsummer to midautumn. ↕ 5–10ft (1.5m–3m), ↔ 36in (90cm). C. and E. North America. Zone 3. **'Golden Fountain'** see 'Goldquelle'. **'Golden Glow'** is very vigorous, bearing fully double flowerheads with yellow ray florets; ↕ to 6ft (2m), ↔ 6–8ft (2–2.5m). **'Goldquelle'** ▣ syn. 'Golden Fountain', is compact, bearing double flowerheads with lemon-yellow ray florets and green disk florets that turn yellow as the flowerheads open; ↕ to 36in (90cm), ↔ 18in (45cm). **var. *hortensia*** is the name applied to all variants with double flowerheads.

Rudbeckia hirta 'Rustic Dwarfs'

Rudbeckia laciniata 'Goldquelle'

Rudbeckia maxima (inset: flowerhead detail)

R. maxima ▣ Upright, stiff perennial with elliptic to spoon-shaped, gray-green basal leaves, to 12in (30cm) long, and progressively smaller stem leaves. Bears slightly drooping flowerheads, 3in (8cm) across, with yellow ray florets and prominent conical centers of brown disk florets, in late summer. ↕ 5–6ft (1.5–2m), ↔ 24in (60cm). North America. Zone 4.

R. newmanii see *R. fulgida* var. *speciosa*.

R. nitida. Upright, rhizomatous, branching, hairless perennial with pinnatisect, mid-green leaves, to 6in (15cm) long. Flowerheads to 4in (10cm) across, with yellow ray florets and conical centers of green disk florets, are produced in late summer and early autumn. ↕ to 6ft (2m), ↔ 36in (90cm). Georgia and Florida to Texas. Zone 3b. **'Autumn Glory'** has gold flowerheads; ↕ to 5ft (1.5m).

R. purpurea see *Echinacea purpurea*.

R. speciosa see *R. fulgida* var. *speciosa*.

R. subtomentosa (Sweet coneflower). Upright, branching, rhizomatous perennial with ovate, softly gray-hairy leaves, ↕ 5in (13cm) long, often borne in threes. Flowerheads to 3in (8cm) across, with yellow ray florets and conical centers of deep brown-purple disk florets, are produced in autumn. ↕ to 28in (70cm), ↔ 12in (30cm). C. US. Zone 5.

R. sullivantii see *R. fulgida* var. *sullivantii.*

R. triloba (Brown-eyed Susan). Usually branching, clump-forming biennial with ovate to oblong-ovate, 3- to 7-lobed leaves, to 5in (13cm) long, hairless or covered with short, stiff hairs. In late summer and autumn, bears numerous flowerheads, 1–1½in (2.5–4cm) across, with yellow to orange ray florets and conical centers of black to purple disk florets. ↕ to 5ft (1.5m), ↔ 36in (90cm). C. and E. US. Zone 5.

RUELLIA

syn. DIPTERACANTHUS

ACANTHACEAE

Diverse genus of about 150 species of evergreen perennials and soft-stemmed or woody shrubs and subshrubs, widely distributed in tropical America, warm parts of North America, and Africa and Asia, where they are found in meadows and at woodland margins. The leaves are opposite and entire, and may be stalked or stalkless. Funnel-shaped flowers are produced singly, in clusters from the leaf axils, or in terminal panicles. The tropical species, in particular, are cultivated for their attractive foliage and flowers, and are suitable for informal

Ruellia devosiana

borders or plantings. Where not hardy, grow in a warm greenhouse.

• **CULTIVATION** Under glass, grow in soilless potting mix in bright filtered light with high humidity. In growth, water freely and apply a balanced liquid fertilizer monthly; water moderately in winter. Pinch out the young shoots to encourage branching. Pruning group 10, after flowering. Outdoors, grow in any fertile, humus-rich, moist soil in a site in full sun or partial shade.

• **PROPAGATION** Sow seed at 66–75°F (19–24°C) in spring. Root softwood cuttings in spring or early summer.

• **PESTS AND DISEASES** Bacterial and fungal leaf spots, rust and root rot occur.

R. amoena see *R. graecizans.*

R. devosiana ■ Hairy shrub with soft, purple-flushed stems and broadly lance-shaped, pale-veined, dark green leaves, to 3in (8cm) long, purple beneath. Bears funnel-shaped, lavender-blue-flushed white flowers, 1½–2in (4–5cm) long, with slender tubes and notched, spreading, purple-veined lobes, singly from the leaf axils from spring to summer. ↕ 18in (45cm), ↔ 12in (30cm). Brazil. ❀ (min. 54°F/12°C)

R. graecizans, syn. *R. amoena.* Bushy shrub with soft, spreading stems and ovate to oblong, hairless, mid-green leaves, to 7in (18cm) long. Funnel-shaped scarlet flowers, 1in (2.5cm) long, each with one enlarged sepal, are borne in axillary clusters on long stalks from spring to summer. ↕ 24in (60cm), ↔ 18in (45cm). South America. ❀ (min. 54°F/12°C)

Ruellia macrantha

R. humilis Erect, slightly bush shrub with midgreen stems and sessile, lance-shaped bright green leaves, to 3–4in (8–10cm) long. Bears single, terminal, pink to lavender, petunia-like flowers 2in (5cm). Grow in borders or rock garden. ↕ 7–12in (28–30cm) ↔ 12in (30cm). Pennsylvania to Texas. Zone 5.

R. macrantha ■ (Christmas pride). Erect, soft-stemmed subshrub with lance-shaped, hairy, dull, dark green leaves, to 6in (15cm) long. From autumn to winter, funnel-shaped but slightly curved, rich purplish pink flowers, to 3in (8cm) long, with darker veins, are produced singly from the leaf axils. ↕ to 6ft (2m), ↔ 18in (45cm). Brazil. ❀ (min. 54°F/12°C)

R. makoyana (Monkey plant, Trailing velvet plant). Slender- and soft-stemmed, spreading, hairy perennial with ovate, silver-veined purple leaves, to 3in (8cm) long, dark purple beneath. In summer, produces funnel-shaped, carmine-pink flowers, 2in (5cm) long, singly from the leaf axils. ↕ to 24in (60cm), ↔ 18in (45cm). Brazil. ❀ (min. 54°F/12°C)

RUMEX

Dock

POLYGONACEAE

Genus of about 200 species of annuals, biennials, and usually taprooted, sometimes rhizomatous perennials from a range of habitats, including mountains, wasteland, cultivated ground, and streamsides in N. temperate regions. Docks have simple, variably shaped, mainly basal leaves, which occasionally have wavy margins. In summer, the tiny, star-shaped, bisexual or unisexual flowers are borne in whorls in usually erect, dense, terminal panicles or racemes. They are followed by small, triangular, brown to red-brown fruit. Some species are invasive weeds; a few are grown for their decorative foliage or as herbs. Grow in a herbaceous or mixed border. All parts of docks may cause mild stomach upset if ingested; contact with the foliage may irritate skin.

Rumex acetosa

Rumex sanguineus

• **CULTIVATION** Grow in moderately fertile, well-drained soil in full sun.

• **PROPAGATION** Sow seed *in situ* in spring. Docks also self-seed freely.

• **PESTS AND DISEASES** Prone to slugs and snails, rust, smut, and leaf spots.

R. acetosa ■ (Sorrel, Dock). Large, taprooted perennial with sturdy stems and arrow-shaped, mid- to dark green leaves, 4–6in (10–15cm) long, with basal lobes that do not curve outward. Bears insignificant greenish flowers in spike-like terminal clusters; papery, reddish seeds follow, which self-sow profusely. Needs well-drained soil in full sun. Grown in gardens and borders for the lemony, tangy leaves, high in Vitamin C, used in salads, soups, and sauces. Deadhead to prevent rampant self-seeding, as plant can be highly invasive. ↕ to 5ft (1.5m)↔ indefinite. Europe. Zone 3b.

R. alpinus (Monk's rhubarb, Mountain rhubarb). Rhizomatous, creeping perennial with upright, red-tinged stems and ovate to rounded, wavy, mid-green basal leaves, 8–16in (20–40cm) long, hairy on the veins beneath. In summer, bears erect, well-branched panicles of tiny, star-shaped, green then red-brown flowers, ⅛in (3mm) across, followed by dark brown fruit. ↕ to 5ft (1.5m), ↔ 5ft (1.5m) or more. Europe. Zone 4.

R. sanguineus ■ (Bloody dock, Red-veined dock). Taprooted, rosette-forming perennial with oblong-lance-shaped, mid- to dark green leaves, 2–6in (5–15cm) long, veined blood-red or dark purple. In early and midsummer, erect, red-tinted flower stems bear panicles of tiny, star-shaped, green then red-brown flowers, ⅛in (3mm) across, followed by dark brown fruit. ↕ to 36in (90cm), ↔ 12in (30cm). Europe, N. Africa, S.W. Asia. Zone 5.

RUMOHRA

DRYOPTERIDACEAE

Genus of 50 species of epiphytic or terrestrial, rock-dwelling, evergreen ferns occurring in cool woodland or scrub in tropical regions of the S. hemisphere. They have scaly, creeping rhizomes covered in golden brown scales, and triangular, pinnate or 2- or 3-pinnate, leathery fronds. Spores are formed in conspicuous, large, circular spots, each covered with a centrally attached indusium. Where not hardy, grow in a warm greenhouse; in warmer areas, grow

Rumohra adiantiformis

epiphytically or in a damp, shady border. The fronds are popular for flower arrangements.

• **CULTIVATION** Under glass, grow epiphytically on bark, or in shallow pots or hanging baskets in a mix of 1 part each of loam, medium-grade bark, and charcoal, 2 parts sharp sand, and 3 parts coarse leaf mold. Provide bright filtered light and moderate humidity. In growth, mist regularly, water freely, and apply a half-strength balanced liquid fertilizer monthly; water sparingly in winter. Outdoors, grow epiphytically or in moist, leafy, open, humus-rich soil in partial or light, dappled shade.

• **PROPAGATION** Sow spores at 70°F (21°C) as soon as ripe, or separate rooted sections of rhizomes in early summer. See also p.51.

• **PESTS AND DISEASES** Prone to fungal leaf spots, blight, and lesion nematode. Caterpillars and aphids occur.

R. adiantiformis ■ (Leather fern). Evergreen, terrestrial or epiphytic fern, variable in size, bearing ovate or triangular, 2- or 3-pinnate, leathery, dark green fronds, ↕ to 36in (90cm) or more; fronds have narrowly diamond-shaped to oblong pinnae. ↕ 20–60in (0.5–1.5m), ↔ indefinite. Tropical and subtropical areas of S. hemisphere. ❀ (min. 50–55°F/10–13°C)

RUSCHIA

AIZOACEAE

Genus of about 350 species of shrubby or stemless, upright or prostrate, perennial succulents from semi-desert regions of Namibia and South Africa. Many species branch freely to form tufts or mats; others become shrubby, ↕ to 3ft (1m) tall. The leaves are arranged in pairs and are often boat-shaped. Axillary or terminal, stalked or stalkless, daisy-like flowers open during the day in summer. In warm, dry climates, grow in a raised bed or desert garden. Where not hardy, grow prostrate species in a temperate greenhouse, or treat as frost-tender annuals and use for bedding, windowboxes, or hanging baskets.

• **CULTIVATION** Under glass, grow in standard cactus potting mix in full light with low humidity. Water moderately from spring to autumn, applying a dilute balanced liquid fertilizer once in late spring and once in late summer; keep dry in winter.

ʀuschia macowanii

)utdoors, grow in poor, gritty, harply drained soil in full sun. ee also pp.48–49.
PROPAGATION Sow seed at 70°F 21°C) in early spring. Plant out eedlings to be grown as annuals when ll danger of frost has passed. Root uttings of stem sections in summer.
PESTS AND DISEASES Prey to nealybugs.

ʀ. acuminata. Shrubby succulent vith erect or almost prostrate, woody tems. Produces pairs of ovoid, bluntly eeled, sometimes toothed leaves, to in (2.5cm) long, with convex sides, arrowing toward the tips. They are oughly papillose, fleshy, and lue-green marked with dull green pots. In summer, bears solitary, erminal or axillary, daisy-like, white or ale pink flowers, 1¼in (3cm) across. 8in (20cm), ↔ 20in (50cm). South frica (Eastern Cape). ❀ (min. 5°F/7°C)
ʀ. derenbergiana see *Ebracteola lerenbergiana.*
ʀ. macowanii ■ Shrubby succulent vith short, prostrate, woody stems and rect, fleshy branches. The fleshy, gray-reen leaves, to 1½in (4cm) long, are oat-shaped to cylindrical, flat above nd keeled beneath. In summer, bears olitary, terminal, daisy-like pink lowers, ¾in (2cm) across, with a darker ink stripe on each petal. ↕ 8in (20cm), ↔ 18in (45cm). South Africa (Western Cape, Northern Cape, Eastern Cape). ❀ (min. 45°F/7°C)
ʀ. pusilla. Tufted, prostrate, almost temless succulent with nearly pherical, fleshy, bright green leaves, ⅛in (3mm) long, keeled beneath. olitary, terminal or axillary, daisy-like, ale pinkish white flowers, ½in 1.5cm) across, are produced in ummer. ↕↔ 3in (8cm). South Africa Western Cape, Northern Cape, Eastern Cape). ❀ (min. 45°F/7°C)
ʀ. pygmaea. Mat-forming, prostrate ucculent with very short, fleshy stems earing 1 or 2 dissimilar pairs of ovoid r ellipsoid, fleshy, bright green leaves, o ¼in (5mm) long, keeled beneath, nd more or less united almost to the ips. The leaf skins gradually shrivel to isclose a second pair of leaves, which re not united, and these become the irst pair of leaves of the following ear's growth. Solitary, terminal or xillary, daisy-like, whitish pink lowers, to ¾in (2cm) across, are borne in summer. ↕↔ 3in (8cm). Namibia, South Africa (Western Cape, Northern Cape, Eastern Cape). ❀ (min. 45°F/7°C)

RUSCUS

LILIACEAE

Genus of 6 species of rhizomatous, evergreen subshrubs from Madeira and the Azores, through Europe and N. Africa to Iran. The tiny, true leaves are replaced by flattened, leaf-like shoots (cladophylls), on which the flowers and showy red fruits are borne. The inconspicuous, star-shaped, green or greenish white flowers, to 1/16in (2mm) across, each have 6 tepals. *Ruscus* species are usually dioecious; however, *R. aculeatus* may bear hermaphrodite, self-fertile flowers. Grow in a dry, shady site. he berries of *R. aculeatus* may cause mild stomach upset if ingested.
• **CULTIVATION** Grow in any but waterlogged soil, in sun or partial or full shade. Individual shoots are short-lived, but new ones are produced annually; cut out dead stems at the base in spring.
• **PROPAGATION** Sow seed in a seedbed, or in containers in a cold frame, as soon as ripe. Divide in spring.
• **PESTS AND DISEASES** Prone to leaf spot.

R. aculeatus (Butcher's broom). Clump-forming, rhizomatous subshrub with upright, branched shoots bearing ovate, spine-tipped, glossy, dark green cladophylls, to 1in (2.5cm) long. From late summer to winter, female plants produce spherical, bright red berries, ⅜in (8mm) across, on the upper sides of the cladophylls. ↕ 30in (75cm), ↔ 3ft (1m). Europe, N. Turkey, N. Africa, Azores. Zone 7b.
R. hypoglossum ■ Clump-forming, rhizomatous subshrub producing arching, unbranched shoots and obovate to broadly ovate, glossy, mid-green cladophylls, to 4in (10cm) long. Female plants bear spherical red berries, ½in (1.5cm) across, on the upper sides of the cladophylls, from autumn to winter. ↕ 18in (45cm), ↔ 3ft (1m). Italy, Czech Republic to Turkey. Zone 7b.
R. hypophyllum. Rhizomatous, clump-forming subshrub with upright shoots and ovate, pointed, dark green cladophylls, to 4in (10cm) long. Female plants bear spherical red berries, ½in (1.5cm) across, on the upper or lower side of the cladophylls, from late summer to winter. Male and female flowers may be borne on the same plant. ↕ 24in (60cm), ↔ 3ft (1m). S.E. France, S. Spain, N. Africa, Sicily. Zone 8.

Ruscus hypoglossum

RUSSELIA

SCROPHULARIACEAE

Genus of about 50 species of evergreen or deciduous shrubs and subshrubs found at forest margins from Mexico and Cuba to Colombia. The pendent, rush-like stems produce opposite or whorled, often scale-like leaves. Showy, tubular, red, pink, or white flowers are produced in axillary cymes, or sometimes singly. Where not hardy, grow as house plants, in a cool or temperate green house or conservatory, or in hanging baskets. In warmer climates, grow at the front of a shrub border or allow to trail over the edges of a raised bed or wall.
• **CULTIVATION** Under glass, grow in soil-based potting mix in full or bright filtered light. When in growth, water moderately and apply a balanced liquid fertilizer monthly; water sparingly in winter. Outdoors, grow in a sheltered site in well-drained, humus-rich, moderately fertile soil in full sun. Pruning group 9.
• **PROPAGATION** Separate layers in spring; root softwood cuttings any time.
• **PESTS AND DISEASES** Infrequent.

R. equisetiformis ■ syn. *R. juncea* (Coral plant, Firecracker plant). Deciduous, branching subshrub with rush-like, erect and pendent, mid-green stems. The elliptic, scale-like, mid-green leaves, to ½in (1.5cm) long, fall early. Tubular scarlet flowers, to 1¼in (3cm) long, are borne in pendent cymes from spring to autumn. ↕ 5ft (1.5m), ↔ 8ft (2.5m). Mexico. ❀ (min. 50°F/10°C)
R. juncea see *R. equisetiformis.*

Russelia equisetiformis

RUTA

RUTACEAE

Genus of 8 species of deciduous or evergreen shrubs, subshrubs and woody-based herbaceous perennials, occurring in dry, rocky habitats in the Canary Islands, the Mediterranean region, N.E. Africa, and S.W. Asia. They are grown for their aromatic foliage and flowers. Leaves are alternate, occasionally opposite, broadly ovate to rounded, and pinnatisect to pinnate. The unusual, 4- or 5-petaled, fringed or toothed yellow flowers are borne in terminal cymes. Rue is suitable for a mixed or herbaceous border, or in a large rock garden or herb garden. Foliage is sometimes used medicinally or very sparingly as a culinary flavoring. All parts of rue may cause severe discomfort if ingested; the foliage may cause severe photodermatitis.
• **CULTIVATION** Grow in moderately fertile, very well-drained soil in full sun or partial shade. Rue will thrive in a hot, dry site. Pruning group 10, in spring or after flowering.
• **PROPAGATION** Sow seed in containers in a cold frame in spring. Root semi-ripe cuttings in summer.
• **PESTS AND DISEASES** *Phytophthora* root rot may be a problem.

R. chalepensis (Fringed rue). Upright subshrub producing broadly ovate, 2- or 3-pinnatisect, aromatic, blue-green leaves, to 5in (13cm) long, with numerous oblong-lance-shaped or obovate lobes. Cup-shaped, dark yellow flowers, ¾in (2cm) across, with 4 petals fringed with long hairs, are borne in open cymes in summer. ↕↔ 24in (60cm). S. Europe, N.E. Africa, S.W. Asia. ❀ (min. 35°F/2°C)
R. graveolens (Common rue). Rounded to erect, evergreen shrub producing alternate, broadly ovate to rounded, 2-pinnatisect, aromatic, glaucous, blue-green leaves, to 6in (15cm) long, with numerous obovate lobes. Cymes of cup-shaped, 4-petaled, dull yellow flowers, ¾in (2cm) across, are produced in summer. ↕ 3ft (1m), ↔ 30in (75cm). S.E. Europe. Zone 5.
'Jackman's Blue' ■ is more compact than the species, and has more intensely glaucous, blue-green foliage; ↕ 24in (60cm). **'Variegata'** produces white-splashed and all-white foliage; it comes true from seed.

Ruta graveolens 'Jackman's Blue'

R

S

SABAL

Palmetto

ARECACEAE

Genus of 14 species of single-stemmed or stemless palms, chiefly from low-lying or swampy areas in tropical forest, from S. US to N. South America, and from the West Indies. They have deeply divided, fan-shaped leaves, which often remain *in situ* when they die, forming a skirt-like bundle just below each crown. Panicles of 3-petaled flowers are borne between the leaves, usually in summer. Where not hardy, grow in a cool to warm greenhouse, in a conservatory, or as houseplants. In warmer areas, plant the trees as lawn specimens and the stemless species in a shrub border.

• **CULTIVATION** Under glass, grow in well-drained, soil-based potting mix in bright indirect light. During the growing season, water moderately and apply a balanced liquid fertilizer monthly. Pot on or top-dress in spring. Mist lightly every day in summer. Keep just moist in winter. Outdoors, grow in moderately fertile, moist but well-drained soil in full sun with some midday shade.

• **PROPAGATION** Sow seed at 66–75°F (19–24°C) in spring.

• **PESTS AND DISEASES** Tar spot, butt rot, false smut, manganese deficiency, and a variety of fungal leaf spots occur. Spider mites and scale insects can be problems under glass.

S. glabra see *S. minor.*
S. guatemalensis see *S. mexicana.*
S. mexicana, syn. *S. guatemalensis, S. texana* (Texas palmetto). Medium-sized palm with a columnar trunk that bears old leaf bases for several years. Fan-shaped, bright green, often yellowish green leaves, 3ft (1m) long, are divided up to halfway into many slender, pointed lobes. Bears cream flowers in panicles as long as or longer than the leaves, usually in summer. ↕ to 60ft (18m), ↔ to 12ft (4m). Texas, Mexico, Guatemala. ❄ (min. 50–55°F/10–13°C)
S. minima see *S. minor.*
S. minor ■ syn. *S. glabra, S. minima, S. pumila* (Dwarf palmetto, Scrub palmetto). Small palm with a short, buried stem (only the tip visible above the ground) and long-stalked, fan-shaped, blue-green leaves, to 3ft (1m) long, divided at least two-thirds into many slender lobes. Cream flowers are borne in erect to arching panicles, to 6ft (2m) long, usually in summer. ↕ 3–6ft (1–2m), ↔ to 10ft (3m). S.E. US. ❄ (min. 37–41°F/3–5°C)
S. palmetto ■ (Blue palmetto, Cabbage palmetto). Large palm with a rough trunk, to 24in (60cm) in diameter.

Sabal minor

Sabal palmetto

Bears compact, spherical heads of many fan-shaped, rich green leaves, to 6ft (2m) long, divided into numerous long, 2-lobed segments with thread-like filaments hanging between them. Cream flowers are borne in panicles just longer than the leaves, usually in summer. ↕ to 100ft (30m), ↔ 15–22ft (5–7m). North Carolina to Florida. ❄ (min. 41–45°F/5–7°C)
S. pumila see *S. minor.*
S. texana see *S. mexicana.*

▷ ***Sabina*** see *Juniperus*

SACCHARUM

syn. ERIANTHUS

Plume grass, Sugar cane

POACEAE

Genus of about 20 species of reed-like, tufted, clump-forming, or rhizomatous, perennial grasses found by riversides and in valley bottoms, widely distributed in warm-temperate and tropical regions. They are grown for their inflorescences and foliage. Leaves are narrowly lance-shaped to linear. Large, plume-like panicles of crowded flower spikes with silky-hairy spikelets are borne in pairs in summer and autumn. Effective at the back of a herbaceous or mixed border, against a warm, sunny wall, or as free-standing specimens. *S. officinarium* 'Pele's Smoke' is attractive in large containers. The cut panicles are useful in fresh and dried arrangements.

• **CULTIVATION** Grow in moderately fertile, well-drained soil in full sun, with shelter from strong winds. Protect crowns during winter with a thick, dry mulch. Remove any flowerheads left for winter effect by early spring.

• **PROPAGATION** Sow seed in containers under glass or in a cold frame in spring. Divide in midspring or early summer.

• **PESTS AND DISEASES** Infrequent.

***S. officinarum* 'Pele's Smoke'.** Robust, densely tufted perennial grass with glossy purple culms and arching, linear, purple leaves, to 6ft (2m) long. Erect stems bear upright, fluffy, plume-like panicles, 12–18in (30–45cm) long, of white to gray flower spikes, in early autumn. Useful as a summer accent plant. Rarely flowers in nontropical climates. ↕ 6ft (2m), ↔ 5–6ft (1.5–2m). ❄ (min. 41°F/5°C)
S. ravennae ■ Robust, densely tufted, perennial grass with arching, linear leaves, 24–36in (60–90cm) long, that

Saccharum ravennae

are gray-green with central white stripes, purple-tinted in autumn. In late summe and autumn, erect stems produce dense, upright panicles, to 24in (60cm) long, o softly hairy, silver-gray to purple flower spikes. ↕ 10–12ft (3–4m) or more, ↔ 4–6ft (1.2–2m). Mediterranean to N. Africa. Zone 7.

SADLERIA

BLECHNACEAE

Genus of 7 species of evergreen, tree-lik ferns from rainforest and exposed sites on lava flows in Hawaii. They bear a thick rhizome, crowned with large, divided fronds. The spores, unlike thos of other tree ferns, such as *Cyathea* and *Dicksonia,* are borne in lines along the midribs of the frond segments. *S. cyatheoides* is the only species generall grown. Where not hardy, grow in a temperate greenhouse, in a conservator or as houseplants. In warmer areas, grov in a shrub border, in a woodland garden, or as a free-standing specimen.

• **CULTIVATION** Under glass, grow in equal parts medium-grade bark, perlite, and charcoal, in bright indirect to moderate light, and with moderate to high humidity. During the growing season, water moderately and apply a balanced liquid fertilizer monthly; keep just moist in winter. Outdoors, grow in moderately fertile, humus-rich, moist but well-drained, acidic to neutral soil i partial to deep shade, with no more tha 6 hours of daily sun. Shelter from cold, dry winds.

• **PROPAGATION** Sow spores at 70°F (21°C) as soon as ripe. See also p.51.

• **PESTS AND DISEASES** Infrequent.

S. cyatheoides. Tree-like fern with ovate, 2-pinnate, leathery fronds, 36in (90cm) long, dark green above, glaucou beneath; they have narrowly oblong pinnae, and numerous linear segments with the margins rolled under. ↕ 5ft (1.5m), ↔ 6ft (1.8m). Hawaii. ❄ (min. 45°F/7°C)

AGINA

earlwort

ARYOPHYLLACEAE

enus of about 20 species of compact, w-growing annuals and perennials und in a wide range of habitats, ktensively distributed throughout the mperate regions of the N. hemisphere. hey have linear to narrowly wedge-aped leaves, arranged in pairs and ined at the bases around the stems. Iinute, 4- or 5-petaled, rarely petalless hite flowers are produced either singly : in few-flowered cymes. The majority f pearlworts are weeds; those described ere are cultivated mainly for their ense mats or cushions of leaves, which rovide effective groundcover. They are itable for growing in a rock garden or wing crevice. Alternatively, grow in an pine house.

CULTIVATION Grow in poor to oderately fertile, acidic to neutral, oist but well-drained soil, in full sun ith some midday shade. *S. boydii* quires very sharply drained, poor soil, nd tolerates partial shade. In an alpine ouse, grow in 3 parts grit or sharp sand nd 1 part peat or leaf mold. Dislikes ot, dry conditions.

PROPAGATION Sow seed in containers a cold frame in autumn. Divide *subulata* in spring. Root individual settes of *S. boydii* in early summer.

PESTS AND DISEASES Prone to aphids : spider mites under glass.

. boydii ■ Very slow-growing, dense, ishion-forming perennial producing owded rosettes of rigid, linear to arrowly wedge-shaped, recurved, ossy, dark green leaves, to ¾in (2cm) ng. Tiny, solitary, normally petalless, id-green flowers are produced in immer. Best in an alpine house. 1in (2.5cm), ↔ 3in (8cm). Scotland. one 5.

***. glabra* 'Aurea'** see *S. subulata* urea'.

***S. subulata* 'Aurea'**, syn. *S. glabra* 'Aurea' (Golden pearlwort). Mat-forming perennial with slender, rooting stems clothed in pointed, linear, yellow-green leaves, to ½in (1.5cm) long. In summer, bears solitary, 5-petaled white flowers, ⅛in (3mm) across, on stems to 1½in (4cm) long. Effective as a low groundcover in a rock garden or between paving stones. ↕ ½in (1.5cm), ↔ 8in (20cm) or more. W. and C. Europe. Zone 4.

agina boydii

SAGITTARIA

Arrowhead

ALISMATACEAE

Genus of 20 species of marginal and submerged, herbaceous aquatic perennials and annuals, found mainly on muddy banks or in shallow water in temperate and tropical Europe, Asia, and North, Central, and South America. The often decorative leaves are aerial, floating, or submerged, and linear to elliptic, lance-shaped, ovate, or arrow-shaped. Panicles or racemes of whorled, 3-petaled, saucer-shaped white flowers are borne in summer. Most are excellent for the margins of a wildlife pool, where their tuberous rootstocks may spread; some (including *S. latifolia* and *S. sagittifolia*) produce walnut-sized tubers that attract waterfowl. Grow *S. subulata* in an aquarium for its attractive submerged leaves. Where not hardy, grow in a pool in a cool or temperate greenhouse.

• **CULTIVATION** Outdoors, grow at the margins of a pool, in water no deeper than 9–12in (22–30cm), in full sun. Trim back spreading growth in late summer, and remove faded flowers to prevent seeding. In an aquarium, grow in groups of 4 or 5 in gravelly soil in bright indirect light, with a minimum temperature of 61°F (16°C). Under glass, grow in containers at the margins of an indoor pool in bright filtered light, with a water temperature of 50°F (10°C). See also pp.52–53.

Sagittaria latifolia

• **PROPAGATION** Sow seed as soon as ripe in containers standing in trays of shallow water. Remove runners, or plant overwintered tubers, in spring.

• **PESTS AND DISEASES** Leaf spots, leaf smut, spider mites, and aphids occur.

S. japonica see *S. sagittifolia* 'Flore Pleno'.

S. lancifolia. Stoloniferous, marginal aquatic perennial producing lance-shaped, leathery, pale green aerial leaves, 6–18in (15–45cm) long. In summer, bears several whorls of white flowers, 1¼–2in (3–5cm) across, on scapes to 6ft (2m) tall. ↕↔ 5ft (1.5m). Tropical and subtropical North, Central, and South America. ❀ (min. 50°F/10°C)

S. latifolia ■ (Duck potato, Wapato). Marginal aquatic perennial with large tubers and variable, mainly arrow-shaped aerial leaves, 4–12in (10–30cm) long. In summer, racemes of whorled white flowers, 1¼–1½in (3–4cm) across, are produced on the triangular flower stems, to 4ft (1.2m) tall. ↕ 18–36in (45–90cm), ↔ 36in (90cm). US. Zone 4.

S. montevidensis (Giant arrowhead, Ruby-eye arrowhead). Emergent aquatic perennial with arrow-shaped, mid-green, aerial leaves, to 16in (40cm) long. In summer, bears racemes of whorled white flowers, to 1in (2.5cm) across, each petal with a ruby-red spot at the base, on scapes to 30in (75cm) tall. ↕↔ to 30in (75cm). Warm-temperate North and South America. ❀ (min. 41°F/5°C)

S. sagittifolia (Japanese arrowhead). Marginal aquatic perennial bearing arrow-shaped aerial leaves, 10in (25cm) long, with 2 long, acute, basal lobes. In deep water, produces ribbon-like floating leaves, to 32in (80cm) long. In summer, scapes to 3ft (1m) tall bear racemes of white flowers, to 1in (2.5cm) across, with a purple spot at the base of each petal. ↕ 36in (90cm), ↔ indefinite. Eurasia. Zone 4. **'Flore Pleno'**, syn. *S. japonica*, is double-flowered.

S. subulata. Stoloniferous aquatic perennial bearing variable, usually linear, frequently bent or crooked submerged leaves, to 3ft (1m) long (depending on the depth of the water), with long, sharp-pointed or rounded tips. In shallow water, produces elliptic floating leaves, 2in (5cm) long. White flowers, ½–¾in (1.5–2cm) across, are borne in floating whorls of 1–3, in summer. ↕ to 24in (60cm), ↔ indefinite. E. US. Zone 6.

SAINTPAULIA

African violet

GESNERIACEAE

Genus of 20 species of low-growing, evergreen perennials found on banks, streamsides, on or among rocks, or as epiphytes on trees in a very small area of tropical E. Africa. Most are virtually stemless or have very short stems, and form rosettes of rounded to elliptic, somewhat succulent, usually hairy leaves with long stalks. Trailing African violets produce the rosettes on extended stems. The flowers of the species normally have 2 smaller petals at the top and 3 larger ones below; those of cultivars occur in several flower shapes (see below). They are borne singly or in cymes.

There are over 2,000 cultivars, mainly derived from *S. ionantha*, with white, pink, red, blue, violet, cream to yellow, bi- or multi-colored flowers, ½–2½in (1–6cm) across, borne throughout the year. A "chimera" flower appears striped; small flecks of color are referred to as "fantasy" markings. Many are edged in white or a contrasting color. They may be single (5-petaled), semi-double (with small crests or lobes in the middle of the 5 petals), or fully double (with two or more layers of petals). Some flowers are star-shaped, with all 5 petals of the same shape and size, or bell-shaped, or shaped like a pansy (*Viola*). Petal edges may be ruffled, rounded, or fringed. The leaves are usually mid- or dark green, and may be subtly feathered or flecked, or subtly to strongly variegated white, pink, or cream; most are broadly ovate to oval, and 1½–8in (4–20cm) long, including the stalks. Grow African violets as houseplants; most greenhouses or conservatories are too hot in summer and often too cold in winter.

African violet cultivars are classified by rosette diameter into 5 groups:

MICRO-MINIATURE	less than 3in (8cm)
MINIATURE	3–6in (8–15cm)
SEMI-MINIATURE	6–8in (15–20cm)
STANDARD	8–16in (20–40cm)
LARGE	over 16in (40cm)

• **CULTIVATION** Under glass, grow in well-drained soilless potting mix in bright filtered light and moderate to high humidity. Provide at least 12 hours of light per day for long-term flowering. Avoid direct summer sun, but position in the brightest light in winter; they are excellent for growing under lights. Water moderately and apply a high-potash, high-phosphate liquid fertilizer every 2 weeks, or add a quarter-strength fertilizer at every watering. Repot at least once a year, keeping to virtually the same container size; do not overpot. The diameter of the pot should be one-third the diameter of the plant. ❀ (min. 65°F/18°C)

• **PROPAGATION** Sow seed at 66–75°F (19–24°C) as soon as ripe. Root leaf cuttings or suckers of cultivars at 75–81°F (24–27°C). Chimeras will not come true from leaf cuttings, but will come true from suckers or from plantlets borne on flower stalks.

• **PESTS AND DISEASES** Prone to aphids, mealybugs, thrips, cyclamen and spider mites, gray mold (*Botrytis*), crown rot, and powdery mildew.

***S.* 'Ballet Snowcone'.** (Miniature group) Rosetted perennial with heart-shaped, mid-green leaves, producing double white flowers.
***S.* 'Blushing Ivory'.** (Standard group) Rosetted perennial with quilted, pointed, scalloped, dark green leaves, and single, ivory, star-shaped flowers, with a wide, rose-orchid-dotted edge.
***S.* 'B-Man's Palma'** ■ (Large group) Perennial with variegated plain quilted, serrated, medium green and white leaves. Bears double medium pink frilled pansy-shaped flower.
***S.* 'Buckeye Blithe Spirit'** ■ (Standard group) Perennial with variegated quilted, serrated, medium green and cream leaves. Bears semi-double flowers in pale lavender ruffled star/darker fantasy with a variable darker edge.
***S.* 'Cherry Glo'** ■ (Miniature group) Rosetted perennial with pointed, mid-green leaves, producing star-shaped, double, cherry-red flowers.
***S.* 'Fancy Pants'** ■ (Standard group) Rosetted perennial bearing mid-green leaves and single white flowers with frilled red margins.
***S.* 'Favorite Child'.** (Standard group) Rosetted perennial with quilted, mid-green leaves. Bears pansy-shaped, ruffled, semi-double white flowers with mid-blue eyes, rays, and margins.
***S.* 'Granger's Wonderland'**, syn. *S.* Wonderland'. (Large group) Rosetted perennial with wavy-margined, olive-green leaves and ruffled, semi-double, light blue flowers.
S. ionantha. Rosette-forming perennial bearing ovate to oblong-ovate, scalloped, mid-green leaves, to 2in (5cm) long, paler beneath, on leaf stalks 2½in (6cm) long. Cymes of 4–5 light to dark blue flowers, 1in (2.5cm) across, are produced throughout the year. ↕ to 4in (10cm), ↔ 12in (30cm). Tanzania.
***S.* 'Irish Flirt'** ■ (Semi-miniature group) Rosetted perennial with wavy, mid-green leaves, bearing star-shaped, frilled, variably green-shaded, double white flowers.

Saintpaulia 'B-Man's Palma'

Saintpaulia 'Buckeye Blithe Spirit'

Saintpaulia 'Fancy Pants'

Saintpaulia 'Irish Flirt'

Saintpaulia 'Ma's Pillow Talk'

Saintpaulia 'Ma's Second Thoughts'

Saintpaulia 'Melodie Kimi'

Saintpaulia 'Ozio'

Saintpaulia 'The Alps'

***S.* 'King's Treasure'.** (Large group) Rosetted perennial with mid-green leaves, bears fully double, dark lavender-blue flowers, margined purple, with a white, often green-tinged line at the edges.
***S.* 'Kiwi Dazzle'.** (Standard group) Rosetted perennial with mid-green leaves. Bears fringed, single, bright red chimera flowers, each petal with a central white stripe.
***S.* 'Kristi Marie'.** (Standard group) Rosetted perennial bearing dark green leaves and producing fully double, dusky-red flowers, with white margins.
***S.* 'Lemon Cream'.** (Standard group) Rosetted perennial with wavy, mid-green leaves. Bears star-shaped, semi-double white flowers with yellow centers and mottling.
***S.* 'Ma's Pillow Talk'** ■ (Standard group) Perennial producing variegated serrated, light-medium green and cream leaves with double white frilled pansy-shaped flower.
***S.* 'Ma's Second Thoughts'** ■ (Standard group) Perennial with variegated quilted, serrated, medium green and white leaves. Bears semi-double dark pink pansy-shaped flowers with a white edge.
***S.* 'Melodie Kimi'** ■ (Standard group) Rosetted perennial with mid-green leaves, bearing semi-double, white flowers with purple-blue top petals and purple-blue-marked lower petals.
***S.* 'Mickey Mouse'.** (Miniature group) Rosetted perennial producing pointed, dark green leaves with red undersides. Bears double, dark blue flowers.
***S.* 'Milky Way Trail'** ■ (Semi-miniature group) Trailing perennial with heart-shaped, quilted, mid-green leaves, bearing pansy-shaped, single to semi-double white flowers.
***S.* 'Ness' Firefly'.** (Semi-miniature group) Rosetted perennial producing glossy, dark green leaves with red unde sides, and pansy-shaped, semi-double fuchsia flowers with lighter margins.
***S.* 'Nortex's Snowkist Haven'.** (Standard group) Rosette-forming perennial producing pointed, quilted, mid-green leaves and bearing fringed, single, white flowers.
***S.* 'Ode to Beauty'.** (Large group) Rosetted perennial with quilted, dark green leaves. Bears star-shaped, semi-double mid-coral flowers with narrow, light magenta bands and white margin.
***S.* 'Optimara Rose Quartz'** see *S.* 'Ro Quartz'.
***S.* 'Ozio'** ■ (Standard group) Perenni bearing quilted, serrated, dark green leaves and double pink star/purple fantasy flowers, with fuchsia frilled edg
***S.* 'Party Print'.** (Large group) Rosette-forming perennial producing heart-shaped, quilted, glossy, mid-gree leaves with maroon undersides. Bears star-shaped, ruffled, semi-double to double pink flowers with lavender-blue fantasy markings.
***S.* 'Picasso'.** (Large group) Rosetted perennial producing white-variegated, mid-green leaves with silver-green undersides. Bears double blue flowers with white fantasy markings.
***S.* 'Pip Squeek'** ■ (Micro-miniature group) Semi-trailing perennial with tin

Saintpaulia 'Cherry Glo'

Saintpaulia 'Milky Way Trail'

Saintpaulia 'Pip Squeek'

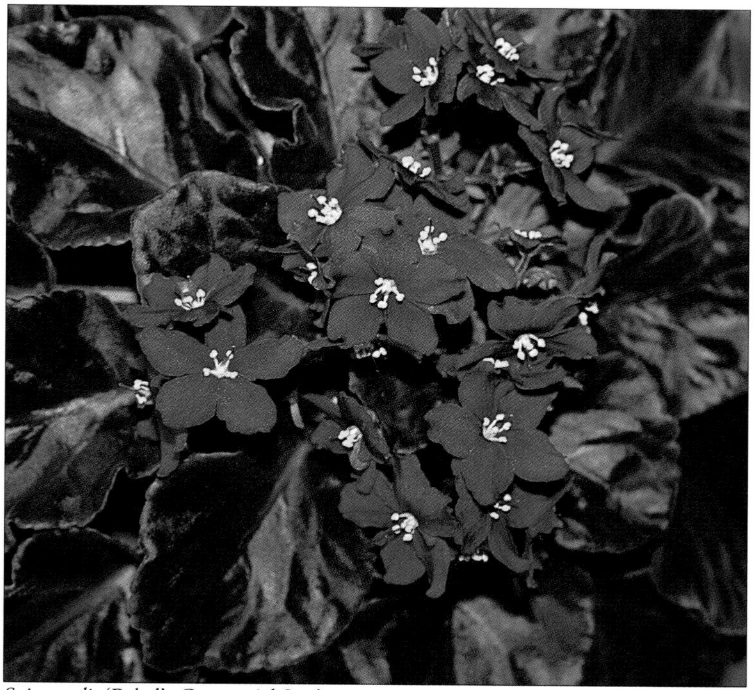
Saintpaulia 'Rebel's Centennial Star'

dark green leaves and bearing single, light pink, bell-shaped flowers.
***S.* 'Rebel's Centennial Star'** ▣ (Standard group) Perennial with pointed, quilted, serrated, medium green leaves with red back. Bears single semi-double flowers with large dark red star.
***S.* 'Rob's Cool Fruit'** ▣ (Semi-miniature group) Perennial with crown variegated pointed, serrated, medium green, white, and yellow leaves. The double white pansy-shaped flower has a rose-pink edge.
***S.* 'Rob's Ice Maiden'.** (Semi-miniature group) Rosetted perennial producing quilted, white-variegated, dark green leaves. Bears semi-double, pale silver-lavender flowers with darker lavender fantasy markings.
***S.* 'Rob's Sticky Wicket'.** (Semi-miniature group) Trailing perennial with pointed, mid-green leaves, bearing semi-double, light fuchsia flowers.
***S.* 'Rose Quartz'**, syn. *S.* 'Optimara Rose Quartz'. (Miniature group) Rosetted perennial with ovate, pointed, glossy, hairy, mid-green leaves. Produces single to semi-double, pink flowers.
***S.* 'Sassy Shirley'.** (Semi-miniature group) Rosetted perennial with white-variegated mid-green leaves, bearing semi-double, light purple flowers.
S. shumensis. Compact, rosette-forming perennial with very short stems. Bears ovate to almost round, slightly serrated leaves, 1½in (4cm) long, often with red-tinged veins beneath. Produces cymes of up to 5 pale blue, almost white flowers, 1in (2.5cm) across, with deep purple eyes, intermittently throughout the year. Leaves may also be variegated, with mottled patterns over the main veins. ↕ 2½–3in (6–8cm), ↔ 3–5in (8–13cm). Tanzania. ❄ (min. 59°F/15°C)
***S.* 'Snuggles'.** (Miniature group) Rosetted perennial with dark green leaves, feathered and margined white. Produces large, semi-double pink flowers.
***S.* 'The Alps'** ▣ (Standard group) Perennial with plain, quilted, medium green leaves. The single semi-double chimera white pansy-shaped flower is marked with a light blue stripe.
***S.* 'Tomahawk'.** (Large group) Rosetted perennial producing dark green leaves and semi-double to fully double, dark red flowers, with fluted petals.
S. tongwensis ▣ Upright, usually single-crowned perennial with narrow, ovate, pointed, hairy, dark green leaves, 3½in (9cm) long. Cymes of up to 5 single, pale violet-blue flowers, 1in (2.5cm) across, are borne intermittently throughout the year. ↕ 6–10in (15–25cm), ↔ up to 10in (25cm). Tanzania. ❄ (min. 59°F/15°C)
S. velutina. Rosette-forming perennial with rounded, velvety, toothed, black-green leaves, 1½in (4cm) long, cupped up or down. Intermittently throughout the year, flower stalks 5in (13cm) long bear cymes of single, often white-tipped, mid-violet flowers, up to 1in (2.5cm) across, with darker eyes. ↕ 10in (25cm), ↔ 12in (30cm). Tanzania. ❄ (min. 59°F/15°C)
***S.* 'Wonderland'** see *S.* 'Granger's Wonderland'.

Saintpaulia 'Rob's Cool Fruit'

Saintpaulia tongwensis

SALIX

Willow

SALICACEAE

Genus of approximately 300 species of normally dioecious, deciduous trees and shrubs found in habitats ranging from lowland meadows and riverbanks to sand dunes and mountain screes worldwide, except in Australia. They have simple, entire or toothed, usually alternate leaves, and bear very small flowers in usually erect catkins, before or with the foliage. Of diverse form, willows are cultivated for their habit (particularly the weeping willows), catkins (of which the males are usually the most striking), foliage, and sometimes colorful winter shoots. The largest willows are suitable only for a garden of large proportions; those with a weeping habit are especially effective by water. Grow smaller willows as specimen trees in a small garden, shrubby willows in a shrub border, and dwarf willows in a rock garden or trough.
• **CULTIVATION** Grow in any deep, moist but well-drained soil in full sun; willows dislike shallow alkaline soil. *S.* 'Erythroflexuosa' needs well-drained soil; the dwarf and alpine species need gritty, sharply drained soil. Pruning group 1 for most; group 7, every 1–3 years, for those grown for colored winter shoots, and to rejuvenate old plants.
• **PROPAGATION** Root softwood cuttings in spring, or hardwood cuttings in winter. Most root very easily.
• **PESTS AND DISEASES** Crown gall, canker and dieback, root knot nematode, powdery mildew, lesion nematode, mushroom root rot, tar spot, rust, twig blight, and heart rot can occur. Pests include caterpillars, borers, aphids, and scale insects.

S. aegyptiaca, syn. *S. medemii* (Musk willow). Strong-growing, bushy shrub or tree with thick, red-purple shoots and oblong, toothed, dark green leaves, to

Salix alba var. *vitellina* 'Britzensis'

6in (15cm) long, with glaucous, hairy undersides. Fragrant gray catkins are produced in early spring, before the leaves: males are up to 1½in (4cm) long, with yellow anthers; females are up to 3in (8cm) long. ↕ 12ft (4m), ↔ 15ft (5m). Turkey, Armenia, Iraq, Iran, Afghanistan. Zone 6.
S. alba (White willow). Very fast-growing, spreading tree with gray-pink to brown shoots and lance-shaped, saw-toothed, slender-pointed, dull green leaves, to 4in (10cm) long, silky-hairy when young, blue-green beneath. Yellow male catkins, to 2in (5cm) long, or stalkless, yellow-green female catkins, 1¼in (3cm) long, are produced in spring, with the leaves. ↕ 80ft (25m), ↔ 30ft (10m). Europe, N. Africa, C. Asia. Zone 4. **f. *argentea*** see var. *sericea*. **var. *caerulea*** (Cricket-bat willow) has upright branches and blue-green leaves. **var. *sericea***, syn. f. *argentea*, 'Sericea', 'Splendens' (Silver willow) has silvery gray leaves; ↕ 50ft (15m), ↔ 25ft (8m). Zone 2. **'Splendens'** see var. *sericea*. **'Tristis'**, syn. *S. vitellina* 'Pendula', has a more weeping habit, and produces only female catkins. **'Tristis' of gardens** see *S.* x *sepulcralis* 'Chrysocoma'. **var. *vitellina*** (Golden willow) produces bright yellow to orange winter shoots. **var. *vitellina* 'Britzensis'** ■ is a male clone, with bright orange-red winter shoots. **var. *vitellina* 'Chermesina'** is a male clone, with carmine-red young winter shoots.
S. arenaria see *S. repens* var. *argentea*.
S. babylonica (Weeping willow). Rounded, weeping tree with slender, pendent, green to brown shoots and lance-shaped, saw-toothed, tapered, mid-green leaves, to 4in (10cm) long, gray-green beneath. Slender, silvery green catkins are produced in spring, with the leaves: the males to 2in (5cm) long with yellow anthers, the females to 1in (2.5cm) long. Largely replaced in gardens by *S.* x *sepulcralis* 'Chrysocoma'. ↕↔ 40ft (12m). N. China. Zone 7. **'Crispa'**, syn. 'Annularis', is slow-growing and upright, and has curiously twisted leaves. **var. *pekinensis* 'Tortuosa'** ■ syn. *S. matsudana* 'Tortuosa' (Dragon-claw willow) is fast-growing and upright. It has curiously twisted shoots that are particularly striking in winter. Bears bright green, twisted leaves and yellow-green catkins; ↕ 50ft (15m), ↔ 25ft (8m).

S

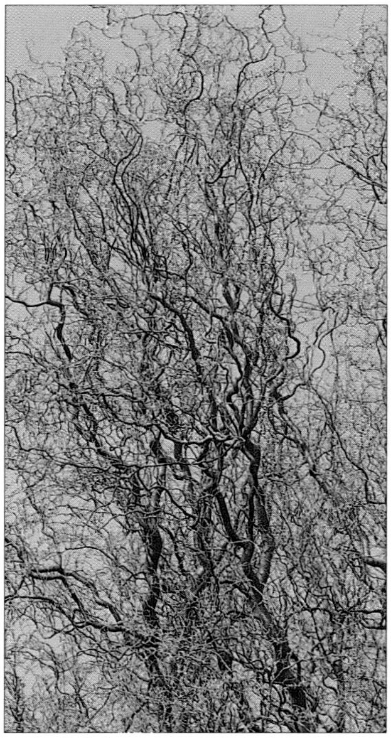

Salix babylonica var. *pekinensis* 'Tortuosa'

***S.* 'Blanda'**, syn. *S.* x *pendulina* var. *blanda* (Wisconsin weeping willow). Spreading tree with weeping shoots and lance-shaped, tapered, glossy, dark green leaves, to 6in (15cm) long. Slender, silvery green, usually female catkins, to 1¼in (3cm) long, are produced in spring, with the leaves. ↕↔ 40ft (12m). Zone 4.
***S.* 'Boydii'** see *S.* x *boydii*.
S.* x *boydii ■ (*S. lapponum* x *S. reticulata*) syn. *S.* 'Boydii'. Very slow-growing, upright shrub with gnarled branches bearing almost rounded, rough-textured, prominently veined, gray-green leaves, ½–¾in (1–2cm) long. Occasionally produces insignificant female catkins on bare branches in early spring. Suitable for a rock garden or trough. ↕ 12in (30cm), ↔ 8in (20cm). Scotland. Zone 5.
***S. caprea* 'Kilmarnock'** ■ syn. *S. caprea* 'Pendula' (Kilmarnock willow). Weeping tree, almost always grown as a grafted standard, with a dense head of thick, yellow-brown shoots and broadly elliptic, toothed leaves, to 4in (10cm) long, dark green above, gray-green beneath. Gray male catkins, 1¼in (3cm) long, studded with yellow anthers, are produced on the bare shoots in mid- and late spring. ↕ 5–6ft (1.5–2m) or more, depending on grafting height, ↔ 6ft (2m). Zone 5.
***S. caprea* 'Pendula'** see *S. caprea* 'Kilmarnock'.
S.* x *chrysocoma see *S.* x *sepulcralis* 'Chrysocoma'.
S. daphnoides (Violet willow). Initially upright, later spreading tree with purple young shoots, which are white-bloomed in winter, and narrowly oblong, saw-toothed, clearly stalked, dark green leaves, to 5in (13cm) long. Silky gray catkins, to 1½in (4cm) long, are produced in late winter and early spring, before the leaves; male catkins have yellow anthers. ↕ 25ft (8m), ↔ 20ft (6m). Europe to C. Asia. Zone 2b. **'Aglaia'** has glossy red shoots.

Salix x *boydii*

S. discolor (Pussy willow). Upright, small tree with deep brown branches and broad-elliptic to oblong, toothed, dark green leaves, 2–4in (5–10cm) long, bluish white beneath. Gray male catkins, ¾–1¼in (2–3cm) long, are produced on the bare shoots in mid- and late spring. ↕ 15–25ft (5–8m), ↔ 12–15ft (4–5m). Wet areas of the E. US. Zone 2.
S. elaeagnos, syn. *S. incana* (Rosemary willow). Dense, upright shrub with slender, gray-velvety, later red-yellow to almost brown shoots. The linear, entire, dark green leaves, to 8in (20cm) long, are gray when young, white-hairy beneath, and turn yellow in autumn. Bears slender green catkins, 1¼–2½in (3–6cm) long, in spring, as the leaves emerge; male catkins have yellow anthers. ↕ 10ft (3m), ↔ 15ft (5m). C. and S. Europe, S.W. Asia. Zone 5.
***S.* 'Erythroflexuosa'**, syn. *S.* 'Golden Curls', *S. matsudana* 'Tortuosa Aureopendula'. Spreading tree with arching branches and spirally twisted, orange-yellow young shoots. The twisted, lance-shaped, glossy, mid-green leaves, to 3in (8cm) long, are glaucous beneath. Produces slender, pale yellow catkins, 1¼–1½in (3–4cm) long, in spring, with the leaves. ↕↔ 15ft (5m). Zone 4b.
S. exigua ■ (Coyote willow). Upright, thicket-forming, suckering shrub with slender shoots and narrowly lance-shaped, tapered, gray-green leaves, to 4in (10cm) long, covered in silky, silvery gray hairs when young. Gray-yellow catkins, the males to 2in (5cm) long, the females to 2½in (6cm) long, are borne in spring, with the leaves. Grows well on

Salix caprea 'Kilmarnock'

sandy soils. ↕ 12ft (4m), ↔ 15ft (5m) or more. W. North America. Zone 3b.
S. fargesii, syn. *S. moupinensis* of gardens. Open, upright, stoutly branched shrub with glossy green young shoots that turn red-brown, and red winter buds. Produces oblong, finely saw-toothed, glossy, dark green leaves, to 7in (18cm) long, silky beneath. Green catkins, the males to 5in (13cm) long, the females to 7in (18cm) long, ar borne in spring, with the leaves. ↕↔ 10ft (3m). C. China. Zone 6.
***S.* 'Flame'**. Oval, compact, densely branched shrub, with orange-red bark i winter; the tips of the branches curl toward the stems. Persistent, elliptic, dark green leaves, to 4in (10cm) long, turn golden yellow in autumn. Does no produce catkins. ↕ 20ft (6m), ↔ 15–20ft (5–6m). Zone 4.
S. fragilis (Crack willow). Spreading tree with brittle, olive-brown shoots. Bears lance-shaped, finely toothed, glossy, dark green leaves, to 6in (15cm) long, blue-green beneath. Produces slender, penden green catkins, to 3in (8cm) long, in early spring, as the leaves emerge; male catkins have yellow anthers. ↕↔ 50ft (15m). Europe, N. Turkey, Russia (W. Siberia). Zone 3b.
***S.* 'Golden Curls'** see *S.* 'Erythroflexuosa'.
S. gracilistyla (Redgold pussy willow). Spreading, bushy shrub with arching shoots, silky-hairy when young, and oval, entire to finely toothed, silky-hairy gray-green leaves, to 4in (10cm) long, turning glossy green. Silvery gray catkins, to 1½in (4cm) long, are produced in early and midspring, before the leaves; male catkins have red anthers that turn bright yellow. ↕ 10ft (3m), ↔ 12ft (4m). E. Asia. Zone 4b. **'Melanostachys'** ■ syn. var. *melanostachys*, *S. melanostachys* (Black pussy willow) is upright in habit and male, and bears black catkins with brick red anthers.
***S. hastata* 'Wehrhahnii'**. Slow-growing, upright shrub with dark purple-brown shoots and oval, entire to finely toothed, bright green leaves, to 2½in (6cm) long. In early spring, bears conspicuous, silvery gray male catkins, to 3in (8cm) long, before the leaves. ↕↔ 3ft (1m). Zone 5.
S. helvetica (Swiss willow). Upright, many-branched shrub with oblong to ovate-lance-shaped, gray-green leaves, ½–1½in (1.5–4cm) long, smooth above silver-downy beneath. In early spring,

Salix exigua

'alix gracilistyla 'Melanostachys'

.lver-gray catkins, to 2in (5cm) long, pen from small golden buds, before the :aves. ↕ 24in (60cm), ↔ 16in (40cm). .lps. Zone 5.

. hylematica of gardens see . *lindleyana.*

. incana see *S. elaeagnos.*

. irrorata. Upright shrub producing .ender purple shoots, which are white- loomed in winter, and narrowly blong, entire to sparsely toothed, short- :alked, bright green leaves, to 4in 10cm) long, glaucous beneath. Gray atkins, to 1in (2.5cm) long, are borne ı early or midspring, before the leaves; ıale catkins have red anthers that turn ellow. ↕ 10ft (3m), ↔ 15ft (5m). .W. US. Zone 6.

. lanata (Woolly willow). Compact, ounded, bushy shrub bearing thick hoots, white-woolly when young. The :aves are broadly rounded, wavy- ıargined, dull, dark green, to 2½in 5cm) long, and covered with silvery ray wool. Golden yellow male catkins, ɔ 2in (5cm) long, or gray-yellow female atkins, to 3in (8cm) long, are produced ı late spring, with the leaves. ↕ 3ft (1m), ↔ 5ft (1.5m). N. Europe. Zone 4.

. lindleyana, syn. *S. hylematica* of ardens, *S. nepalensis.* Dwarf, rocumbent shrub with ovate-spoon- haped, very glossy, pale green leaves, ɔ ½in (1.5cm) long, densely set on hort branchlets. Bears pinkish brown ıale catkins, to ½in (1.5cm) long, or hort female catkins, ¼in (6mm) long, ı spring, with the leaves. Spreads videly in moist, fertile soils, in partial hade. ↕ 1½in (4cm), ↔ 24in (60cm) or ıore. Himalayas. Zone 7b.

'alix reticulata

Salix x *sepulcralis* 'Chrysocoma'

S. magnifica. Broadly upright shrub or tree bearing thick, red-purple shoots and broadly oval, blue-green leaves, to 8in (20cm) long. Slender green catkins, the males to 7in (18cm) long, the females to 10in (25cm) long, are produced in late spring, after the leaves. ↕ 15ft (5m), ↔ 10ft (3m). W. China. Zone 6.

***S. matsudana* 'Tortuosa'** see *S. babylonica* var. *pekinensis* 'Tortuosa'.

***S. matsudana* 'Tortuosa Aureopendula'** see *S.* 'Erythroflexuosa'.

S. medemii see *S. aegyptiaca.*

S. melanostachys see *S. gracilistyla* 'Melanostachys'.

***S. moupinensis* of gardens** see *S. fargesii.*

S. nepalensis see *S. lindleyana.*

S.* x *pendulina* var. *blanda see *S.* 'Blanda'.

S. pentandra (Bay willow, Laurel willow). Spreading, bushy-headed tree with brown-green shoots and oval, finely glandular-toothed leaves, to 5in (13cm) long, glossy, dark green above, pale green beneath. Catkins, 2in (5cm) long, are produced in early summer, after the leaves: male catkins are yellow and very showy, with yellow anthers; female catkins are green. ↕↔ 30ft (10m). Eurasia. Zone 1b.

***S.* 'Prairie Cascade'.** Weeping tree with yellow-brown stems and elliptic, very glossy, mid-green leaves, 3–5in (8–13cm) long. Does not produce catkins. ↕↔ 35–45ft (11–14m). Zone 3.

S. purpurea (Purple osier). Spreading shrub to upright tree with arching, frequently red-tinged shoots and often opposite, oblong, almost entire, dark green to blue-green leaves, to 3in (8cm) long. Slender, silvery green catkins, to 1¼in (3cm) long, are produced in early and midspring, before the leaves; male catkins have purple anthers that turn yellow. ↕↔ 15ft (5m). Europe, N. Africa, C. Asia. Zone 4. **'Nana'**, syn. 'Gracilis', is compact in habit, bearing slender shoots and small, gray-green leaves, to 1½in (4cm) long. Suitable for growing as a low hedge; ↕ 3ft (1m), ↔ 5ft (1.5m).

S. repens (Creeping willow). Prostrate shrub with slender shoots and oblong to oval, gray-green to bright green leaves, to 1½in (4cm) long, silvery beneath. Gray male catkins, to ¾in (2cm) long, with golden yellow anthers, are borne in mid- and late spring, before the leaves. ↕ to 24in (60cm), ↔ 5ft (1.5m) or more. Europe. Zone 1. **var. *argentea***, syn. *S. arenaria,* is spreading, with creeping, initially upright, later arching shoots, and obovate, silky gray leaves, to 1½in (4cm) long. Catkins appear in midspring; ↕ 3ft (1m), ↔ 6ft (2m); N.W. Europe.

S. reticulata ▣ Dwarf, prostrate shrub with rooting stems bearing rounded-ovate, glossy, dark green leaves, ½–1½in (1–4cm) long, conspicuously veined above, white-hairy beneath. In spring, bears slender yellow catkins, 1in (2.5cm) long, with pink tips. ↕ 3in (8cm), ↔ 12in (30cm). N. Europe, N. Asia, North America. Zone 3.

***S. sachalinensis* 'Sekka'** (Fantail willow). Vigorous, spreading shrub, forming large, dense thickets, with lance-shaped, shallowly scalloped, bright green leaves, to 5in (13cm) long. In early spring, bears showy, silvery gray male catkins, to 1½in (4cm) long, with golden anthers, on often curiously flattened, twisted red shoots. ↕ 15ft (5m), ↔ 30ft (10m). Zone 3.

***S.* x *sepulcralis* 'Chrysocoma'** ▣ syn. *S. alba* 'Tristis' of gardens, *S.* x *chrysocoma, S.* x *sepulcralis* var. *chrysocoma* (Golden weeping willow). Fast-growing, wide-spreading tree with slender, golden yellow shoots, pendent to the ground, and narrowly lance-shaped, tapered, bright green leaves, to 5in (13cm) long. Slender catkins, to 2in (5cm) long, both yellow males and green females often present on the same plant, are produced with the leaves, in spring. ↕↔ 50ft (15m). Zone 4.

S.* x *sepulcralis* var. *chrysocoma see *S.* x *sepulcralis* 'Chrysocoma'.

***S. vitellina* 'Pendula'** see *S. alba* 'Tristis'.

SALPIGLOSSIS

Painted tongue

SOLANACEAE

Genus of 2 erect to spreading, bushy, sticky-hairy annuals or short-lived perennials found on disturbed ground, in dry canyons, and on rocky slopes in the southern Andes. They have entire to wavy-margined or lobed, oval to lance-shaped, bright mid-green leaves, and produce funnel-shaped, richly colored, red, yellow, bronze, violet-blue, or purple flowers from summer to autumn. Suitable for an annual, herbaceous, or mixed border where summers are warm, sunny, and reasonably dry. In cool-temperate regions, they are effective long-flowering container plants in a warm greenhouse or conservatory, and may be bedded out in summer.

• **CULTIVATION** Under glass, grow in soilless or soil-based potting mix in full light with shade from hot sun. When in growth, maintain low to moderate humidity, water moderately, and apply a balanced liquid fertilizer every 2 weeks. Keep just moist in winter. Overwinter at 61–64°F (16–18°C). Outdoors, grow in moderately fertile, humus-rich, moist but well-drained soil in full sun.

• **PROPAGATION** Sow seed at 64–75°F (18–24°C) in midspring, or in autumn or late winter for winter- or early spring-flowering container plants. In mild areas, sow *in situ* in midspring.

• **PESTS AND DISEASES** Aphids, gray mold (*Botrytis*), and foot and root rots occur.

S. sinuata. Erect annual with slender, branching stems bearing alternate, long-stalked, narrowly to broadly lance-shaped, wavy-margined leaves, to 4in (10cm) long. From summer to autumn, broadly funnel-shaped, 5-lobed flowers, to 2in (5cm) across, in a wide variety of colors, and heavily veined in deeper or contrasting colors, are produced singly in the leaf axils of flowering stems. ↕ to 24in (60cm), ↔ to 12in (30cm). Peru, Argentina. **Bolero Hybrids** are less floriferous and more straggling than the other cultivars listed, with flowers in shades of blue, orange, purple, red, or yellow. Cultivars of **Casino Series** ▣ have good weather tolerance and are compact, branching freely from the bases. Flowers are blue, purple, red, yellow, or orange, often heavily veined. **'Kew Blue'** has clear purple-blue flowers, conspicuously veined.

Salpiglossis sinuata Casino Series

SALVIA

Sage

LAMIACEAE

Genus of about 900 species of annuals, biennials, herbaceous and evergreen perennials, and shrubs, some rhizomatous or tuberous. Distributed worldwide in temperate and tropical regions (except in very hot, humid areas), they usually grow in sunny sites, including dry meadows, rocky slopes, scrub, light woodland, and moist grassland. They are frequently aromatic and often hairy; some species are very woolly, and others silver in appearance. The usually square stems bear opposite pairs of simple to pinnate, entire, toothed, notched, or scalloped leaves; basal leaves sometimes differ from stem leaves. Flowers are 2-lipped, the upper lips erect and hooded, the lower ones 2-toothed and more spreading. The calyces are sometimes colorful, and tubular to bell- or funnel-shaped; the often leaf-like, colorful bracts are ovate to diamond-shaped. The flowers are borne in panicles, or in axillary whorls on erect stems, forming more or less interrupted terminal spikes or racemes. Sages are effective in a sunny border, light woodland, or wildflower meadow. Annuals, and perennials grown as annuals, provide a wide range of colors and plant habits for bedding, borders, and containers; less hardy sages may be grown in a cool or temperate greenhouse. *S. caespitosa* is suitable for a scree bed or alpine house. Many species attract bees; some, especially *S. elegans*, *S. officinalis*, *S. pratensis*, and *S. sclarea*, have culinary or medicinal uses.

• **CULTIVATION** Under glass, grow in well-drained, soilless or soil-based potting mix in full light with shade from hot sun. During the growing season, water freely and apply a balanced liquid fertilizer monthly; water very sparingly in winter, except *S. canariensis*, *S. elegans* and its cultivars, and *S. leucantha*, which should be watered moderately. Maintain low to moderate humidity. Outdoors, grow in light, moderately fertile, humus-rich, moist but well-drained soil in full sun to light, dappled shade. Species with densely hairy or woolly leaves need sharp drainage and full sun. Protect from excessive winter moisture. Pruning group 9, in spring.

• **PROPAGATION** Sow seed as follows: annuals at 61–64°F (16–18°C) in mid-

Salvia argentea

Salvia cacaliifolia

spring, biennials in containers in a cold frame in summer, and perennials in containers in a cold frame in spring; annuals and biennials may be sown *in situ* after all danger of frost has passed. Divide perennials in spring. For perennials and subshrubs, root basal or softwood cuttings in spring or early summer, or semi-ripe cuttings in late summer or autumn, with bottom heat.

• **PESTS AND DISEASES** Rust, powdery mildew, stem rot, and fungal leaf spots are common. Whiteflies, aphids, mealybugs, and spider mites can be problems.

S. aethiopis. Rosette-forming, monocarpic perennial or biennial with broadly ovate or elliptic to oblong, deeply toothed, white-woolly leaves, to 8in (20cm) long, clasping the erect upper stems. White, sometimes yellow-lipped flowers, ¾in (1.5cm) long, with persistent, broad, spiny bracts, are borne in branching, flat-topped, terminal panicles in mid- and late summer. ↕↔ 24in (60cm). C. and S. Europe to W. Asia. Zone 7b.

S. ambigens see *S. guaranitica* 'Blue Enigma'.

S. angustifolia see *S. azurea.*

Salvia coccinea 'Coral Nymph'

Salvia coccinea 'Lady in Red'

S. argentea ■ (Silver sage). Rosette-forming biennial or short-lived perennial producing ovate to oblong, toothed, silver-woolly leaves, to 8in (20cm) long. In mid- and late summer, bears many-branched, terminal panicles of white or pinkish white flowers, to 1¼in (3cm) long, with gray calyces. ↕ 36in (90cm), ↔ 24in (60cm). S. Europe, N. Africa. Zone 5.

S. azurea, syn. *S. angustifolia* (Blue sage). Erect, woody-based perennial with several to many simple or sparsely branched stems bearing linear, elliptic, or lance-shaped, hairless or softly hairy, sometimes toothed, mid- to deep green leaves, 2–4in (5–10cm) long. From late summer to autumn, pure blue or white flowers, ½–¾in (1.5–2cm) long, are produced in dense, terminal racemes. ↕ to 5ft (1.5m), ↔ 24–36in (60–90cm). S.E. US. Zone 7b. **subsp. *pitcheri*** has very hairy stems; flowers are to 1in (2.5cm) long; Mexico; ❀ (min. 35°F/2°C)

***S. bacheriana* of gardens** see *S. buchananii.*

S. blepharophylla. Spreading, subshrubby, rhizomatous perennial bearing ovate to triangular, irregularly toothed, finely hairy, dark green leaves, 2in (5cm) long. From early summer to early autumn, branched stems bear loose, terminal racemes of bright scarlet flowers, to ¾in (2cm) long, with large lower lips and maroon calyces. ↕ 16in (40cm), ↔ 18in (45cm). Mexico. ❀ (min. 41°F/5°C)

S. buchananii, syn. *S. bacheriana* of gardens. Woody-based perennial, spreading by runners, with erect, branching stems bearing spoon-shaped to ovate-lance-shaped, finely toothed, leathery, dark green leaves, to 3in (8cm) long. Velvety-hairy, magenta-red flowers, to 2in (5cm) long, with dark purplish brown calyces, are borne in loose, terminal racemes from mid-summer to midautumn. ↕ 24in (60cm), ↔ 12in (30cm). Mexico. ❀ (min. 41°F/5°C)

S. cacaliifolia ■ Erect, hairy perennial with more or less triangular, entire, mid-green leaves, to 4in (10cm) long. In early summer, branched stems bear terminal panicles of paired, slightly hairy, deep blue flowers, to ¾in (2cm) long, with much shorter, bell-shaped calyces. ↕ 36in (90cm), ↔ 12in (30cm). Mexico, Guatemala. ❀ (min. 41°F/5°C)

***S. caerulea* of gardens** see *S. guaranitica* 'Black and Blue'.

S. caespitosa. Woody-based, mat-forming perennial or subshrub producing obovate, pinnatisect, silver-hairy leaves, 2in (5cm) long, each with a lance-shaped terminal segment. In summer, bears dense, terminal racemes of wide-tubed, lilac-pink flowers, to 1¼in (3cm) long, with broad lower lips. Resents winter moisture. Suitable for an alpine house; can be grown in a scree bed if overhead protection is provided in winter. ↕ 6in (15cm), ↔ 12in (30cm). Turkey (Anatolia). Zone 7b.

S. canariensis. Erect, open, evergreen shrub with sparsely branched, white-downy stems. Lance-shaped to triangular, entire or notched, mid-green leaves, 2½–6in (6–15cm) long, each have 2 spreading lobes at the bases; they are covered with dense white down, at least beneath. From winter to spring,

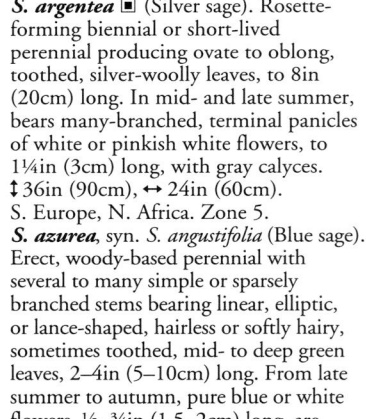

ılvia confertiflora

Salvia farinacea 'Strata'

Salvia fulgens

Salvia guaranitica 'Black and Blue'

ears small, white to violet or purple owers, to ¾in (2cm) long, in terminal nicles or racemes. ↕ 3–6ft (1–2m), 2–4ft (0.6–1.2m). Canary Islands. (min. 45°F/7°C)
cardinalis see *S. fulgens.*
chamaedryoides (Germander sage). ow-growing, woody-based perennial th branching stems. Elliptic, finely alloped, mid- to gray-green leaves, to in (2cm) long, are covered in fine irs, giving them a sage-green pearance. Deep blue flowers, 1in .5cm) long, with widely spreading s, are borne in terminal racemes in e summer. ↕ 12in (30cm), ↔ 24in 0cm). Texas, Mexico. Zone 8.
clevelandii (Jim sage). Dwarf, unded, evergreen shrub, branching ainly from the base, with usually owny stems, and ovate or oblong to liptic or lance-shaped, wrinkled, othed, aromatic, mid-green leaves, to n (2.5cm) long. In summer, white, ue, or violet flowers, ½in (1.5cm) ng, are borne in terminal whorls or ort, simple to branched spikes. 6–24in (40–60cm), ↔ 12–24in 0–60cm). California. Zone 8.
coccinea (Texas sage). Erect, bushy nual with oval to heart-shaped, othed, hairy, dark green leaves, to 2½in cm) long. From summer to autumn, ft cherry-red flowers, to ¾in (2cm) ng, are borne in slender, open, terminal ikes. ↕ 24–30in (60–75cm), ↔ to 12in 0cm). Tropical South America. **'Coral ymph'** ▣ produces coral-pink flowers; 6in (40cm). **'Lady in Red'** ▣ has red owers; ↕ 16in (40cm). **'Snow Nymph'**, n. 'White Lady', bears white flowers.

ılvia discolor

'Starry Eyed' bears white, red, or coral-pink flowers.
***S. concolor* of gardens** see *S. guaranitica.*
S. confertiflora ▣ Woody-based perennial with ovate, scalloped, yellow-green leaves, to 8in (20cm) long, that are densely woolly, especially beneath, and unpleasantly scented if crushed. From late summer to midautumn, the unbranched stems bear terminal spikes of orange-red flowers, ½in (1.5cm) long, with hairy, deep red calyces. ↕ to 4ft (1.2m), ↔ 24in (60cm). Brazil. ❄ (min. 41°F/5°C)
S. deserta see *S.* x *sylvestris.*
S. discolor ▣ Erect perennial with densely white-woolly, branched stems. Oblong-ovate, entire, mid-green leaves, to 2½in (6cm) long, are densely white-woolly beneath, less hairy above. In late summer and early autumn, bears long, terminal racemes of deep indigo-black flowers, to 1in (2.5cm) long, with finely white-hairy calyces. ↕ 18in (45cm), ↔ 12in (30cm). Peru. ❄ (min. 41°F/5°C)
S. elegans. Soft-stemmed herbaceous perennial or subshrub with branching stems and ovate or almost triangular, hairless or softly hairy, toothed, mildly pineapple-scented, mid-green leaves, to 4in (10cm) long. Loose, terminal panicles of bright scarlet flowers, 1in (2.5cm) long, softly hairy inside, are produced from winter to spring. ↕ 6ft (2m), ↔ 3ft (1m). Mexico, Guatemala. Zone 8. **'Scarlet Pineapple'**, syn. *S. rutilans* (Pineapple sage), has leaves that smell strongly of pineapple when crushed, and more densely hairy stems

Salvia farinacea 'Victoria'

than the species; it bears larger flowers, to 1½in (4cm) long; ↕ 36in (90cm), ↔ 24in (60cm).
S. farinacea (Mealycup sage). Erect, bushy perennial, usually grown as an annual, with white-mealy stems bearing pointed, narrowly to broadly lance-shaped, wavy-margined, glossy, mid-green leaves, to 3in (8cm) long, white-hairy beneath. From summer to autumn, produces deep lavender-blue flowers, to ¾in (2cm) long, in tall, slender, dense, purple-stemmed, terminal or axillary spikes. It may be overwintered in barely moist peat, if kept frost-free. ↕ to 24in (60cm), ↔ to 12in (30cm), as an annual. Texas, Mexico. Zone 8. **'Blue Bedder'** has blue flower spikes, to 12in (30cm) long; ↕ 30in (75cm). **'Rhea'** is compact and early-flowering, with intense dark blue flowers; ↕ to 14in (35cm). **'Silver White'** bears pearl-white flowers. **'Strata'** ▣ has blue flowers with white calyces. **'Victoria'** ▣ has deep blue flowers and dense, almost basal branching. **'White Porcelain'** has white flowers.
S. fruticosa, syn. *S. triloba.* Bushy, evergreen shrub or subshrub with white-hairy, branched stems bearing simple or pinnate, mid-green leaves, to 2in (5cm) long; the pinnate leaves each have 3 or 5 oblong-elliptic leaflets. In summer, bears purple, lilac-pink, or pink, rarely white flowers, to 1in (2.5cm) long, in terminal or axillary racemes. ↕ to 4ft (1.2m), ↔ to 32in (80cm). C. and E. Mediterranean. ❄ (min. 35°F/2°C)
S. fulgens ▣ syn. *S. cardinalis.* Woody-based perennial or evergreen subshrub, branching mainly from the base, with ovate to narrowly triangular, toothed or

Salvia greggii

notched leaves, 2½–5in (6–13cm) long, rich green above, densely white-woolly beneath. Terminal or axillary spikes or racemes of red flowers, to 1¼in (3cm) long, with densely downy lower lips, are produced in summer. ↕ 20–39in (50–100cm), ↔ 16–36in (40–90cm). Mexico. ❄ (min. 41°F/5°C)
S. gesneriiflora. Subshrubby perennial bearing ovate, scalloped, hairy, mid-green leaves, to 4in (10cm) long, with heart-shaped bases. From early spring to midautumn, many-branched stems bear terminal racemes of numerous softly hairy red flowers, 2in (5cm) long, with flattened upper lips. ↕ 24in (60cm), ↔ 8in (20cm). Mexico to Colombia. ❄ (min. 41°F/5°C)
S. glutinosa (Jupiter's distaff). Clump-forming, sticky-hairy perennial with branched or unbranched stems and heart-shaped, toothed, mid-green leaves, to 8in (20cm) long. From midsummer to midautumn, bears loose, terminal racemes of softly hairy, pale yellow flowers, to 1½in (4cm) long, heavily spotted maroon and with reddish brown markings on the brighter yellow lower lips. ↕↔ 36in (90cm). C. and S. Europe to W. Asia. Zone 6.
S. grahamii see *S. microphylla.*
S. greggii ▣ (Autumn sage). Dwarf, evergreen shrub or sometimes erect, woody-based perennial, branching mainly from the base, with glandular-hairy stems. Ovate or elliptic to oblong or linear, leathery, entire, mid- to deep green leaves, ¾–1¼in (2–3cm) long, are hairless to softly hairy and dotted with glands. Paired, red to purple, pink, yellow, or violet flowers, ¾in (2cm) long, are borne in terminal racemes from late summer to autumn. ↕↔ 12–20in (30–50cm). Texas, Mexico. Zone 7b. Many color variants are available. **'Raspberry Royal'** has bright raspberry-red flowers; ↕ to 24in (60cm), ↔ 12in (30cm).
S. guaranitica, syn. *S. concolor* of gardens. Subshrubby perennial with branched, dark green stems and ovate, pointed, slightly toothed, hairy, wrinkled, mid-green leaves, to 5in (13cm) long. Deep blue flowers, to 2in (5cm) long, with purplish blue calyces, are borne in terminal or axillary spikes from late summer to late autumn. ↕ 5ft (1.5m), ↔ 24in (60cm). Brazil, Uruguay, Argentina. Zone 8. **'Argentina Skies'** has sky-blue flowers from midsummer to early autumn; ↕ 3ft (1m), ↔ 18in (45cm). **'Black and Blue'** ▣ syn. *S. caerulea* of gardens, bears rich blue

Salvia guaranitica 'Blue Enigma'

flowers with very dark purple-blue calyces; ↕ to 8ft (2.5m), ↔ 36in (90cm). **'Blue Enigma'** ■ syn. *S. ambigens*, bears fragrant, deep blue flowers with bright green calyces; ↔ 36in (90cm).
S. haematodes see *S. pratensis* Haematodes Group.
S. hians. Erect, sticky-hairy, pleasantly scented, somewhat short-lived perennial with ovate, toothed, prominently veined, wrinkled, dark green leaves, to 6in (15cm) long. Branched stems produce terminal spikes of purplish blue flowers, to 1½in (4cm) long, with spreading lips, the lower lips white-marked, from early to late summer. ↕↔ 24in (60cm). Himalayas (mainly Kashmir). Zone 7.
S. hispanica see *S. lavandulifolia.*
S. horminum see *S. viridis.*
***S.* 'Indigo Spires'** ■ Bushy perennial with ovate to oblong, mid-green basal leaves, to 6in (15cm) long. In summer, bears twisting, elongating spikes, to 3ft (1m) long, of purple flowers, ½in (1.5cm) long, with blue bracts. ↕ 3ft (1m), ↔ 12in (30cm). Zone 7b.
S. involucrata. (Rosyleaf sage). Subshrubby perennial with sparsely branched stems and ovate, tapering, entire or notched, softly hairy, rich green leaves, to 5in (13cm) long. From late summer to midautumn, produces dense, terminal racemes of purplish red flowers, to 2in (5cm) long, with prominent pink bracts that fall as the flowers open. ↕ 5ft (1.5m), ↔ 3ft (1m). Mexico. ❀ (min. 41°F/5°C). **'Bethellii'** ■ has slightly larger, more velvety leaves than the species, and produces bright purplish crimson flowers.

S

Salvia 'Indigo Spires'

Salvia involucrata 'Bethellii'

S. x jamensis (*S. greggii* x *S. microphylla*). Bushy shrub with opposite, ovate to elliptic, toothed, mid-green leaves, ¾–1½in (2–4cm) long. In summer and autumn, red, rose-pink, salmon-pink, orange, or rarely creamy yellow flowers, ½–1in (1–2.5cm) long, are borne in opposite pairs in terminal racemes. ↕ 20–39in (0.5–1m), ↔ 20in (50cm). Mexico. ❀ (min. 41°F/5°C). **'Fuego'** bears bright, flame-red flowers. **'La Luna'** bears creamy yellow flowers, the upper lips covered in buff-colored hairs. **'Pat Vlasto'** has ovate-elliptic, entire leaves, ¾in (2cm) long, and pink-suffused orange flowers, ¾–1in (2–2.5cm) long; ↕ 3ft (1m), ↔ 30in (75cm). ❀ (min. 41°F/5°C)
S. jurisicii. Low-growing, hairy perennial with basal rosettes of ovate, scalloped, mid-green leaves, 4in (10cm) long, and many-branched stems producing pinnate leaves, 4in (10cm) long, each divided into 4–6 pairs of linear leaflets. From early to late summer, bears a profusion of terminal racemes of apparently upside-down, violet-blue flowers, to ½in (1.5cm) long, the upper lips covered with long, violet-blue hairs. ↕ to 24in (60cm), ↔ 18in (45cm). Yugoslavia (Serbia), Macedonia. Zone 7.
S. lavandulifolia, syn. *S. hispanica* (Spanish sage). Woody-based perennial with mostly basal, long-stalked, narrowly oblong, entire, gray- to white-woolly leaves, to 1in (2.5cm) long. In midsummer, blue-violet flowers, to 1in (2.5cm) long, are produced in terminal and axillary racemes. ↕ to 20in (50cm), ↔ 24in (60cm). Spain. Zone 6.

Salvia leucantha

S. lemmonii see *S. microphylla var. wislizenii.*
S. leucantha ■ (Mexican bush sage). Bushy, evergreen subshrub with white-downy stems when young, and ovate or lance-shaped to oblong or linear, toothed or scalloped, mid-green leaves, to 6in (15cm) long, wrinkled above, white-downy beneath. From winter to spring, produces terminal racemes of white or purple flowers, to ½–¾in (1.5–2cm) long, with bell-shaped, downy, purple to lavender-blue calyces. ↕ 24–39in (60–100cm), ↔ 16–36in (40–90cm). Mexico, tropical Central America. ❀ (min. 45°F/7°C)
S. microphylla, syn. *S. grahamii.* Moderately bushy, evergreen shrub or shrubby perennial bearing triangular-ovate to elliptic, softly hairy or hairless, mid- to deep green leaves, ½–1½in (1.5–4cm) long, with rounded teeth. From late summer to autumn, paired or whorled, deep crimson or, less commonly, magenta, pink, or purple flowers, 1in (2.5cm) long, are produced in terminal racemes. ↕ 3–4ft (90–120cm), ↔ 24–39in (60–100cm). Arizona, New Mexico, Mexico. ❀ (min. 41°F/5°C). **var. *neurepia*** has pale green leaves, 1¼–2in (3.5–5cm) long, and produces cherry-red flowers, to 1¼in (3cm) long, mainly in autumn. **'Ruth Stungo'** has white-splashed leaves. **var. *wislizenii*,** syn. *S. lemmonii*, is more compact, with triangular leaves, to 1¼in (3cm) long, and dense spikes of vermilion or magenta flowers; ↕↔ 3ft (1m).
S. nemorosa. Erect, many-branched perennial with ovate or lance-shaped to oblong, notched, wrinkled, mid-green leaves, to 4in (10cm) long. From summer to autumn, bears violet to purple, or white to pink flowers, to ½in (1.5cm) long, with violet to purple bracts, in dense, terminal racemes. ↕ to 3ft (1m), ↔ 24in (60cm). Europe to C. Asia. Zone 5. **'East Friesland'** see 'Ostfriesland'. **'Lubecca'**, syn. *S. x superba* 'Lubecca', is dwarf and clump-forming, with grayish green leaves. From midsummer to early autumn, bears violet flowers with reddish purple bracts that persist long after the flowers fall; ↕↔ 18in (45cm). **'Ostfriesland'**, syn. 'East Friesland', has deep blue-violet flowers; ↕ 18in (45cm).
S. officinalis (Common sage, Purple sage). Subshrubby, erect, hairy, evergreen perennial with oblong-ovate,

Salvia officinalis 'Tricolor'

Salvia patens 'Cambridge Blue'

entire, gray-green-woolly, aromatic leaves, to 3in (8cm) long. Branched stems bear terminal or axillary raceme of lilac-blue flowers, ½in (1.5cm) lon in early and midsummer. A popular culinary herb. ↕ to 32in (80cm), ↔ 3ft (1m). Mediterranean, N. Africa. Zone 5b. **'Aurea'** is more compact, with oblong yellow leaves, and bears small spikes of purplish blue flowers i early summer; ↕ 12in (30cm), ↔ 18in (45cm); Zone 6. **'Berggarten'** is compact in habit, with distinctly mor rounded leaves and purple flowers; ↕ 24in (60cm). **'Icterina'** has variegate yellow and green leaves; Zone 6. **'Purpurascens'** has red-purple young leaves; Zone 6. **'Tricolor'** ■ bears gra green leaves, zoned cream and pink to purple; Zone 6.
S. patens (Gentian sage). Tuberous perennial with erect, branched stems bearing ovate, broadly ovate to triangular, or pentagonal, toothed, hairy, mid-green leaves, to 8in (20cm) long, with spear-shaped bases. From midsummer to midautumn, produces few-flowered, loose, sometimes branched, terminal racemes of paired, deep blue flowers, 2in (5cm) long, wit wide-open mouths. ↕ 18–24in (45–60cm), ↔ 18in (45cm). Mexico. Zone 8. **'Cambridge Blue'** ■ produc pale blue flowers.
S. pratensis (Meadow clary). Clump-forming, woody-based perennial with ovate, blunt-tipped, toothed, wrinkled mid-green basal leaves, to 6in (15cm) long, and few smaller stem leaves. In early and midsummer, erect, branched or unbranched, slightly sticky-hairy

Salvia pratensis Haematodes Group

Salvia 'Purple Majesty'

Salvia x *sylvestris* 'Mainacht'

Salvia uliginosa

stems bear terminal spikes of violet, rarely pink or white flowers, ¾–1¼in (2–3cm) long. ↕ to 36in (90cm), ↔ 12in (30cm). Europe, Morocco. Zone 4. Cultivars of **Haematodes Group** ▣ syn. *S. haematodes*, are short-lived plants with basal rosettes of large, broadly ovate, wavy-margined, dark green leaves, to 8in (20cm) long. Branched, reddish brown stems bear loose, spreading panicles of bluish violet flowers, with hairy upper lips and paler throats; Greece. **'Mittsommer'** produces loose spikes of sky-blue flowers with long, arched upper lips and darker blue calyces and bracts, throughout summer.
***S.* 'Purple Majesty'** ▣ Upright perennial with ovate to oblong, mid-green leaves, to 5in (13cm) long. Spikes of royal purple flowers, 2in (5cm) across, are produced in summer. ↕ to 24in (60cm), ↔ 12in (30cm). Zone 8.
S. rutilans see *S. elegans* 'Scarlet Pineapple'.
S. sclarea (Clary sage). Erect, many-branched, glandular-hairy perennial or biennial with ovate to oblong, notched to irregularly toothed, wrinkled, mid-green leaves, to 9in (23cm) long, with heart-shaped or perfoliate bases. From spring to summer, bears many-flowered, terminal panicles or racemes of cream and lilac to pink or blue flowers, to 1¼in (3cm) long, with prominent lilac bracts. ↕ to 3ft (1m), ↔ 12in (30cm). Europe to C. Asia. Zone 5. **var. *turkestanica*** ▣ has pink stems, and produces spikes of pink-flecked white flowers.
S. splendens (Scarlet sage). Erect, bushy perennial, usually grown as an annual, with oval, pointed, toothed, slightly hairy, pale to dark green leaves, to 3in (8cm) long. Long-tubed, bright red flowers, ½–2in (1.5–5cm) long, enclosed in red bracts, are borne in dense, terminal spikes from summer to autumn. ↕ to 16in (40cm), ↔ 9–14in (23–35cm). Brazil. Most modern selections are compact. Grow red cultivars in full sun; pastel shades need shade from hot sun. ❀ (min. 35°F/2°C). **'Blaze of Fire'**, syn. 'Fireball', has pale green leaves and red flowers; ↕ 12–16in (30–40cm). **'Bonfire'** is free-flowering and late-blooming; ↕ 24in (60cm). **'Carabiniere Scarlet'** has rich, deep green leaves and sturdy red flower spikes; ↕ 12–14in (30–35cm). **'Fireball'** see 'Blaze of Fire'. Cultivars of **Firecracker Series** are compact and dwarf, and continuously bloom in bicolors and shades of blue, red, pink, orange, and white; ↕↔ 10–12in (25–30cm). **'Flare'** has dark green leaves and dense, fire-red flower spikes; ↕ 20in (50cm). **'Rambo'** is very tall-growing, vigorous, and bushy, with dark green leaves and scarlet flowers; ↕ to 24in (60cm). **'Red Hot Sally'** bears early, stocky spikes with red flowers, continuing until frost; ↕ 10in (25cm). **'Red Pillar'** has dense spikes, 7–8in (18-20cm) long, of bright scarlet-red flowers in early and midsummer; ↕ 16–18in (40–45cm). **'Scarlet Queen'** bears bright scarlet flowers in early summer; ↕ 10in (25cm). **Sizzler Series** ▣ cultivars bear flowers in bright shades of cerise-red, lavender-blue, salmon-pink, purple, scarlet, or white. They are early-flowering, and available as single colors; ↕ 10–12in (25–30cm). **'St. John's Fire'** is early-blooming; ↕ 12in (30cm).
S.* x *superba (*S. nemorosa* x *S.* x *sylvestris*). Clump-forming, erect, branched perennial with lance-shaped to oblong, scalloped, mid-green leaves, to 4in (10cm) long, slightly hairy beneath; the basal leaves are stalked, the stem leaves stalkless and sometimes stem-clasping. From midsummer to early autumn, bears slender, terminal racemes of bright violet or purple flowers, to ½in (1.5cm) long. ↕ 26–36in (60–90m), ↔ 18–24in (45–60cm). Garden origin. Zone 5. **'Lubecca'** see *S. nemorosa* 'Lubecca'.
S.* x *sylvestris (*S. nemorosa* x *S. pratensis*) syn. *S. deserta*. Clump-forming, erect, branched perennial bearing oblong-lance-shaped, scalloped, wrinkled, softly hairy, mid-green leaves, to 3in (8cm) long. Bears pinkish violet flowers, ½in (1.5cm) long, in dense, terminal racemes in early and midsummer. ↕ 32in (80cm), ↔ 12in (30cm). Garden origin. Zone 4. **'Blauhügel'**, syn. 'Blue Mound', produces pure blue flowers; ↕ 20in (50cm), ↔ 18in (45cm). **'Blaukönigin'**, syn. 'Blue Queen', produces rich blue-violet flowers; ↕ 28in (70cm), ↔ 18in (45cm). **'Blue Mound'** see 'Blauhügel'. **'Blue Queen'** see 'Blaukönigin'. **'Mainacht'** ▣ syn. 'May Night', bears large, indigo-blue flowers, ¾in (2cm) long; ↕ 28in (70cm), ↔ 18in (45cm). **'May Night'** see 'Mainacht'. **'Rose Queen'** has rose-pink flowers and gray-tinted leaves; ↕ 30in (75cm).
S. triloba see *S. fruticosa*.
S. uliginosa ▣ (Bog sage). Clump-forming, moisture-loving, rhizomatous perennial with oblong-lance-shaped, deeply toothed, mid-green leaves, to 3in (8cm) long; they become progressively smaller up the slender, branching stems. From late summer to midautumn, bears short, terminal racemes of clear blue flowers, ¾in (2cm) long. Needs moist soil and full sun. ↕ to 6ft (2m), ↔ 36in (90cm). Brazil, Uruguay, Argentina. Zone 7.

Salvia sclarea var. *turkestanica*

Salvia splendens Sizzler Series

Salvia vanhouttii

S. vanhouttii ■ Mound-forming perennial with diamond-shaped, mid-green leaves, 3in (8cm) long. Bears loose terminal spikes of short-lived, deep orange-red flowers, to 1½in (4cm) long, with burgundy calyces, from late summer to autumn. ↕↔ to 3½ft (1.1m). Brazil. ❄ (min. 41°F/5°C)
S. verticillata. Erect herbaceous perennial with opposite, ovate or elliptic to oblong, softly glandular-hairy, mid-green leaves, to 5in (13cm) long, pinnatifid with a larger terminal lobe. In summer, produces branched racemes of violet to lilac-blue, rarely white flowers, ⅜in (8mm) long, in whorls of 20–40 blooms. ↕ to 36in (90cm), ↔ to 18in (45cm). Europe to W. Asia. Zone 7. **'Purple Rain'** has gray-purple flowers; ↕ 14–20in (35–50cm).
S. viridis, syn. *S. horminum* (Annual clary sage). Erect, bushy annual with ovate to oblong, notched, hairy, mid-green leaves, 2in (5cm) long. In summer, bears terminal spikes of insignificant, whorled, pink to pale purple flowers, ⅜–½in (8–15mm) long, each whorl enclosed in 2 showy, pink, purple, or white bracts, to 1½in (4cm) long, with darker veins. Grow as a cut or dried flower for the very long-lasting bracts. ↕ 18–20in (45–50cm), ↔ 9in (23cm). Mediterranean. **'Claryssa'** ■ is compact and very well-branched, with bracts in rose-pink, blue, purple, or white; also available as single colors; ↕ to 16in (40cm). **'Oxford Blue'** has violet-blue bracts; ↕ 12in (30cm). **'Pink Sundae'** has bright carmine-pink bracts. **'White Swan'** has white bracts with green veins; ↕ 12in (30cm).

Salvia viridis 'Claryssa'

Salvinia natans

SALVINIA

SALVINIACEAE

Genus of 10 species of aquatic annual ferns found in stagnant or slow-moving water, with a wide tropical and subtropical distribution, especially in tropical Africa and Central and South America. They are also naturalized in some warm-temperate areas and have been declared noxious weeds in some areas. Floating, rootless plants, they have very slender, irregularly branched stems, and bear mostly rounded to ovate leaves in pairs, with a third, finely dissected, root-like, submerged leaf. They are useful for an aquarium, where fish fry can hide among the submerged leaves. In tropical areas, grow in an outdoor pool. Where not hardy, grow in an outdoor pool during summer, then lift and store in winter.
• **CULTIVATION** In an aquarium, grow in nutrient-rich water at 64–75°F (18–24°C) in full light. Very invasive, so thin regularly. Outdoors, float on the surface of a still-water pool in full sun. Where not hardy, lift before the first frosts and store in shallow trays of sandy loam covered with 1–2in (2.5–5cm) of water, in a cool or temperate greenhouse. See also pp.52–53.
• **PROPAGATION** Separate in summer.
• **PESTS AND DISEASES** Infrequent.

S. auriculata. Floating aquatic fern with whorls of 3 leaves, each consisting of an opposite pair of oval to ovate floating leaves, 1¼–1½in (3–4cm) long, covered with fine hairs, and one root-like submerged leaf adapted to a root function. ↔ indefinite. Central and South America. ❄ (min. 45°F/7°C)
S. natans ■ Floating aquatic fern bearing paired, elliptic, pale green leaves, to ½in (1.5cm) long, with shiny brown hairs beneath, and a submerged, root-like frond, ¾–3in (2–8cm) long. ↔ indefinite. S. Europe, N. Africa, Asia. ❄ (min. 45°F/7°C)

Sambucus nigra 'Guincho Purple'

SAMBUCUS

Elder

CAPRIFOLIACEAE

Genus of about 25 species of herbaceous perennials and deciduous shrubs and trees from woodland and thickets in temperate and subtropical regions of Eurasia, N. and tropical E. Africa, Australia, and North and South America. They are cultivated for their foliage, flowers, and fruits. They bear opposite, pinnate leaves and dense, flat-topped umbels or panicles of small, white to ivory flowers, followed by red, black, or white fruits. Elders are suitable for a mixed or shrub border, or a wild garden. Those with colored leaves are effective as free-standing specimens. All parts may cause severe discomfort if ingested, although fruits are safe when cooked; contact with the leaves may irritate skin.
• **CULTIVATION** Grow in moderately fertile, humus-rich, moist but well-drained soil in full sun or partial shade; those with colored leaves color well in sun, but retain color best in dappled shade. Pruning group 7, for those grown for their colored or cut leaves; group 1 for the rest. Elders tolerate hard pruning as necessary to restrict size.
• **PROPAGATION** Sow seed in containers in an open frame in autumn. Take hardwood cuttings in winter, or greenwood cuttings in early summer.
• **PESTS AND DISEASES** Powdery mildew, canker and dieback, rust, virus diseases, fungal leaf spots, and borers occur.

S. canadensis (American elder). Upright, stoloniferous shrub with thick shoots and pinnate leaves, to 12in (30cm) long, each composed of 9 or more elliptic to lance-shaped, toothed, light green leaflets. In midsummer, bears small white flowers in flattened panicles, to 8in (20cm) across, followed by spherical, purple-black fruit, to ¼in (6mm) across. ↕↔ 12ft (4m). North America. Zone 3. **'Aurea'** has golden yellow foliage and red fruit.
S. nigra (Black elder, Elderberry, European elder). Upright, bushy shrub with thick shoots. Pinnate leaves, to 10in (25cm) long, each have 5 ovate, toothed mid-green leaflets. Bears musk-scented white flowers in flattened panicles, to 8in (20cm) across, in early summer, followed by spherical, glossy black fruit, to ⅜in (8mm) across. ↕↔ 20ft (6m). Europe, N. Africa, S.W. Asia. Zone 4. **'Aurea'** has golden yellow leaves borne on pink-flushed leaf stalks. **'Aureomarginata'** bears yellow-margined, dark green leaves. **'Guincho Purple'** ■ has dark green leaves, turning blackish purple then red in autumn, and pink-tinged flowers with purple stalks. **'Laciniata'**, syn. f. *laciniata*, has irregularly and finely cut leaflets.
S. racemosa (European red elder). Bushy shrub with arching shoots and pinnate leaves, to 9in (23cm) long, each with usually 5 oval or ovate, toothed, dark green leaflets. In midspring, bears small, creamy yellow flowers in conical panicles, 3in (8cm) long, followed in summer by spherical, glossy red fruit, ⅛in (3mm) across.

Sambucus racemosa 'Plumosa Aurea'

S

↔ 10ft (3m). Europe, Russia W. Siberia). Zone 3. **'Plumosa'** has ›urple new growth and finely cut ›eaflets. **'Plumosa Aurea'** ■ has finely ›ut leaflets, bronze when young, ›urning golden yellow. Foliage may ›urn in hot sun. **'Sutherland Gold'** is ›imilar to 'Plumosa Aurea', but less ›usceptible to sun scorch.

SANCHEZIA

ACANTHACEAE

Genus of about 20 species of soft-stemmed evergreen shrubs and shrubby perennials from tropical rainforest in Central and South America. They have opposite pairs of simple, often entire leaves, and bear terminal or axillary spikes or panicles of tubular, showy, yellow, orange, red, or purple flowers, each with 5 small, rounded lobes, often with colored bracts. Where temperatures drop below 59°F (15°C), grow in a warm greenhouse or conservatory, or as houseplants. In tropical areas, grow in a shrub border.

• **CULTIVATION** Under glass, grow in soil-based potting mix in bright filtered or full light, with shade from hot sun. In growth, water freely and apply a balanced liquid fertilizer every 2 or 3 weeks; water sparingly in winter. Outdoors, grow in moderately fertile, humus-rich, moist but well-drained soil, in full sun with some midday shade, or in light, dappled shade. Pruning group 3; plants under glass may need restrictive pruning in late winter.

• **PROPAGATION** Root softwood cuttings in spring or semi-ripe cuttings in summer, both with gentle bottom heat.

• **PESTS AND DISEASES** Spider mites and scale insects may be problems.

S. glaucophylla see *S. speciosa.*
S. nobilis see *S. speciosa.*
S. speciosa ■ syn. *S. glaucophylla, S. nobilis, S. spectabilis.* Moderately bushy shrub with sparsely branched, sturdy, sometimes obscurely angled, smooth, bright green stems and ovate-elliptic to oblong-lance-shaped, glossy, dark green leaves, 6–12in (15–30cm) long, with yellow-, ivory-, or white-banded midribs and main veins. In summer, bears terminal spikes of 5–10 yellow flowers, 1½–2in (4–5cm) long, with red bracts. ↕4–7ft (1.2–2.2m), ↔ 3–5ft (0.9–1.5m). Ecuador, Peru. ❀ (min. 55–59°F/13–15°C)
S. spectabilis see *S. speciosa.*

Sanchezia speciosa

Sandersonia aurantiaca

SANDERSONIA

LILIACEAE

Genus of one species of tuberous, perennial climber from rocky areas and light woodland in South Africa. It has alternate leaves, often tipped with tendrils, and solitary flowers. Where not hardy, grow in a temperate greenhouse. In frost-free areas, grow in a herbaceous border or among low shrubs.

• **CULTIVATION** Under glass, plant tubers 3–4in (7–10cm) deep in late winter or early spring, in 4 parts soil-based potting mix and 1 part grit, in full light with some midday shade. In growth, water freely and apply a balanced liquid fertilizer every 4 weeks; dry off as leaves fade and keep dry while dormant. Stems need support. Outdoors, grow in moderately fertile to humus-rich, well-drained soil in full sun. Protect from excessive winter moisture. Where not hardy, lift tubers in autumn and store dry and frost-free.

• **PROPAGATION** Sow seed at 64–75°F (18–24°C) as soon as ripe. Divide in autumn or winter.

• **PESTS AND DISEASES** Infrequent.

S. aurantiaca ■ Perennial climber with slender stems bearing scattered, lance-shaped, mid-green leaves, to 4in (10cm) long, some of which are tipped with tendrils. In summer, bears pendent, urn-shaped, bright orange flowers, 1in (2.5cm) long, on downcurved stalks, ¾–1¼in (2–3cm) long, from the upper leaf axils. ↕ to 30in (75cm), PD4in (10cm). South Africa. ❀ (min. 41°F/5°C)

SANGUINARIA

Bloodroot, Red puccoon

PAPAVERACEAE

Genus of one species of rhizomatous perennial occurring in moist woodland in E. North America. It is cultivated for its cup-shaped, white or pink-tinted flowers, which emerge from between the vertically folded leaves as they unfurl, in spring. *S. canadensis* is excellent for growing in a shaded site in a rock garden or wild or woodland garden. The rhizomes exude red sap when cut, giving rise to the common name, bloodroot.

• **CULTIVATION** Grow in moderately fertile, humus-rich, moist but well-drained soil in deep or partial shade. Thrives in part-day sun where soils remain reliably moist.

Sanguinaria canadensis

• **PROPAGATION** Sow seed in containers in a cold frame in autumn, or divide rhizomes immediately after flowering.

• **PESTS AND DISEASES** *Cercospora* leaf spot (and others) may occur.

S. canadensis ■ Rhizomatous perennial producing variably lobed, heart- to kidney-shaped, scalloped, bluish gray-green leaves, 6–12in (15–30cm) across when fully expanded, disappearing by late summer. Solitary, cup-shaped, white, occasionally pink-tinted flowers, to 3in (8cm) across, emerge in spring as the leaves unfold. ↕ 6in (15cm), ↔ 12in (30cm) or more. E. North America. Zone 4. **'Flore Pleno'**, syn. 'Multiplex', 'Plena', produces many-petaled, double white flowers, which are longer-lasting than those of the species. **'Multiplex'** see 'Flore Pleno'. **'Plena'** see 'Flore Pleno'.

SANGUISORBA

Burnet

ROSACEAE

Genus of approximately 18 species of rhizomatous perennials, most occurring in damp meadows, with a few from dry, grassy or rocky sites, in temperate and cooler regions of the N. hemisphere. They produce alternate, pinnate leaves, with mostly oblong to elliptic, toothed, neatly veined leaflets, which in some species are glaucous. The leafy, wiry stems bear dense or loose, bottlebrush-like, terminal spikes of small, fluffy flowers, with red, pink, white, or greenish white sepals and prominent stamens, but no petals. Burnets are suitable for growing in a herbaceous or mixed border, and for naturalizing in a damp meadow garden or by water. Many species provide unusual flowers and foliage for cutting.

• **CULTIVATION** Grow in any moderately fertile, moist but well-drained soil that does not dry out, in full sun or partial shade. Taller species usually require support. *S. canadensis* prefers a waterside site, but may become invasive.

• **PROPAGATION** Sow seed in containers in a cold frame in spring or autumn. Divide in spring or autumn.

• **PESTS AND DISEASES** *Cercospora* leaf spot (and others) may occur.

S. canadensis ■ (Canadian burnet). Spreading, clump-forming, rhizomatous perennial with upright, simple or branched stems and pinnate, hairy leaves, to 10in (25cm) long, each composed of 7–17 oblong-lance-shaped to ovate leaflets. From midsummer to midautumn, long "cones" of green buds open from the bottom up, to form bottlebrush-like spikes, to 8in (20cm) long, of small, fluffy white flowers. ↕ to 6ft (2m), ↔ 3ft (1m). N.E. North America. Zone 3.
S. hakusanensis. Upright, hairless, rhizomatous perennial with pinnate basal leaves, to 2½in (6cm) long, each with 9–13 oblong to ovate-oblong, coarsely toothed leaflets. In summer, bears few, bottlebrush-like, nodding spikes, to 4in (10cm) long, of deep rose-purple flowers. ↕ to 32in (80cm), ↔ to 24in (60cm). Japan, Korea. Zone 7.
S. minor (Salad burnet). Rhizomatous, clump-forming perennial with upright stems bearing pinnate leaves up to 6in (15cm) long, divided into 4–12 pairs of rounded-elliptic, toothed leaflets ¾in (2cm) long. Leaves used in salads for their cucumber flavor. Produces tiny purplish flowers on dense, oblong spikes to 1in (2.5cm) from late spring to late summer. ↕↔ 12–30in (30–90cm). S.W. and C. Europe, N. Africa, Canary Islands, W. and C. Asia. Zone 6.
S. officinalis (Greater burnet). Clump-forming, rhizomatous perennial producing pinnate basal leaves, 20in (50cm) long, each with 7–25 oblong-elliptic leaflets; leaves on the erect, branching, often red stems are smaller. The small, red-brown to maroon flowers are borne in erect, very short, dense, ovoid spikes, ¾–1¼in (1.5–3cm) long, from early summer to midautumn. ↕ to 4ft (1.2m), ↔ 24in (60cm). Europe, N. and W. Asia, North America. Zone 4.
S. tenuifolia. Upright, rhizomatous perennial with pinnate, narrow-linear leaves, 5–20in (13–50cm) long, each with 13–21 deeply toothed, mid-green leaflets. In summer, bears bottlebrush-like spikes, to 3in (8cm) long, of white to purple flowers. ↕ to 4ft (1.2m), ↔ 24in (60cm). China, Japan. Zone 5.

Sanguisorba canadensis

SANSEVIERIA

AGAVACEAE

Genus of about 60 species of usually stemless, xerophytic, rhizomatous, evergreen perennials from dry, rocky habitats in tropical and subtropical Africa, Madagascar, India, and Indonesia. They are mainly grown for their stiff, fleshy, linear to broadly ovate, upright or more or less spreading leaves, which may be flat, concave, or cylindrical; these are produced in clumps or squat rosettes from spreading, underground or partially exposed rhizomes. Mature plants bear racemes or panicles of fragrant, nectar-rich, tubular, 6-lobed flowers in spring. Where not hardy, grow in a warm greenhouse or conservatory, or use as houseplants. In warmer areas, grow in a desert garden, in containers on a patio, or in a small courtyard garden. Many tolerate neglect.

• **CULTIVATION** Under glass, grow in 2 parts soil-based potting mix and 1 part coarse grit, in bright filtered light or indirect light. When in growth, water moderately and apply a half-strength balanced liquid fertilizer monthly; water sparingly in winter. Pot on only when pot-bound; leaf growth may stop if leaf-tips are damaged. Outdoors, grow in poor to moderately fertile, neutral to slightly alkaline, gritty soil in full sun. Protect from excessive winter moisture.

• **PROPAGATION** Remove suckers, or divide, in spring. Root leaf sections from spring to autumn. Offspring from variegated cultivars will lack variegation if raised from leaf cuttings.

• **PESTS AND DISEASES** Vine weevil grubs may be a problem. Mealybugs and spider mites can occur.

S. cylindrica ▣ Very slow-growing, woody, rhizomatous perennial with 2-ranked, erect, cylindrical, fleshy, dark green leaves, to 3ft (1m) or more long, with lighter crossbands. Intermittently bears spike-like racemes, 14–30in (35–75cm) long, of tubular, pink or white flowers, ½–1in (1.5–2.5cm) long, the lobes with margins rolled outward. ↕ to 5ft (1.5m), ↔ 24in (60cm). Angola. ❀ (min. 55°F/13°C)

S. trifasciata (Mother-in-law's tongue, Snake plant). Erect, rhizomatous perennial with pointed, lance-shaped, fleshy leaves, to 4ft (1.2m) or more long, horizontally marbled and banded dark and light green. Bears racemes, 12–30in

Sansevieria cylindrica

Sansevieria trifasciata 'Golden Hahnii'

(30–75cm) long, of tubular, green or greenish white flowers, ¼–½in (6–15mm) long, intermittently. Dwarf cultivars are suitable for growing in bowls and pans. ↕ 4ft (1.2m), ↔ 20in (50cm). W. tropical Africa. ❀ (min. 55°F/13°C). **'Bantel's Sensation'** has variable, slender, slightly spiraled, dark green leaves, to 24in (60cm) long, with intermittent, vertical cream stripes. **'Golden Hahnii'** ▣ forms dwarf rosettes of broad leaves, to 8in (20cm) long, with bold, golden yellow, vertical stripes, particularly at the margins; rarely flowers; ↕↔ 5in (13cm). **'Hahnii'** (Bird's nest) is dwarf, with rosettes of broad, mid-green leaves, 10in (25cm) long, crossbanded with darker green; rarely flowers; ↕ to 6in (15cm), ↔ 7in (18cm). **'Hoop's Pride'** is compact in habit, with fleshy, gray-flecked, deep green leaves. **'Laurentii'** ▣ has upright leaves, 18in (45cm) long, horizontally marbled mid- and dark green, with broad yellow margins; ↕ 3–4ft (1–1.2m). **'Silbersee'** has silver leaves with faint green bands. **'Silver Hahnii'** is dwarf, with rosettes of broad, dark green leaves, to 10in (25cm) long, banded silver; flowers are rarely borne; ↕↔ 5in (13cm).

Sansevieria trifasciata 'Laurentii'

SANTOLINA

ASTERACEAE

Genus of 18 species of evergreen shrubs occurring in dry, rocky habitats in the Mediterranean. They have alternate, entire, pinnatisect, or pinnate, aromatic leaves, and tiny flowers borne in long-stemmed, dense, button-like heads, surrounded by several rows of involucral bracts. Each floret is tubular and yellow or white; there are no ray florets. They are grown mainly for their ornamental and aromatic foliage, and are suitable for a mixed or shrub border, or a rock garden, or as an edging or low hedge.

• **CULTIVATION** Grow in poor to moderately fertile, well-drained soil in full sun. Pruning group 10, in spring; may be cut back severely to maintain compactness.

• **PROPAGATION** Sow seed in containers in a cold frame in autumn or spring. Root semi-ripe cuttings with bottom heat in late summer.

• **PESTS AND DISEASES** Infrequent.

S. chamaecyparissus, syn. *S. incana* (Lavender cotton). Compact, rounded shrub producing white-woolly young shoots, densely covered with slender, narrowly oblong, toothed to pinnatisect, gray-white leaves, to 1½in (4cm) long, with very fine, toothed divisions. Bright yellow flowerheads, to ½in (1cm) across, are borne on slender stems in mid- and late summer. ↕ 20in (50cm), ↔ 3ft (1m). W. and C. Mediterranean. Zone 7. **'Lambrook Silver'** has silver-gray leaves. **'Lemon Queen'** ▣ is compact, with lemon-yellow flowerheads; ↕↔ 24in (60cm). **'Pretty Carol'** is compact, with soft gray foliage; ↕↔ 16in (40cm). **subsp. *tomentosa*** see *S. pinnata*. **'Weston'** is very dwarf, with very silvery foliage; ↕ 6in (15cm), ↔ 8in (20cm).

S. incana see *S. chamaecyparissus*.

S. neapolitana see *S. pinnata* subsp. *neapolitana*.

S. pinnata, syn. *S. chamaecyparissus* subsp. *tomentosa*. Rounded, bushy shrub with slender, pinnate, hairless, slightly aromatic, mid-green leaves, to 1½in (4cm) long, with many cylindrical leaflets. Creamy white flowerheads, ¾in (2cm) across, are borne in midsummer. ↕ 30in (75cm), ↔ 3ft (1m). Italy. ❀ (min. 41°F/5°C). Represented in gardens mainly by the following subspecies and its forms. **subsp. *neapolitana***, syn. *S. neapolitana*, *S. tomentosa*, has aromatic, gray-green foliage and bright yellow flowerheads. **subsp. *neapolitana* 'Edward Bowles'** has gray-green foliage and creamy white flowerheads. **subsp. *neapolitana* 'Sulphurea'** has gray-green foliage and primrose-yellow flowerheads.

S. rosmarinifolia, syn. *S. virens*, *S. viridis*. Dense, rounded, bushy shrub with slender, finely cut, aromatic, bright green leaves, to 2in (5cm) long. Bright yellow flowerheads, ¾in (2cm) across, are produced at the end of slender shoots in midsummer. ↕ 24in (60cm), ↔ 3ft (1m). S.W. Europe. Zone 7. **'Primrose Gem'** has pale yellow flowerheads.

S. tomentosa see *S. pinnata* subsp. *neapolitana*.

S. virens see *S. rosmarinifolia*.

S. viridis see *S. rosmarinifolia*.

Santolina chamaecyparissus 'Lemon Queen'

Sanvitalia procumbens

SANVITALIA

Creeping zinnia

ASTERACEAE

Genus of 7 species of creeping and spreading annuals and perennials from rocky slopes and dry river washes in S.W. US and Mexico. They have opposite, simple, oval leaves, and bear daisy-like, bright yellow, orange, or white flowerheads. Creeping zinnias provide colorful groundcover in an annual or herbaceous border, raised bed, or rock garden, or at the edge of a path. They are also suitable for a trough, or for containers on a patio. Modern cultivars are good for hanging baskets.

• **CULTIVATION** Grow in moderately fertile, humus-rich, well-drained soil in full sun.
• **PROPAGATION** Sow seed *in situ* in autumn or spring. Delay thinning autumn-sown seedlings until spring.
• **PESTS AND DISEASES** Infrequent.

S. procumbens ■ (Creeping zinnia). Prostrate, mat-forming annual with pointed, oval, mid-green leaves, to 2½in (6cm) long. Bears single, black-centered, bright yellow flowerheads, to ¾in (2cm) across, over a long period from early summer to early autumn. ↕ to 8in (20cm), ↔ to 18in (45cm). Mexico. **'Gold Braid'** is compact in habit, producing golden yellow flowerheads; ↕ 2–4in (5–10cm), ↔ 14in (35cm). **'Golden Carpet'** is dwarf, producing dark green leaves and small, lemon-yellow flowerheads; ↕ to 4in (10cm).

Sanvitalia procumbens 'Mandarin Orange'

'Mandarin Orange' ■ is compact, with semi-double orange flowerheads; ↕ to 4in (10cm), ↔ 14in (35cm). **'Yellow Carpet'** is dwarf, with dark green leaves and single, lemon-yellow flowerheads with black centers; ↕ to 4in (10cm).

SAPINDUS

SAPINDACEAE

Genus of 13 species of deciduous or evergreen trees, shrubs, and climbers, widely distributed in woodland and on riverbanks in warm-temperate, subtropical, and tropical regions. They are cultivated for their alternate, simple or pinnate leaves; axillary or terminal racemes or panicles of small, 4- or 5-petaled flowers; and fleshy, spherical fruits. They grow best in a continental climate, with long, hot summers, where they are effective shade trees. Useful for gardens with poor, dry soil.

• **CULTIVATION** Grow in poor to moderately fertile, well-drained soil in full sun, sheltered from cold winds. Pruning group 1.
• **PROPAGATION** Sow seed of hardy species in containers in a cold frame in spring, after cold stratification for 8 weeks. Sow seed of tender species at 61–64°F (16–18°C) in spring.
• **PESTS AND DISEASES** Infrequent.

S. drummondii (Western soapberry). Spreading, deciduous tree producing pinnate leaves, to 16in (40cm) long, with up to 18 lance-shaped, glossy, mid-green leaflets, turning golden yellow in autumn. Small, creamy white flowers are borne in conical, terminal panicles, to 10in (25cm) long, in late spring and early summer; they are followed by spherical, orange-yellow fruit, ½in (1cm) across. ↕ 50ft (15m), ↔ 30ft (10m). S. US, N. Mexico. Zone 8.

SAPIUM

Tallow tree

EUPHORBIACEAE

Genus of over 100 species of monoecious, deciduous trees and shrubs from tropical and subtropical regions. They are grown as shade trees, especially *S. sebiferum*. Commercially, they are grown for their milky sap, used in the production of candles and soap. The leaves are alternate, hairless, and mid-green. The petalless flowers are borne in terminal spikes, with the males in threes beneath the bracts and the females singly at the top of the spikes. Grow at the back of a shrub border or in a lawn as a specimen. Where not hardy, grow in large containers in a cool greenhouse.

• **CULTIVATION** Under glass, grow in soil-based potting mix in full light. When in growth, water freely and apply a balanced liquid fertilizer monthly; water sparingly in winter. Outdoors, grow in fertile, well-drained soil in full sun. They resent transplanting. Pruning group 1.
• **PROPAGATION** Sow seed *in situ* in spring or take semi-ripe cuttings in summer. Propagate selected forms by grafting onto seedling rootstocks.
• **PESTS AND DISEASES** Infrequent.

S. japonicum. Small, hairless, deciduous tree with broadly ovate, short-pointed, dark green leaves, 3–5in (8–13cm) long, blue-green beneath and turning carmine in autumn. Tiny, green-yellow flowers are borne in catkin-like spikes, 2–4in (5–10cm) long, in spring, followed by pendent, flat, cylindrical, brown-spotted, yellow fruit, to ⅜in (8mm) across. ↕ to 25ft (8m), ↔ 10ft (3m). China, Korea, Japan. ❀ (min. 35°F/2°C)

S. sebiferum (Chinese tallow tree, Vegetable tallow tree). Poplar-like tree with ovate-diamond-shaped, long-pointed, mid-green leaves, to 3in (8cm) long, with broadly wedge-shaped or truncated bases and turning yellow-red in autumn. Terminal spikes, 2–4in (5–10cm) long, of tiny, yellow-green flowers are borne in spring, followed by 3-lobed, brown fruit, ½in (1.5cm) across, which open to reveal white-waxy seeds. ↕ to 40ft (12m), ↔ 15–20ft (5–6m). China, Japan. ❀ (min. 35°F/2°C)

SAPONARIA

Soapwort

CARYOPHYLLACEAE

Genus of about 20 species of annuals and perennials, some with a woody rootstock, mostly from meadows or rocky areas in the mountains of Europe and S.W. Asia. Closely related to *Lychnis* and *Silene*, they differ in having flowers with 2 styles rather than 3 or 5. They have opposite, entire, variably shaped, narrow leaves and abundant flat, 5-petaled, clawed flowers, usually in shades of pink, borne in loose or dense heads, panicles, or cymes. The genus includes compact plants, suitable for a rock garden, trough, or raised bed, and taller, spreading plants, useful for a herbaceous or mixed border.

• **CULTIVATION** Grow border perennials in moderately fertile, well-drained, neutral to slightly alkaline soil in full sun. More compact species, such as *S. caespitosa*, require gritty, sharply drained soil. Cut *S. ocymoides* back hard after flowering, to maintain compactness.
• **PROPAGATION** Sow seed in containers in an open frame in autumn or spring. Divide border perennials in autumn or spring. Root softwood cuttings in spring or summer.
• **PESTS AND DISEASES** May be damaged by slugs and snails.

***S.* 'Bressingham'**, syn. *S.* 'Bressingham Hybrid'. Loose, mat-forming perennial with hairy, narrowly ovate-lance-shaped,

Saponaria caespitosa

Saponaria ocymoides

mid-green leaves, to ½in (1.5cm) long. Bears many short-stemmed, panicle-like cymes of brilliant deep pink flowers, to ½in (1cm) across, in summer. Ideal for a trough or rock garden. ↕ 3in (8cm), ↔ 12in (30cm). Zone 6.

***S.* 'Bressingham Hybrid'** see *S.* 'Bressingham'.

S. caespitosa ■ Compact, densely tufted, mat-forming perennial with a woody rootstock and narrowly lance-shaped, mid-green leaves, ¼in (6mm) long. Few-flowered heads of pink to purple flowers, ½in (1cm) across, are borne just above the leaves in summer. ↕↔ 6in (15cm). Pyrenees. Zone 4.

S. × lempergii (*S. cypria* × *S. haussknechtii*). Procumbent perennial with ascending, well-branched stems and lance-shaped, softly hairy, dark green leaves, to ½in (1.5cm) long. Bears axillary, bright carmine-pink flowers, 1in (2.5cm) across, with long, reddish pink calyces, in late summer and early autumn. ↕ 12in (30cm), ↔ 12–18in (30–45cm). Zone 5. **'Max Frei'** bears early, pale pink flowers.

S. ocymoides ■ (Rock soapwort). Spreading, mat-forming, sometimes weakly climbing perennial with ovate-lance-shaped, hairy, bright green leaves, to ½in (1cm) long. A profusion of pink flowers, ½in (1cm) across, open in loose, panicle-like cymes in summer. May swamp smaller plants. ↕ 3in (8cm), ↔ 18in (45cm) or more. Mountainous areas from Spain to Yugoslavia. Zone 3. **'Alba'** is less vigorous than the species, with white flowers. **'Rubra Compacta'** has a neat, dense habit, and dark red flowers.

S. officinalis (Bouncing Bet, Soapwort). Upright perennial, spreading rapidly by rhizomes, with narrowly ovate, rough, prominently veined, mid-green leaves, 1½–3in (4–8cm) long. From summer to autumn, bears panicle-like cymes of pink, red, or white flowers, to ¾in (2cm) across. ↕ 24in (60cm), ↔ 20in (50cm). Europe. Zone 3. **'Alba Plena'** bears abundant, double, white flowers, pink in bud. **'Dazzler'**, syn. 'Taff's Dazzler', 'Variegata', has single pink flowers, and leaves heavily variegated cream. Less invasive than the species. **'Rosea Plena'** produces fragrant, double pink flowers, in late spring and early summer; ↕ 2ft (60cm). **'Rubra Plena'** tends to spread, and has double red flowers that fade to pink. **'Taff's Dazzler'** see 'Dazzler'. **'Variegata'** see 'Dazzler'.

SARCOCAPNOS

PAPAVERACEAE

Genus of 3 or 4 species of dwarf, tufted annuals or perennials from cliff crevices in mountains throughout S.W. Europe and N. Africa. They are grown for their fleshy, simple or 2- or 3-ternate, finely divided leaves, to 6in (15cm) long, and for their terminal racemes of spurred flowers, similar to those of *Corydalis*, which are borne in spring and summer. Grow in a scree bed or raised bed, or in tufa; they are also delicate, short-lived plants for an alpine house.

• **CULTIVATION** Grow in moderately fertile, sharply drained, alkaline soil, in full sun with some midday shade; protect from excessive winter moisture. In an alpine house, grow in a mix of 2 parts grit and 1 part each loam and leaf mold, with additional tufa chips.

• **PROPAGATION** Sow seed in containers in a cold frame as soon as ripe. Plants grown under glass often self-seed.

• **PESTS AND DISEASES** Aphids and spider mites may be a problem under glass.

S. enneaphylla. Tuft-forming annual or short-lived perennial with brittle, branching stems bearing fern-like, 2- or 3-ternate, blue-green leaves, to 4in (10cm) long, consisting of ovate to elliptic leaflets with heart-shaped bases. In spring, produces racemes of 5–15 white or pink flowers, to ¾in (2cm) long, with short spurs. ↕↔ 6in (15cm). S. Spain, Morocco. Zone 7.

SARCOCAULON

GERANIACEAE

Genus of about 15 species of freely branching, deciduous, succulent perennials and subshrubs from very dry areas of Angola, Namibia, and South Africa. Stem branches are armed with usually small thorns and have hard, resinous bark. The opposite leaves are of 2 types: primary, with long stalks that become spines, and secondary, with shorter stalks that may persist as blunt stumps in the axils of the primary leaves. Solitary, trumpet-shaped flowers are borne mostly from winter to summer. Where temperatures fall below 50°F (10°C), grow in a temperate or warm greenhouse or conservatory; in warmer climates, use in a desert garden.

• **CULTIVATION** Under glass, grow in standard cactus potting mix in full light with low humidity. In growth, water moderately, and apply a half-strength balanced liquid fertilizer monthly; water sparingly in winter, but mist lightly on warmer days. Outdoors, grow in poor to moderately fertile, sharply drained soil in full sun. Protect from excessive winter moisture. See also pp.48–49.

• **PROPAGATION** Sow seed at 75°F (24°C) as soon as ripe.

• **PESTS AND DISEASES** Susceptible to mealybugs.

S. herrei. Shrubby, succulent perennial with spreading branches marked with leaf scars, and bearing thorns to 1in (2.5cm) long. Triangular to rounded, fleshy, 2- or 3-pinnatisect leaves, ½–¾in (1.5–2cm) long, are yellowish green with silky hairs. White and yellow flowers, ¾in (2cm) across, are borne in winter. ↕↔ to 12in (30cm). South Africa (Western Cape). ❀ (min. 50°F/10°C)

S. peniculinum. Succulent perennial with grayish white branches and 2- or 3-pinnatisect, woolly, gray-green leaves, ¾in (2cm) long, produced in tufts on old growth. In spring, produces pink flowers, ¾in (2cm) across, opening almost flat. ↕ 4in (10cm), ↔ 6in (15cm). Namibia. ❀ (min. 40°F/4°C)

S. vanderiettia. Low-growing, spreading, succulent perennial with green stems, turning brown with age, and elliptic, shiny, dark green leaves, ½in (1cm) long, notched at the ends. Bears pale pink flowers, 1¼in (3cm) across, opening flat, in spring and summer. ↕ to 4in (10cm), ↔ 12in (30cm). South Africa (Western Cape). ❀ (min. 40°F/4°C)

SARCOCOCCA

Christmas box, Sweet box

BUXACEAE

Genus of about 14 species of monoecious, evergreen, sometimes rhizomatous shrubs found in moist, shady places, forest, and thickets from China to the Himalayas and S.E. Asia. They are grown for their foliage, usually fragrant flowers, and berry-like fruits. The leaves are mainly alternate, rarely opposite, entire, and narrowly lance-shaped to broadly ovate or elliptic. Tiny, fragrant, petalless, white or whitish green male and female flowers, ¼in (6mm) long, are borne in small clusters or spikes in the leaf axils. The male flowers have conspicuous anthers; the females are produced below the males in the inflorescence. Grow as a groundcover in a shade garden, or use as a low, informal hedge.

• **CULTIVATION** Grow in moderately fertile, humus-rich, moist, well-drained soil in deep or partial shade. Full sun is tolerated if the soil remains moist; otherwise, the leaves will go off-color and the plant will lose vigor. Shelter from wind. Pruning group 8.

Sarcococca hookeriana var. *digyna* 'Purple Stem'

Sarcococca humilis

• **PROPAGATION** Sow seed in containers outdoors in autumn or spring. Take semi-ripe cuttings in summer and provide gentle bottom heat. Remove suckers in late winter or early spring.

• **PESTS AND DISEASES** Infrequent.

S. confusa ■ Dense, rounded, bushy shrub with elliptic, tapered, glossy, dark green leaves, to 2½in (6cm) long. Clusters of about 5 very fragrant white flowers are borne in early spring, followed by spherical, glossy black fruit, ¼in (6mm) across. ↕ 6ft (2m), ↔ 3ft (1m). Probably W. China. Zone 7b.

S. hookeriana. Rhizomatous, thicket-forming, suckering, compact shrub with lance-shaped to oblong, mid- to dark green leaves, to 3½in (9cm) long. Clusters of fragrant white flowers are borne in early spring, followed by spherical, black or blue-black fruit, ¼in (6mm) across. ↕ 5ft (1.5m), ↔ 6ft (2m). W. China. Zone 6. **var. *digyna*** has slender, tapered leaves, and male flowers with cream anthers. **var. *digyna* 'Purple Stem'** ■ has young shoots flushed dark purple-pink, and pink-tinged flowers. **var. *humilis*** see *S. humilis.*

Sarcococca confusa

S. humilis ■ syn. *S. hookeriana* var. *humilis.* Dwarf, clump-forming shrub, spreading by suckers, with erect shoots and oblong, glossy, dark green leaves, to 3in (8cm) long. In early spring, bears clusters of fragrant, pink-tinged white flowers, the males with pink anthers, followed by spherical, dark blue-black fruit, ¼in (6mm) across. ↕ 18in (45cm), ↔ 3ft (1m). W. China. Zone 6.

S. ruscifolia. Dense, bushy shrub with arching shoots and ovate, tapered, glossy, dark green leaves, to 2½in (6cm) long. Clusters of fragrant, creamy white flowers are produced in early spring, and are followed by spherical, dark red fruit, ¼in (6mm) across. ↕↔ 3ft (1m). W. and C. China. Zone 8.

S. saligna. Thicket-forming shrub with erect shoots and narrowly lance-shaped, finely tapered leaves, to 5½in (14cm) long, dark green above, pale green beneath. In winter and early spring, bears spikes, to ½in (1.5cm) long, of unscented, greenish white flowers, followed by ovoid purple fruit, to ½in (1cm) long. ↕ 3ft (1m), ↔ 6ft (2m). Afghanistan to Nepal (Himalayas). ❀ (min. 41°F/5°C)

SARITAEA

BIGNONIACEAE

Genus of a single species of woody-stemmed, evergreen tendril climber from woodland in N. South America. It produces opposite pairs of leaves and cyme-like panicles of tubular-bell-shaped flowers, with 5 spreading petal lobes. Where temperatures fall below 50°F (10°C), grow in a temperate or warm greenhouse. In warmer regions, grow over a pergola or arch, or through the branches of a tree.

• **CULTIVATION** Under glass, grow in soil-based potting mix in bright filtered light. When in growth, water freely and apply a balanced liquid fertilizer monthly; maintain moderate to high humidity. Water sparingly in winter. Outdoors, grow in moderately fertile, humus-rich, moist but well-drained soil in full sun with some midday shade, or in partial shade. Pruning group 11, in early spring.

• **PROPAGATION** Sow seed at about 61°F (16°C) in spring. Root semi-ripe cuttings with bottom heat in late summer. Layer in early spring.

• **PESTS AND DISEASES** Spider mites may be a problem under glass.

S. magnifica, syn. *Arrabidaea magnifica.* Vigorous, erect climber with leaves composed of 2 obovate, rich green leaflets, to 4in (10cm) long, those on the main climbing stems having hook-tipped tendrils. Cyme-like panicles of tubular-bell-shaped, pale purple to rose-pink flowers, 3–3½in (7–9cm) across, with light yellow to white, V-shaped markings inside, are borne in several flushes throughout the year. ↕ to 30ft (10m) or more. Colombia, Ecuador. ❄ (min. 50°F/10°C)

SARMIENTA

GESNERIACEAE

Genus of one species of small, shrubby, creeping, evergreen perennial growing epiphytically on trees in cool rainforest in temperate Chile. It has simple leaves in opposite pairs, and 5-lobed, tubular, axillary flowers. Where temperatures fall below 41°F (5°C), grow in a cool or temperate greenhouse, or conservatory. In milder areas, grow over mossy rocks, or epiphytically on a tree.

• **CULTIVATION** Under glass, grow in 2 parts soilless potting mix and 1 part each fine-grade ground bark and leaf mold, or grow epiphytically. Provide bright indirect light. In growth, water freely, applying a balanced liquid fertilizer monthly. Mist daily in summer. Water sparingly in winter. Outdoors, grow in fertile, humus-rich soil, ideally mixed with sphagnum moss, in light, dappled shade or partial shade.

• **PROPAGATION** Sow seed at 61–70°F (16–21°C) in spring. Root stem-tip cuttings in late summer, with bottom heat. Separate rooted stems in spring.

• **PESTS AND DISEASES** Spider mites may infest plants grown under glass.

S. repens, syn. *S. scandens.* Creeping or low-climbing perennial with semi-woody, rooting stems and obovate to elliptic, minutely glandular, light to mid-green leaves, to 1in (2.5cm) long, with 3–5 shallow to deep teeth at the tips. In summer, bears solitary, pendent, tubular scarlet flowers, ¾–1in (2–2.5cm) long. ↕ prostrate, ↔ to 12in (30cm) or more. S. Chile. ❄ (min. 41°F/5°C); tolerates brief periods to 32°F (0°C).
S. scandens see *S. repens.*

SARRACENIA

Pitcher plant

SARRACENIACEAE

Genus of 8 species of evergreen or deciduous, carnivorous perennials found in acidic, nutrient-deficient bogs, as well as less wet sites, from the Canadian Arctic to Florida. Short, thick rhizomes bear sparse, wiry roots and rosettes of phyllodes, some or all of which are modified into nectar-secreting, insect-catching pitchers. The mostly vertical, sometimes horizontal, attractively marked pitchers, 2–36in (5–90cm) long, have lateral wings and hooded lids. Mainly in spring, solitary, nodding or pendent, more or less cup-shaped flowers, with 4 or 5 sepals and 5 petals, are borne above the pitchers. Where temperatures fall below 23°F (-5°C), grow in a cold or cool greenhouse or on a sunny windowsill. In warmer areas, grow in a damp, shaded peat bed or bog garden.

Sarracenia flava

• **CULTIVATION** Under glass, grow in shallow pots of 3 parts sphagnum moss and 1 part each leaf mold and coarse sand or grit, in full light. During the growing season, apply a balanced liquid fertilizer monthly. In summer, stand containers in trays of acidic water. In winter, keep just moist, cool, and well ventilated. Outdoors, grow in humus-rich, wet, acidic soil in full sun. Water often.

• **PROPAGATION** Sow seed of species at 61–70°F (16–21°C) in spring, after cold stratification for 2 weeks; place the pot in a tray of acidic water. Prick out seedlings when 3 tiny pitchers appear. Divide in spring.

• **PESTS AND DISEASES** Prone to scale insects, mealybugs, aphids, and tortrix moth caterpillars.

S. drummondii see *S. leucophylla.*
S. flava ▣ (Yellow pitcher plant). Very variable perennial bearing erect, yellow-green pitchers, 12–36in (30–90cm) long, with round mouths and raised lids, often veined red. Phyllodes that do not produce pitchers are linear, and persist throughout the winter. In spring, bears yellow flowers, to 4in (10cm) across. ↕ 20–39in (50–100cm), ↔ to 3ft (1m). Virginia to Alabama, Florida. Zone 7b. **'Burgundy'** has pitchers plum-colored outside. **'Maxima'** has pitchers 36in (90cm) long, with purple-veined lids and stems.
S. leucophylla, syn. *S. drummondii* (White trumpet). Semi-evergreen perennial bearing erect, slender pitchers, 10–39in (25–100cm) long, with narrow wings and erect lids with wavy margins. The lids and tops are typically white, often with light or heavy purple-red netting, gradually merging into green bases. In spring, bears purple flowers, to 3in (8cm) across. ↕ 20–39in (50–90cm), ↔ to 3ft (1m). Missouri to Florida. Zone 7.
S. purpurea (Common pitcher plant, Huntsman's cup). Very variable perennial bearing nearly horizontal, purple-veined, purple or green pitchers, 2–20in (5–50cm) long, with upcurved ends, broad wings, and erect, entire, smooth, often glossy, broad lids. Dark purple-red and pink to dark red flowers, occasionally yellow, to 2in (5cm) across, are produced in spring. ↕ 4–6in (10–15cm), ↔ 3ft (1m). Canadian Arctic to New Jersey. Zone 2.
subsp. *venosa* has more inflated, rough, green to purple pitchers, with broader, wavy lids that extend beyond the mouths; flowers are purple or rose-pink; New Jersey to Louisiana; Zone 7.

SASA

POACEAE

Genus of 40–50 species of small to medium-sized bamboos, with running rhizomes, closely related to *Sasaella,* to which several species of *Sasa* have now been transferred. They are found in damp hollows and woodland in Japan, Korea, and China. The ascending culms are smooth and cylindrical, with persistent, bristly sheaths and a white-waxy bloom beneath the nodes. Most produce large, usually broad, thick, toothed, and checkered leaves. Some forms turn beige at the margins in

Sasa veitchii

winter, giving a variegated effect. Use as a groundcover under trees, or as a hedge; they tolerate deep shade.

• **CULTIVATION** Grow in fertile, humus-rich, moist but well-drained soil in full sun to deep shade; tolerant of most soils, but avoid dry soils when planting in full sun. To retard spread, plant in containers and plunge into the soil.

• **PROPAGATION** Divide or cut sections of the youngest rhizomes in spring.

• **PESTS AND DISEASES** Emergent shoots may be eaten by slugs.

S. albomarginata see *S. veitchii.*
S. humilis see *Pleioblastus humilis.*
***S. masumuneana* 'Albostriata'**, syn. *Sasaella masumuneana* f. *albostriata.* Low-growing, moderately spreading bamboo with very slender, green or brown culms, producing a single branch at each node. The narrowly elliptic, mid-green leaves, 4–7in (10–18cm) long, are conspicuously white-striped when young, becoming yellow shaded as they mature in autumn, and fading in winter. ↕ to 5ft (1.5m), ↔ indefinite. Zone 7b.
S. palmata* f. *nebulosa. Vigorous bamboo with wide-spreading rhizomes and thick, upward-curved, usually purple-streaked culms that produce a single branch at each node. The broadly elliptic, tapered, smooth, glossy, bright green leaves, 14–16in (35–40cm) long, are paler green beneath, and have yellow midribs. ↕ to 6ft (2m), ↔ indefinite. Japan. Zone 6b.
S. ramosa, syn. *Arundinaria vagans, Sasaella ramosa.* Extremely vigorous, low-growing bamboo with slender, glossy, bright green culms producing a single branch at each node. Elliptic, mid-green leaves, to 8in (20cm) long, have yellow midribs, and wither at the margins and tips in winter. ↕ 2–5ft (0.6–1.5m), ↔ indefinite. Japan. ❄ (min. 35°F/2°C)
S. ruscifolia see *Shibataea kumasasa.*
S. veitchii ▣ syn. *S. albomarginata* (Kuma bamboo grass). Moderately spreading bamboo with slender, glaucous, usually purple culms, producing a single branch at each node. The broadly lance-shaped-ovate, ribbed leaves are glossy, dark green, to 10in (25cm) long. ↕ to 6ft (2m), usually 3–4ft (1–1.2m), ↔ indefinite. Japan. Zone 6.

▷ ***Sasaella masumuneana* f. *albostriata*** see *Sasa masumuneana* 'Albostriata'
▷ ***Sasaella ramosa*** see *Sasa ramosa*

S

Sassafras albidum

SASSAFRAS

LAURACEAE

Genus of 3 species of generally dioecious, deciduous trees from woodland and thickets in China, Taiwan, and North America. They are cultivated for their stately habit and glossy, aromatic foliage, which colors attractively in autumn. They have deeply fissured bark, and produce alternate, often 1- to 3-lobed, elliptic, oval, ovate, or obovate leaves. Clustered racemes of small, yellow-green flowers are borne in spring, either before or as the leaves emerge. Where plants of both sexes are grown together, the flowers on female plants are followed by ovoid fruits. Grow as specimen trees in a woodland garden or at woodland margins.

- **CULTIVATION** Grow in moist but well-drained, moderately fertile, humus-rich, preferably acidic, deep soil in full sun or partial shade. Cut out suckers as they arise to maintain single specimens, or retain suckers to produce a colony. Pruning group 1.
- **PROPAGATION** Sow seed in containers in a cold frame as soon as ripe. Take root cuttings in winter. Difficult to establish from the wild because of its deep taproot and few lateral roots; container-growth is advised until planting in the ground.
- **PESTS AND DISEASES** Infrequent.

S. albidum ■ Irregular to rounded-pyramidal tree, spreading by suckers, sometimes forming large colonies. The elliptic to ovate, entire or shallowly to deeply 3-lobed, aromatic, dark green leaves, to 6in (15cm) long, turn yellow to orange or purple in autumn. Tiny yellow flowers are produced in racemes to 2in (5cm) across, in spring, as the leaves emerge. If pollinated, the flowers on female plants are followed by red-stalked, ovoid, dark blue fruit, ½in (1cm) long. ↕ 80ft (25m), ↔ 50ft (15m). E. North America. Zone 6.

SATUREJA

Savory

LAMIACEAE

Genus of approximately 30 species of annuals, perennials, and subshrubs, widely distributed throughout the N. hemisphere, occurring in dry, sunny sites and often found on cliffs. They are cultivated for their aromatic leaves, which are opposite, linear to lance-shaped, or oblong-obovate to spoon-shaped, and for their cyme-like or spike-like inflorescences; these consist of whorls of stalkless, tubular, 2-lipped flowers, borne in summer, which are attractive to bees and other insects. Suitable for growing in a mixed border or rock garden. *S. hortensis* and *S. montana* are used as culinary herbs.

- **CULTIVATION** Grow in moderately fertile, well-drained, neutral to slightly alkaline soil in full sun. Protect from excessive winter moisture. Cut back old shoots of subshrubs in early spring.
- **PROPAGATION** Sow seed at 55–61°F (13–16°C) in late winter or early spring; seed of *S. hortensis* may be sown *in situ* in spring or, in mild climates, in autumn. Take greenwood cuttings of subshrubs in summer.
- **PESTS AND DISEASES** Infrequent.

S. hortensis (Summer savory). Bushy, aromatic annual with linear to narrowly lance-shaped, fresh green leaves, to 1¼in (3cm) long. In summer, bears crowded or lax, whorl-like spikes of 2–5 white or pink flowers, to ¼in (6mm) long. ↕ 10in (25cm), ↔ to 12in (30cm). S.E. Europe.
S. montana ■ (Winter savory). Dwarf subshrub producing stalkless, linear to inversely lance-shaped, leathery, smooth or sparsely hairy, dark grayish green leaves, ¼–1¼in (0.5–3cm) long. For long periods throughout summer, bears whorls of up to 14 lavender-pink to purple flowers, to ⅜in (8mm) long, in dense, upright spikes. ↕ 16in (40cm), ↔ 8in (20cm). S. Europe. Zone 4b. **'Nana'** is compact in habit; the foliage is purple-tinged in winter. **'Prostrate White'** ■ is compact, with erect white flower spikes; ↕↔ to 6in (15cm).
S. repanda see *S. spicigera.*
S. reptans see *S. spicigera.*
S. spicigera, syn. *S. repanda, S. reptans.* Creeping, aromatic subshrub with procumbent stems and linear to lance-shaped, mid-green leaves, to 1in (2.5cm) long. In summer, bears lax cymes of

Satureja montana

Satureja montana 'Prostrate White'

white flowers, ½in (1cm) long, in whorls of up to 16. Makes an attractive edging. ↕ 6in (15cm), ↔ 12in (30cm). Turkey, Iran, Caucasus. Zone 7b.
S. thymbra. Mound-forming, well-branched shrub with recurved, softly hairy stems and linear to spoon-shaped, mid-green leaves, to ½in (1.5cm) long. In spring, bears lax, dense, whorl-like spikes of many mauve to purple flowers, to ¼in (6mm) long. ↕ to 16in (40cm), ↔ 12in (30cm). Balkans. Zone 7.

SAUROMATUM

ARACEAE

Genus of 2 species of tuberous perennials from woodland and shady cliffs in the Himalayas and E. and W. Africa, cultivated for their large spathes borne in spring or early summer, followed by single, pedate, long-stalked leaves. Where not hardy, grow in a cool greenhouse, or outdoors in summer; elsewhere, grow in a woodland garden.

- **CULTIVATION** Plant tubers 6in (15cm) deep in late winter. Under glass, grow in soil-based potting mix in bright filtered or indirect light. In growth, water moderately; keep completely dry in winter. Tubers will flower on a saucer without soil or water. Outdoors, grow in well-drained, fertile, humus-rich, neutral to slightly acidic soil in partial shade.
- **PROPAGATION** Remove offsets when dormant in winter.
- **PESTS AND DISEASES** Infrequent.

Sauromatum venosum

S. guttatum see *S. venosum.*
S. venosum ■ syn. *S. guttatum* (Monarch of the East, Voodoo lily). Tuberous perennial with an oblong-lance-shaped, yellowish or greenish white spathe, 12–28in (30–70cm) long, heavily spotted purple, with a foul-smelling, greenish purple spadix, to 14in (35cm) long, produced in late spring and early summer. The spathe is followed by a single, rounded leaf, to 14in (35cm) long, with many oblong-lance-shaped segments. ↕ 12–18in (30–45cm), PD6in (15cm). Himalayas. ❄ (min. 41°F/5°C)

SAXEGOTHAEA

PODOCARPACEAE

Genus of one species of monoecious, evergreen, coniferous tree or shrub from dense forest in Chile and Argentina. It has whorled branches with irregularly set, yew-like foliage, and bears fleshy, spherical green female cones and tiny male cones. Grow in a woodland garden among other conifers, or as a free-standing specimen.

- **CULTIVATION** Grow in moderately fertile, well-drained, neutral to slightly acidic soil, in full sun with some midday shade, or in partial shade. Shelter from cold, drying winds.
- **PROPAGATION** Take semi-ripe cuttings in late summer or early autumn.
- **PESTS AND DISEASES** Infrequent.

S. conspicua ■ (Prince Albert's yew). Slender, conical, coniferous tree or shrub, bushy in cold areas, with smooth, purple-brown bark and whorled branches bearing green shoots. Linear to linear-lance-shaped, dark green leaves, to 1¼in (3cm) long, each have 2 silver crossbands beneath, and persist for 5 or 6 years. Fleshy, spherical, prickly, glaucous-green female cones, ½in (1.5cm) across, contain about 6 seeds, and develop from terminal clusters of scales in autumn. Male cones are cylindrical, dark purple, and borne at the bases of the shoots. ↕ to 70ft (20m), ↔ 15–25ft (5–8m). S. Chile to Argentina. ❄ (min. 35°F/2°C)

Saxegothaea conspicua

S

SAXIFRAGA

Saxifrage

SAXIFRAGACEAE

Genus of about 440 species of mostly mat- or cushion-forming, evergreen, semi-evergreen, or deciduous perennials, biennials, and a few annuals, mostly from mountains in the N. hemisphere. Those described are evergreen and perennial unless stated. Varying greatly in habit and leaf form, they produce flat, star-shaped, or shallowly cup-shaped flowers, either singly or in cymes, racemes, or panicles. The rosettes of monocarpic saxifrages die after flowering and are replaced by daughter rosettes. Saxifrages are suitable for rock gardens, mixed borders, and woodland gardens.

Saxifrages are classified botanically into sections, subsections, and series. Those of most horticultural value are as follows.

Section Gymnopera (Robertsonia) Saxifrages with evergreen, rosetted leaves, and flowers in panicles on leafless flower stems. Contains London pride (*S.* x *urbium*) and similar shade lovers.
Section Irregulares (Diptera) Woodland plants with rosettes of basal, usually deciduous leaves (often evergreen under glass); flower panicles, on leafless stems, appear in summer and autumn.
Section Ligulatae (Euaizoonia) The silver or encrusted saxifrages, which have evergreen, monocarpic rosettes with a conspicuous calcareous (lime) encrustation. Cushion- or mat-forming; flower panicles are borne on leafy stems.
Section Porphyrion (Porophyllum) Cushion- or mat-forming, evergreen perennials with rosettes or leafy shoots, usually with lime-encrusted leaves. This section includes the following horticulturally important subsections. ***Engleria*** – saxifrages with rosettes of leaves alternately arranged, the margins translucent. Flower stems are leafy and distinct, with colored bracts, and flowers have erect sepals largely hiding the pink, purple, white, or yellow petals, which have basal fringes of hairs; they are borne singly or in small cymes or racemes. ***Kabschia*** – saxifrages with leafy shoots, and alternate leaves with translucent margins. The leafy flowering stems are short or distinct (with up to 15 flowers), and bear white, pink, purple, or yellow flowers, singly or in small cymes or racemes. ***Oppositifoliae*** – saxifrages with opposite leaves, usually without translucent margins. Purple, pink, or white flowers are borne in short cymes of up to 3. Flowering stems are short and leafy or absent.
Section Saxifraga (Dactyloides) Perennial, rarely annual or biennial, usually evergreen saxifrages, sometimes summer-dormant; they produce bulbils. Of varied habit, they often have leafy shoots that form cushions or mats, with soft, lobed or scalloped leaves, lacking glands. Bears cymes of white, rarely red, pink, or yellow flowers on usually leafy stems. Includes the mossy saxifrages.
Section Xanthizoon are mat- or cushion-forming, evergreen perennials with fleshy, narrow, stalkless leaves, with or without functional glands. Yellow or orange flowers are borne in loose cymes on leafy stems.

Saxifraga x *apiculata*

• **CULTIVATION** Requirements fall broadly into 4 groups.
1. Grow in moist but well-drained, humus-rich soil in deep or partial shade. Suitable for a border or rock garden.
2. Grow in humus-rich, moist but very sharply drained, neutral to alkaline soil in light shade. Suitable for a rock crevice, scree bed, or alpine house.
3. Grow in moderately fertile, very well-drained, neutral to alkaline soil; keep roots moist. Tolerant of full sun in cool areas, but protect from hot sun in warm areas to prevent leaf scorch. Suitable for a rock garden or trough.
4. Grow in moderately fertile, very sharply drained, alkaline soil or scree in full sun. Suitable for a rock garden, trough, alpine house, or tufa. Some are intolerant of excessive winter moisture. In an alpine house, grow in shallow pans in 2 parts soil-based potting mix and 1 part limestone chips.
• **PROPAGATION** Sow seed in autumn in containers in an open frame. Divide herbaceous perennials in spring. Detach individual rosettes and root as cuttings in late spring or early summer.
• **PESTS AND DISEASES** Aphids, slugs, vine weevil grubs, and spider mites occur.

Saxifraga x *boydii* 'Hindhead Seedling'

S. aizoides (Yellow mountain saxifrage). Mat-forming Xanthizoon saxifrage with branching stems bearing tight rosettes of linear to oblong, fleshy, glossy, mid- to dark green leaves, ⅛–¾in (0.4–2cm) long, with 2 short teeth near the tips, and bristly margins. In summer and early autumn, erect, hairy stems bear star-shaped, red-spotted, deep orange flowers, ⅜in (8mm) across, in few-flowered cymes. Cultivation group 2. ↕ 6in (15cm), ↔ 8in (20cm). Arctic, alpine areas of Europe, Asia, North America. Zone 7.
S. aizoon see *S. paniculata.*
S.* x *anglica (*S. aretioides* x *S. lilacina* x *S. media*). Dense, mat- or rosette-forming Kabschia saxifrage with linear-oblong to spoon-shaped, dark green or gray-green to silver, encrusted leaves, ⅛–½in (0.3–1.5cm) long. Cup-shaped, pink to pink-purple flowers, to ¾in (2cm) across, are borne singly or in 2- or 3-flowered cymes in early and midspring. Cultivation group 3 or 4. ↕ ¾–2½in (2–6cm), ↔ 2–12in (5–30cm). Garden origin. Zone 7b. **'Cranbourne'** has linear, gray-green leaves and, in early summer, bears solitary, almost stemless, deep rose-pink flowers; ↕ 1in (2.5cm), ↔ 8in (20cm). **'Myra'**, syn. *S.* 'Myra', is very compact and slow-growing, with narrowly lance-shaped leaves, to ½in (1cm) long. Bears deep red-purple flowers, ½in (1cm) across, in early spring; ↕ 2in (5cm), ↔ 4in (10cm).
S.* x *apiculata ▣ (*S. marginata* x *S. sancta*). Cushion-forming Kabschia saxifrage with tight rosettes of linear-lance-shaped, slightly lime-encrusted, deep green leaves, ½in (1cm) long. Produces cymes of 4–12 cup-shaped yellow flowers, ⅜in (8mm) across, in early spring. Cultivation group 3. ↕ 4in (10cm) ↔ 12in (30cm). Garden origin. Zone 5. **'Gregor Mendel'** has glossy, pale green leaves and pale yellow flowers. Good for a rock garden or wall.
S. aretioides. Compact Kabschia saxifrage bearing rosettes of pointed, oblong-lance-shaped, blue-green leaves, ¼in (6mm) long. Produces flat-topped cymes of up to 5 open cup-shaped yellow flowers, ⅜–½in (9–15mm) across, in early spring. Cultivation group 3. ↕ 3in (8cm), ↔ 6in (15cm). N.W. Spain, Pyrenees. Zone 7.
***S.* 'Bob Hawkins'.** Mossy, mat-forming Saxifraga saxifrage with large, soft rosettes of deeply divided, linear, white-variegated, mid-green leaves, to ¾in (2cm) long. In summer, cymes of 5–12 upturned, cup-shaped, greenish white flowers, to ¾in (2cm) across, are produced on upright stems. Cultivation group 2. ↕ 6in (15cm), ↔ 12in (30cm). Zone 7.
S.* x *boydii (*S. aretioides* x *S. burseriana*). Dense, rosette-forming Kabschia saxifrage with linear to lance-shaped, often pointed, gray-green to silver-green leaves, ⅛–½in (3–15mm) long. In spring, cup-shaped yellow flowers, to ½in (1.5cm) across, are borne singly or in 2- or 3-flowered cymes. Cultivation group 3 or 4. ↕ 1¼–3in (3–8cm), ↔ 6in (15cm). Garden origin. Zone 7. **'Faldonside'** is vigorous, with irregular cymes of star-shaped, bright yellow flowers, to 1in (2.5cm) across; ↕ 2in (5cm). **'Hindhead Seedling'** ▣ syn. *S.* 'Hindhead Seedling', has spiny, blue-green leaves, ¼–½in (6–15mm) long, and mostly solitary, yellow-centered, creamy white flowers, to 1in (2.5cm) across; ↕ 2in (5cm).
S. burseriana ▣ Kabschia saxifrage with firm rosettes of pointed, narrowly lance-shaped, lime-encrusted, gray-green leaves, to ½in (1cm) long. Solitary, cup-shaped white flowers, ½in (1cm) across, open on short red stems in early spring. Cultivation group 3 or 4. ↕ to 2in (5cm), ↔ 6in (15cm). E. Alps. Zone 5. **'Gloria'** produces larger flowers, 1¼in (3cm) across, with yellow centers, on bright red stems.
S. callosa, syn. *S. lingulata.* Rosette-forming Ligulatae saxifrage with linear, lime-encrusted silver leaves, to 3in (8cm) long. In early summer, arching stems bear narrow panicles, 2–8in (5–20cm) long, of 3–7 star-shaped white flowers, ½in (1cm) across. Cultivation group 4. ↕ 10in (25cm), ↔ 8in (20cm). N.E. Spain, S.W. Alps, Apennines to S. Italy, Sicily, Sardinia. Zone 7b.
S. cochlearis (Snail saxifrage). Dense, cushion-forming Ligulatae saxifrage with compact rosettes of spoon-shaped, mid-green leaves, 1½in (4cm) long, with

Saxifraga burseriana

Saxifraga cotyledon

lime-encrusted margins. In early summer, bears densely hairy panicles, 2½–4in (6–10cm) long, of 15–25 (occasionally up to 60) rounded, sometimes red-spotted white flowers, ½in (1cm) or more across. Cultivation group 3 or 4. ↕8in (20cm), ↔6in (15cm). France (Maritime Alps). Zone 7b. **'Minor'** is lower-growing, and has smaller rosettes; ↕4in (10cm).

S. cortusifolia. Deciduous or evergreen Irregulares saxifrage with loose rosettes of kidney-shaped to rounded, 5- or 7-lobed, fleshy, glossy, mid-green leaves, 2–3in (5–8cm) long, with scalloped margins. In late summer, produces pyramidal panicles, to 8in (20cm) long, of cup-shaped white flowers, to 1½in (4cm) across, spotted yellow or red.

Saxifraga exarata subsp. *moschata* 'Cloth of Gold'

Saxifraga fortunei

Saxifraga frederici-augusti subsp. *grisebachii* 'Wisley Variety'

Each flower has 3 or 4 upper petals and 1 or 2 much longer lower petals. Cultivation group 1. ↕6in (15cm), ↔8in (20cm). Japan. Zone 7. **var. *fortunei*** see *S. fortunei.*

S. cotyledon ■ (Jungfrau saxifrage). Rosette-forming Ligulatae saxifrage with oblong to inversely lance-shaped, pale green leaves, to 3in (8cm) long, with lime-encrusted teeth. In late spring and early summer, bears loose, pyramidal panicles, to 28in (70cm) long, of cup-shaped white flowers, to ½in (1cm) across, often marked red. Cultivation group 3 or 4. ↕12–28in (30–70cm), ↔8in (20cm). Iceland, Scandinavia, Alps, Pyrenees. Zone 4.

S. cuneifolia. Mat-forming Gymnopera saxifrage bearing rosettes of stalked, usually wedge-shaped, occasionally ovate to rounded, leathery, fresh green leaves, to 1in (2.5cm) long, purple beneath. In spring and early summer, produces loose panicles, 2–7in (5–18cm) long, of 3–12 (rarely up to 30) star-shaped white flowers, ¼in (6mm) across, frequently spotted yellow, sometimes red, on red-tinted stems. Cultivation group 1. ↕8in (20cm), ↔12in (30cm). Europe (Carpathians to Pyrenees). Zone 7.

S. exarata* subsp. *moschata, syn. *S. moschata.* Mossy, mat- or cushion-forming Saxifraga saxifrage with rosettes of variably shaped, entire or 3-lobed, pale green leaves, ⅛–¾in (0.4–2cm) long. From late spring to early autumn, bears flat-topped cymes of 1–7 star-shaped, cream or yellow, occasionally pink-tinted flowers, to ⅜in (8mm) across. Cultivation group 2. ↕4in (10cm), ↔12in (30cm). C. and S. Europe. Zone 7. **'Cloth of Gold'** ■ has golden foliage; best grown in light shade.

S. ferdinandi-coburgi. Dense, irregular cushion-forming Kabschia saxifrage with rosettes of oblong-lance-shaped, chalk-gray, lime-encrusted leaves, to ⅜in (8mm) long, incurved at the tips. In early spring, produces cymes of 7–12 open cup-shaped, rich yellow flowers, ½in (1cm) across, on red-tinged stems. Cultivation group 3. ↕4in (10cm), ↔6in (15cm). Macedonia, N. Greece, E. Bulgaria. Zone 6.

S. fortunei ■ syn. *S. cortusifolia* var. *fortunei.* Deciduous or semi-evergreen, clump-forming Irregulares saxifrage with kidney-shaped to rounded, 7-lobed, mid-green leaves, 2½–4in (6–10cm) across, often red-purple beneath or purple-tinged with age; they have deeply heart-shaped bases and scalloped margins. In late summer or autumn, bears loose, pendent, red-stemmed panicles, to 20in (50cm) long, of white flowers, ½in (1cm) across, with 3 upper petals and 1 or 2 longer lower petals. Cultivation group 1. ↕↔12in (30cm). Japan. Zone 7. **'Rubrifolia'** is compact, with strongly red-suffused leaves and deep red stems; ↕↔8in (20cm).

S. frederici-augusti. Cushion-forming Engleria saxifrage with flat rosettes of obovate to spoon-shaped, gray-green, usually lime-encrusted leaves, ½–1½in (1.5–4cm) long. The red stems, which bear several leaves, and flower stalks are partially covered in long, bright cherry-red to dark purple, glandular hairs. In late spring, produces slender racemes, 1¼–4in (3–10cm) long, of 15–25 cup-shaped, purplish pink flowers, ¼in (6mm) across. Cultivation group 4. ↕3–8in (7–20cm), ↔ to 6in (15cm). Macedonia, Albania, Greece, Bulgaria. Zone 7. **subsp. *grisebachii* 'Wisley Variety'** ■ has spoon-shaped, silver-gray leaves, arching stems clothed in green-tipped, red-purple bracts, and red-purple flowers; ↕4in (10cm).

S. x geum ■ (*S. hirsuta* x *S. umbrosa*). Mat-forming Gymnopera saxifrage with rosettes of long-stalked, sparsely hairy, spoon-shaped, scalloped, mid-green leaves, to 3in (8cm) long. In summer, bears loose panicles, 2½–8in (6–20cm) long, of 2–12 star-shaped white flowers, ¼–⅜in (7–8mm) across, spotted with red. Cultivation group 1. ↕↔8in (20cm). Pyrenees. Zone 7.

S. granulata ■ (Fair maids of France, Meadow saxifrage). Clump-forming, summer-dormant Saxifraga saxifrage with stem and root bulbils, and loose rosettes of kidney-shaped, toothed or scalloped, pale to mid-green leaves, to 1¼in (3cm) long. In late spring, bears panicles, 3–8in (8–20cm) long, of 10–20 rounded white flowers, to ½in (1.5cm) across, on sticky, erect stems. May be naturalized in grass. Cultivation group 2; tolerates full sun in moist soil. ↕8–14in (20–35cm), ↔12in (30cm). Europe (mostly W.), N. Africa. Zone 7b. **'Plena'** has double flowers.

***S.* 'Hindhead Seedling'** see *S.* x *boydii* 'Hindhead Seedling'.

***S. x irvingii* 'Jenkinsiae'** ■ syn. *S.* x *jenkinsiae.* Dense, mound-forming, slow-growing Kabschia saxifrage with tight rosettes of wedge-shaped, lime-encrusted, gray-green leaves, ¼in (6mm) long. In early spring, bears abundant

Saxifraga x *geum*

Saxifraga granulata

solitary, open cup-shaped, dark-centered, pale pink flowers, to ¾in (2cm) across, on short red stems. Cultivation group 3. ↕2in (5cm), ↔8in (20cm). Zone 6.

S. x jenkinsiae see *S.* x *irvingii* 'Jenkinsiae'.

S. juniperifolia* subsp. *sancta see *S. sancta.*

***S.* 'Kathleen Pinsent'** ■ Rosette-forming Ligulatae saxifrage with narrowly spoon-shaped, silvery leaves, ¾–3in (2–8cm) long, recurved at the tips. In late spring and early summer, bears arching panicles, to 8in (20cm) long, of open cup-shaped, rose-pink flowers, to ¾in (2cm) across. Cultivation group 3 or 4. ↕↔ to 8in (20cm). Zone 6.

S. lingulata see *S. callosa.*

S. longifolia ■ (Pyrenean saxifrage). Ligulatae saxifrage with a single rosette of linear, lime-encrusted silver leaves, 2½–4½in (6–11cm) long, silver-gray beneath. After 3 or 4 years, produces a huge pyramidal panicle, to 28in (70cm) long, of up to 80 rounded, 5-petaled, open cup-shaped white flowers, ½in (1cm) across, in summer. Cultivation group 4. Can only be propagated from seed. ↕24in (60cm), ↔8in (20cm). Pyrenees. Zone 6. **'Tumbling Waters'** see *S.* 'Tumbling Waters'.

S. marginata. Vigorous, cushion- to mat-forming Kabschia saxifrage with rosettes of narrowly elliptic to obovate, lime-encrusted, silver-gray leaves, to ½in (1.5cm) long. Compact panicles, ½–2in (1–5cm) long, of 5–9 open cup-shaped, white, sometimes pink-flushed flowers, to ¾in (2cm) across, are borne in early

Saxifraga x *irvingii* 'Jenkinsiae'

Saxifraga 'Kathleen Pinsent'

spring. Cultivation group 3. ↕ 3in (8cm), ↔ 12in (30cm). S. Italy, Balkans, Romania. Zone 7.
S. moschata see *S. exarata* subsp. *moschata*.
***S.* 'Myra'** see *S.* x *anglica* 'Myra'.
S. oppositifolia ■ (Purple mountain saxifrage). Mat-forming Oppositifoliae saxifrage with rosettes of stiff, oblong or elliptic, dark green leaves, to ¼in (6mm) long, on branching stems. In early summer, bears solitary, almost stemless, cup-shaped, deep red-purple to pale pink or white flowers, to ¾in (2cm) across. Cultivation group 2. ↕ 1in (2.5cm), ↔ 8in (20cm) or more. Arctic, mountains of Europe, W. Asia, North America. Zone 2. **'Ruth Draper'** has large, bright rose-pink flowers, to 1¼in (3cm) across. **'Vaccarina'** has deep red-purple flowers.
S. paniculata, syn. *S. aizoon.* Variable, mat-forming Ligulatae saxifrage bearing rosettes of incurved, broadly linear or narrowly obovate, gray-green leaves, ¼–2½in (0.5–6cm) long, with lime-encrusted margins. In early summer, numerous cup-shaped flowers open in narrow, flat panicles, 1¼–8in (3–20cm) long. The primary branches each have

Saxifraga longifolia

Saxifraga oppositifolia

1–3, rarely 4, rounded, creamy white, rarely pink flowers, to ½in (1cm) across. Cultivation group 4. ↕ 6in (15cm), ↔ 10in (25cm). Norway, C. and S. Europe, Caucasus, Canada, Greenland, Iceland. Zone 2. **var. *baldensis***, syn. 'Baldensis', 'Minutifolia', produces much smaller rosettes and red-tinged flower stems; ↕ 4in (10cm), ↔ 6in (15cm). **'Baldensis'** see var. *baldensis.* **'Minutifolia'** see var. *baldensis.*
S. porophylla* var. *thessalica see *S. sempervivum.*
***S.* 'Primulaize'** see *S.* x *primulaize.*
S.* x *primulaize (*S. aizoides* x *S.* x *urbium* or *S. umbrosa*), syn. *S.* 'Primulaize'. Loose, rosette-forming saxifrage, a hybrid of Section Xanthizoon and Section Gymnopera, resembling a miniature *S.* x *urbium.* Fleshy, narrowly ovate, glossy, mid-green leaves are ¾–2½in (2–6cm) long. In summer, bears loose panicles, 6in (15cm) long, of star-shaped, crimson- or salmon-pink flowers, to ½in (1.5cm) across. Cultivation group 1. ↕ 3in (8cm), ↔ 6in (15cm). Garden origin. Zone 7.
S. primuloides see *S. umbrosa* var. *primuloides.*
S. sancta ■ syn. *S. juniperifolia* subsp. *sancta.* Cushion-forming Kabschia saxifrage with rosettes of narrowly lance-shaped, lime-encrusted, bright green leaves, to ½in (1cm) long. Cymes of 3–7 upward-facing, open cup-shaped, deep yellow flowers, ¼–⅜in (6–8mm) across, with prominent anthers, are borne in spring. Cultivation group 3. ↕ 2in (5cm), ↔ 8in (20cm). N.E. Greece. Zone 7b.
***S. sarmentosa* 'Tricolor'** see *S. stolonifera* 'Tricolor'.

Saxifraga sancta

Saxifraga 'Southside Seedling'

S. scardica. Dense, cushion-forming, slow-growing Kabschia saxifrage with firm rosettes of fleshy, oblong, lime-encrusted, blue-green leaves, to ½in (1.5cm) long. In spring, bears cymes of 4–13 upward-facing, cup-shaped white flowers, to ½in (1.5cm) across, on red-tinted stems. Prefers light, dappled shade. Cultivation group 3. ↕ 3in (8cm), ↔ 6in (15cm). Balkans. Zone 7b.
S. sempervivum, syn. *S. porophylla* var. *thessalica.* Loose, cushion-forming Engleria saxifrage with rosettes of linear, lime-encrusted, silvery green leaves, to ¾in (2cm) long. In spring, crozier-like, silver-hairy stems bear racemes, ¾–3in (2–8cm) long, of 7–20 pendent, open cup-shaped, deep reddish purple flowers, to ¼in (6mm) across. Cultivation group 4. ↕ 4in (10cm), ↔ 8in (20cm). Balkans, N.W. Turkey. Zone 7.
***S.* 'Southside Seedling'** ■ Mat-forming Ligulatae saxifrage similar to, and possibly a cultivar of, *S. cotyledon*, with rosettes of oblong to spoon-shaped, pale green leaves, to 5in (13cm) long. Arching panicles, 12in (30cm) long, of open cup-shaped white flowers, ½in (1cm) across, heavily spotted red, are borne in late spring and early summer. Cultivation group 3 or 4. ↕ 12in (30cm), ↔ 8in (20cm). Zone 6.
S. spruneri. Cushion-forming, slow-growing Kabschia saxifrage. Hairy, oblong or spoon-shaped, lime-encrusted, mid-green leaves, to ¼in (6mm) long, are in small rosettes. In late spring, bears flat-topped cymes of 6–10 star-shaped, yellowish white flowers, to ½in (1cm) across. Cultivation group 3. ↕ 3in (8cm), ↔ 4in (10cm). Balkans. Zone 8.

Saxifraga stolonifera 'Tricolor'

Saxifraga stribrnyi

Saxifraga 'Tumbling Waters'

S. stolonifera (Mother of thousands). Stoloniferous, rosette- or tuft-forming Irregulares saxifrage with kidney-shaped to rounded, deeply cut, mid- to dark green leaves, 1½–3½in (4–9cm) long. In summer, produces loose panicles, 8–16in (20–40cm) long, of white flowers, to 1in (2.5cm) across, spotted yellow or red, with 3 or 4 upper petals and 1 or 2 longer lower petals, on slender, upright stems. Cultivation group 1. ↕↔ to 12in (30cm). Zone 7. **'Magic Carpet'** see 'Tricolor'. **'Tricolor'** ■ syn. *S. sarmentosa* 'Tricolor', 'Magic Carpet', has leaves strongly patterned in red and white; Zone 7.
S. stribrnyi ■ Mound-forming Engleria saxifrage with tight rosettes of pointed, inversely lance-shaped to spoon-shaped, lime-encrusted, blue-green leaves, ½–1in (1–2.5cm) long. Bears branched, arching, crozier-like stems with racemes, ¾–2in (2–5cm) long, of 10–30 open cup-shaped, deep violet-purple flowers, to ½in (1cm) across, in late spring and early summer. Cultivation group 4. ↕ 4in (10cm), ↔ 8in (20cm). Balkans. Zone 7.
***S.* 'Tumbling Waters'** ■ syn. *S. longifolia* 'Tumbling Waters'. Slow-growing Ligulatae perennial with large, clustered rosettes of narrow, linear, lime-encrusted, silvery green leaves, to 6in (15cm) long. Dense, arching, conical panicles, 12–28in (30–70cm) long, of small, open cup-shaped white flowers, to ½in (1cm) across, are borne in spring, after several years. Cultivation group 4. ↕ 18in (45cm), ↔ 12in (30cm). Zone 7.

S. umbrosa* var. *primuloides, syn. *S. primuloides.* Gymnopera saxifrage with neat, compact rosettes of ovate to spoon-shaped, crinkled, regularly scalloped leaves, to 3in (8cm) long, mid-green above, reddish green beneath. Loose panicles, to 10in (25cm) long, of star-shaped, red-spotted white flowers, ¼–⅜in (6–8mm) across, are produced in summer. Cultivation group 1. ↕↔ 12in (30cm). Pyrenees. Zone 3. **'Clarence Elliott'** see 'Elliott's Variety'. **'Elliott's Variety'**, syn. *S. primuloides* 'Clarence Elliott', *S. primuloides* 'Elliott's Variety', *S. umbrosa* var. *primuloides* 'Clarence Elliott', is more compact, with leaves to 2½in (6cm) long, and red-stemmed, rose-pink flowers, ⅜–½in (9–15mm) across; ↕↔ 6in (15cm).
S.* x *urbium (*S. spathularis* x *S. umbrosa*) (London pride). Vigorous, spreading Gymnopera saxifrage with large rosettes of spoon-shaped, toothed, leathery, mid-green leaves, ¾–1½in (2–4cm) across. Upright, branching stems bear loose panicles, to 12in (30cm) long, of tiny, star-shaped, pink-flushed white flowers, to ⅜in (8mm) across, in summer. Good as a groundcover, even in poor soil. Cultivation group 1. ↕ 12in (30cm), ↔ indefinite. Garden origin. Zone 4.

SCABIOSA

Pincushion flower, Scabious

DIPSACACEAE

Genus of about 80 species of annuals, biennials, and perennials from sunny sites, dry meadows, and rocky slopes, mostly in the Mediterranean region, but also in the rest of Europe, the Caucasus, Africa, Asia, and Japan. They have mainly basal leaves, which are simple and entire or lobed, pinnatifid, or pinnatisect, and produce compound or solitary, blue, white, yellow, or pink flowerheads with domed, pincushion-like central florets and larger marginal florets. The smaller perennial species are ideal for a rock garden, while the taller ones are suitable for a sunny herbaceous or mixed border, or a wild garden; the annuals are excellent in borders. Long-flowering species and cultivars are ideal for windowboxes or containers on a patio. Many are also good for cutting. All are attractive to bees and butterflies.
• **CULTIVATION** Grow in moderately fertile, well-drained, neutral to slightly alkaline soil in full sun. Protect from excessive winter moisture. Deadhead to prolong flowering. Divide and replant perennials in fresh or replenished soil every 3 years.
• **PROPAGATION** Sow seed of annuals and biennials at 43–54°F (6–12°C) in early spring, or *in situ* in midspring; sow seed of perennials in containers in a cold frame as soon as ripe or in spring. Divide, or take basal cuttings of perennials, in spring.
• **PESTS AND DISEASES** Infrequent.

Scabiosa atropurpurea 'Blue Cockade'

Scabiosa caucasica 'Clive Greaves'

S. alpina see *Cephalaria alpina.*
S. arvensis see *Knautia arvensis.*
S. atropurpurea (Pincushion flower, Sweet scabious). Erect, branching, wiry-stemmed annual with mid-green leaves, 1¼–5in (3–13cm) long: the basal leaves are oblong-spoon-shaped and entire or coarsely toothed; the stem leaves are pinnatifid, composed of entire or toothed segments. Solitary, fragrant, dark purple to lilac flower-heads, to 2in (5cm) across, are borne in summer. ↕ to 36in (90cm), ↔ to 9in (23cm). S. Europe. **'Blue Cockade'** ■ bears lavender-blue to purple-blue flower-heads, sometimes over 2in (5cm) across. **'Double'** is a mixture with fully double, white, dark purple, blue, or pink flower-heads, which need support. **'Dwarf Double'** is a mixture with fully double flowerheads in white, dark purple, blue, or pink; ↕ to 18in (45cm). **Imperial Giants Mix** cultivars have fragrant, double flowerheads, 2½–3in (6–8cm) across, in shades of crimson, rose, lavender, and white, on strong stems; ↕ 2ft (60cm).
***S.* 'Butterfly Blue'** see *S. columbaria* 'Butterfly Blue'.
***S.* 'Butterfly Pink'** see *S. columbaria* 'Pink Mist'.
S. caucasica. Clump-forming perennial with lance-shaped, entire, gray-green basal leaves, to 6in (15cm) long, with partly winged stalks, and usually unbranched stems bearing pinnatifid leaves. Solitary, pale blue or lavender-blue flowerheads, to 3in (8cm) across, are borne in mid- and late summer. ↕↔ 24in (60cm). Caucasus, N.E. Turkey, N. Iran. Zone 4. **'Clive Greaves'** ■ has lavender-blue flower-heads. **'Fama'** produces sky-blue flowerheads, in summer; ↕ 24in (60cm). **'House's Hybrids'** see 'Isaac House'. **'Isaac House'**, syn. 'House's Hybrids', bears large, shaggy flowerheads, in shades of blue; ↕ 18–24in (45–60cm). **'Miss Willmott'** ■ has white flower-heads; ↕ to 36in (90cm). **'Perfecta Alba'** has pure white flowerheads on strong stems; ↕ to 18in (45cm). **'Spielarten'** has flowerheads with blue marginal florets and white and blue (occasionally pinkish blue) central florets; ↕ to 24in (60cm).

Scabiosa columbaria 'Butterfly Blue'

Scabiosa caucasica 'Miss Willmott' (inset: flower detail)

Scabiosa lucida

S. columbaria (Small scabious). Branched, hairy perennial with long-stalked, ovate to lance-shaped, simple or pinnatifid basal leaves, 2–6in (5–15cm) long, and pinnatifid, 2-pinnatifid, or pinnatisect stem leaves, the uppermost very finely divided; all are light, mid-, or grayish green. Solitary, bluish lilac flowerheads, to 1½in (4cm) across, are produced from summer to early autumn. ↕ 20–28in (50–70cm), ↔ to 3ft (1m) or more. Europe, W. Asia. Zone 4. The following cultivars are probably hybrids of *S. columbaria.* **'Butterfly Blue'** ■ syn. *S.* 'Butterfly Blue', has gray-green leaves, and bears lavender-blue flowerheads in mid- and late summer; ↕↔ to 16in (40cm). **'Pink Mist'**, syn. *S.* 'Butterfly Pink', *S.* 'Pink Mist', is similar to 'Butterfly Blue', with gray-green leaves and deep pink to lavender-pink flowerheads, borne over long periods in summer; ↕↔ to 16in (40cm). Zone 4.
S. gigantea see *Cephalaria gigantea.*
S. graminifolia (Grass-leaved scabious). Evergreen, clump-forming perennial with tufts of silver-hairy, entire, linear-lance-shaped, mid-green leaves, to 6in (15cm) long. In summer, solitary, spherical, lilac to violet flowerheads, to 1½in (4cm) across, are borne on stiff, slender stems. ↕ 10in (25cm), ↔ 12in (30cm). S. Europe. Zone 4.

Scabiosa stellata 'Paper Moon'

S

'Pinkushion' is mat-forming, with rose-pink flowerheads.
S. lucida ■ Clump-forming, occasionally branched perennial with tufts of ovate-lance-shaped, toothed basal leaves and pinnatifid stem leaves; both are silvery green and to 5in (13cm) long. In summer, bears solitary, pale lilac flowerheads, to 1½in (4cm) across, on slender, erect stems. ↕ 8in (20cm), ↔ 12in (30cm). C. Europe. Zone 4.
***S.* 'Pink Mist'** see *S. columbaria* 'Pink Mist'.
S. rumelica see *Knautia macedonica.*
S. stellata. Erect, branching, wiry-stemmed, hairy annual with lance-shaped to ovate, pinnatifid, mid-green leaves, 7in (18cm) long. Solitary, spherical, pale blue flowerheads, to 1¼in (3cm) across, are borne in summer. They are followed by silvery cream seed heads, to 3in (8cm) across, formed by clustered, cup-shaped, green- or maroon-centered bracts, enlarged after flowering. The seed heads are excellent for dried flower arrangements. ↕ to 18in (45cm), ↔ 9in (23cm). S. Europe.
'Drum Stick' has light blue flower-heads, turning bronze; ↕ to 12in (30cm).
'Paper Moon' ■ produces pale, watery blue seed heads. **'Ping Pong'** bears small white seed heads.
S. succisa see *Succisa pratensis.*
S. tatarica see *Cephalaria gigantea.*

SCADOXUS

Blood lily

AMARYLLIDACEAE

Genus of 9 species of bulbous and rhizomatous perennials from rocky cliffs and woodland in tropical regions of Africa and the Arabian Peninsula. They are closely related to *Haemanthus,* but are distinguished by the spiral arrangement of their leaves, and by their rhizomatous bulbs. They are cultivated for their spectacular, crowded, conical to spherical flowerheads of cylindrical red flowers, with 6 spreading or erect tepals, borne on leafless stems from spring to summer, and followed by spherical, yellow, orange, or red berries. Where not hardy, grow blood lilies in a temperate or warm greenhouse or conservatory; elsewhere, use in a border, or at the base of a warm, sunny wall.
• **CULTIVATION** Plant bulbs in autumn or winter with the necks at soil level. Under glass, grow in soil-based potting mix in full light with shade from hot sun. Move into partial shade as buds open. When in growth, water freely and apply a half-strength balanced liquid fertilizer monthly. Dry off completely as leaves fade. Pot on in spring if necessary. Outdoors, grow in moderately fertile, humus-rich, moist but well-drained soil in full sun or light, dappled shade.
• **PROPAGATION** Sow seed at 66–75°F (19–24°C) as soon as ripe. Separate offsets in spring.
• **PESTS AND DISEASES** Infrequent.

Scadoxus multiflorus subsp. *katherinae*

S. multiflorus, syn. *Haemanthus multiflorus* (Blood lily). Bulbous perennial with semi-erect, broad, lance-shaped to ovate, basal leaves, to 12in (30cm) long. In summer, bears spherical heads, 4–6in (10–15cm) across, of up to 200 narrow-tepaled red flowers, with conspicuous stamens, followed by small orange berries, ¼–½in (6–15mm) across. ↕ to 24in (60cm), PD6in (15cm). Tropical Africa, South Africa, Yemen. ❀ (min. 50–59°F/10–15°C). **subsp. *katherinae*** ■ syn. *Haemanthus katherinae* (Catherine wheel) has wavy-margined leaves; ↕ to 4ft (1.2m); E. southern Africa.
S. puniceus, syn. *Haemanthus magnificus, H. natalensis, H. puniceus* (Giant stove brush). Bulbous perennial with semi-erect, elliptic, wavy-margined, basal leaves, to 12in (30cm) long, that form a "stem," to 20in (50cm) long, of sheathed leaf stalks. From spring to summer, bears conical heads, 4in (10cm) across, of up to 100 tiny, yellowish green to pink or scarlet flowers, surrounded by conspicuous red bracts; they are followed by yellow berries, ½in (1cm) across. ↕ 20in (50cm), PD6in (15cm). E. and S. Africa. ❀ (min. 50–59°F/10–15°C)

SCAEVOLA

GOODENIACEAE

Genus of about 96 species of mostly short-lived, mainly evergreen perennials, but also scrambling climbers, shrubs and small trees, occurring in habitats ranging from coastal dunes to damp, subalpine regions in Australia and Polynesia. They have alternate, rarely opposite, rounded to linear, entire or toothed leaves, and produce solitary or few-flowered cymes or racemes of distinctive, fan-shaped flowers. Where not hardy, grow in a cool greenhouse or conservatory, or grow outdoors in containers or hanging baskets during summer. In warmer climates, grow in a border.
• **CULTIVATION** Under glass, grow in soil-based potting mix in bright indirect light. In the growing season, water freely and apply a balanced liquid fertilizer monthly. Keep just moist in winter. Outdoors, grow in moderately fertile, humus-rich, moist but well-drained soil in full sun or light, dappled shade.
• **PROPAGATION** Sow seed at 66–75°F (19–24°C) in spring. Root softwood cuttings in late spring or summer.
• **PESTS AND DISEASES** Infrequent.

S. aemula ■ (Fairy fan-flower) Variable, tufted, evergreen perennial, often grown as an annual, with spoon-shaped, toothed basal leaves, to 3½in (9cm) long, and smaller stem leaves, borne on erect or sometimes procumbent stems, with yellow or brown hairs. Leafy racemes of purple-blue or blue flowers,

Scaevola aemula

to 1in (2.5cm) across, are borne during summer. ↕↔ to 20in (50cm). S. and E. Australia. ❀ (min. 41°F/5°C)
'Blue Wonder' is shrubby, with vigorous, trailing stems and inversely lance-shaped leaves, ½in (1cm) long. Lilac-blue flowers, ½in (1cm) across, are borne almost continuously and in great profusion from spring to autumn; ↕ to 6in (15cm), ↔ to 5ft (1.5m).
***S.* 'Mauve Clusters'.** Vigorous, shrubby, evergreen perennial, often grown as an annual, with a trailing habit and inversely lance-shaped leaves, ½in (1cm) long. Leafy racemes of lilac-mauve flowers, ½in (1cm) across, are borne freely for much of the year, but particularly in summer. ↕ 4–6in (10–15cm), ↔ to 5ft (1.5m). ❀ (min. 41°F/5°C)

SCHEFFLERA *syn.* BRASSAIA

ARALIACEAE

Genus of at least 900 species of mostly evergreen shrubs, trees, and climbers (some epiphytic when juvenile) from warm-temperate and tropical areas of S.E. Asia to the Pacific islands and Central and South America. They are grown mainly for their spiraled, fine, long-stalked, usually rounded, fully divided leaves, each with 3–30 stalked leaflets. In summer, autumn, or winter, mature trees bear compound umbels, panicles, racemes, or spikes of usually tiny flowers with 4 or 5 yellow-green to greenish red petals. The flowers are followed by mostly spherical or ovoid, black or purple fruits. Where not hardy, grow in a warm greenhouse or as houseplants. In warmer areas, grow at the back of a shrub border or as an informal hedge or windbreak.
• **CULTIVATION** Under glass, grow in soil-based potting mix in bright filtered or indirect light. During the growing season, water moderately and apply a balanced liquid fertilizer monthly; keep just moist in winter. Pot on in spring. Outdoors, grow in fertile, humus-rich, moist but well-drained soil in partial to deep shade. Shelter from cold, drying winds. Pruning group 1; clip hedges in late summer.
• **PROPAGATION** Sow seed at 66–75°F (19–24°C) in spring. Root semi-ripe cuttings with bottom heat in summer. Air layer in spring.
• **PESTS AND DISEASES** Scale insects, thrips, and mealybugs may be a problem under glass.

Schefflera actinophylla

S. actinophylla ■ syn. *Brassaia actinophylla* (Australian ivy palm, Octopus tree, Queensland umbrella tree). Erect, large shrub or small tree with stiff, thick, sparsely branched stems. Large leaves, 4–12in (10–30cm) long, divided into 7–16 ovate-oblong, leathery, glossy, deep bright green leaflets, to 12in (30cm) long, are borne in terminal rosettes on the branches. Leaves of juvenile plants have fewer, smaller leaflets than those of adult plants. Upright, terminal, compound panicles, to 32in (80cm) long, of tiny, brownish pink to red flowers are produced in summer, followed by spherical black fruit. Often grown as juvenile plants. ↕ to 40ft (12m), ↔ to 20ft (6m). N. and N.E. Australia, S. and S.E. New Guinea. ❀ (min. 55°F/13°C)
S. arboricola. Upright, hairless shrub with leaves, 4–8in (10–20cm) long, each divided into 7–11 obovate, stalked, short-pointed, semi-glossy, bright green leaflets, to 4½in (11cm) long. Leaves of juvenile plants have short, broadly spaced teeth. In summer, produces upright, terminal, compound panicles, to 12in (30cm) long, of red flowers; these are followed by ovoid orange fruit, to ¼in (6mm) long, becoming black with age. ↕ 5–20ft (1.5–6m), ↔ 3–8ft (1–2.5m). Taiwan. ❀ (min. 55–59°F/13–15°C)
S. elegantissima ■ syn. *Aralia elegantissima, Dizygotheca elegantissima* (False aralia). Erect, sparsely branched, large shrub or small tree with leaves, 3–16in (8–40cm) long, composed of 7–11 linear, deeply toothed leaflets, 6–9in (15–23cm) long; when young,

S

Schefflera elegantissima

they are glossy, dark green above, dark brown-green beneath, with white midribs; adult plants have broader, stiffer, less glossy leaflets. In autumn and winter, bears yellowish green flowers in terminal umbels, to 12in (30cm) long, followed by spherical black fruit. ↕ 25–50ft (8–15m), ↔ 6–10ft (2–3m). New Caledonia. ❀ (min. 55–59°F/13–15°C)
S. heptaphylla, syn. *S. octophylla* (Fukanoki, Ivy tree). Dense, spreading, evergreen or semi-evergreen tree with loose rosettes of leaves, to 5in (13cm) long, each composed of 6–8 elliptic to oblong-elliptic, glossy, deep green leaflets, 4–8in (10–20cm) long, often white beneath. From autumn to early winter, produces yellowish green flowers in terminal panicles, to 12in (30cm) long, followed by spherical, blue-black fruit. ↕ 40–80ft (12–25m), ↔ 15–30ft (5–10m). E. Asia, Philippines. ❀ (min. 55–59°F/13–15°C)
S. octophylla see *S. heptaphylla.*

SCHIMA

THEACEAE

Genus of one very variable species of evergreen tree or shrub extensively distributed in forest from S.W. China and the E. Himalayas to S.E. Asia. It is grown for the attractive spiral arrangement of its simple, glossy leaves, and for its fragrant, camellia-like flowers, usually solitary, sometimes in raceme-like inflorescences. Where not hardy, grow *S. wallichii* in a cool greenhouse; elsewhere, use as a specimen tree in a woodland garden.
• **CULTIVATION** Under glass, grow in acidic potting mix in bright filtered light or indirect light; provide moderate humidity. During the growing season, water freely and apply a balanced liquid fertilizer monthly; keep just moist in winter. Outdoors, grow in humus-rich, leafy, moist but well-drained, neutral to acidic soil in full sun with some midday shade, or in partial shade. Shelter from cold, drying winds. Pruning group 1.
• **PROPAGATION** Sow seed at 43–54°F (6–12°C) in autumn. Root semi-ripe cuttings in late summer.
• **PESTS AND DISEASES** Infrequent.

S. argentea see *S. wallichii.*
S. khasiana see *S. wallichii.*
S. wallichii, syn. *S. argentea*, *S. khasiana.* Broadly conical tree or shrub. The oblong, lance-shaped, ovate, or obovate, tapered leaves are entire, shallowly scalloped, or toothed, 3–10in (8–25cm) long, papery or leathery in texture, and glossy, dark green, with red veins, often reddish beneath. From late summer to autumn, red-tinged buds open to solitary, cup-shaped, fragrant white flowers, to 3in (8cm) across, with 5 or 6 rounded petals. ↕ 30ft (10m), ↔ 20ft (6m). Himalayas to S.E. Asia. ❀ (min. 41°F/5°C)

S

SCHINUS

ANACARDIACEAE

Genus of about 30 species of usually dioecious, evergreen shrubs and trees occurring in woodland from Mexico to Uruguay. They are grown mainly for their alternate leaves, which may be simple or pinnate, entire or toothed. Tiny, 4- or 5-petaled flowers are borne

Schinus molle

in terminal or axillary panicles. When plants of both sexes are grown together, the flowers are followed on female plants by small, red to purple fruits (drupes). Where not hardy, grow *Schinus* species in a temperate greenhouse or conservatory; elsewhere, use smaller species in a shrub border and larger ones as specimen trees.
• **CULTIVATION** Under glass, grow in soil-based potting mix in full light with shade from hot sun. When in active growth, water freely and apply a balanced liquid fertilizer monthly; water sparingly in winter. Outdoors, grow in moderately fertile, humus-rich, moist but well-drained soil in full sun, or with some midday shade. Pruning group 1.
• **PROPAGATION** Sow seed at 66–70°F (19–21°C) in spring. Root semi-ripe cuttings with bottom heat during late summer. Air layer in spring.
• **PESTS AND DISEASES** Scale insects and spider mites may be troublesome.

S. molle ■ (Pepper tree, Peruvian mastic tree). Usually broad-headed tree with slender, pendent branches. The arching or semi-pendent, pinnate leaves, 4–12in (10–30cm) long, are composed of 19–41 narrow, lance-shaped, toothed, glossy, mid- to deep green leaflets. Pendent panicles, 3–8in (8–20cm) long, of tiny, whitish yellow flowers are borne from late winter to summer, followed by rose-pink fruit. ↕ 30–80ft (10–25m), ↔ 10–15ft (3–5m). Mexico, Brazil, Bolivia, Chile, N. Argentina, Paraguay, Uruguay. ❀ (min. 50°F/10°C)
S. terebinthifolius (Brazilian pepper tree, Christmasberry tree). Moderately bushy, large shrub or small tree with erect to spreading stems bearing pinnate leaves, 4–7in (10–18cm) long, with winged midribs and 3–13 (normally 7) oblong, deep green leaflets, which are paler beneath. From summer to autumn, produces panicles, to 6in (15cm) long, of tiny white flowers, followed by red fruit. Highly invasive in parts of California and Florida, where planting it is not recommended. Contact with the seeds may irritate skin and cause respiratory problems. ↕ 15–22ft (5–7m), ↔ 10–15ft (3–5m). Venezuela to Argentina, S. Brazil. ❀ (min. 45°F/7°C)

SCHISANDRA

SCHISANDRACEAE

Genus of about 25 species of twining, woody, monoecious or dioecious, deciduous or evergreen climbers found in woodland in E. Asia, with one species from S.E. US. They are grown for their cup-shaped, red, pink, yellow, or white flowers, borne singly or in clusters or short spikes in the leaf axils, and for their spikes of spherical, brightly colored fruits. Leaves are alternate, entire or toothed, and usually lance-shaped or ovate to elliptic. Both male and female plants of dioecious species must be grown to obtain fruit. Grow over rocks and stumps in woodland, or train on a wall or pergola.
• **CULTIVATION** Grow in fertile, moist but well-drained soil in full sun or partial shade. Tie in shoots of young plants until established. Pruning group 12, in early spring.

Schisandra rubriflora

• **PROPAGATION** Sow seed in containers in a cold frame as soon as ripe. Take greenwood cuttings in early or mid-summer, or semi-ripe cuttings in summer.
• **PESTS AND DISEASES** Infrequent.

S. chinensis (Chinese magnolia vine). Twining, woody, deciduous climber with red shoots and producing elliptic to obovate, minutely toothed, glossy, dark green leaves, to 5½in (14cm) long. From late spring to summer, bears small clusters of cream to pale pink flowers, to ¾in (2cm) across; these are followed, on female plants, by pendent spikes, to 6in (15cm) long, of fleshy, red or pink fruit. ↕ 30ft (10m). E. Asia. Zone 7b.
S. henryi. Twining, woody, deciduous climber with angled shoots, winged when young, and oval, finely toothed, leathery, glossy, mid-green leaves, to 4in (10cm) long. In spring, bears small clusters of white flowers, ½in (1cm) across; these are followed, on female plants, by pendent spikes, to 3in (8cm) long, of fleshy red fruit. ↕ 10–12ft (3–4m). W. China. Zone 7b.
S. rubriflora ■ Twining, woody, deciduous climber with slender red shoots and lance-shaped to narrowly elliptic or inversely lance-shaped, slightly toothed to entire, dark green leaves, to 5in (13cm) long, yellow in autumn. Produces solitary, dark crimson flowers, to 1in (2.5cm) across, from late spring to summer, followed, on female plants, by pendent spikes, to 6in (15cm) long, of fleshy red fruit. ↕ 30ft (10m). India, W. China, Burma. Zone 7b.

SCHIZACHYRIUM

POACEAE

Genus of about 100 species of deciduous, perennial grasses native to grasslands worldwide. Closely related to *Andropogon*, they are distinguished by their solitary, terminal, obliquely branched racemes of stalked spikelets. Suitable for a herbaceous or mixed border. The flowerheads may be dried.
• **CULTIVATION** Grow in moderately fertile, sharply drained soil in full sun. Cut down old stems in early winter.
• **PROPAGATION** Sow seed at 55–59°F (13–15°C), or divide, in spring.
• **PESTS AND DISEASES** Infrequent.

S. scoparium, syn. *Andropogon scoparius* (Little bluestem). Densely tufted, perennial grass, spreading slowly to form clumps of upright stems with linear, mid-green to gray-green leaves, to 18in (45cm) long, that turn purple to orange red in autumn. From late summer to midautumn, bears narrow racemes, to 6in (15cm) long, of wispy, long-awned spikelets. ↕ to 3ft (1m), ↔ 12in (30cm). North America. Zone 6.

SCHIZANTHUS

Butterfly flower, Poor man's orchid

SOLANACEAE

Genus of 12–15 erect to spreading, bushy, soft-stemmed, downy annuals, and some biennials, from dry, rocky slopes and canyons in Chile. They have alternate, pinnatisect to 3-pinnatisect or deeply lobed leaves. They are cultivated for their terminal cymes of showy, 2-lipped flowers of various colors, which are borne from spring to winter. In cool

Schizanthus pinnatus 'Hit Parade'

temperate regions, grow in either a conservatory or cool greenhouse, as marginally hardy annuals in a sheltered annual border, or in containers on a patio or in a courtyard garden. In warmer climates, grow in a border. They provide long-lasting cut flowers.

• **CULTIVATION** Under glass, grow in soil-based potting mix in full light with shade from hot sun, or in bright filtered light. In growth, water moderately, and apply a high-potash liquid fertilizer every 2 weeks. Support flowering stems. Excessive heat above 70°F (21°C) produces elongated plants. Outdoors, grow in fertile, moist but well-drained soil in full sun. Pinch back young plants to promote bushiness.

• **PROPAGATION** Sow seed at 61°F (16°C) in midspring for summer- to autumn-flowering plants. Sow in late summer at 61°F (16°C) for winter-flowering container plants.

• **PESTS AND DISEASES** Aphids may be a problem under glass.

S. pinnatus (Poor man's orchid). Erect annual with almost fern-like, lance-shaped to inversely lance-shaped, pinnatisect to 3-pinnatisect, light green leaves, to 5in (13cm) long. From spring to autumn, bears terminal, open cymes of tubular, then flared, 2-lipped, white, yellow, pink, purple, or red flowers, to 3in (8cm) across; they often have yellow throats with violet markings, further streaked and spotted in contrasting colors. ↕ 8–20in (20–50cm), ↔ 9–12in (23–30cm). Chile. **'Angel's Wings'** bears large flowers, 3–4in (8–10cm) across, in a range of pink, red, and purple shades; ↕ to 18in (45cm). **Disco Hybrids** are compact and vigorous, with a wide range of flower colors; ↕ 12–16in (30–40cm). **Dwarf Bouquet Mixed** cultivars bear a profusion of crimson, amber, pink, and salmon flowers; ↕ 12–16in (30–40cm). **'Hit Parade'** ■ bears flowers with clear, contrasting markings; ↕ 9–12in (23–30cm). **Royal Pierrot Mixed** cultivars are long-blooming, in shades of pink, purple, violet, and white. **'Star Parade'** is compact, with a distinctive pyramidal habit; ↕ 8–10in (20–25cm). **'Sweet Lips'** bears flowers that are picotee-edged, striped, and veined in deep shades of red and pink.

S. x wisetonensis (*S. grahamii* x *S. pinnatus*). Erect annual with lance-shaped to inversely lance-shaped, pinnatisect to 3-pinnatisect, light green leaves, to 5in (13cm) long. From spring to summer, bears terminal, open cymes of tubular, then flared, 2-lipped, white, pale blue, pink, or red-brown flowers, to 3in (8cm) across, often flushed yellow on the central lobe of the upper lips. ↕ to 18in (45cm), ↔ 9–12in (23–30cm). Garden origin.

▷ ***Schizocodon*** see *Shortia*

SCHIZOPETALON

BRASSICACEAE

Genus of about 8 species of erect, slender-stemmed, hairy annuals from rocky slopes and disturbed ground in Chile. They have alternate, wavy-margined, toothed, simple or pinnatifid, linear to ovate leaves. From late spring to early autumn, they bear leafy racemes of star-shaped, white or purple flowers, each with 4 fringed petals. Grow at the edge of a border, in a rock garden or raised bed, or in containers. They are particularly effective grown near a patio or paved area where the evening scent of the blooms may be best appreciated.

• **CULTIVATION** Grow in moderately fertile, well-drained soil in full sun.

• **PROPAGATION** Sow seed at 66–70°F (19–21°C) in midspring.

• **PESTS AND DISEASES** Infrequent.

S. walkeri. Upright, slightly branching annual producing deeply pinnatifid, linear to lance-shaped leaves, to 5½in (14cm) long. Terminal racemes of almond-scented, spreading, deeply cut, star-shaped, pure white flowers, to 1½in (4cm) across, are borne from summer to early autumn. ↕ 6–14in (15–35cm), ↔ 8in (20cm). Chile.

SCHIZOPHRAGMA

HYDRANGEACEAE

Genus of 2 species of woody, deciduous root climbers from woodland and cliffs in China, Korea, and Japan. They bear opposite pairs of simple, long-stalked, entire or toothed, ovate, dark green leaves. Schizophragmas are cultivated for their showy flowerheads, similar to those of lacecap hydrangeas, but with large, conspicuous, bract-like, sterile, outer flowers. Best grown against a wall, fence, or large tree, to which the plant will attach itself by aerial roots.

• **CULTIVATION** Grow in moderately fertile, humus-rich, moist but well-drained soil, in full sun or partial shade. Plant at least 24in (60cm) away from a host plant or support. Tie in to a support and train until established. Pruning group 11, in spring.

• **PROPAGATION** Take greenwood cuttings in early or midsummer; take semi-ripe cuttings in late summer.

• **PESTS AND DISEASES** Infrequent.

S. hydrangeoides (Japanese hydrangea vine). Woody root climber with long-stalked, broadly ovate, sharply toothed, dark green leaves, to 6in (15cm) long. In midsummer, small, slightly fragrant, creamy white flowers are borne in broad, flattened, terminal cymes, to 10in (25cm) across, with conspicuous, ovate, creamy, marginal bracts, to 2½in (6cm) long. ↕ 40ft (12m). Korea, Japan. Zone 6. **'Moonlight'** has silver-glaucous, blue-green leaves with deep green veins. **'Roseum'** has pink bracts.

Schizophragma integrifolium

S. integrifolium ■ Woody root climber with long-stalked, ovate, entire or finely toothed, dark green leaves, to 7in (18cm) long. In midsummer, small, slightly fragrant, creamy white flowers are borne in broad, flattened, terminal cymes, to 12in (30cm) across, with conspicuous, ovate, creamy, marginal bracts, to 3½in (9cm) long. ↕ 40ft (12m). C. and W. China. Zone 5b.

S. viburnoides see *Pileostegia viburnoides.*

SCHIZOSTYLIS

Kaffir lily

IRIDACEAE

Genus of a single species of virtually evergreen, rhizomatous perennial from damp water-meadows and streambanks in southern Africa. Kaffir lilies are cultivated for their showy, gladiolus-like spikes of open cup-shaped flowers, which are produced from late summer to early winter. They are suitable for growing at the front of a herbaceous or mixed border, at the base of a warm, sunny wall, or in a small courtyard garden. *S. coccinea* and its cultivars are also effective grown *en masse* in large containers in a cool greenhouse, where they will flower for long periods during winter. Excellent for cut flowers.

• **CULTIVATION** Grow in moderately fertile, moist but well-drained soil in full sun. Keep the roots moist. Shelter from cold, drying winds. Provide an organic mulch in winter.

• **PROPAGATION** Sow seed at 55–61°F (13–16°C) in spring. Divide species and cultivars in spring.

• **PESTS AND DISEASES** Infrequent.

S. coccinea (Crimson flag). Vigorous, clump-forming, rhizomatous perennial with erect, keeled, narrow, sword-shaped leaves, to 16in (40cm) long, with distinct midribs. Spikes of 4–14 open cup-shaped scarlet flowers, ¾in (2cm) across, are produced in autumn. ↕ to 24in (60cm), ↔ 12in (30cm). South Africa, Lesotho, Swaziland. Zone 7b. **var. *alba*** bears white flowers. **'Grandiflora'** see 'Major'. **'Jennifer'** is robust, bearing large, mid-pink flowers, 2–2½in (5–6cm) across, in late summer. **'Major'** ■ syn. 'Grandiflora', is robust, producing large red flowers, 2–2½in (5–6cm) across, on stiff stems in late summer. **'November Cheer'** has deep pink flowers. **'Pallida'** has very pale pink flowers. **'Sunrise'** ■ syn. 'Sunset', bears large, salmon-pink flowers, 2–2½in (5–6cm) across, in autumn. **'Sunset'** see 'Sunrise'. **'Viscountess Byng'** ■ bears pale pink flowers, 1¼in (3cm) across, with narrow petals, in late autumn; its flowers are particularly vulnerable to damage by frost. **'Zeal Salmon'** has clear, salmon-pink flowers.

Schizostylis coccinea 'Sunrise'

Schizostylis coccinea 'Major'

Schizostylis coccinea 'Viscountess Byng'

SCHLUMBERGERA

Holiday cactus

CACTACEAE

Genus of about 6 species of bushy, epiphytic or rock-dwelling cacti from tropical rainforest in S.E. Brazil, cultivated for their attractive flowers. Erect then pendent, fleshy stems are divided into flattened, oblong or obovate, normally truncate, leaf-like segments, usually with marginal, often prominent notches, almost tooth-like in some species. The areoles often have a few fine bristles; those near the tips of the upper segments bear open trumpet-shaped, narrow-petaled flowers, most in late winter and early spring, others in summer or autumn. Where temperatures fall below 50°F (10°C), grow as houseplants, or in a temperate or warm greenhouse. In warmer areas, use in a raised bed in a courtyard garden.

• **CULTIVATION** Under glass, grow in epiphytic cactus potting mix in bright indirect light. Water moderately and maintain moderate humidity. Apply a high-potash liquid fertilizer every 4 weeks when in growth; keep barely moist after flowering. Repot or pot on every 3 or 4 years in spring. Outdoors, grow in humus-rich, acidic to neutral, moist but well-drained soil, with added leaf mold and grit, in light dappled to partial shade. Protect from excessive rain; shelter from strong winds. Buds may drop in dry conditions or if other environmental conditions suddenly change. See also pp.48–49.

• **PROPAGATION** Sow seed at 66–70°F (19–21°C) in spring, or take cuttings of stem sections in spring or early summer.

• **PESTS AND DISEASES** Susceptible to mealybugs.

Schlumbergera 'Spectabilis'

S. bridgesii see *S.* x *buckleyi.*

***S.* 'Bristol Beauty'.** Epiphytic cactus with oblong, bright green stem segments, 1in (2.5cm) long, with 4–6 marginal notches. In late winter and early spring, produces reddish purple flowers, 3in (8cm) long, with silvery white tubes. ↕ to 14in (35cm), ↔ 12in (30cm). ❄ (min. 50°F/10°C)

S.* x *buckleyi (*S. russelliana* x *S. truncata*) syn. *S. bridgesii* (Christmas cactus). Epiphytic cactus with oblong or obovate, truncate, scalloped, mid-green stem segments, ¾–2in (2–5cm) long. Produces bright red flowers, to 3in (8cm) long, in late winter. ↕ to 24in (60cm), ↔ 3ft (1m). Garden origin. ❄ (min. 50°F/10°C)

***S.* 'Gold Charm'** ■ Epiphytic cactus with oblong, mid-green stem segments, 1¼–2in (3–5cm) long, with 6–8 prominent, tooth-like marginal notches. Flowers, 2½in (6cm) long, are yellow in autumn but may turn pinkish if kept below 57°F (14°C). ↕↔ to 12in (30cm). ❄ (min. 50°F/10°C)

S. opuntioides, syn. *Epiphyllanthus obovatus.* Epiphytic or rock-dwelling cactus with thick, obovate to oblong, deep green stem segments, 2–3in (5–8cm) long, often tinged red, bearing white areoles, with minute spines, on both surfaces and margins. Deep pink flowers, 2½in (6cm) long, are produced in spring. Allow houseplants a brief, dry period after flowering. ↕ to 16in (40cm), ↔ 9in (22cm). S.E. Brazil. ❄ (min. 50°F/10°C)

S. orssichiana. Epiphytic cactus with oblong, dark green stem segments, to 2in (5cm) long, with 4–6 prominent, tooth-like marginal notches, with areoles set in the angles. White flowers, to 3½in (9cm) long, purplish pink toward the petal tips, are borne from late summer to winter. ↕ to 12in (30cm), ↔ to 14in (35cm). S.E. Brazil. ❄ (min. 50°F/10°C)

***S.* 'Spectabilis'** ■ Epiphytic cactus with oblong, dark green stem segments, to 1in (2.5cm) long, with 3–5 tooth-like marginal notches. Bears bright red flowers, to 3in (8cm) long, in late winter and early spring. ↕ to 11in (28cm), ↔ 10in (25cm) or more. ❄ (min. 50°F/10°C)

S. truncata ■ syn. *Zygocactus truncatus* (Crab cactus, Thanksgiving cactus). Epiphytic cactus with oblong, bright green stem segments, 1½–2½in (4–6cm) long, with 4–8 prominent, tooth-like marginal notches. Bears deep pink, red, orange, or white flowers, to 3in (8cm) long, from late autumn to winter. ↕↔ to 12in (30cm). S.E. Brazil. ❄ (min. 50°F/10°C)

***S.* 'Wintermärchen'.** Epiphytic cactus bearing oblong, glossy, mid-green stem segments, 1½in (4cm) long, with 4–6 tooth-like marginal notches. Delicate pale pink, almost white flowers, 2½–3in (6–8cm) long, are produced in late autumn, and turn pinkish white in winter. ↕ to 14in (35cm), ↔ 12in (30cm). ❄ (min. 50°F/10°C)

Schlumbergera 'Gold Charm'

Schlumbergera truncata

Schoenoplectus lacustris subsp. *tabernaemontani* 'Zebrinus'

SCHOENOPLECTUS

CYPERACEAE

Genus, formerly included in *Scirpus*, of 80 species of evergreen, rhizomatous, marginal aquatic perennials and annuals usually found on the banks of lakes and slow-running streams, almost worldwide. Leaves are grass-like and often borne under water. Insignificant flowers are borne in inflorescences on cylindrical or 3-angled stems, in summer. The plant described is grown for its striped stems, and is suitable for cultivation in a bog garden, or as a marginal aquatic plant in still or slow-moving water.

• **CULTIVATION** Grow in fertile, wet soil, or in water up to 12in (30cm) deep, in full sun. In small pools, restrict growth by cutting back the rhizomes annually. See also pp.52–53.

• **PROPAGATION** Root sections of rhizome from midspring to midsummer.

• **PESTS AND DISEASES** Infrequent.

***S. lacustris* subsp. *tabernaemontani* 'Zebrinus'** ■ (Club rush). Rhizomatous perennial with virtually leafless, gray-green stems banded creamy white, arising at intervals along the rhizome. Bears branched clusters, ¼–½in (6–15mm) across, of brown spikelets from early to late summer. Cut reverting stems back to the rhizomes. ↕ 3ft (1m), ↔ 24in (60cm) or more. Zone 5.

SCHOMBURGKIA

ORCHIDACEAE

Genus, closely related to *Laelia*, of about 12–15 species of large, evergreen, epiphytic or lithophytic orchids from rainforest and moist cliffs or rocks, at low to medium altitudes in the West Indies and tropical North and South America. They have thick, elongated, spindle-shaped to cylindrical, sometimes hollow pseudobulbs, each with 1–3 leathery, semi-rigid, ovate to oblong

aves. Racemes or panicles of showy
owers are produced from the tips of
e pseudobulbs, and may reach 6ft
m) in length.
CULTIVATION Intermediate-growing
chids. Grow in epiphytic orchid
otting mix in containers or slatted
askets. In the growing season, water
eely and apply a half-strength balanced
quid fertilizer every 4 weeks; provide
gh humidity and bright indirect light.
ater sparingly and provide full light
winter. See also p.46.
PROPAGATION Divide when the plant
verflows the sides of the container.
emove backbulbs and pot them up in
parate containers.
PESTS AND DISEASES Scale insects,
ider mites, aphids, whiteflies, and
ealybugs may be troublesome.

. tibicinis, syn. *Myrmecophila tibicinis*.
piphytic orchid with stoutly cylindrical,
ollow pseudobulbs and 2 or 3 elliptic
oblong leaves, 18in (45cm) long.
ariable, fragrant, brown to rich purple
owers, 2½in (6cm) across, with
visted, wavy sepals and petals, and
llow, white, and purple lips, are
roduced in extended racemes, 5ft
.5m) or more long, in summer.
↔ 24in (60cm). Mexico to Panama.
(min. 55°F/13°C; max. 86°F/30°C)

SCHOTIA

ABACEAE

enus of 4 or 5 species of deciduous or
mi-evergreen shrubs and trees from
pen deciduous woodland, dry wood-
nd, and scrub in southern Africa. They
e cultivated for their pinnate leaves,
d for their 5-petaled, red or pink
owers, which are borne in summer
axillary or terminal panicles, often
n bare stems and sometimes directly
om older wood. Where temperatures
gularly fall below 32°F (0°C), grow
a cool or temperate greenhouse. In
ilder climates, use in a shrub border
as specimen plants.
CULTIVATION Under glass, grow in
oil-based potting mix in full light.
uring the growing season, water
oderately and apply a balanced liquid
rtilizer monthly; water sparingly in
inter. Outdoors, grow in moderately
rtile, well-drained soil in full sun
ith shelter from cold, drying winds.
runing group 1.
PROPAGATION Sow seed at 55–61°F
3–16°C) in spring. Root semi-ripe
uttings with bottom heat in summer.
PESTS AND DISEASES Whiteflies and
ider mites may be troublesome,
specially under glass.

. brachypetala (African walnut, Tree
uchsia, Weeping boerboon). Spreading
arching, semi-evergreen, large shrub
small tree with red-brown bark and
ray twigs. The pinnate leaves, to 7in
8cm) long, each have 8–15 oblong or
val leaflets, which emerge rose-red and
ature through copper to bright green.
rom summer to late autumn, bears
agrant flowers in nodding to pendent,
sually crowded panicles, to 5in (13cm)
cross, on leafless or almost leafless
vigs; each flower has 5 minute petals
d 4 spreading crimson sepals, to ½in
cm) long. Bean-like pods, 2–7in
–18cm) long, contain large seeds that
are edible when roasted. ↕ 30–50ft (10–15m), ↔ 15–30ft (5–10m). Zimbabwe, Mozambique, South Africa (Northern Transvaal, KwaZulu/Natal), Swaziland. ❀ (min. 45°F/7°C)

SCHWANTESIA

AIZOACEAE

Genus of 10 species of dwarf, compact, cushion-forming, perennial succulents from hillsides and lowlands of Namibia and S. South Africa. They have unequal pairs of fleshy, keeled, bluish green leaves, and bear daisy-like, bright yellow flowers, which open during the day, in summer. Where temperatures fall below 50°F (10°C), grow in a temperate or warm greenhouse; in warmer climates, they are suitable for cultivation in a desert garden.

• **CULTIVATION** Under glass, grow in standard cactus potting mix in full light with shade from hot sun; provide low humidity. During the growing season, water moderately and apply a balanced liquid fertilizer monthly; keep just moist in winter. Outdoors, grow in poor to moderately fertile, humus-rich, sharply drained soil in full sun. Protect from excessive rain in summer and winter. See also pp.48–49.

• **PROPAGATION** Sow seed at 66–70°F (19–21°C) in spring. Divide offsets from spring to early summer.

• **PESTS AND DISEASES** Prone to aphids while flowering.

S. herrei. Cushion-forming, succulent perennial with 2 or 3 pairs of 3-angled, keeled, fleshy, pale blue-green leaves, 1–1½in (2.5–4cm) long, sometimes with a few terminal teeth. Bright yellow flowers, 1½in (4cm) across, are produced in summer. ↕↔ 5½in (14cm). Namibia, South Africa (Northern Cape, Western Cape). ❀ (min. 50°F/10°C).
f. *major* bears flowers to 2½in (6cm) across; Namibia.
S. ruedebuschii ▣ Clump-forming, succulent perennial producing slightly angular, very fleshy, white-mottled, grayish green leaves, 1¼–2in (3–5cm) long, the upper surfaces slightly convex, the lower ones more rounded, and the tips widening and bearing 3–7 thick blue teeth, to ⅛in (3mm) long. Bright pale yellow flowers, to 1½in (4cm) across, are borne in summer. ↕ 4in (10cm), ↔ 6in (15cm). Namibia, South Africa (Northern Cape, Western Cape). ❀ (min. 50°F/10°C)

Schwantesia ruedebuschii

SCIADOPITYS

SCIADOPITYACEAE

Genus of one species of monoecious, evergreen, coniferous tree from forest and very steep, rocky sites in Japan. It has peeling, red-brown bark, and the glossy, linear leaves, sometimes in fused pairs, are borne in whorls at the shoot-tips, like the spokes of an umbrella. Use as a specimen tree for its unusual radiating foliage. *S. verticillata* can add texture to a landscape planting, border, or large rock garden.

• **CULTIVATION** Grow in moderately fertile, moist but well-drained, neutral to slightly acidic soil, in full sun with some midday shade, or in partial shade. May need several years of training to maintain a central leader.

• **PROPAGATION** Sow seed in containers in a cold frame in spring, or take semi-ripe cuttings in late summer. Soak seedlings in water to improve rooting; they are slow to begin growth.

• **PESTS AND DISEASES** Infrequent.

S. verticillata ▣ (Japanese umbrella pine). Conical or columnar-conical tree with red-brown bark, peeling in ribbons, and brown shoots. Linear, grooved, glossy, dark green leaves, 2–5in (5–13cm) long, olive-green beneath, are borne in terminal whorls of 15–25, and persist for 3 or 4 years. Single, ovoid female cones, 2–3in (5–8cm) long, ripen in the second year. Spherical male cones, ⅛–⅜in (3–8mm) across, are borne in clusters. ↕ 30–70ft (10–20m), ↔ to 20–25ft (6–8m). S. Japan. Zone 6.

SCILLA

LILIACEAE

Genus of about 90 species of bulbous perennials found in subalpine meadows, rocky slopes, woodland, and sea shores in Europe, Africa, and Asia. They are grown for their terminal racemes or corymbs of small, usually blue but also pink, purple, or white, bell-shaped to flat, or star-shaped flowers, borne in spring, summer, and autumn. Most have semi-erect, linear to elliptic, sometimes channeled, basal leaves. Naturalize under trees and shrubs or in grass; small species are suitable for an alpine house.

• **CULTIVATION** Plant bulbs 3–4in (8–10cm) deep in autumn. Under glass, grow in 2 parts soil-based potting mix and 1 part each leaf mold and grit. Provide full light. In growth, water freely; keep dry during summer dormancy. *S. peruviana* does not have a natural dormant period, but it may be given a short dormancy period by withholding water in summer. Outdoors, grow in moderately fertile, humus-rich, well-drained soil in full sun or partial shade.

• **PROPAGATION** Sow seed in containers in a cold frame as soon as ripe. Divide and pot up offsets when dormant.

• **PESTS AND DISEASES** Prone to viruses.

S. adlamii see *Ledebouria cooperi.*
S. amethystina see *S. litardierei.*
S. amoena (Star hyacinth). Small, bulbous perennial producing 3–5 flaccid, linear, basal leaves, 6–9in (15–22cm) long, emerging before the small, compact racemes of 3–6 star-

Sciadopitys verticillata (inset: female cone detail)

S

Scilla bifolia

shaped blue flowers, ½–¾in (1.5–2cm) across, in spring. Similar to *S. bithynica* but lacks bracts. Good for naturalizing. ↕ 6–8in (15–20cm), PD2in (5cm). Probably S.E. Europe. Zone 7b.
S. bifolia ▣ Small, bulbous perennial with 2 semi-erect, broadly linear, basal leaves, 2–8in (5–20cm) long, borne in early spring, at the same time as slightly one-sided racemes of up to 10 star-shaped, blue to purple-blue flowers, 1–1½in (2.5–4cm) across. Excellent for naturalizing. ↕ 3–6in (8–15cm), PD2in (5cm). C. and S. Europe, Turkey. Zone 3.
S. bithynica. Small, bulbous perennial with 3–5 flaccid, linear, basal leaves, to 8in (20cm) long, borne in spring, at the same time as compact, conical racemes of 6–12 star-shaped blue flowers, to ¾in (2cm) across. Excellent for naturalizing. ↕ 4–6in (10–15cm), PD3in (8cm). Bulgaria, Turkey. Zone 7.
S. campanulata see *Hyacinthoides hispanica.*
S. chinensis see *S. scilloides.*
S. cilicica. Bulbous perennial producing 3 or 4 erect, broadly linear, basal leaves, 6–10in (15–25cm) long, in autumn. In spring, bears loose racemes of 5–15 star-shaped, pale or lavender-blue flowers, ¾–1¼in (2–3cm) across, with reflexed segments. Easily grown in a bulb frame or alpine house. ↕ 6–14in (15–35cm), PD3in (8cm). Turkey. Zone 7b.
S. cooperi see *Ledebouria cooperi.*
S. hispanica see *Hyacinthoides hispanica.*
S. hohenackeri. Bulbous perennial, similar to *S. cilicica*, with 3–5 flaccid, linear, basal leaves, 4–10in (10–25cm) long, produced in spring, before loose racemes of 4–12 star-shaped, pale blue flowers, ½in (1.5cm) across, with reflexed segments. Easily grown in partial shade. ↕ 4–8in (10–20cm), PD2in (5cm). Azerbaijan, Iran. Zone 7.
S. japonica see *S. scilloides.*
S. liliohyacinthus. Small, clump-forming, bulbous perennial with relatively large, lily-like bulbs, with yellow scales. In late spring, produces a basal cluster of 6–10 erect, inversely lance-shaped, glossy leaves, 6–12in (15–30cm) long, and dense, conical racemes of 5–20 star-shaped, bright lilac-blue to purplish blue, rarely white flowers, ½in (1.5cm) across. Prefers a cool site. ↕ 6–10in (15–25cm), PD3in (8cm). S.W. France, Spain. Zone 7.

Scilla peruviana f. *alba*

Scilla siberica 'Spring Beauty'

S. litardierei, syn. *S. amethystina, S. pratensis.* Clump-forming, bulbous perennial with a basal cluster of 3–6 semi-erect, linear leaves, 6–12in (15–30cm) long, borne in early summer, at the same time as dense racemes of 15–35 star-shaped, pale bluish violet flowers, ¼in (6mm) across. ↕ 4–8in (10–20cm), PD2in (5cm). Coast of former Yugoslavia. Zone 7.
S. mischtschenkoana, syn. *S. tubergeniana.* Dwarf, bulbous perennial with 3–5 semi-erect, linear to inversely lance-shaped, basal leaves, 1½–4in (4–10cm) long, borne in late winter or early spring. At the same time, racemes of 2–6 star-shaped, silvery blue flowers, ¾in (2cm) across, with darker stripes, open just above the ground. Stems and racemes gradually elongate. ↕ 4–6in (10–15cm), PD2in (5cm). Republic of Georgia, Armenia, Azerbaijan, Iran. Zone 3.
S. natalensis. Bulbous perennial with 4–8 semi-erect, lance-shaped, basal leaves, to 8in (20cm) long when they emerge at flowering time, later growing to 12–24in (30–60cm). Tall racemes of up to 100 flattish, light violet-blue, pink, or white flowers, ½in (1.5cm) across, are produced in summer. The flowering stems gradually elongate. ↕ 12–48in (30–120cm), PD3in (8cm). South Africa, Lesotho. ❀ (min. 41°F/5°C)
S. non-scripta see *Hyacinthoides non-scripta.*
S. nutans see *Hyacinthoides non-scripta.*
S. peruviana (Cuban lily, Peruvian jacinth). Virtually evergreen, clump-forming, bulbous perennial with a basal cluster of 5–15 semi-erect, lance-shaped leaves, 16–24in (40–60cm) long, developing in autumn as the older leaves fade. In early summer, produces elongating, conical racemes of 50–100 star-shaped, deep purplish blue or white flowers, ½in (1.5cm) across. ↕ 6–18in (15–45cm), ↔ 8in (20cm). Portugal, Spain, Italy, N. Africa. Zone 8.
f. *alba* ▣ produces large heads of white flowers.
S. pratensis see *S. litardierei.*
S. scilloides, syn. *S. chinensis, S. japonica* (Chinese scilla). Slender, bulbous perennial with 2–7 semi-erect, flaccid, linear, basal leaves, 6–10in (15–25cm) long, borne in late summer and early autumn, with slender racemes of 40–80 star-shaped, mauve-pink flowers, ⅛in (3mm) across. Easily grown in full sun to partial shade. ↕ 6–8in (15–20cm), PD2in (5cm). China, Korea, Taiwan, Japan. Zone 4.
S. siberica (Siberian squill, Spring squill). Bulbous perennial with 2–4 semi-erect, broadly linear, basal leaves, 4–6in (10–15cm) long, produced in spring, at the same time as loose racemes of up to 4 or 5 pendent, bowl-shaped, bright blue flowers, ½in (1.5cm) across. Stems gradually elongate. ↕ 4–8in (10–20cm), ↔ 2in (5cm). Ukraine, Russia, Republic of Georgia, Azerbaijan, N. Iran. Zone 3. **'Alba'** has white flowers. **'Atrocoerulea'** see 'Spring Beauty'. **'Spring Beauty'** ▣ syn. 'Atrocoerulea', has deep blue flowers; ↕ to 8in (20cm).
S. socialis see *Ledebouria socialis.*
S. tubergeniana see *S. mischtschenkoana.*
S. violacea see *Ledebouria socialis.*

▷ ***Scindapsus*** see *Epipremnum*

SCIRPOIDES

CYPERACEAE

Genus, formerly included in *Scirpus*, of one species of deciduous or semi-evergreen, fleshy-rooted, rhizomatous, perennial sedge found in damp, sandy, coastal areas and damp or wet meadow inland, from Europe to S.W. Asia. *S. holoschoenus* has almost leafless stem and produces long-stalked, spherical flowerheads from midsummer to early autumn. Suitable for a wild garden. Grow *S. holoschoenus* 'Variegatus' at th margins of a pool or in a bog garden.
• **CULTIVATION** Grow in moderately fertile, constantly moist soil in full sun Submerge in water to 9in (23cm) deep grown as a marginal aquatic plant. Cu back stems left for winter effect by earl spring. See also pp.52–53.
• **PROPAGATION** Sow seed at 43–54°F (6–12°C) in spring, in permanently moist seed starting mix. Divide betwee midspring and early summer.
• **PESTS AND DISEASES** Infrequent.

S. holoschoenus, syn. *Scirpus holoschoenus* (Round-headed club-rush Tufted perennial with upright, smoot rounded, mid-green stems, to 3ft (1m) long, turning orange-brown in autum they occasionally bear linear, round-tipped, rough-margined, mid-green, basal leaves. From midsummer to early autumn, produces lax, terminal umbel of dense, long-stalked, spherical heads, ½in (1.5cm) long, consisting of ovoid, pale brown spikelets. ↕ 3ft (1m), ↔ 18i (45cm). Europe, S.W. Asia. Zone 7. **'Variegatus'** has leaves and stems that are ringed yellow.

▷ ***Scirpus holoschoenus*** see *Scirpoides holoschoenus*
▷ ***Scirpus lacustris*** **'Spiralis'** see *Juncu effusus* 'Spiralis'

SCLEROCACTUS

syn. ANCISTROCACTUS

CACTACEAE

Genus, closely allied to and sometimes merged with *Pediocactus*, of 3 or 4 species of depressed-spherical to club-shaped or cylindrical cacti from relatively arid areas of the US and Mexico. They have a long, fleshy taproot and deeply notched or warty ribs. The areoles are nectar-secreting a bear prominent spines, the centrals oft

Sclerocactus scheeri

S

lightly hooked; flowering areoles extend n a furrow. Diurnal, trumpet-shaped lowers are borne in summer, followed y juicy, ovoid to cylindrical or club- or arrel-shaped, mid-green fruits, scaly on he upper part, smooth below. Where emperatures fall below 45–50°F 7–10°C), grow in a temperate green-house; elsewhere, use in a desert garden.
• CULTIVATION Under glass, grow in tandard cactus potting mix in full light vith shade from hot sun. When in rowth, water moderately and apply a alf-strength balanced liquid fertilizer nonthly; keep completely dry in winter. Outdoors, grow in poor to moderately ertile, sharply drained, neutral to lightly alkaline soil in full sun with ome midday shade. See also pp.48–49.
• PROPAGATION Sow seed at 61–70°F 16–21°C) in spring. Graft onto *Cereus eruvianus* or *Hylocereus undatus* in late pring or early summer.
• PESTS AND DISEASES Prone to root and tem mealybugs.

S. polyancistrus. Solitary or clustering actus with dense, cylindrical spination bscuring the stems. Tubercles are ormed from 13–17 well-developed, lunt ribs, with 9–11 central hooked pines, 1¼–3¼in (3–8.5cm), 1–18 flat nd straight radial, 2–2½in (5–6cm) cm ong; lower spines are red to reddish rown, upper whitish and flattened. Bear scented, funnel-shaped, rose purple o magenta flowers, 2–2½in (5–6cm) m long, and cylindrical, green fruit that urns tan. ↕ 4–16in (10–40cm), ↔ 2–3½in (5–9cm). S.E. California, S.W. Nevada. ❀ (min. 45°F/7°C)
S. scheeri ■ syn. *Ancistrocactus megarhizus, A. scheeri, Echinocactus cheeri.* Spherical to narrowly club-haped, dark green cactus bearing about 13 ribs with warts that have areoles at he tips, and yellow spines (12–20 radials o ½in (1.5cm) long, and 1–4 centrals to 2in (5cm) long, the lowest hooked). Bears greenish yellow flowers, 1¼in 3cm) across, in summer. ↕ 5in (13cm), ↔ 3in (8cm). Texas, Mexico. ❀ (min. 45–50°F/7–10°C); tolerates brief periods o 20°F (-7°C) if kept dry in winter.
S. uncinatus, syn. *Ancistrocactus uncinatus, Echinocactus uncinatus, Glandulicactus uncinatus, Hamatocactus uncinatus.* Depressed-spherical to short-cylindrical, bluish green cactus with 13 ribs. Hairy areoles bear prominently hooked, reddish brown spines (7–11 radials to 2in (5cm) long; 1–4 centrals, he upper 3, where present, nearly traight or incurved, and to 1in (2.5cm) ong, the lowest strongly hooked, scending, and to 3½in (9cm) long). n summer, bears deep pinkish red to rownish red flowers, 1in (2.5cm) across. ↕ 8in (20cm), ↔ 4in (10cm). Texas, N. to C. Mexico. ❀ (min. 45–50°F/7–10°C); tolerates brief periods o 20°F (-7°C) if kept dry in winter.

SCOLIOPUS

LILIACEAE

Genus, allied to *Trillium,* of 2 species of herbaceous perennials found in woodland in the W. US. They have short, underground stems and usually paired, ovate or oblong to elliptic, boldly veined, basal leaves, sometimes with brown-purple markings. In spring, stalkless umbels of flowers, each with 3 narrow, upright inner tepals and 3 spreading outer tepals, arise directly from buds on the rootstock. Grow for their unusual but malodorous flowers and attractive foliage in a woodland garden, rock garden, or alpine house.
• CULTIVATION Grow in humus-rich, leafy, moist but well-drained, acidic to neutral soil in deep to partial shade. Provide a dry winter mulch. In an alpine house, grow in soilless potting mix with added leaf mold in filtered light.
• PROPAGATION Sow seed in containers in a cold frame as soon as ripe.
• PESTS AND DISEASES Young foliage may be damaged by slugs and snails; aphids and thrips may occur under glass.

Scoliopus bigelovii

S. bigelovii ■ syn. *S. bigelowii* (Footed adder's tongue, Stink pod). Compact herbaceous perennial producing pairs of broadly oblong to elliptic, boldly veined, purple-mottled, dull, dark green leaves, 4–8in (10–20cm) long. In early spring, bears umbels of 3–12 trillium-like flowers, to 2in (5cm) across, with narrow, erect, deep purple inner tepals, and greenish white outer tepals, striped brown-purple. ↕ 4in (10cm), ↔ 6in (15cm). California. Zone 7.
S. bigelowii see *S. bigelovii.*

▷ ***Scolopendrium vulgare*** see *Asplenium scolopendrium*

SCOPOLIA

SOLANACEAE

Genus of 5 species of rhizomatous, creeping perennials from woodland in C. and S. Europe, and Siberia (Russia) to the Himalayas, China, and Japan. Scopolias have alternate, simple, entire, boldly veined leaves. They die back after producing solitary, pendent, bell-shaped flowers in spring. Grow in woodland. All parts are highly toxic if ingested.
• CULTIVATION Grow in humus-rich, leafy, moist but well-drained, neutral to slightly alkaline soil in partial shade.

Scopolia carniolica

• PROPAGATION Sow seed in containers in a cold frame in autumn, or *in situ* in autumn or spring. Divide in spring.
• PESTS AND DISEASES Infrequent.

S. carniolica ■ Creeping, rhizomatous perennial with ovate or ovate-oblong, pointed, veined, wrinkled leaves, to 8in (20cm) long. Solitary, 5-pointed, bell-shaped, brownish purple to red flowers, 1in (2.5cm) long, yellow-green inside, are borne from the leaf axils in mid- and late spring. ↕↔ to 24in (60cm). C. and S.E. Europe, Caucasus. Zone 6. **subsp. *hladnikiana*** has brighter, buff-yellow flowers, greenish yellow inside.

SCROPHULARIA

Figwort

SCROPHULARIACEAE

Genus of about 200 species of subshrubs and herbaceous perennials, mainly found in marshes, moist meadows, woodland, scrub, and drier wasteland in N. temperate regions, with a few species occurring in tropical North and Central America. Often coarse and unpleasantly scented, they have erect, square stems; opposite, simple, entire or toothed, scalloped or lobed leaves; and small, 2-lipped, foxglove-like, greenish yellow, purple, or red flowers, borne in terminal, panicle-like cymes. Suitable for a wild or woodland garden. *S. auriculata* may also be grown as a marginal aquatic plant.
• CULTIVATION Grow in humus-rich, moist but well-drained soil in dappled to partial shade. If *S. auriculata* and its cultivars are grown as marginal aquatic plants, submerge to about 6in (15cm) deep. See also pp.52–53. To maintain *S. auriculata* 'Variegata' as a foliage plant, remove flowering stems as they form.
• PROPAGATION Sow seed of perennials *in situ* in autumn or spring. *S. auriculata* 'Variegata' will not come true from seed. Divide in spring. Root basal cuttings in a cold frame in spring, or root softwood cuttings in summer.
• PESTS AND DISEASES Prone to damage from slugs, caterpillars, and weevils, as well as downy mildew and *Septoria* leaf spot.

Scrophularia auriculata 'Variegata'

S. aquatica see *S. auriculata.*
S. auriculata, syn. *S. aquatica* (Water betony, Water figwort). Marginal aquatic perennial, or moisture-loving herbaceous perennial. Erect, square, winged stems produce lance-shaped, wrinkled, toothed, mid-green leaves, 2–10in (5–25cm) long. Panicle-like cymes of 2-lipped, yellowish green flowers, to ½in (1.5cm) long, each with a brown upper lip, are borne from early summer to early autumn. ↕↔ 36in (90cm). W. Europe. Zone 6. **'Variegata'** ■ bears leaves boldly marked with cream.

SCUTELLARIA

Helmet flower, Skullcap

LAMIACEAE

Genus of about 300 species of erect or spreading annuals, rhizomatous and clump-forming herbaceous perennials, and, more rarely, subshrubs, widespread in temperate regions and on mountains in tropical areas. Leaves are opposite and entire, rarely pinnatifid or toothed. The tubular, 2-lipped, blue, violet, yellow, or white flowers, often with colored bracts, are borne singly or in pairs from the leaf axils, or in terminal spikes or racemes. Grow smaller species in a rock garden or alpine house; use taller species at the front of a herbaceous border.
• CULTIVATION Grow in moderately fertile, light, gravelly, well-drained, neutral to alkaline soil in full sun or light, dappled shade. Where marginally hardy, apply a deep winter mulch. In an alpine house, grow in equal parts loam, leaf mold, and grit.
• PROPAGATION Sow seed in containers in a cold frame in autumn. Divide in autumn or spring. Take basal and soft-wood cuttings in spring or early summer.
• PESTS AND DISEASES Powdery mildew, leaf spot, aphids, and spider mites occur.

S. alpina (Alpine skullcap). Spreading, tuft-forming perennial with ovate, toothed, hairy, gray-green leaves, to 1in (2.5cm) long. In summer, bears erect purple flowers, 1in (2.5cm) long, with yellow-white lower lips, in dense, 4-angled racemes. ↕ 6in (15cm), ↔ 12in (30cm). S. Europe to Russia (Siberia). Zone 5.
S. baicalensis. Bushy perennial with angular, decumbent then erect, purple-tinged stems, and short-stalked, lance-shaped, hairy-margined, mid-green

Scutellaria orientalis

leaves, to 1½in (4cm) long. From early summer to early autumn, bears dense, one-sided racemes of hairy flowers, to 1in (2.5cm) long, upper lips dark blue, lower lips paler. ↕↔ 8–12in (20–30cm). Mongolia, China, Japan. Zone 5.

S. laterifolia (Virginian skullcap, mad dog skullcap). Perennial with slender rhizomes and thin, ovate-lanceolate, toothed leaves, to 3in (8cm) long. Blue, occasionally pink or white flowers are borne in one-sided, mostly axillary racemes in summer. ↕ 6–30in (15–75cm), ↔ to 18in (45cm). N. America. Zone 4.

S. orientalis ▣ Woody-based, rhizomatous perennial with gray-hairy, rooting stems, and ovate-oblong to broadly ovate, deeply toothed to pinnatisect, dark green leaves, ½in (1.5cm) long, gray-woolly beneath. In summer, bears dense, erect, 4-angled racemes of bright yellow flowers, ½–1¼in (1.5–3cm) long, marked red on the lower lips, and with yellow-green or purple-tinted bracts. ↕ 10in (25cm), ↔ 12in (30cm). S.E. Europe. Zone 6.

▷ ***Seaforthia elegans*** see *Ptychosperma elegans*

SECURINEGA

EUPHORBIACEAE

Genus of about 20 species of deciduous, monoecious or dioecious shrubs from temperate and subtropical regions of N.E. Asia to C. China. *Securinega* species are grown for their upright, arching branching habit and alternate, elliptic or ovate to ovate-lance-shaped, bright yellowish green leaves. Grow in a massed screen planting.

• **CULTIVATION** Grow in moderately fertile, well-drained soil in full sun. Pruning group 1; prune in late winter to encourage long shoot increases.

• **PROPAGATION** Take softwood cuttings in spring.

• **PESTS AND DISEASES** Infrequent.

S. suffruticosa. Upright, arching shrub with elliptic to ovate-lance-shaped, bright green leaves, to 2½in (6cm) long, wedge-shaped at the bases. In mid-summer, bears axillary, insignificant, petalless, greenish white flowers, to ¾in (2cm) across, the males in clusters and the females singly. ↕ to 6ft (2m), ↔ to 5ft (1.5m). N.E. Asia to C. China. Zone 4.

▷ ***Sedirea japonica*** see *Aerides japonica*

SEDUM *syn.* HYLOTELEPHIUM

Stonecrop

CRASSULACEAE

Genus of about 400 species of usually succulent annuals and evergreen, semi-evergreen, or deciduous biennials, perennials, subshrubs, and shrubs, a few of which are sometimes included in the genus *Hylotelephium.* They are widely distributed, most found in mountains of the N. hemisphere, but some in arid areas of South America. Stonecrops are very variable, with alternate, opposite, or whorled, fleshy, cylindrical or flattened leaves and usually terminal, often compound, cymes, panicles, or corymbs of generally star-shaped and 5-petaled flowers, borne mostly in summer and autumn. Grow hardy species in a rock garden or at the front of a herbaceous or mixed border. Where not hardy, grow as houseplants, or in a temperate greenhouse or conservatory. All parts of the plants may cause mild stomach upset if ingested; contact with the sap may irritate skin.

• **CULTIVATION** Under glass, grow tender species in a mix of 3 parts soil-based potting mix, 2 parts grit, and 1 part leaf mold, in full light with good ventilation. In the growing season, water moderately and apply a half-strength balanced liquid fertilizer every month; water sparingly in winter. Outdoors, grow in moderately fertile, well-drained, neutral to slightly alkaline soil in full sun. Vigorous species tolerate light shade. Cut back spreading species after flowering to maintain shape. Divide larger, herbaceous species every 3 or 4 years to improve flowering.

• **PROPAGATION** Sow seed of hardy species in containers in a cold frame in autumn. Sow seed of annuals and biennials at 55–61°F (13–16°C) in early spring, or *in situ* in midspring. Sow tender species at 59–64°F (15–18°C) in early spring. Divide in spring. For perennials, subshrubs, and shrubs, take softwood cuttings of non-flowering shoots in early summer. Individual leaves of large species may be rooted in summer.

• **PESTS AND DISEASES** Mealybugs, scale insects, slugs, and snails can be problems.

S. acre (Golden carpet, Golden moss). Vigorous, mat-forming, evergreen perennial with erect or trailing stems densely clothed in overlapping, triangular, mid-green leaves, to ¼in (6mm) long. Flat-topped cymes, ½in (1.5cm) across, of tiny, star-shaped, yellow-green flowers, are produced in abundance in summer. ↕ 2in (5cm), ↔ indefinite. Europe, Turkey, N. Africa. Zone 4. **'Aureum'** ▣ bears bright yellow leaves. **var. *elegans*** produces silver-tipped leaves. **'Minor'** is smaller in habit; ↕ to 1in (2.5cm).

S. aizoon, syn. *S. maximowiczii.* Rhizomatous, deciduous perennial with a thick rootstock and upright, unbranched, hairless stems bearing alternate, stalkless, ovate-lance-shaped, coarsely toothed, light green leaves, to 3in (8cm) long. In summer, produces star-shaped yellow flowers, ½in (1.5cm) across, with conspicuous stamens, in terminal, flattened, cyme-like clusters, to 1½in (4cm) across.

Sedum acre 'Aureum'

↕↔ 18in (45cm). Russia (Siberia), China, Japan. Zone 4. **'Aurantiacum'** produces dark red stems, dark green leaves, and red-tinted buds opening to yellow-orange flowers, followed by spherical to ovoid red fruit. **'Euphorbioides'** is more compact in habit, and has deeper yellow flowers; ↕ 14in (35cm), ↔ 12in (30cm).

S. alboroseum see *S. erythrostictum.*

***S.* 'Autumn Joy'** see *S.* 'Herbstfreude'.

***S.* x 'Bertram Anderson'.** Low-growing, deciduous perennial with upright, then spreading stems, and opposite, rounded to ovate, fleshy, purple leaves, 1–1½in (2.5–4cm) long. Bears rounded corymbs, 1–2in (2.5–5cm) across, of star-shaped, dusky pink flowers, in mid- and late summer. ↕ 6in (15cm), ↔ 12in (30cm). Zone 5.

S. caeruleum. Branching, spreading annual with alternate, spoon-shaped, ovate to oblong-ovate, pale green leaves, ½–¾in (1–2cm) long. In summer, bears star-shaped, 7-petaled, pale blue flowers, ¼in (6mm) across, in cymes to 1in (2.5cm) across. Leaves and stems gradually flush red during flowering. Self-seeds freely. ↕ 4–6in (10–15cm), ↔ to 6in (15cm). France (Corsica), Italy (Sardinia, Sicily), coastal Tunisia and Algeria.

S. cauticola. Trailing, stoloniferous, sometimes woody-based, deciduous perennial with purple-tinged stems bearing opposite, bluntly toothed, rounded to spoon-shaped or obovate, gray-green leaves, to 1in (2.5cm) long. In early autumn, branching stems bear terminal, slightly rounded, panicle-like cymes, to 4in (10cm) across, of star-shaped, pink-purple flowers, to ⅜in (9mm) across, aging to carmine-red. ↕ 3in (8cm), ↔ 12in (30cm). Japan. Zone 5.

S. crassipes see *Rhodiola wallichiana.*

S. dasyphyllum. Mound-forming, evergreen perennial with many horizontal to erect, branching, pink-gray stems and opposite or rarely alternate, overlapping, gray to glaucous, ovoid to obovoid leaves, ⅛–¼in (3–6mm) long. In summer, bears cymes of few pink-streaked, white flowers, ¼in (6mm) across. ↕ to 1¼–4½in (3–11cm), ↔ 12in (30cm). Mediterranean, S.W. US. Zone 7b.

S. erythrostictum, syn. *Hylotelephium roseum, S. alboroseum.* Clump-forming, deciduous perennial, similar to *S. spectabile*, with unbranched, spreading, woody stems bearing usually opposite, ovate, sometimes toothed, glaucous, gray-green leaves, to 3in (8cm) long. In late summer, bears terminal, corymb-like clusters, to 6in (15cm) across, of star-shaped, greenish white flowers, ½in (1.5cm) across, with pink carpels. ↕ 12in (30cm), ↔ 24in (60cm). E. Asia Zone 7. **'Mediovariegatum'** bears larger flower clusters than those of the species, and produces leaves with central, creamy white splashes, especially striking in spring. Grow in partial shade and cut out reverting green shoots; ↔ 18in (45cm).

S. ewersii. Low-branching, deciduous perennial with opposite, stalkless, rounded to broadly ovate, entire or slightly toothed, gray-blue leaves, to ¾in (2cm) long, heart-shaped at the bases. In summer, produces dense, rounded cymes, to 4in (10cm) across, of star-shaped, pinkish red flowers, to ⅜in (9mm) across. Similar to, but often later flowering than *S. cauticola.* ↕ 3in (8cm), ↔ 12in (30cm). C. Asia, Himalayas, Mongolia, China. Zone 6.

S. frutescens. Shrubby, semi-evergreen perennial bearing woody, branching stems, to ½in (1.5cm) thick, clothed in papery, peeling bark. Alternate, pointed, linear-elliptic, bright green leaves, ¾–2½in (2–6cm) long, are usually produced in terminal clusters. In summer, star-shaped white flowers, to ½in (1.5cm) across, are produced in few-flowered, terminal cymes. ↕ to 3ft (1m), ↔ 16in (40cm). Mexico. ❀ (min. 41–45°F/5–7°C)

***S.* 'Herbstfreude'** ▣ syn. *S.* 'Autumn Joy'. Clump-forming, bushy, deciduous perennial with unbranched, glaucous, mid-green stems bearing alternate, oblong to obovate, toothed, glaucous, dark green leaves, to 5in (13cm) long. In early autumn, produces flat corymbs, to 8in (20cm) across, of star-shaped flowers, ¼in (6mm) across, deep pink at first, then turning pinkish bronze to eventually copper-red. ↕↔ to 24in (60cm). Zone 3.

S. heterodontum see *Rhodiola heterodonta.*

Sedum 'Herbstfreude'

Sedum humifusum

S. humifusum ■ Mat-forming, evergreen perennial with creeping, branching stems bearing tight rosettes of overlapping, blunt, obovate, mid-green leaves, ⅛in (3mm) long, aging to red. Solitary, terminal, bright yellow flowers, ⅜in (9mm) across, are borne in early summer. ↕ ½in (1.5cm), ↔ 4in (10cm). Mexico. Zone 4.
S. kamtschaticum. Clump-forming perennial with thick rhizomes and alternate, inversely lance-shaped to spoon-shaped, glossy, deep green leaves, to 1½in (4cm) long, coarsely toothed toward the tips. In late summer, bears short-stemmed, flat cymes, to 2in (5cm) across, of star-shaped, deep golden yellow flowers, ½in (1.5cm) across, opening from pink buds. ↕ 4in (10cm), ↔ 10in (25cm). Russia (Siberia, Kamchatka), N. and C. China, Japan. Zone 3b. **'Rosy Glow'** has rose-blue leaves, and bears pink flowers from late summer to autumn; ↕ 12in (30cm). **'Variegatum'** ■ has pink-tinted, mid-green leaves with cream margins, and yellow flowers, aging to crimson. **'Weihenstephaner Gold'** has a trailing habit, and produces golden yellow flowers, which turn orange with age.

S. lydium ■ Stem-rooting, mat-forming, evergreen perennial with tight rosettes of cylindrical, red-tipped, bright to mid-green leaves, to ¼in (6mm) long. In summer, bears flat-topped, terminal corymbs, 1in (2.5cm) across, of star-shaped white flowers, ¼in (6mm) across. ↕ 2in (5cm), ↔ 8in (20cm). W. and C. Turkey. Zone 4.
S. maximowiczii see *S. aizoon.*
S. middendorffianum. Rhizomatous, creeping perennial with many erect, basally branching stems and alternate, linear, grooved, mid-green leaves, ½–2in (1.5–5cm) long. Ascending, panicle-like cymes of many yellow flowers, ½in (1.5cm) across, are produced in summer. ↕ to 12in (30cm), ↔ 18in (45cm). E. Siberia, Mongolia, Manchuria. Zone 6.
S. 'Mohrchen'. Upright, clump-forming perennial with unbranched, glaucous stems bearing alternate, oblong to obovate, toothed, glaucous, burgundy-red leaves, to 5in (13cm) long, turning ruby-red in fall. From late summer to autumn, bears flat corymbs, to 8in (20cm) across, of star-shaped, pink flowers, to ½in (1.5cm) across. ↕↔ 2ft (60cm). Zone 3.

Sedum morganianum

S. morganianum ■ (Burro's tail). Pendent, evergreen perennial (prostrate in the wild) with fleshy, woody-based stems and bearing alternate, oblong-lance-shaped, fleshy, glaucous, greenish blue leaves, to ¾in (2cm) long. In spring and summer, star-shaped, pale pink to deep scarlet-purple flowers, ½in (1.5cm) across, are produced in cymes to 1in (2.5cm) across. Makes a spectacular hanging basket. ↕↔ 12in (30cm). Mexico. ❄ (min. 41–45°F/5–7°C)
S. obtusatum ■ syn. *S. rubroglaucum.* Evergreen perennial with terminal rosettes of spoon-shaped, blunt-tipped, glaucous, mid-green leaves, ¼–1in (0.5–2.5cm) long, flushed crimson in autumn. In summer, bears star-shaped, bright yellow flowers, to ½in (1.5cm) across, in flat, panicle-like cymes, to 4in (10cm) across. ↕ 2in (5cm), ↔ 8in (20cm). California. Zone 6.
S. oxypetalum. Many-branched, semi-evergreen perennial with fleshy, woody stems, clothed in papery, peeling bark. The alternate, inversely lance-shaped to obovate, minutely papillose, grayish green leaves are 2in (5cm) long. Diurnal, star-shaped, fragrant, pink or dull red flowers, to ½in (1.5cm) across, usually with pink-marked petals, open in cymes 1½in (4cm) across, in summer. ↕ 20–36in (50–90cm), ↔ 18in (45cm). Mexico. ❄ (min. 41–45°F/5–7°C)
S. pilosum. Densely gray-hairy, rosette-forming, evergreen biennial. Incurved, oblong to narrowly spoon-shaped, dark green leaves are to ¾in (2cm) long. Bears dense, flat corymbs, 2in (5cm) across, of many short-stemmed, bell-shaped, rose-red flowers, ⅜in (9mm)

Sedum populifolium

across, in summer. ↕ 3in (8cm), ↔ 6in (15cm). W. Asia (Turkey to Iran). Zone 7b.
S. populifolium ■ Slowly spreading, deciduous subshrub with slightly decumbent, branched, dark brown stems bearing alternate, ovate, toothed, light green leaves, to 1½in (4cm) long, heart-shaped at the bases. Corymb-like cymes, 2in (5cm) across, of star-shaped, fragrant white flowers, ½in (1.5cm) across, each pink-tinged on the reverse, are borne in late summer and early autumn. ↕ 8–12in (20–30cm), ↔ 18in (45cm). Russia (Siberia). Zone 5.
S. reflexum see *S. rupestre.*
S. rhodiola see *Rhodiola rosea.*
S. rosea see *Rhodiola rosea.*
S. rosea var. heterodontum see *Rhodiola heterodonta.*
S. rubroglaucum see *S. obtusatum.*
S. rubrotinctum. Evergreen subshrub with numerous arching, rooting, branching stems bearing alternate, blunt, cylindrical, mid-green leaves, ½in (1.5cm) long, often flushed red. Loose, many-flowered cymes, 1½in (4cm) across, of star-shaped, pale yellow flowers, ½in (1.5cm) across, are borne in winter. ↕ 10in (25cm), ↔ 8in (20cm). Mexico. ❄ (min. 41°F/5°C)
S. 'Ruby Glow' ■ Low-growing deciduous perennial with spreading, unbranched red stems bearing opposite, elliptic, toothed, green-purple leaves, 2in (5cm) long. Numerous loose cymes, 2½in (6cm) across, of star-shaped, ruby-red flowers, ½in (1.5cm) across, are produced from midsummer to early autumn. ↕ 10in (25cm), ↔ 18in (45cm). Zone 3.

S

Sedum kamtschaticum 'Variegatum'

Sedum lydium

Sedum obtusatum

Sedum 'Ruby Glow'

Sedum rupestre

Sedum spathulifolium 'Cape Blanco'

Sedum spathulifolium 'Purpureum'

S. rupestre ■ syn. *S. reflexum* (Stone orpine). Vigorous, mat-forming, evergreen perennial with alternate, pointed, cylindrical, gray-green leaves, to ½–¾in (1–2cm) long. Upright, leafy, woody stems bear terminal, umbel-like cymes, 2½in (6cm) across, of star-shaped yellow flowers, ½in (1.5cm) across, pendent inbud, but erect as they open in summer. Spreads freely; best in a large rock garden. ↕4in (10cm), ↔24in (60cm) or more. Mountains of C. and W. Europe. Zone 6.
S. sarcocaule see *Crassula sarcocaulis.*
S. sempervivoides. Rosette-forming, evergreen biennial producing pointed, ovate to diamond-shaped, hairy, blue-green leaves, to 1¼in (3cm) long, flushed red-purple at the bases. In summer, bears domed, corymb-like panicles, 1½–2in (4–5cm) across, of many star-shaped, carmine-red flowers, ½in (1.5cm) across. Dislikes excessive winter moisture; best in an alpine house. ↕4in (10cm), ↔6in (15cm). Caucasus, Republic of Georgia, N. Iran, S.W. Asia. Zone 6.
S. sieboldii ■ (October daphne). Spreading, tuberous, tufted, deciduous perennial with whorls of 3 rounded, glaucous, blue-green, occasionally purple-tinted leaves, to ¾in (2cm) long, some irregularly toothed and red-margined toward the tips. Star-shaped pink flowers, to ½in (1.5cm) across, are borne in flat-topped cymes, 2½in (6cm) across, in autumn. ↕4in (10cm), ↔8in (20cm). Japan. Zone 5.
'Mediovariegatum', syn. 'Foliis Mediovariegatis', 'Foliis Variegatis', 'Variegatum', has glaucous-blue leaves, marbled cream and with red margins.
S. spathulifolium. Vigorous, mat-forming, evergreen perennial with branching, fleshy stems bearing terminal rosettes of brittle, spoon-shaped, silvery or mid-green leaves, to ¾in (2cm) long, usually tinted bronze-purple. Short-stemmed, star-shaped, bright yellow flowers, ½in (1.5cm) across, are borne in flat cymes, 1in (2.5cm) across, in summer. Tolerates light shade. ↕4in (10cm), ↔24in (60cm). W. North America. Zone 6. **'Cape Blanco'** ■ syn. 'Cappa Blanca', has the innermost leaves of its rosettes heavily powdered with white bloom. **'Purpureum'** ■ has leaves richly suffused reddish purple.
S. spectabile (Everlasting, Showy stonecrop). Clump-forming, deciduous perennial. Upright, unbranched green stems bear opposite or whorled, ovate to elliptic or obovate, slightly scalloped, toothed, gray-green leaves, to 3in (8cm) long. In late summer, star-shaped pink flowers, to ½in (1.5cm) across, with prominent stamens, are borne in dense, flat cymes, to 6in (15cm) across, often causing the plant to open up in the center. Attractive to bees. ↕↔18in (45cm). China, Korea. Zone 4.
'Brilliant' ■ bears flowers with bright pink petals and darker pink carpels and anthers. **'Carmen'** is a slightly darker mauve-pink. **'Iceberg'** has paler green leaves than the species, and pure white flowers; ↕12–18in (30–45cm), ↔14in (35cm). **'Septemberglut'**, syn. 'September Glow', has glowing, rich pink flowers; ↕to 20in (50cm).
S. spurium (Two-row stonecrop). Vigorous, mat-forming, evergreen perennial with branching red stems bearing opposite, obovate, toothed, mid-green leaves, to 1in (2.5cm) long. Star-shaped, pinkish purple or white flowers, ¾in (2cm) across, are produced in rounded corymbs, 1½in (4cm) across, in late summer. ↕4in (10cm), ↔24in (60cm) or more. Caucasus, Armenia,

Sedum sieboldii

Sedum spectabile 'Brilliant'

Sedum telephium subsp. *maximum* 'Atropurpureum'

N. Iran. Zone 4. **'Bronze Carpet'** has bronze leaves, and bears pink flowers, from early to late summer; ↕4in (10cm **'Dragon's Blood'** see 'Schorbuser Blut **'Fuldaglut',** syn. *S.* 'Fuldaglow', has bronze-red leaves and rose-red flowers. **'Golden Carpet'** has light green leaves, and bears golden yellow flowers in early summer; ↕3–4in (8–10cm). **'John Creech'** has pink flowers in early summer; ↕2in (5cm). **'Purple Carpet'** see 'Purpurteppich'. **'Purpurteppich'**, syn. 'Purple Carpet', is compact, with deep plum-purple leaves and dark purplish red flowers. **'Red Carpet'** has red leaves and red flowers, from early to late summer; ↕3–4in (8–10cm). **'Schorbuser Blut'**, syn. 'Dragon's Blood', has green leaves, purple-tinted when mature, and deep pink flowers. **'Tricolor'** has three-colored green, cream-white, and pink leaves, and bear pink flowers from early to late summer ↕4in (10cm).
S. telephium (Orpine). Clump-formin rhizomatous, deciduous perennial. Erect, unbranched, pale green stems bear alternate, oblong to oblong-ovate, toothed, glaucous, gray-green leaves, to

Sedum 'Vera Jameson'

n (8cm) long. Dense, axillary and rminal cymes, to 5in (13cm) across, of ar-shaped, purplish pink flowers, to ½in .5cm) across, are borne in late summer ıd early autumn. ↕ to 24in (60cm), 12in (30cm). Europe, Russia (Siberia), hina, Japan. Zone 3. **subsp. *maximum* tropurpureum'** ▣ has glaucous, very ırk purple stems and leaves, and bears naller cymes of pink flowers with ange-red centers, appearing buff-white; 8–24in (45–60cm). **'Munstead Dark ed'** has purple-tinted, dark green leaves ıd dark purplish red flowers, becoming en darker with age; ↕ to 24in (60cm). **'Vera Jameson'** ▣ Deciduous erennial with spreading purple stems ıd opposite, ovate, toothed, glaucous, ırple-pink leaves, to 4in (10cm) long, ppearing almost pink at flowering time. late summer and early autumn, bears unded cymes, 2½in (6cm) across, star-shaped, soft rose-pink flowers, –½in (6–15mm) across. ↕ 8–12in 0–30cm), ↔ 18in (45cm). Zone 4. ***wallichianum*** see *Rhodiola allichiana.* ***weinbergii*** see *Graptopetalum ıraguayense.*

Seemannia gymnostoma see *Gloxinia gymnostoma*

SELAGINELLA

ELAGINELLACEAE

enus of approximately 700 species of vergreen, rhizomatous perennials found a range of habitats, from semi-desert rainforest, mostly in tropical regions, ith some species in temperate and pine zones. Grown for their foliage, ey vary from small, moss-like tufts to ll, scrambling plants. They have long, eeping, branched stems, often rooting ong their length, which are clothed in ale-like leaves, to ⅛in (3mm) long. pores form in small, leafy, terminal ikes. Use as a groundcover or in anging baskets. Where not hardy, grow a cool, temperate, or warm eenhouse, or as houseplants.

CULTIVATION Under glass, grow in mix of 2 parts soil-based potting mix ıd 1 part leaf mold, in bright filtered indirect light; *S. uncinata* and *willdenovii* are best in bright filtered ght. In growth, water freely and apply balanced liquid fertilizer monthly. Maintain high humidity. Keep just oist in winter. Outdoors, grow in oderately fertile, humus-rich, moist

elaginella kraussiana

Selaginella lepidophylla

but well-drained, neutral to slightly acidic soil in partial shade in a sheltered site. *S. lepidophylla* tolerates drier conditions and prefers alkaline soil.

• **PROPAGATION** Sow spores at 70°F (21°C) as soon as ripe. Divide rhizomes or rooted stems in spring.

• **PESTS AND DISEASES** Leaf spots and stem rots may occur.

S. braunii (Chinese lace fern). Erect, spreading perennial with erect, simple, lower stems, much-branched upper stems, and ovate to diamond-shaped, dark green leaves. ↕ 12–18in (30–45cm), ↔ indefinite. W. China. ❄ (min. 35°F/2°C)
S. emmeliana see *S. pallescens.*
S. kraussiana ▣ (Trailing spikemoss). Mat-forming perennial producing trailing stems clothed in pinnatisect, bright green foliage. ↕ 1in (2.5cm), ↔ indefinite. Tropical and southern Africa, Azores. ❄ (min. 45°F/7°C). **'Aurea'** has yellow-green foliage. **'Brownii'** forms small cushions; ↕ 2in (5cm), ↔ 6in (15cm). **'Variegata'** produces cream-splashed foliage.
S. lepidophylla ▣ (Resurrection plant, Rose of Jericho). Small, spreading

Selaginella willdenovii

perennial with dense tufts of dark green leaves. When dry, curls into a ball that opens into a flat rosette when soaked with water. Dry plants are often sold as curiosities. ↕ to 3in (8cm), ↔ 6in (15cm). Arizona, Texas to Peru. ❄ (min. 35°F/2°C)
S. martensii. Trailing perennial with many-branched stems bearing frond-like, glossy, bright green foliage. ↕ to 6in (15cm), ↔ 8in (20cm). Central America. ❄ (min. 45°F/7°C). **'Variegata'** has white-flecked foliage.
S. pallescens, syn. *S. emmeliana.* Perennial with a densely tufted stem, branching from the base, with short, much-divided branches. Leaves are light yellow-green, white beneath. ↕ to 6in (15cm), ↔ 12in (30cm). North America to N. Colombia and Venezuela. ❄ (min. 45°F/7°C)
S. uncinata (Peacock moss). Perennial with slender, trailing, rooting stems bearing alternate, short, pinnate branches and leaves with a distinct metallic blue sheen. ↕ 1–2in (2.5–5cm), ↔ indefinite. China. Zone 7b.
S. willdenovii ▣ (Peacock fern). Perennial climber with a nearly leafless stem bearing densely branched, leafy sideshoots. Leaves are mid-green, aging to pinkish yellow or plum, with a metallic blue sheen. ↕ 10–20ft (3–6m) or more. Himalayas to S. China and Indonesia. ❄ (min. 45°F/7°C)

SELAGO

SCROPHULARIACEAE

Genus of about 150 species of evergreen shrubs, subshrubs, and annuals from grassland, rocky places, moist sites, and forest margins in tropical Africa and South Africa. Their simple, often very narrow leaves are usually clustered or solitary, and borne at alternate nodes or occasionally in opposite pairs. They are grown mainly for their heads, spikes, corymbs, or panicles of usually small, tubular flowers, each with 5 spreading petal lobes. Where not hardy, grow in a temperate greenhouse. In milder areas, grow at the front of a shrub border, in a raised bed, or at the base of a warm, sunny wall. *S. serrata* is also effective grown in a container.

• **CULTIVATION** Under glass, grow in soil-based potting mix in full light with shade from hot sun, or in bright filtered light. In growth, water freely, and apply a balanced liquid fertilizer monthly; maintain low to moderate humidity. Keep just moist in winter. Outdoors, grow in moderately fertile, humus-rich, moist but well-drained soil in full sun. Deadhead regularly. Pruning group 9.

• **PROPAGATION** Sow seed at 55–59°F (13–15°C) in spring. Root softwood cuttings in spring or early summer, with bottom heat. Layer or air layer in spring or early summer.

• **PESTS AND DISEASES** Spider mites may be a problem under glass.

S. serrata. Initially erect, then spreading to decumbent, evergreen shrub with crowded, stalkless, obovate or oblong, boldly toothed, firm, deep green leaves, to 1in (2.5cm) long. Fragrant purple to pale blue flowers are borne in compact corymbs, to 2in (5cm) across, in summer. ↕↔ 12–36in (30–90cm). South Africa. ❄ (min. 41°F/5°C); tolerates brief periods to 32°F (0°C).

SELENICEREUS

CACTACEAE

Genus of approximately 20 species of mostly scandent or semi-pendent, epiphytic or rock-dwelling cacti from forest and woody areas of Texas, Mexico, Central America, Colombia, and the West Indies. They produce short-hairy, generally spiny areoles, and most have aerial roots. Stems are slender, ribbed, or, more rarely, angled or flattened. The large, trumpet-shaped, strangely scented, mainly nocturnal flowers are usually borne in summer. They do not flower well until mature, but they are fast growing. In areas where temperatures fall below 59°F (15°C), grow in a warm greenhouse, in hanging baskets, or in containers with support for climbing stems. In warmer climates, grow in containers or at the base of a warm, sunny wall.

• **CULTIVATION** Under glass, grow in epiphytic cactus potting mix in bright indirect to moderate light. In the growing season, water freely and apply a half-strength balanced liquid fertilizer monthly; keep just moist in winter. Maintain moderate to high humidity. Outdoors, grow in moderately fertile, humus-rich, moist but sharply drained, neutral to slightly alkaline soil, with additional grit and leaf mold, in light dappled to partial shade. See also pp.48–49.

• **PROPAGATION** Sow seed at 61–66°F (16–19°C) as soon as ripe or in spring. Root cuttings of stem segments in a closed, slightly shaded propagating case in spring or summer.

• **PESTS AND DISEASES** Scale insects and mealybugs may be a problem.

S. anthonyanus, syn. *Cryptocereus anthonyanus.* Semi-pendent, scandent, epiphytic cactus with flattened, leaf-like, bright green stems, 3–6in (7–15cm) across, with prominent marginal notches, 1¾in (4.5cm) deep, forming lobes. The areoles bear 2–4 short, pale brown spines. In summer, produces nocturnal, fragrant, yellowish or creamy white flowers, 5in (13cm) long, with maroon-red outer segments. ↕ to 30in (75cm), ↔ indefinite. S.E. Mexico. ❄ (min. 59°F/15°C)
S. chrysocardium see *Epiphyllum chrysocardium.*
S. grandiflorus ▣ (Queen of the night). Scandent, epiphytic cactus producing 5-

Selenicereus grandiflorus

Selinum wallichianum

to 8-ribbed, mid-green stems, ½–1in (1–2.5cm) thick, with areoles bearing 6–18 yellow spines that turn gray. The nocturnal, fragrant white flowers, 12in (30cm) long, with spreading, pale yellowish brown outer segments, are borne in summer. ↕ 15ft (5m). Mexico, West Indies. ❀ (min. 59°F/15°C)
S. hamatus. Scandent, epiphytic cactus with 3- or 4-angled, dark green stems, ½in (1.5cm) thick, bearing hooked warts. The areoles have 5–9 white or brown spines. The nocturnal, scented white flowers are 8–14in (20–35cm) long, with yellow and red outer segments, are produced during summer. ↕ 12ft (4m). Mexico, West Indies. ❀ (min. 59°F/15°C)
S. innesii. Scandent or trailing, epiphytic cactus with 4- or 5-ribbed, mid-green stems, ½in (1.5cm) thick, and woolly areoles bearing 1 or 2 thick, pale yellow spines and 3–7 slender ones. In summer, produces diurnal white flowers, 1½–2in (4–5cm) long, with extended petals, to 2½in (6cm) across, the outer petals tinged magenta-pink; some plants produce only male flowers, others produce only females. ↕ to 6ft (2m). West Indies (St. Vincent). ❀ (min. 59°F/15°C)
S. pteranthus (Princess of the night). Scandent, epiphytic cactus with 4- to 6-angled, purplish green stems, 1–2in (2.5–5cm) thick, and white-woolly areoles bearing 6–12 thick, yellowish gray spines. Nocturnal, white or pale cream flowers, 12in (30cm) long, with long, slender, recurved, pale purple outer segments, are produced during summer. ↕ 12ft (4m). Mexico. ❀ (min. 59°F/15°C)
S. wercklei. Semi-pendent, freely branching, epiphytic cactus with mid-green stems, ½in (1.5cm) thick, each with up to 12 shallow ribs. Areoles are mostly spineless, but a few brown spines form on the flower tubes. Nocturnal white flowers, 6in (15cm) long, with red outer segments, are produced in summer. ↕ 30in (75cm), ↔ indefinite. Costa Rica. ❀ (min. 59°F/15°C)

SELINUM

APIACEAE

Genus of 6 species of taprooted perennials from rocky slopes, mountain meadows, and scrub in temperate areas of Europe and the Himalayas. Few species are grown, but *S. wallichianum* is suitable for an informal, mixed or shrub border or a woodland garden, and is effective as a specimen plant because of the tiered effect of its floral umbels.
• **CULTIVATION** Grow in moderately fertile, moist but well-drained soil in full sun or partial shade. Tolerant of a wide range of conditions.
• **PROPAGATION** Sow seed in containers in a cold frame as soon as ripe; prick out into deep containers as soon as possible to avoid taproot damage. Divide carefully in early spring.
• **PESTS AND DISEASES** Overwintering buds are especially prone to slug and snail damage. Powdery mildew may be a problem in dry conditions.

S. tenuifolium see *S. wallichianum.*
S. wallichianum ■ syn. *S. tenuifolium.* Clump-forming perennial with erect, branched stems, usually shaded or lined reddish purple, as are the leaf stalks, which are 8–12in (20–30cm) long. Triangular leaf blades, to 20in (50cm) long, are 2- or 3-pinnate, the final segments elliptic and toothed. Tiny, star-shaped white flowers are borne in terminal umbels, to 8in (20cm) across, from midsummer to early autumn. ↕ to 6ft (1.8m), ↔ 24in (60cm). W. Pakistan, Himalayas, India. ❀ (min. 35°F/2°C)

SEMELE

Climbing butcher's broom

LILIACEAE

Genus of one species of evergreen, woody climber from laurel forest in S. Spain, S.E. France, Sicily, N. Africa, and the Canary Islands. The true leaves are scale-like, their function taken over by leaf-like stems, on which clusters of tiny, star-shaped, 6-tepaled flowers are borne in late spring and early summer. These are sometimes followed by single-seeded, orange-red berries. Where not hardy, grow as a foliage plant in a cool greenhouse. In warmer climates, use to provide handsome foliage cover on a warm, sunny wall.
• **CULTIVATION** Under glass, grow in soil-based potting mix in full light with shade from hot sun, or in bright filtered light. In growth, water moderately and apply a balanced liquid fertilizer monthly; water sparingly in winter. Maintain low to moderate humidity. Outdoors, grow in moderately fertile, well-drained soil in full sun. Provide the stems with support. Pruning group 11, in late winter or early spring.
• **PROPAGATION** Sow seed at 61–66°F (16–19°C) in spring. Divide in spring.
• **PESTS AND DISEASES** Infrequent.

S. androgyna. Moderately bushy, twining climber, with the main stems arising at ground level, bearing lance-shaped to ovate, sometimes shallowly lobed, glossy, mid-green, leaf-like stems, to 1in (2.5cm) long. Clusters of 2–6 tiny, star-shaped cream flowers are produced in late spring and early summer; the females are ¼in (6mm) across, the males ⅜in (9mm) across. ↕ 15–22ft (5–7m). S. Spain, S.E. France (Hyères Isles), Sicily, N. Africa, Canary Islands. ❀ (min. 41°F/5°C)

SEMIAQUILEGIA

RANUNCULACEAE

Genus of one species of small, sometimes short-lived perennials from the forests of China, Korea, and Japan. It resembles columbines (*Aquilegia*), but has spurless flowers, swollen or pouched at the bases, borne in corymb-like panicles in spring or summer. Leaves are ternate, and often further divided. This plant is most effective when grown in a rock garden.
• **CULTIVATION** Grow in moderately fertile, humus-rich, moist but well-drained, neutral to slightly acidic soil in full sun with some midday shade, or in partial shade. Provide shelter from cold, drying winds.
• **PROPAGATION** Sow seed in containers in a cold frame as soon as ripe.
• **PESTS AND DISEASES** Susceptible to damage by slugs and snails.

S. adoxoides. Perennial, with ternately compound basal leaves, leaflets flabellate to reniform-obovate and ½–1in (1–2.5cm) long. Stems occasionally branched, with smaller, flabellate leaves. Flowers very small, nodding, with narrow, oblong-elliptic sepals white or light pink, ¼in (5mm) long. ↕↔ 4–12in (10–30cm). E. Asia. Zone 6.

SEMIARUNDINARIA

POACEAE

Genus of 10–20 species of tall, upright bamboos from deciduous woodland, upland slopes, and ravines in China and Japan. They generally have running rhizomes, but form dense clumps in cool climates. Smooth, cylindrical culms, with short-lived, sometimes persistent, sheaths, some with upper internodes grooved or flattened, produce 3–7 branches at each node, with

Semiarundinaria fastuosa

checkered, narrowly lance-shaped leave Grow in a woodland garden, as a specimen plant, or as an informal hedg
• **CULTIVATION** Grow in moderately fertile, humus-rich, moist but well-drained soil in full sun or dappled shad
• **PROPAGATION** Divide, or cut up sections of youngest rhizomes, in sprin
• **PESTS AND DISEASES** Young shoots may be damaged by slugs.

S. fastuosa ■ syn. *Arundinaria fastuosa* (Narihira bamboo). Tall, erect, tree-like bamboo with spreading rhizomes. The shining, mid-green culms are striped purple-brown, markedly so when youn culm sheaths open to reveal polished, deep red-purple interiors. Bears lance-shaped, glossy, mid-green leaves, 5–6in (12–15cm) long, mainly on the upper part of the plant. ↕ to 22ft (7m), ↔ 6ft (2m) or more. Japan. Zone 7.

SEMPERVIVUM

Hens and chicks, Houseleek

CRASSULACEAE

Genus of about 40 species of dense, mat-forming, evergreen succulent perennials, mainly from the mountains of Europe and Asia. They bear rosettes of thick, pointed leaves, often with bristle-fringed margins, and sometimes covered with a web of white hairs. Flat, branching, terminal, panicle-like cymes of star-shaped, white, yellow, red, or purple flowers are borne on upright stems in summer. The rosettes die after flowering, but are replaced by new, offset rosettes, borne on lateral runners. Numerous cultivars are available. Grow

Sempervivum arachnoideum

Sempervivum ciliosum

n a rock garden, scree bed, wall crevice, r trough, or in an alpine house.
CULTIVATION Grow in poor to moderately fertile, sharply drained soil, vith added grit, in full sun. Some, articularly softly hairy species, resent vinter moisture, and are best grown in n alpine house in areas with wet vinters. In an alpine house, grow in a nix of equal parts soil-based potting nix and grit. See also pp.48–49.
PROPAGATION Sow seed in containers n a cold frame in spring. Root offsets in pring or early summer.
PESTS AND DISEASES May be affected y *Endophyllum* rust.

S. arachnoideum ▣ (Cobweb house-eek). Mat-forming, rosetted succulent vith fleshy, obovate, mid-green to red eaves, to ½in (1.5cm) long. The rosettes, ½–1in (1–2.5cm) across, are cobwebbed vith white hairs. In summer, bears flat ymes, to 1in (2.5cm) across, of reddish ink flowers on leafy stems. ↕ 3in (8cm), ↔ 12in (30cm). Europe (Alps, Apennines, Carpathians). Zone 4.
S. arboreum see *Aeonium arboreum.*
S. ciliosum ▣ Mat-forming succulent vith very hairy rosettes, to 2in (5cm) across, of incurved, inversely lance-shaped, gray-green leaves, 1in (2.5cm) long, convex on both surfaces. Bears flat, compact cymes, 1in (2.5cm) across, of greenish yellow flowers in summer. Best in an alpine house. ↕ 3in (8cm), ↔ 12in (30cm). Former Yugoslavia, Bulgaria, N.W. Greece. Zone 7.
S. 'Commander Hay'. Succulent, similar to *S. tectorum*, bearing rosettes, to 4in (10cm) across, of inversely lance-shaped, glossy, deep red-purple leaves, to 1½in (4cm) long, with mid-green tips. In summer, produces cymes, 2–4in (5–10cm) across, of greenish red flowers. ↕ 4in (10cm), ↔ 12in (30cm). Zone 4.
S. complanatum see *Aeonium tabuliforme.*
S. giuseppii ▣ Vigorous, mat-forming succulent with rosettes, 1–1½in (2.5–4cm) across, of ovate, pea-green leaves, ½in (1.5cm) long, hairy when young, and dark-spotted at the tips. Red flowers are produced in cymes, 1½in (4cm) across, in summer. ↕ 3in (8cm), ↔ 12in (30cm). Spain. Zone 4.
S. grandiflorum. Variable, mat-forming succulent bearing rosettes, 2–4in (5–10cm) across, of sharp-pointed, oblong-triangular, very hairy, dark green leaves, 1–2in (2.5–5cm) long, which are often tipped with brown. In summer, bears yellow flowers, stained purple at the bases, in cymes 4in (10cm) across. Prefers acidic soil. ↕ 4in (10cm), ↔ 12in (30cm). Europe (W. and C. Alps). Zone 4.

Sempervivum giuseppii

Sempervivum montanum

Sempervivum tectorum 'Pacific Hawk'

S. haworthii see *Aeonium haworthii.*
S. helveticum see *S. montanum.*
S. hirtum see *Jovibarba hirta.*
S. masferreri see *Aeonium sedifolium.*
S. montanum ▣ syn. *S. helveticum.* Vigorous, mat-forming succulent with clustered, open rosettes, ¾–3in (2–8cm) across, of sharp-pointed, inversely lance-shaped, finely hairy, fleshy, dull, dark green leaves, to ½in (1.5cm) long. Bears red-purple flowers in loose cymes, to 2½in (6cm) across, in summer. Hybridizes freely. ↕ 4in (10cm), ↔ 12in (30cm) or more. C. Europe. Zone 4. **'Lloyd Praeger'** has slightly flattened rosettes and leaves tipped dark brown. **'Minima'** produces green rosettes, ¼in (6mm) across, tinged red when dormant.
S. nobile see *Aeonium nobile.*
S. patens see *Jovibarba heuffelii.*
S. soboliferum see *Jovibarba sobolifera.*
S. tectorum (Hens and chicks, Roof houseleek). Mat-forming succulent with open rosettes, to 4in (10cm) across, of thick, obovate to narrowly oblong, bristle-tipped, blue-green leaves, to 1½in (4cm) long, often suffused red-purple. In summer, bears cymes, 2–4in (5–10cm) across, of red-purple flowers on upright, hairy stems. ↕ 6in (15cm), ↔ 20in (50cm). Mountains of S. Europe. Zone 4. **'Atropurpureum'** has dark violet leaves. **'Boissieri'** produces bronze-green leaves with red-brown tips. **'Limelight'** has rosettes of chartreuse leaves, tipped with dusk-pink. **'Nigrum'** has green leaves with red-purple tips. **'Oddity'** produces rosettes, 2–5in (5–13cm) across, of quilled, bright green leaves with black-edged tips. **'Pacific Hawk'** ▣ bears rosettes, 2in (5cm) across, of red leaves with fine white hairs. **'Red Flush'** has red-tinged leaves. **'Red-Purple'** has rosettes of deep olive-green leaves with red and purple shading. **'Royanum'** produces rosettes with yellow-green leaves and red tips. **'Silverine'** has rosettes of silver-blue leaves, shaded pink, carrying offsets at the ends of red stolons. **'Sunset'** produces rosettes of bright, light green leaves, shaded deep red and orange. **'Triste'** produces red-brown flowers.

SENECIO

ASTERACEAE

Large genus of more than 1,000 species of annuals, biennials, herbaceous perennials, climbers, shrubs, and small trees, some of which are succulent. They are found worldwide in habitats ranging from mountains to seashores, and in dry to moist soils. Basal leaves are entire or variably lobed, sometimes white or silver; stem leaves, if present, are smaller and alternate. The flowerheads, either solitary or borne in corymbs, are usually terminal and daisy-like (some species lack ray florets), and yellow, white, red, blue, or purple, sometimes orange; they mainly have yellow, sometimes purple disk florets. Use annuals as bedding plants, or in containers; grow small perennials in a scree bed or rock garden, and tall ones in a border or wild garden. Tender species should be grown in a cool or temperate green-house. All parts of the plant may cause severe discomfort if ingested.

• **CULTIVATION** For ease of reference, cultivation has been grouped as follows:
1. Grow in poor, gritty, sharply drained soil in full sun.
2. Grow in moderately fertile, well-drained soil in full sun.
3. Grow in moderately fertile, moist to boggy soil (such as in a bog garden) in full sun or partial shade.
4. Under glass, grow in a mix of 2 parts soil-based potting mix and 1 part each leaf mold and grit, in full light with good ventilation. When in growth, water moderately and apply a balanced liquid fertilizer monthly. Maintain moderate humidity. Keep just moist in winter. Outdoors, in frost-free areas, grow as for group 2.
5. Under glass, grow in a mix of 2 parts soil-based potting mix and 1 part each leaf mold and grit, in full light with good ventilation. When in growth, water moderately, maintain low humidity, and apply a half-strength balanced liquid fertilizer monthly. Keep just moist in winter at a minimum temperature of 45–50°F (7–10°C). Outdoors, in frost-free areas, grow as for group 1, in neutral to slightly alkaline soil.
Pruning group 8 or 9 for shrubs; group 11, after flowering, for climbers.

• **PROPAGATION** Sow seed in spring: for cultivation groups 2, 4, and 5, at 66–75°F (19–24°C); for groups 1 and 3 in containers in a cold frame. Divide groups 1 and 3, and *S. doronicum* in spring; take basal cuttings in early spring. Divide groups 4 and 5 as growth begins; take softwood cuttings in early summer or semi-ripe cuttings in mid- or late summer. Take semi-ripe cuttings of silver and white forms of group 2 in mid- or late summer.

• **PESTS AND DISEASES** Prone to rust, particularly *S. cineraria* and its cultivars. Whiteflies, aphids, and spider mites may be problems under glass.

S. abrotanifolius. Evergreen subshrub with spreading or erect, hairless or downy stems, and 2- or 3-pinnatisect, glossy, dark green leaves, to 3in (8cm) long, the upper leaves less divided. From midsummer to early autumn, bears yellow to orange-scarlet flowerheads, to 1½in (4cm) across, singly or in few-flowered corymbs. Cultivation group 1.

Senecio articulatus 'Variegatus'

↕6–18in (15–45cm), ↔ 12in (30cm). Mountains of C. and E. Europe. Zone 5.
S. articulatus (Candle plant). Erect, perennial succulent with cylindrical, jointed, fleshy, gray-veined, silvery blue stems, each segment up to 6in (15cm) long. Bears ovate, 3- to 5-lobed, stalked, blue-green leaves, to 2in (5cm) long. Yellow flowerheads, approximately ½in (1.5cm) across, are borne in small corymbs from spring to autumn. Cultivation group 5. ↕ to 24in (60cm), ↔ indefinite. South Africa. ❄ (min. 45°F/7°C). **'Variegatus'** ▣ has bold, pink or cream marks and shading on the leaves and flowerheads.
S. bicolor* subsp. *cineraria see *S. cineraria.*
S. candicans see *S. cineraria.*
S. cineraria, syn. *S. bicolor* subsp. *cineraria, S. candicans, S. maritimus* (Dusty miller). Mound-forming, evergreen subshrub or shrub, usually grown as an annual, with ovate to lance-shaped or elliptic, shallowly to deeply pinnatisect or pinnate, felted, silvery gray leaves, to 6in (15cm) long. Loose corymbs of mustard-yellow flowerheads, to 1in (2.5cm) across, are produced in midsummer, in the second year if the plants overwinter. Cultivation group 2. ↕↔ to 24in (60cm). W. and C. Mediterranean. Zone 7b. Dwarf cultivars, with a range of foliage characteristics, are popular. **'Alice'** has deeply cut, silver-stained white leaves; ↕↔ 12in (30cm). **'Cirrus'** ▣ produces elliptic, finely toothed or lobed, silvery green to white leaves; ↕↔ 12in (30cm). **'Silver Dust'** ▣ has deeply pinnatisect, lacy, almost white leaves; ↕↔ 12in (30cm). **'Silver Queen'** is compact in habit and has lacy, silver-white leaves; ↕ to 8in (20cm). **'White Diamond'** has deeply divided, almost oak-like, gray-white leaves; usually grown as a perennial; ↕12–16in (30–40cm), ↔ 12in (30cm).
S. clivorum see *Ligularia dentata.*
S. compactus see *Brachyglottis compacta.*

Senecio cineraria 'Cirrus'

S. confusus ▣ syn. *Pseudogynoxys chenopodioides.* Moderately bushy, evergreen, twining climber with lance-shaped to narrowly ovate, thick, toothed, mid-green leaves, to 3in (8cm) long. Fragrant flowerheads, 2in (5cm) across, are bright orange fading to red, and are profusely borne in small, axillary and terminal corymbs, mainly in summer. Cultivation group 4. ↕ to 20ft (6m) or more. Mexico to Honduras. ❄ (min. 45–50°F/7–10°C)
S. cruentus see *Pericallis* x *hybrida.*
S. doronicum (Leopard's bane ragwort). Clump-forming, deciduous perennial with upright, sometimes branched stems and ovate to lance-shaped or elliptic, toothed, dark green leaves, to 10in (25cm) long, cobweb-hairy beneath. Bright orange-yellow to rich yellow flowerheads, to 2½in (6cm) across, are borne singly or in loose corymbs in early and midsummer. Cultivation group 2. ↕6–16in (15–40cm), ↔ 12in (30cm). Mountainous regions of C. and S. Europe. Zone 6.
***S.* Dunedin Hybrids** see *Brachyglottis* Dunedin Hybrids.
S. elaeagnifolius see *Brachyglottis elaeagnifolia.*

Senecio confusus

S. elegans (Purple ragwort). Erect annual with branched stems and oblong-ovate, pinnately lobed or coarsely toothed, deep green leaves, to 3in (8cm) long. In summer, bears corymbs of flowerheads, 1in (2.5cm) across, with yellow disk florets and purple, reddish purple, or occasionally white ray florets. Cultivation group 2. ↕ to 24in (60cm), ↔ to 14in (35cm). South Africa.
S. grandifolius ▣ syn. *Telanthophora grandifolia.* Evergreen shrub, rounded when young, but becoming erect, with very thick, sparsely branched, purple-downy stems bearing ovate to elliptic, usually wavy-lobed, sometimes toothed, semi-lustrous, mid- to deep green leaves, 8–18in (20–45cm) long, downy, rust-brown beneath. Small, 5-rayed, bright yellow flowerheads, to ½in (1.5cm) across, are borne in dense, widely domed corymbs, to 12in (30cm) across, mainly in winter. Cultivation group 4. ↕↔ 6–10ft (2–3m), sometimes more. Mexico. ❄ (min. 45–50°F/7–10°C)
S. greyi see *Brachyglottis greyi.*
***S. greyi* of gardens** see *Brachyglottis* Dunedin Hybrids.

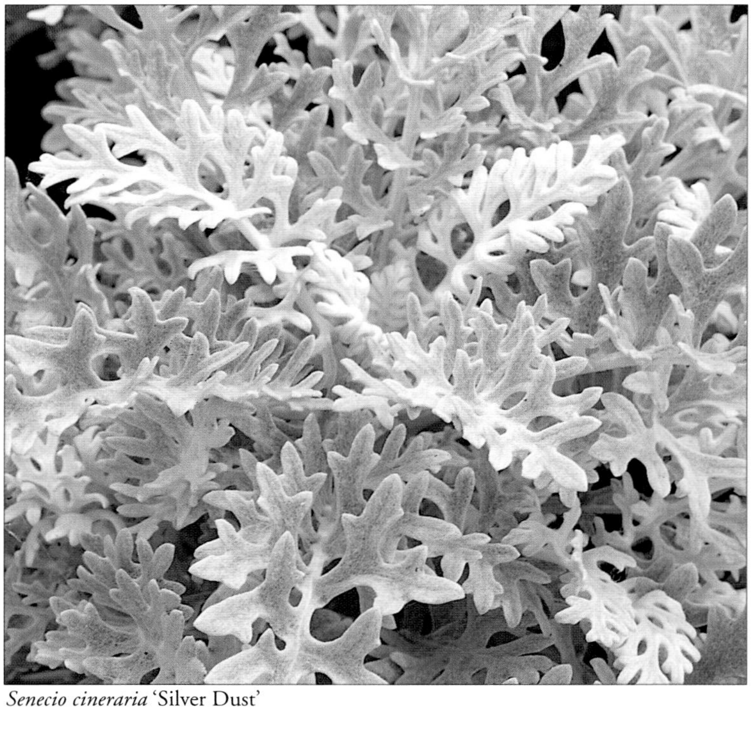
Senecio cineraria 'Silver Dust'

Senecio grandifolius

S. hectoris see *Brachyglottis hectoris.*
S. huntii see *Brachyglottis huntii.*
S.* x *hybridus see *Pericallis* x *hybrida.*
S. laxifolius see *Brachyglottis laxifolia.*
***S. laxifolius* of gardens** see *Brachyglott*. Dunedin Hybrids.
S. leucostachys see *S. viravira.*
S. macroglossus (Cape ivy, Natal ivy). Evergreen, twining climber with semi-succulent growth at first, then eventual woody stems, which branch moderately. Triangular to spear-shaped, mid-green leaves, to 3in (8cm) long, have 3–5 pointed lobes. Flowerheads, 2–2½in (5–6cm) across, with white to pale yellow ray florets, are usually produced singly, but sometimes in twos or threes, in summer and winter. Cultivation group 4, with shade from midday sun. ↕ to 10ft (3m), sometimes more. Zimbabwe to Mozambique, E. South Africa. ❄ (min. 41–45°F/5–7°C). **'Variegatus'** ▣ has foliage with irregula. cream to light yellow margins.
S. maritimus see *S. cineraria.*
S. mikanioides, syn. *Delairea odorata* (German ivy, Parlor ivy). Evergreen, twining climber with succulent young stems, woody when mature. Fleshy, bright green leaves, 3–4in (8–10cm) across, are triangular to triangular-ovate, with 5–7 broad, pointed lobes. Small yellow flowerheads, ⅜in (9mm) across, without ray florets, are produced in dense axillary and terminal corymbs, 3in (8cm) across, from autumn to early winter. Cultivation group 4. ↕ to 20ft (6m). South Africa. ❄ (min. 37–41°F/3–5°C)
***S.* 'Moira Read'** see *Brachyglottis* Dunedin Hybrids 'Moira Read'.
S. monroi see *Brachyglottis monroi.*

Senecio macroglossus 'Variegatus'

Senecio pulcher

S. przewalskii see *Ligularia przewalskii.*
S. pulcher ■ Erect, deciduous or semi-evergreen perennial, woolly in early growth, becoming hairless, with leathery, mid-green leaves, to 8in (20cm) long. Basal leaves are elliptic with scalloped margins; stem leaves are lance-shaped with toothed margins. Solitary corymbs of carmine-purple flowerheads, 2–3in (5–8cm) across, are produced in mid- and late autumn. Cultivation group 4; may survive outdoors in a sheltered, sunny site, in cool, deep, fertile soil, but severe weather harms leaves and flowers. ↕ 18–24in (45–60cm), ↔ 20in (50cm). S. Brazil, Uruguay, Argentina. ❄ (min. 35°F/2°C)
S. radicans. Mat-forming, perennial succulent with prostrate, rooting stems and cylindrical, straight or slightly curved, fleshy, glaucous, mid-green leaves, to 1in (2.5cm) long, each with a darker stripe down the middle. Solitary or paired white flowerheads, ⅛–¼in (3–6mm) across, are borne sporadically during the year. Cultivation group 5. ↕ 3–4in (8–10cm), ↔ 6–12in (15–30cm). South Africa. ❄ (min. 35°F/2°C)
S. reinholdii see *Brachyglottis rotundifolia.*

Senecio rowleyanus

Senecio smithii

S. rotundifolius see *Brachyglottis rotundifolia.*
S. rowleyanus ■ syn. *Kleinia rowleyana* (String of beads). Pendent or creeping, perennial succulent with adventitious roots on the stems and spherical mid-green leaves, to ½in (1.5cm) long. Bears solitary, funnel-shaped, cinnamon-scented white flowerheads, to ½in (1.5cm) long, with protruding brown stamens, in summer. Cultivation group 5. ↕ 24in (60cm) or more, ↔ indefinite. S.W. Africa. ❄ (min. 45–50°F/7–10°C)
S. scandens. Evergreen, twining climber, woody-based and usually bushy when mature, with ovate or narrowly triangular, almost entire to sharply toothed or lobed, bright green leaves, to 4in (10cm) long. From autumn to winter, bears yellow flowerheads, ½in (1.5cm) across, in panicle-like corymbs, 5in (13cm) across. Cultivation group 4. ↕ 8–15ft (2.5–5m). E. Asia. ❄ (min. 45°F/7°C)
S. serpens, syn. *Kleinia repens* (Blue chalksticks). Shrubby, perennial succulent with semi-erect, fleshy, blue-frosted shoots, ¼in (6mm) thick. Cylindrical, fleshy, waxy, bluish gray leaves, to 1¼in (3cm) long, grooved on the upper surfaces, are crowded at the stem and branch tips. In summer, bears whitish yellow flowerheads, ½in (1.5cm) long, lacking ray florets. Cultivation group 5. ↕↔ 12in (30cm). South Africa. ❄ (min. 45°F/7°C)
S. smithii ■ Vigorous, deciduous, clump-forming, woolly perennial with oblong-ovate, toothed, leathery, glossy, dark gray-green basal and stem leaves, to 12in (30cm) long. From early to late summer, thick, upright, unbranched stems bear large corymbs, 4–6in (10–15cm) across, of numerous yellow-centered white flowerheads, to 2in (5cm) across. Cultivation group 3, but best in moist soil. ↕ to 4ft (1.2m), ↔ 24in (60cm). S. Chile, W. Argentina, Falkland Islands. Zone 7b.
S. stapeliiformis see *Kleinia stapeliiformis.*
S. 'Sunshine' see *Brachyglottis* Dunedin Hybrids 'Sunshine'.
S. tanguticus, syn. *Ligularia tangutica, Sinacalia tangutica* (Chinese groundsel). Clump-forming, deciduous perennial with upright, unbranched black stems and ovate, deeply pinnatisect, dark green leaves, to 7in (18cm) long. In early and midautumn, bears pyramidal panicles of yellow flowerheads, 1⁄16in (2mm) across. Cultivation group 3; invasive, so best in a wild garden, near water. ↕ to 4ft (1.2m) or more, ↔ 3½ft (1.1m). N.W. China. Zone 6.
S. viravira ■ syn. *S. leucostachys* (Dusty miller). Open, spreading, evergreen subshrub with densely white-hairy shoots and deeply pinnatisect, silvery white leaves, to 3in (8cm) long, with 5–9 linear lobes that are usually further divided. Loose corymbs of small, pale yellow flowerheads, ¼in (6mm) across, without ray florets, are produced from summer to autumn. Cultivation group 2. ↕ 24in (60cm), ↔ 3ft (1m). Argentina. ❄ (min. 35°F/2°C)

Senecio viravira

SENNA

FABACEAE

Genus, often included in *Cassia*, of about 260 species of evergreen and deciduous trees, shrubs, and perennials from semi-desert, scrub, and savanna in dry, tropical and warm-temperate regions. Leaves are alternate and pinnate, with linear to nearly rounded leaflets. Sennas are cultivated for their yellow or rarely white, pea-like flowers, borne in terminal or axillary racemes, corymbs, or panicles. Where not hardy, grow in a temperate or warm greenhouse. In frost-free areas, grow in a shrub border.
• **CULTIVATION** Under glass, grow in soil-based potting mix in full light and moderate humidity. During the growing season, water moderately and apply a balanced liquid fertilizer monthly; water sparingly in winter. Outdoors, grow in moist but well-drained, moderately fertile soil in full sun. Pruning group 1; may need restrictive pruning under glass.
• **PROPAGATION** Sow seed at 64–75°F (18–24°C) in spring. Divide perennials in spring. Root semi-ripe cuttings with bottom heat in summer.
• **PESTS AND DISEASES** Infrequent.

S. alata, syn. *Cassia alata* (Empress candle plant). Erect to spreading, evergreen shrub or small tree. Broadly oblong to obovate, pinnate leaves, 8–30in (20–75cm) long, have 14–28 oblong, bright green leaflets. Bears numerous bright yellow flowers, to 1in (2.5cm) across, in tall, erect, axillary racemes, 6–24in (15–60cm) long, mainly from late summer to autumn; flowers are protected by broad, yellowish green bracts when in bud. ↕ 6–30ft (2–10m), ↔ 6–15ft (2–5m). Africa to S.E. Asia, Pacific islands, tropical America. ❄ (min. 41–45°F/5–7°C)

Senna artemisioides

S. artemisioides ■ syn. *Cassia artemisioides* (Silver cassia). Erect to spreading, evergreen shrub with pinnate leaves, 1¼–2½in (3–6cm) long, composed of 6–8 short, narrowly linear, thickly downy, gray-green leaflets. Stems are covered in ash-white hairs. Bears axillary racemes, to 3in (8cm) long, of 4–12 fragrant, pale to rich yellow flowers, to ½in (1.5cm) across, intermittently throughout the year. ↕ 3–6ft (1–2m), ↔ 3ft (1m). Northern Territory, South Australia, New South Wales. ❄ (min. 50–55°F/10–13°C)
S. corymbosa ■ syn. *Cassia corymbosa.* Erect to spreading, evergreen shrub producing pinnate, yellowish green leaves, 16–36in (40–90cm) long, with 6–8 oblong-lance-shaped leaflets. Axillary corymbs, 4in (10cm) across, of up to 20 yellow flowers, to ¾in (2cm) across, are borne in summer. ↕ 6–12ft (2–4m), ↔ 5–10ft (1.5–3m). Argentina, Uruguay. ❄ (min. 41–45°F/5–7°C)
S. didymobotrya, syn. *Cassia didymobotrya.* Erect to spreading, evergreen shrub or small tree with pinnate, mid-green leaves, 4–20in (10–50cm) long, composed of 16–32 elliptic-obovate leaflets. Bears golden yellow

Senna corymbosa

flowers, to 1¼in (3cm) across, with brown bracts covering the buds, in tall, erect, terminal or axillary racemes, 6–24in (15–60cm) long, from late summer to autumn. ↕ 8ft (2.5m), ↔ 5–10ft (1.5–3m). Tropical Africa. ❄ (min. 55°F/13°C)

S. x floribunda (*S. multiglandulosa* x *S. septentrionalis*) syn. *Cassia corymbosa* var. *plurijuga, C. floribunda* of gardens, *C.* x *floribunda.* Many-branched, evergreen or deciduous shrub with pinnate, mid-green leaves, 2½–3in (6–8cm) long, consisting of 12 oblong-elliptic leaflets. From summer to winter, often-branched, axillary racemes, 4in (10cm) long, produce up to 20 rich yellow flowers, to ¾in (2cm) across. ↕ 3–10ft (1–3m), ↔ 3–8ft (1–2.5m). Garden origin. ❄ (min. 45°F/7°C)

S. siamea, syn. *Cassia siamea* (Kassod tree). Open, fast-growing, evergreen tree. Pinnate, deep yellow-green leaves, 4–14in (10–35cm) long, each have 14–24 narrowly elliptic to oblong leaflets. Dense, erect, terminal, corymb-like panicles, 6–14in (15–35cm) long, of 10–60 yellow flowers, to ¾in (2cm) across, are produced from spring to summer. ↕ 30ft (10m), ↔ 22ft (7m). Indonesia, Malay Peninsula. ❄ (min. 61–64°F/16–18°C)

S. sturtii. Spreading or rounded, evergreen shrub. Pinnate, mid-green leaves, 1½–2in (4–5cm) long, each consist of 4–16 linear to elliptic leaflets. In early summer, bears short, axillary racemes, to 4in (10cm) across, of 4 or 5 yellow flowers, ½in (1.5cm) across. ↕ 3–6ft (1–2m), ↔ 3–5ft (1–1.5m). Australia. ❄ (min. 50°F/10°C)

SEQUOIA

TAXODIACEAE

Genus of one species of very tall, fast-growing, monoecious, evergreen, coniferous tree from coastal forest in California and Oregon. It has thick, soft bark, whorled branches when young, and yew-like foliage. Useful where a tall, evergreen tree is needed quickly; it thrives in climates with cool, damp summers, and is tolerant of pollution and wind. It is one of the few conifers that will coppice, or make new shoots from the base if cut down. The genus contains the tallest tree and also some of the oldest trees in the world.

• **CULTIVATION** Grow in moderately fertile, moist but well-drained soil in full sun to light, dappled shade.

• **PROPAGATION** Sow seed in containers in a cold frame in spring. Root softwood cuttings in summer, or semi-ripe cuttings in late summer or autumn.

• **PESTS AND DISEASES** Infrequent.

S. sempervirens ▣ (Coast redwood). Columnar-conical tree with horizontal or downcurved branches; thick, fissured, soft, red-brown bark; and mid-green, later red-brown shoots with decurrent leaf bases. The hard, linear, sharp-pointed, deep green leaves, ¾in (2cm) long, silvery white beneath, are 2-ranked. On very strong shoots, the leaves are scale-like. Cones are spherical-cylindrical: the terminal, mid-green female cones, 1¼in (3cm) long, ripen in their first autumn; the tiny, terminal and axillary, brownish green male cones are to ⅛in (3mm) long. ↕ to 365ft (112m), but mainly 70–100ft (20–30m), ↔ 20–28ft (6–9m). Coastal California and Oregon. Zone 7; best in mild climates. **'Adpressa'** has short, broad leaves, to ½in (1.5cm) long, creamy white when young and lying flat along the shoots; ↕ 20–28ft (6–9m), ↔ 12–20ft (4–6m). **'Aptos Blue'** bears dark bluish green leaves with very horizontal branches and pendulous branchlets. **'Pendula'** produces arching branches with pendent branchlets. **'Prostrata'** is dwarf, with spreading branches and broader, glaucous, dark green leaves; ↕ to 5ft (1.5m), ↔ 6–10ft (2–3m). **'Santa Cruz'** is sharply conical in shape, has a horizontal branching habit, and bears soft, pale green leaves. **'Soquel'** is pyramidal, with dark green leaves, bluish green beneath.

SEQUOIADENDRON

TAXODIACEAE

Genus of one species of monoecious, evergreen, coniferous tree from forest in the mountains of California. It is related to *Sequoia* but has narrowly wedge-shaped leaves and thicker, harder bark, and cones that ripen in the second year rather than the first; it thrives in a cooler, drier atmosphere than *Sequoia.* An excellent, but very tall specimen tree.

• **CULTIVATION** Grow in moderately fertile, well-drained soil in full sun or light, dappled shade.

• **PROPAGATION** Sow seed in containers in a cold frame in spring. Root softwood cuttings in summer, or semi-ripe cuttings in late summer.

• **PESTS AND DISEASES** Mushroom root rot, butt rot, dieback, and needle blight may occur.

S. giganteum ▣ (Big tree, Giant redwood). Conical tree, becoming flat-topped or columnar, with downcurved branches, very thick, fissured, red-brown bark, and mid-green, later red-brown shoots. Awl-shaped, gray-green leaves, to ¼in (6mm) long, are arranged radially and point forward on the shoots. Bears ovoid, mid-green female cones, 1¾in (4.5cm) long, ripening brown and persisting for several years. ↕ 80–260ft (25–80m), ↔ 22–30ft (7–10m). California (Sierra Nevada). Zone 6b. **'Pendulum'** has pendent side branches, giving a curtain-like effect.

SERIPHIDIUM

ASTERACEAE

Genus of 60–130 species of annuals, herbaceous or evergreen perennials, and mainly evergreen subshrubs from dry steppes, chaparral, and rocky or stony ground in Europe, N. Africa, temperate Asia, and North America. They are grown for their silver or gray, alternate, simple, pinnatisect, often aromatic leaves. Yellow to purple flowerheads, consisting only of disk florets, are borne in terminal or axillary spikes, panicles, or racemes in summer or autumn. Grow in a shrub border. Tolerant of adverse conditions and neglect.

• **CULTIVATION** Grow in poor to moderately fertile, dry, sharply drained soil in full sun. Pruning group 9.

• **PROPAGATION** Sow seed in containers in a cold frame in spring. Root semi-ripe cuttings in late summer.

• **PESTS AND DISEASES** Infrequent.

S. nutans, syn. *Artemisia nutans.* Woody-based, evergreen perennial producing 2- or 3-pinnatisect, aromatic, silvery gray leaves, 2–4in (5–10cm) long, with small, linear lobes. In late summer and early autumn, bears pale yellow flowerheads, ¼in (6mm) across, in dense, leafy, pyramidal panicles, to 5in (13cm) long. ↕ to 3ft (1m), ↔ 24in (60cm). S.E. Russia. Zone 6.

S. tridentatum ▣ syn. *Artemisia tridentata* (Sagebrush). Woody-based, evergreen perennial or spreading subshrub with a short trunk or few stems, white-woolly at first, becoming pale brown as bark forms. Densely clustered, wedge-shaped, aromatic, silvery gray-

Sequoia sempervirens (inset: leaf and cone detail)

Sequoiadendron giganteum

Seriphidium tridentatum

lowny leaves, ½–1½in (1–4cm) long, ›ften have 3-toothed tips. In mid- ıutumn, bears feathery, grayish white ›r yellow flowerheads, to ⅛in (3mm) ıcross, in slender panicles, to 18in 45cm) long. ↕↔ to 8ft (2.5m). ›. California. Zone 8.

ƩERISSA

ʀUBIACEAE

Ɉenus of one species of small, evergreen hrub from moist, open woodland in ›.E. Asia. Its leaves are simple, borne in ›pposite pairs, and fetid when crushed. ›mall, funnel-shaped flowers, with ubular calyces and 4–6 spreading petal obes, are borne singly or in clusters in ummer. Where temperatures fall below ‹5°F (7°C), grow in a temperate green- ıouse, mainly as a foliage plant or ›onsai. In warmer areas, grow at the ›ase of a house wall, in a shrub border, ›r as a low hedge.

CULTIVATION Under glass, grow in oil-based potting mix in full light vith shade from hot sun. When in ;rowth, water moderately and apply balanced liquid fertilizer monthly; vater sparingly in winter. Outdoors, ;row in moderately fertile, moist but vell-drained soil in full sun. Shelter rom cold, drying winds. Pruning ;roup 9. Trim hedges after flowering ›r in late winter.

PROPAGATION Root softwood cuttings n spring or early summer, or semi-ripe uttings in late summer, both with ›ottom heat. Layer in spring.

PESTS AND DISEASES Scale insects may ›e a problem under glass.

. foetida, syn. *S. japonica.* Wiry- ɛtemmed, eventually domed, bushy shrub ›roducing crowded, tiny, ovate, leathery, leep green leaves, to ¾in (2cm) long. In ummer, pink buds open to star-shaped vhite flowers, to ½in (1.5cm) across. 12–24in (30–60cm), ↔ 12–30in 30–75cm). S.E. Asia. ❀ (min. 5°F/7°C). **'Flore Pleno'** is smaller, with louble flowers; ↕ to 18in (45cm), ↔ 12in 30cm). **'Kyoto'** has tiny, closely set, ark green leaves and produces tiny, louble, white flowers. **'Mt. Fuji'** has iny, dark green leaves, heavily edged and treaked white. **'Variegata'** has leaves vith cream margins. **'Variegated Pink'** ıas cream-margined foliage and bears a ›rofusion of pink flowers.
. japonica see *S. foetida.*

ƩERRURIA

ROTEACEAE

Ɉenus, related to *Protea*, of about 55 ›pecies of evergreen shrubs from dry ıeathland scrub in South Africa. They ıave alternate, usually finely divided ɛaves, and from early spring to autumn, ›ear dense heads of small, 4-petaled lowers, surrounded in *S. florida* by howy, petal-like bracts. Where they re not hardy, grow in a temperate reenhouse. In warmer areas, grow in a hrub border or at the base of a warm, unny wall.

CULTIVATION Under glass, grow in part soil-based potting mix and 3 parts 0/50 mix of perlite and peat (or coir) n full light, with good ventilation.)uring the growing season, water noderately; after the first year, apply a

Serruria florida

half-strength phosphate-free liquid fertilizer monthly. Water sparingly in winter. Outdoors, grow in poor to moderately fertile, well-drained, neutral to slightly acidic soil in full sun. May become chlorotic if deficient in magnesium. Pruning group 1; may need restrictive pruning under glass.

• **PROPAGATION** Sow seed singly in pots at 61–70°F (16–21°C) as soon as ripe or in spring. Root semi-ripe cuttings in late summer, with bottom heat.

• **PESTS AND DISEASES** Infrequent.

S. florida ▣ (Blushing bride). Airy shrub with erect, purple-tinged branches bearing pinnate or 2-pinnate, grayish green leaves, 1½–2½in (4–6cm) long, with numerous almost cylindrical, sharp-pointed leaflets. Salmon-pink flowerheads, ¾–1in (2–2.5cm) across, each with a cup-shaped ring of pink-tinted white bracts, are produced from spring to autumn. ↕ 5–6ft (1.5–2m), ↔ 3–5ft (1–1.5m). South Africa (Western Cape, Eastern Cape). ❀ (min. 45–50°F/7–10°C); tolerates brief periods to 32°F (0°C).

SESBANIA *syn.* DAUBENTONIA

FABACEAE

Genus of about 50 species of short-lived, evergreen perennials, shrubs, and small trees found on streambanks and on moist soils in tropical and subtropical regions worldwide. Sesbanias are cultivated for their showy, pea-like flowers, borne in loose racemes from the leaf axils in summer. The leaves are alternate and pinnate, with many leaflets, each leaf terminating in a short extension of the axis. Where not hardy, grow in a cool to warm greenhouse, or in a conservatory. In warmer areas, grow in a shrub border, or at the base of a warm, sunny wall.

• **CULTIVATION** Under glass, grow in soil-based potting mix in full light. In growth, water freely and apply a balanced liquid fertilizer monthly. Water sparingly in winter. Outdoors, grow in moderately fertile, moist but well-drained soil in full sun. Pruning group 9.

• **PROPAGATION** Sow seed at 59–66°F (15–19°C) in spring. Root semi-ripe cuttings in late summer.

• **PESTS AND DISEASES** Spider mites, whiteflies, fungal leaf spots, and powdery mildew occur.

S. punicea, syn. *Daubentonia punicea.* Erect to spreading, large shrub or small tree. Pinnate leaves, 8–12in (20–30cm) long, have 6–20 pairs of oblong, mid- to deep green leaflets. In summer, bears pea-like, red-purple flowers, ¾in (2cm) across, in racemes to 4in (10cm) long. ↕ 6–12ft (2–4m), ↔ 5–8ft (1.5–2.5m). S. Brazil, N.E. Argentina, Uruguay. ❀ (min. 41°F/5°C)

SESLERIA

POACEAE

Genus of 33 species of tufted or clump-forming, evergreen, perennial grasses found mainly in damp or dry grasslands in the hills and mountains of Europe. They bear narrow, usually linear leaves and dense, spherical to cylindrical, spike-like panicles of flowers. Cultivated mainly for their colorful foliage, they are suitable for the front of a herbaceous or mixed border, in a rock garden, or in a wildflower meadow.

• **CULTIVATION** Grow in moderately fertile, well-drained, neutral to slightly alkaline soil in full sun or dappled shade.

• **PROPAGATION** Sow seed in containers in a cold frame in spring or autumn. Divide in spring.

• **PESTS AND DISEASES** Infrequent.

S. albicans, syn. *S. caerulea* subsp. *calcarea* (Blue moor grass). Vigorous, densely tufted, mound-forming, evergreen perennial with round-tipped, flat or channeled, linear, pale blue-gray leaves, to 12in (30cm) long, glossy, dark green beneath. Bears bluish purple, rarely greenish white spikelets, in dense, ovoid panicles, to ½–1¼in (1–3cm) long, just above the foliage from mid-spring to early summer. ↕ to 12in (30cm), ↔ 10in (25cm). Europe. Zone 5.
S. caerulea* subsp. *calcarea see *S. albicans.*
S. heufleriana (Balkan moor grass). Densely tufted, mound-forming, ever-green perennial with linear, bright green leaves, to 18in (45cm) long, grayish green beneath, and initially glaucous. White spikelets, aging to deep purple, are borne in panicles ½–1¼in (1–3cm) long, from late spring to late summer. ↕ to 24in (60cm), ↔ 18in (45cm). S.E. Europe. Zone 5.
S. nitida ▣ (Nest moor grass). Densely tufted, mound-forming, evergreen perennial with smooth, linear, sharp-pointed, pale gray-green to gray-blue leaves, to 18in (45cm) long. In late spring and early summer, long stems bear panicles, ¾–1¼in (2–3cm) long, of whitish green spikelets. ↕ to 24in (60cm), ↔ 16in (40cm). C. and S. Italy. Zone 5.

Sesleria nitida

SETARIA

POACEAE

Genus of about 100 species of annual or perennial grasses growing naturally in grasslands and woodlands of the tropics, subtropics, and warm-temperate zones. The leaves are elliptic to ovate, or rarely arrow-shaped. They have long, narrow spikes of flowers that arch up and away from the foliage. Setarias are suitable for a herbaceous or mixed border, or a subtropical perennial border. They are also useful in dried flower arrangements. Where not hardy, grow in a temperate greenhouse.

• **CULTIVATION** Outdoors, grow in any well-drained soil in full sun to partial shade. Under glass, grow in soil-based potting mix in full light. When in growth, water freely and apply a balanced liquid fertilizer every 2 weeks. Water moderately in winter.

• **PROPAGATION** For annual grasses, sow seed *in situ* in spring. Divide perennials in spring. Root stem cuttings with small pieces of shoot attached in spring.

• **PESTS AND DISEASES** Spider mites, caterpillars, and rust occur.

S. palmifolia (Palm grass). Upright to spreading, dense, clump-forming perennial grass with elliptic-lance-shaped, longitudinally pleated, mid-green leaves, to 18in (45cm) long. Bears arching, narrow stems with bottlebrush-like spikes, 3–5in (8–13cm) long, of green to beige flowers, in late summer. ↕↔ 3–6ft (1–2m). Africa, India. ❀ (min. 41°F/5°C). **'Rubra'** ▣ has purple-red midribs and leaf sheaths.

▷ ***Setcreasea purpurea*** see *Tradescantia pallida* 'Purpurea'
▷ ***Setcreasea striata*** see *Callisia elegans*

Setaria palmifolia 'Rubra'

SHEPHERDIA

ELAEAGNACEAE

Genus of 3 species of dioecious, evergreen or deciduous shrubs or small trees found in rocky and sandy habitats, and on streambanks, in North America. They have opposite, simple, ovate or oblong leaves and, in spring, before the leaves appear, bear short spikes or racemes of tiny, tubular, petalless flowers, each with a 4-lobed calyx. On female plants, the flowers are followed by spherical or ovoid, red or yellowish red fruits. Valued for their ornamental fruit and foliage, they are suitable for the back of a mixed or shrub border; they are particularly useful on poor, dry soils, and excellent for sites in exposed coastal regions. Male and female plants must be grown together to obtain fruit.

• **CULTIVATION** Grow in moderately fertile, well-drained, neutral to slightly alkaline soil in full sun. Pruning group 1.

• **PROPAGATION** Sow seed in containers in a cold frame in autumn. Root greenwood cuttings in early summer, with gentle bottom heat.

• **PESTS AND DISEASES** Powdery mildew, rust, white heart rot, and *Septoria* leaf spot can be problems.

S. argentea (Silver buffaloberry). Upright, bushy, deciduous shrub, often tree-like, with oblong leaves, to 2in (5cm) long, covered in silvery scales. In spring, produces insignificant, yellow-green flowers, followed on female plants by ovoid, sour-tasting, bright red fruit, ¼in (6mm) long. ↕↔ 12ft (4m). North America. Zone 1.

SHIBATAEA

POACEAE

Genus of about 5 species of low-growing, spreading, evergreen bamboos from deciduous woodland and valley slopes in China and Japan. They have slowly spreading rhizomes and slender culms, slightly flattened on one side and slightly bent at the nodes, creating a zigzag effect. Each node bears 2–5 short branches with narrowly ovate to elliptic, checkered leaves. Some have fragrant foliage. Grow for their foliage in a mixed border, a gravel garden, or a container on a patio, or, if densely planted, as a groundcover.

• **CULTIVATION** Grow in moderately fertile, moist but well-drained or damp soil in partial shade, or in full sun where soil stays damp in spring and summer.

• **PROPAGATION** Divide or transplant sections of young rhizomes in spring.

• **PESTS AND DISEASES** Young shoots may be damaged by slugs.

S. kumasasa ■ syn. *Sasa ruscifolia.* Evergreen, clump-forming bamboo with short-jointed, greenish brown culms and abundant, long-stalked, broadly lance-shaped, taper-pointed, rich dark green leaves, 2–4½in (5–11cm) long. New shoots appear in late spring. ↕ 2–5ft (0.6–1.5m), ↔ 24in (60cm). Japan. Zone 7.

Shibataea kumasasa

SHORTIA *syn.* SCHIZOCODON

DIAPENSIACEAE

Genus of 6 species of evergreen perennials, spreading by runners, from woodland in E. Asia, with one species from North America. The rounded, heart-shaped, or elliptic, toothed, leathery, glossy, usually dark green leaves often turn red in autumn and winter. Bell-, trumpet-, or funnel-shaped, white or deep pink flowers, with toothed or deeply fringed petals, are borne either singly or in terminal racemes, in spring. These attractive, shade-loving plants are suitable for cultivation in a rock garden, open glade in a woodland garden, or an alpine house. They grow best in areas with cool, damp summers.

• **CULTIVATION** Grow in humus-rich, leafy, moist but well-drained, acidic soil in deep to partial shade. Difficult to grow in dry climates, even with frequent watering. Under glass, grow in acidic potting mix, and keep cool and well ventilated, with moderate to high humidity.

• **PROPAGATION** Sow seed in containers in a cold frame as soon as ripe; keep moist at all times. Remove small, rooted runners carefully in spring; shortias dislike root disturbance. Take basal cuttings in early summer.

• **PESTS AND DISEASES** Prone to slugs and snails outdoors; may be infested with aphids under glass.

S. galacifolia (Oconee bells). Clump-forming perennial with rounded, blunt-toothed, glossy, dark green leaves, ¾–3in (2–8cm) long, with wavy margins, turning bronze-red in autumn. In late spring, bears solitary, funnel-shaped white flowers, to 1in (2.5cm) across, often flushed pink, with toothed petals and pink calyces. ↕ 6in (15cm), ↔ 10in (25cm). E. US. Zone 7.

Shortia uniflora 'Grandiflora'

S. soldanelloides (Fringed galax). Mat-forming perennial producing ovate to rounded, coarsely toothed, glossy, dark green leaves, 2in (5cm) long, rounded or heart-shaped at the bases. In late spring, bears narrowly trumpet-shaped, deep pink flowers, to 1in (2.5cm) across, with deeply fringed petals, usually in one-sided racemes. ↕ 4–12in (10–30cm), ↔ 10in (25cm). Japan. Zone 6.

var. *ilicifolia* has smaller leaves with triangular teeth, and white or rarely pink flowers.

***S. uniflora* 'Grandiflora'** ■ (Nippon bells). Vigorous, mat-forming perennial with rounded, toothed, glossy, mid-green leaves, ¾–3in (2–8cm) long, heart-shaped at the bases and with wavy margins. In spring, bears a profusion of solitary, widely bell-shaped, shell-pink flowers, 2in (5cm) across, with toothed petals. ↕ 6in (15cm), ↔ 10in (25cm). Japan. Zone 6.

SIBIRAEA

ROSACEAE

Genus, closely related to *Spiraea*, of one species of deciduous shrub found on cliffs and in rocky places in E. Europe, Russia (Siberia), and China. The leaves are alternate (occasionally appearing whorled on short, lateral shoots), entire, linear-oblong to narrowly obovate, and mid- or blue-green. Racemes of tiny, cup-shaped, white or yellowish green flowers are produced in summer; the flowers are usually either male or female. Grow *S. laevigata* for its foliage and flowers in a mixed or shrub border.

• **CULTIVATION** Grow in moderately fertile, well-drained, neutral to slightly alkaline soil in full sun. Pruning group 2 or 4.

• **PROPAGATION** Sow seed in containers in a cold frame in autumn or spring. Root softwood cuttings in spring or summer, with gentle bottom heat.

• **PESTS AND DISEASES** Infrequent.

S. altaiensis see *S. laevigata.*

S. laevigata, syn. *S. altaiensis.* Spreading, sparsely branched shrub with thick, purple-brown shoots and linear-oblong to narrowly obovate, mid- or blue-green leaves, to 4in (10cm) long. Tiny, cup-shaped, white or yellowish green flowers are borne in terminal racemes, to 5in (13cm) long, in early summer. ↕ 3ft (1m), ↔ 5ft (1.5m). Russia (Siberia), Balkans, W. China. Zone 6.

SIDALCEA

False mallow, Prairie mallow

MALVACEAE

Genus of approximately 20–25 species of annuals and perennials, some rhizomatous, occurring in grassland, woodland glades, and on mountain streamsides in W. and C. North America. They form clumps of rounded to kidney-shaped, palmately lobed or toothed, mid-green basal leaves, from which arise erect, sometimes branched, stiff, flowering stems. The flowering stems produce palmately lobed, mid-green stem leaves and long-lasting, hollyhock-like, white, pink, or purple-pink flowers in dense, upright, terminal racemes. Each flower has 5 spreading, sometimes fringed, silky petals and numerous prominent stamens. They are suitable for growing in a mixed or herbaceous border, and provide good cut flowers.

Sidalcea malviflora 'Elsie Heugh'

• **CULTIVATION** Grow in moderately fertile, humus-rich, moist but well-drained, light, sandy, neutral to slightly acidic soil in full sun. Sidalceas will tolerate a wide range of soil conditions, but resent waterlogging. Provide a dry winter mulch during winters without protective snow cover. Cut stems back hard after flowering, to prevent seed formation and to encourage a further flush of blooms.

• **PROPAGATION** Sow seed in containers in a cold frame in autumn or spring. Divide cultivars in autumn or spring.

• **PESTS AND DISEASES** Prone to damage from slugs, Japanese beetles, and rust.

S. candida. Rhizomatous perennial with rounded, 7-lobed basal leaves, to 8in (20cm) long, and smaller, rounded leaves on the erect, unbranched stems. Dense racemes of open funnel-shaped, white or cream flowers, to 1in (2.5cm) across, are produced in mid- and late

Sidalcea malviflora 'Oberon'

ımmer. ↕ 12–32in (30–80cm), ↔ 18in
ł5cm). Wyoming, Nevada, Utah,
:olorado, New Mexico. Zone 6.
. ***malviflora*** (Checkerbloom). Erect to
ightly decumbent perennial producing
›unded to kidney-shaped, shallowly
›bed basal leaves, 1½–3in (4–8cm)
›ng, and more deeply lobed stem
aves. In early and midsummer, bears
ıcemes of funnel-shaped, pink or lilac-
:nk flowers, 2in (5cm) across. ↕ to 4ft
(.2m), ↔ 18in (45cm). Oregon,
:alifornia, Mexico (Baja California).
one 6. Most of the cultivars described
:e hybrids between *S. candida* and
. *malviflora.* **'Brilliant'** has carmine-red
›owers; ↕ 2½ft (75cm). **'Croftway Red'**
as rich reddish pink flowers; ↕ 36in
›0cm). **'Elsie Heugh'** ■ has large,
ıtin-textured, purple-pink flowers, the
etals fringed; ↕ 36in (90cm). **'Listeri'**
as pearly pink flowers. **'Loveliness'** is
›mpact, with pale pink flowers; ↕ 30in
75cm). **'Oberon'** ■ has clear rose-pink
›owers. **'Puck'** is compact and upright,
earing deep pink flowers in mid-
ımmer; ↕ to 16in (40cm). **'Reverend
age Roberts'** has silvery, pale rose-pink
owers. **'Scarlet Beauty'** has deep
ırple flowers. **Stark's Hybrid Mixed**
ıltivars are erect, clump-forming, and
ear rose-red flowers, to 1¼in (3cm)
:ross; ↕ 5ft (1.5m). **'Sussex Beauty'**
as satin-textured, clear pink flowers.
Villiam Smith' has deep rose-pink
owers, tinted salmon-pink;
36in (90cm).
. **'Party Girl'.** Clump-forming, stiffly
:ect perennial with rounded to kidney-
ıaped, gray-green leaves, 1½–3in
ł–8cm) long. Bright pink flowers, to
½in (4cm) across, are borne in spikes,
4–36in (60–90cm) long, from
ıidsummer to autumn. ↕ 24–36in
50–90cm), ↔ 18in (45cm). Zone 4.

›IDERITIS

AMIACEAE

ienus of about 100 species of annuals, erennials, and evergreen shrubs and ıbshrubs from coastal plains to forest r laurel-covered clifftops in the Iediterranean and Atlantic islands. 'hey are grown mainly for their simple, ften softly hairy or white-woolly leaves, :ranged in opposite pairs. Tubular to ell-shaped, 2-lipped flowers are borne ı whorled spikes in summer. They need ›ng, hot summers to thrive. In warm, ry climates, grow at the front of a ıixed or shrub border, or in a small ›urtyard garden. Where winters are ›ld and damp, grow as foliage plants in cool greenhouse.
CULTIVATION Under glass, grow in ›il-based potting mix in full light. Vhen in growth, water moderately and ›pply a balanced liquid fertilizer ıonthly; water sparingly in winter.)utdoors, grow in moderately fertile, ıarply drained, neutral to slightly kaline soil in full sun. Provide a dry 'inter mulch. Pruning group 9.
PROPAGATION Sow seed of tender ›ecies at 55–61°F (13–16°C) in spring; ›w seed of hardier species in containers ı a cold frame in spring. Divide erennials in early spring. Root soft-ood cuttings of shrubs in late spring, ith bottom heat; take semi-ripe ıttings in late summer.
PESTS AND DISEASES Infrequent.

S. candicans. Erect to spreading, many-branched shrub with ovate to heart-shaped, densely white-woolly, scalloped leaves, 2–4in (5–10cm) long. In summer, bears erect, terminal spikes, 6–11in (15–28cm) long, of 20–30 small, light yellow flowers, ⅜in (9mm) long, tipped orange and red-brown. ↕ 24–36in (60–90cm), ↔ 18–32in (45–80cm). Canary Islands (Tenerife). ❅ (min. 41°F/5°C)

▷ ***Sieversia reptans*** see *Geum reptans*
▷ ***Sigmatostalix radicans*** see *Ornithophora radicans*

SILENE

Campion, Catchfly

CARYOPHYLLACEAE

Genus of about 500 species of annuals, biennials, and deciduous or evergreen perennials, some subshrubby, widely distributed in habitats ranging from open woodland to meadows and mountain screes in the N. hemisphere; most occur around the Mediterranean, but some are found in the mountains of tropical Africa and in South America. The variable leaves are opposite, linear to ovate or obovate, and entire. The flowers have 5 often notched or split, clawed petals and a tubular, often conspicuously inflated calyx; they are borne singly or in sprays, clusters, broad or narrow panicle-like cymes, or corymb-like panicles. Most silenes are easily grown, and often self-seed freely. Smaller perennials are excellent for a rock garden, and taller ones for the front of a herbaceous border, or for a wild garden. Use annuals as bedding in mixed or annual borders. Some silenes resent winter moisture and are best grown in a scree bed or alpine house.
• **CULTIVATION** Grow in moderately fertile, well-drained, neutral to slightly alkaline soil in full sun or light, dappled shade. *S. hookeri* needs acidic soil. *S. dioica* 'Rosea Plena' needs moist but well-drained soil in light, dappled shade.

Silene alpestris

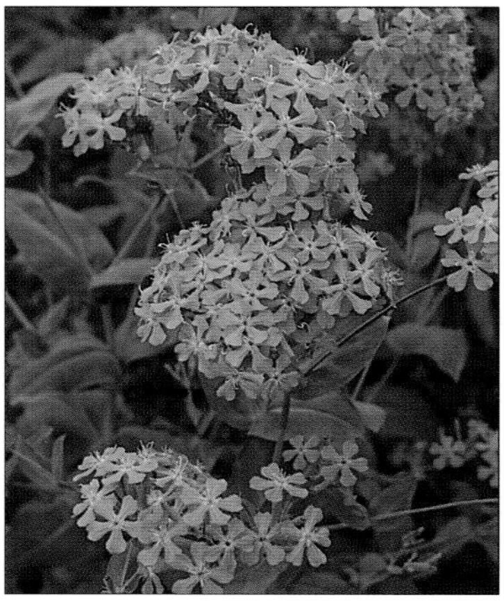

Silene armeria 'Electra'

Grow smaller alpine species in sharply drained, gritty soil in a scree bed, or in a mix of equal parts soil-based potting mix and sharp grit, in containers in an alpine house.
• **PROPAGATION** Sow seed of perennials in containers in a cold frame in autumn. Sow seed of hardy annuals *in situ* in autumn or spring; sow tender annuals at 61–66°F (16–19°C) in spring and harden off before planting out after last frosts. Divide rooted offshoots of *S. dioica* 'Rosea Plena' from midsummer to autumn. Root basal cuttings of perennials in spring.
• **PESTS AND DISEASES** Slugs, snails, whiteflies, spider mites, and aphids can be problems. Rust, smut, and a few stem and leaf fungi occur.

S. acaulis (Moss campion). Very dwarf, evergreen perennial forming moss-like cushions of tiny, linear, bright green leaves, ¼–½in (6–15mm) long. In summer, produces solitary, almost stemless, deep pink, sometimes white flowers, to ½in (1.5cm) across, with entire or notched petals. Suitable for a scree bed, but rarely bears abundant flowers in cultivation. ↕ 2in (5cm), ↔ 8in (20cm). Arctic, mountains of Eurasia, North America. Zone 3.
S. alpestris ■ syn. *Heliosperma alpestris.* Loosely tufted, branching, evergreen perennial with linear-lance-shaped, mid-green leaves, to 1¼in (3cm) long. In early summer, bears open sprays of rounded, white, sometimes pink-flushed flowers, ½in (1.5cm) across, with fringed petals. ↕ 6in (15cm), ↔ 8in (20cm). Europe (E. Alps). Zone 4.
S. armeria (Sweet William catchfly). Sticky-stemmed annual with upright stems. Produces gray-green leaves, ½–1½in (1–4cm) long, the basal leaves spoon-shaped, the stem leaves lance-shaped. In late summer, bears broad, dense, rounded, corymb-like panicles of deep carmine-pink flowers, to ½in (1.5cm) across, with shallowly notched petals. ↕ 12in (30cm), ↔ 6in (15cm). C. and S. Europe. **'Electra'** ■ is very free-flowering.
S. caroliniana. Tuft-forming, hairy, evergreen perennial with spoon-shaped, mid-green basal leaves and linear-lance-shaped stem leaves, to 3in (8cm) long. Corymbs of large, short-stalked, pink flowers, to 1in (2.5cm) across, are borne in summer. ↕ to 8in (20cm), ↔ 6in (15cm). C. and E. North America. Zone 5.

Silene coeli-rosa

S. coeli-rosa ■ syn. *Agrostemma coeli-rosa, Lychnis coeli-rosa, Viscaria elegans* (Rose of heaven). Erect, slender, hairless annual with oblong to lance-shaped, gray-green leaves, ½–2in (1–5cm) long. In summer, bears loose, long-stalked clusters of spreading, white-centered, rose-pink flowers, to 1in (2.5cm) across, with deeply notched petals and prominently toothed calyces. Good for cut flowers. ↕ to 20in (50cm), ↔ to 6in (15cm). Mediterranean. **Angel Series** cultivars flower in 2 separate, soft, clear colors; ↕ 10–12in (25–30cm). **'Rose Angel'** bears deep pink-magenta flowers.
***S. conica* 'Balletje Balletje'.** Erect, slender, sticky-stemmed annual with narrowly lance-shaped, gray-green leaves, ½–1½in (1–4cm) long. In summer, produces cymes of 5–30 rose-pink flowers, to ¼in (6mm) across, but is grown for its oval, sticky-hairy, gray-green calyces, with bright green ribs. ↕ 6–20in (15–50cm), ↔ to 6in (15cm).
***S. dioica* 'Rosea Plena'.** Clump-forming, semi-evergreen perennial with erect, branched flowering stems. Bears dark green leaves, most to 3½in (9cm) long, the basal leaves obovate, the stem leaves oblong-obovate, becoming smaller and almost stalkless toward the stem tips. From late spring to midsummer, produces loosely branched, panicle-like cymes of large, rounded, double flowers, 1½in (4cm) across, with notched, dusky pink petals, white at the bases. ↕ to 32in (80cm), ↔ 18in (45cm). Zone 5.
S. elisabethae, syn. *Melandrium elisabethae.* Tufted, semi-evergreen perennial with loose rosettes of lance-shaped, glossy, mid-green leaves, 2½in (6cm) long. In early summer, spreading stems bear usually solitary, large, deep red-purple flowers, 2in (5cm) across, with 2-lobed petals. Resents winter moisture. ↕ to 10in (25cm), ↔ 6in (15cm). Limestone screes in the Italian Alps. Zone 7b.
S. hookeri. Tufted, prostrate, deciduous perennial with lance-shaped, gray-hairy, mid-green leaves, 2–3in (5–8cm) long. In late summer, bears solitary, clear pale pink to salmon-pink flowers, to 2½in (6cm) across, with very deeply lobed white petals. Resents winter moisture; needs acidic soil. ↕ to 2in (5cm), ↔ to 6in (15cm). California. Zone 5.
S. keiskei* var. *minor. Tufted, evergreen perennial, similar to *S. elisabethae*, with hairy, narrowly lance-shaped, dark green leaves, to 1¼in (3cm) long, on slender stems. Bears loosely branching sprays of

deep rose-pink flowers, ¾–1¼in (2–3cm) across, with shallowly notched petals, in late summer. ↕4in (10cm), ↔ 8in (20cm). Japan. Zone 6.
S. laciniata. Lax-stemmed, hairy-glandular perennial with linear to lance-shaped, mid-green leaves, 1–5in (2.5–13cm) long. Bears loose clusters of few to many scarlet flowers, to 1in (2.5cm) across, in summer. ↕ to 16in (40cm), ↔ 24in (60cm). California, Mexico. Zone 7.
***S. maritima* 'Flore Pleno'** see *S. uniflora* 'Flore Pleno'.
S. pendula (Nodding catchfly). Erect to spreading, glandular-hairy, bushy annual with ovate to lance-shaped, hairy, mid-green leaves, to 2½in (6cm) long. In summer, bears loose clusters of slightly pendent, single or double, pale pink flowers, to ½in (1.5cm) across, with prominently toothed calyces. ↕↔ 6–9in (15–23cm). Mediterranean. **'Peach Blossom'** has double flowers, opening deep rose-pink and maturing through pale pink to white, showing a range of colors at the same time on a single plant; ↕ 6in (15cm). **'Snowball'** has double white flowers.
S. schafta. Clump-forming, slender-stemmed, semi-evergreen perennial with lance-shaped, bright green leaves, ½–¾in (1–2cm) long. Profusely bears sprays of long-tubed, deep magenta flowers, ¾in (2cm) across, with notched petals, from late summer to autumn. Suitable for a rock garden. ↕ 10in (25cm), ↔ 12in (30cm). W. Asia. Zone 3b.
***S. uniflora* 'Flore Pleno'**, syn. *S. maritima* 'Flore Pleno', *S. vulgaris* subsp. *maritima* 'Flore Pleno' (Double bladder campion). Lax, prostrate, deeply rooting, semi-evergreen perennial with fleshy, lance-shaped, gray-green leaves, to ¾in (2cm) long, fringed with fine hairs. In summer, erect, branching stems produce double white flowers, to 1in (2.5cm) across, with deeply cut petals, either singly or in few-flowered clusters. ↕ 6in (15cm), ↔ 8in (20cm). Zone 4.
***S. vulgaris* subsp. *maritima* 'Flore Pleno'** see *S. uniflora* 'Flore Pleno'.

SILPHIUM

Prairie dock, Rosinweed

ASTERACEAE

Genus of about 20 species of tall herbaceous perennials from fields, prairies, and open woodland and scrub (some in moister areas) in Canada and C. and E. US. Their erect, sparsely branched stems exude resinous sap with a strong turpentine-like scent. The opposite or alternate, coarse leaves, sometimes all basal, are lance-shaped to ovate or triangular, some toothed or pinnatifid. Sunflower-like yellow flowerheads are borne in branching corymbs. Excellent for naturalizing in a wild or woodland garden, or for the back of a herbaceous border.
• **CULTIVATION** Grow in moderately fertile, moist, deep, neutral to slightly alkaline soil in full sun or partial shade; best in heavy soil. *S. perfoliatum* prefers damper soil.
• **PROPAGATION** Sow seed in containers as soon as ripe. Divide in spring.
• **PESTS AND DISEASES** Downy mildew, rust, and *Cercospora* leaf spot are sometimes problems.

S

Silphium perfoliatum

S. integrifolium. Erect, finely woolly to bristly perennial with usually opposite, lance-shaped to ovate or elliptic, stalkless, entire or toothed, bristly, mid-green leaves, 6in (15cm) long, densely woolly to hairless beneath. In summer, bears yellow flowerheads, to 2in (5cm) across, in loose or dense corymb-like inflorescences. ↕ 18–60in (45–150cm), ↔ 36in (90cm). C. and E. US. Zone 5.
S. laciniatum (Compass plant, Pilot plant, Polar plant). Upright, clump-forming perennial with stiffly hairy stems bearing alternate, erect, pinnatifid or 2-pinnatifid, fern-like, hairy leaves, to 20in (50cm) long, becoming smaller up the stems; the flat sides face east and west, hence the plant's common names. In late summer and early autumn, bears terminal, narrow, raceme-like corymbs of nodding yellow, eastward-facing flowerheads, to 5in (13cm) across, with darker disk florets. ↕ to 10ft (3m), ↔ 24in (60cm). E. and C. US. Zone 6.
S. perfoliatum ▣ (Cup plant). Erect, hairless or nearly hairless, clump-forming perennial producing opposite, triangular-ovate, coarsely toothed, bristly leaves, to 14in (35cm) long, with winged stalks. The upper leaves are perfoliate. From midsummer to early autumn, bears terminal, open-branched, corymb-like inflorescences of yellow flowerheads, to 3in (8cm) across, with darker disk florets. ↕ to 8ft (2.5m), ↔ 3ft (1m). Ontario to Oklahoma and Georgia. Zone 6.
S. terebinthinaceum. Erect perennial with ovate, oblong, or elliptic, sharply toothed to pinnatifid, long-stalked, mid-green, mostly basal leaves, to 24in (60cm) long. Bears many yellow flowerheads, 3in (8cm) across, in open corymbs, in summer. ↕ to 10ft (3m), ↔ 4–6ft (1.2–2m). E. Canada to S.E. US. Zone 4.

SILYBUM

ASTERACEAE

Genus of 2 species of erect, rosette-forming, thistle-like annuals or biennials from the mountains of E. Africa and from stony slopes, steppes, and thickets in W. Africa, the Mediterranean, and Europe to C. Asia. They have broad, shallowly to deeply lobed, obovate to inversely lance-shaped, spiny, light to dark green leaves, and bear spherical, single, purple-pink flowerheads,

Silybum marianum

enclosed in spiny bracts. Cultivated for their foliage and flowers, they are suitable for growing in a mixed or herbaceous border or a gravel garden.
• **CULTIVATION** Grow in poor to moderately fertile, well-drained, neutral to slightly alkaline soil in full sun. Protect from excessive winter moisture. Carefully remove flowering stems as they form, to retain foliage effect.
• **PROPAGATION** Sow seed *in situ* in late spring or early summer, and thin seedlings to 24in (60cm) apart. To grow for foliage effect alone, sow in a cold greenhouse in late winter or very early spring; prick out into 3½in (9cm) containers and grow on to plant out in late spring.
• **PESTS AND DISEASES** Prone to damage by caterpillars, slugs, and snails.

S. marianum ▣ (Mary's thistle). Rosette-forming biennial with a flat, basal rosette of deeply lobed, obovate, spiny, heavily white-veined and marbled, glossy, dark green leaves, to 20in (50cm) long. In the second year after sowing, bears thistle-like, slightly scented, purple-pink flowerheads, to 2in (5cm) across, from summer to autumn. ↕ to 5ft (1.5m), ↔ 24–36in (60–90cm). S.W. Europe to Afghanistan, N. Africa. Zone 5.

▷ ***Sinacalia tangutica*** see *Senecio tanguticus*
▷ ***Sinarundinaria jaunsarensis*** see *Yushania anceps*
▷ ***Sinarundinaria murieliae*** see *Fargesia murieliae*
▷ ***Sinarundinaria nitida*** see *Fargesia nitida*

SIMMONDSIA

Jojoba

SIMMONDSIACEAE

Genus of one species of woody, evergreen dioecious shrub growing naturally in desert areas of S.W. US and N. Mexico. The leaves are opposite and oblong-ovate. It is grown commercially for its edible, nutlike fruit, which yields oil. Jojoba is highly suitable for erosion control, hedging, or a desert garden.
• **CULTIVATION** Grow in poor, dry soil with added sand in full sun. Pruning group 10.
• **PROPAGATION** Sow seed in containers or *in situ* in summer. Take ripe or hardwood cuttings in spring, with bottom heat at over 90°F (32°C).
• **PESTS AND DISEASES** Infrequent.

S. chinensis (Goat nut, Jojoba). Stiff-branched, multi-stemmed shrub with oblong-ovate, green or yellow-green to blue-green leaves, to 1½in (4cm) long. I early spring, bears clusters of tiny, yellow male flowers, to ¼in (6mm) long or pal green female flowers, to ½in (15mm) long, followed by an ovoid, brown nutlike fruit, to ¾in (2cm) long. ↕ 3–4ft (1–1.2m), ↔ 3–5ft (1–1.5m). S.W. US, N. Mexico. ❀ (min. 45°F/7°C)

SINNINGIA

GESNERIACEAE

Genus, including species formerly classified under *Gloxinia* and *Rechsteineria*, of about 40 species of tuberous perennials and deciduous or evergreen, low-growing shrubs from tropical forest in Central and South America. They have usually ovate to elliptic, fleshy leaves, in opposite pairs or in whorls of 6 or more, often crowded at the stem bases. They are grown for their showy, solitary or clustered, tubular, trumpet-shaped, or bell-shaped flowers, generally borne in summer. Where not hardy or in areas with high winter rainfall, grow as houseplants or in a warm greenhouse o conservatory. In frost-free areas, they a suitable for a trough, raised bed, terrac or woodland garden.
• **CULTIVATION** Under glass, grow in soilless potting mix in bright filtered o indirect light. Most are best maintaine at 64–75°F (18–24°C) with high humidity; grow *S. cardinalis* and *S. pusilla* at 66°F (19°C) or more. In the growing season, water moderately and apply a half-strength high-potash fertilizer every 2 weeks. Dry off tubers in autumn and keep completely dry in winter; *S. pusilla* and micro-miniature cultivars generally remain evergreen, sending up new crowns periodically. Start into growth in early spring in shallow trays of peat; pot up individua into 3½–4in (9–10cm) containers when young shoots are 2–3in (5–8cm) long. Outdoors, grow in moist but we drained, humus-rich, acidic to neutral soil in light dappled or partial shade.
• **PROPAGATION** Surface-sow seed at 59–70°F (15–21°C) in spring. Divide tubers in spring. Take stem-tip cutting of miniature species and cultivars in la spring or early summer. Root leaf cuttings in spring or summer, with bottom heat.
• **PESTS AND DISEASES** Pests include cyclamen mites, aphids, whiteflies, leaf miners, and thrips. The most commo diseases are crown rot, viruses, and nematodes.

S. canescens ▣ syn. *Rechsteineria leucotricha*, *S. leucotricha* (Brazilian edelweiss, Queen of the abyss). Upright, densely woolly, tuberous perennial. Whorls of obovate, sage-green leaves, to 6in (15cm) long, are covered with silvery white hairs. In spring, short-lived, nodding, narrowly tubular, pinkish orange-red to rose-pink flowers, 1in (2.5cm) long, are produced in clusters of 3–5 or more. ↕ 12in (30cm), ↔ 14in (35cm) or mor Brazil. ❀ (min. 59°F/15°C)
S. cardinalis ▣ (Cardinal flower, Helmet flower). Tuberous perennial with short white hairs covering both t

Sinningia canescens

stems and the pairs of ovate, scalloped, mid-green leaves, 3–6in (7–15cm) long. Clustered, upwardly angled, hooded, tubular, blood-red flowers, 2in (5cm) long, open in succession for up to 3 months from late summer to autumn. ↕↔ to 12in (30cm). Brazil. ❄ (min. 59°F/15°C)

***S.* 'Cherry Chips'.** Miniature tuberous perennial with rosettes of rounded, scalloped, dark green leaves, 1¼in (3cm) long. In summer, bears solitary, trumpet-shaped, cherry-red flowers, 1in (2.5cm) long, each with small dots over a white throat. ↕↔ 3in (8cm). ❄ (min. 59°F/15°C)

S. conspicua. Upright, tuberous perennial with rosettes of heart-shaped-ovate, scalloped, hairy, light green leaves, 4in (10cm) long. Solitary or clustered, nodding, bell-shaped, slightly fragrant, light yellow flowers, 1½in (4cm) long, are borne in spring and summer. ↕ 12in (30cm), ↔ 10in (25cm). Brazil. ❄ (min. 59°F/15°C)

S. eumorpha. Upright, tuberous perennial with rosettes of heart-shaped-ovate, scalloped, mid-green leaves, 4in (10cm) long. In summer, produces solitary or clustered, nodding, bell-shaped, pale-violet-edged, lavender-flushed, white flowers, 1½in (4cm) long, each with a red-spotted yellow band inside the tube. ↕ 12in (30cm), ↔ 10in (25cm). ❄ (min. 59°F/15°C)

S. leucotricha see *S. canescens.*

S. pusilla. Miniature perennial with pea-sized tubers, bearing pairs of ovate, hairy, dark olive-green leaves, to ½in (1.5cm) long, red-veined beneath. Solitary, nodding, tubular lilac flowers, ¾in (2cm) long, with white throats, are produced on hairy stalks, ½in (1.5cm) long, almost continuously, especially in a terrarium. Parent of several micro-miniature cultivars. ↕↔ 1–2in (2.5–5cm). Brazil. ❄ (min. 59°F/15°C). **'White Sprite'** bears white flowers.

S. regina (Cinderella slippers). Tuberous perennial with pairs of ovate to elliptic, finely scalloped, dark green leaves, 4–8in (10–20cm) long, velvety above and pale green in the vein areas. Clusters of 4–6 nodding, trumpet-shaped, rich purple flowers, 2in (5cm) long, each with a pale yellow band, are produced in summer. ↕ 8in (20cm), ↔ 14in (35cm). Brazil. ❄ (min. 59°F/15°C)

S. speciosa, syn. *Gloxinia speciosa* (Florists' gloxinia). Tuberous perennial with rosettes of ovate to oblong, scalloped, dark green leaves, 8–12in (20–30cm) long, covered with velvety hairs, and red-flushed beneath. Produces solitary or clustered, nodding, tubular-bell-shaped, red, violet-blue, or white flowers, 1½in (4cm) long, in summer. ↕↔ 12in (30cm). Brazil. ❄ (min. 59°F/15°C). Many single and double cultivars are available, with larger, upward-facing, trumpet-shaped flowers, to 3in (8cm) long, in a wide color range.

***S.* 'Switzerland'** ■ Tuberous perennial with rosettes of ovate, velvety, mid-green leaves, 8–10in (20–25cm) long. In summer, produces solitary, upright, trumpet-shaped, bright scarlet flowers, 1½in (4cm) long, with wavy white margins. ↕ to 12in (30cm), ↔ 18in (45cm). ❄ (min. 59°F/15°C)

Sinningia cardinalis

Sinningia 'Switzerland'

▷ ***Sinocalamus giganteus*** see *Dendrocalamus giganteus*

SINOCALYCANTHUS

CALYCANTHACEAE

Genus of one species of deciduous shrub, related to *Calycanthus*, occurring in woodland in China. It produces simple, opposite leaves, and is grown for its showy, single white flowers, borne in early summer. Use in a shrub border or wild garden.

- **CULTIVATION** Grow in moderately fertile, humus-rich, moist but well-drained soil in full sun, or with some midday shade. Shelter from cold, drying winds. Pruning group 1.
- **PROPAGATION** Sow seed in containers in a cold frame in autumn. Root softwood cuttings in late spring or early summer, with bottom heat.
- **PESTS AND DISEASES** Infrequent.

S. chinensis, syn. *Calycanthus chinensis.* Spreading shrub with broadly oval, short-tapered, glossy, mid-green leaves, to 6in (15cm) long. Cup-shaped, slightly pink-flushed white flowers, 3in (8cm) across, marked white and maroon inside, are produced singly, close to the shoot tips, in early summer. ↕ 10ft (3m), ↔ 12ft (4m). E. China. Zone 7.

SINOFRANCHETIA

LARDIZABALACEAE

Genus of one species of twining, woody, dioecious, deciduous climber occurring in woodland in China. It has alternate, 3-palmate leaves, and produces pendent racemes of tiny white flowers; on female plants, these are followed by grape-like berries. Cultivated for its attractive foliage and fruit, it may be grown through a tree, over a large shrub, or against a wall to quickly cover an unsightly feature. Female plants can bear fruit without a male.

- **CULTIVATION** Grow in moderately fertile, humus-rich, moist but well-drained soil in full sun or partial shade. Pruning group 11, in spring.
- **PROPAGATION** Sow seed in containers in a cold frame in autumn. Root softwood cuttings in spring or early summer.
- **PESTS AND DISEASES** Infrequent.

S. chinensis. Twining, woody climber with glaucous, purple-spotted stems and long-stalked leaves, to 6in (15cm) long, composed of 3 ovate, dark green leaflets, glaucous beneath. In late spring, bears tiny white flowers in pendent racemes, to 4in (10cm) long. In summer, female plants produce spherical, grape-like purple berries, to ¾in (2cm) long. ↕ 40ft (12m). W. and C. China. Zone 7b.

SINOJACKIA

STYRACACEAE

Genus of 2 species of deciduous shrubs or small trees from woodland in China. They are valued for their small racemes of white flowers, which are borne close to the tips of short, leafy shoots in late spring and early summer. The leaves are simple and alternate. Grow sinojackia species in a woodland garden among other trees and shrubs. *S. xylocarpa* may also be used as a specimen tree in a lawn planting.

- **CULTIVATION** Grow in moderately fertile, humus-rich, moist but well-drained, acidic soil in full sun with some midday shade, or in partial shade. Avoid very exposed sites. Pruning group 1.
- **PROPAGATION** Sow seed in containers in a cold frame in autumn. Root greenwood cuttings in early summer, with bottom heat.
- **PESTS AND DISEASES** Infrequent.

S. rehderiana ■ Bushy shrub, or sometimes spreading tree, with elliptic to elliptic-obovate, glossy, dark green leaves, to 3½in (9cm) long. In late spring and early summer, produces pendent, star-shaped white flowers, ¾in (2cm) across, with yellow stamens. ↕↔ to 15ft (5m). E. China. Zone 7.

S. xylocarpa. Bushy shrub, or sometimes spreading tree, with obovate, glossy, dark green leaves, to 3in (8cm) long, wedge-shaped at the bases and with pointed tips. Star-shaped white flowers, 1in (2.5cm) across, with yellow stamens, are borne in late spring and early summer. ↕↔ to 20ft (6m). E. China. Zone 7b.

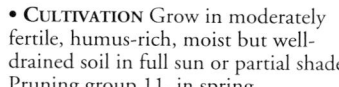

Sinojackia rehderiana

SINOWILSONIA

HAMAMELIDACEAE

Genus of one species of monoecious, deciduous shrub or small tree, related to witch hazels (*Hamamelis*), found on streambanks in the mountains of China. It has simple, alternate leaves, and is mainly cultivated for its catkin-like racemes of small flowers, borne in late spring before the leaves. Grow in a shrub border or woodland garden.

• **CULTIVATION** Grow in moist but well-drained, moderately fertile, humus-rich, acidic soil, in full sun with some midday shade, or in partial shade. Pruning group 1.

• **PROPAGATION** Sow seed in containers in a cold frame in autumn. Root greenwood cuttings with bottom heat in early summer.

• **PESTS AND DISEASES** Infrequent.

S. henryi. Spreading shrub or small tree with broadly oval to elliptic, tapered, bristle-toothed leaves, to 7in (18cm) long. In late spring, bears catkin-like racemes of small green flowers: males are 2½in (6cm) long; females are to 1¼in (3cm) long, and elongate to 6in (15cm) in fruit. The fruit are woody, 2-valved capsules, ¾in (2cm) across. ↕25ft (8m), ↔ 15ft (5m). C. and W. China. Zone 7.

▷ ***Siphonosmanthus delavayi*** see *Osmanthus delavayi*

SISYRINCHIUM

IRIDACEAE

Genus of about 90 species of annuals and rhizomatous perennials, some of which are semi-evergreen. Native to North and South America (although some are widely naturalized elsewhere), they thrive in habitats ranging from mountainous areas to meadows and coastal sands. They produce clumps of linear to sword-shaped, mostly basal leaves, often forming fans. In spring and summer, upright, often winged stems bear star-, cup-, or shallowly trumpet-shaped, blue, yellow, mauve, white, or rarely pink flowers, either singly or in umbel-like clusters of 2–8; each cluster is enclosed in a pair of spathe bracts. Grow smaller species in a rock garden or gravel planting, taller species in a herbaceous border. Where not hardy, grow in a cool greenhouse or alpine

Sisyrinchium 'E.K. Balls'

Sisyrinchium graminoides

house. Some species self-seed freely. A few species, especially the larger perennials, are shallow rooted, and may die suddenly after several years.

• **CULTIVATION** Grow in poor to moderately fertile, well-drained, neutral to slightly alkaline soil in full sun. Protect from excessive winter moisture.

• **PROPAGATION** Sow seed in containers in a cold frame in autumn or early spring. Divide in spring.

• **PESTS AND DISEASES** Rust, as well as aphids and spider mites, can occur.

S. angustifolium see *S. graminoides.*
***S.* 'Ball's Mauve'** see *S.* 'E.K. Balls'.
***S. bellum* of gardens** see *S. idahoense.*
S. bermudiana see *S. graminoides.*
***S. birameum* of gardens** see *S. graminoides.*
***S.* 'Biscutella'.** Clump-forming, semi-evergreen perennial with linear leaves, to 7in (18cm) long. In summer, upright stems bear a succession of individually short-lived, shallowly trumpet-shaped, dull yellow flowers, ¾in (2cm) across, heavily veined and suffused brownish purple. ↕12in (30cm), ↔ 6in (15cm). Zone 7b.
S. boreale see *S. californicum.*
S. brachypus see *S. californicum.*
S. californicum, syn. *S. boreale, S. brachypus* (Golden-eyed grass). Short-lived, semi-evergreen perennial with sword-shaped, gray-green leaves, to 6in (15cm) long. In summer, broadly winged stems bear a succession of star-shaped, dark-veined, bright yellow flowers, ½–¾in (1–2cm) across. Self-seeds freely. ↕24in (60cm), ↔ to 6in (15cm). British Columbia to California. Zone 8.
S. douglasii see *Olsynium douglasii.*
***S.* 'E.K. Balls'** ■ syn. *S.* 'Ball's Mauve'. Clump-forming, semi-evergreen perennial with fans of narrow, sword-shaped leaves, to 10in (25cm) long. Erect stems bear individually short-lived, star-shaped mauve flowers, ¾in (2cm) across, in summer. ↕10in (25cm), ↔ 6in (15cm). Zone 6.
S. graminoides ■ syn. *S. angustifolium, S. bermudiana, S. birameum* of gardens (Blue-eyed grass). Clump-forming, semi-evergreen perennial with linear leaves, to 20in (50cm) long. In summer, erect stems bear a long succession of individually short-lived, iris-like, deep blue, yellow-throated flowers, ¾in (2cm) across. Self-seeds freely. ↕20in (50cm), ↔ 6in (15cm). North America. Zone 5.

Sisyrinchium striatum

S. grandiflorum see *Olsynium douglasii.*
S. idahoense, syn. *S. bellum* of gardens, *S. macounii* (California blue-eyed grass). Clump-forming, semi-evergreen perennial with narrowly linear leaves, 3–12in (7–30cm) long. Upright stems bear star-shaped, deep violet-blue flowers, 1in (2.5cm) across, with yellow throats, during summer. Self-seeds freely. ↕5in (13cm), ↔ 6in (15cm). Washington and Idaho to California. Zone 8. **'Album'**, syn. *S.* 'May Snow', has white flowers with yellow throats.
S. macounii see *S. idahoense.*
***S.* 'May Snow'** see *S. idahoense* 'Album'.
***S.* 'North Star'** see *S.* 'Pole Star'.
S. odoratissimum see *Olsynium biflorum.*
***S.* 'Pole Star'**, syn. *S.* 'North Star'. Clump-forming, semi-evergreen perennial with linear leaves, to 16in (40cm) long. In summer, erect stems bear a succession of star-shaped white flowers, to 1¼in (3cm) across. ↕↔ to 6in (15cm). Zone 6.
***S.* 'Quaint and Queer'.** Tufted semi-evergreen perennial with narrow, linear leaves, to 12in (30cm) long. Upright stems bear star-shaped, apricot flowers, ½in (1.5cm) across, with maroon throats, in summer. ↕↔ 12in (30cm). Zone 6.
S. striatum ■ syn. *Phaiophleps nigricans.* Clump-forming, evergreen perennial with linear to lance-shaped, iris-like but 2-ranked, stiff, grayish green leaves, to 16in (40cm) long. In early and midsummer, unbranched stems bear stalkless clusters of open cup-shaped, pale yellow flowers, 1in (2.5cm) across, with tepal backs striped purple-brown. ↕ to 36in (90cm), ↔ 10in (25cm). Chile, Argentina. Zone 7. **'Aunt May'** ■ syn. 'Variegatum', is less vigorous, with leaves striped creamy yellow; ↕ to 20in (50cm). **'Variegatum'** see 'Aunt May'.

Sisyrinchium striatum 'Aunt May'

SKIMMIA

RUTACEAE

Genus of 4 species of monoecious or dioecious, occasionally hermaphrodite, evergreen shrubs and trees found in woodland from the Himalayas to S.E. Asia, China, and Japan. They are grown for their attractive leaves, flowers, and fruits. Leaves are alternate, simple, aromatic, obovate to inversely lance-shaped or elliptic, and mainly borne in terminal clusters. In spring, they bear terminal panicles of star-shaped flowers, strongly scented in some species, followed, on female and hermaphrodite plants, by fleshy, spherical, red or black fruits. Skimmias are suitable for a shrub border or woodland garden. With dioecious species, both male and female plants are needed to obtain fruit. Skimmias tolerate shade, atmospheric pollution, and neglect. The fruits may cause mild stomach upset if ingested.

Skimmia x *confusa* 'Kew Green'

Skimmia japonica

kimmia japonica 'Bronze Knight'

CULTIVATION Grow in moderately rtile, humus-rich, moist but well-ained soil in light, dappled shade to eep shade; *S.* x *confusa* 'Kew Green' lerates almost full sun. May become ılorotic on poor, dry soil or if over-posed to sun. Pruning group 8, necessary.

PROPAGATION Sow seed in containers a cold frame in autumn. Root semi-pe cuttings with bottom heat in mid-d late summer.

PESTS AND DISEASES Prone to scale sects and aphids.

anquetilia. Creeping or erect, dome-aped shrub producing inversely lance-aped to oblong-elliptic, leathery, omatic, dark or yellowish green leaves, 7in (18cm) long. In mid- and late ring, bears small, yellow-green flowers, in (3mm) across, in compact, nearly herical panicles, 2in (5cm) across, llowed on female plants by scarlet uit, ½in (1.5cm) across. ↕↔ 6ft (2m). . Himalayas. Zone 7b.

x *confusa* 'Kew Green' ■ Compact, me-shaped shrub with inversely lance-aped to elliptic, pointed, aromatic, id-green leaves, to 4½in (11cm) long. agrant, creamy white male flowers, –¼in (3–6mm) across, open in dense, nical panicles, to 6in (15cm) long, in ring. ↕ 1½–10ft (0.5–3m), ↔ 5ft .5m). Zone 7.

x *foremanii* of gardens see *japonica* 'Veitchii'.

japonica ■ (Japanese skimmia). ome-shaped to erect or creeping shrub th oval to obovate or inversely lance-aped, slightly aromatic, dark green

Skimmia japonica subsp. *reevesiana*

leaves, to 4in (10cm) long. Fragrant white flowers, ¼in (6mm) across, sometimes tinged pink or red, often opening from red buds, are borne in dense panicles, to 3in (8cm) long, in mid- and late spring; they are followed on female plants by red fruit, ⅜in (8mm) across. ↕↔ to 20ft (6m). China, Japan, S.E. Asia. Zone 7. **'Bowles' Dwarf'** is compact, with leaves to 1½in (4cm) long, and red winter flower buds; both male and female clones are available; ↕ 6in (15cm), ↔ 18in (45cm). **'Bronze Knight'** ■ is a male clone of open habit, with dark red winter buds. **'Cecilia Brown'** has large fruit clusters. **'Foremanii'** see 'Veitchii'. **'Fragrans'**, syn. *S. laureola* 'Fragrant Cloud', is an erect, compact, free-flowering male clone, with narrowly oval leaves; ↕↔ 3ft (1m). **'Fructu Albo'** ■ has green flower buds and white fruit; ↕ 24in (60cm), ↔ 3ft (1m). **'Nymans'** is a spreading female clone, with inversely lance-shaped leaves; ↕ 3ft (1m), ↔ 6ft (2m). **subsp. *reevesiana*** ■ syn. *S. reevesiana*, is hermaphrodite, with narrowly elliptic, tapered leaves and ovoid fruit; ↕ to 18–24in (45–60cm), ↔ 24–36in (60–90cm); China, Taiwan. **subsp. *reevesiana* 'Robert Fortune'** is hermaphrodite, with pale green leaves margined dark green. **'Rogersii'** is a dense female clone, with thick, twisted leaves and abundant fruit; ↕↔ 30in (75cm). **'Rubella'** ■ is a compact male clone, with red-margined leaves, and dark red flower buds in autumn and winter. **'Veitchii'**, syn. *S.* x *foremanii* of gardens, 'Foremanii', is a vigorous, upright female clone. **'Wakehurst White'** has white fruit.

***S. laureola* 'Fragrant Cloud'** see *S. japonica* 'Fragrans'.

S. reevesiana see *S. japonica* subsp. *reevesiana*.

SMILACINA

LILIACEAE

Genus of 25 species of mainly rhizomatous perennials from woodland in Asia and North and Central America. Similar to Solomon's seal (*Polygonatum*), they have unbranched, often arching stems with alternate, ovate-lance-shaped, stalkless or short-stalked leaves, and bear terminal racemes or panicles of star-shaped, short-stalked, scented, creamy white flowers, followed by green berries, usually ripening to red. Excellent in a woodland garden or shaded border.

• **CULTIVATION** Grow in moderately fertile, humus-rich, acidic, moist but well-drained soil in light, dappled shade or deep shade.

• **PROPAGATION** Sow seed in containers in a cold frame in autumn. Divide rhizomes in spring.

• **PESTS AND DISEASES** Rust and a variety of leaf spots occur.

S. racemosa ■ syn. *Maianthemum racemosum* (False Solomon's seal). Clump-forming, rhizomatous perennial with narrowly ovate or elliptic, pointed, prominently veined, mid-green leaves, to 6in (15cm) long, downy beneath and yellow in autumn. Terminal panicles of many white to creamy white, sometimes green-tinged flowers, ¼in (6mm) across,

Smilacina racemosa

are produced in mid- and late spring, followed by green, later red berries. ↕ to 36in (90cm), ↔ 24in (60cm). North America, Mexico. Zone 4.

S. stellata (Star-flowered lily-of-the-valley, Starflower). Clump-forming, rhizomatous perennial with downy stems and stalkless, lance-shaped to oblong-lance-shaped, pointed, glaucous, mid-green leaves, to 6in (15cm) long, minutely softly hairy beneath. In summer, bears crowded terminal racemes of 6–20 white or white-green flowers, ¼in (6mm) across, followed by blue-black-striped, green, later dark red or dark blue berries. ↕ 8–24in (20–60cm), ↔ to 24in (60cm). North America, Mexico. Zone 4.

SMILAX

LILIACEAE

Genus of about 200 species of usually dioecious, woody, deciduous or evergreen climbers, and herbaceous perennials, grown for their foliage and fruits. They are widespread in tropical and temperate regions, often making nearly impenetrable thickets in woodland. The alternate, simple, sometimes shallowly lobed leaves are lance-shaped to elliptic, or broadly ovate to rounded, some truncate or heart-shaped at the bases; they have curled tendrils, and are often borne on prickly stems. The small, star-shaped flowers are green, greenish white, yellow, or brown, and are followed by spherical, black or red berries. Train onto a tree or pillar, or against a warm, sunny wall. Where not hardy, grow in a temperate or warm greenhouse.

• **CULTIVATION** Grow against a support in moderately fertile, well-drained soil in full sun or partial shade. Pruning group 11, after flowering.

• **PROPAGATION** Sow seed in containers in a cold frame in autumn. Divide in autumn or spring.

• **PESTS AND DISEASES** Rust and a variety of leaf spots occur.

S. china. Scrambling, woody, deciduous climber with sparsely prickly shoots and broadly ovate to rounded, tapered, dark green leaves, to 3in (8cm) long. Small umbels of tiny, yellow-green flowers, ¹⁄₁₆–⅛in (2–3mm) across, are borne in spring, followed on female plants by spherical, bright red berries, ⅜in (8mm) across, in autumn. ↕ 15ft (5m). China, Korea, Japan. Zone 7b.

immia japonica 'Fructu Albo'

Skimmia japonica 'Rubella'

SMITHIANTHA

Temple bells

GESNERIACEAE

Genus of 4 species of rhizomatous perennials from moist, tropical woodland and rocks in Mexico, grown for their flowers and foliage. They have opposite, heart-shaped, fleshy leaves, with a velvet sheen of fine, red or purple hairs. Terminal racemes of nodding, tubular to tubular-bell-shaped, red, orange, or yellow flowers are borne in summer and autumn. Where not hardy, grow in a temperate or warm greenhouse, in a conservatory, or as houseplants. In frost-free areas, grow in a border or lightly shaded raised bed; they grow best in areas with dry winters.
• **CULTIVATION** Under glass, grow in shallow pots of well-drained, soilless potting mix. Provide high humidity and bright filtered to indirect light. In the growing season, water moderately and apply a quarter-strength high-potash liquid fertilizer at each watering; maintain at 66°F (19°C). Keep completely dry when dormant in winter. Divide and repot each spring, and water sparingly until in full growth. Do not overwater. Outdoors, grow in moderately fertile, humus-rich, moist but well-drained, neutral to slightly acidic soil, in full sun with some midday shade, or in light, dappled shade. Protect from winter moisture.
• **PROPAGATION** Sow seed at 59–64°F (15–18°C), or divide rhizomes, in spring.
• **PESTS AND DISEASES** Prone to aphids.

S. cinnabarina, syn. *Naegelia cinnabarina*. Rhizomatous perennial with stem-sheathing, heart-shaped, densely red-hairy, deep green leaves, 6in (15cm) long, marked purple along the veins. From summer to autumn, bears brick-red flowers, 1½in (4cm) long, paler or white-spotted in the throats. ↕ to 18in (45cm), ↔ 12in (30cm). Mexico. ❀ (min. 50°F/10°C)
***S.* 'Orange King'** ▣ Rhizomatous perennial with heart-shaped, scalloped, densely red-purple-hairy, rich mid-green leaves, 6in (15cm) long, marked dark red along the veins. From summer to autumn, bears orange flowers, 1¼–1½in (3–4cm) long, with red-spotted throats and yellow lips. ↕↔ 24in (60cm). ❀ (min. 50°F/10°C)
S. zebrina, syn. *Gesneria zebrina*, *Naegelia zebrina*. Rhizomatous perennial producing heart-shaped, deep green leaves, 7in (18cm) long, marked darker green and purple-brown along the veins. Scarlet and yellow flowers, 1½in (4cm) long, with red-spotted yellow throats, are borne in summer. ↕ to 30in (75cm), ↔ 14in (35cm). Mexico. ❀ (min. 50°F/10°C)

Smithiantha 'Orange King'

SMYRNIUM

APIACEAE

Genus of about 8 erect, branching biennials or short-lived, monocarpic perennials found in rocky places, scrub, fields, and at woodland margins in Europe, Africa, and W. Asia. They have broadly oblong, divided basal leaves and rounded, usually entire upper leaves. In late spring and early summer, they bear branched, terminal umbels of numerous tiny, greenish yellow flowers. Ideal for naturalizing in a large border or in a wild or woodland garden. They also provide unusual, long-lasting cut flowers.
• **CULTIVATION** Grow in moderately fertile, moist but well-drained soil in full sun to partial shade. Will also naturalize well in grass.
• **PROPAGATION** Sow seed *in situ* in autumn or late spring, or in containers in a cold frame in spring; transplant while still small to lessen root disturbance. Germination is often erratic.
• **PESTS AND DISEASES** Infrequent.

S. perfoliatum ▣ (Perfoliate Alexanders). Upright biennial with thick, ribbed stems, pinnate or 2-pinnate basal leaves, 2–8in (5–20cm) long, and perfoliate, simple, rounded, bract-like, bright yellow-green upper leaves, 1¼–4in (3–10cm) long, borne on the flowering stems. Many tiny flowers are produced in dome-shaped, 7- to 12-rayed umbels, to 4in (10cm) across, in spring of the second year after germination. ↕ 2–5ft (0.6–1.5m), ↔ 24in (60cm). N. Czech Republic, Slovakia, S. Europe, N. Africa, S.W. Asia. Zone 7.

Smyrnium perfoliatum

SOBRALIA

ORCHIDACEAE

Genus of about 35 species of mostly tall, evergreen, terrestrial, occasionally epiphytic orchids from Central America and tropical South America, occurring at altitudes of up to 11,300ft (3,400m), sometimes on rocks by streams. They have slender, cane-like stems, with foliage borne along almost all the stem length. The leathery, mid-green leaves are oblong to broadly oval or lance-shaped, and often folded. Short-lived, cattleya-like blooms, with a delicate, papery texture, are borne in succession every 3–4 days, at the stem tips.
• **CULTIVATION** Cool-growing orchids. Grow in containers of terrestrial orchid potting mix in bright filtered light, and maintain moderate to high humidity. When in active growth, water freely, mist the foliage daily, and apply a quarter-strength balanced liquid fertilizer monthly. Water sparingly in winter. Pot on when the plant fills the container and flows over the sides. See also p.46.
• **PROPAGATION** Divide after flowering. Offshoots may be rooted in spring.
• **PESTS AND DISEASES** Spider mites, aphids, whiteflies, and mealybugs may be troublesome.

S. leucoxantha. Terrestrial or sometimes epiphytic orchid with reedy stems and lance-shaped, leathery, mid-green leaves, to 12in (30cm) long. In late summer, bears papery, pure white flowers, 3in (8cm) across, with brown-striped, golden throats. ↕ 3ft (90cm), ↔ 12–18in (30–45cm). Costa Rica, Panama. ❀ (min. 52–55°F/11–13°C; max. 86°F/30°C)
S. macrantha. Terrestrial or epiphytic orchid producing lance-shaped leaves, 6–12in (15–30cm) long. Delicate, papery, white to pink-purple flowers, 6–7in (15–18cm) across, with yellow on the lips, are borne from spring to summer. ↕ 6ft (2m), ↔ 4ft (1.2m). Mexico to Costa Rica. ❀ (min. 52–55°F/11–13°C; max. 86°F/30°C)

SOLANDRA

Chalice vine

SOLANACEAE

Genus of 8 species of woody-stemmed, evergreen, scrambling climbers found in tropical forest in Mexico, the West Indies, and South America. They are grown for their large, solitary, funnel- or trumpet-shaped, night-scented flowers, each with 5 reflexed lobes. The lustrous, rich green leaves are alternate, simple, ovate to obovate, and usually leathery. Where temperatures fall below 45–50°F (7–10°C), grow in a temperate greenhouse. In warmer climates, use to clothe a pergola, arch, or wall.
• **CULTIVATION** Under glass, grow in soil-based potting mix in full light with shade from hot sun. When in growth, water moderately and apply a balanced liquid fertilizer every 4 weeks. Water more sparingly in winter. Outdoors, grow in moderately fertile, humus-rich, moist but well-drained soil in full sun. Provide support for the climbing stems. Pruning group 11, in late winter or early spring, if necessary to restrict size.
• **PROPAGATION** Sow seed at 61–64°F (16–18°C) in spring. Root semi-ripe cuttings with bottom heat in summer. Air layer in spring.
• **PESTS AND DISEASES** Spider mites and scale insects may be troublesome.

Solandra maxima

S. grandiflora. Vigorous, semi-scande climber with robust, sparsely branched stems clothed in elliptic to obovate leaves, to 5in (13cm) long. In spring, produces funnel-shaped, violet-tinged white flowers, 6–10in (15–25cm) long which become tawny yellow with age. ↕ to 40ft (12m) or more. Jamaica. ❀ (min. 45–50°F/7–10°C)
S. hartwegii see *S. maxima.*
S. maxima ▣ syn. *S. hartwegii*, *S. nitida* (Cup of gold). Scandent, moderately dense climber with branching stems clothed in elliptic leaves, to 6in (15cm) long. Trumpet-shaped yellow flowers, 6–8in (15–20cm) long, with purple vein are produced in summer; the inside of each flower is marked with purple ridges ↕ to 40ft (12m). Mexico to Colombia an Venezuela. ❀ (min. 45–50°F/7–10°C)
S. nitida see *S. maxima.*

SOLANUM syn. LYCIANTHES

SOLANACEAE

Genus of about 1,400 species of annuals biennials, herbaceous perennials, and evergreen, semi-evergreen, and deciduou shrubs, trees, and twining climbers from range of habitats worldwide. The genus includes a number of vegetables, such as potato (*S. tuberosum*) and eggplant (*S. melongena*), and also ornamental plants, described below, which are cultivated for their flowers and decorativ fruits. The leaves are alternate, and entir lobed, or pinnately divided. The small, 5-petaled, bell- or shallowly trumpet-shaped, sometimes star-shaped, blue, purple, or white, yellow-anthered flower are borne singly or in cymes, cyme-like umbels, corymbs, or panicles, from spri to autumn, later followed by fruits. Trai climbers on a warm, sunny wall. Shrubs are suitable for a sheltered border. Whe not hardy, grow in a cool or temperate greenhouse. All parts of most species, especially the fruits of *S. capsicastrum* an *S. pseudocapsicum*, can cause severe discomfort if ingested.
• **CULTIVATION** Under glass, grow in so based potting mix in full light with shad from hot sun, or in bright indirect light When in growth, water freely, apply a balanced liquid fertilizer monthly, mist daily, and maintain moderate humidity Apply a high-potash liquid fertilizer eve

S

or 3 weeks to *S. capsicastrum* and *pseudocapsicum* until fruit ripens. Water aringly when dormant. Outdoors, grow moderately fertile, moist but well-ained, neutral to slightly alkaline soil in ll sun. Support plants and tie in young oots regularly. Pruning group 9 r shrubs; group 12 for climbers, ter flowering.
PROPAGATION Sow seed at 64–68°F 8–20°C) in spring. Root semi-ripe ttings of shrubs and climbers with ntle bottom heat from summer to rly autumn.
PESTS AND DISEASES Late blight, mping off, powdery mildew, stem ight and rot, early blight, gray mold *Botrytis*), virus diseases, and aphids and rips can occur.

aviculare (Kangaroo apple). Erect to reading, open, evergreen, hairless shrub th narrowly lance-shaped, simple to egularly pinnatifid, deep green leaves, -8in (12–20cm) long. In spring and mmer, bears axillary cymes, 2–5in –13cm) across, of 3–8 shallowly lobed, ue-purple or white flowers, 1¼–1½in –4cm) across, followed by ovoid green uit, ½in (1.5cm) long, ripening llow. ↕ 6–11ft (1.8–3.5m), ↔ 5–8ft .5–2.5m). Queensland to Tasmania, ew Zealand. ❄ (min. 45°F/7°C)
capsicastrum (False Jerusalem cherry, inter cherry). Erect, bushy, evergreen, wny-stemmed shrub, often grown as a nter-fruiting annual. Oblong to lance-aped, wavy-margined leaves, 2–3in -8cm) long, are downy, dark green. In mmer, bears axillary cymes, 2in (5cm) ng, of star-shaped white flowers, to in (1.5cm) across, followed by oblong-ipsoid to ovoid, pointed, red or ange-red fruit, ¾in (2cm) or more ng. ↕↔ 12–24in (30–60cm), in ntainers. Brazil. ❄ (min. 41°F/5°C)
crispum (Chilean potato vine). Fast-owing, scrambling, evergreen or semi-ergreen climber with ovate, dark green ves, to 5in (13cm) long. In summer, ars fragrant, lilac- to purple-blue wers, 1in (2.5cm) across, in terminal rymbs, to 6in (15cm) across; they are lowed by yellowish white fruit, ¼–⅜in -9mm) across. ↕ 20ft (6m). Peru, Chile. (min. 41°F/5°C). **'Glasnevin'** ■ syn. utumnale', bears deep purple-blue wers from summer to autumn.
jasminoides (Potato vine). rambling, evergreen or semi-evergreen mber with narrowly ovate to lance-aped, glossy, dark green leaves, to 2in

Solanum jasminoides 'Album'

(5cm) long, sometimes 3- to 5-lobed or with separate ovate leaflets at the bases. In summer and autumn, fragrant, blue-white flowers, 1in (2.5cm) across, with yellow anthers, are produced in terminal and axillary clusters, 2–3in (5–8cm) across, followed by ovoid black fruit, ⅜in (9mm) across. ↕ 20ft (6m). Brazil. ❄ (min. 35°F/2°C). **'Album'** ■ bears pure white flowers with yellow anthers.
S. melongena (Eggplant). Short-lived perennials, but usually grown as annuals. Erect, shrubby plant with green to gray simple leaves to 8in (20cm) across. Bears drooping violet flowers, 1½in (4cm) across, in late spring followed in summer by white to purple fruit, 3–15in (8–37.5cm). Grow indoors from seed, transplant 18–24in (45–60cm) apart in rows when soil is warm. Grow in full sun. Ripens in 65 days 16–24 weeks after sowing. Africa, Asia. ↕ 24–36in (60–90cm), ↔ 12–24in (30–60cm).
S. pseudocapsicum (Christmas cherry, Jerusalem cherry, Winter cherry). Erect, bushy, evergreen shrub, often grown as a winter-fruiting annual. Wavy-margined, elliptic leaves, to 3in (8cm) long, are glossy, dark green. In summer, bears axillary cymes, 2in (5cm) across, of up to 3 star-shaped white flowers, to ½in (1.5cm) across, followed by long-lasting, spherical, red, yellow, or orange-red fruit, ½–¾in (1.5–2cm) across. ↕↔ 12–18in (30–45cm), in containers. E. South America. ❄ (min. 41°F/5°C). **'Cherry Jubilee'** has white, yellow, or orange fruit. **'Fancy'** is compact, with bright scarlet fruit; ↕ to 12in (30cm). **'Joker'** is dwarf, with yellow fruit turning orange and red; ↕↔ 8in (20cm). **'Jubilee'** is dwarf, with pale lime-green fruit, ripening deep orange; ↕↔ 6in (15cm). **'Red Giant'** ■ has large, orange-red fruit, to 1in (2.5cm) across.
S. rantonnetii, syn. *Lycianthes rantonnetii* (Blue potato bush). Lax, evergreen shrub, usually many-branched when mature, producing ovate to lance-shaped, often wavy-margined, smooth, mid- to deep green leaves, 2½–4in (6–10cm) long. In summer and autumn, bears axillary clusters, to 2½in (6cm) across, of 2–5 shallowly trumpet-shaped, dark blue to violet-blue or pale blue flowers, ½–1in (1–2.5cm) across, with paler blue or yellow-tinged centers, followed by ovoid red fruit, 1in (2.5cm) long. ↕↔ 3–6ft (1–2m). Paraguay,

Solanum wendlandii

Argentina. ❄ (min. 45°F/7°C). **'Royal Robe'** ■ has slightly fragrant, deep violet-blue flowers with yellow centers.
S. seaforthianum (Italian jasmine, St. Vincent lilac). Spreading, evergreen, hairless, scandent climber with broadly elliptic, rich green leaves, 4–8in (10–20cm) long, either entire or pinnatifid with 3–9 lobes. In summer, bears blue, purple, pink, or white flowers, to ¾in (2cm) across, in pendent panicles, to 6in (15cm) across, followed by ovoid red fruit, ¼–½in (6–10mm) across. ↕ to 20ft (6m). Tropical South America. ❄ (min. 45–50°F/7–10°C)
S. wendlandii ■ (Paradise flower, Potato vine). Spreading, evergreen or semi-evergreen, scrambling climber with hooked barbs on the stems and foliage. Bright green leaves, 4–10in (10–25cm) long, are pinnate (with 8–13 leaflets), oblong with heart-shaped bases, or 3-palmate. In summer, bears shallowly trumpet-shaped, lilac-blue flowers, 1½–2½in (4–6cm) across, in terminal, pendent, cyme-like panicles, to 6in (15cm) long, followed by spherical to ovoid orange fruit, 3–4in (8–10cm) across. ↕ 15ft (5m) or more. Costa Rica. ❄ (min. 45–50°F/7–10°C). **'Albescens'** has off-white flowers.

SOLDANELLA
Snowbell

PRIMULACEAE

Genus of about 10 species of small, spring-flowering, evergreen perennials from the mountains of Europe, usually found in alpine turf or among rocks, often flowering through the melting snow. They have basal rosettes of long-stalked, rounded or kidney-shaped, leathery leaves. The nodding to pendent, funnel- or bell-shaped, purple to white flowers have fringed petals and are borne in umbels, rarely singly. Grow in a rock garden or alpine house.
• **CULTIVATION** Grow in humus-rich, moist, sharply drained soil in full sun with some midday shade, or in partial shade in warm areas. Top-dress with sharp grit, and protect from excessive winter moisture. Under glass, grow in shallow pans of equal parts acidic potting mix, leaf mold, and grit.
• **PROPAGATION** Sow seed as soon as ripe in containers in a cold frame. Divide in early spring.
• **PESTS AND DISEASES** Young growth is prone to slug and snail damage.

lanum crispum 'Glasnevin'

Solanum pseudocapsicum 'Red Giant'

Solanum rantonnetii 'Royal Robe'

S

S. alpina ■ (Alpine snowbell). Clump-forming perennial with thick, rounded to kidney-shaped, dark green leaves, 1½in (4cm) long. In early spring, each erect scape bears 2–5 nodding, funnel-shaped, bluish violet flowers, to ½in (1.5cm) long, with fringed petals cut to half their lengths, and marked red inside. ↕↔ 5in (13cm). C. and S. Europe. Zone 5.
S. carpatica. Clump-forming perennial with rounded, dark green leaves, 2in (5cm) long, violet-purple beneath. In early spring, each scape bears 2–5 funnel-shaped, violet-blue flowers, to ½in (1.5cm) across, resembling those of *S. alpina*, but more freely borne, with fringed petals cut to two-thirds of their lengths. ↕↔ 6in (15cm). E. Europe (W. Carpathians). Zone 5.
S. minima (Least snowbell). Dwarf, clump-forming perennial with rounded, glossy, mid-green leaves, ½in (1.5cm) long. In early spring, scapes bear usually solitary, narrowly bell-shaped, white or pale blue flowers, to ½in (1.5cm) long, with darker streaks, the fringed petals cut to a quarter of their lengths. ↕ 4in (10cm), ↔ 8in (20cm). S. central Europe (E. Alps, C. Apennines). Zone 5.
S. montana. Mound-forming perennial producing shallowly toothed, rounded or kidney-shaped, bright green leaves, ¾–3in (2–8cm) long, violet-tinted beneath. In early spring, each scape bears 3–10 pendent, bell-shaped, lavender-blue flowers, to ¾in (2cm) long, with fringed petals cut to three-quarters of their lengths. ↕ 12in (30cm), ↔ 8in (20cm). S. central Europe. Zone 5.
S. villosa. Vigorous, clump-forming perennial with rounded, hairy-stalked, mid-green leaves, 3in (8cm) long, paler green beneath. In early spring, each scape bears 3 or 4 nodding, bell-shaped violet flowers, ½in (1.5cm) long, with fringed petals cut to three-quarters of their lengths. Relatively easy to grow. ↕ 12in (30cm), ↔ 8in (20cm). S.W. Europe (W. Pyrenees). Zone 5.

Soldanella alpina

Soleirolia soleirolii

SOLEIROLIA *syn.* HELXINE

URTICACEAE

Genus of one species of vigorous, dwarf, monoecious, evergreen perennial from moist, shaded sites in W. Mediterranean islands. It is cultivated for its fresh green foliage, and tolerates a wide range of conditions. Where temperatures fall below 23°F (-5°C), grow as a houseplant, in a terrarium, or in a cool to warm greenhouse or conservatory. In warmer areas, it provides groundcover in difficult sites outdoors, but is often invasive; it is difficult to eradicate.

• **CULTIVATION** Under glass, grow in soil-based potting mix with added grit, in full light with shade from hot sun, or in partial shade. When in growth, water freely; water sparingly in winter. Outdoors, grow in any soil in sun or shade. May be damaged by light frost, but quickly recovers in spring.
• **PROPAGATION** Divide in late spring.
• **PESTS AND DISEASES** Infrequent.

S. soleirolii ■ syn. *Helxine soleirolii* (Baby's tears, Irish moss, Mind-your-own-business). Slender, mat-forming perennial with branched, translucent, pale green, sometimes pink-tinted stems and alternate, rounded, minutely hairy, short-stalked leaves, 1/16–¼in (2–6mm) long. Produces tiny, solitary, tubular, 4-lobed, pink-tinged white flowers from the leaf axils in summer. ↕ 2in (5cm), ↔ indefinite. W. Mediterranean islands. ❀ (min. 45°F/7°C); will become deciduous if temperatures fall below 32°F (0°C). **'Aurea'**, syn. 'Golden Queen', has gold-green leaves. **'Golden Queen'** see 'Aurea'. **'Silver Queen'** see 'Variegata'. **'Variegata'**, syn. 'Silver Queen', has silver-variegated leaves.

SOLENOPSIS *syn.* ISOTOMA

CAMPANULACEAE

Genus of about 25 species of annuals and perennials from dry, exposed sites in Australia as well as Central and South America. They have alternate, lobed to pinnatisect, linear to ovate or oblong leaves, and bear solitary, terminal or axillary, long-tubed, salverform flowers, each with 5 usually narrow, star-like petal lobes. Where not hardy, grow in a temperate or warm greenhouse, in containers, or use for summer bedding. In warmer climates, grow as accent plants in a border or for bedding.

Solenopsis axillaris

• **CULTIVATION** Under glass, grow in soil-based potting mix in full light. When in growth, water moderately and apply a balanced liquid fertilizer every 4 weeks; maintain low humidity. Water sparingly in winter. Outdoors, grow in moderately fertile, well-drained soil in full sun. Where not hardy, plant out after last frosts. Deadhead regularly.
• **PROPAGATION** Sow seed at 61–64°F (16–18°C) in spring. Root softwood cuttings in summer.
• **PESTS AND DISEASES** Aphids may be a problem in hot, dry conditions.

S. axillaris ■ syn. *Isotoma axillaris, Laurentia axillaris.* Woody-based perennial with erect, branched stems bearing ovate, pinnatisect leaves, 1¼–5in (3–13cm) long, with very narrow lobes. Star-shaped, pale to deep blue flowers, to 1½in (4cm) across, are borne in great abundance from spring to late autumn. ↕↔ 12in (30cm). Australia. ❀ (min. 45°F/7°C)

SOLENOSTEMON

LAMIACEAE

Genus of about 60 species of evergreen, bushy, erect to spreading, subshrubby perennials from forest in tropical Africa and Asia. They are mainly cultivated for their opposite, coarsely toothed, often hairy, generally ovate, colorful leaves. Throughout the year, they bear raceme-like whorls of tiny, tubular, 2-lipped, blue, white, or purple flowers. Where not hardy, grow in a temperate greenhouse or as houseplants, or use outdoors as summer bedding or in hanging baskets or containers. In warmer areas, they are good bedding plants for sunny or shady positions.

• **CULTIVATION** Under glass, grow in soil-based potting mix in bright filtered to moderate light. In growth, water freely and apply a high-nitrogen fertilizer every 2 weeks. Keep just moist in winter. Pot on annually in spring, or repropagate to produce the strongest-growing plants. Outdoors, grow in humus-rich, moist but well-drained soil, enriched with well-rotted organic matter. Provide a sheltered position in full sun or partial shade. Water freely in dry weather. Pinch out young shoots to promote bushiness.
• **PROPAGATION** Surface-sow seed at 72–75°F (22–24°C) in early spring. Root softwood cuttings from late sprin to autumn.
• **PESTS AND DISEASES** Mealybugs, scal insects, and whiteflies may be a proble under glass.

***S. scutellarioides* cultivars**, syn. *Coleu blumei* var. *verschaffeltii* (Coleus, Flam nettle, Painted nettle). Finely hairy, evergreen perennials, usually grown as annuals or short-lived perennials for their foliage. Semi-succulent, 4-angled stems bear broadly to narrowly ovate t irregular, toothed, sometimes frilly-margined, multi-colored leaves, generally 1–6in (2.5–15cm) long, ofte heart-shaped at the bases and slightly hairy beneath. Terminal, whorled racemes, to 6in (15cm) long, of tiny, blue or white flowers, ½in (1.5cm) lon are borne at any time of year. Pinch ou to maintain foliage color and compact habit, especially seed-grown series. Mo cutting-propagated, named cultivars ar reluctant to flower and thus are easier to maintain as attractive, compact plan with selective pinching. ↕↔ to 36in (90cm), in containers. Originally S.E. Asia (including Malaysia). ❀ (min 50°F/10°C). **'Bronze Pagoda'** produc bright red leaves edged gold with red spots. **'Caladium'** produces white-centered leaves with fresh green markings radiating out toward the margins. **'Cinders'** bears light green leaves speckled with dark red and brig yellow. **'Defiance'** is dense and compa in habit, bearing spear-shaped, bright red leaves edged gold. **'El Brighto'** produces scalloped, intense pink-red leaves edged with mid-green and brigh yellow. **'India Frills'** is self-branching, spreading, and compact, bearing irregularly lobed, green-marked, dark red leaves, to 1in (2.5cm) long, variab edged with bright yellow and green; ↕ 6in (15cm). **'Inky Fingers'** spreads more widely

Solenostemon scutellarioides 'Pineapple Queen'

S

Solenostemon scutellarioides 'The Line'

than most other cultivars; it bears mid-green, irregularly lobed leaves, to 1in (2.5cm) long, with a dark black-red mark in the centers. **'Kiwi Fern'** produces pinnatifid, dark red to red-purple leaves, 3in (8cm) long and ½in (1.5cm) wide, edged bright yellow and green. **'Max Levering'** bears bright green-gold leaves with red splashes. **'Night Skies'** bears dark red leaves dotted with light yellow-green. **'Olive'** bears mid-olive-green leaves, to 3in (8cm) long, with light purplish green undersides. **'Pineapple Queen'** ■ is vigorous, with yellow-green leaves that turn gold, and with brown-purple markings at the leaf bases and on the stems; excellent for training into pyramids or standards. **'Purple Emperor'** is open-growing, producing black-purple leaves with ruffly and lacy margins, sometimes finely edged with light green. **'Saturn'** bears maroon leaves with a vivid green central blotch and random green spots. **'The Line'** ■ produces bright gold leaves with dark purple midribs and main veins. The seed-grown **Wizard Series** ■ produces compact plants, branched from the base; ↕↔ to 8in (20cm).

Solenostemon scutellarioides Wizard Series

SOLIDAGO

Goldenrod

ASTERACEAE

Genus of about 100 species of woody-based perennials occurring on roadsides, prairies, and riverbanks; most are found in North America, a few in South America and Eurasia. They are valued for their small, elongated flowerheads, mostly borne in one-sided, upward-facing racemes or spike-like panicles. Stiff, branched stems bear alternate, narrowly elliptic to lance-shaped, entire or toothed, prominently veined, usually mid-green leaves, 4–12in (10–30cm) or more long. Most species are coarse and invasive, and are best grown in a wild garden, although *S. virgaurea* subsp. *minuta* is suitable for a rock garden. Named hybrids are robust, less invasive, and more colorful, with slightly larger flowerheads. They are ideal for a late-summer border or wild garden, and provide good cut flowers. Site them carefully, for they can overwhelm less vigorous plants. Goldenrods are not a cause of hayfever; ragweeds (*Ambrosia* species), which bloom at the same time, are the primary allergen in autumn.

• **CULTIVATION** Grow in poor to moderately fertile, preferably sandy, well-drained soil in full sun. Remove flowered stems to prevent seeding.

• **PROPAGATION** Divide in midautumn or early spring.

• **PESTS AND DISEASES** Spot anthracnose, powdery mildew, rust, and a few fungal spots are common.

***S.* 'Crown of Rays'**, syn. *S.* 'Strahlenkrone'. Erect, clump-forming perennial with mid-green leaves. Bears golden yellow flowerheads in flattened, radiating, corymb-like panicles, to 10in (25cm) long, in mid- and late summer. ↕24in (60cm), ↔ 18in (45cm). Zone 4.

***S.* 'Golden Baby'.** Compact, dwarf perennial with mid-green leaves. Bears

Solidago 'Goldenmosa'

Solidago sphacelata 'Golden Fleece'

plume-like panicles, 6–8in (15–20cm) long, of golden yellow flowerheads in late summer. ↕24in (60cm), ↔ 18in (45cm). Zone 4.

***S.* 'Goldenmosa'** ■ Compact, bushy perennial with wrinkled, mid-green leaves. In late summer and early autumn, bears yellow-stalked, bright yellow flowerheads in conical panicles, to 12in (30cm) long. ↕ to 30in (75cm), ↔ 18in (45cm). Zone 4.

***S.* 'Golden Wings'.** Erect perennial with mid-green leaves, and spreading, corymb-like panicles, to 10in (25cm) long, of golden yellow flowerheads, borne in late summer and early autumn. Thrives in poor soil. ↕ to 6ft (1.8m), ↔ 36in (90cm). Zone 4.

***S.* 'Lemore'** see x *Solidaster luteus* 'Lemore'.

***S.* 'Loddon Gold'.** Erect perennial with mid-green leaves. In late summer and early autumn, bears deep yellow flowerheads in conical panicles, to 8in (20cm) long. ↕ to 36in (90cm), ↔ 18in (45cm). Zone 4.

***S. sphacelata* 'Golden Fleece'** ■ Clump-forming perennial with branching stems and lance-shaped, mid-green leaves, to 12in (30cm) long. In autumn, bears open panicles, to 10in (25cm) long, of golden yellow flowerheads. Tolerant of dry soil. ↕18in (45cm), ↔ 2ft (60cm). Zone 4.

***S.* 'Strahlenkrone'** see *S.* 'Crown of Rays'.

S. virgaurea* subsp. *alpestris see *S. virgaurea* subsp. *minuta*.

S. virgaurea* subsp. *minuta, syn. *S. virgaurea* subsp. *alpestris*. Mound-forming perennial with leathery, lance-shaped, toothed, mid-green leaves, ¾–4in (2–10cm) long. From late summer to autumn, bears compact, erect, spike-like racemes, 1¼in (3cm) long, of deep yellow flowerheads, ¼–⅜in (6–8mm) across. Good for a rock garden, in moist soil. ↕2–8in (5–20cm), ↔ 8in (20cm). N., C., and E. Europe. Zone 4.

x SOLIDASTER

ASTERACEAE

Hybrid genus of one clump-forming perennial, possibly the result of a cross between *Solidago canadensis* and *Aster ptarmicoides*. It is valued for its daisy-like yellow flowerheads, profusely borne from midsummer to early autumn. The leaves are alternate, and lance-shaped to linear-elliptic or narrowly inversely

x *Solidaster luteus*

lance-shaped. Suitable for a mixed or herbaceous border; the flowers are good for cutting.

• **CULTIVATION** Grow in moderately fertile, well-drained soil in full sun.

• **PROPAGATION** Divide, or take basal cuttings, in spring.

• **PESTS AND DISEASES** Prone to powdery mildew in dry summers.

x *S. hybridus* see x *S. luteus*.

x *S. luteus* ■ syn. x *S. hybridus*. Clump-forming perennial with erect, branched stems bearing leaves to 6in (15cm) long, toothed at the tips. From midsummer to early autumn, bears branched, corymb-like panicles of daisy-like flowerheads, to ½in (1.5cm) across, with pale yellow ray florets and golden yellow disk florets. ↕ to 36in (90cm), ↔ 12in (30cm). Garden origin. Zone 5. **'Lemore'** syn. *Solidago* 'Lemore', has pale lemon ray florets; ↕↔ to 32in (80cm).

SOLLYA

PITTOSPORACEAE

Genus, related to *Billardiera*, of 3 species of evergreen, twining climbers or scandent shrubs or subshrubs found in light woodland in Australia. They are cultivated for their 5-petaled, bell-shaped, usually blue flowers, which are terminally borne, either singly or in pendent cymes, from summer to autumn. Stalkless, narrow, entire or slightly wavy-margined, oblong to ovate or obovate leaves are arranged alternately or in spirals. Where temperatures fall below 41°F (5°C), grow in a cool or temperate greenhouse. In warmer areas, train over an arch, pergola, or shrub.

• **CULTIVATION** Under glass, grow in soil-based potting mix in full light with shade from hot sun, or in bright filtered light. During the growing season, water moderately and apply a balanced liquid fertilizer monthly; maintain low to moderate humidity. Water sparingly in winter. Outdoors, grow in moderately fertile, humus-rich, moist but well-drained soil in full sun with some midday shade, or in light, dappled shade. Apply a dry winter mulch. Support the climbing stems. Pruning group 12, in late winter or early spring.

• **PROPAGATION** Sow seed at 50–61°F (10–16°C) in spring. Root softwood cuttings in late spring or early summer.

• **PESTS AND DISEASES** Spider mites may be troublesome under glass.

S

Sollya heterophylla

S. fusiformis see *S. heterophylla.*
S. heterophylla ■ syn. *S. fusiformis* (Bluebell creeper). Weak-stemmed, eventually bushy, twining climber with ovate to narrowly oblong or obovate, mid- to deep green leaves, 1–2in (2.5–5cm) long, paler beneath. Bell-shaped light to mid-blue flowers, ½in (1.5cm) across, are borne singly or in cymes of 4–8 or more, from early summer to autumn; they are followed by edible, cylindrical blue berries, to 1in (2.5cm) long. ↕ 5–6ft (1.5–2m). Western Australia. ❄ (min. 45°F/7°C)

SONERILA

MELASTOMATACEAE

Genus of about 175 species of evergreen perennials and small shrubs from tropical woodland in Asia, cultivated for their foliage and flowers. The leaves are opposite, whorled, or in basal rosettes, and mainly oval to elliptic, with bold veins. Flowers are star-, saucer-, or cup-shaped, and are borne in curved, spike-like racemes or corymbs. Where not hardy, grow in a warm greenhouse or conservatory, as houseplants, or in a terrarium. In warmer climates, use as a groundcover among shrubs.
• **CULTIVATION** Under glass, grow in half pots or shallow pans of soilless potting mix with added fine-grade, ground bark, in bright filtered light. Maintain steady temperatures and high humidity to prevent leaf drop. When in growth, water moderately and apply a half-strength balanced liquid fertilizer monthly. Keep just moist in winter. Pot on in spring; trim regularly to maintain dense growth. Outdoors, grow in humus-rich, moist but well-drained, acidic to neutral soil with added leaf mold and grit, in light dappled to partial shade.
• **PROPAGATION** Root softwood cuttings with bottom heat in spring or summer.
• **PESTS AND DISEASES** Infrequent.

S. margaritacea. Evergreen perennial with weak, 4-angled red stems bearing opposite, ovate to lance-shaped, glossy, dark green leaves, 4in (10cm) long, with numerous oval, pearl-white spots above, purple veins beneath, and purple-red leaf stalks. Racemes of 8–10 star-shaped, 3-petaled, reddish pink flowers, ½in (1.5cm) long, are borne from summer to autumn. ↕↔ 10in (25cm). Burma to Indonesia (Java). ❄ (min. 66°F/19°C). **'Argentea'** (Pearly sonerila) has claret-red leaves, densely spotted silver. **'Hendersonii'** ■ has dark olive-green leaves, covered with white spots above, and purple-red beneath.

Sonerila margaritacea 'Hendersonii'

SOPHORA

FABACEAE

Genus of about 50 species of herbaceous perennials and deciduous and evergreen trees and shrubs, widely distributed in tropical and temperate regions, found mostly in dry valleys and woodland, and on rocky slopes of hills and mountains. They are cultivated for their elegant, alternate, pinnate leaves and racemes or panicles of pea-like flowers, with upright standards or with all petals forward-pointing. Grow in a shrub border, or as specimen plants. Where marginally hardy, grow at the base of a warm, sunny wall, or in a temperate or warm greenhouse. They need long, hot summers to flower well.
• **CULTIVATION** Grow in moderately fertile, well-drained soil in full sun. Pruning group 1.
• **PROPAGATION** Sow seed in containers in a cold frame as soon as ripe. Root semi-ripe cuttings of evergreen species with bottom heat in summer or autumn. Graft *S. japonica* cultivars in late winter.
• **PESTS AND DISEASES** Twig blight, *Verticillium* wilt, canker, and rust can be problems.

S. arizonica. Slow-growing, evergreen shrub with pinnate leaves, to 6in (15cm) long, composed of up to 10 ovate or elliptic-oblong, gray-green leaflets. Bears drooping racemes of pea-like, lavender flowers, 1in (2.5cm) across, in late spring. ↕ to 6–10ft (2–3m), ↔ 4–5ft (1.2–1.5m). S.W. US. ❄ (min. 41°F/5°C)
S. davidii ■ syn. *S. viciifolia.* Bushy or spreading, deciduous shrub with pinnate leaves, to 3½in (9cm) long, each composed of up to 17 oval or obovate, gray-green leaflets. In late spring and early summer, produces terminal racemes, to 6in (15cm) long, of small, pea-like, purple-blue and white flowers, to ¾in (2cm) long. ↕ 8ft (2.5m), ↔ 10ft (3m). China. Zone 7.
S. japonica ■ (Japanese pagoda tree). Spreading, deciduous tree with pinnate leaves, to 10in (25cm) long, each with up to 17 ovate to lance-shaped, glossy, dark green leaflets that turn yellow in autumn. In summer, bears abundant, small, fragrant, pea-like, creamy white flowers, ½in (1.5cm) long, in terminal panicles to 12in (30cm) long. ↕ to 100ft (30m), ↔ 70ft (20m). China, Korea. Zone 6. **'Pendula'** has long, pendent, sometimes twisted branches, and rarely flowers; ↕↔ 10ft (3m). **'Regent'** has an oval-rounded crown, grows faster, and blooms at an earlier age. **'Violacea'** has white flowers tinged lilac-pink.
S. microphylla, syn. *Edwardia microphylla.* Spreading, evergreen, small tree or shrub producing pinnate leaves, to 6in (15cm) long, each with up to 40 pairs of ovate or elliptic-oblong, dark green leaflets, borne on silky shoots. In spring, bears small, axillary, pendent racemes, to 2in (5cm) long, of pea-like, dark yellow flowers, 2in (5cm) long, with all petals pointing forward. ↕↔ 25ft (8m). New Zealand, Chile. ❄ (min. 35°F/2°C). **'Sun King'** ■ is bushy, and bears long-lasting flowers in late winter and early spring; ↕↔ 10ft (3m).
S. secundiflora (Mescal bean, Texas mountain laurel). Evergreen tree with pinnate leaves, 4–6in (10–15cm) long, each composed of 3–5 pairs of oblong to obovate, notched, mid-green leaflets, silky beneath. In spring, bears terminal racemes, 1¼–2in (3–5cm) long, of pea-like, fragrant, violet-blue flowers, 1in (2.5cm) long, followed by bright red seeds. ↕ 25–35ft (8–11m), ↔ 15–20ft (5–6m). Texas, N. Mexico. Zone 7b.
S. tetraptera (Kowhai). Spreading, evergreen tree or shrub with pinnate leaves, to 7in (18cm) long, each with up to 20 pairs of ovate or elliptic-oblong, dark green leaflets. In late spring, produces racemes, to 2½in (6cm) long, of 4–10 golden yellow flowers, to 2in (5cm) long, with all the petals pointing forward. ↕ 30ft (10m), ↔ 15ft (5m). New Zealand. ❄ (min. 41°F/5°C)
S. viciifolia see *S. davidii.*

Sophora davidii

Sophora japonica

Sophora microphylla 'Sun King'

SOPHROLAELIO-CATTLEYA

ORCHIDACEAE

Trigeneric hybrid genus of evergreen orchids derived from crosses between *Sophronitis, Laelia,* and *Cattleya.* They are vegetatively similar to laeliocattleyas and brassolaeliocattleyas, and all are loosely referred to as cattleyas. The spindle-shaped or elongated pseudobulbs support 1 or 2 semi-rigid, elliptic leaves, to 6in (15cm) long. Flowers up to 4in (10cm) across, in a range of rich colors from vibrant reds to fiery oranges and yellows, are borne singly or in racemes of up to 6 blooms; they are produced from the tops of the pseudobulbs at any time of year.
• **CULTIVATION** Intermediate-growing orchids. Grow in containers of porous, terrestrial orchid potting mix. During the growing season, provide bright indirect light, and water freely; apply a half-strength balanced liquid fertilizer monthly; mist daily and maintain high humidity. In winter, provide full light and water sparingly. See also p.46.
• **PROPAGATION** Divide when the plant overflows the container. Separate backbulbs into groups of at least 3 and and pot them up.
• **PESTS AND DISEASES** Scale insects, spider mites, aphids, and mealybugs may be troublesome.

S. **Hazel Boyd 'Apricot Glow'** ■ Evergreen orchid with spindle-shaped pseudobulbs and elliptic leaves, 4in (10cm) long. Bears racemes of 3 or more rich orange-red flowers, marked red on the lips, at any time of year. ↕ 8in (20cm), ↔ 12in (30cm). ❄ (min. 55°F/13°C; max. 86°F/30°C)
S. **Jewel Box 'Dark Waters'.** Evergreen orchid with spindle-shaped pseudobulbs and elliptic-ovate leaves, 4in (10cm) long. Produces racemes of 3 or more deep vibrant red flowers at any time of year. ↕↔ 12in (30cm). ❄ (min. 55°F/13°C; max. 86°F/30°C)
S. **Trizac 'Purple Emperor'.** Evergreen orchid with spindle-shaped pseudobulbs and elliptic leaves, 4in (10cm) long. Bears racemes of deep purple flowers at any time of year. ↕↔ 12in (30cm). ❄ (min. 55°F/13°C; max. 86°F/30°C)

Sophrolaeliocattleya Hazel Boyd Apricot Glow'

S. Paprika 'Black Magic'. Evergreen orchid with spindle-shaped pseudobulbs and elliptic leaves, 4in (10cm) long. Bears racemes of up to 4 black-red flowers, at any time of the year. ↕ 12in (30cm), ↔ 8–12in (20–30cm). ❀ (min. 55°F/13°C; max. 86°F/30°C)

SOPHRONITIS

ORCHIDACEAE

Genus of 7 species of small, evergreen, epiphytic or lithophytic orchids from E. Brazil and Paraguay, found at medium altitudes in humid, shady cloud forest. They have small, elongated to oval, often clustered pseudobulbs, each with a single leathery, ovate to elliptic or oblong, purple-tinted, dark green leaf. Richly colored flowers are borne singly, or in short-stemmed racemes of up to 8 flowers, at any time of year. The plants resemble miniature cattleyas, and will interbreed with them and other related genera to produce brilliantly colored hybrids, such as the sophrolaeliocattleyas.

• **CULTIVATION** Cool-growing orchids. Grow in epiphytic orchid potting mix in small containers or wooden slatted baskets, or epiphytically on bark. In growth, provide bright indirect light, water moderately, and maintain high humidity; apply a half-strength balanced liquid fertilizer monthly. In winter, admit full light and water more sparingly. See also p.46.

• **PROPAGATION** Divide when the plant overflows the sides of the container.

• **PESTS AND DISEASES** Prone to spider mites, aphids, and mealybugs.

S. cernua. Small epiphytic orchid with oval pseudobulbs and ovate, leathery, sometimes purple-spotted, dark green leaves, 1in (2.5cm) long. In winter, bears racemes of 4 to 8 pink to deep red flowers, 1½in (4cm) across, resembling small cattleyas or laelias. ↕↔ 2–3in (5–8cm). E. Brazil (Rio de Janeiro). ❀ (min. 50°F/10°C; max. 86°F/30°C)

S. coccinea syn. *S. grandiflora.* Epiphytic orchid with small, oval or spindle-shaped pseudobulbs and elliptic to ovate, purple-tinted, sometimes glaucous, dark green leaves, 1¼–2½in (3–6cm) long. Bears yellow to red or pinkish red flowers, 2½–3in (6–8cm) across, at any time of year. ↕ 2in (5cm), ↔ 4in (10cm). E. Brazil. ❀ (min. 52–55°F/11–13°C; max. 86°F/30°C)

S. grandiflora see *S. coccinea.*

SORBARIA

False spirea

ROSACEAE

Genus of 10 species of suckering, deciduous shrubs, often with star-shaped hairs, mainly occurring on riverbanks from the Himalayas to E. Asia. They are cultivated for their elegant foliage and flowers. The leaves are alternate and pinnate; the 5-petaled, star-like white flowers are borne in large, conical, terminal panicles in mid- and late summer. Sorbarias are good for a large shrub border, a wild or woodland garden, where they may form thickets, or for a waterside planting.

• **CULTIVATION** Grow in moderately fertile, moist but well-drained, neutral to slightly alkaline soil in full sun to partial shade. Remove excess suckers to restrict spread. Pruning group 2 or 6.

• **PROPAGATION** Sow seed in containers in a cold frame in autumn. Take semi-ripe cuttings in midsummer. Transplant rooted suckers in autumn or winter.

• **PESTS AND DISEASES** Can be affected by fireblight.

S. aitchisonii see *S. tomentosa* var. *angustifolia.*

S. arborea see *S. kirilowii.*

S. kirilowii ▣ syn. *S. arborea, Spiraea arborea.* Vigorous, spreading shrub with arching shoots and pinnate leaves, to 12in (30cm) long, each composed of 13–17 (rarely 9) lance-shaped, tapered, dark green leaflets. In mid- and late summer, bears white flowers, to ¼in (6mm) across, in terminal, arching, conical panicles, to 16in (40cm) long. ↕↔ 4½–25ft (1.3–8m). W. China, S.E. Tibet. Zone 5.

S. lindleyana see *S. tomentosa.*

S. sorbifolia ▣ syn. *Spiraea sorbifolia* (Ural false spirea). Upright, thicket-forming shrub with erect branches and pinnate leaves, to 10in (25cm) long, each with up to 25 lance-shaped or oblong, tapered, dark green leaflets. In mid- and late summer, produces small white flowers, to ⅜in (8mm) across, in erect, terminal, conical panicles, to 10in (25cm) long. ↕ 6ft (2m), ↔ 10ft (3m). N. Asia, Japan. Zone 2.

S. tomentosa, syn. *S. lindleyana* (Kashmir false spirea). Strong-growing, spreading shrub with pinnate leaves, to 18in (45cm) long, composed of up to 23 lance-shaped, tapered, dark green leaflets. In mid- and late summer, bears small, creamy white flowers, ¼in (6mm) across, in terminal, conical panicles, to 16in (40cm) long. ↕↔ 20ft (6m). Himalayas. Zone 8.

var. *angustifolia*, syn *S. aitchisonii, Spiraea aitchisonii,* is shorter than the species, with red shoots and slender leaflets; ↕↔ 10ft (3m); Afghanistan to W. Nepal; Zone 4.

Sorbaria kirilowii

Sorbaria sorbifolia

SORBUS

ROSACEAE

Genus of about 100 species of deciduous trees and shrubs, widely distributed in N. temperate regions, found in woodland, on hills and mountains, and on scree. *Sorbus* species and cultivars are valued for their ornamental leaves, which are alternate, variable, and either simple and toothed to lobed, or pinnate; they often color well in autumn. They are also grown for their terminal, sometimes panicle-like corymbs of small, white, rarely pink flowers, ⅜–¾in (0.8–2cm) across, borne in spring or early summer, and for their mostly spherical, white, yellow, orange, red, or brown fruits (berries). Tolerant of atmospheric pollution, they are ideal as specimen trees in a small garden, or wild or woodland garden. The raw fruit may cause mild stomach upset if ingested.

• **CULTIVATION** Grow in moderately fertile, humus-rich, well-drained soil in full sun or light, dappled shade. *Sorbus* species and cultivars with pinnate leaves grow best in moist but well-drained, acidic to neutral soil. *S. aria* will thrive on dry, alkaline soil as well as on acidic soil. Pruning group 1, if necessary.

Sorbus americana

• **PROPAGATION** Sow seed in containers in a cold frame in autumn. Take greenwood cuttings in early summer; not all will root readily. Bud in summer. Graft in winter.

• **PESTS AND DISEASES** Fireblight, dieback, powdery mildew, anthracnose, wood rot, borers, sawfly, scale insects, and aphids are common.

S. alnifolia ▣ (Korean mountain ash). Broadly conical tree with simple, ovate to lance-shaped, toothed, dark green leaves, to 4in (10cm) long, turning yellow to orange or red in autumn. In midspring, bears dense corymbs, 3in (8cm) across, of small white flowers, followed in autumn by spherical, deep pink to red berries, ½in (1.5cm) across. ↕ 70ft (20m), ↔ 25ft (8m). E. Asia. Zone 4b.

S. americana ▣ (American mountain ash, Dogberry). Rounded tree or shrub producing pinnate leaves, to 10in (25cm) long, each with up to 15 oblong to lance-shaped, toothed, light green leaflets, turning yellow or red in autumn. In late spring and early summer, bears dense corymbs, 5½in (14cm) across, of white flowers, followed by spherical, orange-red berries, ⅜in (8mm) across. ↕ 30ft (10m), ↔ 22ft (7m). E. North America. Zone 3.

S. aria (Whitebeam). Broadly columnar tree producing simple, elliptic to broadly ovate or obovate, toothed, glossy, dark green leaves, to 5in (13cm) long, white-hairy beneath. White flowers are borne in corymbs 3in (8cm) across, in late spring; they are followed by ovoid to

Sorbus alnifolia

S

Sorbus aria 'Lutescens' (inset: flower detail)

spherical, brown-speckled, dark red berries, ½in (1.5cm) across. ↕ 30–80ft (10–25m), ↔ 30ft (10m). Europe. Zone 4. **'Chrysophylla'** has golden yellow juvenile leaves; ↕ 30ft (10m), ↔ 22ft (7m). **'Decaisneana'** see 'Majestica'. **'Lutescens'** ■ is compact in habit, with silvery gray, later gray-green foliage; ↕ 30ft (10m), ↔ 25ft (8m). **'Magnifica'** has large, very glossy leaves, to 5in (13cm) long. **'Majestica'**, syn. 'Decaisneana', has leaves to 6in (15cm) or more long.

S. aucuparia ■ (European mountain ash, Rowan). Broadly conical to rounded tree with mid- to dark green leaves, turning red or yellow in autumn. Leaves are oblong-lance-shaped to elliptic, to 8in (20cm) long, with 1 or 2 pairs of separate leaflets at the bases, or pinnate, with up to 12 oblong-lance-shaped, sharply toothed leaflets. In late spring, bears white flowers in corymbs to 5in (13cm) across, followed by spherical, orange-red berries, ⅜in (8mm) across. Does not grow well in areas with hot summers. ↕ 50ft (15m), ↔ 22ft (7m). Europe, Asia. Zone 3. **'Apricot Queen'** bears yellow-orange berries. **'Aspleniifolia'** has leaflets pinnately divided at the bases. **'Beissneri'**, syn. *S. moravica* 'Laciniata', is upright, with coppery bark, and red shoots and leaf stalks; yellow-green leaves turn yellow in autumn; ↕ 30ft (10m), ↔ 15ft (5m). **'Black Hawk'** is upright and bears orange fruit; ↕ 30ft (10m), ↔ 20ft (6m). **'Cardinal Royal'** is upright and vigorous, and fruits profusely. **'Fastigiata'**, syn. *S. decora* var. *nana*, *S. scopulina* of gardens, is dense in habit, with upright branches, conical when mature; it bears dark red berries, ½in (1.5cm) across; ↕ 25ft (8m), ↔ 15ft (5m). **'Fructu Luteo'**, syn. 'Xanthocarpa', is spreading, with orange-yellow berries; ↕↔ 25ft (8m). **var. *pluripinnata*** see *S. scalaris*. **'Xanthocarpa'** see 'Fructu Luteo'.

S. cashmiriana ■ Spreading tree or shrub with pinnate leaves, to 8in (20cm) long, composed of 17–21 lance-shaped, dark green leaflets. In late spring, bears pink or white flowers in corymbs 5in (13cm) across, followed by spherical white berries, to ½in (1.5cm) across, pink-tinged at first. ↕ 25ft (8m), ↔ 22ft (7m). W. Himalayas. Zone 6.

***S.* 'Chinese Lace'.** Upright tree with pinnate leaves, to 8in (20cm) long, composed of numerous deeply cut, elliptic to oblong, dark green leaflets. Small white flowers, in corymbs to 6in (15cm) across, are produced in late spring, followed by spherical, orange-red berries, ½in (1.5cm) across. ↕ 20ft (6m), ↔ 15ft (5m). Zone 6.

S. commixta ■ syn. *S. discolor* of gardens, *S. reflexipetala*. Compact, broadly conical tree or shrub with erect branches and pinnate leaves, to 10in (25cm) long, each with up to 17 elliptic to lance-shaped, tapered, dark green leaflets, turning yellow to red or purple in autumn. In late spring, bears white flowers in corymbs 6in (15cm) across, followed by spherical, orange-red or red berries, ⅜in (8mm) across. ↕ 30ft (10m), ↔ 22ft (7m). Korea, Japan. Zone 3b. **'Embley'** has bright red leaves in late autumn, and fruits profusely.

S. conradinae see *S. esserteauana*.

Sorbus aucuparia

***S. conradinae* of gardens** see *S. pohuashanensis*.

S. cuspidata see *S. vestita*.

S. decora ■ (Showy mountain ash). Upright tree or shrub with pinnate leaves, to 6in (15cm) long, composed of up to 15 elliptic to oval-lance-shaped, dark blue-green leaflets, turning orange-red in autumn. In late spring, bears white flowers in corymbs to 4in (10cm) across, followed by spherical, bright red berries, ½in (1.5cm) across. ↕ 25ft (8m), ↔ 15ft (5m). Newfoundland, Greenland, N.E. US. Zone 2. **var. *nana*** see *S. aucuparia* 'Fastigiata'.

***S. discolor* of gardens** see *S. commixta*.

S. domestica. Broadly columnar tree with pinnate leaves, to 8in (20cm) long, composed of up to 21 narrowly oblong, dark green leaflets, turning yellow or red in autumn. In late spring, bears white flowers in conical corymbs, 4in (10cm) across; these are followed by spherical or pear-shaped, yellow-green, red-flushed berries, to 1¼in (3cm) across. ↕ 70ft (20m), ↔ 40ft (12m). C. and S. Europe, N. Africa, Turkey, Caucasus, Ukraine (Crimea), Moldavia. Zone 6. **f. *pomifera***, syn. 'Maliformis', bears spherical berries. **f. *pyriformis*** ■ syn. var. *pyrifera*, 'Pyriformis', produces pear-shaped berries.

Sorbus cashmiriana

S. esserteauana, syn. *S. conradinae*. Spreading tree with large, pinnate leaves, to 10in (25cm) long, composed of up to 15 oblong-lance-shaped, tapered, dark green leaflets, white-felted beneath, turning red in autumn. In late spring, bears white flowers in corymbs 5in (13cm) across, followed by spherical, dark red berries, ⅜in (8mm) across. ↕↔ 30ft (10m). China (W. Sichuan). Zone 4. **'Flava'** produces orange-yellow berries.

***S. folgneri* 'Lemon Drop'.** Arching tree with slightly pendent branches and simple, narrowly ovate, dark green leaves, to 4in (10cm) long, white beneath. In late spring, white flowers, are produced in corymbs 4in (10cm) across, followed by ovoid, bright yellow berries, ½in (1.5cm) across. ↕↔ 25ft (8m). Zone 4b.

S. forrestii. Spreading tree with pinnate leaves, to 8in (20cm) long, composed of up to 19 elliptic-oblong, dark blue-green leaflets. In late spring, bears white flowers in corymbs 4in (10cm) across, followed by spherical white berries, ½in (1.5cm) across, tinged dark pink at the tips. ↕↔ 20ft (6m). China (N.W. Yunnan). Zone 7b.

S. glabrescens see *S. hupehensis*.

S. hupehensis, syn. *S. glabrescens* (Hubei mountain ash). Broadly columnar tree with pinnate leaves, to 6in (15cm) long, each with up to 15 ovate, blue-green leaflets, turning red in autumn. In late spring, bears pyramidal, panicle-like corymbs, to 5in (13cm) long, of white flowers, followed by spherical white berries, ⅜in (8mm) across, slightly flushed pink. ↕↔ to 25ft (8m). China (Hubei). Zone 4. **'Coral Fire'** has dark green leaves, which turn bright red in autumn, and bears coral-red berries. **var. *obtusa*** ■ syn. 'Rosea', has berries ripening dark pink.

***S.* x *hybrida* of gardens** see *S.* x *thuringiaca*.

S. intermedia (Swedish whitebeam). Compact, rounded tree with elliptic to oblong-elliptic, toothed, dark green leaves, to 5in (13cm) long, lobed near the bases. In late spring, bears dense corymbs, 5in (13cm) across, of white flowers, followed by ovoid-oblong, bright red berries, ½in (1.5cm) long. ↕↔ 40ft (12m). N.W. Europe. Zone 4.

***S.* 'Joseph Rock'** ■ Broadly upright tree with pinnate leaves, to 6in (15cm)

Sorbus commixta

S

Sorbus decora (inset: fruit detail)

long, composed of up to 21 narrowly oblong, sharply toothed, bright green leaflets, turning orange, red, and purple in autumn. In late spring, bears white flowers, in corymbs 4in (10cm) across, followed by spherical, pale yellow, later orange-yellow berries, ½in (1.5cm) across. Especially prone to fireblight. ↕30ft (10m), ↔ 22ft (7m). Zone 7.
S.* x *kewensis (*S. pohuashanensis* x *S. aucuparia*) syn. *S. pohuashanensis* of gardens. Slow-growing, rounded, shrubby tree with pinnate leaves, to 12in (30cm) long, composed of 4–9 pairs of oblong-elliptic or oblong-lance-shaped, coarsely toothed, mid-green leaflets. In late spring, bears white flowers in corymbs 5in (13cm) across, followed by ovoid, bright red berries, ⅜in (8mm) across. ↕8ft (2.5m), ↔ 6ft (2m). Garden origin. Zone 7.
S. koehneana. Spreading, small tree or shrub with pinnate leaves, to 6in (15cm) long, composed of up to 25 or more oblong to ovate, sharply toothed, dark green leaflets. In late spring, produces small corymbs, 3in (8cm) across, of white flowers, followed by small, spherical, mid-green berries, ¼in (6mm) across, ripening to white, on red stalks.

Sorbus domestica f. *pyriformis*

Often confused with *S. fruticosa*, which is very similar but only grows to 6ft (2m) in height. ↕15ft (5m), ↔ 20ft (6m). China. Zone 5.
***S. lanata* of gardens** see *S. vestita*.
S. latifolia. Broadly columnar tree with broadly elliptic, sharply toothed, glossy, dark green leaves, to 4in (10cm) long, lobed toward the bases. In late spring, bears white flowers in corymbs 3in (8cm) across, followed by spherical, yellow-brown berries, ½in (1.5cm) across. ↕30–70ft (10–20m), ↔ 15–25ft (5–8m). W. Europe. Zone 6.
S. megalocarpa. Spreading tree or shrub with arching branches and oval, finely toothed, dark green leaves, to 10in (25cm) long, red when young and in autumn. In early spring, bears pungent,

Sorbus hupehensis var. *obtusa*

Sorbus 'Joseph Rock'

creamy white flowers in dense corymbs, to 6in (15cm) across, before or with the young leaves, followed by ovoid, russet-brown berries, 1¼in (3cm) long. ↕25ft (8m), ↔ 30ft (10m). C. to S. China. Zone 7.
S. microphylla. Elegant, spreading tree or shrub with pinnate leaves, to 7in (18cm) long, each with up to 33 oblong, sharply toothed, dark green leaflets, red in autumn. In late spring, bears small corymbs, to 3in (8cm) across, of pale pink to almost crimson flowers, followed by spherical, white or pink berries, ⅜in (8mm) across. ↕↔ 20ft (6m). W. China, E. Himalayas. Zone 7.
***S.* 'Mitchellii'** see *S. thibetica* 'John Mitchell'.
***S. moravica* 'Laciniata'** see *S. aucuparia* 'Beissneri'.
***S.* 'Pearly King'.** Spreading tree with slender shoots and pinnate leaves, to 6in (15cm) long, each consisting of up to 17 elliptic, glossy, dark green leaflets, turning yellow or red in autumn. In late spring, produces white flowers in corymbs 4in (10cm) across, followed by spherical pink, later white-flushed berries, ½in (1.5cm) across. ↕↔ 20ft (6m). Zone 5.
S. pohuashanensis, syn. *S. conradinae* of gardens. Spreading tree with pinnate leaves, to 7in (18cm) long, composed of up to 15 elliptic to oblong-lance-shaped, dark green leaflets. In late spring, produces dense corymbs, to 5in (13cm) across, of white flowers, followed by spherical red berries, ⅜in (8mm) across. ↕ to 70ft (20m), ↔ 25ft (8m). Probably N. China. Zone 3b.

Sorbus prattii

Sorbus reducta

***S. pohuashanensis* of gardens** see *S.* x *kewensis*.
S. prattii ■ Spreading tree with pinnate leaves, to 6in (15cm) long, composed of up to 31 oblong, sharply toothed, dark green leaflets. In late spring, bears small corymbs, 3in (8cm) across, of white flowers, followed by spherical green berries, ⅜in (8mm) across, ripening to white. ↕↔ 20ft (6m). China (Sichuan). Zone 7.
S. reducta ■ Thicket-forming, usually suckering shrub with upright shoots. Pinnate leaves, to 4in (10cm) long, composed of up to 15 ovate, glossy, dark green leaflets, turn red and purple in autumn. In late spring, bears white flowers in small, open corymbs, to 3in (8cm) across, followed by spherical, crimson then white berries, ½in (1.5cm) across. ↕3–5ft (1–1.5m), ↔ 6ft (2m) or more. W. China. Zone 6.
S. reflexipetala see *S. commixta*.
S. sargentiana ■ Broadly upright, slow-growing tree with thick shoots and large, sticky red winter buds. Large, pinnate leaves, to 14in (35cm) long, each with up to 13 oblong-lance-shaped, dark green leaflets, turn orange and red in autumn. In early summer, bears white

Sorbus sargentiana

Sorbus scalaris

flowers in broad corymbs, 8in (20cm) across, followed by spherical red berries, ⅜in (8mm) across. ↕↔ 30ft (10m). W. China. Zone 6.
S. scalaris ■ syn. *S. aucuparia* var. *pluripinnata*. Spreading tree with pinnate leaves, to 8in (20cm) long, composed of up to 33 narrowly oblong, glossy, dark green leaflets, turning red and purple in late autumn. In late spring and early summer, bears flattened corymbs, 6in (15cm) across, of white flowers, followed by spherical red berries, ¼in (6mm) across. ↕↔ 30ft (10m). China (W. Sichuan). Zone 7.
S. scopulina. Erect shrub with pinnate leaves, 1¾–2½in (3–6cm) long, each composed of up to 15 oblong-lance-shaped, dark green leaflets. In late spring and early summer, bears white flowers in corymbs to 4in (10cm) across, followed by spherical, glossy red berries, ½in (1.5cm) across. ↕ to 6ft (2m), ↔ 5ft (1.5m). British Columbia to New Mexico. Zone 4.
***S. scopulina* of gardens** see *S. aucuparia* 'Fastigiata'.
S. thibetica. Broadly conical tree with elliptic to rounded, sharply toothed, dark green leaves, to 5in (13cm) long, densely white-hairy when young, remaining white-hairy beneath when mature. In late spring and early summer, bears white flowers in corymbs to 2½in (6cm) across, followed by spherical to pear-shaped green berries, ½in (1.5cm) across, ripening orange or yellow. ↕ 70ft (20m), ↔ 50ft (15m). S.W. China, Himalayas. Zone 6. **'John Mitchell'**, syn. *S.* 'Mitchellii', produces broadly rounded leaves.

Sorbus x *thuringiaca*

Sorbus vilmorinii

S.* x *thuringiaca ■ (*S. aria* x *S. aucuparia*) syn. *S.* x *hybrida* of gardens. Compact, broadly conical tree with ovate to elliptic, deeply lobed, glossy, dark green leaves, to 6in (15cm) long, often with separate leaflets at the bases. In late spring, bears white flowers in corymbs to 5in (13cm) across, followed by spherical to ellipsoid, bright red berries, ½in (1.5cm) across. ↕ to 50ft (15m), ↔ 25ft (8m). Europe. Zone 5. **'Fastigiata'** is very compact and narrowly upright, becoming broadly conical with age.
S. vestita, syn. *S. cuspidata*, *S. lanata* of gardens. Broadly conical tree with simple, elliptic, sharply toothed, sometimes shallowly lobed leaves, to 8in (20cm) long. Leaves are white-hairy when young; mature leaves are glossy, dark green above, white-hairy beneath. In late spring, bears white-woolly corymbs, to 3in (8cm) across, of white flowers, followed by spherical, brown-speckled, yellow-green berries, ¾in (2cm) across. ↕ to 80ft (25m), ↔ 30ft (10m). Himalayas, N. Burma. Zone 7.
S. vilmorinii ■ Spreading shrub or tree with arching branches and pinnate leaves, to 6in (15cm) long, composed of up to 29 glossy, dark green leaflets. In late spring and early summer, bears white flowers in corymbs 4in (10cm) across, followed by spherical, dark red berries, ½in (1.5cm) across, aging pink then white. ↕↔ 15ft (5m). S.W. China. Zone 7.
***S.* 'Wilfrid Fox'.** Upright tree, broadly conical when mature, with elliptic, glossy, dark green leaves, to 5in (13cm) long, densely white-hairy beneath. White flowers are produced in corymbs 4in (10cm) across, in late spring, followed by spherical, yellow-brown, red-flushed berries, to ½in (1.5cm) across. ↕ 50ft (15m), ↔ 30ft (10m). Zone 6.

SORGHASTRUM

POACEAE

Genus of about 16 species of clump-forming, annual and perennial grasses from prairies and savanna in Africa and tropical and temperate North, Central, and South America. They are cultivated for their open or narrow, terminal panicles of late-summer flowerheads (which may be dried and dyed), and for their linear, flat or rolled leaves. Suitable for a mixed or herbaceous border.
• **CULTIVATION** Grow in moderately fertile, well-drained soil in full sun. Protect from excessive winter moisture.
• **PROPAGATION** Sow seed in containers in a cold frame in spring. Divide in midspring or early summer.
• **PESTS AND DISEASES** Sometimes affected by rust, leaf smut, and leaf spots.

S. avenaceum see *S. nutans*.
S. nutans, syn. *S. avenaceum* (Indian grass, Wood grass). Slowly spreading, perennial grass forming loose clumps of erect stems with arching, broadly linear, bluish green leaves, to 24in (60cm) long. From summer to autumn, produces narrow, terminal panicles, to 14in (35cm) long, of golden brown spikelets. ↕ 4ft (1.2m), ↔ 24in (60cm). E. and C. US. Zone 6. **'Sioux Blue'** is strongly erect in habit, with metallic blue-green leaves, turning purple in autumn, and glossy, red-brown spikelets with yellow anthers.

SPARAXIS

Harlequin flower

IRIDACEAE

Genus of 6 species of cormous perennials from moist, rocky sites in South Africa. They are grown for their loose spikes of up to 5 widely funnel-shaped, brightly colored flowers, borne in spring or summer. The sword-, sickle-, or lance-shaped, ribbed leaves are often produced in an erect, basal fan. Where not hardy, grow in a cool greenhouse, or outdoors at the base of a warm, sunny wall in summer. In warmer areas, use in a raised bed or at the front of a border.
• **CULTIVATION** Plant corms 4in (10cm) deep. Under glass, plant in early to late autumn in soil-based potting mix, with added sand and leaf mold, in full light with shade from hot sun. Water sparingly when in growth, and keep cool; dry off as flowers fade. Keep completely dry when dormant.

Sparaxis tricolor

Outdoors, plant in late autumn in moderately fertile, well-drained soil in full sun and provide a dry winter mulch. Where not hardy, plant in spring and lift in autumn. Store in a frost-free place.
• **PROPAGATION** Sow seed in containers in a cold frame as soon as ripe. Remove offsets when corms are dormant.
• **PESTS AND DISEASES** Infrequent.

S. elegans, syn. *Streptanthera cuprea*, *Streptanthera elegans*. Cormous perennial with basal fans of sword-shaped leaves, 3–10in (8–25cm) long. In spring and summer, bears up to 5 stems, each with a spike of up to 5 widely funnel-shaped, orange or red, rarely white flowers, 1½in (4cm) long, fading to pink, marked with yellow and violet. ↕ 4–12in (10–30cm), PD3in (8cm). South Africa (Western Cape). ❄ (min. 45°F/7°C). **'Coccinea'** has orange-red flowers with near-black centers.
S. fragrans. Cormous perennial with basal fans of lance- or sickle-shaped leaves, to 12in (30cm) long. In spring and summer, bears spikes of up to 6 flattish, widely funnel-shaped flowers, 2–2½in (5–6cm) long, with cream, yellow, red-purple, or violet-purple lobes, sometimes with darker markings, and yellow, purple, or black tubes. ↕ 3–18in (8–45cm), PD3in (8cm). South Africa (Western Cape). ❄ (min. 45°F/7°C). **subsp. *grandiflora***, syn. *S. grandiflora*, is less vigorous, bearing reddish purple flowers with yellow tubes.
S. grandiflora see *S. fragrans* subsp. *grandiflora*.
S. pillansii. Cormous perennial with basal fans of 8 or 10 narrowly sword-shaped leaves, to 14in (35cm) long. In spring, bears 2–4 stems, each with spikes of 4–9 flattish, widely funnel-shaped flowers, to 2½in (6cm) across, with rose-pink lobes, marked yellow and purple-edged at the bases, and yellow tubes. ↕ to 24in (60cm), PD3in (8cm). South Africa (Western Cape, Northern Cape). ❄ (min. 45°F/7°C)
S. tricolor ■ Cormous perennial with basal fans of erect, lance-shaped leaves, to 12in (30cm) long. From spring to early summer, produces 1–5 stems that bear 2–5 widely funnel-shaped, orange, red, or purple flowers, 2–3in (5–8cm) across, each with a black or dark red central mark. ↕ 4–16in (10–40cm), PD3in (8cm). South Africa (Western Cape). ❄ (min. 45°F/7°C)

SPARGANIUM

Burr reed

SPARGANIACEAE

Genus of 21 species of deciduous or semi-evergreen, rhizomatous, marginal aquatic perennials, widely distributed in temperate regions worldwide, where they form vigorous stands of lush growth at the edges of lakes and rivers. Strong rhizomes support erect, linear, deep green, sometimes brown-green leaves, and produce spikes or racemes of inconspicuous, spherical, male and female flowerheads, followed by fleshy, burr-like fruits. Best grown in the shallows of a large wildlife pool.
• **CULTIVATION** Grow in large drifts in a shallow pool margin, to 18in (45cm) deep, in full sun or partial shade. In winter, leave the foliage to provide

shelter for wildlife. Remove dead foliage in spring. See also pp.52–53.
• **PROPAGATION** Sow seed at 59°F (15°C) as soon as ripe. Divide in spring.
• **PESTS AND DISEASES** Infrequent.

S. emersum. Vigorous, submerged, floating, or erect, semi-evergreen, marginal aquatic perennial with erect, boldly keeled, linear leaves, 8–20in (20–50cm) long, longer and wider on sterile plants. In summer, erect, unbranched flower spikes, 8–32in (20–80cm) long, bear densely packed, spherical, white to yellow-green flowerheads, to 1in (2.5cm) across, followed by ellipsoid, spiky brown fruit, ⅛–¼in (4–6mm) across. ↕ 10–28in (20–70cm), ↔ indefinite. Eurasia, North America. Zone 6.
S. erectum, syn. *S. ramosum.* Vigorous, erect, rarely floating or submerged, semi-evergreen, marginal aquatic perennial with keeled, linear leaves, 5ft (1.5m) long. In summer, branched flower spikes, 8–39in (20–100cm) long, bear spherical, greenish brown flowerheads, ½–¾in (1–2cm) across, followed by ellipsoid to conical, prickly brown fruit, ¼–⅜in (6–9mm) across. ↕ 5ft (1.5m), ↔ indefinite. Eurasia. Zone 6.
S. minimum see *S. natans.*
S. natans, syn. *S. minimum.* Slender, floating, deciduous or semi-evergreen, marginal aquatic perennial with thin, flat, translucent, dark green, submerged, sometimes floating leaves, 2½–16in (6–40cm) long. In summer, floating stems, 3–16in (8–40cm) long, bear unbranched spikes, 20–60in (50–150cm) or more long, of spherical, brownish green flowerheads, ½–¾in (1–2cm) across, followed by ovoid, spiky, green or brown fruit, ¼–½in (6–10mm) across. ↔ indefinite. Arctic, Eurasia, North America. Zone 6.
S. ramosum see *S. erectum.*

▷ ***Sparmannia*** see *Sparrmannia*

SPARRMANNIA
syn. SPARMANNIA

TILIACEAE

Genus of 3–7 species of evergreen shrubs and small trees found in open woodland in tropical Africa, South Africa, and Madagascar. They are grown for their 4-petaled, white or pink to purple flowers, each with a showy boss of stamens, produced in long-stalked umbels from the upper leaf axils. Leaves are alternate, simple or palmately 3- to 7-lobed, toothed, narrow to broadly ovate, and often heart-shaped at the bases. Where not hardy, grow in a cool or temperate greenhouse. In warmer areas, grow in a shrub border.
• **CULTIVATION** Under glass, grow in soil-based potting mix in full light. In the growing season, water freely and apply a balanced liquid fertilizer monthly. Water sparingly in winter. Outdoors, grow in fertile, moist but well-drained soil in full sun. Pruning group 9, in late winter. Needs restrictive pruning under glass.
• **PROPAGATION** Sow seed at 59–64°F (15–18°C) in spring. Root semi-ripe cuttings with bottom heat in summer. Air layer in spring.
• **PESTS AND DISEASES** Whiteflies and spider mites may be troublesome.

Sparrmannia africana

S. africana ▣ (African hemp). Large shrub or small, upright tree with vigorous, many-branched, hairy stems. Produces long-stalked, ovate to broadly ovate or rounded, shallowly palmately lobed, hairy, light green leaves, to 8in (20cm) long. In late spring and early summer, bears umbels of up to 20 cup-shaped white flowers, 1¼–1½in (3–4cm) across, with long, yellow and red-purple stamens. ↕ 10–20ft (3–6m), ↔ 6–12ft (2–4m). South Africa. ❀ (min. 45°F/7°C). **'Flore Pleno'**, syn. 'Plena', produces double flowers. **'Plena'** see 'Flore Pleno'. **'Variegata'** has leaves marked with white.

SPARTINA
Cord grass, Marsh grass

POACEAE

Genus of about 15 species of rhizomatous perennial grasses, from swamps, salt marshes, and prairies in North America, W. Europe, and N.W. Africa. They have tough, flat to rolled, narrowly linear leaves, and finger-like racemes of flattened, wedge-shaped spikelets. *S. pectinata* is tolerant of saline soils, and may be grown in a wild garden, bog garden, or at a pond- or streamside; *S. pectinata* 'Aureomarginata' is also suitable for the back of a herbaceous or mixed border. The graceful inflorescences, particularly in their yellow autumn color, are suitable for dried flower arrangements.
• **CULTIVATION** Grow in moist but well-drained soil in full sun. If necessary, pull out rhizomes from the edge of the clump to keep in bounds. Cut back dead material in winter.
• **PROPAGATION** Separate rooted sections of the rhizomes from midspring to early summer.
• **PESTS AND DISEASES** Infrequent.

S. pectinata (Prairie cord grass, Freshwater cord grass, Slough grass). Rhizomatous, deciduous perennial forming loose, spreading clumps of erect stems bearing flat, arching, linear, mid-green leaves, to 4ft (1.2m) long, turning bright yellow in autumn. Compact, narrow, spike-like inflorescences, to 4in (10cm) long, of pale green spikelets with purple anthers, are produced in late summer and early autumn. ↕ 5ft (1.5m), ↔ 3ft (90cm) or more. North America. Zone 4. **'Aureomarginata'**, syn. 'Aureovariegata', 'Variegata', has olive-green leaves edged with golden yellow.

Spartium junceum

SPARTIUM
Broom, Spanish broom

FABACEAE

Genus of a single species of deciduous shrub occurring in dry places, open woodland, and on roadsides mainly in the Mediterranean region, including Portugal. *S. junceum* is cultivated for its terminal racemes of fragrant, pea-like yellow flowers, and rich dark green, broom-like stems. The leaves are sparse, alternate, simple, and dark green. It is suitable for a shrub border, or for growing against a warm, sunny wall.
• **CULTIVATION** Grow in moderately fertile, well-drained soil in full sun. Thrives in coastal situations and on alkaline soils. Pruning group 9. To renovate older specimens, cut back to the ground in spring.
• **PROPAGATION** Sow seed in containers in a cold frame in autumn or spring. May self-seed.
• **PESTS AND DISEASES** Young plants may be damaged by rabbits.

S. junceum ▣ (Spanish broom). Upright shrub with slender, dark green shoots and few linear-oblong to narrowly lance-shaped, dark green leaves, to 1¼in (3cm) long, silky-hairy beneath. A profusion of fragrant, pea-like, golden yellow flowers, 1in (2.5cm) long, is borne in terminal racemes, to 18in (45cm) long, from early summer to early autumn; flowers are followed by flattened, dark brown seed pods, to 3in (8cm) long. ↕↔ 10ft (3m). S. Europe, Ukraine (Crimea), Turkey, Syria, N. Africa. Zone 8.

SPATHIPHYLLUM

ARACEAE

Genus of 36 species of rhizomatous, evergreen perennials occurring in damp tropical forest in Indonesia, the Philippines, and tropical North, Central, and South America. They are cultivated for their stately, long-stemmed, white or cream-colored spathes, set against dark green, lance-shaped, inversely lance-shaped, or oblong-ovate leaves with prominent midribs. Where not hardy, grow in a warm greenhouse or in a conservatory. In warmer regions, they are suitable for a humid, shady border. Some *Spathiphyllum* species can be grown as houseplants. All parts of the plants may cause mild stomach upset if

Spathiphyllum 'Mauna Loa'

ingested, and contact with the sap may irritate skin.
• **CULTIVATION** Under glass, grow in well-drained, soilless potting mix or soil-based potting mix. Water freely in growth, applying a balanced liquid fertilizer monthly; maintain high humidity. Provide bright indirect light throughout the year. Pot on when root growth has overfilled the container. Outdoors, grow in moist but well-drained, humus-rich soil in deep shade.
• **PROPAGATION** Sow seed at 73–81°F (23–27°C) as soon as ripe, or in spring, on sphagnum moss. Divide in winter or immediately after flowering.
• **PESTS AND DISEASES** Often affected by root rot, leaf spots, and bacterial soft rot.

S. 'Mauna Loa' ▣ Vigorous but compact, rhizomatous perennial with inversely lance-shaped, glossy, dark green leaves, to 12in (30cm) long. Oval, fragrant, pure white spathes, to 8in (20cm) long, surrounding green and white spadices, to 3in (8cm) long, are produced in spring and summer. ↕ 3ft (1m), ↔ 24in (60cm). ❀ (min. 59°F/15°C)
S. wallisii ▣ Rhizomatous perennial with lance-shaped-elliptic to oblong-elliptic, wavy-margined, dark green leaves, to 14in (35cm) long. Ovate to oblong-elliptic, fragrant white spathes, to 7in (18cm) long, aging to green, and surrounding green and white spadices, to 4in (10cm) long, are borne above the foliage in spring and summer. ↕ 26in (65cm), ↔ 20in (50cm). Costa Rica, Panama, Colombia, Venezuela. ❀ (min. 50°F/10°C)

Spathiphyllum wallisii

SPATHODEA

African tulip tree

BIGNONIACEAE

Genus of one species of usually evergreen tree from forest margins and gorges in tropical Africa. It is grown for its showy, bell-shaped flowers; large, pinnate leaves; and deeply fissured bark. Where temperatures fall below 55°F (13°C), grow *S. campanulata* in a warm greenhouse; it seldom blooms in containers. In tropical climates, use as a specimen tree.

• **CULTIVATION** Under glass, grow in large containers or in a greenhouse border, in soil-based potting mix in full light. When in growth, water freely and apply a balanced liquid fertilizer monthly; water sparingly in winter. Outdoors, grow in fertile, moist soil in full sun. Pruning group 1; needs restrictive pruning under glass, in late winter or after flowering.

• **PROPAGATION** Sow seed at 64–75°F (18–24°C) in spring. Root semi-ripe cuttings with bottom heat in summer. Air layer in spring.

• **PESTS AND DISEASES** Spider mites may be troublesome under glass.

S. campanulata ▣ Moderately branched, open, leafy tree with opposite, pinnate leaves, to 18in (45cm) long, each consisting of 9–19 oblong to ovate, leathery, deep green leaflets. Terminal racemes or panicles of asymmetrical, bell-shaped, yellow-rimmed, scarlet to blood-red flowers, 2–4in (5–10cm) long, yellowish green inside, are produced mainly in spring and summer; they have a crepe-like texture, musky scent, and abundant nectar. Large, woody, canoe-shaped seed pods release papery-winged seeds. ↕60–80ft (18–25m), ↔30–60ft (10–18m). Tropical Africa. ❀ (min. 55–59°F/13–15°C)

▷ ***Specularia speculum-veneris*** see *Legousia speculum-veneris*

Spathodea campanulata (inset: flower detail)

SPHAERALCEA

syn. ILIAMNA

False mallow, Globe mallow

MALVACEAE

Genus of about 60 species of downy annuals, perennials, and deciduous or evergreen subshrubs and shrubs that are found in well-drained sites (many on mountain slopes, in wasteland, or in scrub) in warmer regions of North America, with a few in South America and southern Africa. The upright or decumbent stems bear spirally arranged, linear-lance-shaped to rounded, simple or lobed to palmate, toothed leaves. Saucer- or cup-shaped, mallow-like flowers, the stamens joined into a column around the styles, are produced either singly or in racemes or panicles from summer to autumn. These plants are suitable for a gravel garden, raised bed, or stony bank if there is protection from excessive winter moisture; may also be grown in a cold greenhouse.

• **CULTIVATION** Outdoors, grow in moderately fertile, sharply drained, gravelly soil in full sun; in colder areas, plant in a warm, dry, sheltered position, and protect from winter moisture. Under glass, grow in soil-based potting mix with added grit, in full light. When in growth, water moderately and apply a balanced liquid fertilizer monthly. Water sparingly in winter. Repot annually in early spring.

• **PROPAGATION** Sow seed at 55°F (13°C) in spring. Divide perennials as growth begins in spring. Root basal or softwood cuttings with bottom heat in spring or early summer.

• **PESTS AND DISEASES** Hollyhock rust may be a problem.

S. munroana ▣ Gray-hairy perennial with upright, unbranched stems and ovate to almost diamond-shaped, shallowly 3- to 5-lobed or scalloped, mid-green leaves, to 2½in (6cm) long.

Sphaeralcea munroana

Saucer-shaped, reddish orange flowers, 1in (2.5cm) across, are produced in many-flowered, axillary and terminal panicles, from midsummer to early autumn. ↕to 32in (80cm), ↔18in (45cm). W. North America. ❀ (min. 41°F/5°C)

SPIGELIA

Pink root, Worm grass

LOGANIACEAE

Genus of about 50 species of annuals or perennials occurring in moist woods and thickets of North and South America. The leaves are opposite, hairless or softly hairy, entire, and ovate. Spigelias are valued for their tubular-funnel-shaped, red, yellow, or purple flowers, borne in cymes. Grow *S. marilandica* in a bed, border, or woodland garden.

• **CULTIVATION** Grow in any fertile, well-drained soil in partial shade, or in full sun if soil remains moist.

• **PROPAGATION** Sow seed *in situ* as soon as ripe; divide clumps in spring.

• **PESTS AND DISEASES** Powdery mildew and leaf spots occur occasionally.

S. marilandica ▣ (Indian pink, Maryland pinkroot). Clump-forming perennial with stalkless, ovate-lance-shaped, mid-green leaves, to 4in (10cm) long. Bears one-sided cymes of tubular-funnel-shaped red flowers, to 2in (5cm) long, with yellow insides, from spring to summer. ↕24in (60cm), ↔18in (45cm). S.E. US. Zone 7b.

▷ ***Spiloxene capensis*** see *Hypoxis capensis*

Spigelia marilandica

SPINACIA

CHENOPODIACEAE

Genus of 4 species of fast-growing, bushy annuals, grown for its highly nutritious, smooth or crinkled, round or pointed leaves. Leaves are highly variable in size and can be eaten raw in salads or cooked until just tender. Grows best in a cool climate or as an early spring vegetable.

• **CULTIVATION** Vegetable garden plant, grows best in a wide range of soils, in full sun and with adequate water.

• **PROPAGATION** Sow seed *in situ*, every 10 days to insure continuous crop.

• **PESTS AND DISEASES** Cut worms, downy mildew, cucumber mosaic virus.

S. oleracea (Spinach). Leaves are simple, 2–12in (5–30cm) long. Flowers are not evident. Spinach will not germinate in temperatures above 86°F (30°C). Sow seeds in rows, 1in (2.5cm) apart. Thin early to about 3in (7cm). Harvest leaves 5–10 weeks after sowing, when plants are about 2in (5cm) tall, or cut rosette heads when about 1in (2.5cm) above ground and let them resprout. Harvest plants before they bolt to seed. ↕6–8in (15–20cm), ↔1–2ft (30–61cm). SW Asia. Zone 6.

SPIRAEA

Spirea

ROSACEAE

Genus of about 80 species of deciduous or semi-evergreen shrubs found in rocky places, thickets, woodland, at woodland margins, and on riverbanks, widely distributed in N. temperate regions of Europe, Asia, and North America, including Mexico. The alternate leaves are entire, toothed, or lobed, and are decorative in some species. Spireas are cultivated mainly for their terminal, umbel-like racemes, panicles, cymes, or corymbs of small, mostly saucer-, cup-, or bowl-shaped, white, yellow, pink, or purple flowers; these are ¼–½in (0.6–1.5cm) across, sometimes slightly larger, and are profusely borne in spring or summer. Grow in a mixed or shrub border. Compact spireas are ideal for a rock garden; use low-growing variants of *S. japonica* as a groundcover; use taller spireas as informal hedging.

• **CULTIVATION** Grow in fertile, moist but well-drained soil in full sun. Pruning group 2 for those flowering on previous year's wood; group 6 for those flowering on current season's wood (*S.* x *billiardii*, many *S. japonica* selections, and *S. douglasii*).

• **PROPAGATION** Take greenwood cuttings in summer. Divide suckering species, such as *S.* x *billiardii* and *S. douglasii*, in late autumn or early spring.

• **PESTS AND DISEASES** Can be affected by dieback, fireblight, powdery mildew, and *Cylindrocladium* leaf spot. Weevils, scale insects, and aphids can occur.

S. aitchisonii see *Sorbaria tomentosa* var. *angustifolia*.
S. albiflora see *S. japonica* var. *albiflora*.
S. arborea see *Sorbaria kirilowii*.
S. aruncus see *Aruncus dioicus*.
S.* x *billiardii (*S. douglasii* x *S. salicifolia*). Upright, thicket-forming, suckering, deciduous shrub with oval to narrowly oblong, toothed, mid- or dark

Spiraea canescens

green leaves, to 4in (10cm) long. Bears cup-shaped, purple-pink flowers in dense, terminal panicles, to 8in (20cm) long, in mid- and late summer. ↕ 3–6ft (1–2m), ↔ to 6ft (2m). Garden origin. Zone 4. **'Triumphans'** has dark green leaves, 2½in (6cm) long; ↕↔ 8ft (2.5m).
S.* x *bumalda see *S. japonica* 'Bumalda'.
S. canescens ■ Upright, deciduous shrub with arching shoots and elliptic to obovate, gray-green leaves, to 1in (2.5cm) long, toothed at the tips. Bowl-shaped, creamy white flowers, in corymbs to 2in (5cm) across, are borne at the tips of short, lateral shoots in mid- and late summer. ↕ 10ft (3m), ↔ 6ft (2m). Himalayas. Zone 7b.
S. cantoniensis ■ Spreading, deciduous or semi-evergreen shrub with arching shoots and lance-shaped, toothed, blue-green leaves, to 2½in (6cm) long. In early summer, short, lateral shoots bear corymbs, to 2in (5cm) across, of bowl-shaped white flowers. ↕ 6ft (2m), ↔ 10ft (3m). Zone 7b. **'Flore Pleno'**, syn. 'Lanceata', has double white flowers.
S. crispifolia see *S. japonica* 'Bullata'.
S. douglasii. Vigorous, suckering, erect, thicket-forming, deciduous shrub with narrowly oblong, dark green leaves, to 4in (10cm) long, toothed at the tips and densely gray-felted beneath. In early and midsummer, bears bowl-shaped, purple-pink flowers in dense, terminal panicles, to 8in (20cm) long. ↕ 8ft (2.5m), ↔ 5ft (1.5m). W. North America. Zone 4. **subsp. *menziesii***, syn. *S. menziesii*, has leaves without felt beneath and bears pink flowers.
S. japonica (Japanese spirea). Clump-forming, deciduous shrub with erect shoots. Ovate to lance-shaped, sharply toothed, dark green leaves, to 5in (13cm) long, are gray-green beneath. In mid- and late summer, bears bowl-shaped, pink or white flowers in terminal corymbs, to 8in (20cm) across. ↕ 6ft (2m), ↔ 5ft (1.5m). China, Japan. Zone 2b. **'Alba'** see var. *albiflora*. **var. *albiflora***, syn. 'Alba', *S. albiflora*, has pale green leaves, and white flowers in corymbs 4in (10cm) across; ↕ 24in (60cm), ↔ 36in (90cm). Zone 5. **'Alpina'** is low-growing and spreading, with light blue-green leaves, ½–1in (1.5–2.5cm) long, and pink flowers in late spring; ↕ 16–30in (40–75cm), ↔ 6ft (2m). **'Anthony Waterer'** ■ has dark pink flowers, and leaves occasionally margined creamy white, bronze-red when young; ↕ to 5ft (1.5m). **'Bullata'**, syn. *S. crispifolia*, is slow-growing and compact, with small, puckered, very dark green leaves, to 1in (2.5cm) long, and deep pink flowers in corymbs 3in (8cm) across; ↕ to 16in (40cm), ↔ to 20in (50cm). Zone 5. **'Bumalda'** syn. *S.* x *bumalda*, has bronze young leaves and dark pink flowers; ↕↔ 3ft (1m). **'Froebelii'** ■ has bronze-red young leaves and large corymbs of deep pink flowers. **'Golden Princess'** ■ has bronze-red, later bright yellow leaves, red in autumn, and bright purplish pink flowers. Zone 5. **'Goldflame'** ■ has bronze-red young leaves, turning bright yellow then mid-green, then orange, red, and yellow in autumn, and dark pink flowers; ↕↔ 30in (75cm). **'Goldmound'** has yellow leaves, aging to yellow-green, and bears pink flowers in late spring and early summer; ↕ 30–42in (75–110cm), ↔ 3–4ft (1–1.2m). **'Limemound'** has lime-green leaves that turn orange-red in autumn. **'Little Princess'** ■ forms a dense mound, with small leaves, 1in (2.5cm) long, and rose-pink flowers in corymbs 1½in (4cm) across; ↕ 20in (50cm), ↔ 3ft (1m). **'Nana'**, syn. 'Nyewoods', forms a dwarf mound, with small leaves, to ½in (1.5cm) long, and dark pink flowers in corymbs 1in (2.5cm) across; ↕ 18in (45cm), ↔ 24in (60cm). **'Nyewoods'** see 'Nana'. **'Shiburi'** see 'Shirobana'. **'Shirobana'**, syn. 'Shiburi', produces both dark pink and white flowers on each plant; ↕↔ 24in (60cm). Zone 5.
S. menziesii see *S. douglasii* subsp. *menziesii*.
S. nipponica. Upright to spreading, deciduous shrub with arching branches and ovate to rounded, dark green leaves, ½–1¼in (1.5–3cm) long, entire or with a few teeth at the tips, bluish green beneath. In midsummer, bowl-shaped white flowers open in terminal corymbs, 1–1½in (2.5–4cm) across. ↕↔ 4–8ft (1.2–2.5m). Japan. Zone 3. **'Halward's Silver'** is erect but compact, and flowers freely; ↕↔ 3ft (1m). **'Snowmound'** ■ syn. var. *tosaensis* of gardens, is fast-growing and spreading; ↔ 3–5ft (1–1.5m). **var. *tosaensis* of gardens** see 'Snowmound'.
S. opulifolius see *Physocarpus opulifolius*.
S. palmata see *Filipendula palmata*.
S. prunifolia, syn. *S. prunifolia* 'Plena' (Bridalwreath). Arching, deciduous shrub with ovate, finely toothed leaves, to 1¾in (4.5cm) long, glossy, bright green above, gray-downy beneath, turning bronze-yellow to red in autumn.

Spiraea japonica 'Froebelii'

Spiraea japonica 'Goldflame'

Spiraea japonica 'Little Princess'

Spiraea cantoniensis

Spiraea japonica 'Anthony Waterer'

Spiraea japonica 'Golden Princess'

Spiraea nipponica 'Snowmound'

S

Spiraea x *vanhouttei*

Double white flowers are produced in stalkless corymbs, to 2½in (6cm) across, on short laterals along the shoots, in mid- and late spring. ‡↔ 6ft (2m). China, Taiwan, Japan. Zone 6.
***S.* 'Snow White'**, syn. *S. trichocarpa* 'Snow White'. Bushy, deciduous shrub with arching shoots and ovate, bright mid-green leaves, to 2in (5cm) long, with a few teeth at the tips. Small, cup-shaped white flowers are borne in dense corymbs, to 2in (5cm) across, on short laterals, in late spring and early summer. ‡↔ 6ft (2m). Zone 2b.
S. sorbifolia see *Sorbaria sorbifolia.*
S. thunbergii. Dense, bushy, deciduous or semi-evergreen shrub with arching branches and slender, lance-shaped, sparsely toothed, light green leaves, to 1½in (4cm) long. In spring and early summer, bears bowl- or saucer-shaped white flowers in stalkless corymbs, to 2in (5cm) across, on short laterals along the shoots. ‡ 5ft (1.5m), ↔ 6ft (2m). China, Japan. Zone 3.
***S. trichocarpa* 'Snow White'** see *S.* 'Snow White'.
***S. trilobata* 'Fairy Queen'.** Dense, compact, deciduous shrub with spreading branches and rounded, 3-lobed, dark green leaves, ½–1in (1.5–2.5cm) long. In spring and early summer, bears profuse, bowl-shaped white flowers in dense corymbs, ¾–1½in (2–4cm) across. ‡↔ 3ft (1m). Zone 3.
S. ulmaria see *Filipendula ulmaria.*
S.* x *vanhouttei ▣ (*S. cantoniensis* x *S. trilobata*) (Van Houtte spirea). Compact, bushy, deciduous shrub with slender, arching shoots. The diamond-shaped to obovate leaves, to 1¾in (4.5cm) long, are scalloped or coarsely toothed, occasionally 3- to 5-lobed at the tips, and dark green above, blue-green beneath. Bowl-shaped white flowers are borne in dense corymbs, to 2in (5cm) across, on short laterals along the shoots, in early summer. ‡ 6ft (2m), ↔ 5ft (1.5m). Garden origin. Zone 3. **'Pink Ice'** is slow-growing, with white-flecked leaves.
S. veitchii. Upright, deciduous shrub with long, arching shoots, red when young, and elliptic to oblong, entire, mid-green leaves, to 2in (5cm) long, glaucous beneath. In early and mid-summer, bears bowl-shaped white flowers in dense corymbs, 2½in (6cm) across, on short laterals along the shoots. ‡ 12ft (4m), ↔ 10ft (3m). W. and C. China. Zone 5.

SPIRANTHES

ORCHIDACEAE

Genus of about 50 species of usually small, evergreen or deciduous, terrestrial or rarely epiphytic orchids from grassland or woodland habitats, often close to water, in temperate and tropical regions, mainly in North America, with a few in Europe and Asia. They have tuberous roots and basal rosettes of papery or fleshy, lance-shaped or ovate to almost rounded leaves. Tiny white flowers are borne in spiral racemes along erect stems. May form large colonies outdoors.
• **CULTIVATION** Cool-growing orchids. Under glass, grow in terrestrial orchid potting mix in bright filtered light. In growth, water freely and apply fertilizer at every third watering. Keep almost dry and frost-free when dormant. Outdoors, plant hardy species, when dormant, in moist but well-drained, fertile, humus-rich, leafy soil in a sheltered site in partial shade. Provide a deep, dry winter mulch where marginally hardy. See also p.46.
• **PROPAGATION** Divide tubers when dormant. Seed propagation is difficult.
• **PESTS AND DISEASES** Susceptible to spider mites and aphids under glass.

S. cernua ▣ (Nodding ladies' tresses). Deciduous, terrestrial orchid producing broadly linear, acute leaves, 2–10in (5–25cm) long. Racemes of almost translucent white flowers, ¼in (6mm) long, with yellow centers, are produced in autumn. ‡ 24in (60cm), ↔ 3in (8cm). E. Canada to Texas and Florida. Zone 4.

Spiranthes cernua

▷ ***Spironema fragrans*** see *Callisia fragrans*

SPOROBOLUS

Dropseed, Rushgrass

POACEAE

Genus of about 100 species of annual and perennial grasses from the central valley grasslands and prairies of W. North America. They are grown for their narrow leaves and cloud-like panicles of flowers. Dropseeds are useful as a groundcover and for erosion control, due to extreme heat and drought tolerance. They are attractive as accents in a perennial border and for use in dried flower arrangements.
• **CULTIVATION** Grow in any well-drained soil in full sun.
• **PROPAGATION** Sow seed *in situ* in spring or autumn; divide established clumps in spring or autumn.
• **PESTS AND DISEASES** Root rot, rust, seed smut, and a variety of leaf spots and blotches can be problems.

S. airoides (Alkali dropseed). Clump-forming perennial grass with linear, slightly sharp-edged, gray-green leaves, 12–24in (30–60cm) long. In mid-summer, produces small pink flowers in panicles 5–10in (13–25cm) long, on stems 24–36in (60–90cm) above the foliage. ‡↔ 24–36in (60–90cm). C. and S.W. US, Mexico. Zone 7b.
S. heterolepsis (Prairie dropseed). Slow-growing, clump-forming perennial grass with linear, scented, emerald-green leaves, 24–36in (60–90cm) long, turning golden yellow in autumn. In late summer, bears airy panicles, 5–10in (13–25cm) long, of small, drooping, fragrant, pale pink flowers, on stems 30–42in (75–110cm) above the foliage. ‡ 18–24in (45–60cm), ↔ 24in (60cm). Canada to Texas. Zone 4.

SPREKELIA

AMARYLLIDACEAE

Genus of a single species of bulbous perennial occurring on rocky slopes in Mexico and Guatemala. It has semi-erect, strap-shaped, basal leaves, and is grown for its large, showy, 6-tepaled red flowers, sometimes marked or striped yellow, borne in spring. Where not hardy, grow in a temperate greenhouse. Elsewhere, grow in a sunny border.

Sprekelia formosissima

• **CULTIVATION** Plant in autumn with the neck and shoulders of the bulb above soil level. Under glass, grow in soil-based potting mix in full light. When in growth, water moderately and apply a half-strength balanced liquid fertilizer every 2 weeks after flowering. Reduce water as foliage fades; keep almost dry when dormant. Repot every 2–3 years. Outdoors, grow in well-drained, moderately fertile soil in full sun. Roots resent disturbance.
• **PROPAGATION** Separate offsets when dormant in early autumn.
• **PESTS AND DISEASES** Infrequent.

S. formosissima ▣ (Aztec lily, Jacobean lily). Bulbous perennial with strap-shaped, mid-green leaves, to 20in (50cm) long. In spring, produces solitary, bright scarlet to deep crimson flowers, 5in (13cm) across, each with a broad, erect upper tepal, 2 narrower, horizontal tepals, and 3 narrow, pendent tepals. ‡ 6–14in (15–35cm), PD6in (15cm). Mexico, Guatemala. ❀ (min. 45–50°F/7–10°C)

STACHYS *syn.* BETONICA

Betony, Hedge nettle, Woundwort

LAMIACEAE

Genus of about 300 species of annuals, mostly rhizomatous and stoloniferous perennials, and a few evergreen shrubs, widely distributed in a range of habitats, including mountains, dry, rocky hills, scrub, wasteland, meadows, forest clearings, and streamsides, especially in N. temperate regions. The leaves on the square stems are short-stalked or stalkless, and opposite, and become progressively smaller up the stems; basal leaves are lance-shaped or elliptic to ovate, entire to scalloped or toothed, wrinkled, prominently veined, hairy, and stalked. Many species are aromatic, occasionally unpleasantly so. The tubular, 2-lipped, often hooded, usually white, yellow, pink, red, or purple flowers are borne in racemes or spikes of axillary whorls. Most are attractive to bees and butterflies. Grow taller perennials in a mixed or herbaceous border. *S. byzantina* is ideal as edging or as a groundcover. Low-growing, hairy-leaved species, such as *S. candida*, *S. citrina*, and *S. lavandulifolia*, are suitable for a dry bank, gravel garden, raised bed, or rock garden, but need protection from excessive winter moisture; they are best grown in an alpine house. Grow *S. sylvatica* in a wild garden.

Stachys byzantina

Stachys byzantina 'Big Ears'

• **CULTIVATION** Outdoors, grow in well-drained, moderately fertile soil in full sun; *S. macrantha*, *S. officinalis*, and *S. sylvatica* tolerate partial shade. Grow rock-garden species in sharply drained, gritty soil in a sunny site; protect from excessive winter moisture. In an alpine house, grow in soil-based potting mix with added grit, in full light.
• **PROPAGATION** Sow seed in containers in a cold frame in autumn or spring. Divide or remove rooted sections of perennials in spring as growth begins. Take greenwood cuttings of shrubs and subshrubs in early summer.
• **PESTS AND DISEASES** Prone to powdery mildew and sometimes rust and leaf spot. Slugs and caterpillars can be troublesome.

S. betonica see *S. officinalis.*
S. byzantina ■ syn. *S. lanata*, *S. olympica* (Lambs' ears, Woolly betony). Mat-forming, densely white-woolly perennial with rosettes of entire, oblong-elliptic to lance-shaped, thick, wrinkled, veined, gray-green leaves, to 4in (10cm) long. Erect stems bear interrupted spikes of woolly, pink-purple flowers, ½in (1.5cm) long, from early summer to early autumn. ↕ 18in (45cm), ↔ 24in (60cm). Caucasus to Iran. Zone 3b. **'Big Ears'** ■ has large, grayish white-felted, mid-green leaves, 10in (25cm) long, and purple flowers. **'Cotton Boll'**, syn. 'Sheila McQueen', has leaves 4½in (11cm) long, and clusters of modified flowers forming cotton-like balls along the stems. **'Margery Fish'** has silver leaves and mauve flowers. **'Primrose Heron'** ■ syn. *S.* 'Primrose Heron', has yellowish gray leaves. **'Sheila McQueen'** see 'Cotton Boll'. **'Silver Carpet'** ■ syn. *S.* 'Silver Carpet', is a non-flowering cultivar, and has intensely silvered, grayish white leaves.
S. candida ■ Spreading subshrub producing rounded, white-felted, gray-green leaves, to 1in (2.5cm) long. In summer, bears leafy spikes of hooded white flowers, ½in (1.5cm) or more long, streaked and spotted purple. ↕ 6in (15cm), ↔ 12in (30cm). S. Greece. Zone 6.
S. citrina. Spreading, woody-based perennial producing elliptic to ovate-oblong, minutely round-toothed, gray-hairy, soft, lime-green leaves, to 2in (5cm) long. Short, dense, sometimes

Stachys byzantina 'Primrose Heron'

Stachys byzantina 'Silver Carpet'

Stachys candida

interrupted spikes of sulfur-yellow flowers, ¾–1in (2–2.5cm) long, are borne in summer. ↕ 8in (20cm), ↔ 12in (30cm). Turkey. Zone 6.
S. coccinea. Spreading, softly hairy perennial with entire, ovate-lance-shaped or oblong-triangular, wrinkled, veined, mid-green leaves, to 3in (7cm) long. Upright stems bear slender spikes of narrow scarlet flowers, to ¾in (2cm) long, from midspring to midautumn. ↕ 24in (60cm), ↔ 18in (45cm). Arizona, Texas to Mexico. Zone 7b.
S. grandiflora see *S. macrantha.*
S. lanata see *S. byzantina.*
S. lavandulifolia. Spreading, woody-based perennial with oblong-lance-shaped, toothed, gray-hairy, gray-green leaves, ¾–2½in (2–6cm) long. Bears upright spikes of purple-pink flowers, to ½in (1.5cm) long, in summer. ↕↔ 12in (30cm). Turkey, Iraq. Zone 6.
S. macrantha, syn. *S. grandiflora*, *S. spicata* (Big betony). Erect, hairy perennial with rosettes of broadly ovate, scalloped, wrinkled, veined, dark green leaves, to 3in (7cm) long, heart-shaped at the bases. Dense spikes of hooded, pinkish purple flowers, 1¼in (3cm) long, are produced on erect stems from early summer to early autumn. ↕ 24in (60cm), ↔ 12in (30cm). Caucasus, N.E. Turkey, N.W. Iran. Zone 5. **'Superba'** ■ has slightly deeper pinkish purple flowers.
S. officinalis ■ syn. *Betonica officinalis*, *S. betonica* (Bishop's wort, Wood betony). Erect, almost hairless to densely hairy perennial with rosettes of ovate-oblong to oblong, scalloped, wrinkled, veined, mid-green leaves, to 5in (13cm)

Stachys macrantha 'Superba'

Stachys officinalis

long, heart-shaped at the bases. Upright stems bear dense, oblong spikes of reddish purple, pink, or white flowers, to ½in (1.5cm) long, from early summer to early autumn. ↕ 24in (60cm), ↔ 12in (30cm). Europe. Zone 6. **'Rosea Superba'** has rose-pink flowers and slightly paler green leaves.
S. olympica see *S. byzantina.*
***S.* 'Primrose Heron'** see *S. byzantina* 'Primrose Heron'.
***S.* 'Silver Carpet'** see *S. byzantina* 'Silver Carpet'.
S. spicata see *S. macrantha.*
S. sylvatica (Hedge woundwort). Unpleasant-smelling, creeping, glandular-hairy perennial producing heart- to lance-shaped, toothed, mid-green leaves, 1½–5½in (4–14cm) long. Spikes of usually white-marked, dull reddish purple, occasionally pink or white flowers, to ½in (1.5cm) long, are borne from summer to autumn. ↕ to 3ft (1m), ↔ 16–48in (40–120cm). Europe, W. Asia. Zone 6.

STACHYURUS

STACHYURACEAE

Genus of about 6 species of deciduous or semi-evergreen shrubs, occasionally small trees, found in woodland and thickets in the Himalayas and E. Asia. They are cultivated for their pendent racemes of small, 4-petaled flowers, produced from the leaf axils on bare shoots, before the leaves emerge. The alternate, simple, usually lance-shaped-oblong to broadly ovate, toothed leaves are borne on slender, glossy, red-brown shoots. Suitable for a shrub border, or for growing in a woodland garden or against a wall.
• **CULTIVATION** Grow in light, moist but well-drained, humus-rich, fertile, acidic soil in full sun or partial shade, with shelter from cold, drying winds. Pruning group 1; cut out flowered shoots to the base on mature plants, after flowering.
• **PROPAGATION** Sow seed in containers in a cold frame in autumn. Take heeled, semi-ripe cuttings in summer.
• **PESTS AND DISEASES** Infrequent.

S. chinensis. Spreading, deciduous shrub with arching shoots and ovate, abruptly pointed, dark green leaves, to 5in (13cm) long. Bell-shaped, pale yellow flowers, ⅜in (8mm) across, are borne in racemes to 5in (13cm) long, in late winter and early spring. ↕ 6ft (2m), ↔ 12ft (4m). China. Zone 7b.

S

Stachyurus praecox 'Magpie' (inset: flower detail)

S. praecox. Open, spreading, deciduous shrub with arching, red-purple shoots and ovate, tapered, mid-green leaves, to 7in (18cm) long. Bell-shaped, pale yellow-green flowers, 3/8in (8mm) across, are borne in racemes to 4in (10cm) long, in late winter and early spring. ↕3–12ft (1–4m), ↔ 10ft (3m). Japan. Zone 7b. **'Magpie'** ▣ is less vigorous than the species, with broad, creamy white margins on the leaves; ↕5ft (1.5m), ↔ 6ft (2m).

STANGERIA

STANGERIACEAE

Genus of one species of fern-like cycad found in dry, open woodland and scrub in South Africa. It has a swollen, woody, largely underground stem, from the tip of which it produces rosettes of oval to oblong, pinnate leaves, which lack the leathery texture typical of cycads. Separate male and female, cone-like spikes ("cones") of flowers are borne from the centers of the rosettes, usually in summer. Where not hardy, grow *S. eriopus* in a warm greenhouse or as a houseplant. In warmer climates, grow in a border or as a specimen plant.

Stangeria eriopus

• **CULTIVATION** Under glass, grow in a mix of equal parts loam, grit, coarse bark, and leaf mold, in bright filtered light with high humidity. In growth, water freely and apply a foliar fertilizer monthly. Water sparingly in winter. Pot on or top-dress in spring. Outdoors, grow in fertile, humus-rich, moist but well-drained soil in dappled shade.

• **PROPAGATION** Surface-sow seed on damp sand at 75–86°F (24–30°C) in spring. Pot up as soon as the taproot begins to form.

• **PESTS AND DISEASES** Susceptible to mealybugs and scale insects under glass.

S. eriopus ▣ Fern-like cycad with a cylindrical to turnip-shaped stem or trunk, to 4in (10cm) across, with only the tip above ground. Bears one to several rosettes of long-stalked, pinnate leaves, 3/4–6ft (0.25–2m) long, each with 10–40 lance-shaped to oblong, wavy, often papery, olive- to deep green leaflets, with entire or toothed margins. Cylindrical, felted, gray to yellow-brown flowering cones, to 7in (18cm) long, are produced mainly in summer. ↕ to 3ft (1m) or more, ↔ 3–6ft (1–2m). South Africa (Eastern Cape, KwaZulu/Natal). ❀ (min. 59°F/15°C)

STANHOPEA

ORCHIDACEAE

Genus of about 30 species of evergreen, epiphytic orchids from moist forest, 3,250–7,000ft (1,000–2,000m) high, in Mexico and Central and South America. The conical, ribbed pseudobulbs each bear a single, large, semi-rigid, folded, elliptic to oblong-lance-shaped leaf. Pendent racemes of 2–10 very fragrant, short-lived flowers arise from the bases of the pseudobulbs over a long period.

• **CULTIVATION** Cool- to intermediate-growing orchids. Grow epiphytically on bark, or in epiphytic orchid potting mix in moss-lined, slatted baskets, to allow the pendent racemes to spread freely downward through the potting mix and

Stanhopea tigrina

out the bottom of the basket. Provide high humidity and bright filtered light in summer, and full light in winter. In full growth, water and mist freely, and apply a half-strength balanced liquid fertilizer monthly. Water sparingly when inactive, which may be in early summer. See also p.46.

• **PROPAGATION** Divide when the plants overflow their containers, or remove backbulbs and pot up separately.

• **PESTS AND DISEASES** Pests include spider mites, aphids, whiteflies, and mealybugs. Anthracnose, bacterial brown spot, and a variety of viruses are common.

S. oculata. Epiphytic orchid with one broadly elliptic or broadly lance-shaped leaf, 18in (45cm) long. Pendent racemes of fragrant, waxy, maroon-spotted, light yellow, orange, or white flowers, 5in (13cm) across, are borne in summer or autumn. ↕18in (45cm), ↔ 24in (60cm). S. Mexico to Venezuela, N. Peru. ❀ (min. 52–55°F/11–13°C; max. 86°F/30°C)

S. tigrina ▣ Epiphytic orchid with one broad, oblong leaf, 16in (40cm) long. Pendent racemes of fleshy yellow flowers, 6in (15cm) across, with extensive dark red markings, are borne from summer to autumn. ↕18in (45cm), ↔ 24in (60cm). Mexico. ❀ (min. 52–55°F/11–13°C; max. 86°F/30°C)

S. wardii. Epiphytic orchid with one elliptic leaf, 12–18in (30–45cm) long. In summer, bears pendent racemes of yellow-orange flowers, 5in (13cm) across, lightly spotted purple. ↕18in (45cm), ↔ 24in (60cm). S. Mexico to Venezuela, N. Peru. ❀ (min. 52–55°F/11–13°C; max. 86°F/30°C)

STAPELIA

Carrion flower

ASCLEPIADACEAE

Genus of about 45 species of perennial succulents from low, hilly, often rocky terrain, mainly in tropical and southern Africa. They have generally erect, angular, coarsely toothed, fleshy stems, which branch from the bases to form large clumps. The rudimentary, fleshy leaves are borne at the tips of the stem teeth. Diurnal, star-shaped, often foul-smelling, solitary or clustered flowers, pollinated by flies, are produced in summer, usually from the stem bases. Where temperatures fall below 52°F (11°C), grow in a temperate or warm

Stapelia gigantea

greenhouse. In warm, dry areas, grow in a raised bed or desert garden. Many species originally included in *Stapelia* are now classified under *Orbea*, *Orbeopsis*, *Huernia*, and other genera.

• **CULTIVATION** Under glass, grow in a mix of equal parts soil-based potting mix and grit; top-dress with grit. Provide full light with shade from hot sun, and low humidity. When in growth, water moderately and apply a low-nitrogen fertilizer monthly. Water very sparingly at other times. Outdoors, grow in moderately fertile, gritty, sharply drained soil, in full sun with some midday shade. See also pp.48–49.

• **PROPAGATION** Sow seed at 64–70°F (18–21°C) in spring. Separate rooted sections, or take cuttings of stem sections, from spring to summer.

• **PESTS AND DISEASES** Bacterial and fungal stem rots may occur. Also affected by mealybugs.

S. europaea see *Caralluma europaea*.
S. flavirostris see *S. grandiflora*.
S. gigantea ▣ syn. *S. nobilis*. Very variable, clump-forming succulent with erect, 4-angled, velvety, light green stems, 1¼in (3cm) thick, with small teeth. During summer, produces malodorous, pale ochre-yellow and dark red flowers, 10–14in (25–35cm) across, with silky red hairs, numerous minute, transverse red wrinkles, and petals with white-hairy margins. ↕ to 8in (20cm), ↔ indefinite. E. southern Africa. ❀ (min. 52°F/11°C). **'Schwankart'** has unscented flowers.
S. grandiflora ▣ syn. *S. flavirostris*. Clump-forming succulent with erect,

Stapelia grandiflora

toothed, mid-green stems, ¾–1¼in (2–3cm) thick, with slightly winged angles, and covered with minute, velvety hairs. In summer, bears dull, purplish red flowers, to 9in (23cm) across, with hairy margins and wrinkled lobes, lined with purple and yellow, becoming rich dull purple at the tips. ↕ to 12in (30cm), ↔ indefinite. South Africa (Western Cape, Eastern Cape), Lesotho. ❀ (min. 52°F/11°C)

S. leendertziae. Clump-forming succulent with 4-angled, concavely sided, dull green stems, ¾in (2cm) thick. In summer, bears malodorous, deeply bell-shaped, dark purple flowers, 3in (8cm) across. ↕ 6in (15cm), ↔ 12in (30cm) or more. South Africa (Transvaal). ❀ (min. 40°F/4°C)

S. nobilis see *S. gigantea.*

S. variegata see *Orbea variegata.*

STAPELIANTHUS

ASCLEPIADACEAE

Genus, closely related to *Huernia*, of about 8 species of perennial succulents from hilly lowlands in S. and S.W. Madagascar. They have often prostrate, 4- to 8-angled, fleshy, branching stems, which root down as the plant spreads; the stems sometimes have rudimentary leaves. Diurnal flowers are borne singly or in clusters from leaf axils at the bases of the stems in summer; each flower has a corona forming an erect, 5-lobed head above the staminal column. Where temperatures fall below 50°F (10°C), grow in a temperate or warm greenhouse. In warm, dry climates, use in a desert garden.

• **CULTIVATION** Under glass, grow in shallow pans in a mix of equal parts soil-based potting mix and grit; top-dress with grit. Provide bright filtered light and low humidity. When in growth, water moderately and apply a low-nitrogen fertilizer monthly. Water sparingly at other times. Outdoors, grow in gritty, sharply drained, moderately fertile soil in full sun with some midday shade. See also pp.48–49.

• **PROPAGATION** Sow seed at 64–70°F (18–21°C) in spring. Germination occurs within a few days, and seedlings should be acclimated by being kept lightly shaded for a few months before potting on. Take cuttings of stem sections in spring and summer.

• **PESTS AND DISEASES** Infrequent.

S. hardyi. Mat-forming succulent with prostrate, 4- to 6-angled, grayish green stems, ⅜in (8mm) thick, producing small, rudimentary leaves at the tips. Bell-shaped, fleshy, yellowish pink and purplish brown flowers, ½in (1.5cm) across, with triangular, pointed lobes, densely covered in soft, purplish brown hairs, are produced in summer. ↕ 3in (8cm), ↔ 6in (15cm). Madagascar. ❀ (min. 50°F/10°C)

S. madagascariensis. Semi-erect or creeping succulent with 6- to 8-angled, red-spotted, gray-green stems, to ⅜in (8mm) thick, with tubercles producing small, thin, linear, scale-like leaves. In summer, bears bell-shaped, pale yellow, red-marked flowers, to ¾in (2cm) across; they have triangular, broadly spreading lobes with red papillae on the upper surfaces. ↕ to 2in (5cm), ↔ 5in (13cm). Madagascar. ❀ (min. 50°F/10°C)

STAPELIOPSIS

ASCLEPIADACEAE

Genus of 5 or 6 species of perennial succulents from hilly lowlands of Namibia and South Africa. They have 4-angled, fleshy, minutely hairy, usually toothed, purple-spotted, mid-green stems; in some species, these bear tiny leaves. Diurnal, stalked, urn-shaped flowers develop from the bases of new shoots in summer. Where temperatures fall below 50°F (10°C), grow in a temperate or warm greenhouse. In warm, dry areas, use in a desert garden.

• **CULTIVATION** Under glass, grow in shallow pans in a mix of equal parts soil-based potting mix and grit; top-dress with grit. Provide bright filtered light and low humidity. In the growing season, water moderately and apply a low-nitrogen fertilizer monthly. Water sparingly at other times. Outdoors, grow in moderately fertile, gritty, sharply drained soil in full sun, with midday shade. See also pp.48–49.

• **PROPAGATION** Sow seed at 64–70°F (18–21°C) in spring. Take cuttings of stem sections in spring and summer.

• **PESTS AND DISEASES** Mealybugs may be a problem.

S. pillansii, syn. *Pectinaria pillansii.* Clustering succulent with usually prostrate, 4-angled, dark green stems, ½in (1.5cm) thick, with brown teeth. Red flowers, ¼in (6mm) across, pale red inside, with watery papillae, are borne at ground level in summer. ↕ 3in (8cm), ↔ 7in (18cm). South Africa (Eastern Cape). ❀ (min. 50°F/10°C)

S. urniflora. Clump-forming succulent with prostrate, brown-marked, rounded, 4-angled, minutely papillose, grayish green, partially subterranean stems, ¾in (2cm) thick. The stems have laterally compressed teeth and tiny, scale-like, deciduous leaves, to 1⁄16in (2mm) long. Red flowers, ½in (1.5cm) across, hairless outside, densely hairy and papillose inside, are borne in summer. ↕↔ to 3in (8cm). Namibia. ❀ (min. 50°F/10°C)

STAPHYLEA

Bladdernut

STAPHYLEACEAE

Genus of about 11 species of deciduous shrubs or small trees found in woodland and thickets in N. temperate regions. They are grown for their bell- or cup-shaped, white, cream, or pink flowers, borne in terminal panicles, and for their curious, bladder-like, 2- or 3-lobed fruits. The opposite leaves are pinnate or 3- to 5-palmate. Suitable for a shrub border or woodland garden.

• **CULTIVATION** Grow in any moist but well-drained soil in full sun or partial shade. Pruning group 1 or 2.

• **PROPAGATION** Sow seed in containers in a cold frame in autumn. Root greenwood cuttings in early summer, or semi-ripe cuttings in midsummer.

• **PESTS AND DISEASES** Can be affected by twig blight and leaf spot.

S. colchica. Upright shrub with thick shoots and pinnate, glossy, mid-green leaves, each with 3–5 ovate-oblong leaflets, 1½–3½in (4–9cm) long. In late spring, bears bell-shaped, fragrant white

Staphylea pinnata

flowers, to ¾in (2cm) long, in panicles to 5in (13cm) long; they are followed by greenish white fruit, to 4in (10cm) long. ↕↔ 11ft (4m). Caucasus. Zone 5.

S. holocarpa. Upright shrub or spreading, small tree bearing 3-palmate, blue-green leaves with oblong to lance-shaped leaflets, 1¼–4in (3–10cm) long. Bell-shaped, white to pink flowers, to ½in (1.5cm) long, are borne in nodding panicles, to 4in (10cm) long, in mid- and late spring, before the leaves; they are followed by greenish white fruit, to 2in (5cm) long. ↕ 30ft (10m), ↔ 20ft (6m). China. Zone 7. **'Rosea'** has bronze young leaves and pink flowers.

S. pinnata ▣ (European bladdernut). Upright shrub with thick shoots and pinnate leaves, each composed of 5–7 ovate-oblong leaflets, 2–4in (5–10cm) long, dark green above, slightly glaucous beneath. In late spring and early summer, bears bell-shaped, fragrant, pink-tinged white flowers, ½in (1.5cm) long, in pendent panicles, to 4in (10cm) long; they are followed by greenish white fruit, to 1½in (4cm) long. ↕↔ 15ft (5m). Europe, Turkey, Caucasus. Zone 7.

S. trifolia (American bladdernut). Upright, suckering shrub with smooth, striped bark and pinnate leaves, each consisting of 3 ovate to broadly ovate, sharply pointed, toothed, dark green leaflets, 2–4in (5–10cm) long, softly hairy beneath. In early spring, bears abundant, bell-shaped, greenish white flowers, ½in (1.5cm) long, in pendent panicles, 1½–2in (4–5cm) long, followed by pale green fruit, 1–1½in (2.5–4cm) long. ↕ 10–15ft (3–5m), ↔ 6–8ft (2–2.5m). Ontario and Quebec to Missouri and Georgia. Zone 4.

▷ ***Statice bellidifolia*** see *Limonium bellidifolium*

▷ ***Statice minuta*** see *Limonium minutum*

▷ ***Statice spicata*** see *Psylliostachys spicata*

▷ ***Statice suworowii*** see *Psylliostachys suworowii*

Stauntonia hexaphylla

STAUNTONIA

LARDIZABALACEAE

Genus of up to 16 species of twining, woody, mostly dioecious, evergreen climbers occurring in woodland from Burma to Taiwan and Japan. They are cultivated for their handsome, alternate, palmate leaves; for their bell-shaped flowers, borne in few-flowered, axillary racemes; and for their ellipsoid, edible fruits. Grow over a large shrub or through a tree, or train on wires against a wall. Where not hardy, grow stauntonias in a cool greenhouse.

• **CULTIVATION** Under glass, grow in soil-based potting mix in full light, with shade from hot sun. When in full growth, water freely and apply a balanced liquid fertilizer every 4 weeks. Water sparingly in winter. Outdoors, grow in fertile, well-drained soil, in a warm, sheltered site in full sun or partial shade, with suitable support. Pruning group 11, in early spring.

• **PROPAGATION** Sow seed at 55–61°F (13–16°C) in spring. Take semi-ripe cuttings in summer.

• **PESTS AND DISEASES** Infrequent.

S. hexaphylla ▣ Fast-growing, dioecious, evergreen climber producing 3- to 7-palmate, mid- to dark green leaves, to 6in (15cm) long, with oval to elliptic, leathery leaflets. Racemes of cup-shaped, fragrant, violet-tinged white flowers, ¾in (2cm) across, are borne in spring. If pollinated, females produce ellipsoid, edible purple fruit, 2in (5cm) long. ↕ 30ft (10m) or more. S. Korea, Japan. ❀ (min. 41°F/5°C)

▷ ***Steironema ciliata*** see *Lysimachia ciliata*

STENANTHIUM

LILIACEAE

Genus of about 5 species of bulbous perennials from moist slopes in grassland or open woodland on Sakhalin Island (Russia), and in North America. They have arching, grass-like, mostly basal leaves and erect, slender stems bearing terminal racemes or panicles of small, bell- or star-shaped flowers. Grow in a border or in woodland.

• **CULTIVATION** Plant bulbs 4in (10cm) deep in autumn, in moist but well-drained, moderately fertile, humus-rich, neutral to acidic soil, in a sheltered site

S

in partial shade. They dislike hot, dry conditions.
• **PROPAGATION** Sow seed in containers in a cold frame as soon as ripe.
• **PESTS AND DISEASES** Infrequent.

S. angustifolium see *S. gramineum*.
S. gramineum, syn. *S. angustifolium*. Bulbous perennial with 4 erect, linear, keeled, channeled, bright green, basal leaves, 12–16in (30–40cm) long. In summer, produces star-shaped, fragrant, white or greenish white to purple flowers, to ¾in (2cm) across, in dense, often arching panicles, to 24in (60cm) long. ↕ 3–6ft (1–2m), PD12in (30cm). S.E. US. Zone 7b. **var. *robustum***, syn. *S. robustum*, has broader leaves and white or green flowers; ↕ to 6ft (1.8m).
S. robustum see *S. gramineum* var. *robustum*.

STENOCACTUS

syn. ECHINOFOSSULOCACTUS

CACTACEAE

Genus of about 10 species of variable, solitary, rarely clustering, spherical cacti from shaded lowlands in Mexico. The stems have numerous, frequently undulating ribs, often with tubercles, and well-spaced areoles bearing variable spines, which are curved or straight, sometimes flat and dagger-like. Bell- or funnel-shaped, sometimes striped flowers develop from the crowns in spring, often in clusters. Where not hardy, grow as houseplants or in a temperate greenhouse. In warm, dry climates, use in a desert garden.
• **CULTIVATION** Under glass, grow in standard cactus potting mix in full light with low humidity. When in growth, water moderately and apply a low-nitrogen liquid fertilizer at every third or fourth watering. Keep almost dry at other times. Outdoors, grow in poor, humus-rich, gritty, sharply drained soil in full sun, with some midday shade. See also pp.48–49.
• **PROPAGATION** Sow seed at 70°F (21°C) in early spring.
• **PESTS AND DISEASES** Susceptible to aphids while flowering.

S. coptonogonus ▣ syn. *Echinofossulocactus coptonogonus*. Solitary cactus producing a depressed-spherical to spherical, gray to blue-green stem with 10–14 deeply scalloped, acute ribs. White areoles bear 3–5 flat, upward-curving, pale brownish red spines, fading

Stenocactus coptonogonus

Stenocactus obvallatus

to very pale brown, the upper spines to 1¼in (3cm) long, the lower ones to ½in (1.5cm). In spring, bears clusters of funnel-shaped, white to purple flowers, 1¼in (3cm) long, with a pink-purple or violet midstripe on each petal. ↕ to 4in (10cm), ↔ 6in (15cm). C. Mexico. ❄ (min. 45°F/7°C); tolerates brief periods to 20°F (-7°C).
S. crispatus, syn. *Echinofossulocactus lamellosus*. Solitary or clustering cactus with spherical, dark green to blue-green stems, each of which has 26–60 wavy ribs. White-woolly areoles bear brown-tipped white spines: 6–10 flat, straight radials, to 1¾in (2cm) long; 3 or 4 flattened, slightly curved centrals, 1½in (4cm) long. Solitary, funnel-shaped, carmine-red flowers, 1½in (4cm) long, are produced in spring. ↕ 4in (10cm), ↔ 3in (8cm). C. to S. Mexico. ❄ (min. 45°F/7°C); tolerates brief periods to 20°F (-7°C).
S. multicostatus, syn. *Echinofossulocactus multicostatus*. Solitary or clustering cactus producing flattened-spherical to spherical, pale green stems with 100 or more wavy ribs; each rib bears about 2 white-woolly areoles with 6–18 flat, straight or curved, yellow or gray spines, the upper ones to 3in (8cm) long, the lower to ½in (1.5cm). In spring, bears clusters of funnel-shaped flowers, 1in (2.5cm) long, pinkish purple or white with a purplish violet or faint pink stripe on each petal. ↕↔ 4in (10cm). N.E. Mexico. ❄ (min. 45°F/7°C); tolerates brief periods to 20°F (-7°C).
S. obvallatus ▣ syn. *Echinofossulocactus pentacanthus*, *E. violaciflorus*. Solitary cactus producing a spherical, grayish blue-green stem with 20–50 wavy-margined ribs. White areoles bear 5–12 flat, straight or curved, grayish brown spines, the upper and lateral ones to 2in (5cm) long, the lower to ½in (1.5cm). In spring, bears solitary, funnel-shaped, pale yellow or pale pink flowers, ¾in (2cm) long, with a purplish red stripe on each petal. ↕↔ 3in (8cm). N. and E. central Mexico. ❄ (min. 45°F/7°C); tolerates brief periods to 20°F (-7°C).

STENOCARPUS

PROTEACEAE

Genus of up to 22 species of evergreen shrubs and trees from Malaysia, New Caledonia, and Australia. The trees usually grow in rainforest; the shrubs are found in open scrub, often along water-courses. They have alternate, simple to pinnatifid leaves and, in summer, bear axillary umbels of tubular, cream to red flowers, each with a knob-shaped stigma protruding through a split on the lower side of the tube. Where not hardy, use in a temperate greenhouse as foliage plants (flowering is rare in containers). In warmer areas, use as specimen plants.
• **CULTIVATION** Under glass, grow in soil-based potting mix in full light, shaded from hot sun. During the growing season, water moderately and apply a balanced liquid fertilizer every month. Water sparingly in winter. Outdoors, grow in fertile, humus-rich, moist but well-drained soil in full sun, with some midday shade; shelter from cold, drying winds. Pruning group 1; larger species need restrictive pruning under glass.

Stenocarpus sinuatus

• **PROPAGATION** Sow seed at 59–68°F (15–20°C) as soon as ripe or in spring (seedlings take about 7 years to flower). Root semi-ripe cuttings with bottom heat in summer.
• **PESTS AND DISEASES** Infrequent.

S. sinuatus ▣ (Firewheel tree). Slow-growing, columnar tree with erect branches and branchlets. The leathery, wavy-margined, glossy, deep green leaves, 24in (60cm) long, are sometimes red beneath, and may be oblong-lance-shaped or deeply lobed, with up to 8 lance-shaped lobes, to 4in (10cm) long. Plants over 10ft (3m) tall bear wheel-like umbels of 12–20 scarlet flowers, to 1in (2.5cm) long, in summer. ↕ 70–100ft (20–30m), ↔ 15–50ft (5–15m). Queensland, New South Wales. ❄ (min. 45–50°F/7–10°C); tolerates brief periods to 32°F (0°C).

STENOCEREUS

CACTACEAE

Genus of about 25 species of tree-like or shrubby, sometimes clump-forming cacti found on low hillsides in Arizona, Mexico, Central America, Colombia, Venezuela, and the West Indies. The prominently ribbed stems are often densely spined. The funnel- or bell-shaped, usually nocturnal flowers, produced in spring or summer, are followed by ovoid, fleshy, spiny fruits. Where temperatures fall below 55°F (13°C), grow in a warm greenhouse. In warmer climates, use in a desert garden.
• **CULTIVATION** Under glass, grow in a mix of 3 parts standard cactus potting mix and 1 part leaf mold, in full light with low humidity. From midspring to early autumn, water moderately and apply a low-nitrogen liquid fertilizer monthly. Keep completely dry at other times. Outdoors, grow in poor to moderately fertile, humus-rich, sharply drained, gritty soil in full sun. See also pp.48–49.
• **PROPAGATION** Sow seed at 70°F (21°C) in spring. Take cuttings of stem sections in summer.
• **PESTS AND DISEASES** Prone to scale insects and aphids while flowering.

S. eruca ▣ syn. *Machaerocereus eruca* (Creeping devil). Bushy, creeping cactus rooting all along its prostrate, 10- to 12-ribbed, mid-green stems, 1½–4in (4–10cm) thick, with only the stem tips erect. Brown areoles bear pale yellow

Stenocereus eruca

to white spines (about 20 radials, 1 flattened, dagger-like central). In spring, produces nocturnal, funnel-shaped, white or pale yellow, sometimes pink-tinged flowers, 4–5½in (10–14cm) long. ↕ to 12in (30cm), ↔ indefinite. N.W. Mexico. ❀ (min. 55°F/13°C)

S. marginatus, syn. *Marginatocereus marginatus* (Mexican fencepost). Tree-like cactus with erect, freely branching, 5- to 7-ribbed, dark grayish green stems, to 12in (30cm) thick. Brown-woolly areoles bear brown spines (7–9 radials, 1 or 2 centrals), which fall as the plant matures. Diurnal, bell-shaped white flowers, red outside, 1½–2in (4–5cm) long, are produced at the stem tips in summer. ↕↔ 20ft (6m). C. and S. Mexico. ❀ (min. 55°F/13°C)

S. thurberi, syn. *Lemaireocereus thurberi* (Organpipe cactus). Columnar, clump-forming cactus, with erect, grayish green stems, 4–8in (10–20cm) thick, with 12–19 prominent ribs. Brown areoles bear almost black or brown spines (7–10 radials, 1–3 longer centrals). Mainly nocturnal, funnel-shaped, purple or pink flowers, 2½–3in (6–8cm) long, with red sepals, are borne in summer. ↕ 10–22ft (3–7m), ↔ 3ft (1m). Arizona, Mexico (Baja California). ❀ (min. 55°F/13°C)

> ***Stenolobium stans*** see *Tecoma stans*

STENOMESSON

syn. URCEOLINA

AMARYLLIDACEAE

Genus of about 20 species of bulbous perennials from rocky, upland slopes and meadows in the Andes, South America. They are grown for their umbels of pendent, tubular, brightly colored flowers, borne on solid, sometimes 4-angled stems mainly from spring to summer. The semi-erect, linear to lance-shaped, occasionally channeled or keeled, basal leaves often elongate after flowering. Where not hardy, grow in a temperate greenhouse or conservatory. In warmer areas, grow in a border.

- **CULTIVATION** Plant in autumn with the neck and shoulders of the bulb above soil level. Under glass, grow in soil-based potting mix in full light, shaded from hot sun. Water sparingly until in active growth, then water moderately and apply a balanced liquid fertilizer every 2 weeks. Reduce water as leaves wither, and keep barely moist when dormant. Pot on every 3 years. Outdoors, grow in well-drained, moderately fertile soil in a sheltered site in full sun; provide a winter mulch.
- **PROPAGATION** Sow seed at 61–64°F (16–18°C) in spring. Divide in autumn.
- **PESTS AND DISEASES** Infrequent.

Stenomesson miniatum

S. coccineum. Bulbous perennial with narrow, strap-shaped leaves, to 12in (30cm) long, which appear as the flowers open, and then elongate. Umbels of 4–8 nodding, tubular, bright crimson flowers, 1½in (4cm) long, are produced from spring to summer. ↕ 12in (30cm), PD6in (15cm). Peru. ❀ (min. 45–50°F/7–10°C)

S. incarnatum see *S. variegatum.*

S. miniatum ▣ syn. *Urceolina pendula, U. peruviana.* Bulbous perennial bearing umbels of 3–6 pendent, tubular, bright red or orange flowers, 1¼–1½in (3–4cm) long, with protruding stamens, from spring to summer. Narrow, strap-shaped leaves, to 16in (40cm) long, develop after the flowers. ↕ 12in (30cm), PD6in (15cm). Peru, Bolivia. ❀ (min. 45–50°F/7–10°C)

S. variegatum, syn. *S. incarnatum.* Bulbous perennial with strap-shaped leaves elongating to 24–30in (60–75cm) long after flowering. In spring, usually 4-angled stems bear umbels of up to 6 pendent, tubular, white, yellow, pink, or scarlet flowers, to 5in (13cm) long, sometimes with bands of another color, all with a green mark on each tepal. ↕ 16–24in (40–60cm), PD10in (25cm). Ecuador, Peru, Bolivia. ❀ (min. 45–50°F/7–10°C)

STENOTAPHRUM

POACEAE

Genus of about 6 species of annual and perennial grasses, widespread in tropical and subtropical regions worldwide, on seashores or near the coast, occasionally inland. The creeping or ascending stems root at the nodes, and bear linear to lance-shaped, flat or folded, upright leaves, sheathing at the bases. Greenish brown spikelets are borne in axillary and terminal racemes. *S. secundatum* and *S. secundatum* 'Variegatum' are the most commonly grown, and are valued for their foliage. Where not hardy, treat perennials as annuals, or grow in a cool greenhouse as a groundcover or in hanging baskets. Use as lawn grasses in tropical and subtropical climates; *S. secundatum* 'Variegatum' is also suitable for a border.

- **CULTIVATION** Under glass, grow in soil-based potting mix in full light. When in growth, water freely and apply a balanced liquid fertilizer every 2 weeks. Water sparingly in winter. Container-grown plants thrive and continue to look attractive if given a winter minimum temperature of 54°F (12°C). Outdoors, grow in moist but well-drained, fertile soil in full sun. Where not hardy, plant out only when danger of frost has passed.
- **PROPAGATION** Divide in spring. Take nodal cuttings in spring or summer.
- **PESTS AND DISEASES** Affected by downy mildew, rust, brown patch, leaf blight, and gray leaf spot (blast).

S. secundatum (Buffalo grass, St. Augustine grass). Stoloniferous, prostrate, evergreen, perennial grass. Almost rigid, flattened, branching stems bear linear-oblong, flat to folded, bluish green leaves, to 6in (15cm) long. In late summer and early autumn, produces greenish brown, flattened, spike-like racemes, to 4in (10cm) long. ↕ 6in (15cm), ↔ indefinite. Central America, tropical South America. ❀ (min. 41°F/5°C). **'Variegatum'** has pale green leaves with ivory-white stripes.

STENOTUS

ASTERACEAE

Genus of 18 species of tufted, evergreen subshrubs found in dry, rocky places in W. North America. They produce mainly basal, alternate, leathery, simple, entire leaves and solitary, daisy-like flowerheads. Grow in a rock garden.

- **CULTIVATION** Grow in gritty, poor to moderately fertile, sharply drained soil in full sun.
- **PROPAGATION** Sow seed in containers in a cold frame in spring.
- **PESTS AND DISEASES** Infrequent.

S. acaulis, syn. *Haplopappus acaulis.* Mat-forming subshrub producing erect, slender stems and inversely lance-shaped, tapered, dark green leaves, to 2½in (6cm) long. In summer, bears solitary, daisy-like yellow flowerheads, to 1in (2.5cm) across. ↕ 6in (15cm), ↔ 18in (45cm). W. US. Zone 4.

STEPHANANDRA

ROSACEAE

Genus, related to *Spiraea*, of 4 species of suckering, deciduous shrubs occurring in thickets and at woodland margins in E. Asia. They have attractive leaves, which are alternate, narrowly ovate to ovate, lobed, and sharply toothed, with good autumn color. The tiny, star-shaped, greenish white or yellow-green flowers are produced in terminal, corymb-like panicles during summer. Suitable for a shrub border. Stems root wherver they touch the ground, spreading it well beyond its anticipated borders.

Stephanandra tanakae

- **CULTIVATION** Grow in moist but well-drained, fertile soil in full sun or partial shade. Pruning group 2.
- **PROPAGATION** Separate rooted suckers from autumn to early spring. Take greenwood cuttings in early summer, semi-ripe cuttings in summer, or hardwood cuttings in late autumn.
- **PESTS AND DISEASES** Infrequent.

S. incisa (Cutleaf stephanandra). Thicket-forming shrub with arching shoots, rich brown in winter, and ovate, sharply lobed, toothed, mid-green leaves, to 3in (8cm) long, turning orange-yellow in autumn. Greenish white flowers are produced in panicles, to 3in (8cm) long, in early summer. ↕ to 6ft (2m), ↔ 10ft (3m). Korea, Japan, Taiwan. Zone 5. **'Crispa'** ▣ has deeply lobed, wavy-margined leaves; ↕ 24in (60cm).

S. tanakae ▣ Thicket-forming shrub with arching, orange-brown shoots and broadly ovate, 3- to 5-lobed, sharply toothed, mid-green leaves, to 5in (13cm) long, turning orange and yellow in autumn. In early and midsummer, bears yellow-green flowers in panicles to 4in (10cm) long. ↕↔ 10ft (3m). Japan. Zone 7.

Stephanandra incisa 'Crispa'

S

STEPHANOCEREUS

CACTACEAE

Genus of one species of columnar, rarely branching, ribbed cactus from stony, rocky sites in E. Brazil. The stems, with rings of bristles at the joints, eventually develop woolly cephaliums at the tips; during summer, the tips bear tubular, nocturnal flowers, followed by ovoid, mid-green fruit, 2in (5cm) long, which take many weeks to ripen. Where temperatures fall below 55°F (13°C), grow *S. leucostele* in a warm greenhouse. In warmer areas, use in a desert garden.

• **CULTIVATION** Under glass, grow in standard cactus potting mix with added limestone chips, in full light with low humidity. In spring and summer, water moderately and apply a low-nitrogen liquid fertilizer every 4–5 weeks. Water sparingly at other times. Outdoors, grow in sharply drained, gritty, poor, humus-rich, neutral to alkaline soil in full sun. See also pp.48–49.

• **PROPAGATION** Sow seed at 75°F (24°C) in spring.

• **PESTS AND DISEASES** Infrequent.

S. leucostele. Erect, columnar cactus with 12– to 18-ribbed, blue-green stems, to 4in (10cm) thick. Close-set, white-hairy areoles each bear about 22 spines (20 white to yellow radials, 1 or 2 longer yellow centrals). In summer, the densely wooly cephalium produces white flowers, to 3in (7cm) long, with scaly yellow tubes. ↕ to 10ft (3m), ↔ 18in (45cm). E. Brazil. ❀ (min. 55°F/13°C)

STEPHANOTIS

ASCLEPIADACEAE

Genus of 5–15 species of evergreen, woody-stemmed climbers from tropical woodland in Africa, Madagascar, and Asia. They are grown for their strongly perfumed, waxy, tubular, usually white flowers, each with 5 spreading lobes, borne in short-stalked, axillary cymes. Leaves are opposite, ovate to elliptic, and leathery. Where temperatures fall below 59°F (15°C), grow in a warm greenhouse or as houseplants. In warmer areas, train over a pergola or on a wall.

• **CULTIVATION** Under glass, grow in soilless or soil-based potting mix in full light, with shade from hot sun. In the growing season, water and mist freely, and apply a balanced liquid fertilizer every 2 or 3 weeks. Water sparingly in winter. Outdoors, grow in moderately fertile, humus-rich, moist but well-drained soil in full sun, with some midday shade. Support climbing stems. Pruning group 11, in late winter or early spring.

• **PROPAGATION** Sow seed at 64–70°F (18–21°C) in spring. Root semi-ripe cuttings with bottom heat in summer.

• **PESTS AND DISEASES** Scale insects, mealybugs, and virus diseases may be problems.

S. floribunda ▣ syn. *S. jasminoides* (Floradora, Madagascar jasmine). Sparsely branched, twining climber with oval to broadly elliptic, thick, glossy, mid- to deep green leaves, to 4in (10cm) or more long. From spring to autumn, bears cymes of 3–6 fragrant, waxy white flowers, 1½–2½in (4–6cm) long. ↕ 10–20ft (3–6m) or more. Madagascar. ❀ (min. 59°F/15°C)

S. jasminoides see *S. floribunda.*

▷ ***Sterculia acerifolia*** see *Brachychiton acerifolius*

▷ ***Sterculia diversifolia*** see *Brachychiton populneus*

▷ ***Sterculia platanifolia*** see *Firmiana simplex*

Stephanotis floribunda

STERNBERGIA

Autumn daffodil

AMARYLLIDACEAE

Genus of about 8 species of bulbous perennials found on stony hillsides, in fields, and in sparse scrub or pine woodland from S. Europe and Turkey to C. Asia. They are cultivated for their crocus-like, mainly solitary, funnel- or goblet-shaped, occasionally narrow-tepaled and star-like, usually bright yellow flowers, borne on leafless stems. The erect, basal leaves are linear or strap-shaped to narrowly lance-shaped. Grow in a sunny rock garden. Where not hardy, grow all species except *S. lutea* and *S. sicula* in an alpine house or bulb frame; most sternbergias are intolerant of winter moisture.

• **CULTIVATION** Plant bulbs 6in (15cm) deep in late summer; plant *S. candida* and *S. fischeriana* 8in (20cm) deep. Under glass, grow in equal parts loam, leaf mold, and sharp sand, in full light. Water sparingly in growth, reduce water as leaves wither, and keep completely dry when dormant. Outdoors, grow in sharply drained, moderately fertile soil in full sun. Allow large clumps to form; divide only if flowering is impaired.

• **PROPAGATION** Sow seed at 55–61°F (13–16°C) as soon as ripe. Separate offsets when dormant.

• **PESTS AND DISEASES** Prone to narcissus viruses. May be infested with large and small narcissus bulb flies and nematodes.

S. candida ▣ Bulbous perennial with lance- to strap-shaped, gray-green leaves, 6in (15cm) long, followed in late winter and early spring by cup-, goblet-, or funnel-shaped, fragrant white flowers, 2in (5cm) across. ↕ 4–8in (10–20cm), PD4in (10cm). S.W. Turkey. ❀ (min. 35°F/2°C)

S. clusiana, syn. *S. macrantha.* Bulbous perennial producing funnel-shaped yellow flowers, 3in (7cm) across, in autumn, before the strap-shaped, gray-green leaves, to 12in (30cm) long, develop. ↕ 4in (10cm), PD3in (8cm). Turkey, Israel, Jordan, Iran. Zone 7b.

Sternbergia candida

S. fischeriana. Bulbous perennial with goblet-shaped, pale yellow flowers, 1½in (4cm) across, in winter, after the strap-shaped, glossy, dark gray-green leaves, to 14in (35cm) long. Tends to divide into small, non-flowering bulbs. ↕ 3–6in (8–15cm), PD3in (8cm). Caucasus to India (Kashmir). Zone 7b.

S. lutea ▣ (Winter daffodil). Bulbous perennial producing goblet-shaped, deep yellow flowers, 1½in (4cm) across, in autumn, with the narrowly lance-shaped, deep green leaves, to 12in (30cm) long. ↕ 6in (15cm), PD3in (8cm). Spain to Afghanistan. Zone 7b.

S. macrantha see *S. clusiana.*

S. sicula. Variable, bulbous perennial with very narrow, strap-shaped, dark green leaves, 10in (25cm) long, with central gray stripes; these emerge before or with the star-shaped, deep yellow flowers, ½–1½in (1.5–4cm) across, with rounded or pointed segments, in autumn. ↕ 3in (7cm), PD2in (5cm). Italy (including Sicily), Greece (including Aegean Islands, Crete), W. Turkey. Zone 7.

Sternbergia lutea

STEWARTIA *syn.* STUARTIA

THEACEAE

Genus of 15–20 species of deciduous or evergreen trees and shrubs from woodland in E. Asia and S.E. US. They are grown for their often peeling bark; their simple, usually toothed leaves, which color well in autumn; and their cup-shaped white flowers, borne in the leaf axils. Use as specimens.

• **CULTIVATION** Grow in moist but well-drained, moderately fertile, humus-rich, neutral to acidic soil in full sun or light, dappled shade, with shelter from strong winds. Older plants resent transplanting. Pruning group 1.

• **PROPAGATION** Sow seed in containers in a cold frame in autumn. Take greenwood cuttings in early summer, or semi-ripe cuttings in mid- to late summer. Layer in autumn.

• **PESTS AND DISEASES** Infrequent.

S. koreana see *S. pseudocamellia* Koreana Group.

S. malacodendron (Silky stewartia). Broadly columnar, deciduous tree or upright, bushy shrub with ovate, finely toothed, dark green leaves, to 4in (10cm) long, downy beneath. Rose-like white flowers, 4in (10cm) across, cup-shaped at first, with purple stamens and often purple streaks on the petals, are borne singly along the shoots in midsummer. ↕ 22ft (7m), ↔ 10ft (3m). S.E. US. Zone 7b.

S. monadelpha ▣ (Tall stewartia). Broadly columnar to conical, deciduous tree or shrub with peeling, gray and red-brown bark. Ovate, elliptic, or lance-shaped, toothed, glossy, dark green leaves, to 4in (10cm) long, turn orange and red in autumn. In midsummer, cup-shaped white flowers, 1½in (4cm) across, with creamy filaments and violet anthers, are borne singly or in pairs along the shoots. ↕ to 80ft (25m), ↔ 25ft (8m). Korea, S. Japan. Zone 7.

S. ovata (Mountain stewartia). Broadly upright, bushy, deciduous shrub bearing ovate to lance-shaped, toothed or entire dark green leaves, to 6in (15cm) long, red-tinged when young, downy beneath, turning orange and red in autumn. Rose-like, cup-shaped white flowers, to 4in (10cm) across, with creamy yellow or rose-pink stamens, are produced singly along the shoots in mid- and late summer. ↕ 20ft (6m), ↔ 12ft (4m). S.E. US. Zone 6.

Stewartia monadelpha

S

Stewartia pseudocamellia

S. pseudocamellia ▣ (Japanese stewartia). Broadly columnar, deciduous tree with peeling, pink to red-brown and gray bark. Ovate to elliptic, finely toothed, dark green leaves, to 4in (10cm) long, turn yellow to orange and red in autumn. Rose-like, cup-shaped white flowers, 2½in (6cm) across, with creamy yellow stamens, are borne singly or in pairs along the shoots in midsummer. ↕70ft (20m), ↔ 25ft (8m). Japan. Zone 5b. **Koreana Group**, syn. *S. koreana*, *S. pseudocamellia* var. *koreana*, has flowers that open more widely, to 3in (7cm) across; Korea.
S. sinensis. Broadly conical, deciduous tree with peeling, red-brown bark and ovate or elliptic, toothed, dark green leaves, to 4in (10cm) long, turning brilliant red in autumn. Rose-like, cup-shaped, fragrant white flowers, 2in (5cm) across, are borne singly along the shoots in midsummer. ↕70ft (20m), ↔ 22ft (7m). C. and E. China. Zone 7.

STIGMAPHYLLON

MALPIGHIACEAE

Genus of about 110 species of evergreen, woody-stemmed climbers, shrubs, and perennials occurring in tropical woodland in Central and South America and the Caribbean, with one species from West Africa. They have simple or lobed, sometimes toothed leaves, borne in opposite pairs or nearly alternately. From spring to autumn, wide open, 5-petaled flowers are produced in short, dense, corymb-like racemes. Where not hardy, grow in a temperate greenhouse. In warmer climates, grow over a pergola or arch, or allow to cascade from a tree.

Stigmaphyllon ciliatum

• **CULTIVATION** Under glass, grow in soilless or soil-based potting mix in full light, shaded from hot sun. In growth, water freely and apply a balanced liquid fertilizer every 4 weeks. Water sparingly in winter. Outdoors, grow in fertile, moist soil in full sun with some shade. Support climbing stems. Pruning group 11, in late winter.
• **PROPAGATION** Root semi-ripe cuttings with bottom heat in summer. Layer in autumn or spring.
• **PESTS AND DISEASES** Infrequent.

S. ciliatum ▣ Twining, evergreen climber with slender, branched stems and broadly ovate, hairy-margined, light green leaves, 1½–4in (4–10cm) long, each with 2 ear-shaped lobes at the bases. Axillary, corymb-like racemes of 3–7 saucer-shaped, rich bright yellow flowers, 1¼–1½in (3–4cm) across, are produced in autumn; each flower has 1 small and 4 large, rounded, clawed, fringed petals. ↕15–25ft (5–8m). Belize to Uruguay. ❀ (min. 45–50°F/7–10°C)

STIPA *syn.* ACHNATHERUM

Feather grass, Needle grass, Spear grass

POACEAE

Genus of about 300 species of bristly, tufted, evergreen or deciduous, perennial (rarely annual) grasses from open woodland and stony slopes in temperate and warm-temperate regions worldwide. They have linear, pleated, inrolled, occasionally flat leaves, and bear narrow panicles of flattened spikelets, often with long, feathery or bristly awns, from early summer to autumn. They are grown for their habit, and also for their attractive inflorescences, which may be dried and dyed for use in flower arrangements. Use in a mixed or shrub border.
• **CULTIVATION** Grow in moderately fertile, medium to light, well-drained soil in full sun; *S. arundinacea* tolerates heavier soils and partial shade. Cut back deciduous species in early winter; remove dead leaves on evergreens in early spring.

Stipa calamagrostis

• **PROPAGATION** Sow seed in containers in a cold frame in spring. Divide from midspring to early summer.
• **PESTS AND DISEASES** Damping off, rust, smut, brown patch, brown stripe, and eye spot can occur.

S. arundinacea ▣ (Pheasant's tail grass). Loosely tufted, rhizomatous, evergreen perennial producing arching, linear, flat or inrolled, leathery, dark green leaves, to 12in (30cm) long, streaked orange-brown in summer, and turning orange-brown all over in winter. From midsummer to early autumn, bears pendent panicles, to 30in (75cm) long, of purplish green spikelets. ↕3ft (1m), ↔ 4ft (1.2m). New Zealand. Zone 8.
S. calamagrostis ▣ syn. *S. lasiogrostis.* Densely tufted, deciduous perennial with mounds of arching, linear, inrolled, blue-green leaves, to 12in (30cm) long. In summer, bears silvery, purple-tinted to buff spikelets in nodding, feathery, lax panicles, to 32in (80cm) long. ↕3ft (1m), ↔ 4ft (1.2m). S. Europe. Zone 7.
S. gigantea ▣ (Giant feather grass, Golden oats). Densely tufted, evergreen or semi-evergreen perennial forming lax

Stipa gigantea

clumps of linear, inrolled, mid-green leaves, to 28in (70cm) long. Bristled, silvery, purplish green spikelets, turning gold when ripe, are borne in long-stemmed, oat-like panicles, to 20in (50cm) long, in summer. ↕to 8ft (2.5m), ↔ 4ft (1.2m). Spain, Portugal. Zone 8.
S. lasiogrostis see *S. calamagrostis.*
S. splendens. Densely tufted, deciduous perennial forming large mounds of arching, linear, pleated, dark green leaves, to 20in (50cm) long. Purple-tinted white spikelets, in large, loose panicles, to 20in (50cm) long, are borne above the foliage in early and midsummer. ↕to 8ft (2.5m), ↔ 4ft (1.2m). C. Asia, Russia, Chile. Zone 7b.
S. tenuissima ▣ Densely tufted, deciduous perennial with erect, narrowly linear to filament-like, tightly inrolled, bright green leaves, 12in (30cm) or more long. Throughout summer, bears a profusion of narrow, nodding, softly feathery panicles, to 12in (30cm) long, greenish white at first, becoming buff. The whole plant billows in the slightest breeze. ↕24in (60cm), ↔ 12in (30cm). Texas, New Mexico, Mexico, Argentina. Zone 7.

Stipa arundinacea

Stipa tenuissima

Stokesia laevis

Stomatium agninum var. *integrifolium*

STOKESIA

Stokes' aster

ASTERACEAE

Genus of one species of erect perennial from conifer woods on moist, acidic soil in S.E. US. The evergreen, simple, smooth leaves are entire, sometimes with spines toward the bases, and are borne in basal rosettes. The long-lasting, colorful, terminal, cornflower-like flowerheads are solitary or produced in few- to many-flowered corymbs; they are good for cutting. Grow in a warm position in a herbaceous border.

• **CULTIVATION** Grow in light, fertile, moist but well-drained, acidic soil in full sun. Liable to rot in damp, heavy soils. Provide twiggy support. Deadhead to prolong flowering.

• **PROPAGATION** Sow seed in containers in a cold frame in autumn. Divide in spring, or take root cuttings in late winter or early spring.

• **PESTS AND DISEASES** Leaf spot and caterpillars can be problems.

S. laevis ▣ Rosette-forming, evergreen perennial with elliptic to lance-shaped, mid-green basal leaves, to 8in (20cm) long, slightly spiny near the bases, and with conspicuous, pale greenish white midribs. From midsummer to early autumn, upright stems, with smaller, stalkless leaves, bear solitary, terminal, cornflower-like flowerheads, to 4in (10cm) across; these have spreading, fringed ray florets in purplish blue, pink, or white, and disk florets in paler or darker shades of the same colors. ↕ to 24in (60cm), ↔ 18in (45cm). S.E. US. Zone 5. **'Blue Danube'** has very large, mid-blue flowerheads; ↕ 12–16in (30–40cm). **'Blue Star'** has large, light blue flowerheads with whitish blue disk florets. **'Silver Moon'** has silvery white flowerheads.

STOMATIUM

AIZOACEAE

Genus of about 40 species of mainly mat-forming, perennial succulents from semi-desert areas of Botswana and South Africa. They have very short stems and unequal pairs of angular or rounded, often keeled, rough, fleshy leaves, sometimes with marginal teeth and white or transparent dots. Solitary, daisy-like, scented flowers are borne in the middle of the stems in summer; they often open in late afternoon and stay open all night. Where not hardy, grow in a temperate greenhouse. In warm, dry areas, use in a desert garden or raised bed.

• **CULTIVATION** Under glass, grow in standard cactus potting mix in full light. From spring to summer, apply a low-nitrogen fertilizer monthly and water moderately. Water very sparingly at other times. Outdoors, grow in sandy, poor, humus-rich, sharply drained soil in full sun. See also pp.48–49.

• **PROPAGATION** Sow seed at 66–75°F (19–24°C), or take cuttings of stem sections, from spring to summer.

• **PESTS AND DISEASES** Susceptible to aphids while flowering.

S. agninum (Lamb's tongue). Clustering succulent with pairs of 3-angled to semi-cylindrical, oblong, obtuse, very convex and keeled, dull gray-green leaves, 1½–2in (4–5cm) long, roughened by green papillae, and sometimes with 3–5 short, marginal teeth. In summer, bears pale yellow flowers, ¾–1in (2–2.5cm) across, that open in late afternoon or early evening. ↕ 2in (5cm), ↔ 18in (45cm). South Africa (Western Cape). ❄ (min. 45°F/7°C). **var. *integrifolium*** ▣ has smooth leaves.
S. patulum. Clustering succulent with crowded pairs of 3-angled to semi-cylindrical, pale grayish green leaves, ¾in (2cm) long, with rough white dots, and with 2–9 pointed tubercles on the upper surfaces. Produces pale yellow flowers, ¾in (2cm) across,which open in the evening in summer. ↕ 1¼in (3cm), ↔ 18in (45cm). South Africa. ❄ (min. 45°F/7°C)

▷ ***Strangweja spicata*** see *Bellevalia hyacinthoides*
▷ ***Stranvaesia*** see *Photinia*

STRATIOTES

HYDROCHARITACEAE

Genus of one species of vigorous, dioecious, submerged aquatic perennial found in still and slow-moving water in Eurasia. It has rosettes of narrow, prickly, saw-toothed, submerged leaves, which rise to the surface at flowering time. An attractive foliage plant for a sunny pool, it acts to some extent as a filter and oxygenator, but must be kept in check.

• **CULTIVATION** In summer, scatter new plants into a pool of slightly alkaline water over 12in (30cm) deep. Remove runners as necessary to control spread.

• **PROPAGATION** Detach winter buds or young plantlets in spring.

• **PESTS AND DISEASES** Infrequent.

S. aloides (Water soldier). Aquatic perennial with short runners producing stalkless rosettes of linear to lance-shaped, sharp-pointed, toothed, deep olive-green leaves, to 20in (50cm) long. In midsummer, bears cup-shaped, white, sometimes pink-tinged flowers, 1¼in (3cm) across, from 2-leaved bracts: the males in pairs or threes, the females solitary. ↔ indefinite. Eurasia. Zone 6.

STRELITZIA

Bird of paradise

STRELITZIACEAE

Genus of about 5 species of clump-forming, evergreen perennials found in habitats ranging from riverbanks to open glades in the bush of South Africa. They have large, long-stalked, mostly oblong to lance-shaped leaves with woody bases forming a "trunk" that may reach 30ft (10m) tall. Their exotic inflorescences, produced intermittently from the leaf axils, consist of usually horizontal, waxy, stiff, boat-shaped spathes, from the top of which crest-like flowers arise sequentially, often in contrasting colors; they are very long-lasting when cut. Where not hardy, grow in a warm greenhouse; move outdoors in summer. In warmer areas, grow as specimen plants.

• **CULTIVATION** Under glass, grow in large containers or in a greenhouse border in soil-based potting mix. Provide full light with shade from hot sun, and ventilate freely when temperatures exceed 68°F (20°C). In the growing season, water freely and apply a balanced liquid fertilizer monthly. Water sparingly in winter. Top-dress annually and repot every second year. Outdoors, grow in fertile, moist but well-drained soil in full sun or partial shade, with shelter from strong winds.

Strelitzia nicolai

Strelitzia reginae

• **PROPAGATION** Sow seed at 64–70°F (18–21°C), or divide rooted suckers, in spring. Seed-raised plants may take 3 o more years to flower.

• **PESTS AND DISEASES** Prone to fungal and bacterial spot, and scale insects.

S. alba. Clump-forming perennial wit oblong to lance-shaped leaf blades, 6ft (2m) long, on leaf stalks 3ft (1m) long. Bears purple-glaucous spathes, 10–12ir (25–30cm) long, with white flowers, 8i (20cm) long, usually in spring. ↕ to 30f (10m), ↔ to 10ft (3m). South Africa (Western Cape, Northern Cape, Easter Cape). ❄ (min. 50°F/10°C)
S. juncea, syn. *S. reginae* var. *juncea.* Clump-forming perennial with rush-lik leaves, 20in (50cm) long, without leaf blades. From winter to spring, produce green spathes, 5in (13cm) long, and flowers, 1¼–1½in (3–4cm) long, with orange calyces and blue corollas. ↕ to 5f (1.5m), ↔ 3ft (1m). South Africa (Eastern Cape). ❄ (min. 50°F/10°C)
S. nicolai ▣ (Tree bird of paradise). Clump-forming perennial with oblong leaf blades, 5ft (1.5m) long, rounded o heart-shaped at the bases, on leaf stalks 6ft (2m) long. In spring, produces 3–5 brownish red spathes, 16–18in (40–45cm) long, and white flowers, 8i (20cm) long, with light purplish blue corollas. Needs ample space. ↕ to 30ft (10m), ↔ to 15ft (5m). South Africa (Northern Cape, Eastern Cape, KwaZulu/Natal). ❄ (min. 50°F/10°C)
S. reginae ▣ (Bird of paradise, Crane flower). Clump-forming perennial with oblong-lance-shaped leaf blades, to 20in (50cm) long, with round or tapered bases, on stalks to 3ft (1m) long. From winter to spring, bears purple- and orange-flushed green spathes, 5in (13cm) long, and flowers 4in (10cm) long, with orange or yellow calyces and blue corollas. ↕ to 6ft (2m), ↔ to 3ft (1m). South Africa. ❄ (min. 50°F/10°C). **'Glauca'** produces glaucous, oblong-lance-shaped leaves. **'Humilis'**, syn. 'Pygmaea', is dwarf, forming dense clumps, and has ovate-oblong leaves; it grows well in containers; ↕ 32in (80cm). **var. *juncea*** see *S. juncea.* **'Ovata'** has ovate leaves with heart-shaped bases and short leaf stalks. **'Pygmaea'** see 'Humilis'. **'Rutilans'** has leaves with red or purple midribs and bears bright flowers.

▷ ***Streptanthera elegans*** see *Sparaxis elegans*

STREPTOCARPUS

Cape primrose

GESNERIACEAE

Genus of about 130 species of annuals and perennials, some monocarpic, or rarely subshrubs, often found in rainforest, sometimes as epiphytes, and on damp banks and rocks or in grassland. They occur from tropical to southern Africa, in Madagascar, and in China, with 4 species from S.E. Asia. Linear to rounded, hairy, often mid-green, veined, wrinkled leaves are borne singly or in opposite pairs on erect, fleshy stems (subgenus *Streptocarpella*), or in stemless rosettes (subgenus *Streptocarpus*). Cymes of tubular, often 2-lipped flowers, with 5 spreading lobes, are axillary or borne from the leaf rosettes. Where not hardy, grow in a temperate or warm greenhouse. Use in a humid, shady border in warmer areas.

• **CULTIVATION** Under glass, grow in soilless potting mix in bright filtered light, with shade from hot sun. When in growth, water freely, allowing soil mix to dry out between waterings (overwatering results in basal rot); apply a high-potash fertilizer every 2 weeks. Reduce humidity and keep just moist in winter. Repot annually in spring. Remove faded flowers and stalks to discourage seeding. Outdoors, grow in fertile, leafy, humus-rich, moist but well-drained soil in partial shade.

• **PROPAGATION** Surface-sow seed in late winter or spring, at 64°F (18°C). Divide, or take leaf cuttings, in spring or early summer. Root stem-tip cuttings, 2–3in (5–8cm) long, of bushy and trailing plants in spring, with bottom heat.

• **PESTS AND DISEASES** Can be affected by mealybugs, aphids, and some of the diseases that attack African violets.

S. 'Albatross'. Robust perennial with rosettes of broad, strap-shaped, finely hairy leaves, 10in (25cm) long. Cymes of up to 5 yellow-throated white flowers, 2½in (6cm) across, open from spring to autumn. ↕ 12in (30cm), ↔ 22in (55cm). ❀ (min. 50°F/10°C)

S. caulescens ■ Erect perennial with fleshy, deep brown stems and opposite, elliptic to ovate, softly hairy leaves, 2½in (6cm) long. Cymes of 6–12 violet or white flowers, ½–¾in (1.5–2cm) across, with purple throats, are borne throughout the year. ↕↔ to 24in (60cm). Kenya, Tanzania. ❀ (min. 50°F/10°C)

S. 'Concord Blue'. Erect, bushy perennial producing fleshy stems and opposite, rounded, softly hairy leaves, 1in (2.5cm) long. Cymes of many mid-blue flowers, ¾in (2cm) across, open from spring to autumn. ↕ 12in (30cm), ↔ 20in (50cm). ❀ (min. 50°F/10°C)

S. 'Constant Nymph' ■ Stemless perennial with rosettes of lance-shaped, finely hairy leaves, to 12in (30cm) long. From spring to autumn, produces cymes of up to 5 blue flowers, 2½in (6cm) across, with pale yellow throats and deep violet veins on the 3 lower lobes. ↕ 12in (30cm), ↔ 24in (60cm). ❀ (min. 50°F/10°C)

S. 'Heidi'. Perennial with rosettes of strap-shaped, finely hairy leaves, to 9in (23cm) long. From spring to autumn, bears cymes of up to 5 clear blue flowers, 2½in (6cm) across, with purple markings on the lower 3 lobes. ↕ 10in (25cm), ↔ 18in (45cm). ❀ (min. 50°F/10°C)

S. 'Joanna'. Vigorous perennial producing rosettes of strap-shaped, finely hairy leaves, 14in (35cm) long. From spring to autumn, bears cymes of up to 5 frilled, deep velvet-red flowers, 3in (8cm) across, with darker markings. ↕ 12in (30cm), ↔ 30in (75cm). ❀ (min. 50°F/10°C)

S. 'Kim' ■ Perennial with rosettes of strap-shaped, finely hairy leaves, 6in (15cm) long. From spring to summer, bears cymes of many dark purple flowers, 1½in (4cm) across, with white throats. ↕ 8in (20cm), ↔ 14in (35cm). ❀ (min. 50°F/10°C)

S. 'Lisa' ■ Perennial with rosettes of strap-shaped, finely hairy leaves, 12in (30cm) long. Many cymes of up to 5 white-throated, shell-pink flowers, 2½in (6cm) across, open from spring to autumn. ↕ 14in (35cm), ↔ 26in (65cm). ❀ (min. 50°F/10°C)

S. 'Mighty Mouse'. Rosette-forming perennial producing strap-shaped, finely hairy, mid- to dark green leaves, 8in (20cm) long. From spring to autumn, bears cymes of up to 10 white-throated, light blue flowers, ¾in (2cm) across, with dark purple lines from the throats to the lobes. ↕ 6in (15cm), ↔ 10in (25cm). ❀ (min. 50°F/10°C)

S. 'Nicola' ■ Perennial with erect rosettes of strap-shaped, finely hairy leaves, 8in (20cm) long. From spring to autumn, bears many cymes of up to 5 semi-double, deep pink flowers, 1¼in (3cm) across. ↕ 14in (35cm), ↔ 18in (45cm). ❀ (min. 50°F/10°C)

S. rexii. Perennial with rosettes of strap-shaped, blunt-tipped, finely hairy leaves, to 12in (30cm) long. Violet-tinged white, or violet flowers, 1½–1¾in (4–4.5cm) across, with violet lines on the lower lobes, are produced usually singly or in pairs, or in cymes of up to 6, from spring to autumn. ↕ to 10in (25cm), ↔ to 20in (50cm). South Africa (Western Cape, Eastern Cape, S. KwaZulu/Natal). ❀ (min. 50°F/10°C)

S. saxorum ■ Prostrate, sparsely branched, woody-based perennial producing opposite, elliptic to ovate, finely hairy, thick, gray-green leaves, 1in (2.5cm) long. Axillary, pale lilac, white-throated flowers, 1¼in (3cm) across, are borne singly or in pairs, in spring and early summer. ↕ 6in (15cm), ↔ 24in (60cm). E. Africa. ❀ (min. 50°F/10°C)

S. 'Susie'. Rosette-forming perennial with strap-shaped, finely hairy leaves, to 10in (25cm) long. Cymes of up to 4 yellow-throated, fuchsia-red flowers, 2in (5cm) across, open from spring to autumn. ↕ 10in (25cm), ↔ 18in (45cm). ❀ (min. 50°F/10°C)

Streptocarpus 'Constant Nymph'

Streptocarpus 'Lisa'

Streptocarpus 'Nicola'

Streptocarpus caulescens

Streptocarpus 'Kim'

Streptocarpus saxorum

S

STREPTOSOLEN

SOLANACEAE

Genus of one species of evergreen shrub found in open woodland from Colombia to Peru and Ecuador, grown for its clusters of colorful, salverform flowers. It is loosely scrambling, with alternate, simple leaves. Below 45°F (7°C), grow in a cool or temperate greenhouse; may be grown in pots, in hanging baskets, or as a standard. In warmer areas, grow against a wall or among other shrubs.

• **CULTIVATION** Under glass, grow in soil-based potting mix in full light with shade from hot sun. When in growth, water freely and apply a balanced liquid fertilizer monthly. Water sparingly in winter. Outdoors, grow in fertile, moist but well-drained soil in full sun. Pruning group 8 or 9, in late winter or early spring; group 13 if wall-trained; may need restrictive pruning under glass.

• **PROPAGATION** Root softwood cuttings in early summer, or semi-ripe cuttings in mid- or late summer, both with bottom heat. Layer in late summer.

• **PESTS AND DISEASES** Whiteflies, spider mites, and aphids may be troublesome under glass.

S. jamesonii ▣ (Marmalade bush). Tall, slender-stemmed shrub, semi-scandent unless annually pruned, with ovate to elliptic, finely wrinkled, mid- to deep green leaves, 1–2in (2.5–5cm) long. From late spring to late summer, produces yellow to orange-yellow flowers, 1¼–1½in (3–4cm) long, with slender, twisted tubes and spreading petal lobes, in large, terminal corymbs, to 6in (15cm) across. ↕ 6–10ft (2–3m), ↔ 3–8ft (1–2.5m). Colombia, Ecuador, Peru. ❀ (min. 45°F/7°C)

Streptosolen jamesonii

STROBILANTHES

ACANTHACEAE

Genus of 250 species of evergreen or deciduous perennials or soft-stemmed shrubs from woodland margins in Asia and Madagascar. They are grown for their tubular to funnel-shaped, 2-lipped, often hooded, 5-lobed, blue to purple, white, or rarely yellow flowers, borne in terminal or axillary, usually cone-shaped inflorescences, sometimes loose panicles or spikes. The leaves are opposite, ovate to lance-shaped or elliptic, and entire or toothed, often in unequal pairs. Grow hardy species in a herbaceous border; grow tender species as summer bedding, in a border, or in a warm greenhouse.

• **CULTIVATION** Under glass, grow in soil-based potting mix in full light with shade from hot sun. During the growing season, water freely; apply a balanced liquid fertilizer every 4 weeks. Water moderately in winter. Outdoors, grow in light, fertile, free-draining soil in full sun or partial shade. Pinch to induce bushiness. Where marginally hardy, protect *S. atropurpureus* with a dry winter mulch. Pruning group 9 for shrubby species; they may need restrictive pruning under glass.

• **PROPAGATION** Sow seed at 55–64°F (13–18°C) in spring. Root basal or softwood cuttings in spring or early summer, with bottom heat.

Strobilanthes atropurpureus

• **PESTS AND DISEASES** Sometimes affected by root rot and spider mites.

S. anisophyllus. Small subshrub with unequal pairs of lance-shaped, toothed, dark green leaves, 3½in (9cm) long. Tubular, lavender-blue flowers, 1in (2.5cm) long, with curved corolla tubes, are borne in cone-shaped inflorescences in spring and winter. ↕ 3–6ft (1–2m), ↔ 30in (75cm). Himalayas. ❀ (min. 54°F/12°C)

S. atropurpureus ▣ Erect, branching perennial with long-stalked, ovate, toothed, dark green leaves, 4in (10cm) long. Bears dense spikes of tubular, indigo or purple flowers, 1½in (4cm) long, in summer. ↕ 4ft (1.2m), ↔ 3ft (1m). N. India. Zone 6.

S. dyerianus (Persian shield). Soft-stemmed shrub with unequal pairs of elliptic, toothed, dark green leaves, to 6in (15cm) long, flushed purple with an iridescent silver overlay above, dark purple beneath. Short spikes of funnel-shaped, pale blue flowers, 1¼in (3cm) long, are produced in autumn. ↕ 4ft (1.2m), ↔ 3ft (1m). Burma. ❀ (min. 54°F/12°C)

STROMANTHE

MARANTACEAE

Genus of 13 species of evergreen, rhizomatous herbaceous perennials from forest floors and clearings in Central and South America. They are grown for their foliage and showy flower bracts. Obovate, ovate, elliptic, or lance-shaped to linear-lance-shaped leaves are borne basally and on the slender, often many-branched stems. Cup-shaped, yellow, red, or white flowers, with colorful bracts, are borne in racemes or panicles, often several on a stem, in winter, spring, and summer. Where not hardy, grow in a warm greenhouse. In warmer areas, use in a damp, humid border.

• **CULTIVATION** Under glass, grow in a greenhouse border in soilless or soil-based potting mix in bright filtered light, allowing a free root run. In growth, water freely, maintain high humidity, and apply a low-nitrogen liquid fertilizer every 2 or 3 weeks. Water moderately in winter. Outdoors, grow in moist, fertile soil in full sun or dappled shade.

• **PROPAGATION** Sow seed at 64°F (18°C) in early spring. Divide when dormant or after flowering, minimizing root damage.

• **PESTS AND DISEASES** Affected by mino element toxicity, mealybugs, spider mites, and root rot.

S. jacquinii, syn. *S. lutea.* Rhizomatous perennial with branching stems and oblong-ovate to elliptic, mid-green leaves, 14in (35cm) long. In winter and spring, bears pale yellow flowers, ⅜in (9mm) long, with bright yellow bracts, in panicles 2–3in (5–8cm) across. ↕ 10ft (3m), ↔ 3ft (1m). Panama, Colombia, Venezuela. ❀ (min. 50°F/10°C)

S. lutea see *S. jacquinii.*

S. sanguinea. Erect, rhizomatous perennial. Branching stems bear lance-shaped to linear-lance-shaped, dark olive-green leaves, 20in (50cm) long, rec beneath and 2-ranked at the bases. Bears white-petaled flowers, to ½in (1.5cm) long, with orange-red sepals, among red bracts, in panicles 2–3in (5–8cm) across in winter and spring. ↕ to 5ft (1.5m), ↔ 3ft (1m). Brazil. ❀ (min. 50°F/10°C)

STROMBOCACTUS

CACTACEAE

Genus of one species of cactus from rocky fissures in C. Mexico. It has a mainly flattened-spherical stem, with ribs divided into prominent tubercles, spirally arranged; the areoles produce a few bristles, which fall as the plant matures. It produces solitary, funnel-shaped flowers from the crown in summer, followed by thin-walled, dry fruit containing minute seeds. Where temperatures drop below 50°F (10°C), grow in a warm greenhouse; in warmer climates, use in a desert garden.

• **CULTIVATION** Under glass, grow in standard cactus potting mix, with added limestone chips, in full light and low humidity. Water moderately in spring and summer, applying a balanced liquid fertilizer every 3 or 4 weeks. Keep completely dry at other times. Outdoors, grow in gritty, sharply drained, poor, humus-rich, preferably neutral to slightly alkaline soil in full sun. See also pp.48–49.

• **PROPAGATION** Sow seed at 70°F (21°C) in spring; seedlings may be difficult to establish.

• **PESTS AND DISEASES** Infrequent.

S. disciformis ▣ Solitary, occasionally offsetting, flattened-spherical, grayish green cactus, bearing a few persistent, off-white, dark-tipped spines at the crown and 12–18 ribs closely set with

Strombocactus disciformis

diamond-shaped tubercles. Each tubercle has a central white areole bearing 1–5 bristly white radial spines (there are no centrals). Produces funnel-shaped, white or yellow flowers, with red throats, 1¼in (3cm) across, by day in summer. ↕↔ to 5in (13cm). C. Mexico. ❀ (min. 50°F/10°C)

STRONGYLODON

FABACEAE

Genus of about 20 species of evergreen shrubs or woody-stemmed, twining climbers from tropical woodland in S.E. Asia and the Pacific islands. Alternate, 3-palmate leaves have lance-shaped to rounded leaflets, the terminal one largest. From winter to summer, they bear pendent racemes of pea-like, red, orange, blue, or bluish green flowers with pointed, upturned keel petals. Below 59°F (15°C), grow in a warm greenhouse. In warmer areas, train over an arch or pergola.

• **CULTIVATION** Under glass, grow in soil-based potting mix in full light with shade from hot sun. In growth, water freely; apply a balanced liquid fertilizer every 2 or 3 weeks. Water moderately to sparingly in winter. Outdoors, grow in fertile, humus-rich, neutral to acidic soil in full sun or partial shade. Support climbing stems. Pruning group 11; or 12, after flowering.

• **PROPAGATION** Sow seed at 81–86°F (27–30°C) as soon as ripe. Root semi-ripe stem sections in summer, with bottom heat. Air layer in spring.

• **PESTS AND DISEASES** Scale insects may be troublesome under glass.

Strongylodon macrobotrys

S. macrobotrys ■ (Emerald creeper, Jade vine). Strong-growing, evergreen, twining climber. Leaves, to 6in (15cm) long, with 3 oblong to elliptic leaflets, are pinkish bronze, turning glossy, rich green. From winter to spring, rarely in summer, bears pea-like, luminous, blue-green flowers, 3in (8cm) long, in dense racemes, 16–36in (40–90cm) long. ↕ to 70ft (20m). Philippines. ❀ (min. 59°F/15°C)

▷ ***Stuartia*** see *Stewartia*

STYLIDIUM

STYLIDIACEAE

Genus of about 150 species of annuals, herbaceous perennials, and subshrubs from dry scrub in Australia (one species from New Zealand). They are grown for their glossy, grass-like foliage and their flowers. The usually very narrow leaves, to 20in (50cm) long, are alternate or in basal rosettes. Pink, white, yellow, or purple flowers are borne in racemes, panicles, or corymbs in summer. The flowers are asymmetrical: each has 5 petals, one very small, with a central column combining stamens and style. A trigger action in the stamens aids insect pollination. Where not hardy, grow in a cool to temperate greenhouse. In warmer areas, use in a sunny border.

• **CULTIVATION** Under glass, grow in soilless or soil-based potting mix in full light. When in full growth, water sparingly and apply a balanced liquid fertilizer monthly. Keep almost dry in winter. Outdoors, grow in well-drained, fertile soil in full sun.

• **PROPAGATION** Sow seed at 55–64°F (13–18°C), or divide, in spring.

• **PESTS AND DISEASES** Infrequent.

S. graminifolium (Trigger plant). Tufted perennial with basal rosettes of stiffly erect to arching, linear leaves, to 10in (25cm) long. Produces tiny, pink to magenta flowers in terminal, erect, narrow racemes, to 12in (30cm) long, in summer. ↕ 12in (30cm), ↔ 18in (45cm). Australia. ❀ (min. 45°F/7°C)

STYLOPHORUM

PAPAVERACEAE

Genus of 3 species of herbaceous perennials from woodland in E. Asia and E. North America. The pinnatisect leaves have long stalks in the basal rosettes, and are stalkless on the upright, branching, ridged stems. The flowers are saucer-shaped, poppy-like, and yellow or orange, borne in terminal umbels in spring and summer. They are attractive plants for a woodland garden, a shady border among shrubs, or a large rock garden. They may become weedy.

• **CULTIVATION** Grow in moist, moderately fertile, humus-rich soil in deep or partial shade; will become scorched in direct sun.

Stylophorum diphyllum

• **PROPAGATION** Sow seed in containers in a cold frame in autumn. Divide in spring; may be slow to re-establish, but easily transplants.

• **PESTS AND DISEASES** May be attacked by slugs and snails.

S. diphyllum ■ (Celandine poppy, Flaming poppy). Downy, rosette-forming perennial with deeply incised, hairy, mid-green leaves, 8–12in (20–30cm) long, each with 5–7 oblong-obovate, irregularly scalloped and toothed lobes. Bright golden yellow flowers, to 1in (2.5cm) across, are borne in summer. ↕↔ to 12in (30cm). E. US. Zone 7.

STYPHELIA

EPACRIDACEAE

Genus of 12 species of wiry-stemmed, evergreen shrubs from dry forest and woodland; they occur in Australia, except for one species found in New Guinea. They have small, simple, aromatic, rigidly leathery leaves, arranged alternately or in spirals. Long, slender, tubular flowers, each with 5 reflexed or rolled-back lobes, are borne singly or in small groups from the upper leaf axils in summer. Where not hardy, grow in a cool greenhouse. In milder climates, grow in a shrub border.

• **CULTIVATION** Under glass, grow in acidic potting mix in full light with good ventilation. In the growing season, water moderately and apply a balanced liquid fertilizer monthly. Water sparingly in winter. Outdoors, grow in fertile, humus-rich, neutral to acidic soil in full sun. Pruning group 10, after flowering.

• **PROPAGATION** Sow seed at 43–54°F (6–12°C) as soon as ripe or in spring. Root semi-ripe cuttings in summer, with bottom heat. Layer in spring.

• **PESTS AND DISEASES** Infrequent.

S. colensoi see *Cyathodes colensoi*.
S. triflora (Pink fivecorner). Erect, moderately dense shrub bearing elliptic to oblong-elliptic leaves, ½–1¼in (1.5–3cm) long, with sharp points. In summer, bears tubular, 5-angled, usually pink to red, occasionally cream or pale yellow-green flowers, ¾in (2cm) long, with strongly rolled-back lobes, singly or in twos or threes. ↕ 16–72in (0.4–2m), ↔ 24–36in (60–90cm). S.W. Australia. ❀ (min. 35°F/2°C)

STYRAX

STYRACACEAE

Genus of approximately 100 species of deciduous or evergreen shrubs and small trees found in woodland and thickets in Europe, Asia, and North America, including Mexico. Of graceful habit, they have alternate, short-stalked, variably shaped, entire or toothed leaves. The dainty, nodding, bell-shaped or cup-shaped, fragrant white flowers may be solitary, borne in pendent, terminal or axillary racemes or panicles, or produced in clusters on short branchlets; they appear on the previous year's wood in spring or summer. Grow as specimens or in a woodland garden.

• **CULTIVATION** Grow in moist but well-drained, fertile, humus-rich, neutral to acidic soil in full sun or partial shade, with shelter from wind. Pruning group 1.

• **PROPAGATION** Sow seed as soon as ripe; keep at 59°F (15°C) for 3 months, then at 32–41°F (0–5°C) for 3 months. Take greenwood cuttings in summer.

• **PESTS AND DISEASES** Infrequent.

S. americanus (American snowbell). Rounded, deciduous shrub with elliptic to oblong, entire or toothed, dark green leaves, to 3in (8cm) long. Nodding, bell-shaped white flowers, ¾in (2cm) long, with narrow, backward-curving petals, are produced singly or in small clusters of up to 4 from the leaf axils, in early and midsummer. ↕ 10ft (3m), ↔ 8ft (2.5m). S.E. US. Zone 7.
S. grandifolius (Bigleaf snowbell). Spreading, deciduous shrub with slightly rounded to broadly ovate, dark green leaves, 2½–7in (6–18cm) long, gray-woolly beneath. In early summer, bears pendent racemes, 4–8in (10–20cm) long, of 7–12 bell-shaped, fragrant white flowers, ¾–1in (2–2.5cm) across. ↕ 8–12ft (2.5–4m), ↔ 6ft (2m). Virginia to Georgia. Zone 7b.
S. hemsleyanus. Broadly columnar, deciduous tree with oval to obovate, toothed, dark green leaves, to 5in (13cm) long. Bell-shaped white flowers, ½in (1.5cm) long, are borne in terminal racemes or few-branched panicles, to 6in (15cm) long, in early summer. ↕ 25ft (8m), ↔ 15ft (5m). C. China. Zone 7b.
S. japonicus ■ (Japanese snowbell). Graceful, spreading, deciduous tree bearing elliptic-oblong, minutely

Styrax japonicus

Styrax obassia (inset: flower detail)

toothed, mid- to dark green leaves, to 3in (8cm) long, rarely turning yellow or red in autumn. Bell-shaped, white, sometimes pink-tinged flowers, ½in (1.5cm) long, are produced singly or in clusters of 2–6 along the undersides of the branches, in late spring. ↕ 30ft (10m), ↔ 25ft (8m). China, Korea, Japan. Zone 5b. **'Pendula'** bears pendulous branches; ↕↔ 8–12ft (2.5–4m). **'Pink Chimes'** bears a profusion of pink flowers. **'Rosea'** is upright in habit, with pink flowers; ↕ 4ft (1.2m). **'Sohuksan'** bears leaves that are more leathery and darker green.

S. obassia ▣ (Fragrant snowbell). Broadly columnar, deciduous tree bearing elliptic to rounded, dark green leaves, 3–6in (7–15cm) long, distinctly toothed except toward the bases, and blue-gray beneath, turning yellow in autumn. Bell-shaped white flowers, 1in (2.5cm) long, are produced in pendent, terminal racemes, to 8in (20cm) long, in early summer. ↕ 40ft (12m), ↔ 22ft (7m). N. China, Korea, Japan. Zone 6.

S. officinalis ▣ (Storax). Spreading, deciduous shrub or tree with ovate, entire, dark green leaves, gray-white beneath, to 3in (8cm) long. Bell-shaped white flowers, 1in (2.5cm) long, are produced in pendent clusters of 3–8 near the shoot tips, in early summer. ↕ 20ft (6m), ↔ 15ft (5m). S. Europe, S.W. Asia. ❀ (min. 41°F/5°C)

S. wilsonii. Rounded, bushy, deciduous shrub with slender shoots and oval to diamond-shaped, dark green leaves, to 1in (2.5cm) long, with a few teeth near the tips. Broadly bell-shaped white flowers, ½in (1.5cm) across, are borne singly or in clusters of up to 4 along the shoots, in early summer. ↕↔ 8ft (2.5m). W. China. Zone 7b.

Styrax officinalis

S

SUCCISA

DIPSACACEAE

Genus of one species of perennial found in boggy meadows and moorland from Europe to W. Siberia, and in N.W. Africa. Minutely hairy, it bears rosettes of obovate to elliptic basal leaves and erect or decumbent stems with smaller, narrower leaves. Its pincushion-like flowerheads, late- and long-flowering, are similar to those of *Scabiosa.* Grow in a damp wild garden or meadow.

• **CULTIVATION** Grow in poor to moderately fertile, peaty soil that is moist at least through the growing season, in full sun or partial shade.

• **PROPAGATION** Sow seed in containers in a cold frame in autumn or spring. Root basal cuttings in spring.

• **PESTS AND DISEASES** Infrequent.

S. pratensis, syn. *Scabiosa succisa* (Blue buttons, Devil's bit scabious). Rosette-forming, rhizomatous perennial with thin, branched, softly hairy stems and obovate to elliptic, usually entire, mainly basal leaves, to 12in (30cm) long. From midsummer to late autumn, bears solitary, pincushion-like, violet, rarely white or pink flowerheads, to 1in (2.5cm) across. ↕ 6–24in (15–60cm), ↔ to 24in (60cm). Europe, N.W. Africa, Caucasus, Russia (W. Siberia). Zone 5.

▷ ***Sulcorebutia*** see *Rebutia*

SUTERA

SCROPHULARIACEAE

Genus of 130 species of annuals, soft-stemmed perennials, and small, woody, evergreen shrubs, mostly from woodland margins in South Africa. They have opposite, toothed, scalloped, or lobed leaves. From summer to autumn, white, pale mauve, or blue, salverform flowers, with tubular corollas and 5 spreading lobes, are produced singly from the leaf axils or in axillary or terminal cymes, racemes, spikes, or panicles. Where not hardy, use as summer bedding or grow in a temperate greenhouse. In warmer areas, grow as border edging.

• **CULTIVATION** Under glass, grow in soil-based potting mix in full light. When in growth, water freely and apply a balanced liquid fertilizer every 4 weeks. Water sparingly in winter. Outdoors, grow in well-drained, fertile soil in full sun.

• **PROPAGATION** Sow seed at 55–64°F (13–18°C), or divide, in spring. Root stem-tip cuttings in spring or summer, with bottom heat.

• **PESTS AND DISEASES** Prone to aphids.

S. grandiflora (Purple glory plant). Many-branched perennial, woody at the base, with elliptic, deeply scalloped leaves, 1in (2.5cm) long. From summer to autumn, bears racemes, 12in (30cm) long, of salverform, lavender-blue, white-throated flowers, ¾–1¼in (2–3cm) long. ↕ 3ft (1m), ↔ 24in (60cm). South Africa. ❀ (min. 41°F/5°C)

Sutherlandia frutescens

SUTHERLANDIA

FABACEAE

Genus of 5 species of evergreen shrubs found on dry slopes and grassland in southern Africa. They are grown for their showy, pea-like, red to purple flowers, borne in slender, axillary racemes from late spring to summer, and for their bladder-like fruits. Leaves are alternate and pinnate. Where not hardy, grow in a cool greenhouse; in milder areas, plant at the base of a sunny wall.

• **CULTIVATION** Under glass, grow in soil-based potting mix, with added sharp sand, in full light. During growth, water moderately and apply a balanced liquid fertilizer monthly. Water sparingly in winter. Outdoors, grow in well-drained, poor to moderately fertile soil in full sun; dry soils are tolerated. Pruning group 8; may need restrictive pruning under glass, in late winter.

• **PROPAGATION** Sow seed at 59°F (15°C) in spring. Root semi-ripe cuttings in summer, with bottom heat.

• **PESTS AND DISEASES** Earwigs and spider mites may be problems.

S. frutescens ▣ (Balloon pea, Duck plant). Evergreen shrub with slender, erect, twiggy, white-downy stems and pinnate, hairy, gray-green leaves, 2½–4in (6–10cm) long, each composed of 13–21 small, oblong to linear-elliptic leaflets on densely white-downy midribs. From late spring to summer, bears racemes, to 3in (8cm) long, of pea-like, bright red flowers, 1–2in (2.5–5cm) long, followed by inflated, broadly ellipsoid, greenish yellow seed pods, to 2in (5cm) long. ↕ 2–6ft (0.6–2m), ↔ 3–5ft (1–1.5m). Southern Africa. ❀ (min. 45°F/7°C)

SWAINSONA

syn. SWAINSONIA

FABACEAE

Genus of 50 species of annuals, perennials, and subshrubs occurring on stony slopes and grassland and in open woodland in Australia (one species in New Zealand). They have alternate, pinnate leaves and pea-like, usually purple, sometimes white, pink, yellow, orange, or red flowers, with very broad standard petals, borne in erect, axillary racemes from spring to summer. Where not hardy, grow in a cool greenhouse. Elsewhere, use in a border.

Swainsona galegifolia

Syagrus flexuosa

Sycopsis sinensis

• **CULTIVATION** Under glass, grow in soil-based potting mix, with added sharp sand, in full light. In growth, water moderately and apply a low-phosphate fertilizer monthly. Water sparingly in winter. Outdoors, grow in sharply drained, moderately fertile soil in full sun. Pruning group 10, after flowering (or late winter, if under glass).
• **PROPAGATION** Sow pre-soaked seed at 59°F (15°C) in spring. Root semi-ripe cuttings in summer, with bottom heat.
• **PESTS AND DISEASES** Spider mites may be a problem under glass.

S. galegifolia ▣ (Darling pea, Swan flower). Loose, evergreen subshrub with spreading to semi-scandent stems. Pinnate leaves, 2–3in (5–8cm) long, have 11–21 small, oblong, gray- to deep green leaflets. From spring to summer, bears racemes, 3–6in (8–15cm) long, of red, pink, purple, or blue flowers, ½in (1.5cm) long. ↕↔3–6ft (1–2m). Queensland, New South Wales. ❄ (min. 41–45°F/5–7°C). **'Albiflora'** has pure white flowers and light green leaves.

▷ ***Swainsonia*** see *Swainsona*

SYAGRUS syn. ARECASTRUM

ARECACEAE

Genus of 32 species of often low-growing, single- or cluster-stemmed, sometimes stemless palms, from habitats including shrubby vegetation to woodland, often on rocky ridges, in South America. Leaves are pinnate, arranged in spiraling, terminal tufts; the ovoid, 3-petaled flowers appear in spikes or panicles between them. Where not hardy, grow *Syagrus* species in a temperate or warm greenhouse, or as houseplants. In warmer areas, use tall species as lawn specimens, and smaller ones in a shrub border.
• **CULTIVATION** Under glass, grow in soil-based potting mix in bright filtered light. During the growing season, water freely; apply a balanced liquid fertilizer monthly. Water sparingly in winter. Pot on or top-dress in spring. Outdoors, grow in fertile, moist but well-drained soil in full sun or partial shade.
• **PROPAGATION** Sow seed at 81°F (27°C) in spring.
• **PESTS AND DISEASES** Spider mites, scale insects, and mealybugs can be problems on seedlings. Tar spot, butt rot, pink rot, false smut, and several other leaf spots can be severe.

S. flexuosa ▣ (Palmito do campo). Small palm with slender, single or clustered stems bearing pinnate leaves, 3–6ft (1–2m) long, composed of many linear, mid- to deep green leaflets each side. Green flowers appear in panicles, to 18in (45cm) or more long, usually in summer. ↕6–15ft (2–5m), ↔ 6–12ft (2–4m). Brazil. ❄ (min. 55°F/13°C)
S. petraea. Usually stemless palm with pinnate leaves, to 3ft (1m) long, composed of many linear, rich green leaflets in 2 flat ranks. Green flowers are borne in simple or branched spikes, to 12in (30cm) long, usually in summer. ↕ to 3ft (1m), ↔ 6ft (2m) or more. Bolivia, Brazil. ❄ (min. 55°F/13°C)

S. romanzoffiana, syn. *Arecastrum romanzoffianum* (Queen palm). Small to medium-sized palm with a sturdy trunk, sometimes swollen around the middle. Pinnate leaves are 10–15ft (3–5m) long, each with many linear, mid-green leaflets, borne singly or in clusters of 2–5. Orange-glanded green flowers are borne in panicles, to 3ft (1m) long, usually in summer. ↕ to 70ft (20m), ↔ 20–30ft (6–10m). Brazil. ❄ (min. 55°F/13°C)

x SYCOPARROTIA

HAMAMELIDACEAE

Hybrid genus of one species of semi-evergreen shrub with alternate, simple, glossy, dark green leaves and dense clusters of flowers. It is grown for its unusually colored flowers, which appear reddish-brown from a distance. Grow in a shrub border, as a specimen plant on a lawn, or in light woodland.
• **CULTIVATION** Grow in moderately fertile, moist but well-drained, neutral to acidic soil in partial shade. Pruning group 1.
• **PROPAGATION** Take semi-ripe cuttings in summer.
• **PESTS AND DISEASES** Infrequent.

x *S. semidecidua* (*Sycopsis sinensis* x *Parrotia persica*). Spreading shrub with oblong-elliptic, glossy, dark green leaves, to 3in (8cm) long; some may turn yellow in autumn. In spring, brown-woolly flower buds open to reveal dense clusters, 1in (2.5cm) across, of bright red anthers surrounded by small brown bracts. ↕12ft (4m), ↔ 20ft (6m). Garden origin. Zone 7b.

SYCOPSIS

HAMAMELIDACEAE

Genus of 7 species of evergreen shrubs and trees from woodland in China, the Himalayas, and S.E. Asia. They bear alternate, simple, ovate to oblong, entire or finely toothed leaves and, in spring, racemes or heads of small, petalless, male or bisexual flowers. Only *S. sinensis* is generally cultivated, for its flowers; use in a shrub border or woodland garden.
• **CULTIVATION** Grow in moist but well-drained, moderately fertile, humus-rich, neutral to acidic soil in full sun or partial shade, sheltered from wind. Pruning group 1.
• **PROPAGATION** Sow seed as soon as ripe, in acidic seed starting mix in containers in a cold frame. Take semi-ripe cuttings in summer.
• **PESTS AND DISEASES** Infrequent.

S. sinensis ▣ Conical shrub with upright branches and oblong, leathery, dark green leaves, to 4in (10cm) long, pale green beneath. In spring, short, dense clusters, 1in (2.5cm) across, of brown-felted buds open to reveal petalless flowers with red anthers and yellow filaments. ↕20ft (6m), ↔ 12ft (4m). C. China. ❄ (min. 35°F/2°C)

SYMPHORICARPOS

Snowberry

CAPRIFOLIACEAE

Genus of about 17 species of deciduous shrubs found in woodland and thickets and on prairies and plains in W. China and North and Central America. They are grown for their spherical or ovoid, fleshy, white to pink, or dark blue or purple fruits, which last well into winter, and their tiny, bell- or funnel-shaped, nectar-rich, white to pink flowers, which attract bees. The flowers are borne singly or in terminal or axillary clusters, spikes, or dense racemes. The leaves are simple and opposite. Very hardy, and tolerant of poor soil, pollution, and exposed sites. Good for a shrub border, screen, or informal hedge. Use *S.* x *chenaultii* 'Hancock' as a groundcover. Fruits may cause mild stomach upset if ingested; contact with them may irritate skin.
• **CULTIVATION** Grow in any fertile, reasonably well-drained soil in full sun or partial shade. Pruning group 1 or 2.
• **PROPAGATION** Divide in autumn if suckering. Take greenwood cuttings in

Symphoricarpos albus var. *laevigatus*

Symphoricarpos x *doorenbosii* 'White Hedge'

summer, or take hardwood cuttings in late autumn.
• **PESTS AND DISEASES** May be affected by anthracnose and powdery mildew.

S. albus* var. *laevigatus ■ syn. *S. rivularis* (Snowberry). Thicket-forming shrub with upright, arching shoots and oval to oval-oblong, rarely lobed, dark green leaves, to 2in (5cm) long. Tiny, bell-shaped pink flowers are produced in pairs on spike-like racemes in summer, followed by spherical, pure white fruit, ½in (1.5cm) across. ↕↔ 6ft (2m). W. North America. Zone 2.
S.* x *chenaultii (*S. microphyllus* x *S. orbiculatus*). Upright, many-branched shrub with ovate, dark green leaves, to 1in (2.5cm) long, glaucous and densely hairy beneath. In late summer, bears short spikes of small, open bell-shaped, greenish white flowers, followed by spherical, red-stippled white fruit, ¼in (6mm) across. ↕ 6ft (2m), ↔ 4ft (1.2m). Garden origin. Zone 5b. **'Hancock'** is low and spreading in habit, and self-layering to form a broad mound; bears white flowers and sparse, dark pink fruit; ↕↔ 10ft (3m).
S.* x *doorenbosii (*S. albus* var. *laevigatus* x *S.* x *chenaultii*). Thicket-forming shrub with elliptic to broadly ovate, dark green leaves, ¾–1½in (2–4cm) long, lighter beneath. In mid- and late summer, bears short racemes of small, bell-shaped, greenish white flowers, followed by dense clusters of spherical white fruit, to ½in (1.5cm) across, with a pink blush. ↕ 6ft (2m), ↔ indefinite. Garden origin. Zone 5. **'Mother of**

Symphoricarpos orbiculatus 'Foliis Variegatis'

Pearl' has arching shoots bearing dense crops of white fruit. **'White Hedge'** ■ is compact and upright, with white fruit; ↕ 5ft (1.5m).
S. microphyllus. Upright shrub with ovate, blue-green leaves, to 2½in (6cm) long, with pointed tips, softly hairy beneath. In late summer, bears small, cup-shaped white flowers, which are solitary, in axillary pairs, or in short, terminal spikes, followed by spherical, semi-translucent, pink or white fruit, ⅜in (8mm) across. ↕ 3–6ft (1–2m), ↔ 2–4ft (0.6–1.2m). Mexico. ❄ (min. 35°F/2°C)
S. orbiculatus (Coralberry, Indian currant). Dense, bushy shrub with broadly elliptic to ovate, dark green leaves, to 1¼in (3cm) long. In late summer and early autumn, bears dense clusters of tiny, bell-shaped, white, sometimes pink-tinged flowers, followed by ovoid-spherical, dark purple-red fruit, ¼in (6mm) across. ↕↔ 6ft (2m). E. US, Mexico. Zone 2b.
'Foliis Variegatis' ■ syn. 'Variegatus', has irregularly yellow-margined leaves.
S. rivularis see *S. albus* var. *laevigatus.*

SYMPHYANDRA

CAMPANULACEAE

Genus of about 12 species of often monocarpic, sometimes rhizomatous perennials from mountains in the E. Mediterranean and the Caucasus to C. Asia and Korea. They are grown for their tubular-bell-shaped or bell-shaped flowers, borne on branched stems in racemes, corymbs, or panicles over long

Symphyandra hofmannii

Symphyandra wanneri

periods in summer. Leaves are long-stalked, often heart-shaped, toothed, hairy, and mainly basal. Grow in a herbaceous or mixed border, or rock garden. They are very free-flowering, but usually short-lived. May self-seed.
• **CULTIVATION** Grow in light, fertile, well-drained soil in full sun or light, dappled shade. Often die after flowering; collect seed and propagate regularly.
• **PROPAGATION** Sow seed at 55°F (13°C) in winter or early spring, or in containers in a cold frame when ripe.
• **PESTS AND DISEASES** Susceptible to slugs and snails, especially new growth.

S. armena. Upright or spreading, densely hairy, rhizomatous perennial with long-stalked, pointed, heart-shaped, velvety-hairy, irregularly lobed and toothed leaves, to 10in (25cm) long. During summer, produces pendent, bell-shaped, velvet-textured, white or pale blue flowers, to ¾in (2cm) long, usually in terminal corymbs, sometimes solitary. ↕ to 20in (50cm), ↔ to 12in (30cm). Caucasus, Turkey, Iran. Zone 7b.
S. hofmannii ■ Rosette-forming, usually short-lived, often monocarpic perennial with ovate to lance-shaped, toothed basal leaves, 6in (15cm) long, with winged stalks. Erect stems produce a few alternate, shorter-stalked leaves, and, from early to late summer, they bear terminal racemes of long-lasting, pendent, tubular-bell-shaped, hairy, white to cream flowers, to 1¼in (3cm) long. ↕ 12–24in (30–60cm), ↔ 12in (30cm). Bosnia and Herzegovina. Zone 4.
S. pendula, syn. *Campanula ossetica.* Arching, spreading, often woody-based perennial with broadly ovate, hairy, pale green leaves, to 6in (15cm) long, heart-shaped at the bases, and with round-toothed margins. In summer, bears short panicles of bell-shaped, velvet-textured, creamy white flowers, to 2in (5cm) long. ↕ to 20in (50cm), ↔ to 12in (30cm). Caucasus. Zone 7.

S. wanneri ■ syn. *Campanula wanneri.* Upright, downy, monocarpic perennial with rosettes of lance-shaped, roughly hairy, irregularly toothed leaves, to 4in (10cm) long, stalkless or with winged stalks. Bears pendent, narrowly bell-shaped, deep violet-blue flowers, to 1½in (4cm) long, in pyramidal, terminal or axillary panicles, over long periods in summer. ↕↔ to 12in (30cm). Mountains of Romania, Bulgaria, Serbia, Montenegro, Macedonia. Zone 7b.

SYMPHYTUM

Comfrey

BORAGINACEAE

Genus of 25–35 species of coarse, sometimes invasive, bristly or hairy, rhizomatous perennials from damp, often shady habitats, including woodland, scrub, wasteland, streamsides, and roadsides, in Europe, N. Africa, and W. Asia. Some are used medicinally or for liquid plant food or green manure. They have fleshy roots and long-stalked, oblong- to ovate-lance-shaped or elliptic, wrinkled, prominently veined, mostly basal leaves. Erect, usually branched stems often become decumbent; they bear smaller, more or less stalkless leaves and terminal cymes of pendent, tubular flowers in blue, purple, pink, yellowish white, or white. Excellent groundcover plants for a shady border or woodland garden, but they can be rampant. *S. officinale* is used in healing creams, teas, and other herbal medicines, but is legally restricted in certain countries. Roots and leaves may cause severe discomfort if ingested; contact with foliage may irritate skin.
• **CULTIVATION** Grow in moist, moderately fertile soil in full sun or partial shade. Site carefully, since all but variegated cultivars may be very invasive; even small pieces of detached root will form new plants. To keep the foliage attractive, remove flower stems of variegated cultivars as they form. For plant food, grow *S. officinale* and *S.* x *uplandicum* in a permanent, sunny site in a vegetable garden; mulch with well-rotted manure in spring; compost the leaves, or steep in water until decayed, in summer; then use the liquid diluted 1:20.
• **PROPAGATION** Sow seed in containers in a cold frame in autumn or spring. Divide in spring. Take root cuttings in early winter.
• **PESTS AND DISEASES** Infrequent.

Symphytum caucasicum

S

. *caucasicum* ■ (Caucasian
›mfrey).Clump-forming, hairy,
ıizomatous perennial with rosettes of
ɔlong-lance-shaped to ovate-lance-
ıaped, mid-green leaves, to 10in (25cm)
›ng. Bears cymes of bright blue flowers,
› ½in (1.5cm) long, on erect then
ecumbent stems, early to late summer.
→ 24in (60cm), later spreading widely.
:aucasus, Iran. Zone 4. **'Eminence'** is
›w-growing, spreading, with gray-
ınted leaves, and rich blue flowers in
ırly summer; ↕ to 18in (45cm).
. **'Goldsmith'** ■ syn. *S. ibericum*
ıubilee', *S. ibericum* 'Variegatum', *S.*
ıubilee'. Spreading, hairy, rhizomatous
erennial with ovate-lance-shaped, dark
·een leaves, to 10in (25cm) long, with
›ld and cream markings. Bears cymes
f pale blue, cream, or pink flowers, to
:in (1.5cm) long, in mid- and late
›ring. ↕↔ 12in (30cm). Zone 6.
. ***grandiflorum* of gardens** see
ibericum.
. **'Hidcote Blue'.** Erect then decum-
ent, hairy, rhizomatous perennial with
›vate to elliptic, mid-green leaves, to 10in
!5cm) long. In mid- and late spring,
/mes of red buds open to pale blue
owers, to ½in (1.5cm) long, fading
ith age. ↕↔ 18in (45cm). Zone 6.
. **'Hidcote Pink'**, syn. *S.* 'Roseum'.
rect then decumbent, hairy, rhizo-
ıatous perennial with ovate to elliptic,
ıid-green leaves, to 10in (25cm) long.
ymes of pale pink and white flowers,
› ½in (1.5cm) long, fading with age,
·e produced in mid- and late spring.
→ 18in (45cm). Zone 6.
. ***ibericum***, syn. *S. grandiflorum* of
ırdens. Erect then decumbent, hairy,

Symphytum tuberosum

rhizomatous perennial. Ovate to elliptic or ovate-lance-shaped, mid-green leaves, are to 10in (25cm) long. In late spring and early summer, cymes of red-tipped buds open to pale yellow flowers, to ½in (1.5cm) long. ↕ 16in (40cm), ↔ 24in (60cm), later more. Turkey (N.E. Anatolia), Republic of Georgia. Zone 6.
'Jubilee' see *S.* 'Goldsmith'.
'Variegatum' see *S.* 'Goldsmith'.
***S.* 'Jubilee'** see *S.* 'Goldsmith'.
S. officinale (Common comfrey). Vigorous, clump-forming perennial with winged, upright stems and coarse, hairy, ovate to lance-shaped, dark green leaves, 10in (25cm) long, with winged stalks. From late spring to summer, bears forked cymes of purple-violet, pink, or creamy yellow flowers, to ¾in (2cm) long. ↕ to 5ft (1.5m), ↔ to 6ft (2m) or more. Europe, W. Asia. Zone 4. Non-invasive, sterile clones, such as **'Bocking'**, are available. **'Variegatum'** produces leaves with white margins.
***S. peregrinum* of gardens** see *S.* x *uplandicum.*
***S.* 'Roseum'** see *S.* 'Hidcote Pink'.
S. rubrum. Decumbent, rhizomatous perennial with ovate to lance-shaped, softly hairy, dark green leaves, to 10in (25cm) long. Bears pendent cymes of dark red flowers, ½in (1.5cm) across, in early and midsummer. ↕↔ 20in (50cm). Europe, W. Asia. Zone 6.
S. tuberosum ■ (Tuberous comfrey). Coarse, creeping perennial producing tuberous rhizomes. Upright, hairy stems bear ovate to lance-shaped, dark green leaves, to 10in (25cm) long, and in early summer, produce spiraled cymes of pale yellow flowers, ½–¾in (1.5–2cm) long. ↕ 16–24in (40–60cm), ↔ to 3ft (1m). Europe (Pyrenees to Balkans), N.W. Turkey. Zone 6.
S.* x *uplandicum (*S. asperum* x *S. officinale*), syn. *S. peregrinum* of gardens (Russian comfrey). Erect, bristly perennial bearing oblong to elliptic-lance-shaped, mid-green, basal leaves, to 14in (35cm) long, decurrent at the bases. From late spring to late summer, many-branched stems bear cymes of pinkish blue buds, opening to blue-purple flowers, to ¾in (2cm) long. ↕ 6ft (2m), ↔ 4ft (1.2m) or more. Garden origin. Zone 4. **'Variegatum'** ■ has grayish green leaves with broad and irregular cream margins, and pale lilac-pink flowers. Liable to revert, especially if roots are damaged or in poor soil; ↕ 36in (90cm), ↔ 24in (60cm).

Symplocos paniculata

SYMPLOCOS

SYMPLOCACEAE

Genus of about 250 species of evergreen or deciduous trees and shrubs widely distributed, mainly in woodland, from E. Asia to Australasia and in North and South America. Leaves are alternate and simple. Star-shaped, 5-petaled, usually yellow or white flowers are produced singly or in racemes, panicles, or spikes, followed by blue, black, purple, or white ovoid fruits. Only *S. paniculata* is generally cultivated, for its flowers and fruit; grow in a shrub border. It fruits best when several seedlings are planted together.
• **CULTIVATION** Grow in fertile, moist but well-drained, neutral to acidic soil in full sun. Pruning group 1.
• **PROPAGATION** Sow seed in containers in a cold frame in autumn. Take greenwood cuttings in summer.
• **PESTS AND DISEASES** Infrequent.

S. paniculata ■ (Sapphireberry). Deciduous, upright, bushy shrub or spreading tree with elliptic to oblong-obovate, finely toothed, sparsely hairy, dark green leaves, to 3in (8cm) long. In late spring and early summer, small, star-shaped, fragrant white flowers, with many prominent stamens, are borne in terminal panicles, to 3in (8cm) long, followed by ovoid, bright blue fruit, ⅜in (8mm) across. ↕↔ 15ft (5m), rarely to 40ft (12m). Himalayas, E. Asia. Zone 6.

SYNADENIUM

EUPHORBIACEAE

Genus of about 20 species of evergreen shrubs and small trees from dry slopes and banks in tropical Africa to the Mascarene Islands. Their smooth, fleshy stems contain a milky sap. Leaves are alternate, simple, obovate or lance-shaped, and fleshy; insignificant, petal-less flowers are borne from the upper leaf axils. *S. compactum* var. *rubrum* is most often grown, for its foliage. Where temperatures fall below 50°F (10°C), grow in a temperate or warm greenhouse, as a houseplant, or as summer bedding. In warmer, dry areas, grow in a shrub border. All parts of *Synadenium* species are highly toxic if ingested; sap may irritate skin.
• **CULTIVATION** Under glass, grow in soil-based potting mix, with added sharp

ymphytum 'Goldsmith'

Symphytum x *uplandicum* 'Variegatum'

sand, in full light. In growth, water moderately and apply a balanced liquid fertilizer monthly. Water sparingly in winter. Outdoors, grow in moderately fertile, well-drained soil in full sun. Pruning group 9; may need restrictive pruning under glass.
• **PROPAGATION** Sow seed at 59–68°F (15–20°C) in spring. Root semi-ripe cuttings in summer, with bottom heat.
• **PESTS AND DISEASES** Root mealybugs may be a problem under glass.

S. compactum* var. *rubrum, syn. *S. grantii* 'Rubrum', *S. grantii* var. *rubrum*. Erect, succulent shrub, eventually moderately bushy, with obovate, finely toothed red leaves, 3–7in (8–18cm) long, red-purple beneath. Throughout the year, bears cup-shaped, yellow-green floral bracts with red glands, in cymes 4–6in (10–15cm) long. ↕ to 10ft (3m), ↔ to 6ft (2m). ❀ (min. 50°F/10°C)
***S. grantii* 'Rubrum'** see *S. compactum* var. *rubrum*.
S. grantii* var. *rubrum see *S. compactum* var. *rubrum*.

SYNEILESIS

ASTERACEAE

Genus of 3 species of perennials from open, sunny areas of cool-temperate regions in China, Korea, and Japan. They are grown for their clustered, palmate, deeply incised, hairy to hairless, light green, gray-green, to dark green leaves, covered with a cobweb-like substance when young. Inconspicuous, white to greenish white flowers are produced in corymbs or panicles, and are papery-textured when mature. Cultivate *S. palmata* as a specimen or massed in a border.
• **CULTIVATION** Grow in fertile, well-drained, slightly acidic soil in partial shade to full sun.
• **PROPAGATION** Sow seed when ripe in autumn. Divide in early spring or early autumn.
• **PESTS AND DISEASES** Infrequent.

S. palmata. Stout perennial with glaucous stems, silky-hairy when young, and 7- to 9-palmate, rounded, white-hairy leaves, 14–20in (35–50cm) across, each borne in a closed-umbrella-like shape when young, unfurling as a broad, open-umbrella-like leaf, fading to gray-green. Inconspicuous white flowers, to ¼in (6mm) across, are borne in spike-like panicles, 12–24in (30–60cm) long, from midsummer to autumn. ↕ 28–48in (70–120cm) long, ↔ 12–24in (30–60cm). Korea. Zone 6.

S

SYNGONIUM

ARACEAE

Genus of 33 species of evergreen, root climbers from woodland in tropical Central and South America. The alternate leaves are initially simple and ovate to triangular, becoming larger, long-stalked, arrow-shaped, then 3- to 5-lobed or pedate as the plants mature. Tiny, petalless flowers are borne on spadices surrounded by pale green and cream to purplish green spathes, which often become bright red at fruiting time. They rarely flower in cultivation, and are grown for their foliage. Where

Syngonium podophyllum

temperatures fall below 59°F (15°C), grow in a warm greenhouse or as houseplants. In warmer climates, use as a groundcover, or to clothe a wall. All parts may cause mild stomach upset if ingested; contact with the sap may irritate skin.
• **CULTIVATION** Under glass, grow in soilless potting mix, in bright indirect light for green-leaved species, or in bright filtered light for variegated ones. Provide moderate humidity. When in growth, water freely and apply a balanced liquid fertilizer every 3 or 4 weeks. Water moderately in winter. Support with a moss pole. Outdoors, grow in fertile, moist soil in light dappled or partial shade. Pruning group 11, in late winter or early spring.
• **PROPAGATION** Root stem-tip cuttings or leaf-bud cuttings in summer.
• **PESTS AND DISEASES** Prone to bacterial leaf spot, soft rot, and a variety of fungal diseases. Spider mites, mealybugs, aphids, and scale insects can be problems.

S. auritum, syn. *Philodendron auritum* of gardens, *P. trifoliatum* (Five fingers). Sparsely branched trailer or climber. Juvenile leaves are ovate to triangular, often arrow-shaped, glossy, mid- to deep green, and to 6in (15cm) long; mature leaves are pedate, each with usually 3 or 5 elliptic, deep green leaflets, the central one broadly elliptic and 4–12in (10–30cm) long, the others much smaller. In summer, green and cream spathes, to 3½in (9cm) long, are borne in groups from the leaf axils. ↕ to 10ft (3m) or more. Cuba, Jamaica, Haiti, Dominican Republic. ❀ (min. 59°F/15°C). **'Fantasy'** has white-mottled leaves.
S. erythrophyllum. Sparsely branched climber with ovate juvenile leaves, heart-shaped at the bases, to 4in (10cm) long; adult leaves are each composed of 3 elliptic leaflets, the central one largest, 4–9in (10–23cm) long, pale at first, then very dark green above and purple-flushed beneath. Green and white

Syngonium podophyllum 'Trileaf Wonder'

spathes, 3–4½in (8–11cm) long, with longer spadices, are produced from the leaf axils in summer. ↕ 6–10ft (2–3m) or more. Panama. ❀ (min. 59°F/15°C)
S. macrophyllum. Sparsely branched climber with broadly ovate, mid-green juvenile leaves, to 6in (15cm) long; mature leaves are composed of 3 oblong-lance-shaped, light green segments, the middle one the largest, 7–18in (18–45cm) long. In summer, green spathes, to 4½in (11cm) long, later cream, are borne in groups of 4–8 from the leaf axils. ↕ 6–10ft (2–3m) or more. Mexico to Ecuador. ❀ (min. 59°F/15°C)
S. podophyllum ■ syn. *Nephthytis triphylla* of gardens (Arrowhead vine, Goosefoot). Sparsely branched climber, compact or trailing when young. Juvenile leaves, 3–5½in (7–14cm) long, are ovate with heart-shaped bases; when mature, they are arrow-shaped, later pedate, each with 5–11 elliptic leaflets, the largest leaflet 6–16in (16–40cm) long; all are dark green above, sometimes with gray-green markings, paler beneath. In summer, green and greenish white to cream or, more rarely, yellow spathes, 4½in (11cm) long, are borne in groups of 4–11 from the leaf axils. ↕ 3–6ft (1–2m) or more. Mexico to Brazil. ❀ (min. 59°F/15°C). **'Albolineatum'** has heart-shaped young leaves with white centers and veins. **'Emerald Gem'** has arrow-shaped, fleshy, shiny, dark green juvenile leaves. **'Imperial White'** has white-veined, blue-tinted leaves. **'Silver Knight'** produces silver-green leaves. **'Trileaf Wonder'** ■ has silvery gray-veined leaves. **'Variegatum'** produces arrow-shaped leaves, splashed creamy white.

SYNNOTIA

IRIDACEAE

Genus, sometimes included in *Sparaxis*, of 5 species of small, spring-flowering, cormous perennials from low-altitude grassland and scrub in South Africa. They have basal fans of 2-ranked, linear or oblong to lance-shaped leaves. Branched or unbranched stems bear short spikes of funnel-shaped, cream, yellow, lilac, or mauve flowers, hooded like gladioli. Where not hardy, grow in a cool greenhouse or bulb frame. In warmer areas, grow in a sunny border.
• **CULTIVATION** Plant corms in autumn, 4in (10cm) deep. Under glass, grow in soil-based potting mix, with added sand and leaf mold, in full light. Keep cool and only slightly moist until roots are well developed. Water sparingly when in growth, and dry off as the leaves wither; keep dry and frost-free when dormant in summer. Outdoors, grow in a warm, sheltered site in moderately fertile, well-drained soil in full sun. Provide a dry winter mulch, and keep dry in summer.
• **PROPAGATION** Sow seed at 61°F (16°C) as soon as ripe, or in spring. Remove offsets when dormant.
• **PESTS AND DISEASES** Infrequent.

S. variegata. Cormous perennial with fan of oblong, basal leaves, each to 6in (15cm) long. In spring, an unbranched or 1- to 3-branched stem produces up to 7 hooded flowers, 1¼in (3cm) across, evenly colored yellow and violet, or lavender-blue to deep purple with yellow stripes on the lower lips and in the throats. ↕ 6–16in (15–40cm), PD3in (8cm). South Africa (Western Cape). ❀ (min. 41°F/5°C). **var. *metelerkampiae*** has a branched stem, each branch bearing a sparse spike of violet flowers, marked orange on each of the lower 3 petals.

SYNTHYRIS

SCROPHULARIACEAE

Genus of about 14 species of tufted, low-growing, usually rhizomatous perennials, mainly from woodland in W. and C. North America. They have radical, heart-shaped, kidney-shaped, or pinnatifid leaves. Unbranched, leafy, upright stems produce narrow, upright spike-like racemes of small, tubular to bell-shaped, violet to blue, or rarely pink or white flowers, mainly in spring. Grow in a woodland or rock garden, or at the front of a shady, herbaceous border. Grow *S. pinnatifida* var. *lanuginosa* in a scree bed or alpine house; it is difficult to grow, and flower buds often abort.
• **CULTIVATION** Grow in fertile, moist but well-drained, humus-rich soil in partial or deep shade. For *S. pinnatifida* var. *lanuginosa*: in a scree bed, grow in gritty, poor to moderately fertile, humus-rich soil in full sun with some midday shade; in an alpine house, use a mix of equal parts loam, leaf mold, and grit, water moderately when in growth, and keep just moist in winter.
• **PROPAGATION** Sow seed in containers in an open frame in autumn. Divide in early spring as growth begins.

Synthyris missurica

Synthyris stellata

• **PESTS AND DISEASES** Prone to attack by slugs and snails. Aphids and spider mites may damage *S. pinnatifida* var. *lanuginosa* under glass.

S. missurica ■ Clump-forming herbaceous perennial with rounded-heart-shaped to kidney-shaped, shallowly lobed, bluntly toothed, leathery, dark green leaves, to 2in (5cm) across. Over long periods in spring, bears tubular-bell-shaped, deep lavender-blue flowers, to ¾in (2cm) long, with prominent styles and anthers, in abundant dense, upright, spike-like racemes, 2–4in (5–10cm) long. ↕ to 10in (25cm), ↔ to 12in (30cm). Arctic Canada to N. and C. US. Zone 2.
S. pinnatifida. Clump-forming herbaceous perennial bearing ovate, pinnate, mid-green leaves, to 4in (10cm) long, with linear, toothed segments. Bears racemes 4–6in (10–15cm) long, of tubular, lavender-blue flowers, to 2in (5cm) long, with silver calyces, in spring. ↕↔ to 6in (15cm). Washington. Zone 7b. **var. *lanuginosa*** forms a low mound, with silvery gray leaves, and bears deep blue flowers, to ¾in (2cm) long, in racemes 1¼–2½in (3–6cm) long; ↕ to 4in (10cm).
S. reniformis. Clump-forming, evergreen perennial with shallowly round-lobed, rounded-heart-shaped, dark green leaves, to 2in (5cm) long, paler beneath. In spring, bears bell-shaped, blue, pink, or white flowers, to ⅜in (9mm) long, in short racemes, to 1¼in (3cm) long. ↕ to 6in (15cm), ↔ to 10in (25cm). Washington, Oregon. Zone 7b.
S. stellata ■ Clump-forming herbaceous perennial with rounded-heart-shaped, hairy, dark green leaves, to 2in (5cm) across, deeply and doubly toothed. From spring to early summer, bears dense, spike-like racemes, 3–6in (8–15cm) long, of bell-shaped, violet-blue flowers, to ¼in (6mm) long, with conspicuous, sharply toothed bracts. ↕ to 6in (15cm), ↔ to 10in (25cm). Washington, Oregon. Zone 7b.

SYRINGA

Lilac

OLEACEAE

Genus of about 20 species of deciduous shrubs and small trees found in woodland and scrub from S.E. Europe to E. Asia. They are grown for their often pyramidal or conical panicles of small, tubular, usually fragrant flowers, which may be white, pink, almost red to magenta, lilac (light purplish pink), or blue. They have opposite, entire, lance-shaped to rounded, usually ovate, rarely pinnate leaves.

• **CULTIVATION** Grow in a shrub border or as specimens in fertile, humus-rich, well-drained, neutral to alkaline soil in full sun. Mulch regularly. Deadhead newly planted lilacs before fruits form. Pruning group 1; *S. vulgaris* tolerates hard renovation pruning.

• **PROPAGATION** Sow seed in containers in a cold frame as soon as ripe or in spring. Take greenwood cuttings, or layer, in early summer. Graft in winter or bud in midsummer.

• **PESTS AND DISEASES** Powdery mildew, dieback, leafroll virus, MLO (mycoplasma-like organisms), root knot nematode, *Verticillium* wilt, witches' broom, bacterial leaf spot, and anthracnose can be problems. Borers, scale insects, and caterpillars also occur regularly.

S. afghanica see *S. protolaciniata.*
S.* x *chinensis (*S.* x *persica* x *S. vulgaris*) (Chinese lilac, Rouen lilac). Bushy shrub with arching to spreading branches and oval leaves, to 3in (8cm) long. In late spring, bears fragrant, lilac-purple flowers in abundant, slightly nodding panicles, to 6in (15cm) long. ↕↔ 15ft (5m). Garden origin. Zone 2b. **'Alba'** ■ bears pale pink to white flowers. **'Saugeana'** has lilac-red flowers.
S. emodi (Himalayan lilac). Vigorous, upright shrub with thick shoots and elliptic-oblong leaves, to 6in (15cm) long. Unpleasantly scented, pale lilac flowers borne in large, upright panicles, to 6in (15cm) long, in early summer. ↕ 15ft (5m), ↔ 12ft (4m). Afghanistan, Himalayas. Zone 5.
S.* x *hyacinthiflora (*S. oblata* x *S. vulgaris*). Spreading shrub, upright when young, with broadly heart-shaped leaves, bronze when young, sometimes purple in autumn. In mid- and late spring, produces fragrant, single or double, variably colored flowers, in large panicles, to 5in (13cm) long. ↕↔ 15ft (5m). Garden origin. Zone 2b. **'Alice Eastwood'** bears double, claret-purple flowers in slender panicles. **'Assessippi'** bears early, fragrant, pale lavender flowers. **'Blanche Sweet'** has early, whitish blue flowers with pink-tinged petals, blue in bud. **'Esther Staley'** is vigorous, with profuse single, lilac-pink flowers opening from mauve-red buds. **'Evangeline'** ■ flowers early, bearing semi-double, coral-pink buds that open to pale pink; ↕↔ 12ft (4m). **'Mount Baker'** has leaves with purple autumn color and single white flowers. **'Maiden Blush'** is compact, with burgundy autumn leaf color and blush-pink flowers, rose-pink in bud. **'Pocahontas'** ■ bears single, distinctive, very bright magenta-pink flowers, early in the season; ↕ 10ft (3m), ↔ 12ft (4m). **'Sister Justena'** ■ flowers early; bears fragrant single, white flowers; ↕ 15ft (5m), ↔ 12ft (4m).

Syringa x *chinensis* 'Alba' (inset: flower detail)

S.* x *josiflexa (*S. josikaea* x *S. komarowii* subsp. *reflexa*). Upright shrub with ovate to oblong-lance-shaped, mid-green leaves, 3–6in (8–15cm) long, white-hairy beneath. In early summer, bears fragrant, lavender-pink flowers in conical to cylindrical panicles, 4–8in (10–20cm) long. ↕ 10ft (3m), ↔ 6ft (2m). Garden origin. Zone 4b. **'Royalty'** ■ bears single, fragrant, open flowers that are darker on the outside, in midseason; magenta buds open to light pink; ↕ 15ft (5m), ↔ 12ft (4m).
S.* x *laciniata ■ (*S. protolaciniata* x *S. vulgaris*). Spreading shrub with lance-shaped to pinnate leaves, to 3in (8cm) long, composed of up to 9 narrowly elliptic, dark green leaflets. Fragrant lilac flowers, in panicles to 4in (10cm) long, are produced in late spring. ↕ 6ft (2m), ↔ 10ft (3m). Garden origin. Zone 4b.
S. meyeri. Compact, rounded shrub with oval leaves, ½–1¼in (1–3cm) long. Bears fragrant, bluish pink or lavender-pink flowers in small panicles, 1¼–3in (3–8cm) long, in late spring and early summer. ↕ 5–6ft (1.5–2m), ↔ 4ft (1.2m). Zone 2b. **'Palibin'** ■ syn. *S. palibiniana* of gardens, *S. patula* of

Syringa x *hyacinthiflora* 'Evangeline'

Syringa x *hyacinthiflora* 'Pocahontas'

Syringa x *hyacinthiflora* 'Sister Justena'

Syringa x *josiflexa* 'Royalty'

Syringa x *laciniata*

Syringa meyeri 'Palibin'

S

Syringa pubescens subsp. *patula* 'Miss Kim'

gardens, *S. velutina* of gardens (Dwarf Korean lilac) is slower-growing, with lavender-pink flowers in dense panicles, to 4in (10cm) long; ↔ 5ft (1½m).
S. microphylla see *S. pubescens* subsp. *microphylla*.
***S. oblata* var. *dilatata*.** Vigorous, upright, later spreading shrub or small tree with broadly heart-shaped, tapered leaves, to 3in (8cm) long, bronze when young, then glossy, mid-green, turning purple in autumn. Fragrant, pale lilac flowers, in broad panicles, to 5in (13cm) long, are produced in midspring. ↕↔ 15ft (5m). Korea. Zone 3.
***S. palibiniana* of gardens** see *S. meyeri* 'Palibin'.
S. patula see *S. pubescens* subsp. *patula*.
***S. patula* of gardens** see *S. meyeri* 'Palibin'.
S. pekinensis see *S. reticulata* subsp. *pekinensis*.
S.* x *persica (*S. afghanica* x *S. laciniata*) (Persian lilac). Compact, bushy shrub with lance-shaped, rarely 3-lobed, dark green leaves, to 2½in (6cm) long. In late spring, profusely bears fragrant purple flowers in small, dense panicles, to 2in (5cm) long. ↕↔ 6ft (2m). Garden origin. Zone 2b. **'Alba'** bears white flowers.
***S. pinnatifolia*.** Open, upright shrub with peeling bark on older branches. Each pinnate leaf, to 2½in (6cm) long, has up to 11 ovate to lance-shaped, green leaflets. In late spring, bears fragrant, lilac-flushed white flowers, in panicles to 3in (8cm) long. ↕ to 12ft (4m), ↔ 8ft (2½m). W. China. Zone 4b.
S.* x *prestoniae (*S. reflexa* x *S. villosa*) (Preston lilac). Vigorous, upright shrub or small tree with oval, dark green leaves, to 6in (15cm) long. In early summer, bears fragrant, white, pink, lavender-pink, lavender-blue, violet, magenta, or deep purple flowers in large, erect to nodding panicles, 4–6in (10–15cm) long. ↕↔ 12ft (4m). Garden origin. Zone 2. **'Coral'** bears pale pink flowers, fading to nearly white. **'Donald Wyman'** bears tubular, fragrant flowers in dense clusters with dull, hairy, mid-green leaves; single, rose-pink buds open to paler pink. **'James MacFarlane'** bears single, fragrant, pale pink flowers with an arching habit, and dull, hairy, mid-green leaves. **'Minuet'** *(S. josiflexa x prestoniae)* bears single, fragrant, open pale pink flowers, from magenta-pink buds. **'Miss Canada'** bears two-tone flowers with near-white petal tips and rough, bright green leaves; single, bright rose buds open to pink, with dark pink throat, late in the season. **'Nocturne'** bears single, fragrant, lilac buds that open to a lavender-blue, with hairy, dull green leaves late in the season.
S. protolaciniata, syn. *S. afghanica*. Graceful, open, spreading shrub with slender, purplish brown shoots and pinnate leaves, to 3in (8cm) long; 3–9 narrowly elliptic to lance-shaped, green leaflets. Bears fragrant lilac flowers, in panicles to 3in (8cm) long. ↕ 10ft (3m), ↔ 5ft (1.5m). W. China. Zone 4.
S. pubescens*.** Erect, spreading, often bushy shrub with slender branches, red-green when young, and lance-shaped to ovate or elliptic, glossy, green leaves, to 3½in (9cm) long, densely gray-white-hairy beneath. Bears strongly scented, white-throated, purplish lilac flowers, in panicles to 5in (13cm) long. ↕↔ to 20ft (6m). N. central China. Zone 3. **subsp. *microphylla, syn. *S. microphylla* (Littleleaf lilac), is conical and spreading or upright; bears lilac-pink flowers in small panicles, to 3in (8cm) long, in summer, often again in autumn; W. China. **subsp. *microphylla* 'Superba'** ▣ bears rose-pink flowers. After initial flowering, blooms irregularly until autumn. **subsp. *patula***, syn. *S. patula*, has dull green leaves, 2–4½in (5–11cm) long, with purple

Syringa reticulata (inset: flower detail)

young shoots. Purplish lilac flowers, in nodding panicles, open from lilac buds. N. China, Korea. **subsp. *patula* 'Miss Kim'** ▣ is mound-forming, with erect panicles of pale lilac-blue flowers; leaves may turn purple in autumn; ↕ 8ft (2.5m), ↔ 10ft (3m).
S. reflexa (Nodding lilac). Vigorous, upright shrub with thick shoots and oval, green leaves, to 6in (15cm) long. Bears rich purple-pink flowers in slender, nodding panicles, to 6in (15cm) long. ↕↔ 12ft (4m). C. China. Zone 5.
S. reticulata ▣ (Japanese tree lilac). Upright shrub or broadly conical tree with an oval crown and reddish brown, shining bark when young. Leaves are lance-shaped to ovate, sharp-pointed, and to 6in (15cm) long. Bears fragrant, creamy white flowers, in panicles, to 8in (20cm) long, in summer. ↕ 30ft (10m), ↔ 20ft (6m). Japan. Zone 2. **'Ivory Silk'** is compact, and flowers profusely, even when young; ↕ 10–12ft (3–4m), ↔ 6ft (2m). **subsp. *pekinensis***, syn. *S. pekinensis* (Peking lilac), is spreading, with arching branches and dark green leaves, to 3in (8cm) long; ↕↔ 15ft (5m); Mongolia, N. China.
S.* x *swegiflexa (*S. reflexa* x *S. sweginzowii*). Upright shrub with purple-gray young stems and oblong-

S

Syringa pubescens subsp. *microphylla* 'Superba'

Syringa sweginzowii

Syringa vulgaris 'Agincourt Beauty'

Syringa vulgaris 'Charles Joly'

Syringa vulgaris 'Congo'

Syringa vulgaris 'Dappled Dawn'

Syringa vulgaris 'Katherine Havemeyer'

Syringa vulgaris 'Mme. Florent Stepman'

Syringa vulgaris 'Mrs. Edward Harding'

Syringa vulgaris 'Primrose'

Syringa vulgaris 'Sarah Sands'

Syringa yunnanensis

yringa vulgaris 'Président Grévy'

ınce-shaped to oval leaves, 2–5in 5–13cm) long. In late spring and ımmer, bears fragrant pink flowers, pening from deep red buds, in nearly ylindrical, nodding panicles, 4–8in 10–20cm) long. ↕ 12ft (4m), ↔ 8ft 2.5m). Garden origin. Zone 4.
. sweginzowii ■ Upright shrub with ed-purple shoots and elliptic-oblong to ınce-shaped leaves, to 4in (10cm) long. ears fragrant, pale pink to lilac-pink or hite flowers, in upright panicles, to 8in 20cm) long, in late spring and early ımmer. ↕ 12ft (4m), ↔ 8ft (2.5m). .W. China. Zone 4.
velutina **of gardens** see *S. meyeri* 'alibin'.
villosa (Late lilac). Compact, ounded shrub with upright shoots and vate to oblong leaves, to 8in (20cm) ng. Bears fragrant pink flowers, in rge, conical panicles, to 8in (20cm) ng, in late spring and early summer. ↔ 12ft (4m). N. China. Zone 3.
. vulgaris (Common lilac, French lac). Suckering, spreading shrub or nall tree, with heart-shaped to ovate aves, to 4in (10cm) long. Bears agrant, single or double lilac flowers e borne in dense, conical panicles, to –8in (10–20cm) long, in late spring nd early summer. ↕↔ 22ft (7m). E. urope. Zone 2. **'Agincourt Beauty'** ■ ears large, fragrant, single, individual eep purple flowers with a white petal ase; ↕↔ 20ft (6m). **'Albert F. Holden'** compact, bearing deep violet flowers ith silvery reverses; ↕ to 7ft (2.2m). **lphonse Lavallée'** produces double, ac-blue flowers, from purple buds. **nnabel'** bears double, bright pink ıds that open to a light pink; ↕↔ 20ft 5m). **'Andenken an Ludwig Späth'**, n. 'Souvenir de Louis Spaeth', bears ender panicles, to 12in (30cm) long, of ngle, dark purple-red flowers. **'Belle de ancy'** produces large panicles of ouble, mauve-pink flowers, from ırple buds. **'Charles Joly'** ■ bears ouble, dark purple flowers. **'Charles X'** oduces single, purple-red flowers.
'Congo' ■ bears large, single, dark lilac-purple flowers, from purple-red buds. **'Dappled Dawn'** ■ has variegated, mid-green foliage, splashed and spotted with creamy yellow. **'Edith Cavell'** bears panicles, to 12in (30cm) long, of large, double, creamy white flowers. **'Firmament'** produces single, light blue flowers. **'Flamingo'**, syn. 'Edward J. Gardner', has short, dense spikes of blooms; double, bright pink buds open slightly paler. **'Glory of Horstenstein'** see 'Ruhm von Horstenstein'. **'Katherine Havemeyer'** ■ is vigorous and bears double, lavender-blue flowers, from purple buds. **'Krasavitsa Moskvy'**, syn. 'Pride of Moscow', has very fragrant, double white flowers, from pink buds. **'Leon Gambetta'** is upright, with double, deep purple flowers, pink in bud; mildew resistant. **'Lucie Baltet'** bears single, pale pink flowers, from purple-pink buds. **'Maréchal Lannes'** bears double, pale violet flowers. **'Marie Francis'** bears single, pink, flowers. **'Masséna'** bears loose panicles of large, single, dark purple flowers. **'Michel Buchner'** bears large panicles, to 12in (30cm) long, of double, rose-lilac, white-centered flowers. **'Miss Ellen**

Syringa vulgaris 'Sensation'

Willmott' has late, double, fragrant, creamy white flowers. **'Mme. Florent Stepman'** ■ produces large panicles, to 10in (25cm) long, of single white flowers. **'Mme. F. Morel'** bears large panicles of single, dark mauve-pink flowers. **'Mme. Lemoine'** bears compact panicles of large, double white flowers, from creamy buds. **'Monge'** bears a profusion of very large, single, dark purple-red flowers. **'Montaigne'** bears double, pale pink flowers, from purple-pink buds. **'Mont Blanc'** produces large panicles, to 14in (35cm) long, of single white flowers. **'Mrs. Edward Harding'** ■ bears large panicles, to 10in (25cm) long, of double, purple-red flowers. **'Nadezhda'** bears double, pale pink buds that open blue with a lavender tinge. **'Night'** bears single, dark purple flowers. **'Olivier de Serres'** bears large panicles, to 14in (35cm) long, of large, double, lavender-blue flowers, from purple-blue buds. **'Paul Thirion'** produces double, lilac-pink flowers, from dark purple-red buds. **'Président Grévy'** ■ bears very large panicles, to 10in (25cm) long, of double, lilac-blue flowers, from red-violet buds. **'President Lincoln'** has fragrant, single, deep blue flowers. **'Président Poincaré'** has large flower spikes; flowers are double, fragrant, magenta buds that open paler. **'Pride of Moscow'** see 'Krasavitsa Moskvy'. **'Primrose'** ■ bears small panicles of single, pale creamy yellow flowers. **'Ruhm von Horstenstein'**, syn. 'Glory of Horstenstein', is vigorous, with compact panicles of single, dark lilac-red flowers. **'Sarah Sands'** ■ bears large, multiple-truss heads of single, fragrant, dark magenta flowers, late in the season. **Sensation'** ■ bears single, purple flowers with distinct white edges. **'Souvenir de Louis Spaeth'** see 'Andenken an Ludwig Späth'. **'Vestale'** bears many single, pure white flowers. **'Victor Lemoine'** bears slender panicles of double, pale lavender-pink to lilac-blue flowers. **'Violetta'** bears long, slim panicles of double, dark violet flowers. **'Wedgwood Blue'** is compact, with single, pale blue flowers, lilac-pink in bud; ↕ 6ft (2m). **'Yankee Doodle'** is compact, and bears profuse, deep, dark purple flowers; ↕ 8ft (2.5m).
S. yunnanensis ■ Upright shrub with elliptic-oblong leaves, to 4in (10cm) long. Fragrant, pale pink to nearly white flowers, in large, upright or semi-pendent panicles, to 6in (15cm) long, are borne in early summer. ↕ 10ft (3m), ↔ 8ft (2.5m). W. China. Zone 3.

SYZYGIUM

MYRTACEAE

Genus of 400–500 species of aromatic, evergreen shrubs and trees, mostly from woodland and rainforest throughout tropical regions. They have opposite, leathery leaves and terminal or axillary cymes or panicles of saucer-shaped, 4- or 5-petaled flowers, each with a prominent boss of stamens. Bears fleshy, spherical to pear-shaped or oblong, red, purple, or white berries. Dried flower buds of *S. aromaticum* are the cloves of commerce.

• **CULTIVATION** Under glass, grow in soil-based potting mix in full or bright indirect light. In spring and summer, water moderately; apply a balanced liquid fertilizer monthly. Water sparingly

Syzygium aromaticum

in winter. Outdoors, grow in deep, fertile, moist, but well-drained soil in full sun or partial shade. Pruning group 1.

• **PROPAGATION** Sow seed at 59–64°F (15–18°C), or 81°F (27°C) in spring. Root greenwood cuttings in early summer, or semi-ripe cuttings in mid- to late summer, both with bottom heat. Air layer in spring.

• **PESTS AND DISEASES** Leaf spots and root rot can occur.

S. aromaticum ■ syn. *Eugenia aromatica* (Clove). Small, bushy, roughly conical to columnar tree, with oval-lance-shaped, clove-scented leaves, to 5in (13cm) long; pink-flushed when young, then lustrous, deep green above. In late summer, bears terminal panicles of 3–20 flowers, to ¾in (2cm) long, with tiny, pink-tinted petals, which fall on opening, and a small brush of slender yellow stamens; flowers are followed by ellipsoid purple fruit, ⅜in (8mm) long. ↕ to 50ft (15m), ↔ 10–15ft (3–5m). Indonesia (Moluccas). ❀ (min. 72–77°F/22–25°C)
S. paniculatum ■ syn. *Eugenia australis* of gardens, *E. paniculata* (Brush cherry). Erect to spreading, bushy, large shrub or small tree with flaky, patterned, cream, pink, and light brown bark. Obovate to elliptic or lance-shaped leaves, to 3½in (9cm) long, reddish bronze when young, become shiny, deep green above. In summer, bears a few small white flowers, to 1in (2½cm) long, with many yellow stamens, in terminal and axillary panicles, followed by ovoid, pink, red, purple, or white fruit, to ¾in (2cm) long. ↕ to 30ft (10m) or more, ↔ 10–30ft (3–10m). Queensland. ❀ (min. 45°F/7°C)

S

Syzygium paniculatum

T

TABEBUIA

BIGNONIACEAE

Genus of about 100 species of evergreen or deciduous trees and shrubs found in a variety of habitats, from swamp margins to thickets and rainforest, in Central and South America, and the West Indies. They are grown mainly for their foliage, although flowers may form once plants reach about 10ft (3m) tall. They have mostly opposite, long-stalked, simple or fully divided, 3- to 7-palmate leaves, with the central leaflet longer than the others. The 3- to 5-lobed, tubular to bell-shaped flowers are produced in showy, terminal panicles, usually in spring. Where temperatures fall below 46–59°F (8–15°C), grow in a temperate or warm greenhouse or conservatory. In warmer areas, grow the larger species as specimens, the shrubby ones in a border. *Tabebuia* species are excellent as shade trees in a lawn planting or as street trees. Plants with salt spray resistance can be used in coastal borders.

• **CULTIVATION** Under glass, grow in soil-based potting mix, in full light with shade from hot sun. When in growth, water freely and apply a balanced liquid fertilizer monthly; water sparingly in winter. Outdoors, grow in fertile, moist soil in full sun. Pruning group 1; may need restrictive pruning under glass.

• **PROPAGATION** Sow seed at 61°F (16°C) as soon as ripe or in spring. Insert semi-ripe cuttings with bottom heat in summer. Air layer in spring.

• **PESTS AND DISEASES** Sometimes affected by leaf spot and dieback, with spider mites a problem under glass.

T. chrysantha ■ (Golden trumpet tree). Rounded to spreading, deciduous tree bearing 5-palmate leaves, consisting of lance-shaped to obovate, entire or toothed leaflets, the central ones to 7in (18cm) long; the leaflets are mid-green, with a light covering of star-shaped hairs on the upper surfaces, more densely hairy beneath. Trumpet-shaped, sweetly scented, golden yellow flowers, 1–3in (2.5–8cm) long, are produced in panicles in spring. ↕80ft (25m), ↔ 60ft (18m). Mexico to Colombia, Venezuela. ❄ (min. 46°F/8°C)

Tabebuia chrysantha

Tabebuia serratifolia

T. donnell-smithii see *Cybistax donnell-smithii.*

T. impetiginosa. Broadly upright deciduous tree with smooth gray bark. The 5- to 7-palmate leaves have ovate to oblong-ovate, entire or finely toothed, papery, scaly mid-green leaflets, 1–7in (2.5–18cm) long. Bears panicles of 5-lobed, tubular-bell-shaped, rose to deep purple flowers, to 2in (5cm) long, with yellow throats, darkening to purple, in spring. ↕ to 70ft (20m), ↔ 30–50ft (10–15m). N. Mexico to Argentina. ❄ (min. 45°F/7°C)

***T. pentaphylla* of gardens** see *T. rosea.*

T. rosea, syn. *T. pentaphylla* of gardens (Pink poui, Pink tecoma, Rosy trumpet tree). Broadly upright, evergreen or deciduous tree with a long, smooth trunk, branching near the top. The 5-palmate leaves have oblong to ovate-elliptic, leathery, scaly, mid- to dark green leaflets, the central ones to 12in (30cm) long. Funnel-shaped, white, pink, or lilac flowers, 2–4in (5–10cm) long, with yellow eyes fading to white, are produced in pairs in dense panicles, in spring. ↕70–80ft (20–25m), ↔ 30–50ft (10–15m). Mexico to Colombia, Venezuela. ❄ (min. 50–59°F/10–15°C)

T. serratifolia ■ (Guayacan polvillo, Yellow poui). Ascending to spreading, deciduous shrub or medium-sized tree bearing 3- to 5-palmate leaves with oblong-lance-shaped, mid-green leaflets, to 7in (18cm) long, with rounded teeth. From winter to spring, produces dense panicles of funnel-shaped yellow flowers, 2–2½in (5–6cm) long, each with 5 crimped lobes. ↕ to 40ft (12m) (but slow-growing), ↔ to 70ft (20m). Trinidad, Colombia, Venezuela. ❄ (min. 50–59°F/10–15°C)

TABERNAEMONTANA

APOCYNACEAE

Genus of at least 100 species of rounded to upright, evergreen trees and shrubs found in tropical areas worldwide, in a variety of habitats, from rocky coppices to forests. They have opposite, simple, usually oblong to elliptic leaves, and are grown for their salverform flowers, each with 5 wide-spreading lobes, produced in sparsely branched, terminal cymes over a long period in summer. In areas where temperatures fall below 50–55°F (10–13°C), grow in a temperate or warm greenhouse. Elsewhere, grow in a shrub border or small courtyard garden.

• **CULTIVATION** Under glass, grow in soil-based potting mix in full light. In the growing season, water moderately and apply a balanced liquid fertilizer monthly; water sparingly in winter. Outdoors, grow in moist, fertile soil in full sun. Pruning group 9, in early spring.

• **PROPAGATION** Sow seed at 61–68°F (16–20°C) in spring. Insert semi-ripe cuttings in summer, with bottom heat in cool areas. Layer or air layer in spring.

• **PESTS AND DISEASES** Leaf spot and root rot sometimes occur. Aphids and scale insects can be occur under glass.

T. coronaria see *T. divaricata.*

T. divaricata, syn. *Ervatamia coronaria, T. coronaria* (Crepe jasmine, East Indian rosebay, Paper gardenia). Spreading, bushy, many-branched shrub with elliptic-oblong, wavy-margined, thin, glossy, mid- to dark green leaves, 3–6in (7–15cm) long, paler beneath. In summer, bears cymes of 4–6 salverform, waxy, pure white flowers, 2in (5cm) across, fragrant at dusk and after dark. ↕6–10ft (2–3m) or more, ↔ 5–8ft (1.5–2.5m). India to China (Yunnan), Thailand. ❄ (min. 50–55°F/10–13°C). **'Flore Pleno'** has double flowers.

TACCA

TACCACEAE

Genus of 10 species of stemless perennials, with solid tubers or upright, scarred rhizomes, from semi-evergreen, monsoon forest in West Africa and S.E. Asia, grown for their handsome foliage and unusual flowers. Lance-shaped to elliptic or obovate, entire or palmately or pinnately lobed leaves, often with purplish green leaf stalks, are widely spaced or crowded on the rootstock.

Tacca chantrierei

Nodding, bell-shaped flowers are borne in umbels, each umbel surrounded by 4 leaf-like floral bracts. Each flower also has a distinctive, narrow, thread-like appendage, to 10in (25cm) long. When not hardy, grow in a warm greenhouse; elsewhere, grow in a shady border.

• **CULTIVATION** Under glass, grow in a mix of equal parts leaf mold and coarse bark, with added slow-release fertilizer, in bright filtered light. Water freely all year; in summer, mist regularly and apply a half-strength foliar fertilizer monthly. Pot on every 2 or 3 years, removing old, decaying rhizomes. Outdoors, grow in fertile, moist but well-drained, leafy, acidic soil in partial shade.

• **PROPAGATION** Surface-sow seed at 72–81°F (22–27°C) in spring. Divide, or take transverse sections of rhizomes with at least one bud, in spring. Dust cut surfaces with fungicide.

• **PESTS AND DISEASES** Spider mites, tarsonemid mites, and gray mold (*Botrytis*) may be a problem.

T. chantrierei ■ (Bat flower, Cat's whiskers, Devil flower). Erect, rhizomatous perennial with oblong or lance-shaped leaves, 7–22in (17–55cm) long, dark green above and paler beneath. In summer, umbels of 5-petaled green flowers, each with 2 pairs of green, brown, or black floral bracts and dark green, maroon, or black thread-like appendages, 10in (25cm) long, are borne on scapes to 26in (65cm) long. ↕↔ 3ft (1m). N.E. India, S.E. Asia. ❄ (min. 55°F/13°C)

T. integrifolia (Bat flower). Erect, rhizomatous perennial with oblong or lance-shaped leaves, 3–26in (7–65cm) long, dark green above and mid-green beneath. In summer, umbels of purple-red or brown flowers, surrounded by 4 green or deep purple floral bracts, are borne on scapes to 3ft (1m) long; the inner 2 flowers are white, green, or purple, with pale green, thread-like appendages, 8in (20cm) long, suffused violet and darkening with age. ↕ to 4ft (1.2m), ↔ 30in (75cm). E. India to S. China, Thailand, Malaysia, Indonesia (Sumatra, Java), Borneo. ❄ (min. 55°F/13°C)

▷ ***Tacitus bellus*** see *Graptopetalum bellum*

▷ ***Tacsonia*** see *Passiflora*

T. x exonsiensis see *Passiflora* x *exoniensis*

T. van-volxemii see *P. antioquiensis*

TAGETES

Marigold

ASTERACEAE

Genus of about 50 species of erect, bushy, strongly aromatic annuals and herbaceous perennials. They are found on hot, dry slopes and in valley bottoms from New Mexico to Argentina; one species occurs in Africa. The many hybrids and cultivars are derived mainly from *T. erecta, T. patula,* and *T. tenuifolia.* The almost fern-like leaves are usually opposite, pinnatifid to pinnate, with conspicuous glands, and mid- to dark green. Daisy-like or double, carnation-like flowerheads are produced singly or in cyme-like clusters from late spring to autumn.

'agetes Antigua Series 'Antigua Gold'

ermination from the large, easily andled seeds is rapid, and blooms ppear within a few weeks of sowing. 'he African marigolds are excellent for ɔrmal bedding, whereas the French, 'riploid, and Signet marigolds are more ıitable for the edge of a mixed border. ll are good in containers and provide ng-lasting cut flowers. Contact with e foliage may aggravate skin allergies. our main hybrid groups are in ıltivation:

frican marigolds (African Group) :ompact annuals, derived from *T. erecta,* so known as American marigolds, with ngular, hairless stems and pinnate, arsely glandular leaves, 2–4in 5–10cm) long, each with 11–17 arrowly lance-shaped, pointed, sharply oothed leaflets, to 2in (5cm) long. arge, densely double, pompon-like, rminal flowerheads, usually to 5in 13cm) across, each with 5–8 or more y florets and numerous orange to ellow disk florets, are produced om late spring to autumn. ↔ to 8in (45cm).

rench marigolds (French Group) :ompact annuals, derived from *. patula,* with hairless, purple-tinged ems and pinnate leaves, to 4in (10cm) ng, with lance-shaped to narrowly nce-shaped, toothed leaflets, to 1¼in 3cm) long. Solitary, usually double owerheads, typically to 2in (5cm) cross, with few to many red-brown, ellow, orange, or multi-colored ray orets and usually several disk florets in wide range of colors, are borne singly r in cyme-like inflorescences from late oring to autumn. ↔ to 12in (30cm).

'agetes Boy Series

Triploid marigolds (Triploid Group) Bushy annuals, derived from crosses of *T. erecta* and *T. patula,* with angular to rounded stems, branched and sometimes stained purple, and pinnate leaves, 2–5in (5–13cm) long, with lance-shaped leaflets, to 2in (5cm) long. Numerous small, single or double, yellow or orange flowerheads, usually 1–2½in (2.5–6cm) across, often marked red-brown, are borne singly or in cyme-like inflorescences from late spring to autumn. ↔ 12–16in (30–40cm).

Signet marigolds (Signet Group) Upright annuals, derived from *T. tenuifolia,* with cylindrical, simple or many-branched stems and pinnate leaves, 2–5in (5–13cm) long, with narrowly lance-shaped, toothed leaflets, to ¾in (2cm) long. Many single flowerheads, usually to 1in (2.5cm) across, with yellow or orange florets (few ray florets and several disk florets), are borne in cyme-like inflorescences from late spring to autumn. ↔ to 16in (40cm).

• CULTIVATION Grow in moderately fertile, well-drained soil in full sun. Deadhead to prolong flowering, and water freely during drought. The densely double flowerheads of the African marigolds tend to rot in wet weather. In containers, use a soil-based potting mix; during the growing season, water freely and apply a balanced liquid fertilizer weekly.

• PROPAGATION Sow seed *in situ* in late spring, or at 70°F (21°C) in early spring.

• PESTS AND DISEASES Prone to gray mold (*Botrytis*), bacterial leaf spot, powdery mildew, *Alternaria* leaf spot, damping off, and root rot. Leaf miners, spider mites, and whiteflies may be problems, especially under glass.

***T.* Antigua Series.** African marigolds producing orange, lemon-yellow, golden yellow, or primrose-yellow flowerheads, from late spring to early autumn. ↕ to 12in (30cm). **'Antigua Gold'** ▣ has rich golden yellow flowerheads.

Tagetes Gem Series 'Lemon Gem'

***T.* Aurora Series.** French marigolds bearing densely double, broad-petaled, light to golden yellow, orange, or mahogany-red flowerheads, with some unusual bicolors, from late spring to early autumn. ↕ 8–10in (20–25cm).

***T.* Bonanza Series.** French marigolds that produce double flowerheads in combinations of yellow, orange, and mahogany, in summer. ↕ 12in (30cm).

***T.* Boy Series** ▣ Compact French marigolds that produce double, crested flowerheads in a range of colors, including shades of golden yellow, yellow, orange, or reddish brown, with deep orange or yellow crests, in late spring or early summer. ↕ to 6in (15cm). **'Boy O'Boy'** is available as a mixture. **'Golden Boy'** has deep red flowerheads with orange crests.

***T.* Climax Series.** African marigolds producing fully double, ruffled flowerheads, 4½in (11cm) across, in shades of yellow and orange, from midsummer to late autumn. ↕ 18–36in (45–90cm).

***T.* Crackerjack Series.** African marigolds producing fully double flowerheads, 5in (13cm) across, in shades of yellow, gold, and orange, from late spring to early autumn. ↕ 30in (75cm).

***T.* Crush Series.** African marigolds producing fully double flowerheads, 3½–4in (9–10cm) across, in shades of orange, gold, and yellow, from late spring to early autumn. ↕ 10–12in (25–30cm). **'Guys and Dolls'** is a mixture of Crush Series.

***T.* Disco Series.** French marigolds that produce single, weather-resistant flowerheads in a range of colors, including yellow, golden yellow, mahogany, golden red, and red-orange, from late spring to early autumn. ↕ 8–10in (20–25cm).

***T.* Discovery Series.** African marigolds that produce early, double, long-lasting flowerheads in a range of colors, from yellow to orange, from late spring to early autumn. ↕ 12in (30cm).

***T.* Excel Series.** African marigolds bearing primrose-yellow, yellow, golden yellow, or orange flowerheads, from late spring to early autumn. ↕ to 12in (30cm).

***T.* Gem Series.** Signet marigolds that bear flowerheads in lemon-yellow, deep orange, or bright orange with darker markings, from late spring to early autumn. ↕ to 9in (23cm). **'Lemon Gem'** ▣ produces lemon-yellow flowerheads. **'Tangerine Gem'** has deep orange flowerheads.

***T.* Gold Coin Series.** African marigolds producing large double flowerheads, 5in (13cm) across, in shades of yellow, orange, and gold, in late summer. ↕ 18in (45cm).

***T.* Hero Series.** French marigolds that produce large, double flowerheads, to 2½in (6cm) across, in yellow, golden yellow, orange, red, or mahogany, with crested yellow centers, from late spring to early autumn. ↕ 8–10in (20–25cm). **'Hero Spry'** ▣ bears flowerheads with mahogany outer petals and crested yellow centers.

***T.* Inca Series.** African marigolds producing early, fully double flowerheads in shades of yellow, gold, and orange, from late spring to early autumn. ↕ 14–16in (35–40cm).

Tagetes Hero Series 'Hero Spry'

***T.* Janie Series.** French marigolds bearing crested flowerheads in shades of yellow, orange, and mahogany-red, from late spring to early autumn. Among the earliest French marigolds to bloom. ↕ 8in (20cm).

***T.* Jubilee Series.** African marigolds producing early, fully double flowerheads in shades of gold and orange. ↕ 22in (55cm).

***T.* Lady Series.** African marigolds bearing orange, primrose-yellow, yellow, or golden yellow flowerheads, from late spring to early autumn. ↕ 16–18in (40–45cm). The series includes **'First Lady'**, with clear yellow flowerheads.

***T.* 'Lemon Drop'.** French marigold producing early-blooming, yellow flowerheads, in late spring or early summer. ↕ 8in (20cm).

T. lucida (Mexican tarragon, Sweet mace). Woody-based perennial with linear to oblong, anise-scented, sharply toothed, mid-green leaves, to 4in (10cm) long. From late summer to early autumn, bears terminal cymes of many yellow flowerheads, to ⅜in (9mm) across. Used as a culinary herb. ↕ 14–30in (35–75cm), ↔ 18in (45cm). Mexico, Guatemala. ❀ (min. 35°F/2°C)

***T.* Marvel Series.** Compact African marigolds bearing densely double flowerheads in gold, orange, yellow, or lemon-yellow, or in a formula mixture of colors, from late spring to early autumn. ↕ 18in (45cm).

***T.* 'Naughty Marietta'** ▣ French marigold producing single, deep yellow flowerheads, with maroon-red markings at the petal centers, from late spring to early autumn. ↕ 12–16in (30–40cm).

Tagetes 'Naughty Marietta'

Tagetes Safari Series 'Safari Tangerine'

***T.* Nugget Series.** Triploid marigolds producing compact, double flowerheads, 2in (5cm) across, in shades of yellow, orange, red, and gold, from late spring to early autumn. ↕ 12in (30cm).
***T.* Perfection Series.** African marigolds with fully double flowerheads in shades of yellow, gold, and orange, from late spring to early autumn. ↕ 14in (35cm).
***T.* 'Queen Sophia'.** French marigold bearing double, russet-red flowerheads, each with a gold-edged rim on the petals, in summer. ↕ 10in (25cm).
***T.* 'Royal King'.** French marigold bearing fully double flowerheads, to 3in (8cm) across, in blends of orange and red, in summer. ↕ to 12in (30cm).
***T.* Safari Series.** French marigolds bearing double, broad-petaled flowerheads in a range of colors, including golden yellow with mahogany-red splashes, soft pale yellow, tangerine-orange, and scarlet, from late spring to early autumn. ↕ 8–10in (20–25cm). **'Safari Bolero'** has maroon flowerheads with gold centers. **'Safari Tangerine'** ▣ has rich tangerine-orange flowerheads.
***T.* Solar Series.** Triploid marigolds bearing large, densely double flowerheads, to 3in (8cm) across, in colors including orange with red flecking, sulfur-yellow, and golden yellow, some with crested centers, from late spring to early autumn. ↕ 14in (35cm). **'Solar Gold'** has abundant non-crested, golden yellow flowerheads.
***T.* 'Spanish Brocade'.** French marigold bearing semi-double, flat, crested flowerheads in yellow and gold shades, with red flecks, from late spring to early autumn. ↕ 12in (30cm).

Tagetes 'Vanilla'

***T.* 'Starfire'.** Signet marigold producing flowerheads in a range of colors that include yellow, golden yellow, and red, with some bicolors, in late spring and early summer. ↕ 6–8in (15–20cm).
***T.* 'Vanilla'** ▣ African marigold producing creamy white flowerheads, from late spring to early autumn. ↕ to 14in (35cm).
***T.* Voyager Series.** Compact African marigolds producing large, yellow or orange flowerheads, to 4in (10cm) across, from late spring to early autumn. ↕ 12–14in (30–35cm).
***T.* Zenith Series.** Triploid marigolds producing crested flowerheads in yellow, golden yellow, lemon-yellow, red, or orange, from late spring to early autumn. ↕ 12in (30cm).

▷ ***Talbotia elegans*** see *Vellozia elegans*

TALINUM
Fameflower
PORTULACACEAE

Genus of 50 species of annuals, biennials, and often succulent and woody-based perennials, found in dry grassland and scrub in tropical and subtropical regions of Africa and North and Central America. The smooth, often succulent, usually deciduous but sometimes semi-evergreen leaves are arranged in attractive rosettes or in opposite pairs on short or elongated stems arising from a tuberous or fleshy rootstock. Showy, cup- to saucer-shaped flowers are borne singly or in cymes or panicles; although short-lived, they may be produced over a long period in summer. Grow in a rock garden; *T. paniculatum* is suitable for a mixed border. In cool areas, grow tender species in a temperate or warm greenhouse, or on a sunny windowsill.
• **CULTIVATION** Under glass, grow in standard cactus potting mix in full light and with good ventilation. In the growing season, water moderately, applying a balanced liquid fertilizer once or twice; keep just moist at other times. Outdoors, grow in well-drained, poor to moderately fertile soil in full sun.
• **PROPAGATION** Sow seed at 59–64°F (15–18°C) in spring or as soon as ripe. Divide mat- or rosette-forming species in spring.
• **PESTS AND DISEASES** Aphids occur.

T. caffrum. Succulent, deciduous perennial, sometimes biennial, with a thickened, tuberous, caudex-like rootstock; short, erect or prostrate stems; and inversely lance-shaped, linear, or oval, fleshy, mid-green leaves, 1–5in (2.5–13cm) long. Solitary, cup-shaped, pale lemon-yellow flowers, ½–¾in (1–2cm) across, open during daytime in summer. ↕↔ 6in (15cm). Namibia and Angola to Kenya. ❀ (min. 50°F/10°C)
T. guadalupense. Succulent, deciduous perennial with fleshy, thickened, spherical or irregularly cylindrical, peeling, gray-skinned stems and ovate-spoon-shaped to spoon-shaped, red-edged, blue-green leaves, 1½–2½in (4–6cm) long, produced on the ends of the branches in rosettes of 10–15 together. Panicles of saucer-shaped pink flowers, 1in (2.5cm) across, are borne in summer. ↕ 12–24in (30–60cm), ↔ to 24in (60cm). Mexico, Guadalupe. ❀ (min. 40°F/4°C)

Talinum okanoganense

T. okanoganense ▣ Prostrate, mat- or cushion-forming, semi-evergreen perennial with succulent stems bearing cylindrical, fleshy, gray-green leaves, to ½in (1.5cm) long. The basal portions of the leaf midribs are retained as bristles in winter. Solitary, short-stemmed, saucer-shaped white flowers, to ¾in (2cm) across, tinged pink or yellow and with yellow stamens, are borne over several weeks in summer. Grow in an alpine house or trough. ↕ to 2in (5cm), ↔ to 8in (20cm). W. North America. Zone 8.
T. paniculatum (Jewels of Opar). Tuberous-rooted, deciduous perennial, often grown as an annual, with erect, usually unbranched stems, becoming somewhat woody with age, and elliptic or obovate, mid-green leaves, to 4in (10cm) long. In summer, bears terminal panicles of many bowl-shaped, red or yellow flowers, to 1in (2.5cm) across. ↕ 3ft (1m), ↔ 24in (60cm). S. US to Central America. ❀ (min. 59°F/15°C)
T. spinescens. Dense, cushion-forming, semi-evergreen perennial with succulent stems, clothed in spines and thickening with age; cylindrical, fleshy, gray-green leaves, ½–1¼in (1–3cm) long. The basal portions of the leaf midribs are usually retained as bristles in winter. In summer, bears 1–5 short-stemmed, saucer-shaped, dark magenta flowers, to ½in (1.5cm) across, in loose, cyme-like panicles. ↕ to 4in (10cm), ↔ to 6in (15cm). W. North America. Zone 8.

TAMARIX
Tamarisk
TAMARICACEAE

Genus of 54 species of deciduous shrubs and small trees from coastal sites and dry or marshy, often salt-rich areas inland, from W. Europe and the Mediterranean to E. Asia and India. They are grown for their attractive, feathery foliage, consisting of small, scale- or needle-like leaves, and their plume-like, often leafy racemes of small flowers. They are useful for a shrub border in an inland garden, but may also be used as a windbreak or hedge in an exposed coastal area, and for growing on light, sandy soils.
• **CULTIVATION** Grow in full sun, in well-drained soil in coastal areas, or in moister soil inland. Shelter from cold, drying winds in inland gardens; in coastal areas, they are resistant to strong winds. Prune regularly, or they may become top-heavy and unstable. Cut

Tamarix ramosissima 'Pink Cascade'

back young plants almost to ground level after planting. Pruning group 2 fo spring-flowering species; group 6 for those flowering in late summer.
• **PROPAGATION** Sow seed as soon as ripe in containers in a cold frame. Take hardwood cuttings in winter or semi-ripe cuttings in summer.
• **PESTS AND DISEASES** Infrequent.

T. parviflora. (Small-flowered tamarisk). Spreading shrub with archin purple shoots and pointed leaves, ⅛in (3mm) long. In late spring, 4-petaled, pale pink flowers are produced in dense lateral racemes, to 2in (5cm) long, on the old shoots. ↕ 15ft (5m), ↔ 20ft (6m). S.E. Europe. Zone 4.
T. pentandra see *T. ramosissima.*
T. ramosissima, syn. *T. pentandra* (Five-stamen tamarisk). Graceful shrub or small tree with arching, red-brown shoots and pointed leaves, to ⅛in (3mm) long. In late summer and early autumn, 5-petaled pink flowers are produced in dense racemes, to 3in (8cm) long, on the new shoots. ↕↔ 15ft (5m). S.E. Europe to Asia. Zone 3. **'Pink Cascade'** ▣ has rich pink flower
T. tetrandra. Shrub or small tree with arching, purple-brown shoots and needle- or scale-like leaves, to ⅛in (3mm) long. In mid- and late spring, 4-petaled, light pink flowers are produced in lateral racemes, to 2in (5cm) long, on the old shoots. ↕↔ 10ft (3m). E. Balkans, W. Asia, S. former USSR. Zone 6.

TANACETUM
syn. BALSAMITA, PYRETHRUM
ASTERACEAE

Genus of about 70 species of annuals and evergreen and herbaceous perennia and subshrubs from mountains, cliffs, meadows, and dry slopes in N. temperat regions. They have simple or pinnate to 3-pinnate, entire, toothed, or scalloped, mostly aromatic, mainly basal leaves th are sparsely to densely hairy and sometimes silver. Stem leaves, where present are spirally arranged, usually smaller an less divided, and may be stalkless. Thei terminal, daisy- or button-like flowerheads, borne singly or in corymbs, have yellow disk florets and sometimes barel discernible, white, red, or yellow ray florets. This diverse genus includes species suitable for a rock garden, an her garden, or border edging. *T. coccineum* and its cultivars are suitable for a borde

Tanacetum argenteum

and produce good cut flowers. Some have aromatic foliage, which may be dried for use in potpourri; several have medicinal qualities. Contact with the foliage may aggravate skin allergies.

• **CULTIVATION** Grow in well-drained, preferably sandy soil in full sun, although most will tolerate any soil that is not wet and heavy. *T. balsamita* produces leafier growth in partial shade. Grow mound-forming, dwarf, white- or silver-leaved species in sharply drained, poor to moderately fertile soil. Cut back *T. coccineum* and its cultivars as the flowers fade, in order to encourage a second flowering. *T. parthenium* and its cultivars self-seed prolifically.

• **PROPAGATION** Sow seed at 50–55°F (10–13°C) in late winter or early spring.

Tanacetum coccineum 'Eileen May Robinson'

Divide perennials, or root basal cuttings, in spring. Insert softwood cuttings of *T. parthenium* and *T. ptarmiciflorum* in early summer; in winter, young plants of *T. ptarmiciflorum* are best kept in a cool greenhouse.

• **PESTS AND DISEASES** Aphids, chrysanthemum nematode, and leaf miners may be a problem.

T. argenteum ■ syn. *Achillea argentea.* Mat-forming, usually evergreen, woody-based perennial with branching, densely white-woolly stems. Ovate, 2-pinnate, bright silvery white leaves, ¾–3in (2–8cm) long, have 5–9 pairs of divided to narrowly lance-shaped leaflets. In summer, daisy-like white flowerheads, ⅛in (3mm) across, are borne singly or in corymbs. Suitable for a rock garden or border edging. ↕ to 8in (20cm), ↔ to 12in (30cm). Mediterranean. Zone 6.

T. balsamita, syn. *Balsamita major, Chrysanthemum balsamita* (Alecost, Costmary). Mat-forming, woody-based, rhizomatous perennial with oblong to elliptic, scalloped, softly silver-hairy basal leaves, to 12in (30cm) long, and

Tanacetum densum subsp. *amani*

smaller, stalkless leaves on erect stems. Numerous flowerheads to ½in (1.5cm) across, with tiny white ray florets and yellow disk florets, are borne in corymbs in late summer and early autumn. Grown for its balsam-scented foliage (used in potpourri), and suitable for an herb garden. ↕ to 36in (90cm), ↔ 18in (45cm). Europe to C. Asia. Zone 7.

T. coccineum, syn. *Chrysanthemum coccineum, Pyrethrum coccineum, P. roseum* (Painted daisy, Pyrethrum). Bushy, hairless, herbaceous perennial with erect stems and elliptic-oblong, pinnatisect or 2-pinnatisect, dark green, mainly basal leaves, to 5in (13cm) long, consisting of 10–14 narrowly lance-shaped, toothed segments. Daisy-like flowerheads to 3in (8cm) across, with white, pink, or red ray florets and yellow disk florets, are borne in early summer. ↕ 18–30in (45–75cm), ↔ 18in (45cm). Caucasus, S.W. Asia. Zone 5. **'Brenda'** ■ bears deep cerise-pink flowerheads; ↕ 28–32in (70–80cm). **'Eileen May Robinson'** ■ has pale, rich pink flowerheads; ↕ 28–32in (70–80cm). **'James Kelway'** produces brilliant, deep crimson-pink flowerheads; ↕ 24in (60cm). **Robinson's Hybrids** cultivars are very hardy, and bear flowerheads in a wide range of colors; ↕ 18in (45cm). **'Snow Cloud'** produces white flowerheads; ↕ 24in (60cm).

T. corymbosum. Clump-forming, woody-based perennial with elliptic-oblong, pinnatisect, mid-green basal leaves, composed of 6–10 pairs of ovate-lance-shaped, softly hairy, toothed segments, ½–1¼in (1.5–3cm) long; stem leaves are smaller, less-divided, and stalkless. In summer, bears corymbs of white flowerheads, to ½in (1.5cm) across. ↕ to 36in (90cm), ↔ 18in (45cm). S. and C. Europe, C. Russia. Zone 7.

T. densum* subsp. *amani ■ syn. *Chrysanthemum densum.* Mound-forming, usually evergreen, woody-based perennial with white-downy stems and ovate to broadly elliptic, 2-pinnatisect, downy, gray-white leaves, ¾–2in (2–5cm) long, finely cut into 10–25 inversely lance-shaped segments. In summer, bears flat corymbs of 3–7 daisy-like yellow flowerheads, ¼–½in (5–15mm) across, each with 12–15 yellow ray florets, to ⅛in (3mm) long. *T. densum* is similar to *T. haradjanii*, but female ray florets are absent on the latter. Grow in a rock garden. ↕ to 10in (25cm), ↔ to 8in (20cm). Turkey. Zone 7.

T. haradjanii, syn. *Chrysanthemum haradjanii.* Mat-forming, woody-based, evergreen perennial with silver-white, downy stems. Oblong-elliptic to ovate, 2- or 3-pinnatisect, silvery gray leaves, to 2in (5cm) long, are composed of 4 or 5 pairs of narrowly lance-shaped, entire or further divided segments. Daisy-like yellow flowerheads, 1/16–⅛in (2–3mm) across, are borne in loose corymbs in late summer. Suitable for a rock garden. ↕ to 6in (15cm), ↔ to 8in (20cm). Syria, Turkey. Zone 7.

T. parthenium ■ syn. *Chrysanthemum parthenium, Matricaria parthenium, Pyrethrum parthenium* (Feverfew). Short-lived, bushy, aromatic, woody-based perennial, often grown as an annual, with ovate, pinnatisect or 2-pinnatisect, softly hairy basal leaves, to 3in (8cm) long, with 3–5 paired, scalloped or entire segments; smaller, less-divided, shorter-stalked leaves are produced on the erect stems. Daisy-like flowerheads, to 1in (2.5cm) across, with yellow disk florets and white ray florets, are produced in dense corymbs in summer. Suitable for borders. ↕ 18–24in (45–60cm), ↔ 12in (30cm). Europe, Caucasus. Zone 3. **'Aureum'** has golden yellow leaves and bears single, yellow-tinted white flowerheads. **'Ball's Double White'** has double white flowerheads. **'Butterball'** bears double yellow flowerheads. **'Golden Ball'** has rounded, golden yellow flowerheads; ↕↔ 9in (23cm). **'Golden Moss'** ■ is dwarf and mat-forming, with moss-like yellow leaves; ↕ to 4in (10cm). **'Plenum'** has fully

Tanacetum coccineum 'Brenda'

Tanacetum parthenium

Tanacetum parthenium 'Golden Moss'

T

Tanacetum parthenium 'Snowball'

Tanacetum ptarmiciflorum

double white flowerheads; ↕ 14in (35cm). **'Santana'** is dwarf, producing double flowerheads, and will flower at any time of year when grown in containers; ↕ 8in (20cm), ↔ 6in (15cm). **'Silver Ball'** is dwarf and compact in habit, and produces pure white flowerheads; ↕ to 12in (30cm). **'Sissinghurst'** bears double, pompon-like, pure white flowerheads; ↕ to 24in (60cm). **'Snowball'** ■ produces pompon-like, fully double, ivory-white flowerheads; ↕ 12in (30cm), ↔ 6in (15cm). **'Tom Thumb White Stars'** has pompon-like, double white flowerheads with broad outer petals; ↕↔ 9in (23cm). **'White Bonnet'** is tall, bearing white, conical flowerheads, each surrounded by a ring of broad petals; ↕ to 24in (60cm).

T. ptarmiciflorum ■ syn. *Pyrethrum ptarmiciflorum.* Woody-based perennial, often grown as an annual, with erect stems. Elliptic to oblong-ovate, 2- or 3-pinnatisect, silver-hairy basal and stem leaves, to 4in (10cm) long, have 8–22 linear-elliptic, scalloped segments. Daisy-like white flowerheads, to 1in (2.5cm) across, with yellow disk florets, are borne in dense corymbs in late summer. Suitable for edging a border. ↕ 24in (60cm), ↔ 16in (40cm). Canary Islands (Gran Canaria). Zone 8.

T. vulgare, syn. *Chrysanthemum vulgare* (Common tansy). Vigorous, erect, deciduous perennial with alternate, oblong, pinnate leaves, to 4in (10cm) long, composed of up to 12 oblong or lance-shaped, pinnately lobed or toothed leaflets. Bears button-shaped, bright yellow flowerheads, to ½in (1.5cm) across, in flat-topped corymbs, to 5½in (14cm) across, in summer. Suitable for an herb garden. ↕ 24–36in (60–90cm), ↔ 18in (45cm). Europe. Zone 4. **'Crispum'** (Curly tansy) is compact in habit, with fern-like, lacy, crinkled, camphor-scented leaves and button-like, golden yellow flowerheads, in late summer; ↕ 36in (90cm).

TANAKAEA *syn.* TANAKEA

Japanese foam flower

SAXIFRAGACEAE

Genus of one species of dioecious, rhizomatous, evergreen perennial from wet, rocky, shaded sites in Japan. *T. radicans* is an attractive creeping plant, with basal leaf rosettes and upright, leafless stems bearing dense panicles of minute white flowers in late spring and early summer. Grow in a moist, shaded site in a woodland or rock garden.

- **CULTIVATION** Grow in moist, humus-rich, peaty soil in full or partial shade.
- **PROPAGATION** Separate rooted portions of rhizome in spring.
- **PESTS AND DISEASES** Infrequent.

T. radicans. Dense, spreading perennial with basal rosettes of ovate to broadly lance-shaped or oblong, leathery leaves, ¾–3in (2–8cm) long, rounded or heart-shaped at the bases, dark green above, paler beneath. In late spring and early summer, mainly unisexual, star-shaped white flowers, to ⅛in (3mm) across, with prominent anthers, are borne in dense panicles, 2–6in (5–15cm) long. ↕ to 4in (10cm), ↔ to 12in (30cm). Japan (Shikoku, Kyushu). Zone 7.

▷ ***Tanakea*** see *Tanakaea*

▷ ***Tasmannia*** see *Drimys*

TARAXAEUM

Common dandelion

COMPOSITAE

Genus of about 20,000 species of hardy, herbaceous, perennial weeds. The basal leaves are 2–16in (5–40cm) long, deeply and irregularly toothed. The yellow and numerous-rayed flowerhead is produced on a single stalk. The milky sap in the stem is toxic. Dandelions are highly invasive weeds, but the leaves are used raw in salads; the flowers are used in jellies and wines.

- **CULTIVATION** Grow in small gardens or containers in well-drained, nitrogen-rich soil.
- **PROPAGATION** Sow in spring in seed trays for transplanting, or *in situ*, spacing 14in (35cm) apart. Blanch in succession from late summer, covering dry plants with a large, lightproof bucket.
- **PESTS AND DISEASES** Infrequent.

T. officinale. The dandelion can be successfully grown from seed, with full sun and adequate moisture. ↕ 6–12in (15–30cm), ↔ 6–8in (15–20cm). Eurasia, escaped in North America. Zone 3.

TAXODIUM

TAXODIACEAE

Genus of 2 species of upright, conical, monoecious, deciduous or semi-evergreen, coniferous trees found in swampy forest or by river margins from S.E. US to Guatemala. The shoots are of 2 types: deciduous (without buds), which fall in autumn, and persistent (with buds), from which only the leaves fall. The narrowly lance-shaped or linear leaves are arranged alternately, radially, or in 2 ranks. Male cones occur in groups; female cones are scattered. They are late to come into leaf and to assume the attractive autumn colors for which they are valued. Grow as specimen trees; they are especially suited to very wet sites, where they produce aerial roots at water level.

- **CULTIVATION** Grow in any moist to wet, preferably acidic soil in full or partial shade.
- **PROPAGATION** Sow seed in containers in a cold frame in spring. Graft cultivars in late winter.
- **PESTS AND DISEASES** Leaf spot, bark beetle, and wood rot can occur.

T. ascendens see *T. distichum* var. *imbricarium.*

T. distichum ■ (Bald cypress, Swamp cypress). Conical tree, columnar and often ragged with age, with pale brown, shallowly fissured bark. On deciduous shoots, leaves are ¾in (2cm) long, alternate (almost opposite), 2-ranked, narrowly lance-shaped, and bright green, turning rust-brown in autumn. On persistent shoots, leaves are small and scale-like. Spherical green female cones, 1¼in (3cm) across, ripen to brown in autumn; pendent red male cones expand in late winter. ↕ 70–130ft (20–40m), ↔ 20–28ft (6–9m). S.E. US. Zone 5. **var. *imbricarium***, syn. *T. ascendens*, var. *imbricatum* (Pond cypress) is narrowly conical, with dull

Taxodium distichum

Taxodium distichum var. *imbricarium* 'Nutans'

brown bark and radial leaves, ¼–½in (5–15mm) long, lying flat on erect shoots; ↕ 30–70ft (10–20m), ↔ to 20ft (6m). **var. *imbricarium* 'Nutans'** ■ has erect foliage shoots, becoming pendent when mature. **var. *imbricarium* 'Prairie Sentinel'** has very soft, fine-textured leaves; ↕ 60ft (18m), ↔ 10ft (3m). **'Shawnee Brave'** is narrowly pyramidal; ↕ 70ft (20m), ↔ 15ft (5m). **var. *imbricatum*** see var. *imbricarium.*

TAXUS

Yew

TAXACEAE

Genus of 5–10 species of broadly rounded to upright, dioecious, evergreen, coniferous, large shrubs or small trees found in forest extending from N. temperate areas to the Philippines and Central America. Yews are grown for their linear, dark green leaves, often paler beneath; these are spirally arranged but often appear 2-ranked. On the female plants, single-seeded, oblong-ovoid fruits are produced in open, fleshy arils. Grow as specimen plants or use as hedges and topiary; the prostrate forms make a good groundcover, even in dense, dry shade. Most tolerate coastal exposure, dry soils, and urban pollution. All parts (except the fleshy red seed coats) are highly toxic if ingested.

- **CULTIVATION** Grow in any well-drained, fertile soil, including alkaline or acidic soils, in sun or deep shade. Trim hedges in summer and early fall. Can withstand renovation pruning.
- **PROPAGATION** Sow seed as soon as ripe in containers in a cold frame, or in a seedbed; seed may take 2 or more years to germinate. Insert semi-ripe cuttings in late summer or early autumn; take cuttings from strongly upright shoots (except for prostrate cultivars), otherwise they may not form a strong leading shoot. Graft cultivars in early autumn.
- **PESTS AND DISEASES** Black vine weevil, mealybugs, mites, and scale insects can

Taxus baccata 'Adpressa'

be troublesome. *Phtyophthora* dieback, root rot, and needle blights sometimes occur.

T. baccata (English yew). Broadly conical tree with spreading, horizontal branches, scaly, purple-brown bark, and shoots that remain green for several years. Linear, glossy or matte, dark green leaves, ¾–1¼in (2–3cm) long, paler beneath, are 2-ranked and parted either side of the shoots. Yellow male cones are borne in spring. Fruit consist of single green seeds with juicy, sweet, usually red arils, ½in (1.5cm) across. ↕ 30–70ft (10–20m), ↔ 25–30ft (8–10m). Europe, N. Africa to Iran. Zone 6. **'Adpressa'** ■ is a dense, spreading, female shrub, with short, wide, abruptly pointed leaves, to ½in (1.5cm) long; ↕ 20ft (6m), ↔ 12ft (4m). **'Dovastonii Aurea'** ■ is a small, female tree, with spreading branches, pendent branchlets, and yellow-margined leaves borne on golden yellow shoots; ↕ 10–15ft (3–5m), ↔ 6ft (2m). **'Fastigiata'** ■ (Irish yew) is columnar and female, with radially set leaves; ↕ to 30ft (10m), ↔ 20ft (6m). **'Repandens'** is female, and spreads over the ground, forming a mound; ↕ to 24in (60cm), ↔ 15ft (5m).
T. cuspidata (Japanese yew). Broadly columnar shrub or small tree with linear, spiny-tipped, dark green leaves, ½–1in (1.5–2.5cm) long, tawny or yellow-green beneath, turning red-green over winter, and narrowly parted either side of the shoots. Scarlet arils are ¼–½in (0.6–1.5cm) across. ↕ 30–50ft (10–15m), ↔ 20–25ft (6–8m). N.E. China, Japan. Zone 4.

Taxus baccata 'Dovastonii Aurea'

Taxus baccata 'Fastigiata'

'Capitata' is pyramidal in habit; ↕ 40ft (12m). **f. *nana*** is a spreading shrub, with erect shoots and radial leaves, and is mainly male in cultivation; ↕ 6–12ft (2–4m); Japan (Honshu). **f. *nana* 'Densa'** is a low-growing, broad, flattened, female shrub; ↕ 4ft (1.2m), ↔ to 20ft (6m).
T.* x *media (*T. baccata* x *T. cuspidata*). Rounded to upright tree, usually grown as a shrub in its cultivars, combining the vigor of *T. baccata* with the hardiness of *T. cuspidata*. The distinctly 2-ranked, oblong to needle-like, pointed, flat, olive- to dark green leaves, ½–1¼in (1.5–3cm) long, have prominent white midribs and are slightly red-flushed in winter. Scarlet arils are ¼–½in (5–15mm) across. ↕↔ to 20–25ft (6–8m). Garden origin. Zone 5. **'Brownii'** is female, dense, and spherical, with short, parted, widely spaced, dark green leaves, ½–¾in (1.5–2cm) long; ↕ to 8ft (2.5m), ↔ to 11ft (3.5m). **'Densiformis'** is bushy and dense, with bright green leaves; ↕ 3–4ft (1–1.2m), ↔ 4–6ft (1.2–2m). **'Everlow'** is low-growing and spreading, with dark green leaves; wind tolerant; ↕ 18in (45cm), ↔ 4–5ft (1.2–1.5m). **'Green Wave'** is mound-forming and spreading, with arching branches and dark green leaves; ↕ 3–4ft (1–1.2m), ↔ 4–5ft (1.2–1.5m). **'Hatfieldii'** has a dense, broadly pyramidal habit, and dark green leaves; ↕ 12ft (4m), ↔ 10ft (3m). **'Hicksii'** ■ is probably male, and columnar in habit, similar to *T. baccata* 'Fastigiata' but more open, with more radially set, dark green leaves; ↕ 20–25ft (6–8m), ↔ 6–10ft (2–3m), later to 20ft (6m). **'Kelseyi'** is upright in habit, with very dark green leaves and abundant fruit; ↕ 12ft (4m), ↔ 9ft (2.5m). **'Nigra'** is compact, becoming broad and spreading, with black-green leaves; ↕↔ 4–5ft (1.2–1.5m).**'Tauntonii'** is slow-growing and spherical; resists winter burn and tolerates heat; ↕ 3–4ft (1–1.2m), ↔ 4–6ft (1.2–2m). **'Wardii'** is wide-spreading and flat-topped, with dark green leaves; ↕ 6ft (2m), ↔ 20ft (6m).

Taxus x *media* 'Hicksii'

TECOMA *syn.* TECOMARIA

BIGNONIACEAE

Genus of about 12 species of evergreen climbers, scrambling shrubs, and upright trees, found on rocky slopes and in valleys in southern Africa and from S. US to Argentina. The opposite leaves are pinnate or sometimes 3-pinnate, with ovate-oblong to rounded leaflets. Narrowly bell- to funnel-shaped, 5-lobed, yellow, orange, or red flowers are produced in dense, terminal racemes or panicles between winter and summer. Where not hardy, grow in a cool or temperate greenhouse or conservatory. In warmer climates, grow as specimen plants; the scrambling species may be trained over an arch.
• **CULTIVATION** Under glass, plant directly into a border, or grow in large pots of soil-based potting mix in full light. During the growing season, water freely and apply a half-strength balanced liquid fertilizer monthly; water sparingly in winter. Outdoors, grow in moist but well-drained, fertile soil in full sun. Pruning group 8 for early-flowering species; group 9 for late-flowering species, in early spring. Plants under glass need restrictive pruning and benefit from thinning of overcrowded stems.
• **PROPAGATION** Sow seed at 64–70°F (18–21°C) in spring. Insert semi-ripe cuttings with bottom heat in summer. Layer *T. capensis* in spring or autumn.
• **PESTS AND DISEASES** Spider mites and whiteflies may occur under glass.

T. australis see *Pandorea pandorana.*
T. capensis, syn. *Bignonia capensis, Tecomaria capensis, T. petersii* (Cape honeysuckle). Erect, scrambling, evergreen shrub with slender stems and pinnate, lustrous, mid- to dark green leaves, to 6in (15cm) long, each with 5–7 elliptic-ovate to roughly diamond-shaped, toothed leaflets. Racemes, to 6in (15cm) long, of slender, tubular, orange to scarlet flowers, 2½–3in (6–8cm) long, are produced mainly in summer. ↕ 6–22ft (2–7m), ↔ 3–10ft (1–3m). Southern Africa. ❅ (min. 41°F/5°C); tolerates brief periods to 32°F (0°C). **'Apricot'** is compact, with vivid apricot-orange flowers; ↕ to 5ft (1.5m), ↔ 3ft (1m). **'Aurea'** bears yellow flowers, to 2in (5cm) long; ↕ 12ft (4m), ↔ 6ft (2m). **'Lutea'** is slow-growing, with dark yellow flowers; ↕ 6ft (2m), ↔ 3ft (1m).

Tecoma stans

T. grandiflora see *Campsis grandiflora.*
T. radicans see *Campsis radicans.*
T. ricasoliana see *Podranea ricasoliana.*
T. stans ■ syn. *Bignonia stans, Stenolobium stans* (Trumpet bush, Yellow bells, Yellow elder). Open, ascending, large shrub or small tree, often with several slim trunks if grown as a tree. Pinnate leaves, to 14in (35cm) long, each have 5–13 oblong-ovate to lance-shaped, toothed, bright green leaflets. Funnel-shaped, bright yellow flowers, 2in (5cm) long, are produced in terminal racemes or panicles, to 6in (15cm) long, from late winter to summer. ↕ 15–28ft (5–9m), ↔ 10–15ft (3–5m). S. US to Guatemala, Argentina. ❅ (min. 45–50°F/7–10°C)

TECOMANTHE

BIGNONIACEAE

Genus of 5 species of woody-stemmed, evergreen, twining climbers from tropical woodland in Indonesia, New Guinea, the Solomon Islands, and Australasia. They are grown for their funnel-shaped, 5-lobed flowers, borne in pendent racemes from the bare branches, below the leafy stems. The opposite leaves are pinnate or sometimes 3-palmate. Where temperatures fall below 59°F (15°C), grow in a warm greenhouse. In tropical areas, train over an arch or pergola, or grow against a warm wall.
• **CULTIVATION** Under glass, grow in soil-based potting mix in full light with shade from hot sun. Provide strong support. In growing season, water freely, applying a balanced liquid fertilizer monthly; water sparingly in winter. Outdoors, grow in fertile, moist but well-drained soil, in full sun with some midday shade. Pruning group 11, in spring.
• **PROPAGATION** Sow seed at 64–70°F (18–21°C) in spring. Insert semi-ripe cuttings with bottom heat in summer. Layer in spring.
• **PESTS AND DISEASES** Spider mites and mealybugs may occur under glass.

T. dendrophila. Evergreen, twining climber with sparsely branched stems, and pinnate leaves, 3in (8cm) long, each consisting of 3–5 ovate or oblong-lance-shaped, rich green leaflets. In summer, produces racemes of 1–12 flowers, 3–4½in (7–11cm) long, with deep pink to rose-purple tubes, becoming yellow at the top, and yellow lobes, suffused and veined pink or purple. ‡ to 50ft (15m) or more. Indonesia (Moluccas), New Guinea, Solomon Islands. ❀ (min. 55–59°F/13–15°C)

T. speciosa. Evergreen, twining climber with sparsely branched stems when young, and pinnate leaves, to 2½in (6cm) long, each with 5 broadly obovate, thick, lustrous, deep green leaflets. In autumn, bears light, almost luminous, yellow-green flowers, 2½–3in (6–8cm) long, with downy lobes, in dense racemes of 1–10. ‡ 30ft (10m) or more. New Zealand (Three Kings Islands). ❀ (min. 55–59°F/13–15°C)

▷ ***Tecomaria*** see *Tecoma*

TECOPHILAEA

LILIACEAE

Genus of 2 species of cormous perennials, originally from subalpine grassland in South America but probably now extinct in the wild. They have narrowly lance-shaped, basal leaves, and bear crocus-like, brilliantly colored flowers on leafless stems in spring. They are suitable for a rock garden or raised bed, but, in all except completely frost-free areas, should be grown in a bulb frame, cold greenhouse, or alpine house.

• **CULTIVATION** Under glass, plant 2in (5cm) deep, in a mix of equal parts soil-based potting mix and sharp sand, in full light. In the growing season, water moderately; reduce water gradually as the leaves die down. Outdoors, grow in well-drained, sandy soil in full sun.

• **PROPAGATION** Sow seed in containers in a frost-free frame, in autumn or as soon as ripe. Remove offsets in late summer.

• **PESTS AND DISEASES** Infrequent.

T. cyanocrocus ■ (Chilean blue crocus). Small, cormous perennial with semi-erect, narrowly lance-shaped, basal leaves, to 5in (13cm) long. In spring, produces 1 or 2 open funnel-shaped, intense gentian-blue flowers, 1½–2in (4–5cm) long, with white throats and faint white veins. ‡ 3–4in (8–10cm), PD2in (5cm). Chile. Zone 7b.
var. *leichtlinii* has pale blue flowers with large white centers. **var. *violacea*** produces deep violet flowers.

▷ ***Telanthophora grandifolia*** see *Senecio grandifolius*

TELEKIA

ASTERACEAE

Genus of 2 species of imposing, erect, herbaceous perennials found in moist woodland and beside streams in scrub, from C. and S. Europe to the Caucasus, Turkey, Ukraine, Belorussia, and Russia. The basal leaves are long-stalked, ovate, and coarsely toothed; the alternate stem leaves have shorter stalks. Solitary flowerheads, with long, narrow yellow ray florets, tubular yellow disk florets, aging to brown, and 3 or 4 rows of overlapping involucral bracts, are produced in branching sprays from early summer to early autumn. *Telekia* species make effective specimen plants for a woodland, wild garden, or beside water.

Tecophilaea cyanocrocus

• **CULTIVATION** Grow in moist, not too fertile soil, in partial shade with shelter from strong winds. They may self-seed.

• **PROPAGATION** Sow seed in containers as soon as ripe. Divide in spring.

• **PESTS AND DISEASES** Young leaves may be damaged by slugs.

T. speciosa, syn. *Buphthalmum speciosum.* Spreading, rhizomatous perennial with ovate, coarsely scalloped to toothed, aromatic, somewhat limp leaves, 12in (30cm) or more long, heart-shaped at the bases, on stalks to 8in (20cm) long. The coarse, upright stems have smaller, almost clasping leaves. In late summer and early autumn, loose, branching sprays of solitary, daisy-like yellow flowerheads, 2½–3½in (6–9cm) across, are produced on long peduncles. ‡ to 6ft (2m), ↔ 3ft (1m). S.E. Europe, Caucasus, Ukraine, Belorussia, Russia. Zone 5b.

▷ ***Telesonix jamesii*** see *Boykinia jamesii*

TELEPHIUM

CARYOPHYLLACEAE

Genus of 6 species of procumbent perennials found in warm, open sites among limestone rocks or sandy, gravelly soils in the Mediterranean, N. Africa, Madagascar, and S.W. Asia. They are grown for their white inflorescences with unusual knob-shaped tips. Grow on a sunny slope in a rock garden.

• **CULTIVATION** Grow in perfectly drained soil in full sun.

• **PROPAGATION** Sow seed *in situ* as soon as ripe. Take cuttings in early autumn.

• **PESTS AND DISEASES** Infrequent.

T. imperati. Rhizomatous, woody, trailing to upright perennial with alternate, obovate, fleshy, glaucous, mid-green leaves, to ½in (1.5cm) long. In spring, produces knob-tipped cymes of 5–50 white flowers, to ¾in (2cm) across, with green sepals. ‡ to 6in (15cm), ↔ to 16in (40cm). S. Europe. Zone 7b.

TELLIMA

Fringe cups

SAXIFRAGACEAE

Genus of one species of rosette-forming, hairy herbaceous perennial from cool, moist woodland in W. North America. The mainly basal leaves are heart-shaped or triangular to kidney-shaped, scalloped or toothed, and 5- to 7-lobed. Small, bell-shaped flowers, with 5 tiny petals, fringed into linear segments, relatively large calyces, and 10 stamens, are borne in terminal racemes in late spring and midsummer. Fringe cups are drought-tolerant and suitable as a groundcover in a shrub border or woodland garden.

• **CULTIVATION** Grow in moist, humus-rich soil in partial shade; will tolerate dry soil and full sun. Self-seeds freely.

• **PROPAGATION** Sow seed in containers in a cold frame as soon as ripe or in spring. Divide in spring.

• **PESTS AND DISEASES** Leaves may be attacked by slugs.

T. grandiflora ■ Rosette-forming perennial with hairy, heart-shaped or triangular to kidney-shaped, 5- to 7-

Tellima grandiflora

lobed, scalloped leaves, 2–4in (5–10cm long. From late spring to midsummer, erect, hairy stems bear terminal raceme to 12in (30cm) long, of 15–30 white to greenish white flowers, to ⅜in (9mm) long, with greenish white calyces. ‡ to 32in (80cm), ↔ 12in (30cm). North America (Alaska to California). Zone 4. **'Perky'** has smaller leaves than the species, and bears red flowers; ‡ to 16in (40cm), ↔ 10in (25cm).
'Purpurteppich' has leaves tinged purplish red in summer, dark purple le stalks, and pink-fringed green flowers; ‡ to 24in (60cm). **var. *rubra*** has reddis purple leaves.

TELOPEA

Waratah

PROTEACEAE

Genus of 4 species of evergreen shrubs small trees occurring in drought-prone woodland in Australia. The alternate leaves are simple, leathery, and sometime toothed or lobed. *Telopea* species are cultivated mainly for their paired, tubular flowers, ¾–1in (2–2.5cm) long which are split on the lower sides. Each flower has 4 short lobes, with the margins rolled under, and a prominent stigma. The flowers are surrounded by overlapping, colored bracts and are produced in dense, terminal, umbel-like heads in spring or summer; they are followed by boat-shaped, woody seed pods. Where not hardy, grow in a cool greenhouse. In warmer areas, they are suitable for a shrub border.

• **CULTIVATION** Under glass, grow in soil-based potting mix, with additional sharp sand, in full light or bright filtere light. During the growing season, water freely and apply a low-nitrate, low-phosphate fertilizer monthly; water sparingly in winter. Outdoors, grow in moist but well-drained, sandy, slightly acidic soil in full sun or partial shade. Pruning group 8.

• **PROPAGATION** Sow seed in containers in a cold frame as soon as ripe. Insert semi-ripe or leaf-bud cuttings with bottom heat in summer.

• **PESTS AND DISEASES** Infrequent.

T. mongaensis ■ (Braidwood waratah, Monga waratah). Erect, bushy shrub producing inversely lance-shaped, round tipped, matte, dark green leaves, 4–6in (10–15cm) long. From late spring to summer, produces flowerheads, 3–4in (8–10cm) across, each consisting of a

T

Telopea mongaensis (inset: flowerhead detail)

ring of pale green to pale pink bracts and abundant tubular red flowers. ↕ 6–10ft (2–3m) or more, ↔ 5–8ft (1.5–2.5m). New South Wales. ❀ (min. 45°F/7°C)

T. oreades ▣ (Gippsland waratah, Victorian waratah). Large, moderately bushy shrub or sometimes small, broadly upright tree with inversely lance-shaped to obovate, matte, dark green leaves, 6–8in (15–20cm) long, with pointed tips. In late spring and summer, bears flowerheads, 3½in (9cm) across, each consisting of a ring of light green or pink bracts and tubular red flowers. ↕ to 10ft (3m) as a shrub, to 30ft (10m) as a tree, ↔ 5–10ft (1.5–3m) or more. Victoria. ❀ (min. 45°F/7°C)

T. speciosissima (Common waratah, Sydney waratah). Large shrub, bushy when young, often becoming untidy with age, with narrowly obovate, round-tipped, mid-green leaves, to 10in (25cm) long, usually toothed above the middle. Flowerheads, 4–6in (10–15cm) across, each consisting of a ring of red bracts and many tubular red flowers, the outer flowers maturing first, are borne in spring. ↕ 10ft (3m), ↔ 5–6ft (1.5–2m). New South Wales. ❀ (min. 45°F/7°C)

Telopea oreades

TEMPLETONIA

FABACEAE

Genus of 11 species of upright to rounded, evergreen shrubs and sub-shrubs found in dry, open scrub and drought-prone woodland in Australia. Angular or grooved, sometimes spiny branches bear alternate, simple, obovate to oblong leaves. They are grown for their pea-like flowers, borne singly or in clusters from the leaf axils, between autumn and spring. Where temperatures fall below 41–45°F (5–7°C), grow in a cool or temperate greenhouse. Elsewhere, grow in a shrub border.

• **CULTIVATION** Under glass, grow in soil-based potting mix in full light. In growth, water freely, applying a balanced liquid fertilizer monthly; water sparingly in winter. Outdoors, grow in moist but well-drained, fertile soil in full sun. Pruning group 8; plants under glass may need restrictive pruning.

• **PROPAGATION** Sow pre-soaked seed at 61°F (16°C) in spring. Insert semi-ripe cuttings in summer. Layer in spring.

• **PESTS AND DISEASES** Spider mites may be troublesome under glass.

Templetonia retusa

T. retusa ▣ (Cockies' tongues, Coral bush, Flamebush). Evergreen shrub, bushy when young, with alternate, obovate to oblong, leathery, glaucous, deep green leaves, ½–1½in (1.5–4cm) long. Crimson, sometimes pink or yellow-white flowers, 1¼–2in (3–5cm) long, are borne singly from the leaf axils from winter to spring. ↕ 3–10ft (1–3m), ↔ 3–6ft (1–2m). S. and W. Australia. ❀ (min. 41–45°F/5–7°C)

TEPHROCACTUS

CACTACEAE

Genus of 5 or 6 species of small, shrubby, cactus, from the desert of Argentina. Stem joints are distinctly segmented, with small, cylindrical, early deciduous leaves. Apically borne flowers are in a range of white, pinkish white, yellow, to red. The dehiscent fruit is dry, with glochids, and contains no pulp.

• **CULTIVATION** Under glass, grow in standard cactus potting mix in full light or bright filtered light. Large species are best planted directly into a greenhouse border. From early spring to midautumn, water only when approaching dryness and apply a balanced liquid fertilizer 3 or 4 times; this should be diluted from ¼ to ½ strength. Keep reasonably dry at other times. Outdoors, grow in moderately fertile, well drained, gritty, humus-rich soil infull sun. See also pp. 48-49.

• **PROPAGATION** Sow pre-soaked seed at 70ºF (21ºC) in spring. Separate, detach, and root stem segments.

• **PESTS AND DISEASES** : Cladode rots, zonate leaf spot, black spot, mealybugs, and scale insects, are common. Bacterial soft rot and several viruses also occur.

T. articulatus. Erect, loosely branching cactus from various parts of Argentina. Stem segments are subglobose to short cylindrical, to 4in (10cm) long; with 3–40 or more areoles, those on the upper half are covered with flattened, flexible spines, to 4in (10cm) long. Produces white to pinkish flowers, to 1¾in (4.5cm) long; pericarpels are covered with areoles, yet spineless. Barrel-shaped fruit is obconical, dry, and thin-walled. ❀ (min. 50°F/10°C)

TERMINALIA

COMBRETACEAE

Genus of 200 species of deciduous and evergreen trees, frequently buttressed, found in tropical woodland worldwide. The broadly obovate to oblong or elliptic leaves are either transparent or minutely pitted with transparent spots, and arranged alternately, in spirals, or in nearly opposite pairs. Petalless, tubular flowers are borne in axillary or terminal spikes or panicles, followed by one-seeded fruits.

• **CULTIVATION** Under glass, grow in soil-based potting mix, with additional sharp sand, in full light. During the growing season, water moderately and apply a balanced liquid fertilizer monthly; water sparingly in winter. Outdoors, grow in moderately fertile, sandy soil in full sun. Pruning group 1; plants grown under glass need restrictive pruning.

• **PROPAGATION** Sow seed at 64–75°F (18–24°C) in spring. Layer in spring.

• **PESTS AND DISEASES** Leaf spot occurs.

T. catappa (Indian almond). Dense, spreading, deciduous tree, the branches of young specimens forming horizontal whorls. Broadly obovate to obovate, lustrous, dark green leaves, to 10in (25cm) long, borne in rosette-like clusters at the branch tips, turn red before falling. Petalless flowers have white calyces, with tubes to ½in (1.5cm) long, and are borne in axillary spikes, to 6in (15cm) long, in summer; they are followed by narrowly winged, ellipsoid, red, yellow, or green fruit, 2–3in (5–8cm) long, with edible seeds. ↕ 70–120ft (20–35m), ↔ 50–70ft (15–20m). Tropical Asia, Malaysia, N. Australia, Polynesia. ❀ (min. 55–59°F/13–15°C)

TERNSTROEMIA

THEACEAE

Genus of 85 species of evergreen trees and shrubs occurring in woodland in mainly tropical regions of Asia, Africa, and North and South America. They are cultivated for their handsome, usually entire, leathery leaves; their many-stamened flowers, produced singly or sometimes in small clusters; and their usually pendent, spherical, fleshy, greenish yellow then bright red fruit. *T. gymnanthera* is the most commonly cultivated species. Grow as a specimen plant or for hedging, in a shrub border, or against a shady wall. Where not hardy, grow in a cool greenhouse.

• **CULTIVATION** Under glass, grow in acidic soil mix in bright filtered light. In the growing season, water freely, applying a balanced liquid fertilizer monthly; water sparingly in winter. Outdoors, grow in moist but well-drained, humus-rich, acidic soil in partial shade. Pruning group 8; plants grown under glass may need restrictive pruning. Trim hedges after flowering.

• **PROPAGATION** Sow seed as soon as ripe in containers in a cold frame. Insert semi-ripe cuttings with bottom heat in late summer.

• **PESTS AND DISEASES** Infrequent.

T. gymnanthera, syn. *T. japonica.* Rounded, evergreen shrub. Elliptic to inversely lance-shaped, leathery, glossy, very dark green leaves, to 4in (10cm) long, turning bronze in cold weather, are usually clustered at the shoot tips. White flowers, ½in (1.5cm) across, are produced singly or in small clusters from the leaf axils, in late spring and early summer; they are followed by spherical, greenish yellow berries, 1in (2.5cm) long, ripening to red. ↕↔ 10ft (3m). China, Taiwan, Japan. ❀ (min. 35°F/2°C). **'Variegata'** has leaves margined with creamy white, and tinged pink in winter; ❀ (min. 35°F/2°C)

T. japonica see *T. gymnanthera.*

▷ ***Testudinaria elephantipes*** see *Dioscorea elephantipes*

TETRADIUM

syn. EUODIA, EVODIA

Bee tree

RUTACEAE

Genus of 9 species of upright to rounded, deciduous or evergreen trees and shrubs found in woodland from the Himalayas to E. and S.E. Asia, and cultivated for their attractive foliage, flowers (highly attractive to bees), and dense clusters of fruit. They have

T

Tetradium daniellii

opposite, usually pinnate leaves. Cup-shaped flowers, each with 4 or 5 usually hooded petals, are borne in terminal or axillary corymbs or panicles. Oval to pear-shaped or spherical green fruits, with 1–5 follicles, each 1- or 2-seeded, are produced in late summer or autumn. Tetradiums make handsome specimen trees for a lawn or woodland garden.
• **CULTIVATION** Grow in well-drained soil in full sun or partial shade. Pruning group 1.
• **PROPAGATION** Sow seed in a seedbed in autumn. Insert root cuttings in midwinter.
• **PESTS AND DISEASES** Infrequent.

T. daniellii ■ syn. *Euodia daniellii, E. hupehensis.* Spreading, deciduous tree bearing pinnate leaves, to 16in (40cm) or more long, each with up to 11 elliptic, ovate, or lance-shaped, glossy, dark green leaflets, turning yellow in autumn. Small, aromatic white flowers, with yellow anthers, are produced in domed, terminal corymbs, to 6in (15cm) across, in late summer and early autumn; they are followed by dense clusters of angular-spherical, red-brown fruit, ⅜in (9mm) across, containing hard, shiny black seeds. ↕↔ 50ft (15m). S.W. China, Korea. Zone 6.

TETRANEMA

SCROPHULARIACEAE

Genus of 2 species of shrubby, evergreen perennials from moist, shady altitudes in Mexico and Guatemala. Cultivated for their decorative flowers, they are borne over a long period in summer. Flower stems bear terminal clusters of trumpet-shaped, 2-lipped, violet, lilac, or mauve flowers, the upper lips 2-lobed, the lower ones 3-lobed; the stems arise from neat rosettes of obovate or oblong, scalloped, leathery leaves. Where not hardy, grow in a warm greenhouse or as houseplants. In warmer areas, grow in a shady border.
• **CULTIVATION** Under glass, grow in soil-based potting mix in bright filtered light with moderate to high humidity. In summer, water freely and apply a balanced liquid fertilizer monthly; water moderately at other times. Pot on in spring. Outdoors, grow in well-drained soil in partial shade.
• **PROPAGATION** Sow seed at 64–70°F (18–21°C) as soon as ripe or in spring. Divide established clumps in spring.
• **PESTS AND DISEASES** Aphids and thrips may be problems.

Tetranema roseum

T. mexicanum see *T. roseum.*
T. roseum ■ syn. *T. mexicanum* (Mexican foxglove, Mexican violet). Evergreen perennial with obovate, dark green leaves, to 5in (13cm) long. In summer, trumpet-shaped, 2-lipped, lilac or mauve flowers, ½in (1.5cm) across, with darker markings, are borne on stems to 8in (20cm) long. ↕ 8in (20cm), ↔ 6in (15cm). Mexico. ❁ (min. 55°F/13°C). **'Alba'** bears white flowers.

TETRANEURIS

ASTERACEAE

Genus of about 35 species of aromatic annuals and short-lived herbaceous perennials from plains, prairies, and mountain screes in W. and C. US. They are grown for their aromatic foliage and flowers. Alternate, narrowly linear to lance-shaped or inversely lance-shaped, occasionally lobed, very hairy leaves are usually arranged in basal rosettes. The mostly solitary, daisy-like yellow flowerheads are borne in early summer.
• **CULTIVATION** Outdoors, grow in well drained, gritty soil in full sun, protected from excessive winter moisture. In an alpine house, use a mix of 2 parts grit and 1 part each loam and leaf mold. Water moderately when in growth, avoiding the foliage; water sparingly in winter.
• **PROPAGATION** Sow seed as soon as ripe in an open frame.
• **PESTS AND DISEASES** Aphids and spider mites may be troublesome under glass.

T. acaulis, syn. *Hymenoxys acaulis.* Tap-rooted perennial with crowded, basal rosettes of narrowly inversely lance-shaped, very hairy, gray-green leaves, ¼–3in (2–8cm) long. Usually solitary yellow flowerheads, to 2in (5cm) across, are produced on upright, hairy stems in early summer. ↕↔ to 6in (15cm). Idaho to N. Dakota, Texas, and New Mexico. Zone 4.

TETRAPANAX

ARALIACEAE

Genus of one species of suckering, evergreen shrub or small tree occurring in woodland in S. China and Taiwan. It is grown for its large, alternate, palmately lobed leaves; its umbels of flowers, borne in panicle-like, woolly inflorescences with conspicuous bracts; and its clusters of black fruit. Where not hardy, grow against a warm wall, in a container moved under cover in winter, or in a cool greenhouse. In warmer climates, grow in a sheltered border. The flowers are attractive to bees. Contact with foliage may irritate skin.
• **CULTIVATION** Under glass, grow in soil-based potting mix, in full light with shade from hot sun. During the growing season, water freely and apply a balanced liquid fertilizer monthly; water sparingly in winter. Outdoors, grow in any well-drained soil in full sun, sheltered from strong winds. In order to restrict the spread of established clumps, remove suckers at the extremities. Where top-growth is killed by frost, *T. papyrifer* becomes herbaceous, growing again from below ground. Pruning group 1 or 7.
• **PROPAGATION** Sow seed in containers in a cold frame in autumn. Remove suckers in spring or summer.
• **PESTS AND DISEASES** Infrequent.

T. papyrifer, syn. *Aralia papyrifer, Fatsia papyrifera, T. papyriferus* (Rice-paper plant). Thicket-forming, sparsely branched, evergreen shrub or small tree with thick shoots. The 5- to 11-lobed leaves, to 20in (50cm) or more across, scaly, mid-green above and felted pale green beneath, are clustered at the shoot tips. In autumn, produces umbels, ½in (1.5cm) across, of white flowers in panicle-like inflorescences, to 20in (50cm) long, followed by spherical fruit, to ⅛in (3mm) across. ↕↔ 15ft (5m) or more. S. China, Taiwan. Zone 7.
T. papyriferus see *T. papyrifer.*

TETRASTIGMA

VITACEAE

Genus of about 90 species of evergreen and deciduous tendril climbers found in tropical woodland from Indonesia and Malaysia to N. Australia. They are grown mainly for their alternate, mostly fully divided, sometimes lobed, palmate to pedate leaves. Tiny, 4-petaled flowers are borne in cyme-like, axillary umbels or clusters in summer, followed by grape-like black berries. In areas where temperatures fall below 59°F (15°C), grow in a warm greenhouse or as houseplants. In tropical climates, train over a wall or a tree stump.
• **CULTIVATION** Under glass, grow in soil-based potting mix, with additional leaf mold, in bright filtered or bright indirect light, with moderate to high humidity. In the growing season, water freely, applying a balanced liquid fertilizer monthly; water moderately in winter. Outdoors, grow in moist, fertile soil in partial or dappled shade. Pruning group 11, in spring.
• **PROPAGATION** Insert semi-ripe cuttings in summer. Layer in spring.
• **PESTS AND DISEASES** Spider mites may be a problem under glass.

Tetrastigma voinierianum

T. voinierianum ■ syn. *Cissus voinieriana, Vitis voinieriana* (Chestnut vine, Lizard plant). Strong-growing, evergreen climber with sturdy, hairy, densely red-brown stems. Leaves are 3- to 5-palmate, 6–16in (15–40cm) long, with broadly diamond-shaped to obovate, coarsely toothed leaflets, to 10in (25cm) long, lustrous, dark green above and brownish yellow-hairy beneath. Yellowish green flowers are borne in dense, axillary umbels or clusters, 2in (5cm) across, on mature plants in summer; they are followed by small, acidic berries. ↕ to 50ft (15m) or more. Laos. ❁ (min. 59°F/15°C)

TETRATHECA

TREMANDRACEAE

Genus of at least 20 species of small, evergreen shrubs from heathland and drought-prone forest in Australia, grown for their flowers and attractive, heather-like habit. The tiny linear to rounded leaves are arranged alternately, in whorls, or in opposite pairs. Solitary, nodding, cross-, star-, or cup-shaped, 4- or 5-petaled flowers are produced from the upper leaf axils in spring and summer. Where not hardy, grow in a cool greenhouse. In milder areas, grow in a shrub border.
• **CULTIVATION** Under glass, grow in acidic potting mix in full light, with shade from hot sun. In growth, water freely and apply a half-strength balanced liquid fertilizer monthly; water sparingly in winter. Outdoors, grow in humus-rich, neutral to acidic soil in full sun with some midday shade. Pruning group 10,after flowering.
• **PROPAGATION** Surface-sow seed at 55–61°F (13–16°C) in spring. Insert semi-ripe cuttings with bottom heat in summer. Air layer in spring.
• **PESTS AND DISEASES** Infrequent.

T. ciliare. Twiggy, tufted shrub with wiry, densely hairy stems and whorls of 3 broadly ovate, mid- to dark green leaves, ¼in (6mm) long, fringed with hairs. From spring to summer, cup-shaped, rose-pink flowers, ½–¾in (1–2cm) across, with 4 oblong petals, are produced from the upper leaf axils. ↕↔ 16–20in (40–50cm). S. Australia. ❀ (min. 41°F/5°C)

TEUCRIUM

LAMIACEAE

Genus of approximately 100 species of herbaceous perennials and evergreen and deciduous shrubs and subshrubs, found mainly in thickets, woodland, dry, rocky places, and mountainous areas worldwide, especially in the Mediterranean region. Teucriums are grown for their attractive habit, aromatic foliage, and whorled clusters or racemes of 2–6 tubular to bell-shaped, sometimes 2-lipped flowers. The leaves, arranged in opposite pairs, are simple or lobed, and entire or toothed. Teucriums have a variety of garden uses: the small species, to 12in (30cm) tall, are suitable for a rock garden, low hedge, knot garden, raised bed, or trough; the shrubs, such as *T. fruticans*, are best grown in a sheltered border or against a warm, sunny wall and, in mild areas, may be used as a hedge. *T. fruticans* may also be trained into topiary.

• **CULTIVATION** Grow in well-drained, preferably neutral to alkaline soil in full sun; the smallest species retain their compact habit better on poor, gritty soil. Pruning group 7 for *T. fruticans.*

• **PROPAGATION** Sow seed in containers in a cold frame as soon as ripe. Insert softwood cuttings in early summer or semi-ripe cuttings in midsummer, both with bottom heat. Overwinter young plants of tender species in a cool greenhouse, then root softwood cuttings in late winter or early spring.

• **PESTS AND DISEASES** Infrequent.

T. aroanium, syn. *T. aroanum.* Low-growing, evergreen subshrub producing branching, stoloniferous, densely hairy

Teucrium polium

stems and ovate or elliptic to oblong, aromatic, silver-hairy leaves, to ¾in (2cm) long. In summer, 2-lipped purple flowers, to ¾in (2cm) long, are borne in short-stemmed, axillary clusters. ↕ to 3in (8cm), ↔ to 8in (20cm). S. Greece. Zone 7.

T. aroanum see *T. aroanium.*

T. chamaedrys (Wall germander). Evergreen or deciduous subshrub with oblong-ovate, glossy, entire to toothed, dark green leaves, ¾in (2cm) long. In summer and early autumn, bears loose to dense, terminal racemes of 2-lipped, pale pink to deep purple flowers. May be cut to within 1–2in (2.5–5cm) of ground level in spring to maintain compact habit. Excellent as a low hedge or knot garden plant. ↕ 12–20in (30–50cm), ↔ 12in (30cm). Europe and S.W. Asia. Zone 4.

T. fruticans ▣ (Shrubby germander, Tree germander). Bushy, evergreen shrub with arching, white-woolly shoots and aromatic, ovate to lance-shaped, gray-green leaves, to ¾in (2cm) long, white-woolly beneath. In summer, whorls of pale blue flowers, 1in (2.5cm) long, with prominent stamens, are produced in terminal racemes, to 4in (10cm) long. ↕ 24–39in (60–100cm), ↔ 12ft (4m). W. Mediterranean. Zone 7b. **'Azureum'** produces dark blue flowers.

T. polium ▣ Mound-forming, deciduous subshrub with decumbent to erect, white- to tawny-woolly stems. Bears stemless, linear or oblong to lance-shaped, wrinkled, white-woolly, gray-green leaves, to 1½in (4cm) long. In summer, 2-lipped, purple or yellow flowers, to ½in (1.5cm) long, are borne in abundant dense, flat-topped, terminal clusters. ↕↔ 12in (30cm). Mediterranean to W. Asia. Zone 8.

T. subspinosum. Shrubby perennial with ascending, twisted, branching, white-woolly stems, with short spines on the branchlets, and diamond-shaped to lance-shaped or linear, gray-green leaves, to ¼in (6mm) long, often densely white-woolly beneath. In summer, 2-lipped pink flowers, to ⅜in (9mm) long, are produced in loose, terminal racemes, to 2in (5cm) long. ↕↔ 8in (20cm). Balearic Islands (Majorca). Zone 8.

Teucrium fruticans

THALIA

MARANTACEAE

Genus of 12 species of evergreen or herbaceous, marginal aquatic perennials found at the swampy margins of lakes and ponds from S.E. US to Argentina, including the West Indies, with one species in tropical Africa. They have handsome, long-stalked, ovate-lance-shaped leaves, and bear unusual violet flowers, with enlarged staminodes, in 2 ranks in long-stalked, branched panicles. Where not hardy, grow in a pool in a cool greenhouse. In warmer areas, grow as specimen plants in and around a tropical pool or bog garden.

• **CULTIVATION** Grow in a large aquatic container of fertile, loamy soil, or in deep, humus-rich mud in water up to 6in (15cm) deep, at the edge of a sunny pool. In summer, apply a commercial aquatic plant fertilizer monthly. Remove old leaves and flowers regularly. Under glass, grow in aquatic containers of loamy soil in full light, with a minimum temperature of 50°F (10°C). See also pp.52–53.

• **PROPAGATION** Sow seed at 61–70°F (16–21°C) in moist propagating soil mix, as soon as ripe or in spring. Divide in spring.

• **PESTS AND DISEASES** Leaf-rolling caterpillars may attack.

Thalia dealbata

T. dealbata ▣ Evergreen, marginal aquatic perennial producing ovate to lance-shaped, white-floury, gray-green leaves, 20in (50cm) long, on leaf stalks 12–24in (30–60cm) long. In summer, violet flowers, ½–¾in (1.5–2cm) across, are borne in slender panicles, to 8in (20cm) long. ↕ 6–10ft (2–3m), ↔ 6ft (2m). S. US, Mexico. Zone 7b.

T. geniculata. Evergreen, marginal aquatic perennial bearing ovate to lance-shaped, gray-green leaves, to 24in (60cm) long, on leaf stalks to 6ft (1.8m) long. In summer, bears violet flowers, ½–¾in (1.5–2cm) across, in lax, pendent panicles, to 8in (20cm) long. ↕↔ 6ft (2m). Tropical Africa, Florida to Argentina, West Indies. ❀ (min. 41°F/5°C)

THALICTRUM

Meadow rue

RANUNCULACEAE

Genus of about 130 species of rhizomatous or tuberous perennials found by streams, in meadows, and in moist, shady, often mountainous areas worldwide (except Australasia), mainly in N. temperate regions. The usually erect stems bear alternate, ternate to 4-ternate or 2- to 4-pinnate, sometimes glaucous leaves with lobed or toothed leaflets, the end leaflet longer than the others. The many tiny, petalless flowers are borne in axillary or terminal corymbs, racemes, or panicles; they have petal-like sepals and often numerous showy stamens and pistils in white, yellow, pink, lilac-pink, or violet, giving a fluffy effect. Grown for their attractive foliage and flowers, the taller species are excellent background plants for a border, or a wild or woodland garden; the smaller species are suitable for a shady rock garden or alpine house. Except for *T. aquilegiifolium* and *T. flavum*, most grow better in areas with cool, damp summers. Where not hardy, grow in a cool greenhouse.

• **CULTIVATION** Grow in moist, humus-rich soil in partial shade; *T. flavum* subsp. *glaucum* tolerates drier soil and more sun. Grow smaller, alpine species in moist, humus-rich, acidic soil in cool, partial shade. Tall species and cultivars need staking. Divide and replant *T. delavayi* 'Hewitt's Double' every 2 or 3 years to maintain vigor. All start into growth in mid- or late spring, so take care to avoid damage to dormant plants when cultivating earlier in the year.

• **PROPAGATION** Sow seed in containers in a cold frame as soon as ripe or in early spring. Divide as new growth begins in spring; divisions may be slow to re-establish. *T. delavayi* 'Hewitt's Double' is sterile, and so may be increased only by division.

• **PESTS AND DISEASES** Powdery mildew, rust, white smut, and some leaf spots may occur. Slugs and some insects may be problems.

T. aquilegiifolium. Erect, clump-forming, rhizomatous perennial with 2- or 3-pinnate, hairless leaves, to 12in (30cm) long, composed of obovate, wavy-margined leaflets. Clustered, fluffy flowers, ⅜–½in (8–15mm) long, with greenish white sepals, falling to reveal numerous bright purple-pink or white stamens, are produced in spreading, flat-topped, terminal panicles on glaucous stems in early summer. ↕ to 3ft (1m), ↔ 18in (45cm). Europe to temperate Asia. Zone 5. **'Album'** has white stamens. **'Purple Cloud'** see 'Thundercloud'. **'Thundercloud'**, syn. 'Purple Cloud', has flowers with dark purple stamens. **'White Cloud'** has yellow-tipped white stamens.

T. chelidonii. Erect, clump-forming, rhizomatous perennial bearing 2- or 3-pinnate or ternate, hairless leaves, to 18in (45cm) long, with ovate to almost rounded, many-toothed leaflets. During late summer and early autumn, fluffy flowers, to 1in (2.5cm) across, with conspicuous mauve sepals and shorter, pendent yellow stamens, are produced in terminal and axillary panicles. ↕ 1–8ft (0.3–2.5m), ↔ 24in (60cm). C. and E. Himalayas. Zone 6.

T. dasycarpum. Erect, clump-forming perennial with purple stems and finely dissected, 2- or 3-pinnate, prominently veined leaves, to 4in (10cm) long, softly hairy beneath, with oblong, mid-green leaflets. In summer, bears panicles of purple-tinged, white flowers, ⅜in (3mm) long. ↕ to 6ft (2m), ↔ 24in (60cm). Alberta and Ontario south to Arizona and Ohio. Zone 4.

T. delavayi, syn. *T. dipterocarpum* of gardens (Yunnan meadow rue). Erect, hairless, clump-forming, rhizomatous perennial with slender stems, shaded dark purple, and usually 2- or 3-pinnate or ternate leaves, to 14in (35cm) long, with entire or 3-lobed leaflets. From midsummer to early autumn, numerous long-stalked, fluffy flowers, to 1in (2.5cm) across, with large, lilac to white sepals, ½in (1.5cm) long, and clusters of yellowish white stamens, are borne in widely branching, pyramidal, terminal and axillary panicles. ↕ 4ft (1.2m) or more, ↔ 24in (60cm). E. Tibet to W. China. Zone 5. **'Album'** ▣ has white sepals. **'Hewitt's Double'** ▣ lacks stamens but has numerous mauve sepals, forming pompon-like flowers.

T. diffusiflorum. Erect, clump-forming, rhizomatous perennial, similar to

Thalictrum delavayi 'Album'

Thalictrum delavayi 'Hewitt's Double'

T. chelidonii, bearing 2- or 3-pinnate or ternate, grayish green, basal leaves, to 8in (20cm) long, with rounded, almost circular, slightly toothed, finely hairy leaflets. In summer, bears fluffy flowers, 1¼in (2.5cm) across, with light pinkish mauve sepals and much shorter, pendent yellow stamens, in loose, few- to many-flowered, axillary and terminal panicles. ↕ 36in (90cm) or more, ↔ 12in (30cm). S.E. Tibet. Zone 6.

T. dioicum (Early meadow rue, Quicksilver weed). Clump-forming perennial, erect in habit, with 1- to 3-pinnate, hairless leaves, 3–4in (8–10cm) long, with kidney-shaped to obovate, bluntly lobed or toothed, mid-green leaflets. In summer, produces terminal and axillary panicles, to 4in (10cm) long, of tiny flowers with green or purple sepals. ↕ to 30in (75cm), ↔ 24in (60cm). North Dakota to Quebec, south to Missouri and Georgia. Zone 5.

***T. dipterocarpum* of gardens** see *T. delavayi.*

T. flavum (Yellow meadow rue). Clump-forming, rhizomatous perennial producing 2- or 3-pinnate, hairless leaves, to 16in (40cm) long, composed of obovate, 3- or 4-lobed leaflets. In summer, numerous fragrant flowers, ¼in (6mm) long, with small yellow sepals and longer, erect, bright yellow stamens, are produced in erect, compact, narrowly ovoid, axillary and terminal panicles on thick, furrowed stems. ↕ to 3ft (1m), ↔ 18in (45cm). Europe to Caucasus, Russia (Siberia). Zone 5. **subsp. *glaucum*** ▣ syn. *T. speciosissimum* (Dusty meadow rue) has distinctively

Thalictrum flavum subsp. *glaucum*

Thalictrum kiusianum

glaucous stems and foliage, the leaflets with prominent veins beneath, and larger panicles of paler, luminous, sulfur-yellow flowers; ↔ 24in (60cm); Portugal, Spain, N.W. Africa. **'Illuminator'** produces bright green leaves, emerging yellow-green, and bears lemon-yellow flowers; ↕ 4ft (1.2m).

T. kiusianum ▣ Mat-forming perennial with short rhizomes and fern-like, ternate or 2-ternate, dark blue-green leaves, to 5in (13cm) long, with ovate, 3- to 5-lobed leaflets. Pale pinkish mauve flowers, to ½in (1.5cm) across, with conspicuous stamens, are borne in few-flowered, short-stemmed corymbs in early summer. Grow in a damp, shady bed, trough, rock garden, or alpine house. Prefers peaty soil. ↕ to 4in (10cm), ↔ to 12in (30cm). Japan. Zone 4.

***T. minus* 'Adiantifolium'.** Tufted, rhizomatous perennial with fern-like, 3- to 4-pinnate, hairless, finely cut, leaves, 4–5in (10–13cm) long, with rounded to ovate, slightly glaucous, mid-green leaflets. In summer, bears loose panicles, 6–8in (15–20cm) long, of tiny yellow-green flowers that turn brown and are persistent for many

Thalictrum rochebruneanum

months. Excellent as a dried flower. ↕ 36in (90cm), ↔ 24in (60cm). Zone 5.

T. orientale. Slow-growing, clump-forming, rhizomatous perennial with fern-like, 2-ternate, blue-green leaves, to 5in (13cm) long, with rounded, 3-lobed leaflets. Deep pinkish blue flowers, ½in (1.5cm) long, are produced in few-flowered, wiry-stemmed corymbs in late spring and early summer. Difficult to propagate. ↕↔ to 12in (30cm). Greece to Caucasus. Zone 6.

T. rochebruneanum ▣ Upright, hairless, clump-forming, rhizomatous perennial with 3- or 4-ternate leaves, to 18in (45cm) long, composed of obovate to elliptic, entire or lobed leaflets. White or lavender-pink flowers, ½in (1.5cm) long, with pendent stamens, are produced in loose panicles in summer. ↕ 36in (90cm), ↔ 12in (30cm). Japan. Zone 5. **'Lavender Mist'** has purple flower stems, frosted with yellow, and bears single, deep lavender flowers. Excellent for cutting; ↕ 5ft (1.5m).

T. speciosissimum see *T. flavum* subsp. *glaucum.*

▷ ***Thamnocalamus falconeri*** see *Himalayacalamus falconeri*

▷ ***Thamnocalamus spathaceus* of gardens** see *Fargesia murieliae*

THELESPERMA

Greenthreads

ASTERACEAE

Genus of about 12 species of annuals and perennials from open fields of W. North America and S. South America. The leaves are usually opposite and are pinnate, with linear leaflets. Greenthreads are cultivated for their daisy-like, yellow to brown-red flowerheads with red to purple disk florets. Grow *Thelesperma* species in a herbaceous border or wild garden.

• **CULTIVATION** Grow in any moderately fertile soil in full sun.

• **PROPAGATION** Sow seed *in situ* in spring.

• **PESTS AND DISEASES** Infrequent.

T. burridgeanum. Branching annual with pinnate leaves, to 4in (10cm) long, composed of linear mid-green leaflets. In summer, bears daisy-like, red-brown flowerheads, to 1¼in (3cm) across, yellow-orange at the apexes, with purple-brown disk florets. ↕ to 32in (80cm), ↔ to 24in (60cm). Texas.

THELOCACTUS

CACTACEAE

Genus of about 11 species of spherical to short-cylindrical, ribbed or warty cacti occurring in arid regions of S.W. US and C., E., and N. Mexico. In summer, large, funnel- to bell-shaped, diurnal flowers are borne on or near the slightly depressed crowns. In areas where temperatures fall below 45°F (7°C), grow *Thelocactus* species as houseplants, or in a cool or temperate greenhouse. In warm, dry climates, they are suitable for a border with other cacti and succulents, or for a desert garden.

• **CULTIVATION** Under glass, grow in standard cactus potting mix in full light, with low humidity. From midspring to early autumn, water moderately,

Thelocactus bicolor

pplying fertilizer 2 or 3 times; keep ompletely dry at other times of year. Outdoors, grow in poor to moderately ertile, gritty, sharply drained soil in full un. See also pp.48–49.
PROPAGATION Sow seed at 70°F 21°C) in spring. Detach offsets in pring or early summer.
PESTS AND DISEASES Mealybugs may e a problem.

T. bicolor ▣ syn. *Ferocactus bicolor* Glory of Texas). Solitary, rarely lustering cactus bearing spherical, often ightly elongated, bluish green stems. Each rib has 8–13 straight or spirally rranged, warty ribs. Areoles, which ave nectar-secreting glands, produce ed, yellow, or white spines (8–18 adials and 4 slightly longer centrals, the ppermost of which is flat). Funnel-haped, red-throated, dark purple-pink owers, 1½–3in (4–8cm) across, are roduced in summer. ↕6–8in 15–20cm), ↔ 4in (10cm). Texas, N. and E. Mexico. ❀ (min. 45°F/7°C)
T. leucacanthus. Often offsetting cactus roducing spherical to cylindrical, pale reen stems, each bearing 7–14 straight r slightly spiraling, conical, warty ribs. reoles with nectar-secreting glands roduce yellow, red, gray, or black pines (6–20 yellow, sometimes ed-tinged radials and 1–3 yellow, red, r black centrals). Short-tubed, unnel-shaped, pale to deep yellow to nagenta flowers, 1½–2in (4–5cm) cross, are produced in summer. ↕ to 6in 15cm), ↔ to 8in (20cm). C. Mexico. ❀ (min. 45°F/7°C)
T. macdowellii, syn. *Echinomastus macdowelli.* Sometimes clustering cactus roducing spherical to club-shaped, ale green stems, each bearing 20–25 onical, warty ribs. The white-felted reoles are densely arranged, and roduce glassy, transparent, white or ale yellow spines (15–20 radials and or 4 yellowish white centrals, the entrals longer than the radials). Funnel-haped magenta flowers, 2in (5cm) or more across, are produced in summer. to 6in (15cm), ↔ 4in (10cm). N.E. Mexico. ❀ (min. 45°F/7°C)
T. setispinus, syn. *Ferocactus setispinus, Hamatocactus setispinus.* Solitary cactus, ter offsetting, producing spherical to hort-cylindrical, dark green stems. Each em has 12–15 notched, often wavy bs. Rounded to elliptic, straw-colored reoles produce white or brown spines)–17 white or red-tinged radials and 1 pale yellow, sometimes red-tinged, hooked central). Funnel-shaped, red-throated yellow flowers, to 2in (5cm) across, are produced from summer to autumn. ↕ 8in (20cm), ↔ 5in (13cm). Texas, N.E. Mexico. ❀ (min. 45°F/7°C)

THELYPTERIS

THELYPTERIDACEAE

Genus, often considered synonymous in part with *Phegopteris*, of 500 species of deciduous, terrestrial ferns found in swamps and bogs in temperate regions throughout the world. The lance-shaped, pinnate fronds, consisting of deeply lobed pinnae, arise from creeping rhizomes. Sori, which have no protective indusia, form on the undersides of the fronds. Suitable for a moist border or for planting at the edge of a pond; *T. palustris* may be invasive.
• **CULTIVATION** Grow in any moist, moderately fertile soil in full sun or partial shade.
• **PROPAGATION** Sow spores at 59°F (15°C) as soon as ripe. Divide in spring or summer. See also p.51.
• **PESTS AND DISEASES** Rust, scale insects, and leaf curl sometimes occur.

T. decursive-pinnata see *Phegopteris decursive-pinnata.*
T. hexagonoptera see *Phegopteris hexagonoptera.*
T. noveboracensis (New York fern). Upright, spreading, deciduous, terrestrial fern producing long, creeping rhizomes with pale golden brown scales. Erect, lance-shaped, pinnate, mid-green sterile fronds, to 18in (45cm) long, each have up to 25 pairs of lance-shaped pinnae, abruptly tapering to long points in the lower third of the frond, then reduced to lobes on the lowest pinnae. ↕ 18in (45cm), ↔ indefinite. Newfoundland to Georgia, Alabama, and Tennessee. Zone 3.
T. palustris ▣ (Marsh fern). Deciduous fern producing long, creeping rhizomes and long-stalked, erect, lance-shaped, pinnate, pale green sterile fronds, to 16in (40cm) long, each consisting of up to 25 pairs of narrowly lance-shaped, deeply lobed pinnae. Fertile fronds, 36in (90cm) long, which are produced only in good light, have pinnae with narrower lobes. The abundant sori may produce a brown haze over the colony in late summer. ↕ 24in (60cm), ↔ to 3ft (1m). Europe, Asia. Zone 4.
T. phegopteris see *Phegopteris connectilis.*

Thelypteris palustris

THERMOPSIS

FABACEAE

Genus of approximately 20 species of rhizomatous perennials from grassy mountainsides, light woodland, and streamsides in Siberia (Russia), N. India, E. Asia, and North America. They are cultivated for their attractive foliage and lupine-like flowers. Erect stems bear alternate, stalked, 3-palmate leaves, some silver-hairy, with persistent, leafy stipules; the similar basal leaves are produced in smaller numbers. Pea-like, yellow or purple flowers, with rounded standard petals and roughly equal-sized keel and wing petals, are borne in terminal or axillary racemes. Suitable for a mixed or herbaceous border, or a wild-flower garden; *T. rhombifolia* is invasive and best grown in a wild garden. The flowers are attractive to bees.
• **CULTIVATION** Grow in light, well-drained, fertile, loamy soil in full sun or partial shade, although they will tolerate a range of conditions. Usually long-lived, they resent root disturbance.
• **PROPAGATION** Sow seed at 50–55°F (10–13°C) in spring, transplanting seedlings to their final position as soon as possible. Division is difficult, and divisions are slow to re-establish.
• **PESTS AND DISEASES** Slugs, aphids, powdery mildew, and leaf spot occur.

T. caroliniana see *T. villosa.*
T. montana see *T. rhombifolia.*
T. rhombifolia, syn. *T. montana* (Mountain false lupine). Rhizomatous perennial producing unbranched stems and 3-palmate leaves, to 4½in (11cm) long, with broadly ovate leaflets. The stems and lower leaf surfaces are softly silver-hairy. In early summer, yellow flowers, 1in (2.5cm) long, are produced in erect, terminal racemes. ↕ 36in (90cm), ↔ 24in (60cm). Rocky Mountains to New Mexico. Zone 2.
T. villosa ▣ syn. *T. caroliniana* (Carolina lupine). Rhizomatous perennial with thick, few-branched or branchless, hairless stems. The 3-palmate leaves, to 4in (10cm) long, have elliptic, obovate, or lance-shaped leaflets, hairless above, glaucous and silky-hairy beneath. In late spring and early summer, downy yellow flowers, to ¾in (2cm) long, are produced in erect, compact, terminal racemes. ↕ 3–5ft (1–1.5m), ↔ 24in (60cm). North Carolina to Georgia. Zone 5.

Thermopsis villosa

THESPESIA

MALVACEAE

Genus of 17 species of mainly evergreen shrubs and trees, closely allied to *Hibiscus*, occurring throughout the world in a wide range of habitats, often in coastal areas of tropical regions. They are grown for their cup-shaped flowers, each with 5 spreading petals, produced singly or in clusters from the leaf axils. The leaves are alternate, simple, mainly lance-shaped to broadly ovate, or palmately 5- to 9-lobed. In areas where temperatures fall below 55–59°F (13–15°C), grow in a warm greenhouse. In tropical climates, grow as specimen plants or windbreaks, especially in coastal areas. *Thespesia* species are relatively carefree; grow with other plants to create an informal screen.
• **CULTIVATION** Under glass, grow in soil-based potting mix in full light. In growth, water freely, applying a balanced liquid fertilizer monthly; water sparingly in winter. Outdoors, grow in moist but well-drained, fertile soil in full sun. Pruning group 1; plants under glass may need restrictive pruning.
• **PROPAGATION** Sow seed at 61°F (16°C) in spring. Insert semi-ripe cuttings with bottom heat in summer. Air layer in spring or summer.
• **PESTS AND DISEASES** Susceptible to spider mites and whiteflies under glass.

T. populnea (Portia tree). Erect to spreading, bushy, evergreen tree bearing long-stalked, heart-shaped to ovate, light to mid-green leaves, 2½–5in (6–13cm) long, with nectar-bearing zones at the bases of the midribs. Solitary yellow flowers, 2–3in (5–8cm) across, with maroon-marked centers, open in sequence throughout the year in warm areas; they fade to dull purple. ↕ 30–50ft (10–15m), ↔ 15–25ft (5–8m). Coastal tropics. ❀ (min. 55–59°F/13–15°C)

THEVETIA

APOCYNACEAE

Genus of 8 species of evergreen shrubs and small trees from woodland, often near coastal areas, in tropical North and South America and the West Indies. They are cultivated for their showy, funnel-shaped flowers, with 5 over-lapping petals, produced singly or in cymes from spring to autumn. They have alternate, simple, mostly linear to ovate leaves. Where temperatures fall below 55–59°F (13–15°C), grow in a temperate or warm greenhouse. In warmer climates, grow in a shrub border. The seeds are highly toxic if ingested.
• **CULTIVATION** Under glass, grow in soil-based potting mix in full light and with good ventilation. During the growing season, water freely and apply a balanced liquid fertilizer monthly; withhold water for a short period after flowering. Water sparingly in winter. Outdoors, grow in moist but well-drained, fertile soil in full sun. Pruning group 1; plants under glass need restrictive pruning.
• **PROPAGATION** Sow seed at 64–70°F (18–21°C) in spring. Insert semi-ripe cuttings with bottom heat in summer.
• **PESTS AND DISEASES** Infrequent.

Thevetia peruviana

T. neriifolia see *T. peruviana.*
T. peruviana ▣ syn. *T. neriifolia* (Be-still tree). Erect, open shrub or small tree bearing narrowly lance-shaped, lustrous, mid- to dark green leaves, 3–6in (8–15cm) long. Fragrant, apricot-yellow flowers, to 3in (8cm) long, are produced in few-flowered cymes near the shoot tips from spring to autumn; they are followed by triangular-ovoid, semi-fleshy, red, later black seed pods, each of which contains 1 or 2 nut-like seeds. ↕ 6–25ft (2–8m), ↔ 3–10ft (1–3m). Tropical America. ❄ (min. 55–59°F/13–15°C)

THLASPI

BRASSICACEAE

Genus of about 60 species of annuals, biennials, and short-lived perennials found in alpine pasture, in mountain woodland, or among rocks and screes in N. temperate regions. They produce oblong or spoon-shaped to broadly ovate or rounded, entire or toothed leaves, usually in rosettes, and are grown for their racemes of 4-petaled, cross-shaped flowers, borne from spring to early summer. Suitable for a sunny rock garden, scree bed, or alpine house.
• **CULTIVATION** Grow in gritty, humus-rich, sharply drained soil in full sun with some midday shade. In an alpine house, use a mix of equal parts loam, leaf mold, and sharp grit.
• **PROPAGATION** Sow seed as soon as ripe in containers in an open frame.
• **PESTS AND DISEASES** White and brown rusts, slugs, and snails can be problems.

T

T. bulbosum. Tufted, tuberous-rooted perennial with rosettes of ovate to ovate-oblong or rounded, entire or toothed, glaucous, dark green leaves, to 1in (2.5cm) long. Deep purple-violet flowers, ¼–⅜in (6–9mm) across, with spoon-shaped petals, are produced in loose, spike-like racemes in spring. ↕ to 4in (10cm), ↔ to 8in (20cm). C. Greece, Aegean Islands. Zone 8.
T. cepaeifolium* subsp. *rotundifolium. Short-lived, tufted perennial producing broadly ovate to almost rounded, deep green leaves, to ½in (1.5cm) long. From spring to early summer, fragrant, deep violet-blue flowers, ½in (1.5cm) long, are borne in short-stemmed, congested, head-like racemes. ↕↔ to 4in (10cm). Europe (Alps, Apennines). Zone 7.
T. macrophyllum see *Pachyphragma macrophyllum.*

THRINAX

Thatch palm

ARECACEAE

Genus of 7 species of single-stemmed palms, found in forested areas on well-drained, often limestone soils, from sea level to 4,000ft (1,200m), in Florida, Mexico, Belize, and the Caribbean islands. The long-stalked, fan-shaped, palmately lobed leaves are borne in a terminal, almost spherical head. Small, cup-shaped flowers, each composed of a fused, 3-lobed calyx and a 3-lobed corolla, are borne in panicles between the leaves. Where not hardy, grow in a warm greenhouse or as houseplants. In tropical regions, grow in a shrub border or as specimen plants on a lawn.
• **CULTIVATION** Under glass, grow in soil-based potting mix in full light or bright filtered light. During growth, water freely and apply a balanced liquid fertilizer monthly; water sparingly in winter. Pot on or top-dress in spring. Outdoors, grow in moist but well-drained, fertile soil in full sun.
• **PROPAGATION** Sow seed at 81°F (27°C) in spring.
• **PESTS AND DISEASES** Sometimes affected by *Stigmina* leaf spot and spider mites.

T. bahamensis see *T. morrisii.*
T. microcarpa see *T. morrisii.*
T. morrisii ▣ syn. *T. bahamensis, T. microcarpa, T. ponceana* (Brittle thatch, Buffalo thatch, Key palm). Small palm with a slim, erect stem. Leaves, 30in (75cm) long, are divided to halfway into 33–58 narrow lobes, densely white- to tan-scaly beneath when young, then glabrous blue-green above; they have fibrous-based leaf stalks, to 32in (80cm) long. White to yellow or orange flowers are borne in loose, arching panicles, to 5ft (1.5m) long, usually in summer. ↕ 15–30ft (5–10m), ↔ 6–11ft (2–3.5m). Florida, Cuba, West Indies. ❄ (min. 61°F/16°C)

Thrinax morrisii

T. parviflora (Florida thatch palm). Small to medium-sized palm with a slim stem. Leaves, to 3ft (1m) long, are divided to halfway into 35–60 narrow lobes, sparsely scaly beneath, rich green above; they have leaf stalks 16–54in (40–130cm) long. Fragrant, cream to yellow flowers are produced in panicles, 20–66in (0.5–1.7m) long, usually in summer. ↕ 20–43ft (6–13m), ↔ 5–11ft (1.5–3.5m). Jamaica. ❄ (min. 61°F/16°C)
T. ponceana see *T. morrisii.*

THRYPTOMENE

Heath myrtle

MYRTACEAE

Genus of 25 species of upright to spreading, evergreen shrubs, found on rocky slopes and heathland in Australia, and grown for their flowers and foliage. The wiry stems bear small, simple, oblong or obovate to inversely lance-shaped leaves in opposite pairs, and produce an abundance of saucer-shaped flowers, each with 5 petals and 5 tepals, from winter to summer. Where not hardy, grow in a cool greenhouse. In milder climates, grow heath myrtles in a shrub border.
• **CULTIVATION** Under glass, grow in acidic potting mix in full light with good ventilation. During the growing season, water moderately and apply a half-strength, balanced liquid fertilizer monthly; water sparingly in winter. Outdoors, grow in light, well-drained, moderately fertile, neutral to acidic soil in full sun. Pruning group 10, after flowering.
• **PROPAGATION** Surface-sow seed at 55°F (13°C) in spring. Insert semi-ripe cuttings with bottom heat in summer.
• **PESTS AND DISEASES** Infrequent.

T. calycina. Spreading, bushy shrub with crowded, tiny, oblong to inversely lance-shaped, aromatic, dark green leaves, ⅜–½in (0.8–1.5cm) long. From winter to spring, axillary, white, pink, or pink and white flowers, ¼in (6mm) across, with yellow centers that age to red, are borne singly or in clusters of 2 or 3. ↕↔ 5–8ft (1.5–2.5m). Victoria. ❄ (min. 39–41°F/4–5°C)

THUJA syn. PLATYCLADUS

Arborvitae

CUPRESSACEAE

Genus of 6 species of narrowly to broadly conical, sometimes columnar, monoecious, evergreen, coniferous trees found in forest in E. Asia and North America. Scale-like, narrowly wedge- to diamond-shaped leaves, borne in 2 ranks of opposite pairs, are usually aromatic when bruised, and may turn brown in winter. The small, erect, variably shaped female cones have scales that hinge from the base; male cones are small and ovoid. Grow as specimen trees or shrubs; most are suitable for hedging. The dwarf cultivars may be grown in a rock garden. Contact with the foliage may aggravate skin allergies.
• **CULTIVATION** Grow in deep, moist but well-drained soil in full sun. Trim hedges in spring and late summer.
• **PROPAGATION** Sow seed in late winter in containers in a cold frame. Insert semi-ripe cuttings in late summer.
• **PESTS AND DISEASES** Caterpillars (including bagworms), bark beetle, weevils, mites, and scale insects are common pests. Butt rot, twig dieback, gray mold (*Botrytis*), mushroom root rot, and needle blights are also common.

T. koraiensis ▣ (Korean arborvitae). Small, conical tree with often trailing branchlets and flattened shoots. Scale-like leaves are triangular on the main shoots and diamond-shaped on the young shoots, bright mid-green above and vivid silver beneath. Ellipsoid brown female cones, ⅜–½in (0.8–1.5cm) long, each have 4 pairs of scales. ↕ to 30ft (10m), ↔ to 15ft (5m). N.E. China, Korea. Zone 5b.
T. occidentalis (American arborvitae, Eastern arborvitae, White cedar). Small, rounded, conical tree with billowing branches and shredding, orange-brown bark. Scale-like, ovate, yellowish green leaves, pale or grayish green beneath, each with a prominent, raised dorsal gland, are distinctively scented and turn brown in winter. Ovoid female cones, ½in (1.5cm) long, each have 8–10 pairs of smooth scales. ↕ 30–60ft (10–18m), ↔ 10–15ft (3–5m). E. North America. Zone 3. **'Boothii'** is dwarf and spherical, flat-topped when mature; ↕ 6–10ft (2–3m). **'Caespitosa'** ▣ is a very slow-growing, cushion- or bun-shaped shrub; ↕ to 12in (30cm), ↔ to 16in (40cm). **'Douglas Pyramidalis'** see 'Pyramidalis'. **'Elegantissima'** is narrowly pyramidal, with yellow-tipped dark green leaves, bronze in winter; ↕ 10–15ft (3–5m), ↔ 4–5ft (1.2–1.5m). **'Ellwangeriana Aurea'** see 'Rheingold'.

Thuja koraiensis

Thuja occidentalis 'Caespitosa'

Thuja occidentalis 'Rheingold'

Thuja occidentalis 'Techny'

Thujopsis dolabrata 'Variegata'

'Emerald' see 'Smaragd'. **'Filiformis'** is mound-forming, with pendent, whip-like shoots; ↕ to 25ft (8m). **'Golden Globe'** is a dwarf, spherical shrub, with bright golden yellow leaves; ↕↔ 3ft (1m). **'Hetz Midget'** ■ is a slow-growing, spherical, dwarf bush; ↕↔ 32in (80cm). **'Hetz Wintergreen'** has a narrowly pyramidal habit and keeps its bright green color all winter; ↕ 20–30ft (6–10m), ↔ 5–10ft (1.5–3m). **'Holmstrup'** is a dense, conical bush, with vertical sprays of mid-green leaves; ↕ to 12ft (4m). **'Little Gem'** is dwarf and spherical, with dark green leaves; ↕ 3ft (1m), ↔ 4½–6ft (1.4–2m). **'Little Giant'** is slow-growing and spherical, with rich green leaves. **'Nigra'** is a pyramidal shrub with dark green leaves; ↕ 20–30ft (6–10m), ↔ 4–5ft (1.2–1.5m). **'Pyramidalis'**, syn. 'Douglas Pyramidalis', is narrowly pyramidal, with soft-textured, bright green leaves. **'Rheingold'** ■ syn. 'Ellwangeriana Aurea', is a conical bush, with golden yellow leaves, pink-tinted when young; ↕ 3–6ft (1–2m). **'Smaragd'**, syn. 'Emerald', is a dwarf, conical, compact shrub, with bright green leaves; ↕ 3ft (1m), ↔ 32in (80cm). **'Techny'** ■ is a slow-growing, broadly pyramidal shrub with leaves that remain dark green all year; ↕ 10–15ft (3–5m), ↔ 6–8ft (2–2.5m). **'Wansdyke Silver'** is dwarf and conical, with variegated, silver-white leaves; ↕ 5ft (1.5m), ↔ 24in (60cm). **'Wareana'** is dense and pyramidal, and bears bright green leaves; ↕ 8ft (2.5m). **'Woodwardii'** is spherical, with dark green leaves; ↕ 8ft (2.5m), ↔ 15ft (5m).

T. orientalis, syn. *Biota orientalis, Platycladus orientalis* (Oriental arborvitae). Conical or irregularly crowned tree with fibrous, red-brown bark and flat, vertical, irregularly arranged sprays of scale-like, blunt, triangular, unscented, mid-green or yellow-green leaves, which often turn bronze in winter. Upright, flask-shaped, gray-bloomed female cones, ¾in (2cm) long, have 3 or 4 pairs of scales, each with 2 prominent, dorsal, reflexed hooks. ↕ to 50ft (15m), ↔ to 20ft (6m). China, Iran. Zone 6. **'Aurea Nana'** is dwarf, with yellow-green leaves, fading to bronze in winter; ↕ to 24in (60cm). **'Elegantissima'** is a conical bush, with golden yellow leaves that slowly age to yellow-green and turn bronze over winter; ↕ to 15ft (5m). **'Semperaurea'** is an ovoid bush, with gold-yellow new growth; ↕ to 10ft (3m). **'Sunkist'** is dwarf, with dense, flat, gold-tipped leaves; ↕↔ 24in (60cm).

T. plicata (Western red cedar). Tall, columnar-conical tree, developing billowing lower branches with fissured, red-brown bark and flat, horizontal or hanging sprays of foliage. Scale-like, ovate, mid- to dark green leaves, whitish green beneath, have small dorsal glands. Oblong-ellipsoid female cones, to ½in (1.5cm) long, have 4 or 5 pairs of scales, with a small, terminal hook on each scale. ↕ 70–120ft (20–35m), ↔ 20–30ft (6–9m). W. North America. Zone 7. All of the following, except 'Zebrina', are shrubs. **'Atrovirens'** is good for hedging, and has very dark green leaves. **'Aurea'** has gold-yellow leaves. **'Cuprea'** is a slow-growing, broadly pyramidal, dwarf shrub with golden yellow-tipped, bronze-green leaves; ↕↔ 3ft (1m). **'Hillieri'** is dwarf, with blue-green leaves; ↕↔ 6–10ft (2–3m). **'Stoneham Gold'** is conical, with bright gold new leaves, aging to dark green; ↕↔ to 6ft (2m). **'Zebrina'** is broadly conical, with yellow-striped leaves; ↕ 40–50ft (12–15m), ↔ 12ft (4m).

THUJOPSIS

CUPRESSACEAE

Genus of one species of monoecious, slow-growing, evergreen, coniferous tree, related to *Thuja*, found in forest in Japan. *T. dolabrata* has shredding bark, 4-ranked, scale-like leaves, and a large, prominent, central prickle on each cone scale. A fine specimen plant in woodland.

- **CULTIVATION** Grow in moist but well-drained, fertile, humus-rich soil in full sun with shelter from cold, dry winds.
- **PROPAGATION** Sow seed in containers in a cold frame in early spring. Insert semi-ripe cuttings in late summer.
- **PESTS AND DISEASES** Infrequent.

T. dolabrata (Hiba arborvitae). Conical to cylindrical tree with brown bark, shredding in gray strips, and 4-ranked, thick, scale-like, shiny-margined, glossy, dark green leaves, silvery white beneath; spreading side leaves are hatchet- or boat-shaped. Spherical, blue-gray female cones, ½in (1.5cm) across, with leathery scales, ripen to brown; cylindrical male cones are dark violet. ↕ to 70ft (20m), ↔ 20–30ft (6–9m). Japan. Zone 6. **'Nana'** ■ is dwarf, with lighter leaves; ↕ 3ft (1m), ↔ 32in (80cm). **'Variegata'** ■ has mid-green foliage with white patches; ↕ 30ft (10m), ↔ 12ft (4m).

THUNBERGIA

ACANTHACEAE

Genus of about 100 species of annuals, evergreen perennials, including many twining climbers, and some shrubs, from tropical and southern Africa, Madagascar, and warm to tropical Asia. They occur on forest floors or in rocky areas, or climb through forest trees or shrubs. They are grown for their often showy, salverform to trumpet-shaped, blue, yellow, orange, red, or white flowers, each with 5 usually spreading lobes, borne singly from the leaf axils or in terminal racemes, mainly in summer. The opposite, elliptic or ovate to almost

Thuja occidentalis 'Hetz Midget' (inset: leaf detail)

Thujopsis dolabrata 'Nana'

rounded leaves are sometimes lobed or toothed. Where not hardy, grow in a temperate or warm greenhouse; *T. alata*, *T. gregorii*, and their cultivars may be grown outdoors as annuals in a sheltered site. In warmer areas, grow shrubs and perennials in a border; the climbers are suitable for training over an arch, pergola, or tree.

• **CULTIVATION** Under glass, grow in soil-based potting mix in full light with shade from hot sun. Support the climbing stems. In growth, water freely, applying a balanced liquid fertilizer monthly; water sparingly in winter. Outdoors, grow in moist but well-drained, fertile soil in full sun. Tropical climbers require partial shade. Pruning group 11 for climbers, in early spring; group 9 for shrubs. All may need restrictive pruning under glass.

• **PROPAGATION** Sow seed at 61–64°F (16–18°C) in spring. Insert greenwood cuttings in early summer, or semi-ripe cuttings in mid- or late summer, both with bottom heat. Layer in spring.

• **PESTS AND DISEASES** Spider mites, whiteflies, and scale insects may be problems under glass.

T. alata ▣ (Black-eyed Susan vine). Evergreen, perennial, twining climber, often grown as an annual, with ovate-triangular, toothed, mid-green leaves, to 3in (8cm) long, usually with angular basal lobes and narrowly winged stalks. From summer to autumn, bears numerous axillary, solitary, salverform flowers, 1¼–1½in (3–4cm) across, usually bright orange or yellow, sometimes creamy white, with or without chocolate-purple centers. ↕ to 8ft (2.5m) as a perennial, 5–8ft (1.5–2m) as an annual. Tropical Africa. ❄ (min. 45–50°F/7–10°C). **'Alba'** has white flowers with dark purple-brown centers. **'Bakeri'** produces snow-white flowers with white centers. **Suzie Hybrids** produce dark-centered, orange-yellow or white flowers.

T. coccinea. Moderately to sparsely branched, evergreen, perennial, twining climber with narrowly elliptic-ovate, toothed, dark green leaves, to 8in (20cm) long. Tubular, orange-red flowers, 1in (2.5cm) long, with reflexed lobes, are borne in loose, pendent racemes, 6–18in (15–45cm) long, from winter to spring. ↕ 10–25ft (3–8m). India, Burma. ❄ (min. 50–55°F/10–13°C)

T. erecta (Bush clock vine, King's mantle). Often creeping or mat-forming, evergreen perennial or bushy, spreading shrub, with ovate to oblong, semi-lustrous, dark green leaves, 1¼–3in (3–8cm) long, sometimes with a few broad teeth. Solitary, trumpet-shaped, creamy yellow flowers, to 3in (8cm) long, with deep blue-purple lobes, are produced from the leaf axils in summer. ↕↔ to 6ft (2m). Tropical W. Africa to South Africa. ❄ (min. 45°F/7°C)

T. gibsonii see *T. gregorii.*

T. grandiflora ▣ (Blue trumpet vine, Sky vine). Vigorous, woody-stemmed, evergreen, perennial, twining climber. Ovate-elliptic to heart-shaped, toothed or lobed, dark green leaves, 4–8in (10–20cm) long, are softly hairy. Bears trumpet-shaped, lavender-blue to violet-blue, occasionally white flowers, 3in (8cm) long, with yellow throats, singly or in pendent racemes, to 4in (10cm) long, in summer. ↕ 15–30ft (5–10m). N. India. ❄ (min. 50–55°F/10–13°C)

T. gregorii ▣ syn. *T. gibsonii.* Woody-based, evergreen, perennial, twining climber, often grown as an annual, with slender, bristly-hairy stems and ovate-triangular, softly hairy, mid-green leaves, to 3in (8cm) long. In summer, bears solitary, salverform, clear orange flowers, 1¾in (4.5cm) across. ↕ to 12ft (4m) or more as a perennial, to 7ft (2.2m) as an annual. Tropical Africa. ❄ (min. 50–55°F/10–13°C)

T. mysorensis ▣ Vigorous, woody-stemmed, evergreen, perennial, twining climber with slender, sparsely branched shoots, at least when young. Narrowly elliptic, slender-pointed, toothed, dark green leaves, 4–6in (10–15cm) long, are prominently veined. In spring, hooded, 2-lipped yellow flowers, 2in (5cm) long, with brownish red to purple tubes, and almost erect, arching, tongue-like upper lips, are produced in pendent racemes, to 7in (18cm) long. ↕ to 20ft (6m) or more. India. ❄ (min. 55–59°F/13–15°C)

Thunbergia grandiflora

Thunbergia mysorensis

THYMOPHYLLA

ASTERACEAE

Genus of 10–12 species of erect to spreading, bushy, strongly aromatic annuals, biennials, perennials, and subshrubs from dry slopes and prairies in the US, Mexico, and Central America. Alternate or opposite leaves are entire to pinnatisect. The abundant small, daisy-like, bright yellow or orange flowerheads are borne from spring to summer. Use *T. tenuiloba*, the most commonly grown species, for summer bedding, or grow in a container or hanging basket.

• **CULTIVATION** Grow in well-drained, moderately fertile soil in full sun.

• **PROPAGATION** Sow seed at 50–55°F (10–13°C) in midspring, and plant out after last frosts. Alternatively, sow seed *in situ* in mid- to late spring.

• **PESTS AND DISEASES** Infrequent.

T. tenuiloba ▣ syn. *Dyssodia tenuiloba* (Dahlberg daisy, Golden fleece, Shooting star). Branching annual, rarely a short-lived perennial, with almost fern-like, pinnatisect, pungent leaves, ⅜–1in (0.8–2.5cm) long, with 7–15 long, linear lobes. From spring to summer, produces upturned, star-shaped, bright yellow flowerheads, to ½in (1.5cm) across. ↕↔ to 12in (30cm). Texas, Mexico.

THYMUS

Thyme

LAMIACEAE

Genus of approximately 350 species of woody-based, aromatic, evergreen perennials, shrubs, and subshrubs, found mainly on calcareous soils and in dry grassland throughout Eurasia. They have small, opposite, oval to linear leaves. In summer, they produce usually terminal, whorled racemes, heads, or clusters of tubular, 2-lipped, usually pink, purple, or white flowers, mostly ⅛–⅜in (4–9mm) long, often with conspicuous bracts. Some thymes, such as *T.* x *citriodorus*, *T. herba-barona*, and *T. vulgaris*, have culinary uses, and are traditionally grown in herb gardens. Most are ideal low shrubs or mat-forming plants for a sunny border or rock garden. The prostrate species, such as *T. polytrichus* or *T. serpyllum*, are suitable for planting in paving crevices, where they release their fragrance when walked on. Some, such as *T. cilicicus*, need protection from winter moisture and are best grown in an alpine house. All are attractive to bees.

• **CULTIVATION** Grow in well-drained, neutral to alkaline soil in full sun. In an alpine house, use a mix of equal parts loam, leaf mold, and grit. Pruning group 10, in spring, for upright, shrubby species. Cut back hard in early spring and trim lightly after flowering to retain compactness.

• **PROPAGATION** Sow seed in containers in a cold frame in spring; thymes hybridize readily and may not come true from seed. Divide in spring. Insert semi-ripe cuttings in mid- or late summer, or softwood cuttings in early summer. Separate rooted stem sections in spring or summer, and pot up, and grow on until re-established.

• **PESTS AND DISEASES** Gray mold (*Botrytis*) and root rot rarely occur.

T. azoricus see *T. caespititius.*

T. caespititius, syn. *T. azoricus*, *T. micans.* Dense, mat- or mound-forming subshrub with branching, woody stems and hairy, narrowly spoon-shaped, dark green leaves, to ½in (1.5cm) long. In late spring and early summer, bears whorled heads of pale rose-pink, lilac, or white flowers, pressed against the foliage. ↕ to 2in (5cm), ↔ to 12in (30cm). Spain, Portugal. Zone 5.

T. cilicicus ▣ (Cilician thyme). Compact, cushion- to tussock-forming subshrub with upright, minutely hairy shoots bearing stalkless, linear, prominently veined, dark green leaves, to ½in (1.5cm) long, finely hairy beneath and at the margins. In early summer, bears lilac or mauve flowers in dense, hemispherical heads. ↕ to 6in (15cm), ↔ to 8in (20cm). Turkey. Zone 6.

T.* x *citriodorus (*T. pulegioides* x *T. vulgaris*) (Lemon-scented thyme). Bushy, rounded shrub with branching stems and narrow, oval-diamond-shaped to lance-shaped, more or less hairless, lemon-scented, mid-green leaves, to ½in (1.5cm) long. In summer, pale lavender-pink flowers, with leaf-like bracts, are borne in irregular, oblong heads. ↕ to 12in (30cm), ↔ to 10in (25cm). Garden origin. Zone 5. **'Anderson's Gold'** see 'Bertram Anderson'. **'Archer's Gold'**

Thunbergia alata

Thunbergia gregorii

Thymophylla tenuiloba

as mid-green leaves with narrow, olden yellow margins. **'Argenteus'** has ilver-edged leaves. **'Aureus'** ▣ has gold-appled leaves. **'Bertram Anderson'** ▣ yn. 'Anderson's Gold', produces gray-reen leaves, strongly suffused yellow. **Golden King'** is upright in habit, with old-margined leaves; ↕ 10in (25cm), ↔ to 18in (45cm). **'Silver Queen'** roduces cream-variegated leaves.
T. doerfleri. Compact, spreading sub-hrub with prostrate, hairy stems and near, slightly fragrant, mid- to dark reen, hairy leaves, ⅜–½in (0.8–1.5cm) ong. Purplish pink flowers are produced n whorled racemes in summer. Requires harp drainage; best in a rock garden. 6in (15cm), ↔ 18in (45cm). Albania. Zone 5. **'Bressingham'** ▣ is prostrate nd mat-forming, with gray-reen leaves and clear pink flowers; 4in (10cm), ↔ 14in (35cm).
***T.* 'Doone Valley'** ▣ Mat-forming ubshrub with lance-shaped, dark olive-reen leaves, to ½in (1.5cm) long, with ellow spots. Lavender-pink flowers, rimson-red in bud, are borne in ounded heads in summer. ↕ 5in (13cm), ↔ 14in (35cm). Zone 5b.
T. herba-barona (Caraway thyme, Herb baron). Dwarf, loosely mat-orming, wiry-branched subshrub earing ovate to lance-shaped, caraway-cented, dark green leaves, to ¼in 5mm) long. Pale pink flowers are roduced in loose, irregular, oblong o hemispherical heads in midsummer. to 4in (10cm), ↔ to 8in (20cm). Corsica, Sardinia. Zone 5.
T. leucotrichus ▣ Dwarf, creeping ubshrub with narrowly lance-shaped, airy, strongly scented, gray-green eaves, ⅛–⅜in (4–9mm) long. Whorled lusters of pale purplish pink flowers re produced in spring. ↕ to 6in (15cm), ↔ to 8in (20cm). Greece, Turkey. Zone 6.
T. longiflorus ▣ Densely branched ubshrub with ascending, hairy shoots earing hairy, narrowly elliptic to linear, ray-green leaves, to ½in (1.5cm) long, vith the margins rolled under. Pink lowers with ovate, leathery, greenish urple bracts are borne in spike-like vhorls in summer. ↕ to 12in (30cm), ↔ to 10in (25cm). S. Spain. Zone 6.
T. mastichina. Vigorous, erect sub-hrub with upright, hairy shoots and

Thymus pulegioides

ovate to elliptic-lance-shaped, often shallowly scalloped, mid-green leaves, ½in (1.5cm) long. In summer, bears spherical heads of abundant white flowers. ↕ to 12in (30cm), ↔ to 16in (40cm). Spain, Portugal. Zone 7b.
T. membranaceus. Spreading, rounded shrub with ascending shoots and linear, gray-green leaves, to ½in (1.5cm) long. In summer, bears ovoid heads of long-tubed white flowers, to ½in (1.5cm) long, with conspicuous, greenish white bracts. Grow in an alpine house or a warm garden. Cut back immediately after flowering. ↕↔ to 8in (20cm). S. Spain. Zone 7b.
T. micans see *T. caespititius.*
T. polytrichus, syn. *T.* 'Porlock', *T. praecox.* Dense, compact subshrub with woody, prostrate, branching stems and narrowly obovate, dark green leaves, ⅜in (9mm) long, fringed with minute hairs. Pale to deep purple, occasionally off-white flowers are borne in terminal heads in summer. ↕ to 2in (5cm), ↔ to 24in (60cm) or more. S. Europe. Zone 6. **subsp. *britannicus* var. *albus***, syn. *T. praecox* subsp. *arcticus* var. *albus*, has softly hairy stems, obovate leaves, and white flowers.
***T.* 'Porlock'** see *T. polytrichus.*
T. praecox see *T. polytrichus.*
T. praecox* subsp. *arcticus* var. *albus see *T. polytrichus* subsp. *britannicus* var. *albus.*
***T. praecox* 'Coccineus'** see *T. serpyllum* var. *coccineus.*
T. pulegioides ▣ (Mother of thyme). Spreading subshrub with semi-erect, 4-angled stems and oblong-lance-shaped, strongly aromatic, mid-green leaves, ¼–¾in (0.6–2cm) long. In late spring and early summer, bears short, irregular, whorled racemes of pink to purple flowers. ↕ 2–10in (5–25cm), ↔ 12in (30cm). Europe; naturalized in North America. Zone 5.
T. richardii. Spreading to loosely mat-forming subshrub with ovate, aromatic, mid-green leaves, ⅜–½in (0.9–1.5cm) long. Whorled racemes of purple flowers are produced in late spring. ↕ 5in (13cm), ↔ 12in (30cm). Spain (Balearic Islands), Italy (Sicily), Croatia. Zone 7. **subsp. *nitidus*** has narrowly ovate leaves, to ½in (1.5cm) long; Italy (Sicily). **subsp. *nitidus* 'Peter Davis'** ▣ is bushy, with gray-green leaves, to ⅜in (9mm) long, and numerous pink flowers; ↕ 6in (15cm), ↔ 2in (5cm).
T. serpyllum (Mother of thyme, Wild thyme, Serpolet). Mat-forming subshrub with finely hairy, trailing stems and linear to elliptic or elliptic-ovate, aromatic, mid-green leaves, ⅛–⅜in (3–9mm) long. Purple flowers are borne in congested whorls in summer. ↕ 10in (25cm), ↔ 18in (45cm). Europe. Zone 4. Some cultivars are probably of hybrid origin, and their status is botanically uncertain. **'Annie Hall'** ▣ has pale purple-pink flowers. **'Aureus'** is creeping, with gold leaves. **'Carol Ann'** is mat-forming, and bears gold-variegated leaves and lilac flowers. **var. *coccineus*** ▣ syn. *T. praecox* 'Coccineus', has crimson-pink flowers. **'Elfin'** ▣ forms dense mounds of foliage, and seldom flowers freely; ↕ to 3in (8cm), ↔ to 4in (10cm). **'Minimus'** is compact, producing lance-shaped leaves, to ⅛in (3mm) long, and pink flowers; ↕ 2in (5cm), ↔ 4in (10cm). **'Minor'** is compact, with lance-shaped leaves, to ¼in (6mm) long, and pink flowers; ↕ 5in (13cm). **'Mountain'** is creeping, with glossy leaves, and deep plum flowers. **'Pink Chintz'** has gray-green leaves and flesh-pink flowers. **'Snowdrift'** bears clear white flowers.
T. villosus. Upright, woody subshrub with linear to lance-shaped, woolly, mid-green leaves, to ½in (1.5cm) long. In summer and early autumn, bears conical heads of purple flowers with green bracts. ↕ to 12in (30cm), ↔ to 10in (25cm). Spain, Portugal. Zone 6.
T. vulgaris (Common thyme, Garden thyme). Bushy, cushion-forming, spreading subshrub with linear to elliptic, finely hairy, aromatic, gray-green leaves, ¼–½in (0.6–1.5cm) long. In late spring and early summer, bright purple to white flowers are produced in whorled racemes. ↕ 6–12in (15–30cm), ↔ 16in (40cm). W. Mediterranean to S. Italy. Zone 4. **'Aureus'** has leaves suffused yellow. **'Orange Balsam'** has orange-scented foliage. **'Silver Posie'** ▣ has white-margined leaves.

Thymus cilicicus

Thymus x *citriodorus* 'Aureus'

Thymus x *citriodorus* 'Bertram Anderson'

Thymus doerfleri 'Bressingham'

Thymus 'Doone Valley'

Thymus leucotrichus

Thymus longiflorus

Thymus richardii subsp. *nitidus* 'Peter Davis'

Thymus serpyllum 'Annie Hall'

Thymus serpyllum var. *coccineus*

Thymus serpyllum 'Elfin'

Thymus vulgaris 'Silver Posie'

T

TIARELLA

Foam flower

SAXIFRAGACEAE

Genus of about 7 species of rhizomatous herbaceous perennials from woodland and streambanks in E. Asia and North America. The mainly basal, ovate to heart-shaped or rounded, toothed, sometimes long-stalked leaves are simple or palmately 3- to 5-lobed, occasionally 7-lobed, or 3-palmate; they are pale to mid-green, often turning shades of reddish copper in autumn and winter, and have conspicuous veins and sparse, bristly hairs. The tiny, star-shaped, fluffy, white or pinkish white flowers, ¼–½in (5–15mm) across, are borne in terminal panicles or racemes over a long period from spring to summer. Grow as a groundcover in a woodland garden or shady border; *T. cordifolia* spreads freely.
• **CULTIVATION** Grow ideally in cool, moist, humus-rich soil, although they tolerate a wide range of soil conditions. Provide deep or partial shade. Protect from excessive winter moisture.
• **PROPAGATION** Sow seed in containers in a cold frame in spring or as soon as ripe. Divide in spring.
• **PESTS AND DISEASES** Prone to rust and slugs.

T. cordifolia ▣ Vigorous, rhizomatous perennial, spreading by stolons, with hairy, 3- to 5-lobed, ovate, pale green leaves, to 4in (10cm) long, heart-shaped at the bases, tinted bronze-red in autumn. In summer, bears creamy white flowers in a profusion of upright, spike-like racemes, 4–12in (10–30cm) long. ↕ 4–12in (10–30cm), ↔ to 12in (30cm) or more. North America. Zone 4. **var. *collina*** see *T. wherryi.* **'Marmorata'** has bronze leaves, turning dark green with purple flecks, and maroon flowers. **'Slickrock'** has deeply dissected, dark green leaves and fragrant, pink flowers.
***T.* 'Maple Leaf'.** Clump-forming, herbaceous or semi-evergreen perennial, without stolons, producing rosettes of broadly ovate, 5-lobed, mid-green, red-flushed leaves, 2–5in (5–13cm) long. From late spring to midsummer, bears white, pink-flushed flowers in racemes, 6–12in (15–30cm) long. ↕↔ to 12in (30cm). Zone 5.
T. polyphylla. Clump-forming, rhizomatous perennial, spreading by stolons, with 5-lobed, heart-shaped, scalloped basal leaves, ¾–2½in (2–8cm)

Tiarella cordifolia

Tiarella wherryi 'Oakleaf'

across, with mid-green leaflets, and 2 or 3 minutely stalked stem leaves. Bears racemes, 9in (23cm) long, of several nodding, white-tinged, pink flowers, in mid- and late summer. ↕ 12–24in (30–60cm), ↔ 12in (30cm). Himalayas. Zone 5.
T. trifoliata. Clump-forming, rhizomatous perennial, without stolons, producing 3-palmate basal leaves, to 3in (8cm) long, with 3-lobed, hairy, mid-green leaflets, veined dark green; the 2 or 3 stem leaves have short stalks. Pendent white flowers are produced in loose panicles, 6–20in (15–50cm) long, opening from pinkish white buds from late spring to midsummer. ↕ to 20in (50cm), ↔ 12in (30cm). Alaska to Oregon. Zone 5. **'Incarnadine'** bears pink flowers.
T. unifoliata. Clump-forming, rhizomatous perennial, without stolons, producing ovate, 3- to 5-lobed, hairy, pointed, scalloped, mid-green leaves, to 3in (8cm) long. In mid- and late summer, bears narrow panicles, to 18in (45cm) long, of pendent white flowers with twisted petal tips, pinkish white in bud. ↕ to 18in (45cm), ↔ 12in (30cm). S. Alaska to W. Montana. Zone 3.
T. wherryi, syn. *T. cordifolia* var. *collina.* Compact, slow-growing, clump-forming perennial, without stolons, producing hairy, ovate, sharply 3-lobed, maroon-tinted, pale green leaves, to 5½in (14cm) long, heart-shaped at the bases. White, sometimes pink-tinged flowers are produced in brown-stemmed, slender, spike-like racemes, 6–14in (15–35cm) long, in late spring and early summer. Prefers moist shade. ↕ to 8in (20cm), ↔ to 6in (15cm). E. US (Appalachians). Zone 3b. **'Bronze Beauty'** has dark red-bronze foliage and light pinkish white flowers. **'Eco Red Heart'** has light green leaves marked with a heart-shaped, red zone, and bears pink flowers. **'Oakleaf'** ▣ is fast-growing, densely clump-forming, and has lobed, toothed, dark green leaves and profuse, deep pink flowers.

Tibouchina urvilleana

TIBOUCHINA

MELASTOMATACEAE

Genus of about 350 species of evergreen shrubs and subshrubs or herbaceous perennials, some of them climbing, found in rainforest in Mexico, the West Indies, and from tropical South America to N. Argentina (mainly Brazil). Large, elliptic, ovate, or lance-shaped, leathery leaves, usually with 1–3 pairs of prominent, primary veins, are borne in opposite pairs. Saucer- to cup-shaped, mostly 5-petaled flowers are produced singly, in threes, or in long panicles. Where temperatures fall below 45°F (7°C), grow in a cool or temperate greenhouse. In warmer areas, grow in a shrub border.
• **CULTIVATION** Under glass, grow in soil-based potting mix in full light with shade from hot sun. During the growing season, water freely and apply a balanced liquid fertilizer monthly; water sparingly in winter. Outdoors, grow in moist, fertile soil in full sun. Pruning group 9; plants grown under glass need restrictive pruning in late winter.
• **PROPAGATION** Sow seed at 61°F (16°C) in spring. Root softwood cuttings in late spring or semi-ripe cuttings in summer, both with bottom heat.
• **PESTS AND DISEASES** Gray mold, mushroom root rot, leaf spots, and root rot of seedlings can occur. Spider mites may be a problem under glass.

T. organensis, syn. *T. semidecandra* subsp. *floribunda* of gardens (Glory bush). Open, erect shrub with 4-angled, hairy stems and ovate-oblong, velvety-hairy, grayish green leaves, to 6in (15cm) long, sometimes maturing to bright scarlet. From summer to autumn, produces open, leafy panicles of satin-textured, saucer-shaped, bluish purple flowers, 4in (10cm) or more across. ↕ 10–20ft (3–6m), ↔ 6–10ft (2–3m). S.E. Brazil. ❀ (min. 41–45°F/5–7°C)
***T. semidecandra* of gardens** see *T. urvilleana.*
***T. semidecandra* subsp. *floribunda* of gardens** see *T. organensis.*
T. urvilleana ▣ syn. *Pleroma macrantha, T. semidecandra* of gardens (Brazilian spider flower, Glory bush). Erect to spreading shrub with 4-angled, red-hairy stems and oblong-ovate to ovate or elliptic, velvety-hairy, mid- to dark green leaves, 2–3in (5–8cm) long. From summer to autumn, bears leafy panicles of satin-textured, saucer-shaped deep purple flowers, 2in (5cm) across, with dark, hooked stamens. ↕ 10–20ft (3–6m), ↔ 6–10ft (2–3m). Brazil. ❀ (min. 39–41°F/3–5°C)

TIGRIDIA

Peacock flower, Tiger flower

IRIDACEAE

Genus of 23 species of bulbous perennials from seasonally dry sands and grassland, occasionally among rocks in Mexico and Guatemala. They have mostly basal, narrowly lance-shaped to sword-shaped leaves. The attractive, short-lived, brightly colored summer flowers open in succession on long stems. They are either upright and iris-like or pendent and bell-shaped, with 3 large, spreading outer segments and 3 shorter inner ones. In frost-free climates grow in a border; where not hardy, grow outdoors and lift in autumn, or grow permanently as container plants in a cool greenhouse or conservatory.
• **CULTIVATION** Plant 4in (10cm) deep. Outdoors, grow in well-drained, preferably sandy, fertile soil in full sun. In cold areas, lift bulbs after flowering and overwinter in dry sand at about 50°F (10°C). Under glass, grow in soil-based potting mix, with added sharp sand. Water freely when in growth and keep dry when dormant; repot annually in spring.
• **PROPAGATION** Sow seed at 55–64°F (13–18°C) in spring. Separate offsets when dormant (taking care to avoid plants affected by viruses).
• **PESTS AND DISEASES** Prone to viruses.

T. meleagris. Bulbous perennial with branched stems bearing 1 or 2 lance-shaped leaves, 8–12in (20–30cm) long; basal leaves are only rarely produced. In summer, bears 2–6 pendent, widely bell shaped, pale pink to maroon flowers, 1¼in (3cm) across, with darker spots. ↕ 10–24in (25–60cm), PD4in (10cm). Mexico. ❀ (min. 46–54°F/8–12°C)
T. pavonia ▣ (Peacock flower, Tiger flower). Bulbous perennial with lance-shaped leaves, 8–20in (20–50cm) long, borne in a basal fan. In summer, bears occasionally branched stems, each with 1–3 stem leaves and a succession of iris-like, orange to pink, red, yellow, or white flowers, 4–6in (10–15cm) across, mostly with contrasting central marks. ↕ 5ft (1.5m), PD4in (10cm). Mexico. ❀ (min. 46–54°F/8–12°C)

Tigridia pavonia

TILIA

inden

ILIACEAE

enus of 20–45 species of deciduous rees occurring in woodland in Europe, sia, and North America. They are ultivated for their stately habit, their oliage and flowers, and, in some cases, or their colorful winter shoots. The vate to rounded leaves, arranged lternately on slender stalks, are toothed r lobed, with tapered to pointed tips nd heart-shaped bases. On old trees, he smooth, silver-gray bark becomes issured. Small, cup-shaped, fragrant, reamy white to yellow flowers are orne in slender, axillary cymes with ong stalks; the stalks are fused with the pper surfaces of large, narrowly elliptic r inversely lance-shaped, membranous racts, usually pale yellow or green, to in (15cm) long. The flowers are ollowed by dry, nut-like fruits. Grow as ree-standing specimens or street trees. he flowers attract bees, although the ectar of *T. tomentosa* and *T.* 'Petiolaris' nay be toxic, especially to bumblebees.

CULTIVATION Grow in moist but well-rained soil in full sun or partial shade. void very dry conditions and exposure o strong winds. Lindens prefer alkaline r neutral soil, but they tolerate acidic oil. Several species produce dense hickets of shoots from the base and rom burrs on the trunk; control these y cutting back in early spring and again n late summer. Pruning group 1.

PROPAGATION Stratify seed for 3–5 nonths and sow in containers in a cold frame in spring, or sow as soon as ripe in a seedbed in autumn; garden-collected seed may yield hybrids of variable quality. Bud in late summer.

• **PESTS AND DISEASES** Anthracnose, butt rot and canker, powdery mildew, bacterial leaf spot, caterpillars (including gypsy moth larvae), lace bugs, aphids, borers, Japanese beetle, and mites occur.

T. americana (American linden, Basswood). Broadly columnar tree with broadly ovate to rounded, dark green leaves, matte above, glossy beneath, to 8in (20cm) long. Pendent cymes of 10–15 yellow flowers, ½in (1.5cm) across, are produced in midsummer. ↕ 80ft (25m), ↔ 50ft (15m). C. and E. North America. Zone 2b. **'Fastigiata'** is conical, with upright branches; ↔ 25ft (8m). **'Redmond'**, syn. *T.* x *euchlora* 'Redmond', is dense and broadly pyramidal; ↕ 46ft (14m), ↔ 22ft (7m).

T. caroliniana (Carolina basswood). Dense, rounded tree with ovate, dark green leaves, to 3½in (9cm) long, paler and hairy beneath. In early summer, bears pale yellow flowers, ½in (1.5cm) across, in pendent cymes of 10–15. ↕ 30–40ft (10–12m), ↔ 25ft (8m). S.E. US. Zone 7b.

T. cordata (Littleleaf linden). Broadly pyramidal tree with rounded, lustrous, dark green leaves, to 3in (8cm) long, blue-green and smooth beneath except for tufts of brown hairs in the leaf axils; leaves turn yellow in autumn. Produces cymes of up to 10 pale yellow flowers, ¾in (2cm) across, in midsummer. ↕ 90ft (25m), ↔ 50ft (15m). Europe, Caucasus. Zone 3. **'Glenleven'** is fast-growing and open, with leaves to 4in (10cm) long; ↕ 50ft (15m), ↔ 35ft (11m). **'Greenspire'** ■ is vigorous and conical; ↕ 50ft (15m), ↔ 22ft (7m). **'Prestige'** is fast-growing, with a uniformly oval shape, uniform radial branching, and glossy, bright green leaves; ↕ 60ft (18m), ↔ 40ft (12m). **'Rancho'** is open in habit when young, becoming narrowly oval, with glossy leaves; ↕ 50ft (15m), ↔ 25ft (8m). **'Salem'** has a rounded crown, upright branches, and deep green leaves; ↕ 35ft (11m), ↔ 25–30ft (8–10m).

Tilia cordata 'Greenspire' (inset: flower detail)

***T. dasystyla* of gardens** see *T.* x *euchlora.*

T.* x *euchlora, syn. *T. dasystyla* of gardens (Crimean linden). Rounded tree with branches that become slightly pendent with age. The rounded to broadly ovate, toothed leaves, 2–4in (5–10cm) long, are heart-shaped at the bases, glossy, dark green above and pale green with tufts of hairs in the axils of the veins beneath. Cymes of 3–7 yellowish white flowers, ½in (1.5cm) across, are borne in midsummer. Remains free of aphids, and therefore also of sticky honeydew. ↕ 70ft (20m), ↔ 50ft (15m). Garden origin. Zone 3. **'Laurelhurst'** is vigorous in habit, with a straight trunk and broadly pyramidal crown. **'Redmond'** see *T. americana* 'Redmond'.

T.* x *europaea (*T. cordata* x *T. platyphyllos*) syn. *T. intermedia*, *T.* x *vulgaris* (European linden). Broadly columnar tree with broadly ovate to rounded, dark green leaves, to 4in (10cm) long, paler beneath. Cymes of up to 10 pale yellow flowers, ¾in (2cm) across, are borne in midsummer. ↕ 120ft (35m), ↔ 50ft (15m). Europe. Zone 4. **'Wratislaviensis'** has bright yellow young leaves, turning yellowish green; ↕ 70ft (20m), ↔ 40ft (12m).

T. henryana ■ Spreading tree with broadly ovate, glossy, bright green leaves, to 5in (13cm) long, brown-hairy and paler beneath, red-tinged when young, and with long, bristle-like teeth. In late summer and early autumn, bears cymes of up to 25 small, creamy white flowers, ½in (1.5cm) across. ↕↔ to 80ft (25m). C. China. Zone 7.

T. intermedia see *T.* x *europaea.*

T. mongolica (Mongolian linden). Rounded tree or shrub with glossy, dark green leaves, to 1½in (4cm) long, blue-green beneath, and red when young; they are rounded to triangular, and deeply cut into 3 sharply toothed lobes, often with 2 lateral lobes. Pale yellow flowers, ¾in (2cm) across, are produced in pendent cymes of up to 30 in early summer. ↕ 60ft (18m), ↔ 40ft (12m). Mongolia, N. China. Zone 3b.

T. petiolaris see *T.* 'Petiolaris'.

***T.* 'Petiolaris'**, syn. *T. petiolaris*, *T. tomentosa* 'Petiolaris' (Weeping silver linden). Broadly columnar tree with weeping branches, pendent shoots, and long-stalked, rounded, dark green leaves, to 3in (8cm) long, densely white-hairy beneath. Bears pendent cymes of up to 10 fragrant, pale yellow flowers, to ½in (1.5cm) across, in late summer. ↕ 100ft (30m), ↔ 70ft (20m). Zone 4b.

T. platyphyllos ■ (Large-leaved linden). Broadly columnar tree with rounded to broadly ovate, dark green leaves, 3–6in (8–15cm) long, paler and usually densely hairy beneath, turning yellow in autumn. Produces pendent cymes of 3–5 pale yellow flowers, ¾in (2cm) across, in midsummer. ↕ 100ft (30m), ↔ 70ft (20m). Europe. Zone 5. **'Princes Street'** is upright, with bright red winter shoots. **'Rubra'** (Red-twigged linden) has red winter shoots.

Tilia henryana

T. tomentosa (European white linden, Silver linden). Broadly columnar tree with rounded to broadly ovate, sometimes lobed, dark green leaves, to 4in (10cm) long, densely white-hairy beneath. In summer, bears cymes of up to 10 very fragrant white flowers, to ½in (1.5cm) across. ↕ 100ft (30m), ↔ 70ft (20m). S.E. Europe, S.W. Asia. Zone 4b. **'Green Mountain'** is fast-growing, with leaves that are silver-green beneath; heat and drought tolerant. **'Petiolaris'** see *T.* 'Petiolaris'. **'Princeton'** is broadly pyramidal in shape, aging to pyramidal-oval, with dark green leaves, silver-green beneath, turning yellow in autumn; ↕ 50–60ft (15–18m), ↔ 30–40ft (10–12m). **'Sterling'** has a broadly pyramidal crown, gray bark, and silver-green young leaves, aging to dark green, silver-green beneath; resistant to Japanese beetle and gypsy moth; ↕ 50ft (15m), ↔ 25ft (8m).

T.* x *vulgaris see *T.* x *europaea.*

Tilia platyphyllos

TILLANDSIA

Air plant

BROMELIACEAE

Genus of over 400 species of epiphytic, terrestrial, or rock-dwelling, evergreen perennials (bromeliads) from scrub and woodland in S. US, the West Indies, and Central and South America. The entire, often scaly leaves are strap-shaped to narrowly triangular to linear, sometimes tapering to fine threads; they are mainly borne in rosettes, with a few along the slender stems, and sometimes have prominent sheaths. Most species have tubular to funnel-shaped flowers, each with 3 sepals and 3 petals, often with spreading terminal lobes; they are borne among usually colorful floral bracts, generally opening in daytime in spring or autumn. The flowers may be solitary but are usually in 2 or more opposite rows, forming small, dense racemes or spikes, which are sometimes grouped into compound inflorescences; the flowers are borne mainly at the ends of scapes that have sometimes dense or colorful bracts. Where temperatures fall below 45°F (7°C), grow in a temperate greenhouse or conservatory, or as houseplants. In warmer areas, grow the epiphytic species on a tree; the rock-dwelling and terrestrial species may also be grown in a rock garden, on bark or tree branches placed on the ground, or beneath trees or shrubs.

• **CULTIVATION** Under glass, grow epiphytically in bright indirect light, with moderate to high humidity; rock-dwelling species prefer full light with shade from hot sun, and will tolerate low humidity. Constant air movement is essential. From late spring to mid-autumn, mist daily and apply a quarter-strength low-nitrogen liquid fertilizer monthly. In winter, mist once or twice a week. Grow terrestrial species, and *T. cyanea* and *T. lindenii*, in containers of terrestrial bromeliad potting mix, with the bases of the leaves at or just above the surface, in bright filtered light. In growth, water freely and apply a half-strength, low-nitrogen fertilizer monthly; keep just moist in winter. Outdoors, grow epiphytic species in a tree in moist, partial shade. Grow terrestrial and rock-dwelling species in coarse, open, leafy soil in partial or dappled shade. Many are hardy outdoors in Zone 9 if kept dry in winter. See also p.47.

Tillandsia fuchsii

Tillandsia brachycaulos

• **PROPAGATION** Sow seed at 81°F (27°C) in spring, onto bundles of conifer twigs and sphagnum moss; mist daily. Detach offsets in spring.

• **PESTS AND DISEASES** Prone to *Fusarium* rot, scale insects, and mealybugs.

T. aeranthos, syn. *T. dianthoidea.* Epiphytic, cushion-forming perennial with fine-scaly stems bearing narrowly lance-shaped, often keeled, rigid, densely gray-scaly, mid-green leaves, 4in (10cm) or more long. In spring, bears cylindrical spikes of 5–20 slender, funnel-shaped, dark blue flowers, 1in (2.5cm) long, with bright rose-pink floral bracts. ↕↔ to 12in (30cm). S. Brazil, N.E. Argentina, Paraguay, Uruguay. ❄ (min. 45°F/7°C)

T. bergeri. Rock-dwelling perennial with rosettes of narrowly triangular, gray-scaly, mid-green leaves, 4in (10cm) long. In spring, produces simple spikes of 7–12 funnel-shaped, blue and white flowers, 1¼in (3cm) long, fading to rose-pink, with gray-green floral bracts. Requires very bright light to bloom. ↕ to 7in (18cm), ↔ 6in (15cm). Argentina. ❄ (min. 45°F/7°C)

T. brachycaulos ▣ Stemless, epiphytic perennial with rosettes of slender, linear to lance-shaped, arching, densely green-scaly or silver-gray-scaly, dark green leaves, 5–10in (12–25cm) long, with thread-like tips and prominent sheaths, turning bright red when in flower. In spring, bears short spikes of 1 or 2 erect, tubular violet flowers, to 3in (8cm) long, with red floral bracts, clustered into a head. ↕↔ 10in (25cm). S. Mexico, Central America. ❄ (min. 45°F/7°C)

T. caput-medusae ▣ Stemless, epiphytic perennial with rosettes of narrowly awl-shaped, tapered, recurved, pale green leaves, 6in (15cm) or more long; the leaf blades are covered with spreading, coarse, silver-gray hairs, and have ovate sheaths inflated to form hollow pseudobulbs. Suberect or curved spikes of 6–12 slender, tubular blue flowers, 1¼–1½in (3–4cm) long, with red floral bracts, are produced in late spring. ↕ 6–16in (15–40cm), ↔ to 10in (25cm). Mexico, Central America. ❄ (min. 45°F/7°C)

T. crocata. Short-stemmed, untidy, sometimes branched, epiphytic or rock-dwelling perennial with 2 rows of linear, coarse, gray-hairy, mid-green leaves, 4–6in (10–15cm) long. In spring or autumn, produces simple spikes of 3 or 4 funnel-shaped, fragrant, bright canary-yellow flowers, ¾in (2cm) long, with green, heavily gray-scaled floral bracts. ↕ to 8in (20cm), ↔ to 6in (15cm). Brazil, Argentina. ❄ (min. 45°F/7°C)

Tillandsia caput-medusae

T. cyanea ▣ Epiphytic perennial with stemless rosettes of linear-triangular, semi-erect then recurved, dark green leaves, to 14in (35cm) long, red-striped near the bases. Flattened, paddle-shaped, almost stalkless spikes of 20 funnel-shaped, rich violet flowers, to 1¼in (3cm) long, with spreading petals and rose-pink floral bracts, are produced in late spring or autumn. ↕ to 12in (30cm), ↔ to 16in (40cm). Ecuador. ❄ (min. 45°F/7°C)

T. dianthoidea see *T. aeranthos.*

T. fasciculata ▣ (Wild pineapple). Epiphytic perennial with stemless rosettes of narrowly triangular, spreading, sparsely hairy or silver-gray-hairy, brittle, pale gray-green leaves, to 12in (30cm) long, with brown sheaths. In late spring, spikes of red to yellow floral bracts and erect, tubular, white and purple flowers, to 2½in (6cm) long, usually 3 or 4 at a time, are borne in compound inflorescences. ↕↔ 12in (30cm) or more. S. US, West Indies, Mexico to Colombia and Peru. ❄ (min. 45°F/7°C)

T. fuchsii ▣ Epiphytic perennial with rhizomatous, curved, short, branched stem bearing dense rosettes of narrowly linear, silvery white-scaly, pale green leaves, 2½–3½in (6–9cm) long. Bears simple spikes of 6–8 tubular, bright red or blue flowers, 1¼in (3cm) long, with salmon-pink floral bracts, in spring.

Tillandsia cyanea

Tillandsia fasciculata

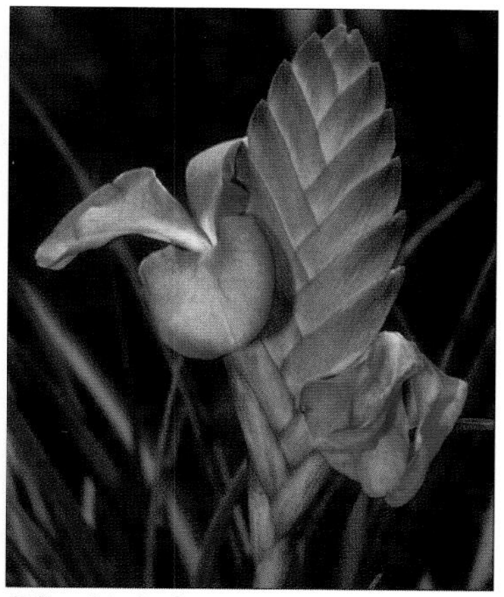
Tillandsia lindenii

↕↔ to 10in (25cm). Mexico, Guatemala. ❄ (min. 45°F/7°C)
T. gardneri. Epiphytic or rock-dwelling perennial bearing dense rosettes of narrowly triangular, densely scaly, silver-gray leaves, 4–11in (10–28cm) long, the lower ones recurved. Compound inflorescences, each consisting of 4–12 spikes of 3–12 slender, funnel-shaped, rose-pink to pale lavender-pink flowers, to ¾in (2cm) long, with green to pink floral bracts, are produced in late spring. ↕↔ 10in (25cm). Colombia to E. Brazil, Trinidad. ❄ (min. 45°F/7°C)
T. imperialis. Stemless, epiphytic or rock-dwelling perennial producing dense rosettes of slender, lance-shaped, sparsely scaly, mid-green or slightly purple leaves, to 16in (40cm) long. In autumn, spikes of 3 or 4 erect, tubular violet flowers, to 2½in (6cm) long, with brilliant red floral bracts, are borne in compound, cone-shaped inflorescences. ↕↔ 20in (50cm). C. and S. Mexico. ❄ (min. 45°F/7°C)
T. ionantha. Freely clustering, epiphytic or lithophytic perennial with dense rosettes of linear, incurved or recurved, coarsely scaly, grayish green leaves, to 1½in (4cm) long, turning red in late spring. Solitary, tubular, violet-blue and white flowers, to 1¾in (4.5cm) long, with white floral bracts, are borne in simple spikes in spring. ↕ 5in (13cm), ↔ 4in (10cm) or more. Mexico, Central America. ❄ (min. 45°F/7°C)
T. leiboldiana. Stemless, epiphytic perennial with funnel-shaped rosettes of slender, lance-shaped, mid-green leaves, to 6in (15cm) long, with flat, brown-scaly sheaths. Branched spikes of 3–8

Tillandsia stricta

tubular violet flowers, 1¼in (3cm) long, with red or purple floral bracts, are produced in late spring. ↕↔ 12–24in (30–60cm). Mexico, Central America. ❄ (min. 45°F/7°C)
T. lindenii ■ (Blue-flowered torch). Epiphytic perennial with funnel-shaped rosettes of linear-triangular, arching, dark green leaves, 16in (40cm) long, striped reddish purple. In late spring or autumn, green to purple-pink floral bracts and funnel-shaped, fragrant, white-eyed, deep purple-blue flowers, 3in (8cm) long, with spreading petals, are borne in lance-shaped spikes, each with 2 ranks of up to 20 flowers. ↕ 16in (40cm), ↔ 24in (60cm). N.W. Peru. ❄ (min. 45°F/7°C)
T. multicaulis ■ Epiphytic perennial with dense, funnel-shaped rosettes of linear, pale brown-scaly, mid-green leaves, 12–16in (30–40cm) long. In late spring, simple, sword-shaped spikes of 9–12 tubular blue flowers, 3in (8cm) long, with greenish white sepals and red floral bracts, are produced from the leaf axils on scapes with green bracts. ↕↔ 16in (40cm). Mexico, Central America. ❄ (min. 45°F/7°C)
T. punctulata (Mexican black torch). Stemless, epiphytic perennial forming symmetrical rosettes of linear, bright green and purplish green leaves, to 18in (45cm) long, with almost black sheaths. In late spring, bears erect spikes of 4–6 tubular, white-tipped violet flowers, 1¼–2in (3–5cm) long, with green floral bracts, sometimes grouped into compound inflorescences; scapes have red bracts. ↕↔ 18in (45cm). Mexico to Panama. ❄ (min. 45°F/7°C)

Tillandsia multicaulis

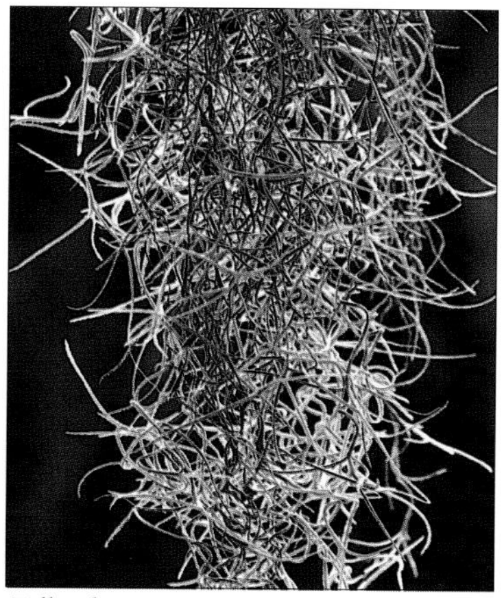
Tillandsia usneoides

T. recurvata (Ball moss). Epiphytic or lithophytic perennial with simple or branched stems bearing linear, recurved, gray-scaly, mid-green leaves, 1¼–7in (3–18cm) long, in 2 rows. In autumn, produces simple spikes of 1–5 slender, funnel-shaped, erect, pale violet or white flowers, to ½in (1.5cm) long, with green sepals and green or silver, gray-scaly floral bracts. ↕↔ 4–8in (10–20cm). Arizona and Texas to Central and South America. ❄ (min. 45°F/7°C); hardy in Zone 8 if kept dry in winter.
T. stricta ■ Clump-forming, short-stemmed, epiphytic perennial with dense rosettes of narrowly triangular, gray-scaly, pale green leaves, 2½–7in (6–18cm) long. In spring, bears slender, pendent, cone-shaped spikes of 40 or more slender, funnel-shaped, blue or purple flowers, ¾in (2cm) or more long, with yellowish white to rose-pink floral bracts. ↕↔ 4–8in (10–20cm). Venezuela and Trinidad to N. Argentina. ❄ (min. 45°F/7°C)
T. usneoides ■ (Spanish moss). Pendent, epiphytic perennial with branching, rootless, wiry stems, to ⅛in (3mm) thick, bearing cylindrical, densely gray-scaly, gray-green leaves, 1–2in (2.5–5cm) long. Solitary, tubular, fragrant, greenish yellow flowers, to ½in (1.5cm) long, with green or silver, gray-scaly floral bracts, are produced in late spring or autumn. ↕ 25ft (8m), ↔ indefinite. S. US, Central and South America, West Indies. ❄ (min. 41°F/5°C)

TIPUANA

Tipu tree

FABACEAE

Genus of one species of semi-evergreen tree found in tropical forest in South America, and cultivated for its attractive habit and flowers. *T. tipu* has mainly alternate, pinnate leaves and arching to pendent, terminal or axillary racemes or panicles of pea-like flowers. Where temperatures fall below 50°F (10°C), grow in a cool or temperate greenhouse; flowers are seldom produced when grown in a container. In warmer areas, grow as a shade or street tree.

• **CULTIVATION** Under glass, grow in soil-based potting mix in full light. From late spring to early autumn, water freely and apply a balanced liquid fertilizer monthly; water sparingly in winter. Outdoors, grow in moist but well-drained, fertile soil in full sun. Pruning group 1; plants grown under glass need restrictive pruning after flowering.

• **PROPAGATION** Sow seed at 59°F (15°C) in spring.

• **PESTS AND DISEASES** Prone to root rot at seedling age. Spider mites may be troublesome under glass.

T. speciosa see *T. tipu.*
T. tipu, syn. *T. speciosa* (Brazilian rosewood, Pride of Bolivia, Tipu tree). Freely branching, rounded tree bearing pinnate leaves, to 18in (45cm) long, with 9–25 oblong to elliptic, mid- to bright green leaflets with notched tips, downy beneath. In spring, pea-like flowers, ¾–1in (2–2.5cm) across, with crimped, bright yellow to apricot petals, veined rust-red, are borne in racemes to 12in (30cm) long, followed by broadly winged, short, ovoid, woody seed pods. ↕ 30–100ft (10–30m), ↔ 25–50ft (8–15m). Bolivia, Brazil, Argentina. ❄ (min. 45–50°F/7–10°C)

TITANOPSIS

AIZOACEAE

Genus of 5 or 6 species of short-stemmed, fleshy-rooted, succulent herbaceous perennials, forming dense mats or clumps, found in semi-desert areas of Namibia and South Africa. The erect, spoon-shaped to 3-angled, fleshy leaves, crowded with tubercles at the tips, are arranged in basal rosettes. Solitary, daisy-like, yellow or orange flowers are borne during daytime from late summer to early spring. In areas where temperatures fall below 50°F (10°C), grow in a warm greenhouse. In warmer climates, grow in a desert garden.

• **CULTIVATION** Under glass, grow in deep containers in a mix of 3 parts standard cactus potting mix and 1 part limestone chips; provide full light and low humidity. From spring to late summer, water moderately, applying a balanced liquid fertilizer 3 or 4 times; keep almost dry at other times. Outdoors, grow in sharply drained, gritty, alkaline soil in full sun. See also pp.48–49.

• **PROPAGATION** Sow seed at 70°F (21°C) in spring or early summer.

• **PESTS AND DISEASES** Vulnerable to aphids while flowering.

T. calcarea ■ (Jewel box, Jewel plant). Clump-forming succulent with crowded, basal rosettes of spoon-shaped, bluish green, sometimes white-tinged

Titanopsis calcarea

leaves, 2½–3in (6–8cm) long, with reddish or grayish white tubercles. Produces bright golden yellow to orange flowers, ¾in (2cm) across, from late summer to autumn. ↕ 1¼in (3cm), ↔ 4in (10cm). South Africa (Western Cape). ❄ (min. 50°F/10°C); tolerates brief periods to 25°F (-4°C) if kept dry.
T. hugo-schlechteri. Clump-forming succulent with basal rosettes of spoon-shaped, red-tinged, gray-green to brownish leaves, to ½in (15mm) long, with rounded bases, 3-angled tips, and bronze tubercles. Yellow flowers, to ½in (1.5cm) across, are borne in late autumn. ↕ ½in (1.5cm), ↔ to 2in (5cm). Namibia. ❄ (min. 50°F/10°C); tolerates brief periods to 25°F (-4°C) if kept dry.
T. schwantesii (White jewel plant). Clump-forming succulent with basal rosettes of spoon-shaped, light gray-blue, sometimes red-tinged leaves, 1¼in (3cm) long, with rounded bases, 3-angled tips, and yellowish brown tubercles. Pale yellow flowers, to ¾in (2cm) across, are borne from autumn to early winter. ↕ 1¼in (3cm), ↔ 4in (10cm). Namibia. ❄ (min. 50°F/10°C); tolerates brief periods to 25°F (-4°C) if kept dry.

TITHONIA
Mexican sunflower
ASTERACEAE

Genus of 10 erect, bushy, thick-stemmed, sometimes woody-based, frequently hairy annuals, perennials, and shrubs, found in thickets and scrub in Mexico and Central America. Alternate, occasionally opposite, entire or lobed leaves each have 3 prominent veins. Large, long-stemmed, mostly solitary flowerheads are borne from late summer to autumn. *T. rotundifolia*, the most commonly grown species, gives height to a mixed or annual border and provides long-lasting cut flowers.
• **CULTIVATION** Grow in well-drained, moderately fertile soil in full sun, with shelter from strong winds. Support tall cultivars, water in dry weather, and deadhead to prolong flowering. They grow poorly in cool, overcast weather.
• **PROPAGATION** Sow seed at 55–64°F (13–18°C) in mid- or late spring. Plant out when all danger of frost has passed. Alternatively, sow seed *in situ* in late spring. Leaves turn yellow if seedlings are subjected to cold.
• **PESTS AND DISEASES** Young foliage may be attacked by slugs and snails.

T

Tithonia rotundifolia 'Torch'

T. rotundifolia (Mexican sunflower). Robust, branching annual with long, triangular-ovate, entire or occasionally 3-lobed, toothed leaves, 3–12in (8–30cm) long, hairy beneath. Bright orange or orange-red flowerheads, to 3in (8cm) across, similar to those of single-flowered dahlias, are borne from late summer to autumn. ↕ to 6ft (2m), ↔ 12in (30cm). Mexico to Central America. **'Goldfinger'** is compact, with vivid, rich orange flowerheads; ↕ to 30in (75cm). **'Sundance'** has bright orange flowerheads. **'Torch'** ■ has vivid red or orange-red flowerheads.

TODEA
OSMUNDACEAE

Genus of 2 species of large, terrestrial, evergreen ferns found in open places in tropical and warm-temperate rainforest in South Africa, Australia, New Guinea, and New Zealand. Massive, erect, hairy rhizomes bear crowns of upright 2-pinnate, leathery fronds, with spores along the veins. Where not hardy, grow *T. barbara* in a temperate or warm greenhouse. In warmer areas, grow as a specimen plant or in light woodland.
• **CULTIVATION** Under glass, grow in 1 part each of loam, medium-grade bark, and charcoal, 2 parts sharp sand, and 3 parts leaf mold, in bright filtered light, with moderate humidity. In growth, water freely and apply a balanced liquid fertilizer monthly; water moderately to sparingly in winter. Outdoors, grow in moist, fertile soil in partial shade.
• **PROPAGATION** Sow spores at 70°F (21°C) as soon as ripe. Divide in early summer, but only after several trunks have developed. See also p.51.
• **PESTS AND DISEASES** Susceptible to mealybugs under glass.

T. barbara. Tree-like fern with thick black rhizomes and short, thick trunks, to 32in (80cm) tall. Glossy, bright green fronds, to 6ft (2m) long, have lance-shaped, pinnatifid pinnae. ↕ to 6ft (2m), ↔ to 5ft (1.5m). South Africa, Australia, New Zealand. ❄ (min. 45°F/7°C)

TOLMIEA
SAXIFRAGACEAE

Genus of one species of fast-spreading, herbaceous perennial from coniferous woodland in W. North America. Young plants are produced on the leaves, where leaf stalk and blade meet. Leafy stems bear erect racemes of small, cup-shaped, greenish purple flowers with 3 stamens. Grow as a groundcover in a woodland garden, or as a houseplant.
• **CULTIVATION** Grow in cool, moist, humus-rich soil in partial or deep shade. Sun will scorch the leaves, especially of *T. menziesii* 'Taff's Gold'. Under glass, grow in fertile, soil-based potting mix in bright filtered or indirect light. During the growing season, water freely and apply a balanced liquid fertilizer monthly; water sparingly in winter.
• **PROPAGATION** Sow seed in containers in a cold frame in autumn. Divide in spring. Remove and pot up plantlets from the leaves in mid- or late summer, or peg leaves into potting mix and remove plantlets when rooted.
• **PESTS AND DISEASES** Susceptible to anthracnose, mealybugs, and rust.

Tolmiea menziesii 'Taff's Gold'

T. menziesii (Piggyback plant, Thousand mothers, Youth-on-age). Clump-forming, hairy perennial with creeping rhizomes and mainly basal, long-stalked, triangular, shallowly lobed, toothed, conspicuously veined, pale to lime-green leaves, to 5in (13cm) long. In late spring and early summer, produces one-sided racemes of 20–50 slightly scented flowers, to ½in (1.5cm) long, with orange anthers; the sepals are pale green, heavily shaded and lined purple-brown, with thread-like, purple-brown petals recurved between them. ↕ 12–24in (30–60cm), ↔ 3–6ft (1–2m). W. North America. Zone 7.
'Maculata' see 'Taff's Gold'.
'Taff's Gold' ■ syn. 'Maculata', has paler green leaves, spotted and mottled cream and pale yellow.

TOLPIS
ASTERACEAE

Genus of 20 frequently mat-forming annuals and perennials from dry, sandy areas in the Azores and the Canary Islands, the Mediterranean region, N.E. Africa, and Ethiopia. The mainly ovate to lance-shaped, toothed or lobed, bright green basal leaves are usually arranged in rosettes, while the branching stems support pinnate or lobed leaves. Leaves and stems contain a milky latex. Daisy-like, bright yellow flowerheads emerge over a long period from spring to summer. Suitable for the front of a mixed or annual border.
• **CULTIVATION** Grow in well-drained, light, moderately fertile soil in full sun. Deadhead to prolong flowering.

Tolpis barbata

• **PROPAGATION** Sow seed *in situ* in early or midspring.
• **PESTS AND DISEASES** Infrequent.

T. barbata ■ Annual with mostly basal, lance-shaped to oblong, toothed, hairy, bright green leaves, ¾–4in (2–10cm) long. From spring to summer solitary or clustered, bright yellow flowerheads, ½–1¼in (1–3cm) across, with fringed margins and dark maroon centers, are borne singly or in clusters, on sparsely leaved, branching stems. ↕ to 24in (60cm), usually less, ↔ 12in (30cm). Mediterranean.

TOONA
MELIACEAE

Genus of about 6 species of deciduous or semi-evergreen trees found in woodland from E. Asia to Australasia. They are grown for their alternate, pinnate leaves and small, cup-shaped, fragrant, greenish white or white flowers, which are borne in large, terminal or axillary panicles. *T. sinensis* is the most common species in cultivation. It grows best in areas with hot summers, where it is a useful shade or street tree.
• **CULTIVATION** Grow in fertile, well-drained soil in full sun. Pruning group 1
• **PROPAGATION** Sow seed in containers in a cold frame in autumn. Insert root cuttings in late winter.
• **PESTS AND DISEASES** Infrequent.

T. sinensis ■ syn. *Cedrela sinensis.* Broadly columnar, often suckering, deciduous tree with peeling brown bark Aromatic leaves, to 24in (60cm) long, have up to 26 ovate-lance-shaped to oblong, papery leaflets, bronze-red to pink when young, turning yellow in autumn. In midsummer, bears small, fragrant, white or greenish white flowers in pendent, terminal panicles, to 12in (30cm) long. ↕ 50ft (15m), ↔ 30ft (10m). China. Zone 7. **'Flamingo'** has vivid pink young leaves, turning creamy yellow then bright green.

Toona sinensis

Torenia fournieri

TORENIA

Wishbone flower

SCROPHULARIACEAE

Genus of 40–50 erect to spreading, bushy, sometimes softly hairy annuals and perennials found in woodland, at altitudes up to 10,000ft (3,000m), in tropical Africa and Asia. They are grown for their short, showy, terminal or axillary racemes of tubular then flaring, 2-lipped flowers, the upper lips slightly 2-lobed, the lower ones markedly 3-lobed, produced in summer. The opposite leaves are mostly broadly to narrowly ovate or lance-shaped, and may be entire or toothed. *T. fournieri* is the most commonly cultivated species: use for summer bedding, or grow at the front of an annual or mixed border; it is also grown as a summer-flowering houseplant or cool-greenhouse plant.

- **CULTIVATION** Under glass, grow in soil-based potting mix in bright filtered light, providing good ventilation. During the growing season, water freely and apply a high-potash liquid fertilizer every 2 or 3 weeks. Pinch out stem tips to promote bushiness. Outdoors, grow in fertile, moist but well-drained soil in partial shade.
- **PROPAGATION** Sow seed at 64°F (18°C) in midspring; plant out when all danger of frost has passed.
- **PESTS AND DISEASES** Sometimes affected by root rot, gray mold (*Botrytis*), and powdery mildew.

T. fournieri ▣ (Bluewings, Wishbone flower). Erect, smooth annual with long-stalked, pointed, ovate to narrowly ovate, toothed, pale green leaves, 1½–2in (4–5cm) long. In summer, produces abundant lilac-blue flowers, to 1½in (4cm) long, the lower lips deep purple and the throats marked yellow. ↕ 12in (30cm), ↔ 6–9in (15–23cm). Tropical Asia. Cultivars of **Clown Series** ▣ are compact, and produce white, pink, deep purple, or lavender-blue flowers; ↕ 8–10in (20–25cm). **Panda Series** cultivars are more compact, producing white, pink, purple, or lavender-blue flowers; ↕ 4–8in (10–20cm).

TORREYA

Nutmeg yew

TAXACEAE

Genus of 7 species of dioecious, evergreen, coniferous shrubs or trees found in woodland in Asia and North America. The flattened, lance-shaped, 2-ranked leaves are yew-like, but hard and spine-tipped. The common name refers to the single-seeded, ovoid or ovoid-ellipsoid female, cone-like structures ("cones"); they may take 2 years to ripen, maturing to olive- or plum-like fruits. The male cones are white and spherical. Nutmeg yews are vigorous, small to medium-sized specimen trees. *T. californica* thrives in areas with cool, damp summers; other species grow best in areas with summers that are warm and humid.

- **CULTIVATION** Grow in fertile, moist but well-drained soil in full sun or light, dappled shade. Shelter from wind.

Torenia fournieri Clown Series

Torreya californica

- **PROPAGATION** Sow seed in containers in a cold frame or in a seedbed, as soon as ripe; the seed may take 2 or more years to germinate. Insert semi-ripe cuttings in late summer; use cuttings from strongly upright growth to form leading shoots.
- **PESTS AND DISEASES** Root rot and needle blight sometimes occur.

T. californica ▣ (California nutmeg). Broadly conical tree with whorled branches, red-brown or brown bark, becoming scaly, and green shoots with pointed buds. Produces spreading, 2-ranked, narrowly lance-shaped, tapered, yellowish green leaves, 1¼–2in (3–5cm) long, and ellipsoid or obovoid, purplish green female cones, to 1½in (4cm) long. ↕ to 80ft (25m), ↔ to 25ft (8m). C. California. Zone 7b.

T. nucifera (Japanese torreya, Kaya). Upright to broadly conical tree with opposite branchlets and linear, glossy, dark green leaves, ¾–1¼in (2–3cm) long, in 2 opposite ranks, separated by a broad, V-shaped channel. Ellipsoid female cones are olive-green, 1in (2.5cm) long. ↕ to 50ft (15m), ↔ 25ft (8m). S. Japan. Zone 7.

▷ ***Tovara*** see *Persicaria*

TOWNSENDIA

ASTERACEAE

Genus of about 20 species of compact, occasionally stemless annuals and evergreen, often monocarpic perennials found in open, freely draining habitats in mountainous areas of W. North America. The alternate leaves are linear to spoon-shaped, entire, and smooth to densely hairy. They are grown for their solitary, short-stemmed, aster-like flowerheads, produced in summer. *Townsendia* species are suitable for a rock garden, trough, or alpine house.

- **CULTIVATION** Grow in gritty, sharply drained soil in full sun. Immediately upon germination, transfer to individual pots to avoid taproot damage; seedlings will not survive transplanting. Pinch to prevent flowering the first year. Protect from excessive winter moisture. In an alpine house, grow in a mix of equal parts loam, leaf mold, and sharp sand.
- **PROPAGATION** Sow seed as soon as ripe in containers in a cold frame. Propagate regularly; plants are often short-lived.
- **PESTS AND DISEASES** Susceptible to aphids and spider mites under glass.

Townsendia formosa

T. formosa ▣ Upright, clump-forming, rhizomatous perennial with spoon-shaped to inversely lance-shaped leaves, to 3in (8cm) long, with finely hairy midribs and margins. In summer, one to several solitary flowerheads, 1¼in (3cm) across, with pale violet ray florets, mauve beneath, and yellow disk florets, are produced on upright stems, 4in (10cm) long. ↕ to 24in (60cm), ↔ to 6in (15cm). S.W. US. Zone 7.

T. parryi. Clump-forming, short-lived perennial with spoon-shaped, slightly fleshy leaves, to 4in (10cm) long, smooth above and bristly-hairy beneath. One to several solitary flowerheads, to 1¼in (3cm) across, with violet-blue or lavender-blue ray florets and yellow disk florets, are borne on upright stems, 2–6in (5–15cm) long, in early summer. ↕ to 6in (15cm), ↔ to 4in (10cm). N.W. North America. Zone 5.

▷ ***Toxicodendron*** see *Rhus*

TRACHELIUM

syn. DIOSPHAERA

CAMPANULACEAE

Genus of about 7 species of small, sometimes cushion-forming, often woody-based perennials, usually found in calcareous soils in the Mediterranean region. The tiny, narrowly lance-shaped to oblong or almost rounded leaves are alternate and simple. Tubular flowers, each with 5 spreading petal lobes, are solitary or, more usually, produced in corymbs. Grow *T. caeruleum* and other tall species and cultivars in an annual, mixed, or herbaceous border; their flowers are excellent for cutting. Dwarf species, such as *T. asperuloides*, are suitable for a rock garden, scree bed, trough, or alpine house.

- **CULTIVATION** Grow in well-drained soil in full sun with some midday shade. *T. asperuloides* prefers more sharply drained, alkaline soil, and needs protection from excessive winter moisture. In an alpine house, grow in deep containers in a mix of equal parts loam, leaf mold, and sharp sand.
- **PROPAGATION** Sow seed of marginally hardy or tender species at 55–61°F (13–16°C) in early spring, or *in situ* in late spring. Sow seed of hardy species as soon as ripe in containers in a cold frame. Insert softwood cuttings in early summer.
- **PESTS AND DISEASES** Aphids and spider mites may occur under glass.

Trachelium asperuloides

T. asperuloides ■ syn. *Diosphaera asperuloides.* Dense, cushion-forming perennial with thread-like stems bearing minute, overlapping, ovate-rounded, glossy, mid-green leaves, ¼in (6mm) long. In late summer, bears abundant, tubular, lavender-blue or white flowers, ¼in (6mm) across, singly or in corymbs of up to 5, on very short flower stalks in the upper leaf axils. ↕ to 2in (5cm), ↔ to 6in (15cm). S. Greece. ❄ (min. 35°F/2°C)

T. caeruleum (Blue throatwort). Erect perennial, grown as an annual where not hardy, with pointed, oval to lance-shaped, toothed, mid-green leaves, 3in (8cm) long. In summer, bears lightly scented, deep violet-blue or white flowers, to ¼in (6mm) across, in dense, dome-shaped, terminal corymbs on long, branching, red-flushed stalks. ↕ 3–4ft (1–1.2m), ↔ 12in (30cm). W. and C. Mediterranean. ❄ (min. 35°F/2°C). **'Purple Umbrella'** has deep purple flowers. **'White Veil'** has white flowers.

TRACHELOSPERMUM

APOCYNACEAE

Genus of about 20 species of woody, evergreen, twining climbers found in woodland from India to Japan. They are grown for their attractive foliage and fragrant flowers. Opposite, lance-shaped to broadly ovate leaves are borne on stems that contain a milky latex. Small, salverform flowers, with cylindrical tubes and 5 spreading, slightly twisted lobes, are produced in terminal or axillary cymes, followed by pendent, pod-like fruits (seldom borne in areas with cool summers). Where marginally hardy, grow against a warm, sunny wall; where not hardy, grow in a cool greenhouse or as houseplants.

• **CULTIVATION** Outdoors, grow in fertile, well-drained soil in full sun or partial shade; provide shelter from cold, drying winds. Under glass, grow in soil-based potting mix in full light with shade from hot sun. During the growing season, water freely and apply a balanced liquid fertilizer monthly. Water sparingly in winter. Pruning group 11, in early spring.

• **PROPAGATION** Insert semi-ripe cuttings in summer. Layer in autumn.

• **PESTS AND DISEASES** Mushroom root rot and leaf spot sometimes occur.

T. asiaticum. Woody, evergreen, twining climber bearing oval, glossy,

Trachelospermum jasminoides

dark green leaves, to 2in (5cm) long. Fragrant, creamy white flowers, ¾in (2cm) across, which age to yellow, are produced in terminal cymes in mid- and late summer. ↕ 20ft (6m). Korea, Japan. ❄ (min. 35°F/2°C)

T. jasminoides ■ (Confederate jasmine, Star jasmine). Woody, evergreen, twining climber with oval, glossy, dark green leaves, to 4in (10cm) long, turning bronze-red in winter. In summer, fragrant, pure white flowers, 1in (2.5cm) across, are produced in terminal and axillary cymes. ↕ 28ft (9m). China, Korea, Japan. ❄ (min. 35°F/2°C). **'Variegatum'** produces white-marked foliage.

TRACHYCARPUS

ARECACEAE

Genus of 6 species of usually single-stemmed, sometimes clustering, dioecious, evergreen palms occurring in temperate and mountain forest in subtropical Asia. They are cultivated for their attractive habit; their terminal, fan-shaped leaves, palmately lobed to half their length or more; and their cup-shaped flowers, surrounded by bowl-shaped, white or brown bracts. The flowers are followed by spherical or kidney-shaped fruits. Fan palms are small enough to be grown in a restricted area, such as a courtyard; they are also effective specimen trees.

• **CULTIVATION** Grow in well-drained, fertile soil in full sun or light, dappled shade, sheltered from strong or cold, drying winds.

• **PROPAGATION** Sow seed in spring or autumn at 75°F (24°C).

Trachycarpus fortunei

• **PESTS AND DISEASES** Leaf spots and root rot may occur on seedlings. Spider mites and scale insects can be problems under glass.

T. fortunei ■ (Chusan palm, Windmill palm). Unbranched, single-stemmed, evergreen palm with a head of fan-shaped, dark green leaves, 18–30in (45–75cm) long, with numerous pointed segments variously lobed to half their length or more. Bears small yellow flowers in large, pendent panicles, 24in (60cm) or more long; they emerge from close to the leaf bases in early summer. Female plants bear spherical, blue-black fruit, ½in (1.5cm) across. ↕ to 70ft (20m), ↔ 8ft (2.5m). Origin unknown. Zone 7b. **'Nanus'** has a short or almost non-existent trunk and stiffer leaf blades, to 12in (30cm) long.

TRACHYMENE

syn. DIDISCUS

APIACEAE

Genus of 12 or more species of erect, branching annuals, biennials, and perennials from moist woodland and swamps to dry sandhills and subalpine areas in Australia and the W. Pacific. The lacy leaves are ternate or 2-ternate, usually with linear leaflets, or rarely with 2 leaflets or palmately divided. Dainty, terminal umbels of tiny, star-shaped, white, pink, or blue flowers are borne in summer. Grow *T. coerulea,* the species most commonly cultivated, at the front of an annual or mixed border, or in a cool greenhouse. It provides long-lasting cut flowers.

• **CULTIVATION** Under glass, grow in soil-based potting mix in full light with shade from hot sun. In summer, water moderately and apply a high-potash liquid fertilizer every 2 or 3 weeks. Outdoors, grow in light, well-drained, moderately fertile soil in a sheltered site in full sun. Provide twiggy support.

• **PROPAGATION** Sow seed at 59°F (15°C) in midspring, or sow *in situ* in late spring. Germination is slow.

• **PESTS AND DISEASES** Infrequent.

T. coerulea, syn. *Didiscus coeruleus* (Blue lace flower). Stiff-stemmed annual or biennial with pale green leaves, to 4in (10cm) long, divided into 2 or 3 narrow, 3-lobed leaflets. Lightly scented, lavender-blue flowers are produced in long-stemmed, rounded umbels, to 2in (5cm) across, in summer. ↕ to 24in (60cm), ↔ 9in (23cm). W. Australia.

TRADESCANTIA

COMMELINACEAE

Genus of about 65 species of creeping, trailing, or tuft-forming, fibrous- or tuberous-rooted, evergreen perennials from woodland, scrub, or disturbed ground in North, Central, and South America. The leaves are alternate, usually fleshy, lance-shaped to ovate, often purple-flushed or variegated, and hairy or hairless. Short-lived, spreading, usually saucer-shaped flowers, each with 3 petals and 3 sepals, are produced in terminal or axillary cymes, which are fused in pairs, with paired, boat-shaped bracts. Hardy tradescantias are suitable for a mixed or herbaceous border. In warm regions, grow the tender species

Tradescantia Andersoniana Group 'J.C. Weguelin'

beneath shrubs or as a groundcover; where not hardy, grow in a temperate or cool greenhouse, as houseplants, or in a conservatory; they are especially effective in hanging baskets. Contact with the foliage may irritate skin.

• **CULTIVATION** Under glass, grow in soilless or soil-based potting mix in bright filtered light. When in active growth, water moderately and apply a balanced liquid fertilizer every 4 weeks; water sparingly in winter. Pinch growing tips to encourage bushiness, and remove plain green foliage from variegated cultivars. Pot on or repropagate each spring. Outdoors, grow in moist, fertile soil in full sun or partial shade. After flowering, cut back flowered stems to prevent seeding and to encourage further flowers.

• **PROPAGATION** Insert stem-tip cuttings, 2–3in (5–8cm) long, of the tender tradescantias at any time; root in soil mix or water, then pot up into soil-based mix. Divide hardy species and cultivars in autumn or spring.

• **PESTS AND DISEASES** May be affected by viruses, aphids, and spider mites.

T. albiflora **'Albovittata'** see *T. fluminensis* 'Albovittata'.

T. albiflora **'Variegata'** see *T. fluminensis* 'Variegata'.

T.* x *andersoniana see *T.* Andersoniana Group.

***T.* Andersoniana Group**, syn. *T.* x *andersoniana* (Spiderwort). Tufted, clump-forming perennials with erect, branching stems and arching, narrowly lance-shaped, pointed, hairless, slightly fleshy, mid-green, often purple-tinted leaves, to 14in (35cm) long. Blue, purple, rose-pink to rose-red, or white flowers, 1–1½in (2.5–4cm) across, each have 3 wide-open, triangular petals and fluffy-hairy stamen hairs; they are borne in succession in paired, terminal cymes from early summer to early autumn. ↕ 16–24in (40–60cm), ↔ 18–24in (45–60cm). Zone 3b. **'Blue Stone'** has clear blue flowers; ↕ 24in (60cm). **'Carmine Glow'** see 'Karminglut'. **'Innocence'** has pure white flowers; ↕ 24in (60cm). **'Iris Prichard'** has white flowers, shaded pale blue. **'Isis'** has dark blue flowers. **'J.C. Weguelin'** ■ bears pale blue flowers. **'Karminglut'**, syn. 'Carmine Glow', bears carmine-red flowers. **'Osprey'** ■ produces white flowers with blue stamen filaments. **'Pauline'** bears orchid-pink flowers;

T

Tradescantia Andersoniana Group 'Osprey'

↕24in (60cm). **'Purewell Giant'** ■ produces purple to rose-red flowers; ↕↔ 18in (45cm). **'Purple Dome'** ■ has rich purple flowers. **'Red Cloud'** has cerise-red flowers; ↕↔ 18in (45cm). **'Snowcap'** has unusually large white flowers; ↕18in (45cm). **'Zwanenburg Blue'** produces dark blue flowers.
T. blossfeldiana see *T. cerinthoides.*
T. cerinthoides, syn. *T. blossfeldiana.* Vigorous, creeping or ascending perennial with thick, branching stems and elliptic-oblong to narrowly ovate, very fleshy, deep green leaves, 6in (15cm) long, hairless above, and deep purple and densely hairy beneath. Paired, terminal or axillary cymes of pink and white flowers are produced intermittently throughout the year.

Tradescantia Andersoniana Group 'Purple Dome'

↕36in (90cm), ↔ 18in (45cm). Brazil. ❀ (min. 50–61°F/10–16°C).
'Variegata' has leaves with bold buff stripes, light pink above.
T. fluminensis (Wandering Jew). Trailing perennial with thin, pointed, ovate to ovate-oblong, usually hairless, light green leaves, ¾–4in (2–10cm) long, stained purple beneath. White flowers are produced in paired, terminal or axillary cymes intermittently throughout the year. ↕6in (15cm), ↔ 8in (20cm). Brazil to N. Argentina. ❀ (min. 50–61°F/10–16°C).
'Albovittata' ■ syn. *T. albiflora* 'Albovittata', has light green leaves with white longitudinal stripes, and purple undersides that partially show through the almost transparent upper surfaces.

Tradescantia Andersoniana Group 'Purewell Giant'

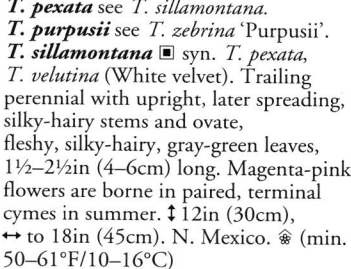

Tradescantia fluminensis 'Albovittata'

'Aurea' has yellow-striped leaves.
'Variegata' ■ syn. *T. albiflora* 'Variegata', has leaves variably striped green, white, purple, or cream.
T. navicularis see *Callisia navicularis.*
***T. pallida* 'Purple Heart'** see *T. pallida* 'Purpurea'.
***T. pallida* 'Purpurea'** ■ syn. *Setcreasea purpurea, T. pallida* 'Purple Heart'. Trailing perennial producing ascending purple stems. Large, pointed, narrowly oblong leaves, 3–6in (8–15cm) long, are V-shaped in section, and fleshy, hairless, rich violet-purple. In summer, bears bright pink flowers in paired, terminal cymes. Leaves color best in bright sunlight and when the root zone is slightly dry and cramped. ↕8in (20cm), ↔ to 16in (40cm). E. Mexico. ❀ (min. 50–61°F/10–16°C)
T. pexata see *T. sillamontana.*
T. purpusii see *T. zebrina* 'Purpusii'.
T. sillamontana ■ syn. *T. pexata, T. velutina* (White velvet). Trailing perennial with upright, later spreading, silky-hairy stems and ovate, fleshy, silky-hairy, gray-green leaves, 1½–2½in (4–6cm) long. Magenta-pink flowers are borne in paired, terminal cymes in summer. ↕12in (30cm), ↔ to 18in (45cm). N. Mexico. ❀ (min. 50–61°F/10–16°C)
T. spathacea ■ syn. *Rhoeo discolor, R. spathacea* (Moses-in-the-cradle, Three-men-in-a-boat). Clump-forming perennial with rosettes of semi-erect, linear-lance-shaped, fleshy, hairless leaves, 8–14in (20–35cm) long, dark green above and deep purple beneath.

Tradescantia fluminensis 'Variegata'

Tradescantia pallida 'Purpurea'

White flowers are produced in paired, axillary cymes, which are surrounded by prominent, long-lasting purple bracts, throughout the year. ↕↔ 12in (30cm). Central America. ❀ (min. 50–61°F/10–16°C). **'Vittata'** has leaves with longitudinal yellow stripes.
T. velutina see *T. sillamontana.*
T. zanonia, syn. *Campelia zanonia.* Clump-forming perennial with erect or decumbent stems and broadly elliptic to inversely lance-shaped, hairless, membranous, dark green leaves, 10in (25cm) long. White flowers are borne in paired, axillary cymes, surrounded by 2 leafy bracts, from summer to winter. ↕7ft (2.2m), ↔ 3ft (1m). Mexico to Brazil, West Indies. ❀ (min. 50–61°F/10–16°C)

Tradescantia sillamontana

Tradescantia spathacea

Tradescantia zebrina

Tradescantia zebrina 'Purpusii'

T. zebrina ■ syn. *Zebrina pendula* (Wandering Jew). Trailing perennial with ovate-oblong to broadly ovate, fleshy, hairless, bluish green leaves, to 4in (10cm) long; 2 longitudinal stripes, silver-green above and rich purple beneath, mark each leaf. Purple-pink to purple-blue flowers are produced in paired, terminal cymes intermittently throughout the year. ↕ 6in (15cm), ↔ 8in (20cm). S. Mexico. ❅ (min. 50–61°F/10–16°C). **'Purpusii'** ■ syn. *T. purpusii*, *Zebrina purpusii*, has rich bronze-purple-marked leaves and pink flowers. **'Quadricolor'** has leaves striped green, cream, pink, and silver.

TRAPA

Water chestnut

TRAPACEAE

Genus of about 30 species of submerged aquatic annuals from still or slow-moving water in C. Europe, E. Asia, and Africa. The creeping, floating stems bear linear submerged leaves and rosettes of ovate or almost triangular to diamond-shaped, toothed, mottled floating leaves, hairy beneath, with spongy, swollen leaf stalks. Small, solitary, tubular, white or lilac flowers are followed by inflated, spiny fruits. Where not hardy, grow in containers in a cold-greenhouse pool, or float rosettes on the surface of an outdoor pool after last frost. In warmer climates, grow in an outdoor pool.

• **CULTIVATION** Plant in aquatic containers of loamy soil in full light, at no less than 50°F (10°C); or float rosettes on still, shallow, nutrient-rich water in full sun. See also pp.52–53.

Trapa natans

• **PROPAGATION** Collect seed in autumn. Store frost-free in water or wet moss over winter; sow in spring, at 55–64°F (13–18°C), in wet soil mix.

• **PESTS AND DISEASES** Infrequent.

T. natans ■ (Jesuit's nut, Water caltrops, Water chestnut). Clump-forming, aquatic annual. Roughly diamond-shaped, floating leaves, 1in (2.5cm) across, have red-tinged leaf stalks, 2–3in (5–8cm) long. White flowers are borne from the leaf axils in summer, followed by 4-angled, spiny, hard black fruit, to 2in (5cm) across. ↔ indefinite. Eurasia, Africa.

▷ ***Trichinium manglesii*** see *Ptilotus manglesii*

▷ ***Trichocereus*** see *Echinopsis*

TRICHODIADEMA

AIZOACEAE

Genus of about 30 species of mainly small, tuberous, fibrous, or woody-based, shrubby, succulent perennials found in dry, hilly areas in Namibia, South Africa, and Ethiopia. The long-lasting, solitary, short-stalked, daisy-like, terminal flowers are borne on long or short stems in daytime, from spring to autumn. Semi-cylindrical to cylindrical leaves are sparsely covered with minute papillae, producing a glistening effect, and the leaf tips bear clusters of stiff, spreading or erect, shiny bristles. Below 45°F (7°C), grow in a temperate greenhouse. In warm, dry areas, grow in a border with other succulents.

• **CULTIVATION** Under glass, grow in standard cactus potting mix in full light, with low humidity. In growth, water moderately and apply a low-nitrogen fertilizer every 3 or 4 weeks; keep dry at other times. Outdoors, grow in gritty, sharply drained, poor to moderately fertile soil in full sun. See also pp.48–49.

• **PROPAGATION** Sow seed at 66–75°F (19–24°C), or insert cuttings of stem sections, in spring or summer.

• **PESTS AND DISEASES** Mealybugs occur.

T. bulbosum. Semi-erect, short- to long-stemmed succulent with an almost caudex-like, tuberous rootstock and semi-cylindrical, gray-papillose leaves, to ⅜in (9mm) long, with white bristles. Deep red flowers, ¾in (2cm) across, are borne from spring to autumn. ↕ 8in (20cm), ↔ 12in (30cm). South Africa (Eastern Cape). ❅ (min. 45°F/7°C)

Trichodiadema mirabile

T. mirabile ■ Short-stemmed, often prostrate succulent with a fibrous rootstock, and stems covered with bristly white hairs. Semi-cylindrical, finger-like leaves, to 1in (2.5cm) long, are flat above, and have blunt tips with stiff, dark brown bristles. White flowers, 1½in (4cm) across, are produced in summer. ↕ 4in (10cm), ↔ 5in (13cm) or more. South Africa (Eastern Cape, Karoo). ❅ (min. 45°F/7°C)

TRICHOSANTHES

CUCURBITACEAE

Genus of 15 species of monoecious or dioecious, annual and perennial tendril climbers found in woodland and scrub from Indonesia and Malaysia to the Pacific islands. They are grown mainly for their colorful, ornamental, mostly ovoid or spherical gourd-like fruits, which are edible when young. The alternate leaves are ovate to rounded, and simple or palmately 3- to 9-lobed. Parasol-like, fringed, 5-lobed flowers are produced from the upper leaf axils in summer, the females singly, the males in racemes or, rarely, singly. Where not hardy, grow in a warm greenhouse; elsewhere, train over a pergola, arch, or tree stump.

• **CULTIVATION** Under glass, grow in soil-based potting mix in full light with shade from hot sun, with high humidity. During growth, water freely and apply a balanced liquid fertilizer every 2 weeks. Water sparingly in winter. For good fruit production, carefully pollinate female flowers by hand. Outdoors, grow in moist but well-drained, fertile soil in full sun. Provide support for climbing stems.

• **PROPAGATION** Sow seed at 68°F (20°C) in spring. Insert softwood cuttings with bottom heat in summer.

• **PESTS AND DISEASES** Susceptible to spider mites and whiteflies under glass.

T. anguina see *T. cucumerina* var. *anguina*.

T. cucumerina (Serpent cucumber, Snake gourd). Dioecious, annual climber with slender, 5-angled stems and rounded-kidney-shaped to broadly ovate, 5- to 7-lobed, toothed, rich green leaves, 2½–5in (6–13cm) long. Bears pure white flowers, 2in (5cm) across, in summer. Ovoid to conical fruit, 2½in (6cm) long, are yellowish green with red seeds. ↕ 10–15ft (3–5m) or more. India to Malaysia and N. Australia. ❅ (min. 59°F/15°C). **var. *anguina***, syn. *T. anguina* (Serpent cucumber, Snake gourd), has shallowly to deeply 3- to 7-lobed leaves, to 6in (15cm) long, and bears slender, twisted, pointed fruit, 1–6ft (0.3–2m) long, white-striped when young, orange when ripe; Pakistan to India.

▷ ***Tricuspidaria lanceolata*** see *Crinodendron hookerianum*

TRICYRTIS

Toad lily

LILIACEAE

Genus of about 16 species of rhizomatous or stoloniferous herbaceous perennials occurring in moist woodland and on mountains and cliffs from the E. Himalayas to the Philippines. Erect or arching, usually hairy stems bear alternate, sometimes 2-ranked, oblong to lance-shaped, pointed, pale to dark green, usually stem-clasping leaves; they are often glossy, sometimes spotted darker green, and have prominent veins. The flowers are star-shaped, open bell-shaped, or funnel-shaped with the tips opened out. They each have 6 tepals, the outer 3 with basal bulges, and are borne singly or in clusters from the leaf axils, or in terminal or axillary cymes. Toad lilies are suitable for a woodland garden or a shady border.

• **CULTIVATION** Grow in moist but well-drained, humus-rich soil in deep or partial shade. *T. latifolia* tolerates drier conditions and may spread widely. *T. macrantha* and *T. macrantha* subsp. *macranthopsis* prefer deep shade and very moist soil. In colder areas, grow the late-blooming species in a sheltered, warm but not sunny position to encourage flowering before frosts. Provide a deep, loose winter mulch in areas where prolonged cold is not accompanied by snow cover.

• **PROPAGATION** Sow seed as soon as ripe in containers in a cold frame; where winters are severe, overwinter young plants in a cold greenhouse for the first winter. Divide in early spring, when dormant.

• **PESTS AND DISEASES** Slugs and snails may attack young spring growth.

T. bakeri see *T. latifolia*.

T. flava. Clump-forming perennial with short rhizomes, erect, softly hairy stems, and broadly ovate, veined, mid-green leaves, to 5½in (14cm) long, often with

Tricyrtis formosana

Tricyrtis hirta var. *alba*

dark purplish green spots. In early autumn, upward-facing, star-shaped yellow flowers, to 1in (2.5cm) across, spotted brownish purple, are borne singly or in clusters from the upper leaf axils. ↕12–20in (30–50cm), ↔ 12in (30cm). Japan. Zone 7. **subsp. *ohsumiensis*** see *T. ohsumiensis.*

T. formosana ■ syn. *T. stolonifera.* Rhizomatous perennial, spreading by stolons, with erect, somewhat zig-zagging, softly hairy stems, and inversely lance-shaped to ovate, veined, glossy, dark green leaves, to 5in (13cm) long, spotted darker purplish green. In early autumn, produces branched, terminal cymes of upward-facing, star-shaped, white to pinkish white or pinkish purple flowers, 1–1¼in (2.5–3cm) across; they are spotted reddish purple inside, with yellow tepal bases and heavily red-spotted white stigmas. ↕ to 32in (80cm), ↔ 18in (45cm). Taiwan. Zone 4. **'Amethystina'** bears lavender-blue flowers with cream-white throats and tiny mahogany-red spots; ↕ 24–36in (60–90cm).

T. hirta, syn. *T. japonica.* Clump-forming, rhizomatous perennial with densely hairy stems and lance-shaped, veined, hairy, pale green leaves, to 6in (15cm) long, heart-shaped at the bases. From late summer to midautumn, erect, funnel-shaped, purple-spotted white flowers, to 1¼in (3cm) long, with purple stigmas and spreading then recurved tepals, are produced singly or in clusters from the leaf axils, or in terminal or axillary cymes. ↕ to 32in (80cm), ↔ 24in (60cm). Japan. Zone 5. **var. *alba*** ■ has green-flushed white flowers with pink-tinged anthers. **'Miyazaki'** bears white flowers, spotted lilac-purple, in the leaf axils all along the stems; ↕ to 36in (90cm), ↔ 18in (45cm). **'Variegata'** has leaves narrowly edged in yellow-gold. **'White Towers'** has erect stems, and bears upward-facing white flowers, with pink-tinged stamens, in most of the leaf axils; ↕ to 24in (60cm), ↔ 12in (30cm).

T. japonica see *T. hirta.*

T. latifolia, syn. *T. bakeri.* Spreading, clump-forming perennial with short rhizomes, erect to arching, hairy stems, and broadly ovate-oblong, veined, glossy, mid-green leaves, to 6in (15cm) long, with heart-shaped bases, spotted darker green when young. In early and midsummer, produces upward-facing, trumpet- then star-shaped flowers, to 1in (2.5cm) across, with spreading,

Tricyrtis macrantha subsp. *macranthopsis*

brown-spotted tepals, yellow inside and greenish yellow outside, in branched, terminal cymes. ↕ to 32in (80cm), ↔ 36in (90cm). China, Japan. Zone 6.

T. macrantha. Tufted perennial with short rhizomes, arching or decumbent, brown-hairy stems, and ovate to lance-shaped, veined, glossy, dark green leaves, 4–6in (10–15cm) long, heart-shaped at the bases. In early and midautumn, bears pendent, bell-shaped, deep yellow flowers, 1¼–1½in (3–4cm) long, with thick, fleshy tepals, spotted red-brown inside, in few-flowered cymes from the upper leaf axils. ↕ 16–32in (40–80cm), ↔ 12in (30cm). Japan. Zone 8. **subsp. *macranthopsis*** ■ syn. *T. macranthopsis,* has hairless stems, with leaves to 7in (18cm) long, and bears axillary or terminal cymes in mid- and late autumn.

T. macranthopsis see *T. macrantha* subsp. *macranthopsis.*

T. ohsumiensis ■ syn. *T. flava* subsp. *ohsumiensis.* Clump-forming perennial with short rhizomes, erect to arching, hairy stems, and oblong-lance-shaped, veined, pale green leaves, 2–8in (5–20cm) long, marked darker green, the lower ones larger and elliptic-oblong. In early autumn, upward-facing, broadly bell-shaped yellow flowers, 1–1¼in (2.5–3cm) long, faintly brown-spotted inside, especially the stigmas, are borne singly or in axillary clusters. ↕ to 20in (50cm), ↔ 9in (23cm). Japan. Zone 7.

T. stolonifera see *T. formosana.*

TRIFOLIUM

Clover

FABACEAE

Genus of about 240 species of erect or creeping annuals, biennials, and herbaceous perennials, usually found on scree or in grassy meadows or scrub worldwide, except in Australasia, and mainly in the N. hemisphere. The 3-palmate leaves, rarely up to 7-palmate, have entire or toothed leaflets, usually with stipules. Small, pea-like flowers are produced in heads or in short, terminal or axillary spike-like racemes (or, rarely, singly), in spring or summer, and are attractive to bees. Although many clovers are invasive weeds, they are sometimes an ingredient in commercial grass-seed mixes. Their aggressive behavior may choke out more desirable species. Less invasive clovers are suitable for a border or a wildflower garden.

• **CULTIVATION** Grow in moist but well-drained, neutral soil in full sun.

• **PROPAGATION** Sow seed in containers in a cold frame in spring. Divide, or detach and replant rooted stems, in spring.

• **PESTS AND DISEASES** Prone to viruses, sooty leaf blotch, powdery mildew, stem canker, rust, anthracnose, and a wide variety of fungal spots.

T. incarnatum (Crimson clover, Italian clover). Erect, bushy, downy-stemmed annual with 3-palmate leaves, to 1¼in (3cm) long, with obovate-wedge-shaped leaflets, finely toothed toward the tips. In spring and summer, bears oblong, spike-like racemes, to ½in (1.5cm) across, of 5–8 deep red to creamy yellow

Tricyrtis ohsumiensis

Trifolium repens 'Purpurascens Quadrifolium'

flowers. ↕↔ 8–20in (20–50cm). S. and W. Europe.

***T. pratense* 'Dolly North'** see *T. pratense* 'Susan Smith'.

***T. pratense* 'Goldnet'** see *T. pratense* 'Susan Smith'.

***T. pratense* 'Susan Smith',** syn. *T. pratense* 'Dolly North', *T. pratense* 'Goldnet'. Mat-forming perennial with 3-palmate leaves, to 1½in (4cm) long, with obovate to broadly elliptic, entire leaflets, usually notched at the tips, with vein-like gold markings, hairy beneath. In early and midsummer, bears dense, spherical to ovoid, axillary, spike-like racemes, to ¾in (2cm) across, of 5–9 pink flowers. ↕ 6in (15cm), ↔ 18in (45cm). Zone 7.

T. repens (Dutch clover, Shamrock, White clover). The species is very invasive, rarely cultivated as an annual, and often a weed of lawns. **'Purpurascens Quadrifolium'** ■ is a vigorous, rhizomatous, stem-rooting perennial with 4-palmate leaves, ¾–1¼in (2–3cm) long, divided into inversely heart-shaped leaflets with deep purple maroon centers and narrow, mid-green margins. Small, pea-like white flowers are produced in dense, umbel-like racemes, ½–¾in (1.5–2cm) across, in summer. ↕ to 4in (10cm), ↔ indefinite. Europe. Zone 4.

TRIGONELLA

LEGUMINOSAE

Genus of 70 species of hardy, annual herbs grown as a cultivated medicinal plant, as a spice, a leafy vegetable, and for forage. Leaves are alternate and three ovate, white to purple pea-like flowers emerge in early summer and develop into long, slender green pods.

• **CULTIVATION** Grow in full sun, in reasonably fertile, well-drained soil.

• **PROPAGATION** Easily grown from seed. May be used as a forage crop.

• **PESTS AND DISEASES** Aphids and powdery mildew.

T. foenum-graecum (Fenugreek). Erect, bushy annual with ¾–1in (2–2.5cm) long leaves. In summer, bears triangular or pea-like flowers, followed by long, slender green pods, which ripen to brown. When mature, the pods hold 20 small yellow to brown seeds, which have a maple or vanilla taste. ↕ 12–24in (30–61cm), ↔ 6–8in (15–20cm). S. Europe and Asia.

TRILLIUM

Trinity flower, Wakerobin, Wood lily

LILIACEAE

Genus of about 30 species of rhizomatous, deciduous perennials occurring mainly in woodland and scrub in North America, with a few species in the W. Himalayas and N.E. Asia. Erect, rarely procumbent, short stems each bear an apical whorl of 3 lance-shaped or elliptic to ovate or diamond-shaped, net-veined, often silver- or purple-marbled leaves. Upright or nodding, terminal, solitary, funnel- or cup-shaped flowers, with whorls of 3 leaf-like, often reflexed outer sepals, and 3 inner petals, are either stalkless and surrounded by the leaves, or stalked and borne above or below the leaves. Suitable for a moist, shady border or woodland garden. Grow the smallest species, *T. nivale* and *T. rivale*, in a pocket in a rock garden.

• **CULTIVATION** Grow in moist but well-drained, deep, humus-rich, preferably acidic to neutral soil, although some will grow in moderately alkaline soils, in deep or partial shade. Mulch annually in autumn with leaf mold.

• **PROPAGATION** Sow seed as soon as ripe in containers in a shaded cold frame; leaves will not usually appear until the second spring, and plants take 5–7 years to reach flowering size. Divide rhizomes after flowering; divisions may be slow to re-establish. Alternatively, cut out the growing point from the rhizome after flowering, which stimulates formation of offsets.

• **PESTS AND DISEASES** Rust, smut, and fungal spots sometimes occur. Young growth can be damaged by slugs and snails.

T. catesbaei, syn. *T. catesbyi*, *T. nervosum*, *T. stylosum* (Rosy wakerobin). Slender, clump-forming perennial with red-pink-tinted stems and almost stalkless, elliptic to ovate, deeply veined leaves, to 3in (8cm) long.

Trillium cernuum

Trillium chloropetalum

Stalked, nodding, pale to deep pink flowers, with ovate to heart-shaped petals, to 2in (5cm) long, reflexed, mid-green sepals, and pale green ovaries, are borne beneath or among the leaves in spring and summer. ↕ to 20in (50cm), ↔ to 6in (15cm). S.E. US. Zone 8.

T. catesbyi see *T. catesbaei*.

T. cernuum ■ (Nodding trillium). Clump-forming perennial with short-stalked, broadly diamond-shaped, abruptly pointed, mid-green leaves, 2–6in (5–15cm) long, with moderately conspicuous veining. Pale pink, sometimes reddish brown, occasionally white flowers, with recurved, wavy petals, to ¾in (2cm) long, prominent purple stamens, and dark red ovaries, are borne on reflexed, pendent stalks, beneath or among the leaves, in spring. ↕ to 24in (60cm), ↔ to 10in (25cm). E. North America. Zone 6. **f. *album*** has white flowers.

T. chloropetalum ■ Robust, clump-forming perennial with thick, hairless, red-green stems. Stalkless, broadly ovate to diamond-shaped, dark green leaves, 4–8in (10–20cm) long, are variably marbled grayish cream or maroon. Upright, stalkless, fragrant flowers, with obovate, greenish white, yellow, or brownish purple petals, 2–4in (5–10cm) long, and spreading, lance-shaped sepals, are borne above or among the leaves, in spring. ↕ to 16in (40cm), ↔ to 8in (20cm). California. Zone 6.

T. cuneatum, syn. *T. sessile* of gardens (Whippoorwill flower). Robust, upright, clump-forming perennial with stalkless, broadly ovate-rounded, often pointed, mid-green leaves, to 8in (20cm) long, marked pale or silver-green. In spring, upright, stalkless, musk-scented, dark maroon flowers, with wedge-shaped petals, 2in (5cm) or more long, and purple-tipped, olive-green sepals, are borne above the leaves. Similar to *T. sessile*; often offered under that name. ↕ 12–24in (30–60cm), ↔ to 12in (30cm). S.E. US. Zone 7.

T. erectum ■ (Purple trillium, Stinking Benjamin). Vigorous, upright perennial with stalkless, broadly ovate, mid-green leaves, to 8in (20cm) long. In spring, stalked, upright or outward-facing flowers, with pointed, elliptic, spreading or incurved petals, to 3in (8cm) long, are borne above the leaves; flowers are deep red-purple, occasionally white or yellow, with purple-tinted green sepals and purple ovaries. ↕ to 20in (50cm), ↔ to 12in (30cm). E. North America.

Trillium erectum

Zone 4. **f. *albiflorum*** has flowers with white or pale pink petals and dark purple ovaries.

T. grandiflorum ■ (Great white trillium, White wakerobin). Vigorous, clump-forming perennial with almost stalkless, ovate to rounded, dark green leaves, to 12in (30cm) long. In mid-spring, pure white flowers, often fading to pink, with green sepals, are produced above the leaves; they are stalked, erect or outward-facing, cupped at first, then opening widely, with broadly ovate, slightly wavy petals, to 3in (8cm) long, reflexing near the tips. ↕ to 16in (40cm), ↔ 12in (30cm) or more. E. North America. Zone 4. **'Flore Pleno'** is slower-growing, with very attractive, formal double flowers. Several variants with slightly differing double flowers are

Trillium luteum

grown under this name. **var. *roseum*** has bright pink flowers.

T. kamtschaticum. Upright perennial with stalkless, ovate to diamond-shaped, abruptly pointed, dark green leaves, to 6in (15cm) long. Stalked, upright flowers, with ovate white petals, to 1¾in (4.5cm) long, sometimes purple-flushed with age, and dark green sepals, are produced above the leaves in late spring and early summer. ↕ to 10in (25cm), ↔ to 8in (20cm). E. Asia. Zone 6.

T. luteum ■ (Yellow trillium). Upright, clump-forming perennial with stalkless, elliptic to broadly ovate, abruptly pointed, mid-green leaves, to 6in (15cm) long, heavily marked paler green. Stalkless, upright, sweet-scented, golden- or bronze-green flowers, with

Trillium grandiflorum

Trillium ovatum

inversely lance-shaped to obovate or narrowly elliptic petals, to 3½in (9cm) long, and lance-shaped, mid-green sepals, are produced above the leaves in spring. ↕ to 16in (40cm), ↔ to 12in (30cm). S.E. US. Zone 6b.

T. nervosum see *T. catesbaei.*

T. nivale (Dwarf white wood lily, Snow trillium). Compact, clump-forming perennial with stalked, ovate, dark bluish green leaves, to 1½in (4cm) long. Short-stalked, upright, pure white flowers, with oblong petals, to 1½in (4cm) long, and green sepals and ovaries, are borne above the leaves in early spring. ↕ to 5in (13cm), ↔ to 4in (10cm). S.E. US. Zone 6.

T. ovatum ▣ (Coast trillium). Clump-forming perennial with red-green stems and stalkless, diamond-shaped, pointed, dark green leaves, to 6in (15cm) long, each with 5 conspicuous sunken veins. In spring, stalked, upright, musk-scented, pure white flowers, fading to pink or red, with spreading, ovate petals, 1–3in (2.5–8cm) long, and green sepals, are borne above the leaves. ↕ to 20in (50cm), ↔ to 8in (20cm). W. North America. Zone 6.

T. recurvatum (Bloody butcher, Purple wakerobin). Upright, clump-forming perennial with lance-shaped to elliptic, mottled, mid-green leaves, to 3in (8cm) ong, tapering to short stalks. In spring, upright, stalkless, deep maroon, occasionally white or yellow flowers are produced above the leaves; they have ance-shaped to ovate petals, to 2in (5cm) ong, clawed at the bases, and strongly recurving green sepals. ↕ to 16in (40cm), ↔ to 12in (30cm). E. US. Zone 6.

rillium rivale

Trillium sessile

T. rivale ▣ Dwarf, upright perennial with stalked, ovate, pointed, mid-green leaves, to 1¼in (3cm) long. In spring, stalked, upright, white or pale pink flowers, spotted purple at the bases, with diamond-shaped to ovate petals, to 1in (2.5cm) long, and green sepals, are produced above the leaves. Similar to *T. nivale*, but generally easier to grow. ↕ to 5in (13cm), ↔ to 6in (15cm). W. US. Zone 6.

T. sessile ▣ (Toadshade, Wakerobin). Upright, clump-forming perennial with stalkless, broadly elliptic to rounded, deep green leaves, to 5in (13cm) long, marbled pale green, gray-white, and bronze-maroon. Stalkless, upright, red-maroon, rarely greenish yellow flowers, with lance-shaped petals, to 1¾in (4.5cm) long, and spreading, maroon-flushed green sepals, are borne above the leaves in late spring. ↕ to 12in (30cm), ↔ to 8in (20cm). N.E. US. Zone 5b.

***T. sessile* of gardens** see *T. cuneatum.*

T. stylosum see *T. catesbaei.*

T. undulatum (Painted trillium, Painted wood lily). Graceful, clump-forming perennial with erect, pale green stems, flushed pink at the bases, and stalked, narrowly ovate, tapered, dark blue-green leaves, to 6in (15cm) long. In late spring, stalked, upright, white or very pale pink flowers, with wavy petals, to 1¼in (3cm) long, with dark red, V-shaped marks at the bases and maroon-margined, dark green sepals, are borne above the leaves. ↕ to 12in (30cm), ↔ to 6in (15cm). E. US. Zone 4.

T. viride (Wood trillium). Upright perennial with sometimes downy stems, and stalkless, lance-shaped to elliptic, mid-green leaves, 3–6in (8–15cm) long, spotted white above. Stalkless, upright, malodorous, yellow-green flowers, sometimes maroon at the bases, occasionally completely maroon, with narrowly lance-shaped petals, to 3in (8cm) long, and green sepals, are borne above the leaves in spring. ↕ to 16in (40cm), ↔ to 8in (20cm). Illinois, Missouri. Zone 5.

TRIPETALEIA

ERICACEAE

Genus of 2 species of deciduous shrubs found in mountain woodland in Japan. They are cultivated for their terminal panicles of attractive, 3-petaled, sometimes 4- or 5-petaled flowers. Grow in a woodland garden.

• **CULTIVATION** Grow in moist but well-drained, humus-rich, acidic soil in partial shade. Pruning group 1.

• **PROPAGATION** Sow seed in containers in a cold frame in autumn. Insert softwood cuttings in summer.

• **PESTS AND DISEASES** Infrequent.

T. paniculata. Upright, deciduous shrub with alternate, obovate to narrowly ovate-elliptic, dark green leaves, to 2½in (6cm) long. From midsummer to early autumn, pink-tinged white flowers, ¾in (2cm) across, with 3 or 5 narrow, twisted petals, are borne in upright, terminal panicles, to 6in (15cm) long. ↕↔ 5ft (1.5m). Japan. Zone 7.

TRIPTERYGIUM

CELASTRACEAE

Genus of 2 or 3 species of deciduous, scrambling to twining climbers from deciduous woodland in E. Asia. They have large, alternate, ovate or broadly ovate to elliptic leaves. Abundant tiny, 5-petaled, saucer-shaped flowers are borne in terminal panicles, followed by prominently winged fruits. *T. regelii*, the most commonly cultivated species, is suitable for training on a house wall or over a pergola, tree, or tall tree stump. Where not hardy, grow in a cool greenhouse.

• **CULTIVATION** Grow in moist but well-drained, fertile soil in full sun. Pruning group 11, in spring.

• **PROPAGATION** Sow seed in containers in a cold frame as soon as ripe. Root semi-ripe cuttings in summer with bottom heat. Layer in early spring.

• **PESTS AND DISEASES** Infrequent.

T. regelii. Bushy, twining climber, often loosely shrubby when young, producing slightly angled, warty stems and long-stalked, ovate or broadly ovate to elliptic, slender-pointed, toothed, bright green leaves, 3–5in (8–13cm) long. In summer, small, saucer-shaped, green-tinted white flowers are borne in leafy panicles, to 10in (25cm) long, followed by 3-winged, pale green to light brown fruit, ½–¾in (1.5–2cm) long. ↕ to 30ft (10m). China, Korea, Japan. Zone 6.

▷ ***Tristagma*** see *Ipheion*

▷ ***Tristania conferta*** see *Lophostemon confertus*

TRITELEIA

LILIACEAE

Genus of about 15 species of cormous perennials, closely related to *Brodiaea*, mainly found in grassland, chaparral, and pine woodland in W. US. They are cultivated for their umbels of funnel-shaped flowers, borne on leafless stems. The semi-erect, narrowly linear, basal leaves usually die away by flowering time. Suitable for a warm, sunny, mixed or herbaceous border. In areas with severe winters, grow in a cold greenhouse or alpine house.

• **CULTIVATION** Plant corms 3in (8cm) deep in autumn. Outdoors, grow in light, sandy, fertile soil in full sun. Under glass, grow in soil-based potting mix, with added sharp sand, in full light. After planting, water sparingly until leaves appear. In growth, water freely

Triteleia hyacinthina

and apply a half-strength balanced liquid fertilizer monthly. Reduce water gradually after flowering; keep warm and dry when dormant.

• **PROPAGATION** Sow seed at 55–61°F (13–16°C) as soon as ripe or in early spring; seed-grown plants take 3–5 years to reach maturity. Separate corms when dormant.

• **PESTS AND DISEASES** Rust may occur.

T. hyacinthina ▣ syn. *Brodiaea hyacinthina, B. lactea* (Wild hyacinth). Cormous perennial with linear, basal leaves, 4–16in (10–40cm) long. Flat umbels, 4in (10cm) across, of up to 20 or more white or pale blue flowers, ½in (1.5cm) long, are produced in late spring and early summer. ↕ to 28in (70cm), PD2in (5cm). W. US. Zone 7b.

T. ixioides, syn. *Brodiaea ixioides, B. lutea* (Pretty face). Cormous perennial with linear, basal leaves, 4–16in (10–40cm) long. Open umbels, 5in (13cm) across, of up to 25 yellow flowers, ½–1in (1–2.5cm) long, with purple midribs, are produced in early summer. ↕ to 24in (60cm), PD3in (8cm). W. US. Zone 7b.

T. laxa ▣ syn. *Brodiaea laxa* (Grass nut). Showy, cormous perennial with linear, basal leaves, 8–16in (20–40cm) long. In early summer, produces loose umbels, 6in (15cm) across, of up to 25 pale to deep purple-blue flowers, ¾–2in (2–5cm) long, rarely white or shading to white at the bases. ↕ to 28in (70cm), PD2in (5cm). W. US. Zone 7.

'Koningin Fabiola', syn. 'Queen Fabiola', has purple-blue flowers, 2in (5cm) long.

Triteleia laxa

TRITONIA

IRIDACEAE

Genus of 28 species of cormous perennials, closely related to *Crocosmia*, found mainly on grassy or stony hillsides in South Africa and Swaziland. They are grown for their slender spikes of funnel- or cup-shaped, colorful flowers. The 2-ranked leaves are usually linear to lance-shaped. Grow in a warm, sunny, mixed or herbaceous border. Where not hardy, grow in a cool greenhouse.

• **CULTIVATION** Plant 4in (10cm) deep. Under glass, grow in soil-based potting mix, with added sharp sand, in full light. After flowering, water sparingly, until leaves appear; in full growth, water freely. As leaves wither after flowering, reduce water gradually to ensure a warm, dry dormancy. Repot annually. Outdoors, grow in light, well-drained, preferably sandy soil, in a sheltered site in full sun. Provide a deep, dry winter mulch. Avoid excessive moisture.

• **PROPAGATION** Sow seed at 55–61°F (13–16°C) as soon as ripe. Remove offsets when dormant

• **PESTS AND DISEASES** Infrequent.

T. crocata, syn. *T. fenestrata*, *T. hyalina*. Cormous perennial with erect, lance-shaped, basal leaves, 2–12in (5–30cm) long. Spikes of up to 10 cup-shaped, orange to pinkish red flowers, ½in (1.5cm) long, are borne on arching, wiry stems in spring. ↕ 8–20in (20–50cm), PD3in (8cm). South Africa (Western Cape, Eastern Cape). ❀ (min. 35°F/2°C). **'Princess Beatrix'** ▣ bears brilliant orange-red flowers. **'White Glory'** has amber-tinged white flowers.

T. disticha, syn. *Crocosmia rosea*. Cormous perennial with erect, linear or lance- or sword-shaped, basal leaves, 10–28in (25–70cm) long. In mid- and late summer, irregular, funnel-shaped, orange-red, red, or pink flowers, ¾in (2cm) long, are borne in many-flowered spikes, on arching, branched stems. ↕ 20–39in (50–100cm), PD2in (5cm). South Africa (Western Cape, Eastern Cape, Kwazulu/Natal). ❀ (min. 41°F/5°C). **subsp. *rubrolucens*** ▣ syn. *T. rosea*, *T. rubrolucens*, bears a succession of open funnel-shaped pink flowers, 1–1½in (2.5–4cm) across, in one-sided spikes on wiry stems; South Africa (Eastern Cape, Orange Free State, Kwazulu/Natal, Eastern Transvaal), Swaziland.

Tritonia crocata 'Princess Beatrix'

Tritonia disticha subsp. *rubrolucens*

T. fenestrata see *T. crocata*.
T. hyalina see *T. crocata*.
T. longiflora see *Ixia paniculata*.
T. rosea see *T. disticha* subsp. *rubrolucens*.
T. rubrolucens see *T. disticha* subsp. *rubrolucens*.

TROCHODENDRON

TROCHODENDRACEAE

Genus of one species of evergreen tree or large shrub from forest in Japan, Korea, and Taiwan. *T. aralioides* is grown for its handsome growth habit, its spirally arranged leaves, and its racemes of unusual, vivid green flowers. Grow in a woodland garden among other trees and shrubs, or as a specimen.

• **CULTIVATION** Grow in moist but well-drained, neutral to slightly acidic soil in full sun or dappled shade. Shelter from cold, drying winds. Pruning group 1.

• **PROPAGATION** Sow seed in containers in a cold frame in autumn. Insert semi-ripe cuttings in summer.

• **PESTS AND DISEASES** Infrequent.

T. aralioides ▣ (Wheel tree). Broadly columnar tree or large, rounded shrub with broadly ovate to elliptic, tapered, glossy, dark green leaves, to 5in (12cm) long. Racemes, to 5in (12cm) long, of 10–20 or more flowers are borne at the shoot tips in late spring and early summer; the petalless, bright green flowers, ¾in (2cm) across, each consist of numerous stamens radiating from a central green disk. ↕ 30ft (10m), ↔ 25ft (8m). Japan (including Ryukyu Islands), Korea, Taiwan. Zone 7.

Trochodendron aralioides

TROLLIUS

Globeflower

RANUNCULACEAE

Genus of about 24 species of buttercup-like, hairless, clump-forming herbaceous perennials from moist or wet meadows in cool-temperate areas of Europe, Asia, and North America. They produce numerous fibrous roots, and basal rosettes of stalked, palmately lobed leaves, the lobes further divided or toothed. Erect stems usually bear a few mainly stalkless leaves. Both the basal and stem leaves are usually mid-green, sometimes glossy. Terminal, solitary, spherical to bowl-shaped flowers, with reduced or linear, petal-like sepals, nectary-bearing petals, and numerous stamens, are borne in spring or summer. Grow in a moist border or bog garden, or beside a pond or stream; naturalize in a damp meadow garden; or force for flowers in a temperate greenhouse.

• **CULTIVATION** Grow in moist, deep, fertile, preferably heavy soil that does not dry out, in full sun or partial shade. Cut stems back hard after the first flush of flowers; apply a balanced liquid fertilizer to encourage further blooming.

• **PROPAGATION** Sow seed in containers in a cold frame as soon as ripe or in spring; seed may take 2 years to germinate. Divide as new growth begins or immediately after flowering.

• **PESTS AND DISEASES** Powdery mildew may be a problem.

T. chinensis ▣ syn. *T. ledebourii* of gardens (Chinese globeflower). Clump-forming perennial bearing 5-lobed basal leaves, to 5in (12cm) long, with broadly lance-shaped lobes divided into sharply toothed segments; the stem leaves are smaller. In midsummer, shallowly bowl-shaped, light orange-yellow flowers, 2in (5cm) across, with long petals, are produced on thick, furrowed stems. ↕ to 36in (90cm), ↔ 18in (45cm). N.E. China. Zone 5.

Trollius chinensis

Trollius x *cultorum* 'Alabaster'

***T. x cultorum* cultivars.** Clump-forming perennials bearing 5-lobed, toothed, glossy basal leaves, 7in (18cm) long, with lance-shaped lobes divided into toothed segments; stem leaves are smaller and more finely divided. Bowl-shaped flowers, 1–2½in (2.5–6cm) across, are borne from midspring to midsummer. ↕ to 36in (90cm), ↔ 18in (45cm). Zone 3b. **'Alabaster'** ▣ bears pale primrose-yellow flowers in mid- and late spring; ↕ to 24in (60cm), ↔ to 16in (40cm). **'Canary Bird'** bears pale lemon-yellow flowers over a long perio[d]. **'Earliest of All'** ▣ bears clear yellow flowers, 3in (8cm) across, in midspring; ↕ 20in (50cm), ↔ 16in (40cm). **'Feuertroll'**, syn. 'Fireglobe', produces rich orange-yellow flowers, with deeper orange stamens, in late spring; ↕ to 26in (65cm), ↔ 16in (40cm). **'Fireglobe'** see 'Feuertroll'. **'Golden Queen'** produces tangerine-orange flowers, 2in (5cm) across, that open flat, in early and midsummer; ↕ 24in (60cm). **'Gold Fountain'** see 'Goldquelle'. **'Goldquelle'**, syn. 'Gold Fountain', bears yellow flowers, 3in (8cm) across, in early and midsummer; ↕ to 28in (70cm). **'Lemon Queen'** bears pale

Trollius x *cultorum* 'Earliest of All'

T

Trollius x *cultorum* 'Orange Princess'

yellow flowers, 3in (8cm) across, in late spring and early summer; ↕ 24in (60cm). **'Orange Globe'** has orange flowers, in late spring or early summer; ↕ 30in (75cm). **'Orange Princess'** ■ bears orange-gold flowers in late spring and early summer.

T. europaeus (Common European globeflower). Clump-forming, very variable perennial bearing 5-lobed basal leaves, to 5in (12cm) long, with wedge-shaped, deeply divided and toothed lobes. Erect, rarely branched stems produce smaller leaves and spherical, lemon-yellow flowers, 2in (5cm) across, in early and midsummer. ↕ 32in (80cm), ↔ 18in (45cm). Europe, Caucasus, North America. Zone 5. **'Superbus'** has huge, sulfur-yellow flowers, to 4in (10cm) across; ↕ 24in (60cm).

***T. ledebourii* of gardens** see *T. chinensis.*

T. pumilus ■ Clump-forming, tufted perennial bearing 5-lobed, glossy basal leaves, ¾–3in (2–8cm) long, with oblong to lance-shaped, toothed lobes. In late spring and early summer, bears cup-shaped, deep golden yellow flowers, ¾–1½in (2–4cm) across, often red or purple-crimson on the outside. ↕ to 12in (30cm), ↔ to 8in (20cm). Himalayas, E. Tibet, China. Zone 5.

T. yunnanensis. Clump-forming, tufted perennial bearing 3- to 5-lobed, glossy basal leaves, 2–5in (5–12cm) long, with ovate, toothed lobes; the stem leaves are similar but smaller. In late spring and early summer, produces cup-shaped, golden yellow flowers, ¾–2½in (2–6cm) across. ↕ to 28in (70cm), ↔ to 12in (30cm). S.W. China. Zone 5.

Trollius pumilus

TROPAEOLUM

TROPAEOLACEAE

Genus of 80–90 species of hairless, climbing, trailing, or bushy annuals and herbaceous perennials, many with tuberous roots, found mainly in cool, mountainous areas in Central and South America. The alternate, rounded, peltate leaves are entire or palmately lobed to palmate, with 5–7 lobes or leaflets; they have long leaf stalks, which are used as the method of attachment in climbing species. Roughly funnel-shaped flowers, with 5 showy, clawed petals, often with prominent spurs, and 5 inconspicuous, pointed sepals, are borne singly from the leaf axils. Grow climbing species over a fence, trellis, pergola, or non-flowering shrub, or allow to trail on a bank or dry wall. *T. polyphyllum* is suitable for a raised or scree bed, or a large rock garden. The dwarf, bushy *T. majus* hybrids and cultivars are effective in an annual bed or border; the trailing or semi-trailing variants are excellent for hanging baskets or other containers. Where not hardy, grow tender perennials in a cool greenhouse or conservatory. The leaves and flowers of annuals are edible, and the young fruits of *T. majus* can be pickled.

• **CULTIVATION** Grow in moist but well-drained, moderately fertile soil in full sun. *T. majus* and its hybrids and cultivars flower best in poorer soils; *T. speciosum* prefers moist, humus-rich, neutral to acidic soil in full sun or partial shade, with the roots and lower stems in cool shade. Support the climbing stems. Where not hardy, lift tubers and store in a frost-free place until the following spring. Under glass, grow in soil-based potting mix, with added fine grit, in full light with shade from hot sun. Plant those with running rootstocks directly into a border; tuberous species need deep containers. During growth, water freely and apply a balanced liquid fertilizer monthly; reduce water as leaves wither, and keep barely moist when dormant. *T. azureum* and *T. tricolorum* are both dormant in summer; start into growth in early autumn, and water sparingly in autumn and winter.

• **PROPAGATION** Sow seed of annuals at 55–61°F (13–16°C) in early spring, or *in situ* in midspring. Sow seed of perennials in containers in a cold frame as soon as ripe; germination is often erratic. Separate tubers in autumn, when dormant. Divide *T. speciosum* carefully in early spring. Insert stem-tip cuttings in late summer with bottom heat. Root basal or stem-tip cuttings of selected cultivars, such as *T. majus* 'Hermine Grasshoff', in spring or early summer.

• **PESTS AND DISEASES** Caterpillars of cabbage white butterflies, flea beetles, black aphids, and slugs occur. *T. majus* and its hybrids and cultivars are susceptible to whiteflies and viruses.

T. aduncum see *T. peregrinum.*

***T.* Alaska Series** ■ Dwarf, bushy annuals, derived from *T. majus*, with light green leaves, speckled and marked creamy white. Single flowers, in shades of yellow, orange, mahogany, or cream, are borne from summer to autumn. ↕ to 12in (30cm), ↔ to 18in (45cm). **'Burpeei'** has fully double flowers.

Tropaeolum Alaska Series

T. azureum. Perennial climber with an ovoid tuber and 5- to 9-palmate or palmately lobed, pale or mid-green leaves, ¾in (2cm) across, with lance-shaped leaflets or lobes. Short-spurred, sky-blue flowers, ½–¾in (1.5–2cm) across, with whitish cream or yellow centers, are borne in late spring. ↕ 24–39in (60–100cm). Chile. ❀ (min. 41°F/5°C)

T. canariense see *T. peregrinum.*

***T.* 'Empress of India'.** Dwarf, bushy annual, derived from *T. majus*, with purple-green leaves. From summer to autumn, produces semi-double, velvety, rich scarlet flowers. ↕ to 12in (30cm), ↔ to 18in (45cm).

***T.* Gleam Series.** Vigorous, semi-trailing annuals, derived from *T. majus*, bearing semi-double flowers in scarlet, orange, yellow, or pastel shades, from summer to autumn. ↕ to 16in (40cm), ↔ to 24in (60cm). A non-climbing, compact strain is sometimes offered, under various names.

***T.* Jewel Series** ■ Dwarf, bushy annuals, derived from *T. majus*, bearing semi-double and double, yellow, pink-orange, scarlet, or crimson flowers from early summer to autumn; flowers are sometimes covered by the foliage. ↕ to 12in (30cm), ↔ to 18in (45cm).

T. majus (Indian cress, Nasturtium). Strong-growing, annual climber, sometimes scrambling, with rounded to kidney-shaped, wavy-margined, light green leaves, 1–2½in (2.5–6cm) long. From summer to autumn, produces long-spurred, red, orange, or yellow flowers, 2–2½in (5–6cm) across. Many cultivars often attributed to *T. majus*, and with characteristics similar to the species, are of hybrid origin, and are described in this book under their cultivar names. ↕ 3–10ft (1–3m), ↔ 5–15ft (1.5–5m). Bolivia to Colombia. **'Hermine Grasshof'** has double, bright red flowers, and may be propagated only by stem-tip cuttings. **'Salmon Baby'** is compact, with fringed, deep salmon-pink flowers. **'Variegatus'** is trailing, with variegated leaves and red or orange flowers.

***T.* 'Peach Melba'** ■ Dwarf, bushy annual, derived from *T. majus*, bearing semi-double, creamy yellow flowers with orange-red centers, from summer to autumn. Best in a container. ↕ 9–12in (23–30cm), ↔ to 18in (45cm).

Tropaeolum Jewel Series

Tropaeolum 'Peach Melba'

Tropaeolum peregrinum (inset: flower detail)

T. peregrinum ■ syn. *T. aduncum, T. canariense* (Canary creeper). Strong-growing, annual or perennial climber with 5-lobed, light to grayish green leaves, 1–2in (2.5–5cm) long. From summer to autumn, produces hook-spurred, bright yellow flowers, 1in (2.5cm) across; they have 3 tiny lower petals and 2 large, erect upper ones, which are toothed and fringed like tiny birds' wings. ↕ 8–12ft (2.5–4m). Ecuador, Peru. ❀ (min. 41°F/5°C)

T. polyphyllum ■ Trailing herbaceous annual or perennial with an elongated, rhizome-like tuber and deeply 5- to 9-lobed, glaucous, blue-green leaves, to 3in (8cm) long. Bears long-spurred, rich yellow to orange flowers, 1½in (4cm) across, among long, trailing masses of foliage over a long period in summer. ↕ 2–3in (5–8cm), ↔ to 3ft (1m). Chile, Argentina. ❀ (min. 35°F/2°C)

T. speciosum ■ (Flame nasturtium, Scottish flame flower). Slender, perennial climber with deep-rooting, long, thin, fleshy white rhizomes. The 5- to 7-palmate, mid- to dark green leaves, 1½in (4cm) long, are composed of obovate to wedge-shaped leaflets. From summer to autumn, bears long-spurred, bright vermilion flowers, ¾in (2cm) across, with long-clawed petals, the lower 3 of which are larger than the others; flowers are followed by spherical blue fruit with persistent red calyces. ↕ to 10ft (3m) or more. Chile. Zone 8.

***T.* Tom Thumb Series.** Dwarf, bushy annuals, derived from *T. majus*, bearing single, yellow, orange, red, salmon-pink, or rose-pink flowers from summer to autumn; flowers are sometimes covered by the foliage. ↕ to 10in (25cm), ↔ to 14in (35cm).

T. tricolor see *T. tricolorum.*

T. tricolorum, syn. *T. tricolor*. Tuberous-rooted, perennial climber with ovoid, often irregular tubers. Very slender stems bear rounded, 5- to 7-palmate, light green leaves, to 1½in (4cm) long, with narrowly elliptic to narrowly obovate, 5- to 7-lobed leaflets. From winter to early summer, bears flowers, 1¼in (3cm) long, with lantern-shaped, maroon-tipped, orange-scarlet calyces, short, orange to yellow petals, and long, upturned, red to yellow or purple spurs. ↕ 3–6ft (1–2m). Chile. ❀ (min. 35°F/2°C)

T. tuberosum. Perennial climber with large, purple-marbled yellow tubers and

Tropaeolum polyphyllum

Tropaeolum speciosum

Tropaeolum tuberosum var. *lineamaculatum* 'Ken Aslet'

3- to 6-lobed, grayish green leaves, 2in (5cm) long. Long-spurred, cup-shaped flowers, 1¼–1½in (3–4cm) long, with orange-red sepals and deep yellow to orange-yellow petals, with brown veins inside, are produced from midsummer to autumn. ↕ 6–12ft (2–4m). Colombia, Ecuador, Peru, Bolivia. ❀ (min. 35°F/2°C). **var. *lineamaculatum* 'Ken Aslet'** ■ is the most common cultivar, and has orange flowers. **var. *piliferum* 'Sidney'** has more slender, rhizome-like tubers, and bears orange flowers, ¾–1¼in (2–3cm) long.

***T.* Whirlybird Series.** Dwarf, bushy annuals, derived from *T. majus*. Non-spurred, single to semi-double flowers, in colors including reds, pinks, yellows, and oranges, are produced well above the foliage, from summer to autumn. ↕ to 10in (25cm), ↔ to 14in (35cm). **'Whirlybird Cream'** bears creamy yellow flowers.

TSUGA

Hemlock

PINACEAE

Genus of 10 or 11 species of evergreen, monoecious, coniferous trees found in forest from the Himalayas to N. Burma, W. Vietnam, China, Taiwan, and Japan, and in North America. Flattened, usually linear leaves, with silvery white bands beneath, are radially arranged or 2-ranked, and vary in length along the shoots. The small, ovoid-oblong to almost spherical, terminal, pale to mid-brown female cones become pendent, similar to those of *Picea*, but with few scales; male cones are almost spherical, ⅛–¼in (3–6mm) across, and borne at the tips of lateral shoots. The leading shoot is pendent. Excellent specimen trees and very shade-tolerant, especially when young; many are suitable for hedging. Dwarf cultivars are all suitable for bonsai work and shady rock gardens.

• **CULTIVATION** Grow in humus-rich, moist but well-drained, acidic to slightly alkaline soil in full sun or partial shade. Trim hedges from early to late summer.

• **PROPAGATION** Sow seed in containers in a cold frame in spring. Root semi-ripe cuttings in late summer or early autumn.

• **PESTS AND DISEASES** Gray mold (*Botrytis*), butt rot, rust, needle blights, snow blight, weevils, mites, and aphids can cause problems. Simultaneous infestation by woolly adelgid, mites, and scale is becoming increasingly common.

T. canadensis ■ (Canada hemlock). Broadly conical tree, often having several trunks, with deeply furrowed, purplish gray bark and small-budded, slender, gray-hairy shoots. Linear, finely toothed, mid-green leaves, to ¾in (2cm) long, taper from the bases and are 2-ranked with a wide parting below; a few very short leaves lie flat along the shoots, with their silver undersides positioned face up. Oblong-conical female cones are ¾in (2cm) long. ↕ to 80ft (25m), ↔ to 30ft (10m). E. North America. Zone 4. **'Aurea'** is compact and slow-growing, with golden yellow young foliage, turning greener with age; ↕ 25ft (8m), ↔ 12ft (4m). **'Bennett'** is dwarf and vase-shaped, forming a central depression, with short, light green leaves; ↕ 5ft (1.5m), ↔ 6ft (2m). **'Cole's Prostrate'**, syn. 'Coles', is low-growing and suitable as a groundcover; ↕ 12in (30cm), ↔ 3ft (1m). **'Gentsch's White'** is nest-shaped and slow-growing, with silver-tipped, mid-green leaves; ↕↔ 4ft (1.2m). **'Jeddeloh'** ■ is hemispherical, and similar to 'Bennett', with bright green leaves; ↕ 5ft (1.5m), ↔ 6ft (2m). **'Jervis'** is slow-growing, densely branched, and irregular in habit, with dark green leaves arranged closely together; ↕↔ 14in (35cm). **'Macrophylla'** is slow-growing, dense, and bears dark green leaves. **'Minuta'** is dwarf and slow-growing, with soft chartreuse new leaves, turning dark green; ↕↔ to 12in (30cm). **'Pendula'** ■ syn. f. *pendula* (Sargent's weeping hemlock), is a slow-growing, spreading, mound-forming shrub, with pendent branches, and is very attractive hanging over a bank or wall; ↕ to 12ft (4m), ↔ to 25ft (8m). **Westonigra Strain** has very dark green leaves.

T. caroliniana ■ (Carolina hemlock). Conical or ovoid, twiggy tree with shallowly fissured, red-brown bark and shiny, red-brown shoots with short hairs in the grooves. Round-tipped, entire, dark green leaves, ½–¾in (1–2cm) long, are 2-ranked, widely parted above, and somewhat irregular and sparse. Ovoid to ellipsoid female cones are 1–1½in (2.5–4cm) long. ↕ 50–70ft (15–20m), ↔ to 25ft (8m). Appalachians from Virginia to Georgia. Zone 6b.

T. chinensis (Chinese hemlock). Broadly conical to domed tree with peeling, deeply fissured, buff-pink bark and green-yellow shoots, becoming yellow-tinged gray. Linear, entire, sometimes toothed, slightly tapered,

Tsuga canadensis

Tsuga canadensis 'Jeddeloh'

glossy, dark green leaves, ¼–1in (0.6–2.5cm) long, are 2-ranked, with light green to white bands beneath. Ovoid-oblong female cones are ½–1in (1.5–2.5cm) long. ↕ to 140ft (45m), ↔ 80–100ft (25–30m). C. China. Zone 6b.

T. diversifolia (Northern Japanese hemlock). Broadly conical, later domed tree, usually having several stems, with orange-brown bark and orange shoots with short, fine hairs. Linear leaves are very glossy, dark green, ¼–½in (0.5–1.5cm) long, and 2-ranked, broader and more densely packed toward the rounded, notched shoot tips. Ovoid female cones are up to ¾in (2cm) long. ↕ to 50ft (15m), ↔ to 25ft (8m). N. Japan. Zone 6.

T. heterophylla (Western hemlock). Narrowly conical tree with cracked, purple-brown bark, horizontal branches with pendent tips, and brownish gray shoots with long brown hairs. Blunt, round-tipped, narrowly elliptic-oblong, finely toothed, very glossy, dark green leaves, ¼–¾in (0.5–2cm) long, are 2-ranked with a wide parting beneath. Ovoid female cones are ¾in (2cm) long. Very shade-tolerant and requires shelter

Tsuga caroliniana

from wind. ↕ 70–130ft (20–40m), ↔ 20–30ft (6–10m). Alaska to California. Zone 6.

T. mertensiana (Mountain hemlock). Columnar-conical tree with scaly, purple to red-brown bark and hairy, red-brown shoots. Thick, blunt-tipped, linear, entire, glaucous blue or gray-green leaves, ½–1in (1.5–2.5cm) long, are convex on both sides, and radially arranged. Female cones are oblong-cylindrical, 1½–3in (4–8cm) long, and have reflexed scales when fully open. ↕ 50ft (15m), ↔ 20ft (6m). Alaska to California. Zone 7. **'Glauca'** is slow-growing and dwarf in habit, with glaucous, silver-gray foliage; ↕ 10ft (3m), ↔ 6ft (2m).

T. sieboldii (Southern Japanese hemlock). Broadly conical tree having several stems, with smooth, dark gray bark, later cracked, and stiff, shiny, buff shoots. Linear, entire leaves, ¼–¾in (0.7–2cm) long, with notched tips, glossy, dark green above and pale green or dull white beneath, are variable in length and arrangement. Ovoid female cones are 1in (2.5cm) long. ↕ 50ft (15m), ↔ to 25ft (8m). S. Japan. Zone 7.

Tsuga canadensis 'Pendula' (inset: leaf detail)

TSUSIOPHYLLUM

ERICACEAE

Genus of one species of dwarf, semi-evergreen shrub found in woodland in Japan. It is cultivated for its umbel-like clusters of small, tubular-bell-shaped white flowers, borne in early summer, and is an attractive addition to a woodland garden.

• **CULTIVATION** Grow in moist, humus-rich, acidic soil in partial shade. Provide shelter from cold, drying winds. Pruning group 8.

• **PROPAGATION** Sow seed as soon as ripe in containers in a cold frame. Insert semi-ripe cuttings in summer.

• **PESTS AND DISEASES** Infrequent.

T. tanakae. Prostrate, spreading shrub with short, hairy branches and alternate, ovate to lance-shaped or inversely lance-shaped, very hairy, dark green leaves, ½–1¼in (1–3cm) or more long. Dense clusters of 2–6 silky-hairy white flowers, ¼–½in (0.6–1.5cm) long, each with 4 or 5 spreading petal lobes, are produced at the shoot tips in early summer. ↕ to 20in (50cm), ↔ to 8in (20cm). Japan (Honshu). Zone 7.

TUBERARIA

CISTACEAE

Genus of about 12 species of annuals and perennials from scrub, heath, and woodland in C. and S. Europe. The simple, lance-shaped to almost rounded leaves are borne in basal rosettes, and occasionally on the upright flowering stems. Terminal cymes of shallowly cup-shaped yellow flowers, sometimes with purple or red spots, are borne in late spring and summer. Grow annuals at the front of a mixed or annual border, and perennials in a sunny border or warm rock garden. Tuberarias can also be used in a wall crevice or gravel bed.

• **CULTIVATION** Grow in any well-drained soil in full sun. Prune back woody species after flowering for a second flush of growth.

• **PROPAGATION** Sow seed at 55–61°F (13–16°C) in early spring. Seed of annuals may also be sown *in situ* in mid- to late spring. Separate rooted rosettes, or take rosettes as cuttings, in spring.

• **PESTS AND DISEASES** Leaves may be damaged by slugs and snails.

T. guttata, syn. *Helianthemum guttatum.* Erect, rosette-forming, hairy annual with wavy-margined, mid-green, prominently 3-veined leaves, 1–3in (2.5–8cm) long; the basal leaves are elliptic or obovate, the stem leaves linear-oblong or linear-lance-shaped. In summer, bears terminal cymes of short-lived, long-stalked, cup-shaped yellow flowers, to 1¼in (3cm) across, each petal spotted maroon-red at the base. ↕↔ to 12in (30cm). C. and S. Europe.

T. lignosa, syn. *Helianthemum tuberaria.* Spreading, rosette-forming, woody-based perennial with hairy, obovate to lance-shaped or elliptic, dark green leaves, to 2½in (6cm) long. Loose, terminal cymes of bright yellow flowers, 1–1¼in (2.5–3cm) across, without spots, are produced from early to late summer. ↕ to 16in (40cm), ↔ 16in (40cm). W. Mediterranean. ❀ (min. 35°F/2°C)

Tulbaghia simmleri

TULBAGHIA

LILIACEAE

Genus of about 24 species of clump-forming, mainly deciduous, rhizomatous or bulbous perennials found in various habitats in tropical and temperate southern Africa. Basal, strap-shaped to linear, hairless, sometimes gray-green leaves have a smell similar to that of onions or garlic. Umbels of dainty, usually purple or white flowers, sometimes fragrant, especially at night, are borne over a long period between late spring and autumn. The flowers are tubular, each with 6 spreading tepals and a small, trumpet-like corona. Grow in a sunny border or rock garden. Where not hardy, grow in a cool greenhouse or conservatory.

• **CULTIVATION** Under glass, grow in well-drained, soil-based potting mix in full light. Water freely during the growing season; reduce water when in flower, and again as the leaves wither; keep almost dry when dormant. Outdoors, grow in well-drained, moderately fertile, humus-rich, loamy soil in full sun.

• **PROPAGATION** Sow seed in containers in a cold frame as soon as ripe, or in spring. Divide most species in spring.

• **PESTS AND DISEASES** Aphids, whiteflies, root rots, leaf spots, and Southern blight can occur.

T. fragrans see *T. simmleri.*
T. pulchella see *T. simmleri.*
T. simmleri ▣ syn. *T. fragrans, T. pulchella.* Bulbous perennial with clusters of linear leaves, 12–24in (30–60cm) long. Large, terminal umbels of fragrant, light to deep purple flowers, to ¾in (2cm) long, are produced in early and midsummer. ↕ to 24in (60cm), PD10in (25cm). South Africa (Eastern Transvaal). Zone 7b.

T. violacea (Pink agapanthus, Society garlic, Sweet garlic). Vigorous, clump-forming perennial with corm-like rhizomes and narrowly linear, grayish green leaves, to 12in (30cm) long. Large, terminal umbels of fragrant lilac flowers, ¾in (2cm) long, are produced from midsummer to early autumn. ↕ 18–24in (45–60cm), PD10in (25cm). South Africa (Eastern Cape, KwaZulu/Natal, Eastern Transvaal). Zone 7. **'Silver Lace'**, syn. 'Variegata', has cream-striped leaves and larger flowers, ¾–1½in (2–4cm) long.

TULIPA

Tulip

LILIACEAE

Genus of about 100 species of spring-flowering bulbous perennials found in habitats with dry summers and cold winters, from sea level and steppes to alpine areas, in temperate Europe, Asia and the Middle East; they are at their most diverse in C. Asia. Tulips have linear to broadly ovate, either hairy or hairless, sometimes channeled or wavy-margined, mostly mid- or gray-green leaves; they are borne at the base or are arranged alternately on the usually hairless, sometimes hairy or downy flower stems (scapes), and decrease in size up the stem. The upright, terminal flowers, usually with 6 tepals (often referred to as petals), are borne singly or in clusters of up to 12. Tulip cultivars have single or double flowers, mainly ovoid or goblet- to bowl-shaped or lily-like, sometimes fringed (see panel below), and are available in a wide range of single, mixed, or variegated colors. Variegation (i.e., breaks in color) may be caused by a virus; however, healthy tulips may also be variegated.

Tulips are excellent in beds and borders; many are suitable for forcing, especially those that bloom early. Many of the species are suitable for a rock garden. Contact with any part may aggravate skin allergies.

For horticultural purposes, tulips are divided into the following groups, which are chiefly defined by their flower characteristics. These replace the older divisions (given in parentheses below).

Single Early Group (Division 1)
Cup-shaped single flowers, to 3in (8cm) across, are white to dark purple, often margined, flamed, or flecked with a contrasting color. Early and midseason-flowering. Leaves are 4–14in (10–35cm) long. Suitable for bedding or a mixed border; use low-growing cultivars in containers. ↕6–18in (15–45cm).

Double Early Group (Division 2)
Fully double, bowl-shaped flowers, to 3in (8cm) across, are dark red to yellow or white, often margined or flecked with another color. Midseason-flowering. Leaves are 4–14in (10–35cm) long. Suitable for bedding and containers. ↕12–16in (30–40cm).

Triumph Group (Division 3)
Single, cup-shaped flowers, to 2½in (6cm) across, are produced in a wide range of colors, including dark purple to red, pink, yellow, or white, often margined or flecked with a contrasting color. Mid- or late-season-flowering. Leaves are 4–14in (10–35cm) long. Suitable for bedding, and good for cut flowers. ↕14–24in (35–60cm).

Darwin Hybrid Group (Division 4)
Single, ovoid flowers, to 3in (8cm) across, are often very brightly colored in shades of yellow, pink, orange, or red, usually flushed, flamed, or margined with a different color, and often with contrasting bases. Mid- or late-season-flowering. Leaves are upright, 4–14in (10–35cm) long. Not to be confused with the old Darwin tulips (see Single Late Group). Suitable for bedding, and good for cut flowers. ↕20–28in (50–70cm).

Single Late Group (Division 5)
Cup- or goblet-shaped flowers, to 3in (8cm) across, sometimes several to a stem, are white to yellow, pink, red, or almost black, often with contrasting margins. Late-season-flowering. Leaves are 4–14in (10–35cm) long. Includes the old Darwin and cottage tulips. Suitable for bedding, and good for cut flowers. ↕18–30in (45–75cm).

Lily-flowered Group (Division 6)
Elegant, single, goblet-shaped flowers, to 3in (8cm) across, with reflexed, pointed tips to the tepals, are white to yellow, or pink to shades of red and magenta, sometimes margined, flamed, or flushed with a contrasting color. Late-season-flowering. Leaves are 4–16in (10–40cm) long. Excellent for formal bedding. ↕18–26in (45–65cm).

Fringed Group (Division 7)
Single, cup-shaped flowers, to 3in (8cm) across, are white, yellow, pink, red, or violet, with fringed margins, usually in a different color. Late-season-flowering. Leaves are 4–16in (10–40cm) long. Suitable for a border, and good for cut flowers. ↕14–26in (35–65cm).

Viridiflora Group (Division 8)
Single, cup- or almost closed bowl-shaped flowers, to 3in (8cm) across, are sometimes entirely green, margined with another color, or white to yellow, red, or purple, flamed or striped green, with contrasting centers. Late-season-flowering. Leaves are 4–16in (10–40cm) long. Ideal for a mixed border, and good for cut flowers. ↕16–22in (40–55cm).

Rembrandt Group (Division 9)
Of historical interest; they are no longer commercially available. Single, cup-shaped flowers, to 3in (8cm) across, are white, yellow, or red, with black, brown, bronze, purple, red, or pink stripes or "feathers," caused by a virus. Often termed "broken" tulips. Late-season-flowering. Leaves are 4–14in (10–35cm) long. ↕18–26in (45–65cm).

Parrot Group (Division 10)
Single, cup-shaped flowers, to 4in (10cm) across, are white to pink or violet-blue, often unevenly striped with different colors, including green. The tepals are finely and irregularly cut. Late-season-flowering. Leaves are 4–14in (10–35cm) long. Good for cut flowers. ↕14–26in (35–65cm).

Double Late Group (peony-flowered) (Division 11)
Fully double, bowl-shaped flowers, to 5in (12cm) across, are white to purple, sometimes margined or flamed in a different color. Late-season-flowering. Leaves are 4–16in (10–40cm) long. Suitable for bedding or a border. ↕14–24in (35–60cm).

Kaufmanniana Group (Division 12)
T. kaufmanniana and hybrids mainly derived from it. Single, bowl-shaped flowers, 3–4in (8–10cm) across, are frequently multicolored, usually with distinctively colored bases. Early- or midseason-flowering. Leaves, 3–10in (8–25cm) long, are sometimes marked bronze, red, or purple. Ideal for a rock garden or border. ↕6–12in (15–30cm).

Fosteriana Group (Division 13)
T. fosteriana and hybrids mainly derived from it. Single, bowl-shaped flowers, to 5in (12cm) across, are white to yellow or dark red, sometimes margined or flamed in another color, and with contrasting bases. Midseason-flowering.

Tulipa 'Abba'

Tulipa acuminata

Tulipa 'African Queen'

Tulipa 'Ancilla'

Tulipa 'Angélique'

Tulipa 'Apeldoorn'

Leaves, 2–12in (5–30cm) long, are usually light bright green to dark green, sometimes marked red-purple. Suitable for a border. ↕8–26in (20–65cm).

Greigii Group (Division 14)
T. greigii and hybrids mainly derived from it. Single, bowl-shaped flowers, to 4in (10cm) across, are yellow to red, sometimes flamed or margined in a different color, and with contrasting bases. Usually early- or midseason-flowering. Broad, spreading, usually wavy-margined, blue-gray leaves, 2–7in (5–18cm) long, have dark bluish maroon markings. Grow in a rock garden or border. ↕6–12in (15–30cm).

Miscellaneous Group (Division 15)
All species and hybrids not included in other divisions. There are two informal sections: low-growing, 4–8in (10–20cm) tall, with star-shaped flowers, 2–3in (5–8cm) across, with pointed tepals; and taller-growing, 8–14in (20–35cm) or more tall, with mainly bowl-shaped flowers, 2½–6in (6–15cm) across, mostly with rounded bases and tepals. Very early- to late-season-flowering. Grow in a rock garden or border. Keep dry in summer. The smallest ones may also be grown in a bulb frame or alpine house. *T. sylvestris* is suitable for naturalizing in fine grass.

• **HARDINESS** See CULTIVATION.

• **CULTIVATION** Select tulip cultivars and species based on hardiness zones. Most tulips require a long winter and thrive from Zones 4 to 8. Grow in fertile, well-drained, neutral to slightly acidic soil in full or afternoon sun. Where summers are hot, planting named hybrids 9–12in (22–30cm) deep, rather than 6in (15cm) will keep the bulbs flowering for several years.

T. tarda prefers humus-rich, peaty soil; rock garden species and cultivars prefer more sharply drained soil. All dislike excessive moisture. Plant most cultivars at a depth of 8in (20cm) to the base of the bulb; most species should be planted 4in (10cm) deep or less. The optimum season to plant depends on hardiness zone, ranging from early autumn (Zone 4) to early winter (Zone 8). Depending on the desired effect, plant nearly bulb-to-bulb or allow for a spread of 1–3in (2.5–8cm) for most tulips, and 5–6in (13–15cm) for Greigii and Kaufmanniana Group tulips, which have spreading leaves. If perennial flowering is desired, apply a balanced fertilizer after planting. Deadhead after flowering. Allow the foliage to yellow for about 6 weeks after flowering before removing it. The bulbs

TULIP FLOWERS

Tulips are valued for their brightly colored, upright flowers, mainly produced in spring. The flowers may be single or double, and vary in shape from simple cups, bowls, and goblets to more complex forms produced by twisted or rounded tepals.

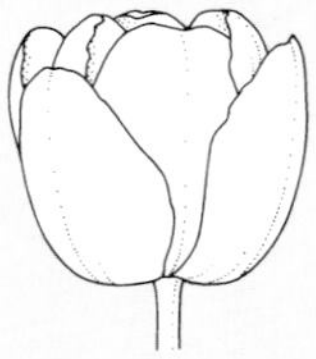
SINGLE, CUP-SHAPED

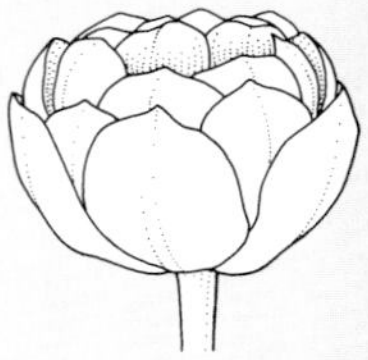
DOUBLE, BOWL-SHAPED

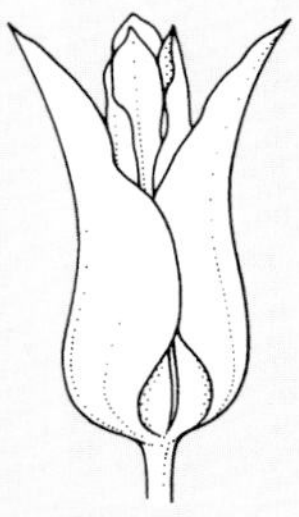
GOBLET-SHAPED

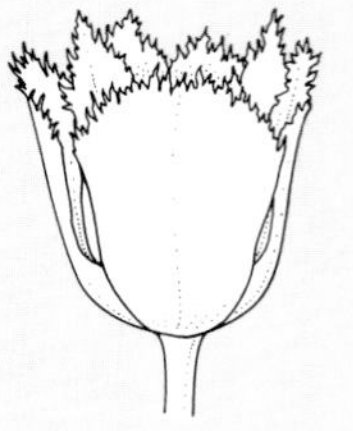
FRINGED

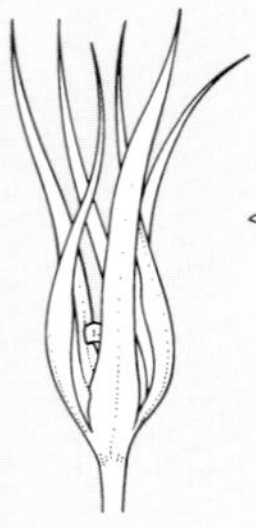
LONG, SLENDER-TEPALLED

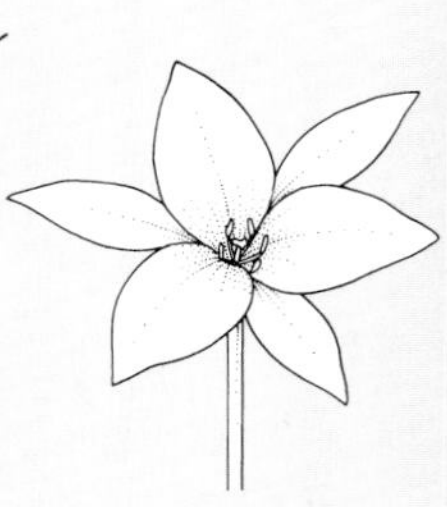
STAR-SHAPED

T

Tulipa 'Apricot Beauty'

Tulipa 'Arabian Mystery'

Tulipa 'Attila'

Tulipa 'Balalaika'

Tulipa 'Ballade'

Tulipa batalinii

Tulipa biflora

Tulipa 'Bing Crosby'

Tulipa 'Bird of Paradise'

Tulipa 'Blue Heron'

Tulipa 'Blue Parrot'

Tulipa 'Burns'

of species, and many Greigii and Kaufmanniana Group tulips, may be left in the ground for several years. For those belonging to other groups, they may be lifted annually, once the leaves have died down, and ripened in a warm, dry place but this is not usually necessary. Replant the largest bulbs. Smaller tulips may be grown in containers in a bulb frame or alpine house, in a mix of equal parts loam, leaf mold, and sharp sand. When in growth, water moderately, applying a balanced liquid fertilizer weekly for 3 or 4 weeks after flowering; keep dry in summer, and repot annually.
• **PROPAGATION** Sow seed of species in containers in a cold greenhouse or frame in autumn; it may take 4–7 years for flowers to be produced. Separate offsets of species and cultivars after lifting in summer, replant, and grow on.
• **PESTS AND DISEASES** Root and bulb rots are common in wet or poorly drained soil. Gray mold, slugs, snails, aphids, and nematodes are problems.

***T.* 'Abba'** ■ Double Early Group tulip producing glowing tomato-red flowers, flushed dull cardinal-red and sometimes irregularly feathered yellow. Midseason-flowering. ↕10–12in (25–30cm).
T. acuminata ■ Miscellaneous Group tulip with 2–7 linear to lance-shaped, sometimes wavy-margined, hairless, glaucous, gray-green leaves, to 12in (30cm) long. Solitary flowers, 4in (10cm) long, with long, pointed tepals and rounded bases, are produced on hairless or finely downy stems in midseason. Flowers are pale red or yellow, usually tinged red or green. Stamens have reddish brown anthers and yellow or white filaments. ↕16–18in (40–45cm). Garden origin.
***T.* 'African Queen'** ■ Triumph Group tulip bearing dark purplish red flowers, fading at the margins, with purple-margined, primrose-yellow basal marks, in midseason. Insides are dark ruby-red with yellow-white or white margins and purple anthers. ↕14–16in (35–40cm).
T. aitchisonii see *T. clusiana.*
***T.* 'Aladdin'.** Lily-flowered Group tulip bearing yellow-margined scarlet flowers in mid- and late season. ↕16–18in (40–45cm).
***T.* 'Ancilla'** ■ Kaufmanniana Group tulip producing soft pink flowers, flushed rose-red, with red inner and outer basal rings. Midseason-flowering. ↕6–8in (15–20cm).
***T.* 'Angélique'** ■ Double Late Group tulip with pale pink flowers, flushed with paler and darker shades of pink, with lighter margins and, occasionally, green or yellow bases. Mid- and late-season-flowering. ↕12–14in (30–35cm).
***T.* 'Apeldoorn'** ■ Darwin Hybrid Group tulip bearing cherry-red flowers with signal-red margins. Insides are signal-red with yellow-bordered black marks and black anthers. Midseason-flowering. ↕14–18in (35–45cm).
***T.* 'Apeldoorn's Elite'.** Darwin Hybrid Group tulip with red-feathered, buttercup-yellow flowers, flushed yellowish green at the bases outside, with black anthers and black basal marks inside. Midseason-flowering. ↕14–18in (35–45cm).
***T.* 'Apricot Beauty'** ■ Single Early Group tulip producing soft salmon-pink flowers, later with orange margins, in midseason. Excellent tulip for forcing, as well as for culture outdoors. ↕10–12in (25–30cm).
***T.* 'Arabian Mystery'** ■ Triumph Group tulip bearing dark purple flowers, with white margins, in midseason. ↕12–14in (30–35cm).
***T.* 'Artist'** ■ Viridiflora Group tulip bearing purple and salmon-pink flowers, green-flushed salmon-pink inside, late in the season. ↕8–10in (20–25cm).
***T.* 'Attila'** ■ Triumph Group tulip bearing light purplish violet flowers in midseason. ↕12–14in (30–35cm).

Tulipa 'Artist'

T. aucheriana. Miscellaneous Group tulip with 2–5 linear, channeled, hairless, glaucous, mid-green leaves, to 6in (15cm) long. In midseason, bears star-shaped pink flowers, to 3in (8cm) across, with yellow centers and stamens, singly or, occasionally, in twos or threes. ↕6–8in (15–20cm). Iran.
T. australis see *T. sylvestris.*
***T.* 'Avignon'.** Single Late Group tulip with red flowers, fire-red toward the margins and flushed yellowish white at the bases. Insides are tomato-red with yellow basal marks, greenish red at the margins, and with yellow anthers. Late-season-flowering. ↕14–16in (35–40cm).
T. bakeri see *T. saxatilis.*
***T.* 'Balalaika'** ■ Single Late Group tulip bearing glowing bright red flowers with yellow basal marks inside and black anthers. Late-season-flowering. ↕16–22in (40–55cm).
***T.* 'Ballade'** ■ Lily-flowered Group tulip bearing white-margined, reddish magenta flowers with white-margined yellow basal marks inside. Late-season-flowering. ↕14–16in (35–40cm).
***T.* 'Ballerina'.** Lily-flowered Group tulip producing lemon-yellow flowers with blood-red flames, orange-yellow veins at the margins, and star-shaped yellow bases. Insides are capsicum-red, feathered marigold-orange, with pale golden yellow anthers. Late-season-flowering. ↕16–22in (40–55cm).
***T.* 'Baronesse'.** Single Late Group tulip producing rose-red flowers with broad white margins and bluish white bases. Insides are white with red feathers, pale blue and yellow basal marks, and dark brown anthers. Midseason-flowering. ↕14–16in (35–40cm).
T. batalinii ■ Miscellaneous Group tulip with 3–9 linear, sickle-shaped, hairless, gray-green leaves, to 6in (15cm) long, with wavy red margins. Late in the season, bears solitary, bowl-shaped, pale yellow flowers, to 3in (8cm) across, with rounded bases and dark yellow or bronze marks inside. Stamens have yellow anthers and black or yellow filaments. ↕8–10in (20–25cm). Uzbekistan.
***T.* 'Bellona'.** Triumph Group tulip bearing scented, golden yellow flowers in midseason. ↕10–14in (25–35cm).
***T.* 'Bestseller'.** Single Early Group tulip producing bright copper-orange flowers in midseason. ↕10–12in (25–30cm).
***T.* 'Bienvenue'.** Darwin Hybrid Group tulip bearing canary-yellow flowers with dark pink flames and yellow-green bases. Insides are bright yellow, flamed red, with black basal marks. Midseason-flowering. ↕14–18in (35–45cm).
T. biflora ■ syn. *T. polychroma.* Miscellaneous Group tulip with 1 or 2 linear, hairless, gray-green leaves, to 7in (18cm) long. Star-shaped, fragrant, red-margined white flowers, to 1½in (4cm) across, have yellow bases, and are flushed greenish gray or greenish pink outside. Stamens have yellow anthers, often tipped dark purple or black, and yellow filaments. Flowers are borne singly or in twos or threes, on upright stems early in the season. ↕4–5in (10–13cm). Kazakhstan, E. Turkey, Iran, Afghanistan, Tajikistan.
***T.* 'Bing Crosby'** ■ Triumph Group tulip producing glowing scarlet flowers in midseason. ↕10–14in (25–35cm).
***T.* 'Bird of Paradise'** ■ Parrot Group tulip with orange-margined, cardinal-red flowers. Insides are scarlet, feathered dark red, with bright yellow bases and purple anthers. Late-season-flowering. ↕22in (55cm).
***T.* 'Blue Heron'** ■ Fringed Group tulip producing purple-fringed, violet-purple flowers. Insides are cobalt-violet with white stripes and bases, and black anthers. Late-season-flowering. ↕16–22in (40–55cm).
***T.* 'Blue Parrot'** ■ Parrot Group tulip with bright violet-blue flowers, bronze-purple inside. Late-season-flowering. ↕12–14in (30–35cm).
***T.* 'Bright Gem'.** Miscellaneous Group tulip bearing orange-flushed, sulfur-yellow flowers with bronze-orange basal marks. Late-season-flowering. ↕8–10in (20–25cm).
***T.* 'Brilliant Star'.** Single Early Group tulip bearing bright vermilion flowers early in the season. ↕8–10in (20–25cm).
***T.* 'Burgundy Lace'.** Fringed Group tulip bearing fringed, wine-red flowers late in the season. ↕16–22in (40–55cm).
***T.* 'Burns'** ■ Fringed Group tulip bearing bright light pink flowers, with grayish white bases outside, late in the season. Insides are pinkish red with ivory-white bases, violet margins, and yellow anthers. ↕14–16in (35–40cm).
***T.* 'Buttercup'.** Greigii Group tulip bearing yellow-margined, carmine-red

Tulipa 'Candela'

Tulipa 'Cape Cod'

Tulipa 'Carnaval de Nice'

Tulipa 'China Pink'

Tulipa 'Clara Butt'

Tulipa clusiana

Tulipa clusiana var. *chrysantha*

Tulipa 'Don Quichotte'

Tulipa 'Dreamboat'

Tulipa 'Dreaming Maid'

Tulipa 'Estella Rijnveld'

Tulipa 'Flaming Parrot'

flowers, dark golden yellow inside, with red-marked yellow bases. Midseason-flowering. ↕8–10in (20–25cm).

***T.* 'Candela'** ■ Fosteriana Group tulip producing large, pure yellow flowers, with black anthers, early in the season. ↕8–10in (20–25cm).

***T.* 'Cape Cod'** ■ Greigii Group tulip bearing apricot-yellow flowers, with red central stripes on the tepals, in mid-season. Leaves are marked dark bluish maroon. ↕7–9in (18–23cm).

***T.* 'Carnaval de Nice'** ■ Double Late Group tulip bearing white flowers, with dark red feathers and markings, in mid-season. ↕10–14in (25–35cm).

***T.* 'China Pink'** ■ Lily-flowered Group tulip bearing pink flowers, with white bases inside, in midseason. ↕14–16in (35–40cm).

T. chrysantha see *T. clusiana* var. *chrysantha.*

***T.* 'Clara Butt'** ■ Single Late Group tulip bearing deep salmon-pink flowers late in the season. ↕18–22in (45–55cm).

T. clusiana ■ syn. *T. aitchisonii* (Lady tulip). Miscellaneous Group tulip with 2–5 linear, hairless, glaucous, gray-green leaves, to 6in (15cm) long, sometimes wavy-margined. Bowl-shaped, later star-shaped flowers, to 4in (10cm) across, with rounded bases, are produced singly or in pairs in early and midseason. Flowers are white, striped dark pink outside, with purple or crimson basal marks and purple stamens. Persistent in borders if not disturbed. ↕10–12in (25–30cm). Iran to Himalayas. **var. *chrysantha*** ■ syn. *T. chrysantha, T. stellata* var. *chrysantha*, has up to 3 yellow flowers, tinged red or brownish purple outside, with yellow anthers. **var. *stellata***, syn. *T. stellata*, has star-shaped flowers with yellow basal marks.

***T.* 'Cordell Hull'.** Single Late Group tulip bearing white-flamed red flowers late in the season. ↕12–14in (30–35cm).

***T.* 'Corona'.** Kaufmanniana Group tulip bearing red flowers, pale yellow inside, in midseason. Leaves are marked purple. ↕8–10in (20–25cm).

***T.* 'Corsage'.** Greigii Group tulip bearing rose-pink flowers, with yellow margins and bronze bases, in midseason. Insides are rose-red with golden yellow feathers. Leaves are marked dark bluish maroon. ↕8–10in (20–25cm).

***T.* 'Couleur Cardinal'.** Triumph Group tulip producing plum-purple flowers, dark crimson-scarlet inside, in midseason. ↕8–10in (20–25cm).

T. dasystemon see *T. tarda.*

***T.* 'Dawnglow'.** Darwin Hybrid Group tulip bearing pale apricot flowers, flushed carmine-pink, with greenish yellow bases. Insides are yellow-orange with purple anthers. Midseason-flowering. ↕16–20in (40–50cm).

***T.* 'Destiny'.** Parrot Group tulip producing carmine-pink flowers, with creamy white bases and bronze anthers, late in the season. ↕12–14in (30–35cm).

***T.* 'Diana'.** Single Early Group tulip producing white flowers in midseason. ↕8–12in (20–30cm).

***T.* 'Don Quichotte'** ■ Triumph Group tulip producing cherry-pink flowers in midseason. ↕14–16in (35–40cm).

***T.* 'Dreamboat'** ■ Greigii Group tulip producing red-tinged, amber-yellow flowers with red-marked, green-bronze bases. Midseason-flowering. Leaves are marked dark bluish maroon. ↕6–8in (15–20cm).

***T.* 'Dreaming Maid'** ■ Triumph Group tulip producing white-margined violet flowers in midseason. ↕12–14in (30–35cm).

***T.* 'Dreamland'** ■ Single Late Group tulip producing cream-flamed red flowers. Insides are pinkish red with white bases and yellow anthers. Late-season-flowering. ↕24in (60cm).

***T.* 'Early Harvest'.** Kaufmanniana Group tulip bearing dark pinkish red flowers with yellow margins and bases, and bronze-green basal marks. Insides are yellow with vivid, reddish orange markings and pale yellow anthers. Midseason-flowering. Leaves are marked purple. ↕8–10in (20–25cm).

T. edulis, syn. *Amana edulis.* Miscellaneous Group tulip with 6 linear, hairless, mid-green leaves, 6–10in (15–25cm) long. Early in the season, star-shaped white flowers, 2½in (6cm) across, veined reddish brown or purple outside, with yellow-margined, dark purple basal marks, are borne singly or in pairs. The linear flower bracts distinguish it from other species. ↕6–8in (15–20cm). N.E. China, Korea, Japan.

***T.* 'Elizabeth Arden'.** Darwin Hybrid Group tulip producing violet-flushed, dark salmon-pink flowers with yellow and white bases. Midseason-flowering. ↕12–14in (30–35cm).

***T.* 'Engadin'.** Greigii Group tulip bearing yellow-margined, blood-red flowers, dark golden yellow with blood-red stripes inside. Midseason-flowering. Leaves are marked dark bluish maroon. ↕6–8in (15–20cm).

***T.* 'Esperanto'.** Viridiflora Group tulip bearing pinkish red flowers with green-flamed midveins that fade to reddish brown, greenish brown bases, and greenish yellow anthers. Late-season-flowering. Leaves are margined white. ↕14–16in (35–40cm).

***T.* 'Estella Rijnveld'** ■ syn. *T.* 'Gay Presto'. Parrot Group tulip producing fringed, white-flamed red flowers late in the season. ↕10–12in (25–30cm).

***T.* 'Fancy Frills'.** Fringed Group tulip producing deep rose-red flowers with whitish pink fringes, ivory-white bases, and pale yellow anthers. Late-season-flowering. ↕14–16in (35–40cm).

***T.* 'Flaming Parrot'** ■ Parrot Group tulip with deep yellow flowers, flamed dark red, and with primrose-yellow bases. Insides are primrose-yellow with glowing blood-red flames, and purple-black anthers. Late-season-flowering. ↕14–16in (35–40cm).

T. fosteriana. Fosteriana Group tulip with 3–6 oblong to broadly ovate, light

Tulipa 'Dreamland'

T

Tulipa 'Fringed Beauty'

Tulipa 'Fringed Elegance'

Tulipa 'Generaal de Wet'

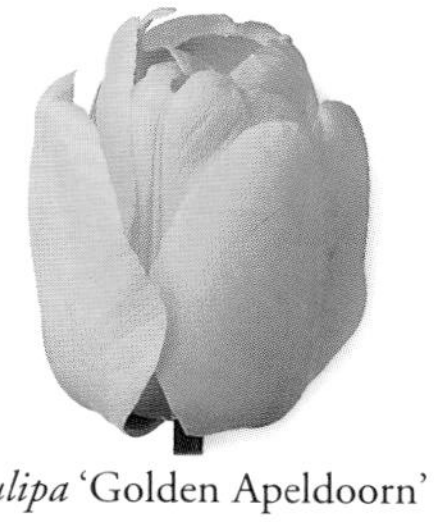
Tulipa 'Golden Apeldoorn'

Tulipa 'Golden Artist'

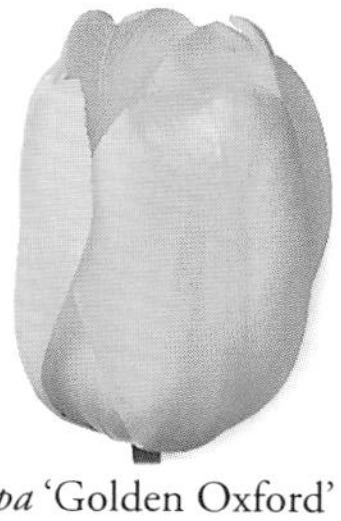
Tulipa 'Golden Oxford'

Tulipa 'Gordon Cooper'

Tulipa 'Groenland'

Tulipa 'Gudoshnik'

Tulipa hageri 'Splendens'

Tulipa 'Hamilton'

Tulipa humilis

gray-green leaves, to 12in (30cm) long, downy above. Bowl-shaped, slightly fragrant flowers, to 8in (20cm) across, with rounded bases, are borne singly on slightly downy stems in early and mid-season. Flowers are bright red with yellow-margined, purplish black basal marks. Stamens have purplish black anthers and black or yellow filaments. ↕6–10in (15–25cm). Kazakhstan, Uzbekistan, Tajikistan. **'Princeps'** has orange-scarlet flowers, scarlet inside, with greenish bronze basal marks.

***T.* 'Fringed Beauty'** ■ Fringed Group tulip producing vermilion flowers, with golden yellow fringes, late in the season. ↕12–14in (30–35cm).

***T.* 'Fringed Elegance'** ■ Fringed Group tulip bearing primrose-yellow flowers, with paler fringes, and sometimes with pink markings, late in the season. Insides are brilliant greenish yellow with bronze-green basal marks and purple anthers. ↕12–14in (30–35cm).

***T.* 'Garden Party'.** Triumph Group tulip bearing white flowers, carmine-red at the margins. Insides are feathered carmine-red with white bases. Midseason-flowering. ↕12–14in (30–35cm).

***T.* 'Gay Presto'** see *T.* 'Estella Rijnveld'.

***T.* 'Generaal de Wet'** ■ syn. *T.* 'General de Wet'. Single Early Group tulip bearing fragrant, golden orange flowers, with dark orange shading, in early and midseason. ↕8–10in (20–25cm).

***T.* 'General de Wet'** see *T.* 'Generaal de Wet'.

***T.* 'Georgette'.** Single Late Group tulip producing red-margined yellow flowers, several per stem, late in the season. ↕10–14in (25–35cm).

***T.* 'Gerbrand Kieft'.** Double Late Group tulip bearing glowing purple-red flowers, with pure white margins, late in the season. ↕10–12in (25–30cm).

T. gesneriana. Miscellaneous Group tulip with 2–7 lance-shaped to ovate-lance-shaped, hairless or finely downy, mid-green leaves, to 12in (30cm) long. Solitary flowers, to 5in (12cm) across, cup-shaped at first, opening to star-shaped, with rounded bases, are borne on hairless or finely downy stems from early to late in the season. Flowers are red, orange, yellow, or purplish red, sometimes marked yellow or black at the bases, with purple or yellow stamens. The original parent of many garden cultivars. ↕18in (45cm). Probably garden origin; naturalized in parts of the Mediterranean.

***T.* 'Giuseppe Verdi'** ■ Kaufmanniana Group tulip bearing yellow-margined, carmine-red flowers, golden yellow with small red marks inside, early in the season. Leaves are marked purple. ↕7–9in (18–23cm).

***T.* 'Golden Apeldoorn'** ■ Darwin Hybrid Group tulip producing golden yellow flowers, with black anthers, in midseason. Inside, star-shaped black bases have bronze-green borders. ↕14–18in (35–45cm).

***T.* 'Golden Artist'** ■ Viridiflora Group tulip producing golden orange flowers, with green stripes on the tepals, late in the season. ↕14–16in (35–40cm).

***T.* 'Golden Mirjoran'.** Triumph Group tulip producing dark rose-red flowers, with light yellow margins, in midseason. Insides are sulfur-yellow with broad,

Tulipa 'Giuseppe Verdi'

cherry-red margins and purple-brown anthers. ↕8–12in (20–30cm).

***T.* 'Golden Oxford'** ■ syn. *T.* 'Topic'. Darwin Hybrid Group tulip producing pure yellow flowers, sometimes narrowly margined red, with black anthers, in midseason. ↕12–14in (30–35cm).

***T.* 'Golden Parade'.** Darwin Hybrid Group tulip producing pale buttercup-yellow flowers, with black anthers, in midseason. Insides are golden yellow with black basal marks. ↕16–20in (40–50cm).

***T.* 'Gordon Cooper'** ■ Darwin Hybrid Group tulip with red flowers, maturing to pink, with signal-red margins and bluish black and yellow basal marks. Insides are glowing signal-red with black anthers. Midseason-flowering. ↕14–18in (35–45cm).

***T.* 'Grand Duc'** see *T.* 'Keizerskroon'.

***T.* 'Greenland'** see *T.* 'Groenland'.

T. greigii. Greigii Group tulip with 2–7 oblong-lance-shaped to lance-shaped, sometimes wavy-margined, glaucous, gray-green leaves, to 10in (25cm) long, streaked or marked reddish or dark purple, and often downy above. Early in the season, densely downy, pink- or brown-tinged stems bear solitary, bowl-shaped, red or yellow flowers, to 5½in (14cm) across; they are often orange-stained outside, with yellow-rimmed, blackish purple basal marks and black stamens. ↕20in (50cm). Tajikistan.

***T.* 'Greuze'.** Single Late Group tulip producing violet-purple flowers late in the season. ↕14–16in (35–40cm).

***T.* 'Groenland'** ■ syn. *T.* 'Greenland'. Viridiflora Group tulip producing green flowers, with rose-pink margins, late in the season. ↕14–18in (35–45cm).

***T.* 'Gudoshnik'** ■ Darwin Hybrid Group tulip bearing yellow flowers with red spots, rose-pink flames, bluish black basal marks, and black anthers. Midseason-flowering. ↕14–16in (35–40cm).

T. hageri. Miscellaneous Group tulip with 2–7 lance-shaped, hairless, light green leaves, to 8in (20cm) long, often margined reddish purple. In early and midseason, bears star-shaped flowers, 2½–3½in (6–9cm) across, singly or in clusters of up to 4, on hairless stems. The buff flowers are mostly green-tinged outside. Inside, they are dull red with black, sometimes yellow-margined basal marks, dark green or brown anthers, and green filaments, sometimes tinged purple. ↕8–10in (20–25cm). Bulgaria, Greece, W. Turkey. **var. *nitens*** has orange-scarlet flowers and glaucous leaves. **'Splendens'** ■ has crimson-scarlet flowers, brownish red inside.

***T.* 'Hamilton'** ■ Fringed Group tulip producing buttercup-yellow flowers, with darker yellow fringes and anthers, late in the season. ↕14–16in (35–40cm).

***T.* 'Hans Mayer'.** Darwin Hybrid Group tulip bearing buttercup-yellow flowers, flamed translucent vermilion, with light green bases. Insides are golden yellow with vermilion flames and dark brown bases. Brown anthers have a violet glow. Midseason-flowering. ↕14–18in (35–45cm).

***T.* 'Heart's Delight'.** Kaufmanniana Group tulip bearing dark rose-red flowers with pale rose-pink margins and red-marked, golden yellow bases. Insides are ivory-white. Early-season-flowering. Leaves are marked purple. ↕7–9in (18–23cm).

***T.* 'Hollywood'.** Viridiflora Group tulip producing green-tinged red flowers, with yellow basal marks, late in the season. ↕14–16in (35–45cm).

T. humilis ■ Miscellaneous Group tulip with 2–5 linear, channeled, hairless, glaucous, gray-green leaves, to 6in (15cm) long. In early and midseason, star-shaped flowers, to 3in (8cm) across, are produced singly, or sometimes in twos or threes. Flowers are pale pink to purplish pink or magenta, often tinged grayish green outside, with yellow, olive-green, or blue-black basal marks, and frequently margined yellow or white. Stamens have yellow, brown, purple, or black anthers and yellow filaments. ↕to 8–10in (20–25cm). S. and E. Turkey, N. Iraq, N. and W. Iran, Azerbaijan.

***T.* 'Ile de France'.** Triumph Group tulip producing cardinal-red flowers with dark bronze-green basal marks and narrow, yellowish brown margins. Insides are blood-red. Midseason-flowering. ↕14–16in (35–40cm).

***T.* 'Inzell'.** Triumph Group tulip producing ivory-white flowers, with yellow anthers, in midseason. ↕12–14in (30–35cm).

***T.* 'Jewel of Spring'.** Darwin Hybrid Group tulip producing red-margined, sulfur-yellow flowers, with greenish black bases and black anthers, in midseason. ↕14–16in (35–40cm).

Tulipa 'Juan'

Tulipa linifolia

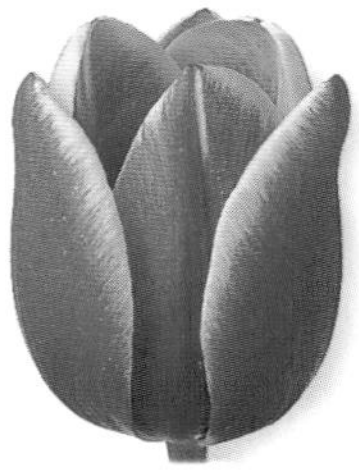
Tulipa 'Lustige Witwe'

Tulipa 'Margot Fonteyn'

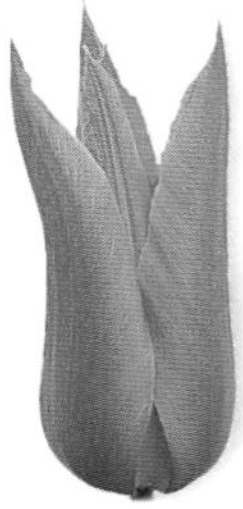
Tulipa 'Mariette'

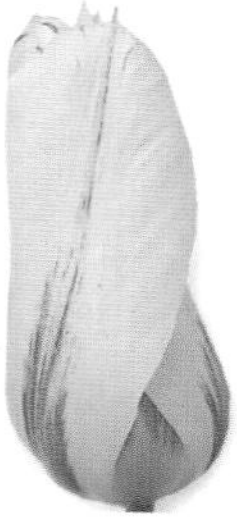
Tulipa 'Marilyn'

Tulipa marjolletii

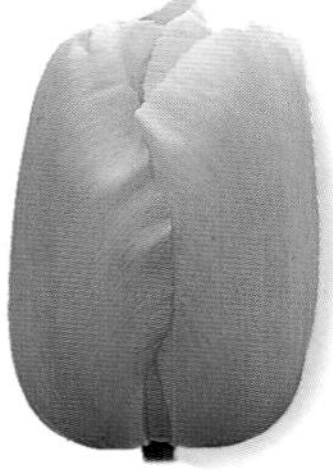
Tulipa 'Menton'

Tulipa 'Mme. Lefeber'

Tulipa 'Orange Monarch'

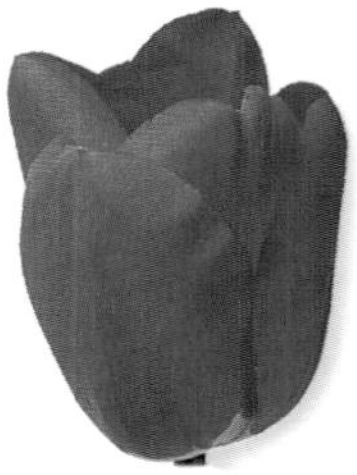
Tulipa 'Oxford'

Tulipa 'Page Polka'

***T.* 'Johann Strauss'.** Kaufmanniana Group tulip bearing currant-red flowers, margined sulfur-yellow, with golden yellow bases. Insides are ivory-white. Early-season-flowering. Leaves are marked purple. ↕6–8in (15–20cm).
***T.* 'Juan'** ■ Fosteriana Group tulip producing pink-tinged, dark orange flowers, with yellow bases and anthers, in midseason. Leaves are marked reddish brown. ↕10in (25cm).
T. kaufmanniana (Waterlily tulip). Kaufmanniana Group tulip with 3–5 lance-shaped to inversely lance-shaped, slightly wavy-margined, hairless, gray-green leaves, to 10in (25cm) long. Bowl-shaped flowers, 1¼–5in (3–12cm) across, are borne singly or in clusters of up to 5, on slightly downy, often red-tinged stems in early and midseason. Flowers are cream or yellow, flushed pink or grayish green outside, or pink, orange, or red, often with contrasting basal marks. Stamens are yellow with twisted anthers. ↕to 10in (25cm). Kazakhstan, Uzbekistan, Tajikistan, Kyrgyzstan.
***T.* 'Kees Nelis'.** Triumph Group tulip bearing blood-red flowers, with orange-yellow margins, in midseason. ↕10–14in (25–35cm).
***T.* 'Keizerskroon'** ■ syn. *T.* 'Grand Duc'. Single Early Group tulip bearing broadly yellow-margined scarlet flowers in early and midseason. ↕8–10in (20–25cm).
***T.* 'Kingsblood'.** Single Late Group tulip bearing cherry-red flowers, with scarlet margins, late in the season. ↕14–16in (35–40cm).
T. kolpakowskiana. Miscellaneous Group tulip with 2–4 erect, linear, deeply channeled, hairless, wavy-margined, gray-green leaves, to 8in (20cm) long. In early and midseason, bowl-shaped yellow flowers, 1½–3in (3.5–8cm) across, marked crimson, orange, or olive-green outside, with yellow stamens, are produced singly or in clusters of up to 4. ↕6–8in (15–20cm). Uzbekistan, Afghanistan.
***T.* 'Leen van der Mark'** ■ Triumph Group tulip bearing cardinal-red flowers with white edges. Insides are blood-red with broad, white edges, pale yellow-spotted, ivory-white bases, and green-yellow anthers. Midseason-flowering. ↕12–14in (30–35cm).
T. linifolia ■ Miscellaneous Group tulip with 3–9 linear-sickle-shaped, hairless, gray-green leaves, to 3in (8cm) long, with wavy red margins. Bowl-shaped red flowers, to 3in (8cm) across, are produced in early and midseason. The rounded flower bases have blackish purple, often yellow-margined marks; stamens have dark purple or yellow anthers and black or yellow filaments. ↕6–8in (15–20cm). Uzbekistan, N. Iran, Afghanistan.
***T.* 'Lustige Witwe'** ■ syn. *T.* 'Merry Widow'. Triumph Group tulip bearing glowing dark red flowers, margined pure white, in midseason. ↕10–14in (25–35cm).
***T.* 'Magician'** see *T.* 'Magier'.
***T.* 'Magier'**, syn. *T.* 'Magician'. Single Late Group tulip bearing white flowers, with violet-blue margins, late in the season. ↕16–20in (40–50cm).
***T.* 'Maja'.** Fringed Group tulip bearing fringed, pale mimosa-yellow flowers, brilliant greenish yellow inside, with bronze-yellow bases and yellow anthers, late in the season. ↕14–16in (35–40cm).

Tulipa 'Keizerskroon'

***T.* 'Margot Fonteyn'** ■ Triumph Group tulip bearing yellow-margined, cardinal-red flowers with yellow bases. Insides are bright red with lighter margins and black anthers. Midseason-flowering. ↕10–12in (25–30cm).
***T.* 'Mariette'** ■ Lily-flowered Group tulip bearing satin-textured, dark rose-pink flowers, with white bases inside, late in the season. ↕14–16in (35–40cm).
***T.* 'Marilyn'** ■ Lily-flowered Group tulip bearing white flowers with purple flames. Insides are ivory-white with red flames, white bases, and canary-yellow to dark brown anthers. Late-season-flowering. ↕20in (50cm).
T. marjolettii see *T. marjolletii.*
T. marjolletii ■ syn. *T. marjolettii.* Miscellaneous Group tulip with 2–7 lance-shaped to ovate-lance-shaped, hairless, gray-green leaves, to 12in (30cm) long. In early and midseason, hairless stems bear solitary, bowl-shaped, creamy white flowers, to 5in (12cm) across, with rounded bases, margined dark pink and flushed purple on the outside. Stamens have yellow anthers and blue-black filaments. ↕18in (45cm). Probably garden origin; naturalized in S.W. Europe.
***T.* 'Maytime'.** Lily-flowered Group tulip bearing reddish violet flowers, with narrowly white-margined yellow bases, late in the season. ↕12–14in (30–35cm).
***T.* 'Menton'** ■ Single Late Group tulip bearing pinkish red flowers with pale orange stripes at the margins, and green-marked, yellow and white bases. Insides are poppy-red with white veins and yellow anthers. Late-season-flowering. ↕16–20in (40–50cm).
***T.* 'Merry Widow'** see *T.* 'Lustige Witwe'.
***T.* 'Mme. Lefeber'** ■ syn. *T.* 'Red Emperor'. Fosteriana Group tulip bearing fire-red flowers early in the season. ↕8–10in (20–25cm).
***T.* 'Monte Carlo'.** Double Early Group tulip producing sulfur-yellow flowers, with small red feathers, in midseason. ↕8–10in (20–30cm).
***T.* 'Mount Tacoma'.** Double Late Group tulip with pure white flowers late in the season. ↕10–12in (25–30cm).
***T.* 'Negrita'** ■ Triumph Group tulip producing purple flowers with beet-purple veins and bluish gray outer bases. Insides are purple with clear blue basal marks, yellowish white edges, and green-yellow anthers. Midseason-flowering. ↕12–14in (30–35cm).
***T.* 'New Design'.** Triumph Group tulip bearing light yellow flowers, the outsides fading to pinkish white, with pale fuchsia-red margins. Insides have apricot flames, buttercup-yellow bases, and dark brown anthers. Midseason-flowering. Leaves have pinkish white margins. ↕12–14in (30–35cm).
***T.* 'Noranda'.** Fringed Group tulip bearing dark blood-red flowers with fringed, orange-tinted margins, green-yellow bases, and black anthers. Late-season-flowering. ↕14–16in (35–40cm).
***T.* 'Orange Emperor'.** Fosteriana Group tulip bearing carrot-orange flowers with yellow bases and black anthers, in midseason. ↕10–12in (25–30cm).
***T.* 'Orange Favorite'.** Parrot Group tulip producing fragrant, green-marked orange flowers, with yellow bases, late in the season. ↕12–16in (30–40cm).
***T.* 'Orange Monarch'** ■ Triumph Group tulip bearing orange flowers, tinged red-pink, with orange-yellow bases. Insides are apricot-orange with purple anthers. Midseason-flowering. ↕10–12in (25–30cm).
***T.* 'Oranje Nassau'.** Double Early Group tulip bearing blood-red flowers, flushed fire-red, in midseason. ↕8–10in (20–25cm).
***T.* 'Oratorio'.** Greigii Group tulip bearing rose-pink flowers, with black bases, early in the season. Insides are apricot-pink. Leaves are marked dark bluish purple. ↕6–8in (15–20cm).

Tulipa 'Leen van der Mark'

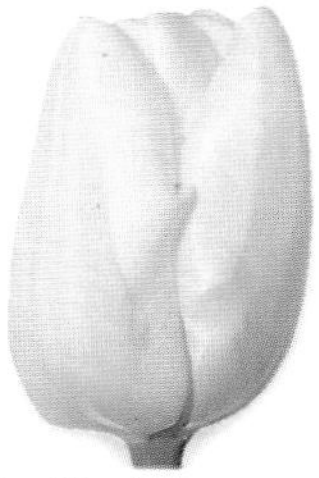
Tulipa 'Pax'

Tulipa 'Peach Blossom'

Tulipa 'Pink Diamond'

Tulipa 'Plaisir'

Tulipa praestans 'Van Tubergen's Variety'

Tulipa 'Prinses Irene'

Tulipa 'Purple Prince'

Tulipa 'Queen of Night'

Tulipa 'Queen of Sheba'

Tulipa 'Red Riding Hood'

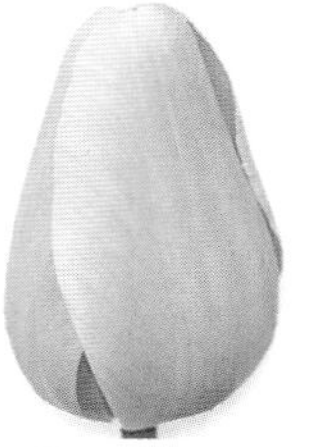
Tulipa 'Rosalie'

Tulipa saxatilis

***T.* 'Oxford'** ■ Darwin Hybrid Group tulip producing scarlet flowers, flushed purple-red, with sulfur-yellow bases. Insides are capsicum-red. Midseason-flowering. ↕ 12–14in (30–35cm).
***T.* 'Page Polka'** ■ Triumph Group tulip producing dark red flowers, striped white outside, with white basal marks and yellow anthers. Midseason-flowering. ↕ 8–10in (20–25cm).
***T.* 'Palestrina'.** Triumph Group tulip bearing salmon-pink flowers, green-tinged outside, late in the season. ↕ 8–10in (20–25cm).
***T.* 'Parade'.** Darwin Hybrid Group tulip bearing bright red flowers with black bases, yellow edges, and black anthers, in midseason. ↕ 16–20in (40–50cm).
***T.* 'Pax'** ■ Triumph Group tulip bearing pure white flowers in early and midseason. ↕ 14–16in (40–45cm).
***T.* 'Peach Blossom'** ■ Double Early Group tulip producing dark rose-pink flowers early in the season. Young flowers often have greenish white bases. ↕ 7–9in (18–23cm).
***T.* 'Peer Gynt'.** Triumph Group tulip bearing purple-margined, bright rose-pink flowers with yellow-spotted white bases. Insides are pink with purple-gray anthers. Midseason-flowering. ↕ 14–16in (35–40cm).
***T.* 'Pink Diamond'** ■ Single Late Group tulip producing pink-purple flowers with paler margins. Insides are bright mid-pink with gray-yellow bases and yellow-green anthers. Late-season-flowering. ↕ 16–22in (40–55cm).

Tulipa 'Negrita'

***T.* 'Pink Impression'.** Darwin Hybrid Group tulip bearing pale rose flowers with darker rose veins, mid-pink flames, light red edges, and green-yellow and bluish black outer basal marks. Insides are bright claret-rose on a pale rose background with black bases, narrow pale yellow edges, and black anthers. Midseason-flowering. ↕ 20–22in (50–55cm).
***T.* 'Plaisir'** ■ Greigii Group tulip bearing carmine-red flowers with sulfur-yellow margins and black and yellow bases. Insides are vermilion with sulfur-yellow margins. Early- and midseason-flowering. Leaves are marked dark bluish maroon. ↕ 6–8in (15–20cm).
T. polychroma see *T. biflora.*
T. praestans. Miscellaneous Group tulip with 3–6 erect, oblong or lance-shaped, keeled, downy, gray-green leaves, to 8in (20cm) long. Early in the season, bowl-shaped, scarlet-orange flowers, 4–5in (10–12cm) across, are produced singly or in clusters of up to 5 on each of the minutely downy stems; stamens have yellow or purplish red anthers, and red filaments shading to yellow at the bases. Easily grown. ↕ 8–12in (20–30cm). Kazakhstan (Pamir Altai), Tajikistan. **'Fusilier'** produces several very bright red flowers. **'Unicum'** ■ has variegated leaves with creamy white margins, and bears up to 5 capsicum-red flowers with small, light yellow bases and blue-black anthers. **'Van Tubergen's Variety'** ■ has up to 3 larger, bright orange-scarlet flowers, flushed yellow at the bases, with reddish brown anthers.

Tulipa praestans 'Unicum'

***T.* 'Prinses Irene'** ■ Triumph Group tulip producing unusual, orange and purple flowers in midseason. ↕ 8–10in (20–25cm).
T. pulchella. Miscellaneous Group tulip with 2–5 linear, hairless, glaucous, gray-green leaves, to 6in (15cm) long. In early and midseason, star-shaped, light crimson or purple flowers, to 3in (8cm) across, with blue-black basal marks, are produced singly or sometimes in twos or threes. Stamens have purple anthers and blue filaments. ↕ 10–12in (25–30cm). Turkey, N. Iran, Turkmenistan, Uzbekistan, Afghanistan. **'Odalisque'** bears pale purple flowers with yellow basal marks. **'Persian Pearl'** produces rose-red flowers with yellow basal marks.
***T.* 'Purissima'** ■ syn. *T.* 'White Emperor'. Fosteriana Group tulip that produces pure white flowers in early and midseason. ↕ 10–12in (25–30cm).
***T.* 'Purple Prince'** ■ Single Early Group tulip producing purple flowers with dull lilac flames, and greenish white outer basal marks. Insides are beet-purple with star-shaped, gold bases, and chrome-yellow anthers. Early-season-flowering. ↕ 10–12in (25–30cm).
***T.* 'Queen of Night'** ■ Single Late Group tulip producing velvety, dark maroon flowers late in the season. ↕ 14–16in (35–40cm).
***T.* 'Queen of Sheba'** ■ Lily-flowered Group tulip that produces glowing brownish red flowers, with orange margins, in midseason. ↕ 14–16in (35–40cm).
***T.* 'Red Emperor'** see *T.* 'Mme. Lefeber'.
***T.* 'Red Parrot'.** Parrot Group tulip producing raspberry-red flowers late in the season. ↕ 14–16in (35–40cm).
***T.* 'Red Riding Hood'** ■ Greigii Group tulip producing carmine-red flowers, scarlet inside, with black bases, in midseason. Leaves are marked dark bluish maroon. ↕ 6–8in (15–20cm).
***T.* 'Renown'.** Single Late Group tulip producing light carmine-red flowers with paler margins and blue-margined yellow bases. Late-season-flowering. ↕ 14–18in (35–45cm).
***T.* 'Rococo'.** Parrot Group tulip bearing carmine-red flowers, margined fire-red, late in the season. ↕ 10–12in (25–30cm).

***T.* 'Rosalie'** ■ Triumph Group tulip bearing phlox-pink flowers on rose grounds. Insides are red-flamed with canary-yellow bases and lemon-yellow anthers. Late-season-flowering. ↕ 16–20in (40–50cm).
***T.* 'Rosario'.** Triumph Group tulip producing dark pink flowers with large white bases. Insides are rose-pink with smaller, ivory-white bases. Midseason-flowering. ↕ 14–16in (35–40cm).
T. saxatilis ■ syn. *T. bakeri.* Miscellaneous Group tulip, spreading by runners, with 2–4 linear, hairless, shiny, mid-green leaves, to 12in (30cm) long. In mid- and late season, star-shaped, fragrant flowers, 2½–3in (6–8cm) across, are borne singly or in clusters of up to 4. Flowers are pink to lilac-purple with white-margined yellow marks. Stamens have yellow, purple, or brown anthers and yellow filaments. Tulips grown as *T. bakeri* are darker pink. ↕ 8–10in (20–25cm). Crete, W. Turkey.
***T.* 'Schoonoord'.** Double Early Group tulip bearing pure white flowers in midseason. ↕ 8–10in (20–25cm).

Tulipa 'Purissima'

T

Tulipa sprengeri

Tulipa 'Spring Green'

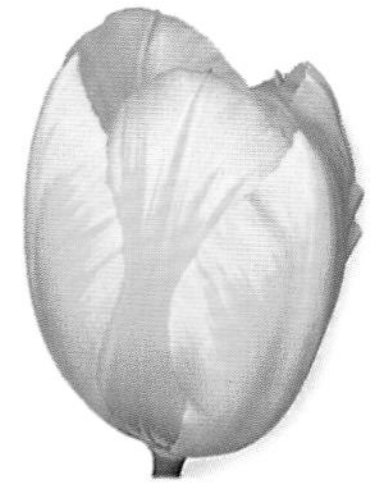
Tulipa 'Sweetheart'

Tulipa sylvestris

Tulipa tarda

Tulipa turkestanica

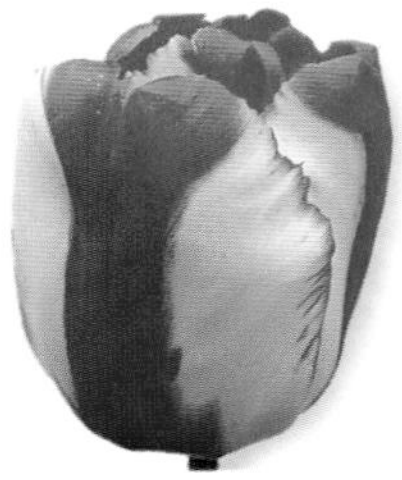
Tulipa 'Union Jack'

Tulipa violacea

Tulipa 'West Point'

Tulipa 'White Parrot'

Tulipa whittallii

Tulipa 'Yokohama'

***T.* 'Shakespeare'.** Kaufmanniana Group tulip bearing carmine-red flowers, with salmon-pink margins and golden yellow bases, in midseason. Insides are scarlet-flushed salmon-pink. ↕ 8–10in (20–25cm).

***T.* 'Shirley'.** Triumph Group tulip bearing ivory-white flowers, with narrow purple margins, white bases spotted pale purple, and brownish violet anthers, in midseason. ↕ 10–14in (25–35cm).

***T.* 'Solva'.** Fosteriana Group tulip bearing pale vermilion flowers, yellow at the bases, in midseason. ↕ 8–10in (20–25cm).

***T.* 'Sorbet'.** Single Late Group tulip bearing pinkish white flowers, creamy white at the bases, late in the season. Insides are white with carmine-red flames and yellow anthers. ↕ 14–16in (35–40cm).

T. sprengeri ■ Miscellaneous Group tulip with 5 or 6 linear, hairless, shiny, erect, mid-green leaves, to 10in (25cm) long. Late in the season, bears solitary, goblet-shaped, red to orange-red flowers, 1¾–2½in (4.5–6cm) long, with yellow-buff bases, yellow anthers, and red filaments, on smooth stems. One of the latest tulips to flower. Will self-seed and naturalize in sun or light woodland. ↕ 12–14in (30–35cm). Turkey (but no longer known in the wild).

***T.* 'Spring Green'** ■ Viridiflora Group tulip bearing green-feathered, ivory-white flowers, with light green anthers, late in the season. ↕ 12–14in (30–35cm).

T. stellata see *T. clusiana* var. *stellata*.

T. stellata* var. *chrysantha see *T. clusiana* var. *chrysantha*.

***T.* 'Sweetheart'** ■ Fosteriana Group tulip bearing ivory-white flowers with lemon-yellow flames, broad, ivory-white margins, and yellow bases. Insides are deep yellow with ivory-white margins and yellow anthers. Midseason-flowering. ↕ 8–10in (20–25cm).

***T.* 'Sweet Lady'.** Greigii Group tulip bearing peach-pink flowers with yellow-tinged, bronze-green bases and yellow anthers. Midseason-flowering. Leaves are marked dark bluish maroon. ↕ 6–8in (15–20cm).

T. sylvestris ■ syn. *T. australis.* Miscellaneous Group tulip with 2–4 linear, channeled, glaucous, light green leaves, to 8in (20cm) long. In midseason, star-shaped, fragrant flowers, 2½–3in (6–8cm) across, pendent in bud then erect, are produced singly or in pairs. Flowers are yellow, occasionally cream, with green-flushed bases outside and yellow anthers. Easily grown. ↕ 14–16in (35–40cm). Origin unknown; naturalized in Europe and from N. Africa to the Middle East and Russia (Siberia).

T. tarda ■ syn. *T. dasystemon.* Miscellaneous Group tulip with 3–7 lance-shaped, recurved, often finely fringed, shiny, bright green leaves, to 5in (12cm) long. Produces 4–6 star-shaped flowers, to 2½in (6cm) across, in midseason. Flowers are white with a green tinge, sometimes red-tinged outside and yellow on the lower half inside. Stamens are yellow. ↕ 4–6in (10–15cm). C. Asia (Tien Shan).

***T.* 'Texas Gold'.** Parrot Group tulip producing red-margined, bright golden yellow flowers. Late-season-flowering. ↕ 10–14in (25–35cm).

***T.* 'Topic'** see *T.* 'Golden Oxford'.

***T.* 'Toronto'.** Greigii Group tulip bearing vermilion-tinged, pinkish red flowers, several to a stem, early in the season; insides are tangerine-red with buttercup-yellow bases, tinged bronze-green, and bronze anthers. Leaves are marked dark bluish maroon. ↕ 8–10in (20–25cm).

T. turkestanica ■ Miscellaneous Group tulip with 2–4 linear, gray-green leaves, to 6in (15cm) long. In early and midseason, up to 12 star-shaped, malodorous white flowers, 1¼–2in (3–5cm) across, flushed greenish gray or greenish pink outside, yellow or orange at the centers, are borne on hairy stems. Stamens have purple, brown, or purple-tipped yellow anthers, and yellow filaments. ↕ 8–10in (20–25cm). Kazakhstan, Tajikistan, N.W. China.

***T.* 'Union Jack'** ■ Single Late Group tulip bearing ivory-white flowers, with raspberry-red flames and blue-margined white bases, late in the season. ↕ 16–22in (40–55cm).

T. urumiensis. Miscellaneous Group tulip with 2–4 linear, sometimes slightly glaucous, mid-green leaves, to 5in (12cm) long. Star-shaped yellow flowers, 2–3in (5–8cm) across, flushed lilac or reddish brown outside, with yellow stamens, are produced singly or in pairs early in the season. ↕ 4–6in (10–15cm). N.W. Iran.

***T.* 'Viking'.** Double Early Group tulip bearing scarlet-flamed, greenish red flowers. Insides are signal-red with slight yellow feathering, canary-yellow bases, and purple anthers. Midseason-flowering. ↕ 8–10in (20–25cm).

T. violacea ■ Miscellaneous Group tulip with 2–5 linear, channeled, hairless, glaucous, gray-green leaves, to 6in (15cm) long. Produces star-shaped violet-purple flowers, 3in (8cm) across, with yellow or blue-black basal marks and purple stamens, singly or sometimes in clusters of 3, in early and midseason. ↕ 8–10in (20–25cm). S. and E. Turkey, N. Iraq, N. and W. Iran, Azerbaijan.

T. vvedenskyi. Miscellaneous Group tulip with 4 or 5 lance-shaped, reflexed, often very finely downy, glaucous, gray-green, crimped leaves, to 12in (30cm) long. Solitary, bowl-shaped flowers, to 8in (20cm) across, with rounded bases, are produced on bristly, sometimes purple-tinged stems in early and midseason. Flowers are red with black or yellow basal marks, violet or yellow anthers, and brown or yellow filaments. ↕ 10–12in (20–25cm). Kazakhstan, C. Asia (Tien Shan). **'Tangerine Beauty'** has bright red flowers, orange inside, with pale yellow basal marks; stamens have purple anthers and yellow filaments.

***T.* 'West Point'** ■ Lily-flowered Group tulip producing primrose-yellow flowers late in the season. ↕ 12–16in (30–40cm).

***T.* 'White Emperor'** see *T.* 'Purissima'.

***T.* 'White Parrot'** ■ Parrot Group tulip producing pure white flowers late in the season. ↕ 14–16in (35–40cm).

T. whittallii ■ Miscellaneous Group tulip with 2–7 lance-shaped, hairless, mid-green leaves, to 8in (20cm) long, often with reddish purple margins. In early and midseason, bears star-shaped flowers, 1¼–2½in (3–6cm) across, singly or in clusters of up to 4 on hairless stems. Flowers are bright bronze-orange, usually green-tinged outside, with black, sometimes yellow-margined basal marks inside. Stamens have dark green or brown anthers, and purple or green filaments. ↕ 8–10in (20–25cm). Bulgaria, Greece, W. Turkey.

***T.* 'Willemsoord'.** Double Early Group tulip bearing carmine-red and white flowers in midseason. ↕ 12in (30cm).

***T.* 'Wirosa'.** Double Late Group tulip producing cream-margined, wine-red flowers in midseason. ↕ 8–10in (20–25cm).

***T.* 'Yellow Purissima'.** Fosteriana Group tulip with canary-yellow flowers, broadly flamed deep yellow. Insides are bright golden yellow with greenish yellow anthers. Midseason-flowering. ↕ 8–10in (20–25cm).

***T.* 'Yokohama'** ■ Single Early Group tulip producing tapered yellow flowers, with yellow anthers, in midseason. ↕ 8–10in (20–25cm).

***T.* 'Zampa'.** Greigii Group tulip producing primrose-yellow flowers, with bronze and green bases, in midseason. Leaves are marked dark bluish maroon. ↕ 8–10in (20–25cm).

▷ ***Tunica saxifraga*** see *Petrorhagia saxifraga*

TURBINICARPUS

CACTACEAE

Genus of 24 or 25 species of diminutive, usually globose, sometimes clustering, cacti. Mostly solitary, they prefer limestone or gypsum soils, rock rubble on slightly hilly terrain, or desert conditions. Ribs are either absent or divided into distinct tubercles. Diurnal flowers in white, rose, or magenta, arise from the stem tips; the pericarpels may be naked or may have a few scales. The berry-like fruit is dehiscent. N. Mexico south into Guanajuato,

• **CULTIVATION** Under glass, grow in a mix of 4 parts standard cactus potting mix and 1 part limestone chips, in full light. From spring to summer, water freely and apply a balanced liquid fertilizer every 4–5 weeks. Keep nearly dry at other times. Outdoors, grow in moderately fertile, slightly alkaline, sharply drained, humus-rich soil in full sun. See also pp.48–49.

• **PROPAGATION** Sow seed at 70°F (21°C) in spring or summer.

• **PESTS AND DISEASES** Scale occurs.

T. laui. Solitary, flattened globose, yellowish green succulent with broad, conical tubercles, ⅛–⅕in (3–5mm) high. All 6–8 spines are radial, brownish white, radiating, mostly straight, ½–¾in (12–22mm) long. Flowers are white; midribs are with brownish midribs, ⅔–1in (1.8–2.5cm) long. Greenish brown slightly elongate fruit is ⅕–¼in (5–7mm) long. ↕ ⅕–½in (0.5–1.5cm), ↔ ½–1⅜in (1.2–3.5cm).

South of Villa Juarez, San Luis Potosi, Mexico. ❀ (min. 50°F/10°C)

T. pseudomacrochele. Slow-growing, small, cylindrical succulent, usually solitary, sometimes clustering, and quite spiny. Stems are pale green to blue green, tuberculate with wooly tips, ↕ ¾–1½in (2–4 cm) tall, ↔ 1–1⅜in (2.5–3.5cm). Central and radial spines are indistinguishable, 5–8 yellowish brown when young, gray at maturity; to about 1in (2.5cm) long. In late winter to early spring, areoles bear flowers ranging from magenta to reddish purple to yellow-green to white, ↕↔ 1–1⅜in (2.5–3.5cm). Hidalgo, Querétaro, Mexico. ❀ (min. 50°F/10°C)

T. schmiedickeanus. Solitary, globose to flattened globose, dull to blue-green to gray-green succulent. Tubercles are either conical, elongate conical, or broad and rounded, spines, usually 0–10; these can be thickened and spongy, flattened and paper-like, or flexible and slightly curved or twisted. Bears white, cream, greenish yellow, or magenta flowers, ½–1in (1.5–2.5cm) long, and rounded fruit that is somewhat fleshy at maturity. ↕ ⅜–1¼in (1–3cm), ↔ ½–2in (1.5–5cm). Nuevo Leon, Tamaulipas, San Luis Potosi, Mexico. ❀ (min. 50°F/10°C)

TWEEDIA *syn.* OXYPETALUM

ASCLEPIADACEAE

Genus of one species of evergreen, twining, scrambling subshrub from scrub and rocky areas in S. Brazil and Uruguay. It has simple, opposite leaves and bears stalked, axillary and terminal cymes of short, tubular, 5-petaled, salverform flowers. Where not hardy, grow as bedding or container annuals, or in a cool greenhouse. In warmer areas, grow in a border or with other small shrubs.

• **CULTIVATION** Under glass, grow in soil-based potting mix in full light. In the growing season, water freely and apply a balanced liquid fertilizer monthly; water sparingly in winter. Outdoors, grow in moist but well-drained, fertile soil in full sun. Support the climbing stems. Pruning group 13, in early spring.

• **PROPAGATION** Sow seed at 15°C (59°F) in spring. Insert softwood cuttings with bottom heat in summer.

• **PESTS AND DISEASES** Infrequent.

T. caerulea ▣ syn. *Amblyopetalum caeruleum, Oxypetalum caeruleum.* Erect, evergreen subshrub with twining, white-hairy stems and oblong-lance-shaped, downy, light green leaves, 2–4in (5–10cm) long, usually heart-shaped at the bases. From summer to early autumn, oblong-petaled, sky-blue flowers, ¾–1in (2–2.5cm) across, pink-flushed in bud and aging to purple, are borne in small, 3- or 4-flowered cymes. ↕ 24–39in (60–100cm). S. Brazil to Uruguay. ❀ (min. 39–41°F/3–5°C)

TYLECODON

CRASSULACEAE

Genus of 20–30 species of bushy, succulent, deciduous shrubs, similar to *Cotyledon* and at one time included in that genus. They are found in deserts and partially shaded areas of Namibia and South Africa. The linear to ovate, spoon-shaped, or almost cylindrical leaves are alternate or borne in crowded spirals. Mainly bell-shaped, upright to pendent flowers have calyces with club-shaped hairs, and are borne in complex, many-branched, panicle-like cymes. In warm, dry, winter-rainfall areas, they are summer-dormant, suitable for a border with other succulents. In areas where temperatures fall below 45°F (7°C), grow in a temperate greenhouse. The leaves of several species are highly toxic if ingested.

• **CULTIVATION** Under glass, grow in standard cactus potting mix in full light, with low humidity. In the growing season, water moderately and apply a half-strength, low-nitrogen liquid fertilizer every 4–6 weeks; keep dry when leafless, and water moderately as growth resumes. Pot on as or just before new growth begins. Outdoors, grow in sharply drained, humus-rich, sandy or gritty soil in full sun. Pruning group 1. See also pp.48–49.

• **PROPAGATION** Sow seed at 66–75°F (19–24°C), or insert cuttings of stem sections, in late spring or summer.

• **PESTS AND DISEASES** Prey to mealybugs.

T. paniculatus, syn. *Cotyledon paniculata* (Botterbom, Butter tree). Succulent shrub bears soft, swollen, fleshy stems and short, thick, fleshy, warty branches, all covered with papery yellow bark. Obovate-spoon-shaped, fleshy, bright green leaves, to 4½in (11cm) long, are initially hairy with smooth margins, becoming completely hairless before falling. In spring, nodding, yellow-striped, dark reddish brown flowers, ½in (1.5cm) long, are borne in panicle-like cymes, 24in (60cm) long. ↕ to 6ft (2m), ↔ 3ft (1m). Namibia, South Africa (Northern Cape, Western Cape, Eastern Cape). ❀ (min. 45°F/7°C)

T. reticulatus ▣ syn. *Cotyledon reticulata* (Barbed-wire plant). Stumpy, succulent shrub with short, thick, fleshy stems, covered with peeling gray-brown bark, and soft, spongy branches covered in leaf scars. Linear to almost cylindrical, downy, soft, brown-tipped, yellowish green leaves, ½–2in (1.5–5cm) long, are compressed or grooved above. In winter, bears erect, yellowish green flowers, ½in (1.5cm) long, in panicle-like cymes, to 12in (30cm) long. Dead inflorescences persist, forming a tangle of weak, silvery thorns that envelops the plant. ↕↔ 12in (30cm). Namibia, South Africa (Western Cape, Karoo). ❀ (min. 45°F/7°C)

T. wallichii see *T. papillaris* subsp. *wallichii*

TYPHA

Cattail

TYPHACEAE

Genus of 10–15 species of monoecious, marginal aquatic herbaceous perennials from temperate and tropical regions worldwide. They form dense, robust stands of vegetation around lakes and large ponds. Thick rhizomes spread in shallow water, producing long, linear, mostly basal leaves and poker-like brown flower spikes, borne among the foliage but overtopped by the leaf tips. Clusters of male and female flowers are produced on the same spike. Cattails are usually suitable for planting only around a large wildlife pool, where deep water prevents their spread; *T. minima* is the only species suitable for a small pool or barrel. They are invasive in earth-bottom ponds. The flower spikes are used in dried flower arrangements.

• **CULTIVATION** Grow in water to 12–16in (30–40cm) deep, with ample space and depth of mud for the root system. Thin pond liners may be punctured by the rhizome tips of the larger species.

• **PROPAGATION** Divide in spring.

• **PESTS AND DISEASES** Spots on culms and leaves can occur.

Typha latifolia 'Variegata'

T. laxmannii (Graceful Cattail). Aquatic herbaceous perennial with green linear leaves. Bears yellow (male) and green (female) flowers July–November. Catkins grow to 3in ((8cm). May be invasive, but is attractive to insects and birds. Suitable for bogs and water gardens; ↕ 3–5ft (1–1.5m), ↔ 18–36in (45–90cm). Eurasia. Zone 5.

T. latifolia ▣ (Cattail). Aquatic perennial with strap-shaped leaves, to 6ft (2m) or more long, with open-sheathed bases. Dark brown flower spikes, 6–9in (15–23cm) long, are borne in summer; male and female flowers are close together, the females becoming white-mottled with age. ↕ 6ft (2m) or more, ↔ indefinite. Europe, Asia, N. Africa, North America. Zone 3. **'Variegata'** ▣ is much less vigorous, and has leaves with longitudinal cream stripes; ↕ 3–4ft (0.9–1.2m).

T. minima ▣ (Dwarf cattail, Least cattail). Slender, aquatic perennial with narrowly linear leaves, 8–30in (20–75cm) long. Dark brown flowers are borne in cylindrical spikes, ½–2in (1.5–5cm) long, the female flowers borne above the males, in mid- and late summer. ↕ to 30in (75cm), ↔ 12–18in (30–45cm). Eurasia. Zone 4.

Tweedia caerulea

Tylecodon reticulatus

Typha latifolia

Typha minima

U

UEBELMANNIA

CACTACEAE

Genus of 3–5 species of solitary cacti found in humid, moist areas in the mountains of E. Brazil. The mostly spherical to cylindrical stems have smooth or finely warty, sometimes scaly ribs, and spiny areoles. Diurnal, solitary, funnel-shaped yellow flowers are produced near the crown in summer. In areas where temperatures drop below 59°F (15°C), grow in a warm greenhouse; in warmer climates, they are useful in a border.

• **CULTIVATION** Under glass, grow in acidic standard cactus potting mix in full light. From midspring to early autumn, water moderately and apply a low-nitrogen liquid fertilizer every 6–8 weeks. Mist daily in summer. In winter, keep completely dry, but mist frequently on warm days. Outdoors, grow in gritty, moderately fertile, sharply drained, acidic soil in full sun. See also pp.48–49.

• **PROPAGATION** Sow seed at 75°F (24°C) in spring. Often difficult to grow unless grafted.

• **PESTS AND DISEASES** Infrequent.

U. buiningii. Cactus with spherical, sometimes slightly elongated, greenish red-brown to deep chocolate bodies, each with about 18 ribs, totally covered with minute, waxy scales. Close-set areoles each bear 6–8 semi-erect (some slightly curved), black-tipped, yellow-brown spines. Funnel-shaped, bright yellow flowers, ¾in (2cm) across, are produced in summer. ↕ 4–5in (10–13cm), ↔ 3in (8cm). E. Brazil. ❄ (min. 59°F/15°C)

U. pectinifera ■ Cactus with spherical to cylindrical, reddish green to reddish brown bodies, later elongating, each with 15–20 prominently margined, smooth ribs and minute, off-white scales (sometimes absent in cultivation). Close-set areoles each bear 3–6 comb-like, light gray to nearly black spines. Funnel-shaped yellow flowers, to ½in (1.5cm) across, are borne in summer. ↕ 20–32in (50–80cm), ↔ 6in (15cm). E. Brazil. ❄ (min. 59°F/15°C)

Uebelmannia pectinifera

UGNI

MYRTACEAE

Genus of 5–15 species of densely leafy, evergreen shrubs or trees found in forest and scrub in South America. They have opposite, small, elliptic to ovate, simple, leathery leaves, and produce solitary, cup- or bowl-shaped flowers from the leaf axils of young shoots, followed by edible, spherical berries. *U. molinae*, the only species usually cultivated, is valued for its foliage, flowers, and fruit. Grow in a border or as a hedge. Where not hardy, grow in a cool greenhouse.

• **CULTIVATION** Grow in any moist but well-drained soil in full sun or partial shade. Pruning group 1.

• **PROPAGATION** Root semi-ripe cuttings in late summer, with bottom heat.

• **PESTS AND DISEASES** Infrequent.

U. molinae, syn. *Eugenia ugni, Myrtus ugni* (Chilean guava). Upright shrub or tree with elliptic to ovate, glossy, dark green leaves, to 1½in (4cm) long. Axillary, nodding, bowl-shaped, fragrant, pink-tinged white flowers, ½in (1.5cm) across, are borne singly in late spring, followed by spherical, aromatic, dark red berries, ½in (1.5cm) across, in autumn. ↕ 5ft (1.5m), ↔ 3ft (1m). Chile, W. Argentina. ❄ (min. 41°F/5°C)

ULEX

Furze, Gorse

FABACEAE

Genus of about 20 species of spiny, evergreen shrubs from heaths and hill-sides, woodland margins, and rocky sites in W. and C. Europe and N. Africa. As young seedlings, they have alternate leaves, which are quickly replaced by long-lasting green spines. They are grown for their axillary, pea-like yellow flowers, borne singly, in clusters, or in racemes, virtually all year round in mild climates. Suitable for a shrub border and as a low hedge. The seeds may cause mild stomach upset if ingested.

• **CULTIVATION** Grow in poor, sandy, acidic to neutral, well-drained soil in full sun. May become very leggy on rich soil. Pruning group 10, after flowering, every 2 or 3 years.

• **PROPAGATION** Sow seed in containers in a cold frame in autumn or spring. Take semi-ripe cuttings in summer.

• **PESTS AND DISEASES** Infrequent.

U. europaeus ■ (Furze, Gorse, Whin). Upright to rounded, densely bushy shrub with spine-tipped green shoots and rigid leaves reduced to deeply grooved spines, to 1in (2.5cm) long. Solitary, axillary, pea-like, coconut-scented, bright yellow flowers, ¾in (2cm) long, are produced intermittently throughout the year but mainly over a long period in spring. Dark brown seed pods, to ¾in (2cm) long, are borne in summer. ↕ to 8ft (2.5m), ↔ 6ft (2m). W. and C. Europe. Zone 7. **'Flore Pleno'** has double flowers and no fruit. **'Strictus'** (Irish gorse) is less spiny, with upright shoots.

Ulex europaeus

U. gallii (Dwarf gorse). Spreading shrub with spine-tipped green shoots and rigid leaves reduced to slightly grooved spines, to 1in (2.5cm) long. From late summer to autumn, bears solitary, axillary, pea-like, bright yellow flowers, ½in (1.5cm) long; dark brown seed pods, to ½in (1.5cm) long, are produced in spring. ↕ 5–6ft (1.5–2m), ↔ 5ft (1.5m). W. Europe. ❄ (min. 35°F/2°C)

ULMUS

Elm

ULMACEAE

Genus of about 45 species of deciduous, rarely semi-evergreen trees and, very rarely, shrubs, occurring in woodland, thickets, and hedgerows in N. temperate regions. They have alternate, ovate to elliptic, obovate, or rounded, toothed leaves, usually with unequally sized bases, and often attractively colored in autumn. Clusters of tiny, bell-shaped flowers, each with 4–9 segments joined at the bases, are usually produced from axillary buds in spring, but sometimes from leafy buds in autumn; the flowers are very quickly followed by fruits, each consisting of a seed surrounded by a green to brown, rounded to elliptic, membranous wing. Cultivated for their habit and foliage, elms are mainly grown as specimen trees. *U.* x *hollandica* 'Jacqueline Hillier' is suitable for a shrub border and for hedging.

• **CULTIVATION** Grow in any well-drained soil in full sun or partial shade. Pruning group 1.

• **PROPAGATION** Sow seed in containers outdoors in autumn or spring. Take greenwood cuttings in summer, or remove rooted suckers in autumn. Bud weeping trees in summer, or graft in winter.

• **PESTS AND DISEASES** Dutch elm disease, spread by bark beetles and natural root grafts, has destroyed hundreds of thousands of American elms. *U.* x *hollandica* 'Jacqueline Hillier', *U. parvifolia* and its cultivars, *U. pumila*, and *U.* 'Sapporo Autumn Gold' are partially resistant. A number of Asiatic species are, at present, the most disease-resistant, although breeding and selection programs are producing progressively more resistant American elms. Borers, beetles, caterpillars, mealybugs, scale insects, leaf hoppers, mushroom root rot, dieback and canker, *Verticillium* wilt, wood rot, and elm yellows also affect elms.

Ulmus americana

U. americana ■ (American elm). Graceful, usually vase-shaped, deciduous tree with pendent branch tips and ovate to elliptic, toothed, dark green leaves, to 6in (15cm) long, turning bright yellow in autumn. Tiny red flowers are borne in early spring, followed in mid- and late spring by winged green fruit, ½in (1.5cm) across. ↕↔ 100ft (30m). E. North America (E. of the Rocky Mountains). Zone 2. **'Homestead'** is upright, arching, and narrowly oval; resistant to phloem necrosis and Dutch elm disease. **'Liberty'** shows resistance to Dutch elm disease. **'Pioneer'** is rounded; resistant to phloem necrosis and Dutch elm disease.

U. angustifolia see *U. minor* subsp. *angustifolia*.

***U.* 'Camperdownii'** see *U. glabra* 'Camperdownii'.

U. carpinifolia see *U. minor*.

U. carpinifolia* var. *sarniensis see *U. minor* 'Sarniensis'.

***U.* 'Commelin'** see *U.* x *hollandica* 'Commelin'.

***U.* x *elegantissima* 'Jacqueline Hillier'** see *U.* x *hollandica* 'Jacqueline Hillier'.

U. glabra (Dutch elm, Wych elm). Rounded, deciduous tree with broadly obovate, double-toothed, dark green leaves, to 6in (15cm) long, lobed at the tips, and rough above, downy beneath, turning yellow in autumn. Tiny red flowers are produced in early spring, followed by clustered, winged green fruit, 1in (2.5cm) across, in late spring. ↕ 120–130ft (35–40m), ↔ 80ft (25m). Europe, S.W. Asia. Zone 4b. **'Camperdownii'** ■ syn. *U.* 'Camperdownii' (Camperdown elm), is weeping, with twisted branches and toothed to double-toothed, dark matte green leaves, to 8in (20cm) long; ↕↔ 25ft (8m). **'Exoniensis'** ■ (Exeter elm) is narrowly columnar when young, broadening with age, and has upright branches bearing clustered, twisted, and folded leaves; ↕ 50ft (15m), ↔ 25ft (8m)

U.* x *hollandica (probably *U. glabra* x *U. minor*) (Holland elm). Broadly columnar, deciduous tree with a short trunk and wide-spreading to often arching or pendent branches. Broadly elliptic, pointed, double-toothed, dark green leaves, 3–5in (7–13cm) long, initially rough above, becoming glossy, turn yellow in autumn. Tiny red flowers are produced in early spring, followed by winged green fruit, ¾in (2cm) across in late spring. ↕ 120ft (35m), ↔ 80ft (25m). Europe. Zone 5.

Ulmus glabra 'Camperdownii'

'Commelin', syn. *U.* 'Commelin', is narrower in habit, with more upright branches and oval, toothed, bright green leaves, to 4in (10cm) long, smooth above, downy beneath, turning yellow in autumn. Flowers are produced in late spring, followed by fruit ½in (1.5cm) across, in late summer. ↕ 80ft (25m), ↔ 50ft (15m). **'Groenveldt'** has a uniform, boxy crown and is resistant to Dutch elm disease; ↕ 65ft (20m). **'Jacqueline Hillier'**, syn. *U.* x *elegantissima* 'Jacqueline Hillier', is a slow-growing, rounded, bushy shrub with elliptic-lance-shaped, double-toothed leaves, to 1½in (4cm) long, rough above, densely arranged in 2 rows along the shoots, and lasting until early winter; flowers are not usually produced. ↕↔ 8ft (2.5m).

Ulmus glabra 'Exoniensis'

'Vegeta', syn. *U.* 'Vegeta', is fast-growing and broadly upright, with erect branches, pendent outer shoots, and elliptic to obovate, toothed, slightly rough leaves that turn yellow in autumn; ↕ 120ft (35m).
U. minor, syn. *U. carpinifolia* (European field elm, Smooth-leaf elm). Broadly columnar, deciduous tree with arching branches and pendent shoots. Bears ovate, glossy, mid-green leaves, to 4in (10cm) long, smooth above, downy along the veins beneath and in the vein axils, and with double-toothed margins; they turn yellow in autumn. Very small red flowers are produced in early and midspring, followed by winged green fruit, ½in (1.5cm) across, in late spring. ↕ 100ft (30m), ↔ 70ft (20m). Europe, N. Africa, S.W. Asia. Zone 5.

Ulmus parvifolia

subsp. *angustifolia*, syn. *U. angustifolia*, has a rounded canopy and elliptic or obovate to inversely lance-shaped, double-toothed, glossy, mid- to deep green leaves, 2–5in (5–13cm) long, paler beneath. Flowers are borne in early spring, followed by fruit to ½in (1.5cm) across, in summer; S. Europe, N. Africa, S.W. Asia. **'Sarniensis'**, syn. *U. carpinifolia* var. *sarniensis* (Jersey elm), is compact and conical, with upright branches and broadly elliptic to obovate, toothed, smooth, glossy, mid-green leaves, to 3in (8cm) long; bears flowers in early spring; ↔ 30ft (10m).
U. parvifolia ■ (Chinese elm, Lacebark elm). Spreading, deciduous or semi-evergreen tree with a rounded crown, pendent shoots, and flaking bark marked orange and brown. Elliptic, toothed, leathery, glossy, dark green leaves, to 2½in (6cm) long, with bases of almost equal size with matted hair beneath, may turn yellow or red in late autumn or early winter. Tiny red flowers are produced from late summer to autumn; they are followed by winged green fruit, ⅜in (9mm) across, in late autumn. Tough; tolerant of urban soils. ↕ 60ft (18m), ↔ 25–40ft (8–12m). China, Korea, Japan. Zone 5. **'Emerald Isle'** is rounded; highly resistant to Dutch elm disease; ↕ 30ft (10m), ↔ 55ft (17m). **'Emerald Vase'** is upright to spreading in habit, and highly resistant to Dutch elm disease; ↕ 70ft (20m), ↔ 60ft (18m). **'Frosty'** is slow-growing and shrubby, with small, white-margined leaves, less than 1in (2.5cm) long; ↕↔ 8ft (2.5m). **'Hokkaido'**, syn. var. *pygmaea*, is slow-growing, with small leaves, to 1½in (4cm) long, and corky bark. **'Sempervirens'** is a name of questionable standing for evergreen to semi-evergreen forms; habit is round-headed, with widely arching branches, weeping slightly at the ends; ↕↔ 40–50ft (12–15m); Zone 7b.
U. procera (English elm). Broadly upright, deciduous tree with a dense crown, broadest at the top. Broadly ovate to obovate, dark green leaves, to 4in (10cm) long, are rough above, paler and thinly hairy beneath, with coarsely double-toothed margins; they turn yellow in late autumn. Tiny red flowers are produced in early spring, followed by winged green fruit, to ½in (1.5cm) across, in late spring. ↕ 130ft (40m), ↔ 50ft (15m). UK. Zone 6.
U. pumila (Siberian elm). Broadly upright, deciduous tree with narrowly elliptic to lance-shaped or ovate, tapered, toothed, dark green leaves, 1¼–4in (3–10cm) long, smooth above, hairy beneath, especially when young. Tiny red flowers are produced in early spring, followed by winged green fruit, ½in (1.5cm) across, in late spring. Fast-growing but weak-wooded. ↕ 70–100ft (20–30m), ↔ 40ft (12m). Russia (E. Siberia), S. Kazakhstan, N. China. Zone 3b.
***U.* 'Sapporo Autumn Gold'.** Fast-growing, broadly conical, deciduous tree with upright branches. Oval, toothed, smooth, glossy, dark green leaves, to 3in (8cm) long, red-tinged when young, turn yellow-green in autumn. Flowers are not usually produced. ↕ 60ft (18m), ↔ 40ft (12m). Zone 5.
***U.* 'Vegeta'** see *U.* x *hollandica* 'Vegeta'.

Umbellularia californica

UMBELLULARIA

LAURACEAE

Genus of one species of evergreen tree, with alternate, entire leaves, from coniferous forest in W. US. It is grown for its aromatic foliage, densely covering the stems to the ground when grown as a multi-stemmed shrub. The scent of the crushed leaves may induce headaches and nausea in some people. Grow as a specimen tree or as a hedge or screen.
• **CULTIVATION** Grow in any well-drained, acidic soil in full sun. Where not hardy, shelter from cold, drying winds. Pruning group 1.
• **PROPAGATION** Sow seed in containers in a cold frame in autumn. Insert semi-ripe cuttings in summer.
• **PESTS AND DISEASES** Anthracnose, dieback and canker, bacterial leaf spot, and wood rot can be problems. Aphids, whiteflies, and scale insects also occur.

U. californica ■ (California laurel, Headache tree). Rounded, evergreen tree with elliptic to oblong, leathery, very aromatic, bright green leaves, to 4in (10cm) long. Umbels of up to 10 small, salverform, yellow-green flowers, ½in (1.5cm) across, are borne from the leaf axils in late winter and spring, followed by ovoid purple berries, 1in (2.5cm) long. ↕ 60ft (18m), ↔ 40ft (12m). S. Oregon, N. California. Zone 7b.

UNCINIA

Hook sedge

CYPERACEAE

Genus of about 35–45 species of tufted, evergreen, monoecious perennials, some rhizomatous, occurring in damp, tussocky grassland, moist woodland, or swamps throughout S. temperate zones, except southern Africa. They have smooth, 3-angled to cylindrical stems and flat or shallowly channeled, grass-like leaves. The flowering stems bear spikes, with the male flowers at the top of the spike and the females beneath. The female flowers give rise to hooked, nut-like fruits. Several species are grown for their colorful leaves; they are suitable for the front of a border, or for gravel plantings. Where not hardy, grow frost-tender species in a cool greenhouse.
• **PROPAGATION** Sow seed at 55°F (13°C) in spring. Divide between late spring and midsummer.
• **PESTS AND DISEASES** Infrequent.

Uncinia rubra

U. rubra ■ Evergreen perennial, loosely tufted or with short rhizomes. Rigid, upright, 3-angled stems bear flat or inrolled, sharply pointed, shiny leaves, to 14in (35cm) long; both stems and leaves are greenish red to rich reddish brown. Dark brown to black flowers are produced in narrow spikes, to 2½in (6cm) long, in mid- and late summer. ↕ 12in (30cm), ↔ 14in (35cm). New Zealand. ❀ (min. 35°F/2°C)
U. uncinata. Densely tufted, evergreen perennial, with rigid, upright stems and flat, rough-margined, pale brown to red-brown leaves, 2–4in (5–10cm) long. Bears dark brown flowers in narrow spikes, 6in (15cm) long, in mid- and late summer. ↕ 10in (25cm), ↔ 12in (30cm). New Zealand. ❀ (min. 35°F/2°C)

▷ ***Uniola*** see *Chasmanthium*
▷ ***Urceolina*** see *Stenomesson*

URGINEA

LILIACEAE

Genus of about 100 species of bulbous perennials found on dry, rocky hillsides, on sandy soils near coasts, or on plains or savanna, mostly in tropical Africa, with a few in the Mediterranean. They have narrowly linear, basal leaves, and are grown for their star- or saucer-shaped flowers, produced in long, erect, dense racemes on leafless stems in summer and autumn. Grow in a sunny border. Where not hardy, grow in a cool greenhouse.
• **CULTIVATION** Under glass, grow in soil-based potting mix, with added sharp sand, in full light. Water freely in the growing season. Keep just moist when dormant. Outdoors, grow in sandy or stony, poor to moderately fertile, sharply drained soil in full sun. Protect from winter moisture.
• **PROPAGATION** Sow seed at 55–64°F (13–18°C) when ripe. Remove offsets in summer.
• **PESTS AND DISEASES** Infrequent.

U. maritima (Red squill, Sea onion). Bulbous perennial producing dense racemes, 12in (30cm) or more long, of many tiny, star-shaped white flowers, ¼in (6mm) across, with green or purple midveins, in late summer and early autumn. Erect, narrow, basal leaves, 12–39in (30–100cm) long, appear in autumn, after the flowers. ↕ 5ft (1.5m), PD12in (30cm). Mediterranean. ❀ (min. 45°F/7°C)

URSINIA

ASTERACEAE

Genus of about 40 species of annuals and evergreen perennials and subshrubs from dry savanna in South Africa, Namibia, Botswana, and Ethiopia. They are cultivated mainly for their flowers; a few species are grown for their foliage. The alternate leaves may occasionally be simple, but are usually pinnatifid, pinnatisect, or pinnate, often hairy or downy, and frequently aromatic. Daisy-like, yellow, orange, or red flowerheads, usually solitary, sometimes in corymbs, are borne on long stalks well above the foliage. Grow annual species at the front of a border or at the base of a house wall. Where winter temperatures fall below 32°F (0°C), grow perennials and subshrubs in a cool greenhouse or treat as annuals. Alternatively, lift before the first frosts and overwinter in frost-free conditions. In milder areas, grow in a border or small courtyard garden.
• **CULTIVATION** Under glass, grow in soil-based potting mix in full light. In growth, water freely and apply a balanced liquid fertilizer every 4 weeks. Water sparingly in winter. Outdoors, grow in sandy, fertile, well-drained soil in full sun.
• **PROPAGATION** Sow seed at 55–64°F (13–18°C) in spring. Take softwood cuttings in summer.
• **PESTS AND DISEASES** Infrequent.

U. anthemoides ■ Erect, bushy annual with pinnatisect, slightly hairy, scented, light green leaves, ¾–1½in (2–6cm) long, with slender, flat or thread-like lobes. In summer, bears solitary, purple-centered, yellow-orange flowerheads, to 2½in (6cm) across, each ray floret zoned in maroon-red or copper-purple on the underside. ↕ to 16in (40cm), ↔ to 12in (30cm). South Africa (Northern Cape, Western Cape, Eastern Cape).
U. chrysanthemoides. Erect, spreading, woody-based, evergreen, short-lived perennial, sometimes grown as an annual, with rooting stems. Bears softly hairy or hairless, scented, silvery gray-green leaves, 2in (5cm) long, which may be pinnate, 2-pinnate, or occasionally entire, all on the same plant. Produces solitary flowerheads, 1¼–2½in (3–6cm) across, with yellow or occasionally red or white ray florets, sometimes copper-tinted beneath, mainly in summer. ↕ 12–18in (30–45cm), ↔ 24–30in (60–75cm). South Africa (Northern Cape, Western Cape, Eastern Cape). ❀ (min. 41–45°F/5–7°C). **var. *geyeri*,** syn. 'Geyeri', *U. geyeri*, has dull green leaves, very white-woolly at first. Rich crimson-red flowerheads, 1–2½in (2.5–6cm) across, with red-black disk florets, are produced in summer; ↕ to 36in (90cm), ↔ to 12in (30cm).
U. geyeri see *U. chrysanthemoides* var. *geyeri.*
U. sericea. Bushy, evergreen subshrub with pinnate or pinnatisect, silver-silky-hairy leaves, to 3in (8cm) long. In summer, bears solitary yellow flowerheads, to 1¼in (3cm) across, on very long stalks. ↕↔ to 30in (70cm). South Africa (Northern Cape, Western Cape, Eastern Cape). ❀ (min. 41–45°F/5–7°C)

Ursinia anthemoides

URTICA

Nettle

URTICACEAE

Genus of about 50 species of annual and perennial herbs native to Europe and Asia; widespread in temperate regions. Familiar weed that thrives in deep, rich soils along streams, mountain slopes, and woodland clearings. Leaves, stems, and flowers are sparsely to moderately covered with long, stinging hairs. Raw leaves contain high levels of irritants. Some species contain substances toxic enough to cause death.
• **CULTIVATION** Grow in moist, nitrogen-rich soil in sun or in partial shade.
• **PROPAGATION** Sow seeds outdoors, in full sun or partial shade, in the fall.
• **PESTS AND DISEASES** Infrequent.

U. dioica (Stinging nettle). Coarse, erect, perennial with creeping yellow roots and ovate, toothed leaves covered with long, bristly, stinging hairs. Mature leaves have long, stinging hairs; younger leaves usually have both long and short hairs. In summer produces small green to yellowish flowers in pendulous clusters, to 4in (10cm) long. ↕ 6ft (2m). Europe and Asia. Zone 3.

UTRICULARIA

Bladderwort

LENTIBULARIACEAE

Genus of approximately 180 species of terrestrial, epiphytic, or free-floating aquatic annuals and perennials found worldwide in stagnant, shallow water, or growing on rainforest trees. They are insectivorous, and thrive in water that attracts mosquito larvae. Generally rootless, they have mainly submerged stems, either loosely anchored or free-floating, and thread-like or linear to rounded leaves with traps (bladders) adapted to catch and absorb insects and other water animals. The flowers, solitary or in racemes, are usually borne on leafless stems above the water, and are supported by a whorl of spongy, floating leaves. Grow in an outdoor pool. Where not hardy, grow in a warm aquarium. The hardy species may also be grown in a cold-water aquarium.
• **CULTIVATION** Outdoors, grow in acidic water that warms up quickly in spring, in full sun. In an aquarium, grow in full light; frost-tender species need a water temperature of 66°F (19°C), hardy species 54–59°F (12–15°C). The potting mix should be very loose, consisting of 2 parts orchid bark, 2 parts peat moss, 1 part perlite, and a little sand. See also pp.52–53.
• **PROPAGATION** Collect buds that sink to the bottom of the pool or aquarium after flowering and replant. Divide mats of floating foliage in summer.
• **PESTS AND DISEASES** Infrequent.

U. exoleta see *U. gibba.*
U. gibba, syn. *U. exoleta.* Floating aquatic annual or perennial with mat-forming stolons. Slender stems produce feathery, bladder-bearing leaves, to 3in (8cm) long. In midsummer, pouched, red-veined yellow flowers, to ¼in (6mm) long, are borne above the water, either singly or in a 2- to 5-flowered raceme, 8in (20cm) long. ↔ 8in (20cm). Spain, Portugal, Israel, southern Africa, China, Japan, Australia, New Zealand, North America, Argentina. ❀ (min. 45°F/7°C)

UVULARIA

Merrybells

LILIACEAE

Genus of 5 species of rhizomatous perennials from woodland in E. North America. They have erect, simple or branched stems, the upper parts bearing alternate, stalkless or perfoliate, ovate to lance-shaped, hairless or downy leaves. Pendent, tubular-bell-shaped, 6-tepaled yellow flowers are produced on long, slender stalks, and are usually solitary and terminal. Excellent for a shady border or woodland garden.
• **CULTIVATION** Grow in fertile, humus-rich, moist but well-drained soil in deep or partial shade.
• **PROPAGATION** Sow seed in containers in a cold frame as soon as ripe. Divide in early spring.
• **PESTS AND DISEASES** Rust, *Phyllosticta* leaf spot, slugs, and snails occur.

U. grandiflora ■ (Large merrybells). Slowly spreading, rhizomatous perennial with sometimes 2-branched stems bearing ovate-lance-shaped, downward-pointing, perfoliate, mid-green leaves, to 5in (13cm) long, softly hairy beneath. Solitary or paired, pendent, tubular bell-shaped, sometimes green-tinted, yellow flowers, 2in (5cm) long, with free, slightly twisted tepals, and stamens longer than styles, are borne in mid- and late spring. ↕ to 30in (75cm), ↔ 12in (30cm). E. North America. Zone 3.

Uvularia grandiflora

U

V

VACCINIUM

Blueberry, Cranberry, Huckleberry

ERICACEAE

Genus of about 450 species of evergreen, semi-evergreen, or deciduous shrubs and trees, widely distributed throughout arctic and tropical regions, occurring in a variety of habitats, from heath and moorland to bogs and woodland. They are valued for their ornamental foliage, flowers, and berries. The leathery leaves are alternate, and may be lance-shaped to elliptic, ovate, or rounded, with entire or toothed margins; in some of the deciduous species, the leaves provide brilliant autumn color. The small, urn- or bell-shaped to cylindrical flowers are white, green, pink, or red, and are produced either singly in the leaf axils or in terminal or axillary racemes, in spring and summer. The flowers are followed by edible, usually spherical berries; some species, including *V. angustifolium* var. *laevifolium*, *V. ashei*, *V. corymbosum*, and *V. macrocarpon*, are grown primarily for their fruits (blueberries and cranberries). Vacciniums are useful for a shrub border, woodland garden, or rock garden.

• **CULTIVATION** Grow in acidic, peaty or sandy, moist but well-drained soil in full sun or partial shade. Pruning group 1 for deciduous species; group 8 for evergreens.

• **PROPAGATION** Sow seed in containers in a cold frame in autumn. Take greenwood cuttings of deciduous species in early summer, and semi-ripe cuttings of evergreens in mid- to late summer. Layer in late summer.

• **PESTS AND DISEASES** Caterpillars, scale insects, gray mold (*Botrytis*), leaf and bud gall, dieback, *Phytophthora* crown and root rot, powdery mildew, rust, and witches' broom may cause problems.

V. angustifolium* var. *laevifolium ■ (Lowbush blueberry). Spreading, densely branched, deciduous shrub with

Vaccinium angustifolium var. *laevifolium*

Vaccinium arctostaphylos

lance-shaped, minutely toothed, glossy, dark green leaves, to 1½in (4cm) long, turning red in autumn. Bell-shaped, white, sometimes pink-tinged flowers, ½in (1.5cm) long, are borne in pendent, axillary and terminal racemes, to 2in (5cm) long, in mid- and late spring; they are followed by edible, sweet, spherical, blue-black berries, to ½in (1.5cm) across. ↕↔ 4–24in (10–60cm). E. North America. Zone 2.

V. arctostaphylos ■ (Caucasian whortleberry). Erect, densely branched, deciduous shrub with red-brown young shoots and elliptic, entire, dark green leaves, to 4in (10cm) long, colored red and purple in autumn. Bell-shaped, pink-tinged white flowers, ⅜in (9mm) long, are produced in pendent, axillary racemes, to 2in (5cm) long, in early summer; they are followed by edible, spherical, purple-black berries, ⅜in (9mm) across. ↕ 10ft (3m), ↔ 6ft (2m). Bulgaria, Turkey, Caucasus. Zone 7.

V. ashei (Rabbiteye blueberry). Deciduous or sometimes semi-evergreen or evergreen shrub with broadly elliptic to broadly ovate, entire or toothed, often slightly blue-tinged, mid-green leaves, 1½–3in (4–8cm) long, densely glandular and softly hairy to hairless beneath. In late spring or early summer, bears broadly urn-shaped, white or light pink to red flowers, ½in (1.5cm) across, in pendent racemes, followed by black berries, ⅜–½in (0.9–1.5cm) across. ↕ 3–15ft (1–5m), ↔ 3–10ft (1–3m). S.E. US. Zone 8. **'Climax'** is upright and open, and bears early, dark blue berries. **'Tifblue'** is vigorous and upright, with large, light blue berries.

Vaccinium corymbosum

Vaccinium glaucoalbum

V. caespitosum (Dwarf bilberry). Low-growing, rapidly spreading, densely branched, deciduous shrub with elliptic to obovate, entire or toothed, dark green leaves, ½–1½in (1.5–4cm) long. In late spring and early summer, produces pendent, urn-shaped, white to pink flowers, ¼in (6mm) long, singly from the leaf axils; flowers are followed by edible, spherical, blue-black fruit, ¼in (6mm) across. ↕ to 6in (15cm), ↔ 24in (60cm) or more. N. and W. North America. Zone 2.

V. corymbosum ■ (Highbush blueberry, Swamp blueberry). Upright, dense, many-branched, deciduous shrub with arching shoots and lance-shaped to elliptic, entire or toothed, mid-green leaves, to 3½in (9cm) long, turning yellow or red in autumn. In late spring and early summer, produces pendent, terminal racemes, to 2in (5cm) long, of cylindrical, white, sometimes pink-tinged flowers, ½in (1.5cm) long; they are followed by edible, sweet, spherical, white-bloomed, blue-black berries, to ½in (1.5cm) across. ↕↔ 5ft (1.5m). E. North America. Zone 4. Many cultivars have been selected. **'Bluecrop'** ripens in midseason and is more drought resistant than the species. **'Earliblue'** is upright and vigorous, with early-ripening fruit. **'Jersey'** is vigorous and upright, with large, late-ripening, light blue fruit, to ½in (1.5cm) across.

V. crassifolium (Creeping blueberry). Vigorous, procumbent, mat-forming, evergreen shrub with oval-elliptic to rounded, finely toothed, thick, leathery, dark green leaves, ⅜–½in (0.8–1.5cm) long, paler beneath. In late spring and early summer, bears pendent, urn-shaped, white to pink or rose-red flowers, ⅛in (3mm) long, in loose, terminal and axillary racemes, to 2in (5cm) long; they are followed by edible, spherical, purple-black fruit, to ½in (1.5cm) across. ↕ to 18in (45cm), ↔ 3ft (1m). S.E. US. Zone 7. **'Well's Delight'** is looser and broader, and prefers partial shade; ↕ to 8in (20cm), ↔ 24in (60cm) or more.

V. delavayi. Compact, spreading, evergreen shrub with densely arranged, obovate to elliptic, entire, leathery, dark green leaves, to ½in (1.5cm) long, red-tinged when young. Tiny, pendent, urn-shaped, pink-flushed, creamy white flowers, ¼in (6mm) long, are produced singly or in clusters of 2–4 from the leaf axils in early summer; they are followed by edible, spherical, deep red berries, ¼in (6mm) across. ↕ 24in (60cm), ↔ 36in (90cm). S.W. China. Zone 7b.

V. floribundum, syn. *V. mortinia* (Mortiña). Spreading, evergreen shrub bearing arching shoots densely covered with ovate, glandular-toothed, dark green leaves, to ½in (1.5cm) long, red when young. In early summer, produces dense, pendent, axillary racemes, to 2in (5cm) long, of cylindrical pink flowers, ¼in (6mm) long; they are followed by edible, spherical red berries, ¼in (6mm) across. ↕ 3ft (1m), ↔ 6ft (2m). Ecuador, Peru. ❄ (min. 41°F/5°C)

V. glaucoalbum ■ Spreading, mound-forming, dense, evergreen shrub producing elliptic, dark green leaves, to 2½in (6cm) long, bright bluish white beneath, either entire or with bristle-like teeth. Cylindrical, pink-tinged white flowers, ¼in (6mm) long, are borne in pendent, axillary racemes, to 3in (8cm) long, in late spring and early summer; they are followed by edible, spherical, white-bloomed, blue-black berries, ⅜in (9mm) across. ↕ 20–48in (50–120cm), ↔ 3ft (1m). E. Himalayas to China, Tibet, N. Burma. ❄ (min. 41°F/5°C)

V. macrocarpon (Cranberry). Prostrate, mat-forming, evergreen shrub with slender shoots and elliptic-oblong, entire, dark green leaves, to ¾in (2cm) long, bronze in winter. In summer, pendent, slender-stalked, bell-shaped pink flowers, ½in (1.5cm) across, with 4 slender, reflexed lobes, are produced singly from the leaf axils or in clusters of 2–10; they are followed by edible, spherical red berries, to ¾in (2cm) across. Best in cool, moist to wet soil in sun. ↕ 6in (15cm), ↔ indefinite.

Vaccinium myrtillus

E. North America. Zone 3.
'Hamilton' is dwarf, with dense foliage, and bears pink flowers in summer.
V. mortinia see *V. floribundum.*
V. moupinense. Compact, rounded, evergreen shrub with densely arranged, elliptic-oblong to obovate, entire, leathery, glossy, dark green leaves, to ½in (1.5cm) long. Bears tiny, urn-shaped, dark red-brown flowers, ¼in (6mm) long, in pendent, axillary racemes, to 1in (2.5cm) long, in late spring and early summer, followed by edible, spherical, purple-black berries, ¼in (6mm) across. ↕ 24in (60cm), ↔ 36in (90cm). W. China. ❄ (min. 41°F/5°C)
V. myrtillus ■ (Sourtop blueberry). Vigorous, creeping, deciduous shrub with dense, upright stems and oval-elliptic, finely toothed, glossy, bright green leaves, ½–1¼in (1–3cm) long, often coloring red in autumn. In late spring and early summer, bears pendent, axillary, rounded, urn-shaped pink flowers, ¼in (6mm) long, singly or in pairs, followed by edible, spherical, blue-black berries, ¼–½in (6–15mm) across. May be invasive in fertile soils. ↕ to 12in (30cm), ↔ indefinite. Europe to N. Asia. Zone 6.

Vaccinium vitis-idaea subsp. *minus*

V. nummularia. Spreading, low-growing, evergreen shrub with arching, brown-bristly stems. Rounded to elliptic, finely toothed, leathery, wrinkled, glossy, bright green leaves, ½–1in (1–2.5cm) long, are margined with red-brown bristles. In late spring, urn-shaped, red-tipped, pale pink flowers, ¼in (6mm) long, are produced in pendent racemes, to 2in (5cm) long, from leaf axils near the shoot tips; they are followed by edible, broadly ovoid black berries, ¼in (6mm) across. ↕ to 12in (30cm), ↔ to 24in (60cm). Himalayas (Sikkim, Bhutan). Zone 7b.
V. ovatum (Box blueberry, California huckleberry). Upright, bushy, evergreen shrub with arching shoots and densely arranged, ovate, finely toothed, leathery, glossy, dark green leaves, to 1¼in (3cm) long, bronze when young. In late spring and early summer, cylindrical or urn-shaped, pink-flushed white flowers, ¼in (6mm) long, are produced in dense, nodding, axillary racemes, 1in (2.5cm) long. The flowers are followed by edible, spherical, glossy black berries, ¼in (6mm) across. ↕ 12ft (4m), ↔ 10ft (3m). British Columbia to California. Zone 7b.

Vaccinium vitis-idaea 'Koralle' (inset: fruit detail)

V. parvifolium (Red whortleberry). Upright, deciduous shrub with oblong, entire, blue-green leaves, to 1¼in (3cm) long, turning brilliant red in autumn. Small, rounded, urn-shaped, white, sometimes pink-tinged flowers, ⅛–¼in (4–6mm) long, are produced singly or in pairs from the leaf axils in late spring and early summer. Flowers are followed by edible, spherical, coral-red berries, ½in (1.5cm) across. ↕ 10ft (3m), ↔ 6ft (2m). Alaska to California. Zone 6.
V. vitis-idaea (Cowberry). Creeping, evergreen shrub, spreading by means of underground rhizomes, and bearing obovate, glossy, dark green leaves, to 1in (2.5cm) long, often shallowly notched at the tips. In late spring and early summer, produces bell-shaped, white to deep pink flowers, ¼in (6mm) long, in dense, nodding, terminal racemes, to 1in (2.5cm) long; they are followed by edible but acidic, spherical, bright red berries, ¼in (6mm) across. ↕ 10in (25cm), ↔ indefinite. Arctic and alpine regions of N. Eurasia, Japan, North America. Zone 2. **'Koralle'** ■ bears abundant fruit, to ⅜in (9mm) across. **subsp. *minus*** ■ (Lingberry) is shorter, with smaller leaves, to ½in (1.5cm) long, and deep pink flowers; ↕ 8in (20cm); Arctic and alpine North America.

VALERIANA

Valerian

VALERIANACEAE

Genus of 200 or more species of annuals, often rhizomatous or taprooted herbaceous perennials, semi-evergreen subshrubs, and usually evergreen shrubs. They are found throughout the world, except in Australasia, and occur in moist woodland, meadows, or at streamsides, often in mountainous regions; the alpine species grow in scree or rock crevices. The opposite leaves are often aromatic, but not always pleasantly so; they are generally simple, although the non-shrubby species often produce pinnate or pinnatifid stem leaves as well as basal rosettes of simple leaves. The small, unisexual or bisexual, salverform flowers are pink to lavender-pink, white, or yellow, and are borne in terminal, panicle- or corymb-like cymes in summer. The few species in cultivation are herbaceous perennials, grown for their attractive flowers. Valerians are suitable for growing in an informal, cottage-style garden, herbaceous border, or herb garden, or for naturalizing in a wild garden.
• **CULTIVATION** Grow in any, preferably moist, soil in full sun or dappled shade. Tall-stemmed species and cultivars may require support.
• **PROPAGATION** Sow seed in containers outdoors, or take basal cuttings, in spring. Divide in spring or autumn.
• **PESTS AND DISEASES** Powdery mildew, rust, and a few leaf spots can occur.

V. officinalis (All heal, Common valerian, Garden heliotrope). Upright, clump-forming perennial with short rhizomes producing fleshy, branching stems. The aromatic, bright green, basal and stem leaves are pinnate, to 8in (20cm) long, each with 7–10 pairs of lance-shaped, toothed leaflets. Branched, rounded, corymb-like cymes of salverform, bisexual, pink or white flowers, to

Valeriana phu 'Aurea'

¼in (6mm) long, are borne throughout summer. ↕ 4–6ft (1.2–2m), ↔ 16–32in (40–80cm). W. Europe. Zone 4.
***V. phu* 'Aurea'** ■ Clump-forming, rhizomatous perennial with simple or pinnatifid, elliptic to inversely lance-shaped, aromatic basal leaves, to 8in (20cm) long, and pinnatifid, pinnatisect, or pinnate stem leaves; pinnate leaves have 3 or 4 pairs of elliptic leaflets. All leaves are soft yellow in spring, turning lime- to mid-green by summer. In early summer, branching stems bear panicle-like corymbs of small, salverform, bisexual white flowers, ⅛in (3mm) long. ↕ to 5ft (1.5m), ↔ 24in (60cm). Zone 6.

VALLEA

ELAEOCARPACEAE

Genus of one species of evergreen shrub or tree found in scrub in the Andes from Colombia to Bolivia. It has spirally arranged, simple or occasionally lobed leaves, and produces cup-shaped flowers, each with 5 sepals and 5 petals, in small, axillary and terminal cymes. Where temperatures fall below 32°F (0°C), grow in a cool greenhouse. In warmer areas, use in a courtyard garden or border, or plant against a warm, sunny wall.
• **CULTIVATION** Under glass, grow in acidic potting mix in full or bright filtered light. In the growing season, water moderately and apply a balanced liquid fertilizer monthly. Water sparingly in winter. Outdoors, grow in moderately fertile, neutral to acidic, moist but well-drained soil in full sun or partial shade. Pruning group 9.
• **PROPAGATION** Sow seed at 43–54°F (6–12°C) as soon as ripe. Root semi-ripe cuttings in mid- or late summer.
• **PESTS AND DISEASES** Spider mites may be a problem under glass.

V. stipularis. Erect to spreading shrub or tree, freely branching, at least when mature. Almost fleshy, leathery, deep green leaves, 1¼–5in (3–13cm) long, are lance-shaped to broadly ovate, rounded to heart-shaped at the bases, and sometimes lobed. Cymes of cup-shaped, crimson to dark rose-red flowers, ¾–1in (2–2.5cm) across, with darker veins, are produced from spring to summer. ↕ 10–15ft (3–5m), ↔ 6–12ft (2–4m). N. South America (Colombia to Bolivia). ❄ (min. 41°F/5°C)

▷ ***Vallota speciosa*** see *Cyrtanthus elatus*

VANCOUVERIA

BERBERIDACEAE

Genus, closely allied to *Epimedium*, of about 3 species of creeping, rhizomatous perennials, some of them evergreen, from rocky hillside scrub or coniferous woodland in W. US. They are grown for their ternate or 2-ternate, thick, sometimes leathery, basal leaves, and for their loose panicles of nodding flowers, each with 6 reflexed petals and 12 sepals, borne on wiry stems in late spring and summer. Suitable as a groundcover in a large rock garden or woodland garden.
• **CULTIVATION** Grow in moderately fertile, humus-rich, leafy, moist but well-drained soil in partial shade.
• **PROPAGATION** Sow seed in containers in a cold frame as soon as ripe. Divide in spring.
• **PESTS AND DISEASES** Vine weevil may be a problem.

V. chrysantha. Creeping, evergreen, rhizomatous perennial with ternate or 2-ternate, thick, leathery, glossy, dark green, basal leaves, to 18in (45cm) long, glaucous and paler beneath, composed of usually 9, rarely 3 or 5, rounded, diamond-shaped leaflets, 1½in (4cm) long, with thickened, wavy margins. From late spring to summer, leafless stems bear loose panicles of 4–15 yellow flowers, to ½in (1.5cm) long. ↕ to 12in (30cm), ↔ to 24in (60cm) or more. S.W. Oregon, N. California. Zone 6b.
V. hexandra ▣ Creeping, deciduous, rhizomatous perennial with 2-ternate, normally basal leaves, to 18in (45cm) long, each composed of 9 or more variable, ovate, smooth-textured, bright green leaflets, 3in (8cm) long, white-hairy when young. In late spring and early summer, leafless stems bear loose panicles of 6–45 white flowers, to ½in (1.5cm) long. Seldom spreads as widely as *V. chrysantha*. ↕↔ to 16in (40cm). Washington to California. Zone 6.
V. planipetala. Creeping, evergreen, rhizomatous perennial with 2-ternate leaves, to 18in (45cm) long, divided into leathery, marginally thickened, glossy, dark green ovate leaflets, to 1½in (4cm) long, sparsely hairy and glaucous beneath. In late spring and early summer, leafless stems bear loose panicles of bell-shaped, lavender-tinged white flowers, ½in (1.5cm) long. ↕ 8in (20cm), ↔ 16in (40cm). Oregon to California. Zone 6b.

Vancouveria hexandra

Vanda Rothschildiana

VANDA

ORCHIDACEAE

Genus of 30–40 species of evergreen, epiphytic, monopodial orchids found in exposed sites in scrub forest, at altitudes of 5,000ft (1,500m), from India to S.E. Asia and the Philippines, and south to Australia. They have thick, simple stems, the tips of which bear 2-ranked, strap-shaped to linear, leathery, semi-rigid, mid-green leaves, often lobed or toothed at the tips. Aerial roots form on the lower part of the stems. The flowers, borne in axillary, occasionally terminal racemes, are often large, showy, and intricately colored on their sepals, with small lips. A range of richly colored hybrids is available, including blue shades rarely found in the Orchidaceae.
• **CULTIVATION** Intermediate-growing orchids. Grow in epiphytic orchid potting mix in slatted baskets, in full light with shade from hot sun. In summer, water freely, apply fertilizer at every third watering, and mist plants twice daily. Water moderately in winter. See also p.46.
• **PROPAGATION** Remove offsets that arise at the base of the plants, or root cuttings of stem sections, in spring.
• **PESTS AND DISEASES** Leaf spots, petal blight, bacterial soft rot, and viruses occur. Spider mites, aphids, whiteflies, and mealybugs are common.

V. caerulea (Blue orchid). Unbranched, epiphytic orchid producing curved, linear leaves, to 10in (25cm) long. In autumn and winter, bears long, erect to arching racemes of clear blue flowers, 2–4in (5–10cm) across, often checkered darker blue; the lips are dark violet-blue with whitish blue lateral lobes. ↕ 24in (60cm), ↔ 12in (30cm). India, Burma, Thailand. ❀ (min. 55–61°F/13–16°C; max. 86°F/30°C)
***V.* Kasem's Delight** (*V.* Sun Tan x *V.* Thospol). Unbranched, epiphytic orchid producing linear leaves, 6in (15cm) long. Flowers, 4in (10cm) across, in a combination of deep mauve and indigo, are borne in long, pendent racemes intermittently throughout the year. ↕ 24in (60cm), ↔ 12in (30cm). ❀ (min. 55–61°F/13–16°C; max. 86°F/30°C)
***V.* 'Miss Joaquin'** (*V. hookerianum* x *V. teres*). Unbranched, epiphytic orchid with curved, linear leaves, 8in (20cm) long. In summer, this orchid bears upright racemes of pinkish purple flowers, 2in (5cm) across. ↕ 36in (90cm), ↔ 10in (25cm). ❀ (min. 55–61°F/13–16°C; max. 86°F/30°C)
***V.* Rothschildiana** ▣ (*Euanthe sanderiana* x *V. caerulea*). Unbranched, epiphytic orchid with curved, linear leaves, 6in (15cm) long. Dark-veined, violet-blue flowers, 4in (10cm) across, are borne in long, pendent racemes intermittently throughout the year. ↕ 24in (60cm), ↔ 12in (30cm). ❀ (min. 55–61°F/13–16°C; max. 86°F/30°C)
V. tessellata. Unbranched, epiphytic orchid with curved, linear leaves, to 18in (45cm) long. In autumn, produces long, pendent racemes of variable flowers, 2in (5cm) across, yellow-green or very pale blue, checkered brown, with white-margined, violet to blue lips. ↕ 24in (60cm), ↔ 12in (30cm). India, Sri Lanka, Burma, Malaysia. ❀ (min. 55–61°F/13–16°C; max. 86°F/30°C)
V. tricolor. Unbranched, epiphytic orchid with curved, linear leaves, 18in (45cm) long. Fragrant flowers, 2–3in (5–8cm) across, are usually pale yellow, heavily patterned red-brown, with purple-striped, violet-red lips; they are borne in long, erect to spreading racemes in winter. ↕ 3ft (1m), ↔ 12in (30cm). Laos, Indonesia (Java). ❀ (min. 55–61°F/13–16°C; max. 86°F/30°C)

VANILLA

ORCHIDACEAE

Genus of about 100 climbing, monopodial, terrestrial orchids growing on trees and shrubs from warm, moist forest in the tropics and subtropics. They have thick, adventitious roots with succulent, jointed, green or brown stems that climb or trail and bear stalkless or short-stalked, sometimes absent, ovate to oblong, fleshy leaves. Bears racemes or panicles of few to many, very fragrant, waxy, white, yellow, or green flowers. *V. planifolia* is cultivated commercially for vanilla flavoring, extracted from its cylindrical seed pods.
• **CULTIVATION** Intermediate to warm-growing orchids. Grow in containers of terrestrial orchid potting mix with bark and added organic mix. In summer, provide moist, shady conditions, water freely, feed at every third watering, and mist twice daily. In winter, water freely. Provide support. See also p.46.
• **PROPAGATION** Not suitable for division, although cuttings may be rooted successfully if taken after a period of dormancy and kept dry for 2–3 weeks before inserted.
• **PESTS AND DISEASES** Aphids, scale insects, and spider mites may be troublesome under glass.

V. planifolia (Vanilla). Climbing, branching, terrestrial orchid, often bearing a leaf and root at each node, with oblong, fleshy, mid-green leaves, 6in (15cm) long. In spring, bears axillary racemes of many yellow-green flowers, ¾in (2cm) across, with yellow-haired lips, followed by pendulous, cylindrical, brown seed pods, 6–10in (15–25cm) long. ↕ 10–30ft (3–10m). Florida, West Indies, Central and South America. ❀ (min. 59–64°F/15–18°C; max. 86°F/30°C). **'Albo-marginata'** produces mid-green leaves with white variegation; ↕ 10–12ft (3–4m).

VEITCHIA

ARECACEAE

Genus of 18 species of single-stemmed palms found in tropical rainforest, from sea level to 2,100ft (650m), from the Philippines and New Caledonia to Fiji and the New Hebrides. Oblong, pinnate leaves are produced in terminal tufts above a conspicuous, distinctive crownshaft, often with black-brown scales. Bowl-shaped, 3-petaled, male and female flowers with up to 100 stamens each are borne in panicles just beneath the foliage, and are followed by showy, red to orange fruits. Where not hardy, grow in a warm greenhouse or as houseplants. In warmer areas, use small species in a courtyard or border, and grow tall species on a lawn.
• **CULTIVATION** Under glass, grow in soil-based potting mix with added peat and sharp sand, in full light. Pot on or top-dress in spring. When in growth, water freely and apply a balanced liquid fertilizer monthly. Water sparingly in winter. Outdoors, grow in fertile, moist but well-drained soil in full sun.
• **PROPAGATION** Sow seed at 75°F (24°C) in spring.
• **PESTS AND DISEASES** Spider mites may be troublesome under glass.

V. merrillii ▣ syn. *Adonidia merrillii* (Christmas palm, Manila palm). Small palm with a slender trunk, to 10in (25cm) across, which tapers toward the crownshaft. Strongly arching, matte, mid- to deep green leaves, 3–6ft (1–2m) long, each have 40–60 strap-shaped leaflets, pale green and scaly beneath. Green to yellow-green flowers, ¾in (2cm) across, are borne in panicles to 3ft (1m) long, usually in summer; they are followed by ovoid crimson fruit, to 1¼in (3cm) long, which are at their most colorful during winter. ↕ to 15–20ft (5–6m), ↔ 6–11ft (2–3.5m). Philippines (Palawan Islands). ❀ (min. 59°F/15°C)

Veitchia merrillii

VELLOZIA

VELLOZIACEAE

Genus of 124 species of xerophytic, sometimes tree-like, evergreen perennials occurring on rocky, windswept cliffs or outcrops in scrub or woodland in tropical Africa, Madagascar, and tropical N., C., and S. America. They are grown for their fragrant, white, yellow, blue, purple, or violet flowers, which are bell-, funnel-, or star-shaped, and borne singly on long stalks. The narrowly elliptic to lance-shaped, toothed, rigid, often sharp-edged leaves are produced in tufts at the tops of woody stems, which can reach 12ft (4m) high. Where not hardy, grow in a warm greenhouse in containers or in hanging baskets. In dry, tropical areas, grow in a rock garden or desert garden. They often appear dead in drought conditions but quickly bear new leaves after watering or rainfall.

• **CULTIVATION** Under glass, grow in soil-based potting mix with added peat and sharp sand, in full light. Water sparingly during the growing season; keep almost dry in winter. Outdoors, grow in moderately fertile, sharply drained soil in full sun.

• **PROPAGATION** Sow seed at 66–75°F (19–24°C), or divide, in spring.

• **PESTS AND DISEASES** Infrequent.

V. elegans, syn. *Barbacenia elegans, Talbotia elegans.* Evergreen perennial with firm, arching stems and narrow, lance-shaped, mid-green leaves, to 8in (20cm) long, with slender points. Pale lilac buds open to solitary, star-shaped, pure white flowers, 1¼in (3cm) across, in spring. ↕ 6–8in (15–20cm), ↔ 8in (20cm). South Africa (KwaZulu/Natal). ❀ (min. 61°F/16°C)

VELTHEIMIA

LILIACEAE

Genus of 2 species of bulbous perennials from grassy and rocky hillsides in South Africa. They are grown for their rosettes of thick, wavy leaves, and for their terminal racemes of pendent, spring flowers, similar in form to those of red-hot pokers (*Kniphofia*). Where not hardy, grow in a temperate greenhouse or as houseplants. In warmer areas, grow in a warm, sunny border.

• **CULTIVATION** Plant in autumn with the neck of each bulb just above the soil surface. Under glass, grow in soil-based potting mix with added sharp sand, in full sun. In growth, water moderately and apply a low-nitrogen liquid fertilizer every 2 weeks. Reduce watering as the leaves fade, and keep just moist when dormant. Repot only when congested, to avoid root disturbance. Outdoors, grow in moderately fertile, well-drained soil in full sun.

• **PROPAGATION** Sow seed at 66–75°F (19–24°C) in autumn. Remove offsets in late summer.

• **PESTS AND DISEASES** Infrequent.

Veltheimia bracteata

V. bracteata ■ syn. *V. capensis* of gardens, *V. undulata, V. viridifolia.* Robust, bulbous perennial with basal rosettes of broad, strap-shaped, thick, spreading, wavy, glossy, dark green leaves, to 14in (35cm) long and 4in (10cm) across. In spring, bears dense, terminal racemes of up to 60 pendent, tubular, yellow-spotted, pinkish purple flowers, 1½in (4cm) long, on thick, erect, yellow-spotted purple stems. ↕ 18in (45cm), PD12in (30cm). South Africa. ❀ (min. 41–45°F/5–7°C). **'Rosalba'** has red-tinted yellow flowers.

V. capensis, syn. *V. glauca, V. roodeae, V. viridifolia* of gardens. Bulbous perennial producing basal rosettes of erect, narrowly lance-shaped, thick, glaucous, bluish green leaves, to 12in (30cm) long and 1½in (4cm) across, with wavy margins. In spring, thick green stems, flecked with purple, bear terminal racemes of pendent, tubular flowers, ¾–1¼in (2–3cm) long, varying from white with red spots to pink with green or red markings. Similar to *V. bracteata*, but more delicate and less easy to grow. ↕ 18in (45cm), PD12in (30cm). South Africa (Western Cape). ❀ (min. 41–45°F/5–7°C)

***V. capensis* of gardens** see *V. bracteata.*

V. glauca see *V. capensis.*

V. roodeae see *V. capensis.*

V. undulata see *V. bracteata.*

V. viridifolia see *V. bracteata.*

***V. viridifolia* of gardens** see *V. capensis.*

▷ **x *Venidioarctotis*** see *Arctotis*

▷ ***Venidium*** see *Arctotis*

VERATRUM

LILIACEAE

Genus of about 45 species of imposing, vigorous perennials, with poisonous black rhizomes, from damp meadows and open woodland throughout the N. hemisphere. The alternate, pleated, prominently veined, mid- to dark green leaves are broadly elliptic to ovate at the bases of the thick, erect stems, usually becoming smaller and more lance-shaped further up the stems. Numerous small, star-shaped, white, green, reddish brown, or almost black flowers are borne in summer, followed by spherical seed heads. The flowers are borne in large, terminal panicles, with unisexual (male) and bisexual flowers in the same inflorescence. Grow veratrums in a moist, shady site in a mixed or herbaceous border, or a woodland or wild garden. All parts are highly toxic if ingested. Contact with the foliage may irritate the skin.

• **CULTIVATION** Grow in deep, fertile, moist but well-drained soil, with added well-rotted organic matter, in a site in partial shade, or in full sun where the soil does not dry out; *V. viride* tolerates wet soil. Provide shelter from cold, drying winds.

• **PROPAGATION** Sow seed in containers in a cold frame as soon as ripe. Divide in autumn or early spring.

• **PESTS AND DISEASES** Prone to rust and fungal leaf spots. Slugs and snails may damage young plants.

Veratrum album

V. album ■ (False hellebore, White hellebore). Rhizomatous perennial with ovate to broadly elliptic, pleated basal leaves, to 12in (30cm) long, and a few stem leaves. All leaves are hairless above, hairy-veined beneath. In early and midsummer, bears numerous star-shaped, greenish white to white flowers, ½–¾in (1.5–2cm) across, in erect, terminal, freely branched panicles, to 24in (60cm) long. ↕ to 6ft (2m), ↔ 24in (60cm). Europe, N. Africa, N. Asia. Zone 6.

V. nigrum ■ (Black hellebore). Rhizomatous perennial producing broadly elliptic, pleated basal leaves, to 14in (35cm) long, and a few stem leaves. All foliage is hairless. In mid- and late summer, numerous star-shaped, unpleasantly scented, reddish brown to almost black flowers, ½in (1.5cm) across, with green-striped backs, are borne in terminal panicles, 18in (45cm) long; the lower branches are often horizontal or slightly pendent. ↕ 24–48in (60–120cm), ↔ 24in (60cm). Europe to Russia (Siberia), China, Korea. Zone 5b.

Veratrum nigrum

V. viride (Indian poke). Rhizomatous perennial with ovate to broadly elliptic, pleated basal leaves, to 12in (30cm) long, and a few stem leaves. All leaves are hairless above and hairy beneath. In early and midsummer, numerous star-shaped, green to yellowish green flowers to ¾in (2cm) across, are produced in terminal panicles, to 24in (60cm) long, with slightly pendent lower branches. ↕ to 6ft (2m), ↔ 24in (60cm). E. North America. Zone 3b.

VERBASCUM syn. CELSIA

Mullein

SCROPHULARIACEAE

Genus of 360 species, most of which are biennials, with a few annuals, perennials and subshrubs, some semi-evergreen or evergreen. They are found mainly on dry, stony hillsides, wasteland, and in open woodland in Europe, N. Africa, and W. and C. Asia. Usually hairy, sometimes woolly plants, they have large, alternate, simple, entire, scalloped lobed, or toothed, soft-textured basal leaves, which often form large rosettes, and smaller, often stalkless stem leaves. Most produce one or a few tall, erect stems bearing flowers in dense spikes or racemes, but some may have flowers clustered within the rosette centers. The generally short-stemmed or stemless, outward-facing, saucer-shaped flowers are usually yellow, occasionally purple, red, brownish red, or white; each has a short tube with 5 wide-spreading lobes, and sometimes colored filament hairs. Individual flowers are short-lived, but they are very numerous, and flowering takes place over a long period. Semi-evergreen species are grown as much for their overwintering rosettes of white-woolly leaves, built up during the first year, as for their flowers.

Most cultivated mulleins are hybrids. Rosette-forming and short-lived, they have ovate to oblong, mid- to grayish green leaves, and generally bear large, showy, saucer-shaped flowers, to 1½in (4cm) across, in more or less branched racemes, 12–39in (30–100cm) long.

Hybrids and larger species are good for growing in a large, mixed or herbaceous border or gravel bed, or for naturalizing in a wild or woodland garden. Smaller species, including *V. dumulosum, V. pestallozae,* and *V. spinosum,* are suitable for a rock garden or alpine house.

• **CULTIVATION** Grow in alkaline, poor, well-drained soil in full sun. In fertile soil, they grow larger and need support. Protect alpines from winter moisture. In an alpine house, use a mix of equal parts soil-based potting mix and grit.

• **PROPAGATION** Sow seed of biennials and perennials in containers in a cold frame in late spring or early summer; biennials sown at 55–64°F (13–18°C) in early spring may flower and die in their first year. Divide perennials in spring, or take root cuttings in winter. Take semi-ripe cuttings of shrubby species in late summer.

V

Verbascum chaixii f. *album*

• **PESTS AND DISEASES** Powdery mildew and a variety of fungal leaf spots are common, as well as caterpillars.

V. acaule, syn. *Celsia acaulis*. Rosette-forming, evergreen perennial producing ovate, rough, gray-green, basal leaves, to 2in (5cm) long, with coarsely toothed margins. In midsummer, bears saucer-shaped yellow flowers, ¾in (2cm) across, either singly or in clusters, from the centers of the rosettes. Best in a dry wall or alpine house. ↕ to 2in (5cm), ↔ to 6in (15cm). Mediterranean. Zone 7.
V. blattaria (Moth mullein). Rosette-forming biennial or annual with oblong to lance-shaped, stalkless or short-stalked, hairless, mid-green leaves, 3–10in (8–25cm) long. In summer, bears saucer-shaped yellow flowers, 1in (2.5cm) across, in lax racemes, to 6ft (2m) long. ↕ 5–7ft (1.5–2.2m), ↔ 24in (60cm). Europe, W. and C. Asia. Zone 7.
V. bombyciferum, syn. *V. broussa* (Turkish mullein). Rosette-forming biennial or short-lived, evergreen perennial covered with silky silver hairs. It has ovate-oblong, densely white-woolly, basal leaves, to 14in (35cm) long. Saucer-shaped, sulfur-yellow flowers, to 1½in (4cm) across, are borne in erect, dense, sparsely branched spikes, 24–48in (60–120cm) long, in summer. ↕ to 8ft (1.8m), ↔ to 24in (60cm). Turkey. Zone 4. **'Arctic Summer'** has heavily felted, silver-white leaves and yellow flowers; ↕ 5ft (1.5m). **'Silver Lining'**, often cultivated as an annual, has silvery white, very silky-hairy foliage.
V. broussa see *V. bombyciferum*.
V. chaixii (Nettle-leaved mullein). Rosette-forming, semi-evergreen perennial producing long-stalked, ovate-oblong, gray-hairy, mid-green basal leaves, 2–10in (5–25cm) long, with scalloped margins, and sometimes lobed toward the bases. Densely white-woolly stems bear short-stalked leaves on the middle section of the stem, and more rounded, stalkless upper leaves. Saucer-shaped, pale yellow flowers, to 1in (2.5cm) across, with purple filament hairs, are borne in slender panicles, to 16in (40cm) long, in mid- and late summer. ↕ to 36in (90cm), ↔ 18in (45cm). C., E., and S. Europe. Zone 6. **f. *album*** ■ produces white flowers with mauve centers.
***V.* 'Cotswold Queen'** ■ Erect, semi-evergreen perennial with ovate to lance-

Verbascum 'Cotswold Queen'

Verbascum dumulosum

shaped, wrinkled, gray-green leaves, to 8in (20cm) long. From early to late summer, bears erect, unbranched spikes, 12–24in (30–60cm) long, of saucer-shaped yellow flowers, to 1½in (4cm) across, with purple filament hairs. ↕ 4ft (1.2m), ↔ 12in (30cm). Zone 5.
V. densiflorum, syn. *V. thapsiforme*. Rosette-forming biennial or short-lived, semi-evergreen perennial with a dense covering of gray-yellow hairs and oblong to elliptic, wavy-margined, mid- to dark green, basal leaves, to 18in (45cm) long. In summer, produces erect, branching spikes, 24–36in (60–90cm) long, of closely set clusters of saucer-shaped, bright yellow, sometimes white flowers, to 2in (5cm) across. ↕ 4–5ft (1.2–1.5m), ↔ to 24in (60cm). Europe, Russia (Siberia). Zone 6.
V. dumulosum ■ Spreading, evergreen subshrub with white-downy stems and elliptic, entire to scalloped, felted-hairy, gray or gray-green leaves, ½–2in (1.5–5cm) long. In late spring and early summer, produces a succession of short racemes, to 6in (15cm) long, of saucer-shaped yellow flowers, to ½in (1.5cm) across, with small, red-purple eyes. Grow on its side in a wall crevice, or in a gravel or scree bed. ↕ to 10in (25cm), ↔ to 16in (40cm). S.W. Turkey. Zone 6.
***V.* 'Gainsborough'**. Rosette-forming, semi-evergreen perennial with ovate to elliptic, wrinkled, gray-green leaves, 10in (25cm) long. From early to late summer, bears pyramidal panicles, to 30in (75cm) long, of saucer-shaped, soft yellow flowers, 1in (2.5cm) across. ↕ to 4ft (1.2m), ↔ 12in (30cm). Zone 5.
***V.* 'Letitia'** ■ Dense, rounded, evergreen subshrub with stiff, branching stems bearing oblong-lance-shaped, irregularly toothed or lobed, gray-green leaves, 1¼in (3cm) long. Produces an abundance of almost flat, clear yellow flowers, ½in (1.5cm) across, with reddish purple centers, in short racemes, 4in (10cm) long, over long periods in summer. Suitable for a raised bed, rock garden, or alpine house. Needs sharply drained soil. ↕ to 12in (30cm), ↔ to 9in (23cm). Zone 5.
V. longifolium* var. *pannosum see *V. olympicum*.
V. lychnitis (White mullein). Rosette-forming biennial with ovate-oblong-lance-shaped to oblong, entire or coarsely scalloped, mid-green leaves, 6–12in (15–30cm) long, white-hairy

Verbascum 'Letitia'

beneath. In summer, bears narrow panicles, 24–72in (60–150cm) long, of many saucer-shaped, bright yellow or white flowers, ½–¾in (1.5–2cm) across. ↕ to 5ft (1.5m), ↔ 24in (60cm). Europe, W. Asia. Zone 6.
***V.* 'Mont Blanc'**. Rosette-forming, semi-evergreen perennial producing ovate to lance-shaped, wrinkled, finely white-downy, pale gray-green, basal leaves, to 12in (30cm) long. Upright, unbranched, slender racemes, to 20in (50cm) long, of saucer-shaped, pure white flowers, to 1¼in (3cm) across, are borne from early to late summer. ↕ 36in (90cm), ↔ 12in (30cm). Zone 5.
V. nigrum ■ (Dark mullein). Rosette-forming, deciduous or semi-evergreen perennial with ovate-oblong, scalloped, long-stalked, mid- to dark green basal leaves, 6–16in (15–40cm) long; the leaves become progressively shorter-stalked up the stems, then stalkless and more rounded; all leaves are heart-shaped at the bases, hairless above, and slightly gray-woolly beneath. From midsummer to early autumn, usually unbranched, ridged stems, with long hairs, bear slender racemes, 20in (50cm) long, of clustered, saucer-shaped, dark yellow

Verbascum nigrum

V

flowers, to 1in (2.5cm) across, with violet filament hairs. ↕ 36in (90cm), ↔ 24in (60cm). Europe to Russia (Siberia). Zone 3.
V. olympicum ■ syn. *V. longifolium* var. *pannosum.* Rosette-forming, densely gray-white-woolly, often monocarpic perennial with broadly lance-shaped, entire, short-stalked, mid-green, mainly basal leaves, usually 6in (15cm) long, sometimes to 24in (60cm). Branching stems, which form a candelabra shape, bear stalkless leaves; from early to late summer of the second or third year, they bear panicles, to 30in (75cm) or more long, of clustered, saucer-shaped, golden yellow flowers, 1¼in (3cm) across, with yellowish white filament hairs. Often dies after flowering. ↕ to 6ft (2m), ↔ 24in (60cm). Greece. Zone 5.
V. pestallozae. Dwarf, many-branched, evergreen subshrub with stems and mid-green leaves clothed in densely felted, white, yellow, or tawny brown hairs. In summer, bears elliptic to lance-shaped, entire, basal leaves, 1–1½in (2.5–4cm) long, and short racemes, to 6in (15cm) long, of saucer-shaped yellow flowers, ¾in (2cm) across. ↕ to 10in (25cm), ↔ to 16in (40cm). Turkey. Zone 7b.
V. phoeniceum (Purple mullein). Rosette-forming biennial or short-lived, evergreen perennial with short-stalked, ovate, slightly scalloped, wrinkled, conspicuously veined, dark green basal leaves, to 6in (15cm) long, sparsely softly hairy or hairless, and a few stalkless stem leaves. In late spring and early summer, bears slender racemes, 30in (75cm) long, of saucer-shaped, white, pink, or violet to dark purple flowers, to 1¼in (3cm) across, with violet filament hairs. ↕ to 4ft (1.2m), ↔ 18in (45cm). S. Europe, N. Africa to C. Asia (Altai Mountains). Zone 4.
***V.* 'Pink Domino'.** Rosette-forming, semi-evergreen perennial with ovate to lance-shaped, wrinkled, dark purplish green leaves, 8in (20cm) long. From early to late summer, produces saucer-shaped, deep rose-pink flowers, 1¼in

Verbascum olympicum

(3cm) long, with darker purple filament hairs, in erect, unbranched spikes, 28in (70cm) long. ↕ 4ft (1.2m), ↔ 12in (30cm). Zone 5.
***V.* 'Silver Candelabra'** see *V.* 'Silberkandelaber'.
***V.* 'Silberkandelaber'**, syn. *V.* 'Silver Candelabra'. Rosette-forming, evergreen perennial with elliptic, softly hairy, silver-white leaves, to 6in (15cm) long. Bears tall, candelabra-like spikes of saucer-shaped yellow flowers, to 1in (2.5cm) across, in mid- and late summer. ↕ 5–7ft (1.5–2.2m), ↔ 24in (60cm). Zone 5.
V. spinosum. Slow-growing, hummock-forming, intricately branched, semi-evergreen subshrub with woody gray shoots terminating in sharp spines. The oblong-lance-shaped, woolly, gray-white leaves, ½–2in (1.5–5cm) long, are irregularly toothed or lobed. In summer, bears twiggy panicles, to 2in (5cm) long, of saucer-shaped yellow flowers, to ¾in (2cm) across, with short lilac filament hairs. ↕ to 10in (25cm), ↔ to 16in (40cm) or more. Greece (Crete). Zone 8.
V. thapsiforme see *V. densiflorum.*
V. thapsus (Aaron's rod, Common mullein, Flannel plant). Robust, gray- or white-woolly, rosette-forming biennial with elliptic to oblong, entire or finely scalloped, mid-green, basal leaves, to 20in (50cm) long. In the summer of the second year, produces a thick, erect, usually unbranched, densely woolly stem, terminating in a spike-like raceme, to 30in (75cm) long, of saucer-shaped yellow flowers, to 1¼in (3cm) across; the stem often persists through winter. ↕ 4–6ft (1.2–2m), ↔ to 18in (45cm). Eurasia. Zone 4.
V. wiedemannianum. Rosette-forming, evergreen biennial, with a covering of cobweb-like, gray-white hairs, and elliptic to lance-shaped, tapered, mid-green leaves, 3–5in (8–13cm) long. In summer, bears branched racemes, 14–48in (35–120cm) long, of saucer-shaped, indigo-blue to violet flowers, 1½in (4cm) across, with purple stamens. ↕ 3ft (1m), ↔ 24in (60cm). Turkey. Zone 7.

VERBENA *syn.* GLANDULARIA

VERBENACEAE

Genus of about 250 species of annuals, perennials, and subshrubs, some of them tuberous or rhizomatous, occurring in usually open and sunny habitats, such as prairies, wasteland, and roadsides, and in open woodland (some species prefer dry sites, others moist). Almost all are from tropical and temperate regions of North, Central, and South America; a few are from S. Europe. The erect or procumbent, square stems have usually opposite, toothed, sometimes lobed to pinnatifid leaves, and bear small flowers in dense, terminal spikes, panicles, cymes, or corymbs, occasionally singly. The flowers, often brightly colored, are salverform, each with a tubular corolla spreading at the mouth, and slightly 2-lipped, with 2 upper petals and 3 lower ones. Verbenas are long-flowering. There are numerous hybrids, which are ideal for an annual border, for edging, or for growing in containers, including hanging baskets; some are suitable for a herbaceous border.

Verbena bonariensis

• **CULTIVATION** In containers, grow in soil-based potting mix with added sharp sand, in full sun. Water freely in growth, and apply a balanced liquid fertilizer monthly. Water more sparingly in winter. Outdoors, grow in moist but well-drained, moderately fertile soil in full sun. Where marginally hardy, protect with a dry winter mulch.
• **PROPAGATION** Sow seed at 64–70°F (18–21°C) in autumn or early spring. Divide perennials in spring. Take stem-tip cuttings in late summer.
• **PESTS AND DISEASES** Prone to aphids, whiteflies, slugs, snails, scale insects, spider mites, powdery mildew, *Septoria* leaf spot, and rust.

***V. alpina* of gardens** see *V.* x *maonettii.*
V. bipinnatifida (Dakota verbena). Spreading, prostrate, stiff bristly-haired perennial with 2- or 3-pinnatisect, triangular, mid-green leaves, to 2in (5cm) long. In summer, bears dense, hairy spikes, 2–3in (5–8cm) long, of salverform, lilac-purple flowers, to ½in (1.5cm) across, on ascending stems. ↕ 16in (40cm), ↔ 18in (45cm). South Dakota to N.W. Mexico to Alabama. Zone 5.

Verbena corymbosa

Verbena x *hybrida* 'Imagination'

V. bonariensis ■ syn. *V. patagonica.* Stiff, upright, open clump-forming perennial, often grown as an annual in colder areas, with rough, branching stems bearing a few oblong-lance-shaped, wrinkled, clasping leaves, to 5in (13cm) long, with toothed margins, and hairy beneath. Salverform, lilac-purple flowers, ¼in (6mm) across, are borne in panicle-like cymes, to 2in (5cm) across, from midsummer to frost. ↕ to 6ft (2m), ↔ 18in (45cm). South America (Brazil to Argentina). Zone 7b.
V. canadensis (Rose vervain). Spreading annual or perennial with ascending, branching stems and pinnatifid, ovate to oblong-ovate, irregularly toothed, hairless, mid-green leaves, 3½in (9cm) long. Bears dense, terminal panicles, 2½in (6cm) across, of rose-pink flowers, ½in (1.5cm) across, in summer. ↕ 8–16in (20–40cm), ↔ 1½–3ft (45–90cm). S. central to S.E. North America. Zone 4. **'Homestead Purple'** has glossy leaves, and bears purple flowers in summer; mildew resistant; ↕ 18in (45cm).
V. chamaedrifolia see *V. peruviana.*
V. chamaedrioides see *V. peruviana.*
V. corymbosa ■ Spreading, rhizomatous perennial with erect, branched stems and stalkless, oblong or ovate, toothed, rough leaves, 1–2½in (2.5–6cm) long, often lobed at the bases. From early to late summer, bears salverform, red-purple flowers, ½in (1.5cm) across, in dense, corymb-like panicles, 2–3in (5–8cm) across. ↕ 3–6ft (1–2m), ↔ 24in (60cm). South America (S. Chile, Argentina). ❄ (min. 41°F/5°C)
V. goodingii. Upright or ascending, glandular or hairy perennial with pinnate leaves, to 2in (5cm) long, and ovate, mid-green leaflets. Bears dense, terminal spikes, to 3in (8cm) long, of salverform, pink, lavender, or blue-violet flowers, ½in (1.5cm) across, in summer. ↕ to 24in (60cm), ↔ 18in (45cm). US, N. Mexico. ❄ (min. 35°F/2°C)
V. hastata (Blue vervain). Upright, clump-forming perennial with stems sometimes branched near the top. Bears stalked, mainly lance-shaped, pointed, toothed leaves, to 6in (15cm) long, the lowest ones spear-shaped. From early summer to early autumn, produces stiff panicles, 2–4in (5–10cm) across, of numerous salverform, violet-blue to pinkish purple, occasionally white flowers, ¼in (6mm) across. ↕ to 5ft (1.5m), ↔ 24in (60cm). E. North America. Zone 4.

V

Verbena x *hybrida* 'Peaches and Cream'

V.* x *hortensis see *V.* x *hybrida* cultivars.
***V.* x *hybrida* cultivars**, syn. *V.* x *hortensis*. Erect and bushy, or spreading and mat-forming, hairy perennials, usually grown as annuals, with ovate to oblong, toothed, rough, mid- to dark green leaves, 2–4in (5–10cm) long, either stalkless or with short stalks. In summer and autumn, they bear tight, corymb-like panicles, to 3in (8cm) or more across, of tiny, salverform, sometimes scented, white, pink, red, yellow, or purple-blue flowers, ½–1in (1.5–2.5cm) across, each usually with a white eye. ↕ to 18in (45cm), ↔ 12–20in (30–50cm). ❀ (min. 35°F/2°C). **'Amethyst'** has small blue flowers with white eyes. **'Blaze'** is mound-forming, with scarlet-red flowers; ↕ 9in (23cm). **'Blue Lagoon'** is mound-forming, and bears light, sky-blue flowers without eyes; ↕ 10in (25cm). **'Imagination'** ▣ is spreading and mound-forming, with pinnatifid leaves and deep violet-blue flowers; good for hanging baskets. It is sometimes listed under *V. speciosa*. Cultivars of **Novalis Series** are erect and bushy, with almost spherical corymbs, 2–3in (5–8cm) across, of white-eyed flowers in rose-pink, deep blue, pinkish red, and scarlet, as well as single colors in bright scarlet, white, or rose-pink; ↕ to 10in (25cm). **'Peaches and Cream'** ▣ is spreading and branching, bearing pastel orange-pink flowers, aging to apricot-yellow, then creamy yellow. Cultivars of **Romance Series** are erect and bushy, producing white-eyed flowers in deep wine-red, intense scarlet, carmine-rose-red, and blue-purple, as well as single colors of white, bright scarlet, dark rose, or lavender-pink; ↕ to 10in (25cm). **Sandy Series** ▣ cultivars are compact and erect, with flowers in rose-pink, rose-pink with white eyes, magenta, scarlet, or white; color mixtures are available. **'Showtime'** is bushy and fairly slow-growing, bearing flowers in a wide range of colors.
***V.* 'Mahonettii'** see *V.* x *maonettii*.
V.* x *maonettii, syn. *V. alpina* of gardens, *V.* 'Mahonetti' (Italian verbena). Spreading, prostrate perennial with finely cut, pinnatifid leaves, to 1in (2.5cm) long. Produces short spikes of red-violet flowers, to ½in (1.5cm) across, with white-margined lobes, in summer. ↕ to 2in (5cm), ↔ to 12in (30cm). Zone 7b.
V. patagonica see *V. bonariensis*.
V. peruviana, syn. *V. chamaedrifolia*, *V. chamaedrioides*. Fast-growing, mat-forming, semi-evergreen perennial with slender, ascending stems clothed in closely set, oblong-lance-shaped, toothed leaves, 2in (5cm) long, with short stalks. From summer to autumn, bears salverform, rich scarlet flowers, ½in (1.5cm) across, in flat-topped, corymb-like spikes, 2in (5cm) across. ↕ to 3in (8cm), ↔ 3ft (1m). South America (S. Brazil to Argentina). ❀ (min. 41°F/5°C). **'Alba'** has white flowers.

Verbena x *hybrida* Sandy Series

V. rigida, syn. *V. venosa* (Vervain). Erect to spreading, hairy, tuberous perennial, often grown as an annual, with stalkless, oblong, toothed, rough leaves, to 3in (8cm) long. In summer, bears salverform, fragrant, bright purple or magenta flowers, ¼in (6mm) across, in lax corymbs, to 2in (5cm) across, gradually lengthening and becoming spike-like with age. ↕ 18–24in (45–60cm), ↔ to 16in (40cm). South America (S. Brazil, Argentina). ❀ (min. 35°F/2°C). **'Flame'** is low-growing and mound-forming, with scarlet-red flowers; ↕ 4in (10cm). **'Lilacina'** has violet-blue flowers. **'Polaris'** forms dense clumps, and has rigid leaves to 3in (8cm) long; from early summer to early autumn, bears silver-blue flowers, ⅜in (9mm) across, in corymbs 2in (5cm) across; ↕ to 24in (60cm), ↔ 12in (30cm).
***V.* 'Saint Paul'** see *V.* 'Sissinghurst'.
***V.* 'Silver Anne'.** Upright, spreading perennial with ovate-oblong, shallowly cut, rough, stalked leaves, 4in (10cm) long. Corymbs, 1½in (4cm) across, of salverform, sweetly scented flowers, ½in (1.5cm) across, bright pink at first and fading to silver-white with age, open in succession in summer and autumn, giving a multitoned effect. ↕ to 12in (30cm), ↔ 24in (60cm). ❀ (min. 35°F/2°C)
***V.* 'Sissinghurst'** ▣ syn. *V.* 'Saint Paul'. Mat-forming perennial with ovate, pinnatifid, dark green leaves, to 1¼in (3cm) long. Salverform, magenta-pink flowers, ½in (1.5cm) across, are borne in corymbs, 1in (2.5cm) across, from late spring to autumn, but most prolifically in summer. ↕ to 8in (20cm), ↔ to 3ft (1m). Zone 8.
V. stricta (Hoary vervain). Upright, clump-forming perennial with densely softly hairy stems and variable, narrowly elliptic to broadly ovate to rounded, rough, toothed, mid-green leaves, to 4in (10cm) long, densely gray-white-hairy beneath. In summer, bears upright, dense, hairy spikes, to 12in (30cm) long, of salverform, deep lavender or purple flowers, to ½in (1.5cm) across. ↕ to 3ft (1m), ↔ 18in (45cm). North America. Zone 4.

Verbena 'Sissinghurst'

V. tenuisecta. (Moss verbena). Usually prostrate to decumbent, sometimes erect, aromatic annual or perennial with 3-lobed leaves, to 1½in (4cm) long, the lobes pinnatifid, with linear, entire or toothed segments. Salverform, lilac, mauve, purple, white, or blue flowers are produced in corymb-like spikes, to 2in (5cm) across, from summer to autumn. ↕ to 20in (50cm), ↔ to 9in (23cm). S. South America. ❀ (min. 35°F/2°C). **'Alba'** bears finely dissected leaves and many clusters of pure white flowers; ↕ 6in (15cm).
V. venosa see *V. rigida*.

VERNONIA

Ironweed

ASTERACEAE

Genus of about 1,000 species of annuals, perennials, climbers, subshrubs, shrubs, and trees from mainly tropical and subtropical habitats, ranging from moist meadows to dry woodland. Most occur in South America, some in Africa, Asia, Australasia, and North America. Species from more northerly habitats are usually annuals or herbaceous perennials; those from the tropics are mainly woody. Generally, only the perennials are cultivated. They have upright stems bearing alternate, simple, entire or toothed, stalkless leaves, and flat, corymb-like cymes of tubular, purple or reddish pink, rarely white flowerheads, becoming rust-colored with age. Grow in a wild garden or mixed border.

- **CULTIVATION** Grow in any light, moderately fertile, moist soil in full sun or partial shade. Deadhead regularly.
- **PROPAGATION** Sow seed in containers in a cold frame in spring. Divide in spring or autumn.
- **PESTS AND DISEASES** Powdery mildew, rust, and *Cercospora* leaf spot are common. Slugs and snails may damage young growth.

V. noveboracensis ▣ (Ironweed) Upright herbaceous perennial with branching stems bearing lance-shaped, entire to toothed leaves, to 8in (20cm) long. From late summer to midautumn, bears loose, flat, corymb-like cymes of tubular, red-purple or white florets, in fluffy heads, ½in (1.5cm) across. ↕ to 6ft (2m), ↔ 24in (60cm). Massachusetts to Mississippi and Georgia. Zone 5.

Vernonia noveboracensis

VERONICA

Speedwell

SCROPHULARIACEAE

Genus of about 250 species of annuals, perennials (including some marginal aquatics), and mostly deciduous subshrubs, some of them rhizomatous. They occur in swamps and moist meadows and grassland, or in open woodland to dry, sunny meadows, rocky hills, and scree, mainly in Europe. The linear to broadly lance-shaped, or oblong to rounded, entire or toothed, stalkless or short-stalked leaves are usually produced in opposite pairs, although those on the flowering stems can be alternate or whorled. Small, outward-facing flowers, ¼–½in (5–15mm) across, in purple, blue, pink, or white, are borne in long, axillary or terminal racemes or spikes, or singly from the leaf axils, from spring to autumn. The petals form a short tube, with 4 or 5 spreading, often unequally sized lobes; each flower has only 2 functional stamens. Good for a mixed or herbaceous border. Use cushion- or mat-forming veronicas in a rock garden; grow less vigorous species and cultivars in a trough or in an alpine house.

• **CULTIVATION** Outdoors, grow alpines and rock garden veronicas in poor to moderately fertile, well-drained soil in full sun. Protect species with felted leaves from winter moisture. In an alpine house, grow in a mix of equal parts loam, leaf mold, and grit. Grow border veronicas in loamy, moderately fertile, moist but well-drained soil in full sun or partial shade. Grow *V. beccabunga* in wet soil, or in water to 5in (13cm) deep, in full sun; see also pp.52–53.

• **PROPAGATION** Sow seed in containers in a cold frame in autumn. Divide perennials in autumn or spring; for *V. beccabunga*, divide, or take stem-tip cuttings, in summer. Take softwood cuttings of subshrubs in spring.

• **PESTS AND DISEASES** Scale insects, downy mildew, powdery mildew, rust, leaf smut, and root rot occur.

Veronica gentianoides

Veronica peduncularis

Veronica prostrata 'Trehane'

Veronica austriaca subsp. *teucrium* 'Crater Lake Blue'

Veronica beccabunga

V. austriaca* subsp. *teucrium, syn. *V. teucrium*. Mat-forming perennial with ovate to oblong, scalloped or deeply toothed, hairy, grayish green leaves, to 3in (8cm) long. Upright stems bear abundant erect, terminal, spike-like racemes, 4–6in (10–15cm) long, of saucer-shaped, deep bright blue flowers over a long period in summer. ↕ to 36in (90cm), ↔ to 24in (60cm). N. temperate Europe. Zone 5. **'Crater Lake Blue'** ■ produces deep, gentian-blue flowers in early summer; ↕ 12–18in (30–45cm). **'Kapitän'** has gentian-blue flowers; ↕ to 12in (30cm), ↔ to 16in (40cm). **'Shirley Blue'** produces erect racemes, 2½–4in (6–10cm) long, of vivid blue flowers from late spring to midsummer; ↕ to 10in (25cm), ↔ 12in (30cm).

V. beccabunga ■ (Brooklime). Usually evergreen, marginal aquatic perennial with creeping, branching, hollow, fleshy stems, rooting at the nodes, and ovate to rounded, entire or toothed, fleshy mid-green leaves, ½–1½in (1–4cm) long. Bears saucer-shaped, white-centered blue flowers in loose, erect, axillary racemes, to 5in (13cm) long, from late spring to late summer. ↕ 4in (10cm), ↔ indefinite. Eurasia. Zone 5. **'Blue Spire'** bears intensely blue flowers.

V. chamaedrys (Germander speedwell). Spreading, slender-stemmed, branching, rhizomatous perennial with stalkless, ovate to lance-shaped, toothed, bright green leaves, to 1½in (4cm) long. From summer to autumn, bears saucer-shaped, white-eyed, bright blue flowers in erect, slender, paired, axillary racemes, 3–6in (8–15cm) long. ↕ 12–20in (30–50cm), ↔ 20–32in (50–80cm). Europe, Caucasus, Russia (Siberia). Zone 4.

V. cinerea. Woody-based, white-felted, subshrubby, evergreen perennial with prostrate, branching stems and linear, entire, mid-green, densely silvery white-woolly leaves, to ½in (1.5cm) long. In early summer, bears abundant terminal racemes, ¾–1¼in (2–3cm) long, of saucer-shaped, deep blue or blue-purple flowers. ↕ to 6in (15cm), ↔ to 12in (30cm). E. Mediterranean, Turkey. Zone 5.

V. fruticans, syn. *V. saxatilis* (Rock speedwell). Mat-forming, woody-based, branching perennial or subshrub with obovate to narrowly oblong, entire or slightly scalloped, mid-green leaves, to ¾in (2cm) long. In summer, produces erect, terminal racemes, to 2in (5cm) long, of saucer-shaped, deep blue flowers with dark red eyes. ↕ to 3in (8cm), ↔ to 8in (20cm). N.W. Europe, mountains of Spain to C. Europe, Balkans. Zone 6.

V. gentianoides ■ Mat-forming perennial with basal rosettes of broadly lance-shaped, entire or slightly scalloped, thick, dark green leaves, to 3in (8cm) long. In early summer, bears shallowly cup-shaped, pale blue, rarely darker blue or white flowers in erect, terminal racemes, 3–10in (8–25cm) long. ↕↔ 18in (45cm). Ukraine (Crimea), N. and C. Turkey, Caucasus. Zone 4. **'Variegata'** has white-variegated leaves and blue flowers.

V. incana see *V. spicata* subsp. *incana*.

***V. incana* 'Saraband'** see *V. spicata* subsp. *incana* 'Saraband'.

***V. incana* 'Wendy'** see *V. spicata* subsp. *incana* 'Wendy'.

V. kellereri see *V. spicata*.

V. longifolia. Variable, upright perennial with lance-shaped to linear, pointed, toothed, mid-green leaves, to 5in (13cm) long, either opposite or in whorls of 3, usually on unbranched stems. In late summer and early autumn, bears tubular, 5-lobed, lilac-blue flowers in dense, erect, terminal racemes, to 10in (25cm) long. ↕ to 4ft (1.2m), ↔ 12in (30cm). N. and C. Europe to Russia (Siberia), E. Asia. Zone 4. **'Blauriesin'**, syn. 'Foerster's Blue', is bushy, with bright, deep blue flowers; ↕ to 30in (75cm). **'Foerster's Blue'** see 'Blauriesin'.

V. pectinata. Dense, mat-forming, evergreen, subshrubby perennial with elliptic to oblong, deeply toothed, gray leaves, to 1in (2.5cm) long. Saucer-shaped, white-eyed, deep blue flowers are borne in short, erect, axillary racemes, 2½–10in (6–25cm) long, in summer. ↕ to 3in (8cm), ↔ to 8in (20cm). E. Balkans, Turkey. Zone 4. **'Rosea'** has pink flowers.

V. peduncularis ■ Mat-forming perennial with branching rhizomes and prostrate to ascending, freely branched stems bearing ovate to lance-shaped, toothed, glossy, purple-tinged, mid-green leaves, ¼–1in (0.5–2.5cm) long. Produces abundant erect, axillary racemes, 1½–3in (4–8cm) long, of saucer-shaped, deep blue flowers, with small white eyes, over a long period from early spring to summer. ↕ to 4in (10cm), ↔ 24in (60cm) or more. Turkey, Caucasus, Ukraine. Zone 7. **'Georgia Blue'**, syn. 'Oxford Blue', is vigorous, very free-flowering, and easily grown. **'Oxford Blue'** see 'Georgia Blue'.

V. perfoliata see *Parahebe perfoliata*.

V. prostrata ■ syn. *V. rupestris* (Prostrate speedwell). Mat-forming perennial with short, branched, decumbent stems bearing linear-oblong to ovate, toothed, bright to mid-green leaves, ⅜–1in (0.8–2.5cm) long. In early

Veronica prostrata

Veronica spicata subsp. *incana*

V

'eronica spicata 'Rotfuchs'

ummer, produces erect, terminal, spike-
ke racemes, ¾–1½in (2–4cm) long, of
aucer-shaped, pale to deep blue flowers.
to 6in (15cm), ↔ to 16in (40cm).
urope. Zone 4. **'Heavenly Blue'** is
rostrate and bears brilliant, gentian-
lue flowers in spring; ↕ 3in (8cm).
Loddon Blue' bears bright blue
owers; ↕ to 8in (20cm). **'Mrs. Holt'**
ears pale pink flowers. **'Trehane'** ■
as yellow-green or golden leaves and
eep blue flowers.
'. rupestris see *V. prostrata.*
'. saxatilis see *V. fruticans.*
'. spicata, syn. *V. kellereri* (Spike
peedwell). Mat-forming perennial with
ecumbent, simple, rooting stems, and
scending to erect, flowering stems
earing oblong-lance-shaped to linear,
oothed, hairy leaves, to 3in (8cm) long.
tar-shaped, bright blue flowers, with
ong purple stamens, open in erect,
ense, pyramidal, terminal racemes, to
2in (30cm) long, from early to late
ummer. ↕ 12–24in (30–60cm), ↔ 18in
45cm). Europe to Turkey, C. and
. Asia. Zone 3. **'Alba'** bears white
owers in midsummer; ↕ to 16in
40cm). **'Barcarolle'** freely produces
ink flowers; ↕ 12in (30cm). **'Blue

'eronica 'Sunny Border Blue'

Charm'** has pale, lavender-blue flowers in early summer; ↕ 30–36in (75–90cm). **'Blue Peter'** bears deep navy-blue flowers in mid- and late summer; ↕ 18–24in (45–60cm). **'Caerulea'** has sky-blue flowers. **'Erica'** produces pink flowers; ↕ to 12in (30cm). **'Goodness Grows'** bears dark blue flowers all summer long; ↕ 12–16in (30–40cm). **'Heidekind'** has silver-gray leaves and short spikes of raspberry-pink flowers; ↕ 12in (30cm). **'Icicle'**, syn. 'White Icicle', has white flowers; ↕ 24in (60cm). **subsp. *incana*** ■ syn. *V. incana* (Silver speedwell), is entirely silver-hairy, and produces purple-blue flowers; ↕↔ 12in (30cm); Russia. **subsp. *incana* 'Saraband'**, syn. *V. incana* 'Saraband', has violet-blue flowers above densely hairy, silver-gray foliage. **subsp. *incana* 'Silver Slippers'** is mat-forming and produces oblong to lance-shaped, gray leaves, 2in (5cm) long, and does not bear flowers; excellent for the front of a border or a rock garden; ↕ to ½in (1.5cm), ↔ to 18in (45cm). **subsp. *incana* 'Wendy'**, syn. *V. incana* 'Wendy', has a looser habit, with gray leaves and bright blue flowers; ↕ 18in (45cm). **'Minuet'** has gray leaves, and bears pink flowers in late spring; ↕ 10–16in (25–40cm). **subsp. *nana* 'Blauteppich'** is compact and bears bright indigo-blue flowers, in summer; ↕ 4–6in (10–15cm). **'Noah Williams'** has white-edged, mid-green leaves and white flowers. **'Red Fox'** see 'Rotfuchs'. **'Romiley Purple'** is bushy, with lateral racemes of dark violet flowers; ↕ 18in (45cm). **'Rotfuchs'** ■ syn. 'Red Fox', has very deep pink flowers; ↕↔ 12in (30cm). **'White Icicle'** see 'Icicle'.
***V.* 'Sunny Border Blue'** ■ Clump-forming perennial with lance-shaped, crinkled, toothed, glossy, dark green leaves, 2–3in (5–8cm) long. Bears erect, sturdy spikes, to 7in (18cm) long, of tubular, dark violet-blue flowers, from early summer to late autumn. ↕ 18–20in (45–50cm), ↔ 12in (30cm). Zone 4.
V. teucrium see *V. austriaca* subsp. *teucrium.*
V. virginica see *Veronicastrum virginicum.*

VERONICASTRUM

SCROPHULARIACEAE

Genus of 2 species of erect perennials, one from Siberia, one from North America, occurring in open woodland, scrub, prairies, meadows, and grassy mountain sites. Imposing in stature, they have whorls of 3–7 more or less horizontal, simple, toothed leaves. They bear veronica-like racemes of salverform, white to pale pink or bluish purple flowers, terminally and from the upper leaf axils; each flower has a long, slender tube and 4 or 5 short lobes. Use to add height to a mixed summer border.
• **CULTIVATION** Grow in moderately fertile, humus-rich, moist soil in full sun or partial shade.
• **PROPAGATION** Sow seed in containers in a cold frame in autumn. Divide in spring or autumn.
• **PESTS AND DISEASES** Prone to downy mildew, powdery mildew, and leaf spot.

V. virginicum, syn. *Veronica virginica* (Culver's root). Erect, usually hairless perennial with unbranched stems bearing lance-shaped to inversely lance-

Veronicastrum virginicum f. *album*

shaped, pointed, toothed, dark green leaves, to 6in (15cm) long, in whorls of 3–7. From midsummer to early autumn, produces tubular, white to pink or bluish purple flowers, ¼in (6mm) long, with protruding stamens, in slender, dense, terminal and axillary racemes. ↕ to 6ft (2m), ↔ 18in (45cm). Ontario to Texas. Zone 3. **f. *album*** ■ has white flowers.

VERTICORDIA

MYRTACEAE

Genus of about 50 species of heath-like, evergreen shrubs from usually sandy or gravel heathland in Australia. They are grown for their leafy racemes or corymbs of showy flowers, produced terminally or from the upper leaf axils; each flower has 5 feathery, often colored sepals and 5 entire or toothed petals. The leathery leaves are small, simple, and usually borne in opposite pairs. Where winter temperatures fall below 45°F (7°C), grow in a temperate greenhouse. In warmer, dry climates, use in a border.
• **CULTIVATION** Under glass, grow in acidic potting mix with added sharp sand, in full light. In growth, water moderately and apply a low-phosphate, low-nitrogen fertilizer monthly. Water sparingly in winter. Outdoors, grow in moderately fertile, neutral to acidic, sharply drained soil in full sun. Pruning group 8 or 9; may need restrictive pruning under glass.
• **PROPAGATION** Sow seed at 55–64°F (13–18°C) in spring. Take semi-ripe cuttings in summer.

Verticordia plumosa

• **PESTS AND DISEASES** Spider mites may be a problem under glass.

V. grandis (Scarlet featherflower). Usually erect, sparsely branched, open shrub with crowded, rounded, semi-glossy, grayish to deep green leaves, ⅜–½in (0.8–1.5cm) long. From spring to summer, bears deep bright scarlet to pink flowers, ¾–1in (2–2.5cm) across, in dense corymbs, to 5in (13cm) across, either terminally or from the upper leaf axils. ↕↔ 3–6ft (1–2m). W. Australia. ❄ (min. 45°F/7°C)
V. plumosa ■ (Featherflower). Erect, bushy shrub with crowded, linear, cylindrical, gray-green leaves, ½in (1.5cm) long. Terminal corymbs, 1¼in (3cm) across, of many pink or white flowers, to ⅜in (9mm) wide, are borne from spring to autumn. ↕↔ to 36in (90cm). Granite outcrops in S.W. Australia. ❄ (min. 45°F/7°C)

VESTIA

SOLANACEAE

Genus of one species of evergreen shrub found in woodland in Chile, cultivated for its attractive but malodorous foliage and flowers. The leaves are alternate, obovate to elliptic, and glossy, dark green. The pendent, pale yellow flowers are borne singly or in clusters. Grow in a sheltered border or against a sunny wall where marginally hardy. Where temperatures fall much below 23°F (-5°C), grow in a cool greenhouse.
• **CULTIVATION** Under glass, grow in soil-based potting mix in full light, shaded from hot sun. In the growing season, water moderately and apply a balanced liquid fertilizer monthly. Water sparingly in winter. Outdoors, grow in any well-drained soil in full sun. Where marginally hardy, provide winter protection. Pruning group 8.
• **PROPAGATION** Sow seed in containers in a cold frame in autumn, or take semi-ripe cuttings in summer.
• **PESTS AND DISEASES** Infrequent.

V. foetida ■ syn. *V. lycioides.* Erect, evergreen shrub with glossy, dark green leaves, to 2in (5cm) long, unpleasantly scented when crushed. Bears pendent, tubular, pale yellow flowers, to 1¼in (3cm) long, with protruding stamens, singly or in clusters from the leaf axils midspring to midsummer. ↕ 6ft (2m), ↔ 5ft (1.5m). Chile. ❄ (min. 35°F/2°C)
V. lycioides see *V. foetida.*

Vestia foetida

VIBURNUM

CAPRIFOLIACEAE

Genus of 150 or more species of evergreen, semi-evergreen, and deciduous shrubs, sometimes trees, from thickets and woodland, mainly in N. temperate regions, but extending to S.E. Asia and South America. They are cultivated for their foliage, flowers, and fruits. The mostly lance-shaped to rounded, entire or toothed, sometimes lobed leaves are arranged in opposite pairs, occasionally in whorls of 3; they are often rough and prominently veined, and, in most deciduous species, color attractively in autumn. The sometimes fragrant, white or cream, pink-flushed, or wholly pink flowers are salverform to tubular, or tubular-trumpet-shaped, each with 5 usually spreading lobes. They are borne in terminal or axillary panicles, clusters, corymbs, or cymes, which are often spherical or domed. Some species have flowers in flattened heads, similar to those of "lacecap" hydrangeas, in which the small, fertile central flowers are surrounded by larger, flat or saucer-shaped, sterile ray florets. The ornamental fruits are usually spherical or ovoid, and may be red, blue, or black.

Viburnums are suitable for a shrub border or woodland garden, and for attracting wildlife. Many show self-incompatibility; fruiting is often best if several seedlings of the same species are planted together so that cross-pollination can occur. The fruits of viburnums may cause mild stomach upset if ingested.

• **CULTIVATION** Grow in any moderately fertile, moist but well-drained soil in full sun or partial shade. *V. lantanoides* needs acidic soil. Where not hardy, shelter evergreen viburnums from cold, drying winds. Pruning group 1 for evergreens; group 8 for deciduous viburnums. *V. tinus* and most deciduous viburnums tolerate hard pruning.

• **PROPAGATION** Sow seed in containers in a cold frame, or in a seedbed, in autumn. Take greenwood cuttings of deciduous viburnums, and semi-ripe cuttings of evergreens, in summer.

• **PESTS AND DISEASES** Gray mold (*Botrytis*), rust, downy mildew, powdery mildew, wood rot, *Verticillium* wilt, leaf spots, and dieback occur. Aphids, scale insects, weevils, Japanese beetles, mealybugs, and tree hoppers are common.

V. acerifolium ■ (Mapleleaf viburnum, Possumhaw). Upright, deciduous shrub with maple-like, 3-lobed, dark green leaves, to 5in (13cm) long, turning orange, red, and purple in autumn. In early summer, bears small, tubular white flowers, ¼in (6mm) across, in long-stalked cymes, 3in (8cm) across, at the shoot tips. Ovoid red fruit, ⅜in (9mm) long, ripen to purple-black. ↕ 3–6ft (1–2m), ↔ 4ft (1.2m). E. North America. Zone 5b.
V. alnifolium see *V. lantanoides.*
V. x bodnantense (*V. farreri* x *V. grandiflorum*). Upright, deciduous shrub with ovate to oblong, toothed, dark green leaves, to 4in (10cm) long, bronze when young. Heavily scented, tubular, rich rose-red to white-pink flowers, to ½in (1.5cm) across, are borne in dense, terminal and axillary clusters, to 3in (8cm) across, on bare wood, in late winter and early spring. Virtually sterile, producing a few small, spherical, blue-black or purple fruit, ⅛–¼in (3–6mm) across. ↕ 10ft (3m), ↔ 6ft (2m). Garden origin. Zone 7. Mainly grown as the following cultivars. **'Charles Lamont'** bears bright pink flowers. **'Dawn'** ■ has dark pink flowers, aging to white, strongly flushed pink. **'Deben'** bears white flowers, faintly pink-flushed in winter.
V. x burkwoodii (*V. carlesii* x *V. utile*). Open, rounded, bushy, evergreen to deciduous shrub producing ovate, sparsely toothed, glossy, dark green leaves, to 4in (10cm) long. Tubular, fragrant white flowers, ½in (1.5cm) across, in domed, terminal corymbs, to 3½in (9cm) across, open from pink buds in mid- and late spring; they are followed by flattened, ellipsoid red fruit, ½in (1.5cm) long, ripening to black in autumn. ↕↔ 8ft (2.5m). Garden origin. Zone 6. **'Anne Russell'** is compact and deciduous, with fragrant flowers; ↕ 6ft (2m), ↔ 5ft (1.5m). **'Chenaultii'** is compact, with pale pink flowers and leaves that turn bronze in autumn; ↕↔ 5ft (1.5m). **'Fulbrook'**, syn. *V.* 'Fulbrook', has very fragrant white flowers. **'Mohawk'** ■ is compact, with leaves that turn orange-red in autumn, and abundant, dark red flower buds that open to white petals with red-blotched reverses. Resistant to bacterial leaf spot and powdery mildew. **'Park Farm Hybrid'** produces dark pink flowers, fading to white, in broad corymbs, to 5in (13cm) across; some leaves turn orange and red in autumn.
V. x carlcephalum ■ (*V. carlesii* x *V. macrocephalum*). Rounded, bushy, deciduous shrub with broadly heart-shaped, irregularly toothed, dark green leaves, 5in (13cm) long, turning red in autumn. Tubular-trumpet-shaped, fragrant white flowers, ½in (1.5cm) across, in domed, terminal corymbs, 6in (15cm) across, open from pink buds in late spring. ↕↔ 10ft (3m). Garden origin. Zone 6.
V. carlesii (Koreanspice viburnum). Dense, bushy, deciduous shrub with ovate, irregularly toothed, dark green leaves, to 4in (10cm) long, often turning red in autumn. In mid- and late spring, pink buds open to tubular, very fragrant, white or pink-flushed white flowers, ½in (1.5cm) across, produced in domed, terminal corymbs, to 3in (8cm) across; they are followed by ellipsoid red fruit, ¼in (6mm) long,

Viburnum acerifolium

Viburnum x *bodnantense* 'Dawn'

ripening to black. ↕↔ 6ft (2m). Korea, Japan (Tsushima Island). Zone 5b. **'Compactum'** is compact in habit; ↕ to 3½ft (1.1m).
***V.* 'Cayuga'.** Compact, spreading, upright, deciduous shrub with broadly ovate to elliptic, scalloped, dark green leaves, 1–3in (2.5–8cm) long. In early spring, pink buds open to salverform, waxy, fragrant white flowers, ½in (1.5cm) across, starting from one side of each hemispherical cyme, 2–3in (5–8cm) across; nearly all cymes bear buds and flowers simultaneously. ↕ to 5ft (1.5m), ↔ to 4ft (1.2m). Zone 5.
***V.* 'Chesapeake'** ■ Compact, dense mound-forming, semi-evergreen shrub with ovate, slightly wavy-margined, leathery, glossy, dark green leaves, to 4in (10cm) long. Pink buds open to salverform, fragrant white flowers, ½in (1.5cm) across, borne in domed, terminal corymbs, 3½in (9cm) across, in mid- and late spring. Virtually sterile. ↕ 6ft (2m), ↔ 10ft (3m). Zone 5.
V. davidii ■ Dome-shaped, compact, evergreen shrub with oval, indistinctly toothed, 3-veined, dark green leaves, to 6in (15cm) long. Tiny, tubular white flowers, ⅛in (3mm) across, are borne in flattened, terminal cymes, 3in (8cm) across, in late spring; they are followed by ovoid, metallic-blue fruit, ¼in (6mm) long. Both male and female plants are needed to produce fruit. ↕↔ 3–5ft (1–1.5m). W. China. Zone 7.
V. dentatum ■ (Arrow-wood). Upright, deciduous shrub with arching branches and ovate to rounded, coarsely toothed, dark green leaves, to 4½in (11cm) long, turning yellow or red in

Viburnum x *burkwoodii* 'Mohawk'

Viburnum x *carlcephalum*

autumn. Tiny, tubular white flowers, ⅛in (3mm) across, are borne in flattened, terminal corymbs, 4in (10cm) across, in late spring and early summer; they are followed by ovoid, blue-black fruit, ⅜in (9mm) long. ↕↔ 10ft (3m). E. North America. Zone 3.
V. dilatatum ■ (Linden viburnum). Upright, deciduous shrub producing broadly ovate to rounded or obovate, coarsely toothed, dark green leaves, to 5in (13cm) long, turning bronze to red in autumn. Small, salverform white flowers, ¼in (6mm) across, are borne in domed, terminal corymbs, to 5in (13cm) across, in late spring and early summer. The flowers are followed by showy, ovoid, bright red fruit, ⅜in (9mm) long. ↕ 10ft (3m), ↔ 6ft (2m). China, Japan. Zone 5. **'Catskill'** is compact, with leaves turning yellow, orange, and red in autumn, and bears dark red fruit; ↕ 5ft (1.5m), ↔ 8ft (2.5m). **'Erie'** is mound-forming, bearing large cymes, to 6in (15cm) across, and a profusion of coral-red fruit turning pink in winter; ↕ 6ft (2m), ↔ 10ft (3m). **'Iroquois'** ■ is a dense, exceptionally heavy-fruited form. **'Xanthocarpum'** bears yellow fruit.
***V.* 'Eskimo'.** Mound-forming, compact semi-evergreen shrub producing ovate, leathery, glossy, dark green leaves, to 4in (10cm) long. In mid- and late spring, pink-tinged cream buds open to tubular pure white flowers, ½in (1.5cm) across, borne in dense, terminal, almost spherical corymbs, 4in (10cm) across. ↕↔ 5ft (1.5m). Zone 6b.
V. farreri, syn. *V. fragrans*. Erect, deciduous shrub with oval, toothed,

Viburnum 'Chesapeake'

V

Viburnum davidii

Viburnum dilatatum

Viburnum macrocephalum

dark green leaves, to 4in (10cm) long, bronze when young, turning red-purple in autumn. Tubular, fragrant, white or pink-tinged white flowers, ½in (1.5cm) long, are borne in dense, terminal and lateral clusters, to 2in (5cm) across, in mild weather, in winter and early spring on bare stems; they are followed by spherical, bright red fruit, ¼in (6mm) long. ↕ 10ft (3m), ↔ 8ft (2.5m). N. China. Zone 5b. **'Album'** see 'Candidissimum'. **'Candidissimum'**, syn. 'Album', has leaves that are pale green when young, and white flowers, followed by pale yellow fruit. **'Nanum'** forms a dense mound, but is not free-flowering; ↕ 30in (75cm), ↔ 3ft (1m).
V. foetens. Upright, deciduous shrub with oblong, dark green leaves, to 4in (10cm) long. From late autumn to early spring, produces tubular, fragrant, white or pink-tinged white flowers, 2in (5cm) long, in flattened, terminal clusters, to 2in (5cm) across, on bare stems; they are followed by ovoid red fruit, to ½in (1.5cm) long, ripening to black. ↕↔ 6ft (2m). Himalayas. Zone 7.
V. fragrans see *V. farreri.*
***V.* 'Fulbrook'** see *V.* x *burkwoodii* 'Fulbrook'.
V. grandiflorum. Open, upright, deciduous shrub with thick shoots and elliptic, finely and irregularly toothed, dark green leaves, to 4in (10cm) long, turning dark purple in autumn. From winter to early spring, tubular, fragrant, pink-flushed white flowers, to ¾in (2cm) across, are borne on bare stems in flattened, terminal clusters, to 3in (8cm) across; they are followed by ovoid, black-purple fruit, to ¾in (2cm) long. ↕↔ 6ft (2m). Himalayas, W. China. Zone 7b. **'Snow White'** has white flowers, flushed pink on the backs of the lobes, opening from dark pink buds.
V. japonicum. Rounded, evergreen shrub with thick shoots and ovate to rounded, leathery, sparsely toothed, glossy, dark green leaves, to 6in (15cm) long. Small, tubular, fragrant white flowers, ½in (1.5cm) across, in spherical cymes, to 4in (10cm) across, are borne in early summer, followed by ovoid, bright red fruit, ⅜in (9mm) long, which last into winter. ↕ 6ft (2m), ↔ 8ft (2.5m). Japan. Zone 8.
V.* x *juddii ■ (*V. bitchiuense* x *V. carlesii*). Rounded, bushy, deciduous shrub with oval, dark green leaves, to 2½in (6cm) long, sometimes turning red in autumn. Small, salverform, fragrant, pink-tinged white flowers, ¼in (6mm) across, in almost spherical corymbs, to 3½in (9cm) across, open from pink buds in mid- and late spring. ↕ 4ft (1.2m), ↔ 5ft (1.5m). Garden origin. Zone 5.
V. lantana (Wayfaring tree). Vigorous, upright, deciduous shrub with broadly ovate, finely toothed, gray-green leaves, to 5in (13cm) long, often turning red in autumn. Small, tubular white flowers, ¼in (6mm) across, in loosely domed cymes, to 4in (10cm) across, are borne in late spring and early summer; they are followed by ovoid-oblong red fruit, ⅜in (9mm) long, ripening to black. ↕ 15ft (5m), ↔ 12ft (4m). Europe, N. Africa, S.W. Asia. Zone 2b. **'Mohican'** is compact, with dark green foliage and orange-red fruit; resists bacterial leaf spot; ↕↔ 8ft (2.5m).
V. lantanoides, syn. *V. alnifolium* (Hobble bush). Spreading, deciduous shrub, the outer branches prostrate and rooting in the soil. Broadly ovate to rounded, irregularly toothed, dark green leaves, to 8in (20cm) long, turn yellow to red or purple in autumn. In late spring and early summer, bears lacecap-like, terminal cymes, to 5in (13cm) wide, of tubular, white, fertile central flowers, ⅛in (3mm) across, surrounded by saucer-shaped, white, sterile ray florets, to 1in (2.5cm) across; they are followed by ovoid red fruit, ⅜in (9mm) long, ripening to black-purple. Prefers partial shade. ↕ 8ft (2.5m), ↔ 12ft (4m). E. North America. Zone 3.
V. lentago (Nannyberry, Sheepberry). Vigorous, upright, deciduous shrub or small tree, producing oval, finely toothed, glossy, dark green leaves, to 4in (10cm) long, turning red and purple in autumn. Small, tubular, fragrant, creamy white flowers, to ¼in (6mm) across, are borne in flattened, terminal cymes, to 4½in (11cm) across, in late spring and early summer, followed by ovoid, blue-black fruit, ½in (1.5cm) long. ↕ 12ft (4m), ↔ 10ft (3m). E. North America. Zone 2.
V. macrocephalum ■ (Chinese snowball). Rounded shrub, sometimes tree-like, semi-evergreen or evergreen in mild climates, deciduous where winters are severe, with ovate to elliptic, toothed, dark green leaves, to 4in (10cm) long. In late spring, salverform, sterile white flowers, 1¼in (3cm) across, are borne in dense, terminal cymes, to 6in (15cm) across. Does not bear fruit. ↕↔ 15ft (5m). Garden origin. Zone 7b.
V. mariesii see *V. plicatum* 'Mariesii'.
V. nudum (Smooth witherod). Spreading, bushy, deciduous shrub with elliptic to oblong, very glossy, dark green leaves, 1½–3½in (4–9cm) long, turning red to reddish purple in the fall. In early summer, bears white flowers, ¼in (6mm) across, in cymes, 2–5in (5–13cm) across; these are followed by ovoid, pink to blue fruit, ⅜in (9mm) long, that ripens to black. ↕ 12–15ft (4–5m), ↔ 6ft (2m). New York to Louisiana. Zone 5b. **'Winterthur'** ■ has leaves that turn a brighter red than the species, and abundant fruit.
V. odoratissimum (Sweet viburnum). Vigorous, bushy, evergreen shrub with oval, glossy, dark green leaves, to 8in (20cm) long. Small, tubular, fragrant white flowers, ¼in (6mm) across, are produced in broadly conical panicles, 3–4in (8–10cm) long, in late spring, followed by ovoid red fruit, ½in (1.5cm) long, ripening to black. ↕↔ 15ft (5m). India, China, Burma, Philippines, Japan. ❀ (min. 35°F/2°C)
***V.* 'Oneida'.** Upright, wide-spreading, deciduous shrub with thin, rounded, broadly ovate, or broadly obovate, coarsely toothed, shiny, softly hairy, dark green leaves, 2–5in (5–13cm) long, turning pale yellow and orange-red in autumn. In late spring and sporadically throughout the summer, bears flat, lacecap-like cymes, 3–5in (8–13cm) across, of abundant, salverform, creamy white flowers, ¼in (6mm) across, followed by ovoid, glossy, persistent, dark red fruit, ⅜in (9mm) long. ↕ 10ft (3m), ↔ 9ft (2.5m). Zone 5.

Viburnum dentatum

Viburnum dilatatum 'Iroquois'

Viburnum x *juddii*

Viburnum nudum 'Winterthur'

V

Viburnum opulus

Viburnum plicatum f. *plicatum* 'Roseum'

Viburnum plicatum f. *tomentosum* 'Pink Beauty'

Viburnum rhytidophyllum

V. opulus ■ (European cranberry bush, Guelder rose). Vigorous, bushy, deciduous shrub with maple-like, usually 3-lobed, dark green leaves, to 4in (10cm) long, turning red in autumn. In late spring and early summer, bears flat, lacecap-like, terminal cymes, to 3in (8cm) across, composed of tubular, white, fertile central flowers, ¾in (2cm) across, surrounded by showy, flat, white, sterile ray florets, to ¾in (2cm) across; they are followed by spherical, fleshy, bright red fruit, ⅜in (9mm) across. ↕15ft (5m), ↔12ft (4m). Europe, N. Africa, C. Asia. Zone 2b. **'Compactum'** is slow-growing and dense; ↕↔5ft (1.5m). **'Roseum'**, syn. 'Sterile' (Snowball bush), has a rounded habit, with leaves that become purple-tinted in autumn; it bears large, white or green-tinted white, sterile flowers, ½in (1.5cm) long, sometimes turning pink, in spherical cymes, 2–2½in (5–6cm) across; ↕↔ to 12ft (4m). **'Sterile'** see 'Roseum'. **'Xanthocarpum'** ■ produces bright yellow fruit.
V. plicatum* f. *plicatum (Japanese snowball bush). Spreading, bushy, deciduous shrub with heart-shaped, tapered, toothed, deeply veined, dark green leaves, to 4in (10cm) long, turning red-purple in autumn. In late spring, bears saucer-shaped, sterile white flowers, to 1¼in (3cm) across, in dense, spherical, terminal cymes, 3in (8cm) across. Does not produce fruit. ↕10ft (3m), ↔12ft (4m). Garden origin. Zone 6. **'Grandiflorum'** has larger flowerheads, to 4in (10cm) across. **'Roseum'** ■ bears pink-tinted flowerheads.
V. plicatum* f. *tomentosum ■ syn. *V. tomentosum* (Doublefile viburnum). Horizontally branched, deciduous shrub with broadly ovate to oblong-ovate, toothed, dark green leaves, 2–4in (5–10cm) long, softly hairy beneath. In midspring, produces double rows of flattened, lacecap-like cymes, to 4in (10cm) across, with tiny, fertile central flowers and larger, sterile outer florets, to 1¼in (3cm) across. Ovoid red fruit, ⅜in (9mm) long, ripen to black. ↕10ft (3m), ↔12ft (4m). China, Japan. Zone 5. **'Lanarth'** has large, sterile florets, to 2in (5cm) or more across, and bears few fruit. **'Mariesii'**, syn. *V. mariesii*, has distinctly layered, tiered branches, and few fruit. **'Nanum Semperflorens'**, syn. 'Nanum', 'Watanabei', *V. semperflorens, V. watanabei*, is low-growing and compact, blooming from late spring to autumn; ↕6ft (2m), ↔5ft (1.5m). **'Pink Beauty'** ■ produces white sterile florets maturing to pink. **'Shasta'** is lower-growing, but has wide-spreading, horizontal branches and bears many large inflorescences, 4–6in (10–15cm) across, of white flowers, to 2in (5cm) across, in late spring and early summer; ↕6ft (2m), ↔10–12ft (3–4m). **'Shoshoni'** is compact; ↕5ft (1.5m), ↔8ft (2.5m). **'Watanabei'** see 'Nanum Semperflorens'.
***V.* 'Pragense'**. Rounded, bushy, evergreen shrub with elliptic, deeply veined, wrinkled, wavy-margined, glossy, dark green leaves, to 4in (10cm) long. Tubular white flowers, ¼–⅜in (6–9mm) across, opening from pink buds, are produced in domed, terminal, umbel-like cymes, to 4in (10cm) across, in late spring. ↕↔10ft (3m). Zone 7.
V. propinquum. Compact, bushy, evergreen shrub with ovate-lance-shaped to elliptic, sparsely toothed, 3-veined, glossy, dark green leaves, to 3½in (9cm) long. Bears tiny, tubular, greenish white flowers, ⅛in (3mm) across, in flattened, terminal cymes, to 3in (8cm) across, in late spring, sometimes followed by ovoid, blue-black fruit, ¼in (6mm long. ↕10ft (3m), ↔6ft (2m). C. and W. China, Taiwan, Philippines. ❀ (min. 35°F/2°C)
V. prunifolium ■ (Blackhaw viburnum). Round-headed tree or stiffly branched, deciduous shrub with broadly elliptic to ovate, toothed, hairless, shiny, dark green leaves, 1½–3½in (4–9cm) long, pale green beneath, turning purple to reddish purple in autumn. In late spring, bears flattened cymes, 2–4in (5–10cm) across, of salverform, creamy white flowers, to 1in (2.5cm) across, followed by ovoid, glaucous, edible, pink-rose fruit, to ½in (1.5cm) long, ripening to bluish black. ↕12–15ft (4–5m), ↔8–12ft (2.5–4m). Michigan and Connecticut south to Texas and Florida. Zone 3.
V. x rhytidophylloides (*V. lantana* x *V. rhytidophyllum*). Spreading, semi-evergreen shrub with arching shoots clothed in oblong, wavy-margined, dark green leaves, to 8in (20cm) long. In late spring, small, tubular, creamy white flowers, ¼in (6mm) across, are borne in flattened, terminal, umbel-like cymes, to 4in (10cm) across; they are followed by ovoid red fruit, ⅜in (9mm) long, which ripen to black. ↕10ft (3m), ↔12ft (4m). Garden origin. Zone 5. **'Alleghany'** is dense and rounded, with darker green leaves and abundant, yellowish white flowers. **'Willowwood'** has deeply veined, glossy leaves.
V. rhytidophyllum ■ (Leatherleaf viburnum). Vigorous, erect, evergreen shrub with oblong to lance-shaped, wavy-margined, very deeply veined, glossy, dark green leaves, 8in (20cm) or more long. In late spring, bears small, tubular, creamy white flowers, ¼in (6mm) across, in dense, domed, terminal, umbel-like cymes, to 8in (20cm) across, followed by ovoid red fruit, ⅜in (9mm) long, ripening to glossy black. ↕15ft (5m), ↔12ft (4m). C. and W. China. Zone 5b.
V. sargentii (Sargent viburnum). Bushy, deciduous shrub with maple-like, 3-lobed, toothed leaves, to 5in (13cm) long, bronze when young, often turning yellow or red in autumn. Flat, lacecap-like cymes, to 4in (10cm) across, with a central mass of tiny, tubular, white, fertile flowers surrounded by saucer-shaped, white, sterile ray florets, ¾in (2cm) across, are borne in late spring. The flowers are followed by spherical, bright red fruit, ½in (1.5cm) across. ↕↔10ft (3m). N.E. Asia. Zone 3b. **'Onondaga'** ■ is upright, with dark bronze-purple foliage aging to dark green, turning red-purple in autumn. Fertile flowers are dark red in bud, opening pink-flushed white; ↔6ft (2m). **'Susquehanna'** is broad-spreading, with thick, heavy branches and abundant flowers; ↕↔12–15ft (4–5m).

Viburnum opulus 'Xanthocarpum'

Viburnum plicatum f. *tomentosum*

Viburnum prunifolium

Viburnum sargentii 'Onondaga'

Viburnum setigerum

V. semperflorens see *V. plicatum* 'Nanum Semperflorens'.
V. setigerum ■ (Tea viburnum). Upright, bushy, deciduous shrub, often leggy at the base, with ovate-oblong, slightly toothed, blue-green to dark green leaves, 3–6in (8–15cm) long. In spring, bears flat-topped cymes, 1–2in (2.5–5cm) across, of white flowers, followed by abundant, ovoid, bright red fruit, ⅓in (9mm) long. ↕ 8–12ft (2.5–4m), ↔ 5–8ft (1.5–2.5m). C. and W. China. Zone 6. **'Aurantiacum'** bears orange fruit.
V. sieboldii. Large, deciduous shrub or small tree with arching shoots and elliptic to obovate, coarsely toothed, unpleasantly scented, glossy, dark green leaves, to 5in (13cm) long. Small, tubular white flowers, ¼in (6mm) across, are borne in flattened, terminal cymes, to 4in (10cm) across, in late spring, and followed by ovoid, rose-red, showy fruit, ½in (1.5cm) long, which ripen to black. ↕ 12ft (4m), ↔ 20ft (6m). Japan. Zone 4. **'Seneca'** is tree-like, with abundant red fruit on persistent, showy red flower stalks.
V. tinus. (Laurustinus). Compact, bushy, evergreen shrub with narrowly ovate to oblong, dark green leaves, to 4in (10cm) long. Bears small, salverform white flowers, ¼in (6mm) across, in flattened, terminal cymes, to 4in (10cm) across, over a long period in late winter and spring; they are followed by ovoid, dark blue-black fruit, ¼in (6mm) long. ↕↔ 10ft (3m). Mediterranean. Zone 7b. **'Eve Price'** ■ is dense, with leaves to 3in (8cm) long, and pink flower buds. **'Gwenllian'** bears a profusion of pink-

Viburnum tinus 'Eve Price'

Viburnum tinus 'Variegatum'

flushed white flowers opening from dark pink buds, and fruits freely. **'Lucidum'** is vigorous, with very glossy leaves; each flower is ½in (1.5cm) across. **'Pink Prelude'** has white flowers opening from pink buds and aging to pink. **'Purpureum'** has young foliage tinged dark bronze-purple. **'Variegatum'** ■ has leaves broadly margined with creamy yellow; needs more shelter than green-leaved forms.
V. tomentosum see *V. plicatum* f. *tomentosum.*
V. trilobum (American cranberry bush). Dense, rounded, deciduous shrub producing maple-like, 3-lobed, dark green leaves, to 5in (13cm) long, bronze when young, turning yellow to red in autumn. In late spring, bears flattened, lacecap-like, terminal cymes, to 4in (10cm) across, of tiny, tubular, white, fertile central flowers, ¾in (2cm) across, surrounded by showy, flat, white, sterile florets, to ¾in (2cm) across. The flowers are followed by edible, spherical red fruit, ⅜in (9mm) across. ↕ 15ft (5m), ↔ 12ft (4m). North America. Zone 2. **'Alfredo'** is dense and broad in habit, with brilliant red autumn color; ↕ 5–6ft (1.5–2m). **'Andrews'** produces fruit that ripen early. **'Hahs'** bears fruit in midseason. **'Wentworth'** has rich red autumn leaf color and produces yellow-red fruit that ripen to bright red, late in the season.
V. watanabei see *V. plicatum* 'Nanum Semperflorens'.

VICIA

LEGUMINACEAE

Genus of 150 species of annual and perennial beans, native to N. Africa and S.W. Asia. Many climb by tendrils at the tips of the leaves. They bear violet-blotched flowers, and 1–3 pairs of leaves, to 4in (10cm). The plump fruit is 12in (30cm) long and more than 1in (2.5cm) wide.
• **CULTIVATION** Requires moist conditions and full sun.
• **PROPAGATION** Sow seed 1in (2.5cm) deep, 4–6in (10–15cm) apart.
• **PESTS AND DISEASES** Susceptible to aphids and viral disease.

V. faba (Fava bean, Bread bean, Horse bean). An upright annual having divided leaves and no tendrils. White flowers, with purple splotch, are borne in the leaf axils, followed by oblong edible seed pods. ↕ to 6ft (2m), ↔ to 12in (30cm). N. Africa, S.W. Asia.

VICTORIA

Giant waterlily

NYMPHAEACEAE

Genus of 2 species of rhizomatous, submerged, deep-water aquatic annuals or perennials occurring in tropical South America, in the slow-moving backwaters of the Amazon. Their thick rhizomes support enormous, rounded, floating leaves, and bear night-blooming, pineapple-scented, waterlily-like flowers. In tropical gardens, grow giant waterlilies in a large pool; elsewhere, grow as long-season annuals in a heated pool in a warm greenhouse.
• **CULTIVATION** Outdoors, grow in a pool at least 3ft (1m) deep in full sun; grow in aquatic containers, 3ft (1m) across and 24in (60cm) deep, of rich, loamy soil, with added well-rotted organic matter. Under glass, grow in containers of loamy soil in an indoor pool with a water temperature of 70–75°F (21–24°C) in summer; provide full light. During the growing season, add pellets of slow-release fertilizer to the growing medium every 2 weeks. See also pp.52–53.
• **PROPAGATION** Collect seeds when ripe and overwinter in water. In late winter, sow at 84–90°F (29–32°C), covering seeds with 2–3in (5–8cm) of water.
• **PESTS AND DISEASES** Infrequent.

V. amazonica ■ (Amazon waterlily, Royal waterlily). Submerged, deep-water aquatic annual or perennial with thick rhizomes supporting rounded, mid-green, floating leaves, to 6ft (2m) long, reddish purple beneath; they have large prickles and vertical rims, to 6in (15cm) high. In summer, bears many-petaled, waterlily-like white flowers, to 12in (30cm) across, aging pink, with prickly sepals. ↔ 20ft (6m). South America (Amazon). ❀ (min. 77°F/25°C to remain perennial)
V. cruziana, syn. *V. trickeri* (Santa Cruz waterlily). Submerged, deep-water aquatic annual or perennial with thick rhizomes supporting rounded, floating leaves, to 4½ft (1.4m) long, with vertical rims, to 8in (20cm) high. Leaves are mid-green above, densely softly hairy and reddish purple beneath, but the undersides are less highly colored than those of *V. amazonica.* Many-petaled, waterlily-like white flowers, to 4in (10cm) across, are produced during summer, the sepals with basal prickles only. ↔ 20ft (6m). South America (Bolivia, Brazil, N. Argentina, Paraguay). ❀ (min. 72–77°F/22–25°C to remain perennial)
***V.* 'Longwood Hybrid'** (*V. amazonica* x *V. cruziana*). Submerged, deep-water aquatic annual or perennial with a thick rhizome supporting rounded, mid-green, floating leaves, to 8ft (2.5m) long, with reddish purple outer margins on the upturned rims. In summer, produces many-petaled, waterlily-like white flowers, to 12in (30cm) across, the sepals with basal prickles only. More free-flowering and hardier than its parents. ↔ 22ft (7m). Garden origin. ❀ (min. 72°F/22°C to remain perennial)
V. trickeri see *V. cruziana.*

Victoria amazonica

VIGNA

FABACEAE

Genus of about 150 species of erect and climbing or trailing annuals and evergreen perennials from woodland, scrub, and rocky areas in tropical regions of Africa, Asia, S. US, and Central and South America. Most are cultivated as agricultural crops, for their edible pods and seeds (beans); the climbers are also grown as ornamentals, for their flowers, foliage, and seed pods. The alternate leaves are palmately lobed or 3-palmate with entire leaflets. Pea-like flowers with distinctive, coiled keel petals are borne in axillary clusters or racemes, often in alternate pairs, followed by linear, straight or curved pods. Where summer temperatures average less than 61°F (16°C), grow as annuals in a warm greenhouse. Elsewhere, grow over a pergola, arch, or tall tree stump.

• **CULTIVATION** Under glass, grow in soil-based potting mix in full light. In the growing season, water freely and apply a balanced liquid fertilizer monthly; water sparingly in winter. Outdoors, grow in fertile, moist but well-drained soil in full sun. Support climbing stems. Pruning group 11.

• **PROPAGATION** Sow seed at 55–64°F (13–18°C) in autumn or spring.

• **PESTS AND DISEASES** Can be affected by powdery mildew, gray mold (*Botrytis*), rust, leaf spots, damping off, and root rot. Spider mites and whiteflies are common under glass.

V. unguiculata (Cowpea, Black-eyed pea). Trailing or bushy, vigorous-growing annual vine with oval to heart-shaped leaves, to 6in (15cm) long, and flattened pods. Bears large, dark-"eyed" seeds. ↕ to 12ft (4m). C. Africa, India.

▷ ***Villarsia nymphoides*** see *Nymphoides peltata*

VIGUIERA

ASTERACEAE

Genus of about 150 species of annuals or tender perennials and shrubs from the US to South America. The leaves are usually opposite, linear to ovate or rounded, entire to toothed, or pinnatisect. They are grown for their flowerheads, which are usually yellow, with ovate to elliptic ray florets. Grow in a mixed border. Where not hardy, treat as annuals.

• **CULTIVATION** Grow in any fertile, well-drained soil, in full sun.

• **PROPAGATION** Sow seed *in situ* as soon as ripe, divide, or take basal cuttings.

• **PESTS AND DISEASES** Rust is common; spider mites may occur.

V. multiflora. Branching perennial with lance-shaped to ovate-lance-shaped, entire or slightly toothed, mid-green leaves, to 1½in (4cm) long, opposite in the lower half of the plant, alternate above. In summer, produces yellow flowerheads with yellow disk florets, to 2in (5cm) across, in loose panicles. ↕ to 3ft (1m), ↔ 24in (60cm). S. central to S.W. US. ❄ (min. 45°F/7°C)

VINCA

Periwinkle

APOCYNACEAE

Genus of 7 species of slender-stemmed, evergreen subshrubs and herbaceous perennials from woodland in Europe, N. Africa, and C. Asia. They are grown for their opposite, simple, lance-shaped to elliptic or ovate, often variegated leaves, and for their showy, long-stalked, star-like or salverform flowers, each with 5 petal lobes, borne singly in the leaf axils. Useful groundcover for a woodland garden, shrub border, or shady bank, but may be invasive. All parts may cause mild stomach upset if ingested.

• **CULTIVATION** Grow in any but very dry soil, in full sun (for best flowering) or partial shade. To restrict growth, cut back hard in early spring.

• **PROPAGATION** Divide in early spring or mid- or late autumn. Take semi-ripe cuttings in summer.

• **PESTS AND DISEASES** May be attacked by leafhoppers, scale insects, aphids, leaf spot, and dieback.

V. difformis ■ Prostrate, evergreen subshrub with usually narrowly lance-shaped, glossy, dark green leaves, to 3in (8cm) long. In late winter and early spring, upright shoots produce pale blue to nearly white flowers, to 1½in (4cm) across. ↕ 12in (30cm), ↔ indefinite. S.W. Europe, N. Africa. ❄ (min. 35°F/2°C)
***V. herbacea* 'Hidcote Purple'** see *V. major* var. *oxyloba.*
***V. hirsuta* of gardens** see *V. major* var. *oxyloba.*
V. major (Blue buttons, Greater periwinkle). Prostrate, evergreen, trailing subshrub with arching shoots and ovate to lance-shaped, dark green leaves, to 3½in (9cm) long. Blue-violet or dark violet flowers, to 2in (5cm) across, are produced over a long period from midspring to autumn. Useful for windowboxes and tall containers. ↕ 18in (45cm), ↔ indefinite. W. Mediterranean. Zone 7. **'Dartington Star'** see var. *oxyloba.* **'Elegantissima'** see 'Variegata'. **subsp. *hirsuta*,** syn. var. *pubescens*, produces lance-shaped, distinctly hairy leaves; Republic of Georgia, Turkey. **'Maculata'** has leaves with yellow-green

Vinca difformis

Vinca major 'Variegata'

centers. **var. *oxyloba*,** syn. 'Dartington Star', *V. herbacea* 'Hidcote Purple', *V. hirsuta* of gardens, produces dark violet-blue flowers with narrow, pointed lobes. **var. *pubescens*** see subsp. *hirsuta.* **'Reticulata'** has leaves conspicuously veined with yellow or cream when young, later dark green. **'Variegata'** ■ syn. 'Elegantissima' (Vinca vine) has leaves irregularly margined creamy white.
V. minor ■ (Creeping myrtle, Lesser periwinkle). Prostrate, mat-forming, evergreen subshrub with long, trailing shoots and elliptic or lance-shaped, sometimes ovate, dark green leaves, to 2in (5cm) long. Over a long period from midspring to autumn, bears usually blue-violet, sometimes pale blue, reddish purple, or white flowers, 1–1¼in (2.5–3cm) across. ↕ 4–8in (10–20cm), ↔ indefinite. Europe, S. Russia, N. Caucasus. Zone 4. **f. *alba*** has white flowers. **'Alba Variegata',** syn. 'Alba Aureavariegata', has leaves with pale yellow margins, and bears white flowers. **'Argenteovariegata'** syn. 'Variegata', has leaves with creamy white margins, and produces light violet-blue flowers. **'Atropurpurea',** syn. 'Purpurea', 'Rubra', has dark plum-purple flowers. **'Azurea Flore Pleno',** syn. 'Caerulea Plena', has double, sky-blue flowers. **'Bowles' Blue'** see 'La Grave'. **'Bowles' Variety'** see 'La Grave'. **'Bowles' White'** bears white flowers, opening from pinkish white buds. **'Caerulea Plena'** see 'Azurea Flore Pleno'. **'Double Burgundy'** see 'Multiplex'. **'Gertrude Jekyll'** is very compact, and profusely bears white

Vinca minor

flowers. **'La Grave',** syn. 'Bowles' Blue', 'Bowles' Variety', produces lavender-blue flowers, 1¼in (3cm) across. **'Multiplex',** syn. 'Double Burgundy', produces double, plum-purple flowers. **'Purpurea'** see 'Atropurpurea'. **'Rubra'** see 'Atropurpurea'. **'Variegata'** see 'Argenteovariegata'.
V. rosea see *Catharanthus roseus.*

VIOLA *syn.* ERPETION

Pansy, Violet

VIOLACEAE

Genus of about 500 species of annuals, biennials, evergreen, semi-evergreen, and deciduous perennials (some tufted or rhizomatous), and a few deciduous subshrubs, found in varied habitats in temperate regions worldwide. They have variable, entire to finely pinnatisect, mostly mid-green leaves with stipules. Some South American species are rosette-forming, and are very similar to sempervivums. The mostly unscented flowers, borne in the leaf axils, are usually solitary, rarely paired. Each has 5 petals: a spurred lower petal, 2 lateral petals, and 2 upward-facing upper petals. Most flower profusely over long periods in summer, and may self-seed freely and become weedy.

Many cultivars within the genus are informally referred to as garden pansies, violas, or violettas; they are all derived from the complex hybridization of *V. tricolor*, *V. lutea*, *V. cornuta*, and other species. Garden pansies (*V.* x *wittrockiana* cultivars) are very short-lived perennials, with faintly scented or unscented, more or less rounded flowers, often with patterned "faces." They have a single-stemmed root system. Violas, sometimes referred to as tufted pansies, are compact, tufted perennials with usually scented, more or less rounded, often patterned flowers with rays (lines in a deeper or contrasting color), and a multi-stemmed root system. Violettas are similar to violas, but are even more compact, with small, sweetly fragrant, oval flowers, each with a central yellow mark and no rays.

The perennials and subshrubs are suitable for a rock garden, a scree bed, or the front of a border; a few are best in an alpine house. Treat garden pansies as annuals, biennials, or short-lived perennials. They are good for containers; some are suitable for bedding. Others are winter- or spring-flowering, and are ideal for planting with spring-flowering bulbs.

• **CULTIVATION** Grow in fertile, humus-rich, moist but well-drained soil in full sun or partial shade. In a rock garden, grow in poor to moderately fertile, gritty, sharply drained soil in full sun or partial shade; protect from winter moisture. In an alpine house, use a mix of equal parts loam, leaf mold, and grit or tufa chips. Deadhead to prolong flowering. After flowering, cut back vigorous plants, especially *V. cornuta*, to keep compact.

• **PROPAGATION** Sow seed in containers in a cold frame as soon as ripe or in spring; for garden pansies, sow seed in late winter for early spring and summer flowering, or in summer for winter flowering. Divide *V. biflora*, *V. cornuta*, *V. elatior*, *V. glabella*, *V. hederacea*,

Viola biflora

V. obliqua, and *V. odorata* in spring or autumn. Take stem-tip cuttings of perennials and subshrubs in spring or late summer. Many species are short-lived, so propagate them regularly.
• **PESTS AND DISEASES** Prone to mosaic viruses, downy mildew, powdery mildew, crown and root rot, rust, gray mold (*Botrytis*), spot anthracnose, and other fungal leaf spots. Slugs and snails are common, as well as aphids and violet leaf midge.

V. adunca (Hooked-spur violet, Western dog violet). Compact, tuft-forming, semi-evergreen perennial with procumbent stems bearing ovate to broadly ovate, finely toothed, smooth to slightly hairy leaves, to 1½in (4cm) long. In spring, bears scented, violet to lavender-blue flowers, ¾in (2cm) across, with white spurs, to ¾in (2cm) long, and white eyes. Suitable for a rock garden; self-seeds freely. ↕↔ to 3in (8cm). N. US. Zone 4. **var. *minor*** see *V. labradorica*.
V. aetolica. Neat, clump-forming, short-lived, evergreen perennial with short, spreading stems and ovate to lance-shaped, scalloped leaves, to ¾in (2cm) long. In late spring and early summer, produces yellow flowers, to ¾in (2cm) across; the slightly darker lower petals have spurs to ¼in (6mm) long. ↕ to 3in (8cm), ↔ to 6in (15cm). E. Europe. Zone 7.
V. beckwithii (Great Basin violet). Small, tufted, evergreen perennial with spreading stems and palmately 3-lobed, hairy, conspicuously veined leaves, 1¼in (3cm) long, each lobe pinnatifid with linear segments. In spring, bears solitary, slightly scented flowers, ¾in (2cm) across, with spurs to 1/16in (2mm) long; the 2 upper petals are deep reddish violet, the 3 lower ones pale lavender-blue with purple-veined yellow bases. Best in an alpine house; difficult to grow. ↕ 2–5in (5–13cm), ↔ to 4in (10cm). North America (Great Basin area). Zone 6.

V. biflora ▣ (Twin-flowered violet). Dwarf, creeping herbaceous perennial with slender rhizomes and thin stems bearing kidney- to heart-shaped, toothed, pale green leaves, 1¼–1½in (3–4cm) long, with scalloped margins. In late spring and summer, bears solitary or paired, deep lemon flowers, ½in (1.5cm) across, veined dark purple-brown on the lower petals and with spurs to ⅛in (3mm) long. Prefers moist soil in partial shade. ↕ to 3in (8cm), ↔ to 8in (20cm). Europe to N. Asia, Alaska, Rocky Mountains. Zone 4.
V. canina (Dog violet, Heath violet). Rhizomatous, semi-evergreen perennial with decumbent to erect stems and ovate to ovate-lance-shaped, entire leaves, ½–¾in (1–2cm) long, shallowly heart-shaped at the bases. In spring and early summer, bears solitary, bright blue or violet flowers, to 1in (2.5cm) across, each with a straight, pale yellowish green or white spur, ½in (1.5cm) long. ↕↔ 6–12in (15–30cm). Temperate Europe and W. Asia. Zone 6b.
V. cazorlensis ▣ Dwarf, woody-based, evergreen perennial with crowded, upright stems bearing very narrow, linear to inversely lance-shaped, entire leaves, to ½in (1.5cm) long. In late spring and early summer, produces narrow-petaled, pinkish purple flowers, ¾in (2cm) across, with notched lower petals, and slender spurs, to 1¼in (3cm) long. Difficult to grow; best in tufa or in an alpine house. ↕ to 3in (8cm), ↔ to 4in (10cm). S.E. Spain. ❄ (min. 35°F/2°C)

Viola cazorlensis

V. cornuta ▣ (Horned violet, Viola). Spreading, rhizomatous, evergreen perennial with ascending stems and ovate, toothed leaves, ¾–2in (2–5cm) long, truncate at the bases. From spring to summer, produces abundant slightly scented flowers, to 1½in (4cm) across; they have widely separated, usually violet to lilac-blue petals, the lower ones with white markings, and slender spurs, to ½in (1.5cm) long. ↕ to 6in (15cm), ↔ to 16in (40cm) or more. Spain (Pyrenees). Zone 7b. **'Chantryland'** has deep apricot flowers; ↕ 6–8in (15–20cm). **var. *minor*** is smaller in all its parts, and produces white or lavender-blue flowers, ½–¾in (1.5–2cm) across; ↕ to 3in (8cm), ↔ to 8in (20cm).
V. cucullata see *V. obliqua*.
V. elatior, syn. *V. erecta*. Upright, sparsely branched, subshrubby perennial with deciduous, lance-shaped, toothed leaves, to 3½in (9cm) long, slightly heart-shaped at the bases. Bears scented, pale lavender-blue flowers, 1in (2.5cm) across, with spurs 1/16–⅛in (2–3mm) long, over long periods in late spring and early summer. Easily grown in moist soil. ↕ to 12in (30cm), ↔ to 6in (15cm). C., S., and E. Europe to W. Asia. Zone 6.
V. erecta see *V. elatior*.
***V.* 'Etain'** ▣ Clump-forming evergreen perennial with spreading stems and ovate, toothed, bright green leaves, to 1in (2.5cm) long. In spring, bears pale lemon-yellow flowers, 1¾in (4.5cm) across, with lavender margins and short spurs, ⅛–¼in (4–6mm) long. ↕ 6–8in (15–20cm), ↔ 8in (20cm). Zone 5.
V. glabella (Stream violet). Vigorous, spreading, rhizomatous, deciduous or semi-evergreen perennial with upright or spreading stems and long-stalked, ovate or rounded, toothed, bright green leaves, 1¼–3½in (3–9cm) long, with heart-shaped bases. In late spring, bears deep yellow flowers, 1in (2.5cm) across, veined purple on the lower petals, and with short spurs, 1/16in (2mm) long. Prefers partial shade. ↕ to 8in (20cm), ↔ to 12in (30cm) or more. N.E. Asia, N.W. US. Zone 6.

Viola cornuta

Viola 'Etain'

V. gracilis, syn. *V. velutina*. Mat-forming, evergreen perennial with erect or ascending stems and oblong to broadly ovate, variably toothed leaves, ¾–1¼in (2–3cm) long, with finely divided stipules. In summer, produces yellow-eyed, deep violet, occasionally yellow flowers, to 1¼in (3cm) across, with slender spurs, to ¼in (6mm) long. Needs full sun. ↕ to 4in (10cm), ↔ to 8in (20cm). Balkan Peninsula, Greece, Turkey. Zone 6.
***V.* 'Haslemere'** see *V.* 'Nellie Britton'.
V. hederacea, syn. *Erpetion hederaceum, E. reniforme, V. reniforme* (Australian violet, Ivy-leaved violet, Trailing violet). Mat-forming, evergreen perennial with slender stolons and short, erect, tufted stems bearing broadly ovate to kidney-shaped, entire or coarsely toothed, dark green leaves, to 1½in (4cm) long, with scalloped margins. In late summer, bears sometimes slightly scented flowers, to 1in (2.5cm) across, either spurless or with inconspicuous spurs, and with a rather flattened appearance; they may be white, cream, pale to dark violet, or sometimes white with violet patches. Best in an alpine house; prefers partial shade. Very vigorous; good groundcover in warm climates. ↕ to 4in (10cm), ↔ 8–12in (20–30cm). Australia. ❄ (min. 35°F/2°C)
***V.* 'Huntercombe Purple'** ▣ Spreading, clump-forming, evergreen perennial with upright stems and ovate, toothed leaves, to 1in (2.5cm) long. In spring and late summer, produces abundant deep violet-purple flowers, to 1in (2.5cm) across, with spurs ⅛–¼in (4–6mm) long. ↕ to 6in (15cm), ↔ to 12in (30cm). Zone 6.

Viola 'Huntercombe Purple'

V

Viola hybrida

V. hybrida ■ Clumping, short-lived, fragrant annual with spreading stems, heart-shaped leaves, and velvety flowers in a wide variety of colors. Grow in any well-drained soil, in full sun to partial shade. Excellent for borders, rock gardens, and containers or window boxes. ↕↔ 6–8in (15–20cm). Zone 4.

***V.* 'Irish Molly'.** Evergreen, usually short-lived perennial with spreading stems and broadly ovate, deeply cut leaves, to 1¼in (3cm) long. In summer, produces a long succession of dark gold flowers, to 1¼in (3cm) across, with brown centers, and spurs ⅛–¼in (4–6mm) long. Propagate regularly. ↕ to 6in (15cm), ↔ to 8in (20cm). Zone 6.

***V.* 'Jackanapes'.** Robust, clump-forming, evergreen perennial with spreading stems and ovate, toothed, bright green leaves, to 1in (2.5cm) long. In late spring and summer, bears flowers to ¾in (2cm) across, the upper petals deep violet-purple to almost brown, the lower ones golden yellow, streaked purple at the centers, and with spurs ½in (1.5cm) long. Propagate regularly. ↕ to 5in (13cm), ↔ to 12in (30cm). Zone 5.

V. labradorica, syn. *V. adunca* var. *minor* (Labrador violet). Spreading, clump-forming, semi-evergreen perennial with prostrate stems and heart- to kidney-shaped, finely toothed, dark green leaves, ¾in (2cm) long, flushed bronze-purple when young. Solitary, pale purple flowers, ½in (1.5cm) across, with short spurs, ¼in (6mm) long, are borne in spring and summer. ↕ to 3in (8cm), ↔ indefinite. Canada, N. US, Greenland. Zone 3. **var. *purpurea* of gardens** see *V. riviniana* 'Purpurea'.

V. lutea, syn. *V. lutea* subsp. *elegans* (Mountain pansy). Slender, creeping, rhizomatous, evergreen perennial bearing ovate lower stem leaves and ovate to lance-shaped, shallowly scalloped or almost entire upper leaves, to ¾in (2cm) long. In late spring and early summer, bears flowers to 1¼in (3cm) across, in bright yellow, blue-violet, or red-violet, or all three colors combined, and with short spurs, ⅛–¼in (3–6mm) long. ↕↔ 3–6in (7–15cm). W. and C. Europe. Zone 5. **subsp. *elegans*** see *V. lutea*.

***V.* 'Nellie Britton'** ■ syn. *V.* 'Haslemere'. Clump-forming, evergreen perennial with spreading stems bearing ovate to lance-shaped, toothed, glossy leaves, 1¼in (3cm) long. Pinkish mauve flowers, to 1in (2.5cm) across, with spurs ½in (1.5cm) long, are profusely borne over long periods in summer. ↕ to 6in (15cm), ↔ to 12in (30cm). Zone 6.

V. obliqua, syn. *V. cucullata* (Marsh blue violet). Spreading, stemless, rhizomatous, deciduous perennial with heart-shaped, toothed leaves, to 3½in (9cm) long. In late spring, solitary, blue-violet flowers, to ¾in (2cm) across, with short spurs, to 1⁄16in (2mm) long, are borne above the leaves. Occasionally produces white flowers with blue eyes and blue veins. ↕ to 3in (8cm), ↔ to 10in (25cm). North America. Zone 5.

V. odorata (English violet, Garden violet, Sweet violet). Rhizomatous, semi-evergreen perennial with slender stolons and short, erect stems that bear tufts of heart-shaped to rounded, toothed, bright green leaves, to 2½in (6cm) long. In late winter and early spring, produces sweetly scented, blue or white flowers, ¾in (2cm) or more across, with spurs to ¼in (6mm) long. Self-seeds freely; excellent for a wild or woodland garden. ↕ to 8in (20cm), ↔ 12in (30cm) or more. Probably W. and S. Europe; widely naturalized elsewhere. Zone 5. **'Queen Charlotte'** bears dark blue flowers. **'Royal Robe'** produces fragrant, deep violet flowers, in spring and again in autumn; ↕ 6in (15cm). **'White Czar'** has large white flowers with delicately streaked, purple markings on the throats, in late spring; ↕ 4–6in (10–15cm).

V. papilionacea see *V. sororia*.

V. pedata ■ (Bird's-foot violet, Crow-foot violet). Stemless, clump-forming, semi-evergreen perennial with short, thick rhizomes and 3-lobed leaves, to 1¼in (3cm) long, the 2 lateral lobes themselves divided into 3–5 linear or spoon-shaped lobes. In late spring and early summer, bears yellow-centered, pale violet flowers, 1¼in (3cm) across, with widely spaced petals and short spurs, to 1⁄16in (2mm) long. Flowers are sometimes white or bicolored, with deep purple upper petals and pale lavender-blue or white lower ones. Needs well-drained, peaty, sandy soil. ↕ to 2in (5cm), ↔ to 4in (10cm). E. North America. Zone 4.

V. pedatifida (Larkspur violet, Purple prairie violet). Small, clump-forming, semi-evergreen to deciduous perennial with 5- to 11-palmate leaves, to 1¼in (3cm) long, with very narrow leaflets. In spring and summer, bears deep violet-blue flowers, to ¾in (2cm) across, with bearded lower petals and short spurs, ⅛in (3mm) long. Self-seeds freely. ↕ to 5in (13cm), ↔ to 6in (15cm). C. North America. Zone 2.

Viola sororia 'Freckles'

V. reniforme see *V. hederacea*.

V. riviniana (Dog violet, Wood violet). Tufted, semi-evergreen perennial with basal tufts of ovate-rounded, toothed leaves, to 1½in (4cm) long, deeply heart-shaped at the bases. In late spring and early summer, bears pale violet-blue flowers, ½–1in (1.5–2.5cm) across, with notched, white or pale purple spurs, to ¼in (6mm) long. Suitable for a wild garden, in deep or partial shade. ↕ 4–8in (10–20cm), ↔ 8–16in (20–40cm). Europe, N. Africa. Zone 6. **'Purpurea'** ■ syn. *V. labradorica* var. *purpurea* of gardens, has dark purplish green leaves. Invasive, but excellent in a wild or woodland garden.

V. sororia, syn. *V. papilionacea* (Woolly blue violet). Stemless, rhizomatous herbaceous perennial with ovate to rounded, sharp-pointed, scalloped leaves, to 4in (10cm) long, densely hairy beneath. In spring and summer, bears flowers to ¾in (2cm) across, with short spurs, to ⅛in (3mm) long. The flowers are sometimes deep violet-blue, but usually white, heavily speckled and streaked violet-blue around the centers. Self-seeds freely. ↕ to 4in (10cm), ↔ to 8in (20cm). E. North America. Zone 4.

Viola 'Nellie Britton'

Viola pedata

Viola riviniana 'Purpurea'

Viola tricolor

Viola tricolor 'Molly Sanderson'

Viola x *wittrockiana* Forerunner Series

Viola x *wittrockiana* 'Padparadja'

'Freckles' ■ bears white flowers, speckled violet-purple.
V. tricolor ■ (Heartsease, Johnny-ump-up, Love-in-idleness). Tufted annual, biennial, or short-lived, evergreen perennial, sometimes hizomatous, with spreading stems and ovate to heart-shaped, toothed leaves, to 1¼in (3cm) long. From spring to autumn, bears flowers, 1in (2.5cm) or more across, in shades of purple, avender-blue, white, or yellow, with usually dark purple upper petals, lower petals often streaked dark purple, and spurs to ¼in (6mm) long. Short-lived, but self-seeds prolifically. ↕ to 3–5in (8–13cm), ↔ to 4–6in (10–15cm). Europe, Asia. Zone 4. **'Bowles' Black'** has velvety, almost black flowers with small, golden yellow eyes. Seeds freely and comes almost true from seed; ↕ to 4in (10cm), ↔ to 8in (20cm). **'Helen Mount'** has large flowers, 1½in (4cm) across, in spring and summer. **'Molly Sanderson'** ■ has black flowers and blooms over a long period; ↕ 6–8in (15–20cm). **'Prince Henry'** bears small, very dark purple flowers, ½–¾in (1.5–2cm) across, from spring to summer. **'Prince John'** bears small, bright yellow flowers, ½–¾in (1.5–2cm) across, from spring to summer.
V. velutina see *V. gracilis.*
***V. x wittrockiana* cultivars** (Pansy). Erect, bushy evergreen perennials, grown as annuals or biennials, derived from cross-breeding *V. altaica*, *V. cornuta*, *V. lutea*, and *V. tricolor*; they are usually larger and more robust than their parents. They have spreading stems and ovate to almost heart-shaped, shallowly lobed, shiny, mid- to deep green leaves, to 1½in (4cm) or more long. Flowers are 2½–4in (6–10cm) across, with the lateral petals overlapping the lower and upper petals, and with very short spurs. They may be either self-colored, usually in blue, white, yellow, orange, pink, red, or purple; bicolored; or the more traditional pansy type, bicolored with central, face-like markings. Flowers are produced mainly from early spring to summer, some from autumn to winter. Other, usually smaller-flowered cultivars have been bred for winter and early spring flowering, and are excellent bedding and container plants. ↕ 6–9in (16–23cm), ↔ 9–12in (23–30cm). Zone 5. **Allegro Series** cultivars bear large flowers in a broad color range, with or without markings, in winter and spring. **'Baby Lucia'** produces small, yellow-eyed, clear blue flowers in spring and summer. **'Bambini'** has small flowers, borne in spring and summer, in a wide color range, most with contrasting white or yellow faces and "whiskered" central markings. **'Beaconsfield'** produces winter-blooming flowers with pale blue upper petals and deep blue lower petals. **Bingo Series** cultivars flower in winter and spring, producing large blooms in a broad color range, some with darker markings. **'Black Prince'** bears black flowers with yellow eyes. **'Bruno'** has mahogany-red flowers with yellow margins. **Clear Crystal Series** cultivars bear medium-sized flowers in summer, in a wide range of clear, single colors, without central markings. **Color Festival Hybrids** bloom earlier than most, and all colors have faces; ↕ 7–8in (18–20cm). **'Cornetto'** produces small, very long-spurred, clear white flowers in spring and summer. **Crown Series** cultivars produce large flowers in a broad range of clear colors, in early spring and summer. Cultivars of **Crystal Bowl Series** are compact in habit, and bear medium-sized, unmarked flowers in a wide range of clear colors, including white, in summer; ↕ 9in (23cm), ↔ 12in (30cm). **'Cuty'** bears small, yellow-eyed white flowers, with deep violet-purple upper petals, from spring to summer. Cultivars of **Delta Series** are compact and robust, bearing large flowers in a wide range of colors, some with darker markings, in early spring. **Faces Series** cultivars bear large flowers, 2½–3in (6–8cm) across, in shades of blue, purple, red, orange, yellow, and white, all with contrasting faces or blotches. **Fama Series** ■ cultivars produce large flowers in winter and spring, in a wide range of single colors and in mixed colors. Cultivars of **Fanfare Series** are compact, producing medium-sized flowers in winter and spring, available in a broad range of single colors and bicolors; excellent for hanging baskets. Cultivars of **Forerunner Series** ■ bloom in winter and spring, bearing medium-sized flowers in a range of bright single colors and bicolors. **'Gemini'** has purple flowers with ivory margins. Cultivars of **Imperial Series** bear large flowers in a broad color range, almost all with a deeper central mark, in winter and early spring; **'Imperial Frosty Rose'** is an unusual rose-pink with a deeper central mark; **'Imperial Gold Princess'** is bicolored yellow and red. **Jewel Series** cultivars are compact and free-flowering, bearing small blooms in winter and spring, in yellow, blue, purple with pansy faces, and white with pansy faces. Cultivars of **Joker Series** produce medium-sized, bicolored flowers in light blue, mahogany-gold, violet-gold, and mixed colors, with very strongly marked pansy faces, in summer; **'Jolly Joker'** ■ blooms in spring and summer, and has medium-sized orange flowers, with deep purple upper petals and purple-margined lower petals. **Maxim Series** cultivars have flowers, to 3in (8cm) across, with contrasting face colors, including orange and black, red and yellow, white and purple, and white and blue. **'Padparadja'** ■ has dark orange flowers, 2in (5cm) across, without faces. **'Pretty'** bears small yellow flowers, with rich mahogany-red upper petals, in spring and summer. **Princess Series** ■ cultivars are neat in habit, and produce small flowers in blue, cream, dark purple, bicolored purple and white, or yellow, in spring and summer. Cultivars of **Rally Series** are free-flowering, producing medium-sized blooms in a broad range of colors, in winter and spring. **Regal Series** cultivars are compact in habit, producing medium-sized flowers in a wide range of separate colors and a mixture of colors, all with darker markings, in winter and spring. Cultivars of **Roc Series** bear flowers, 3½in (9cm) across, in red shades and contrasting bicolors, such as yellow and black, blue and light blue, and blue and black; ↕ 7in (18cm). **Super Chalon Giants** bear medium-sized to large, bicolored flowers, with wavy, ruffled margins, in summer. **Swiss Giants Hybrids** are robust, and produce larger flowers in shades of red, blue, yellow, and white, many with contrasting blotches. **Ultima Series** cultivars, blooming in winter and spring, have medium-sized flowers in a very broad range of colors, including bicolors. **Universal Series** cultivars bear medium-sized flowers in winter and spring, in a broad range of colors, including bicolors, and sometimes with patterned faces. **Velours Series** cultivars have a neat habit, and bear small flowers in violet-blue, pale blue with deep blue markings, purple, and yellow, in spring and summer.

Viola x *wittrockiana* Fama Series

Viola x *wittrockiana*
Joker Series 'Jolly Joker'

Viola x *wittrockiana* Princess Series

VIRGILIA

FABACEAE

Genus of 2 species of small, evergreen trees from forest edges and river valleys in coastal areas of South Africa. They have alternate, pinnate leaves, and are grown for their abundant pea-like flowers, borne in axillary or terminal racemes, occasionally in panicles. Where winter temperatures fall below 41–45°F (5–7°C), grow in a cool greenhouse. In milder areas, use as specimen trees.
• **CULTIVATION** Under glass, grow in acidic potting mix with added sharp sand, in full light. In growth, water moderately and apply a balanced liquid fertilizer every month; water sparingly in

V

Virgilia oroboides

winter. Outdoors, grow in neutral to acidic, poor to moderately fertile, moist but well-drained soil in full sun. Pruning group 1; may need restrictive pruning under glass.
• **PROPAGATION** Sow seed at about 59°F (15°C) in spring, after soaking in hot water or after scarification.
• **PESTS AND DISEASES** Infrequent.

V. capensis see *V. oroboides.*
V. oroboides ■ syn. *V. capensis.* Fast-growing shrub or small, rounded to broadly columnar tree, usually with several main stems, and with red-downy young growth. Pinnate leaves, 4–8in (10–20cm) long, each have 13–21 narrowly oblong, leathery, mid- to deep green leaflets, pale and densely woolly beneath, with thorn-like points. From spring to summer, bears racemes of up to 12 pea-like, fragrant, white, pink, purple, or crimson flowers, to ¾in (2cm) across. ↕ 15–28ft (5–9m), ↔ 10–15ft (3–5m). South Africa (Western Cape, Eastern Cape). ❀ (min. 45°F/7°C)

▷ ***Viscaria*** see *Lychnis*
V. elegans see *Silene coeli-rosa*

VITALIANA *syn.* DOUGLASIA

PRIMULACEAE

Genus of one species of tufted, mat- or cushion-forming, evergreen perennial, occurring in alpine and subalpine screes, rocks, and meadows in the mountains of C. and S. Europe. It has rosettes of small leaves, and is cultivated for its solitary flowers, produced in spring. Grow in a rock garden, scree bed, or alpine house.

Vitaliana primuliflora

• **CULTIVATION** Grow in leafy, moderately fertile, gritty, moist but sharply drained soil in full sun. Protect from winter moisture. In an alpine house, grow in a mix of 1 part each loam and leaf mold, and 3 parts grit.
• **PROPAGATION** Sow seed in containers in an open frame as soon as ripe. Detach and root offsets in mid- and late spring and early summer.
• **PESTS AND DISEASES** Susceptible to aphids and spider mites under glass.

V. primuliflora ■ syn. *Androsace vitaliana, Douglasia vitaliana.* Tufted, mat- or cushion-forming, evergreen perennial with creeping stems and tight rosettes of linear to oblong-lance-shaped, pointed, usually hairy, pale green leaves, to ½in (1.5cm) long, with silver margins. In spring, bears solitary, almost stemless, tubular yellow flowers, to ¾in (2cm) across, with 5 spreading lobes. ↕ to 1in (2.5cm), ↔ to 10in (25cm). Mountains of S.W. and C. Europe, to S.E. Alps, and C. Apennines. Zone 5.

VITEX

VERBENACEAE

Widespread genus of 250 species of deciduous or evergreen trees and shrubs, occurring mainly in tropical regions, often in woodland or dry river beds. They have opposite, fully divided, 3- to 7-palmate leaves, and produce terminal panicles, racemes, or cymes of tubular, 2-lipped flowers. *V. agnus-castus* and *V. negundo* are cultivated for their elegant foliage and summer flowers, and may be grown in a shrub border or against a wall. Where not hardy, grow in a warm greenhouse.
• **CULTIVATION** Grow in any well-drained soil in full sun. Pruning group 6 or 7.
• **PROPAGATION** Sow seed at 43–54°F (6–12°C) in autumn or spring. Take semi-ripe cuttings in summer.
• **PESTS AND DISEASES** Sometimes affected by leaf spot, root rot, and scale insects.

V. agnus-castus (Chaste tree). Open, spreading, deciduous shrub with 5- or 7-palmate leaves composed of slender, narrowly elliptic, pointed, entire or slightly toothed, aromatic, dark green leaflets, to 4in (10cm) or more long. Small, tubular, fragrant, lilac- to dark blue, sometimes white flowers are borne in slender upright, terminal panicles, to 5–7in (13–18cm) long, in early and midautumn. ↕↔ 6–25ft (2–8m). Mediterranean to C. Asia. Zone 7. **var. *latifolia*** ■ is more vigorous than the species, with broader leaflets. **'Silver Spire'** is vigorous in habit and produces white flowers.

Vitex agnus-castus var. *latifolia*

V. negundo (Chaste tree). Bushy, deciduous shrub with 3- to 5-palmate, dark green leaves composed of lance-shaped, pointed, sharply toothed or entire leaflets, to 4in (10cm) long. In late summer and early autumn, bears small, tubular, pale violet-blue flowers in terminal panicles, to 9in (23cm) long. ↕↔ 10ft (3m). E. Africa, E. Asia. Zone 6b. **'Heterophylla'** has leaves with deeply cut leaflets.
V. rotundifolia. Sprawling, prostrate shrub with broadly oblong or obovate-spoon-shaped, softly hairy, mid-green leaves, to 1¾in (4.5cm) long. In late summer and early autumn, tubular, fragrant, blue to purple flowers are produced in usually terminal panicles, to 8in (20cm) long. ↕ 3–5ft (1–1.5m), ↔ 6–8ft (2–2.5m). Asia, Australia. ❀ (min. 35°F/2°C)

VITIS

Grape

VITACEAE

Genus of about 65 species of woody, deciduous tendril climbers, occasionally shrubs, occurring in woodland, woodland margins, and thickets in N. temperate regions. They have flaking bark and alternate, simple to lobed, sometimes toothed leaves. Tiny green flowers are produced in panicles from the leaf axils in summer, and are followed by fruits (grapes), which in some species are edible or are used to make wine. The ornamental grapes are cultivated for their foliage and fruits; grow over a trellis, pergola, or fence, or through a large shrub or tree, or train against a wall.
• **CULTIVATION** Grow in well-drained, preferably neutral to alkaline, humus-rich soil in full sun or partial shade. Pruning group 11, in midwinter, and again in midsummer if necessary, to restrict growth; pruning group 12, if more formal training is required.
• **PROPAGATION** Sow seed in containers in a cold frame in autumn or spring. Take hardwood cuttings in late winter, or root "vine eye" cuttings (with a single bud) in early spring. Layer in autumn.
• **PESTS AND DISEASES** Downy mildew, canker and dieback, gray mold (*Botrytis*), Pierce's disease, black rot, powdery mildew, mushroom root rot, and various leaf spots occur. Grape leaf skeletonizer, Japanese beetle, scale insects, and mealybugs cause problems.

V. aconitifolia see *Ampelopsis aconitifolia.*
V. amurensis (Amur grape). Vigorous, woody, deciduous climber, sometimes a shrub, with red-tinged young shoots and broadly ovate, often shallowly 3-lobed, sharply toothed, dark green leaves, to 12in (30cm) long, heart-shaped at the bases, and turning red and purple in autumn. Bears small, unpalatable, ovoid, white-bloomed black grapes, ½in (1.5cm) across, in late summer. ↕ 50ft (15m). China, Korea, Japan. Zone 3b.

Vitis coignetiae

***V.* 'Brant'.** Vigorous, woody, deciduou climber with rounded, palmately 3- to 5-lobed, toothed, bright green leaves, tc 9in (23cm) long, which turn bronze-re with green veins in autumn. In autumn produces large bunches of edible, spherical, blue-black grapes, ½in (1.5cm) across. ↕ 22ft (7m) or more. Zone 6.
V. capensis see *Rhoicissus capensis.*
V. coignetiae ■ (Crimson glory vine). Vigorous, woody, deciduous climber with large, heart-shaped, shallowly 3- to 5-lobed, shallowly to coarsely toothed, dark green leaves, to 12in (30cm) long, with impressed veins above and brown-felted beneath; they turn bright red in autumn. Small, unpalatable, spherical, blue-black grapes, ½in (1.5cm) across, are produced in autumn. ↕ 50ft (15m). Korea, Japan. Zone 5.
V. davidii. Woody, deciduous climber producing young shoots densely covere with short, rigid spines. Heart-shaped, shallowly lobed, toothed, glossy, dark green leaves, to 10in (25cm) long, blue-green or blue-gray beneath, turn scarlet in autumn. Produces edible, spherical black grapes, ½in (1.5cm) across, in

Vitis vinifera 'Purpurea'

V

autumn. ↕25ft (8m) or more. China. Zone 7b.
V. henryana see *Parthenocissus henryana.*
V. heterophylla see *Ampelopsis brevipedunculata* var. *maximowiczii.*
V. quinquefolia see *Parthenocissus quinquefolia.*
V. striata see *Cissus striata.*
V. thomsonii see *Parthenocissus thomsonii.*
***V. vinifera* 'Purpurea'** ▣ (Purpleleaf grape). Woody, deciduous climber with rounded, 3- to 5-lobed, toothed leaves, to 6in (15cm) long, gray-hairy at first, turning plum-purple, then dark purple in autumn. In autumn, produces small, unpalatable, spherical purple grapes, to ¾in (2cm) across. ↕22ft (7m). Zone 6.
V. voinieriana see *Tetrastigma voinierianum.*

VRIESEA

BROMELIACEAE

Genus of about 250 species of rosette-forming, evergreen, mostly epiphytic perennials (bromeliads), closely related to *Tillandsia.* They occur in forested and rocky areas, to 8,000ft (2,500m) high, in Mexico, Central America, the West Indies, and South America. The mostly lance-shaped or linear leaves have smooth margins, are often finely scaly, and frequently have colored cross-bands and other markings. Bract-like sheaths, sometimes colorful, are present at the leaf bases. The short-stalked flowers are variously shaped, with petals free or fused into a tube, often shorter than the sepals, each petal with 2 scales at the base on the inner surface; the flowers are usually borne in flattened, 2-ranked, spike-like racemes or panicles, with prominent floral bracts, produced on more or less erect scapes from the centers of the rosettes, in summer or autumn. Where temperatures drop below 59°F (15°C), grow in a warm greenhouse or as houseplants, although some species, including those native to eastern Brazil, are hardy to 45°F (7°C). In tropical gardens, grow epiphytically in a tree, or on mossy rocks.
• **CULTIVATION** Under glass, grow attached to pieces of bark or tree branches, or in containers of standard epiphytic bromeliad potting mix, in moderate light. During the growing season, keep the rosette centers filled with water, mist daily, and apply quarter-strength foliar fertilizer every 4–5 weeks. Keep just moist in winter. Outdoors, grow epiphytically in partial shade. See also p.47.
• **PROPAGATION** Sow seed at 66–75°F (19–24°C) when ripe. Remove offsets in spring.
• **PESTS AND DISEASES** Susceptible to scale insects, mealybugs, leaf spots caused by drying, and crown rot (especially during propagation).

Vriesea hieroglyphica

Vriesea carinata

Vriesea platynema

V. carinata ▣ (Lobster claw, Painted feather). Epiphytic bromeliad with funnel-shaped rosettes of arching, lance-shaped, pale green leaves, to 8in (20cm) long, broadly acute or rounded at the tips, and with broadly elliptic, red-tinged sheaths, 2–2½in (5–6cm) long. In summer or autumn, scapes with green, purple, or red bracts bear spike-like racemes, 1½–2in (4–5cm) long, of tubular flowers, to 2in (5cm) long; the flowers have green-tipped yellow petals, keeled sepals, and red-based, yellow-green floral bracts. ↕ to 12in (30cm), ↔ 6–8in (15–20cm). Brazil. ❀ (min. 59°F/15°C)
V. fenestralis. Rock-dwelling or epiphytic bromeliad with funnel-shaped rosettes of recurved or arching, broadly linear, pale green leaves, to 16in (40cm) long, with rounded tips, each with a recurved spine; the leaf blades have dark green lines and purple circles beneath, and the broadly oval, yellowish green sheaths, 3½–4in (9–10cm) long, are spotted reddish brown. In summer, bears loose, spike-like racemes, to 12in (30cm) long, of green floral bracts and spreading, yellowish green or greenish white flowers, 2½–3in (6–8cm) long. ↕ to 3ft (1m), ↔ 14–20in (35–50cm). Brazil. ❀ (min. 59°F/15°C)
V. fosteriana. Epiphytic, probably also terrestrial bromeliad with stiff, dense, funnel-shaped rosettes of arching, broadly tongue-shaped, yellowish to deep green leaves, to 28in (70cm) long; they are cross-banded with purple or maroon, especially beneath, and have broadly oval, dark brown sheaths, 4–6in (10–15cm) long. In summer, bears loose, spike-like racemes, 16in (40cm) or more long, of yellow floral bracts and tubular flowers, 1¾in (4.5cm) long, with yellow petals and green sepals, all with reddish brown tips. ↕ to 5ft (1.5m), ↔ 3ft (1m). Brazil. ❀ (min. 59°F/15°C)
V. hieroglyphica ▣ Epiphytic bromeliad with dense, funnel-shaped rosettes of arching, strap-shaped, minutely scaly, yellowish green leaves, 20–32in (50–80cm) long, marked dark green above, purplish brown beneath; dark brown sheaths are 3–4in (8–10cm) long. In summer, bears greenish yellow floral bracts and tubular-trumpet-shaped, sulfur-yellow flowers, to 2½in (6cm) long, in branching, spike-like racemes or panicles, to 32in (80cm) long. ↕ to 3ft (1m), ↔ 32–39in (80–100cm). E. Brazil. ❀ (min. 59°F/15°C)
V. platynema ▣ Variable, epiphytic bromeliad with very dense, funnel-shaped rosettes of flaccid, strap-shaped, violet-tipped, dull green, often violet-striped leaves, 24in (60cm) long, often margined purple, and with broadly oval, dark brown sheaths, to 5in (13cm) long. In summer, bears loose, spike-like racemes, to 16in (40cm) long, of red or yellow floral bracts and tubular green flowers, to 1¾in (4.5cm) long, with yellow sepals. ↕ to 3ft (1m), ↔ 24in (60cm). West Indies, E. South America. ❀ (min. 59°F/15°C)
V. psittacina. Variable, epiphytic bromeliad with broadly funnel-shaped rosettes of arching, strap-shaped, pale green leaves, 20in (50cm) long; the leaves have elliptic, green or pale brown sheaths, 3–3½in (7–9cm) long. In summer, produces slender, erect, spike-like racemes, to 12in (30cm) long, of yellow-tipped red, or entirely red or green floral bracts, and spreading, sometimes green-tipped yellow flowers, 2½in (6cm) long. ↕ to 24in (60cm), ↔ 16–24in (40–60cm). Brazil, Paraguay. ❀ (min. 59°F/15°C)
V. saundersii. Rock-dwelling bromeliad with dense rosettes of arching, linear, spine-tipped, gray-scaly, gray-green leaves, 12in (30cm) long; they have fine maroon spots beneath, and oval, yellowish brown sheaths, to 6in (15cm) long, with reddish brown spots. In summer, bears dense, spike-like racemes or panicles, 5½in (14cm) long, of pale or yellowish green floral bracts and tubular yellow flowers, 1½in (4cm) long, with pale or yellowish green sepals. ↕24–28in (60–70cm), ↔ 16in (40cm). E. Brazil. ❀ (min. 59°F/15°C)
V. splendens ▣ (Flaming sword). Variable, terrestrial or epiphytic bromeliad producing dense, funnel-shaped rosettes of arching, linear, bluish green leaves, to 32in (80cm) long, with broad, dark green, purple, or reddish brown cross-banding, and with indistinct sheaths. In summer, bears lance-shaped, spike-like racemes, to 22in (55cm) long, of thin, bright red floral bracts and tubular yellow flowers, 3in (8cm) long, with often red-tipped, yellow sepals. ↕ to 3ft (1m), ↔ 12in (30cm). E. Venezuela to French Guiana. ❀ (min. 59°F/15°C)

Vriesea splendens

W

WACHENDORFIA

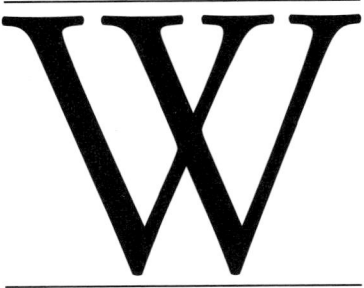

HAEMODORACEAE

Genus of about 25 species of tuberous, evergreen perennials found on grassy slopes in South Africa. They have bright red tubers and large, broadly linear, pleated, parallel-veined, erect, basal leaves, sheathing one another at their bases and arranged in 2 opposite rows. They are grown for their large, terminal panicles of irregular, flat, star-shaped yellow flowers, with 6 tepals, borne on leafless stems. Where not hardy, grow in a cool greenhouse; for best flowering, plant directly into a greenhouse border. In frost-free areas, grow in a border.

• **CULTIVATION** Under glass, grow in soil-based potting mix, with additional sharp sand and peat or leaf mold, in full light. During the growing season, water freely and apply a balanced liquid fertilizer every month. Keep just moist when dormant. Outdoors, grow in fertile, reliably moist soil in full sun.

• **PROPAGATION** Sow seed at 55–64°F (13–18°C) in autumn or spring. Separate tubers in spring.

Wachendorfia thyrsiflora

• **PESTS AND DISEASES** Susceptible to slug and snail damage, and to aphids and spider mites under glass.

W. thyrsiflora ■ Clump-forming, tuberous perennial with furry red roots and tubers. Arching, broadly linear, pleated, parallel-veined, basal leaves, to 3ft (1m) long, are hairless and fairly brittle. In early summer, produces dense panicles of star-shaped yellow flowers, to 1¼in (3cm) across. ↕ 5–6ft (1.5–2m), PD18in (45cm). South Africa (Northern Cape, Western Cape, Eastern Cape). ❀ (min. 41°F/5°C)

WAHLENBERGIA

CAMPANULACEAE

Genus of about 150 species of mat-forming to upright annuals and perennials from mountains in Europe, South Africa, and Australasia. They have variable, usually alternate leaves, and are grown for their conspicuous, funnel-, bell-, saucer-, or star-shaped, usually violet, blue, or white flowers, borne singly or in cymes, in summer. Grow in a rock garden or alpine house.

• **CULTIVATION** Grow in well-drained, sandy, humus-rich soil in a sheltered site in partial shade. In an alpine house, grow in a mix of equal parts loam, leaf mold, and sharp sand.

• **PROPAGATION** Sow seed at 55–59°F (13–15°C) in early spring. Divide in spring. Propagate regularly.

• **PESTS AND DISEASES** May be damaged by slugs and snails.

W. albomarginata (New Zealand bluebell). Tufted, spreading, short-lived, rhizomatous perennial producing basal rosettes of elliptic to lance-shaped or ovate-spoon-shaped, hairy, leathery, mid-green leaves, to ¾in (2cm) long, with reddish brown margins, often purplish green beneath. Solitary, slender-stemmed, upward-facing, bell-shaped, blue, sometimes white flowers, 1in (2.5cm) across, usually with green veins, are produced in summer. ↕ 2–8in (5–20cm), ↔ to 8in (20cm). New Zealand. Zone 7. **'Blue Mist'** bears gray-blue flowers.

W. congesta. Creeping, branched, mat-forming, rhizomatous perennial with basal rosettes of rounded to elliptic-spoon-shaped, hairless, mid-green leaves, to 1in (2.5cm) long. Solitary, bell-shaped, pale blue to white flowers, to ⅜in (9mm) across, are produced in summer. ↕ 2–4in (5–10cm), ↔ to 8in (20cm). New Zealand. ❀ (min. 35°F/2°C)

Wahlenbergia gloriosa

W. gloriosa ■ Tufted, rhizomatous perennial bearing lance-shaped, thick, dark green leaves, ¾–1¼in (2–3cm) long, with wavy, toothed margins. Solitary, upward-facing, widely bell-shaped, deep violet-blue flowers, ¾in (2cm) across, with darker veins, are produced in summer. ↕ to 2in (5cm), ↔ to 6in (15cm). Australia. ❀ (min. 35°F/2°C)

W. matthewsii. Tufted, hairless, woody, rhizomatous perennial with many congested, basal rosettes of narrowly oblong, entire or toothed, leathery, mid-green leaves, to 1½in (4cm) long. Solitary, upward-facing, bell-shaped, white to pale mauve flowers, to ½in (1.5cm) across, are borne in summer and autumn. ↕ 2–6in (5–15cm), ↔ to 8in (20cm). New Zealand. ❀ (min. 35°F/2°C)

W. pumilio see *Edraianthus pumilio.*

W. serpyllifolia see *Edraianthus serpyllifolius.*

WALDSTEINIA

ROSACEAE

Genus of about 6 species of tufted, rhizomatous, herbaceous perennials found in woodland throughout N. temperate regions. They are grown mainly for their alternate, 3-palmate or palmately 3- to 7-lobed leaves, and for their saucer-shaped yellow flowers, borne singly or in cymes in late spring and early summer. Waldsteinias provide a good groundcover for a woodland garden, on dry, shady banks, or at the front of a herbaceous border, but may be invasive.

• **CULTIVATION** Grow in any moderately fertile soil in full or partial shade.

• **PROPAGATION** Sow seed in containers in a cold frame in autumn or spring. Divide in early spring.

• **PESTS AND DISEASES** Infrequent.

W. fragariodes (Barren strawberry). Mat-forming, rhizomatous perennial with 3-palmate, bronze leaves, to 6in (15cm) long, consisting of obovate, hairy, scalloped leaflets, to 3in (8cm) long. In spring and summer, bears cymes of 3–8 saucer-shaped, bright yellow flowers, to ¾in (2cm) across. ↕ 8–10in (20–25cm), ↔ 24in (60cm). Virginia, Tennessee, Alabama, Georgia. Zone 5.

W. geoides. Creeping perennial with short rhizomes and upright or nearly upright stems. Stem leaves, to 10in (25cm) long, are diamond-shaped, shallowly lobed, and mid-green; basal leaves, 3–10in (8–25cm) long, are broadly heart-shaped, coarsely scalloped, and densely softly hairy. In spring, bears lax cymes of few, saucer-shaped, bright yellow flowers, ¾in (2cm) across. ↕ to 10in (25cm), ↔ 8in (20cm). C. Europe, Balkans, Turkey. Zone 5.

W. parviflora. Hairy or hairless, creeping perennial with 3-lobed basal leaves, to 12in (30cm) long, consisting of wedge-shaped-obovate to broadly diamond-shaped, coarsely and irregularly scalloped or lobed, mid-green leaflets, to 3in (8cm) long. In spring, produces usually nodding, saucer-shaped, bright yellow flowers, to ¼in (6mm) across, singly or in cymes of up to 7. ↕ to 10in (25cm), ↔ 8in (20cm). S.W. Virginia, Tennessee, North Carolina, Georgia. Zone 7.

Waldsteinia ternata

W. ternata ■ syn. *W. trifolia.* Vigorous, semi-evergreen perennial, spreading by rhizomes and stolons, with 3-palmate, shallowly lobed and toothed leaves, to 2½in (6cm) long, each composed of 2 almost diamond-shaped lateral leaflets and a rounded terminal leaflet. In late spring and early summer, bears loose cymes of 3–7 saucer-shaped, bright yellow flowers, ½in (1.5cm) across. ↕ to 4in (10cm), ↔ 24in (60cm) or more. C., E., and S. Europe, Russia (E. Siberia), China, Japan. Zone 4.

W. trifolia see *W. ternata.*

WASHINGTONIA

ARECACEAE

Genus of 2 species of single-stemmed palms from rocky, arid areas in S.W. US and N. Mexico. Deeply lobed, fan-shaped leaves are borne in terminal heads that form a dense, shaggy thatch on the trunk as they die back. Because of the fire risk, this dead material is often removed in cultivation. Tubular, creamy white or creamy pink flowers, each with 3 petal lobes, are borne in slender, arching panicles between the leaves. Where not hardy, grow young plants as houseplants or in a temperate or warm greenhouse. In warmer areas, use as lawn specimens or as street trees.

• **CULTIVATION** Under glass, grow in soil-based potting mix, with added leaf mold and sharp sand, in full light. When in growth, water moderately and apply a balanced liquid fertilizer monthly; keep almost dry in winter.

Washingtonia robusta

Outdoors, grow in fertile, well-drained soil in full sun.
• **PROPAGATION** Sow seed at 75°F (24°C) in spring.
• **PESTS AND DISEASES** Prone to scale insects and spider mites under glass. Viruses, pink rot, bud rot, butt rot, and a wide variety of leaf spots occur.

W. filamentosa see *W. filifera.*
W. filifera, syn. *W. filamentosa* (Desert fan palm, Northern washingtonia). Medium-sized to large palm with a robust, columnar trunk. Leaf stalks are sharply toothed at the bases, and the fan-shaped, gray-green blades, 5–10ft (1.5–3m) long, are erect at first, then spreading and arching, with filaments hanging from the slender lobes. Dead foliage forms an even skirt that clothes the trunk from top to bottom. Bears tubular, creamy white flowers in panicles to 15ft (5m) long, usually in summer. ↕ 50–70ft (15–20m), ↔ 10–20ft (3–6m). S. California, S. Arizona. ❄ (min. 46–50°F/8–10°C)
W. robusta ▣ (Thread palm). Tall, fast-growing palm with a slender trunk that gradually tapers from ground level to the crown. Leaf stalks are sharply toothed throughout their length, and the fan-shaped, bright green blades, to 3ft (1m) long, have arching lobe tips, with inconspicuous or no filaments. Dead foliage forms a shaggy skirt that clothes the trunk. Tubular, creamy pink flowers are borne in panicles to 10ft (3m) long, usually in summer. Suitable for coastal gardens. ↕ to 80ft (25m), ↔ 8–15ft (2.5–5m). N. Mexico. ❄ (min. 46–50°F/8–10°C)

WATSONIA

IRIDACEAE

Genus of about 60 species of cormous perennials, usually from rocky or grassy slopes and plateaus in South Africa and Madagascar. They have erect, usually sword-shaped, basal leaves, and are cultivated for their showy spikes of horizontal, tubular, red, orange, pink, or white flowers, with curved tubes and 6 tepal lobes, borne on erect stems at various times of the year. *Watsonia* species are suitable for outdoor cultivation only in areas where there is little or no frost. Where not hardy, grow in a cool greenhouse or conservatory; spring- and summer-growing species may be used in a border outdoors, and

Watsonia pillansii

Watsonia
'Stanford Scarlet'

lifted in autumn for storage in a dry, frost-free place.
• **CULTIVATION** Under glass, grow in soil-based potting mix, with added sharp sand and leaf mold, in full sun. When in growth, water freely and apply a balanced liquid fertilizer every month. Keep just moist when dormant. Outdoors, grow in light, well-drained soil that does not dry out in summer. Where frost is likely, protect with a dry winter mulch.
• **PROPAGATION** Sow seed at 55–64°F (13–18°C) in autumn. Divide in spring.
• **PESTS AND DISEASES** Infrequent.

W. aletroides. Clump-forming, cormous perennial with sword-shaped, glossy leaves, 8–16in (20–40cm) long, overtopped from late winter to spring by unbranched spikes of up to 12 tubular, orange-red flowers, 2in (5cm) long, the tepal lobes not spreading. ↕ 24in (60cm), PD4in (10cm). South Africa (Western Cape). ❄ (min. 41°F/5°C)
W. ardernei see *W. borbonica* subsp. *ardernei.*
W. beatricis see *W. pillansii.*
W. borbonica, syn. *W. pyramidata.* Clump-forming, cormous perennial with narrowly sword-shaped leaves, to 30in (75cm) long. In summer, bears branched spikes of up to 20 slightly irregular, bright pink flowers, 1¼in (3cm) long, with spreading tepal lobes and white lines at the base of each tepal. ↕ 3–5ft (1–1.5m), PD4in (10cm). South Africa (Western Cape). ❄ (min. 41°F/5°C).
subsp. *ardernei*, syn. *W. ardernei*, has usually white, rarely pink flowers.
W. bulbillifera see *W. meriana* 'Bulbillifera'.
W. fourcadei. Robust, clump-forming, cormous perennial with sword-shaped leaves, 12–24in (30–60cm) long. Dense, branched spikes of 20–40 tubular, pink, orange, or red flowers, 2½in (6cm) long, are produced in spring and summer. ↕ 5ft (1.5m), PD4in (10cm). South Africa (Western Cape). ❄ (min. 41°F/5°C)
W. humilis. Slender, clump-forming, cormous perennial with lance-shaped leaves, to 12in (30cm) long. In spring or early summer, produces unbranched spikes of up to 12 tubular flowers, 1¼–1¾in (3–4.5cm) long, either white with pink outside, or pink with darker pink outside. ↕ 12in (30cm), PD3in (8cm). South Africa (Western Cape). ❄ (min. 41°F/5°C)
W. marginata. Clump-forming, cormous perennial with sword-shaped leaves, 30in (75cm) long. From spring to early summer, bears dense, branched spikes of few to many tubular, mauve-pink flowers, ¾in (2cm) long, with spreading tepal lobes and white and purple markings. ↕ to 6ft (2m), PD6in (15cm). South Africa (Western Cape). ❄ (min. 41°F/5°C)
W. meriana. Clump-forming, cormous perennial with sword-shaped leaves, 12–24in (30–60cm) long. In summer, produces branched spikes of up to 25 tubular flowers, ¾–1in (2–2.5cm) long, with spreading tepal lobes, in bright rose-red, rarely scarlet or white. ↕ 1¾–6ft (0.5–2m), PD6in (15cm). South Africa (Eastern Cape, Western Cape, KwaZulu/Natal). ❄ (min. 41°F/5°C).
'Bulbillifera', syn. *W. bulbillifera*, has flowers 1¼in (3cm) long, and produces bulbils among the flower spikes.
W. pillansii ▣ syn. *W. beatricis.* Slender, clump-forming, cormous perennial producing sword-shaped leaves, 10–24in (25–60cm) long. From summer to autumn, bears branched spikes of 20–25 tubular, bright orange to orange-red flowers, to 2in (5cm) long, with spreading tepal lobes. ↕ 20–48in (50–120cm), PD4in (10cm). South Africa (Western Cape, Eastern Cape, KwaZulu/Natal, Eastern Transvaal). ❄ (min. 41°F/5°C)
W. pyramidata see *W. borbonica.*
***W.* 'Stanford Scarlet'** ▣ Slender, clump-forming, cormous perennial with sword-shaped leaves, 16–39in (40–100cm) long. Bears unbranched spikes of 10–12 tubular scarlet flowers, 1¼in (3cm) long, with spreading tepal lobes, in late spring or summer. ↕ 32–54in (80–140cm), PD6in (15cm). ❄ (min. 41°F/5°C)

▷ ***Wattakaka*** see *Dregea*

WEBEROCEREUS

CACTACEAE

Genus of about 5 species of climbing or pendent, epiphytic or rock-dwelling cacti from mostly rainforest habitats in Mexico, Guatemala, Nicaragua, Costa Rica, and Panama. They have aerial roots and spiny, fleshy stems that may be 3- or 4-angled, slender and cylindrical, or flat and leaf-like with scalloped margins. Nocturnal, cup- or funnel-shaped, pink or greenish or yellowish white flowers are produced in midsummer, followed by spherical to oblong, warty fruits with short, spiny or hairy areoles. Where temperatures drop below 59°F (15°C), grow in a warm greenhouse; in warmer climates, use outdoors in a courtyard garden or against a wall.
• **CULTIVATION** Under glass, grow in epiphytic cactus potting mix, with added leaf mold, in bright filtered light and high humidity. From spring to early autumn, water freely, apply a half-strength, balanced liquid fertilizer every 4 or 5 weeks, and mist daily with tepid water. Keep winter-flowering species dry in late summer. Keep just moist at other times. Outdoors, grow in gritty, moderately fertile, sharply drained, acidic soil in partial shade. See also pp.48–49.
• **PROPAGATION** Sow seed at 66–75°F (19–24°C), or take cuttings of stem sections, both in spring or summer.
• **PESTS AND DISEASES** Scale insects may attack plants if kept too dry.

Weberocereus biolleyi

W. biolleyi ■ Mainly pendent cactus with cylindrical or irregularly 4-angled stems, ¼in (6mm) thick, sometimes branching. Small, white-woolly areoles occasionally bear 1–3 very short, fine yellow spines. Funnel-shaped, whitish pink flowers, 1¼–2in (3–5cm) long, with dark pink outer petals, are borne in midsummer. ↕ 32in (80cm), ↔ 12in (30cm). Costa Rica. ❀ (min. 59°F/15°C)
W. bradei, syn. *Eccremocactus bradei.* Pendent cactus with flat, leaf-like, wavy-margined, jointed branches, to 4in (10cm) across; these produce small, pale brown-woolly areoles, each with one dark brown spine. Funnel-shaped white flowers, 2½–3in (6–8cm) long, with slightly expanding, fleshy petals, pale pink outside, are borne from the upper areoles from spring to autumn. ↕↔ 24in (60cm). Costa Rica. ❀ (min. 59°F/15°C)
W. glaber, syn. *Werckleocereus glaber.* Climbing cactus with 3-angled, toothed, pale green stems, 1–1¾in (2.5–4.5cm) thick. Small, brown-woolly areoles bear 2–4 yellow or brown spines. Cup-shaped white flowers, 4–5in (10–13cm) long, with pale greenish brown outer petals, are borne in midsummer. ↕ 10ft (3m), ↔ 24in (60cm). Mexico, Guatemala, Costa Rica. ❀ (min. 59°F/15°C)

WEDELIA

ASTERACEAE

Genus of about 70 species of erect, prostrate, or climbing, hairy annuals, evergreen perennials, and soft-stemmed or woody shrubs, found near coasts in tropical and subtropical regions. They have opposite, usually oblong to elliptic or obovate, toothed or lobed leaves, and are grown for their daisy-like yellow flowerheads, borne either singly or in few-headed clusters in summer. Where not hardy, grow as houseplants, or in a warm greenhouse, or use outdoors in summer in containers. In warmer areas, *W. trilobata* is a rampant groundcover, and is particularly useful for growing in dry shade under trees.

• **CULTIVATION** Grow in any well-drained soil or potting mix.
• **PROPAGATION** Sow seed at 64°F (18°C), divide, or root stem-tip cuttings, at any time.
• **PESTS AND DISEASES** Leaf spots and powdery mildew can occur.

W. trilobata ■ Creeping, evergreen perennial, rooting at the leaf nodes and spreading widely. The elliptic or

Wedelia trilobata

obovate, mid- to dark green leaves, 5in (13cm) long, are usually 3-lobed, sometimes entire or barely lobed. Solitary, daisy-like yellow flowerheads, ¾in (2cm) across, are borne from late spring to autumn. ↕ 6–8in (15–20cm), ↔ 6ft (2m) or more. Florida, West Indies, Central America, tropical South America. ❀ (min. 55°F/13°C)

WEIGELA

CAPRIFOLIACEAE

Genus of 12 species of mostly spreading to upright, deciduous shrubs found in scrub and woodland margins in E. Asia. They have opposite, oblong to ovate or elliptic, toothed leaves, usually up to 4in (10cm) long. Weigelas are cultivated for their showy, bell- to funnel-shaped, pink to red, sometimes white or yellow flowers; these are usually 1½in (4cm) long, and are borne singly or in corymbs or cymes of 3 or 4, usually on short lateral twigs on the previous year's branches; many are sparingly remontant. Suitable for a mixed or shrub border, or for open woodland. The flowers attract hummingbirds.

• **CULTIVATION** Grow in any fertile, well-drained soil in full sun or partial shade. Pruning group 2.
• **PROPAGATION** Sow seed in containers in a cold frame in autumn; weigelas hybridize readily, so seed may not come true. Root greenwood cuttings in early summer; semi-ripe cuttings with bottom heat in midsummer; and hardwood cuttings from autumn to winter.
• **PESTS AND DISEASES** Root knot nematode, Japanese beetle, scale insects, *Verticillium* wilt, and twig dieback can be problems.

***W.* 'Abel Carrière'.** Spreading shrub with oval, dark green leaves. Bell-shaped, dark pinkish red flowers, with yellow-spotted throats, open from purple-red buds in late spring and early summer. ↕↔ 6ft (2m). Zone 6.
***W.* 'Briant Rubidor'**, syn. *W.* 'Olympiade'. Spreading shrub with oval leaves, to 3in (8cm) long, yellow-green at first, turning bright yellow or sometimes becoming margined with yellow. In late spring and early summer, bears bell-shaped, dark ruby-red flowers, 1¼in (3cm) long. Best in partial shade. ↕↔ 6ft (2m). Zone 5.
***W.* 'Bristol Ruby'.** Vigorous, upright shrub with oval, dark green leaves and usually bell-shaped, dark red flowers,

Weigela 'Eva Rathke' (inset: flower detail)

opening from very dark red buds, in late spring and early summer. ↕ 8ft (2.5m), ↔ 6ft (2m). Zone 5.
***W.* 'Bristol Snowflake'** see *W.* 'Snowflake'.
***W.* 'Candida'.** Spreading, bushy shrub with oval, bright green leaves and bell-shaped, pure white flowers, borne in late spring and early summer. ↕↔ 8ft (2.5m). Zone 4.
***W.* 'Carnaval'.** Vigorous, upright shrub with oval, dark green leaves, to 4in (10cm) or more long. Bell-shaped flowers, to 2in (5cm) long, in a combination of pale pink, white, and dark pink, are borne in late spring and early summer. ↕ 8ft (2.5m), ↔ 6ft (2m). Zone 4.
***W.* 'Eva Rathke'** ■ Compact, upright shrub with oval, dark green leaves and broadly funnel-shaped, dark crimson flowers, opening from dark red buds in late spring and early summer. ↕↔ 5ft (1.5m). Zone 5.
W. florida. Spreading shrub with arching shoots and oval, tapered, dark green leaves. Produces corymbs of funnel-shaped, dark pink flowers, 1¼in (3cm) long, pale pink to nearly white inside, in late spring and early

Weigela florida 'Foliis Purpureis'

summer. ↕↔ 8ft (2.5m). N. China, Korea. Zone 5. **'Foliis Purpureis'** ■ syn. 'Java Red', has bronze-green foliage; ↕ 3ft (1m), ↔ 5ft (1.5m). **'Java Red'** see 'Foliis Purpureis'. **'Lucifer'** is compact in habit, producing dark green leaves and large, deep red flowers, 1¾in (4.5cm) long; ↕ 3–5ft (1–1.5m). **'Variegata'** ■ is compact, and has yellow to creamy white-edged, gray-green leaves, and deep rose flowers; ↕↔ 4–6ft (1.2–2m).
***W.* 'Looymansii Aurea'** ■ Slow-growing, spreading shrub with arching shoots and oval, golden yellow leaves, 3in (8cm) long, narrowly margined with red. Bears bell-shaped, pale pink flowers in late spring and early summer. Best in partial shade. ↕↔ 5ft (1.5m). Zone 5.

Weigela florida 'Variegata'

Weigela 'Looymansii Aurea'

W. middendorffiana. Upright shrub with oval, bright green leaves, to 3in (8cm) long. Bell-shaped, pale yellow flowers, often with conspicuous, orange or red throat markings, are borne in terminal cymes from midspring to midsummer. ↕↔ 5ft (1.5m). N.E. Russia, N. China, Korea, Japan. Zone 4.
***W.* 'Minuet'.** Compact, spreading shrub with oval, bronze-green leaves, to 3in (8cm) long. Bell-shaped, slightly fragrant, dark pink flowers, with yellow throats, are produced in late spring and early summer. ↕ 30in (75cm), ↔ 4ft (1.2m). Zone 4.
***W.* 'Newport Red'**, syn. *W.* 'Vanicek'. Vigorous, upright shrub with oblong-ovate to obovate, mid-green leaves, 2–4½in (5–11cm) long. Bears bell-shaped, purple-red flowers with yellow anthers, in late spring and early summer. ↕↔ 5ft (1.5m). Zone 5.
***W.* 'Olympiade'** see *W.* 'Briant Rubidor'.
***W.* 'Pink Princess'.** Spreading, open shrub with oblong-ovate to obovate, mid-green leaves, 2–4½in (5–11cm) long. Bears bell-shaped, lavender-pink flowers in late spring and early summer. ↕ 5–6ft (1.5–2m), ↔ 4–5ft (1.2–1.5m). Zone 5.
***W.* 'Polka'.** Vigorous, spreading shrub with oblong-ovate to obovate, dark green leaves, 2½–3in (6–8cm) long. Bears bell-shaped pink flowers with yellow throats, from early summer to early autumn. ↕ 3–4ft (1–1.2m), ↔ 4–5ft (1.2–1.5m). Zone 4.
W. praecox. Upright shrub with oval, dark green leaves, hairy beneath. In late spring and early summer, bears corymbs of funnel-shaped, fragrant pink flowers with yellow throats. ↕ 8ft (2.5m), ↔ 6ft (2m). N.E. Russia, Korea, Japan. Zone 4. **'Variegata'** produces leaves with creamy yellow margins that turn white with age.
***W.* 'Red Prince'.** Upright shrub with oblong-ovate to obovate, mid-green leaves, 2–4½in (5–11cm) long. Bell-shaped red flowers, which do not fade, are borne in early summer and again in late summer. ↕ 5–6ft (1.5–2m), ↔ 4–5ft (1.2–1.5m). Zone 5.
***W.* 'Rumba'.** Vigorous, compact, spreading shrub with oblong-ovate to obovate, purple-edged, yellow-green leaves, 3in (8cm) long. From early summer to early autumn, bears bell-shaped, dark red flowers with yellow throats. ↕ 3ft (1m), ↔ 3½ft (1.1m). Zone 3b.
***W.* 'Samba'.** Vigorous, compact, spreading shrub with oblong-ovate to obovate, dark green leaves, 2½–3in (6–8cm) long, with purple tips and edges. In late spring and early summer, bears bell-shaped, red flowers with yellow throats. ↕↔ 3ft (1m). Zone 4.
***W.* 'Snowflake'**, syn. *W.* 'Bristol Snowflake'. Spreading shrub with ovate, dark green leaves and bell-shaped, pure white flowers, borne profusely in late spring and early summer. ↕ 4ft (1.2m), ↔ 5ft (1.5m). Zone 5.
***W.* 'Tango'.** Compact shrub with oblong-ovate to obovate, purple-green leaves, 2½–5in (6–13cm) long, dark green beneath. In late spring and early summer, bears bell-shaped red flowers with yellow throats. ↕ 24in (60cm), ↔ 30in (75cm). Zone 4.
***W.* 'Vanicek'** see *W.* 'Newport Red'.

▷ ***Weingartia*** see *Rebutia*

WELDENIA

COMMELINACEAE

Genus of one species of tuberous perennial occurring in the mountains of Mexico and Guatemala. *W. candida* is grown for its rosettes of large, simple leaves and its stalkless cymes of cup-shaped white flowers. Grow in a raised bed; in regions with cool, damp winters, it is best grown in an alpine house.

• **CULTIVATION** Grow in gritty, moderately fertile, sharply drained soil in full sun. Protect from excessive winter moisture. In an alpine house, grow in deep containers in a mix of equal parts loam, leaf mold, and grit. Water freely during the growing season; reduce water as leaves wither, and keep barely moist when dormant in winter. Repot annually in autumn.
• **PROPAGATION** Sow seed as soon as ripe in containers in a cold frame. Divide in spring. Take root cuttings in winter.
• **PESTS AND DISEASES** Aphids and whiteflies may be problems under glass.

Weldenia candida

W. candida ▣ Tuberous perennial with rosettes of lance-shaped, pointed, wavy-margined, slightly leathery leaves, 2–8in (5–20cm) long. In late spring and early summer, bears a long succession of upright, cup-shaped, pure white flowers, to 1¼in (3cm) across. ↕↔ to 6in (15cm). Mexico, Guatemala. ❄ (min. 41°F/5°C)

WELWITSCHIA

WELWITSCHIACEAE

Genus of one species of prostrate, dioecious, evergreen perennial from deserts, mainly coastal, in Angola and Namibia. It has a large but relatively shallow taproot with many lateral roots just below ground level. The fleshy, leathery, mid- or gray-green leaves are strap-shaped, and the inflorescences are cone-like. In their natural habitat, male plants produce masses of pollen, which is carried on the wind to female plants. In summer, females can produce up to 100 conical to spherical floral cones. Where not hardy, grow in a warm greenhouse; in warmer climates, use in a desert garden. Its adaptation to the extreme conditions of its natural habitat makes it difficult to cultivate.

• **CULTIVATION** Under glass, grow in a mixture of 2 parts sharp, granitic sand and 1 part each soil-based potting mix, peat, and leaf mold. Provide full light and low humidity. Grow in deep containers, or in a clay drainpipe, and top-dress with crushed limestone. From spring to autumn, water moderately and apply a balanced liquid fertilizer every 6–8 weeks. Keep completely dry in winter. Outdoors, grow in gritty, poor, sharply drained soil, with added leaf mold, in full sun. See also pp.48–49.
• **PROPAGATION** Sow seed at 66–75°F (19–24°C) as soon as ripe; sow in tall, narrow containers that allow for the growth of the taproot.
• **PESTS AND DISEASES** Infrequent.

W. bainesii see *W. mirabilis.*
W. mirabilis ▣ syn. *W. bainesii.* Prostrate, dioecious, evergreen perennial with a short, conical caudex becoming swollen with age, often 3ft (1m) across in very old plants, and divided in half by a groove. The 2 strap-shaped, often curling, leathery, fleshy, mid- or gray-green leaves, 6ft (2m) or more long, grow from marginal grooves on the crown. Cones are produced in axillary cymes from the top of the caudex in summer: female cones, 2in (5cm) long, are brownish green; male cones, 1¼in (3cm) long, are reddish brown. ↕ 18in (45cm) or more, ↔ 12ft (4m). Angola, Namibia. ❄ (min. 66°F/19°C)

Welwitschia mirabilis

▷ ***Werckleocereus glaber*** see *Weberocereus glaber*

WESTRINGIA

LAMIACEAE

Genus of about 25 species of rounded to erect, evergreen shrubs from dry coastal heathland, scrub, sands, and dry forest in Australia. They are cultivated for their flowers and foliage. The crowded, narrowly linear to ovate, rosemary-like leaves are produced in whorls of 3–5. The tubular, white to pale blue or mauve flowers are 2-lipped, the upper lip longer, erect and 2-lobed, the lower lip divided into 3 spreading lobes; the flowers are borne singly in the uppermost leaf axils or in terminal clusters. Where not hardy, grow in a cool greenhouse. In milder regions, use in a border, or as a hedge or screen.

• **CULTIVATION** Under glass, grow in soil-based potting mix, with added leaf mold and sharp sand, in full light. When in growth, water moderately and apply a balanced liquid fertilizer monthly. Water sparingly in winter. Outdoors, grow in moderately fertile, moist but well-drained soil in full sun. Pruning group 9; trim hedges in late spring and late summer. May need restrictive pruning under glass.
• **PROPAGATION** Sow seed at 55–64°F (13–18°C) in spring. Root greenwood cuttings in early summer, or semi-ripe cuttings in midsummer.
• **PESTS AND DISEASES** Leaf spots and root rot occur.

W. fruticosa ▣ syn. *W. rosmariniformis* (Australian rosemary, Victorian rosemary). Erect, bushy, rounded shrub, at least when young, becoming more open as it matures, with linear to narrowly lance-shaped leaves, ½–1in (1.5–2.5cm) long, mid- to deep green above, white-felted beneath. Solitary, tubular, white to very pale blue flowers, ½in (1.5cm) across, with darker freckling in the throats, are borne in axillary cymes from late spring to early autumn. Excellent topiary subject. ↕↔ 3–5ft (1–1.5m). New South Wales. ❄ (min. 41°F/5°C). **'Morning Light'** produces cream-edged leaves; ↕↔ 3–4ft (1–1.2m).
W. rosmariniformis see *W. fruticosa.*

Westringia fruticosa

WIDDRINGTONIA

African cypress

CUPRESSACEAE

Genus of 3 species of upright, spreading, evergreen trees or shrubs native to Southern Africa. They are grown for their exfoliating, red-tinged gray bark, and blue-green foliage. African cypresses are very flammable and should not be planted in residential areas threatened by brush fires. Use as a specimen tree or in a large shrub border. Where not hardy, grow in a cool greenhouse or indoors as a bonsai.

• **CULTIVATION** Under glass, grow in soil-based potting mix in full light. Water moderately in growth, sparingly in winter. Apply a balanced liquid fertilizer when in growth. Outdoors, grow in sharply drained, loam-based soil in full sun. Pruning group 1.

• **PROPAGATION** Sow seed *in situ* as soon as ripe or take cuttings.

• **PESTS AND DISEASES** Infrequent.

W. cedarbergensis see *W. juniperoides*.

W. juniperoides, syn. *W. cedarbergensis* (Clanwilliam cedar). Cone-shaped evergreen tree with rust-gray bark, red-brown twigs, and blue-green leaves, to ¾in (2cm) long. Juvenile leaves are arranged in whorls, linear, sharp, flat, and blue-green; mature leaves are opposite and scale-like. Bears clustered, spherical, black-brown cones, to 1in (2.5cm) across, with woody, warty, spurred scales. ↕ to 22ft (7m), ↔ 12–15ft (4–5m). South Africa. ❄ (min. 41°F/5°C)

WIGANDIA

HYDROPHYLLACEAE

Genus of 5 species of evergreen, upright to spreading perennials, subshrubs, shrubs, and small trees occurring in woodland and roadsides in tropical US, Central America, and South America. They are cultivated for their flowers and foliage. The large, alternate, simple, oblong to broadly ovate, toothed leaves are covered in stinging hairs. Tubular-based, bell-shaped, usually lilac to violet flowers, with 5 broad, wide-spreading lobes, are borne in terminal panicles. Where temperatures fall below 41–45°F (5–7°C) in winter, grow *Wigandia* species in a cool or temperate greenhouse, or use as annuals for summer bedding. In milder regions, grow as specimen plants. Contact with foliage may aggravate skin allergies.

• **CULTIVATION** Under glass, grow in soil-based potting mix in full light. During the growing season, water moderately and apply a balanced liquid fertilizer monthly. Water sparingly in winter. Outdoors, grow in fertile, moist but well-drained soil in full sun. Pruning group 1; may need restrictive pruning under glass.

• **PROPAGATION** Sow seed at 55–64°F (13–18°C) in spring. Take greenwood cuttings in early summer.

• **PESTS AND DISEASES** Spider mites may be troublesome under glass.

W. caracasana ▣ syn. *W. macrophylla*. Open, soft-stemmed, evergreen sub-shrub with robust, sparsely branched, yellow- to white-woolly stems. Long-stalked, ovate, coarsely toothed leaves,

Wigandia caracasana

12–24in (30–60cm) long, heart-shaped at the bases, are mid- to deep green above, hoary beneath. Bears bell-shaped, white-tubed, light violet flowers, ¾in (2cm) across, in large, terminal panicles, to 12in (30cm) or more long, mainly in summer. ↕ 10–12ft (3–4m), ↔ 6–11ft (2–3.5m). Mexico to Colombia. ❄ (min. 45°F/7°C)

W. macrophylla see *W. caracasana*.

▷ ***Wigginsia*** see *Parodia*
W. vorwerkiana see *P. erinacea*

WIKSTROEMIA

THYMELAEACEAE

Genus of approximately 70 species of deciduous or evergreen, spreading to upright shrubs and trees, closely related to *Daphne*. They are usually found in habitats ranging from dry slopes to wet woodland in mountainous areas from the Himalayas to E. Asia, Sri Lanka, Australia, and the Pacific islands. The alternate or opposite leaves are oblong-lance-shaped to broadly ovate. Tubular or salverform, usually yellow flowers are produced in terminal spikes, racemes, cymes, or, occasionally, panicles. They are seldom cultivated, but *W. canescens*, valued for its flowers, will grow in a sheltered position in a woodland garden or informal shrub border. Where not hardy, grow the tender species in a cool or temperate greenhouse.

• **CULTIVATION** Grow in any well-drained but moisture-retentive soil in full sun to partial shade, providing shade during the hottest part of the day. Where not hardy, shelter from cold, drying winds. Pruning group 1.

• **PROPAGATION** Sow seed in containers in a cold frame in autumn.

• **PESTS AND DISEASES** Infrequent.

W. canescens. Upright, deciduous shrub with slender, arching shoots. Alternate to nearly opposite, elliptic leaves are up to 3in (8cm) long. In late summer and early autumn, purple flower buds open to tubular, yellow to greenish yellow flowers, ½in (1.5cm) long, each with a slender, slightly curved tube and 4 short lobes, in terminal cymes. ↕ 6ft (1.8m), ↔ 5ft (1.5m). Sri Lanka, Himalayas, China. ❄ (min. 45°F/7°C)

▷ ***Wilcoxia albiflora*** see *Echinocereus leucanthus*

▷ ***Wilcoxia schmollii*** see *Echinocereus schmollii*

WILSONARA

ORCHIDACEAE

Hybrid genus of evergreen orchids, derived from crosses between *Cochlioda*, *Odontoglossum*, and *Oncidium*. Conical, flattened pseudobulbs grow from a rhizome, each pseudobulb producing 1 or 2 soft, linear to lance-shaped leaves at its apex. The inflorescences, either tall panicles with 100 or more flowers, or shorter panicles of larger flowers, are produced from the bases of the pseudobulbs. The rounded, sometimes star-shaped flowers are very variably colored, often having conspicuous markings.

• **CULTIVATION** Cool-growing orchids. Grow in epiphytic orchid potting mix in containers that restrict the roots. In summer, provide bright filtered light and high humidity, water freely, apply a fertilizer at every third watering, and mist twice daily. In winter, admit full light, water sparingly, provide moderate humidity, and mist daily. See also p.46.

• **PROPAGATION** Divide every 2 years or when plants fill their containers and flow over the sides.

• **PESTS AND DISEASES** Aphids, spider mites, and mealybugs may be problems.

***W.* Hambühren Stern 'Cheam'** ▣ (*Oncidium tigrinum* x *Odontioda* Lippestern). Evergreen orchid with 1 or 2 linear leaves, 9in (23cm) long. Almost circular flowers, 2½in (6cm) across, are rich brown and yellow, and are borne in long panicles at any time of year. ↕ 24in (60cm), ↔ 12in (30cm). ❄ (min. 50°F/10°C; max. 86°F/30°C)

***W.* Widecombe Fair.** Evergreen orchid with 1 or 2 linear leaves, 9in (23cm) long. At any time of the year, bears almost circular white flowers, to 2in (5cm) across, with deep mauve spots, in large, branching panicles. ↕ 24in (60cm), ↔ 12in (30cm). ❄ (min. 50°F/10°C; max. 86°F/30°C)

▷ ***Wintera aromatica*** see *Drimys winteri*

Wilsonara Hambühren Stern 'Cheam'

WISTERIA

FABACEAE

Genus of about 10 species of twining, woody, deciduous climbers found in moist woodland and on streambanks in China, Korea, Japan, and C. and S. US. They have alternate, pinnate, dark green leaves, to 14in (35cm) or more long, with ovate to lance-shaped or elliptic leaflets. They are cultivated for their showy, pea-like, fragrant flowers, borne in usually pendent racemes in spring or summer, followed by pendent, bean-like green seed pods. Train against a wall, into a large tree, over a sturdy arch or pergola, or as a standard. All parts may cause severe discomfort if ingested.

• **CULTIVATION** Grow in fertile, moist but well-drained soil in full sun or partial shade. To train formally, after planting, prune back the leading shoot to 30–36in (75–90cm) above ground level. During the first growing season, tie in lateral shoots to the framework and cut back sublaterals to 2 or 3 buds. In the first winter, cut back laterals by one-third of their length, and sublaterals to 2 or 3 buds; cut back the leading shoot again, to 30–36in (75–90cm) above the point from which the topmost laterals branch. In subsequent years, repeat the pruning of the leader and selection of lateral shoots until the framework has been completed. Once established, in late summer cut back all shoots not needed to extend the framework, to within 6in (15cm) of the main branches; leave 4–6 leaves on each shoot. In late winter, reduce these spurs further to 3–4in (8–10cm), leaving only 2 or 3 buds.

• **PROPAGATION** Take basal cuttings from side shoots in early to midsummer and root with bottom heat. Layer in autumn, or graft in winter.

• **PESTS AND DISEASES** Dieback, crown gall, leaf spots, virus diseases, Japanese beetle, aphids, leaf miners, scale insects, and mealybugs can be problems.

W. brachybotrys, syn. *W. venusta* (Silky wisteria). Twining climber with pinnate, softly hairy leaves, to 14in (35cm) long, each composed of 9–13 ovate to lance-shaped leaflets. Pea-like, fragrant, yellow-marked, violet to white flowers are produced in racemes, to 6in (15cm) long, in early summer; they are followed by bean-like, velvety green seed pods, to 8in (20cm) long. ↕ 28ft (9m) or more.

Wisteria brachybotrys 'Shiro Kapitan'

Wisteria floribunda 'Alba'

Japan. Zone 7. **'Alba'** see 'Shiro Kapitan'. **f. *alba*** see 'Shiro Kapitan'. **'Alba Plena'** see 'Shiro Kapitan'. **'Murasaki Kapitan'**, syn. *W. venusta* 'Violacea', *W. venusta* f. *violacea*, produces deep blue-violet flowers with prominent white, slightly yellow-tinged markings on the standards. **f. *plena*** see 'Shiro Kapitan'. **'Shiro Kapitan'** ▣ syn. 'Alba', f. *alba*, 'Alba Plena', f. *plena*, *W. venusta*, *W. venusta* 'Alba', *W. venusta* f. *alba*, *W. venusta* 'Alba Plena', produces white, sometimes double, flowers with yellow markings.
W. chinensis see *W. sinensis*.
W. floribunda (Japanese wisteria). Vigorous, twining climber with pinnate leaves, each composed of 11–19 ovate to lance-shaped leaflets. In late spring, pea-like, fragrant, blue to violet, pink, or

Wisteria floribunda 'Macrobotrys'

white flowers, the standards marked with white and yellow, are produced in pendent racemes, to 12in (30cm) or more long, the flowers opening gradually from the bases to the tips before or as the leaves emerge; they are often followed by bean-like, velvety green seed pods, to 6in (15cm) long. Has escaped from cultivation and become weedy in many areas. ↕ 28ft (9m) or more. Japan. Zone 6. **'Alba'** ▣ syn. 'Shiro Noda', bears white flowers in racemes to 24in (60cm) long. **'Black Dragon'** see 'Royal Purple'. **'Double Black Dragon'** see 'Violacea Plena'. **'Honbeni'**, syn. 'Honko', 'Rosea', f. *rosea*, has pink flowers in racemes to 18in (45cm) long. **'Honko'** see 'Honbeni'. **'Kokuryu'** see 'Royal Purple'. **'Kyushaku'** see 'Macrobotrys'. **'Lawrence'** has violet-blue flowers in racemes 18in (45cm) long. Zone 5. **'Macrobotrys'** ▣ syn. 'Kyushaku', 'Multijuga', 'Naga Noda', has lilac-blue flowers in racemes 3–4ft (0.9–1.2m) long. **'Multijuga'** see 'Macrobotrys'. **'Naga Noda'** see 'Macrobotrys'. **'Rosea'** see 'Honbeni'. **f. *rosea*** see 'Honbeni'. **'Royal Purple'**, syn. 'Black Dragon', 'Kokuryu', has racemes, 12–20in (30–50cm) long, with purple-violet flowers. **'Shiro Noda'** see 'Alba'. **'Violacea Plena'**, syn. 'Double Black Dragon', 'Yae Kokyuryu', has double, violet-blue flowers. **'Yae Kokyuryu'** see 'Violacea Plena'.
W. sinensis, syn. *W. chinensis* (Chinese wisteria). Vigorous, twining climber with pinnate leaves, each composed of 7–13 elliptic or ovate leaflets. In late spring, bears pea-like, fragrant, lilac-blue

Wisteria sinensis 'Alba'

to white flowers, in dense, pendent racemes to 12in (30cm) long, opening more or less simultaneously, and with the leaves; they are often followed by bean-like, velvety green seed pods, to 6in (15cm) long. ↕ 28ft (9m) or more. China. Zone 6. **'Alba'** ▣ produces white flowers. **'Prolific'** bears many lilac-blue to pale violet-blue flowers. **'Sierra Madre'** has very fragrant, lavender-violet flowers with white-flushed standards.
W. venusta and its related forms and cultivars see *W. brachybotrys*.

WITHANIA

SOLANACEAE

Genus of about 10 species of mostly evergreen shrubs distributed mainly in Asia and Africa, with two species in Europe. *W. somnifera* occurs in stony areas up to 5,500ft (1,700m), and as a weed near habitation. Like most other members of the nightshade family (Solanaceae), they are rich in alkaloids and all parts should be regarded as toxic.
• **CULTIVATION** Dry, stony soil in sun or partial shade. Cut back plants in early spring.
• **PROPAGATION** By seed sown in spring; by greenwood cuttings with a heel in late spring.
• **PESTS AND DISEASES** Infrequent.

W. somnifera ▣ (Winter cherry, ashwagandha). Upright, evergreen shrub with mealy stems and ovate leaves, to 4in (10cm) long. Green to yellow inconspicuous flowers grow in clusters in the leaf axils all year, followed by globse, orange-red berries, ¼in (6mm)

Withania somnifera

across, enclosed in a papery, inflated calyx. ↕ 2–6ft (60cm–2m), ↔ 1–3ft (30cm–1m). Mediterranean and Middle East to India and Sri Lanka. ❄ (min. 59°F/15°C)

▷ ***Wittia amazonica*** see *Disocactus amazonicus*
▷ ***Wittiocactus amazonicus*** see *Disocactus amazonicus*

WITTROCKIA

BROMELIACEAE

Genus, closely related to *Nidularium*, of 7 species of rosetted, stemless, evergreen, terrestrial, epiphytic, or rock-dwelling perennials (bromeliads) from coastal to highland areas, to 3,000ft (900m) high, in Brazil. The linear, spiny-margined, scaly leaves, smooth near the tips, are often wide and colorful. In summer, spikes of tubular, usually blue flowers, with 3 separate sepals and 3 petals joined only at their tips, are produced among clusters of leaf-like bracts within the leaf rosettes. In areas where temperatures drop below 64°F (18°C), grow as houseplants or in a warm greenhouse; in warmer climates, use in a humid, moist border.
• **CULTIVATION** Under glass, grow in standard epiphytic or terrestrial bromeliad potting mix in bright filtered light. From late spring to early autumn, mist daily with tepid water to maintain moderate humidity, and apply a low-nitrogen liquid fertilizer every 3 or 4 weeks. Outdoors, grow in peaty, leafy, moderately fertile, moist but well-drained soil in a site in partial shade. See also p.47.
• **PROPAGATION** Sow seed at 66–75°F (19–24°C) in spring. Detach offsets in spring or summer.
• **PESTS AND DISEASES** Susceptible to damage from mealybugs, aphids, slugs, and snails.

W. superba ▣ Terrestrial, epiphytic, or rock-dwelling, evergreen bromeliad producing linear, pointed, mid-green leaves, to 3ft (1m) long, narrower at the bases, and with brown scales, red tips, and spiny, red or green teeth. Compact, sunken inflorescences, 5in (13cm) wide, consisting of cone-shaped spikes of tubular blue flowers with pointed petals, surrounded by red bracts, are produced on very short scapes in summer. ↕↔ 3ft (1m) or more. E. Brazil. ❄ (min. 64°F/18°C)

Wittrockia superba

Wolffia arrhiza

Woodsia polystichoides

Woodwardia radicans

WOLFFIA

LEMNACEAE

Genus of 8 species of semi-evergreen, floating aquatic perennials, similar to duckweeds (*Lemna*) but much smaller and lacking a root, with a wide distribution in Europe, Africa, W. Asia, India, Australia, North America, and E. Brazil. They are the smallest known flowering plants, grown mainly for their curiosity value. Where not hardy, grow in an aquarium. In warmer climates, grow in an outdoor pool.
• **CULTIVATION** In an outdoor pool, grow in full sun. In an aquarium, grow at 59–82°F (15–28°C) in full light. See also pp.52–53.
• **PROPAGATION** Remove and relocate a number of plants.
• **PESTS AND DISEASES** Infrequent.

W. arrhiza ▣ Semi-evergreen, floating aquatic perennial with rootless, rounded, bright green fronds, 1/16in (2mm) across. Insignificant, green-tinged white flowers are produced in summer. ↔ indefinite. Europe, Africa, W. Asia, Australia. ❄ (min. 35°F/2°C)

WOODSIA

DRYOPTERIDACEAE

Genus of approximately 25 species of small, tufted, deciduous, terrestrial or rock-dwelling ferns occurring in upland and mountainous regions, mainly in the N. hemisphere. They have erect, short rhizomes, and pinnate to 2-pinnate fronds, with the pinnae sometimes pinnatifid. Sporangia are in cup-shaped indusia, which have often deeply cut fringes. Suitable for a shady rock garden.
• **CULTIVATION** Grow in sharply drained but moist, fertile soil in partial shade. Position crowns above soil level and surround with small stones. *W. ilvensis* prefers acidic soil.
• **PROPAGATION** Sow spores at 59–61°F (15–16°C) as soon as ripe. Divide when dormant. See also p.51.
• **PESTS AND DISEASES** Infrequent.

W. ilvensis (Rusty woodsia). Dwarf, tufted, terrestrial or rock-dwelling fern. In early spring, produces lance-shaped to oblong, pinnate, dull green fronds, to 6in (15cm) long, each composed of 7–25 pairs of ovate to lance-shaped, lobed pinnae, clothed with reddish brown hairs and scales. ↕ 6in (15cm), ↔ 4in (10cm). Arctic, Europe, North America. Zone 3.
W. obtusa (Blunt-lobed woodsia, Common woodsia, Large woodsia). Tufted, terrestrial or rock-dwelling fern. In early spring, produces ovate to oblong, pinnate, dull green fronds, to 24in (60cm) long, each composed of 8–17 pairs of triangular to lance-shaped pinnae, with notched margins. ↕ to 24in (60cm), ↔ 10–16in (25–40cm). Quebec to Florida. Zone 4.
W. polystichoides ▣ (Holly-fern woodsia). Tufted, terrestrial or rock-dwelling fern. In early spring, produces lance-shaped, pinnate, pale green fronds, to 14in (35cm) long, softly hairy on both surfaces and scaly beneath; each is composed of 15–30 pairs of narrowly sickle-shaped or oblong pinnae, with slightly toothed margins. ↕ 4–12in (10–30cm), ↔ 8–16in (20–40cm). E. Asia. Zone 5.

WOODWARDIA

Chain fern

BLECHNACEAE

Genus of approximately 10 species of evergreen or deciduous, terrestrial ferns found in damp, sheltered places in warm-temperate regions of Eurasia and North America. Some are creeping plants, found in acidic bogs. Most are large, often with spreading and arching, usually pinnate fronds with pinnatifid pinnae, unfurling in spring; bulbils may be produced toward the tips of the fronds or on their upper surfaces. The chain-like arrangement of the sori on the undersides of the pinnae gives rise to the common name. Use to clothe a moist, shady bank, ideally near water.
• **CULTIVATION** Grow in neutral, moderately fertile, damp soil in partial shade. Where marginally hardy, shelter from wind and protect in winter with a dry mulch.
• **PROPAGATION** Sow spores at 61°F (16°C) in late summer or early autumn. Remove bulbils in autumn. Divide in spring. See also p.51.
• **PESTS AND DISEASES** Rust can occur.

W. areolata, syn. *Lorinsaria areolata* (Netted chain fern). Upright, clump-forming, deciduous fern producing upright, ovate-lance-shaped, mid-green fronds, 18in (45cm) long. The erect, narrowly elliptic to oblong, thin, papery pinnae, are pinnate at the bases and pinnatifid at the tips, and have narrowly linear, scalloped or shallowly lobed segments. ↕↔ 18in (45cm). E. North America. Zone 3.
W. fimbriata (Giant chain fern). Sprawling, rosette-forming, deciduous fern producing elliptic-lance-shaped, pinnate-pinnatifid, mid-green fronds, 5ft (1.5m) long. The oblong-lance-shaped, pinnatifid pinnae have narrowly triangular to linear, tapered, long-pointed, scalloped or shallowly lobed segments. ↕ 3ft (1m), ↔ 3–9ft (1–3m). S. British Columbia to S. California. Zone 8.
W. orientalis Evergreen, horizontally arching fern. Thick, leathery, glossy, ovate blades are densely covered with proliferous bulbils, which drop off and rapidly produce new plants. New growth is a glowing deep red. ↕ 4–6ft (1.2–2m). Asia. **var. *formosana*** has a less glossy, coarser texture overall, and larger pinnules.
W. radicans ▣ (European chain fern). Evergreen fern with arching, broadly lance-shaped, pinnate, dark green fronds, to 6ft (2m) tall, producing bulbils near the tips; the pinnatifid pinnae, to 12in (30cm) long, are ovate-lance-shaped, with curved, lance-shaped, finely toothed segments. ↕ 6ft (1.8m), ↔ 10ft (3m). Atlantic islands, S.W. Europe. Zone 8.
W. unigemmata (Asian chain fern). Evergreen fern very similar to *W. radicans*. New foliage emerges brilliant red and fades to brown then green. ↕ 3ft (1m), ↔ 10ft (3m). Himalayas, E. Asia. ❄ (min. 35°F/2°C)

WORSLEYA

Blue amaryllis

AMARYLLIDACEAE

Genus of one species of bulbous, evergreen perennial from moist mountain forests in Brazil. It has strap-shaped leaves, and is grown for its large umbels of funnel-shaped flowers, borne on leafless stems in winter. Where not hardy, it is suitable for a warm greenhouse or conservatory, although it does not readily flower. In warmer climates, grow in a warm, sunny border.
• **CULTIVATION** Plant bulbs with the bottom few inches below soil level. Under glass, grow in soil-based potting mix, with added leaf mold and bark chips or sharp sand, in full light. In the growing season, water freely and apply a balanced liquid fertilizer monthly. Keep barely moist in winter, but do not allow the soil mix to dry out. Outdoors, grow in fertile, reliably moist but sharply drained soil in full sun.
• **PROPAGATION** Sow seed at 66–75°F (19–24°C) in spring.
• **PESTS AND DISEASES** Infrequent.

W. procera see *W. rayneri.*
W. rayneri, syn. *Hippeastrum procerum, W. procera.* Robust, bulbous, evergreen perennial with arching, strap-shaped leaves, to 3ft (1m) long. In winter, bears umbels of up to 14 funnel-shaped flowers, lilac-blue to white at the bases, 1½in (4cm) across, speckled mauve within; the tubes are ¾in (2cm) long, the curving lobes to 6in (15cm) long. ↕ 3–4ft (1–1.2m), PD12in (30cm). Brazil. ❄ (min. 59°F/15°C)

WULFENIA

SCROPHULARIACEAE

Genus of about 6 species of rosette-forming, evergreen perennials from alpine meadows in C. and S.E. Europe, W. Asia, and the Himalayas. They are grown mainly for their spike-like racemes of tubular, 2-lipped, blue to pinkish purple or occasionally white flowers, borne in summer. Leaves are inversely lance-shaped to broadly ovate or oblong. Suitable for a rock garden or wall crevice.
• **CULTIVATION** Grow in gritty, humus-rich, moist but well-drained soil in full sun. Protect from winter moisture.
• **PROPAGATION** Sow seed in containers in a cold frame in spring or autumn. Divide in spring.
• **PESTS AND DISEASES** Infrequent.

W. amherstiana ▣ Evergreen perennial with rosettes of obovate-oblong, coarsely scalloped, conspicuously veined, dark green leaves, 2–6in (5–15cm) long, sparsely hairy beneath. In summer, produces erect stems bearing lax, one-sided racemes, 1½–8in (4–20cm) long, of many small, narrowly tubular, pinkish purple flowers. ↕↔ to 8in (20cm). Afghanistan, W. Himalayas. Zone 6.
W. carinthiaca. Evergreen perennial with rosettes of scalloped, inversely lance-shaped to obovate, shiny, dark green leaves, to 8in (20cm) long. In summer, bears dense, one-sided racemes, 2½–4in (6–10cm) long, of small, narrowly tubular, deep violet-blue flowers on erect stems. ↕↔ 10in (25cm) or more. S.E. Alps, Albania. Zone 6.

Wulfenia amherstiana

X

XANTHOCERAS

SAPINDACEAE

Genus of one species of erect, deciduous, suckering shrub found in scrub and at woodland margins in N. China. An unusual plant and rare in gardens, *X. sorbifolium* is grown for its alternate, pinnate leaves and attractive, star-shaped, 5-petaled, sweetly scented white flowers, borne in late spring. Suitable as a specimen, for a shrub border, for training against a wall, or for a sunny position in a woodland garden.
• **CULTIVATION** Grow in moderately fertile to fertile, well-drained soil in full sun; grows best in areas with hot summers and cold winters. Pruning group 1.
• **PROPAGATION** Sow seed in containers outdoors in autumn. Take root cuttings, or remove rooted suckers, in winter.
• **PESTS AND DISEASES** May be affected by coral spot.

X. sorbifolium ▣ (Yellowhorn). Upright, deciduous shrub with thick shoots and pinnate leaves, to 12in (30cm) long, composed of up to 17 narrowly elliptic to lance-shaped, toothed, glossy, dark green leaflets. As the young leaves emerge in late spring, star-shaped, basally yellow-green-flushed white flowers, 1¼in (3cm) across, are borne in upright, terminal panicles, 6–8in (15–20cm) long; yellow-green marks at the petal bases mature to red-brown. ↕ 12ft (4m), ↔ 10ft (3m). N. China. Zone 5.

Xanthoceras sorbifolium

Xanthorhiza simplicissima

XANTHORHIZA

RANUNCULACEAE

Genus of one species of suckering, deciduous shrub found in moist woodland and on streambanks in E. US. It is cultivated for its alternate, pinnate leaves, clustered at the shoot tips. Tiny, star-shaped, brown-purple flowers are produced in spring. Use as a groundcover in woodland or on a bank.
• **CULTIVATION** Grow in moist but not waterlogged soil in sun to partial shade. Pruning group 1 or 3.
• **PROPAGATION** Sow seed in containers outdoors in autumn. Divide in spring. Root semi-ripe cuttings in summer.
• **PESTS AND DISEASES** Infrequent.

X. apiifolia see *X. simplicissima.*
X. simplicissima ▣ syn. *X. apiifolia* (Yellowroot). Thicket-forming shrub with erect shoots and bright green leaves to 12in (30cm) long, bronze at first, often yellow and red-purple in autumn, each with 3–5 ovate, deeply lobed, irregularly toothed leaflets. In spring, bears tiny, brownish purple flowers in pendent racemes, to 4in (10cm) long, as the leaves emerge. ↕ 24in (60cm), ↔ 5ft (1.5m) or more. E. US. Zone 4.

XANTHOSOMA

Yautia

ARACEAE

Genus of up to 50 species of tuberous or thick-stemmed perennials from forest clearings in tropical US and in Central and South America. They are grown for their edible, fleshy, long-stalked leaves, which may be arrow- to spear-shaped or pedately divided into 3–18 segments. Their cylindrical or spherical tubers or corms, which are white, orange, pink, or purple inside, are also edible, as are some of the stems. Inflorescences consist of a spadix within a taller spathe, and are borne intermittently throughout the year. Where not hardy, grow in a warm greenhouse or conservatory. In warmer areas, grow in a shady border.
• **CULTIVATION** Under glass, grow in large containers, in soil-based potting mix, with added leaf mold, in moderate light. In growth, water freely and apply a balanced liquid fertilizer every 2–3 weeks. Water moderately in winter. Outdoors, grow in slightly acidic, leafy, humus-rich, fertile, well-drained soil in partial shade. Avoid waterlogging.

Xanthosoma violaceum

• **PROPAGATION** Separate tubers at any time of year. Take soft-tip cuttings from young plants from spring to autumn.
• **PESTS AND DISEASES** Fungal spots, bacterial spot, and virus disease can be problems.

X. sagittifolium. Thick-stemmed, non-tuberous perennial with arrow-shaped, often white-spotted leaves, to 28in (70cm) long, with broad basal lobes, and leaf stalks 3ft (1m) long. Greenish white spathes, 9in (23cm) long, surrounding white spadices, are borne intermittently. Stems are edible. ↕↔ 3ft (1m). Tropical US, Central America, South America. ❀ (min. 55°F/13°C)
X. violaceum ▣ (Blue taro). Tuberous perennial, stemless above ground. Arrow-shaped leaves, 28in (70cm) long, with almost triangular lobes, and dark purple leaf stalks, 12–34in (30–85cm) long, have creamy white veins above, purple veins beneath and at the margins. Intermittently bears pale yellow spathes, 12in (30cm) long, around violet, dark red, or white spadices. Edible tubers are pink inside. ↕ 8ft (2.5m), ↔ 6ft (2m). Widely naturalized. ❀ (min. 55°F/13°C)

XERANTHEMUM

ASTERACEAE

Genus of 6 species of erect, white-woolly, branching annuals from steppes and stony banks in the Mediterranean to S.W. Asia. They have linear to linear-elliptic, entire leaves, and are cultivated for their alternate, daisy-like, crimson-red, pink, white, lilac-blue, or mauve-blue flowerheads, enclosed within papery bracts, borne in summer and autumn. They are suitable for an annual border, and provide long-lasting cut flowers for both fresh and dried arrangements.
• **CULTIVATION** Grow in moderately fertile, well-drained soil in full sun. Provide light support in exposed sites. Cut flowers for drying before they have fully opened, and hang upside down in a cool, dark, well-ventilated area.
• **PROPAGATION** Sow seed at 61°F (16°C) in spring.
• **PESTS AND DISEASES** Infrequent.

Xeranthemum annuum

X. annuum ▣ (Immortelle). Slender, upright annual, branched at the bases of the wiry stems, bearing linear-elliptic, entire, woolly, silver-green leaves, ¾–2½in (2–6cm) long. Branched heads of delicate, daisy-like, single to double, white, bright pink, crimson-red, or deep purple flowerheads, to 2in (5cm) across, are produced from summer to autumn. ↕ 10–30in (25–75cm), ↔ 18in (45cm). S.E. Europe to Caucasus, Iran.
'Snow Lady' produces single white flowerheads.

XEROPHYLLUM

LILIACEAE

Genus of 2 or 3 species of upright, rhizomatous, clump-forming perennials from dry slopes and open woodland in hilly and mountainous areas of North America. They are cultivated for their flowers and bold, architectural foliage. Woody, stem-like rhizomes produce numerous densely tufted, linear, finely tapered leaves, mid-green above and glaucous, blue-green beneath, with hard, rough or finely toothed margins. The leaves become progressively smaller toward the tips of the unbranched stems, each of which bears a dense, terminal raceme of small, funnel-shaped, white or yellowish white flowers in summer. They are suitable for growing in a sunny herbaceous border, in a Mediterranean garden, or in a native plant collection.
• **CULTIVATION** Grow in moderately fertile, moist but well-drained soil in full sun. Where marginally hardy, protect crowns with a dry winter mulch. Plants will form colonies if the rhizomes are left undisturbed.
• **PROPAGATION** Sow seed in containers in a cold frame in autumn or spring. Divide crowns just before growth commences in spring.
• **PESTS AND DISEASES** Infrequent.

X. asphodeloides. Upright perennial with linear leaves, to 18in (45cm) long, mid-green above, glaucous, blue-green beneath, with rough margins. During summer, bears funnel-shaped, fragrant, yellow-white flowers, ½in (1.5cm) across, in dense, broad, rounded racemes, to 12in (30cm) long. ↕ to 5ft (1.5m), ↔ to 24in (60cm). E. Canada to Tennessee, Georgia. Zone 6.
X. tenax (Bear grass). Upright perennial with tufted, linear, stiff leaves, to 36in (90cm) long, mid-green above, glaucous, blue-green beneath, with rough margins. Produces funnel-shaped, white to cream flowers, ¼in (6mm) across, in dense racemes, to 24in (60cm) long, in summer. ↕↔ 30in (75cm). W. North America. Zone 6.

Y

YUCCA *syn.* HESPEROYUCCA

AGAVACEAE

Genus of about 40 species of rosette-forming or woody-based perennials (some species monocarpic), evergreen shrubs, and erect, eventually spreading, evergreen trees from hot, dry places, such as deserts, sand dunes, and plains, in North and Central America and the West Indies. They are cultivated for their bold, linear to lance-shaped or inversely lance-shaped, neatly or loosely rosetted leaves, and for their erect or, rarely, pendent panicles of bell-shaped to hemispherical, usually white flowers. Use as architectural specimens in a border or courtyard, or in containers. Where not hardy, grow tender yuccas in a cool or temperate greenhouse, or in a conservatory.

• **CULTIVATION** Under glass, grow in soil-based potting mix in full light. When in growth, water moderately and apply a balanced liquid fertilizer monthly. Water sparingly in winter. Outdoors, grow in any well-drained soil in full sun. Flowers may require hand-pollination to set seed. Remove spent flowering stems.

Yucca filamentosa 'Bright Edge'

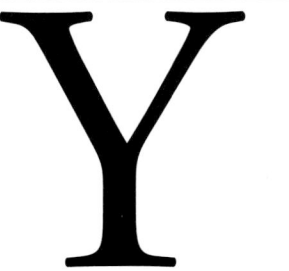

• **PROPAGATION** Sow seed in spring, at 55–64°F (13–18°C) for hardy yuccas, or at 66–75°F (19–24°C) for tender ones. Remove rooted suckers in spring. Take root cuttings in winter.

• **PESTS AND DISEASES** Cane borers, scale insects, and fungal leaf spots occur.

Y. aloifolia (Dagger plant, Spanish bayonet). Slow-growing, rounded shrub or small tree with a simple or branched stem and densely arranged, linear to narrowly lance-shaped, toothed, dark green leaves, to 20in (50cm) long, each ending in a sharp, stiff point. From summer to autumn, bears thick, erect panicles, to 18in (45cm) long, of pendent, bell-shaped, white, sometimes purple-tinged flowers, 1¼in (3cm) long, held above the foliage. ↕ 25ft (8m), ↔ 12–15ft (4–5m). S.E. US, Mexico, West Indies. ❄ (min. 45°F/7°C)

Y. elephantipes, syn. *Y. guatemalensis* (Giant yucca, Spineless yucca). Large, upright shrub or usually small tree with several to many sparsely branched trunks arising near ground level. Narrowly lance-shaped, light to mid-green leaves, 24–39in (60–100cm) long, are stiffly leathery, with toothed margins. On mature plants, pendent, hemispherical, white to cream flowers, 1¼–1½in (3–4cm) long, are borne in dense, erect panicles, to 3ft (1m) long, from summer to autumn. ↕ to 30ft (10m), ↔ 15–25ft (5–8m). Mexico. ❄ (min. 50°F/10°C). **'Variegata'** ▣ has creamy-white-margined leaves.

Y. filamentosa (Adam's needle). Clump-forming shrub, stemless or almost so, with basal rosettes of inversely lance-shaped, rigid, dark green leaves, to 30in (75cm) long, margined with curly white threads. Nodding, bell-shaped white flowers, 2in (5cm) long, tinged green or cream, are borne in upright panicles, to 6ft (2m) or more long, in mid- and late summer. ↕ 30in (75cm), ↔ 5ft (1.5m). New Jersey to Florida. Zone 4. **'Bright Edge'** ▣ has leaves with broad yellow margins. **'Golden Sword'** has yellow-centered leaves. **'Variegata'** has white-margined, blue-green leaves, tinged pink in winter.

Y. flaccida. Clump-forming, almost stemless shrub bearing basal rosettes of lance-shaped, dark blue-green leaves, to 22in (55cm) long, fringed with curly or straight threads. Bears nodding, bell-shaped white flowers, 2in (5cm) long, in upright panicles, to 5ft (1.5m) or more long, in mid- and late summer. ↕ 22in (55cm), ↔ 5ft (1.5m). North Carolina to Alabama. Zone 4. **'Ivory Tower'** bears a profusion of spreading, green-tinged, creamy white flowers.

Y. gloriosa ▣ (Spanish dagger). Erect shrub with a thick stem, simple at first, later sparsely branched, bearing terminal tufts of narrowly lance-shaped, stiffly pointed, arching, leaves, to 24in (60cm) long, blue-green maturing to dark green, with entire to few-toothed margins. From late summer to autumn, produces pendent, bell-shaped, sometimes purple-tinged, white flowers, 2in (5cm) long, in upright panicles, to 8ft (2.5m) long. ↕↔ 6ft (2m). North Carolina to Florida. Zone 7b. **'Variegata'** has yellow-margined leaves.

Y. guatemalensis see *Y. elephantipes.*

Y. parviflora see *Hesperaloe parviflora.*

Y. recurvifolia. Robust, tree-like shrub, sometimes with several trunk-like stems, sparsely branched with age. Bears lance-shaped, arching to strongly recurved, stiffly leathery, mid- to deep green leaves, to 36in (90cm) long, blue-green when young, with entire to slightly toothed margins. Pendent, bell-shaped cream flowers, 2½–3in (6–8cm) long, open in upright panicles, to 6ft (2m) long, from late summer to autumn. ↕ 5–8ft (1.5–2.5m), ↔ 4–6ft (1.2–2m). Georgia to Missouri. Zone 7.

Y. whipplei. Clump-forming, stemless, monocarpic shrub with dense tufts of slender, linear, finely toothed, rigid, gray-green leaves, to 36in (90cm) long. Pendent, bell-shaped or hemispherical, fragrant, creamy white, sometimes purple-tinged flowers, 1½in (4cm) long, are borne in summer in upright panicles, to 6ft (2m) or more long. Propagate by seed; it may take many years to flower. ↕ 3ft (1m), ↔ 4ft (1.2m). S. California, Arizona, N.W. Mexico. Zone 6b.

Yucca elephantipes 'Variegata'

Yucca gloriosa

YUSHANIA

Anceps bamboo

POACEAE

Genus of 2 species of tall, evergreen, clump-forming bamboos found at high altitudes in the N.W. and C. Himalayas, Taiwan, and the Philippines. Cultivated for their lance-shaped to linear leaves, they are suitable for use as hedging or screening, or as specimens, but they can be invasive.

• **CULTIVATION** Grow in fertile, humus-rich, moist but well-drained soil in full sun or partial shade. Shelter from cold winds. Plant in large containers plunged into the soil to restrict spread.

• **PROPAGATION** Divide in spring.

• **PESTS AND DISEASES** Young shoots may be damaged by slugs.

Y. anceps, syn. *Arundinaria anceps, A. jaunsarensis, Sinarundinaria jaunsarensis* (Anceps bamboo). Tall, evergreen, rhizomatous bamboo forming dense, scattered clumps of shiny, dark green culms, straight and erect at first, arching with age. Pendent branchlets bear narrowly lance-shaped, mid-green leaves, 2½–5½in (6–14cm) long, rounded at the bases, with purple-tinted stalks. ↕ 10–25ft (3–8m), ↔ indefinite. N.W. and C. Himalayas. ❄ (min. 35°F/2°C)

Z

ZALUZIANSKYA

SCROPHULARIACEAE

Genus of about 35 species of sticky, low-growing annuals and evergreen perennials or subshrubs from grassland and rocky slopes in South Africa. They are grown for their terminal spikes of tubular, salverform, heavily scented flowers, with 5 spreading petal lobes; the flowers are usually deep red in bud, opening to white with red petal backs. The variably shaped leaves are entire or toothed, the lower ones opposite, the upper ones alternate. Suitable in a sunny rock garden or border, or in a container or alpine house.

• **CULTIVATION** Grow in moist but sharply drained, humus-rich soil in full sun. Cut back hard after flowering. In an alpine house, grow in a mix of equal parts loam, leaf mold, and grit. Water freely when in growth. Keep barely moist in winter.

• **PROPAGATION** Propagate regularly, since plants are short-lived. Take stem-tip cuttings in summer, overwinter in frost-free conditions, and plant out in spring. Seed is not regularly produced in gardens; if available, sow at 50–55°F (10–13°C) as soon as ripe or in spring.

• **PESTS AND DISEASES** Aphids and spider mites may be troublesome under glass.

Z. ovata ■ Clump-forming, evergreen perennial, sometimes grown as an annual, with branching, brittle stems bearing ovate, toothed, sticky, gray-green leaves, 1½in (4cm) long. Produces terminal spikes of salverform, crimson-backed white flowers, ¾–1in (2–2.5cm) across, each with 5 petal lobes, cleft into 2 further lobes; they open in sunshine, and are produced over a long period in summer. ↕ to 10in (25cm), ↔ to 24in (60cm). South Africa (Western Cape, Northern Cape, Eastern Cape, KwaZulu/Natal, Orange Free State), Lesotho. ❀ (min. 41°F/5°C)

Zaluzianskya ovata

ZAMIA

ZAMIACEAE

Genus of about 30 species of mainly small, dioecious cycads found in scrub and pine woodland, and on dry slopes from North to South America. Most have short, swollen stems, some similar to palms; others, with tuberous, underground stems, resemble ferns. Zamias are grown for their habit and pinnate leaves, borne in terminal whorls or rosettes and often composed of many narrow, oblong or linear to ovate leaflets. They produce usually felted, single-sexed, cone-like flower spikes (cones), with male and female flowers borne on separate plants; the insignificant male cones are cylindrical, the females ovoid. Where not hardy, grow in a warm greenhouse or as houseplants. In tropical areas, site large species on a lawn and small ones in a shrub border.

• **CULTIVATION** Under glass, grow in soil-based potting mix, with added leaf mold and sharp sand, in full light with shade from hot sun. During the growing season, water freely and apply a balanced liquid fertilizer monthly. Water sparingly in winter. Outdoors, grow in fertile, moist but well-drained soil in full sun with some midday shade, or in partial shade.

• **PROPAGATION** Sow seed at 75°F (24°C) in spring.

• **PESTS AND DISEASES** Leaf spots, scale insects, and mealybugs can be problems.

Z. floridana see *Z. pumila.*

Z. furfuracea. Small cycad with a partly underground, simple or rarely branched, cylindrical trunk. Bears terminal whorls of semi-erect to spreading, pinnate leaves, to 3ft (1m) long, each with up to 24 oblong or inversely lance-shaped to obovate, stiff, pale green leaflets, later olive-green, with red-brown hairs. Produces felted, red-brown female flower cones, 4–5in (10–13cm) long, usually in summer. ↕ to 3ft (1m), ↔ to 6ft (2m). Coast of E. Mexico. ❀ (min. 59°F/15°C)

Z. integrifolia see *Z. pumila.*

Z. loddigesii. Small cycad with a largely underground, sometimes branching trunk. Bears terminal whorls of semi-erect to spreading, pinnate leaves, to 3ft (1m) long, each with up to 54 narrowly lance-shaped, lustrous, bright green leaflets, toothed on their upper halves. Brownish green female flower cones, 2in (5cm) or more long, are generally produced in summer. ↕ 5ft (1.5m), ↔ to 5½ft (1.7m). Mexico, Guatemala. ❀ (min. 59°F/15°C). **var. *latifolia*** has lance-shaped to obovate leaflets.

Z. pumila ■ syn. *Z. floridana, Z. integrifolia* (Florida arrowroot, Guayiga, Seminole bread). Small cycad with a mainly underground, unbranched or branched trunk. Bears terminal rosettes of ascending to spreading, pinnate leaves, 24–48in (60–120cm) long, each with up to 60 linear to inversely lance-shaped, leathery, deep green leaflets, frequently toothed on their upper halves. Large, russet-green female flower cones, to 6in (15cm) long, are usually produced in summer. ↕ to 4ft (1.2m), ↔ 4–6ft (1.2–2m). Florida, Cuba, West Indies. ❀ (min. 59°F/15°C)

Zamia pumila

ZANTEDESCHIA

Calla lily

ARACEAE

Genus of 6 species of perennials, with tuberous rhizomes, found in moist soils, swamps, or lake margins in southern and E. Africa. They are grown for their unusual, white or brightly colored spathes, borne in spring and summer. Most bear lance-shaped or narrowly to broadly arrow- or heart-shaped leaves. A number of hybrids have been developed. **Elliottiana hybrids** have broadly heart-shaped, usually mid- to dark green leaves, most covered with translucent white dots, and usually yellow spathes, 6in (15cm) long, surrounding golden yellow spadices. **Rehmannii hybrids** have lance-shaped, rarely spotted, mid- to dark green leaves, and white to pink or dark purple spathes, 5in (13cm) long, surrounding yellow spadices.

Z. aethiopica may be cultivated as a marginal aquatic. Where temperatures fall below 50°F (10°C), grow less hardy calla lilies in a warm greenhouse or as houseplants, or plant out in summer. All parts may cause mild stomach upset if ingested, and contact with the sap may irritate the skin.

• **CULTIVATION** Under glass, grow in soil-based potting mix in full light. In growth, water freely and apply a balanced liquid fertilizer every 2 weeks until the flowers have faded. Keep just moist in winter. Outdoors, grow in humus-rich, moist soil in full sun. As a marginal aquatic, grow *Z. aethiopica* in an aquatic container 10–12in (25–30cm) across, filled with heavy loam soil, in water up to 12in (30cm) deep; see also pp.52–53.

• **PROPAGATION** Sow seed at 70–81°F (21–27°C) when ripe. Divide in spring.

• **PESTS AND DISEASES** Rhizome rot, bacterial soft rot, gray mold (*Botrytis*), rust, and virus diseases are common.

Z. aethiopica. Clump-forming, rhizomatous perennial, evergreen in mild areas, with semi-erect, arrow-shaped, glossy, bright green leaves, to 16in (40cm) long. From late spring to midsummer, produces a succession of large, pure white spathes, to 10in (25cm) long, with creamy yellow spadices. ↕ 36in (90cm), ↔ 24in (60cm). South Africa, Lesotho. ❀ (min. 35°F/2°C). **'Apple Court Babe'** is much shorter than the species; ↕ 24in (60cm). **'Crowborough'** ■ has spathes 4–6in (10–15cm) long; it is reported to be hardier than the species. **'Green Goddess'** ■ has dull green leaves and white-marked, bright green spathes, 6–8in (15–20cm) long. **'Little Gem'** is dwarf and floriferous; ↕ 18in (45cm). **'White Sails'** has open white spathes, 4in (10cm) long.

Zantedeschia aethiopica 'Crowborough'

Z. albomaculata, syn. *Z. melanoleuca* (Spotted calla). Rhizomatous perennial with semi-erect, arrow-shaped, mid-green, basal leaves, to 18in (45cm) long, with translucent white spots. In summer, bears white to cream, pale yellow, or pale pink spathes, to 5in (13cm) long, each with a purple mark inside at the base, surrounding yellow spadices. ↕ 12–16in (30–40cm), ↔ 8in (20cm). Tropical Africa, South Africa, E. Africa. ❀ (min. 50°F/10°C)

Z. angustiloba see *Z. pentlandii.*

Z. 'Aztec Gold'. Elliottiana hybrid with unspotted leaves. Golden yellow spathes are borne in summer, maturing to burnt orange. ↕ 22in (55cm), ↔ 8in (20cm). ❀ (min. 50°F/10°C)

Z. 'Black-eyed Beauty'. Elliottiana hybrid with heavily white-spotted leaves. In summer, produces cream spathes, each with a black central mark in the

Zantedeschia aethiopica 'Green Goddess'

Zantedeschia elliottiana

throat. ↕ 12–16in (30–40cm), ↔ 6in (15cm). ❀ (min. 50°F/10°C)
Z. 'Black Magic'. Elliottiana hybrid with heavily white-mottled leaves. Bears yellow spathes, with black throats, in summer. ↕ 30in (75cm), ↔ 8in (20cm). ❀ (min. 50°F/10°C)
Z. 'Dusty Pink'. Rehmannii hybrid bearing rounded, mauve-pink spathes, with darker throats, in summer. ↕ 28in (70cm), ↔ 8in (20cm). ❀ (min. 50°F/10°C)
Z. elliottiana ▣ (Golden calla, Yellow calla). Rhizomatous perennial with erect, heart-shaped, dark green, basal leaves, to 18in (45cm) long, covered with translucent white spots. In summer, bears golden yellow spathes, 6in (15cm) long, with golden yellow spadices. ↕ 24–36in (60–90cm), ↔ 8in (20cm). Origin unknown. ❀ (min. 50°F/10°C)
Z. 'Golden Affair'. Elliottiana hybrid with unspotted leaves. In summer, bears bright yellow spathes. ↕ 24in (60cm), ↔ 8in (20cm). ❀ (min. 50°F/10°C)
Z. 'Majestic Red'. Elliottiana hybrid with unspotted leaves, and pointed, crimson spathes, borne in summer. ↕ 26in (65cm), ↔ 8in (20cm). ❀ (min. 50°F/10°C)
Z. melanoleuca see *Z. albomaculata.*
Z. pentlandii, syn. *Z. angustiloba.* Upright, rhizomatous perennial with erect, oblong-elliptic to oblong-lance-shaped, mid- to dark green, rarely spotted leaves, to 12in (30cm) long, arrow- or heart-shaped at the bases. In summer, bears bright golden to lemon-yellow spathes, to 5in (13cm) long, each marked dark purple inside at the base, with golden yellow spadices. ↕ 24–36in (60–90cm), ↔ 8in (20cm). ❀ (min. 35°F/2°C)
Z. rehmannii (Pink calla). Rhizomatous perennial with semi-erect, lance-shaped, dark green, basal leaves. In summer, bears slender, white to pink or dark purple spathes, 5in (13cm) long, with yellow spadices. ↕ 16in (40cm), ↔ 11in (28cm). South Africa (Northern Transvaal, Eastern Transvaal), Swaziland. ❀ (min. 50°F/10°C)

ZANTHOXYLUM

RUTACEAE

Genus of about 250 species of broadly rounded to upright, spiny, deciduous or evergreen trees and shrubs, mainly from forest in Asia, Australia, North to South America, and Africa, usually in warmer regions. They have aromatic bark, and are grown for their alternate, usually pinnate leaves, dotted with minute glands, and for their fruits, which split to reveal often black seeds attached by short threads. They bear cymes or panicles of small, cup-shaped, green or yellowish green flowers from spring to summer; individual plants may be dioecious, or produce both unisexual and bisexual flowers. Suitable for use in a shrub border or as specimen trees. Where not hardy, grow in a cool greenhouse.
• **CULTIVATION** Grow in fertile, well-drained soil in full sun or light, dappled shade. Pruning group 1.
• **PROPAGATION** Sow seed in containers in a cold frame in autumn. Root semi-ripe cuttings in midsummer. Take root cuttings in late winter.
• **PESTS AND DISEASES** Powdery mildew, rust, and a few leaf spots can occur.

Z. americanum. Spreading, deciduous, aromatic tree or shrub with pinnate, mid-green leaves, to 12in (30cm) long, each with 5–11 ovate to oblong, dark green leaflets, pale green and softly hairy beneath. In early spring, bears axillary, stalkless cymes, 2in (5cm) across, of small, cup-shaped, yellow-green flowers; they are followed by spherical to ellipsoid, warty red fruit, to ¼in (6mm) across. ↕ to 25ft (8m), ↔ 10–12ft (3–4m). E. North America. Zone 4.
Z. piperitum ▣ (Japan pepper). Bushy, spiny, deciduous shrub with pinnate, aromatic, glossy, dark green leaves, to 6in (15cm) long, each with 11–23 ovate, toothed leaflets, turning yellow in autumn. In early summer, bears panicles,

Zanthoxylum piperitum

Zanthoxylum simulans

2in (5cm) long, of small, cup-shaped, yellow-green flowers from the leaf axils, followed by tiny, spherical, berry-like red fruit. ↕↔ 8ft (2.5m). China, Korea, Japan, Taiwan. Zone 7.
Z. simulans ▣ (Prickly ash). Spreading, deciduous shrub or small tree with broad spines, sometimes with pendent shoots. Pinnate leaves, to 8in (20cm) long, each with up to 11 ovate-oblong, saw-toothed, glossy, dark green leaflets, become yellow to reddish yellow in autumn. In early summer, bears tiny, cup-shaped green flowers in cymes 2in (5cm) across, followed by showy, spherical, warty red fruit, ¼in (6mm) across. ↕ 20ft (6m), ↔ 15ft (5m). China, Japan, Taiwan. Zone 7.

ZAUSCHNERIA

California fuchsia

ONAGRACEAE

Genus of 4 species of subshrubby, evergreen or deciduous perennials, sometimes included in *Epilobium*, from dry slopes and chaparral or coastal sage brush in W. North America. The small, opposite or alternate, linear-lance-shaped to broadly ovate leaves are stalkless or virtually so. California fuchsias are grown for their profusion of tubular to funnel-shaped, usually scarlet flowers, borne in terminal racemes in late summer and autumn. Providing color late in the season, they are suitable for a rock garden or dry-stone wall, or for a mixed or herbaceous border.
• **CULTIVATION** Grow in moderately fertile, well-drained soil in full sun, with shelter from wind.
• **PROPAGATION** Sow seed in containers in a cold frame in spring. Root basal cuttings in spring, with bottom heat.
• **PESTS AND DISEASES** Young growth may be damaged by slugs.

Z. californica, syn. *Epilobium californicum.* Clump-forming, woody-based, evergreen or semi-evergreen, rhizomatous perennial producing lance-shaped to linear-lance-shaped, hairy, gray-green leaves, ½–1½in (1–4cm) long. Racemes of tubular, brilliant scarlet flowers, 1–1½in (2.5–4cm) long, are terminally borne over long periods in late summer and early autumn. ↕ to 12in (30cm), ↔ to 20in (50cm). California. ❀ (min. 35°F/2°C). **subsp. *angustifolia*** has linear, densely woolly leaves, and slightly shorter flowers; ↕ to 20in (50cm). **subsp. *cana***, syn. *Epilobium canum, Z. cana*, is deciduous, with linear to oblong, gray-woolly to white silky-hairy leaves, and funnel-shaped, vermilion to scarlet flowers; ↕ to 24in (60cm), ↔ 18in (45cm). **subsp. *cana* 'Dublin'** ▣ is deciduous, with bright red flowers; ↕ to 10in (25cm), ↔ to 12in (30cm). **subsp. *cana* 'Etteri'** is deciduous and mat-forming; ↕ 6in (15cm). **subsp. *latifolia*** is spreading, with a non-woody base, and ovate to lance-shaped-ovate, finely hairy, mid-green to grayish green leaves. **'Solidarity Pink'** is less vigorous, and produces pale pink flowers; ↔ to 12in (30cm).
Z. cana see *Z. californica* subsp. *cana.*

ZEA

POACEAE

Genus of 4 species of annual, rarely perennial grasses found along field margins and on disturbed ground in Central America. The sturdy stems bear lance-shaped leaves in 2 ranks. They produce terminal, spike-like male panicles (the tassels); axillary female inflorescences (the ears) consist of numerous flowers arranged in longitudinal rows on a thickened axis (the cob). The female flowers, each with a long, silky style, are enclosed within spathe bracts (the husks) and mature into fleshy kernels. *Z. mays* (corn) is an important cereal crop in tropical and temperate regions. A number of ornamental cultivars are valued for their brightly variegated leaves and for their multi-colored ears. Grow in a mixed border or as accent plants in summer bedding designs.

Zauschneria californica subsp. *cana* 'Dublin'

Zea mays 'Strawberry Corn'

• **CULTIVATION** Grow in a warm, sheltered site in fertile, moist but well-drained soil in full sun.
• **PROPAGATION** Sow seed in individual pots at 64°F (18°C) in early spring, or *in situ* in late spring.
• **PESTS AND DISEASES** Can be affected by downy mildew, damping off, rust, smut, and a wide variety of fungal spots. Corn earworm and other caterpillars, aphids, and many other insect pests are frequent problems on some cultivars.

Z. mays (Corn). Robust, erect, annual grass with pointed, lance-shaped, arching, wavy leaves, to 36in (90cm) long. In midsummer, produces a terminal panicle of spike-like male racemes, to 8in (20cm) long, and female inflorescences, also to 8in (20cm) long, enclosed within spathe bracts. The female flowers are followed in late summer and early autumn by ears with flattened, usually yellow, sweet-tasting, edible kernels, to ½in (1.5cm) long. ↕ to 12ft (4m), ↔ 24in (60cm) or more. Mexico. **var. everta** (Popcorn) Long, pointed leaves, to 4ft (1.2m). Flowers are generally blue and spikey. Produces a wide variety of kernel sizes and husk colors, one ear per plant, in late summer. Sow seed 6in (15cm) apart. Matures in 100–120 days. ↕ 4–10ft (1.5–3m), ↔ 24in (60cm). Temperate to warm areas of North America. **'Harlequin'** has foliage striped green, red, and white, and ears with deep red kernels; ↕ 4ft (1.2m). **var. *japonica*** (Ornamental corn) Produces the typical, multicolored cobs, from white to yellow to red and black, and in multicolors. Available in standard and miniature cob sizes. Harvested kernels can also be ground for corn meal and flour. Matures in 106–116 days. ↕ 4–10ft (1.5–3m). Temperate to warm areas of North America. **var. *saccharata*** (Sweet corn) Long, leathery leaves, to 4ft (1.2m). Yellow to creamy white kernels in three types: normal sugar, sugar enhanced, and shrunken. Super sweet strains will germinate in cold soils and will produce early crops. ↕ 8–10ft (2.5–3m). Temperate to warm areas of North America. **'Strawberry Corn'** ■ produces ears with small, yellow to burgundy-red kernels enclosed within yellow-green spathe bracts; ↕ 4ft (1.2m). **'Variegata'** has leaves boldly striped with creamy white; ↕ 36in (90cm).

▷ ***Zebrina pendula*** see *Tradescantia zebrina*
▷ ***Zebrina purpusii*** see *Tradescantia zebrina* 'Purpusii'

ZELKOVA

ULMACEAE

Genus of about 6 species of deciduous, monoecious or hermaphrodite trees, occasionally shrubby, occurring in scrub and woodland in Sicily (Italy), Crete (Greece), N.E. Turkey, the Caucasus, N. Iran, and E. Asia. They are grown for their attractive habit and alternate, oval-oblong to ovate or elliptic, toothed, dark green leaves, which change color to yellow, then orange-brown or red, in autumn. *Zelkova* species are closely related to, and often confused with elms (*Ulmus*), differing in their unwinged fruits and in their leaves, which are not uneven at the bases. The very small, inconspicuous, male or hermaphrodite green flowers are borne singly or in small clusters in spring, the males from the lower axils of the shoots, the hermaphrodites higher up; the flowers are followed by small, spherical green fruits. *Zelkova* species and cultivars are handsome specimen and street trees, most of them suitable for open parkland and larger gardens; *Z. abelicea* and dwarf cultivars of *Z. serrata* are better suited for use in smaller gardens.
• **CULTIVATION** Grow in deep, fertile, moist but well-drained soil in sun or partial shade. Pruning group 1.
• **PROPAGATION** Sow seed in containers outdoors in autumn. Take greenwood cuttings in summer (preferably from young plants). Graft in winter. Remove rooted suckers in winter.
• **PESTS AND DISEASES** Prone to bacterial canker, Dutch elm disease, elm-leaf beetle, and horse-chestnut scale.

Zelkova serrata

Z. carpinifolia ■ (Caucasian elm). Broadly upright tree, normally with a short, thick trunk, from which arise many erect branches. Ovate, dark green leaves, slightly rough above, to 4in (10cm) long, each with about 10 broad teeth on either side, are orange-brown in autumn. ↕ 100ft (30m), ↔ 80ft (25m). Caucasus, N.E. Turkey, N. Iran. Zone 6.
Z. keaki see *Z. serrata.*
Z. serrata ■ syn. *Z. keaki* (Japanese zelkova). Spreading tree, often vase-shaped when young, with smooth gray bark, peeling to reveal orange patches. Thin, narrowly ovate, tapered leaves, to 5in (13cm) long, each with up to 16 teeth on either side, are dark green, becoming yellow, orange, or red in autumn. ↕ to 100ft (30m), ↔ 60ft (18m). S. Korea, Japan, Taiwan. Zone 5b. **'Goblin'** is dwarf and slow-growing, forming a dense, bushy shrub; ↕↔ 3ft (1m). **'Green Vase'** is vase-shaped, fast-growing, and graceful, with upright, arching branches, and leaves that turn orange-brown to bronze-red in autumn. **'Village Green'** is fast-growing, with red autumn coloration; it is resistant to Dutch elm disease.

Zelkova carpinifolia (inset: leaf detail)

ZENOBIA

ERICACEAE

Genus of one species of spreading, deciduous or semi-evergreen shrub occurring in moist, sandy places and bogs in S.E. US. It has oblong-ovate, toothed leaves, and is grown for its bell-shaped, fragrant white flowers. Suitable for a moist woodland garden.
• **CULTIVATION** Grow in a sheltered site, in acidic, humus-rich, moist soil in sun or partial shade. Plant in shade in areas where the soil dries out in summer. Pruning group 2 or 5, in midsummer.
• **PROPAGATION** Sow seed in containers outdoors in late winter. Take semi-ripe cuttings in summer.
• **PESTS AND DISEASES** Infrequent.

Z. pulverulenta ■ Spreading shrub with slender, arching shoots producing alternate, oblong-ovate, glaucous,

Zenobia pulverulenta

blue-green to glossy, dark green leaves, to 3in (8cm) long, with toothed margins. Pendent, bell-shaped, scented white flowers, ½in (1.2cm) long, are borne in erect racemes, to 8in (20cm) long, in early and midsummer. ↕ 6ft (2m), ↔ 5ft (1.5m). Virginia to South Carolina. Zone 6.

ZEPHYRANTHES

syn. COOPERIA
Rainflower, Rain lily, Zephyr lily
AMARYLLIDACEAE

Genus of about 70 species of bulbous perennials, some evergreen, found in grassland from North to South America. Closely related to *Habranthus,* they are grown for their erect, funnel-shaped to tubular, often crocus-like, white, yellow, pink, or red flowers, borne from spring to autumn, usually when the linear leaves emerge, and often a few days after rainstorms. Where not hardy, grow in containers or in an alpine house or cool greenhouse. Elsewhere, use in a rock garden or at the front of a sunny border.
• **CULTIVATION** Under glass, grow 4in (10cm) deep in soil-based potting mix, with added sharp sand, in full light. When in growth, water freely and apply a balanced liquid fertilizer every 4 weeks. Keep just moist in winter. Outdoors, grow in moist but well-drained soil in full sun. Protect from excessive winter moisture.
• **PROPAGATION** Sow seed at 55–64°F (13–18°C) as soon as ripe. Separate offsets in spring.
• **PESTS AND DISEASES** Infrequent.

Z. andersonii see *Habranthus tubispathus.*
Z. atamasco (Atamasco lily). Deciduous, bulbous perennial with semi-erect, strap-shaped, basal leaves, to 16in (40cm) long. In spring or summer, bears funnel-shaped white flowers, 3in (7cm) long, the petals sometimes flushed with purple. ↕ 8–12in (20–30cm), PD2in (5cm). S.E. US. ❀ (min. 45°F/7°C)
Z. carinata see *Z. grandiflora.*
Z. citrina. Deciduous, bulbous perennial producing crocus-like, bright yellow flowers, 2in (5cm) long, above the erect, basal leaves, to 12in (30cm) long, in autumn. ↕ 4–6in (10–15cm), PD2in (5cm). Tropical South America. ❀ (min. 45°F/7°C)
Z. grandiflora ■ syn. *Z. carinata, Z. rosea* of gardens. Deciduous, bulbous perennial with semi-erect, slender, linear, glossy, basal leaves, to 12in (30cm) long. In late summer and early autumn, bears funnel-shaped, bright pink flowers, 3in (7cm) long. An attractive greenhouse container plant. ↕ 8–12in (20–30cm), PD2in (5cm). Central America. ❀ (min. 45°F/7°C)
Z. robusta see *Habranthus robustus.*
***Z. rosea* of gardens** see *Z. grandiflora.*

Zephyranthes grandiflora

ZIGADENUS

LILIACEAE

Genus of 18 species of bulbous or rhizomatous, deciduous perennials from grassland and open woodland in North America, Mexico, and N.E. Asia. They are cultivated for their upright, terminal racemes or panicles of small, star-shaped, 6-tepaled, greenish white or yellowish white flowers, produced in summer. The leaves are mainly basal and linear, and often folded or keeled. Good for a shady border or woodland garden; grow *Z. fremontii* in a bulb frame. All parts are highly toxic if ingested.
• **CULTIVATION** Grow in deep, fertile, moist but well-drained soil in full sun or partial shade; *Z. fremontii* prefers full sun. In a bulb frame, grow 6–8in (15–20cm) deep in equal parts soil-based potting mix and grit.
• **PROPAGATION** Sow seed at 55–64°F (13–18°C) when ripe or in spring. Divide in spring or autumn.
• **PESTS AND DISEASES** Rust can occur.

Z. fremontii ■ (Star lily). Robust, bulbous perennial with semi-erect, narrowly linear, grayish green, basal leaves, to 24in (60cm) long. Racemes or panicles of many star-shaped, creamy white flowers, ½in (1.5cm) across, are borne in early summer. Requires dry summer dormancy; best in a bulb frame. ↕ 28in (70cm), PD3in (8cm). S. Oregon to Mexico (N. Baja California). Zone 8.
Z. glaucus. Bulbous perennial with semi-erect, narrowly linear, grayish green, basal leaves, to 12in (30cm) long. In summer, bears racemes or panicles of many star-shaped, creamy white flowers, to ½in (1.5cm) across, suffused brown or purple. ↕ to 24in (60cm), ↔ to 3in (8cm). E. Canada, N.E. US. Zone 4.
Z. venenosus (Death camas). Bulbous perennial with semi-erect, narrowly linear, mid- to dark green, basal leaves, to 12in (30cm) long. In summer, produces slender racemes of numerous small, star-shaped, off-white flowers, ⅛–¼in (3–6mm) across. ↕ 28in (70cm), PD3in (8cm). W. Canada to Utah and New Mexico. Zone 5.

ZINNIA

ASTERACEAE

Genus of 20 species of spreading to erect annuals, perennials, and subshrubs from scrub and desert grassland, mainly in Mexico, but also in S.W. US, and Central and South America. They have branching, angled or rounded stems and opposite, stalkless or almost stalkless, linear to ovate or elliptic, pale to mid-green leaves. Zinnias are cultivated for their solitary, long-stemmed, daisy-like, terminal flowerheads in a wide range of colors, including white, yellow, orange, red, purple, and lilac, some with contrasting eyes. In some, the flower-

Zigadenus fremontii

heads resemble formal decorative dahlias (referred to as "dahlia-flowered"); others resemble cactus-flowered dahlias (referred to as "cactus-flowered"). Use in an annual or mixed border, and for cutting. Smaller cultivars are suitable for edging, and for windowboxes or other containers.
• **CULTIVATION** Grow in fertile, humus-rich, well-drained soil in full sun. Deadhead to prolong flowering.
• **PROPAGATION** Sow seed at 55–64°F (13–18°C) in early spring, or *in situ* in late spring. Sow in succession for a longer flowering display.
• **PESTS AND DISEASES** Bacterial and fungal spots, powdery mildew, bacterial wilt, Southern blight, and stem rots are common. Caterpillars, mealybugs, and spider mites also cause problems.

***Z. angustifolia* of gardens** see *Z. haageana.*
***Z. angustifolia* 'Orange Star'** see *Z. haageana* 'Orange Star'.
***Z. angustifolia* 'Persian Carpet'** see *Z. haageana* 'Persian Carpet'.
Z. elegans. Upright, bushy annual bearing lightly hairy, ovate to lance-shaped leaves, to 3in (8cm) long. Daisy-like, broad-petaled purple flowerheads, to 1¾in (4.5cm) across, are produced in summer. ↕ 24–30in (60–75cm), ↔ 12in (30cm). Mexico. ❀ (min. 50°F/10°C). **Button Box Series** cultivars are dwarf and dahlia-flowered, bearing fully double flowerheads, 1½in (4cm) across, in a wide color range; ↕↔ 10–12in (25–30cm). **California Giants** is a standard, dahlia-flowered strain, with bushy plants and semi-double to double flowerheads, 3–5in (8–13cm) across, in a wide range of colors; ↕ 36in (90cm), ↔ 24in (60cm). **Dasher Series** cultivars are dwarf and long-lasting, bearing early, double flowerheads, 3½in (9cm) across, in shades of red, pink, orange, yellow, and white; ↕ 10–12in (25–30cm). Cultivars of **Dreamland Series** are dwarf and compact, with fully double flowerheads, to 4in (10cm) across, in a wide color range; ↕ 8–12in (20–30cm); **'Dreamland Scarlet'** ■ has scarlet-orange flowerheads. **'Envy'** ■ has semi-double, chartreuse-green flowerheads; benefits from some shade, especially in hot areas; ↕ to 30in (75cm). **'Fantastic Light Pink'** bears profuse, fully double, light pink flowerheads. **Lilliput Series** cultivars bear small, double flowerheads, 2in (5cm) across, in crimson, rose, pink, yellow, lavender, and white; ↕ 24in (60cm). Cultivars of **Peter Pan Series** are dwarf and compact, with early, large flowerheads, to 4in (10cm) across; use in containers or as bedding plants; ↕ 12in (30cm); **'Peter Pan Gold'** ■ has golden yellow flowerheads. **Pinwheel Series** cultivars are mildew resistant and compact, with single flowerheads, 2in (5cm) across, in shades of rose-pink, salmon-pink, and white; ↕ 12in (30cm). **Pulcino Series** cultivars bear double flowerheads, 2–3in (5–8cm) across, in shades of red, pink, salmon, yellow, orange, and white; more disease tolerant than most zinnias; ↕ 12–16in (30–40cm). **Ruffles Series** cultivars are dahlia-flowered, bearing ruffled, fully double flowerheads, 3–3½in (8–9cm) across, in a wide color range; good for cut flowers; ↕ to 24in (60cm). Cultivars of **Small World Series** are dwarf, with double flowerheads in a wide color range, including pale pink; ↕ to 12–14in (30–35cm). **State Fair Series** cultivars are tall-growing, vigorous, and dahlia-flowered, with large, double, lavender, rose-pink, orange, purple, or scarlet flowerheads, to 3in (8cm) across; ↕ to 30in (75cm). **Sun Series** cultivars have huge, double, flowerheads,

Zinnia elegans Dreamland Series 'Dreamland Scarlet'

Zinnia elegans 'Envy'

Z

Zinnia elegans
Peter Pan Series 'Peter Pan Gold'

4–5in (10–13cm) across, in a range of red, gold, white, and bright rose-pink; ↕ 20in (50cm). **Thumbelina Series** ■ cultivars are dwarf and spreading, with single or semi-double, weather-resistant, yellow, orange, red, magenta, lavender, or pale pink flowerheads, 1¼in (3cm) across; ↕ to 6in (15cm). **Whirligig Series** cultivars are cactus-flowered, bearing fully double flowerheads, 3–4½in (8–11cm) across, with the ends of the petals strongly marked in a contrasting color, in combinations of yellow-crimson, red-white, pink-white, and bronze-red; ↕ 18–24in (45–60cm). **Zenith Series** cultivars are cactus-flowered, with huge flowerheads, 6in (15cm) across, in a range of red, white, pink, yellow, and orange; ↕ 30in (75cm).
Z. haageana, syn. *Z. angustifolia* of gardens, *Z. mexicana* (Mexican zinnia). Erect, bushy annual with oblong to linear or linear-lance-shaped leaves, to 3in (7cm) long, lightly covered in bristly hairs. In summer, produces daisy-like, broad-petaled, bright orange flowerheads, to 1½in (4cm) across. ↕ to 24in (60cm), ↔ to 12in (30cm). S.E. US, Mexico. **'Chippendale'** has deep red flowerheads with golden yellow petal tips; ↕ 24in (60cm). **'Classic'** see 'Orange Star'. **'Orange Star'** ■ syn. 'Classic', *Z. angustifolia* 'Orange Star', is dwarf and bushy, with orange flowerheads; mildew-resistant and a good groundcover; ↕ to 10in (25cm). **'Persian Carpet'** ■ syn. *Z. angustifolia* 'Persian Carpet', is dwarf, compact, and spreading in habit, with small, semi-double and double, weather-resistant flowerheads, to 1½in (4cm) across, in a wide range of bicolors and tricolors; excellent for summer bedding; ↕ to 16in (40cm). **'Star White'** has white flowerheads with golden yellow centers.
Z. mexicana see *Z. haageana.*

Zinnia elegans Thumbelina Series

Zinnia haageana 'Orange Star'

ZIZANIA

Water oats, Wild rice

POACEAE

Genus of 3 species of annual or perennial, marginal aquatic grasses from marshland and lake margins in E. Asia and North America. They are cultivated for their flat, linear leaves, produced on tall, reedy stems. Conical or pyramidal, feathery panicles of spikelets are borne from summer to autumn, followed by edible, rice-like seeds. Suitable for a large pond or wildlife pool. Where not hardy, grow in a warm greenhouse.
• **CULTIVATION** Outdoors, grow at the edges of a large pool in full sun, in water to 9in (23cm) deep. See also pp.52–53.
• **PROPAGATION** Overwinter seed in trays of damp loam, and sow at 64°F (18°C) in early spring. As the seedlings emerge, cover with 2in (5cm) of water and maintain at the same temperature. Plant out when danger of frost has passed.
• **PESTS AND DISEASES** Leaf smut, ergot, and fungal spots occur.

Z. aquatica (Annual wild rice, Canadian wild rice, Water rice). Marginal aquatic annual with grass-like, linear, deep green leaves, to 4ft (1.2m) long. Pale green flowers are borne in pyramidal panicles, to 30in (75cm) long, in summer, followed by edible, rice-like seeds. ↕ 10ft (3m), ↔ 18in (45cm). North America. Zone 4.

Zinnia haageana 'Persian Carpet'

ZOYSIA

Zoysiagrass

POACEAE

Genus of 5 species of Asian perennial grasses with both stolons and rhizomes. They are green during the growing season from spring through autumn, but turn brown after the first frost. Stiff due to a high silica content, they range from fine to coarse-textured. They have deep root systems and so are drought-resistant and do well in full sun or partial shade.
• **CULTIVATION** Cut with a reel mower at ½–1in (1–2.5cm). Occasional watering and fertilizing necessary, and should be thinned out every 2–3 years.
• **PROPAGATION** Planted both by clones and seed.
• **PESTS AND DISEASES** New cultivars are disease- and insect resistance, but susceptible to nematodes.

Z. japonica (Korean lawngrass, Japanese lawngrass) is the most cold-tolerant of the zoysiagrasses, the coarsest in texture, and is the only one of the three that can be seeded. Zone 8.
Z. matrella (Manillagrass). Forms a thick mat; must be propagated from sprigs and is slow to become established. In tropical climates, retains its color throughout the year. ❄ (min. 35°F/2°C)
Z. tenuifolia (Mascarene grass, Korean velvet). The finest textured and least cold-hardy. ❄ (min. 41°F/5°C)

▷ ***Zygocactus truncatus*** see *Schlumbergera truncata*

ZYGOPETALUM

Caper bean

ORCHIDACEAE

Genus of about 40 species of medium-sized, evergreen, epiphytic or terrestrial orchids native to South America, occurring in warm, moist rainforest, sometimes on rocky outcrops or in leaf litter. They have conical to ovoid pseudobulbs, from the tops of which are produced 2 or more narrowly elongated, lance-shaped, folded, leathery or fleshy leaves. Racemes of delicate, highly fragrant flowers, most of which are richly colored with an attractive combination of green-brown and indigo-blue, arise from the bases of the pseudobulbs from autumn to spring.
• **CULTIVATION** Cool- to intermediate-growing orchids. Grow in standard epiphytic orchid potting mix in containers that will easily accommodate the root system, or in slatted baskets. When in growth, provide high humidity and bright filtered light; water freely, and apply a quarter- to half-strength balanced liquid fertilizer at every third watering. In winter, admit full light and water sparingly. See also p.46.
• **PROPAGATION** Divide when the roots of the plant fill the container and flow over the sides. Alternatively, remove backbulbs and pot them up separately.
• **PESTS AND DISEASES** May be attacked by spider mites, aphids, and mealybugs.

Z. mackaii ■ syn. *Z. mackayi.* Epiphytic orchid with fleshy, ovoid pseudobulbs and 2 or 3 pendent, lance-shaped, leathery, apical leaves, 12–20in (30–50cm) long. Upright racemes of 5–7 green flowers, to 3in (8cm) across, each one strongly barred in brown and with a heavily veined indigo-blue lip, are produced from autumn to winter. ↕ 12in (30cm), ↔ 18in (45cm). Brazil. ❄ (min. 52–55°F/11–13°C; max. 86°F/30°C)
Z. mackayi see *Z. mackaii.*
***Z.* Perrenoudii** (*Z. intermedium* x *Z. maxillare*). Epiphytic orchid with fleshy, ovoid pseudobulbs and 2 pendent, lance-shaped, leathery, apical leaves, 12in (30cm) long. Upright racemes of 5–12 green flowers, 2–3in (5–7cm) across, each lightly barred in brown and with a heavily veined indigo lip, are produced from autumn to spring. ↕↔ 12in (30cm). ❄ (min. 52–55°F/11–13°C; max. 86°F/30°C)

Zygopetalum mackaii

GLOSSARY OF TERMS

This glossary provides concise definitions of terms used throughout this encyclopedia, as well as a number of others commonly found in horticulture. For the sake of clarity, many of the terms are narrowly defined here, but may be interpreted differently in non-horticultural contexts. For an illustrated account of plant botany, cultivation, and ornamental plant groups, see the introductory pages (pp.10–54).

A

Accent plant Plant used in a formal bed or border to emphasize contrasts of height, color, and/or texture.
Acicular *see* Linear, Needle.
Acidic With a pH value below 7.
Acuminate With a long, tapering point.
Acute Ending in a short, sharp point.
Adpressed Pressed flat to the axis to which it is attached.
Adventitious Refers to a plant organ that occurs in an unusual location.
Aeration Loosening of the soil structure to allow free circulation of air.
Aerial root Root that emerges from the stem above ground level.
Air-layering Method of propagation whereby a cut in an aerial stem is covered with moist sphagnum moss and sealed in a plastic sleeve in order to induce rooting. *See also p.28.*
Alkaline With a pH value above 7.
Alpine 1. High-altitude plant from above the tree line and usually snow-covered in winter. 2. Loosely, any plant suitable for a rock garden. *See also pp.40–41.*
Alpine house Minimally heated, well-ventilated greenhouse used to grow alpines and other perennial plants.
Alternate Describes organs, usually leaves, borne singly at each node, in 2 vertical rows, on either side of an axis.
Angiosperm Flowering plant that bears ovules, later seeds, enclosed in ovaries (as opposed to a gymnosperm that bears naked ovules, then seeds, in cones). *See also p.10.*
Annual Plant that completes its life cycle in one growing season. *See also pp.42–43.*
Annulus 1. Corona (inner rim) of the corolla in members of the Asclepiadaceae. 2. In ferns, the part of the sporangium involved in spore dispersal.
Anther Part of the stamen that releases pollen; usually borne on a filament.
Apex (*pl.* apexes; *adj.* apical) Tip or growing point of an organ.
Apomixis (*adj.* apomictic) Asexual production of ripe seed. Offspring are clones, genetically identical to the parent.
Aquatic plant Plant that lives in water; free-floating, submerged, or rooted on the bottom with the leaves and flowers above water. *See also pp.52–53.*
Areole 1. Depressed or raised area bearing spines, branches, or flowers in cacti. 2. Small space outlined on a surface, such as an area of leaf between veins.
Aril Coat covering some seeds, often fleshy and brightly colored.
Aroid Member of the Araceae, characterized by an inflorescence composed of a spadix and spathe.
Arrow-shaped (sagittate) With a narrow, blunt or pointed tip, and widening at the base into 2 acute, downward-pointing lobes.
Asexual reproduction Process of producing new individuals by apomixis or vegetative propagation. *See also* Reproduction.
Auricle (*adj.* auricular) Ear-like lobe, often in pairs at the base of an organ.
Awn Stiff, bristle-like projection often found on grass seeds and spikelets.
Axil Upper angle between a part of a plant and the stem that bears it.
Axillary Borne in an axil. *See also* Terminal.
Axis (*pl.* axes) Rachis, stalk, or stem on which organs such as flowers, leaves, or leaflets are arranged.
Azalea pot Container that is half as tall as it is wide.

B

Backbulb Dormant pseudobulb unique to orchids.
Balled-and burlapped A plant with its rootball dug out of the soil and wrapped in burlap or similar material for transplanting.
Bamboo Woody-stemmed plant belonging to the Poaceae. *See also p.54.*
Bare-root A plant with its roots free of soil. Usually used of plants offered for sale.
Bark Outermost layers of a woody stem, including all the living and non-living tissues outside the cambium.
Basal At the base of an organ or structure.
Basal leaf Leaf that grows from the lowest part of the stem.
Basal stem cutting Cutting taken from the base of a (usually herbaceous) plant, in spring.
Beard 1. Awn. 2. Tuft or zone of hairlike structures.
Bed Area of ground, often set into or alongside a lawn, in which plants are grown.
Bedding plant Any plant set into the ground to provide a temporary display of foliage and/or flowers.
Bell-shaped (campanulate) Describes a flower with a broad tube terminating in flared lobes.
Berry Fruit with soft flesh surrounding one or more seeds.
Bicolored With 2 distinct colors.
Biennial Plant that completes its life cycle in 2 years, growing in the first year, and flowering and fruiting in the second. *See also pp.10, 42–43.*
Bigeneric hybrid Offspring derived from crossing 2 different genera.
Binomial Two-part scientific name consisting of a genus name and a species, cultivar, group, series, or hybrid epithet, denoting an individual within a genus. *See also p.11.*
Bipinnate *see* Pinnate.
Bisexual (hermaphrodite) Refers to a flower that bears both male and female reproductive organs.
Bleed To weep sap.
Blind 1. Refers to a plant in which the growing point has been damaged. 2. Refers to plants, particularly bulbs, that do not flower.
Bloom 1. Flower or blossom. 2. Fine, waxy, whitish or bluish white coating. *See also* Glaucous, White-frosted.
Bog garden Waterlogged area used to grow plants found in bogs, marshes, wet pasture, and at water margins.
Bolt To produce flowers and seed prematurely.
Bonsai Production of dwarf trees or shrubs by pruning and root restriction.
Boss A dense group of stamens.
Bottom heat Warmth radiated from below, usually via electrical cables, used in propagating units to assist the rooting of cuttings and the germination of seed.
Bowl-shaped Describes a flower that is hemispherical with the sides straight or very slightly spreading at the tips.
Bract Modified leaf at the base of a flower or flowerhead. May be small and scale-like; or large, brightly colored, and petal-like; or resemble normal foliage.
Bracteole Secondary bract sheathing a flower in an inflorescence, itself enclosed within a primary bract.
Branch Division of a stem, a trunk, or the axis of an inflorescence.
Branched-head standard Standard tree with a clear stem of 6ft (1.8m); the leader is cut back to develop an open crown. *See also p.33.*
Break To produce new growth as a result of pinching out or renovation.
Broad-leaved Describes trees and shrubs that have broad, flat, usually deciduous leaves – in contrast to the narrow, linear, usually evergreen needles of conifers.
Broken Type of marking in which the ground color is striped with one or more contrasting colors, usually caused by viral infection; particularly applied to tulips.
Bromeliad Member of the Bromeliaceae, characterized by showy inflorescences, frequently with brightly colored bracts, and rosettes of often colorful leaves. *See also p.47.*
Bud Immature organ or shoot enclosing an embryonic branch, leaf, inflorescence, or flower.
Budding Method of propagation in which a vegetative bud of one plant is grafted onto another plant.
Bulb Modified, subterranean bud, with a short, thick stem and fleshy scale leaves or leaf bases.
Bulb frame 1. Glass or plastic frame used to provide a dry environment for bulbs during dormancy. 2. Deep cold frame for storing potted bulbs before forcing.
Bulbil Small, bulb-like organ borne in the axil of a leaf, bract, or occasionally flowerhead.
Bulblet Small bulb produced at the base of a parent bulb, often inside the tunic.
Bulbous 1. Describes a stem that is swollen at the base, usually underground. 2. Describes a plant with bulbs. 3. Loosely, refers to a plant with an underground storage organ such as a bulb, corm, tuber, or rhizome. *See also pp.44–45.*
Burr 1. Prickly, spiny, or hooked fruit, seed head, or flowerhead. 2. Woody outgrowth on the trunk of some trees.
Buttress root Fluted or swollen tree trunk that aids stability in shallow rooting conditions. *See also* Stilt root.

C

Cactus (*pl.* cacti) Stem succulent, member of the Cactaceae. *See also pp.48–49.*
Calcareous Refers to soil with a high content of calcium carbonate (chalk) or magnesium carbonate. *See also* Lime.
Callus Thickened tissue that is formed by the cambium layer to aid healing around a wound.
Calyx (*pl.* calyces) Collective name for sepals, joined or separate, which form the outer whorl of the perianth.
Cambium Growth tissue of woody

plants; its increase adds to the girth and length of roots and stems.
Campanulate *see* Bell-shaped.
Capitulum *see* Flowerhead.
Capsule Dry fruit that splits open to disperse ripe seed.
Carnivorous (insectivorous) Applied to a plant that obtains nutrients by trapping and ingesting insects or other creatures.
Carpel Female part of a flower consisting of a style, a stigma, and an ovary. *See also* Pistil.
Catkin Form of inflorescence, often pendent, consisting of scale-like bracts and tiny, unisexual, usually petalless flowers arranged in a spike.
Caudex (*pl.* caudices; *adj.* caudiciform) Swollen stem base of a woody-based plant such as a palm, a cycad, or some succulents.
Caudiciform Resembling or possessing a caudex.
Central Spine of a cactus, growing from the center of an areole.
Central-leader standard Standard tree with a clear stem of 6ft (1.8m) or more, and lateral branches that taper from an erect central leader. *See also p.33.*
Central vein *see* Midrib.
Cephalium Woody, flower-bearing, densely spined area at the stem apex of some cacti. *See also* Pseudocephalium.
Chalky *see* Calcareous.
Channeled Lined with one or more longitudinal grooves.
Checkered With a bold, checkerboard-like pattern that contrasts with the ground color; usually describes corolla markings.
Chimera Plant composed of 2 or more genetically different tissues; the result of a mutation or of a graft hybrid.
Chipping *see* Scarify.
Chlorophyll Green pigment that absorbs energy from sunlight. *See also* Photosynthesis.
Chlorosis Loss of chlorophyll, and consequently the loss of green leaf coloration, caused by mineral deficiency, poor light levels, or disease.
Cladode *see* Phylloclade.
Cladophyll *see* Phylloclade.
Clay Very fertile, heavy, moisture-retentive soil, prone to compaction and surface capping.
Clay granules Moisture-retentive pellets of expanded clay. In hot, dry weather, the evaporation of water poured on to these granules increases humidity around houseplants. They may also be used as a growing medium.
Cleft Divided almost halfway to the center. *See also* Sinus.
Climber Plant that climbs or clings by means of modified stems, roots, leaves, or leaf stalks, using other plants or objects as support. *See also pp.36–37,* Scandent, Tendril.
Cloche Structure of glass or plastic panes or plastic sheeting, mainly used for cold-weather protection or for forcing early crops in open ground.
Clone A genetically identical group of plants derived from one individual by vegetative propagation or apomixis.
Cluster (fascicle) Arrangement of several inflorescences, leaves, stems, roots, or flowers that arise from a single point, or appear to do so.
Cold frame Protective structure used for growing and propagating plants, usually situated outdoors.
Cold greenhouse Minimally heated, frost-free greenhouse. *See also p.24.*
Column Flower organ, mainly found in orchids, consisting of fused male and female reproductive parts.
Compaction Compression of soil, particularly saturated clay and silt soils, resulting in poor aeration. *See also* Surface-capping.
Compost Material formed by the decay of organic matter. Used as a mulch or to improve soil structure and content.
Compound Consisting of several parts, but still identifiable as single unit, such as a leaf divided into 2 or more leaflets.
Cone Woody, seed-bearing structure in gymnosperms, generally composed of an axis with many lateral scales.
Conifer (*adj.* coniferous) Mostly evergreen trees or shrubs, usually with needle-like, linear leaves, and seeds borne naked on the scales of cones. Often from cool-temperate zones.
Conservatory Glazed, heated or unheated structure attached to a house; often has poorer ventilation than a greenhouse. *See also p.24.*
Continental climate Weather conditions in the center of a landmass, distant from coastal areas; the seasons are well defined, with hot summers and cold winters. *See also pp.18–19.*
Contractile Describes a root that is able to draw a bulb, corm, rhizome, or seedling deeper into the soil or closer to the surface.
Cool greenhouse Greenhouse with a minimum temperature of 35°F (2°C). *See also p.24.*
Cool-temperate Refers to a temperate climate with cold winters and warm summers.
Coppice (stool) To prune trees or shrubs close to ground level periodically to promote strong growth.
Cordate *see* Heart-shaped.
Cordon Trained plant (usually a fruit tree) generally restricted to one main stem, occasionally 2–4 stems, by a careful system of training and pruning.
Corm (*adj.* cormous) Subterranean storage organ consisting of a solid stem or stem base, often enclosed in a tunic. Corms are replaced annually.
Cormlet Small corm that arises at or near the base of a mature one.
Corolla 1. Collective name for petals. 2. Inner whorl of perianth segments in some monocotyledons.
Corona A crown- or cup-like structure of a flower, between the corolla and the stamens, formed either by fused stamen filaments or from the perianth segments.
Corymb Broad, flat-topped or domed inflorescence of stalked flowers or flowerheads arising at different levels on alternate sides of an axis.
Cotyledon (seed leaf) A leaf-like structure in a seed that functions as a leaf before the true leaves emerge. *See also* Dicotyledon, Monocotyledon.
Crenate *see* Scalloped.
Crest 1. Tuft of hairs or soft bristles. 2. Raised ridge on a surface. *See also* Beard.
Crisped With edges finely waved or ruffled.
Cristate 1. Crested, or with a terminal tuft of hairs or other tissue. 2. Describes ferns with ruffled, usually forked fronds. 3. Referring to succulents whose bodies have mutated into twisted, compacted shapes.
Crocks Broken pieces of clay pot, used to cover drainage holes in containers in order to modify drainage and improve air circulation to the roots.
Cross To interbreed. *See also* Hybrid.
Cross-pollination When the stigma of a flower on one plant is dusted with the pollen from a different plant.
Cross-shaped (cruciform) Describes a flower with 4 petals, usually set at right angles to each other in the form of a cross when viewed from above.
Crown 1. Growing point of a plant from which new shoots arise, at or just below the soil surface, at the junction with the roots. 2. Uppermost part of a tree or shrub. 3. Corona of a flower.
Crown bud Central flower bud growing at the tip of a shoot among other, usually smaller buds.
Crownshaft Upper section of a palm or cycad trunk, bearing leaves and inflorescences.
Crozier Coiled juvenile frond of a fern, similar in form to a bishop's staff.
Cruciform *see* Cross-shaped.
Culm Hollow, slender, jointed stem, particularly characteristic of bamboos.
Cultivar (*abbrev.* cv., contraction of "cultivated variety") Plant raised or selected in cultivation that retains distinct, uniform characteristics when propagated by appropriate means. *See also p.11, 42.*
Cuneate *see* Wedge-shaped.
Cup Corona of *Narcissus,* but only when shorter than the surrounding tepals.
Cup-shaped Describes a flower that is hemispherical with the sides straight or very slightly spreading at the tips; slightly narrower than bowl-shaped.
Cupule Cup-shaped whorl of hard, fused bracts surrounding the base of a fruit, as in beech nuts (*Fagus*).
Cutting Section of leaf, stem, or root separated from a plant and used for propagation. *See also p.29.*
Cutting soil mix Free-draining, low-nutrient soil mix that is used to root cuttings; usually based on fine-grade ground bark, soil, peat (or peat substitute), perlite, or sand.
Cyathium (*pl.* cyathia) Inflorescence of *Euphorbia,* in which a cup-like involucre surrounds a single pistil and several male flowers, each with a single stamen; flowers are sometimes bisexual.
Cycad Member of the Cycadaceae, mainly with stiff, palm-like leaves borne terminally from a short, thick trunk. *See also p.50.*
Cyme Flat or round-topped, branched inflorescence with each axis ending in a flower, the oldest at the center, and the youngest arising in succession from the axils of bracteoles.

D

Damp down To wet the floor and staging in a greenhouse in order to raise humidity and lower the temperature. *See also* Mist.
Damping off Collapse of seedlings and young plants caused by fungi, which rot the bases of stems and roots.
Deadhead To remove spent flowerheads in order to prolong flowering and prevent self-seeding.
Deciduous 1. Shedding leaves annually at the end of the growing season. 2. Falling away when no longer functional, as with the petals of many flowers.
Decumbent Growing close to the ground but usually with upward-growing tips.
Decurrent Extending downward from the point of attachment; often used to describe the attachment of a leaf to a stem.
Decussate *see* Rank.
Deep-water aquatic Plant that roots in water 12–36in (30–90cm) deep, and produces foliage and flowers at or above surface level.
Deltoid *see* Triangular.
Dentate *see* Toothed.
Depressed Describes a flattened, solid form.
Diamond-shaped (rhomboidal) Roughly oval but with acute angles at the base and tip, and obtuse angles midway down both sides.
Dicotyledon Angiosperm with 2 seed leaves, net-veined leaves, a cambium layer (in many species), and floral parts usually in fours or fives. *See also* Monocotyledon.
Die-back Death of a shoot, beginning at the tip, due to damage or disease.
Digitate *see* Palmate.
Dioecious Bearing male and female flowers on separate plants, so that both male and female plants must be grown if fruit is desired.
Disbud To remove surplus buds so that better-quality flowers or fruit are borne.
Disk floret Tiny, usually tubular flower,

one of many that normally comprise the center of a (composite) flowerhead.
Dissected *see* Divided.
Distichous *see* Rank.
Diurnal With activity taking place only in daylight, e.g. a flower that opens only during the day.
Divide To propagate a plant by splitting it into 2 or more parts, each with its own section of root system and one or more shoots or dormant buds.
Divided (dissected) Deeply cut into segments or lobes.
Dormancy (*adj.* dormant) Suspension of active growth during unfavorable conditions.
Double Describes a flower with more petals than in the normal wild state and with few, if any, stamens.
Drainage 1. Movement of excess water through the soil or soil mix. 2. System designed to remove excess water rapidly from the soil.
Drill Narrow, straight furrow in the soil, into which seeds are sown.
Drupe Fruit consisting of one or several hard seeds (stones) surrounded by a fleshy outer covering.
Dwarf Small or slow-growing variant of a species resulting from hybridization, mutation, or specific cultivation methods. *See also* Bonsai.

E

Ellipsoid Describes a solid form, broadest at the center, tapering toward each end; length is 2 times the width. It is wider than a spindle-shaped form, with the sides more curved.
Elliptic Describes a flat structure, broadest at the center, tapering toward each end; length is 2 times the width.
Embryo Part of a seed from which a new plant develops.
Ensiform *see* Strap-shaped.
Entire Describes a continuous, untoothed, and unlobed margin, usually of a leaf.
Epicalyx (*pl.* epicalyces) 1. Whorl of bracts surrounding the calyx. 2. False calyx.
Epicormic Refers to shoots that develop from latent or adventitious buds under the bark of a tree or shrub, often close to pruning cuts or wounds.
Epiphyte (*adj.* epiphytic) Plant that grows on another plant without obtaining food from it.
Erect Upright; perpendicular to the ground or to the point of attachment.
Ericaceous 1. Belonging to the Ericaceae. 2. Describes potting mix with a pH of 6.5 or less, suitable for growing acid-loving plants.
Espalier Fruit tree with pairs of branches trained horizontally from the central stem, in a single plane.
Etiolated Describes a plant that has abnormally elongated, often pale shoots as a result of poor light levels.
Evergreen 1. Retaining leaves for more than one growing season. 2. Plant with the above characteristic.
Exfoliate To shed bark in flakes, patches, or strips.
Eye Center of a flower, usually contrasting with the ground color.

F

F_1 hybrid Vigorous and uniform, first-generation offspring, derived from crossing 2 distinct, pure-bred lines. F_2 hybrids result from self-pollination within a population of F_1 hybrids; they do not come true.
Falcate *see* Sickle-shaped.
Fall Semi-pendent or spreading tepal of an *Iris* flower.
Family Primary category in plant classification, between order and genus, encompassing genera that have natural characteristics that group them together. *See also p.11.*
Fancy Describes a flower that is flaked, flecked, or striped in contrast to the ground color.
Fan palm Palm with fan-like, palmate rather than pinnate leaves.
Fan-shaped (flabellate) Wedge-shaped or semi-circular, with a pleated or boldly veined surface.
Farina (*adj.* farinaceous, farinose) *see* White-mealy.
Fascicle *see* Cluster.
Feathered 1. Describes a standard tree with a stem or trunk that is branched to the base with lateral "feathers." *See also p.33.* 2. Describes a flower with feather-like markings contrasting with the ground color, particularly of some tulips.
Fern Non-flowering, vascular plant, often with feather-like fronds. *See also p.51.*
Fertile 1. Refers to organs that produce functional pollen, spores, or viable seed. 2. Describes soil with a high content of nutrients essential to plant growth.
Fertilization Sexual fusion of male and female elements, initiating seed development. *See also* Reproduction.
Fertilizer Nutrients added to soil or potting mix to promote the vigor of a plant. Nitrogen (N), phosphorus (P), and potassium (K) are the chief elements in fertilizers. Organic fertilizers are based on plant or animal matter.
Filament 1. Stalk of the stamen attached to the anther. 2. Thread-like extension or hair.
Filiform *see* Linear.
Flabellate *see* Fan-shaped.
Flaked Describes a flower in which another color overlies the ground color in large splashes; particularly applied to some carnations (*Dianthus*) and tulips.
Floret Tiny, individual flower within a dense inflorescence, such as a grass flower in a spikelet, or a disk- or ray floret in a (composite) flowerhead.
Flower Reproductive structure of angiosperms, usually consisting of an ovary or stamens, or both, most frequently encircled by a perianth of differentiated petals and sepals or undifferentiated tepals, and usually borne on a flower stalk. *See also pp.16–17.*
Flowerhead (capitulum) Inflorescence consisting of a central group of tiny disk florets, usually ringed by ray florets, borne on a compressed axis or stem. Also referred to as a composite flowerhead.
Flowering plant *see* Angiosperm.
Flower stalk (pedicel) Stalk supporting an individual flower or fruit singly or in an inflorescence.
Fluted With long, rounded, vertical grooves.
Foliar feed Dilute solution of fertilizer applied to leaves.
Follicle Dry fruit, formed from a single carpel, that splits along one side to release one or more seeds.
Force To induce unseasonal growth, flowering, or fruiting of a plant, usually under glass; achieved by manipulating the plant's environment.
Forma (*abbrev.* f.) Variant of a species, ranked below *varietas* (var.) in the nomenclatural hierarchy, distinguished by minor characteristics such as habit or the color of the leaves, flowers, or fruits. *See also p.11.*
Formative pruning Training of young trees or shrubs to produce a framework of strong, evenly spaced stems or branches. *See also p.25.*
Frame Structure with a glass or plastic cover used for forcing, hardening off, propagation, or winter protection. *See also* Bulb frame, Cold frame, Propagating frame.
Free-tipped Refers to a conifer needle that is pressed flat to an axis with the tip extending beyond it.
Frond 1. Leaf of a fern. 2. Loosely, a large, compound leaf, such as a palm leaf.
Fruit Ripened ovary and any attached structures that ripen with it.
Fungus (*pl.* fungi; *adj.* fungal) Non-vascular, non-photosynthetic organism, such as a mold or mushroom, that obtains nutrients by absorbing organic compounds from its surroundings.
Funnel-shaped Describes a flower in which the perianth widens gradually from the base into a spreading, often lobed mouth, like a funnel.
Fusiform *see* Spindle-shaped.

G

Garden origin Applied to a plant that has been artificially bred or selected, rather than occurring in the wild.
Garigue Exposed Mediterranean habitat covered with scrub vegetation.
Genus (*pl.* genera; *adj.* generic) Primary category in plant classification, ranked between family and species. Encompasses species that share a wide range of characteristics. *See also p.11,* Binomial.
Germination Physical and chemical changes that occur as a seed begins to develop into a young plant.
Glabrous Smooth and hairless.
Gland Cell, organ, or pore that secretes oils or other substances.
Glandular-hairy With gland-tipped hairs.
Glaucous With a blue-green, blue-gray, gray, or white bloom; usually refers to stems and leaves.
Globose *see* Spherical.
Globular *see* Spherical.
Glochid Small, barbed bristle or hair borne on the areole of a cactus.
Glume Thin, dry, membrane-like bract in the inflorescence of a grass or sedge, usually arranged in 2 ranks; may be a perianth segment, or support a spikelet or flower, depending on the species.
Graft hybrid Plant resulting from the combination of tissues from both scion and rootstock after grafting. *See also* Chimera.
Grafting Method of propagation by which the scion of one plant and rootstock of another are artificially united so that they eventually function as one plant.
Ground bark Bark ground to fine, medium, or coarse grade, often used in potting mix.
Grass Member of the Poaceae family, with round, hollow, or solid stems that have usually regularly spaced, solid nodes. The basic inflorescence is a spikelet, grouped into a panicle, raceme, or spike. *See also p.54.*
Greenhouse Structure glazed with glass or plastic, providing a controlled environment for the cultivation of plants.
Green manure Quick-growing crops, such as clover (*Trifolium*) and rye (*Festuca*) that are turned over into the soil to improve the organic content.
Greenwood cutting Cutting taken from the shoot-tip of a plant once the initial flush of spring growth has slowed; stems are slightly harder than those used for softwood cuttings.
Grex A collective term applied to all the progeny of an artificial cross from known parents of different taxa. Mainly applied to orchids. *See also p.11.*
Grit Coarse material (usually sand or gravel) used to assist drainage, usually in containers, in the potting mix or on the surface.

Ground color The predominant color of (usually) a flower part.
Groundcover Applied to (usually) low-growing plants that quickly spread over the soil surface, helping to suppress weeds.
Ground frost Climatic effect when the temperature at or just beneath the surface of the soil falls to 32°F (0°C) or below.
Group Category of cultivated plants that denotes a collection of similar, named cultivars. *See also p.11,* Series.
Growing point (shoot-tip) Tip of a shoot from which new extension growth develops.
Growing season Part of the year when a plant is in active growth.
Grow on To grow young plants to a stage where they are ready to plant out or flower.
Growth habit *see* Habit.
Gymnosperm Tree or shrub, generally evergreen, that bears naked seeds in cones rather than enclosed in ovaries, such as conifers and cycads. *See also p.10.*

H

Habit Characteristic form, appearance, or mode of growth of a plant.
Habitat Natural environment in which a plant occurs in the wild.
Haft Narrowed or constricted base of an organ, particularly on the fall petals of *Iris* flowers.
Half-pot Container that is half the depth of a standard plant pot.
Half-standard Standard tree or shrub with a clear stem of 3–5ft (1–1.5m) from ground level to the lowest lateral branches.
Harden off To gradually acclimatize young plants reared in a protective environment to harsher conditions.
Hardiness Capacity of a cultivated plant to withstand adverse conditions; in general usage, its tolerance of low temperatures. *See pp.18–19.*
Hardwood Mature wood for cuttings.
Hardwood cutting Cutting taken from mature wood from early autumn (after leaf fall) to early winter.
Hardy Able to withstand the climate of a given area. *See also p.18.*
Hastate *see* Spear-shaped.
Heart-shaped (cordate) 1. Roughly ovate, pointed at the tip, and with a deep cleft at the center of a rounded base. 2. Describes a base that is rounded with a deep cleft at the center.
Heel cutting Cutting consisting of a vigorous sideshoot from a stem of the current season's growth, with a small piece of bark or older wood at the base.
Herb 1. Plant with practical properties, such as for culinary or medicinal use. 2. Botanically, any herbaceous plant.
Herbaceous border Area of land set aside for the cultivation of herbaceous plants.
Herbaceous plant Non-woody plant that dies back (loses top-growth and becomes dormant) at the end of the growing season, usually in autumn, overwintering by means of underground rootstocks. Some may develop a woody base. Growth resumes in spring.
Herbicide Chemical used to control or eradicate weeds.
Hermaphrodite *see* Bisexual.
Hill up To draw soil up around a plant to exclude light, promote the formation of roots from the stem, or provide winter protection.
Hip Fleshy fruit of a rose.
Hose-in-hose Describes a double flower in which the corolla or calyx is duplicated, with one within the throat of the other.
Houseplant Any plant grown for long periods indoors, often frost-tender species that would not survive outside in cold climates.
Humidity Measure of the air's moisture content as a percentage of saturated air (relative humidity/RH). In this encyclopedia, low humidity is below 50% RH; moderate humidity is 51–60% RH; high humidity is 61% RH and above. *See also p.24.*
Humus Highly decomposed organic material found in soil; often refers to compost, leaf mold, or other less decomposed organic matter.
Hybrid (cross) Naturally or artificially produced offspring of genetically distinct parents of different taxa. Hybrids show new combinations of characteristics and are often vigorous in growth. *See also* F_1 hybrid, Graft hybrid, Intergeneric hybrid, Interspecific hybrid, Multigeneric hybrid, Trigeneric hybrid.

I

Incised Deeply, irregularly, and sharply toothed or lobed.
Incurved Bending inward.
Indumentum Covering of hair or, more rarely, scales.
Indusium (*pl.* indusia) Tissue covering a sorus on a fern frond.
Infertile 1. Refers to a soil that is very low in nutrients. 2. More loosely, applied to plants that do not flower or fruit for various reasons, but may do so if the conditions are right. *See also* Sterile.
Inflorescence Arrangement of flowers on a single axis. *See also* Catkin, Cluster, Corymb, Cyme, Flowerhead, Panicle, Raceme, Spadix, Spike, Umbel.
Infructescence A matured inflorescence. Commonly called seed head or fruit cluster.
Insecticide Chemical used to control or eradicate insect pests.
Insectivorous *see* Carnivorous.
Insert To place cuttings in a growing medium.
Intergeneric hybrid Result of crossing plants of 2 distinct, usually closely related genera.
Internode Section of stem between 2 nodes.
Interrupted Refers to a structure, usually an inflorescence, that is not continuous, such as the inflorescences of *Salvia* species.
Interspecific hybrid Result of crossing 2 species within the same genus.
Invasive Describes a vigorous plant that rapidly overwhelms more delicate neighbors, unless restricted in spread.
Inversely heart-shaped (obcordate) Inversely ovate, with a deep cleft at the center of a rounded tip, and pointed at the base.
Inversely lance-shaped (oblanceolate) Broadest above the center, tapering to a narrow basal point; length is 3–6 times the width.
Involucre (*adj.* involucral) Ring of crowded bracts (sometimes only one), sometimes conspicuous and often overlapping, around the base of a flowerhead or umbel.

K

Keel 1. Prominent longitudinal ridge, usually on the underside of an organ such as a leaf, similar to the keel of a boat. 2. Two lower, fused petals of a pea-like flower.
Kidney-shaped (reniform) Roughly quarter-moon-shaped with blunt ends (on a leaf, the stalk is attached at the notched center of the concave margin).

L

Labellum Lip, particularly applied to prominent third petal of orchid flowers. *See also* Lip.
Laced 1. Describes a flower (e.g. *Dianthus*) in which the color of the petal margins and center contrast with the ground color. 2. Laciniate.
Laciniate Describes a margin that is finely and irregularly cut or fringed, as in some daylilies and irises.
Lamina *see* Leaf blade.
Lanceolate *see* Lance-shaped.
Lance-shaped (lanceolate) Broadest below the center, tapering to a narrow tip; length is 3–6 times the width.
Lateral 1. Located on or to the side of an axis or organ, such as lateral veins that arise from the midrib on a leaf surface. 2. Side-shoot from the stem of a plant.
Latex Milky-white sap or fluid that bleeds from some plants when the stem is cut or damaged; may be irritant.
Lath house Structure composed of thin strips of wood (laths) or trellis work used to protect plants from sun, wind, and rain and to acclimatize young, usually woody, plants before planting out in the garden.
Lax Loose and open, not compact.
Layering Method of propagation whereby a stem is pegged to the soil while still attached to the parent plant, to induce rooting. *See also* Air-layering, Mound-layering.
Leaching Removal of soluble nutrients from soil by the passage of water.
Leader 1. Main, usually central stem of a plant. *See also* Central-leader standard. 2. Terminal shoot of a main branch.
Leaf Plant organ, usually flattened and green, borne on a stem or branch, that fulfills the functions of photosynthesis, respiration, and transpiration. *See also pp.14–15.*
Leaf axil Angle formed between a leaf or leaf stalk and the stem of a plant.
Leaf blade (lamina) Thin, usually flat part of a leaf, excluding the leaf stalk.
Leaf-bud cutting Cutting taken from a stem section, including a leaf bud and leaf stalk.
Leaf cutting Cutting taken from a leaf or section of a leaf.
Leaflet Single division of a compound leaf. Botanically, a pinna.
Leaf mold Fibrous, flaky, organic material composed of decayed leaves. May be used in soil mixes as a peat substitute. *See also* Humus.
Leaf node Point at which a leaf arises from a stem.
Leaf scar Marked area on a tree trunk, branch, or twig, where a leaf once grew.
Leaf stalk (petiole) Part of a leaf, attached to the base or center of the leaf blade, that connects it to a stem or branch.
Legume *see* Pod.
Lenticel Raised pore on the surface of bark or some fruits, which provides access for air to the inner tissues.
Ligulate *see* Strap-shaped.
Limb 1. Broadened, flattened, and expanded part of a plant organ, usually a leaf or flower, extending from a narrower base. 2. Larger branch of a tree.
Lime Loosely, refers to compounds of calcium. Calcium content is used to measure soil pH. *See also* Calcareous.
Lime-tolerant Capable of growing in calcareous soil.
Linear (acicular, filiform) Long and narrow, with parallel margins, or almost so; length is 12 or more times the width.
Lingulate *see* Strap-shaped.
Lip Prominent lower lobe on a flower, formed by one or more fused petals or sepals. *See also* Labellum.
Lithophytic (saxicolous) Growing on or among rocks or stones.
Loam Highly fertile, well-drained but moisture-retentive soil, usually high in organic matter, and containing more or less equal parts of clay, sand, and silt.
Lobe Usually rounded segment, separated from adjacent segments by clefts extending

halfway or less to the center of an organ, such as a leaf. *See also* Palmately lobed.
Lorate *see* Strap-shaped.

M

Maquis Habitat consisting of dense shrub thickets, particular to Corsican and other Mediterranean coastlines.
Marginal aquatic Plant that requires permanently moist conditions, from mud to water 12–18in (30–45cm) deep.
Maritime climate Weather conditions experienced in coastal areas. Proximity to the sea or ocean brings exposure to strong winds, but usually moderates seasonal temperatures; rainfall occurs regularly throughout the year. *See also pp.18–19.*
Meristem Tip of a shoot or root in which cell division takes place. Undifferentiated cells are formed or differentiated into tissues that eventually become leaves, flowers, stems, or even whole plants.
Mesic Pertaining to conditions of moderate moisture or water supply; used of organisms occupying moist habitats.
Midrib (midvein) Primary, usually central vein running from the stalk to the tip of a leaf or leaflet.
Midvein *see* Midrib.
Mist To increase humidity under glass in summer by spraying very fine droplets of water into the air. *See also* Damp down.
Mixed border Area of ground in which herbaceous plants, annuals, bulbs, and shrubs are grown.
Monocarpic Refers to plants that flower and fruit once and then die. Monocarpic perennials may grow for a few to many years before flowering.
Monocotyledon Angiosperm with a single seed leaf, parallel-veined leaves, no cambium layer, and floral parts usually in threes. *See also* Dicotyledon.
Monoecious With separate male and female flowers borne on the same plant.
Monopodial Refers to a stem or rhizome growing indefinitely from an apical or terminal bud, not usually producing secondary branches.
Monotypic Having only one component, e.g. a genus containing a single species.
Mound-layering Method of propagation whereby the basal section of a stem is hilled up to induce rooting.
Mulch Layer of material spread on the top of the soil around plants. Loose mulches, such as leaf mold and compost, retain moisture, insulate roots, and can improve soil structure and add nutrients. Sheet mulches, such as black plastic and landscape fabric, suppress weeds and also conserve moisture. *See also p.21.*
Multigeneric hybrid Result of crossing 3 or more genera.
Mutation *see* Sport.

Mycorrhizal Refers to a mutually beneficial association between a fungus and the roots of a plant.

N

Native Species that naturally grows wild in a particular area.
Naturalized Describes a species that apparently grows wild in a particular area, but is introduced and not native.
Nectar Sugary, liquid secretion that attracts some pollinators.
Nectary Gland, often a modified sepal, petal, or stamen, that secretes nectar.
Needle Stiff, linear leaf of a conifer.
Neutral Neither acid nor alkaline.
Node Point on a stem, sometimes swollen, at which leaves, leaf buds, and shoots arise.
Nodule Small, rounded swelling.
Nomenclature Standard system of naming plants and providing for the formation and use of the names. Cultivated plants are named in accordance with the International Code of Nomenclature for Cultivated Plants and the International Code for Botanical Nomenclature. *See also p.11.*
Non-vascular Describes plants that lack conductive tissue for the circulation of water and nutrients, for example mosses. *See also p.10.*
Non-woody *see* Soft-stemmed.
Nut Dry, non-splitting fruit with a hard or leathery shell surrounding a single seed (kernel).
Nutrients Minerals necessary for healthy metabolism and growth.

O

Obcordate *see* Inversely heart-shaped.
Oblanceolate *see* Inversely lance-shaped.
Oblong With 2 parallel sides of roughly equal length; length is 2–4 times the width.
Oblong-ovate Roughly oblong, rounded at both ends, and broader at one end than the other.
Obovate Refers to a flat form, egg-shaped in outline and broadest above the middle; length is 1½–2 times the width.
Obovoid Refers to a solid form that is egg-shaped and broadest above the middle; length is 1½ times the width.
Offset Small plant that arises naturally by vegetative increase, as with many bulbous plants and succulents.
Of gardens Term used after the Latin name of a plant to denote that the name is commonly but incorrectly used.
Opposite Describes organs, usually leaves, borne in pairs at each node, in the same plane but on opposite sides of an axis.
Orbicular *see* Rounded.
Organic 1. Carbon-based matter of plant or animal origin. 2. Gardening practices using natural materials and environmentally aware techniques.
Osmunda fiber Chopped, dried roots of the fern genus *Osmunda*, often used in orchid cultivation.
Oval Broadly elliptic, rounded at both ends, with slightly parallel sides in the middle; length is 1½–2 times the width.
Ovary Female organ of a flower, containing ovules.
Ovate Refers to a flat form, egg-shaped in outline and broadest below the middle; length is 1½ times the width.
Ovoid Refers to a solid form, egg-shaped, and broadest below the middle.
Ovule Part of the ovary from which a seed develops after fertilization.

PQ

Palate The inner portion of the upper part of a two-lipped flower, as in many members of the Menthaceae and Scrophulariaceae.
Palmate leaf Describes a compound leaf that is fully divided into leaflets arising from a single basal point; it is often also used loosely to mean lobed in a hand-like form. 3-palmate leaves are divided into 3 leaflets, and are often also referred to as trifoliolate, ternate, or, incorrectly, trifoliate. 5-palmate leaves are divided into 5 leaflets, and may also be described as digitate.
Palmately lobed Describes a leaf that is deeply divided into 3–7, sometimes more, lobes. It is distinct from a palmate leaf in that the divisions do not extend to the basal point and so are lobes (not leaflets).
Pan Shallow pot used for growing alpine plants and bulbs and sowing seed; often set into a raised bed.
Panicle Branched raceme. Loosely applied to freely branched, corymb-like or cyme-like inflorescences.
Papilla (*pl.* papillae, *adj.* papillose) Small, soft, wart-like projection, common in lilies (*Lilium*).
Parasite Organism that derives nutrients directly from a host species, often to the detriment of the latter.
Pea-like Describes a flower structure found in many genera of the Fabaceae, with an erect standard petal, 2 large, usually lateral wing petals, and 2 lower, keeled petals that may be fused at the base or on the lower side, enclosing the stamens and pistil.
Peat Moisture-retentive, humus-rich, acidic, partially decayed organic matter, with a pH up to 6.5. Used mainly in potting mixes and as a mulch. Derived from sedges (sedge peat) or sphagnum moss (sphagnum peat) and occurring in boggy, waterlogged conditions. Peat substitutes can be used where appropriate; they include coconut fiber (coir), compost, ground bark, and leaf mold.
Peat bed A highly specialized growing area edged with peat blocks and filled with peaty soil, for growing acid-loving plants.
Pectinate Arrangement of plant organs, usually leaves, in regular, comb-like rows, either in a single row or 2-ranked.
Pedate Describes a palmate or palmately divided leaf in which the basal lobes or leaflets are themselves lobed.
Pedicel *see* Flower stalk.
Peduncle Stalk of an inflorescence.
Peltate Attached to the stalk at the center or other point on the underside of a structure, such as a leaf, rather than at the margin.
Pendent Hanging downward. Used synonymously with pendulous.
Perennial Plant that lives for more than 2 growing seasons; in horticulure, usually applied only to non-woody plants. *See also pp.10, 38–39.*
Perfoliate Describes stalkless leaves, arranged singly or in opposite pairs, with the bases united around the stem.
Perianth Collective term for the corolla and calyx, whether these are distinct from each other or undifferentiated.
Perianth segment Undifferentiated petal or sepal.
Perlite Light granules of volcanic minerals added to soil or to potting and seed starting mix to improve aeration.
Permeability Ease with which water passes through soil.
Perpetual-flowering Describes a plant that bears flowers more or less continuously throughout the growing season or year. *See also* Remontant.
Persistent Remaining attached.
Pesticide Chemical used to control or eradicate pests, diseases, or weeds.
Pests Loosely, animals that feed on plants and often transmit disease. *See also pp.30–31.*
Petal Modified leaf that makes up the corolla of a flower; generally brightly colored. *See also* Perianth segment, Tepal.
Petaloid Similar to a petal in color shape and texture. *See also* Perianth segment, Tepal.
Petiole *see* Leaf stalk.
pH Measure of acidity or alkalinity. Many garden plants prefer neutral to slightly acidic soil with pH5.5–7.5. *See also* Acidic, Alkaline, Neutral.
Photosynthesis Complex series of chemical reactions in green plants and some bacteria, in which energy from sunlight is absorbed by chlorophyll, and carbon dioxide and water are converted into sugar and oxygen.
Phylloclade (cladode, cladophyll) Stem that looks like and takes on the functions of a leaf.

Phyllode Expanded leaf stalk that takes on the functions of a leaf.
Picotee Describes a flower narrowly edged in a color that contrasts with the ground color.
Pinch out (stop) To remove soft growing points to encourage the bushy growth of sideshoots.
Pinna (*pl.* pinnae) Leaflet of a pinnate leaf or of a fern frond. *See also* Pinnate.
Pinnate Describes a compound leaf with leaflets (pinnae) arranged alternately or in opposite pairs on a central axis, with or without a terminal leaflet. 2-pinnate (bipinnate) leaves have pinnately divided leaflets. 3-pinnate (tripinnate) leaves have pinnately divided leaflets that are themselves pinnately divided.
Pinnatifid Describes a simple leaf with usually opposite pairs of lobes cut no deeper than half way to the midrib.
Pinnatisect Describes a simple leaf with usually opposite pairs of deep lobes cut almost to the midrib.
Pinnule *see* Segment.
Pistil Female reproductive organ of a flower, composed of one or several fused or separate carpels.
Plantlet 1. Older seedling. 2. Young, small plant that develops on a mature plant. *See also* Offset, Viviparous.
Pleach To intertwine the branches of a tree or shrub to form a hedge or screen.
Plumose 1. Feather-like, with long, fine, often branched hairs. 2. Applied to plume-like, finely branched inflorescences.
Plunge To sink a container to its rim in peat, sand, soil, or similar material to insulate the roots and prevent the plant from drying out.
Pod (legume) 1. One-chambered fruit of the Fabaceae that splits along 2 sides to disperse ripe seed. 2. Loosely, any dry fruit that splits to disperse seed.
Pollard To cut branches back hard to the main trunk (or to a framework of several main branches) of a tree in order to restrict growth or to promote long, unbranched shoots.
Pollen Grains released from anthers containing the male cells necessary for fertilization.
Pollination Transfer of pollen from the anthers to the stigma of the same or a different flower. Can be performed by animals, insects, wind, or water, and, in the garden, by hand.
Pompon Describes a roughly spherical flower with tightly packed florets that are often curved inward.
Pot on To remove a plant (usually a cutting or seedling) from an outgrown container, and place it with fresh soil mix in a larger container, with room for further growth.
Potting mix (soil mix) Well-drained but moisture-retentive growing medium used mainly for container-grown plants. Soil-based potting mix is based on loam mixed with peat (or substitute), and perlite, vermiculite, or sharp sand. Soilless potting mixes are based on peat (or substitute), mixed with perlite or vermiculite. *See also p.24.*
Pot up To insert a seedling or rooted cutting in potting mix in a container.
Pre-chill *see* Stratify.
Pre-soak To soak seed in recently boiled water for between 10 minutes and 72 hours, depending on the species, to soften the seedcoat prior to sowing.
Prick out To transfer seedlings from where they have been germinated into appropriate containers and soil mix, where they have room to grow.
Procumbent *see* Prostrate.
Propagate To increase plants by seed or by vegetative means. *See also pp.28–29,* Vegetative propagation.
Propagating case (propagator) Small, closed case with a transparent lid, used to provide a humid atmosphere under glass, usually with bottom heat, for rooting cuttings, or germinating seed.
Propagating frame Large case, normally unheated, used outdoors to root cuttings, germinate seed, or raise plants.
Propagator *see* Propagating case.
Prostrate (procumbent) Describes a plant with spreading or trailing stems lying flat on the ground.
Pruinose *see* White-frosted.
Prune To remove twigs or branches from woody plants in order to maintain health, control size, train to a desired shape, or stimulate growth or the production of flowers or fruit. *See also pp.25–27,* Formative pruning, Renovation pruning, Restrictive pruning.
Pseudobulb Swollen, bulb-like stem, sometimes jointed, that acts as a storage organ for some sympodial orchids. *See also* Backbulb.
Pseudocephalium Woody, flower-bearing, densely spined area near the apex of some cacti. *See also* Cephalium.
Quilled Describes a flowerhead consisting of narrow, tubular ray florets.

R

Raceme Inflorescence of stalked flowers radiating from a single, unbranched axis, the youngest flowers near the tip.
Rachis Main axis of a compound leaf or inflorescence.
Radial Spine at the perimeter of an areole on a cactus.
Radical Refers to basal leaves that grow from or near ground level. *See also* Rosette.
Rank Refers to a linear arrangement of leaves. 2-ranked (distichous) leaves are arranged in opposite pairs along a stem. 4-ranked (decussate) leaves are arranged in opposite pairs, each pair at right angles to the pair next to it.
Ray floret Tiny, usually strap-shaped, tubular-based, outer flower of a (composite) flowerhead.
Receptacle Enlarged or elongated tip of the stem from which all parts of a simple flower arise.
Recurved Arched backward.
Reflexed Arched or bent sharply back.
Remontant Refers to a plant that flowers more than once within a growing season, at distinct times. *See also* Perpetual-flowering.
Renewal pruning *see* Renovation pruning.
Reniform *see* Kidney-shaped.
Renovation pruning (renewal pruning) Hard pruning to rejuvenate an old or overgrown shrub. *See also p.25.*
Repot 1. To return a plant to its original container after shaving off some roots and/or replacing the top few inches with fresh soil mix. Often done to older plants growing in large containers. 2. To move into a larger container.
Reproduction Process of producing new individuals by either sexual or asexual (vegetative) methods.
Respiration Absorption of oxygen and breakdown of carbohydrates within cells, releasing carbon dioxide and water and providing energy for metabolism.
Resting period *see* Dormancy.
Restrictive pruning Periodic pruning to limit growth. *See also p.25.*
Reversion Genetic change within a sport or chimera in which a plant or part of a plant reverts to its original character, especially leaves and flowers.
Rhizome (*adj.* rhizomatous) Horizontal, usually branching and fleshy stem, growing underground or at ground level.
Rhomboidal *see* Diamond-shaped.
Rib 1. Ridge, normally vertical, formed on the stem of a cactus. 2. Refers to the primary vein on a leaf.
Ripening 1. Maturing of fruit. 2. Maturing of young shoots (wood) on trees and shrubs, or of bulbs.
Ripewood cutting Cutting of a mature shoot taken from an evergreen plant, from late summer to early winter.
Rock-dwelling *see* Lithophytic.
Rock garden Area for growing alpines and rock plants among rocks, ideally to resemble natural outcrops.
Rock plant Any small plant grown in association with alpines, and with similar cultivation requirements. *See also p.40–41.*
Root 1. Part of a plant, usually underground, that anchors it and absorbs water and nutrients from the soil. 2. To produce roots (on a cutting). *See also pp.12–13,* Aerial root, Buttress root, Stilt root, Taproot.
Root ball Mass of roots and soil or soil mix attached to them, formed by a plant in a container or in the ground.
Root cutting Cutting taken from a vigorous, young root during winter.
Rootstock 1. Underground part of a plant. 2. Loosely, the crown and root system of any herbaceous perennial, from which new plants arise. 3. Plant upon which a scion is grafted.
Rosette 1. Dense whorl of leaves arising from the central point or crown of a plant, usually at or near ground level. 2. Whorled arrangement of petals or tepals.
Rounded (orbicular) Roughly or fully circular in outline.
Runner 1. Trailing stem, growing above ground and rooting at the nodes, where plantlets are produced.
2. Underground, spreading shoot producing upright shoots that form new plants at intervals.

S

Sac Space or chamber inside an ovary, anther, or fruit.
Sagittate *see* Arrow-shaped.
Salverform Describes a flower with a long, slim, tubular corolla that spreads out into flat lobes.
Sandy Describes dry, light, free-draining soil, low in nutrients, derived from quartz or sandstone.
Sap Complex liquid that flows through conductive tissue of vascular plants.
Sapling Young tree.
Saprophyte Plant, usually lacking in chlorophyll, that absorbs nutrients from dead or decaying organic matter.
Saucer-shaped Describes a flat flower with the corolla lobes slightly upturned at the tips.
Savanna Flat, dry grassland habitat covered with low shrubs and dotted with small trees.
Saxicolous *see* Lithophytic.
Scale 1. Flat, membranous structure.
2. Dry leaf or bract, usually pressed flat to the axis to which it is attached.
Scalloped (crenate) Refers to a margin, generally of a leaf, with shallow, rounded teeth.
Scandent Describes a plant that climbs by means of flexible stems that grow over or through supports, attaching themselves loosely, if at all. *See also pp.36–37,* Climber.
Scape Leafless stem of a solitary flower or inflorescence, as in daylilies and irises.
Scarify 1. To treate chemically or abrade the hard outer casing of a seed before sowing, to increase rate of water uptake and thus rate of germination. 2. To remove moss and old grass from a lawn by raking. *See also p.28.*
Scion Shoot or part of a shoot that is joined to the rootstock of a second plant by grafting.
Scree 1. Slope of unstable, rocky fragments, retaining little moisture, at the bottom of a cliff. 2. In gardens, a deep layer of stone chips with a small

proportion of soil, providing very sharp drainage for alpines and rock plants.
Scrub Habitat with poor or dry soil, covered with shrubs and small trees.
Seed Ripened, fertilized ovule containing a dormant embryo capable of developing into an adult plant.
Seedbed Area of ground that has been dug over, raked, and firmed in preparation for sowing seed.
Seedcoat Outer casing of seed. *See also* Aril.
Seed-starting mix Fine-textured, low-nutrient, moisture-retentive soil mix, formulated for the healthy germination and development of seedlings; also used for rooting cuttings.
Seed head Infructescence.
Seed leaf *see* Cotyledon.
Seedling Young plant raised from seed.
Segment 1. Subdivision of pinna on a pinnate leaf or frond; botanically known as a pinnule. 2. Any division of an organ, such as the lobe of a leaf or flower.
Self *see* Self-colored.
Self-colored (self) Describes a flower with a uniform color.
Self-fertile (self-setting) Describes a plant that does not need pollen from a second individual in order to fertilize and set fruit. *See also* Self-pollinate.
Self-pollinate Process whereby pollen from the anthers of one flower reaches the stigma of a second flower on the same plant. *See also* Self-fertile.
Self-seed To regenerate from seed that is dispersed in the garden without human intervention.
Self-setting *see* Self-fertile.
Self-sterile Describes a plant that requires pollen from a second individual of the species, but not the same clone, to fertilize its flowers.
Semi-deciduous *see* Semi-evergreen.
Semi-double Describes a flower with 2 or 3 times the number of petals of a single flower, usually arranged in 2 or 3 rows.
Semi-evergreen Describes a plant that retains most or some of its foliage throughout the year.
Semi-ripe cutting Cutting taken from semi-mature wood in mid- or late summer, occasionally in early autumn.
Semi-ripe wood Refers to stems or shoots that have slowed down in growth and become semi-woody.
Sepal One part of the calyx, when it is composed of separate parts. Usually green and smaller than petals, but sometimes colorful and petal-like.
Series Name applied to a group of cultivars of annuals that share most of the same characteristics but differ from one another by one character (rarely more), usually color. *See also pp.11, 42.*
Serrate Describes a finely toothed margin, usually of a leaf, with the teeth slightly curved as in a saw blade.
Sessile Refers to a stalkless or almost stalkless plant organ.
Set Refers to fertilized flowers that have developed fruit.
Sharp drainage Very free movement of excess water through the soil.
Sheath Tubular structure around a part of plant, such as a leaf base around a stem.
Shoot 1. First, erect growth of a seedling, before it becomes a stem. 2. Loosely applied to side-growths, twigs, or branches. *See also* Branch, Sideshoot, Stem.
Shoot-tip *see* Growing point.
Shrub Deciduous or evergreen perennial with multiple woody stems or branches, generally bearing branches from or near its base. *See also pp.34–35.*
Shrub border Area of ground set aside for the cultivation of shrubs.
Shrublet *see* Subshrub.
Shy-flowering 1. Reluctant to come into flower. 2. Bearing few blooms.
Sickle-shaped (falcate) Curving sideways in the manner of a sickle or scythe.
Sideshoot Lateral shoot that develops from the side of a main shoot.
Silt Moderately fertile, moisture-retentive soil, prone to compaction and surface-capping. Has larger soil particles than clay.
Simple Not divided into secondary units; for example, a leaf with a continuous surface, not cut into leaflets.
Single Describes a flower with the normal number of petals or tepals for the species, arranged in a single whorl. Also applied to (composite) flowerheads that have a single row of outer ray florets with the center filled with disk florets.
Sinus Space between 2 lobes.
Slipper-shaped Describes a flower in which the corolla has a pouch-like form.
Soft-stemmed With a non-woody stem.
Soft-tip cutting *see* Stem-tip cutting.
Softwood Young, soft, unripened shoots of woody plants.
Softwood cutting Cutting taken from young, non-woody growth, from spring to early summer.
Soilless medium Growing medium based on substances other than soil. *See also* Clay granules, Perlite, Vermiculite.
Soil mix *see* Potting mix.
Solitary Flower borne singly rather than in an inflorescence.
Sorus (*pl.* sori) Cluster of sporangia usually on the underside of a fern frond, almost always surrounded or covered by an indusium.
Spadix (*pl.* spadices) Fleshy axis of a spike or spike-like inflorescence, embedded with tiny sessile flowers, usually borne within a spathe.
Spathe Often prominent, fleshy, hood-like bract, surrounding a spadix.
Spathulate *see* Spoon-shaped.
Spear-shaped (hastate) Triangular, with 2 equal, roughly triangular, outward-pointing, basal lobes.
Species Basic category in plant classification, ranked below genus and consisting of similar individual plants that breed true in the wild. Characterized by a binomial. *See also p.11.*
Specimen plant Ornamental plant, normally a tree or shrub, grown usually in a prominent position, where it may be viewed from different angles.
Speculum Glossy raised area, varying from square- to diamond- or horseshoe-shaped, on the lip of some orchid flowers.
Sphagnum Genus of mosses which, when decomposed in bog conditions, is called sphagnum (or moss) peat. In fresh form, it is used to line hanging baskets, or is finely chopped and added to potting mixes.
Spherical (globose, globular) Applied to a round or almost round solid form.
Spike Inflorescence in which stalkless flowers occur on an unbranched axis.
Spikelet Small spike forming part of a compound inflorescence, particularly in grasses and bromeliads.
Spindle-shaped (fusiform) Applied to a solid form, broadest at the center, tapering toward each end (narrower and with straighter sides than ellipsoid forms).
Spine Stiff, sharp-tipped, modified leaf or stem.
Spiny (spinose) Bearing stiff, sharp-tipped spines.
Spoon-shaped (spathulate) Narrow at the base, gradually broadening into a blunt, rounded tip.
Sporangium (*pl.* sporangia) Spore-producing organ on the underside of the fronds of all ferns (and other members of the order Pteridophyta). *See also p.51.*
Spore Basic unit of reproduction in many non-flowering plants, such as ferns and mosses. *See also p.51.*
Sporeling Young, spore-raised plant.
Sport (mutation) Natural or induced genetic change, often exhibited as a variegated shoot or flower from the parent plant. Sports may be vegetatively propagated to give rise to new cultivars. *See also p.11.*
Spray Cluster of flowers or flowerheads arranged on a single, branched stem.
Spur 1. Modified petal with a hollow, basal projection, often containing nectar. 2. Short branches or branchlets along the main branches, on which flowers and fruit are produced.
Stalk Stem-like organ joining a leaf, flower, flowerhead, or inflorescence to the stem of a plant. *See also* Flower stalk, Leaf stalk, Peduncle, Sessile.
Stamen Male part of a flower, composed of an anther, normally borne on a filament.
Staminode Sterile, modified stamen, either inconspicuous or resembling a petal.
Standard 1. Tree or shrub trained to form a rounded head of branches at the top of a clear stem. *See also* Branched-head standard, Central-leader standard, Half-standard. 2. Uppermost petal of a pea-like flower, often large and brightly colored.
3. Erect inner tepal of an *Iris* flower.
Standard pot A pot roughly twice as tall as it is wide.
Star-shaped (stellate) Refers to a flower with widely spaced, narrow petals, tepals, or lobes that radiate from a common central point.
Stellate *see* Star-shaped.
Stem Main axis of a plant, usually above ground, that supports structures such as branches, leaves, flowers, and fruit.
Stem-tip cutting (soft-tip cutting) Cutting taken from the soft tip of a non-flowering stem, usually from spring to autumn.
Sterile 1. Refers to any flower that is incapable of producing seeds. 2. Refers to soils that have been deliberately treated with a chemical to kill weed seeds, pests, and diseases.
Stigma Tip of pistil, which receives pollen to fertilize the ovules.
Stilt root Stabilizing adventitious root produced from the trunks of trees adapted to shallow or waterlogged soil. *See also* Buttress root.
Stipule Leaf-like or bract-like structure borne, usually in pairs, at the point where a leaf stalk arises from a stem.
Stolon (*adj.* stoloniferous) Arching, horizontal or trailing stem producing roots and new shoots at its tips.
Stomata Microscopic pores in the surface of the aerial parts of plants, allowing gaseous exchange. *See also* Transpiration.
Stool *see* Coppice.
Stop *see* Pinch out.
Strap-shaped (ensiform, ligulate, lingulate, lorate) Narrow, with straight or curving sides; length is 6 (or more) times the width.
Stratify (pre-chill) To expose seed to cold in order to break dormancy, either by refrigeration before sowing, or by sowing outdoors in autumn or winter.
Strobilus (*pl.* strobili) Reproductive organ of a conifer. Male strobili resemble catkins; female ones resemble mature cones in miniature.
Style Part of the carpel or pistil connecting the ovary and the stigma.
Subalpine Applied to mountain areas between the foothills and the alpine slopes.
Submerged aquatic Plant that remains totally submerged below water.
Subshrub (shrublet) 1. Woody-based plant with soft-wooded stems. 2. Low-growing, woody-stemmed plant.
Subsoil Layer of soil below the topsoil, usually less fertile and of poor structure.
Subspecies (*abbrev.* subsp.) Category of plant classification, below species but higher in rank than *varietas* or *forma. See also p.11.*

Subtropical Refers to the high-temperature zone located between tropical and temperate regions. Rainfall occurs mainly as heavy downpours during the monsoon season.
Succulent Plant with fleshy leaves, roots, or stems (not bulbs, corms, rhizomes, or tubers) that are adapted for water storage; often native to arid areas. *See also pp.48–49.*
Sucker 1. Adventitious shoot arising below soil level, usually from the roots rather than from the stem or crown of the plant. 2. Shoot that arises from the stock of a grafted or budded plant.
Surface-capping Plate-like structures occurring when the soil surface bakes dry in summer, especially on clay and silt soils, resulting in poor aeration. *See also* Compaction.
Synonym Name or epithet that is not the accepted one for the plant. *See also p.11.*
Sympodial Form of growth in which the terminal bud dies or ends in an inflorescence, and growth continues from lateral buds.

T

Taproot 1. Primary, normally swollen, downward-growing root of a plant from which the root system extends.
Taxon (*pl.* taxa) Named group of organisms that is defined by a set of shared characters.
Taxonomy The science of classification, nomenclature, and identification of organisms. *See also p.10–11.*
Temperate Refers to zones located between the subtropics and the polar circles, which experience distinct seasons, without temperature extremes. Precipitation occurs throughout the year. *See also* Cool-temperate, Warm-temperate.
Temperate greenhouse Greenhouse with a minimum temperature of 45°F (7°C). *See also p.24.*
Tender Applied to plants that are damaged by temperatures below 41°F (5°C).
Tendril Coiling, thread-like, modified leaf, leaflet, inflorescence, or shoot used by a climbing plant to attach itself to an adjacent support.
Tepal Petal or sepal of a flower, where the calyx and corolla are not clearly distinguished. *See also* Perianth segment, Petaloid.
Terminal Located at the end of a stem, shoot, or other organ. *See also* Axillary.
Ternate Arranged in groups of 3 around a common axis. *See also* Palmate.
Terrarium An enclosed, glass or plastic container in which plants are grown.
Terrestrial Describes a land plant that grows in soil, rather than epiphytically, parasitically, or aquatically.
Thin To remove a number of buds, flowers, seedlings, or shoots to improve the growth and quality of remaining ones.
Throat Opening of the tubular part of a flower, from where the petals or tepals spread.
Toothed (dentate) Describes a margin, usually of a leaf, with tooth-like, triangular indentations. Double-toothed margins have alternate large and small teeth.
Top-dress 1. To apply fertilizers or mulches to the soil surface around plants. 2. To apply organic and inorganic dressing to lawns to feed and improve the texture of the grass. 3. To apply material such as stone or grit, usually decorative, to the surface of the soil or potting mix around a plant, in order to improve drainage and reduce moisture loss. 4. To renew the upper layers of potting mix.
Topiary Clipping and training of shrubs or trees into free, geometric, or representational forms.
Topsoil Uppermost layer of the soil, usually the most fertile.
Trademark name Name legally licensed for commercial use, and distinct from a registered cultivar name.
Trailing *see* Climber.
Train To prune and shape the growth of a plant.
Transpiration Evaporation of water from the leaves and stems of plants (mostly through stomata).
Tree Woody perennial with a crown of branches developing from the top of a usually single stem or trunk. *See also pp.32–33.*
Tree fern Large fern that develops a trunk-like rhizome. *See also p.51.*
Triangular (deltoid) With 3 sides of equal length, as in leaves or petals.
Trifoliolate *see* Palmate.
Trigeneric hybrid Offspring of 3 genera, crossed over 2 generations.
Tripartite Divided almost to the base into 3 lobes or segments.
Tripinnate (3-pinnate) *see* Pinnate.
Tropical Refers to the zone between the Tropics of Cancer and Capricorn, with a hot, steamy climate that encourages lush plant growth. Rainfall may occur throughout the year or mainly during a monsoon season. *See also* Subtropical.
True (true-breeding) Term applied to plants that, when raised from seed, virtually reproduce the characteristics of the parents.
Trumpet-shaped Refers to a flower with a long, narrow tube, flaring at the throat into corolla lobes, which are usually arched backward.
Truncate Ending abruptly as though cut off at a right angle.
Trunk Rigid, woody, bark-covered stem of a tree.
Truss Compact cluster of flowers or fruit, particularly of rhododendrons.
Tuber (*adj.* tuberous) Swollen root or underground stem with storage tissue.
Tubercle (*adj.* tuberculate) Small, wart-like projection.
Tubular Refers to a plant organ, usually a flower, with perianth segments fully or partially fused to form a hollow tube.
Tufa Porous, moisture-retentive limestone rock, used for the cultivation of alkaline-loving, rock-dwelling alpines.
Tunic Membrane covering bulbs and corms, often papery but sometimes thick and leathery.
Turion Detached, often fleshy bud of an aquatic plant that overwinters at the bottom of a pond, regenerating in spring.
Twining *see* Climber.

UV

Umbel Flat- or round-topped inflorescence in which numerous stalked flowers are terminally borne from a single point.
Unisexual Applied to a flower that is either male or female only, requiring pollination from a flower of the other sex.
Upright *see* Erect.
Urceolate *see* Urn-shaped.
Urn-shaped (urceolate) Describes a spherical to cylindrical or tubular flower contracted at or just below the mouth.
Variant Plant form that varies to some degree from the norm. Often loosely applied to any naturally occurring or artificially selected form of species.
Variegation Irregular arrangement of pigments, usually as result of mutation or sometimes disease.
Varietas (variety; *abbrev.* var.) Naturally occurring variant of a species, ranked taxonomically between subspecies and *forma. See also p.11.*
Variety *see* Varietas.
Vascular Containing conductive tissue, enabling sap to flow throughout the plant. *See also p.10,* Non-vascular.
Vegetative propagation Asexual techniques for increasing plants, by cuttings, division, grafting, or layering.
Vein Fibrous strand of vascular tissue that conducts sap through the plant.
Venation Pattern of leaf veins.
Ventilation Control of air movement under glass to avoid atmospheric stagnation and regulate temperature.
Vermiculite Light, mica-derived mineral added to potting mix to improve aeration and moisture retention.
Viable Applied to seed capable of germination.
Viviparous Describes plant that forms plantlets on leaves, inflorescences, or stems. Also applied loosely to plants that produce bulbils or bulblets on these organs.

WX

Warm greenhouse Greenhouse with a minimum temperature of 55°F (13°C). *See also p.24.*
Warm-temperate Refers to a temperate climate with mild winters and hot summers.
Waterlogged Refers to soil that is saturated as a result of excessive rainfall, overwatering, or proximity to a water source, and which often drains very slowly.
Water plant *see* Aquatic plant.
Wedge-shaped (cuneate) Inversely triangular, or with straight sides tapering to the base.
Weed 1. Vigorous, invasive, or self-seeding plant competing with desired garden plants for moisture and nutrients. 2. Any plant growing where it is not wanted.
Weeping Describes a tree or shrub that is pendent in habit.
White-frosted (pruinose) With a whitish bloom. *See also* Glaucous.
White-mealy (farinaceous, farinose) With a white or yellow, floury or starchy texture.
Whorl Circular arrangement of 3 or more flowers, parts of a flower, leaves, or shoots, arising from a single point.
Wildflower garden Informal garden used to grow mainly indigenous (native) plants.
Wild garden Informal area intended to resemble a natural habitat, such as a woodland or alpine meadow. *See also* Wildflower garden, Woodland garden.
Wing 1. Thin, flat or membranous extension of an organ. 2. Lateral petal in many orchids and members of the Fabaceae. *See also* Pea-like.
Woodland garden Woodland in which native and non-indigenous trees and shrubs are grown with underplantings of shade-loving herbaceous plants and bulbs, and often with artificially created open glades.
Woody Describes the fibrous stems of certain perennials, such as trees and shrubs, that persist above ground throughout the year.
Woody-based perennial Perennial with a woody base but herbaceous stems.
Xerophytic Describes a plant adapted to survive in arid conditions, either by the reduction of stems and leaves to minimize water loss, or by having water-storage tissue, as in cacti and other succulents.

VISUAL GLOSSARY: FLOWERS

STRUCTURE OF A FLOWER

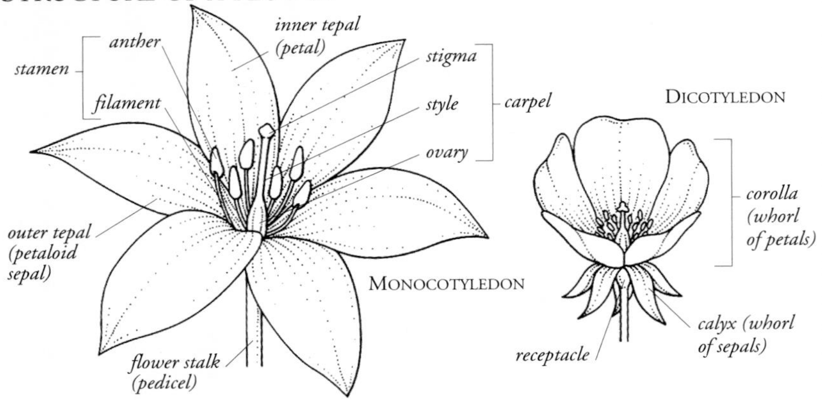

DIFFERENT STRUCTURES

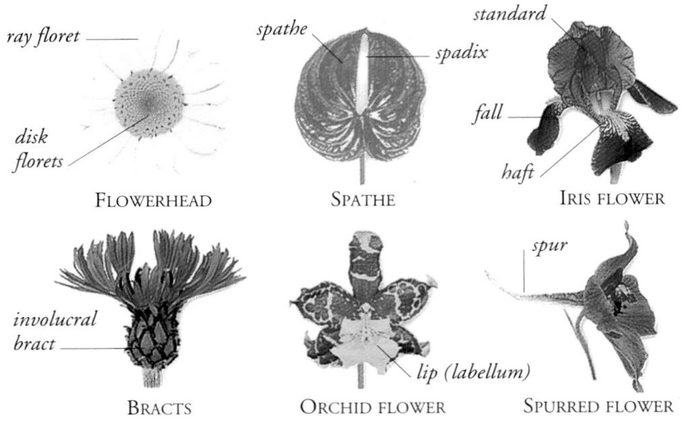

INFLORESCENCES

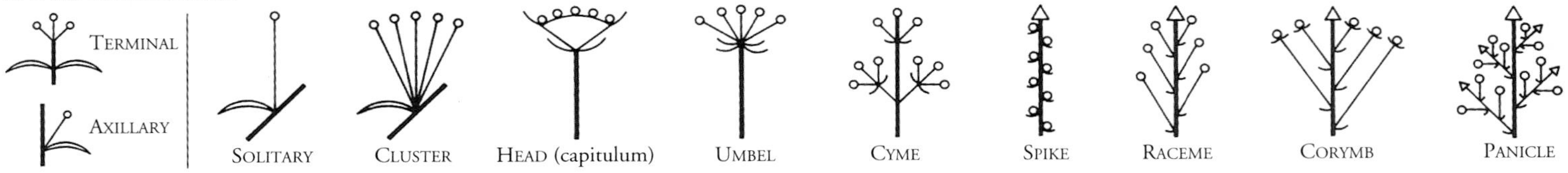

HABITS

SHAPES

PETALS

GROWTH HABITS

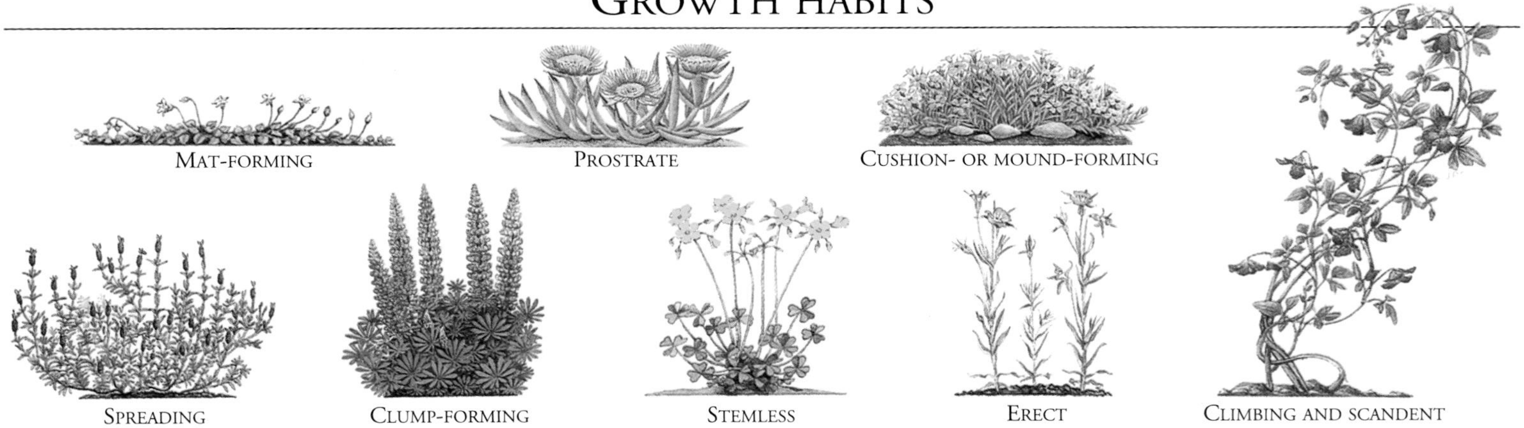

VISUAL GLOSSARY: LEAVES

STRUCTURE OF A LEAF

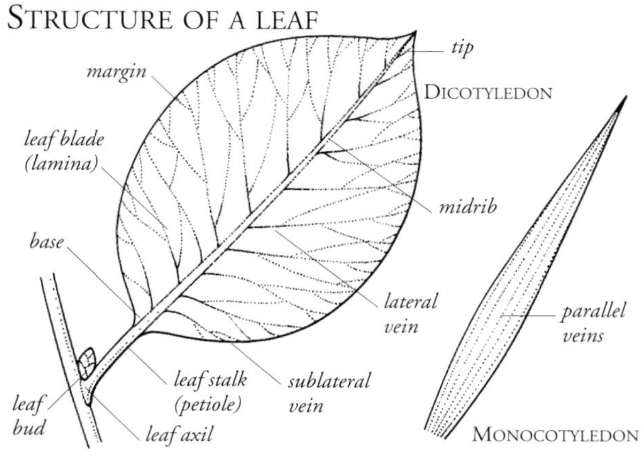

ARRANGEMENTS

CONIFEROUS LEAVES

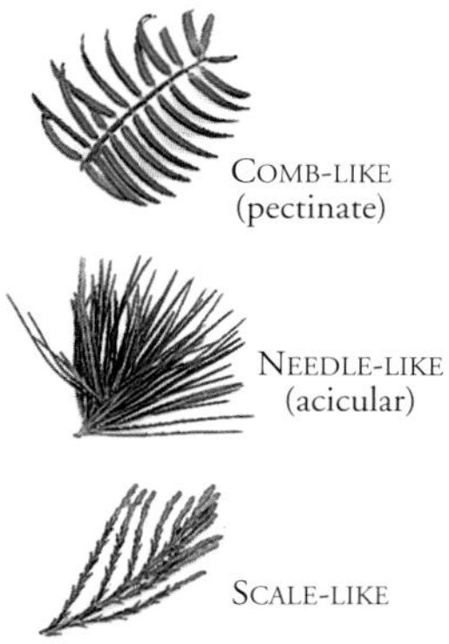

LOBING AND DIVISION

SHAPES

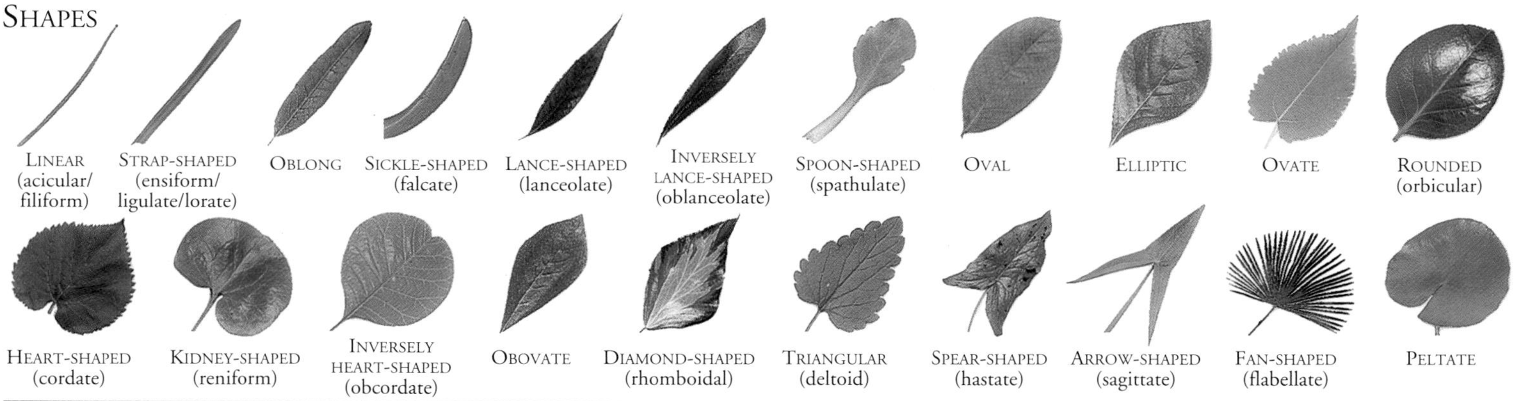

MARGINS

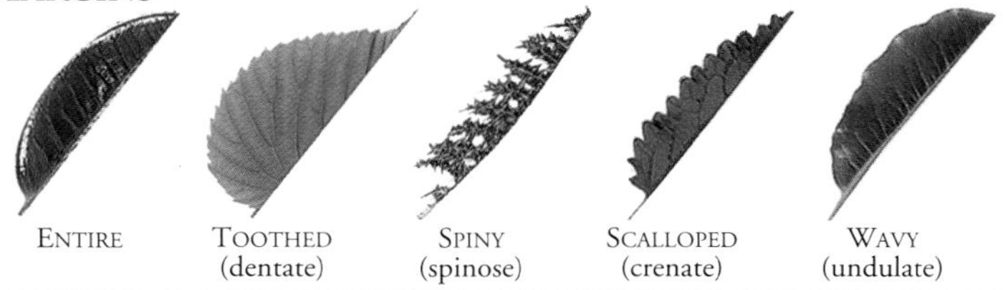

TIPS

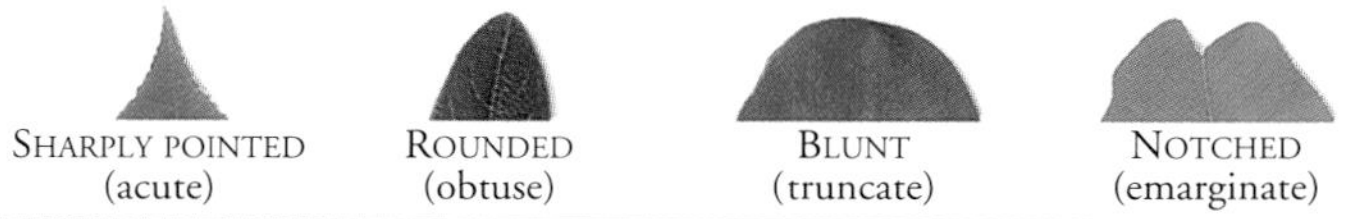

BASES

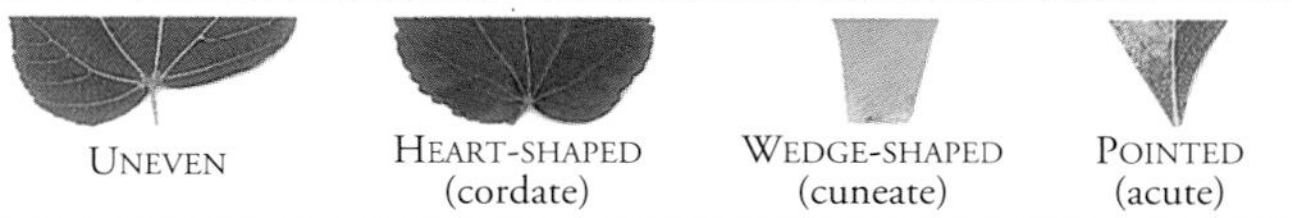

KEY TO SYMBOLS

MISCELLANEOUS	PLANT DIMENSIONS
▷ Cross-reference	↕ Typical height
▣ Plant is pictured (on same page as entry or facing page)	↔ Typical spread
Zones and minimum temperatures, see far right and below	↕↔ Typical height and spread (if the same)
HARDINESS RATINGS	
❀ Plant is tender and may be damaged by temperatures below freezing.	PD Suggested planting distance between bulbs (including corms, rhizomes, and tubers)

HARDINESS RATINGS

A NOTE ON PLANT HARDINESS

Except for annuals and tender plants, all plants in this book are given hardiness zones based on the map produced in 2000 by Natural Resources Canada and Agriculture and Agri-Food Canada. For example, "Zone 5b" occurring at the end of an entry means the plant has the best chance of survival if planted in Canadian hardiness zone 5b or in a milder zone.

The Canadian plant hardiness zones map is presented on the endpapers of this book. Hardiness is explained in greater detail on pages 18–19.

All hardiness zones are intended as approximate guides and should not be considered definitive, especially with perennial plants whose hardiness is influenced by the depth and persistence of snow cover.

COMMON NAME INDEX

Star-leaved see *Begonia heracleifolia*
Stitched-leaf see *Begonia mazae* f. *viridis*
Trailing watermelon see *Elatostema repens*
Winter see *Bergenia ciliata*
Belle de nuit see *Ipomoea alba*
Bellflower see **Campanula**
Adriatic see *Campanula garganica*
Bearded see *Campanula barbata*
Canary see *Canarina canariensis*
Chilean see **Lapageria**
Chimney see *Campanula pyramidalis*
Clustered see *Campanula glomerata*
Dalmatian see *Campanula portenschlagiana*
Giant see **Ostrowskia**
Italian see *Campanula isophylla*
Milky see *Campanula lactiflora*
Nettle-leaved see *Campanula trachelium*
Peach-leaved see *Campanula persicifolia*
Bells of Ireland see *Moluccella laevis*
Bent see **Agrostis**
Brown see *A. canina*
Colonial see *A. tenuis*
Creeping see *A. stolonifera*
Rhode Island see *A. tenuis*
Velvet see *A. canina*
Bergamot see **Monarda**
Bermudagrass see **Cynodon**
Betony see **Stachys**
Big see *Stachys macrantha*
Water see *Scrophularia auriculata*
Wood see *Stachys officinalis*
Woolly see *Stachys byzantina*
Bidi-bidi see **Acaena**
Big tree see *Sequoiadendron giganteum*
Bilberry, Dwarf see *Vaccinium caespitosum*
Billy buttons see **Craspedia**
Bindweed see **Convolvulus**
Birch see **Betula**
Arctic see *B. nana*
Asian white see *B. platyphylla* var. *japonica*
Black see *B. nigra*
Canoe see *B. papyrifera*
Cherry see *B. lenta*
Chinese paper see *B. albosinensis*
Downy see *B. pubescens*
Dwarf see *B. nana*
Erman's see *B. ermanii*
European white see *B. pendula*
Gray see *B. populifolia*
Himalayan see *B. utilis*
Japanese cherry see *B. grossa*
Monarch see *B. maximowicziana*
Paper see *B. papyrifera*
River see *B. nigra*
Schmidt see *B. schmidtii*
Sweet see *B. lenta*
Szechuan see *B. szechuanica*
Transcaucasian see *B. medwedewii*
White-barked Himalayan see *B. utilis* var. *jaquemontii*
Yellow see *B. alleghaniensis*
Bird-catcher tree see *Pisonia umbellifera*
Bird of paradise see **Strelitzia**, *S. reginae*
Tree see *S. nicolai*
Bird of paradise shrub see *Caesalpinia gilliesii*
Bird's eye bush see **Ochna**
Bird's eyes see *Gilia tricolor*
Bird's nest see *Sansevieria trifasciata* 'Hahnii'
Birthwort see *Aristolochia clematitis*
Bishop's cap see *Astrophytum myriostigma*, **Mitella**
Bishop's weed see **Aegopodium**, *Ammi majus*
Bishop's wort see *Stachys officinalis*
Bistort see *Persicaria amplexicaulis, P. bistorta*
Bitter-bark see *Pinckneya pubens*
Bittercress see **Cardamine**
Bitternut see *Carya cordiformis*
Bitterroot see *Lewisia rediviva*
Bittersweet see **Celastrus**
Bitterwort see *Gentiana lutea*
Black-eyed pea see *Vigna unguiculata*
Black-eyed Susan see *Rudbeckia fulgida, R. hirta*
Black-eyed Susan vine see *Thunbergia alata*
Blackwood see *Acacia melanoxylon*
Bladdernut see **Staphylea**
Bladderpod see **Physaria**
Bladderwort see **Utricularia**
Blanket flower see **Gaillardia**, *G. pulchella*
Blazing star see **Liatris**, *Mentzelia lindleyi*
Bleeding heart see **Dicentra**
Blood flower see *Asclepias curassavica*
Blood leaf see *Iresine lindenii*
Bloodroot see **Sanguinaria**
Bloody butcher see *Trillium recurvatum*
Bluebell see *Campanula rotundifolia*, **Hyacinthoides**
California see *Phacelia campanularia*
English see *Hyacinthoides non-scripta*
New Zealand see *Wahlenbergia albomarginata*
Spanish see *Hyacinthoides hispanica*
Texan see *Eustoma grandiflorum*
Virginia see *Mertensia pulmonarioides*
Bluebell creeper see *Sollya heterophylla*
Blueberry see **Vaccinium**
Box see *Vaccinium ovatum*
Climbing see *Billardiera longiflora*
Creeping see *Vaccinium crassifolium*
Highbush see *Vaccinium corymbosum*
Lowbush see *Vaccinium angustifolium* var. *laevifolium*
Rabbiteye see *Vaccinium ashei*
Sourtop see *Vaccinium myrtillus*
Swamp see *Vaccinium corymbosum*
Blueblossom see *Ceanothus thyrsiflorus*
Creeping see *C. thyrsiflorus* var. *repens*
Bluebonnet, Texas see *Lupinus texensis*
Bluebottle see *Centaurea cyanus*
Blue buttons see *Knautia arvensis, Succisa pratensis, Vinca major*
Blue candle see *Myrtillocactus geometrizans*
Blue chalksticks see *Senecio serpens*
Blue cupidone see **Catananche**
Blue-dicks see *Dichelostemma pulchellum*
Blue-eyed Mary see *Omphalodes verna*
Blue lily, African see **Agapanthus**
Bluestar see *Amsonia ciliata*
Bluestem see **Andropogon**
Big see *Andropogon gerardii*
Cane see *Bothriochloa barbinoides*
Little see *Schizachyrium scoparium*
Yellow see *Bothriochloa ischaemum*
Bluet, Mountain see *Centaurea montana*
Blueweed see *Echium vulgare*
Bluewings see *Torenia fournieri*
Blushing bride see *Serruria florida*
Bobie-bobie see *Phebalium squameum*
Boerboon, Weeping see *Schotia brachypetala*
Bog star see **Parnassia**
Bogbean see *Menyanthes trifoliata*
Boneset see *Eupatorium perfoliatum*
Boojum tree see *Fouquieria columnaris*
Borage see *Borago officinalis*
Botanical wonder see x *Fatshedera lizei*
Bo tree see *Ficus religiosa*
Bottlebrush see **Callistemon**
Albany see *Callistemon speciosus*
Alpine see *Callistemon pityoides, C. sieberi*
Crimson see *Callistemon citrinus*
Granite see *Melaleuca elliptica*
Green see *Callistemon viridiflorus*
Lemon see *Callistemon pallidus*
Narrow-leaved see *Callistemon linearis*
Natal see *Greyia sutherlandii*
One-sided see **Calothamnus**
Pine see *Callistemon pinifolius*
Scarlet see *Callistemon macropunctatus*
Stiff see *Callistemon rigidus*
Swamp see *Beaufortia sparsa*
Tonghi see *Callistemon subulatus*
Weeping see *Callistemon viminalis*
White see *Callistemon salignus*
Willow see *Callistemon salignus*
Bottle plant see *Jatropha podagrica*
Bouncing Bet see *Saponaria officinalis*
Bower plant see *Pandorea jasminoides*
Bowman's root see *Gillenia trifoliata*
Box see **Buxus**
Brush see *Lophostemon confertus*
Christmas see **Sarcococca**
Red see *Eucalyptus polyanthemos*
Running see *Mitchella repens*
Sweet see **Sarcococca**
Box elder see *Acer negundo*
Boxwood see **Buxus**
African see *Myrsine africana*
Balearic see *Buxus balearica*
Common see *Buxus sempervirens*
Himalayan see *Buxus wallichiana*
Japanese see *Buxus harlandii* of gardens
Oregon see *Paxistima myrtifolia*
Small-leaved see *Buxus microphylla*
Brake see **Pteris**
Bramble, Ghost see *Rubus cockburnianus*
Brass buttons see *Cotula coronopifolia*
Brazilian firecracker see *Manettia luteorubra*
Brazilian plume see *Justicia carnea*
Brazilian red cloak see *Megaskepasma erythrochlamys*
Breadfruit, Mexican see *Monstera deliciosa*
Bridal bouquet see *Porana paniculata*
Bridal wreath see **Francoa**, *Spiraea* 'Arguta', *Spiraea prunifolia*
Bride's bonnet see *Clintonia uniflora*
Brittlebrush see *Encelia farinosa*
Broadleaf see *Griselinia littoralis*
Broad-leaved kindling bark see *Eucalyptus dalrympleana*
Brodiaea, Twining see *Dichelostemma volubile*
Bromeliad,
Bird's-nest see **Nidularium**
Blushing see *Neoregelia carolinae, Nidularium fulgens*
Brooklime see *Veronica beccabunga*
Broom see **Cytisus**, **Genista**, **Spartium**
Butcher's see *Ruscus aculeatus*
Climbing butcher's see **Semele**
Hedgehog see *Erinacea anthyllis*
Mount Etna see *Genista aetnensis*
Normandy see *Cytisus scoparius* f. *andreanus*
Pineapple see *Cytisus battandieri*
Pink see **Notospartium**
Portuguese see *Cytisus multiflorus*
Purple see *Chamaecytisus purpureus*
Scotch see *Cytisus scoparius*
Spanish see *Genista hispanica*, **Spartium**
Warminster see *Cytisus* x *praecox* 'Warminster'
White Spanish see *Cytisus multiflorus*
Brown-eyed Susan see *Rudbeckia triloba*
Buckeye see **Aesculus**
Bottlebrush see *A. parviflora*
California see *A. californica*
Ohio see *A. glabra*
Red see *A. pavia*
Yellow see *A. flava*
Buckthorn,
Alder see *Rhamnus frangula*
Common see *Rhamnus cathartica*
Italian see *Rhamnus alaternus*
Sea see *Hippophae rhamnoides*
Tallhedge see *Rhamnus frangula* 'Columnaris'
Buckwheat, Saffron see *Eriogonum crocatum*
Wild see **Eriogonum**
Buffaloberry, Silver see *Shepherdia argentea*
Buffalo-wood see **Burchellia**
Bugbane see **Cimicifuga**
Buglevine, Red see *Aeschynanthus lobbianus*
Bugleweed see **Ajuga**
Bugloss,
Blue see *Anchusa azurea*
Siberian see *Brunnera macrophylla*
Bunchberry see *Cornus canadensis*
Bunny ears see *Opuntia microdasys* var. *pallida*
Bunya-bunya see *Araucaria bidwillii*
Burnet see **Sanguisorba**
Canadian see *Sanguisorba canadensis*
Greater see *Pimpinella major, Sanguisorba officinalis*
Salad see *Sanguisorba minor*
Burning bush see *Bassia scoparia* f. *trichophylla, Dictamnus albus, Euonymus alatus*
Burr, New Zealand see **Acaena**
Burrawong see *Macrozamia communis*
Burro's tail see *Sedum morganianum*
Busy Lizzie see **Impatiens**, *Impatiens walleriana*
Butter and eggs see *Linaria vulgaris*
Butterbur see **Petasites**
Buttercup see **Ranunculus**
Bulbous see *R. asiaticus*
Double creeping see *R. parnassiifolius* var. *pleniflorus*
Giant see *R. lyallii*
Persian see *R. asiaticus*
Tall see *R. acris*
Butterfly bush see *Buddleja davidii*
Butterfly flower see **Schizanthus**
Butterfly weed see *Asclepias tuberosa*
Butternut see *Juglans cinerea*
Butterwort see **Pinguicula**
Buttonbush see *Cephalanthus occidentalis*
Buttonwood see *Platanus occidentalis*

C

Cabbage, Skunk see **Lysichiton**
Cabbage tree see **Cordyline**
Cactus,
Agave see *Leuchtenbergia principis*
Apple see *Cereus uruguayanus*
Beavertail see *Opuntia basilaris*
Bird's-nest see *Mammillaria camptotricha*
Chain see *Rhipsalis paradoxa*
Chain-link see *Opuntia imbricata*
Christmas see *Schlumbergera* x *buckleyi*
Coral see *Rhipsalis cereuscula*
Cotton-pole see *Opuntia vestita*
Crab see *Schlumbergera truncata*
Dutchman's pipe see *Epiphyllum oxypetalum*
Easter see *Hatiora rosea*
Eve's-pin see *Opuntia subulata*
Feather see *Mammillaria plumosa*
Fishhook see *Ferocactus wislizenii*
Flapjack see *Opuntia chlorotica*
Goat's horn see *Astrophytum capricorne*
Gold lace see *Mammillaria elongata*
Golden barrel see *Echinocactus grusonii*
Grizzly bear see *Opuntia erinacea* var. *ursina*
Hairbrush see *Pachycereus pecten-aboriginum*
Lace see *Echinocereus reichenbachii*
Mistletoe see *Rhipsalis baccifera*
Mule-crippler see *Echinocactus horizonthalonius*
Old lady see *Mammillaria hahniana*
Old man see *Opuntia vestita, Cephalocereus senilis*
Orchid see **Epiphyllum**
Organpipe see *Stenocereus thurberi*
Polka-dot see *Opuntia microdasys* var. *albispina*
Rat's tail see **Aporocactus**
Rose see *Pereskia grandifolia*
Sand dollar see *Astrophytum asterias*
Scarlet ball see *Parodia haselbergii*
Sea urchin see *Astrophytum asterias*
Silver ball see *Parodia scopa*
Snowball see *Mammillaria bocasana, Pediocactus simpsonii*
Snowball cushion see *Mammilloydia candida*
Starfish see *Orbea variegata*
Thanksgiving see *Schlumbergera truncata*
Toad see *Orbea variegata*
Turk's cap see **Melocactus**
Calamint see **Acinos**, **Calamintha**
Alpine see *Acinos alpinus*
Lesser see *Calamintha nepeta*
Calamondin see x *Citrofortunella microcarpa*
Calico bush see *Kalmia latifolia*
Calico flower see *Aristolochia littoralis*
Calico hearts see *Adromischus maculatus*
Calico plant see *Alternanthera bettzichiana*
Calla see **Zantedeschia**
Calliopsis see *Coreopsis tinctoria*
Caltrops, Water see *Trapa natans*
Camass see *Camassia cusickii*
Death see *Zigadenus venosus*
Camellia,
Common see *Camellia japonica*
Snow see *Camellia rusticana*
Camphor tree see *Cinnamomum camphora*
Campion see **Lychnis**, **Silene**
Alpine see *Lychnis alpina*
Moss see *Silene acaulis*
Rose see *Lychnis coronaria*
Canary bush see *Crotalaria agatiflora*
Canary creeper see *Tropaeolum peregrinum*
Candelabra plant see *Aloe arborescens, Isolatocereus dumorteiri*
Candle plant see *Plectranthus oertendahlii, Senecio articulatus*
Empress see *Senna alata*
Candlewood see *Rothmannia capensis*
Candytuft see **Iberis**
Canebrake see *Arundinaria gigantea*
Cankerroot see *Coptis trifolia* subsp. *groenlandica*
Canterbury bells see *Campanula medium*
Caraway see **Carum**, *C. carvi*
Cardamom see *Elettaria cardamomum*
Cardinal climber see *Ipomoea* x *multifida*
Cardinal flower see *Lobelia cardinalis, Sinningia cardinalis*
Blue see *Lobelia siphilitica*
Cardinal's guard see *Pachystachys coccinea*
Cardo-del-valle see *Centaurea americana*
Cardoon see *Cynara cardunculus*
Caricature plant see *Graptophyllum pictum*
Carnation see **Dianthus**
Wild see *D. caryophyllus*
Carrion flower see **Stapelia**
Carrot see **Daucus,** *D. carota*
Cassia,
Purging see *Cassia fistula*
Silver see *Senna artemisioides*
Cast-iron plant see *Aspidistra elatior*
Catchfly see **Lychnis**, **Silene**
Alpine see *Lychnis alpina*
German see *Lychnis viscaria*

Pussy-toes see **Antennaria**
Pussy willow see *Salix discolor*
Black see *S. gracilistyla* 'Melanostachys'
Redgold see *S. gracilistyla*
Pyramid tree, Queensland see *Lagunaria patersonia*
Pyrethrum see *Tanacetum coccineum*

Q

Quaker ladies see *Hedyotis caerulea*
Quamash see **Camassia**, *C. quamash*
Quassia see *Picrasma quassioides*
Queen Anne's lace see *Anthriscus sylvestris*
Queen Anne's thimbles see *Gilia capitata*
Queencup see *Clintonia uniflora*
Queen of the abyss see *Sinningia canescens*
Queen of the meadow see *Filipendula ulmaria*
Queen of the night see *Hylocereus undatus, Selenicereus grandiflorus*
Queen of the prairie see *Filipendula rubra*
Queen's tears see *Billbergia nutans*
Queen's wreath see **Antigonon**, *Petrea volubilis*
Quicksilver weed see *Thalictrum dioicum*
Quince see **Cydonia**
Common see *Cydonia oblonga*
Flowering see **Chaenomeles**
Japanese flowering see *Chaenomeles japonica*

R

Rabbit's foot see *Maranta leuconeura* 'Kerchoveana'
Rabbit's tracks see *Maranta leuconeura* 'Kerchoveana'
Radiator plant see *Peperomia maculosa*
Radish see *Raphanus sativus*
Raffia see **Raphia**
Ragged robin see *Lychnis flos-cuculi*
Ragwort,
Leopard's bane see *Senecio doronicum*
Purple see *Senecio elegans*
Rainbow star see *Cryptanthus bromelioides*
Rainbow vine see *Elatostema pulchra*
Rainflower see **Zephyranthes**
Raisin tree see *Hovenia dulcis*
Ram's horn see *Proboscidea louisianica*
Rangoon creeper see *Quisqualis indica*
Raripila, Red see *Mentha* x *smithiana*
Raspberry see **Rubus**
Black see *R. occidentalis*
Flowering see *R. odoratus*
Red see *R. idaeus*
Rata see **Metrosideros**
Ratstripper see *Paxistima canbyi*
Rattail see *Crassula muscosa*
Rattan cane see *Calamus rotang*
Rattan vine see *Berchemia scandens*
Rattlebox see **Crotalaria**
Rattlesnake plant see *Calathea lancifolia*
Rattlesnake-master see *Eryngium yuccifolium*
Rauli see *Nothofagus procera*
Redbud see **Cercis**
Red crown see *Rebutia minuscula*
Red-hot cat's-tail see *Acalypha hispida*
Red-hot poker see **Kniphofia**
Red ink plant see *Phytolacca americana*
Red ironbark see *Eucalyptus sideroxylon*
Redmaids see *Calandrinia ciliata*
Redroot see *Ceanothus americanus*
Redshanks see *Adenostoma sparsifolium*
Red tree see *Peperomia metallica*
Redwood,
Coast see *Sequoia sempervirens*
Dawn see *Metasequoia glyptostroboides*
Giant see *Sequoiadendron giganteum*
Reed see **Phragmites**
Burr see **Sparganium**
Giant see *Phragmites australis, Arundo donax*
Reed canary grass see *Phalaris arundinacea*
Restharrow see **Ononis**
Resurrection plant see *Selaginella lepidophylla*
Rewarewa see *Knightia excelsa*
Rhododendron,
Honeybell see *Rhododendron campylocarpum*
Indian see *Melastoma malabathricum*
Rosebay see *Rhododendron maximum*
Tree see *Rhododendron arboreum*
Wilson see *Rhododendron* x *laetevirens*
Rhubarb see **Rheum**
Chinese see *R. officinale*
Indian see *R. officinale*
Ornamental see *R. acuminatum*
Pieplant see *R. rhabarbarum*
Ribbon bush see **Homalocladium**, *Hypoestes aristata*
Ribbon gum see *Eucalyptus viminalis*
Ribbon plant see *Chlorophytum comosum, Dracaena sanderiana*
Ribbonwood see *Adenostoma sparsifolium, Hoheria sexstylosa*
Rice see **Oryza**
Water see *Zizania aquatica*
Wild see **Zizania**
Rice-paper plant see *Tetrapanax papyrifer*
Rimu see *Dacrydium cupressinum*
Robert Ougon-chiku see *Phyllostachys sulphurea*
Roblé see *Nothofagus obliqua*
Rockspray see *Cotoneaster horizontalis*
Rooistompie see *Mimetes cucullatus*
Rose see **Rosa**
Alpine see *Rhododendron ferrugineum*
Apothecary's see *Rosa gallica* var. *officinalis*
Austrian briar see *Rosa foetida*
Austrian copper see *Rosa foetida* 'Bicolor'
Austrian yellow see *Rosa foetida*
Autumn damask see *Rosa* x *damascena* var. *semperflorens*
Burnet see *Rosa pimpinellifolia*
Burr see *Rosa roxburghii*
Cabbage see *Rosa* x *centifolia*
Camellia see *Rosa laevigata*
Cherokee see *Rosa laevigata*
Chestnut see *Rosa roxburghii*
Chickasaw see *Rosa bracteata*
Chinquapin see *Rosa roxburghii*
Christmas see *Helleborus niger*
Cotton see *Hibiscus mutabilis*
Crimson damask see *Rosa gallica* var. *officinalis*
Damask see *Rosa* x *damascena*
Desert see **Adenium**
Double velvet see *Rosa* 'Tuscany Superb'
Double white banksian see *Rosa banksiae*
Eglantine see *Rosa eglanteria*
Father Hugo's see *Rosa xanthina* f. *hugonis*
Fen see **Kosteletzkya**
Fortune's double yellow see *Rosa* x *odorata* 'Pseudindica'
Four seasons see *Rosa* x *damascena* var. *semperflorens*
Great double white see *Rosa* 'Alba Maxima'
Green see *Rosa* x *odorata* 'Viridiflora'
Guelder see *Viburnum opulus*
Hedgehog see *Rosa rugosa*
Incense see *Rosa primula*
Japanese see *Rosa rugosa*
Lenten see *Helleborus orientalis*
Macartney see *Rosa bracteata*
Memorial see *Rosa wichurana*
Montpellier rock see *Cistus monspeliensis*
Moss see *Portulaca grandiflora*
Musk see *Rosa moschata*
Myrrh-scented see *Rosa* 'Splendens'
Nutka see *Rosa nutkana*
Old black see *Rosa* 'Nuits de Young'
Old blush China see *Rosa* x *odorata* 'Pallida'
Old glory see *Rosa* 'Gloire de Dijon'
Painted damask see *Rosa* 'Leda'
Parsons' pink China see *Rosa* x *odorata* 'Pallida'
Persian yellow see *Rosa foetida* 'Persiana'
Pompon see *Rosa* 'De Meaux'
Portland see *Rosa* 'Portlandica'
Provence see *Rosa* x *centifolia*
Provins see *Rosa gallica* var. *officinalis*
Ramanas see *Rosa rugosa*
Red moss see *Rosa* 'Henri Martin'
Rock see **Cistus**, **Helianthemum**
Rosa mundi see *Rosa gallica* var. *officinalis* 'Versicolor'
Sacramento see *Rosa stellata* var. *mirifica*
Sand see *Anacampseros telephiastrum*
Scotch see *Rosa pimpinellifolia*
Scots see *Rosa pimpinellifolia*
Single white banksian see *Rosa banksiae* var. *normalis*
Slater's crimson China see *Rosa* x *odorata* 'Semperflorens'
Sun see **Cistus**, **Helianthemum**
Sydney rock see *Boronia serrulata*
Thornless see *Rosa* 'Zéphirine Drouhin'
Velvet see *Aeonium canariense*
Winged-thorn see *Rosa sericea* subsp. *omeiensis* f. *pteracantha*
Wood see *Merremia tuberosa*
Yellow banksian see *Rosa banksiae* 'Lutea'
York and Lancaster see *Rosa* x *damascena* 'Versicolor'
Rosebay,
East Indian see *Tabernaemontana divaricata*
Mountain see *Rhododendron catawbiense*
Rose mallow,
Common see *Hibiscus moscheutos*
Confederate see *Hibiscus mutabilis*
Swamp see *Hibiscus moscheutos*
Rosemary see **Rosmarinus**, *Rosmarinus officinalis*
Australian see *Westringia fruticosa*
Bog see **Andromeda**
Common bog see *Andromeda polifolia*
Victorian see *Westringia fruticosa*
Wild see *Dampiera rosmarinifolia, Ledum palustre*
Rose of Castille see *Rosa* x *damascena* var. *semperflorens*
Rose of China see *Hibiscus rosa-sinensis*
Golden see *Rosa xanthina* f. *hugonis*
Rose of Jericho see *Selaginella lepidophylla*
Rose of Lancaster, Red see *Rosa gallica* var. *officinalis*
Rose of Sharon see *Hibiscus syriacus, Hypericum calycinum*
Rose of Venezuela see *Brownea ariza*
Roseroot see **Rhodiola**
Rosewood, Brazilian see *Tipuana tipu*
Rosinweed see **Grindelia**, **Silphium**
Rowan see *Sorbus aucuparia*
Rubber plant see *Ficus elastica*
Rubber tree,
Baby see *Peperomia obtusifolia*
Hardy see *Eucommia ulmoides*
India see *Ficus elastica*
Rue see **Ruta**
Common see *Ruta graveolens*
Early meadow see *Thalictrum dioicum*
Fringed see *Ruta chalepensis*
Goat's see **Galega**
Meadow see **Thalictrum**
Yellow meadow see *Thalictrum flavum*
Yunnan meadow see *Thalictrum delavayi*
Rue anemone see *Anemonella thalictroides*
False see **Isopyrum**
Running postman see *Kennedia prostrata*
Rush see **Juncus**
Club see *Schoenoplectus lacustris* subsp. *tabernaemontani* 'Zebrinus'
Corkscrew see *Juncus effusus* 'Spiralis'
Dwarf Japanese see *Acorus gramineus* 'Pusillus'
Egyptian paper see *Cyperus papyrus*
Flowering see **Butomus**
Hard see *Juncus inflexus* 'Afro'
Japanese see *Acorus gramineus* 'Ogon'
Jointed see *Juncus articulatus*
Mat see **Lomandra**
Pale mat see *Lomandra glauca*
Spike see **Eleocharis**
Spiny-headed mat see *Lomandra longifolia*
Variegated Japanese see *Acorus gramineus* 'Variegatus'
Rushgrass see **Sporobolus**
Russian vine see *Fallopia baldschuanica*
Rusty leaf see *Menziesia ferruginea*
Ryegrass see **Lolium**
Italian see *L. multiflorum*
Perennial see *L. perenne*
Rye, Wild see **Elymus**

S

Sacred flower of the Incas see *Cantua buxifolia*
Safflower see **Carthamus**, *C. tinctorius*
Saffron,
False see *Carthamnus tinctorius*
Meadow see **Colchicum**, *C. autumnale*
Spring meadow see *Bulbocodium vernum*
Saffron-spike see *Aphelandra squarrosa*
Sage see **Salvia**
Annual clary see *Salvia viridis*
Autumn see *Salvia greggii*
Bethlehem see *Pulmonaria saccharata*
Blue see *Eranthemum pulchellum, Salvia azurea*
Bog see *Salvia uliginosa*
Clary see *Salvia sclarea*
Common see *Salvia officinalis*
Gentian see *Salvia patens*
Germander see *Salvia chamaedryoides*
Goldleaf Jerusalem see *Phlomis chrysophylla*
Greek Jerusalem see *Phlomis samia*
Jerusalem see *Phlomis fruticosa*
Jim see *Salvia clevelandii*
Mealycup see *Salvia farinacea*
Mexican bush see *Salvia leucantha*
Purple see *Salvia officinalis*
Rosyleaf see *Salvia involucrata*
Russian see *Perovskia atriplicifolia*
Scarlet see *Salvia splendens*
Silver see *Salvia argentea*
Spanish see *Salvia lavandulifolia*
Sticky Jerusalem see *Phlomis russeliana*
Texas see *Leucophyllum frutescens, Salvia coccinea*
Sagebrush see **Artemisia**, *Seriphidium tridentatum*
Sagewood, South African see *Buddleja salviifolia*
Sago, False see *Cycas circinalis*
Saguaro see **Carnegiea**, *C. gigantea*
Sarana, Black see *Fritillaria camschatcensis*
Salal see *Gaultheria shallon*
Saltbush, Four-wing see *Atriplex canescens*
Salt tree see *Halimodendron halodendron*
Sandwort see **Arenaria**
Sang see *Panax quinquefolius*
Sapphire flower see *Browallia speciosa*
Sapphireberry see *Symplocos paniculata*
Saskatoon see *Amelanchier alnifolia*
Sassafras, Australian see *Atherosperma moschatum*
Satin flower see *Clarkia amoena*
Satinwood see *Phebalium squameum*
Sausage tree see **Kigelia**
Savory see **Satureja**
Saxifrage see **Saxifraga**
Golden see **Chrysosplenium**
Jungfrau see *Saxifraga cotyledon*
Meadow see *Saxifraga granulata*
Purple mountain see *Saxifraga oppositifolia*
Pyrenean see *Saxifraga longifolia*
Snail see *Saxifraga cochlearis*
Yellow mountain see *Saxifraga aizoides*
Scabious see **Scabiosa**
Devil's bit see *Succisa pratensis*
Giant see *Cephalaria gigantea*
Grass-leaved see *Scabiosa graminifolia*
Small see *Scabiosa columbaria*
Sweet see *Scabiosa atropurpurea*
Yellow see *Cephalaria gigantea*
Scarlet plume see *Euphorbia fulgens*
Scarlet runner see *Kennedia prostrata*
Sea coral see *Maihueniopsis clavariodes*
Sea holly see **Eryngium**
Sedge see **Carex**
Bird's foot see *Carex ornithopoda*
Bowles' golden see *Carex elata* 'Aurea'
Drooping see *Carex pendula*
Forest see *Carex sylvatica*
Gray's see *Carex grayi*
Hook see **Uncinia**
Leatherleaf see *Carex buchananii*
New England hair see *Carex comans*
Palm branch see *Carex muskingumensis*
Pendulous see *Carex pendula*
Silver variegated Japanese see *Carex morrowii* 'Variegata'
Weeping see *Carex pendula*
Wood see *Carex sylvatica*
Selfheal see **Prunella**
Seminole bread see *Zamia pumila*
Seneca see **Polygala**
Senna,
Appleblossom see *Cassia javanica*
Bladder see **Colutea**
Bladder see *Colutea arborescens*
Scorpion see *Coronilla emerus*
Wild see *Cassia marilandica*
Sensitive plant see *Mimosa pudica*
September bells see *Rothmannia globosa*
Serpolet see *Thymus serpyllum*
Serviceberry see **Amelanchier**
Sevenbark see *Hydrangea arborescens*
Shadblow see *Amelanchier canadensis*
Shadbush see **Amelanchier**, *A. canadensis*
Shallon see *Gaultheria shallon*
Shamrock see **Oxalis**
Irish see *O. acetosella* var. *subpurpurascens*
Shaving brush plant see *Haemanthus albiflos*
Sheepberry see *Viburnum lentago*
Sheep's bit see **Jasione**
Shell flower see *Moluccella laevis*, **Pistia**
Shingle plant see *Rhaphidophora celatocaulis*
Shinleaf see **Pyrola**
Shoo-fly see **Nicandra**, *N. physalodes*
Shooting star see *Thymophylla tenuiloba*
Shooting stars see **Dodecatheon**
Shower tree, Golden see *Cassia fistula*
Shrimp bush see *Justicia brandegeeana*

ACKNOWLEDGMENTS

Special thanks to the following specialists:

Terry Aitken, Tim Alderton, Kathryn S. Andersen, Ph.D., Jane Aspden, Duke Benadom, Dick Bir, Edward Buyarski, Brenda Cole, Richard Craig, Arabella Dane, John T. Dickman, Ph.D., Joyce Fingerut, Alan A. Fisher, Brent Heath, Judith I. Jones, Richard Koogle, Victoria Koogle, Anthony Liberta, Ph.D., Michael Ludwig, Harry E. Luther, Edith M. Malek, Susan Martin, Mark Miller, Ned Nash, Robert Nold, Susanne Warner Pierot, Ruth Rumsey, Luke Senior, Ann Walton, Russell Windle.

Additional editorial assistance

Louise Abbott, Cathy Buchanan, Rebecca Davies, Laurie B. Eichengreen, Claire Folkard, Robert Graham, Jill Hamilton, Lindsay Harber, Eleanor Hoffman, Lesley Malkin, Andrew Mikolajski, Irene Pavitt, Gillian Emerson Roberts, Lyn Saville, Julee Binder Shapiro, Sue Spielberg, Leslie Sterling, June Sussman, Kristin Ward, Agnes Wolff.

Additional design assistance

Esther Beaton, David Bruce, Caroline Fanshawe, Lisa Gould, Frances Hutchison, Stephen Josland, Geoff Manders, Ros Searle, Alistair Wardle.

Additional consultants

Patricia K. Alholm, Dr. Darrell Apps, Dr. Allan M. Armitage, Margaret Askern, David Bar-Zvi, Bob Beach, Mary S. Beasley, Alan D. Bradshaw, Nicola Brown, Tony Clements, Charles O. Cresson, Margaret DePhillippo, Michael Dodge, Philip Eden, Gene Eisenbeiss, Barbara W. Ellis, Benjamin Fay, Richard Felger, Martin F. Gardner, Will Gibbs, Robert Gilman, Jack Golding, Barney Gonsalves, Galen L. Goss, Mark Griffiths, A.P. Hamilton, Dr. Edward R. Hasselkus, Bob Hays, Ronald Hedge, Robert Hobbs, Leon Hubbard, P. Francis Hunt, John Ingles, Elizabeth Kassab, Sally Kington, Alan Leslie, Sylvia Lin, Dr. Seymour Linden, Mark MacDougall, James B. Martin, Tovah Martin, Scott Massey, Suzanne Maxwell, Robert B. McCartney, Dr. John Mickel, Susanne Mitchell, Kathy Musial, Walter W. Oakes, Diana Percy, Dr. Warren I. Pollock, James E. Richardson, Michael A. Riley, Harry A. Rissetto, Stephen Scanniello, Dr. Johan van Scheepen, Nancy Schmieder, Nicola J. Sinclair, Dr. Herbert Spady, Dr. Harold Sweetman, Nancy Szmuriga, Charles P. Thomas, Philip Thomas, Millie Thompson, John Trager, Dr. Arthur Tucker, Peter Valder, Olive Rice Waters, Jim Watson, Nona E. Wolfram-Koivula, Christopher Woods.

Additional photographers

Bill Balham, Paul Barker, Peter Chadwick, Paul Goff, Steve Gorton, David Harding, Dr. Alan Hemsley, Julian Holland, David Karonides, Jonathan Metcalf, Roger Scruton, Darryl Sweetland, Alex Watson.

PHOTO CREDITS

African Violet Society of America: 922/1 • 922/2 • 922/5 • 922/6 922/8 922/9 • 923/2 • 923/3

T.Aitken/www.flowerfantasy.net: 559/8 559/9 • 559/12 • 559/15 560/2 560/3 560/6 • 560/16 560/19 • 562/7 • 562/10 562/13 562/14 • 562/21 • 564/4 • 564/8 564/9 • 564/11 • 564/18 • 565/1

The Alpine Garden Society: 533/10 • 569/1 • 721/1

American Camellia Society: 214/6 •215/1 215/13 • 216/10 217/7 • 218/4

American Clematis Society/Edith Malek: 275/11 •276/1 • 276/22 • 278/2 278/13 278/14 • 279/1• 279/2

American Dahlia Society: 339/5 • 339/8 339/11 • 339/13 339/15 • 340/3 • 340/6 • 340/8 340/11 • 340/12 • 341/2 341/4 341/6 • 341/8 • 341/13 342/6 • 342/8 342/11 • 342/13 • 342/18 • 343/2 • 343/5 343/6 • 343/7 • 343/10 • 343/11 343/13 343/15 • 343/16

American Iris Society: 563/1

American Ivy Society/ Rachel Cobb: 498/4 • 498/9 • 498/14 500/1

Miles Anderson: 153/6 • 441/3 • 668/2

Peter Anderson: 35/1 • 49/1

Tony Avent/Plant Delights Nursery: 528/1 529/2 •592/8 592/9 • 530/1 • 530/2 531/16 532/1

Rich Baer: 900/12 • 912/9

Bailey Nurseries/ Michelle Meyer: 539/5 743/2

Ball Horticultural Company: 764/14 764/15

Gillian Beckett: 104/6 256/2 • 348/3 381/1 399/1 489/1 • 517/3 543/3 968/2

Duke Benadom: 80/4 • 98/2 157/4 387/5 • 661/3 • 727/4 727/5 • 738/1 772/3 • 1061/3

Biofotos: 10/5 • 18/1 • 40/3 56/1 • 61/1 73/5 • 109/2 296/2 • 535/4 • 686/3 919/1

Dick Bir: 540/3

Michael Booher: 1046/1

Brent and Becky's Bulbs/ Brent Heath: 690/4• 690/6 • 690/8 691/3 • 691/10 691/11 691/12• 692/5 • 692/13 • 693/3 693/5 • 693/6 • 693/9• 694/2 694/3 694/7 • 694/8 • 695/4 695/7

Christopher Brickell: 87/2 174/6 • 175/3 220/4• 259/2 299/2 • 362/3 • 384/1 931/3 970/4

Pat Brindley: 359/4 • 436/4 618/1

Richard Brooks: 875/6

Eric Catterall: 168/7

Dennis Cathcart/www.tropiflora.com: 320/3• 484/4 • 701/1 • 856/3

David Cavagnaro: 689/1 805/1 • 928/2 930/1

Trevor Cole: 742/3 • 742/7 744/12 895/4• 899/12 • 911/1 993/3 • 993/5 993/6 • 994/4 994/7 • 994/12

Bruce Coleman Limited: 18/2

Cotswold Garden Flowers: 684/5 • 737/3

Christopher DeRosa: 159/2

Davesgarden.com: 466/3

Jack Elliott: 142/1 • 281/5 415/4 • 460/6 • 560/9 • 672/1 735/2 • 1053/3

Nigel Farr: 266/7

Philippe Faucon/www.desert-tropicals.com: 483/2 • 487/1 649/3 • 727/3 • 814/3

John Fielding: 156/7 • 352/7

Fischer USA: 762/1 • 762/8 762/10 763/8

Fleurmerc B.V.: 83/3 • 296/1 547/1 586/3• 646/9 • 676/4

John Galbally: 359/8 • 360/1

Garden Matters and Wildlife Photo Library
560/5 • 611/4

Garden Picture Library: 35/2 40/2 42/2 • 43/1 • 46/2 • 48/2 51/3 • 52/2 92/1 • 138/2 196/3 • 220/6 • 293/4 343/1 • 433/2 • 464/1 • 617/2 •663/3 678/3 • 710/3 • 767/5 830/9 • 972/4 978/4 • 981/1

John Glover: 44/2 • 127/1 307/2 322/2

Goldsmith Seeds: 759/5 • 761/10

Derek Gould: 172/3 • 313/2 371/2 376/1 378/1 • 507/2 567/1 • 569/2 571/4 • 583/7 663/2 • 924/3 • 1065/2

Hans Hansen/Shady Oaks Nursery: 529/10 • 533/13

Peter Harkness: 890/1 • 890/5 890/13 893/10 • 896/3 897/8 • 900/5 • 902/6 903/3 903/4 903/5 • 903/6 • 905/9 907/4 907/12 • 908/6 908/11 • 909/11 911/13 913/1

Jerry Harpur: 36/2 • 38/1 43/2 • 54/6

Jessie Harris: 150/11 • 443/3 707/1 880/2 • 1047/2

Richard Hartlage: 341/1

Richard Havens: 693/3

Heirloom Roses: 892/12 898/12

Derek Hewlett: 339/11 341/13 • 342/2

Neil Holmes: 648/5

Horticopia: 932/1

Clive Innes: 58/6 • 188/4 383/2 • 387/1 391/1 427/2 428/1 • 485/3 • 492/2 527/2 536/2 • 536/3 • 536/4 • 591/3 708/5 • 714/1 • 714/2 • 752/1 980/4 1015/2

International Flower Bulb Centre: 471/9 472/4 • 473/4

Jackson & Perkins: 903/4 903/8 • 912/10 913/7

PHOTOGRAPHY CREDITS

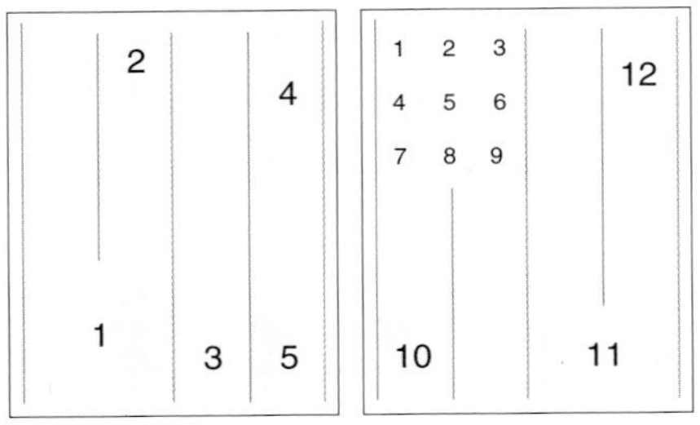

How to use the photography grid (above)
Photographs are numbered from top to bottom within each column of text, then left to right across the page. In the feature panels, photographs are numbered from left to right across each row, working from the top row to the bottom row (see panel on right-hand page above).

With the exception of those listed below, all photographs in the encyclopedia were taken by the photographers listed on p.6. Dorling Kindersley is grateful to the following agencies and photographers for their kind permission to reproduce images in the encyclopedia. To locate the photographs credited below, use the reference numbers given. The first in each pair of numbers is the page number on which the photograph appears; the second is its position number, determined by the order of photographs on each page (see left).

Judith I. Jones/Fancy Fronds Nursery: 819/2 • 819/4 • 819/5

T. Kelso: 832/7

Klehm's Song Sparrow Perennial Farm: 742/2 • 742/18

C. Paul Kneebone: 285/2

Andrew Lawson: 44/3 • 124/1 128/4 192/3 224/1 • 243/5 255/2 • 273/1 274/1 • 386/1 413/2 • 417/2 • 616/8 621/2 744/3 • 745/1 864/2 • 883/1 1067/2

Lilypons Water Gardens: 711/7 • 711/8 711/12 • 712/3 • 712/5 • 712/13

The Lily Nook/www.lilynook.mb.ca: 614/11 • 614/13 • 616/4 • 614/17

Jay Lunn: 827/7

Robert Marcy III: 217/11 218/4

Brian Mathew: 121/2

Peter Maynard: 558/2 • 562/4 562/8

Nora Melzer: 272/1

J. Mertzweiller: 562/14

Paul Meyer: 300/2 • 645/13

Diana Miller: 45/1

Missouri Botanical Garden: 531/9

Monrovia Nursery: 539/8 741/1 • 993/4

National Auricula & Primula Society Northern Section/T. Mitchell: 828/10

Netherlands Flower Bulb Information Center: 614/4

Clive Nichols: 34/2 • 53/1 54/7 • 224/3 349/2

O. David Niswonger: 559/7

Oglevee Ltd.: 761/8 • 761/11 762/9 764/4 • 764/6

Vincent Page: 896/8 • 904/12 907/1 913/3

Ralph Parks: 265/9

Peonygarden.com: 742/12

Peonymeadows.com: 742/8

J.S. Peterson @ USDA-NRCS PLANTS : 916/1

Photos Horticultural: 75/3 76/3 • 78/1 83/1 • 86/3 106/2 • 107/3 • 139/4 • 140/1 141/7 • 213/2 • 230/3 • 272/2 288/2 • 292/5 • 293/2 • 297/2 336/1 361/10 • 368/3 • 375/1 384/2 • 386/2 390/1 • 398/1 411/1 • 420/2 • 432/2 436/2 438/2 • 440/3 • 495/6 • 496/3 516/8 • 520/1 • 524/1 • 527/1 535/1 535/3 • 551/2 • 552/3 553/4 • 555/2 562/18 • 564/6 574/1 579/5 • 605/2 645/8 661/2 • 664/1 • 670/3 681/1 686/1 • 772/4 • 856/4 • 871/6 930/3 936/2 • 939/2 • 1000/1 1003/4 • 1005/1 1011/3 1011/12 • 1017/4 • 1062/1

Larry and Nancy Pitts: 215/10 216/11 217/1

Planet Earth Pictures: 47/2 50/2

Plant Portraits Worldwide: 61/5 • 73/1 74/3 • 77/2 • 91/2 102/2 • 109/1 • 113/4 • 118/1 121/1 • 138/1 • 138/3 138/4 157/3 • 158/2 • 161/3 • 176/1 190/1 • 193/1 • 206/3 • 222/3 259/4 273/2 • 288/3 • 311/2 319/2 • 325/1 348/1 • 350/1 350/2 • 368/4 • 376/2 377/1 379/3 • 382/2 • 420/7 • 461/1 474/10 • 485/4 • 506/4 • 524/3 • 541/2 542/2 • 609/1 • 639/2 649/3 • 685/4 697/2 • 704/6 731/2 • 747/2 • 750/1 751/1 791/2 • 805/3 • 815/3 • 1054/5

David Rankin: 832/3

Martin Rickard: 817/4

Rogers Plants, Ltd: 892/7 895/8 • 904/1 • 911/5 912/5

Barbara Rothenberger: 549/14

Les Saucier: 232/2 • 540/9 819/1 • 974/4

Sakata Seeds: 432/1

Schreiner's Garden: 560/13

Richard Shiell: 444/4 • 633/4 1048/3

Howard Shockey: 560/20

Christine Skelmersdale: 317/12 • 887/3 982/2

Bob Skowron/Rocky Mountain Rare Plants: 128/2 • 793/1

Harry Smith Collection: 63/1 73/2 77/4 • 122/3 • 125/4 • 128/2 134/4 161/1 • 178/4 183/2 187/3 • 191/3 203/4 • 204/4 227/4 243/1 • 283/2 288/1 343/11 • 366/6 • 373/1 • 375/2 408/9 • 413/3 • 436/3 • 463/11 • 464/2 468/5 • 507/4 • 521/4 560/17 • 573/3 598/1 • 616/4 616/19 • 627/4 • 663/4 701/2 742/14 • 742/17 • 768/2 778/1 893/3 • 936/3 • 957/1 961/2 • 965/3 999/3 • 1031/12 • 1071/2

Bob Solberg/Green Hill Farm: 529/1 531/5 • 531/13 • 531/20

Spring Meadow Nursery: 539/9

Star Roses: 901/7 • 905/1

Marco Polo Stufano: 547/5

Sabina Mueller Sulgrove: 498/5 • 498/7 498/11 • 498/12 499/3 • 499/5 • 499/9 499/10 500/2 • 500/3 • 500/5

Samuel Roberts Noble Foundation, Inc., ©2000 : 194/3

Michael Thompson:559/14

Thompson and Morgan Seeds: 1054/1

James Tolland: 215/5

Robbie Tucker: 895/13

Van Staaveren Aalsmeer B.V.: 446/1 • 446/2

Weeks Roses: 891/11 • 891/12 904/3

Alun Whitehead/Auldenfarm.co.uk: 516/2 516/5

Dave Wilson Nursery: 650/2 652/1

Patrick Worley: 72/6